Family Guide to the Bible

Reader's Digest

Family Guide to the Bible

A Concordance and Reference Companion to the King James Version

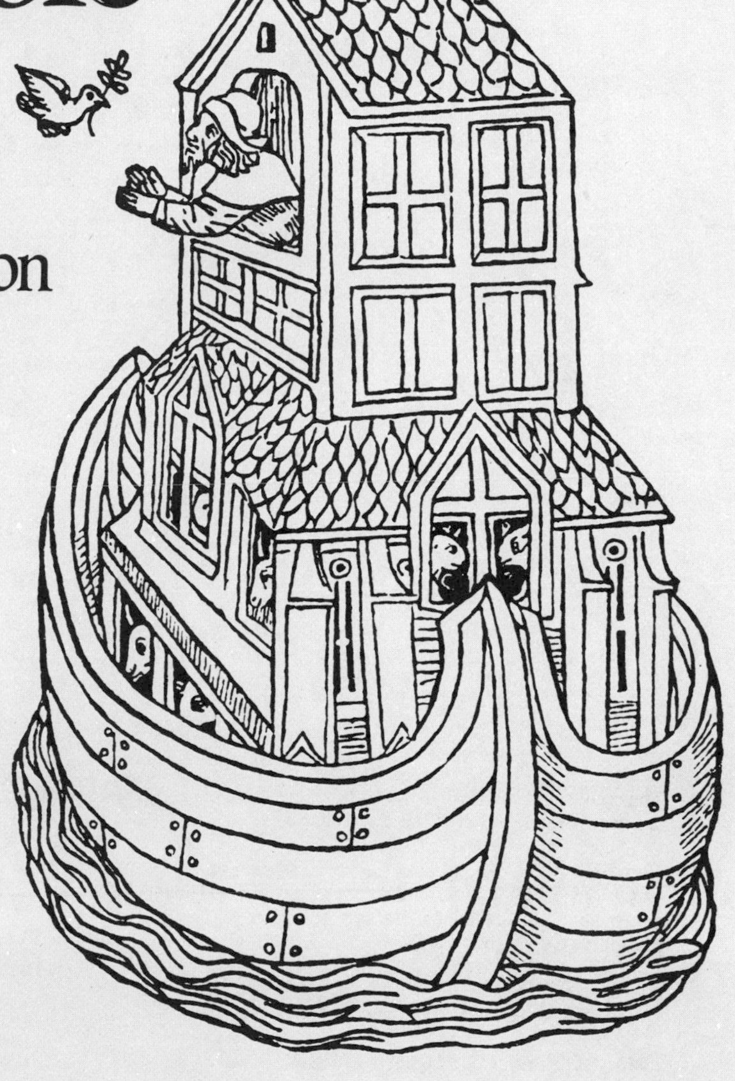

The Reader's Digest Association, Inc.
Pleasantville, New York / Montreal

The credits and acknowledgments that appear on page 832
are hereby made a part of this copyright page.

Library of Congress Cataloging in Publication Data
Main entry under title:

Reader's Digest Family guide to the Bible.

1. Bible—Concordances, English. 2. Bible—
Outlines, syllabi, etc. I. Reader's digest.
II. Bible. English. Authorized. III. Title:
Family guide to the Bible.
BS425.R43 1984 220.5'2033 84-13261
ISBN 0-89577-192-6

READER'S DIGEST and the Pegasus colophon are registered trademarks
of The Reader's Digest Association, Inc.

Printed in the United States of America

Family Guide to the Bible

Project Editor: James Cassidy
Project Art Editor: Kenneth Chaya

Senior Editors: Monica Borrowman, David Rattray
Research Editor: Tanya Strage
Special Typesetting: Grace Del Bagno

Group Editor, General Reference: Joseph L. Gardner

Contributing Researchers: Mary Lyn Maiscott, Nathalie Laguerre
Contributing Picture Researcher: Natalie Goldstein
Contributing Copy Editors: May Dikeman, Kendra K. Ho
Contributing Writers: Bryce Walker, Charles Flowers

PRINCIPAL CONSULTANT

David Noel Freedman
Director, Program on Studies in Religion
The University of Michigan

SPECIAL CONTRIBUTORS AND CONSULTANTS

The editors are deeply indebted to the board of scholars assembled by Geoffrey F. Green of T. & T. Clark Ltd, Edinburgh, Scotland, whose efforts were instrumental in the preparation of this book.

Editors

John C. L. Gibson
Head of Department of Hebrew and Old Testament Studies
New College, Edinburgh

Ian A. Moir
Senior Lecturer in New Testament (Retired)
New College, Edinburgh

Consultant Editor

R. McL. Wilson
Emeritus Professor of Biblical Criticism
St. Mary's College, St. Andrews

Contributors

Kenneth T. Aitken
Lecturer in Hebrew and Semitic Languages
King's College, Old Aberdeen

John Ashton
Former Head of Department of Biblical Studies
Heythrop College, London;
Former Lecturer in Old and New Testament
New College, Edinburgh

A. Graeme Auld
Lecturer in Hebrew and Old Testament Studies
New College, Edinburgh

J. Gordon McConville
Lecturer in Old Testament Studies
Trinity College, Bristol

Roy A. Stewart
Retired Parish and Overseas Minister

Alastair H. Symington
Minister of Craiglockhart, Edinburgh

About This Book

FAMILY GUIDE TO THE BIBLE is, first and foremost, a concordance keyed for use with the King James Version. One of the essential tools of Bible study, a concordance serves as an alphabetical index to words and names that appear in the Scriptures, showing where they occur and in what contexts. To locate a specific phrase or quotation anywhere in the Bible, the reader simply looks up any of the significant words in that phrase. For example, someone wishing to find the famous passage that speaks of turning swords into plowshares can turn to the entry SWORDS, scan the context lines, and find the one that reads,

Isa 2. 4 shall beat their *s* into plowshares,

then open the Bible to the Book of Isaiah, Chapter 2, Verse 4, to read the complete passage. The same result can be obtained by looking up one of the other keywords in this passage, BEAT or PLOWSHARES. The concordance thus enables a reader to locate a favorite verse, check the exact wording of a passage, learn where a particular person or event is described, and trace the recurrence of key phrases and ideas through the Old and New Testaments.

Traditionally, Bible concordances have tended to fall into two categories: at one extreme, exhaustive concordances that list virtually every occurrence of every word; at the other, the modest selections included as appendixes in many editions of the Bible. One of the goals of this volume is to provide readers with an alternative that is comprehensive in scope and depth of coverage—nearly 7,000 keywords and more than 160,000 context lines—yet not so unwieldy that it becomes impractical for quick, everyday use.

In preparing FAMILY GUIDE TO THE BIBLE, the editors first made a careful analysis of *Strong's Exhaustive Concordance of the Bible,* the monumental work compiled over a period of more than 30 years in the late 19th century by the American scholar Dr. James Strong of Drew Theological Seminary. Under the supervision of expert consultants in the United States and Britain, an entry-by-entry review of that volume was conducted to determine how best to reduce the massive text to a more manageable size.

In the end, it was agreed that a considerable number of entries in *Strong's* should be deleted altogether. These included prepositions, pronouns, and most forms of such ubiquitous verbs as *to be, to go, to have,* and *to say*—terms that appear hundreds or thousands of times in the Bible but are relatively unimportant in themselves and serve little use in a concordance. In the illustration above, for instance, it would be foolhardy to search for the passage in Isaiah by looking up *shall, their,* or *into*; the listings of such words would be vast, forcing the reader to conduct a needle-in-the-haystack hunt that would defeat the purpose of this book.

A number of other keyword entries in Strong's text were retained with selective rather than complete references, edited to eliminate repetitive or insignificant citations. It was considered desirable, however, to preserve important entries intact wherever possible; consequently, most of the keywords in this volume appear with complete context listings.

The entire text was freshly typeset in order to produce an attractive, easily readable format (readers familiar with other concordances will appreciate the difference). The output was then subjected to multiple proofreadings to filter out technical and typographical errors—including, as an unexpected bonus, a number of errors that had gone uncorrected for nearly a century in *Strong's Concordance.*

Citations

The citation style used in the references is simple and consistent: as in the sample line above, the abbreviated name of the book is followed by the chapter and verse numbers. (A complete list of abbreviations appears on page 49.)

Readers will encounter occasional variations in this style, the most common of which is a multiple verse reference. When a phrase occurs more than once in the same chapter, the verse numbers are listed together before the context line to avoid repeating the same line for each occurrence. For example, the entry ELEVEN includes the line,

2Ch 36. 5, 11 and he reigned *e* years in

indicating that the same phrase occurs twice in 2 Chronicles, Chapter 36—in Verses 5 and 11.

Most references to the Book of Psalms follow the standard form—Ps 52.12, for instance, signifying Psalm 52, Verse 12. In some cases, however, the reader will notice a citation such as Ps 52(T). This is a reference to the titles that precede individual Psalms in some editions of the Bible; strictly speaking, they are not part of the biblical text, but those of traditional interest have been retained.

A similar but less frequent variation is the use of *sub.* where chapter and verse numbers normally appear. This indicates a subscript added at the end of an Epistle in some Bible editions; for instance, Php *sub.* refers to the subscript following the Epistle to the Philippians.

Spelling and Typography

For the sake of familiarity, the spelling of certain words in the concordance has been changed from British to American style, as has been done in some American editions of the King James Version. For example, *colour* appears here as *color* and *favour* as *favor*. In the rare instances where these changes cause an alphabetical repositioning of a word, such as *enquire* becoming *inquire,* a note appears in the appropriate location.

An exception has been made in the case of a few words with spellings that, though considered archaic in both England and America—*heretick*, for example, and *cloke* instead of *cloak*—preserve some of the distinctive flavor of the language as it was used when the King James Version appeared.

The King James and many other Bibles differentiate typographically between two Hebrew terms for the Deity. The word *Adonai* is usually rendered as "Lord," while the sacred name of God, *Yahweh,* is designated by large and small capitals: "LORD." Since that distinction, although linguistically and theologically important, is not vital to the purposes of this book, the single form "Lord" is used throughout.

Most editions of the King James Version also italicize words that do not have equivalents in the original Hebrew and Greek texts but were added by the translators for the sake of clarity or continuity. Again, since such distinctions are not essential to a concordance, those words are printed here in standard roman type.

Finally, personal pronouns referring to God—*he, him, his*—appear here uncapitalized, following the style of the King James text.

Special Features

In addition to the main concordance listings, FAMILY GUIDE TO THE BIBLE includes a variety of special features designed to broaden and enrich its usefulness as a reference volume.

Two types of features, thematic boxes and biographical entries, are distributed alphabetically throughout the concordance section, which begins on page 51. The thematic boxes present collections of scriptural quotations on topics of lasting importance and interest. They cannot attempt to include everything the Bible has to say on a given subject, of course, but the selections have been made in an effort to reflect the great breadth and diversity of biblical teachings. (A listing of the thematic boxes appears on page 9.) The biographical entries supplement the regular concordance listings with capsule accounts of the lives of more than 60 prominent biblical figures.

Another useful reference tool is the overview of the Bible that begins on page 14, providing a synopsis of each book in the Old and New Testaments and a brief analysis of its historical background and theological significance.

Finally, readers will find an assortment of other features on topics ranging from the long process by which the Bible assumed its present form to a catalog of everyday phrases that originated in the King James Version. All of these, together with the illustrations, maps, and charts that appear throughout its 832 pages, have been prepared with the single goal of making FAMILY GUIDE TO THE BIBLE a versatile, informative, and truly helpful book.

—THE EDITORS

Contents

Thematic Boxes in the Concordance

A
Ability
Absence
Adversity
Age
Anger
Animals

B
Baptism
Beauty
Birth
Blessings
Body
Brotherhood

C
Change
Christ
Church
Compassion
Conscience
Courage

D
Danger
Death
Desire
Devotion
Dishonesty
Doubt
Duty

E
Earth
Education
Envy

F
Faith
Fall
Family
Fate
Fear
Food and Drink
Forgiveness

G
Generosity
God
Good and Evil
Greed
Grief
Guilt

H
Happiness
Health and Sickness
Heaven
Hell
Home
Hope
Hospitality

I
Idolatry
Immortality
Innocence

J
Justice

K
Knowledge

L
Last Things
Law
Liberty
Light and Darkness
Loneliness
Love

M
Man
Marriage
Master and Servant
Memory
Ministry
Music

N
Nation
Nature

O
Offering
Oppression

P
Peace
Plants
Prayer
Pride and Humility
Prosperity
Providence
Prudence

R
Redemption
Reputation
Revelation
Reward and Punishment

S
Salvation
Satan
Sea
Sin
Spirit
Suffering

T
Temptation
Thanksgiving
Time
Tradition
Truth and Falsehood

V
Vigilance
Vows

W
War
Weakness and Strength
Wealth and Poverty
Woman
Work
Worship

Y
Youth

Z
Zeal

The thematic boxes are located alphabetically with the exception of "Animals," which appears on page 106.

A History of the Bible

From generation to generation, the descendants of the patriarch Abraham retold the story of his covenant with the Lord and the promises made to Abraham's children. After the settlement of Canaan, these descendants forsook the life of wandering herdsmen and began to adopt the arts of city-dwellers—writing, among other things. By the time of King David (about 1000 B.C.), scribes and copyists were committing the sacred traditions to papyrus and skin scrolls in the alphabetic system now known as the Early Hebrew.

But this was not the beginning. An ancient tradition ascribes the authorship of the first five books of the Old Testament to Moses. This is unlikely, although Moses had had the training and professional experience of a scribe in Egypt. Most scholars today agree that the early written Scriptures must have gone through a number of preliminary stages impossible to reconstruct at this distance in time. The connection between writing and the Jewish Law is inextricable, from the handing down of the Ten Commandments onward through the generations. (Indeed, the Bible contains hundreds of references to writing or written documents.)

Between the 8th and 6th centuries B.C., the Jewish people suffered two shattering blows: the destruction of the northern kingdom of Israel by the Assyrians and the southern kingdom of Judah by the Babylonians. Mass deportations and destruction followed in each case. When King Cyrus of Persia began his repatriation program, sending thousands of Jews back to Palestine, many other Jews elected to remain in Babylonia under Cyrus; still others had already traveled to other lands, especially Egypt. Aramaic came to replace Hebrew as the common language of the Jews. The Scriptures, however, continued to be written in Hebrew, and great care was taken to ensure the accuracy of the text. "Book correctors" at the newly rebuilt version of Solomon's temple in Jerusalem were on the watch for any additions or deletions in the sacred writings.

The conquests of Alexander the Great in the 4th century B.C. made Greek the paramount language of the Mediterranean, so it seemed a natural step to translate the Scriptures into Greek for the benefit of non-Hebrew-speaking Jews. This translation, known as the Septuagint (Latin for "seventy") after the 70 legendary scholars who started it, was begun shortly after 300 B.C. in Alexandria. It would pose problems later on because it was based on an earlier and different Hebrew text from the standard or Masoretic text of the rabbis, which was not finalized until the 2nd century A.D. And the earlier scholars sometimes made odd choices of words in the actual translation; for example, they translated the Hebrew word for "covenant" as "testament"—the origin of the names later applied to the two parts of the Christian Bible.

Prominent in the background of the decision to produce a Greek translation was the prevailing climate of Hellenism, a world view inherited from the visionary ideas and policies of Alexander the Great. Inseparable from Hellenism was an attitude of enlightened outreach and transcendence of ethnic and religious boundaries. For the first time in history, such notions as the "brotherhood of man" gained popular currency. According to some students of antiquity, the Septuagint translation was in part a missionary effort aimed at the conversion of the pagan world. As matters turned out, it may have done more to Hellenize Jews than to convert Hellenes. To Palestinian rabbis of a later age, the day on which the Septuagint was completed was "as unlucky a day for Israel as the day of the fabrication of the golden calf."

The transmission of the New Testament proceeded in much the same way, although at a much faster pace. The Epistles of Paul were the first to be gathered together, before the end of the 1st century; the four gospels did not appear as a single collection until about A.D. 140. Soon the Christian church began to make use of codices, a codex being sheets of parchment or papyrus folded and sewn together like a book, rather than being rolled up in a scroll.

Over the years, countless copies of the writing of the early leaders of the church went into circulation, suffering from copyists' mistakes, editorial changes, and individual interpretations. In 367, to clarify this confusing state of affairs, Bishop Athanasius of Alexandria established the order of the 27 New Testament books out of a large body of writing, rejecting some that were considered questionable, such as the apocryphal gospels of Thomas and Philip. This became the "canonical" order of the New Testament, after the Greek word *canon*, meaning a measuring rod. But this firm reorganization was not enough. At the request of Pope Damasus I, the matter was taken in hand by Saint Jerome, an extraordinary linguist and scholar.

Recognizing the variant texts that lay behind the Septuagint, Jerome retranslated the Old Testament from the Hebrew text used by the rabbis into Latin. To this new version he added a definitive revision of the New Testament, eliminating as far as possible all introduced errors. This new Bible, later called the Vulgate (the Latin form of this word means "standard" or "common"), became the standard version for Western Christianity until the Reformation, while the Greek-speaking Eastern Church continued to use the Septuagint.

Other early translators were at work too. The Bible was put into several Coptic dialects for the Egyptian churches; the Goths had their own Gothic version; there were Bibles in the Syriac (an Aramaic dialect), Armenian, Georgian, Arabic, and Ethiopic languages.

Although the New Testament had reached England around A.D. 600, hundreds of years were to elapse before a complete English Bible was in use. Translation of the New Testament appeared in the form of glosses, with the Latin text on one line and an Anglo-Saxon version beneath; the most famous of these is a beautifully illuminated Latin manuscript known as the Lindisfarne Gospels, dating from about A.D. 700, with the Anglo-Saxon gloss added in about 950. Psalters or psalm books with interlinear translations were also in use.

The 14th-century reformer and theologian John Wycliffe was responsible for the first Bible translation in English. More than 150 manuscript copies of this pioneering effort still exist. The book was marred by some striking mistakes—"The Lord shall dread his adversaries" instead of "His adversaries shall dread the Lord"—but a subsequent revision, completed between 1388 and 1395, corrected the mistakes and improved the overly literal quality of the first translation.

For more than a century thereafter, the Wycliffe Bible was the only vernacular edition available in England. Wycliffe and his followers had been branded as heretics and his movement was forced underground. But elsewhere, significant events were reshaping the world. First, Constantinople fell to the Turks in 1453 and its scholars fled to the West, bringing with them a long tradition of Byzantine learning. Then, about 1455, Johann Gutenberg's printing press in Mainz produced its first important book, a Bible (the Latin Vulgate). The combination of the increase in the store of learning and the means of disseminating it was the real start of the Renaissance. Before long, vernacular editions of the Bible were being published in French, Italian, Spanish, and German.

One of the outstanding scholars of the "new learning" was the Dutch priest Erasmus, who remains best known today for his famous *Praise of Folly*, in which he pokes fun at the narrow-mindedness and rigidity of the Church in his day. Hankering for a return to the simplicity and purity of primitive Christianity, he studied the Gospels in the original Greek and in 1516 published a Greek New Testament with a Latin pony. Martin Luther, who had for some years differed from Rome on points of doctrine, based his German translation of the New Testament (1522) on Erasmus's Greek text. This marked the first significant departure from the sole use of Jerome's now 1100-year-old Vulgate. Twelve years later Luther completed his work with a translation of the Old Testament from a Hebrew edition that had been published in 1495. This work of Luther's was a milestone in biblical translation. It meant that even those who could read the vernacular but not the classical languages could still have access to an accurate and artistic rendering of the ancient texts.

As the tide of reform surged from the Continent to England, a scholar named William Tyndale tried to convince Church authorities of the need for a printed English Bible. When he failed, he took his translation of Erasmus to Germany for printing. He shipped the books back to England but Henry VIII had the seized copies publicly burned in London as "untrue translations." As Tyndale continued to publish new editions and revisions from abroad, he also began work on the Old Testament, which was only partially completed before his arrest and execution as a heretic by Dutch authorities in 1536. Because of its scholarly accuracy and flowing idiom, Tyndale's translation of the New Testament was heavily mined by the later compilers of the King James Version.

In 1535, Miles Coverdale published the first complete English Bible, based partly on Tyndale's work and partly on translations of German versions by Luther and the Swiss reformer Ulrich Zwingli. Dedicated to Henry VIII, now head of an independent Church of England, it did not get royal approval but was at least spared burning. Just four years later, Coverdale was called on for an authorized version to be placed in every church. Known as the "Great Bible," it was in fact only a reworking of a reworking, not a fresh translation.

When the Catholic Queen Mary came to the throne several years later, succeeding her half-brother Edward VI, a Protestant, she forbade the printing of the English Bible and condemned its use in parish churches. The Bible still had to be in Latin, and explained by the clergy to the faithful. Religious refugees in Geneva promptly undertook another revision of the Great Bible to be smuggled back to England. Known as the Geneva Bible, it achieved enormous popularity among Protestants. It was easy to read, being set in Roman type rath-

This 11th-century Greek Bible is open to Chapter 1 of the Gospel of Mark, which describes the preaching of John the Baptist. The illustration depicts Mark and, above, the baptism of Jesus at the Jordan River and the sudden descent of the Holy Spirit in the form of a dove (Mk 1.9-10).

Isaiah prophesied that "there shall come forth a rod out of the stem of Jesse, and a Branch shall grow out of his roots" (Isa 11.1), and the Church interpreted this as a prophecy of the coming of Jesus Christ. The concept is illustrated on this page of a medieval manuscript containing the Isaiah commentary of St. Jerome, who originated the interpretation.

er than the old heavy Gothic type, and was the first English version to use numbered verses in each chapter.

On succeeding her half-sister in 1558, Queen Elizabeth ordered that an English translation of the Bible again be placed in every parish church. A 1572 revision of this Bible was the basis for the King James edition. Queen Elizabeth's ardent Protestantism produced its own crop of refugees, as Catholics fled to France and Flanders. The English college at Douay in France produced a translation of the Vulgate between 1582 and 1610 that would become the only version authorized for use by English-speaking Catholics for more than 300 years.

King James himself, who assumed the throne in 1603, was the prime mover for the edition of the Bible that bears his name. He disliked the Geneva Bible, saying "I profess I could never yet see a Bible well translated into English, but I think, that of all, that of Geneva is the worst." He wanted a moderate version that would reconcile the quarreling Puritan and Anglican factions within his kingdom.

The King and his ministers appointed 54 scholars, the finest linguists of their time, to set about the project. Working from Cambridge, Oxford, and Westminster, the teams were assigned individual sections of the Bible, read and considered the work of the other teams, and submitted their differences at a general meeting held in London. The result, published in 1611, became the best-known and best-loved version of the English-speaking world. The King James Bible combined great learning with a mastery of style, something all the more remarkable since it was the work of a committee.

During the course of two and one-half centuries, only unauthorized revisions of the King James Version were made, principally to modernize or colloquialize the archaic quality of the original, but none of these achieved much popularity. By 1870, however, there had been advances in scholarship that could affect some readings, so a Revised Version was commissioned. It was completed in 1885, and its textual accuracy was indisputably an improvement on that of its predecessor. But the King James Version, accuracy notwithstanding, retained its unchallenged supremacy.

Several colloquial editions subsequently appeared, particularly in the United States, with the aim of making the Bible more accessible to lay readers. In 1952 the National Council of Churches of Christ produced the influential Revised Standard Version, which sought to preserve the literary tone of the King James translation while incorporating the findings of further linguistic research. Other notable Christian Bibles of recent years include The Amplified Bible (1964), The Jerusalem Bible (1966), The New English Bible with Apocrypha (1970), The New American Bible (1970), The New American Standard Bible (1971), The Living Bible (1971), Good News Bible (1976), and the New International Version (1978). The standard English-language Jewish Bible in the United States remains The Holy Scriptures According to the Masoretic Text (1917; newly translated in 1982).

From its origins in the distant past, the Bible has endured as a legacy that lives on in all the synagogues, churches, and homes of the Judeo-Christian world. Before the invention of the printing press, the Bible had already been translated into 33 languages, seven of them Asiatic and four African. By the end of the 19th century, translations numbered 71, including three American Indian languages. The number of complete translations is now approaching 300, with partial translations in more than a thousand languages and dialects—a tribute to the translators, the "laborers in the vineyard," as well as to the powerful message the Bible bears.

The Dead Sea Scrolls

The 20th century's most astonishing development in Bible history began in the Valley of Qumran west of the Dead Sea, where in 1947 a Bedouin shepherd boy looking for a stray goat chanced upon a cave that may have remained undisturbed for almost 2,000 years. Inside, he found a number of cylindrical jars containing linen-wrapped leather scrolls. These were the first of the famous Dead Sea Scrolls, which eventually added up to hundreds of items as ten more caves yielded their caches, including a unique copper scroll.

Most scholars agree that the writings formed the literature of an ascetic Jewish sect, the Essenes. Their strictly organized community at Qumran, excavated since 1951, was the site of an ancient abandoned city which the brotherhood rebuilt and enlarged during the 2nd century B.C. A monastic center of workshops and communal facilities surrounded by strong walls, it was destroyed by an earthquake in 31 B.C. and left uninhabited until the death of Herod the Great in 4 B.C. Resettled, the community apparently flourished again, only to be razed finally in A.D. 68, when the Tenth Roman Legion marched into the region to put down the first Jewish revolt.

Theories about the Essenes, their beliefs and their possible connection to the early Christian church have been adventurous. Some have felt that John the Baptist must have been an Essene. Others have speculated that Jesus was influenced by Essene teaching or is the Messiah mentioned in Essene texts. In fact, the evidence of the scrolls indicates that the Essenes were a distinct group of puritanical believers whose principles were different from and even antithetical to those of the early followers of Jesus. No direct links between the Essenes and the beginnings of Christianity have been found. They were, however, on the same general fringe—both groups believed that the last days were at hand in a soon-to-culminate battle between the powers of light and darkness, and both believed in the imminent coming of a Messiah.

The scrolls, written generally in Hebrew in a beautiful hand, form a Bible library including a number of nearly complete Old Testament texts and hundreds of fragmentary documents, together with Apocryphal and Essene writings, some of which were known before the discovery of the scrolls only in Latin, Greek, Syriac, Ethiopic, and other translations. Translators have also found important commentaries on Biblical texts and *florilegia*, or collections of sacred texts.

Among the most significant scrolls are those which give the history of the Qumran community and detail its monastic rules: the Habakkuk Commentary, the War Scroll, and the Manual of Discipline. The Habakkuk Commentary relates Essene history to the prophecies contained in the biblical Book of Habakkuk. A Right-Teacher, who reveals God's plan to destroy all but those who are faithful to the Torah and join a community led by the teacher himself, comes into conflict with the Wicked Priest, presumably the high priest at Jerusalem. The Wicked Priest drives the Right-Teacher and his sect into exile. Soon, this priest is destroyed and the nation falls to the conquering Kittim—who, scholars believe, may have been the Greeks, both of Syria (the Seleucids) and of Egypt (the Ptolemies). Later, the Romans may also have been so designated. If the Right-Teacher and the Wicked Priest were actual historical figures—a distinct possibility—their identities were unfortunately not preserved.

In the War Scroll, Essene writers describe the final conflict to come between the forces of good and evil, an apocalyptic vision ending with God's judgment. The holy war, which lasts 40 years, will see both victory and defeat in turn for the Children of Light, who will eventually vanquish all of the enemies of Israel—Edom, Moab, Ammon, the Philistines, the "Kittim of Assur" (that is, the Seleucids), the "Kittim of Egypt" (the Ptolemies), and the "kings of the North." Curiously, the War Scroll gives the rules for very realistic, contemporary military equipment and tactics—for example, such Roman innovations as the wedge formation, the scissors formation, and the *testudo* ("tortoise") formation of interlocked shields.

Our most dependable insights into the character of the Essene brotherhood come from the prescriptions of the Manual of Discipline, of which fragments of eleven manuscripts have come to light. Believing themselves to represent the true covenant of God, the Essenes were convinced that they alone had found the correct interpretation of Old Testament Law and must therefore live in communities separate from all other Jews. A novice was expected to undergo years of instruction and severe examination. Purification rites, morning and evening prayers, sacred meals, and other rituals are prescribed in the Manual.

Above, part of a scroll containing a nearly complete Hebrew text of Isaiah, and two earthenware jars in which some of the scrolls were found in the Qumran caves.

From the Manual and other Essene writings, scholars have assembled a picture of a community which aimed to lead a life of continuous worship but which understood the importance of addressing practical matters as well. A financial administrator distributed the communal property and earnings according to individual needs. A priest-president-general governed the sect; the brotherhood was symbolically divided into 12 tribes, and then into smaller units down to the basic group of ten led by a priest-president. Evidently, these scrolls present the ideal toward which the desert community aspired.

In addition to various collections of hymns, prayers, and Biblical commentaries, the Dead Sea caves also concealed a copper scroll listing the hiding places of an enormous treasure scattered all over Palestine. Some scholars think the list is imaginary, but others feel it might indicate actual caches of precious objects and money from the temple.

When the scrolls were first discovered, it was widely expected that they would revolutionize our understanding of the New Testament and even provide a "missing link" between Judaism and Christianity. This was too much to expect. Nevertheless, the Scrolls do shed important new light on accepted Scripture. In addition to telling us about the Essenes in their own words, they provide insights into the text of the Hebrew Bible and its history, enabling us to reconstruct older forms of the original text. Further, they offer information on the Judaism of the intertestamental period, the 200-year span between the writing of the last canonical book of the Old Testament and the writing of the New Testament books. This was the era that saw the history of the last independent Jewish state before modern Israel—the Maccabean kingdom of the 2nd and 1st centuries B.C.—the subsequent Roman occupation, and the destruction of Jerusalem in A.D. 70.

Finally, the Scrolls evidence indirect but important links with early Christianity in terms of doctrines, scriptural interpretation, and other matters. The two groups, the Qumran nonconformists and the infant church, lived in a similar social environment, both standing apart from Judea's religious and cultural mainstream. While the most sensational claims and speculations have been discounted, therefore, the Scrolls' value to biblical scholarship is clear and considerable, and they remain one of the century's luckiest discoveries.

The Books of the Bible

The original Hebrew Bible consists of 24 books, traditionally categorized under three basic headings: the Torah, or Law (5 books, Genesis through Deuteronomy), the Prophets (8 books), and the Writings (11 books). The Prophets are classified as Former (Joshua, Judges, Samuel, and Kings; the division into 1 and 2 Samuel and 1 and 2 Kings appears only in the Christian Bible) and Latter (Isaiah, Jeremiah, and Ezekiel, the three "major prophets"; and the Book of the Twelve, the "minor prophets" that appear individually in the Christian Bible as Hosea through Malachi). The remaining books are the Writings; Ezra and Nehemiah form one book, as do 1 and 2 Chronicles. The 24 books of the Hebrew Bible are divided and rearranged into the 39 books of the Protestant Old Testament. The Catholic Old Testament likewise contains these 39 books and, in addition, includes seven books from the body of writings that appears in a separate, non-canonical section in many Protestant Bibles as the Apocrypha (see page 28). The Greek Orthodox Bible follows the Catholic canon with some further additions.

The Old Testament took shape over a long period of time; more than a thousand years separate its earliest and latest books. The history of the Israelites contained in the Torah (also called the Pentateuch, Greek for "five books") was already a centuries-old oral tradition when it was written down sometime after 1000 B.C. A number of the books were composed after the return from the Babylonian captivity in the 6th century B.C. And the story of Daniel, an exile prophet in Babylon, was not set down in writing until about 165 B.C.

A literary work of almost infinite variety, the Old Testament has been described as containing "prose and poetry, myth and legend, folk tale and history, sacred hymns and a superb love song, religious and secular laws, proverbs of the wise and oracles of the prophets, epic poems, laments, parables, and allegories." Its majestic and unifying theme, of course, the message that has resounded through the ages, is the belief in one God, a God of justice and mercy.

GENESIS

The first five books of the Bible—Genesis, Exodus, Leviticus, Numbers, and Deuteronomy—are uniquely important in Scripture. Known collectively as the Torah, or Law, in Jewish tradition and as the Pentateuch by Christians, they lay a foundation of belief for two great religions. Scribes compiled the books over time by drawing upon the oral tradition of the early Israelites as handed down through generations. (Another common designation, the Books of Moses, refers to the fact that Moses, as the principal lawgiver, is their protagonist.) The books embrace an enormous variety of material: moral doctrine, rituals of worship, laws and customs, tribal genealogies, and stirring historical narrative. But all point to one essential theme: the special relationship between the God of Israel and his Chosen People.

The Book of Genesis, or "origins," is largely narrative and falls into two main sections: a collection of epic tales about the world from its creation through the time of Noah and the Flood (Gen 1–11); and the early history of the Israelites, as told through the lives of their tribal patriarchs, Abraham, Isaac, Jacob, and Joseph (Gen 12–50).

The creation story tells how God shaped the world from chaos, made Adam and Eve, and placed them at its choicest spot, the Garden of Eden (Gen 1–2). But Adam's attachment to Eve soon leads him to disobey God's orders. He eats forbidden fruit from the tree of knowledge, and as punishment God expels him and Eve from the garden (Gen 3). Out in the world Eve bears the couple's two sons; Cain, the elder, angry at God's rejection of his sacrifice, slays his brother, Abel, and is condemned to a fugitive's life (Gen 4). Adam's descendants populate the earth (Gen 5), founding cities and developing the arts of civilization. But mankind's impulse to misbehave persists. Finally God, in frustration and anger, sends a great flood to sweep away the evildoers, sparing only Noah and his family in their ark filled with representative wildlife. When the waters recede, God promises Noah he will never again inflict such watery vengeance upon mankind and confirms the promise with a rainbow (Gen 6–9).

In the centuries that follow, Noah's progeny replenish the earth (Gen 10), only to fall once again into error. They raise a lofty pyramid, the tower of Babel, hoping to reach heaven. God sees this as a rebellious attempt to usurp his place and confounds the builders by causing them to speak in mutually incomprehensible languages (Gen 11). As with the other parables in this opening section, the meaning is clear: God intends mankind to live in quiet harmony upon the good and fruitful earth, but man's natural wickedness has always worked to upset this plan. So God must continually intervene in hopes of regaining man's loyalty and obedience.

The second section of Genesis, more clearly historical, takes place in the Near East during the 2nd millennium B.C. and begins with the story of Abraham, a pastoral wanderer who is the first of Israel's patriarchs. At God's bidding Abraham leaves his homeland in Mesopotamia to roam the area we know as the Fertile Crescent (Gen 12–25). He arrives in Canaan, goes to Egypt because of a famine, then returns to Canaan. Along the way God offers him a covenant: the promise of a glorious destiny, a land of his own, and a multitude of descendants to live in it—if he keeps God's faith and obeys his will in all things. Years go by, however, before Abraham can produce an heir by his aged, presumably barren wife Sarah. Finally God gives them a son, Isaac. But as the boy grows toward manhood, God orders Abraham to sacrifice his son as a burnt offering. At the very last moment God stops the patriarch and reaffirms the covenant. "I will bless thee, and in multiplying, I will multiply thy seed as the stars of heaven," the Lord declares, ". . . and in thy seed shall all the nations of the earth be blessed, because thou hast obeyed my voice."

Isaac's heirs are his twin sons, Esau and Jacob (Gen 26–36). To modern readers Jacob may appear to be a sly and even mean-spirited man; he steals his brother's birthright and then his father's sacred blessing. Even so, God loves Jacob. In a dream in which angels ascend and descend a ladder into heaven, God speaks again of the covenant, with its promise of land and a powerful nation of descendants. Jacob travels to Aram, the land of his uncle, where he stays 14 years tending his uncle's flocks. He weds his two cousins, Leah and Rachel, who together with their handmaidens Bilhah and Zilpah bear him 12 sons—the founding fathers of Israel's 12 tribes.

The final chapters (Gen 37–50) contain the story of Joseph and his 11 brothers, a superb narrative in which God's benevolent hand is seen to guide the destinies of the protagonists. Joseph, sold into slavery in Egypt by the treachery of his brothers, gains Pharaoh's favor and rises to the powerful post of grand vizier. When a great famine sweeps the Near East, Joseph takes in his brethren and feeds them from Egypt's well-stocked granaries. Genesis closes on a note of hope, with the implication that God will provide for his Chosen People until the time his promises to Abraham begin to take effect.

EXODUS

The Book of Exodus carries the Old Testament narrative to a new level of significance; no longer the tale of a single family, it now becomes the chronicle of a nation—the people of Israel. It also marks the arrival of Moses, the supreme hero of the Pentateuch, who leads the descendants of Abraham, Isaac, and Jacob out of Egypt (Ex 1–18) and into the Sinai; there a new covenant is made and laws are handed down governing life and worship (Ex 19–40).

As the story opens, the Israelites are held in bondage by the Egyptians, who use them as slaves. Pharaoh, disturbed by their growing numbers, orders that all newborn Israelite males be put to death (Ex 1). But the baby Moses, hidden among the bulrushes of the Nile, escapes. He is found by Pharaoh's daughter, who adopts him as her own son. Upon reaching manhood, he leaves Egypt to escape punishment for killing an Egyptian and goes to the land of Midian, in present-day Arabia (Ex 2). One day, while tending sheep in the desert, Moses hears God speaking out of a burning bush. God appoints him as emissary to Pharaoh, with instructions to demand the release of his people from servitude (Ex 3–4). When Pharaoh refuses, God sends a series of plagues, designed to force Pharaoh's compliance (Ex 5–10). The Egyptian ruler remains obdurate until, in a final scourge, God slays every first-born Egyptian child. Miraculously, no child of the Israelites is harmed—a deliverance that is celebrated in the first Passover feast (Ex 11–13).

With the Israelites now freed from Pharaoh's yoke, Moses leads them out of Egypt and into the desert in search of the rich and fertile land that God had promised to their forefather Abraham. When they reach the Red Sea, the waters miraculously part—and then close abruptly to engulf an army that Pharaoh, in a last-minute change of heart, has sent to bring his former vassals back (Ex 14–15). The Israelites continue their journey through the wilderness. The way is bitterly hard, however, causing them to murmur and complain. God sends food—manna from heaven—and water from a rock that Moses smites with his staff (Ex 16–18).

When the travelers reach the Sinai, the Exodus story shifts from straight narrative to an exposition of God's law. As this section opens, God offers a new covenant, which the Israelites accept; in confirmation, God displays his power and magnificence with thunder, lightning, and a trumpet blast from atop Mount Sinai (Ex 19). God then summons Moses to the mountaintop, where he reveals the covenant law. Its essence is contained in the Ten Commandments (Ex 20), which are further spelled out in more detailed ordinances (Ex 21–23). The covenant is sealed by a sprinkling of blood, as the people pledge their obedience (Ex 24). God then recalls Moses to deliver instructions for building a tabernacle (Ex 25–31).

But no sooner has Moses departed for this second conference on the mountaintop than the people relapse into sin. Melting down their jewelry and coin, they fashion a golden calf and proceed to worship it. When Moses returns and sees what has happened, he falls into a fury. God's covenant has been inscribed on a pair of stone tablets, and these he now smashes upon the ground—thus delivering a graphic lesson on the fruits of apostasy. God's punishment, harsh and bloody, quickly follows. Moses intercedes, however, and the covenant and tablets are replaced (Ex 32–34).

Exodus closes with a detailed description of the tabernacle and its furnishings, as built according to God's earlier instructions (Ex 35–40). The intent is to stress God's continued presence among his people: a god who is holy yet approachable.

The stirring epic recounted in Exodus provides the basis of Israel's life and faith. A proud but oppressed people, held captive in an alien land, is singled out by God and redeemed through his mighty acts. A relationship of mutual dedication is established and sealed with a covenant. Israel's history as the community of God in the world is thus set upon its course.

But there is another side to the story. Though filled with miraculous incidents, the narrative of Exodus displays a keen, all too realistic sense of human frailty and sinfulness. No sooner do the Israelites escape into the desert than they yearn for the comforts they have left behind in Egypt; no sooner do they reach a formal agreement with God than they break it. A pattern of behavior begins to emerge: entering into a covenant opens up the possibility of rebelling against it, with a consequent provoking of divine wrath, judgment, and finally, in God's grace, renewal. This sequence will repeat itself time after time throughout Israel's history and will lead future prophets to look forward to a day when God again intervenes, leading his people once more out of exile in a new exodus and declaring an even newer covenant.

LEVITICUS

Leviticus continues the body of law and instruction begun in Exodus, with particular emphasis on the rituals of worship. It deals with the nature of the tabernacle, wherein God dwells among the people yet preserves his sanctity behind a protective wall of clearly defined religious observances. The book's title, in fact, refers to the Levitical priests who minister at the tabernacle and the sacred area around it. Its contents are: laws of sacrifices (Lev 1–7), of the priesthood (Lev 8–10), of cleanness and uncleanness (Lev 11–15); observances for the Day of Atonement (Lev 16); and miscellaneous laws focused on the theme of holiness (Lev 17–27). These are presented as the ritual and practice of Mosaic times, though most scholars believe they reflect the later period of the First Temple, after numerous additions over many generations of worship.

Central to the thinking of Leviticus is the concept of ritual purity. In Old Testament belief reality exists under three conditions: the unclean, that is, people or things unfit to participate in communal or religious activity; the clean, or people and things that are thus fit; and the holy, or that which is specifically designated as belonging to God. More precisely, only that which is clean may remain within the "camp," while only that which is holy may enter the tabernacle. Holy objects, moreover, must be handled only by priests, while only the high priest may penetrate to the inner sanctum—and then only once a year. People can become temporarily unclean through such circumstances as illness or certain sexual conditions; they can also, through a process of atonement, regain their purity. The very concept of ritual uncleanness may seem bewildering to most Westerners—but it persists to this day in various Middle Eastern cultures. The relevant point for Israel was that the nation must be holy because God is holy; any uncleanness threatened the relationship of God to his people and had to be prevented or rectified for the common good.

Regulations for sacrifice occupy a prominent place in Leviticus. Three broad categories of sacrifice are described: burnt offerings of slain animals, which are fully consumed on the altar; peace offerings, of which parts are burned and parts set aside as payment to the priests; and cereal offerings, which consist of grain or unleavened bread and which also are divided into a portion for the priests and a portion to be set afire for God. Each of the types tends to carry a specific meaning. Thus a burnt offering might symbolize the giver's total dedication, while a peace offering would speak to the close relationship between God and the community. Beyond this, all sacrifice is seen as a plea for atonement—a bid to restore the giver to ritual cleanness, or to wipe out the blemish of some past sin or moral guilt. Indeed, as so often in Leviticus, the two conditions—sinfulness and ritual impurity—are treated as being closely analogous.

The Israelites understood the difference between religious observance and ethics in general but believed that both were important and necessary to establish and maintain the correct relationship to God. To them, the commands of God had a basic unity. And so Leviticus, filled as it is with ceremonial regulations, is also permeated with a high moral tone.

NUMBERS

The Book of Numbers returns to the narrative epic of the Israelites' wilderness journey, carrying them from Mount Sinai to the very edge of Canaan—the Promised Land. It is a lengthy, often discouraging pilgrimage. Time and again the travelers come near to losing their faith in God's purpose. Only the prompt intervention of Moses, backed by God's guiding, disciplinary hand, brings them back to their destined path. In summary, it is the beginning of the fulfillment of God's great promise of nationhood.

The opening section describes the preparations for leaving Mount Sinai (Nu 1–10). These include a detailed census of the 12 Israelite tribes—thus the book's title—along with various ceremonies of departure. The tribes set out, at the command of Moses, the Ark of the Covenant carried before them.

In the book's second section, the travelers make their way to the oasis of Kadesh-barnea, just south of the Negeb (Nu 11–20). They have come to within striking distance of Canaan, and Moses sends out a party of scouts to survey the territory. When the spies return with distressing reports of Canaan's great military strength, the people murmur against their leaders, saying it would be better to be back in Egypt. Nonetheless, the Israelites attack—without Moses and the Ark—and are defeated. As further punishment for their weakness, God condemns them to wander another 40 years in the desert and decrees that no member of the adult generation shall live to see the Promised Land. Only Caleb and Joshua, two scouts who had urged an immediate attack on Canaan despite the odds, are exempted.

Weary and discouraged, the Israelites make their way back into the desert and then swing north through present-day Jordan. And under God's protection their fortunes begin to turn as they win heated battles against the Amorites. By the end of the third section (Nu 21–36), they have reached the Plains of Moab, where they can look out across the Jordan River to Jericho and, at long last, the Promised Land of Canaan.

Embedded in this narrative are lengthy recitations of Mosaic law, much of it suggested by events on the journey. Thus a part of the first section—the departure from Mount Sinai—lists the duties of the Levitical priests who will officiate (Nu 3–4), along with various conditions for observing the Passover (Nu 9). As the travelers near Canaan, regulations are proposed for taking possession of the land. Provisions are made for inheriting property (Nu 27) and for dividing the territory among the various tribes (Nu 32–35). Some of the laws appear to be extraordinarily harsh; a man caught gathering firewood on the Sabbath is, on God's orders, stoned to death (Nu 15). Yet in a chapter on punishments for homicide, care is taken to protect the suspect from tribal vengeance and to bring him safely to trial (Nu 35).

The overriding theme in Numbers is God's total commitment to his people—despite their frequent lapses from faith. He deals swiftly with their shortcomings; when a number of Moses' followers attempt a mutiny, for example, God opens the earth and swallows them up (Nu 16). Then, often as not, he steps in to defend the Israelites from their enemies. The confrontation with Balak, king of Moab, is a case in point. When the king hires the sorcerer Balaam to lay a curse on Israel, God intervenes to win over the magician. Instead of a curse, Israel receives Balaam's heartfelt blessing (Nu 22–24). All through the wilderness, in fact, God's presence is felt, until the journey's hardships are seen as a testing and strengthening for the final occupation of Canaan.

DEUTERONOMY

Deuteronomy, meaning "second lawgiving," expands and redefines the Mosaic tradition established thus far in the Pentateuch. Containing both moral instruction and a lengthy code of statutes and religious ordinances, it consists of three sermons by Moses, for the benefit of the younger generation that has reached adulthood during the period of wandering.

The book opens as Moses, encamped near the Jordan River on the Plains of Moab, recalls the wilderness journey from Mount Sinai: the sending of scouts into Canaan, the 40 years in the desert, the victories in Jordan against Kings Sihon and Og, the apportioning of the land among various tribes, and the designation of Joshua as his successor (Dt 1–3). There follows an extended review of the encounter with God on Mount Sinai, along with further explanation of his teaching (Dt 4). The Ten Commandments are restated in a slightly different form (Dt 5). The heart of the next chapter—"Thou shalt love the Lord thy God with all thine heart, and with all thy soul"—has deeply influenced Jewish piety in daily prayer and practice (Dt 6). Warnings are then given against ingratitude and apostasy when the Israelites reach the Promised Land (Dt 7–8), followed by a recitation of the golden calf incident at Sinai (Dt 9) and sundry other misdemeanors (Dt 10–11).

Next comes a detailed code of the laws themselves. It begins by insisting on a divinely appointed central sanctuary for offerings and sacrifice (Dt 12). Apostasy is never to be countenanced, even at the instigation of a successful diviner or prophet (Dt 13). Clean and unclean meats are defined (Dt 14), then circumstances for releasing debtors from their obligations, and a statement of God's claim to the firstborn goat or calf from each herd (Dt 15). That leads to rules for the Passover and the other great annual festivals (Dt 16). The duties of officials are detailed—judges, the king, priests and Levites, and prophets (Dt 16–18). Standards for administering justice (Dt 19) and for making war (Dt 20) are laid down; both themes are then developed (Dt 21). Proper respect is decreed for all life and for family relationships in particular (Dt 22). Miscellaneous rules of purity follow (Dt 23), then various broadly humanitarian provisions (Dt 24–25). The end of the legislation matches the beginning, with the appointment of two brief liturgies for use at the chosen sanctuary (Dt 26).

Moses offers the people a choice: benefits for those who observe the code that follows, penalties for those who disobey. Blessings are far outnumbered by curses, several of them depicting the horrors of invasion, depopulation, and exile (Dt 27–29). But after disaster a future is envisaged: divine compassion and a return to obedience. And for those who choose to obey God's word, a future of abundance and prosperity is pictured (Dt 30).

In its final section Deuteronomy returns to history. It concludes with Joshua installed (Dt 31); two farewell poems by Moses: a "song" (Dt 32) and a "blessing" (Dt 33); and the report of Moses' death as the aging patriarch looks west across the Jordan to the Promised Land (Dt 34).

With the death of Moses the five books of the Pentateuch come to an end. Israel's history now enters a new and triumphant phase, with the conquest of Canaan and the building of a mighty kingdom under David and Solomon. All this occurs in the next sequence of Old Testament works, known collectively as the Prophets.

JOSHUA

In the Book of Joshua—the first of the so-called Prophets—the narrative of the Old Testament reaches a historic turning point, the culmination of past events and a prologue for future ones. Moses, the great lawgiver, has died, having brought his people out of Egypt and, after 40 years of wandering, to the very threshold of Canaan. It now falls to Joshua, his longtime aide and chosen successor, to lead them across the Jordan River and take possession of the land. In so doing, Joshua will fulfill God's ancient promise to Abraham and at the same time set the stage for the epic drama of Israel yet to unfold.

The book falls into three parts: the conquest of Canaan (Jos 1–12), the division of land among the tribes of Israel (Jos 13–22), and Joshua's farewell and death (Jos 23–24).

In the opening section Joshua prepares by sending two spies into the walled city of Jericho, where they are aided by the harlot Rahab in return for a pledge that her family will be spared (Jos 1–2). After they report back to Joshua, the flow of the Jordan is miraculously halted, permitting the Ark to be carried across the dry riverbed. All the Israelites follow, and on Joshua's orders a memorial of stones is erected at Gilgal and all the males born in the wilderness are circumcised (Jos 3–5). Shortly, in the first and most famous military encounter, the walls of Jericho collapse at the sound of the Israelites' shouts and trumpets; all its inhabitants, except Rahab's family, are slain, and all objects of value seized as an offering to God (Jos 6). It is soon learned, however, that an Israelite named Achan kept some of the treasure for himself—a transgression for which he and his family are executed (Jos 7). The city of Ai is the next to fall, followed by victories against the kings of five other cities and a final consolidation of power in southern Canaan. Only the Gibeonites escape destruction, thanks to a ruse through which they elicit a pledge of alliance from Joshua before he learns their true identity (Jos 8–10). A subsequent campaign in the north, including the burning of Hazor, concludes Joshua's military exploits, which are recapitulated in a listing of 31 vanquished kings (Jos 11–12).

The second section details the distribution of territory among the various tribes, including the establishment of the Lord's tabernacle at Shiloh and the building of a second altar by the Jordan River (Jos 13–22).

After the passage of many years the aging Joshua makes a farewell address to the people of Israel, exhorting them to follow the law of Moses and to renew their covenant with the Lord. He dies at the age of 110 and is buried in Mount Ephraim (Jos 23–24).

The Book of Joshua offers a vivid historical narrative, rich in graphic detail about the conquest and territorial division of Canaan. Nevertheless, it is better understood as a theological document—a powerful reassertion of the laws and traditions set forth in the Pentateuch—than as a factual account of events in the 13th century B.C. Modern archeological research, while corroborating certain incidents such as the destruction of Hazor, has tended to support what many biblical scholars had already concluded from the Book of Judges and other scriptural evidence: that the Israelites' occupation of the Promised Land was not nearly so swift or complete as the Joshua story suggests. It was actually a process that took place unevenly over many generations. But the editors of the book's final version, which probably dates from the 6th century B.C., compressed and streamlined earlier narratives—presumably to dramatize their fundamental belief that this was the fulfillment of God's promise, made possible only by divine assistance. The same point is implied by the recurrence of miraculous incidents: the halting of the Jordan's flow, the collapse of Jericho's walls, the lethal storm of hailstones, and the sun's standing still in the sky. In effect, the message in Joshua is that the conquest was God's victory, not the Israelites'—and that only through strict adherence to their covenant would they continue to enjoy God's special protection.

JUDGES

The Israelites' triumphant entry into Canaan, led by Joshua, by no means secured their future in the Promised Land. Many battles had yet to be fought against various local kingdoms before each tribe could take possession of its allotted territory. The Book of Judges is the story of these conflicts. It contains a riveting collection of military folk epics, each centered on the exploits of a particular tribal hero—the judges of the title, who act as warriors, sages, and religious leaders.

The book opens with a brief reprise of the early settlement in Canaan under Joshua, along with a moralizing reference to God's covenant and the dire consequences of breaking it (Jdg 1–2). Three minor judges then emerge: Othniel; Ehud, who slays the king of the Moabites; and Shamgar, who demolishes 600 Philistines with an ox goad (Jdg 3). The next judge is a woman, the prophet Deborah, who inspires Israel to overcome the Canaanites; right after the battle another heroic female, Jael, the wife of Heber, dispatches the Canaanite general by driving a tent peg through his temple (Jdg 4–5).

The next great tribal champion, Gideon, is one of the book's most appealing figures. Fierce in battle—he routs a huge army of Midianites with just 300 carefully chosen men—he is offered the kingship of all Israel, but modestly declines. "The Lord shall rule over you," he says. And he retires to his house to sire 70 sons (Jdg 6–8).

Upon Gideon's death, the tribes of Israel fall to bickering among themselves. One of his sons, Abimelech, names himself judge in Shechem, murdering most of his brethren to secure his claim. The people rebel, and in the ensuing battle Abimelech is mortally wounded (Jdg 9). Then another mighty warrior emerges, Jephthah of Gilead, who delivers his people from oppression by the powerful Ammonites. He pays a terrible price, however. To ensure victory, he has sworn to offer up in sacrifice whatsoever first comes to meet him on his return home. That unfortunate creature turns out to be his only daughter—and he must keep his vow. Nor are his troubles over: a dispute breaks out between his tribe and the people of Ephraim, and he is forced into battle against his fellow Israelites (Jdg 10–12).

The best known of the book's stories is that of Samson, the ultimate strong man and a worthy defender of Israel against the Philistines (Jdg 13–16). Dedicated from birth to God's service, Samson suffers a fatal weakness—his passion for the Philistine woman Delilah. In an intimate moment he tells her the secret of his great prowess—no razor has ever touched his head—and Delilah quickly summons confederates who lop off his hair. Thus drained of strength, Samson is blinded and enslaved. But in captivity his hair grows back, and with it his former powers. Offering a final prayer to God, he heaves down the main pillars of the Philistine temple, where most of his enemies have gathered for a feast. Samson dies in the rubble, taking large numbers of Philistines with him.

Disputes continue to break out among the Israelites as the various tribes seek to establish themselves in Canaan. The people of Dan, driven north by the Philistines, trek through the lands of Ephraim to a new area, and on the way they make off with an Ephraimite priest (Jdg 17–18). Another Ephraimite holy man journeys through territory belonging to the tribe of Benjamin, where some unruly townsmen rape and murder his favorite concubine. Crying vengeance, the other tribes band together to assault the Benjamites, all but destroying them (Jdg 19–21).

On this discordant note the book ends, with the rueful observation that "In those days there was no king in Israel: every man did that which was right in his own eyes." A cyclical pattern emerges from the events described in Judges: as the people settle on the land, they fall into error and are punished by an enemy sent against them by God; after they suffer, repent, and cry out for help, God sends them a savior in the person of a judge who leads them to victory against their oppressors; they settle in peace—only to fall again into error as the cycle begins again. Thus Judges uses history to underscore the same moral lesson propounded in Deuteronomy: whenever the Israelites obey God's commandments, they gain victory and prosperity; but when they fall short, there is disaster.

RUTH

The Book of Ruth, with its mood of quiet romance, tells one of the Bible's most charming stories. Though set in the same period as Judges, it has a warmth and an intimacy that is in sharp contrast to the strife of those days.

On one level the book is a simple country idyll about family loyalty. Famine drives a couple and their two sons from Judah to Moab, across the Dead Sea. Elimelech, the father, dies. Both sons marry local women, and themselves die. Their mother, Naomi, finds herself bereft in a strange land. She urges both young widows to make a fresh start among their own people; but Ruth insists on accompanying her back to Bethlehem, where there is now a report of food (Ru 1).

Once in Bethlehem the two women still have no means of support. So Ruth, claiming the prerogative of the destitute, goes to glean the leftover grain from the barley harvest. She catches the eye of a prosperous field owner, Boaz, who is also a kinsman of her late husband. Boaz encourages her, matching his generosity to his admiration for her loyalty to Naomi (Ru 2). Naomi responds by sending Ruth, on the night of the harvest feast, to seek from Boaz her widow's right of a child by her husband's relative (Ru 3). And though Ruth is an alien—and a Moabite at that—Boaz takes her as his legal wife. In time she bears him a son, Obed, whose grandson in turn will become King David (Ru 4)—thus giving Israel's great king a Moabite ancestor.

But beyond the parable of loyalty and love, Ruth can be read as a tale in sharp contrast to the strictures against marriage outside the clan that are found in the Pentateuch and were so rigidly enforced in the time of Ezra and Nehemiah.

1 and 2 SAMUEL

The Books of Samuel—once a single volume—recount the period in Israel's history from the birth of the prophet Samuel to the rise and reign of King David. This was a time of critical, often painful transition, which would see Israel transformed from a confederacy of independent, often divided tribes, separately ruled by judges though bound together by a common religious loyalty, to a unified state under a dynastic monarchy. The first book chronicles the emergence of Samuel, the last of the judges, and the choice of Saul as Israel's first king (1Sa 1–12); then Saul's early reign and his rejection by God for disobedience (1Sa 13–15); and finally Saul's decline and David's rise (1Sa 16–31). The second book gives the story of David's reign (2Sa 1–24).

The narrative begins with a description of Samuel's birth and his dedication to serve under the priest Eli in the temple at Shiloh. There he is called by God and in time wins recognition throughout all Israel as his prophet (1Sa 1–3). Hereafter Samuel will play the leading role in guiding Israel through the troubled times of transition.

A shattering military defeat at Aphek (1Sa 4) marks the beginning of the end of the era of the judges. Here the victorious Philistines gain a political supremacy that threatens Israel's very existence. Even worse, they capture the Ark of God and destroy the sanctuary at Shiloh, thus depriving the Israelites of the focus of their common religious life. Later, when plagues break out among the Philistines, the Ark is hurriedly returned (1Sa 5–6); but the shock to Israel's religious and political well-being leaves the old system of tribal confederacy all but exhausted. Only Samuel's firm leadership prevents its total collapse. Summoning the people to repentance, he rallies them to a victory over the Philistines (1Sa 7).

But Samuel's judgeship can only postpone, not avert, the changes about to take place, and he is soon obliged to appoint the handsome young Saul as Israel's first king (1Sa 8–12). Two conflicting accounts are given of Saul's accession, undoubtedly reflecting the Israelites' deeply mixed feelings about the shift into monarchy. In one, the people's request for a king is seen as an act of rebellion against God, and warning is given of its possibly dire consequences; but the request is granted, and Saul is selected by lot at Mizpeh (1Sa 8, 10). In the other account, Saul is seen as God's chosen prince and is anointed by Samuel on divine instructions; Saul then gains a notable victory over the Ammonites and is acclaimed king of the Israelites at Gilgal (1Sa 9, 11).

The second part of 1 Samuel (1Sa 13–15) details Saul's campaigns against the Philistines and the Amalekites and summarizes his considerable military achievements. His successes are marred, however, by Saul's tendency to stray from God's commandments, as conveyed to him through Samuel. When ordered to exterminate the Amalekites and their livestock, for example, Saul spares their king, Agag, and their prize sheep and cattle. As a result, he finds himself rebuked and his kingship revoked.

In the third section (1Sa 16–31) the stories of Saul and David are intertwined—the one rejected and the other anointed as his divinely chosen successor. For Saul it is a tragic account of decline: brooding over his sins, deprived of Samuel's prophetic support, consumed with jealousy of David, and thus distracted from the larger affairs of his kingdom. But for David it is a steady march to greatness, beginning with the moment Samuel seeks him out as a young shepherd lad to anoint him in God's name (1Sa 16). Taken into Saul's service, he achieves his first triumph—slaying Goliath, the 10-foot-tall Philistine, with a single stone from his slingshot (1Sa 17). He wins Saul's daughter as his wife and the king's son Jonathan as a blood brother (1Sa 18). But as David's popularity increases, Saul grows bitterly envious, forcing David to flee for his life (1Sa 19–21). Out in the wilderness David rallies a band of outlaws to defend himself; but, twice given the opportunity to kill the king, he twice refuses to strike at the anointed of the Lord even though Saul is trying to kill him (1Sa 22–26). David then crosses over to the land of the Philistines, where he bides his time in relative safety.

Saul, meanwhile, is told an alarming prophecy by the witch of Endor: he will lose his kingdom to David and die in battle with the Philistines. And so it happens. The next day, after the Philistines attack and slay Jonathan and two other of his sons, Saul takes his own life (1Sa 27–31).

The story of David in 2 Samuel describes the establishment of his kingdom (2Sa 1–10), followed by an account of events at court during his 40-year reign (2Sa 11–24). It begins as David learns of the deaths of Saul and Jonathan and delivers a moving elegy on the two (2Sa 1). Following God's bidding, he journeys to Hebron, where he is anointed king of Judah—the southern part of Israel (2Sa 2). War then breaks out between David and Saul's son Ishbosheth, the ruler of northern Israel (2Sa 3–4); but with Ishbosheth's death David becomes king of a united kingdom (2Sa 5.1 ff.). Three events of far-reaching significance now occur: the removal of his capital from Hebron to Jerusalem (2Sa 5.6 ff.), the transference of the Ark of God to Jerusalem (2Sa 6), and God's covenant with David announced by the prophet Nathan (2Sa 7). Thereby Jerusalem becomes the religious as well as the political center of Israel's life, and the Davidic monarchy gains legitimacy as the divinely appointed successor of the old tribal order. His throne secure, David expands his domain in a string of military victories, beginning with a defense against the Philistines and ending with the creation of an empire (2Sa 8–10).

The story now shifts to a vivid, down-to-earth account of David's domestic troubles during the latter half of his reign. They begin when the king surprises a beautiful young woman, Bath-sheba, at her bath. David takes her to bed and sends her husband, Uriah, who is one of his soldiers, to the front lines to be killed (2Sa 11–12). God in his displeasure tells David, "I will raise up evil against thee out of thine own house" (2Sa 12.11). And soon the evils come in rapid succession. David's eldest son, Amnon, rapes his half sister Tamar and is murdered in revenge by another son, Absalom, Tamar's full brother (2Sa 13). The king becomes estranged from Absalom but is later reconciled. Absalom, however, seeks to displace his father on the throne, raises a rebellion, and meets an untimely death (2Sa 14–18).

The book's final chapters (2Sa 19–24) contain notices of minor events—a sudden revolt quickly put down, a brief epidemic. They also record David's psalm of thanksgiving (2Sa 22) and a poem introduced as his "last words" (2Sa 23.1-7).

1 and 2 KINGS

The two Books of Kings, like those of Samuel, were originally one. Compiled mainly from state annals and temple archives, they survey Israel's history from the time of Solomon down to the end of the monarchy, with the destruction of Jerusalem and the exile of the people to Babylon. Adding color and meaning to this material are graphic stories of individual kings and holy men, particularly the prophets Elijah and Elisha.

The books divide into three major parts. The first (1Ki 1–11) describes the death of David and the accession of his son Solomon (1Ki 1–2) and is followed by an account of Solomon's reign. Solomon's great wisdom takes a prime position, along with his love of God (1Ki 3). Thus under him the kingdom prospers, and he himself acquires enormous wealth (1Ki 4), most of which goes to build a royal palace and a lavish temple at Jerusalem (1Ki 5–9). The queen of Sheba, hearing of the splendors of Solomon's court, comes to visit (1Ki 10). But a cloud begins to overshadow Israel, for the king has taken a number of foreign wives, and they persuade him to build sanctuaries to alien deities. In the face of this apostasy, God announces that on Solomon's death the kingdom will be rent asunder (1Ki 11).

As the second and longest part (1Ki 12–2Ki 17) opens, Solomon is dead and the kingdom is once more divided into two independent states: Judah in the south and Israel in the north. Solomon's son Rehoboam is acclaimed ruler in Judah, but his rival Jeroboam sets up a new capital in the north (1Ki 12). The story now alternates between the two kingdoms, with particular emphasis on the evil ways of Israel. For events in the north rapidly deteriorate, as Jeroboam raises up idolatrous bull images in the sanctuaries of Dan and Bethel and commits other abominations (1Ki 12–14). His successors are no better; the chronicler contrasts their sinful doings with the relatively more devout ways of the rulers in Judah (1Ki 15–16). The worst of all is Ahab, who, led on by his consort Jezebel, institutes the worship of Baal. This affront to the deity brings the prophet Elijah into vehement opposition (1Ki 17–19, 21). Ahab dies in battle (1Ki 22), and shortly afterward Elijah is carried to heaven in a fiery chariot. But before departing, he bequeaths his mantle to Elisha, who carries on his work of prophecy and condemnation against Ahab's successors (2Ki 2–8). Throughout this period the northern kingdom is racked by numerous bloody coups d'état that plunge it time and time again into political chaos and sometimes even into civil war (1Ki 15.27 ff., 16.8-22; 2Ki 9–10, 15.8-30). Finally, during the reign of Hoshea in 721 B.C., the kingdom of Israel falls to the imperial armies of Assyria (2Ki 17).

The last part (2Ki 18–25) gives the remaining history of Judah. Also under assault by the Assyrians, it nevertheless manages to hold out. The virtuous King Hezekiah, guided by the prophet Isaiah—and considerably helped by the Lord's angel, who reputedly slays 185,000 enemy warriors in one night's work—turns back the Assyrian emperor Sennacherib, and the crisis is averted (2Ki 18–20). Thereafter the kingdom maintains its existence for another century, one that sees the proliferation of idolatrous practices under King Manasseh (2Ki 21) and the reforms of King Josiah (2Ki 22–23), before it too is extinguished by the Babylonians, the successors of Assyria to empire. In 587 B.C. Jerusalem is leveled, the temple is set to the torch, and the people are taken into exile in Babylon under Nebuchadnezzar (2Ki 24–25).

Throughout this epic chronicle the writer is careful to assess the performance of each king—but not so much for qualities of statesmanship as for fidelity to God and his covenant. The rulers of Israel are invariably condemned for frequenting the sanctuaries of Dan and Bethel with their idolatrous bull images—Israel's cardinal sin. Those of Judah get mixed evaluations—some, such as the idolater Manasseh, being condemned outright (2Ki 21.2), while others, like Jehoshaphat, receive qualified approval (1Ki 22.43). And Hezekiah and Josiah, both religious reformers, win high praise (2Ki 18.3 ff., 22.2). The greatest space is devoted to reigns where important religious issues are at stake. Accordingly, the Israelite kings Omri and Jeroboam II—politically two of Israel's most effective rulers—share a mere 15 verses (1Ki 16.21-28; 2Ki 14.23-29). But the antagonism between Elijah and the apostate Ahab merits roughly six chapters (1Ki 16.29–22.40), and the accord of Hezekiah and Isaiah embraces three more (2Ki 18–20). The Book of Kings is thus a theological and religious evaluation of the history of the monarchy. And since king and subjects were as one, it is also an evaluation of the people's relation to God during this period.

Like all other Old Testament historians, the author is concerned not only with the past, but with the lessons that can be drawn from it. The turbulent times of Jerusalem's fall and the Babylonian exile were a shattering experience, and they raised acutely the question *why*. Why should a people put their faith in a God who, having delivered them from Egypt and entered into a solemn covenant with them, has now seemingly abandoned them in their hour of trial? The writer's concern is to provide an answer: the exile is God's righteous judgment upon his people for their sins, made inevitable by their stubborn refusal to listen to their prophets. He also offers a method of recovery, as shown by the worthy example of King Josiah (2Ki 23–24). Devout repentance and a renewal of their fidelity to God's covenant are needed to bring about the restoration of God's people.

1 and 2 CHRONICLES

Also once a single work, the two Books of Chronicles cover the same historical period as Samuel and Kings but with an even stronger ritual emphasis. In the Hebrew Bible they stand in the final position, presumably having been written in the latest part of the Old Testament period, up to 200 years after the exile. As the author looks back on the reigns of David and Solomon in particular, he sees in them an idealized radiance, their shortcomings quickly glossed over and their glories enhanced. It is as though he were offering them up as shining examples of the perfect kingdom under God. Echoing this theme, the author devotes much space to matters of religious observance—the organization of priests, Levites, temple singers, custodians, and the like.

Chronicles opens with a lengthy genealogy, which traces the Israelite heritage from Adam (1Ch 1–9). The nation and its monarchy are thus firmly set in the context of God's divine plan. The narrative begins with the death of Saul, adding a cautionary note that he lost his life and his kingdom because he failed to keep faith with the Lord (1Ch 10). The rest of 1 Chronicles devotes itself to David, extolling his virtues and enumerating his achievements (1Ch 11–29). Chief among these is the establishment of the Ark in Jerusalem after years of neglect (1Ch 13, 15–16). David's military feats are proudly hailed, including his triumphs against the Philistines, the Syrians, and the Ammonites (1Ch 14, 18–20). "Thus the Lord preserved David whithersoever he went," the chronicler notes (1Ch 18.6), presumably because of his attentiveness to God's wishes. God promises David that his son Solomon will succeed him as king and will build the great temple in Jerusalem. But to David falls the task of preparation—choosing the temple site (1Ch 21), providing the materials (1Ch 22), organizing the duties of the priests and Levites (1Ch 23–27), and handing over detailed ground plans to his successor (1Ch 28). Then David dies, and Solomon becomes king (1Ch 29).

The second book opens with Solomon enthroned in splendor and then moves quickly to the building and dedication of the temple (2Ch 1–9). The details of construction are lovingly told (2Ch 3–4), as is the transfer of the Ark to its permanent place in the sanctuary (2Ch 5). Solomon offers up a prayer that the temple will become God's true house, and therefore a place of blessing (2Ch 6); God in his reply promises blessing to a penitent people but warns of what will happen should anyone break his commandments (2Ch 7). Attention then turns to Solomon's great wealth and to the awe in which he is held by the rulers of other nations—both seen as rewards for his faithfulness to God (2Ch 8–9).

The book's final part (2Ch 10–36) outlines the split between Judah and Israel but tells the story of the southern kingdom only, since the north is held to have been in rebellion against the house of David. The judgment passed on each king follows the predictable Old Testament pattern: faithfulness to God brings security, land, wealth, and prestige, while disobedience results in calamity for the nation. The exile to Babylon is presented as simply the last in a long line of similar, if less drastic punishments.

Like other Old Testament writings, Chronicles is not intended as a straightforward and objective history, but rather as a reflection upon past events for the benefit of its present readers. Even the opening genealogies show a special interest in the tribes that constituted the restoration community—Judah, Benjamin, and Levi. The function of the genealogies is to show, by way of encouragement, that the small, weak, harassed, and politically impotent Judah of the Persian Empire is still the people of God, in whom are to be found his great plans for world redemption.

Hand in hand with encouragement, however, goes exhortation. The stories of the kings are told as parables to show how God has consistently dealt—and therefore will continue to deal—with his people. If contemporary Judah will only seek its God in truth, paying proper attention to the service of the temple and making it a real house of prayer, then Judah can again possess the power and wealth that reflect God's commitment to and concern for its well-being and success.

EZRA and NEHEMIAH

Continuing the history set down in Chronicles, these two books were most probably compiled by the same author as a supplement to Chronicles, and they once formed, along with Chronicles, a larger work. Telling the story of the Israelites' return from exile in Babylon and of the two great religious reformers who helped lead the way and rebuild the nation, the narratives of Ezra and Nehemiah are closely intertwined, and in the Hebrew Bible they appear as a single book.

A half century after the Babylonians conquered Judah in 587 B.C., they were conquered in turn by the Persians under Cyrus the Great. Since it was Persian policy to let subject peoples dwell in their own lands and follow their own customs, Cyrus in 538 B.C. issued a decree allowing and encouraging the Jews to move back to Jerusalem and rebuild their temple. The return took place in stages, with a vanguard led by Sheshbazzar of Judah arriving first. There were problems from the start, however. Not all Jews had been exiled to Babylon, and those who stayed behind had intermarried with other local peoples and had inevitably grown lax in religious matters. These backsliders now caused such trouble that work on the temple came to a halt. Not until the reign of Darius I, when a second group of exiles returned under the leadership of Zerubbabel and Jeshua, did construction resume. Urged on in their efforts by the prophets Haggai and Zechariah, the people completed the temple in 515 B.C.

So much is straight history, as related in the first part of the Book of Ezra (Ezr 1–6) and confirmed by outside sources. The order of events now turns more speculative as the individual accounts of Ezra and Nehemiah are given; both stories are told in the first person, and they overlap in a way that makes it difficult to reconstruct the chronological sequence of events. Most authorities believe that both men were active during the reign of Artaxerxes I (465–424 B.C.). Each one brought a large group of exiles back to Jerusalem and exhorted the people to stricter obedience to God's covenant.

Ezra is the first to speak. A scribe who is commissioned to reestablish the laws of Moses in their original purity (Ezr 7), he sets out for Jerusalem with a party of compatriots, whom he lists by name (Ezr 8). Once in the Judean capital, he begins to preach, urging public repentance and renewal of the covenant with God (Ezr 9). He then orders the Jews to give up their foreign wives and thenceforth to marry only within the covenant community itself (Ezr 10).

Nehemiah is a high official in the Persian court who in 445 B.C. takes leave to visit Jerusalem and rebuild the city walls (Neh 1–2). In spite of dissension within and opposition from without, he completes the work handily (Neh 3–6) and then takes a census of the Jewish community (Neh 7). Then Nehemiah's account breaks off, abruptly giving way to a long passage on Ezra and his efforts at covenant renewal (Neh 8–10). After this, Nehemiah takes up the narrative again with yet another listing of names, a dedication of the new city walls, and a further account of various reform measures (Neh 11–13).

Much significance has been given to the strictures in both Ezra and Nehemiah against marriage with Gentiles, which fostered the exclusiveness so notable in Judaism for centuries afterward. At the time these measures were perhaps essential. Only by restoring the rigid bonds of family and tribe were the returning exiles able to assert their sense of national identity and to reaffirm their position as God's Chosen People.

ESTHER

After the exile, while large numbers of Jews were returning to their ancestral homes, others decided to remain in foreign lands. One of the cities toward which they gravitated was Susa (Shushan), capital of the Persian Empire, and it is here that the story of Esther takes place. Jewish communities abroad have always existed in a precarious balance, subject to grave peril on one hand while open to high achievement on the other. The Book of Esther demonstrates both possibilities.

Esther is a beautiful Jewish maiden who gains the favor of the emperor, becomes his queen, and in this capacity saves her people from annihilation. As the book opens, the emperor Ahasuerus—history's Xerxes I, who reigned from 486 to 465 B.C.—casts aside his present queen, Vashti (Est 1), and has his eunuchs search out a maiden to replace her. A minor court official, the Benjamite Mordecai, proposes Esther, who is his cousin. The king is smitten with love and quickly takes her into a lofty position in his harem (Est 2). Now the king's grand vizier, Haman, belongs to a tribal group that is a traditional blood enemy of the Benjamite Jews. And while Haman is not aware of Esther's origins, he knows about Mordecai's. When Mordecai refuses to make proper obeisance to him, Haman has the excuse he needs to order a pogrom against the entire Jewish community (Est 3). Mordecai hears of the plot and tells Esther. The queen, seeking a way to avert the slaughter, invites both Haman and the king to a banquet in her quarters. During that feast and at another the following night, she uncovers Haman's scheme. The king is enraged, cancels the pogrom, and has Haman hanged upon the gallows that has been erected to receive Mordecai (Est 4–7). All Haman's lands and property are given to Mordecai, who has been elevated to a high government post, and Jews throughout the empire are given leave to exact a prompt and bloody vengeance against all their enemies (Est 8–10).

The book is notable in Scripture in that it contains no mention of God or religion, though the Greek translation added passages to give it a religious flavor (additions to Esther in the Apocrypha). It is best seen as a folk tale of passion and triumph in which God's implicit will for his people is carried out. There is one passage of lasting import, however. In celebrating their deliverance from Haman's evil plot, the people of Judah held the first feast of Purim (Est 9.23-28), still an annual observance in the Jewish faith.

JOB

Why, if God is just, do even virtuous people sometimes suffer great misfortune? The Book of Job addresses this age-old problem with compelling power and insight. Based on an ancient folk tale and expanded by an anonymous poet of the 6th century B.C., the book explores the issues of suffering and innocence, doubt and faith, in a passionate debate that achieves new levels of understanding.

In most Old Testament writings, suffering is seen as a punishment for sin. But Job is a man of unquestioned righteousness—so much so that God, to test his devotion, allows Satan to afflict him with a series of almost unbearable hardships. Job, not knowing of this agreement, cannot understand why he is being tormented. But he accepts his lot uncomplainingly and scolds his wife for suggesting that, in defiance, he "Curse God, and die" (Job 1–2). At this point three friends come along to console him.

Here the story breaks off, with the prose of the folk tale giving way to verse as the friends arrive, and there is a sudden and perturbing switch of roles. In the ensuing dialogue (Job 3–31) the friends take the stance of pious orthodoxy hitherto maintained by Job, while Job lashes out in a vitriolic attack on God's providence. The friends tell Job to stop complaining and to appeal instead to God's mercy, but Job continues his tirade. The debate between them lasts until chapter 31, but well before that the friends give up in exasperation. Job has to finish the argument by himself, citing his innocence, lamenting his misfortunes, and demanding to know why God has abandoned him. Only toward the end, in a magnificent soliloquy on man's ignorance in the face of God's infinite wisdom (Job 28), does his anger seem to abate.

God's reply is tantalizingly delayed as a younger visitor, Elihu, intervenes with a lengthy hymn to God's omnipotence (Job 32–37). Then God at last begins to speak, his voice rising "out of the whirlwind," in a set of stirring rhetorical questions that emphasize the extent and complexity of his mighty creation (Job 38–39). He goes on to describe two awesome beasts, behemoth and leviathan, which represent the powers of darkness and disorder that God himself has built into the fabric of the world (Job 40–41). "Yes," he says in effect to Job, "there is evil in the world, but I can contain it." These four remarkable chapters, among the most majestic in all Scripture, accomplish what the pious arguments of the friends could not: they bring a defiant Job to his knees in adoration and remorse, and God, ever forgiving, restores Job's fortunes to twice their previous state (Job 42).

For all its dramatic power, the book leaves a number of questions open. God reprimands the three friends, for example, even though they have defended him. Is it because, in explaining God's ways to Job, they display an unseemly arrogance? Job's anger, which often approaches blasphemy, seems more to God's liking. Is it because Job cares so deeply about justice and suffering, while the friends simply mouth platitudes? No one knows for sure. But certainly the Book of Job probes more deeply into the agonies and perplexities of human existence—and into the mysterious ways of divine providence—than almost any other work of Scripture. It is a unique masterpiece both of poetry and of theology.

PSALMS

Since the most ancient times the Book of Psalms has been the basic hymnal of the Hebrew faith, and subsequently of Christendom. These intensely lyric verses, collected during the return from exile for use in the rebuilt temple, have a timeless appeal that cuts across denominational boundaries and that few other works of Scripture can match.

Though the original Hebrew title means "praises," the Psalms speak to a broad range of emotions: praise, to be sure, but also supplication, thanksgiving, contrition, and even revenge. Some are messianic in tone and are quoted in this light by New Testament writers. As written down by the ancient editors they are organized into five separate books, but the division is arbitrary. Biblical authorities now classify them under six traditional headings, which occasionally overlap; thus, a particular psalm may fall under more than one heading. The categories are:

Laments, the largest group, in which the worshiper seeks deliverance in time of need or danger. Some of the Laments have a bitter, vituperative tone, upbraiding the deity for his seeming neglect or ringing down curses on unnamed enemies. But most always the complaint is resolved, and the psalm ends on a note of confidence and trust in God. The Laments include Psalms 3–7, 9, 10–14, 16, 17, 22, 23, 25–28, 31, 35, 36,

38, 39, 41–44, 51–64, 69–71, 74, 77, 79, 80, 83, 85, 86, 88, 90, 94, 102, 106, 109, 120, 125, 129, 130, 131, 137, 140–143.

Psalms of Thanksgiving, in which the singer praises God for his divine assistance. Examples are Psalms 18, 30, 32, 34, 40, 75, 92, 107, 116, 124, 138.

Hymns of Praise, in which God's majesty and providence are extolled for their own sake. They are Psalms 8, 19, 29, 33, 47, 65, 66, 93, 95–100, 103–105, 111, 113, 114, 117, 134, 135, 136, 139, 145–150.

Royal Psalms, designed for use at coronations or royal weddings, and which usually celebrate the monarch in Israel's life and worship. Psalms 2, 18, 20, 21, 45, 72, 89, 91, 101, 110, and 144 fall into this category.

Worship, or *Liturgical*, *Psalms*, many of which were composed for a specific religious occasion. The Songs of Zion (46, 48, 76, 84, 87, 132), which celebrate Jerusalem or its temple, belong in this group. So do the Songs of Ascents (120–134), associated with pilgrimages to the Holy City. Also included in this category are miscellaneous verses on a variety of topics, including Psalms 50, 67, 78, 81, 82, 108, 115.

Psalms of Wisdom, which deal with problems of ethics or behavior in language similar to that of Job or Proverbs, and which include Psalms 1, 37, 49, 73, 112, 119, 127, 128, 133.

Nearly half the psalms have a heading attributing them to David, though he was probably not their author. Some scholars speculate that the heading may refer to any reigning monarch belonging to David's line. Other headings include Hebrew terms whose significance is not fully understood. Some are names referring perhaps to individual scribes or musicians; others may be musical instructions indicating the style of recitation or the instruments to be used.

The Psalms in all their lyric beauty and wisdom reach beyond the doctrines of Israel's theologians, the regulations of its lawgivers, the thunderings of its prophets, the advice of its sages, and allow us to hear the beating of its heart. Rooted in the worship of a time long past, they transcend their ancient origins, ringing down through the ages to speak to the hopes and anxieties and the need for faith of people everywhere.

PROVERBS

A collection of maxims, admonitions, and moral instructions, the Book of Proverbs belongs to a category of Old Testament writings known as Wisdom Literature, which also includes the Books of Job, Ecclesiastes, and several of the Psalms. Traditionally ascribed to King Solomon, Proverbs was compiled by professional sages of a later time, though possibly based on collections already made at Solomon's court. The work was copied out by the men of Hezekiah about 700 B.C. One passage (Pr 22.17–24.22) appears to have been based on an Egyptian book of wisdom that dates back as far as 1000 B.C. And though Proverbs is firmly grounded in religious belief—"fear of the Lord is the beginning of knowledge," runs its most famous line (Pr 1.7)—its tone is distinctly worldly. It offers counsel and observation on the ordinary business of daily life, designed to convert its hearers into worthy and capable citizens of the community.

The book can be divided into two main sections and a postscript. The first part (Pr 1–9) is a selection of discourses on individual topics, often dramatized as exhortations of a father to his son. Besides counseling against rash pledges and indolence (Pr 6.1-5; 6-11), stern warning is given to avoid bad company (Pr 1.10-19; 4.14-19) and especially to guard against the allurements of loose women (Pr 5.1-23; 6.20-35; 7.1-27; 9.13-18). Such conduct brings on misery and ruin, the listener is told, but upright behavior will lead to the rewards of long life, happiness, riches, and honor (Pr 3.13-18; 4.8-9; 8.18-21).

The book's largest section (Pr 10–29) is a collection of proverbial sayings, each giving a short, crisp formulation of a theme, usually within a single verse. They cover a multiplicity of topics: laziness (Pr 24.30-34), pride (Pr 16.18), drunkenness (Pr 23.29-35), the upbringing of children (Pr 23.13-14), regard for the poor (Pr 21.13), the acquiring of wealth (Pr 13.11), even table manners (Pr 23.1-3), and much more besides, all of which reflect the wide-ranging concerns of the ancient sages of Israel.

The final two chapters (Pr 30–31) appear as an appendix to the earlier sections. They include a dialogue between a skeptic and a believer in the style of the Book of Job (Pr 30.1-9); another small collection of proverbial sayings (Pr 30.10-33); a queen mother's words of advice to her son, the king (Pr 31.1-9); and finally a dissertation on what qualities make an ideal wife (Pr 31.10-31).

ECCLESIASTES

No other book in Scripture—and few in literature of any sort—are as deeply pessimistic as this one. "Vanity of vanities, saith the Preacher . . . all is vanity": on this doleful note Ecclesiastes begins (Ec 1.2), and on this note it concludes (Ec 12.8), save for a brief postscript. In between, the author ruminates, in words of extraordinary power, on life's frustrations and on the pointlessness of trying to explain them. God's ways are inscrutable, he declares, and man's greatest achievements are largely exercises in futility.

The author's reflections develop in no particular order, with the same themes recurring throughout. Man is caught in a relentless cycle of activity leading nowhere (Ec 1.4-11), for "that which is done is that which shall be done: and there is no new thing under the sun" (Ec 1.9). He lives in the perpetual shadow of his own death (Ec 3.19-21; 7.2), which may occur at any hour (Ec 9.11-12), which none can resist (Ec 8.8), which comes alike to the wise and foolish (Ec 2.14-15), the righteous and wicked (Ec 9.2), and which thus brings all endeavor to no account (Ec 2.12-23). The pursuit of wisdom results in grief (Ec 1.12-18); the search for pleasure and wealth is profitless (Ec 2.1-11; 5.10-17); even the pursuit of morality is of little comfort (Ec 7.15).

In the face of such cosmic futility, the Preacher recommends a stoic acceptance. Life, however fleeting and imperfect, is good in itself (Ec 9.4); we must take it as it comes, finding enjoyment in the benefits God sees fit to send (Ec 2.24; 5.18-20). As a practical guide to living, wisdom is to be preferred to folly (Ec 1.13; 7.1-29; 9.13–10.20), and moderation is advised in all things (Ec 7.16-17). Above all, we must revere the Lord, baffling though his intentions may be (Ec 3.11; 6.10; 8.17; 9.1). "Remember now thy Creator in the days of thy youth," the Preacher counsels, before the onset of age (Ec 12.1-7). And, he concludes, "Fear God, and keep his commandments: for this is the whole duty of man" (Ec 12.13).

The author, an anonymous sage writing in the 5th or 4th century B.C., styles himself as David's son Solomon—a literary device to lend weight to his words. But his pessimism argues against the neat, orthodox solutions offered by Israel's earlier scribes and historians. Probing more deeply into the mysteries of human existence, he finds them to be beyond easy or rational explanation.

THE SONG OF SOLOMON

The Song of Solomon is an anomaly in biblical literature—a collection of love poetry that contains no outright mention of religion and in which the name of God does not occur even once. Its single theme is human love and courtship, expressed in part as dialogue between two lovers (SS 1.5-17, for example) and in part as a soliloquy on the beauties of the loved one (SS 2.8-17 and elsewhere). The poetry is graceful, sensuous, rich in pastoral imagery, and often frankly erotic. Some 25 different poems or poetic fragments are included.

Despite its great literary merit and its unquestioned place in Jewish folk tradition, the book's acceptance in Scripture can be justified only by ascribing a mystical symbolism to its picturesque, often explicit language. It has been described as an allegory of God's love for Israel, with the figure of the Lord as the "husband" of his people. In the Christian canon it can be interpreted as an ode on Christ's love for the church or on the mystical embrace of divine love and the human soul.

Also known as the Song of Songs or the Canticles, the book has been attributed by tradition to Solomon. As in so many Old Testament works, this is simply a literary device. Modern scholars see it as a product of the 5th or 4th century B.C.

ISAIAH

The first of the Bible's truly prophetic books is also perhaps its richest and most complex. Like many of the lengthier Old Testament writings, it is the product of an extended period of composition and growth. It has at least two different authors, in fact: Isaiah of Jerusalem, who lived in the 8th century B.C. at a time when the northern kingdom of Israel was under the threat of the Assyrians and was then conquered by them, after which Judah itself was left as an uneasy tributary threatened by the same fate; and an unknown poet of Judah's exile in Babylon, the so-called Second Isaiah, who wrote during the 6th century B.C.

The resounding prophecies of Isaiah I fill the book's first half (Isa 1–33, 36–39; it is generally agreed that Isaiah II is the author of chapters 34–35). The writer opens with a series of vivid warnings addressed chiefly to Jerusalem's upper classes, urging them to mend their profligate ways or else suffer the consequences (Isa 1–5). He interrupts himself to describe his call to prophecy—an astonishing vision at Jerusalem's temple in which the angel of the Lord cleanses his lips with a live coal from the altar (Isa 6). But Isaiah is both a visionary and a man with access to ruling circles, and he now tells of his dealings with the Jerusalem court. Faced with an invasion from northern Israel and Syria (Aram), Judah appeals to Assyria (Isa 7.1–9.7). Woven into the political account are two stirring passages beloved of Christian piety, since they foretell the coming of the Messiah: a prophecy that a maiden shall bear a child called Immanuel (Isa 7.14-16), who will redeem his people (Isa 9.6-7). After some additional warnings, the prophet goes on to note that the menace from without, though very real, is in God's hands (Isa 10.5-34); he then delivers a further messianic promise (Isa 11) and a glorious hymn of praise to God (Isa 12). In this opening section a pattern emerges that will continue through Isaiah I. Almost every passage moves from judgment to promise, from a vision of stark devastation to one of peace and redemption, in a way that distinguishes Isaiah as one of the most hopeful prophets in all Scripture.

The next part of Isaiah I (Isa 13–23) is largely invective, in which the prophet foresees the collapse of Israel's foreign enemies: Babylon (Isa 13–14, 21), Moab (Isa 15–16), Damascus (Isa 17), Ethiopia and Egypt (Isa 18–20), Tyre and Sidon (Isa 23), all fallen into ruin. Then in a section called the Isaiah Apocalypse (Isa 24–27) the writer predicts destruction in more general terms, followed by renewal and salvation in the distant future.

Isaiah then returns to the most immediate political threat of his day—the aggressive imperialism of Assyria (Isa 28–33). The administration in Jerusalem hoped to avert it by signing a defense pact with Egypt, much to Isaiah's distress. The prophet attacks the priests and officials of Jerusalem, then the pact itself; and he advocates reliance on God, not entangling alliances, to preserve the city. Typically, throughout this section he interjects verses on the benevolence of the Lord, who gives men skill (Isa 28.23-29) and understanding (Isa 29.22-24), and who will discomfit the Assyrian and rescue Zion.

The next few chapters form an editorial bridge between the two large divisions of the book. Written by anonymous scribes of various periods, it includes a verbal attack on Edom (Isa 34), an idyllic vision of redemption (Isa 35, typical of Isaiah II), and a historical account of Isaiah's dealings with King Hezekiah (Isa 36–39).

A distinct shift in style and tone occurs in the section ascribed to the Second Isaiah (Isa 40–55). The theme of judgment fades into the background, and that of blessing and renewal sounds out with clarion force. The writing takes no narrative direction; it is simply a collection of poetic oracles on recurring topics as seen in the context of the Babylonian exile, along with the poet's joyful anticipation of his people's return to Zion. "Comfort ye my people," the poet begins (Isa 40.1), and he continues with unflagging optimism: "O Zion, that bringest good tidings, get thee up into the high mountain" (Isa 40.9). The most explicit hero of these verses is King Cyrus of Persia, who is hailed as Judah's champion against the Babylonians (Isa 44.24–45.13)—and, in language normally reserved for David's royal line, as God's "anointed." But there is a more shadowy figure, an unnamed servant of the Lord (Isa 42.1-4; 49.1-6; 50.4-11), who assumes far greater importance in the Christian canon. "Despised and rejected of men," then exalted by God (Isa 52.13–53.12), he is seen as yet another of this book's prophecies of the coming Christ.

The book's closing chapters (Isa 56–66) are believed by some scholars to have been written later than the 6th-century visions of Isaiah II, though others see them as dating to the same period. They appear to be more of a collection than a sustained piece. A keynote is struck in the opening words: not all the bright hopes kindled earlier have yet been fulfilled, and only just and righteous behavior can bring them to fruition. There is also an insistence that God's promise—and his commandments—are not for Israel alone, but for men everywhere. In all, right standards and rich mercy are nowhere in as fine a balance as they are throughout this best loved of all the prophetic writings.

JEREMIAH

More is known about the life of Jeremiah than about any other Old Testament prophet. Called by God in 627 B.C., 40 years before the fall of Jerusalem, he eloquently warned of the coming disaster. Hoping to avert it, he summoned the people of Judah to moral reform, bidding them to give up false gods, repent, and cultivate purity of heart. He aroused the hostility of Jerusalem's establishment and was eventually thrown into prison. There he continued to preach, his words being taken down by his secretary, Baruch, to be read aloud to the people.

The Book of Jeremiah can be divided into two main parts, with a short historical appendix at the end. The first section is a collection of oracles as recorded by Baruch and generally arranged in chronological order (Jer 1–25). In the second, Baruch outlines Jeremiah's later preaching career (Jer 26–45) and records still more oracles (Jer 46–51). Two great themes predominate: God's intent to spread his word to all nations through the agency of his true prophet, Jeremiah; and his determination to punish the people of Jerusalem for their sins, so that the city may be restored in purity and righteousness under a new generation.

Jeremiah from the first is a reluctant prophet, called as a mere youth to a task that seems utterly beyond him. But God reassures him, setting him "over the nations and over the kingdoms . . . to destroy, and to throw down, to build, and to plant" (Jer 1). So Jeremiah embarks on his mission, warning of the dangers to Judah, which are seen at first as coming from Assyria in the north. He castigates the nation for its sins (Jer 2–3) and paints a vision of destruction that amounts to the very undoing of creation itself (Jer 4–6). The blasts of rhetoric continue with a sermon at the temple (Jer 7) and in the chapters that follow (Jer 8–20). No note of hope, as in Isaiah, sounds through the message of doom.

Scattered amid these censures are poignant reminders that Jeremiah is an unwilling herald of doom. In a series of so-called confessions (Jer 11.18–12.6; 15.15-21; 17.14-18; 20.7-18), he laments his role and complains vehemently to God. He would rather intercede for his people than pronounce judgment upon them. When the Lord turns him down (Jer 14.1–15.4), he declares, "Cursed be the day wherein I was born!" (Jer 20.14).

For all his unwelcome words, Jeremiah is sometimes consulted by the government on God's intentions. The reply is usually bleak. When King Zedekiah asks about the military threat from Babylon, he answers that God will give the Babylonians victory and that Judah should not resist (Jer 21). Various criticisms of the royal house follow (Jer 22); but they end in a rare word of comfort, with the promise of a future "branch" of David worthy to be called "The Lord our righteousness"—a pun in Hebrew on Zedekiah's name. Next comes an extended reproach against false prophets for their lies and apostasy, for deserting God for Baal, and for speaking without awaiting the divine impulse (Jer 23.9-40). This part of the book ends with a vision in which God shows Jeremiah two baskets of figs, one good and one so bad it must be discarded—a reference to the rottenness at Judah's heart (Jer 24). The result is punishment at the hand of Babylon, which will last 70 years (Jer 25.1-14).

The narrative in the book's second half opens with another account of Jeremiah's temple sermon—and the consequences of giving it. A mob, spurred on by the priests, assaults him, and he is saved only by the intervention of the nation's elders (Jer 26). Then, as an object lesson to the people, God instructs Jeremiah to fashion and wear a yoke of the type used to harness oxen: it is a symbol of Judah's subservience to Babylon. The prophet Hananiah predicts that the yoke will soon be broken, but Jeremiah cautions that prophets of good tidings should be viewed with suspicion; oracles of doom proved to be more reliable in the past (Jer 27–28). Jerusalem had been captured by Nebuchadnezzar in 597 and the king, the high priest, and a number of leading citizens taken in captivity to Babylon. Jeremiah now urges the exiles to build houses, plant gardens, and seek the welfare of the city where they are held (Jer 29).

The next several chapters gather together the rare hopeful elements in the prophet's message (Jer 30–33). He looks forward to a change in fortune, with the people of Judah returning to rebuild Jerusalem, and with a new covenant written not on stone but in the hearts of men. The scene then moves back to Jerusalem in the years before its final fall to Babylon, with the stories of Jeremiah's purchase of land in Anathoth as an act of faith in the future (Jer 32) and the perfidy of the Jerusalemites in freeing and then reclaiming their slaves (Jer 34). Barred from the temple for sedition, Jeremiah has Baruch write down his words to read in the sanctuary (Jer 36); when King Jehoiakim has the scroll cut up and burned, another is prepared. After Zedekiah's accession, Jeremiah is imprisoned yet secretly consulted by the king (Jer 37–38). When Jerusalem is taken in 587 B.C., Jeremiah is freed (Jer 39–40). Then, when the governor appointed by Babylon is killed in an uprising, the rebels ask his counsel. He tells them to stay in Judah, but instead they flee to Egypt, taking the now aged prophet with them (Jer 41–45).

A series of oracles against other nations follows; doom is predicted for Egypt, Philistia, Moab, Ammon, Edom, Damascus, Elam (Jer 46–49), and finally for Babylon itself (Jer 50–51). The final section of the book (Jer 52) is almost identical with the concluding chapter of Kings (2Ki 25); it summarizes the dire events that it was Jeremiah's unenviable task to announce as God's judgment.

Despite the harshness of his message, Jeremiah is a sensitive and sympathetic figure. One of the high points of his teaching is his promise of a new covenant in which there will be no need for sanctions, enforcement procedures, or penalties because obedience will come from the heart. This is the gleam of hope in a book that on the surface seems so bleak.

LAMENTATIONS

Part of the great poetic outpouring of the exile period, these five poignant laments express the writer's grief at the sacking of Jerusalem in 587 B.C. and at other sufferings inflicted on his people by their Babylonian captors. Why has God deserted Judah, he asks; when will it be restored to its former glory?

Tradition assigns these verses to Jeremiah, but their literary style is so distinctively unlike the prophet's known writings that they are most certainly by another, unnamed lyricist. The first four (La 1–4) are structured as alphabetic acrostics, with a stanza for each of the 22 letters in the Hebrew alphabet; the third has three verses for each letter. The last poem (La 5), modeled on other liturgies written for use in times of national crisis, is also 22 lines long and based on the acrostic pattern, though its lines are longer and do not follow the alphabetic sequence of the other four.

Throughout, as the poet moves from dirge to national prayer, he displays a vivid, eyewitness eloquence on the horrors of war, famine, and exile. Adding to his pain is his sense of astonishment that God should have allowed Jerusalem to fall in the first place (La 4.2) and that such a fate should have been suffered by the royal house of David (La 4.20).

Composed for public recitation, the five lamentations are read today in synagogues on the ninth of Ab (which falls in July or August), the traditional date of Jerusalem's fall to Babylon in 587 B.C.—and centuries later, in A.D. 70, of its capitulation to the legions of imperial Rome.

EZEKIEL

Ezekiel, a younger contemporary of Jeremiah with a similar stern and apocalyptic message, was among those taken into captivity to Babylon after the initial capture of Jerusalem by Nebuchadnezzar in 597 B.C. Jeremiah had heralded the exile, God's harshest punishment upon his people for their waywardness; Ezekiel prophesied from Babylon itself. While Jerusalem still stood as the capital of Judah, the nation had already come under Babylonian suzerainty. This perspective governs the prophet's message, which has three main thrusts: 1) because of deep-seated sinfulness, Jerusalem will be totally laid waste by Babylon, the agent of God's wrath; 2) all contemporary Israel, including the exiles, must yet repent; 3) the Lord nevertheless intends a glorious restoration of his people.

The book opens with Ezekiel's call (Eze 1). His remarkable vision of God, enthroned amid cherubim and transported by a magical system of interlocking wheels, convinces Ezekiel of the Lord's majesty not only in Jerusalem but in Babylon as well. The terms of the vision can largely be explained by Ezekiel's background as a priest. In the Jerusalem temple where he had served, carved winged cherubim surmounted the Ark of the Covenant; and in earlier centuries this holy of holies had been moved about on wheeled carriages. So the message becomes clear: God is on the move again, in a way that expresses his sovereignty over all the world.

The theme of Jerusalem's transgressions and her impending punishment dominates the book's first major division (Eze 2–24). To dramatize the city's fate, Ezekiel builds a clay model surrounded with siege towers and lies down before it (Eze 4). Then, shaving the hair from his head, he sets fire to a third of it, slashes a third of it with his sword, and scatters the rest in the wind—as the people of Judah will be ravaged, cut down, and scattered (Eze 5). A vivid portrayal of idolatry within the temple (Eze 8–11)—one of Jerusalem's chronic sins, apparently—culminates in the departure of the Lord, borne by the cherubim, from the temple and city, toward Babylon (Eze 11.22-25). The indictment continues as Ezekiel condemns the false prophets who have allowed Judah to remain complacent (Eze 13). Jerusalem, in her faithlessness to God, is a harlot of the worst sort, he declares, and in the end she will be savaged by her lovers (Eze 16.15-43).

The prophet addresses this tirade to the exiles in Babylon, calling them to repentance and pointing out that the events they have experienced, and must yet experience, are a punishment by God for the nation's earlier misdeeds. They must learn to settle for a life of alienation. But at the same time that he persuades them that the judgment is real, he also implies that it is not necessarily final. Two passages are significant here, both stressing the importance of an individual's responsibility for his own actions. In the first (Eze 14.12-20), he declares that no father, no matter how righteous, can save a sinful son. In the second (Eze 18), he cites a well-known proverb of despair—"The fathers have eaten sour grapes, and the children's teeth are set on edge"—and refutes it. No man needs to suffer for the sins of his forefathers, he declares.

The next major division (Eze 25–32) consists of oracles against various foreign nations such as Moab, Edom, Tyre, and Egypt. It is designed to show that Judah is not alone under God's judgment. After it, the book's third major section opens with the dreaded event that Ezekiel has foretold: word comes to the exiles that Jerusalem has at last fallen to Babylon (Eze 33.21). These tidings that God's judgment has been carried out mark a turning point in the prophecy, for the next few chapters (Eze 33–37) contain oracles of hope and renewal. The Lord is seen as a good shepherd to his people, caring and providing for them and protecting them from the beasts of the wilderness (Eze 34). In one passage reminiscent of Jeremiah's new covenant, God promises, "A new heart . . . will I give you, and a new spirit will I put within you . . ." (Eze 36.26-28). Chapter 37 contains the most famous of Ezekiel's visionary images. God leads the prophet into a valley covered with dry bones. "Can these bones live?" he asks. "O Lord God, thou knowest," Ezekiel answers. With that the bones assemble themselves into skeletons, grow flesh, and become the resurrected people of Israel and Judah. Then comes an oracle on the destruction of King Gog of Magog, an unidentified, perhaps mythical empire representing Babylon (Eze 38–39). A cataclysmic war among the nations heralds a new age.

The Lord takes his place once more among his people, who are restored to their former homes in Judah (Eze 40–48). A new temple is built, as glorious as the one destroyed, and the Lord reenters it in triumph. The building is half real, half metaphorical; a sacred river flows from each portal, symbolizing the rejuvenation of the land and of Israel's spiritual life (Eze 47). And in the very last verse (Eze 48.35), the restored capital city is given a new name, "The Lord is there," which in Hebrew is a play on the word *Jerusalem*.

DANIEL

The miraculous stories of Daniel, an exile prophet in Babylon, are as familiar as any in Scripture. Each one, from the hero's oracles for King Nebuchadnezzar to his escape from the lions' den, is a parable of fortitude in time of oppression. Written down by a pious Jewish scribe around 165 B.C., centuries after Daniel's death, they offer solace and inspiration during a similar period of national travail, when Israel had fallen under the yoke of the Hellenistic tyrant Antiochus IV.

As the book opens, Nebuchadnezzar has just conquered Jerusalem and taken a number of young men, Daniel among them, to serve in his court. Urged to feast on the king's rich food, Daniel declines to break the Jewish dietary laws (Dan 1). Nebuchadnezzar has a dream that none of his sages can guess at or interpret; but Daniel, inspired by God, both recounts the dream and tells the king that it depicts the rise of a great new kingdom under the Lord (Dan 2). Then Nebuchadnezzar erects a 90-foot gold idol and commands all his subjects to worship it. Three of Daniel's companions—Shadrach, Meshach, and Abednego—refuse and as punishment are cast into a fiery furnace. But the flames do not burn them, for they are protected by an angel (Dan 3). Daniel then interprets another of the king's dreams, prophesying that Nebuchadnezzar, for his pride, will go mad for seven years, living like a beast. So it happens, until at the end of the predicted time the king accepts God, and his sanity is restored (Dan 4).

The next story occurs during the reign of a subsequent monarch, Belshazzar. There is a great feast at the palace, and as the revels reach their height a ghostly hand writes mysterious words on the wall: *mene*, *mene*, *tekel*, *upharsin*. Only Daniel can read their meaning, which foretells the destruction of Babylon at the hands of the Persians (Dan 5). Again, it happens as prophesied. And under the Persian emperor (misidentified as Darius the Median; it was Cyrus of Persia who overthrew the Babylonians), the prophet achieves his greatest triumph. The new ruler issues an ordinance forbidding the worship of any foreign gods. But Daniel is caught praying toward Jerusalem, as is his custom, and is thrown into the lions' den. However, the Lord protects him, he emerges unscathed, and his accusers are tossed to the lions instead (Dan 6). The moral is clear: acceptance of martyrdom is better than apostasy; faithfulness will be rewarded with deliverance.

The book now shifts from religious anecdote to a sequence of densely symbolic visions, all prophesying the triumph of God over Israel's oppressors (Dan 7–12). Though presented as dreams of Daniel, they refer directly to the persecution of Israel at the time the book was written, for Antiochus IV, a 2nd-century successor to Alexander the Great, slaughtered large numbers of Jews for refusing to abandon their ancient religious customs. The first vision sets the style (Dan 7). Four great beasts, representing the empires of Babylon, Media, Persia, and Alexander's Greece, arise one after the other from the sea. The last and most terrible sprouts a little horn—Antiochus—which boasts great things and makes war upon the whole earth. The scene then shifts to a heavenly court, presided over by the Ancient of days, where the beast is judged and destroyed. Then another figure appears, "one like the Son of man," who represents the people of God, and he is given a universal and everlasting kingdom.

The following visions are a variation on this same theme. The kingdom of Antiochus is going to be destroyed, to be replaced by the kingdom of God. In the final one (Dan 11–12), the writer traces in less apocalyptic language the course of events from the Persian Empire, to the division of the Hellenistic Empire after Alexander, through the subsequent rivalries between his successors, down to the reign of Antiochus. He details Antiochus' savage treatment of the Jews and the beginnings of a rebellion by the Jewish Maccabees and foretells the ruler's doom at "the time of the end." Assurance is given that God's people will be delivered and that the dead will be resurrected to everlasting bliss or contempt, depending on their adherence to God's word. Through these chapters—and in the earlier parables of Daniel and his fellows—the writer seeks to encourage God's hard-pressed people to stand firm in their faith, confident in the sovereignty of their God over the tide of history.

HOSEA

The last 12 books of the Old Testament, known as the Minor Prophets because of their brevity, quickly review the teaching of a dozen holy men from various periods. They begin with Hosea, who lived in the northern kingdom of Israel in the 8th century B.C. at a time of political crisis. The country was engaged in a losing war with the Assyrians and had fallen into a state of near anarchy. Against this background Hosea upbraids Israel's leaders for idolatry, for oppressing the poor, and for general faithlessness to God. He calls them to repentance, and as an object lesson in God's forgiveness he offers the example of his own tumultuous domestic life.

Hosea's family troubles take up the book's first section (Hos 1–3). At God's behest he weds the prostitute Gomer, who bears three children with names that symbolize God's displeasure. They are not his own children, Hosea says, and he will not accept them as such unless Gomer reforms. She does and is forgiven—and the point is made that God will take back his people if they only let him.

In the chapters that follow, Hosea draws out the parallel (Hos 4–11). The people of Israel "play the harlot" with God (Hos 4.15), her leaders have defiled his covenant, "they have sown the wind, and they shall reap the whirlwind" (Hos 8.7); but God's love is all-encompassing (Hos 11). The prophet cites Israel's earliest history—the birth of Jacob, his wrestling match with the Lord, the deliverance from Egypt "by a prophet"—all pointing to God's continuing concern for his people (Hos 12–13). And Hosea delivers God's promise that should his people repent, he will be "as the dew unto Israel," bringing it rich new life (Hos 14.5).

JOEL

In three powerful chapters, the prophet Joel beats a drum roll of terrible apocalypse. A plague of locusts has swept across Israel and Judah, and he takes it as a warning of imminent judgment. "For the day of the Lord is at hand," he writes, "and as a destruction from the Almighty shall it come" (Joel 1.15). Prayers, fasting, and repentance are called for. They will usher in a time of plenty when God "will restore to you the years that the locust hath eaten" (Joel 2.25). And with judgment there will also come a day of Pentecost, when God promises "that I will pour out my spirit upon all flesh; and your sons and your daughters shall prophesy, your old men shall dream dreams, your young men shall see visions" (Joel 2.28). Finally, there is a call to arms—"beat your plowshares into swords, and your pruning hooks into spears," Joel commands (Joel 3.10)—and a prediction of disaster for two ancient enemies, Egypt and Edom.

Almost nothing is known about Joel personally, though some of his imagery suggests he may have been a priest in the rebuilt temple at Jerusalem following the return from exile.

AMOS

No matter how eloquent, a prophet's words in times of prosperity are likely to fall on deaf ears. Such was the obstacle facing Amos, a Judean shepherd who was called to preach to the northern kingdom of Israel around 760 B.C. Under the long, peaceful reign of Jeroboam II the nation had reached its apogee of power and affluence. At the same time it was riddled with social injustice, corruption, hypocrisy, and religious indifference, all of which Amos now passionately denounces.

He begins by calling down a fiery destruction on Israel's neighbors for their various transgressions (Am 1–2.5). Then he turns to Israel itself. Its leaders have "sold the righteous for silver, and the poor for a pair of shoes," he declares (Am 2.6), and then goes on to paint a graphic picture of the nation's comeuppance (Am 2.7–5). "Let judgment run down as waters," he commands, "and righteousness as a mighty stream" (Am 5.24). As Israel is the first among nations, it will be led first into captivity (Am 6). The seer then records the first three of five prophetic visions of God's judgment: a plague of locusts, a catastrophic fire, and an episode where God measures Israel with a plumb line and finds it leaning crookedly into corruption (Am 7.1-9).

The warnings are too much for Israel's authorities, who ban Amos from the royal sanctuary at Bethel and forbid him to preach (Am 7.10-13). Amos presumably returns to Judah, where he continues to speak out (Am 8–9). He issues another prediction of Israel's exile and then ends on the book's only hopeful note. Not all Jacob's line will be destroyed, he says, and after the exile Israel will enjoy a rich future under David's heirs (Am 9.11-15).

OBADIAH

This shortest of Old Testament books—it is only one chapter long—delivers a stinging diatribe against the kingdom of Edom. When Jerusalem fell to Babylon in 587 B.C., its leaders sought aid from the Edomites, who were their supposed allies. The Edomites not only refused, they also joined Judah's enemies in carving up its territory and seizing booty from the captured and looted cities. For this lapse they must expect divine retribution; indeed, after the exiled Israelites return to the Promised Land, they will rule over Edom as well.

Scholars know nothing about Obadiah and even question his authorship of certain verses, but it is assumed that he lived during the period of the Babylonian exile.

JONAH

One of the storytelling masterpieces of the Bible, the Book of Jonah is unusual on two counts: it is pure biography with almost no doomsday rhetoric; and its hero preaches not to the Israelites, but to the Gentile population of Nineveh.

Nineveh was the capital of the Assyrian Empire, and thus Israel's archenemy. So when God calls Jonah to preach there, the prophet shows little enthusiasm. Seeking to escape his mission, Jonah embarks on a ship headed in the opposite direction. God pursues him in the shape of a tempest. As the ship begins to founder, the terrified sailors draw lots to see who is causing the elements to rage so dangerously. The lot falls on Jonah, who admits he is in flight from the Lord. At his own behest the sailors cast him overboard—reluctantly, to be sure, for they fear they will be held guilty of his death—and the seas quickly grow calm. To save his prophet from drowning, God sends a great fish to swallow him up (Jon 1).

From the fish's belly Jonah offers a psalm of thanksgiving for his miraculous rescue and the fish vomits him onto dry land (Jon 2). Thus chastened, the prophet now heads for Nineveh. His message is simple and direct: in 40 days the city will be overthrown. All Nineveh repents, putting on sackcloth by order of the king, and God suspends his punishment (Jon 3).

Everyone is delighted—except for Jonah, who becomes angry because he has been made the instrument of Nineveh's salvation rather than its destruction. The prophet goes into a sulk, setting up camp outside the city to see if perhaps God will change his mind. Instead, God has another lesson for Jonah. He causes a melon vine to sprout up and shade Jonah's campsite; then he sends a worm to eat the vine. Jonah is furious. Why should God make this wanton attack on his leafy bower, he wants to know. And the Lord answers with a message of gentle tolerance: "Thou hast had pity on the gourd, for the which thou hast not labored. . . . And should not I spare Nineveh, that great city, wherein are more than sixscore thousand persons . . . ?" (Jon 4.11).

The protagonist of this artful morality tale was a minor prophet from Galilee during the reign of Jeroboam II (786–746 B.C.), but the book itself is assigned to the postexilic period, perhaps the 4th or 3rd century B.C. It suggests that God's word applies to Jew and Gentile alike and that Israel's mission is to proclaim this truth to all nations. The New Testament makes reference to the "sign of Jonah" (Mt 12.39, 16.4; Lk 11.29), interpreting the seer's rescue from the giant fish as a prophecy of Christ's resurrection.

MICAH

A doomsaying prophet from a small country town in Judah, Micah was a contemporary of Isaiah who preached at Jerusalem in the late 8th century B.C. Samaria, capital of the northern kingdom, was being overrun by the Assyrians; Judah itself would soon come under attack and be left as a weak vassal state. Micah warns of the disaster and at the same time predicts a glorious national revival in the distant future.

Micah's brief, pungent oracles are assembled in no particular order. Samaria's ruin is vividly depicted and held up as a warning to Judah (Mic 1). The nation's authorities are charged with immorality and social injustice (Mic 2); in consequence, Zion shall "be plowed as a field, and Jerusalem shall become heaps" (Mic 3.12), a prophecy that would be quoted at the trial of Jeremiah. Then in an abrupt shift of tone the prophet offers a vision of peace and salvation, when men "shall beat their swords into plowshares, and their spears into pruning hooks," and the nations of the earth "shall not . . . learn war any more" (Mic 4.1-3; the same three verses appear in Isa 2.2-4). He speaks of a shepherd-king from Bethlehem, who will emerge to champion Israel against her enemies (Mic 5.2-5)—a passage seen in the Christian canon as a prophecy of Christ. There is another call for reform, with Micah urging the Israelites "to do justly, and to love mercy, and to walk humbly with thy God" (Mic 6.6-8). And he looks forward a second time to a new era of salvation (Mic 7.8-20).

NAHUM

In a rapid, fervent style that reveals his keen sense of God's power, Nahum announces the coming destruction of Nineveh, the Assyrian capital. His opening words give a vivid, boldly metaphorical description of God's majesty, expressed in storm and drought, earthquake and volcanic fire; slow to anger, but now roused to full fury, God is a scourge to his enemies—but a stronghold to those who trust in him (Na 1.2-8). And since Nineveh, the object of his wrath, is Israel's current oppressor, the tidings of its downfall are seen as a prophecy of peace and liberation for Israel (Na 1.9-15).

In the next chapter the assault on the city by the Medes is portrayed with great vigor and effectiveness: the scarlet-clad soldiers, the jostling of chariots, the breach of the ramparts, the spread of panic, and the plundering of its treasures (Na 2.1-9)—the predator has become the prey (Na 2.10-13).

Nahum repeats his prediction in the final chapter. Nineveh is doomed to terrible slaughter (Na 3.1-3). Likened to a harlot who has seduced other nations, it will be stripped bare and exposed to public ridicule (Na 3.5-7). As the mighty city No Amon (Thebes) once fell to Assyria, so will Nineveh fall, its people will be scattered, and the world will rejoice (Na 3.8-19). Shortly after Nahum's prophecy, Nineveh was in fact besieged and destroyed by the Medes, in 612 B.C. Nahum's book makes clear that national politics founded on cruelty and militarism is self-destructive, and that even great nations are responsible to God and must submit to his judgment.

HABAKKUK

This sharply questioning work belongs to the close of the 7th century B.C., when Babylon dominated the ancient world and was threatening to gobble up Judah. For Habakkuk this raised the age-old dilemma of God's justice: Does history serve the ends of righteousness or of brute force?

The book opens with a dialogue between the prophet and God (Hab 1.1–2.5). Violence and injustice spread throughout the world, Habakkuk complains; yet God remains silent and seemingly indifferent (Hab 1.2-4). God replies that he is acting in a new way: he is raising up the proud and terrible Chaldeans (i.e., the Babylonians) to punish the wicked (Hab 1.5-11). But the prophet is unsatisfied. How can a God who is just use such a savagely wicked nation as his instrument, allowing it to devour people who are basically more righteous (Hab 1.12-17)? The prophet retires to brood in his watchtower (Hab 2.1), and there the divine resolution is made known: The tyranny of the Chaldeans will be their undoing, God declares, and the faithfulness of the righteous will be their wellbeing. God's vindication is assured: "Though it tarry, wait for it; because it will surely come" (Hab 2.2-4).

The seer now intones five prophetic denunciations of the Chaldean oppressor. Its doom is sealed, for the rapacious destroyer of nations will itself be destroyed (Hab 2.5-20).

The book concludes with the Psalm of Habakkuk, a magnificent poem celebrating the advent of God in judgment and salvation. Its forceful, allusive language evokes the ancient story of Exodus, where God's guiding hand delivered the Israelites from servitude. And in quiet confidence it declares that God in his own good time will perform the same miracle against the proud Chaldeans, coming once again to save his people (Hab 3.17-19).

ZEPHANIAH

No prophet of doomsday spells out the event more powerfully or precisely than Zephaniah, possibly a descendant of the royal house of Judah who preached during the reign of Josiah (640–609 B.C.). "The great day of the Lord is near, it is near, and hasteth greatly," he shouts (Zep 1.14). A trumpet will sound, nations will fall, and God will sweep all living creatures from the face of the earth. Judgment will fall on Judah in particular, for it is proud and rebellious and sunk in idolatry and corruption (Zep 1.2–2.3; 3.1-8). Other nations will suffer as well—Gaza and Canaan, Philistia and Moab, Assyria and even Ethiopia (Zep 2.4-15).

The occasion for Zephaniah's warnings may have been a threatened invasion by Scythian hordes from the north—one that in fact never took place. But God's judgment is inevitable, nonetheless; Judah is doomed. Of this the prophet has no doubt. Yet even at the eleventh hour there is hope for those humble enough to seize it: "Seek ye the Lord, all ye meek of the earth . . . seek righteousness, seek meekness; it may be ye shall be hid in the day of the Lord's anger" (Zep 2.3). And in the book's closing section (Zep 3.8-20) this ray of promise breaks into full light as the prophet looks beyond judgment to Israel's salvation and to the dawn of a better day. For God comes in compassion as well as in anger; he brings cleansing and renewal as well as destruction.

HAGGAI

With the fall of Babylon to Cyrus the Great in 538 B.C., the exile came to an end. Cyrus issued an edict allowing the Jews to return to Jerusalem and to rebuild the temple, which had been destroyed by Nebuchadnezzar some 50 years earlier. But while the returnees industriously put up fine houses for themselves, they allowed construction of the Lord's house to languish. So in 520 B.C. the prophet Haggai, in five brief addresses, exhorted the community to get to work.

In his first two speeches Haggai urges Zerubbabel, the governor (a grandson of King Jehoiachin), and his high priest Joshua to take personal charge of the construction (Hag 1). He then promises that the new temple will be even more splendid than the old (Hag 2.1-9). In his next address the prophet implies that the community, because it has so long neglected the Lord's work, is spiritually unclean; but as the new temple rises, God's blessing will flow down upon it (Hag 2.10-19). Finally, he predicts the imminent arrival of God's kingdom, with Zerubbabel as the rightful ruler (Hag 2.20-23).

ZECHARIAH

The prophet Zechariah, like his contemporary Haggai, sought to inspire the exiles on their return to Jerusalem and to urge them forward in rebuilding the temple. But his message is broader and its style more vividly allegorical. In a sequence of densely symbolic visions, he assures the Judeans that God, their champion, will restore them to glory and salvation.

The visions make up the book's first half (Zec 1–8). After an introductory call to repentance, Zechariah pictures God as a divine horseman patrolling the earth on Judah's behalf (Zec 1.7-17). He sees Judah's enemies, in the guise of four disembodied horns, overthrown (Zec 1.18-21). A surveyor measures Jerusalem in preparation for God's triumphal entry (Zec 2.1-5). Satan and Joshua, the high priest, stand in judgment before God, and Joshua is elevated (Zec 3.1-10). Another allegory shows Zerubbabel completing the temple (Zec 4.1-14); in yet another, God's word is a scroll flying through the air to curse evildoers (Zec 5.1-4).

Throughout these passages Zechariah speaks with a gentleness of tone unusual in the early prophets. "Show mercy and compassions every man to his brother," he advises, "and oppress not the widow, nor the fatherless, the stranger, nor the poor" (Zec 7.9-10). And his predicted new Jerusalem is a reassuringly joyful place with "boys and girls playing in the streets thereof" (Zec 8.5).

Most authorities agree that Zechariah did not write the book's remaining chapters (Zec 9–14), though they mirror his concerns and employ some of his highly figurative language. The main theme is the restoration of Judah, its victory over its enemies, and the arrival of a messianic age. The new era is ushered in by a Prince of Peace mounted humbly on a donkey (Zec 9.9-10)—a passage that prefigures Jesus' entry into Jerusalem on Palm Sunday. There is a lengthy allegory on the "foolish shepherds" who have led Judah in the past (Zec 10–11) and another centered around an unnamed person whose sacrificial death will cleanse the people of their sins and idolatry (Zec 12–13). The Day of the Lord will arrive shortly thereafter; he will stand in judgment and establish his universal reign (Zec 14).

MALACHI

The Hebrew word *Malachi* means "my messenger" and may not be the actual name of the prophet who wrote this book. Whoever he was, most scholars assign his work to the 5th century B.C., some years after the Jews returned from exile. And like much postexilic literature, it lays heavy emphasis upon the traditional aspects of Israel's religion.

The writer affirms God's love for Israel (Mal 1.1-5) and then expands on all the ways that Israel has betrayed God's covenant. The nation offers up polluted sacrifices (Mal 1.7-14), its priests have failed to teach God's laws (Mal 2.1-10), the people abuse the sanctity of marriage (Mal 2.10-16), and they cheat in their tithe-giving to the temple (Mal 3.6-12). In all, their sins pervert the good things God has given them.

In response, Malachi promises a day of judgment with blessings for those who fear and honor the Lord and divine wrath for those who do not. God will appear, preceded by another "messenger"—or by an angel; the Hebrew word can mean either. His arrival will be terrible indeed. "Who may abide the day of his coming?" the writer asks (Mal 3.2). And at that time, when the wicked will be cast into flames and the God-fearing saved, "shall the Sun of righteousness arise with healing in his wings" (Mal 4.2). In a final promise, Malachi predicts that Elijah—who centuries earlier had been carried alive to heaven in a whirlwind (2Ki 2.11)—will return to herald "the great and dreadful day of the Lord" (Mal 4.5).

Not surprisingly, the early Christians laid great significance on these particular verses. They equated both Elijah and the second messenger with John the Baptist, and they saw the "Sun of righteousness" as Jesus himself.

THE APOCRYPHA

In addition to the 66 books in the basic Protestant Bible, there are some closely related writings that have never won full acceptance as authentic, divinely inspired Scripture. Among these are various books and book fragments that appear in early Greek-language editions of the Old Testament but not in the original Hebrew. They are known collectively as The Apocrypha, from the Greek word for "hidden." For one reason or another—perhaps because temple scribes doubted their veracity, perhaps because they were deemed too complex to be understood by laymen—they were omitted from the original Jewish canon.

Christian scholars over the centuries have been of two minds about these Apocryphal works. Saint Jerome, the great 4th-century editor of the Latin Vulgate, incorporated them into the Old Testament—although taking note of their special status—and in time they came to be recognized as part of the Roman Catholic canon. Protestants, on the other hand, followed the Jewish tradition. Both Martin Luther and John Calvin, while allowing the Apocrypha's usefulness for instruction, denied it status as God-inspired. Thus, Protestant Bibles either omit these works or put them in a separate appendix (see page 37).

Despite their ambiguous status, the books of the Apocrypha are rich in historic and inspirational value. Written mostly in the late pre-Christian era, from 200 B.C. up to several decades after Jesus' crucifixion, they include psalms, prayers, prophecies, historical narrative, and didactic wisdom similar to that found in Proverbs and Ecclesiastes.

Much of the Apocrypha consists of additions to other Old Testament books. The First Book of Esdras, for example, is simply a Greek rendition of the stories of Ezra and Nehemiah, the charismatic leaders who brought the Judeans back to

Jerusalem after their exile in Babylon. Second Esdras is a later embellishment, recounting seven apocalyptic visions supposedly granted to Ezra while he dwelt in Babylon. By the same token, The Prayer of Azariah and the Song of the Three Young Men fits neatly into the Book of Daniel; it records the hymns sung by Daniel's three friends as they walked in the fiery furnace. Susanna and Bel and the Dragon both tell anecdotes affirming the wisdom and piety of Daniel himself. Another Apocryphal work, Additions to the Book of Esther, attempts to inject a religious theme into what is basically a secular tale. Two others—Baruch and The Letter of Jeremiah—relate to the prophet Jeremiah.

Perhaps most interesting from a historical point of view are the two Books of the Maccabees. In the 2nd century B.C. the Syrian despot Antiochus Epiphanes launched a savage campaign against the Jewish inhabitants of his vassal state. Persecution bred resistance: Mattathias of Modein and his five sons—the Maccabees—raised a guerrilla army to drive out the oppressors. At the death of Mattathias his eldest son, Judas Maccabaeus, assumed command. When a Syrian sword took Judas, another brother stepped in. Eventually the Jewish rebels, though heavily outnumbered, fought their way to victory. Once again the Lord's Chosen People, with the help of their God, had thrown off an alien yoke.

While no one questions the veracity of Maccabees, the Books of Judith and Tobit have little basis in historical fact. Judith is a tale of heroism set during the wars with Assyria in the 6th century B.C. The Assyrian general Holofernes invites the widow Judith into his tent on the eve of battle. When he falls into a drunken sleep, she seizes the general's own scimitar to chop off his head—thus saving the beleaguered Israelites from a vastly superior army. The story is a vivid and inspiring one, but it is also replete with errors in names, dates, and locale.

Tobit, likewise, is a parable of hope for the distressed. A pious Jew living in exile in Babylon, Tobit for no accountable reason goes suddenly blind. He seems headed for a dark and dismal old age until his son Tobias embarks on a long and dangerous quest to a neighboring kingdom. There Tobias discovers a magic potion that restores his father's sight. The story, immensely popular in its day, is an ancient Middle Eastern folk tale dressed up in Jewish garb. Like Judith, it is better read as enthralling fiction than as true Scripture.

Most of the remaining Apocryphal books fall into the category of wisdom writing—didactic verses designed to instruct readers in matters of faith and morality. In The Wisdom of Solomon, a Hellenistic Jew of the 1st century B.C. invokes the name of Israel's most powerful monarch to rekindle a genuine zeal for God and his law. Some of the writing is trenchant and apt, some less so. Most theologians give greater weight to Ecclesiasticus, or the Wisdom of Jesus the Son of Sirach. A lengthy tract written in 180 B.C. by a respected Jewish sage, it employs the aphoristic style of Proverbs to examine questions of mortality, free will, sin, worldliness, and spirituality. The most highly esteemed of all Apocryphal writings, it stands as an important source for knowledge of Jewish faith and customs of the period.

THE NEW TESTAMENT

Unlike the Old Testament, which was compiled over centuries, all 27 books of the New Testament were written at nearly the same moment in history, from about A.D. 51 to 95. The four Gospels, which appear first in the traditional biblical order, give biographical accounts of Jesus' life and teachings—his birth, ministry, death, and resurrection, along with a record of his various parables and other sayings. Three of them—Matthew, Mark, and Luke—are known as the Synoptic Gospels (*synoptic,* from the Greek, means "seen together," or "from the same point of view") because they share common sources and tell many of the same stories. The Gospel according to John, based on other sources, offers somewhat different material.

Immediately following the Gospels, the Acts of the Apostles traces the growth and development of the early Christian church. Then comes a selection of 21 letters, the Epistles, which were written by the church fathers to help guide converts in the Christian way of life. The last book, Revelation, is in the form of apocalyptic prophecy. With elaborate, often ambiguous symbolism, it discloses God's will for the future and the working out of his divine purpose.

MATTHEW

No one knows the true author of the Gospel according to Matthew. Written more than three decades after Jesus' death, it draws much of its content from the Gospel of Mark, which preceded it by several years. It may also include material from a number of Jesus' sayings that, by tradition, were collected by the apostle Matthew. Whoever its author, its purpose is clear: to show through Jesus' life and teachings that he is Israel's true Messiah—the Christ (from *christos,* Greek for "the anointed")—who has come to fulfill the promises of the Old Testament prophets.

Matthew establishes Jesus' prominence at the very start, tracing his ancestry from Abraham and David and so asserting his right to be "King of Israel" (Mt 1.1-17). The author moves quickly to the story of Jesus' birth at Bethlehem, the visit of the wise men, and the Holy Family's flight into Egypt to escape the tyrant Herod, who is so jealous of a newborn rival king that he orders a massacre of Bethlehem's children (Mt 1.18–2.23). Wherever possible, each incident is referred to as the fulfillment of an Old Testament prophecy.

The story shifts briefly to John the Baptist and his message of the coming Messiah. Jesus appears and is baptized (Mt 3). Retiring into the desert to meditate, he confronts Satan, who tries three times, unsuccessfully, to tempt him away from his mission (Mt 4.1–11). Instead, Jesus returns to Galilee and recruits his first two disciples, Peter and Andrew (Mt 4.12-22).

Besides stressing Jesus' place within the Jewish tradition, Matthew gives the fullest possible account of his teachings. Thus, in chronicling the events of Jesus' ministry, the writer pauses to quote him at considerable length. There are five lengthy verbatim discourses, each expanding on a particular topic. The most notable and familiar is presented first. It is the Sermon on the Mount (Mt 5–7), which lays the cornerstone of all moral Christian teaching.

The narrative picks up again with a detailed account of Jesus' early ministry in Galilee, including a series of miraculous healings. A leper is cleansed, a man is cured of paralysis, a dead girl is revived, two blind men regain their sight (Mt 8–9). All the while Jesus is gathering disciples. And in his second major discourse, he instructs his followers on their duties as preachers of the Gospel (Mt 10).

Jesus' teachings are gaining widespread popularity, but they provoke considerable enmity within the religious establishment. News comes that John the Baptist has been imprisoned, and Jesus takes the occasion to point out the virtues of John's dedicated life, and to rebuke the cities of Galilee for their unrepentant ways (Mt 11). He tells his listeners, "Come unto me, all ye that labor and are heavy laden . . . for my yoke is easy, and my burden is light" (Mt 11.28-30). He disputes at length with the scribes and Pharisees, who look for a way to discredit him (Mt 12). Then, in his third discourse, he offers parables of the kingdom of heaven (Mt 13.1-52).

Jesus returns from Galilee to Judea, where his reception at the synagogue is openly hostile: "A prophet is not without honor, save in his own country," he wryly observes (Mt 13.57). Then, hearing that John the Baptist has been killed by Herod's soldiers (Mt 14.1-12), Jesus in his grief goes into the desert to be alone. He is followed by a multitude of admirers, however; with five loaves and two fishes, he feeds them all and sends them away. His disciples are caught in a storm on Lake Galilee, and he walks across the water to save them (Mt 14.13-36). Further confrontations occur with the Pharisees, and again Jesus feeds the multitude with a handful of bread and fish (Mt 15–16). In a moment of revelation at Caesarea Philippi, the disciple Peter calls his leader "the Son of the living God," and Jesus says of Peter, "Upon this rock I will build my church" (Mt 16.16-18). To Peter's sorrow, Jesus foretells his own death but adds that he will be raised on the third day (Mt 16.21-28). And, in an act linking him to Moses and Elijah, he stands transfigured before his disciples (Mt 17.1-8).

Jesus' fourth major discourse is offered next (Mt 18). Unique to Matthew, it stresses the humility and dedication that mark a good Christian. "Except ye be converted, and become as little children, ye shall not enter into the kingdom of heaven," he declares (Mt 18.3).

The narrative gathers drama and intensity as Jesus travels toward Jerusalem and his coming crucifixion (Mt 19–23). There are more parables and teachings, including the so-called Great Commandment: "Thou shalt love the Lord thy God with all thy heart, and with all thy soul, and with all thy mind," adding "Thou shalt love thy neighbor as thyself" (Mt 22.37-39). Jesus delivers another dressing down to the Pharisees (Mt 23) and an impassioned final discourse on the Last Judgment and the Messiah's second coming (Mt 24–25). And so the Gospel moves toward its inevitable conclusion. It tells the story of the Last Supper, of Judas's betrayal, of Peter's denial, of Jesus' death on the cross (Mt 26–27). But that is not the end, for in the last chapter Jesus rises from the dead and returns to his disciples. "Teach all nations, baptizing them in the name of the Father, and of the Son, and of the Holy Ghost," he instructs. "I am with you always, even unto the end of the world" (Mt 28.19-20).

With its emphasis on Jewish law and prophecy, Matthew is clearly addressed to the people of Israel. Yet its attitude is strangely ambiguous. In his disputes with the Pharisees, Jesus often seems to sabotage the ancient religious strictures. Rather than confine his message to Israel, Jesus bids his disciples to preach to all nations, Jews and Gentiles alike. And Matthew lays heavy stress on the guilt of the Jews in Jesus' crucifixion. "His blood be on us and on our children," cries the mob in Jerusalem (Mt 27.25).

Was Jesus a dangerous rebel who put himself above the law? The answer in Matthew is that he came not to break the law but to fulfill it, bringing with him a new covenant superior to the old. He stands personified as a new Moses and a new Israel, the visible proof that the promises contained in the Law and the Prophets have been triumphantly achieved.

MARK

Widely thought to be the earliest of the four Gospels, Mark was written between A.D. 65 and 70, possibly in Rome, by a disciple of Peter's named John Mark. Predominantly narrative in form, it is the most concise of the four Gospels. In Mark it is Jesus' deeds, more than his words, that are offered as signs of God's power and presence, and of his own messianic role. And since Mark appears to have been the basic source of the two other Synoptic Gospels, most of the events he relates also appear in the narratives of Matthew and Luke.

Mark contains one distinctive element, however; it continually stresses the ease with which Jesus' central message can be misconstrued. Neither Jesus' family, nor his disciples, nor the world at large comprehend what it means to be God's Messiah, any more than they can grasp the essential nature of God's kingdom. Only in two climactic moments does awareness break through: at Caesarea Philippi, when Peter confesses, "Thou art the Christ" (Mk 8.29); and when a Roman centurion at Jesus' crucifixion declares, "Truly this man was the Son of God" (Mk 15.39). Between these events, Jesus' ministry is a constant struggle to make himself understood.

Mark opens with two prophecies of the Messiah, one from Isaiah and the other by John the Baptist (Mk 1.1-8). Then, omitting all mention of Jesus' birth, and skimming quickly past his baptism and his temptations by Satan (Mk 1.9-13), it plunges directly into Jesus' ministry (Mk 1.14–9.50). "The kingdom of God is at hand: repent ye, and believe," Jesus says (Mk 1.15). He calls his first disciples (Mk 1.16-20) and performs his first miracles (Mk 1.21–2.12). And from the very beginning he runs afoul of the Pharisees, who seek to destroy him (Mk 2.13–3.6). But he continues to gather followers, naming the 12 apostles and proclaiming all believers to be his brothers (Mk 3).

Jesus' teachings in Mark largely take the form of parables—brief, simple stories told to illustrate a particular moral point. Sometimes he speaks them to his followers (Mk 4), sometimes in disputes with the Pharisees (Mk 7). They punctuate the accounts of his many miracles—his healing of the sick, his quelling of a storm at sea, his feeding of the multitudes. Their purpose is at once to hide and to reveal, "that seeing they may see, and not perceive; and hearing they may hear, and not understand" (Mk 4.12), an adaptation of Isa 6.9-10. And when perception does occur, it requires a leap of faith—as when Peter makes his confession at Caesarea Philippi (Mk 8.29), or when Jesus, healing a blind man, declares: "Go thy way; thy faith hath made thee whole" (Mk 10.52).

The account of Jesus' ministry continues with his journey from Galilee to Judea (Mk 10) and leads to his triumphant entry into Jerusalem, where he is greeted with hosannas by the crowd (Mk 11.1-10). Jesus drives the money changers from the temple and curses a barren fig tree, adroitly turning this act into a parable of faith and forgiveness (Mk 11.11-26). More controversy and teaching follow, along with a warning against the Pharisees (Mk 11.26–12.44). Jesus then delivers an oracle predicting the destruction of the temple, the end of the world, and the coming of the Son of Man (Mk 13). Thus the evangelist introduces the concluding events of Jesus' life: the Last Supper, the Passion and Crucifixion, and an assurance of his Resurrection (Mk 14–16). The book's final verses (Mk 16.9-20), describing Jesus' reappearance to Mary Magdalene and the disciples, were added to Mark's original manuscript by a later hand.

Mark's central message, expressed through Jesus' deeds and parables, is seen in the tension between faith and doubt, and between awareness and incomprehension. His messianic secret, so difficult of access, is the unexpected nature of Jesus' messiahship and the purpose of his coming: "For the Son of man came not to be ministered unto, but to minister, and to give his life a ransom for many" (Mk 10.45).

LUKE

Scholars differ as to the identity of Luke, possibly "the beloved physician" (Col 4.14; 2Ti 4.11) who was Paul's companion, and possibly a Gentile convert first to Judaism and then to Christianity. At any rate, it is Luke who offers the broadest perspective of any New Testament author. Writing with thoughtful eloquence and weaving together material from several different sources, he presents Jesus as the universal Saviour, whose message applies equally to all peoples. He stresses Jesus' compassion and forgiveness, his concern for the sick, the needy, the downtrodden, the outcast. Only the proud and self-seeking are sternly judged. And of all the evangelists, Luke lays greatest emphasis on the Holy Ghost as representative of God's continuing presence on earth.

After a brief introduction, Luke tells two stories unique to his Gospel—the annunciations of John the Baptist and of Jesus. He also records two memorable Christian psalms. The first, the Magnificat, is sung by Mary when she learns she will bear the Christ Child; then in the Benedictus, John's father, Zechariah, delivers a prophecy of redemption (Lk 1). There is a full account of Jesus' birth, his dedication at the temple, and one of the few recorded episodes from his youth: a precocious boy Jesus engaging the temple priests in learned discourse (Lk 2). The story continues with John's preaching, Jesus' baptism, and his triple temptation in the desert; there is also a digression in which Luke traces Jesus' ancestry back to Adam (Lk 3.1–4.13). Luke then relates Jesus' ministry in Galilee, closely paralleling the accounts of healings, exorcisms, miracles, and confrontations with Pharisees that are given in the other two Synoptic Gospels (Lk 4.14–9.50). For example, Matthew's Sermon on the Mount becomes, in Luke, a more abbreviated Sermon on the Plain (Lk 6.17-49).

The Gospel's next section, chronicling Jesus' final journey to Jerusalem (Lk 9.51–19.27), contains material found only in Luke. This includes some of Jesus' best-loved parables: the good Samaritan, who helped an enemy in trouble (Lk 10.29-37); a father's happiness at the return of his prodigal son (Lk 15.11-32); and the rich man and Lazarus, one going at death to Hades and the other, a pauper, being taken up to heaven (Lk 16.19-31). Jesus' love of the destitute is nowhere made plainer. There are also teachings derived from Mark and Matthew on such topics as the Son of Man, the kingdom of heaven, and Jesus' prediction of his coming Passion.

Jesus' entry into Jerusalem begins the third section (Lk 19.28–21.28). Here Luke describes the events of Jesus' last week—his driving the money changers from the temple, his disputes with the scribes and other authorities, a prediction of Jerusalem's fall. Then, with the Last Supper, presented here as a Passover feast, the Gospel moves toward its familiar denouement (Lk 22–24). Luke's account of the Crucifixion is less tragically despairing than that of the other Synoptics; Jesus' last words, rather than "My God, my God, why hast thou forsaken me?" (Mt 27.46; Mk 15.34), here become "Father, into thy hands I commend my spirit" (Lk 23.46). Luke carefully builds toward the climax of Jesus' Resurrection and tells in masterful detail how Jesus appeared to his disciples on the road to Emmaus. Finally, Jesus delivers his blessing and ascends into heaven, while his followers return to Jerusalem to sing God's praises (Lk 24.51-53).

JOHN

John differs markedly in style, in vocabulary, and often in content from the other three Gospels. Drawn largely from other sources, it goes beyond the events of Jesus' life to explore the nature and significance of his divinity. There are no parables in the Synoptic sense and only seven miracles. Instead, the evangelist interprets Jesus' teaching largely through allegory and philosophical discourse. Tradition ascribes the book to the "beloved" apostle John; more likely, it was written toward the end of the 1st century by an unknown convert to Christianity who, with a group of fellow believers, had recently broken away from the synagogue.

A powerful introductory section sets the Gospel's high spiritual tone (Jn 1.1-18). "In the beginning was the Word, and the Word was with God, and the Word was God," runs the opening verse. Making a key point of theology, the evangelist declares, "the Word was made flesh, and dwelt among us" (Jn 1.14); he gives no other account of Jesus' birth.

The Gospel's narrative portion divides neatly into two halves: the so-called Book of Signs, which describes and interprets Jesus' miracles and also recounts his early ministry in Judea and Galilee (Jn 1.19–12.50); and the Book of Glory, which tells the drama of his last days, his death, and resurrection (Jn 13–20). The final chapter (Jn 21) is an appendix added by another member of the evangelist's group.

The narrative begins with John the Baptist's prophecies of the coming Messiah and cuts quickly to Jesus picking his first disciples—Peter, Andrew, Philip, and finally Nathanael (Jn 1.19-51). The first "sign," or miracle, follows. At a marriage feast in Cana, Jesus transforms the water in six stone jugs into wine (Jn 2.1-11)—a feat recounted in no other Gospel. He then visits Jerusalem and prophesies the destruction and restoration of the temple, thus prefiguring his own fate (Jn 2.12-22). The Pharisee Nicodemus comes to visit Jesus, sparking a profound discussion on the need for spiritual rebirth and the nature of judgment (Jn 3). "Except a man be born again, he cannot see the kingdom of God," Jesus says (Jn 3.3).

Jesus spends time among the Samaritans, a people despised by the Jews; in a discourse with a woman drawing water from a well, he reveals himself to be the Messiah (Jn 4.1-42). Next he effects two miraculous cures: of a nobleman's son (Jn 4.46-54) and of a cripple by the Sheep Gate in Jerusalem. The latter, performed on the Sabbath, arouses the hostility of the Jews; but Jesus maintains that the twin powers of judging and of bestowing life have been given to him by his heavenly Father (Jn 5). Jesus' miracle of the loaves and fishes, in which he feeds five thousand people, introduces a discourse on the bread of life, another symbol of revelation (Jn 6).

A series of controversies erupts between Jesus and the Jewish authorities (Jn 7–8). Jesus accuses them of being the children of the devil and proclaims his own special status: "Before Abraham was, I am" (Jn 8.58). Then, with the healing of a blind man, he pointedly illustrates the willful blindness of those who reject his message (Jn 9). To emphasize his role, he offers one of his most famous allegories, describing himself as the good shepherd who is willing to die for his sheep. For what they consider his blasphemy in claiming equality with God, the conservative Jews threaten to stone him (Jn 10). In a final miracle Jesus raises Lazarus from the dead and draws a lesson from it: "I am the resurrection and the life" (Jn 11.25). Then the Book of Signs concludes with Jesus' final, triumphant entry into Jerusalem (Jn 12).

The Book of Glory, after a solemn introduction, shows Jesus at the Last Supper, washing his disciples' feet as an example of service to God (Jn 13). After Judas leaves, his coming treachery known, Jesus intones a long farewell discourse and prayer (Jn 14–17). He gives his disciples a "new commandment"—to love one another "as I have loved you" (Jn 13.34). He warns of his coming departure and prays for perfect unity among his followers when he is gone (Jn 17.20-23).

John's Passion narrative (Jn 18–19) differs in important particulars from the other Gospels. It omits Jesus' agony in the garden of Gethsemane and includes a dialogue with Pilate in which Jesus discloses the nature of his kingly rule, based on the authority of truth. Jesus is seen as firmly in command throughout, up to the final "It is finished" upon the cross (Jn 19.30). Jesus appears, resurrected, to Mary, the disciples, and to doubting Thomas (Jn 20), and he offers a summary of all Beatitudes: "Blessed are they that have not seen, and yet have believed" (Jn 20.29). The appendix (Jn 21) tells of one further appearance, on the shore of the sea of Tiberias, and of Peter's commission: "Feed my sheep" (Jn 21.16).

THE ACTS OF THE APOSTLES

The Book of Acts, a continuation of the narrative of Luke's Gospel, offers a gripping account of early church history, describing the rapid spread of Christianity in the years immediately following Jesus' death and resurrection. Its two protagonists are Peter and Paul, the first preaching mostly in Jerusalem and the second carrying Jesus' teachings to the Gentiles. Inspiring both is an even greater presence, the Holy Spirit, who keeps watch over the growing church and guides its apostles and their converts.

In a brief introduction Luke recalls the risen Christ, who gives this last commission to his followers: "Ye shall be witnesses unto me both in Jerusalem, and in all Judea, and in Samaria, and unto the uttermost parts of the earth" (Ac 1.8). Luke's history traces the church's expansion in roughly the same geographic sequence. Its first section tells of the apostles' deeds in the Holy Land—and of their frequent persecution by the Jewish authorities (Ac 1–12). The second half concentrates almost entirely on Paul's ministry to the Gentiles, first in Asia Minor, then Greece, and finally in Rome (Ac 13–28). The point is made that the Jews, by rejecting Jesus a second time, have forced his followers to turn to a much wider audience, so that Christians everywhere now become the authentic heirs to the promises given in the Old Testament.

The church in Jerusalem takes shape immediately after Jesus' ascension. The disciples meet to plan their ministry and to elect a 12th member, Matthias, to replace the traitor Judas (Ac 1). On the day of Pentecost the Holy Spirit descends, empowering the apostles to speak "in tongues," and Peter delivers a long oration that wins many converts (Ac 2). Peter heals a cripple—the first apostolic miracle (Ac 3). More miracles follow, provoking hostility from Jerusalem's powerful religious establishment and leading to arrests and imprisonments of adherents to the new faith (Ac 4–5). At the same time the Christian community grows closer in spirit, worshiping daily together in the temple, breaking bread in one another's homes, holding their goods in common.

Seven deacons are appointed to distribute food to the needy. One of these, Stephen, is arraigned for blasphemy before the Jewish religious tribunal and, though he speaks with great eloquence in his own defense, is stoned to death, thus becoming the first Christian martyr (Ac 6–7). Another deacon named Philip goes to Samaria, where he fares much better, making many converts (Ac 8).

Among the church's most violent adversaries is one Saul of Tarsus, who had consented to the stoning of Stephen and sent Christians to prison. While traveling to Damascus, Saul sees a vision so intensely brilliant that it blinds him for three days afterward. In this period of enforced darkness he repents and converts to Christ (Ac 9). Henceforth Saul, known more familiarly as Paul, devotes all his considerable energies to bringing others into the church.

It is Peter who makes the first Gentile convert, however. With much reluctance, and only after being persuaded by a vision direct from God, Peter baptizes the Roman centurion Cornelius at Caesarea (Ac 10–11). Soon afterward Peter is arrested by Herod Agrippa, who is hostile to the Christians; he escapes, and Herod is struck down by God (Ac 12).

Paul now embarks on the first of his missionary journeys, traveling to Cyprus and through parts of Asia Minor (Ac 13–14). He returns full of enthusiasm at his success, which, paradoxically, raises doubts among some of his fellow believers. Can non-Jews, who do not follow the laws of Moses, become real Christians? The answer, decided at a council of church elders at Jerusalem, is an emphatic yes (Ac 15.1-35). Peter, leading the argument for admitting Gentiles, makes his last appearance in the text.

Paul's second mission takes him again through Asia Minor and then, guided by the Holy Spirit, on to Greece. He founds Christian communities at Philippi, Thessalonica, and Corinth, before returning to his base at Antioch in Syria (Ac 16–18).

The apostle does not stay quiet for long. A third and final mission begins with a trip to Ephesus in Asia Minor. Paul spends two years there, converting so many of the city's pagan inhabitants that the silversmiths, who make idols for pagan worship, riot over the lost business (Ac 19). After a brief side trip to Greece, he returns through Macedonia, pausing at Miletus to deliver a farewell address (Ac 20).

The remainder of Acts tells of Paul's troubles with the authorities, both religious and civil. Returning to Jerusalem, he is assaulted in the temple by conservative Jews from Asia Minor. Arrested, he defends himself in a moving speech to the people (Ac 21–22). He carries his plea to the council of priests, to the provincial governor, and finally to Herod Agrippa II (Ac 23–26). Because he has also appealed to Caesar, he is sent to Rome. On the way he is shipwrecked, survives, and on arriving at the imperial capital is put under house arrest. Nonetheless, he continues to preach the Gospel unhindered (Ac 27–28).

Throughout his account of the church's beginnings, Luke implies a parallel between its struggles and persecutions and those of Christ himself. He also hopes to show that the early Christians, for all their fervor, pose no political threat either to the Roman Empire or to the honored institutions of Judaism. And in ending his account with Paul, he provides a natural transition, in the New Testament canon, to the Epistles of Paul that immediately follow.

ROMANS

Of the 21 Epistles, nearly two-thirds are by the apostle Paul. Addressed for the most part to the members of Christian communities Paul himself had founded, they contain further guidance in matters of faith and morality. His Epistle to the Romans is one of the few he intended to be read by strangers. The Roman church was already thriving when Paul planned his first visit there, and this letter, written around A.D. 58, was sent ahead by way of introduction.

Romans is the longest of Paul's Epistles and the weightiest—more theological discourse than letter. In it he offers his interpretation of the central Gospel message, particularly in regard to Christ's role as universal redeemer.

After a salutation and thanksgiving, Paul tells of his intended journey to Rome (Ro 1.1-15). He then moves straight to his Gospel theme: "It is the power of God unto salvation to every one that believeth; to the Jew first, and also to the Greek" (Ro 1.16). He builds his argument thoughtfully and systematically: the world is in sore need of redemption (Ro 1.19–3.20); redemption will come not merely through good deeds or obedience to Mosaic law, but through faith in God (Ro 3.21–4.25), and the vehicle of this faith is Christ, who died for the sins of all mankind (Ro 5–8). In this section the apostle explains the rite of baptism as a symbol of Christ's death and resurrection. He describes the wretchedness of the human condition before the advent of Christianity and emphasizes the powers of Christ's saving grace. "The Spirit of life in Christ Jesus hath made me free from the law of sin and death," he declares (Ro 8.2).

Having made this central point, Paul takes up the problem of Israel's lack of faith (Ro 9–11). If the Jews are God's Chosen People, how can they reject him? The answer is that God's plan of salvation applies not to Israel's physical descendants but to its spiritual ones, and that Israel's reluctance has allowed God to display his merciful grace to the Gentiles.

Paul now explains the ethical consequences of accepting God's word (Ro 12–15). Each Christian convert must demonstrate his state of spiritual renewal according to his own particular gifts, and also through the general qualities of love, patience, and generosity. Christian duty includes paying taxes, abiding by the law, and respecting the scruples of others. Paul then reviews his reasons for writing. He closes with a number of personal messages (Ro 16.1-23), including a note introducing Sister Phebe, a deaconess who is traveling to Rome from one of the Greek churches.

1 CORINTHIANS

Shortly after Paul implanted the faith at Corinth, in Greece, word came to him that the young church was experiencing problems. Quarrels over doctrine had split the membership into factions. Some of the faithful were claiming superior "wisdom" and showing undue pride in their ability to speak with tongues. Flagrant moral lapses had occurred. In two long, thoughtful Epistles, Paul exhorts the Corinthians to mend their differences and return to the good Christian life.

Paul begins his first letter with a powerful expression of dismay over the squabbles at Corinth. "Is Christ divided?" he asks (1Co 1.13). He then builds a strong case for unity and for simplicity in doctrine (1Co 1–4). "Hath not God made foolish the wisdom of this world?" he demands (1Co 1.20). Paul's own message contains no subtle turns of rhetoric, he says; it is simply the news of "Jesus Christ, and him crucified" (1Co 2.2). God's wisdom is addressed not to philosophers but to "babes in Christ" (1Co 3.1). Paul warns against false and prideful teachers, portraying the apostles as mere stewards of God's mysteries (1Co 4.1-13).

The letter's next section is concerned mostly with ethics and morality (1Co 5–10). A member of the congregation has married his stepmother, and Paul is horrified. The faithful should not associate with idolaters and drunkards, he cautions (1Co 5). Nor should they take their grievances with each other to pagan courts (1Co 6). Paul has been asked about the advantages of celibacy, which he heartily endorses; but for those who cannot contain themselves, "it is better to marry than to burn" (1Co 7.9). Should Christians eat food that has been consecrated to a pagan god—often available in the Corinth market? Paul says that while doing so is no sin, the practice might offend others and so is best avoided (1Co 8). Paul himself exercises moral self-restraint, waiving his apostolic freedoms for the common good (1Co 9–10). "All things are lawful," he affirms, but not all things are helpful (1Co 10.23).

Advice in matters of public worship takes up the Epistle's next section (1Co 11–14). The Lord's Supper, he says, should not be an excuse for private parties (1Co 11.17-34); its celebration should follow the example set by Jesus himself, when, serving bread to his disciples on the night of his betrayal, he said, "Take, eat: this is my body, which is broken for you: this do in remembrance of me" (1Co 11.24). Paul insists that the church preserve its unity, no matter how varied the spiritual practices of its members (1Co 12). The greatest of all spiritual gifts, surpassing the ability to prophesy or work miracles, is Christian love. "Though I speak with the tongues of men and of angels, and have not charity, I am become as sounding brass" (1Co 13.1), the apostle declares. He then delivers some cautionary words on speaking with tongues (1Co 14).

Paul's last concern is to put to rest various doubts concerning the Resurrection (1Co 15). Jesus most assuredly was raised from the dead and seen afterward by some 500 witnesses. Likewise, on the Day of Judgment, all true Christians will be revived, though perhaps not in a familiar or recognizable form. "For the trumpet shall sound, and the dead shall be raised incorruptible, and we shall be changed," Paul writes (1Co 15.52). And he asks a question resonant with triumph: "O death, where is thy sting? O grave, where is thy victory?" (1Co 15.55). The letter concludes with personal messages.

2 CORINTHIANS

Paul followed his first Corinthian letter with a visit, and he found the church in even greater trouble than he had anticipated. He wrote another, severely critical document, which has been lost. Then word arrived that matters had improved. In joy and gratitude, he composed this Epistle to explain his actions and to give further news of his own work.

After the customary greeting and thanksgiving, Paul reviews his relations with the Corinth church. Its problems have given him much anguish, he says; even so, his reprimands were delivered not in anger but out of love (2Co 1–2). He speaks of a new covenant, represented in part by the Corinthians themselves and written "not in tablets of stone, but in fleshy tablets of the heart" (2Co 3.3). Offering encouragement to the young church, he cites his own sufferings: "We are troubled on every side, yet not distressed; we are perplexed, but not in despair" (2Co 4.8). And through his afflictions, he looks forward to an "eternal weight of glory" (2Co 4.17). After expanding further on the problems of his own ministry (2Co 5–6), he declares his renewed confidence in the Corinthians (2Co 7).

One of Paul's tasks is to raise money for needy Christians and for the church in Jerusalem in particular. He adroitly solicits from the Corinthians, equating generosity with high spiritual worth (2Co 8–9). Christ, "though he was rich, yet for your sakes he became poor, that ye through his poverty might be rich," the apostle notes (2Co 8.9). "God loveth a cheerful giver," he adds (2Co 9.7).

The Epistle's final section (2Co 10–13), a vigorous defense of Paul's ministry, may have been written as a separate letter. In it the apostle lashes out at certain unnamed detractors, who have complained that he lacks personal forcefulness. "Bear with me," he pleads, "for I am jealous over you with godly jealousy" (2Co 11.1-2). He mentions the perils he has undergone in his journeys to spread the Gospel—once stoned, thrice beaten with sticks, thrice shipwrecked. "When I am weak, then am I strong," he claims (2Co 12.10). And after he declares his readiness to make a third visit to Corinth (2Co 12.14–13.10), he closes with a final blessing to the church there (2Co 13.11-14).

GALATIANS

In this letter to the churches of Galatia in Asia Minor, Paul addresses the central issue of early Christianity: must a Gentile first become a Jew before he converts to the new faith? Paul's answer is an emphatic no. Conservative teachers had been visiting Christian churches, demanding that its members follow the laws of Moses; Paul, horrified, now writes an impassioned rebuttal.

The apostle begins by reviewing his call to God's ministry and his work among the Gentiles (Gal 1–2). From the very first the status of non-Jewish converts was a point of dispute, resulting in a confrontation between Paul and Cephas—another name for the apostle Peter. Must all Christians be circumcised and honor Jewish religious and dietary customs? "A man is not justified by the works of the law," Paul responds, "but by the faith of Jesus Christ" (Gal 2.16).

Paul appeals to Scripture to show that faith has always taken precedence over Mosaic law (Gal 3–4). The laws were written to curb certain transgressions, he admits, but they have imposed a bondage of the spirit. Christ has set men free, however (Gal 5). With freedom come other obligations beyond mere obedience—gentleness, compassion, mercy, and love for others (Gal 6).

Despite its brevity, Galatians is among the most important of Paul's Epistles, often called the Magna Charta of Christian liberty. It contains a major doctrinal statement: salvation comes from faith in Christ, not obedience to the law. It helped transform what might otherwise have been a minor Jewish sect into a great world religion.

EPHESIANS

Perhaps the most sublimely expressive of all Paul's writings, Ephesians reads more like a meditation than a letter to a specific church—and indeed the earliest manuscript makes no mention of Ephesus. It may have been meant for distribution among all the Christian missions—an early form of encyclical.

From a majestic opening hymn of praise and thanksgiving (Eph 1), the Epistle moves on to speak of Christ as redeemer and of the church's unity (Eph 2). The wall between Jew and Gentile has been broken down, and a new temple of the spirit has been raised, with "Jesus Christ himself being the chief cornerstone" (Eph 2.20). A deeply felt prayer follows (Eph 3.14-21), in which Paul begs God to grant his readers strength "to know the love of Christ, which passeth knowledge, that ye might be filled with all the fullness of God" (Eph 3.19).

Words of general advice on good Christian behavior make up the Epistle's second half. Lead a worthy life, "forbearing one another in love," the apostle enjoins (Eph 4.2). Put off "the old man" and put on the new, renouncing all pagan ways—lying, profanity, lust, anger, and the like (Eph 4). Instead, "walk as children of light," he advises (Eph 5.8). Wives are urged to be obedient and husbands loving, on the model of Christ's relationship with his church (Eph 5.21-33). More advice follows—to children, fathers, slaves, and masters (Eph 6.1-9). In the battle against sin, good Christians should don appropriate armor—the girdle of truth, "the breastplate of righteousness" (Eph 6.14). The letter ends with a commendation of its bearer, Tychicus, and a blessing (Eph 6.21-24).

PHILIPPIANS

Paul was being held in prison, possibly at Rome, when he wrote this brief missive to the church at Philippi, in Macedonia. Even so, it is the most joyous of his letters, breathing serenity and a sense of fellowship.

After a salutation expressing his deep affection for his readers, Paul outlines his own situation (Php 1.1-26). He is confident that his imprisonment has furthered the Gospel's spread, and he prays for courage to see the ordeal through to the end. He urges the Philippi congregation to keep steadfast in its faith and remember how Jesus became man, "obedient unto death, even the death of the cross" (Php 1.27–2.18).

Even in prison, Paul worries that the old-line Mosaic teachers will undercut his Gospel of tolerance, and he sternly warns against them (Php 3). Though a Jew himself, all his old values were overturned when he found Christ, the apostle declares. He is now prepared to share Christ's sufferings and hopes also to share his resurrection.

More encouragement follows (Php 4). The Philippians should seek whatever is true, honest, just, pure, and lovely. Follow my example, Paul says, "and the God of peace shall be with you" (Php 4.9). He ends with a note of gratitude for aid the community has sent him and for the concern they have shown him (Php 4.10-23).

COLOSSIANS

The church at Colossae, a small town in western Asia Minor, was founded by Epaphras, one of Paul's disciples. And while Paul was never able to visit it himself, he felt a strong paternal interest in its well-being. This letter, probably written during his Roman imprisonment, expresses that concern.

Paul follows his customary greeting and thanksgiving with a dissertation on Christ's universal supremacy (Col 1). He is "the image of the invisible God, the firstborn of every creature" (Col 1.15), a prime force in the world's creation whose appearance on earth has reconciled all things to the Father. God's church is a new creation, and its members at Colossae are exhorted to continue in the faith. Paul's own role in spreading the faith is briefly mentioned.

The apostle then warns against false teachings—apparently widespread throughout the early church (Col 2). The heresy at Colossae seems to have been an excessive devotion to ritual, the worship of angels rather than God, and an undue tendency toward asceticism. The antidote, Paul suggests, is a heightened spirituality based on the ethic of Christian love.

Practical admonitions to the Colossians make up the letter's second half (Col 3–4). The faithful are urged to give up their pagan ways and to take on a new persona of humility, meekness, and mercy. "The word of Christ" is to dwell among them, governing their life and worship. Wives, husbands, children, masters, and servants should perform their duties "as to the Lord, and not unto men" (Col 3.23). Prayer, wisdom, and decorum in speech are commended. Various personal messages and salutations close the letter.

1 THESSALONIANS

Written from Corinth in A.D. 51, this is the earliest of Paul's letters and probably the oldest surviving document in the New Testament. Paul had stopped at Thessalonica, the capital of Macedonia, during his first missionary journey, to preach in the synagogue there. He made so many converts that the local Jewish authorities became alarmed and drove him out of town. But, despite strong official opposition, the new congregation flourished, attracting both Jews and Gentiles. Here Paul follows up his visit with a characteristic message of encouragement and instruction.

The apostle's warm concern for the Thessalonians pervades his opening statement (1Th 1). He defends himself against his enemies, who have charged him with heresy, greed, and guile (1Th 2.1–16), and he reiterates his love for his new followers (1Th 2.17–3.13). Reminding them of his earlier lessons in holiness and chastity (1Th 4.1-12), he then addresses a question of doctrine that seems to perplex them (1Th 4.13–5.11). At the time of the Lord's Second Coming, will the dead in fact be raised with the living? Assuredly so, Paul declares, and he bids his readers, as they await that hoped-for event, to "watch and be sober" and to put on the armor of Christian faith and love (1Th 5.6-8). He ends with brief injunctions urging peace, patience, generosity, joy, prayer, thankfulness, and steadfastness (1Th 5.11-22).

2 THESSALONIANS

Concerned about continuing persecution, Paul wrote a second letter of encouragement, urging the congregation to remain steadfast and promising that in due course its enemies will meet with God's just vengeance (2Th 1).

Another problem regarding the Second Coming of Christ has also arisen. Some church members apparently think the great day is imminent or may even have occurred; others are so taken with the notion of instant salvation that they have laid off work to wait for it (2Th 2–3). Paul quickly disabuses them of both ideas. The Day of the Lord will not arrive until after a rebellion by a "man of sin, the son of perdition"—an Antichrist, in effect (2Th 2.3-11). And as for those idle brethren who "walk among you disorderly, working not at all, but are busybodies," they should not only be shunned but exhorted to return to work (2Th 3.6-12).

1 and 2 TIMOTHY, TITUS (The Pastoral Letters)

The so-called Pastoral Letters—two to Timothy and one to Titus—are addressed to individual church pastors. Timothy, the son of a Greek father and a Jewish mother who had converted to Christianity, was already well versed in the faith when Paul visited his home town in Asia Minor; Titus, a Greek, is thought to have been one of Paul's first Gentile converts. Both men accompanied the apostle on various of his missionary journeys and then went on to minister to their own parishes. These letters were intended to serve them as practical guides in church administration and doctrine.

Marked differences in style and vocabulary from Paul's other writings suggest that the final text of the Pastoral Letters is not by the apostle himself, however. Some scholars think that a loyal disciple may have collected—and heavily edited—several previously unpublished messages. In any event, all three closely reflect the apostle's typical ongoing concerns.

There is a strong insistence on preserving and protecting Paul's basic gospel. "Keep that which is committed to thy trust," the writer admonishes (1Ti 6.20; cf. 2Ti 1.12-14). False teachers, who are to be shunned, constitute an especial threat, "being abominable, and disobedient, and unto every good work reprobate" (Tit 1.16). Some communicants err by saying that the general resurrection of the dead has already happened (2Ti 2.18); others show a wayward bent by prohibiting marriage and the use of certain foods (1Ti 4.3-4).

The writer lays great stress on the proper relationship between a pastor and his flock. He suggests rules of conduct for bishops (1Ti 3.1-7; Tit 1.7-9), for deacons (1Ti 3.8-13), elders (1Ti 5.17-19), even for widows, who occupied a special place in these communities (1Ti 5.3-16). Apart from warnings against cupidity (1Ti 6.6-10) and dissension (2Ti 2.23; Tit 3.9-11), much of the moral teaching is addressed to particular groups, such as women (1Ti 2.9-15) and servants (Tit 2.9-10; cf. 1Ti 6.1-2). Yet the bright personal touches enliven these instructions: "Use a little wine for thy stomach's sake," the writer advises Timothy (1Ti 5.23), and he makes fond mention of Timothy's mother and grandmother (2Ti 1.5). There is a general tone of optimism. God our Saviour "will have all men to be saved, and to come unto the knowledge of the truth," the writer affirms (1Ti 2.4), and he holds out the hope of eternal life, "which God, that cannot lie, promised before the world began" (Tit 1.2).

PHILEMON

Philemon was a well-to-do member of the church at Colossae whose fugitive slave, Onesimus, had somehow met up with Paul, who was being held under house arrest in Rome. Under the apostle's influence, Onesimus had repented of his crime (possibly also including theft of his master's property), converted to Christianity, and promised to return to his former master. Paul, in his briefest and most personal Epistle, makes a plea for tolerance, urging Philemon to forgive and welcome back his slave as a fellow brother in Christ—hinting perhaps (Phm 21) that Philemon should give Onesimus his freedom.

Slavery was deeply entrenched in the ancient world, sanctioned by law, and runaways were subject to severe penalties. Paul could do nothing to overturn so basic an institution. But in the Gospel all men are equal under Christ; and so Paul tactfully tries to soften the effects of slavery. Many generations would pass before slavery was ended, but this letter shows how the Christian message of love and forgiveness would begin to subvert the harshness of the old order.

HEBREWS

From its style and vocabulary, most authorities agree that Hebrews was written not by Paul, but by some other leader of the early church. More tract than Epistle, it offers a closely reasoned argument to prove the pre-eminence of Christianity over Judaism. Presumably it was addressed to Christianized Jews who, faced with persecution from the temple, were wavering in their faith. Its date is put several years before the fall of Jerusalem in A.D. 70.

To win his readers back to Christ, the author emphasizes three points: the superiority of Jesus over his Old Testament predecessors, including the prophets, the angels, and Moses himself (Heb 1.1–3.6); the supremacy of Christ's ministry over that of the traditional Levite priests (Heb 4.14–7.28); and the overwhelming importance of Christ's sacrificial death compared to the ritual sacrifices offered by the Levites (Heb 8.1–10.39). Woven into this argument are passages of earnest exhortation in which the author urges his readers to remain steadfast in their beliefs.

The author sees Christ as God's only son, purified through sacrifice and elevated to a position higher than the angels. He is "crowned with glory and honor . . . that he by the grace of God might taste death for every man," the writer reasons (Heb 2.9). Because Jesus endured temptation on earth, he "is able to succor them that are tempted" (Heb 2.18). His fidelity to God, greater than that of Moses in the desert, serves as a model to his followers—but woe to those who stray, as did the Israelites on their way to Canaan (Heb 3.1–4.13).

The author drives home his argument with frequent references to Old Testament writings. He compares Christ's ministry with that of Melchisedec, a shadowy figure mentioned briefly in Genesis and in Psalm 110, whom he describes as being "a priest forever" (Heb 5.6). He speaks of Christ's new covenant, reminding readers of Jeremiah's prophecy that the old covenant has grown obsolete and should be replaced (Heb 8; 10.1-18). In one of the book's most resonant passages, the writer exhorts his readers to faith ("the substance of things hoped for, the evidence of things not seen") by citing examples from the full sweep of Israelite history, from Abel to Abraham and on down to David (Heb 11). Having invoked this great "cloud of witnesses," he then turns back to Jesus, who for his faith in the future joys of heaven willingly endured the cross (Heb 12).

Hebrews concludes with particular exhortations, blessings, and greetings focused, like all that precedes, upon the person of Christ, "the same yesterday, and today, and forever" (Heb 13.8). At the very end (Heb 13.22-24) is a reference to Paul's companion Timothy and a closing that sounds much like those of Paul's letters.

JAMES

More like a sermon than a letter, James is a collection of forcefully worded homilies on proper conduct. It is addressed, in the briefest of salutations, to Christianized Jews scattered throughout the ancient world.

Christians, the writer says, should rejoice in suffering because it engenders strength of purpose. He urges single-mindedness, endurance, humility, faith in God, and such charitable acts as visiting orphans and widows (Jas 1). The rich deserve no more respect than the poor, for God himself shows no partiality (Jas 2.1-7). Heed all God's commandments with equal devotion (Jas 2.8-14). Faith, essential though it may be, is no more important than good works (Jas 2.14–26).

The admonitions continue in no particular order. Curb the tongue, "a world of iniquity," and cultivate true wisdom instead, James enjoins (Jas 3). Since pride and enmity lead to killing and strife, "God resisteth the proud, but giveth grace unto the humble" (Jas 4.1-12). The future is unknowable, and God's will supreme (Jas 4.13-17). The rich, enemies of the righteous, are doomed; thus it is best to wait patiently for the Lord (Jas 5.7-11). The letter concludes with a number of additional exhortations: spend time in prayer, in anointing the sick, in the mutual confession of sins, and above all in converting the wayward—an act which "shall hide a multitude of sins" (Jas 5.8-20). Tradition ascribes this letter to Jesus' brother James, writing about A.D. 45. But modern opinion is uncertain and differs widely on both origin and date.

1 PETER

Addressed to Christians living in the Roman-occupied provinces of Asia Minor, this letter offers encouragement in difficult times. The early church has already suffered opposition from Jewish religious leaders; now it is threatened by a more disastrous persecution at the hands of the Romans.

The letter opens by stressing the promise of salvation held out in Jesus' death and resurrection and by praising the purifying virtues of suffering for Christ (1Pe 1.1–10). In a plea for godliness the writer urges the faithful to live up to their calling as "a royal priesthood, an holy nation," which has been called out of the darkness into light (1Pe 1.11–2.10).

The author then discusses the obligations of Christians during times of persecution, frequently citing the example of Christ himself. He tells his readers to win the respect of the Gentiles among whom they live. "Honor all men," he declares. "Love the brotherhood. Fear God. Honor the king" (1Pe 2.11-18). When oppressed by an unjust master, a Christian should not resist but should imitate Christ, the Suffering Servant, for "by his stripes ye were healed" (1Pe 2.19-25).

By the same token, wives should behave submissively to their husbands, and husbands considerately toward their wives (1Pe 3.1-12). Good Christians should keep their consciences clear even when abused, for if God so wills it is better to "suffer for well doing, than for evil doing" (1Pe 3.13-17). Christ himself, innocent as he was, suffered in order to bring men to God, the writer notes. Avoid temptation, he advises, and cultivate brotherly love, thus preparing the way for Christ's Second Coming; for "the end of all things is at hand: be ye therefore sober, and watch . . . that God in all things may be glorified through Jesus Christ" (1Pe 4.1-11).

The letter concludes with a second set of exhortations similar to the first, but possibly written at a later date. The author tells his readers to rejoice that they share in Christ's sufferings (1Pe 4.12-19). The church elders should be eager and unstinting shepherds of their flock, and everyone must guard against the devil, who "as a roaring lion, walketh about, seeking whom he may devour." Christ himself, the writer assures them, will see them through their troubles (1Pe 5.1-11).

The true authorship of this Epistle is open to question. By tradition, it was written from Rome by the apostle Peter, possibly during the persecution of Christians by the emperor Nero that started in A.D. 64. The scribe Sylvanus (1Pe 5.12) also served as assistant to Paul (1 and 2Th 1.1) and has been identified as Silas (Ac 15.22, 40; 16.19; 17.4). The letter's elegant Greek style suggests a different hand at work, and some scholars put it around the turn of the 1st century during a later period of oppression under the emperor Domitian.

2 PETER

The case against Peter's authorship of this letter is even stronger than that against 1 Peter. Most biblical scholars agree that this brief letter was composed in Peter's name by one of his disciples and published toward the end of the 1st century—making it in all likelihood the latest-written book in the New Testament. Its author's purpose is twofold: to warn against false doctrine and to reinforce his readers' belief in the Second Coming of Christ.

The writer begins with an exhortation to maintain holiness and good character, at the same time establishing his own credentials as an eyewitness to Christ's transfiguration (2Pe 1). Then he attacks the teachings of false prophets, which lead to sinfulness and God's due punishment (2Pe 2).

Among the worst transgressors are those who scoff at the doctrine of the Second Coming, and the author turns forcefully to defend it (2Pe 3). Just as God once destroyed the earth in a flood, he will do so again by fire. He will do so in his own good time, arriving suddenly, "as a thief in the night," to dissolve the entire universe in flame. But those who zealously await God's arrival, living blamelessly and at peace, will win the Lord's forgiveness and eternal salvation.

THE EPISTLES OF JOHN

These three short letters are traditionally associated with John the Evangelist, author of the fourth Gospel. They may have been written by John himself or by some other influential church figure who had taken up John's message. For both in style of expression and in spiritual outlook the letters closely mirror the Evangelist's known work.

The first letter, and the most important one, is virtually a commentary on John's Gospel, aimed at correcting certain questionable interpretations of it. One Christian sect, the Gnostics, had come to deny that Jesus could be both God and man. John's first letter resolutely denounces this heresy. The author expands on Christ's mystical persona as deity, as redeemer, and as mortal man. "We have an advocate with the Father, Jesus Christ the righteous: and he is the propitiation for our sins," he affirms (1Jn 2.1-2).

Readers are warned against false teachers—Antichrists who have come to subvert the Gospel (1Jn 2.18-26). The writer gives supreme importance to the twin themes of faith and love: shun sin, obey God, "believe in the name of his Son Jesus Christ, and love one another," he commands (1Jn 3). With faith in Christ and love of the Father, the true believer becomes a child of God, and so overcomes the world and its troubles (1Jn 5).

The second and third letters are brief personal notes. One, addressed to an unidentified local church, reaffirms John's message of love and faith (2Jn). The other commends an influential church member, Gaius, for his Christian hospitality to all men (3Jn).

JUDE

The intent of this short, forceful letter is to denounce certain false teachers who were infiltrating the early church. The writer does not specify the nature of their heresy except to describe it as a denial of Christ. Instead, he makes a direct attack on the teachers themselves. He calls them murmurers, complainers, mockers, and worldly people "having not the Spirit" (Jude 19). They will suffer dire punishment, he predicts, similar to that visited on Sodom and Gomorrah or on the rebellious angels that God keeps chained in eternal gloom.

The letter's date and destination are uncertain, and even its true authorship remains unknown, though it was long attributed to Jude, a brother of James and Jesus. It closes with a beautiful and moving hymn of praise (Jude 24–25).

REVELATION

In its powerful imagery and glorious poetic cadences, Revelation brings the New Testament to a fitting conclusion. Its author was a Christian holy man named John, who was exiled to the rocky island of Patmos in the Aegean, tradition says, for refusing to worship an image of the Roman emperor Domitian (A.D. 81–96). There is strong scholarly opinion, however, that the core of the book dates to the time of Nero and before the fall of Jerusalem in A.D. 70. At any rate, it was on Patmos that John experienced a series of remarkable visions—some beautiful, some horrifying, all highly symbolic. Upon his release, he wrote them down as an affirmation of faith in the imminent triumph of Christianity.

As with much other writing in time of persecution, the symbolism in Revelation is purposefully obscure—full of strange beasts, apocalyptic figures, and a complex numerical code, the key to which is now lost. Much of the imagery is derived from the Old Testament prophets Ezekiel and Daniel and might have appeared meaningless to any Roman official who happened to obtain a copy of the manuscript.

The book's prologue is clear, however. John addresses the seven Christian churches in the Roman province of Asia Minor, exhorting each to perseverance and repentance (Rev 1–3). Then come the visions. "I looked, and, behold, a door was opened in heaven," the seer declares (Rev 4.1). Behind the door a fantastic new world appears—a heavenly court with a throne in the center, surrounded by 24 other thrones and fronted by a sea of glass. Four symbolic creatures borrowed from Ezekiel—lion, ox, man, and eagle—stand attendance (Rev 4). God, seated on the central throne, holds a book with seven seals. In front of him Christ, in the shape of a heavenly lamb, proceeds to open the seals (Rev 5).

From each of the first four seals a horse springs out, the last, pale in color, being ridden by Death. The souls of the Christian martyrs emerge from the next seal, and then, with the breaking of the sixth seal, a terrible earthquake strikes (Rev 6). The day of judgment is at hand. It arrives when the seventh seal is opened (Rev 8–9). Seven angels appear, blowing seven trumpets and announcing various universal cataclysms. Then, as the seventh angel sounds his trumpet, a voice cries out that the kingdom of God has arrived (Rev 11.14-19).

A great battle now rages in heaven between a dragon and the archangel Michael (Rev 12). Two enormous beasts, symbolizing Rome and worship of its emperor, rise up to terrorize the earth (Rev 13). Finally, the Lamb of God appears on Mount Zion, symbolizing the victory of Christ (Rev 14).

Images of judgment fill the prophet's gaze (Rev 15–16). He hears a sentence of doom pronounced upon a great whore "drunken with the blood of the saints"—a reference to the cruelties of the Roman Empire (Rev 17). He witnesses the fall of Babylon—that is, Rome (Rev 18). Then, with God's enemies vanquished, a heavenly choir sings a canticle of praise: "Alleluia: for the Lord God omnipotent reigneth" (Rev 19.6). Satan is bound in chains and cast into a bottomless pit. And the reign of the Messiah begins, to last for a thousand years (Rev 20).

The seer now offers a vision of the new Jerusalem, where God himself will "wipe away all tears from their eyes; and there shall be no more death, neither sorrow, nor crying, neither shall there be any more pain" (Rev 21.4). So radiant is this heavenly city that it has "no need of the sun, neither of the moon, to shine in it: for the glory of God did lighten it, and the Lamb is the light thereof" (Rev 21.23). And on this triumphant note the New Testament draws to a close.

The Hebrew Bible

The Law
Genesis
Exodus
Leviticus
Numbers
Deuteronomy

The Prophets
Former Prophets
Joshua
Judges
Samuel
Kings

Latter Prophets
Isaiah
Jeremiah
Ezekiel
The Twelve
(Hosea, Joel, Amos,
Obadiah, Jonah, Micah,
Nahum, Habakkuk, Zephaniah,
Haggai, Zechariah, Malachi)

The Writings
Psalms
Proverbs
Job
Song of Songs
Ruth
Lamentations
Ecclesiastes
Esther
Daniel
Ezra-Nehemiah
Chronicles

The Apocrypha

*Books or sections of books recognized as part of the Old Testament canon in Roman Catholic Bibles.

1 Esdras
2 Esdras
Tobit*
Judith*
Additions to Esther*
Wisdom of Solomon*
Ecclesiasticus (Sirach)*
Baruch*
Letter of Jeremiah*
(included in Baruch)
Prayer of Azariah and the Song
of the Three Young Men*
Susanna*
Bel and the Dragon*
(included in Daniel)
Prayer of Manasseh
1 Maccabees*
2 Maccabees*

The Biblical Cosmos

Genesis means "beginning," and the Book of Genesis is principally an account of the beginnings of mankind, from Adam down to the age of the Patriarchs, setting the stage for Israel's emergence as a people and a nation. But Genesis also deals with ultimate beginnings: the origin of the earth, the sun, and the stars—the whole of the physical universe.

Through the ages, many have maintained that the scriptural passages referring to the Creation describe the cosmos in precise, literal terms—in other words, that the Bible offers a true cosmology, or picture of the structure and workings of the universe. In certain periods, religious authorities have disparaged or even suppressed scientific theories that seemed to contradict Old Testament descriptions of the earth and heavens. At other times, attempts have been made to reconcile the apparent conflicts between the images of Scripture and the observations of scientists. The debate has persisted into our own time, though with inevitable differences in tone and perspective—as well as some surprising developments.

What does the Bible actually say about the physical universe? The Creation narrative in Genesis is thought to be a blend of two different traditions. In the second (and reputedly older) version, beginning at Genesis 2.4, man is the focus of attention. The main cosmological detail is a subterranean flood that waters the earth; significantly, agriculture in Mesopotamia depended less on rain than on water from springs. This account, which was probably committed to writing around the 10th century B.C., emphasizes man's function as God's gardener, created to tend and till the earth. Man is made from clay and woman is created from one of his ribs. Their relationship to the universe is not explored.

The other Genesis account, however, deals with the birth of the entire cosmos, from the creation of light on the first day to the appearance of man on the sixth. This version (Gen 1.1–2.4) is thought to date from the 6th century B.C. and is considered more comprehensive and sophisticated than the other. Many aspects seem not to be in accord with modern scientific knowledge, however. Light appears before there is a sun, the heavenly bodies are created after the earth, and birds precede the appearance of any land animals. In addition, this version of creation, augmented by references in other books of the Old Testament, assumes a specific model of the universe: a flat, disk-like earth surrounded by the oceans; a sky (called "the firmament"), which like a dome ("hard as a molten mirror," Job 37.18) holds back the waters above it; and a complementary bowl beneath the earth (*Sheol*, the nether region of the dead). In the view of most scholars today, the passages describing the universe or its constituent parts generally reflect the beliefs that prevailed at the time they were written.

Cosmology, in any case, was not a primary concern of the Old Testament writers. The total picture to be assembled from the scattered references—chiefly in Genesis, Job, Proverbs, and Isaiah—is incomplete, fragmentary, and at times contradictory. Some of the references may well have been intended by the authors as poetic conceptions rather than as literal descriptions; human reason, it was believed, simply could not comprehend anything so vast as the creation and structuring of the cosmos. Indeed, no single passage in the Bible attempts to describe the universe as a whole.

Nor did the authors of the New Testament feel impelled to add any important cosmological ideas to the existing accounts. Nevertheless, in the centuries that followed, acceptance of the Old Testament portrayals as literally true was to become an article of faith for the leaders of the church. It may be that the political chaos resulting from the decline of the Roman Empire was at least partially responsible for the tendency of church fathers in the 3rd and 4th centuries to insist on literal interpretation of the Scriptures. They were intent on eradicating beliefs and traditions of all kinds that echoed the paganism of Greece and Rome. Consequently, the Greek models of a universe with a spherical earth at its center, though based on actual observation and the use of reason, were rejected. To be sure, not all Christian thinkers were ready to dismiss completely the accomplishments of such pagan philosophers as Plato, who pictured a well-ordered geocentric (earth-centered) universe, and Aristotle, who described the movements of the stars and planets around the earth. In the main, however, the church fathers strove to suppress rather than to assimilate the teachings of the Greeks.

Many, for example, insisted that, as indicated in Genesis, the vault of heaven indeed held up literal waters. The explanation offered for this phenomenon was the need to cool the firmament and protect the earth from devastation by celestial fire. In addition, a popular Christian model of the universe had the shape of a tabernacle, the flat earth being surmounted by a two-storied heaven. The lower heaven sent down the heat and light of the heavenly bodies, while the upper heaven, invisible to man, contained only fire; it was this structure that restrained the supercelestial waters.

Against the Greek notions of cosmology, arguments continued to be fierce, contemptuous, and often ingenious. It was said that the earth was so heavy that it obviously had to be at the bottom of the universe rather than in the center. It was argued that a spherical earth, which implied the existence of people standing upside down on the other side of the globe, could not logically exist. In various forms, the basic ideas of a flat earth and a firmament holding back waters were to have some currency throughout the Middle Ages. How, in this model, did the sun set? According to a 7th-century geographer, whose view was typical, it disappeared each night behind a wall of high mountains that had never been seen by man because God willed them to be inaccessible.

Slowly, however, educated people came to realize that the earth must be spherical—even if they did not see fit to propagate this knowledge. Early in the 8th century, England's renowned scholar, the Venerable Bede, reproduced—often almost verbatim—the geocentric model proposed by the Roman Pliny not long after the time of Jesus. In 999, the ascension to the papal throne of an accomplished mathematician, Sylvester II, led to acceptance of the ideas that the earth is round and that the planets circle around it. Increasingly, Latin scientific writings, or Greek writings in Latin translation, were being revived. Indeed, by the 12th century, the Norman William of Conches found it possible to challenge the Genesis picture of water held above the firmament as irrational, suggesting that the passage be construed instead as an allegory.

Meanwhile, in the Arab countries to the east, original Greek texts had been translated, studied, and commented upon during their long period of eclipse in the West. Chiefly through the work of the great 12th-century Islamic scholar Averroes, the theories of Aristotle began to reappear. Still banned early in the 13th century, Aristotelian thought won the church's support by midcentury and became a mainstay of philosophic training at every major seat of Christian learning for the next 400 years. Owing to the tenacity of such men as Thomas Aquinas, classical science became recognized as an ally rather than a rebuttal of scriptural cosmology.

Mankind ventures through an opening in the crystalline dome of the firmament—the outer limit of the cosmos as described in the Bible and preserved in church tradition—to discover a vast, astonishing universe of spheres and gyres in this early 16th-century woodcut.

Aquinas, a professor of theology at the University of Paris, is still considered one of the great philosophers of all time. He was a Scholastic, like other medieval masters such as Albertus Magnus and Roger Bacon. They all stressed that reason could be used to prove the truth of the scriptures, but it was Aquinas who most elegantly and persuasively showed that it was possible to reconcile the religious beliefs inspired by divine revelation with the insights resulting from the direct, systematic observation of nature. He was not disturbed when reason and revelation seemed to arrive at contrary conclusions. Scientific knowledge and biblical doctrine, he was convinced, ultimately spring from the same source; they are distinct forms of truth, superficially inconsistent, perhaps, but separately true nonetheless. In effect, his commentaries brought to a conclusion the debate over the acceptance of Aristotelian cosmology. Possibly, Aquinas suggested, the non-scientific aspects of the Genesis creation story had been necessary in ancient times to communicate the essence of complex ideas to the peoples who first heard the word of God.

Once reinstated in the mainstream of western thought, Aristotle's model of the universe was to reign supreme. His earth-centered cosmos was compounded of five elements—ether, earth, fire, air, and water. Surrounding the spherical earth were numerous celestial spheres which moved the five known planets as well as the sun, the moon, and the stars. Enclosing the spheres was the *primum mobile,* or first mover, which kept them all in motion. To explain irregularities observed in the orbits of the heavenly bodies, Aristotle had suggested as many as 55 spheres. Subsequent scholars were to decrease this number, but the basic Aristotelian concepts would not be challenged for generations.

Aristotle had speculated, for example, that the motions of the spheres were controlled by separate intelligences. This fit well with Aquinas' view that angels, acting under divine control, moved the heavenly bodies. Both agreed that there was a basic difference between the perfect, eternal matter of the heavens and the flawed, transitory matter of earth. It followed that celestial bodies, being perfect, were unique (while earth had many individuals of each type); they also moved in a circle—the most nearly perfect of motions, since the object returned to its starting point. Absolute perfection, to both Aristotle and Aquinas, would be complete immobility.

This cosmology was not simply a theoretical picture. It was accepted as an accurate portrayal of the physical universe. It

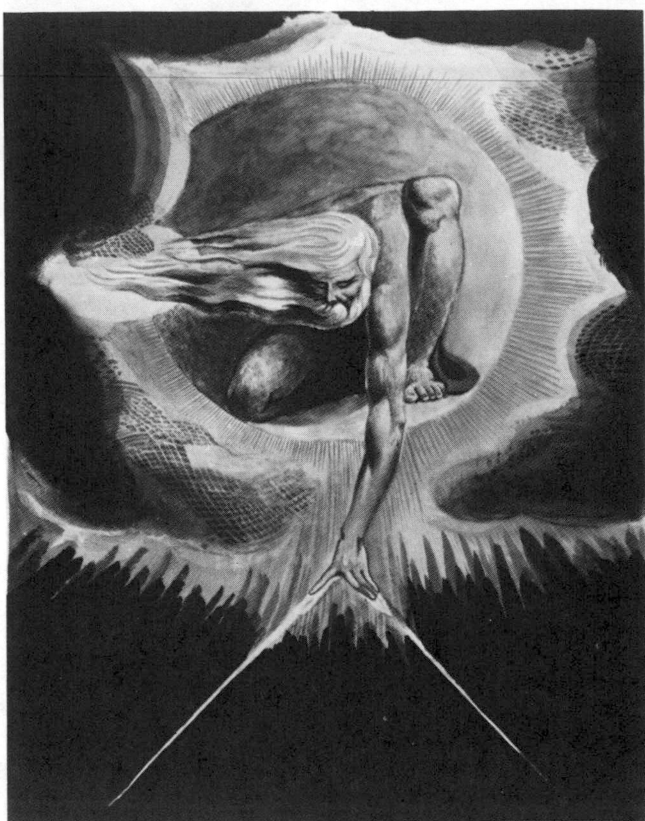

The Ancient of Days *by William Blake (1757-1827) vividly illustrates the conception of God as architect of the cosmos, the master builder who "set a compass upon the face of the depth" (Pr 8.27).*

helped the faithful Christian understand how to view the world and see God manifested therein. Moreover, the cosmological model that Aquinas refined from Aristotle had crucial implications for everyday life. Through the actions of the heavenly bodies, God worked his will; in other words, nearly all material events were affected by these celestial bodies. The implied justification of astrology had to be qualified by Aquinas, who insisted that this science had no relationship to those events which involve man's free will. The essential concept was that the universe was the instrument of God's plan. As the great Italian poet Dante would write, it was "love that moves the sun and the other stars." In such a view of the world, man was at the center, the recipient of divine love, the focal point of divine creation.

From the most ancient times, of course, the sun and stars have been universally viewed as a key to the structure of the cosmos. The connectedness of all things was vividly set forth in the Talmud: "There is not a blade of grass that has not its star in the heavens to strike it and say to it: grow!" For Jews and early Christians, the fountainhead of such studies was Mesopotamia, homeland of Babylonian, Chaldean, and Persian astronomy and astrology. There was actually no strict division among the ancients between these two disciplines—nor was there to be such a divison anywhere, in fact, until the 17th century in Europe.

In the Bible proper, there are only a few references to astrology. Most relate to Babylonian "star-gazers." Then, of course, there are the Magi—Eastern astrologers, possibly Persian—who in the New Testament followed the star to Bethlehem in order to render homage to the infant Jesus. There was a very strong current of popular belief in astrology among ancient Jews, but biblical authority—from the Deuteronomic prohibition of worshipping the sun, moon, and stars (Dt 4.19) on through the scoffing references to astrology in Isaiah and Jeremiah (Isa 47.13; Jer 10.2)—ran counter to this belief because it could all too easily lead to idolatry. However, the current persisted, and medieval Christian literature made frequent references to learned Jews who were the possessors of a cosmological system including astrology and an occult, Kabbalistic interpretation of the Scriptures. Such was the background of the medieval Christian belief in astrology.

It was Dante's masterpiece, *The Divine Comedy*, written in the early 1300s, that most beautifully summed up the dominant medieval view of the universe. Profoundly immersed in the scientific learning of his time, the poet placed hell precisely in the center of a spherical earth, and purgatory was a mountain diametrically opposite to Jerusalem. His celestial spheres increased in perfection and glory until he reached the tenth, or Empyrean, where the Deity ruled.

In nature, then, there was a hierarchy, a logical progression from the lower to the higher. To the medieval Christian this hierarchy was an image of supernatural truth. Thanks in part to the influence of the newly rediscovered Greeks, Christian theologians began to stress the value of direct observation of nature as a kind of worship; to see nature, to plumb its secrets, was to acknowledge the majesty of God and to begin to appreciate his infinite wisdom. As the Apostle Paul had written, it was possible for the believer to come to know God and his attributes through created things. Study of the cosmos was thus integrated into the Christian belief that God had created the universe; indeed, its orderliness was powerful proof of God's existence.

It was not until 1543, when the Polish astronomer Copernicus published his epochal *Concerning the Revolutions of the Celestial Spheres*, that Christian cosmology began to change so as to accommodate the discovery that the earth revolves around the sun. Although the church would prohibit Copernicus' work on the heliocentric (sun-centered) system for 200 years and persecute Galileo in the 17th century for publicizing telescopic observations that supported the Copernican theory, eventually the heliocentric model was to become accepted in Christian cosmology.

In our own time, the Christian world has increasingly come to accept the findings of science, turning to astronomers and physicists rather than to theologians for a literal understanding of the structure of the universe. The cosmological passages of the Bible have been interpreted as being poetically or symbolically edifying—a mirror of moral if not objective reality. Ironically, though, recent thinking among physicists suggests that at least part of the Genesis version of the creation is scientifically quite plausible. The so-called "Big Bang" theory of the origin of the universe, now accepted by most scientists, is based on evidence indicating that the universe was born at a definite moment in time in a flash of energy and light. This great cosmic fireball, which occurred perhaps 20 billion years ago, would have destroyed anything that had existed before and would have produced the elements for everything which has existed since. In other words, as the astrophysicist Robert Jastrow has pointed out, the Genesis concept of a universe with a definite beginning is borne out by scientific study—as is the impossibility of looking past that instant to see what, if anything, might have existed before.

The relationship between the Scriptures and the scientific view of the universe may not yet be fully understood. Some argue that scientific truth is somehow hidden in the sacred texts, to be revealed to the faithful who possess the key. Others, in the tradition of Aquinas, contend that the apparent conflicts between biblical and scientific cosmologies need not distress the believer. There are those who believe that mankind should strive to uncover the secrets of creation, and those who warn against impious curiosity—as one person, according to Saint Augustine, did when considering what the Creator might have been doing before time began: "He was creating Hell for people who asked questions like that."

Today, even as most would concur that science has accurately pictured the physical structure of the universe, discoveries emerge that are ever more difficult to imagine concretely: space that curves, parallel lines that converge, light trapped by gravity in a black hole. How can these concepts be represented in a cosmological model? Will expanded knowledge of physical principles find unexpected resonance in the Bible's few, but compelling, passages of ancient cosmology? These questions will be considered cautiously both by scientists of faith and by rationalist theologians so long as Christians believe that the Scriptures may have been intended to portray in inspired words the physical truth of the universe.

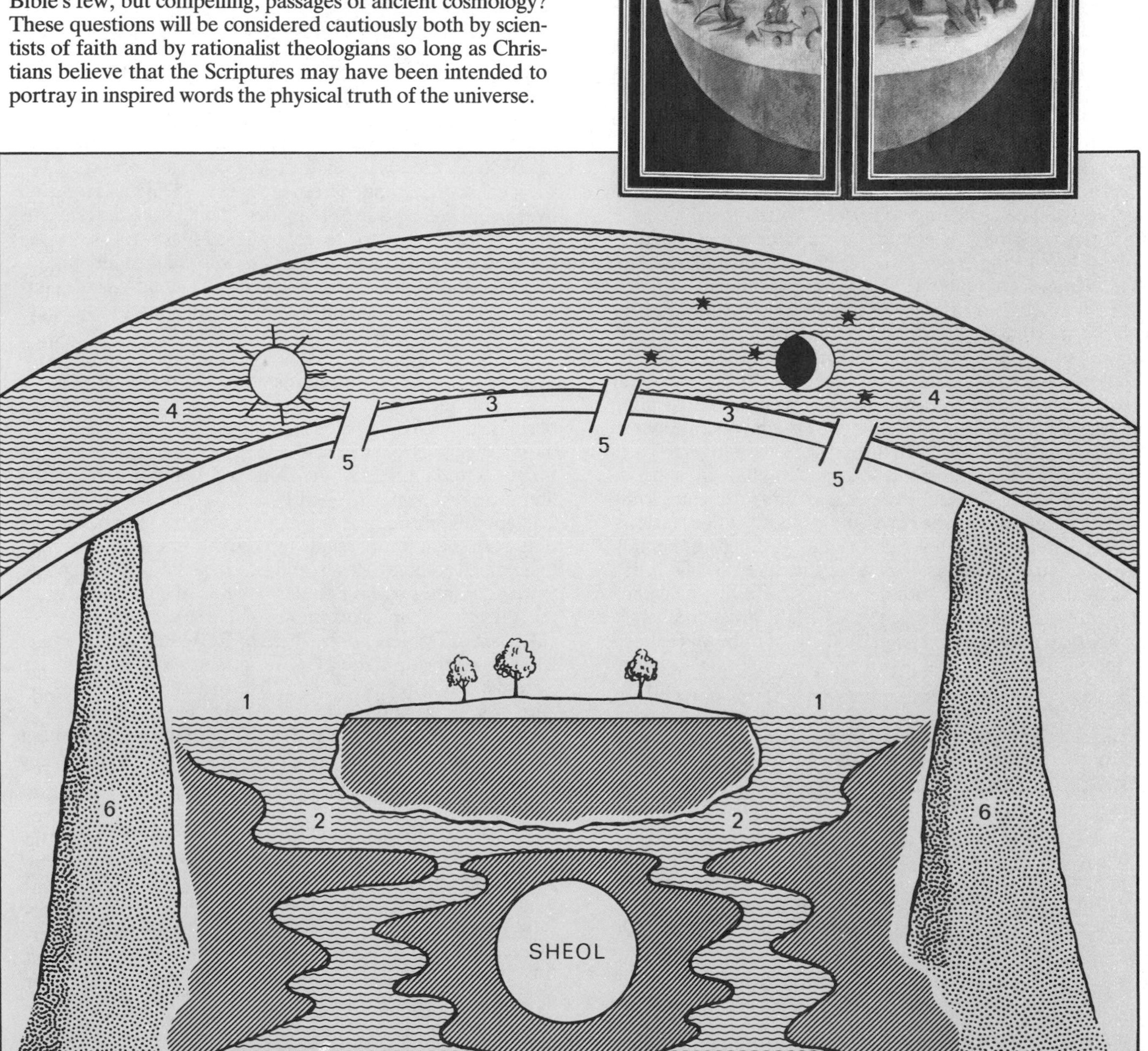

In this schematic rendering of the Old Testament cosmos, the circular disc of the earth is bounded by seas (1) fed from vast subterranean waters (2), in the midst of which is Sheol, resting place of the dead. Arcing over the earth, the dome of the firmament (3) holds back the waters above (4), permitting rain to fall through windowlike openings (5). Above the firmament, the sun, moon, and stars move in their courses, and the heavens ascend to their uppermost level, the abode of God. The earth and firmamant both rest on mysterious pillars (6), invisible to man, rising out of the watery chaos. Above right, the third day of Creation—in which dry land was separated from the seas and the first plant life appeared—as visualized by the Dutch artist Hieronymus Bosch (c. 1450-1516).

Prophecy: The Lion's Roar

The lion hath roared, who will not fear? the Lord God hath spoken, who can but prophecy? (Amos 3.8)

From its beginnings, Judeo-Christian tradition has revered prophecy as a living medium of the word of God. As early as the 11th century B.C., two kinds of prophet were known in Israel—ecstatic promulgators of Yahwistic faith, some of whom lived communally and traveled in music-making bands, and the solitary seer, gifted with the ability to foretell the future.

The aim and character of Old Testament prophecy were first to be typified, however, by Samuel. A charismatic preacher who stressed the critical importance of God's word and insisted that fidelity to moral law should supplant sacrifice as a test of virtue, Samuel advised and chastised King Saul. Prophets subsequently took on a significant political role: a true prophet, it was believed, could read the future, judge even a king's personal behavior, and capably give advice on matters of national policy. Characteristically, the relationship between prophet and king was close, if often troubled, as in the famous encounters between David and Nathan. The duty of the prophet in such cases was to ensure that Israel's anointed leader perform God's will in day-to-day affairs.

Gradually, the prophet's role expanded to include the mission of exhorting all Jews, not just their royal representative. Coming to the fore in periods of crisis, prophets urged the people to repent before God punished them for their sins. For example, Amos, Hosea, and Isaiah predicted the Assyrian victory that would lead to captivity of the northern tribes in 721 B.C. The fall of Jerusalem to Babylon's armies in 587 B.C. was prophesied by Jeremiah, Ezekiel, Zephaniah, and Habakkuk. During the Babylonian captivity, the comforting promise of release and the restoration of both nation and temple was first announced by Ezekiel and, just before its fulfillment, by the anonymous prophet of the exile, Second Isaiah (so called for being the author, scholars believe, of chapters 40–66 of the Book of Isaiah). The last of the great prophets in the classical period were Haggai and Zechariah, who exhorted the discouraged Jews, worn out by economic hardships and regional hostilities, to fulfill God's redemptive purpose by rebuilding the temple.

This lengthy, vigorous age of prophetic intervention in the affairs of men was dominated by uniquely individual figures—the aristocratic Isaiah, the angrily pessimistic Jeremiah, the intensely empathetic Hosea who married a prostitute to symbolize God's steadfast love for the "whoring" nation of Israel. Some, like Habakkuk, were even capable of turning a wary eye on the divine will itself, asking, "Wherefore lookest thou upon them that deal treacherously, and holdest thy tongue when the wicked devoureth the man that is more righteous than he?" What each prophet had experienced was a decisive "call" to serve the will of God. Some accepted this call with enthusiasm, some with hesitation, but all were to feel the urgency of a compulsion to spread the word as well as unshakable confidence in the righteousness of their message, no matter how fierce the opposition they encountered.

Although each prophet addressed the distinct problems of his own time, several themes reappeared through the ages. A true prophet saw God in everything, actively giving religious meaning to historical events. Much Old Testament prophecy centered particularly on the fate of Jerusalem: to be spared in the 8th century B.C. (Isaiah); to be destroyed in the 6th century (Jeremiah, Ezekiel); to be rebuilt along with the temple, also in the 6th century (Haggai and Zechariah). A similar theme was to run through the much later New Testament and rabbinical writings concerning the destruction of the temple and city, which was interpreted as an act of divine judgment by both Christians and Jews, though in different ways.

Throughout the classical Old Testament period, it was considered that, whereas Israel's priests could ably teach religious law, the prophet alone had access to the divine word. That could be a destructive force, as when Isaiah predicted Israel's fall because of idolatry, but it could also offer comfort, as when Second Isaiah promised, "The grass withereth, the flower fadeth: but the word of our God shall stand for ever" (Isa 40.8). Another key prophetic theme was the supremacy of moral righteousness. Micah asked, "what doth the Lord require of thee, but to do justly, and to love mercy, and to walk humbly with thy God?" (Mic 6.8). Finally, the classical prophets looked to God's ultimate victory over evil in the future. Three types of messianic figure came to be predicted—the ideal king descended from the house of David, as foretold by Isaiah; Daniel's Son of Man, descending from the heavens to rule forever; and the teacher of God's law, the "suffering servant" described in Second Isaiah, who would endure hardship and death for the sake of others. The hundreds of references in the Old Testament to such a figure were, of course, to become central elements of Christian belief.

After a period of decline, Jewish prophecy sprang to vibrant life again in the 2nd century B.C. The new genre known as Apocalyptic (from the Greek *apokalupsis*, "unveiling") developed chiefly in response to the national crisis lasting almost 250 years, from the Maccabean period until the destruction of Jerusalem in A.D. 70. Little wonder that it inspired a literature of apocalypse—visionary, cryptic, doom-ridden. The apocalyptic authors wrote what purported to be revelations of the near future as told by God centuries earlier to such figures as Abraham, Moses, and Daniel. Although the apocalyptic tradition proved popular down to the early Christian era, only two complete examples of it exist in today's Bible—the Book of Daniel and the Book of Revelation. It nevertheless echoes through the New Testament writings, as in the Transfiguration scene of Mt 17.1-8, paralleled in Mk 9.2-8 and Lk 9.28-36, and in various passages in the Epistles. The same is true of the Dead Sea Scrolls, which include a number of manuscripts belonging to apocalyptic prophecy, especially that of the War of the Children of Light.

Probably borrowing from Persian beliefs, the apocalyptic writers introduced into Judaism the concept of reward or punishment after death and the idea of a continuing war between good and evil on the cosmic scale. They saw the history of man and of the universe as a battle between the demonic forces of evil and the righteous forces of heaven. In their view, divine intervention would bring about a crisis ending in victory over evil and the arrival of an age of peace and plenty, an eternal Sabbath. In expounding these themes, fantastic images and symbols were often invoked, such as charging rams, portents of blood in the heavens, Death mounted on a pale horse. The apocalyptic author, himself experiencing a vision, might reinterpret imagery that had been used by others before him—the malformed beast thought to represent Greece during the age of Hellenistic domination, for example, became a symbol for Rome when she conquered the Holy Land.

At the beginning of the Christian era, prophecy dramatically became actual history in the eyes of Jesus' followers. He was seen as the Messiah whose advent had been foretold by

A mystical wheel painted in Florence about 1450, echoing Ezekiel's vision of wheels of fire (Eze 1). Old Testament figures fill the outer circle, New Testament figures the inner; in the corners are Ezekiel and Pope Gregory I, author of the 6th-century Homilies on Ezekiel.

the classical prophets of the Old Testament. Skeptics may have objected that the ancient prophecies portrayed a king, but the authors of the New Testament believed that certain passages should be read in a broader sense, taking into account not merely the human author's limited understanding, but the full import of divinely intended meaning. For the faithful, the Crucifixion had not been a setback of Jesus' mission. On the contrary, this physical suffering had initiated those events that would lead to the end of the ages. His Resurrection was a further step toward the day of God's final judgment. Jesus had promised to return. Expectation of the Second Coming would fuel religious debate from apostolic times down to the present. Could the date be predicted, on the basis of scriptural prophecy? Was it impious or reckless to try to do so? Even among the early fathers of the church it was a subject of sharp disagreement. Some confidently expected that Jesus would return within their lifetimes, while others, like Paul, who modified his view as time went on, cautioned that the believer should be prepared but not impatient.

The role of prophecy, therefore, continues to be a source of intellectual debate and spiritual involvement. Much as in Old Testament days, many of the faithful look for signs so that they may better understand divine intent. Christianity, it has been said, is characterized by a belief in the fulfillment of promise. Those who believe that the life and teachings of Jesus brought the Old Testament to fruition may reasonably conclude, as well, that the life to come will be a fulfillment of New Testament prophecy. In that regard, most biblical scholars would agree that the primary aim of prophecy is not to assign specific dates; rather, its purpose is to remind man of God's grace, and to encourage him to live his life as a reflection of that grace.

The Parables of Jesus

A king invites poor people in from the streets to his son's wedding banquet . . . a shepherd leaves an entire flock grazing in the hills to save a single lost sheep . . . a passing Samaritan rescues a man who might despise him as an inferior. These simple but profound stories are known as "parables," an ancient form of wisdom teaching practiced throughout the lands of the Near East and the Mediterranean. In the three Synoptic Gospels—Matthew, Mark, and Luke—Jesus is shown to have been supremely skilled in the use of this emotionally moving and intellectually provocative device.

Many theologians consider the parables the most authentic of Jesus' recorded words, often giving us extraordinary insights into the workings of his mind. We must remember, though, that these stories were originally spoken aloud, not composed for the written page. Their true effectiveness was in persuading members of large outdoor audiences to change their spiritually arid or unthinkingly selfish lives. Gently but insistently, the messages are underscored: God's judgment may be imminent; God's mercy is infinite toward those who repent; positive discipleship requires both decision and action; the sincerity of the heart is more significant than strict adherence to legalism.

Scholars of the Bible disagree on the actual number of parables: depending on how they are counted, there are between 30 and 60 in the New Testament. (Parables figure in the Old Testament too, of course; a well-known example is Nathan's pointed story of the rich man and the poor man, told to David in 2Sa 12.) Some would define only a complete, rounded narrative as a parable; others cite the numerous parable-like sayings or metaphors used to illustrate spiritual ideas in a vivid, concrete way. Generally, however, there is agreement on a traditional core of 35 to 40 stories, many of which have become essential to Christian discourse as well as to Western ethics, art, and literature. Even in casual speech, it is hardly surprising to encounter references to the Prodigal Son, the Good Samaritan, or the Lost Sheep.

It was Mark who wrote that there was a parable in all that Jesus taught: "Without a parable spake he not unto them" (Mk 4.34). About a third of Jesus' teachings, as documented in the Gospels, are in parable form. It was also Mark who suggested that parables were a form of teaching designed to be understood only by the enlightened inner circle of disciples (Mk 4.11-12). Some scholars, however, believe that Mark simply meant that a hearer's own unwillingness to grasp the implied message of a parable would keep him in the dark.

In either event, the Gospels of Matthew and Luke clearly reflect the view that parables are created not to obscure but to reveal. The parables in their writings are set down succinctly and dramatically; the single idea that informs the tale is forcefully illustrated. We hear a Jesus who draws from the everyday world familiar to his listeners, an inspired teacher who does not condescend to his audience. Indeed, the parables are so completely a product of time and place that historians view them as an especially fertile source of information on the way ordinary people lived and worked in the Holy Land at the beginning of the Christian era.

Contemporary theologians warn that, while the meaning of most of Jesus' parables is abundantly clear, there are some that contain ambiguities beneath the outward simplicity. Because the message of a parable is indirect, relying on suggested meaning rather than literal statement, one scholar cautions that, in some cases, "we must simply be willing to settle for something less than absolute precision and certainty."

A possible complicating factor is that the Gospels were written decades after Jesus' death. Although it was a tradition of the age that disciples committed their teacher's words to memory exactly as they were spoken, it is reasonable to assume that time would bring about some changes as parables were transmitted orally through the growing network of Christian congregations. In addition, to retain the parables' function as a spiritual teaching device, the evangelists doubtless made editorial alterations to ensure that the message would be accessible to audiences living in different places. The parables as recorded in the New Testament certainly remain true to Jesus' teaching, but occasionally they may also reflect the outlooks or particular needs of the evangelists who wrote them down.

The most beloved parables are characterized by simplicity, emotional directness, and spontaneity. They bridge the gap between the mundane and the spiritual by sparking the listener's imagination, by inspiring him or her to embark upon a personal search for meaning. As the following examples make clear, the parables express in unmistakably human terms the central truths of Jesus' message, truths that know no bounds of time or place.

The Good Samaritan: To Jesus, love of God and of one's neighbor was the essence of faith. Love was, in fact, the single most important attribute he required of his disciples. In this famous parable, a Jew is left for dead by robbers. A priest and a Levite, both members of the Jerusalem religious establishment, see him on the lonely road but pass him by. It is the Samaritan, neither Jew nor Gentile, hated and considered heretical, who stops, binds up the victim's wounds, and carries him to safety. A man who (despite centuries-old racial and religious antagonisms) helps another is a true *neighbor,* living out the principles enunciated in the Sermon on the Mount (Mt 5) and exemplified in Jesus' encounter with the Samaritan woman (Jn 4). Jesus concludes this message with the simple injunction, "Go and do thou likewise" (Lk 10.29-37).

The Lost Sheep: Jesus taught that God, like an earthly father, loves his children, no matter how far they might stray from the paths of righteousness. Prideful religious people might write off sinners as of small account, but God wants them to be saved and rejoices in their salvation. In this parable, a concerned shepherd leaves ninety-nine sheep behind to find the one that is lost in the wilds. When he succeeds, he rouses his friends and neighbors to celebrate. The message, Jesus explains, is that "Likewise joy shall be in heaven over one sinner that repenteth than over ninety and nine just persons, which need no repentance" (Mt 18.12-14; Lk 15.3-7).

The Prodigal Son: Celebration, too, is the conclusion of this parable, in which a wastrel son repents of his evil ways and comes home. This spoiled younger son, contemptuous of advice and eager for the pleasures of the world, takes his inheritance and squanders it far from home. Reduced to disgraceful poverty, he at last recognizes the depth of his foolishness and repents. He fully intends, as a man "no more worthy to be called" his father's son, to work as a hired servant. The father, however, forgives him without hesitation, reinstates him in the family and orders a great feast. In other words, a defeated, helpless sinner is restored by the love of a father. God's mercy and love, Jesus implies, are of an incomparably greater magnitude. As the father in the parable explains to his older son, "It was meet that we should make merry and be glad: for this thy brother was dead, and is alive again; and was lost, and is found" (Lk 15.11-32).

The Ten Virgins: An essential theme in Jesus' teaching is the need to prepare for the coming day of God's judgment. There may be a little time to repent and to put that repentance into useful action. In this tale, ten maidens await the appearance of a bridegroom for a nighttime wedding feast. He is delayed, and all fall asleep. A midnight cry signals the young man's arrival, but five of the women have let their lamps run out of oil and must go off to buy more to participate in the celebratory procession. By the time they return, the door to the marriage feast is already barred. Jesus ends this parable with the warning: "Watch therefore, for ye know neither the day nor the hour" (Mt 25.1-13).

The Mustard Seed: Understandably, the disciples frequently asked Jesus for explanations of the meaning and nature of the Kingdom of Heaven that his teaching promised. Perhaps one of the most engaging of his was the parable of the mustard seed, which can be found in all three Synoptic Gospels. His father's kingdom, Jesus explains in Mark's account, "is like a grain of mustard seed which when sown in the earth, is less than all the seeds that be in the earth; but when it is sown it groweth up and becometh greater than all herbs, and shooteth out great branches, so that the fowls of the air may lodge under the shadow of it." The mustard, strictly speaking, is a bush, not a great tree, nor is its seed the smallest of seeds. The point is clear enough, however: the reign of God, which will comprehend all creation, is beginning, even as Jesus speaks, in a small and humble way in their common homeland.
(Mt 13.31-32; Mk 4.30-32; Lk 13.18-19)

The Unmerciful Servant: God's just wrath as well as his mercy is also captured in the parables. For example, there is the dark, unsettling story Matthew records of punishment for those who are forgiven but cannot themselves forgive. A huge sum of money is hopelessly owed by a servant to his king. His pleas for mercy move the king, who out of pity forgives the debt. Immediately afterward, however, the servant encounters a fellow servant, who owes him a relatively small sum. When this second servant, also unable to pay, begs for mercy, his creditor has him thrown into prison. Outraged friends tell the king, who summons the unmerciful servant, berates him for his cruelty, and has him jailed until the impossible debt can be paid. Jesus explains, "So likewise shall my heavenly Father do also unto you, if ye from your hearts forgive not every one his brother from their trespasses" (Mt 18.23-35).

The Pharisee and the Publican: It is the heart that counts in this important parable as well, for Jesus often emphasized the difference between outward appearance and inner truth. In the temple, two men pray. A Pharisee, self-satisfied and contemptuous of lesser mortals, thanks God while praising himself for fulfilling such religious obligations as tithing and ritual fasting. Nearby, his eyes cast down, a remorseful publican, or tax collector, desperately begs forgiveness for his sins. Tax collecting itself was considered as dishonest as thievery; to make amends, he would have to pay back more than he had earned in this way, bringing his family to financial ruin. "God, be merciful to me a sinner!" he cries, and Jesus explains, "I tell you, this man went down to his house justified rather than the other: for every one that exalteth himself will be abased; but he that humbleth himself shall be exalted" (Lk 18.9-14).

The Sower: Despite the moral and emotional appeal of Jesus' teachings, the impatient may have wondered why they must wait for the coming of the promised kingdom. To explain how God's will must be developed in the world, there is the parable of the farmer sowing seed for his crops. Some of the seed is eaten by birds, some falls on rocky soil and produces plants that are too weak to live, some falls among thorns and the plants that spring up are too choked to produce grain, but other seeds fall into good soil and bring yields of as much as "a hundredfold." Jesus, putting some of the burden of interpretation on the listener, warns, "Who hath ears to hear, let him hear." He does go on, however, to explain that the parable refers to the message of God as it is being spread in the world. The last group of seeds represents those among us "which, in an honest and good heart, having heard the word, keep it, and bring forth fruit with patience." In time, he is saying, all that he has promised will indeed come to pass.
(Mt 13.3-23; Mk 4.3-20; Lk 8.5-15)

An Index to the Parables

The Candle under a Bushel *(Mt 5.15-16; Mk 4.21-22; Lk 8.16-17)*
The House Built on Rock and Sand *(Mt 7.24; Lk 6.48)*
New Cloth on an Old Garment *(Mt 9.16; Mk 2.21; Lk 5.36)*
New Wine and Old Bottles *(Mt 9.17; Mk 2.22; Lk 5.37-38)*
The Sower *(Mt 13.3-23; Mk 4.3-20; Lk 8.5-15)*
The Tares *(Mt 13.24-30)*
The Mustard Seed *(Mt 13.31-32; Mk 4.31-32; Lk 13.18-19)*
The Leaven *(Mt 13.33; Lk 13.20)*
The Hidden Treasure *(Mt 13.44)*
The Pearl of Great Price *(Mt 13.45-46)*
The Draw-net *(Mt 13.47-50)*
The Lost Sheep *(Mt 18.12-14; Lk 15.3-7)*
The Unmerciful Servant *(Mt 18.23-35)*
The Laborers in the Vineyard *(Mt 20.1-16)*
The Father and Two Sons *(Mt 21.28-32)*
The Vineyard and Husbandmen *(Mt 21.33-44; Mk 12.1-12; Lk 20.9-18)*
The Marriage of the King's Son *(Mt 22.2-14)*
The Fig Tree *(Mt 24.32-35; Mk 13.28-31; Lk 21.29-33)*
The Ten Virgins *(Mt 25.1-13)*
The Talents *(Mt 25.14-30)*
The Sheep and Goats *(Mt 25.31-46)*
The Seed Growing Secretly *(Mk 4.26-29)*
The Household Watching *(Mk 13.34-36)*
The Two Debtors *(Lk 7.36-50)*
The Good Samaritan *(Lk 10.29-37)*
The Importunate Friend *(Lk 11.5-13)*
The Rich Man *(Lk 12.16-21)*
The Servants Watching *(Lk 12.35-40)*
The Faithful and Wicked Stewards *(Lk 12.42-48)*
The Barren Fig Tree *(Lk 13.6-9)*
The Wedding Feast *(Lk 14.8-11)*
The Great Supper *(Lk 14.16-24)*
The Tower and the Warring King *(Lk 14.28-33)*
The Lost Piece of Silver *(Lk 15.8-10)*
The Prodigal Son *(Lk 15.11-32)*
The Unjust Steward *(Lk 16.1-13)*
The Rich Man and Lazarus *(Lk 16.19-31)*
The Master and Servant *(Lk 17.7-10)*
The Judge and the Widow *(Lk 18.1-8)*
The Pharisee and the Publican *(Lk 18.9-14)*
The Ten Pounds *(Lk 19.12-27)*

Fishers of Men: The Apostles of Jesus

"Behold, I send you forth as sheep in the midst of wolves" (Mt 10.16), said Jesus to the twelve young disciples he had selected from among a much larger following to be his personal envoys to the world—(the word *apostle* comes from a Greek word meaning "messenger," or "ambassador"). Some of them came from the poorest, least educated, least influential segments of Jewish society, but they were to be the founders of a new faith, charged by Jesus to act in his stead, just as he had represented God the Father.

Anger, cowardice, vengefulness—the failings of the individual apostles were the failings of ordinary human beings. Their achievements, however, are seen by believers as proof of the transforming power of the Christian message. After the Resurrection and Ascension, these inspired followers fulfilled a complex and often dangerous mission. Traveling out across the world, they spread the Gospel, gave heart to wavering converts, and established the first fledgling congregations. Abused, imprisoned, ridiculed, and tortured, they remained true to the faith. All but John, according to later traditions, died as martyrs, following in the footsteps of their Master. Each in his separate way bore witness to the conviction that what matters most in the kingdom of heaven is not birth, social position, or education, but purity and tenacity of spirit.

The New Testament lists the apostles' names in four places: Matthew 10.2-4, Mark 3.16-19, Luke 6.14-16, and Acts 1.13.

Peter, an engraving from a work by Guido Reni (1575-1642)

Peter: The hot-tempered, uncouth Simon of Galilee was the predominant if the most paradoxical figure among the apostles. It was he who first recognized the divinity of Jesus, and it was he who denied Jesus three times on the eve of the crucifixion. The Master renamed him in the famous passage, "thou art Peter, and upon this rock I will build my church," (Mt 16.18) but it was Jesus, too, who challenged this flamboyant disciple by asking him three times in succession, "Simon, son of Jonas, lovest thou me?" To each positive reply, Jesus countered, "Feed my sheep" (Jn 21.15-17). Peter would indeed do so, in the spiritual sense, for his missionary work was critical. He was apparently in charge when the disciples met in the upper room on the day of Pentecost and the Holy Spirit descended to give them divine inspiration. He immediately faced a hostile crowd in the streets of Jerusalem and converted 3,000. He performed the first miracle of healing, was once released from imprisonment by an angel, and guided the delicate decision to accept the first Gentile converts. Traditional belief holds that Peter, after leading the church in Rome for many years, was martyred in the gardens of Nero. At his own request, he was crucified head downward, because he deemed himself unworthy to be crucified as Jesus had been.

Andrew: Brother of Simon Peter, Andrew was the first apostle to follow Jesus. An early disciple of John the Baptist, he had immediately understood when the latter pointed to Jesus and said, "Behold the Lamb of God!" (Jn 1.29). He brought the news to his brother; it was after some time that the Master found the two fishing on the Sea of Galilee and called them to follow him and become "fishers of men" (Mt 4.19). According to tradition, Andrew's ministry after Jesus' resurrection took him through Greece and to Byzantium. It is said that he died slowly on an X-shaped cross, bound rather than nailed, and preaching the faith until he lost consciousness. He was later chosen to be the patron saint of Scotland and Russia.

John: "Woman, behold thy son" (Jn 19.26), the dying Jesus said to his mother Mary; for John, known as the "disciple whom Jesus loved," was the only apostle to appear at the foot of the Cross. Called by Jesus as they were mending their fishing nets, John and his elder brother James angered the other apostles by asking to be placed at the Master's right hand in heaven; but if John was rash in his youth, this youngest of the apostles was to become the most beloved of patriarchs. His writings, thought to include a Gospel and three Epistles, are characterized by a spirit of charity. It is believed that in his last years, before he died peacefully at age 94, he would often be carried into a church service and say simply to the congregation, "My little children, love one another."

James: John's brother, too, had to learn the lesson of meekness through his relationship with Jesus—the Master referred to the pair as Boanerges, "Sons of Thunder." Only James, John, and Peter were allowed to see the Transfiguration of Jesus or to accompany him closely during his ordeal in Gethsemane. There is a tradition that James evangelized in Spain; he did become its patron saint. The first apostle to be martyred, he was beheaded during the persecutions initiated by Herod Agrippa I.

Philip: Only the Gospel of John furnishes any details about this apostle, who is portrayed as an amiable, literal-minded fellow. He seems to have questioned Jesus' ability to feed 5,000 with only "two hundred pennyworth of bread" (Jn 6.7), and may have been the unnamed disciple who asked leave to bury his father before following the Master. "Let the dead bury their dead" (Lk 9.60), Jesus replied in his famous and spiritually significant rebuke. Tradition holds that Philip, like Peter, was crucified head downward.

Bartholomew: Scarcely mentioned in the Bible, this apostle may also have been known as Nathanael, the Galilean whose behavior caused Jesus to exclaim, "Behold an Israelite indeed, in whom there is no guile" (Jn 1.47). Under either name, he is usually linked with Philip, and there is some indication that, alone among the apostles, he was born to the nobility. Legends attest that he preached in such far-flung lands as Egypt, Persia, Mesopotamia, and India. Traditional belief also holds that he was flayed alive for the faith.

Thomas: Remembered proverbially as the doubter who insisted upon feeling Jesus' wounds before he would believe in the Resurrection, Thomas was in fact second to none in his devotion to his Lord. On one occasion, when others warned Jesus to avoid a potentially dangerous situation, Thomas exclaimed, "Let us also go, that we may die with him" (Jn 11.16), and it was he at the Last Supper who elicited Jesus' summation of Christian belief: "I am the way, the truth, and the life: no man cometh unto the Father but by me" (Jn 14.6). Saint Augustine placed the role of Thomas in a clear perspective: "He doubted in order that we might not doubt." Thomas' missonary activities are uncertain, but important traditions place him in India, where native Christians on the Malabar Coast are still known as "the Christians of Saint Thomas."

Matthew: Traditionally credited as author of the first Gospel, the publican Matthew collected taxes for the Roman authorities before his conversion—a role that made him an outcast in traditional Jewish society. It was in response to the Pharisees' criticism of his association with such "publicans and sinners" that Jesus declared, "I came not to call the righteous, but sinners to repentance" (Lk 5.32). Traditions concerning Matthew's subsequent activities are contradictory, some holding that he died of natural causes after a career of evangelism, others that he was martyred by beheading or fire.

James: Identified only as the son of Alpheus, this apostle is not specifically named as a participant in any events in the New Testament. Various traditions have associated him with James "the less" (Mk 15.40), son of Mary and perhaps a cousin of Jesus, or with James, the brother of Jesus (Mt 13.55; Mk 6.3), whose prominence in the early Jerusalem church is made clear in the Epistles and who, according to the Jewish historian Josephus, was stoned to death in A.D. 62.

Thaddeus: The apostle called by this name in the Gospels of Matthew and Mark was probably the same one known in Luke and Acts as Judas, the son (or brother) of James; the different name may have been adopted to distinguish him from Judas the betrayer. The time and place of his conversion are not recorded, but it was "Judas . . . not Iscariot" who asked Jesus at the Last Supper, "Lord, how is it that thou wilt manifest thyself unto us, and not unto the world?" His question produced Jesus' memorable response, "If a man love me, he will keep my words: and my Father will love him, and we will come unto him" (Jn 14.22-23).

Simon: The accounts in the New Testament tell us only that Simon was chosen as an apostle and might have been a member of the Zealots, a politically radical Jewish sect (Luke and Acts call him Simon Zelotes, while Matthew and Mark refer to him only as Simon the Canaanite). Tradition is divided as to his missionary life. Some believe that he died peacefully at Edessa in northwestern Mesopotamia, others that he evangelized in Egypt and was later martyred in Persia.

Judas Iscariot: For thirty pieces of silver offered by Jesus' enemies, the chief priests, Judas Iscariot led Roman soldiers to the Master as he prayed in the garden of Gethsemane, identifying Jesus by kissing him on the cheek. Judas' motives for the betrayal, apart from simple greed, are not examined in the Gospels. According to Matthew, he soon repented and hanged himself from a tree (in later legend a redbud, the "Judas tree") after flinging the blood money at the priests' feet when they refused to take it back. In a different account, Judas bought a field with the money and died there soon afterward in a violent fall (Ac 1.16-19).

Matthias: At Peter's suggestion, the apostles chose a replacement for Judas. It had to be someone who had known Jesus "from the baptism of John, unto that same day that he was taken up from us," and had been "a witness with us of his resurrection" (Ac 1.22). Two men were found to fit the qualifications. Lots were cast, and one of them, named Matthias, was chosen. Little is known about his ministry; according to one tradition, he suffered martyrdom by stoning.

Paul, also engraved from a work by Guido Reni

Paul: Although he did not meet the qualifications cited above to be named an apostle Paul considered himself one: "Am I not an apostle? have I not seen Jesus our Lord?" (1Co 9.1). On the road to Damascus, this zealous persecutor of Christians was converted when the risen Christ appeared to him. Paul may have truly believed himself to be, as he put it, "the least of the apostles," but he felt that Jesus' commission gave him apostolic authority. Well educated, intellectually acute, and physically brave, Paul worked so vigorously in spreading the Gospel that about half of the Acts of the Apostles concerns his work. Many of the Epistles, in addition, were written by Paul, who provided crucial guidance and encouragement to the infant church. It has long been believed that Paul was beheaded in or near Rome; according to one tradition, his martyrdom took place during Nero's persecution of A.D. 64, while another holds that he first evangelized in Spain and then was brought back to Rome, tried, and executed.

A Treasury of Language

If the King James Bible is one of the pillars of Christian worship in the English-speaking world, scarcely less can be said of its importance to the English language itself. Written at a time when British life and letters were bursting with vitality—the same age that produced Shakespeare—the Authorized Version, as it was called in England, emerged not only as a monument of religious scholarship but also as one of the world's supreme literary masterpieces. Newer translations may offer more technically accurate or colloquially up-to-date renderings of various passages, but none can approach the beauty, vigor, and resonance of the King James Version. So thoroughly is it woven into the fabric of our language that, after more than 350 years, the phrases and figures of speech it produced live on in modern English idiom—used every day by millions of people who probably never suspect that they are quoting directly from the Bible. The examples presented below, listed in their biblical order, are all drawn verbatim from the King James text.

gave up the ghost *(Gen 25.8)*
the fat of the land *(Gen 45.18)*
a land flowing with milk and honey *(Ex 3.8)*
what hath God wrought? *(Nu 23.23)*
man doth not live by bread only *(Dt 8.3; Mt 4.4; Mk 4.4)*
smote them hip and thigh *(Jdg 15.8)*
a man after his own heart *(1Sa 13.14)*
I have played the fool *(1Sa 26.21)*
how are the mighty fallen *(2Sa 1.25)*
far be it from me *(2Sa 20.20)*
gird up thy loins *(2Ki 4.29)*
chariots of fire *(2Ki 6.17)*
the skin of my teeth *(Job 19.20)*
out of the mouths of babes *(Ps 8.2)*
the apple of the eye *(Ps 17.8)*
his heart's desire *(Ps 21.2)*
my cup runneth over *(Ps 23.5)*
the young lions *(Ps 34.8)*
tender mercies *(Ps 51.1)*
angels' food *(Ps 78.25)*
from strength to strength *(Ps 84.7)*
make a joyful noise *(Ps 98.4)*
at their wit's end *(Ps 107.27)*
the beginning of wisdom *(Ps 111.10)*
inherit the wind *(Pr 11.29)*
he that spareth his rod hateth his son *(Pr 13.24)*
pride goeth before . . . a fall *(Pr 16.18)*
there is no new thing under the sun *(Ec 1.9)*
a time to be born, and a time to die *(Ec 3.2)*
vanity of vanities; all is vanity *(Ec 1.3)*
the race is not to the swift *(Ec 9.11)*
come . . . let us reason together *(Isa 1.18)*
for unto us a child is born *(Isa 9.6)*
a little child shall lead them *(Isa 11.7)*
a covenant with death *(Isa 28.15)*
a drop of a bucket *(Isa 40.15)*
see eye to eye *(Isa 52.8)*
a lamb to the slaughter *(Isa 53.7)*
sackcloth and ashes *(Isa 58.5)*
from time to time *(Eze 4.10)*
the fathers have eaten sour grapes, and the children's teeth are set on edge *(Eze 18.2)*
the salt of the earth *(Mt 5.13)*
an eye for an eye *(Mt 5.39)*
whosoever shall smite thee on thy right cheek, turn to him the other also *(Mt 5.39)*
pearls before swine *(Mt 7.6)*
seek, and ye shall find *(Mt 7.7)*
strait is the gate, and narrow is the way *(Mt 7.14)*
false prophets . . . come to you in sheep's clothing, but inwardly they are ravening wolves *(Mt 7.15)*
what manner of man is this *(Mt 8.27)*
he that is not for me is against me *(Mt 12.30)*
pearl of great price *(Mt 13.46)*
the blind lead the blind *(Mt 15.14)*
signs of the times *(Mt 16.3)*
the keys of the kingdom *(Mt 16.19)*
what . . . God hath joined together, let not man put asunder *(Mt 19.6)*
a den of thieves *(Mt 21.13)*
many are called, but few are chosen *(Mt 22.14)*
the spirit . . . is willing, but the flesh is weak *(Mt 26.41)*
they that take the sword shall perish with the sword *(Mt 26.52)*
held his peace *(Mt 26.63)*
the potter's field *(Mt 27.7)*
a house divided *(Mk 3.5)*
in his right mind *(Mk 5.15)*
voice . . . crying in the wilderness *(Lk 3.4)*
generation of vipers *(Lk 3.7)*
eat, drink, and be merry *(Lk 12.19)*
not of this world *(Jn 8.23)*
the truth shall make you free *(Jn 8.32)*
greater love hath no man *(Jn 15.13)*
fare ye well *(Ac 15.29)*
turned the world upside down *(Ac 17.6)*
it is more blessed to give than to receive *(Ac 20.35)*
a law unto themselves *(Ro 2.14)*
in due time *(Ro 5.6)*
the wages of sin *(Ro 6.23)*
a short work will the Lord make *(Ro 9.28)*
the powers that be *(Ro 13.1)*
it is high time *(Ro 13.11)*
all things to all men *(1Co 9.22)*
through a glass, darkly *(1Co 13.12)*
faith, hope, charity *(1Co 13.13)*
in the twinkling of an eye *(1Co 15.52)*
O death, where is thy sting? *(1Co 15.55)*
bear with him *(2Co 11.4)*
whatsoever a man soweth, that shall he also reap *(Gal 6.7)*
world without end *(Eph 3.21)*
flesh and blood *(Eph 6.12)*
fear and trembling *(Php 2.12)*
hearts and minds *(Php 4.7)*
in word and deed *(Col 3.17)*
labor of love *(1Th 1.3)*
filthy lucre *(1Ti 3.8)*
old wives' fables *(1Ti 4.7)*
love of money is the root of all evil *(1Ti 6.10)*
fight the good fight *(1Ti 6.12)*
the patience of Job *(Jas 5.11)*
charity shall cover the multitude of sins *(1Pe 4.8)*
a thief in the night *(2Pe 3.10)*
the seventh seal *(Rev 8.1)*
fire and brimstone *(Rev 14.10)*
the measure of a man *(Rev 21.17)*
clear as crystal *(Rev 22.1)*

Abbreviations of the Books of the Bible

The Old Testament

Book	Abbr.	Book	Abbr.	Book	Abbr.
Genesis	Gen	2 Chronicles	2Ch	Daniel	Dan
Exodus	Ex	Ezra	Ezr	Hosea	Hos
Leviticus	Lev	Nehemiah	Neh	Joel	Joel
Numbers	Nu	Esther	Est	Amos	Am
Deuteronomy	Dt	Job	Job	Obadiah	Ob
Joshua	Jos	Psalms	Ps	Jonah	Jon
Judges	Jdg	Proverbs	Pr	Micah	Mic
Ruth	Ru	Ecclesiastes	Ec	Nahum	Na
1 Samuel	1Sa	Song of Solomon	SS	Habakkuk	Hab
2 Samuel	2Sa	Isaiah	Isa	Zephaniah	Zep
1 Kings	1Ki	Jeremiah	Jer	Haggai	Hag
2 Kings	2Ki	Lamentations	La	Zechariah	Zec
1 Chronicles	1Ch	Ezekiel	Eze	Malachi	Mal

The New Testament

Book	Abbr.	Book	Abbr.	Book	Abbr.
Matthew	Mt	Ephesians	Eph	Hebrews	Heb
Mark	Mk	Philippians	Php	James	Jas
Luke	Lk	Colossians	Col	1 Peter	1Pe
John	Jn	1 Thessalonians	1Th	2 Peter	2Pe
Acts	Ac	2 Thessalonians	2Th	1 John	1Jn
Romans	Ro	1 Timothy	1Ti	2 John	2Jn
1 Corinthians	1Co	2 Timothy	2Ti	3 John	3Jn
2 Corinthians	2Co	Titus	Tit	Jude	Jude
Galatians	Gal	Philemon	Phm	Revelation	Rev

AARON

Ex 4.14 Is not *A* the Levite thy brother?
27 the Lord said to *A*, Go into the
28 Moses told *A* all the words of the
29 Moses and *A* went and gathered
30 *A* spake all the words which the
5. 1 afterward Moses and *A* went in,
4 Wherefore do ye, Moses and *A*, let
20 they met Moses and *A*, who stood
6.13 Lord spake unto Moses and unto *A*,
20 and she bare him *A* and Moses:
23 *A* took him Elisheba, daughter of
26 These are that *A* and Moses, to
27 these are that Moses and *A*.
7. 1 and *A* thy brother shall be thy
2 and *A* thy brother shall speak
6 Moses and *A* did as the Lord
7 and *A* fourscore and three years
8 Lord spake unto Moses and unto *A*,
9 then thou shalt say unto *A*, Take
10 And Moses and *A* went in unto
10 and *A* cast down his rod before
19 Lord spake unto Moses, Say unto *A*,
20 Moses and *A* did so, as the Lord
8. 5 Say unto *A*, Stretch forth thine
6 *A* stretched out his hand over the
8 Pharaoh called for Moses and *A*,
12 Moses and *A* went out from
16 Say unto *A*, Stretch out thy rod,
17 for *A* stretched out his hand with
25 Pharaoh called for Moses and for *A*,
9. 8 Lord said unto Moses and unto *A*,
27 sent, and called for Moses and *A*,
10. 3 Moses and *A* came in unto
8 Moses and *A* were brought again
16 Pharaoh called for Moses and *A* in
11.10 Moses and *A* did all these wonders
12. 1 the Lord spake unto Moses and *A*
28 Lord had commanded Moses and *A*,
31 he called for Moses and *A* by night,
43 the Lord said unto Moses and *A*,
50 the Lord commanded Moses and *A*,
15.20 the prophetess, the sister of *A*,
16. 2 murmured against Moses and *A*
6 Moses and *A* said unto all the
9 Moses spake unto *A*, Say unto all
10 as *A* spake unto the whole
33 Moses said unto *A*, Take a pot,
34 so *A* laid it up before the
17.10 and Moses, *A*, and Hur went up
12 and *A* and Hur stayed up his
18.12 and *A* came, and all the elders of
19.24 thou shalt come up, thou, and *A*
24. 1 up unto the Lord thou and *A*,
9 Then went up Moses, and *A*,
14 and, behold, *A* and Hur are with
27.21 *A* and his sons shall order it from
28. 1 take thou unto thee *A* thy
1 in the priest's office, even *A*,
2 shalt make holy garments for *A*
4 shall make holy garments for *A*
12 and *A* shall bear their names
29 *A* shall bear the names of the
30 and *A* shall bear the judgment of
35 And it shall be upon *A* to minister
38 that *A* may bear the iniquity of
41 thou shalt put them upon *A* thy
43 they shall be upon *A*, and upon
29. 4 *A* and his sons thou shalt bring
5 and put upon *A* the coat, and the
9 shalt gird them with girdles, *A*
9 thou shalt consecrate *A* and his
10, 15, 19 *A* and his sons shall put their
20 upon the tip of the right ear of *A*,
21 and sprinkle it upon *A*, and upon
24 shalt put all in the hands of *A*,
27 even of that which is for *A*, and
29 the holy garments of *A* shall be
32 *A* and his sons shall eat the flesh
35 thus shalt thou do unto *A*, and to
44 I will sanctify also both *A* and
30. 7 *A* shall burn thereon sweet
8 when *A* lighteth the lamps at even,
10 *A* shall make an atonement upon
19 For *A* and his sons shall wash
30 thou shalt anoint *A* and his sons,
31.10 and the holy garments for *A* the
32. 1 themselves together unto *A*, and
2 *A* said unto them, Break off the
3 and brought them unto *A*,
5 when *A* saw it he built an altar
5 *A* made proclamation, and said,
21 Moses said unto *A*, What did this
22 *A* said, Let not the anger of my
25 (for *A* had made them naked unto
35 they made the calf, which *A* made.
34.30 when *A* and all the children of
31 *A* and all the rulers of the
35.19 the holy garments for *A*, the
38.21 by the hand of Ithamar, son to *A*
39. 1 made the holy garments for *A*;
27 fine linen of woven work for *A*,
41 and the holy garments for *A* the
40.12 thou shalt bring *A* and his sons
13 thou shalt put upon *A* the holy
31 Moses and *A* and his sons washed
Lev 1. 7 the sons of *A* the priest shall put
3.13 the sons of *A* shall sprinkle the
6. 9 Command *A* and his sons, saying,
14 the sons of *A* shall offer it before
16 the remainder thereof shall *A*
18 males among the children of *A*
20 This is the offering of *A* and of
25 Speak unto *A* and to his sons,
7.10 and dry, shall all the sons of *A*
33 He among the sons of *A*, that
34 and have given them unto *A* the
35 the portion of the anointing of *A*,
8. 2 Take *A* and his sons with him,
6 Moses brought *A* and his sons,
14, 18 *A* and his sons laid their hands
22 the ram of consecration: and *A*
30 and sprinkled it upon *A*, and
30 sanctified *A*, and his garments,
31 Moses said unto *A*, and to his
31 as I commanded, saying, *A* and
36 So *A* and his sons did all things
9. 1 the eighth day, that Moses called *A*
2 he said unto *A*, Take thee a young
7 Moses said unto *A*, Go into the
8 *A* therefore went unto the altar,
9 the sons of *A* brought the blood
21 And the right shoulder *A* waved
22 *A* lifted up his right hand toward
23 Moses and *A* went into the
10. 1 Nadab and Abihu, the sons of *A*,
3 Moses said unto *A*, This is it that
3 And *A* held his peace.
4 the sons of Uzziel the uncle of *A*,
6 Moses said unto *A* and unto
8 the Lord spake unto *A*, saying,
12 Moses spake unto *A* and unto
16 the sons of *A* which were left
19 *A* said unto Moses, Behold, this
11. 1 Lord spake unto Moses and to *A*,
13. 1 the Lord spake unto Moses and *A*,
2 then he shall be brought unto *A*
14.33 Lord spake unto Moses and unto *A*,
15. 1 Lord spake unto Moses and to *A*,
16. 1 the death of the two sons of *A*,
2 Speak unto *A* thy brother, that
3 Thus shall *A* come into the holy
6 *A* shall offer his bullock of the sin
8 *A* shall cast lots upon the two goats
9 *A* shall bring the goat upon which
11 *A* shall bring the bullock of the sin
21 *A* shall lay both his hands upon the
23 *A* shall come into the tabernacle
17. 2 Speak unto *A*, and unto his sons,
21. 1 unto the priests the sons of *A*, and
17 Speak unto *A*, saying, Whosoever
21 hath a blemish of the seed of *A* the
24 Moses told it unto *A*, and to his
22. 2 Speak unto *A* and to his sons, that
4 What man soever of the seed of *A*
18 Speak unto *A*, and to his sons, and
24. 3 Shall *A* order it from the evening
Nu 1. 3 thou and *A* shall number them by
17 Moses and *A* took these men which
44 which Moses and *A* numbered, and
2. 1 Lord spake unto Moses and unto *A*,
3. 1 also are the generations of *A* and
2, 3 are the names of the sons of *A*
4 the priest's office in the sight of *A*
6 and present them before *A* the
9 thou shalt give the Levites unto *A*
10 thou shalt appoint *A* and his sons
32 Eleazar the son of *A* the priest
38 shall be Moses, and *A* and his sons
39 which Moses and *A* numbered at
48 is to be redeemed, unto *A* and to
51 that were redeemed unto *A* and to
4. 1 Lord spake unto Moses and unto *A*,
5 when the camp setteth forward, *A*
15 when *A* and his sons have made an
16 the office of Eleazar the son of *A*
17 Lord spake unto Moses and unto *A*,
19 *A* and his sons shall go in, and
27 At the appointment of *A* and his
28, 33 hand of Ithamar the son of *A*
34 Moses and *A* and the chief of the
37 which Moses and *A* did number
41 whom Moses and *A* did number
45 whom Moses and *A* numbered
46 whom Moses and *A* and the chief
6.23 Speak unto *A* and unto his sons,
7. 8 the hand of Ithamar the son of *A*
8. 2 Speak unto *A*, and say unto him,
3 *A* did so; he lighted the lamps
11 *A* shall offer the Levites before the
13 shalt set the Levites before *A*, and
19 given the Levites as a gift to *A* and
20 And Moses, and *A*, and all the
21 and *A* offered them as an offering
21 *A* made an atonement for them
22 of the congregation before *A*, and
9. 6 came before Moses and before *A*
10. 8 the sons of *A*, the priests, shall
12. 1 And Miriam and *A* spake against
4 suddenly unto Moses, and unto *A*,
5 and called *A* and Miriam:
10 and *A* looked upon Miriam, and,
11 *A* said unto Moses, Alas, my lord,
13.26 and came to Moses, and to *A*, and
14. 2 against Moses and against *A*: and
5 Moses and *A* fell on their faces
26 Lord spake unto Moses and unto *A*,
15.33 brought him unto Moses and *A*,
16. 3 against Moses and against *A*, and
11 and what is *A*, that ye murmur
16 thou, and they, and *A*, to morrow:
17 and *A*, each of you his censer.
18 congregation with Moses and *A*.
20 Lord spake unto Moses and unto *A*,
37 Speak unto Eleazar the son of *A*
40 which is not of the seed of *A*, come
41, 42 against Moses and against *A*,
43 And Moses and *A* came before the

Nu 16.46 Moses said unto *A*, Take a censer
47 *A* took as Moses commanded, and
50 *A* returned unto Moses unto the
17. 6 the rod of *A* was among their rods.
8 the rod of *A* for the house of Levi
18. 1 the Lord said unto *A*, Thou and
8 the Lord spake unto *A*, Behold, I
20 the Lord spake unto *A*, Thou
28 the Lord's heave offering to *A* the
19. 1 Lord spake unto Moses and unto *A*,
20. 2 against Moses and against *A*.
6 And Moses and *A* went from the
8 thou and *A* thy brother, and speak
10 And Moses and *A* gathered the
12, 23 Lord spake unto Moses and *A*,
24 *A* shall be gathered unto his people
25 Take *A* and Eleazar his son, and
26 strip *A* of his garments, and put
26 and *A* shall be gathered unto his
28 Moses stripped *A* of his garments
28 and *A* died there in the top of the
29 congregation saw that *A* was dead,
29 they mourned for *A* thirty days
25. 7 the son of Eleazar, the son of *A* the
11 the son of *A* the priest, hath turned
26. 1 and unto Eleazar the son of *A* the
9 and against *A* in the company of
59 and she bare unto Amram *A* and
60 And unto *A* was born Nadab and
64 a man of them whom Moses and *A*
27.13 as *A* thy brother was gathered.
33. 1 under the hand of Moses and *A*.
38 *A* the priest went up into mount
39 *A* was a hundred and twenty and
Dt 9.20 Lord was very angry with *A* to
20 and I prayed for *A* also the
10. 6 there *A* died, and there he was
32.50 as *A* thy brother died in mount
Jos 21. 4 and the children of *A* the priest,
10 Which the children of *A*, being of
13 Thus they gave to the children of *A*
19 All the cities of the children of *A*,
24. 5 I sent Moses also and *A*, and I
33 And Eleazar the son of *A* died;
Jdg 20.28 the son of *A*, stood before it in
1Sa 12. 6 Lord that advanced Moses and *A*,
8 then the Lord sent Moses and *A*,
1Ch 6. 3 the children of Amram; *A*, and
3 The sons also of *A*; Nadab and
49 But *A* and his sons offered upon
50 these are the sons of *A*; Eleazar
54 of the sons of *A*, of the families of
57 And to the sons of *A* they gave the
15. 4 David assembled the children of *A*,
23.13 of Amram; *A* and Moses: and *A*
28 office was to wait on the sons of *A*
32 and the charge of the sons of *A*
24. 1 are the divisions of the sons of *A*.
1 The sons of *A*; Nadab and
19 to their manner, under *A* their
31 their brethren the sons of *A* in the
2Ch 13. 9 the sons of *A*, and the Levites, and
10 unto the Lord, are the sons of *A*,
26.18 but to the priests the sons of *A*,
29.21 the priests the sons of *A* to offer
31.19 Also of the sons of *A* the priests,
35.14 because the priests the sons of *A*
14 and for the priests the sons of *A*.
Ezr 7. 5 Eleazar, the son of *A* the chief
Neh 10.38 the priest the son of *A* shall be
12.47 them unto the children of *A*.
Ps 77.20 flock by the hand of Moses and *A*.
99. 6 Moses and *A* among his priests,
105.26 He sent Moses his servant; and *A*
106.16 Moses also in the camp, and *A*
115.10 O house of *A*, trust in the Lord:
12 he will bless the house of *A*.
118. 3 Let the house of *A* now say, that
135.19 bless the Lord, O house of *A*;
Mic 6. 4 I sent before thee Moses, *A*, and
Lk 1. 5 wife was of the daughters of *A*,
Ac 7.40 Saying unto *A*, Make us gods to
Heb 5. 4 that is called of God, as was *A*.
7.11 not be called after the order of *A*?
10 Bring *A* rod again before the
Ps 133. 2 upon the beard, even *A* beard:
Heb 9. 4 pot that had manna, and *A* rod

AARON

Older brother of Moses and first High Priest of Israel, 13th century B.C.; on Moses' return from Midian is appointed his spokesman (Ex 4); accompanies Moses before Pharaoh and with him is rebuffed (Ex 5); on their next audience casts rod before Pharaoh and it turns into a serpent; when Pharaoh is unimpressed, stretches the rod over the Nile and changes its waters to blood (Ex 7); accompanies Moses in subsequent audiences when the other plagues are announced (Ex 8–11); is with Moses when the people complain in the wilderness (Ex 16); supports Moses' upraised hands when the Amalekites are defeated (Ex 17); appointed Moses' deputy while he is on Mount Sinai (Ex 24); accedes to the people's request and supervises the making of the golden calf; tries to excuse himself, but stands with the Levites "on the Lord's side" when Moses issues his challenge (Ex 32); he and his sons anointed to the priestly office (Ex 40); his sons Nadab and Abihu slain for offering unauthorized sacrifices and he himself warned against unfaithfulness (Lev 10); given the words of the Aaronic blessing (Nu 6); sides with his sister Miriam against Moses and intercedes for her when she is stricken with leprosy (Nu 12); makes atonement for the people after the rebellion of Korah (Nu 16); his rod blossoms miraculously (Nu 17); is told at Mount Hor that for sharing the doubts of the people neither he nor Moses will enter the promised land; dies and is succeeded as High Priest by his son Eleazar (Nu 20).

AARONITES

1Ch 12.27 Jehoiada was the leader of the *A*,
27.17 the sons of Kemuel: of the *A*,

AARON'S

Ex 6.25 Eleazar *A* son took him one of the
7.12 but *A* rod swallowed up their rods.
28. 1 Eleazar and Ithamar, *A* sons.
3 that they may make *A* garments
30 and they shall be upon *A* heart,
38 And it shall be upon *A* forehead
40 for *A* sons thou shalt make coats,
29.26 of the ram of *A* consecration,
28 it shall be *A* and his sons' by a
Lev 1. 5 the priests, *A* sons, shall bring
8 the priests, *A* sons, shall lay the
11 the priests, *A* sons, shall sprinkle
2. 2 he shall bring it to *A* sons the
3, 10 of the meat offering shall be *A*
3. 2 *A* sons the priests shall sprinkle
5 *A* sons shall burn it on the altar
8 *A* sons shall sprinkle the blood
7.31 but the breast shall be *A* and his
8.12 the anointing oil upon *A* head,
13 Moses brought *A* sons, and put
23 put it upon the tip of *A* right ear,
24 he brought *A* sons, and Moses
27 he put all upon *A* hands, and
9.12, 18 and *A* sons presented unto him
24. 9 it shall be *A* and his sons'; and
Nu 17. 3 thou shalt write *A* name upon

ABASE

Job 40.11 every one that is proud, and *a*
Isa 31. 4 nor *a* himself for the noise of
Eze 21.26 is low, and *a* him that is high.
Dan 4.37 that walk in pride he is able to *a*.

ABASED

Mt 23.12 shall exalt himself shall be *a*;
Lk 14.11 that exalteth himself shall be *a*:
18.14 that exalteth himself shall be *a*;
Php 4.12 I know both how to be *a*, and I

ABASING

2Co 11. 7 *a* myself that ye might be exalted,

ABATED

Gen 8. 3 and fifty days the waters were *a*.
8 him to see if the waters were *a*
11 nor knew that the waters were *a*
Lev 27.18 shall be *a* from thy estimation
Dt 34. 7 not dim, nor his natural force *a*
Jdg 8. 3 their anger was *a* towards him

ABBA

Mk 14.36 And he said, *A*, Father, all things
Ro 8.15 of adoption, whereby we cry, *A*,
Gal 4. 6 into your hearts, crying, *A*, Father.

ABED-NEGO

Dan 1. 7 Meshach; and to Azariah, of *A*.
2.49 Shadrach, Meshach, and *A*, over
3.12, 13, 14, 16, 19, 20, 22, 23, 26, 26, 28,
29, 30 Shadrach, Meshach, and *A*

ABEL

Gen 4. 2 bare his brother *A*. And *A* was
4 And *A*, he also brought of the
4 the Lord had respect unto *A* and
8 Cain talked with *A* his brother:
8 that Cain rose up against *A* his
9 Lord said unto Cain, Where is *A*
25 me another seed instead of *A*,
1Sa 6.18 even unto the great stone of *A*,
2Sa 20.14 all the tribes of Israel unto *A*,
15 they came and besieged him in *A*
18 They shall surely ask counsel at *A*:
Mt 23.35 from the blood of righteous *A* unto
Lk 11.51 From the blood of *A* unto the
Heb 11. 4 by faith *A* offered unto God a more
12.24 better things than that of *A*.

ABHOR

Lev 26.11 and my soul shall not *a* you.
15 if your soul *a* my judgments, so
30 your idols, and my soul shall *a* you.
44 neither will I *a* them, to destroy
Dt 7.26 thou shalt utterly *a* it; for it is a
23. 7 Thou shalt not *a* an Edomite;
7 thou shalt not *a* an Egyptian;
1Sa 27.12 his people Israel utterly to *a* him
Job 9.31 and mine own clothes shall *a* me.
30.10 They *a* me, they flee far from me,
42. 6 Wherefore I *a* myself, and repent
Ps 5. 6 the Lord will *a* the bloody and
119.163 I hate and *a* lying: but thy
Pr 24.24 the people curse, nations shall *a*
Jer 14.21 Do not *a* us, for thy name's sake,
Am 5.10 and they *a* him that speaketh
6. 8 I *a* the excellency of Jacob, and
Mic 3. 9 Israel, that *a* judgment, and
Ro 12. 9 *A* that which is evil; cleave to

ABHORRED

Ex 5.21 ye have made our savor to be *a*
Lev 20.23 things, and therefore I *a* them.
26.43 because their soul *a* my statutes.
Dt 32.19 when the Lord saw it, he *a* them,

1Sa 2.17 men *a* the offering of the Lord.
2Sa 16.21 shall hear that thou art *a* of thy
1Ki 11.25 and he *a* Israel, and reigned
Job 19.19 All my inward friends *a* me:
Ps 22.24 he hath not despised nor *a* the
78.59 was wroth, and greatly *a* Israel:
89.38 thou hast cast off and *a*, thou
106.40 that he *a* his own inheritance.
Pro 22.14 he that is *a* of the Lord shall fall
La 2. 7 he hath *a* his sanctuary, he hath
Eze 16.25 hast made thy beauty to be *a*,
Zec 11. 8 and their soul also *a* me.

ABHORREST

Isa 7.16 the land that thou *a* shall be
Ro 2.22 that *a* idols, dost thou commit

ABHORRETH

Job 33.20 So that his life *a* bread, and
Ps 10. 3 the covetous, whom the Lord *a*.
36. 4 that is not good; he *a* not evil.
107.18 Their soul *a* all manner of meat;
Isa 49. 7 to him whom the nation *a*, to a

ABHORRING

Isa 66.24 they shall be an *a* unto all flesh.

ABIATHAR

1Sa 22.20 son of Ahitub, named *A*, escaped,
21 And *A* shewed David that Saul had
22 David said unto *A*, I knew it that
23. 6 when *A* the son of Ahimelech fled
9 and he said to *A* the priest, Bring
30. 7 And David said to *A* the priest,
7 And *A* brought thither the ephod
2Sa 8.17 and Ahimelech the son of *A*, were
15.24 *A* went up, until all the people
27 and Jonathan the son of *A*.
29 Zadok therefore and *A* carried the
35 not there with thee Zadok and *A*
35 thou shalt tell it to Zadok and *A*
17.15 said Hushai unto Zadok and to *A*
19.11 king David sent to Zadok and to *A*
20.25 and Zadok and *A* were the priests:
1Ki 1. 7 the son of Zeruiah, and with *A*
19 sons of the king, and *A* the priest,
25 the captains of the host, and *A* the
42 Jonathan the son of *A* the priest
2.22 for him, and for *A* the priest,
26 unto *A* the priest said the king,
27 Solomon thrust out *A* from being
35 did the king put in the room of *A*.
4. 4 and Zadok and *A* were the priests:
1Ch 15.11 And David called for Zadok and *A*
18.16 and Abimelech the son of *A*, were
24. 6 priest, and Ahimelech the son of *A*,
27.34 the son of Benaiah, and *A*:
Mk 2.26 in the days of *A* the high priest,

ABIDE

Gen 19. 2 we will *a* in the street all night.
22. 5 *A* ye here with the ass;
24.55 Let the damsel *a* with us a few
29.19 *a* with me.
Ex 16.29 *a* ye every man in his place,
Lev 8.35 Therefore shall ye *a* at the door of
19.13 shall not *a* with thee all night
Nu 22. 5 they *a* over against me:
31.19 *a* without the camp seven days:
23 Every thing that may *a* the fire,
35.25 he shall *a* in it unto the death of
Dt 3.19 *a* in your cities which I have
Jos 18. 5 Judah shall *a* in their coast on
5 Joseph shall *a* in their coasts on
Ru 2. 8 *a* here fast by my maidens:
1Sa 1.22 and there *a* for ever.
5. 7 God of Israel shall not *a* with us:
19. 2 and *a* in a secret place, and hide
22. 5 *A* not in the hold;
23 *A* thou with me, fear not:
30.21 whom they had made also to *a* at
2Sa 11.11 the ark, and Israel, and Judah, *a*
15.19 return to thy place, and *a* with
16.18 with him will I *a*.
1Ki 8.13 a settled place for thee to *a* in
2Ch 25.19 *a* now at home;
32.10 ye *a* in the siege in Jerusalem?
Job 24.13 nor *a* in the paths thereof.
38.40 and *a* in the covert to lie in wait?
39. 9 to serve thee, or *a* by thy crib?
Ps 15. 1 who shall *a* in thy tabernacle?
61. 4 I will *a* in thy tabernacle
7 He shall *a* before God for ever:
91. 1 shall *a* under the shadow
Pr 7.11 her feet *a* not in her house:
19.23 he that hath it shall *a* satisfied;
Ec 8.15 shall *a* with him of his labor
Jer 10.10 the nations shall not be able to *a*
42.10 If ye will still *a* in this land,
49.18 no man shall *a* there,
33 there shall no man *a* there,
50.40 so shall no man *a* there,
Hos 3. 3 Thou shalt *a* for me many days;
4 children of Israel shall *a* many
11. 6 the sword shall *a* on his cities,
Joel 2.11 and who can *a* it?
Mic 5. 4 and they shall *a*:
Na 1. 6 who can *a* in the fierceness of his
Mal 3. 2 may *a* the day of his coming?
Mt 10.11 and there *a* till ye go thence.
Mk 6.10 *a* till ye depart from that place.
Lk 9. 4 there *a*, and thence depart.
19. 5 for to-day I must *a* at thy house.
24.29 constrained him, saying, *A* with
Jn 12.46 believeth on me should not *a* in
14.16 that he may *a* with you for ever;
15. 4 *A* in me, and I in you.
4 except it *a* in the vine;
4 no more can ye, except ye *a* in me.
6 If a man *a* not in me, he is cast
7 If ye *a* in me, and my words *a* in
10 ye shall *a* in my love;
10 and *a* in his love.
Ac 34 it pleased Silas to *a* there still.
16.15 come into my house, and *a* there.
20.23 and afflictions *a* me.
27.31 Except these *a* in the ship,
Ro 11.23 if they *a* not still in unbelief,
1Co 3.14 any man's work *a* which he hath
7. 8 if they *a* even as I.
20 every man *a* in the same calling
24 every man,...therein *a* with God.
40 she is happier if she so *a*,
16. 6 And it may be that I will *a*, yea,
Php 1.24 to *a* in the flesh is more needful
25 know that I shall *a* and continue
1Ti 1. 3 to *a* still at Ephesus,
1Jn 2.24 Let that therefore *a* in you,
27 ye shall *a* in him.
28 little children, *a* in him;

ABIDETH

Nu 31.23 all that *a* not the fire ye shall
2Sa 16. 3 he *a* at Jerusalem:
Job 39.28 She dwelleth and *a* on the rock,
Ps 49.12 man being in honor *a* not:
55.19 even he that *a* of old.
119.90 established the earth, and it *a*.
125. 1 cannot be removed, but *a* for ever.
Pr 15.31 reproof of life *a* among the wise.
Ec 1. 4 the earth *a* for ever.
Jer 21. 9 He that *a* in this city shall die
Jn 3.36 the wrath of God *a* on him.
8.35 the servant *a* not in the house for
35 but the Son *a* ever.
12.24 ground and die, it *a* alone:
34 of the law that Christ *a* for ever:
15. 5 He that *a* in me, and I in him,
1Co 13.13 now *a* faith, hope, charity,
2Ti 2.13 he *a* faithful: he cannot deny
Heb 7. 3 *a* a priest continually.
1Pe 1.23 which liveth and *a* for ever.
1Jn 2. 6 He that saith he *a* in him
10 *a* in the light,
14 the word of God *a* in you,
17 doeth the will of God *a* for ever.
27 received of him *a* in you,
3. 6 Whosoever *a* in him sinneth not:
14 He that loveth not his brother *a* in
24 hereby we know that he *a* in us,
2Jn 1. 9 *a* not in the doctrine of Christ,
9 He that *a* in the doctrine

ABIDING

Nu 24. 2 he saw Israel *a* in his tents
Jdg 16. 9 *a* with her in the chamber.
12 *a* in the chamber.
1Sa 26.19 driven me out this day from *a*
1Ch 29.15 there is none *a*.
Lk 2. 8 shepherds *a* in the field,
Jn 5.38 ye have not his word *a* in you:
Ac 16.12 were in that city *a* certain days.
1Jn 3.15 no murderer hath eternal life *a*

ABIGAIL

1Sa 25. 3 Nabal: and the name of his wife *A*:
14 But one of the young men told *A*,
18 Then *A* made haste, and took two
23 when *A* saw David, she hasted,
32 David said to *A*, Blessed be the Lord
36 And *A* came to Nabal; and, behold,
39 David sent and communed with *A*,
40 servants of David were come to *A*
42 And *A* hasted, and arose, and rode
27. 3 *A* the Carmelitess, Nabal's wife.
30. 5 *A* the wife of Nabal the Carmelite.
2Sa 2. 2 and *A* Nabal's wife the Carmelite.
3. 3 *A* the wife of Nabal the Carmelite;
17.25 in to *A* the daughter of Nahash,
1Ch 2.16 Whose sisters were Zeruiah, and *A*.
17 and *A* bare Amasa: and the father
3. 1 the second Daniel, of *A* the

ABILITY

Lev 27. 8 according to his *a* that vowed
Ezr 2.69 They gave after their *a*
Neh 5. 8 We after our *a* have redeemed
Dan 1. 4 such as had *a* in them
Mt 25.15 according to his several *a*;
Ac 11.29 every man according to his *a*,
1Pe 4.11 as of the *a* which God giveth;
(See box on page 54)

ABIMAEL

Gen 10.28 And Obal, and *A*, and Sheba,
1Ch 1.22 And Ebal, and *A*, and Sheba,

ABIMELECH

Gen 20. 2 and *A* king of Gerar sent, and took
3 But God came to *A* in a dream
4 But *A* had not come near her:
8 *A* rose early in the morning,
9 Then *A* called Abraham, and said
10 *A* said unto Abraham, What sawest
14 And *A* took sheep, and oxen, and
15 *A* said, Behold, my land is before
17 and God healed *A*, and his wife,
18 all the wombs of the house of *A*,
21.22 that *A* and Phichol the chief captain
25 And Abraham reproved *A* because
26 *A* said, I wot not who hath done
27 and oxen, and gave them unto *A*;
29 *A* said unto Abraham, What mean
32 then *A* rose up, and Phichol the
26. 1 And Isaac went unto *A* king of the
8 *A* king of the Philistines looked
9 And *A* called Isaac, and said,
10 *A* said, What is this thou hast done
11 *A* charged all his people, saying,
16 And *A* said unto Isaac, Go from us;
26 Then *A* went to him from Gerar,
Jdg 8.31 a son, whose name he called *A*.

Biblical Themes

ABILITY

Jubal . . . was the father of all such as handle the harp and organ . . . Tubal-cain, an instructer of every artificer in brass and iron. Gen 4.21-22

And thou shalt make an hanging for the door of the tent, of blue, and purple, and scarlet, and fine twined linen, wrought with needlework. Ex 26.36

And thou shalt make it an oil of holy ointment, an ointment compound after the art of the apothecary. Ex 30.25

And the Lord spake unto Moses, saying . . . I have filled [Bezaleel] with the spirit of God, in wisdom, and in understanding, and in knowledge, and in all manner of workmanship, to devise cunning works, to work in gold, and in silver, and in brass, and in cutting of stones, to set them, and in carving of timber, to work in all manner of workmanship. Ex 31.1, 3-5

[Hiram] was . . . a worker in brass: and he was filled with wisdom, and understanding, and cunning to work all works in brass. And he came to king Solomon, and wrought all his work. 1Ki 7.14

And Chenaniah, chief of the Levites, was for song: he instructed about the song, because he was skilful. 1Ch 15.22

If I forget thee, O Jerusalem, let my right hand forget her cunning. Ps 137.5

Trust in the Lord with all thine heart; and lean not unto thine own understanding. Pr 3.5

She layeth her hands to the spindle, and her hands hold the distaff. Pr 31.19

Whatsoever thy hand findeth to do, do it with thy might; for there is no work, nor device, nor knowledge, nor wisdom, in the grave, whither thou goest. . . . the race is not to the swift, nor the battle to the strong, neither yet bread to the wise, nor yet riches to men of understanding, nor yet favor to men of skill; but time and chance happeneth to them all. Ec 9.10-11

Then I went down to the potter's house, and, behold, he wrought a work on the wheels. Jer 18.3

As for these four children, God gave them knowledge and skill in all learning and wisdom: and Daniel had understanding in all visions and dreams. Dan 1.17

All things are possible to him that believeth. Mk 9.23

Unto whomsoever much is given, of him shall be much required. Lk 12.48

Without me ye can do nothing. Jn 15.5

Paul departed from Athens, and came to Corinth; and found a certain Jew named Aquila . . . with his wife Priscilla. . . . And because he was of the same craft, he abode with them, and wrought: for by their occupation they were tentmakers. Ac 18.1-3

Hath not the potter power over the clay? Ro 9.21

Where is the wise? where is the scribe? where is the disputer of this world? hath not God made foolish the wisdom of this world? 1Co 1.20

There are diversities of gifts, but the same Spirit. . . . to one is given by the Spirit the word of wisdom; to another the word of knowledge . . . to another faith by the same Spirit; to another the gifts of healing . . . but all these worketh that one and the selfsame Spirit, dividing to every man severally as he will. 1Co 12.4-11

I can do all things through Christ which strengtheneth me. Php 4.13

Neglect not the gift that is in thee. 1Ti 4.14

If any man minister, let him do it as of the ability which God giveth: that God in all things may be glorified. 1Pe 4.11

Jdg 9. 1 And *A* the son of Jerubbaal went
3 their hearts inclined to follow *A*;
4 *A* hired vain and light persons,
6 and went, and made *A* king,
16 in that ye have made *A* king,
18 made *A*, the son of his maidservant,
19 then rejoice ye in *A*, and let him
20 But if not, let fire come out from *A*,
20 the house of Millo, and devour *A*.
21 and dwelt there, for fear of *A* his
22 When *A* had reigned three years
23 God sent an evil spirit between *A*
23 dealt treacherously with *A*:
24 *A* their brother, which slew them;
25 way by them: and it was told *A*.
27 did eat and drink, and cursed *A*.
28 Who is *A*, and who is Shechem,
29 my hand! then would I remove *A*.
29 he said to *A*, Increase thine army,
31 he sent messengers unto *A* privily,
34 And *A* rose up, and all the people
35 And *A* rose up, and the people that
38 Who is *A*, that we should serve him?
39 of Shechem, and fought with *A*.
40 *A* chased him, and he fled before
41 And *A* dwelt at Arumah: and Zebul
42 out into the field; and they told *A*.
44 *A*, and the company that was with
45 And *A* fought against the city all
47 And it was told *A*, that all the men
48 *A* gat him up to mount Zalmon,
48 and *A* took an axe in his hand,
49 and followed *A*, and put them to the
50 went *A* to Thebez, and encamped
52 And *A* came unto the tower,
55 men of Israel saw that *A* was dead,
56 God rendered the wickedness of *A*,
10. 1 after *A* there arose to defend Israel
2Sa 11.21 smote *A* the son of Jerubbesheth?
1Ch 18.16 and *A* the son of Abiathar,
Ps 34(T) changed his behavior before *A*;

ABIMELECH'S

Gen 21.25 *A* servants had violently taken
Jdg 9.53 a piece of a millstone upon *A* head,

ABIRAM

Nu 16. 1 Dathan and *A*, the sons of Eliab,
12 Moses sent to call Dathan and *A*,
24 tabernacle of Korah, Dathan, and *A*.
25 up and went unto Dathan and *A*;
27 tabernacle of Korah, Dathan, and *A*,
27 Dathan and *A* came out, and stood
26. 9 Eliab; Nemuel, and Dathan, and *A*.
9 Dathan and *A*, which were famous
Dt 11. 6 what he did unto Dathan and *A*,
1Ki 16.34 he laid the foundations thereof in *A*
Ps 106.17 and covered the company of *A*.

ABISHAG

1Ki 1. 3 and found *A* a Shunammite,
15 and *A* the Shunammite ministered
2.17 give me *A* the Shunammite to wife.
21 she said, Let *A* the Shunammite be
22 dost thou ask *A* the Shunammite

ABISHAI

1Sa 26. 6 and to *A* the son of Zeruiah,
6 *A* said, I will go down with thee.
7 So David and *A* came to the people
8 said *A* to David, God hath delivered
9 David said to *A*, Destroy him not:
2Sa 2.18 sons of Zeruiah there, Joab, and *A*,
24 also and *A* pursued after Abner:
3.30 Joab and *A* his brother slew Abner,
10.10 he delivered into the hand of *A*
14 then fled they also before *A*,
16. 9 Then said *A* the son of Zeruiah unto
11 David said to *A*, and to all his
18. 2 a third part under the hand of *A*
5 the king commanded Joab and *A*
12 hearing the king charged thee and *A*
19.21 But *A* the son of Zeruiah answered
20. 6 David said to *A*, Now shall Sheba
10 So Joab and *A* his brother pursued
21.17 *A* the son of Zeruiah succored him,
23.18 And *A*, the brother of Joab, the son
1Ch 2.16 the sons of Zeruiah; *A*, and Joab,
11.20 *A* the brother of Joab, he was chief
18.12 *A* the son of Zeruiah slew of the
19.11 he delivered unto the hand of *A*
15 likewise fled before *A* his brother,

ABIUD

Mt 1.13 Zorobabel begat *A*; and *A* begat

ABLE

Gen 13. 6 the land was not *a* to bear them,
15. 5 if thou be *a* to number them:
33.14 and the children be *a* to endure,
Ex 10. 5 one cannot be *a* to see the earth:
18.18 thou art not *a* to perform it
21 provide out of all the people *a*
23 then thou shalt be *a* to endure,
25 Moses chose *a* men out of all

40.35 Moses was not *a* to enter into the
Lev 5. 7 be not *a* to bring a lamb,
11 he be not *a*
12. 8 be not *a* to bring a lamb,
14.22 such as he is *a* to get;
31 such as he is *a* to get, the one for
32 whose hand is not *a* to get that
25.26 himself be *a* to redeem it;
28 if he be not *a* to restore it
49 he be *a*, he may redeem himself.
Nu 1. 3 all that are *a* to go forth to war
20, 22, 24, 26, 28, 30, 32, 34, 36, 38, 40,
42, 45 all that were *a* to go forth to war
11.14 I am not *a* to bear all this people
13.30 we are well *a* to overcome it.
31 not *a* to go up against the people;
14.16 the Lord was not *a* to bring this
22.11 I shall be *a* to overcome them,
37 am I not *a* indeed to promote thee
26. 2 all that are *a* to go to war
Dt 1. 9 am not *a* to bear you myself alone:
7.24 no man be *a* to stand before thee,
9.28 Lord was not *a* to bring them
11.25 no man be *a* to stand before you:
14.24 thou art not *a* to carry it;
16.17 man shall give as he is *a*,
Jos 1. 5 There shall not any man be *a* to
14.12 I shall be *a* to drive them out,
23. 9 hath been *a* to stand before you
Jdg 8. 3 what was I *a* to do
1Sa 6.20 Who is *a* to stand before this holy
17. 9 If he be *a* to fight with me,
33 Thou art not *a* to go against this
1Ki 3. 9 *a* to judge this thy so great people?
9.21 children of Israel also were not *a*
2Ki 3.21 all that were *a* to put on armor,
18.23 thou be *a* on thy part to set riders
29 he shall not be *a* to deliver you
1Ch 5.18 men *a* to bear buckler and sword,
9.13 *a* men for the work of the service
26. 8 *a* men for strength for the service,
29.14 that we should be *a* to offer
2Ch 2. 6 is *a* to build him an house,
7. 7 *a* to receive the burnt offerings,
20. 6 that none is *a* to withstand thee?
37 they were not *a* to go to Tarshish.
25. 5 choice men, *a* to go forth to war,
9 Lord is *a* to give thee much more
32.13 any ways *a* to deliver their lands
14 your God should be *a* to deliver
15 was *a* to deliver his people
Ezr 10.13 we are not *a* to stand without,
Neh 4.10 we are not *a* to build the wall.
Job 41.10 who then is *a* to stand before me?
Ps 18.38 that they were not *a* to rise:
21.11 they are not *a* to perform.
36.12 shall not be *a* to rise.
40.12 I am not *a* to look up;
Pro 27. 4 who is *a* to stand before envy?
Ec 8.17 yet shall he not be *a* to find it.
Isa 36. 8 thou be *a* on thy part to set riders
14 he shall not be *a* to deliver you.
47.11 thou shalt not be *a* to put it off:
12 if so be thou shalt be *a* to profit,
Jer 10.10 the nations shall not be *a* to abide
11.11 they shall not be *a* to escape;
49.10 he shall not be *a* to hide himself:
La 1.14 I am not *a* to rise up.
Eze 7.19 their gold shall not be *a* to deliver
33.12 shall the righteous be *a* to live
46. 5 as he shall be *a* to give,
11 the lambs as he is *a* to give,
Dan 2.26 Art thou *a* to make known unto
3.17 God whom we serve is *a* to deliver
4.18 not *a* to make known unto me the
18 but thou art *a*; for the spirit of
37 walk in pride he is *a* to abase.
6.20 *a* to deliver thee from the lions?
Am 7.10 land is not *a* to bear all his words.
Zep 1.18 nor their gold shall be *a* to deliver
Mt 3. 9 God is *a* of these stones to raise
9.28 Believe ye that I am *a* to do this?
10.28 but are not *a* to kill the soul:
28 fear him which is *a* to destroy
19.12 He that is *a* to receive it, let him
20.22 Are ye *a* to drink of the cup that I
22 They say unto him, We are *a*.
22.46 no man was *a* to answer him
26.61 am *a* to destroy the temple of God,
Mk 4.33 as they were *a* to hear
Lk 1.20 shalt be dumb, and not *a* to speak,
3. 8 God is *a* of these stones to raise
12.26 ye then be not *a* to do that thing
13.24 to enter in, and shall not be *a*.
14.29 is not *a* to finish it, all that behold
30 began to build, and was not *a* to
31 whether he be *a* with ten
21.15 not be *a* to gainsay nor resist.
Jn 10.29 no man is *a* to pluck them out of
21. 6 now they were not *a* to draw it
Ac 6.10 were not *a* to resist the wisdom
15.10 neither our fathers nor we were *a*
20.32 the word of his grace, which is *a*
25. 5 which among you are *a*, go down
Ro 4.21 what he had promised, he was *a*
8.39 shall be *a* to separate us from the
11.23 God is *a* to graff them in again.
14. 4 for God is *a* to make him stand.
15.14 *a* also to admonish one another.
1Co 3. 2 hitherto ye were not *a* to bear it,
2 neither yet now are ye *a*.
6. 5 not one that shall be *a* to judge
10.13 to be tempted above that ye are *a*;
13 that ye may be *a* to bear it.
2Co 1. 4 may be *a* to comfort them which
3. 6 hath made us *a* ministers of the
9. 8 God is *a* to make all grace abound
Eph 3.18 *a* to comprehend with all saints
20 Now unto him that is *a* to do
6.11 that ye may be *a* to stand against
13 that ye may be *a* to withstand in
16 ye shall be *a* to quench all the
Php 3.21 he is *a* even to subdue all things
2Ti 1.12 persuaded that he is *a* to keep
2. 2 shall be *a* to teach others also.
3. 7 never *a* to come to the knowledge
15 scriptures, which are *a* to make
Tit 1. 9 he may be *a* by sound doctrine
Heb 2.18 he is *a* to succor them that are
5. 7 was *a* to save him from death,
7.25 Wherefore he is *a* also to save
11.19 that God was *a* to raise him up,
Jas 1.21 which is *a* to save your souls.
3. 2 *a* also to bridle the whole body.
4.12 lawgiver, who is *a* to save and to
2Pe 1.15 ye may be *a* after my decease to
Jude 24 Now unto him that is *a* to keep
Rev 5. 3 was *a* to open the book, neither
6.17 who shall be *a* to stand?
13. 4 who is *a* to make war with him?
15. 8 was *a* to enter into the temple,

ABNER

1Sa 14.50 of the captain of his host was *A*,
51 Ner the father of *A* was the son of
17.55 said unto *A*, the captain of the host,
55 *A*, whose son is this youth?
55 *A* said, As thy soul liveth, O king,
57 *A* took him, and brought him
20.25 and Jonathan arose, and *A* sat by
26. 5 and *A* the son of Ner, the captain
7 *A* and the people lay round about
14 David cried to the people, and to *A*
14 saying, Answerest thou not, *A*?
14 *A* answered and said, Who are thou
15 David said to *A*, Art not thou a
2Sa 2. 8 *A* the son of Ner, captain of Saul's
12 *A* the son of Ner, and the servants
14 *A* said to Joab, Let the young men
17 *A* was beaten, and the men of Israel,
19 And Asahel pursued after *A*; and
19 nor to the left from following *A*.
20 *A* looked behind him, and said,
21 And *A* said to him, Turn thee aside
22 *A* said again to Asahel, Turn thee
23 *A* with the hinder end of the spear
24 also and Abishai pursued after *A*:
25 themselves together after *A*,
26 Then *A* called to Joab, and said,
29 *A* and his men walked all that
30 Joab returned from following *A*:
3. 6 that *A* made himself strong for the
7 Ishbosheth said to *A*, Wherefore
8 Then was *A* very wroth for the
9 So do God to *A*, and more also,
11 And he could not answer *A* a word
12 And *A* sent messengers to David
16 Then said *A* unto him, Go, return.
17 And *A* had communication with
19 And *A* also spake in the ears of
19 *A* went also to speak in the ears of
20 So *A* came to David to Hebron,
20 David made *A* and the men that
21 *A* said unto David, I will arise and
21 David sent *A* away; and he went in
22 *A* was not with David in Hebron;
23 *A* the son of Ner came to the king,
24 behold, *A* came unto thee; why is
25 Thou knowest *A* the son of Ner,
26 he sent messengers after *A*, which
27 when *A* was returned to Hebron,
28 for ever from the blood of *A* the
30 and Abishai his brother slew *A*,
31 sackcloth, and mourn before *A*.
32 And they buried *A* in Hebron: and
32 voice, and wept at the grave of *A*;
33 the king lamented over *A*, and said,
33 Died *A* as a fool dieth?
37 that it was not of the king to slay *A*
4. 1 Saul's son heard that *A* was dead
12 and buried it in the sepulcher of *A*
1Ki 2. 5 unto *A* the son of Ner, and unto
32 to wit, *A* the son of Ner, captain of
1Ch 26.28 Saul the son of Kish, and *A* the son
27.21 of Benjamin, Jaasiel the son of *A*:

ABNER'S

2Sa 2.31 of Benjamin, and of *A* men, so that

ABOARD

Ac 21. 2 we went *a*, and set forth.

ABODE

Gen 29.14 *a* with him the space of a month,
49.24 But his bow *a* in strength, and
Ex 24.16 glory of the Lord *a* upon mount
40.35 because the cloud *a* thereon,
Nu 9.17 the place where the cloud *a*, there
18 as long as the cloud *a* upon the
20 *a* in their tents, and according
21 when the cloud *a* from even
22 the children of Israel *a* in their
11.35 unto Hazeroth; and *a* at
20. 1 and the people *a* in Kadesh;
22. 8 princes of Moab *a* with Balaam.
25. 1 And Israel *a* in Shittim, and the
Dt 1.46 So ye *a* in Kadesh many days,
46 according unto the days that ye *a*
3.29 So we *a* in the valley over against
9. 9 then I *a* in the mount forty days
Jos 2.22 and *a* there three days, until the
5. 8 they *a* in their places in the camp,
8. 9 and *a* between Beth-el and Ai,
Jdg 5.17 Gilead *a* beyond Jordan:
17 and *a* in his breaches.
11.17 and Israel *a* in Kadesh.
19. 4 and he *a* with him three days:
20.47 *a* in the rock Rimmon four months.
21. 2 and *a* there till even before God,
1Sa 1.23 the woman *a*, and gave her son
7. 2 while the ark *a* in Kirjath-jearim,
13.16 *a* in Gibeah of Benjamin:
22. 6 Saul *a* in Gibeah under a tree

1Sa 23.14 David *a* in the wilderness
18 and David *a* in the wood,
25 and *a* in the wilderness of Maon.
25.13 two hundred *a* by the stuff.
26. 3 David *a* in the wilderness, and he
30.10 for two hundred *a* behind, which
2Sa 1. 1 David had *a* two days in Ziklag;
11.12 Uriah *a* in Jerusalem that day,
15. 8 while I *a* in Geshur in Syria,
1Ki 17.19 him up into a loft, where he *a*,
2Ki 19.27 I know thy *a*, and thy going out,
Ezr 8.15 there *a* we in tents three days:
32 came to Jerusalem, and *a* there
Isa 37.28 I know thy *a*, and thy going out,
Jer 38.28 So Jeremiah *a* in the court of the
Mt 17.22 while they *a* in Galilee, Jesus
Lk 1.56 *a* with her about three months,
8.27 *a* in any house, but in the tombs,
21.37 he went out, and *a* in the mount
Jn 1.32 like a dove, and it *a* upon him.
39 saw where he dwelt, and *a* with
4.40 he *a* there two days.
7. 9 he *a* still in Galilee.
8.44 *a* not in the truth, because there
10.40 and there he *a*.
11. 6 *a* two days still in the same place
14.23 and make our *a* with him.
Ac 1.13 where *a* both Peter, and James,
12.19 Judea to Caesarea, and there *a*.
14. 3 Long time therefore *a* they
28 *a* long time with the disciples,
17.14 Silas and Timotheus *a* there still.
18. 3 he *a* with them, and wrought:
20. 3 And there *a* three months.
6 where we *a* seven days.
21. 7 saluted the brethren, and *a* with
8 one of the seven, and *a* with him.
Gal 1.18 see Peter, and *a* with him fifteen
2Ti 4.20 Erastus *a* at Corinth:

ABOLISH
Isa 2.18 the idols he shall utterly *a*.

ABOLISHED
Isa 51. 6 my righteousness shall not be *a*.
Eze 6. 6 and your works may be *a*.
2Co 3.13 to the end of that which is *a*:
Eph 2.15 Having *a* in his flesh the enmity,
2Ti 1.10 Christ, who hath *a* death,

ABOMINABLE
Lev 7.21 or any *a* unclean thing,
11.43 ye shall not make yourselves *a*
18.30 not any one of these *a* customs,
19. 7 it is *a*; it shall not be accepted.
20.25 ye shall not make your souls *a*
Dt 14. 3 Thou shalt not eat any *a* thing.
1Ch 21. 6 the king's word was *a* to Joab.
2Ch 15. 8 put away the *a* idols out of all
Job 15.16 How much more *a* and filthy is
Ps 14. 1 they have done *a* works,
53. 1 and have done *a* iniquity:
Isa 14.19 thy grave like an *a* branch,
65. 4 of *a* things is in their vessels;
Jer 16.18 detestable and *a* things.
44. 4 do not this *a* thing that I hate.
Eze 4.14 neither came there *a* flesh into
8.10 and *a* beasts, and all the idols
16.52 thou hast committed more *a* than
Mic 6.10 the scant measure that is *a*?
Na 3. 6 I will cast *a* filth upon thee,
Tit 1.16 him, being *a*, and disobedient,
1Pe 4. 3 banquetings, and *a* idolatries:
Rev 21. 8 unbelieving, and the *a*, and

ABOMINABLY
1Ki 21.26 he did very *a* in following idols,

ABOMINATION
Gen 43.32 is an *a* unto the Egyptians.
46.34 every shepherd is an *a* unto the
Ex 8.26, 26 the *a* of the Egyptians
Lev 7.18 it shall be an *a*,
11.10 they shall be an *a* unto you:
11 be even an *a* unto you;
11 ye shall have their carcases in *a*.
12 that shall be an *a*
13 shall have in *a* among the fowls;
13 they are an *a*:
20 an *a* unto you.
23 four feet, shall be an *a* unto you.
41 the earth shall be an *a*;
42 shall not eat; for they are an *a*.
18.22 with womankind: it is *a*.
20.13 of them have committed an *a*:
Dt 7.25 for it is an *a* to the Lord thy God.
26 shalt thou bring an *a* into thine
12.31 for every *a* to the Lord, which he
13.14 such *a* is wrought among you;
17. 1 an *a* unto the Lord
4 such *a* is wrought in Israel:
18.12 these things are an *a* unto the
22. 5 all that do so are *a* unto the
23.18 both these are *a* unto the Lord
24. 4 that is *a* before the Lord:
25.16 unrighteously, are an *a* unto
27.15 molten image, an *a* unto
1Sa 13. 4 Israel also was had in *a*
1Ki 11. 5 the *a* of the Ammonites.
7 the *a* of Moab,
7 the *a* of the children of Ammon.
2Ki 23.13 the *a* of the Zidonians, and for
13 Chemosh the *a* of the Moabites,
13 Milcom the *a* of the children
Ps 88. 8 thou hast made me an *a* unto
Pr 3.32 the froward is *a* to the Lord:
6.16 seven are an *a* unto him:
8. 7 and wickedness is an *a* to my lips.
11. 1 false balance is *a* to the Lord:
20 are of a froward heart are *a* to
12.22 Lying lips are *a* to the Lord:
13.19 it is *a* to fools to depart from evil.
15. 8 wicked is an *a* to the Lord:
9 way of the wicked is an *a* unto the
26 thoughts of the wicked are an *a* to
16. 5 proud in heart is an *a* to
12 *a* to kings to commit wickedness:
17.15 both are *a* to the Lord.
20.10 both of them are alike *a* to the
23 Divers weights are an *a* unto
21.27 sacrifice of the wicked is *a*:
24. 9 and the scorner is an *a* to men.
28. 9 even his prayer shall be *a*.
29.27 An unjust man is an *a* to the just:
27 is upright in the way is *a* to the
Isa 1.13 incense is an *a* unto me;
41.24 an *a* is he that chooseth you.
44.19 make the residue thereof an *a*?
66.17 eating swine's flesh, and the *a*,
Jer 2. 7 made mine heritage an *a*.
6.15 when they had committed *a*?
8.12 when they had committed *a*?
32.35 do this *a*, to cause Judah to sin.
Eze 16.50 were haughty, and committed *a*
18.12 the idols, hath committed *a*,
22.11 *a* with his neighbor's wife;
33.26 ye work *a*, and ye defile every
Dan 11.31 place the *a* that maketh desolate.
12.11 the *a* that maketh desolate set up,
Mal 2.11 and an *a* is committed in Israel
Mt 24.15 see the *a* of desolation,
Mk 13.14 shall see the *a* of desolation,
Lk 16.15 is *a* in the sight of God.
Rev 21.27 worketh *a*, or maketh a lie:

ABOUND
Pr 28.20 A faithful man shall *a* with
Mt 24.12 because iniquity shall *a*,
Ro 5.20 the offense might *a*. But where
20 grace did much more *a*:
6. 1 that grace may *a*?
15.13 that ye may *a* in hope, through
2Co 1. 5 sufferings of Christ *a* in us, so our
8. 7 as ye *a* in every thing, in faith,
7 that ye *a* in this grace also.
9. 8 to make all grace *a* toward you:
8 may *a* to every good work:
Php 1. 9 that your love may *a* yet more
4.12 and I know how to *a*:
12 both to *a* and to suffer need.
17 that may *a* to your account.
18 I have all and *a*:
1Th 3.12 make you to increase and *a* in
4. 1 so ye would *a* more and more.
2Pe 1. 8 if these things be in you, and *a*,

ABOUNDED
Ro 3. 7 hath more *a* through my lie unto
5.15 hath *a* unto many.
20 But where sin *a*, grace did much
2Co 8. 2 *a* unto the riches of their liberality
Eph 1. 8 Wherein he hath *a* toward us in

ABOUNDETH
Pr 29.22 a furious man *a* in transgression.
2Co 1. 5 consolation also *a* by Christ.
2Th 1. 3 all toward each other *a*;

ABRAHAM

Tribal leader from Mesopotamia traditionally regarded as forefather of the Hebrews (through Isaac) and of the Arabs (through Ishmael); celebrated for his faith; at first called Abram; confronted by God at Haran and commanded to leave his homeland for a new land; also told that, though his wife Sarai is barren, his descendants will become a great nation (Gen 11.27–12.3); obeys God's call and arrives in Canaan (Gen 12.4-9); pretends on a visit to Egypt that Sarai is his sister, when Pharaoh has designs on her, and only escapes through God's intervention (Gen 12.10-20); parts from his nephew Lot and lets him choose the fertile plain of Sodom and Gomorrah (Gen 13); rescues Lot from invading army (Gen 14); in an attempt to safeguard his posterity, appoints his servant as his heir, but is told that his own son will succeed him; believes God and is taken into covenant by him (Gen 15); takes Sarai's maid Hagar as a concubine but stands aside when Sarai drives her away (Gen 16); when Hagar returns and Ishmael is born, thinks that he is the son of promise but is told that Sarai will have a son in her old age, and laughs; God renews his covenant with him, its sign being circumcision, and his and his wife's names are changed to Abraham and Sarah (Gen 17); hearing of the fate decreed for Sodom and Gomorrah, intercedes for the wicked cities, but to no avail (Gen 18); the cities are destroyed but Lot's life is spared (Gen 19); at Gerar again pretends that Sarah is his sister and again God's intervention is needed (Gen 20); Isaac is born and for a second time Sarah wishes to drive Hagar away; Abraham this time protests, but at God's bidding acquiesces (Gen 21); sorrowfully obeys God's command to sacrifice Isaac, but at the last moment is permitted to offer a ram instead (Gen 22); buries Sarah (Gen 23) and before his own death sends servant to Mesopotamia to find a wife for Isaac (Gen 24).

ABOUNDING

Pr 8.24 no fountains *a* with water.
1Co 15.58 always *a* in the work of the Lord,
Col 2. 7 *a* therein with thanksgiving

ABRAHAM

Gen 17. 5 but thy name shall be *A*;
9 God said unto *A*, Thou shalt keep
15 God said unto *A*, As for Sarai thy
17 *A* fell upon his face, and laughed,
18 *A* said unto God, Oh that Ishmael
22 and God went up from *A*.
23 And *A* took Ishmael his son, and
24 *A* was ninety years old and nine,
26 selfsame day was *A* circumcised,
18. 6 *A* hastened into the tent unto
7 *A* ran unto the herd, and fetcht
11 *A* and Sarah were old and well
13 the Lord said unto *A*, Wherefore
16 *A* went with them to bring them
17 Shall I hide from *A* that thing
18 Seeing that *A* shall surely become
19 that the Lord may bring upon *A*
22 but *A* stood yet before the Lord.
23 *A* drew near, and said, Wilt thou
27 *A* answered and said, Behold now,
33 as he had left communing with *A*:
33 and *A* returned unto his place.
19.27 *A* gat up early in the morning to
29 God remembered *A*, and sent Lot
20. 1 *A* journeyed from thence toward
2 *A* said of Sarah his wife, She is my
9 Abimelech called *A*, and said unto
10 Abimelech said unto *A*, What
11 *A* said, Because I thought, surely
14 gave them unto *A*, and restored
17 So *A* prayed unto God: and God
21. 2 and bare *A* a son in his old age,
3 *A* called the name of his son that
4 *A* circumcised his son Isaac
5 *A* was an hundred years old, when
7 Who would have said unto *A*, that
8 *A* made a great feast the same day
9 which she had born unto *A*,
10 she said unto *A*, Cast out this
12 God said unto *A*, Let it not be
14 *A* rose up early in the morning,
22 captain of his host spake unto *A*,
24 And *A* said, I will swear.
25 *A* reproved Abimelech because of a
27 *A* took sheep and oxen, and gave
28 *A* set seven ewe lambs of the flock
29 Abimelech said unto *A*, What mean
33 *A* planted a grove in Beer-sheba,
34 *A* sojourned in the Philistines' land
22. 1 that God did tempt *A*, and said
1 unto him, *A*: and he said, Behold,
3 *A* rose up early in the morning,
4 day *A* lifted up his eyes, and saw
5 *A* said unto his young men, Abide
6 *A* took the wood of the burnt
7 Isaac spake unto *A* his father, and
8 *A* said, My son, God will provide
9 *A* built an altar there, and laid the
10 *A* stretched forth his hand, and
11 him out of heaven, and said, *A*, *A*:
13 *A* lifted up his eyes, and looked,
13 *A* went and took the ram, and
14 *A* called the name of that place
15 the angel of the Lord called unto *A*
19 So *A* returned unto his young men,
20 it was told *A*, saying, Behold,
23. 2 and *A* came to mourn for Sarah,
3 *A* stood up from before his dead,
5 the children of Heth answered *A*,
7 *A* stood up, and bowed himself to
10 Ephron the Hittite answered *A*
12 *A* bowed down himself before the
14 Ephron answered *A*, saying unto
16 And *A* hearkened unto Ephron;
16 *A* weighed to Ephron the silver,

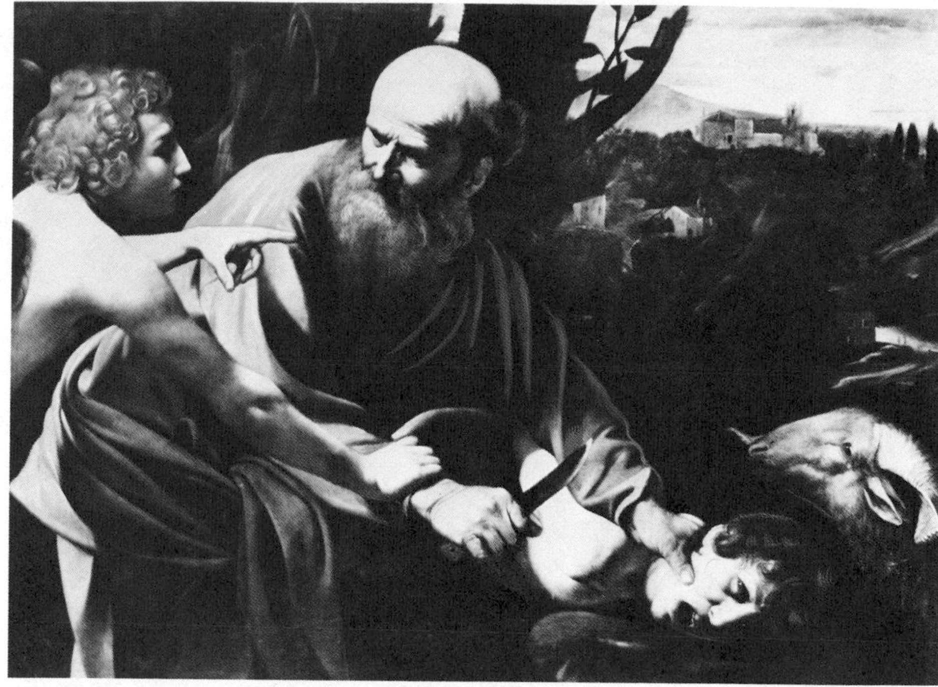

Abraham's hand is stayed by the angel of the Lord in the Sacrifice of Isaac, *by Caravaggio (1573-1610).*

18 Unto *A* for a possession in the
19 after this, *A* buried Sarah his wife
20 made sure into *A* for a possession
24. 1 *A* was old, and well stricken in age:
1 Lord had blessed *A* in all things.
2 *A* said unto his eldest servant of
6 *A* said unto him, Beware thou that
9 put his hand under the thigh of *A*
12 O Lord God of my master *A*, I pray
12 shew kindness unto my master *A*
27 be the Lord God of my master *A*,
42 said, O Lord God of my master *A*,
48 the Lord God of my master *A*,
25. 1 Then again *A* took a wife, and her
5 *A* gave all that he had unto Isaac
6 concubines, which *A* had, *A* gave
8 Then *A* gave up the ghost, and died
10 The field which *A* purchased of the
10 there was *A* buried, and Sarah his
11 the death of *A*, that God blessed
12 Sarah's handmaid, bare unto *A*:
19 *A* begat Isaac:
26. 1 famine that was in the days of *A*.
3 the oath which I swear unto *A*
5 Because that *A* obeyed my voice,
15 had digged in the days of *A*
18 they had digged in the days of *A*
18 stopped them after the death of *A*:
24 and said, I am the God of *A* thy
28. 4 And give thee the blessing of *A*,
4 a stranger, which God gave unto *A*.
13 I am the Lord God of *A* thy father,
31.42 the God of my father, the God of *A*,
53 The God of *A*, and the God of Nahor,
32. 9 Jacob said, O God of my father *A*,
35.12 the land which I gave *A* and Isaac,
27 which is Hebron, where *A* and
48.15 before whom my fathers *A* and
16 and the name of my fathers *A* and
49.30 which *A* bought with the field of
31 There they buried *A* and Sarah his
50.13 which *A* bought with the field for a
24 unto the land which he sware to *A*,
Ex 2.24 remembered his covenant with *A*,
3. 6 the God of thy father, the God of *A*,
15 God of your fathers, the God of *A*,
16 God of *A*, of Isaac, and of Jacob,

4. 5 God of their fathers, the God of *A*,
6. 3 I appeared unto *A*, unto Isaac, and
8 which I did swear to give it to *A*,
32.13 Remember *A*, Isaac, and Israel,
33. 1 the land which I swear unto *A*,
Lev 26.42 also my covenant with *A* will I
Nu 32.11 see the land which I sware unto *A*,
Dt 1. 8 Lord sware unto your fathers, *A*,
6.10 he sware unto thy fathers, to *A*,
9. 5 Lord sware unto thy fathers, *A*,
27 Remember thy servants, *A*, Isaac,
29.13 hath sworn unto thy fathers, to *A*,
30.20 Lord sware unto thy fathers, to *A*,
34. 4 is the land which I sware unto *A*,
Jos 24. 2 even Terah, the father of *A*,
3 I took your father *A* from the
1Ki 18.36 came near, and said, Lord God of *A*,
2Ki 13.23 because of his covenant with *A*,
1Ch 1.27 Abram; the same is *A*.
28 The sons of *A*; Isaac, and Ishmael.
34 And *A* begat Isaac. The sons of
16.16 covenant which he made with *A*,
29.18 O Lord God of *A*, Isaac, and of
2Ch 20. 7 and gavest it to the seed of *A*
30. 6 again unto the Lord God of *A*,
Neh 9. 7 and gavest him the name of *A*;
Ps 47. 9 even the people of the God of *A*:
105. 6 O ye seed of *A* his servant,
9 Which covenant he made with *A*,
42 his holy promise, and *A*
Isa 29.22 saith the Lord, who redeemed *A*,
41. 8 the seed of *A* my friend.
51. 2 Look unto *A* your father, and unto
63.16 though *A* be ignorant of us,
Jer 33.26 to be rulers over the seed of *A*,
Eze 33.24 *A* was one, and he inherited the
Mic 7.20 truth to Jacob, and the mercy to *A*,
Mt 1. 1 the son of David, the son of *A*.
2 *A* begat Isaac; and Isaac begat
17 the generations from *A* to David
3. 9 We have *A* to our father:
9 to raise up children unto *A*.
8.11 shall sit down with *A*,
22.32 I am the God of *A*, and the God of
Mk 12.26 I am the God of *A*,
Lk 1.55 As he spake to our fathers, to *A*,
73 he sware to our father *A*,

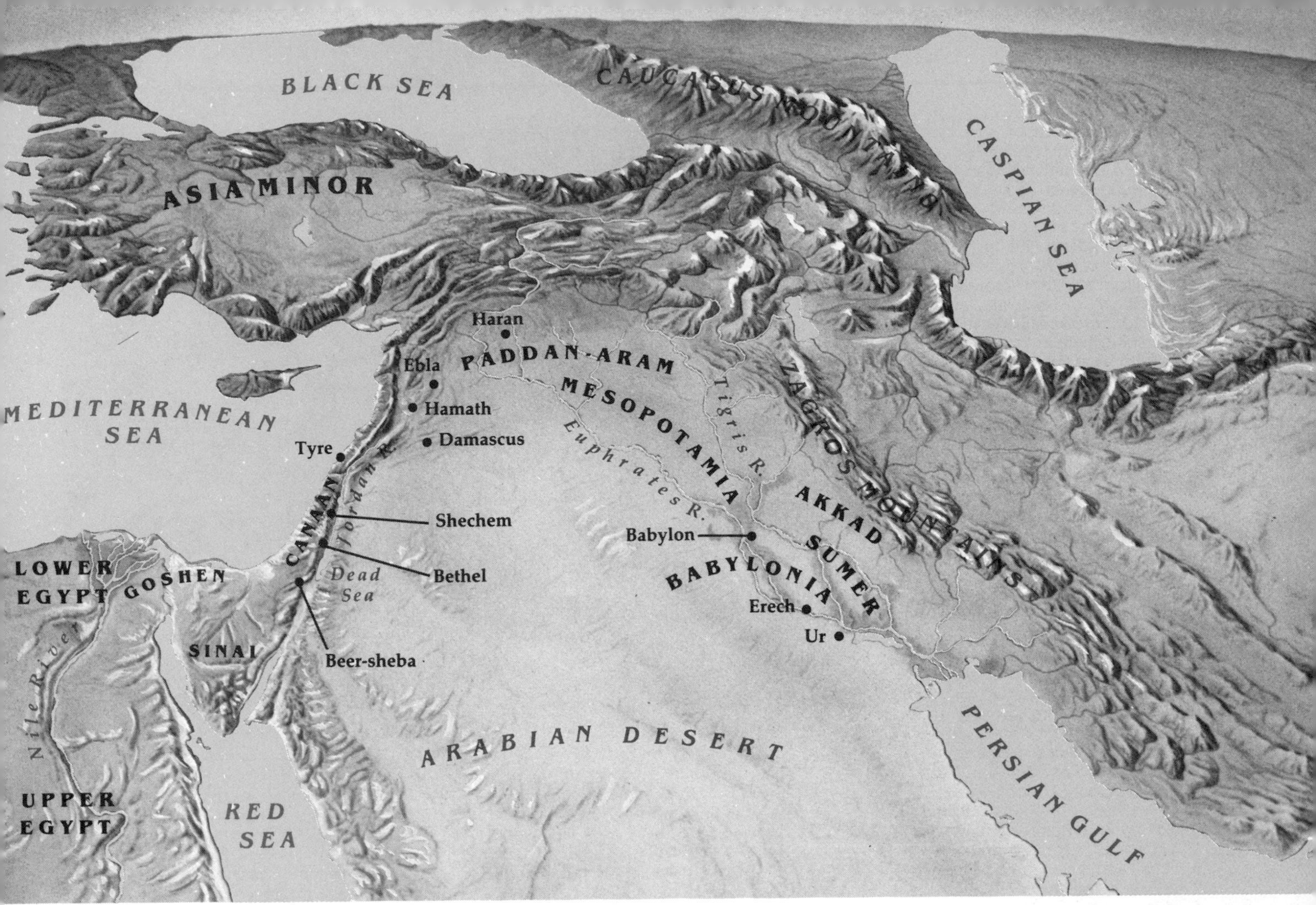

***The travels of Abraham** took him first from Ur, his ancestral home on the Euphrates, to Haran 600 miles to the northwest, where his clan sojourned on the long trek to Canaan. He then led them southward to the Promised Land, erecting an altar at Shechem; famine forced them to press on into Egypt, but in time they returned. It was at Beer-sheba that Abraham was commanded to sacrifice Isaac, and at Bethel that he was buried next to his beloved Sarah.*

Lk 3. 8 We have *A* to our father:
8 to raise up children unto *A*.
34 which was the son of *A*,
13.16 this woman, being a daughter of *A*,
28 when ye shall see *A*, and Isaac,
16.23 and seeth *A* afar off,
24 Father *A*, have mercy on me,
25 But *A* said, Son, remember that
29 *A* saith unto him, They have Moses
30 Nay, father *A*: but if one went
19. 9 forsomuch as he also is a son of *A*.
20.37 he calleth the Lord the God of *A*,
Jn 8.39 answered and said unto him, *A* is
39 ye would do the works of *A*.
40 this did not *A*.
52 *A* is dead, and the prophets;
53 Art thou greater than our father *A*,
56 *A* rejoiced to see my day:
57 and hast thou seen *A*?
58 Before *A* was, I am.
Ac 3.13 The God of *A*, and of Isaac,
25 saying unto *A*, And in thy seed
7. 2 appeared unto our father *A*,
8 circumcision: and so *A* begat
16 the sepulcher that *A* bought
17 which God had sworn to *A*,
32 God of thy fathers, the God of *A*,
13.26 children of the stock of *A*,
Ro 4. 1 *A* our father, as pertaining
2 if *A* were justified by works,
3 *A* believed God, and it was counted
9 faith was reckoned to *A* for
12 that faith of our father *A*,
13 not to *A*, or to his seed, through
16 which is of the faith of *A*;
9. 7 because they are the seed of *A*,
11. 1 of the seed of *A*, of the tribe of
2Co 11.22 Are they the seed of *A*? so am I.
Gal 3. 6 Even as *A* believed God,
7 are the children of *A*.
8 preached before the gospel unto *A*,
9 blessed with faithful *A*.
14 the blessing of *A* might come
16 to *A* and his seed were the
18 God gave it to *A* by promise.
4.22 *A* had two sons, the one by
Heb 2.16 but he took on him the seed of *A*.
6.13 when God made promise to *A*,
7. 1 *A* returning from the slaughter
2 To whom also *A* gave a tenth
4 *A* gave the tenth of the spoils.
5 they come out of the loins of *A*:
6 received tithes of *A*,
9 payed tithes in *A*.
11. 8 By faith *A*, when he was called to
17 By faith *A*, when he was tried,
Jas 2.21 Was not *A* our father justified by
23 *A* believed God, and it was imputed
1Pe 3. 6 Sara obeyed *A*, calling him lord:

ABRAHAM'S

Gen 17.23 every male among the men of *A*
20.18 because of Sarah *A* wife.
21.11 thing was very grievous in *A* sight
22.23 eight Milcah did bear to Nahor, *A*
24.15 son of Milcah, the wife of Nahor, *A*
34 And he said, I am *A* servant.
52 when *A* servant heard their words,
59 and her nurse, and *A* servant, and
25. 7 these are the days of the years of *A*
12 are the generations of Ishmael, *A*
19 are the generations of Isaac, *A*
26.24 multiply thy seed for my servant *A*
28. 9 the daughter of Ishmael *A*
1Ch 1.32 the sons of Keturah, *A* concubine:
Lk 16.22 carried by the angels into *A* bosom:
Jn 8.33 We be *A* seed, and were never in
37 I know that ye are *A* seed;
39 If ye were *A* children, ye would do
Gal 3.29 then are ye *A* seed, and heirs

ABRAM

Gen 11.26 lived seventy years, and begat *A*,
27 Terah begat *A*, Nahor, and Haran;
29 And *A* and Nahor took them wives:
31 And Terah took *A* his son, and Lot
12. 1 the Lord had said unto *A*, Get thee
4 So *A* departed, as the Lord had
4 *A* was seventy and five years old
5 *A* took Sarai his wife, and Lot
6 *A* passed through the land unto
7 Lord appeared unto *A*, and said,
9 *A* journeyed, going on still toward
10 and *A* went down into Egypt to
14 when *A* was come into Egypt, the
16 And he entreated *A* well for her
18 Pharaoh called *A*, and said, What
13. 1 *A* went up out of Egypt, he, and
2 And *A* was very rich in cattle,
4 and there *A* called on the name of
5 Lot also, which went with *A*, had
8 *A* said unto Lot, Let there be no
12 *A* dwelled in the land of Canaan,
14 the Lord said unto *A*, after that
18 Then *A* removed his tent, and

14.13 one that had escaped, and told *A*
13 and these were confederate with *A*.
14 when *A* heard that his brother was
19 Blessed be *A* of the most high God,
21 the king of Sodom said unto *A*,
22 *A* said to the king of Sodom,
23 thou shouldest say, I have made *A*
15. 1 the word of the Lord came unto *A*
1 in a vision, saying, Fear not, *A*:
2 *A* said, Lord God, what wilt thou
3 *A* said, Behold, to me thou hast
11 came down upon the carcasses, *A*
12 a deep sleep fell upon *A*;
13 he said unto *A*, Know of a surety
18 the Lord made a covenant with *A*,
16. 2 Sarai said unto *A*, Behold now, the
2 And *A* hearkened to the voice of
3 after *A* had dwelt ten years in the
3 and gave her to her husband *A*
5 Sarai said unto *A*, My wrong be
6 *A* said unto Sarai, Behold, thy
15 Hagar bare *A* a son: and *A* called
16 *A* was fourscore and six years old,
16 when Hagar bare Ishmael to *A*.
17. 1 when *A* was ninety years old and
1 the Lord appeared to *A*,
3 *A* fell on his face: and God talked
5 thy name any more be called *A*,
1Ch 1.27 *A*; the same is Abraham.
Neh 9. 7 Lord the God, who didst choose *A*,

ABRAM'S

Gen 11.29 the name of *A* wife was Sarai;
31 his daughter in law, his son *A* wife;
12.17 because of Sarai, *A* wife.
13. 7 a strife between the herdmen of *A*
14.12 they took Lot, *A* brother's son,
16. 1 Now Sarai, *A* wife, bare him no
3 And Sarai, *A* wife, took Hagar her

ABSALOM

2Sa 3. 3 the third, *A* the son of Maacah
13. 1 that *A* the son of David had a fair
20 And *A* her brother said unto her,
22 And *A* spake unto his brother
22 Amnon neither good nor bad: for *A*
23 *A* had sheepshearers in Baal-hazor,
23 and *A* invited all the king's
24 And *A* came to the king, and said,
25 the king said to *A*, Nay, my son,
26 Then said *A*, If not, I pray thee,
27 *A* pressed him, that he let Amnon
28 Now *A* had commanded his
29 And the servants of *A* did unto
29 Amnon as *A* had commanded.
30 *A* hath slain all the king's sons,
32 by the appointment of *A* this hath
34 But *A* fled. And the young man
37 But *A* fled, and went to Talmai,
38 So *A* fled, and went to Geshur,
39 David longed to go forth unto *A*:
14. 1 that the king's heart was toward *A*.
21 bring the young man *A* again.
23 went to Geshur, and brought *A* to
24 So *A* returned to his own house,
25 much praised as *A* for his beauty:
27 unto *A* there were born three sons,
28 *A* dwelt two full years in Jerusalem,
29 *A* sent for Joab, to have sent him
31 Then Joab arose, and came to *A*
32 *A* answered Joab, Behold, I sent
33 when he had called for *A*, he came
33 the king: and the king kissed *A*.
15. 1 that *A* prepared him chariots and
2 And *A* rose up early, and stood
2 then *A* called unto him, and said,
3 *A* said unto him, See, thy matters
4 *A* said moreover, Oh that I were
6 on this manner did *A* to all Israel
6 so *A* stole the hearts of the men of
7 *A* said unto the king, I pray thee,
10 But *A* sent spies throughout all the
10 ye shall say, *A* reigneth in Hebron.
11 and with *A* went two hundred men
12 *A* sent for Ahithophel the Gilonite,
12 people increased continually with *A*
13 of the men of Israel are after *A*.
14 for we shall not else escape from *A*:
31 is among the conspirators with *A*.
34 say unto *A*, I will be thy servant,
37 came into the city, and *A* came into
16. 8 the kingdom into the hand of *A*
15 And *A*, and all the people the men
16 David's friend, was come unto *A*,
16 Hushai said unto *A*, God save the
17 *A* said to Hushai, Is this thy
18 Hushai said unto *A*, Nay; but whom
20 said *A* to Ahithophel, Give counsel
21 Ahithophel said unto *A*, Go in unto
22 So they spread *A* a tent upon the
22 and *A* went in unto his father's
23 both with David and with *A*.
17. 1 Ahithophel said unto *A*, Let me
4 And the saying pleased *A* well,
5 Then said *A*, Call now Hushai
6 When Hushai was come to *A*, *A*
7 Hushai said unto *A*, The counsel
9 among the people that follow *A*.
14 *A* and all the men of Israel said,
14 the Lord might bring evil upon *A*.
15 and thus did Ahithophel counsel *A*
18 a lad saw them, and told *A*:
24 And *A* passed over Jordan, he and
25 *A* made Amasa captain of the host
26 Israel and *A* pitched in the land of
18. 5 with the young man, even with *A*.
5 the captains charge concerning *A*.
9 and *A* met the servants of David.
9 And *A* rode upon a mule,
10 Behold, I saw *A* hanged in an oak.
12 that none touch the young man *A*.
14 them through the heart of *A*,
15 about and smote *A*, and slew him.
17 they took *A*, and cast him into a
18 Now, *A* in his life time had taken
29 said, Is the young man *A* safe?

ABSALOM

Third son of King David, 10th century B.C., his mother being a Geshurite princess (2Sa 3.3); when his sister Tamar is violated by their half-brother Amnon, gives her protection and, waiting his opportunity, slays Amnon (2Sa 13); flees for sanctuary to his mother's homeland but is recalled to Jerusalem by David through the good offices of Joab and the wise woman of Tekoa (2Sa 14); courts popularity in the country and harbors thoughts of usurping the throne, finally arranging to have himself declared king in Hebron; David flees and abandons the capital to him (2Sa 15); on the advice of Ahithophel, David's former counsellor, takes over the king's harem, thus making reconciliation impossible (2Sa 16); however, refuses Ahithophel's advice to pursue David immediately, preferring the advice of Hushai, another counsellor secretly loyal to David, to postpone action until he can enlarge his army (2Sa 17); after this fatal delay, is defeated in battle by David's forces, flees from the field, is caught in the branches of a tree, and run through by Joab, despite the king's orders that he should not be killed; deeply mourned by his father (2Sa 18).

32 Cushi, Is the young man *A* safe?
33 O my son *A*, my son, my son *A*!
33 died for thee, O *A*, my son, my son!
19. 1 king weepeth and mourneth for *A*.
4 with a loud voice, O my son *A*,
4 O *A*, my son, my son!
6 I perceive, that if *A* had lived,
9 now he is fled out of the land for *A*.
10 And *A*, whom we anointed over us,
20. 6 do us more harm than did *A*:
1Ki 1. 6 and his mother bare him after *A*.
2. 7 I fled because of *A* thy brother.
28 though he turned not after *A*.
1Ch 3. 2 The third, *A* the son of Maachah
2Ch 11.20 took Maachah the daughter of *A*;
21 loved Maachah the daughter of *A*
Ps 3(T) Psalm of David, when he fled from *A*

ABSENCE

Lk 22. 6 in the *a* of the multitude.
Php 2.12 now much more in my *a*,
(See box on page 60)

ABSENT

Gen 31.49 when we are *a* one from another.
1Co 5. 3 For I verily, as *a* in body, but
2Co 5. 6 we are *a* from the Lord:
8 rather to be *a* from the body,
9 that, whether present or *a*,
10. 1 being *a* am bold toward you:
11 by letters when we are *a*, such
13. 2 *a* now I write to them
10 write these things being *a*,
Php 1.27 come and see you, or else be *a*,
Col 2. 5 though I be *a* in the flesh,

ABSTAIN

Ac 15.20 they *a* from pollutions of idols,
29 ye *a* from meats offered to idols,
1Th 4. 3 that ye should *a* from fornication:
5.22 *A* from all appearance of evil.
1Ti 4. 3 commanding to *a* from meats,
1Pe 2.11 *a* from fleshly lusts, which war

ABSTINENCE

Ac 27.21 after long *a* Paul stood forth in

ABUSE

1Sa 31. 4 thrust me through, and *a* me.
1Ch 10. 4 these uncircumcised come and *a*
1Co 9.18 I *a* not my power in the gospel.

ABUSED

Jdg 19.25 they knew her, and *a* her

ABUSERS

1Co 6. 9 *a* of themselves with mankind,

ABUSING

1Co 7.31 that use this world, as not *a* it:

ACCEPT

Gen 32.20 peradventure he will *a* of me.
Ex 22.11 the owner of it shall *a* thereof,
Lev 26.41 they then *a* of the punishment
43 they shall *a* of the punishment
Dt 33.11 *a* the work of his hands:
1Sa 26.19 me, let him *a* an offering:
2Sa 24.23 The Lord thy God *a* thee.
Job 13. 8 Will ye *a* his person? will ye
10 If ye do secretly *a* persons.
32.21 Let me not, I pray you, *a* any
42. 8 for him will I *a*:
Ps 20. 3 *a* thy burnt sacrifice;
82. 2 *a* the persons of the wicked?
119.108 *A*, I beseech thee, the freewill
Pr 18. 5 to *a* the person of the wicked,
Jer 14.10 the Lord doth not *a* them;
12 I will not *a* them:
Eze 20.40 there will I *a* them, and there will
41 will *a* you with your sweet savor,

Biblical Themes

ABSENCE

And Jacob vowed a vow, saying, If God will be with me, and will keep me in this way that I go, and will give me bread to eat, and raiment to put on, so that I come again to my father's house in peace; then shall the Lord be my God.
Gen 28.20-21

The Lord watch between me and thee, when we are absent one from another.
Gen 31.49

And Moses went . . . to Jethro his father in law, and said unto him, Let me go, I pray thee, and return unto my brethren which are in Egypt, and see whether they be yet alive. Ex 4.18

Saul answered, I am sore distressed; for the Philistines make war against me, and God is departed from me, and answereth me no more. 1Sa 28.15

And David longed, and said, Oh that one would give me drink of the water of the well of Bethlehem, which is by the gate! 2Sa 23.15

By the rivers of Babylon . . . we wept, when we remembered Zion . . . There they that carried us away captive required of us a song; and they that wasted us required of us mirth, saying, Sing us one of the songs of Zion. How shall we sing the Lord's song in a strange land? If I forget thee, O Jerusalem, let my right hand forget her cunning. If I do not remember thee, let my tongue cleave to the roof of my mouth; if I prefer not Jerusalem above my chief joy.
Ps 137.1-6

Whither shall I go from thy spirit? or whither shall I flee from thy presence? If I ascend up into heaven, thou art there: if I make my bed in hell, behold, thou art there. If I take the wings of the morning, and dwell in the uttermost parts of the sea; even there shall thy hand lead me, and thy right hand shall hold me. Ps 139.7-10

The Lord is nigh unto all them that call upon him, to all that call upon him in truth. Ps 145.18

I opened to my beloved; but my beloved had withdrawn himself, and was gone: my soul failed when he spake: I sought him, but I could not find him; I called him, but he gave me no answer.
SS 5.6

Remember the Lord afar off, and let Jerusalem come into your mind.
Jer 51.50

And Jesus said unto them, Can the children of the bridechamber mourn, as long as the bridegroom is with them? but the days will come, when the bridegroom shall be taken from them, and then shall they fast. Mt 9.15

The poor always ye have with you; but me ye have not always. Jn 12.8

A little while, and ye shall not see me: and again, a little while, and ye shall see me, because I go to the Father.
Jn 16.16

God is my witness . . . that without ceasing I make mention of you always in my prayers; making request, if by any means now at length I might have a prosperous journey by the will of God to come unto you. For I long to see you.
Ro 1.9-11

Absent in body, but present in spirit.
1Co 5.3

Therefore we are always confident, knowing that, whilst we are at home in the body, we are absent from the Lord: (for we walk by faith, not by sight:) we are confident, I say, and willing rather to be absent from the body, and to be present with the Lord.
2Co 5.6-8

Prepare me also a lodging: for I trust that through your prayers I shall be given unto you. Phm 22

Here have we no continuing city, but we seek one to come. Heb 13.14

Even so, come, Lord Jesus.
Rev 22.20

Eze 43.27 I will *a* you, saith the Lord God.
Am 5.22 meat offerings, I will not *a* them;
Mal 1. 8 pleased with thee, or *a* thy
10 neither will I *a* an offering at
13 should I *a* this of your hand?
Ac 24. 3 We *a* it always, and in all places,

ACCEPTED

Gen 4. 7 doest well, shalt thou not be *a*?
19.21 I have *a* thee concerning this
Ex 28.38 they may be *a* before the Lord.
Lev 1. 4 and it shall be *a* for him to make
7.18 the third day, it shall not be *a*,
10.19 been *a* in the sight of the Lord?
19. 7 is abominable; it shall not be *a*.
22.21 shall be perfect to be *a*;
23 for a vow it shall not be *a*.
25 they shall not be *a* for you.
27 it shall be *a* for an offering made
23.11 before the Lord, to be *a* for you:
1Sa 18. 5 and he was *a* in the sight of all
25.35 and have *a* thy person.
Est 10. 3 and *a* of the multitude of his
Job 42. 9 the Lord also *a* Job.
Isa 56. 7 their sacrifices shall be *a* upon
Jer 37.20 let my supplication...be *a*
42. 2 Let...our supplication be *a*
Lk 4.24 No prophet is *a* in his own
Ac 10.35 worketh righteousness, is *a*
Ro 15.31 may be *a* of the saints;
2Co 5. 9 we may be *a* of him.
6. 2 I have heard thee in a time *a*,
2 behold, now is the *a* time;
8.12 it is *a* according to that a man
17 For indeed he *a* the exhortation;
11. 4 gospel, which ye have not *a*,
Eph 1. 6 wherein he hath made us *a* in

ACCEPTEST

Lk 20.21 neither *a* thou the person of any,

ACCEPTETH

Job 34.19 him that *a* not the persons of
Ec 9. 7 God now *a* thy works.
Hos 8.13 the Lord *a* them not;
Gal 2. 6 God *a* no man's person:)

ACCEPTING

Heb 11.35 were tortured, not *a* deliverance;

ACCESS

Ro 5. 2 we have *a* by faith into this grace
Eph 2.18 we both have *a* by one Spirit
3.12 *a* with confidence by the faith of

ACCOMPANIED

Ac 10.23 brethren from Joppa *a* him.
11.12 these six brethren *a* me,
20. 4 *a* him into Asia Sopater of Berea;
38 And they *a* him unto the ship.

ACCOMPANY

Heb 6. 9 things that *a* salvation,

ACCOMPANYING

2Sa 6. 4 *a* the ark of God:

ACCOMPLISH

Lev 22.21 to *a* his vow,
1Ki 5. 9 and thou shalt *a* my desire,
Job 14. 6 till he shall *a*, as an hireling,
Ps 64. 6 they *a* a diligent search:
Isa 55.11 it shall *a* that which I please,
Jer 44.25 ye will surely *a* your vows,
Eze 6.12 thus will I *a* my fury upon them.
7. 8 and *a* mine anger upon thee:
13.15 Thus will I *a* my wrath upon the
20. 8, 21 to *a* my anger against them
Dan 9. 2 that he would *a* seventy years in
Lk 9.31 which he should *a* at Jerusalem.

ACCOMPLISHED

2Ch 36.22 word of the Lord...might be *a*,
Est 2.12 days of their purifications *a*,
Job 15.32 It shall be *a* before his time,
Pr 13.19 The desire *a* is sweet to the soul:
Isa 40. 2 her warfare is *a*, that her
Jer 25.12 when seventy years are *a*, that I
34 and of your dispersions are *a*;
29.10 after seventy years be *a* at
39.16 and they shall be *a* in that
La 4.11 The Lord hath *a* his fury;
22 punishment of thine iniquity is *a*,
Eze 4. 6 And when thou hast *a* them,
5.13 Thus shall mine anger be *a*,
13 when I have *a* my fury in them.
Dan 11.36 till the indignation be *a*:
12. 7 and when he shall have *a* to
Lk 1.23 days of his ministration were *a*,
2. 6 the days were *a* that she should
21 eight days were *a*
22 when the days...were *a*,
12.50 straitened till it be *a*!

18.31 the Son of man shall be *a*.
22.37 must yet be *a* in me,
Jn 19.28 all things were now *a*,
Ac 21. 5 when we had *a* those days,
1Pe 5. 9 are *a* in your brethren

ACCOMPLISHING
Heb 9. 6 *a* the service of God.

ACCOMPLISHMENT
Ac 21.26 the *a* of the days of purification,

ACCORD
Lev 25. 5 which groweth of its own *a*
Jos 9. 2 and with Israel, with one *a*.
Ac 1.14 continued with one *a* in prayer
2. 1 were all with one *a* in one place.
46 daily with one *a* in the temple,
4.24 up their voice to God with one *a*,
5.12 they were all with one *a* in
7.57 and ran upon him with one *a*,
8. 6 the people with one *a* gave heed
12.10 opened to them of his own *a*:
20 but they came with one *a* to him,
15.25 being assembled with one *a*, to
18.12 made insurrection with one *a*
19.29 rushed with one *a* into the
2Co 8.17 of his own *a* he went unto you.
Php 2. 2 love, being of one *a*, of one mind.

ACCOUNT
2Ki 12. 4 of every one that passeth the *a*,
1Ch 27.24 was the number put in the *a* of
2Ch 26.11 number of their *a* by the hand
Job 33.13 he giveth not *a* of any of his
Ps 144. 3 son of man, that thou makest *a*
Ec 7.27 one by one, to find out the *a*;
Mt 12.36 they shall give *a* thereof in the
18.23 would take *a* of his servants.
Lk 16. 2 give an *a* of thy stewardship;
Ac 19.40 whereby we may give an *a* of this
Ro 14.12 every one of us shall give *a* of
1Co 4. 1 Let a man so *a* of us, as of the
Php 4.17 fruit that may abound to your *a*.
Phm 18 put that on mine *a*;
Heb 13.17 as they that must give *a*,
1Pe 4. 5 shall give *a* to him that is ready
2Pe 3.15 And *a* that the longsuffering

ACCOUNTED
Dt 2.11 Which also were *a* giants, as the
20 (That also was *a* a land of giants:
1Ki 10.21 it was nothing *a* of in the days
2Ch 9.20 of silver; it was not any thing *a*
Ps 22.30 it shall be *a* to the Lord for a
Isa 2.22 wherein is he to be *a* of?
Mk 10.42 they which are *a* to rule over
Lk 20.35 which shall be *a* worthy to
21.36 that ye may be *a* worthy to
22.24 which of them should be *a* the
Ro 8.36 we are *a* as sheep for the
Gal 3. 6 it was *a* to him for righteousness.

ACCOUNTING
Heb 11.19 *A* that God was able to raise

ACCOUNTS
Dan 6. 2 that the princes might give *a*

ACCURSED
Dt 21.23 he that is hanged is *a* of God;)
Jos 6.17 the city shall be *a*,
18 keep yourselves from the *a*
18 lest ye make yourselves *a*,
18 when ye take of the *a* thing, and
7. 1 a trespass in the *a* thing:
1 took of the *a* thing:
11 have even taken of the *a* thing,
12 because they were *a*:
12 except ye destroy the *a* from
13 an *a* thing in the midst of thee,
13 until ye take away the *a* thing
15 taken with the *a* thing shall be
22.20 commit a trespass in the *a* thing,
1Ch 2. 7 who transgressed in the thing *a*.
Isa 65.20 an hundred years old shall be *a*.
Ro 9. 3 that myself were *a* from Christ
1Co 12. 3 calleth Jesus *a*: and that no man
Gal 1. 8 preached unto you, let him be *a*.
9 have received, let him be *a*

ACCUSATION
Ezr 4. 6 wrote they unto him an *a* against
Mt 27.37 over his head his *a* written,
Mk 15.26 his *a* was written over,
Lk 6. 7 might find an *a* against him.
19. 8 thing from any man by false *a*,
Jn 18.29 What *a* bring ye against this
Ac 25.18 they brought none *a* of such
1Ti 5.19 receive not an *a*, but before two
2Pe 2.11 bring not railing *a* against them
Jude 9 a railing *a*, but said, The Lord

ACCUSE
Pr 30.10 *A* not a servant unto his master,
Mt 12.10 that they might *a* him.
Mk 3. 2 sabbath day; that they might *a*
Lk 3.14 neither *a* any falsely; and be
11.54 his mouth, that they might *a*
23. 2 they began to *a* him,
14 whereof ye *a* him:
Jn 5.45 Do not think that I will *a* you to
8. 6 that they might have to *a* him.
Ac 24. 2 Tertullus began to *a* him,
8 these things, whereof we *a* him.
13 whereof they now *a* me.
25. 5 go down with me, and *a* this man,
11 whereof these *a* me, no man may
28.19 ought to *a* my nation of.
1Pe 3.16 ashamed that falsely *a* your

ACCUSED
Dan 3. 8 Chaldeans came near, and *a*
6.24 those men which had *a*
Mt 27.12 he was *a* of the chief priests
Mk 15. 3 the chief priests *a* him of many
Lk 16. 1 the same was *a* unto him that he
23.10 scribes stood and vehemently *a*
Ac 22.30 wherefore he was *a* of the Jews,
23.28 the cause wherefore they *a* him,
29 be *a* of questions of their law,
25.16 before that he which is *a* have
26. 2 things whereof I am *a* of the
7 king Agrippa, I am *a* of the Jews.
Tit 1. 6 children not *a* of riot, or
Rev 12.10 which *a* them before our God

ACCUSER
Rev 12.10 for the *a* of our brethren is cast

ACCUSERS
Jn 8.10 where are those thine *a*?
Ac 23.30 gave commandment to his *a*
35 when thine *a* are also come.
24. 8 Commanding his *a* to come unto
25.16 have the *a* face to face,
18 when the *a* stood up,
2Ti 3. 3 trucebreakers, false *a*,
Tit 2. 3 not false *a*, not given to much

ACCUSETH
Jn 5.45 there is one that *a* you, even

ACCUSING
Ro 2.15 their thoughts the mean while *a*

ACCUSTOMED
Jer 13.23 that are *a* to do evil.

ACELDAMA
Ac 1.19 *A*, that is to say, The field of

ACHAIA
Ac 18.12 Gallio was the deputy of *A*,
27 to pass into *A*, the brethren wrote,
19.21 passed through Macedonia and *A*,
Ro 15.26 them of Macedonia and *A* to make
16. 5 who is the firstfruits of *A* unto
1Co 16.15 firstfruits of *A*, and that they have
2Co 1. 1 saints which are in all *A*:
9. 2 *A* was ready a year ago;
11.10 of boasting in the regions of *A*.
1Th 1. 7 that believe in Macedonia and *A*.
8 not only in Macedonia and *A*, but

ACHAN
Jos 7. 1 for *A*, the son of Carmi, the son
18 his household man by man; and *A*,
19 And Joshua said unto *A*, My son,
20 And *A* answered Joshua, and said,
24 and all Israel with him, took *A*
22.20 Did not *A* the son of Zerah

ACHAZ
Mt 1. 9 Joatham begat *A*;
9 and *A* begat Ezekias;

ACHIM
Mt 1.14 and Sadoc begat *A*;
14 and *A* begat Eliud;

ACHOR
Jos 7.24 them unto the valley of *A*.
26 was called, The valley of *A*, unto
15. 7 toward Debir from the valley of *A*,
Isa 65.10 and the valley of *A* a place for the
Hos 2.15 and the valley of *A* for a door of

ACKNOWLEDGE
Dt 21.17 he shall *a* the son of the hated
33. 9 neither did he *a* his brethren,
Ps 51. 3 I *a* my transgressions:
Pr 3. 6 In all thy ways *a* him,
Isa 33.13 ye that are near, *a* my might.
61. 9 all that see them shall *a* them,
63.16 Israel *a* us not:
Jer 3.13 Only *a* thine iniquity,
14.20 We *a*, O Lord, our wickedness,
24. 5 so will I *a* them that are carried
Dan 11.39 a strange god, whom he shall *a*
Hos 5.15 till they *a* their offense,
1Co 14.37 let him *a* that the things that I
16.18 therefore *a* ye them that are such.
2Co 1.13 than what ye read or *a*;
13 ye shall *a* even to the end;

ACKNOWLEDGED
Gen 38.26 And Judah *a* them,
Ps 32. 5 I *a* my sin unto thee, and mine
2Co 1.14 ye have *a* us in part,

ACKNOWLEDGETH
1Jn 2.23 he that *a* the Son hath the Father

ACKNOWLEDGING
2Ti 2.25 repentance to the *a* of the truth;
Tit 1. 1 and the *a* of the truth which is
Phm 6 by the *a* of every good thing

ACKNOWLEDGMENT
Col 2. 2 to the *a* of the mystery of God,

ACQUAINT
Job 22.21 *A* now thyself with him,

ACQUAINTANCE
2Ki 12. 5 it to them, every man of his *a*:
7 receive no more money of your *a*,
Job 19.13 and mine *a* are verily estranged
42.11 all they that had been of his *a*
Ps 31.11 a fear to mine *a*:
55.13 my guide, and mine *a*.
88. 8 Thou hast put away mine *a*

Ps 88.18 mine *a* into darkness.
Lk 2.44 among their kinsfolk and *a*.
23.49 all his *a*, and the women that
Ac 24.23 he should forbid none of his *a*

ACQUAINTED
Ps 139. 3 and art *a* with all my ways.
Isa 53. 3 man of sorrows, and *a* with grief:

ACQUAINTING
Ec 2. 3 *a* mine heart with wisdom;

ACQUIT
Job 10.14 thou wilt not *a* me from mine
Na 1. 3 will not at all *a* the wicked:

ACT
Isa 28.21 to pass his *a*, his strange *a*.
59. 6 *a* of violence is in their hands.
Jn 8. 4 taken in adultery, in the very *a*.

ACTIONS
1Sa 2. 3 by him *a* are weighed.

ACTIVITY
Gen 47. 6 if thou knowest any men of *a*

ADAM
Gen 2.19 brought them unto *A* to see what
19 whatsoever *A* called every living
20 *A* gave names to all cattle,
20 but for *A* there was not found an
21 a deep sleep to fall upon *A*,
23 *A* said, This is now bone of my
3. 8 *A* and his wife hid themselves
9 And the Lord God called unto *A*,
17 And unto *A* he said, Because
20 *A* called his wife's name Eve;
21 Unto *A* also and to his wife did the
4. 1 And *A* knew Eve his wife;
25 *A* knew his wife again;
5. 1 the book of the generations of *A*.
2 called their name *A*, in the day
3 *A* lived an hundred and thirty years,
4 And the days of *A* after he had
5 the days that *A* lived
Dt 32. 8 when he separated the sons *A*,

This classic Adam and Eve *was painted by Lucas Cranach (1472-1553), a friend of Martin Luther.*

Jos 3.16 very far from the city *A*,
1Ch 1. 1 *A*, Sheth, Enosh,
Job 31.33 I covered my transgressions as *A*,
Lk 3.38 which was the son of *A*,
Ro 5.14 death reigned from *A* to Moses,
1Co 15.22 as in *A* all die, even so in Christ
45 The first man *A* was made a
45 the last *A* was made
1Ti 2.13 For *A* was first formed,
14 And *A* was not deceived,
Jude 14 Enoch also, the seventh from *A*.

ADAMANT
Eze 3. 9 As an *a* harder than flint
Zec 7.12 made their hearts as an *a* stone,

ADAM'S
Ro 5.14 similitude of *A* transgression,

ADD
Gen 30.24 Lord shall *a* to me another son.
Lev 5.16 shall *a* the fifth part thereto, and
6. 5 shall *a* the fifth part more thereto,
27.13 then he shall *a* a fifth part
15, 19 then he shall *a* the fifth part
27 and shall *a* a fifth part
31 he shall *a* thereto the fifth part
Nu 5. 7 *a* unto it the fifth part thereof,
35. 6 to them ye shall *a* forty and two
Dt 4. 2 Ye shall not *a* unto the word
12.32 thou shalt not *a* thereto, nor
19. 9 then shalt thou *a* three cities
29.19 to *a* drunkenness to thirst:
2Sa 24. 3 Now the Lord thy God *a* unto the
1Ki 12.11 I will *a* to your yoke:
14 heavy, and I will *a* to your yoke:
2Ki 20. 6 And I will *a* unto thy days fifteen
1Ch 22.14 thou mayest *a* thereto.
2Ch 10.14 I will *a* thereto: my father
28.13 ye intend to *a* more to our sins
Ps 69.27 *A* iniquity unto their iniquity:
Pr 3. 2 peace, shall they *a* to thee.
30. 6 *A* thou not unto his words, lest he
Isa 29. 1 *a* ye year to year;
30. 1 that they may *a* sin to sin:
38. 5 I will *a* unto thy days fifteen
Mt 6.27 can *a* one cubit unto his stature?
Lk 12.25 can *a* to his statue one cubit?
Php 1.16 to *a* affliction to my bonds:
2Pe 1. 5 *a* to your faith virtue;
Rev 22.18 If any man shall *a* unto these,
18 God shall *a* unto him the

ADDED
Dt 5.22 great voice: and he *a* no more.
1Sa 12.19 we have *a* unto all our sins this
Jer 36.32 there were *a* besides unto them
45. 3 Lord hath *a* grief to my sorrow;
Dan 4.36 excellent majesty was *a* unto me.
Mt 6.33 these things shall be *a* unto you.
Lk 3.20 *A* yet this above all, that he shut
12.31 these things shall be *a* unto you.
19.11 he *a* and spake a parable,
Ac 2.41 there were *a* unto them about
47 And the Lord *a* to the church
5.14 believers were the more *a* to the
11.24 much people was *a* unto the Lord.
Gal 2. 6 in conference *a* nothing to me:
3.19 was *a* because of transgressions,

ADDER
Gen 49.17 serpent by the way, an *a* in the
Ps 58. 4 the deaf *a* that stoppeth her ear;
91.13 shalt tread upon the lion and *a*:
Pr 23.32 a serpent, and stingeth like an *a*.

ADDERS'
Ps 140. 3 *a* poison is under their lips.

ADDETH
Job 34.37 he *a* rebellion unto his sin,

Pr 10.22 he *a* no sorrow with it.
16.23 *a* learning to his lips.
Gal 3.15 no man disannulleth, or *a*

ADDICTED
1Co 16.15 they have *a* themselves to the

ADJURE
1Ki 22.16 How many times shall I *a* thee
2Ch 18.15 How many times shall I *a* thee
Mt 26.63 I *a* thee by the living God,
Mk 5. 7 I *a* thee by God, that thou
Ac 19.13 We *a* you by Jesus whom Paul

ADJURED
Jos 6.26 Joshua *a* them at that time,
1Sa 14.24 for Saul had *a* the people,

ADMINISTERED
2Co 8.19 which is *a* by us to the glory of
20 abundance which is *a* by us:

ADMINISTRATION
2Co 9.12 For the *a* of this service

ADMINISTRATIONS
1Co 12. 5 are differences of *a*, but the

ADMIRATION
Jude 16 having men's persons in *a*
Rev 17. 6 her, I wondered with great *a*.

ADMIRED
2Th 1.10 to be *a* in all them that believe

ADMONISH
Ro 15.14 able also to *a* one another.
1Th 5.12 over you in the Lord, and *a* you;
2Th 3.15 but *a* him as a brother.

ADMONISHED
Ec 4.13 who will no more be *a*.
12.12 by these, my son, be *a*:
Jer 42.19 know certainly that I have *a*
Ac 27. 9 already past, Paul *a* them,
Heb 8. 5 as Moses was *a* of God when

ADMONISHING
Col 3.16 *a* one another in psalms and

ADMONITION
1Co 10.11 they are written for our *a*,
Eph 6. 4 the nurture and *a* of the Lord.
Tit 3.10 after the first and second *a* reject;

ADO
Mk 5.39 Why make ye this *a*, and weep?

ADONIJAH
2Sa 3. 4 the fourth, *A* the son of Haggith;
1Ki 1. 5 *A* the son of Haggith exalted
7 and they following *A* helped him.
8 belonged to David, were not with *A*
9 And *A* slew sheep and oxen and
11 Hast thou not heard that *A* the son
13 why then doth *A* reign?
18 And now, behold, *A* reigneth;
24 hast thou said, *A* shall reign after
25 and say, God save king *A*.
41 And *A* and all the guests that were
42 and *A* said unto him, Come in;
43 Jonathan answered and said to *A*,
49 guests that were with *A* were afraid,
50 *A* feared because of Solomon,
51 Behold, *A* feareth king Solomon:
2.13 And *A* the son of Haggith came to
19 to speak unto him for *A*.
21 the Shunammite be given to *A*
22 ask Abishag the Shunammite for *A*?
23 if *A* have not spoken this word
24 *A* shall be put to death this day.

28 for Joab had turned after *A*,
1Ch 3. 2 the fourth, *A* the son of Haggith:
2Ch 17. 8 Jehonathan, and *A*, and Tobijah,
Neh 10.16 *A*, Bigvai, Adin,

ADOPTION
Ro 8.15 ye have received the Spirit of *a*,
23 waiting for the *a*, to wit, the
9. 4 to whom pertaineth the *a*, and
Gal 4. 5 we might receive the *a* of sons.
Eph 1. 5 unto the *a* of children by Jesus

ADORN
1Ti 2. 9 that women *a* themselves in
Tit 2.10 they may *a* the doctrine of God

ADORNED
Jer 31. 4 thou shalt again be *a* with thy
Lk 21. 5 how it was *a* with goodly stones
1Pe 3. 5 *a* themselves, being in subjection
Rev 21. 2 as a bride *a* for her husband.

ADORNETH
Isa 61.10 a bride *a* herself with her jewels.

ADORNING
1Pe 3. 3 *a* let it not be that outward *a*

ADULLAM
Jos 12.15 of Libnah, one; the king of *A*,
15.35 Jarmuth, and *A*, Socoh, and
1Sa 22. 1 and escaped to the cave *A*: and
2Sa 23.13 harvest time unto the cave of *A*:
1Ch 11.15 rock to David, into the cave of *A*;
2Ch 11. 7 And Beth-zur, and Shoco, and *A*,
Neh 11.30 Zanoah, *A*, and in their villages,
Mic 1.15 he shall come unto *A* the glory

ADULLAMITE
Gen 38. 1 turned in to a certain *A*, whose
12 he and his friend Hirah the *A*.
20 by the hand of his friend the *A*,

ADULTERER
Lev 20.10 the *a* and the adulteress shall
Job 24.15 the eye also of the *a* waiteth for
Isa 57. 3 the seed of the *a*

ADULTERERS
Ps 50.18 hast been partaker with *a*.
Jer 9. 2 they be all *a*,
23.10 the land is full of *a*;
Hos 7. 4 They are all *a*,
Mal 3. 5 the sorcerers, and against the *a*,
Lk 18.11 extortioners, unjust, *a*,
1Co 6. 9 nor idolaters, nor *a*,
Heb 13. 4 whoremongers and *a* God will
Jas 4. 4 Ye *a* and adulteresses,

ADULTERESS
Lev 20.10 adulterer and the *a* shall surely
Pr 6.26 and the *a* will hunt for the
Hos 3. 1 beloved of her friend, yet an *a*,
Ro 7. 3 she shall be called an *a*:
3 so that she is no *a*,

ADULTERESSES
Eze 23.45 after the manner of *a*,
45 because they are *a*,
Jas 4. 4 Ye adulterers and *a*,

ADULTERIES
Jer 13.27 I have seen thine *a*,
Eze 23.43 her that was old in *a*,
Hos 2. 2 out of her sight, and her *a*
Mt 15.19 murders, *a*, fornications,
Mk 7.21 evil thoughts, *a*, fornications,

ADULTEROUS
Pr 30.20 such is the way of an *a* woman;
Mt 12.39 An evil and *a* generation seeketh
16. 4 A wicked and *a* generation
Mk 8.38 in this *a* and sinful generation;

ADULTERY
Ex 20.14 Thou shalt not commit *a*.
Lev 20.10 the man that committeth *a*
10 he that committeth *a*
Dt 5.18 Neither shalt thou commit *a*.
Pr 6.32 committeth *a* with a woman
Jer 3. 8 backsliding Israel committed *a*
9 and committed *a* with stones
5. 7 they then committed *a*, and
7. 9 ye steal, murder, and commit *a*,
23.14 they commit *a*, and walk in lies:
29.23 in Israel, and have committed *a*
Eze 16.32 a wife that committeth *a*,
23.37 they have committed *a*, and blood
37 their idols have they committed *a*,
Hos 4. 2 stealing, and committing *a*,
13 your spouses shall commit *a*.
14 when they commit *a*:
Mt 5.27 Thou shalt not commit *a*:
28 hath committed *a* with her
32 causeth her to commit *a*:
32 that is divorced committeth *a*.
19. 9 marry another, committeth *a*:
9 is put away doth commit *a*.
18 Thou shall not commit *a*,
Mk 10.11 committeth *a* against her.
12 to another, she committeth *a*.
19 Do not commit *a*,
Lk 16.18 marrieth another, committeth *a*:
18 from her husband committeth *a*.
18.20 Do not commit *a*, Do not kill,
Jn 8. 3 unto him a woman taken in *a*;
4 was taken in *a*, in the very act.
Ro 2.22 should not commit *a*,
22 dost thou commit *a*?
13. 9 Thou shalt not commit *a*, Thou
Gal 5.19 *A*, fornication, uncleanness,
Jas 2.11 Do not commit *a*, said also
11 Now if thou commit no *a*,
2Pe 2.14 Having eyes full of *a*,
Rev 2.22 and them that commit *a* with her

ADVANCED
1Sa 12. 6 Lord that *a* Moses and Aaron,
Est 3. 1 and *a* him, and set his seat above
5.11 he had *a* him above the princes
10. 2 whereunto the king *a* him,

ADVANTAGE
Job 35. 3 thou saidst, What *a* will it be
Ro 3. 1 What *a* then hath the Jew?
2Co 2.11 Lest Satan should get an *a* of us:
Jude 16 in admiration because of *a*.

ADVANTAGED
Lk 9.25 For what is a man *a*,

ADVANTAGETH
1Co 15.32 what *a* it me, if the dead rise

ADVENTURE
Dt 28.56 would not *a* to set the sole of her
Ac 19.31 not *a* himself into the theater.

ADVERSARIES
Ex 23.22 and an adversary unto thine *a*.
Dt 32.27 *a* should behave themselves
43 render vengeance to his *a*,
Jos 5.13 Art thou for us, or for our *a*?
1Sa 2.10 *a* of the Lord shall be broken to
2Sa 19.22 should this day be *a* unto me?
Ezr 4. 1 the *a* of Judah and Benjamin
Neh 4.11 And our *a* said, They shall not
Ps 38.20 render evil for good are mine *a*;
69.19 mine *a* are all before thee.
71.13 *a* to my soul;
81.14 turned my hand against their *a*.
89.42 hast set the right hand of his *a*;
109. 4 For my love they are my *a*:
20 the reward of mine *a*
29 Let mine *a* be clothed with
Isa 1.24 I will ease me of mine *a*,
9.11 shall set up the *a* of Rezin against
11.13 and the *a* of Judah shall be cut
59.18 he will repay, fury to his *a*,
63.18 our *a* have trodden down thy
64. 2 make thy name known to thine *a*,
Jer 30.16 devoured; and all thine *a*,
46.10 avenge him of his *a*:
50. 7 and their *a* said, We offend not,
La 1. 5 Her *a* are the chief,
7 the *a* saw her, and did mock
17 his *a* should be round about him:
2.17 set up the horn of thine *a*.
Mic 5. 9 lifted up upon thine *a*,
Na 1. 2 Lord will take vengeance on his *a*,
Lk 13.17 all his *a* were ashamed:
21.15 which all your *a* shall not be able
1Co 16. 9 unto me, and there are many *a*.
Php 1.28 in nothing terrified by your *a*:
Heb 10.27 which shall devour the *a*.

ADVERSARY
Ex 23.22 and an *a* unto thine adversaries.
Nu 22.22 stood in the way for an *a* against
1Sa 1. 6 her *a* also provoked her sore,
29. 4 lest in the battle he be an *a*
1Ki 5. 4 is neither *a* nor evil occurrent.
11.14 the Lord stirred up an *a* unto
23 God stirred him up another *a*,
25 he was an *a* to Israel all the days
Est 7. 6 The *a* and enemy is this wicked
Job 31.35 mine *a* had written a book.
Ps 74.10 how long shall the *a* reproach?
Isa 50. 8 who is mine *a*?
La 1.10 The *a* hath spread out his hand
2. 4 with his right hand as an *a*,
4.12 have believed that the *a* and the
Am 3.11 An *a* there shall be even round
Mt 5.25 Agree with thine *a* quickly,
25 at any time the *a* deliver
Lk 12.58 with thine *a* to the magistrate,
18. 3 saying, Avenge me of mine *a*.
1Ti 5.14 give none occasion to the *a*
1Pe 5. 8 because your *a* the devil,

ADVERSITIES
1Sa 10.19 saved you out of all your *a*
Ps 31. 7 hast known my soul in *a*;

ADVERSITY
2Sa 4. 9 redeemed my soul out of all *a*,
2Ch 15. 6 God did vex them with all *a*.
Ps 10. 6 I shall never be in *a*.
35.15 But in mine *a* they rejoiced,
94.13 give him rest from the days of *a*,
Pr 17.17 a brother is born for *a*.
24.10 If thou faint in the day of *a*,
Ec 7.14 in the day of *a* consider:
Isa 30.20 the Lord give you the bread of *a*,
Heb 13. 3 and them which suffer *a*,
(See box on page 64)

ADVERTISE
Nu 24.14 I will *a* thee what this people
Ru 4. 4 And I thought to *a* thee,

ADVICE
Jdg 19.30 consider of it, take *a*, and speak
20. 7 give here your *a* and counsel.
1Sa 25.33 blessed be thy *a*, and blessed be
2Sa 19.43 that our *a* should not be first had
2Ch 10. 9 What *a* give ye that we may
14 answered them after the *a* of
25.17 Amaziah king of Judah took *a*,
Pr 20.18 and with good *a* make war.
2Co 8.10 herein I give my *a*: for this is

BIBLICAL THEMES

ADVERSITY

I have surely seen the affliction of my people which are in Egypt, and have heard their cry by reason of their taskmasters, for I know their sorrows; and I am come down to deliver them. Ex 3.7-8

Shall we receive good at the hand of God, and shall we not receive evil? Job 2.10

Man that is born of a woman is of few days, and full of trouble. Job 14.1

Wait on the Lord: be of good courage, and he shall strengthen thine heart: wait, I say, on the Lord. Ps 27.14

Many are the afflictions of the righteous: but the Lord delivereth him out of them all. Ps 34.19

God is our refuge and strength, a very present help in trouble. Ps 46.1

Cast thy burden upon the Lord, and he shall sustain thee. Ps 55.22

If thou faint in the day of adversity, thy strength is small. Pr 24.10

In the day of prosperity be joyful, but in the day of adversity consider. Ec 7.14

When thou passest through the waters, I will be with thee; and through the rivers, they shall not overflow thee. Isa 43.2

Come, and let us return unto the Lord: for he hath torn, and he will heal us; he hath smitten, and he will bind us up. Hos 6.1

Come unto me, all ye that labor and are heavy laden, and I will give you rest. Take my yoke upon you, and learn of me; for I am meek and lowly in heart: and ye shall find rest unto your souls. Mt 11.28-29

O my Father, if it be possible, let this cup pass from me: nevertheless not as I will, but as thou wilt. Mt 26.39

In the world ye shall have tribulation: but be of good cheer; I have overcome the world. Jn 16.33

Who shall separate us from the love of Christ? shall tribulation, or distress, or persecution, or famine, or nakedness, or peril, or sword? . . . Nay, in all these things we are more than conquerors through him that loved us. For I am persuaded, that neither death, nor life, nor angels, nor principalities, nor powers, nor things present, nor things to come, nor height, nor depth, nor any other creature, shall be able to separate us from the love of God, which is in Christ Jesus our Lord. Ro 8.35-39

We are troubled on every side, yet not distressed; we are perplexed, but not in despair; persecuted, but not forsaken; cast down, but not destroyed. 2Co 4.8-9

Without were fightings, within were fears. 2Co 7.5

Endure hardness, as a good soldier of Jesus Christ. 2Ti 2.3

Whom the Lord loveth he chasteneth. Heb 12.6

He hath said, I will never leave thee, nor forsake thee. So that we may boldly say, The Lord is my helper, and I will not fear what man shall do unto me. Heb 13.5-6

Casting all your care upon him; for he careth for you. 1Pe 5.7

These are they which came out of great tribulation, and have washed their robes, and made them white in the blood of the Lamb. Rev 7.14

ADVISE

2Sa 24.13 *a*, and see what answer I shall
1Ki 12. 6 How do ye *a* that I may answer
1Ch 21.12 *a* thyself what word I shall

ADVISED

Pr 13.10 with the well *a* is wisdom.
Ac 27.12 the more part *a* to depart

ADVOCATE

1Jn 2. 1 *a* with the Father, Jesus Christ

AENEAS

Ac 9.33 found a certain man named *A*,
34 And Peter said unto him, *A*,

AFAR

Gen 22. 4 Abraham...saw the place *a* off.
37.18 when they saw him *a* off,
Ex 2. 4 his sister stood *a* off,
20.18 they removed, and stood *a* off.
21 the people stood *a* off, and Moses
24. 1 worship ye *a* off.
Ex 33. 7 pitched it without the camp, *a* off
Nu 9.10 in a journey *a* off,
1Sa 26.13 Stood on the top of a hill *a* off;
2Ki 2. 7 went, and stood to view *a* off:
4.25 when the man of God saw her *a* off
Ezr 3.13 the noise was heard *a* off.
Neh 12.43 Jerusalem was heard even *a* off.
Job 2.12 they lifted up their eyes *a* off,
36. 3 I will fetch my knowledge from *a*,
25 man may behold it *a* off.
39.25 and he smelleth the battle *a* off,
29 her eyes behold *a* off.
Ps 10. 1 Why standest thou *a* off, O Lord?
38.11 my kinsmen stand *a* off.
65. 5 them that are *a* off upon the sea:
138. 6 the proud he knoweth *a* off.
139. 2 understandest my thought *a* off.
Pr 31.14 she bringeth her food from *a*.
Isa 23. 7 her own feet shall carry her *a* off
59.14 justice standeth *a* off:
66.19 isles *a* off, that have not heard
Jer 23.23 saith the Lord, and not a God *a*
30.10 I will save thee from *a*,
31.10 declare it in the isles *a* off,
46.27 I will save thee from *a* off,
51.50 remember the Lord *a* off,
Mic 4. 3 rebuke strong nations *a* off;
Mt 26.58 Peter followed him *a* off
27.55 women were there beholding *a*
Mk 5. 6 when he saw Jesus *a* off,
11.13 seeing a fig tree *a* off
14.54 Peter followed him *a* off,
15.40 women looking on *a* off:
Lk 16.23 and seeth Abraham *a* off,
17.12 lepers, which stood *a* off:
18.13 the publican, standing *a* off,
22.54 Peter followed *a* off.
23.49 stood *a* off, beholding these
Ac 2.39 and to all that are *a* off,
Eph 2.17 peace to you which were *a* off,
Heb 11.13 but having seen them *a* off,
2Pe 1. 9 is blind, and cannot see *a* off,
Rev 18.10 Standing *a* off for the fear of her
15 shall stand *a* off for the fear of
17 as many as trade by sea, stood *a*

AFFAIRS

1Ch 26.32 pertaining to God, and *a* of the
Ps 112. 5 he will guide his *a*
Dan 2.49 the *a* of the province of Babylon:
3.12 whom thou hast set over the *a* of
Eph 6.21 also may know my *a*,
22 ye might know our *a*,
Php 1.27 I may hear of your *a*, that ye
2Ti 2. 4 entangleth himself with the *a* of

AFFECT

Gal 4.17 They zealously *a* you, but not
17 that ye might *a* them.

AFFECTED

Ac 14. 2 and made their minds evil *a*
Gal 4.18 be zealously *a* always in a good

AFFECTETH

La 3.51 Mine eye *a* mine heart

AFFECTION

1Ch 29. 3 because I have set my *a* to the
Ro 1.31 without natural *a*, implacable,
2Co 7.15 his inward *a* is more abundant
Col 3. 2 Set your *a* on things above,
5 uncleanness, inordinate *a*,
2Ti 3. 3 Without natural *a*, trucebreakers,

AFFECTIONATELY

1Th 2. 8 So being *a* desirous of you, we

AFFECTIONED

Ro 12.10 Be kindly *a* one to another

AFFECTIONS

Ro 1.26 God gave them up unto vile *a*:
Gal 5.24 crucified the flesh with the *a*

AFFINITY

1Ki 3. 1 Solomon made *a* with Pharaoh
2Ch 18. 1 and joined *a* with Ahab.
Ezr 9.14 and join in *a* with the people

AFFIRM
Ro 3. 8 and as some *a* that we say,)
1Ti 1. 7 they say, nor whereof they *a*.
Tit 3. 8 I will that thou *a* constantly,

AFFIRMED
Lk 22.59 another confidently *a*, saying,
Ac 12.15 she constantly *a* that it was even
25.19 whom Paul *a* to be alive.

AFFLICT
Gen 15.13 they shall *a* them four hundred
31.50 If thou shalt *a* my daughters,
Ex 1.11 over them taskmasters to *a* them
22.22 Ye shall not *a* any widow,
23 If thou *a* them in any wise,
Lev 16.29 ye shall *a* your souls,
31 you, and ye shall *a* your souls,
23.27 ye shall *a* your souls, and offer an
32 ye shall *a* your souls: in the ninth
Nu 24.24 shall *a* Asshur, and shall *a* Eber,
29. 7 and ye shall *a* your souls:
30.13 every binding oath to *a* the soul,
Jdg 16. 5 that we may bind him to *a* him:
6 thou mightest be bound to *a* thee.
19 and she began to *a* him,
2Sa 7.10 shall the children of wickedness *a*
1Ki 11.39 I will for this *a* the seed of David,
2Ch 6.26 when thou dost *a* them;
Ezr 8.21 *a* ourselves before our God,
Job 37.23 plenty of justice: he will not *a*.
Ps 44. 2 how thou didst *a* the people,
55.19 God shall hear, and *a* them,
89.22 nor the son of wickedness *a* him.
94. 5 and *a* thine heritage.
143.12 destroy all them that *a* my soul:
Isa 9. 1 afterward did more grievously *a*
51.23 into the hand of them that *a*
58. 5 a day for a man to *a* his soul?
64.12 hold thy peace, and *a* us very sore?
Jer 31.28 down, and to destroy, and to *a*;
La 3.33 For he doth not *a* willingly
Am 5.12 they *a* the just, they take a bribe,
6.14 and they shall *a* you
Na 1.12 I will *a* thee no more.
Zep 3.19 I will undo all that *a* thee:

AFFLICTED
Ex 1.12 But the more they *a* them, the
Lev 23.29 shall not be *a* in that same day,
Nu 11.11 Wherefore hast thou *a* thy
Dt 26. 6 evil entreated us, and *a* us,
Ru 1.21 the Almighty hath *a* me?
2Sa 22.28 the *a* people thou wilt save:
1Ki 2.26 thou hast been *a* in all
26 wherein my father was *a*.
2Ki 17.20 all the seed of Israel, and *a* them.
Job 6.14 To him that is *a* pity should be
30.11 he hath loosed my cord, and *a*
34.28 and he heareth the cry of the *a*.
Ps 18.27 thou wilt save the *a* people;
22.24 abhorred the affliction of the *a*;
25.16 me; for I am desolate and *a*.
82. 3 do justice to the *a* and needy.
88. 7 hast *a* me with all thy waves.
15 I am *a* and ready to die from my
90.15 thou hast *a* us,
102(T) A prayer of the *a*, when he
107.17 because of their iniquities, are *a*.
116.10 I was greatly *a*:
119.67 Before I was *a* I went astray:
71 good for me that I have been *a*;
75 thou in faithfulness hast *a* me.
107 I am *a* very much:
129. 1, 2 Many a time have they *a* me
140.12 maintain the cause of the *a*, and
Pr 15.15 All the days of the *a* are evil:
22.22 neither oppress the *a* in the gate:
26.28 hateth those that are *a* by it;
31. 5 the judgment of any of the *a*.
Isa 9. 1 lightly *a* the land of Zebulun,
49.13 and will have mercy upon his *a*.
51.21 Therefore hear now this, thou *a*,
53. 4 smitten of God, and *a*.
7 He was oppressed, and he was *a*,
54.11 O thou *a*, tossed with tempest,
58. 3 wherefore have we *a* our soul,
10 satisfy the *a* soul;
60.14 The sons also of them that *a* thee
63. 9 In all their affliction he was *a*,
La 1. 4 priests sigh, her virgins are *a*,
5 for the Lord hath *a* her for the
12 wherewith the Lord hath *a* me
Mic 4. 6 her that I have *a*;
Na 1.12 Though I have *a* thee,
Zep 3.12 of thee an *a* and poor people,
Mt 24. 9 they deliver you up to be *a*,
2Co 1. 6 And whether we be *a*,
1Ti 5.10 if she have relieved the *a*,
Heb 11.37 being destitute, *a*, tormented;
Jas 4. 9 Be *a*, and mourn, and weep:
5.13 Is any among you *a*?

AFFLICTEST
1Ki 8.35 their sin, when thou *a* them:

AFFLICTION
Gen 16.11 the Lord hath heard thy *a*.
29.32 the Lord hath looked upon my *a*;
31.42 God hath seen mine *a*
41.52 in the land of my *a*.
Ex 3. 7 surely seen the *a* of my people
17 bring you up out of the *a* of Egypt
4.31 he had looked upon their *a*,
Dt 16. 3 the bread of *a*;
26. 7 and looked on our *a*,
1Sa 1.11 look on the *a* of thine handmaid,
2Sa 16.12 the Lord will look on mine *a*,
1Ki 22.27 feed him with bread of *a*
27 and with water of *a*,
2Ki 14.26 the Lord saw the *a* of Israel,
2Ch 18.26 feed him with bread of *a*
26 and with water of *a*,
20. 9 and cry unto thee in our *a*,
33.12 when he was in *a*, he besought
Neh 1. 3 in great *a* and reproach:
9. 9 didst see the *a* of our fathers
Job 5. 6 *a* cometh not forth of the dust,
10.15 see thou mine *a*;
30.16 days of *a* have taken hold upon
27 the days of *a* prevented me.
36. 8 in cords of *a*;
15 He delivereth the poor in his *a*,
21 hast thou chosen rather than *a*.
Ps 22.24 the *a* of the afflicted;
25.18 Look upon mine *a* and my pain;
44.24 our *a* and our oppression?
66.11 thou laidst *a* upon our loins.
88. 9 eye mourneth by reason of *a*:
106.44 he regarded their *a*,
107.10 bound in *a* and iron;
39 through oppression, *a*, and
41 he the poor on high from *a*,
119.50 my comfort in my *a*:
92 then have perished in mine *a*.
153 Consider mine *a*,
Isa 30.20 water of *a*, yet shall not
48.10 in the furnace of *a*.
63. 9 In all their *a* he was afflicted,
Jer 4.15 *a* from mount Ephraim.
15.11 of evil and in the time of *a*.
16.19 my refuge in the day of *a*,
30.15 Why criest thou for thine *a*?
48.16 and his *a* hasteth fast.
La 1. 3 gone into captivity because of *a*,
7 remembered in the days of her *a*
9 O Lord, behold my *a*:
3. 1 I am the man that hath seen *a*
19 Remembering mine *a* and my
Hos 5.15 in their *a* they will seek me early.
Am 6. 6 not grieved for the *a* of Joseph.
Ob 13 not have looked on their *a*
Jon 2. 2 reason of mine *a* unto the Lord,
Na 1. 9 *a* shall not rise up the second time.
Hab 3. 7 I saw the tents of Cushan in *a*:
Zec 1.15 they helped forward the *a*.
8.10 out or came in because of the *a*:
10.11 pass through the sea with *a*,
Mk 4.17 when *a* or persecution ariseth
13.19 in those days shall be *a*,
Ac 7.11 Egypt and Chanaan, and great *a*:
34 I have seen the *a* of my people
2Co 2. 4 out of much *a* and anguish of
4.17 light *a*, which is but for a moment,
8. 2 How that in a great trial of *a*
Php 1.16 to add *a* to my bonds:
4.14 ye did communicate with my *a*.
1Th 1. 6 the word in much *a*,
3. 7 our *a* and distress by your faith:
Heb 11.25 Choosing rather to suffer *a* with
Jas 1.27 and widows in their *a*,
5.10 an example of suffering *a*, and

AFFLICTIONS
Ps 34.19 Many are the *a* of the righteous:
132. 1 remember David, and all his *a*:
Ac 7.10 delivered him out of all his *a*,
20.23 bonds and *a* abide me.
2Co 6. 4 in *a*, in necessities, in distresses,
Col 1.24 which is behind of the *a* of Christ
1Th 3. 3 man should be moved by these *a*:
2Ti 1. 8 partaker of the *a* of the gospel
3.11 Persecutions, *a*, which came
4. 5 *a*, do the work of an evangelist,
Heb 10.32 endured a great fight of *a*;
33 both by reproaches and *a*;
1Pe 5. 9 the same *a* are accomplished

AFFORDING
Ps 144.13 That our garners may be full, *a*

AFFRIGHT
2Ch 32.18 to *a* them, and to trouble them;

AFFRIGHTED
Dt 7.21 Thou shalt not be *a* at them:
Job 18.20 that went before were *a*.
39.22 He mocketh at fear, and is not *a*;
Isa 21. 4 fearfulness *a* me:
Jer 51.32 and the men of war are *a*.
Mk 16. 5 white garment; and they were *a*.
6 And he saith unto them, Be not *a*:
Lk 24.37 But they were terrified and *a*,
Rev 11.13 remnant were *a*, and gave glory

AFOOT
Mk 6.33 ran *a* thither out of all cities,
Ac 20.13 minding himself to go *a*.

AFORE
2Ki 20. 4 came to pass, *a* Isaiah was gone
Ps 129. 6 which withereth *a* it groweth up:
Isa 18. 5 *a* the harvest, when the bud is
Eze 33.22 *a* he that was escaped came:
Ro 1. 2 had promised *a* by his prophets
9.23 he had *a* prepared unto glory,
Eph 3. 3 (as I wrote *a* in few words,

AFOREHAND
Mk 14. 8 she is come *a* to anoint my body

AFORETIME
Neh 13. 5 *a* they laid the meat offerings,
Job 17. 6 *a* I was as a tabret.
Isa 52. 4 My people went down *a* into
Jer 30.20 Their children also shall be as *a*,
Dan 6.10 his God, as he did *a*.
Jn 9.13 him that *a* was blind.
Ro 15. 4 things were written *a* were

AFRAID
Gen 3.10 I was *a*, because I was naked;
18.15 I laughed not; for she was *a*.

Gen 20. 8 and the men were sore *a*.
28.17 And he was *a*, and said,
31.31 Because I was *a*: for I said,
32. 7 Then Jacob was greatly *a* and
42.28 failed them, and they were *a*,
35 bundles of money, they were *a*.
43.18 And the men were *a*, because
Ex 3. 6 he was *a* to look upon God.
14.10 and they were sore *a*: and the
15.14 people shall hear, and be *a*:
34.30 they were *a* to come nigh him.
Lev 26. 6 none shall make you *a*:
Nu 12. 8 then were ye not *a* to speak
22. 3 Moab was sore *a* of the people,
Dt 1.17 ye shall not be *a* of the face of man;
29 Dread not, neither be *a* of them.
2. 4 and they shall be *a* of you:
5. 5 ye were *a* by reason of the fire,
7.18 Thou shalt not be *a* of them: but
19 all the people of whom thou art *a*.
9.19 For I was *a* of the anger and hot
18.22 thou shalt not be *a* of him.
20. 1 be not *a* of them: for the Lord
28.10 and they shall be *a* of thee.
60 of Egypt, which thou wast *a* of;
31. 6 fear not, nor be *a* of them:
Jos 1. 9 not *a*, neither be thou dismayed
9.24 we were sore *a* of our lives
11. 6 Be not *a* because of them:
Jdg 7. 3 Whosoever is fearful and *a*,
Ru 3. 8 that the man was *a*, and turned
1Sa 4. 7 And the Philistines were *a*, for
7. 7 they were *a* of the Philistines.
17.11 were dismayed, and greatly *a*.
24 fled from him, and were sore *a*.
18.12 And Saul was *a* of David,
15 very wisely, he was *a* of him.
29 Saul was yet the more *a* of David;
21. 1 Ahimelech was *a* at the meeting
12 was sore *a* of Achish the king of
23. 3 we be *a* here in Judah:
28. 5 he was *a*, and his heart
13 the king said unto her, Be not *a*:
20 was sore *a*, because of the words
31. 4 would not: for he was sore *a*.
2Sa 1.14 How wast thou not *a* to stretch
6. 9 David was *a* of the Lord that day,
14.15 the people have made me *a*:
17. 2 and will make him *a*:
22. 5 of ungodly men made me *a*;
46 they shall be *a* out of their close
1Ki 1.49 that were with Adonijah were *a*,
2Ki 1.15 down with him: be not *a* of him.
10. 4 But they were exceedingly *a*,
19. 6 Be not *a* of the words which thou
25.26 they were *a* of the Chaldees.
1Ch 10. 4 would not; for he was sore *a*.
13.12 David was *a* of God that day,
21.30 he was *a* because of the sword
2Ch 20.15 Be not *a* nor dismayed by reason
32. 7 be not *a* nor dismayed for the
Neh 2. 2 Then I was very sore *a*,
4.14 Be not ye *a* of them:
6. 9 they all made us *a*, saying,
13 was he hired, that I should be *a*,
Est 7. 6 Haman was *a* before the king
Job 3.25 which I was *a* of is come unto me.
5.21 shalt thou be *a* of destruction
22 neither shalt thou be *a* of the
6.21 see my casting down, and are *a*.
9.28 I am *a* of all my sorrows, I
11.19 none shall make thee *a*;
13.11 not his excellency make you *a*?
21 let not thy dread make me *a*.
15.24 anguish shall make him *a*;
18.11 Terrors shall make him *a* on every
19.29 Be ye *a* of the sword:
21. 6 when I remember I am *a*,
23.15 when I consider, I am *a* of him.
32. 6 wherefore I was *a*, and durst
33. 7 my terror shall not make thee *a*,
39.20 Canst thou make him *a* as a
41.25 the mighty are *a*:
Ps 3. 6 I will not be *a* of ten thousands
18. 4 floods of ungodly men made me *a*.
45 shall fade away, and be *a*
27. 1 of whom shall I be *a*?
49.16 Be not thou *a* when one is made
56. 3 time I am *a*, I will trust in thee.
11 not be *a* what man can do unto me.
65. 8 in the uttermost parts are *a* at
77.16 they were *a*: the depths also
83.15 make them *a* with thy storm.
91. 5 Thou shalt not be *a* for the
112. 7 He shall not be *a* of evil tidings:
8 is established, he shall not be *a*,
119.120 I am *a* of thy judgments.
Pr 3.24 thou shalt not be *a*:
25 Be not *a* of sudden fear,
31.21 She is not *a* of the snow for her
Ec 12. 5 they shall be *a* of that which is
Isa 8.12 fear ye their fear, nor be *a*.
10.24 be not *a* of the Assyrian:
29 Ramah is *a*; Gibeah of Saul is
12. 2 I will trust, and not be *a*:
13. 8 And they shall be *a*: pangs and
17. 2 none shall make them *a*.
19.16 and it shall be *a* and fear because
17 mention thereof shall be *a* in
20. 5 they shall be *a* and ashamed
31. 4 he will not be *a* of their voice,
9 princes shall be *a* of the ensign,
33.14 The sinners in Zion are *a*;
37. 6 Be not *a* of the words
40. 9 lift it up, be not *a*;
41. 5 the ends of the earth were *a*,
44. 8 Fear ye not, neither be *a*:
51. 7 neither be ye *a* of their revilings.
12 that thou shouldest be *a* of a man
57.11 of whom hast thou been *a* or
Jer 1. 8 Be not *a* of their faces:
2.12 be horribly *a*, be ye very desolate,
10. 5 Be not *a* of them; for they cannot
26.21 he was *a*, and fled, and went into
30.10 none shall make him *a*.
36.16 heard all the words, they were *a*
24 Yet they were not *a*,
38.19 I am *a* of the Jews
39.17 of the men of whom thou art *a*.
41.18 *a* of them, because of Ishmael
42.11 Be not *a* of the king of Babylon,
11 of whom ye are *a*;
11 be not *a* of him, saith the Lord
16 the famine, whereof ye were *a*,
46.27 and none shall make him *a*.
Eze 2. 6 son of man, be not *a* of them,
6 neither be *a* of their words,
6 be not *a* of their words,
27.35 their kings shall be sore *a*,
30. 9 make the careless Ethiopians *a*,
32.10 their kings shall be horribly *a*
34.28 none shall make them *a*.
39.26 none made them *a*.
Dan 4. 5 I saw a dream which made me *a*,
8.17 when he came, I was *a*,
Joel 2.22 Be not *a*, ye beasts of the field:
Am 3. 6 the people not be *a*?
Jon 1. 5 Then the mariners were *a*,
10 Then were the men exceedingly *a*,
Mic 4. 4 none shall make them *a*:
7.17 they shall be *a* of the Lord
Na 2.11 none made them *a*?
Hab 2.17 beasts, which made them *a*,
3. 2 heard thy speech, and was *a*:
Zep 3.13 none shall make them *a*.
Mal 2. 5 was *a* before my name.
Mt 2.22 he was *a* to go thither:
14.27 it is I; be not *a*.
30 the wind boisterous, he was *a*;
17. 6 fell on their face, and were sore *a*.
7 Arise, and be not *a*.
25.25 And I was *a*, and went and hid
28.10 Be not *a*: go tell my brethren
Mk 5.15 his right mind: and they were *a*.
36 Be not *a*, only believe.
6.50 it is I; be not *a*.
9. 6 to say; for they were sore *a*.
32 and were *a* to ask him.
10.32 and as they followed, they were *a*.
16. 8 any man; for they were *a*.
Lk 2. 9 and they were sore *a*.
8.25 And they being *a* wondered,
35 and they were *a*.
12. 4 Be not *a* of them that kill the body,
24. 5 as they were *a*, and bowed down
Jn 6.19 unto the ship: and they were *a*.
20 It is I; be not *a*,
14.27 be troubled, neither let it be *a*.
19. 8 he was the more *a*;
Ac 9.26 but they were all *a* of him,
10. 4 looked on him, he was *a*,
18. 9 Be not *a*, but speak, and hold
22. 9 saw indeed the light, and were *a*;
29 and the chief captain also was *a*,
Ro 13. 3 Wilt thou then not be *a* of the
4 if thou do that which is evil, be *a*;
Gal 4.11 I am *a* of you, lest I have bestowed
Heb 11.23 and they were not *a* of the king's
1Pe 3. 6 are not *a* with any amazement.
14 and be not *a* of their terror,
2Pe 2.10 they are not *a* to speak evil of

AFRESH

Heb 6. 6 to themselves the Son of God *a*,

AFTERNOON

Jdg 19. 8 they tarried until *a*, and

AGAG

Nu 24. 7 his king shall be higher than *A*,
1Sa 15. 8 took *A* the king of the Amalekites
9 But Saul and the people spared *A*,
20 have brought *A* the king of Amalek,
32 Bring ye hither to me *A* the king
32 And *A* came unto him delicately.
32 *A* said, Surely the bitterness of
33 And Samuel hewed *A* in pieces

AGE

Gen 15.15 shalt be buried in a good old *a*.
18.11 well stricken in *a*; and it ceased
21. 2 bare Abraham a son in his old *a*,
7 have born him a son in his old *a*,
24. 1 was old, and well stricken in *a*:
25. 8 Abraham ...died in a good old *a*,
37. 3 he was the son of his old *a*:
44.20 child of his old *a*, a little one;
47.28 whole *a* of Jacob was an hundred
48.10 the eyes of Israel were dim for *a*,
Nu 8.25 And from the *a* of fifty years
Jos 23. 1 waxed old and stricken in *a*.
2 I am old and stricken in *a*:
Jdg 8.32 Gideon... died in a good old *a*,
Ru 4.15 and a nourisher of thine old *a*:
1Sa 2.33 shall die in the flower of their *a*.
1Ki 14. 4 eyes were set by reason of his *a*.
15.23 in the time of his old *a* he was
1Ch 23. 3 from the *a* of thirty years and
24 from the *a* of twenty years and
29.28 died in a good old *a*, full of days,
2Ch 36.17 or him that stooped for *a*:
Job 5.26 come to thy grave in a full *a*,
8. 8 I pray thee, of the former *a*,
11.17 And thine *a* shall be clearer
30. 2 in whom old *a* was perished?
Ps 39. 5 mine *a* is as nothing before thee:
71. 9 me not off in the time of old *a*;
92.14 still bring forth fruit in old *a*;
Isa 38.12 Mine *a* is departed, and is
46. 4 even to your old *a* I am he;
Zec 8. 4 his staff in his hand for very *a*.
Mk 5.42 she was of the *a* of twelve years.
Lk 1.36 also conceived a son in her old *a*:

BIBLICAL THEMES

AGE

And all the days of Methuselah were nine hundred sixty and nine years: and he died. Gen 5.27

Honor thy father and thy mother: that thy days may be long upon the land which the Lord thy God giveth thee. Ex 20.12

And Moses was an hundred and twenty years old when he died: his eye was not dim, nor his natural force abated. Dt 34.7

Thou shalt come to thy grave in a full age, like as a shock of corn cometh in in his season. Job 5.26

With the ancient is wisdom; and in length of days understanding. Job 12.12

I have been young, and now am old; yet have I not seen the righteous forsaken, nor his seed begging bread. Ps 37.25

Cast me not off in the time of old age; forsake me not when my strength faileth. Ps 71.9

We spend our years as a tale that is told. The days of our years are threescore years and ten; and if by reason of strength they be fourscore years, yet is their strength labor and sorrow; for it is soon cut off, and we fly away. Ps 90.9-10

The hoary head is a crown of glory, if it be found in the way of righteousness. Pr 16.31

Truly the light is sweet, and a pleasant thing it is for the eyes to behold the sun: But if a man live many years, and rejoice in them all; yet let him remember the days of darkness; for they shall be many. Ec 11.7-8

Remember now thy Creator in the days of thy youth, while the evil days come not, nor the years draw nigh, when thou shalt say, I have no pleasure in them; while the sun, or the light, or the moon, or the stars, be not darkened, nor the clouds return after the rain: in the day when the keepers of the house shall tremble, and the strong men shall bow themselves, and the grinders cease because they are few, and those that look out of the windows be darkened, and the doors shall be shut in the streets, when the sound of the grinding is low, and he shall rise up at the voice of the bird, and all the daughters of musick shall be brought low; also when they shall be afraid of that which is high, and fears shall be in the way, and the almond tree shall flourish, and the grasshopper shall be a burden, and desire shall fail: because man goeth to his long home, and the mourners go about the streets: or ever the silver cord be loosed, or the golden bowl be broken, or the pitcher be broken at the fountain, or the wheel broken at the cistern. Then shall the dust return to the earth as it was: and the spirit shall return unto God who gave it. Ec 12.1-7

Even to your old age I am he; and even to hoar hairs will I carry you: I have made, and I will bear; even I will carry, and will deliver you. Isa 46.4

[Anna] was a widow of about fourscore and four years, which departed not from the temple, but served God with fastings and prayers night and day. Lk 2.37

Verily, verily, I say unto thee, When thou wast young, thou girdedst thyself, and walkedst whither thou wouldest: but when thou shalt be old, thou shalt stretch forth thy hands, and another shall gird thee, and carry thee whither thou wouldest not. Jn 21.18

That the aged men be sober, grave, temperate, sound in faith, in charity, in patience. The aged women likewise, that they be in behavior as becometh holiness. Tit 2.2-3

For he that will love life, and see good days, let him refrain his tongue from evil, and his lips that they speak no guile. 1Pe 3.10

2.36 was of a great *a*, and had lived
3.23 about thirty years of *a*, being (as
Jn 9.21 we know not: he is of *a*;
23 said his parents, He is of *a*;
1Co 7.36 she pass the flower of her *a*,
Heb 5.14 to them that are of full *a*,
11.11 when she was past *a*, because she

AGED
2Sa 19.32 Barzillai was a very *a* man,
Job 12.20 away the understanding of the *a*.
15.10 the grayheaded and very *a* men,
29. 8 and the *a* arose, and stood up.
32. 9 neither do the *a* understand
Jer 6.11 *a* with him that is full of days.
Tit 2. 2 That the *a* men be sober, grave,
3 The *a* women likewise, that they
Phm 9 being such an one as Paul the *a*,

AGES
Eph 2. 7 That in the *a* to come he might
3. 5 Which in other *a* was not made
21 throughout all *a*, world without
Col 1.26 hid from *a* and from generations,

AGONY
Lk 22.44 being in an *a* he prayed more

AGREE
Mt 5.25 *A* with thine adversary quickly,
18.19 That if two of you shall *a* on
20.13 didst not thou *a* with me for a
Mk 14.59 neither so did their witness *a*
Ac 15.15 *a* the words of the prophets;
1Jn 5. 8 blood: and these three *a* in one.
Rev 17.17 fulfil his will, and to *a*,

AGREED
Am 3. 3 walk together, except they be *a*?
Mt 20. 2 And when he had *a* with the
Mk 14.56 their witness *a* not together.
Jn 9.22 for the Jews had *a* already,
Ac 5. 9 How is it that ye have *a* together
40 And to him they *a*:
23.20 The Jews have *a* to desire thee
28.25 they *a* not among themselves,

AGREEMENT
2Ki 18.31 an *a* with me by a present,
Isa 28.15 with hell are we at *a*;
18 and your *a* with hell shall not
36.16 Assyria, Make an *a* with me by
Dan 11. 6 king of the north to make an *a*:
2Co 6.16 what *a* hath the temple of God

AGREETH
Mk 14.70 and thy speech *a* thereto.
Lk 5.36 *a* not with the old.

AGRIPPA
Ac 25.13 king *A* and Bernice came
22 Then *A* said unto Festus,
23 when *A* was come,
24 And Festus said, King *A*,
26 specially before thee, O king *A*, that
26. 1 Then *A* said unto Paul,
2 I think myself happy, king *A*,
7 For which hope's sake, king *A*,
19 Whereupon, O king *A*,
27 King *A*, believest thou the prophets?
28 Then *A* said unto Paul,
32 Then said *A* unto Festus,

AGROUND
Ac 27.41 they ran the ship *a*;

AHAB
1Ki 16.28 and *A* his son reigned in his stead.
29 began *A* the son of Omri to reign
29 and *A* the son of Omri reigned
30 *A* the son of Omri did evil
33 *A* made a grove; and *A* did more
17. 1 said unto *A*, As the Lord God of
18. 1 Go, shew thyself unto *A*; and I will
2 Elijah went to shew himself unto *A*.
3 *A* called Obadiah, which was the
5 *A* said unto Obadiah, Go into the
6 *A* went one way by himself, and
9 thy servant into the hand of *A*,
12 and so when I come and tell *A*,
16 So Obadiah went to meet *A*, and
16 and *A* went to meet Elijah.
17 it came to pass, when *A* saw Elijah,
17 that *A* said unto him, Art thou he
20 So *A* sent unto all the children of
41 Elijah said unto *A*, Get thee up, eat
42 So *A* went up to eat and to drink.
44 And he said, Go up, say unto *A*,
45 And *A* rode, and went to Jezreel
46 and ran before *A* to the entrance
19. 1 *A* told Jezebel all that Elijah had
20. 2 sent messengers to *A* king of Israel
13 there came a prophet unto *A*.

AHAB

King of Israel in the time of the prophet Elijah, 9th century B.C.; for reasons of state contracts a marriage with Jezebel, a princess of Tyre, and with her encouragement accords favored status to the Tyrian religion (1Ki 16.29-33); is present at the contest between Elijah and the prophets of the Tyrian Baal on Mount Carmel but, in spite of Elijah's triumph, refuses to change his policy (1Ki 18); after a victory over the king of Syria makes peace with the enemy and is rebuked by an unnamed prophet (1Ki 20); permits Jezebel to have Naboth condemned to death on false charges in order to seize Naboth's vineyard; is confronted by Elijah, who prophesies the end of Ahab's dynasty, though he himself is spared for his repentance (1Ki 21); however, in a later encounter with Syria ignores the warnings of the prophet Micaiah and is slain in battle (1Ki 22).

1Ki 20.14 *A* said, By whom? And he said,
34 Then said *A*, I will send thee away
21. 1 the palace of *A* king of Samaria.
2 *A* spake unto Naboth, saying,
3 Naboth said to *A*, The Lord forbid
4 *A* came into his house heavy and
15 Jezebel said to *A*, Arise, take
16 *A* heard that Naboth was dead,
16 that *A* rose up
18 go down to meet *A* king of Israel,
20 *A* said to Elijah, Hast thou found
21 and will cut off from *A* him
24 Him that dieth of *A* in the city
25 But there was none like unto *A*,
27 to pass, when *A* heard those words,
29 Seest thou how *A* humbleth himself
22.20 Lord said, Who shall persuade *A*,
39 Now the rest of the acts of *A*,
40 So *A* slept with his fathers;
41 the fourth year of *A* king of Israel.
49 said Ahaziah the son of *A* unto
51 Ahaziah the son of *A* began to reign
2Ki 1. 1 against Israel after the death of *A*.
3. 1 Jehoram the son of *A* began to reign
5 it came to pass, when *A* was dead,
8.16 the fifth year of Joram the son of *A*
18 as did the house of *A*;
18 for the daughter of *A* was his wife:
25 twelfth year of Joram the son of *A*
27 walked in the way of the house of *A*,
27 as did the house of *A*: for he was
27 the son in law of the house of *A*.
28 he went with Joram the son of *A*
29 see Joram the son of *A* in Jezreel,
9. 7 thou shalt smite the house of *A*
8 the whole house of *A* shall perish:
8 and I will cut off from *A* him
9 I will make the house of *A* like the
25 I and thou rode together after *A*
29 year of Joram the son of *A*
10. 1 *A* had seventy sons in Samaria.
10 spake concerning the house of *A*:
11 all that remained of the house of *A*
17 he slew all that remained unto *A*
18 unto them, *A* served Baal a little;
30 and hast done unto the house of *A*
21. 3 and made a grove, as did *A*
13 and the plummet of the house of *A*:
2Ch 18. 1 and joined affinity with *A*.
2 certain years he went down to *A*
2 *A* killed sheep and oxen for him
3 *A* king of Israel said unto
19 Who shall entice *A* king of Israel,
21. 6 like as did the house of *A*:
6 he had the daughter of *A* to wife:
13 to the whoredoms of the house of *A*,
22. 3 in the ways of the house of *A*:
4 of the Lord like the house of *A*:
5 went with Jehoram the son of *A*
6 down to see Jehoram the son of *A*
7 anointed to cut off the house of *A*.
8 judgment upon the house of *A*,
Jer 29.21 of *A* the son of Kolaiah, and of
22 make thee like Zedekiah and like *A*,
Mic 6.16 all the works of the house of *A*,

AHAB'S

1Ki 21. 8 So she wrote letters in *A* name,
2Ki 10. 1 them that brought up *A* children,

AHASUERUS

Ezr 4. 6 in the reign of *A*, in the beginning
Est 1. 1 in the days of *A*,
1 (this is *A* which reigned from India
2 when the king *A* sat on the throne
9 house which belonged to king *A*.
10 in the presence of *A* the king,
15 the commandment of the king *A*
16 in all the provinces of the king *A*.
17 The king *A* commanded Vashti
19 Vashti come no more before king *A*;
2. 1 the wrath of king *A* was appeased,
12 turn was come to go in to king *A*,
16 So Esther was taken unto king *A*
21 sought to lay hand on the king *A*.
3. 1 After these things did king *A*
6 throughout the whole kingdom of *A*,
7 in the twelfth year of king *A*, they
8 Haman said unto king *A*, There
12 in the name of king *A* was it
6. 2 sought to lay hand on the king *A*.
7. 5 Then the king *A* answered and
8. 1 On that day did the king *A* give
7 Then the king *A* said unto Esther
12 day in all the provinces of king *A*,
9. 2 all the provinces of the king *A*,
20 the provinces of the king *A*, both
30 of the kingdom of *A*, with words
10. 1 the king *A* laid a tribute upon the
3 the Jew was next unto king *A*,
Dan 9. 1 first year of Darius the son of *A*,

AHAZ

2Ki 15.38 *A* his son reigned in his stead.
16. 1 *A* the son of Jotham king of Judah
2 Twenty years old was *A* when he
5 they besieged *A*, but could not
7 So *A* sent messengers to
8 *A* took the silver and gold that was
10 king *A* went to Damascus to meet
10 king *A* sent to Urijah the priest
11 king *A* had sent from Damascus:
11 priest made it against king *A* came
15 king *A* commanded Urijah the
16 to all that king *A* commanded.
17 *A* cut off the borders of the bases,
19 rest of the acts of *A* which he did,
20 *A* slept with his fathers, and was
17. 1 In the twelfth year of *A* king of
18. 1 of *A* king of Judah began to reign.
20.11 it had gone down in the dial of *A*.
23.12 the top of the upper chamber of *A*,
1Ch 3.13 *A* his son, Hezekiah his son,
8.35 and Melech, and Tarea, and *A*.
36 And *A* begat Jehoiadah; and
9.41 and Melech, and Tahrea, and *A*.
42 And *A* begat Jarah; and Jarah
2Ch 27. 9 *A* his son reigned in his stead.
28. 1 *A* was twenty years old when he
16 At that time did king *A* send unto
19 brought Judah low because of *A*
21 *A* took away a portion out of the
22 against the Lord: this is that king *A*.
24 *A* gathered together the vessels of
27 And *A* slept with his fathers, and
29.19 all the vessels, which king *A* in his
Isa 1. 1 in the days of Uzziah, Jotham, *A*,
7. 1 the days of *A* the son of Jotham,
3 Go forth now to meet *A*, thou,
10 the Lord spake again unto *A*,
12 But *A* said, I will not ask,
14.28 that king *A* died was this burden.
38. 8 is gone down in the sun dial of *A*,
Hos 1. 1 *A*, and Hezekiah, kings of Judah,
Mic 1. 1 in the days of Jotham, *A*, and

AHAZIAH

1Ki 22.40 *A* his son reigned in his stead.
49 Then said *A* the son of Ahab unto
51 *A* the son of Ahab began to reign
2Ki 1. 2 And *A* fell down through a lattice
18 rest of the acts of *A* which he did,
8.24 and *A* his son reigned in his stead.
25 did *A* the son of Jehoram king of
26 Two and twenty years old was *A*
29 *A* the son of Jehoram king of Judah
9.16 *A* king of Judah was come down
21 and *A* king of Judah went out,
23 his hands, and fled, and said to *A*,
23 There is treachery, O *A*.
27 when *A* king of Judah saw this,
29 began *A* to reign over Judah.
10.13 Jehu met with the brethren of *A*
13 answered, We are the brethren of *A*;
11. 1 the mother of *A* saw that her son
2 daughter of king Joram, sister of *A*,
2 took Joash the son of *A*,
12.18 and *A*, his fathers, kings of Judah,
13. 1 twentieth year of Joash the son of *A*
14.13 the son of Jehoash the son of *A*,
1Ch 3.11 Joram his son, *A* his son, Joash
2Ch 20.35 join himself with *A* king of Israel,
37 thou hast joined thyself with *A*,
22. 1 made *A* his youngest son king in
1 So *A* the son of Jehoram king of
2 Forty and two years old was *A*
7 the destruction of *A* was of God
8 and the sons of the brethren of *A*,
8 that ministered to *A*,
9 he sought *A*: and they caught him,
9 So the house of *A* had no power
10 Athaliah the mother of *A* saw that
11 the king, took Joash the son of *A*,
11 (for she was the sister of *A*,) hid

AHIMAAZ

1Sa 14.50 was Ahinoam, the daughter of *A*:
2Sa 15.27 *A* thy son, and Jonathan the son
36 *A* Zadok's son, and Jonathan
17.17 Jonathan and *A* stayed by
20 Where is *A* and Jonathan?
18.19 Then said *A* the son of Zadok, Let
22 Then said *A* the son of Zadok yet
23 *A* ran by the way of the plain,
27 foremost is like the running of *A*
28 *A* called, and said unto the king,
29 *A* answered, When Joab sent the
1Ki 4.15 *A* was in Naphtali; he also took
1Ch 6. 8 begat Zadok, and Zadok begat *A*,
9 *A* begat Azariah, and Azariah
53 Zadok his son, *A* his son.

AHIMELECH

1Sa 21. 1 came David to Nob to *A* the priest:
1 *A* was afraid at the meeting of
2 David said unto *A* the priest, The
8 David said unto *A*, And is there
22. 9 coming to Nob, to *A* the son of
11 Then the king sent to call *A* the
14 Then *A* answered the king, and
16 king said, Thou shalt surely die, *A*,
20 one of the sons of *A* the son of
23. 6 when Abiathar the son of *A* fled

26. 6 answered David and said to *A*
2Sa 8.17 Ahitub, and *A*, the son of Abiathar,
1Ch 24. 3 and *A* of the sons of Ithamar,
6 *A* the son of Abiathar, and before
31 David the king, and Zadok, and *A*,
Ps 52(T) David is come to the house of *A*.

AILED

Ps 114. 5 What *a* thee, O thou sea, that

AILETH

Gen 21.17 said unto her, What *a* thee, Hagar?
Jdg 18.23 said unto Micah, What *a* thee,
24 ye say unto me, What *a* thee?
1Sa 11. 5 What *a* the people that they weep?
2Sa 14. 5 king said unto her, What *a* thee?
2Ki 6.28 king said unto her, What *a* thee
Isa 22. 1 What *a* thee now, that thou art

AIR

Gen 1.26, 28 the fowl of the *a*, and over
30 every fowl of the *a*, and to every
2.19 the field, and every fowl of the *a*;
20 gave names...to the fowl of the *a*,
6. 7 fowls of the *a*; for it repenteth me
7. 3 Of fowls also of the *a* by sevens,
9. 2 upon every fowl of the *a*,
Dt 4.17 winged fowl that flieth in the *a*,
28.26 all fowls of the *a*, and unto the
1Sa 17.44 thy flesh unto the fowls of the *a*,
46 carcases...unto the fowls of the *a*,
2Sa 21.10 the birds of the *a* to rest on them
1Ki 14.11 shall the fowls of the *a* eat:
16. 4 shall the fowls of the *a* eat.
21.24 field shall the fowls of the *a* eat.
Job 12. 7 fowls of the *a*, and they shall tell
28.21 kept close from the fowls of the *a*.
41.16 no *a* can come between them.
Ps 8. 8 The fowl of the *a*, and the fish of
Pr 30.19 The way of an eagle in the *a*;
Ec 10.20 bird of the *a* shall carry the voice,
Mt 6.26 Behold the fowls of the *a*:
8.20 the birds of the *a* have nests;
13.32 birds of the *a* come and lodge in
Mk 4. 4 the fowls of the *a* came and
32 fowls of the *a* may lodge under
Lk 8. 5 the fowls of the *a* devoured it.
9.58 and birds of the *a* have nests;
13.19 the fowls of the *a* lodged in the
Ac 10.12 things, and fowls of the *a*.
11. 6 and fowls of the *a*.
22.23 clothes, and threw dust into the *a*,
1Co 9.26 not as one that beateth the *a*:
14. 9 for ye shall speak into the *a*.
Eph 2. 2 prince of the power of the *a*,
1Th 4.17 to meet the Lord in the *a*: and
Rev 9. 2 the sun and the *a* were darkened
16.17 poured out his vial into the *a*;

ALABASTER

Mt 26. 7 having an *a* box of very precious
Mk 14. 3 having an *a* box of ointment
Lk 7.37 brought an *a* box of ointment,

ALARM

Nu 10. 5 When ye blow an *a*, then the
6 When ye blow an *a* the second
6 they shall blow an *a* for their
7 blow, ye shall not sound an *a*.
9 blow an *a* with the trumpets;
2Ch 13.12 with sounding trumpets to cry *a*
Jer 4.19 sound of the trumpet, the *a* of war.
49. 2 I will cause an *a* of war to be heard
Joel 2. 1 sound an *a* in my holy mountain:
Zep 1.16 A day of the trumpet and *a*

ALAS

Nu 12.11 Aaron said unto Moses, *A*, my,
24.23 *A*, who shall live when God doeth
Jos 7. 7 Joshua said, *A*, O Lord
Jdg 6.22 Gideon said, *A*, O Lord God!
11.35 *A*, my daughter! thou hast
1Ki 13.30 mourned over him, saying, *A*, my
2Ki 3.10 the king of Israel said, *A*!
6. 5 *A*, master! for it was borrowed.
15 *A*, my master! how shall we do?
Jer 30. 7 *A*! for that day is great,
Eze 6.11 *A* for all the evil abominations
Joel 1.15 *A* for the day! for the day of the
Am 5.16 say in all the highways, *A*! *a*!
Rev 18.10 *A a*, that great city Babylon,
16 *A*, *a* that great city, that was
19 *A*, *a* that great city, wherein

ALEXANDER

Mk 15.21 the father of *A* and Rufus,
Ac 4. 6 John, and *A*, and as many as were
19.33 they drew *A* out of the multitude,
33 *A* beckoned with the hand,
1Ti 1.20 Of whom is Hymenaeus and *A*;
2Ti 4.14 *A* the coppersmith did me much

ALEXANDRIA

Ac 18.24 Apollos, born at *A*, an eloquent
27. 6 a ship of *A* sailing into Italy;
28.11 we departed in a ship of *A*,

ALEXANDRIANS

Ac 6. 9 *A*, and of them of Cilicia and of

ALIEN

Ex 18. 3 I have been an *a* in a strange
Dt 14.21 thou mayest sell it unto an *a*:
Job 19.15 I am an *a* in their sight.
Ps 69. 8 an *a* unto my mother's children.
Isa 61. 5 the *a* shall be your plowmen

ALIENATE

Eze 48.14 nor *a* the first fruits of the land:

ALIENATED

Eze 23.17 and her mind was *a* from them.
18 then my mind was *a* from her,
18 like as my mind was *a* from her
22 whom thy mind is *a*, and I will
28 them from whom thy mind is *a*:
Eph 4.18 being *a* from the life of God
Col 1.21 that were sometime *a* and enemies

ALIENS

La 5. 2 our houses to *a*.
Eph 2.12 being *a* from the commonwealth
Heb 11.34 to flight the armies of the *a*.

ALIVE

Gen 6.19 to keep them *a* with thee;
20 come unto thee, to keep them *a*.
7. 3 to keep seed *a* upon the face of
23 and Noah only remained *a*, and
12.12 but they will save thee *a*.
43. 7 Is your father yet *a*?
27 of whom ye spake? Is he yet *a*?
28 he is yet *a*.
45.26 told him, saying, Joseph is yet *a*,
28 Joseph my son is yet *a*:
46.30 because thou art yet *a*.
50.20 to save much people *a*.
Ex 1.17 but saved the men children *a*.
18 have saved the men children *a*?
22 every daughter ye shall save *a*.
4.18 see whether they be yet *a*.
22. 4 be certainly found in his hand *a*,
Lev 10.16 sons of Aaron which were left *a*,
14. 4 cleansed two birds *a* and clean,
16.10 be presented *a* before the Lord,
26.36 And upon them that are left *a*
Nu 16.33 went down *a* into the pit, and the
21.35 until there was none left him *a*:
22.33 I had slain thee, and saved her *a*.
31.15 Have ye saved all the women *a*?
18 keep *a* for yourselves.
Dt 4. 4 *a* every one of you this day.
5. 3 who are all of us here *a* this day.
6.24 that he might preserve us *a*,
20.16 save *a* nothing that breatheth:
31.27 while I am yet *a* with you this
32.39 I kill, and I make *a*; I wound,
Jos 2.13 And that ye will save *a* my father,
6.25 Joshua saved Rahab the harlot *a*,
8.23 the king of Ai they took *a*,
14.10 the Lord hath kept me *a*,
Jdg 8.19 if ye had saved them *a*, I would
21.14 which they had saved *a* of the
1Sa 2. 6 The Lord killeth, and maketh *a*:
15. 8 Agag the king of the Amalekites *a*,
27. 9 left neither man nor woman *a*,
11 saved neither man nor woman *a*,
2Sa 8. 2 with one full line to keep *a*.
12.18 while the child was yet *a*,
21 weep for the child, while it was *a*;
22 While the child was yet *a*, I fasted
18.14 while he was yet *a* in the midst of
1Ki 18. 5 to save the horses and mules *a*,
20.18 come out for peace, take them *a*;
18 be come out for war, take them *a*.
32 said, Is he yet *a*? he is my brother.
21.15 for Naboth is not *a*, but dead.
2Ki 5. 7 Am I God, to kill and to make *a*,
7. 4 if they save us *a*, we shall live;
12 catch them *a*, and get into the
10.14 he said, Take them *a*.
14 And they took them *a*,
2Ch 25.12 other ten thousand left *a*
Ps 22.29 none can keep *a* his own soul.
30. 3 thou hast kept me *a*,
33.19 and to keep them *a* in famine.
41. 2 will preserve him, and keep him *a*;
Pr 1.12 swallow them up *a* as the grave;
Ec 4. 2 than the living which are yet *a*.
Jer 49.11 I will preserve them *a*;
Eze 7.13 although they were yet *a*:
13.18 save the souls *a* that come unto
19 save the souls *a* that should not
18.27 he shall save his soul *a*.
Dan 5.19 whom he would he kept *a*;
Mt 27.63 said, while he was yet *a*, After
Mk 16.11 when they had heard that he was *a*,
Lk 15.24 my son was dead, and is *a* again;
32 brother was dead, and is *a* again;
24.23 angels, which said that he was *a*.
Ac 1. 3 he shewed himself *a* after his
9.41 and widows, presented her *a*.
20.12 they brought the young man *a*.
25.19 whom Paul affirmed to be *a*.
Ro 6.11 dead indeed unto sin, but *a* unto
13 as those that are *a* from the dead,
7. 9 I was *a* without the law once:
1Co 15.22 so in Christ shall all be made *a*.
1Th 4.15 we which are *a* and remain
17 are *a* and remain shall be caught
Rev 1.18 behold, I am *a* for evermore,
2. 8 which was dead, and is *a*;
19.20 both were cast *a* into a lake of fire

ALLEGING

Ac 17. 3 Opening and *a*, that Christ

ALLEGORY

Gal 4.24 Which things are an *a*: for these

ALLELUIA

Rev 19. 1 people in heaven, saying, *A*;
3 they said, *A*. And her
4 the throne, saying, Amen; *A*.
6 mighty thunderings, saying, *A*:

ALLOW

Lk 11.48 ye *a* the deeds of your fathers:
Ac 24.15 which they themselves also *a*,
Ro 7.15 that which I do I *a* not:

ALLOWANCE

2Ki 25.30 And his *a* was a continual *a*

ALLOWED
1Th 2. 4 But as we were *a* of God to be

ALLOWETH
Ro 14.22 in that thing which he *a*.

ALLURE
Hos 2.14 I will *a* her, and bring her into
2Pe 2.18 *a* through the lusts of the flesh,

ALMIGHTY
Gen 17. 1 said unto him, I am the *A* God;
28. 3 And God *A* bless thee,
35.11 God said unto him, I am God *A*:
43.14 God *A* give you mercy
48. 3 God *A* appeared unto me at Luz
49.25 and by the *A*, who shall bless thee
Ex 6. 3 by the name of God *A*,
Nu 24. 4, 16 which saw the vision of the *A*,
Ru 1.20 *A* hath dealt very bitterly with me.
21 and the *A* hath afflicted me?
Job 5.17 not thou the chastening of the *A*:
6. 4 arrows of the *A* are within me,
14 he forsaketh the fear of the *A*.
8. 3 doth the *A* pervert justice?
5 make thy supplication to the *A*;
11. 7 find out the *A* unto perfection?
13. 3 Surely I would speak to the *A*,
15.25 himself against the *A*.
21.15 What is the *A*, that we should
20 shall drink of the wrath of the *A*.
22. 3 Is it any pleasure to the *A*,
17 what can the *A* do for them?
23 If thou return to the *A*,
25 the *A* shall be thy defense,
26 have thy delight in the *A*,
23.16 and the *A* troubleth me:
24. 1 times are not hidden from the *A*,
27. 2 the *A*, who hath vexed my soul;
10 Will he delight himself in the *A*?
11 with the *A* will I not conceal.
13 they shall receive of the *A*.
29. 5 When the *A* was yet with me,
31. 2 inheritance of the *A* from on high?
35 that the *A* would answer me,
32. 8 inspiration of the *A* giveth them
33. 4 breath of the *A* hath given me life.
34.10 and from the *A*, that he should
12 will the *A* pervert judgment.
35.13 neither will the *A* regard it.
37.23 the *A*, we cannot find him out:
40. 2 he that contendeth with the *A*
Ps 68.14 When the *A* scattered kings
91. 1 under the shadow of the *A*.
Isa 13. 6 as a destruction from the *A*.
Eze 1.24 as the voice of the *A*,
10. 5 the *A* God when he speaketh.
Joel 1.15 as a destruction from the *A*
2Co 6.18 saith the Lord *A*.
Rev 1. 8 and which is to come, the *A*.
4. 8 Holy, holy, holy, Lord God *A*,
11.17 O Lord God *A*, which art, and wast,
15. 3 thy works, Lord God *A*;
16. 7 Lord God *A*, true and righteous
14 that great day of God *A*.
19.15 and wrath of *A* God.
21.22 the Lord God *A* and the Lamb are

ALMOND
Ec 12. 5 the *a* tree shall flourish,
Jer 1.11 I see a rod of an *a* tree.

ALMONDS
Gen 43.11 myrrh, nuts, and *a*:
Ex 25.33 Three bowls made like unto *a*,
33 bowls made like *a*
34 four bowls made like unto *a*,
37.19 made after the fashion of *a*
19 three bowls made like *a*

ALMSDEEDS
Ac 9.36 full of good works and *a* which

ALOES
Nu 24. 6 as the trees of lign *a* which the
Ps 45. 8 garments smell of myrrh, and *a*,
Pr 7.17 perfumed my bed with myrrh, *a*,
SS 4.14 and *a*, with all the chief spices:
Jn 19.39 brought a mixture of myrrh and *a*,

ALONE
Gen 2.18 good that the man should be *a*;
32.24 And Jacob was left *a*; and there
42.38 brother is dead, and he is left *a*:
44.20 brother is dead, and he *a* is left
Ex 14.12 thee in Egypt, saying, Let us *a*,
18.14 why sittest thou thyself *a*,
18 art not able to perform it thyself *a*.
24. 2 And Moses *a* shall come near the
32.10 Now therefore let me *a*,
Lev 13.46 shall dwell *a*; without the camp
Nu 11.14 able to bear all this people *a*,
17 that thou bear it not thyself *a*,
23. 9 the people shall dwell *a*,
Dt 1. 9 not able to bear you myself *a*:
12 How can I myself *a* bear your
9.14 me *a*, that I may destroy them,
32.12 the Lord *a* did lead him,
33.28 Israel then shall dwell in safety *a*:
Jos 22.20 man perished not *a* in his iniquity.
Jdg 3.20 which he had for himself *a*.
11.37 let me *a* two months,
1Sa 21. 1 Why art thou *a*, and no man with
2Sa 16.11 let him *a*, and let him curse;
18.24 and behold a man running *a*.
25 And the king said, If he be *a*,
26 Behold another man running *a*.
1Ki 11.29 and they two were *a* in the field:
2Ki 4.27 Let her *a*; for her soul is vexed
19.15 thou art the God, even thou *a*, of
23.18 And he said, Let him *a*;
18 So they let his bones *a*,
1Ch 29. 1 my son, whom *a* God hath chosen,
Ezr 6. 7 the work of this house of God *a*;
Neh 9. 6 Thou, even thou, art Lord *a*;
Est 3. 6 scorn to lay hands on Mordecai *a*;
Job 1.15, 16, 17, 19 am escaped *a* to tell thee.
7.16 let me *a*; for my days are vanity.
19 let me *a* till I swallow down my
9. 8 *a* spreadeth out the heavens,
10.20 let me *a*, that I may take comfort
13.13 Hold your peace, let me *a*, that I
15.19 whom *a* the earth was given,
31.17 have eaten my morsel myself *a*,
Ps 83.18 thou, whose name *a* is Jehovah,
86.10 wondrous things: thou art God *a*.
102. 7 as a sparrow *a* upon the housetop.
136. 4 him who *a* doeth great wonders:
148.13 Lord: for his name *a* is excellent;
Pr 9.12 scornest, thou *a* shalt bear it.
Ec 4. 8 There is one *a*, and there is not a
10 him that is *a* when he falleth;
11 but how can one be warm *a*?
Isa 2.11, 17 Lord *a* shall be exalted in that
5. 8 placed *a* in the midst of the earth!
14.31 none shall be *a* in his appointed
37.16 thou art the God, even thou *a*,
44.24 stretcheth forth the heavens *a*;
49.21 Behold, I was left *a*; these, where
51. 2 I called him *a*, and blessed him,
63. 3 I have trodden the winepress *a*;
Jer 15.17 I sat *a* because of thy hand:
49.31 which dwell *a*.
La 3.28 He sitteth *a* and keepeth silence,
Dan 10. 7 And I Daniel *a* saw the vision:
8 Therefore I was left *a*, and saw
Hos 4.17 is joined to idols: let him *a*.
8. 9 a wild ass *a* by himself:
Mt 4. 4 shall not live by bread *a*,
14.23 he was there *a*.
15.14 Let them *a*: they be blind leaders
18.15 between thee and him *a*:
Mk 1.24 Saying, Let us *a*: what have we
4.10 And when he was *a*,
34 and when they were *a*,
6.47 and he *a* on the land.
14. 6 Let her *a*; why trouble ye her?
15.36 saying, Let *a*; let us see whether
Lk 4. 4 not live by bread *a*, but by every
34 Saying, Let us *a*; what have we
5.21 Who can forgive sins, but God *a*?
6. 4 but for the priests *a*?
9.18 as he was *a* praying,
36 Jesus was found *a*.
10.40 hath left me to serve *a*?
13. 8 Lord, let it *a* this year also,
Jn 6.15 into a mountain himself *a*.
22 his disciples were gone away *a*;
8. 9 and Jesus was left *a*,
16 for I am not *a*, but I and the
29 the Father hath not left me *a*;
11.48 If we let him thus *a*, all men will
12. 7 Then said Jesus, Let her *a*:
24 and die, it abideth *a*:
16.32 and shall leave me *a*:
32 and yet I am not *a*, because the
17.20 pray I for these *a*, but for
Ac 5.38 from these men, and let them *a*:
19.26 not *a* at Ephesus, but almost
Ro 4.23 for his sake *a*, that it was
11. 3 and I am left *a*, and they seek
Gal 6. 4 have rejoicing in himself *a*,
1Th 3. 1 to be left at Athens *a*;
Heb 9. 7 went the high priest *a* once every
Jas 2.17 not works, is dead, being *a*.

ALOOF
Ps 38.11 friends stand *a* from my sore;

ALOUD
Gen 45. 2 And he wept *a*:
1Ki 18.27 Cry *a*: for he is a god;
28 they cried *a*, and cut
Ezr 3.12 many shouted *a* for joy:
Job 19. 7 I cry *a*, but there is no
Ps 51.14 my tongue shall sing *a* of thy
55.17 will I pray, and cry *a*: and he
59.16 yea, I will sing *a* of thy mercy
81. 1 Sing *a* unto God our strength:
132.16 her saints shall shout *a* for joy.
149. 5 let them sing *a* upon their beds.
Isa 24.14 they shall cry *a* from the sea.
54. 1 break forth into singing and cry *a*,
58. 1 Cry *a*, spare not, lift up thy voice
Dan 3. 4 Then an herald cried *a*, To you
4.14 He cried *a*, and said thus, Hew
5. 7 The king cried *a* to bring in the
Hos 5. 8 cry *a* at Beth-aven,
Mic 4. 9 thou cry out *a*? is there no king
Mk 15. 8 the multitude crying *a* began to

ALPHA
Rev 1. 8 I am *A* and Omega, the
11 I am *A* and Omega, the first and
21. 6 I am *A* and Omega, the beginning
22.13 I am *A* and Omega, the beginning

ALPHAEUS
Mt 10. 3 James the son of *A*,
Mk 2.14 Levi the son of *A* sitting
3.18 James the son of *A*,
Lk 6.15 James the son of *A*,
Ac 1.13 James the son of *A*,

ALTAR
Gen 8.20 Noah builded an *a* unto the Lord
20 offered burnt offerings on the *a*.
12. 7 there builded he an *a*
8 there he builded an *a*
13. 4 Unto the place of the *a*,
18 built there an *a* unto the Lord.
22. 9 Abraham built an *a* there,

Incense was burned on this 22-inch-high carved stone altar, found at Megiddo and dating from the time of Samuel, about 1000 B.C.

9 laid him on the *a*
26.25 he builded an *a* there,
33.20 And he erected there an *a*,
35. 1 make there an *a* unto God,
3 I will make there an *a*
7 he built there an *a*,
Ex 17.15 And Moses built an *a*,
20.24 An *a* of earth thou shalt make
25 if thou wilt make me an *a* of stone,
26 go up by steps unto mine *a*,
21.14 thou shalt take him from mine *a*,
24. 4 builded an *a* under the hill,
6 the blood he sprinkled on the *a*.
27. 1 thou shalt make an *a*
1 the *a* shall be foursquare:
5 compass of the *a* beneath, that
5 may be even to the midst of the *a*.
6 thou shalt make staves for the *a*,
7 be upon the two sides of the *a*,
28.43 when they come near unto the *a*
29.12 put it upon the horns of the *a*
12 beside the bottom of the *a*.
13 burn them upon the *a*.
16 sprinkle it round about upon the *a*.
18 burn the whole ram upon the *a*:
20 sprinkle the blood upon the *a*
21 the blood that is upon the *a*,
25 burn them upon the *a*
36 thou shalt cleanse the *a*,
37 an atonement for the *a*, and
37 and it shall be an *a* most holy:
37 toucheth the *a* shall be holy.
38 thou shalt offer upon the *a*;
44 the congregation, and the *a*:
30. 1 thou shalt make an *a* to burn
18 the congregation and the *a*,
20 when they come near to the *a*
27 and the *a* of incense,
28 the *a* of burnt offering
31. 8 the *a* of incense,
9 the *a* of burnt offering
32. 5 he built an *a* before it;
35.15 the incense *a*, and his staves,
16 The *a* of burnt offering,
37.25 he made the incense *a*
38. 1 he made the *a* of burnt offering
3 he made all the vessels of the *a*,
4 he made for the *a* a brasen grate
7 the rings on the sides of the *a*,
7 made the *a* hollow with boards.
30 and the brasen *a*,
30 all the vessels of the *a*.
39.38 the golden *a*, and the anointing
39 The brasen *a*, and his grate
40. 5 thou shalt set the *a* of gold
6 the *a* of the burnt offering
7 of the congregation and the *a*,
10 shalt anoint the *a* of the burnt
10 all his vessels, and sanctify the *a*:
10 and it shall be an *a* most holy.
26 he put the golden *a* in the tent
29 he put the *a* of burnt offering
30 tent of the congregation and the *a*,
32 they came near unto the *a*,
33 about the tabernacle and the *a*,
Lev 1. 5 blood round about upon the *a*
7 shall put fire upon the *a*,
8 the fire which is upon the *a*:
9 the priest shall burn all on the *a*,
11 kill it on the side of the *a*
11 blood round about upon the *a*.
12 the fire which is upon the *a*:
13 burn it upon the *a*:
15 the priest shall bring it unto the *a*,
15 burn it on the *a*; and the blood
15 wrung out at the side of the *a*:
16 cast it beside the *a*
17 the priest shall burn it upon the *a*,
2. 2 burn the memorial of it upon the *a*,
8 he shall bring it unto the *a*.
9 shall burn it upon the *a*:
12 shall not be burnt on the *a*
3. 2 shall sprinkle the blood upon the *a*
5 shall burn it on the *a*
8 round about upon the *a*.
11 the priest shall burn it upon the *a*:
13 upon the *a* round about.
16 priest shall burn them upon the *a*:
4. 7 blood upon the horns of the *a*
7 the bullock at the bottom of the *a*
10 shall burn them upon the *a*
18 blood upon the horns of the *a*
18 the blood at the bottom of the *a*
19 burn it upon the *a*.
25 it upon the horns of the *a*
25 blood at the bottom of the *a*
26 burn all his fat upon the *a*,
30 it upon the horns of the *a*
30 thereof at the bottom of the *a*.
31 shall burn it upon the *a*
34 it upon the horns of the *a*
34 thereof at the bottom of the *a*:
35 shall burn them upon the *a*,
5. 9 upon the side of the *a*;
9 out at the bottom of the *a*:
12 burn it on the *a*,
6. 9 the burning upon the *a*
9 the fire of the *a* shall be burning
10 with the burnt offering on the *a*,
10 and he shall put them beside the *a*.
12 the fire upon the *a* shall be
13 shall ever be burning upon the *a*;
14 before the Lord, before the *a*.
15 shall burn it upon the *a*
7. 2 sprinkle round about upon the *a*.
5 priest shall burn them upon the *a*
31 shall burn the fat upon the *a*:
8.11 he sprinkled thereof upon the *a*
11 and anointed the *a* and all
15 put it upon the horns of the *a*
15 and purified the *a*, and poured
15 blood at the bottom of the *a*,
16 Moses burnt it upon the *a*.
19 sprinkled the blood upon the *a*
21 burnt the whole ram upon the *a*:
24 sprinkled the blood upon the *a*
28 burnt them on the *a*
30 the blood which was upon the *a*,
9. 7 Go unto the *a*,
8 Aaron therefore went unto the *a*,
9 put it upon the horns of the *a*,
9 the blood at the bottom of the *a*:
10 he burnt upon the *a*;
12 sprinkled round about upon the *a*.
13 and he burnt them upon the *a*.
14 the burnt offering on the *a*.
17 burnt it upon the *a*,
18 which he sprinkled upon the *a*
20 he burnt the fat upon the *a*:
24 upon the *a* the burnt offering
10.12 eat it without leaven beside the *a*:
14.20 the meat offering upon the *a*:
16.12 burning coals of fire from off the *a*
18 he shall go out unto the *a*
18 put it upon the horns of the *a*
20 the *a*, he shall bring the live goat:
25 shall he burn upon the *a*,
33 of the congregation, and for the *a*,
17. 6 sprinkle the blood upon the *a*
11 to you upon the *a*
21.23 nor come nigh unto the *a*,
22.22 offering by fire of them upon the *a*
Nu 3.26 by the *a* round about,
4.11 golden *a* they shall spread a cloth
13 take away the ashes from the *a*,
14 all the vessels of the *a*;
26 by the *a* round about,
5.25 offer it upon the *a*:
26 and burn it upon the *a*,
7. 1 both the *a* and all the vessels
10 offered for dedicating of the *a*
10 offered their offering before the *a*.
11 for the dedicating of the *a*.
84 This was the dedication of the *a*,
88 the dedication of the *a*, after that
16.38, 39 plates for a covering of the *a*:
46 put fire therein from off the *a*,
18. 3 vessels of the sanctuary and the *a*,
5 the charge of the *a*:
7 for everything of the *a*,
17 sprinkle their blood upon the *a*,
23. 2 on every *a* a bullock and a ram.
4 upon every *a* a bullock and a ram.
14 bullock and a ram on every *a*.
30 a bullock and a ram on every *a*.
Dt 12.27 upon the *a* of the Lord thy God:
27 shall be poured out upon the *a*
16.21 trees near unto the *a* of the Lord
26. 4 set it down before the *a*
27. 5 shalt thou build an *a*
5 an *a* of stones:
6 build the *a* of the Lord thy God
33.10 burnt sacrifice upon thine *a*.
Jos 8.30 Then Joshua built an *a*
31 an *a* of whole stones,
9.27 and for the *a* of the Lord,
22.10 there an *a* by Jordan, a great *a*
11 have built an *a* over against
16 in that ye have builded you an *a*,
19 in building you an *a*
19 beside the *a* of the Lord
23 That we have built us an *a*
26 prepare to build us an *a*,
28 Behold the pattern of the *a* of
29 to build an *a* for burnt offerings,
29 beside the *a* of the Lord
34 called the *a* Ed:
Jdg 6.24 Then Gideon built an *a* there
25 throw down the *a* of Baal
26 and build an *a* unto the Lord
28 the *a* of Baal was cast down,
28 offered upon the *a* that was built
30 he hath cast down the *a* of Baal,
31 because one hath cast down his *a*.
32 because he hath thrown down his *a*.
13.20 toward heaven from off the *a*,

Jdg 13.20 in the flame of the *a*.
21. 4 built there an *a*,
1Sa 2.28 to offer upon mine *a*,
33 I shall not cut off from mine *a*,
7.17 and there he built an *a*
14.35 And Saul built an *a*
35 the same was the first *a*
2Sa 24.18 rear an *a* unto the Lord
21 to build an *a* unto the Lord,
25 David built there an *a*
1Ki 1.50 caught hold on the horns of the *a*.
51 on the horns of the *a*, saying, Let
53 they brought him down from the *a*.
2.28 caught hold on the horns of the *a*.
29 behold, he is by the *a*.
3. 4 did Solomon offer upon that *a*.
6.20 and so covered the *a*
22 also the whole *a*
7.48 the *a* of gold, and the table of gold,
8.22 Solomon stood before the *a* of the
31 the oath come before thine *a*
54 he arose from before the *a*
64 the brasen *a* that was before the
9.25 upon the *a* which he built
25 he burnt incense upon the *a* that
12.32 he offered upon the *a*.
33 So he offered upon the *a* which he
33 he offered upon the *a*, and burnt
13. 1 Jeroboam stood by the *a*
2 he cried against the *a* in the word
2 and said, O *a*, *a*,
3 the *a* shall be rent,
4 which had cried against the *a* in
4 he put forth his hand from the *a*,
5 the *a* also was rent, and
5 the ashes poured out from the *a*,
32 against the *a* in Beth-el,
16.32 he reared up an *a* for Baal
18.26 they leaped upon the *a*
30 he repaired the *a* of the Lord
32 And with the stones he built an *a*
32 he made a trench about the *a*,
35 the water ran round about the *a*;
2Ki 11.11 by the *a* and the temple.
12. 9 set it beside the *a*,
16.10 saw an *a* that was at Damascus:
10 the fashion of the *a*,
11 And Urijah the priest built an *a*
12 the king saw the *a*: and
12 the king approached to the *a*,
13 his peace offerings, upon the *a*.
14 he brought also the brasen *a*,
14 from between the *a*
14 put it on the north side of the *a*.
15 Upon the great *a* burn
15 and the brasen *a* shall be for me
18.22 Ye shall worship before this *a*
23. 9 came not up to the *a* of the Lord
15 the *a* that was at Beth-el,
15 both that *a* and the high place
16 burned them upon the *a*,
17 hast done against the *a* of Beth-el.
1Ch 6.49 and his sons offered upon the *a*
49 and on the *a* of incense,
16.40 upon the *a* of the burnt offering
21.18 set up an *a* unto the Lord
22 that I may build an *a*
26 built there an *a* unto the Lord
26 fire upon the *a* of burnt offering.
29 and the *a* of the burnt offering,
22. 1 this is the *a* of the burnt offering
28.18 And for the *a* of incense
2Ch 1. 5 the brasen *a*, that Bezaleel
6 went up thither to the brasen *a*
4. 1 Moreover he made an *a* of brass,
19 the golden *a* also,
5.12 stood at the east end of the *a*,
6.12 he stood before the *a* of the Lord
22 and the oath come before thine *a*
7. 7 brasen *a* which Solomon had made
9 kept the dedication of the *a* seven
8.12 on the *a* of the Lord,
15. 8 renewed the *a* of the Lord,
23.10 along by the *a* and the temple,
26.16 incense upon the *a* of incense.
19 from beside the incense *a*.
29.18 the *a* of burnt offering,
19 they are before the *a* of the Lord.
21 to offer them on the *a* of the Lord.
22 sprinkled it on the *a*:
22 upon the *a*: they killed also the
22 sprinkled the blood upon the *a*.
24 their blood upon the *a*,
27 the burnt offering upon the *a*.
32.12 Ye shall worship before one *a*,
33.16 he repaired the *a* of the Lord,
35.16 to offer burnt offerings upon the *a*
Ezr 3. 2 builded the *a* of the God of Israel,
3 they set the *a* upon his bases;
7.17 and offer them upon the *a*
Neh 10.34 to burn upon the *a* of the Lord
Ps 26. 6 so will I compass thine *a*,
43. 4 Then will I go unto the *a* of God,
51.19 they offer bullocks upon thine *a*.
118.27 unto the horns of the *a*.
Isa 6. 6 with the tongs from off the *a*:
19.19 in that day shall there be an *a*
27. 9 maketh all the stones of the *a*
36. 7 Ye shall worship before this *a*?
56. 7 accepted upon mine *a*;
60. 7 with acceptance on mine *a*,
La 2. 7 The Lord hath cast off his *a*,
Eze 8. 5 at the gate of the *a* this image
16 between the porch and the *a*,
9. 2 stood beside the brasen *a*.
40.46 the keepers of the charge of the *a*:
47 the *a* that was before the house.
41.22 The *a* of wood was three cubits
43.13 measures of the *a* after the cubits:
13 the higher place of the *a*.
15 So the *a* shall be four cubits;
15 and from the *a* and upward
16 And the *a* shall be twelve cubits
18 are the ordinances of the *a*
22 they shall cleanse the *a*,
26 Seven days shall they purge the *a*
27 your burnt offerings upon the *a*,
45.19 four corners of the settle of the *a*,
47. 1 at the south side of the *a*.
Joel 1.13 howl, ye ministers of the *a*:
2.17 weep between the porch and the *a*,
Am 2. 8 laid to pledge by every *a*,
3.14 the horns of the *a* shall be cut off,
9. 1 the Lord standing upon the *a*:
Zec 9.15 as the corners of the *a*.
14.20 be like the bowls before the *a*.
Mal 1. 7 offer polluted bread upon mine *a*;
10 do ye kindle fire on mine *a* for
2.13 covering the *a* of the Lord with
Mt 5.23 bring thy gift to the *a*,
24 thy gift before the *a*,
23.18 shall swear by the *a*,
19 the gift, or the *a*
20 shall swear by the *a*,
35 the temple and the *a*.
Lk 1.11 of the *a* of incense.
11.51 between the *a* and the temple:
Ac 17.23 I found an *a* with this inscription,
1Co 9.13 and they which wait at the *a*
13 partakers with the *a*?
10.18 partakers of the *a*?
Heb 7.13 no man gave attendance at the *a*.
13.10 We have an *a*, whereof
Jas 2.21 offered Isaac his son upon the *a*?
Rev 6. 9 under the *a* the souls
8. 3 stood at the *a*, having a golden
3 of all saints upon the golden *a*
5 filled it with fire of the *a*,
9.13 horns of the golden *a*
11. 1 the temple of God, and the *a*,
14.18 another angel came out from the *a*,
16. 7 I heard another out of the *a* say,

ALTARS

Ex 34.13 But ye shall destroy their *a*,
Nu 3.31 the candlestick, and the *a*,
23. 1 Build me here seven *a*,
4 I have prepared seven *a*,
14 and built seven *a*,
29 Build me here seven *a*, and prepare
Dt 7. 5 ye shall destroy their *a*,
12. 3 ye shall overthrow their *a*,
Jdg 2. 2 ye shall throw down their *a*:
1Ki 19.10, 14 thrown down thine *a*,
2Ki 11.18 his *a* and his images
18 the priest of Baal before the *a*.
18.22 whose *a* Hezekiah hath taken
21. 3 he reared up *a* for Baal,
4 he built *a* in the house of the Lord,
5 built *a* for all the host of heaven
23.12 the *a* that were on the top
12 the *a* which Manasseh had made
20 that were there upon the *a*,
2Ch 14. 3 he took away the *a* of the strange
23.17 brake his *a* and his images
17 the priest of Baal before the *a*.
28.24 *a* in every corner of Jerusalem.
30.14 they arose and took away the *a*
14 the *a* for incense took they away,
31. 1 the *a* out of all Judah
32.12 away his high places and his *a*,
33. 3 he reared up *a* for Baalim,
4 Also he built *a* in the house
5 built *a* for all the host of heaven
15 all the *a* that he had built
34. 4 they brake down the *a* of Baalim
5 bones of the priests upon their *a*,
7 when he had broken down the *a*
Ps 84. 3 even thine *a*, O Lord of hosts,
Isa 17. 8 he shall not look to the *a*,
36. 7 whose *a* Hezekiah hath taken
65. 3 burneth incense upon *a* of brick;
Jer 11.13 set up *a* to that shameful thing,
13 even *a* to burn incense unto Baal.
17. 1 upon the horns of your *a*;
2 their children remember their *a*
Eze 6. 4 your *a* shall be desolate,
5 your bones round about your *a*.
6 that your *a* may be laid waste
13 round about their *a*,
Hos 8.11 Ephraim hath made many *a* to sin,
11 *a* shall be unto him to sin.
10. 1 he hath increased the *a*;
2 he shall break down their *a*,
8 shall come up on their *a*;
12.11 their *a* are as heaps
Am 3.14 I will also visit the *a* of Beth-el:
Ro 11. 3 and digged down thine *a*;

ALTER

Lev 27.10 He shall not *a* it, nor change it,
Ezr 6.11 that whosoever shall *a* this word,
12 that shall put to their hand to *a*
Ps 89.34 covenant will I not break, nor *a*

ALTERED

Est 1.19 it be not *a*, That Vashti come
Lk 9.29 of his countenance was *a*,

ALTERETH

Dan 6. 8, 12 and Persians, which *a* not.

ALTHOUGH

Ex 13.17 *a* that was near; for God said,
Jos 22.17 *a* there was a plague in the
2Sa 23. 5 *A* my house be not so with God;
5 *a* he make it not to grow.
1Ki 20. 5 *A* I have sent unto thee, saying,
Est 7. 4 held my tongue, *a* the enemy
Job 2. 3 integrity, *a* thou movedst me
5. 6 *A* affliction cometh not forth
35.14 *A* thou sayest thou shalt
Jer 31.32 *a* I was an husband unto them,
Eze 7.13 is sold, *a* they were yet alive:

11.16 *A* I have cast them far off
16 and *a* I have scattered them
Hab 3.17 *A* the fig tree shall not blossom,
Mk 14.29 *A* all shall be offended,
Heb 4. 3 *a* the works were finished

AMAZED
Ex 15.15 the dukes of Edom shall be *a*;
Jdg 20.41 the men of Benjamin were *a*:
Job 32.15 They were *a*, they answered no
Isa 13. 8 they shall be *a* one at another;
Eze 32.10 will make many people *a* at thee,
Mt 12.23 all the people were *a*,
19.25 they were exceedingly *a*,
Mk 1.27 And they were all *a*,
2.12 insomuch that they were all *a*,
6.51 they were sore *a* in themselves,
9.15 they beheld him, were greatly *a*,
10.32 and they were *a*;
14.33 began to be sore *a*,
16. 8 for they trembled and were *a*:
Lk 2.48 they saw him, they were *a*:
4.36 And they were all *a*,
5.26 And they were all *a*,
9.43 *a* at the mighty power of God.
Ac 2. 7 they were all *a* and marvelled,
12 were all *a*, and were in doubt,
9.21 all that heard him were *a*.

AMAZEMENT
Ac 3.10 filled with wonder and *a*
1Pe 3. 6 and are not afraid with any *a*.

AMBASSADOR
Pr 13.17 but a faithful *a* is health.
Jer 49.14 an *a* is sent unto the heathen,
Ob 1 an *a* is sent among the heathen,
Eph 6.20 For which I am an *a* in bonds:

AMBASSADORS
Jos 9. 4 and made as if they had been *a*,
2Ch 32.31 in the business of the *a* of the
35.21 he sent *a* to him,
Isa 18. 2 That sendeth *a* by the sea,
30. 4 and his *a* came to Hanes.
33. 7 the *a* of peace shall weep bitterly.
Eze 17.15 in sending his *a* into Egypt,
2Co 5.20 we are *a* for Christ,

AMBASSAGE
Lk 14.32 he sendeth an *a*,

AMBUSH
Jos 8. 2 lay thee an *a* for the city
7 ye shall rise up from the *a*,
9 they went to lie in *a*,
12 set them to lie in *a* between
14 liers in *a* against him
19 And the *a* arose quickly
21 saw that the *a* had taken the city,

AMBUSHES
Jer 51.12 up the watchmen, prepare the *a*:

AMBUSHMENT
2Ch 13.13 Jeroboam caused an *a*
13 and the *a* was behind them.

AMBUSHMENTS
2Ch 20.22 the Lord set *a*

AMEN
Nu 5.22 And the woman shall say, *A*, *a*.
Dt 27.15, 16 people shall answer and say, *A*.
17, 18, 19, 20, 21, 22, 23, 24, 25, 26 And all the people shall say, *A*.
1Ki 1.36 answered the king, and said, *A*:
1Ch 16.36 And all the people said, *A*,
Neh 5.13 all the congregation said, *A*,
8. 6 the people answered, *A*, *A*,
Ps 41.13 to everlasting. *A*, and *A*.
72.19 filled with his glory; *A*, and *A*.
89.52 for evermore. *A*, and *A*.
106.48 *A*. Praise ye the Lord.
Jer 28. 6 the prophet Jeremiah said, *A*:
Mt 6.13 and the glory, for ever. *A*.
28.20 unto the end of the world, *A*.
Mk 16.20 the word with signs following. *A*.
Lk 24.53 praising and blessing God. *A*.
Jn 21.25 books that should be written. *A*.
Ro 1.25 Creator, who is blessed for ever. *A*.
9. 5 over all, God blessed for ever. *A*.
11.36 to whom be glory for ever. *A*.
15.33 God of peace be with you all. *A*.
16.20 Jesus Christ be with you. *A*.
24 Jesus Christ be with you all. *A*.
27 through Jesus Christ for ever. *A*.
1Co 14.16 unlearned say *A* at thy giving of
16.24 with you all in Christ Jesus. *A*.
2Co 1.20 yea, and in him *A*, unto the glory
13.14 Holy Ghost, be with you all. *A*.
Gal 1. 5 be glory for ever and ever. *A*.
6.18 Christ be with your spirit. *A*.
Eph 3.21 all ages, world without end. *A*.
6.24 Jesus Christ in sincerity. *A*.
Php 4.20 be glory for ever and ever. *A*.
23 Jesus Christ be with you all. *A*.
Col 4.18 my bonds. Grace be with you. *A*.
1Th 5.28 of...Christ be with you. *A*.
2Th 3.18 of...Christ be with you all. *A*.
1Ti 1.17 and glory for ever and ever. *A*.
6.16 honor and power everlasting. *A*.
21 Grace be with thee. *A*.
2Ti 4.18 be glory for ever and ever. *A*.
22 Grace be with you. *A*.
Tit 3.15 Grace be with you all. *A*.
Phm 25 Christ be with your spirit. *A*.
Heb 13.21 be glory for ever and ever. *A*.
25 Grace be with you all. *A*.
1Pe 4.11 dominion for ever and ever. *A*.
5.11 dominion for ever and ever. *A*.
14 all that are in Christ Jesus. *A*.
2Pe 3.18 glory both now and for ever. *A*.
1Jn 5.21 keep yourselves from idols. *A*.
2Jn 13 of thy elect sister greet thee. *A*.
Jude 25 and power, both now and ever. *A*.
Rev 1. 6 dominion for ever and ever. *A*.
7 wail because of him. Even so, *A*.
18 I am alive for evermore, *A*;
3.14 These things saith the *A*,
5.14 And the four beasts said, *A*.
7.12 Saying, *A*: Blessing, and glory,
12 unto our God for ever and ever. *A*.
19. 4 Sat on the throne, saying, *A*;
22.20 *A*. Even so, come, Lord Jesus.
21 Jesus Christ be with you all. *A*.

AMEND
2Ch 34.10 to repair and *a* the house:
Jer 7. 3 *A* your ways and your doings,
5 if ye throughly *a* your ways
26.13 *a* your ways and your doings,
35.15 and *a* your doings,
Jn 4.52 hour when he began to *a*.

AMENDS
Lev 5.16 he shall make *a* for the harm

AMETHYST
Ex 28.19 a ligure, an agate, and an *a*.
39.12 a ligure, an agate, and an *a*.
Rev 21.20 a jacinth; the twelfth, an *a*.

AMIABLE
Ps 84. 1 How *a* are thy tabernacles,

AMISS
2Ch 6.37 We have sinned, we have done *a*,
Dan 3.29 speak anything *a* against the God
Lk 23.41 this man hath done nothing *a*.
Jas 4. 3 receive not, because ye ask *a*,

AMMON
Gen 19.38 the children of *A* unto this day.
Nu 21.24 even unto the children of *A*:
24 of the children of *A* was strong.
Dt 2.19 over against the children of *A*,
19 the children of *A* any possession;
37 of the children of *A* thou camest
3.11 in Rabbath of the children of *A*?
16 is the border of the children of *A*;
Jos 12. 2 the border of the children of *A*;
13.10 the border of the children of *A*;
25 half the land of the children of *A*,
Jdg 3.13 unto him the children of *A*
10. 6 and the gods of the children of *A*,
7 into the hands of the children of *A*.
9 children of *A* passed over Jordan
11 Amorites, from the children of *A*,
17 the children of *A* were gathered
18 to fight against the children of *A*?
11. 4 children of *A* made against Israel.
5 when the children of *A* made war
6 we may fight with the children of *A*.
8, 9 against the children of *A*,
12 king of the children of *A*, saying,
13 king of the children of *A* answered
14 unto the king of the children of *A*:
15 nor the land of the children of *A*:
27 of Israel and the children of *A*.
28 the king of the children of *A*
29 passed over unto the children of *A*.
30 children of *A* into mine hands,
31 in peace from the children of *A*,
32 passed over unto the children of *A*
33 the children of *A* were subdued
36 enemies, even of the children of *A*.
12. 1 against the children of *A*,
2 great strife with the children of *A*;
3 over against the children of *A*,
1Sa 12.12 the king of the children of *A*
14.47 against the children of *A*,
2Sa 8.12 of Moab, and of the children of *A*,
10. 1 the king of the children of *A* died,
2 into the land of the children of *A*.
3 the princes of the children of *A*
6 when the children of *A* saw that
6 the children of *A* sent and hired
8 And the children of *A* came out,
10 array against the children of *A*.
11 if the children of *A* be too strong
14 when the children of *A* saw that
14 returned from the children of *A*,
19 feared to help the children of *A*
11. 1 they destroy the children of *A*,
12. 9 with the sword of the children of *A*.
26 of *A*, and took the royal city.
31 all the cities of the children of *A*.
17.27 of Rabbah of the children of *A*,
1Ki 11. 7 abomination of the children of *A*.
33 the god of the children of *A*,
2Ki 23.13 abomination of the children of *A*,
24. 2 and bands of the children of *A*,
1Ch 18.11 and from the children of *A*,
19. 1 the king of the children of *A* died,
2 into the land of the children of *A*
3 princes of the children of *A* said
6 of *A* saw that they had made
6 of *A* sent a thousand talents of
7 of *A* gathered themselves together
9 of *A* came out, and put the battle
11 array against the children of *A*.
12 of *A* be too strong for thee, then
15 of *A* saw that the Syrians were
19 the Syrians help the children of *A*
20. 1 of *A*, and came and besieged
3 all the cities of the children of *A*.
2Ch 20. 1 of *A*, and with them other beside
10 the children of *A* and Moab,
22 against the children of *A*,
23 children of *A* and Moab stood up
27. 5 of *A* gave him the same year an
5 So much did the children of *A* pay

Neh 13.23 married wives of Ashdod, of *A*,
Ps 83. 7 Gebal, and *A*, and Amalek;
Isa 11.14 the children of *A* shall obey them.
Jer 9.26 of *A*, and Moab, and all that are
25.21 and Moab, and the children of *A*,
49. 6 the captivity of the children of *A*,
Dan 11.41 and the chief of the children of *A*.
Am 1.13 transgressions of the children of *A*,
Zep 2. 8 the revilings of the children of *A*,
9 of *A* as Gomorrah, even the

AMMONITE

Dt 23. 3 An *A* or Moabite shall not enter
1Sa 11. 1 the *A* came up, and encamped
2 Nahash the *A* answered them,
2Sa 23.37 Zelek the *A*, Naharai the
1Ch 11.39 Zelek the *A*, Naharai the
Neh 2.10 and Tobiah the servant, the *A*,
19 the *A*, and Geshem the Arabian,
4. 3 Now Tobiah the *A* was by him,
13. 1 the *A* and the Moabite should not

AMMONITES

Dt 2.20 the *A* call them Zamzummims;
1Sa 11.11 slew the *A* until the heat of the
1Ki 11. 1 women of the Moabites, *A*,
5 Milcom the abomination of the *A*.
2Ch 20. 1 and with them other beside the *A*,
26. 8 the *A* gave gifts to Uzziah:
27. 5 fought also with the king of the *A*,
Ezr 9. 1 the Perizzites, the Jebusites, the *A*,
Neh 4. 7 and the Arabians, and the *A*,
Jer 27. 3 to the king of the *A*, and to the
40.11 among the *A*, and in Edom,
14 Baalis the king of the *A* hath
41.10 departed to go over to the *A*.
15 eight men, and went to the *A*.
49. 1 Concerning the *A*, thus saith
2 to be heard in Rabbah of the *A*;
Eze 21.20 come to Rabbath of the *A*,
28 concerning the *A*, and
25. 2 set thy face against the *A*,
3 unto the *A*, Hear the word
5 *A* a couchingplace for flocks;
10 men of the east with the *A*,
10 *A* may not be remembered

AMMONITESS

1Ki 14.21 mother's name was Naamah an *A*.
31 was Naamah an *A*. And Abijam
2Ch 12.13 mother's name was Naamah an *A*.
24.26 Zabad the son of Shimeath, an *A*,

AMON

1Ki 22.26 and carry him back unto *A* the
2Ki 21.18 and *A* his son reigned in his stead.
19 *A* was twenty and two years old
23 the servants of *A* conspired against
24 that had conspired against king *A*;
25 the rest of the acts of *A* which he
1Ch 3.14 *A* his son, Josiah his son.
2Ch 18.25 carry him back to *A* the governor
33.20 and *A* his son reigned in his stead.
21 *A* was two and twenty years old
22 *A* sacrificed unto all the carved
23 but *A* trespassed more and more.
25 that had conspired against king *A*;
Neh 7.59 of Zebaim, the children of *A*.
Jer 1. 2 in the days of Josiah the son of *A*
25. 3 year of Josiah the son of *A*
Zep 1. 1 the son of *A*, king of Judah.
Mt 1.10 Manasses begat *A*;
10 and *A* begat Josias;

AMORITE

Gen 10.16 And the Jebusite, and the *A*,
14.13 dwelt in the plain of Mamre the *A*,
48.22 I took out of the hand of the *A*
Ex 33. 2 will drive out the Canaanite, the *A*,
34.11 I drive out before thee the *A*,
Nu 32.39 dispossessed the *A* which was in it.
Dt 2.24 given into thine hand Sihon the *A*,
Jos 9. 1 Hittite, and the *A*, the Canaanite,
11. 3 east and on the west, and to the *A*,
1Ch 1.14 The Jebusite also, and the *A*,
Eze 16. 3 thy father was an *A*, and thy
45 was a Hittite, and your father an *A*.
Am 2. 9 destroyed I the *A* before them,
10 to possess the land of the *A*.

AMORITES

Gen 14. 7 and also the *A*, that dwelt in
15.16 iniquity of the *A* is not yet full.
21 And the *A* and the Canaanites,
Ex 3. 8 and the Hittites, and the *A*,
17 and the *A*, and the Perizzites,
13. 5 and the *A*, and the Hivites,
23.23 and bring thee in unto the *A*,
Nu 13.29 the *A*, dwell in the mountains:
21.13 cometh out of the coasts of the *A*:
13 between Moab and the *A*.
21 unto Sihon king of the *A*,
25 dwelt in all the cities of the *A*,
26 city of Sihon the king of the *A*,
29 captivity unto Sihon king of the *A*.
31 Israel dwelt in the land of the *A*.
32 drove out the *A* that were there.
34 didst unto Sihon king of the *A*,
22. 2 all that Israel had done to the *A*.
32.33 the kingdom of Sihon king of the *A*,
Dt 1. 4 had slain Sihon the king of the *A*,
7 and go to the mount of the *A*,
19 the way of the mountain of the *A*,
20 come unto the mountain of the *A*,
27 deliver us into the hand of the *A*,
44 *A*, which dwell in that mountain,
3. 2 of the *A*, which dwelt at Heshbon.
8 the hand of the two kings of the *A*
9 and the *A* call it Shenir;)
4.46 in the land of Sihon king of the *A*,
47 two kings of the *A*, which were on
7. 1 and the Girgashites, and the *A*,
20.17 namely, the Hittites, and the *A*,
31. 4 to Sihon and to Og, kings of the *A*,
Jos 2.10 ye did unto the two kings of the *A*,
3.10 and the *A*, and the Jebusites,
5. 1 when all the kings of the *A*,
7. 7 deliver us into the hand of the *A*,
9.10 the two kings of the *A*, that were
10. 5 Therefore the five kings of the *A*,
6 all the kings of the *A* that dwell
12 when the Lord delivered up the *A*
12. 2 Sihon king of the *A*, who dwelt in
8 the *A*, and the Canaanites,
13. 4 unto Aphek, to the borders of the *A*:
10 Sihon king of the *A*, which reigned
21 kingdom of Sihon king of the *A*,
24. 8 brought you into the land of the *A*,
11 fought against you, the *A*,
12 even the two kings of the *A*;
15 or the gods of the *A*, in whose land
18 even the *A* which dwelt in the land:
Jdg 1.34 the *A* forced the children of Dan
35 *A* would dwell in mount Heres
36 the coast of the *A* was from the
3. 5 the Canaanites, Hittites, and *A*,
6.10 fear not the gods of the *A*,
10. 8 Jordan in the land of the *A*,
11 the Egyptians, and from the *A*,
11.19 Sihon king of the *A*, the king of
21 *A*, the inhabitants of that country.
22 possessed all the coasts of the *A*,
23 of Israel hath dispossessed the *A*
1Sa 7.14 peace between Israel and the *A*.
2Sa 21. 2 but of the remnant of the *A*;
1Ki 4.19 the country of Sihon king of the *A*,
9.20 the people that were left of the *A*,
21.26 according to all things as did the *A*,
2Ki 21.11 wickedly above all that the *A* did,
2Ch 8. 7 of the Hittites, and the *A*,
Ezr 9. 1 Moabites, the Egyptians, and the *A*.
Neh 9. 8 the *A*, and the Perizzites,
Ps 135.11 Sihon king of the *A*, and Og
136.19 Sihon king of the *A*: for his mercy

AMOS

Am 1. 1 The words of *A*, who was among
7. 8 And the Lord said unto me, *A*,
10 saying, *A* hath conspired against
11 thus *A* saith, Jeroboam shall die
12 Amaziah said unto *A*, O thou seer,
14 answered *A*, and said to Amaziah,
8. 2 And he said, *A*, what seest thou?
Lk 3.25 which was the son of *A*,

AMOUNTING

2Ch 3. 8 gold, *a* to six hundred talents.

AMOZ

2Ki 19. 2 to Isaiah the prophet the son of *A*.
20 the son of *A* sent to Hezekiah,
20. 1 the son of *A* came to him, and said
2Ch 26.22 did Isaiah the prophet, the son of *A*,
32.20 the son of *A*, prayed and cried to
32 Isaiah the prophet, the son of *A*,
Isa 1. 1 The vision of Isaiah the son of *A*,
2. 1 The word that Isaiah the son of *A*
13. 1 which Isaiah the son of *A* did see.
20. 2 the Lord by Isaiah the son of *A*,
37. 2 Isaiah the prophet the son of *A*.
21 the son of *A* sent unto Hezekiah,
38. 1 son of *A* came unto him, and said

AMPHIPOLIS

Ac 17. 1 when they had passed through *A*

AMPLIAS

Ro 16. 8 Greet *A* my beloved in the Lord.

ANAK

Nu 13.22 and Talmai, the children of *A*,
28 we saw the children of *A* there.
33 we saw the giants, the sons of *A*,
Dt 9. 2 stand before the children of *A*!
Jos 15.13 the city of Arba the father of *A*,
14 drove thence the three sons of *A*,
14 and Talmai, the children of *A*.
21.11 the city of Arba the father of *A*,
Jdg 1.20 expelled thence the three sons of *A*.

ANAKIMS

Dt 1.28 seen the sons of the *A* there.
2.10 and many, and tall, as the *A*;
11 were accounted giants, as the *A*;
21 as the *A*; but the Lord destroyed
9. 2 and tall, the children of the *A*,
Jos 11.21 cut off the *A* from the mountains,
22 There was none of the *A* left
14.12 heardest in that day how the *A*
15 was a great man among the *A*.

ANANIAS

Ac 5. 1 a certain man named *A*,
3 But Peter said, *A*, why hath Satan
5 *A* hearing these words fell down,
9.10 disciple at Damascus, named *A*;
10 said the Lord in a vision, *A*.
12 a vision a man named *A* coming
13 Then *A* answered, Lord,
17 *A* went his way, and entered into
22.12 *A*, a devout man according to the
23. 2 the high priest *A* commanded
24. 1 after five days *A* the high priest

ANATHEMA

1Co 16.22 let him be *A* Maran-atha.

ANCHOR

Heb 6.19 hope we have as an *a* of the soul,

ANCHORS

Ac 27.29 they cast four *a* out of the stern,
30 have cast *a* out of the foreship
40 they had taken up the *a*,

ANDREW

Disciple remembered for bringing others to Jesus; follower of John the Baptist when first attracted to the new teacher; brings his brother Simon Peter to him (Jn 1.35-42); summoned with Simon to leave their nets and become fishers of men (Mt 4.18-20; Mk 1.16-18; Lk 5.1-11); finds the boy with the loaves and fishes and takes him to Jesus, who then feeds the five thousand (Jn 6.1-14); with Philip introduces some Greek inquirers to Jesus (Jn 12.20-22); in later tradition associated with a mission to Scythia, and chosen as the patron saint of Russia and Scotland.

ANCLE

Ac 3. 7 feet and *a* bones received strength.

ANCLES

Eze 47. 3 the waters were to the *a*.

ANDREW

Mt 4.18 Simon called Peter, and *A* his
10. 2 called Peter, and *A* his brother;
Mk 1.16 Simon and *A* his brother casting
29 into the house of Simon and *A*,
3.18 *A*, and Philip, and Bartholomew,
13. 3 John and *A* asked him privately,
Lk 6.14 named Peter,) and *A* his brother,
Jn 1.40 *A*, Simon Peter's brother.
44 Bethsaida, the city of *A* and Peter.
6. 8 One of his disciples, *A*, Simon
12.22 Philip cometh and telleth *A*:
22 and again *A* and Philip tell Jesus.
Ac 1.13 *A*, Philip, and Thomas,

ANDRONICUS

Ro 16. 7 Salute *A* and Junia, my kinsmen,

ANGEL

Gen 16. 7 the *a* of the Lord found her by a
9 the *a* of the Lord said unto her,
10 *a* of the Lord said unto her, I will
11 the *a* of the Lord said unto her,
21.17 the *a* of God called to Hagar out
22.11 the *a* of the Lord called unto him
15 *a* of the Lord called unto Abraham
24. 7 he shall send his *a* before thee
40 will send his *a* with thee,
31.11 the *a* of God spake unto me in a
48.16 The *A* which redeemed me from
Ex 3. 2 *a* of the Lord appeared unto him,
14.19 the *a* of God, which went before
23.20 Behold, I send an *A* before thee,
23 mine *A* shall go before thee,
32.34 mine *A* shall go before thee:
33. 2 I will send an *a* before thee;
Nu 20.16 he heard our voice, and sent an *a*,
22.22 the *a* of the Lord stood in the way
23 the ass saw the *a* of the Lord
24 the *a* of the Lord stood in a path
25 And when the ass saw the *a* of the
26 the *a* of the Lord went further,
27 the *a* of the Lord, she fell down
31 he saw the *a* of the Lord standing
32 the *a* of the Lord said unto him,
34 Balaam said unto the *a* of the
35 *a* of the Lord said unto Balaam,
Jdg 2. 1 an *a* of the Lord came up from
4 when the *a* of the Lord spake
5.23 Meroz, said the *a* of the Lord,
6.11 there came an *a* of the Lord,
12 *a* of the Lord appeared unto him,
20 the *a* of God said unto him, Take
21 *a* of the Lord put forth the end
21 Then the *a* of the Lord departed
22 perceived that he was an *a*
22 I have seen an *a* of the Lord
13. 3 the *a* of the Lord appeared unto
6 like the countenance of an *a*
9 the *a* of God came again unto the
13, 16 the *a* of the Lord said unto
15, 17 Manoah said unto the *a* of the
16 Manoah knew not that he was an *a*
18 And the *a* of the Lord said
19 and the *a* did wondrously;
20 the *a* of the Lord ascended in the
21 *a* of the Lord did no more appear
21 Manoah knew that he was an *a*
1Sa 29. 9 good in my sight, as an *a* of God:
2Sa 14.17 *a* of God, so is my lord the king
20 to the wisdom of an *a* of God,
19.27 the king is as an *a* of God:
24.16 when the *a* stretched out his hand
16 to the *a* that destroyed the people,
16 *a* of the Lord was by the threshing
17 the *a* that smote the people,
1Ki 13.18 and an *a* spake unto me by the
19. 5 an *a* touched him, and said unto
7 the *a* of the Lord came again
2Ki 1. 3 the *a* of the Lord said to Elijah
15 the *a* of the Lord said unto Elijah,
19.35 the *a* of the Lord went out,
1Ch 21.12 and the *a* of the Lord destroying
15 God sent an *a* unto Jerusalem
15 *a* that destroyed, It is enough,
15 And the *a* of the Lord stood by
16 saw the *a* of the Lord stand
18 the *a* of the Lord commanded
20 Ornan turned back, and saw the *a*;
27 And the Lord commanded the *a*;
30 the sword of the *a* of the Lord.
2Ch 32.21 the Lord sent an *a*, which cut off
Ps 34. 7 The *a* of the Lord encampeth
35. 5 let the *a* of the Lord chase them.
6 let the *a* of the Lord persecute
Ec 5. 6 neither say thou before the *a*,
Isa 37.36 the *a* of the Lord went forth,
63. 9 the *a* of his presence saved them:
Dan 3.28 who hath sent his *a*, and delivered
6.22 My God hath sent his *a*, and hath
Hos 12. 4 he had power over the *a*,
Zec 1. 9 the *a* that talked with me
11 they answered the *a* of the Lord
12 *a* of the Lord answered and said,
13 the Lord answered the *a* that
14 the *a* that communed with me
19 I said unto the *a* that talked
2. 3 *a* that talked with me went forth,
3 and another *a* went out
3. 1 the *a* of the Lord, and Satan
3 stood before the *a*.
5 And the *a* of the Lord stood by.
6 the *a* of the Lord protested unto
4. 1 *a* that talked with me came again,
4 spake to the *a* that talked with
5 *a* that talked with me answered
5. 5 *a* that talked with me went forth,
10 said I to the *a* that talked with me,
6. 4 I answered and said unto the *a*
5 the *a* answered and said unto me,
12. 8 as the *a* of the Lord before them.
Mt 1.20 *a* of the Lord appeared unto him
24 did as the *a* of the Lord had bidden
2.13 *a* of the Lord appeareth to
19 behold, an *a* of the Lord appeareth
28. 2 for the *a* of the Lord descended
5 the *a* answered and said unto the
Lk 1.11 appeared unto him an *a* of the Lord
13 the *a* said unto him, Fear not,
18 Zacharias said unto the *a*,
19 the *a* answering said unto him,
26 the *a* Gabriel was sent from God
28 And the *a* came in unto her,
30 *a* said unto her, Fear not, Mary:
34 Then said Mary unto the *a*,
35 the *a* answered and said unto her,
38 And the *a* departed from her.
2. 9 the *a* of the Lord came upon them,
10 the *a* said unto them, Fear not:
13 *a* a multitude of the heavenly
21 which was so named of the *a*
22.43 there appeared an *a* unto him
Jn 5. 4 *a* went down at a certain season
12.29 others said, An *a* spake to him.
Ac 5.19 the *a* of the Lord by night opened
6.15 as it had been the face of an *a*.
7.30 an *a* of the Lord in a flame
35 the hand of the *a* which appeared
38 with the *a* which spake to him
8.26 *a* of the Lord spake unto Philip,
10. 3 an *a* of God coming in to him,
7 the *a* which spake unto Cornelius
22 warned from God by an holy *a*
11.13 how he had seen an *a* in his house,
12. 7 the *a* of the Lord came upon him,
8 the *a* said unto him, Gird thyself,
9 which was done by the *a*;
10 forthwith the *a* departed
11 the Lord hath sent his *a*,
15 said they, It is his *a*.
23 the *a* of the Lord smote him,
23. 8 resurrection, neither *a*, nor spirit:
9 if a spirit or an *a* hath spoken
27.23 by me this night the *a* of God,
2Co 11.14 transformed into an *a* of light.
Gal 1. 8 we, or an *a* from heaven, preach
4.14 received me as an *a* of God,
Rev 1. 1 he sent and signified it by his *a*
2. 1 the *a* of the church of Ephesus
8 the *a* of the church in Smyrna
12 to the *a* of the church in Pergamos
18 the *a* of the church in Thyatira
3. 1 unto the *a* of the church in Sardis
7 the *a* of the church in Philadelphia
14 unto the *a* of the church of the
5. 2 I saw a strong *a* proclaiming
7. 2 another *a* ascending from the east,
8. 3 *a* came and stood at the altar,
5 the *a* took the censer, and filled it
7 The first *a* sounded, and there
8 the second *a* sounded, and as it
10 the third *a* sounded, and there fell
12 the fourth *a* sounded, and the
13 an *a* flying through the midst
9. 1 the fifth *a* sounded, and I saw
11 which is the *a* of the bottomless pit,
13 and the sixth *a* sounded,
14 saying to the sixth *a* which had the
10. 1 And I saw another mighty *a* come
5 *a* which I saw stand upon the sea
7 of the voice of the seventh *a*,
8 open in the hand of the *a*
9 I went unto the *a*, and said unto
11. 1 and the *a* stood, saying, Rise,
15 and the seventh *a* sounded;
14. 6 I saw another *a* fly in the midst
8 and there followed another *a*,
9 the third *a* followed them,
15, 17 *a* came out of the temple
18 another *a* came out from the altar,
19 *a* thrust in his sickle into the earth,
16. 3 the second *a* poured out his vial
4 the third *a* poured out his vial
5 I heard the *a* of the waters say,
8 the fourth *a* poured out his vial
10 the fifth *a* poured out his vial
12 the sixth *a* poured out his vial
17 the seventh *a* poured out his vial
17. 7 and the *a* said unto me,
18. 1 I saw another *a* come down from
21 a mighty *a* took up a stone
19.17 I saw an *a* standing in the sun;
20. 1 and I saw an *a* come down
21.17 measure of a man, that is, of the *a*.

Hagar, Ishmael, and the Angel in the Wilderness, *by Pietro da Cortona (1596-1669). Biblical angels were messengers of God, typically appearing in the form of young men; later tradition gave them wings.*

Rev 22. 6 his *a* to shew unto his servants
8 before the feet of the *a*
16 have sent mine *a* to testify unto

ANGEL'S

Rev 8. 4 before God out of the *a* hand.
10.10 the little book out of the *a* hand,

ANGELS

Gen 19. 1 there came two *a* to Sodom
15 then the *a* hastened Lot,
28.12 the *a* of God ascending
32. 1 way, and the *a* of God met him.
Job 4.18 and his *a* he charged with folly:
Ps 8. 5 him a little lower than the *a*,
68.17 thousand, even thousands of *a*:
78.49 by sending evil *a* among them.
91.11 shall give his *a* charge over thee,
103.20 Bless the Lord, ye his *a*,
104. 4 Who maketh his *a* spirits;
148. 2 Praise ye him, all his *a*:
Mt 4. 6 He shall give his *a* charge
11 *a* came and ministered unto him.
13.39 and the reapers are the *a*.
41 Son of man shall send forth his *a*,
49 the *a* shall come forth, and sever
16.27 the glory of his Father with his *a*;
18.10 That in heaven their *a* do always
22.30 are as the *a* of God in heaven.
24.31 And he shall send his *a* with a great
36 no, not the *a* of heaven,
25.31 all the holy *a* with him,
41 prepared for the devil and his *a*:
26.53 more than twelve legions of *a*?
Mk 1.13 and the *a* ministered unto him.
8.38 glory of his Father with the holy *a*.
12.25 are as the *a* which are in heaven.
13.27 then shall he send his *a*,
32 not the *a* which are in heaven,
Lk 2.15 as the *a* were gone away from
4.10 He shall give his *a* charge over thee,
9.26 in his Father's, and of the holy *a*.
12. 8 confess before the *a* of God:
9 denied before the *a* of God.
15.10 in the presence of the *a* of God
16.22 carried by the *a* into Abraham's
20.36 for they are equal unto the *a*;
24.23 had also seen a vision of *a*,
Jn 1.51 the *a* of God ascending and
20.12 seeth two *a* in white sitting, the
Ac 7.53 the law by the disposition of *a*,
Ro 8.38 nor life, nor *a*, nor principalities,
1Co 4. 9 world, and to *a*, and to men.
6. 3 Know ye not that we shall judge *a*?
11.10 on her head because of the *a*.
13. 1 the tongues of men and of *a*,
Gal 3.19 and it was ordained by *a* in the
Col 2.18 humility and worshipping of *a*,
2Th 1. 7 from heaven with his mighty *a*,
1Ti 3.16 in the Spirit, seen of *a*, preached
5.21 Jesus Christ, and the elect *a*,
Heb 1. 4 made so much better than the *a*,
5 unto which of the *a* said he at
6 let all the *a* of God worship him.
7 of the *a* he saith,
7 Who maketh his *a* spirits,
13 to which of the *a* said he at any
2. 2 if the word spoken by *a* was
5 unto the *a* hath he not put in
7 a little lower than the *a*;
9 made a little lower than the *a*
16 not on him the nature of *a*;
12.22 an innumerable company of *a*,
13. 2 some have entertained *a* unawares.
1Pe 1.12 things the *a* desire to look into.
3.22 *a* and authorities and powers being
2Pe 2. 4 spared not the *a* that sinned,
11 Whereas *a*, which are greater
Jude 6 *a* which kept not their first estate,
Rev 1.20 the *a* of the seven churches:
3. 5 my Father, and before his *a*.
5.11 I heard the voice of many *a* round
7. 1 I saw four *a* standing on the four
2 with a loud voice to the four *a*,
11 all the *a* stood round about the
8. 2 I saw the seven *a* which stood
6 *a* which had the seven trumpets
13 the trumpet of the three *a*, which
9.14 Loose the four *a* which are bound
15 and the four *a* were loosed,
12. 7 Michael and his *a* fought against
7 and the dragon fought and his *a*,
9 his *a* were cast out with him.
14.10 in the presence of the holy *a*,
15. 1 seven *a* having the seven last
6 seven *a* came out of the temple,
7 gave unto the seven *a* seven golden
8 of the seven *a* were fulfilled.
16. 1 saying to the seven *a*, Go your
17. 1 one of the seven *a* which had the
21. 9 unto me one of the seven *a* which
12 at the gates twelve *a*,

ANGELS'

Ps 78.25 Man did eat *a* food:

ANGER

Gen 27.45 Until thy brother's *a* turn away
30. 2 Jacob's *a* was kindled against
44.18 thine *a* burn against thy servant:
49. 6 in their *a* they slew a man,
7 Cursed be their *a*, for it was fierce;
Ex 4.14 the *a* of the Lord was kindled
11. 8 out from Pharaoh in a great *a*.
32.19 Moses' *a* waxed hot, and he cast
22 Let not the *a* of my lord wax hot;
Nu 11. 1 heard it; and his *a* was kindled;
10 the *a* of the Lord was kindled
12. 9 *a* of the Lord was kindled against
22.22 God's *a* was kindled because he
27 Balaam's *a* was kindled, and he
24.10 Balak's *a* was kindled against
25. 3 the *a* of the Lord was kindled
4 that the fierce *a* of the Lord may
32.10, 13 the Lord's *a* was kindled
14 to augment yet the fierce *a* of the
Dt 4.25 Lord thy God, to provoke him to *a*:
6.15 lest the *a* of the Lord thy God be
7. 4 will the *a* of the Lord be kindled
9.18 the Lord, to provoke him to *a*.
19 I was afraid of the *a* and hot
13.17 turn from the fierceness of his *a*,
29.20 *a* of the Lord and his jealousy
23 which the Lord overthrew in his *a*,
24 meaneth the heat of this great *a*?
27 the *a* of the Lord was kindled
28 rooted them out of their land in *a*,
31.17 Then my *a* shall be kindled
29 to provoke him to *a* through the
32.16 provoked they him to *a*.
21 they have provoked me to *a* with
21 I will provoke them to *a* with a
22 For a fire is kindled in mine *a*,
Jos 7. 1 the *a* of the Lord was kindled
26 turned from the fierceness of his *a*.
23.16 then shall the *a* of the Lord be
Jdg 2.12 and provoked the Lord to *a*.
14 the *a* of the Lord was hot against
20 And the *a* of the Lord was hot
3. 8 *a* of the Lord was hot against Israel,
6.39 Let not thine *a* be hot against me,
8. 3 their *a* was abated toward him,
9.30 son of Ebed, his *a* was kindled.
10. 7 the *a* of the Lord was hot against
14.19 his *a* was kindled, and he went up
1Sa 11. 6 his *a* was kindled greatly.
17.28 Eliab's *a* was kindled against
20.30 Saul's *a* was kindled against
34 arose from the table in fierce *a*,
2Sa 6. 7 the *a* of the Lord was kindled
12. 5 David's *a* was greatly kindled
24. 1 again the *a* of the Lord was
1Ki 14. 9 images, to provoke me to *a*,
15 groves, provoking the Lord to *a*.
15.30 the Lord God of Israel to *a*.
16. 2 provoke me to *a* with their sins;
7 provoking him to *a* with the work

Biblical Themes

ANGER

The Lord had respect unto Abel and to his offering: but unto Cain and to his offering he had not respect. And Cain was very wroth, and his countenance fell.
Gen 4.4-5

Now therefore, my son . . . arise, flee thou to Laban my brother to Haran; and tarry with him a few days, until thy brother's fury turn away; until thy brother's anger turn away from thee, and he forget that which thou hast done to him: then I will send, and fetch thee from thence: why should I be deprived also of you both in one day?
Gen 27.43-45

And the Lord's anger was kindled against Israel, and he made them wander in the wilderness forty years, until all the generation, that had done evil in the sight of the Lord, was consumed.
Nu 32.13

For wrath killeth the foolish man, and envy slayeth the silly one. Job 5.2

God judgeth the righteous, and God is angry with the wicked every day.
Ps 7.11

The Lord is merciful and gracious, slow to anger, and plenteous in mercy. He will not always chide: neither will he keep his anger for ever. Ps 103.8-9

A soft answer turneth away wrath: but grievous words stir up anger. Pr 15.1

He that is slow to anger is better than the mighty; and he that ruleth his spirit than he that taketh a city. Pr 16.32

Proud and haughty scorner is his name, who dealeth in proud wrath. Pr 21.24

Make no friendship with an angry man; and with a furious man thou shalt not go. Pr 22.24

Surely the churning of milk bringeth forth butter, and the wringing of the nose bringeth forth blood: so the forcing of wrath bringeth forth strife.
Pr 30.33

In a little wrath I hid my face from thee for a moment; but with everlasting kindness will I have mercy on thee.
Isa 54.8

But who may abide the day of his coming? and who shall stand when he appeareth? Mal 3.2

Whosoever is angry with his brother without a cause shall be in danger of the judgment. Mt 5.22

And when the chief priests and scribes saw the wonderful things that he did, and the children crying in the temple, and saying, Hosanna to the son of David; they were sore displeased.
Mt 21.15

When the king heard thereof, he was wroth: and he sent forth his armies, and destroyed those murderers, and burned up their city. Then saith he to his servants, The wedding is ready, but they which were bidden were not worthy. Go ye therefore into the highways, and as many as ye shall find, bid to the marriage. Mt 22.7-9

Then said he to the multitude that came forth to be baptized of him, O generation of vipers, who hath warned you to flee from the wrath to come? Lk 3.7

And he went into the temple, and began to cast out them that sold therein, and them that bought; saying unto them, It is written, My house is the house of prayer: but ye have made it a den of thieves. Lk 19.45-46

And the high priest Ananias commanded them that stood by him to smite him on the mouth. Then said Paul unto him, God shall smite thee, thou whited wall: for sittest thou to judge me after the law, and commandest me to be smitten contrary to the law? Ac 23.2-3

Be ye angry, and sin not: let not the sun go down upon your wrath. Eph 4.26

Let every man be swift to hear, slow to speak, slow to wrath. Jas 1.19

13 the Lord God of Israel to *a*
26 provoke the Lord God of Israel to *a*
33 Israel to *a* than all the kings of
21.22 thou hast provoked me to *a*,
22.53 and provoked to *a* the Lord God
2Ki 13. 3 the *a* of the Lord was kindled
17.11 things to provoke the Lord to *a*:
17 the Lord, to provoke him to *a*.
21. 6 to provoke him to *a*.
15 provoked me to *a*, since the day
22.17 that they might provoke me to *a*

23.19 made to provoke the Lord to *a*,
26 wherewith his *a* was kindled
24.20 through the *a* of the Lord it came
1Ch 13.10 the *a* of the Lord was kindled
2Ch 25.10 wherefore their *a* was greatly
10 they returned home in great *a*.
15 the *a* of the Lord was kindled
28.25 and provoked to *a* the Lord God
33. 6 to provoke him to *a*.
34.25 that they might provoke me to *a*
Neh 4. 5 they have provoked thee to *a*

9.17 merciful, slow to *a*, and of great
Est 1.12 and his *a* burned in him.
Job 9. 5 which overturneth them in his *a*.
13 God will not withdraw his *a*,
18. 4 He teareth himself in his *a*:
21.17 God distributeth sorrows in his *a*.
35.15 is not so, he hath visited in his *a*;
Ps 6. 1 O Lord, rebuke me not in thine *a*,
7. 6 Arise, O Lord, in thine *a*, lift up
21. 9 fiery oven in the time of thine *a*:
27. 9 put not thy servant away in *a*:
30. 5 his *a* endureth but a moment;
37. 8 Cease from *a*, and forsake wrath:
38. 3 in my flesh because of thine *a*;
56. 7 in thine *a* cast down the people,
69.24 let thy wrathful *a* take hold of
74. 1 doth thine *a* smoke against the
77. 9 in *a* shut up his tender mercies?
78.21 *a* also came up against Israel;
38 many a time turned he his *a* away,
49 upon them the fierceness of his *a*,
50 He made a way to his *a*;
58 For they provoked him to *a* with
85. 3 from the fierceness of thine *a*.
4 cause thine *a* toward us to cease.
5 out thine *a* to all generations?
90. 7 we are consumed by thine *a*,
11 Who knoweth the power of thine *a*?
103. 8 gracious, slow to *a*, and plenteous
103. 9 neither will he keep his *a* for ever.
106.29 Thus they provoked him to *a*
145. 8 slow to *a*, and of great mercy.
Pr 15. 1 grievous words stir up *a*.
18 that is slow to *a* appeaseth strife.
16.32 slow to *a* is better than the mighty,
19.11 discretion of a man deferreth his *a*;
20. 2 whoso provoketh him to *a* sinneth
21.14 A gift in secret pacifieth *a*:
22. 8 the rod of his *a* shall fail.
27. 4 is cruel, and *a* is outrageous;
Ec 7. 9 *a* resteth in the bosom of fools.
Isa 1. 4 the Holy One of Israel unto *a*,
5.25 the *a* of the Lord kindled against
25 all this his *a* is not turned away,
7. 4 the fierce *a* of Rezin with Syria,
9.12 all this his *a* is not turned away,
17 his *a* is not turned away, but his
21 against Judah. For all this his *a*
10. 4 under the slain. For all this his *a*
5 O Assyrian, the rod of mine *a*,
25 and mine *a* in their destruction.
12. 1 thine *a* is turned away, and thou
13. 3 called my mighty ones for mine *a*,
9 both with wrath and fierce *a*,
13 in the day of his fierce *a*.
14. 6 he that ruled the nations in *a*,
30.27 from far burning with his *a*,
30 with the indignation of his *a*,
42.25 poured upon him the fury of his *a*,
48. 9 name's sake will I defer mine *a*,
63. 3 for I will tread them in mine *a*,
6 tread down the people in mine *a*,
65. 3 A people that provoketh me to *a*
66.15 to render his *a* with fury, and his
Jer 2.35 surely his *a* shall turn from me.
3. 5 Will he reserve his *a* forever?
12 not cause mine *a* to fall upon you:
12 and I will not keep *a* forever.
4. 8 for the fierce *a* of the Lord is not
26 presence of the Lord by his fierce *a*.
7.18 that they may provoke me to *a*.
19 Do they provoke me to *a*?
20 mine *a* and my fury shall be poured
8.19 Why have they provoked me to *a*
10.24 not in thine *a*, lest thou bring me
11.17 to provoke me to *a* in offering
12.13 because of the fierce *a* of the Lord.
15.14 for a fire is kindled in mine *a*,
17. 4 have kindled a fire in mine *a*,
18.23 with them in the time of thine *a*.
21. 5 *a*, and in fury, and in great wrath.

Jer 23.20 The *a* of the Lord shall not return,
25. 6 provoke me not to *a* with the
7 that ye might provoke me to *a*
37 because of the fierce *a* of the Lord.
38 because of his fierce *a*.
30.24 *a* of the Lord shall not return,
32.29 other gods, to provoke me to *a*.
30 provoked me to *a* with the work .
31 to me as a provocation of mine *a*
32 provoke me to *a*, they, their kings.
37 I have driven them in mine *a*,
33. 5 whom I have slain in mine *a*
36. 7 for great is the *a* and the fury
42.18 As mine *a* and my fury hath been
44. 3 provoke me to *a*, in that they
6 and mine *a* was poured forth,
49.37 evil upon them, even my fierce *a*,
51.45 from the fierce *a* of the Lord.
52. 3 through the *a* of the Lord it came
La 1.12 me in the day of his fierce *a*.
2. 1 with a cloud in his *a*,
1 his footstool in the day of his *a*!
3 He hath cut off in his fierce *a*
6 of his *a* the king and the priest.
21 slain them in the day of thine *a*;
22 day of the Lord's *a* none escaped
3.43 covered with *a*, and persecuted us:
66 Persecute and destroy them in *a*
4.11 he hath poured out his fierce *a*,
16 *a* of the Lord hath divided them;
Eze 5.13 shall mine *a* be accomplished,
15 in *a* and in fury and in furious
7. 3 I will send mine *a* upon thee,
8 accomplish mine *a* upon thee:
8.17 returned to provoke me to *a*:
13.13 overflowing shower in mine *a*,
16.26 whoredoms, to provoke me to *a*.
20. 8 to accomplish my *a* against them
21 to accomplish my *a* against them
22.20 so will I gather you in mine *a*
25.14 in Edom according to mine *a*
35.11 I will even do according to thine *a*,
43. 8 I have consumed them in mine *a*.
Dan 9.16 let thine *a* and thy fury be turned
11.20 neither in *a*, nor in battle.
Hos 8. 5 mine *a* is kindled against them:
11. 9 execute the fierceness of mine *a*,
12.14 provoked him to *a* most bitterly:
13.11 I gave thee a king in mine *a*,
14. 4 for mine *a* is turned away from him.
Joel 2.13 slow to *a*, and of great kindness,
Am 1.11 his *a* did tear perpetually,
Jon 3. 9 turn away from his fierce *a*,
4. 2 slow to *a*, and of great kindness,
Mic 5.15 I will execute vengeance in *a*
7.18 he retaineth not his *a* for ever,
Na 1. 3 The Lord is slow to *a*, and great
6 abide in the fierceness of his *a*?
Hab 3. 8 thine *a* against the rivers?
12 thou didst thresh the heathen in *a*.
Zep 2. 2 before the fierce *a* of the Lord
2 before the day of the Lord's *a* come
3 hid in the day of the Lord's *a*.
3. 8 even all my fierce *a*:
Zec 10. 3 Mine *a* was kindled against the
Mk 3. 5 on them with *a*, being grieved
Ro 10.19 by a foolish nation I will *a* you.
Eph 4.31 and wrath, and *a*, and clamor,
Col 3. 8 put off all these; *a*, wrath, malice,
21 provoke not your children to *a*

ANGERED

Ps 106.32 *a* him also at the waters of strife,

ANGRY

Gen 18.30, 32 Oh let not the Lord be *a*, and
45. 5 grieved, nor *a* with yourselves,
Lev 10.16 was *a* with Eleazar and Ithamar,
Dt 1.37 was *a* with me for your sakes,
4.21 was *a* with me for your sakes,
9. 8 so that the Lord was *a* with you
20 the Lord was very *a* with Aaron
Jdg 18.25 lest *a* fellows run upon thee,
2Sa 19.42 then be ye *a* for this matter?
1Ki 8.46 and thou be *a* with them, and
11. 9 And the Lord was *a* with Solomon,
2Ki 17.18 the Lord was very *a* with Israel,
2Ch 6.36 be *a* with them, and deliver them
Ezr 9.14 wouldest not thou be *a* with us
Neh 5. 6 very *a* when I heard their cry
Ps 2.12 Kiss the Son, lest he be *a*, and
7.11 God is *a* with the wicked every
76. 7 in thy sight when once thou art *a*?
79. 5 wilt thou be *a* for ever? shall thy
80. 4 how long wilt thou be *a* against
85. 5 Wilt thou be *a* with us for ever?
Pr 14.17 that is soon *a* dealeth foolishly:
21.19 a contentious and an *a* woman.
22.24 no friendship with an *a* man;
25.23 so doth an *a* countenance a
29.22 An *a* man stirreth up strife,
Ec 5. 6 should God be *a* at thy voice,
7. 9 Be not hasty in thy spirit to be *a*:
SS 1. 6 my mother's children were *a*
Isa 12. 1 though thou wast *a* with me,
Eze 16.42 be quiet and will be no more *a*.
Dan 2.12 the king was *a* and very furious,
Jon 4. 1 and he was very *a*.
4 Lord, Doest thou well to be *a*?
9 thou well to be *a* for the gourd?
9 I do well to be *a*, even unto death.
Mt 5.22 whosoever is *a* with his brother
Lk 14.21 the master of the house being *a*
15.28 he was *a*, and would not go in:
Jn 7.23 are ye *a* at me, because I have
Eph 4.26 Be ye *a*, and sin not: let not the
Tit 1. 7 not soon *a*, not given to wine,
Rev 11.18 nations were *a*, and thy wrath

ANGUISH

Gen 42.21 we saw the *a* of his soul, when
Ex 6. 9 hearkened not...for *a* of spirit,
Dt 2.25 and be in *a* because of thee.
2Sa 1. 9 *a* is come upon me, because my
Job 7.11 I will speak in the *a* of my spirit;
15.24 and *a* shall make him afraid;
Ps 119.143 Trouble and *a* have taken hold
Pr 1.27 distress and *a* cometh upon you.
Isa 8.22 and darkness, dimness of *a*;
30. 6 the land of trouble and *a*,
Jer 4.31 the *a* as of her that bringeth
6.24 *a* hath taken hold of us,
49.24 *a* and sorrows have taken her,
50.43 *a* took hold of him, and pangs as
Jn 16.21 she remembereth no more the *a*,
Ro 2. 9 and *a*, upon every soul of man
2Co 2. 4 of much affliction and *a* of heart

ANISE

Mt 23.23 tithe of mint, and *a* and cummin,

ANNA

Lk 2.36 there was one *A*, a prophetess,

ANNAS

Lk 3. 2 *A* and Caiaphas being the high
Jn 18.13 led him away to *A* first;
24 *A* had sent him bound unto
Ac 4. 6 *A* the high priest, and Caiaphas,

ANOINT

Ex 28.41 *a* them, and consecrate them,
29. 7 pour it upon his head, and *a* him.
36 and thou shalt *a* it, to sanctify it.
30.26 And thou shalt *a* the tabernacle
30 thou shalt *a* Aaron and his sons,
40. 9 *a* the tabernacle, and all that is
10 *a* the altar of the burnt offering,
11 thou shalt *a* the laver and his foot,
13 the holy garments, and *a* him,
15 And thou shalt *a* them,
15 as thou didst *a* their father,
Lev 16.32 And the priest, whom he shall *a*,
Dt 28.40 shalt not *a* thyself with the oil;
Jdg 9. 8 trees went forth on a time to *a*
15 If in truth ye *a* me king over you,
Ru 3. 3 Wash thyself therefore, and *a*
1Sa 9.16 *a* him to be captain over my
15. 1 The Lord sent me to *a* thee
16. 3 shalt *a* unto me him whom I name
12 the Lord said, Arise, *a* him:
2Sa 14. 2 *a* not thyself with oil,
1Ki 1.34 and Nathan the prophet *a* him
19.15 *a* Hazael to be king over Syria:
16 the son of Nimshi shalt thou *a*
16 Elisha...shalt thou *a* to be prophet
Isa 21. 5 arise, ye princes, and *a* the shield.
Dan 9.24 and to *a* the most Holy.
10. 3 neither did I *a* myself at all,
Am 6. 6 *a* themselves with the chief
Mic 6.15 thou shalt not *a* thee with oil;
Mt 6.17 *a* thine head, and wash thy face;
Mk 14. 8 to *a* my body to the burying.
16. 1 they might come and *a* him.
Lk 7.46 My head with oil thou didst not *a*:
Rev 3.18 *a* thine eyes with eyesalve, that

ANOINTED

Ex 29. 2 wafers unleavened *a* with oil:
29 *a* therein, and to be consecrated
Lev 2. 4 unleavened wafers *a* with oil.
4. 3 If the priest that is *a* do sin
5 And the priest that is *a* shall
16 is *a* shall bring of the bullock's
6.20 the Lord in the day when he is *a*;
22 the priest of his sons that is *a* in
7.12 *a* with oil, and cakes mingled
36 in the day that he *a* them,
8.10 *a* the tabernacle and all that was
11 *a* the altar and all his vessels,
12 and *a* him, to sanctify him.
Nu 3. 3 of Aaron, the priests which were *a*,
6.15 wafers of unleavened bread *a*
7. 1 set up the tabernacle, and had *a* it,
1 vessels thereof, and had *a* them,
10 the altar in the day that it was *a*,
84 it was *a*, by the princes of Israel;
88 of the altar after that it was *a*.
35.25 which was *a* with the holy oil.
1Sa 2.10 and exalt the horn of his *a*,
35 shall walk before mine *a* for ever.
10. 1 Lord hath *a* thee to be captain
12. 3 before the Lord, and before his *a*:
5 his *a* is witness this day,
15.17 the Lord *a* thee king over Israel?
16. 6 Surely the Lord's *a* is before him.
13 *a* him in the midst of his brethren.
24. 6 unto my master, the Lord's *a*,
6 he is the *a* of the Lord.
10 he is the Lord's *a*.
26. 9 his hand against the Lord's *a*,
11 mine hand against the Lord's *a*:
16 kept your master, the Lord's *a*.
23 against the Lord's *a*.
2Sa 1.14 to destroy the Lord's *a*?
16 I have slain the Lord's *a*.
21 as though he had not been *a* with
2. 4 and there they *a* David king
7 house of Judah have *a* me king
3.39 this day weak, though *a* king;
5. 3 they *a* David king over Israel.
17 heard that they had *a* David king
12. 7 I *a* thee king over Israel,
20 earth and washed, and *a* himself,
19.10 Absalom, whom we *a* over us,
21 because he cursed the Lord's *a*?
22.51 sheweth mercy to his *a*,
23. 1 the *a* of the God of Jacob,
1Ki 1.39 the tabernacle, and *a* Solomon.
45 and Nathan...have *a* him king
5. 1 *a* him king in the room of his
2Ki 9. 3 I have *a* thee king over Israel.
6 have *a* thee king over the people

12 Thus saith the Lord, I have *a* thee
11.12 they made him king, and *a* him;
23.30 and *a* him, and made him king
1Ch 11. 3 they *a* David king over Israel,
14. 8 David was *a* king over all Israel,
16.22 Touch not mine *a*, and do my
29.22 and *a* him unto the Lord
2Ch 6.42 turn not away the face of thine *a*:
22. 7 *a* to cut off the house of Ahab.
23.11 Jehoiada and his sons *a* him,
28.15 to eat and to drink, and *a* them,
Ps 2. 2 the Lord, and against his *a*,
18.50 sheweth mercy to his *a*,
20. 6 the Lord saveth his *a*;
28. 8 he is the saving strength of his *a*.
45. 7 thy God, hath *a* thee with the oil
84. 9 look upon the face of thine *a*.
89.20 with my holy oil have I *a* him:
38 hast been wroth with thine *a*.
51 reproached the footsteps of thine *a*.
92.10 I shall be *a* with fresh oil.
105.15 Touch not mine *a*,
132.10 turn not away the face of thine *a*.
17 I have ordained a lamp for mine *a*.
Isa 45. 1 Thus saith the Lord to his *a*,
61. 1 the Lord hath *a* me to preach
La 4.20 *a* of the Lord, was taken in their
Eze 16. 9 and I *a* thee with oil.
28.14 art the *a* cherub that covereth;
Hab 3.13 for salvation with thine *a*;
Zec 4.14 the two *a* ones, that stand
Mk 6.13 *a* with oil many that were sick,
Lk 4.18 hath *a* me to preach the gospel
7.38 *a* them with the ointment.
46 hath *a* my feet with ointment.
Jn 9. 6 *a* the eyes of the blind man
11 made clay and *a* mine eyes,
11. 2 was that Mary which *a* the Lord
12. 3 *a* the feet of Jesus, and wiped
Ac 4.27 child Jesus, whom thou hast *a*,
10.38 How God *a* Jesus of Nazareth
2Co 1.21 and hath *a* us is God.
Heb 1. 9 *a* thee with the oil of gladness

ANOINTEDST
Gen 31.13 Bethel, where thou *a* the pillar,

ANOINTEST
Ps 23. 5 thou *a* my head with oil; my

ANOINTING
Ex 25. 6 spices for *a* oil, and for sweet
29. 7 Then shalt thou take the *a* oil,
21 and of the *a* oil, and sprinkle it
30.25 it shall be an holy *a* oil.
31 This shall be an holy *a* oil unto
31.11 And the *a* oil, and sweet incense
35. 8 the light, and spices for the *a* oil,
15 and his staves, and the *a* oil,
28 and for the *a* oil,
37.29 he made the holy *a* oil,
39.38 the golden altar and the *a* oil,
40. 9 thou shalt take the *a* oil,
15 *a* shall surely be an everlasting
Lev 7.35 is the portion of the *a* of Aaron,
35 and of the *a* of his sons,
8. 2 and the *a* oil, and a bullock for
10 Moses took the *a* oil, and anointed
12 he poured of the *a* oil upon
30 Moses took the *a* oil,
10. 7 the *a* oil of the Lord is upon you.
21.10 whose head the *a* oil was poured,
12 the crown of the *a* oil is of his
Nu 4.16 daily meat offering, and the *a* oil,
18. 8 given them by reason of the *a*,
Isa 10.27 be destroyed because of the *a*.
Jas 5.14 *a* him with oil in the name of the
1Jn 2.27 But the *a* which ye have received
27 same *a* teacheth you of all things,

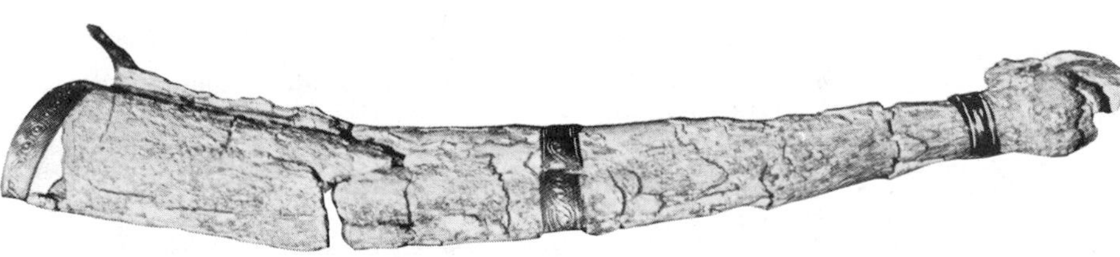

Ancient anointing horn. The large end was sealed tight, and the pointed end had a small hole to drip oil.

ANSWER
Gen 30.33 shall my righteousness *a* for me
41.16 God shall give Pharaoh an *a* of
45. 3 his brethren could not *a* him;
Dt 20.11 if it make thee *a* of peace,
21. 7 And they shall *a* and say,
25. 9 shall *a* and say, So shall it be done
27.15 the people shall *a* and say, Amen.
Jos 4. 7 Then ye shall *a* them, That the
Jdg 5.29 yea, she returned *a* to herself,
1Sa 2.16 then he would *a* him, Nay;
20.10 if thy father *a* thee roughly?
2Sa 3.11 he could not *a* Abner a word
24.13 see what *a* I shall return to him
1Ki 9. 9 And they shall *a*, Because they
12. 6 do ye advise, that I may *a*
7 and wilt serve them, and *a* them,
9 that we may *a* this people,
18.29 neither voice, nor any to *a*,
2Ki 4.29 if any salute thee, *a* him not
18.36 commandment was, saying, *A*
2Ch 10. 6 to return *a* to this people?
9 we may return *a* to this people,
10 Thus shalt thou *a* the people
Ezr 4.17 sent the king an *a* unto Rehum
5. 5 then they returned *a* by letter
11 And thus they returned us *a*,
Neh 5. 8 peace, and found nothing to *a*.
Est 4.13 commanded to *a* Esther,
15 bade them return Mordecai this *a*,
Job 5. 1 if there be any that will *a* thee;
9. 3 cannot *a* him one of a thousand.
14 How much less shall I *a* him,
15 would I not *a*, but I would make
32 I should *a* him, and we should
13.22 Then call thou, and I will *a*:
22 let me speak, and *a* thou me.
14.15 Thou shalt call, and I will *a* thee:
19.16 servant, and he gave me no *a*;
20. 2 do my thoughts cause me to *a*,
3 understanding causeth me to *a*.
23. 5 the words which he would *a* me,
31.14 when he visiteth, what shall I *a*
35 that the Almighty would *a* me,
32. 1 these three men ceased to *a* Job,
3 they had found no *a*, and yet had
5 saw that there was no *a*
14 will I *a* him with your speeches.
17 I said, I will *a* also my part,
20 I will open my lips and *a*.
33. 5 If thou canst *a* me, set thy
12 I will *a* thee, that God is greater
32 If thou hast any thing to say, *a*
35. 4 I will *a* thee and thy
12 there they cry, but none giveth *a*,
38. 3 demand of thee, and *a* thou me.
40. 2 he that reproveth God, let him *a*
4 vile; what shall I *a* thee?
5 have I spoken; but I will not *a*:
Ps 27. 7 mercy also upon me, and *a* me.
65. 5 wilt thou *a* us, O God
86. 7 call upon thee: for thou wilt *a* me.
91.15 call upon me, and I will *a* him:
102. 2 the day when I call *a* me speedily.
108. 6 with thy right hand, and *a* me.
119.42 to *a* him that reproacheth me:
143. 1 in thy faithfulness *a* me, and in
Pr 1.28 call upon me, but I will not *a*;
15. 1 A soft *a* turneth away wrath:
23 hath joy by the *a* of his mouth:
28 of the righteous studieth to *a*:
16. 1 *a* of the tongue, is from the Lord
22.21 mightest *a* the words of truth
24.26 his lips that giveth a right *a*.
26. 4 *A* not a fool according to his
5 *A* a fool according to his folly,
27.11 *a* him that reproacheth me.
29.19 he understand he will not *a*.
SS 5. 6 called him, but he gave me no *a*
Isa 14.32 shall one then *a* the messengers
30.19 he shall hear it, he will *a* thee.
36.21 was, saying, *A* him not.
41.28 I asked of them, could *a*
46. 7 yet can he not *a*, nor save him
50. 2 I called, was there none to *a*?
58. 9 thou call, and the Lord shall *a*;
65.12 when I called, ye did not *a*;
24 before they call, I will *a*;
66. 4 when I called, none did *a*;
Jer 5.19 then shalt thou *a* them, Like as
7.27 they will not *a* thee.
22. 9 Then they shall *a*, Because they
33. 3 Call unto me, and I will *a* thee,
42. 4 the Lord shall *a* you,
44.20 which had given him that *a*,
Eze 14. 4 I the Lord will *a* him that cometh
7 I the Lord will *a* him by myself:
21. 7 thou shalt *a*, For the tidings;
Dan 3.16 careful to *a* thee in this matter,
Joel 2.19 Yea, the Lord will *a* and say
Mic 3. 7 for there is no *a* of God.
Hab 2. 1 what I shall *a* when I am
11 beam out of the timber shall *a*
Zec 13. 6 Then he shall *a*, Those with
Mt 22.46 no man was able to *a* him a word,
25.37 Then shall the righteous *a* him,
40 King shall *a* and say unto them,
44 Then shall they also *a* him,
45 Then shall he *a* them,
Mk 11.29 ask of you one question, and *a* me,
30 from heaven, or of men? *a* me.
14.40 wist they what to *a* him.
Lk 11. 7 shall *a* and say, Trouble me not:
12.11 how or what thing ye shall *a*,
13.25 he shall *a* and say unto you,
14. 6 could not *a* him again to these
20. 3 ask you one thing; and *a* me:
26 they marvelled at his *a*, and held
21.14 meditate before what ye shall *a*:
22.68 ye will not *a* me, nor let me go.
Jn 1.22 give an *a* to them that sent us.
19. 9 Jesus gave him no *a*.
Ac 24.10 more cheerfully *a* for myself:
25.16 have license to *a* for himself
26. 2 *a* for myself this day before thee
Ro 11. 4 what saith the *a* of God unto him?
1Co 9. 3 *a* to them that do examine me
2Co 5.12 somewhat to *a* them which glory
Col 4. 6 how ye ought to *a* every man.
2Ti 4.16 first *a* no man stood with me,
1Pe 3.15 *a* to every man that asketh you
21 *a* of a good conscience toward

ANSWERABLE
Ex 38.18 *a* to the hangings of the court.

ANSWERED

Gen 18.27 And Abraham *a* and said,
23. 5 the children of Heth *a* Abraham,
10 and Ephron the Hittite *a* Abraham
14 and Ephron *a* Abraham, saying
24.50 Laban and Bethuel *a* and said,
27.37 And Isaac *a* and said unto Esau,
39 And Isaac his father *a* and said
31.14 And Rachel and Leah *a* and said
31, 36 Jacob *a* and said to Laban,
43 And Laban *a* and said unto Jacob,
34.13 And the sons of Jacob *a* Shechem
35. 3 unto God, who *a* me in the day of
40.18 And Joseph *a* and said, This is
41.16 And Joseph *a* Pharaoh, saying,
42.22 And Reuben *a* them, saying,
43.28 they *a*, Thy servant our father is
Ex 4. 1 Moses *a* and said, But, behold,
15.21 And Miriam *a* them,
19. 8 And all the people *a* together,
19 and God *a* him by a voice.
24. 3 and all the people *a* with one voice,
Nu 11.28 And Joshua the son of Nun,...*a*
22.18 And Balaam *a* and said unto the
23.12 and he *a* and said,
26 But Balaam *a* and said unto Balak,
32.31 And the children of Gad...*a*,
Dt 1.14 And ye *a* me, and said,
41 Then ye *a* and said unto me,
Jos 1.16 And they *a* Joshua, saying,
2.14 men *a* her, Our life for yours,
7.20 And Achan *a* Joshua,
9.24 And they *a* Joshua,
15.19 Who *a*, Give me a blessing;
17.15 Joshua *a* them, If thou be a great
22.21 the half tribe of Manasseh *a*,
24.16 the people *a* and said, God forbid
Jdg 5.29 Her wise ladies *a* her,
7.14 And his fellow *a* and said,
8. 8 and the men of Penuel *a* him
8 as the men of Succoth had *a* him.
18 they *a*, As thou art, so were they;
25 they *a*, We will willingly give them.
11.13 of Ammon *a* unto the messengers
15. 6 they *a*, Samson, the son in law
10 And they *a*, To bind Samson
18.14 *a* the five men that went to spy
19.28 and let us be going. But none *a*.
20. 4 And the Levite...*a* and said,
Ru 2. 4 they *a* him, The Lord bless thee.
6 And the servant...*a* and said,
11 And Boaz *a* and said unto her,
3. 9 she *a*, I am Ruth thine handmaid;
1Sa 1.15 Hannah *a* and said, No, my lord,
17 Then Eli *a* and said, Go in peace:
3. 4 and he *a*, Here am I.
6 And he *a*, I called not, my son;
10 Then Samuel *a*, Speak; for thy
16 And he *a*, Here am I.
4.17 And the messenger *a* and said,
20 she *a* not, neither did she regard it.
5. 8 And they *a*, Let the ark of the God
6. 4 They *a*, Five golden emerods,
9. 8 the servant *a* Saul again,
12 and they *a* them, and said,
19 And Samuel *a* Saul, and said,
21 And Saul *a*, and said,
10.12 And one of the same place *a*
22 the Lord *a*, Behold, he hath hid
11. 2 Nahash the Ammonite *a* them,
12. 5 And they *a*, He is witness.
14.12 men of the garrison *a* Jonathan
28 Then *a* one of the people,
37 he *a* him not that day.
39 among all the people that *a* him.
44 Saul *a*, God do so and more:
16.18 Then *a* one of the servants,
17.27 people *a* him after this manner,
30 the people *a* him again after
58 David *a*, I am the son of thy servant
18. 7 the women *a* one another as
19.17 Michal *a* Saul, He said unto me,
20.28 And Jonathan *a* Saul, David
32 And Jonathan *a* Saul his father,
21. 4 And the priest *a* David,
5 And David *a* the priest,
22. 9 Then *a* Doeg the Edomite,
12 And he *a*, Here I am, my lord.
14 Then Ahimelech *a* the king,
23. 4 the Lord *a* him and said, Arise,
25.10 And Nabal *a* David's servants,
26. 6 *a* David and said to Ahimelech
14 Abner *a* and said, Who art thou
22 David *a* and said, Behold the king's
28. 6 the Lord *a* him not, neither by
15 Saul *a*, I am sore distressed;
29. 9 And Achish *a* and said to David,
30. 8 And he *a* him, Pursue:
22 Then *a* all the wicked men
2Sa 1. 4 And he *a*, That the people are fled
7 And I *a*, Here am I.
8 I *a* him, I am an Amalekite.
13 he *a*, I am the son of a stranger,
2.20 Art thou Ashel? And he *a*, I am.
4. 9 David *a* Rechab and Baanah his
9. 6 And he *a*, Behold thy servant!
13.12 she *a* him, Nay, my brother,
32 And Jonadab,...David's brother, *a*
14. 5 she *a*, I am indeed a widow woman,
18 king *a* and said unto the woman,
19 And the woman *a* and said,
32 Absalom *a* Joab, Behold, I sent
15.21 And Ittai *a* the king, and said,
18. 3 people *a*, Thou shalt not go
29 And Ahimaaz *a*, When Joab sent
32 Cushi *a*, The enemies of my lord
19.21 But Abishai the son of Zeruiah *a*
26 he *a*, My lord, O king, my servant
38 the king *a*, Chimham shall go over
42 men of Judah *a* the men of Israel,
43 men of Israel *a* the men of Judah,
20.17 he *a*, I am he. Then she said
17 And he *a*, I do hear.
20 And Joab *a* and said, Far be it,
21. 1 And the Lord *a*, It is for Saul,
5 And they *a* the king, The man
22.42 the Lord, but he *a* them not.
1Ki 1.28 Then king David *a* and said,
36 And Benaiah...*a* the king,
43 Jonathan *a* and said to Adonijah,
2.22 And king Solomon *a* and said
30 Thus said Joab, and thus he *a* me.
3.27 Then the king *a* and said,
11.22 he *a*, Nothing: howbeit let me go
12.13 the king *a* the people roughly,
16 people *a* the king, saying,
13. 6 king *a* and said unto the man of
18. 8 And he *a* him, I am:
18 he *a*, I have not troubled Israel;
21 the people *a* him not a word.
24 people *a* and said, It is well spoken.
26 was no voice, nor any that *a*.
20. 4 And the king of Israel *a* and
11 *a* and said, Tell him, Let not him
14 And he *a*, Thou.
21. 6 *a*, I will not give thee my vineyard.
20 And he *a*, I have found thee:
22.15 he *a* him, Go, and prosper:
2Ki 1. 8 they *a* him, He was a hairy man,
10 Elijah *a* and said to the captain
11 And he *a* and said unto him,
12 And Elijah *a* and said unto them,
2. 5 And he *a*, Yea, I know it; hold
3. 8 *a*, The way through the wilderness
11 of the king of Israel's servants *a*
4.13 she *a*, I dwell among mine own
14 Gehazi *a*, Verily she hath no child,
26 the child? And she *a*, It is well.
6. 2 And he *a*, Go ye.
3 thy servants. And he *a*, I will go.
16 And he *a*, Fear not: for they that
22 he *a*, Thou shalt not smite them:
28 she *a*, This woman said unto me,
7. 2 king leaned *a* the man of God,
13 one of his servants *a* and said,
19 And that lord *a* the man of God,
8.12 he *a*, Because I know the evil
13 Elisha *a*, The Lord hath shewed
14 And he *a*, He told me that thou
9.19 And Jehu *a*, What hast thou to do
22 And he *a*, What peace, so long as
10.13 And they *a*, We are the brethren
15 And Jehonadab *a*, It is. If it be,
18.36 and *a* him not a word:
20.10 Hezekiah *a*, It is a light thing
15 And Hezekiah *a*, All the things
1Ch 12.17 David went out...and *a* and
21. 3 And Joab *a*, The Lord make his
26 he *a* him from heaven by fire
28 the Lord had answered him in
2Ch 2.11 the king of Tyre *a* in writing,
7.22 And it shall be *a*, Because they
10.13 And the king *a* them roughly;
14 And *a* them after the advice of
16 when...the people *a* the king,
18. 3 And he *a* him, I am as thou art,
25. 9 the man of God *a*, The Lord is able
29.31 Then Hezekiah *a* and said,
31.10 priest of the house of Zadok *a*
34.15 Hilkiah *a* and said to Shaphan
23 she *a* them, Thus saith the Lord
Ezr 10. 2 sons of Elam, *a* and said unto
12 all the congregation *a* and said
Neh 2.20 Then *a* I them, and said unto
6. 4 I *a* them after the same manner.
8. 6 all the people *a*, Amen, Amen.
Est 1.16 And Memucan *a* before the king
5. 4 Esther *a*, If it seem good unto
7 Then *a* Esther, and said, My
6. 7 And Haman *a* the king, For the
7. 3 Esther the queen *a* and said,
5 the king Ahasuerus *a* and said
Job 1. 7, 9 Satan *a* the Lord and said,
2. 2, 4 Satan *a* the Lord, and said,
4. 1 Eliphaz the Temanite *a* and said,
6. 1 But Job *a* and said,
8. 1 Then *a* Bildad the Shuhite,
9. 1 Then Job *a* and said,
16 If I had called, and he had *a* me;
11. 1 *a* Zophar the Naamathite,
2 not the multitude of words be *a*?
12. 1 And Job *a* and said,
15. 1 Then *a* Eliphaz the Temanite,
16. 1 Then Job *a* and said,
18. 1 Then *a* Bildad the Shuhite,
19. 1 Then Job *a* and said,
20. 1 Then *a* Zophar the Naamathite,
21. 1 But Job *a* and said,
22. 1 Then Eliphaz the Temanite *a*
23. 1 Then Job *a* and said,
25. 1 Then *a* Bildad the Shuhite,
26. 1 But Job *a* and said,
32. 6 the son of Barachel the Buzite *a*
12 convinced Job, or that *a* his words:
15 were amazed they *a* no more:
16 stood still, and *a* no more,
34. 1 Furthermore Elihu *a* and said,
38. 1 Lord *a* Job out of the whirlwind,
40. 1 Moreover the Lord *a* Job,
3 Then Job *a* the Lord, and said,
6 Then *a* the Lord unto Job
42. 1 Then Job *a* the Lord,
Ps 18.41 the Lord, but he *a* them not.
81. 7 I *a* thee in the secret place of
99. 6 upon the Lord, and he *a* them.
118. 5 Lord *a* me, and set me in a large
Isa 6.11 And he *a*, Until the cities
21. 9 he *a* and said, Babylon is fallen,
36.21 peace, and *a* him not a word:
39. 4 Hezekiah *a*, All that is in mine
Jer 7.13 I called you, but ye *a* not;
11. 5 Then *a* I, and said, so be it, O Lord.
23.35 What hath the Lord *a*?

37 What hath the Lord *a* thee?
35.17 unto them, but they have not *a*.
36.18 Then Baruch *a* them,
44.15 all the men...*a* Jeremiah,
Eze 24.20 I *a* them, The word of the Lord
37. 3 I *a*, O Lord God, thou knowest.
Dan 2. 5 king *a* and said to the Chaldeans,
7 *a* again and said, Let the king tell
8 *a* and said, I know of certainty
10 Chaldeans *a* before the king, and
14 *a* with counsel and wisdom to
15 He *a* and said to Arioch
20 Daniel *a* and said, Blessed be the
26 The king *a* and said to Daniel,
27 *a* in the presence of the king,
47 The king *a* unto Daniel,
3.16 *a* and said to the king,
24 They *a* and said unto the king,
25 He *a* and said, Lo, I see four men
4.19 Belteshazzar *a* and said, My lord,
5.17 Daniel *a* and said before the king,
6.12 king *a* and said, The thing is true,
Am 7.14 *a* Amos, and said to Amaziah,
Mic 6. 5 Balaam the son of Beor *a* him,
Hab 2. 2 And the Lord *a* me, and said,
Hag 2.12 And the priests *a* and said, No.
13 the priests *a* and said, It shall be
14 Then *a* Haggai, and said,
Zec 1.10 the man that stood...*a* and said,
11 And they *a* the angel of the Lord
12 Then the angel of the Lord *a*
13 And the Lord *a* the angel
19 And he *a* me, These are the horns
3. 4 And he *a* and spake
4. 4 So I *a* and spake to the angel
5 the angel that talked with me *a*
6 Then he *a* and spake unto me,
11 Then *a* I, and said unto him,
12 And I *a* again, and said unto him,
13 And he *a* me and said,
5. 2 And I *a*, I see a flying roll;
6. 4 Then I *a* and said unto the angel
5 the angel *a* and said unto me,
Mt 4. 4 he *a* and said, It is written,
8. 8 The centurion *a* and said, Lord,
11. 4 Jesus *a* and said unto them,
25 At that time Jesus *a* and said,
12.38 scribes and of the Pharisees *a*,
39 he *a* and said unto them,
48 he *a* and said unto him that told
13.11, 37 He *a* and said unto them,
14.28 Peter *a* him and said, Lord,
15. 3 he *a* and said unto them,
13 he *a* and said, Every plant,
15 Then *a* Peter and said unto him,
23 he *a* her not a word.
24 he *a* and said, I am not sent
26 he *a* and said, It is not meet
28 Then Jesus *a* and said unto her,
16. 2 He *a* and said unto them,
16 Simon Peter *a* and said,
17 Jesus *a* and said unto him,
17. 4 Then *a* Peter, and said unto
11 Jesus *a* and said unto them,
17 Then Jesus *a* and said, O faithless
19. 4 he *a* and said unto them,
27 Then *a* Peter and said unto him,
20.13 he *a* one of them, and said,
22 Jesus *a* and said, Ye know
21.21, 24 Jesus *a* and said unto them,
27 they *a* Jesus, and said, We cannot
29 He *a* and said, I will not:
30 he *a* and said, I go, sir:
22. 1 Jesus *a* and spake unto them again
29 Jesus *a* and said unto them,
24. 4 Jesus *a* and said unto them,
25. 9 the wise *a*, saying, Not so;
12 he *a* and said, Verily I say unto
26 His lord *a* and said unto him,
26.23 he *a* and said, He that dippeth his
25 which betrayed him, *a* and said,
33 Peter *a* and said unto him,
63 the high priest *a* and said unto
66 *a* and said, He is guilty of death.
27.12 priests and elders, he *a* nothing.
14 he *a* him to never a word;
21 The governor *a* and said unto them,
25 Then *a* all the people, and said,
28. 5 the angel *a* and said unto the
Mk 3.33 he *a* them, saying, Who is my
5. 9 he *a*, saying, My name is Legion:
6.37 He *a* and said unto them,
7. 6 He *a* and said unto them,
28 she *a* and said unto him,
8. 4 his disciples *a* him,
28 they *a*, John the Baptist:
9. 5 Peter *a* and said to Jesus,
12 he *a* and told them, Elias verily
17 one of the multitude *a* and said,
38 John *a* him, saying, Master,
10. 3 he *a* and said unto them,
5 Jesus *a* and said unto them,
20 he *a* and said unto him, Master,
29 Jesus *a* and said, Verily I say
51 Jesus *a* and said unto him,
11.14 Jesus *a* and said unto it,
29 Jesus *a* and said unto them,
33 they *a* and said unto Jesus, We
12.28 perceiving that he had *a* them well,
29 Jesus *a* him, The first of all the
34 saw that he *a* discreetly,
35 Jesus *a* and said, while he taught
14.20 he *a* and said unto them,
48 Jesus *a* and said unto them,
61 held his peace and *a* nothing.
15. 3 many things: but he *a* nothing.
5 Jesus yet *a* nothing; so that Pilate
9 Pilate *a* them, saying,
12 Pilate *a* and said again unto them
Lk 1.35 the angel *a* and said unto her,
60 his mother *a* and said,
3.16 John *a*, saying unto them all,
4. 4 Jesus *a* him, saying,
8 Jesus *a* and said unto him,
7.43 Simon *a* and said, I suppose that
8.21 he *a* and said unto them,
50 he *a* him, saying, Fear not:
9.49 John *a* and said, Master, we saw
10.28 unto him, Thou hast *a* right:
41 Jesus *a* and said unto her,
11.45 Then *a* one of the lawyers, and
13.14 the ruler of the synagogue *a*
15 The Lord then *a* him, and said,
14. 5 *a* them, saying, Which of you
17.20 he *a* them and said,
37 they *a* and said unto him,
19.40 he *a* and said unto them,
20. 3 he *a* and said unto them,
7 they *a*, that they could not tell
24 They *a* and said, Caesar's.
22.51 Jesus *a* and said, Suffer ye thus
23. 3 he *a* him and said, Thou sayest it.
9 he *a* him nothing.
Jn 1.21 thou that prophet? And he *a*, No.
26 John *a* them, saying, I baptize
48 Jesus *a* and said unto him,
49 Nathanael *a* and saith
50 Jesus *a* and said unto him,
2.18 Then *a* the Jews and said
19 Jesus *a* and said unto them,
3. 3 Jesus *a* and said unto him,
5 Jesus *a*, Verily, verily,
9 Nicodemus *a* and said
10 Jesus *a* and said unto him, Art
27 John *a* and said, A man can
4.10, 13 Jesus *a* and said unto her,
17 *a* and said, I have no husband.
5. 7 The impotent man *a*
11 He *a* them, He that made me
17 Jesus *a* them, My Father worketh
19 Then *a* Jesus and said unto them,
6. 7 Philip *a* him, Two hundred
26 Jesus *a* them and said,
29 Jesus *a* and said unto them,
43 Jesus therefore *a* and said
68 Then Simon Peter *a* him,
70 Jesus *a* them, Have not I chosen
7.16 Jesus *a* them, and said,
20 The people *a* and said,
21 Jesus *a* and said unto them,
46 The officers *a*, Never man
47 Then *a* them the Pharisees,
52 They *a* and said unto him,
8.14 Jesus *a* and said unto them,
19 Jesus *a*, Ye neither know me,
33 *a* him, We be Abraham's seed,
34 Jesus *a* them, Verily,
39 They *a* and said unto him,
48 Then *a* the Jews, and said
49 Jesus *a*, I have not a devil;
54 Jesus *a*, If I honor myself, my
9. 3 Jesus *a*, Neither hath this man
11 He *a* and said, A man that is
20 His parents *a* them
25 He *a* and said, Whether he be a
27 He *a* them, I have told
30 The man *a* and said unto them,
34 They *a* and said unto him,
36 He *a* and said, Who is he,
10.25 Jesus *a* them, I told you, and ye
32 Jesus *a* them, Many good works
33 The Jews *a* him, saying,
34 Jesus *a* them, Is it not
11. 9 Jesus *a*, Are there not twelve
12.23 Jesus *a* them, saying,
30 Jesus *a* and said, This voice
34 The people *a* him, We have heard
13. 7 Jesus *a* and said unto him,
8 Jesus *a* him, If I wash thee not,
26 Jesus *a*, He it is, to whom
36 Jesus *a* him, Whither I go,
38 Jesus *a* him, Wilt thou lay
14.23 Jesus *a* and said unto him,
16.31 Jesus *a* them, Do ye now believe?
18. 5 They *a* him, Jesus of Nazareth.
8 Jesus *a*, I have told you that I am
20 Jesus *a* him, I spake openly to
23 Jesus *a* him, If I have spoken evil,
30 They *a* and said unto him,
34 Jesus *a* him, Sayest thou this
35 Pilate *a*, Am I a Jew?
36 Jesus *a*, My kingdom is not of
37 Jesus *a*, Thou sayest that I am
19. 7 The Jews *a* him, We have a law,
11 Jesus *a*, Thou couldest have no
15 chief priests *a*, We have no king
22 Pilate *a*, What I have written,
20.28 Thomas *a* and said unto
21. 5 They *a* him, No.
Ac 3.12 he *a* unto the people, ye men of
4.19 Peter and John *a* and said unto
5. 8 Peter *a* unto her, Tell me
29 and the other apostles *a* and said,
8.24 Then *a* Simon, and said, Pray ye,
34 the eunuch *a* Philip, and said,
37 he *a* and said, I believe
9.13 Ananias *a*, Lord, I have heard
10.46 magnify God. Then *a* Peter,
11. 9 the voice *a* me again from heaven,
15.13 James *a*, saying, Men,
19.15 the evil spirit *a* and said,
21.13 Then Paul *a*, What mean ye to
22. 8 I *a*, Who art thou, Lord?
28 chief captain *a*, With a great sum
24.10 answered, Forasmuch as I know
25 trembled, and *a*, Go thy way
25. 4 Festus *a*, that Paul should be
8 While he *a* for himself,
9 *a* Paul, and said, Wilt thou go up
12 *a*, Hast thou appealed unto
16 whom I *a*, It is not the manner
26. 1 the hand, and *a* for himself:
Rev 7.13 one of the elders *a*, saying unto

ANSWEREDST
Ps 99. 8 Thou *a* them, O Lord our God:
138. 3 the day when I cried thou *a* me,

ANSWEREST
1Sa 26.14 *A* thou not, Abner?
Job 16. 3 emboldeneth thee that thou *a*?
Mt 26.62 unto him, *A* thou nothing?
Mk 14.60 saying, *A* thou nothing?
15. 4 him, saying, *a* thou nothing?
Jn 18.22 *A* thou the high priest so?

ANSWERETH
1Sa 28.15 and *a* me no more, neither by
1Ki 18.24 the God that *a* by fire, let him
Job 12. 4 upon God, and he *a* him:
Pr 18.13 He that *a* a matter before
23 intreaties; but the rich *a* roughly.
27.19 As in water, face *a* to face, so
Ec 5.20 God *a* him in the joy of his
10.19 but money *a* all things.
Mk 8.29 And Peter *a* and saith unto
9.19 He *a* him, and saith, O faithless
10.24 But Jesus *a* again, and saith unto
Lk 3.11 He *a* and saith unto them,
Gal 4.25 and *a* to Jerusalem which now is,

ANSWERING
Mt 3.15 Jesus *a* said unto him,
Mk 11.22 And Jesus *a* saith unto them,
33 Jesus *a* saith unto them,
12.17 Jesus *a* said unto them,
24 Jesus *a* said unto them,
13. 2 Jesus *a* said unto him,
5 Jesus *a* them, began to say,
15. 2 he *a* said unto him, Thou sayest it.
Lk 1.19 the angel *a* said unto him,
4.12 Jesus *a* said unto him,
5. 5 Simon *a* said unto him, Master,
22 *a* said unto them, What reason
31 Jesus *a* said unto them,
6. 3 Jesus *a* them said, Have ye not
7.22 Then Jesus *a* said unto
40 Jesus *a* said unto him,
9.19 They *a* said, John the Baptist;
20 Peter *a* said, The Christ of God.
41 Jesus *a* said, O faithless
10.27 he *a* said, Thou shalt love the
30 And Jesus *a* said, A certain man
13. 2 Jesus *a* said unto them,
8 he *a* said unto him, Lord,
14. 3 Jesus *a* spake unto the lawyers
15.29 he *a* said to his father,
17.17 Jesus *a* said, Were there not ten
20.34 Jesus *a* said unto them,
39 certain of the scribes *a* said,
23.40 the other *a* rebuked him,
24.18 Cleopas, *a* said unto him,
Tit 2. 9 well in *a* things; not *a* again;

ANSWERS
Job 21.34 *a* there remaineth falsehood?
34.36 of his *a* for wicked men.
Lk 2.47 at his understanding and *a*.

ANT
Pr 6. 6 Go to the *a*, thou sluggard;

ANTICHRIST
1Jn 2.18 ye have heard that *a* shall come,
22 He is *a*, that denieth the Father
4. 3 this is that spirit of *a*, whereof
2Jn 7 This is a deceiver and an *a*.

ANTICHRISTS
1Jn 2.18 come, even now are there many *a*;

ANTIOCH
Ac 6. 5 and Nicolas a proselyte of *A*:
11.19 far as Phenice, and Cyprus, and *A*,
20 when they were come to *A*,
22 that he should go as far as *A*.
26 brought him unto *A*.
26 were called Christians first in *A*.
27 from Jerusalem unto *A*.
13. 1 in the church that was at *A*
14 they came to *A* in Pisidia,
14.19 certain Jews from *A* and Iconium,
21 Iconium, and *A*,
26 and thence sailed to *A*,
15.22 men of their own company to *A*
23 Gentiles in *A* and Syria
30 were dismissed, they came to *A*:
35 Barnabas continued in *A*, teaching
18.22 the church, he went down to *A*.
Gal 2.11 when Peter was come to *A*,
2Ti 3.11 which came unto me at *A*,

ANTIPAS
Rev 2.13 *A* was my faithful martyr,

ANTIPATRIS
Ac 23.31 and brought him by night to *A*.

ANTS
Pr 30.25 The *a* are a people not strong,

ANVIL
Isa 41. 7 hammer him that smote the *a*,

APART
Ex 13.12 thou shalt set *a* unto the Lord
Lev 15.19 she shall be put *a* seven days:
18.19 as long as she is put *a* for her
Ps 4. 3 the Lord hath set *a* him that is
Eze 22.10 they humbled her that was set *a*
Zec 12.12 land shall mourn, every family *a*;
12 the family of the house of David *a*,
12 and their wives *a*;
12 family of the house of Nathan *a*;
12 and their wives *a*;
13 The family of...Levi *a*,
13 and their wives *a*;
13 the family of Shimei *a*,
13 and their wives *a*;
14 every family *a*,
14 and their wives *a*.
Mt 14.13 into a desert place *a*:
23 into a mountain *a* to pray:
17. 1 into an high mountain *a*,
19 the disciples to Jesus *a*,
20.17 took the twelve disciples *a* in
Mk 6.31 ye yourselves *a* into a desert
9. 2 mountain *a* by themselves:
Jas 1.21 Wherefore lay *a* all filthiness

APELLES
Ro 16.10 Salute *A* approved in Christ.

APIECE
Nu 3.47 take five shekels *a* by the poll.
7.86 ten shekels *a*, after the shekel
17. 6 their princes gave him a rod *a*,
1Ki 7.15 eighteen cubits high *a*:
Eze 10.21 Every one had four faces *a*,
41.24 and the doors had two leaves *a*,
Lk 9. 3 money, neither have two coats *a*.
Jn 2. 6 containing two or three firkins *a*.

APOLLONIA
Ac 17. 1 through Amphipolis and *A*,

APOLLOS
Ac 18.24 a certain Jew named *A*,
19. 1 while *A* was at Corinth,
1Co 1.12 and I of *A*; and I of Cephas;
3. 4 another, I am of *A*; are ye not
5 Who then is Paul, and who is *A*,
6 *A* watered; but God gave the
22 Whether Paul, or *A*, or Cephas.
4. 6 and to *A* for your sakes;
16.12 touching our brother *A*,
Tit 3.13 Bring Zenas the lawyer and *A*

APOLLYON
Rev 9.11 Greek tongue hath this name *A*.

APOSTLE
Ro 1. 1 called to be an *a*, separated unto
11.13 as I am the *a* of the Gentiles,
1Co 1. 1 called to be an *a* of Jesus Christ
9. 1 Am I not an *a*? am I not free?
2 If I be not an *a* unto others,
15. 9 not meet to be called an *a*,
2Co 1. 1 Paul, an *a* of Jesus Christ by the
12.12 the signs of an *a* were wrought
Gal 1. 1 Paul, an *a*, (not of men, neither by
Eph 1. 1 Paul, an *a* of Jesus Christ
Col 1. 1 Paul, an *a* of Jesus Christ by the
1Ti 1. 1 Paul, an *a* of Jesus Christ by the
2. 7 am ordained a preacher, and an *a*,
2Ti 1. 1 Paul, an *a* of Jesus Christ
11 appointed a preacher, and an *a*,
Tit 1. 1 an *a* of Jesus Christ, according to
Heb 3. 1 consider the *A* and High Priest
1Pe 1. 1 Peter, an *a* of Jesus Christ, to the
2Pe 1. 1 a servant and an *a* of Jesus

APOSTLES
Mt 10. 2 names of the twelve *a* are these;
Mk 6.30 the *a* gathered themselves together
Lk 6.13 whom also he named *a*;
9.10 the *a*, when they were returned,
11.49 I will send them prophets and *a*,
17. 5 the *a* said unto the Lord,
22.14 the twelve *a* with him.
24.10 told these things unto the *a*.
Ac 1. 2 commandments unto the *a* whom
26 numbered with the eleven *a*.
2.37 Peter, and to the rest of the *a*,
43 and signs were done by the *a*.
4.33 the *a* witness of the resurrection
36 by the *a* was surnamed Barnabas,
5.12 hands of the *a* were many signs
18 laid their hands on the *a*,
29 Peter and the other *a* answered
34 to put the *a* forth a little space;
40 called the *a*, and beaten them,
6. 6 Whom they set before the *a*:
8. 1 Judea and Samaria, except the *a*.
14 the *a* which were at Jerusalem
9.27 him and brought him to the *a*,
11. 1 *a* and brethren that were in Judea,
14. 4 with the Jews, and part with the *a*.
14 when the *a*, Barnabas and Paul,
15. 2 unto the *a* and elders about this
4 of the *a* and elders, and they
6 the *a* and elders came together
22 Then pleased it the *a* and elders,
23 The *a* and elders and brethren
33 the brethren unto the *a*.
16. 4 were ordained of the *a* and elders
Ro 16. 7 who are of note among the *a*,
1Co 4. 9 God hath set forth us the *a* last,
9. 5 as well as other *a*, and as the
12.28 first *a*, secondarily prophets,
29 Are all *a*? are all prophets?
15. 7 of James; then of all the *a*.
9 I am the least of the *a*, that am
2Co 11. 5 a whit behind the very chiefest *a*
13 are false *a*, deceitful workers,
13 themselves into the *a* of Christ.
12.11 the very chiefest *a*, though I be
Gal 1.17 to them which were *a* before me;
19 other of the *a* saw I none,
Eph 2.20 foundation of the *a* and prophets,
3. 5 revealed unto his holy *a*
4.11 gave some, *a*; and some, prophets;
1Th 2. 6 burdensome, as the *a* of Christ.
2Pe 3. 2 the *a* of the Lord and Saviour:
Jude 17 before of the *a* of our Lord Jesus
Rev 2. 2 them which say they are *a*,
18.20 ye holy *a* and prophets;
21.14 names of the twelve *a* of the Lamb.

APOSTLES'

Ac 2.42 in the *a* doctrine and fellowship,
4.35 laid them down at the *a* feet:
37 the money, and laid it at the *a* feet.
5. 2 part, and laid it at the *a* feet.
8.18 through laying on of the *a* hands

APOSTLESHIP

Ac 1.25 take part of this ministry and *a*,
Ro 1. 5 received grace and *a*, for obedience
1Co 9. 2 seal of mine *a* are ye in the Lord.
Gal 2. 8 to the *a* of the circumcision,

APPARENTLY

Nu 12. 8 speak mouth to mouth, even *a*,

APPEAL

Ac 25.11 I *a* unto Caesar.
28.19 constrained to *a* unto Caesar;

APPEALED

Ac 25.12 Hast thou *a* unto Caesar?
21 when Paul had *a* to be reserved
25 himself hath *a* to Augustus,
26.32 if he had not *a* unto Caesar.

APPEAR

Gen 1. 9 let the dry land *a*: and it was so.
30.37 made the white *a* which was in
Ex 23.15 none shall *a* before me empty:)
17 all thy males shall *a* before
34.20 none shall *a* before me empty.
23 menchildren *a* before the Lord
24 to *a* before the Lord thy God
Lev 9. 4 to day the Lord will *a* unto you.
6 glory of the Lord shall *a* unto you.
13.57 if it *a* still in the garment,
16. 2 I will *a* in the cloud upon the
Dt 16.16 males *a* before the Lord thy God
16 they shall not *a*...empty:
31.11 Israel is come to *a* before the Lord
Jdg 13.21 angel of the Lord did no more *a*
1Sa 1.22 that he may *a* before the Lord,
2.27 Did I plainly *a* unto the house of
2Ch 1. 7 night did God *a* unto Solomon,
Ps 42. 2 shall I come and *a* before God?
90.16 thy work *a* unto thy servants,
102.16 he shall *a* in his glory.
SS 2.12 The flowers *a* on the earth;
4. 1 goats, that *a* from mount Gilead.
6. 5 of goats that *a* from Gilead.
7.12 whether the tender grape *a*,
Isa 1.12 When ye come to *a* before me,
66. 5 but he shall *a* to your joy, and
Jer 13.26 that thy shame may *a*.
Eze 21.24 so that...your sins do *a*;
Mt 6.16 they may *a* unto men to fast.
18 thou *a* not unto men to fast,
23.27 which indeed *a* beautiful outward,
28 ye also outwardly *a* righteous
24.30 shall *a* the sign of the Son of man
Lk 11.44 are as graves which *a* not,
19.11 of God should immediately *a*.
Ac 22.30 and all their council to *a*,
26.16 in the which I will *a* unto thee;
Ro 7.13 But sin, that it might *a* sin,
2Co 5.10 all *a* before the judgment seat
7.12 sight of God might *a* unto you.
13. 7 not that we should *a* approved,
Col 3. 4 Christ, who is our life, shall *a*,
4 then shall ye also *a* with him in
1Ti 4.15 that thy profiting may *a*
Heb 9.24 *a* in the presence of God for us.
28 them that look for him shall he *a*
11. 3 not made of things which do *a*.
1Pe 4.18 the ungodly and the sinner *a*?
5. 4 when the chief Shepherd shall *a*,
1Jn 2.28 when he shall *a*, we may have
3. 2 doth not yet *a* what we shall be:
2 when he shall *a*, we shall be like
Rev 3.18 of thy nakedness do not *a*;

APPEARANCE

Nu 9.15 as it were the *a* of fire.
16 and the *a* of fire by night.
1Sa 16. 7 man looketh on the outward *a*,
Eze 1. 5 this was their *a*; they had the
13 their *a* was like burning coals
13 and like the *a* of lamps:
14 as the *a* of a flash of lightning.
16 The *a* of the wheels
16 and their *a* and their work
26 as the *a* of a sapphire
26 as the *a* of a man above it.
27 as the *a* of fire round about
27 the *a* of his loins even upward,
27 the *a* of his loins even downward,
27 as it were the *a* of fire,
28 *a* of the bow that is in the cloud
28 *a* of the brightness round about.
28 This was the *a* of the likeness
8. 2 a likeness as the *a* of fire:
2 from the *a* of his loins
2 as the *a* of brightness, as the
10. 1 the *a* of the likeness of a throne.
9 and the *a* of the wheels
40. 3 whose *a* was like the *a* of brass,
41.21 *a* of the one as the *a* of the other.
42.11 like the *a* of the chambers
43. 3 according to the *a* of the vision,
Dan 8.15 as the *a* of a man.
10. 6 his face as the *a* of lightning,
18 like the *a* of a man, and he
Joel 2. 4 *a* of them is as the *a* of horses;
Jn 7.24 Judge not according to the *a*,
2Co 5.12 glory in *a*, and not in heart.
10. 7 on things after the outward *a*?
1Th 5.22 Abstain from all *a* of evil.

APPEARANCES

Eze 10.10 And as for their *a*, they four had
22 Chebar, their *a* and themselves:

APPEARED

Gen 12. 7 And the Lord *a* unto Abram,
7 unto the Lord, who *a* unto him.
17. 1 And when...the Lord *a* to Abram,
18. 1 And the Lord *a* unto him in the
26. 2 And the Lord *a* unto him,
24 *a* unto him the same night,
35. 1 God, that *a* unto thee when thou
7 because there God *a* unto him,
9 And God *a* unto Jacob again,
48. 3 God Almighty *a* unto me at Luz
Ex 3. 2 And the angel of the Lord *a*
16 The Lord God of your fathers,...*a*
4. 1 The Lord hath not *a* unto thee.
5 God of Jacob, hath *a* unto thee.
6. 3 And I *a* unto Abraham,
14.27 strength when the morning *a*;
16.10 glory of the Lord *a* in the cloud.
Lev 9.23 and the glory of the Lord *a* unto
Nu 14.10 the glory of the Lord *a* in the
16.19 Lord *a* unto all the congregation.
42 and the glory of the Lord *a*.
20. 6 the glory of the Lord *a* unto them.
Dt 31.15 And the Lord *a* in the tabernacle
Jdg 6.12 the angel of the Lord *a* unto him,
13. 3 *a* unto the woman, and said unto
10 the man hath *a* unto me,
1Sa 3.21 the Lord *a* again in Shiloh:
2Sa 22.16 And the channels of the sea *a*,
1Ki 3. 5 In Gibeon the Lord *a* to Solomon
9. 2 the Lord *a* to Solomon the second
2 as he had *a* unto him at Gibeon.
11. 9 Lord God of Israel, which had *a*
2Ki 2.11 behold, there *a* a chariot of fire,
2Ch 3. 1 where the Lord *a* unto David
7.12 the Lord *a* to Solomon by night,
Neh 4.21 of the morning till the stars *a*.
Jer 31. 3 The Lord hath *a* of old
Eze 10. 1 there *a* over them as it were a
8 And there *a* in the cherubims
19.11 and she *a* in her height
Dan 1.15 countenances *a* fairer and fatter
8. 1 *a* unto me,...after that which *a*
Mt 1.20 behold, the angel of the Lord *a*
2. 7 what time the star *a*.
13.26 then *a* the tares also.
17. 3 *a* unto them Moses and Elias
27.53 into the holy city, and *a* unto
Mk 9. 4 *a* unto them Elias with Moses:
16. 9 he *a* first to Mary Magdalene,
12 *a* in another form unto two of
14 Afterward he *a* unto the eleven
Lk 1.11 there *a* unto him an angel
9. 8 of some, that Elias had *a*;
31 Who *a* in glory, and spake of his
22.43 And there *a* an angel unto him
24.34 and hath *a* to Simon.
Ac 2. 3 there *a* unto them cloven tongues
7. 2 God of glory *a* unto our father
30 there *a* to him in the wilderness.
35 angel which *a* to him in the bush.
9.17 Jesus, that *a* unto thee in the way
16. 9 a vision *a* to Paul in the night;
26.16 I *a* unto thee for this purpose,
27.20 nor stars in many days *a*,
Tit 2.11 salvation hath *a* to all men.
3. 4 of God our Saviour toward man *a*,
Heb 9.26 hath he *a* to put away sin by
Rev 12. 1 *a* a great wonder in heaven,
3 *a* another wonder in heaven;

APPEARETH

Lev 13.14 when raw flesh *a* in him,
43 *a* in the skin of the flesh;
Dt 2.30 into thy hands, as *a* this day.
Ps 84. 7 every one of them in Zion *a*
Pr 27.25 The hay *a*, and the tender grass
Jer 6. 1 evil *a* out of the north,
Mal 3. 2 who shall stand when he *a*?
Mt 2.13 angel of the Lord *a* to Joseph in
19 *a* in a dream to Joseph in Egypt,
Jas 4.14 a vapor, that *a* for a little time,

APPEARING

1Ti 6.14 the *a* of our Lord Jesus Christ:
2Ti 1.10 the *a* of our Saviour Jesus Christ,
4. 1 at his *a* and his kingdom;
8 them also that love his *a*.
Tit 2.13 the glorious *a* of the great God
1Pe 1. 7 glory at the *a* of Jesus Christ:

APPHIA

Phm 2 to our beloved *A*, and Archippus

APPII

Ac 28.15 to meet us as far as *A* forum,

APPLE

Dt 32.10 he kept him as the *a* of his eye.
Ps 17. 8 Keep me as the *a* of the eye,
Pr 7. 2 my law as the *a* of thine eye.
SS 2. 3 as the *a* tree among the trees
8. 5 I raised thee up under the *a* tree:
La 2.18 not the *a* of thine eye cease.
Joel 1.12 palm tree also, and the *a* tree,
Zec 2. 8 toucheth the *a* of his eye.

APPLES

Pr 25.11 A word fitly spoken is like *a* of
SS 2. 5 flagons, comfort me with *a*:
7. 8 the smell of thy nose like *a*;

APPLIED

Ec 7.25 I *a* mine heart to know, and
8. 9 and *a* my heart unto every work
16 I *a* mine heart to know wisdom,

APPLY

Ps 90.12 may *a* our hearts unto wisdom.
Pr 2. 2 *a* thine heart to understanding;
22.17 *a* thine heart unto my
23.12 *A* thine heart unto instruction,

APPOINT

Gen 30.28 *A* me thy wages, and I will give
41.34 him *a* officers over the land,
Ex 21.13 then I will *a* thee a place,
30.16 and shalt *a* it for the service of
Lev 26.16 I will even *a* over you terror,
Nu 1.50 thou shalt *a* the Levites over
3.10 And thou shalt *a* Aaron
4.19 and *a* them every one to his
27 ye shall *a* unto them in charge
35. 6 ye shall *a* for the manslayer,
11 Then ye shall *a* you cities to be
Jos 20. 2 *A* out for you cities of refuge,
1Sa 8.11 and *a* them for himself, for his
12 And he will *a* him captains
2Sa 6.21 to *a* me ruler over the people
7.10 I will *a* a place for my people
15.15 my lord the king shall *a*:
1Ki 5. 6 all that thou shalt *a*:
9 the place that thou shalt *a* me,
1Ch 15.16 the Levites to *a* their brethren
Neh 7. 3 *a* watches of the inhabitants
Est 2. 3 And let the king *a* officers
Job 14.13 thou wouldst *a* me a set time,
Isa 26. 1 salvation will God *a* for walls
61. 3 To *a* unto them that mourn in
Jer 15. 3 I will *a* over them four kinds,
49.19 that I may *a* over her?
19 who will *a* me the time?
50.44 man, that I may *a* over her?
44 and who will *a* me the time?
51.27 *a* a captain against her;
Eze 21.19 son of man, *a* thee two ways,
20 *A* a way, that the sword may
22 to *a* captains, and to open the
22 to *a* battering rams against the
45. 6 ye shall *a* the possession of the
Hos 1.11 and *a* themselves one head,
Mt 24.51 and *a* him his portion with
Lk 12.46 and will *a* him his portion with
22.29 I *a* unto you a kingdom, as my
Ac 6. 3 we may *a* over this business.

APPOINTED

Gen 4.25 said she, hath *a* me another seed
18.14 At the time *a* I will return
24.14 hast *a* for thy servant Isaac;
44 woman whom the Lord hath *a*
Ex 9. 5 And the Lord *a* a set time,
23.15 the time *a* of the month Abib;
Nu 9. 2 keep the passover at his *a* season.
3 ye shall keep it in his *a* season:
7 in his *a* season among the children
13 of the Lord in his *a* season,
Jos 8.14 at a time *a*, before the plain;
20. 7 And they *a* Kedesh in Galilee
9 These were the cities *a* for all
Jdg 18.11 men *a* with weapons of war.
16 the six hundred men *a*
17 men that were *a* with weapons
20.38 there was an *a* sign between
1Sa 13. 8 set time that Samuel had *a*:
11 camest not within the days *a*,
19.20 Samuel standing as *a* over
20.35 field at the time *a* with David,
21. 2 I have *a* my servants to such
25.30 and shall have *a* thee ruler over
29. 4 his place which thou hast *a* him,
2Sa 17.14 Lord had *a* to defeat the good
20. 5 the set time which he had *a* him,
24.15 the morning even to the time *a*:
1Ki 1.35 I have *a* him to be ruler
11.18 *a* him victuals, and gave him
12.12 as the king had *a*, saying,
20.42 whom I *a* to utter destruction,
2Ki 7.17 king *a* the lord on whose hand
8. 6 king *a* unto her a certain officer,
10.24 Jehu *a* fourscore men without,
11.18 And the priest *a* officers over the
18.14 the king of Assyria *a* unto
1Ch 6.48 Levites were *a* unto all manner
49 and were *a* for all the work
9.29 were *a* to oversee the vessels,
15.17 So the Levites *a* Heman
19 And Ethan, were *a* to sound
16. 4 And he *a* certain of the Levites
2Ch 8.14 And he *a*, according to the order
20.21 he *a* singers unto the Lord,
23.18 Jehoiada *a* the officers of the
31. 2 And Hezekiah *a* the courses
3 He *a* also the king's portion
33. 8 which I have *a* for your fathers;
34.22 king had *a*, went to Huldah
Ezr 3. 8 and *a* the Levites, from twenty
8.20 David and the princes had *a*
10.14 come at *a* times, and with them
Neh 5.14 I was *a* to be their governor
6. 7 thou hast also *a* prophets to
7. 1 singers and the Levites were *a*,
9.17 in their rebellion *a* a captain
10.34 at times *a* year by year
12.31 and *a* two great companies
44 were some *a* over the chambers
13.30 and *a* the wards of the priests
31 for the wood offering, at times *a*,
Est 1. 8 king had *a* to all the officers
2.15 the keeper of the women, *a*.
4. 5 whom he had *a* to attend
9.27 and according to their *a* time
31 days of Purim in their times *a*,
Job 7. 1 *a* time to man upon the earth?
3 wearisome nights are *a* to me,
14. 5 thou hast *a* his bounds that he
14 days of my *a* time will I wait,
20.29 the heritage *a* unto him by God.
23.14 the thing that is *a* for me:
30.23 the house *a* for all living.
Ps 44.11 given us like sheep *a* for meat;
78. 5 *a* a law in Israel, which he
79.11 preserve thou those that are *a*
81. 3 in the new moon, in the time *a*,
102.20 loose those that are *a* to death;
104.19 He *a* the moon for seasons:
Pr 7.20 will come home at the day *a*.
8.29 when he *a* the foundations of
31. 8 all such as are *a* to destruction.
Isa 1.14 new moons and your *a* feasts
14.31 shall be alone in his *a* times.
28.25 wheat and the *a* barley
44. 7 since I *a* the ancient people?
Jer 5.24 reserveth unto us the *a* weeks
8. 7 the stork...knoweth her *a* times;
33.25 if I have not *a* the ordinances
46.17 he hath passed the time *a*.
47. 7 there hath he *a* it.
Eze 4. 6 have *a* thee each day for a year.
36. 5 have *a* my land into their
43.21 he shall burn it in the *a* place
Dan 1. 5 And the king *a* them a daily
10 who hath *a* your meat, and
8.19 at the time *a* the end shall be.
10. 1 but the time *a* was long:
11.27 the end shall be at the time *a*.
29 At the time *a* he shall return,
35 it is yet for a time *a*.
Mic 6. 9 the rod, and who hath *a* it.
Hab 2. 3 the vision is yet for an *a* time,
Mt 26.19 disciples did as Jesus had *a* them;
27.10 as the Lord *a* me.
28.16 where Jesus had *a* them.
Lk 3.13 than that which is *a* you.
10. 1 the Lord *a* other seventy also,
22.29 as my Father hath *a* unto me;
Ac 1.23 *a* two, Joseph called Barsabas,
7.44 as he had *a*, speaking unto Moses,
17.26 determined the times before *a*,
31 Because he hath *a* a day,
20.13 for so he had *a*, minding himself
22.10 which are *a* for thee to do.
28.23 And when they had *a* him a day,
1Co 4. 9 as it were *a* to death;
Gal 4. 2 until the time *a* of the father.
1Th 3. 3 know that we are *a* thereunto.
5. 9 God hath not *a* us to wrath,
2Ti 1.11 Whereunto I am *a* a preacher,
Tit 1. 5 as I had *a* thee:
Heb 1. 2 he hath *a* heir of all things,
3. 2 faithful to him that *a* him,
9.27 as it is *a* unto men once to die,
1Pe 2. 8 whereunto also they were *a*.

APPOINTETH

Dan 5.21 he *a* over it whomsoever he will.

APPOINTMENT

Nu 4.27 At the *a* of Aaron and his sons
2Sa 13.32 by the *a* of Absalom this hath
Ezr 6. 9 according to the *a* of the priests
Job 2.11 for they had made an *a* together

APPREHEND

2Co 11.32 desirous to *a* me:
Php 3.12 if that I may *a* that for which

APPREHENDED

Ac 12. 4 when he had *a* him,
Php 3.12 for which also I am *a* of Christ
13 I count not myself to have *a*:

APPROACH

Lev 18. 6 None of you shall *a* to any that
14 thou shalt not *a* to his wife:
19 thou shalt not *a* unto a woman
20.16 if a woman *a* unto any beast,
21.17 let him not *a* to offer the bread
18 hath a blemish, he shall not *a*:
Nu 4.19 they *a* unto the most holy things:
Dt 20. 2 that the priest shall *a* and speak
3 Israel, ye *a* this day unto battle
31.14 thy days *a* that thou must die:
Jos 8. 5 people that are with me will *a*
Job 40.19 make his sword to *a* unto him.
Ps 65. 4 thou choosest and causest to *a*
Jer 30.21 and he shall *a* unto me:
21 engaged his heart to *a* unto me?
Eze 42.13 the priests that *a* unto the Lord
14 shall *a* to those things which are
43.19 the Levites...which *a* unto me,
1Ti 6.16 in the light which no man can *a*

APPROACHED

2Sa 11.20 Wherefore *a* ye so nigh unto the
2Ki 16.12 and the king *a* to the altar,

APPROACHETH

Lk 12.33 where no thief *a*, neither moth

APPROACHING

Isa 58. 2 they take delight in *a* to God.
Heb 10.25 the more, as ye see the day *a*.

APPROVE

Ps 49.13 their posterity *a* their sayings.
1Co 16. 3 whosoever ye shall *a* by...letters
Php 1.10 may *a* things that are excellent;

APPROVED

Ac 2.22 a man *a* of God among you by
Ro 14.18 acceptable to God, and *a* of men.
16.10 Salute Apelles *a* in Christ.
1Co 11.19 which...*a* may be made manifest
2Co 7.11 ye have *a* yourselves to be clear
10.18 he that commendeth himself is *a*,
13. 7 not that we should appear *a*,
2Ti 2.15 Study to shew thyself *a* unto God,

APPROVEST

Ro 2.18 *a* the things that are more

APPROVETH

La 3.36 in his cause, the Lord *a* not.

APPROVING

2Co 6. 4 *a* ourselves as the ministers of

APRONS

Gen 3. 7 together, and made themselves *a*.
Ac 19.12 handkerchiefs or *a*, and the

APT

2Ki 24.16 all that were strong and *a* for war,
1Ch 7.40 that were *a* to the war and to
1Ti 3. 2 given to hospitality, *a* to teach;
2Ti 2.24 unto all men, *a* to teach, patient,

AQUILA

Ac 18. 2 a certain Jew named *A*, born in
18 with him Priscilla and *A*;
26 when *A* and Priscilla had heard,
Ro 16. 3 Greet Priscilla and *A* my helpers
1Co 16.19 *A* and Priscilla salute you much
2Ti 4.19 Salute Prisca and *A*,

ARABIA

1Ki 10.15 of all the kings of *A*, and of the
2Ch 9.14 all the kings of *A* and governors
Isa 21.13 The burden upon *A*. In the forest
13 In the forest in *A* shall ye lodge,
Jer 25.24 And all the kings of *A*, and all
Eze 27.21 *A*, and all the princes of Kedar,
Gal 1.17 I went into *A*, and returned
4.25 this Agar is mount Sinai in *A*,

ARABIAN

Neh 2.19 and Geshem the *A*, heard it, they
6. 1 Geshem the *A*, and the rest of
Isa 13.20 neither shall the *A* pitch tent
Jer 3. 2 thou sat for them, as the *A* in the

ARABIANS

2Ch 17.11 and the *A* brought him flocks,
21.16 of the Philistines, and of the *A*,
22. 1 band of men that came with the *A*,
26. 7 the *A* that dwelt in Gur-baal,
Neh 4. 7 and the *A*, and the Ammonites,
Ac 2.11 Cretes and *A*, we do hear them

ARAM

Gen 10.22 and Arphaxad, and Lud, and *A*.
23 the children of *A*: Uz, and Hul,
22.21 and Kemuel the father of *A*,
Nu 23. 7 of Moab that brought me from *A*,
1Ch 1.17 Arphaxad, and Lud, and *A*, and Uz,
2.23 he took Geshur, and *A*, with the
7.34 Rohgah, Jehubbah, and *A*.
Mt 1. 3 Esrom begat *A*;
4 *A* begat Aminadab;
Lk 3.33 which was the son of *A*,

ARARAT

Gen 8. 4 upon the mountains of *A*.
Jer 51.27 against her the kingdoms of *A*.

ARCHANGEL

1Th 4.16 with the voice of the *a*,
Jude 9 Michael the *a*, when contending

ARCHELAUS

Mt 2.22 heard that *A* did reign in Judea

ARCHER

Gen 21.20 he grew...and became an *a*.
Jer 51. 3 let the *a* bend his bow,

ARCHERS

Gen 49.23 *a* have sorely grieved him,
Jdg 5.11 are delivered from the noise of *a*
1Sa 31. 3 the *a* hit him; and he
3 sore wounded of the *a*.
1Ch 8.40 mighty men of valor, *a*,
10. 3 the *a* hit him,
3 he was wounded of the *a*.
2Ch 35.23 the *a* shot at king Josiah;
Job 16.13 His *a* compass me round about,
Isa 21.17 the residue of the number of *a*,

Noah's ark, shown in Cologne Bible (1478). Some details are fanciful—there are no mermaids in the Bible.

22. 3 they are bound by the *a*:
Jer 50.29 Call together the *a* against

ARCHES

Eze 40.16 about, and likewise to the *a*:
21 posts thereof and the *a* thereof
22 their windows, and their *a*,
24 and the *a* thereof according to
25 windows in it and in the *a* thereof
26 the *a* thereof were before them:
29 and the posts thereof, and the *a*
29 the *a* thereof round about: it was
30 *a* round about were five and twenty
31 *a* thereof were toward the outer
33 *a* thereof, were according to these
33 windows therein and in the *a*
34 the *a* thereof were toward the
36 and the *a* thereof, and the windows

ARCHIPPUS

Col 4.17 say to *A*, Take heed to the
Phm 2 *A* our fellowsoldier,

ARCTURUS

Job 9. 9 maketh *A*, Orion, and Pleiades,
38.32 thou guide *A* with his sons?

ARGUING

Job 6.25 what doth your *a* reprove?

ARGUMENTS

Job 23. 4 fill my mouth with *a*.

ARIGHT

Ps 50.23 that ordereth his conversation *a*
78. 8 that set not their heart *a*,
Pr 15. 2 of the wise useth knowledge *a*:
23.31 the cup, when it moveth itself *a*.
Jer 8. 6 heard, but they spake not *a*:

ARIMATHAEA

Mt 27.57 there came a rich man of *A*,
Mk 15.43 Joseph of *A*, an honorable
Lk 23.51 *A*, a city of the Jews:
Jn 19.38 Joseph of *A*, being a disciple of

ARISTARCHUS

Ac 19.29 having caught Gaius and *A*,
20. 4 Thessalonians, *A* and Secundus;
27. 2 *A*, a Macedonian of Thessalonica,
Col 4.10 *A* my fellowprisoner saluteth you,
Phm 24 Marcus, *A*, Demas,

ARK

Gen 6.14 Make thee an *a* of gopher wood;
7. 1 thou and all thy house into the *a*;
8. 4 the *a* rested in the seventh month,
16 Go forth of the *a*,
Ex 2. 3 she took for him an *a* of bulrushes,
Nu 14.44 nevertheless the *a* of the covenant
Jos 3. 6 Take up the *a* of the covenant,
1Sa 4.11 And the *a* of God was taken;
13 his heart trembled for the *a* of God.
6. 2 What shall we do to the *a* of
2Ch 5. 4 the Levites took up the *a*.
Jer 3.16 The *a* of the covenant of the Lord:
Mt 24.38 day that Noe entered into the *a*,
Lk 17.27 Noe entered into the *a*, and the
Heb 9. 4 censer, and the *a* of the covenant
11. 7 prepared an *a* to the saving of
1Pe 3.20 while the *a* was a preparing
Rev 11.19 was seen in his temple the *a* of

ARM

Ex 6. 6 you with a stretched out *a*,
15.16 by the greatness of thine *a*
Nu 31. 3 *A* some of yourselves unto the
Dt 4.34 and by a stretched out *a*, and by
5.15 hand and by a stretched out *a*:
7.19 and the stretched out *a*,
9.29 and by thy stretched out *a*.
11. 2 hand, and his stretched out *a*,
26. 8 and with an outstretched *a*,
33.20 teareth the *a* with the crown of
1Sa 2.31 that I will cut off thine *a*, and
31 the *a* of thy father's house,
2Sa 1.10 the bracelet that was on his *a*,
1Ki 8.42 and of thy stretched out *a*;)
2Ki 17.36 great power and a stretched out *a*,
2Ch 6.32 and thy stretched out *a*;
32. 8 With him is an *a* of flesh;
Job 26. 2 the *a* that hath no strength?
31.22 *a* fall from my shoulder blade,
22 mine *a* be broken from the bone.
35. 9 by reason of the *a* of the mighty.
38.15 and the high *a* shall be broken.
40. 9 Hast thou an *a* like God?
Ps 10.15 Break thou the *a* of the wicked
44. 3 neither did their own *a* save them:
3 but thy right hand, and thine *a*,
77.15 with thine *a* redeemed thy people,
89.10 thine enemies with thy strong *a*.
13 Thou hast a mighty *a*:
21 mine *a* also shall strengthen him.
98. 1 *a*, hath gotten him the victory.

Ps 136.12 and with a stretched out *a*:)
SS 8. 6 as a seal upon thine *a*:
Isa 9.20 every man the flesh of his own *a*:
17. 5 and reapeth the ears with his *a*;
30.30 shew the lighting down of his *a*,
33. 2 be thou their *a* every morning,
40.10 and his *a* shall rule for him:
11 shall gather the lambs with his *a*,
48.14 his *a* shall be on the Chaldeans.
51. 5 on mine *a* shall they trust.
9 put on strength, O *a* of the Lord;
52.10 Lord hath made bare his holy *a*
53. 1 to whom is the *a* of the Lord
59.16 his *a* brought salvation unto him;
62. 8 and by the *a* of his strength,
63. 5 own *a* brought salvation unto me;
12 Moses with his glorious *a*, dividing
Jer 17. 5 and maketh flesh his *a*,
21. 5 and with a strong *a*,
27. 5 and by my outstretched *a*,
32.17 great power and stretched out *a*,
21 and with a stretched out *a*,
48.25 his *a* is broken, saith the Lord.
Eze 4. 7 and thine *a* shall be uncovered,
20.33 with a stretched out *a*, and with
34 hand, and with a stretched out *a*,
30.21 I have broken the *a* of Pharaoh
31.17 and they that were his *a*,
Dan 11. 6 not retain the power of the *a*;
6 neither shall he stand, nor his *a*:
Zec 11.17 the sword shall be upon his *a*,
17 his *a* shall be clean dried up,
Lk 1.51 hath shewed strength with his *a*;
Jn 12.38 to whom hath the *a* of the Lord
Ac 13.17 with an high *a* brought he them
1Pe 4. 1 *a* yourselves likewise with the

ARMAGEDDON

Rev 16.16 in the Hebrew tongue *A*.

ARMED

Gen 14.14 when...he *a* his trained servants,
Nu 31. 5 twelve thousand *a* for war.
32.17 we ourselves will go ready *a*
20 if ye will go *a* before the Lord
21 go all of you *a* over Jordan
27 every man *a* for war,
29 every man *a* to battle,
30 they will not pass over with you *a*,
32 will pass over *a* before the Lord
Dt 3.18 pass over *a* before your brethren
Jos 1.14 pass before your brethren *a*,
4.12 Manasseh, passed over *a* before
6. 7 that is *a* pass on before the ark
9 the *a* men went before the priests
13 the *a* men went before them; but
Jdg 7.11 the *a* men that were in the host.
1Sa 17. 5 he was *a* with a coat of mail;
38 Saul *a* David with his armor,
38 also he *a* him with a coat of mail.
1Ch 12. 2 They were *a* with bows,
23 that were ready *a* to the war,
24 ready *a* to the war.
2Ch 17.17 *a* men with bow and shield
28.14 the *a* men left the captives and
Job 39.21 he goeth on to meet the *a* men.
Ps 78. 9 The children of Ephraim, being *a*,
Pr 6.11 and thy want as an *a* man.
24.34 and thy want as an *a* man.
Isa 15. 4 *a* soldiers of Moab shall cry out
Lk 11.21 strong man *a* keepeth his palace,

ARMENIA

2Ki 19.37 they escaped into the land of *A*:
Isa 37.38 they escaped into the land of *A*:

ARMHOLES

Jer 38.12 rotten rags under thine *a*
Eze 13.18 sew pillows to all *a*,

ARMIES

Ex 6.26 from...Egypt according to their *a*.
7. 4 forth mine *a*, and my people
12.17 your *a* out of the land of Egypt:
51 of the land of Egypt by their *a*.
Nu 1. 3 number them by their *a*.
2. 3 pitch throughout their *a*: and
9 throughout their *a*. These shall
10 of Reuben according to their *a*:
16 throughout their *a*. And they
18 of Ephraim according to their *a*:
24 throughout their *a*. And they
25 on the north side by their *a*:
10.14, 18 according to their *a*: and
22 according to his *a*; and over his
28 of Israel according to their *a*,
33. 1 their *a* under the hand of Moses
Dt 20. 9 make captains of the *a* to lead
1Sa 17. 1 together their *a* to battle,
8 and cried unto the *a* of Israel,
10 I defy the *a* of Israel this day;
23 out of the *a* of the Philistines,
26 defy the *a* of the living God?
36 defied the *a* of the living God.
45 the God of the *a* of Israel,
23. 3 against the *a* of the Philistines?
28. 1 the Philistines gathered their *a*
29. 1 together all their *a* to Aphek:
2Ki 25.23 the captains of the *a*, they and
26 captains of the *a*, arose, and
1Ch 11.26 the valiant men of the *a* were,
2Ch 16. 4 of his *a* against the cities
Job 25. 3 Is there any number of his *a*?
Ps 44. 9 goest not forth with our *a*.
60.10 didst not go out with our *a*?
68.12 Kings of *a* did flee apace: and
SS 6.13 As it were the company of two *a*.
Isa 34. 2 his fury upon all their *a*: he
Mt 22. 7 he sent forth his *a*, and destroyed
Lk 21.20 Jerusalem compassed with *a*,
Heb 11.34 turned to flight the *a* of the aliens.
Rev 19.14 And the *a* which were in heaven
19 and their *a*, gathered together

ARMOR

1Sa 14. 1 the young man that bare his *a*,
6 that bare his *a*, Come, and let us
17.38 Saul armed David with his *a*,
39 girded his sword upon his *a*,
54 he put his *a* in his tent.
31. 9 his head, and stripped off his *a*,
10 his *a* in the house of Ashtaroth:
2Sa 2.21 take thee his *a*. But Asahel would
18.15 young men that bare Joab's *a*
1Ki 10.25 garments, and *a*, and spices,
22.38 they washed his *a*; according
2Ki 3.21 all that were able to put on *a*,
10. 2 horses, a fenced city also, and *a*;
20.13 of his *a*, and all that was found
1Ch 10. 9 they took his head, and his *a*,
10 his *a* in the house of their gods,
Isa 22. 8 the *a* of the house of the forest.
39. 2 the house of his *a*, and all that
Eze 38. 4 clothed with all sorts of *a*, even
Lk 11.22 him all his *a* wherein he trusted,
Ro 13.12 let us put on the *a* of light.
2Co 6. 7 by the *a* of righteousness on the
Eph 6.11 Put on the whole *a* of God, that
13 take unto you the whole *a* of God,

ARMORBEARER

Jdg 9.54 the young man his *a*,
1Sa 14. 7 his *a* said unto him,
12 Jonathan and his *a*, and said,
12 Jonathan said unto his *a*,
13 and his *a* after him:
13 and his *a* slew after him.
14 Jonathan and his *a* made,
17 Jonathan and his *a* were not
16.21 he became his *a*.
31. 4 Then said Saul unto his *a*,
4 his *a* would not; for he was
5 *a* saw that Saul was dead,
6 Saul died,...and his *a*, and
2Sa 23.37 *a* to Joab the son of Zeruiah,
1Ch 10. 4 Then said Saul to his *a*,
4 his *a* would not;
5 his *a* saw that Saul was dead,
11.39 *a* of Joab the son of Zeruiah,

ARMORY

Neh 3.19 going up to the *a* at the turning
SS 4. 4 builded for an *a*, whereon there
Jer 50.25 The Lord hath opened his *a*,

ARMS

Gen 49.24 the *a* of his hands were made
Dt 33.27 underneath are the everlasting *a*:
Jdg 15.14 the cords that were upon his *a*
16.12 he brake them from off his *a* like
2Sa 22.35 bow of steel is broken by mine *a*.
2Ki 9.24 smote Jehoram between his *a*,
Job 22. 9 the *a* of the fatherless have been
Ps 18.34 bow of steel is broken by mine *a*.
37.17 For the *a* of the wicked shall be
Pr 31.17 strength, and strengtheneth her *a*.
Isa 44.12 it with the strength of his *a*:
49.22 bring thy sons in their *a*, and thy
51. 5 mine *a* shall judge the people;
Eze 13.20 I will tear them from your *a*,
30.22 of Egypt, and will break his *a*,
24 I will strengthen the *a* of the king
24 but I will break Pharaoh's *a*,
25 I will strengthen the *a* of the king
25 the *a* of Pharaoh shall fall down;
Dan 2.32 his breast and his *a* of silver,
10. 6 his *a* and his feet like in color
11.15 and the *a* of the south shall not
22 with the *a* of a flood shall they be
31 And *a* shall stand on his part,
Hos 7.15 bound and strengthened their *a*,
11. 3 taking them by their *a*; but they
Mk 9.36 when he had taken him in his *a*,
10.16 he took them up in his *a*, put his
Lk 2.28 took he him up in his *a*,

ARMY

Gen 26.26 the chief captain of his *a*.
Ex 14. 9 and his horsemen, and his *a*,
Dt 11. 4 what he did unto the *a* of Egypt,
Jdg 4. 7 Sisera, the captain of Jabin's *a*,
8. 6 should give bread unto thine *a*?
9.29 Increase thine *a*, and come out.
1Sa 4. 2 they slew of the *a* in the field
12 a man of Benjamin out of the *a*,
16 I am he that came out of the *a*,
16 I fled to day out of the *a*.
17.21 battle in array, *a* against *a*.
22 and ran into the *a*, and came and
48 David hasted, and ran toward the *a*
1Ki 20.19 and the *a* which followed them.
25 number thee an *a*,
25 like the *a* that thou hast lost,
2Ki 25. 5 the *a* of the Chaldees pursued
5 all his *a* were scattered from him.
10 And all the *a* of the Chaldees,
1Ch 20. 1 Joab led forth the power of the *a*,
27.34 the general of the king's *a*
2Ch 13. 3 in array with an *a* of valiant
14. 8 Asa had an *a* of men that bare
20.21 they went out before the *a*,
24.24 *a* of the Syrians came with a
25. 7 let not the *a* of Israel go with
9 I have given to the *a* of Israel?
10 the *a* that was come to him out of
13 But the soldiers of the *a* which
26.13 under their hand was an *a*,
Neh 2. 9 had sent captains of the *a*
4. 2 the *a* of Samaria, and said, What
Job 29.25 dwelt as a king in the *a*,
SS 6. 4, 10 terrible as an *a* with banners.
Isa 36. 2 king Hezekiah with a great *a*.

43.17 horse, the *a* and the power;
Jer 32. 2 Babylon's *a* besieged Jerusalem:
34. 1 king of Babylon, and all his *a*,
7 the king of Babylon's *a* fought
21 hand of the king of Babylon's *a*,
35.11 for fear of the *a* of the Chaldeans,
11 for fear of the *a* of the Syrians:
37. 5 Pharaoh's *a* was come forth out
7 Pharaoh's *a*, which is come
10 ye had smitten the whole *a* of
11 when the *a* of the Chaldeans was
11 for fear of Pharaoh's *a*,
38. 3 the king of Babylon's *a*,
39. 1 all his *a* against Jerusalem,
5 Chaldeans' *a* pursued after them,
46. 2 against the *a* of Pharaoh-necho
22 they shall march with an *a*,
52. 4 he and all his *a*, against Jerusalem,
8 *a* of the Chaldeans pursued after
8 all his *a* was scattered from him.
14 all the *a* of the Chaldeans,
Eze 17.17 Pharaoh with his mighty *a*
27.10 Lud and Phut were in thine *a*,
11 The men of Arvad with thine *a*
29.18 caused his *a* to serve a great service
18 yet had he no wages, nor his *a*,
19 and it shall be the wages for his *a*,
32.31 Pharaoh and all his *a* slain by
37.10 an exceeding great *a*.
38. 4 all thine *a*, horses and horsemen,
15 a great company, and a mighty *a*:
Dan 3.20 mighty men that were in his *a*
4.35 according to his will in the *a* of
11. 7 which shall come with an *a*,
13 after certain years with a great *a*
25 of the south with a great *a*;
25 with a very great and mighty *a*;
26 and his *a* shall overflow:
Joel 2.11 shall utter his voice before his *a*:
20 far off from you the northern *a*,
25 my great *a* which I sent among
Zec 9. 8 mine house because of the *a*,
Ac 23.27 then came I with an *a*, and
Rev 9.16 number of the *a* of the horsemen
19.19 sat on the horse, and against his *a*.

AROSE

Gen 19.15 when the morning *a*, then the
33 she lay down, nor when she *a*.
35 and the younger *a*, and lay with
35 she lay down, nor when she *a*.
24.10 he *a*, and went to Mesopotamia,
61 And Rebekah *a*, and her damsels,
37. 7 my sheaf *a*, and also stood upright;
38.19 And she *a*, and went away,
Ex 1. 8 there *a* up a new king over Egypt,
Dt 34.10 there *a* not a prophet since in
Jos 8. 3 So Joshua *a*, and all the people
19 the ambush *a* quickly out of their
18. 8 And the men *a*, and went away:
24. 9 *a* and warred against Israel,
Jdg 2.10 *a* another generation after them,
3.20 And he *a* out of his seat.
4. 9 Deborah *a*, and went with Barak
5. 7 until that I Deborah *a*,
7 that I *a* a mother in Israel.
6.28 when the men of the city *a* early
8.21 And Gideon *a*, and slew Zebah
10. 1 after Abimelech there *a* to defend
3 And after him *a* Jair, a Gileadite,
13.11 And Manoah *a*, and went after
16. 3 Samson lay till midnight, and *a* at
19. 3 her husband *a*, and went after her,
5 they *a* early in the morning,
8 And he *a* early in the morning on
20. 8 And all the people *a* as one man,
18 And the children of Israel *a*,
Ru 1. 6 she *a* with her daughters in law,
1Sa 3. 6 And Samuel *a* and went to Eli,
8 And he *a* and went to Eli,
5. 3 And when they of Ashdod *a* early
4 when they *a* early on the morrow
9.26 And they *a* early: and it came
26 Saul *a*, and they went out both
13.15 Samuel *a*, and gat him up from
17.35 he *a* against me, I caught him
48 came to pass, when the Philistine *a*,
52 the men of Israel and of Judah *a*,
18.27 Wherefore David *a* and went,
20.25 Jonathan *a*, and Abner sat by
34 *a* from the table in fierce anger,
41 soon as the lad was gone, David *a*
42 And he *a* and departed:
21.10 And David *a*, and fled that day
23.13 David...*a* and departed out of
16 And Jonathan Saul's son *a*,
24 *a*, and went to Ziph before Saul:
24. 4 Then David *a*, and cut off the skirt
8 David also *a* afterward, and went
25. 1 And David *a*, and went down to
41 And she *a*, and bowed herself
42 Abigail hasted, and *a*,
26. 2 Then Saul *a*, and went down
5 David *a*, and came to the place
27. 2 David *a*, and he passed over with
28.23 hearkened unto their voice. So he *a*
31.12 All the valiant men *a*,
2Sa 2.15 Then there *a* and went over by
6. 2 And David *a*, and went with all
11. 2 that David *a* from off his bed,
12.17 And the elders of his house *a*.
20 Then David *a* from the earth,
13.29 Then all the king's sons *a*,
31 the king *a*, and tare his garments,
14.23 So Joab *a*, and went to Geshur,
31 Then Joab *a*, and came to Absalom
15. 9 So he *a*, and went to Hebron.
17.22 Then David *a*, and all the people
23 he saddled his ass, and *a*,
19. 8 the king *a*, and sat in the gate,
23.10 He *a*, and smote the Philistines
1Ki 1.50 and *a*, and went, and caught hold
2.40 Shimei *a*, and saddled his ass,
3.20 And she *a* at midnight,
8.54 he *a* from before the altar of the
11.18 And they *a* out of Midian,
40 Jeroboam *a*, and fled into Egypt,
14. 4 Jeroboam's wife did so, and *a*,
17 Jeroboam's wife *a*, and departed,
17.10 So he *a* and went to Zarephath.
19. 3 And when he saw that, he *a*,
8 And he *a*, and did eat and drink,
21 Then he *a*, and went after Elijah,
2Ki 1.15 he *a*, and went down with him
4.30 And he *a*, and followed her.
7. 7 they *a* and fled in the twilight,
12 And the king *a* in the night,
8. 2 woman *a*, and did after the saying
9. 6 he *a*, and went into the house;
10.12 And he *a* and departed.
11. 1 she *a* and destroyed all the seed
12.20 servants *a*, and made a conspiracy,
19.35 they *a* early in the morning,
23.25 after him *a* there any like him.
25.26 the captains of the armies, *a*,
1Ch 10.12 They *a*, all the valiant men,
20. 4 *a* war at Gezer with the
2Ch 22.10 she *a* and destroyed all the seed
29.12 Then the Levites *a*, Mahath the
30.14 they *a* and took away the altars
27 Then the priests the Levites *a*
36.16 the wrath of the Lord *a* against
Ezr 9. 5 I *a* up from my heaviness;
10. 5 *a* Ezra, and made the chief priest,
Neh 2.12 And I *a* in the night,
Est 8. 4 Esther *a*, and stood before the
Job 1.20 Then Job *a*, and rent his mantle,
19.18 I *a*, and they spake against me.
29. 8 the aged *a*, and stood up.
Ps 76. 9 When God *a* to judgment,
Ec 1. 5 hasteth to his place where he *a*.
Isa 37.36 when they *a* early in the morning,
Jer 41. 2 *a* Ishmael the son of Nethaniah,
Eze 3.23 Then I *a*, and went forth into the
Dan 6.19 king *a* very early in the morning,
Jon 3. 3 Jonah *a*, and went unto Nineveh,
6 and he *a* from his throne,
Mt 2.14 he *a* he took the young child and
21 he *a*, and took the young child
8.15 she *a*, and ministered unto them.
24 there *a* a great tempest in the sea,
26 he *a*, and rebuked the winds
9. 7 he *a*, and departed to his house.
9 And he *a*, and followed him.
19 Jesus *a*, and followed him,
25 her by the hand, and the maid *a*.
25. 7 all those virgins *a*, and trimmed
26.62 the high priest *a*, and said
27.52 of the saints which slept *a*,
Mk 2.12 immediately he *a*, took up the bed,
14 And he *a* and followed him.
4.37 there *a* a great storm of wind,
39 he *a*, and rebuked the wind,
5.42 the damsel *a*, and walked;
7.24 he *a*, and went into the borders
9.27 lifted him up; and he *a*.
10. 1 he *a* from thence, and cometh
14.57 *a* certain, and bare false witness,
Lk 1.39 And Mary *a* in those days, and
4.38 he *a* out of the synagogue,
39 she *a* and ministered unto them.
6. 8 he *a* and stood forth.
48 *a*, the stream beat vehemently
8.24 he *a*, and rebuked the wind
55 again, and she *a* straightway:
9.46 there *a* a reasoning among them,
15.14 *a* a mighty famine in that land;
20 he *a*, and came to his father.
23. 1 the whole multitude of them *a*,
24.12 *a* Peter, and ran unto the sepulcher;
Jn 3.25 there *a* a question between some
6.18 sea *a* by reason of a great wind
11.29 she *a* quickly, and came unto him.
Ac 5. 6 the young men *a*, wound him
6. 1 *a* a murmuring of the Grecians
9 there *a* certain of the synagogue,
7.18 king *a*, which knew not Joseph.
8.27 he *a* and went: and, behold, a
9. 8 Saul *a* from the earth; and when
18 *a*, and was baptized.
34 thy bed. And he *a* immediately.
39 Then Peter *a* and went with them.
11.19 persecution that *a* about Stephen
19.23 same time there *a* no small stir,
23. 7 there *a* a dissension between the
9 *a* a great cry: and the scribes
9 of the Pharisees' part *a*, and
10 when there *a* a great dissension
27.14 *a* against it a tempestuous wind
Rev 9. 2 there *a* a smoke out of the pit,

ARPAD

2Ki 18.34 the gods of Hamath, and of *A*?
19.13 of Hamath, and the king of *A*,
Isa 10. 9 not Hamath as *A*? is not Samaria
Jer 49.23 Hamath is confounded, and *A*:

ARPHAD

Isa 36.19 are the gods of Hamath and *A*?
37.13 of Hamath, and the king of *A*,

ARPHAXAD

Gen 10.22 Elam, and Asshur, and *A*, and
24 *A* begat Salah; and Salah begat
11.10 begat *A* two years after the flood:
11 Shem lived after he begat *A* five
12 *A* lived five and thirty years,
13 *A* lived after he begat Salah four
1Ch 1.17 *A*, and Lud, and Aram,
18 *A* begat Shelah, and Shelah
24 Shem, *A*, Shelah,
Lk 3.36 which was the son of *A*,

ARRAYED
Gen 41.42 *a* him in vestures of fine linen,
2Ch 5.12 *a* in white linen, having cymbals
28.15 and *a* them, and shod them).
Est 6.11 *a* Mordecai, and brought him on
Mt 6.29 was not *a* like one of these.
Lk 12.27 was not *a* like one of these.
23.11 *a* him in a gorgeous robe, and
Ac 12.21 Herod, *a* in royal apparel,
Rev 7.13 these which are *a* in white robes?
17. 4 And the woman was *a* in purple
19. 8 she should be *a* in fine linen,

ARRIVED
Lk 8.26 *a* at the country of the Gadarenes,
Ac 20.15 and the next day we *a* at Samos,

ARROW
1Sa 20.36 he shot an *a* beyond him.
37 was come to the place of the *a*
37 is not the *a* beyond thee?
2Ki 9.24 the *a* went out at his heart,
13.17 The *a* of the Lord's deliverance,
17 and the *a* of deliverance
19.32 nor shoot an *a* there,
Job 41.28 *a* cannot make him flee:
Ps 11. 2 they make ready their *a*
64. 7 God shall shoot at them with an *a*;
91. 5 for the *a* that flieth by day;
Pr 25.18 a sword, and a sharp *a*.
Isa 37.33 nor shoot an arrow there,
Jer 9. 8 Their tongue is as an *a*
La 3.12 set me as a mark for the *a*.
Zec 9.14 his *a* shall go forth

ARROWS
Nu 24. 8 pierce them through with his *a*.
Dt 32.23 I will spend mine *a* upon them.
42 make mine *a* drunk with blood,
1Sa 20.20 I will shoot three *a* on the side
21 Go, find out the *a*.
21 the *a* are on this side of thee,
22 the *a* are beyond thee;
36 find out now the *a* which I shoot.
38 Jonathan's lad gathered up the *a*,
2Sa 22.15 he sent out *a*, and scattered them;
2Ki 13.15 Take bow and *a*.
15 And he took unto him bow and *a*.
18 he said, Take the *a*.
1Ch 12. 2 in hurling stones and shooting *a*
2Ch 26.15 to shoot *a* and great stones
Job 6. 4 For the *a* of the Almighty are
Ps 7.13 he ordaineth his *a* against the
18.14 Yea, he sent out his *a*,
21.12 ready thine *a* upon thy strings
38. 2 For thine *a* stick fast in me,
45. 5 Thine *a* are sharp in the heart
57. 4 whose teeth are spears and *a*,
58. 7 bendeth his bow to shoot his *a*,
64. 3 bend their bows to shoot their *a*,
76. 3 brake he the *a* of the bow,
77.17 thine *a* also went abroad.
120. 4 Sharp *a* of the mighty,
127. 4 As *a* are in the hand of a mighty
144. 6 shoot out thine *a*, and destroy
Pr 26.18 casteth firebrands, *a*, and death,
Isa 5.28 Whose *a* are sharp,
7.24 With *a* and with bows shall men
Jer 50. 9 their *a* shall be as of a mighty
14 shoot at her, spare no *a*:
51.11 Make bright the *a*;
La 3.13 hath caused the *a* of his quiver
Eze 5.16 send upon them the evil *a* of
21.21 he made his *a* bright, he
39. 3 and will cause thine *a* to fall
9 the bows and the *a*, and the
Hab 3.11 at the light of thine *a* they went,

ARTAXERXES
Ezr 4. 7 in the days of *A*, wrote Bishlam,
7 unto *A* king of Persia; and the
8 to *A* the king in this sort:
11 they sent unto him, even unto *A*
6.14 and Darius, and *A* king of Persia.
7. 1 in the reign of *A* king of Persia,
7 in the seventh year of *A* the king.
11 that the king *A* gave unto Ezra
12 *A*, king of kings, unto Ezra the
21 And I, even I *A* the king,
8. 1 in the reign of *A*, the king,
Neh 2. 1 in the twentieth year of *A* the king,
5.14 the two and thirtieth year of *A*
13. 6 in the two and thirtieth year of *A*

ARTAXERXES'
Ezr 4.23 the copy of king *A* letter was read

ARTEMAS
Tit 3.12 When I shall send *A* unto thee,

ARTIFICERS
1Ch 29. 5 by the hands of *a*.
2Ch 34.11 Even to the *a* and builders

ARTS
Ac 19.19 them also which used curious *a*

ASCEND
Jos 6. 5 and the people shall *a* up
Ps 24. 3 Who shall *a* into the hill of the
135. 7 He causeth the vapors to *a*
139. 8 If I *a* up into heaven,
Isa 14.13 I will *a* into heaven,
14 I will *a* above the heights of the
Jer 10.13 and he causeth the vapors to *a*
51.16 and he causeth the vapors to *a*
Eze 38. 9 Thou shalt *a* and come like a
Jn 6.62 ye shall see the Son of man *a* up
20.17 I *a* unto my Father, and your
Ro 10. 6 Who shall *a* into heaven?
Rev 17. 8 shall *a* out of the bottomless pit,

ASCENDED
Ex 19.18 and the smoke thereof *a*
Nu 13.22 And they *a* by the south,
Jos 8.20 the smoke of the city *a* up
21 the smoke of the city *a*,
10. 7 So Joshua *a* from Gilgal,
15. 3 and *a* up on the south side
Jdg 13.20 that the angel of the Lord *a* in
20.40 flame of the city *a* up to heaven,
Ps 68.18 Thou hast *a* on high,
Pr 30. 4 Who hath *a* up into heaven,
Jn 3.13 no man hath *a* up to heaven,
20.17 for I am not yet *a* to my Father:
Ac 2.34 David is not *a* into the heavens:
25. 1 *a* from Caesarea to Jerusalem
Eph 4. 8 When he *a* up on high,
9 (Now that he *a*, what is it
10 is the same also that *a* up
Rev 8. 4 *a* up before God out of the angel's
11.12 they *a* up to heaven in a cloud;

ASCENDETH
Rev 11. 7 that *a* out of the bottomless pit
14.11 their torment *a* up for ever

ASCENDING
Gen 28.12 angels of God *a* and descending
1Sa 28.13 I saw gods *a* out of the earth.
Lk 19.28 went before, *a* up to Jerusalem.
Jn 1.51 angels of God *a* and descending
Rev 7. 2 another angel *a* from the east,

ASCENT
Nu 34. 4 to the *a* of Akbrabim,
2Sa 15.30 up by the *a* of mount Olivet,
1Ki 10. 5 and his *a* by which he went up
2Ch 9. 4 and his *a* by which he went up

ASCRIBE
Dt 32. 3 *a* ye greatness unto our God.
Job 36. 3 *a* righteousness to my Maker.
Ps 68.34 *A* ye strength unto God:

ASCRIBED
1Sa 18. 8 They have *a* unto David
8 to me they have *a* but thousands:

ASER
Lk 2.36 of the tribe of *A*:
Rev 7. 6 Of the tribe of *A* were sealed

ASH
Isa 44.14 he planteth an *a*, and the rain

ASHAMED
Gen 2.25 and were not *a*.
Nu 12.14 should she not be *a* seven days?
Jdg 3.25 they tarried till they were *a*:
2Sa 10. 5 because the men were greatly *a*:
19. 3 as people being *a* steal away
2Ki 2.17 they urged him till he was *a*,
8.11 until he was *a*: and the man of
1Ch 19. 5 the men were greatly *a*.
2Ch 30.15 and the Levites were *a*,
Ezr 8.22 I was *a* to require of the king
9. 6 I am *a* and blush to lift up my face
Job 6.20 they came thither, and were *a*.
11. 3 shall no man make thee *a*?
19. 3 ye are not *a* that ye make
Ps 6.10 Let all mine enemies be *a*
10 them return and be *a* suddenly.
25. 2 I trust in thee: let me not be *a*,
3 let none that wait on thee be *a*:
3 let them be *a* which transgress
20 let me not be *a*; for I put
31. 1 let me never be *a*:
17 Let me not be *a*, O Lord;
17 let the wicked be *a*,
34. 5 their faces were not *a*.
35.26 be *a* and brought to confusion
37.19 shall not be *a* in the evil time:
40.14 Let them be *a* and confounded
69. 6 them that wait on thee,...be *a*
70. 2 Let them be *a* and confounded
74.21 let not the oppressed return *a*:
86.17 may see it, and be *a*:
109.28 them be *a*; but let thy servant
119. 6 Then shall I not be *a*,
46 and will not be *a*.
78 Let the proud be *a*;
80 that I be not *a*.
116 let me not be *a* of my hope.
127. 5 they shall not be *a*,
Pr 12. 4 she that maketh *a* is as rottenness
Isa 1.29 For they shall be *a* of the oaks
20. 5 shall be afraid and *a* of Ethiopia
23. 4 Be thou *a*, O Zidon:
24.23 and the sun *a*,
26.11 be *a* for their envy at the people;
29.22 Jacob shall not now be *a*,
30. 5 They were all *a* of a people
33. 9 Lebanon is *a* and hewn down:
41.11 shall be *a* and confounded:
42.17 they shall be greatly *a*,
44. 9 that they may be *a*.
11 all his fellows shall be *a*:
11 they shall be *a* together.
45.16 shall be *a*, and also confounded,
17 shall not be *a* nor confounded
24 incensed against him shall be *a*.
49.23 shall not be *a* that wait for me.
50. 7 that I shall not be *a*.
54. 4 for thou shalt not be *a*:
65.13 but ye shall be *a*:
66. 5 they shall be *a*.
Jer 2.26 the thief is *a* when he is found,
26 so is the house of Israel *a*;
36 thou also shalt be *a* of Egypt,
36 as thou wast *a* of Assyria.
3. 3 thou refusedst to be *a*.
6.15 Were they *a* when they had

15 they were not at all *a*,
8. 9 The wise men are *a*,
12 Were they *a* when they
12 at all *a*, neither could they blush:
12.13 they shall be *a* of your enemies
14. 3 they were *a* and confounded,
4 the plowmen were *a*,
15. 9 hath been *a* and confounded,
17.13 all that forsake thee shall be *a*,
20.11 they shall be greatly *a*;
22.22 surely then shalt thou be *a*
31.19 I was *a*, yea, even confounded
48.13 And Moab shall be *a* of Chemosh,
13 house of Israel was *a* of Beth-el
50.12 she that bare you shall be *a*:
Eze 16.27 of the Philistines, which are *a*
61 remember thy ways, and be *a*,
32.30 they are *a* of their might;
36.32 be *a* and confounded for your own
43.10 they may be *a* of their iniquities:
11 if they be *a* of all that
Hos 4.19 and they shall be *a*
10. 6 Israel shall be *a* of his own counsel.
Joel 1.11 Be ye *a*, O ye husbandmen;
2.26, 27 My people shall never be *a*.
Mic 3. 7 the seers be *a*, and the diviners
Zep 3.11 In that day shalt thou not be *a*
Zec 9. 5 her expectation shall be *a*;
13. 4 the prophets shall be *a* every one
Mk 8.38 therefore shall be *a* of me
38 shall the Son of man be *a*,
Lk 9.26 whosoever shall be *a* of me
26 of him shall the Son of man be *a*,
13.17 all his adversaries were *a*:
16. 3 I cannot dig; to beg I am *a*.
Ro 1.16 am not *a* of the gospel of Christ:
5. 5 hope maketh not *a*; because
6.21 whereof ye are now *a*?
9.33 believeth on him shall not be *a*.
10.11 on him shall not be *a*.
2Co 7.14 I am not *a*;
9. 4 we...should be *a* in this same
10. 8 destruction, I should not be *a*:
Php 1.20 in nothing I shall be *a*,
2Th 3.14 with him, that he may be *a*.
2Ti 1. 8 thou therefore *a* of the testimony
12 nevertheless I am not *a*:
16 and was not *a* of my chain:
2.15 workman that needeth not to be *a*,
Tit 2. 8 the contrary part may be *a*,
Heb 2.11 is not *a* to call them brethren,
11.16 is not *a* to be called their God:
1Pe 3.16 as of evildoers, they may be *a*
4.16 a Christian, let him not be *a*;
1Jn 2.28 not be *a* before him.

ASHES

Gen 18.27 which am but dust and *a*:
Ex 9. 8 you handfuls of *a* of the furnace,
10 And they took *a* of the furnace,
27. 3 pans to receive his *a*,
Lev 1.16 by the place of the *a*:
4.12 where the *a* are poured out, and
12 where the *a* are poured out shall
6.10 take up the *a*
11 carry forth the *a*
Nu 4.13 And they shall take away the *a*
19. 9 the *a* of the heifer,
10 he that gathereth the *a* of
17 they shall take of the *a* of the
2Sa 13.19 Tamar put *a* on her head,
1Ki 13. 3 the *a* that are upon it
5 the *a* poured out from the altar,
20.38 disguised himself with *a* upon
41 took the *a* away from his face;
2Ki 23. 4 the *a* of them unto Beth-el.
Est 4. 1 put on sackcloth with *a*,
3 many lay in sackcloth and *a*.
Job 2. 8 he sat down among the *a*.
13.12 remembrances are like unto *a*,
30.19 I am become like dust and *a*,
42. 6 repent in dust and *a*.
Ps 102. 9 For I have eaten *a* like bread,
147.16 he scattereth the hoarfrost like *a*.
Isa 44.20 He feedeth on *a*:
58. 5 spread sackcloth and *a* under him?
61. 3 to give unto them beauty for *a*,
Jer 6.26 wallow thyself in *a*:
25.34 and wallow yourselves in the *a*, ye
31.40 and of the *a*, and all the fields
La 3.16 he hath covered me with *a*.
Eze 27.30 wallow themselves in the *a*:
28.18 I will bring thee to *a*
Dan 9. 3 with fasting, and sackcloth, and *a*:
Jon 3. 6 and sat in *a*.
Mal 4. 3 for they shall be *a*
Mt 11.21 long ago in sackcloth and *a*.
Lk 10.13 sitting in sackcloth and *a*.
Heb 9.13 the *a* of an heifer sprinkling the
2Pe 2. 6 Sodom and Gomorrha into *a*

ASHKELON

Jdg 14.19 and he went down to *A*, and slew
Jer 25.20 *A*, and Azzah, and Ekron,
47. 5 *A* is cut off with the remnant
7 *A*, and against the sea shore?
Am 1. 8 that holdeth the scepter from *A*,
Zep 2. 4 Gaza shall be forsaken, and *A*
7 houses of *A* shall they lie down
Zec 9. 5 *A* shall see it, and fear;
5 and *A* shall not be inhabited.

ASHTAROTH

Jos 9.10 king of Bashan, which was at *A*.
12. 4 that dwelt at *A* and at Edrei,
13.12 Og in Bashan, which reigned in *A*
31 half Gilead, and *A*, and Edrei,
Jdg 2.13 the Lord, and served Baal and *A*.
10. 6 served Baalim, and *A*, and the
1Sa 7. 3 put away the strange gods and *A*
4 Israel did put away Baalim and *A*,
12.10 and have served Baalim and *A*:
31.10 put his armor in the house of *A*;
1Ch 6.71 and *A* with her suburbs:

ASHTORETH

1Ki 11. 5 Solomon went after *A* the
33 *A* the goddess of the Sidonians,
2Ki 23.13 for *A* the abomination of the

ASIA

Ac 2. 9 Pontus, and *A*,
6. 9 them of Cilicia, and of *A*,
16. 6 to preach the word in *A*,
19.10 all they which dwelt in *A*
22 stayed in *A* for a season.
26 but almost throughout all *A*,
27 all *A* and the world worshippeth.
31 certain of the chief of *A*,
20. 4 accompanied him into *A*
4 of *A*, Tychicus and Trophimus.
16 would not spend the time in *A*:
18 that I came into *A*,
21.27 the Jews which were of *A*,
24.18 certain Jews from *A*
27. 2 by the coasts of *A*;
1Co 16.19 The churches of *A* salute you.
2Co 1. 8 which came to us in *A*,
2Ti 1.15 all they which are in *A*
1Pe 1. 1 *A* and Bithynia,
Rev 1. 4 seven churches which are in *A*:
11 seven churches which are in *A*;

ASIDE

Ex 3. 3 I will now turn *a*, and see this
4 the Lord saw that he turned *a*
32. 8 They have turned *a* quickly out
Nu 5.12 If any man's wife go *a*,
19 if thou hast not gone *a*
20 if thou hast gone *a*
29 when a wife goeth *a*
22.23 and the ass turned *a*
Dt 5.32 ye shall not turn *a* to the right
9.12 they are quickly turned *a* out of
16 ye had turned *a* quickly out of
11.16 ye turn *a*, and serve other gods,
28 but turn *a* out of the way
17.20 that he turn not *a* from the
28.14 thou shalt not go *a* from any
31.29 corrupt yourselves, and turn *a*
Jos 23. 6 that ye turn not *a* therefrom
Jdg 14. 8 he turned *a* to see the carcase
19.12 We will not turn *a* hither into
15 And they turned *a* thither, to go
Ru 4. 1 Ho, such a one! turn *a*, sit down
1 And he turned *a*, and sat down,
1Sa 6.12 turned not *a* to the right hand
8. 3 but turned *a* after lucre,
12.20 turn not *a* from following the
21 turn ye not *a*: for then
2Sa 2.21 Turn thee *a* to thy right hand, or
21 But Asahel would not turn *a*
22 Turn thee *a* from following me:
23 Howbeit he refused to turn *a*:
3.27 And when...Joab took him *a* in
6.10 but David carried it *a*
18.30 Turn *a*, and stand here.
30 And he turned *a*, and stood still.
1Ki 15. 5 turned not *a* from any thing
20.39 behold, a man turned *a*,
22.32 And they turned *a* to fight
43 he turned not *a* from it,
2Ki 4. 4 thou shalt set *a* that which is
22. 2 turned not *a* to the right hand
1Ch 13.13 but carried it *a* into the house of
Job 6.18 paths of their way are turned *a*;
Ps 14. 3 They are all gone *a*,
40. 4 nor such as turn *a* to lies.
78.57 were turned *a* like a deceitful
101. 3 the work of them that turn *a*;
125. 5 As for such as turn *a* unto their
SS 1. 7 should I be as one that turneth *a*
6. 1 whither is thy beloved turned *a*?
Isa 10. 2 To turn *a* the needy from
29.21 and turn *a* the just for a thing of
30.11 turn *a* out of the path,
44.20 heart hath turned him *a*,
Jer 14. 8 a wayfaring man that turneth *a*
15. 5 who shall go *a* to ask how thou
La 3.11 He hath turned *a* my ways,
35 To turn *a* the right of a man
Am 2. 7 and turn *a* the way of the meek:
5.12 they turn *a* the poor
Mal 3. 5 and that turn *a* the stranger
Mt 2.22 he turned *a* into the parts of
Mk 7. 8 laying *a* the commandment of
33 *a* from the multitude,
Lk 9.10 and went *a* privately
Jn 13. 4 and laid *a* his garments;
Ac 4.15 commanded them to go *a* out of
23.19 went with him *a* privately, and
26.31 when they were gone *a*, they
1Ti 1. 6 turned *a* unto vain jangling;
5.15 some are already turned *a* after
Heb 12. 1 let us lay *a* every weight, and
1Pe 2. 1 Wherefore laying *a* all malice,

ASK

Gen 32.29 thou dost *a* after my name?
34.12 *A* me never so much dowry and
Nu 27.21 who shall *a* counsel for him
Dt 4.32 *a* now of the days that are past,
32 *a* from the one side of heaven
13.14 inquire, and make search, and *a*
32. 7 *a* thy father, and he will shew
Jos 4. 6 your children *a* their fathers
21 When your children shall *a*
15.18 she moved him to *a* of her
Jdg 1.14 she moved him to *a* of her
18. 5 *A* counsel, we pray thee, of God,
1Sa 12.19 our sins this evil, to *a* us a king.
25. 8 *A* thy young men, and they will
28.16 Wherefore then dost thou *a* of me,

2Sa 14.18 thee, the thing that I shall *a* thee.
20.18 shall surely *a* counsel at Abel;
1Ki 2.16 I *a* one petition of thee,
20 the king said unto her, *A* on, my
22 why dost thou *a* Abishag
22 *a* for him the kingdom also;
3. 5 *A* what I shall give thee.
14. 5 cometh to *a* a thing of thee for
2Ki 2. 9 *A* what I shall do for thee,
2Ch 1. 7 *A* what I shall give thee.
20. 4 to *a* help of the Lord:
Job 12. 7 *a* now the beasts, and they shall
Ps 2. 8 *A* of me, and I shall give thee
Isa 7.11 *A* thee a sign of the Lord
11 *a* it either in the depth, or in the
12 Ahaz said, I will not *a*,
45.11 *A* me of things to come
58. 2 *a* of me the ordinances of justice;
Jer 6.16 and *a* for the old paths,
15. 5 who shall go aside to *a* how thou
18.13 *A* ye now among the heathen,
23.33 prophet, or a priest, shall *a* thee,
30. 6 *A* ye now, and see
38.14 I will *a* thee a thing;
48.19 *a* him that fleeth,
50. 5 They shall *a* the way to Zion
La 4. 4 the young children *a* bread,
Dan 6. 7 whosoever shall *a* a petition of
12 every man that shall *a* a petition
Hos 4.12 My people *a* counsel at their
Hag 2.11 *A* now the priests concerning
Zec 10. 1 *A* ye of the Lord rain
Mt 6. 8 have need of, before ye *a* him.
7. 7 *A*, and it shall be given you;
9 if his son *a* bread, will he give
10 Or if he *a* a fish, will he give him
11 good things to them that *a* him?
14. 7 give her whatsoever she would *a*.
18.19 any thing that they shall *a*,
20.22 said, Ye know not what ye *a*.
21.22 whatsoever ye shall *a* in prayer
24 I also will *a* you one thing,
22.46 *a* him any more questions.
27.20 that they should *a* Barabbas,
Mk 6.22 *A* of me whatsoever thou wilt;
23 Whatsoever thou shalt *a* of me,
24 unto her mother, What shall I *a*?
9.32 saying, and were afraid to *a* him.
10.38 Ye know not what ye *a*:
11.29 I will also *a* of you one question,
12.34 And no man after that durst *a*
Lk 6. 9 I will *a* you one thing; Is it
30 away thy goods *a* them not
9.45 they feared to *a* him of that
11. 9 *A*, and it shall be given you;
11 If a son shall *a* bread of any
11 if he *a* a fish will he for a fish
12 Or if he shall *a* an egg, will
13 Holy Spirit to them that *a* him?
12.48 of him they will *a* the more.
19.31 if any man *a* you,
20. 3 I will also *a* you one thing;
40 they durst not *a* him any
22.68 And if I also *a* you,
Jn 1.19 from Jerusalem to *a* him, Who
9.21 he is of age; *a* him: he shall
23 his parents, He is of age; *a* him.
11.22 whatsoever thou wilt *a* of God,
13.24 that he should *a* who it should
14.13 whatsoever ye shall *a* in my
14 If ye shall *a* any thing in my
15. 7 abide in you, ye shall *a* what
16 whatsoever ye shall *a* of the
16.19 they were desirous to *a* him,
23 ye shall *a* me nothing.
23 Whatsoever ye shall *a* the
24 *a*, and ye shall receive, that your
26 At that day ye shall *a* in my name:
30 that any man should *a* thee:
18.21 Why askest thou me? *a* them
21.12 none of the disciples durst *a*
Ac 3. 2 to *a* alms of them that entered
10.29 I *a* therefore for what intent
1Co 14.35 let them *a* their husbands at
Eph 3.20 above all that we *a* or think,
Jas 1. 5 you lack wisdom, let him *a* of
6 But let him *a* in faith, nothing
4. 2 ye have not, because ye *a* not.
3 Ye *a*, and receive not, because
3 ye *a* amiss, that ye may
1Jn 3.22 whatsoever we *a*, we receive
5.14 if we *a* any thing according to his
15 we *a*, we know that we have the
16 not unto death, he shall *a*, and

ASKED

Gen 24.47 And I *a* her, and said,
26. 7 the men of the place *a* him of
32.29 And Jacob *a* him,
37.15 and the man *a* him,
38.21 Then he *a* the men of that place,
40. 7 And he *a* Pharaoh's officers
43. 7 The man *a* us straitly
27 And he *a* them of their welfare,
44.19 My lord *a* his servants,
Ex 18. 7 they *a* each other of their welfare;
Jos 9.14 *a* not counsel at the mouth of the
19.50 gave him the city which he *a*,
Jdg 1. 1 that the children of Israel *a*
5.25 *a* water, and she gave him milk;
6.29 And when they inquired and *a*,
13. 6 I *a* him not whence he was,
20.18 and *a* counsel of God,
23 and *a* counsel of the Lord,
1Sa 1.17 thy petition that thou hast *a*
20 I have *a* him of the Lord.
27 my petition which I *a* of him:
8.10 the people that *a* of him a king.
14.37 And Saul *a* counsel of God,
19.22 and he *a* and said,
20. 6 David earnestly *a* leave
28 *a* leave of me to go to Bethlehem:
1Ki 3.10 Solomon had *a* this thing.
11 Because thou hast *a* this thing,
11 hast not *a* for thyself long life;
11 neither hast *a* riches for thyself,
11 hast *a* the life of thine enemies;
11 hast *a* for thyself understanding
13 thee that which thou hast not *a*,
10.13 whatsoever she *a*,
2Ki 2.10 Thou hast *a* a hard thing:
8. 6 when the king *a* the woman,
2Ch 1.11 thou hast not *a* riches,
11 neither yet hast *a* long life;
11 hast *a* wisdom and knowledge
9.12 all her desire, whatsoever she *a*,
Ezr 5. 9 Then *a* we those elders,
10 We *a* their names also,
Neh 1. 2 and I *a* them concerning the Jews
Job 21.29 Have ye not *a* them that go by
Ps 21. 4 He *a* life of thee,
105.40 The people *a*, and he brought
Isa 30. 2 have not *a* at my mouth;
41.28 when I *a* of them, could answer
65. 1 I am sought of them that *a* not
Jer 36.17 they *a* Baruch,
37.17 the king *a* him secretly in his
38.27 the princes unto Jeremiah, and *a*
Dan 2.10 *a* such things at any magician,
7.16 and *a* him the truth of all this.
Mt 12.10 they *a* him, saying,
16.13 he *a* his disciples, saying, Whom
17.10 his disciples *a* him, saying,
22.23 is no resurrection, and *a* him,
35 them, which was a lawyer, *a* him
41 gathered together, Jesus *a* them,
27.11 and the governor *a* him, saying,
Mk 4.10 about him with the twelve *a* of
5. 9 And he *a* him, What is thy name?
6.25 unto the king, and *a*, saying,
7. 5 Pharisees and scribes *a* him,
17 his disciples *a* him concerning the
8. 5 he *a* them, How many loaves
23 he *a* him if he saw ought.
27 by the way he *a* his disciples,
9.11 And they *a* him saying, Why say
16 And he *a* the scribes, What
21 And he *a* his father, How long is it
28 his disciples *a* him privately, Why
33 being in the house he *a* them,
10. 2 Pharisees came to him, and *a* him,
10 disciples *a* him again of the same
17 and *a* him, Good Master, what
12.18 no resurrection; and they *a* him,
28 *a* him, Which is the first
13. 3 John and Andrew *a* him privately,
14.60 the midst, and *a* Jesus, saying,
61 Again the high priest *a* him, and
15. 2 And Pilate *a* him, Art thou the
4 And Pilate *a* him again, saying,
44 he *a* him whether he had been
Lk 1.63 he *a* for a writing table, and wrote,
3.10 And the people *a* him, saying,
8. 9 And his disciples *a* him, saying,
30 And Jesus *a* him, saying, What is
9.18 and he *a* them, saying, Whom say
15.26 and *a* what these things meant.
18.18 a certain ruler *a* him, saying,
36 pass by, he *a* what it meant.
40 he was come near, he *a* him,
20.21 they *a* him, saying, Master, we
27 any resurrection; and they *a* him,
21. 7 And they *a* him, saying, Master,
22.64 and *a* him, saying, Prophesy, who
23. 3 And Pilate *a* him, saying, Art
6 he *a* whether the man were a
Jn 1.21 And they *a* him, What then?
25 they *a* him, and said
4.10 thou wouldest have *a* of him,
5.12 Then *a* they him, What man is
9. 2 his disciples *a* him,
15 the Pharisees also *a* him
19 *a* them, saying, Is this your son,
16.24 have ye *a* nothing in my name:
18. 7 Then *a* he them again, Whom
19 The high priest then *a* Jesus of
Ac 1. 6 they *a* of him, saying, Lord, wilt
3. 3 to go into the temple *a* an alms.
4. 7 they *a*, By what power, or by
5.27 and the high priest *a* them,
10.18 and *a* whether Simon,
23.19 aside privately, and *a* him,
34 he *a* of what province he was.
25.20 I *a* him whether he would go
Ro 10.20 unto them that *a* not after me.

ASKEST

Jdg 13.18 Why *a* thou thus after my name,
Jn 4. 9 being a Jew, *a* drink of me,
18.21 Why *a* thou me? ask them which

ASKETH

Gen 32.17 my brother meeteth thee, and *a*
Ex 13.14 when thy son *a* thee
Dt 6.20 thy son *a* thee in time to come,
Mic 7. 3 hands earnestly, the prince *a*,
3 and the judge *a* for a reward;
Mt 5.42 Give to him that *a* thee, and
7. 8 every one that *a* receiveth:
Lk 6.30 Give to every man that *a* of thee;
11.10 every one that *a* receiveth;
Jn 16. 5 none of you *a* me,
1Pe 3.15 every man that *a* you a reason

ASKING

1Sa 12.17 in *a* you a king.
1Ch 10.13 for *a* counsel of one that had a
Ps 78.18 tempted God in their heart by *a*
Lk 2.46 them, and *a* them questions.
Jn 8. 7 So when they continued *a* him,
1Co 10.25 *a* no question for conscience sake:
27 eat, *a* no question for conscience

ASKELON

Jdg 1.18 and *A* with the coast thereof,
1Sa 6.17 for Gaza one, for *A* one, for Gath
2Sa 1.20 publish it not in the streets of *A*;

ASLEEP

Jdg 4.21 he was fast *a* and weary.
1Sa 26.12 for they were all *a*;
SS 7. 9 those that are *a* to speak.
Jon 1. 5 and he lay, and was fast *a*.
Mt 8.24 but he was *a*.
26.40 and findeth them *a*,
43 came and found them *a* again:
Mk 4.38 *a* on a pillow: and they awake
14.40 he found them *a* again,
Lk 8.23 as they sailed he fell *a*:
Ac 7.60 when he had said this, he fell *a*.
1Co 15. 6 but some are fallen *a*.
18 also which are fallen *a* in Christ
1Th 4.13 concerning them which are *a*,
15 not prevent them which are *a*.
2Pe 3. 4 since the fathers fell *a*, all things

ASP

Isa 11. 8 shall play on the hole of the *a*,

ASPS

Dt 32.33 and the cruel venom of *a*.
Job 20.14 the gall of *a* within him.
16 He shall suck the poison of *a*:
Ro 3.13 poison of *a* is under their lips:

ASS

Gen 22. 3 saddled his *a*, and took two of
5 Abide ye here with the *a*;
42.27 give his *a* provender in the inn,
44.13 laded every man his *a*,
49.14 Issachar is a strong *a* couching
Ex 4.20 set them upon an *a*,
13.13 every firstling of an *a* thou shalt
20.17 nor his ox, nor his *a*, nor anything
21.33 an ox or an *a* fall therein;
22. 4 whether it be ox, or *a*, or sheep;
9 for ox, for *a*, for sheep,
10 deliver unto his neighbor an *a*,
23. 4 thine enemy's ox or his *a* going
5 If thou see the *a* of him that
12 thine ox and thine *a* may rest,
34.20 firstling of an *a* thou shalt redeem
Nu 16.15 I have not taken one *a* from them,
22.21 and saddled his *a*, and went with
22 Now he was riding upon his *a*,
23 the *a* saw the angel of the Lord
23 the *a* turned aside out of the way,
23 Balaam smote the *a*, to turn her
25, 27 the *a* saw the angel of the Lord,
27 he smote the *a* with a staff.
28 Lord opened the mouth of the *a*,
29 Balaam said unto the *a*,
30 the *a* said unto Balaam,
30 Am not I thine *a*,
32 hast thou smitten thine *a*
33 And the *a* saw me, and turned
Dt 5.14 nor thine ox, nor thine *a*,
21 his ox, or his *a*, or any thing
22. 3 shalt thou do with his *a*;
4 see thy brother's *a* or his ox fall
10 plow with an ox and an *a* together
28.31 thine *a* shall be violently taken
Jos 6.21 ox, and sheep, and *a*, with the
15.18 she lighted off her *a*;
Jdg 1.14 she lighted from off her *a*;
6. 4 neither sheep, nor ox, nor *a*.
10. 4 sons that rode on thirty *a* colts,
12.14 threescore and ten *a* colts:
15.15 found a new jawbone of an *a*,
16 With the jawbone of an *a*,
16 upon heaps, with the jaw of an *a*
19.28 the man took her up upon an *a*,
1Sa 12. 3 or whose *a* have I taken?
15. 3 ox and sheep, camel and *a*.
16.20 Jesse took an *a* laden with bread,
25.20 she rode on the *a*,
23 hasted, and lighted off the *a*,
42 arose, and rode upon an *a*,
2Sa 17.23 he saddled his *a*, and arose,
19.26 I will saddle me an *a*,
1Ki 2.40 Shimei arose, and saddled his *a*,
13.13 Saddle me the *a*.
13 So they saddled him the *a*:
23 that he saddled for him the *a*,
24 cast in the way, and the *a* stood by
27 Saddle me the *a*.
28 and the *a* and the lion standing
28 the carcase, nor torn the *a*.
29 laid it upon the *a*,
2Ki 4.24 Then she saddled an *a*,
Job 6. 5 Doth the wild *a* bray
24. 3 away the *a* of the fatherless,
39. 5 hath sent out the wild *a* free?
5 loosed the bands of the wild *a*?
Pr 26. 3 a bridle for the *a*,
Isa 1. 3 and the *a* his master's crib:
32.20 the feet of the ox and the *a*.
Jer 2.24 A wild *a* used to the wilderness,
22.19 buried with the burial of an *a*,
Hos 8. 9 a wild *a* alone by himself:
Zec 9. 9 lowly, and riding upon an *a*,
9 and upon a colt the foal of an *a*.
14.15 mule, of the camel, and of the *a*,
Mt 21. 2 ye shall find an *a* tied,
5 meek, and sitting upon an *a*,
5 and a colt the foal of an *a*.
7 And brought the *a*, and the colt,
Lk 13.15 loose his ox or his *a* from the stall,
14. 5 Which of you shall have an *a* or
Jn 12.14 when he had found a young *a*,
2Pe 2.16 *a* speaking with man's voice

ASSAULT

Est 8.11 the people...that would *a* them,
Ac 14. 5 when there was an *a* made

ASSAULTED

Ac 17. 5 *a* the house of Jason, and sought

ASSAYED

Dt 4.34 hath God *a* to go and take him
1Sa 17.39 and he *a* to go; for he had not
Ac 9.26 *a* to join himself to the disciples:
16. 7 they *a* to go into Bithynia:

ASSAYING

Heb 11.29 Egyptians *a* to do were

ASSEMBLED

Ex 38. 8 *a* at the door of the tabernacle
Nu 1.18 they *a* all the congregation
Jos 18. 1 congregation...*a* together at
Jdg 10.17 of Israel *a* themselves together,
1Sa 2.22 *a* at the door of the tabernacle
14.20 all the people...*a* themselves,
1Ki 8. 1 Solomon *a* the elders of Israel,
2 *a* themselves unto king Solomon
5 that were *a* unto him,
12.21 he *a* all the house of Judah,
1Ch 15. 4 David *a* the children of Aaron,
28. 1 David *a* all the princes of Israel,
2Ch 5. 2 Solomon *a* the elders of Israel.
3 all the men of Israel *a* themselves
6 were *a* unto him before the ark,
20.26 they *a* themselves in the valley
30.13 *a* at Jerusalem much people,
Ezr 9. 4 Then were *a* unto me every one
10. 1 there *a* unto him...a very great
Neh 9. 1 the children of Israel were *a*
Est 9.18 that were at Shushan *a* together
Ps 48. 4 kings were *a*, they passed by
Isa 43. 9 and let the people be *a*:
Jer 5. 7 and *a* themselves by troops
Eze 38. 7 company that are *a* unto thee,
Dan 6. 6 presidents and princes *a* together
11 these men *a*, and found Daniel
15 Then these men *a* unto the king,
Mt 26. 3 *a* together the chief priests,
57 scribes and the elders were *a*.
28.12 they were *a* with the elders,
Mk 14.53 were *a* all the chief priests,
Jn 20.19 where the disciples were *a*
Ac 1. 4 And being *a* together with them,
4.31 where they were *a* together;
11.26 *a* themselves with the church,
15.25 being *a* with one accord,

ASSEMBLIES

Ps 86.14 and the *a* of violent men
Ec 12.11 fastened by the masters of *a*,
Isa 1.13 calling of *a*, I cannot away with;
4. 5 her *a*, a cloud of smoke by day,
Eze 44.24 my statutes in all mine *a*;
Am 5.21 not smell in your solemn *a*.

ASSEMBLING

Ex 38. 8 lookingglasses of the women *a*,
Heb 10.25 the *a* of ourselves together,

ASSEMBLY

Gen 49. 6 into their secret; unto their *a*,
Ex 12. 6 *a* of the congregation of Israel
16. 3 kill this whole *a* with hunger.
Lev 4.13 be hid from the eyes of the *a*,
8. 4 the *a* was gathered together
23.36 it is a solemn *a*;
Nu 8. 9 thou shalt gather the whole *a*
10. 2 the calling of the *a*, and for the
3 *a* shall assemble themselves to
14. 5 on their faces before all the *a*
16. 2 princes of the *a*, famous
20. 6 went from the presence of the *a*
8 gather thou the *a* together,
29.35 ye shall have a solemn *a*:
Dt 5.22 the Lord spake unto all your *a*
9.10 fire in the day of the *a*.
10. 4 of the fire, in the day of the *a*
16. 8 a solemn *a* to the Lord thy God:
18.16 Horeb in the day of the *a*,
Jdg 20. 2 themselves in the *a* of the people,
21. 8 from Jabesh-gilead to the *a*.
1Sa 17.47 this *a* shall know that the Lord
2Ki 10.20 Proclaim a solemn *a* for Baal.
2Ch 7. 9 they made a solemn *a*:
30.23 the whole *a* took counsel
Neh 5. 7 And I set a great *a* against them.
8.18 the eighth day was a solemn *a*,
Ps 22.16 *a* of the wicked have inclosed me:
89. 7 to be feared in the *a* of the saints,
107.32 and praise him in the *a* of the
111. 1 in the *a* of the upright,
Pr 5.14 midst of the congregation and *a*.
Jer 6.11 the *a* of young men together:
9. 2 an *a* of treacherous men.
15.17 I sat not in the *a* of the mockers,
26.17 spake to all the *a* of the people,
50. 9 Babylon an *a* of great nations,
La 1.15 he hath called an *a* against me,
2. 6 destroyed his places of the *a*:
Eze 13. 9 not be in the *a* of my people,
23.24 and with an *a* of people,
Joel 1.14 call a solemn *a*, gather the elders
2.15 sanctify a fast, call a solemn *a*:
Zep 3.18 are sorrowful for the solemn *a*,
Ac 19.32 for the *a* was confused;
39 determined in a lawful *a*.
41 thus spoken, he dismissed the *a*.
Heb 12.23 *a* and church of the firstborn,
Jas 2. 2 there come unto your *a* a man

ASSENTED

Ac 24. 9 And the Jews also *a*, saying

ASS'S

Gen 49.11 his *a* colt unto the choice vine;
2Ki 6.25 an *a* head was sold for fourscore

Job 11.12 man be born like a wild *a* colt.
Jn 12.15 King cometh, sitting on an *a* colt.

ASSES

Gen 12.16 he *a*, and menservants,
16 and maidservants, and she *a*,
24.35 maidservants, and camels, and *a*:
30.43 menservants, and camels, and *a*.
32. 5 I have oxen, and *a*, flocks,
15 twenty she *a*, and ten foals.
34.28 their oxen, and their *a*,
36.24 as he fed the *a* of Zibeon
42.26 they laded their *a* with the corn,
43.18 take us for bondmen, and our *a*.
24 he gave their *a* provender.
44. 3 sent away, they and their *a*.
45.23 ten *a* laden with the good things
23 she *a* laden with corn and bread
47.17 herds, and for the *a*:
Ex 9. 3 upon the horses, upon the *a*,
Nu 31.28 of the beeves, and of the *a*,
30 of the *a*, and of the flocks,
34 threescore and one thousand *a*,
39 And the *a* were thirty thousand
45 thousand *a* and five hundred,
Jos 7.24 his oxen, and his *a*,
9. 4 took old sacks upon their *a*,
Jdg 5.10 speak, ye that ride on white *a*.
19. 3 with him, and a couple of *a*:
10 with him two *a* saddled,
19 straw and provender for our *a*;
21 gave provender unto the *a*:
1Sa 8.16 goodliest young men, and your *a*,
9. 3 *a* of Kish, Saul's father were lost.
3 arise, go seek the *a*.
5 leave caring for the *a*,
20 And as for thine *a* that were lost
10. 2 The *a* which thou wentest to seek
2 hath left the care of the *a*,
14 And he said, To seek the *a*:
16 plainly that the *a* were found.
22.19 oxen, and *a*, and sheep,
25.18 laid them on *a*.
27. 9 oxen, and the *a*, and the camels,
2Sa 16. 1 with a couple of *a* saddled,
2 The *a* be for the king's household
2Ki 4.22 the young men, and one of the *a*,
7. 7 their horses, and their *a*,
10 horses tied, and *a* tied,
1Ch 5.21 and of *a* two thousand,
12.40 brought bread on *a*,
27.30 and over the *a* was Jehdeiah
2Ch 28.15 all the feeble of them upon *a*,
Ezr 2.67 *a*, six thousand seven hundred
Neh 7.69 seven hundred and twenty *a*.
13.15 bringing in sheaves, and lading *a*;
Job 1. 3 five hundred she *a*,
14 and the *a* feeding beside them
24. 5 as wild *a* in the desert,
42.12 a thousand she *a*.
Ps 104.11 the wild *a* quench their thirst.
Isa 21. 7 a chariot of *a*, and a chariot of
30. 6 upon the shoulders of young *a*,
24 the young *a* that ear the ground
32.14 joy of wild *a*, a pasture of flocks;
Jer 14. 6 *a* did stand in the high places,
Eze 23.20 whose flesh is as the flesh of *a*,
Dan 5.21 his dwelling was with the wild *a*:

ASSIST

Ro 16. 2 and that ye *a* her in whatsoever

ASSOS

Ac 20.13 sailed unto *A*, there intending to
14 he met with us at *A*,

ASSURANCE

Dt 28.66 shalt have none *a* of thy life:
Isa 32.17 quietness and *a* for ever.
Ac 17.31 he hath given *a* unto all men,
Col 2. 2 of the full *a* of understanding,
1Th 1. 5 and in much *a*; as ye know
Heb 6.11 the full *a* of hope unto the end:
10.22 in full *a* of faith, having our

ASSURE

1Jn 3.19 and shall *a* our hearts before him.

ASSURED

Lev 27.19 and it shall be *a* to him.
Jer 14.13 *a* peace in this place.
2Ti 3.14 and hast been *a* of,

ASSUREDLY

1Sa 28. 1 know thou *a*, that thou shalt go
1Ki 1.13 *A* Solomon thy son shall reign
17, 30 saying, *A* Solomon thy son
Jer 32.41 *a* with my whole heart
38.17 wilt *a* go forth unto the king
49.12 of the cup have *a* drunken;
Ac 2.36 house of Israel know *a*,
16.10 *a* gathering that the Lord had

ASSYRIA

Gen 2.14 which goeth toward the east of *A*.
25.18 Egypt, as thou goest toward *A*:
2Ki 15.19 Pul the king of *A* came against
20 of silver, to give to the king of *A*.
20 So the king of *A* turned back,
29 came Tiglath-pileser king of *A*,
29 and carried them captive to *A*.
16. 7 to Tiglath-pileser king of *A*,
8 for a present to the king of *A*.
9 the king of *A* hearkened unto him:
9 of *A* went up against Damascus,
10 to meet Tiglath-pileser king of *A*,
18 of the Lord for the king of *A*.
17. 3 came up Shalmaneser king of *A*;
4 the king of *A* found conspiracy
4 brought no present to the king of *A*,
4 therefore the king of *A* shut him up,
5 Then the king of *A* came up
6 the king of *A* took Samaria,
6 and carried Israel away into *A*,
23 away out of their own land to *A*
24 the king of *A* brought men from
26 they spake to the king of *A*,
27 Then the king of *A* commanded,
18. 7 he rebelled against the king of *A*,
9 Shalmaneser king of *A* came up
11 And the king of *A* did carry away
11 did carry away Israel unto *A*,
13 did Sennacherib king of *A* come
14 sent to the king of *A* to Lachish,
14 king of *A* appointed unto Hezekiah
16 and gave it to the king of *A*.
17 the king of *A* sent Tartan and
19 the great king, the king of *A*,
23 pledges to my lord the king of *A*,
28 of the great king, the king of *A*:
30 into the hand of the king of *A*.
31 for thus saith the king of *A*,
33 out of the hand of the king of *A*?
19. 4 whom the king of *A* his master
6 the servants of the king of *A* have
8 and found the king of *A* warring
10 into the hand of the king of *A*.
11 what the kings of *A* have done
17 the kings of *A* have destroyed the
20 against Sennacherib king of *A* I
32 Lord concerning the king of *A*,
36 Sennacherib king of *A* departed,
20. 6 out of the hand of the king of *A*;
23.29 went up against the king of *A*
1Ch 5. 6 whom Tilgath-pileser king of *A*
26 up the spirit of Pul king of *A*,
26 spirit of Tilgath-pileser king of *A*,
2Ch 28.16 Ahaz send unto the kings of *A* to
20 Tilgath-pileser king of *A* came
21 and gave it unto the king of *A*:
30. 6 out of the hand of the kings of *A*.
32. 1 Sennacherib king of *A* came,
4 Why should the kings of *A* come,
7 nor dismayed for the king of *A*,
9 did Sennacherib king of *A* send
10 Thus saith Sennacherib king of *A*,
11 out of the hand of the king of *A*?
21 in the camp of the king of *A*.
22 hand of Sennacherib the king of *A*,
33.11 of the host of the king of *A*,
Ezr 6.22 turned the heart of the king of *A*
Neh 9.32 since the time of the kings of *A*
Isa 7.17 from Judah; even the king of *A*.
18 the bee that is in the land of *A*.
20 beyond the river, by the king of *A*.
8. 4 taken away before the king of *A*,
7 the king of *A*, and all his glory:
10.12 of the stout heart of the king of *A*,
11.11 which shall be left, from *A*, and
16 which shall be left, from *A*; like as
19.23 a highway out of Egypt to *A*,
23 and the Egyptian into *A*, and the
24 the third with Egypt and with *A*,
25 and *A* the work of my hands,
20. 1 Sargon the king of *A* sent him,)
4 So shall the king of *A* lead away
6 be delivered from the king of *A*:
27.13 ready to perish in the land of *A*,
36. 1 that Sennacherib king of *A* came
2 the king of *A* sent Rabshakeh
4 the king of *A*, What confidence
8 thee, to my master the king of *A*,
13 of the great king, the king of *A*.
15 into the hand of the king of *A*.
16 for thus saith the king of *A*,
18 out of the hand of the king of *A*?
37. 4 whom the king of *A* his master hath
6 the servants of the king of *A* have
8 and found the king of *A* warring
10 into the hand of the king of *A*.
11 what the kings of *A* have done
18 the kings of *A* have laid waste all
21 me against Sennacherib king of *A*:
33 Lord concerning the king of *A*,
37 Sennacherib king of *A* departed,
38. 6 out of the hand of the king of *A*:
Jer 2.18 hast thou to do in the way of *A*,
36 Egypt, as thou wast ashamed of *A*.
50.17 the king of *A* hath devoured him;
18 as I have punished the king of *A*.
Eze 23. 7 that were the chosen men of *A*,
Hos 7.11 they called to Egypt, they go of *A*.
8. 9 For they are gone up to *A*, a wild
9. 3 they shall eat unclean things in *A*.
10. 6 It shall be also carried unto *A*
11.11 as a dove out of the land of *A*:
Mic 5. 6 they shall waste the land of *A*
7.12 shall come even to thee from *A*,
Na 3.18 shepherds slumber, O king of *A*:
Zep 2.13 against the north, and destroy *A*;
Zec 10.10 Egypt, and gather them out of *A*;
11 pride of *A* shall be brought down,

ASSYRIAN

Isa 10. 5 O *A*, the rod of mine anger,
24 in Zion, be not afraid of the *A*:
14.25 I will break the *A* in my land,
19.23 and the *A* shall come into Egypt,
23.13 till the *A* founded it for them that
30.31 shall the *A* be beaten down,
31. 8 shall the *A* fall with the sword,
52. 4 *A* oppressed them without cause.
Eze 31. 3 the *A* was a cedar in Lebanon with
Hos 5.13 then went Ephraim to the *A*,
11. 5 but the *A* shall be his king,
Mic 5. 5 the *A* shall come into our land:
6 thus shall he deliver us from the *A*,

ASSYRIANS

2Ki 19.35 and smote in the camp of the *A*
Isa 19.23 shall serve with the *A*.
37.36 and smote in the camp of the *A*
La 5. 6 and to the *A*, to be satisfied with

Eze 16.28 the whore also with the *A*,
23. 5 her lovers, on the *A* her neighbors,
9 into the hand of the *A*, upon
12 upon the *A* her neighbors,
23 and Koa, and all the *A* with them:
Hos 12. 1 do make a covenant with the *A*,

ASTONIED
Ezr 9. 3 of my beard, and sat down *a*.
4 sat *a* until the evening sacrifice.
Job 17. 8 upright men shall be *a* at this,
18.20 that come after him shall be *a*
Isa 52.14 As many were *a* at thee;
Jer 14. 9 shouldest thou be as a man *a*,
Eze 4.17 *a* one with another, and
Dan 3.24 Nebuchadnezzar the king was *a*,
4.19 Daniel,...was *a* for one hour.
5. 9 in him, and his lords were *a*.

ASTONISHED
Lev 26.32 and your enemies...shall be *a*
1Ki 9. 8 passeth by it shall be *a*,
Job 21. 5 Mark me, and be *a*, and lay your
26.11 and are *a* at his reproof.
Jer 2.12 Be *a*, O ye heavens, at this,
4. 9 and the priests shall be *a*,
18.16 that passeth thereby shall be *a*,
19. 8 that passeth thereby shall be *a*
49.17 that goeth by it shall be *a*,
50.13 that goeth by Babylon shall be *a*,
Eze 3.15 remained there *a* among them
26.16 every moment, and be *a* at thee.
27.35 inhabitants of the isles shall be *a*
28.19 the people shall be *a* at thee:
Dan 8.27 and I was *a* at the vision,
Mt 7.28 the people were *a* at his doctrine:
13.54 insomuch that they were *a*,
22.33 they were *a* at his doctrine.
Mk 1.22 they were *a* at his doctrine:
5.42 *a* with a great astonishment.
6. 2 many hearing him were *a*,
7.37 were beyond measure *a*,
10.24 disciples were *a* at his words.
26 they were *a* out of measure,
11.18 the people was *a* at his doctrine.
Lk 2.47 were *a* at his understanding
4.32 they were *a* at his doctrine:
5. 9 For he was *a*, and all that
8.56 her parents were *a*:
24.22 made us *a*, which were early
Ac 9. 6 And he trembling and *a* said,
10.45 were *a*, as many as came with
12.16 saw him, they were *a*.
13.12 *a* at the doctrine of the Lord.

ASTONISHMENT
Dt 28.28 and *a* of heart:
37 thou shalt become an *a*,
2Ch 7.21 shall be an *a* to every one
29. 8 to trouble, to *a*, and to hissing,
Ps 60. 3 made us to drink the wine of *a*.
Jer 8.21 *a* hath taken hold on me.
25. 9 make them an *a*, and an hissing,
11 desolation, and an *a*;
18 a desolation, an *a*, an hissing,
29.18 a curse, and an *a*,
42.18 execration, and an *a*,
44.12 an *a*, and a curse,
22 desolation, and an *a*,
51.37 an *a*, and an hissing,
41 Babylon become an *a*.
Eze 4.16 water by measure, and with *a*:
5.15 instruction and an *a*
12.19 and drink their water with *a*,
23.33 with the cup of *a* and desolation,
Zec 12. 4 smite every horse with *a*,
Mk 5.42 astonished with a great *a*.

ASTRAY
Ex 23. 4 enemy's ox or his ass going *a*,
Dt 22. 1 not see thy brother's ox...go *a*,
Ps 58. 3 they go *a* as soon as they be born,
119.67 Before I was afflicted I went *a*:
176 I have gone *a* like a lost sheep;
Pr 5.23 of his folly he shall go *a*.
7.25 go not *a* in her paths.
28.10 causeth the righteous to go *a*
Isa 53. 6 All we like sheep have gone *a*;
Jer 50. 6 have caused them to go *a*,
Eze 14.11 Israel may go no more *a* from me,
44.10 when Israel went *a*,
10 which went *a* away from me
15 the children of Israel went *a*,
48.11 which went not *a*
11 when the children of Israel went *a*,
11 as the Levites went *a*.
Mt 18.12 and one of them be gone *a*,
12 and seeketh that which is gone *a*?
13 ninety and nine which went not *a*.
1Pe 2.25 ye were as sheep going *a*;
2Pe 2.15 and are gone *a*, following the way

ASTROLOGER
Dan 2.10 things at any magician, or *a*,

ASTROLOGERS
Isa 47.13 now the *a*, the stargazers,
Dan 1.20 *a* that were in all his realm,
2. 2 the magicians, and the *a*,
27 cannot the wise men, the *a*,
4. 7 came in the magicians, the *a*,
5. 7 cried aloud to bring in the *a*,
11 master of the magicians, *a*,
15 the *a*, have been brought in

ASUNDER
Lev 1.17 shall not divide it *a*:
5. 8 his neck, but shall not divide it *a*:
Nu 16.31 the ground clave *a* that was
2Ki 2.11 and parted them both *a*;
Job 16.12 but he hath broken me *a*: he hath
13 about, he cleaveth my reins *a*,
Ps 2. 3 Let us break their bands *a*, and
129. 4 he hath cut *a* the cords of the
Jer 50.23 hammer of the whole earth cut *a*
Eze 30.16 No shall be rent *a*,
Hab 3. 6 and drove *a* the nations;
Zec 11.10 and cut it *a*, that I might break
14 Then I cut *a* mine other staff,
Mt 19. 6 together, let not man put *a*.
24.51 shall cut him *a*, and appoint him
Mk 5. 4 had been plucked *a* by him,
10. 9 let not man put *a*.
Ac 1.18 he burst *a* in the midst,
15.39 they departed *a* one from the
Heb 4.12 even to the dividing *a* of soul and
11.37 they were sawn *a*, were tempted,

ATHALIAH
2Ki 8.26 and his mother's name was *A*,
11. 1 And when *A*, the mother of
2 from *A*, so that he was not slain.
3 And *A* did reign over the land.
13 when *A* heard the noise of the
14 and *A* rent her clothes, and cried
20 and they slew *A* with the sword
1Ch 8.26 and Shehariah, and *A*,
2Ch 22. 2 was *A* the daughter of Omri.
10 when *A* the mother of Ahaziah
11 hid him from *A*, so that she slew
12 house of God in six years: and *A*
23.12 Now when *A* heard the noise
13 *A* rent her clothes, and said,
21 they had slain *A* with the sword.
24. 7 sons of *A*, that wicked woman,
Ezr 8. 7 of Elam; Jeshaiah the son of *A*,

ATHENIANS
Ac 17.21 (For all the *A* and strangers

ATHENS
Ac 17.15 brought him unto *A*:
16 while Paul waited for them at *A*,
22 Ye men of *A*, I perceive
18. 1 Paul departed from *A*,
1Th 3. 1 it good to be left at *A* alone;

ATHIRST
Jdg 15.18 he was sore *a*, and called on the
Ru 2. 9 thou art *a*, go unto the vessels,
Mt 25.44 saw we thee an hungered, or *a*,
Rev 21. 6 I will give to him that is *a*
22.17 let him that is *a* come.

ATONEMENT
Ex 29.33 wherewith the *a* was made,
36 a bullock for a sin offering for *a*:
36 when thou hast made an *a* for it,
37 shalt make an *a* for the altar,
30.10 shall make an *a* upon the horns
10 once in the year shall he make *a*
15 to make *a* for your souls.
16 take the *a* money of the children
16 to make an *a* for your souls.
32.30 I shall make an *a* for your sin.
Lev 1. 4 to make *a* for him.
4.20 priest shall make an *a* for them,
26 and the priest shall make an *a*
31 priest shall make an *a* for him,
35 shall make an *a* for his sin
5. 6, 10, 13 shall make an *a* for him
16 the priest shall make an *a*
18 an *a* for him concerning his
6. 7 an *a* for him before the Lord:
7. 7 the priest that maketh *a*
8.34 to make an *a* for you.
9. 7 and make an *a* for thyself,
7 and make an *a* for them;
10.17 make *a* for them before the Lord?
12. 7 and make an *a* for her;
8 priest shall make an *a* for her,
14.18 and the priest shall make an *a*
19 and make an *a* for him
20 and the priest shall make an *a*
21, 29 to make an *a* for him,
31 and the priest shall make an *a*
53 and make an *a* for the house:
15.15, 30 the priest shall make an *a* for
16. 6 and make an *a* for himself,
10 to make an *a* with him,
11 and shall make an *a* for himself,
16 shall make an *a* for the holy place,
17 to make an *a* in the holy place,
17 and have made an *a* for himself,
18 and make an *a* for it;
24 and make an *a* for himself,
27 blood was brought in to make *a*
30 the priest make an *a* for you,
32 And the priest,...shall make the *a*,
33 make an *a* for the holy sanctuary,
33 shall make an *a* for the tabernacle
33 and he shall make an *a* for the
34 an *a* for the children of Israel.
17.11 to make an *a* for your souls:
11 the blood that maketh an *a* for
19.22 the priest shall make an *a* for
23.27 there shall be a day of *a*:
28 it is a day of *a*,
28 to make an *a* for you
25. 9 the day of *a* shall ye make the
Nu 5. 8 the ram of the *a*,
8 an *a* shall be made for him.
6.11 and make an *a* for him,
8.12 to make an *a* for the Levites.
19 and to make an *a* for the children
21 and Aaron made an *a*
15.25 And the priest shall make an *a*
28 shall make an *a* for the soul
28 to make an *a* for him;
16.46 and make an *a* for them:
47 and made an *a* for the people.
25.13 an *a* for the children of Israel.
28.22 sin offering, to make an *a* for you.
30 the goats; to make an *a* for you.

Nu 29. 5 offering to make an *a* for you:
11 the sin offering of *a*,
31.50 to make an *a* for our souls
2Sa 21. 3 wherewith shall I make the *a*,
1Ch 6.49 and to make an *a* for Israel,
2Ch 29.24 to make an *a* for all Israel:
Neh 10.33 to make an *a* for Israel,
Ro 5.11 we have now received the *a*.

ATONEMENTS
Ex 30.10 the sin offering of *a*:

ATTAIN
Ps 139. 6 it is high, I cannot *a* unto it.
Pr 1. 5 a man of understanding shall *a*
Eze 46. 7 as his hand shall *a* unto,
Hos 8. 5 will it be ere they *a* to innocency?
Ac 27.12 means they might *a* to Phenice,
Php 3.11 I might *a* unto the resurrection

ATTAINED
Gen 47. 9 not *a* unto the days of the years
2Sa 23.19 he *a* not unto the first three:
23 he *a* not to the first
1Ch 11.21 howbeit he *a* not to the first three.
25 but *a* not to the first three.
Ro 9.30 have *a* to righteousness,
31 not *a* to the law of righteousness.
Php 3.12 Not as though I had already *a*,
16 whereto we have already *a*,
1Ti 4. 6 whereunto thou hast *a*.
Ac 14.25 they went down into *A*:

ATTEND
Est 4. 5 he had appointed to *a* upon her,
Ps 17. 1 *a* unto my cry, give ear unto my
55. 2 *A* unto me, and hear me:
61. 1 *a* unto my prayer.
86. 6 *a* to the voice of my supplications.
142. 6 *A* unto my cry; for I am brought
Pr 4. 1 and *a* to know understanding.
20 My son, *a* to my words;
5. 1 My son, *a* unto my wisdom,
7.24 and *a* to the words of my mouth.
1Co 7.35 that ye may *a* upon the Lord

ATTENDANCE
1Ki 10. 5 and the *a* of his ministers,
2Ch 9. 4 and the *a* of his ministers,
1Ti 4.13 Till I come, give *a* to reading,
Heb 7.13 no man gave *a* at the altar.

ATTENDED
Job 32.12 Yea, I *a* unto you, and, behold,
Ps 66.19 hath *a* to the voice of my prayer.
Ac 16.14 she *a* unto the things which were

ATTENDING
Ro 13. 6 *a* continually upon this very thing.

ATTENT
2Ch 6.40 thine ears be *a* unto the prayer
7.15 mine ears *a* unto the prayer

ATTENTIVE
Neh 1. 6 let now thine ear be *a*,
11 now thine ear be *a* to the prayer
8. 3 were *a* unto the book of the law.
Ps 130. 2 let thine ears be *a* to the voice
Lk 19.48 were very *a* to hear him.

ATTENTIVELY
Job 37. 2 Hear *a* the noise of his voice,

ATTIRE
Pr 7.10 the *a* of an harlot,
Jer 2.32 her ornaments, or a bride her *a*?
Eze 23.15 in dyed *a* upon their heads,

ATTIRED
Lev 16. 4 the linen miter shall he be *a*:

AUDIENCE
Gen 23.10 in the *a* of the children of Heth,
13 in the *a* of the people of the land,
16 named in the *a* of the sons of Heth,
Ex 24. 7 read in the *a* of the people:
1Sa 25.24 in thine *a*, and hear the words
1Ch 28. 8 and in the *a* of our God,
Neh 13. 1 in the *a* of the people;
Lk 7. 1 sayings in the *a* of the people,
20.45 in the *a* of all the people he said
Ac 13.16 ye that fear God, give *a*.
15.12 and gave *a* to Barnabas and
22.22 they gave him *a* unto this word,

AUGUSTUS
Lk 2. 1 a decree from Caesar *A*,
Ac 25.21 reserved unto the hearing of *A*,
25 himself hath appealed to *A*,

AUGUSTUS'
Ac 27. 1 a centurion of *A* band.

AUL
Ex 21. 6 bore his ear through with an *a*;
Dt 15.17 Then thou shalt take an *a*,

AUNT
Lev 18.14 she is thine *a*.

AUSTERE
Lk 19.21 because thou art an *a* man:
22 that I was an *a* man,

AUTHOR
1Co 14.33 God is not the *a* of confusion, but
Heb 5. 9 became the *a* of eternal salvation
12. 2 the *a* and finisher of our faith;

AUTHORITIES
1Pe 3.22 *a* and powers being made subject

AUTHORITY
Est 9.29 Mordecai the Jew,...with all *a*,
Pr 29. 2 When the righteous are in *a*, the
Mt 7.29 taught them as one having *a*,
8. 9 For I am a man under *a*,
20.25 that are great exercise *a* upon
21.23 what *a* doest thou these things?
23 and who gave thee this *a*
24, 27 by what *a* I do these things.
Mk 1.22 as one that had *a*,
27 for with *a* commandeth he even
10.42 their great ones exercise *a* upon
11.28 what *a* doest thou these things?
28 and who gave thee this *a*
29, 33 by what *a* I do these things.
13.34 gave *a* to his servants,
Lk 4.36 with *a* and power he commandeth
7. 8 am a man set under *a*,
9. 1 gave them power and *a* over all
19.17 have thou *a* over ten cities.
20. 2 what *a* doest thou these things?
2 who is he that gave thee this *a*?
8 by what *a* I do these things.
20 power and *a* of the governor.
22.25 that exercise *a* upon them are
Jn 5.27 hath given him *a* to execute
Ac 8.27 eunuch of great *a* under Candace
9.14 he hath *a* from the chief priests
26.10 having received *a* from the chief
12 went to Damascus with *a* and
1Co 15.24 all rule and all *a* and power.
2Co 10. 8 somewhat more of our *a*,
1Ti 2. 2 and for all that are in *a*;
12 nor to usurp *a* over the man, but
Tit 2.15 exhort, and rebuke with all *a*.
Rev 13. 2 power, and his seat, and great *a*.

AVAILETH
Est 5.13 all this *a* me nothing,
Gal 5. 6 neither circumcision *a* any thing,
6.15 neither circumcision *a* any thing,
Jas 5.16 prayer of a righteous man *a* much.

AVENGE
Lev 19.18 Thou shalt not *a*, nor bear any
26.25 a sword...that shall *a* the quarrel
Nu 31. 2 *A* the children of Israel of
3 and *a* the Lord of Midian.
Dt 32.43 will *a* the blood of his servants,
1Sa 24.12 and the Lord *a* me of thee:
2Ki 9. 7 I may *a* the blood of my servants
Est 8.13 to *a* themselves on their enemies.
Isa 1.24 and *a* me of mine enemies:
Jer 46.10 he may *a* him of his adversaries:
Hos 1. 4 and I will *a* the blood of Jezreel
Lk 18. 3 saying, *A* me of mine adversary.
5 I will *a* her, lest by her continual
7 not God *a* his own elect,
8 he will *a* them speedily.
Ro 12.19 Dearly beloved, *a* not yourselves,
Rev 6.10 dost thou not judge and *a* our

AVENGED
Gen 4.24 If Cain shall be *a* sevenfold,
Jos 10.13 the people had *a* themselves
Jdg 15. 7 yet will I be *a* of you,
16.28 that I may be at once *a* of the
1Sa 14.24 that I may be *a* on mine enemies.
18.25 to be *a* of the king's enemies.
25.31 or that my Lord hath *a* himself:
2Sa 4. 8 the Lord hath *a* my lord
18.19 hath *a* him of his enemies.
31 Lord hath *a* thee this day of all
Jer 5. 9, 29 shall not my soul be *a* on such
9. 9 shall not my soul be *a* on such
Ac 7.24 *a* him that was oppressed,
Rev 18.20 God hath *a* you on her.
19. 2 hath *a* the blood of his servants

AVENGER
Nu 35.12 for refuge from the *a*; that the
Dt 19. 6 Lest the *a* of the blood pursue the
12 into the hand of the *a* of blood,
Jos 20. 3 your refuge from the *a* of blood.
5 if the *a* of blood pursue after him,
9 by the hand of the *a* of blood,
Ps 8. 2 still the enemy and the *a*.
44.16 by reason of the enemy and *a*.
1Th 4. 6 the Lord is the *a* of all such,

AVENGETH
2Sa 22.48 It is God that *a* me,
Ps 18.47 It is God that *a* me,

AVENGING
Jdg 5. 2 Praise ye the Lord for the *a*
1Sa 25.26 from *a* thyself with thine own
33 from *a* myself with mine own

AVERSE
Mic 2. 8 by securely as men *a* from war.

AVOID
Pr 4.15 *A* it, pass not by it, turn from it,
Ro 16.17 which ye have learned; and *a*
1Co 7. 2 Nevertheless, to *a* fornication,
2Ti 2.23 and unlearned questions *a*,
Tit 3. 9 But *a* foolish questions, and

AVOIDED
1Sa 18.11 And David *a* out of his presence

AVOIDING
2Co 8.20 *A* this, that no man should
1Ti 6.20 *a* profane and vain babblings,

AWAIT
Ac 9.24 laying *a* was known of Saul.

AWAKE
Jdg 5.12 *A*, *a*, Deborah; *a*, *a*, utter a
Job 8. 6 surely now he would *a* for thee,

14.12 they shall not *a*, nor be raised
Ps 7. 6 and *a* for me to the judgment
17.15 I shall be satisfied, when I *a*, with
35.23 Stir up thyself, and *a* to my
44.23 *A*, why sleepest thou, O Lord?
57. 8 *A* up, my glory,
8 *a*, psaltery and harp:
8 I myself will *a* early.
59. 4 *a* to help me, and behold.
5 *a* to visit all the heathen:
108. 2 *A*, psaltery and harp:
2 I myself will *a* early.
139.18 when I *a*, I am still with thee.
Pr 23.35 when shall I *a*? I will seek it yet
SS 2. 7 nor *a* my love, till he please.
3. 5 not up, nor *a* my love, till he
4.16 *A*, O north wind; and come,
8. 4 ye stir not up, nor *a* my love,
Isa 26.19 *A* and sing, ye that dwell in dust:
51. 9 *A*, *a*, put on strength, O arm of
9 the Lord; *a*, as in the ancient
17 *A*, *a*; stand up, O Jerusalem,
52. 1 *A*, *a*; put on thy strength,
Dan 12. 2 in the dust of the earth shall *a*,
Joel 1. 5 *A*, ye drunkards, and weep;
Hab 2. 7 and *a* that shall vex thee,
19 him that saith to the wood, *A*;
Zec 13. 7 *A*, O sword, against my shepherd,
Mk 4.38 they *a* him, and say unto him,
Lk 9.32 when they were *a*, they saw his
Jn 11.11 that I may *a* him out of sleep.
Ro 13.11 is high time to *a* out of sleep:
1Co 15.34 *A* to righteousness, and sin not;
Eph 5.14 *A* thou that sleepest, and arise

AWAKED
Gen 28.16 And Jacob *a* out of his sleep,
Jdg 16.14 And he *a* out of his sleep,
1Sa 26.12 saw it, nor knew it, neither *a*:
1Ki 18.27 he sleepeth, and must be *a*.
2Ki 4.31 The child is not *a*.
Ps 3. 5 I *a*; for the Lord sustained me.
78.65 the Lord *a* as one out of sleep,
Jer 31.26 Upon this I *a*, and beheld;

AWAKEST
Ps 73.20 when thou *a*, thou shalt despise
Pr 6.22 when thou *a*, it shall talk with

AWAKETH
Ps 73.20 As a dream when one *a*;
Isa 29. 8 but he *a*, and his soul is empty:
8 but he *a*, and, behold, he is faint,

AWAKING
Ac 16.27 *a* out of his sleep, and

AWARE
SS 6.12 Or ever I was *a*, my soul made
Jer 50.24 thou wast not *a*: thou art found,
Mt 24.50 in an hour that he is not *a* of,
Lk 11.44 over them are not *a* of them.
12.46 and at an hour when he is not *a*,

AWE
Ps 4. 4 Stand in *a*, and sin not:
33. 8 of the world stand in *a*
119.161 heart standeth in *a* of thy word.

AWOKE
Gen 9.24 And Noah *a* from his wine,
41. 4 and fat kine. So Pharaoh *a*.
7 and Pharaoh *a*, and, behold, it
21 as at the beginning. So I *a*.
Jdg 16.20 And he *a* out of his sleep,
1Ki 3.15 And Solomon *a*; and, behold, it
Mt 8.25 *a* him, saying, Lord, save us:
Lk 8.24 they came to him, and *a* him,

AX
Dt 19. 5 with the *a* to cut down the tree,
20.19 by forcing an *a* against them:
Jdg 9.48 Abimelech took an *a* in his hand,
1Sa 13.20 to sharpen every man...his *a*,
1Ki 6. 7 neither hammer nor *a* nor any
2Ki 6. 5 the *a* head fell into the water:
Isa 10.15 Shall the *a* boast itself
Jer 10. 3 of the workman, with the *a*.
51.20 Thou art my battle *a* and
Mt 3.10 now also the *a* is laid unto the

AXE
Lk 3. 9 now also the *a* is laid unto the

AXES
1Sa 13.21 for the forks, and for the *a*,
2Sa 12.31 and under *a* of iron,
1Ch 20. 3 with harrows of iron, and with *a*.
Ps 74. 5 he had lifted up *a* upon the thick
6 with *a* and hammers.
Jer 46.22 and come against her with *a*,
Eze 26. 9 with his *a* he shall break down

AXLETREES
1Ki 7.32 and the *a* of the wheels
33 their *a*, and their naves,

AZOTUS
Ac 8.40 But Philip was found at *A*:

B

Baal, great rain and fertility god of the Canaanites

BAAL

Nu 22.41 up into the high places of *B*,
Jdg 2.13 Lord, and served *B* and Ashtaroth.
6.25 and throw down the altar of *B*
28 the altar of *B* was cast down,
30 hath cast down the altar of *B*,
31 Will ye plead for *B*? will ye save
32 Let *B* plead against him, because
1Ki 16.31 and served *B*, and worshipped
32 he reared up an altar for *B*
32 in the house of *B*,
18.19 the prophets of *B* four hundred
21 but if *B*, then follow him.
25 Elijah said unto the prophets of *B*,
26 and called on the name of *B*
26 saying, O *B*, hear us.
40 them, Take the prophets of *B*;
19.18 which have not bowed unto *B*,
22.53 For he served *B*, and worshipped
2Ki 3. 2 for he put away the image of *B*
10.18 unto them, Ahab served *B* a little;
19 unto me all the prophets of *B*,
19 have a great sacrifice to do to *B*;
19 destroy the worshippers of *B*.
20 Proclaim a solemn assembly for *B*.
21 all the worshippers of *B* came,
21 they came into the house of *B*;
21 and the house of *B* was full
22 for all the worshippers of *B*.
23 into the house of *B*,
23 said unto the worshippers of *B*,
23 but the worshippers of *B* only.
25 went to the city of the house of *B*.
26 the images out of the house of *B*,
27 they brake down the image of *B*,
27 and brake down the house of *B*,
28 Jehu destroyed *B* out of Israel.
11.18 the land went into the house of *B*,
18 and slew Mattan the priest of *B*
17.16 the host of heaven, and served *B*.
21. 3 and he reared up altars for *B*,
23. 4 the vessels that were made for *B*,
5 also that burned incense unto *B*,
1Ch 4.33 about the same cities, unto *B*.
5. 5 Reaia his son, *B* his son,
8.30 and Kish, and *B*, and Nadab,
9.36 Kish, and *B*, and Ner, and Nadab,
2Ch 23.17 the people went to the house of *B*,
17 and slew Mattan the priest of *B*
Jer 2. 8 the prophets prophesied by *B*,
7. 9 falsely, and burn incense unto *B*,
11.13 altars to burn incense unto *B*.
17 anger in offering incense unto *B*.
12.16 taught my people to swear by *B*;
19. 5 built also the high places of *B*,
5 fire for burnt offerings unto *B*,
23.13 they prophesied in *B*, and caused
27 have forgotten my name for *B*.
32.29 they have offered incense unto *B*,
35 they build the high places of *B*,
Hos 2. 8 gold, which they prepared for *B*.
13. 1 when he offended in *B*, he died.
Zep 1. 4 I will cut off the remnant of *B*
Ro 11. 4 bowed the knee to the image of *B*.

BAALIM

Jdg 2.11 sight of the Lord, and served *B*:
3. 7 and served *B* and the groves.
8.33 went a whoring after *B*, and made
10. 6 and served *B*, and Ashtaroth,
10 our God, and also served *B*.
1Sa 7. 4 children of Israel did put away *B*
12.10 have served *B* and Ashtaroth:
1Ki 18.18 and thou hast followed *B*.
2Ch 17. 3 David, and sought not unto *B*;
24. 7 Lord did they bestow upon *B*.
28. 2 made also molten images for *B*.
33. 3 and he reared up altars for *B*,
34. 4 they brake down the altars of *B*
Jer 2.23 polluted, I have not gone after *B*?
9.14 after *B*, which their fathers
Hos 2.13 I will visit upon her the days of *B*,
17 I will take away the names of *B*
11. 2 sacrificed unto *B*, and burned

BAAL'S

1Ki 18.22 but *B* prophets are four hundred

BAAL-ZEBUB

2Ki 1. 2 Go, inquire of *B* the god of Ekron
3 that ye go to inquire of *B* the god
6 that thou sendest to inquire of *B*
16 sent messengers to inquire of *B*

BABBLER

Ec 10.11 and a *b* is no better.
Ac 17.18 said, What will this *b* say?

BABBLING

Pr 23.29 who hath *b*? who hath wounds

BABBLINGS

1Ti 6.20 avoiding profane and vain *b*,
2Ti 2.16 shun profane and vain *b*: for

BABE

Ex 2. 6 behold, the *b* wept.
Lk 1.41 the *b* leaped in her womb;
44 the *b* leaped in my womb for joy.
2.12 the *b* wrapt in swaddling clothes,
16 Mary, and Joseph, and the *b* lying
Heb 5.13 of righteousness: for he is a *b*.

BABEL

Gen 10.10 beginning of his kingdom was *B*,
11. 9 is the name of it called *B*;

BABES

Ps 8. 2 of the mouth of *b* and sucklings
17.14 rest of their substance to their *b*.
Isa 3. 4 and *b* shall rule over them.
Mt 11.25 hast revealed them unto *b*.
21.16 Out of the mouth of *b*
Lk 10.21 hast revealed them unto *b*:
Ro 2.20 teacher of *b*, which hast the form
1Co 3. 1 as unto *b* in Christ.
1Pe 2. 2 As newborn *b*, desire the sincere

BABYLON

2Ki 17.24 of Assyria brought men from *B*,
30 men of *B* made Succoth-benoth,
20.12 son of Baladan, king of *B*, sent
14 from a far country, even from *B*.
17 this day, shall be carried unto *B*:
18 in the palace of the king of *B*.
24. 1 king of *B* came up, and Jehoiakim
7 the king of *B* had taken from
10 of *B* came up against Jerusalem,
11 king of *B* came against the city,
12 Judah went out to the king of *B*,
12 king of *B* took him in the eighth
15 he carried away Jehoiachin to *B*,
15 into captivity from Jerusalem to *B*.
16 king of *B* brought captive to *B*.
17 the king of *B* made Mattaniah his
20 rebelled against the king of *B*.
25. 1 of *B* came, he, and all his host,
6 him up to the king of *B* to Riblah;
7 of brass, and carried him to *B*,
8 of king Nebuchadnezzar king of *B*,
8 a servant of the king of *B*, unto
11 that fell away to the king of *B*,
13 carried the brass of them to *B*.
20 them to the king of *B* to Riblah:
21 king of *B* smote them, and slew
22 Nebuchadnezzar king of *B* had
23 of *B* had made Gedaliah governor,
24 the land, and serve the king of *B*;
27 Evil-merodach king of *B* in the

The Tower of Babel in a 17th-century engraving

28 kings that were with him in *B*;
1Ch 9. 1 away to *B* for their transgression.
2Ch 32.31 ambassadors of the princes of *B*,
33.11 with fetters, and carried him to *B*.
36. 6 up Nebuchadnezzar king of *B*,
6 him in fetters, to carry him to *B*.
7 of the house of the Lord to *B*,
7 put them in his temple at *B*.
10 brought him to *B*, with the goodly
18 all these he brought to *B*.
20 the sword carried he away to *B*;
Ezr 1.11 up from *B* unto Jerusalem.
2. 1 of *B* had carried away unto *B*,
5.12 the king of *B*, the Chaldean, who
12 carried the people away into *B*.
13 first year of Cyrus the king of *B*
14 brought them into the temple of *B*,
14 king take out of the temple of *B*,
17 treasure house, which is there at *B*,
6. 1 the treasures were laid up in *B*.
5 and brought unto *B*, be restored,
7. 6 This Ezra went up from *B*; and
9 began he to go up from *B*, and on
16 canst find in all the province of *B*,
8. 1 that went up with me from *B*,
Neh 7. 6 the king of *B* had carried away,
13. 6 of Artaxerxes king of *B* came I
Est 2. 6 the king of *B* had carried away.
Ps 87. 4 make mention of Rahab and *B*
137. 1 the rivers of *B*, there we sat down,
8 O daughter of *B*, who art to be
Isa 13. 1 The burden of *B*, which Isaiah
19 And *B*, the glory of kingdoms,
14. 4 this proverb against the king of *B*,
22 and cut off from *B* the name,
21. 9 and said, *B* is fallen, is fallen;
39. 1 king of *B*, sent letters and a
3 far country unto me, even from *B*.
6 this day, shall be carried to *B*:
7 in the palace of the king of *B*.
43.14 For your sake I have sent to *B*,
47. 1 O virgin daughter of *B*, sit on the
48.14 he will do his pleasure on *B*,
20 Go ye forth of *B*, flee ye from the
Jer 20. 4 into the hand of the king of *B*.
4 he shall carry them captive into *B*,
5 take them, and carry them to *B*.
6 and thou shalt come to *B*, and
21. 2 Nebuchadrezzar king of *B*
4 ye fight against the king of *B*,
7 of Nebuchadrezzar king of *B*,
10 into the hand of the king of *B*,
22.25 king of *B*, and into the hand of the
24. 1 king of *B* had carried away
1 and had brought them to *B*.
25. 1 of Nebuchadrezzar king of *B*;
9 the king of *B*, my servant, and
11 serve the king of *B* seventy years.
12 I will punish the king of *B*,
27. 6 the king of *B*, my servant; and
8 the king of *B*, and that will not
8 under the yoke of the king of *B*,
9 Ye shall not serve the king of *B*:
11, 12 under the yoke of the king of *B*,
13 that will not serve the king of *B*?
14 Ye shall not serve the king of *B*:
16 shortly be brought again from *B*:
17 serve the king of *B*, and live:
18 and at Jerusalem, go not to *B*.
20 Nebuchadnezzar king of *B* took
20 from Jerusalem to *B*, and all the
22 They shall be carried to *B*,
28. 2 broken the yoke of the king of *B*.
3 Nebuchadnezzar king of *B* took
3 and carried them to *B*:
4 of Judah, that went into *B*,
4 break the yoke of the king of *B*.
6 captive, from *B* into this place.
11 king of *B* from the neck of all
14 serve Nebuchadnezzar king of *B*;
29. 1 away captive from Jerusalem to *B*;

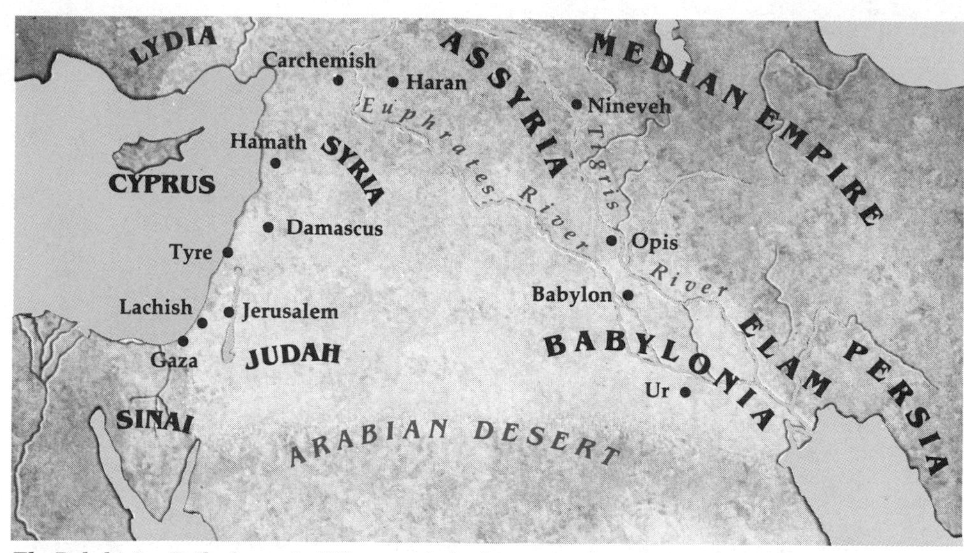

The Babylonian Exile, *begun in 597* B.C. *with the deportation by Nebuchadnezzar of more than 3,000 families from Judah to Babylonia, ended in 538 when the newly triumphant King Cyrus of Persia released the captive Jews and provided them with funds to begin the rebuilding of their temple in Jerusalem.*

3 king of Judah sent unto *B*
3 to Nebuchadnezzar king of *B*)
4 away from Jerusalem unto *B*;
10 years be accomplished at *B*
15 hath raised us up prophets in *B*;
20 I have sent from Jerusalem to *B*:
21 king of *B*; and he shall slay them
22 of Judah which are in *B*, saying,
22 the king of *B* roasted in the fire;
28 therefore he sent unto us in *B*,
32. 3 the king of *B*, and he shall take it;
4 of the king of *B*, and shall speak
5 he shall lead Zedekiah to *B*,
28 Nebuchadrezzar king of *B*,
36 of the king of *B* by the sword,
34. 1 king of *B*, and all his army,
2 the king of *B*, and he shall burn it
3 behold the eyes of the king of *B*,
3 to mouth, and thou shalt go to *B*.
35.11 Nebuchadrezzar king of *B* came up
36.29 king of *B* shall certainly come.
37. 1 Nebuchadrezzar king of *B* made
17 into the hand of the king of *B*.
19 The king of *B* shall not come
38.23 by the hand of the king of *B*:
39. 1 came Nebuchadrezzar king of *B*
3 princes of the king of *B* came in,
3 of the princes of the king of *B*.
5 up to Nebuchadnezzar king of *B*
6 Then the king of *B* slew the sons
6 the king of *B* slew all the nobles
7 with chains, to carry him to *B*.
9 guard carried away captive into *B*
11 king of *B* gave charge concerning
40. 1 were carried away captive unto *B*.
4 unto thee to come with me into *B*,
4 unto thee to come with me into *B*,
5 whom the king of *B* hath made
7 the king of *B* had made Gedaliah
7 not carried away captive to *B*;
9 and serve the king of *B*, and it
11 the king of *B* had left a remnant
41. 2 and slew him, whom the king of *B*
18 Ahikam, whom the king of *B* made
42.11 Be not afraid of the king of *B*,
43. 3 and carry us away captives into *B*.
10 Nebuchadrezzar the king of *B*,
44.30 king of *B*, his enemy, and that
46. 2 king of *B* smote in the fourth year
13 Nebuchadrezzar king of *B* should
26 hand of Nebuchadrezzar king of *B*,

49.28 which Nebuchadrezzar king of *B*
30 king of *B* hath taken counsel
50. 1 that the Lord spake against *B*
2 *B* is taken, Bel is confounded,
8 Remove out of the midst of *B*,
9 and cause to come up against *B*
13 goeth by *B* shall be astonished,
14 Put yourselves in array against *B*
16 Cut off the sower from *B*,
17 king of *B* hath broken his bones.
18 I will punish the king of *B* and
23 how is *B* become a desolation
24 and thou art also taken, O *B*,
28 and escape out of the land of *B*,
29 together the archers against *B*:
34 and disquiet the inhabitants of *B*.
35 and upon the inhabitants of *B*,
42 against thee, O daughter of *B*.
43 king of *B* hath heard the report.
45 that he hath taken against *B*;
46 At the noise of the taking of *B*
51. 1 Behold, I will raise up against *B*,
2 and will send unto *B* fanners,
6 Flee out of the midst of *B*,
7 *B* hath been a golden cup
8 *B* is suddenly fallen and destroyed:
9 We would have healed *B*, but she
11 for his device is against *B*,
12 the standard upon the walls of *B*,
12 spake against the inhabitants of *B*.
24 I will render unto *B* and to all
29 shall be performed against *B*,
29 make the land of *B* a desolation
30 mighty men of *B* have forborn
31 shew the king of *B* that his city
33 of *B* is like a threshing floor,
34 the king of *B* hath devoured me,
35 and to my flesh be upon *B*,
37 *B* shall become heaps, a dwelling
41 how is *B* become an astonishment
42 The sea is come up upon *B*:
44 I will punish Bel in *B*,
44 yea, the wall of *B* shall fall.
47 upon the graven images of *B*:
48 that is therein, shall sing for *B*:
49 As *B* hath caused the slain of
49 so at *B* shall fall the slain of all
53 *B* should mount up to heaven,
54 A sound of a cry cometh from *B*,
55 Because the Lord hath spoiled *B*,
56 is come upon her, even upon *B*,

Jer 51.58 walls of *B* shall be utterly broken,
59 *B* in the fourth year of his reign.
60 evil that should come upon *B*,
60 words that are written against *B*.
61 When thou comest to *B*, and shalt
64 Thus shall *B* sink, and shall not
52. 3 rebelled against the king of *B*.
4 king of *B* came, he and all his
9 carried him up unto the king of *B*
10 king of *B* slew the sons of Zedekiah
11 the king of *B* bound him in chains,
11 and carried him to *B*,
12 year of Nebuchadrezzar king of *B*,
12 which served the king of *B*, into
15 that fell to the king of *B*,
17 carried all the brass of them to *B*.
26 them to the king of *B* to Riblah.
27 the king of *B* smote them, and
31 Evil-merodach king of *B*, in the
32 of the kings that were with him in *B*,
34 diet given him of the king of *B*,
Eze 12.13 I will bring him to *B* to the land
17.12 tell them, Behold, the king of *B*
12 and led them with him to *B*;
16 in the midst of *B* he shall die.
20 I will bring him to *B*, and will
19. 9 and brought him to the king of *B*:
21.19 the sword of the king of *B* may
21 the king of *B* stood at the parting
24. 2 the king of *B* set himself against
26. 7 Nebuchadrezzar king of *B*, a king
29.18 of man, Nebuchadrezzar king of *B*
19 unto Nebuchadrezzar king of *B*;
30.10 of Nebuchadrezzar king of *B*.
24 the arms of the king of *B*,
25 the king of *B*, and the arms of
25 of the king of *B*, and he shall
32.11 The sword of the king of *B*
Dan 1. 1 Nebuchadnezzar king of *B*
2.12 to destroy all the wise men of *B*.
14 to slay the wise men of *B*:
18 with the rest of the wise men of *B*.
24 to destroy the wise men of *B*:
24 Destroy not the wise men of *B*:
48 ruler over the whole province of *B*,
48 over all the wise men of *B*.
49 the affairs of the province of *B*:
3. 1 of Dura, in the province of *B*.
12 the affairs of the province of *B*,
30 Abed-nego, in the province of *B*.
4. 6 to bring in all the wise men of *B*
29 in the palace of the kingdom of *B*.
30 Is not this great *B*, that I have
5. 7 and said to the wise men of *B*,
7. 1 first year of Belshazzar king of *B*
Mic 4.10 and thou shall go even to *B*;
Zec 2. 7 with the daughter of *B*.
6.10 which are come from *B*,
Mt 1.11 they were carried away to *B*:
12 after they were brought to *B*,
17 the carrying away into *B*
17 carrying away into *B* unto Christ
Ac 7.43 carry you away beyond *B*.
1Pe 5.13 The church that is at *B*,
Rev 14. 8 *B* is fallen, is fallen,
16.19 great *B* came in remembrance
17. 5 *B* the great, the mother of
18. 2 *B* the great is fallen,
10 that great city *B*, that mighty city!
21 great city *B* be thrown down,

BACKBONE
Lev 3. 9 it shall he take off hard by the *b*;

BACKS
Ex 23.27 all thine enemies turn their *b*
Jos 7. 8 when Israel turneth their *b*
12 their *b* before their enemies,
Jdg 20.42 Therefore they turned their *b*
2Ch 29. 6 of the Lord, and turned their *b*.
Neh 9.26 cast thy law behind their *b*,
Eze 8.16 with their *b* toward the temple
10.12 and their *b*, and their hands,

BACKSIDE
Ex 3. 1 flock to the *b* of the desert, and
26.12 over the *b* of the tabernacle.
Rev 5. 1 book written within and on the *b*,

BACKSLIDER
Pr 14.14 The *b* in heart shall be filled

BACKSLIDING
Jer 3. 6 that which *b* Israel hath done?
8 *b* Israel committed adultery
11 The *b* Israel hath justified herself
12 Return, thou *b* Israel, saith the
14 Turn, O *b* children, saith the
22 Return, ye *b* children, and I will
8. 5 slidden back by a perpetual *b*?
31.22 O thou *b* daughter?
49. 4 thy flowing valley, O *b* daughter?
Hos 4.16 Israel slideth back as a *b* heifer:
11. 7 my people are bent to *b* from me:
14. 4 I will heal their *b*,

BACKSLIDINGS
Jer 2.19 and thy *b* shall reprove thee:
3.22 and I will heal your *b*.
5. 6 their *b* are increased.
14. 7 our *b* are many;

BACKWARD
Gen 9.23 both their shoulders, and went *b*,
23 and their faces were *b*, and they
49.17 so that his rider shall fall *b*.
1Sa 4.18 he fell from off the seat *b*
2Ki 20.10 shadow return *b* ten degrees.
11 brought the shadow ten degrees *b*,
Job 23. 8 and *b*, but I cannot perceive
Ps 40.14 them be driven *b* and put to shame
70. 2 be turned *b*, and put to confusion,
Isa 1. 4 unto anger, they are gone away *b*.
28.13 that they might go, and fall *b*.
38. 8 sun dial of Ahaz, ten degrees *b*.
44.25 that turneth wise men *b*,
59.14 judgment is turned away *b*,
Jer 7.24 went *b*, and not forward.
15. 6 saith the Lord, thou art gone *b*:
La 1. 8 she sigheth, and turneth *b*.
Jn 18. 6 they went *b*, and fell to

BAD
Gen 24.50 cannot speak unto thee *b* or good.
31.24, 29 not to Jacob either good or *b*.
Lev 27.10 nor change it, a good for a *b*,
10 or a *b* for a good: and if he
12 value it, whether it be good or *b*:
14 estimate it, whether it be good or *b*,
33 not search whether it be good or *b*,
Nu 13.19 whether it be good or *b*; and what
24.13 good or *b* of mine own mind;
2Sa 13.22 brother Amnon neither good nor *b*:
14.17 the king to discern good and *b*:
1Ki 3. 9 discern between good and *b*:
Ezr 4.12 the rebellious and the *b* city,
Jer 24. 2 not be eaten, they were so *b*.
Mt 13.48 into vessels, but cast the *b* away.
22.10 as they found, both *b* and good:
2Co 5.10 done, whether it be good or *b*.

BADE
Gen 43.17 did as Joseph *b*; and the man
Ex 16.24 up till the morning, as Moses *b*:
Nu 14.10 congregation *b* stone them with
Jos 11. 9 unto them as the Lord *b* him:
Ru 3. 6 all that her mother in law *b* her.
1Sa 24.10 and some *b* me kill thee: but
2Sa 1.18 *b* them teach the children of Judah
14.19 thy servant Joab, he *b* me, and
2Ch 10.12 the king *b*, saying, Come again
Est 4.15 Then Esther *b* them return
Mt 16.12 they how that he *b* them not
Lk 14. 9 And he that *b* thee and him come
10 when he that *b* thee cometh, he
12 said he also to him that *b* him,
16 made a great supper, and *b* many:
Ac 11.12 the spirit *b* me go with them,
18.21 *b* them farewell, saying, I must
22.24 *b* that he should be examined

BADEST
Gen 27.19 done according as thou *b* me:

BADGERS'
Ex 2. 5 *b* skins, and shittim wood,
26.14 a covering above of *b* skins.
35. 7 dyed red, and *b* skins, and
23 red skins of rams, and *b* skins,
36.19 a covering of *b* skins above that
39.34 the covering of *b* skins,
Nu 4. 6 the covering of *b* skins,
8 with a covering of *b* skins,
10 within a covering of *b* skins,
11 with a covering of *b* skins,
12 a covering of *b* skins, and shall
14 upon it a covering of *b* skins,
25 the covering of the *b* skins
Eze 16.10 shod thee with *b* skin,

BADNESS
Gen 41.19 in all the land of Egypt for *b*:

BAG
Dt 2.13 not have in thy *b* divers weights,
1Sa 17.40 in a shepherd's *b* which he had,
49 David put his hand in his *b*,
Job 14.17 transgression is sealed up in a *b*,
Pr 7.20 taken a *b* of money with him,
16.11 weights of the *b* are his work.
Isa 46. 6 They lavish gold out of the *b*,
Mic 6.11 with the *b* of deceitful weights?
Hag 1. 6 to put it into a *b* with holes.
Jn 1. 6 he was a thief, and had the *b*,
13.29 thought, because Judas had the *b*,

BAGS
2Ki 5.23 two talents of silver in two *b*,
12.10 they put up in *b*, and told the
Lk 1.33 provide yourselves *b* which wax

BAKE
Gen 19. 3 did *b* unleavened bread, and they
Ex 1.23 *b* that which ye will *b*
Lev 24. 5 and *b* twelve cakes thereof:
26.26 ten women shall *b* your bread in
1Sa 28.24 did *b* unleavened bread thereof:
2Sa 13. 8 in his sight, and did *b* the cakes.
Eze 4.12 thou shalt *b* it with dung that
46.20 they shall *b* the meat offering;

BAKED
Ex 11.39 And they *b* unleavened cakes
Nu 11. 8 *b* it in pans, and made cakes
1Ch 23.29 and for that which is *b* in the pan,
Isa 44.19 I have *b* bread upon the coals

BAKEMEATS
Gen 40.17 of *b* for Pharaoh;

BAKEN
Lev 2. 4 a meat offering *b* in the oven,
5 be a meat offering *b* in a pan,
7 offering *b* in the frying pan,
6.17 It shall not be *b* with leaven.
21 when it is *b*, thou shalt
21 the *b* pieces of the meat offering
7. 9 all the meat offering that is *b*
23.17 they shall be *b* with leaven;
1Ki 19. 6 there was a cake *b* on the coals,

BAKETH
Isa 44.15 he kindleth it, and *b* bread;

BAKER

Gen 40. 1 and his *b* had offended their lord
5 and the *b* of the king of Egypt,
16 When the chief *b* saw that the
20 of the chief *b* among his servants.
22 But he hanged the chief *b*:
41.10 both me and the chief *b*:
Hos 7. 4 as an oven heated by the *b*,
6 their *b* sleepeth all the night;

BAKERS

Gen 40. 2 against the chief of the *b*.
1Sa 8.13 and to be cooks, and to be *b*.

BAKERS'

Jer 37.21 piece of bread out of the *b* street,

BALAAM

Nu 22. 5 therefore unto *B* the son of Beor
7 and they came unto *B*, and spake
8 princes of Moab abode with *B*.
9 And God came unto *B*, and said,
10 And *B* said unto God, Balak the
12 God said unto *B*, Thou shalt not
13 *B* rose up in the morning, and said
14 said, *B* refuseth to come with us.
16 they came to *B*, and said to him,
18 *B* answered and said unto the
20 And God came unto *B* at night,
21 And *B* rose up in the morning,
23 and *B* smote the ass, to turn her
27 fell down under *B*: and Balaam's
28 she said unto *B*, What have I done
29 And *B* said unto the ass, Because
30 ass said unto *B*, Am not I thine
31 the Lord opened the eyes of *B*,
34 *B* said unto the angel of the Lord,
35 angel of the Lord said unto *B*, Go
35 *B* went with the princes of Balak.
36 Balak heard that *B* was come,
37 And Balak said unto *B*, Did I not
38 *B* said unto Balak, Lo, I am come
39 *B* went with Balak, and they came
40 sent to *B*, and to the princes
41 Balak took *B*, and brought him
23. 1 And *B* said unto Balak, Build me
2 Balak did as *B* had spoken;

BALAAM

Renowned seer from Pethor in northern Syria; summoned by Balak, king of Moab, to curse Israel as she moves toward the promised land, but on God's command refuses invitation (Nu 22:1-14); **on being offered a greater reward accepts, though with reluctance** (Nu 22:15-21); **God is angry and sends angel to bar the way; Balaam's ass sees the angel and turns aside, and Balaam beats her** (Nu 22:22-30); **Balaam's eyes are opened and he too sees the angel, who warns him to say to Balak only what he is told** (Nu 22:31-35); **Balak takes him to a high place to pronounce his curse, but in a trance he blesses Israel instead** (Nu 22:36–23:10); **he takes him to a better vantage point, with the same result** (Nu 23:11-26); **a third time Balak implores him to curse the incomers but, seeing the tents of Israel spread out before him, he pronounces an even stronger blessing** (Nu 23:27–24:9); **Balak in a rage dismisses him but before Balaam goes he blesses Israel for a fourth time, prophesying a glorious future for her, including victory over Balak's own nation** (Nu 24:10-25).

2 Balak and *B* offered on every altar
3 *B* said unto Balak, Stand by thy
4 And God met *B*: and he said unto
11 Balak said unto *B*, What hast thou
16 the Lord met *B*, and put a word
25 Balak said unto *B*, Neither curse
26 *B* answered and said unto Balak,
27 Balak said unto *B*, Come, I pray
28 brought *B* unto the top of Peor,
29 *B* said unto Balak, Build me here
30 And Balak did as *B* had said,
24. 1 *B* saw that it pleased the Lord
2 And *B* lifted up his eyes, and he
3 and said, *B* the son of Beor
10 anger was kindled against *B*,
10 Balak said unto *B*, I called thee
12 *B* said unto Balak, Spake I not
15 said, *B* the son of Beor hath said,
25 *B* rose up, and went and returned
31. 8 *B* also the son of Beor they slew
16 through the counsel of *B*,
Dt 23. 4 they hired against thee *B* the son
5 God would not hearken unto *B*;
Jos 13.22 *B* also the son of Beor, the
24. 9 sent and called *B* the son of Beor
10 But I would not hearken unto *B*;
Neh 13. 2 water, but hired *B* against them,
Mic 6. 5 what *B* the son of Beor answered
2Pe 2.15 following the way of *B* the son of
Jude 11 the error of *B* for reward)
Rev 2.14 doctrine of *B*, who taught Balac

BALAK

Nu 22. 2 *B* the son of Zippor saw all that
4 *B* the son of Zippor was king of
7 spake unto him the words of *B*.
10 *B* the son of Zippor, king of
13 and said unto the princes of *B*,
14 went unto *B*, and said, Balaam
15 And *B* sent yet again princes,
16 Thus saith *B* the son of Zippor,
18 unto the servants of *B*,
18 If *B* would give me
35 went with the princes of *B*.
36 *B* heard that Balaam was come,
37 *B* said unto Balaam, Did I not
38 Balaam said unto *B*, Lo, I am
39 Balaam went with *B*, and they
40 And *B* offered oxen and sheep,
41 *B* took Balaam, and brought him
23. 1 Balaam said unto *B*, Build me
2 *B* did as Balaam had spoken;
2 *B* and Balaam offered on every
3 Balaam said unto *B*, Stand by thy
5 Return unto *B*, and thus thou
7 and said, *B* the king of Moab
11 *B* said unto Balaam, What hast
13 *B* said unto him, Come, I pray
15 said unto *B*, Stand here by thy
16 Go again unto *B*, and say thus.
17 *B* said unto him, What hath the
18 and said, Rise up, *B*, and hear;
25 And *B* said unto Balaam,
26 and said unto *B*, Told not I thee,
27 *B* said unto Balaam, Come, I pray
28 *B* brought Balaam unto the top
29 Balaam said unto *B*, Build me
30 *B* did as Balaam had said,
24.10 *B* said unto Balaam, I called thee
12 Balaam said unto *B*, Spake I not
13 If *B* would give me his house
25 to his place: and *B* also went
Jos 24. 9 Then *B* the son of Zippor, king of
Jdg 11.25 art thou anything better than *B*
Mic 6. 5 what *B* king of Moab consulted,

BALANCE

Job 31. 6 Let me be weighed in an even *b*,
Ps 62. 9 to be laid in the *b*, they are
Pr 11. 1 false *b* is abomination to the
16.11 just weight and *b* are the Lord's:
20.23 and a false *b* is not good.
Isa 40.12 and the hills in a *b*?
15 count as the small dust of the *b*:
46. 6 weigh silver in the *b* and hire a

BALANCES

Lev 19.36 Just *b*, just weights, a just
Job 6. 2 my calamity laid in the *b* together!
Jer 32.10 weighed him the money in the *b*.
Eze 5. 1 then take thee *b* to weigh, and
45.10 Ye shall have just *b*,
Dan 5.27 Thou art weighed in the *b*,
Hos 12. 7 the *b* of deceit are in his hand:
Am 8. 5 falsifying the *b* by deceit?
Mic 6.11 pure with the wicked *b*,
Rev 6. 5 had a pair of *b* in his hand.

BALANCINGS

Job 37.16 thou know the *b* of the clouds,

BALD

Lev 11.22 the *b* locust after his kind, and
13.40 he is *b*; yet is he clean.
41 he is forehead *b*: yet is he clean.
42 if there be in the *b* head,
42 or *b* forehead, a white
42 leprosy sprung up in his *b* head,
42 head or his *b* forehead.
43 be white reddish in his *b* head,
43 or in her *b* forehead,
2Ki 2.23 *b* head; go up, thou *b* head.
Jer 16. 6 make themselves *b* for them:
48.37 every head shall be *b*, and every
Eze 27.31 themselves utterly *b* for thee,
29.18 every head was made *b*, and every
Mic 1.16 Make thee *b*, and poll thee for thy

BALDNESS

Lev 21. 5 They shall not make *b* upon their
Dt 14. 1 nor make any *b* between your
Isa 3.24 instead of well set hair *b*;
15. 2 on all their heads shall be *b*,
22.12 to mourning, and to *b*,
Jer 47. 5 *B* is come upon Gaza;
Eze 7.18 *b* upon all their heads.
Am 8.10 *b* upon every head; and I will
Mic 1.16 enlarge thy *b* as the eagle;

BALL

Isa 22.18 and toss thee like a *b* into a

BALM

Gen 37.25 spicery and *b* and myrrh, going
43.11 a little *b*, and a little honey,
Jer 8.22 Is there no *b* in Gilead;
46.11 Go up into Gilead, and take *b*,
51. 8 take *b* for her pain, if so be she
Eze 27.17 and honey, and oil, and *b*.

BANISHED

2Sa 14.13 doth not fetch home again his *b*.
14 that his *b* be not expelled

BANISHMENT

Ezr 7.26 it be unto death, or to *b*,
La 2.14 false burdens and causes of *b*.

BANK

Gen 41.17 I stood upon the *b* of the river:
Dt 4.48 is by the *b* of the river Arnon,
Jos 12. 2 upon the *b* of the river Arnon,
13. 9 is upon the *b* of the river Arnon,
16 is on the *b* of the river Arnon,
2Sa 20.15 cast up a *b* against the city,
2Ki 2.13 and stood by the *b* of Jordan;
19.32 shield, nor cast a *b* against it.
Isa 37.33 shields, nor cast a *b* against it.
Eze 47. 7 at the *b* of the river were very
12 by the river upon the *b* thereof,
Dan 12. 5 this side of the *b* of the river,
5 other on that side of the *b* of
Lk 19.23 money into the *b*, that at my

BANKS
Jos 3.15 overfloweth all his *b* all the time
4.18 flowed over all his *b*, as they did
1Ch 12.15 it had overflown all his *b*;
Isa 8. 7 channels, and go over all his *b*:
Dan 8.16 man's voice between the *b* of Ulai,

BANNER
Ps 60. 4 given a *b* to them that fear
SS 2. 4 and his *b* over me was love.
Isa 13. 2 Lift ye up a *b* upon the high

BANNERS
Ps 20. 5 set up our *b*: the Lord fulfil all
SS 6. 4 terrible as an army with *b*.
10 and terrible as an army with *b*?

BANQUETINGS
1Pe 4. 3 *b*, and abominable idolatries:

BAPTISM
Mt 3. 7 and Sadducees come to his *b*,
20.22 the *b* that I am baptized with?
23 be baptized with the *b* that I am
21.25 The *b* of John, whence was it?
Mk 1. 4 preach the *b* of repentance for
10.38 the *b* that I am baptized with?
39 with the *b* that I am baptized
11.30 The *b* of John, was it from heaven,
Lk 3. 3 preaching the *b* of repentance
7.29 being baptized with the *b* of John.
12.50 I have a *b* to be baptized with,
20. 4 The *b* of John, was it from heaven,
Ac 1.22 Beginning from the *b* of John,
10.37 after the *b* which John preached;
13.24 the *b* of repentance to all the people
18.25 Lord, knowing only the *b* of John.
19. 3 And they said, Unto John's *b*.
4 with the *b* of repentance, saying
Ro 6. 4 buried with him by *b* into death:
Eph 4. 5 One Lord, one faith, one *b*,
Col 2.12 Buried with him in *b*, wherein
1Pe 3.21 even *b* doth also now save us

BAPTISMS
Heb 6. 2 Of the doctrine of *b*, and of laying

Giovanni Bellini's The Baptism of Christ *(1502)*

BAPTIST
Mt 3. 1 In those days came John the *B*,
11.11 risen a greater than John the *B*:
12 from the days of John the *B* until
14. 2 This is John the *B*; he is risen
16.14 Some say that thou art John the *B*:
17.13 he spake unto them of John the *B*.
Mk 6.14 That John the *B* was risen from
24 she said, The head of John the *B*.
25 a charger the head of John the *B*.
8.28 they answered, John the *B*:
Lk 7.20 John *B* hath sent us unto thee,
28 greater prophet than John the *B*:
33 John the *B* came neither eating
9.19 answering said, John the *B*;

BAPTIST'S
Mt 14. 8 Give me here John *B* head in

BAPTIZE
Mt 3.11 I indeed *b* you with water
11 he shall *b* you with the Holy Ghost,
Mk 1. 4 John did *b* in the wilderness,
8 he shall *b* you with the Holy Ghost
Lk 3.16 I indeed *b* you with water;
16 he shall *b* you with the Holy Ghost
Jn 1.26 saying, I *b* with water: but
33 he that sent me to *b* with water,
1Co 1.17 Christ sent me not to *b*, but to

BAPTIZED
Mt 3. 6 And were *b* of him in Jordan,
13 Jordan unto John, to be *b* of him.
14 I have need to be *b* of thee, and
16 Jesus, when he was *b*, went up
20.22 I shall drink of, and to be *b*,
22 the baptism that I am *b* with?
23 and be *b* with the baptism
23 that I am *b* with:
Mk 1. 5 all *b* of him in the river of Jordan,
8 I indeed have *b* you with water:
9 and was *b* of John in Jordan.
10.38 and be *b* with the baptism
38 that I am *b* with?
39 and with the baptism that I am *b*
39 withal shall ye be *b*:
16.16 believeth and is *b* shall be saved;
Lk 3. 7 came forth to be *b* of him,
12 Then came also publicans to be *b*,
21 when all the people were *b*, it came
21 that Jesus also being *b*,
7.29 being *b* with the baptism of John.
30 themselves, being not *b* of him.
12.50 I have a baptism to be *b* with:
Jn 3.22 there he tarried with them, and *b*.
23 and they came, and were *b*.
4. 1 Jesus made and *b* more disciples
2 (Though Jesus himself *b* not,
10.40 place where John at first *b*;
Ac 1. 5 John truly *b* with water;
5 ye shall be *b* with the Holy Ghost
2.38 Repent, and be *b* every one of you
41 gladly received his word were *b*:
8.12 were *b*, both men and women.
13 he was *b*, he continued with Philip,
16 only they were *b* in the name
36 what doth hinder me to be *b*?
38 and the eunuch; and he *b* him.
9.18 forthwith, and arose, and was *b*.
10.47 water, that these should not be *b*,
48 commanded them to be *b* in the
11.16 John indeed *b* with water;
16 ye shall be *b* with the Holy Ghost.
16.15 when she was *b*, and her household,
33 was *b*, he and all his, straightway.
18. 8 hearing believed, and were *b*.
19. 3 Unto what then were ye *b*?
4 John verily *b* with the baptism of
5 heard this, they were *b* in the name
22.16 and be *b*, and wash away thy sins,
Ro 6. 3 of us as were *b* into Jesus Christ
3 were *b* into his death?
1Co 1.13 or were ye *b* in the name of Paul?
14 I thank God that I *b* none of you.
15 say that I had *b* in mine own name.
16 I *b* also the household of Stephanas:
16 I know not whether I *b* any other.
10. 2 were all *b* unto Moses in the cloud
12.13 For by one Spirit are we all *b* into
15.29 they do which are *b* for the dead,
29 why are they then *b* for the dead?
Gal 3.27 as have been *b* into Christ have put

BAPTIZEST
Jn 1.25 said unto him, Why *b* thou then,

BAPTIZETH
Jn 1.33 is he which *b* with the Holy Ghost.
3.26 behold, the same *b*, and all men

BAPTIZING
Mt 28.19 *b* them in the name of the Father,
Jn 1.28 Jordan, where John was *b*,
31 therefore am I come *b* with water.
3.23 John also was *b* in Aenon

BAR
Ex 26.28 And the middle *b* in the midst of
36.33 he made the middle *b* to shoot
Nu 4.10 skins, and shall put it upon a *b*.
12 skins, and shall put them on a *b*:
Jdg 16. 3 away with them, *b* and all, and
Neh 7. 3 them shut the doors, and *b* them:
Am 1. 5 break also the *b* of Damascus,

BARABBAS
Mt 27.16 a notable prisoner, called *B*.
17 *B*, or Jesus which is called Christ?
20 should ask *B*, and destroy Jesus.
21 release unto you? They said, *B*.
26 Then released he *B* unto them:
Mk 15. 7 And there was one named *B*,
11 that he should rather release *B*
15 released *B* unto them, and delivered
Lk 23.18 this man, and release unto us *B*:
Jn 18.40 Not this man, but *B*.
40 Now *B* was a robber,

BARACHIAS
Mt 23.35 Zacharias son of *B*, whom ye slew

BARBARIAN
1Co 14.11 unto him that speaketh a *b*,
11 that speaketh shall be a *b* unto me.
Col 3.11 *B*, Scythian, bond nor free:

BARBARIANS
Ac 28. 4 when the *b* saw the venomous
Ro 1.14 to the Greeks, and to the *B*;

BARBAROUS
Ac 28. 2 the *b* people shewed us no little

BARBER'S
Eze 5. 1 sharp knife, take thee a *b* rasor,

BARE
Gen 4. 1 she conceived, and *b* Cain, and
2 she again *b* his brother Abel.
17 she conceived, and *b* Enoch:
20 Adah *b* Jabal: he was the father
22 And Zillah, she also *b* Tubal-cain,
25 *b* a son, and called his name Seth:
6. 4 and they *b* children to them,
7.17 increased, and *b* up the ark,
16. 1 Abram's wife, *b* him no children:
15 And Hagar *b* Abram a son: and
15 his son's name, which Hagar *b*,
16 when Hagar *b* Ishmael to Abram.
19.37 the firstborn *b* a son, and called
38 And the younger, she also *b* a son,
20.17 maidservants; and they *b* children.

Biblical Themes

BAPTISM

I will pour water upon him that is thirsty, and floods upon the dry ground: I will pour my spirit upon thy seed, and my blessing upon thine offspring.
Isa 44.3

And it shall come to pass afterward, that I will pour out my spirit upon all flesh; and your sons and your daughters shall prophesy. Joel 2.28

I indeed baptize you with water unto repentance: but he that cometh after me is mightier than I . . . he shall baptize you with the Holy Ghost, and with fire.
Mt 3.11

Then cometh Jesus from Galilee to Jordan unto John, to be baptized of him. But John forbad him, saying, I have need to be baptized of thee, and comest thou to me? And Jesus answering said unto him, Suffer it to be so now: for thus it becometh us to fulfil all righteousness. Then he suffered him.
Mt 3.13-15

But Jesus answered and said, Ye know not what ye ask. Are ye able to drink of the cup that I shall drink of, and to be baptized with the baptism that I am baptized with? Mt 20.22

Go ye therefore, and teach all nations, baptizing them in the name of the Father, and of the Son, and of the Holy Ghost. Mt 28.19

He that believeth and is baptized shall be saved; but he that believeth not shall be damned. Mk 16.16

I have a baptism to be baptized with; and how am I straitened till it be accomplished! Lk 12.50

Except a man be born of water and of the Spirit, he cannot enter into the kingdom of God.
Jn 3.5

Then Peter said unto them, Repent, and be baptized every one of you in the name of Jesus Christ for the remission of sins, and ye shall receive the gift of the Holy Ghost. . . . Then they that gladly received his word were baptized: and the same day there were added unto them about three thousand souls.
Ac 2.38, 41

Can any man forbid water, that these should not be baptized, which have received the Holy Ghost as well as we?
Ac 10.47

She was baptized, and her household.
Ac 16.15

Christ sent me not to baptize, but to preach the gospel. 1Co 1.17

For by one Spirit are we all baptized into one body. 1Co 12.13

Ye are all the children of God by faith in Christ Jesus. For as many of you as have been baptized into Christ have put on Christ. There is neither Jew nor Greek, there is neither bond nor free, there is neither male nor female: for ye are all one in Christ Jesus. And if ye be Christ's, then are ye Abraham's seed, and heirs according to the promise.
Gal 3.26-29

One Lord, one faith, one baptism.
Eph 4.5

Christ . . . loved the church, and gave himself for it; that he might sanctify and cleanse it with the washing of water by the word. Eph 5.25-26

Buried with him in baptism. Col 2.12

Not by works of righteousness which we have done, but according to his mercy he saved us, by the washing of regeneration, and renewing of the Holy Ghost.
Tit 3.5

21. 2 Sarah conceived, and *b* Abraham a
3 whom Sarah *b* to him, Isaac.
22.24 she *b* also Tebah, and Gaham,
24.24 Milcah, which she *b* unto Nahor.
36 wife *b* a son to my master
47 son, whom Milcah *b* unto him:
25. 2 she *b* him Zimran, and Jokshan,
12 handmaid, *b* unto Abraham:
26 threescore years old when she *b*
29.32 And Leah conceived, and *b* a son,
33, 34, 35 conceived again, and *b* a
30. 1 saw that she *b* Jacob no children,
5 conceived, and *b* Jacob a son.
7 maid conceived again, and *b* Jacob
10 Zilpah Leah's maid *b* Jacob a son.
12 Leah's maid *b* Jacob a second
17 she conceived, and *b* Jacob a fifth
19 again, and *b* Jacob the sixth son.
21 And afterwards she *b* a daughter,
23 And she conceived, and *b* a son;
31. 8 then all the cattle *b* speckled:
8 then *b* all the cattle ringstraked.
39 I *b* the loss of it; of my hand
34. 1 which she *b* unto Jacob, went
36. 4 Adah *b* to Esau Eliphaz;
4 and Bashemath *b* Reuel;
5 Aholibamah *b* Jeush, and Jaalam,
12 and she *b* to Eliphaz Amalek:
14 she *b* to Esau Jeush, and Jaalam,
38. 3 And she conceived, and *b* a son;
4 she conceived again, and *b* a son;
5 yet again conceived, and *b* a son;
5 was at Chezib, when she *b* him.
41.50 Poti-pherah priest of On *b* unto
44.27 Ye know that my wife *b* me two
46.15 she *b* unto Jacob in Padan-aram,
18 and these she *b* unto Jacob,
20 priest of On *b* unto him.
25 and she *b* these unto Jacob:
Ex 2. 2 the woman conceived, and *b* a son:
22 And she *b* him a son, and he called
6.20 and she *b* him Aaron and Moses:
23 and she *b* him Nadab, and Abihu,
25 and she *b* him Phinehas: these are
19. 4 and how I *b* you on eagles' wings,
Lev 13.45 and his head *b*, and he shall put
55 whether it be *b* within or
Nu 13.23 and they *b* it between two
26.59 her mother *b* to Levi in Egypt:
59 and she *b* unto Amram Aaron
Dt 1.31 how that the Lord thy God *b* thee,
31. 9 the sons of Levi, which *b* the ark
25 the Levites, which *b* the ark
Jos 3.15 they that *b* the ark were come
15 and the feet of the priests that *b*
17 the priests that *b* the ark
4. 9 which *b* the ark of the covenant
10 the priest which *b* the ark stood
18 when the priests that *b* the ark
8.33 the Levites, which *b* the ark
Jdg 3.18 the people that *b* the present.
8.31 she also *b* him a son, whose
11. 2 And Gilead's wife *b* him sons;
13. 2 his wife was barren, and *b* not.
24 And the woman *b* a son.
Ru 4.12 Pharez whom Tamar *b* unto
13 her conception and she *b* a son.
1Sa 1.20 Hannah had conceived that she *b*
2.21 she conceived, and *b* three sons
14. 1 unto the young man that *b* his
6 the young man that *b* his armor,
17.41 man that *b* the shield went before
2Sa 6.13 they that *b* the ark of the Lord.
11.27 became his wife, and *b* him a
12.15 the child that Uriah's wife *b*
24 and she *b* a son, and he called
18.15 ten young men that *b* Joab's
21. 8 Aiah, whom she *b* unto Saul,
1Ki 1. 6 his mother *b* him after Absalom.
5.15 and ten thousand that *b* burdens,
9.23 five hundred and fifty which *b*
10. 2 camels that *b* spices, and very
11.20 the sister of Tahpenes *b* him
14.28 the guard *b* them, and brought
2Ki 4.17 the woman conceived, and *b* a son
5.23 and they *b* them before him.
1Ch 1.32 she *b* Zimran, and Jokshan,
2. 4 Tamar, his daughter in law, *b* him
17 Abigail *b* Amasa; and the father
19 Ephrath, which *b* him Hur.
21 and she *b* him Segub.
24 then Abiah Hezron's wife *b* him
29 and she *b* him Ahban, and Molid.
35 servant to wife; and she *b* him
46 Ephah, Caleb's concubine, *b*
48 Maachah, Caleb's concubine, *b*
49 she *b* also Shaaph the father
4. 6 And Naarah *b* him Ahuzam, and
9 saying, Because I *b* him with
17 and she *b* Miriam, and Shammai,
18 And his wife Jehudijah *b* Jered
7.14 Ashriel, whom she *b*; but his
14 concubine the Aramitess *b* Machir
16 Maachah the wife of Machir *b* a
18 his sister Hammoleketh *b* Ishod,
23 she conceived, and *b* a son, and he
12.24 children of Judah that *b* shield
15.15 children of the Levites *b* the ark
26 the Levites that *b* the ark of the
27 and all the Levites that *b* the ark,
2Ch 8.10 two hundred and fifty, that *b* rule
9. 1 camels that *b* spices and gold in
11.19 Which *b* him children; Jeush,

2Ch 11.20 which *b* him Abijah, and Attai,
14. 8 an army of men that *b* targets
8 out of Benjamin, that *b* shields
Neh 4.17 and they that *b* burdens, with the
5.15 even their servants *b* rule
Pr 17.25 and bitterness to her that *b* him.
23.25 she that *b* thee shall rejoice.
SS 6. 9 is the choice one of her that *b* her.
8. 5 brought thee forth that *b* thee.
Isa 8. 3 she conceived, and *b* a son.
22. 6 Elam *b* the quiver with chariots
32.11 strip you, and make you *b*, and
47. 2 make *b* the leg, uncover the
51. 2 father, unto Sarah that *b* you:
52.10 Lord hath made *b* his holy arm
53.12 and he *b* the sin of many, and
63. 9 and he *b* them, and carried them
Jer 13.22 discovered, and thy heels made *b*.
16. 3 concerning their mothers that *b*
20.14 day wherein my mother *b* me be
22.26 out, and thy mother that *b* thee,
49.10 I have made Esau *b*, I have
50.12 she that *b* you shall be ashamed:
Eze 12. 7 I *b* it upon my shoulder in their
16. 7 whereas thou wast naked and *b*.
22 when thou wast naked and *b*,
39 jewels, and leave thee naked and *b*.
19.11 the scepters of them that *b* rule,
23. 4 and they *b* sons and daughters.
29 shall leave thee naked and *b*:
37 their sons, whom they *b* unto me,
Hos 1. 3 which conceived, and *b* him a son.
6 she conceived again, and *b* him a
8 she conceived, and *b* a son.
Joel 1. 7 he hath made clean *b*, and cast it
Mt 8.17 our infirmities, and *b* our
Mk 14.56 For many *b* false witness against
57 and *b* false witness against him,
Lk 4.22 all *b* him witness, and wondered
7.14 they that *b* him stood still.
8. 8 and sprang up, and *b* fruit an
11.27 Blessed is the womb that *b* thee,
23.29 and the wombs that never *b*,
Jn 1.15 John *b* witness of him, and cried,
32 And John *b* record, saying, I saw
34 I saw, and *b* record that this
2. 8 of the feast. And they *b* it.
5.33 and he *b* witness unto the truth.
12. 6 had the bag, and *b* what was put
17 from the dead, *b* record.
19.35 he that saw it *b* record, and his
Ac 15. 8 *b* them witness, giving them the
1Co 15.37 body that shall be, but *b* grain,
1Pe 2.24 who his own self *b* our sins in his
Rev 1. 2 Who *b* record of the word of God,
22. 2 which *b* twelve manner of fruits,

BAREFOOT

2Sa 15.30 head covered, and he went *b*:
Isa 20. 2 he did so, walking naked and *b*.
3 Isaiah hath walked naked and *b*
4 young and old, naked and *b*,

BAREST

1Ki 2.26 because thou *b* the ark of the
Isa 63.19 thou never *b* rule over them:
Jn 3.26 to whom thou *b* witness, behold,

BAR-JESUS

Ac 13. 6 a Jew, whose name was *B*:

BAR-JONA

Mt 16.17 Blessed art thou, Simon *B*:

BARK

Isa 56.10 all dumb dogs, they cannot *b*;

BARLEY

Ex 9.31 the flax and the *b* was smitten:
31 for the *b* was in the ear.
Lev 27.16 an homer of *b* seed shall be valued
Nu 5.15 tenth part of an ephah of *b* meal;
Dt 8. 8 A land of wheat, and *b*, and vines,
Jdg 7.13 and, lo, a cake of *b* bread tumbled
Ru 1.22 in the beginning of *b* harvest.
2.17 and it was about an ephah of *b*.
23 to glean unto the end of *b* harvest
3. 2 he winnoweth *b* to-night in the
15 he measured six measures of *b*.
17 six measures of *b* gave he me;
2Sa 14.30 he hath *b* there; go and set it on
17.28 wheat, and *b*, and flour
21. 9 beginning of *b* harvest.
1Ki 4.28 *B* also and straw for the horses
2Ki 4.42 twenty loaves of *b*, and full ears
7. 1 two measures of *b* for a shekel,
16 two measures of *b* for a shekel,
18 saying, Two measures of *b* for a
1Ch 11.13 parcel of ground full of *b*;
2Ch 2.10 twenty thousand measures of *b*,
15 and the *b*, the oil, and the wine,
27. 5 of wheat, and ten thousand of *b*,
Job 31.40 cockle instead of *b*. The words
Isa 28.25 and the appointed *b* and the rie
Jer 41. 8 of wheat, and of *b*, and of oil,
Eze 4. 9 unto thee wheat, and *b*, and beans,
12 thou shalt eat it as *b* cakes,
13.19 for handfuls of *b*, and for pieces
45.13 part of an ephah of an homer of *b*:
Hos 3. 2 and for an homer of *b*,
2 and an half homer of *b*:
Joel 1.11 for the wheat and for the *b*;
Jn 6. 9 which hath five *b* loaves and two
13 the fragments of the five *b* loaves,
Rev 6. 6 three measures of *b* for a penny;

BARN

Job 39.12 seed, and gather it into thy *b*?
Hag 2.19 Is the seed yet in the *b*?
Mt 13.30 but gather the wheat into my *b*.
Lk 12.24 neither have storehouses nor *b*;

BARNABAS

Ac 4.36 by the apostles was surnamed *B*,
9.27 But *B* took him and brought him
11.22 and they sent forth *B*, that he
25 Then departed *B* to Tarsus,
30 it to the elders by the hands of *B*
12.25 And *B* and Saul returned from
13. 1 as *B*, and Simeon that was called
2 Separate me *B* and Saul for the
7 called for *B* and Saul, and desired
43 proselytes followed Paul and *B*;
46 Then Paul and *B* waxed bold,
50 persecution against Paul and *B*,
14.12 And they called *B*, Jupiter;
14 when the apostles, *B* and Paul,
20 he departed with *B* to Derbe.
15. 2 When therefore Paul and *B* had
2 they determined that Paul and *B*,
12 and gave audience to *B* and Paul,
22 to Antioch with Paul and *B*;
25 with our beloved *B* and Paul,
35 also and *B* continued in Antioch,
36 some days after, Paul said unto *B*,
37 *B* determined to take with them
39 and so *B* took Mark, and sailed
1Co 9. 6 Or I only and *B*, have not we
Gal 2. 1 up again to Jerusalem with *B*,
9 gave to me and *B* the right hands
13 that *B* also was carried away
Co 4.10 and Marcus, sister's son to *B*,

BARNS

Pr 3.10 shall thy *b* be filled with plenty,
Joel 1.17 the *b* are broken down;
Mt 6.26 do they reap, nor gather into *b*;
Lk 12.18 I will pull down my *b*, and build

BARREL

1Ki 17.12 a handful of meal in a *b*, and a

BARNABAS

Companion of the Apostle Paul; Diaspora Jew of Levitical descent, born in Cyprus but first encountered in Jerusalem as a well-to-do member of the believing community following Pentecost; sells some land and lays the proceeds at the apostles' feet (Ac 4.36-37); introduces Saul (the future Paul) to the disciples when he visits Jerusalem after his conversion (Ac 9.26-27); commissioned by the Jerusalem Church to look after the new converts in Antioch, and invites Saul to join him (Ac 11.22-26); he and Saul take relief funds to Jerusalem during a famine (Ac 11.27-30); back in Antioch, the two are assigned to missionary work (Ac 13.1-3); with his young relative John Mark (Col 4.10) accompanies Saul (now called Paul) on his first missionary journey (Ac 13–14); the journey takes in Cyprus, his homeland, and several cities in Asia Minor, including Perga, where John Mark leaves them (Ac 13.13), Antioch in Pisidia, from which they are summarily ejected (Ac 13.50), and Lystra, where after a healing miracle the people think they are gods, comparing Barnabas to Jupiter and Paul to Mercury (Ac 14.12); supports Paul at the council in Jerusalem which rules that Gentile converts need not be circumcised, though they must keep certain Jewish laws (Ac 15.1-35), but later quarrels with him over John Mark, whom Paul refuses to take back, and they separate (Ac 15.36-38); Barnabas sails with John Mark for Cyprus, while Paul takes Silas on his second missionary journey (Ac 15.39-41).

14 The *b* of meal shall not waste,
16 the barrel of meal wasted not,

BARRELS

1Ki 18.33 Fill four *b* with water, and pour

BARREN

Gen 11.30 Sarai was *b*; she had no child.
25.21 for his wife, because she was *b*:
29.31 but Rachel was *b*.
Ex 23.26 nothing cast their young, nor be *b*,
Dt 7.14 shall not be male or female *b*
Jdg 13. 2 his wife was *b*, and bare not.
3 Behold now, thou art *b*,
1Sa 2. 5 so that the *b* hath born seven;
2Ki 2.19 is naught, and the ground *b*.
21 any more death or *b* land.
Job 24.21 He evil entreateth the *b* that
39. 6 and the *b* land his dwellings.
Ps 113. 9 maketh the *b* woman to keep
Pr 30.16 The grave; and the *b* womb;
SS 4. 2 and none is *b* among them.
6. 6 there is not one *b* among them.
Isa 54. 1 Sing, O *b*, thou that didst not
Joel 2.20 him into a land *b* and desolate,
Lk 1. 7 because that Elisabeth was *b*,
36 month with her, who was called *b*.
23.29 Blessed are the *b*, and the wombs
Gal 4.27 Rejoice, thou *b* that bearest not;
2Pe 1. 8 neither be *b* nor unfruitful in the

BARRENNESS

Ps 107.34 A fruitful land into *b*, for the

BARS

Ex 26.26 shalt make *b* of shittim wood;
27 *b* for the boards of the other side
27 for the boards of the side of
29 rings of gold for places for the *b*:
29 thou shalt overlay the *b* with gold.
35.11 his *b*, his pillars, and his sockets;
36.31 And he made *b* of shittim wood;
32 five *b* for the boards of the other
32 *b* for the boards of the tabernacle
34 rings of gold to be places for the *b*,
34 and overlaid the *b* with gold.
39.33 his *b*, and is pillars, and his
40.18 put in the *b* thereof, and reared up
Nu 3.36 and the *b* thereof, and the pillars
4.31 boards of the tabernacle, and the *b*
Dt 3. 5 with high walls, gates, and *b*;
1Sa 23. 7 a town that hath gates and *b*.
1Ki 4.13 cities with walls and brasen *b*:
2Ch 8. 5 cities, with walls, gates, and *b*;
14. 7 walls, and towers, gates, and *b*.
Neh 3. 3 locks thereof, and the *b* thereof.
6 and the *b* thereof.
13 and the *b* thereof, and a thousand
14 and the *b* thereof.
15 and the *b* thereof, and the wall of
Job 17.16 shall go down to the *b* of the pit,
38.10 place, and set *b* and doors,
40.18 his bones are like *b* of iron.
Ps 107.16 and cut the *b* of iron in sunder.
147.13 strengthen the *b* of thy gates;
Pr 18.19 are like the *b* of a castle.
Isa 45. 2 and cut in sunder the *b* of iron:
Jer 49.31 which have neither gates nor *b*,
51.30 dwellingplaces; her *b* are broken.
La 2. 9 hath destroyed and broken her *b*:
Eze 38.11 having neither *b* nor gates,
Jon 2. 6 the earth with her *b* was about me
Na 3.13 the fire shall devour thy *b*.

BARSABAS

Ac 1.23 *B*, who was surnamed Justus,
15.22 namely, Judas surnamed *B*,

BARTHOLOMEW

Mt 10. 3 Philip, and *B*; Thomas,
Mk 3.18 Philip, and *B*, and Matthew,
Lk 6.14 Philip and *B*,
Ac 1.13 Philip, and Thomas, *B*,

BARZILLAI

2Sa 17.27 and *B* the Gileadite of Rogelim,
19.31 *B* the Gileadite came down from
32 Now *B* was a very aged man,
33 the king said unto *B*, Come thou
34 *B* said unto the king, How long
39 king kissed *B*, and blessed him;
21. 8 brought up for Adriel the son of *B*
1Ki 2. 7 shew kindness unto the sons of *B*
Ezr 2.61 children of Koz, the children of *B*;
61 took a wife of the daughters of *B*
Neh 7.63 the children of *B*, which took
63 one of the daughters of *B*

BASE

2Sa 6.22 will be *b* in mine own sight:
1Ki 7.27 cubits was the length of one *b*,
29 upon the ledges there was a *b*
30 every *b* had four brasen wheels,
31 work of the *b*, a cubit and a
32 axletrees...were joined to the *b*:
34 the four corners of one *b*:
34 undersetters were of the very *b*
35 in the top of the *b* was there a
35 and on the top of the *b* the ledges
Job 30. 8 yea, children of *b* men:
Isa 3. 5 the *b* against the honorable.
Eze 17.14 That the kingdom might be *b*,
29.14 they shall be there a *b* kingdom.
Zec 5.11 and set there upon her own *b*.
Mal 2. 9 and *b* before all the people,

1Co 1.28 And *b* things of the world,
2Co 10. 1 who in presence am *b* among

BASER

Ac 17. 5 lewd fellows of the *b* sort,

BASES

1Ki 7.27 And he made ten *b* of brass;
28 the work of the *b* was on this
37 this manner he made the ten *b*:
38 upon every one of the ten *b* one
39 he put five *b* on the right side of
43 And the ten *b*,
43 and ten lavers on the *b*;
2Ki 16.17 Ahaz cut off the borders of the *b*,
25.13 and the *b*, and the brasen sea
16 the *b* which Solomon had made
2Ch 4.14 He made also *b*,
14 and lavers made he upon the *b*;
Ezr 3. 3 they set the altar upon his *b*;
Jer 27.19 concerning the *b*, and concerning
52.17 and the *b*, and the brasen sea
20 bulls that were under the *b*,

BASEST

Eze 29.15 shall be the *b* of the kingdoms;
Dan 4.17 setteth up over it the *b* of men.

BASKET

Gen 40.17 And in the uppermost *b* there
17 birds did eat them out of the *b*
Ex 29. 3 thou shalt put them into one *b*,
3 and bring them in the *b*,
23 wafer out of the *b* of unleavened
32 and the bread that is in the *b*,
Lev 8. 2 and a *b* of unleavened bread;
26 out of the *b* of unleavened bread,
31 that is in the *b* of consecrations,
Nu 6.15 And a *b* of unleavened bread,
17 with the *b* of unleavened bread:
19 one unleavened cake out of the *b*,
Dt 26. 2 shalt put it in a *b*, and shalt go
4 the priest shall take the *b* out of
28. 5 Blessed shall be thy *b* and thy
17 Cursed shall be thy *b* and thy
Jdg 6.19 the flesh he put in a *b*, and he
Jer 24. 2 One *b* had very good figs,
2 other *b* had very naughty figs,
Am 8. 1 behold a *b* of summer fruit.
2 And I said, A *b* of summer fruit.
Ac 9.25 let him down by the wall in a *b*.
2Co 11.33 in a *b* was I let down by the wall,

BASKETS

Gen 40.16 I had three white *b* on my head:
18 The three *b* are three days:
2Ki 10. 7 put their heads in *b*, and sent
Jer 6. 9 as a grapegatherer into the *b*.
24. 1 two *b* of figs were set before the
Mt 14.20 that remained twelve *b* full.
15.37 meat that was left seven *b* full.
16. 9 and how many *b* ye took up?
10 and how many *b* ye took up?
Mk 6.43 twelve *b* full of the fragments,
8. 8 meat that was left seven *b*.
19 how many *b* full of fragments
20 how many *b* full of fragments
Lk 9.17 remained to them twelve *b*.
Jn 6.13 and filled twelve *b* with the

BASON

Ex 12.22 in the blood that is in the *b*,
22 with the blood that is in the *b*;
1Ch 28.17 gave gold by weight for every *b*;
17 silver by weight for every *b* of
Jn 13. 5 that he poureth water into a *b*,

BASONS

Ex 24. 6 half of the blood, and put it in *b*;
27. 3 ashes, and his shovels, and his *b*,
38. 3 the shovels, and the *b*, and the

Nu 4.14 the shovels, and the *b*, all the
2Sa 17.28 beds, and *b*, and earthen vessels,
1Ki 7.40 the shovels, and the *b*. So Hiram
45 and the *b*: and all these vessels,
50 the snuffers, and the *b*, and the
2Ki 12.13 bowls of silver, snuffers, *b*,
1Ch 28.17 for the golden *b* he gave gold by
2Ch 4. 8 he made an hundred *b* of gold.
11 pots, and the shovels, and the *b*.
22 the snuffers, and the *b*, and the
Ezr 1.10 Thirty *b* of gold,
10 silver *b* of a second sort
8.27 Also twenty *b* of gold, of a
Neh 7.70 thousand drams of gold, fifty *b*.
Jer 52.19 the *b*, and the firepans, and the

BASTARD

Dt 23. 2 A *b* shall not enter into the
Zec 9. 6 and a *b* shall dwell in Ashdod,

BASTARDS

Heb 12. 8 then are ye *b*, and not sons.

BAT

Lev 11.19 kind, and the lapwing, and the *b*.
Dt 14.18 the lapwing, and the *b*.

BATH

Isa 5.10 of vineyard shall yield one *b*,
Eze 45.10 a just ephah, and a just *b*.
11 the *b* shall be of one measure,
11 that the *b* may contain
14 the *b* of oil, ye shall
14 offer the tenth part of a *b*

BATHE

Lev 15. 5 and *b* himself in water, and be
6 wash his clothes, and *b* himself
7 *b* himself in water, and be unclean
8 wash his clothes, and *b* himself
10 *b* himself in water, and be unclean
11 wash his clothes, and *b* himself
13 and *b* his flesh in running water,
18 shall both *b* themselves in water
21 wash his clothes, and *b* himself
22 *b* himself in water, and be unclean
27 wash his clothes, and *b* himself
16.26 *b* his flesh in water, and afterward
28 clothes, and *b* his flesh in water,
17.15 *b* himself in water, and be unclean
16 nor *b* his flesh;
Nu 19. 7 he shall *b* his flesh in water,
8 *b* his flesh in water, and shall be
19 clothes, and *b* himself in water,

BATHED

Isa 34. 5 my sword shall be *b* in heaven:

BATHSHEBA

Wife of Uriah the Hittite, a mercenary of David, 10th century B.C.; one evening from his palace roof David sees her bathing, is captivated by her beauty, sends for her, seduces her, and arranges for Uriah's death in battle, then marries her (2Sa 11); after the prophet Nathan confronts David with his sin and their first son dies as foretold by him, becomes the mother of Solomon (2Sa 12); later when David is dying and his eldest surviving son, Adonijah, is preparing to seize the throne, persuades the ailing king to pronounce in favor of Solomon (1Ki 1); promises as queen-mother to speak for Adonijah before the new king but, despite her intercession, Solomon has him executed (1Ki 2).

BATHS

1Ki 7.26 it contained two thousand *b*.
38 one laver contained forty *b*:
2Ch 2.10 twenty thousand *b* of wine,
10 and twenty thousand *b* of oil.
4. 5 received and held three thousand *b*.
Ezr 7.22 and to an hundred *b* of wine,
22 and to an hundred *b* of oil,
Eze 45.14 an homer of ten *b*;
14 for ten *b* are an homer.

BATHSHEBA

2Sa 11. 3 one said, Is not this *B*, the
12.24 David comforted *B* his wife,
1Ki 1.11 Nathan spake unto *B* the
15 And *B* went in unto the king
16 And *B* bowed, and did obeisance
28 answered and said, Call me *B*.
31 Then *B* bowed with her face to
2.13 came to *B* the mother of Solomon.
18 And *B* said, Well; I will speak
19 *B* therefore went unto king
Ps 51(T) him, after he had gone in to *B*.
(See box on page 103)

BATS

Isa 2.20 to the moles and to the *b*;

BATTERED

2Sa 20.15 *b* the wall, to throw it down.

BATTERING

Eze 4. 2 set *b* rams against it
21.22 appoint *b* rams against the gates,

BATTLE

Gen 14. 8 they joined *b* with them in the
Nu 21.33 all his people, to the *b* at Edrei.
31.14 which came from the *b*.
21 men of war which went to the *b*,
27 upon them, who went out to *b*,
28 men of war which went out to *b*:
32.27 before the Lord to *b*, as my lord
29 man armed to *b*, before the Lord,
Dt 2. 9 neither contend with them in *b*:
24 and contend with him in *b*.
3. 1 and all his people, to *b* at Edrei.
20. 1 When thou goest out to *b* against
2 ye are come nigh unto the *b*,
3 ye approach this day unto *b*
5, 6 his house, lest he die in the *b*,
7 lest he die in the *b*, and another
29. 7 came out against us unto *b*,
Jos 4.13 unto *b*, to the plains of Jericho.
8.14 went out against Israel to *b*,
11.19 of Gibeon: all other they took in *b*.
20 should come against Israel in *b*,
22.33 to go up against them in *b*, to
Jdg 8.13 the son of Joash returned from *b*
20.14 unto Gibeah, to go out to *b*
18 of us shall go up first to the *b*
20 the men of Israel went out to *b*
22 and set their *b* again in array
23 Shall I go up again to *b*
28 Shall I yet again go out to *b*
34 of all Israel, and the *b* was sore:
39 the men of Israel retired in the *b*,
39 as in the first *b*.
42 but the *b* overtook them; and
1Sa 4. 1 out against the Philistines to *b*,
2 they joined *b*, Israel was smitten
7.10 the Philistines drew near to *b*
13.22 So it came to pass in the day of *b*,
14.20 themselves, and they came to the *b*:
22 followed hard after them in the *b*.
23 the *b* passed over unto Beth-aven.
17. 1 together their armies to *b*,
2 and set the *b* in array against
8 come out to set your *b* in array?
13 went and followed Saul to the *b*:
13 three sons that went to the *b*
20 the fight, and shouted for the *b*.
21 had put the *b* in array,
28 that thou mightest see the *b*.
47 for the *b* is the Lord's, and he
26.10 he shall descend into *b*, and perish.
28. 1 thou shalt go out with me to *b*,
29. 4 not go down with us to *b*,
4 lest in the *b* he be an adversary
9 He shall not go up with us to the *b*.
30.24 part is that goeth down to the *b*,
31. 3 the *b* went sore against Saul,
2Sa 1. 4 the people are fled from the *b*,
25 fallen in the midst of the *b*!
2.17 there was a very sore *b* that day;
3.30 brother Asahel at Gibeon in the *b*.
10. 8 put the *b* in array at the entering
9 Joab saw that the front of the *b*
13 unto the *b* against the Syrians:
11. 1 the time when kings go forth to *b*,
15 in the forefront of the hottest *b*,
25 make thy *b* more strong against
17.11 go to *b* in thine own person.
18. 6 *b* was in the wood of Ephraim;
8 the *b* was there scattered
19. 3 steal away when they flee in *b*.
10 anointed over us, is dead in *b*.
21.17 go no more out with us to *b*,
18 that there was again a *b* with the
19 there was again a *b* in Gob
20 And there was yet a *b* in Gath,
22.40 girded me with strength to *b*:
23. 9 gathered together to *b*, and the
1Ki 8.44 go out to *b* against their enemy,
20.14 Who shall order the *b*? And he
29 the seventh day the *b* was joined:
39 went out into the midst of the *b*;
22. 4 Wilt thou go with me to *b*
6 I go against Ramoth-gilead to *b*,
15 go against Ramoth-gilead to *b*,
30 enter into the *b*; but put thou on
30 himself, and went into the *b*.
35 the *b* increased that day: and the
2Ki 3. 7 go with me against Moab to *b*?
26 the king of Moab saw that the *b*
1Ch 5.20 they cried to God in the *b*, and he
7.11 fit to go out for war and *b*.
40 were apt to the war and to *b*
10. 3 the *b* went sore against Saul,
11.13 were gathered together to *b*,
12. 8 men of war fit for the *b*, that
19 Philistines against Saul to *b*:
33 Zebulun, such as went forth to *b*,
36 of Asher, such as went forth to *b*,
37 of instruments of war for the *b*,
14.15 then thou shalt go out to *b*:
19. 7 from their cities, and came to *b*.
9 came out, and put the *b* in array
10 Joab saw that the *b* was set
14 before the Syrians unto the *b*;

Battle scene in a contemporary Assyrian relief of Sennacherib's invasion of Judah, about 700 B.C.

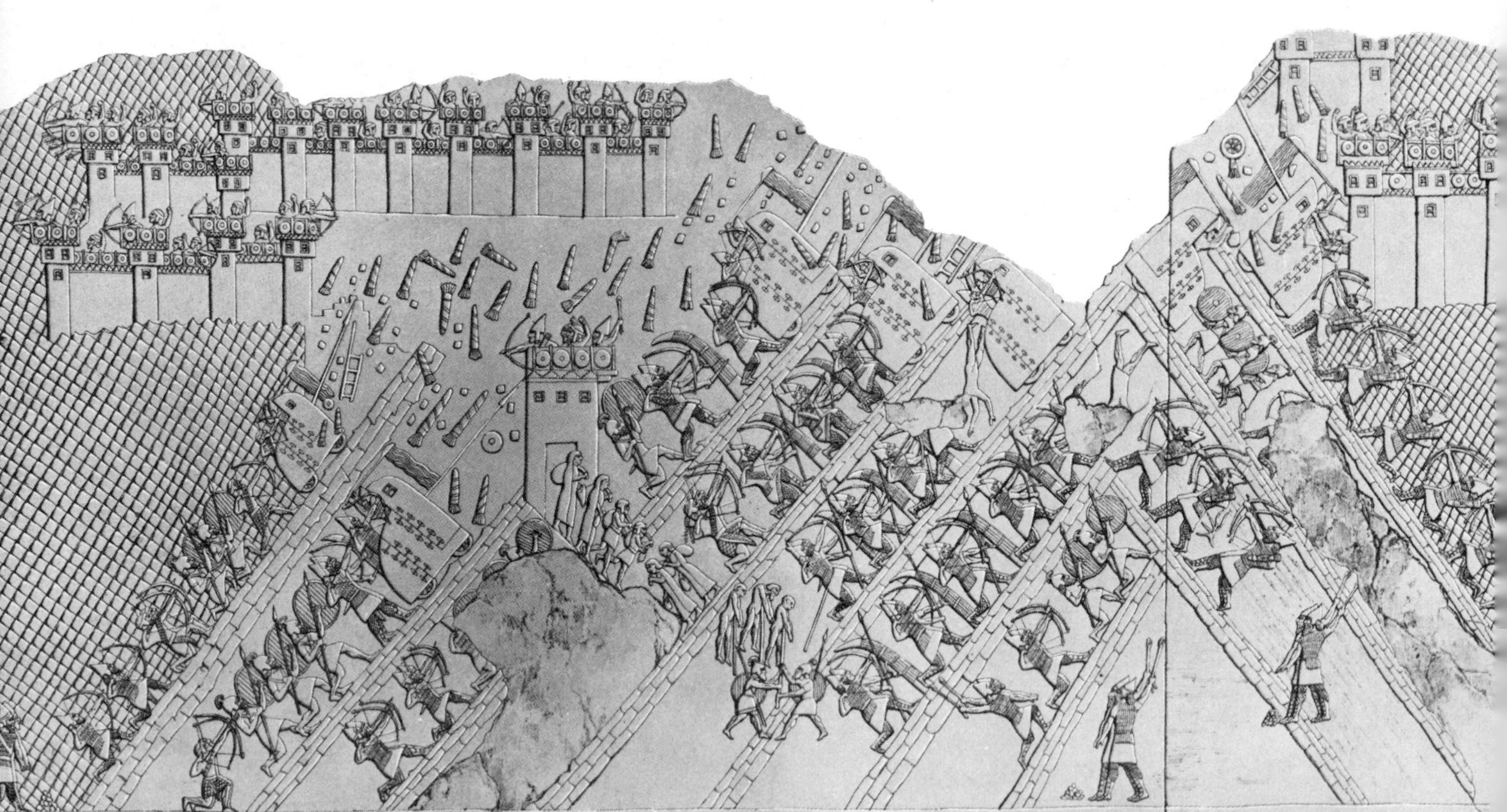

17 set the *b* in array against them.
17 David had put the *b* in array
20. 1 the time that kings go out to *b*,
2Ch 13. 3 Abijah set the *b* in array with an
3 Jeroboam also set the *b* in array
14 the *b* was before and behind:
14.10 set the *b* in array in the valley
18. 5 we go to Ramoth-gilead to *b*,
14 shall we go to Ramoth-gilead to *b*,
29 myself, and will go to the *b*;
29 himself, and they went to the *b*.
34 And the *b* increased that day:
20. 1 I came against Jehoshaphat to *b*.
15 for the *b* is not yours, but God's.
17 shall not need to fight in this *b*:
25. 8 will go, do it, be strong for the *b*:
13 they should not go with him to *b*,
Job 15.24 him, as a king ready to the *b*.
38.23 against the day of *b* and war?
39.25 he smelleth the *b* afar off,
41. 8 remember the *b*, do no more.
Ps 18.39 me with strength unto the *b*:
24. 8 mighty, the Lord mighty in *b*.
55.18 my soul in peace from the *b*
76. 3 shield, and the sword, and the *b*.
78. 9 turned back in the day of *b*.
89.43 not made him to stand in the *b*.
140. 7 covered my head in the day of *b*.
Pr 21.31 is prepared against the day of *b*:
Ec 9.11 nor the *b* to the strong, neither
Isa 9. 5 For every *b* of the warrior is
13. 4 mustereth the host of the *b*.
22. 2 with the sword, nor dead in *b*.
27. 4 and thorns against me in *b*?
28. 6 strength to them that turn the *b*
42.25 the strength of *b*: and it hath set
Jer 8. 6 as the horse rusheth into the *b*.
18.21 men be slain by the sword in *b*.
46. 3 and shield, and draw near to *b*.
49.14 against her, and rise up to the *b*.
50.22 A sound of *b* is in the land,
42 like a man to the *b*, against thee.
51.20 Thou art my *b* axe and weapons
Eze 7.14 none goeth to the *b*: for my
13. 5 to stand in the *b* in the day
Dan 11.20 neither in anger, nor in *b*.
25 stirred up to *b* with a very great
Hos 1. 7 by bow, nor by sword, nor by *b*,
2.18 the bow and the sword and the *b*
10. 9 *b* in Gibeah against the children
14 spoiled Beth-arbel in the day of *b*:
Joel 2. 5 a strong people set in *b* array.
Am 1.14 with shouting in the day of *b*,
Ob 1 let us rise up against her in *b*.
Zec 9.10 and the *b* bow shall be cut off:
10. 3 them as his goodly horse in the *b*.
4 out of him the *b* bow, out of him
5 down their enemies...in the *b*:
14. 2 nations against Jerusalem to *b*;
3 when he fought in the day of *b*.
1Co 14. 8 shall prepare himself to the *b*?
Rev 9. 7 horses prepared unto *b*; and on
9 of many horses running to *b*.
16.14 to the *b* of that great day of God
20. 8 to gather them together to *b*:

BATTLEMENT
Dt 22. 8 thou shalt make a *b* for thy roof,

BATTLEMENTS
Jer 5.10 take away her *b*; for they are

BATTLES
1Sa 8.20 go out before us, and fight our *b*.
18.17 and fight the Lord's *b*. For Saul
25.28 my lord fighteth the *b* of the Lord,
1Ch 26.27 spoils won in *b* did they dedicate
2Ch 32. 8 and to fight our *b*. And the people
Isa 30.32 and in *b* of shaking will he fight

BAY
Jos 15. 2 the *b* that looketh southward:
5 the *b* of the sea at the uttermost
18.19 the north *b* of the salt sea
Ps 37.35 himself like a green *b* tree.
Zec 6. 3 fourth chariot grisled and *b* horses.
7 And the *b* went forth, and sought

BEAM
Jdg 16.14 went away with the pin of the *b*,
1Sa 17. 7 of his spear was like a weaver's *b*;
2Sa 21.19 whose spear was like a weaver's *b*.
1Ki 7. 6 the thick *b* were before them.
2Ki 6. 2 take thence every man a *b*, and
5 as one was felling a *b*, the axe head
1Ch 11.23 was a spear like a weaver's *b*:
20. 5 spear staff was like a weaver's *b*.
Hab 2.11 *b* out of the timber shall answer
Mt 7. 3 considerest not the *b* that is in
4 behold, a *b* is in thine own eye?
5 cast out the *b* out of thine own eye;
Lk 6.41 perceivest not the *b* that is in
42 beholdest not the *b* that is in
42 cast out first the *b* out of thine

BEAMS
1Ki 6. 6 that the *b* should not be fastened
9 covered the house with *b* and
36 stone, and a row of cedar *b*.
7. 2 with cedar *b* upon the pillars.
3 with cedar above upon the *b*,
12 a row of cedar *b*, both for the
2Ch 3. 7 the *b*, the posts, and the walls
Neh 2. 8 give me timber to make *b* for the
3. 3 who also laid the *b* thereof, and
6 they laid the *b* thereof, and set up
Ps 104. 3 Who layeth the *b* of his chambers
SS 1.17 The *b* of our house are cedar,

BEARD
Lev 13.29 plague upon the head or the *b*;
30 a leprosy upon the head or *b*.
14. 9 head and his *b* and his eyebrows,
19.27 thou mar the corners of thy *b*.
21. 5 shave off the corner of their *b*,
1Sa 17.35 him by his *b*, and smote him
21.13 his spittle fall down upon his *b*.
2Sa 19.24 his feet, nor trimmed his *b*,
20. 9 And Joab took Amasa by the *b*
Ezr 9. 3 of my *b*, and sat down astonied
Ps 133. 2 that ran down upon the *b*,
2 even Aaron's *b*: that went down
Isa 7.20 and it shall also consume the *b*.
15. 2 be baldness, and every *b* cut off.
Jer 48.37 shall be bald and every *b* clipped:
Eze 5. 1 upon thine head and upon thy *b*:

BEARDS
2Sa 10. 4 shaved off the one half of their *b*,
5 at Jericho until your *b* be grown,
1Ch 19. 5 Jericho until your *b* be grown,
Jer 41. 5 *b* shaven, and their clothes rent,

BEARERS
2Ch 2.18 of them to be *b* of burdens,
34.13 they were over the *b* of burdens,
Neh 4.10 of the *b* of burdens is decayed,

BEAREST
Jdg 13. 3 thou art barren and *b* not:
Ps 106. 4 the favor that thou *b* unto thy
Jn 8.13 Thou *b* record of thyself; thy
Ro 11.18 thou *b* not the root, but the root
Gal 4.27 Rejoice, thou barren that *b* not;

BEARETH
Lev 11.25 whosoever *b* ought of the
28 he that *b* the carcase of them
40 he also that *b* the carcase of it
15.10 and he that *b* any of those things
Nu 11.12 a nursing father *b* the sucking
Dt 25. 6 the firstborn which she *b* shall
29.18 a root that *b* gall and wormwood;
23 is not sown, nor *b*, nor any grass
32.11 *b* them on her wings:
Job 16. 8 rising up in me *b* witness
24.21 entreateth the barren that *b* not:
Pr 25.18 A man that *b* false witness
29. 2 but when the wicked *b* rule,
SS 6. 6 every one *b* twins, and there is
Joel 2.22 tree that *b* her fruit, the fig tree
Mt 13.23 also *b* fruit, and bringeth forth,
Jn 5.32 another that *b* witness of me:
8.18 that sent me *b* witness of me.
15. 2 branch in me that *b* not fruit
2 branch that *b* fruit, he purgeth it,
Ro 8.16 The Spirit itself *b* witness with
13. 4 for he *b* not the sword in vain:
1Co 13. 7 *B* all things, believeth all things,
Heb 6. 8 that which *b* thorns and briers
1Jn 5. 6 it is the Spirit that *b* witness,

BEARING
Gen 1.29 given you every herb *b* seed,
16. 2 Lord hath restrained me from *b*:
29.35 his name Judah; and left *b*.
30. 9 Leah saw that she had left *b*,
37.25 *b* spicery and balm and myrrh,
Nu 10.17 set forward, *b* the tabernacle,
21 set forward, *b* the sanctuary:
Jos 3. 3 the priests the Levites *b* it,
14 priests *b* the ark of the covenant
6. 8 seven priests *b* the seven trumpets
13 seven priests *b* seven trumpets
1Sa 17. 7 one *b* a shield went before him.
2Sa 15.24 *b* the ark of the covenant of God:
Ps 126. 6 *b* precious seed, shall doubtless
Mk 14.13 a man *b* a pitcher of water:
Lk 22.10 meet you, *b* a pitcher of water;
Jn 19.17 *b* his cross went forth
Ro 2.15 conscience also *b* witness, and
9. 1 conscience also *b* me witness
2Co 4.10 Always *b* about in the body the
Heb 2. 4 God also *b* them witness both
13.13 without the camp, *b* his reproach.

BEARS
2Ki 2.24 forth two she *b* out of the wood,
Isa 59.11 We roar all like *b*, and mourn

BEAST
Gen 1.24 and *b* of the earth after his kind:
25 God made the *b* of the earth
30 And to every *b* of the earth,
2.19 God formed every *b* of the field,
20 every *b* of the field; but for Adam
3. 1 subtil than any *b* of the field
14 above every *b* of the field;
6. 7 man, and *b*, and the creeping
7. 2 Of every clean *b* thou shalt take
14 every *b* after his kind, and all the
21 of *b*, and of every creeping thing
8.19 Every *b*, every creeping thing, and
20 clean *b*, and of every clean fowl,
9. 2 be upon every *b* of the earth,
5 hand of every *b* will I require it,
10 every *b* of the earth with you;
10 to every *b* of the earth.
34.23 every *b* of theirs be ours?
37.20 Some evil *b* hath devoured him:
33 an evil *b* hath devoured him;
Ex 8.17 became lice in man, and in *b*;
18 were lice upon man, and upon *b*.
9. 9 blains upon man, and upon *b*,
10 blains upon man, and upon *b*.
19 every man and *b* which shall be
22 man, and upon *b*, and upon every
25 was in the field, both man and *b*;
11. 7 his tongue, against man or *b*:
12.12 land of Egypt, both man and *b*;
13. 2 of man and of *b*: it is mine.
12 cometh of a *b* which thou hast;

BIBLICAL THEMES

ANIMALS

And God made the beast of the earth after his kind, and cattle after their kind, and every thing that creepeth upon the earth after his kind: and God saw that it was good. Gen 1.25

Now the serpent was more subtil than any beast of the field. Gen 3.1

Let him go for a scapegoat into the wilderness. Lev 16.10

And there we saw the giants . . . And we were in our own sight as grasshoppers, and so we were in their sight. Nu 13.33

As the hart panteth after the water brooks, so panteth my soul after thee, O God. Ps 42.1

Every beast of the forest is mine, and the cattle upon a thousand hills. Ps 50.10

Yea, the sparrow hath found an house, and the swallow a nest for herself, where she may lay her young, even thine altars, O Lord of hosts. Ps 84.3

I am like a pelican of the wilderness . . . an owl of the desert . . . a sparrow alone upon the house top. Ps 102.6-7

The young lions roar after their prey, and seek their meat from God. Ps 104.21

The mountains skipped like rams, and the little hills like lambs. Ps 114.4

Go to the ant, thou sluggard; consider her ways, and be wise. Pr 6.6

There be four things which are little upon the earth, but they are exceeding wise: the ants are a people not strong, yet they prepare their meat in the summer; the conies are but a feeble folk, yet make they their houses in the rocks; the locusts have no king, yet go they forth all of them by bands; the spider taketh hold with her hands, and is in kings' palaces. Pr 30.24-28

The wolf also shall dwell with the lamb, and the leopard shall lie down with the kid; and the calf and the young lion and the fatling together; and a little child shall lead them. Isa 11.6

He shall feed his flock like a shepherd: he shall gather the lambs with his arm, and carry them in his bosom, and shall gently lead those that are with young. Isa 40.11

All we like sheep have gone astray. Isa 53.6

I will restore to you the years that the locust hath eaten. Joel 2.25

Behold the fowls of the air: for they sow not, neither do they reap, nor gather into barns; yet your heavenly Father feedeth them. Mt 6.26

Beware of false prophets, which come to you in sheep's clothing, but inwardly they are ravening wolves. Mt 7.15

The foxes have holes, and the birds of the air have nests; but the Son of man hath not where to lay his head. Mt 8.20

Behold, I send you forth as sheep in the midst of wolves: be ye therefore wise as serpents, and harmless as doves. Mt 10.16

Are not two sparrows sold for a farthing? and one of them shall not fall on the ground without your Father. Mt 10.29

Ye blind guides, which strain at a gnat, and swallow a camel. Mt 23.24

How often would I have gathered thy children together, even as a hen gathereth her chickens under her wings, and ye would not! Mt 23.37

Yes, Lord: yet the dogs under the table eat of the children's crumbs. Mk 7.28

Wheresoever the body is, thither will the eagles be gathered together. Lk 17.37

Ex 13.15 of man, and the firstborn of *b*:
19.13 whether it be *b* or man,
21.34 them; and the dead *b* shall be his.
22. 5 shall put in his *b*, and shall feed
10 or an ox, or a sheep, or any *b*,
19 lieth with a *b* shall surely
23.29 the *b* of the field multiply against
Lev 5. 2 the carcase of an unclean *b*,
7.21 unclean *b*, or any abominable
24 fat of the *b* that dieth of itself
25 whosoever eateth the fat of the *b*,
26 or of *b*, in any of your dwellings.
11.26 every *b* which divideth the hoof,
39 if any *b*, of which ye may eat, die;
47 between the *b* that may be eaten
47 the *b* that may not be eaten.
17.13 hunteth and catcheth any *b*
18.23 Neither shalt thou lie with any *b*
23 shall any woman stand before a *b*
20.15 And if a man lie with a *b*,
15 and ye shall slay the *b*.
16 if a woman approach unto any *b*,
16 kill the woman and the *b*:
25 make your souls abominable by *b*,
24.18 that killeth a *b* shall make it
18 good; *b* for *b*.
21 that killeth a *b*, he shall restore it.
25. 7 cattle, and for the *b* that are
27. 9 And if it be a *b*, whereof men
10 if he shall at all change *b* for *b*,
11 if it be any unclean *b*, of which
11 present the *b* before the priest:
27 if it be an unclean *b*,
28 of man and *b*, and of the field
Nu 3.13 firstborn in Israel, both man and *b*:
8.17 Israel are mine, both man and *b*:
31.26 man and of *b*, thou, and Eleazar
47 of man and of *b*, and gave them
Dt 4.17 likeness of any *b*...on the earth,
14. 6 And every *b* that parteth the hoof,
27.21 that lieth with any manner of *b*.
Jdg 20.48 the men of every city, as the *b*,
2Ki 14. 9 passed by a wild *b* that was in
2Ch 25.18 passed by a wild *b* that was in
Neh 2.12 neither was there any *b* with me,
12 save the *b* that I rode upon.
14 for the *b* that was under me to pass.
Job 39.15 that the wild *b* may break them.
Ps 36. 6 thou preservest man and *b*.
50.10 every *b* of the forest is mine,
73.22 I was as a *b* before thee.
80.13 wild *b* of the field doth devour it.
104.11 give drink to every *b* of the field:
135. 8 of Egypt, both of man and *b*.
147. 9 He giveth to the *b* his food,
Pr 12.10 regardeth the life of his *b*:
Ec 3.19 hath no preeminence above a *b*:
21 the spirit of the *b* that goeth
Isa 35. 9 nor any ravenous *b* shall go up
43.20 The *b* of the field shall honor
46. 1 they are a burden to the weary *b*.
63.14 As a *b* goeth down into the valley,
Jer 7.20 upon man, and upon *b*, and upon
9.10 the fowl of the heavens and the *b*
21. 6 of this city, both man and *b*:
27. 5 the *b* that are upon the ground,
31.27 of man, and with the seed of *b*.
32.43 desolate without man or *b*;
33.10 without man and without *b*,
10 without inhabitant, and without *b*,
12 without man and without *b*,
36.29 to cease from thence man and *b*?
50. 3 shall depart, both man and *b*.
51.62 neither man nor *b*, but that it shall
Eze 14.13 will cut off man and *b* from it:
17 so that I cut off man and *b*
19 to cut off from it man and *b*:
21 the famine, and the noisome *b*,
21 to cut off from it man and *b*?
25.13 and will cut off man and *b*
29. 8 cut off man and *b* out of thee.
11 nor foot of *b* shall pass through it,
34. 8 meat to every *b* of the field,
28 neither shall the *b* of the land
36.11 multiply upon you man and *b*;
39.17 to every *b* of the field, Assemble
44.31 or torn, whether it be fowl or *b*.
Dan 7. 5 And behold another *b*, a second,
6 the *b* had also four heads;
7 behold a fourth *b*, dreadful and
11 I beheld even till the *b* was slain,
19 know the truth of the fourth *b*,
23 The fourth *b* shall be the fourth
Hos 13. 8 the wild *b* shall tear them.
Jon 3. 7 Let neither man nor *b*, herd nor
8 But let man and *b* be covered
Mic 1.13 bind the chariot to the swift *b*:
Zep 1. 3 I will consume man and *b*:
Zec 8.10 no hire for man, nor any hire for *b*;
Lk 10.34 and set him on his own *b*, and
Ac 28. 4 the venomous *b* hang on his hand,
5 shook off the beast into the fire,
Heb 12.20 And if so much as a *b* touch the

Rev 4. 7 the first *b* was like a lion,
7 and the second *b* like a calf,
7 third *b* had a face as a man
7 and the fourth *b* was like a
6. 3 I heard the second *b* say,
5 I heard the third *b* say, Come
7 the voice of the fourth *b* say,
11. 7 the *b* that ascendeth out of the
13. 1 saw a beast rise up out of the sea,
2 the *b* which I saw was like
3 the world wondered after the *b*.
4 power unto the *b*: and they
4 worshipped the *b*, saying,
4 Who is like unto the *b*?
11 I beheld another *b* coming up
12 all the power of the first *b* before
12 therein to worship the first *b*,
14 to do in the sight of the *b*;
14 should make an image to the *b*,
15 unto the image of the *b*, that the
15 image of the *b* should both speak,
15 worship the image of the *b*
17 or the name of the *b*, or the
18 count the number of the *b*:
14. 9 If any man worship the *b* and his
11 who worship the *b* and his image
15. 2 the victory over the *b*, and over
16. 2 the mark of the *b*, and upon them
10 his vial upon the seat of the *b*;
13 and out of the mouth of the *b*,
17. 3 upon a scarlet colored *b*,
7 of the *b* that carrieth her, which
8 The *b* that thou sawest was
8 the *b* that was, and is not,
11 And the *b* that was and is not,
12 as kings one hour with the *b*.
13 power and strength unto the *b*.
16 which thou sawest upon the *b*,
17 give their kingdom unto the *b*,
19.19 And I saw the *b*, and the kings
20 And the *b* was taken,
20 had received the mark of the *b*,
20. 4 had not worshipped the *b*,
10 where the *b* and the false prophet

BEAST'S
Dan 4.16 and let a *b* heart be given unto

BEASTS
Gen 7. 2 of *b* that are not clean by two,
8 Of clean *b*, and of *b* that are not
31.39 That which was torn of *b* I
36. 6 and all his *b*, and all his
45.17 lade your *b*, and go, get you
Ex 11. 5 and all the firstborn of *b*.
22.31 flesh that is torn of *b* in the field;
23.11 what they leave the *b* of the field
Lev 7.24 fat of that which is torn with *b*,
11. 2 These are the *b* which ye shall
2 among all the *b* that are on
3 cheweth the cud, among the *b*,
27 among all manner of *b* that go
46 This is the law of the *b*, and of
17.15 or that which was torn with *b*,
20.25 between clean *b* and unclean,
22. 8 or is torn with *b*, he shall not eat
26. 6 I will rid evil *b* out of the land,
22 I will also send wild *b* among
27.26 Only the firstling of the *b*,
Nu 18.15 whether it be of men or *b*,
15 the firstling of unclean *b* shalt
20. 8 congregation and their *b* drink.
11 drank, and their beasts also.
31.11 prey, both of men and of *b*.
30 of all manner of *b* and give
35. 3 their goods, and for all their *b*.
Dt 7.22 lest the *b* of the field increase
14. 4 These are the *b* which ye shall
6 cheweth the cud among the *b*,
28.26 and unto the *b* of the earth,
32.24 I will also send the teeth of *b* upon

1Sa 17.44 of the air, and to the *b* of the field.
46 and to the wild *b* of the earth;
2Sa 21.10 nor the *b* of the field by night.
1Ki 4.33 he spake also of *b*, and of fowl,
18. 5 that we lose not all the *b*.
2Ki 3.17 and your cattle, and your *b*.
2Ch 32.28 stalls for all manner of *b*,
Ezr 1. 4 with goods, and with *b*, beside
6 with goods, and with *b*, and with
Job 5.22 shalt thou be afraid of the *b* of
23 and the *b* of the field shall be at
12. 7 But ask now the *b*, and they shall
18. 3 Wherefore are we counted as *b*,
35.11 teacheth us more than the *b* of
37. 8 Then the *b* go into dens, and
40.20 where all the *b* of the field play.
Ps 8. 7 oxen, yea, and the *b* of the field;
49.12 he is like the *b* that perish.
20 is like the *b* that perish.
50.11 the wild *b* of the field are mine.
79. 2 saints unto the *b* of the earth.
104.20 all the *b* of the forest do creep
25 both small and great *b*.
148.10 *B*, and all cattle; creeping things,
Pr 9. 2 She hath killed her *b*; she hath
30.30 lion which is strongest among *b*,
Ec 3.18 see that they themselves are *b*.
19 the sons of men befalleth *b*;
Isa 1.11 the fat of fed *b*; and I delight
13.21 wild *b* of the desert shall lie
22 wild *b* of the islands shall cry
18. 6 and to the *b* of the earth:
6 the *b* of the earth shall winter
30. 6 The burden of the beasts of the
34.14 The wild *b* of the desert shall
14 with the wild *b* of the island,
40.16 nor the *b* thereof sufficient for a
46. 1 their idols were upon the *b*,
56. 9 ye *b* of the field, come to devour,
9 all ye *b* in the forest.
66.20 upon mules, and upon swift *b*,
Jer 7.33 and for the *b* of the earth;
12. 4 the *b* are consumed, and the birds;
9 assemble all the *b* of the field,
15. 3 the *b* of the earth, to devour
16. 4 and for the *b* of the earth.
19. 7 for the *b* of the earth.
27. 6 the *b* of the field have I given him
28.14 given him the *b* of the field also.
34.20 heaven, and to the *b* of the earth.
50.39 Therefore the wild *b* of the
39 with the wild *b* of the islands
Eze 5.17 send upon you famine and evil *b*,
8.10 and abominable *b*, and all the
14.15 cause noisome *b* to pass through
15 pass through because of the *b*:
29. 5 for meat to the *b* of the field
31. 6 under his branches did all the *b* of
13 all the *b* of the field shall be upon
32. 4 I will fill the *b* of the whole earth
13 destroy also all the *b* thereof
13 nor the hoofs of *b* trouble them.
33.27 will I give to the *b* to be devoured,
34. 5 became meat to all the *b* of the
25 the evil *b* to cease out of the land:
38.20 and the *b* of the field, and all
39. 4 and to the *b* of the field, to be
Dan 2.38 the *b* of the field and the fowls
4.12 the *b* of the field had shadow
14 let the *b* get away from under it,
15 let his portion be with the *b*
21 under which the *b* of the field dwelt,
23 let his portion be with the *b* of
25 dwelling shall be with the *b* of the
32 shall be with the *b* of the field:
5.21 his heart was made like the *b*,
7. 3 four great *b* came up from the sea,
7 from all the *b* that were before it;
12 concerning the rest of the *b*,
17 These great *b*, which are four,
8. 4 no *b* might stand before him,

Hos 2.12 the *b* of the field shall eat them.
18 a covenant for them with the *b* of
4. 3 with the *b* of the field, and with
Joel 1.18 How do the *b* groan! the herds of
20 The *b* of the field cry also
2.22 Be not afraid, ye *b* of the field:
Am 5.22 the peace offerings of your fat *b*.
Mic 5. 8 a lion among the *b* of the forest,
Hab 2.17 the spoil of *b*, which made them
Zep 2.14 of her, all the *b* of the nations:
15 a place for *b* to lie down in!
Zec 14.15 all the *b* that shall be in these
Mk 1.13 was with the wild *b*; and the
Ac 7.42 have ye offered to me slain *b*
10.12 all manner of fourfooted *b*
12 of the earth, and wild *b*,
11. 6 and saw fourfooted *b* of the earth,
6 and wild *b*, and creeping things,
23.24 And provide them *b*, that they
Ro 1.23 fourfooted *b*, and creeping things.
1Co 15.32 I have fought with *b* at Ephesus,
39 another flesh of *b*, another of
Tit 1.12 alway liars, evil *b*, slow bellies.
Heb 13.11 of those *b*, whose blood is brought
Jas 3. 7 Every kind of *b*, and of birds,
2Pe 2.12 as natural brute *b*, made to be
Jude 10 they know naturally, as brute *b*,
Rev 4. 6 were four *b* full of eyes
8 And the four *b* had each of them
9 those *b* give glory and honor
5. 6 of the throne and of the four *b*,
8 the four *b* and four and twenty
11 round about the throne and the *b*,
14 And the four *b* said, Amen.
6. 1 one of the four *b* saying, Come
6 voice in the midst of the four *b*
8 death, and with the *b* of the earth.
7.11 about the elders and the four *b*,
14. 3 before the four *b*, and the elders:
15. 7 one of the four *b* gave unto the
18.13 and *b*, and sheep, and horses,
19. 4 elders and the four *b* fell down

BEAT
Ex 30.36 shalt *b* some of it very small,
39. 3 did *b* the gold into thin plates,
Nu 11. 8 it in mills, or *b* it in a mortar,
Dt 25. 3 and *b* him above these with
Jdg 8.17 he *b* down the tower of Penuel,
9.45 and *b* down the city, and sowed
19.22 *b* at the door, and spake to the
Ru 2.17 and *b* out that she had gleaned:
2Sa 22.43 Then did I *b* them as small as
2Ki 3.25 they *b* down the cities, and on
13.25 Three times did Joash *b* him,
23.12 did the king *b* down, and brake
Ps 18.42 did I *b* them small as the dust
89.23 *b* down his foes before his face,
Pr 23.14 Thou shalt *b* him with the rod,
Isa 2. 4 *b* their swords into plowshares,
3.15 ye *b* my people to pieces, and
27.12 Lord shall *b* off from the channel
41.15 and *b* them small, and shalt make
Joel 3.10 *B* your plowshares into swords,
Jon 4. 8 the sun *b* upon the head of Jonah,
Mic 4. 3 *b* their swords into plowshares,
13 shalt *b* in pieces many people:
Mt 7.25 winds blew, and *b* upon that
27 *b* upon that house; and it fell:
21.35 took his servants, and *b* one,
Mk 4.37 and the waves *b* into the ship,
12. 3 they caught him, and *b* him,
Lk 6.48 stream *b* vehemently upon that
49 against which the stream did *b*
12.45 shall begin to *b* the menservants
20.10 the husbandmen *b* him, and
11 servant: and they *b* him also,
Ac 16.22 and commanded to *b* them.
18.17 *b* him before the judgment seat.
22.19 and *b* in every synagogue

BEATEN

Ex 5.14 had set over them, were *b*,
16 and, behold, thy servants are *b*;
25.18 of *b* work shalt thou make them,
31 of *b* work shall the candlestick
36 one *b* work of pure gold.
27.20 pure oil olive *b* for the light,
29.40 fourth part of an hin of *b* oil;
37. 7 of gold, *b* out of one piece
17 *b* work made he the candlestick;
22 it was one *b* work of pure gold.
Lev 2.14 even corn *b* out of full ears.
16 of the *b* corn thereof, and part
16.12 full of sweet incense *b* small,
24. 2 pure oil olive *b* for the light,
Nu 8. 4 the candlestick was of *b* gold,
4 the flowers thereof, was *b* work:
28. 5 fourth part of an hin of *b* oil.
Dt 25. 2 the wicked man be worthy to be *b*,
2 and to be *b* before his face,
Jos 8.15 made as if they were *b* before
2Sa 2.17 and Abner was *b*, and the men
1Ki 10.16 two hundred targets of *b* gold:
17 three hundred shields of *b* gold;
2Ch 2.10 measures of *b* wheat,
9.15 two hundred targets of *b* gold:
15 hundred shekels of *b* gold
16 three hundred shields made he of *b*
34. 7 *b* the graven images into powder,
Pr 23.35 they have *b* me, and I felt it not:
Isa 27. 9 chalkstones that are *b* in sunder,
28.27 the fitches are *b* out with a staff,
30.31 shall the Assyrian be *b* down,
Jer 46. 5 and their mighty ones are *b* down,
Mic 1. 7 images thereof shall be *b* to pieces,
Mk 13. 9 in the synagogues ye shall be *b*:
Lk 12.47 shall be *b* with many stripes.
48 shall be *b* with few stripes.
Ac 5.40 called the apostles, and *b* them,
16.37 have *b* us openly uncondemned
2Co 11.25 Thrice was I *b* with rods, once

BEATEST

Dt 24.20 When thou *b* thine olive tree,
Pr 23.13 if thou *b* him with the rod,

BEATETH

1Co 9.26 not as one that *b* the air:

BEATING

1Sa 14.16 went on *b* down one another.
Mk 12. 5 others; *b* some, and killing some.
Ac 21.32 the soldiers, they left *b* of Paul.

BEAUTIES

Ps 110. 3 in the *b* of holiness from the

BEAUTIFUL

Gen 29.17 Rachel was *b* and well
Dt 21.11 among the captives a *b* woman,
1Sa 16.12 withal of a *b* countenance,
25. 3 and of a *b* countenance:
2Sa 11. 2 was very *b* to look upon.
Est 2. 7 the maid was fair and *b*;
Ps 48. 2 *B* for situation, the joy of the
Ec 3.11 made every thing *b* in his time:
SS 6. 4 Thou art *b*, O my love,
7. 1 How *b* are thy feet with shoes,
Isa 4. 2 shall the branch of the Lord be *b*
52. 1 put on thy *b* garments, O
7 How *b* upon the mountains are
64.11 Our holy and our *b* house,
Jer 13.20 was given thee, thy *b* flock?
48.17 strong staff broken, and the *b* rod!
Eze 16.12 a *b* crown upon thine head.
13 thou wast exceeding *b*, and thou
23.42 *b* crowns upon their heads.
Mt 23.27 which indeed appear *b* outward,
Ac 3. 2 the temple which is called *B*,
10 sat for alms at the *B* gate
Ro 10.15 How *b* are the feet of them that

Biblical Themes

BEAUTY

And it came to pass, when men began to multiply on the face of the earth, and daughters were born unto them, that the sons of God saw the daughters of men that they were fair; and they took them wives of all which they chose.
Gen 6.1-2

Leah was tender eyed; but Rachel was beautiful and well favored.
Gen 29.17

And it came to pass in an eveningtide, that David arose from off his bed, and walked upon the roof of the king's house: and from the roof he saw a woman washing herself; and the woman was very beautiful to look upon. 2Sa 11.2

Jezebel . . . painted her face, and tired her head, and looked out at a window.
2Ki 9.30

One thing have I desired of the Lord . . . that I may dwell in the house of the Lord all the days of my life, to behold the beauty of the Lord. Ps 27.4

Worship the Lord in the beauty of holiness. Ps 29.2

Out of Zion, the perfection of beauty, God hath shined. Ps 50.2

The Lord taketh pleasure in his people: he will beautify the meek with salvation. Ps 149.4

As a jewel of gold in a swine's snout, so is a fair woman which is without discretion. Pr 11.22

Favor is deceitful, and beauty is vain: but a woman that feareth the Lord, she shall be praised. Pr 31.30

Behold, thou art fair, my love; behold, thou art fair; thou hast doves' eyes. Behold, thou art fair, my beloved, yea, pleasant. SS 1.15-16

His mouth is most sweet: yea, he is altogether lovely. This is my beloved.
SS 5.16

How beautiful upon the mountains are the feet of him that bringeth good tidings. Isa 52.7

And I put a jewel on thy forehead, and earrings in thine ears, and a beautiful crown upon thine head. . . . And thy renown went forth among the heathen for thy beauty: for it was perfect through my comeliness, which I had put upon thee, saith the Lord God. But thou didst trust in thine own beauty, and playedst the harlot because of thy renown. Eze 16.12, 14-15.

Consider the lilies of the field, how they grow; they toil not, neither do they spin: and yet I say unto you, That even Solomon in all his glory was not arrayed like one of these.
Mt 6.28-29

And as he prayed, the fashion of his countenance was altered, and his raiment was white and glistering.
Lk 9.29

And the Word was made flesh, and dwelt among us, (and we beheld his glory, the glory as of the only begotten of the Father,) full of grace and truth.
Jn 1.14

Finally, brethren, whatsoever things are true, whatsoever things are honest, whatsoever things are just, whatsoever things are pure, whatsoever things are lovely, whatsoever things are of good report; if there be any virtue, and if there be any praise, think on these things. Php 4.8

And I John saw the holy city, new Jerusalem, coming down from God out of heaven, prepared as a bride adorned for her husband. Rev 21.2

BEAUTIFY

Ezr 7.27 to *b* the house of the Lord
Ps 149. 4 he will *b* the meek with salvation,
Isa 60.13 to *b* the place of my sanctuary;

BEAUTY

Ex 28. 2 thy brother, for glory and for *b*.
40 for them, for glory and for *b*.
2Sa 1.19 The *b* of Israel is slain upon thy
14.25 praised as Absalom for his *b*:
1Ch 16.29 the Lord in the *b* of holiness.
2Ch 3. 6 house with precious stones for *b*:
20.21 should praise the *b* of holiness,
Est 1.11 the people and the princes her *b*:
Job 40.10 array thyself with glory and *b*.
Ps 27. 4 to behold the *b* of the Lord,
29. 2 the Lord in the *b* of holiness.
39.11 makest his *b* to consume away
45.11 the king greatly desire thy *b*:
49.14 and their *b* shall consume in the
50. 2 out of Zion, the perfection of *b*,
90.17 let the *b* of the Lord our God
96. 6 and *b* are in his sanctuary.
9 the Lord in the *b* of holiness:
Pr 6.25 Lust not after her *b* in thine
20.29 *b* of old men is the gray head.
31.30 Favor is deceitful, and *b* is vain:
Isa 3.24 burning instead of *b*.
13.19 the *b* of the Chaldees' excellency,
28. 1 glorious *b* is a fading flower,
4 glorious *b*, which is on the head
5 of glory, and for a diadem of *b*,

33.17 eyes shall see the king in his *b*:
44.13 according to the *b* of a man;
53. 2 no *b* that we should desire him.
61. 3 to give unto them *b* for ashes,
La 1. 6 her *b* is departed: her princes
2. 1 the *b* of Israel, and remembered
15 the perfection of *b*, The joy of
Eze 7.20 As for the *b* of his ornament,
16.14 among the heathen for thy *b*:
15 thou didst trust in thine own *b*,
25 hast made thy *b* to be abhorred,
27. 3 thou hast said, I am of perfect *b*.
4 thy builders have perfected thy *b*.
11 they have made thy *b* perfect.
28. 7 against the *b* of thy wisdom,
12 full of wisdom, and perfect in *b*.
17 was lifted up because of thy *b*,
31. 8 God was like unto him in his *b*.
32.19 Whom dost thou pass in *b*?
Hos 14. 6 his *b* shall be as the olive tree,
Zec 9.17 goodness, how great is his *b*!
11. 7 the one I called *B*, and the other
10 I took my staff, even *B*, and cut

BECKONED
Lk 1.22 he *b* unto them, and remained
5. 7 they *b* unto their partners,
Jn 13.24 Peter therefore *b* to him, that
Ac 19.33 Alexander *b* with the hand, and
21.40 *b* with the hand unto the people.
24.10 after that the governor had *b*

BECKONING
Ac 12.17 *b* unto them with the hand
13.16 and *b* with his hand, said

BED
Gen 48. 2 himself, and sat upon the *b*.
49. 4 thou wentest up to thy father's *b*;
33 gathered up his feet into the *b*,
Ex 8. 3 bedchamber, and upon thy *b*,
21.18 he die not, but keepeth his *b*:
Lev 15. 4 Every *b*, whereon he lieth that
5 whosoever toucheth his *b* shall
21 whosoever toucheth her *b* shall
23 if it be on her *b*, or on any
24 all the *b* whereon he lieth shall be
26 Every *b* whereon she lieth all the
26 her as the *b* of her separation:
1Sa 19.13 an image, and laid it in the *b*,
15 Bring him up to me in the *b*,
16 there was an image in the *b*,
28.23 the earth, and sat upon the *b*.
2Sa 4. 5 who lay on a *b* at noon.
7 lay on his *b* in his bedchamber,
11 in his own house upon his *b*?
11. 2 David arose from off his *b*,
13 he went out to lie on his *b*
13. 5 Lay thee down on thy *b*, and
1Ki 1.47 king bowed himself upon the *b*.
17.19 and laid him upon his own *b*.
21. 4 he laid him down upon his *b*,
2Ki 1. 4 that *b* on which thou art gone up,
6 shalt not come down from that *b*
16 shalt not come down off that *b*
4.10 let us set for him there a *b*,
21 him on the *b* of the man of God,
32 was dead, and laid upon his *b*.
1Ch 5. 1 he defiled his father's *b*, his
2Ch 16.14 laid him in the *b* which was
24.25 slew him on his *b*, and he died:
Est 7. 8 Haman was fallen upon the *b*
Job 7.13 My *b* shall comfort me, my couch
17.13 made my *b* in the darkness.
33.15 men, in slumberings upon the *b*;
19 also with pain upon his *b*,
Ps 4. 4 with your own heart upon your *b*,
6. 6 the night make I my *b* to swim;
36. 4 He deviseth mischief upon his *b*;
41. 3 strengthen him upon the *b* of
3 make all his *b* in his sickness,
63. 6 I remember thee upon my *b*,
132. 3 my house, nor go up into my *b*;
139. 8 if I make my *b* in hell, behold,
Pr 7.16 decked my *b* with coverings
17 perfumed my *b* with myrrh,
22.27 why should he take away thy *b*
26.14 So doth the slothful upon his *b*.
SS 1.16 pleasant: also our *b* is green.
3. 1 By night on my *b* I sought him
7 his *b*, which is Solomon's;
5.13 His cheeks are as a *b* of spices,
Isa 28.20 the *b* is shorter than that a man
57. 7 mountain hast thou set thy *b*:
8 thou hast enlarged thy *b*,
8 their *b* where thou sawest it.
Eze 23.17 came to her into the *b* of love,
41 And satest upon a stately *b*,
32.25 They have set her a *b* in the
Dan 2.28 visions of thy head upon thy *b*,
29 came into thy mind upon thy *b*,
4. 5 and the thoughts upon my *b*
10 the visions of mine head in my *b*;
13 the visions of my head upon my *b*,
7. 1 visions of his head upon his *b*:
Am 3.12 in Samaria in the corner of a *b*,
Mt 9. 2 sick of the palsy, lying on a *b*:
6 take up thy *b*, and go unto thine
Mk 2. 4 they let down the *b* wherein
9 Arise, and take up thy *b*,
11 Arise, and take up thy *b*, and go
12 he arose, took up the *b*, and went
4.21 under a bushel, or under a *b*?
7.30 and her daughter laid upon the *b*.
Lk 5.18 men brought in a *b* a man which
8.16 putteth it under a *b*; but setteth
11. 7 my children are with me in *b*;
17.34 there shall be two men in one *b*;
Jn 5. 8 Rise, take up thy *b*, and walk.
9 and took up his *b*, and walked:
10 lawful for thee to carry thy *b*.
11 unto me, Take up thy *b*, and walk.
12 Take up thy *b*, and walk?
Ac 9.33 Aeneas, which had kept his *b*
34 arise, and make thy *b*. And he
Heb 13. 4 *b* undefiled: but whoremongers
Rev 2.22 Behold, I will cast her into a *b*,

BEDCHAMBER
Ex 8. 3 into thy *b*, and upon thy bed,
2Sa 4. 7 he lay on his bed in his *b*,
2Ki 6.12 that thou speakest in thy *b*.
11. 2 in the *b* from Athalia,
2Ch 22.11 put him and his nurse in a *b*.
Ec 10.20 curse not the rich in thy *b*:

BED'S
Gen 47.31 bowed himself upon the *b* head.

BEDS
2Sa 17.28 *b*, and basons, and earthen
Est 1. 6 the *b* were of gold and silver,
Ps 149. 5 let them sing aloud upon their *b*.
SS 6. 2 to the *b* of spices, to feed in
Isa 57. 2 they shall rest in their *b*, each
Hos 7.14 they howled upon their *b*:
Am 6. 4 That lie upon *b* of ivory,
Mic 2. 1 and work evil upon their *b*!
Mk 6.55 and began to carry about in *b*
Ac 5.15 and laid them on *b* and couches,

BEDSTEAD
Dt 3.11 his *b* was a *b* of iron;

BEE
Isa 7.18 and for the *b* that is in the land

BEELZEBUB
Mt 10.25 called the master of the house *B*,
12.24 but by *B* the prince of the devils.
27 And if I by *B* cast out devils,
Mk 3.22 said, He hath *B*, and by the prince
Lk 11.15 He casteth out devils through *B*
18 I cast out devils through *B*.
19 And if I by *B* cast out devils,

BEES
Dt 1.44 you, as *b* do, and destroyed you
Jdg 14. 8 of *b* and honey in the carcase
Ps 118.12 They compassed me about like *b*;

BEG
Ps 109.10 be continually vagabonds, and *b*:
Pr 20. 4 therefore shall he *b* in the harvest,
Lk 16. 3 cannot dig; to *b* I am ashamed.

BEGAN
Gen 4.26 then *b* men to call upon the name
6. 1 when men *b* to multiply on the
9.20 And Noah *b* to be an husbandman,
10. 8 *b* to be a mighty one in the earth.
41.54 seven years of dearth *b* to come,
44.12 he searched, and *b* at the eldest,
Nu 25. 1 people *b* to commit whoredom
Dt 1. 5 *b* Moses to declare this law,
Jdg 13.25 the Spirit of the Lord *b* to move
16.19 and she *b* to afflict him, and his
22 the hair of his head *b* to grow
19.25 when the day *b* to spring, they
20.31 they *b* to smite of the people,
39 Benjamin *b* to smite and kill
40 when the flame *b* to arise up out
1Sa 3. 2 his eyes *b* to wax dim, that he
2Sa 2.10 old when he *b* to reign over Israel,
5. 4 years old when he *b* to reign,
1Ki 6. 1 *b* to build the house of the Lord.
14.21 when he *b* to reign, and he
15.25 son of Jeroboam *b* to reign over
33 *b* Baasha the son of Ahijah to
16. 8 *b* Elah the son of Baasha to reign
11 when he *b* to reign, as soon as
23 *b* Omri to reign over Israel,
29 *b* Ahab the son of Omri to reign
22.41 son of Asa *b* to reign over Judah
42 when he *b* to reign; and he
51 the son of Ahab *b* to reign over
2Ki 3. 1 the son of Ahab *b* to reign over
8.16 king of Judah *b* to reign.
17 when he *b* to reign; and he
26 when he *b* to reign; and he
9.29 *b* Ahaziah to reign over Judah.
10.32 the Lord *b* to cut Israel short:
11.21 Jehoash when he *b* to reign.
12. 1 Jehoash *b* to reign; and forty
13. 1 the son of Jehu *b* to reign
10 *b* Jehoash the son of Jehoahaz
14. 2 when he *b* to reign, and reigned
23 Joash king of Israel *b* to reign
15. 1 *b* Azariah son of Amaziah king
2 old was he when he *b* to reign,
13 the son of Jabesh *b* to reign
17 *b* Menahem the son of Gadi to reign
23 the son of Menahem *b* to reign
27 the son of Remaliah *b* to reign
32 *b* Jotham the son of Uzziah king
33 old was he when he *b* to reign,
37 In those days the Lord *b* to send
16. 1 Jotham king of Judah *b* to reign.
2 Ahaz when he *b* to reign, and
17. 1 *b* Hoshea the son of Elah to reign
18. 1 of Ahaz king of Judah *b* to reign.
2 when he *b* to reign; and he
21. 1 years old when he *b* to reign,
19 twenty and two years old when he *b*
22. 1 years old when he *b* to reign,
23.31 years old when he *b* to reign,
36 twenty and five years old when he *b*
24. 8 years old when he *b* to reign,
18 twenty and one years old when he *b*
25.27 in the year that he *b* to reign did
1Ch 1.10 *b* to be mighty upon the earth.
27.24 the son of Zeruiah *b* to number,

2Ch 3. 1 Solomon *b* to build the house
2 And he *b* to build in the second
12.13 years old when he *b* to reign,
13. 1 *b* Abijah to reign over Judah.
20.22 when they *b* to sing and to praise,
31 years old when he *b* to reign,
21. 5 years old when he *b* to reign,
20 years old was he when he *b* to
22. 2 was Ahaziah when he *b* to reign,
24. 1 seven years old when he *b* to reign,
25. 1 years old when he *b* to reign,
26. 3 was Uzziah when he *b* to reign,
27. 1 twenty and five years old when he *b*
8 years old when he *b* to reign,
28. 1 years old when he *b* to reign,
29. 1 Hezekiah *b* to reign when he was
17 Now they *b* on the first day of
27 when the burnt offering *b*,
27 the song of the Lord *b*
31. 7 they *b* to lay the foundation of
10 Since the people *b* to bring the
21 And in every work that he *b*
33. 1 twelve years old when he *b* to
21 years old when he *b* to reign,
34. 1 eight years old when he *b* to reign,
3 *b* to seek after the God of David
3 in the twelfth year he *b* to purge
36. 2 twenty and three years old when he *b*
5 twenty and five years old when he *b*
9 eight years old when he *b* to reign,
11 one and twenty years old when he *b*
Ezr 3. 6 *b* they to offer burnt offerings
8 *b* Zerubbabel the son of Shealtiel
5. 2 and *b* to build the house of God
7. 9 of the first month *b* he to go up
Neh 4. 7 that the breaches *b* to be stopped,
13.19 gates of Jerusalem *b* to be dark
Jer 52. 1 years old when he *b* to reign,
Eze 9. 6 Then they *b* at the ancient men
Jon 3. 4 Jonah *b* to enter into the city
Mt 4.17 Jesus *b* to preach, and to say,
11. 7 Jesus *b* to say unto the multitudes
20 Then *b* he to upbraid the cities
12. 1 *b* to pluck the ears of corn, and to
16.21 *b* Jesus to shew unto his disciples,
22 *b* to rebuke him, saying, Be it far
26.22 *b* every one of them to say unto
37 *b* to be sorrowful and very heavy.
74 Then *b* he to curse and to swear,
28. 1 as it *b* to dawn toward the first
Mk 1.45 *b* to publish it much, and to
2.23 his disciples *b*, as they went,
4. 1 he *b* again to teach by the sea side:
5.17 they *b* to pray him to depart
20 *b* to publish in Decapolis how great
6. 2 he *b* to teach in the synagogue:
7 *b* to send them forth by two and
34 he *b* to teach them many things.
55 *b* to carry about in beds those
8.11 *b* to question with him, seeking
31 he *b* to teach them, that the Son of
32 Peter took him, and *b* to rebuke
10.28 Then Peter *b* to say unto him,
32 *b* to tell them what things should
41 they *b* to be much displeased
47 he *b* to cry out, and say, Jesus,
11.15 *b* to cast out them that sold and
12. 1 *b* to speak unto them by parables.
13. 5 Jesus answering them *b* to say,
14.19 they *b* to be sorrowful, and to
33 *b* to be sore amazed, and to be
65 some *b* to spit on him, and to cover
69 *b* to say to them that stood by,
71 he *b* to curse and to swear, saying,
15. 8 crying aloud, *b* to desire him to do
18 *b* to salute him, Hail, king of the
Lk 1.70 have been since the world *b*:
3.23 Jesus himself *b* to be about thirty
4.21 he *b* to say unto them, This day
5. 7 the ships, so that they *b* to sink.
21 scribes and the Pharisees *b* to
7.15 he that was dead sat up, and *b* to
24 he *b* to speak unto the people
38 *b* to wash his feet with tears, and
49 *b* to say within themselves, Who is
9.12 when the day *b* to wear away, then
11.29 gathered thick together, he *b* to
53 scribes and the Pharisees *b* to
12. 1 he *b* to say unto his disciples first
14.18 with one consent *b* to make excuse.
30 Saying, This man *b* to build, and
15.14 famine in that land, and he *b* to be
24 And they *b* to be merry.
19.37 multitude of the disciples *b* to
45 *b* to cast out them that sold
20. 9 Then *b* he to speak to the people
22.23 they *b* to inquire among themselves
23. 2 they *b* to accuse him, saying,
Jn 4.52 when he *b* to amend. And they
9.32 Since the world *b* was it not heard
13. 5 *b* to wash the disciples' feet, and
Ac 1. 1 all that Jesus *b* both to do and
2. 4 *b* to speak with other tongues, as
3.21 holy prophets since the world *b*.
8.35 *b* at the same scripture, and
10.37 *b* from Galilee, after the baptism
11.15 as I *b* to speak, the Holy Ghost fell
18.26 he *b* to speak boldly in the
24. 2 Tertullus *b* to accuse him, saying,
27.35 when he had broken it, he *b* to eat
Ro 16.25 kept secret since the world *b*,
2Ti 1. 9 Christ Jesus before the world *b*;
Tit 1. 2 promised before the world *b*.
Heb 2. 3 which at the first *b* to be

BEGGAR

1Sa 2. 8 up the *b* from the dunghill,
Lk 16.20 was a certain *b* named Lazarus,
22 that the *b* died, and was carried

BEGGARLY

Gal 4. 9 to the weak and *b* elements,

BEGGED

Mt 27.58 Pilate, and *b* the body of Jesus.
Lk 23.52 Pilate, and *b* the body of Jesus.
Jn 9. 8 Is not this he that sat and *b*?

BEGGING

Ps 37.25 forsaken, nor his and *b* bread.
Mk 10.46 sat by the highway side *b*.
Lk 18.35 man sat by the wayside *b*:

BEGIN

Gen 11. 6 this they *b* to do: and now
Dt 2.24 *b* to possess it, and contend
25 will I *b* to put the dread of thee
31 his land before thee: *b* to possess,
16. 9 *b* to number the seven weeks
Jos 3. 7 This day will I *b* to magnify thee
Jdg 10.18 What man is he that will *b*
13. 5 he shall *b* to deliver Israel
1Sa 3.12 I *b*, I will also make an end.
22.15 Did I then *b* to inquire of God
2Ki 8.25 Jeroham king of Judah *b* to reign.
Neh 11.17 to *b* the thanksgiving in prayer:
Jer 25.29 I *b* to bring evil on the city
Eze 9. 6 and *b* at my sanctuary.
Mt 24.49 *b* to smite his fellowservants,
Lk 3. 8 *b* not to say within yourselves,
12.45 shall *b* to beat the menservants
13.25 ye *b* to stand without, and to knock
26 Then shall ye *b* to say, We have
14. 9 thou *b* with shame to take the
29 behold it *b* to mock him,
21.28 these things *b* to come to pass,
23.30 they *b* to say to the mountains,
2Co 3. 1 Do we *b* again to commend
1Pe 4.17 must *b* at the house of God:
17 and if it first *b* at us, what shall
Rev 10. 7 he shall *b* to sound, the mystery

BEGINNEST

Dt 16. 9 from such time as thou *b* to put

BEGINNING

Gen 1. 1 In the *b* God created the heaven
10.10 the *b* of his kingdom was Babel,
13. 3 his tent had been at the *b*,
41.21 still ill favored, as at the *b*.
49. 3 might, and the *b* of my strength,
Ex 12. 2 the *b* of months: it shall be the
Dt 11.12 the *b* of the year even unto the
21.17 for he is the *b* of his strength;
32.42 *b* of revenges upon the enemy.
Jdg 7.19 in the *b* of the middle watch;
Ru 1.22 Bethlehem in the *b* of barley
3.10 in the latter end than at the *b*,
2Sa 21. 9 in the *b* of barley harvest.
10 from the *b* of harvest until water
2Ki 17.25 was at the *b* of their dwelling
1Ch 17. 9 them any more, as at the *b*,
Ezr 4. 6 Ahasuerus, in the *b* of his reign,
Job 8. 7 Though thy *b* was small, yet thy
42.12 end of Job more than his *b*:
Ps 111.10 of the Lord is the *b* of wisdom:
119.160 is true from the *b*: and every
Pr 1. 7 the *b* of knowledge: but fools
8.22 possessed me in the *b* of his
23 up from everlasting, from the *b*,
9.10 fear of the Lord is the *b* of
17.14 The *b* of strife is as when
20.21 hastily at the *b*; but the end
Ec 3.11 that God maketh from the *b*
7. 8 end of a thing than the *b* thereof:
10.13 The *b* of the words of his mouth
Isa 1.26 thy counsellors as at the *b*:
18. 2 terrible from their *b* hitherto; a
7 a people terrible from their *b*
40.21 you from the *b*? have ye not
41. 4 the generations from the *b*?
26 Who hath declared from the *b*,
46.10 Declaring the end from the *b*,
48. 3 the former things from the *b*:
5 I have even from the *b* declared
7 now, and not from the *b*; even
16 not spoken in secret from the *b*;
64. 4 For since the *b* of the world men
Jer 17.12 glorious high throne from the *b*
26. 1 the *b* of the reign of
27. 1 the *b* of the reign of Jehoiakim
28. 1 in the *b* of the reign of Zedekiah
49.34 Elam in the *b* of the reign
La 2.19 in the *b* of the watches pour out
Eze 40. 1 in the *b* of the year of our
Dan 9.21 seen in the vision at the *b*,
23 At the *b* of my supplications
Hos 1. 2 The *b* of the word of the Lord
Am 7. 1 poured grasshoppers in the *b* of
Mic 1.13 the *b* of the sin to the daughter
Mt 14.30 *b* to sink, he cried, saying,
19. 4 which made them at the *b*
8 from the *b* it was not so.
20. 8 *b* from the last unto the first.
24. 8 these are the *b* of sorrows.
21 since the *b* of the world to this
Mk 1. 1 The *b* of the gospel of Jesus
10. 6 from the *b* of the creation
13.19 such as was not from the *b*
Lk 1. 2 from the *b* were eyewitnesses,
5 *b* from Galilee to this place.
24.27 *b* at Moses and all the prophets,
47 among all nations, *b* at Jerusalem,
Jn 1. 1 In the *b* was the Word, and the
2 The same was in the *b* with God.
2.10 man at the *b* doth set forth
11 This *b* of miracles did Jesus
6.64 Jesus knew from the *b* who
8. 9 *b* at the eldest, even unto the last:
25 I said unto you from the *b*.
44 was a murderer from the *b*,
15.27 ye have been with me from the *b*.
16. 4 not unto you at the *b*, because I

Ac 1.22 *B* from the baptism of John,
11. 4 rehearsed the matter from the *b*,
15 fell on them, as on us at the *b*.
15.18 his works from the *b* of the
26. 5 Which knew me from the *b*,
Eph 3. 9 which from the *b* of the world
Php 4.15 that in the *b* of the gospel,
Col 1.18 who is the *b*, the firstborn
2Th 2.13 God hath from the *b* chosen you
Heb 1.10 Thou, Lord, in the *b* hast laid
3.14 if we hold the *b* of our confidence
7. 3 having neither *b* of days, nor end
2Pe 2.20 is worse with them than the *b*.
3. 4 were from the *b* of the creation.
1Jn 1. 1 That which was from the *b*,
2. 7 which ye had from the *b*.
7 ye have heard from the *b*.
13 him that is from the *b*.
14 known him that is from the *b*.
24 which ye have heard from the *b*.
24 ye have heard from the *b*
3. 8 the devil sinneth from the *b*.
11 that ye heard from the *b*,
2Jn 5 which we had from the *b*,
6 as ye have heard from the *b*,
Rev 1. 8 the *b* and the ending,
3.14 the *b* of the creation of God;
21. 6 the *b* and the end. I will
22.13 Alpha and Omega, the *b* and the

BEGOTTEN
Gen 5. 4 days of Adam after he had *b* Seth
Lev 18.11 *b* of thy father, she is thy sister,
Nu 11.12 I *b* them, that thou shouldest
Dt 23. 8 The children that are *b* of them
Jdg 8.30 and ten sons of his body *b*:
Job 38.28 who hath *b* the drops of dew?
Ps 2. 7 my son; this day have I *b* thee.
Isa 49.21 Who hath *b* me these, seeing I
Hos 5. 7 for they have *b* strange children:
Jn 1.14 as of the only *b* of the Father,)
18 the only *b* Son, which is
3.16 his only *b* Son, that whosoever
18 name of the only *b* Son of God.
Ac 13.33 my Son, this day have I *b* thee.
1Co 4.15 I have *b* you through the gospel.
Phm 10 whom I have *b* in my bonds:
Heb 1. 5 my Son, this day have I *b* thee?
5. 5 my Son, to day have I *b* thee.
11.17 offered up his only *b* son,
1Pe 1. 3 *b* us again unto a lively hope
1Jn 4. 9 God sent his only *b* Son
5. 1 loveth him also that is *b* of him.
18 but he that is *b* of God keepeth
Rev 1. 5 first *b* of the dead, and the prince

BEGUILE
Col 2. 4 lest any man should *b* you with
18 Let no man *b* you of your reward

BEGUILED
Gen 3.13 The serpent *b* me, and I did eat.
29.25 wherefore then hast thou *b* me?
Nu 25.18 they have *b* you in the matter of
Jos 9.22 Wherefore have ye *b* us, saying,
2Co 11. 3 as the serpent *b* Eve through his

BEGUILING
2Pe 2.14 *b* unstable souls: an heart they

BEGUN
Nu 16.46 from the Lord; the plague is *b*.
47 plague was *b* among the people:
Dt 2.31 I have *b* to give Sihon and his
3.24 thou hast *b* to shew thy servant
Est 6.13 before whom thou hast *b* to fall,
9.23 undertook to do as they had *b*,
Mt 18.24 when he had *b* to reckon, one was
2Co 8. 6 that as he had *b*, so he would also
10 who have *b* before, not only to do,
Gal 3. 3 having *b* in the Spirit, are ye now
Php 1. 6 that he which hath *b* a good
1Ti 5.11 when they have *b* to wax wanton

BEHAVE
Dt 32.27 lest their adversaries should *b*
1Ch 19.13 and let us *b* ourselves violently
Ps 101. 2 I will *b* myself wisely in a perfect
Isa 3. 5 the child shall *b* himself proudly
1Co 13. 5 Doth not *b* itself unseemly,
1Ti 3.15 to *b* thyself in the house of God,

BEHAVED
1Sa 18. 5 sent him, and *b* himself wisely:
14 David *b* himself wisely in all his
15 saw that he *b* himself very wisely,
30 David *b* himself more wisely than
Ps 35.14 I *b* myself as though he had been
131. 2 I have *b* and quieted myself
Mic 3. 4 as they have *b* themselves ill
1Th 2.10 unblameably we *b* ourselves
2Th 3. 7 for we *b* not ourselves disorderly

BEHAVETH
1Co 7.36 think that he *b* himself uncomely

BEHAVIOR
1Sa 21.13 he changed his *b* before them,
Ps 34(T) when he changed his *b* before
1Ti 3. 2 vigilant, sober, of good *b*,
Tit 2. 3 that they be in *b* as becometh

BEHEADED
Dt 21. 6 the heifer that is *b* in the valley:
2Sa 4. 7 and slew him, and *b* him,
Mt 14.10 he sent, and *b* John in the prison,
Mk 6.16 It is John, whom I *b*:
27 he went and *b* him in the prison.
Lk 9. 9 Herod said, John have I *b*;
Rev 20. 4 the souls of them that were *b*

BEHEMOTH
Job 40.15 Behold now *b*, which I made

BEHIND
Gen 18.10 in the tent door, which was *b* him.
19.17 look not *b* thee, neither stay thou
26 his wife looked back from *b* him,
22.13 *b* him a ram, caught in a thicket
32.18 and, behold, also he is *b* us.
20 Behold, thy servant Jacob is *b* us.
Ex 10.26 there shall not an hoof be left *b*;
11. 5 the maidservant that is *b* the mill;
14.19 removed and went *b* them; and the
19 before their face, and stood *b* them:
Lev 25.51 If there be yet many years *b*,
Nu 3.23 pitch *b* the tabernacle westward.
Dt 25.18 even all that were feeble *b* thee,
Jos 8. 2 lay thee an ambush for the city *b*
4 *b* the city: go not very far from
14 in ambush against him *b* the city.
20 when the men of Ai looked *b* them,
Jdg 18.12 behold, it is *b* Kirjath-jearim.
20.40 the Benjamites looked *b* them,
1Sa 21. 9 wrapped in a cloth *b* the ephod:
24. 8 when Saul looked *b* him, David
30. 9 those that were left *b* stayed.
10 for two hundred abode *b*, which
2Sa 1. 7 when he looked *b* him, he saw
2.20 Then Abner looked *b* him,
23 the spear came out *b* him; and he
3.16 weeping *b* her to Bahurim.
5.23 fetch a compass *b* them, and come
10. 9 was against him before and *b*,
13.34 by the way of the hill side *b* him.
1Ki 10.19 top of the throne was round *b*:
14. 9 and hast cast me *b* thy back:
2Ki 6.32 sound of his master's feet *b* him?
9.18, 19 do with peace? turn thee *b* me.
11. 6 third part at the gate *b* the guard:
1Ch 19.10 was set against him before and *b*,
2Ch 13.13 an ambushment to come about *b*
13 the ambushment was *b* them.
14 the battle was before and *b*:
Neh 4.13 in the lower places *b* the wall,
16 the rulers were *b* all the house
9.26 cast thy law *b* their backs, and slew
Ps 50.17 and castest my words *b* thee.
139. 5 Thou hast beset me *b* and before,
SS 2. 9 he standeth *b* our wall, he looketh
Isa 9.12 before, and the Philistines *b*;
30.21 Ears shall hear a word *b*,
38.17 hast cast all my sins *b* thy back.
57. 8 *B* the doors also and the posts
66.17 *b* one tree in the midst, eating
Eze 3.12 I heard *b* me a voice of a great
23.35 and cast me *b* thy back, therefore
41.15 separate place which was *b* it,
Joel 2. 3 and *b* them a flame burneth:
3 and *b* them a desolate wilderness;
14 leave a blessing *b* him; even a
Zec 1. 8 and *b* him were there red horses,
Mt 9.20 came *b* him, and touched the hem
16.23 Get thee *b* me, Satan: thou art
Mk 5.27 came in the press *b*, and touched
8.33 Get thee *b* me, Satan: for thou
12.19 brother die, and leave his wife *b*,
Lk 2.43 Jesus tarried *b* in Jerusalem;
4. 8 Get thee *b* me, Satan: for it is
7.38 And stood at his feet *b* him
8.44 Came *b* him, and touched the
1Co 1. 7 So that ye come *b* in no gift;
2Co 11. 5 I suppose I was not a whit *b* the
12.11 for in nothing am I *b* the very
Php 3.13 those things which are *b*,
Col 1.24 that which is *b* of the afflictions
Rev 1.10 and heard *b* me a great voice,
4. 6 beasts full of eyes before and *b*.

BEHOVED
Lk 24.46 thus it *b* Christ to suffer, and
Heb 2.17 in all things it *b* him to be made

BELIAL
Dt 13.13 the children of *B*, are gone out
Jdg 19.22 certain sons of *B*, beset the
20.13 the children of *B*, which are in
1Sa 1.16 handmaid for a daughter of *B*:
2.12 the sons of Eli were sons of *B*;
10.27 But the children of *B* said, How
25.17 for he is such a son of *B*, that a
25 pray thee, regard this man of *B*,
30.22 men of *B*, of those that went
2Sa 16. 7 man, and thou man of *B*:
20. 1 there a man of *B*, whose name
23. 6 the sons of *B* shall be all of
1Ki 21.10 set two men, sons of *B*, before
13 came in two men, children of *B*,
13 the men of *B* witnessed against
2Ch 13. 7 him vain men, the children of *B*,
2Co 6.15 what concord hath Christ with *B*?

BELIEF
2Th 2.13 of the Spirit and *b* of the truth:

BELIEVE
Ex 4. 1 they will not *b* me, nor hearken
5 That they may *b* that the Lord
8 if they will not *b* thee, neither
8 that they will *b* the voice of the
9 if they will not *b* also these two
19. 9 with thee, and *b* thee for ever.
Nu 14.11 how long will it be ere they *b* me,
Dt 1.32 ye did not *b* the Lord your God,
2Ki 17.14 that did not *b* in the Lord their
2Ch 20.20 *B* in the Lord your God, so shall
20 *b* his prophets, so shall ye prosper.
32.15 on this manner, neither yet *b* him:
Job 9.16 I not *b* that he had hearkened
39.12 Wilt thou *b* him, that he will
Pr 26.25 When he speaketh fair, *b* him not:
Isa 7. 9 If ye will not *b*, surely ye shall not
43.10 that ye may know and *b* me, and

Jer 12. 6 *b* them not, though they speak
Hab 1. 5 ye will not *b*, though it be told
Mt 9.28 *B* ye that I am able to do this?
18. 6 little ones which *b* in me, it were
21.25 Why did ye not then *b* him?
32 afterwards, that ye might *b* him.
24.23 here is Christ, or there, *b* it not.
26 in the secret chambers; *b* it not.
27.42 and we will *b* him.
Mk 1.15 repent ye, and *b* the gospel.
5.36 Be not afraid, only *b*.
9.23 If thou canst *b*, all things are
24 Lord, I *b*; help thou mine
42 little ones that *b* in me,
11.23 but shall *b* that those things which
24 *b* that ye receive them, and ye
31 say, Why then did ye not *b* him?
13.21 or, lo, he is there; *b* him not:
15.32 that we may see and *b*. And they
16.17 signs shall follow them that *b*;
Lk 8.12 lest they should *b* and be saved.
13 which for a while *b*, and in time
50 *b* only, and she shall be made
22.67 ye will not *b*:
24.25 fools, and slow of heart to *b*
Jn 1. 7 all men through him might *b*.
12 even to them that *b* on his name:
3.12 and ye *b* not,
12 how shall ye *b*, if I tell you of
4.21 Woman, *b* me, the hour cometh,
42 Now we *b*, not because of thy
48 signs and wonders, ye will not *b*.
5.38 whom he hath sent, him ye *b* not.
44 How can ye *b*, which receive
47 But if ye *b* not his writings,
47 how shall ye *b* my words?
6.29 ye *b* on him whom he hath sent.
30 that we may see, and *b* thee?
36 ye also have seen me, and *b* not.
64 there are some of you that *b* not.
69 And we *b* and are sure that thou
7. 5 neither did his brethren *b* in him.
39 which they that *b* on him should
8.24 if ye *b* not that I am he, ye shall
45 I tell you the truth, ye *b* me not.
46 the truth, why do ye not *b* me?
9.18 the Jews did not *b* concerning
35 Dost thou *b* on the Son of God?
36 he, Lord, that I might *b* on him?
38 Lord, I *b*. And he worshipped
10.26 But ye *b* not, because ye are not
37 the works of my Father, *b* me not.
38 though ye *b* not me,
38 *b* the works; that ye may know,
38 and *b*, that the Father
11.15 to the intent ye may *b*; nevertheless
27 I *b* that thou art the Christ, the
40 thou wouldest *b*, thou shouldest
42 by I said it, that they may *b* that
48 thus alone, all men will *b* on him:
12.36 *b* in the light, that ye may be
39 Therefore they could not *b*,
47 man hear my words, and *b* not,
13.19 come to pass, ye may *b* that I am he.
14. 1 ye *b* in God, *b* also in me.
11 *B* me that I am in the Father,
11 else *b* me for the very works' sake.
29 it is come to pass, ye might *b*.
16. 9 because they *b* not on me;
30 by this we *b* that thou camest
31 answered them, Do ye now *b*?
17.20 for them also which shall *b* on me
21 that the world may *b* that thou
19.35 he saith true, that ye might *b*.
20.25 my hand into his side, I will not *b*.
31 might *b* that Jesus is the Christ,
Ac 8.37 I *b* that Jesus Christ is the Son of
13.39 by him all that *b* are justified
41 which ye shall in no wise *b*,
15. 7 hear the word of the gospel, and *b*.
11 But we *b* that through the grace
16.31 *B* on the Lord Jesus Christ, and
19. 4 that they should *b* on him which
21.20 of Jews there are which *b*;
25 touching the Gentiles which *b*,
27.25 for I *b* God, that it shall be even
Ro 3. 3 For what if some did not *b*?
22 unto all and upon all them that *b*:
4.11 be the father of all them that *b*,
24 if we *b* on him that raised up
6. 8 we *b* that we shall also live with
10. 9 shalt *b* in thine heart that God
14 not believed? and how shall they *b*
15.31 them that do not *b* in Judæa;
1Co 1.21 preaching to save them that *b*.
10.27 If any of them that *b* not bid you
11.18 and I partly *b* it.
14.22 not to them that *b*,
22 but to them that *b* not:
22 serveth not for them that *b* not,
22 but for them which *b*.
2Co 4. 4 minds of them which *b* not,
13 spoken; we also *b*, and therefore
Gal 3.22 might be given to them that *b*.
Eph 1.19 to us-ward who *b*, according to
Php 1.29 not only to *b* on him, but also to
1Th 1. 7 were ensamples to all that *b*
2.10 ourselves among you that *b*:
13 worketh also in you that *b*.
4.14 if we *b* that Jesus died and rose
2Th 1.10 be admired in all them that *b*
2.11 delusion, that they should *b* a lie:
1Ti 1.16 should hereafter *b* on him to life
4. 3 them which *b* and know the truth.
10 all men, specially of those that *b*.
2Ti 2.13 If we *b* not, yet he abideth
Heb 10.39 of them that *b* to the saving
11. 6 must *b* that he is, and that he is
Jas 2.19 the devils also *b*, and tremble.
1Pe 1.21 Who by him do *b* in God, that
2. 7 Unto you therefore which *b* he is
1Jn 3.23 That we should *b* on the name of
4. 1 Beloved, *b* not every spirit, but
5.13 unto you that *b* on the name of
13 ye may *b* on the name of the Son

BELIEVED

Gen 15. 6 And he *b* in the Lord; and he
45.26 Jacob's heart fainted, for he *b*
Ex 4.31 And the people *b*: and when they
14.31 and *b* the Lord, and his servant
Nu 20.12 Because ye *b* me not, to sanctify
Dt 9.23 and ye *b* him not, nor hearkened
1Sa 27.12 And Achish *b* David, saying, He
1Ki 10. 7 Howbeit I *b* not the words, until
2Ch 9. 6 Howbeit I *b* not their words, until
Job 29.24 I laughed on them, they *b* it not;
Ps 27.13 unless I had *b* to see the goodness
78.22 Because they *b* not in God, and
32 *b* not for his wondrous works.
106.12 Then *b* they his words; they sang
24 pleasant land they *b* not his word:
116.10 I *b*, therefore have I spoken: I
119.66 for I have *b* thy commandments.
Isa 53. 1 Who hath *b* our report? and to
Jer 40.14 the son of Ahikam, *b* them not.
La 4.12 of the world, would not have *b* that
Dan 6.23 upon him, because he *b* in his
Jon 3. 5 So the people of Nineveh *b* God,
Mt 8.13 and as thou hast *b*, so be it
21.32 and ye *b* him not; but the
32 publicans and the harlots *b* him:
Mk 16.11 and had been seen of her, *b* not.
13 unto the residue: neither *b* they
14 because they *b* not them which
Lk 1. 1 things which are most surely *b*
45 blessed is she that *b*: for there
20. 5 say, Why then *b* ye him not?
24.11 idle tales, and they *b* them not.
41 while they yet *b* not for joy, and
Jn 2.11 his disciples *b* on him.
22 and they *b* the scripture, and the
23 many *b* in his name, when they
3.18 already, because he hath not *b*
4.39 of the Samaritans of that city *b* on
41 many more *b* because of his own
50 the man *b* the word that Jesus had
53 himself *b*, and his whole house.
5.46 had ye *b* Moses,
46 ye would have *b* me.
6.64 who they were that *b* not, and who
7.31 And many of the people *b* on him,
48 or of the Pharisees *b* on him?
8.30 spake these words, many *b* on
31 to those Jews which *b* on him,
10.25 ye *b* not: the works that I do
42 And many *b* on him there.
11.45 things which Jesus did, *b* on him
12.11 of the Jews went away, and *b* on
37 before them, yet they *b* not on him:
38 Lord, who hath *b* our report?
42 chief rulers also many *b* on him;
16.27 have *b* that I came out from God.
17. 8 and they have *b* that thou didst
20. 8 the sepulchre, and he saw, and *b*
29 thou hast *b*: blessed are they
29 have not seen, and yet have *b*.
Ac 2.44 And all that *b* were together,
4. 4 of them which heard the word *b*;
32 of them that *b* were of one heart
8.12 But when they *b* Philip preaching
13 Then Simon himself *b* also:
9.26 and *b* not that he was a disciple.
42 Joppa; and many *b* in the Lord.
10.45 they of the circumcision which *b*
11.17 who *b* on the Lord Jesus Christ;
21 a great number *b*, and turned
13.12 when he saw what was done, *b*,
48 as were ordained to eternal life *b*.
14. 1 Jews and also of the Greeks *b*.
23 them to the Lord, on whom they *b*.
15. 5 of the Pharisees which *b*, saying,
16. 1 which was a Jewess, and *b*;
17. 4 And some of them *b*, and
5 the Jews which *b* not, moved
12 Therefore many of them *b*; also
34 certain men clave unto him, and *b*:
18. 8 *b* on the Lord with all his house;
8 of the Corinthians hearing *b*,
27 helped them much which had *b*
19. 2 received the Holy Ghost since ye *b*?
9 divers were hardened, and *b* not,
18 And many that *b* came, and
22.19 every synagogue them that *b* on
27.11 the centurion *b* the master and
28.24 And some *b* the things which
24 were spoken, and some *b* not.
Ro 4. 3 Abraham *b* God, and it was
17 before him whom he *b*, even God,
18 who against hope *b* in hope,
10.14 on him in whom they have not *b*?
16 saith, Lord, who hath *b* our report?
11.30 ye in times past have not *b* God,
31 so have these also now not *b*,
13.11 salvation nearer than when we *b*.
1Co 3. 5 ministers by whom ye *b*, even as
15. 2 unless ye have *b* in vain.
11 or they, so we preach, and so ye *b*.
2Co 4.13 I *b*, and therefore have I spoken;
Gal 2.16 even we have *b* in Jesus Christ,
3. 6 as Abraham *b* God, and it was
Eph 1.13 in whom also after that ye *b*,
2Th 1.10 our testimony among you was *b*)
2.12 who *b* not the truth, but had
1Ti 3.16 *b* on in the world, received up into
2Ti 1.12 I know whom I have *b*, and am
Tit 3. 8 that they which have *b* in God
Heb 3.18 his rest, but to them that *b* not?
4. 3 which have *b* do enter into rest,
11.31 perished not with them that *b*
Jas 2.23 Abraham *b* God, and it was
1Jn 4.16 we have known and *b* the love
Jude 5 destroyed them that *b* not.

BELIEVERS
Ac 5.14 And *b* were the more added
1Ti 4.12 be thou an example of the *b*, in

BELIEVEST
Lk 1.20 because thou *b* not my words,
Jn 1.50 thee under the fig tree, *b* thou?
11.26 in me shall never die. *B* thou
14.10 *B* thou not that I am in the
Ac 8.37 If thou *b* with all thine heart,
26.27 King Agrippa, *b* thou the prophets?
27 I know that thou *b*.
Jas 2.19 Thou *b* that there is one God;

BELIEVETH
Job 15.22 He *b* not that he shall return
39.24 neither *b* he that it is the sound
Pr 14.15 The simple *b* every word:
Isa 28.16 he that *b* shall not make haste.
Mk 9.23 are possible to him that *b*.
16.16 He that *b* and is baptized shall
16 he that *b* not shall be damned.
Jn 3.15, 16 whosoever *b* in him should
18 He that *b* on him is not
18 but he that *b* not is condemned
36 He that *b* on the Son hath
36 that *b* not the Son shall not see
5.24 and *b* on him that sent me,
6.35 he that *b* on me shall never thirst.
40 and *b* on him, may have
47 He that *b* on me hath everlasting
7.38 He that *b* on me, as the scripture
11.25 he that *b* in me, though he were
26 and *b* in me shall never die.
12.44 He that *b* on me, *b* not on me, but
46 that whosoever *b* on me should not
14.12 He that *b* on me, the works that I
Ac 10.43 whosoever *b* in him shall receive
Ro 1.16 unto salvation to every one that *b*;
3.26 justifier of him which *b* in
4. 5 but *b* on him that justifieth the
9.33 whosoever *b* on him shall not be
10. 4 righteousness to every one that *b*.
10 For with the heart man *b* unto
11 Whosoever *b* on him shall not be
14. 2 For one *b* that he may eat all
1Co 7.12 hath a wife, that *b* not, and she
13 hath an husband that *b* not, and
13. 7 *b* all things, hopeth all things,
14.24 there come in one that *b* not, or
2Co 6.15 hath he that *b* with an infidel?
1Ti 5.16 If any man or woman that *b*
1Pe 2. 6 and he that *b* on him shall not be
1Jn 5. 1 Whosoever *b* that Jesus is the
5 he that *b* that Jesus is the Son
10 He that *b* on the Son of God
10 he that *b* not God hath made
10 because he *b* not the record

BELIEVING
Mt 21.22 ye shall ask in prayer, *b*, ye shall
Jn 20.27 and he not faithless, but *b*.
31 and that *b* ye might have life
Ac 16.34 rejoiced, *b* in God with all his
24.14 *b* all things which are written
Ro 15.13 you with all joy and peace in *b*,
1Ti 6. 2 And they that have *b* masters,
1Pe 1. 8 yet *b*, ye rejoice with joy

BELL
Ex 28.34 *b* and a pomegranate,
34 a golden *b*
39.26 A *b* and a pomegranate, a *b*

BELLIES
Tit 1.12 always liars, evil beasts, slow *b*.

BELLS
Ex 28.33 and *b* of gold between them
39.25 *b* of pure gold, and put the *b*
Zec 14.20 there be upon the *b* of the horses,

BELLY
Gen 3.14 upon thy *b* shalt thou go, and
Lev 11.42 goeth upon the *b*, and whatsoever
Nu 5.21 thy thigh to rot, and thy *b* to
22 to make thy *b* to swell, and thy
27 her *b* shall swell, and her thigh
25. 8 and the woman through her *b*.
Jdg 3.21 thrust it into his *b*:
22 not draw the dagger out of his *b*;
1Ki 7.20 over against the *b* which was by
Job 3.11 ghost when I came out of the *b*?
15. 2 and fill his *b* with the east wind?
35 vanity, and their *b* prepareth
20.15 God shall cast them out of his *b*.
20 shall not feel quietness in his *b*,
23 he is about to fill his *b*, God
32.19 *b* is as wine which hath no vent;
40.16 his force is in the navel of his *b*.
Ps 17.14 whose *b* thou fillest with thy hid
22.10 art my God from my mother's *b*.
31. 9 grief, yea, my soul and my *b*.
44.25 to the dust, our *b* cleaveth unto
Pr 13.25 but the *b* of the wicked shall want.
18. 8 the innermost parts of the *b*.
20 A man's *b* shall be satisfied with
20.27 all the inward parts of the *b*.
30 stripes the inward parts of the *b*.
26.22 into the innermost parts of the *b*.
SS 5.14 his *b* is as bright ivory, overlaid
7. 2 thy *b* is like an heap of wheat set
Isa 46. 3 borne by me from the *b*, which
Jer 1. 5 Before I formed thee in the *b* I
51.34 he hath filled his *b* with my
Eze 3. 3 cause thy *b* to eat, and fill thy
Dan 2.32 arms of silver, his *b* and his
Jon 1.17 in the *b* of the fish three days
2. 1 Lord his God out of the fish's *b*,
2 out of the *b* of hell cried I, and
Hab 3.16 my *b* trembled; my lips quivered
Mt 12.40 three nights in the whale's *b*;
15.17 in at the mouth goeth into the *b*,
Mk 7.19 but into the *b*, and goeth out into
Lk 15.16 he would fain have filled his *b*
Jn 7.38 out of his *b* shall flow rivers of
Ro 16.18 Jesus Christ, but their own *b*;
1Co 6.13 Meats for the *b*,
13 and the *b* for meats:
Php 3.19 whose God is their *b*, and whose
Rev 10. 9 it shall make thy *b* bitter, but it
10 as I had eaten it, my *b* was bitter.

BELOVED
Dt 21.15 wives, one *b*, and another hated,
15 both the *b* and the hated;
16 not make the son of the *b* firstborn
33.12 The *b* of the Lord shall dwell in
Neh 13.26 was *b* of his God, and God made
Ps 60. 5 That thy *b* may be delivered;
108. 6 That thy *b* may be delivered:
127. 2 for so he giveth his *b* sleep.
Pr 4. 3 only *b* in the sight of my mother.
SS 1.14 My *b* is unto me as a cluster
16 Behold, thou art fair, my *b*,
2. 3 so is my *b* among the sons.
8 The voice of my *b*! behold, he
9 My *b* is like a roe or a young hart:
10 My *b* spake, and said unto me,
16 My *b* is mine, and I am his:
17 turn, my *b*, and be thou like a roe
4.16 *b* come into his garden, and eat
5. 1 yea, drink abundantly, O *b*.
2 the voice of my *b* that knocketh,
4 My *b* put in his hand by the hole
5 rose up to open to my *b*; and my
6 to my *b*; but my *b* had withdrawn
8 if ye find my *b*, that ye tell him,
9 thy *b* more than another *b*, O thou
9 *b* more than another *b*, that thou
10 my *b* is white and ruddy, the
16 This is my *b*, and this is my friend,
6. 1 Whither is thy *b* gone, O thou
1 whither is thy *b* turned aside?
2 My *b* is gone down into his garden,
3 my beloved's, and my *b* is mine:
7. 9 the best wine for my *b* that goeth,
11 come my *b*, let us go forth
13 I have laid up for thee, O my *b*.
8. 5 the wilderness, leaning upon her *b*?
14 Make haste, my *b*, and be thou like
Isa 5. 1 to my wellbeloved a song of my *b*
Jer 11.15 hath my *b* to do in mine house,
12. 7 dearly *b* of my soul into the hand
Dan 9.23 greatly *b*: therefore understand
10.11 a man greatly *b*, understand the
19 said, O man greatly *b*, fear not:
Hos 3. 1 yet, love a woman *b* of her friend,
9.16 even the *b* fruit of their womb.
Mt 3.17 saying, This is my *b* Son, in whom
12.18 I have chosen; my *b* in whom,
17. 5 which said, This is my *b* Son,
Mk 1.11 Thou art my *b* Son, in whom
9. 7 saying, This is my *b* Son: hear him.
Lk 3.22 which said, Thou art my *b* Son;
9.35 saying, This is my *b* Son: hear
20.13 shall I do? I will send my *b* son:
Ac 15.25 chosen men unto you with our *b*
Ro 1. 7 To all that be in Rome, *b* of God,
9.25 and her *b*, which was not *b*.
11.28 touching the election, they are *b*
12.19 Dearly *b*, avenge not yourselves,
16. 8 Greet Amplias my *b* in the Lord.
9 helper in Christ, and Stachys my *b*.
12 Salute the *b* Persis, which labored
1Co 4.14 but as my *b* sons I warn you.
17 who is my *b* son, and faithful in the
10.14 my dearly *b*, flee from idolatry.
15.58 Therefore, my *b* brethren, be ye
2Co 7. 1 dearly *b*, let us cleanse ourselves
12.19 we do all things, dearly *b*, for your
Eph 1. 6 he hath made us accepted in the *b*.
6.21 a *b* brother and faithful minister
Php 2.12 Wherefore, my *b*, as ye have
4. 1 brethren dearly *b* and longed for,
1 stand fast in the Lord, my dearly *b*.
Col 3.12 as the elect of God, holy and *b*,
4. 7 declare unto you, who is a *b* brother
9 Onesimus, a faithful and *b* brother,
14 Luke, the *b* physician, and Demas,
1Th 1. 4 Knowing, brethren *b*, your election
2Th 2.13 for you, brethren *b* of the Lord,
1Ti 6. 2 because they are faithful and *b*,
2Ti 1. 2 To Timothy, my dearly *b* son:
Phm 1 unto Philemon our dearly *b*, and
2 to our *b* Apphia, and Archippus
16 but above a servant, a brother *b*,
Heb 6. 9 *b*, we are persuaded better things
Jas 1.16 Do not err, my *b* brethren.
19 Wherefore, my *b* brethren, let every
2. 5 Hearken, my *b* brethren, Hath not
1Pe 2.11 *b*, I beseech you as strangers
4.12 *B*, think it not strange concerning
2Pe 1.17 This is my *b* Son, in whom I am
3. 1 This second epistle, *b*, I now write
8 But, *b*, be not ignorant of this
14 Wherefore, *b*, seeing that ye look
15 our *b* brother Paul also according
17 Ye therefore, *b*, seeing ye know
1Jn 3. 2 *B*, now are we the sons of God,
21 *B*, if our heart condemn us not,
4. 1 *B*, believe not every spirit, but try
7 *B*, let us love one another: for love
11 *B*, if God so loved us, we ought also
3Jn 2 *B*, I wish above all things that
5 *B*, thou doest faithfully whatsoever
11 *B*, follow not that which is evil,
Jude 3 *B*, when I gave all diligence to
17 *b*, remember ye the words which
20 But ye, *b*, building up yourselves
Rev 20. 9 of the saints about, and the *b* city:

BELOVED'S
SS 6. 3 my *b*, and my beloved is mine:

SS 7.10 I am my *b*, and his desire is

BENEATH

Gen 35. 8 and she was buried *b* Beth-el.
Ex 20. 4 or that is in the earth *b*, or that
26.24 they shall be coupled together *b*,
27. 5 under the compass of the altar *b*,
28.33 And *b* upon the hem of it thou
32.19 and brake them *b* the mount.
36.29 they were coupled *b*, and coupled
38. 4 thereof, *b* unto the midst of it.
Dt 4.18 that is in the waters *b* the earth:
39 upon the earth *b*: there is none
5. 8 or that is in the earth *b*,
8 or that is in the waters *b*
28.13 above only, thou shalt not be *b*;
33.13 and for the deep that coucheth *b*,
Jos 2.11 in heaven above, and in earth *b*.
Jdg 7. 8 the host of Midian was *b* him
1Ki 4.12 which is by Zartanah *b* Jezreel,
7.29 and *b* the lions and oxen were
8.23 in heaven above, or on earth *b*,
Job 18.16 His roots shall be dried up *b*, and
Pr 15.24 that he may depart from hell *b*.
Isa 14. 9 Hell from *b* is moved for thee to
51. 6 and look upon the earth *b*:
Jer 31.37 of the earth searched out *b*,
Am 2. 9 from above, and his roots from *b*.
Mk 14.66 And as Peter was *b* in the palace,
Jn 8.23 Ye are from *b*; I am from above:
Ac 2.19 and signs in the earth *b*; blood,

BENEFACTORS

Lk 12.25 authority upon them are called *b*.

BENEFIT

2Ch 32.25 according to the *b* done unto
Jer 18.10 wherewith I said I would *b* them.
2Co 1.15 that ye might have a second *b*;
1Ti 6. 2 and beloved, partakers of the *b*.
Phm 14 that thy *b* should not be as it

BENEFITS

Ps 68.19 who daily loadeth us with *b*,
103. 2 and forget not all his *b*:
116.12 Lord for all his *b* toward me?

BENEVOLENCE

1Co 7. 3 render unto the wife due *b*:

BENJAMIN

Gen 35.18 but his father called him *B*.
24 sons of Rachel; Joseph, and *B*:
42. 4 *B*, Joseph's brother, Jacob sent
36 and ye will take *B* away:
43.14 away your other brother, and *B*.
15 money in their hand, and *B*;
16 Joseph saw *B* with them, he said
29 saw his brother *B*, his mother's
45.12 and the eyes of my brother *B*,
14 and wept; and *B* wept upon
22 But to *B* he gave three hundred
46.19 Jacob's wife; Joseph, and *B*.
21 sons of *B* were Belah, and Becher,
49.27 *B* shall ravin as a wolf: in the
Ex 1. 3 Issachar, Zebulun, and *B*,
Nu 1.11 Of *B*; Abidan the son of Gideoni.
36 Of the children of *B*, by their
37 even of the tribe of *B*, were thirty
2.22 Then the tribe of *B*:
22 the captain of the sons of *B*,
7.60 prince of the children of *B*, offered:
10.24 the children of *B* was Abidan the
13. 9 Of the tribe of *B*, Palti the son of
26.38 The sons of *B* after their families:
41 *B* after their families: and they
34.21 Of the tribe of *B*, Elidad the son
Dt 27.12 and Issachar, and Joseph, and *B*:
34.12 And of *B* he said, The beloved of
Jos 18.11 children of *B* came up according
20 children of *B*, by the coasts
21 *B* according to their families were
28 inheritance of the children of *B*
21. 4 of the tribe of *B*, thirteen cities.
17 of *B*, Gibeon with her suburbs,
Jdg 1.21 *B* did not drive out the Jebusites
21 of *B* in Jerusalem unto this day.
5.14 after thee, *B*, among thy people;
10. 9 against Judah, and against *B*,
19.14 by Gibeah, which belongeth to *B*.
20. 3 children of *B* heard that the
4 belongeth to *B*, I and my
10 come to Gibeah of *B*, according to
12 men through all the tribe of *B*,
13 *B* would not hearken to the voice
14 children of *B* gathered themselves
15 of *B* were numbered at that time
17 Israel, beside *B*, were numbered
18 against the children of *B*?
20 went out to battle against *B*;
21 of *B* came forth out of Gibeah,
23 of *B* my brother? And the Lord
24 near against the children of *B*
25 *B* went forth against them out of
28 against the children of *B* my
30 against the children of *B* on the
31 *B* went out against the people,
32 *B* said, They are smitten down
35 the Lord smote *B* before Israel:
36 So the children of *B* saw that they
39 in the battle, *B* began to smite
41 the men of *B* were amazed:
44 fell of *B* eighteen thousand men;
46 fell that day of *B* were twenty and
48 upon the children of *B*, and smote
21. 1 give his daughter unto *B* to wife.
6 Israel repented them for *B* their
13 speak to the children of *B* that
14 And *B* came again at that time;
15 repented them for *B*, because the
16 women are destroyed out of *B*?
17 that be escaped of *B*, that a tribe
18 be he that giveth a wife to *B*.
20 commanded the children of *B*,
21 Shiloh, and go to the land of *B*.
23 children of *B* did so, and took
1Sa 4.12 ran a man of *B* out of the army,
9. 1 a man of *B*, whose name was Kish,
16 man out of the land of *B*, and thou
21 the families of the tribe of *B*?
10. 2 in the border of *B* at Zelzah;
20 near, the tribe of *B* was taken.
21 tribe of *B* to come near by their
13. 2 with Jonathan in Gibeah of *B*:
15 up from Gilgal unto Gibeah of *B*.
16 with them, abode in Gibeah of *B*:
14.16 watchmen of Saul in Gibeah of *B*
2Sa 2. 9 and over Ephraim, and over *B*,
15 went over by number twelve of *B*,
25 children of *B* gathered themselves
31 of David had smitten of *B*, and
3.19 Abner also spake in the ears of *B*:
19 good to the whole house of *B*.
4. 2 Beerothite, of the children of *B*:
2 Beeroth also was reckoned to *B*:
19.17 thousand men of *B* with him,
21.14 in the country of *B* in Zelah,
23.29 of Gibeah of the children of *B*,
1Ki 4.18 Shimei the son of Elah, in *B*:
12.21 Judah, with the tribe of *B*, an
23 unto all the house of Judah and *B*,
15.22 Asa built with them Geba of *B*,
1Ch 2. 2 Dan, Joseph, and *B*, Naphtali,
6.60 And out of the tribe of *B*; Geba
65 children of *B*, these cities, which
7. 6 The sons of *B*; Bela, and Becher,
10 Jeush, and *B*, and Ehud, and
8. 1 Now *B* begat Bela his firstborn,
40 All these are of the sons of *B*.
9. 3 children of *B*, and of the children
7 And of the sons of *B*; Sallu the
11.31 to the children of *B*, Benaiah
12. 2 even of Saul's brethren of *B*.
16 came of the children of *B* and
29 children of *B*, the kindred of
21. 6 But Levi and *B* counted he not
27.21 of *B*, Jaasiel the son of Abner:
2Ch 11. 1 house of Judah and *B* an hundred
3 all Israel in Judah and *B*, saying,
10 which are in Judah and in *B*
12 having Judah and *B* on his side.
23 all the countries of Judah and *B*,
14. 8 and out of *B*, that bare shields
15. 2 ye me, Asa, and all Judah and *B*;
8 land of Judah and *B*, and out of
9 gathered all Judah and *B*, and
17.17 And of *B*; Eliada a mighty man
25. 5 throughout all Judah and *B*:
31. 1 the altars out of all Judah and *B*,
34. 9 and all Judah and *B*; and they
32 were present in Jerusalem and *B*
Ezr 1. 5 fathers of Judah and *B*, and the
4. 1 adversaries of Judah and *B* heard
10. 9 men of Judah and *B* gathered
32 *B*, Malluch, and Shemariah.
Neh 3.23 After him repaired *B* and Hashub
11. 4 of Judah, and of the children of *B*.
7 All these are the sons of *B*; Sallu
31 The children also of *B* from Geba
36 were divisions in Judah, and in *B*.
12.34 Judah, and *B*, and Shemaiah,
Ps 68.27 There is little *B* with their ruler,
80. 2 Before Ephraim and *B* and
Jer 1. 1 in Anathoth in the land of *B*:
6. 1 O ye children of *B*, gather
17.26 and from the land of *B*,
20. 2 that were in the high gate of *B*,
32. 8 which is in the country of *B*:
44 take witnesses in the land of *B*,
33.13 and in the land of *B*, and in the
37.12 to go into the land of *B*, to
13 was in the gate of *B*, a captain of
38. 7 king then sitting in the gate of *B*;
Eze 48.22 of Judah and the border of *B*,
23 west side, *B* shall have a portion.
24 by the border of *B*, from the east
32 one gate of Joseph, one gate of *B*,
Hos 5. 8 at Beth-aven, after thee, O *B*.
Ob 19 Samaria; and *B* shall possess
Ac 13.21 a man of the tribe of *B*, by the
Ro 11. 1 of Abraham, of the tribe of *B*.
Php 3. 5 of the tribe of *B*, an Hebrew of
Rev 7. 8 Of the tribe of *B* were sealed

BEREA

Ac 17.10 Paul and Silas by night unto *B*:
13 was preached of Paul at *B*, they
20. 4 him into Asia Sopater of *B*;

BEREAVE

Ec 4. 8 I labor and *b* my soul of good?
Jer 15. 7 I will *b* them of children, I will
Eze 5.17 beasts, and they shall *b* thee:
36.12 no more henceforth *b* them of
14 neither *b* thy nations any
Hos 9.12 yet will I *b* them, that there shall

BEREAVED

Gen 42.36 Me have ye *b* of my children:
43.14 I be *b* of my children, I am *b*.
Jer 18.21 wives be *b* of their children,
Eze 36.13 up men, and hast *b* thy nations;
Hos 13. 8 as a bear that is *b* of her whelps,

BEREAVETH

La 1.20 abroad the sword *b*, at home

BERNICE

Ac 25.13 and *B* came unto Cæsarea to
23 come, and *B*, with great pomp,
26.30 *B*, and they that sat with them:

BERYL

Ex 28.20 the fourth row a *b*, and an onyx,
39.13 a *b*, an onyx, and a jasper: they
SS 5.14 are as gold rings set with the *b*:
Eze 1.16 was like unto the color of a *b*:
10. 9 was as the color of a *b* stone.
28.13 topaz, and the diamond, the *b*,
Dan 10. 6 His body also was like the *b*,
Rev 21.20 seventh, chrysolyte; the eighth, *b*;

BESET

Jdg 19.22 Belial, *b* the house round about,
20. 5 and *b* the house round about
Ps 22.12 of Bashan have *b* me round.
139. 5 hast *b* me behind and before,
Hos 7. 2 own doings have *b* them about;
Heb 12. 1 the sin which doth so easily *b* us,

BEST

Gen 43.11 take of the *b* fruits in the land in
47. 6 in the *b* of the land make thy
11 Egypt, in the *b* of the land, in the
Ex 22. 5 of the *b* of his own field, and of
5 the *b* of his own vineyard,
Nu 18.12 All the *b* of the oil,
12 and all the *b* of the wine,
29 of all the *b* thereof, even the
30 when ye have heaved the *b*
32 ye have heaved from it the *b* of it:
36. 6 to whom they think *b*;
Dt 23.16 where it liketh him *b*: thou
1Sa 8.14 your oliveyards, even the *b* of
15. 9 the *b* of the sheep, and of the
15 for the people spared the *b* of the
2Sa 18. 4 What seemeth you *b* I will do.
1Ki 10.18 and overlaid it with the *b* gold.
2Ki 10. 3 Look even out the *b* and meetest
Est 2. 9 her maids unto the *b* place of the
Ps 39. 5 man at his *b* state is altogether
SS 7. 9 roof of thy mouth like the *b* wine
Eze 31.16 the choice and *b* of Lebanon,
Mic 7. 4 the *b* of them is as a brier: the
Lk 15.22 Bring forth the *b* robe, and put
1Co 12.31 but covet earnestly the *b* gifts:

BESTOW

Ex 32.29 he may *b* upon you a blessing
Dt 14.26 And thou shalt *b* that money for
2Ch 24. 7 of the Lord did they *b* upon
Ezr 7.20 thou shalt have occasion to *b*,
20 *b* it out of the king's treasure
Lk 12.17 I have no more room where to *b*
18 there will I *b* all my fruits and my
1Co 12.23 upon these we *b* more abundant
13. 3 And though I *b* all my goods to

BESTOWED

1Ki 10.26 horsemen, whom he *b* in the
2Ki 5.24 their hand, and *b* them in the
12.15 the money to be *b* on workmen:
1Ch 29.25 *b* upon him such royal majesty
2Ch 9.25 whom he *b* in the chariot cities,
Isa 63. 7 to all that the Lord hath *b* on us,
7 he hath *b* on them according
Jn 4.38 whereon ye *b* no labor: other
Ro 16. 6 Mary, who *b* much labor on us.
1Co 15.10 his grace which was *b* upon me
2Co 1.11 that for the gift *b* upon us by the
8. 1 grace of God *b* on the churches
Gal 4.11 lest I have *b* upon you labor in
1Jn 3. 1 of love the Father hath *b* on us.

BETHABARA

Jn 1.28 These things were done in *B*

BETHANY

Mt 21.17 and went out of the city into *B*;
26. 6 Now when Jesus was in *B*, in the
Mk 11. 1 unto Bethphage and *B*, at the
11 he went out unto *B* with the
12 when they were come from *B*, he

The ancient town of Bethlehem, home of David and birthplace of Jesus, as it appeared in the 19th century

14. 3 And being in *B* in the house of
Lk 19.29 come nigh to Bethphage and *B*,
24.50 he led them out as far as to *B*,
Jn 11. 1 named Lazarus, of *B*, the town
18 Now *B* was nigh unto Jerusalem,
12. 1 before the passover came to *B*,

BETHESDA

Jn 5. 2 is called in the Hebrew tongue *B*,

BETHLEHEM

Gen 35.19 the way to Ephrath, which is *B*.
48. 7 way of Ephrath; the same is *B*.
Jos 19.15 Shimron, and Idalah, and *B*:
Jdg 12. 8 after him Ibzan of *B* judged Israel.
10 died Ibzan, and was buried at *B*.
Ru 1.19 two went until they came to *B*.
19 they were come to *B*, that all
22 came to *B* in the beginning of
2. 4 Boaz came from *B*, and said
4.11 in Ephratah, and be famous in *B*:
1Sa 16. 4 and came to *B*. And the elders
17.15 to feed his father's sheep at *B*.
20. 6 that he might run to *B* his city:
28 asked leave of me to go to *B*:
2Sa 2.32 of his father, which was in *B*.
23.14 of the Philistines was then in *B*.
15 the water of the well of *B*, which
16 drew water out of the well of *B*,
24 Elhanan the son of Dodo of *B*,
1Ch 2.51 the father of *B*, Hareph the
54 Salma; *B*, and the Netophathites,
4. 4 of Ephratah, the father of *B*.
11.16 Philistines' garrison was then at *B*.
17 the well of *B*, that is at the gate!
18 drew water out of the well of *B*,
26 Elhanan the son of Dodo of *B*,
2Ch 11. 6 He built even *B*, and Etam, and
Ezr 2.21 children of *B*, an hundred twenty
Neh 7.26 The men of *B* and Netophah,
Jer 41.17 of Chimham, which is by *B*, to go
Mic 5. 2 thou, *B* Ephratah, though thou
Mt 2. 1 Jesus was born in *B* of Judea
5 In *B* of Judea: for thus it is
6 And thou *B*, in the land of Juda,
8 And he sent them to *B*, and said,
16 all the children that were in *B*,
Lk 2. 4 city of David, which is called *B*;
15 Let us now go even unto *B*, and see
Jn 7.42 and out of the town of *B*, where

BETHPHAGE

Mt 21. 1 were come to *B*, unto the mount
Mk 11. 1 Jerusalem, unto *B* and Bethany,
Lk 19.29 was come nigh to *B* and Bethany,

BETHSAIDA

Mt 11.21 woe unto thee, *B*! for if the
Mk 6.45 go to the other side before unto *B*,
8.22 And he cometh to *B*; and they
Lk 9.10 belonging to the city called *B*.
10.13 woe unto thee, *B*! for if the mighty
Jn 1.44 Now Philip was of *B*, the city of
12.21 therefore to Philip, which was of *B*

BETRAY

1Ch 12.17 but if ye be come to *b* me to
Mt 24.10 and shall *b* one another, and
26.16 he sought opportunity to *b* him.
21 one of you shall *b* me.
23 in the dish, the same shall *b* me.
46 he is at hand that doth *b* me.
Mk 13.12 the brother shall *b* the brother
14.10 the chief priests, to *b* him unto
11 he might conveniently *b* him.
18 eateth with me shall *b* me.
Lk 22. 4 how he might *b* him unto them.
6 sought opportunity to *b* him
Jn 6.64 not, and who should *b* him.
71 he it was that should *b* him, being
12. 4 Simon's son, which should *b* him,
13. 2 Iscariot, Simon's son, to *b* him;
11 For he knew who should *b* him;
21 you, that one of you shall *b* me.

BETRAYED

Mt 10. 4 Judas Iscariot, who also *b* him.
17.22 The Son of man shall be *b* into
20.18 The Son of man shall be *b* unto
26. 2 Son of man is *b* to be crucified.
24 by whom the Son of man is *b*!
25 Then Judas, which *b* him,
45 Son of man is *b* into the hands of
48 Now he that *b* him gave them a
27. 3 Then Judas, which had *b* him,
4 I have sinned in that I have *b*
Mk 3.19 Judas Iscariot, which also *b* him:
14.21 by whom the Son of man is *b*!
41 the Son of man is *b* into the hands
44 And he that *b* him had given them
Lk 21.16 And ye shall be *b* both by
22.22 unto that man by whom he is *b*!
Jn 18. 2 And Judas also, which *b* him,
5 Judas also, which *b* him, stood
1Co 11.23 night in which he was *b* took

BETRAYERS

Ac 7.52 ye have been now the *b* and

BETRAYEST

Lk 22.48 *b* thou the Son of man with a

BETRAYETH

Mk 14.42 lo, he that *b* me is at hand.
Lk 22.21 the hand of him that *b* me is with
Jn 21.20 Lord, which is he that *b* thee?

BETROTH

Dt 28.30 Thou shalt *b* a wife, and another
Hos 2.19 And I will *b* thee unto me for ever;
19 yea, I will *b* thee unto me in
20 I will even *b* thee unto me in

BETROTHED

Ex 21. 8 who hath *b* her to himself,
9 And if he have *b* her unto his
22.16 maid that is not *b*, and lie with
Lev 19.20 that is a bondmaid, *b* to an
Dt 20. 7 that hath *b* a wife, and hath not
22.23 that is a virgin be *b* unto an
25 But if a man find a *b* damsel in the
27 the *b* damsel cried, and there was
28 which is not *b*, and lay hold on her,

BETTER

Gen 29.19 *b* that I give her to thee, than
Ex 14.12 been *b* for us to serve the
Nu 14. 3 not *b* for us to return into Egypt?
Jdg 8. 2 the grapes of Ephraim *b* than the
9. 2 Whether is *b* for you, either that
11.25 now art thou any thing *b* than
18.19 is it *b* for thee to be a priest unto
Ru 4.15 which is *b* to thee than seven sons,
1Sa 1. 8 am not I *b* to thee than ten sons?
15.22 Behold, to obey is *b* than sacrifice,
28 neighbor of thine, that is *b* than
27. 1 nothing *b* for me than that I
2Sa 17.14 *b* than the counsel of Ahithophel.
18. 3 *b* that thou succor us out of the
1Ki 1.47 God make the name of Solomon *b*
2.32 more righteous and *b* than he,
19. 4 for I am not *b* than my fathers.
21. 2 I will give thee for it a *b* vineyard
2Ki 5.12 *b* than all the waters of Israel?
2Ch 21.13 which were *b* than thyself:
Est 1.19 estate unto another that is *b* than
Ps 37.16 *b* than the riches of many wicked
63. 3 loving kindness is *b* than life, my
69.31 This also shall please the Lord *b*
84.10 a day in thy courts is *b* than a
118. 8, 9 *b* to trust in the Lord than to
119.72 the law of thy mouth is *b* unto me
Pr 3.14 *b* than the merchandise of silver,
8.11 For wisdom is *b* than rubies;
19 My fruit is *b* than gold, yea,
12. 9 is *b* than he that honoreth
15.16 *B* is little with the fear of the
17 *B* is a dinner of herbs where love
16. 8 *B* is a little with righteousness
16 how much *b* is it to get wisdom
19 *B* it is to be of an humble spirit
32 slow to anger is *b* than the mighty
17. 1 *B* is a dry morsel, and quietness
19. 1 *B* is the poor that walketh in his
22 and a poor man is *b* than a liar.
21. 9 *b* to dwell in a corner of the
19 *b* to dwell in the wilderness,
25. 7 *b* it is that it be said unto thee,
24 It is *b* to dwell in the corner
27. 5 Open rebuke is *b* than secret love.
10 *b* is a neighbor that is near than
28. 6 *B* is the poor that walketh in his
Ec 2.24 nothing *b* for a man, than that he
3.22 I perceive that there is nothing *b*,
4. 3 Yea, *b* is he than both they, which
6 *B* is an handful with quietness,
9 Two are *b* than one; because they
13 *B* is a poor and a wise child than
5. 5 *B* is it that thou shouldest not
6. 3 an untimely birth is *b* than he.
9 *B* is the sight of the eyes than the
11 what is man the *b*?
7. 1 A good name is *b* than
2 *b* to go to the house of mourning,
3 Sorrow is *b* than laughter: for by
3 countenance the heart is made *b*.
5 *b* to hear the rebuke of the wise,
8 *B* is the end of a thing than the
8 spirit is *b* than the proud in spirit.
10 cause that the former days were *b*
8.15 hath no *b* thing under the sun,
9. 4 a living dog is *b* than a dead lion.
16 said I, Wisdom is *b* than strength:
18 Wisdom is *b* than weapons of war:
10.11 and a babbler is no *b*.
SS 1. 2 for thy love is *b* than wine.
4.10 how much *b* is thy love than wine!
Isa 56. 5 *b* than of sons and of daughters:
La 4. 9 *b* than they that be slain with
Eze 36.11 will do *b* unto you than at your
Dan 1.20 ten times *b* than all the magicians
Hos 2. 7 then it was *b* with me than now.
Am 6. 2 be they *b* than these kingdoms?
Jon 4. 3, 8 it is *b* for me to die than to live.
Na 3. 8 Art thou *b* than populous No,
Mt 6.26 Are ye not much *b* than they?
12.12 then is a man *b* than a sheep?
18. 6 it were *b* for him that a millstone
8, 9 it is *b* for thee to enter into life
Mk 9.42 is *b* for him that a millstone
43 it is *b* for thee to enter into life
45 it is *b* for thee to enter halt
47 it is *b* for thee to enter into the
Lk 5.39 for he saith, The old is *b*.
12.24 more are ye *b* than the fowls?
17. 2 were *b* for him that a millstone
Ro 3. 9 What then? are we *b* than they?
1Co 7. 9 it is *b* to marry than to burn.
38 her not in marriage doeth *b*.
8. 8 neither, if we eat, are we the *b*;
9.15 it were *b* for me to die,
11.17 not for the *b*, but for the worse.
Php 1.23 to be with Christ; which is far *b*:
2. 3 esteem other *b* than themselves.
Heb 1. 4 made so much *b* than the angels,
6. 9 we are persuaded *b* things of you,
7. 7 the less is blessed of the *b*.
19 but the bringing in of a *b* hope
22 made a surety of a *b* testament.
8. 6 the mediator of a *b* covenant,
6 was established upon *b* promises.
9.23 with *b* sacrifices than these.
10.34 in heaven a *b* and an enduring
11.16 But now they desire a *b* country,
35 they might obtain a *b* resurrection:
40 provided some *b* thing for us,
12.24 *b* things than that of Abel.
1Pe 3.17 it is *b*, if the will of God be so,
2Pe 2.21 For it had been *b* for them not to

BETTERED

Mk 5.26 nothing *b*, but rather grew worse,

BEULAH

Isa 62. 4 and thy land *B*: for the Lord

BEWAIL

Lev 10. 6 the whole house of Israel, *b*
Dt 21.13 and *b* her father and her mother
Jdg 11.37 and *b* my virginity, I and my
Isa 16. 9 I will *b* with the weeping
2Co 12.21 and that I shall *b* many which
Rev 18. 9 shall *b* her, and lament for her,

BEWAILED

Jdg 11.38 companions, and *b* her virginity
Lk 8.52 And all wept, and *b* her: but he
23.27 which also *b* and lamented

BEWARE

Gen 24. 6 *B* thou that thou bring not my
Ex 23.21 *B* of him, and obey his voice,
Dt 6.12 Then *b* lest thou forget the Lord,
8.11 *B* that thou forget not the Lord
15. 9 *B* that there be not a thought in
Jdg 13. 4 Now therefore *b*, I pray thee,
13 I said unto the woman let her *b*.
2Sa 18.12 *B* that none touch the young man
2Ki 6. 9 *B* that thou pass not such a place;
Job 36.18 Because there is wrath, *b* lest
Pr 19.25 a scorner, and the simple will *b*:
Isa 36.18 *B* lest Hezekiah persuade you,
Mt 7.15 *B* of false prophets, which come
10.17 But *b* of men: for they will
16. 6 Take heed and *b* of the leaven
11 that ye should *b* of the leaven
12 not *b* of the leaven of bread, but
Mk 8.15 Take heed, *b* of the leaven of the
12.38 *B* of the scribes, which love to go
Lk 12. 1 *B* ye of the leaven of the
15 heed, and *b* of covetousness:
20.46 *B* of the scribes, which desire
Ac 13.40 *B* therefore, lest that come
Php 3. 2 *B* of dogs, *b* of evil workers,
2 *b* of the concision.
Col 2. 8 *B* lest any man spoil you
2Pe 3.17 ye know these things before, *b*

BEWITCHED

Ac 8. 9 *b* the people of Samaria, giving
11 he had *b* them with sorceries.
Gal 3. 1 foolish Galatians, who hath *b*

BEWRAYETH

Pr 27.16 of his right hand, which *b* itself.
29.24 heareth cursing, and *b* it not.
Mt 26.73 for thy speech *b* thee.

BID

Nu 15.38 and *b* them that they make them
Jos 6.10 until the day I *b* you shout;
1Sa 9.27 *B* the servant pass on before us,
2Sa 2.26 long shall it be then, ere thou *b*
2Ki 4.24 riding for me, except I *b* thee.
5.13 if the prophet had *b* thee do
10. 5 will do all that thou shalt *b* us;
Jon 3. 2 the preaching that I *b* thee.
Zep 1. 7 prepared a sacrifice, he hath *b*
Mt 14.28 *b* me come unto thee on the
22. 9 ye shall find, *b* to the marriage.
23. 3 therefore whatsoever they *b* you
Lk 9.61 let me first go *b* them farewell,
10.40 *b* her therefore that she help me.
14.12 lest they also *b* thee again, and
1Co 10.27 any of them that believe not *b*
2Jn 10 house, neither *b* him God speed:

BIDDEN

1Sa 9.13 afterwards they eat that be *b*.
22 among them that were *b*, which
2Sa 16.11 for the Lord hath *b* him.
Mt 1.24 angel of the Lord had *b* him,
22. 3 to call them that were *b*
4 Tell them which are *b*, Behold, I
8 which were *b* were not worthy.
Lk 7.39 the Pharisee which had *b* him
14. 7 a parable to those which were *b*,
8 When thou art *b* of any man
8 man than thou be *b* of him;
10 when thou art *b*, go and sit down
17 to say to them that were *b*,
24 none of those men which were *b*

BIDDETH

2Jn 11 For he that *b* him God speed

BIDDING

1Sa 22.14 and goeth at thy *b*, and is

BILL

Dt 24. 1 write her a *b* of divorcement,
3 and write her a *b* of divorcement,

Isa 50. 1 Where is the *b* of your mother's
Jer 3. 8 and given her a *b* of divorce;
Mk 10. 4 to write a *b* of divorcement,
Lk 16. 6, 7 he said unto him, Take thy *b*,

BILLOWS
Ps 42. 7 all thy waves and thy *b* are
Jon 2. 3 all thy *b* and thy waves passed

BIND
Ex 28.28 they shall *b* the breastplate
39.21 And they did *b* the breastplate
Nu 30. 2 swear an oath to *b* his soul
3 Lord, and *b* herself by a bond,
Dt 6. 8 thou shalt *b* them for a sign
11.18 and *b* them for a sign upon
14.25 *b* up the money in thine hand,
Jos 2.18 thou shalt *b* this line of scarlet
Jdg 15.10 To *b* Samson are we come up,
12 We are come down to *b* thee,
13 but we will *b* thee fast, and
16. 5 that we may *b* him to afflict him:
7 they *b* me with seven green withs
11 If they *b* me fast with new ropes
Job 31.36 and *b* it as a crown to me.
38.31 Canst thou *b* the sweet
39.10 Canst thou *b* the unicorn with
40.13 and *b* their faces in secret.
41. 5 or wilt thou *b* him for thy
Ps 105.22 To *b* his princes at his pleasure;
118.27 *b* the sacrifice with cords, even
149. 8 To *b* their kings with chains,
Pr 3. 3 *b* them about thy neck; write
6.21 *B* them continually upon thine
7. 3 *B* them upon thy fingers, write
Isa 8.16 *B* up the testimony, seal the law
49.18 and *b* them on thee, as a bride
61. 1 to *b* up the brokenhearted,
Jer 51.63 thou shalt *b* a stone to it, and
Eze 3.25 and shall *b* thee with them, and
5. 3 and *b* them in thy skirts.
24.17 *b* the tire of thine head upon
30.21 to put a roller to *b* it, to make
34.16 *b* up that which was broken,
Dan 3.20 were in his army to *b* Shadrach,
Hos 6. 1 smitten, and he will *b* us up.
10.10 when they shall *b* themselves
Mic 1.13 *b* the chariot to the swift beast:
Mt 12.29 except he first *b* the strong man?
13.30 *b* them in bundles to burn them:
16.19 whatsoever thou shalt *b* on earth
18.18 shall *b* on earth shall be bound in
22.13 *B* him hand and foot, and take
23. 4 For they *b* heavy burdens and
Mk 3.27 he will first *b* the strong man;
5. 3 no man could *b* him, no, not with
Ac 9.14 to *b* all that call on thy name.
12. 8 thyself, and *b* on thy sandals.
21.11 the Jews at Jerusalem *b* the man

BINDETH
Job 5.18 for he maketh sore, and *b* up:
26. 8 He *b* up the waters in his thick
28.11 *b* the floods from overflowing;
30.18 it *b* me about as the collar of my
36.13 they cry not when he *b* them.
Ps 129. 7 nor he that *b* sheaves his bosom.
147. 3 in heart, and *b* up their wounds.
Pr 26. 8 As he that *b* a stone in a sling,
Isa 30.26 that the Lord *b* up the breach

BINDING
Gen 37. 7 For, behold, we were *b* sheaves
49.11 *B* his foal unto the vine, and his
Ex 28.32 it shall have a *b* of woven work
Nu 30.13 every *b* oath to afflict the soul,
Ac 22. 4 *b* and delivering into prisons

BIRD
Gen 7.14 his kind, every *b* of every sort.
Lev 14. 6 As for the living *b*, he shall take
6 the living *b* in the blood of the *b*
7 and shall let the living *b* loose
51 and the scarlet, and the living *b*,
51 them in the blood of the slain *b*,
52 the house with the blood of the *b*,
52 living *b*, and with the cedar wood,
53 But he shall let go the living *b*
Job 41. 5 thou play with him as with a *b*?
Ps 11. 1 Flee as a *b* to your mountain?
124. 7 *b* out of the snare of the fowlers:
Pr 1.17 spread in the sight of any *b*.
6. 5 a *b* from the hand of the fowler.
7.23 as a *b* hasteth to the snare, and
26. 2 As the *b* by wandering, as the
27. 8 As a *b* that wandereth from
Ec 10.20 *b* of the air shall carry the voice,
12. 4 the voice of the *b*, and all the
Isa 16. 2 wandering *b* cast out of the nest,
46.11 a ravenous *b* from the east,
Jer 12. 9 heritage is unto me as a speckled *b*,
La 3.52 enemies chased me sore, like a *b*,
Hos 9.11 their glory shall fly away like a *b*,
11.11 shall tremble as a *b* out of Egypt,
Am 3. 5 Can a *b* fall in a snare upon the
Rev 18. 2 of every unclean and hateful *b*.

BIRD'S
Dt 22. 6 *b* nest chance to be before thee

BIRDS
Gen 15.10 another: but the *b* divided he not.
40.17 and the *b* did eat them out of the
19 *b* shall eat thy flesh from off thee.
Lev 14. 4 cleansed two *b* alive and clean,
5 that one of the *b* be killed
49 take to cleanse the house two *b*,
50 and he shall kill the one of the *b*
Dt 14.11 Of all clean *b* ye shall eat.
2Sa 21.10 neither the *b* of the air to rest
Ps 104.17 Where the *b* make their nests:
Ec 9.12 and as the *b* that are caught in
SS 2.12 time of the singing of *b* is come,
Isa 31. 5 As *b* flying, so will the Lord of
Jer 4.25 the *b* of the heavens were fled.
5.27 As a cage is full of *b*, so are their
12. 4 beasts are consumed, and the *b*;
9 as a speckled bird, the *b* round
Eze 39. 4 give thee unto the ravenous *b*
Mt 8.20 and the *b* of the air have nests;
13.32 so that the *b* of the air come
Lk 9.58 holes, and *b* of the air have nests;
Ro 1.23 like to corruptible man, and to *b*,
1Co 15.39 of fishes, and another of *b*.
Jas 3. 7 every kind of beasts, and of *b*,

BIRDS'
Dan 4.33 and his nails like *b* claws.

BIRTH
Ex 28.10 other stone, according to their *b*.
2Ki 19. 3 for the children are come to the *b*,
Job 3.16 untimely *b* I had not been;
Ps 58. 8 like the untimely *b* of a woman,
Ec 6. 3 an untimely *b* is better than he.
7. 1 of death than the day of one's *b*.
Isa 37. 3 the children are come to the *b*,
66. 9 I bring to the *b*, and not cause
Eze 16. 3 Thy *b* and thy nativity is of the
Hos 9.11 from the *b*, and from the womb,
Mt 1.18 the *b* of Jesus Christ was on this
Lk 1.14 and many shall rejoice at his *b*.
Jn 9. 1 man which was blind from his *b*.
Gal 4.19 I travail in *b* again until Christ
Rev 12. 2 cried, travailing in *b*, and pained
(See box on page 118)

BIRTHDAY
Gen 40.20 which was Pharaoh's b,
Mt 14. 6 when Herod's *b* was kept, the
Mk 6.21 Herod on his *b* made a supper

BIRTHRIGHT
Gen 25.31 said, Sell me this day thy *b*.
32 what profit shall this *b* do to me?
33 and he sold his *b* unto Jacob.
34 way; thus Esau despised his *b*.
27.36 he took away my *b*; and, behold,
43.33 the firstborn according to his *b*,
1Ch 5. 1 his *b* was given unto the sons
1 is not to be reckoned after the *b*.
2 ruler; but the *b* was Joseph's:)
Heb 12.16 for one morsel of meat sold his *b*.

BISHOP
1Ti 3. 1 If a man desire the office of a *b*,
2 A *b* then must be blameless, the
Tit 1. 7 For a *b* must be blameless, as the
1Pe 2.25 Shepherd and *B* of your souls.

BISHOPRICK
Ac 1.20 therein: and his *b* let another

BISHOPS
Php 1. 1 Philippi, with the *b* and deacons:

BIT
Nu 21. 6 people, and they *b* the people;
Ps 32. 9 be held in with *b* and bridle,
Am 5.19 on the wall, and a serpent *b* him.

BITE
Ec 10. 8 an hedge, a serpent shall *b* him.
11 will *b* without enchantment;
Jer 8.17 be charmed, and they shall *b* you,
Am 9. 3 the serpent, and he shall *b* them:
Mic 3. 5 that *b* with their teeth, and cry,
Hab 2. 7 up suddenly that shall *b* thee,
Gal 5.15 if ye *b* and devour one another,

BITETH
Gen 49.17 the path, that *b* the horse heels,
Pr 23.32 it *b* like a serpent, and stingeth

BITHYNIA
Ac 16. 7 Mysia, they assayed to go into *B*:
1Pe 1. 1 Galatia, Cappadocia, Asia, and *B*,

BITS
Jas 3. 3 we put *b* in the horses' mouths,

BITTER
Gen 27.34 with a great and exceeding *b* cry,
Ex 1.14 made their lives *b* with hard
12. 8 with *b* herbs they shall eat it.
15.23 waters of Marah, for they were *b*:
Nu 5.18 *b* water that causeth the curse:
19 be thou free from this *b* water
23 blot them out with the *b* water:
24 drink the *b* water that causeth
24 enter into her, and become *b*.
27 into her, and become *b*, and her
9.11 unleavened bread and *b* herbs.
Dt 32.24 heat, and with *b* destruction:
32 of gall, their clusters are *b*:
2Ki 14.26 of Israel, that it was very *b*
Est 4. 1 cried with a loud and a *b* cry;
Job 3.20 and life unto the *b* in soul;
13.26 thou writest *b* things against me,
23. 2 Even to day is my complaint *b*:
Ps 64. 3 to shoot their arrows, even *b*
Pr 5. 4 her end is *b* as wormwood, sharp
27. 7 to the hungry soul every *b* thing
Ec 7.26 more *b* than death the woman,
Isa 5.20 put *b* for sweet, and sweet for *b*!
24. 9 strong drink shall be *b* to them
Jer 2.19 it is an evil thing and *b*, that thou
4.18 is thy wickedness, because it is *b*,
6.26 an only son, most *b* lamentation:
31.15 in Ramah, lamentation, and *b*
Eze 27.31 bitterness of heart and *b* wailing.
Am 8.10 and the end therefore as a *b* day.
Hab 1. 6 Chaldeans, that *b* and hasty

BIBLICAL THEMES

BIRTH

Unto the woman he said, I will greatly multiply thy sorrow and thy conception; in sorrow thou shalt bring forth children. Gen 3.16

And Adam knew Eve his wife; and she conceived, and bare Cain, and said, I have gotten a man from the Lord. And she again bare his brother Abel. Gen 4.1-2

And the Lord said unto Abraham, Wherefore did Sarah laugh, saying, Shall I of a surety bear a child, which am old? Is any thing too hard for the Lord? Gen 18.13-14

And God remembered Rachel, and God hearkened to her, and opened her womb. And she conceived, and bare a son; and said, God hath taken away my reproach. Gen 30.22-23

Israel is my son, even my firstborn. Ex 4.22

Hannah . . . bare a son, and called his name Samuel, saying, Because I have asked him of the Lord. 1Sa 1.20

Job . . . cursed his day . . . and said, Let the day perish wherein I was born . . . because it shut not up the doors of my mother's womb, nor hid sorrow from mine eyes. Job 3.1-3, 10

Yet man is born unto trouble, as the sparks fly upward. Job 5.7

How then can man be justified with God? or how can he be clean that is born of a woman? Job 25.4

Hath the rain a father? or who hath begotten the drops of dew? Job 38.28

Behold, I was shapen in iniquity; and in sin did my mother conceive me. Ps 51.5

By thee have I been holden up from the womb: thou art he that took me out of my mother's bowels: my praise shall be continually of thee. Ps 71.6

A time to be born, and a time to die. Ec 3.2

Behold, a virgin shall be with child, and shall bring forth a son, and they shall call his name Emmanuel, which being interpreted is, God with us. Mt 1.23

And she brought forth her firstborn son, and wrapped him in swaddling clothes, and laid him in a manger. Lk 2.7

That which is born of the flesh is flesh; and that which is born of the Spirit is spirit. Marvel not that I said unto thee, Ye must be born again. Jn 3.6-7

A woman when she is in travail hath sorrow, because her hour is come: but as soon as she is delivered of the child, she remembereth no more the anguish, for joy that a man is born into the world. Jn 16.21

For it is written, Rejoice, thou barren that bearest not; break forth and cry, thou that travailest not: for the desolate hath many more children than she which hath an husband. Gal 4.27

Being born again, not of corruptible seed, but of incorruptible, by the word of God, which liveth and abideth for ever. 1Pe 1.23

Col 3.19 wives, and be not *b* against them.
Jas 3.11 same place sweet water and *b*?
14 if ye have *b* envying and strife
Rev 8.11 waters, because they were made *b*.
10. 9 it shall make thy belly *b*, but it
10 I had eaten it, my belly was *b*.

BITTERLY

Jdg 5.23 curse ye *b* the inhabitants thereof;
Ru 1.20 Almighty hath dealt very *b* with
Isa 22. 4 I will weep *b*, labor not to comfort
33. 7 of peace shall weep *b*.
Eze 27.30 and shall cry *b*, and shall cast up
Hos 12.14 provoked him to anger most *b*:
Zep 1.14 the mighty man shall cry there *b*.
Mt 26.75 And he went out, and wept *b*.
Lk 22.62 Peter went out, and wept *b*.

BITTERNESS

1Sa 1.10 she was in *b* of soul, and prayed
15.32 said, Surely the *b* of death is past.
2Sa 2.26 that it will be *b* in the latter end?
Job 7.11 I will complain in the *b* of my
9.18 breath, but filleth me with *b*.
10. 1 I will speak in the *b* of my soul,
21.25 another dieth in the *b* of his soul,
Pr 14.10 The heart knoweth his own *b*;
17.25 father, and *b* to her that bare
Isa 38.15 my years in the *b* of my soul.
17 Behold, for peace I had great *b*:
La 1. 4 are afflicted, and she is in *b*.
3.15 He hath filled me with *b*,
Eze 3.14 took me away, and I went in *b*,
21. 6 and with *b* sigh before their eyes.
27.31 they shall weep for thee with *b*
Zec 12.10 and shall be in *b* for him,
10 as one that is in *b*
Ac 8.23 thou art in the gall of *b*, and in
Ro 3.14 mouth is full of cursing and *b*:
Eph 4.31 Let all *b*, and wrath, and anger,
Heb 12.15 lest any root of *b* springing up

BLACK

Lev 13.31 that there is no *b* hair in it;
37 there is *b* hair grown up therein;
1Ki 18.45 heaven was *b* with clouds and
Est 1. 6 of red, and blue, and white, and *b*,
Job 30.30 My skin is *b* upon me, and my
Pr 7. 9 in the evening, in the *b* and
SS 1. 5 I am *b*, but comely, O ye
6 not upon me, because I am *b*,
5.11 his locks are bushy, and *b* as a
Jer 4.28 and the heavens above be *b*:
8.21 I am *b*; astonishment hath taken
14. 2 they are *b* unto the ground; and
La 5.10 Our skin was *b* like an oven
Zec 6. 2 in the second chariot *b* horses;
6 The *b* horses which are therein
Mt 5.36 not make one hair white or *b*.
Rev 6. 5 And I beheld, and lo a *b* horse;
12 sun became *b* as sackcloth of

BLACKER

La 4. 8 Their visage is *b* than a coal;

BLACKNESS

Job 3. 5 let the *b* of the day terrify it.
Isa 50. 3 I clothe the heavens with *b*,
Joel 2. 6 pained: all faces shall gather *b*.
Na 2.10 the faces of them all gather *b*.
Heb 12.18 nor unto *b*, and darkness, and
Jude 13 to whom is reserved the *b* of

BLADE

Jdg 3.22 the haft also went in after the *b*;
22 and the fat closed upon the *b*,
Job 31.22 arm fall from my shoulder *b*,
Mt 13.26 But when the *b* was sprung up,
Mk 4.28 first the *b*, then the ear, after that

BLAME

Gen 43. 9 then let me bear the *b* for ever:
44.32 then I shall bear the *b* to my
2Co 8.20 that no man should *b* us in this
Eph 1. 4 be holy and without *b*

BLAMED

2Co 6. 3 that the ministry be not *b*:
Gal 2.11 the face, because he was to be *b*.

BLAMELESS

Gen 44.10 my servant; and ye shall be *b*.
Jos 2.17 We will be *b* of this thine oath
Jdg 15. 3 Now shall I be more *b* than the
Mt 12. 5 profane the sabbath, and are *b*?
Lk 1. 6 and ordinances of the Lord *b*.
1Co 1. 8 that ye may be *b* in the day of
Php 2.15 that ye may be *b* and harmless,
3. 6 which is in the law, *b*.
1Th 5.23 be preserved *b* unto the coming
1Ti 3. 2 a bishop then must be *b*, the
10 office of a deacon, being found *b*.
5. 7 in charge, that they may be *b*.
Tit 1. 6 if any be *b*, the husband of one
7 For a bishop must be *b*, as the
2Pe 3.14 in peace, without spot, and *b*.

BLASPHEME

2Sa 12.14 the enemies of the Lord to *b*,
1Ki 21.10 Thou didst *b* God and the king.
13 Naboth did *b* God and the king.
Ps 74.10 shall the enemy *b* thy name for
Mk 3.28 wherewith soever they shall *b*:
29 he that shall *b* against the Holy
Ac 26.11 and compelled them to *b*;
1Ti 1.20 that they may learn not to *b*.
Jas 2. 7 Do not they *b* that worthy name
Rev 13. 6 to *b* his name, and his tabernacle,

BLASPHEMED

Lev 24.11 Israelitish woman's son *b* the
2Ki 19. 6 of the king of Assyria have *b* me.
22 has thou reproached and *b*?
Ps 74.18 the foolish people have *b* thy
Isa 37. 6 of the king of Assyria have *b* me.

23 hast thou reproached and *b*?
52. 5 name continually every day is *b*.
65. 7 upon the mountains, and *b* me
Eze 20.27 in this your fathers have *b* me,
Ac 18. 6 they opposed themselves, and *b*,
Ro 2.24 the name of God is *b* among the
1Ti 6. 1 God and his doctrine be not *b*.
Tit 2. 5 that the word of God be not *b*.
Rev 16. 9 heat, and *b* the name of God,
11 *b* the God of heaven because of
21 men *b* God because of the plague

BLASPHEMER
1Ti 1.13 Who was before a *b*, and a

BLASPHEMERS
Ac 19.37 churches, nor yet *b* of your
2Ti 3. 2 covetous, boasters, proud, *b*,

BLASPHEMEST
Jn 10.36 Thou *b*; because I said, I am the

BLASPHEMETH
Lev 24.16 he that *b* the name of the Lord,
16 when he *b* the name of the Lord,
Ps 44.16 of him that reproacheth and *b*;
Mt 9. 3 within themselves, This man *b*.
Lk 12.10 unto him that *b* against the Holy

BLASPHEMIES
Eze 35.12 I have heard all thy *b* which thou
Mt 15.19 thefts, false witness, *b*:
Mk 2. 7 Why doth this man thus speak *b*?
3.28 *b* wherewith soever they shall
Lk 5.21 Who is this which speaketh *b*?
Rev 13. 5 mouth speaking great things and *b*;

BLASPHEMING
Ac 13.45 by Paul, contradicting and *b*.

BLASPHEMOUS
Ac 6.11 we have heard him speak *b* words
13 ceaseth not to speak *b* words

BLASPHEMOUSLY
Lk 22.65 things *b* spake they against him.

BLASPHEMY
2Ki 19. 3 of trouble, and of rebuke, and *b*:
Isa 37. 3 trouble, and of rebuke, and of *b*:
Mt 12.31 All manner of sin and *b* shall be
31 the *b* against the Holy Ghost
26.65 clothes, saying, He hath spoken *b*;
65 behold, now ye have heard his *b*.
Mk 7.22 an evil eye, *b*, pride, foolishness:
14.64 Ye have heard the *b*: what think
Jn 10.33 for *b*; and because that thou,
Col 3. 8 anger, wrath, malice, *b*, filthy
Rev 2. 9 I know the *b* of them which say
13. 1 and upon his heads the name of *b*.
6 And he opened his mouth in *b*
17. 3 full of names of *b*, having seven

BLAST
Ex 15. 8 And with the *b* of thy nostrils
Jos 6. 5 when they make a long *b* with the
2Sa 22.16 at the *b* of the breath of his
2Ki 19. 7 I will send a *b* upon him, and he
Job 4. 9 By the *b* of God they perish, and
Ps 18.15 at the *b* of the breath of thy
Isa 25. 4 when the *b* of the terrible ones
37. 7 I will send a *b* upon him, and he

BLAZE
Mk 1.45 and to *b* abroad the matter,

BLEMISHES
Lev 22.25 corruption in them, and *b* be in
2Pe 2.13 Spots they are and *b*, sporting

BLESS
Gen 12. 2 and I will *b* thee, and make thy
3 And I will *b* them that *b* thee,
17.16 And I will *b* her, and give thee a
16 son also of her: yea, I will *b* her,
22.17 in blessing I will *b* thee, and in
26. 3 be with thee, and will *b* thee: for
24 for I am with thee, and will *b* thee,
27. 4 that my soul may *b* thee before I
7 and *b* thee before the Lord before
10 he may eat, and that he may *b* thee
19 venison, that thy soul may *b* me.
25 venison, that my soul may *b* thee.
31 venison, that thy soul may *b* me.
34 *B* me, even me also, O my father.
38 *b* me, even me also, O my father.
28. 3 God Almighty *b* thee, and make
32.26 let thee go, except thou *b* me.
48. 9 thee, unto me, and I will *b* them.
16 me from all evil, *b* the lads;
20 In thee shall Israel *b*, saying, God
49.25 the Almighty, who shall *b* thee
Ex 12.32 said, and be gone; and *b* me also.
20.24 come unto thee, and I will *b* thee.
23.25 and he shall *b* thy bread, and thy
Nu 6.23 on this wise ye shall *b* the children
24 The Lord *b* thee, and keep thee:
27 children of Israel; and I will *b*
23.20 have received commandment to *b*:
25 Neither curse them at all, nor *b*
24. 1 it pleased the Lord to *b* Israel, he
Dt 1.11 and *b* you, as he hath promised
7.13 will love thee, and *b* thee, and
13 he will also *b* the fruit of thy
8.10 then thou shalt *b* the Lord thy
10. 8 unto him, and to *b* in his name,
14.29 the Lord thy God may *b* thee in all
15. 4 the Lord shall greatly *b* thee in
10 thy God shall *b* thee in all thy
18 thy God shall *b* thee in all that
16.15 the Lord thy God shall *b* thee in
21. 5 unto him, and to *b* in the name of
23.20 the Lord thy God may *b* thee in all
24.13 sleep in his own raiment, and *b*
19 thy God may *b* thee in all the work
26.15 from heaven, and *b* thy people
27.12 upon mount Gerizim to *b* the
28. 8 and he shall *b* thee in the land
12 and to *b* all the work of thine
29.19 that he *b* himself in his heart,
30.16 and the Lord thy God shall *b*
33.11 *B*, Lord, his substance, and accept
Jos 8.33 that they should *b* the people of
Jdg 5. 9 among the people. *B* ye the Lord.
Ru 2. 4 answered him, the Lord *b* thee.
1Sa 9.13 because he doth *b* the sacrifice;
2Sa 6.20 Then David returned to *b* his
7.29 let it please thee to *b* the house of
8.10 to salute him, and to *b* him,
21. 3 that ye may *b* the inheritance of
1Ki 1.47 servants came to *b* our lord king
1Ch 4.10 Oh that thou wouldest *b* me
16.43 house: and David returned to *b*
17.27 to *b* the house of thy servant, that
23.13 minister unto him, and to *b* in his
29.20 the congregation, Now *b* the Lord
Neh 9. 5 *b* the Lord your God for ever and
Ps 5.12 For thou, Lord, wilt *b* the
16. 7 I will *b* the Lord, who hath given
26.12 in the congregations will I *b* the
28. 9 Save thy people, and *b* thine
29.11 the Lord will *b* his people with
34. 1 I will *b* the Lord at all times: his
62. 4 they *b* with their mouth, but they
63. 4 Thus will I *b* thee while I live:
66. 8 O *b* our God, ye people, and make
67. 1 God be merciful unto us and *b* us;
6 God, even our own God, shall *b* us.
7 God shall *b* us; and all the ends of
68.26 *B* ye God in the congregations,
96. 2 Sing unto the Lord, *b* his name;
100. 4 be thankful unto him, and *b* his
103. 1 *B* the Lord, O my soul, and all
1 that is within me, *b* his holy
2 *B* the Lord, O my soul, and
20 *B* the Lord, ye his angels, that
21 *B* ye the Lord, all ye his hosts; ye
22 *B* the Lord, all his works in all
22 places of his dominion; *b* the Lord,
104. 1 *B* the Lord, O my soul, O Lord,
35 *B* thou the Lord, O my soul.
109.28 Let them curse, but *b* thou: when
115.12 he will *b* us; he will *b* the house
12 of Israel; he will *b* the house of
13 He will *b* them that fear the Lord,
18 But we will *b* the Lord from this
128. 5 The Lord shall *b* thee out of Zion:
129. 8 upon you: we *b* you in the name
132.15 I will abundantly *b* her provision:
134. 1 *b* ye the Lord, all ye servants of
2 in the sanctuary, and *b* the Lord.
3 heaven and earth *b* thee out of
135.19 *B* the Lord, O house of Israel:
19 *b* the Lord, O house of Aaron:
20 *B* the Lord, O house of Levi:
20 ye that fear the Lord, *b* the Lord.
145. 1 and I will *b* thy name for ever
2 Every day will I *b* thee; and I will
10 Lord; and thy saints shall *b* thee.
21 and let all flesh *b* his holy name
Pr 30.11 and doth not *b* their mother.
Isa 19.25 Whom the Lord of hosts shall *b*.
65.16 shall *b* himself in the God of truth;
Jer 4. 2 and the nations shall *b* themselves
31.23 The Lord *b* thee, O habitation of
Hag 2.19 forth: from this day will I *b* you.
Mt 5.44 *b* them that curse you, do good
Lk 6.28 *B* them that curse you, and pray
Ac 3.26 sent him to *b* you, in turning
Ro 12.14 *B* them which persecute you: *b*,
1Co 4.12 being reviled, we *b*; being
10.16 The cup of blessing which we *b*,
14.16 Else, when thou shalt *b* with the
Heb 6.14 Surely blessing I will *b* thee, and
Jas 3. 9 Therewith *b* we God, even the

BLESSED
Gen 1.22 And God *b* them, saying,
28 God *b* them, and God said unto
2. 3 And God *b* the seventh day, and
5. 2 created he them; and *b* them,
9. 1 And God *b* Noah and his sons,
26 *B* be the Lord God of Shem;
12. 3 shall all families of the earth be *b*.
14.19 And he *b* him, and said,
19 *B* be Abram of the most high
20 And *b* the most high God, which
17.20 Behold, I have *b* him, and will
18.18 the nations of the earth shall be *b*
22.18 all the nations of the earth be *b*;
24. 1 and the Lord had *b* Abraham in
27 *B* be the Lord God of my master
31 Come in, thou *b* of the Lord;
35 Lord hath *b* my master greatly;
48 and *b* the Lord God of my master
60 And they *b* Rebekah, and said unto
25.11 Abraham, that God *b* his son Isaac;
26. 4 the nations of the earth be *b*;
12 hundredfold: and the Lord *b* him.
29 thou art now the *b* of the Lord.
27.23 brother Esau's hands: so he *b* him.
27 and *b* him, and said, See, the smell
27 of a field which the Lord hath *b*:
29 and *b* be he that blesseth thee.
33 thou camest, and have *b* him?
33 yea, and he shall be *b*.
41 wherewith his father *b* him:
28. 1 Isaac called Jacob, and *b* him,
6 Esau saw that Isaac had *b* Jacob,
6 and that as he *b* him he gave him
14 all the families of the earth be *b*.
30.13 for the daughters will call me *b*:
27 that the Lord hath *b* me for thy
30 and the Lord hath *b* thee since my

Gen 31.55 and *b* them: and Laban departed,
32.29 my name? And he *b* him there.
35. 9 out of Padan-aram, and *b* him.
39. 5 the Lord *b* the Egyptian's house
47. 7 Pharaoh: and Jacob *b* Pharaoh.
10 Jacob *b* Pharaoh, and went out
48. 3 in the land of Canaan, and *b* me,
15 And he *b* Joseph, and said, God,
20 And he *b* them that day, saying,
49.28 spake unto them, and *b* them;
28 according to his blessing he *b* them.
Ex 18.10 Jethro said, *B* be the Lord,
20.11 the Lord *b* the sabbath day, and
39.43 they done it: and Moses *b* them.
Lev 9.22 toward the people, and *b* them,
23 and came out, and *b* the people:
Nu 22. 6 that he whom thou blessest is *b*,
12 curse the people: for they are *b*.
23.11 thou hast *b* them altogether.
20 he hath *b*; and I cannot reverse it.
24. 9 *B* is he that blesseth thee, and
10 thou has altogether *b* them these
Dt 2. 7 the Lord thy God hath *b* thee in
7.14 Thou shalt be *b* above all people:
12. 7 the Lord thy God hath *b* thee.
14.24 the Lord thy God hath *b* thee:
15.14 the Lord thy God hath *b* thee
16.10 the Lord thy God hath *b* thee:
28. 3 *B* shalt thou be in the city,
3 and *b* shalt thou be in the field.
4 *B* shall be the fruit of thy body,
5 *B* shall be thy basket and thy
6 *B* shalt thou be when thou comest
6 and *b* shalt thou be when thou
33. 1 Moses the man of God *b* the
13 *B* of the Lord be his land, for
20 *B* be he that enlargeth Gad: he
24 Let Asher be *b* with children;
Jos 14.13 And Joshua *b* him, and gave unto
17.14 forasmuch as the Lord hath *b* me
22. 6 So Joshua *b* them, and sent them
7 unto their tents, then he *b* them,
33 and the children of Israel *b* God,
24.10 Balaam; therefore he *b* you still:
Jdg 5.24 *B* above women shall Jael the wife
24 *b* shall be above women
13.24 child grew, and the Lord *b* him.
17. 2 *B* be thou of the Lord, my son.
Ru 2.19 *b* be he that did take knowledge
20 *B* be he of the Lord, who hath not
3.10 *B* be thou of the Lord, my
4.14 *B* be the Lord, which hath not
1Sa 2.20 And Eli *b* Elkanah and his wife,
15.13 *B* be thou of the Lord: I have
23.21 *B* be ye of the Lord; for ye have
25.32 *B* be the Lord God of Israel,
33 And *b* be thy advice.
33 and *b* be thou, which hast kept.
39 *B* be the Lord, that hath pleaded
26.25 *B* be thou, my son David: thou
2Sa 2. 5 *B* be ye of the Lord, that ye have
6.11 and the Lord *b* Obed-edom, and
12 The Lord hath *b* the house of
18 he *b* the people in the name of the
7.29 house of thy servant be *b* forever.
13.25 he would not go, but *b* him.
18.28 *B* be the Lord thy God, which hath
19.39 king kissed Barzillai, and *b* him;
22.47 the Lord liveth; and *b* be my rock;
1Ki 1.48 *B* be the Lord God of Israel,
2.45 and king Solomon shall be *b*,
5. 7 *B* be the Lord this day, which
8.14 and *b* all the congregation of
15 *B* be the Lord God of Israel, which
55 stood, and *b* all the congregation
56 *B* be the Lord, that hath given
66 and they *b* the king, and went
10. 9 *B* be the Lord thy God, which
1Ch 13.14 And the Lord *b* the house of
16. 2 he *b* the people in the name of the
36 *B* be the Lord God of Israel for
17.27 O Lord, and it shall be *b* for ever.
26. 5 the eighth: for God *b* him.
29.10 Wherefore David *b* the Lord
10 *B* be thou, Lord God of Israel our
20 all the congregation *b* the Lord
2Ch 2.12 *B* be the Lord God of Israel, that
6. 3 and *b* the whole congregation of
4 *B* be the Lord God of Israel, who
9. 8 *B* be the Lord thy God, which
20.26 for there they *b* the Lord:
30.27 Levites arose and *b* the people:
31. 8 they *b* the Lord, and his people
10 for the Lord hath *b* his people;
Ezr 7.27 *B* be the Lord God of our fathers,
Neh 8. 6 Ezra *b* the Lord, the great God.
9. 5 and *b* be thy glorious name, which
11. 2 And the people *b* all the men,
Job 1.10 hast *b* the work of his hands,
21 *b* be the name of the Lord.
29.11 the ear heard me, then it *b* me;
31.20 If his loins have not *b* me, and if
42.12 So the Lord *b* the latter end of
Ps 1. 1 *B* is the man that walketh not
2.12 *B* are all they that put their
18.46 Lord liveth; and *b* be my rock;
21. 6 hast made him most *b* for ever:
28. 6 *B* be the Lord, because he hath
31.21 *B* be the Lord: for he hath
32. 1 *B* is he whose transgression is
2 *B* is the man unto whom the Lord
33.12 *B* is the nation whose God is the
34. 8 *b* is the man that trusteth in him.
37.22 For such as be *b* of him shall
26 and lendeth; and his seed is *b*.
40. 4 *B* is that man that maketh the
41. 1 *B* is he that considereth the poor:
2 and he shall be *b* upon the earth:
13 *B* be the Lord God of Israel
45. 2 therefore God hath *b* thee for ever.
49.18 while he lived he *b* his soul: and
65. 4 *B* is the man whom thou choosest,
66.20 *B* be God, which hath not turned
68.19 *B* be the Lord, who daily loadeth
35 power unto his people. *B* be God.
72.17 sun: and men shall be *b* in him:
17 him: all nations shall call him *b*.
18 *B* be the Lord God, the God of
19 *b* be his glorious name for ever:
84. 4 *B* are they that dwell in thy house:
5 *B* is the man whose strength is in
12 *b* is the man that trusteth in thee.
89.15 *B* is the people that know the
52 *B* be the Lord for evermore.
94.12 *B* is the man whom thou
106. 3 *B* are they that keep judgment,
48 *B* be the Lord God of Israel from
112. 1 *B* is the man that feareth the Lord,
2 of the upright shall be *b*.
113. 2 *B* be the name of the Lord from
115.15 Ye are *b* of the Lord which made
118.26 *B* be he that cometh in the name
26 we have *b* you out of the house of
119. 1 *B* are the undefiled in the way,
2 *B* are they that keep his
12 *B* art thou, O Lord: teach me
124. 6 *B* be the Lord, who hath not
128. 1 *B* is every one that feareth the
4 thus shall the man be *b* that
135.21 *B* be the Lord out of Zion, which
144. 1 *B* be the Lord my strength,
147.13 he hath *b* thy children within
Pr 5.18 Let thy fountain be *b*: and rejoice
8.32 for *b* are they that keep my ways.
34 *B* is the man that heareth me,
10. 7 The memory of the just is *b*: but
20. 7 his children are *b* after him.
21 the end thereof shall not be *b*.
22. 9 hath a bountiful eye shall be *b*;
31.28 children arise up, and call her *b*;
Ec 10.17 *B* art thou, O land, when thy
SS 6. 9 daughters saw her, and *b* her;
Isa 19.25 *B* be Egypt my people,
30.18 *b* are all they that wait for him.
32.20 *B* are ye that sow beside all
51. 2 I called him alone, and *b* him,
56. 2 *B* is the man that doeth this,
61. 9 the seed which the Lord hath *b*.
65.23 the seed of the *b* of the Lord,
66. 3 incense, as if he *b* an idol.
Jer 17. 7 *B* is the man that trusteth in the
20.14 wherein my mother bare me be *b*.
Eze 3.12 *B* be the glory of the Lord from
Dan 2.19 Then Daniel *b* the God of heaven.
20 *B* be the name of God forever
3.28 *B* be the God of Shadrach,
4.34 I *b* the most High, and I praised
12.12 *B* is he that waiteth, and cometh
Zec 11. 5 that sell them say, *B* be the Lord;
Mal 3.12 And all nations shall call you *b*:
Mt 5. 3 *B* are the poor in spirit:
4 *B* are they that mourn: for they
5 *B* are the meek: for they shall
6 *B* are they which do hunger and
7 *B* are the merciful: for they shall
8 *B* are the pure in heart: for they
9 *B* are the peacemakers: for they
10 *B* are they which are persecuted
11 *B* are ye, when men shall revile
11. 6 And *b* is he, whosoever shall not
13.16 But *b* are your eyes, for they see:
14.19 he *b*, and brake, and gave
16.17 said unto him, *B* art thou, Simon
21. 9 *B* is he that cometh in the name
23.39 *B* is he that cometh in the name
24.46 *B* is that servant, whom his lord
25.34 ye *b* of my Father, inherit the
26.26 *b* it, and brake it, and gave it to
Mk 6.41 he looked up to heaven, and *b*,
8. 7 and he *b*, and commanded to set
10.16 hands upon them, and *b* them.
11. 9 *B* is he that cometh in the name
10 *B* be the kingdom of our father
14.22 and *b*, and brake it, and gave to
61 thou the Christ, the Son of the *B*?
Lk 1.28 thee: *b* art thou among women,
42 *B* art thou among women,
42 and *b* is the fruit of thy womb.
45 *b* is she that believed: for there
48 all generations shall call me *b*.
68 *B* be the Lord God of Israel;
2.28 him up in his arms, and *b* God,
34 And Simeon *b* them, and said
6.20 disciples, and said, *B* be ye poor:
21 *B* are ye that hunger now: for ye
21 *B* are ye that weep now: for ye
22 *B* are ye, when men shall hate
7.23 And *b* is he, whosoever shall not
9.16 he *b* them, and brake, and gave
10.23 *B* are the eyes which see the
11.27 *B* is the womb that bare thee,
28 Yea rather, *b* are they that hear
12.37 *B* are those servants, whom the
38 *b* are those servants.
43 *B* is that servant, whom his lord
13.35 *B* is he that cometh in the name
14.14 thou shalt be *b*; for they cannot
15 *B* is he that shall eat bread in
19.38 *B* be the king that cometh
23.29 they shall say, *B* are the barren,
24.30 took bread, and *b* it, and brake,
50 he lifted up his hands, and *b* them.
51 while he *b* them, he was parted
Jn 12.13 *B* is the King of Israel that
20.29 *b* are they that have not seen,
Ac 3.25 all the kindreds of the earth be *b*.
20.35 more *b* to give than to receive.
Ro 1.25 the Creator, who is *b* for ever.
4. 7 *B* are they whose iniquities are
8 *B* is the man to whom the Lord
9. 5 who is over all, God *b* for ever.
2Co 1. 3 *B* be God, even the Father of our
11.31 Jesus Christ, which is *b* for

Gal 3. 8 In thee shall all nations be *b*.
9 are *b* with faithful Abraham.
Eph 1. 3 *B* be the God and Father of our
3 *b* us with all spiritual blessings
1Ti 1.11 the glorious gospel of the *b* God,
6.15 *b* and only Potentate, the King
Tit 2.13 Looking for that *b* hope, and the
Heb 7. 1 slaughter of the kings, and *b* him;
6 *b* him that had the promises.
7 contradiction the less is *b* of
11.20 By faith Isaac *b* Jacob and Esau
21 Jacob, when he was a dying, *b*
Jas 1.12 *B* is the man that endureth
25 this man shall be *b* in his deed.
1Pe 1. 3 *B* be the God and Father of our
Rev 1. 3 *B* is he that readeth, and they
14.13 *B* are the dead which die in the
16.15 *B* is he that watcheth, and
19. 9 *B* are they which are called
20. 6 *B* and holy is he that hath part
22. 7 *b* is he that keepeth the sayings
14 *B* are they that do his

BLESSEDNESS

Ro 4. 6 also describeth the *b* of the man,
9 Cometh this *b* then upon the
Gal 4.15 Where is then the *b* ye spake of?

BLESSEST

Nu 22. 6 that he, whom thou *b* is blessed,
1Ch 17.27 for thou *b*, O Lord, and it shall
Ps 65.10 it soft with showers: thou *b* the

BLESSETH

Gen 27.29 and blessed be he that *b* thee.
Nu 24. 9 Blessed is he that *b* thee, and
Dt 15. 6 the Lord thy God *b* thee, as he
Ps 10. 3 *b* the covetous, whom the Lord
107.38 He *b* them also, so that they are
Pr 3.33 but he *b* the habitation of the just.
27.14 that *b* his friend with a loud voice,
Isa 65.16 That he who *b* himself in the earth

BLESSING

Gen 12. 2 great; and thou shalt be a *b*:
22.17 That in *b* I will bless thee, and in
27.12 a curse upon me, and not a *b*.
30 Isaac had made an end of *b*
35 and hath taken away thy *b*.
36 hath taken away my *b*. And he
36 Hast thou not reserved a *b*
38 Hast thou but one *b*, my father?
41 because of the *b* wherewith his
28. 4 and give thee the *b* of Abraham,
33.11 Take, I pray thee, my *b* that is
39. 5 the *b* of the Lord was upon all
49.28 every one according to his *b* he
Ex 32.29 he may bestow upon you a *b*
Lev 25.21 I will command my *b* upon you
Dt 11.26 you this day a *b* and a curse;
27 A *b*, if ye obey the commandments
29 thou shalt put the *b* upon mount
12.15 according to the *b* of the Lord
16.17 according to the *b* of the Lord
23. 5 thy God turned the curse into a *b*
28. 8 The Lord shall command the *b*
30. 1 the *b* and the curse, which I have
19 life and death, *b* and cursing:
33. 1 this is the *b* wherewith Moses
7 And this is the *b* of Judah:
16 *b* come upon the head of Joseph,
23 and full with the *b* of the Lord:
Jos 15.19 Who answereth, Give me a *b*;
Jdg 1.15 Give me a *b*: for thou hast given
1Sa 25.27 now this *b* with thine handmaid
2Sa 7.29 and with thy *b* let the house of
2Ki 5.15 thee, take a *b* of thy servant.
Neh 9. 5 is exalted above all *b* and praise.
13. 2 God turned the curse into a *b*.
Job 29.13 *b* of him that was ready to perish
Ps 3. 8 thy *b* is upon thy people.
24. 5 shall receive the *b* from the Lord,
109.17 as he delighted not in *b*, so let it
129. 8 The *b* of the Lord be upon you:
133. 3 there the Lord commanded the *b*,
Pr 10.22 The *b* of the Lord, it maketh rich,
11.11 By the *b* of the upright the city is
26 but *b* shall be upon the head of
24.25 a good *b* shall come upon them.
Isa 19.24 even a *b* in the midst of the land:
44. 3 and my *b* upon thine offspring:
65. 8 Destroy it not; for a *b* is in it:
Eze 34.26 places round about my hill a *b*;
26 there shall be showers of *b*.
44.30 that he may cause the *b* to rest
Joel 2.14 repent, and leave a *b* behind him;
Zec 8.13 I save you, and ye shall be a *b*:
Mal 3.10 pour you out a *b*, that there shall
Lk 24.53 in the temple, praising and *b* God.
Ro 15.29 the fulness of the *b* of the gospel
1Co 10.16 The cup of *b* which we bless,
Gal 3.14 the *b* of Abraham might come
Heb 6. 7 is dressed, receiveth *b* from God:
14 Saying, Surely *b* I will bless thee,
12.17 would have inherited the *b*,
Jas 3.10 mouth proceedeth *b* and cursing.
1Pe 3. 9 but contrariwise *b*;
9 that ye should inherit a *b*
Rev 5.12 and honor, and glory, and *b*.
13 *B*, and honor, and glory,
7.12 *B*, and glory, and wisdom,

BIBLICAL THEMES

BLESSINGS

And God blessed them, and God said unto them, Be fruitful, and multiply, and replenish the earth, and subdue it. Gen 1.28

In blessing I will bless thee, and in multiplying I will multiply thy seed as the stars of the heaven, and as the sand which is upon the sea shore; and thy seed shall possess the gate of his enemies; and in thy seed shall all the nations of the earth be blessed; because thou hast obeyed my voice. Gen 22.17-18

And when Esau heard the words of his father, he cried with a great and exceeding bitter cry, and said unto his father, Bless me, even me also, O my father. Gen 27.34

I will not let thee go, except thou bless me. Gen 32.26

The Lord bless thee, and keep thee: The Lord make his face shine upon thee, and be gracious unto thee: The Lord lift up his countenance upon thee, and give thee peace. Nu 6.24-26

I call heaven and earth to record this day against you, that I have set before you life and death, blessing and cursing: therefore choose life, that both thou and thy seed may live. Dt 30.19

Bless the Lord, O my soul: and all that is within me, bless his holy name. Bless the Lord, O my soul, and forget not all his benefits. Ps 103.1-2

Blessed are the poor in spirit: for theirs is the kingdom of heaven.
Blessed are they that mourn: for they shall be comforted.
Blessed are the meek: for they shall inherit the earth.
Blessed are they which do hunger and thirst after righteousness: for they shall be filled.
Blessed are the merciful: for they shall obtain mercy.
Blessed are the pure in heart: for they shall see God.
Blessed are the peacemakers: for they shall be called the children of God.
Blessed are they which are persecuted for righteousness' sake: for theirs is the kingdom of heaven. Mt 5.3-10

And the angel came in unto her, and said, Hail, thou that art highly favored, the Lord is with thee: blessed art thou among women. Lk 1.28

Glory to God in the highest, and on earth peace, good will toward men. Lk 2.14

The grace of the Lord Jesus Christ, and the love of God, and the communion of the Holy Ghost, be with you all. 2Co 13.14

Blessed be the God and Father of our Lord Jesus Christ, who hath blessed us with all spiritual blessings in heavenly places in Christ. Eph 1.3

Now unto the King eternal, immortal, invisible, the only wise God, be honor and glory for ever and ever. 1Ti 1.17

Now unto him that is able to keep you from falling, and to present you faultless before the presence of his glory with exceeding joy, to the only wise God our Savior, be glory and majesty, dominion and power, both now and ever. Jude 24-25

Worthy is the Lamb that was slain to receive power, and riches, and wisdom, and strength, and honor, and glory, and blessing. Rev 5.12

Blessed are they that do his commandments, that they may have right to the tree of life, and may enter in through the gates into the city. Rev 22.14

BLESSINGS

Gen 49.25 bless thee with *b* of heaven above,
25 *b* of the deep that lieth under,
25 *b* of the breasts, and of the womb:
26 The *b* of thy father have prevailed
26 above the *b* of my progenitors
Dt 28. 2 all these *b* shall come on thee,
Jos 8.34 the *b* and cursings, according to
Ps 21. 3 preventest with the *b* of goodness:
Pr 10. 6 *B* are upon the head of the just:
28.20 faithful man shall abound with *b*:
Mal 2. 2 I will curse your *b*: yea, I have
Eph 1. 3 with all spiritual *b* in heavenly

BLIND

Ex 4.11 or deaf, or the seeing, or the *b*?
Lev 19.14 a stumblingblock before the *b*,
21.18 a *b* man, or a lame, or he that
22.22 *B*, or broken, or maimed, or
Dt 15.21 it be lame, or *b*, or have any ill
16.19 a gift doth *b* the eyes of the wise,
27.18 he that maketh the *b* to wander
28.29 *b* gropeth in darkness, and thou
1Sa 12. 3 bribe to *b* mine eyes therewith?
2Sa 5. 6 take away the *b* and the lame,
8 *b*, that are hated of David's soul,
8 The *b* and the lame shall not come
Job 29.15 I was eyes to the *b*, and feet was I
Ps 146. 8 Lord openeth the eyes of the *b*:
Isa 29.18 the *b* shall see out of obscurity,
35. 5 eyes of the *b* shall be opened,
42. 7 open the *b* eyes, to bring out the
16 bring the *b* by a way that they
18 Hear, ye deaf; and look, ye *b*, that
19 Who is *b*, but my servant? or deaf
19 who is *b* as he that is perfect, and
19 *b* as the Lord's servant?
43. 8 forth the *b* people that have eyes,
56.10 His watchmen are *b*: they are all
59.10 for the wall like the *b*, and we
Jer 31. 8 and with them the *b* and the lame,
La 4.14 wandered as *b* men in the streets,
Zep 1.17 walk like *b* men, because they
Mal 1. 8 the *b* for sacrifice, is it not evil?
Mt 9.27 two *b* men followed him, crying,
9.28 the house, the *b* men came to him:
11. 5 The *b* receive their sight, and the
12.22 one possessed with a devil, *b*,
22 that the *b* and dumb both spake
15.14 Let them alone: they be *b*
14 leaders of the *b*. And
14 if the *b* lead the *b*,
30 lame, *b*, dumb, maimed, and many
31 lame to walk, and the *b* to see:
20.30 And, behold, two *b* men sitting by
21.14 the *b* and the lame came to him
23.16 Woe unto you, ye blind guides,
17, 19 Ye fools and *b*: for whether is
24 Ye *b* guides, which strain at a
26 Thou *b* Pharisee, cleanse first that
Mk 8.22 and they bring a *b* man unto him,
23 he took the *b* man by the hand,
10.46 *b* Bartimaeus, the son of Timaeus,
49 they call the *b* man, saying unto
51 The *b* man said unto him, Lord,
Lk 4.18 and recovering of sight to the *b*,
6.39 Can the *b* lead the *b*?
7.21 many that were *b* he gave sight.
22 how that the *b* see, the lame walk,
14.13 the maimed, the lame, the *b*:
21 maimed, and the halt, and the *b*.
18.35 a certain *b* man sat by the way side
Jn 5. 3 *b*, halt, withered, waiting for the
9. 1 which was *b* from his birth.
2 his parents, that he was born *b*?
6 anointed the eyes of the *b* man
8 had seen him that he was *b*,
13 him that aforetime was *b*.
17 They say unto the *b* man again,
18 he had been *b*, and received his
19 your son, who ye say was born *b*?
20 and that he was born *b*:
24 called they the man that was *b*,
25 whereas I was *b*, now I see.
32 the eyes of one that was born *b*.
39 they which see might be made *b*.
40 and said unto him, Are we *b* also?
41 If ye were *b*, ye should have no
10.21 a devil open the eyes of the *b*?
11.37 opened the eyes of the *b*, have
Ac 13.11 shalt be *b*, not seeing the sun
Ro 2.19 thou thyself art a guide of the *b*,
2Pe 1. 9 he that lacketh these things is *b*,
Rev 3.17 and poor, and *b*, and naked:

BLINDED

Jn 12.40 He hath *b* their eyes, and
Ro 11. 7 obtained it, and the rest were *b*
2Co 3.14 But their minds were *b*: for until
4. 4 of this world hath *b* the minds
1Jn 2.11 that darkness hath *b* his eyes.

BLINDFOLDED

Lk 22.64 And when they had *b* him, they

BLINDNESS

Gen 19.11 at the door of the house with *b*,
Dt 28.28 smite thee with madness, and *b*,
2Ki 6.18 this people, I pray thee, with *b*.
18 And he smote them with *b*
Zec 12. 4 every horse of the people with *b*.
Ro 11.25 *b* in part is happened to Israel,
Eph 4.18 because of the *b* of their heart:

BLOOD

Gen 4.10 of thy brother's *b* crieth unto me
11 thy brother's *b* from thy hand;
9. 4 thereof, which is the *b* thereof,
5 surely your *b* of your lives will
6 sheddeth man's *b*....his *b* be shed:
37.22 Shed no *b*, but cast him into
26 our brother, and conceal his *b*?
31 goats, and dipped the coat in the *b*;
42.22 behold, also his *b* is required.
49.11 and his clothes in the *b* of grapes:
Ex 4. 9 become *b* upon the dry land.
7.17 and they shall be turned to *b*.
19 that they may become *b*;
19 and that there may be *b*
20 in the river were turned to *b*.
21 *b* throughout all the land of Egypt.
12. 7 shall take of the *b*, and strike it
13 the *b* shall be to you for a token
13 when I see the *b*, I will pass over
22 dip it in the *b* that is in the bason,
22 the *b* that is in the bason;
23 he seeth the *b* upon the lintel,
22. 2 shall no *b* be shed for him.
3 there shall be *b* shed for him;
23.18 not offer the *b* of my sacrifice
24. 6 took half of the *b* and put it
6 half of the *b* he sprinkled on
8 Moses took the *b*, and sprinkled
8 Behold the *b* of the covenant,
29.12 thou shalt take the *b* of
12 pour all the *b* beside the bottom
16 shalt take his *b* and sprinkle it
20 kill the ram, and take of his *b*,
20 sprinkle the *b* upon the altar
21 shalt take of the *b* that is upon
30.10 with the *b* of the sin offering
34.25 not offer the *b* of my sacrifice
Lev 1. 5 bring the *b*, and sprinkle the *b*
11 sprinkle his *b* round about upon
15 the *b* thereof shall be wrung out
3. 2 sprinkle the *b* upon the altar
8 sons shall sprinkle the *b* thereof
13 Aaron shall sprinkle the *b* thereof
17 that ye eat neither fat nor *b*.
4. 5 shall take of the bullock's *b*, and
6 dip his finger in the *b*, and
6 sprinkle of the *b* seven times
7 some of the *b* upon the horns
7 pour all the *b* of the bullock
16 shall bring of the bullock's *b*
17 dip his finger in some of the *b*,
18 And he shall put some of the *b*
18 pour out all the *b* at the bottom
25 the priest shall take of the *b* of
25 shall pour out his *b* at the bottom
30 shall take of the *b* thereof
30 shall pour out all the *b* thereof
34 priest shall take of the *b* of the
34 shall pour out all the *b* thereof
5. 9 he shall sprinkle of the *b* of the
9 the rest of the *b* shall be wrung out
6.27 is sprinkled of the *b* thereof
30 whereof any of the *b* is brought
7. 2 the *b* thereof shall he sprinkle
14 the priest's that sprinkleth the *b* of
26 ye shall eat no manner of *b*,
27 that eateth any manner of *b*,
33 the *b* of the peace offerings,
8.15 Moses took the *b*, and put it upon
15 poured the *b* at the bottom of the
19 Moses sprinkled the *b* upon the
23 and Moses took of the *b* of it, and
24 Moses put of the *b* upon the tip of
24 the *b* upon the altar round about.
30 the *b* which was upon the altar,
9. 9 brought the *b* unto him: and he
9 dipped his finger in the *b*,
9 poured out the *b* at the bottom of
12, 18 sons presented unto him the *b*,
10.18 Behold, the *b* of it was not brought
12. 4 shall then continue in the *b* of her
5 shall continue in the *b* of her
7 cleansed from the issue of her *b*.
14. 6 the living bird in the *b* of the
14 the *b* of the trespass offering,
17 upon the *b* of the trespass offering:
25 some of the *b* of the trespass
28 upon the place of the *b* of the
51 dip them in the *b* of the slain
52 the house with the *b* of the bird,
15.19 her issue in her flesh be *b*,
25 if a woman have an issue of her *b*
16.14 shall take of the *b* of the bullock,
14 shall he sprinkle of the *b*
15 bring his *b* within the vail,
15 and do with that *b* as he did
15 with the *b* of the bullock,
18 take of the *b* of the bullock,
18 and of the *b* of the goat,
19 And he shall sprinkle of the *b*
27 whose *b* was brought in to make
17. 4 *b* shall be imputed unto that man;
4 he hath shed *b*; and that man
6 the priest shall sprinkle the *b*
10 that eateth any manner of *b*;
10 against that soul that eateth *b*,
11 the life of the flesh is in the *b*:
11 the *b* that maketh an atonement
12 No soul of you shall eat *b*,
12 that sojourneth among you eat *b*.
13 shall even pour out the *b* thereof,
14 the *b* of it is for the life thereof:
14 Ye shall eat the *b* of no manner
14 the life of all flesh is the *b* thereof:
19.16 against the *b* of thy neighbor:
26 shall not eat anything with the *b*:
20. 9 his *b* shall be upon him.
11 their *b* shall be upon them.
12 wrought confusion; their *b* shall
13 their *b* shall be upon them.
16 put to death; their *b* shall be
18 uncovered the fountain of her *b*:
27 their *b* shall be upon them.
Nu 18.17 thou shalt sprinkle their *b* upon
19. 4 take of her *b* with his finger,
4 and sprinkle of her *b*
5 her skin, and her flesh, and her *b*,
23.24 prey, and drink the *b* of the slain.

35.19 The revenger of *b* himself shall
21 the revenger of *b* shall slay
24 the slayer and the revenger of *b*
25 of the hand of the revenger of *b*,
27 And the revenger of *b* find him
27 the revenger of *b* kill the slayer;
27 he shall not be guilty of *b*:
33 for *b* it defileth the land: and the
33 cannot be cleansed of the *b*
33 but by the *b* of him that shed it.
Dt 12.16 Only ye shall not eat the *b*;
23 sure that thou eat not the *b*:
23 for the *b* is the life;
27 the flesh, and the *b*, upon the
27 and the *b* of thy sacrifices shall
15.23 thou shalt not eat the *b* thereof;
17. 8 between *b* and *b*, between plea
19. 6 Lest the avenger of the *b* pursue
10 That innocent *b* be not shed in
10 and so *b* be upon thee.
12 into the hand of the avenger of *b*,
13 of innocent *b* from Israel,
21. 7 Our hands have not shed this *b*,
8 lay not innocent *b* unto thy people
8 And the *b* shall be forgiven them.
9 put away the guilt of innocent *b*
22. 8 that thou bring not *b* upon
32.14 drink the pure *b* of the grape.
42 make mine arrows drunk with *b*,
42 and that with the *b* of the slain
43 will avenge the *b* of his servants,
Jos 2.19 his *b* shall be upon his head,
19 his *b* shall be on our head, if any
20. 3 refuge from the avenger of *b*.
5 if the avenger of *b* pursue after
9 by the hand of the avenger of *b*,
Jdg 9.24 their *b* be laid upon Abimelech
1Sa 14.32 people did eat them with the *b*.
33 Lord, in that they eat with the *b*.
34 the Lord in eating with the *b*.
19. 5 wilt thou sin against innocent *b*,
25.26 thee from coming to shed *b*,
31 either that thou hast shed *b*
33 this day from coming to shed *b*,
26.20 let not my *b* fall to the earth
2Sa 1.16 Thy *b* be upon thy head;
22 From the *b* of the slain,
3.27 that he died, for the *b* of Asahel
28 from the *b* of Abner the son
4.11 therefore now require his *b*
14.11 the revengers of *b* to destroy
16. 8 all the *b* of the house of Saul,
20.12 Amasa wallowed in *b* in the
23.17 the *b* of the men that went in
1Ki 2. 5 shed the *b* of war in peace,
5 put the *b* of war upon his girdle
9 thou down to the grave with *b*,
31 take away the innocent *b*, which
32 the Lord shall return his *b*
33 Their *b* shall therefore return
37 thy *b* shall be upon thine own
18.28 lancets, till the *b* gushed out
21.19 dogs licked the *b* of Naboth
19 shall dogs lick thy *b*,
22.35 and the *b* ran out of the wound
38 and the dogs licked up his *b*;
2Ki 3.22 on the other side as red as *b*:
23 they said, This is *b*: the kings
9. 7 avenge the *b* of my servants
7 and the *b* of all the servants
26 seen yesterday the *b* of Naboth,
26 and the *b* of his sons,
33 and some of her *b* was sprinkled
16.13 sprinkled the *b* of his peace
15 all the *b* of the burnt offering,
15 and all the *b* of the sacrifice:
21.16 shed innocent *b* very much,
24. 4 for the innocent *b* that he shed:
4 filled Jerusalem with innocent *b*;
1Ch 11.19 shall I drink the *b* of these men
22. 8 Thou hast shed *b* abundantly,
8 thou hast shed much *b* upon the
28. 3 man of war, and hast shed *b*.
2Ch 19.10 between *b* and *b*, between law
24.25 conspired against him for the *b*
29.22 the priests received the *b*, and
22 sprinkled the *b* upon the altar:
22 lambs, and they sprinkled the *b*
24 reconciliation with their *b* upon
30.16 the priests sprinkled the *b*, which
35.11 the priests sprinkled the *b* from
Job 16.18 O earth, cover not thou my *b*,
39.30 Her young ones also suck up *b*:
Ps 9.12 he maketh inquisition for *b*,
16. 4 their drink offerings of *b* will I
30. 9 What profit is there in my *b*, when
50.13 of bulls, or drink the *b* of goats?
58.10 his feet in the *b* of the wicked.
68.23 dipped in the *b* of thine enemies,
72.14 precious shall their *b* be in his
78.44 had turned their rivers into *b*;
79. 3 Their *b* have they shed like water
10 revenging of the *b* of thy servants
94.21 and condemn the innocent *b*.
105.29 turned their waters into *b*, and
106.38 shed innocent *b*, even
38 even the *b* of their sons
38 the land was polluted with *b*.
Pr 1.11 let us lay wait for *b*, let us look
16 evil, and make haste to shed *b*.
18 they lay wait for their own *b*;
6.17 and hands that shed innocent *b*,
12. 6 to lie in wait for *b*: but the mouth
28.17 violence to the *b* of any person
30.33 of the nose bringeth forth *b*:
Isa 1.11 delight not in the *b* of bullocks,
15 hear: your hands are full of *b*.
4. 4 have purged the *b* of Jerusalem
9. 5 noise, and garments rolled in *b*;
15. 9 of Dimon shall be full of *b*:
26.21 the earth also shall disclose her *b*,
33.15 his ears from hearing of *b*,
34. 3 shall be melted with their *b*.
6 sword of the Lord is filled with *b*,
6 with the *b* of lambs and goats,
7 their land shall be soaked with *b*,
49.26 be drunken with their own *b*,
59. 3 your hands are defiled with *b*,
7 make haste to shed innocent *b*:
63. 3 their *b* shall be sprinkled upon
66. 3 as if he offered swine's *b*; he that
Jer 2.34 skirts is found the *b* of the souls
7. 6 shed not innocent *b* in this place,
18.21 pour out their *b* by the force
19. 4 this place with the *b* of innocents;
22. 3 neither shed innocent *b* in this
17 and for to shed innocent *b*, and
26.15 shall surely bring innocent *b* upon
46.10 and made drunk with their *b*:
48.10 keepeth back his sword from *b*.
51.35 and my *b* upon the inhabitants of
La 4.13 that have shed the *b* of the just
14 polluted themselves with *b*, so
Eze 3.18, 20 but his *b* will I require at thine
5.17 pestilence and *b* shall pass
9. 9 the land is full of *b*, and the city
14.19 and pour out my fury upon it in *b*,
16. 6 polluted in thine own *b*, I said
6 when thou wast in thy *b*, Live;
6 thee when thou wast in thy *b*,
9 washed away thy *b* from thee, and
22 bare, and wast polluted in thy *b*.
36 and by the *b* of thy children,
38 that break wedlock and shed *b*
38 will give thee *b* in fury and
18.10 that is a robber, a shedder of *b*,
13 surely die; his *b* shall be upon him.
19.10 Thy mother is like a vine in thy *b*,
21.32 thy *b* shall be in the midst of the
22. 3 The city sheddeth *b* in the midst of
4 Thou art become guilty in thy *b*
6 in thee to their power to shed *b*.
9 are men that carry tales to shed *b*:
12 have they taken gifts to shed *b*;
13 at thy *b* which hath been in the
27 to shed *b*, and to destroy souls,
23.37 and *b* is in their hands, and with
45 the manner of women that shed *b*;
45 are adulteresses, and *b* is in their
24. 7 For her *b* is in the midst of her;
8 I have set her *b* upon the top of a
28.23 her pestilence, and *b* into her
32. 6 I will also water with thy *b* the
33. 4 his *b* shall be upon his own head.
5 warning; his *b* shall be upon him.
6 but his *b* will I require at the
8 but his *b* will I require at thine
25 Ye eat with the *b*, and lift up your
25 toward your idols, and shed *b*:
35. 5 shed the *b* of the children of
6 I will prepare thee unto *b*,
6 and *b* shall pursue thee: sith
6 thou hast not hated *b*, even *b* shall
36.18 the *b* that they had shed upon the
38.22 him with pestilence and with *b*;
39.17 that ye may eat flesh, and drink *b*.
18 and drink the *b* of the princes of
19 and drink *b* till ye be drunken, of
43.18 thereon, and to sprinkle *b* thereon.
20 thou shalt take of the *b* thereof,
44. 7 my bread, the fat and the *b*, and
15 offer unto me the fat and the *b*,
45.19 the priest shall take of the *b* of the
Hos 1. 4 I will avenge the *b* of Jezreel upon
4. 2 they break out, and *b* toucheth *b*.
6. 8 iniquity, and is polluted with *b*.
12.14 therefore shall he leave his *b* upon
Joel 2.30 *b*, and fire, and pillars of smoke.
31 darkness, and the moon into *b*,
3.19 they have shed innocent *b* in their
21 For I will cleanse their *b* that I
Jon 1.14 and lay not upon us innocent *b*:
Mic 3.10 They build up Zion with *b*, and
7. 2 they all lie in wait for *b*; they
Hab 2. 8 because of men's *b*, and for the
12 him that buildeth a town with *b*,
17 them afraid, because of men's *b*,
Zep 1.17 and their *b* shall be poured out as
Zec 9. 7 I will take away his *b* out of his
11 by the *b* of thy covenant I have
Mt 9.20 diseased with an issue of *b* twelve
16.17 for flesh and *b* hath not revealed
23.30 with them in the *b* of the prophets.
35 the righteous *b* shed upon the
35 from the *b* of righteous Abel
35 unto the *b* of Zacharias son of
26.28 for this is my *b* of the new
27. 4 I have betrayed the innocent *b*.
6 because it is the price of *b*.
8 was called, The field of *b*, unto this
24 I am innocent of the *b* of this just
25 His *b* be on us, and on our children.
Mk 5.25 which had an issue of *b* twelve
29 the fountain of her *b* was dried up;
14.24 This is my *b* of the new testament,
Lk 8.43 having an issue of *b* twelve years,
44 and immediately her issue of *b*
11.50 the *b* of all the prophets, which
51 From the *b* of Abel
51 unto the *b* of Zacharias,
13. 1 whose *b* Pilate had mingled with
22.20 new testament in my *b*, which is
44 great drops of *b* falling down to
Jn 1.13 Which were born, not of *b*, nor of
6.53 Son of man, and drink his *b*, he
54 eateth my flesh, and drinketh my *b*,
55 is meat indeed, and my *b* is drink
56 eateth my flesh, and drinketh my *b*,
19.34 forthwith came there out *b* and
Ac 1.19 that is to say, The field of *b*.
2.19 *b*, and fire, and vapor of smoke:
20 into darkness, and the moon into *b*,
5.28 intend to bring this man's *b* upon

Ac 15.20 from things strangled, and from *b*.
29 offered to idols, and from *b*, and
17.26 hath made of one *b* all nations of
18. 6 Your *b* be upon your own heads; I
20.26 that I am pure from the *b* of all
28 hath purchased with his own *b*.
21.25 from *b*, and from strangled, and
22.20 the *b* of thy martyr Stephen was
Ro 3.15 Their feet are swift to shed *b*:
25 through faith in his *b*, to declare
5. 9 then, being now justified by his *b*,
1Co 10.16 the communion of the *b* of Christ?
11.25 the new testament in my *b*:
27 of the body and *b* of the Lord.
15.50 that flesh and *b* cannot inherit the
Gal 1.16 I conferred not with flesh and *b*:
Eph 1. 7 have redemption through his *b*, the
2.13 are made nigh by the *b* of Christ.
6.12 wrestle not against flesh and *b*,
Col 1.14 redemption through his *b*, even
20 made peace through the *b* of his
Heb 2.14 partakers of flesh and *b*, he also
9. 7 once every year, not without *b*,
12 neither by the *b* of goats and
12 calves, but by his own *b* he
13 For if the *b* of bulls and of goats,
14 How much more shall the *b* of
18 testament was dedicated without *b*.
19 he took the *b* of calves and of
20 Saying, this is the *b* of the
21 sprinkled with *b* both the
22 are by the law purged with *b*; and
22 without shedding of *b* is no
25 the holy place every year with *b* of
10. 4 that the *b* of bulls and of goats
19 to enter into the holiest by the *b* of
29 and hath counted the *b* of the
11.28 passover, and the sprinkling of *b*,
12. 4 not yet resisted unto *b*, striving
24 to the *b* of sprinkling, that
13.11 those beasts, whose *b* is brought
12 sanctify the people with his own *b*,
20 through the *b* of the everlasting
1Pe 1. 2 sprinkling of the *b* of Jesus Christ:
19 with the precious *b* of Christ, as of
1Jn 1. 7 the *b* of Jesus Christ his Son
5. 6 water and *b*, even Jesus Christ;
6 by water only, but by water and *b*.
8 spirit, and the water, and the *b*:
Rev 1. 5 us from our sins in his own *b*,
5. 9 redeemed us to God by thy *b* out of
6.10 thou not judge and avenge our *b*
12 of hair, and the moon became as *b*;
7.14 them white in the *b* of the Lamb.
8. 7 hail and fire mingled with *b*, and
8 third part of the sea became *b*;
11. 6 over waters to turn them to *b*, and
12.11 by the *b* of the Lamb, and by the
14.20 the city, and *b* came out of the
16. 3 it became as the *b* of a dead man:
4 of waters; and they became *b*.
6 shed the *b* of saints and prophets,
6 thou hast given them *b* to drink;
17. 6 drunken with the *b* of the saints,
6 and with the *b* of the martyrs of
18.24 And in her was found the *b* of
19. 2 avenged the *b* of his servants at
13 clothed with a vesture dipped in *b*:

BLOODY

Ex 4.25 Surely a *b* husband art thou to
26 A *b* husband thou art because of
2Sa 16. 7 come out, thou *b* man, and thou
8 because thou art a *b* man.
21. 1 for Saul, and for his *b* house,
Ps 5. 6 Lord will abhor the *b* and
26. 9 with sinners, nor my life with *b*
55.23 *b* and deceitful men shall not
59. 2 iniquity, and save me from *b*
139.19 depart from me therefore, ye *b*
Eze 7.23 the land is full of *b* crimes, and
22. 2 wilt thou judge the *b* city? yea,
24. 6 Woe to the *b* city, to the pot
9 Woe to the *b* city! I will even
Na 3. 1 Woe to the *b* city! it is all full
Ac 28. 8 lay sick of a fever and of a *b* flux:

BLOSSOM

Nu 17. 5 whom I shall choose, shall *b*:
Isa 5.24 and their *b* shall go up as dust:
27. 6 Israel shall *b* and bud, and fill
35. 1 shall rejoice, and *b* as the rose.
2 It shall *b* abundantly, and rejoice
Hab 3.17 Although the fig tree shall not *b*,

BLOSSOMS

Gen 40.10 it budded, and her *b* shot forth;
Nu 17. 8 and bloomed *b*, and yielded

BLOT

Ex 32.32 *b* me, I pray thee, out of thy book
33 him will I *b* out of my book.
Nu 5.23 and he shall *b* them out with the
Dt 9.14 and *b* out their name from under
25.19 *b* out the remembrance of Amalek
29.20 the Lord shall *b* out his name
2Ki 14.27 he would *b* out the name of Israel
Job 31. 7 if any *b* hath cleaved to mine
Ps 51. 1 mercies *b* out my transgressions.
9 sins, and *b* out all mine iniquities.
Pr 9. 7 wicked man getteth himself a *b*.
Jer 18.23 neither *b* out their sin from thy
Rev 3. 5 I will not *b* out his name out of

BLOTTED

Neh 4. 5 let not their sin be *b* out from
Ps 69.28 Let them be *b* out of the book
109.13 following let their name be *b* out.
14 the sin of his mother be *b* out.
Isa 44.22 *b* out, as a thick cloud, thy
Ac 3.19 your sins may be *b* out, when

BLOTTING

Col 2.14 *B* out the handwriting of

BLOWETH

Isa 18. 3 when he *b* a trumpet, hear ye.
40. 7 the spirit of the Lord *b* upon it:
54.16 the smith that *b* the coals in the
Jn 3. 8 the wind *b* where it listeth,

BLUE

Ex 25. 4 And *b*, and purple, and scarlet,
26. 1 twined linen, and *b*, and purple,
4 thou shalt make loops of *b* upon
31 shalt make a vail of *b*, and purple,
36 for the door of the tent, of *b*,
27.16 an hanging of twenty cubits, of *b*,
28. 5 shall take gold, and *b*, and purple,
6 make the ephod of gold, of *b*,
8 even of gold, of *b*, and purple,
15 thou shalt make it; of gold, of *b*,
28 the ephod with a lace of *b*, that it
31 the robe of the ephod all of *b*.
33 shalt make pomegranates of *b*,
37 thou shalt put it on a *b* lace, that
35. 6 And *b*, and purple, and scarlet,
23 man with whom was found *b*,
25 spun, both of *b*, and of purple,
35 and of the embroiderer, in *b*,
36. 8 twined linen, and *b*, and purple,
11 he made loops of *b* on the edge
35 he made a vail of *b*, and purple,
37 for the tabernacle door of *b*,
38.18 the court was needlework, of *b*,
23 embroiderer in *b*, and in purple,
39. 1 of the *b*, and purple, and scarlet,
2 the ephod of gold, *b*, and purple,
3 it into wires, to work it in the *b*,
5 thereof; of gold, *b*, and purple,
8 of gold, *b*, and purple, and scarlet,
21 the ephod with a lace of *b*, that it
22 ephod of woven work, all of *b*.
24 of the robe pomegranates of *b*,
29 twined linen, and *b*, and purple,
31 they tied unto it a lace of *b*, to
Nu 4. 6 spread over it a cloth wholly of *b*,
7 they shall spread a cloth of *b*,
9 they shall take a cloth of *b*, and
11 spread a cloth of *b*, and cover it
12 and put them in a cloth of *b*,
15.38 of the borders a ribband of *b*:
2Ch 2. 7 in purple, and crimson, and *b*,
14 in *b*, and in fine linen, and in
3.14 he made the vail of *b*, and purple,
Est 1. 6 white, green, and *b*, hangings,
7. 6 *b*, and white, and black, marble.
8.15 the king in royal apparel of *b*
Jer 10. 9 *b* and purple is their clothing:
Eze 23. 6 were clothed with *b*, captains
27. 7 *b* and purple from the isles
24 in *b* clothes, and broidered work,

BLUNT

Ec 10.10 If the iron be *b*, and he do not

BLUSH

Ezr 9. 6 I am ashamed and *b* to lift
Jer 6.15 ashamed, neither could they *b*:
8.12 neither could they *b*: therefore

BOANERGES

Mk 3.17 he surnamed them *B*, which is,

BOAR

Ps 80.13 *b* out of the wood doth waste it,

BOAST

1Ki 20.11 that girdeth on his harness *b*
2Ch 25.19 thine heart lifteth thee up to *b*:
Ps 34. 2 My soul shall make her *b* in the
44. 8 In God we *b* all the day long,
49. 6 trust in their wealth, and *b*
94. 4 workers of iniquity *b* themselves?
97. 7 images, that *b* themselves of
Pr 27. 1 *B* not thyself of to morrow; for
Isa 10.15 Shall the axe *b* itself against him
61. 6 their glory shall ye *b* yourselves.
Ro 2.17 law, and makest thy *b* of God,
23 Thou that makest thy *b* of the
11.18 *B* not against the branches. But
18 if thou *b*, thou bearest not
2Co 9. 2 for which I *b* of you to them of
10. 8 though I should *b* somewhat
13 we will not *b* of things without
16 not to *b* in another man's line
11.16 me, that I may *b* myself a little.
Eph 2. 9 of works, lest any man should *b*.

BOASTED

Eze 35.13 with your mouth ye have *b*
2Co 7.14 I have *b* any thing to him of

BOASTERS

Ro 1.30 despiteful, proud, *b*, inventors
2Ti 3. 2 covetous, *b*, proud, blasphemers,

BOASTETH

Ps 10. 3 wicked *b* of his heart's desire,
Pr 20.14 he is gone his way, then he *b*.
25.14 Whoso *b* himself of a false gift
Jas 3. 5 little member, and *b* great

BOASTING

Ac 5.36 Theudas, *b* himself to be
Ro 3.27 Where is *b* then? It is excluded.
2Co 7.14 even so our *b*, which I made
8.24 love, and of our *b* on your behalf.
9. 3 lest our *b* of you should be in
4 in this same confident *b*.
10.15 Not *b* of things without our
11.10 no man shall stop me of this *b*
17 in this confidence of *b*.

BOAT

2Sa 19.18 And there went over a ferry *b*
Jn 6.22 that there was none other *b* there,
22 with his disciples into the *b*,
Ac 27.16 much work to come by the *b*:
30 when they had let down the *b*
32 cut off the ropes of the *b*, and

BOATS

Jn 6.23 (Howbeit there came other *b*

BODIES

Gen 47.18 lord, but our *b*, and our lands:
1Sa 31.12 body of Saul and the *b* of his
1Ch 10.12 away the body of Saul, and the *b*
2Ch 20.24 they were dead *b* fallen to the
25 riches with the dead *b*, and
Neh 9.37 they have dominion over our *b*,
Job 13.12 ashes, your *b* to *b* of clay.
Ps 79. 2 The dead *b* of thy servants have
110. 6 fill the places with the dead *b*,
Jer 31.40 the whole valley of the dead *b*,
33. 5 the dead *b* of men, whom I have
34.20 and their dead *b* shall be for
41. 9 the dead *b* of the men, whom he
Eze 1.11 another, and two covered their *b*.
23 covered on that side, their *b*.
Dan 3.27 upon whose *b* the fire had no
28 and yielded their *b*, that they
Am 8. 3 there shall be many dead *b* in
Mt 27.52 and many *b* of the saints which
Jn 19.31 the *b* should not remain upon
Ro 1.24 to dishonor their own *b* between
8.11 shall also quicken your mortal *b*
12. 1 that ye present your *b* a living
1Co 6.15 that your *b* are the members of
15.40 also celestial *b*, and *b* terrestrial:
Eph 5.28 to love their wives as their own *b*.
Heb 10.22 and our *b* washed with pure
13.11 For the *b* of those beasts, whose
Rev 11. 8 And their dead *b* shall lie in the
9 shall see their dead *b* three days
9 shall not suffer their dead *b* to be

BODILY

Lk 3.22 Holy Ghost descended in a *b*
2Co 10.10 but his *b* presence is weak, and
Col 2. 9 all the fulness of the Godhead *b*.
1Ti 4. 8 For *b* exercise profiteth little:

BODY

Ex 24.10 and as it were the *b* of heaven in
Lev 21.11 any dead *b*, nor defile himself
Nu 6. 6 Lord he shall come at no dead *b*.
9. 6 defiled by the dead *b* of a man,
7 we are defiled by the dead *b* of a
10 unclean by reason of a dead *b*,
19.11 He that toucheth the dead *b* of
13 Whosoever toucheth the dead *b* of
16 or a dead *b*, or a bone of a man,
Dt 21.23 His *b* shall not remain all
28. 4 Blessed shall be the fruit of thy *b*,
11 in goods, in the fruit of thy *b*,
18 Cursed shall be the fruit of thy *b*,
53 shalt eat the fruit of thine own *b*,
30. 9 in the fruit of thy *b*, and in the
Jdg 8.30 threescore and ten sons of his *b*
1Sa 31.10 they fastened his *b* to the wall of
12 took the *b* of Saul and the bodies
2Ki 8. 5 he had restored a dead *b* to life,
1Ch 10.12 took away the *b* of Saul, and the
Job 19.17 children's sake of mine own *b*.
26 worms destroy this *b*, yet in
20.25 drawn, and cometh out of the *b*;
Ps 132.11 fruit of thy *b*, will I set upon
Pr 5.11 when thy flesh and thy *b* are
Isa 10.18 both soul and *b*: and they shall
26.19 with my dead *b* shall they arise.
51.23 thou hast laid thy *b* as the
Jer 26.23 and cast his dead *b* into the
36.30 and his dead *b* shall be cast out

Biblical Themes

BODY

So God created man in his own image, in the image of God created he him; male and female created he them. Gen 1.27

And the rib, which the Lord God had taken from man, made he a woman, and brought her unto the man. Gen 2.22

Behold, Esau my brother is a hairy man, and I am a smooth man. Gen 27.11

And when he saw that he prevailed not against him, he touched the hollow of his thigh; and the hollow of Jacob's thigh was out of joint, as he wrestled with him. Gen 32.25

And if any mischief follow, then thou shalt give life for life, eye for eye, tooth for tooth, hand for hand, foot for foot. Ex 21.23-24

And he sent, and brought him in. Now he was ruddy, and withal of a beautiful countenance, and goodly to look to. 1Sa 16.12

Nevertheless in the time of his old age he was diseased in his feet. 1Ki 15.23

And though after my skin worms destroy this body, yet in my flesh shall I see God. Job 19.26

How beautiful are thy feet with shoes, O prince's daughter! the joints of thy thighs are like jewels, the work of the hands of a cunning workman. Thy navel is like a round goblet, which wanteth not liquor: thy belly is like an heap of wheat set about with lilies. Thy two breasts are like two young roes that are twins. SS 7.1-3

But the very hairs of your head are all numbered. Mt 10.30

And if thine eye offend thee, pluck it out, and cast it from thee: it is better for thee to enter into life with one eye, rather than having two eyes to be cast into hell fire. Mt 18.9

The spirit indeed is willing, but the flesh is weak. Mt 26.41

And they entered in, and found not the body of the Lord Jesus. Lk 24.3

I beseech you therefore, brethren, by the mercies of God, that ye present your bodies a living sacrifice, holy, acceptable unto God, which is your reasonable service. Ro 12.1

What? know ye not that your body is the temple of the Holy Ghost which is in you, which ye have of God, and ye are not your own? 1Co 6.19

And when he had given thanks, he brake it, and said, Take, eat: this is my body, which is broken for you: this do in remembrance of me. 1Co 11.24

The body is not one member but many. If the foot shall say, Because I am not the hand, I am not of the body; is it therefore not of the body? And if the ear shall say, Because I am not the eye, I am not of the body; is it therefore not of the body? If the whole body were an eye, where were the hearing? If the whole were hearing, where were the smelling? But now hath God set the members every one of them in the body, as it hath pleased him. 1Co 12.14-18

It is sown a natural body; it is raised a spiritual body. 1Co 15.44

There was given to me a thorn in the flesh, the messenger of Satan to buffet me, lest I should be exalted above measure. 2Co 12.7

La 4. 7 they were more ruddy in *b* than
Eze 10.12 And their whole *b*, and their
Dan 4.33 his *b* was wet with the dew of
5.21 his *b* was wet with the dew of
7.11 and his *b* destroyed, and given to
15 in my spirit in the midst of my *b*,
10. 6 His *b* also was like the beryl,
Mic 6. 7 the fruit of my *b* for the sin of
Hag 2.13 unclean by a dead *b* touch any
Mt 5.29 not that thy whole *b* should be
30 that thy whole *b* should be cast
6.22 The light of the *b* is the eye: if
22 thy whole *b* shall be full of light.
23 thy whole *b* shall be full of
25 nor yet for your *b*, what ye shall
25 more than meat, and the *b* than
10.28 fear not them which kill the *b*,
28 able to destroy both soul and *b* in
14.12 came, and took up the *b*, and
26.12 hath poured this ointment on my *b*,
26 and said, Take, eat; this is my *b*.
27.58 begged the *b* of Jesus. Then
58 Pilate commanded the *b* to be
59 when Joseph had taken the *b*,
Mk 5.29 and she felt in her *b* that she was
14. 8 aforehand to anoint my *b* to the
22 and said, Take, eat: this is my *b*.
51 cloth cast about his naked *b*;
15.43 unto Pilate, and craved the *b* of
45 of the centurion, he gave the *b*
Lk 11.34 The light of the *b* is the eye:
11.34 is single, thy whole *b* also is full

Lk 11.34 evil, thy *b* also is full of darkness.
36 If thy whole *b* therefore be full of
12. 4 not afraid of them that kill the *b*,
22 neither for the *b*, what ye shall
23 than meat, and the *b* is more
17.37 Wheresoever the *b* is, thither will
22.19 This is my *b* which is given for
23.52 unto Pilate, and begged the *b* of
55 sepulchre, and how his *b* was laid,
24. 3 and found not the *b* of the Lord
23 when they found not his *b*, they
Jn 2.21 he spake of the temple of his *b*.
19.38 that he might take away the *b* of
38 came therefore, and took the *b*
40 Then took they the *b* of Jesus,
20.12 the feet, where the *b* of Jesus had
Ac 9.40 and turning him to the *b* said,
19.12 So that from his *b* were brought
Ro 4.19 he considered not his own *b* now
6. 6 the *b* of sin might be destroyed,
12 reign in your mortal *b*, that ye
7. 4 dead to the law by the *b* of Christ;
24 shall deliver me from the *b* of this
8.10 the *b* is dead because of sin; but
13 do mortify the deeds of the *b*, ye
23 to wit, the redemption of our *b*.
12. 4 we have many members in one *b*,
5 being many, are one *b* in Christ,
1Co 5. 3 For I verily, as absent in *b*, but
6.13 Now the *b* is not for fornication,
13 and the Lord for the *b*.
16 is joined to an harlot is one *b*?
18 that a man doeth is without the *b*;
18 sinneth against his own *b*.
19 your *b* is the temple of the Holy
20 therefore glorify God in your *b*,
7. 4 wife hath not power of her own *b*,
4 hath not power of his own *b*,
34 she may be holy both in *b* and in
9.27 But I keep under my *b*, and bring
10.16 is it not the communion of the *b*
17 many are one bread, and one *b*:
11.24 Take, eat: this is my *b*, which is
27 shall be guilty of the *b* and blood
29 not discerning the Lord's *b*.
12.12 For as the *b* is one, and hath many
12 the members of that one *b*, being
12 are one *b*: so also is Christ.
13 are we all baptized into one *b*,
14 For the *b* is not one member, but
15 I am not of the *b*; is it
15 therefore not of the *b*?
16 I am not of the *b*; is it
16 therefore not of the *b*?
17 If the whole *b* were an eye, where
18 every one of them in the *b*, as it
19 all one member, where were the *b*?
20 many members, yet but one *b*.
22 those members of the *b* which
23 And those members of the *b*
24 but God hath tempered the *b*
25 should be no schism in the *b*;
27 Now ye are the *b* of Christ, and
13. 3 though I give my *b* to be burned,
15.35 and with what *b* do they come?
37 thou sowest not that *b* that shall
38 But God giveth it a *b* as it hath
38 him, and to every seed his own *b*.
44 It is sown a natural *b*;
44 it is raised a spiritual *b*.
44 There is a natural *b*,
44 and there is a spiritual *b*.
2Co 4.10 bearing about in the *b* the dying
10 might be made manifest in our *b*.
5. 6 whilst we are at home in the *b*, we
8 rather to be absent from the *b*,
10 receive the things done in his *b*,
12. 2 the *b*, I cannot tell;
2 or whether out of the *b*,
3 in the *b*, or out of the *b*, I cannot
Gal 6.17 I bear in my *b* the marks of the
Eph 1.23 Which is his *b*; the fulness of him
2.16 unto God in one *b* by the cross,
3. 6 fellow heirs, and of the same *b*,
4. 4 There is one *b*, and one Spirit,
12 ministry, for the edifying of the *b*
16 From whom the whole *b* fitly
16 maketh increase of the *b* unto
5.23 and he is the saviour of the *b*.
30 For we are members of his *b*, of
Php 1.20 Christ shall be magnified in my *b*,
3.21 Who shall change our vile *b*, that
21 like unto his glorious *b*, according
Col 1.18 And he is the head of the *b*, the
22 In the *b* of his flesh through
2.11 putting off the *b* of the sins of the
17 of things to come; but the *b* is of
19 from which all the *b* by joints and
23 humility, and neglecting of the *b*;
3.15 which also ye are called in one *b*;
1Th 5.23 and *b* be preserved blameless
Heb 10. 5 but a *b* hast thou prepared me:
10 through the offering of the *b* of
13. 3 as being yourselves also in the *b*.
Jas 2.16 things which are needful to the *b*;
26 as the *b* without the spirit is dead,
3. 2 able also to bridle the whole *b*.
3 and to turn about their whole *b*.
6 that it defileth the whole *b*, and
1Pe 2.24 bare our sins in his own *b* on the
Jude 9 he disputed about the *b* of Moses,

BODY'S

Col 1.24 in my flesh for his *b* sake, which

BOILS

Ex 9.11 before Moses because of the *b*;
Job 2. 7 smote Job with sore *b* from the

BOISTEROUS

Mt 14.30 when he saw the wind *b*, he was

BOLD

Pr 28. 1 but the righteous are *b* as a lion.
Ac 13.46 Paul and Barnabas waxed *b*,
Ro 10.20 Esaias is very *b*, and saith, I was
2Co 10. 1 being absent am *b* toward you:
2 that I may not be *b* when I am
2 wherewith I think to be *b* against
11.21 whereinsoever any is *b*, (I speak
21 foolishly,) I am *b* also.
Php 1.14 much more *b* to speak the word
1Th 2. 2 we were *b* in our God to speak
Phm 8 I might be much *b* in Christ

BOLDLY

Gen 34.25 came upon the city *b*, and slew
Mk 15.43 and went in *b* unto Pilate, and
Jn 7.26 But, lo, he speaketh *b*, and they
Ac 9.27 he had preached *b* at Damascus
29 spake *b* in the name of the Lord
14. 3 speaking *b* in the Lord, which
18.26 to speak *b* in the synagogue:
19. 8 spake *b* for the space of three
Ro 15.15 I have written the more *b* unto
Eph 6.19 may open my mouth *b*, to make
20 may speak *b*, as I ought to speak.
Heb 4.16 Let us therefore come *b* unto
13. 6 So that we may *b* say, The Lord

BOLDNESS

Ec 8. 1 the *b* of his face shall be changed.
Ac 4.13 they saw the *b* of Peter and John,
29 all *b* they may speak thy word,
31 they spake the word of God with *b*.
2Co 7. 4 Great is my *b* of speech toward
Eph 3.12 In whom we have *b* and access
Php 1.20 but that with all *b*, as always,
1Ti 3.13 great *b* in the faith which is in
Heb 10.19 *b* to enter into the holiest by the
1Jn 4.17 have *b* in the day of judgment:

BOND

Nu 30. 2 an oath to bind his soul with a *b*;
3 bind herself by a *b*, being in her
4 and her *b* wherewith she hath
4 every *b* wherewith she hath bound
10 bound her soul by a *b* with an oath;
11 and every *b* wherewith she bound
12 or concerning the *b* of her soul,
Job 12.18 He looseth the *b* of kings, and
Eze 20.37 I will bring you into the *b* of the
Lk 13.16 be loosed from this *b* on the
Ac 8.23 bitterness, and in the *b* of
1Co 12.13 whether we be *b* or free; and
Gal 3.28 there is neither *b* nor free, there
Eph 4. 3 of the Spirit in the *b* of peace.
6. 8 Lord, whether he be *b* or free.
Col 3.11 Barbarian, Scythian, *b* nor free:
14 which is the *b* of perfectness.
Rev 13.16 rich and poor, free and *b*, to
19.18 flesh of all men, both free and *b*,

BONDAGE

Ex 1.14 their lives bitter with hard *b*,
2.23 sighed by reason of the *b*,
23 up unto God by reason of the *b*.
6. 5 whom the Egyptians keep in *b*;
6 and I will rid you out of their *b*,
9 anguish of spirit, and for cruel *b*.
13. 3 out of the house of *b*; for by
14 from Egypt, from the house of *b*:
20. 2 of Egypt, out of the house of *b*.
Dt 5. 6 of Egypt, from the house of *b*.
6.12 of Egypt, from the house of *b*.
8.14 of Egypt, from the house of *b*;
13. 5 you out of the house of *b*,
10 of Egypt, from the house of *b*.
26. 6 us, and laid upon us hard *b*:
Jos 24.17 from the house of *b*, and which
Jdg 6. 8 you forth out of the house of *b*;
Ezr 9. 8 give us a little reviving in our *b*.
9 hath not forsaken us in our *b*,
Neh 5. 5 we bring into *b* our sons and our
5 our daughters are brought unto *b*
18 because the *b* was heavy upon
9.17 a captain to return to their *b*:
Isa 14. 3 the hard *b* wherein thou wast
Jn 8.33 and were never in *b* to any man:
Ac 7. 6 they should bring them into *b*,
7 to whom they shall be in *b* will
Ro 8.15 received the spirit of *b* again to
21 shall be delivered from the *b* of
1Co 7.15 a sister is not under *b* in such
2Co 11.20 if a man bring you into *b*,
Gal 2. 4 that they might bring us into *b*:
4. 3 were in *b* under the elements of
9 ye desire again to be in *b*?
24 which gendereth to *b*, which is
25 and is in *b* with her children.
5. 1 again with the yoke of *b*.
Heb 2.15 all their lifetime subject to *b*.
2Pe 2.19 of the same is he brought in *b*.

BONDMAN

Gen 44.33 instead of the lad a *b* to my lord;
Dt 15.15 remember that thou wast a *b* in
16.12 remember that thou wast a *b* in
24.18 thou wast a *b* in Egypt, and the
22 a *b* in the land of Egypt:
Rev 6.15 every *b*, and every free man, hid

BONDS

Nu 30. 5 or of her *b* wherewith she
7 and her *b* wherewith she bound
14 or all her *b*, which are upon her:
Ps 116.16 handmaid: thou hast loosed my *b*.
Jer 5. 5 broken the yoke, and burst the *b*.
27. 2 Make thee *b* and yokes, and put
30. 8 burst thy *b*, and strangers shall
Na 1.13 and will burst thy *b* in sunder.
Ac 20.23 saying that *b* and afflictions
23.29 charge worthy of death or of *b*.

25.14 a certain man left in *b* by Felix:
26.29 such as I am, except these *b*.
31 nothing worthy of death or of *b*.
Eph 6.20 which I am an ambassador in *b*:
Php 1. 7 as both in my *b*, and in the
13 So that my *b* in Christ are
14 waxing confident by my *b*, are
16 to add affliction to my *b*:
Col 4. 3 for which I am also in *b*:
18 Remember my *b*. Grace be with
2Ti 2. 9 as an evil doer, even unto *b*;
Phm 10 whom I have begotten in my *b*:
13 have ministered unto me in the *b*
Heb 10.34 had compassion of me in my *b*,
11.36 moreover of *b* and imprisonment:
13. 3 Remember them that are in *b*,

BONDWOMAN
Gen 21.10 Cast out this *b* and her son: for
10 the son of this *b* shall not be heir
12 because of thy *b*; in all that Sarah
13 the son of the *b* will I make a
Gal 4.23 he who was of the *b* was born
30 Cast out the *b* and her son:
30 for the son of the *b* shall not be
31 children of the *b*, but of the free.

BONE
Gen 2.23 This is now *b* of my bones, and
29.14 thou art my *b* and my flesh.
Ex 12.46 neither shall ye break a *b* thereof.
Nu 9.12 nor break any *b* of it:
19.16 a dead body, or a *b* of a man,
18 him that touched a *b*, or one slain,
Jdg 9. 2 that I am your *b* and your flesh.
2Sa 5. 1 Behold, we are thy *b* and thy flesh.
19.13 Art thou not of my *b*, and of my
1Ch 11. 1 Behold, we are thy *b* and thy flesh.
Job 2. 5 touch his *b* and his flesh, and he
19.20 My *b* cleaveth to my skin and to
31.22 mine arm be broken from the *b*.
Ps 3. 7 all mine enemies upon the cheek *b*;
Eze 37. 7 bones came together, *b* to his *b*.
39.15 when any seeth a man's *b*, then
Jn 19.36 A *b* of him shall not be broken.

BONES
Gen 2.23 bone of my *b*, and flesh of my
50.25 shall carry up my *b* from hence.
Ex 13.19 took the *b* of Joseph with him:
19 ye shall carry up my *b* away hence
Nu 24. 8 break their *b*, and pierce them
Jos 24.32 *b* of Joseph, which the children
Jdg 19.29 divided her, together with her *b*,
1Sa 31.13 took their *b*, and buried them
2Sa 19.12 ye are my *b* and my flesh:
21.12 went and took the *b* of Saul
12 and the *b* of Jonathan
13 *b* of Saul and the *b* of Jonathan
13 the *b* of them that were hanged.
14 the *b* of Saul and Jonathan
1Ki 13. 2 men's *b* shall be burnt upon thee.
31 buried; lay my *b* beside his *b*:
2Ki 13.21 and touched the *b* of Elisha,
23.14 their places with the *b* of men.
16 took the *b* out of the sepulchres,
18 let no man move his *b*. So they let
18 his *b* alone, with the *b* of the
20 men's *b* upon them, and returned
1Ch 10.12 buried their *b* under the oak in
2Ch 34. 5 *b* of the priests upon their altars,
Job 4.14 which made all my *b* to shake.
10.11 fenced me with *b* and sinews.
20.11 His *b* are full of the sin of his
21.24 his *b* are moistened with marrow.
30.17 My *b* are pierced in me in the
30 and my *b* are burned with heat.
33.19 of his *b* with strong pain:
21 *b* that were not seen stick out.
40.18 *b* are as strong as pieces of
18 his *b* are like bars of iron.
Ps 6. 2 heal me; for my *b* are vexed.
22.14 all my *b* are out of joint:
17 all my *b*: they look and stare
31.10 and my *b* are consumed.
32. 3 *b* waxed old through my roaring
34.20 He keepeth all his *b*: not one of
35.10 All my *b* shall say, Lord, who is
38. 3 neither is there any rest in my *b*
42.10 with a sword in my *b*,
51. 8 the *b* which thou hast broken
53. 5 God hath scattered the *b* of him
102. 3 my *b* are burned as an hearth.
5 my *b* cleave to my skin.
109.18 water, and like oil into his *b*.
141. 7 Our *b* are scattered at the grave's
Pr 3. 8 thy navel, and marrow to thy *b*.
12. 4 is as rottenness in his *b*.
14.30 but envy the rottenness of the *b*.
15.30 a good report maketh the *b* fat.
16.24 to the soul and health to the *b*.
17.22 a broken spirit drieth the *b*.
25.15 a soft tongue breaketh the *b*.
Ec 11. 5 how the *b* do grow in the womb
Isa 38.13 lion, so will he break all my *b*:
58.11 drought and make fat thy *b*:
66.14 and your *b* shall flourish like an
Jer 8. 1 the *b* of the kings of Judah,
1 and the *b* of his princes,
1 and the *b* of the priests,
1 and the *b* of the prophets,
1 and the *b* of the inhabitants
20. 9 as a burning fire shut up in my *b*,
23. 9 all my *b* shake; I am like a
50.17 king of Babylon hath broken his *b*.
La 1.13 he sent fire into my *b*, and it
3. 4 made old; he hath broken my *b*.
4. 8 their skin cleaveth to their *b*;
Eze 6. 5 scatter your *b* round about your
24. 4 fill it with the choice *b*.
5 burn also the *b* under it,
5 let them seethe the *b* of it
10 it well, and let the *b* be burned.
32.27 iniquities shall be upon their *b*,
37. 1 the valley which was full of *b*,
3 Son of man, can these *b* live?
4 upon these *b*, and say unto them,
4 O ye dry *b*, hear the word
5 saith the Lord God unto these *b*;
7 *b* came together bone to his bone.
11 these *b* are the whole house of
11 Our *b* are dried, and our hope is
Dan 6.24 and brake all their *b* in pieces or
Am 2. 1 burned the *b* of the king of Edom
6.10 to bring out the *b* out of the house,
Mic 3. 2 their flesh from off their *b*;
3 they break their *b*, and chop them
Hab 3.16 rottenness entered into my *b*, and
Zep 3. 3 gnaw not the *b* till the morrow.
Mt 23.27 full of dead men's *b*, and of all
Lk 24.39 hath not flesh and *b*, as ye see
Ac 3. 7 feet and ankle *b* received
Eph 5.30 body, of his flesh, and of his *b*.
Heb 11.22 commandment concerning his *b*.

BOOK
Gen 5. 1 This is the *b* of the generations of
Ex 17.14 Write this for a memorial in a *b*,
24. 7 he took the *b* of the covenant, and
32.32 blot me, I pray thee, out of thy *b*
33 me, him will I blot out of my *b*.
Nu 5.23 shall write these curses in a *b*,
21.14 it is said in the *b* of the wars of
Dt 17.18 him a copy of this law in a *b* out
28.58 this law that are written in this *b*,
61 which is not written in the *b* of
29.20 curses that are written in this *b*
21 that are written in this *b* of the
27 curses that are written in this *b*:
30.10 statutes which are written in this *b*
31.24 the words of this law in a *b*,
26 Take this *b* of the law and put it
Jos 1. 8 This *b* of the law shall not depart
8.31 it is written in the *b* of the law
34 all that is written in the *b* of the
10.13 Is not this written in the *b* of
18. 9 by cities into seven parts in a *b*,
23. 6 all that is written in the *b* of the
24.26 wrote these words in the *b* of the
1Sa 10.25 wrote it in a *b*, and laid it up
2Sa 1.18 behold, it is written in the *b* of
1Ki 11.41 they not written in the *b* of the
14.19 *b* of the chronicles of...Israel?
29 *b* of the chronicles of...Israel?
15. 7, 23 *b* of the chronicles of...Judah?
2Ki 1.18 *b* of the chronicles of...Israel?
8.23 *b* of the chronicles of...Judah?
13.12 are they not written in the *b* of the
14. 6 which is written in the *b* of the law
22. 8 I have found the *b* of the law in
8 Hilkiah gave the *b* to Shaphan
10 the priest hath delivered me a *b*.
11 king had heard the words of the *b*
13 concerning the words of this *b*
13 hearkened unto the words of this *b*,
16 all the words of the *b* which the
23. 2 all the words of the *b* of the
3 that were written in this *b*.
21 written in the *b* of this covenant.
24 law which were written in the *b*
28 written in the *b* of the chronicles
24. 5 did, are they not written in the *b*
1Ch 9. 1 were written in the *b* of the kings
29.29 behold, they are written in the *b*
29 in the *b* of Nathan the prophet,
29 and in the *b* of Gad the seer,
2Ch 9.29 in the *b* of Nathan the prophet,
12.15 in the *b* of Shemaiah the
16.11 are written in the *b* of the kings
17. 9 had the *b* of the law of the Lord
20.34 in the *b* of Jehu the son of
34 who is mentioned in the *b* of the
24.27 in the story of the *b* of the kings.
25. 4 in the law in the *b* of Moses,
26 in the *b* of the kings of Judah and
27. 7 they are written in the *b* of the
28.26 in the *b* of the kings of Judah and
32.32 in the *b* of the kings of Judah and
33.18 written in the *b* of the kings of
34.14 Hilkiah the priest found a *b* of
15 I have found the *b* of the law in
15 And Hilkiah delivered the *b* to
16 Shaphan carried the *b* to the king,
18 the priest hath given me a *b*.
21 concerning the words of the *b*
21 after all that is written in this *b*.
24 curses that are written in the *b*
30 all the words of the *b* of the
31 which are written in this *b*.
35.12 as it is written in the *b* of Moses.
27 in the *b* of the kings of Israel
36. 8 they are written in the *b* of the
Ezr 4.15 search may be made in the *b* of
15 so shalt thou find it in the *b* of the
6.18 as it is written in the *b* of Moses.
Neh 8. 1 bring the *b* of the law of Moses,
3 people were attentive unto the *b*
5 And Ezra opened the *b* in the
8 they read in the *b* in the law of
18 last day, he read in the *b* of the
9. 3 read in the *b* of the law of the
12.23 written in the *b* of the chronicles,
13. 1 they read in the *b* of Moses in the
Est 2.23 written in the *b* of the chronicles
6. 1 he commanded to bring the *b* of
9.32 Purim; and it was written in the *b*.
10. 2 in the *b* of the chronicles of the
Job 19.23 oh that they were printed in a *b*!
31.35 mine adversary had written a *b*.
Ps 40. 7 in the volume of the *b* it is
56. 8 thy bottle: are they not in thy *b*?
69.28 Let them be blotted out of the *b* of
139.16 in thy *b* all my members were

Isa 29.11 the words of a *b* that is sealed,
12 And the *b* is delivered to him that
18 the deaf hear the words of the *b*,
30. 8 and note it in a *b*, that it may be
34.16 Seek ye out of the *b* of the Lord
Jer 25.13 even all that is written in this *b*,
30. 2 I have spoken unto thee in a *b*.
32.12 subscribed the *b* of the purchase,
36. 2 Take thee a roll of a *b*, and write
4 unto him, upon a roll of a *b*.
8 reading in the *b* the words of the
10 Then read Baruch in the *b* the
11 out of the *b* all the words of the
13 Baruch read the *b* in the ears of
18 I wrote them with ink in the *b*.
32 all the words of the *b* which
45. 1 he had written these words in a *b*
51.60 Jeremiah wrote in a *b* all the evil
63 made an end of reading this *b*,
Eze 2. 9 and, lo, a roll of a *b* was therein;
Dan 12. 1 shall be found written in the *b*.
4 shut up the words, and seal the *b*,
Na 1. 1 The *b* of the vision of Nahum the
Mal 3.16 and a *b* of remembrance was
Mt 1. 1 The *b* of the generation of Jesus
Mk 12.26 have ye not read in the *b* of Moses,
Lk 3. 4 As it is written in the *b* of the
4.17 delivered unto him the *b* of the
17 And when he had opened the *b*, he
20 he closed the *b*, and he gave it
20.42 David himself saith in the *b* of
Jn 20.30 which are not written in this *b*:
Ac 1.20 For it is written in the *b* of
7.42 as it is written in the *b* of the
Gal 3.10 things which are written in the *b*
Php 4. 3 whose names are in the *b* of life.
Heb 9.19 sprinkled both the *b*, and all the
10. 7 (in the volume of the *b* it is
Rev 1.11 What thou seest, write in a *b*, and
3. 5 blot out his name out of the *b* of
5. 1 on the throne a *b* written within
2 Who is worthy to open the *b*, and
3 was able to open the *b*, neither to
4 worthy to open and to read the *b*,
5 hath prevailed to open the *b*, and
7 he came and took the *b* out of the
8 when he had taken the *b*, the four
9 Thou art worthy to take the *b*, and
10. 2 he had in his hand a little *b* open:
8 Go and take the little *b* which
9 said unto him, Give me the little *b*.
10 I took the little *b* out of the
13. 8 not written in the *b* of life of the
17. 8 names were not written in the *b*
20.12 and another *b* was opened,
12 which is the *b* of life:
15 was not found written in the *b*
21.27 written in the Lamb's *b* of life.
22. 7 sayings of the prophecy of this *b*.
9 which keep the sayings of this *b*:
10 sayings of the prophecy of this *b*:
18 words of the prophecy of this *b*,
18 plagues that are written in this *b*:
19 take away from the words of the *b*
19 take away his part out of the *b* of
19 things which are written in this *b*.

BOOKS

Ec 12.12 making many *b* there is no end;
Dan 7.10 judgment was set, and the *b*
9. 2 I Daniel understood by *b* the
Jn 21.25 could not contain the *b* that
Ac 19.19 brought their *b* together, and
2Ti 4.13 bring with thee, and the *b*, but
Rev 20.12 the *b* were opened: and another
12 which were written in the *b*,

BORN

Gen 4.18 And unto Enoch was *b* Irad:
26 to him also there was *b* a son;
6. 1 and daughters were *b* unto them,
10. 1 them were sons *b* after the flood.
21 even to him were children *b*.
25 unto Eber were *b* two sons: the
14.14 *b* in his own house, three
15. 3 one *b* in my house is mine heir.
17.12 he that is *b* in the house, or
13 He that is *b* in thy house, and
17 Shall a child be *b* unto him that
23 all that were *b* in his house,
27 men of his house, *b* in the house,
21. 3 his son that was *b* unto him, whom
5 his son Isaac was *b* unto him.
7 I have *b* him a son in his old age.
9 which she had *b* unto Abraham,
22.20 she hath also *b* children unto
24.15 was *b* to Bethuel, son of Milcah,
29.34 because I have *b* him three sons:
30.20 I have *b* him six sons: and she
25 Rachel had *b* Joseph, that Jacob
31.43 children which they have *b*?
35.26 were *b* to him in Padan-aram.
36. 5 *b* unto him in the land of Canaan.
41.50 And unto Joseph were *b* two sons
46.20 land of Egypt were *b* Manasseh
22 of Rachel, which were *b* to Jacob:
27 which were *b* him in Egypt, were
48. 5 Manasseh, which were *b* unto thee
Ex 1.22 Every son that is *b* ye shall cast
12.19 be a stranger, or *b* in the land.
48 be as one that is *b* in the land.
21. 4 have *b* him sons or daughters;
Lev 12. 2 and *b* a man child, then she
7 law for her that hath *b* a male
18. 9 whether she be *b* at home,
9 or *b* abroad,
19.34 unto you as one *b* among you,
22.11 and he that is *b* in his house:
23.42 all that are Israelites *b* shall
24.16 as he that is *b* in the land, when
Nu 9.14 him that was *b* in the land.
15.13 All that are *b* of the country
29 him that is *b* among the children
30 be *b* in the land, or a stranger,
26.60 unto Aaron was *b* Nadab and
Dt 21.15 and they have *b* him children,
Jos 5. 5 the people that were *b* in the
8.33 as he that was *b* among them;
Jdg 13. 8 do unto the child that shall be *b*.
18.29 father, who was *b* unto Israel:
Ru 4.15 than seven sons, hath *b* him.
17 There is a son *b* to Naomi;
1Sa 2. 5 so that the barren hath *b* seven;
4.20 Fear not, for thou hast *b* a son.
2Sa 3. 2 unto David were sons *b* in Hebron:
5 These were *b* to David in Hebron.
5.13 sons and daughters *b* to David.
14 names of those that were *b* unto
12.14 the child also that is *b* unto thee
14.27 Absalom there were *b* three sons,
21.20 and he also was *b* to the giant.
22 four were *b* to the giant in Gath,
1Ki 13. 2 be *b* unto the house of David,
1Ch 1.19 And unto Eber were *b* two sons:
2. 3 which three were *b* unto him of
9 of Hezron, that were *b* unto him;
3. 1 which were *b* unto him in Hebron;
4 six were *b* unto him in Hebron;
5 were *b* unto him in Jerusalem;
7.21 of Gath that were *b* in that land
20. 8 were *b* unto the giant in Gath;
22. 9 a son shall be *b* to thee, who shall
26. 6 Shemaiah his son were sons *b*,
Ezr 10. 3 such as are *b* of them, according
Job 1. 2 there were *b* unto him seven sons
3. 3 the day perish wherein I was *b*,
5. 7 man is *b* unto trouble, as the
11.12 man be *b* like a wild ass's colt.
14. 1 Man that is *b* of a woman is of
15. 7 Art thou the first man that was *b*?
14 he which is *b* of a woman, that he
25. 4 he be clean that is *b* of a woman?
38.21 thou it, because thou wast then *b*?
Ps 22.31 a people that shall be *b*, that he
58. 3 go astray as soon as they be *b*,
78. 6 the children which should be *b*;
87. 4 Ethiopia; this man was *b* there.
5 that man was *b* in her: and the
6 people, that this man was *b* there,
Pr 17.17 and a brother is *b* for adversity.
Ec 2. 7 and had servants *b* in my house;
3. 2 A time to be *b*, and a time to die;
4.14 is *b* in his kingdom becometh
Isa 9. 6 unto us a child is *b*, unto us a son
66. 8 shall a nation be *b* at once? for as
Jer 16. 3 daughters that are *b* in this place,
20.14 be the day wherein I was *b*:
15 A man child is *b* unto thee;
22.26 country, where ye were not *b*;
Eze 16. 4 in the day thou wast *b* thy
5 in the day that thou wast *b*.
47.22 shall be unto you as *b* in the
Hos 2. 3 her as in the day that she was *b*,
Mt 1.16 of whom was *b* Jesus, who is
2. 1 when Jesus was *b* in Bethlehem
2 is he that is *b* King of the Jews?
4 of them where Christ should be *b*.
11.11 Among them that are *b* of women
19.12 so *b* from their mother's womb:
26.24 that man if he had not been *b*.
Mk 14.21 that man if he had never been *b*.
Lk 1.35 that holy thing which shall be *b*
2.11 For unto you is *b* this day in the
7.28 Among those that are *b* of women
Jn 1.13 Which were *b*, not of blood, nor
3. 3 Except a man be *b* again, he
4 can a man be *b* when he is old?
4 into his mother's womb, and be *b*?
5 Except a man be *b* of water and
6 which is *b* of the flesh is flesh;
6 which is *b* of the Spirit is spirit.
7 unto thee, Ye must be *b* again.
8 every one that is *b* of the Spirit.
8.41 We be not *b* of fornication; we
9. 2 or his parents, that he was *b* blind?
19 your son, who ye say was *b* blind?
20 our son, and that he was *b* blind:
32 the eyes of one that was *b* blind.
34 Thou wast altogether *b* in sins,
16.21 joy that a man is *b* into the world.
18.37 To this end was I *b*, and for this
Ac 2. 8 own tongue, wherein we were *b*?
7.20 In which time Moses was *b*, and
18. 2 Aquila, *b* in Pontus, lately come
24 named Apollos, *b* at Alexandria,
22. 3 which am a Jew, *b* in Tarsus,
28 Paul said, But I was free *b*.
Ro 9.11 (For the children being not yet *b*,
1Co 15. 8 also, as of one *b* out of due time.
Gal 4.23 bondwoman was *b* after the flesh;
29 he that was *b* after the flesh
29 him that was *b* after the Spirit,
Heb 11.23 By faith Moses, when he was *b*,
1Pe 1.23 *b* again not of corruptible seed,
1Jn 2.29 doeth righteousness is *b* of him.
3. 9 Whosoever is *b* of God doth not
9 sin, because he is *b* of God.
4. 7 every one that loveth is *b* of God,
5. 1 Jesus is the Christ is *b* of God:
4 For whatsoever is *b* of God
18 whosoever is *b* of God sinneth not;
Rev 12. 4 her child as soon as it was *b*.

BORNE

Ex 25.14 the ark may be *b* with them.
28 the table may be *b* with them.
Jdg 16.29 and on which it was *b* up,
Job 34.31 I have *b* chastisement, I will not
Ps 55.12 then I could have *b* it: neither
69. 7 I have *b* reproach; shame hath
Isa 46. 3 are *b* by me from the belly,
53. 4 Surely he hath *b* our griefs,
66.12 ye shall be *b* upon her sides,

Jer 10. 5 they must needs be *b*, because
15. 9 that hath *b* seven languisheth:
10 thou hast *b* me a man of strife
La 3.28 because he hath *b* it upon him.
5. 7 and we have *b* their iniquities.
Eze 16.20 daughters, whom thou hast *b*
58 Thou hast *b* thy lewdness
32.24, 25 yet have they *b* their shame
36. 6 ye have *b* the shame of the
39.26 that they have *b* their shame,
Am 5.26 *b* the tabernacle of your Moloch
Mt 20.12 which have *b* the burden and heat
23. 4 burdens and grievous to be *b*,
Mk 2. 3 the palsy, which was *b* of four.
Lk 11.46 with burdens grievous to be *b*,
Jn 5.37 hath sent me, hath *b* witness of me.
20.15 Sir, if thou have *b* him hence,
Ac 21.35 that he was *b* of the soldiers
1Co 15.49 have *b* the image of the earthy,
3Jn 6 have *b* witness of thy charity
Rev 2. 3 And hast *b*, and hast patience,

BORROW
Ex 3.22 woman shall *b* of her neighbor,
11. 2 every man *b* of his neighbor,
22.14 borrow ought of his neighbor,
Dt 15. 6 nations, but thou shalt not *b*;
28.12 nations, and thou shalt not *b*.
2Ki 4. 3 *b* thee vessels abroad of all thy
3 even empty vessels; *b* not a few.
Mt 5.42 from him that would *b* of thee

BORROWED
Ex 12.35 they *b* of the Egyptians jewels
2Ki 6. 5 Alas, master! for it was *b*.
Neh 5. 4 We have *b* money for the king's

BORROWER
Pr 22. 7 the *b* is servant to the lender.
Isa 24. 2 so with the *b*; as with the taker

BORROWETH
Ps 37.21 The wicked *b*, and payeth not

BOSOM
Gen 16. 5 I have given my maid into thy *b*;
Ex 4. 6 Put now thine hand into thy *b*.
6 And he put his hand into his *b*:
7 Put thine hand into thy *b* again.
7 he put his hand into his *b* again;
7 and plucked it out of his *b*,
Nu 11.12 Carry them in thy *b*, as a nursing
Dt 13. 6 or the wife of thy *b*, or thy friend,
28.54 toward the wife of his *b*,
56 evil toward the husband of her *b*,
Ru 4.16 laid it in her *b*, and became nurse
2Sa 12. 3 lay in his *b*, and was unto him
8 thy master's wives into thy *b*,
1Ki 1. 2 let her lie in thy *b*, that my lord
3.20 and laid it in her *b*, and laid her
20 and laid her dead child in my *b*.
17.19 he took him out of her *b*,
Job 31.33 by hiding mine iniquity in my *b*:
Ps 35.13 prayer returned into mine own *b*.
74.11 hand? pluck it out of thy *b*.
79.12 sevenfold into their *b* their
89.50 I do bear in my *b* the reproach of
129. 7 he that bindeth sheaves his *b*.
Pr 5.20 and embrace the *b* of a stranger?
6.27 Can a man take fire in his *b*, and
17.23 man taketh a gift out of the *b* to
19.24 man hideth his hand in his *b*,
21.14 a reward in the *b* strong wrath.
26.15 slothful hideth his hand in his *b*;
Ec 7. 9 anger resteth in the *b* of fools.
Isa 40.11 and carry them in his *b*, and shall
65. 6 even recompense into their *b*,
7 their former work into their *b*.
Jer 32.18 into the *b* of their children after
La 2.12 poured out into their mother's *b*.
Mic 7. 5 from her that lieth in thy *b*.
Lk 6.38 shall men give into your *b*.
16.22 by the angels into Abraham's *b*:
23 afar off, and Lazarus in his *b*.
Jn 1.18 which is in the *b* of the Father,
13.23 leaning on Jesus' *b* one of his

BOTTLE
Gen 21.14 took bread, and a *b* of water,
15 the water was spent in the *b*, and
19 filled the *b* with water, and gave
Jdg 4.19 she opened a *b* of milk, and gave
1Sa 1.24 one ephah of flour, and a *b* of
10. 3 another carrying a *b* of wine:
16.20 and a *b* of wine, and a kid, and
2Sa 16. 1 summer fruits, and a *b* of wine,
Ps 56. 8 put thou my tears into thy *b*:
119.83 am become like a *b* in the smoke;
Jer 13.12 Every *b* shall be filled with wine:
12 not certainly know that every *b*
19. 1 get a potter's earthen *b*, and take
10 Then shalt thou break the *b* in
Hab 2.15 that puttest thy *b* to him, and

BOTTLES
Jos 9. 4 and wine *b*, old, and rent, and
13 these *b* of wine, which we filled,
1Sa 25.18 two *b* of wine, and five sheep
Job 32.19 it is ready to burst like new *b*.
38.37 or who can stay the *b* of heaven,
Jer 48.12 his vessels, and break their *b*.
Hos 7. 5 have made him sick with *b* of
Mt 9.17 put new wine into old *b*:
17 else the *b* break, and the wine
17 runneth out, and the *b* perish:
17 put new wine into new *b*,
Mk 2.22 putteth new wine into old *b*:
22 new wine doth burst the *b*,
22 spilled, and the *b* will be
22 wine must be put into new *b*,
Lk 5.37 putteth new wine into old *b*;
37 new wine will burst the *b*, and
37 spilled, and the *b* shall perish.
38 wine must be put into new *b*;

BOTTOM
Ex 15. 5 they sank into the *b* as a stone.
29.12 blood beside the *b* of the altar.
Lev 4. 7 blood of the bullock at the *b* of
18 blood at the *b* of the altar of the
25 pour out his blood at the *b* of the
30 thereof at the *b* of the altar.
34 thereof at the *b* of the altar:
5. 9 blood shall be wrung out at the *b*
8.15 the blood at the *b* of the altar.
9. 9 poured out the blood at the *b* of
Job 36.30 and covereth the *b* of the sea,
SS 3.10 *b* thereof of gold, the covering
Eze 43.13 even the *b* shall be a cubit, and
14 And from the *b* upon the ground
17 and the *b* thereof shall be a cubit
Dan 6.24 or ever they came at the *b* of the
Am 9. 3 in the *b* of the sea, thence will I
Zec 1. 8 myrtle trees that were in the *b*;
Mt 27.51 from the top to the *b*; and the
Mk 15.38 in twain from the top to the *b*.

BOTTOMLESS
Rev 9. 1 was given the key of the *b* pit.
2 And he opened the *b* pit;
11 the angel of the *b* pit, whose
11. 7 that ascendeth out of the *b* pit
17. 8 and shall ascend out of the *b* pit,
20. 1 having the key of the *b* pit and a
3 cast him into the *b* pit, and shut

BOTTOMS
Jon 2. 6 I went down to the *b* of the

BOUGHT
Gen 17.12 or *b* with money of any stranger,
13 and he that is *b* with thy money,
23 all that were *b* with his money,
27 *b* with money of the stranger,
33.19 And he *b* a parcel of a field,
39. 1 *b* him of the hands of the
47.14 for the corn which they *b*:
20 And Joseph *b* all the land of
22 Only the land of the priests *b* he
23 Behold, I have *b* you this day and
49.30 which Abraham *b* with the field
50.13 which Abraham *b* with the field
Ex 12.44 man's servant that is *b* for
Lev 25.28 hand of him that hath *b* it until
30 to him that *b* it throughout his
50 him that *b* him from the year
51 of the money that he was *b* for.
27.22 field which he hath *b*, which is
24 unto him of whom it was *b*, even
Dt 32. 6 he thy father that hath *b* thee?
Jos 24.32 which Jacob *b* of the sons of
Ru 4. 9 that I have *b* all that was
2Sa 12. 3 which he had *b* and nourished up:
24.24 So David *b* the threshingfloor and
1Ki 16.24 And he *b* the hill Samaria of
Neh 5.16 of this wall, neither *b* we any
Isa 43.24 Thou hast *b* me no sweet cane
Jer 32. 9 And I *b* the field of Hanameel my
43 And fields shall be *b* in this land,
Hos 3. 2 So I *b* her to me for fifteen pieces
Mt 13.46 and sold all that he had, and *b* it.
21.12 sold and *b* in the temple, and
27. 7 *b* with them the potter's field, to
Mk 11.15 cast out them that sold and *b* in
15.46 he *b* fine linen, and took him
16. 1 had *b* sweet spices, that they
Lk 14.18 I have *b* a piece of ground, and I
19 I have *b* five yoke of oxen, and I go
17.28 they did eat, they drank, they *b*,
19.45 that sold therein, and them that *b*;
Ac 7.16 Abraham *b* for a sum of money of
1Co 6.20 For ye are *b* with a price:
7.23 Ye are *b* with a price; be not ye
2Pe 2. 1 denying the Lord that *b* them, and

BOUND
Gen 22. 9 and *b* Isaac his son, and laid
38.28 and *b* upon his hand a scarlet
39.20 where the king's prisoners were *b*:
40. 3 the place where Joseph was *b*.
5 Egypt, which were *b* in the prison.
42.19 let one of your brethren be *b* in
24 Simeon, and *b* him before their
44.30 seeing that his life is *b* up in the
49.26 the utmost *b* of the everlasting
Ex 12.34 their kneadingtroughs being *b*
Lev 8. 7 and *b* it unto him therewith.
Nu 19.15 vessel, which hath no covering *b*
30. 4 her bond wherein she hath *b* her
4 wherewith she hath *b* her soul,
5 bonds wherewith she hath *b* her
6 out of her lips, wherewith she *b*
7 wherewith she *b* her soul shall
8 wherewith she *b* her soul, of none
9 have *b* their souls, shall stand
10 house, or *b* her soul by a bond
11 every bond wherewith she *b* her
Jos 2.21 and she *b* the scarlet line in the
9. 4 wine bottles, old, and rent, and *b*
Jdg 15.13 they *b* him with two new cords,
16. 6 wherewith thou mightest be *b* to
8 not been dried, and she *b* him
10 thee, wherewith thou mightest be *b*.
12 new ropes, and *b* him therewith,
13 me wherewith thou mightest be *b*.
21 and *b* him with fetters of brass;
1Sa 25.29 the soul of my lord shall be *b* in
2Sa 3.34 Thy hands were not *b*, nor thy
2Ki 5.23 and *b* two talents of silver in two
17. 4 of Assyria shut him up, and *b* him
25. 7 and *b* him with fetters of brass,
2Ch 33.11 and *b* him with fetters, and
36. 6 and *b* him in fetters, to carry him

Job 36. 8 if they be *b* in fetters, and be
38.20 to the *b* thereof, and that thou
Ps 68. 6 bringeth out those which are *b*
104. 9 Thou hast set a *b* that they may
107.10 shadow of death, being *b* in
Pr 22.15 Foolishness is *b* in the heart of a
30. 4 who hath *b* the waters in a
Isa 1. 6 have not been closed, neither *b*
22. 3 they are *b* by the archers:
3 all that are found in thee are *b*
61. 1 of the prison to them that are *b*;
Jer 5.22 the *b* of the sea by a perpetual
30.13 thy cause, that thou mayest be *b*
39. 7 and *b* him with chains to carry
40. 1 being *b* in chains among all that
52.11 and the king of Babylon *b* him
La 1.14 yoke of my transgressions is *b* by
Eze 27.24 apparel, *b* with cords, and made
30.21 it shall not be *b* up to be healed,
34. 4 neither have ye *b* up that which
Dan 3.21 Then these men were *b* in their
23 fell down *b* into the midst of the
24 Did not we cast three men *b* into
Hos 4.19 The wind hath *b* her up in her
5.10 them that remove the *b*;
7.15 I have *b* and strengthened their
13.12 The iniquity of Ephraim is *b* up;
Na 3.10 and all her great men were *b* in
Mt 14. 3 laid hold on John, and *b* him,
16.19 on earth shall be *b* in heaven;
18.18 on earth shall be *b* in heaven;
27. 2 when they had *b* him, they led him
Mk 5. 4 had been often *b* with fetters and
6.17 laid hold upon John, and *b* him in
15. 1 and *b* Jesus, and carried him
7 Barabbas, which lay *b* with them
Lk 8.29 he was kept *b* with chains and in
10.34 And went to him, and *b* up his
13.16 whom Satan hath *b*, lo, these
Jn 11.44 *b* hand and foot with
44 his face was *b* about with a
18.12 the Jews took Jesus and *b* him,
24 Now Annas had sent him *b* unto
Ac 9. 2, 21 he might bring them *b* unto
12. 6 *b* with two chains: and the
20.22 I go *b* in the spirit unto
21.11 *b* his own hands and feet, and
13 I am ready not to be *b* only, but
33 commanded him to be *b* with
22. 5 *b* unto Jerusalem, for to be
25 as they *b* him with thongs, Paul
29 a Roman, and because he had *b*
23.12 and *b* themselves under a curse,
14 *b* ourselves under a great curse,
21 have *b* themselves with an oath,
24.27 the Jews a pleasure, left Paul *b*.
28.20 hope of Israel I am *b* with this
Ro 7. 2 which hath an husband is *b* by
1Co 7.27 Art thou *b* unto a wife? seek not
39 The wife is *b* by the law as long as
2Th 1. 3 We are *b* to thank God always
2.13 we are *b* to give thanks alway
2Ti 2. 9 but the word of God is not *b*.
Heb 13. 3 them that are in bonds, as *b*
Rev 9.14 Loose the four angels which are *b*
20. 2 Satan, and *b* him a thousand

BOUNDS

Ex 19.12 thou shalt set *b* unto the people
23 Set *b* about the mount, and
23.31 set thy *b* from the Red sea even
Dt 32. 8 he set the *b* of the people
Job 14. 5 hast appointed his *b* that he
26.10 waters with *b*, until the day
Isa 10.13 removed the *b* of the people,
Ac 17.26 and the *b* of their habitation;

BOUNTIFULLY

Ps 13. 6 he hath dealt *b* with me.
116. 7 the Lord hath dealt *b* with thee.
119.17 Deal *b* with thy servant, that I
142. 7 thou shalt deal *b* with me.
2Co 9. 6 which soweth *b* shall reap also *b*.

BOUNTIFULNESS

2Co 9.11 thing to all *b*, which causeth

BOW

Gen 9.13 I do set my *b* in the cloud, and it
14 the *b* shall be seen in the cloud:
16 And the *b* shall be in the cloud;
27. 3 thy weapons, thy quiver and thy *b*,
29 and nations *b* down to thee:
29 thy mother's sons *b* down to thee:
37.10 come to *b* down ourselves to thee
41.43 cried before him, *B* the knee:
48.22 with my sword and with my *b*.
49. 8 children shall *b* down before thee.
24 his *b* abode in strength, and the
Ex 11. 8 and *b* down themselves unto me,
20. 5 Thou shalt not *b* down thyself
23.24 Thou shalt not *b* down to their
Lev 26. 1 in your land, to *b* down unto it:
Dt 5. 9 Thou shalt not *b* down thyself
Jos 23. 7 nor *b* yourselves unto them:
24.12 with thy sword, nor with thy *b*.
Jdg 2.19 them, and to *b* down unto them;
1Sa 18. 4 and to his *b*, and to his girdle.
2Sa 1.18 of Judah the use of the *b*:
22 the *b* of Jonathan turned not back,
22.35 a *b* of steel is broken by mine
1Ki 22.34 certain man drew a *b* at a venture,
2Ki 5.18 *b* myself in the house of Rimmon:
18 when I *b* down myself in the
6.22 with thy sword and with thy *b*?
9.24 drew a *b* with his full strength,
13.15 said unto him, Take *b* and arrows.
15 he took unto him *b* and arrows.
16 Put thine hand upon the *b*. And
17.35 other gods, nor *b* yourselves to
19.16 Lord, *b* down thine ear and
1Ch 5.18 to shoot with *b*, and skilful in
12. 2 arrows out of a *b*, even of Saul's
2Ch 17.17 armed men with *b* and shield
18.33 certain man drew a *b* at a venture,
Job 20.24 the *b* of steel shall strike him
29.20 my *b* was renewed in my hand.
31.10 and let others *b* down upon her.
39. 3 They *b* themselves, they bring
Ps 7.12 bent his *b*, and made it ready.
11. 2 bend their *b*, they make ready
18.34 a *b* of steel is broken by mine
22.29 go down to the dust shall *b*
31. 2 *B* down thine ear to me; deliver
37.14 have bent their *b*, to cast down
44. 6 I will not trust in my *b*, neither
46. 9 he breaketh the *b*, and cutteth
58. 7 bendeth his *b* to shoot his arrows,
72. 9 wilderness shall *b* before him;
76. 3 the arrows of the *b*, the shield,
78.57 turned aside like a deceitful *b*.
86. 1 *B* down thine ear, O Lord, hear
95. 6 let us worship and *b* down:
144. 5 *B* thy heavens, O Lord, and
Pr 5. 1 *b* thine ear to my understanding:
14.19 The evil *b* before the good; and
22.17 *B* down thine ear, and hear the
Ec 12. 3 strong men shall *b* themselves,
Isa 10. 4 Without me they shall *b* down
21.15 sword, and from the bent *b*,
41. 2 and as driven stubble to his *b*.
45.23 unto me every knee shall *b*, every
46. 2 stoop, they *b* down together;
49.23 *b* down to thee with their face
51.23 *B* down, that we may go over:
58. 5 *b* down his head as a bulrush,
60.14 shall *b* themselves down at the
65.12 all *b* down to the slaughter:
66.19 Pul, and Lud, that draw the *b*,
Jer 6.23 shall lay hold on *b* and spear;
9. 3 bend their tongues like their *b*
46. 9 that handle and bend the *b*.
49.35 I will break the *b* of Elam, the
50.14 all ye that bend the *b*, shoot at
29 all ye that bend the *b*, camp
42 shall hold the *b* and the lance:
51. 3 bend his *b*, and against him
La 2. 4 hath bent his *b* like an enemy:
3.12 He hath bent his *b*, and set me as
Eze 1.28 As the appearance of the *b* that is
39. 3 smite thy *b* out of thy left hand,
Hos 1. 5 I will break the *b* of Israel
7 not save them by *b*, nor by sword,
2.18 and I will break the *b* and the
7.16 they are like a deceitful *b*:
Am 2.15 he stand that handleth the *b*;
Mic 6. 6 *b* myself before the high God?
Hab 3. 6 the perpetual hills did *b*:
9 Thy *b* was made quite naked,
Zec 9.10 and the battle *b* shall be cut off:
13 filled the *b* with Ephraim, and
10. 4 out of him the battle *b*, out of
Ro 11.10 and *b* down their back alway.
14.11 every knee shall *b* to me, and
Eph 3.14 I *b* my knees unto the Father
Php 2.10 of Jesus every knee should *b*,
Rev 6. 2 he that sat on him had a *b*;

BOWELS

Gen 15. 4 of thine own *b* shall be thine
25.23 shall be separated from thy *b*;
43.30 his *b* did yearn upon his brother:
Nu 5.22 the curse shall go into thy *b*,
2Sa 7.12 which shall proceed out of thy *b*,
16.11 which came forth of my *b*,
20.10 and shed out his *b* to the ground,
1Ki 3.26 her *b* yearned upon her son,
2Ch 21.15 of thy *b*, until thy *b* fall out by
18 the Lord smote him in his *b* with
19 his *b* fell out by reason of his
32.21 they that came forth of his own *b*
Job 20.14 his meat in his *b* is turned, it is
30.27 My *b* boiled, and rested not:
Ps 22.14 it is melted in the midst of my *b*.
71. 6 took me out of my mother's *b*:
109.18 into his *b* like water, and like
SS 5. 4 and my *b* were moved for him.
Isa 16.11 my *b* shall sound like an harp for
48.19 the offspring of thy *b* like the
49. 1 from the *b* of my mother hath
63.15 the sounding of my *b* and of thy
Jer 4.19 My *b*, my *b*! I am pained at my
31.20 my *b* are troubled for him;
La 1.20 my *b* are troubled; mine heart
2.11 my *b* are troubled, my liver is
Eze 3. 3 and fill thy *b* with this roll that
7.19 their souls, neither fill their *b*:
Ac 1.18 and all his *b* gushed out.
2Co 6.12 are straightened in your own *b*.
Php 1. 8 you all in the *b* of Jesus Christ.
2. 1 Spirit, if any *b* and mercies,
Col 3.12 *b* of mercies, kindness,
Phm 7 the *b* of the saints are refreshed
12 receive him, that is, mine own *b*:
20 refresh my *b* in the Lord.
1Jn 3.17 shutteth up his *b* of compassion

BOWING

Gen 24.52 worshipped the Lord, *b*
Ps 17.11 have set their eyes *b* down
62. 3 as a *b* wall shall ye be, and as a
Mk 15.19 *b* their knees worshipped him.

BOWS

1Sa 2. 4 *b* of the mighty men are broken,
1Ch 12. 2 They were armed with *b*,
2Ch 14. 8 bare shields and drew *b*,
26.14 helmets, and habergeons, and *b*,
Neh 4.13 swords, their spears, and their *b*.
16 spears, the shields, and the *b*,
Ps 37.15 and their *b* shall be broken.
64. 3 and bend their *b* to shoot their
78. 9 being armed, and carrying *b*,

Isa 5.28 all their *b* bent, their horses
7.24 With arrows and with *b* shall
13.18 Their *b* also shall dash the young
Jer 51.56 every one of their *b* is broken:
Eze 39. 9 bucklers, the *b* and the arrows,

BOX

2Ki 9. 1 take this *b* of oil in thine hand,
3 Then take the *b* of oil, and pour
Isa 41.19 pine, and the *b* tree together:
60.13 and the *b* together, to beautify
Mt 26. 7 having an alabaster *b* of very
Mk 14. 3 having an alabaster *b* of
3 she brake the *b*, and poured it
Lk 7.37 brought an alabaster *b* of

BOY

Joel 3. 3 given a *b* for an harlot, and

BOYS

Gen 25.27 And the *b* grew: and Esau was
Zec 8. 5 *b* and girls playing in the streets

BRAKE

Ex 9.25 *b* every tree of the field.
32. 3 people *b* off the golden earrings
19 and *b* them beneath the mount.
Dt 9.17 and *b* them before your eyes.
Jdg 7.19 the trumpets, and *b* the pitchers
20 the trumpets, and *b* the pitchers,
9.53 head, and all to *b* his skull.
16. 9 And he *b* the withs, as a thread
12 he *b* them from off his arms
1Sa 4.18 and his neck *b*, and he died:
2Sa 23.16 three mighty men *b* through
1Ki 19.11 and *b* in pieces the rocks before
2Ki 10.27 they *b* down the image of Baal,
27 and *b* down the house of Baal,
11.18 house of Baal, and *b* it down;
18 his images *b* they in pieces
14.13 *b* down the wall of Jerusalem
18. 4 and *b* the images, and cut down
4 *b* in pieces the brasen serpent
23. 7 And he *b* down the houses of
8 and *b* down the high places
12 and *b* them down from thence,
14 And he *b* in pieces the images,
15 the high place he *b* down, and
25.10 *b* down the walls of Jerusalem
1Ch 11.18 And the three *b* through the host
2Ch 14. 3 and *b* down the images, and cut
21.17 and *b* into it, and carried away
23.17 the house of Baal, and *b* it down,
17 and *b* his altars and his images
25.23 *b* down the wall of Jerusalem
26. 6 and *b* down the wall of Gath,
31. 1 and *b* the images in pieces,
34. 4 they *b* down the altars of Baalim
4 images, he *b* in pieces,
36.19 *b* down the wall of Jerusalem,
Job 29.17 I *b* the jaws of the wicked,
38. 8 when it *b* forth, as if it had
10 *b* up for it my decreed place,
Ps 76. 3 *b* he the arrows of the bow,
105.16 he *b* the whole staff of bread.
33 and *b* the trees of their coasts.
106.29 inventions: and the plague *b* in
107.14 and *b* their bands in sunder.
Jer 28.10 off...Jeremiah's neck, and *b* it.
31.32 my covenant they *b*, although
39. 8 *b* down the walls of Jerusalem.
52.14 *b* down all the walls of Jerusalem
17 the Chaldeans *b*, and carried
Eze 17.16 whose covenant he *b*, even with
Dan 2. 1 and his sleep *b* from him.
34 and clay, and *b* them to pieces.
45 that it *b* in pieces the iron,
6.24 and *b* all their bones in pieces
7. 7 it devoured and *b* in pieces,
19 which devoured, *b* in pieces,
8. 7 the ram, and *b* his two horns:
Mt 14.19 he blessed, and *b*, and gave
15.36 and gave thanks, and *b* them,
26.26 bread, and blessed it, and *b*
Mk 6.41 and *b* the loaves, and gave them
8. 6 and gave thanks, and *b*, and
19 When I *b* the five loaves among
14. 3 and she *b* the box, and poured
22 took bread, and blessed, and *b*
Lk 5. 6 of fishes: and their net *b*.
8.29 he *b* the bands, and was
9.16 he blessed them, and *b*, and
22.19 and gave thanks, and *b* it,
24.30 and blessed it, and *b*, and gave
Jn 19.32 and *b* the legs of the first, and of
33 already, they *b* not his legs:
1Co 11.24 he *b* it, and said, Take, eat:

BRAKEST

Ex 34. 1 the first tables, which thou *b*.
Dt 10. 2 the first tables which thou *b*,
Ps 74.13 thou *b* the heads of the dragons
14 Thou *b* the heads of leviathan
Eze 29. 7 they leaned upon thee, thou *b*,

BRANCH

Ex 25.33 in one *b*; and three bowls made
33 like almonds in the other *b*,
37.17 his shaft, and his *b*, his bowls,
19 fashion of the almonds in one *b*,
19 made like almonds in another *b*,
Nu 13.23 cut down from thence a *b* with
Job 8.16 *b* shooteth forth in his garden.
14. 7 tender *b* thereof will not cease.
15.32 and his *b* shall not be green.
18.16 above shall his *b* be cut off.
29.19 dew lay all night upon my *b*.
Ps 80.15 the *b* that thou madest strong
Pr 11.28 righteous shall flourish as a *b*.
Isa 4. 2 day shall the *b* of the Lord
9.14 head and tail, *b* and rush,
11. 1 *B* shall grow out of his roots:
14.19 like an abominable *b*, and as the
17. 9 bough, and an uppermost *b*,
19.15 the head or tail, *b* or rush, may
25. 5 the *b* of the terrible ones shall
60.21 the *b* of my planting, the work of
Jer 23. 5 raise unto David a righteous *B*,
33.15 at that time, will I cause the *B* of
Eze 8.17 and, lo, they put the *b* to their
15. 2 a *b* which is among the trees of
17. 3 and took the highest *b* of the
22 the highest *b* of the high cedar,
Dan 11. 7 out of a *b* of her roots shall
Zec 3. 8 bring forth my servant the *B*.
6.12 the man whose name is The *B*;
Mal 4. 1 leave them neither root nor *b*.
Mt 24.32 When his *b* is yet tender, and
Mk 13.28 When her *b* is yet tender, and
Jn 15. 2 Every *b* in me that beareth not
2 and every *b* that beareth fruit,
4 As the *b* cannot bear fruit of
6 he is cast forth as a *b*, and is

BRANCHES

Gen 40.10 And in the vine were three *b*:
12 The three *b* are three days:
49.22 a well; whose *b* run over the
Ex 25.31 his shaft, and his *b*, his bowls,
32 six *b* shall come out of the sides
32 three *b* of the candlestick out of
32 and three *b* of the candlestick
33 so in the six *b* that come out of
35 a knop under two *b* of the same,
35 and a knop under two *b* of the
35 a knop under two *b* of the same,
35 according to the six *b*
36 and their *b* shall be of the same:
37.18 six *b* going out of the sides
18 three *b* of the candlestick out of
18 three *b* of the candlestick out of
19 so throughout the six *b* going out
21 a knop under two *b* of the same,
21 a knop under two *b* of the same,
21 a knop under two *b* of the same,
21 according to the six *b* going out of
22 Their knops and their *b* were of
Lev 23.40 *b* of palm trees, and the boughs
Neh 8.15 and fetch olive *b*, and pine *b*,
15 and myrtle *b*, and palm *b*,
15 and *b* of thick trees,
Job 15.30 the flame shall dry up his *b*, and
Ps 80.11 unto the sea, and her *b* unto the
104.12 which sing among the *b*.
Isa 16. 8 her *b* are stretched out, they
17. 6 in the outmost fruitful *b* thereof,
18. 5 take away and cut down the *b*.
27.10 lie down, and consume the *b*
Jer 11.16 it, and the *b* of it are broken.
Eze 17. 6 whose *b* turned toward him, and
6 brought forth *b*, and shot forth
7 and shot forth her *b* toward him,
8 that it might bring forth *b*, and
23 the shadow of the *b* thereof shall
19.10 fruitful and full of *b* by reason
11 was exalted among the thick *b*,
11 with the multitude of her *b*.
14 fire is gone out of a rod of her *b*,
31. 3 a cedar in Lebanon with fair *b*,
5 his *b* became long because of the
6 under his *b* did all the beasts
7 greatness, in the length of his *b*:
8 chestnut trees were not like his *b*;
9 fair by the multitude of his *b*:
12 in all the valleys his *b* are fallen,
13 of the field shall be upon his *b*:
36. 8 ye shall shoot forth your *b*, and
Dan 4.14 cut off his *b*, shake off his leaves,
14 under it, and the fowls from his *b*:
21 and upon whose *b* the fowls of
Hos 11. 6 consume his *b*, and devour them,
14. 6 His *b* shall spread, and his
Joel 1. 7 the *b* thereof are made white.
Na 2. 2 out, and marred their vine *b*.
Zec 4.12 these two olive *b* which through
Mt 13.32 come and lodge in the *b* thereof.
21. 8 others cut down *b* from the trees,
Mk 4.32 shooteth out great *b*; so that
11. 8 others cut down *b* off the trees,
Lk 13.19 fowls of the air lodged in the *b*
Jn 12.13 Took *b* of palm trees, and went
15. 5 I am the vine, ye are the *b*.
Ro 11.16 if the root be holy so are the *b*.
17 if some of the *b* be broken off,
18 Boast not against the *b*. But if
19 The *b* were broken off, that I
21 if God spared not the natural *b*,
24 these, which be the natural *b*, be

BRAND

Zec 3. 2 is not this a *b* plucked out of the

BRANDS

Jdg 15. 5 when he had set the *b* on fire, he

BRASS

Gen 4.22 of every artificer in *b* and iron:
Ex 25. 3 of them; gold, and silver, and *b*,
26.11 thou shalt make fifty taches of *b*,
37 cast five sockets of *b* for them.
27. 2 and thou shalt overlay it with *b*.
3 thereof thou shalt make of *b*.
4 for it a grate of network of *b*;
6 wood, and overlay them with *b*.
10 their twenty sockets shall be of *b*;
11 and their twenty sockets of *b*;
17 of silver, and their sockets of *b*.
18 twined linen, and their sockets of *b*.
19 the pins of the court, shall be of *b*.
30.18 Thou shalt also make a laver of *b*,
18 and his foot also of *b*,
31. 4 in gold, and in silver, and in *b*,
35. 5 the Lord; gold, and silver, and *b*,

Ex 35.24 an offering of silver and *b*
32 in gold, and in silver, and in *b*,
36.18 he made fifty taches of *b* to couple
38 but their five sockets were of *b*.
38. 2 same: and he overlaid it with *b*.
3 the vessels thereof made he of *b*.
5 the four ends of the grate of *b*,
6 wood, and overlaid them with *b*.
8 he made the laver of *b*,
8 and the foot of it of *b*,
11 and their sockets of *b* twenty;
17 sockets for the pillars were of *b*;
19 four, and their sockets of *b* four;
20 court round about, were of *b*.
29 And the *b* of the offering was
39.39 brasen altar, and his grate of *b*.
Lev 26.19 as iron, and your earth as *b*:
Nu 21. 9 Moses made a serpent of *b*, and
9 when he beheld the serpent of *b*,
31.22 the gold, and the silver, the *b*,
Dt 8. 9 of whose hills thou mayest dig *b*.
28.23 that is over thy head shall be *b*,
33.25 Thy shoes shall be iron and *b*;
Jos 6.19 vessels of *b* and iron, are
24 the vessels of *b* and of iron, they
22. 8 with gold, and with *b*, and with
Jdg 16.21 bound him with fetters of *b*; and
1Sa 17. 5 had an helmet of *b* upon his head,
5 was five thousand shekels of *b*.
6 had greaves of *b* upon his legs,
6 and a target of *b* between his
38 an helmet of *b* upon his head;
2Sa 8. 8 David took exceeding much *b*.
10 vessels of gold, and vessels of *b*:
21.16 three hundred shekels of *b* in
1Ki 7.14 a man of Tyre, a worker in *b*:
14 cunning to work all works in *b*.
15 he cast two pillars of *b*, of
16 two chapiters of molten *b*, to set
27 he made ten bases of *b*; four
30 brasen wheels, and plates of *b*:
38 Then made he ten lavers of *b*:
45 of the Lord, were of bright *b*.
47 the weight of the *b* found out,
2Ki 25. 7 bound him with fetters of *b*, and
13 pillars of *b* that were in the house
13 carried the *b* of them to Babylon.
14 all the vessels of *b* wherewith
16 *b* of all these vessels was without
17 and the chapiter upon it was *b*;
17 the chapiter round about, all of *b*:
1Ch 15.19 to sound with cymbals of *b*;
18. 8 brought David very much *b*,
8 the pillars, and the vessels of *b*.
10 vessels of gold and silver and *b*.
22. 3 *b* in abundance without weight;
14 and of *b* and iron without weight;
16 the gold, the silver, and the *b*,
29. 2 the *b* for things of *b*, the iron for
7 of *b* eighteen thousand talents,
2Ch 2. 7 in silver, and in *b*, and in iron,
14 in gold, and in silver, and in *b*,
4. 1 made an altar of *b*, twenty cubits
9 overlaid the doors of them with *b*.
16 house of the Lord, of bright *b*.
18 the weight of the *b* could not be
12.10 king Reoboham made shields of *b*
24.12 also such as wrought iron and *b*
Job 6.12 of stones? or is my flesh of *b*?
28. 2 *b* is molten out of the stone.
40.18 bones are as strong pieces of *b*;
41.27 as straw, and *b* as rotten wood.
Ps 107.16 he hath broken the gates of *b*,
Isa 45. 2 break in pieces the gates of *b*,
48. 4 is an iron sinew, and thy brow *b*,
60.17 For *b* I will bring gold, and for
16 bring silver, and for wood *b*,
Jer 6.28 they are *b* and iron; they are all
52.17 Also the pillars of *b* that were in
17 and carried all the *b* of them to
18 of *b* wherewith they ministered,
20 the *b* of all these vessels was
22 a chapiter of *b* was upon it; and
22 the chapiters round about, all of *b*.
Eze 1. 7 like the color of burnished *b*.
22.18 all they are *b*, and tin, and iron,
20 they gather silver, and *b*, and iron,
24.11 that the *b* of it may be hot, and
27.13 persons of men and vessels of *b*
40. 3 was like the appearance of *b*,
Dan 2.32 his belly and his thighs of *b*,
35 the clay, the *b*, the silver, and
39 another third kingdom of *b*,
45 the iron, the *b*, the clay, the
4.15, 23 with a band of iron and *b*,
5. 4 gods of gold, and of silver, of *b*,
23 the gods of silver, and gold, of *b*,
7.19 were of iron, and his nails of *b*;
10. 6 feet like in color to polished *b*,
Mic 4.13 I will make thy hoofs *b*: and
Zec 6. 1 mountains were mountains of *b*.
Mt 10. 9 nor silver, nor *b* in your purses,
1Co 13. 1 I am become as sounding *b*,
Rev 1.15 and his feet like unto fine *b*, as
2.18 and his feet are like fine brass;
9.20 idols of gold, and silver, and *b*,
18.12 and of *b*, and iron, and marble,

BRAWLER

1Ti 3. 3 patient, not a *b*, not covetous;

BRAWLERS

Tit 3. 2 evil of no man, to be no *b*, but

BRAWLING

Pr 21. 9 with a *b* woman in a wide house.
25.24 with a *b* woman in a wide house.

BREAD

Gen 3.19 sweat of thy face shalt thou eat *b*,
14.18 Salem brought forth *b* and wine:
18. 5 I will fetch a morsel of *b*,
19. 3 and did bake unleavened *b*,
21.14 and took *b*, and a bottle of water,
25.34 Jacob gave Esau *b* and pottage
27.17 gave the savory meat and the *b*,
28.20 and will give me *b* to eat,
31.54 called his brethren to eat *b*:
54 and they did eat *b*,
37.25 they sat down to eat *b*: and they
39. 6 save the *b* which he did eat.
41.54 all the land of Egypt there was *b*.
55 the people cried to Pharaoh for *b*:
43.25 they heard that they should eat *b*
31 himself, and said, Set on *b*.
32 the Egyptians might not eat *b*
45.23 laden with corn and *b* and meat
47.12 with *b*, according to their
13 And there was no *b* in all the land;
15 unto Joseph, and said, Give us *b*:
17 Joseph gave them *b* in exchange
17 fed them with *b* for all their cattle
19 buy us and our land for *b*, and we
49.20 Out of Asher his *b* shall be fat,
Ex 2.20 call him, that he may eat *b*.
12. 8 roast with fire, and unleavened *b*;
15 shall ye eat unleavened *b*;
15 whosoever eateth leavened *b*
17 observe the feast of unleavened *b*;
18 ye shall eat unleavened *b*, until
20 shall ye eat unleavened *b*.
13. 3 shall no leavened *b* be eaten.
6 thou shalt eat unleavened *b*,
7 Unleavened *b* shall be eaten
7 there shall no leavened *b* be seen
16. 3 when we did eat *b* to the full;
4 I will rain *b* from heaven for you;
8 and in the morning *b* to the full;
12 morning ye shall be filled with *b*;
15 the *b* which the Lord hath given
22 they gathered twice as much *b*,
29 on the sixth day the *b* of two days;
32 the *b* wherewith I have fed you
18.12 to eat *b* with Moses' father in law
23.15 the feast of unleavened *b*:
15 (thou shalt eat unleavened *b*
18 of my sacrifice with leavened *b*;
25 shall bless thy *b*, and thy water;
29. 2 And unleavened *b*, and cakes
23 loaf of *b*, and one cake of oiled *b*,
23 basket of the unleavened *b* that is
32 the *b* that is in the basket, by the
34 of the *b*, remain until the morning,
34.18 The feast of unleavened *b* shalt
18 (thou shalt eat unleavened *b*,
28 he did neither eat *b*, nor drink
40.23 he set the *b* in order upon it
Lev 6.16 with unleavened *b* shall it be
7.13 leavened *b* with the sacrifice of
8. 2 and a basket of unleavened *b*;
26 the basket of unleavened *b*, that
26 a cake of oiled *b*, and one wafer,
31 the *b* that is in the basket of
32 of the *b* shall ye burn with fire.
21. 6 by fire, and the *b* of their God,
8 for he offereth the *b* of thy God:
17 approach to offer the *b* of his God.
21 nigh to offer the *b* of his God.
22 He shall eat the *b* of his God,
22.25 the *b* of your God of any of these;
23. 6 the feast of unleavened *b* unto
6 ye must eat unleavened *b*.
14 ye shall eat neither *b*, nor
18 offer with the *b* seven lambs
20 the *b* of the firstfruits for a wave
24. 7 may be on the *b* for a memorial,
26. 5 ye shall eat your *b* to the full,
26 the staff of your *b*,
26 ten women shall bake your *b*
26 and they shall deliver you your *b*
Nu 4. 7 the continual *b* shall be thereon:
6.15 a basket of unleavened *b*, cakes
15 wafers of unleavened *b* anointed
17 the basket of unleavened *b*:
9.11 eat it with unleavened *b* and bitter
14. 9 they are *b* for us: their defense
15.19 when ye eat of the *b* of the land,
21. 5 for there is no *b*, neither is there
5 our soul loatheth this light *b*.
28. 2 my *b* for my sacrifices made by
17 shall unleavened *b* be eaten.
Dt 8. 3 man doth not live by *b* only,
9 A land wherein thou shalt eat *b*
9. 9 I neither did eat *b* nor drink
18 I did neither eat *b*, nor drink
16. 3 shalt eat no leavened *b* with it;
3 shalt thou eat unleavened *b*
3 even the *b* of affliction; for thou
4 there shall be no leavened *b*
8 thou shalt eat unleavened *b*:
16 the feast of unleavened *b*, and in
23. 4 they met you not with *b* and with
29. 6 Ye have not eaten *b*, neither have
Jos 9. 5 all the *b* of their provision was
12 This our *b* we took hot for our
Jdg 7.13 and, lo, a cake of barley *b*
8. 5 Give, I pray you, loaves of *b*
6 should give *b* unto thine army?
15 we should give *b* unto thy men
13.16 detain me, I will not eat of thy *b*:
19. 5 thine heart with a morsel of *b*,
19 there is *b* and wine also for me,
Ru 1. 6 visited his people in giving them *b*.
2.14 eat of the *b*, and dip thy
1Sa 2. 5 hired out themselves for *b*;
36 and a morsel of *b*, and shall say,
36 that I may eat a piece of *b*.
9. 7 the *b* is spent in our vessels,
10. 3 another carrying three loaves of *b*,
4 and give thee two loaves of *b*;
16.20 an ass laden with *b*, and a bottle
21. 3 give me five loaves of *b* in mine
4 no common *b* under mine hand,

An ancient clay figurine of a baker kneading dough for bread, found in a tomb in Galilee

4 but there is hallowed *b*:
5 the *b* is in a manner common,
6 the priest gave him hallowed *b*:
6 *b* there but the shewbread,
6 to put hot *b* in the day when it
22.13 in that thou hast given him *b*,
25.11 Shall I then take my *b*, and my
28.20 he had eaten no *b* all the day,
22 let me set a morsel of *b* before
24 did bake unleavened *b* thereof:
30.11 to David, and gave him *b*, and he
12 for he had eaten no *b*, nor drunk
2Sa 3.29 on the sword, or that lacketh *b*.
35 if I taste *b*, or ought else, till the
6.19 to every one a cake of *b*, and a
9. 7 thou shalt eat *b* at my table
10 thy master's son shall eat *b* always
12.17 neither did he eat *b* with them.
20 they set *b* before him, and he did
21 dead, thou didst rise and eat *b*.
16. 1 two hundred loaves of *b*, and an
2 *b* and summer fruit for the young
1Ki 13. 8 neither will I eat *b* nor drink
9 Eat no *b*, nor drink water, nor
15 Come home with me, and eat *b*.
16 neither will I eat *b* nor drink
17 Thou shalt eat no *b*, nor drink
18 he may eat *b* and drink water.
19 went back with him, and did eat *b*
22 hast eaten *b* and drunk water in
22 Eat no *b*, and drink no water;
23 after he had eaten *b*, and after he
17. 6 ravens brought him *b* and flesh
6 and *b* and flesh in the evening;
11 me, I pray thee, a morsel of *b*
18. 4 and fed them with *b* and water.)
13 and fed them with *b* and water?
21. 4 away his face, and would eat no *b*.
5 so sad that thou eatest no *b*?
7 arise, and eat *b*, and let thine
22.27 feed him with *b* of affliction and
2Ki 4. 8 and she constrained him to eat *b*.
8 he turned in thither to eat *b*.
42 *b* of the firstfruits, twenty loaves
6.22 set *b* and water before them, that
18.32 a land of *b* and vineyards, a land
23. 9 they did eat of the unleavened *b*
25. 3 there was no *b* for the people of
29 he did eat *b* continually before
1Ch 12.40 *b* on asses, and on camels, and
16. 3 to every one a loaf of *b*, and a
2Ch 8.13 in the feast of unleavened *b*, and
18.26 feed him with *b* of affliction and
30.13 the feast of unleavened *b* in the
21 feast of unleavened *b* seven days
35.17 feast of unleavened *b* seven days.

Ezr 6.22 feast of unleavened *b* seven days
10. 6 he did eat no *b*, nor drink water:
Neh 5.14 brethren have not eaten the *b* of
15 had taken of them *b* and wine,
18 the *b* of the governor, because
9.15 And gavest them *b* from heaven
13. 2 not the children of Israel with *b*
Job 15.23 wandereth abroad for *b*, saying,
22. 7 thou hast withholden *b* from the
27.14 shall not be satisfied with *b*.
28. 5 for the earth, out of it cometh *b*:
33.20 his life abhorreth *b*, and his soul
42.11 and did eat *b* with him in his
Ps 14. 4 up my people as they eat *b*, and
37.25 forsaken, nor his seed begging *b*.
41. 9 which did eat of my *b*, hath lifted
53. 4 eat up my people as they eat *b*:
78.20 he give *b* also? can he provide
80. 5 feedest them with the *b* of tears;
102. 4 grass; so that I forget to eat my *b*.
9 I have eaten ashes like *b*, and
104.15 and *b* which strengtheneth man's
105.16 he brake the whole staff of *b*.
40 and satisfied them with the *b* of
109.10 and beg: let them seek their *b* also
127. 2 to eat the *b* of sorrows: for so
132.15 I will satisfy her poor with *b*.
Pr 4.17 they eat the *b* of wickedness, and
6.26 a man is brought to a piece of *b*:
9. 5 Come, eat of my *b*, and drink of
17 are sweet, and *b* eaten in secret is
12. 9 honoreth himself, and lacketh *b*.
11 his land shall be satisfied with *b*:
20.13 and thou shalt be satisfied with *b*.
17 *B* of deceit is sweet to a man;
22. 9 for he giveth of his *b* to the poor.
23. 6 the *b* of him that hath an evil eye,
25.21 enemy be hungry, give him *b* to
28.19 his land shall have plenty of *b*:
21 For a piece of *b* that man will
31.27 and eateth not the *b* of idleness.
Ec 9. 7 eat thy *b* with joy, and drink
11 neither yet *b* to the wise, nor
11. 1 Cast thy *b* upon the waters: for
Isa 3. 1 the whole stay of *b*, and the whole
7 house is neither *b* nor clothing:
4. 1 We will eat our own *b*, and wear
21.14 they prevented with their *b* him
28.28 *B* corn is bruised; because he
30.20 the *b* of adversity, and the water
23 and *b* of the increase of the earth,
33.16 of rocks: *b* shall be given him;
36.17 wine, a land of *b* and vineyards.
44.15 he kindleth it and baketh *b*; yea,
19 I have baked *b* upon the coals
51.14 pit, nor that his *b* should fail.
55. 2 money for that which is not *b*?
10 seed to the sower, and *b* to the
58. 7 to deal thy *b* to the hungry, and
Jer 5.17 eat up thine harvest, and thy *b*,
37.21 give him daily a piece of *b* out of
21 the bakers' street, until all the *b*
38. 9 for there is no more *b* in the city.
41. 1 they did eat *b* together in Mizpah.
42.14 nor have hunger of *b*; and there
52. 6 there was no *b* for the people of
33 did continually eat *b* before him
La 1.11 All her people sigh, they seek *b*;
4. 4 the young children ask *b*, and no
5. 6 Assyrians, to be satisfied with *b*.
9 We gat our *b* with the peril of
Eze 4. 9 make thee *b* thereof, according
13 their defiled *b* among the Gentiles,
15 thou shalt prepare thy *b*
16 I will break the staff of *b* in
16 and they shall eat *b* by weight,
17 That they may want *b* and water,
5.16 and will break your staff of *b*:
12.18 of man, eat thy *b* with quaking,
19 shall eat their *b* with carefulness,
13.19 of barley and for pieces of *b*,

14.13 will break the staff of the *b*
16.49 fulness of *b*, and abundance of
18. 7 given his *b* to the hungry, and
16 hath given his *b* to the hungry,
24.17 thy lips, and eat not the *b* of men.
22 your lips, nor eat the *b* of men.
44. 3 sit in it to eat *b* before the Lord;
7 when ye offer my *b*, the fat and
45.21 days; unleavened *b* shall be eaten.
Dan 10. 3 I ate no pleasant *b*, neither
Hos 2. 5 give me my *b* and my water,
9. 4 unto them as the *b* of mourners;
4 their *b* for their soul shall not
Am 4. 6 and want of *b* in all your places:
7.12 and there eat *b*, and prophesy
8.11 not a famine of *b*, nor a thirst for
Ob 7 they that eat thy *b* have laid a
Hag 2.12 and with his skirt do touch *b*,
Mal 1. 7 Ye offer polluted *b* upon mine
Mt 4. 3 that these stones be made *b*.
4 Man shall not live by *b* alone,
6.11 Give us this day our daily *b*.
7. 9 whom if his son ask *b*, will he
15. 2 not their hands, when they eat *b*.
26 not meet to take the children's *b*,
33 should we have so much *b* in
16. 5 they had forgotten to take *b*.
7 It is because we have taken no *b*.
8 because ye have brought no *b*?
11 not to you concerning *b*, that
12 not beware of the leaven of *b*, but
26.17 the feast of unleavened *b* the
26 Jesus took *b*, and blessed it, and
Mk 3.20 could not so much as eat *b*.
6. 8 no scrip, no *b*, no money in their
36 villages, and buy themselves *b*:
37 two hundred pennyworth of *b*,
7. 2 saw some of his disciples eat *b*
5 but eat *b* with unwashen hands?
27 not meet to take the children's *b*,
8. 4 satisfy these men with *b* here in
14 disciples had forgotten to take *b*,
16 saying, It is because we have no *b*.
17 reason ye, because ye have no *b*?
14. 1 the passover, and of unleavened *b*:
12 the first day of unleavened *b*.
22 Jesus took *b*, and blessed, and
Lk 4. 3 this stone that it be made *b*.
4 man shall not live by *b* alone, but
7.33 neither eating *b* nor drinking
9. 3 scrip, neither *b*, neither money;
11. 3 Give us day by day our daily *b*.
11 If a son shall ask *b* of any of you
14. 1 to eat *b* on the sabbath day, that
15 he that shall eat *b* in the kingdom
15.17 servants of my father's have *b*
22. 1 Now the feast of unleavened *b* drew
7 came the day of unleavened *b*,
19 he took *b*, and gave thanks, and
24.30 he took *b*, and blessed it, and
35 known of them in breaking of *b*.
Jn 6. 5 Whence shall we buy *b*, that these
7 Two hundred pennyworth of *b*
23 place where they did eat *b*, after
31 He gave them *b* from heaven to
32 Moses gave you not that *b* from
32 my Father giveth you the true *b*
33 For the *b* of God is he which
34 Lord, evermore give us this *b*.
35 I am the *b* of life: he that cometh
41 I am the *b* which came down from
48 I am that *b* of life.
50 This is the *b* which cometh down
51 I am the living *b* which came
51 if any man eat of this *b*, he shall
51 the *b* that I will give is my flesh.
58 This is that *b* which came down
58 he that eateth of this *b* shall live
13.18 He that eateth *b* with me hath
21. 9 there, and fish laid thereon, and *b*.
13 Jesus then cometh, and taketh *b*

Ac 2.42 in breaking of *b*, and in prayers.
46 breaking *b* from house to house,
12. 3 were the days of unleavened *b*.)
20. 6 after the days of unleavened *b*,
7 came together to break *b*, Paul
11 had broken *b*, and eaten, and
27.35 he took *b*, and gave thanks to God
1Co 5. 8 unleavened *b* of sincerity and
10.16 The *b* which we break, is it not
17 we being many are one *b*, and
17 are all partakers of that one *b*,
11.23 which he was betrayed took *b*:
26 as often as ye eat this *b*, and drink
27 whosoever shall eat this *b*, and
28 so let him eat of that *b*, and drink
2Co 9.10 minister *b* for your food, and
2Th 3. 8 Neither did we eat any man's *b*
12 they work, and eat their own *b*.

BREADTH

Gen 6.15 the *b* of it fifty cubits, and the
13.17 the length of it and in the *b* of it;
Ex 25.10 a cubit and a half the *b* thereof,
17 and a cubit and a half the *b*
23 a cubit the *b* thereof, and a cubit
25 border of an hand *b* round
26. 2 and the *b* of one curtain four
8 shall be thirty cubits, and the *b*
16 cubit and a half shall be the *b* of
27.12 And for the *b* of the court on the
13 And the *b* of the court on the
18 and the *b* fifty every where, and
28.16 and a span shall be the *b* thereof.
30. 2 a cubit the *b* thereof; four
36. 9 and the *b* of one curtain four
15 four cubits was the *b* of one
21 the *b* of a board one cubit and a
37. 1 a cubit and a half the *b* of it, and
6 and one cubit and a half the *b*
10 a cubit the *b* thereof, and a cubit
25 the *b* of it a cubit; it was four
38. 1 five cubits the *b* thereof; it was
18 length, and the height in the *b*
39. 9 thereof, and span the *b* thereof,
Dt 2. 5 so much as a foot *b*;
3.11 four cubits the *b* of it, after the
Jdg 20.16 could sling stones at an hair *b*,
1Ki 6. 2 the *b* thereof twenty cubits, and
3 according to the *b* of the house;
3 the *b* thereof before the house.
20 in length, and twenty cubits in *b*,
7. 2 the *b* thereof fifty cubits, and the
6 fifty cubits, and the *b* thereof
26 And it was an hand *b* thick,
27 four cubits the *b* thereof, and
2Ch 3. 3 threescore cubits, and the *b*
4 the *b* of the house, twenty cubits,
8 was according to the *b* of the
8 twenty cubits, and the *b* thereof
4. 1 twenty cubits the *b* thereof, and
Ezr 6. 3 and the *b* thereof threescore
Job 37.10 and the *b* of the waters is
38.18 Hast thou perceived the *b* of the
Isa 8. 8 shall fill the *b* of thy land, O
Eze 40. 5 by the cubit and an hand *b*:
5 he measured the *b* of the
11 the *b* of the entry of the gate, ten
13 the *b* was five and twenty cubits,
19 the *b* from the forefront of
20 the length thereof and the *b*
21, 25, 36 and the *b* five and twenty
48 and the *b* of the gate was three
49 twenty cubits, and the *b* eleven
41. 1 other side, which was the *b* of the
2 And the *b* of the door was ten
2 forty cubits; and the *b*, twenty
3 and the *b* of the door, seven
4 and the *b*, twenty cubits, before
5 and the *b* of every side chamber.
7 therefore the *b* of the house was
11 and the *b* of the place that was
14 Also the *b* of the face of the house
42. 2 north door, and the *b* was fifty
4 a walk of ten cubits *b* inward.
43.13 cubit is a cubit and an hand *b*;
13 and the *b* a cubit, and the border
14 shall be two cubits, and the *b*
14 shall be four cubits, and the *b*
45. 1 and the *b* shall be ten thousand.
2 five hundred in *b*, square round
3 and the *b* of ten thousand: and
5 the ten thousand of *b*, shall also
48. 8 and twenty thousand reeds in *b*,
9 length, and of ten thousand in *b*.
10 the west ten thousand in *b*,
10 the east ten thousand in *b*,
13 and ten thousand in *b*: all the
13 twenty thousand, and the *b* ten
15 in the *b* over against the five
Dan 3. 1 threescore cubits, and the *b*
Hab 1. 6 through the *b* of the land, to
Zec 2. 2 to see what is the *b* thereof, and
5. 2 twenty cubits, and the *b* thereof
Eph 3.18 what is the *b*, and length, and
Rev 20. 9 they went up on the *b* of the
21.16 the length is as large as the *b*:
16 and the *b* and the height of it are

BREAK

Gen 19. 9 even Lot, came near to *b* the
27.40 that thou shalt *b* his yoke from
Ex 12.46 neither shall ye *b* a bone
13.13 then thou shalt *b* his neck: and
19.21 lest they *b* through unto the
22 lest the Lord *b* forth upon them.
24 the people *b* through to come up
24 lest he *b* forth upon them.
22. 6 If fire *b* out, and catch in thorns,
23.24 overthrow them, and quite *b*
32. 2 *B* off the golden earrings, which
24 hath any gold, let them *b* it off.
34.13 *b* their images, and cut down
20 him not, then shalt thou *b* his
Lev 11.33 shall be unclean: and ye shall *b*
13.12 if a leprosy *b* out abroad in the
14.43 and *b* out in the house, after that
45 And he shall *b* down the house,
26.15 but that ye *b* my covenant:
19 I will *b* the pride of your power;
44 to *b* my covenant with them: for
Nu 9.12 of it unto the morning, nor *b*
24. 8 shall *b* their bones, and pierce
30. 2 he shall not *b* his word, he shall
Dt 7. 5 *b* down their images, and cut
12 a border of an hand *b* round
12. 3 and *b* their pillars, and burn
31.16 and *b* my covenant which I have
20 provoke me, and *b* my covenant.
Jdg 2. 1 I will never *b* my covenant with
8. 9 again in peace, I will *b* down this
1Sa 25.10 servants now a days that *b* away
2Sa 2.32 they came to Hebron at *b* of day.
1Ki 15.19 and *b* thy league with Baasha
2Ki 3.26 that drew swords, to *b* through
25.13 did the Chaldees *b* in pieces, and
2Ch 16. 3 go, *b* thy league with Baasha
Ezr 9.14 Should we again *b* thy
Neh 4. 3 he shall even *b* down their
Job 13.25 Wilt thou *b* a leaf driven to and
19. 2 vex my soul, and *b* me in pieces
34.24 He shall *b* in pieces mighty
39.15 that the wild beast may *b* them.
Ps 2. 3 Let us *b* their bands asunder,
9 Thou shalt *b* them with a rod of
10.15 *B* thou the arm of the wicked
58. 6 *B* their teeth, O God, in their
6 *b* out the great teeth of the
72. 4 shall *b* in pieces the oppressor.
74. 6 But now they *b* down the carved
89.31 If they *b* my statutes, and keep
34 My covenant will I not *b*, nor
94. 5 They *b* in pieces thy people,
141. 5 shall not *b* my head: forget my
Ec 3. 3 a time to *b* down, and a time to
SS 2.17 Until the day *b*, and the
4. 6 day *b*, and the shadows flee
Isa 5. 5 and *b* down the wall thereof,
14. 7 and is quiet: they *b* forth into
25 That I will *b* the Assyrian in my
28.24 doth he open and *b* the clods of
28 nor *b* it with the wheel of his
30.14 And he shall *b* it as the breaking
35. 6 in the wilderness shall waters *b*
38.13 as a lion, so will he *b* all my
42. 3 A bruised reed shall he not *b*,
44.23 *b* forth into singing, ye
45. 2 I will *b* in pieces the gates of
49.13 and *b* forth into singing, O
52. 9 *B* forth into joy, sing together,
54. 1 *b* forth into singing, and cry
3 thou shalt *b* forth on the right
55.12 mountains and the hills shall *b*
58. 6 go free, and that ye *b* every yoke?
8 Then shall thy light *b* forth as
Jer 1.14 an evil shall *b* forth upon all the
4. 3 *B* up your fallow ground, and
14.21 remember, *b* not thy covenant
15.12 Shall iron *b* the northern iron
19.10 Then shalt thou *b* the bottle in
11 Even so will I *b* this people and
28. 4 I will *b* the yoke of the king of
11 Even so will I *b* the yoke of
30. 8 I will *b* his yoke from off thy
31.28 to pluck up, and to *b* down,
33.20 If ye can *b* my covenant of the
43.13 He shall *b* also the images of
45. 4 which I have built will I *b* down,
48.12 empty his vessels, and *b* their
49.35 I will *b* the bow of Elam, the
51.20 for with thee will I *b* in pieces
21 And with thee will I *b* in pieces
21 rider; and with thee will I *b* in
22 With thee also will I *b* in pieces
22 and with thee will I *b* in pieces old
22 and with thee will I *b* in pieces
23 I will also *b* in pieces with thee
23 and with thee will I *b* in pieces
23 And with thee will I *b* in pieces
Eze 4.16 I will *b* the staff of bread in
5.16 and will *b* your staff of bread:
13.14 So will I *b* down the wall that ye
14.13 and will *b* the staff of the bread
16.38 women that *b* wedlock and shed
39 shall *b* down thy high places:
17.15 or shall he *b* the covenant, and
23.34 thou shalt *b* the sherds thereof,
26. 4 Tyrus, and *b* down her towers:
9 he shall *b* down thy towers.
12 and they shall *b* down thy walls,
29. 7 thou didst *b*, and rend all their
30.18 when I shall *b* there the yokes of
22 and will *b* his arms, the strong
24 but I will *b* Pharaoh's arms, and
Dan 2.40 all these shall it *b* in pieces
44 it shall *b* in pieces and consume
4.27 *b* off thy sins by righteousness,
7.23 shall tread it down, and *b* it in
Hos 1. 5 that I will *b* the bow of Israel in
2.18 I will *b* the bow and the sword
4. 2 they *b* out, and blood toucheth
10. 2 he shall *b* down their altars, he
11 shall plow, and Jacob shall *b* his
12 mercy; *b* up your fallow ground:
Joel 2. 7 and they shall not *b* their ranks:
Am 1. 5 I will *b* also the bar of Damascus,
5. 6 lest he *b* out like fire in the
Mic 3. 3 they *b* their bones, and chop
Na 1.13 now will I *b* his yoke from off
Zec 11.10 that I might *b* my covenant
14 that I might *b* the brotherhood
Mt 5.19 shall *b* one of these least
6.19 where thieves *b* through and
20 where thieves do not *b* through

9.17 else the bottles *b*, and the wine
12.20 A bruised reed shall he not *b*,
Ac 20. 7 came together to *b* bread, Paul
11 a long while, even to *b* of day,
21.13 What mean ye to weep and to *b*
1Co 10.16 The bread which we *b*, is it not
Gal 4.27 *b* forth and cry, thou that

BREAKER
Mic 2.13 The *b* is come up before them:
Ro 2.25 but if thou be a *b* of the law,

BREAKEST
Ps 48. 7 Thou *b* the ships of Tarshish

BREAKING
Gen 32.24 a man with him until the *b* of
Ex 9. 9 a boil *b* forth with blains upon
10 it became a boil *b* forth with
22. 2 If a thief be found *b* up, and be
1Ch 14.11 like the *b* forth of waters:
Job 30.14 me as a wide *b* in of waters:
Ps 144.14 that there be no *b* in, nor going
Isa 22. 5 *b* down the walls, and of crying
30.13 whose *b* cometh suddenly at an
14 as the *b* of the potters' vessel
Eze 16.59 despised the oath in *b* the
17.18 by *b* the covenant, when, lo, he
21. 6 with the *b* of thy loins; and
Hos 13.13 in the place of the *b* forth of
Lk 24.35 known of them in *b* of bread.
Ac 2.42 in *b* of bread, and in prayers.
46 and *b* bread from house to house,
Ro 2.23 *b* the law dishonorest thou

BREAST
Ex 29.26 thou shalt take the *b* of the
27 sanctify the *b* of the wave
Lev 7.30 the fat with the *b*, it shall he
30 that the *b* may be waved
31 but the *b* shall be Aaron's and his
34 the wave *b* and the heave
8.29 Moses took the *b*, and waved it
10.14 the wave *b* and heave shoulder
15 heave shoulder and the wave *b*
Nu 6.20 priest, with the wave *b* and heave
18.18 as the wave *b* and as the right
Job 24. 9 pluck the fatherless from the *b*,
Isa 60.16 shalt suck the *b* of kings; and
La 4. 3 the sea monsters draw out the *b*,
Dan 2.32 his *b* and his arms of silver, his
Lk 18.13 but smote upon his *b*, saying,
Jn 13.25 He then lying on Jesus' *b* saith
21.20 which also leaned on his *b* at

BREASTPLATE
Ex 25. 7 be set in the ephod, and in the *b*.
28. 4 they shall make; a *b*, and an
15 shalt make the *b* of judgment
22 make upon the *b* chains at the
23 make upon the *b* two rings of
23 two rings on the two ends of the *b*.
24 which are on the ends of the *b*.
26 two ends of the *b* in the border
28 they shall bind the *b* by the rings
28 that the *b* be not loosed from the
29 the children of Israel in the *b* of
30 put in the *b* of judgment the
29. 5 the ephod, and the *b*, and gird
35. 9 set for the ephod, and for the *b*.
27 set, for the ephod, and for the *b*;
39. 8 he made the *b* of cunning work,
9 they made the *b* double:
15 upon the *b* chains at the ends,
16 rings in the two ends of the *b*.
17 two rings on the ends of the *b*.
19 put them on the two ends of the *b*,
21 bind the *b* by his rings unto the
21 that the *b* might not be loosed
Lev 8. 8 he put the *b* upon him:
8 also he put in the *b* the Urim
Isa 59.17 put on righteousness as a *b*,
Eph 6.14 having on the *b* of righteousness;
1Th 5. 8 putting on the *b* of faith and love;

BREASTPLATES
Rev 9. 9 *b*, as it were *b* of iron;
17 *b* of fire, and of jacinth, and

BREASTS
Gen 49.25 blessings of the *b*, and of the
Lev 9.20 they put the fat upon the *b*, and
21 the *b* and the right shoulder
Job 3.12 or why the *b* that I should suck?
21.24 His *b* are full of milk, and his
Ps 22. 9 when I was upon my mother's *b*.
Pr 5.19 let her *b* satisfy thee at all times;
SS 1.13 shall lie all night betwixt my *b*.
4. 5 Thy two *b* are like two young roes
7. 3 thy two *b* are like two young roes
7 and thy *b* to clusters of grapes.
8 thy *b* shall be as clusters of the
8. 1 that sucked the *b* of my mother!
8 little sister, and she hath no *b*:
10 and my *b* like towers: then was
Isa 28. 9 the milk, and drawn from the *b*.
66.11 satisfied with the *b* of her
Eze 16. 7 thy *b* are fashioned, and thine
23. 3 there were their *b* pressed, and
8 bruised the *b* of her virginity,
34 and pluck off thine own *b*:
Hos 2. 2 adulteries from between her *b*;
9.14 miscarrying womb and dry *b*.
Joel 2.16 and those that suck the *b*:
Na 2. 7 of doves, tabering upon their *b*.
Lk 23.48 smote their *b*, and returned.
Rev 15. 6 their *b* girded with golden girdles.

BREATH
Gen 2. 7 into his nostrils the *b* of life;
6.17 wherein is the *b* of life, from
7.15 flesh, wherein is the *b* of life.
22 in whose nostrils was the *b* of life,
2Sa 22.16 at the blast of the *b* of his nostrils.
1Ki 17.17 that there was no *b* left in him.
Job 4. 9 and by the *b* of his nostrils are
9.18 will not suffer me to take my *b*,
12.10 and the *b* of all mankind.
15.30 by the *b* of his mouth shall he go
17. 1 My *b* is corrupt, my days are
19.17 My *b* is strange to my wife,
27. 3 while my *b* is in me, and the
33. 4 and the *b* of the Almighty hath
34.14 unto himself his spirit and his *b*;
37.10 By the *b* of God frost is given:
41.21 His *b* kindleth coals, and a flame
Ps 18.15 the blast of the *b* of thy nostrils.
33. 6 the host of them by the *b* of his
104.29 thou takest away their *b*, they
135.17 neither is there any *b* in their
146. 4 His *b* goeth forth, he returneth
150. 6 every thing that hath *b* praise
Ec 3.19 yea, they have all one *b*; so that
Isa 2.22 from man, whose *b* is in his
11. 4 and with the *b* of his lips shall
30.28 And his *b*, as an overflowing
33 the *b* of the Lord, like a stream
33.11 your *b*, as fire, shall devour you.
42. 5 he that giveth *b* unto the people
Jer 10.14 falsehood, and there is no *b* in
51.17 falsehood, and there is no *b* in
La 4.20 *b* of our nostrils, the anointed
Eze 37. 5 I will cause *b* to enter into you,
6 and put *b* in you, and ye shall
8 but there was no *b* in them.
9 the four winds, O *b*, and breathe
10 the *b* came into them, and they
Dan 5.23 God in whose hand thy *b* is, and
10.17 me, neither is there *b* left in me.
Hab 2.19 there is no *b* at all in the midst
Ac 17.25 he giveth to all life, and *b*, and

BREATHE
Jos 11.11 there was not any left to *b*: and
14 them, neither left they any to *b*.
Ps 27.12 me, and such as *b* out cruelty.
Eze 37. 9 and *b* upon these slain, that

BREATHED
Gen 2. 7 and *b* into his nostrils the breath
Jos 10.40 utterly destroyed all that *b*, as
1Ki 15.29 left not to Jeroboam any that *b*,
Jn 20.22 said this, he *b* on them, and said

BREATHING
La 3.56 hide not thine ear at my *b*, at
Ac 9. 1 Saul, yet *b* out threatenings and

BRIBE
1Sa 12. 3 hand have I received any *b*
Am 5.12 they take a *b*, and they turn aside

BRIBERY
Job 15.34 consume the tabernacles of *b*.

BRIBES
1Sa 8. 3 aside after lucre, and took *b*,
Ps 26.10 and their right hand is full of *b*.
Isa 33.15 his hands from holding of *b*,

BRICK
Gen 11. 3 Go to, let us make *b*, and burn
3 they had *b* for stone, and slime
Ex 1.14 in morter, and in *b*, and in all
5. 7 give the people straw to make *b*,
14 fulfilled your task in making *b*
16 and they say to us, Make *b*: and
Isa 65. 3 burneth incense upon altars of *b*;

BRICKS
Ex 5. 8 the tale of the *b*, which they did
18 yet shall ye deliver the tale of *b*,
19 from your *b* of your daily task.
Isa 9.10 The *b* are fallen down, but we will

BRIDE
Isa 49.18 bind them on thee, as a *b* doeth.
61.10 a *b* adorneth herself with jewels.
62. 5 bridegroom rejoiceth over the *b*,
Jer 2.32 maid forget her ornaments, or a *b*
7.34 bridegroom, and the voice of the *b*:
16. 9 and the voice of the *b*.
25.10 the voice of the *b*, the sound of
33.11 the voice of the *b*, the voice of
Joel 2.16 and the *b* out of her closet.
Jn 3.29 that hath the *b* is the bridegroom:
Rev 18.23 of the *b* shall be heard no more
21. 2 prepared as a *b* adorned for her
9 shew thee the *b*, the Lamb's wife.
22.17 the Spirit of the *b* say, Come.

BRIDECHAMBER
Mt 9.15 Can the children of the *b* mourn,
Mk 2.19 Can the children of the *b* fast,
Lk 5.34 make the children of the *b* fast,

BRIDEGROOM
Ps 19. 5 a *b* coming out of his chamber,
Isa 61.10 as a *b* decketh himself with
62. 5 the *b* rejoiceth over the bride, so
Jer 7.34 the voice of the *b*, and the voice
16. 9 of gladness, the voice of the *b*,
25.10 the voice of the *b*, and the voice
33.11 the voice of the *b*, and the voice
Joel 2.16 let the *b* go forth of his chamber,
Mt 9.15 as long as the *b* is with them?
15 when the *b* shall be taken from
25. 1 and went forth to meet the *b*.
5 While the *b* tarried, they all
6 Behold, the *b* cometh; go ye out
10 they went to buy, the *b* came;
Mk 2.19 while the *b* is with them?
19 as long as they have the *b*

Mk 2.20 when the *b* shall be taken away
Lk 5.34 fast, while the *b* is with them?
35 come, when the *b* shall be taken
Jn 2. 9 governor of the feast called the *b*,
3.29 that hath the bride is the *b*:
29 but the friend of the *b*,
Rev 18.23 and the voice of the *b* and of the

BRIDLE
2Ki 19.28 my *b* in thy lips, and I will turn
Job 30.11 they have also let loose the *b*
41.13 come to him with his double *b*?
Ps 32. 9 must be held in with bit and *b*,
39. 1 I will keep my mouth with a *b*,
Pr 26. 3 a *b* for the ass, and a rod for the
Isa 30.28 be a *b* in the jaws of the people,
37.29 in thy nose, and my *b* in thy lips,
Jas 3. 2 able also to *b* the whole body.

BRIDLES
Rev 14.20 even unto the horse *b*, by the

BRIDLETH
Jas 1.26 *b* not his tongue, but deceiveth

BRIEFLY
Ro 13. 9 *b* comprehended in this saying,
1Pe 5.12 I have written *b*, exhorting

BRIER
Isa 55.13 instead of the *b* shall come up
Eze 28.24 shall be no more a pricking *b*
Mic 7. 4 The best of them is as a *b*: the

BRIGHT
Lev 13. 2 a rising, a scab, or *b* spot, and it
4 If the *b* spot be white in the skin
19 or a *b* spot, white, and somewhat
23 if the *b* spot stay in his place, and
24 have a white *b* spot, somewhat
25 the hair in the *b* spot be turned
26 no white hair in the *b* spot, and it
28 if the *b* spot stay in his place, and
38 in the skin of their flesh *b* spots,
38 even white *b* spots;
39 the *b* spots in the skin of their
14.56 and for a scab, and for a *b* spot:
1Ki 7.45 of the Lord, were of *b* brass.
2Ch 4.16 for the house of the Lord of *b*
Job 37.11 he scattereth his *b* cloud:
21 now men see not the *b* light
SS 5.14 his belly is as *b* ivory overlaid
Jer 51.11 Make *b* the arrows; gather the
Eze 1.13 and the fire was *b*, and out of
21.15 ah! it is made *b*, it is wrapped
21 he made his arrows *b*, he
27.19 *b* iron, cassia, and calamus,
32. 8 All the *b* lights of heaven will I
Na 3. 3 both the *b* sword and the
Zec 10. 1 so the Lord shall make *b* clouds,
Mt 17. 5 behold, a *b* cloud overshadowed
Lk 11.36 as when the *b* shining of a candle
Ac 10.30 stood before me in *b* clothing,
Rev 22.16 and the *b* and morning star.

BRIGHTNESS
2Sa 22.13 Through the *b* before him were
Job 31.26 shined, or the moon walking in *b*;
Ps 18.12 At the *b* that was before him his
Isa 59. 9 for *b*, but we walk in darkness.
60. 3 and kings to the *b* of thy rising.
19 neither for *b* shall the moon give
62. 1 righteousness thereof go forth as *b*
Eze 1. 4 and a *b* was about it, and out of
27 of fire, and it had *b* round about.
28 the appearance of the *b* round
8. 2 as the appearance of *b*, as the
10. 4 the court was full of the *b* of the
28. 7 wisdom, they shall defile thy *b*.
17 thy wisdom by reason of thy *b*:
Dan 2.31 This great image, whose *b* was
4.36 mine honor and *b* returned
12. 3 shall shine as the *b* of the
Am 5.20 even very dark, and no *b* in it?
Hab 3. 4 And his *b* was as the light;
Ac 26.13 light from heaven, above the *b* of
2Th 2. 8 with the *b* of his coming;
Heb 1. 3 Who being the *b* of his glory

BRIM
Jos 3.15 were dipped in the *b* of the
1Ki 7.23 ten cubits from the one *b* to the
24 under the *b* of it round about
26 and the *b* thereof was wrought
26 like the *b* of a cup,
2Ch 4. 2 from *b* to *b*, round in compass,
5 and the *b* of it like the work
5 like the work of the *b* of a cup,
Jn 2. 7 And they filled them up to the *b*.

BRIMSTONE
Gen 19.24 Sodom and upon Gomorrah *b*
Dt 29.23 the whole land thereof is *b*, and
Job 18.15 *b* shall be scattered upon his
Ps 11. 6 he shall rain snares, fire and *b*,
Isa 30.33 like a stream of *b*, doth kindle it.
34. 9 the dust thereof into *b*, and the
Eze 38.22 and great hail stones, fire and *b*.
Lk 17.29 fire and *b* from heaven, and
Rev 9.17 of fire, and of jacinth, and *b*,
17 issued fire and smoke and *b*.
18 the smoke, and by the *b*, which
14.10 with fire and *b* in the presence of
19.20 a lake of fire burning with *b*,
20.10 the lake of fire and *b*, where the
21. 8 lake which burneth with fire and *b*:

BRINGERS
2Ki 10. 5 and the *b* up of the children,

BRINGEST
1Ki 1.42 art a valiant man, and *b* good
Job 14. 3 *b* me into judgment with thee?
Isa 40. 9 O Zion, that *b* good tidings, get
9 O Jerusalem, that *b* good
Ac 17.20 thou *b* certain strange things to

BROAD
Ex 27. 1 five cubits long, and five cubits *b*;
Nu 16.38 let them make them *b* plates for
39 and they were made *b* plates for
1Ki 6. 6 chamber was five cubits *b*,
6 and the middle was six cubits *b*,
6 and the third was seven cubits *b*:
2Ch 6.13 five cubits long, and five cubits *b*,
Neh 3. 8 Jerusalem unto the *b* wall.
12.38 furnaces even unto the *b* wall;
Job 36.16 out of the strait into a *b* place,
Ps 119.96 commandment is exceeding *b*.
SS 3. 2 in the streets, and in the *b* ways
Isa 33.21 of *b* rivers and streams;
Jer 5. 1 seek in the *b* places thereof, if ye
51.58 The *b* walls of Babylon shall be
Eze 40. 6 the gate, which was one reed *b*;
6 the other threshold...one reed *b*.
7 one reed long, and one reed *b*;
29 and five and twenty cubits *b*.
30 cubits long, and five cubits *b*.
33 and five and twenty cubits *b*.
42 and a cubit and a half *b*, and one
43 hooks, an hand *b*, fastened
47 and an hundred cubits *b*, four
41. 1 six cubits *b* on the one side,
1 six cubits *b* on the other side,
12 the west was seventy cubits *b*;
42.11 long as they, and as *b* as they:
20 and five hundred *b*, to make a
43.16 twelve cubits long, twelve *b*,
17 cubits long and fourteen *b* in the
45. 6 of the city five thousand *b*,
46.22 forty cubits long and thirty *b*:
Na 2. 4 against another in the *b* ways:
Mt 7.13 *b* is the way, that leadeth to
23. 5 they make *b* their phylacteries,

BROILED
Lk 24.42 they gave him a piece of a *b* fish,

BROKEN
Gen 7.11 fountains of the great deep *b* up,
17.14 he hath *b* my covenant.
38.29 How hast thou *b* forth? this
Lev 6.28 wherein it is sodden shall be *b*:
11.35 they shall be *b* down: for they
13.20 a plague of leprosy *b* out of the
25 a leprosy *b* out of the burning:
15.12 which hath the issue, shall be *b*:
21.20 scabbed, or hath his stones *b*;
22.22 Blind, or *b*, or maimed, or having
24 bruised, or crushed, or *b*, or cut;
26.13 I have *b* the bands of your yoke,
26 I have *b* the staff of your bread,
Nu 15.31 and hath *b* his commandment,
Jdg 5.22 Then were the horsehoofs *b* by
16. 9 as a thread of tow is *b* when it
1Sa 2. 4 bows of the mighty men are *b*,
10 shall be *b* to pieces; out of
2Sa 5.20 hath *b* forth upon mine enemies
22.35 a bow of steel is *b* by mine arms.
1Ki 18.30 altar of the Lord that was *b*
22.48 the ships were *b* at Ezion-geber.
2Ki 11. 6 the house, that it be not *b* down.
25. 4 And the city was *b* up, and all
1Ch 14.11 God hath *b* in upon mine enemies
2Ch 20.37 the Lord hath *b* thy works.
37 And the ships were *b*, that they
24. 7 that wicked woman, had *b* up
25.12 that they all were *b* in pieces.
32. 5 the wall that was *b*, and raised
33. 3 his father had *b* down, and he
34. 7 when he had *b* down the altars
Neh 1. 3 wall of Jerusalem also is *b* down,
2.13 of Jerusalem, which were *b* down,
Job 4.10 teeth of the young lions, are *b*.
7. 5 my skin is *b*, and become
16.12 but he hath *b* me asunder:
17.11 my purposes are *b* off, even the
22. 9 of the fatherless have been *b*.
24.20 wickedness shall be *b* as a tree.
31.22 mine arm be *b* from the bone.
Ps 3. 7 hast *b* the teeth of the ungodly.
18.34 a bow of steel is *b* by mine arms.
31.12 of mind: I am like a *b* vessel.
34.18 unto them that are of a *b* heart:
20 his bones: not one of them is *b*.
37.15 and their bows shall be *b*.
17 the arms of the wicked shall be *b*:
38. 8 I am feeble and sore *b*: I have
44.19 Though thou hast sore *b* us in
51. 8 the bones which thou hast *b* may
17 sacrifices of God are a *b* spirit:
17 a *b* and a contrite heart,
55.20 him: he hath *b* his covenant.
60. 2 earth to tremble; thou hast *b* it:
69.20 Reproach hath *b* my heart;
80.12 thou then *b* down her hedges,
89.10 Thou hast *b* Rahab in pieces,
40 thou hast *b* down all his hedges;
107.16 he hath *b* the gates of brass,
109.16 might even slay the *b* in heart.
124. 7 snare is *b*, and we are escaped.
147. 3 He healeth the *b* in heart,
Pr 3.20 knowledge the depths are *b* up,
6.15 suddenly shall he be *b* without
15.13 sorrow of the heart the spirit is *b*.
17.22 but a *b* spirit drieth the bones.
24.31 stone wall thereof was *b* down.
25.19 is like a *b* tooth, and a foot out
28 is like a city that is *b* down,
Ec 4.12 a threefold cord is not quickly *b*.
12. 6 or the golden bowl be *b*,
6 the pitcher be *b* at the fountain,
6 or the wheel *b* at the cistern.

Isa 5.27 the latchet of their shoes be *b*:
7. 8 five years shall Ephraim be *b*,
8. 9 people, and ye shall be *b* in pieces;
9 be *b* in pieces; gird yourselves,
9 and ye shall be *b* in pieces.
15 shall stumble, and fall, and be *b*,
9. 4 hast *b* the yoke of his burden,
14. 5 hath *b* the staff of the wicked,
29 rod of him that smote thee is *b*:
16. 8 the heathen have *b* down the
19.10 they shall be *b* in the purposes
21. 9 images of her gods he hath *b*
22.10 and the houses have ye *b* down
24. 5 *b* the everlasting covenant.
10 The city of confusion is *b* down:
19 The earth is utterly *b* down,
27.11 withered, they shall be *b* off:
28.13 and fall backward, and be *b*,
30.14 potters' vessel that is *b* in pieces
33. 8 he hath *b* the covenant, he hath
20 any of the cords thereof be *b*.
36. 6 staff of this *b* reed, on Egypt;
Jer 2.13 *b* cisterns, that can hold no
16 have *b* the crown of thy head.
20 I have *b* thy yoke, and burst thy
4.26 all the cities thereof were *b* down
5. 5 have altogether *b* the yoke,
10.20 all my cords are *b*: my children
11.10 of Judah have *b* my covenant
16 it, and the branches of it are *b*.
14.17 virgin daughter of my people is *b*
22.28 man Coniah a despised *b* idol?
23. 9 Mine heart within me is *b*
28. 2 *b* the yoke of the king of Babylon.
12 had *b* the yoke from off the neck
13 Thou hast *b* the yokes of wood;
33.21 Then may also my covenant be *b*
37.11 the army of the Chaldeans was *b*
39. 2 the month, the city was *b* up.
48.17 How is the strong staff *b*, and
20 for it is *b* down: howl and cry;
25 his arm is *b*, saith the Lord.
38 I have *b* Moab like a vessel
39 howl, saying, How is it *b* down!
50. 2 Merodach is *b* in pieces; her
2 her images are *b* in pieces.
17 king of Babylon hath *b* his bones
23 whole earth cut asunder and *b*!
51.30 dwelling places; her bars are *b*.
56 every one of their bows is *b*:
58 of Babylon shall be utterly *b*,
52. 7 Then the city was *b* up, and all
La 2. 9 destroyed and *b* her bars:
3. 4 made old; he hath *b* my bones.
16 *b* my teeth with gravel stones,
Eze 6. 4 and your images shall be *b*:
6 and your idols may be *b* and
9 I am *b* with their whorish heart,
17.19 and my covenant that he hath *b*,
19.12 her strong rods were *b* and
26. 2 *b* that was the gates of the people:
27.26 the east wind hath *b* thee in the
34 thou shalt be *b* by the seas in
30. 4 her foundations shall be *b*
21 I have *b* the arm of Pharaoh
22 strong, and that which was *b*;
31.12 and his boughs are *b* by all the
32.28 thou shalt be *b* in the midst of
34. 4 ye bound up that which was *b*,
16 will bind up that which was *b*,
27 have *b* the bands of their yoke,
44. 7 and they have *b* my covenant
Dan 2.35 silver, and the gold, *b* to pieces
42 be partly strong, and partly *b*.
8. 8 strong, the great horn was *b*;
22 Now that being *b*, whereas
25 but he shall be *b* without hand.
11. 4 his kingdom shall be *b*, and shall
22 and shall be *b*; yea, also the prince
Hos 5.11 Ephraim is oppressed and *b*
8. 6 Samaria shall be *b* in pieces.
Joel 1.17 the barns are *b* down; for the
Jon 1. 4 that the ship was like to be *b*.
Mic 2.13 they have *b* up, and have passed
Zec 11.11 And it was *b* in that day; and so
16 nor heal that that is *b*, nor feed
Mt 15.37 they took up of the *b* meat that
21.44 fall on this stone shall be *b*:
24.43 suffered his house to be *b* up.
Mk 2. 4 when they had *b* it up, they let
5. 4 and the fetters *b* in pieces:
8. 8 they took up the *b* meat that
Lk 12.39 suffered his house to be *b*
20.18 fall upon that stone shall be *b*;
Jn 5.18 he not only had *b* the sabbath,
7.23 law of Moses should not be *b*;
10.35 and the scripture cannot be *b*;
19.31 that their legs might be *b*,
36 A bone of him shall not be *b*.
21.11 many, yet was not the net *b*.
Ac 13.43 when the congregation was *b*
20.11 and had *b* bread, and eaten,
27.35 when he had *b* it, he began to
41 the hinder part was *b* with the
44 some on *b* pieces of the ship.
Ro 11.17 some of the branches be *b* off,
19 The branches were *b* off, that I
20 because of unbelief they were *b* off,
1Co 11.24 is my body, which is *b* for you:
Eph 2.14 hath *b* down the middle wall
Rev 2.27 of the potter shall they be *b*

BROKENHEARTED

Isa 61. 1 bind up the *b*, to proclaim
Lk 4.18 hath sent me to heal the *b*,

BROOD

Lk 13.34 as a hen doth gather her *b*

BROTHER

Gen 4. 2 And she again bare his *b* Abel.
8 And Cain talked with Abel his *b*:
8 Cain rose up against Abel his *b*,
9 Where is Abel thy *b*?
9. 5 at the hand of every man's *b*
10.21 the *b* of Japheth the elder, even
14.13 *b* of Eschol, and *b* of Aner:
14 Abram heard that his *b* was taken
16 also brought his *b* Lot, and his
20. 5 she herself said, He is my *b*:
13 come, say of me, He is my *b*.
16 Behold, I have given thy *b*
22.20 born children unto thy *b* Nahor;
21 Huz his firstborn, and Buz his *b*,
23 did bear to Nahor, Abraham's *b*.
24.15 the wife of Nahor, Abraham's *b*,
29 Rebekah had a *b*, and his name
53 he gave also to her *b* and to her
55 her *b* and her mother said, Let the
25.26 after that came his *b* out, and his
27. 6 thy father speak unto Esau thy *b*,
11 Esau my *b* is a hairy man, and
23 as his *b* Esau's hands: so he
30 Esau his *b* came in from his
35 Thy *b* came with subtilty,
40 thou live, and shalt serve thy *b*;
41 then will I slay my *b* Jacob.
42 Behold, thy *b* Esau, as touching
43 flee thou to Laban my *b* to Haran;
28. 2 daughters of Laban thy mother's *b*.
5 the Syrian, the *b* of Rebekah,
29.10 daughter of Laban his mother's *b*,
10 sheep of Laban his mother's *b*,
10 the flock of Laban his mother's *b*.
12 Rachel that he was her father's *b*,
15 Because thou art my *b*,
32. 3 before him to Esau his *b*
6 We came to thy *b* Esau, and also
11 from the hand of my *b*, from the
13 hand a present for Esau his *b*;
17 When Esau my *b* meeteth thee,
33. 3 until he came near to his *b*.
9 Esau said, I have enough, my *b*;
35. 1 from the face of Esau thy *b*.
7 he fled from the face of his *b*.
36. 6 from the face of his *b* Jacob.
37.26 is it if we slay our *b*, and conceal
27 for he is our *b* and our flesh:
38. 8 her, and raise up seed to thy *b*.
9 that he should give seed to his *b*.
29 behold, his *b* came out: and she
30 afterward came out his *b*, that
42. 4 But Benjamin, Joseph's *b*,
15 except your youngest *b* come
16 let him fetch your *b*, and ye shall
20 bring your youngest *b* unto me;
21 guilty concerning our *b*, in that
42.34 bring your youngest *b* unto me:
34 I deliver you your *b*, and ye shall
38 his *b* is dead, and he is left alone:
43. 3 face, except your *b* be with you.
4 If thou wilt send our *b* with us, we
5 face, except your *b* be with you.
6 the man whether ye had yet a *b*?
7 have ye another *b*? and we told
7 he would say, Bring your *b* down?
13 Take also your *b*, and arise, and
14 he may send away your other *b*,
29 saw his *b* Benjamin, his mother's
29 Is this your younger *b*, of whom
30 his bowels did yearn upon his *b*:
44.19 saying, Have ye a father, or a *b*?
20 and his *b* is dead, and he alone is
23 Except your youngest *b* come
26 if our youngest *b* be with us, then
26 except our youngest *b* be with us.
45. 4 he said, I am Joseph your *b*, whom
12 the eyes of my *b* Benjamin, that
14 fell upon his *b* Benjamin's neck,
48.19 younger *b* shall be greater than he,
Ex 4.14 Is not Aaron the Levite thy *b*?
7. 1 Aaron thy *b* shall be thy prophet.
2 thy *b* shall speak unto Pharoah,
28. 1 take thou unto thee Aaron thy *b*,
2, 4 holy garments for Aaron thy *b*,
41 put them upon Aaron thy *b*, and
32.27 slay every man his *b*, and every
29 man upon his son, and upon his *b*;
Lev 16. 2 Speak unto Aaron thy *b*, that he
18.14 the nakedness of thy father's *b*,
19.17 Thou shalt not hate thy *b* in thine
21. 2 for his daughter, and for his *b*,
25.25 If thy *b* be waxen poor, and hath
25 he redeem that which his *b* sold.
35 if thy *b* be waxen poor, and fallen
36 God; that thy *b* may live with thee.
39 if thy *b* that dwelleth by thee be
47 *b* that dwelleth by him wax poor,
Nu 6. 7 for his *b*, or for his sister, when
20. 8 thou, and Aaron thy *b*, and speak
14 Thus saith thy *b* Israel, Thou
27.13 as Aaron thy *b* was gathered,
36. 2 our *b* unto his daughters.
Dt 1.16 between every man and his *b*, and
13. 6 If thy *b*, the son of thy mother, or
15. 2 of his neighbor, or of his *b*;
3 that which is thine with thy *b*
7 shut thine hand from thy poor *b*:
9 eye be evil against thy poor *b*, and
11 open thine hand wide unto thy *b*,
12 if thy *b*, an Hebrew man, or an
17.15 over thee, which is not thy *b*.
19.18 hath testified falsely against his *b*;
19 thought to have done unto his *b*:
22. 1 case bring them again unto thy *b*.
2 if thy *b* be not nigh unto thee, or if
2 until thy *b* seek after it, and thou
23. 7 an Edomite; for he is thy *b*:
19 not lend upon usury to thy *b*;
20 unto thy *b* thou shalt not lend upon
24.10 When thou dost lend thy *b*
25. 3 thy *b* should seem vile unto thee.
5 husband's *b* shall go in unto her,

Dt 25. 5 the duty of an husband's *b*
6 shall succeed in the name of his *b*
7 My husband's *b* refuseth to raise
7 his *b* a name in Israel, he will not
7 the duty of my husband's *b*.
28.54 his eye shall be evil toward his *b*,
32.50 Aaron thy *b* died in mount Hor,
Jos 15.17 son of Kenaz, the *b* of Caleb, took
Jdg 1. 3 And Judah said unto Simeon his *b*,
13 son of Kenaz, Caleb's younger *b*,
17 Judah went with Simeon his *b*,
3. 9 son of Kenaz, Caleb's younger *b*.
9. 3 for they said, He is our *b*.
18 Shechem, because he is your *b*;
21 there, for fear of Abimelech his *b*.
24 upon Abimelech their *b*, which
20.23 the children of Benjamin my *b*?
28 of Benjamin my *b*, or shall I cease?
21. 6 repented them for Benjamin their *b*,
Ru 4. 3 which was our *b* Elimelech's:
1Sa 14. 3 the son of Ahitub, I-chabod's *b*,
17.28 Eliab his eldest *b* heard when he
20.29 my *b*, he hath commanded me to
26. 6 the son of Zeruiah, *b* to Joab,
2Sa 1.26 distressed for thee, my *b* Jonathan:
2.22 I hold up my face to Joab thy *b*?
27 every one from following his *b*.
3.27 died, for the blood of Asahel his *b*.
30 Joab and Abishai his *b* slew Abner,
30 because he had slain their *b*
4. 6 Rechab and Baanah his *b* escaped.
9 answered Rechab and Baanah his *b*,
10.10 into the hand of Abishai his *b*,
13. 3 the son of Shimeah David's *b*:
4 Tamar, my *b* Absalom's sister.
7 Go now to thy *b* Amnon's house,
8 Tamar went to her *b* Amnon's
10 into the chamber to Amnon her *b*.
12 she answered him, Nay, my *b*, do
20 Absalom her *b* said unto her, Hath
20 Amnon thy *b* been with thee?
20 peace, my sister: he is thy *b*;
20 desolate in her *b* Absalom's house.
22 Absalom spake unto his *b* Amnon
26 thee, let my *b* Amnon go with us.
32 the son of Shimeah David's *b*,
14. 7 Deliver him that smote his *b*, that
7 life of his *b* whom he slew;
18. 2 the son of Zeruiah, Joab's *b*, and
20. 9 said, Art thou in health, my *b*?
10 Abishai his *b* pursued after Sheba
21.19 slew the *b* of Goliath the Gittite,
21 Shimeah the *b* of David slew him.
23.18 Abishai, the *b* of Joab, the son of
24 Asahel the *b* of Joab was one of
1Ki 1.10 and Solomon his *b*, he called not.
2. 7 I fled because of Absalom thy *b*.
21 be given to Adonijah thy *b* to wife.
22 for he is mine elder *b*; even for
9.13 which thou hast given me, my *b*?
13.30 over him, saying, Alas, my *b*!
20.32 said, Is he yet alive? he is my *b*.
33 Thy *b* Ben-hadad. Then he said,
2Ki 24.17 made Mattaniah his father's *b* king
1Ch 2.32 sons of Jada the *b* of Shammai;
42 sons of Caleb the *b* of Jerahmeel
4.11 Chelub the *b* of Shuah begat Mehir,
6.39 And his *b* Asaph, who stood on
7.16 the name of his *b* was Sheresh;
35 the sons of his *b* Helem; Zophah,
8.39 the sons of Eshek his *b* were, Ulam
11.20 Abishai the *b* of Joab, he was chief
26 Asahel the *b* of Joab, Elhanan
38 Joel the *b* of Nathan, Mibhar the
45 Shimei, and Joha his *b*, the Tizite,
19.11 unto the hand of Abishai his *b*,
15 fled before Abishai his *b*, and
20. 5 Jair slew Lahmi the *b* of Goliath
7 son of Shimea David's *b* slew him.
24.25 The *b* of Michah was Isshiah: of
26.22 Zetham, and Joel his *b*, which
27. 7 Asahel the *b* of Joab, and Zebadiah
2Ch 31.12 and Shimei his *b* was the next.
13 Cononiah and Shimei his *b*, at the
36. 4 Eliakim his *b* king over Judah
4 Necho took Jehoahaz his *b*, and
10 Zedekiah his *b* king over Judah
Neh 5. 7 Ye exact usury, every one of his *b*.
7. 2 That I gave my *b* Hanani, and
Job 22. 6 hast taken a pledge from thy *b*
30.29 I am a *b* to dragons, and a
Ps 35.14 though he had been my friend or *b*:
49. 7 can by any means redeem his *b*,
50.20 sittest and speakest against thy *b*;
Pr 17.17 times, and a *b* is born for adversity.
18. 9 is *b* to him that is a great waster.
19 A *b* offended is harder to be won
24 friend that sticketh closer than a *b*.
27.10 that is near than a *b* far off.
Ec 4. 8 yea, he hath neither child nor *b*:
SS 8. 1 O that thou wert as my *b*, that
Isa 3. 6 a man shall take hold of his *b* of
9.19 the fire: no man shall spare his *b*.
19. 2 fight every one against his *b*, and
41. 6 every one said to his *b*, Be of good
Jer 9. 4 trust ye not in any *b*: for
4 every *b* will utterly supplant,
22.18 saying, Ah my *b*! or, Ah sister!
23.35 every one to his *b*, What hath the
31.34 every man his *b*, saying, Know the
34. 9 of them, to wit, of a Jew his *b*.
14 ye go every man his *b* an Hebrew,
17 liberty, every one to his *b*,
Eze 18.18 spoiled his *b* by violence, and did
33.30 every one to his *b*, saying, Come,
38.21 man's sword shall be against his *b*.
44.25 for son, or for daughter, for *b*, or
Hos 12. 3 He took his *b* by the heel in the
Am 1.11 because he did pursue his *b* with
Ob 10 thy violence against thy *b* Jacob,
12 have looked on the day of thy *b*
Mic 7. 2 hunt every man his *b* with a net.
Hag 2.22 every one by the sword of his *b*.
Zec 7. 9 compassions every man to his *b*:
10 evil against his *b* in your heart.
Mal 1. 2 Was not Esau Jacob's *b*? saith
2.10 every man against his *b*,
Mt 4.18 called Peter, and Andrew his *b*,
21 of Zebedee, and John his *b*,
5.22 whosoever is angry with his *b*
22 whosoever shall say to his *b*, Raca,
23 thy *b* hath ought against thee;
24 first be reconciled to thy *b*, and
7. 4 wilt thou say to thy *b*, Let me
10. 2 called Peter, and Andrew his *b*;
2 son of Zebedee, and John his *b*;
21 *b* shall deliver up the *b* to death,
12.50 the same is my *b*, and sister, and
14. 3 Herodias' sake, his *b* Philip's wife.
17. 1 James, and John his *b*, and
18.15 thy *b* shall trespass against thee,
15 hear thee, thou hast gained thy *b*.
21 how oft shall my *b* sin against me,
35 every one his *b* their trespasses.
22.24 his *b* shall marry his wife,
24 and raise up seed unto his *b*.
25 no issue, left his wife unto his *b*:
Mk 1.16 saw Simon and Andrew his *b*
19 the son of Zebedee and John his *b*,
3.17 and John the *b* of James; and he
35 will of God, the same is my *b*, and
5.37 James, and John the *b* of James.
6. 3 son of Mary, the *b* of James, and
17 Herodias' sake, his *b* Philip's wife:
12.19 If a man's *b* die, and leave his wife
19 that his *b* should take his wife,
19 and raise up seed unto his *b*.
13.12 the *b* shall betray the *b* to death,
Lk 3. 1 and his *b* Philip tetrarch of Ituraea
19 for Herodias his *b* Philip's wife,
6.14 named Peter,) and Andrew his *b*,
16 And Judas the *b* of James, and
42 say to thy *b*, *B*, let me pull out the
12.13 Master, speak to my *b*, that he
15.27 said unto him, Thy *b* is come;
32 for this thy *b* was dead, and is alive
17. 3 If thy *b* trespass against thee,
20.28 If any man's *b* die, having a wife,
28 that his *b* should take his wife,
28 and raise up seed unto his *b*.
Jn 1.40 was Andrew, Simon Peter's *b*.
41 findeth his own *b* Simon, and saith
6. 8 Andrew, Simon Peter's *b*, saith
11. 2 hair, whose *b* Lazarus was sick.)
19 to comfort them concerning their *b*.
21 hadst been here, my *b* had not died.
23 unto her, Thy *b* shall rise again.
32 hadst been here, my *b* had not died.
Ac 1.13 Zelotes, and Judas the *b* of James.
9.17 said, *B* Saul, the Lord, even Jesus,
12. 2 he killed James the *b* of John with
21.20 Thou seest, *b*, how many thousands
22.13 unto me, *B* Saul, receive thy sight.
Ro 14.10 why dost thou judge thy *b*? or why
10 dost thou set at nought thy *b*?
15 if thy *b* be grieved with thy meat,
21 thing whereby thy *b* stumbleth,
16.23 city saluteth you, and Quartus a *b*.
1Co 1. 1 will of God, and Sosthenes our *b*,
5.11 that is called a *b* be a fornicator,
6. 6 *b* goeth to law with *b*, and that
7.12 If any *b* hath a wife that
15 A *b* or a sister is not under
8.11 shall the weak *b* perish, for
13 meat make my *b* to offend,
13 lest I make my *b* to offend.
16.12 As touching our *b* Apollos,
2Co 1. 1 will of God, and Timothy our *b*,
2.13 I found not Titus my *b*: but
8.18 have sent with him the *b*, whose
22 have sent with them our *b*,
12.18 Titus, and with him I sent a *b*.
Gal 1.19 none, save James the Lord's *b*.
Eph 6.21 a beloved *b* and faithful minister
Php 2.25 send to you Epaphroditus, my *b*,
Col 1. 1 will of God, and Timotheus our *b*,
4. 7 you, who is a beloved *b*, and a
9 a faithful and beloved *b*, who is
1Th 3. 2 sent Timotheus, our *b*, and
4. 6 and defraud his *b* in any matter:
2Th 3. 6 from every *b* that walketh
15 but admonish him as a *b*.
Phm 1 Timothy our *b*; unto Philemon
7 the saints are refreshed by thee, *b*.
16 above a servant, a *b* beloved,
20 Yea, *b*, let me have
Heb 8.11 neighbor, and every man his *b*,
13.23 Know ye that our *b* Timothy
Jas 1. 9 Let the *b* of low degree rejoice
2.15 If a *b* or sister be naked, and
4.11 evil of his *b*, and judgeth his *b*,
1Pe 5.12 a faithful *b* unto you, as I suppose,
2Pe 3.15 as our beloved *b* Paul also
1Jn 2. 9 in the light, and hateth his *b*,
10 He that loveth his *b* abideth in the
11 he that hateth his *b* is in darkness,
3.10 neither he that loveth not his *b*.
12 wicked one, and slew his *b*.
14 loveth not his *b* abideth in death.
15 Whosoever hateth his *b* is a
17 seeth his *b* have need, and
4.20 hateth his *b*, he is a liar: for he
20 that loveth not his *b* whom he
21 who loveth God, love his *b* also.
5.16 any man see his *b* sin a sin which
Jude 1 of Jesus Christ, and *b* of James,
Rev 1. 9 I John who also am your *b*, and

BROTHERHOOD

Zec 11.14 the *b* between Judah and Israel.
1Pe 2.17 Love the *b*. Fear God. Honor

Biblical Themes

BROTHERHOOD

And the Lord said unto Cain, Where is Abel thy brother? And he said, I know not: Am I my brother's keeper?
Gen 4.9

And he lifted up his eyes, and saw his brother Benjamin, his mother's son. . . . And Joseph made haste; for his bowels did yearn upon his brother: and he sought where to weep.
Gen 43.29-30

The soul of Jonathan was knit with the soul of David, and Jonathan loved him as his own soul. 1Sa 18.1

I am distressed for thee, my brother Jonathan: very pleasant hast thou been unto me: thy love to me was wonderful, passing the love of women. 2Sa 1.26

Behold, how good and how pleasant it is for brethren to dwell together in unity! Ps 133.1

A friend loveth at all times, and a brother is born for adversity. Pr 17.17

A man that hath friends must shew himself friendly: and there is a friend that sticketh closer than a brother.
Pr 18.24

Can two walk together, except they be agreed? Am 3.3

For thy violence against thy brother Jacob shame shall cover thee, and thou shalt be cut off for ever.
Ob 10

Whosoever is angry with his brother without a cause shall be in danger of the judgment. . . . Therefore if thou bring thy gift to the altar, and there rememberest that thy brother hath ought against thee; leave there thy gift before the altar, and go thy way; first be reconciled to thy brother, and then come and offer thy gift. Mt 5.22-24

Whosoever shall do the will of my Father which is in heaven, the same is my brother, and sister, and mother.
Mt 12.50

And he answering said to his father, Lo, these many years do I serve thee, neither transgressed I at any time thy commandment: and yet thou never gavest me a kid, that I might make merry with my friends: but as soon as this thy son was come, which hath devoured thy living with harlots, thou hast killed for him the fatted calf. And he said unto him, Son, thou art ever with me, and all that I have is thine. It was meet that we should make merry, and be glad: for this thy brother was dead, and is alive again; and was lost, and is found.
Lk 15.29-32

And all that believed were together, and had all things common. Ac 2.44

Let us not therefore judge one another any more: but judge this rather, that no man put a stumblingblock or an occasion to fall in his brother's way. . . . It is good neither to eat flesh, nor to drink wine, nor any thing whereby thy brother stumbleth. Ro 14.13, 21

But brother goeth to law with brother, and that before the unbelievers.
1Co 6.6

Count him not as an enemy, but admonish him as a brother.
2Th 3.15

Perhaps he therefore departed for a season, that thou shouldest receive him for ever; not now as a servant, but above a servant, a brother beloved, specially to me, but how much more unto thee, both in the flesh, and in the Lord? Phm 15-16

Let brotherly love continue. Heb 13.1

Seeing ye have purified your souls in obeying the truth through the Spirit unto unfeigned love of the brethren, see that ye love one another with a pure heart fervently. 1Pe 1.22

Whosoever hateth his brother is a murderer: and ye know that no murderer hath eternal life abiding in him.
1Jn 3.15

BROTHERLY
Am 1. 9 remembered not the *b* covenant:
Ro 12.10 one to another with *b* love;
1Th 4. 9 But as touching *b* love ye need
Heb 13. 1 Let *b* love continue.
2Pe 1. 7 godliness *b* kindness; and to *b*

BROTHER'S
Gen 4. 9 I know not: Am I my *b* keeper?
10 the voice of thy *b* blood crieth
11 her mouth to receive thy *b* blood
21 And his *b* name was Jubal:
10.25 and his *b* name was Joktan.
12. 5 Sarah his wife, and Lot his *b* son,
14.12 And they took Lot, Abram's *b* son,
24.48 to take my master's *b* daughter
27.44 until thy *b* fury turn away;
45 Until thy *b* anger turn away
38. 8 in unto thy *b* wife, and marry her,
9 he went in unto his *b* wife, that he
Lev 18.16 the nakedness of thy *b* wife:
16 it is thy *b* nakedness.
20.21 if a man shall take his *b* wife,
21 hath uncovered his *b* nakedness;
Dt 22. 1 Thou shalt not see thy *b* ox
3 with all lost thing of thy *b*,
4 Thou shalt not see thy *b* ass or
25. 7 like not to take his *b* wife,
7 then let his *b* wife go up to the
9 Then shall his *b* wife come unto
9 will not build up his *b* house
1Ki 2.15 turned about, and is become my *b*:
1Ch 1.19 and his *b* name was Joktan.
Job 1.13 drinking wine in their eldest *b*
18 wine in their eldest *b* house:
Pr 27.10 neither go into thy *b* house in
Mt 7. 3 the mote that is in thy *b* eye,
5 out the mote out of thy *b* eye.
Mk 6.18 lawful for thee to have thy *b* wife,
Lk 6.41 mote that is in thy *b* eye,
42 out the mote that is in thy *b* eye.
Ro 14.13 an occasion to fall in his *b* way.
1Jn 3.12 were evil, and his *b* righteous.

BROW
Isa 48. 4 an iron sinew, and thy *b* brass;
Lk 4.29 and led him unto the *b* of the hill

BRUISE
Gen 3.15 it shall *b* thy head,
15 and thou shalt *b* his heel.
Isa 28.28 cart, nor *b* it with his horsemen.
53.10 Yet it pleased the Lord to *b* him;
Jer 30.12 Thy *b* is incurable, and thy
Dan 2.40 shall it break in pieces and *b*.
Na 3.19 no healing of thy *b*; thy wound
Ro 16.20 *b* Satan under your feet shortly.

BRUISED
Lev 22.24 unto the Lord that which is *b*,
2Ki 18.21 the staff of this *b* reed, even
Isa 28.28 Bread corn is *b*; because he
42. 3 A *b* reed shall he not break, and
53. 5 he was *b* for our iniquities: the
Eze 23. 3 they *b* the teats of their virginity.
8 *b* the breasts of her virginity,
Mt 12.20 A *b* reed shall he not break, and
Lk 4.18 to set at liberty them that are *b*,

BRUTE
2Pe 2.12 these, as natural *b* beasts, made
Jude 10 know naturally, as *b* beasts, in

BUCKET
Isa 40.15 the nations are as a drop of a *b*,

BUDDED
Gen 40.10 it was as though it *b*, and her
Nu 17. 8 Aaron for the house of Levi was *b*,
SS 6.11 and the pomegranates *b*.
Eze 7.10 hath blossomed, pride hath *b*.
Heb 9. 4 Aaron's rod that *b*, and the tables

BUFFET
Mk 14.65 to cover his face, and to *b* him,
2Co 12. 7 messenger of Satan to *b* me, lest

BUFFETED
Mt 26.67 they spit in his face and *b* him;
1Co 4.11 and are *b*, and have no certain
1Pe 2.20 when ye be *b* for your faults, ye

BUILD
Gen 11. 4 Go to, let us *b* us a city and
8 and they left off to *b* the city.
Ex 20.25 thou shalt not *b* it of hewn stone:
Nu 23. 1, 29 *B* me here seven altars, and
32.16 We will *b* sheepfolds here for our
24 *B* you cities for your little ones,
Dt 20.20 and thou shalt *b* bulwarks against
25. 9 will not *b* up his brother's house.
27. 5 there shalt thou *b* an altar unto
6 Thou shalt *b* the altar of the Lord

Dt 28.30 thou shalt *b* an house, and thou
Jos 22.26 Let us now prepare to *b* us an
29 to *b* an altar for burnt offerings,
Jdg 6.26 And *b* an altar unto the Lord
Ru 4.11 two did *b* the house of Israel:
1Sa 2.35 and I will *b* him a sure house;
2Sa 7. 5 Shalt thou *b* me an house for me
7 Why *b* ye not me an house of
13 shall *b* an house for my name,
27 saying, I will *b* thee an house:
24.21 to *b* an altar unto the Lord, that
1Ki 2.36 *B* thee an house in Jerusalem
5. 3 my father could not *b* an house
5 behold, I purpose to *b* an house
5 shall *b* an house unto my name.
18 timber and stones to *b* the house.
6. 1 that he began to *b* the house of
8.16 tribes of Israel to *b* an house,
17 David my father to *b* an house
18 to *b* an house unto my name, thou
19 thou shalt not *b* the house; but
19 shall *b* the house unto my name.
9.15 to *b* the house of the Lord, and
19 which Solomon desired to *b* in
24 built for her: then did he *b* Millo.
11. 7 Then did Solomon *b* an high place
38 and *b* thee a sure house,
16.34 did Hiel the Beth-elite *b* Jericho:
1Ch 14. 1 carpenters, to *b* him an house.
17. 4 Thou shalt not *b* me an house
10 the Lord will *b* thee an house.
12 He shall *b* me an house, and I will
25 that thou wilt *b* him an house:
21.22 that I may *b* an altar therein unto
22. 2 stones to *b* the house of God.
6 him to *b* an house for the Lord
7 it was in my mind to *b* an house
8 thou shalt not *b* an house unto
10 shall *b* an house for my name;
11 *b* the house of the Lord thy God,
19 and *b* the sanctuary of the Lord
28. 2 in mine heart to *b* an house of
3 Thou shalt not *b* an house for my
6 shall *b* my house and my courts,
10 to *b* an house for the sanctuary:
29.16 to *b* thee an house for thine holy
19 and to *b* the palace, for the which
2Ch 2. 1 Solomon determined to *b* an house
3 send him cedars to *b* him an
4 Behold, I *b* an house to the name
5 the house which I *b* is great: for
6 who is able to *b* him an house,
6 that I should *b* him an house,
9 the house which I am about to *b*
12 that might *b* an house for the Lord,
3. 1 Solomon began to *b* the house
2 And he began to *b* in the second
6. 5 to *b* an house in, that my name
7 David my father to *b* an house
8 heart to *b* an house for my name,
9 thou shalt not *b* the house; but
9 he shall *b* the house for my name.
8. 6 desired to *b* in Jerusalem,
14. 7 Let us *b* these cities, and make
35. 3 son of David king of Israel did *b*;
36.23 to *b* him an house in Jerusalem,
Ezr 1. 2 to *b* him an house at Jerusalem,
3 and *b* the house of the Lord God
5 to *b* the house of the Lord which
4. 2 Let us *b* with you: for we seek
3 to *b* an house unto our God;
3 but we ourselves together will *b*
5. 2 and began to *b* the house of God
3 Who hath commanded you to *b*
9 commanded you to *b* this house,
11 and *b* the house that was builded
13 made a decree to *b* this house of
17 was made of Cyrus the king to *b*
6. 7 the elders of the Jews *b* this house
Neh 2. 5 sepulchres, that I may *b* it.
17 let us *b* up the wall of Jerusalem,
18 Let us rise up and *b*. So they
20 we his servants will arise and *b*:
3. 3 did the sons of Hassenaah *b*, who
4. 3 Even that which they *b*, if a fox
10 that we are not able to *b* the wall.
Ps 28. 5 destroy them, and not *b* them up.
51.18 *b* thou the walls of Jerusalem.
69.35 and will *b* the cities of Judah:
89. 4 *b* up thy throne to all generations.
102.16 the Lord shall *b* up Zion, he shall
127. 1 Except the Lord *b* the house, they
1 house, they labor in vain that *b* it:
147. 2 The Lord doth *b* up Jerusalem:
Pr 24.27 and afterwards *b* thine house.
Ec 3. 3 break down, and a time to *b* up;
SS 8. 9 will *b* upon her a palace of silver:
Isa 9.10 but we will *b* with hewn stones:
45.13 he shall *b* my city, and he shall
58.12 they that shall be of thee shall *b*
60.10 the sons of strangers shall *b* up
61. 4 And they shall *b* the old wastes,
65.21 shall *b* houses, and inhabit them;
22 shall not *b*, and another inhabit;
66. 1 where is the house that ye *b* unto
Jer 1.10 to throw down, to *b*, and to plant.
18. 9 concerning a kingdom, to *b* and
22.14 I will *b* me a wide house and large
24. 6 I will *b* them, and not pull them
29. 5, 28 *B* ye houses, and dwell in them;
31. 4 Again I will *b* thee, and thou shalt
28 so will I watch over them, to *b*,
33. 7 and will *b* them, as at the first.
35. 7 Neither shall ye *b* house, nor sow
9 Nor to *b* houses for us to dwell in:
42.10 then will I *b* you, and not pull you
Eze 4. 2 and *b* a fort against it, and cast a
11. 3 let us *b* houses: this city is the
21.22 to cast a mount, and to *b* a fort.
28.26 and shall *b* houses, and plant
36.36 that I the Lord *b* the ruined
Dan 9.25 to restore and to *b* Jerusalem
Am 9.11 I will *b* it as in the days of old:
14 and they shall *b* the waste cities,
Mic 3.10 They *b* up Zion with blood, and
Zep 1.13 they shall also *b* houses, but not
Hag 1. 8 and *b* the house; and I will take
Zec 5.11 To *b* it an house in the land of
6.12 and he shall *b* the temple of the
13 Even he shall *b* the temple of
15 and *b* in the temple of the Lord,
9. 3 Tyrus did *b* herself a strong hold,
Mal 1. 4 return and *b* the desolate places;
4 shall *b*, but I will throw down;
Mt 16.18 upon this rock I will *b* my
23.29 because ye *b* the tombs of the
26.61 God, and to *b* it in three days.
Mk 14.58 within three days I will *b* another
Lk 11.47 *b* the sepulchres of the prophets,
48 them, and ye *b* their sepulchres.
12.18 I will pull down my barns, and *b*
14.28 intending to *b* a tower, sitteth
30 This man began to *b*, and was not
Ac 7.49 what house will ye *b* me? saith
15.16 *b* again the tabernacle of David,
16 I will *b* again the ruins thereof,
20.32 to *b* you up, and to give you an
Ro 15.20 lest I should *b* upon another
1Co 3.12 Now if any man *b* upon this
Gal 2.18 if I *b* again the things which I

BUILDED

Gen 4.17 and he *b* a city, and called the
8.20 Noah *b* an altar unto the Lord;
10.11 and *b* Nineveh, and the city
11. 5 which the children of men *b*.
12. 7 there *b* he an altar unto the Lord,
8 and there he *b* an altar unto the
26.25 And he *b* an altar there, and
Ex 24. 4 and *b* an altar under the hill,
Nu 32.38 unto the cities which they *b*.
Jos 22.16 in that ye have *b* you an altar,
1Ki 8.27 less this house that I have *b*?
43 this house, which I have *b*, is
15.22 thereof, wherewith Baasha had *b*;
2Ki 23.13 Solomon the king of Israel had *b*
1Ch 22. 5 to be *b* for the Lord must be
Ezr 3. 2 and *b* the altar of the God of Israel,
4. 1 children of the captivity *b* the
13 if this city be *b*, and the walls set
16 if this city be *b* again, and the
21 and that this city be not *b*, until
5. 8 which is *b* with great stones,
11 *b* these many years ago, which
11 which a great king of Israel *b* and
15 let the house of God be *b* in this
6. 3 Let the house be *b*, the place
14 And the elders of the Jews *b*,
14 And they *b*, and finished it,
Neh 3. 1 and they *b* the sheep gate;
2 And next unto him *b* the men
2 And next to him *b* Zaccur
4. 1 heard that we *b* the wall, he was
17 They which *b* on the wall, and
18 girded by his side, and so *b*.
6. 1 heard that I had *b* the wall, and
7. 4 and the houses were not *b*.
12.29 the singers had *b* them villages
Job 20.19 away an house which he *b* not;
Ps 122. 3 Jerusalem is *b* as a city that is
Pr 9. 1 Wisdom hath *b* her house, she
24. 3 Through wisdom is an house *b*;
Ec 2. 4 I *b* me houses; I planted me
SS 4. 4 tower of David *b* for an armory,
Jer 30.18 and the city shall be *b* upon
La 3. 5 He hath *b* against me, and
Eze 36.10 and the wastes shall be *b*:
33 cities, and the wastes shall be *b*.
Lk 17.28 they sold, they planted, they *b*;
Eph 2.22 In whom ye also are *b* together
Heb 3. 3 as he who hath *b* the house hath
4 every house is *b* by some man;

BUILDEDST

Dt 6.10 goodly cities, which thou *b* not,

BUILDER

Heb 11.10 whose *b* and maker is God.

BUILDERS

1Ki 5.18 Solomon's *b* and Hiram's *b*
2Ki 12.11 to the carpenters and *b*, that
22. 6 Unto carpenters, and *b*, and
2Ch 34.11 to the artificers and *b* gave they it,
Ezr 3.10 when the *b* laid the foundation
Neh 4. 5 thee to anger before the *b*.
18 For the *b*, every one had his
Ps 118.22 the stone which the *b* refused
Eze 27. 4 thy *b* have perfected thy beauty.
Mt 21.42 The stone which the *b* rejected,
Mk 12.10 The stone which the *b* rejected
Lk 20.17 The stone which the *b* rejected,
Ac 4.11 which was set at nought of you *b*,
1Pe 2. 7 the stone which the *b* disallowed,

BUILDEST

Dt 22. 8 When thou *b* a new house,
Neh 6. 6 which cause thou *b* the wall,
Eze 16.31 In that thou *b* thine eminent
Mt 27.40 temple and *b* it in three days,
Mk 15.29 temple, and *b* it in three days,

BUILDETH

Jos 6.26 and *b* this city Jericho: he shall
Job 27.18 he *b* his house as a moth, and
Pr 14. 1 Every wise woman *b* her house:
Jer 22.13 Woe unto him that *b* his house
Hos 8.14 and *b* temples; and Judah
Am 9. 6 that *b* his stories in the heaven,
Hab 2.12 Woe to him that *b* a town with
1Co 3.10 foundation, and another *b*
10 take heed how he *b* thereupon.

BUILDING

Jos 22.19 in *b* you an altar beside the
1Ki 3. 1 made an end of *b* his own house,
6. 7 when it was in *b*, was built of
7 in the house, while it was in *b*.
12 which thou art in *b*, if thou wilt
38 So was he seven years in *b* it.
7. 1 Solomon was *b* his own house
9. 1 Solomon had finished the *b* of
15.21 that he left off *b* of Ramah,
1Ch 28. 2 and had made ready for the *b*:
2Ch 3. 3 for the *b* of the house of God.
16. 5 that he left off *b* of Ramah,
6 wherewith Baasha was *b*; and
Ezr 4. 4 Judah, and troubled them in *b*,
12 *b* the rebellious and the bad
5. 4 of the men that make this *b*?
16 even until now hath it been in *b*,
6. 8 for the *b* of this house of God:
Ec 10.18 By much slothfulness the *b*
Eze 17.17 and *b* forts, to cut off many
40. 5 the breadth of the *b*, one reed;
41.12 Now the *b* that was before the
12 broad; and the wall of the *b*
13 and the *b*, with the walls thereof,
15 the length of the *b* over against
42. 1 before the *b* toward the north.
5 and than the middlemost of the *b*.
6 therefore the *b* was straitened
10 place, and over against the *b*.
46.23 there was a row of *b* round about
Jn 2.20 was this temple in *b*, and wilt
1Co 3. 9 husbandry, ye are God's *b*.
2Co 5. 1 we have a *b* of God, an house
Eph 2.21 In whom all the *b* fitly framed
Heb 9.11 that is to say, not of this *b*;
Jude 20 *b* up yourselves on your most
Rev 21.18 the *b* of the wall of it was of

BUILDINGS

Mt 24. 1 to shew him the *b* of the temple.
Mk 13. 1 stones and what *b* are here!
2 him, Seest thou these great *b*?

BUILT

Gen 13.18 *b* there an altar unto the Lord.
22. 9 and Abraham *b* an altar there,
33.17 and *b* him an house, and made
35. 7 And he *b* there an altar,
Ex 1.11 *b* for Pharaoh treasure cities,
17.15 And Moses *b* an altar, and called
32. 5 he *b* an altar before it; and Aaron
Nu 13.22 Hebron was *b* seven years before
21.27 let the city of Sihon be *b* and
23.14 and *b* seven altars, and offered
32.34 And the children of Gad *b* Dibon,
37 the children of Reuben *b* Heshbon,
Dt 8.12 and hast *b* goodly houses, and
13.16 for ever; it shall not be *b* again.
20. 5 that hath *b* a new house, and
Jos 8.30 Joshua *b* an altar unto the Lord
19.50 Ephraim: and he *b* the city,
22.10 tribe of Manasseh *b* there an altar
11 *b* an altar over against the land
23 That we have *b* us an altar to
24.13 cities which ye *b* not, and ye
Jdg 1.26 and *b* a city, and called the name
6.24 Then Gideon *b* an altar there
28 offered upon the altar that was *b*.
18.28 And they *b* a city, and dwelt
21. 4 and *b* there an altar, and offered
1Sa 7.17 there he *b* an altar unto the Lord.
14.35 And Saul *b* an altar unto the Lord:
35 same was the first altar that he *b*
2Sa 5. 9 And David *b* round about from
11 and they *b* David an house.
24.25 And David *b* there an altar unto
1Ki 3. 2 *b* unto the name of the Lord,
6. 2 the house which king Solomon *b*
5 against the wall of the house he *b*
7 was *b* of stone made ready before
9 So he *b* the house, and finished it;
10 And then he *b* chambers against
14 So Solomon *b* the house, and
15 And he *b* the walls of the house
16 And he *b* twenty cubits on the
16 with boards of cedar: he even *b*
36 And he *b* the inner court with
7. 2 He *b* also the house of the forest
8.13 I have surely *b* thee an house to
20 promised, and have *b* an house
44 house that I have *b* for thy name:
48 and the house which I have *b*
9. 3 thou hast *b*, to put my name
10 Solomon had *b* the two houses,
17 And Solomon *b* Gezer, and
24 house which Solomon had *b* for
25 altar which he *b* unto the Lord,
10. 4 and the house that he had *b*,
11.27 Solomon *b* Millo, and repaired the
38 a sure house, as I *b* for David,
12.25 Then Jeroboam *b* Shechem in
25 out from thence, and *b* Penuel.
14.23 they also *b* them high places,
15.17 up against Judah, and *b* Ramah,
22 and king Asa *b* with them Geba
23 the cities which he *b*, are they
16.24 and *b* on the hill, and called
24 the name of the city which he *b*,
32 Baal, which he had *b* in Samaria.
18.32 And with the stones he *b* an altar
22.39 made, and all the cities that he *b*,
2Ki 14.22 He *b* Elath, and restored it to
15.35 He *b* the higher gate of the house
16.11 And Urijah the priest *b* an altar
18 that they had *b* in the house, and
17. 9 and they *b* them high places in all
21. 3 he *b* up again the high places
4 And he *b* altars in the house of
5 And he *b* altars for all the host of
25. 1 they *b* forts against it round about.
1Ch 6.10 that Solomon *b* in Jerusalem:)
32 until Solomon had *b* the house of
7.24 who *b* Beth-horon the nether, and
8.12 who *b* Ono, and Lod, with the towns
11. 8 And he *b* the city round about,
17. 6 Why have ye not *b* me an house
21.26 And David *b* there an altar unto
22.19 the house that is to be *b* to the
2Ch 6. 2 I have *b* an house of habitation
10 and have *b* the house for the name
18 less this house which I have *b*!
33 this house which I have *b* is called
34 which I have *b* for thy name;
38 toward the house which I have *b*
8. 1 Solomon had *b* the house of the
2 Solomon *b* them, and caused the
4 he *b* Tadmor in the wilderness,
4 store cities, which he *b* in Hamath.
5 Also he *b* Beth-horon the upper,
11 house that he had *b* for her:
12 which he had *b* before the porch,
9. 3 and the house that he had *b*,
11. 5 *b* cities for defense in Judah.
6 He *b* even Beth-lehem, and Etam,
14. 6 And he *b* fenced cities in Judah:
7 So they *b* and prospered.
16. 1 and *b* Ramah, to the intent that
6 he *b* therewith Geba and Mizpah.
17.12 he *b* in Judah castles, and cities
20. 8 *b* thee a sanctuary therein for thy
26. 2 He *b* Eloth, and restored it to
6 and *b* cities about Ashdod, and
9 Uzziah *b* towers in Jerusalem at
10 Also he *b* towers in the desert,
27. 3 He *b* the high gate of the house of
3 and on the wall of Ophel he *b*
4 he *b* cities in the mountains of
4 and in the forests he *b* castles
32. 5 and *b* up all the wall that was
33. 3 For he *b* again the high places
4 Also he *b* altars in the house of
5 And he *b* altars for all the host of
14 after this he *b* a wall without the
15 all the altars that he had *b* in the
19 places wherein he *b* high places,
Neh 3.13 they *b* it, and set up the doors
14 he *b* it, and set up the doors
15 he *b* it, and covered it, and set up
4. 6 So *b* we the wall; and all the wall
7. 1 when the wall was *b*, and I had set
Job 3.14 *b* desolate places for themselves;
12.14 down, and it cannot be *b* again:
22.23 thou shalt be *b* up, thou shalt put
Ps 78.69 *b* his sanctuary like high palaces,
89. 2 Mercy shall be *b* up for ever: thy
Ec 9.14 and *b* great bulwarks against it:
Isa 5. 2 and *b* a tower in the midst of it,
25. 2 to be no city; it shall never be *b*.
44.26 Ye shall be *b*, and I will raise up
28 Thou shalt be *b*; and to the
Jer 7.31 And they have *b* the high places
12.16 then shall they be *b* in the midst
19. 5 They have *b* also the high places
31. 4 thou shalt be *b*, O virgin of Israel:
38 the city shall be *b* to the Lord
32.31 from the day that they *b* it even
35 And they *b* the high places of Baal,
45. 4 which I have *b* will I break down,
52. 4 and *b* forts against it round about.
Eze 13.10 one *b* up a wall, and, lo, others
16.24 also *b* unto thee an eminent place,
25 Thou hast *b* thy high place at
26.14 thou shalt be *b* no more: for I the
Dan 4.30 I have *b* for the house of the
9.25 the street shall be *b* again,
Am 5.11 ye have *b* houses of hewn stone,
Mic 7.11 the day that thy walls are to be *b*,
Hag 1. 2 that the Lord's house should be *b*.
Zec 1.16 my house shall be *b* in it, saith
8. 9 laid, that the temple might be *b*.
Mt 7.24 which *b* his house upon a rock:
26 which *b* his house upon the sand:
21.33 winepress in it, and *b* a tower,
Mk 12. 1 and *b* a tower, and let it out to
Lk 4.29 whereon their city was *b*, that
6.48 a man which *b* an house, and
49 a man that...*b* an house upon
7. 5 and he hath *b* us a synagogue.
Ac 7.47 But Solomon *b* him an house.
1Co 3.14 abide which he hath *b* thereupon,
Eph 2.20 And are *b* upon the foundation
Col 2. 7 Rooted and *b* up in him, and
Heb 3. 4 but he that *b* all things is God.
1Pe 2. 5 are *b* up a spiritual house,

BULLS

Gen 32.15 forty kine, and ten *b*, twenty
Ps 22.12 Many *b* have compassed me:
12 strong *b* of Bashan have beset me
50.13 Will I eat the flesh of *b*, or drink
68.30 the multitude of the *b*, with the
Isa 34. 7 the bullocks with the *b*; and their
Jer 50.11 heifer at grass, and bellow as *b*;
52.20 and twelve brasen *b* that were
Heb 9.13 if the blood of *b* and of goats,
10. 4 not possible that the blood of *b*

BUNDLE

Gen 42.35 every man's *b* of money was in
1Sa 25.29 bound in the *b* of life with the
SS 1.13 A *b* of myrrh is my wellbeloved
Ac 28. 3 gathered a *b* of sticks, and laid

BUNDLES

Gen 42.35 their father saw the *b* of money,
Mt 13.30 bind them in *b* to burn them:

BURDEN

Ex 18.22 they shall bear the *b* with thee.
23. 5 lying under his *b*, and wouldest
Nu 4.15 the *b* of the sons of Kohath in the
19 one to his service and to his *b*:

Nu 4.31 And this is the charge of their *b*,
32 of the charge of their *b*.
47 service of the *b* in the tabernacle
49 according to his *b*: thus were they
11.11 the *b* of all this people upon me?
17 they shall bear the *b* of the people
Dt 1.12 and your *b*, and your strife?
2Sa 15.33 then thou shalt be a *b* unto me:
19.35 should thy servant be yet a *b*
2Ki 5.17 servant two mules' *b* of earth?
8. 9 forty camels' *b*, and came and
9.25 the Lord laid this *b* upon him;
2Ch 35. 3 not be a *b* upon your shoulders:
Neh 13.19 there should no *b* be brought in
Job 7.20 so that I am a *b* to myself?
Ps 38. 4 as an heavy *b* they are too heavy
55.22 Cast thy *b* upon the Lord, and he
81. 6 removed his shoulder from the *b*:
Ec 12. 5 and the grasshopper shall be a *b*,
Isa 9. 4 broken the yoke of his *b*, and the
10.27 his *b* shall be taken away from off
13. 1 The *b* of Babylon, which Isaiah
14.25 and his *b* depart from off their
28 that king Ahaz died was this *b*.
15. 1 The *b* of Moab. Because in the
17. 1 The *b* of Damascus. Behold,
19. 1 The *b* of Egypt. Behold, the Lord
21. 1 The *b* of the desert of the sea.
11 The *b* of Dumah. He calleth to
13 The *b* upon Arabia. In the forest
22. 1 The *b* of the valley of vision.
25 fall; and the *b* that was upon it
23. 1 The *b* of Tyre. Howl, ye ships
30. 6 The *b* of the beasts of the south:
27 the *b* thereof is heavy: his lips
46. 1 they are a *b* to the weary beast.
2 they could not deliver the *b*, but
Jer 17.21 bear no *b* on the sabbath day,
22 Neither carry forth a *b* out of
24 to bring in no *b* through the gates
27 not to bear a *b*, even entering in at
23.33 saying, What is the *b* of the Lord?
33 then say unto them, What *b*?
34 that shall say, The *b* of the Lord,
36 And the *b* of the Lord shall ye
36 every man's word shall be his *b*;
38 ye say, The *b* of the Lord;
38 this word, The *b* of the Lord,
38 shall not say, The *b* of the Lord;
Eze 12.10 This *b* concerneth the prince
Hos 8.10 for the *b* of the king of princes.
Na 1. 1 The *b* of Nineveh. The book of
Hab 1. 1 *b* which Habakkuk the prophet
Zep 3.18 whom the reproach of it was a *b*.
Zec 9. 1 The *b* of the word of the Lord in
12. 1 The *b* of the word of the Lord
3 all that *b* themselves with it
Mal 1. 1 The *b* of the word of the Lord to
Mt 11.30 yoke is easy, and my *b* is light.
20.12 which have borne the *b* and heat
Ac 15.28 upon you no greater *b* than these
21. 3 the ship was to unlade her *b*.
2Co 12.16 I did not *b* you: nevertheless,
Gal 6. 5 every man shall bear his own *b*.
Rev 2.24 will put upon you none other *b*.

BURDENED

2Co 5. 4 do groan, being *b*: not for that
8.13 other men be eased, and ye *b*:

BURDENS

Gen 49.14 crouching down between two *b*:
Ex 1.11 to afflict them with their *b*.
2.11 looked on their *b*: and he spied
5. 4 their works? get you unto your *b*.
5 ye make them rest from their *b*.
6. 6 from under the *b* of the Egyptians,
7 bringeth you out from under the *b*
Nu 4.24 Gershonites, to serve, and for *b*:
27 the Gershonites, in all their *b*,
27 unto them in charge all their *b*.
1Ki 5.15 and ten thousand that bare *b*,
2Ch 2. 2 ten thousand men to bear *b*,
18 to be bearers of *b*, and fourscore
24.27 the greatness of the *b* laid upon
34.13 over the bearers of *b*, and were
Neh 4.10 The strength of the bearers of *b*
17 and they that bare *b*, with those
13.15 all manner of *b*, which they
Isa 58. 6 to undo the heavy *b*, and to
La 2.14 false *b* and causes of banishment.
Am 5.11 ye take from him *b* of wheat:
Mt 23. 4 For they bind heavy *b* and
Lk 11.46 with *b* grievous to be borne, and
46 ye yourselves touch not the *b*
Gal 6. 2 Bear ye one another's *b*, and

BURDENSOME

Zec 12. 3 will I make Jerusalem a *b* stone
2Co 11. 9 kept myself from being *b* unto
12.13 I myself was not *b* to you?
14 I will not be *b* to you: for I seek
1Th 2. 6 we might have been *b*, as the

BURIAL

2Ch 26.23 in the field of the *b* which
Ec 6. 3 good, and also that ye have no *b*;
Isa 14.20 not be joined with them in *b*,
Jer 22.19 with the *b* of an ass, drawn and
Mt 26.12 my body, she did it for my *b*.
Ac 8. 2 men carried Stephen to his *b*,

BURIED

Gen 15.15 thou shalt be *b* in a good old age.
23.19 Abraham *b* Sarah his wife in the
25. 9 his sons Isaac and Ishmael *b* him
10 there was Abraham *b*, and Sarah
35. 8 nurse died, and she was *b*
19 Rachel died, and was *b* in the
29 his sons Esau and Jacob *b* him.
48. 7 and I *b* her there in the way of
49.31 There they *b* Abraham and Sarah
31 there they *b* Isaac and Rebekah
31 and there I *b* Leah.
50.13 and *b* him in the cave of the field
14 after he had *b* his father.
Nu 11.34 because there they *b* the people
20. 1 Miriam died there, and was *b*
33. 4 For the Egyptians *b* all their
Dt 10. 6 Aaron died, and there he was *b*;
34. 6 And he *b* him in a valley in the
Jos 24.30 And they *b* him in the border of
32 *b* they in Shechem, in a parcel
33 and they *b* him in a hill that
Jdg 2. 9 And they *b* him in the border of
8.32 died in a good old age, and was *b*
10. 2 and died, and was *b* in Shamir.
5 Jair died, and was *b* in Camon.
12. 7 the Gileadite, and was *b* in one of
10 Ibzan, and was *b* at Beth-lehem.
12 died, and was *b* in Aijalon
15 died, and was *b* in Pirathon in
16.31 *b* him between Zorah and Eshtaol
Ru 1.17 and there will I be *b*: the Lord
1Sa 25. 1 and *b* him in his house at Ramah.
28. 3 and *b* him in Ramah, even in
31.13 *b* them under a tree at Jabesh,
2Sa 2. 4 Jabesh-gilead were they that *b*
5 even unto Saul, and have *b* him.
32 and *b* him in the sepulchre of his
3.32 And they *b* Abner in Hebron:
4.12 head of Ish-bosheth, and *b* it
17.23 and was *b* in the sepulchre of his
19.37 be *b* by the grave of my father
21.14 and Jonathan his son *b* they
1Ki 2.10 slept with his fathers, and was *b*
34 and he was *b* in his own house
11.43 slept with his fathers, and was *b*
13.31 after he had *b* him, that he spake
31 wherein the man of God is *b*;
14.18 And they *b* him; and all Israel
31 slept with his fathers, and was *b*
15. 8 they *b* him in the city of David:
24 slept with his fathers, and was *b*
16. 6, 28 with his fathers, and was *b*
22.37 and they *b* the king in Samaria.
50 slept with his fathers, and was *b*
2Ki 8.24 slept with his fathers, and was *b*
9.28 and *b* him in his sepulchre with
10.35 fathers: and they *b* him in
12.21 and they *b* him with his fathers
13. 9 and they *b* him in Samaria: and
13 and Joash was *b* in Samaria with
20 And Elisha died, and they *b* him.
14.16 slept with his fathers, and was *b*
20 and he was *b* at Jerusalem with
15. 7 and they *b* him with his fathers
38 slept with his fathers, and was *b*
16.20 slept with his fathers, and was *b*
21.18 slept with his fathers, and was *b*
26 And he was *b* in his sepulchre
23.30 and *b* him in his own sepulchre.
1Ch 10.12 and *b* their bones under the oak
2Ch 9.31 and he was *b* in the city of David
12.16 slept with his fathers, and was *b*
14. 1 they *b* him in the city of David:
16.14 *b* him in his own sepulchres.
21. 1 slept with his fathers, and was *b*
20 Howbeit they *b* him in the city of
22. 9 they had slain him, they *b* him:
24.16 they *b* him in the city of David
25 and they *b* him in the city of David,
25 they *b* him not in the sepulchres
25.28 and *b* him with his fathers in the
26.23 *b* him with his fathers in the field
27. 9 they *b* him in the city of David:
28.27 and they *b* him in the city, even
32.33 and they *b* him in the chiefest of
33.20 and they *b* him in his own house:
35.24 and was *b* in one of the sepulchres
Job 27.15 remain of him shall be *b* in death:
Ec 8.10 And so I saw the wicked *b*, who
Jer 8. 2 shall not be gathered, nor be *b*;
16. 4 lamented; neither shall they be *b*;
6 they shall not be *b*, neither shall
20. 6 thou shalt die, and shalt be *b*
22.19 He shall be *b* with the burial of an
25.33 lamented, neither gathered, nor *b*;
Eze 39.15 till the buriers have *b* it in the
Mt 14.12 and *b* it, and went and told Jesus.
Lk 16.22 rich man also died, and was *b*;
Ac 2.29 he is both dead and *b*, and his
5. 6 and carried him out, and *b* him.
9 the feet of them which have *b* thy
10 carrying her forth, *b* her by her
Ro 6. 4 we are *b* with him by baptism
1Co 15. 4 And that he was *b*, and that he
Col 2.12 *B* with him in baptism, wherein

BURN

Gen 11. 3 let us make brick, and *b* them
44.18 let not thine anger *b* against thy
Ex 12.10 until the morning ye shall *b* with
27.20 light, to cause the lamp to *b*
29.13 them, and *b* them upon the altar.
14 his dung, shalt thou *b* with fire
18 And thou shalt *b* the whole ram
25 and *b* them upon the altar for a
34 then thou shalt *b* the remainder
30. 1 make an altar to *b* incense upon:
7 And Aaron shall *b* thereon sweet
7 lamps, he shall *b* incense upon it.
8 at even, he shall *b* incense upon
20 to *b* offering made by fire unto
Lev 1. 9 the priest shall *b* all on the altar,
13 and *b* it upon the altar: it is a
15 *b* it on the altar; and the blood
17 the priest shall *b* it upon the altar,
2. 2 the priest shall *b* the memorial
9 and shall *b* it upon the altar:
11 ye shall *b* no leaven, nor any
16 the priest shall *b* the memorial of
3. 5 And Aaron's sons shall *b* it on the

11 And the priest shall *b* it upon the
16 And the priest shall *b* them upon
4.10 and the priest shall *b* them upon
12 are poured out, and *b* him on the
19 from him, and *b* it upon the altar.
21 bullock without the camp, and *b*
26 he shall *b* all his fat upon the
31 and the priest shall *b* it upon the
35 and the priest shall *b* them upon
5.12 and *b* it on the altar, according
6.12 and the priest shall *b* wood on it
12 and he shall *b* thereon the fat
15 and shall *b* it upon the altar
7. 5 the priest shall *b* them upon the
31 And the priest shall *b* the fat
8.32 of the bread shall ye *b* with fire.
13.52 He shall therefore *b* that garment,
55 thou shalt *b* it in the fire;
57 thou shalt *b* that wherein the
16.25 offering shall he *b* upon the altar.
27 and they shall *b* in the fire their
17. 6 and *b* the fat for a sweet savor
24. 2 cause the lamps to *b* continually.
Nu 5.26 and *b* it upon the altar, and
18.17 shalt *b* their fat for an offering
19. 5 And one shall *b* the heifer in his
5 blood, with her dung, shall he *b*:
Dt 5.23 the mountain did *b* with fire,)
7. 5 *b* their graven images with fire.
25 images of their gods shall ye *b*
12. 3 *b* their groves with fire; and ye
13.16 and shalt *b* with fire the city,
32.22 and shall *b* unto the lowest hell,
Jos 11. 6 and *b* their chariots with fire.
13 Hazor only; that did Joshua *b*.
Jdg 9.52 the door of the tower to *b* it
12. 1 we will *b* thine house upon thee
14.15 lest we *b* thee and thy father's
1Sa 2.16 Let them not fail to *b* the fat
28 to *b* incense, to wear an ephod
1Ki 13. 1 stood by the altar to *b* incense.
2 the high places that *b* incense
2Ki 16.15 Upon the great altar *b* the morning
18. 4 children of Israel did *b* incense
23. 5 ordained to *b* incense in the
1Ch 23.13 to *b* incense before the Lord,
2Ch 2. 4 to *b* before him sweet incense,
6 save only to *b* sacrifice before
4.20 that they should *b* after the
13.11 And they *b* unto the Lord
11 to *b* every evening: for we keep
26.16 the temple of the Lord to *b*
18 to *b* incense unto the Lord,
18 that are consecrated to *b* incense:
19 a censer in his hand to *b* incense:
28.25 places to *b* incense unto other
29.11 unto him, and *b* incense.
32.12 altar, and *b* incense upon it?
Neh 10.34 to *b* upon the altar of the Lord
Ps 79. 5 shall thy jealousy *b* like fire?
89.46 shall thy wrath *b* like fire?
Isa 1.31 and they shall both *b* together,
10.17 and it shall *b* and devour his
27. 4 I would *b* them together.
40.16 Lebanon is not sufficient to *b*,
44.15 shall it be for a man to *b*: for he
47.14 the fire shall *b* them; they shall
Jer 4. 4 and *b* that none can quench it,
7. 9 and *b* incense unto Baal, and
20 and it shall *b*, and shall not be
31 *b* their sons and their daughters
11.13 altars to *b* incense unto Baal.
15.14 anger, which shall *b* upon you.
17. 4 anger, which shall *b* for ever.
19. 5 to *b* their sons with fire for
21.10 and he shall *b* it with fire.
12 and *b* that none can quench it,
32.29 and *b* it with the houses, upon
34. 2 and he shall *b* it with fire:
5 so shall they *b* odors for thee;
22 and *b* it with fire: and I will
36.25 that he would not *b* the roll:
37. 8 and take it, and *b* it with fire.
10 and *b* this city with fire.
38.18 and they shall *b* it with fire,
43.12 and he shall *b* them, and carry
13 the Egyptians shall he *b* with fire.
44. 3 in that they went to *b* incense,
5 to *b* no incense unto other gods.
17 to *b* incense unto the queen of
18 since we left off to *b* incense
25 *b* incense to the queen of heaven,
Eze 5. 2 Thou shalt *b* with fire a third
4 and *b* them in the fire; for
16.41 And they shall *b* thine houses
23.47 and *b* up their houses with fire.
24. 5 *b* also the bones under it, and
11 may be hot, and may *b*, and
39. 9 set on fire and *b* the weapons,
9 and they shall *b* them with fire
10 shall *b* the weapons with fire:
43.21 and he shall *b* it in the appointed
Hos 4.13 *b* incense upon the hills,
Na 2.13 and I will *b* her chariots in the
Hab 1.16 and *b* incense unto their drag;
Mal 4. 1 that shall *b* as an oven; and all
1 and the day that cometh shall *b*
Mt 3.12 but he will *b* up the chaff with
13.30 bind them in bundles to *b*
Lk 1. 9 his lot was to *b* incense when
3.17 but the chaff he will *b* with fire
24.32 Did not our heart *b* within us,
1Co 7. 9 it is better to marry than to *b*.
2Co 11.29 who is offended, and I *b* not?
Rev 17.16 and *b* her with fire.

BURNED

Ex 3. 2 the bush *b* with fire, and the
Lev 4.21 him as he *b* the first bullock:
8.16 and Moses *b* it upon the altar.
Dt 4.11 the mountain *b* with fire unto
9.15 and the mount *b* with fire:
Jos 7.25 and *b* them with fire, after
11.13 Israel *b* none of them, save Hazor
1Sa 30. 1 Ziklag, and *b* it with fire;
3 behold, it was *b* with fire; and
14 Caleb; and we *b* Ziklag with fire.
2Sa 5.21 and David and his men *b* them.
23. 7 they shall be utterly *b* with fire
2Ki 10.26 the house of Baal, and *b* them.
15.35 *b* incense still in the high places.
22.17 have *b* incense unto other gods,
23. 4 he *b* them without Jerusalem
5 also that *b* incense unto Baal,
6 and *b* it at the brook Kidron,
8 where the priest had *b* incense,
11 and *b* the chariots of the sun
15 brake down, and *b* the high place,
15 to powder, and *b* the grove.
16 and *b* them upon the altar,
20 and *b* men's bones upon them,
1Ch 14.12 and they were *b* with fire.
2Ch 25.14 them, *b* incense unto them.
29. 7 have not *b* incense nor offered
34.25 have *b* incense unto other gods,
Neh 1. 3 gates thereof are *b* with fire.
2.17 and the gates thereof are *b* with
4. 2 heaps of rubbish which are *b*?
Est 1.12 wroth, and his anger *b* in him.
Job 1.16 and hath *b* up the sheep,
30.30 and my bones are *b* with heat.
Ps 39. 3 while I was musing the fire *b*:
74. 8 have *b* up all the synagogues
80.16 It is *b* with fire, it is cut down:
102. 3 and my bones are *b* as an hearth.
106.18 the flame *b* up the wicked.
Pr 6.27 and his clothes not be *b*?
28 hot coals, and his feet not be *b*?
Isa 1. 7 your cities are *b* with fire: your
24. 6 inhabitants of the earth are *b*,
33.12 as thorns cut up shall they be *b*
42.25 and it *b* him, yet he laid it not
43. 2 thou shalt not be *b*; neither
44.19 I have *b* part of it in the fire;
64.11 is *b* up with fire: and all our
65. 7 *b* incense upon the mountains,
Jer 1.16 have *b* incense unto other gods,
2.15 cities are *b* without inhabitant.
6.29 The bellows are *b*, the lead is
9.10 they are *b* up, so that none can
12 the land perisheth and is *b* up
18.15 they have *b* incense to vanity,
19. 4 *b* incense in it unto other gods,
13 they have *b* incense unto all the
36.27 after that the king had *b* the roll.
28 the king of Judah hath *b*.
29 Thou hast *b* this roll, saying,
32 Jehoiakim king of Judah had *b*
38.17 this city shall not be *b* with fire;
23 cause this city to be *b* with fire.
39. 8 the Chaldeans *b* the king's house,
44.15 wives had *b* incense unto other
19 *b* incense to the queen of heaven,
21 that ye *b* in the cities of Judah,
23 Because ye have *b* incense, and
49. 2 her daughters shall be *b* with fire:
51.30 they have *b* her dwellingplaces;
32 the reeds they have *b* with fire,
58 high gates shall be *b* with fire;
52.13 And *b* the house of the Lord,
13 of the great men, *b* he with fire:
La 2. 3 he *b* against Jacob like a flaming
Eze 15. 4 of it, and the midst of it is *b*.
5 fire hath devoured it, and it is *b*?
20.47 the south to the north shall be *b*
24.10 it well, and let the bones be *b*.
Hos 2.13 wherein she *b* incense to them,
11. 2 and *b* incense to graven images.
Joel 1.19 the flame hath *b* all the trees of
Am 2. 1 *b* the bones of the king of Edom
Mic 1. 7 the hires thereof shall be *b* with
Na 1. 5 the earth is *b* at his presence,
Mt 13.40 the tares are gathered and *b* in
22. 7 murderers, and *b* up their city.
Jn 15. 6 into the fire, and they are *b*.
Ac 19.19 and *b* them before all men: and
Ro 1.27 *b* in their lust one toward
1Co 3.15 If any man's work shall be *b*, he
13. 3 I give my body to be *b*, and have
Heb 6. 8 cursing, whose end is to be *b*.
12.18 and that *b* with fire, nor unto
13.11 high priest for sin, are *b* without
2Pe 3.10 works that are therein shall be *b*
Rev 1.15 as if they *b* in a furnace; and his
18. 8 she shall be utterly *b* with fire:

BURNING

Gen 15.17 a *b* lamp that passed between
Ex 21.25 *B* for *b*, wound for wound,
Lev 6. 9 because of the *b* upon the altar
9 the fire of the altar shall be *b* in
12 the fire upon the altar shall be *b*
13 The fire shall ever be *b* upon
10. 6 *b* which the Lord hath kindled.
13.23 it is a *b* boil; and the priest
24 skin thereof there is a hot *b*,
25 a leprosy broken out of the *b*:
28 a rising of the *b*, and the priest
28 it is an inflammation of the *b*.
16.12 shall take a censer full of *b* coals
26.16 consumption, and the *b* ague,
Nu 16.37 take up the censers out of the *b*,
19. 6 cast it into the midst of the *b* of
Dt 28.22 and with an extreme *b*, and with
29.23 brimstone, and salt, and *b*, that
32.24 devoured with *b* heat, and with
2Ch 16.14 they made a very great *b* for him.
21.19 his people made no *b* for him,
19 like the *b* of his fathers.
Job 41.19 Out of his mouth go *b* lamps,
Ps 140.10 Let *b* coals fall upon them: let
Pr 16.27 in his lips there is as a *b* fire.
26.21 As coals are to *b* coals, and

Pr 26.23 *B* lips and a wicked heart are
Isa 3.24 and *b* instead of beauty.
4. 4 and by the spirit of *b*.
9. 5 but this shall be with *b* and fuel
10.16 kindle a *b* like the *b* of a fire.
30.27 *b* with his anger, and the burden
34. 9 land thereof shall become *b* pitch.
Jer 20. 9 was in mine heart as a *b* fire
36.22 fire on the hearth *b* before him.
44. 8 *b* incense unto other gods in
Eze 1.13 like *b* coals of fire, and like the
Dan 3. 6 into the midst of a *b* fiery furnace.
11 should be cast into the midst of a *b*
15 same hour into the midst of a *b*
17 able to deliver us from the *b* fiery
20 cast them into the *b* fiery furnace.
21, 23 the midst of the *b* fiery furnace.
26 to the mouth of the *b* fiery furnace.
7. 9 flame, and his wheels as *b* fire.
11 and given to the *b* flame.
Am 4.11 firebrand plucked out of the *b*:
Hab 3. 5 *b* coals went forth at his feet.
Lk 12.35 girded about, and your lights *b*;
Jn 5.35 He was a *b* and a shining light:
Jas 1.11 no sooner risen with a *b* heat,
Rev 4. 5 lamps of fire *b* before the throne,
8. 8 a great mountain *b* with fire was
10 *b* as it were a lamp, and it fell
18. 9 they shall see the smoke of her *b*,
18 saw the smoke of her *b*, saying,
19.20 a lake of fire *b* with brimstone.

BURST

Job 32.19 it is ready to *b* like new bottles.
Pr 3.10 and thy presses shall *b* out
Jer 2.20 thy yoke, and *b* thy bands;
5. 5 broken the yoke, and *b* the bonds.
30. 8 and will *b* thy bonds, and
Na 1.13 and will *b* thy bonds in sunder.
Mk 2.22 doth *b* the bottles, and the wine
Lk 5.37 new wine will *b* the bottles,
Ac 1.18 he *b* asunder in the midst,

BURY

Gen 23. 4 I may *b* my dead out of my sight.
6 of our sepulchres *b* thy dead;
6 but that thou mayest *b* thy dead.
8 mind that I should *b* my dead
11 people give I it thee; *b* thy dead.
13 me, and I will *b* my dead there.
15 and thee: *b* therefore thy dead.
47.29 *b* me not, I pray thee, in Egypt:
30 and *b* me in their buryingplace.
49.29 *b* me with my fathers in the
50. 5 Canaan, there shalt thou *b* me.
5 and *b* my father, and I will come
6 Go up, and *b* thy father, according
7 Joseph went up to *b* his father:
14 went up with him to *b* his father,
Dt 21.23 shalt in any wise *b* him that day;
1Ki 2.31 and fall upon him, and *b* him;
11.15 host was gone up to *b* the slain,
13.29 the city, to mourn and to *b* him.
31 When I am dead, then *b* me in
14.13 shall mourn for him, and *b* him:
2Ki 9.10 and there shall be none to *b* her.
34 and *b* her: for she is the king's
35 they went to *b* her: but they
Ps 79. 3 and there was none to *b* them.
Jer 7.32 for they shall *b* in Tophet,
14.16 they shall have none to *b* them,
19.11 they shall *b* them in Tophet,
11 till there be no place to *b*.
Eze 39.11 and there shall they *b* Gog and
13 all the people of the land shall *b*
14 to *b* with the passengers those
Hos 9. 6 them up, Memphis shall *b* them:

Mt 8.21 me first to go and *b* my father.
22 and let the dead *b* their dead.
27. 7 potter's field, to *b* strangers in.
Lk 9.59 me first to go and *b* my father.
60 Let the dead *b* their dead:
Jn 19.40 the manner of the Jews is to *b*.

BURYING

2Ki 13.21 as they were *b* a man, that,
Eze 39.12 house of Israel be *b* of them,
Mk 14. 8 to anoint my body to the *b*,
Jn 12. 7 against the day of my *b* hath she

BUSH

Ex 3. 2 fire out of the midst of a *b*:
2 behold, the *b* burned with fire,
2 and the *b* was not consumed.
3 sight, why the *b* is not burnt.
4 him out of the midst of the *b*,
Dt 33.16 will of him that dwelt in the *b*:
Mk 12.26 how in the *b* God spake unto him,
Lk 6.44 of a bramble *b* gather they grapes.
20.37 even Moses shewed at the *b*,
Ac 7.30 Lord in a flame of fire in a *b*.
35 which appeared to him in the *b*.

BUSHEL

Mt 5.15 a candle, and put it under a *b*,
Mk 4.21 brought to be put under a *b*,
Lk 11.33 neither under a *b*, but on a

BUSINESS

Gen 39.11 went into the house to do his *b*;
Dt 24. 5 shall he be charged with any *b*:
Jos 2.14 yours, if ye utter not this our *b*.
20 if thou utter this our *b*, then we
Jdg 18. 7 and had no *b* with any man.
28 they had no *b* with any man;
1Sa 20.19 when the *b* was in hand,
21. 2 hath commanded me a *b*, and
2 man know any thing of the *b*
8 the king's *b* required haste.
1Ch 26.29 his sons were for the outward *b*
30 westward in all the *b* of the Lord,
2Ch 13.10 the Levites wait upon their *b*:
17.13 much *b* in the cities of Judah:
32.31 in the *b* of the ambassadors of
Neh 11.16 outward *b* of the house of God.
22 over the *b* of the house of God.
13.30 Levites, every one in his *b*;
Est 3. 9 that have the charge of the *b*,
Ps 107.23 ships, that do *b* in great waters;
Pr 22.29 thou a man diligent in his *b*?
Ec 5. 3 through the multitude of *b*;
8.16 the *b* that is done upon the earth:
Dan 8.27 rose up, and did the king's *b*;
Lk 2.49 must be about my father's *b*?
Ac 6. 3 we may appoint over this *b*.
Ro 12.11 Not slothful in *b*; fervent in
16. 2 in whatsoever *b* she hath need of
1Th 4.11 to do your own *b*, and to work

BUSYBODIES

2Th 3.11 working not at all, but are *b*.
1Ti 5.13 but tattlers also and *b*, speaking

BUSYBODY

1Pe 4.15 or as a *b* in other men's matters.

BUTTER

Gen 18. 8 he took *b*, and milk, and the calf
Dt 32.14 *B* of kine, and milk of sheep,
Jdg 5.25 brought forth *b* in a lordly dish.
2Sa 17.29 honey, and *b*, and sheep, and
Job 20.17 floods, the brooks of honey and *b*.
29. 6 When I washed my steps with *b*,

Ps 55.21 his mouth were smoother than *b*,
Pr 30.33 of milk bringeth forth *b*, and the
Isa 7.15 *B* and honey shall he eat, that he
22 they shall give, he shall eat *b*:
22 for *b* and honey shall every one

BUY

Gen 41.57 Egypt to Joseph for to *b* corn;
42. 2 *b* for us from thence; that we
3 went down to *b* corn in Egypt.
5 the sons of Israel came to *b* corn
7 From the land of Canaan to *b* food.
10 to *b* food are thy servants come.
43. 2 Go again, *b* us a little food.
4 we will go down and *b* thee food:
20 down at the first time to *b* food:
22 money have we brought...to *b*
44.25 Go again, and *b* us a little food.
47.19 *b* us and our land for bread,
Ex 21. 2 If thou *b* an Hebrew servant,
Lev 22.11 But if the priest *b* any soul with
25.15 thou shalt *b* of thy neighbor,
44 of them shall ye *b* bondmen
45 of them shall ye *b*, and of their
Dt 2. 6 shall *b* meat of them for money,
6 ye shall also *b* water of them for
28.68 bondwomen, and no man shall *b*
Ru 4. 4 *B* it before the inhabitants,
5 *b* it also of Ruth the Moabitess,
8 said unto Boaz, *B* it for thee.
2Sa 24.21 To *b* the threshingfloor of thee to
24 will surely *b* it of thee at a price:
2Ki 12.12 to *b* timber and hewed stone
22. 6 and to *b* timber and hewn stone
1Ch 21.24 I will verily *b* it for the full price:
2Ch 34.11 to *b* hewn stone, and timber for
Ezr 7.17 *b* speedily with this money
Neh 5. 3 that we might *b* corn, because
10.31 not *b* it of them on the sabbath,
Pr 23.23 *B* the truth, and sell it not;
Isa 55. 1 come ye, *b*, and eat;
1 yea, come, *b* wine and milk
Jer 32. 7 *B* thee my field that is in
7 of redemption is thine to *b* it.
32. 8 *B* my field, I pray thee, that is in
8 is thine; *b* it for thyself.
25 *B* thee the field for money, and
44 Men shall *b* fields for money,
Am 8. 6 That we may *b* the poor for silver,
Mt 14.15 villages, and *b* themselves victuals.
25. 9 that sell, and *b* for yourselves.
10 while they went to *b*, the
Mk 6.36 villages, and *b* themselves bread:
37 *b* two hundred pennyworth
Lk 9.13 go and *b* meat for all this people.
22.36 let him sell his garment, and *b* one.
Jn 4. 8 away unto the city to *b* meat.)
6. 5 Whence shall we *b* bread, that
13.29 *B* those things that we have need
1Co 7.30 they that *b*, as though they
Jas 4.13 and *b* and sell, and get gain:
Rev 3.18 I counsel thee to *b* of me gold
13.17 that no man might *b* or sell,

BUYETH

Pr 31.16 She considereth a field, and *b* it:
Mt 13.44 all that he hath, and *b* that field.
Rev 18.11 for no man *b* their merchandise

BYWORD

Dt 28.37 a *b*, among all nations whither
1Ki 9. 7 and a *b* among all people:
2Ch 7.20 and a *b* among all nations.
Job 17. 6 made me also a *b* of the people;
30. 9 their song, yea, I am their *b*.
Ps 44.14 us a *b* among the heathen,

C

Caesar Augustus, emperor of Rome (27 B.C.–A.D. 14)

CAESAR

Mt 22.17 to give tribute unto *C*, or not?
21 unto *C* the things which are
Mk 12.14 to give tribute to *C*, or not?
17 *C* the things that are Caesar's,
Lk 2. 1 a decree from *C* Augustus,
3. 1 the reign of Tiberius *C*, Pontius
20.22 to give tribute unto *C*, or no?
25 *C* the things which be Caesar's,
23. 2 forbidding to give tribute to *C*,
Jn 19.12 himself a king speaketh against *C*.
15 answered, We have no king but *C*.
Ac 11.28 pass in the days of Claudius *C*.
17. 7 contrary to the decrees of *C*,
25. 8 nor yet against *C*, have I offended
11 unto them. I appeal unto *C*.
12 Hast thou appealed unto *C*?
12 unto *C* shalt thou go.
21 be kept till I might send him to *C*.
26.32 if he had not appealed unto *C*.
27.24 thou must be brought before *C*:
28.19 constrained to appeal unto *C*;

CAESAREA

Mt 16.13 into the coasts of *C* Philippi,
Mk 8.27 into the towns of *C* Philippi:
Ac 8.40 all the cities, till he came to *C*.
9.30 they brought him down to *C*,
10. 1 certain man in *C* called Cornelius,
24 morrow after they entered into *C*.
11.11 I was, sent from *C* unto me.
12.19 went down from Judaea to *C*,
18.22 he had landed at *C*, and gone up,
21. 8 came unto *C*: and we entered
16 of the disciples of *C*, and brought
23.23 soldiers to go to *C*,
33 they came to *C*, and delivered
25. 1 ascended from *C* to Jerusalem.
4 that Paul should be kept at *C*,
6 ten days, he went down unto *C*;
13 Bernice came unto *C* to salute

CAESAR'S

Mt 22.21 They say unto him, *C*. Then
21 Caesar the things which are *C*;
Mk 12.16 And they said unto him, *C*.
17 to Caesar the things that are *C*,
Lk 20.24 They answered and said, *C*.
25 unto Caesar the things which be *C*,
Jn 19.12 thou art not *C* friend: whosoever
Ac 25.10 I stand at *C* judgment seat,
Php 4.22 they that are of *C* household.

CAGE

Jer 5.27 As a *c* is full of birds, so are their
Rev 18. 2 a *c* of every unclean and hateful

CAIAPHAS

Mt 26. 3 high priest, who was called *C*,
57 led him away to *C* the high priest,
Lk 3. 2 Annas and *C* being the high
Jn 11.49 And one of them, named *C*,
18.13 he was father in law to *C*,
14 *C* was he, which gave counsel to
24 Annas had sent him bound unto *C*
28 Then led they Jesus from *C* unto
Ac 4. 6 Annas the high priest, and *C*,

CAIN

Gen 4. 1 and she conceived, and bare *C*,
2 but *C* was a tiller of the ground.
3 pass, that *C* brought of the fruit
5 unto *C* and to his offering he had
5 And *C* was very wroth, and his
6 And the Lord said unto *C*, Why
8 *C* talked with Abel his brother:
8 *C* rose up against Abel his
9 And the Lord said unto *C*, Where
13 And *C* said unto the Lord,
15 Therefore whosoever slayeth *C*,
15 And the Lord set a mark upon *C*,
16 *C* went out from the presence of
17 And *C* knew his wife; and she
24 If *C* shall be avenged seven fold,
25 instead of Abel, whom *C* slew.
Jos 15.57 *C*, Gibeah, and Timnah; ten cities
Heb 11. 4 a more excellent sacrifice than *C*,
1Jn 3.12 Not as *C*, who was of that wicked
Jude 11 gone in the way of *C*, and ran

CALF

Gen 18. 7 fetcht a *c* tender and good,
8 the *c* which he had dressed,
Ex 32. 4 after he had made it a molten *c*:
8 they have made them a molten *c*,
19 he saw the *c*, and the dancing:
20 took the *c* which they had made,
24 fire, and there came out this *c*.
35 made the *c*, which Aaron made
Lev 9. 2 a young *c* for a sin offering,
3 a *c* and a lamb, both of the first
8 slew the *c* of the sin offering,
Dt 9.16 and had made you a molten *c*:
21 the *c* which ye had made, and
1Sa 28.24 woman had a fat *c* in the house;
Neh 9.18 They had made them a molten *c*,
Job 21.10 cow calveth, and casteth not her *c*.
Ps 29. 6 maketh them also to skip like a *c*;
106.19 They made a *c* in Horeb, and
Isa 11. 6 and the *c* and the young lion and
27.10 wilderness: there shall the *c* feed,
Jer 34.18 when they cut the *c* in twain, and
19 passed between the parts of the *c*;
Hos 8. 5 Thy *c*, O Samaria, hath cast thee
6 the *c* of Samaria shall be broken
Lk 15.23 bring hither the fatted *c*, and kill
27 thy father hath killed the fatted *c*,
30 hast killed for him the fatted *c*.
Ac 7.41 they made a *c* in those days, and
Rev 4. 7 the second beast like a *c*, and the
(See illustration on page 146)

CALL

Gen 2.19 to see what he would *c* them:
4.26 began men to *c* upon the name
16.11 shalt *c* his name Ishmael;
17.15 thou shalt not *c* her name Sarai,
19 and thou shalt *c* his name Isaac:

Caesarea, built shortly before the birth of Christ, was administrative capital of Judea under the Romans.

Aaron's calf-idol (Ex 32) figures in The Adoration of the Golden Calf, *by Nicolas Poussin (1594-1665).*

Gen 24.57 We will *c* the damsel, and inquire
30.13 the daughters will *c* me blessed:
46.33 when Pharaoh shall *c* you, and
Ex 2. 7 Shall I go and *c* to thee a nurse
20 *c* him, that he may eat bread.
34.15 *c* thee, and thou eat of his sacrifice;
Nu 16.12 Moses sent to *c* Dathan and
22. 5 of his people, to *c* him, saying,
20 If the men come to *c* thee, rise
37 earnestly send unto thee to *c* thee?
Dt 2.11 but the Moabites *c* them Emims.
20 Ammonites *c* them Zamzummims;
3. 9 Hermon the Sidonians *c* Sirion;
9 and the Amorites *c* it Shenir;)
4. 7 things that we *c* upon him for?
26 I *c* heaven and earth to witness
25. 8 the elders of his city shall *c* him,
30. 1 thou shalt *c* them to mind among
19 I *c* heaven and earth to record
31.14 *c* Joshua, and present yourselves
28 and *c* heaven and earth to record
33.19 *c* the people unto the mountain;
Jdg 12. 1 didst not *c* us to go with thee?
16.25 *C* for Samson, that he may make
21.13 and to *c* peaceably unto them.
Ru 1.20 *C* me not Naomi, *c* me Mara: for
21 why then *c* ye me Naomi, seeing
1Sa 3. 6 Here am I; for thou didst *c* me.
8 for thou didst *c* me. And Eli
9 if he *c* thee, that thou shalt say,
12.17 I will *c* unto the Lord, and he
16. 3 And *c* Jesse to the sacrifice, and I
22.11 Then the king sent to *c* Ahimelech
2Sa 17. 5 *C* now Hushai the Archite also,
22. 4 I will *c* on the Lord, who is worthy
1Ki 1.28 *C* me Bath-sheba. And she came
32 *C* me Zadok the priest, and Nathan
8.52 in all that they *c* for unto thee.
17.18 to *c* my sin to remembrance, and
18.24 *c* ye on the name of your gods,
24 I will *c* on the name of the Lord:
25 and *c* on the name of your gods,
22.13 messenger that was gone to *c*
2Ki 4.12 *C* this Shunammite. And when he
15 And he said, *C* her. And when he
36 and said, *C* this Shunammite.
5.11 *c* on the name of the Lord his
10.19 *c* unto me all the prophets of Baal,
1Ch 16. 8 *c* upon his name, make known his
2Ch 18.12 messenger that went to *c* Micaiah
Job 5. 1 *C* now, if there be any that will
13.22 Then *c* thou, and I will answer:
14.15 Thou shalt *c*, and I will answer
27.10 will he always *c* upon God?
Ps 4. 1 Hear me when I *c*, O God of my
3 the Lord will hear when I *c* unto
14. 4 bread, and *c* not upon the Lord.
18. 3 I will *c* upon the Lord, who is
20. 9 let the king hear us when we *c*.
49.11 *c* their lands after their own names.
50. 4 shall *c* to the heavens from above,
15 *c* upon me in the day of trouble:
55.16 I will *c* upon God; and the Lord
72.17 all nations shall *c* him blessed.
77. 6 I *c* to remembrance my song in
80.18 and we will *c* upon thy name.
86. 5 unto all them that *c* upon thee.
7 In the day of my trouble I will *c*
91.15 He shall *c* upon me, and I will
99. 6 among them that *c* upon his name;
102. 2 day when I *c* answer me speedily.
105. 1 *c* upon his name: make known his
116. 2 therefore will I *c* upon him as long
116.13 and *c* upon the name of the Lord.
17 will *c* upon the name of the Lord.
145.18 unto all them that *c* upon him,
18 to all that *c* upon him
Pr 1.28 Then shall they *c* upon me, but I
7. 4 *c* understanding thy kinswoman:
8. 4 Unto thee, O men, I *c*; and my
9.15 To *c* passengers who go right on
31.28 arise up, and *c* her blessed;
Isa 5.20 that *c* evil good, and good evil;
7.14 and shall *c* his name Immanuel.
8. 3 *C* his name Maher-shalal-hash-baz.
12. 4 Praise the Lord, *c* upon his name,
22.12 Lord God of hosts *c* to weeping,
20 that I will *c* my servant Eliakim
31. 2 will not *c* back his words: but
34.12 They shall *c* the nobles thereof
41.25 shall he *c* upon my name: and
44. 5 *c* himself by the name of Jacob;
7 who, as I, shall *c*, and shall
45. 3 the Lord, which *c* thee by thy name,
48. 2 they *c* themselves of the holy city,
13 when I *c* unto them, they stand
55. 5 *c* a nation that thou knowest not,
6 *c* ye upon him while he is near:
58. 5 wilt thou *c* this a fast, and an
9 thou *c*, and the Lord shall answer;
13 and *c* the sabbath a delight, the
60.14 shall *c* thee, The city of the Lord,
18 thou shalt *c* thy walls Salvation,
61. 6 *c* you the Ministers of our God:
62.12 they shall *c* them, The holy people,
65.15 *c* his servants by another name:
24 and before they *c*, I will answer;
Jer 1.15 I will *c* all the families of the
3.17 *c* Jerusalem the throne of the Lord;
19 Thou shalt *c* me, My father; and
6.30 Reprobate silver shall men *c*
7.27 thou shalt also *c* unto them; but
9.17 and *c* for the mourning women,
10.25 families that *c* not on thy name:
25.29 I will *c* for a sword upon all the
29.12 Then shall ye *c* upon me, and ye
33. 3 *C* unto me, and I will answer
50.29 *C* together the archers against
51.27 *c* together against her the
La 2.15 city that men *c* The perfection of
Eze 21.23 *c* to remembrance the iniquity,
36.29 and I will *c* for the corn, and will
38.21 And I will *c* for a sword against
39.11 shall *c* it The valley of Hamon-gog.
Dan 2. 2 commanded to *c* the magicians,
Hos 1. 4 *C* his name Jezreel; for yet a
6 *C* her name Lo-ruhamah: for I
9 *C* his name Lo-ammi: for ye are
2.16 thou shalt *c* me Ishi;
16 and shalt *c* me no more Baali.
7.11 they *c* to Egypt, they go to Assyria.
Joel 1.14 *c* a solemn assembly, gather the
2.15 a fast, *c* a solemn assembly:
32 whosoever shall *c* on the name of
32 remnant whom the Lord shall *c*.
Am 5.16 and they shall *c* the husbandman
Jon 1. 6 arise, *c* upon thy God, if so be
Zep 3. 9 all *c* upon the name of the Lord,
Zec 3.10 ye *c* every man his neighbor
13. 9 they shall *c* on my name, and I
Mal 1. 4 *c* them, The border of wickedness,
3.12 all nations shall *c* you blessed:
15 now we *c* the proud happy; yea,
Mt 1.21 thou shalt *c* his name Jesus:
23 shall *c* his name Emmanuel,
9.13 I am not come to *c* the righteous,
10.25 shall they *c* them of his household?
20. 8 *C* the laborers, and give them
22. 3 to *c* them that were bidden
43 doth David in spirit *c* him Lord,
45 If David then *c* him Lord, how is
23. 9 And *c* no man your father upon
Mk 2.17 came not to *c* the righteous, but
10.49 they *c* the blind man, saying unto
15.12 whom ye *c* the King of the Jews?
16 and they *c* together the whole
Lk 1.13 thou shalt *c* his name John.
31 son, and shalt *c* his name Jesus.
48 generations shall *c* me blessed.
5.32 I came not to *c* the righteous,
6.46 And why *c* ye me, Lord, Lord,
14.12 *c* not thy friends, nor thy brethren,
13 when thou makest a feast, *c* the
Jn 4.16 Go, *c* thy husband, and come
13.13 Ye *c* me Master and Lord: and ye
15.15 Henceforth I *c* you not servants;
Ac 2.21 whosoever shall *c* on the name of
39 many as the Lord our God shall *c*.
9.14 to bind all that *c* on thy name.
10. 5 to Joppa, and *c* for one Simon
15 that *c* not thou common.
28 I should not *c* any man common
32 *c* hither Simon, whose surname
11. 9 that *c* not thou common.
13 and *c* for Simon, whose surname
19.13 *c* over them which had evil
24.14 *c* heresy, so worship I the God
25 season, I will *c* for thee.
Ro 9.25 I will *c* them my people which

10.12 rich unto all that *c* upon him.
13 whosoever shall *c* upon the name
14 How then shall they *c* on him in
1Co 1. 2 in every place *c* upon the name
2Co 1.23 I *c* God for a record upon my
2Ti 1. 5 When I *c* to remembrance the
2.22 with them that *c* on the Lord
Heb 2.11 not ashamed to *c* them brethren,
10.32 *c* to remembrance the former days,
Jas 5.14 *c* for the elders of the church;
1Pe 1.17 And if ye *c* on the Father, who

CALLED

Gen 1. 5 And God *c* the light Day,
5 and the darkness he *c* Night.
8 God *c* the firmament Heaven.
10 and God *c* the dry land Earth;
10 together of the waters *c* he Seas:
2.19 Adam *c* every living creature,
23 she shall be *c* Woman, because
3. 9 And the Lord God *c* unto Adam,
20 And Adam *c* his wife's name Eve;
4.17 *c* the name of the city, after the
25 and *c* his name Seth:
26 and he *c* his name Enos:
5. 2 and *c* their name Adam,
3 his image; and *c* his name Seth:
29 And he *c* his name Noah,
11. 9 therefore is the name of it *c* Babel;
12. 8 and *c* upon the name of the Lord.
18 And Pharoah *c* Abram, and said,
13. 4 Abram *c* on the name of the Lord.
16.13 And she *c* the name of the Lord
14 the well was *c* Beer-lahai-roi;
15 Abram *c* his son's name, which
17. 5 thy name any more be *c* Abram,
19. 5 And they *c* unto Lot, and said
22 the name of the city was *c* Zoar.
37 and *c* his name Moab:
38 and *c* his name Ben-ammi:
20. 8 and *c* all his servants, and told all
9 Then Abimelech *c* Abraham, and
21. 3 And Abraham *c* the name of his
12 in Isaac shall thy seed be *c*.
17 the angel of God *c* to Hagar
31 he *c* that place Beer-sheba;
33 *c* there on the name of the Lord,
22.11 angel of the Lord *c* unto him out
14 Abraham *c* the name of that place
15 angel of the Lord *c* unto Abraham
24.58 And they *c* Rebekah, and said
25.25 and they *c* his name Esau.
26 and his name was *c* Jacob:
30 therefore was his name *c* Edom.
26. 9 And Abimelech *c* Isaac, and said,
18 he *c* their names after the names
18 by which his father had *c* them.
20 he *c* the name of the well Esek;
21 and he *c* the name of it Sitnah.
22 and he *c* the name of it Rehoboth;
25 and *c* upon the name of the Lord,
33 and he *c* it Shebah:
27. 1 he called Esau his eldest son, and
42 she sent and *c* Jacob
28. 1 Isaac *c* Jacob, and blessed him,
19 *c* the name of that place Beth-el:
19 the name of that city was *c* Luz
29.32 and she *c* his name Reuben:
33 and she *c* his name Simeon.
34 therefore was his name *c* Levi.
35 she *c* his name Judah;
30. 6 therefore *c* she his name Dan.
8 and she *c* his name Naphtali.
11 and she *c* his name Gad.
13 and she *c* his name Asher.
18 and she *c* his name Issachar.
20 and she *c* his name Zebulun.
21 and *c* her name Dinah.
24 And she *c* his name Joseph;
31. 4 Jacob sent and *c* Rachel and Leah
47 And Laban *c* it Jegar-sahadutha:
47 Jacob *c* it Galeed.
31.48 was the name of it *c* Galeed;
54 and *c* his brethren to eat bread:
32. 2 and he *c* the name of that place
28 name shall be *c* no more Jacob,
30 *c* the name of the place Peniel:
33.17 name of the place is *c* Succoth.
20 and *c* it El-elohe-Israel.
35. 7 and *c* the place El-Beth-el:
8 name of it was *c* Allon-bachuth.
10 shall not be *c* any more Jacob,
10 and he *c* his name Israel.
15 And Jacob *c* the name of the place
18 that she *c* his name Ben-oni:
18 his father *c* him Benjamin.
38. 3 and he *c* his name Er.
4 and she *c* his name Onan.
5 and *c* his name Shelah:
29 therefore his name was *c* Pharez.
30 and his name was *c* Zarah.
39.14 she *c* unto the men of her house,
41. 8 and *c* for all the magicians
14 Pharaoh sent and *c* Joseph,
45 And Pharaoh *c* Joseph's name
51 *c* the name of the firstborn
52 of the second *c* he Ephraim:
47.29 and he *c* his son Joseph,
48. 6 *c* after the name of their brethren
49. 1 And Jacob *c* unto his sons,
50.11 name of it was *c* Abel-mizraim,
Ex 1.18 king of Egypt *c* for the midwives,
2. 8 went and *c* the child's mother.
10 And she *c* his name Moses:
22 and he *c* his name Gershom:
3. 4 God *c* unto him out of the midst
7.11 Pharaoh also *c* the wise men
8. 8 Pharaoh *c* for Moses and Aaron,
25 *c* for Moses and for Aaron,
9.27 Pharaoh sent, and *c* for Moses
10.16 Pharaoh *c* for Moses and Aaron
24 And Pharaoh *c* unto Moses,
12.21 Then Moses *c* for all the elders
31 And he *c* for Moses and Aaron
15.23 the name of it was *c* Marah.
16.31 *c* the name thereof Manna:
17. 7 *c* the name of the place Massah,
15 *c* the name of it Jehovah-nissi:
19. 3 *c* unto him out of the mountain,
7 Moses came and *c* for the elders
20 and the Lord *c* Moses up
24.16 the seventh day he *c* unto Moses
31. 2 I have *c* by name Bezaleel
33. 7 and *c* it the Tabernacle of the
34.31 Moses *c* unto them; and Aaron
35.30 the Lord hath *c* by name Bezaleel
36. 2 *c* Bezaleel and Aholiab,
Lev 1. 1 And the Lord *c* unto Moses,
9. 1 Moses *c* Aaron and his sons,
10. 4 Moses *c* Mishael and Elzaphan,
Nu 11. 3 *c* the name of the place Taberah:
34 And he *c* the name of that place
12. 5 and *c* Aaron and Miriam:
13.16 And Moses *c* Oshea the son of Nun
24 The place was *c* the brook Eshcol,
21. 3 *c* the name of the place Hormah.
24.10 I *c* thee to curse mine enemies,
25. 2 *c* the people unto the sacrifices
32.41 and *c* them Havoth-jair.
42 *c* it Nobah, after his own name.
Dt 3.13 which was *c* the land of giants.
14 and *c* them after his own name,
5. 1 *c* all Israel, and said unto them,
15. 2 because it is *c* the Lord's release.
25.10 And his name shall be *c* in Israel,
28.10 art *c* by the name of the Lord;
29. 2 And Moses *c* unto all Israel,
31. 7 And Moses *c* unto Joshua,
Jos 4. 4 Then Joshua *c* the twelve men,
5. 9 the name of the place is *c* Gilgal
6. 6 the son of Nun *c* the priests,
7.26 place was *c*, The valley of Achor,
8.16 *c* together to pursue after them:
9.22 And Joshua *c* for them,
10.24 Joshua *c* for all the men of Israel,
19.47 *c* Leshem, Dan, after the name
22. 1 Then Joshua *c* the Reubenites,
34 and the children of Gad *c* the altar
23. 2 And Joshua *c* for all Israel,
24. 1 and *c* for the elders of Israel.
9 sent and *c* Balaam the son of Beor
Jdg 1.17 name of the city was *c* Hormah.
26 and *c* the name thereof Luz:
2. 5 *c* the name of that place Bochim:
4. 6 *c* Barak the son of Abinoam
10 Barak *c* Zebulun and Naphtali
6.24 and *c* it Jehovah-shalom:
32 on that day he *c* him Jerubbaal,
8.31 son, whose name he *c* Abimelech.
9.54 he *c* hastily unto the young man
10. 4 cities, which are *c* Havoth-jair
12. 2 I *c* you, ye delivered me not
13.24 and *c* his name Samson:
14.15 have ye *c* us to take that we have?
15.17 and *c* that place Ramath-lehi.
18 and *c* on the Lord, and said,
19 *c* the name thereof En-hakkore,
16.18 *c* for the lords of the Philistines,
19 and she *c* for a man, and she
25 *c* for Samson out of the prison
28 And Samson *c* unto the Lord,
18.12 they *c* that place Mahaneh-dan
29 they *c* the name of the city Dan,
Ru 4.17 and they *c* his name Obed:
1Sa 1.20 a son, and *c* his name Samuel,
3. 4 That the Lord *c* Samuel:
5 he said, I *c* not; lie down again.
6 the Lord *c* yet again, Samuel.
6 I *c* not, my son; lie down again.
8 Lord *c* Samuel again the third
8 that the Lord had *c* the child.
10 the Lord came, and stood, and *c*
16 Then Eli *c* Samuel, and said,
6. 2 the Philistines *c* for the priests
7.12 and *c* the name of it Eben-ezer,
9. 9 he that is now *c* a Prophet was
9 beforetime *c* a Seer.)
26 *c* Saul to the top of the house,
10.17 And Samuel *c* the people together
12.18 So Samuel *c* unto the Lord;
13. 4 were *c* together after Saul,
16. 5 and *c* them to the sacrifice.
8 Then Jesse *c* Abinadab, and
19. 7 And Jonathan *c* David, and
23. 8 Saul *c* all the people together
28 *c* that place Sela-hammahlekoth.
28.15 I have *c* thee, that thou mayest
29. 6 Then Achish *c* David, and said
2Sa 1. 7 he saw me, and *c* unto me.
15 David *c* one of the young men,
2.16 place was *c* Helkath-hazzurim,
26 Then Abner *c* to Joab, and said,
5. 9 and *c* it the city of David.
20 he *c* the name of that place
6. 2 whose name is *c* by the name of
8 and he *c* the name of the place
9. 2 when they had *c* him unto David,
9 king *c* to Ziba, Saul's servant,
11.13 David had *c* him, he did eat
12.24 and he *c* his name Solomon:
25 and he *c* his name Jedidiah,
28 and it be *c* after my name.
13.17 Then he *c* his servant that
14.33 he had *c* for Absalom, he came
15. 2 Absalom *c* unto him, and said,
11 out of Jerusalem, that were *c*;
18.18 *c* the pillar after his own name:
18 and it is *c* unto this day,
26 the watchman *c* unto the porter,
28 Ahimaaz *c*, and said unto the king,
21. 2 And the king *c* the Gibeonites,
22. 7 In my distress I *c* upon the Lord,
1Ki 1. 9 *c* all his brethren the king's sons,

1Ki 1.10 Solomon his brother, he *c* not.
19 and hath *c* all the sons of the king,
19 Solomon thy servant hath he not *c*.
25 and hath *c* all the king's sons,
26 servant Solomon, hath he not *c*.
2.36 the king sent and *c* for Shimei,
42 sent and *c* for Shimei, and said
7.21 and *c* the name thereof Jachin:
21 and *c* the name thereof Boaz.
8.43 have builded, is *c* by thy name.
9.13 And he *c* them the land of Cabul
12. 3 and *c* him. And Jeroboam
20 and *c* him unto the congregation,
16.24 and *c* the name of the city
17.10 he *c* to her, and said, Fetch me,
11 he *c* to her, and said, Bring me,
18. 3 And Ahab *c* Obadiah, which was
26 and *c* on the name of Baal
20. 7 the king of Israel *c* all the elders
22. 9 the king of Israel *c* an officer,
2Ki 3.10 that the Lord hath *c* these three
13 for the Lord hath *c* these three
4.12 had *c* her, she stood before him.
15 had *c* her, she stood in the door.
22 And she *c* unto her husband,
36 And he *c* Gehazi, and said, Call
36 this Shunammite. So he *c* her.
6.11 and he *c* his servants, and said
7.10 they came and *c* unto the porter
11 *c* the porters; and they told
8. 1 for the Lord hath *c* for a famine;
9. 1 the prophet *c* one of the children
12. 7 Jehoash *c* for Jehoiada the priest,
14. 7 and *c* the name of it Joktheel
18. 4 and he *c* it Nehushtan.
18 when they had *c* to the king,
1Ch 4. 9 *c* his name Jabez, saying,
10 And Jabez *c* on the God of Israel,
6.65 which are *c* by their names.
7.16 and she *c* his name Peresh;
23 he *c* his name Beriah, because
11. 7 they *c* it the city of David.
13. 6 cherubims, whose name is *c* on it.
11 that place is *c* Perez-uzza
14.11 they *c* the name of that place
15.11 David *c* for Zadok and Abiathar
21.26 and *c* upon the Lord;
22. 6 Then he *c* for Solomon his son,
2Ch 3.17 and *c* the name of that on the
6.33 I have built is *c* by thy name.
7.14 people, which are *c* by my name,
10. 3 And they sent and *c* him.
18. 8 Israel *c* for one of his officers,
20.26 the name of the same place was *c*,
24. 6 And the king *c* for Jehoiada
Ezr 2.61 and was *c* after their name:
Neh 5.12 Then I *c* the priests, and took
7.63 and was *c* after their name.
Est 2.14 that she were *c* by name.
3.12 scribes *c* on the thirteenth day
4. 5 Then *c* Esther for Hatach,
11 who is not *c*, there is one law
11 I have not been *c* to come in
5.10 and *c* for his friends, and
8. 9 king's scribes *c* at that time
9.26 they *c* these days Purim after
Job 1. 4 and *c* for their three sisters to eat
9.16 I had *c*, and he had answered me;
19.16 I *c* my servant, and he gave me
42.14 *c* the name of the first, Jemima;
Ps 17. 6 I have *c* upon thee, for thou
18. 6 In my distress I *c* upon the Lord,
31.17 O Lord; for I have *c* upon thee:
50. 1 Lord hath spoken and *c* the earth
53. 4 they have not *c* upon God.
79. 6 kingdoms that have not *c* upon
88. 9 Lord, I have *c* daily upon thee,
99. 6 they *c* upon the Lord, and he
105.16 *c* for a famine upon the land,
116. 4 *c* I upon the name of the Lord;
118. 5 I *c* upon the Lord in distress: the

Pr 1.24 I have *c*, and ye refused; I have
16.21 wise in heart shall be *c* prudent:
24. 8 be *c* a mischievous person.
SS 5. 6 *c* him, but he gave me no answer.
Isa 1.26 *c*, The city of righteousness,
4. 1 only let us be *c* by thy name,
3 *c* holy, even every one that is
9. 6 his name shall be *c* Wonderful,
13. 3 I have also *c* my mighty ones
19.18 be *c*, The city of destruction,
31. 4 multitude of shepherds is *c* forth
32. 5 person shall be no more *c* liberal,
35. 8 it shall be *c* The way of holiness;
41. 2 man from the east, *c* him
9 *c* thee from the chief men thereof,
42. 6 I the Lord have *c* thee
43. 1 I have *c* thee by thy name;
7 every one that is *c* by my name:
22 thou hast not *c* upon me, O Jacob,
45. 4 I have even *c* thee by thy name:
47. 1 thou shalt no more be *c* tender
5 be *c*, The lady of kingdoms.
48. 1 which are *c* by the name of Israel,
8 and wast *c* a transgressor
12 O Jacob and Israel, my *c*; I am he;
15 yea, I have *c* him: I have
49. 1 The Lord hath *c* me from the
50. 2 I *c*, was there none to answer?
51. 2 I *c* him alone, and blessed him,
54. 5 of the whole earth shall he be *c*.
6 the Lord hath *c* thee as a woman
56. 7 mine house shall be *c* an house of
58.12 and thou shalt be *c*, The repairer
61. 3 might be *c* trees of righteousness,
62. 2 thou shalt be *c* by a new name,
4 thou shalt be *c* Hephzi-bah, and
12 thou shalt be *c*, Sought out,
63.19 they were not *c* by thy name.
65. 1 a nation that was not *c* by my
12 when I *c*, ye did not answer;
66. 4 when I *c*, none did answer;
Jer 7.10 in this house, which is *c* by my
11 Is this house, which is *c* by my
13 I *c* you, but ye answered not;
14 this house, which is *c* by my name,
30 the house which is *c* by my name,
32 it shall no more be *c* Tophet,
11.16 The Lord *c* thy name, A green
12. 6 they have *c* a multitude after
14. 9 we are *c* by thy name; leave us
15.16 I am *c* by thy name, O Lord God
19. 6 place shall no more be *c* Tophet,
20. 3 Lord hath not *c* thy name Pashur,
23. 6 he shall be *c*, The Lord our
25.29 the city which is *c* by my name,
30.17 they *c* thee an Outcast, saying,
32.34 house, which is *c* by my name,
33.16 name wherewith she shall be *c*,
34.15 house which is *c* by my name:
35.17 and I have *c* unto them, but they
36. 4 Then Jeremiah *c* Baruch the
42. 8 Then *c* he Johanan the son of
La 1.15 he hath *c* an assembly against me
19 I *c* for my lovers, but they
21 bring the day that thou hast *c*,
2.22 Thou has *c* as in a solemn day
3.55 I *c* upon thy name, O Lord,
57 in the day that I *c* upon thee:
Eze 9. 3 he *c* to the man clothed with linen,
20.29 And the name thereof is *c* Bamah
Dan 5.12 now let Daniel be *c*, and he will
8.16 which *c*, and said, Gabriel, make
9.18 the city which is *c* by thy name:
19 thy people are *c* by thy name.
10. 1 whose name was *c* Belteshazzar;
Hos 11. 1 *c* my son out of Egypt.
2 As they *c* them, so they went
7 though they *c* them to the most
Am 7. 4 Lord God *c* to contend by fire,
9.12 heathen, which are *c* by my name,
Hag 1.11 And I *c* for a drought upon the

Zec 8. 3 Jerusalem shall be *c* a city of
11. 7 the one I *c* Beauty,
7 and other I *c* Bands;
Mt 1.16 born Jesus, who is *c* Christ.
25 and he *c* his name Jesus.
2. 7 privily *c* the wise men, inquired
15 Out of Egypt have I *c* my son.
23 and dwelt in a city *c* Nazareth:
23 He shall be *c* a Nazarene.
4.18 Simon *c* Peter, and Andrew his
21 mending their nets; and he *c*
5. 9 they shall be *c* the children of God.
19 he shall be *c* the least in the
19 the same shall be *c* great in the
10. 1 And when he had *c* unto him his
2 The first, Simon, who is *c* Peter,
25 If they have *c* the master of the
13.55 is not his mother *c* Mary? and
15.10 And he *c* the multitude, and said
32 Then Jesus *c* his disciples unto
18. 2 Jesus *c* a little child unto him,
32 after that he had *c* him, said
20.16 for many be *c*, but few chosen.
25 But Jesus *c* them unto him, and
32 Jesus stood still, and *c* them,
21.13 My house shall be *c* the house of
22.14 many are *c*, but few are chosen.
23. 7 and to be *c* of men, Rabbi, Rabbi.
8 be not ye *c* Rabbi: for one is your
10 Neither be ye *c* masters: for one
25.14 *c* his own servants, and delivered
26. 3 high priest, who was *c* Caiaphas,
14 Then one of the twelve, *c* Judas
36 unto a place *c* Gethsemane, and
27. 8 that field was *c*, The field of
16 a notable prisoner, *c* Barabbas.
17 or Jesus which is *c* Christ?
22 do then with Jesus which is *c*
33 unto a place *c* Golgotha, that is
Mk 1.20 straightway he *c* them: and they
3.23 And he *c* them unto him, and said
6. 7 And he *c* unto him the twelve,
7.14 when he had *c* all the people unto
8. 1 Jesus *c* his disciples unto him,
34 when he had *c* the people unto
9.35 and *c* the twelve, and saith unto
10.42 But Jesus *c* them to him, and
49 and commanded him to be *c*.
11.17 My house shall be *c* of all nations
12.43 he *c* unto him his disciples, and
14.72 Peter *c* to mind the word that
15.16 into the hall, *c* Praetorium;
Lk 1.32 shall be *c* the Son of the Highest:
35 shall be *c* the Son of God.
36 with her, who was *c* barren.
59 and they *c* him Zacharias, after
60 No so, but he shall be *c* John.
61 kindred that is *c* by this name.
62 father, how he would have him *c*.
76 shalt be *c* the prophet of the
2. 4 David, which is *c* Bethlehem;
21 his name was *c* Jesus, which was
23 shall be *c* holy to the Lord;)
6.13 he *c* unto him his disciples:
15 and Simon *c* Zelotes,
7.11 he went into a city *c* Nain;
8. 2 Mary *c* Magdalene, out of whom
54 and *c*, saying, Maid, arise.
9. 1 *c* his twelve disciples together,
10 belonging to the city *c* Bethsaida.
10.39 she had a sister *c* Mary, which
13.12 he *c* her to him,
15.19 no more worthy to be *c* thy son:
21 no more worthy to be *c* thy son.
26 he *c* one of the servants, and
16. 2 And he *c* him, and said unto
5 So he *c* every one of his lord's
18.16 But Jesus *c* them unto him,
19.13 And he *c* his ten servants, and
15 these servants to be *c* unto him,
29 the mount *c* the mount of Olives,

21.37 that is *c* the mount of Olives.
22. 1 which is *c* the Passover.
25 upon them are *c* benefactors.
47 he that was *c* Judas, one of the
23.13 when he had *c* together the
33 to the place which is *c* Calvary,
24.13 to a village *c* Emmaus, which
Jn 1.42 thou shalt be *c* Cephas, which
48 Before that Philip *c* thee, when
2. 2 Jesus was *c*, and his disciples,
9 governor of the feast *c* the
4. 5 of Samaria, which is *c* Sychar,
25 Messias cometh, which is *c* Christ:
5. 2 which is *c* in the Hebrew tongue
9.11 A man that is *c* Jesus made clay,
18 until they *c* the parents of him
24 Then again *c* they the man that
10.35 If he *c* them gods, unto whom
11.16 Thomas, which is *c* Didymus,
28 and *c* Mary her sister secretly,
54 into a city *c* Ephraim, and there
12.17 when he *c* Lazarus out of his
15.15 but I have *c* you friends;
18.33 *c* Jesus, and said unto him, Art
19.13 in a place that is *c* the Pavement,
17 a place *c* the place of a skull,
17 is *c* in the Hebrew Golgotha:
20.24 one of the twelve, *c* Didymus,
21. 2 and Thomas *c* Didymus, and
Ac 1.12 from the mount *c* Olivet, which
19 insomuch as that field is *c* in
23 Joseph *c* Barsabas, who was
3. 2 gate of the temple which is *c*
11 the porch that is *c* Solomon's,
4.18 they *c* them, and commanded
5.21 and *c* the council together, and
40 when they had *c* the apostles,
6. 2 Then the twelve *c* the multitude
9 of the synagogue, which is *c*
7.14 and *c* his father Jacob to him,
8. 9 a certain man, *c* Simon, which
9.11 the street which is *c* Straight,
11 for one *c* Saul, of Tarsus: for
21 them which *c* on his name in
36 by interpretation is *c* Dorcas:
41 when he had *c* the saints and
10. 1 man in Caesarea *c* Cornelius,
1 of the band *c* the Italian band,
7 *c* two of his household servants,
18 And *c*, and asked whether Simon,
23 Then *c* he them in, and lodged
24 and had *c* together his kinsmen
11.26 the disciples were *c* Christians
13. 1 and Simeon that was *c* Niger,
3 work whereunto I have *c* them.
7 who *c* for Barnabas and Saul,
9 Then Saul, (who also is *c* Paul,)
14.12 they *c* Barnabas, Jupiter; and
15.17 upon whom my name is *c*,
16.10 that the Lord had *c* us for to
29 Then he *c* for a light, and
19.25 Whom he *c* together with the
40 we are in danger to be *c* in
20. 1 Paul *c* unto him the disciples,
17 and *c* the elders of the church.
23. 6 I am *c* in question.
17 *c* one of the centurions unto him,
18 Paul the prisoner *c* me unto him,
23 he *c* unto him two centurions,
24. 2 when he was *c* forth, Tertullus
21 I am *c* in question by you this
27. 8 which is *c* The fair havens;
14 tempestuous wind, *c* Euroclydon.
16 a certain island which is *c* Clauda,
28. 1 knew that the island was *c* Melita.
17 Paul *c* the chief of the Jews
20 have I *c* for you, to see you,
Ro 1. 1 *c* to be an apostle, separated
6 are ye also the *c* of Jesus Christ:
7 *c* to be saints: grace to you
2.17 Behold, thou art *c* a Jew, and
7. 3 she shall be *c* an adulteress:
8.28 to them who are the *c* according
30 them he also *c*: and whom he *c*,
9. 7 In Isaac shall thy seed be *c*.
24 Even us, whom he hath *c*, not of
26 there shall they be *c* the children
1Co 1. 1 *c* to be an apostle of Jesus Christ
2 in Christ Jesus, *c* to be saints,
9 by whom ye were *c* unto the
24 But unto them which are *c*, both
26 mighty, not many noble, are *c*:
5.11 if any man that is *c* a brother
7.15 but God hath *c* us to peace.
17 as the Lord hath *c* every one, so
18 Is any man *c* being circumcised?
18 Is any *c* in uncircumcision? let
20 same calling wherein he was *c*.
21 Art thou *c* being a servant? care
22 For he that is *c* in the Lord, being
22 he that is *c*, being free, is
24 wherein he is *c*, therein abide
8. 5 though there be that are *c* gods,
15. 9 am not meet to be *c* an apostle,
Gal 1. 6 from him that *c* you into the
15 and *c* me by his grace,
5.13 ye have been *c* unto liberty;
Eph 2.11 *c* Uncircumcision by
11 that which is *c* the Circumcision
4. 1 wherewith ye are *c*,
4 even as ye are *c* in one hope
Col 3.15 to the which also ye are *c*
4.11 Jesus, which is *c* Justus, who are
1Th 2.12 worthy of God, who hath *c* you
4. 7 hath not *c* us unto uncleanness,
2Th 2. 4 himself above all that is *c* God,
14 he *c* you by our gospel, to the
1Ti 6.12 life, whereunto thou art also *c*,
20 of science falsely so *c*:
2Ti 1. 9 and *c* us with an holy calling,
Heb 3.13 while it is *c* To day; lest any
5. 4 but he that is *c* of God, as was
10 *C* of God an high priest after
7.11 not be *c* after the order of Aaron?
9. 2 which is *c* the sanctuary.
3 tabernacle which is *c* the Holiest
15 are *c* might receive the promise
11. 8 Abraham, when he was *c* to go
16 not ashamed to be *c* their God:
18 in Isaac shall thy seed be *c*:
24 refused to be *c* the son of
Jas 2. 7 name by the which ye are *c*?
23 he was *c* the Friend of God.
1Pe 1.15 as he which hath *c* you is holy,
2. 9 who hath *c* you out of darkness
21 hereunto were ye *c*: because
3. 9 that ye are thereunto *c*, that ye
5.10 the God of all grace, who hath *c*
2Pe 1. 3 of him that hath *c* us to glory
1Jn 3. 1 we should be *c* the sons of God:
Jude 1 preserved in Jesus Christ, and *c*:
Rev 1. 9 was in the isle that is *c* Patmos,
8.11 name of the star is *c* Wormwood:
11. 8 spiritually is *c* Sodom and Egypt,
12. 9 serpent, *c* the Devil, and Satan,
16.16 *c* in the Hebrew tongue
17.14 they that are with him are *c*,
19. 9 which are *c* unto the marriage
11 him was *c* Faithful and True,
13 his name is *c* The Word of God.

CALLEDST

Jdg 8. 1 that thou *c* us not, when thou
1Sa 3. 5 for thou *c* me. And he said, I
Ps 81. 7 *c* in trouble, and I delivered thee;
Eze 23.21 Thus thou *c* to remembrance the

CALLEST

Mt 19.17 Why *c* thou me good? there is
Mk 10.18 unto him, Why *c* thou me good?
Lk 18.19 Why *c* thou me good? none is

CALLETH

1Ki 8.43 that the stranger *c* to thee for:
2Ch 6.33 that the stranger *c* to thee for;
Job 12. 4 *c* upon God, and he answereth
Ps 42. 7 Deep *c* unto deep at the noise
147. 4 he *c* them all by their names.
Pr 18. 6 and his mouth *c* for strokes.
Isa 21.11 He *c* to me out of Seir, Watchman,
40.26 he *c* them all by names by the
59. 4 None *c* for justice, nor any
64. 7 there is none that *c* upon thy
Hos 7. 7 there is none among them that *c*
Am 5. 8 that *c* for the waters of the sea,
9. 6 he that *c* for the waters of the sea,
Mt 27.47 that, said, This man *c* for Elias.
Mk 3.13 and *c* unto him whom he would:
10.49 of good comfort, rise; he *c* thee.
12.37 therefore himself *c* him Lord;
15.35 heard it, said, Behold, he *c* Elias.
Lk 15. 6 home, he *c* together his friends
9 *c* her friends and her neighbors
20.37 *c* the Lord the God of Abraham,
44 David therefore *c* him Lord, how
Jn 10. 3 and he *c* his own sheep by name,
11.28 The Master is come, and *c* for thee.
Ro 4.17 *c* those things which be not as
9.11 not of works, but of him that *c*;)
1Co 12. 3 *c* Jesus accursed: and that no
Gal 5. 8 cometh not of him that *c* you.
1Th 5.24 Faithful is he that *c* you, who
Rev 2.20 which *c* herself a prophetess, to

CALLING

Nu 10. 2 for the *c* of the assembly, and for
Isa 1.13 the *c* of assemblies, I cannot
41. 4 *c* the generations from the
46.11 *C* a ravenous bird from the east,
Eze 23.19 in *c* to remembrance the days of
Mt 11.16 and *c* unto their fellows,
Mk 3.31 without, sent unto him, *c* him.
11.21 Peter *c* to remembrance saith
15.44 and *c* unto him the centurion, he
Lk 7.19 And John *c* unto him two of his
32 *c* one to another, and saying,
Ac 7.59 stoned Stephen, *c* upon God, and
22.16 sins, *c* on the name of the Lord.
Ro 11.29 gifts and *c* of God are without
1Co 1.26 For ye see your *c*, brethren, how
7.20 abide in the same *c* wherein he
Eph 1.18 what is the hope of his *c*, and
4. 4 are called in one hope of your *c*;
Php 3.14 for the prize of the high *c* of
2Th 1.11 would count you worthy of this *c*,
2Ti 1. 9 us, and called us with an holy *c*,
Heb 3. 1 partakers of the heavenly *c*,
1Pe 3. 6 Even as Sara obeyed Abraham, *c*
2Pe 1.10 give diligence to make your *c*

CALM

Ps 107.29 He maketh the storm a *c*, so that
Jon 1.11 unto thee, that the sea may be *c*
12 so shall the sea be *c* unto you:
Mt 8.26 the sea; and there was a great *c*.
Mk 4.39 ceased, and there was a great *c*.
Lk 8.24 they ceased, and there was a *c*.

CALVARY

Lk 23.33 which is called *C*, there they

CAMEL

Gen 24.64 saw Isaac, she lighted off the *c*.
Lev 11. 4 *c*, because he cheweth the cud,
Dt 14. 7 the *c*, and the hare, and the
1Sa 15. 3 suckling, ox and sheep, *c* and ass.
Zec 14.15 of the mule, of the *c*,
Mt 19.24 easier for a *c* to go through the
23.24 at a gnat, and swallow a *c*.
Mk 10.25 easier for a *c* to go through the
Lk 18.25 easier for a *c* to go through a

CAMEL'S
Gen 31.34 put them in the *c* furniture, and
Mt 3. 4 his raiment of *c* hair, and a
Mk 1. 6 clothed with *c* hair, and with a

CAMP
Ex 14.19 which went before the *c* of Israel,
20 between the *c* of the Egyptians
20 and the *c* of Israel;
16.13 quails came up, and covered the *c*:
19.16 people that was in the *c* trembled.
17 all the people out of the *c* to meet
29.14 burn with fire without the *c*:
32.17 There is a noise of war in the *c*.
19 as he came nigh unto the *c*, that
26 stood in the gate of the *c*, and
27 gate to gate throughout the *c*,
33. 7 without the *c*, afar off from the *c*,
7 which was without the *c*.
11 he turned again into the *c*: but
36. 6 proclaimed throughout the *c*,
Lev 4.12 he carry forth without the *c* unto
21 forth the bullock without the *c*,
6.11 the ashes without the *c* unto a
8.17 he burnt with fire without the *c*;
9.11 he burnt with fire without the *c*.
10. 4 before the sanctuary out of the *c*.
5 their coats out of the *c*; as Moses
13.46 without the *c* shall his habitation
14. 3 shall go forth out of the *c*; and
8 come into the *c*, and shall tarry
16.26 and afterward come into the *c*.
16.27 carry forth without the *c*; and
28 afterward he shall come into the *c*.
17. 3 lamb, or goat, in the *c*, or that
3 killeth it out of the *c*,
24.10 strove together in the *c*;
14 that hath cursed without the *c*;
23 had cursed out of the *c*, and
Nu 1.52 every man by his own *c*, and
2. 3 standard of the *c* of Judah pitch
9 All that were numbered in the *c*
10 the standard of the *c* of Reuben
16 All that were numbered in the *c*
17 with the *c* of the Levites
17 in the midst of the *c*:
18 standard of the *c* of Ephraim
24 that were numbered of the *c* of
25 The standard of the *c* of Dan
31 that were numbered in the *c* of
4. 5 when the *c* setteth forward,
15 as the *c* is to set forward;
5. 2 put out of the *c* every leper,
3 without the *c* shall ye put them;
4 and put them out without the *c*:
10.14 standard of the *c* of the children
18 standard of the *c* of Reuben set
22 *c* of the children of Ephraim set
25 the *c* of the children of Dan set
34 when they went out of the *c*.
11. 1 in the uttermost parts of the *c*.
9 dew fell upon the *c* in the night,
26 remained two of the men in the *c*,
26 and they prophesied in the *c*.
27 and Medad do prophesy in the *c*.
30 Moses gat him into the *c*,
31 let them fall by the *c*, as it were
31 the other side, round about the *c*,
32 themselves round about the *c*.
12.14 let her be shut out from the *c*
15 Miriam was shut out from the *c*
14.44 Moses departed not out of the *c*.
15.35 him with stones without the *c*.
36 brought him without the *c*, and
19. 3 bring her forth without the *c*, and
7 afterward he shall come into the *c*,
9 without the *c* in a clean place,
31.12 unto the *c* at the plains of Moab,
13 forth to meet them without the *c*.
19 do ye abide without the *c* seven
24 afterward ye shall come into the *c*.
Dt 23.10 shall he go abroad out of the *c*,
10 he shall not come within the *c*:
11 he shall come into the *c* again.
12 have a place also without the *c*,
14 God walketh in the midst of thy *c*,
14 therefore shall thy *c* be holy:
29.11 thy stranger that is in thy *c*,
Jos 5. 8 abode in their places in the *c*, till
6.11 into the *c*, and lodged in the *c*.
14 returned into the *c*: so they did
18 make the *c* of Israel a curse, and
23 left them without the *c* of Israel.
9. 6 to Joshua unto the *c* at Gilgal,
10. 6 sent unto Joshua to the *c* to Gilgal,
15 and all Israel with him, unto the *c*
21 all the people returned to the *c* to
43 with him, unto the *c* to Gilgal.
Jdg 7.17 I come to the outside of the *c*,
18 also on every side of all the *c*,
19 came unto the outside of the *c*
21 in his place round about the *c*:
13.25 him at times in the *c* of Dan
21. 8 there came none to the *c* from
12 brought them unto the *c* to Shiloh,
1Sa 4. 3 the people were come into the *c*,
5 of the Lord came into the *c*,
6 noise of this great shout in the *c*
6 of the Lord was come into the *c*.
7 they said, God is come into the *c*.
13.17 out of the *c* of the Philistines
14.21 went up with them into the *c*
17. 4 out of the *c* of the Philistines,
17 run to the *c* to thy brethren;
26. 6 down with me to Saul to the *c*?
2Sa 1. 2 a man came out of the *c* from
3 Out of the *c* of Israel am I
1Ki 16.16 king over Israel that day in the *c*.
2Ki 3.24 when they came to the *c* of Israel,
6. 8 and such a place shall be my *c*.
7. 5 to go unto the *c* of the Syrians:
5 to the uttermost part of the *c*
7 even the *c* as it was, and fled
8 to the uttermost part of the *c*,
10 We came to the *c* of the Syrians,
12 are they gone out of the *c* to hide
19.35 smote in the *c* of the Assyrians
2Ch 22. 1 came with the Arabians to the *c*
32.21 the leaders and captains in the *c*
Ps 78.28 let it fall in the midst of their *c*,
106.16 They envied Moses also in the *c*,
Isa 29. 3 And I will *c* against thee round
37.36 smote in the *c* of the Assyrians
Jer 50.29 *c* against it round about; and
Eze 4. 2 set the *c* also against it, and set
Joel 2.11 for his *c* is very great: for he is
Na 3.17 *c* in the hedges in the cold day,
Heb 13.11 sin, are burned without the *c*.
13 unto him without the *c*, bearing
Rev 20. 9 compassed the *c* of the saints

CANA
Jn 2. 1 in *C* of Galilee; and the mother
11 did Jesus in *C* of Galilee,
4.46 Jesus came again into *C* of
21. 2 Nathanael of *C* in Galilee,

CANAAN
Gen 9.18 and Ham is the father of *C*.
26 God of Shem; and *C* shall be his
10.15 And *C* begat Sidon his firstborn,
11.31 Chaldees, to go into the land of *C*:
13.12 Abram dwelt in the land of *C*,
16. 3 dwelt ten years in the land of *C*,
28. 1 take a wife of the daughters of *C*.
31.18 Isaac his father in the land of *C*.
42. 5 the famine was in the land of *C*.
32 with our father in the land of *C*.
45.17 go, get you unto the land of *C*;
48. 7 Rachel died by me in the land of *C*
Ex 6. 4 them, to give them the land of *C*,
15.15 inhabitants of *C* shall melt away.
16.35 unto the borders of the land of *C*.
Nu 13. 2 they may search the land of *C*.
17 them to spy out the land of *C*,
34.29 children of Israel in the land of *C*.
35.10 over Jordan into the land of *C*:
14 shall ye give in the land of *C*,
Jos 5.12 the fruit of the land of *C* that
14. 1 of Israel inherited the land of *C*,
22. 9 Shiloh, which is in the land of *C*,
11 an altar over against the land of *C*,
Jdg 4.24 had destroyed Jabin king of *C*.
Ps 105.11 Unto thee will I give the land of *C*,
Zep 2. 5 O *C*, the land of the Philistines,
Mt 15.22 behold, a woman of *C* came out

CANDACE
Ac 8.27 under *C* queen of the Ethiopians,

CANDLE
Job 18. 6 and his *c* shall be put out
21.17 is the *c* of the wicked put out!
29. 3 When his *c* shined upon my
Ps 18.28 For thou wilt light my *c*:
Pr 20.27 the *c* of the Lord, searching
24.20 *c* of the wicked shall be put out.
31.18 her *c* goeth not out by night.
Jer 25.10 and the light of the *c*.
Mt 5.15 men light a *c*, and put it under
Mk 4.21 Is a *c* brought to be put under
Lk 8.16 when he hath lighted a *c*,
11.33 when he hath lighted a *c*,
36 the bright shining of a *c* doth
15. 8 doth not light a *c*, and sweep
Rev 18.23 And the light of a *c* shall shine
22. 5 they need no *c*, neither light of

CANDLESTICK
Ex 25.31 thou shalt make a *c* of pure gold:
31 beaten work shall the *c* be made:
32 branches of the *c* out of the one
32 branches of the *c* out of the other
33 branches that come out of the *c*.
34 And in the *c* shall be four bowls
35 branches that proceed out of the *c*.
26.35 the *c* over against the table
30.27 the *c* and his vessels, and the
31. 8 the pure *c* with all his furniture,
35.14 The *c* also for the light,
37.17 he made the *c* of pure gold:
17 of beaten work made he the *c*;
18 *c* out of the one side thereof,
18 and three branches of the *c*
19 six branches going out of the *c*.
20 And in the *c* were four bowls
39.37 The pure *c*, with the lamps
40. 4 thou shalt bring in the *c*,
24 he put the *c* in the tent of the
Lev 24. 4 the lamps upon the pure *c*
Nu 3.31 *c*, and the altars, and the vessels
4. 9 and cover the *c* of the light,
8. 2 give light over against the *c*.
3 over against the *c*, as the Lord
4 work of the *c* was of beaten gold,
4 Moses, so he made the *c*.
2Ki 4.10 a table, a stool, and a *c*:
1Ch 28.15 by weight for every *c*, and for the
15 the *c*, and also for the lamps
15 according to the use of every *c*.
2Ch 13.11 and the *c* of gold with the lamps
Dan 5. 5 and wrote over against the *c*
Zec 4. 2 a *c* all of gold, with a bowl
11 upon the right side of the *c*
Mt 5.15 but on a *c*; and it giveth light
Mk 4.21 abed? and not to be set on a *c*?
Lk 8.16 but setteth it on a *c*, that they
11.33 but on a *c*, that they which
Heb 9. 2 wherein was the *c*, and the table,
Rev 2. 5 remove they *c* out of his place,

CANDLESTICKS
1Ki 7.49 the *c* of pure gold, five on the

1Ch 28.15 the weight for the *c* of gold, and
15 and for the *c* of silver by weight,
2Ch 4. 7 he made ten *c* of gold according
20 the *c* with their lamps, that they
Jer 52.19 the *c*, and the spoons, and the
Rev 1.12 turned, I saw seven golden *c*;
13 in the midst of the seven *c* one
20 hand, and the seven golden *c*.
20 and the seven *c* which thou sawest
2. 1 the midst of the seven golden *c*;
11. 4 and the two *c* standing before the

CANKER

2Ti 2.17 their word will eat as doth a *c*:

CANKERED

Jas 5. 3 Your gold and silver is *c*; and

CAPERNAUM

Mt 4.13 he came and dwelt in *C*, which is
8. 5 when Jesus was entered into *C*,
11.23 And thou, *C*, which art exalted
17.24 were come to *C*, they that
Mk 1.21 they went into *C*: and straightway
2. 1 he entered into *C* after some days;
9.33 he came to *C*: and being in the
Lk 4.23 have heard done in *C*, do also here
31 And came down to *C*, a city of
7. 1 of the people, he entered into *C*.
10.15 And thou, *C*, which art exalted to
Jn 2.12 After this he went down to *C*,
4.46 whose son was sick at *C*.
6.17 and went over the sea toward *C*.
24 came to *C*, seeking for Jesus.
59 synagogue, as he taught in *C*.

CAPPADOCIA

Ac 2. 9 and *C*, in Pontus, and Asia,
1Pe 1. 1 Galatia, *C*, Asia, and Bithynia,

CAPTIVE

Gen 14.14 that his brother was taken *c*,
34.29 their wives took they *c*, and
Ex 12.29 the firstborn of the *c* that was
Nu 24.22 Asshur shall carry thee away *c*.
Dt 21.10 and thou hast taken them *c*,
Jdg 5.12 and lead thy captivity *c*, thou son
1Ki 8.48 enemies, which led them away *c*,
50 who carried them *c*, that they
2Ki 5. 2 and had brought away *c* out of
6.22 those whom thou hast taken *c*
15.29 and carried them *c* to Assyria.
16. 9 and carried the people of it *c* to
24.16 king of Babylon brought *c* to
1Ch 5. 6 king of Assyria carried away *c*:
2Ch 6.37 whither they are carried *c*, and
25.12 children of Judah carry away *c*,
28. 8 carried away *c* of their brethren
11 again, which ye have taken *c*
30. 9 them that lead them *c*, so that
Ps 68.18 thou has led captivity *c*: thou
137. 3 that carried us away *c* required
Isa 49.21 am desolate, a *c*, and removing
24 the mighty, or the lawful *c*
51.14 The *c* exile hasteneth that he
52. 2 thy neck, O *c* daughter of Zion.
Jer 1. 3 carrying away of Jerusalem *c*
13.17 Lord's flock is carried away *c*.
19 shall be carried away *c* all of it,
19 it shall be wholly carried away *c*.
20. 4 and he shall carry them *c* into
22.12 they have led him *c*, and shall
24. 1 had carried away *c* Jeconiah the
5 are carried away *c* of Judah,
27.20 he carried away *c* Jeconiah the
28. 6 all that is carried away *c*, from
29. 1 carried away *c* from Jerusalem
14 caused you to be carried away *c*.
39. 9 carried away *c* into Babylon the
40. 1 all that were carried away *c* of
1 which were carried away *c* unto
7 not carried away *c* to Babylon;
41.10 Then Ishmael carried away *c*
10 carried them away *c*, and
14 Ishmael had carried away *c* from
52.15 carried away *c* certain of the
27 Thus Judah was carried away *c*
28 Nebuchadrezzar carried away *c*:
29 he carried away *c* from Jerusalem
30 carried away *c* of the Jews seven
Am 1. 6 they carried away *c* the whole
6. 7 therefore now shall they go *c* with
7 with the first that go *c*,
7.11 Israel shall surely be led away *c*
Ob 11 the strangers carried away *c*
Na 2. 7 Huzzab shall be led away *c*,
Lk 21.24 shall be led away *c* into all
Eph 4. 8 upon high, he led captivity *c*, and
2Ti 2.26 who are taken *c* by him at his
3. 6 lead *c* silly women laden with

CAPTIVES

Gen 31.26 away my daughters, as *c* taken
Nu 31. 9 took all the women of Midian *c*,
12 they brought the *c*, and the prey,
19 purify both yourselves and your *c*
Dt 21.11 And seest among the *c* a
32.42 blood of the slain and of the *c*,
1Sa 30. 2 And had taken the women *c*,
3 their daughters, were taken *c*.
5 David's two wives were taken *c*,
1Ki 8.46 they carry them away *c* unto
47 whither they were carried *c*,
47 of them that carried them *c*,
2Ki 24.14 ten thousand *c*, and all the
2Ch 6.36 they carry them away *c* unto a
38 they have carried them *c*, and
28. 5 a great multitude of them *c*,
11 deliver the *c* again, which ye
13 Ye shall not bring in the *c* hither:
14 the armed men left the *c* and the
15 by name rose up, and took the *c*,
17 Judah, and carried away *c*.
Ps 106.46 of all those that carried them *c*.
Isa 14. 2 and they shall take them *c*,
2 whose *c* they were; and they shall
20. 4 the Ethiopians *c*, young and old,
45.13 and he shall let go my *c*, not
49.25 the *c* of the mighty shall be
61. 1 to proclaim liberty to the *c*, and
Jer 28. 4 with all the *c* of Judah, that went
29. 1 which were carried away *c*,
4 all that are carried away *c*,
7 caused you to be carried away *c*,
43. 3 death, and carry us away *c* into
12 and carry them away *c*: and he
48.46 thy sons are taken *c*, and
46 and thy daughters *c*.
50.33 and all that took them *c* held
Eze 1. 1 as I was among the *c* by the
6. 9 they shall be carried *c*, because
16.53 captivity of thy *c* in the midst of
Dan 2.25 found a man of the *c* of
11. 8 shall also carry *c* into Egypt
Lk 4.18 to preach deliverance to the *c*.

CAPTIVITY

Nu 21.29 and his daughters, into *c*
Dt 21.13 the raiment of her *c* from off
28.41 them; for they shall go into *c*.
30. 3 the Lord thy God will turn thy *c*,
Jdg 5.12 and lead thy *c* captive, thou son
18.30 Dan until the day of the *c* of the
2Ki 24.15 carried he into *c* from Jerusalem
25.27 thirtieth year of the *c* of
1Ch 5.22 dwelt in their steads until the *c*.
6.15 And Jehozadak went into *c*,
2Ch 6.37 the land of their *c*, saying, We
38 in the land of their *c*, whither
29. 9 daughters and our wives are in *c*
Ezr 1.11 bring up with them of the *c* that
2. 1 that went up out of the *c*,
3. 8 that were come out of the *c* unto
4. 1 that the children of the *c*
6.16 the rest of the children of the *c*,
19 And the children of the *c* kept
20 all the children of the *c*, and for
21 were come again out of *c*, and all
8.35 which were come out of the *c*,
9. 7 to the sword, to *c*, and to a spoil,
10. 7 all the children of the *c*, that
16 the children of the *c* did so. And
Neh 1. 2 escaped, which were left of the *c*,
3 remnant that are left of the *c*
4. 4 them for a prey in the land of *c*:
7. 6 went up out of the *c*, of those
8.17 come again out of the *c* made
Est 2. 6 from Jerusalem with the *c*,
Job 42.10 Lord turned the *c* of Job when
Ps 14. 7 Lord bringeth back the *c* of his
53. 6 God bringeth back the *c* of his
68.18 high, thou hast led *c* captive:
78.61 delivered his strength into *c*, and
85. 1 brought back the *c* of Jacob.
126. 1 the Lord turned again the *c* of
4 Turn again our *c*, O Lord, as the
Isa 5.13 my people are gone into *c*,
22.17 thee away with a mighty *c*,
46. 2 but themselves are gone into *c*.
Jer 15. 2 such as are for the *c*, to the *c*.
20. 6 in thine house, shall go into *c*:
22.22 and thy lovers shall go into *c*:
29.14 and I will turn away your *c*,
16 not gone forth with you into *c*;
20 word of the Lord, all ye of the *c*,
22 a curse by all the *c* of Judah
28 This *c* is long: build ye houses,
31 Send to all them of the *c*, saying,
30. 3 I will bring again the *c* of my
10 seed from the land of their *c*;
16 every one of them, shall go into *c*;
18 will bring again the *c* of Jacob's
31.23 when I shall bring again their *c*;
32.44 I will cause their *c* to return,
33. 7 I will cause the *c* of Judah and the
7 and the *c* of Israel to return,
11 I will cause to return the *c* of the
26 I will cause their *c* to return, and
43.11 and such as are for *c* to *c*;
46.19 furnish thyself to go into *c*:
27 seed from the land of their *c*;
48. 7 Chemosh shall go forth into *c*
11 neither hath he gone into *c*:
47 Yet will I bring again the *c* of
49. 3 their king shall go into *c*, and
6 I will bring again the *c* of the
39 I will bring again the *c* of Elam,
52.31 and thirtieth year of the *c* of
La 1. 3 Judah is gone into *c* because
5 her children are gone into *c*
18 my young men are gone into *c*.
2.14 to turn away thy *c*; but have
4.22 more carry thee away into *c*:
Eze 1. 2 fifth year of king Jehoiachin's *c*,
3.11 get thee to them of the *c*, unto
15 I came to them of the *c* at
11.24 God into Chaldea, to them of the *c*.
25 Then I spake unto them of the *c*
12. 4 as they that go forth into *c*.
7 as stuff for *c*, and in the even
11 they shall remove and go into *c*.
16.53 I shall bring again their *c*,
53 the *c* of Sodom and her daughters,
53 and the *c* of Samaria and her
53 the *c* of thy captives in the midst
25. 3 Judah, when they went into *c*;
29.14 And I will bring again the *c* of
30.17 and these cities shall go into *c*.
18 her daughters shall go into *c*.
33.21 the twelfth year of our *c*, in the
39.23 Israel went into *c* for their
25 will I bring again the *c* of Jacob,
28 them to be led into *c* among the

Eze 40. 1 year of our *c*, in the beginning
Dan 5.13 art of the children of the *c* of
6.13 which is of the children of the *c*
11.33 the sword, and by flame, by *c*,
Hos 6.11 when I returned the *c* of my
Joel 3. 1 shall bring again the *c* of Judah,
Am 1. 5 people of Syria shall go into *c*
6 carried away captive the whole *c*,
9 they delivered up the whole *c* to
15 their king shall go into *c*, he
5. 5 Gilgal shall surely go into *c*, and
27 will I cause you to go into *c*
7.17 Israel shall surely go into *c*
9. 4 though they go into *c* before
14 I will bring again the *c* of my
Ob 20 And the *c* of this host of the
20 and the *c* of Jerusalem, which
Mic 1.16 for they are gone into *c* from
Na 3.10 she went into *c*: her young
Hab 1. 9 they shall gather the *c* as the
Zep 2. 7 them, and turn away their *c*.
3.20 when I turn back your *c* before
Zec 6.10 Take of them of the *c*, even of
14. 2 of the city shall go forth into *c*,
Ro 7.23 bringing me into *c* to the law of
2Co 10. 5 brnging into *c* every thought to
Eph 4. 8 he led *c* captive, and gave gifts
Rev 13.10 that leadeth into *c* shall go into *c*:

CARE

1Sa 10. 2 hath left the *c* of the asses,
2Sa 18. 3 they will not *c* for us;
3 of us die, will they *c* for us:
2Ki 4.13 been careful for us with all this *c*;
Jer 49.31 nation, that dwelleth without *c*,
Eze 4.16 eat bread by weight, and with *c*;
Mt 13.22 the *c* of this world, and the
Lk 10.34 to an inn, and took *c* of him.
35 Take *c* of him; and whatsoever
40 Lord, dost thou not *c* that my
1Co 7.21 being a servant? *c* not for it;
9. 9 Doth God take *c* for oxen?
12.25 the same *c* one for another.
2Co 7.12 or *c* for you in the sight of God
8.16 earnest *c* into the heart of Titus
11.28 daily, the *c* of all the churches.
Php 2.20 will naturally *c* for your state.
4.10 your *c* of me hath flourished
1Ti 3. 5 shall he take *c* of the church of
1Pe 5. 7 Casting all your *c* upon him;

CARED

Ps 142. 4 failed me; no man *c* for my soul.
Jn 12. 6 not that he *c* for the poor;
Ac 18.17 Gallio *c* for none of those things.

CAREFUL

2Ki 4.13 thou hast been *c* for us with all
Jer 17. 8 not be *c* in the year of drought,
Dan 3.16 we are not *c* to answer thee in
Lk 10.41 Martha, thou art *c* and troubled
Php 4. 6 Be *c* for nothing; but in
10 wherein ye were also *c*, but ye
Tit 3. 8 be *c* to maintain good works.

CAREFULLY

Dt 15. 5 Only if thou *c* hearken unto the
Mic 1.12 inhabitant of Maroth waited *c*
Php 2.28 sent him therefore the more *c*,
Heb 12.17 though he sought it *c* with tears.

CAREFULNESS

Eze 12.18 water with trembling and with *c*;
19 eat their bread with *c*, and drink
1Co 7.32 But I would have you without *c*.
2Co 7.11 sort, what *c* it wrought in you,

CARES

Mk 4.19 the *c* of this world, and the
Lk 8.14 are choked with *c* and riches and
21.34 and *c* of this life, and so that day

CAREST

Mt 22.16 neither *c* thou for any man: for
Mk 4.38 Master, *c* thou not that we perish?
12.14 thou art true, and *c* for no man:

CARETH

Dt 11.12 which the Lord thy God *c* for:
Jn 10.13 hireling, and *c* not for the sheep.
1Co 7.32 He that is unmarried *c* for the
33 he that is married *c* for the
34 unmarried woman *c* for the
34 married *c* for the things of the
1Pe 5. 7 upon him, for he *c* for you.

CARNAL

Ro 7.14 but I am *c*, sold under sin.
8. 7 Because the *c* mind is enmity
15.27 to minister unto them in *c* things.
1Co 3. 1 but as unto *c*, even as unto
3 For ye are yet *c*: for whereas
3 are ye not *c*, and walk as men?
4 I am of Apollos; are ye not *c*?
9.11 if we shall reap your *c* things?
2Co 10. 4 weapons of our warfare are not *c*,
Heb 7.16 the law of a *c* commandment,
9.10 and *c* ordinances, imposed on

CARNALLY

Lev 18.20 thou shalt not lie *c* with thy
19.20 whosoever lieth *c* with a
Nu 5.13 And a man lie with her *c*, and
Ro 8. 6 to be *c* minded is death; but to

CARPENTER

Isa 41. 7 the *c* encouraged the goldsmith,
44.13 The *c* stretched out his rule;
Mk 6. 3 Is not this the *c*, the son of

CARPENTER'S

Mt 13.55 Is not this the *c* son? is not his

CARRIAGES

Isa 10.28 Michmash he hath laid up his *c*:
46. 1 your *c* were heavy loaden;
Ac 21.15 we took up our *c*, and went up

CARRIED

Gen 31.18 And he *c* away all his cattle,
26 and *c* away my daughters,
46. 5 of Israel *c* Jacob their father,
50.13 For his sons *c* him into the land
Lev 10. 5 and *c* them in their coats out of
Jos 4. 8 and *c* them over with them
Jdg 16. 3 *c* them up to the top of an hill
1Sa 5. 8 ark of the God of Israel be *c*
8 *c* the ark of the God of Israel
9 so, that, after they had *c* it about,
30. 2 or small, but *c* them away,
18 the Amalekites had *c* away:
2Sa 6.10 David *c* it aside into the house
15.29 and Abiathar *c* the ark of God
1Ki 8.47 whither they were *c* captives,
47 of them that *c* them captives,
50 before them who *c* them captive,
17.19 and *c* him up into a loft,
21.13 *c* him forth out of the city,
2Ki 7. 8 and *c* thence silver, and gold,
8 and *c* thence also, and went
9.28 *c* him in a chariot to Jerusalem,
15.29 and *c* them captive to Assyria.
16. 9 and *c* the people of it captive
17. 6 and *c* Israel away into Assyria,
11 the Lord *c* away before them;
23 So was Israel *c* away out of their
28 had *c* away from Samaria
33 whom they *c* away from thence.
20.17 shall be *c* unto Babylon:
23. 4 *c* the ashes of them unto Beth-el.
30 his servants *c* him in a chariot
24.13 he *c* out thence all the treasures
14 And he *c* away all Jerusalem,
15 And he *c* away Jehoiachin
15 those *c* he into captivity from
25. 7 of brass, and *c* him to Babylon.
13 *c* the brass of them to Babylon.
21 So Judah was *c* away
1Ch 5. 6 king of Assyria *c* away captive:
26 of Assyria, and he *c* them away.
6.15 when the Lord *c* away Judah
9. 1 were *c* away to Babylon
13. 7 And they *c* the ark of God
13 but *c* it aside into the house of
2Ch 6.37 whither they are *c* captive,
38 they have *c* them captives,
12. 9 he *c* away also the shields
14.13 they *c* away very much spoil.
15 and *c* away sheep and camels
16. 6 they *c* away the stones of Ramah,
21.17 and *c* away all the substance
24.11 it, and *c* it to his place again.
28. 5 and they smote him, and *c* away
8 *c* away captive of their brethren
15 and *c* all the feeble of them
17 Judah, and *c* away captives.
33.11 fetters, and *c* him to Babylon.
34.16 Shaphan *c* the book to the king,
36. 4 brother, and *c* him to Egypt.
7 Nebuchadnezzar also *c* of the
20 sword *c* he away to Babylon;
Ezr 2. 1 of those which had been *c* away,
1 king of Babylon had *c* away
5.12 *c* the people away into Babylon.
8.35 those that had been *c* away,
9. 4 those that had been *c* away;
10. 6 them that had been *c* away.
8 those that had been *c* away.
Neh 7. 6 of those that had been *c* away,
6 king of Babylon had *c* away,
Est 2. 6 been *c* away from Jerusalem
6 captivity which had been *c* away
6 king of Babylon had *c* away.
Job 1.17 and have *c* them away, yea,
5.13 of the froward is *c* headlong.
10.19 I should have been *c* from the
Ps 46. 2 though the mountains be *c* into
106.46 those that *c* them captives.
137. 3 they that *c* us away captive
Isa 39. 6 shall be *c* to Babylon: nothing
46. 3 are *c* from the womb:
49.22 thy daughters shall be *c* upon
53. 4 our grief, and *c* our sorrows:
63. 9 and *c* them all the days of old.
Jer 13.17 Lord's flock is *c* away captive.
19 shall be *c* away captive all of
19 shall be wholly *c* away captive,
24. 1 had *c* away captive Jeconiah
5 them that are *c* away captive.
27.20 he *c* away captive Jeconiah the
22 They shall be *c* to Babylon,
28. 3 this place, and *c* them to Babylon:
6 all that is *c* away captive,
29. 1 which were *c* away captives,
1 Nebuchadnezzar had *c* away
4 all that are *c* away captives,
4 whom I have caused to be *c* away
7 caused you to be *c* away captives,
14 caused you to be *c* away captive.
39. 9 the guard *c* away captive into
40. 1 *c* away captive of Jerusalem
1 which were *c* away captive unto
7 that were not *c* away captive
41.10 Then Ishmael *c* away captive
10 *c* them away captive, and
41.14 Ishmael had *c* away captive
52. 9 they took the king and *c* him up
11 and *c* him to Babylon, and put
15, 30 captain of the guard *c* away captive
17 and *c* all the brass of them to
27 Thus Judah was *c* away captive
28 Nebuchadrezzar *c* away captive
29 Nebuchadrezzar he *c* away
Eze 6. 9 they shall be *c* captives,

17. 4 and *c* it into a land of traffick;
37. 1 and *c* me out in the spirit
Dan 1. 2 he *c* into the land of Shinar
2.35 and the wind *c* them away,
Hos 10. 6 It shall be also *c* unto Assyria
12. 1 and oil is *c* into Egypt.
Joel 3. 5 have *c* into your temples
Am 1. 6 because they *c* away captive
Ob 11 the strangers *c* away captive
Na 3.10 Yet was she *c* away, she went
Mt 1.11 the time they were *c* away
Mk 15. 1 bound Jesus, and *c* him away,
Lk 7.12 there was a dead man *c* out,
16.22 was *c* by the angels into
24.51 them, and *c* up into heaven.
Ac 3. 2 from his mother's womb was *c*,
5. 6 up, and *c* him out, and buried
7.16 And were *c* over into Sychem,
8. 2 *c* Stephen to his burial,
21.34 him to be *c* into the castle.
1Co 12. 2 *c* away unto these dumb idols,
Gal 2.13 Barnabas also was *c* away with
Eph 4.14 and *c* about with every wind
Heb 13. 9 Be not *c* about with divers
2Pe 2.17 that are *c* with a tempest;
Jude 12 without water, *c* about of winds;
Rev 12.15 her to be *c* away of the flood.
17. 3 So he *c* me away in the spirit
21.10 *c* me away in the spirit to a great

CARRIEST

Ps 90. 5 *c* them away as with a flood;

CARRIETH

Job 21.18 chaff that the storm *c* away.
27.21 The east wind *c* him away,
Rev 17. 7 and of the beast that *c* her,

CARRY

Gen 37.25 going to *c* it down to Egypt.
42.19 go ye, *c* corn for the famine of
43.11 and *c* down the man a present,
12 sacks, *c* it again in your hand;
44. 1 as much as they can *c*, and put
45.27 which Joseph had sent to *c* him,
46. 5 which Pharaoh had sent to *c* him.
47.30 and thou shalt *c* me out of Egypt,
50.25 shall *c* up my bones from hence.
Ex 12.46 thou shalt not *c* forth ought of
13.19 ye shall *c* up my bones away
14.11 us, to *c* us forth out of Egypt?
33.15 with me, *c* us not up hence.
Lev 4.12 whole bullock shall he *c* forth
21 And he shall *c* forth the bullock
6.11 *c* forth the ashes without the
10. 4 *c* your brethren from before the
14.45 and he shall *c* them forth out of
16.27 shall one *c* forth without the
Nu 11.12 *C* them in thy bosom, as a
24.22 Asshur shall *c* thee away captive.
Dt 14.24 so that thou art not able to *c* it;
28.38 Thou shalt *c* much seed out
Jos 4. 3 ye shall *c* them over with you,
1Sa 17.18 And *c* these ten cheeses unto
20.40 him, Go, *c* them to the city.
2Sa 15.25 *C* back the ark of God into the
19.18 to *c* over the king's household,
1Ki 8.46 *c* them away captives unto the
18.12 the Spirit of the Lord shall *c* thee
21.10 And then *c* him out and stone
22.26 and *c* him back unto Amon
34 Turn thine hand, and *c* me out
2Ki 4.19 *C* him to his mother.
9. 2 and *c* him to an inner chamber;
17.27 *C* thither one of the priests
18.11 the king of Assyria did *c* away
25.11 the captain of the guard *c* away.
1Ch 10. 9 to *c* tidings unto their idols, and
15. 2 None ought to *c* the ark of God
2 the Lord chosen to *c* the ark
23.26 shall no more *c* the tabernacle,
2Ch 2.16 shalt *c* it up to Jerusalem.
6.36 enemies, and they *c* them away
18.25 Micaiah, and *c* him back to Amon
33 mayest *c* me out of the host;
20.25 more than they could *c* away;
25.12 the children of Judah *c* away captives
29. 5 and *c* forth the filthiness out of
16 And the Levites took it, to *c* it
36. 6 in fetters, to *c* him to Babylon.
Ezr 5.15 go, *c* them into the temple that
7.15 And to *c* the silver and gold,
Job 15.12 Why doth thine heart *c* thee
Ps 49.17 he shall *c* nothing away: his glory
Ec 5.15 he may *c* away in his hand.
10.20 a bird of the air shall *c* the voice
Isa 5.29 the prey, and shall *c* it away
15. 7 laid up, shall they *c* away to the
22.17 the Lord will *c* thee away with a
23. 7 her own feet shall *c* her afar off
30. 6 they will *c* their riches upon the
40.11 and *c* them in his bosom, and
41.16 and the wind shall *c* them away,
46. 4 to hoar hairs will I *c* you: I have
4 even I will *c*, and will deliver you.
7 *c* him, and set him in his place,
57.13 the wind shall *c* them all away;
Jer 17.22 Neither *c* forth a burden out of
20. 4 shall *c* them captive into Babylon,
5 them, and *c* them to Babylon.
39. 7 with chains, to *c* him to Babylon.
14 Shaphan, that he should *c* him
43. 3 *c* us away captives into Babylon.
12 and *c* them away captives: and
La 4.22 he will no more *c* thee...into captivity:
Eze 12. 5 their sight, and *c* out thereby.
6 and *c* it forth in the twilight:
12 the wall to *c* out thereby:
22. 9 In thee are men that *c* tales to
38.13 to *c* away silver and gold, to
Dan 11. 8 And shall also *c* captives into
Mk 6.55 to *c* about in beds those that
11.16 any man should *c* any vessel
Lk 10. 4 *C* neither purse, nor scrip, nor
Jn 5.10 it is not lawful for thee to *c* thy
21.18 shall gird thee, and *c* thee whither
Ac 5. 9 at the door, and shall *c* thee out.
7.43 *c* you away beyond Babylon.
1Ti 6. 7 is certain we can *c* nothing out.

CARRYING

1Sa 10. 3 one *c* three kids, and another
3 another *c* three loaves of bread,
3 and another *c* a bottle of wine:
Ps 78. 9 *c* bows, turned back in the day
Jer 1. 3 *c* away of Jerusalem captive
Mt 1.17 from David until the *c* away
17 from the *c* away into Babylon
Ac 5.10 *c* her forth, buried her by her

CASE

Ex 5.19 did see that they were in evil *c*,
Dt 19. 4 this is the *c* of the slayer, which
22. 1 thou shalt in any *c* bring them
24.13 In any *c* thou shalt deliver him
Ps 144.15 that people, that is in such a *c*:
Mt 5.20 ye shall in no *c* enter into the
19.10 If the *c* of the man be so with his
Jn 5. 6 a long time in that *c*, he saith unto

CASES

1Co 7.15 is not under bondage in such *c*:

CAST

Gen 21.10 *C* out this bondwoman and her
15 and she *c* the child under one of
31.38 she goats have not *c* their young,
51 behold this pillar, which I have *c*
37.20 him, and *c* him into some pit,
22 *c* him into this pit that is in the
24 took him, and *c* him into a pit:
39. 7 master's wife *c* her eyes upon
Ex 1.22 is born ye shall *c* into the river,
4. 3 And he said, *C* it on the ground.
3 And he *c* it on the ground,
25 and *c* it at his feet, and said,
7. 9 Take thy rod, and *c* it before
10 and Aaron *c* down his rod before
12 For they *c* down every man his
10.19 locusts, and *c* them into the Red
15. 4 his host hath he *c* into the sea:
25 when he had *c* into the waters,
22.31 ye shall *c* it to the dogs.
23.26 shall nothing *c* their young.
25.12 thou shalt *c* four rings of gold
26.37 thou shalt *c* five sockets of brass
32.19 he *c* the tables out of his hands,
24 then I *c* it into the fire, and
34.24 I will *c* out the nations before
36.36 and he *c* for them four sockets of
37. 3, 13 he *c* for it four rings of gold,
38. 5 he *c* four rings for the four ends
27 hundred talents of silver were *c*
Lev 1.16 and *c* it beside the altar on the
14.40 and they shall *c* them into an
16. 8 Aaron shall *c* lots upon the two
18.24 nations are defiled which I *c* out
20.23 nation, which I *c* out before you:
26.30 and *c* your carcases upon the
44 I will not *c* them away, neither
Nu 19. 6 and *c* it into the midst of the
35.22 or have *c* upon him any thing
23 and *c* it upon him, that he die,
Dt 6.19 To *c* out all thine enemies from
7. 1 hath *c* out many nations before
9. 4 Lord thy God hath *c* them out
17 and *c* them out of my two hands,
21 and I *c* the dust thereof into the
28.40 for thine olive shall *c* his fruit.
29.28 and *c* them into another land, as
Jos 8.29 and *c* it at the entering of the
10.11 the Lord *c* down great stones
27 and *c* them into the cave
13.12 Moses smite, and *c* them out.
18. 6 that I may *c* lots for you here
8 that I may here *c* lots for you
10 And Joshua *c* lots for them
Jdg 6.28 the altar of Baal was *c* down,
30 he hath *c* down the altar of Baal,
31 because one hath *c* down his
8.25 and did *c* therein every man the
9.53 a certain woman *c* a piece of
15.17 that he *c* away the jawbone out
1Sa 14.42 *C* lots between me and Jonathan
18.11 And Saul *c* the javelin; for he
20.33 And Saul *c* a javelin at him to
2Sa 1.21 of the mighty is vilely *c* away,
11.21 did not a woman *c* a piece of a
16. 6 And he *c* stones at David, and at
13 threw stones at him, and *c* dust.
18.17 and *c* him into a great pit in
20.12 and *c* a cloth upon him,
15 *c* up a bank against the city,
22 Bichri, and *c* it out to Joab.
1Ki 7.15 For he *c* two pillars of brass,
24 knops were *c* in two rows,
24 in two rows, when it was *c*.
46 plain of Jordan did the king *c*
9. 7 name, will I *c* out of my sight;
13.24 his carcase was *c* in the way,
25 passed by, and saw the carcase *c*
28 he went and found his carcase *c*
14. 9 and hast *c* me behind thy back:
24 the nations which the Lord *c*
18.42 *c* himself down upon the earth,
19.19 and *c* his mantle upon him.
21.26 whom the Lord *c* out before the
2Ki 2.16 and *c* him upon some mountain
21 and *c* the salt in there, and said,
3.25 *c* every man his stone, and
4.41 And he *c* it into the pot;
6. 6 and *c* it in thither; and the iron
7.15 Syrians had *c* away in their haste.

2Ki 9.25 *c* him in the portion of the field
26 *c* him into the plat of ground,
10.25 and the captain *c* them out,
13.21 *c* the man into the sepulchre
23 neither *c* he them from his
16. 3 whom the Lord *c* out from
17. 8 *c* out from before the children
20 had *c* them out of his sight.
19.18 have *c* their gods into the fire:
32 shield, nor *c* a bank against it.
21. 2 heathen, whom the Lord *c* out
23. 6 and *c* the powder thereof upon
12 and *c* the dust of them into the
27 will *c* off this city Jerusalem
24.20 until he had *c* them out from
1Ch 24.31 These likewise *c* lots over
25. 8 And they *c* lots, hard against
26.13 And they *c* lots, as well the small
14 they *c* lots; and his lot came out
28. 9 thou forsake him, he will *c* thee
2Ch 4. 3 rows of oxen were *c*,
3 when it was *c*.
17 plain of Jordan did the king *c*
7.20 will I *c* out of my sight, and
11.14 and his sons had *c* them off
13. 9 Have ye not *c* out the priests
20.11 to come to *c* us out of thy
24.10 in, and *c* into the chest,
25. 8 power to help, and to *c* down.
12 and *c* them down from the top of
26.14 and bows,and slings to *c* stones.
28. 3 whom the Lord had *c* out
29.19 king Ahaz in his reign did *c*
30.14 and *c* them into the brook
33. 2 whom the Lord had *c* out before
15 and *c* them out of the city.
Neh 1. 9 there were of you *c* out unto
6.16 they were much *c* down in their
9.26 and *c* thy law behind their backs,
10.34 we *c* the lots among the priests,
11. 1 the rest of the people also *c* lots,
13. 8 therefore I *c* forth all the
Est 3. 7 they *c* Pur, that is, the lot,
9.24 and had *c* Pur, that is, the lot,
Job 8. 4 and he have *c* them away for their
20 God will not *c* away a perfect
15.33 and shall *c* off his flower as the
18. 7 his own counsel shall *c* him down.
8 he is *c* into a net by his own
20.15 God shall *c* them out of his belly.
23 God shall *c* the fury of his wrath
22.29 When men are *c* down, then thou
27.22 For God shall *c* upon him, and
29.24 my countenance they *c* not down.
30.19 He hath *c* me into the mire,
39. 3 ones, they *c* out their sorrows.
40.11 *C* abroad the rage of thy wrath:
41. 9 shall not one be *c* down even
Ps 2. 3 and *c* away their cords from us.
5.10 *c* them out in the multitude
17.13 disappoint him, *c* him down:
18.42 I did *c* them out as the dirt
22.10 I was *c* upon thee from the womb:
18 and *c* lots upon my vesture.
36.12 they are *c* down, and shall not
37.14 to *c* down the poor and needy,
24 he shall not be utterly *c* down:
42. 5 Why art thou *c* down, O my soul?
6 my soul is *c* down within me:
11 Why art thou *c* down, O my soul?
43. 2 why dost thou *c* me off?
5 Why art thou *c* down, O my soul?
44. 2 the people, and *c* them out.
9 But thou hast *c* off, and put us
23 arise, *c* us not off for ever.
51.11 *C* me not away from thy presence;
55. 3 they *c* iniquity upon me, and in
22 *C* thy burden upon the Lord,
56. 7 in thine anger *c* down the people,
60. 1 O God, thou hast *c* us off, thou
8 over Edom will I *c* out my shoe:
10 O God, which hadst *c* us off?
62. 4 They only consult to *c* him down
71. 9 *C* me not off in the time of old
74. 1 hast thou *c* us off for ever?
7 have *c* fire into thy sanctuary.
76. 6 the chariot and horse are *c* into
77. 7 Will the Lord *c* off for ever?
78.49 He *c* upon them the fierceness
55 He *c* out the heathen also
80. 8 thou hast *c* out the heathen,
89.38 thou hast *c* off and abhorred,
44 *c* his throne down to the ground.
94.14 Lord will not *c* off his people,
102.10 lifted me up, and *c* me down.
108. 9 over Edom will I *c* out my shoe;
11 O God, who has *c* us off?
140.10 let them be *c* into the fire;
144. 6 *C* forth lightning, and scatter
Pr 1.14 *C* in thy lot among us; let us all
7.26 she hath *c* down many wounded:
16.33 The lot is *c* into the lap; but
22.10 *C* out the scorner, and contention
Ec 3. 5 A time to *c* away stones, and a
6 and a time to *c* away;
11. 1 *C* thy bread upon the waters:
Isa 2.20 a man shall *c* his idols of silver,
5.24 because they have *c* away the
6.13 when they *c* their leaves:
14.19 thou art *c* out of thy grave
16. 2 wandering bird *c* out of the nest,
19. 8 all they that *c* angle into the
25. 7 the covering *c* over all people,
26.19 the earth shall *c* out the dead.
28. 2 shall *c* down to the earth with
25 doth he not *c* abroad the fitches,
25 and *c* in the principal wheat
30.22 gold: thou shalt *c* them away
31. 7 every man shall *c* away his idols
34. 3 Their slain also shall be *c* out,
17 he hath *c* the lot for them,
37.19 have *c* their gods into the fire:
33 nor *c* a bank against it.
38.17 *c* all my sins behind thy back.
41. 9 chosen thee, and not *c* thee away.
57.14 *C* ye up, *c* ye up, prepare the
20 whose waters *c* up mire and
58. 7 poor that are *c* out to thy house?
62.10 *c* up, *c* up the highway;
66. 5 *c* you out for my name's sake,
Jer 6. 6 *c* a mount against Jerusalem:
15 I visit them they shall be *c* down,
7.15 I will *c* you out of my sight,
15 I have *c* out all your brethren,
29 O Jerusalem, and *c* it away,
8.12 visitation, they shall be *c* down,
9.19 our dwellings have *c* us out.
14.16 shall be *c* out in the streets of
15. 1 people: *c* them out of my sight,
16.13 Therefore will I *c* you out of
18.15 in paths, in a way not *c* up;
22. 7 cedars, and *c* them into the fire.
19 burial of an ass, drawn and *c* forth
26 And I will *c* thee out, and thy
28 wherefore are they *c* out, he and
28 and are *c* into a land which
23.39 your fathers, and *c* you out of
26.23 and *c* his dead body into the
28.16 will *c* thee from off the face of
31.37 also *c* off all the seed of Israel
33.24 he hath even *c* them off?
26 I will *c* away the seed of Jacob,
36.23 and *c* it into the fire that was
30 his dead body shall be *c* out in
38. 6 and *c* him into the dungeon
9 whom they have *c* into the
11 took thence old *c* clouts and old
12 Put now these old *c* clouts and
41. 7 and *c* them into the midst of the
9 Ishmael had *c* all the dead
14 from Mizpah *c* about and
50.26 *c* her up as heaps, and destroy
51.34 my delicates, he hath *c* me out.
63 and *c* it into the midst of
52. 3 till he had *c* them out from his
La 2. 1 *c* down from heaven unto the
7 The Lord hath *c* off his altar, he
10 they have *c* up dust upon their
3.31 the Lord will not *c* off for ever:
53 and *c* a stone upon me.
Eze 4. 2 against it, and *c* a mount against
5. 4 and *c* them into the midst of the
6. 4 and I will *c* down your slain
7.19 They shall *c* their silver in the
11.16 I have *c* them far off among the
15. 4 Behold, it is *c* into the fire for
16. 5 but thou wast *c* out in the open
18.31 *C* away from you all your
19.12 in fury, she was *c* down to the
20. 7 *C* ye away every man the
8 they did not every man *c* away
21.22 to *c* a mount, and to build a fort.
23.35 forgotten me, and *c* me behind
26. 8 and *c* a mount against thee,
27.30 shall *c* up dust upon their heads,
28.16 therefore I will *c* thee as profane
17 I will *c* thee to the ground, I will
31.16 when I *c* him down to hell with
32. 4 I will *c* thee forth upon the open
18 of Egypt, and *c* them down, even
36. 5 to *c* it out for a prey.
43.24 and the priests shall *c* salt upon
Dan 3. 6 shall the same hour be *c* into
11 he should be *c* into the midst of
15 ye shall be *c* the same hour into
20 and to *c* them into the burning
21 and were *c* into the midst of the
24 Did not we *c* three men bound
6. 7 he shall be *c* into the den of lions.
12 shall be *c* into the den of lions?
16 they brought Daniel, and *c* him
24 they *c* them into the den of lions,
7. 9 till the thrones were *c* down,
8. 7 but he *c* him down to the
10 and it *c* down some of the host
11 the place of his sanctuary was *c*
12 and it *c* down the truth to the
11.12 and he shall *c* down many ten
15 and *c* up a mount, and take the
Hos 8. 3 Israel hath *c* off the thing that
5 Thy calf, O Samaria, hath *c* thee
9.17 My God will *c* them away,
14. 5 and *c* forth his roots as Lebanon.
Joel 1. 7 made it clean bare, and *c* it away;
3. 3 they have *c* lots for my people;
Am 1.11 and did *c* off all pity, and his
4. 3 and ye shall *c* them into the
8. 3 they shall *c* them forth with
8 and it shall be *c* out and
Ob 11 and *c* lots upon Jerusalem,
Jon 1. 5 and *c* forth the wares that were
7 Come, and let us *c* lots, that we
7 So they *c* lots, and the lot fell
12 and *c* me forth into the sea;
15 and *c* him forth into the sea:
2. 3 For thou hadst *c* me into the
4 I said,I am *c* out of thy sight;
Mic 2. 5 none that shall *c* a cord by lot
9 women of my people have ye *c*
4. 7 and her that was *c* far off a
7.19 and thou wilt *c* all their sins
Na 3. 6 And I will *c* abominable filth
10 they *c* lots for her honorable
Zep 3.15 thy judgments, he hath *c* out
Zec 1.21 *c* out the horns of the Gentiles,
5. 8 And he *c* it into the midst of the
8 and he *c* the weight of lead upon
9. 4 the Lord will *c* her out, and he
10. 6 though I had not *c* them off:
11.13 *C* it unto the potter: a goodly
13 and *c* them to the potter in the
Mal 3.11 shall your vine *c* her fruit before
Mt 3.10 hewn down, and *c* into the fire.

4. 6 the Son of God, *c* thyself down:
12 had heard that John was *c* into
5.13 good for nothing, but to be *c* out,
25 to the officer, and thou be *c* into
29 pluck it out, and *c* it from thee:
29 thy whole body should be *c* into
30 cut it off, and *c* it from thee:
30 that thy whole body should be *c*
6.30 and to morrow is *c* into the oven.
7. 5 first *c* out the beam out of thine
5 see clearly to *c* out the mote out
6 neither *c* ye your pearls before
19 hewn down, and *c* into the fire.
22 in thy name have *c* out devils?
8.12 shall be *c* out into outer darkness;
16 he *c* out the spirits with his word,
31 saying, If thou *c* us out, suffer us
9.33 when the devil was *c* out, the
10. 1 unclean spirits, to *c* them out,
8 lepers, raise the dead, *c* out devils:
12.24 doth not *c* out devils, but by
26 if Satan *c* out Satan, he is divided
27 And if I by Beelzebub *c* out devils,
27 do your children *c* them out?
28 if I *c* out devils by the Spirit
13.42 shall *c* them into a furnace of fire:
47 like unto a net, that was *c* into the
48 good into vessels, but *c* the bad
50 shall *c* them into the furnace of
15.17 and is *c* out into the draft?
26 children's bread, and to *c* it to
30 and *c* them down at Jesus' feet;
17.19 Why could not we *c* him out?
27 go thou to the sea, and *c* an hook,
18. 8 cut them off, and *c* them from thee:
8 feet to be *c* into everlasting fire.
9 pluck it out, and *c* it from thee:
9 having two eyes to be *c* into hell
30 went and *c* him into prison, till he
21.12 *c* out all that sold and bought
21 and be thou *c* into the sea;
39 they caught him, and *c* him out
22.13 and *c* him into outer darkness;
25.30 And *c* ye the unprofitable servant
27. 5 And he *c* down the pieces of
35 upon my vesture did they *c* lots.
44 him, *c* the same in his teeth.
Mk 1.34 and *c* out many devils; and
39 throughout all Galilee, and *c* out
3.15 sicknesses, and to *c* out devils:
23 How can Satan *c* out Satan?
4.26 a man should *c* seed into the
6.13 they *c* out many devils, and
7.26 he would *c* forth the devil out of
27 children's bread, and to *c* it unto
9.18 that they should *c* him out;
22 it hath *c* him into the fire,
28 Why could not we *c* him out?
42 his neck, and he were *c* into the
45 two feet to be *c* into hell, into the
47 two eyes to be *c* into hell fire:
11. 7 and *c* their garments on him;
15 and began to *c* out them that
23 removed, and be thou *c* into the
12. 4 at him they *c* stones, and
8 killed him, and *c* him out of the
41 people *c* money into the treasury:
41 and many that were rich *c* in
43 this poor widow hath *c* more in,
43 than all they which have *c* into
44 they did *c* in of their abundance,
44 but she of her want did *c* in all
14.51 having a linen cloth *c* about his
16. 9 out of whom he had *c* seven
17 In my name shall they *c* out
Lk 1.29 *c* in her mind what manner of
3. 9 is hewn down, and *c* into the fire.
4. 9 Son of God, *c* thyself down from
29 that they might *c* him down
6.22 shall reproach you, and *c* out
42 *c* out first the beam out of thine
9.25 and lose himself, or be *c* away?
40 I besought thy disciples to *c* him
11.18 ye say that I *c* out devils through
19 if I by Beelzebub *c* out devils,
19 by whom do your sons *c* them out?
20 if I with the finger of God *c* out
12. 5 hath power to *c* into hell; yea, I
28 and to morrow is *c* into the oven;
58 and the officer *c* thee into prison.
13.19 a man took, and *c* into his garden;
32 Behold, I *c* out devils, and I do
14.35 for the dunghill; but men *c* it out.
17. 2 about his neck, and he *c* into
19.35 they *c* their garments upon the
43 thine enemies shall *c* a trench
45 began to *c* out them that sold
20.12 wounded him also, and *c* him out.
15 *c* him out of the vineyard, and
21. 3 this poor widow hath *c* in more
4 of their abundance *c* in unto the
4 but she of her penury hath *c* in
22.41 from them about a stone's *c*,
23.19 for murder, was *c* into prison.
25 and murder was *c* into prison,
34 parted his raiment, and *c* lots.
Jn 3.24 John was not yet *c* into prison.
6.37 to me I will in no wise *c* out.
8. 7 let him first *c* a stone at her.
59 took they up stones to *c* at him:
9.34 teach us? And they *c* him out.
35 heard that they had *c* him out;
12.31 the prince of this world be *c* out.
15. 6 he is *c* forth as a branch, and is
6 *c* them into the fire, and they are
19.24 Let us not rend it, but *c* lots for it,
24 and for my vesture they did *c* lots.
21. 6 *C* the net on the right side of the
6 They *c* therefore, and now they
7 and did *c* himself into the sea.
Ac 7.19 they *c* out their young
21 when he was *c* out, Pharaoh's
58 *c* him out of the city, and stoned
12. 8 *C* thy garment about thee, and
16.23 they *c* them into prison, charging
37 have *c* us into prison; and now do
22.23 they cried out, and *c* off their
27.19 we *c* out with our own hands the
26 we must be *c* upon a certain
29 they *c* four anchors out of the
30 as though they would have *c*
38 and *c* out the wheat into the sea.
43 should *c* themselves first into the
Ro 11. 1 Hath God *c* away his people?
2 God hath not *c* away his people
13.12 let us therefore *c* off the works of
1Co 7.35 not that I may *c* a snare upon you,
2Co 4. 9 but not forsaken; *c* down, but
7. 6 comforteth those that are *c* down,
Gal 4.30 *C* out the bondwoman and her
1Ti 5.12 they have *c* off their first faith.
Heb 10.35 *C* not away therefore your
2Pe 2. 4 but *c* them down to hell, and
Rev 2.10 the devil shall *c* some of you into
14 Balac to *c* a stumblingblock
22 Behold, I will *c* her into a bed,
4.10 and *c* their crowns before the
8. 5 *c* it into the earth: and there were
7 they were *c* upon the earth: and
8 burning with fire was *c* into the
12. 4 stars of heaven, and did *c* them to
9 the great dragon was *c* out, that
9 he was *c* out into the earth,
9 and his angels were *c* out with
10 accuser of our brethren is *c* down,
13 dragon saw that he was *c* unto
15 the serpent *c* out of his mouth
16 the dragon *c* out of his mouth.
14.19 *c* it into the great winepress of
18.19 they *c* dust on their heads, and
21 millstone, and *c* it into the sea,
19.20 These both were *c* alive into a
20. 3 *c* him into the bottomless pit, and
10 was *c* into the lake of fire and
14 death and hell were *c* into the
15 was *c* into the lake of fire.

CASTAWAY

1Co 9.27 to others, I myself should be a *c*.

CASTETH

Job 21.10 their cow calveth, and *c* not her
Ps 147. 6 he *c* the wicked down to the
17 He *c* forth his ice like morsels:
Pr 10. 3 but he *c* away the substance of
19.15 Slothfulness *c* into a deep sleep;
21.22 and *c* down the strength of the
26.18 who *c* firebrands, arrows, and
Isa 40.19 with gold, and *c* silver chains,
Jer 6. 7 As a fountain *c* out her waters,
7 so she *c* out her wickedness:
Mt 9.34 He *c* out devils through the prince
Mk 3.22 prince of the devils *c* he out devils.
Lk 11.15 He *c* out devils through Beelzebub
1Jn 4.18 perfect love *c* out fear: because
3Jn 10 and *c* them out of the church.
Rev 6.13 as a fig tree *c* her untimely figs,

CASTING

2Sa 8. 2 *c* them down to the ground;
1Ki 7.37 all of them had one *c*, one
Ezr 10. 1 *c* himself down before the house
Job 6.21 ye see my *c* down, and are afraid.
Ps 74. 7 sanctuary, have they defiled by *c*
89.39 his crown by *c* it to the ground.
Eze 17.17 by *c* up mounts, and building
Mic 6.14 and thy *c* down shall be in the
Mt 4.18 *c* a net into the sea: for they were
27.35 parted his garments, *c* lots: that
Mk 1.16 Andrew his brother *c* a net into
9.38 we saw one *c* out devils in thy
10.50 he, *c* away his garment, rose, and
15.24 parted his garments, *c* lots upon
Lk 9.49 we saw one *c* out devils in thy
11.14 he was *c* out a devil, and it was
21. 1 the rich men *c* their gifts into the
2 a certain poor widow *c* in thither
Ro 11.15 For if the *c* away of them be the
2Co 10. 5 *C* down imaginations, and every
1Pe 5. 7 *C* all your care upon him; for he

CASTLE

1Ch 11. 5 David took the *c* of Zion, which
7 David dwelt in the *c*; therefore
Pr 18.19 contentions are like the bars of a *c*.
Ac 21.34 him to be carried into the *c*.
37 Paul was to be led into the *c*, he
22.24 to be brought into the *c*, and bade
23.10 and to bring him into the *c*.
16 he went and entered into the *c*,
32 and returned to the *c*:

CASTOR

Ac 28.11 whose sign was *C* and Pollux.

CATCH

Ex 22. 6 If fire break out, and *c* in
Jdg 21.21 and *c* you every man his wife of
1Ki 20.33 from him, and did hastily *c* it:
2Ki 7.12 we shall *c* them alive, and get
Ps 10. 9 in wait to *c* the poor: he doth *c*
35. 8 let his net that he hath hid *c*
109.11 Let the extortioner *c* all that he
Jer 5.26 snares; they set a trap, they *c*
Eze 19. 3 it learned to *c* the prey; it
6 and learned to *c* the prey, and
Hab 1.15 they *c* them in their net, and
Mk 12.13 of the Herodians, to *c* him in his
Lk 5.10 henceforth thou shalt *c* men.
11.54 seeking to *c* something out of his

CATCHETH

Lev 17.13 which hunteth and *c* any beast

Mt 13.19 cometh the wicked one, and *c*
Jn 10.12 the wolf *c* them, and scattereth

CAUGHT

Gen 22.13 ram *c* in a thicket by his horns:
39.12 And she *c* him by his garment,
Ex 4. 4 put forth his hand, and *c* it,
Nu 31.32 which the men of war had *c*,
Jdg 1. 6 pursued after him, and *c* him,
8.14 And *c* a young man of the men
15. 4 went and *c* three hundred foxes,
21.23 whom they *c*: and they went
1Sa 17.35 he arose against me, I *c* him
2Sa 2.16 And they *c* every one his fellow
18. 9 and his head *c* hold of the oak,
1Ki 1.50 and *c* hold on the horns of the
51 he hath *c* hold on the horns of
2.28 and *c* hold on the horns of the
11.30 And Ahijah *c* the new garment
2Ki 4.27 she *c* him by the feet: but
2Ch 22. 9 sought Ahaziah: and they *c* him,
Pr 7.13 So she *c* him, and kissed him,
Ec 9.12 birds that are *c* in the snare;
Jer 50.24 thou art found, and also *c*,
Mt 14.31 *c* him, and said unto him,
21.39 they *c* him, and cast him out
Mk 12. 3 And they *c* him and beat him,
Lk 8.29 For oftentimes it had *c* him:
Jn 21. 3 and that night they *c* nothing.
10 the fish which we have now *c*.
Ac 6.12 *c* him, and brought him to the
8.39 Spirit of the Lord *c* away Philip,
16.19 they *c* Paul and Silas, and drew
19.29 *c* Gaius and Aristarchus, men
26.21 the Jews *c* me in the temple,
27.15 And when the ship was *c*,
2Co 12. 2 one *c* up to the third heaven.
4 he was *c* up into paradise,
16 being crafty, I *c* you with guile.
1Th 4.17 shall be *c* up together with
Rev 12. 5 her child was *c* up unto God,

CAUSES

Ex 18.19 that thou mayest bring the *c*
26 hard *c* they brought unto Moses.
Dt 1.16 Hear the *c* between your brethren,
Jer 3. 8 I saw, when for all the *c* whereby
La 2.14 for thee false burdens and *c* of
3.58 O Lord, thou hast pleaded the *c*
Ac 26.21 For these *c* the Jews caught me

CAUSETH

Nu 5.18 the bitter water that *c* the curse:
19 free from this bitter water that *c*
22 this water that *c* the curse shall go
24 the bitter water that *c* the curse:
24 and the water that *c* the curse
27 that the water that *c* the curse shall
Job 12.24 *c* them to wander in a wilderness
20. 3 my understanding *c* me to answer.
37.13 He *c* it to come, whether for
Ps 104.14 He *c* the grass to grow for the cattle,
107.40 *c* them to wander in the wilderness,
135. 7 He *c* the vapors to ascend from the
147.18 he *c* his wind to blow, and the
Pr 10. 5 in harvest is a son that *c* shame.
10 winketh with the eye *c* sorrow:
14.35 wrath is against him that *c* shame.
17. 2 have rule over a son that *c* shame,
18.18 The lot *c* contentions to cease,
19.26 a son that *c* shame, and bringeth
27 hear the instruction that *c* to err
28.10 *c* the righteous to go astray in an
Isa 61.11 the garden *c* the things that are
64. 2 fire burneth, the fire *c* the waters to
Jer 10.13 and he *c* the vapors to ascend from
51.16 in the heavens; and he *c* the vapors
Eze 26. 3 as the sea *c* his waves to come up.
44.18 gird themselves with anything that *c*
Mt 5.32 *c* her to commit adultery: and
2Co 2.14 *c* us to triumph in Christ, and
9.11 *c* through us thanksgiving to
Rev 13.12 beast before him, and *c* the
16 he *c* all, both small and great,

CAVES

Jdg 6. 2 in the mountains, and *c*, and
1Sa 13. 6 people did hide themselves in *c*,
Job 30. 6 cliffs of the valleys, in *c* of the
Isa 2.19 into the *c* of the earth, for fear
Eze 33.27 in the forts and in the *c* shall die
Heb 11.38 mountains, and in dens and *c*

CEASE

Gen 8.22 and day and night shall not *c*.
Ex 9.29 the thunder shall *c*, neither shall
Nu 8.25 years they shall *c* waiting upon
11.25 they prophesied, and did not *c*.
17. 5 and I will make to *c* from me the
Dt 15.11 For the poor shall never *c* out of
32.26 the remembrance of them to *c*
Jos 22.25 children make our children *c*
Jdg 15. 7 of you, and after that I will *c*.
20.28 or shall I *c*? And the Lord said,
1Sa 7. 8 *C* not to cry unto the Lord our
2Ch 16. 5 of Ramah, and let his work *c*.
Ezr 4.21 to cause these men to *c*,
23 and made them to *c* by force and
5. 5 they could not cause them to *c*,
Neh 4.11 them, and cause the work to *c*.
6. 3 why should the work *c*, whilst I
Job 3.17 the wicked *c* from troubling;
10.20 *c* then, and let me alone, that I
14. 7 tender branch thereof will not *c*.
Ps 37. 8 *C* from anger, and forsake
46. 9 He maketh wars to *c* unto the
85. 4 cause thine anger toward us to *c*.
89.44 Thou hast made his glory to *c*,
Pr 18.18 The lot causeth contentions to *c*,
19.27 *C*, my son, to hear the instruction
20. 3 It is an honor for a man to *c*
22.10 yea, strife and reproach shall *c*.
23. 4 *c* from thine own wisdom.
Ec 12. 3 and the grinders *c* because they
Isa 1.16 before mine eyes; *c* to do evil;
2.22 *C* ye from man, whose breath is
10.25 and the indignation shall *c*,
13.11 the arrogancy of the proud to *c*,
16.10 their vintage shouting to *c*.
17. 3 The fortress also shall *c* from
21. 2 sighing thereof have I made to *c*.
30.11 cause the Holy One of Israel to *c*
33. 1 when thou shalt *c* to spoil, thou
Jer 7.34 Then will I cause to *c* from the
14.17 and day, and let them not *c*:
16. 9 I will cause to *c* out of this place
17. 8 drought, neither shall *c* from
31.36 the seed of Israel also shall *c*
36.29 and shall cause to *c* from thence
48.35 I will cause to *c* in Moab, saith
La 2.18 let not the apple of thine eye *c*.
Eze 6. 6 your idols may be broken and *c*,
7.24 the pomp of the strong to *c*;
12.23 I will make this proverb to *c*,
16.41 and I will cause thee to *c* from
23.27 will I make thy lewdness to *c*
48 Thus will I cause lewdness to *c*
26.13 cause the noise of thy songs to *c*;
30.10 make the multitude of Egypt to *c*
13 I will cause their images to *c*,
18 the pomp of her strength shall *c*
33.28 the pomp of her strength shall *c*;
34.10 and cause them to *c* from feeding
25 and will cause the evil beasts to *c*
Dan 9.27 sacrifice and the oblation to *c*,
11.18 reproach offered by him to *c*;
Hos 1. 4 and will cause to *c* the kingdom
2.11 will also cause all her mirth to *c*,
Am 7. 5 O Lord God, *c*, I beseech thee:
Ac 13.10 wilt thou not *c* to pervert the
1Co 13. 8 there be tongues, they shall *c*;
Eph 1.16 *C* not to give thanks for you,
Col 1. 9 do not *c* to pray for you, and to
2Pe 2.14 that cannot *c* from sin; beguiling

CEASED

Gen 18.11 it *c* to be with Sarah after the
Ex 9.33 and the thunders and hail *c*,
34 hail and the thunders were *c*,
Jos 5.12 and the manna *c* on the morrow
Jdg 2.19 *c* not from their own doings,
5. 7 the villages *c*, they *c* in Israel,
1Sa 2. 5 they that were hungry *c*: so that
25. 9 in the name of David, and *c*.
Ezr 4.24 Then *c* the work of the house of
24 So it *c* unto the second year
Job 32. 1 these three men *c* to answer Job,
Ps 35.15 they did tear me, and *c* not:
77. 2 my sore ran in the night, and *c*
Isa 14. 4 How hath the oppressor *c*!
4 the golden city *c*!
La 5.14 The elders have *c* from the gate,
15 The joy of our heart is *c*; our
Jon 1.15 and the sea *c* from her raging.
Mt 14.32 come into the ship, the wind *c*.
Mk 4.39 the wind *c*, and there was a great
6.51 the wind *c*: and they were sore
Lk 7.45 came in hath not *c* to kiss my feet,
8.24 they *c*, and there was a calm.
11. 1 when he *c*, one of his disciples
Ac 5.42 they *c* not to teach and preach
20. 1 And after the uproar was *c*, Paul
31 I *c* not to warn every one night
21.14 not be persuaded, we *c*, saying,
Gal 5.11 then is the offense of the cross *c*.
Heb 4.10 he also hath *c* from his own
10. 2 would they not have *c* to be
1Pe 4. 1 suffered in the flesh hath *c* from

CEASETH

Ps 12. 1 Help, Lord; for the godly man *c*;
49. 8 is precious, and it *c* for ever:)
Pr 26.20 there is no talebearer, the strife *c*.
Isa 16. 4 the spoiler *c*, the oppressors are
24. 8 The mirth of tabrets *c*, the noise
8 endeth, the joy of the harp *c*.
33. 8 lie waste, the wayfaring man *c*:
La 3.49 eye trickleth down, and *c* not,
Hos 7. 4 who *c* from raising after he hath
Ac 6.13 This man *c* not to speak

CEASING

1Sa 12.23 the Lord in *c* to pray for you:
Ac 12. 5 prayer was made without *c* of
Ro 1. 9 that without *c* I make mention of
1Th 1. 3 Remembering without *c* your
2.13 also thank we God without *c*,
5.17 Pray without *c*.
2Ti 1. 3 without *c* I have remembrance

CEDARS

Jdg 9.15 and devour the *c* of Lebanon.
1Ki 7.11 measures of hewed stones, and *c*.
1Ch 14. 1 timber of *c*, with masons and
17. 1 I dwell in an house of *c*, but the
6 ye not built me an house of *c*?
Ps 29. 5 the Lord breaketh the *c*; yea,
80.10 thereof were like the goodly *c*,
Isa 9.10 but we will change them into *c*,
14. 8 the *c* of Lebanon, saying, Since
44.14 He heweth him down *c*, and taketh
Jer 22. 7 shall cut down thy choice *c*, and
23 that makest thy nest in the *c*, how
Eze 31. 8 The *c* in the garden of God could
Am 2. 9 like the height of the *c*, and he
Zec 11. 1 that the fire may devour thy *c*.

CEDRON

Jn 18. 1 over the brook *C*, where was a

CELESTIAL

1Co 15.40 There are also *c* bodies, and
40 but the glory of the *c* is one,

CENTURION

Mt 8. 5 unto him a *c*,beseeching him,
8 The *c* answered and said, Lord,
13 Jesus said unto the *c*, Go thy way;
27.54 *c*, and they that were with him,
Mk 15.39 *c*, which stood over against him,
44 calling unto him the *c*,he asked
45 when he knew it of the *c*, he gave
Lk 7. 6 the *c* sent friends to him, saying
23.47 when the *c* saw what was done,
Ac 10. 1 *c* of the band called the Italian
22 they said, Cornelius the *c*, a just
22.25 Paul said unto the *c* that stood by,
26 When the *c* heard that, he went
24.23 commanded a *c* to keep Paul,
27. 1 Julius, a *c* of Augustus' band.
6 there the *c* found a ship of
11 the *c* believed the master and the
31 Paul said to the *c* and to the
43 the *c*, willing to save Paul, kept
28.16 the *c* delivered the prisoners to

CENTURION'S

Lk 7. 2 a certain *c* servant, who was dear

CENTURIONS

Ac 21.32 immediately took soldiers and *c*,
23.17 Paul called one of the *c* unto him,
23 he called unto him two *c*, saying,

CEPHAS

Jn 1.42 thou shalt be called *C*, which is
1Co 1.12 and I of Apollos; and I of *C*;
3.22 Whether Paul, or Apollos, or *C*,
9. 5 as the brethren of the Lord, and *C*?
15. 5 he was seen of *C*, then of the
Gal 2. 9 And when James, *C*, and John,

CERTAINLY

Gen 26.28 We saw *c* that the Lord was with
43. 7 could we *c* know that he would
44.15 such a man as I can *c* divine?
50.15 will *c* requite us all the evil
Ex 3.12 he said, *C* I will be with thee;
22. 4 If the theft be *c* found in his
Lev 5.19 hath *c* trespassed against the Lord.
24.16 the congregation shall *c* stone him:
Jos 9.24 Because it was *c* told thy
Jdg 14.12 if ye can *c* declare it me within
1Sa 20. 3 Thy father *c* knoweth that I
9 if I knew *c* that evil were
23.10 thy servant hath *c* heard
25.28 the Lord will *c* make my lord a sure
1Ki 1.30 even so will I *c* do this day.
2Ki 8.10 him, Thou mayest *c* recover:
2Ch 18.27 If thou *c* return in peace,
Pr 23. 5 riches *c* make themselves wings;
Jer 8. 8 Lo, *c* in vain made he it;
13.12 Do we not *c* know that every
25.28 Lord of hosts; Ye shall *c* drink.
36.29 king of Babylon shall *c* come
40.14 Dost thou *c* know that Baalis
42.19 know *c* that I have admonished you
22 Now therefore know *c* that ye shall
44.17 we will *c* do whatsoever thing goeth
La 2.16 *c* this is the day that we looked
Dan 11.10 one shall *c* come, and overflow,
13 *c* come after certain years
Lk 23.47 *C* this was a righteous man.

CERTAINTY

Jos 23.13 Know for a *c* that the Lord your God
1Sa 23.23 come ye again to me with the *c*,
Pr 22.21 the *c* of the words of truth; that
Dan 2. 8 I know of *c* that ye would gain
Lk 1. 4 know the *c* of those things,
Ac 21.34 not know the *c* for the tumult,
22.30 he would have known the *c*

CERTIFY

2Sa 15.28 come word from you to *c* me,
Ezr 4.16 We *c* the king that, if this city
5.10 asked their names also, to *c* thee,
7.24 Also we *c* you that touching any
Gal 1.11 But I *c* you, brethren, that the

CHAFF

Job 21.18 *c* that the storm carrieth away.
Ps 1. 4 *c* which the wind driveth away.
35. 5 Let them be as *c* before the wind:
Isa 5.24 and the flame consumeth the *c*,
17.13 chased as the *c* of the mountains
29. 5 the terrible ones shall be as *c*
33.11 Ye shall conceive *c*, ye shall
41.15 and shalt make the hills as *c*.
Jer 23.28 What is the *c* to the wheat?
Dan 2.35 like the *c* of the summer
Hos 13. 3 as the *c* that is driven with the
Zep 2. 2 before the day pass as the *c*,
Mt 3.12 burn up the *c* with unquenchable
Lk 3.17 the *c* he will burn with fire

CHAIN

Gen 41.42 put a gold *c* about his neck;
1Ki 7.17 wreaths of *c* work, for the
Ps 73. 6 compasseth them about as a *c*;
SS 4. 9 eyes, with one *c* of thy neck.
La 3. 7 he hath made my *c* heavy.
Eze 7.23 Make a *c*: for the land is full of
16.11 thy hands, and a *c* on thy neck.
Dan 5. 7 have a *c* of gold about his neck,
16 have a *c* of gold about thy neck,
29 put a *c* of gold about his neck,
Ac 28.20 of Israel I am bound with this *c*.
2Ti 1.16 and was not ashamed of my *c*:
Rev 20. 1 pit and a great *c* in his hand.

CHAINS

Ex 28.14 two *c* of pure gold at the ends;
14 the wreathen *c* to the ouches.
22 upon the breastplate *c* at the ends
24 thou shalt put the two wreathen *c*
25 two ends of the two wreathen *c* thou
39.15 upon the breastplate *c* at the ends,
17 *c* of gold in the two rings
18 the two wreathen *c* they fastened
Nu 31.50 of gold, *c*, and bracelets, rings,
Jdg 8.26 *c* that were about their camels'
1Ki 6.21 made a partition by the *c* of gold
2Ch 3. 5 and set thereon palm trees and *c*.
16 And he made *c*, as in the oracle,
16 and put them on the *c*.
Ps 68. 6 those which are bound with *c*:
149. 8 To bind their kings with *c*,
Pr 1. 9 thy head, and *c* about thy neck.
SS 1.10 jewels, thy neck with *c* of gold.
Isa 3.19 The *c*, and the bracelets, and the
40.19 with gold, and casteth silver *c*.
45.14 in *c* they shall come over,
Jer 39. 7 and bound him with *c*, to carry
40. 1 being bound in *c* among all that
4 I loose thee this day from the *c*
52.11 king of Babylon bound him in *c*,
Eze 19. 4 brought him with *c* unto the land
9 put him in ward in *c*, and
Na 3.10 her great men were bound in *c*.
Mk 5. 3 could bind him, no, not with *c*:
4 often bound with fetters and *c*,
4 the *c* had been plucked asunder
Lk 8.29 he was kept bound with *c* and in
Ac 12. 6 two soldiers, bound with two *c*:
7 And his *c* fell off from his hands.
21.33 him to be bound with two *c*;
2Pe 2. 4 delivered them into *c* of darkness,
Jude 6 hath reserved in everlasting *c*

CHALCEDONY

Rev 21.19 the third, a *c*; the fourth,

CHALDAEANS

Ac 7. 4 out of the land of the *C*,

CHAMBER

Gen 43.30 he entered into his *c*,
Jdg 3.24 covereth his feet in his summer *c*.
15. 1 I will go in to my wife into the *c*.
16. 9 wait, abiding with her in the *c*.
12 were liers in wait abiding in the *c*.
2Sa 13.10 Bring the meat into the *c*, that I
10 brought them into the *c* to
18.33 the *c* over the gate, and wept:
1Ki 1.15 in unto the king into the *c*:
6. 6 The nethermost *c* was five cubits
8 The door for the middle *c* was
8 into the middle *c*, and out of the
14.28 them back into the guard *c*.
17.23 brought him down out of the *c*
20.30 into the city, into an inner *c*.
22.25 when thou shalt go into an inner *c*
2Ki 1. 2 through a lattice in his upper *c*
4.10 Let us make a little *c*, I pray thee,
11 he turned into the *c*, and lay
9. 2 and carry him to an inner *c*;
23.11 the *c* of Nathan-melech the
12 the upper *c* of Ahaz, which the
2Ch 12.11 them again into the guard *c*.
18.24 thou shalt go into an inner *c*
Ezr 10. 6 *c* of Johanan the son of Eliashib:
Neh 3.30 Berechiah over against his *c*.
13. 4 of the *c* of the house of our God,
5 had prepared for him a great *c*,
7 a *c* in the courts of the house
8 stuff of Tobiah out of the *c*.
Ps 19. 5 bridegroom coming out of his *c*,
SS 3. 4 the *c* of her that conceived me.
Jer 35. 4 the *c* of the sons of Hanan,
4 by the *c* of the princes, which
4 was above the *c* of Maaseiah
36.10 in the *c* of Gemariah the son of
12 king's house, into the scribe's *c*:
20 in the *c* of Elishama the scribe,
21 it out of Elishama the scribe's *c*.
Eze 40. 7 every little *c* was one reed long,
13 from the roof of one little *c* to
45 This *c*, whose prospect is toward
46 *c* whose prospect is toward the
41. 5 and the breadth of every side *c*,
7 from the lowest *c* to the highest
9 which was for the side *c* without,
42. 1 into the *c* that was over against
Dan 6.10 windows being open in his *c*
Joel 2.16 the bridegroom go forth of his *c*,
Ac 9.37 they laid her in an upper *c*.
39 they brought him into the upper *c*:
20. 8 were many lights in the upper *c*,

CHAMBERING

Ro 13.13 not in *c* and wantonness, nor in

CHAMBERLAIN

2Ki 23.11 chamber of Nathan-melech the *c*,
Est 2. 3 custody of Hege the king's *c*,
14 of Shaashgaz, the king's *c*, which
15 Hegai the king's *c*, the keeper of
Ac 12.20 Blastus the king's *c*
Ro 16.23 Erastus the *c* of the city saluteth

CHANCE

Dt 22. 6 If a bird's nest *c* to be before thee
1Sa 6. 9 it was a *c* that happened to us.
2Sa 1. 6 I happened by *c* upon mount
Ec 9.11 time and *c* happeneth to them
Lk 10.31 by *c* there came down a certain
1Co 15.37 grain, it may *c* of wheat,

CHANGE

Gen 35. 2 be clean, and *c* your garments:
Lev 27.10 nor *c* it, a good for a bad, or a
10 and if he shall at all *c*
33 neither shall he *c* it:
33 and if he *c* it at all,
33 and the *c* thereof shall be holy;
Jdg 14.12, 13 and thirty *c* of garments:

Jdg 14.19 gave *c* of garments unto them
Job 14.14 time will I wait, till my *c* come.
17.12 They *c* the night into day: and
Ps 102.26 as a vesture shalt thou *c* them,
Pr 24.21 with them that are given to *c*:
Isa 9.10 but we will *c* them into cedars.
Jer 2.36 about so much to *c* thy way?
13.23 Can the Ethiopian *c* his skin, or
Dan 7.25 and think to *c* times and laws:
Hos 4. 7 will I *c* their glory into shame.
Hab 1.11 Then shall his mind *c*, and he
Zec 3. 4 clothe thee with *c* of raiment.
Mal 3. 6 I am the Lord, I *c* not; therefore
Ac 6.14 shall *c* the customs which Moses
Ro 1.26 their women did *c* the natural
Gal 4.20 with you now, and to *c* my voice;
Php 3.21 Who shall *c* our vile body, that it
Heb 7.12 of necessity a *c* also of the law.

CHANGED

Gen 31. 7 and *c* my wages ten times; but
41 thou hast *c* my wages ten times.
41.14 *c* his raiment, and came in unto
Lev 13.16 turn again, and be *c* unto white,
55 the plague have not *c* his color,
Nu 32.38 (their names being *c*,) and
1Sa 21.13 he *c* his behavior before them,
2Sa 12.20 *c* his apparel, and came into the
2Ki 24.17 and *c* his name to Zedekiah.
25.29 *c* his prison garments: and he
Job 30.18 of my disease is my raiment *c*:
Ps 34(T) when he *c* his behavior
102.26 and they shall be *c*:
106.20 Thus they *c* their glory into the
Ec 8. 1 boldness of his face shall be *c*.
Isa 24. 5 have transgressed the laws, *c* the
Jer 2.11 Hath a nation *c* their gods,
11 my people have *c* their glory for
48.11 in him, and his scent is not *c*.
52.33 And *c* his prison garments: and
La 4. 1 how is the most fine gold *c*!
Eze 5. 6 And she had *c* my judgments
Dan 2. 9 before me, till the time be *c*:
3.19 the form of his visage was *c*
27 neither were their coats *c*, nor
28 and have *c* the king's word, and
4.16 Let his heart be *c* from man's, and
5. 6 the king's countenance was *c*, and
9 his countenance was *c* in him,
10 nor let thy countenance be *c*:
6. 8 that it be not *c*, according to the
15 the king establisheth may be *c*.
17 might not be *c* concerning Daniel.
7.28 my countenance *c* in me: but I
Mic 2. 4 hath *c* the portion of my people:
Ac 28. 6 they *c* their minds, and said that
Ro 1.23 *c* the glory of the uncorruptible
25 Who *c* the truth of God into a
1Co 15.51 all sleep, but we shall all be *c*,
52 incorruptible, and we shall be *c*.
2Co 3.18 are *c* into the same image from
Heb 1.12 them up, and they shall be *c*:
7.12 priesthood being *c*, there is made

CHANGERS

Jn 2.14 doves, and the *c* of money sitting:

BIBLICAL THEMES

CHANGE

Then went he [Naaman] down, and dipped himself seven times in Jordan, according to the saying of the man of God: and his flesh came again like unto the flesh of a little child, and he was clean. 2Ki 5.14

If a man die, shall he live again? Job 14.14

My days are like a shadow that declineth; and I am withered like grass. But thou, O Lord, shalt endure for ever; and thy remembrance unto all generations. Ps 102.11-12

Of old hast thou laid the foundation of the earth: and the heavens are the work of thy hands. They shall perish, but thou shalt endure: yea, all of them shall wax old like a garment . . . But thou art the same, and thy years shall have no end. Ps 102.25-27

Can the Ethiopian change his skin, or the leopard his spots? then may ye also do good, that are accustomed to do evil. Jer 13.23

Then will I sprinkle clean water upon you, and ye shall be clean: from all your filthiness, and from all your idols, will I cleanse you. A new heart also will I give you, and a new spirit will I put within you. Eze 36.25-26

I am the Lord, I change not; therefore ye sons of Jacob are not consumed. Mal 3.6

Immediately after the tribulation of those days shall the sun be darkened, and the moon shall not give her light, and the stars shall fall from heaven . . . and then shall appear the sign of the Son of man in heaven. Mt 24.29-30

No man putteth new wine into old bottles: else the new wine doth burst the bottles, and the wine is spilled . . . but new wine must be put into new bottles. Mk 2.22

This my son was dead, and is alive again; he was lost, and is found. Lk 15.24

Repent ye therefore, and be converted, that your sins may be blotted out, when the times of refreshing shall come from the presence of the Lord. Ac 3.19

Behold, I shew you a mystery; We shall not all sleep, but we shall all be changed, in a moment, in the twinkling of an eye, at the last trump: for the trumpet shall sound, and the dead shall be raised incorruptible, and we shall be changed. 1Co 15.51-52

Our light affliction, which is but for a moment, worketh for us a far more exceeding and eternal weight of glory; While we look not at the things which are seen, but at the things which are not seen: for the things which are seen are temporal; but the things which are not seen are eternal. 2Co 4.17-18

For we know that if our earthly house of this tabernacle were dissolved, we have a building of God, an house not made with hands, eternal in the heavens. 2Co 5.1

If any man be in Christ, he is a new creature. 2Co 5.17

Jesus Christ the same yesterday, and to day, and for ever. Heb 13.8

Every good gift and every perfect gift is from above, and cometh down from the Father of lights, with whom is no variableness, neither shadow of turning. Jas 1.17

But the day of the Lord will come as a thief in the night; in the which the heavens shall pass away with a great noise, and the elements shall melt with fervent heat, the earth also and the works that are therein shall be burned up. . . . Nevertheless we . . . look for new heavens and a new earth, wherein dwelleth righteousness. 2Pe 3.10, 13

CHARGE

Gen 26. 5 obeyed my voice, and kept my *c*,
28. 6 he blessed him he gave him a *c*,
Ex 6.13 gave them a *c* unto the children
19.21 *c* the people, lest they break
Lev 8.35 keep the *c* of the Lord, that ye
Nu 1.53 Levites shall keep the *c* of the
3. 7 they shall keep his *c*, and the
7 *c* of the whole congregation
8 the *c* of the children of Israel,
25 And the *c* of the sons of Gershon
28 keeping the *c* of the sanctuary.
31 And their *c* shall be the ark,
32 that keep the *c* of the sanctuary.
36 the custody and *c* of the sons
38 keeping the *c* of the sanctuary for
38 the *c* of the children of Israel;
4.27 unto them in *c* all their burdens.
28 their *c* shall be under the hand of
31 this is the *c* of their burden,
32 instruments of the *c* of their burden.
5.19 the priest shall *c* her by an oath,
21 the priest shall *c* the woman
8.26 congregation, to keep the *c*, and
26 the Levites touching their *c*.
9.19 the children of Israel kept the *c*
23 they kept the *c* of the Lord,
18. 3 shall keep thy *c*, and the *c* of
4 keep the *c* of the tabernacle of
5 keep the *c* of the sanctuary,
5 and the *c* of the altar:
8 I also have given thee the *c* of
27.19 and give him a *c* in their sight.
23 and gave him a *c*, as the Lord
31.30 keep the *c* of the tabernacle of
47 kept the *c* of the tabernacle of
49 which are under our *c*, and
Dt 3.28 *c* Joshua, and encourage him,
11. 1 keep his *c*, and his statutes,
21. 8 unto thy people of Israel's *c*.

31.14 that I may give him a *c*.
23 gave Joshua the son of Nun a *c*,
Jos 22. 3 kept the *c* of the commandment
2Sa 14. 8 I will give *c* concerning thee.
18. 5 the king gave all the captains *c*
1Ki 2. 3 keep the *c* of the Lord thy God,
4.28 every man according to his *c*.
11.28 the *c* of the house of Joseph.
2Ki 7.17 hand he leaned to have the *c*
1Ch 9.27 because the *c* was upon them,
28 And certain of them had the *c*
22.12 give thee *c* concerning Israel,
23.32 the *c* of the tabernacle of the
32 and the *c* of the holy place,
32 and the *c* of the sons of Aaron.
2Ch 13.11 for we keep the *c* of the Lord
30.17 Levites had the *c* of the killing
Neh 7. 2 the palace, *c* over Jerusalem:
10.32 to *c* ourselves yearly with the
Est 3. 9 that have the *c* of the business,
4. 8 to *c* her that she should go in
Job 34.13 Who hath given him a *c* over
Ps 35.11 to my *c* things that I knew not.
91.11 shall give his angels *c* over thee,
SS 2. 7 I *c* you, O ye daughters of
3. 5 I *c* you, O ye daughters of
5. 8 I *c* you, O daughters of
9 beloved, that thou dost so *c* us?
8. 4 I *c* you, O daughters of
Isa 10. 6 of my wrath will I give him a *c*,
Jer 39.11 King of Babylon gave *c* concerning
47. 7 the Lord had given it a *c* against
52.25 which had the *c* of the men
Eze 9. 1 them that have *c* over the city
40.45 keepers of the *c* of the house.
46 the keepers of the *c* of the altar:
44. 8 kept the *c* of mine holy things:
8 but ye have set keepers of my *c*
11 *c* at the gates of the house,
14 keepers of the *c* of the house,
15 kept a *c* of my sanctuary when
16 me, and they shall keep my *c*.
48.11 which have kept my *c*, which
Zec 3. 7 keep my *c*, then thou shalt also
Mt 4. 6 give his angels *c* concerning
Mk 9.25 I *c* thee, come out of him, and
Lk 4.10 shall give his angels *c* over thee,
Ac 7.60 Lord, lay not this sin to their *c*.
8.27 who had the *c* of all her treasure,
16.24 Who, having received such a *c*,
23.29 to have nothing laid to his *c*
Ro 8.33 shall lay anything to the *c* of
1Co 9.18 the gospel of Christ without *c*,
1Th 5.27 I *c* you by the Lord that this
1Ti 1. 3 that thou mightest *c* some that
18 This *c* I commit unto thee, son
5. 7 And these things give in *c*, that
21 I *c* thee before God, and the Lord
6.13 I give thee *c* in the sight of God,
17 *C* them that are rich in this world,
2Ti 4. 1 I *c* thee therefore before God,
16 it may not be laid to their *c*.

CHARGEABLE

2Sa 13.25 now go, lest we be *c* unto thee.
Neh 5.15 before me were *c* unto the people,
2Co 11. 9 I was *c* to no man: for that
1Th 2. 9 not be *c* unto any of you,
2Th 3. 8 that we might not be *c* to any

CHARGED

Gen 26.11 And Abimelech *c* all his people,
28. 1 and *c* him, and said unto him,
40. 4 the captain of the guard *c* Joseph
49.29 he *c* them, and said unto them,
Ex 1.22 Pharaoh *c* all his people, saying,
Dt 1.16 I *c* your judges at that time,
24. 5 be *c* with any business:
27.11 Moses *c* the people the same day,
Jos 18. 8 and Joshua *c* them that went
22. 5 Moses the servant of the Lord *c*
Ru 2. 9 have I not *c* the young men
1Sa 14.27 father *c* the people with the oath:
28 straitly *c* the people with an oath,
2Sa 11.19 And *c* the messenger, saying,
18.12 *c* thee and Abishai and Ittai,
1Ki 2. 1 he *c* Solomon his son, saying,
43 that I have *c* thee with?
13. 9 For so was it *c* me by the word
2Ki 17.15 the Lord had *c* them, that they
35 had made a covenant, and *c* them,
1Ch 22. 6 and *c* him to build an house
13 *c* Moses with concerning Israel:
2Ch 19. 9 *c* them, saying, Thus shall ye do
36.23 hath *c* me to build him an house
Ezr 1. 2 and he hath *c* me to build him
Neh 13.19 *c* that they should not be opened
Est 2.10 Mordecai had *c* her that she
20 Mordecai had *c* her: for Esther
Job 1.22 sinned not, nor *c* God foolishly.
4.18 and his angels he *c* with folly:
Jer 32.13 And I *c* Baruch before them,
35. 8 he hath *c* us, to drink no wine
Mt 9.30 Jesus straitly *c* them, saying,
12.16 And *c* them that they should not
16.20 Then *c* he his disciples that they
17. 9 Jesus *c* them, saying, Tell the
Mk 1.43 he straitly *c* him, and forthwith
3.12 straitly *c* them that they should
5.43 he *c* them straitly that no man
7.36 *c* them that they should tell no
36 but the more he *c* them,
8.15 he *c* them, saying, Take heed,
30 he *c* them that they should tell
9. 9 *c* them that they should tell no man
10.48 And many *c* him that he should
Lk 5.14 And he *c* him to tell no man:
8.56 but he *c* them that they should
9.21 straitly *c* them, and commanded
Ac 23.22 *c* him, See thou tell no man
1Th 2.11 *c* every one of you, as a father
1Ti 5.16 and let not the church be *c*;

CHARGER

Nu 7.13 And his offering was one silver *c*,
19 for his offering one silver *c*,
25, 31, 37, 43, 49, 55, 61, 67, 73, 79, His offering was one silver *c*,
85 *c* of silver weighing an hundred
Mt 14. 8 here John Baptist's head in a *c*.
11 was brought in a *c*, and given to
Mk 6.25 by and by in a *c* the head of John
28 brought his head in a *c*, and gave

CHARGES

2Ch 8.14 the Levites to their *c*, to praise
31.16 service in their *c* according to
17 in their *c* by their courses;
35. 2 And he set the priests in their *c*,
Ac 21.24 *c* with them, that they may shave
1Co 9. 7 warfare any time at his own *c*?

CHARGING

Ac 16.23 *c* the jailor to keep them safely:
2Ti 2.14 *c* them before the Lord that they

CHARIOTS

Gen 50. 9 there went up with him both *c*
Ex 14. 7 he took six hundred chosen *c*,
7 and all the *c* of Egypt,
9 *c* of Pharoah, and his horsemen,
Jos 11. 4 with horses and *c* very many.
6 and burn their *c* with fire.
17.16 have *c* of iron, both they who are
24. 6 *c* and horsemen unto the Red sea.
Jdg 1.19 because they had *c* of iron.
7 Jabin's army, with his *c* and his
13 Sisera gathered together all his *c*,
16 Barak pursued after the *c*, and
1Sa 13. 5 with Israel, thirty thousand *c*,
2Sa 10.18 of seven hundred *c* of the Syrians,
1Ki 1. 5 prepared him *c* and horsemen,

Assyrian chariot dating from reign of Sennacherib

4.26 stalls of horses for his *c*,
9.19 cities for his *c*, and cities for his
10.26 Solomon gathered together *c*
16. 9 Zimri, captain of half his *c*,
2Ki 7. 6 noise of *c*, and a noise of horses,
23.11 burned the *c* of the sun with fire.
Ps 20. 7 trust in *c*, and some in horses:
Isa 22. 6 Elam bare the quiver with *c* of
7 choicest valleys shall be full of *c*,
66.15 with his *c* like a whirlwind, to
Jer 4.13 his *c* shall be as a whirlwind:
22. 4 David, riding in *c* and on horses,
46. 9 rage, ye *c*; and let the mighty
Na 2. 3 *c* shall be with flaming torches
4 The *c* shall rage in the streets,
13 I will burn her *c* in the smoke,
Rev 9. 9 as the sound of *c* of many horses
18.13 and horses, and *c*, and slaves,

CHARITABLY

Ro 14.15 meat, now walkest thou not *c*.

CHARITY

1Co 8. 1 Knowledge puffeth up, but *c*
13. 1 of angels, and have not *c*, I am
2 mountains, and have not *c*,
3 to be burned, and have not *c*.
4 *C* suffereth long, and is kind;
4 *c* envieth not; *c* vaunteth not
8 *C* never faileth: but whether
13 now abideth faith, hope, *c*, these
13 the greatest of these is *c*.
14. 1 Follow after *c*, and desire
16.14 all your things be done with *c*.
Col 3.14 above all these things put on *c*,
1Th 3. 6 good tidings of your faith and *c*,
2Th 1. 3 the *c* of every one of you all
1Ti 1. 5 commandment is *c* out of a
2.15 in faith and *c* and holiness with
4.12 in conversation, in *c*, in spirit, in
2Ti 2.22 follow righteousness, faith, *c*,
3.10 faith, longsuffering, *c*, patience,
Tit 2. 2 temperate, sound in faith, in *c*,
1Pe 4. 8 fervent *c* among yourselves:
8 for *c* shall cover the multitude
5.14 ye one another with a kiss of *c*.
2Pe 1. 7 and to brotherly kindness *c*.
3Jn 6 have borne witness of thy *c*
Jude 12 spots in your feasts of *c*, when
Rev 2.19 I know thy works, and *c*, and

CHARRAN

Ac 7. 2 before he dwelt in *C*,
4 and dwelt in *C*: and from thence,

CHASE
Lev 26. 7 And ye shall *c* your enemies, and
8 And five of you shall *c* an hundred,
36 the sound of a shaken leaf shall *c*
Dt 32.30 How should one *c* a thousand,
Jos 23.10 man of you shall *c* a thousand:
Ps 35. 5 and let the angel of the Lord *c*

CHASTE
2Co 11. 2 present you as a *c* virgin to
Tit 2. 5 discreet, *c*, keepers at home,
1Pe 3. 2 they behold your *c* conversation

CHASTEN
2Sa 7.14 I will *c* him with the rod of men,
Ps 6. 1 neither *c* me in thy hot
38. 1 *c* me in thy hot displeasure.
Pr 19.18 *C* thy son while there is hope,
Dan 10.12 and to *c* thyself before thy God,
Rev 3.19 many as I love, I rebuke and *c*:

CHASTENED
Dt 21.18 when they have *c* him, will not
Job 33.19 He is *c* also with pain upon his
Ps 69.10 When I wept, and *c* my soul
73.14 have I been plagued, and *c* every
118.18 The Lord hath *c* me sore: but he
1Co 11.32 we are *c* of the Lord, that we
2Co 6. 9 as *c*, and not killed;
Heb 12.10 for a few days *c* us after their own

CHASTENEST
Ps 94.12 Blessed is the man whom thou *c*,

CHASTENETH
Dt 8. 5 as a man *c* his son, so
5 the Lord thy God *c* thee.
Pr 13.24 he that loveth him *c* him
Heb 12. 6 For whom the Lord loveth he *c*,
7 son is he whom the father *c* not?

CHASTENING
Job 5.17 therefore despise not thou the *c*
Pr 3.11 despise not the *c* of the Lord;
Isa 26.16 a prayer when thy *c* was upon
Heb 12. 5 despise not thou the *c* of the
7 If ye endure *c*, God dealeth with
11 Now no *c* for the present

CHASTISE
Lev 26.28 and I, even I, will *c* you seven
Dt 22.18 city shall take that man and *c*
1Ki 12.11 but I will *c* you with scorpions.
14 with whips, but I will *c* you with
2Ch 10.11, 14 I will *c* you with scorpions.
Hos 7.12 I will *c* them, as their
10.10 in my desire that I should *c*
Lk 23.16 I will therefore *c* him, and release
22 I will therefore *c* him, and let him

CHASTISED
1Ki 12.11 my father hath *c* you with whips,
14 my father also *c* you with whips,
2Ch 10.11 my father *c* you with whips, but
14 will add thereto: my father *c* you
Jer 31.18 Thou hast *c* me, and I was *c*,

CHASTISEMENT
Dt 11. 2 not seen the *c* of the Lord your
Job 34.31 I have borne *c*, I will not offend
Isa 53. 5 the *c* of our peace was upon
Jer 30.14 the *c* of a cruel one, for the
Heb 12. 8 But if ye be without *c*, whereof

CHEEK
1Ki 22.24 and smote Micaiah on the *c*, and
2Ch 18.23 and smote Micaiah upon the *c*,
Job 16.10 they have smitten me upon the *c*
Ps 3. 7 all mine enemies upon the *c* bone;
La 3.30 He giveth his *c* to him that
Joel 1. 6 hath the *c* teeth of a great lion.
Mic 5. 1 Israel with a rod upon the *c*.
Mt 5.39 smite thee upon thy right *c*,
Lk 6.29 smiteth thee on the one *c*

CHEER
Dt 24. 5 and shall *c* up his wife which he
Ec 11. 9 and let thy heart *c* thee in the
Mt 9. 2 be of good *c*; thy sins be forgiven
14.27 Be of good *c*; it is I; be not afraid.
Mk 6.50 saith unto them, Be of good *c*; it
Jn 16.33 but be of good *c*; I have overcome
Ac 23.11 Be of good *c*, Paul: for as thou
27.22 I exhort you to be of good *c*: for
25 Wherefore, sirs, be of good *c*:
36 Then were they all of good *c*,

CHEERFUL
Pr 15.13 A merry heart maketh a *c*
Zec 8.19 gladness, and *c* feasts; therefore
9.17 shall make the young men *c*,
2Co 9. 7 for God loveth a *c* giver.

CHEERFULLY
Ac 24.10 the more *c* answer for myself:

CHEERFULNESS
Ro 12. 8 he that sheweth mercy, with *c*.

CHERISHETH
Eph 5.29 but nourisheth and *c* it, even
1Th 2. 7 even as a nurse *c* her children:

CHERITH
1Ki 17. 3 and hide thyself by the brook *C*,
5 went and dwelt by the brook *C*,

CHERUB
Ex 25.19 one *c* on the one end,
19 and the other *c* on the other end:
37. 8 One *c* on the end on this side,
8 and another *c* on the other
2Sa 22.11 he rode upon a *c*, and did fly:
1Ki 6.24 the one wing of the *c*, and five
24 cubits the other wing of the *c*:
25 the other *c* was ten cubits: both
26 height of the one *c* was ten cubits,
26 and so was it of the other *c*.
27 of the other *c* touched the wall;
2Ch 3.11 one wing of the one *c* was five
11 to the wing of the other *c*.
12 one wing of the other *c* was five
12 joining to the wing of the other *c*.
Ps 18.10 he rode upon a *c*, and did fly:
Eze 9. 3 was gone up from the *c*,
10. 2 under the *c*, and fill thine hand
4 went up from the *c*, and stood
7 one *c* stretched forth his hand
9 one wheel by one *c*, and another
9 another wheel by another *c*:
14 the first face was the face of a *c*,
28.14 Thou art the anointed *c* that
16 I will destroy thee, O covering *c*,
41.18 between a *c* and a *c*; and
18 every *c* had two faces;

CHERUBIMS
Gen 3.24 of the garden of Eden *C*, and
Ex 25.18 thou shalt make two *c* of gold,
19 mercy seat shall ye make the *c*
20 *c* shall stretch forth their wings
20 seat shall the faces of the *c*
22 between the two *c* which are
26. 1 *c* of cunning work shalt thou
31 work: with *c* shall it be made:
36. 8 *c* of cunning work made he
35 *c* made he it of cunning work.
37. 7 he made two *c* of gold, beaten
8 the mercy seat made he the *c*
9 the *c* spread out their wings on
9 seatward were the faces of the *c*.
Nu 7.89 from between the two *c*:

Winged creatures with animal bodies, cherubims symbolized divine authority in biblical times.

1Sa 4. 4 which dwelleth between the *c*:
2Sa 6. 2 that dwelleth between the *c*.
1Ki 6.23 oracle he made two *c* of olive
25 the *c* were of one measure and
27 set the *c* within the inner house:
27 stretched forth the wings of the *c*,
28 And he overlaid the *c* with gold.
29 about with carved figures of *c*
32 carvings of *c* and palm trees
32 spread gold upon the *c*, and upon
35 carved thereon *c* and palm trees
7.29 ledges were lions, oxen, and *c*:
36 graved *c*, lions, and palm trees,
8. 6 even under the wings of the *c*.
7 *c* spread forth their two wings
7 ark, and the *c* covered the ark
2Ki 19.15 which dwellest between the *c*,
1Ch 13. 6 that dwelleth between the *c*,
28.18 the chariot of the *c*, that spread
2Ch 3. 7 gold; and graved *c* on the walls.
10 he made two *c* of image work,
11 wings of the *c* were twenty
13 The wings of these *c* spread
14 linen, and wrought *c* thereon.
5. 7 even under the wings of the *c*:
8 the *c* spread forth their wings
8 *c* covered the ark and the staves
Ps 80. 1 that dwellest between the *c*,
99. 1 he sitteth between the *c*; let
Isa 37.16 that dwellest between the *c*,
Eze 10. 1 head of the *c* there appeared
2 coals of fire from between the *c*,
3 *c* stood on the right side of the
6 the wheels, from between the *c*;
7 from between the *c* unto the fire
7 the fire that was between the *c*,
8 there appeared in the *c* the form
9 behold the four wheels by the *c*,
15 the *c* were lifted up. This is the
16 when the *c* went, the wheels
16 them: and when the *c* lifted
18 house, and stood over the *c*.
19 the *c* lifted up their wings, and
20 and I knew that they were the *c*.
11.22 the *c* lift up their wings, and the
41.18 was made with *c* and palm trees,
20 door were *c* and palm trees
25 *c* and palm trees, like as were
Heb 9. 5 *c* of glory shadowing the

CHICKENS
Mt 23.37 as a hen gathereth her *c* under

CHIDE
Ex 17. 2 Wherefore the people did *c* with
2 Why *c* ye with me? wherefore
Jdg 8. 1 they did *c* with him sharply.
Ps 103. 9 He will not always *c*: neither will

CHIEFEST
1Sa 2.29 with the *c* of all the offerings
9.22 in the *c* place among them that
21. 7 Edomite, the *c* of the herdmen
2Ch 32.33 they buried him in the *c* of the
SS 5.10 ruddy, the *c* among ten thousand.
Mk 10.44 the *c*, shall be servant of all.
2Co 11. 5 behind the very *c* apostles.
12.11 behind the very *c* apostles,

CHIEFLY
Ro 3. 2 *c*, because that unto them were
Php 4.22 *c* they that are of Caesar's
2Pe 2.10 *c* them that walk after the flesh

CHILD
Gen 11.30 Sarai was barren; she had no *c*.
16.11 her, Behold, thou art with *c*,
17.10 Every man *c* among you shall
12 every man *c* in your generations,
14 the uncircumcised man *c* whose
17 Shall a *c* be born unto him that is an
19.36 both the daughters of Lot with *c*
21. 8 the *c* grew, and was weaned:
14 and the *c*, and sent her away:
15 cast the *c* under one of the shrubs.
16 Let me not see the death of the *c*.
37.30 The *c* is not; and I, whither shall
38.24 she is with *c* by whoredom.
25 am I with *c*: and she said,
42.22 Do not sin against the *c*;
44.20 and a *c* of his old age, a little one;
Ex 2. 2 saw him that he was a goodly *c*,
3 and put the *c* therein; and she
6 had opened it, she saw the *c*:
7 women, that she may nurse the *c*
9 Take this *c* away, and nurse it
9 the woman took the *c*, and nursed
10 And the *c* grew, and she brought
21.22 hurt a woman with *c*, so that her
22.22 afflict any widow, or fatherless *c*.
Lev 12. 2 and born a man *c*: then she shall
5 if she bear a maid *c*, then she
22.13 and have no *c*, and is returned
Nu 11.12 father beareth the sucking *c*,
Dt 25. 5 and have no *c*, the wife of the
Jdg 11.34 she was his only *c*; beside her he
13. 5 for the *c* shall be a Nazarite unto
7 the *c* shall be Nazarite to God
8 what we shall do unto the *c* that
12 How shall we order the *c*, and
24 and the *c* grew, and the Lord
Ru 4.16 Naomi took the *c*, and laid it in
1Sa 1.11 unto thine handmaid a man *c*,
22 I will not go up until the *c* be
24 in Shiloh: and the *c* was young,
25 and brought the *c* to Eli.
27 For this *c* I prayed; and the
2.11 the *c* did minister unto the Lord
18 before the Lord, being a *c*,
21 *c* Samuel grew before the Lord.
26 And the *c* Samuel grew on, and
3. 1 And the *c* Samuel ministered
8 that the Lord had called the *c*.
4.19 Phinehas' wife, was with *c*, near
21 she named the *c* I-chabod,
2Sa 6.23 the daughter of Saul had no *c*
11. 5 told David, and said, I am with *c*.
12.14 the *c* also that is born unto thee
15 And the Lord struck the *c* that
16 therefore besought God for the *c*;
18 the seventh day, that the *c* died.
18 to tell him that the *c* was dead:
18 while the *c* was yet alive, we
18 if we tell him that the *c* is dead?
19 David perceived that the *c* was
19 unto his servants, Is the *c* dead?
21 thou didst fast and weep for the *c*,
21 when the *c* was dead, thou didst
22 While the *c* was yet alive, I fasted
22 gracious to me, that the *c* may live?
1Ki 3. 7 I am but a little *c*: I know not
17 and I was delivered of a *c* with her
19 this woman's *c* died in the night;
20 and laid her dead *c* in my bosom.
21 in the morning to give my *c* suck,
3.25 Divide the living *c* in two, and
26 the woman whose the living *c* was
26 O my Lord, give her the living *c*,
27 Give her the living *c*, and in no
11.17 Egypt; Hadad being yet a little *c*.
13. 2 a *c* shall be born unto the house
14. 3 what shall become of the *c*.
12 enter into the city, the *c* shall die.
17 threshold of the door, the *c* died;
17.21 he stretched himself upon the *c*
22 the soul of the *c* came into him
23 Elijah took the *c*, and brought
2Ki 4.14 Verily she hath no *c*, and her
18 when the *c* was grown, it fell on
26 is it well with the *c*? And she
29 my staff upon the face of the *c*.
30 the mother of the *c* said, As the
31 laid the staff on the face of the *c*;
31 him, saying, The *c* is not awaked.
32 the *c* was dead and laid upon his
34 he went up, and lay upon the *c*,
34 stretched himself upon the *c*;
34 the flesh of the *c* waxed warm.
35 the *c* sneezed seven times,
35 and the *c* opened his eyes.
5.14 like unto the flesh of a little *c*,
8.12 and rip up their women with *c*.
15.16 women therein that were with *c*
Job 3. 3 said, There is a man *c* conceived.
Ps 131. 2 *c* that is weaned of his mother:
2 my soul is even as a weaned *c*.
Pr 20.11 a *c* is known by his doings,
22. 6 Train up a *c* in the way he
15 is bound in the heart of a *c*;
23.13 Withhold not correction from the *c*:
24 he that begetteth a wise *c* shall
29.15 but a *c* left to himself bringeth
21 his servant from a *c* shall have
Ec 4. 8 he hath neither *c* nor brother:
13 Better is a poor and a wise *c*
15 the second *c* that shall stand up
10.16 O land, when thy king is a *c*,
11. 5 in the womb of her that is with *c*:
Isa 3. 5 the *c* shall behave himself
7.16 before the *c* shall know to refuse
8. 4 the *c* shall have knowledge to cry,
9. 6 unto us a *c* is born, unto us a
10.19 shall be few, that a *c* may write
11. 6 and a little *c* shall lead them.
8 the sucking *c* shall play on the
8 and the weaned *c* shall put his
26.17 Like as a woman with *c*, that
18 We have been with *c*, we have
49.15 a woman forget her sucking *c*,
54. 1 that didst not travail with *c*:
65.20 the *c* shall die an hundred years
66. 7 she was delivered of a man *c*.
Jer 1. 6 I cannot speak: for I am a *c*.
7 Say not, I am a *c*: for thou shalt
4.31 that bringeth forth her first *c*,
20.15 A man *c* is born unto thee;
30. 6 a man doth travail with *c*?
31. 8 the lame, the woman with *c*
8 and her that travaileth with *c*
20 dear son? Is he a pleasant *c*?
44. 7 off from you man and woman, *c*
La 4. 4 The tongue of the sucking *c*
Hos 11. 1 When Israel was a *c*, then I
13.16 women with *c* shall be ripped up.
Am 1.13 have ripped up the women with *c*
Mt 1.18 with *c* of the Holy Ghost.
23 a virgin shall be with *c*,
2. 8 search diligently for the young *c*;
9 stood over where the young *c* was.
11 they saw the young *c* with Mary
13 Arise, and take the young *c* and
13 Herod will seek the young *c* to
14 took the young *c* and his mother
20 Arise and take the young *c* and
21 took the young *c* and his mother,
10.21 and the father the *c*: and the
17.18 *c* was cured from that very hour.
18. 2 And Jesus called a little *c* unto
4 humble himself as this little *c*,
5 whoso shall receive one such little *c*
23.15 twofold more the *c* of hell than
24.19 them that are with *c*,
Mk 9.21 unto him? And he said, Of a *c*.
24 straightway the father of the *c*
36 And he took a *c*, and set him in
10.15 the kingdom of God as a little *c*,
13.17 them that are with *c*,
Lk 1. 7 And they had no *c*, because that
59 they came to circumcise the *c*;
66 What manner of *c* shall this be!
76 And thou, *c*, shalt be called the
80 the *c* grew, and waxed strong
2. 5 wife, being great with *c*.
17 was told them concerning this *c*.
21 for the circumcising of the *c*,
27 parents brought in the *c* Jesus,
34 Behold, this *c* is set for the fall
40 And the *c* grew, and waxed strong
43 the *c* Jesus tarried behind
9.38 my son: for he is mine only *c*.
42 and healed the *c*, and delivered
47 their heart, took a *c*, and set him
48 Whosoever shall receive this *c*
18.17 the kingdom of God as a little *c*
21.23 them that are with *c*,
Jn 4.49 Sir, come down ere my *c* die.
16.21 soon as she is delivered of the *c*,
Ac 4.27 against thy holy *c* Jesus, whom
30 by the name of thy holy *c* Jesus.
7. 5 him, when as yet he had no *c*.
13.10 thou *c* of the devil, thou enemy
1Co 13.11 When I was a *c*, I spake as a *c*,
11 I understood as a *c*,
11 I thought as a *c*:
Gal 4. 1 the heir, as long as he is a *c*,
1Th 5. 3 upon a woman with *c*;
2Ti 3.15 from a *c* thou hast known the
Heb 11.11 and was delivered of a *c* when
23 they saw he was a proper *c*;
Rev 12. 2 And she being with *c*
4 to devour her *c* as soon as it
5 she brought forth a man *c*, who
5 her *c* was caught up unto God,
13 which brought forth the man *c*.

CHILDBEARING
1Ti 2.15 she shall be saved in *c*, if they

CHILDISH
1Co 13.11 a man, I put away *c* things.

CHILDLESS
Gen 15. 2 wilt thou give me, seeing I go *c*,
Lev 20.20 bear their sins; they shall die *c*.
21 nakedness; they shall be *c*.
1Sa 15.33 thy sword hath made women *c*,
33 so shall thy mother be *c*
Jer 22.30 Write ye this man *c*, a man that
Lk 20.30 took her to wife, and he died *c*.

CHILDREN
Gen 3.16 sorrow thou shalt bring forth *c*;
11. 5 which the *c* of men builded.
16. 1 Sarai Abram's wife bare him no *c*:
2 that I may obtain *c* by her.
25.22 *c* struggled together within her;

Gen 30. 1 she bare Jacob no *c*, Rachel
1 Give me *c*, or else I die.
3 that I may also have *c* by her.
33. 5 The *c* which God hath graciously
36.31 any king over the *c* of Israel.
37. 3 loved Joseph more than all his *c*,
43.14 If I be bereaved of my *c*, I am
Ex 1.17 but saved the men *c* alive.
18 have saved the men *c* alive?
2. 6 This is one of the Hebrews' *c*.
25 God looked upon the *c* of Israel,
3. 9 the cry of the *c* of Israel is come
14 thou say unto the *c* of Israel, I AM
6. 5 the groaning of the *c* of Israel,
7. 5 bring out the *c* of Israel from
9.35 would he let the *c* of Israel go;
10.20 would not let the *c* of Israel go.
11.10 would not let the *c* of Israel go
12.37 the *c* of Israel journeyed from
13.15 the firstborn of my *c* I redeem.
14. 2 Speak unto the *c* of Israel, that
8 pursued after the *c* of Israel: and
10 the *c* of Israel lifted up their eyes,
10 *c* of Israel cried out unto the Lord
15 *c* of Israel, that they go forward:
16 *c* of Israel shall go on dry ground
15. 1 sang Moses and the *c* of Israel this
16. 2 the *c* of Israel murmured against
35 And the *c* of Israel did eat manna
25. 2 Speak unto the *c* of Israel, that
28.12 stones of memorial unto the *c* of
29.45 I will dwell among the *c* of Israel,
31.16 *c* of Israel shall keep the sabbath,
33. 6 *c* of Israel stripped themselves
34.35 *c* of Israel saw the face of Moses,
Lev 16.21 the iniquities of the *c* of Israel,
34 an atonement for the *c* of Israel
22. 2 the holy things of the *c* of Israel,
27.34 for the *c* of Israel in mount Sinai.
Nu 3.40 of the males of the *c* of Israel
41 firstborn among the *c* of Israel;
6.23 wise ye shall bless the *c* of Israel,
27 put my name upon the *c* of Israel;
8. 6 the Levites from among the *c* of
19 do the service of the *c* of Israel in
19 an atonement for the *c* of Israel:
19 no plague among the *c* of Israel,
9. 2 *c* of Israel also keep the passover
11. 4 and the *c* of Israel also wept
14. 2 *c* of Israel murmured against
3 our wives and our *c* should be a
18 iniquity of the fathers upon the *c*
33 *c* shall wander in the wilderness
16.38 be a sign unto the *c* of Israel.
17. 5 me the murmurings of the *c* of
18. 6 the Levites from among the *c* of
24 But the tithes of the *c* of Israel,
20.13 because the *c* of Israel strove with
25. 8 plague was stayed from the *c* of
13 an atonement for the *c* of Israel.
26.64 they numbered the *c* of Israel in
31. 2 Avenge the *c* of Israel of the
18 But all the women *c*, that have
33. 1 are the journeys of the *c* of Israel,
35. 8 the possession of the *c* of Israel:
15 a refuge, both for the *c* of Israel,
34 Lord dwell among the *c* of Israel.
36. 4 the jubile of the *c* of Israel shall
7 the inheritance of the *c* of Israel
Dt 5. 9 iniquity of the fathers upon the *c*
6. 7 teach them diligently unto thy *c*,
11.19 ye shall teach them your *c*,
24.16 shall not be put to death for the *c*,
16 neither shall the *c* be put to death
54 remnant of his *c* which he shall
55 flesh of his *c* whom he shall eat:
29.29 unto us and to our *c* for ever,
31.12 men, and women, and *c*,
32.20 generation, *c* in whom is no faith.
Jos 4.21 saying, When your *c* shall ask
22 ye shall let your *c* know, saying,
5. 2 circumcise again the *c* of Israel
12 neither had the *c* of Israel manna
7. 1 *c* of Israel committed a trespass
1 kindled against the *c* of Israel.
11.19 made peace with the *c* of Israel,
21. 4 the *c* of Aaron the priest, which
10 of the *c* of Levi, had: for theirs
22.25 so shall your *c* make our *c* cease
27 your *c* may not say to our *c* in time
33 the thing pleased the *c* of Israel;
33 and the *c* of Israel blessed God,
24. 4 Jacob and his *c* went down into
Jdg 2.11 the *c* of Israel did evil in the sight
3. 9 And when the *c* of Israel cried
9 up a deliverer to the *c* of Israel,
4.24 hand of the *c* of Israel prospered,
6. 2 *c* of Israel made them the dens
8 sent a prophet unto the *c* of Israel,
14.16 a riddle unto the *c* of my people,
20.32 the *c* of Israel said, Let us flee,
1Sa 1. 3 but Hannah had no *c*.
7. 4 *c* of Israel did put away Baalim
16.11 unto Jesse, Are here all thy *c*?
1Ki 4.30 the wisdom of all the *c* of the east
8. 9 a covenant with the *c* of Israel,
25 that thy *c* take heed to their way,
63 and all the *c* of Israel dedicated
2Ki 9. 1 one of the *c* of the prophets,
17. 9 the *c* of Israel did secretly those
22 *c* of Israel walked in all the sins
31 Sepharvites burnt their *c* in fire
18. 4 the *c* of Israel did burn incense
19. 3 for the *c* are come to the birth,
1Ch 4.27 multiply, like to the *c* of Judah.
15. 4 David assembled the *c* of Aaron,
15 the *c* of the Levites bare the ark
16.13 ye *c* of Jacob, his chosen ones.
17. 9 neither shall the *c* of wickedness
20. 4 that was of the *c* of the giant:
28. 8 inheritance for your *c* after you
2Ch 5.10 a covenant with the *c* of Israel,
6.30 knowest the hearts of the *c* of men:)
11.23 wisely, and dispersed of all his *c*
25. 4 The fathers shall not die for the *c*,
4 neither shall the *c* die for the
28. 3 burnt his *c* in the fire, after the
33. 6 caused his *c* to pass through the
Ezr 6.16 And the *c* of Israel, the priests,
10. 7 unto all the *c* of the captivity,
16 the *c* of the captivity did so.
Neh 1. 6 confess the sins of the *c* of Israel,
2.10 seek the welfare of the *c* of Israel.
9.23 Their *c* also multipliedst thou
24 *c* went in and possessed the land,
13.16 sabbath unto the *c* of Judah,
24 their *c* spake half in the speech
Est 5.11 and the multitude of his *c*,
Job 8. 4 If thy *c* have sinned against him,
19.18 young *c* despised me; I arose,
20.10 His *c* shall seek to please the poor,
21.11 like a flock, and their *c* dance.
19 layeth up his iniquity for his *c*:
27.14 If his *c* be multiplied, it is for
30. 8 *c* of fools, yea, *c* of base men:
41.34 a king over all the *c* of pride.
Ps 34.11 Come, ye *c*, hearken unto me:
36. 7 the *c* of men put their trust
45. 2 art fairer than the *c* of men:
66. 5 in his doing toward the *c* of men.
69. 8 and an alien unto my mother's *c*.
72. 4 he shall save the *c* of the needy,
78. 5 make them known to their *c*:
82. 6 of you are *c* of the most High.
90. 3 and sayest, Return, ye *c* of men.
103.13 Like as a father pitieth his *c*, so
103.17 righteousness unto children's *c*;
105. 6 ye *c* of Jacob his chosen.
113. 9 and to be a joyful mother of *c*.
115.16 earth hath he given to the *c* of men.
127. 3 Lo, *c* are an heritage of the Lord:
128. 3 thy *c* like olive plants round about
6 thou shalt see thy children's *c*,
132.12 If thy *c* will keep my covenant
12 *c* shall also sit upon the throne
147.13 he hath blessed thy *c* within thee.
149. 2 *c* of Zion be joyful in their king.
Pr 13.22 an inheritance to his children's *c*:
14.26 his *c* shall have a place of refuge.
17. 6 Children's *c* are the crown of old
6 and the glory of *c* are their fathers.
20. 7 his *c* are blessed after him.
31.28 her *c* arise up and call her blessed;
Ec 6. 3 If a man beget an hundred *c*,
SS 1. 6 mother's *c* were angry with me;
Isa 1. 2 I have nourished and brought up *c*,
4 *c* that are corrupters: they have
13.16 *c* also shall be dashed to pieces
18 their eye shall not spare *c*.
23. 4 nor bring forth *c*, neither do I
29.23 he seeth his *c*, the work of mine
30. 1 the rebellious *c*, saith the Lord,
9 lying *c*, that will not hear the
31. 6 *c* of Israel have deeply revolted.
37. 3 for the *c* are come to the birth,
38.19 the *c* shall make known thy truth.
47. 9 day, the loss of *c*, and widowhood:
49.17 Thy *c* shall make haste; thy
21 I have lost my *c*, and am desolate,
54.13 thy *c* shall be taught of the Lord;
13 great shall be the peace of thy *c*.
63. 8 my people, *c* that will not lie:
66. 8 travailed, she brought forth her *c*.
Jer 2.30 In vain have I smitten your *c*;
3.22 Return, ye backsliding *c*, and I
7.18 *c* gather wood, and the fathers
10.20 my *c* are gone forth of me, and
17. 2 their *c* remember their altars
18.21 deliver up their *c* to the famine,
21 wives be bereaved of their *c*,
31.15 Rahel weeping for her *c* refused
15 to be comforted for her *c*,
49.11 Leave thy fatherless *c*, I will preserve
La 4. 4 young *c* ask bread, and no man
Eze 2. 4 are impudent *c* and stiffhearted.
20.21 the *c* rebelled against me: they
23.39 had slain their *c* to their idols,
Hos 4. 6 I will also forget thy *c*.
5. 7 for they have begotten strange *c*:
11.10 the *c* shall tremble from the west.
Joel 1. 3 Tell ye your *c* of it, and
3 let your *c* tell their *c*,
Am 9. 7 Are ye not as *c* of the Ethiopians
Zec 10. 7 their *c* shall see it, and be glad;
Mal 4. 6 the heart of the fathers to the *c*,
6 the heart of the *c* to their fathers,
Mt 2.16 and slew all the *c* that were in
18 Rachel weeping for her *c*, and
3. 9 to raise up *c* unto Abraham.
5. 9 they shall be called the *c* of God.
45 That ye may be the *c* of your
7.11 to give good gifts unto your *c*,
8.12 But the *c* of the kingdom shall be
9.15 Can the *c* of the bridechamber
10.21 and the *c* shall rise up against
11.16 It is like unto *c* sitting in the
19 But wisdom is justified of her *c*.
12.27 by whom do your *c* cast them
13.38 seed are the *c* of the kingdom;
38 tares are the *c* of the wicked
14.21 men, beside women and *c*.
15.38 men, beside women and *c*.
17.25 of their own *c*, or of strangers?
26 saith unto him, Then are the *c*
18. 3 and become as little *c*, ye shall
25 him to be sold, and his wife, and *c*,
19.13 brought unto him little *c*, that
14 Jesus said, Suffer little *c*, and forbid
29 or *c*, or lands, for my name's
20.20 him the mother of Zebedee's *c*
21.15 and the *c* crying in the temple,
22.24 If a man die, having no *c*, his
23.31 that ye are the *c* of them which

37 would I have gathered thy *c*
27. 9 they of the *c* of Israel did value;
25 His blood be on us, and on our *c*.
56 and the mother of Zebedee's *c*.
Mk 2.19 Can the *c* of the bridechamber
7.27 said unto her, Let the *c* first be
9.37 receive one of such *c* in my
10.13 And they brought young *c* to
14 Suffer the little *c* to come unto
24 *C*, how hard is it for them that
29 or wife, or *c*, or lands, for my
30 mothers, and *c*, and lands, with
12.19 and leave no *c*, that his brother
13.12 and *c* shall rise up against their
Lk 1.16 many of the *c* of Israel shall he
17 the hearts of the fathers to the *c*,
3. 8 to raise up *c* unto Abraham.
5.34 Can ye make the *c* of the
6.35 ye shall be the *c* of the Highest:
7.32 like unto *c* sitting in the
35 wisdom is justified of all her *c*.
11. 7 my *c* are with me in bed; I cannot
13 to give good gifts unto your *c*:
13.34 have gathered thy *c* together, as
14.26 *c*, and brethren, and sisters, yea,
16. 8 for the *c* of this world are
8 wiser than the *c* of light.
18.16 Suffer little *c* to come unto me,
29 or wife, or *c*, for the kingdom of
19.44 and thy *c* within thee; and they
20.28 he died without *c*, that his
29 took a wife, and died without *c*.
31 and they left no *c*, and died.
34 The *c* of this world marry, and
36 and are the *c* of God, being
36 the *c* of the resurrection.
23.28 for yourselves, and for your *c*.
Jn 4.12 drank thereof himself, and his *c*,
8.39 If ye were Abraham's *c*, ye would
11.52 *c* of God that were scattered
12.36 that ye may be the *c* of light.
13.33 Little *c*, yet a little while I am
21. 5 Jesus saith unto them, *C*, have ye
Ac 2.39 is unto you, and to your *c*,
3.25 Ye are the *c* of the prophets,
5.21 all the senate of the *c* of Israel,
7.19 they cast out their young *c*, to
23 visit his brethren the *c* of Israel.
37 which said unto the *c* of Israel,
9.15 Gentiles, and kings, and the *c* of
10.36 God sent unto the *c* of Israel,
13.26 *c* of the stock, of Abraham,
33 fulfilled the same unto us their *c*,
21. 5 on our way, with wives and *c*,
21 ought not to circumcise their *c*,
Ro 8.16 spirit, that we are the *c* of God:
17 And if *c*, then heirs; heirs of God.
21 the glorious liberty of the *c* of God.
9. 7 seed of Abraham, are they all *c*:
8 They which are the *c* of the flesh,
8 these are not the *c* of God:
8 the *c* of the promise are counted
11 (For the *c* being not yet born,
26 be called the *c* of the living God.
27 the number of the *c* of Israel be
1Co 7.14 else were your *c* unclean; but
14.20 be not *c* in understanding,
20 howbeit in malice be ye *c*, but
2Co 3. 7 so that the *c* of Israel could not
13 that the *c* of Israel could not
6.13 (I speak as unto my *c*,) be ye also
12.14 the *c* ought not to lay up for the
14 but the parents for the *c*.
Gal 3. 7 the same are the *c* of Abraham.
26 ye are all the *c* of God by faith
4. 3 when we were *c*, were in
19 My little *c*, of whom I travail
25 and is in bondage with her *c*.
27 the desolate hath many more *c*
28 as Isaac was, are the *c* of promise.
31 we are not *c* of the bondwoman,
Eph 1. 5 us unto the adoption of *c* by
2. 2 worketh in the *c* of disobedience:
3 were by nature the *c* of wrath,
4.14 be no more *c*, tossed to and fro,
5. 1 followers of God, as dear *c*;
6 God upon the *c* of disobedience.
8 in the Lord: walk as *c* of light:
6. 1 *C*, obey your parents in the Lord:
4 provoke not your *c* to wrath,
Col 3. 6 cometh on the *c* of disobedience:
20 *C*, obey your parents in all
21 provoke not your *c* to anger,
1Th 2. 7 even as a nurse cherisheth her *c*:
11 as a father doth his *c*,
5. 5 Ye are all the *c* of light,
5 and the *c* of the day:
1Ti 3. 4 having his *c* in subjection with
12 ruling their *c* and their own
5. 4 But if any widow have *c* or
10 if she have brought up *c*, if she
14 younger women marry, bear *c*,
Tit 1. 6 having faithful *c*, not accused of
2. 4 their husbands, to love their *c*,
Heb 2.13 Behold I and the *c* which God
14 then as the *c* are partakers
11.22 of the departing of the *c* of Israel;
12. 5 speaketh unto you as unto *c*,
1Pe 1.14 As obedient *c*, not fashioning
2Pe 2.14 with covetous practices; cursed *c*:
1Jn 2. 1 My little *c*, these things write I
12 I write unto you, little *c*, because
13 I write unto you, little *c*, because
18 Little *c*, it is the last time: and
28 And now, little *c*, abide in him;
3. 7 Little *c*, let no man deceive you:
10 In this the *c* of God are manifest,
10 and the *c* of the devil:
18 My little *c*, let us not love in
4. 4 Ye are of God, little *c*, and have
5. 2 know that we love the *c* of God,
21 Little *c*, keep yourselves from
2Jn 1 unto the elect lady and her *c*,
4 that I found of thy *c* walking in
13 The *c* of thy elect sister greet
3Jn 4 joy I have to hear that my *c* walk
Rev 2.14 before the *c* of Israel, to eat
23 And I will kill her *c* with death;
7. 4 of all the tribes of the *c* of Israel.
21.12 the twelve tribes of the *c* of Israel:

CHILDREN'S

Gen 31.16 father, that is ours, and our *c*:
45.10 thy *c* children, and thy flocks, and
Ex 9. 4 die of all that is the *c* of Israel.
34. 7 the *c* children, unto the third
Jos 14. 9 inheritance, and thy *c* for ever,
2Ki 17.41 children, and their *c* children:
Job 19.17 I entreated for the *c* sake of
Ps 103.17 righteousness unto *c* children;
128. 6 see thy *c* children, and peace
Pro 13.22 leaveth an inheritance to his *c*
17. 6 *C* children are the crown of old men;
Jer 2. 9 and with your *c* children will
31.29 and the *c* teeth are set on edge.
Eze 18. 2 the *c* teeth are set on edge?
37.25 their *c* children for ever: and my
Mt 15.26 It is not meet to take the *c* bread,
Mk 7.27 it is not meet to take the *c* bread,
28 the table eat of the *c* crumbs.

CHILD'S

Ex 2. 8 went and called the *c* mother.
1Ki 17.21 let this *c* soul come into him again.
Job 33.25 flesh shall be fresher than a *c*:
Mt 2.20 which sought the young *c* life.

CHILION

Ru 1. 2 of his two sons Mahlon and *C*,
5 And Mahlon and *C* died also

CHILION'S

Ru 4. 9 Elimelech's, and all that was *C*

CHIMNEY

Hos 13. 3 and as the smoke out of the *c*.

CHIOS

Ac 20.15 the next day over against *C*;

CHLOE

1Co 1.11 which are of the house of *C*,

CHOICE

Gen 23. 6 *c* of our sepulchres bury thy dead;
49.11 his ass's colt unto the *c* vine;
Dt 12.11 your *c* vows which ye vow unto
1Sa 9. 2 a *c* young man, and a goodly:
2Sa 10. 9 chose of all the *c* men of Israel,
2Ki 3.19 fenced city, and every *c* city,
19.23 and the *c* fir trees thereof:
1Ch 7.40 *c* and mighty men of valor,
19.10 all the *c* of Israel, and put them
2Ch 25. 5 three hundred thousand *c* men,
Neh 5.18 one ox and six *c* sheep; also
Pr 8.10 knowledge rather than *c* gold.
19 and my revenue than *c* silver.
10.20 tongue of the just is as *c* silver:
SS 6. 9 is the *c* one of her that bare her.
Isa 37.24 the *c* fir trees thereof: and I will
Jer 22. 7 shall cut down thy *c* cedars,
Eze 24. 4 shoulder, fill it with the *c* bones.
5 Take the *c* of the flock, and burn
31.16 Eden, the *c* and best of Lebanon,
Ac 15. 7 God made *c* among us, that the

CHOICEST

Isa 5. 2 planted it with the *c* vine,
22. 7 *c* valleys shall be full of chariots,

CHOKE

Mt 13.22 deceitfulness of riches, *c* the
Mk 4.19 entering in, *c* the word, and it

CHOKED

Mt 13. 7 thorns sprung up, and *c* them:
Mk 4. 7 *c* it, and it yielded no fruit.
5.13 and were *c* in the sea.
Lk 8. 7 sprang up with it, and *c* it.
14 and are *c* with cares and riches
33 place into the lake, and were *c*.

CHOOSE

Ex 17. 9 *C* us out men, and go out,
Nu 16. 7 the man whom the Lord doth *c*,
17. 5 the man's rod, whom I shall *c*,
Dt 7. 7 nor *c* you, because ye were more
12. 5 the Lord your God shall *c* out
11 God shall *c* to cause his name
14 the place which the Lord shall *c*
18 which the Lord thy God shall *c*,
26 the place which the Lord shall *c*:
14.23 the place which he shall *c* to
24 which the Lord thy God shall *c*
25 which the Lord thy God shall *c*:
15.20 the place which the Lord shall *c*,
16. 2 the place which the Lord shall *c*
6 which the Lord thy God shall *c*
7 which the Lord thy God shall *c*:
15 the place which the Lord shall *c*:
16 in the place which he shall *c*;
17. 8 which the Lord thy God shall *c*;
10 which the Lord shall *c* shall shew
15 whom the Lord thy God shall *c*:
18. 6 the place which the Lord shall *c*;
23.16 that place which he shall *c* in one
26. 2 God shall *c* to place his name
30.19 therefore *c* life, that both
31.11 in the place which he shall *c*,
Jos 9.27 in the place which he should *c*
24.15 *c* you this day whom ye will serve;
1Sa 2.28 did I *c* him out of all the tribes
17. 8 *c* you a man for you, and let
2Sa 16.18 and all the men of Israel, *c*,
17. 1 Let me now *c* out twelve thousand

2Sa 21. 6 of Saul, whom the Lord did *c*.
24.12 *c* thee one of them, that I may do
1Ki 14.21 which the Lord did *c* out of all
18.23 and let them *c* one bullock for
25 *C* you one bullock for yourselves,
1Ch 21.10 *c* thee one of them, that I may
11 Thus saith the Lord, *C* thee
Neh 9. 7 the God, who didst *c* Abram,
Job 9.14 and *c* out my words to reason
34. 4 Let us *c* to us judgment: let us
33 thou refuse, or whether thou *c*;
Ps 25.12 teach in the way that he shall *c*.
47. 4 He shall *c* our inheritance for us,
Pr 1.29 did not *c* the fear of the Lord:
3.31 oppressor, and *c* none of his ways.
Isa 7.15, 16 refuse the evil, and *c* the good,
14. 1 and will yet *c* Israel, and set them
49. 7 of Israel, and he shall *c* thee.
56. 4 and *c* the things that please me,
65.12 *c* that wherein I delighted not.
66. 4 I also will *c* their delusions,
Eze 21.19 *c* thou a place, *c* it at the head
Zec 1.17 Zion, and shall yet *c* Jerusalem.
2.12 and shall *c* Jerusalem again.
Phm 1.22 yet what I shall *c* I wot not.

CHOOSEST

Job 15. 5 thou *c* the tongue of the crafty.
Ps 65. 4 Blessed is the man whom thou *c*,

CHORAZIN

Mt 11.21 Woe unto thee, *C*! woe unto
Lk 10.13 Woe unto thee, *C*! woe unto

CHOSE

Gen 6. 2 them wives of all which they *c*.
13.11 Lot *c* him all the plain of Jordan;
Ex 18.25 Moses *c* able men out of all Israel,
Dt 4.37 therefore he *c* their seed after them,
10.15 and he *c* their seed after them,
Jos 8. 3 Joshua *c* out thirty thousand
Jdg 5. 8 They *c* new gods; then was war in
1Sa 13. 2 Saul *c* him three thousand men
17.40 and *c* him five smooth stones out
2Sa 6.21 which *c* me before thy father,
10. 9 behind, he *c* of all the choice men
1Ki 8.16 I *c* no city out of all the tribes of
16 but I *c* David to be over my people
11.34 David my servant's sake whom I *c*,
1Ch 19.10 *c* out of all the choice of Israel,
28. 4 the Lord God of Israel *c* me before
2Ch 6. 5 I *c* no city among all the tribes
5 neither *c* I any man to be a ruler
Job 29.25 I *c* out their way, and sat chief,
Ps 78.67 and *c* not the tribe of Ephraim:
68 But *c* the tribe of Judah, the
70 He *c* David also his servant,
Isa 66. 4 and *c* that in which I delighted not.
Eze 20. 5 In the day when I *c* Israel,
Lk 6.13 of them he *c* twelve, whom also
14. 7 they *c* out the chief rooms; saying
Ac 6. 5 they *c* Stephen, a man full of faith
13.17 *c* our fathers, and exalted the
15.40 And Paul *c* Silas, and departed,

CHOSEN

Ex 14. 7 he took six hundred *c* chariots,
15. 4 his *c* captains also are drowned
Nu 16. 5 even him whom he hath *c* will
Dt 7. 6 the Lord thy God hath *c* thee to be
12.21 which the Lord thy God hath *c*
14. 2 the Lord hath *c* thee to be a
16.11 the Lord thy God hath *c* to place
18. 5 For the Lord thy God hath *c* him
21. 5 Lord thy God hath *c* to minister
Jos 24.22 that ye have *c* you the Lord to
Jdg 10.14 cry unto the gods which ye have *c*;
20.15 numbered seven hundred *c* men.
16 there were seven hundred *c* men
34 ten thousand *c* men out of all
1Sa 8.18 your king which ye shall have *c*
10.24 See ye him whom the Lord hath *c*,
12.13 the king whom ye have *c*, and
16. 8, 9 Neither hath the Lord *c* this.
10 Jesse, The Lord hath not *c* these.
20.30 that thou hast *c* the son of Jesse
24. 2 Saul took three thousand *c* men
26. 2 having three thousand *c* men of
2Sa 6. 1 together all the *c* men of Israel,
1Ki 3. 8 thy people which thou hast *c*,
8.44 toward the city which thou hast *c*,
48 the city which thou hast *c*, and the
11.13 Jerusalem's sake which I have *c*.
32 sake, the city which I have *c* out of
36 Jerusalem, the city which I have *c*
12.21 hundred and fourscore thousand *c*
2Ki 21. 7 which I have *c* out of all tribes
23.27 Jerusalem, which I have *c*, and the
1Ch 9.22 *c* to be porters in the gates
15. 2 them hath the Lord *c* to carry the
16.13 ye children of Jacob, his *c* ones.
41 the rest that were *c*, who were
28. 4 he hath *c* Judah to be the ruler;
5 he hath *c* Solomon my son to sit
6 I have *c* him to be my son, and I
10 heed now; for the Lord hath *c* thee
29. 1 whom alone God hath *c*, is yet
2Ch 6. 6 But I have *c* Jerusalem, that my
6 and have *c* David to be over my
34 toward this city which thou hast *c*,
38 toward the city which thou hast *c*,
7.12 and have *c* this place to myself for
16 For now have I *c* and sanctified
11. 1 fourscore thousand *c* men which
12.13 which the Lord had *c* out of all
13. 3 four hundred thousand *c* men:
3 eight hundred thousand *c* men,
17 five hundred thousand *c* men.
29.11 Lord hath *c* you to stand before
33. 7 which I have *c* before all the tribes
Neh 1. 9 the place that I have *c* to set
Job 36.21 for this hast thou *c* rather than
Ps 33.12 the people whom he hath *c* for his
78.31 smote down the *c* men of Israel.
89. 3 I have made a covenant with my *c*,
19 exalted one *c* out of the people.
105. 6 servant, ye children of Jacob his *c*.
26 and Aaron whom he had *c*.
43 with joy, and his *c* with gladness:
106. 5 That I may see the good of thy *c*,
23 had not Moses his *c* stood before
119.30 I have *c* the way of truth: thy
173 help me; for I have *c* thy precepts.
132.13 the Lord hath *c* Zion; he hath
135. 4 the Lord hath *c* Jacob unto himself,
Pr 16.16 rather to be *c* than silver!
22. 1 A good name is rather to be *c*
Isa 1.29 for the gardens that ye have *c*.
41. 8 servant, Jacob whom I have *c*,
9 I have *c* thee, and not cast thee
43.10 and my servant whom I have *c*:
20 to give drink to my people, my *c*.
44. 1 Israel, whom I have *c*:
2 and thou, Jesurun, whom I have *c*.
48.10 *c* thee in the furnace of affliction.
58. 5 Is it such a fast that I have *c*?
6 Is not this the fast that I have *c*?
65.15 your name for a curse unto my *c*:
66. 3 they have *c* their own ways, and
Jer 8. 3 death shall be *c* rather than life
33.24 families which the Lord hath *c*,
48.15 and his *c* young men are gone
49.19 and who is a *c* man, that I may
50.44 from her: and who is a *c* man,
Eze 23. 7 with all them that were the *c*
Dan 11.15 neither his *c* people, neither
Hag 2.23 for I have *c* thee, saith the Lord
Zec 3. 2 the Lord that hath *c* Jerusalem
Mt 12.18 my servant, whom I have *c*;
20.16 for many be called, but few *c*.
22.14 many are called, but few are *c*.
Mk 13.20 the elect's sake, whom he hath *c*,
Lk 10.42 Mary hath *c* that good part, which
23.35 if he be Christ, the *c* of God.
Jn 6.70 Have not I *c* you twelve, and one
13.18 I know whom I have *c*:
15.16 Ye have not *c* me,
16 but I have *c* you, and
19 I have *c* you out of the world,
Ac 1. 2 the apostles whom he had *c*:
24 whether of these two thou hast *c*,
9.15 he is a *c* vessel unto me, to bear
10.41 unto witnesses *c* before of God,
15.22 to send *c* men of their own
25 to send *c* men unto you with our
22.14 hath *c* thee, that thou shouldest
Ro 16.13 Salute Rufus *c* in the Lord, and
1Co 1.27 God hath *c* the foolish things of
27 God hath *c* the weak things of
28 which are despised, hath God *c*,
2Co 8.19 who was also *c* of the churches
Eph 1. 4 as he hath *c* us in him before the
2Th 2.13 God hath from the beginning *c*
2Ti 2. 4 he may please him who hath *c*
Jas 2. 5 Hath not God *c* the poor of this
1Pe 2. 4 but *c* of God, and precious,
9 ye are a *c* generation, a royal
Rev 17.14 him are called, and *c*, and faithful.

CHRIST

Mt 1. 1 book of the generation of Jesus *C*,
16 was born Jesus, who is called *C*.
17 unto *C* are fourteen generations.
18 the birth of Jesus *C* was on this
2. 4 of them where *C* should be born.
11. 2 heard in the prison the works of *C*,
16.16 Thou art the *C*, the Son of the
20 no man that he was Jesus the *C*.
22.42 What think ye of *C*? whose son
23. 8 one is your Master, even *C*; and
10 for one is your Master, even *C*.
24. 5 my name, saying, I am *C*; and
23 Lo, here is *C*, or there; believe it
26.63 whether thou be the *C*, the Son
68 Prophesy unto us, thou *C*, Who is
27.17 or Jesus which is called *C*?
22 with Jesus which is called *C*?
Mk 1. 1 of the gospel ofJesus *C*,
8.29 saith unto him, Thou art the *C*.
9.41 because ye belong to *C*, verily I
12.35 How say the scribes that *C* is the
13. 6 saying, I am *C*; and shall
21 Lo, here is *C*; or, lo, he is there;
14.61 Art thou the *C*, the Son of the
15.32 Let *C* the King of Israel descend
Lk 2.11 a Saviour, which is *C* the Lord.
26 before he had seen the Lord's *C*.
3.15 whether he were the *C*, or not;
4.41 Thou art *C* the Son of God.
41 for they knew that he was *C*.
9.20 answering said, The *C* of God.
20.41 say they that *C* is David's son?
21. 8 in my name, saying, I am *C*; and
22.67 Art thou the *C*? tell us. And he
23. 2 saying that he himself is *C* a king.
35 if he be *C*, the chosen of God.
39 saying, If thou be *C*, save thyself
24.26 Ought not *C* to have suffered
46 thus it behoved *C* to suffer, and to
Jn 1.17 grace and truth came by Jesus *C*.
20 but confessed, I am not the *C*.
25 if thou be not that *C*, nor Elias,
41 which is, being interpreted, the *C*.
3.28 said, I am not the *C*, but that I am
4.25 Messiah cometh, which is called *C*:
29 that even I did: is not this the *C*?
42 this is indeed the *C*, the Saviour of
6.69 are sure that thou art that *C*,
7.26 indeed that this is the very *C*?
27 when *C* cometh, no man knoweth
31 When *C* cometh, will he do more
41 Others said, This is the *C*. But
41 Shall *C* come out of Galilee?

BIBLICAL THEMES

CHRIST

Therefore the Lord himself shall give you a sign; Behold, a virgin shall conceive, and bear a son, and shall call his name Immanuel. Isa 7.14

For unto us a child is born, unto us a son is given: and the government shall be upon his shoulder: and his name shall be called Wonderful, Counsellor, The mighty God, The everlasting Father, The Prince of Peace. Isa 9.6

And there shall come forth a rod out of the stem of Jesse, and a Branch shall grow out of his roots: and the spirit of the Lord shall rest upon him, the spirit of wisdom and understanding, the spirit of counsel and might, the spirit of knowledge and of the fear of the Lord. Isa 11.1-2

He is despised and rejected of men; a man of sorrows, and acquainted with grief . . . he was despised, and we esteemed him not. Surely he hath borne our griefs, and carried our sorrows: yet we did esteem him stricken, smitten of God, and afflicted. But he was wounded for our transgressions, he was bruised for our iniquities . . . and with his stripes we are healed. Isa 53.3-5

But thou, Bethlehem . . . out of thee shall he come forth unto me that is to be ruler in Israel. Mic 5.2

The Lord, whom ye seek, shall suddenly come to his temple, even the messenger of the covenant, whom ye delight in. Mal 3.1

And she shall bring forth a son, and thou shalt call his name JESUS: for he shall save his people from their sins. Mt 1.21

And lo a voice from heaven, saying, This is my beloved Son, in whom I am well pleased. Mt 3.17

The men marvelled, saying, What manner of man is this, that even the winds and the sea obey him! Mt 8.27

John . . . sent two of his disciples, and said unto him, Art thou he that should come, or do we look for another? Mt 11.2-3

And he saith unto them, But whom say ye that I am? And Peter answereth and saith unto him, Thou art the Christ. Mk 8.29

Unto you is born this day in the city of David a Savior, which is Christ the Lord. Lk 2.11

And the Word was made flesh, and dwelt among us, (and we beheld his glory, the glory as of the only begotten of the Father,) full of grace and truth. Jn 1.14

Behold the Lamb of God, which taketh away the sin of the world. Jn 1.29

Never man spake like this man. Jn 7.46

And Pilate saith unto them, Behold the man! Jn 19.5

There is none other name under heaven given among men, whereby we must be saved. Ac 4.12

It is Christ that died, yea rather, that is risen again, who is even at the right hand of God, who also maketh intercession for us. Ro 8.34

God, who at sundry times and in divers manners spake in time past unto the fathers by the prophets, hath in these last days spoken unto us by his Son, whom he hath appointed heir of all things, by whom also he made the worlds . . . the brightness of his glory, and the express image of his person. Heb 1.1-3

Whosoever believeth that Jesus is the Christ is born of God. 1Jn 5.1

I am Alpha and Omega, the beginning and the end, the first and the last. Rev 22.13

42 *C* cometh of the seed of David, and
9.22 man did confess that he was *C*,
10.24 If thou be the *C*, tell us plainly.
11.27 I believe that thou art the *C*,
12.34 the law that *C* abideth for ever:
17. 3 Jesus *C*, whom thou hast sent.
20.31 might believe that Jesus is the *C*,
Ac 2.30 raise up *C* to sit on his throne;
31 spake of the resurrection of *C*,
36 ye have crucified, both Lord and *C*.
38 in the name of Jesus *C* for the
3. 6 In the name of Jesus *C* of
18 prophets, that *C* should suffer, he
20 And he shall send Jesus *C*, which
4.10 that by the name of Jesus *C* of
20 the Lord, and against his *C*.
5.42 to teach and preach Jesus *C*.
8. 5 Samaria, and preached *C* unto
12 and the name of Jesus *C*, they were
37 that Jesus *C* is the Son of God,
9.20 preached *C* in the synagogues,
22 proving that this is very *C*.
34 Jesus *C* maketh thee whole:
10.36 peace by Jesus *C*: (he is Lord of
11.17 believed on the Lord Jesus *C*;
15.11 the grace of the Lord Jesus *C*
26 for the name of our Lord Jesus *C*.
16.18 thee in the name of Jesus *C* to
31 Believe on the Lord Jesus *C*, and
17. 3 *C* must needs have suffered, and
3 whom I preach unto you, is *C*.
18. 5 to the Jews that Jesus was *C*.
28 the scriptures that Jesus was *C*.
19. 4 after him, that is, on *C* Jesus.
20.21 faith toward our Lord Jesus *C*.
24.24 him concerning the faith in *C*.
26.23 That *C* should suffer, and that
28.31 which concern the Lord Jesus *C*,
Ro 1. 1 Paul, a servant of Jesus *C*, called
3 Concerning his Son Jesus *C* our
6 ye also the called of Jesus *C*:
7 our Father, and the Lord Jesus *C*.
8 I thank my God through Jesus *C*
16 not ashamed of the gospel of *C*:
2.16 judge the secrets of men by Jesus *C*
3.22 is by faith of Jesus *C* unto all
24 redemption that is in *C* Jesus:
5. 1 God through our Lord Jesus *C*:
6 in due time *C* died for the ungodly.
8 were yet sinners, *C* died for us.
11 through our Lord Jesus *C*, by
15 which is by one man, Jesus *C*,
17 shall reign in life by one, Jesus *C*.)
21 eternal life by Jesus *C* our Lord.
6. 3 were baptized into Jesus *C* were
4 as *C* was raised up from the dead
8 if we be dead with *C*, we believe
9 Knowing that *C* being raised from
11 God, through Jesus *C* our Lord.
23 eternal life through Jesus *C* our
7. 4 dead to the law by the body of *C*;
25 God through Jesus *C* our Lord.
8. 1 to them which are in *C* Jesus,
2 Spirit of life in *C* Jesus hath
9 any man have not the Spirit of *C*,
10 if *C* be in you, the body is dead
11 that raised up *C* from the dead
17 of God, and joint-heirs with *C*;
34 It is *C* that died, yea rather, that
35 separate us from the love of *C*?
39 love of God, which is in *C* Jesus
9. 1 say the truth in *C*, I lie not, my
3 accursed from *C* for my brethren,
5 *C* came, who is over all, God
10. 4 *C* is the end of the law for
6 (that is, to bring *C* down from
7 (that is, to bring up *C* again from
12. 5 being many, are one body in *C*.
13.14 But put ye on the Lord Jesus *C*,
14. 9 *C* both died, and rose, and revived,
10 before the judgment seat of *C*.
15 with thy meat, for whom *C* died.
18 that in these things serveth *C* is
15. 3 For even *C* pleased not himself;
5 another according to *C* Jesus:
6 the Father of our Lord Jesus *C*.
7 as *C* also received us to the glory
8 Jesus *C* was a minister of the
16 minister of Jesus *C* to the Gentiles,
17 I may glory through Jesus *C* in
18 things which *C* hath not wrought
19 fully preached the gospel of *C*.
20 not where *C* was named, lest I
29 the blessing of the gospel of *C*.
16. 3 Aquila my helpers in *C* Jesus:
5 the firstfruits of Achaia unto *C*.
7 who also were in *C* before me.
9 Urbane, our helper in *C*, and
10 Salute Apelles approved in *C*.
16 The churches of *C* salute you.
18 such serve not our Lord Jesus *C*,
20 of our Lord Jesus *C* be with you.
24 our Lord Jesus *C* be with you all.
25 and the preaching of Jesus *C*,
27 wise, be glory through Jesus *C*
1Co 1. 1 apostle of Jesus *C* through the will
2 them that are sanctified in *C* Jesus,

1Co 1. 2 call upon the name of Jesus *C*
3 and from the Lord Jesus *C*.
4 which is given you by Jesus *C*;
6 of *C* was confirmed in you:
7 the coming of our Lord Jesus *C*:
8 in the day of our Lord Jesus *C*.
9 of his Son Jesus *C* our Lord.
10 by the name of our Lord Jesus *C*,
12 and I of Cephas; and I of *C*.
13 Is *C* divided? was Paul crucified
17 *C* sent me not to baptize, but to
17 *C* should be made of none effect.
23 But we preach *C* crucified,
24 *C* the power of God, and the
30 But of him are ye in *C* Jesus,
2. 2 save Jesus *C*, and him crucified.
16 But we have the mind of *C*.
3. 1 even as unto babes in *C*.
11 that is laid, which is Jesus *C*.
23 ye are Christ's; and *C* is God's.
4. 1 ministers of *C*, and stewards of
10 sake, but ye are wise in *C*;
15 ten thousand instructors in *C*, yet
15 for in *C* Jesus I have begotten
17 of my ways which be in *C*,
5. 4 the name of our Lord Jesus *C*,
4 the power of our Lord Jesus *C*,
5. 7 *C* our passover is sacrificed for
6.15 bodies are the members of *C*?
15 I then take the members of *C*,
8. 6 Jesus *C*, by whom are all things,
11 brother perish, for whom *C* died?
12 conscience, ye sin against *C*.
9. 1 have I not seen Jesus *C* our Lord?
12 we should hinder the gospel of *C*.
18 the gospel of *C* without charge,
21 under the law to *C*,) that I might
10. 4 and that rock was *C*.
9 neither let us tempt *C*, as some
16 communion of the blood of *C*?
16 communion of the body of *C*?
11. 1 of me, even as I also am of *C*.
3 that the head of every man is *C*;
3 man; and the head of *C* is God.
12.12 are one body: so also is *C*.
27 are the body of *C*, and members
15. 3 *C* died for our sins according to
12 if *C* be preached that he rose
13 of the dead, then is *C* not risen:
14 if *C* be not risen, then is our
15 of God that he raised up *C*:
16 rise not, then is not *C* raised:
17 *C* be not raised, your faith is vain;
18 also which are fallen asleep in *C*
19 this life only we have hope in *C*,
20 now is *C* risen from the dead,
22 in *C* shall all be made alive.
23 *C* the firstfruits; afterward they
31 which I have in *C* Jesus our Lord,
57 victory through our Lord Jesus *C*.
16.22 man love not the Lord Jesus *C*,
23 of our Lord Jesus *C* be with you.
24 love be with you all in *C* Jesus.
2Co 1. 1 of Jesus *C* by the will of God,
2 and from the Lord Jesus *C*.
3 the Father of our Lord Jesus *C*,
5 sufferings of *C* abound in us,
5 consolation also aboundeth by *C*.
19 *C*, who was preached among you
21 stablisheth us with you in *C*,
2.10 forgave I it in the person of *C*;
14 always causeth us to triumph in *C*,
15 unto God a sweet savor of *C*,
17 in the sight of God speak we in *C*.
3. 3 the epistle of *C* ministered by us,
4 have we through *C* to God-ward:
14 which vail is done away in *C*.
4. 4 light of the glorious gospel of *C*,
5 ourselves, but *C* Jesus the Lord;
6 glory of God in the face of Jesus *C*.
5.10 judgment seat of *C*; that every
14 For the love of *C* constraineth us;
16 we have known *C* after the flesh,
17 if any man be in *C*, he is a new
18 us to himself by Jesus *C*, and hath
19 God was in *C*, reconciling the
20 we are ambassadors for *C*, as
6.15 what concord hath *C* with Belial?
8. 9 the grace of our Lord Jesus *C*,
23 the churches, and the glory of *C*.
9.13 subjection unto the gospel of *C*,
10. 1 meekness and gentleness of *C*,
5 thought to the obedience of *C*;
14 in preaching the gospel of *C*:
11. 2 you as a chaste virgin to *C*.
3 from the simplicity that is in *C*.
10 truth of *C* is in me, no man shall
13 themselves into the apostles of *C*.
23 Are they ministers of *C*? (I speak
31 the Father of our Lord Jesus *C*,
12. 2 a man in *C* above fourteen years
9 power of *C* may rest upon me.
19 we speak before God in *C*: but
13. 3 seek a proof of *C* speaking in me,
5 Jesus *C* is in you, except ye be
14 grace of the Lord Jesus *C*, and
Gal 1. 1 neither by man, but by Jesus *C*,
3 and from our Lord Jesus *C*,
6 grace of *C* unto another gospel:
7 would pervert the gospel of *C*.
10 should not be the servant of *C*.
12 but by the revelation of Jesus *C*.
22 of Judea which were in *C*:
2. 4 in *C* Jesus, that they might bring
16 law, but by the faith of Jesus *C*,
16 we have believed in Jesus *C*,
16 be justified by the faith of *C*,
17 we seek to be justified by *C*,
17 is therefore *C* the minister of sin?
20 I am crucified with *C*:
20 yet not I, but *C* liveth in me:
21 by the law, then *C* is dead in vain.
3. 1 *C* hath been evidently set forth,
13 *C* hath redeemed us from the
14 on the Gentiles through Jesus *C*;
16 one, And to thy seed, which is *C*.
17 confirmed before of God in *C*,
22 promise by faith of Jesus *C*
24 schoolmaster to bring us unto *C*,
26 of God by faith in *C* Jesus.
27 baptized into *C* have put on *C*.
28 for ye are all one in *C* Jesus.
4. 7 then an heir of God through *C*.
14 angel of God, even as *C* Jesus.
19 in birth again until *C* be formed
5. 1 wherewith *C* hath made us free,
2 *C* shall profit you nothing.
4 *C* is become of no effect unto you,
6 in Jesus *C* neither circumcision
6. 2 burdens, and so fulfil the law of *C*.
12 persecution for the cross of *C*.
14 cross of our Lord Jesus *C*, by
6.15 in *C* Jesus neither circumcision
18 Lord Jesus *C* be with your spirit.
Eph 1. 1 Paul, an apostle of Jesus *C* by the
1 and to the faithful in *C* Jesus:
2 and from the Lord Jesus *C*.
3 Father of our Lord Jesus *C*, who
3 in heavenly places in *C*:
5 children by Jesus *C* to himself,
10 all things in *C*, both which are in
12 his glory, who first trusted in *C*.
17 God of our Lord Jesus *C*, the
20 Which he wrought in *C*, when he
2. 5 quickened us together with *C*,
6 in heavenly places in *C* Jesus:
7 toward us through *C* Jesus.
10 in *C* Jesus unto good works,
12 without *C*, being aliens from the
13 now in *C* Jesus, ye who sometimes
13 are made nigh by the blood of *C*.
20 *C* himself being the chief corner
3. 1 prisoner of Jesus *C* for you
4 knowledge in the mystery of *C*)
6 his promise in *C* by the gospel:
8 the unsearchable riches of *C*;
9 created all things by Jesus *C*:
11 which he purposed in *C* Jesus
14 Father of our Lord Jesus *C*,
17 *C* may dwell in your hearts by
19 the love of *C*, which passeth
21 by *C* Jesus throughout all ages,
4. 7 to the measure of the gift of *C*.
12 for the edifying of the body of *C*:
13 of the stature of the fulness of *C*:
15 which is the head, even *C*:
20 ye have not so learned *C*;
5. 2 as *C* also hath loved us, and hath
5 in the kingdom of *C* and of God.
14 dead, and *C* shall give thee light.
20 in the name of our Lord Jesus *C*;
23 *C* is the head of the church:
24 as the church is subject unto *C*,
25 even as *C* also loved the church,
32 concerning *C* and the church.
6. 5 of your heart, as unto *C*;
6 the servants of *C*, doing the will
23 Father and the Lord Jesus *C*.
24 our Lord Jesus *C* in sincerity.
Php 1. 1 the servants of Jesus *C*, to all
1 to all the saints in *C* Jesus
2 Father, and from the Lord Jesus *C*.
6 perform it until the day of Jesus *C*:
8 you all in the bowels of Jesus *C*.
10 without offense till the day of *C*;
11 are by Jesus *C*, unto the glory
13 my bonds in *C* are manifest in all
15 indeed preach *C* even of envy and
16 The one preach *C* of contention,
18 or in truth, *C* is preached;
19 supply of the Spirit of Jesus *C*,
20 *C* shall be magnified in my body,
21 For me to live is *C*, and to die is
23 to depart, and to be with *C*;
26 may be more abundant in Jesus *C*
27 as it becometh the gospel of *C*:
29 it is given in the behalf of *C*, not
2. 1 be therefore any consolation in *C*,
5 you, which was also in *C* Jesus:
11 Jesus *C* is Lord, to the glory of God
16 I may rejoice in the day of *C*,
30 for the work of *C* he was nigh
3. 3 rejoice in *C* Jesus, and have no
7 those I counted loss for *C*.
8 knowledge of *C* Jesus my Lord:
8 but dung, that I may win *C*,
9 which is through the faith of *C*,
12 I am apprehended of *C* Jesus.
14 the high calling of God in *C* Jesus.
18 are the enemies of the cross of *C*:
20 for the Saviour, the Lord Jesus *C*:
4. 7 hearts and minds through *C* Jesus.
13 *C* which strengtheneth me.
19 to his riches in glory by *C* Jesus.
21 Salute every saint in *C* Jesus.
23 The grace of our Lord Jesus *C* be
Col 1. 1 an apostle of Jesus *C* by the will
2 saints and faithful brethren in *C*
2 Father and the Lord Jesus *C*.
3 the Father of our Lord Jesus *C*,
4 we heard of your faith in *C* Jesus,
7 for you a faithful minister of *C*;
24 the afflictions of *C* in my flesh for
27 is *C* in you, the hope of glory:
28 every man perfect in *C* Jesus:
2. 2 and of the Father, and of *C*;
5 stedfastness of your faith in *C*.
6 therefore received *C* Jesus the
8 of the world, and not after *C*.
11 flesh by the circumcision of *C*:
17 but the body is of *C*.
20 dead with *C* from the rudiments
3. 1 If ye then be risen with *C*,

1 where *C* sitteth on the right hand
3 your life is hid with *C* in God.
4 *C*, who is our life, shall appear,
11 but *C* is all, and in all.
13 as *C* forgave you, so also do ye.
16 the word of *C* dwell in you richly
24 for ye serve the Lord *C*.
4. 3 speak the mystery of *C*, for which
12 a servant of *C*, saluteth you,
1Th 1. 1 Father and in the Lord Jesus *C*:
1 Father, and the Lord Jesus *C*.
3 hope in our Lord Jesus *C*, in
2. 6 burdensome, as the apostles of *C*.
14 which in Judea are in *C* Jesus:
19 our Lord Jesus *C* at his coming?
3. 2 fellowlaborer in the gospel of *C*,
11 Lord Jesus *C*, direct our way
13 the coming of our Lord Jesus *C*
4.16 the dead in *C* shall rise first:
5. 9 salvation by our Lord Jesus *C*,
18 this is the will of God in *C* Jesus
23 the coming of our Lord Jesus *C*.
28 The grace of our Lord Jesus *C* be
2Th 1. 1 our Father and the Lord Jesus *C*:
2 our Father and the Lord Jesus *C*.
8 the gospel of our Lord Jesus *C*:
12 the name of our Lord Jesus *C*
12 of our God and the Lord Jesus *C*.
2. 1 the coming of our Lord Jesus *C*,
2 as that the day of *C* is at hand.
14 the glory of our Lord Jesus *C*.
16 Now our Lord Jesus *C* himself,
3. 5 into the patient waiting for *C*.
6 in the name of our Lord Jesus *C*,
12 and exhort by our Lord Jesus *C*,
18 The grace of our Lord Jesus *C* be
1Ti 1. 1 Paul, an apostle of Jesus *C* by the
1 our Saviour, and Lord Jesus *C*,
2 our Father and Jesus *C* our Lord.
12 thank *C* Jesus our Lord, who hath
14 and love which is in *C* Jesus.
15 that *C* Jesus came into the world
16 first Jesus *C* might shew forth
2. 5 and men, the man *C* Jesus;
7 speak the truth in *C*, and lie not;)
3.13 in the faith which is in *C* Jesus.
4. 6 be a good minister of Jesus *C*,
5.11 begun to wax wanton against *C*,
21 before God, and the Lord Jesus *C*,
6. 3 the words of our Lord Jesus *C*,
13 *C* Jesus, who before Pontius Pilate
14 appearing of our Lord Jesus *C*:
2Ti 1. 1 an apostle of Jesus *C* by the will
1 promise of life which is in *C* Jesus,
2 the Father and *C* Jesus our Lord.
9 in *C* Jesus before the world began,
10 appearing of our Saviour Jesus *C*,
13 and love which is in *C* Jesus.
2. 1 in the grace that is in *C* Jesus.
3 as a good soldier of Jesus *C*.
8 Remember that Jesus *C* of the
10 is in *C* Jesus with eternal glory.
19 that nameth the name of *C*
3.12 live godly in *C* Jesus shall suffer
15 through faith which is in *C* Jesus.
4. 1 Lord Jesus *C*, who shall judge
22 Lord Jesus *C* be with thy spirit.
Tit 1. 1 an apostle of Jesus *C*, according to
4 and the Lord Jesus *C* our Saviour.
2.13 great God and our Saviour Jesus *C*;
3. 6 through Jesus *C* our Saviour;
Phm 1 Paul, a prisoner of Jesus *C*,
3 our Father and the Lord Jesus *C*.
6 thing which is in you in *C* Jesus.
8 be much bold in *C* to enjoin thee
9 now also a prisoner of Jesus *C*.
23 my fellowprisoner in *C* Jesus;
25 grace of our Lord Jesus *C* be with
Heb 3. 1 Priest of our profession, *C* Jesus:
6 *C* as a son over his own house;
14 For we are made partakers of *C*,
5. 5 also *C* glorified not himself to be
6. 1 the principles of the doctrine of *C*,
9.11 But *C* being come an high priest
14 much more shall the blood of *C*,
24 *C* is not entered in to the holy places
28 *C* was once offered to bear the sins
10.10 of the body of Jesus *C* once for all.
11.26 the reproach of *C* greater riches
13. 8 Jesus *C* the same yesterday, and
21 in his sight, through Jesus *C*;
Jas 1. 1 Lord Jesus *C*, to the twelve tribes
2. 1 faith of our Lord Jesus *C*, the Lord
1Pe 1. 1 Peter, an apostle of Jesus *C*, to
2 sprinkling of the blood of Jesus *C*:
3 and Father of our Lord Jesus *C*,
3 resurrection of Jesus *C* from the
7 glory at the appearing of Jesus *C*:
11 the spirit of *C* which was in them
11 beforehand the sufferings of *C*,
13 you at the revelation of Jesus *C*;
19 precious blood of *C*, as of a lamb
2. 5 acceptable to God by Jesus *C*.
21 because *C* also suffered for us,
3.16 your good conversation in *C*.
18 *C* also hath once suffered for sins,
21 by the resurrection of Jesus *C*:
4. 1 Forasmuch then as *C* hath suffered
11 may be glorified through Jesus *C*,
14 be reproached for the name of *C*,
5. 1 a witness of the sufferings of *C*,
10 his eternal glory by *C* Jesus,
14 with you all that are in *C* Jesus.
2Pe 1. 1 Peter, an apostle of Jesus *C*, to
1 of God and our Saviour Jesus *C*:
8 knowledge of our Lord Jesus *C*.
11 of our Lord and Saviour Jesus *C*.
14 as our Lord Jesus *C* hath shewed
16 and coming of our Lord Jesus *C*,
2.20 of the Lord and Saviour Jesus *C*,
3.18 of our Lord and Saviour Jesus *C*.
1Jn 1. 3 Father, and with his Son Jesus *C*.
7 and the blood of Jesus *C* his Son
2. 1 the Father, Jesus *C* the righteous:
22 that denieth that Jesus is the *C*?
3.23 on the name of his son Jesus *C*.
4. 2 that Jesus *C* is come in the flesh
3 confesseth not that Jesus *C* is
5. 1 believeth that Jesus is the *C* is
6 water and blood, even Jesus *C*;
20 is true, even in his Son Jesus *C*.
2Jn 3 Lord Jesus *C*, the son of the Father,
7 that Jesus *C* is come in the flesh.
9 abideth not in the doctrine of *C*,
9 that abideth in the doctrine of *C*,
Jude 1 the servant of Jesus *C*, and brother
1 preserved in Jesus *C*, and called:
4 Lord God, and our Lord Jesus *C*.
17 the apostles of our Lord Jesus *C*;
21 the mercy of our Lord Jesus *C*
Rev 1. 1 Revelation of Jesus *C* which God
2 testimony of Jesus *C*, and of all
5 from Jesus *C*, who is the faithful
9 kingdom and patience of Jesus *C*,
9 and for the testimony of Jesus *C*.
11.15 of our Lord, and of his *C*;
12.10 our God, and the power of his *C*:
17 have the testimony of Jesus *C*.
20. 4 reigned with *C* a thousand years.
6 shall be priests of God and of *C*,
22.21 Lord Jesus *C* be with you all.

CHRIST'S
Ro 15.30 for the Lord Jesus *C* sake, and
1Co 3.23 ye are *C*; and Christ is God's.
4.10 for *C* sake, but ye are wise in
7.22 is called, being free, is *C* servant.
15.23 fruits; afterward they that are *C*
2Co 2.12 *C* gospel, and a door was opened
5.20 in *C* stead, be ye reconciled to
10. 7 man trust to himself that he is *C*,
7 think this again, that, as he is *C*,
7 even so are we *C*.
12.10 in distresses for *C* sake:
Gal 3.29 if ye be *C*, then are ye Abraham's
5.24 are *C* have crucified the flesh
Eph 4.32 God for *C* sake hath forgiven
Php 2.21 not the things which are Jesus *C*.
1Pe 4.13 as ye are partakers of *C*

CHRISTS
Mt 24.24 For there shall arise false *C*, and
Mk 13.22 For false *C* and false prophets

CHRISTIAN
Ac 26.28 thou persuadest me to be a *C*.
1Pe 4.16 if any man suffer as a *C*, let him

CHRISTIANS
Ac 11.26 disciples were called *C* first in

CHRYSOLITE
Rev 21.20 the seventh, *c*; the eighth, beryl:

CHRYSOPRASUS
Rev 21.20 the tenth, a *c*; the eleventh, a

CHURCH
Mt 16.18 upon this rock I will build my *c*;
18.17 tell it unto the *c*:
17 but if he neglect to hear the *c*,
Ac 2.47 the Lord added to the *c* daily
5.11 fear came upon all the *c*, and
7.38 he, that was in the *c* in the
8. 1 against the *c* which was at
3 he made havock of the *c*,
11.22 the *c* which was in Jerusalem:
26 assembled themselves with the *c*,
12. 1 his hands to vex certain of the *c*.
5 without ceasing of the *c* unto God
13. 1 Now there were in the *c* that was
14.23 ordained them elders in every *c*,
27 and had gathered the *c* together,
15. 3 brought on their way by the *c*,
4 they were received of the *c*, and of
22 and elders, with the whole *c*,
18.22 gone up, and saluted the *c*, he
20.17 and called the elders of the *c*.
28 overseers, to feed the *c* of God,
Ro 16. 1 is a servant of the *c* which is at
5 greet the *c* that is in their house.
23 mine host, and of the whole *c*,
1Co 1. 2 Unto the *c* of God which is at
4.17 I teach everywhere in every *c*.
6. 4 who are least esteemed in the *c*.
10.32 Gentiles; nor to the *c* of God:
11.18 when ye come together in the *c*,
22 or despise ye the *c* of God, and
12.28 God hath set some in the *c*,
14. 4 that prophesieth edifieth the *c*.
5 interpret, that the *c* may receive
12 excel to the edifying of the *c*.
19 in the *c* I had rather speak five
23 therefore the whole *c* be come
28 let him keep silence in the *c*;
35 for women to speak in the *c*.
15. 9 I persecuted the *c* of God.
16.19 with the *c* that is in their house.
2Co 1. 1 unto the *c* of God which is
Gal 1.13 I persecuted the *c* of God, and
Eph 1.22 the head over all things to the *c*,
3.10 might be known by the *c* the
21 glory in the *c* by Christ Jesus
5.23 Christ is the head of the *c*:
24 Therefore as the *c* is subject unto
25 as Christ also loved the *c*, and
27 present it to himself a glorious *c*,
29 even as the Lord the *c*:
32 concerning Christ and the *c*,
Php 3. 6 Concerning zeal, persecuting the *c*;
4.15 no *c* communicated with me
Col 1.18 the head of the body, the *c*:
24 for his body's sake, which is the *c*:

BIBLICAL THEMES

CHURCH

Ye have seen what I did unto the Egyptians, and how I bare you on eagles' wings, and brought you unto myself. Now therefore, if ye will obey my voice indeed, and keep my covenant, then ye shall be a peculiar treasure unto me above all people: for all the earth is mine: and ye shall be unto me a kingdom of priests, and an holy nation. Ex 19.4-6

[Elijah] said . . . I, even I only, am left. . . . And the Lord said . . . Yet I have left me seven thousand in Israel, all the knees which have not bowed unto Baal, and every mouth which hath not kissed him. 1Ki 19.14-15, 18

Ask of me, and I shall give thee the heathen for thine inheritance, and the uttermost parts of the earth for thy possession. Ps 2.8

I will praise the Lord with my whole heart, in the assembly of the upright, and in the congregation. Ps 111.1

Behold, I lay in Zion for a foundation a stone, a tried stone, a precious corner stone, a sure foundation. Isa 28.16

O Lord, save thy people, the remnant of Israel. Jer 31.7

Jerusalem shall be called a city of truth; and the mountain of the Lord of hosts the holy mountain. Zec 8.3

Thou art Peter, and upon this rock I will build my church; and the gates of hell shall not prevail against it. And I will give unto thee the keys of the kingdom of heaven: and whatsoever thou shalt bind on earth shall be bound in heaven: and whatsoever thou shalt loose on earth shall be loosed in heaven. Mt 16.18-19

Thou art not far from the kingdom of God. Mk 12.34

The kingdom of God is within you. Lk 17.21

I pray not for the world, but for them which thou hast given me; for they are thine. And all mine are thine, and thine are mine; and I am glorified in them. Jn 17.9-10

There is neither Jew nor Greek, there is neither bond nor free, there is neither male nor female: for ye are all one in Christ Jesus. Gal 3.28

The Israel of God. Gal 6.16

Husbands, love your wives, even as Christ also loved the church, and gave himself for it; that he might sanctify and cleanse it with the washing of water by the word, that he might present it to himself a glorious church, not having spot, or wrinkle, or any such thing; but that it should be holy and without blemish. Eph 5.25-27

Giving thanks unto the Father, which hath made us meet to be partakers of the inheritance of the saints in light: who hath delivered us from the power of darkness, and hath translated us into the kingdom of his dear Son. Col 1.12-13

Ye are come unto mount Sion, and unto the city of the living God, the heavenly Jerusalem, and to an innumerable company of angels, to the general assembly and church of the firstborn, which are written in heaven, and to God the Judge of all, and to the spirits of just men made perfect. Heb 12.22-23

And I saw no temple therein: for the Lord God Almighty and the Lamb are the temple of it. Rev 21.22

The Spirit and the bride say, Come. Rev 22.17

Col 4.15 and the *c* which is in his house.
16 it be read also in the *c* of the
1Th 1. 1 unto the *c* of the Thessalonians
2Th 1. 1 unto the *c* of the Thessalonians
1Ti 3. 5 take care of the *c* of God?)
15 the *c* of the living God, the pillar
5.16 let not the *c* be charged;
Phm 2 to the *c* in thy house:
Heb 2.12 in the midst of the *c* will I sing
12.23 general assembly and *c* of the
Jas 5.14 call for the elders of the *c*;
1Pe 5.13 The *c* that is at Babylon, elected
3Jn 6 of thy charity before the *c*:
9 I wrote unto the *c*: but
10 and casteth them out of the *c*.
Rev 2. 1 the angel of the *c* of Ephesus
8 the angel of the *c* in Smyrna
12 to the angel of the *c* in Pergamos
18 the angel of the *c* in Thyatira.
3. 1 the angel of the *c* in Sardis write;
7 the angel of the *c* in Philadelphia
14 the angel of the *c* of the Laodiceans

CHURCHES
Ac 9.31 Then had the *c* rest throughout
15.41 and Cilicia, confirming the *c*.
16. 5 so were the *c* established in the
19.37 which are neither robbers of *c*,
Ro 16. 4 but also all the *c* of the Gentiles.
16 The *c* of Christ salute you.
1Co 7.17 And so ordain I in all *c*.
11.16 custom, neither the *c* of God.
14.33 of peace, as in all *c* of the saints.
34 your women keep silence in the *c*:
16. 1 I have given order to the *c* of
19 The *c* of Asia salute you.
2Co 8. 1 bestowed on the *c* of Macedonia;
18 gospel throughout all the *c*;
19 was also chosen of the *c* to travel
23 they are the messengers of the *c*,
24 ye to them, and before the *c*,
11. 8 I robbed other *c*, taking wages of
28 me daily, the care of all the *c*.
12.13 ye were inferior to other *c*,
Gal 1. 2 unto the *c* of Galatia:
22 unto the *c* of Judea which were
1Th 2.14 became followers of the *c* of God
2Th 1. 4 glory in you in the *c* of God
Rev 1. 4 John to the seven *c* which are in
11 and send it unto the seven *c*
20 are the angels of the seven *c*:
20 which thou sawest are the seven *c*.
2. 7 what the Spirit saith unto the *c*;
11 the Spirit saith unto the *c*; He
17 the Spirit saith unto the *c*; To
23 all the *c* shall know that I am he
29 what the Spirit saith unto the *c*.
3. 6, 13, 22 the Spirit saith unto the *c*.
22.16 unto you these things in the *c*.

CILICIA
Ac 6. 9 and of them of *C* and of Asia,
15.23 in Antioch and Syria and *C*:
41 And he went through Syria and *C*,
21.39 am a Jew of Tarsus, a city in *C*,
22. 3 born in Tarsus, a city in *C*,
23.34 he understood that he was of *C*;
27. 5 we had sailed over the sea of *C*
Gal 1.21 into the regions of Syria and *C*;

CINNAMON
Ex 30.23 and of sweet *c* half so much,
Pr 7.17 my bed with myrrh, aloes, and *c*.
SS 4.14 calamus and *c*, with all trees of
Rev 18.13 *c*, and odors, and ointments,

CIRCLE
Isa 40.22 sitteth upon the *c* of the earth,

CIRCUIT
1Sa 7.16 he went from year to year in *c*
Job 22.14 he walketh in the *c* of heaven.
Ps 19. 6 and his *c* unto the ends of it:

CIRCUMCISE
Gen 17.11 shall *c* the flesh of your foreskin;
Dt 10.16 *C* therefore the foreskin of your
30. 6 And the Lord thy God will *c* thine
Jos 5. 2 *c* again the children of Israel the
4 is the cause why Joshua did *c*:
Jer 4. 4 *C* yourselves to the Lord, and take
Lk 1.59 day they came to *c* the child;
Jn 7.22 ye on the sabbath day *c* a man.
Ac 15. 5 That it was needful to *c* them,
21.21 saying that they ought not to *c*

CIRCUMCISED
Gen 17.10 man child among you shall be *c*.
12 that is eight days old shall be *c*
13 must needs be *c*:
14 whose flesh of his foreskin is not *c*,
23 and *c* the flesh of their foreskin
24 was *c* in the flesh of his foreskin.
25 when he was *c* in the flesh of his
26 the selfsame day was Abraham *c*,
27 the stranger, were *c* with him.
21. 4 And Abraham *c* his son Isaac
34.15 that every male of you be *c*;
17 will not hearken unto us, to be *c*;
22 if every male among us be *c*,
22 as they are *c*.
24 and every male was *c*, all that
Ex 12.44 when thou hast *c* him, then shall

48 let all his males be *c*, and then let
Lev 12. 3 flesh of his foreskin shall be *c*.
Jos 5. 3 *c* the children of Israel at the hill
5 the people that came out were *c*.
5 of Egypt, them they had not *c*.
7 them Joshua *c*: for they were
7 they had not *c* them by the way.
Jer 9.25 all them which are *c* with the
Ac 7. 8 Isaac, and *c* him the eighth day;
15. 1 be *c* after the manner of Moses,
24 Ye must be *c*, and keep the law:
16. 3 and took and *c* him because of
Ro 4.11 believe, though they be not *c*;
1Co 7.18 Is any man called being *c*?
18 let him not be *c*.
Gal 2. 3 a Greek, was compelled to be *c*:
5. 2 if ye be *c*, Christ shall profit you
3 again to every man that is *c*,
6.12 they constrain you to be *c*; only
13 they themselves who are *c* keep
13 desire to have you *c*, that they may
Php 3. 5 *C* the eighth day, of the stock of
Col 2.11 In whom also ye are *c* with the

CIRCUMCISING

Jos 5. 8 they had done *c* all the people,
Lk 2.21 accomplished for the *c* of the

CIRCUMCISION

Ex 4.26 husband thou art, because of the *c*.
Jn 7.22 Moses therefore gave unto you *c*;
23 man on the sabbath day receive *c*,
Ac 7. 8 he gave him the covenant of *c*:
10.45 they of the *c* which believed
11. 2 they that were of the *c* contended
Ro 2.25 For *c* verily profiteth, if thou keep
25 thy *c* is made uncircumcision.
26 uncircumcision be counted for *c*?
27 the letter and *c* dost transgress
28 is that *c*, which is outward in the
29 *c* is that of the heart, in the spirit,
3. 1 what profit is there of *c*?
30 shall justify the *c* by faith, and
4. 9 blessedness then upon the *c* only,
10 when he was in *c*, or in
10 Not in *c*, but in uncircumcision.
11 And he received the sign of *c*,
12 the father of *c* to them who are not
12 them who are not of the *c* only,
15. 8 a minister of the *c* for the truth
1Co 7.19 *C* is nothing, and uncircumcision
Gal 2. 7 gospel of the *c* was unto Peter;
8 Peter to the apostleship of the *c*,
9 heathen, and they unto the *c*.
12 fearing them which were of the *c*.
5. 6 neither *c* availeth any thing,
11 if I yet preach *c*, why do I yet
6.15 neither *c* availeth any thing,
Eph 2.11 *C* in the flesh made by hands;
Php 3. 3 For we are the *c*, which worship
Col 2.11 with the *c* made without hands,
11 sins of the flesh by the *c* of Christ:
3.11 *c* nor uncircumcision, Barbarian,
4.11 called Justus, who are of the *c*.
Tit 1.10 deceivers, specially they of the *c*:

CIRCUMSPECTLY

Eph 5.15 that ye walk *c*, not as fools,

CISTERN

2Ki 18.31 every one the waters of his *c*:
Pr 5.15 Drink waters out of thine own *c*,
Ec 12. 6 or the wheel broken at the *c*.
Isa 36.16 every one the waters of his own *c*;

CISTERNS

Jer 2.13 hewed them out *c*, broken *c*,

CITIZEN

Lk 15.15 himself to a *c* of that country;
Ac 21.39 in Cilicia, a *c* of no mean city:

CITIZENS

Lk 19.14 But his *c* hated him, and sent a

CLAMOR

Eph 4.31 anger, and *c*, and evil speaking,

CLAP

Job 27.23 Men shall *c* their hands at him,
Ps 47. 1 O *c* your hands, all ye people;
98. 8 Let the floods *c* their hands: let
Isa 55.12 of the field shall *c* their hands.
La 2.15 pass by *c* their hands at thee;
Na 3.19 shall *c* the hands over thee:

CLAPPED

2Ki 11.12 and they *c* their hands, and said,
Eze 25. 6 thou hast *c* thine hands, and

CLAPPETH

Job 34.37 he *c* his hands among us, and

CLAUDIA

2Ti 4.21 and *C*, and all the brethren.

CLAUDIUS

Ac 11.28 to pass in the days of *C* Caesar.
18. 2 *C* had commanded all Jews to
23.26 *C* Lysias unto the most excellent

CLAVE

Gen 22. 3 and *c* the wood for the burnt
34. 3 And his soul *c* unto Dinah the
Nu 16.31 ground *c* asunder that was under
Jdg 15.19 But God *c* an hollow place that
Ru 1.14 but Ruth *c* unto her.
1Sa 6.14 and they *c* the wood of the cart,
2Sa 20. 2 men of Judah *c* unto their king,
23.10 and his hand *c* unto the sword:
1Ki 11. 2 Solomon *c* unto these in love.
2Ki 18. 6 he *c* to the Lord, and departed not
Neh 10.29 They *c* to their brethren, their
Ps 78.15 He *c* the rocks in the wilderness,
Isa 48.21 he *c* the rock also, and the
Ac 17.34 men *c* unto him, and believed:

CLAY

1Ki 7.46 king cast them, in the *c* ground
2Ch 4.17 in the *c* ground between Succoth
Job 4.19 them that dwell in houses of *c*,
10. 9 thou hast made me as the *c*; and
13.12 ashes, your bodies to bodies of *c*,
27.16 and prepare raiment as the *c*;
33. 6 I also am formed out of the *c*.
38.14 It is turned as *c* to the seal; and
Ps 40. 2 out of the miry *c*, and set my feet
Isa 29.16 be esteemed as the potter's *c*:
41.25 and as the potter treadeth *c*.
45. 9 *c* say to him that fashioneth it,
64. 8 thou art our father; we are the *c*,
Jer 18. 4 that he made of *c* was marred
6 as the *c* is in the potter's hand, so
43. 9 them in the *c* in the brickkiln,
Dan 2.33 feet part of iron and part of *c*.
34 were of iron and *c*, and brake them
35 iron, the *c*, the brass, the silver,
41 part of potter's *c*, and part of iron,
41 sawest the iron mixed with miry *c*.
42 were part of iron, and part of *c*,
43 sawest iron mixed with miry *c*,
43 even as iron is not mixed with *c*.
45 in pieces the iron, the brass, the *c*,
Na 3.14 go into *c*, and tread the morter,
Hab 2. 6 that ladeth himself with thick *c*!
Jn 9. 6 and made *c* of the spittle, and he
6 eyes of the blind man with the *c*,
11 man that is called Jesus made *c*,
14 when Jesus made the *c*, and
15 He put *c* upon mine eyes, and
Ro 9.21 not the potter power over the *c*,

CLEAN

Gen 7. 2 Of every *c* beast thou shalt take
2 of beasts that are not *c* by two,
8 Of *c* beasts, and of
8 beasts that are not *c*,
8.20 every *c* beast, and of every *c* fowl,
35. 2 go *c*, and change your garments:
Lev 4.12 a *c* place where the ashes are
6.11 without the camp unto a *c* place.
7.19 all that be *c* shall eat thereof.
10.10 and between unclean and *c*;
14 shoulder shall ye eat in a *c* place;
11.36 is plenty of water, shall be *c*:
37 which is to be sown, it shall be *c*.
47 between the unclean and the *c*,
12. 8 for her, and she shall be *c*.
13. 6 the priest shall pronounce him *c*:
6 he shall wash his clothes, and be *c*.
13 he shall pronounce him *c* that
13 it is all turned white: he is *c*.
17 the priest shall pronounce him *c*
17 that hath the plague: he is *c*.
23 the priest shall pronounce him *c*.
28 the priest shall pronounce him *c*:
34 pronounce him *c*: and he shall
34 wash his clothes, and be *c*.
37 the scall is healed, he is *c*:
37 the priest shall pronounce him *c*.
39 groweth in the skin; he is *c*.
40 he is bald; yet is he *c*.
41 he is forehead bald: yet is he *c*.
58 the second time, and shall be *c*.
59 to pronounce it *c*, or to pronounce
14. 4 be cleansed two birds alive and *c*,
7 and shall pronounce him *c*, and
8 himself in water, that he may be *c*:
9 flesh in water, and he shall be *c*.
11 the priest that maketh him *c*
11 the man that is to be made *c*, and
20 for him, and he shall be *c*.
48 priest shall pronounce the house *c*,
53 for the house: and it shall be *c*.
57 unclean, and when it is *c*: this is
15. 8 spit upon him that is *c*; then he
13 in running water, and shall be *c*.
28 days, and after that she shall be *c*.
16.30 ye may be *c* from all your sins
17.15 until the even: then shall he be *c*.
20.25 between *c* beasts and unclean,
25 and between unclean fowls and *c*:
22. 4 of the holy things, until he be *c*.
7 the sun is down, he shall be *c*,
23.22 thou shalt not make *c* riddance
Nu 5.28 woman be not defiled, but be *c*;
8. 7 and so make themselves *c*.
9.13 But the man that is *c*, and is not
18.11 every one that is *c* in thy house
13 every one that is *c* in thine house
19. 9 a man that is *c* shall gather up
9 up without the camp in a *c* place,
12 on the seventh day he shall be *c*:
12 the seventh day he shall not be *c*.
18 a *c* person shall take hyssop, and
19 and the *c* person shall sprinkle
19 himself in water, and shall be *c*
31.23 through the fire, and it shall be *c*:
24 and ye shall be *c*, and afterward
Dt 12.15 the unclean and the *c* may eat
22 the unclean and the *c* shall eat of
14.11 Of all *c* birds ye shall eat.
20 But of all *c* fowls ye may eat.
15.22 unclean and the *c* person shall
23.10 not *c* by reason of uncleanness
Jos 3.17 all the people were passed *c* over
4. 1 people were *c* passed over Jordan,
11 people were *c* passed over, that
1Sa 20.26 he is not *c*; surely he is not *c*.
2Ki 5.10 again to thee, and thou shalt be *c*.
12 may I not wash in them, and be *c*?
13 he saith to thee, Wash, and be *c*?
14 of a little child, and he was *c*.

2Ch 30.17 for every one that was not *c*, to
Job 9.30 and make my hands never so *c*;
11. 4 doctrine is pure, and I am *c* in
14. 4 Who can bring a *c* thing out of an
15.14 What is man, that he should be *c*?
15 the heavens are not *c* in his sight.
17. 9 and he that hath *c* hands shall
25. 4 or how can he be *c* that is born
33. 9 I am *c* without transgression, I
Ps 19. 9 The fear of the Lord is *c*,
24. 4 He that hath *c* hands, and a pure
51. 7 me with hyssop, and I shall be *c*:
10 Create in me a *c* heart, O God;
73. 1 even to such as are of a *c* heart.
77. 8 Is his mercy *c* gone for ever?
Pr 14. 4 Where no oxen are, the crib is *c*:
16. 2 ways of a man are *c* in his own
20. 9 can say, I have made my heart *c*,
Ec 9. 2 to the good and to the *c*, and to
Isa 1.16 Wash you, make you *c*; put away
24.19 broken down, the earth is *c*
28. 8 so that there is no place *c*.
30.24 that ear the ground shall eat *c*
52.11 be ye *c*, that bear the vessels of
66.20 bring an offering in a *c* vessel
Jer 13.27 wilt thou not be made *c*?
Eze 22.26 between the unclean and the *c*,
36.25 Then will I sprinkle *c* water
25 and ye shall be *c*: from all your
44.23 between the unclean and the *c*.
Joel 1. 7 he hath made it *c* bare, and cast
Zec 11.17 his arm shall be *c* dried up, and
Mt 8. 2 thou wilt, thou canst make me *c*.
3 him, saying, I will; be thou *c*.
23.25 for ye make *c* the outside of the
26 the outside of them may be *c*.
27.59 the body, he wrapped it in a *c*
Mk 1.40 wilt, thou canst make me *c*.
41 saith unto him, I will; be thou *c*.
Lk 5.12 thou wilt, thou canst make me *c*.
13 him, saying, I will: be thou *c*.
11.39 Now do ye Pharisees make *c*
41 behold, all things are *c* unto you.
Jn 13.10 but is *c* every whit:
10 and ye are *c*, but not all.
11 therefore said he, Ye are not all *c*.
15. 3 Now ye are *c* through the word
Ac 18. 6 upon your own heads; I am *c*:
2Pe 2.18 those that were *c* escaped from
Rev 19. 8 arrayed in fine linen, *c* and white:
14 clothed in fine linen, white and *c*.

CLEANSE

Ex 29.36 and thou shalt *c* the altar, when
Lev 14.49 he shall take to *c* the house two
52 And he shall *c* the house with the
16.19 seven times, and *c* it, and hallow
30 an atonement for you, to *c* you,
Nu 8. 6 children of Israel, and *c* them.
7 shalt thou do unto them, to *c*
15 and thou shalt *c* them, and offer
21 an atonement for them to *c* them.
2Ch 29.15 of the Lord, to *c* the house of the
16 house of the Lord, to *c* it,
Neh 13.22 the Levites that they should *c*
Ps 19.12 *c* thou me from secret faults.
51. 2 mine iniquity, and *c* me from my
119. 9 Wherewithal shall a young man *c*
Jer 4.11 people, not to fan, nor to *c*,
33. 8 And I will *c* them from all their
Eze 36.25 from all your idols, will I *c* you.
37.23 they have sinned, and will *c* them:
39.12 of them, that they may *c* the land.
14 upon the face of the earth, to *c* it:
16 Thus shall they *c* the land.
43.20 thus shalt thou *c* and purge it.
22 and they shall *c* the altar,
22 as they did *c* it with the bullock.
45.18 blemish, and *c* the sanctuary:
Joel 3.21 For I will *c* their blood that I
Mt 10. 8 *c* the lepers, raise the dead, cast
23.26 *c* first that which is within the
2Co 7. 1 let us *c* ourselves from all
Eph 5.26 That he might sanctify and *c* it
Jas 4. 8 *C* your hands, ye sinners; and
1Jn 1. 9 to *c* us from all unrighteousness.

CLEANSED

Lev 11.32 until the even; so it shall be *c*
12. 7 and she shall be *c* from
14. 4 take for him that is to be *c* two
7 upon him that is to be *c* from the
8 he that is to be *c* shall wash his
14, 17 right ear of him that is to be *c*,
18 the head of him that is to be *c*:
19 for him that is to be *c* from his
25, 28 right ear of him that is to be *c*,
29 the head of him that is to be *c*, to
31 atonement for him that is to be *c*
15.13 when he that hath an issue is *c*
28 if she be *c* of her issue, then she
Nu 35.33 the land cannot be *c* of the blood
Jos 22.17 which we are not *c* until this day,
2Ch 29.18 have *c* all the house of the Lord,
30.18 not *c* themselves, yet did they eat
19 though he be not *c* according to
34. 5 their altars, and *c* Judah and
Neh 13. 9 and they *c* the chambers:
30 Thus *c* I them from all strangers,
Job 35. 3 I have, if I be *c* from my sin?
Ps 73.13 Verily I have *c* my heart in vain,
Eze 22.24 Thou art the land that is not *c*,
36.33 In the day that I shall have *c* you
44.26 after he is *c*, they shall reckon
Dan 8.14 then shall the sanctuary be *c*.
Joel 3.21 their blood that I have not *c*;
Mt 8. 3 immediately his leprosy was *c*.
11. 5 lepers are *c*, and the deaf hear,
Mk 1.42 departed from him and he was *c*.
Lk 4.27 and none of them was *c*, saving
7.22 the lepers are *c*, the deaf hear,
17.14 to pass, as they went, they were *c*.
17 Were there not ten *c*? but where
Ac 10.15 What God hath *c*, that call not thou
11. 9 What God hath *c*, that call not thou

CLEANSETH

Job 37.21 the wind passeth, and *c* them.
Pr 20.30 blueness of a wound *c* away evil:
1Jn 1. 7 blood of Jesus Christ his Son *c* us

CLEANSING

Lev 13. 7 been seen of the priest for his *c*,
35 much in the skin after his *c*;
14. 2 law of the leper in the day of his *c*:
23 them on the eighth day for his *c*
32 get that which pertaineth to his *c*.
15.13 to himself seven days for his *c*,
Nu 6. 9 shave his head in the day of his *c*,
Eze 43.23 When thou hast made an end of *c*
Mk 1.44 and offer for thy *c* those things
Lk 5.14 and offer for thy *c*, according as

CLEAR

Gen 24. 8 shalt be *c* from this my oath:
41 shalt thou be *c* from this my oath,
41 thou shalt be *c* from my oath.
44.16 or how shall we *c* ourselves?
Ex 34. 7 will by no means *c* the guilty;
2Sa 23. 4 the earth by *c* shining after rain.
Ps 51. 4 speakest, and be *c* when thou
SS 6.10 fair as the moon, *c* as the sun,
Isa 18. 4 like a *c* heat upon herbs, and like
Am 8. 9 will darken the earth in the *c* day:
Zec 14. 6 the light shall not be *c*, nor dark:
2Co 7.11 approved yourselves to be *c* in
Rev 21.11 like a jasper stone, *c* as crystal;
18 was pure gold, like unto *c* glass.
22. 1 river of water of life, *c* as crystal,

CLEARING

Nu 14.18 no means *c* the guilty, visiting
2Co 7.11 in you, yea, what *c* of yourselves,

CLEARLY

Job 33. 3 my lips shall utter knowledge *c*.
Mt 7. 5 then shalt thou see *c* to cast out
Mk 8.25 restored, and saw every man *c*.
Lk 6.42 then shalt thou see *c* to pull out
Ro 1.20 are *c* seen, being understood by

CLEAVE

Gen 2.24 shall *c* unto his wife: and they
Lev 1.17 shall *c* it with the wings thereof,
Dt 4. 4 But ye that did *c* unto the Lord
10.20 to him shalt thou *c*, and swear by
11.22 in all his ways, and to *c* unto him;
13. 4 shall serve him, and *c* unto him.
17 shall *c* nought of the cursed thing
28.21 make the pestilence *c* unto thee,
60 they shall *c* unto thee.
30.20 and that thou mayest *c* unto him:
Jos 22. 5 to *c* unto him and to serve him,
23. 8 But *c* unto the Lord your God, as
12 and *c* unto the remnant of these
2Ki 5.27 of Naaman shall *c* unto thee,
Job 38.38 and the clods *c* fast together?
Ps 74.15 *c* the fountain and the flood:
101. 3 it shall not *c* to me.
102. 5 groaning my bones *c* to my skin.
137. 6 tongue *c* to the roof of my mouth;
Isa 14. 1 they shall *c* to the house of Jacob.
Jer 13.11 so have I caused to *c* unto me the
Eze 3.26 tongue *c* to the roof of thy mouth,
Dan 2.43 they shall not *c* one to another,
11.34 shall *c* to them with flatteries.
Hab 3. 9 didst *c* the earth with rivers.
Zec 14. 4 of Olives shall *c* in the midst
Mt 19. 5 *c* to his wife: and they twain
Mk 10. 7 and mother, and *c* to his wife;
Ac 11.23 they would *c* unto the Lord.
Ro 12. 9 *c* to that which is good.

CLEAVED

2Ki 3. 3 Nevertheless he *c* unto the sins
Job 29.10 tongue *c* to the roof of their
31. 7 if any blot hath *c* to mine hands;

CLEAVETH

Dt 14. 6 and *c* the cleft into two claws,
Job 16.13 he *c* my reins asunder, and doth
19.20 My bone *c* to my skin and to my
Ps 22.15 and my tongue *c* to my jaws;
41. 8 disease, say they, *c* fast unto him:
44.25 our belly *c* unto the earth.
119.25 My soul *c* unto the dust: quicken
141. 7 when one cutteth and *c* wood
Ec 10. 9 that *c* wood shall be endangered
Jer 13.11 the girdle *c* to the loins of a man,
La 4. 4 The tongue of the sucking child *c*
8 their skin *c* to their bones; it is
Lk 10.11 dust of your city, which *c* on us,

CLEMENCY

Ac 24. 4 hear us of thy *c* a few words.

CLEMENT

Php 4. 3 in the gospel, with *C* also, and

CLEOPAS

Lk 24.18 one of them, whose name was *C*,

CLEOPHAS

Jn 19.25 Mary the wife of *C*, and Mary

CLIMB

Jer 4.29 and *c* up upon the rocks:
Joel 2. 7 shall *c* the wall like men of war;
9 they shall *c* up upon the houses;
Am 9. 2 though they *c* up to heaven,

CLIMBED

1Sa 14.13 Jonathan *c* up upon his hands
Lk 19. 4 *c* up into a sycamore tree to see

CLIMBETH
Jn 10. 1 *c* up some other way, the same

CLOKE
Isa 59.17 was clad with zeal as a *c*.
Mt 5.40 thy coat, let him have thy *c* also.
Lk 6.29 him that taketh away thy *c*
Jn 15.22 they have no *c* for their sin
1Th 2. 5 nor a *c* of covetousness; God is
2Ti 4.13 The *c* that I left at Troas with
1Pe 2.16 liberty for a *c* of maliciousness,

CLOSE
Nu 5.13 of her husband, and be kept *c*,
2Sa 22.46 be afraid out of their *c* places.
1Ch 12. 1 he yet kept himself *c* because of
Job 28.21 kept *c* from the fowls of the air.
41.15 shut up together as with a *c* seal.
Ps 18.45 be afraid out of their *c* places.
Jer 42.16 *c* after you there in Egypt;
Dan 8. 7 saw him come *c* unto the ram,
Am 9.11 and *c* up the breaches thereof;
Lk 9.36 And they kept it *c*, and told no
Ac 27.13 thence, they sailed *c* by Crete.

CLOSED
Gen 2.21 *c* up the flesh instead thereof;
20.18 the Lord had fast *c* up all the
Nu 16.33 and the earth *c* upon them:
Jdg 3.22 and the fat *c* upon the blade,
Isa 1. 6 they have not been *c*, neither
29.10 sleep, and hath *c* your eyes:
Dan 12. 9 the words are *c* up and sealed
Jon 2. 5 the depth *c* me round about,
Mt 13.15 their eyes they have *c*; lest at
Lk 4.20 *c* the book, and he gave it again
Ac 28.27 their eyes have they *c*; lest they

CLOSER
Pr 18.24 that sticketh *c* than a brother.

CLOSET
Joel 2.16 and the bride out of her *c*.
Mt 6. 6 thou prayest, enter into thy *c*,

CLOSETS
Lk 12. 3 ye have spoken in the ear in *c*

CLOTH
Nu 4. 6 spread over it a *c* wholly of blue,
7 they shall spread a *c* of blue,
8 spread upon them a *c* of scarlet,
9 they shall take a *c* of blue,
11 they shall spread a *c* of blue,
12 put them in a *c* of blue, and cover
13 and spread a purple *c* thereon:
Dt 22.17 spread the *c* before the elders
1Sa 19.13 bolster, and covered it with a *c*.
21. 9 wrapped in a *c* behind the ephod:
2Sa 20.12 cast a *c* upon him, when he saw
2Ki 8.15 he took a thick *c*, and dipped it
Isa 30.22 them away as a menstruous *c*;
Mt 9.16 of new *c* unto an old garment,
27.59 wrapped it in a clean linen *c*,
Mk 2.21 of new *c* on an old garment:
14.51 linen *c* cast about his naked body;
52 And he left the linen *c*, and fled

CLOTHE
Ex 40.14 his sons, and *c* them with coats:
Est 4. 4 she sent raiment to *c* Mordecai,
Ps 132.16 also *c* her priests with salvation:
18 His enemies will I *c* with shame:
Pr 23.21 shall *c* a man with rags.
Isa 22.21 And I will *c* him with thy robe,
49.18 shalt surely *c* thee with them all,
50. 3 I *c* the heavens with blackness,
Eze 26.16 *c* themselves with trembling;
34. 3 ye *c* you with the wool, ye kill them
Hag 1. 6 ye *c* you, but there is none warm;
Zec 3. 4 *c* thee with change of raiment.
Mt 6.30 if God so *c* the grass of the field,
30 shall he not much more *c* you,
Lk 12.28 If then God so *c* the grass, which
28 how much more will he *c* you,

CLOTHED
Gen 3.21 make coats of skins, and *c* them.
Lev 8. 7 and *c* him with the robe, and put
2Sa 1.24 over Saul, who *c* you in scarlet,
1Ch 15.27 was *c* with a robe of fine linen,
21.16 the elders of Israel, who were *c*
2Ch 6.41 thy priests...be *c* with salvation,
18. 9 *c* in their robes, and they sat
28.15 *c* all that were naked among them,
Est 4. 2 the king's gate *c* with sackcloth.
Job 7. 5 My flesh is *c* with worms and
8.22 hate thee shall be *c* with shame;
10.11 hast *c* me with skin and flesh,
29.14 on righteousness, and it *c* me:
39.19 thou *c* his neck with thunder?
Ps 35.26 let them be *c* with shame and
65.13 The pastures are *c* with flocks;
93. 1 he is *c* with majesty;
1 the Lord is *c* with strength,
104. 1 art *c* with honor and majesty.
109.18 As he *c* himself with cursing
29 mine adversaries be *c* with shame,
132. 9 priests be *c* with righteousness;
Pr 31.21 her household are *c* with scarlet.
Isa 61.10 he hath *c* me with the garments of
Eze 7.27 prince shall be *c* with desolation,
9. 2 among them was *c* with linen,
3 called to the man *c* with linen,
11 And, behold, the man *c* with linen,
10. 2 spake unto the man *c* with linen,
6 commanded the man *c* with linen,
7 of him that was *c* with linen:
16.10 *c* thee also with broidered work,
23. 6 *c* with blue, captains and rulers,
12 and rulers *c* most gorgeously,
38. 4 *c* with all sorts of armor,
44.17 shall be *c* with linen garments;
Dan 5. 7 shall be *c* with scarlet, and have
16 thou shalt be *c* with scarlet,
29 and they *c* Daniel with scarlet,
10. 5 behold a certain man *c* in linen,
12. 6 one said to the man *c* in linen,
7 I heard the man *c* in linen,
Zep 1. 8 as are *c* with strange apparel.
Zec 3. 3 Joshua was *c* with filthy garments,
5 head, and *c* him with garments.
Mt 6.31 or, Wherewithal shall we be *c*?
11. 8 A man *c* in soft raiment?
25.36 Naked, and ye *c* me: I was sick,
38 thee in? or naked, and *c* thee?
43 naked and ye *c* me not: sick,
Mk 1. 6 And John was *c* with camel's hair,
5.15 and *c*, and in his right mind:
15.17 *c* him with purple, and platted
16. 5 *c* in a long white garment;
Lk 7.25 see? A man *c* in soft raiment?
8.35 at the feet of Jesus, *c*, and in his
16.19 was *c* in purple and fine linen,
2Co 5. 2 earnestly desiring to be *c* upon
3 being *c* we shall not be found
4 would be unclothed, but *c* upon,
1Pe 5. 5 be *c* with humility: for God
Rev 1.13 *c* with a garment down to the
3. 5 shall be *c* in white raiment;
18 raiment, that thou mayest be *c*,
4. 4 sitting, *c* in white raiment;
7. 9 *c* with white robes, and palms in
10. 1 from heaven, *c* with a cloud:
11. 3 threescore days, *c* in sackcloth.
12. 1 a woman *c* with the sun, and the
15. 6 *c* in pure and white linen, and
18.16 city, that was *c* in fine linen,
19.13 *c* with a vesture dipped in blood:
14 *c* in fine linen, white and clean.

CLOTHES
Gen 37.29 in the pit; and he rent his *c*.
34 And Jacob rent his *c*, and put
44.13 Then they rent their *c*, and
49.11 in wine, and his *c* in the blood
Ex 12.34 being bound up in their *c* upon
19.10 let them wash their *c*,
14 people, and they washed their *c*.
Lev 10. 6 your heads, neither rend your *c*;
11.25 shall wash his *c*, and be unclean
28 carcase of them shall wash his *c*,
40 carcase of it shall wash his *c*,
40 shall wash his *c*, and be unclean
13. 6, 34 shall wash his *c*, and be clean.
45 *c* shall be rent, and his head bare,
14. 8 wash his *c*, and shave off all his hair,
9 he shall wash his *c*, also he shall
47 lieth in the house shall wash his *c*;
47 eateth in the house shall wash his *c*.
15. 5, 6, 7, 8, 10, 11, 13, 21, 22, 27 wash his *c*,
16.26, 28 shall wash his *c*, and bathe
32 shall put on the linen *c*, even
17.15 he shall both wash his *c*, and
21.10 uncover his head, nor rend his *c*;
Nu 8. 7 let them wash their *c*, and so make
21 purified, and they washed their *c*;
14. 6 that searched the land, rent their *c*:
19. 7 Then the priest shall wash his *c*,
8 that burneth her shall wash his *c*
10 of the heifer shall wash his *c*,
19 purify himself, and wash his *c*,
21 of separation shall wash his *c*;
21.24 wash your *c* on the seventh day,
Dt 29. 5 *c* are not waxen old upon you,
Jos 7. 6 Joshua rent his *c*, and fell to the
Jdg 11.35 that he rent his *c*, and said, Alas,
1Sa 4.12 with his *c* rent, and with earth
19.24 he stripped off his *c* also, and
2Sa 1. 2 camp from Saul with his *c* rent,
11 David took hold on his *c*, and rent
3.31 Rend your *c*, and gird you with
13.31 servants stood by with their *c* rent.
19.24 nor washed his *c*, from the day the
1Ki 1. 1 they covered him with *c*, but he gat
21.27 that he rent his *c*, and put
2Ki 2.12 he took hold of his own *c*, and
5. 7 that he rent his *c*, and said, Am I
8 the king of Israel had rent his *c*,
8 hast thou rent they *c*? let him come
6.30 the woman, that he rent his *c*;
11.14 Athaliah rent her *c*, and cried,
18.37 to Hezekiah with their *c* rent,
19. 1 rent his *c*, and covered himself
22.11 book of the law, that he rent his *c*.
19 hast rent thy *c*, and wept before
2Ch 23.13 Then Athaliah rent her *c*, and said,
34.19 words of the law, that he rent his *c*.
27 before me, and didst rend thy *c*,
Neh 4.23 none of us put off our *c*, saving
9.21 their *c* waxed not old, and their
Est 4. 1 Mordecai rent his *c*, and put on
Job 9.31 and mine own *c* shall abhor me.
Pr 6.27 bosom, and his *c* not be burned?
Isa 36.22 to Hezekiah with their *c* rent,
37. 1 heard it, that he rent his *c*,
Jer 41. 5 and their *c* rent, and having cut
Eze 16.39 shall strip thee also of thy *c*,
23.26 strip thee out of thy *c*, and take
27.20 in precious *c* for chariots.
24 in blue *c*, and broidered work,
Am 2. 8 lay themselves down upon *c* laid
Mt 21. 7 put on them their *c*, and they
24.18 field return back to take his *c*.
26.65 Then the high priest rent his *c*,
Mk 5.28 If I may but touch his *c*, I shall
30 and said, Who touched my *c*?
14.63 Then the high priest rent his *c*,
15.20 and put his own *c* on him,
Lk 2. 7 and wrapped him in swaddling *c*,
12 the babe wrapped in swaddling *c*,
8.27 and ware no *c*, neither abode in

Lk 19.36 they spread their *c* in the way.
24.12 the linen *c* laid by themselves,
Jn 19.40 and wound it in linen *c* with the
20. 5 looking in, saw the linen *c* lying;
6 and seeth the linen *c* lie,
7 not lying with the linen *c*, but
Ac 7.58 the witnesses laid down their *c*
14.14 rent their *c*, and ran in among
16.22 the magistrates rent off their *c*,
22.23 cast off their *c*, and threw dust

CLOTHING

Job 22. 6 and stripped the naked of their *c*.
24. 7 the naked to lodge naked without *c*,
10 cause him to go naked without *c*,
31.19 seen any perish for want of *c*,
Ps 35.13 were sick, my *c* was sackcloth:
45.13 within: her *c* is of wrought gold.
Pr 27.26 lambs are for thy *c*, and the goats
31.22 her *c* is silk and purple.
25 Strength and honor are her *c*;
Isa 3. 6 Thou hast *c*, be thou our ruler,
7 my house is neither bread nor *c*:
23.18 sufficiently, and for durable *c*.
59.17 the garments of vengeance for *c*,
Jer 10. 9 blue and purple is their *c*: they
Mt 7.15 come to you in sheep's *c*, but
11. 8 wear soft *c* are in kings' houses.
Mk 12.38 which love to go in long *c*, and
Ac 10.30 stood before me in bright *c*,
Jas 2. 3 to him that weareth the gay *c*,

CLOUD

Gen 9.13 I do set my bow in the *c*, and it
14 when I bring a *c* over the earth,
14 the bow shall be seen in the *c*:
16 And the bow shall be in the *c*;
Ex 13.21 them by day in a pillar of a *c*,
22 took not away the pillar of the *c*
14.19 the *c* went from before their face,
20 it was a *c* and darkness to them,
24 the pillar of fire and of the *c*,
16.10 of the Lord appeared in the *c*.
19. 9 I come unto thee in a thick *c*,
16 and a thick *c* upon the mount,
24.15 a *c* covered the mount.
16 the *c* covered it six days: and
16 Moses out of the midst of the *c*.
18 went into the midst of the *c*,
34. 5 And the Lord descended in the *c*,
40.34 a *c* covered the tent of the
35 *c* abode thereon, and the glory
36 when the *c* was taken up from
37 But if the *c* were not taken up,
38 the *c* of the Lord was upon the
Lev 16. 2 in the *c* upon the mercy seat.
13 that the *c* of the incense may
Nu 9.15 the *c* covered the tabernacle,
16 the *c* covered it by day, and the
17 And when the *c* was taken up
17 in the place where the *c* abode,
18 as long as the *c* abode upon the
19 *c* tarried long upon the tabernacle
20 when the *c* was a few days upon
21 when the *c* abode from even unto
21 *c* was taken up in the morning,
21 by night that the *c* was taken up,
22 the *c* tarried upon the tabernacle,
10.11 that the *c* was taken up
12 the *c* rested in the wilderness of
34 the *c* of the Lord was upon them
11.25 And the Lord came down in a *c*,
12. 5 came down in the pillar of the *c*,
10 And the *c* departed from off the
14.14 that thy *c* standeth over them,
14 by day time in a pillar of a *c*,
16.42 behold, the *c* covered it, and the
Dt 1.33 ye should go, and in a *c* by day.
5.22 the *c*, and of the thick darkness,
31.15 the tabernacle in a pillar of a *c*:
15 and the pillar of the *c* stood over
1Ki 8.10 the *c* filled the house of the Lord,
11 stand to minister because of the *c*:
18.44 ariseth a little *c* out of the sea,
2Ch 5.13 the house was filled with a *c*,
14 to minister by reason of the *c*:
Neh 9.19 the pillar of the *c* departed not
Job 3. 5 let a *c* dwell upon it; let the
7. 9 *c* is consumed and vanisheth away:
22.13 he judge through the dark *c*?
26. 8 the *c* is not rent under them.
9 and spreadeth his *c* upon it.
30.15 my welfare passeth away as a *c*.
36.32 by the *c* that cometh betwixt.
37.11 he wearieth the thick *c*:
11 he scattereth his bright *c*:
15 caused the light of his *c* to shine?
38. 9 made the *c* the garment thereof,
Ps 78.14 daytime also he led them with a *c*,
105.39 He spread a *c* for a covering; and
Pr 16.15 favor is as a *c* of the latter rain.
Isa 4. 5 a *c* and smoke by day, and the
18. 4 a *c* of dew in the heat of harvest.
19. 1 the Lord rideth upon a swift *c*,
25. 5 the heat with the shadow of a *c*:
44.22 I have blotted out, as a thick *c*,
22 as a *c*, thy sins: return unto me;
60. 8 Who are these that fly as a *c*,
La 2. 1 the daughter of Zion with a *c*
3.44 hast covered thyself with a *c*,
Eze 1. 4 a great *c*, and a fire infolding itself,
28 that is in the *c* in the day of rain,
8.11 and a thick *c* of incense went up.
10. 3 and the *c* filled the inner court.
4 the house was filled with the *c*,
30.18 as for her, a *c* shall cover her,
32. 7 I will cover the sun with a *c*, and
38. 9 shalt be like a *c* to cover the land,
16 as a *c* to cover the land; it shall
Hos 6. 4 your goodness is as a morning *c*,
13. 3 they shall be as the morning *c*,
Mt 17. 5 a bright *c* overshadowed them:
5 and behold a voice out of the *c*,
Mk 9. 7 a *c* that overshadowed them:
7 and a voice came out of the *c*,
Lk 9.34 a *c*, and overshadowed them:
34 as they entered into the *c*.
35 there came a voice out of the *c*,
12.54 ye see a *c* rise out of the west,
21.27 in a *c* with power and great glory.
Ac 1. 9 a *c* received him out of their sight.
1Co 10. 1 all our fathers were under the *c*,
2 Moses in the *c* and in the sea;
Heb 12. 1 with so great a *c* of witnesses,
Rev 10. 1 from heaven, clothed with a *c*:
11.12 ascended up to heaven in a *c*;
14.14 and behold a white *c*, and upon the
14 upon the *c* one sat like unto the Son
15 to him that sat on the *c*, Thrust
16 sat on the *c* thrust in his sickle

CLOUDS

Dt 4.11 darkness, *c*, and thick darkness.
Jdg 5. 4 the *c* also dropped water.
2Sa 22.12 waters, and thick *c* of the skies,
23. 4 even a morning without *c*;
1Ki 18.45 was black with *c* and wind,
Job 20. 6 and his head reach unto the *c*;
22.14 Thick *c* are a covering to him,
26. 8 up the waters in his thick *c*;
35. 5 *c* which are higher than thou.
36.28 *c* do drop and distil upon man
29 the spreadings of the *c*,
32 With *c* he covereth the light;
37.16 know the balancings of the *c*,
21 bright light which is in the *c*:
38.34 thou lift up thy voice to the *c*,
37 can number the *c* in wisdom?
Ps 18.11 waters and thick *c* of the skies.
12 before him his thick *c* passed,
36. 5 faithfulness reacheth unto the *c*.
57.10 and thy truth unto the *c*.
68.34 and his strength is in the *c*.
77.17 The *c* poured out water: the
78.23 commanded the *c* from above,
97. 2 *C* and darkness are round about
104. 3 who maketh the *c* his chariot:
108. 4 thy truth reacheth unto the *c*.
147. 8 Who covereth the heaven with *c*.
Pr 3.20 and the *c* drop down the dew.
8.28 When he established the *c* above:
25.14 is like *c* and wind without rain.
Ec 11. 3 If the *c* be full of rain, they empty
4 regardeth the *c* shall not reap.
12. 2 nor the *c* return after the rain:
Isa 5. 6 I will also command the *c* that
14.14 ascend above the heights of the *c*;
Jer 4.13 he shall come up as *c*, and his
Dan 7.13 of man came with the *c* of heaven,
Joel 2. 2 a day of *c* and of thick darkness,
Na 1. 3 and the *c* are the dust of his feet.
Zep 1.15 a day of *c* and thick darkness,
Zec 10. 1 the Lord shall make bright *c*,
Mt 24.30 in the *c* of heaven with power
26.64 and coming in the *c* of heaven.
Mk 13.26 the Son of man coming in the *c*
14.62 and coming in the *c* of heaven.
1Th 4.17 up together with them in the *c*,
2Pe 2.17 *c* that are carried with a
Jude 12 *c* they are without water, carried
Rev 1. 7 Behold he cometh with *c*; and

CLOUDY

Ex 33. 9 *c* pillar descended, and stood
10 the people saw the *c* pillar stand
Neh 9.12 them in the day by a *c* pillar;
Ps 99. 7 spake unto them in the *c* pillar:
Eze 30. 3 day of the Lord is near, a *c* day;
34.12 scattered in the *c* and dark day.

COAL

2Sa 14. 7 so they shall quench my *c* which
Isa 6. 6 having a live *c* in his hand,
47.14 there shall not be a *c* to warm at,
La 4. 8 Their visage is blacker than a *c*;

COALS

Lev 16.12 take a censer full of burning *c*
2Sa 22. 9 devoured: *c* were kindled by it.
13 before him were *c* of fire
1Ki 19. 6 there was a cake baken on the *c*,
Job 41.21 His breath kindleth *c*, and a
Ps 18. 8 devoured: *c* were kindled by it.
12 passed, hail stones and *c* of fire.
13 his voice; hail stones and *c* of fire.
120. 4 of the mighty, with *c* of juniper.
140.10 let burning *c* fall upon them: let
Pr 6.28 Can one go upon hot *c*, and his
25.22 thou shalt heap *c* of fire upon his
26.21 As *c* are to burning
21 are to burning *c*, and wood to
SS 8. 6 the *c* thereof are *c* of fire, which
Isa 44.12 the tongs both worketh in the *c*,
19 baked bread upon the *c* thereof;
54.16 the smith that bloweth the *c*
Eze 1.13 was like burning *c* of fire,
10. 2 and fill thine hand with *c* of fire
24.11 Then set it empty upon the *c*
Hab 3. 5 and burning *c* went forth at his
Jn 18.18 who had made a fire of *c*; for it
21. 9 they saw a fire of *c* there, and fish
Ro 12.20 thou shalt heap *c* of fire on his

COAT

Gen 37. 3 made him a *c* of many colors.
23 out of his *c*, his *c* of many colors
31 they took Joseph's *c*, and killed
31 and dipped the *c* in the blood;
32 they sent the *c* of many colors,
32 whether it be thy son's *c* or no.
33 it, and said, It is my son's *c*;
Ex 28. 4 and a broidered *c*, a miter, and
39 embroider the *c* of fine linen,

29. 5 put upon Aaron the *c*, and the
Lev 8. 7 he put upon him the *c*, and
16. 4 He shall put on the holy linen *c*,
1Sa 2.19 his mother made him a little *c*,
17. 5 he was armed with a *c* of mail;
5 and the weight of the *c* was
38 he armed him with a *c* of mail.
2Sa 15.32 came to meet him with his *c* rent,
Job 30.18 me about as the collar of my *c*.
SS 5. 3 I have put off my *c*; how shall I
Mt 5.40 at the law, and take away thy *c*,
Lk 6.29 forbid not to take thy *c* also.
Jn 19.23 and also his *c*: now the *c* was
21. 7 he girt his fisher's *c* unto him,

COATS
Gen 3.21 did the Lord God make *c* of skins,
Ex 28.40 Aaron's sons thou shalt make *c*,
29. 8 his sons, and put *c* upon them.
39.27 they made *c* of fine linen of
40.14 sons, and clothe them with *c*:
Lev 8.13 put *c* upon them, and girded them
10. 5 carried them in their *c* out of the
Dan 3.21 bound in their *c*, their hosen
27 neither were their *c* changed,
Mt 10.10 neither two *c*, neither shoes,
Mk 6. 9 sandals; and not put on two *c*.
Lk 3.11 He that hath two *c*, let him
9. 3 money; neither have two *c* apiece.
Ac 9.39 shewing the *c* and garments which

COCK
Mt 26.34 this night, before the *c* crow, thou
74 And immediately the *c* crew.
75 Before the *c* crow, thou shalt deny
Mk 14.30 before the *c* crow twice, thou shalt
68 into the porch; and the *c* crew.
72 the second time the *c* crew.
72 said unto him, Before the *c* crow
Lk 22.34 the *c* shall not crow this day,
60 while he yet spake, the *c* crew.
61 Before the *c* crow, thou shalt deny
Jn 13.38 The *c* shall not crow, till thou hast
18.27 and immediately the *c* crew.

COCKCROWING
Mk 13.35 at midnight, or at the *c*, or in the

COLD
Gen 8.22 and *c* and heat, and summer
Job 24. 7 they have no covering in the *c*.
37. 9 whirlwind: and *c* out of the north.
Ps 147.17 who can stand before his *c*?
Pr 20. 4 will not plow by reason of the *c*;
25.13 As the *c* of snow in the time of
20 away a garment in *c* weather,
25 *c* waters to a thirsty soul, so is
Jer 18.14 shall the *c* flowing waters that
Na 3.17 camp in the hedges in the *c* day,
Mt 10.42 these little ones a cup of *c* water
24.12 the love of many shall wax *c*.
Jn 18.18 made a fire of coals; for it was *c*:
Ac 28. 2 present rain, and because of the *c*.
2Co 11.27 in fastings often, in *c* and
Rev 3.15 that thou art neither *c* nor hot:
15 I would thou wert *c* or hot.
16 and neither *c* nor hot, I will spue

COLLECTION
2Ch 24. 6 out of Jerusalem the *c*, according
9 to the Lord the *c* that Moses
1Co 16. 1 concerning the *c* for the saints,

COLONY
Ac 16.12 part of Macedonia, and a *c*:

COLOR
Lev 13.55 plague have not changed his *c*,
Nu 11. 7 *c* thereof as the *c* of bdellium.
Pr 23.31 when it giveth his *c* in the cup,
Eze 1. 4 midst thereof as the *c* of amber,
7 like the *c* of burnished brass.
16 was like unto the *c* of a beryl:
22 as the *c* of the terrible crystal,
27 And I saw as *c* of amber, as
8. 2 of brightness, as the *c* of amber.
10. 9 wheels was as the *c* of a beryl
Dan 10. 6 feet like in *c* to polished brass,
Ac 27.30 under *c* as though they would
Rev 17. 4 arrayed in purple and scarlet *c*,

COLORED
Rev 17. 3 sit upon a scarlet *c* beast,

COLORS
Gen 37. 3 he made him a coat of many *c*.
23 coat of many *c* that was on him;
32 And they sent the coat of many *c*,
Jdg 5.30 to Sisera a prey of divers *c*,
30 a prey of divers *c* of needlework,
30 of divers *c* of needlework on both
2Sa 13.18 a garment of divers *c* upon her:
19 rent her garment of divers *c*
1Ch 29. 2 glistering stones, and of divers *c*,
Isa 54.11 I will lay thy stones with fair *c*,
Eze 16.16 thy high places with divers *c*,
17. 3 of feathers, which had divers *c*,

COLOSSE
Col 1. 2 in Christ which are at *C*:

COLT
Gen 49.11 ass's *c* unto the choice vine;
Job 11.12 man be born like a wild ass's *c*.
Zec 9. 9 and upon a *c* the foal of an ass.
Mt 21. 2 find an ass tied, and a *c* with her:
5 an ass, and a *c* the foal of an ass.
7 brought the ass, and the *c*, and put
Mk 11. 2 ye shall find a *c* tied, whereon
4 and found the *c* tied by the door
5 them, What do ye, loosing the *c*?
7 brought the ass *c* to Jesus, and cast
Lk 19.30 entering ye shall find a *c* tied,
33 as they were loosing the *c*, the
33 unto them, Why loose ye the *c*?
35 cast their garments upon the *c*,
Jn 12.15 king cometh, sitting on an ass's *c*.

COLTS
Gen 32.15 milch camels with their *c*, forty
Jdg 10. 4 sons that rode on thirty ass *c*,
12.14 rode on threescore and ten ass *c*:

COMELINESS
Isa 53. 2 he hath no form nor *c*; and when
Eze 16.14 for it was perfect through my *c*,
27.10 they set forth thy *c*.
Dan 10. 8 for my *c* was turned in me into
1Co 12.23 parts have more abundant *c*.

COMELY
1Sa 16.18 in matters, and a *c* person,
Job 41.12 his power, nor his *c* proportion.
Ps 33. 1 for praise is *c* for the upright.
147. 1 for it is pleasant; and praise is *c*.
Pr 30.29 go well, yea, four are *c* in going:
Ec 5.18 it is good and *c* for one to eat and
SS 1. 5 I am black, but *c*, O ye daughters
10 Thy cheeks are *c* with rows of
2.14 voice, and thy countenance is *c*.
4. 3 thy speech is *c*: thy temples are
6. 4 love, as Tirzah, *c* as Jerusalem,
Isa 4. 2 earth shall be excellent and *c* for
Jer 6. 2 daughter of Zion to a *c* and
1Co 7.35 you, but for that which is *c*,
11.13 is it *c* that a woman pray unto
12.24 For our *c* parts have no need: but

COMFORT
Gen 5.29 shall *c* us concerning our work
18. 5 and *c* ye your hearts; after that
27.42 *c* himself, purposing to kill thee.
37.35 all his daughters rose up to *c* him;
Jdg 19. 5 *C* thine heart with a morsel of
8 said, *C* thine heart, I pray thee.
2Sa 10. 2 David sent to *c* him by the hand
1Ch 7.22 and his brethren came to *c* him.
19. 2 David sent messengers to *c* him
2 of Ammon to Hanun, to *c* him.
Job 2.11 to mourn with him and to *c* him.
6.10 should I yet have *c*; yea, I would
7.13 My bed shall *c* me, my couch
9.27 my heaviness, and *c* myself:
10.20 alone, that I may take *c* a little,
21.34 How then *c* ye me in vain, seeing
Ps 23. 4 thy rod and thy staff they *c* me.
71.21 and *c* me on every side.
119.50 This is my *c* in my affliction: for
76 merciful kindness be for my *c*,
82 saying, When wilt thou *c* me?
SS 2. 5 with flagons, *c* me with apples:
Isa 22. 4 to *c* me, because of the spoiling
40. 1 *C* ye, *c* ye my people, saith your
51. 3 the Lord shall *c* Zion:
3 he will *c* all her waste places;
19 by whom shall I *c* thee?
57. 6 Should I receive *c* in these?
61. 2 to *c* all that mourn;
66.13 comforteth, so will I *c* you;
Jer 8.18 I would *c* myself against sorrow,
16. 7 to *c* them for the dead; neither
31.13 into joy, and will *c* them,
La 1. 2 none to *c* her: all her friends
17 is none to *c* her: the Lord hath
21 I sigh: there is none to *c* me:
2.13 I may *c* thee, O virgin daughter
Eze 14.23 And they shall *c* you, when ye see
16.54 in that thou art a *c* unto them.
Zec 1.17 and the Lord shall yet *c* Zion,
10. 2 they *c* in vain: therefore they
Mt 9.22 Daughter, be of good *c*; thy faith
Mk 10.49 of good *c*, rise; he calleth thee
Lk 8.48 Daughter, be of good *c*: thy faith
Jn 11.19 to Martha and Mary, to *c* them
Ac 9.31 and in the *c* of the Holy Ghost,
Ro 15. 4 patience and *c* of the scriptures
1Co 14. 3 and exhortation, and *c*.
2Co 1. 3 of mercies, and the God of all *c*;
4 that we may be able to *c* them
4 by the *c* wherewith we ourselves
2. 7 to forgive him, and *c* him, lest
7. 4 I am filled with *c*, I am exceeding
13 we were comforted in your *c*:
13.11 Be perfect, be of good *c*, be of
Eph 6.22 and that he might *c* your hearts.
Php 2. 1 if any *c* of love, if any fellowship
19 that I also may be of good *c*,
Col 4. 8 your estate, and *c* your hearts;
11 which have been a *c* unto me.
1Th 3. 2 to *c* you concerning your faith:
4.18 *c* one another with these words.
5.11 *c* yourselves together, and edify
14 *c* the feebleminded, support the
2Th 2.17 *C* your hearts, and stablish you

COMFORTABLY
2Sa 19. 7 speak *c* unto thy servants:
2Ch 30.22 spake *c* unto all the Levites
3.26 spake *c* to them, saying,
Isa 40. 2 Speak ye *c* to Jerusalem,
Hos 2.14 speak *c* unto her.

COMFORTED
Gen 24.67 Isaac was *c* after his mother's
37.35 he refused to be *c*; and he said,
38.12 wife died; and Judah was *c*,
50.21 And he *c* them, and spake kindly
Ru 2.13 for that thou hast *c* me, and for
2Sa 12.24 And David *c* Bath–sheba his wife,
13.39 he was *c* concerning Amnon,
Job 42.11 they bemoaned him, and *c* him
Ps 77. 2 not: my soul refused to be *c*.
86.17 Lord, hast holpen me, and *c* me.

Ps 119.52 of old, O Lord; and have *c* myself.
Isa 49.13 the Lord hath *c* his people, and
52. 9 the Lord hath *c* his people, he
54.11 tossed with tempest, and not *c*,
66.13 ye shall be *c* in Jerusalem.
Jer 31.15 children refused to be *c* for her
Eze 5.13 rest upon them, and I will be *c*:
14.22 and ye shall be *c* concerning
31.16 shall be *c* in the nether parts
32.31 shall be *c* over all his multitude,
Mt 2.18 would not be *c*, because they
5. 4 that mourn: for they shall be *c*.
Lk 16.25 but now he is *c*, and thou art
Jn 11.31 in the house, and *c* her, when
Ac 16.40 the brethren, they *c* them, and
20.12 alive, and were not a little *c*.
Ro 1.12 that I may be *c* together with you.
1Co 14.31 may learn, and all may be *c*.
2Co 1. 4 wherewith we ourselves are *c*
6 or whether we be *c*, it is for your
7. 6 down, *c* us by the coming of Titus;
7 wherewith he was *c* in you,
13 we were *c* in your comfort: yea,
Col 2. 2 That their hearts might be *c*,
1Th 2.11 ye know how we exhorted and *c*
3. 7 we were *c* over you in all our

COMFORTEDST
Isa 12. 1 is turned away, and thou *c* me.

COMFORTER
Ec 4. 1 oppressed, and they had no *c*;
1 was power; but they had no *c*.
La 1. 9 down wonderfully: she had no *c*.
16 the *c* that should relieve my soul
Jn 14.16 and he shall give you another *C*,
26 the *C*, which is the Holy Ghost,
15.26 But when the *C* is come, whom I
16. 7 the *C* will not come unto you; but

COMFORTERS
2Sa 10. 3 that he hath sent *c* unto thee?
1Ch 19. 3 he hath sent *c* unto thee? are not
Job 16. 2 miserable *c* are ye all.
Ps 69.20 none; and for *c*, but I found none,
Na 3. 7 whence shall I seek *c* for thee?

COMFORTETH
Job 29.25 as one that *c* the mourners.
Isa 51.12 I, even I, am he that *c* you:
66.13 As one whom his mother *c*, so will
2Co 1. 4 Who *c* us in all our tribulation,
7. 6 that *c* those that are cast down,

COMFORTLESS
Jn 14.18 I will not leave you *c*: I will

COMING
Gen 24.63 and, behold, the camels were *c*.
30.30 hath blessed thee since my *c*:
Nu 22.16 hinder them from *c* unto me:
33.40 of the *c* of the children of Israel.
Jdg 5.28 Why is his chariot so long in *c*?
1Sa 10. 5 a company of prophets *c* down
16. 4 of the town trembled at his *c*,
22. 4 saw the son of Jesse *c* to Nob,
25.26 withholden thee from *c* to shed
33 me this day from *c* to shed blood,
29. 6 thy going out and thy *c* in with me
6 of thy *c* unto me unto this day:
2Sa 3.25 know thy going out and thy *c* in,
24.20 saw the king and his servants *c*
2Ki 10.15 son of Rechab *c* to meet him:
13.20 invaded the land at the *c* in of the
19.27 and thy going out, and thy *c* in,
2Ch 22. 7 was of God by *c* to Joram: for
Ezr 3. 8 in the second year of their *c* unto
Ps 19. 5 bridegroom *c* out of his chamber,
37.13 for he seeth that his day is *c*.
121. 8 and thy *c* in from this time forth,
Pr 8. 3 city, at the *c* in at the doors.
Isa 14. 9 to meet thee at thy *c*: it stirreth
32.19 When it shall hail, *c* down on
37.28 and thy *c* in, and thy rage against
44. 7 and the things that are *c*, and
Jer 8. 7 swallow observe the time of their *c*:
Dan 4.23 watcher and an holy one *c* down
Mic 7.15 According to the days of thy *c*
Hab 3. 4 he had horns *c* out of his hand:
Mal 3. 2 who may abide the day of his *c*?
4. 5 before the *c* of the great and
Mt 8.28 devils, *c* out of the tombs,
16.28 the Son of man *c* in his kingdom.
24. 3 what shall be the sign of thy *c*,
27 also the *c* of the Son of man be.
30 they shall see the Son of man *c*
37, 39 also the *c* of the Son of man
48 heart, My lord delayeth his *c*;
25.27 at my *c* I should have received
26.64 and *c* in the clouds of heaven.
Mk 1.10 straightway *c* up out of the water,
6.31 for there were many *c* and going,
13.26 see the Son of man *c* in the clouds
36 *c* suddenly he find you sleeping.
14.62 and *c* in the clouds of heaven.
15.21 passed by, *c* out of the country,
Lk 2.38 she *c* in that instant gave thanks
9.42 And as he was yet a *c*, the devil
12.45 My lord delayeth his *c*; and
18. 5 by her continual *c* she weary me.
19.23 at my *c* I might have required
21.26 things which are *c* on the earth:
27 shall they see the Son of man *c*
23.26 a Cyrenian, *c* out of the country.
29 behold, the days are *c*, in the which
36 *c* to him, and offering him
Jn 1.27 *c* after me is preferred before me,
29 John seeth Jesus *c* unto him,
47 Jesus saw Nathanael *c* to him,
5. 7 but while I am *c*, another steppeth
25 The hour is *c*, and now is, when
28 for the hour is *c*, in the which all
10.12 seeth the wolf *c*, and leaveth the
11.20 as she heard that Jesus was *c*,
12.12 that Jesus was *c* to Jerusalem,
Ac 7.52 before of the *c* of the Just One;
9.12 a man named Ananias *c* in,
28 with them *c* in and going out
10. 3 an angel of God *c* in to him,
25 as Peter was *c* in, Cornelius met
13.24 had first preached before his *c*
17.10 Berea: who *c* thither went into
27.33 while the day was *c* on,
Ro 15.22 much hindered from *c* to you.
1Co 1. 7 waiting for the *c* of our Lord
15.23 they that are Christ's at his *c*.
16.17 glad of the *c* of Stephanus and
2Co 7. 6 comforted us by the *c* of Titus;
7 And not by his *c* only, but by the
13. 1 This is the third time I am *c*
Php 1.26 for me by my *c* to you again.
1Th 2.19 our Lord Jesus Christ at his *c*?
3.13 at the *c* of our Lord Jesus Christ
4.15 remain unto the *c* of the Lord
5.23 the *c* of our Lord Jesus Christ.
2Th 2. 1 by the *c* of our Lord Jesus
8 with the brightness of his *c*:
9 him, whose *c* is after the working
Jas 5. 7 brethren, unto the *c* of the Lord.
8 the *c* of the Lord draweth nigh.
1Pe 2. 4 To whom *c*, as unto a living stone,
2Pe 1.16 power and *c* of our Lord Jesus
3. 4 Where is the promise of his *c*?
12 unto the *c* of the day of God,
1Jn 2.28 be ashamed before him at his *c*.
Rev 13.11 beast *c* up out of the earth;
21. 2 new Jerusalem, *c* down from God

COMMAND
Gen 27. 8 according to that which I *c* thee.
Ex 18.23 do this thing, and God *c* thee
Nu 9. 8 the Lord will *c* concerning you.
Dt 4. 2 add unto the word which I *c* you,
40 I *c* thee this day, that it may go
7.11 judgments, which I *c* thee this
8.11 statutes, which I *c* thee this day:
12.32 What thing soever I *c* you,
27. 4 set up these stones, which I *c* you
32.46 shall *c* your children to observe to
Ps 42. 8 Lord will *c* his lovingkindness
Mt 4. 3 *c* that these stones be made bread.
Mk 10. 3 unto them, What did Moses *c* you?
Lk 4. 3 *c* this stone that it be made bread.
9.54 wilt thou that we *c* fire to come
Jn 15.14 if ye do whatsoever I *c* you.
17 These things I *c* you, that ye love
Ac 15. 5 *c* them to keep the law of Moses.
16.18 I *c* thee in the name of Jesus
1Co 7.10 unto the married I *c*, yet not I,
2Th 3. 6 we *c* you, brethren, in the name
1Ti 4.11 These things *c* and teach.

COMMANDED
Gen 2.16 And the Lord God *c* the man,
3.11 the tree, whereof I *c* thee that
6.22 all that God *c* him, so did he.
21. 4 eight days old, as God had *c* him.
Ex 7.10 Aaron did so as the Lord had *c*:
16.16 the Lord hath *c*, Gather of it every
Lev 7.38 the Lord *c* Moses in mount Sinai,
8. 5 thing which the Lord *c* to be done.
Nu 1.19 the Lord *c* Moses, so he numbered
31.31 the priest did as the Lord *c* Moses.
34.13 Lord *c* to give unto the nine tribes,
29 Lord *c* to divide the inheritance
Dt 1.41 all that the Lord our God *c* us.
5.15 the Lord thy God *c* thee to keep
13. 5 the Lord thy God *c* thee to walk
27. 1 *c* the people, saying, Keep all the
31. 5 commandments which I have *c* you.
33. 4 Moses *c* us a law, even the
Jos 4.17 Joshua therefore *c* the priests,
7.11 my covenant which I *c* them: for
8. 8 See, I have *c* you.
11.15 As the Lord *c* Moses his servant,
1Ki 17. 4 I have *c* the ravens to feed thee
9 I have *c* a widow woman there to
1Ch 14.16 David therefore did as God *c* him:
17.10 I *c* judges to be over my people
21.18 Then the angel of the Lord *c* Gad
Ezr 7.23 Whatsoever is *c* by the God
Est 6. 1 he *c* to bring the book of records
Job 38.12 Hast thou *c* the morning since
Ps 33. 9 was done; he *c*, and it stood fast.
68.28 Thy God hath *c* thy strength:
78. 5 he *c* our fathers, that they should
23 Though he had *c* the clouds from
111. 9 he hath *c* his covenant for ever:
148. 5 for he *c*, and they were created.
Jer 17.22 sabbath day, as I *c* your fathers.
35.14 he *c* his sons not to drink wine,
Dan 2. 2 the king *c* to call the magicians,
Am 2.12 *c* the prophets, saying, Prophesy
Zec 1. 6 I *c* my servants the prophets,
Mt 8. 4 offer the gift that Moses *c*, for a
14.19 he *c* the multitude to sit down on
15. 4 For God *c*, saying, Honor thy
35 he *c* the multitude to sit down
18.25 his lord *c* him to be sold, and his
21. 6 went, and did as Jesus *c* them,
27.58 Pilate *c* the body to be delivered.
28.20 whatsoever I have *c* you: and, lo,
Mk 1.44 those things which Moses *c*, for
6.39 he *c* them to make all sit down
8. 6 And he *c* the people to sit down
Lk 5.14 according as Moses *c*, for a
8.55 and he *c* to give her meat.
9.21 and *c* them to tell no man
14.22 it is done as thou hast *c*, and yet
17. 9 he did the things that were *c* him?
10 those things which are *c* you, say,
Jn 8. 5 Now Moses in the law *c* us,
Ac 4.18 and *c* them not to speak at all nor

10.42 he *c* us to preach unto the people,
48 he *c* them to be baptized in the
18. 2 Claudius had *c* all Jews to depart
23.35 he *c* him to be kept in Herod's
24.23 he *c* a centurion to keep Paul,
25.21 *c* him to be kept till I might send
2Co 4. 6 For God, who *c* the light to shine
2Th 3.10 this we *c* you, that if any would

COMMANDER

Isa 55. 4 a leader and *c* to the people.

COMMANDEST

Jos 1.16 All that thou *c* us we will do,
18 thy word in all that thou *c* him,
Ac 23. 3 and *c* me to be smitten contrary

COMMANDETH

Ex 16.32 is the thing which the Lord *c*,
Nu 32.25 Thy servants will do as my lord *c*.
Job 9. 7 Which *c* the sun, and it riseth not;
36.10 *c* that they return from iniquity.
32 and *c* it not to shine by the cloud
37.12 they may do whatsoever he *c*
Ps 107.25 For he *c*, and raiseth the stormy
La 3.37 to pass, when the Lord *c* it not?
Am 6.11 the Lord *c*, and he will smite
Mk 1.27 *c* he even the unclean spirits,
Lk 4.36 power he *c* the unclean spirits
8.25 he *c* even the winds and water,
Ac 17.30 but now *c* all men every where to

COMMANDING

Gen 49.33 Jacob had made an end of *c* his
Mt 11. 1 an end of *c* his twelve disciples,
Ac 24. 8 *C* his accusers to come unto
1Ti 4. 3 *c* to abstain from meats, which

COMMANDMENT

Nu 3.39 numbered at the *c* of the Lord,
9.18 Israel journeyed, and at the *c* of
20 the tabernacle; according to the *c*
23 At the *c* of the Lord they rested
14.41 do ye transgress the *c* of the Lord?
15.31 hath broken his *c*, that soul shall
27.14 ye rebelled against my *c* in the
Dt 17.20 that he turn not aside from the *c*,
Jos 22. 5 But take diligent heed to do the *c*
1Sa 12.14 and not rebel against the *c* of the
15.24 transgressed the *c* of the Lord,
1Ki 13.21 not kept the *c* which the Lord
Ezr 6.14 according to the *c* of the God of
6.14 and according to the *c* of Cyrus,
10. 3 that trembles at the *c* of our God;
Neh 12.24 the *c* of David the man of God,
Est 1.12 refused to come at the king's *c*
3. 3 transgressest thou the king's *c*?
Ps 19. 8 *c* of the Lord is pure, enlightening
119.96 but thy *c* is exceeding broad.
147.15 sendeth forth his *c* upon earth:
Pr 6.20 keep thy father's *c*, and forsake
23 *c* is a lamp; and the law is light;
8.29 the waters should not pass his *c*:
Dan 3.22 because the king's *c* was urgent,
Mal 2. 1 O ye priests, this *c* is for you.
Mt 15. 3 Why do ye also transgress the *c*
6 made the *c* of God of none effect
22.36 which is the great *c* in the law?
38 This is the first and great *c*.
Mk 7. 8 laying aside the *c* of God, ye hold
9 Full well ye reject the *c* of God,
12.28 Which is the first *c* of all?
30 strength: this is the first *c*.
31 there is none other *c* greater than
Lk 15.29 transgressed I at any time thy *c*:
23.56 the sabbath day according to the *c*.
Jn 10.18 This *c* have I received of my
13.34 A new *c* I give unto you, that ye
14.31 as the Father gave me *c*, even so
15.12 This is my *c*, That ye love
Ac 25.23 at Festus' *c* Paul was brought

Ro 7. 8 taking occasion by the *c*, wrought
9 but when the *c* came, sin revived
10 And the *c*, which was ordained
11 taking occasion by the *c*, deceived
12 the *c* holy, and just, and good.
13 that sin by the *c* might appear
13. 9 and if there be any other *c*,
16.26 the *c* of the everlasting God,
1Co 7.25 I have no *c* of the Lord: yet I give
2Co 8. 8 I speak not by *c*, but by occasion
Eph 6. 2 which is the first *c* with promise;
1Ti 1. 1 by the *c* of God our Saviour,
5 Now the end of the *c* is charity
6.14 That thou keep this *c* without
Tit 1. 3 according to the *c* of God our
Heb 7.18 disannulling of the *c* going before
1Jn 2. 7 I write no new *c* unto you,
7 but an old *c* which ye had from the
7 The old *c* is the word which ye
8 Again, a new *c* I write unto you,
3.23 And this is his *c*, That we should
23 love one another, as he gave us *c*.
4.21 And this *c* have we from him, That
2Jn 4 have received a *c* from the Father.
5 though I wrote a new *c* unto thee,
6 This is the *c*, That, as ye have

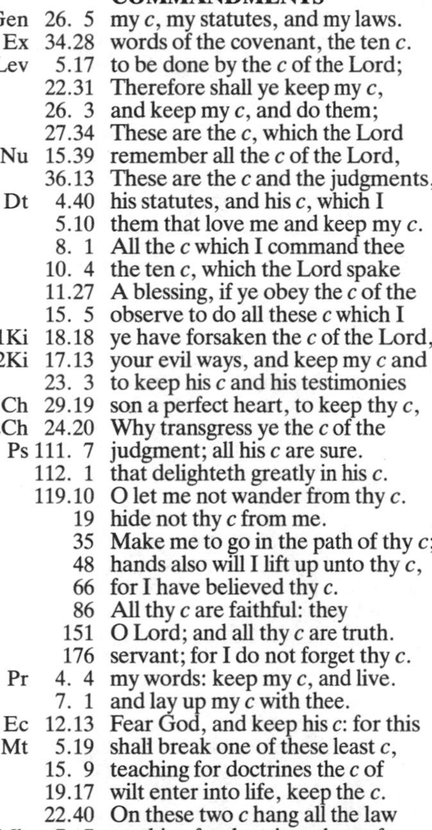

COMMANDMENTS

Gen 26. 5 my *c*, my statutes, and my laws.
Ex 34.28 words of the covenant, the ten *c*.
Lev 5.17 to be done by the *c* of the Lord;
22.31 Therefore shall ye keep my *c*,
26. 3 and keep my *c*, and do them;
27.34 These are the *c*, which the Lord
Nu 15.39 remember all the *c* of the Lord,
36.13 These are the *c* and the judgments,
Dt 4.40 his statutes, and his *c*, which I
5.10 them that love me and keep my *c*.
8. 1 All the *c* which I command thee
10. 4 the ten *c*, which the Lord spake
11.27 A blessing, if ye obey the *c* of the
15. 5 observe to do all these *c* which I
1Ki 18.18 ye have forsaken the *c* of the Lord,
2Ki 17.13 your evil ways, and keep my *c* and
23. 3 to keep his *c* and his testimonies
1Ch 29.19 son a perfect heart, to keep thy *c*,
2Ch 24.20 Why transgress ye the *c* of the
Ps 111. 7 judgment; all his *c* are sure.
112. 1 that delighteth greatly in his *c*.
119.10 O let me not wander from thy *c*.
19 hide not thy *c* from me.
35 Make me to go in the path of thy *c*;
48 hands also will I lift up unto thy *c*,
66 for I have believed thy *c*.
86 All thy *c* are faithful: they
151 O Lord; and all thy *c* are truth.
176 servant; for I do not forget thy *c*.
Pr 4. 4 my words: keep my *c*, and live.
7. 1 and lay up my *c* with thee.
Ec 12.13 Fear God, and keep his *c*: for this
Mt 5.19 shall break one of these least *c*,
15. 9 teaching for doctrines the *c* of
19.17 wilt enter into life, keep the *c*.
22.40 On these two *c* hang all the law
Mk 7. 7 teaching for doctrines the *c* of
10.19 Thou knowest the *c*, Do not kill,
12.29 of all the *c* is, Hear, O Israel;
Lk 1. 6 in all the *c* and ordinances of the
18.20 Thou knowest the *c*, Do not commit
Jn 14.15 If ye love me, keep my *c*.
21 He that hath my *c*, and keepeth
15.10 If ye keep my *c*, ye shall abide in
10 kept my Father's *c*, and abide in
Eph 2.15 law of *c* contained in ordinances;
Col 2.22 after the *c* and doctrines of men?
4.10 touching whom ye received *c*:
Tit 1.14 Jewish fables, and *c* of men,
1Jn 2. 3 that we know him, if we keep his *c*.
4 and keepeth not his *c*, is a liar,
3.22 because we keep his *c*, and do those
24 he that keepeth his *c* dwelleth in

Moses with the Commandments *by Gustave Doré*

5. 2 when we love God, and keep his *c*.
3 love of God, that we keep his *c*:
3 and his *c* are not grievous.
2Jn 6 this is love, that we walk after his *c*.
Rev 12.17 her seed, which keep the *c* of God,
14.12 here are that keep the *c* of God,
22.14 Blessed are they that do his *c*,

COMMEND

Lk 23.46 into thy hands I *c* my spirit:
Ac 20.32 brethren, I *c* you to God, and to
Ro 3. 5 But if our unrighteousness *c* the
16. 1 I *c* unto you Phebe our sister,
2Co 3. 1 Do we begin again to *c* ourselves?
5.12 *c* not ourselves again unto you,
10.12 with some that *c* themselves:

COMMENDATION

2Co 3. 1 some others, epistles of *c* to you,
1 or letters of *c* from you?

COMMENDED

Gen 12.15 her, and *c* her before Pharaoh:
Pr 12. 8 be *c* according to his wisdom:
Ec 8.15 Then I *c* mirth, because a man
Lk 16. 8 the lord *c* the unjust steward,
Ac 14.23 they *c* them to the Lord, on whom
2Co 12.11 I ought to have been *c* of you:

COMMENDETH

Ro 5. 8 But God *c* his love towards us,
1Co 8. 8 But meat *c* us not to God:
2Co 10.18 not he that *c* himself is approved,
18 but whom the Lord *c*.

COMMENDING

2Co 4. 2 truth *c* ourselves to every man's

COMMISSION

Ac 26.12 with authority and *c* from the

COMMIT

Ex 20.14 Thou shalt not *c* adultery.
Lev 5.15 If a soul *c* a trespass, and sin
17 and *c* any of these things which
6. 2 If a soul sin, and *c* a trespass

Lev 18.26 and shall not *c* any of these
29 whosoever shall *c* any of these
29 the souls that *c* them shall be
30 that ye *c* not any one of these
20. 5 to *c* whoredom with Molech,
Nu 5. 6 When a man or woman shall *c*
6 any sin that men *c*, to do a
12 and *c* a trespass against him,
25. 1 the people began to *c* whoredom
31.26 to *c* trespass against the Lord
Dt 5.18 Neither shalt thou *c* adultery.
19.20 *c* no more any such evil among
Jos 22.20 the son of Zerah *c* a trespass
2Sa 7.14 If he *c* iniquity, I will chasten
2Ch 21.11 of Jerusalem to *c* fornication,
Job 5. 8 unto God would I *c* my cause:
34.10 from the Almighty, that he should *c*
Ps 31. 5 Into thine hand I *c* my spirit:
37. 5 *C* thy way unto the Lord; trust
Pr 16. 3 *C* thy works unto the Lord,
12 to kings to *c* wickedness: for the
Isa 22.21 *c* thy government into his hand:
23.17 and shall *c* fornication with
Jer 7. 9 ye steal, murder, and *c* adultery,
9. 5 weary themselves to *c* iniquity.
23.14 they *c* adultery, and walk in lies:
37.21 should *c* Jeremiah into the court
44. 7 Wherefore *c* ye this great evil
Eze 3.20 his righteousness, and *c* iniquity,
8.17 that they *c* the abominations
17 which they *c* here?
16.17 didst *c* whoredom with them,
34 followeth thee to *c* whoredoms:
43 thou shalt not *c* this lewdness
20.30 and *c* ye whoredom after their
22. 9 midst of thee they *c* lewdness.
23.43 Will they now *c* whoredoms with
33.13 and *c* iniquity, all his
Hos 4.10 they shall *c* whoredom, and
13 daughters shall *c* whoredom,
13 your spouses shall *c* adultery.
14 when they *c* whoredom, nor your
14 spouses when they *c* adultery:
6. 9 consent: for they *c* lewdness.
7. 1 they *c* falsehood; and the thief
Mt 5.27 Thou shalt not *c* adultery:
32 causeth her to *c* adultery:
19. 9 which is put away doth *c* adultery.
18 Thou shalt not *c* adultery,
Mk 10.19 Do not *c* adultery,
Lk 12.48 did *c* things worthy of stripes,
16.11 *c* to your trust the true riches?
18.20 Do not *c* adultery,
Jn 2.24 Jesus did not *c* himself unto
Ro 1.32 which *c* such things are worthy
2. 2 them which *c* such things.
22 a man should not *c* adultery,
22 dost thou *c* adultery?
22 idols, dost thou *c* sacrilege?
13. 9 Thou shalt not *c* adultery,
1Co 10. 8 Neither let us *c* fornication,
1Ti 1.18 This charge I *c* unto thee,
2Ti 2. 2 the same *c* thou to faithful men,
Jas 2. 9 ye *c* sin, and are convinced of the
11 that said, Do not *c* adultery,
11 Now if thou *c* no adultery,
1Pe 4.19 *c* the keeping of their souls to
1Jn 3. 9 is born of God doth not *c* sin;
Rev 2.14 unto idols, and to *c* fornication.
20 to *c* fornication, and to eat things

COMMITTED

Gen 39. 8 he hath *c* all that he hath to my
22 of the prison *c* to Joseph's hand
Lev 4.35 for his sin that he hath *c*, it
5. 7 his trespass, which he hath *c*,
18.30 which were *c* before you,
20.13 of them have *c* an abomination:
23 for they *c* all these things, and
Nu 15.24 be *c* by ignorance without the
Dt 17. 5 or that woman, which have *c*
21.22 man have *c* a sin worthy of death,
Jos 7. 1 children of Israel *c* a trespass
22.16 that ye have *c* against the God
31 *c* this trespass against the Lord:
Jdg 20. 6 *c* lewdness and folly in Israel.
1Ki 8.47 we have *c* wickedness;
14.22 with their sins which they had *c*,
27 and *c* them unto the hands of the
1Ch 10.13 for his transgression which he *c*
2Ch 12.10 shields of brass, and *c* them
34.16 All that was *c* to thy servants,
Ps 106. 6 we have *c* iniquity, we have done
Jer 2.13 For my people have *c* two evils;
3. 8 backsliding Israel *c* adultery
9 and *c* adultery with stones and
5. 7 then *c* adultery, and assembled
30 horrible thing is *c* in the land;
6.15 when they had *c* abomination?
8.12 they had *c* abomination? nay,
16.10 that we have *c* against the Lord
29.23 they have *c* villany in Israel, and
39.14 and *c* him unto Gedaliah the son
40. 7 *c* unto him men, and women,
41.10 of the guard had *c* to Gedaliah
44. 3 wickedness which they have *c* to
9 which they have *c* in the land
22 abominations which ye have *c*;
Eze 6. 9 the evils which they have *c* in all
15. 8 have *c* a trespass, saith the Lord
16.26 *c* fornication with the Egyptians
50 and *c* abomination before me:
51 hath Samaria *c* half of thy sins;
52 *c* more abominable than they:
18.12 to the idols, hath *c* abomination,
21 from all his sins that he hath *c*,
22 his transgressions that he hath *c*,
27 his wickedness that he hath *c*,
28 his transgressions that he hath *c*,
20.27 have *c* a trespass against me.
43 for all your evils that ye have *c*.
22.11 And one hath *c* abomination with
23. 3 they *c* whoredoms in Egypt;
3 *c* whoredoms in their youth:
7 she *c* her whoredoms with them,
37 they have *c* adultery, and blood
37 their idols have they *c* adultery,
33.13 for his iniquity that he hath *c*,
16 None of his sins that he hath *c*
29 abominations which they have *c*.
43. 8 abominations that they have *c*:
44.13 abominations which they have *c*.
Dan 9. 5 sinned, and have *c* iniquity,
Hos 1. 2 land hath *c* great whoredom,
4.18 have *c* whoredom continually:
Mal 2.11 an abomination is *c* in Israel
Mt 5.28 hath *c* adultery with her already
Mk 15. 7 *c* murder in the insurrection.
Lk 12.48 to whom men have *c* much, of
Jn 5.22 *c* all judgment unto the Son:
Ac 8. 3 men and women *c* them to prison.
25.11 or have *c* any thing worthy of
25 he had *c* nothing worthy of death,
27.40 they *c* themselves unto the sea,
28.17 *c* nothing against the people,
Ro 3. 2 them were *c* the oracles of God.
1Co 9.17 a dispensation of the gospel is *c*
10. 8 fornication, as some of them *c*,
2Co 5.19 and hath *c* unto us the word of
11. 7 I *c* an offense in abasing myself
12.21 lasciviousness which they have *c*,
Gal 2. 7 uncircumcision was *c* unto me,
1Ti 1.11 which was *c* to my trust.
6.20 keep that which is *c* to thy trust,
2Ti 1.12 able to keep that which I have *c*
14 That good thing which was *c* unto
Tit 1. 3 preaching, which is *c* unto me
Jas 5.15 if he have *c* sins, they shall be
1Pe 2.23 but *c* himself to him that judgeth
Jude 15 deeds which they have ungodly *c*,
Rev 17. 2 of the earth have *c* fornication,
18. 3 have *c* fornication with her, and
9 who have *c* fornication and lived

COMMITTETH

Lev 20.10 man that *c* adultery with another
10 *c* adultery with his neighbor's
Ps 10.14 the poor *c* himself unto thee;
Pr 6.32 whoso *c* adultery with a woman
Eze 8. 6 that the house of Israel *c* here,
16.32 But as a wife that *c* adultery,
18.24 *c* iniquity, and doeth according
26 and *c* iniquity, and dieth in them;
33.18 and *c* iniquity, he shall even die
Mt 5.32 her that is divorced *c* adultery.
19. 9 marry another, *c* adultery: and
Mk 10.11 another, *c* adultery against her.
12 married to another, she *c* adultery.
Lk 16.18 marrieth another *c* adultery:
18 away from her husband *c* adultery.
Jn 8.34 *c* sin is the servant of sin.
1Co 6.18 but he that *c* fornication sinneth
1Jn 3. 4 Whosoever *c* sin transgresseth
8 He that *c* sin is of the devil; for

COMMITTING

Eze 33.15 without *c* iniquity; he shall
Hos 4. 2 stealing, and *c* adultery, they

COMMODIOUS

Ac 27.12 the haven was not *c* to winter in,

COMMON

Lev 4.27 *c* people sin through ignorance,
Nu 16.29 If these men die the *c* death of
1Sa 21. 4 is no *c* bread under mine hand,
5 and the bread is in a manner *c*,
Ec 6. 1 and it is *c* among men:
Jer 26.23 into the graves of the *c* people.
31. 5 and shall eat them as *c* things.
Eze 23.42 men of the *c* sort were brought
Mt 27.27 took Jesus into the *c* hall, and
Mk 12.37 the *c* people heard him gladly.
Ac 2.44 and had all things *c*;
4.32 but they had all things *c*.
5.18 put them in the *c* prison.
10.14 any thing that is *c* or unclean.
15 cleansed, that call not thou *c*.
28 not call any man *c* or unclean.
11. 8 for nothing *c* or unclean hath at
9 cleansed, that call not thou *c*.
1Co 10.13 you but such as is *c* to man:
Tit 1. 4 mine own son after the *c* faith:
Jude 3 write unto you of the *c* salvation,

COMMONLY

Mt 28.15 is *c* reported among the Jews
1Co 5. 1 It is reported *c* that there is

COMMONWEALTH

Eph 2.12 being aliens from the *c* of Israel,

COMMOTIONS

Lk 21. 9 ye shall hear of wars and *c*,

COMMUNED

Gen 23. 8 And he *c* with them, saying, If it
34. 8 And Hamor *c* with them, saying,
20 and *c* with the men of their city,
42.24 and *c* with them, and took from
43.19 and they *c* with him at the door
Jdg 9. 1 and *c* with them, and with all
1Sa 9.25 Samuel *c* with Saul upon the top
25.39 David sent and *c* with Abigail,
1Ki 10. 2 she was come to Solomon, she *c*
2Ki 22.14 and they *c* with her.
2Ch 9. 1 she was come to Solomon, she *c*
Ec 1.16 I *c* with mine own heart, saying,
Dan 1.19 And the king *c* with them; and
Zec 1.14 that *c* with me said unto me,
Lk 6.11 *c* one with another what they
22. 4 and *c* with the chief priests and

24.15 they *c* together and reasoned,
Ac 24.26 him the oftener, and *c* with him.

COMMUNICATE
Gal 6. 6 *c* unto him that teacheth in all
Php 4.14 that ye did *c* with my affliction.
1Ti 6.18 ready to distribute, willing to *c*;
Heb 13.16 to do good and to *c* forget not:

COMMUNICATED
Gal 2. 2 *c* unto them that gospel which I
Php 4.15 church *c* with me as concerning

COMMUNICATION
2Sa 3.17 And Abner had *c* with the elders
2Ki 9.11 Ye know the man, and his *c*.
Mt 5.37 your *c* be, Yea, yea; Nay, nay:
Eph 4.29 Let no corrupt *c* proceed out of
Col 3. 8 filthy *c* out of your mouth.
Phm 6 The *c* of thy faith may become

COMMUNICATIONS
Lk 24.17 What manner of *c* are these that
1Co 15.33 evil *c* corrupt good manners.

COMMUNION
1Co 10.16 not the *c* of the blood of Christ?
16 it not the *c* of the body of Christ?
2Co 6.14 what *c* hath light with darkness?
13.14 the *c* of the Holy Ghost, be with

COMPACT
Ps 122. 3 as a city that is *c* together:

COMPACTED
Eph 4.16 and *c* by that which every joint

COMPANIED
Ac 1.21 these men which have *c* with us

COMPANIES
Jdg 7.16 three hundred men into three *c*,
20 the three *c* blew the trumpets,
9.34 wait against Shechem in four *c*.
43 divided them into three *c*, and
44 other *c* ran upon all the people
1Sa 11.11 Saul put the people in three *c*;
13.17 camp of the Philistines in three *c*:
2Ki 5. 2 the Syrians had gone out by *c*,
1Ch 9.18 they were porters in the *c* of the
28. 1 *c* that ministered to the king by
Neh 12.31 two great *c* of them that gave thanks,
40 So stood the two *c* of them that gave
Job 6.19 the *c* of Sheba waited for them.
Isa 21.13 O ye travelling *c* of Dedanim.
57.13 criest, let thy *c* deliver thee;
Eze 26. 7 with horsemen, and *c*, and much
Mk 6.39 sat down by *c* upon the green

COMPANION
Ex 32.27 brother, and every man his *c*,
Jdg 14.20 Samson's wife was given to his *c*,
15. 2 I gave her to thy *c*: is not her
6 his wife, and given her to his *c*.
1Ch 27.33 the Archite was the king's *c*:
Job 30.29 brother to dragons, and a *c* to owls
Ps 119.63 am a *c* of all them that fear thee,
Pr 13.20 but a *c* of fools shall be destroyed.
28. 7 but he that is a *c* of riotous men
24 the same is the *c* of a destroyer.
Mal 2.14 yet is she thy *c*, and the wife of
Php 2.25 my brother, and *c* in labor,
Rev 1. 9 and *c* in tribulation, and in the

COMPANIONS
Jdg 11.38 she went with her *c*, and bewailed
14.11 they brought thirty *c* to be with
Ezr 4. 7 Tabeel, and the rest of their *c*,
9 the rest of their *c*; the Dinaites,
17 the rest of their *c* that dwell in
23 Shimshai the scribe, and their *c*,
5. 3 Shethar–boznai, and their *c*, and
6 Shethar–boznai, and his *c* the
6. 6 Shethar–boznai, and your *c* the
13 Shethar–boznai, and their *c*,
Job 35. 4 will answer thee, and thy *c* with
41. 6 Shall the *c* make a banquet of
Ps 45.14 the virgins her *c* that follow her
SS 1. 7 aside by the flocks of thy *c*?
8.13 the *c* hearken to thy voice:
Isa 1.23 are rebellious, and *c* of thieves:
Eze 37.16 and for the children of Israel his *c*:
16 for all the house of Israel his *c*:
Dan 2.17 Mishael, and Azariah, his *c*:
Ac 19.29 of Macedonia, Paul's *c* in travel,
Heb 10.33 ye became *c* of them that were so

COMPANIONS'
Ps 122. 8 For my brethren and *c* sakes,

COMPANY
Gen 32. 8 If Esau come to the one *c*,
8 then the other *c* which is left
21 himself lodged that night in the *c*.
35.11 a *c* of nations shall be of thee,
37.25 a *c* of Ishmeelites came from
50. 9 and it was a very great *c*.
Nu 14. 7 they spake unto all the *c* of the
16. 5 unto all his *c*, saying, Even
6 you censers, Korah, and all his *c*;
11 thou and all thy *c* are gathered
16 and all thy *c* before the Lord.
40 he be not as Korah, and as his *c*:
22. 4 Now shall this *c* lick up all that
26. 9 in the *c* of Korah, when they
10 when that *c* died, what time the
27. 3 in the *c* of them that gathered
3 against the Lord in the *c* of Korah;
Jdg 9.37 and another *c* come along by the
44 Abimelech, and the *c* that was
18.23 that thou comest with such a *c*?
1Sa 10. 5 thou shalt meet a *c* of prophets
10 behold, a *c* of prophets met him;
13.17 one *c* turned unto the way that
18 And another *c* turned the way to
18 Beth–horon: and another *c* turned
19.20 they saw the *c* of the prophets
30.15 thou bring me down to this *c*?
15 I will bring thee down to this *c*.
23 the *c* that came against us into
2Ki 5.15 he and all his *c*, and came,
9.17 he spied the *c* of Jehu as he came,
17 and said, I see a *c*. And Joram
2Ch 9. 1 with a very great *c*, and camels
20.12 have no might against this great *c*
24.24 Syrians came with a small *c* of
Neh 12.38 And the other *c* of them that
Job 16. 7 thou hast made desolate all my *c*.
34. 8 Which goeth in *c* with the
Ps 55.14 unto the house of God in *c*.
68.11 great was the *c* of those that
30 Rebuke the *c* of spearmen, the
106.17 and covered the *c* of Abiram.
18 And a fire was kindled in their *c*;
Pr 29. 3 he that keepeth *c* with harlots
SS 1. 9 *c* of horses in Pharaoh's chariots.
6.13 As it were the *c* of two armies.
Jer 31. 8 a great *c* shall return thither.
Eze 16.40 They shall also bring up a *c*
17.17 with his mighty army and great *c*
23.46 I will bring up a *c* upon them,
47 And the *c* shall stone them with
27. 6 the *c* of the Ashurites have made
27 in all thy *c* which is in the midst
34 all thy *c* in the midst of thee shall
32. 3 my net over thee with a *c* of many
22 Asshur is there and all her *c*: his
23 and her *c* is round about her
38. 4 great *c* with bucklers and shields,
7 all thy *c* that are assembled unto
13 hast thou gathered thy *c* to take a
15 horses, a great *c*, and a mighty
Hos 6. 9 *c* of priests murder in the way
Lk 2.44 him to have been in the *c*, went
5.29 *c* of publicans and of others that
6.17 and the *c* of his disciples, and a
22 shall separate you from their *c*,
9.14 them sit down by fifties in a *c*.
38 a man of the *c* cried out, saying,
11.27 certain woman of the *c* lifted up
12.13 And one of the *c* said unto him,
23.27 great *c* of people, and of women,
24.22 certain women also of our *c* made us
Jn 6. 5 saw a great *c* come unto him,
Ac 4.23 go, they went to their own *c*,
6. 7 and a great *c* of the priests were
10.28 is a Jew to keep *c*, or come unto
13.13 when Paul and his *c* loosed
15.22 chosen men of their own *c*
17. 5 gathered a *c*, and set all the city
21. 8 day we that were of Paul's *c*
Ro 15.24 somewhat filled with your *c*.
1Co 5. 9 epistle not to *c* with fornicators:
11 written unto you not to keep *c*,
2Th 3.14 that man, and have no *c* with him,
Heb 12.22 to an innumerable *c* of angels,
Rev 18.17 all the *c* in ships, and sailors,

COMPARE
Isa 40.18 what likeness will ye *c* unto him?
46. 5 and *c* me, that we may be like?
Mk 4.30 what comparison shall we *c* it?
2Co 10.12 or *c* ourselves with some that

COMPARED
Ps 89. 6 who in the heaven can be *c* unto
Pr 3.15 thou canst desire are not to be *c*
8.11 may be desired are not to be *c* to
SS 1. 9 I have *c* thee, O my love, to a
Ro 8.18 not worthy to be *c* with the glory

COMPARING
1Co 2.13 *c* spiritual things with spiritual.
2Co 10.12 *c* themselves among themselves,

COMPARISON
Jdg 8. 2 have I done now in *c* of you?
3 what was I able to do in *c* of you?
Hag 2. 3 is it not in your eyes in *c* of it as
Mk 4.30 or with what *c* shall we compare

COMPASSION
Ex 2. 6 And she had *c* on him, and said,
Dt 13.17 thee mercy, and have *c* upon thee,
30. 3 captivity, and have *c* upon thee,
1Sa 23.21 of the Lord: for ye have *c* on me.
1Ki 8.50 *c* before them who carried them
50 that they may have *c* on them:
2Ki 13.23 had *c* on them, and had respect
2Ch 30. 9 children shall find *c* before them
36.15 because he had *c* on his people,
17 had no *c* on young man or maiden,
Ps 78.38 he, being full of *c*, forgave their
86.15 a God full of *c*, and gracious,
111. 4 Lord is gracious and full of *c*.
112. 4 and full of *c*, and righteous,
145. 8 Lord is gracious, and full of *c*;
Isa 49.15 she should not have *c* on the son
Jer 12.15 I will return, and have *c* on them,
La 3.32 will he have *c* according to the
Eze 16. 5 to have *c* upon thee; but thou
Mic 7.19 he will have *c* upon us; he will
Mt 9.36 he was moved with *c* on them,
14.14 was moved with *c* toward them,
15.32 I have *c* on the multitude, because
18.27 was moved with *c*, and loosed him,
33 have had *c* on thy fellow servant,
20.34 Jesus had *c* on them, and touched
Mk 1.41 Jesus, moved with *c*, put forth
5.19 for thee, and hath had *c* on thee.
6.34 was moved with *c* toward them,
8. 2 I have *c* on the multitude, because
9.22 have *c* on us, and help us.

Biblical Themes

COMPASSION

The Lord was with Joseph, and shewed him mercy, and gave him favor in the sight of the keeper of the prison. Gen 39.21

When she saw the ark among the flags, she sent her maid to fetch it. And when she had opened it, she saw the child: and, behold, the babe wept. And she had compassion on him, and said, This is one of the Hebrews' children. Ex 2.5-6

I . . . will be gracious to whom I will be gracious, and will shew mercy on whom I will shew mercy. Ex 33.19

Have pity upon me, have pity upon me, O ye my friends; for the hand of God hath touched me. Job 19.21

Reproach hath broken my heart; and I am full of heaviness: and I looked for some to take pity, but there was none; and for comforters, but I found none. Ps 69.20

Like as a father pitieth his children, so the Lord pitieth them that fear him. For he knoweth our frame; he remembereth that we are dust. Ps 103.13-14

Praise ye the Lord. O give thanks unto the Lord; for he is good: for his mercy endureth for ever. Ps 106.1

A righteous man regardeth the life of his beast: but the tender mercies of the wicked are cruel. Pr 12.10

He that hath pity upon the poor lendeth unto the Lord; and that which he hath given will he pay him again. Pr 19.17

Should not I spare Nineveh, that great city, wherein are more than sixscore thousand persons that cannot discern between their right hand and their left hand . . . ? Jon 4.11

He hath shewed thee, O man, what is good; and what doth the Lord require of thee, but to do justly, and to love mercy, and to walk humbly with thy God? Mic 6.8

Blessed are the merciful: for they shall obtain mercy. Mt 5.7

And whosoever shall give to drink unto one of these little ones a cup of cold water . . . verily I say unto you, he shall in no wise lose his reward. Mt 10.42

And Jesus, when he came out, saw much people, and was moved with compassion toward them, because they were as sheep not having a shepherd: and he began to teach them many things. Mk 6.34

And by chance there came down a certain priest that way: and when he saw him, he passed by on the other side. And likewise a Levite, when he was at the place, came and looked on him, and passed by on the other side. But a certain Samaritan, as he journeyed, came where he was: and when he saw him, he had compassion on him, and went to him, and bound up his wounds, pouring in oil and wine, and set him on his own beast, and brought him to an inn, and took care of him. Lk 10.31-34

God, who is rich in mercy, for his great love wherewith he loved us, even when we were dead in sins, hath quickened us together with Christ, (by grace ye are saved;) and hath raised us up together, and made us sit together in heavenly places in Christ Jesus: That in the ages to come he might shew the exceeding riches of his grace in his kindness toward us through Christ Jesus. Eph 2.4-7

He shall have judgment without mercy, that hath shewed no mercy. Jas 2.13

Lk 7.13 he had *c* on her, and said unto her,
10.33 when he saw him, he had *c* on him,
15.20 his father saw him, and had *c*,
Ro 9.15 will have *c* on whom I will have *c*.
Heb 5. 2 Who can have *c* on the ignorant,
10.34 For ye had *c* of me in my bonds,
1Pe 3. 8 having *c* one of another, love
1Jn 3.17 shutteth up his bowels of *c* from him,
Jude 22 have *c*, making a difference:

COMPASSIONS

La 3.22 consumed, because his *c* fail not.
Zec 7. 9 shew mercy and *c* every man to

COMPEL

Lev 25.39 thou shalt not *c* him to serve as
Est 1. 8 none did *c*: for so the king had
Mt 5.41 shall *c* thee to go a mile, go with
Mk 15.21 they *c* one Simon a Cyrenian, who
Lk 14.23 *c* them to come in, that my house

COMPELLED

1Sa 28.23 together with the woman, *c* him;
2Ch 21.11 fornication, and *c* Judah thereto.
Mt 27.32 him they *c* to bear his cross.
Ac 26.11 and *c* them to blaspheme; and
2Co 12.11 a fool in glorying; ye have *c* me:
Gal 2. 3 a Greek, was *c* to be circumcised:

COMPELLEST

Gal 2.14 why *c* thou the Gentiles to live

COMPLAIN

Jdg 21.22 come unto us to *c*, that we will say
Job 7.11 *c* in the bitterness of my soul.
31.38 the furrows likewise thereof *c*;
La 3.39 Wherefore doth a living man *c*,

COMPLAINED

Nu 11. 1 when the people *c*, it displeased
Ps 77. 3 I *c*, and my spirit was

COMPLAINERS

Jude 16 are murmurers, *c*, walking after

COMPLAINING

Ps 144.14 that there be no *c* in our streets.

COMPLAINTS

Ac 25. 7 and grievous *c* against Paul,

COMPLETE

Lev 23.15 seven sabbaths shall be *c*:
Col 2.10 are *c* in him, which is the head
4.12 perfect and *c* in all the will of God.

COMPREHEND

Job 37. 5 doeth he, which we cannot *c*.
Eph 3.18 able to *c* with all saints what is

COMPREHENDED

Isa 40.12 and *c* the dust of the earth in a
Jn 1. 5 and the darkness *c* it not.
Ro 13. 9 it is briefly *c* in this saying,

CONCEIT

Pr 18.11 and as an high wall in his own *c*.
26. 5 lest he be wise in his own *c*.
12 thou a man wise in his own *c*?
16 The sluggard is wiser in his own *c*

CONCEITS

Ro 11.25 be wise in your own *c*;
12.16 Be not wise in your own *c*.

CONCEIVE

Gen 30.38 should *c* when they came to drink.
41 cattle did *c*, that Jacob laid
41 that they might *c* among the rods.
Nu 5.28 shall be free, and shall *c* seed.
Jdg 13. 3 but thou shalt *c*, and bear a son.
5 lo, thou shalt *c*, and bear a son;
7 thou shalt *c*, and bear a son;
Job 15.35 They *c* mischief, and bring forth
Ps 51. 5 and in sin did my mother *c* me.
Isa 7.14 a virgin shall *c*, and bear a son,
33.11 shall *c* chaff, ye shall bring forth
59. 4 *c* mischief, and bring forth iniquity.
Lk 1.31 thou shalt *c* in thy womb, and
Heb 11.11 received strength to *c* seed,

CONCEIVED

Gen 4. 1 and she *c*, and bare Cain, and
17 and she *c*, and bare Enoch: and
16. 4 went in unto Hagar, and she *c*:
4 when she saw that she had *c*, her
5 when she saw that she had *c*, I
21. 2 Sarah *c*, and bare Abraham a son
25.21 and Rebekah his wife *c*.
29.32 And Leah *c*, and bare a son,
33, 34 she *c* again, and bare a son;
35 And she *c* again, and bare a son:
30. 5 Bilhah *c*, and bare Jacob a son.
7 And Bilhah Rachel's maid *c* again,
17 she *c* and bare Jacob the fifth son.
19 And Leah *c* again, and bare Jacob
23 And she *c*, and bare a son:
39 And the flocks *c* before the rods,
31.10 pass at the time that the cattle *c*,
38. 3 And she *c*, and bare a son;
4 and she *c* again, and bare a son;
5 And she yet again *c*, and bare
18 in unto her, and she *c* by him.

Ex 2. 2 the woman *c*, and bare a son:
Lev 12. 2 If a woman have *c* seed, and
Nu 11.12 Have I *c* all this people? have I
1Sa 1.20 after Hannah had *c*, that she bare
1Sa 2.21 that she *c*, and bare three sons
2Sa 11. 5 And the woman *c*, and sent and
2Ki 4.17 And the woman *c*, and bare a son
1Ch 7.23 she *c*, and bare a son, and he
Job 3. 3 was said, There is a man child *c*.
Ps 7.14 and hath *c* mischief, and brought
SS 3. 4 into the chamber of her that *c* me.
Isa 8. 3 and she *c*, and bare a son.
Jer 49.30 hath *c* a purpose against you.
Hos 1. 3 which *c*, and bare him a son.
6 she *c* again, and bare a daughter.
8 Loruhamah, she *c*, and bare a son.
2. 5 harlot: she that *c* them hath done
Mt 1.20 that which is *c* in her is of the
Lk 1.24 his wife Elisabeth *c*, and hid
36 hath also *c* a son in her old age:
2.21 before he was *c* in the womb.
Ac 5. 4 why hast thou *c* this thing in
Ro 9.10 when Rebecca also had *c*
Jas 1.15 Then when lust hath *c*, it bringeth

CONCEPTION
Gen 3.16 multiply thy sorrow and thy *c*;
Ru 4.13 the Lord gave her *c*, and she bare
Hos 9.11 from the womb, and from the *c*.

CONCERN
Ac 28.31 things which *c* the Lord Jesus
2Co 11.30 glory of the things which *c* mine

CONCISION
Php 3. 2 of evil workers, beware of the *c*.

CONCLUDE
Ro 3.28 Therefore we *c* that a man is

CONCLUDED
Ac 21.25 we have written and *c* that they
Ro 11.32 For God hath *c* them all in
Gal 3.22 the scripture hath *c* all under

CONCLUSION
Ec 12.13 Let us hear the *c* of the whole

CONCORD
2Co 6.15 And what *c* hath Christ with

CONCOURSE
Pr 1.21 She crieth in the chief place of *c*,
Ac 19.40 we may give an account of this *c*.

CONCUPISCENCE
Ro 7. 8 wrought in me all manner of *c*.
Col 3. 5 evil *c*, and covetousness, which
1Th 4. 5 Not in the lust of *c*, even as the

CONDEMN
Ex 22. 9 whom the judges shall *c*, he shall
Dt 25. 1 the righteous, and *c* the wicked.
Job 9.20 mine own mouth shall *c* me:
10. 2 Do not *c* me; shew me wherefore
34.17 wilt thou *c* him that is most just?
40. 8 wilt thou *c* me, that thou mayest
Ps 37.33 in his hand, nor *c* him when he is
94.21 the righteous, and *c* the innocent
109.31 him from those that *c* his soul.
Pr 12. 2 a man of wicked devices will he *c*.
Isa 50. 9 who is he that shall *c* me? lo, they
54.17 in judgment thou shalt *c*. This is
Mt 12.41 and shall *c* it: because they
42 and shall *c* it: for she came from
20.18 they shall *c* him to death,
Mk 10.33 they shall *c* him to death, and shall
Lk 6.37 *c* not, and ye shall not be
11.31 of this generation, and *c* them:
32 with this generation, and shall *c* it
Jn 3.17 Son into the world to *c* the world;
8.11 Neither do I *c* thee: go, and sin
2Co 7. 3 I speak not this to *c* you: for I
1Jn 3.20 For if our heart *c* us, God is
21 if our heart *c* us not, then have

CONDEMNATION
Lk 23.40 seeing thou art in the same *c*?
Jn 3.19 And this is the *c*, that light is
5.24 shall not come into *c*; but is
Ro 5.16 for the judgment was by one to *c*,
18 judgment came upon all men to *c*;
8. 1 now no *c* to them which are in
1Co 11.34 ye come not together unto *c*.
2Co 3. 9 For if the administration of *c* be
1Ti 3. 6 he fall into the *c* of the devil.
Jas 3. 1 we shall receive the greater *c*.
5.12 your way, nay; lest ye fall into *c*.
Jude 4 before of old ordained to this *c*,

CONDEMNED
2Ch 36. 3 and *c* the land in an hundred
Job 32. 3 no answer, and yet had *c* Job.
Ps 109. 7 be judged, let him be *c*:
Am 2. 8 drink the wine of the *c* in the
Mt 12. 7 ye would not have *c* the guiltless.
37 and by thy words thou shalt be *c*.
27. 3 when he saw that he was *c*,
Mk 14.64 they all *c* him to be guilty of death.
Lk 6.37 and ye shall not be *c*: forgive,
24.20 delivered him to be *c* to
Jn 3.18 believeth on him is not *c*: but he
18 that believeth not is *c* already,
8.10 hath no man *c* thee?
Ro 8. 3 *c* sin in the flesh:
1Co 11.32 that we should not be *c* with
Tit 2. 8 Sound speech, that cannot be *c*;
3.11 and sinneth, being *c* of himself.
Heb 11. 7 by the which he *c* the world, and
Jas 5. 6 Ye have *c* and killed the just;
9 lest ye be *c*; behold, the judge
2Pe 2. 6 *c* them with an overthrow,

CONDEMNEST
Ro 2. 1 judgest another, thou *c* thyself;

CONDEMNETH
Job 15. 6 Thine own mouth *c* thee, and
Pr 17.15 and he that *c* the just, even they
Ro 8.34 Who is he that *c*? It is Christ
14.22 Happy is he that *c* not himself

CONDEMNING
1Ki 8.32 *c* the wicked, to bring his way
Ac 13.27 they have fulfilled them in *c* him.

CONDESCEND
Ro 12.16 but *c* to men of low estate.

CONDITIONS
Lk 14.32 and desireth *c* of peace.

CONDUCT
2Sa 19.15 king, to *c* the king over Jordan.
31 the king, to *c* him over Jordan.
1Co 16.11 but *c* him forth in peace, that he

CONDUCTED
2Sa 19.40 the people of Judah *c* the king,
Ac 17.15 *c* Paul brought him unto Athens:

CONFERENCE
Gal 2. 6 in *c* added nothing to me:

CONFERRED
1Ki 1. 7 And he *c* with Joab the son
Ac 4.15 they *c* among themselves.
25.12 Then Festus, when he had *c* with
Gal 1.16 I *c* not with flesh and blood:

CONFESS
Lev 5. 5 he shall *c* that he hath sinned
16.21 and *c* over him all the iniquities
26.40 If they shall *c* their iniquity, and
Nu 5. 7 *c* their sin which they have done:
1Ki 8.33 and *c* thy name, and pray, and
35 and *c* thy name, and turn from
2Ch 6.24 *c* thy name, and pray and make
26 toward this place, and *c* thy name,
Neh 1. 6 *c* the sins of the children of Israel,
Job 40.14 Then will I also *c* unto thee that
Ps 32. 5 I will *c* my transgressions unto
Mt 10.32 shall *c* me before men, him will I
32 will I *c* also before my Father
Lk 12. 8 shall see me before men, him
8 shall the Son of man also *c* before
Jn 9.22 any man did *c* that he was Christ,
12.42 the Pharisees they did not *c* him,
Ac 23. 8 but the Pharisees *c* both.
24.14 But this I *c* unto thee, that after
Ro 10. 9 *c* with thy mouth the Lord Jesus,
14.11 and every tongue shall *c* to God.
15. 9 *c* to thee among the Gentiles,
Php 2.11 should *c* that Jesus Christ is Lord,
Jas 5.16 *C* your faults one to another, and
1Jn 1. 9 If we *c* our sins, he is faithful and
4.15 *c* that Jesus is the Son of God,
2Jn 7 who *c* not that Jesus Christ is
Rev 3. 5 will *c* his name before my Father,

CONFESSED
Ezr 10. 1 when he had *c*, weeping and
Neh 9. 2 stood and *c* their sins, and the
3 another fourth part they *c*, and
Jn 1.20 he *c*, and denied not: but
20 *c*, I am not the Christ.
Ac 19.18 and *c*, and showed their deeds.
Heb 11.13 and *c* that they were strangers

CONFESSETH
Pr 28.13 *c* and forsaketh them shall have
1Jn 4. 2 Every spirit that *c* that Jesus
3 every spirit that *c* not that Jesus

CONFESSING
Dan 9.20 praying, and *c* my sin and the
Mt 3. 6 of him in Jordan, *c* their sins.
Mk 1. 5 in the river of Jordan, *c* their sins.

CONFESSION
Jos 7.19 make *c* unto him; and tell me
2Ch 30.22 and making *c* to the Lord God of
Ezr 10.11 make *c* unto the Lord God of
Dan 9. 4 Lord my God, and made my *c*,
Ro 10.10 mouth *c* is made unto salvation;
1Ti 6.13 Pontius Pilate witnessed a good *c*:

CONFIDENCE
Jdg 9.26 men of Shechem put their *c* in
2Ki 18.19 *c* is this wherein thou trustest?
Job 4. 6 not this thy fear, thy *c*, thy hope,
18.14 His *c* shall be rooted out of his
31.24 to the fine gold, Thou art my *c*;
Ps 65. 5 the *c* of all the ends of the earth,
118. 8 in the Lord than to put *c* in man.
9 the Lord than to put *c* in princes.
Pr 3.26 the Lord shall be thy *c*, and
14.26 the fear of the Lord is strong *c*:
21.22 the strength of the *c* thereof.
25.19 *C* in an unfaithful man in time of
Isa 30.15 and in *c* shall be your strength:
36. 4 *c* is this wherein thou trustest?
Jer 48.13 was ashamed of Beth–el their *c*.
Eze 28.26 they shall dwell with *c*, when I
29.16 be no more the *c* of the house
Mic 7. 5 a friend, put ye not *c* in a guide:
Ac 28.31 with all *c*, no man forbidding
2Co 1.15 in this *c* I was minded to come
2. 3 having *c* in you all, that my joy
7.16 I have *c* in you in all things.
8.22 the great *c* which I have in you.
10. 2 *c*, wherewith I think to be bold
11.17 foolishly, in this *c* of boasting.

Gal 5.10 have *c* in you through the Lord,
Eph 3.12 and access with *c* by the faith
Php 1.25 And having this *c*, I know that I
3. 3 and have no *c* in the flesh.
3. 4 might also have *c* in the flesh.
2Th 3. 4 have *c* in the Lord touching you,
Phm 21 Having *c* in thy obedience I wrote
Heb 3. 6 if we hold fast the *c* and the
14 if we hold the beginning of our *c*
10.35 therefore your *c*, which hath
1Jn 2.28 we may have *c*, and not be
3.21 then have we *c* toward God.
5.14 is the *c* that we have in him,

CONFIDENCES

Jer 2.37 the Lord hath rejected thy *c*, and

CONFIDENT

Ps 27. 3 against me, in this will I be *c*.
Pr 14.16 but the fool rageth, and is *c*.
Ro 2.19 *c* that thou thyself art a guide
2Co 5. 6 Therefore we are always *c*,
8 are *c*, I say, and willing rather
9. 4 in this same *c* boasting.
Php 1. 6 Being *c* of this very thing, that
14 waxing *c* by my bonds, are much

CONFIDENTLY

Lk 22.59 another *c* affirmed, saying, Of a

CONFIRM

Ru 4. 7 changing, for to *c* all things;
1Ki 1.14 in after thee, and *c* thy words.
2Ki 15.19 be with him to *c* the kingdom
Est 9.29 to *c* this second letter of Purim.
31 To *c* these days of Purim in their
Ps 68. 9 thou didst *c* thine inheritance,
Isa 35. 3 and *c* the feeble knees.
Eze 13. 6 hope that they would *c* the word.
Dan 9.27 And he shall *c* the covenant
11. 1 stood to *c* and to strengthen him.
Ro 15. 8 to *c* the promises made unto the
1Co 1. 8 Who shall also *c* you unto the end,
2Co 2. 8 would *c* your love toward him.

CONFIRMATION

Php 1. 7 in the defense and *c* of the gospel,
Heb 6.16 an oath for *c* is to them an end of

CONFIRMED

2Sa 7.24 thou hast *c* to thyself thy people
2Ki 14. 5 the kingdom was *c* in his hand,
1Ch 14. 2 Lord had *c* him king over Israel,
16.17 And hath *c* the same to Jacob
Est 9.32 Esther *c* these matters of Purim;
Ps 105.10 *c* the same unto Jacob for a law,
Dan 9.12 And he hath *c* his words, which
Ac 15.32 with many words, and *c* them.
1Co 1. 6 testimony of Christ was *c* in you:
Gal 3.15 a man's covenant, yet if it be *c*,
17 that was *c* before of God in Christ,
Heb 2. 3 *c* unto us by them that heard him;
6.17 of his counsel, *c* it by an oath:

CONFIRMING

Mk 16.20 *c* the word with signs following.
Ac 14.22 *C* the souls of the disciples, and
15.41 Syria and Cilicia, *c* the churches.

CONFLICT

Php 1.30 the same *c* which ye saw in me,
Col 2. 1 knew what great *c* I have for you,

CONFORMABLE

Php 3.10 being made *c* unto his death;

CONFORMED

Ro 8.29 to be *c* to the image of his Son,
12. 2 And be not *c* to this world: but

CONFUSED

Isa 9. 5 of the warrior is with *c* noise,
Ac 19.32 for the assembly was *c*;

CONFUSION

Lev 18.23 to lie down thereto: it is *c*.
20.12 they have wrought *c*; their blood
1Sa 20.30 to thine own *c*, and unto the *c* of
Ezr 9. 7 and to *c* of face, as it is this day.
Job 10.15 I am full of *c*; therefore see
Ps 35. 4 be turned back and brought to *c*
26 be ashamed and brought to *c*
44.15 My *c* is continually before me,
70. 2 and put to *c*, that desire my hurt.
71. 1 let me never be put to *c*.
109.29 themselves with their own *c*,
Isa 24.10 The city of *c* is broken down:
30. 3 in the shadow of Egypt your *c*.
34.11 stretch out upon it the line of *c*,
41.29 molten images are wind and *c*.
45.16 they shall go to *c* together that
61. 7 and for *c* they shall rejoice
Jer 3.25 our *c* covereth us: for we have
7.19 to the *c* of their own faces?
20.11 their everlasting *c* shall never
Dan 9. 7 but unto us *c* of faces, as at this
8 Lord, to us belongeth *c* of face,
Ac 19.29 the whole city was filled with *c*:
1Co 14.33 For God is not the author of *c*,
Jas 3.16 there is *c* and every evil work.

CONGEALED

Ex 15. 8 the depths were *c* in the heart of

CONGRATULATE

1Ch 18.10 and to *c* him, because he had

CONGREGATION

Ex 12. 3 Speak ye unto all the *c* of Israel,
6 whole assembly of the *c* of Israel
19 be cut off from the *c* of Israel,
47 All the *c* of Israel shall keep it.
16. 1 the *c* of the children of Israel came
2 And the whole *c* of the children of
9 Say unto all the *c* of the children
10 Aaron spake unto the whole *c* of
22 all the rulers of the *c* came and
17. 1 all the *c* of the children of Israel
34.31 all the rulers of the *c* returned
35. 1 And Moses gathered all the *c* of the
4 spake unto all the *c* of the children
20 *c* of the children of Israel departed
Lev 4.13 And if the whole *c* of Israel sin
14 the *c* shall offer a young bullock,
15 And the elders of the *c* shall lay
21 it is a sin offering for the *c*.
8. 5 And Moses said unto the *c*,
10.17 the iniquity of the *c*, to make
16.17 and for all the *c* of Israel.
19. 2 Speak unto all the *c* of the
21 door of the tabernacle of the *c*,
24. 3 in the tabernacle of the *c*, shall
14 and let all the *c* stone him.
16 the *c* shall certainly stone him:
Nu 1. 1 Sinai, in the tabernacle of the *c*,
2 Take ye the sum of all the *c*
16 were the renowned of the *c*,
18 they assembled all the *c* together
53 there be no wrath upon the *c*
4.34 the chief of the *c* numbered the
13.26 all the *c* of the children of Israel,
26 and unto all the *c*, and shewed
14. 1 And all the *c* lifted up their voice,
2 And the whole *c* said unto them,
5 assembly of the *c* of the children
10 all the *c* bade stone them with
10 the tabernacle of the *c* before all
27 shall I bear with this evil *c*,
35 surely do it unto all this evil *c*,
36 made all the *c* to murmur against
15.15 shall be both for you of the *c*,
24 without the knowledge of the *c*,
24 that all the *c* shall offer one young
25 for the *c* of the children of Israel,
26 forgiven all the *c* of the children
33 and Aaron, and unto all the *c*.
35 the *c* shall stone him with stones
36 *c* brought him without the camp,
16. 2 the assembly, famous in the *c*,
3 seeing all the *c* are holy, every
3 lift ye up yourselves above the *c*
9 separated you from the *c* of Israel,
9 to stand before the *c* to minister
19 Korah gathered all the *c* against
19 door of the tabernacle of the *c*:
19 the Lord appeared unto all the *c*.
21 yourselves from among this *c*,
22 thou be wroth with all the *c*?
24 Speak unto the *c*, saying, Get you
26 he spake unto the *c*, saying,
33 they perished from among the *c*.
41 morrow all the *c* of the children
42 where the *c* was gathered against
42 toward the tabernacle of the *c*:
43 before the tabernacle of the *c*.
45 Get you up from among this *c*,
46 go quickly unto the *c*, and make
47 and ran into the midst of the *c*;
19. 9 for the *c* of the children of Israel
20 shall be cut off from among the *c*,
20. 1 even the whole *c*, into the desert
2 And there was no water for the *c*:
4 have ye brought up the *c* of the
8 thou shalt give the *c* and their
10 Moses and Aaron gathered the *c*
11 the *c* drank, and their beasts
12 ye shall not bring this *c* into the
22 even the whole *c*, journeyed from
27 mount Hor in the sight of all the *c*.
29 when all the *c* saw that Aaron
25. 6 in the sight of all the *c* of the
7 he rose up from among the *c*,
26. 2 Take the sum of all the *c* of the
9 which were famous in the *c*, who
27. 2 the princes and all the *c*,
2 door of the tabernacle of the *c*,
14 in the strife of the *c*, to sanctify
16 set a man over the *c*,
17 the *c* of the Lord be not as sheep
19 and before all the *c*; and give him
20 the *c* of the children of Israel may
21 Israel with him, even all the *c*.
22 and before all the *c*:
31.12 unto the *c* of the children of Israel,
13 all the princes of the *c*, went forth
16 was a plague among the *c* of the
26 and the chief fathers of the *c*:
27 to battle, and between all the *c*:
43 half that pertained unto the *c*
32. 2 and unto the princes of the *c*,
4 before the *c* of Israel, is a land for
35.12 until he stand before the *c* in
24 *c* shall judge between the slayer
25 *c* shall deliver the slayer out of
25 the *c* shall restore him to the city
Dt 23. 1, 2 shall not enter into the *c* of the
2 shall he not enter into the *c* of the
3 Moabite shall not enter into the *c*
3 shall they not enter into the *c* of
8 of them shall enter into the *c*
31.30 spake in the ears of all the *c* of
33. 4 even the inheritance of the *c* of
Jos 8.35 Joshua read not before all the *c*
9.15 the princes of the *c* sware unto
18 because the princes of the *c* had
18 all the *c* murmured against the
19 all the princes said unto all the *c*,
21 drawers of water unto all the *c*;
27 drawers of water for the *c*, and for
18. 1 whole *c* of the children of Israel
1 set up the tabernacle of the *c*
19.51 door of the tabernacle of the *c*.

20. 6 until he stand before the *c* for
9 until he stood before the *c*.
22.12 *c* of the children of Israel gathered
16 Thus saith the whole *c* of the Lord,
17 was a plague in the *c* of the Lord,
18 will be wroth with the whole *c* of
20 wrath fell on all the *c* of Israel?
30 the princes of the *c* and heads of
Jdg 20. 1 *c* was gathered together as one
21. 5 came not up with the *c* unto the
10 *c* sent thither twelve thousand
13 the whole *c* sent some to speak
16 elders of the *c* said, How shall we
1Ki 8. 5 *c* of Israel, that were assembled
14 blessed all the *c* of Israel:
14 (and all the *c* of Israel stood;)
22 in the presence of all the *c* of
55 blessed all the *c* of Israel with a
65 all Israel with him, a great *c*,
12. 3 Jeroboam and all the *c* of Israel
20 sent and called him unto the *c*,
1Ch 13. 2 David said unto all the *c* of
4 the *c* said that they would do so:
28. 8 of all Israel the *c* of the Lord,
29. 1 the king said unto all the *c*,
10 blessed the Lord before all the *c*:
20 David said to all the *c*, Now bless
20 all the *c* blessed the Lord God
2Ch 1. 3 Solomon, and all the *c* with him,
5 Solomon and the *c* sought unto it.
5. 6 *c* of Israel that were assembled
6. 3 blessed the whole *c* of Israel:
3 and all the *c* of Israel stood.
12 the presence of all the *c* of Israel,
13 upon his knees before all the *c* of
7. 8 Israel with him, a very great *c*,
20. 5 stood in the *c* of Judah and
14 of the Lord in the midst of the *c*;
23. 3 all the *c* made a covenant with
24. 6 and of the *c* of Israel, for the
28.14 before the princes and all the *c*.
29.23 offering before the king and the *c*;
28 all the *c* worshipped, and the
31 the *c* brought in sacrifices and
32 burnt offerings, which the *c* brought,
30. 2 all the *c* in Jerusalem, to keep
4 pleased the king and all the *c*.
13 the second month, a very great *c*.
17 there were many in the *c* that
24 give to the *c* a thousand bullocks
24 princes gave to the *c* a thousand
25 all the *c* of Judah, with the priests
25 all the *c* that came out of Israel,
31.18 their daughters, through all the *c*:
Ezr 2.64 whole *c* together was forty and two
10. 1 a very great *c* of men and women
8 himself separated from the *c* of
12 Then all the *c* answered and said
14 now our rulers of all the *c* stand,
Neh 5.13 all the *c* said, Amen, and praised
7.66 whole *c* together was forty and two
8. 2 brought the law before the *c* both
17 all the *c* of them that were come
13. 1 not come into the *c* of God
Job 15.34 *c* of hypocrites shall be desolate,
30.28 I stood up, and I cried in the *c*.
Ps 1. 5 sinners in the *c* of the righteous.
7. 7 shall the *c* of the people compass
22.22 midst of the *c* will I praise thee.
25 shall be of thee in the great *c*:
26. 5 have hated the *c* of evil doers;
35.18 give thee thanks in the great *c*:
40. 9 righteousness in the great *c*:
10 and thy truth from the great *c*.
58. 1 speak righteousness, O *c*?
68.10 Thy *c* hath dwelt therein: thou,
74. 2 Remember thy *c*, which thou hast
19 forget not the *c* of thy poor
75. 2 When I shall receive the *c* I will
82. 1 God standeth in the *c* of the
89. 5 faithfulness also in the *c* of the
107.32 him also in the *c* of the people,
111. 1 of the upright, and in the *c*.
149. 1 and his praise in the *c* of saints.
Pr 5.14 in all evil in the midst of the *c*
21.16 shall remain in the *c* of the dead.
26.26 be shewed before the whole *c*.
Isa 14.13 sit also upon the mount of the *c*,
Jer 6.18 know, O *c*, what is among them.
30.20 and their *c* shall be established
La 1.10 they should not enter into thy *c*.
Hos 7.12 chastise them, as their *c* hath
Joel 2.16 Gather the people, sanctify the *c*,
Mic 2. 5 a cord by lot in the *c* of the Lord,
Ac 13.43 Now when the *c* was broken up,

CONQUER

Rev 6. 2 went forth conquering, and to *c*.

CONQUERORS

Ro 8.37 we are more than *c* through him

CONSCIENCE

Jn 8. 9 being convicted by their own *c*,
Ac 23. 1 have lived in all good *c* before God
24.16 to have always a *c* void of offense
Ro 2.15 their *c* also bearing witness, and
9. 1 my *c* also bearing me witness.
13. 5 for wrath, but also for *c* sake.
1Co 8. 7 for some with *c* of the idol unto
7 and their *c* being weak is defiled.
10 shall not the *c* of him which is weak
12 and wound their weak *c*, ye sin
10.25 eat, asking no question for *c* sake:
27 eat, asking no question for *c* sake.
28 sake that showed it, and for *c* sake:
29 *C*, I say, not thine own, but of the
29 liberty judged of another man's *c*?
2Co 1.12 is this, the testimony of our *c*,
4. 2 ourselves to every man's *c* in the
1Th 1. 5 a good *c*, and of faith unfeigned:
19 Holding faith, and a good *c*;
3. 9 mystery of the faith in a pure *c*.
4. 2 their *c* seared with a hot iron;
2Ti 1. 3 from my forefathers with pure *c*,
Tit 1.15 even their mind and *c* is defiled.
Heb 9. 9 perfect, as pertaining to the *c*;
14 purge your *c* from dead works
10. 2 should have had no more *c* of sins.
22 hearts sprinkled from an evil *c*,
13.18 we trust we have a good *c*,
1Pe 2.19 if a man for *c* toward God endure
3.16 Having a good *c*; that whereas
21 answer of a good *c* toward God,)
(See box on page 182)

CONSCIENCES

2Co 5.11 also are made manifest in your *c*.

CONSECRATE

Ex 28. 3 make Aaron's garments to *c* him,
41 anoint them, and *c* them,
29. 9 shalt *c* Aaron and his sons.
33 to *c* and to sanctify them:
35 seven days shalt thou *c* them.
30.30 Aaron and his sons, and *c* them,
32.29 *C* yourselves to day to the
Lev 8.33 for seven days shall he *c* you.
16.32 he shall *c* to minister in
Nu 6.12 And he shall *c* unto the Lord the
1Ch 29. 5 *c* his service this day unto
2Ch 13. 9 to *c* himself with a young
Eze 43.26 and they shall *c* themselves.
Mic 4.13 and I will *c* their gain unto the

CONSECRATED

Ex 29.29 anointed therein, and to be *c*
Lev 21.10 and that is *c* to put on the
Nu 3. 3 whom he *c* to minister in the
Jos 6.19 of brass and iron, are *c* unto the
Jdg 17. 5 and *c* one of his sons,
12 And Micah *c* the Levite;
1Ki 13.33 he *c* him, and he became one
2Ch 26.18 Aaron, that are *c* to burn incense:
29.31 have *c* yourselves unto the
33 the *c* things were six hundred
31. 6 which were *c* unto the Lord their
Ezr 3. 5 set feasts of the Lord that were *c*,
Heb 7.28 the Son, who is *c* for evermore.
10.20 way, which he hath *c* for us.

CONSECRATION

Ex 29.22 for it is a ram of *c*:
26 breast of the ram of Aaron's *c*,
27 of the ram of the *c*, even of that
31 thou shalt take the ram of the *c*,
Lev 8.22 the other ram, the ram of *c*:
29 of the ram of *c* it was Moses' part;
33 until the days of your *c* be at an
Nu 6. 7 because the *c* of his God is upon
9 he hath defiled the head of his *c*;

CONSECRATIONS

Ex 29.34 And if ought of the flesh of the *c*,
Lev 7.37 and of the *c*, and of the sacrifice
8.28 they were *c* for a sweet savor:
31 bread that is in the basket of *c*,

CONSENT

Gen 34.15 But in this will we *c* unto you:
22 Only herein will the men *c* unto us
23 only let us *c* unto them, and they
Dt 13. 8 Thou shalt not *c* unto him,
Jdg 11.17 but he would not *c*:
1Sa 11. 7 and they came out with one *c*.
1Ki 20. 8 him, Hearken not unto him, nor *c*.
Ps 83. 5 consulted together with one *c*:
Pr 1.10 if sinners entice thee, *c* thou not.
Hos 6. 9 priests murder in the way by *c*:
Zep 3. 9 the Lord, to serve him with one *c*.
Lk 14.18 with one *c* began to make excuse.
Ro 7.16 I *c* unto the law that it is good.
1Co 7. 5 except it be with *c* for a time,
1Ti 6. 3 and *c* not to wholesome words,

CONSENTED

2Ki 12. 8 the priests *c* to receive no more
Dan 1.14 So he *c* to them in this matter,
Lk 23.51 same had not *c* to the counsel and
Ac 18.20 longer time with them, he *c* not;

CONSENTING

Ac 8. 1 And Saul was *c* unto his death.
22.20 standing by, and *c* unto his death,

CONSIDER

Ex 33.13 and *c* that this nation is thy
Lev 13.13 Then the priest shall *c*: and,
Dt 4.39 Know therefore this day, and *c*
8. 5 Thou shalt also *c* in thine heart,
32. 7 *c* the years of many generations:
29 that they would *c* their latter end!
Jdg 18.14 now therefore *c* what ye have to
19.30 *c* of it, take advice, and speak
1Sa 12.24 for *c* how great things he hath
25.17 therefore know and *c* what thou
2Ki 5. 7 wherefore *c*, I pray you, and see
Job 11.11 wickedness also; will he not then *c*
23.15 when I *c*, I am afraid of him.
34.27 and would not *c* any of his ways:
37.14 and *c* the wondrous works of God.
Ps 5. 1 O Lord, *c* my meditation.
8. 3 When I *c* thy heavens, the work
9.13 *c* my trouble which I suffer of
13. 3 *C* and hear me, O Lord my God:
25.19 *C* mine enemies; for they are
37.10 thou shalt diligently *c* his place,
45.10 Hearken, O daughter, and *c*,
48.13 well her bulwarks, *c* her palaces;
50.22 Now *c* this, ye that forget God,
64. 9 they shall wisely *c* of his doing.
119.95 I will *c* thy testimonies.
153 *C* mine affliction, and deliver me:

BIBLICAL THEMES

CONSCIENCE

And he said, I heard thy voice in the garden, and I was afraid, because I was naked; and I hid myself. Gen 3.10

And the Lord said unto Cain, Where is Abel thy brother? And he said, I know not: Am I my brother's keeper? Gen 4.9

And Judah said, What shall we say unto my lord? what shall we speak? or how shall we clear ourselves? God hath found out the iniquity of thy servants. Gen 44.16

And Moses feared, and said, Surely this thing is known. Ex 2.14

Then thou shalt say before the Lord thy God . . . I have not transgressed thy commandments, neither have I forgotten them. Dt 26.13

And David said unto Nathan, I have sinned against the Lord. 2Sa 12.13

O Lord, thou hast searched me, and known me. Thou knowest my downsitting and mine uprising, thou understandest my thought afar off. Thou compassest my path and my lying down, and art acquainted with all my ways. For there is not a word in my tongue, but, lo, O Lord, thou knowest it altogether. Ps 139.1-4

The wicked flee when no man pursueth: but the righteous are bold as a lion. Pr 28.1

Then said I, Woe is me! for I am undone; because I am a man of unclean lips. Isa 6.5

Were they ashamed when they had committed abomination? nay, they were not at all ashamed, neither could they blush. Jer 6.15

When Pilate saw that he could prevail nothing, but that rather a tumult was made, he took water, and washed his hands before the multitude, saying, I am innocent of the blood of this just person. Mt 27.24

And when he came to himself, he said, How many hired servants of my father's have bread enough and to spare, and I perish with hunger! I will arise and go to my father, and will say unto him, Father, I have sinned against heaven, and before thee, and am no more worthy to be called thy son: make me as one of thy hired servants. And he arose, and came to his father. Lk 15.17-20

And the Lord turned, and looked upon Peter. And Peter remembered the word of the Lord, how he had said unto him, Before the cock crow, thou shalt deny me thrice. And Peter went out, and wept bitterly. Lk 22.61-62

And they which heard it, being convicted by their own conscience, went out one by one, beginning at the eldest, even unto the last: and Jesus was left alone, and the woman standing in the midst. Jn 8.9

Herein do I exercise myself, to have always a conscience void of offense toward God, and toward men. Ac 24.16

I am not ashamed of the gospel of Christ. Ro 1.16

Holding the mystery of the faith in a pure conscience. 1Ti 3.9

The word of God is quick, and powerful, and sharper than any twoedged sword, piercing even to the dividing asunder of soul and spirit, and of the joints and marrow, and is a discerner of the thoughts and intents of the heart. Neither is there any creature that is not manifest in his sight: but all things are naked and opened unto the eyes of him with whom we have to do. Heb 4.12-13

Pray for us: for we trust we have a good conscience, in all things willing to live honestly. Heb 13.18

The time is come that judgment must begin at the house of God: and if it first begin at us, what shall the end be of them that obey not the gospel of God? 1Pe 4.17

Ps 119.159 *C* how I love thy precepts:
Pr 6. 6 the ant, thou sluggard; *c* her ways,
23. 1 *c* diligently what is before thee:
24.12 he that pondereth the heart *c* it?
Ec 5. 1 for they *c* not that they do evil.
7.13 *C* the work of God: for who
14 in the day of adversity *c*: God also
Isa 1. 3 not know, my people doth not *c*.
5.12 neither *c* the operation of his
14.16 narrowly look upon thee, and *c* thee
18. 4 I will *c* in my dwelling place
41.20 they may see, and know, and *c*,
22 that we may *c* them, and
43.18 neither *c* the things of old.
52.15 they had not heard shall they *c*.
Jer 2.10 and *c* diligently, and see if there
9.17 *C* ye, and call for the mourning
23.20 in the latter days ye shall *c* it
30.24 in the latter days ye shall *c* it.
La 1.11 see, O Lord, and *c*; for I am
2.20 Behold, O Lord, and *c* to whom
5. 1 *c*, and behold our reproach.
Eze 12. 3 may be they will *c*, though they
Dan 9.23 the matter, and *c* the vision.
Hos 7. 2 they *c* not in their hearts that I
Hag 1. 5, 7 hosts; *C* your ways.
2.15 *c* from this day and upward,
18 *C* now from this day and
18 Lord's temple was laid, *c* it.
Mt 6.28 *C* the lilies of the field, how they
Lk 12.24 *C* the ravens: for they neither
27 *C* the lilies how they grow: they
Jn 11.50 Nor *c* that it is expedient for us,
Ac 15. 6 came together for to *c* of this
2Ti 2. 7 *C* what I say; and the Lord give
Heb 3. 1 *c* the Apostle and High Priest
7. 4 Now *c* how great this man was,
10.24 let us *c* one another to provoke
12. 3 For *c* him that endured such

CONSIDERED

1Ki 3.21 but when I had *c* it in the morning,
5. 8 I have *c* the things which thou
Job 1. 8 Hast thou *c* my servant Job,
2. 3 Hast thou *c* my servant Job,
Ps 31. 7 thou hast *c* my trouble; thou
77. 5 have *c* the days of old, the years
Pr 24.32 I saw, and *c* it well: I looked
Ec 4. 1 and *c* all the oppressions that
4 Again, I *c* all travail, and every
15 I *c* all the living which walk
9. 1 I *c* in my heart even to declare
Dan 7. 8 I *c* the horns, and, behold, there
Mk 6.52 For they *c* not the miracle of the
Ac 11. 6 I *c*, and saw fourfooted beasts
12.12 And when he had *c* the thing,
Ro 4.19 he *c* not his own body now dead,

CONSIDERETH

Ps 33.15 hearts alike; he *c* all their works.
41. 1 Blessed is he that *c* the poor:
Pr 21.12 wisely *c* the house of the wicked:
28.22 *c* not that poverty shall come
29. 7 The righteous *c* the cause of the
31.16 She *c* a field, and buyeth it:
Isa 44.19 none *c* in his heart, neither is
Eze 18.14 and *c*, and doeth not such like,
28 Because he *c*, and turneth away

CONSIDERING

Isa 57. 1 none *c* that the righteous is taken
Dan 8. 5 I was *c*, behold, an he goat came
Ga 6. 1 *c* thyself, lest thou also be
Heb 13. 7 *c* the end of their conversation.

CONSIST

Col 1.17 things, and by him all things *c*.

CONSISTETH

Lk 12.15 man's life *c* not in the abundance

CONSOLATION

Jer 16. 7 give them the cup of *c* to drink
Lk 2.25 waiting for the *c* of Israel;
6.24 for ye have received your *c*.
Ac 4.36 being interpreted. The son of *c*,)
15.31 had read, they rejoiced for the *c*.
Ro 15. 5 the God of patience and *c* grant
2Co 1. 5 in us, so our *c* also aboundeth
6 it is for your *c* and salvation,
6 we be comforted, it is for your *c*
7 so shall ye be also of the *c*.
7. 7 but by the *c* wherewith he was
Php 2. 1 any *c* in Christ, if any comfort
2Th 2.16 given us everlasting *c* and good
Phm 7 we have great joy and *c* in thy
Heb 6.18 we might have a strong *c*, who

CONSORTED

Ac 17. 4 believed, and *c* with Paul and

CONSPIRACY

2Sa 15.12 the *c* was strong; for the people
2Ki 12.20 servants arose, and made a *c*, and

14.19 Now they made a *c* against
15.15 acts of Shallum, and his *c*
30 the son of Elah made a *c*
17. 4 the king of Assyria found *c* in
2Ch 25.27 they made a *c* against him
Jer 11. 9 the Lord said unto me, A *c* is
Eze 22.25 There is a *c* of her prophets in the
Ac 23.13 than forty which had made this *c*.

CONSTANTLY
Pr 21.28 man that heareth speaketh *c*.
Ac 12.15 she *c* affirmed that it was even
Tit 3. 8 things I will that thou affirm *c*,

CONSTRAIN
Gal 6.12 they *c* you to be circumcised;

CONSTRAINED
2Ki 4. 8 she *c* him to eat bread. And so
Mt 14.22 Jesus *c* his disciples to get into a
Mk 6.45 straightway he *c* his disciples to
Lk 24.29 But they *c* him, saying, Abide
Ac 16.15 And she *c* us.
28.19 I was *c* to appeal unto Caesar;

CONSTRAINETH
Job 32.18 the spirit within me *c* me.
2Co 5.14 the love of Christ *c* us; because

CONSTRAINT
1Pe 5. 2 thereof, not by *c*, but willingly;

CONSULTATION
Mk 15. 1 priests held a *c* with the elders

CONSULTED
1Ki 12. 6 Rehoboam *c* with the old men,
8 and *c* with the young men that
1Ch 13. 1 And David *c* with the captains of
2Ch 20.21 when he had *c* with the people,
Neh 5. 7 Then I *c* with myself, and I
Ps 83. 3 and *c* against thy hidden ones.
5 have *c* together with one consent:
Eze 21.21 he *c* with images, he looked in
Dan 6. 7 have *c* together to establish a
Mic 6. 5 now what Balak, king of Moab *c*,
Hab 2.10 Thou hast *c* shame to thy house
Mt 26. 4 *c* that they might take Jesus by
Jn 12.10 the chief priests *c* that they

CONSULTETH
Lk 14.31 *c* whether he be able with ten

CONSUMING
Dt 4.24 the Lord thy God is a *c* fire,
9. 3 as a *c* fire he shall destroy them,
Heb 12.29 For our God is a *c* fire.

CONTAIN
1Ki 8.27 heaven of heavens cannot *c* thee;
18.32 great as would *c* two measures of
2Ch 2. 6 heaven of heavens cannot *c* him?
6.18 heaven of heavens cannot *c* thee;
Eze 45.11 that the bath may *c* the tenth
Jn 21.25 even the world itself could not *c*
1Co 7. 9 if they cannot *c*, let them marry:

CONTAINED
1Ki 7.26 of lilies: it *c* two thousand baths.
38 of brass: one laver *c* forty baths:
Ro 2.14 by nature the things *c* in the law,
Eph 2.15 of commandments *c* in ordinances;
1Pe 2. 6 also it is *c* in the scripture,

CONTAINING
Jn 2. 6 of the Jews, *c* two or three firkins

CONTEMPTIBLE
Mal 1. 7 ye say, The table of the Lord is *c*.
12 the fruit thereof, even his meat, is *c*.
2. 9 have I also made you *c* and base
2Co 10.10 is weak, and his speech *c*.

CONTEMPTUOUSLY
Ps 31.18 and *c* against the righteous.

CONTEND
Dt 2. 9 neither *c* with them in battle:
24 possess it, and *c* with him in battle.
Job 9. 3 If he will *c* with him, he cannot
13. 8 his person? will ye *c* for God?
Pr 28. 4 such as keep the law *c* with them.
Ec 6.10 neither may he *c* with him that
Isa 49.25 I will *c* with him that contendeth
50. 8 who will *c* with me? let us stand
57.16 I will not *c* for ever, neither will I
Jer 12. 5 how canst thou *c* with horses?
18.19 the voice of them that *c* with me.
Am 7. 4 the Lord God called to *c* by fire,
Mic 6. 1 *c* thou before the mountains, and
Jude 3 ye should earnestly *c* for the faith

CONTENDED
Neh 13.11 Then *c* I with the rulers, and
17 Then I *c* with the nobles of Judah,
25 I *c* with them, and cursed them,
Job 31.13 when they *c* with me:
Isa 41.12 them, even them that *c* with thee:
Ac 11. 2 of the circumcision *c* with him,

CONTENDING
Jude 9 when *c* with the devil he disputed

CONTENT
Gen 37.27 flesh. And his brethren were *c*.
Ex 2.21 And Moses was *c* to dwell with
Lev 10.20 Moses heard that he was *c*.
Jos 7. 7 would to God we had been *c*, and
Jdg 17.11 And the Levite was *c* to dwell
19. 6 Be *c*, I pray thee, and tarry all
2Ki 5.23 Naaman said, Be *c*, take two
6. 3 one said, Be *c*, I pray thee, and go
Job 6.28 Now therefore be *c*, look upon
Pr 6.35 neither will he rest *c*, though thou
Mk 15.15 Pilate, willing to *c* the
Lk 3.14 and be *c* with your wages.
Php 4.11 state I am, therewith to be *c*.
1Ti 6. 8 raiment let us be therewith *c*.
Heb 13. 5 be *c* with such things as ye have:
3Jn 10 with malicious words: and not *c*

CONTENTION
Pr 13.10 by pride cometh *c*: but with the
17.14 leave off *c*, before it be meddled
18. 6 A fool's lips enter into *c*, and his
22.10 out the scorner, and *c* shall go out;
Jer 15.10 a man of *c* to the whole earth!
Hab 1. 3 there are that raise up strife and *c*.
Ac 15.39 And the *c* was so sharp between
Php 1.16 The one preach Christ of *c*, not
1Th 2. 2 the gospel of God with much *c*.

CONTENTIONS
Pr 18.18 The lot causeth *c* to cease, and
19 and their *c* are like the bars of a
19.13 the *c* of a wife are a continual
23.29 who hath *c*? who hath babbling?
1Co 1.11 that there are *c* among you.
Tit 3. 9 genealogies, and *c*, and strivings

CONTENTIOUS
Pr 21.19 with a *c* and an angry woman.
26.21 so is a *c* man to kindle strife.
27.15 rainy day and a *c* woman are alike.
Ro 2. 8 But unto them that are *c*,
1Co 11.16 But if any man seem to be *c*,

CONTENTMENT
1Ti 6. 6 godliness with *c* is great gain.

CONTINUANCE
Dt 28.59 great plagues, and of long *c*,
59 and sore sicknesses, and of long *c*.
Ps 139.16 which in *c* were fashioned,
Isa 64. 5 in those is *c*, and we shall be
Ro 2. 7 by patient *c* in well doing seek

CONTINUE
Ex 21.21 if he *c* a day or two, he shall not
Lev 12. 4 she shall then *c* in the blood of
5 she shall *c* in the blood of her
1Sa 12.14 *c* following the Lord your God:
13.14 now thy kingdom shall not *c*:
2Sa 7.29 it may *c* for ever before thee:
1Ki 2. 4 That the Lord may *c* his word
Job 15.29 neither shall his substance *c*,
17. 2 doth not mine eye *c* in their
Ps 36.10 *c* thy lovingkindness unto them
49.11 is, that their houses shall *c* for ever,
102.28 children of thy servants shall *c*,
119.91 They *c* this day according to
Isa 5.11 that *c* until night, till wine
Jer 32.14 that they may *c* many days.
Dan 11. 8 shall *c* more years than the king
Mt 15.32 they *c* with me now three days,
Jn 8.31 If ye *c* in my word, then are ye
15. 9 I loved you: *c* ye in my love.
Ac 13.43 them to *c* in the grace of God.
14.22 exhorting them to *c* in the faith,
26.22 I *c* unto this day, witnessing
Ro 6. 1 Shall we *c* in sin, that grace
11.22 if thou *c* in his goodness:
Gal 2. 5 of the gospel might *c* with you.
Php 1.25 I shall abide and *c* with you all
Col 1.23 If ye *c* in the faith grounded
4. 2 *C* in prayer, and watch in the
1Ti 2.15 if they *c* in faith and charity
4.16 *c* in them: for in doing this thou
2Ti 3.14 *c* thou in the things which thou
Heb 7.23 suffered to *c* by reason of death:
13. 1 Let brotherly love *c*.
Jas 4.13 and *c* there a year, and buy,
2Pe 3. 4 all things *c* as they were from
1Jn 2.24 remain in you, ye also shall *c*
Rev 13. 5 him to *c* forty and two months.
17.10 cometh, he must *c* a short space.

CONTINUED
Gen 40. 4 and they *c* a season in ward.
Jdg 5.17 Asher *c* on the seashore,
Ru 1. 2 country of Moab, and *c* there.
2. 7 hath *c* even from the morning
1Sa 1.12 she *c* praying before the Lord,
2Sa 6.11 ark of the Lord *c* in the house
1Ki 22. 1 they *c* three years without war
2Ch 29.28 this *c* until the burnt offering
Neh 5.16 also I *c* in the work of this wall,
Job 27. 1 Moreover Job *c* his parable, and
29. 1 Moreover Job *c* his parable, and
Ps 72.17 shall be *c* as long as the sun:
Dan 1.21 And Daniel *c* even unto the
Lk 6.12 and *c* all night in prayer to God.
22.28 *c* with me in my temptations
Jn 2.12 they *c* there not many days.
8. 7 So when they *c* asking him,
11.54 and there *c* with his disciples.
Ac 1.14 all *c* with one accord in prayer
2.42 they *c* steadfastly in the apostles'
8.13 he *c* with Philip, and wondered,
12.16 But Peter *c* knocking, and when
15.35 Paul also and Barnabas *c* in
18.11 *c* there a year and six months,
19.10 *c* by the space of two years;
20. 7 and *c* his speech until midnight.
27.33 *c* fasting, having taken nothing.
Heb 8. 9 they *c* not in my covenant,
1Jn 2.19 would no doubt have *c* with us:

CONTINUETH
Job 14. 2 fleeth also as a shadow, and *c* not.
Gal 3.10 every one that *c* not in all things
1Ti 5. 5 *c* in supplications and prayers
Heb 7.24 this man, because he *c* ever,
Jas 1.25 law of liberty, and *c* therein,

CONTINUING
Jer 30.23 a *c* whirlwind: it shall fall with
Ac 2.46 And they, *c* daily with one accord
Ro 12.12 tribulations; *c* instant in prayer;
Heb 13.14 here have we no *c* city, but we

CONTRADICTING
Ac 13.45 were spoken by Paul, *c* and

CONTRADICTION
Heb 7. 7 without all *c* the less is blessed
12. 3 *c* of sinners against himself,

CONTRARIWISE
2Co 2. 7 that *c* ye ought rather to forgive
Gal 2. 7 But *c*, when they saw that the
1Pe 3. 9 railing for railing: but *c* blessing;

CONTRARY
Lev 26.21 if ye walk *c* unto me, and will
23 but will walk *c* unto me;
24 Then will I also walk *c* unto you,
27 but walk *c* unto me;
28 I will walk *c* unto you also in fury;
40 and that also they have walked *c*
41 I also have walked *c* unto them,
Est 9. 1 (though it was turned to the *c*,
Eze 16.34 the *c* is in thee from other women
34 unto thee, therefore thou art *c*.
Mt 14.24 for the wind was *c*.
Mk 6.48 for the wind was *c* unto them:
Ac 17. 7 these all do *c* to the decrees of
18.13 men to worship God *c* to the law.
23. 3 commandest me to be smitten *c* to
26. 9 many things *c* to the name of
27. 4 Cyprus, because the winds were *c*.
Ro 11.24 graffed *c* to nature into a good
16.17 *c* to the doctrine which ye have
Gal 5.17 these are *c* the one to the other:
Col 2.14 which was *c* to us, and took it out
1Th 2.15 not God, and are *c* to all men:
1Ti 1.10 thing that is *c* to sound doctrine;
Tit 2. 8 is of the *c* part may be ashamed,

CONTRIBUTION
Ro 15.26 to make a certain *c* for the poor

CONTRITE
Ps 34.18 saveth such as be of a *c* spirit.
51.17 a broken and a *c* heart, O God,
Isa 57.15 also that is of a *c* and humble
15 to revive the heart of the *c* ones.
66. 2 him that is poor and of a *c* spirit,

CONTROVERSY
Dt 17. 8 being matters of *c* within thy
19.17 the men, between whom the *c* is,
21. 5 by their word shall every *c* and
25. 1 If there be a *c* between men,
2Sa 15. 2 any man that had a *c* came to
Isa 34. 8 year of recompences for the *c* of
Jer 25.31 Lord hath a *c* with the nations,
Eze 44.24 in *c* they shall stand in judgment;
Hos 4. 1 the Lord hath a *c* with the
12. 2 Lord hath also a *c* with Judah,
Mic 6. 2 Hear ye, O mountains, the Lord's *c*,
2 the Lord hath a *c* with his people,
1Ti 3.16 without *c* great is the mystery

CONVENIENT
Pr 30. 8 feed me with food *c* for me:
Jer 40. 4 whither it seemeth good and *c*
5 go wheresoever it seemeth *c* unto
Mk 6.21 And when a *c* day was come,
Ac 24.25 when I have a *c* season, I will call
Ro 1.28 do those things which are not *c*;
1Co 16.12 come when he shall have *c* time.
Eph 5. 4 nor jesting, which are not *c*:
Phm 8 to enjoin thee that which is *c*,

CONVENIENTLY
Mk 14.11 he sought how he might *c* betray

CONVERSATION
Ps 37.14 to slay such as be of upright *c*.
50.23 him that ordereth his *c* aright
2Co 1.12 we have had our *c* in the world,
Gal 1.13 ye have heard of my *c* in time
Eph 2. 3 we all had our *c* in times past
4.22 put off concerning the former *c*
Php 1.27 let your *c* be as it becometh the
3.20 our *c* is in heaven; from whence
1Ti 4.12 in word, in *c*, in charity, in spirit,
Heb 13. 5 your *c* be without covetousness;
7 considering the end of their *c*.
Jas 3.13 shew out of a good *c* his works
1Pe 1.15 so be ye holy in all manner of *c*;
18 from your vain *c* received by
2.12 Having your *c* honest among
3. 1 be won by the *c* of the wives;
2 While they behold your chaste *c*
16 falsely accuse your good *c* in
2Pe 2. 7 with the filthy *c* of the wicked:
3.11 be in all holy *c* and godliness,

CONVERSION
Ac 15. 3 declaring the *c* of the Gentiles:

CONVERT
Isa 6.10 with their heart, and *c*, and be
Jas 5.19 from the truth, and one *c* him;

CONVERTED
Ps 51.13 and sinners shall be *c* unto thee.
Isa 60. 5 of the sea shall be *c* unto thee.
Mt 13.15 and should be *c*, and I should
18. 3 Except ye be *c*, and become as
Mk 4.12 they should be *c*, and their sins
Lk 22.32 and when thou art *c*, strengthen
Jn 12.40 and be *c*, and I should heal them.
Ac 3.19 Repent ye therefore, and be *c*,
28.27 Should be *c*, and I should heal

CONVERTETH
Jas 5.20 he which *c* the sinner from the

CONVERTING
Ps 19. 7 of the Lord is perfect, *c* the soul:

CONVERTS
Isa 1.27 with judgment, and her *c* with

CONVEY
1Ki 5. 9 will *c* them by sea in floats unto
Neh 2. 7 river, that they may *c* me over

CONVEYED
Jn 5.13 for Jesus had *c* himself away,

CONVICTED
Jn 8. 9 being *c* by their own conscience,

CONVINCE
Tit 1. 9 exhort and to *c* the gainsayers.
Jude 15 to *c* all that are ungodly among

CONVINCED
Job 32.12 there was none of you that *c* Job,
Ac 18.28 For he mightily *c* the Jews.
1Co 14.24 unlearned, he is *c* of all, he is
Jas 2. 9 *c* of the law as transgressors.

CONVINCETH
Jn 8.46 Which of you *c* me of sin?

COOL
Gen 3. 8 in the garden in the *c* of the day;
Lk 16.24 finger in water, and *c* my tongue;

COPPER
Ezr 8.27 two vessels of fine *c*, precious as

COPPERSMITH
2Ti 4.14 Alexander the *c* did me much

CORBAN
Mk 7.11 It is *C*, that is to say, a gift,

CORD
Jos 2.15 down by a *c* through the window:
Job 30.11 hath loosed my *c*, and afflicted
41. 1 or his tongue with a *c* which
Ec 4.12 threefold *c* is not quickly broken.
12. 6 Or ever the silver *c* be loosed, or
Mic 2. 5 cast a *c* by lot in the congregation

CORDS
Ex 35.18 the pins of the court, and their *c*,
39.40 his *c*, and his pins, and all the
Nu 3.26 *c* of it for all the service thereof.
37 sockets, their pins, and their *c*.
4.26 their *c*, and all the instruments of
32 their pins, and their *c*, with all
Jdg 15.13 they bound him with two new *c*,
14 the *c* that were upon his arms
Est 1. 6 fastened with *c* of fine linen and
Job 36. 8 and be holden in *c* of affliction;
Ps 2. 3 and cast away their *c* from us.
118.27 with *c*, even unto the horns
129. 4 cut asunder the *c* of the wicked.
140. 5 have hid a snare for me, and *c*;
Pr 5.22 be holden with the *c* of his sins.
Isa 5.18 that draw iniquity with *c* of vanity,
33.20 any of the *c* thereof be broken.
54. 2 lengthen thy *c*, and strengthen
Jer 10.20 is spoiled, all my *c* are broken:
38. 6 they let down Jeremiah with *c*.
11 them down by *c* into the dungeon
12 under thine armholes under the *c*.
13 they drew up Jeremiah with *c*,
Eze 27.24 of rich apparel, bound with *c*,
Hos 11. 4 I drew them with *c* of a man, with
Jn 2.15 he had made a scourge of small *c*,

CORE
Jude 11 perished in the gainsaying of *C*.

CORINTH
Ac 18. 1 from Athens, and came to *C*;
19. 1 while Apollos was at *C*, Paul
1Co 1. 2 the church of God which is at *C*, to
2Co 1. 1 church of God which is at *C*, with
23 spare you I came not as yet unto *C*.
2Ti 4.20 Erastus abode at *C*: but

CORINTHIANS
Ac 18. 8 many of the *C* hearing believed,
2Co 6.11 O ye *C*, our mouth is open unto

CORNELIUS
Ac 10. 1 *C*, a centurion of the band
3 to him, and saying unto him, *C*.
7 which spake unto *C* was departed,
17 the men which were sent from *C*
21 which were sent unto him from *C*;
22 said, *C* the centurion, a just man,
24 *C* waited for them, and had called
25 *C* met him, and fell down at his
30 *C* said, Four days ago I was fasting
31 *C*, thy prayer is heard, and thine

CORNER
Ex 36.25 north *c*, he made twenty boards,
Lev 21. 5 shave off the *c* of their beard,
Jos 18.14 the *c* of the sea southward, from
2Ki 11.11 from the right *c* of the temple
11 to the left *c* of the temple,
14.13 gate of Ephraim unto the *c* gate,
2Ch 25.23 gate of Ephraim to the *c* gate,
26. 9 towers in Jerusalem at the *c* gate,
28.24 altars in every *c* of Jerusalem.
Neh 3.24 of the wall, even unto the *c*.
31 and to the going up of the *c*.
32 between the going up of the *c*
Job 38. 6 or who laid the *c* stone thereof;
Ps 118.22 become the head stone of the *c*.

144.12 daughters may be as *c* stones,
Pr 7. 8 through the street near her *c*;
12 and lieth in wait at every *c*.)
21. 9 to dwell in a *c* of the housetop,
25.24 to dwell in the *c* of the housetop,
Isa 28.16 precious *c* stone, a sure foundation:
30.20 thy teachers be removed into a *c*
Jer 31.38 Hananeel unto the gate of the *c*.
40 unto the *c* of the horse gate
48.45 shall devour the *c* of Moab, and
51.26 not take of thee a stone for a *c*,
Eze 46.21 behold, in every *c* of the court
Am 3.12 in Samaria in the *c* of a bed,
10. 4 Out of him came forth the *c*,
14.10 the *c* gate, and from the tower
Mt 21.42 same is become the head of the *c*:
Mk 12.10 is become the head of the *c*:
Lk 20.17 same is become the head of the *c*?
Ac 4.11 which is become the head of the *c*.
26.26 for this thing was not done in a *c*.
Eph 2.20 Christ himself being the chief *c*
1Pe 2. 6 I lay in Sion a chief *c* stone, elect,
7 same is made the head of the *c*,

CORNERS

Ex 25.12 put them in the four *c* thereof;
26 the rings in the four *c* that are
26.23 make for the *c* of the tabernacle
24 both; they shall be for the two *c*.
27. 2 horns of it upon the four *c* thereof:
4 brasen rings in the four *c* thereof.
30. 4 by the two *c* thereof, upon the
36.28 made he for the *c* of the tabernacle
29 did to both of them in both the *c*.
37. 3 gold, to be set by the four *c* of it;
13 put the rings upon the four *c* that
27 by the two *c* of it, upon the two
38. 2 horns thereof on the four *c* of it;
Lev 19. 9 not wholly reap the *c* of thy field,
27 shall not round the *c* of your heads,
27 shalt thou mar the *c* of thy beard.
23.22 riddance of the *c* of thy field
Nu 24.17 and shall smite the *c* of Moab,
Dt 32.26 said, I would scatter them into *c*,
1Ki 7.30 four *c* thereof had undersetters:
34 to the four *c* of one base: and the
Neh 9.22 and didst divide them into *c*:
Job 1.19 smote the four *c* of the house,
Isa 11.12 from the four *c* of the earth.
Jer 9.26 are in the utmost *c*, that dwell
25.23 all that are in the utmost *c*,
49.32 them that are in the utmost *c*;
Eze 7. 2 come upon the four *c* of the land.
41.22 and the *c* thereof, and the length
43.20 and on the four *c* of the settle,
45.19 upon the four *c* of the settle of the
46.21 to pass by the four *c* of the court;
22 In the four *c* of the court there
22 these four *c* were of one measure.
Zec 9.15 bowls, and as the *c* of the altar.
Mt 6. 5 in the *c* of the streets, that they
Ac 10.11 knit at the four *c*, and let down
11. 5 let down from heaven by four *c*;
Rev 7. 1 standing on the four *c* of the earth,

CORPSE

Mk 6.29 they came and took up his *c*,

CORRECTED

Pr 29.19 A servant will not be *c* by words:
Heb 12. 9 fathers of our flesh which *c* us,

CORRECTETH

Job 5.17 happy is the man whom God *c*:
Pr 3.12 For whom the Lord loveth he *c*;

CORRECTION

Job 37.13 wheher for *c*, or for his land,
Pr 3.11 neither be weary of his *c*:
7.22 as a fool to the *c* of the stocks;
15.10 *C* is grievous unto him that
22.15 rod of *c* shall drive it far from him.
23.13 Withhold not *c* from the child:
Jer 2.30 they received no *c*: your own
5. 3 they have refused to receive *c*:
7.28 nor receiveth *c*: truth is perished,
Hab 1.12 thou hast established them for *c*.
Zep 3. 2 she received not *c*; she trusted
2Ti 3.16 for reproof, for *c*, for instruction

CORRUPT

Gen 6.11 The earth also was *c* before God,
12 it was *c*; for all flesh had corrupted
Dt 4.16 Lest ye *c* yourselves, and make you
25 and shall *c* yourselves, and make a
31.29 ye will utterly *c* yourselves,
Job 17. 1 breath is *c*, my days are extinct,
Ps 14. 1 They are *c*, they have done
38. 5 My wounds stink and are *c*
53. 1 *C* are they, and have done
73. 8 They are *c*, and speak wickedly
Pr 25.26 troubled fountain, and a *c* spring.
Eze 20.44 according to your *c* doings, O ye
23.11 was more *c* in her inordinate love
Dan 2. 9 have prepared lying and *c* words
11.32 shall he *c* by flatteries: but the
Mal 1.14 sacrificeth unto the Lord a *c*
2. 3 I will *c* your seed, and spread
Mt 6.19 where moth and rust doth *c*, and
20 neither moth nor dust doth *c*,
7.17 a *c* tree bringeth forth evil fruit.
18 neither can a *c* tree bring forth
12.33 make the tree *c*, and his fruit *c*:
Lk 6.43 tree bringeth not forth *c* fruit;
43 neither doth a *c* tree bring forth
1Co 15.33 evil communications *c* good
2Co 2.17 many, which *c* the word of God:
Eph 4.22 old man, which is *c* according to
29 Let no *c* communication proceed
1Ti 6. 5 disputings of men of *c* minds,
2Ti 3. 8 men of *c* minds, reprobate
Jude 10 those things they *c* themselves.
Rev 19. 2 which did *c* the earth with her

CORRUPTED

Gen 6.12 flesh had *c* his way upon the earth.
Ex 8.24 land was *c* by reason of the swarm
32. 7 out of Egypt, have *c* themselves:
Dt 9.12 out of Egypt have *c* themselves;
32. 5 They have *c* themselves, their
Jdg 2.19 *c* themselves more than their
Eze 16.47 wast *c* more than they in all thy
28.17 thou hast *c* thy wisdom by reason
Hos 9. 9 They have deeply *c* themselves,
Zep 3. 7 rose early, and *c* all their doings.
Mal 2. 8 ye have *c* the covenant of Levi,
2Co 7. 2 we have *c* no man, we have
11. 3 your minds should be *c* from the
Jas 5. 2 Your riches are *c*, and your

CORRUPTETH

Lk 12.33 approacheth, neither moth *c*.

CORRUPTIBLE

Ro 1.23 into an image made like to *c* man,
1Co 9.25 they do it to obtain a *c* crown;
15.53 this *c* must put on incorruption,
54 So when this *c* shall have put on
1Pe 1.18 were not redeemed with *c* things,
23 not of *c* seed, but of incorruptible,
3. 4 in that which is not *c*, even the

CORRUPTION

Lev 22.25 their *c* is in them, and blemishes
2Ki 23.13 the right hand of the mount of *c*,
Job 17.14 said to *c*, Thou art my father:
Ps 16.10 suffer thine Holy One to see *c*.
49. 9 still live for ever, and not see *c*.
Isa 38.17 delivered it from the pit of *c*:
Dan 10. 8 was turned in me into *c*, and I
Jon 2. 6 thou brought up my life from *c*,
Ac 2.27 suffer thine Holy One to see *c*.
31 in hell, neither his flesh did see *c*.
13.34 to return to *c*, he said on this wise,
35 not suffer thine Holy One to see *c*.
36 laid unto his fathers, and saw *c*:
37 whom God raised again, saw no *c*.
Ro 8.21 delivered from the bondage of *c*
1Co 15.42 It is sown in *c*; it is raised in
50 neither doth *c* inherit incorruption.
Gal 6. 8 shall of the flesh reap *c*; but he
2Pe 1. 4 escaped the *c* that is in the world
2.12 utterly perish in their own *c*;
19 themselves are the servants of *c*:

COST

2Sa 19.42 have we eaten at all of the king's *c*?
24.24 of that which doth *c* me nothing.
1Ch 21.24 nor offer burnt offerings without *c*.
Lk 14.28 not down first, and counteth the *c*,

COSTLINESS

Rev 18.19 ships in the sea by reason of her *c*!

COSTLY

1Ki 5.17 *c* stones, and hewed stones,
7. 9 All these were of *c* stones,
10 the foundation was of *c* stones,
11 And above were *c* stones, after the
Jn 12. 3 of ointment of spikenard, very *c*,
1Ti 2. 9 or gold, or pearls, or *c* array;

COUCH

Gen 49. 4 thou it: he went up to my *c*.
Job 7.13 my *c* shall ease my complaint;
38.40 When they *c* in their dens, and
Ps 6. 6 I water my *c* with my tears.
Am 3.12 of a bed, and in Damascus in a *c*.
Lk 5.19 through the tiling with his *c* into
24 take up thy *c*, and go unto thine

COUCHES

Am 6. 4 stretch themselves upon their *c*,
Ac 5.15 and laid them on beds and *c*,

COULDEST

Jer 3. 5 and done evil things as thou *c*.
Eze 16.28 and yet *c* not be satisfied.
Dan 2.47 seeing thou *c* reveal this secret.
Mk 14.37 *c* not thou watch one hour?
Jn 19.11 Thou *c* have no power at all

COUNCIL

Ps 68.27 princes of Judah and their *c*,
Mt 5.22 Raca, shall be in danger of the *c*:
12.14 Pharisees went out, and held a *c*
26.59 and elders, and all the *c*, sought
Mk 14.55 chief priests and all the *c* sought
15. 1 and scribes and the whole *c*, and
Lk 22.66 and led him into their *c*, saying,
Jn 11.47 chief priests and the Pharisees a *c*,
Ac 4.15 to go aside out of the *c*, they
5.21 and called the *c* together, and all
27 they set them before the *c*:
34 Then stood there up one in the *c*,
41 from the presence of the *c*,
6.12 him, and brought him to the *c*,
15 And all that sat in the *c*, looking
22.30 and all their *c* to appear, and
23. 1 Paul, earnestly beholding the *c*,
6 he cried out in the *c*, Men and
15 Now therefore ye with the *c* signify
20 down Paul to morrow into the *c*,
28 I brought him forth into their *c*:
24.20 while I stood before the *c*,
25.12 he had conferred with the *c*,

COUNCILS

Mt 10.17 they will deliver you up to the *c*,
Mk 13. 9 they shall deliver you up to *c*;

COUNSELLER

2Sa 15.12 David's *c*, from his city, even

1Ch 26.14 for Zechariah his son, a wise *c*,
27.32 Jonathan David's uncle was a *c*,
33 Ahithophel was the king's *c*:
2Ch 22. 3 mother was his *c* to do wickedly.
Isa 3. 3 the *c*, and the cunning artificer,
9. 6 shall be called Wonderful, *C*,
40.13 Who being his *c* hath taught him?
41.28 there was no *c*, that, when I asked
Mic 4. 9 is thy *c* perished? for pangs have
Na 1.11 against the Lord, a wicked *c*.

COUNSELLOR

Mk 15.43 of Arimathaea, an honorable *c*,
Lk 23.50 was a man named Joseph, a *c*;
Ro 11.34 or who hath been his *c*?

COUNT

Ex 12. 4 shall make your *c* for the lamb.
Lev 19.23 *c* the fruit thereof as uncircumcised:
23.15 *c* unto you from the morrow
25.27 *c* the years of the sale thereof,
52 then he shall *c* with him,
Nu 23.10 Who can *c* the dust of Jacob,
1Sa 1.16 *C* not thine handmaid for a
Job 19.15 my maids, *c* me for a stranger:
31. 4 see my ways, and *c* all my steps?
Ps 87. 6 The Lord shall *c*, when he writeth
139.18 If I should *c* them, they are
22 I *c* them mine enemies.
Mic 6.11 Shall I *c* them pure with the
Ac 20.24 neither *c* I my life dear unto
Php 3. 8 I *c* all things but loss for the
8 do *c* them but dung, that I may
13 Brethren, I *c* not myself to have
2Th 1.11 God would *c* you worthy of this
3.15 *c* him not as an enemy, but
1Ti 6. 1 *c* their own masters worthy of
Phm 17 If thou *c* me therefore a partner,
Jas 1. 2 *c* it all joy when ye fall into
5.11 we *c* them happy which endure.
2Pe 2.13 as they that *c* it pleasure to riot
3. 9 as some men *c* slackness; but is
Rev 13.18 hath understanding *c* the number

COUNTED

Gen 15. 6 he *c* it to him for righteousness.
30.33 that shall be *c* stolen with me.
31.15 Are we not *c* of him strangers?
Ex 38.21 as it was *c*, according to the
Lev 25.31 shall be *c* as the fields of the
Nu 18.30 it shall be *c* unto the Levites
Jos 13. 3 is *c* to the Canaanite: five lords
1Ki 1.21 son Solomon shall be *c* offenders.
3. 8 be numbered nor *c* for multitude.
1Ch 21. 6 But Levi and Benjamin *c* he not
23.24 they were *c* by number of names
Neh 13.13 they were *c* faithful, and their
Job 18. 3 Wherefore are we *c* as beasts,
41.29 Darts are *c* as stubble: he
Ps 44.22 we are *c* as sheep for the slaughter.
Ps 88. 4 I am *c* with them that go down
106.31 was *c* unto him for righteousness
Pr 17.28 he holdeth his peace, is *c* wise:
27.14 it shall be *c* a curse to him.
Isa 5.28 horses' hoofs shall be *c* like flint,
32.15 the fruitful field be *c* for a forest.
33.18 where is he that *c* the towers?
40.15 are *c* as the small dust of the
17 are *c* to him less than nothing,
Hos 8.12 they were *c* as a strange thing.
Mt 14. 5 because they *c* him as a prophet
Mk 11.32 men *c* John, that he was a prophet.
Ac 5.41 that they were *c* worthy to suffer
19.19 they *c* the price of them, and found
Ro 2.26 shall not his uncircumcision be *c*
4. 3 *c* unto him for righteousness.
5 his faith is *c* for righteousness
9. 8 of the promise are *c* for the seed.
Php 3. 7 gain to me, those I *c* loss for
2Th 1. 5 may be *c* worthy of the kingdom
1Ti 1.12 that he *c* me faithful, putting me
5.17 well be *c* worthy of double honor,
Heb 3. 3 was *c* worthy of more glory than
7. 6 whose descent is not *c* from them
10.29 hath *c* the blood of the covenant,

COUNTETH

Job 19.11 he *c* me unto him as one of his
33.10 he *c* me for his enemy,
Lk 14.28 and *c* the cost, whether he hath

COUNTRYMEN

2Co 11.26 in perils by mine own *c*, in perils
1Th 2.14 suffered like things of your own *c*,

COURAGE

Nu 13.20 And be ye of good *c*, and bring
Dt 31. 6 Be strong and of a good *c*, fear not
7, 23 Be strong and of a good *c*: for
Jos 1. 6 Be strong and of a good *c*: for unto
9 Be strong and of a good *c*; be not
18 only be strong and of a good *c*.
2.11 did there remain any more *c*
10.25 be strong and of good *c*: for thus
2Sa 10.12 Be of good *c*, and let us play the
1Ch 19.13 Be of good *c*, and let us behave
22.13 be strong, and of good *c*; dread not,
28.20 Be strong and of good *c*, and do it:
2Ch 15. 8 Oded the prophet, he took *c*, and
Ezr 10. 4 with thee: be of good *c*, and do it.
Ps 27.14 Wait on the Lord: be of good *c*,
31.24 Be of good *c*, and he shall
Isa 41. 6 said to his brother, Be of good *c*.

Biblical Themes

COURAGE

And Moses said unto the people, Fear ye not, stand still, and see the salvation of the Lord, which he will shew to you to day: for the Egyptians whom ye have seen to day, ye shall see them again no more for ever. Ex 14.13

Have not I commanded thee? Be strong and of a good courage; be not afraid, neither be thou dismayed: for the Lord thy God is with thee whithersoever thou goest. Jos 1.9

And Samson called unto the Lord, and said, O Lord God, remember me, I pray thee, and strengthen me, I pray thee, only this once, O God, that I may be at once avenged of the Philistines for my two eyes. Jdg 16.28

And David said to Saul, Let no man's heart fail because of him; thy servant will go and fight with this Philistine. 1Sa 17.32

The wicked flee when no man pursueth: but the righteous are bold as a lion. Pr 28.1

The fear of man bringeth a snare: but whoso putteth his trust in the Lord shall be safe. Pr 29.25

Fear thou not; for I am with thee: be not dismayed; for I am thy God: I will strengthen thee; yea, I will help thee; yea, I will uphold thee with the right hand of my righteousness. Isa 41.10

O man greatly beloved, fear not: peace be unto thee, be strong, yea, be strong. And when he had spoken unto me, I was strengthened, and said, Let my lord speak; for thou hast strengthened me. Dan 10.19

Then said Jesus unto him, Put up again thy sword into his place: for all they that take the sword shall perish with the sword. Mt 26.52

Now when they saw the boldness of Peter and John, and perceived that they were unlearned and ignorant men, they marvelled; and they took knowledge of them, that they had been with Jesus. Ac 4.13

They set them before the council: and the high priest asked them, saying, Did not we straitly command you that ye should not teach in this name? and, behold, ye have filled Jerusalem with your doctrine, and intend to bring this man's blood upon us. Then Peter and the other apostles answered and said, We ought to obey God rather than men. Ac 5.27-29

But [Stephen], being full of the Holy Ghost, looked up stedfastly into heaven, and saw the glory of God. Ac 7.55

And at midnight Paul and Silas prayed, and sang praises unto God: and the prisoners heard them. Ac 16.25

For there stood by me this night the angel of God, whose I am, and whom I serve, saying, Fear not. Ac 27.23-24

Finally, my brethren, be strong in the Lord, and in the power of his might. . . . Take unto you the whole armor of God, that ye may be able to withstand in the evil day, and having done all, to stand. Stand therefore, having your loins girt about with truth, and having on the breastplate of righteousness; and your feet shod with the preparation of the gospel of peace; above all, taking the shield of faith, wherewith ye shall be able to quench all the fiery darts of the wicked. And take the helmet of salvation, and the sword of the Spirit, which is the word of God. Eph 6.10, 13-17

He that overcometh shall inherit all things. Rev 21.7

Dan 11.25 shall stir up his power and his *c*
Ac 28.15 saw, he thanked God, and took *c*.

COURSE
2Ch 5.11 and did not then wait by *c*:
Ezr 3.11 And they sang together by *c* in
Ps 82. 5 of the earth are out of *c*.
Jer 8. 6 every one turned to his *c*, as the
23.10 their *c* is evil, and their force is
Lk 1. 5 Zacharias, of the *c* of Abia:
8 before God in the order of his *c*,
Ac 13.25 as John fulfilled his *c*, he said,
16.11 we came with a straight *c* to
20.24 that I might finish my *c* with joy,
21. 1 we came with a straight *c* unto
7 when we had finished our *c* from
1Co 14.27 three, and that by *c*; and let one
Eph 2. 2 according to the *c* of this world,
2Th 3. 1 word of the Lord may have free *c*,
2Ti 4. 7 I have finished my *c*, I have kept
Jas 3. 6 setteth on fire the *c* of nature;

COURTEOUS
1Pe 3. 8 as brethren, be pitiful, be *c*:

COURTEOUSLY
Ac 27. 3 Julius *c* entreated Paul,
28. 7 us, and lodged us three days *c*.

COUSIN
Lk 1.36 And, behold, thy *c* Elizabeth,

COUSINS
Lk 1.58 her neighbors and her *c* heard

COVENANT
Gen 6.18 with thee will I establish my *c*;
9. 9 behold, I establish my *c* with you,
11 I will establish my *c* with you;
12 This is the token of the *c* which
13 shall be for a token of a *c* between
15 I will remember my *c*, which is
16 the everlasting *c* between God
17 This is the token of the *c*, which
15.18 the Lord made a *c* with Abram,
17. 2 I will make my *c* between me and
4 for me, behold, my *c* is with thee,
7 I will establish my *c* between me
7 for an everlasting *c*, to be a God
9 Thou shalt keep my *c* therefore,
10 This is my *c*, which ye shall keep,
11 a token of the *c* betwixt me and
13 and my *c* shall be in your flesh
13 in your flesh for an everlasting *c*.
14 his people; he hath broken my *c*.
19 I will establish my *c* with him
19 with him for an everlasting *c*,
21 my *c* will I establish with Isaac,
21.27 and both of them made a *c*.
32 Thus they made a *c* at Beer–sheba:
26.28 and let us make a *c* with thee;
31.44 let us make a *c*, I and thou;
Ex 2.24 God remembered his *c* with
6. 4 I have also established my *c* with
5 and I have remembered my *c*.
19. 5 and keep my *c*, then ye shall be
23.32 Thou shalt make no *c* with them,
24. 7 And he took the book of the *c*,
8 Behold, the blood of the *c*, which
31.16 generations, for a perpetual *c*.
34.10 Behold, I make a *c*: before all
12 lest thou make a *c* with the
15 Lest thou make a *c* with the
27 of these words I have made a *c*
28 upon the tables the words of the *c*,
Lev 2.13 the salt of the *c* of thy God to be
24. 8 of Israel by an everlasting *c*.
26. 9 and establish my *c* with you.
15 but that ye break my *c*:
25 shall avenge the quarrel of my *c*:
42 will I remember my *c* with Jacob,
42 and also my *c* with Isaac,
42 and also my *c* with Abraham
44 and to break my *c* with them: for
45 remember the *c* of their ancestors,
Nu 10.33 the ark of the *c* of the Lord went
14.44 the ark of the *c* of the Lord, and
18.19 it is a *c* of salt for ever before the
25.12 I give unto him my *c* of peace:
13 the *c* of an everlasting priesthood;
Dt 4.13 And he declared unto you his *c*,
23 lest ye forget the *c* of the Lord
31 nor forget the *c* of thy fathers
5. 2 Lord our God made a *c* with us in
3 The Lord made not this *c* with our
7. 2 thou shalt make no *c* with them,
9 keepeth *c* and mercy with them
12 God shall keep unto thee the *c* and
8.18 that he may establish his *c* which
9. 9 the tables of the *c* which the Lord
11 stone, even the tables of the *c*.
15 the two tables of the *c* were in my
10. 8 to bear the ark of the *c* of the Lord,
17. 2 in transgressing his *c*,
29. 1 These are the words of the *c*,
1 the *c* which he made with them
9 Keep therefore the words of this *c*,
12 That thou shouldest enter into *c*
14 with you only do I make this *c*
21 curses of the *c* that are written
25 have forsaken the *c* of the Lord
31. 9 which bare the ark of the *c* of the
16 break my *c* which I have made
20 and provoke me, and break my *c*.
25 which bare the ark of the *c* of the
26 in the side of the ark of the *c* of
33. 9 thy word, and kept thy *c*.
Jos 3. 3 When ye see the ark of the *c* of
6 Take up the ark of the *c*, and pass
6 they took up the ark of the *c*,
8 that bear the ark of the *c*, saying,
11 the ark of the *c* of the Lord of the
14 bearing the ark of the *c* before the
17 priests that bare the ark of the *c*
4. 7 cut off before the ark of the *c* of
9 which bare the ark of the *c* stood:
18 bare the ark of the *c* of the Lord
6. 6 Take up the ark of the *c*,
8 and the ark of the *c* of the Lord
7.11 also transgressed my *c* which I
15 he hath transgressed the *c* of the
8.33 which bare the ark of the *c* of
23.16 When ye have transgressed the *c*
24.25 Joshua made a *c* with the people
Jdg 2. 1 I will never break my *c* with you.
20 people hath transgressed my *c*
20.27 the ark of the *c* of God was there
1Sa 4. 3 Let us fetch the ark of the *c* of the
4 from thence the ark of the *c* of the
4 there with the ark of the *c* of God.
5 the ark of the *c* of the Lord came
11. 1 Make a *c* with us, and we will
2 condition will I make a *c* with you,
18. 3 Jonathan and David made a *c*,
20. 8 brought thy servant into a *c* of the
16 Jonathan made a *c* with the house
23.18 two made a *c* before the Lord:
2Sa 15.24 bearing the ark of the *c* of God:
23. 5 made with me an everlasting *c*,
1Ki 3.15 and stood before the ark of the *c*
6.19 there the ark of the *c* of the Lord.
8. 1 might bring up the ark of the *c* of
6 brought in the ark of the *c* of the
9 when the Lord made a *c* with the
21 wherein is the *c* of the Lord,
23 who keepest *c* and mercy with
11.11 thou hast not kept my *c* and my
19.10, 14 of Israel have forsaken thy *c*,
20.34 send thee away with this *c*.
34 So he made a *c* with him,
2Ki 11. 4 and made a *c* with them, and took
17 Jehoiada made a *c* between the
13.23 because of his *c* with Abraham,
17.15 *c* that he made with their fathers,
35 With whom the Lord had made a *c*,
38 the *c* that I have made with you
18.12 but transgressed his *c*, and all
23. 2 words of the book of the *c* which
3 made a *c* before the Lord, to walk
3 words of this *c* that were written
3 And all the people stood to the *c*.
21 it is written in the book of this *c*.
1Ch 11. 3 David made a *c* with them in
15.25 went to bring up the ark of the *c*
26 Levites that bare the ark of the *c*
28 Israel brought up the ark of the *c*
29 the ark of the *c* of the Lord came
16. 6 before the ark of the *c* of God.
15 Be ye mindful always of his *c*;
16 Even of the *c* which he made
17 to Israel for an everlasting *c*,
37 before the ark of the *c* of the Lord
17. 1 but the ark of the *c* of the Lord
22.19 bring the ark of the *c* of the Lord,
28. 2 house of rest for the ark of the *c*
18 and covered the ark of the *c* of
2Ch 5. 2 the ark of the *c* of the Lord out
7 brought in the ark of the *c* of
10 when the Lord made a *c* with
6.11 wherein is the *c* of the Lord,
14 which keepest *c*, and shewest
13. 5 and to his sons by a *c* of salt?
15.12 into a *c* to seek the Lord
21. 7 because of the *c* that he had made
23. 1 son of Zichri, into *c* with him.
3 congregation made a *c* with the
16 Jehoiada made a *c* between him,
29.10 a *c* with the Lord God of Israel,
34.30 the book of the *c* that was found
31 made a *c* before the Lord,
31 to perform the words of the *c*
32 did according to the *c* of God,
Ezr 10. 3 let us make a *c* with our God
Neh 1. 5 that keepeth *c* and mercy for them
9. 8 madest a *c* with him to give the land
32 God, who keepest *c* and mercy,
38 we make a sure *c*, and write
13.29 and the *c* of the priesthood, and
Job 31. 1 I made a *c* with mine eyes; why
41. 4 Will he make a *c* with thee?
Ps 25.10 as keep his *c* and his testimonies.
14 and he will shew them his *c*.
44.17 have we dealt falsely in thy *c*.
50. 5 made a *c* with me by sacrifice.
16 shouldest take my *c* in thy mouth?
55.20 with him: he hath broken his *c*.
74.20 have respect unto the *c*: for
78.10 They kept not the *c* of God, and
37 neither were they stedfast in his *c*.
89. 3 I have made a *c* with my chosen,
28 my *c* shall stand fast with him.
34 My *c* will I not break, nor alter
39 made void the *c* of thy servant:
103.18 To such as keep his *c*, and to those
105. 8 hath remembered his *c* for ever,
9 Which *c* he made with Abraham,
10 and to Israel for an everlasting *c*:
106.45 he remembered for them his *c*,
111. 5 he will ever be mindful of his *c*.
9 he hath commanded his *c* for ever:
132.12 If thy children will keep my *c* and
Pr 2.17 and forgetteth the *c* of her God.
Isa 24. 5 ordinance, broken the everlasting *c*.
28.15 We have made a *c* with death, and
18 *c* with death shall be disannulled,
33. 8 he hath broken the *c*, he hath
42. 6 give thee for a *c* of the people, for
49. 8 give thee for a *c* of the people, to
54.10 neither shall the *c* of my peace be
55. 3 make an everlasting *c* with you,
56. 4 please me, and take hold of my *c*;
6 and taketh hold of my *c*;
57. 8 and made thee a *c* with them;

Isa 59.21 As for me, this is my *c* with them,
61. 8 make an everlasting *c* with them.
Jer 3.16 The ark of the *c* of the Lord:
11. 2 Hear ye the words of this *c*, and
3 obeyeth not the words of this *c*,
6 Hear ye the words of this *c*, and do
8 upon them all the words of this *c*,
10 of Judah having broken my *c*
14.21 remember, break not thy *c* with us.
22. 9 Because they have forsaken the *c*
31.31 will make a new *c* with the house
32 Not according to the *c* that I made
32 which my *c* they brake, although I
33 shall be the *c* that I will make
32.40 I will make an everlasting *c* with
33.20 If ye can break my *c* of the day,
20 and my *c* of the night,
21 also my *c* be broken with David
25 If my *c* be not with day and night,
34. 8 had made a *c* with all the people
10 which had entered into the *c*,
13 a *c* with your fathers in the day
15 made a *c* before me in the house
18 men that have transgressed my *c*,
18 not performed the words of the *c*
50. 5 to the Lord in a perpetual *c* that
Eze 16. 8 and entered into a *c* with thee, saith
59 despised the oath in breaking the *c*.
60 I will remember my *c* with thee in
60 establish unto thee an everlasting *c*.
61 for daughters, but not by thy *c*.
62 I will establish my *c* with thee;
17.13 and made a *c* with him, and hath
14 by keeping of his *c* it might stand.
15 he break the *c*, and be delivered?
16 whose *c* he brake, even with him
18 despised the oath by breaking the *c*,
19 and my *c* that he hath broken,
20.37 bring you into the bond of the *c*:
34.25 will make with them a *c* of peace,
37.26 will make a *c* of peace with them;
26 shall be an everlasting *c* with them:
44. 7 they have broken my *c* because
Dan 9. 4 keeping the *c* and mercy to them
27 he shall confirm the *c* with many
11.22 yea, also the prince of the *c*.
28 heart shall be against the holy *c*;
30 indignation against the holy *c*:
30 with them that forsake the holy *c*.
32 such as do wickedly against the *c*
Hos 2.18 in that day will I make a *c* for them
6. 7 like men have transgressed the *c*:
8. 1 they have transgressed my *c*,
10. 4 swearing falsely in making a *c*:
12. 1 do make a *c* with the Assyrians,
Am 1. 9 remembered not the brotherly *c*:
Zec 9.11 by the blood of thy *c* I have sent
11.10 that I might break my *c* which I
Mal 2. 4 that my *c* might be with Levi,
5 My *c* was with him of life and
8 ye have corrupted the *c* of Levi,
10 by profaning the *c* of our fathers?
14 companion, and the wife of thy *c*.
3. 1 the messenger of the *c*, whom ye
Lk 1.72 to remember his holy *c*;
Ac 3.25 *c* which God made with our fathers,
7. 8 And he gave him the *c* of
Ro 11.27 this is my *c* unto them, when I shall
Gal 3.15 Though it be but a man's *c*,
17 the *c*, that was confirmed before
Heb 8. 6 he is the mediator of a better *c*,
7 if that first *c* had been faultless,
8 will make a new *c* with the house
9 Not according to the *c* that I made
9 they continued not in my *c*, and
10 this is the *c* that I will make with
13 In that he saith, A new *c*, he
9. 1 Then verily the first *c* had also
4 the ark of the *c* overlaid round
4 and the tables of the *c*;
10.16 This is the *c* that I will make with
29 the blood of the *c*, wherewith he
12.24 Jesus the mediator of the new *c*,
13.20 the blood of the everlasting *c*,

COVENANTBREAKERS

Ro 1.31 *c*, without natural affection.

COVENANTED

2Ch 7.18 as I have *c* with David thy father
Hag 2. 5 I *c* with you when ye came out of
Mt 26.15 they *c* with him for thirty pieces
Lk 22. 5 glad, and *c* to give him money.

COVENANTS

Ro 9. 4 glory, and the *c*, and the giving
Gal 4.24 for these are the two *c*; the one
Eph 2.12 strangers from the *c* of promise,

COVET

Ex 20.17 shalt not *c* thy neighbor's house,
17 shalt not *c* thy neighbor's wife,
Dt 5.21 shalt thou *c* thy neighbor's house,
Mic 2. 2 And they *c* fields, and take them
Ro 7. 7 law had said, Thou shall not *c*.
13. 9 Thou shalt not *c*; and if there be
1Co 12.31 But *c* earnestly the best gifts:
14.39 *c* to prophesy, and forbid not to

COVETED

Jos 7.21 then I *c* them, and took them;
Ac 20.33 I have *c* no man's silver, or gold,
1Ti 6.10 while some *c* after, they have

COVETOUS

Ps 10. 3 blesseth the *c*, whom the Lord
Lk 16.14 the Pharisees also, who were *c*,
1Co 5.10 or with the *c*, or extortioners, or
11 or *c*, or an idolator, or a railer, or
6.10 nor *c*, nor drunkards, nor revilers,
Eph 5. 5 nor *c* man, who is an idolater,
1Ti 3. 3 patient, not a brawler, not *c*;
2Ti 3. 2 lovers of their own selves, *c*,
2Pe 2.14 have exercised with *c* practices;

COVETOUSNESS

Ex 18.21 fear God, men of truth, hating *c*;
Ps 119.36 thy testimonies, and not to *c*.
Pr 28.16 hateth *c* shall prolong his days.
Isa 57.17 the iniquity of his *c* was I wroth,
Jer 6.13 them every one is given to *c*; and
8.10 the greatest is given to *c*, from
22.17 are not but for *c*, and for to shed
51.13 is come, and the measure of thy *c*.
Eze 33.31 their heart goeth after their *c*.
Hab 2. 9 coveteth an evil *c* to his house,
Mk 7.22 Thefts, *c*, wickedness, deceit,
Lk 12.15 Take heed, and beware of *c*:
Ro 1.20 wickedness, *c*, maliciousness;
2Co 9. 5 of bounty, and not as of *c*.
Eph 5. 3 all uncleanness, or *c*, let it not be
Col 3. 5 and *c*, which is idolatry:
1Th 2. 5 as ye know, nor a cloke of *c*;
Heb 13. 5 your conversation be without *c*;
2Pe 2. 3 through *c* shall they with feigned

CRACKLING

Ec 7. 6 as the *c* of thorns under a pot,

CRAFT

Dan 8.25 cause *c* to prosper in his hand;
Mk 14. 1 how they might take him by *c*,
Ac 18. 3 because he was of the same *c*,
19.25 by this *c* we have our wealth.
27 not only this our *c* is in danger
Rev 18.22 craftsman, of whatsoever *c* he be,

CRAFTINESS

Job 5.13 taketh the wise in their own *c*:
Lk 20.23 But he perceived their *c*, and
1Co 3.19 He taketh the wise in their own *c*.
2Co 4. 2 not walking in *c*, nor handling the
Eph 4.14 the sleight of men, and cunning *c*,

CRAFTSMAN

Dt 27.15 the work of the hands of the *c*,
Rev 18.22 no *c*, of whatsoever craft he be,

CRAFTSMEN

2Ki 24.14 and all the *c* and smiths: none
16 and *c* and smiths a thousand, all
1Ch 4.14 of Charashim; for they were *c*.
Neh 11.35 Lod, and Ono, the valley of *c*.
Hos 13. 2 all of it the work of the *c*:
Ac 19.24 brought no small gain unto the *c*;
38 and the *c* which are with him,

CRAFTY

Job 5.12 disappointeth the devices of the *c*,
15. 5 thou choosest the tongue of the *c*.
Ps 83. 3 They have taken *c* counsel against
Co 12.16 being *c*, I caught you with guile.

CRAVED

Mk 15.43 Pilate, and *c* the body of Jesus.

CREATE

Ps 51.10 *C* in me a clean heart, O God;
Isa 4. 5 Lord will *c* upon every dwelling
45. 7 I form the light, and *c* darkness:
7 I make peace, and *c* evil:
57.19 I *c* the fruit of the lips; Peace,
65.17 I *c* new heavens and a new earth:
18 rejoice for ever in that which I *c*:
18 behold, I *c* Jerusalem a rejoicing,

CREATED

Gen 1. 1 God *c* the heaven and the earth.
21 And God *c* great whales, and every
27 So God *c* man in his own image,
27 in the image of God *c* he him;
27 male and female *c* he them.
2. 3 his work which God *c* and made.
4 and of the earth, when they were *c*,
5. 1 In the day that God *c* man, in the
2 Male and female *c* he them; and
2 in the day when they were *c*.
6. 7 I will destroy man whom I have *c*
Dt 4.32 that God *c* man upon the earth,
Ps 89.12 and the south thou hast *c* them:
102.18 the people which shall be *c* shall
104.30 sendest forth thy spirit, they are *c*:
148. 5 he commanded, and they were *c*.
Isa 40.26 behold who hath *c* these things,
41.20 the Holy One of Israel hath *c* it.
42. 5 he that *c* the heavens, and
43. 1 thus saith the Lord that *c* thee,
7 I have *c* him for my glory, I have
45. 8 I the Lord have *c* it.
12 made the earth, and *c* man upon it:
18 the Lord that *c* the heavens; God
18 he *c* it not in vain, he formed it to
48. 7 They are *c* now, and not from the
54.16 *c* the smith that bloweth the coals
16 I have *c* the waster to destroy.
Jer 31.22 hath *c* a new thing in the earth,
Eze 21.30 in the place where thou wast *c*,
28.13 thee in the day that thou wast *c*.
15 from the day that thou wast *c*, till
Mal 2.10 hath not one God *c* us? why do we
Mk 13.19 which God *c* unto this time, neither
1Co 11. 9 was the man *c* for the woman; but
Eph 2.10 *c* in Christ Jesus unto good works,
3. 9 in God, who *c* all things by Jesus
4.24 after God is *c* in righteousness
Col 1.16 by him were things *c*, that are in
16 all things were *c* by him, and for
3.10 after the image of him that *c* him:
1Ti 4. 3 which God hath *c* to be received
Rev 4.11 for thou hast *c* all things, and for
11 thy pleasure they are and were *c*.
10. 6 who *c* heaven, and the things that

The Creation narrative has inspired many masterpieces—here, Raphael's The Creation of the Animals.

CREATION
Mk 10. 6 But from the beginning of the *c*
13.19 not from the beginning of the *c*
Ro 1.20 from the *c* of the world are clearly
8.22 that the whole *c* groaneth and
2Pe 3. 4 were from the beginning of the *c*
Rev 3.14 the beginning of the *c* of God;

CREATOR
Ec 12. 1 Remember now thy *C* in the days
Isa 40.28 the *C* of the ends of the earth,
43.15 your Holy One, the *c* of Israel,
Ro 1.25 more than the *C*, who is blessed
1Pe 4.19 well doing, as unto a faithful *C*.

CREATURE
Gen 1.20 the moving *c* that hath life, and
21 every living *c* that moveth, which
24 the earth bring forth the living *c*
2.19 called every living *c*, that was the
9.10 every living *c* that is with you, of
12 me and you and every living *c*
15 and every living *c* of all flesh;
16 between God and every living *c*
Lev 11.46 every living *c* that moveth in the
46 every *c* that creepeth upon the
Eze 1.20, 21 spirit of the living *c* was in the
22 upon the heads of the living *c*
10.15 This is the living *c* that I saw by
17 spirit of the living *c* was in them.
20 This is the living *c* that I saw by
Mk 16.15 and preach the gospel to every *c*.
Ro 1.25 and served the *c* more than the
8.19 the earnest expectation of the *c*
20 For the *c* was made subject to
21 Because the *c* itself also shall be
39 nor any other *c*, shall be able to
2Co 5.17 he is a new *c*: old things are
Gal 6.15 uncircumcision, but a new *c*.
Col 1.15 God, the firstborn of every *c*:
23 which was preached to every *c*
1Ti 4. 4 For every *c* of God is good and
Heb 4.13 Neither is there any *c* that is not
Rev 5.13 And every *c* which is in heaven,

CREDITOR
Dt 15. 2 Every *c* that lendeth
2Ki 4. 1 and the *c* is come to take unto
Lk 7.41 There was a certain *c* which had

CREEK
Ac 27.39 they discovered a certain *c* with

CREEP
Lev 11.20 All fowls that *c*, going upon all
29 the creeping things that *c* upon
31 unclean to you among all that *c*:
42 all creeping things that *c* upon
Ps 104.20 the beasts of the forest do *c* forth
Eze 38.20 and all creeping things that *c*
2Ti 3. 6 are they which *c* into houses,

CREPT
Jude 4 For there are certain men *c* in

CRETE
Ac 27. 7 suffering us, we sailed under *C*,
12 which is an haven of *C*, and lieth
13 thence, they sailed close by *C*.
21 me, and not have loosed from *C*,
Tit 1. 5 For this cause left I thee in *C*,

CRETES
Ac 2.11 *C* and Arabians, we do hear

CRETIANS
Tit 1.12 The *C* are always liars, evil

CREW
Mt 26.74 And immediately the cock *c*.
Mk 14.68 out into the porch; and the cock *c*.
72 And the second time the cock *c*.
Lk 22.60 while he yet spake, the cock *c*.
Jn 18.27 again: and immediately the cock *c*.

CRIB
Job 39. 9 to serve thee, or abide by thy *c*?
Pr 14. 4 Where no oxen are, the *c* is clean:
Isa 1. 3 owner, and the ass his master's *c*:

CRIME
Job 31.11 For this is an heinous *c*; yea,
Ac 25.16 concerning the *c* laid against him.

CRIMES
Eze 7.23 for the land is full of bloody *c*,
Ac 25.27 signify the *c* laid against him.

CRIPPLE
Ac 14. 8 a *c* from his mother's womb,

CRISPUS
Ac 18. 8 And *C*, the chief ruler of the
1Co 1.14 I baptized none of you, but *C* and

CROOKED
Dt 32. 5 are a perverse and *c* generation.
Job 26.13 hand hath formed the *c* serpent.
Ps 125. 5 turn aside unto their *c* ways,
Pr 2.15 Whose ways are *c*, and they
Ec 1.15 is *c* cannot be made straight:
7.13 straight, which he hath made *c*?
Isa 27. 1 even leviathan that *c* serpent;
40. 4 and the *c* shall be made straight,
42.16 them, and *c* things straight.
45. 2 and make the *c* places straight:
59. 8 they have made them *c* paths:
La 3. 9 he hath made my paths *c*.
Lk 3. 5 the *c* shall be made straight,
Php 2.15 midst of a *c* and perverse nation,

CROSS
Mt 10.38 And he that taketh not his *c*,
16.24 deny himself, and take up his *c*,
27.32 him they compelled to bear his *c*.
40 Son of God, come down from the *c*.
42 let him now come down from the *c*,
Mk 8.34 deny himself, and take up his *c*,
10.21 take up the *c*, and follow me.
15.21 and Rufus, to bear his *c*.
30 and come down from the *c*.
32 descend now from the *c*, that we
Lk 9.23 himself, and take up his *c* daily,
14.27 whosoever doth not bear his *c*,
23.26 and on him they laid the *c*, that
Jn 19.17 And he bearing his *c* went forth
19 wrote a title, and put it on the *c*.
25 stood by the *c* of Jesus his mother,
31 should not remain upon the *c* on
1Co 1.17 lest the *c* of Christ should be made
18 the preaching of the *c* is to them
Gal 5.11 then is the offense of the *c* ceased.
6.12 should suffer persecution for the *c*
14 save in the *c* of our Lord Jesus
Eph 2.16 unto God in one body by the *c*,
Php 2. 8 death, even the death of the *c*.
3.18 are the enemies of the *c* of Christ:
Col 1.20 peace through the blood of his *c*,
2.14 out of the way, nailing it to his *c*;
Heb 12. 2 endured the *c*, despising the shame,

CROW
Mt 26.34 this night, before the cock *c*, thou
75 Before the cock *c*, thou shalt deny
Mk 14.30 before the cock *c* twice, thou shalt
72 him, Before the *c* crow twice, thou
Lk 22.34 the cock shall not *c* this day, before
61 him, Before the cock *c*, thou shalt
Jn 13.38 The cock shall not *c*, till thou hast

CROWN
Gen 49.26 and on the *c* of the head of him
Ex 25.11 make upon it a *c* of gold round
24 and make thereto a *c* of gold
25 make a golden *c* to the border.
29. 6 put the holy *c* upon the miter.
30. 3 shalt make unto it a *c* of gold
4 thou make to it under the *c* of it,
37. 2 and made a *c* of gold to it round
11 and made thereunto a *c* of gold
12 made a *c* of gold for the border
26 also he made unto it a *c* of gold
27 of gold for it under the *c* thereof,
39.30 they made the plate of the holy *c*
Lev 8. 9 put the golden plate, the holy *c*;
21.12 *c* of the anointing oil of his God
Dt 33.20 the arm with the *c* of the head.
2Sa 1.10 took the *c* that was upon his head,
12.30 And he took their king's *c* from
14.25 his foot even to the *c* of his head
2Ki 11.12 and put the *c* upon him,
1Ch 20. 2 David took the *c* of their king
2Ch 23.11 son, and put upon him the *c*,
Est 1.11 queen before the king with the *c*
2.17 he set the royal *c* upon her head,
6. 8 *c* royal which is set upon his head.

Est 8.15 and with a great *c* of gold,
Job 2. 7 the sole of his foot unto his *c*.
19. 9 and taken the *c* from my head.
31.36 and bind it as a *c* to me.
Ps 21. 3 a *c* of pure gold on his head.
89.39 hast profaned his *c* by casting it
132.18 upon himself shall his *c* flourish.
Pr 4. 9 a *c* of glory shall she deliver to
12. 4 woman is a *c* to her husband:
14.24 The *c* of the wise is their riches:
16.31 The hoary head is a *c* of glory,
17. 6 Children's children are the *c* of
27.24 the *c* endure to every generation?
SS 3.11 behold king Solomon with the *c*
Isa 3.17 Lord will smite with a scab the *c*
28. 1 the *c* of pride, to the drunkards
3 The *c* of pride, the drunkards of
5 Lord of hosts be for a *c* of glory,
62. 3 Thou shalt also be a *c* of glory
Jer 2.16 have broken the *c* of thy head.
13.18 down, even the *c* of your glory.
48.45 *c* of the head of the tumultuous
La 5.16 The *c* is fallen from our head:
Eze 16.12 and a beautiful *c* upon thine head.
21.26 the diadem, and take off the *c*:
Zec 9.16 shall be as the stones of a *c*,
Mt 27.29 they had platted a *c* of thorns,
Mk 15.17 and platted a *c* of thorns,
Jn 19. 2 the soldiers platted a *c* of thorns,
5 wearing the *c* of thorns, and the
1Co 9.25 to obtain a corruptible *c*; but we
Php 4. 1 and longed for, my joy and *c*,
1Th 2.19 hope, or joy, or *c* of rejoicing?
2Ti 4. 8 up for me a *c* of righteousness,
Jas 1.12 he shall receive the *c* of life,
1Pe 5. 4 a *c* of glory that fadeth not away.
Rev 2.10 and I will give thee a *c* of life.
3.11 thou hast, that no man take thy *c*.
6. 2 and a *c* was given unto him:
12. 1 upon her head a *c* of twelve stars:
14.14 having on his head a golden *c*,

CROWNED

Ps 8. 5 *c* him with glory and honor.
Pr 14.18 prudent are *c* with knowledge.
SS 3.11 wherewith his mother *c* him in
Na 3.17 Thy *c* are as the locusts, and thy
2Ti 2. 5 yet is he not *c*, except he strive
Heb 2. 9 death, *c* with glory and honor;

CROWNEDST

Heb 2. 7 thou *c* him with glory and honor,

CROWNEST

Ps 65.11 *c* the year with thy goodness;

CROWNETH

Ps 103. 4 who *c* thee with lovingkindness

CROWNS

Eze 23.42 and beautiful *c* upon their heads.
Zec 6.11 take silver and gold, and make *c*,
14 And the *c* shall be to Hellem,
Rev 4. 4 they had on their heads *c* of gold.
10 and cast their *c* before the throne,
9. 7 heads were as it were *c* like gold,
12. 3 and seven *c* upon his heads.
13. 1 and upon his horns ten *c*, and
19.12 and on his head were many *c*;

CRUCIFIED

Mt 26. 2 Son of man is betrayed to be *c*.
27.22 all say unto him, Let him be *c*.
23 out the more, saying, Let him be *c*.
26 he delivered him to be *c*.
35 And they *c* him, and parted his
38 were there two thieves *c* with him,
44 also, which were *c* with him,
28. 5 that ye seek Jesus, which was *c*.
Mk 15.15 when he had scourged him, to be *c*.
24 when they had *c* him, they parted
25 was the third hour, and they *c* him.
32 that were *c* with him reviled him.
16. 6 Jesus of Nazareth, which was *c*:
Lk 23.23 requiring that he might be *c*.
33 called Calvary, there they *c* him,
24. 7 and be *c*, and the third day rise
20 to death, and have *c* him.
Jn 19.16 him therefore unto them to be *c*.
18 Where they *c* him, and two others
20 place where Jesus was *c* was nigh
23 soldiers, when they had *c* Jesus,
32 the other which was *c* with him.
41 Now in the place where he was *c*
Ac 2.23 wicked hands have *c* and slain:
36 same Jesus, whom ye have *c*,
4.10 Christ of Nazareth, whom ye *c*,
Ro 6. 6 that our old man is *c* with him,
1Co 1.13 was Paul *c* for you? or were ye
23 we preach Christ *c*, unto the Jews
2 .2 you, save Jesus Christ, and him *c*.
8 would not have *c* the Lord of glory.
2Co 13. 4 he was *c* through weakness,
Gal 2.20 I am *c* with Christ: nevertheless
3. 1 evidently set forth, *c* among you?
5.24 have *c* the flesh with the affections
6.14 by whom the world is *c* unto me,
Rev 11. 8 Egypt, where also our Lord was *c*.

CRUCIFY

Mt 20.19 and to scourge, and to *c* him:
23.34 some of them ye shall kill and *c*;
27.31 and led him away to *c* him.
Mk 15.13 they cried out again, *C* him.
14 out the more exceedingly, *C* him.
20 and led him out to *c* him.
27 And with him they *c* two thieves;
Lk 23.21 they cried, saying, *C* him, *c* him.
Jn 19. 6 cried out, saying, *C* him, *c* him.
6 Take ye him, and *c* him: for I find
10 not that I have power to *c* thee.
15 away with him, *c* him. Pilate saith
15 Shall I *c* your King? The chief
Heb 6. 6 they *c* to themselves the Son of God

CRUEL

Gen 49. 7 and their wrath, for it was *c*:
Ex 6. 9 of spirit, and for *c* bondage.
Dt 32.33 dragons, and the *c* venom of asps.
Job 30.21 Thou art become *c* to me: with thy
Ps 25.19 and they hate me with *c* hatred.
71. 4 of the unrighteous and *c* man.
Pr 5. 9 others, and thy years unto the *c*:
11.17 he that is *c* troubleth his own flesh.
12.10 tender mercies of the wicked are *c*.
17.11 a *c* messenger shall be sent against
27. 4 is *c*, and anger is outrageous;
SS 8. 6 jealousy is *c* as the grave: the coals
Isa 13. 9 Lord cometh, *c* both with wrath
19. 4 over into the hand of a *c* lord;
Jer 6.23 they are *c*, and have no mercy;
30.14 the chastisement of a *c* one, for
50.42 they are *c*, and will not shew mercy:
La 4. 3 daughter of my people is become *c*,
Heb 11.36 others had trial of *c* mockings

CRUMBS

Mt 15.27 dogs eat of the *c* which fall from
Mk 7.28 the table eat of the children's *c*.
Lk 16.21 to be fed with the *c* which fell

CRUSH

Job 39.15 that the foot may *c* them, or that
La 1.15 against me to *c* my young men:
3.34 *c* under his feet all the prisoners
Am 4. 1 which *c* the needy, which say to

CRYING

1Sa 4.14 Eli heard the noise of the *c*,
2Sa 13.19 hand on her head, and went on *c*.
Job 39. 7 regardeth he the *c* of the driver.
Ps 69. 3 I am weary of my *c*: my throat
Pr 19.18 let not thy soul spare for his *c*.
30.15 hath two daughters, *c*, Give, give.
Isa 22. 5 walls, and of *c* to the mountains.
24.11 is a *c* for wine in the streets;
65.19 heard in her, nor the voice of *c*.
Jer 48. 3 of *c* shall be from Horonaim,
Zec 4. 7 thereof with shoutings, *c*, Grace,
Mal 2.13 with weeping, and with *c* out,
Mt 3. 3 voice of one *c* in the wilderness,
9.27 *c*, and saying, Thou son of David,
21.15 and the children *c* in the temple,
Mk 1. 3 voice of one *c* in the wilderness,
5. 5 and in the tombs, *c*, and cutting
15. 8 the multitude *c* aloud began to
Lk 3. 4 voice of one *c* in the wilderness,
4.41 out of many, *c* out, and saying,
Jn 1.23 the voice of one *c* in the wilderness,
Ac 8. 7 unclean spirits, *c* with loud voice,
14.14 ran in among the people, *c* out,
17. 6 unto the rulers of the city, *c*,
21.28 *C* out, Men of Israel, help: This
36 followed after, *c*, Away with him.
25.24 *c* that he ought not to live any
Gal 4. 6 into your hearts, *c*, Abba, Father.
Heb 5. 7 with strong *c* and tears unto him
Rev 14.15 *c* with a loud voice to him that
21. 4 neither sorrow, nor *c*, neither

CRYSTAL

Job 28.17 The gold and the *c* cannot equal
Eze 1.22 as the color of the terrible *c*,
Rev 4. 6 was a sea of glass like unto *c*:
21.11 like a jasper stone, clear as *c*;
22. 1 river of water of life, clear as *c*,

CUCUMBERS

Nu 11. 5 freely; the *c*, and the melons,
Isa 1. 8 as a lodge in a garden of *c*,

CUMBERED

Lk 10.40 But Martha was *c* about much

CUMBERETH

Lk 13. 7 cut it down; why *c* it the ground?

CUMMIN

Isa 28.25 and scatter the *c*, and cast in the
27 wheel turned about upon the *c*;
27 with a staff, and the *c* with a rod.
Mt 23.23 pay tithe of mint and anise and *c*,

CUNNINGLY

2Pe 1.16 have not followed *c* devised fables,

CUP

Gen 40.11 and Pharaoh's *c* was in my hand:
11 pressed them into Pharaoh's *c*,
11 I gave the *c* into Pharaoh's hand.
13 deliver Pharaoh's *c* into his hand,
21 he gave the *c* into Pharaoh's hand:
44. 2 And put my *c*, the silver *c*, in the
12 *c* was found in Benjamin's sack.
16 he also with whom the *c* is found.
17 man in whose hand the *c* is found,
2Sa 12. 3 and drank of his own *c*, and lay
1Ki 7.26 was wrought like the brim of a *c*,
2Ch 4. 5 like the work of the brim of a *c*,
Ps 11. 6 this shall be the portion of their *c*.
16. 5 of mine inheritance and of my *c*:
23. 5 head with oil; my *c* runneth over.
73.10 and waters of a full *c* are wrung out
75. 8 hand of the Lord there is a *c*,
116.13 I will take the *c* of salvation, and
Pr 23.31 when it giveth his color in the *c*,
Isa 51.17 of the Lord the *c* of his fury;
17 the dregs of the *c* of trembling,
22 of thine hand the *c* of trembling,
22 even the dregs of the *c* of my fury;
Jer 16. 7 the *c* of consolation to drink for
25.15 the wine *c* of this fury at my hand,
17 took I the *c* at the Lord's hand,

Cup found in Pompeii, from the first century A.D.

28 take the *c* at thine hand to drink,
49.12 judgment was not to drink of the *c*
51. 7 Babylon hath been a golden *c* in
La 4.21 the *c* also shall pass through unto
Eze 23.31 will I give her *c* into thine hand.
32 of thy sister's *c* deep and large:
33 *c* of astonishment and desolation,
33 with the *c* of thy sister Samaria.
Hab 2.16 *c* of the Lord's right hand shall be
Zec 12. 2 make Jerusalem a *c* of trembling
Mt 10.42 *c* of cold water only in the name
20.22 drink of the *c* that I shall drink of,
23 Ye shall drink indeed of my *c*, and
23.25 outside of the *c* and of the platter,
26 first that which is within the *c*
26.27 he took the *c*, and gave thanks,
39 possible, let this *c* pass from me:
42 this *c* may not pass away from me,
Mk 9.41 give you a *c* of water to drink
10.38 ye drink of the *c* that I drink of?
39 indeed drink of the *c* that I drink
14.23 And he took the *c*, and when he
36 take away this *c* from me:
Lk 11.39 make clean the outside of the *c*
22.17 he took the *c*, and gave thanks,
20 Likewise also the *c* after supper,
20 This *c* is the new testament in my
42 if thou be willing, remove this *c*
Jn 18.11 *c* which my Father hath given me,
1Co 10.16 The *c* of blessing which we bless,
21 Ye cannot drink the *c* of the Lord,
21 and the *c* of devils:
11.25 same manner also he took the *c*,
25 This *c* is the new testament in my
26 and drink this *c*, ye do show
27 drink this *c* of the Lord, unworthily,
28 of that bread, and drink of that *c*.
Rev 14.10 into the *c* of his indignation;
16.19 the *c* of the wine of the fierceness
17. 4 having a golden *c* in her hand full
18. 6 in the *c* which she hath filled, fill

CUPS

1Ch 28.17 and the bowls, and the *c*:
Isa 22.24 from the vessels of *c*, even to all
Jer 35. 5 pots full of wine, and *c*, and I
52.19 and the spoons, and the *c*; that
Mk 7. 4 as the washing of *c*, and pots,
8 as the washing of pots and *c*:

CURE

Jer 33. 6 I will bring it health and *c*,
6 and I will *c* them, and will reveal
Hos 5.13 you, nor *c* you of your wound.
Mt 17.16 and they could not *c* him.
Lk 9. 1 over all devils, and to *c* diseases.

CURED

Jer 46.11 for thou shalt not be *c*.
Mt 17.18 child was *c* from that very hour.
Lk 7.21 he *c* many of their infirmities and
Jn 5.10 said unto him that was *c*, It is the

CURES

Lk 13.32 and I do *c* to day and to morrow,

CURIOUS

Ex 28. 8 And the *c* girdle of the ephod,
27, 28 above the *c* girdle of the
29. 5 with the *c* girdle of the ephod:
35.32 devise *c* works, to work in gold,
39. 5 And the *c* girdle of his ephod,
20, 21 above the *c* girdle of the
Lev 8. 7 with the *c* girdle of the ephod,
Ac 19.19 used *c* arts brought their books

CURIOUSLY

Ps 139.15 *c* wrought in the lowest parts

CURSE

Gen 8.21 I will not again *c* the ground any
12. 3 and *c* him that curseth thee: and in
27.12 I shall bring a *c* upon me, and not
13 Upon me be thy *c*, my son:
Ex 22.28 gods, nor *c* the ruler of thy people.
Lev 19.14 Thou shalt not *c* the deaf, nor
Nu 5.18, 19 bitter water that causeth the *c*:
21 Lord make thee a *c* and an oath
22 water that causeth the *c* shall go
24 bitter water that causeth the *c*:
24, 27 water that causeth the *c* shall
27 woman shall be a *c* among her
22. 6 I pray thee, *c* me this people:
11 come now, *c* me them;
12 shalt not *c* the people: for they
17 I pray thee, *c* me this people.
23. 7 Come, *c* me Jacob, and come,
8 How shall I *c*, whom God hath not
11 I took thee to *c* mine enemies,
13 all: and *c* me them from thence.
25 *c* them at all, nor bless them at all.
27 mayest *c* me them from thence.
24.10 I called thee to *c* mine enemies,
Dt 11.26 you this day a blessing and a *c*;
28 a *c*, if ye will not obey the
29 and the *c* upon mount Ebal.
23. 4 Pethor of Mesopotamia, to *c* thee.
5 God turned the *c* into a blessing
27.13 shall stand upon mount Ebal to *c*;
29.19 he heareth the words of this *c*,
30. 1 the blessing and the *c*, which I
Jos 6.18 and make the camp of Israel a *c*,
24. 9 Balaam the son of Beor to *c* you:
Jdg 5.23 *C* ye Meroz, said the angel
23 *c* ye bitterly the inhabitants
9.57 upon them came the *c* of Jotham
2Sa 16. 9 should this dead dog *c* my lord
10 let him *c*, because the Lord hath
10 Lord hath said unto him, *C* David.
11 let him alone, and let him *c*: for
1Ki 2. 8 a grievous *c* in the day when I
2Ki 22.19 should become a desolation and a *c*,
Neh 10.29 entered into a *c*, and into an oath,
13. 2 against them, that he should *c*
2 God turned the *c* into a blessing.
Job 1.11 and he will *c* thee to thy face.
2. 5 and he will *c* thee to thy face.
9 *c* God, and die.
3. 8 Let them *c* it that
8 that *c* the day, who are
31.30 to sin by wishing a *c* to his soul.
Ps 62. 4 their mouth, but they *c* inwardly.
109.28 Let them *c*, but bless thou:
Pr 3.33 The *c* of the Lord is in the house
11.26 corn, the people shall *c* him: but
24.24 him shall the people *c*, nations
26. 2 the *c* causeless shall not come.
27.14 morning, it shall be counted a *c*
28.27 his eyes shall have many a *c*.
30.10 lest he *c* thee, and thou be found
Ec 7.21 lest thou hear thy servant *c* thee:
10.20 *C* not the king, no not in thy
20 *c* not the rich in thy bedchamber:
Isa 8.21 and *c* their king and their God,
24. 6 hath the *c* devoured the earth,
34. 5 and upon the people of my *c*, to
43.28 given Jacob to the *c*, and Israel
65.15 ye shall leave your name for a *c*
Jer 15.10 every one of them doth *c* me.
24. 9 and a proverb, a taunt and a *c*,
25.18 astonishment, an hissing, and a *c*;
26. 6 will make this city a *c* to all the
29.18 to be a *c*, and an astonishment,
22 them shall be taken up a *c* by all
42.18 an astonishment, and a *c*, and a
44. 8 ye might be a *c* and a reproach
12 an astonishment, and a *c*, and a
22 astonishment, and a *c*, without an
49.13 a reproach, a waste, and a *c*; and
La 3.65 sorrow of heart, thy *c* unto them.
Dan 9.11 the *c* is poured upon us, and the
Zec 5. 3 is the *c* that goeth forth over the
8.13 ye were a *c* among the heathen,
Mal 2. 2 I will even send a *c* upon you,
2 and I will *c* your blessings:
3. 9 are cursed with a *c*: for ye have
4. 6 come and smite the earth with a *c*.
Mt 5.44 bless them that *c* you, do good to
26.74 Then began he to *c* and to swear,
Mk 14.71 But he began to *c* and to swear,
Lk 6.28 Bless them that *c* you, and pray
Ac 23.12 and bound themselves under a *c*,
14 bound ourselves under a great *c*,
Ro 12.14 persecute you: bless, and *c* not.
Gal 3.10 works of the law are under the *c*:
13 redeemed us from the *c* of the
13 law, being made a *c* for us:
Jas 3. 9 therewith *c* we men, which are
Rev 22. 3 there shall be no more *c*: but the

CURSED

Gen 3.14 thou art *c* above all cattle, and
17 *c* is the ground for thy sake; in
4.11 now art thou *c* from the earth,
5.29 ground which the Lord hath *c*.
9.25 he said, *C* be Canaan; a servant of
27.29 *c* be every one that curseth thee,
49. 7 *C* be their anger, for it was fierce:
Lev 20. 9 hath *c* his father or his mother;
24.11 the name of the Lord, and *c*.
14 forth him that hath *c* without the
23 forth him that had *c* out of the
Nu 22. 6 and he whom thou cursest is *c*.
23. 8 I curse, whom God hath not *c*?
24. 9 and *c* is he that curseth thee.
Dt 7.26 lest thou be a *c* thing like it:
26 abhor it; for it is a *c* thing.
13.17 cleave nought of the *c* thing to
27.15 *C* be the man that maketh any
16 *C* be he that setteth light by his
17 *C* be he that removeth his
18 *C* be he that maketh the blind to
19 *C* be he that perverteth the
20 *C* be he that lieth with his father's
21 *C* be he that lieth with any manner
22 *C* be he that lieth with his sister,
23 *C* be he that lieth with his mother
24 *C* be he that smiteth his neighbor
25 *C* be he that taketh reward to slay
26 *C* be he that confirmeth not all the
28.16 *C* shalt thou be in the city,
16 and *c* shalt thou be in the field.
17 *C* shall be thy basket and thy store.
18 *C* shall be the fruit of thy body,
19 *C* shalt thou be when thou comest
19 *c* shalt thou be when thou goest
Jos 6.26 *C* be the man before the Lord, that
9.23 therefore ye are *c*, and there shall
Jdg 9.27 eat and drink, and *c* Abimelech.

Jdg 21.18 *C* be he that giveth a wife to
1Sa 14.24, 28 *C* be the man that eateth any
17.43 Philistine *c* David by his gods:
26.19 of men, *c* be they before the Lord;
2Sa 16. 5 came forth, and *c* still as he came.
7 said Shimei when he *c*, Come out,
13 and *c* as he went, and threw stones
19.21 because he *c* the Lord's anointed?
1Ki 2. 8 which *c* me with a grievous curse
2Ki 2.24 *c* them in the name of the Lord.
9.34 now this *c* woman, and bury her:
Neh 13.25 contended with them, and *c* them,
Job 1. 5 sinned, and *c* God in their hearts.
3. 1 Job his mouth, and *c* his day.
5. 3 but suddenly I *c* his habitation.
24.18 their portion is *c* in the earth: he
Ps 37.22 they that be *c* of him shall be cut
119.21 hast rebuked the proud that are *c*,
Ec 7.22 thyself likewise hast *c* others.
Jer 11. 3 *C* be the man that obeyeth not the
17. 5 *C* be the man that trusteth in man,
20.14 *C* be the day wherein I was born:
15 *C* be the man who brought tidings
48.10 *C* be he that doeth the work
10 *c* be he that keepeth back his
Mal 1.14 *c* be the deceiver, which hath in
2. 2 yea, I have *c* them already, because
3. 9 Ye are *c* with a curse: for ye have
Mt 25.41 Depart from me, ye *c*, into
Jn 7.49 who knoweth not the law are *c*.
Gal 3.10 *C* is every one that continueth
13 *C* is every one that hangeth on a
2Pe 2.14 covetous practices; *c* children:

CURSEDST

Jdg 17. 2 about which thou *c*, and spakest
Mk 11.21 behold, the fig tree which thou *c*

CURSETH

Gen 12. 3 and curse him that *c* thee: and in
27.29 cursed be every one that *c* thee,
Ex 21.17 And he that *c* his father, or his
Lev 20. 9 every one that *c* his father or his
24.15 Whosoever *c* his God shall bear
Nu 24. 9 thee, and cursed is he that *c* thee.
Pr 20.20 Whoso *c* his father or his mother,
30.11 There is a generation that *c* their
Mt 25. 4 He that *c* father or mother, let
Mk 7.10 Whoso *c* father or mother, let him

CURSING

Nu 5.21 the woman with an oath of *c*,
Dt 28.20 The Lord shall send upon thee *c*,
30.19 life and death, blessing and *c*:
2Sa 16.12 will requite me good for his *c*
Ps 10. 7 His mouth is full of *c* and deceit
59.12 for *c* and lying which they speak.
109.17 As he loved *c*, so let it come unto
18 he clothed himself with *c* like as
Pr 29.24 he heareth *c*, and bewrayeth it
Ro 3.14 Whose mouth is full of *c* and
Heb 6. 8 nigh unto *c*; whose end is to be
Jas 3.10 mouth proceedeth blessing and *c*.

CUSTOM

Gen 31.35 for the *c* of women is upon me.
Jdg 11.39 And it was a *c* in Israel,
1Sa 2.13 priest's *c* with the people was,
Ezr 3. 4 according to the *c*, as the duty
4.13 they not pay toll, tribute, and *c*,
20 and toll, tribute, and *c*, was paid
7.24 toll, tribute, or *c*, upon them.
Jer 32.11 sealed according to the law and *c*,
Mt 9. 9 sitting at the receipt of *c*:
17.25 of the earth take *c* or tribute?
Mk 2.14 sitting at the receipt of *c*,
Lk 1. 9 to the *c* of the priest's office, his
2.27 do for him after the *c* of the law,
42 Jerusalem after the *c* of the feast,
4.16 as his *c* was, he went into
5.27 Levi, sitting at the receipt of *c*:
Jn 18.39 ye have a *c*, that I should release
Ro 13. 7 is due; *c* to whom *c*; fear to whom
1Co 11.16 we have no such *c*, neither the

CUSTOMS

Lev 18.30 any one of these abominable *c*,
Jer 10. 3 the *c* of the people are vain:
Ac 6.14 the *c* which Moses delivered us.
16.21 teach *c* which are not lawful for us
21.21 neither to walk after the *c*.
26. 3 to be expert in all *c* and questions
28.17 the people, or *c* of our fathers,

CUTTING

Ex 31. 5 And in *c* of stones, to set them,
35.33 And in the *c* of stones, to set them,
Isa 38.10 I said in the *c* off of my days,
Hab 2.10 thy house by *c* off many people,
Mk 5. 5 crying, and *c* himself with stones.

CYMBAL

1Co 13. 1 sounding brass, or a tinkling *c*.

CYPRUS

Ac 4.36 Levite, and of the country of *C*.
11.19 and *C*, and Antioch, preaching
20 them were men of *C* and Cyrene,
13. 4 and from thence they sailed to *C*.
15.39 took Mark, and sailed unto *C*;
21. 3 when we had discovered *C*, we left
16 with them one Mnason of *C*,
27. 4 we sailed under *C*, because the

CYRENE

Mt 27.32 a man of *C*, Simon by name:
Ac 2.10 of Libya about *C*, and strangers
11.20 were men of Cyprus and *C*, which
13. 1 and Lucius of *C*, and Manaen,

CYRENIAN

Mk 15.21 compel one Simon a *C*, who
Lk 23.26 laid hold upon one Simon, a *C*,

CYRENIANS

Ac 6. 9 of the Libertines, and *C*, and

CYRENIUS

Lk 2. 2 when *C* was governor of Syria.)

CYRUS

2Ch 36.22 the first year of *C* king of Persia,
22 the Lord stirred up the spirit of *C*
23 Thus saith *C* king of Persia,
Ezr 1. 1 the first year of *C* king of Persia,
1 the Lord stirred up the spirit of *C*
2 Thus saith *C* king of Persia,
7 *C* the king brought forth the
8 those did *C* king of Persia bring
3. 7 to the grant that they had of *C*
4. 3 as king *C* the king of Persia hath
5 all the days of *C* king of Persia,
5.13 first year of *C* the king of Babylon
13 the same king *C* made a decree
14 those did *C* the king take out of
17 was made of *C* the king to build
6. 3 year of *C* the king the same *C*
14 to the commandment of *C*,
Isa 44.28 saith of *C*, He is my shepherd,
45. 1 the Lord to his anointed, to *C*,
Dan 1.21 even unto the first year of king *C*.
6.28 and in the reign of *C* the Persian.
10. 1 the third year of *C* king of Persia

CYRUS THE GREAT

Originally king of a small vassal-state in the powerful and expanding Median Empire; in the year 550 B.C. he ousted the emperor Astyages, becoming ruler of a domain that included much of the former Assyrian Empire. Cyrus added conquests in Greece and Asia Minor to his realm before turning to Babylon, Assyria's immediate successor to hegemony in Mesopotamia.

Cyrus' conquest of Babylon in 539 B.C. brought him into biblical history, for in that year there was still a community of Jewish exiles there, deported by Nebuchadnezzar earlier in the same century. These Jews benefited from a dramatic policy change decreed by the new emperor: Cyrus determined to resettle the Jewish exiles in their former territory, and even to provide funds for the rebuilding of their temple in Jerusalem. The edict is recorded in Ezr 1.2-4 and 6.3-5.

Cyrus' conquests, therefore, coincide with an event of immense significance for the Jews. The theology of his act of deliverance is found in the latter half of the Book of Isaiah ("Second Isaiah"), where he is called the Lord's "shepherd" (44.28) and even his "anointed" (45.1) for having demonstrated God's power to dispose over all nations for the benefit of his people.

D

DAILY
Ex 5.13 Fulfill your works, your *d* tasks,
19 your bricks of your *d* tasks.
16. 5 twice as much as they gather *d*.
Nu 4.16 the *d* meat offering, and the
28.24 this manner ye shall offer *d*,
29. 6 *d* burnt offering, and his meat
Jdg 16.16 pressed him *d* with her words,
2Ki 25.30 a *d* rate for every day,
2Ch 31.16 his *d* portion for their service
Ezr 3. 4 the *d* burnt offerings by number,
Neh 5.18 prepared for me *d* was one
Est 3. 4 when they spake *d* unto him,
Ps 13. 2 having sorrow in my heart *d*?
42.10 while they say *d* unto me,
56. 1 he fighting *d* oppresseth me.
2 enemies would *d* swallow me
61. 8 I may *d* perform my vows.
68.19 who *d* loadeth us with benefits,
72.15 and *d* shall he be praised.
74.22 foolish...reproacheth thee *d*.
86. 3 O Lord for I cry unto thee *d*
88. 9 Lord, I...called *d* upon thee,
17 They came round about me *d*
Pr 8.30 and I was *d* his delight,
34 watching *d* at my gates,
Isa 58. 2 Yet they seek me *d*, and delight
Jer 7.25 *d* rising up early and sending
20. 7 I am in derision *d*, every one
8 unto me and a derision, *d*.
37.21 *d* a piece of bread out of the
Eze 30.16 Noph shall have distresses *d*.
45.23 without blemish *d* the seven days;
23 and a kid of the goats *d*
46.13 shalt *d* prepare a burnt offering
Dan 1. 5 appointed them a *d* provision
8.11 the *d* sacrifice was taken away,
12 given him against the *d* sacrifice
13 vision concerning the *d* sacrifice,
11.31 shall take away the *d* sacrifice,
12.11 *d* sacrifice shall be taken away,
Hos 12. 1 *d* increaseth lies and
Mt 6.11 Give us this day our *d* bread.
26.55 I sat *d* with you teaching
Mk 14.49 was *d* with you in the temple
Lk 9.23 and take up his cross *d*,
11. 3 us day by day our *d* bread.
19.47 he taught *d* in the temple.
22.53 *d* with you in the temple,
Ac 2.46 continuing *d* with one accord
47 Lord added to the church *d*
3. 2 whom they laid *d* at the gate
5.42 And *d* in the temple, and in
6. 1 neglected in the *d* ministration.
16. 5 increased in number *d*.
17.11 searched the scriptures *d*,
17 the market *d* with them
19. 9 disputing *d* in the school
1Co 15.31 Jesus our Lord, I die *d*.
2Co 11.28 which cometh upon me *d*,
Heb 3.13 exhort one another *d*,
7.27 Who needeth not *d*, as
10.11 priest standeth *d* ministering
Jas 2.15 naked, and destitute of *d* food,

DAINTY
Job 33.20 abhorreth bread, and his soul *d*
Pr 23. 6 neither desire thou his *d* meats:
Rev 18.14 things which were *d* and goodly

DALMANUTHA
Mk 8.10 and came into the parts of *D*.

DALMATIA
2Ti 4.10 Crescens to Galatia, Titus unto *D*.

DAMAGE
Ezr 4.22 why should *d* grow to the hurt
Est 7. 4 not countervail the king's *d*.
Pr 26. 6 off the feet, and drinketh *d*.
Dan 6. 2 and the king should have no *d*.
Ac 27.10 will be with hurt and much *d*,
2Co 7. 9 that ye might receive *d* by us in

DAMARIS
Ac 17.34 and a woman named *D*, and

DAMASCENES
2Co 11.32 the king kept the city of the *D*

DAMNABLE
2Pe 2. 1 privily shall bring in *d* heresies,

DAMNATION
Mt 23.14 ye shall receive the greater *d*.
33 how can ye escape the *d* of hell?
Mk 3.29 but is in danger of eternal *d*:
12.40 these shall receive greater *d*.
Lk 20.47 the same shall receive greater *d*.
Jn 5.29 unto the resurrection of *d*.
Ro 3. 8 good may come? whose *d* is just.
13. 2 shall receive to themselves *d*.
1Co 11.29 eateth and drinketh *d* to himself,
1Ti 5.12 Having *d*, because they have cast
2Pe 2. 3 not, and their *d* slumbereth not.

DAMNED
Mk 16.16 he that believeth not shall be *d*.
Ro 14.23 he that doubteth is *d* if he eat,
2Th 2.12 That they all might be *d* who

DAMSEL
Gen 24.14 the *d* to whom I shall say,
16 And the *d* was very fair to look
28 And the *d* ran, and told them of
55 Let the *d* abide with us a few
57 We will call the *d*, and inquire
34. 3 and he loved the *d*, and
3 spake kindly unto the *d*.
4 saying, Get me this *d* to wife.
12 unto me: but give me the *d* to
Dt 22.15 father of the *d*, and her mother,
19 unto the father of the *d*, because
20 of virginity be not found for the *d*:
21 they shall bring out the *d* to the
23 a *d* that is a virgin be betrothed
24 the *d*, because she cried not,
25 if a man find a betrothed *d* in the
26 unto the *d* thou shalt do nothing;
26 there is in the *d* no sin
27 the betrothed *d* cried, and there
28 If a man find a *d* that is a virgin,
Jdg 5.30 to every man a *d* or two;
19. 3 the father of the *d* saw him,
Ru 2. 5 over the reapers, Whose *d* is this?
6 It is the Moabitish *d* that came
1Ki 1. 3 So they sought for a fair *d*
4 And the *d* was very fair,
Mt 14.11 in a charger, and given to the *d*:
26.69 and a *d* came unto him, saying,
Mk 5.39 the *d* is not dead, but sleepeth.
40 father and the mother of the *d*,
40 and entereth in where the *d* was
41 he took the *d* by the hand,
41 interpreted, *D*, I say unto thee,
42 the *d* arose, and walked; for she
6.22 the king said unto the *d*, Ask of
28 and gave it to the *d*: and
28 the *d* gave it to her mother.
Jn 18.17 Then saith the *d* that kept the
Ac 12.13 a *d* came to hearken, named
16.16 a certain *d* possessed with a

DANCE
Jdg 21.21 of Shiloh come out to *d* in dances,
Job 21.11 like a flock, and their children *d*.
Ps 149. 3 praise his name in the *d*: let
150. 4 Praise him with the timbrel and *d*:
Ec 3. 4 a time to mourn, and a time to *d*;
Isa 13.21 there, and satyrs shall *d* there.
Jer 31.13 shall the virgin rejoice in the *d*,
La 5.15 our *d* is turned into mourning.

DANCED
Jdg 21.23 to their number, of them that *d*,
2Sa 6.14 David *d* before the Lord with all
Mt 11.17 unto you, and ye have not *d*;
14. 6 the daughter of Herodias *d* before
Mk 6.22 the said Herodias came in, and *d*,
Lk 7.32 unto you, and ye have not *d*;

DANCES
Ex 15.20 her with timbrels and with *d*.
Jdg 11.34 him with timbrels and with *d*:
21.21 of Shiloh come out to dance in *d*,
1Sa 21.11 sing one to another of him in *d*,
29. 5 they sang one to another in *d*,
Jer 31. 4 shalt go forth in the *d* of them

DANCING
Ex 32.19 that he saw the calf, and the *d*:
1Sa 18. 6 singing and *d*, to meet king Saul.
30.16 eating and drinking, and *d*,
2Sa 6.16 saw king David leaping and *d*
1Ch 15.29 saw king David *d* and playing:
Ps 30.11 for me my mourning into *d*:
Lk 15.25 the house, he heard musick and *d*.

DANGER
Mt 5.21, 22 shall be in *d* of the judgment:
22 shall be in *d* of the council: but
22 thou fool, shall be in *d* of hell fire.
Mk 3.29 is in *d* of eternal damnation:
Ac 19.27 not only this our craft is in *d*
40 we are in *d* to be called in question
(See box on page 194)

DANGEROUS
Ac 27. 9 when sailing was now *d*,

DANIEL
1Ch 3. 1 *D*, of Abigail the Carmelitess:
Ezr 8. 2 of the sons of Ithamar; *D*: of the
Neh 10. 6 *D*, Ginnethon, Baruch,
Eze 14.14 three men, Noah, *D*, and Job,
20 Noah, *D*, and Job, were in it,
28. 3 Behold, thou art wiser than *D*;
Dan 1. 6 children of Judah, *D*, Hananiah,
7 for he gave unto *D* the name of
8 But *D* purposed in his heart that
9 God had brought *D* into favor
10 prince of the eunuchs said unto *D*,
11 said *D* to Melzar, whom the prince
11 of the eunuchs had set over *D*,
17 *D* had understanding in all visions
19 them all was found none like *D*,
21 *D* continued even unto the first
2.13 they sought *D* and his fellows
14 Then *D* answered with counsel
15 made the thing known to *D*.
16 Then *D* went in, and desired of the
17 Then *D* went to his house, and
18 that *D* and his fellows should not
19 was the secret revealed unto *D*
19 Then *D* blessed the God of heaven,
20 *D* answered and said, Blessed be
24 Therefore *D* went in unto Arioch,
25 Then Arioch brought in *D* before
26 The king answered and said to *D*,

BIBLICAL THEMES

DANGER

And Lot went out, and spake unto his sons in law . . . and said, Up, get you out of this place; for the Lord will destroy this city. But he seemed as one that mocked unto his sons in law.
Gen 19.14

Then said David to the Philistine, Thou comest to me with a sword, and with a spear, and with a shield: but I come to thee in the name of the Lord of hosts, the God of the armies of Israel, whom thou hast defied. 1Sa 17.45

And the evil spirit from the Lord was upon Saul, as he sat in his house with his javelin in his hand: and David played with his hand. And Saul sought to smite David even to the wall with the javelin; but he slipped away out of Saul's presence. 1Sa 19.9-10

Fearfulness and trembling are come upon me, and horror hath overwhelmed me. And I said, Oh that I had wings like a dove! for then would I fly away, and be at rest.
Ps 55.5-6

My soul is among lions: and I lie even among them that are set on fire, even the sons of men, whose teeth are spears and arrows, and their tongue a sharp sword. Ps 57.4

Deliver me, O Lord, from mine enemies: I flee unto thee to hide me.
Ps 143.9

Then the king commanded, and they brought Daniel, and cast him into the den of lions. . . . So Daniel was taken up out of the den, and no manner of hurt was found upon him, because he believed in his God.
Dan 6.16, 23

And when they were departed, behold, the angel of the Lord appeareth to Joseph in a dream, saying, Arise, and take the young child and his mother, and flee into Egypt, and be thou there until I bring thee word: for Herod will seek the young child to destroy him. Mt 2.13

Go your ways: behold, I send you forth as lambs among wolves. Lk 10.3

And we being exceedingly tossed with a tempest, the next day they lightened the ship; and the third day we cast out with our own hands the tackling of the ship. . . . But . . . Paul stood forth in the midst of them, and said, Sirs . . . I exhort you to be of good cheer: for there shall be no loss of any man's life. . . . For there stood by me this night the angel of God, whose I am, and whom I serve. Ac 27.18-19, 21-23

Are they ministers of Christ? (I speak as a fool) I am more. . . . Thrice was I beaten with rods, once was I stoned, thrice I suffered shipwreck, a night and a day I have been in the deep; in journeyings often, in perils of waters, in perils of robbers, in perils by mine own countrymen, in perils by the heathen, in perils in the city, in perils in the wilderness, in perils in the sea, in perils among false brethren; in weariness and painfulness, in watchings often, in hunger and thirst, in fastings often, in cold and nakedness. 2Co 11.23, 25-27

This know also, that in the last days perilous times shall come. . . . Yea, and all that will live godly in Christ Jesus shall suffer persecution. . . . But continue thou in the things which thou hast learned and hast been assured of, knowing of whom thou hast learned them. 2Ti 3.1, 12, 14

Dan 2.27 *D* answered in the presence of the
46 upon his face, and worshipped *D*,
47 king answered unto *D*, and said,
48 the king made *D* a great man,
49 Then *D* requested of the king, and
49 but *D* sat in the gate of the king.
4. 8 at the last *D* came in before me,
19 *D*, whose name was Belteshazzar,
5.12 in the same *D*, whom the king
12 now let *D* be called, and he will
13 was *D* brought in before the king.
13 the king spake and said unto *D*,
13 Art thou that *D*, which art of
17 Then *D* answered and said before
29 and they clothed *D* with scarlet,
6. 2 presidents; of whom *D* was first:
3 Then this *D* was preferred above
4 sought to find occasion against *D*
5 find any occasion against this *D*,
10 when *D* knew that the writing was
11 and found *D* praying and making
13 *D*, which is of the children of the
14 set his heart on *D* to deliver him:
16 and they brought *D*, and cast him
16 the king spake and said unto *D*,
17 not be changed concerning *D*.
20 with a lamentable voice unto *D*:
20 and the king spake and said to *D*,
20 O *D*, servant of the living God,
21 Then said *D* unto the king, O king,
23 that they should take *D* up out of
23 the den. So *D* was taken up
24 those men which had accused *D*,
26 and fear before the God of *D*:
27 hath delivered *D* from the power
28 *D* prospered in the reign of Darius,
7. 1 *D* had a dream and visions of
2 *D* spake and said, I saw in my
15 I *D* was grieved in my spirit
28 As for me *D*, my cogitations much
8. 1 unto me, even unto me *D*,
15 it came to pass, when I, even I *D*,
27 And I *D* fainted, and was sick
9. 2 In the first year of his reign I *D*
22 and said, O *D*, I am now come forth
10. 1 a thing was revealed unto *D*,
2 In those days I *D* was mourning
7 And I *D* alone saw the vision:
11 he said unto me, O *D*, a man
12 Then said he unto me, Fear not, *D*:
12. 4 But thou, O *D*, shut up the words,
5 *D* looked, and behold, there stood
9 And he said, Go thy way, *D*:
Mt 24.15 spoken of by *D* the prophet,
Mk 13.14 spoken of by *D* the prophet,

DARE

Job 41.10 None is so fierce that *d* stir him
Ro 5. 7 man some would even *d* to die.
15.18 For I will not *d* to speak of
1Co 6. 1 *D* any of you, having a matter
2Co 10.12 For we *d* not make ourselves

DARK

Gen 15.17 the sun went down, and it was *d*,
Lev 13. 6 if the plague be somewhat *d*,
21 the skin, but be somewhat *d*;
26 other skin, but be somewhat *d*;
28 the skin, but it be somewhat *d*;
56 the plague be somewhat *d* after
Nu 12. 8 apparently, and not in *d* speeches;
Jos 2. 5 when it was *d*, that the men went
2Sa 22.12 round about him, *d* waters,
Neh 13.19 gates of Jerusalem began to be *d*
Job 3. 9 stars of the twilight thereof be *d*;
12.25 grope in the *d* without light,
18. 6 light shall be *d* in his tabernacle,
22.13 he judge through the *d* cloud?
24.16 In the *d* they dig through houses,
Ps 18.11 round about him were *d* waters
35. 6 Let their way be *d* and slippery:
49. 4 open my *d* saying upon the harp.
74.20 the *d* places of the earth are full

DANIEL

The hero and, by tradition, the author of the book named after him; as a youth of noble descent, is taken captive to Babylon in the 6th century B.C.; because of his intellectual gifts is chosen to train for the king's service and is given the Babylonian name Belteshazzar; in time is presented before the king and proves himself preeminent in wisdom (Dan 1); **makes known to Nebuchadnezzar his dream and its interpretation, thereby saving the lives of the wise men of Babylon who had failed; is richly rewarded and promoted over the governors and wise men** (Dan 2); **once again only Daniel can interpret the king's dream** (Dan 4); **interprets the writing on the wall foretelling the fall of the Babylonian Empire to the Medes and Persians, and is further elevated in the kingdom** (Dan 5); **later his jealous colleagues contrive to make his custom of praying three times daily an offense against Persian law, and reluctantly King Darius commands that he be thrown into a den of lions; is later found miraculously unharmed and the conspirators are cast into the den** (Dan 6); **has visions foretelling the history of his people through the remaining centuries of the Old Testament era and beyond, culminating in the final establishment of God's kingdom on earth** (Dan 7–12).

78. 2 I will utter *d* sayings of old:
88.12 thy wonders be known in the *d*?
105.28 He sent darkness, and made it *d*;
Pr 1. 6 of the wise, and their *d* sayings.
7. 9 evening, in the black and *d* night:
Isa 29.15 their works are in the *d*, and they
45.19 secret, in a *d* place of the earth:
Jer 13.16 stumble upon the *d* mountains,
La 3. 6 He hath sent me in *d* places,
Eze 8.12 the house of Israel do in the *d*,
32. 7 and make the stars thereof *d*;
8 of heaven will I make *d* over thee,
34.12 scattered in the cloudy and *d* day.
Dan 8.23 and understanding *d* sentences,
Joel 2.10 the sun and the moon shall be *d*,
Am 5. 8 maketh the day *d* with night:
20 very *d*, and no brightness in it?
Mic 3. 6 and it shall be *d* unto you, that
6 and the day shall be *d* over them.
Zec 14. 6 light shall not be clear, nor *d*:
Lk 11.36 full of light, having no part *d*,
Jn 6.17 And it was now *d*, and Jesus was
20. 1 Magdalene early, when it was yet *d*,
2Pe 1.19 light that shineth in a *d* place,

DARKEN
Am 8. 9 will *d* the earth in the clear day:

DARKENED
Ex 10.15 earth, so that the land was *d*;
Ps 69.23 Let their eyes be *d*, that they see
Ec 12. 2 stars, be not *d*, nor the clouds
3 that look out of the windows be *d*,
Isa 5.30 light is *d* in the heavens thereof.
9.19 the Lord of hosts is the land *d*,
13.10 sun shall be *d* in his going forth,
24.11 all joy is *d*, the mirth of the
Eze 30.18 shall be *d*, when I shall break
Joel 3.15 sun and the moon shall be *d*,
Zec 11.17 his right eye shall be utterly *d*.
Mt 24.29 of those days shall the sun be *d*,
Mk 13.24 the sun shall be *d*, and the moon
Lk 23.45 And the sun was *d*, and the veil
Ro 1.21 and their foolish heart was *d*.
11.10 Let their eyes be *d*, that they may
Eph 4.18 Having the understanding *d*,
Rev 8.12 so as the third part of them was *d*,
9. 2 and the sun and the air were *d*

DARKENETH
Job 38. 2 Who is this that *d* counsel by

DARKLY
1Co 13.12 we see through a glass, *d*;

DARKNESS
Gen 1. 2 *d* was upon the face of the deep.
4 God divided the light from the *d*.
5 Day, and the *d* he called Night.
18 and to divide the light from the *d*:
15.12 horror of great *d* fell upon him.
Ex 10.21 may be *d* over the land of Egypt,
21 even *d* which may be felt.
22 there was a thick *d* in all the land
14.20 it was a cloud and *d* to them,
20.21 drew near unto the thick *d*
Dt 4.11 unto the midst of heaven, with *d*,
11 clouds, and thick *d*.
5.22 the cloud, and of the thick *d*, with
23 voice out of the midst of the *d*,
28.29 as the blind gropeth in *d*,
Jos 24. 7 *d* between you and the Egyptians,
1Sa 2. 9 the wicked shall be silent in *d*;
2Sa 22.10 and *d* was under his feet.
12 he made *d* pavilions round about
29 and the Lord will lighten my *d*.
1Ki 8.12 he would dwell in the thick *d*.
2Ch 6. 1 he would dwell in the thick *d*.
Job 3. 4 Let that day be *d*; let not God
5 Let *d* and the shadow of death
6 for that night, let *d* seize upon it;

Daniel *from Michelangelo's famed murals on the ceiling of the Sistine Chapel, completed in 1512*

5.14 meet with *d* in the day time,
10.21 Even to the land of *d*, and the
22 A land of *d*, as
22 as *d* itself; and of the shadow
22 and where the light is as *d*.
12.22 discovereth deep things out of *d*,
15.22 that he shall return out of *d*,
23 knoweth that the day of *d* is ready
30 He shall not depart out of *d*;
17.12 the light is short because of *d*.
13 I have made my bed in the *d*.
18.18 be driven from light into *d*, and
19. 8 he hath set *d* in my paths.
20.26 *d* shall be hid in his secret places:
22.11 Or *d*, that thou canst not see;
23.17 I was not cut off before the *d*,
17 neither hath he covered the *d*
28. 3 He setteth an end to *d*, and
3 the stones of *d*, and the
29. 3 by his light I walked through *d*;
30.26 I waited for light, there came *d*.
34.22 There is no *d*, nor shadow of
37.19 order our speech by reason of *d*
38. 9 thick *d* a swaddlingband for it,
19 and as for *d*, where is the place
Ps 18. 9 and *d* was under his feet.
11 He made *d* his secret place;
28 my God will enlighten my *d*.
82. 5 understand; they walk on in *d*:
88. 6 lowest pit, in *d*, in the deeps.
18 me, and mine acquaintance into *d*.
91. 6 the pestilence that walketh in *d*;
97. 2 and *d* are round about him:

104.20 Thou makest *d*, and it is night:
105.28 He sent *d*, and made it dark;
107.10 Such as sit in *d* and in the shadow
14 He brought them out of *d* and the
112. 4 upright there ariseth light in the *d*:
139.11 I say, Surely the *d* shall cover me;
12 Yea, the *d* hideth not from thee;
12 *d* and the light are both alike to
143. 3 he hath made me to dwell in *d*,
Pr 2.13 to walk in the ways of *d*;
4.19 The way of the wicked is as *d*:
20.20 shall be put out in obscure *d*.
Ec 2.13 folly, as far as light excelleth *d*.
14 head; but the fool walketh in *d*:
5.17 All his days also he eateth in *d*,
6. 4 vanity, and departeth in *d*, and
4 his name shall be covered with *d*.
11. 8 let him remember the days of *d*;
Isa 5.20 put *d* for light, and light for *d*;
30 behold *d* and sorrow, and the light
8.22 behold trouble and *d*, dimness of
22 and they shall be driven to *d*.
9. 2 The people that walked in *d* have
29.18 out of obscurity, and out of *d*.
42. 7 them that sit in *d* out of the prison
16 I will make *d* light before them,
45. 3 I will give thee the treasures of *d*,
7 I form the light, and create *d*:
47. 5 Sit thou silent, and get thee into *d*,
49. 9 to them that are in *d*, Shew
50.10 walketh in *d*, and hath no light?
58.10 and thy *d* be as the noon day:
59. 9 for brightness, but we walk in *d*.

Isa 60. 2 the *d* shall cover the earth,
2 and gross *d* the people:
Jer 2.31 unto Israel? a land of *d*?
13.16 before he cause *d*, and before
16 of death, and make it gross *d*.
23.12 as slippery ways in the *d*:
La 3. 2 led me, and brought me into *d*,
Eze 32. 8 over thee, and set *d* upon thy land,
Dan 2.22 he knoweth what is in the *d*,
Joel 2. 2 A day of *d* and of gloominess,
2 a day of clouds and of thick *d*,
31 The sun shall be turned into *d*,
Am 4.13 that maketh the morning *d*, and
5.18 the day of the Lord is *d*, and not
20 shall not the day of the Lord be *d*,
Mic 7. 8 I sit in *d*, the Lord shall be a light
Na 1. 8 and *d* shall pursue his enemies.
Zep 1.15 a day of *d* and gloominess,
15 a day of clouds and thick *d*.
Mt 4.16 The people which sat in *d* saw
6.23 thy whole body shall be full of *d*.
23 in thee be *d*, how great is that *d*!
8.12 shall be cast out into outer *d*:
10.27 What I tell you in *d*, that speak
22.13 away, and cast him into outer *d*;
25.30 unprofitable servant into outer *d*:
27.45 there was *d* over all the land
Mk 15.33 there was *d* over the whole land
Lk 1.79 To give light to them that sit in *d*
11.34 is evil, thy body also is full of *d*.
35 light which is in thee be not *d*.
12. 3 whatsoever ye have spoken in *d*
22.53 is your hour, and the power of *d*.
23.44 there was a *d* over all the earth
Jn 1. 5 And the light shineth in *d*; and
5 and the *d* comprehended it not.
3.19 men loved *d* rather than light,
8.12 followeth me shall not walk in *d*,
12.35 the light, lest *d* come upon you:
35 for he that walketh in *d* knoweth
46 on me should not abide in *d*.
Ac 2.20 The sun shall be turned into *d*,
13.11 there fell on him a mist and a *d*;
26.18 to turn them from *d* to light,
Ro 2.19 a light of them which are in *d*,
13.12 cast off the works of *d*, and let us
1Co 4. 5 to light the hidden things of *d*,
2Co 4. 6 the light to shine out of *d*, hath
6.14 communion hath light with *d*?
Eph 5. 8 ye were sometimes *d*, but now are
11 with the unfruitful works of *d*,
6.12 the rulers of the *d* of this world,
Col 1.13 delivered us from the power of *d*,
1Th 5. 4 But ye, brethren, are not in *d*,
5 we are not of the night, not of *d*.
Heb 12.18 nor unto blackness, and *d*, and
1Pe 2. 9 hath called you out of *d* into his
2Pe 2. 4 delivered them into chains of *d*,
17 the mist of *d* is reserved for ever.
1Jn 1. 5 light, and in him is no *d* at all.
6 and walk in *d*, we lie, and do not
2. 8 because the *d* is past, and the
9 brother, is in *d* even until now.
11 is in *d*, and walketh in *d*, and
11 goeth, because that *d* hath blinded
Jude 6 in everlasting chains under *d*
13 the blackness of *d* for ever.
Rev 16.10 and his kingdom was full of *d*;

DARLING

Ps 22.20 my *d* from the power of the dog.
35.17 my *d* from the lions.

DART

Job 41.26 spear, the *d*, nor the habergeon.
Pr 7.23 Till a *d* strike through his liver;
Heb 12.20 or thrust through with a *d*:

DARTS

2Sa 18.14 he took three *d* in his hand,
2Ch 32. 5 *d* and shields in abundance.
Job 41.29 *D* are counted as stubble: he
Eph 6.16 all the fiery *d* of the wicked.

DASH

2Ki 8.12 wilt *d* their children, and rip up
Ps 2. 9 thou shalt *d* them in pieces like
91.12 thou *d* thy foot against a stone.
Isa 13.18 shall *d* the young men to pieces;
Jer 13.14 *d* them one against another,
Mt 4. 6 thou *d* thy foot against a stone.
Lk 4.11 thou *d* thy foot against a stone.

DASHED

Ex 15. 6 hand, O Lord, hath *d* in pieces
Isa 13.16 children also shall be *d* to pieces
Hos 10.14 the mother was *d* in pieces upon
13.16 their infants shall be *d* in pieces,
Na 3.10 children also were *d* in pieces

DASHETH

Ps 137. 9 that taketh and *d* thy little ones
Na 2. 1 He that *d* in pieces is come

DAUGHTER

Gen 20.12 she is the *d* of my father,
12 but not the *d* of my mother;
24.23 Whose *d* art thou: tell me, I pray
29. 6 his *d* cometh with the sheep.
10 Jacob saw Rachel the *d* of Laban
18 years for Rachel thy younger *d*.
23 took Leah his *d*, and brought her
24 gave unto his *d* Leah Zilpah his
28 gave him Rachel his *d* to wife also.
29 Laban gave to Rachel his *d*
30.21 afterwards she bare a *d*, and
34. 1 And Dinah the *d* of Leah,
3 clave unto Dinah the *d* of Jacob,
5 that he had defiled Dinah his *d*:
7 Israel in lying with Jacob's *d*;
8 son Shechem longeth for your *d*:
17 then will we take our *d*, and we
19 he had delight in Jacob's *d*:
38. 2 there a *d* of a certain Canaanite,
11 said Judah to Tamar his *d* in law,
12 the *d* of Shuah Judah's wife died;
16 not that she was his *d* in law.)
24 Tamar thy *d* in law hath played
41.45 gave him to wife Asenath the *d* of
50 Asenath the *d* of Poti-pherah
46.15 with his *d* Dinah: all the souls of
18 whom Laban gave to Leah his *d*,
25 Laban gave unto Rachel his *d*,
Ex 1.16 but if it be a *d*, then she shall live.
22 every *d* ye shall save alive.
2. 1 took to wife a *d* of Levi.
5 And the *d* of Pharaoh came down
7 said his sister to Pharaoh's *d*,
8 And Pharaoh's *d* said to her, Go.
9 Pharaoh's *d* said unto her, Take
10 she brought him unto Pharaoh's *d*,
21 he gave Moses Zipporah his *d*.
6.23 Elisheba, *d* of Amminadab, sister
20.10 thou, nor thy son, nor thy *d*,
21. 7 man sell his *d* to be a maidservant,
31 a son, or have gored a *d*,
Lev 12. 6 or for a *d*, she shall bring
18. 9 *d* of thy father, or *d* of thy mother,
10 The nakedness of thy son's *d*,
10 or of thy daughter's *d*,
11 nakedness of thy father's wife's *d*,
15 the nakedness of thy *d* in law:
17 nakedness of a woman and her *d*,
17 shalt thou take her son's *d*,
17 or her daughter's *d*,
19.29 Do not prostitute thy *d*, to cause
20.12 if a man lie with his *d* in law,
17 take his sister, his father's *d*,
17 or his mother's *d*,
21. 2 for his son, and for his *d*, and for
9 *d* of any priest, if she profane
22.12 if the priest's *d* also be married
13 But if the priest's *d* be a widow,
Nu 27. 8 his inheritance to pass unto his *d*.
9 if he have no *d*, then he shall give
30.16 between the father and his *d*,
36. 8 every *d*, that possesseth an
Dt 5.14 work, thou, nor thy son, nor thy *d*,
7. 3 *d* thou shalt not give unto his son,
3 *d* shalt thou take unto thy son.
12.18 thou, and thy son, and thy *d*,
13. 6 thy mother, or thy son, or thy *d*,
16.11 thy *d*, and thy manservant, and
14 thou, and thy son, and thy *d*,
18.10 his son or his *d* to pass through
22.16 I gave my *d* unto this man to wife,
17 I found not thy *d* a maid; and yet
27.22 the *d* of his father, or the *d* of his
28.56 toward her son, and toward her *d*,
Jos 15.16 will I give Achsah his *d* to wife.
17 he gave him Achsah my *d* to wife.
Jdg 1.12 will I give Achsah my *d* to wife.
13 he gave him Achsah his *d* to wife.
11.34 his *d* came out to meet him
34 her he had neither son nor *d*.
35 Alas, my *d*! thou hast brought me
40 yearly to lament the *d* of Jephthah
19.24 Behold, here is my *d* a maiden,
21. 1 any of us give his *d* unto Benjamin
Ru 1.22 the Moabitess, her *d* in law, with
2. 2 she said unto her, Go, my *d*.
8 unto Ruth, Hearest thou not, my *d*?
20 Naomi said unto her *d* in law,
22 Naomi said unto Ruth her *d* in law,
22 It is good, my *d*, that thou go
3. 1 My *d*, shall I not seek rest for thee,
10 Blessed be thou of the Lord, my *d*:
11 And now, my *d*, fear not; I will do
16 Who art thou, my *d*? And she told
18 Then said she, Sit still, my *d*,
4.15 thy *d* in law, which loveth thee,
1Sa 1.16 thine handmaid for a *d* of Belial:
4.19 And his *d* in law, Phinehas' wife.
14.50 was Ahinoam, the *d* of Ahimaaz:
17.25 riches, and will give him his *d*,
18.17 Behold my elder *d* Merab, her will
19 Saul's *d* should have been given
20 And Michal Saul's *d* loved David:
27 gave him Michal his *d* to wife.
28 that Michal Saul's *d* loved him.
25.44 But Saul had given Michal his *d*,
2Sa 3.13 thou first bring Michal Saul's *d*,
6.16 Michal Saul's *d* looked through a
20 And Michal the *d* of Saul come out
23 Michal the *d* of Saul had no child
11. 3 this Bath-sheba, the *d* of Eliam,
12. 3 bosom, and was unto him as a *d*.
14.27 three sons, and one *d*, whose name
1Ki 3. 1 took Pharaoh's *d*, and brought her
7. 8 also an house for Pharaoh's *d*,
9.16 given it for a present unto his *d*,
24 Pharaoh's *d* came up out of the
11. 1 together with the *d* of Pharaoh,
16.31 to wife Jezebel the *d* of Ethbaal
22.42 name was Azubah the *d* of Shilhi.
2Ki 8.18 for the *d* of Ahab was his wife:
9.34 bury her for she is a king's *d*.
11. 2 Jehosheba the *d* of king Joram,
14. 9 Give thy *d* to my son to wife:
19.21 virgin the *d* of Zion hath despised
21 the *d* of Jerusalem hath shaken
23.10 or his *d* to pass through the fire
1Ch 2. 4 Tamar his *d* in law bare him
4.18 the *d* of Pharaoh, which Mered
7.24 (And his *d* was Sherah, who built
15.29 Michal the *d* of Saul looking out at
2Ch 8.11 Solomon brought up the *d* of
11.20 took Maachah the *d* of Absalom;
21 the *d* of Absalom above all his
25.18 Give thy *d* to my son to wife:
Neh 6.18 had taken the *d* of Meshullam
Est 2. 7 that is, Esther, his uncle's *d*:
7 were dead, took for his own *d*.

15 who had taken her for his *d*,
9.29 Esther the queen, the *d* of Abihail,
Ps 9.14 in the gates of the *d* of Zion:
45.10 Hearken, O *d*, and consider, and
12 And the *d* of Tyre shall be there
13 The king's *d* is all glorious within:
137. 8 O *d* of Babylon, who art to be
SS 7. 1 O prince's *d*! the joints of thy
Isa 1. 8 the *d* of Zion is left as a cottage
10.30 Lift up thy voice, O *d* of Gallim:
32 against the mount of the *d* of Zion.
16. 1 unto the mount of the *d* of Zion.
22. 4 the spoiling of the *d* of my people.
23.10 *d* of Tarshish: there is no more
12 thou oppressed virgin, *d* of Zidon:
37.22 virgin, the *d* of Zion, hath despised
22 the *d* of Jerusalem hath shaken
47. 1 O virgin *d* of Babylon, sit on the
1 no throne, O *d* of the Chaldeans:
5 darkness, O *d* of the Chaldeans:
52. 2 of thy neck, O captive *d* of Zion.
62.11 Say ye to the *d* of Zion,
Jer 4.11 wilderness toward the *d* of my
31 the voice of the *d* of Zion,
6. 2 I have likened the *d* of Zion
14 the hurt of the *d* of my people
23 war against thee, O *d* of Zion.
26 O *d* of my people, gird thee
8.11 hurt of the *d* of my people slightly,
19 the cry of the *d* of my people
21 the hurt of the *d* of my people
22 the health of the *d* of my people
9. 1 the slain of the *d* of my people!
7 I do for the *d* of my people?
14.17 for the virgin *d* of my people is
31.22 go about, O thou backsliding *d*?
46.11 balm, O virgin, the *d* of Egypt:
19 O thou *d* dwelling in Egypt,
24 *d* of Egypt shall be confounded;
48.18 Thou *d* that dost inhabit Dibon,
49. 4 O backsliding *d*? that trusted
50.42 against thee, O *d* of Babylon.
51.33 The *d* of Babylon is like a
52. 1 the *d* of Jeremiah of Libnah.
La 1. 6 from the *d* of Zion all her beauty
15 the virgin, the *d* of Judah,
2. 1 the Lord covered the *d* of Zion
2 strongholds of the *d* of Judah;
4 the tabernacle of the *d* of Zion:
5 hath increased in the *d* of Judah
8 destroy the wall of the *d* of Zion:
10 The elders of the *d* of Zion sit
11 destruction of the *d* of my people;
13 liken to thee, O *d* of Jerusalem?
13 comfort thee, O virgin *d* of Zion?
15 their head at the *d* of Jerusalem,
18 O wall of the *d* of Zion, let tears
3.48 destruction of the *d* of my people.
4. 3 the *d* of my people is become cruel,
6 the iniquity of the *d* of my people
10 destruction of the *d* of my people.
21 and be glad, O *d* of Edom,
22 is accomplished, O *d* of Zion;
22 O *d* of Edom; he will discover thy
Eze 14.20 shall deliver neither son nor *d*;
16.44 As is the mother, so is her *d*.
45 Thou art thy mother's *d*, that
22.11 hath lewdly defiled his *d* in law;
11 humbled his sister, his father's *d*.
44.25 for son, or for *d*, for brother,
Dan 11. 6 for the king's *d* of the south
17 shall give him the *d* of women,
Hos 1. 3 took Gomer the *d* of Diblaim;
6 conceived again, and bare a *d*.
Mic 1.13 of the sin to the *d* of Zion:
4. 8 the strong hold of the *d* of Zion,
8 shall come to the *d* of Jerusalem.
10 O *d* of Zion, like a woman in travail:
13 Arise and thresh, O *d* of Zion:
5. 1 thyself in troops, O *d* of troops:
7. 6 *d* riseth up against her mother,
6 *d* in law against her mother in
Zep 3.10 even the *d* of my dispersed, shall
14 Sing, O *d* of Zion; shout, O Israel;
14 all the heart, O *d* of Jerusalem.
Zec 2. 7 dwellest with the *d* of Babylon.
10 Sing and rejoice, O *d* of Zion:
9. 9 Rejoice greatly, O *d* of Zion;
9 shout, O *d* of Jerusalem:
Mal 2.11 hath married the *d* of a strange god.
Mt 9.18 My *d* is even now dead: but
22 *D*, be of good comfort; thy faith
10.35 and the *d* against her mother,
35 and the *d* in law against her
37 loveth son or *d* more than me
14. 6 the *d* of Herodias danced before
15.22 my *d* is grievously vexed with a
28 And her *d* was made whole from
21. 5 Tell ye the *d* of Sion, Behold,
Mk 5.23 little *d* lieth at the point of death:
34 *D*, thy faith hath made thee whole;
35 Thy *d* is dead: why troublest thou
6.22 the *d* of the said Herodias came
7.25 young *d* had an unclean spirit,
26 cast forth the devil out of her *d*.
29 the devil is gone out of thy *d*.
30 and her *d* laid upon the bed.
Lk 2.36 the *d* of Phanuel, of the tribe of
8.42 he had one only *d*, about twelve
48 *D*, be of good comfort: thy faith
49 Thy *d* is dead; trouble not the
12.53 against the *d*, and the *d* against
53 *d* in law, and the *d* in law against
13.16 a *d* of Abraham, whom Satan
Jn 12.15 Fear not, *d* of Sion: behold, thy
Ac 7.21 Pharaoh's *d* took him up and
Heb 11.24 be called the son of Pharaoh's *d*;

DAUGHTERS

Gen 6. 1 earth, and *d* were born unto them.
2 the sons of God saw the *d* of men
4 came in unto the *d* of men, and they
19. 8 have two *d* which have not known
12 in law, and thy sons, and thy *d*,
14 sons in law, which married his *d*,
15 and thy two *d*, which are here;
16 and upon the hand of his two *d*;
30 in the mountain, and his two *d*
30 dwelt in a cave, he and his two *d*.
36 Thus were both the *d* of Lot with
24. 3 my son of the *d* of the Canaanites,
13 and the *d* of the men of the city
37 *d* of the Canaanites, in whose land
27.46 my life because of the *d* of Heth:
46 these which are of the *d* of the land,
28. 1 not take a wife of the *d* of Canaan.
2 *d* of Laban thy mother's brother.
6 not take a wife of the *d* of Canaan;
8 Esau seeing that the *d* of Canaan
30.13 for the *d* will call me blessed:
31.26 carried away my *d*, as captives
28 me to kiss my sons and my *d*?
31 take by force thy *d* from me.
41 thee fourteen years for thy two *d*,
43 These *d* are my *d*, and these
43 can I do this day unto these my *d*,
50 If thou shalt afflict my *d*, or if thou
50 shalt take other wives beside my *d*,
55 and kissed his sons and his *d*,
34. 1 went out to see the *d* of the land.
9 and give your *d* unto us, and take
9 and take our *d* unto you.
16 Then we will give our *d* unto you,
16 and we will take your *d* unto us,
21 let us take their *d* to us for wives,
21 and let us give them our *d*.
37.35 and his *d* rose up to comfort
Ex 2.16 the priest of Midian had seven *d*:
20 And he said unto his *d*, And where
3.22 upon your sons, and upon your *d*;
6.25 took him one of the *d* of Putiel to
10. 9 with our sons and with our *d*,
21. 4 she have born him sons or *d*;
9 with her after the manner of *d*.
32. 2 wives, of your sons, and of your *d*,
34.16 take of their *d* unto thy sons,
16 and their *d* go a whoring after
Lev 10.14 and thy sons, and thy *d* with thee:
26.29 the flesh of your *d* shall ye eat.
Nu 18.11 to thy sons and to thy *d* with thee,
19 and thy sons and thy *d* with thee,
21.29 and his *d*, into captivity unto Sihon
25. 1 whoredom with the *d* of Moab.
27. 7 The *d* of Zelophehad speak right:
36. 2 Zelophehad our brother unto his *d*.
11 the *d* of Zelophehad, were married
Dt 12.12 ye, and your sons, and your *d*,
31 sons and their *d* they have burnt
23.17 be no whore of the *d* of Israel,
28.32 Thy sons and thy *d* shall be given
41 Thou shalt beget sons and *d*, but
53 the flesh of thy sons and of thy *d*,
32.19 provoking of his sons, and of his *d*.
Jos 7.24 of gold, and his sons, and his *d*,
17. 3 had no sons, but *d*: and these
3 and these are the names of his *d*,
6 Because the *d* of Manasseh had an
Jdg 3. 6 they took their *d* to be their wives,
6 and gave their *d* to their sons,
11.40 *d* of Israel went yearly to lament
14. 1, 2 of the *d* of the Philistines:
3 among the *d* of thy brethren, or
21. 7 give them of our *d* to wives?
18 may not give them wives of our *d*:
21 the *d* of Shiloh come out to dance
21 man his wife of the *d* of Shiloh,
Ru 1. 6 she arose with her *d* in law,
7 her two *d* in law with her;
8 Naomi said unto her two *d* in law,
11 my *d*: why will ye go with me?
12 Turn again, my *d*, go your way;
13 nay, my *d*; for it grieveth me
1Sa 1. 4 to all her sons and her *d*, portions:
8.13 And he will take your *d* to be
30. 3 their sons, and their *d*, were taken
6 man for his sons and for his *d*:
19 neither sons nor *d*, neither spoil,
2Sa 1.20 lest the *d* of the Philistines rejoice,
20 *d* of the uncircumcised triumph.
24 Ye *d* of Israel, weep over Saul,
5.13 were yet sons and *d* born to David.
13.18 with such robes were the king's *d*
19. 5 the lives of thy sons and of thy *d*,
2Ki 17.17 their *d* to pass through the fire,
2Ch 2.14 son of a woman of the *d* of Dan,
29. 9 our sons and our *d* and our wives
31.18 their sons, and their *d*, through all
Ezr 9. 2 taken of their *d* for themselves,
12 give not your *d* unto their sons,
12 neither take their *d* unto your sons,
Neh 3.12 part of Jerusalem, he and his *d*.
4.14 your sons, and your *d*, your wives,
5. 2 our sons, and our *d*, are many:
5 our sons and our *d* to be servants,
5 our *d* are brought unto bondage
10.28 their sons, and their *d*, every one
30 our *d* unto the people of the land,
30 nor take their *d* for our sons:
13.25 not give your *d* unto their sons,
25 nor take their *d* unto your sons,
Job 1. 2 unto him seven sons and three *d*.
13 his sons and his *d* were eating and
18 Thy sons and thy *d* were eating
42.13 had also seven sons and three *d*.
15 found so fair as the *d* of Job:
Ps 45. 9 Kings' *d* were among thy
48.11 let the *d* of Judah be glad,
97. 8 the *d* of Judah rejoiced because of
106.37 sacrificed their sons and their *d*
38 blood of their sons and of their *d*,
144.12 that our *d* may be as corner stones,
Pr 30.15 horseleach hath two *d*, crying,
31.29 Many *d* have done virtuously, but

Ec 12. 4 *d* of musick shall be brought low,
SS 1. 5 O ye *d* of Jerusalem, as the tents
2. 2 so is my love among the *d*.
7 I charge you, O ye *d* of Jerusalem,
3. 5 I charge you, O ye *d* of Jerusalem,
10 with love, for the *d* of Jerusalem.
11 Go forth, O ye *d* of Zion, and
5. 8 I charge you, O *d* of Jerusalem,
16 is my friend, O *d* of Jerusalem.
6. 9 The *d* saw her, and blessed her;
8. 4 I charge you, O *d* of Jerusalem,
Isa 3.16 Because the *d* of Zion are haughty,
17 crown of the head of the *d* of Zion,
4. 4 away the filth of the *d* of Zion,
16. 2 the *d* of Moab shall be at the fords
32. 9 hear my voice, ye careless *d*;
43. 6 and my *d* from the ends of the earth;
49.22 thy *d* shall be carried upon their
56. 5 name better than of sons and of *d*:
60. 4 thy *d* shall be nursed at thy side.
Jer 3.24 their herds, their sons and their *d*.
5.17 which thy sons and thy *d* should eat:
7.31 their sons and their *d* in the fire;
9.20 teach your *d* wailing, and every
11.22 and their *d* shall die by famine:
14.16 wives, nor their sons, nor their *d*:
16. 2 neither shalt thou have sons or *d*
3 concerning the *d* that are born in
19. 9 flesh of their *d*, and they shall eat
29. 6 beget sons and *d*; and take wives
6 and give your *d* to husbands,
6 that they may bear sons and *d*;
32.35 their *d* to pass through the fire
35. 8 our wives, our sons, nor our *d*;
41.10 the king's *d*, and all the people
43. 6 and the king's *d*, and every person
48.46 taken captives, and thy *d* captives.
49. 2 her *d* shall be burned with fire:
3 cry, ye *d* of Rabbah, gird you with
La 3.51 because of all the *d* of my city.
Eze 13.17 against the *d* of thy people, which
14.16 deliver neither sons nor *d*; they
18 deliver neither sons nor *d*, but they
22 both sons and *d*: behold, they shall
16.20 thou hast taken thy sons and thy *d*,
27 the *d* of the Philistines, which are
46 Samaria, she and her *d* that dwell
46 thy right hand, is Sodom and her *d*.
48 hast not done, she nor her *d*, as
48 thou hast done, thou and thy *d*.
49 idleness was in her and in her *d*,
53 the captivity of Sodom and her *d*,
53 the captivity of Samaria and her *d*,
55 When thy sisters, Sodom and her *d*,
55 Samaria and her *d*, shall return
55 then thou and thy *d* shall return
57 of thy reproach of the *d* of Syria,
57 about her, the *d* of the Philistines,
61 I will give them unto thee for *d*,
23. 2 two women, the *d* of one mother:
4 mine, and they bare sons and *d*.
10 they took her sons and her *d*, and
25 they shall take thy sons and thy *d*;
47 shall slay their sons and their *d*,
24.21 your sons and your *d* whom ye
25 their minds, their sons and their *d*,
26. 6 And her *d* which are in the field
8 He shall slay with the sword thy *d*
30.18 and her *d* shall go into captivity.
32.16 the *d* of the nations shall lament
18 and the *d* of the famous nations,
Hos 4.13 your *d* shall commit whoredom,
14 I will not punish your *d* when they
Joel 2.28 sons and your *d* shall prophesy,
3. 8 I will sell your sons and *d* into the
Am 7.17 and thy *d* shall fall by the sword,
Lk 1. 5 his wife was of the *d* of Aaron,
23.28 *D* of Jerusalem, weep not for me,
Ac 2.17 sons and your *d* shall prophesy,
21. 9 four *d*, virgins, which did prophesy.
2Co 6.18 ye shall be my sons and *d*, saith
1Pe 3. 6 whose *d* ye are, as long as ye do

DAVID

Ru 4.17 father of Jesse, the father of *D*.
22 begat Jesse, and Jesse begat *D*.
1Sa 16.13 the Spirit of the Lord came upon *D*
19 Send me *D* thy son, which is with
20 sent them by *D* his son unto Saul.
21 *D* came to Saul, and stood before
22 Let *D*, I pray thee, stand before
23 *D* took a harp, and played with his
17.12 Now *D* was the son of that
14 *D* was the youngest: and the three
15 *D* went and returned from Saul
17 Jesse said unto *D* his son, Take
20 *D* rose up early in the morning,
22 *D* left his carriage in the hand of
23 same words: and *D* heard them.
26 *D* spake to the men that stood by
28 anger was kindled against *D*,
29 *D* said, What have I now done?
31 words were heard which *D* spake,
32 *D* said to Saul, Let no man's heart
33 Saul said to *D*, Thou art not able
34 *D* said unto Saul, Thy servant
37 *D* said moreover, The Lord that
37 Saul said unto *D*, Go, and the
38 Saul armed *D* with his armor,
39 *D* girded his sword upon his
39 *D* said unto Saul, I cannot go
39 And *D* put them off him.
41 came on and drew near unto *D*;
42 looked about, and saw *D*,

DAVID

Israel's second and greatest king, 10th century B.C.; youngest son of Jesse of Bethlehem; is quietly anointed by Samuel; becomes King Saul's minstrel and armor-bearer (1Sa 16); **slays Goliath** (1Sa 17); **marries Saul's daughter Michal and becomes close friend of his son Jonathan, but is forced to flee for his life when Saul becomes jealous of his popularity** (1Sa 18–20); **gathers together a band of malcontents; is relentlessly pursued by Saul but twice spares Saul's life to demonstrate his innocence** (1Sa 21–24, 26); **is dissuaded from slaying Nabal by Abigail and marries her after Nabal's sudden death** (1Sa 25); **flees beyond Saul's reach, living among Philistines while secretly warring against Judah's southern enemies** (1Sa 27–29); **avenges an Amalekite raid and rescues his wives** (1Sa 30); **laments the deaths of Saul and Jonathan in battle with the Philistines** (2Sa 1); **becomes king of Judah at Hebron** (2Sa 2); **after civil war becomes king of all Israel; seizes Jerusalem as new capital** (2Sa 3–5); **brings the ark of God into Jerusalem** (2Sa 6); **though he is not allowed to build the temple, God makes a covenant with him** (2Sa 7); **extends his kingdom** (2Sa 8–10); **commits adultery with Bathsheba; arranges for the death of Uriah, her husband, and then marries her** (2Sa 11); **is reproved by Nathan and confesses his sin** (2Sa 12); **flees rebellion led by son Absalom** (2Sa 13–16); **returns to Jerusalem after Absalom's death** (2Sa 17–19); **suppresses Sheba's rebellion** (2Sa 20); **delivers song of praise to God** (2Sa 21–23); **secures Solomon's succession; dies after 40-year reign** (1Ki 1–2).

43 the Philistine said unto *D*, Am I a
43 Philistine cursed *D* by his gods.
44 the Philistine said to *D*, Come to
45 Then said *D* to the Philistine,
48 and came and drew nigh to meet *D*,
48 that *D* hasted and ran toward the
49 *D* put his hand in his bag, and
50 So *D* prevailed over the Philistine
50 was no sword in the hand of *D*.
51 Therefore *D* ran, and stood upon
54 *D* took the head of the Philistine,
55 when Saul saw *D* go forth against
57 as *D* returned from the slaughter
58 *D* answered, I am the son of thy
18. 1 was knit with the soul of *D*, and
3 Jonathan and *D* made a covenant,
4 and gave it to *D*, and his garments,
5 *D* went out whithersoever Saul
6 when *D* was returned from the
7 slain his thousands, and *D* his ten
8 They have ascribed unto *D* ten
9 Saul eyed *D* from that day and
10 and *D* played with his hand, as at
11 I will smite *D* even to the wall
11 And *D* avoided out of his presence
12 Saul was afraid of *D*, because the
14 *D* behaved himself wisely in all
16 But all Israel and Judah loved *D*,
17 Saul said to *D*, Behold my elder
18 *D* said unto Saul, Who am I? and
19 should have been given to *D*, that
20 Michal Saul's daughter loved *D*:
21 Wherefore Saul said to *D*, Thou
22 Commune with *D* secretly, and say,
23 spake these words in the ears of *D*.
23 And *D* said, Seemeth it to you a
24 On this manner spake *D*.
25 Thus shall ye say to *D*, The king
25 Saul thought to make *D* fall by the
26 when his servants told *D* these
26 it pleased *D* well to be the king's
27 Wherefore *D* arose and went, he
27 *D* brought their foreskins, and
28 knew that the Lord was with *D*,
29 Saul was yet the more afraid of *D*;
30 *D* behaved himself more wisely
19. 1 servants, that they should kill *D*.
2 Saul's son delighted much in *D*:
2 Jonathan told *D*, saying, Saul my
4 Jonathan spake good of *D* unto
4 sin against his servant, against *D*;
5 against innocent blood, to slay *D*
7 Jonathan called *D*, and Jonathan
7 Jonathan brought *D* to Saul, and
8 and *D* went out, and fought with
9 hand: and *D* played with his hand.
10 Saul sought to smite *D* even to the
10 and *D* fled, and escaped that night,
12 So Michal let *D* down through a
14 Saul sent messengers to take *D*,
15 the messengers again to see *D*,
18 So *D* fled, and escaped, and came
19 Behold, *D* is at Naioth in Ramah.
20 Saul sent messengers to take *D*:
22 said, Where are Samuel and *D*?
20. 1 *D* fled from Naioth in Ramah, and
3 *D* sware moreover, and said, Thy
4 Then said Jonathan unto *D*,
5 *D* said unto Jonathan, Behold,
6 *D* earnestly asked leave of me that
10 Then said *D* to Jonathan, Who
11 Jonathan said unto *D*, Come, and
12 Jonathan said unto *D*, O Lord God
12 if there be good toward *D*, and I
15 Lord hath cut off the enemies of *D*
16 a covenant with the house of *D*,
17 Jonathan caused *D* to swear again,
18 Jonathan said to *D*, To morrow
24 So *D* hid himself in the field: and
28 And Jonathan answered Saul, *D*
33 determined of his father to slay *D*.

34 for he was grieved for *D*, because
35 at the time appointed with *D*, and
39 only Jonathan and *D* knew the
41 *D* arose out of a place toward the
41 with another, until *D* exceeded.
42 Jonathan said to *D*, Go in peace,
21. 1 Then came *D* to Nob to Ahimelech
1 was afraid at the meeting of *D*,
2 *D* said unto Ahimelech the priest,
4 the priest answered *D*, and said,
5 *D* answered the priest, and said
8 *D* said unto Ahimelech, And is
9 *D* said, There is none like that;
10 *D* arose, and fled that day for fear
11 Is not this *D* the king of the land?
11 slain his thousands, and *D* his ten
12 *D* laid up these words in his heart,
22. 1 *D* therefore departed thence, and
3 *D* went thence to Mizpeh of Moab:
4 the while that *D* was in the hold.
5 the prophet Gad said unto *D*,
5 Then *D* departed, and came into
6 Saul heard that *D* was discovered,
14 among all thy servants as *D*,
17 because their hand also is with *D*,
20 Abiathar, escaped, and fled after *D*.
21 Abiathar shewed *D* that Saul had
22 *D* said unto Abiathar, I knew it
23. 1 Then they told *D*, saying, Behold,
2 Therefore *D* inquired of the Lord,
2 the Lord said unto *D*, Go, and
4 *D* inquired of the Lord yet again.
5 So *D* and his men went to Keilah,
5 *D* saved the inhabitants of Keilah.
6 the son of Ahimelech fled to *D*
7 it was told Saul that *D* was come
8 to Keilah, to besiege *D* and his
9 *D* knew that Saul secretly practised
10 Then said *D*, O Lord God of Israel,
12 Then said *D*, Will the men of
13 Then *D* and his men, which were
13 was told Saul that *D* was escaped
14 *D* abode in the wilderness in
15 *D* saw that Saul was come out to
15 *D* was in the wilderness of Ziph
16 arose, and went to *D* into the wood,
18 and *D* abode in the wood, and
19 Doth not *D* hide himself with us
24 but *D* and his men were in the
25 they told *D*: wherefore he came
25 pursued after *D* in the wilderness
26 and *D* and his men on that side of
26 and *D* made haste to get away
26 Saul and his men compassed *D*
28 returned from pursuing after *D*,
29 *D* went up from thence, and dwelt
24. 1 *D* is in the wilderness of En-gedi.
2 and went to seek *D* and his men
3 *D* and his men remained in the
4 the men of *D* said unto him,
4 *D* arose, and cut off the skirt of
7 So *D* stayed his servants with
8 *D* also arose afterward, and went
8 *D* stooped with his face to the
9 *D* said to Saul, Wherefore hearest
9 saying, Behold, *D* seeketh thy
16 when *D* had made an end of
16 said, Is this thy voice, my son *D*?
17 he said to *D*, Thou art more
22 And *D* sware unto Saul. And Saul
22 but *D* and his men gat them up
25. 1 *D* arose, and went down to the
4 *D* heard in the wilderness that
5 And *D* sent out ten young men,
5 and *D* said unto the ten young
8 unto thy servants, and to thy son *D*.
9 words in the name of *D*, and ceased.
10 Who is *D*? and who is the son of
13 *D* said unto his men, Gird ye on
13 and *D* also girded on his sword:
13 went up after *D* about four hundred

14 *D* sent messengers out of the
20 *D* and his men came down against
21 *D* had said, Surely in vain have I
22 also do God unto the enemies of *D*,
23 when Abigail saw *D*, she hasted,
23 lighted off the ass, and fell before *D*
32 *D* said to Abigail, Blessed be the
35 So *D* received of her hand that
39 when *D* heard that Nabal was dead,
39 And *D* sent and communed with
40 when the servants of *D* were come
40 *D* sent us unto thee, to take thee
42 went after the messengers of *D*,
43 *D* also took Ahinoam to Jezreel;
26. 1 Doth not *D* hide himself in the
2 to seek *D* in the wilderness of Ziph.
3 But *D* abode in the wilderness, and
4 *D* therefore sent out spies, and
5 *D* arose, and came to the place
5 *D* beheld the place where Saul lay,
6 Then answered *D* and said to
7 *D* and Abishai came to the people
8 Then said Abishai to *D*, God hath
9 *D* said to Abishai, Destroy him not:
10 *D* said furthermore, As the Lord
12 So *D* took the spear and the cruse
13 Then *D* went over to the other side,
14 *D* cried to the people, and to Abner
15 *D* said to Abner, Art not thou a
17 Is this thy voice, my son *D*?
17 And *D* said, It is my voice, my lord,
21 I have sinned: return, my son *D*;
22 *D* answered and said, Behold the
25 Then Saul said to *D*,
25 Blessed be thou, my son *D*:
25 So *D* went on his way, and Saul
27. 1 *D* said in his heart, I shall now
2 *D* arose, and he passed over with
3 *D* dwelt with Achish at Gath,
3 even *D* with his two wives,
4 it was told Saul that *D* was fled to
5 *D* said unto Achish, If I have now
7 And the time that *D* dwelt in the
8 *D* and his men went up, and
9 *D* smote the land, and left neither
10 *D* said, Against the south of Judah,
11 *D* saved neither man nor woman
11 So did *D*, and so will be his
12 Achish believed *D*, saying, He hath
28. 1 Achish said unto *D*, Know thou
2 *D* said to Achish, Surely thou
2 Achish said to *D*, Therefore will I
17 given it to thy neighbor, even to *D*:
29. 2 *D* and his men passed on in the
3 Is not this *D*, the servant of Saul
5 Is not this *D*, of whom they sang
5 slew his thousands, and *D* his ten
6 Then Achish called *D*, and said
8 *D* said unto Achish, But what
9 Achish answered and said to *D*, I
11 So *D* and his men rose up early
30. 1 when *D* and his men were come to
3 So *D* and his men came to the
4 Then *D* and the people that were
6 *D* was greatly distressed; for the
6 *D* encouraged himself in the Lord
7 *D* said to Abiathar the priest,
7 brought thither the ephod to *D*.
8 *D* inquired at the Lord, saying,
9 So *D* went, he and the six hundred
10 *D* pursued, he and four hundred
11 and brought him to *D*, and gave
13 And *D* said unto him, To whom
15 *D* said to him, Canst thou bring
17 *D* smote them from the twilight
18 *D* recovered all that the
18 and *D* rescued his two wives.
19 taken to them: *D* recovered all.
20 *D* took all the flocks and the herds
21 *D* came to the two hundred men,
21 faint that they could not follow *D*,

21 and they went forth to meet *D*,
21 when *D* came near to the people,
22 Belial, of those that went with *D*,
23 Then said *D*, Ye shall not do so,
26 when *D* came to Ziklag, he sent of
31 where *D* himself and his men were
2Sa 1. 1 *D* was returned from the slaughter
1 *D* had abode two days in Ziklag;
2 And so it was, when he came to *D*,
3 *D* said unto him, From whence
4 *D* said unto him, How went the
5 *D* said unto the young man that
11 Then *D* took hold on his clothes,
13 *D* said unto the young man that
14 *D* said unto him, How wast thou
15 *D* called one of the young men,
16 *D* said unto him, Thy blood be
17 *D* lamented with this lamentation
2. 1 *D* inquired of the Lord, saying,
1 *D* said, Whither shall I go up?
2 *D* went up thither, and his two
3 were with him did *D* bring up,
4 And there they anointed *D* king
4 they told *D*, saying, That the men
5 *D* sent messengers unto the men
10 the house of Judah followed *D*.
11 time that *D* was king in Hebron
13 of Zeruiah, and the servants of *D*,
15 and twelve of the servants of *D*,
17 Israel, before the servants of *D*,
31 the servants of *D* had smitten of
3. 1 house of Saul and the house of *D*:
1 *D* waxed stronger and stronger,
2 unto *D* were sons born in Hebron:
5 These were born to *D* in Hebron.
6 house of Saul and the house of *D*,
8 delivered thee into the hand of *D*,
9 as the Lord hath sworn to *D*, even
10 set up the throne of *D* over Israel
12 sent messengers to *D* on his behalf,
14 *D* sent messengers to Ish-bosheth
17 Ye sought for *D* in times past to
18 for the Lord hath spoken of *D*,
18 By the hand of my servant *D* I will
19 went also to speak in the ears of *D*
20 So Abner came to *D* to Hebron,
20 *D* made Abner and the men that
21 Abner said unto *D*, I will arise and
21 *D* sent Abner away; and he went
22 the servants of *D* and Joab came
22 Abner was not with *D* in Hebron;
26 when Joab was come out from *D*,
26 well of Sirah: but *D* knew it not.
28 afterward when *D* heard it, he said,
31 And *D* said to Joab, and to all the
31 king *D* himself followed the bier.
35 people came to cause *D* to eat
35 while it was yet day, *D* sware,
4. 8 the head of Ish-bosheth unto *D*
9 And *D* answered Rechab and
12 *D* commanded his young men, and
5. 1 came all the tribes of Israel to *D*
3 king *D* made a league with them
3 they anointed *D* king over Israel.
4 *D* was thirty years old when he
6 spake unto *D*, saying, Except thou
6 thinking, *D* cannot come in hither.
7 *D* took the strong hold of Zion:
7 the same is the city of *D*.
8 *D* said on that day, Whosoever
9 So *D* dwelt in the fort,
9 and called it the city of *D*.
9 *D* built round about from Millo
10 *D* went on, and grew great,
11 king of Tyre sent messengers to *D*,
11 and they built *D* an house.
12 *D* perceived that the Lord had
13 *D* took him more concubines and
13 yet sons and daughters born to *D*.
17 had anointed *D* king over Israel,
17 Philistines came up to seek *D*;

2Sa 5.17 and *D* heard of it, and went
19 *D* inquired of the Lord, saying,
19 the Lord said unto *D*, Go up:
20 And *D* came to Baal-perazim,
20 and *D* smote them there,
21 and *D* and his men burned them.
23 when *D* inquired of the Lord, he
25 And *D* did so, as the Lord had
6. 1 *D* gathered together all the chosen
2 *D* arose, and went with all the
5 And *D* and all the house of Israel
8 *D* was displeased, because the
9 *D* was afraid of the Lord that day,
10 *D* would not remove the ark of the
10 Lord unto him in the city of *D*:
10 but *D* carried it aside into the
12 was told king *D*, saying, The Lord
12 So *D* went and brought up the ark
12 into the city of *D* with gladness.
14 *D* danced before the Lord with all
14 and *D* was girded with a linen
15 So *D* and all the house of Israel
16 the Lord came into the city of *D*,
16 saw king *D* leaping and dancing
17 tabernacle that *D* had pitched for
17 and *D* offered burnt offerings
18 as *D* had made an end of offering
20 *D* returned to bless his household.
20 daughter of Saul came to meet *D*,
21 *D* said unto Michal, It was before
7. 5 Go and tell my servant *D*, Thus
8 shalt thou say unto my servant *D*,
17 so did Nathan speak unto *D*.
18 Then went king *D* in, and sat
20 what can *D* say more unto thee?
26 of thy servant *D* be established
8. 1 *D* smote the Philistines, and
1 *D* took Metheg-ammah out of the
3 *D* smote also Hadadezer, the son
4 *D* took from him a thousand
4 *D* houghed all the chariot horses,
5 *D* slew of the Syrians two and
6 *D* put garrisons in Syria of
6 the Syrians became servants to *D*,
6 preserved *D* whithersoever he
7 *D* took the shields of gold that
8 king *D* took exceeding much brass.
9 Toi king of Hamath heard that *D*
10 sent Joram his son unto king *D*,
11 Which also king *D* did dedicate
13 *D* gat him a name when he
14 And the Lord preserved *D*
15 And *D* reigned over all Israel;
15 *D* executed judgment and justice
9. 1 *D* said, Is there yet any that is left
2 when they had called him unto *D*,
5 Then king *D* sent, and fetched
6 come unto *D*, he fell on his face,
6 And *D* said, Mephibosheth.
7 *D* said unto him, Fear not: for I
10. 2 Then said *D*, I will shew kindness
2 *D* sent to comfort him by the hand
3 that *D* doth honor thy father,
3 hath not *D* rather sent his servants
5 When they told it unto *D*, he sent
6 saw that they stank before *D*,
7 when *D* heard of it, he sent Joab,
17 was told *D*, he gathered all Israel
17 set themselves in array against *D*,
18 *D* slew the men of seven hundred
11. 1 *D* sent Joab, and all his servants
1 But *D* tarried still at Jerusalem.
2 that *D* arose from off his bed, and
3 *D* sent and inquired after the
4 *D* sent messengers, and took her;
5 conceived, and sent and told *D*,
6 *D* sent to Joab, saying, Send me
6 And Joab sent Uriah to *D*.
7 *D* demanded of him how Joab did,
8 *D* said to Uriah, Go down to thy
10 had told *D*, saying, Uriah went

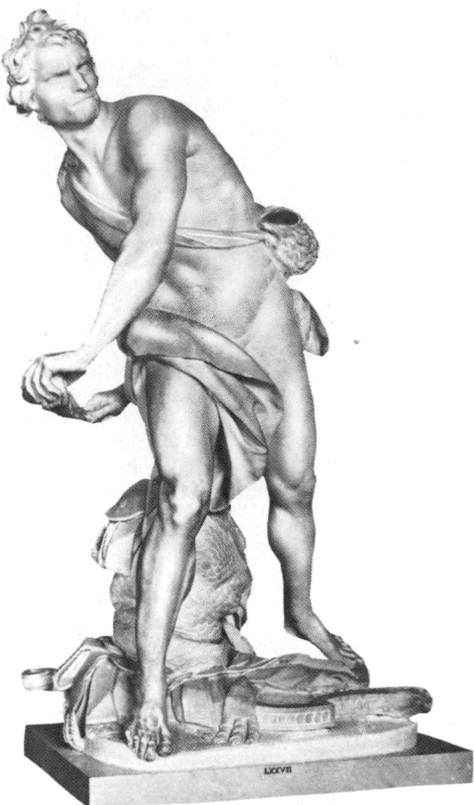

David, *the dramatic statue by Bernini (1598-1680)*

10 *D* said unto Uriah, camest thou
11 Uriah said unto *D*, The ark, and
12 And *D* said to Uriah, Tarry here
13 when *D* had called him, he did eat
14 *D* wrote a letter to Joab, and sent
17 of the people of the servants of *D*;
18 Joab sent and told *D* all the things
22 come and shewed *D* all that Joab
23 messenger said unto *D*, Surely the
25 Then *D* said unto the messenger,
27 the mourning was passed, *D* sent
27 thing that *D* had done displeased
12. 1 the Lord sent Nathan unto *D*.
7 Nathan said to *D*, Thou art the
13 *D* said unto Nathan, I have sinned
13 Nathan said unto *D*, The Lord
15 that Uriah's wife bare unto *D*,
16 *D* therefore besought God for the
16 and *D* fasted, and went in,
18 servants of *D* feared to tell him
19 *D* saw that his servants whispered,
19 *D* perceived that the child was
19 *D* said unto his servants, Is the
20 Then *D* arose from the earth, and
24 *D* comforted Bath-sheba his wife,
27 Joab sent messengers to *D*, and
29 *D* gathered all the people together,
31 So *D* and all the people returned
13. 1 Absalom the son of *D* had a fair
1 Amnon the son of *D* loved her.
7 Then *D* sent home to Tamar,
21 king *D* heard of all these things,
30 came to *D*, saying, Absalom hath
37 *D* mourned for his son every day.
39 the soul of king *D* longed to go
15.13 came a messenger to *D*, saying,
14 *D* said unto all his servants that
22 *D* said to Ittai, Go and pass over.
30 *D* went up by the ascent of mount
31 told *D*, saying, Ahithophel is among
31 *D* said, O Lord, I pray thee, turn
32 when *D* was come up to the top of
33 Unto whom *D* said, If thou passest
16. 1 when *D* was a little past the top of
5 when king *D* came to Bahurim,
6 And he cast stones at *D*, and
6 at all the servants of king *D*:
10 Lord hath said unto him, Curse *D*.
11 *D* said to Abishai, and to all his
13 as *D* and his men went by the way,
23 of Ahithophel both with *D* and
17. 1 I will arise and pursue after *D*
16 and tell *D*, saying, Lodge not this
17 and they went and told king *D*.
21 and told king *D*, and said unto
21 said unto *D*, Arise, and pass quickly
22 Then *D* arose, and all the people
24 *D* came to Mahanaim. And Absalom
27 when *D* was come to Mahanaim,
29 sheep, and cheese of kine, for *D*,
18. 1 *D* numbered the people that were
2 *D* sent forth a third part of the
7 slain before the servants of *D*,
9 Absalom met the servants of *D*.
24 *D* sat between the two gates: and
19.11 *D* sent to Zadok and to Abiathar
16 the men of Judah to meet king *D*.
22 *D* said, What have I to do with
43 have also more right in *D* than ye:
20. 1 We have no part in *D*, neither
2 man of Israel went up from after *D*,
3 *D* came to his house at Jerusalem;
6 *D* said to Abishai, Now shall Sheba
11 favoreth Joab, and he that is for *D*,
21 against the king, even against *D*:
26 Jairite was a chief ruler about *D*.
21. 1 was a famine in the days of *D*
1 and *D* inquired of the Lord. And
3 *D* said unto the Gibeonites, What
7 *D* and Jonathan the son of Saul.
11 it was told *D* what Rizpah the
12 *D* went and took the bones of Saul
15 *D* went down, and his servants
15 Philistines: and *D* waxed faint.
16 new sword, thought to have slain *D*.
17 the men of *D* sware unto him,
21 the brother of *D* slew him.
22 and fell by the hand of *D*, and by
22. 1 *D* spake unto the Lord the words
51 mercy to his anointed, unto *D*,
23. 1 these be the last words of *D*.
1 *D* the son of Jesse said, and the
8 of the mighty men whom *D* had:
9 of the three mighty men with *D*,
13 came to *D* in the harvest time
14 *D* was then in an hold, and the
15 *D* longed, and said, Oh that one
16 and took it, and brought it to *D*,
23 And *D* set him over his guard,
24. 1 he moved *D* against them to say,
10 *D* said unto the Lord, I have
11 when *D* was up in the morning,
12 Go and say unto *D*, Thus saith the
13 So Gad came to *D*, and told him,
14 *D* said unto Gad, I am in a great
17 *D* spake unto the Lord when he
18 Gad came that day to *D*, and said
19 *D*, according to the saying of Gad,
21 *D* said, To buy the threshingfloor
22 Araunah said unto *D*, Let my lord
24 So *D* bought the threshingfloor
25 *D* built there an altar unto the
1Ki 1. 1 Now king *D* was old and stricken
8 mighty men which belonged to *D*,
11 and *D* our lord knoweth it not?
13 Go and get thee in unto king *D*,
28 Then king *D* answered and said,
31 Let my lord king *D* live for ever.
32 *D* said, Call me Zadok the priest,
37 than the throne of my lord king *D*.
43 king *D* hath made Solomon king.
47 came to bless our lord king *D*,

2. 1 of *D* drew nigh that he should die;
10 So *D* slept with his fathers,
10 and was buried in the city of *D*.
11 the days that *D* reigned over Israel
12 sat Solomon upon the throne of *D*
24 and set me on the throne of *D*
26 the ark of the Lord God before *D*
32 my father *D* not knowing thereof,
33 but upon *D*, and upon his seed,
44 that thou didst to *D* my father:
45 throne of *D* shall be established
3. 1 and brought her into the city of *D*,
3 in the statutes of *D* his father:
6 hast shewed unto thy servant *D*
7 made thy servant king instead of *D*
14 as thy father *D* did walk, then I
5. 1 for Hiram was ever a lover of *D*.
3 Thou knowest how that *D* my
5 the Lord spake unto *D* my father,
7 hath given unto *D* a wise son
6.12 which I spake unto *D* thy father:
7.51 which *D* his father had dedicated;
8. 1 out of the city of *D*, which is Zion.
15 which spake with his mouth unto *D*
16 but I chose *D* to be over my people
17 it was in the heart of *D* my father
18 the Lord said unto *D* my father,
20 I am risen up in the room of *D*
24 Who hast kept with thy servant *D*
25 keep with thy servant *D* my father
26 thou spakest unto thy servant *D*
66 that the Lord had done for *D* his
9. 4 *D* thy father walked, in integrity
5 I promised to *D* thy father, saying,
24 came up out of the city of *D* unto
11. 4 as was the heart of *D* his father.
6 not fully after the Lord, as did *D*
12 not do it for *D* thy father's sake:
13 to thy son for *D* my servant's sake,
15 to pass, when *D* was in Edom,
21 Hadad heard in Egypt that *D* slept
24 when *D* slew them of Zobah:
27 the breaches of the city of *D*
33 my judgments, as did *D* his father
34 *D* my servant's sake, whom I chose,
36 *D* my servant may have a light
38 commandments, as *D* my servant
38 thee a sure house, as I built for *D*,
39 I will for this afflict the seed of *D*,
43 buried in the city of *D* his father:
12.16 What portion have we in *D*?
16 now see to thine own house, *D*.
19 rebelled against the house of *D*
20 none that followed the house of *D*,
26 kingdom return to the house of *D*:
13. 2 shall be born unto the house of *D*,
14. 8 kingdom away from the house of *D*,
8 hast not been as my servant *D*,
31 with his fathers in the city of *D*.
15. 3 Lord his God, as the heart of *D*
5 *D* did that which was right in the
8 they buried him in the city of *D*
11 in the eyes of the Lord, as did *D*
24 of *D* his father: and Jehoshaphat
22.50 fathers in the city of *D* his father:
2Ki 8.19 Judah for *D* his servant's sake.
24 with his fathers in the city of *D*:
9.28 with his fathers in the city of *D*.
12.21 with his fathers in the city of *D*:
14. 3 yet not like *D* his father: he did
20 with his fathers in the city of *D*.
15. 7 with his fathers in the city of *D*:
38 fathers in the city of *D* his father
16. 2 Lord his God, like *D* his father.
20 with his fathers in the city of *D*:
17.21 rent Israel from the house of *D*;
18. 3 according to all that *D* his father
20. 5 Thus saith the Lord, the God of *D*
21. 7 house, of which the Lord said to *D*,
22. 2 and walked in all the way of *D*
1Ch 2.15 Ozem the sixth, *D* the seventh

3. 1 these were the sons of *D*, which
9 These were all the sons of *D*,
4.31 their cities unto the reign of *D*.
6.31 *D* set over the service of song
7. 2 whose number was in the days of *D*
9.22 *D* and Samuel the seer did ordain
10.14 and turned the kingdom unto *D*
11. 1 Israel gathered themselves to *D*
3 and *D* made a covenant with them
3 they anointed *D* king over Israel,
4 *D* and all Israel went to Jerusalem,
5 the inhabitants of Jebus said to *D*,
5 Nevertheless *D* took the castle
5 of Zion, which is the city of *D*.
6 *D* said, Whosoever smiteth the
7 *D* dwelt in the castle; therefore
7 they called it the city of *D*.
9 So *D* waxed greater and greater:
10 chief of the mighty men whom *D*
11 number of the mighty men whom *D*
13 He was with *D* at Pas-dammim,
15 went down to the rock to *D*,
16 *D* was then in the hold, and the
17 *D* longed, and said, Oh that one
18 and took it, and brought it to *D*:
18 but *D* would not drink of it,
25 and *D* set him over his guard.
12. 1 they that came to *D* to Ziklag,
8 there separated themselves unto *D*
16 and Judah to the hold unto *D*.
17 *D* went out to meet them, and
18 Thine are we, *D*, and on thy side,
18 *D* received them, and made them
19 there fell some of Manasseh to *D*,
21 *D* against the band of the rovers:
22 day there came to *D* to help him,
23 came to *D* to Hebron, to turn the
31 name, to come and make *D* king.
38 to make *D* king over all Israel:
38 were of one heart to make *D* king.
39 there they were with *D* three days,
13. 1 *D* consulted with the captains of
2 *D* said unto all the congregation
5 So *D* gathered all Israel together,
6 *D* went up, and all Israel, to
8 *D* and all Israel played before God
11 *D* was displeased, because the
12 *D* was afraid of God that day,
13 So *D* brought not the ark home
13 to himself to the city of *D*,
14. 1 king of Tyre sent messengers to *D*,
2 *D* perceived that the Lord had
3 *D* took more wives at Jerusalem:
3 *D* begat more sons and daughters.
8 when the Philistines heard that *D*
8 the Philistines went up to seek *D*.
8 And *D* heard of it, and went out
10 *D* inquired of God, saying, Shall I
11 and *D* smote them there. Then
11 *D* said, God hath broken in upon
12 *D* gave a commandment, and they
14 Therefore *D* inquired again of God;
16 *D* therefore did as God commanded
17 fame of *D* went out into all lands;
15. 1 *D* made him houses in the city
1 houses in the city of *D*,
2 Then *D* said, None ought to carry
3 *D* gathered all Israel together to
4 *D* assembled the children of Aaron,
11 *D* called for Zadok and Abiathar
16 *D* spake to the chief of the Levites
25 So *D*, and the elders of Israel, and
27 *D* was clothed with a robe of fine
27 *D* also had upon him an ephod of
29 came to the city of *D*, that Michal
29 at a window saw king *D* dancing
16. 1 the tent that *D* had pitched for it:
2 *D* had made an end of offering
7 day *D* delivered first this psalm
43 *D* returned to bless his house.
17. 1 to pass, as *D* sat in his house,

1 that *D* said to Nathan the prophet,
2 Nathan said unto *D*, Do all that is
4 Go and tell *D* my servant, Thus
7 shalt thou say unto my servant *D*,
15 so did Nathan speak unto *D*.
16 *D* the king came and sat before
18 What can *D* speak more to thee
24 let the house of *D* thy servant be
18. 1 pass, that *D* smote the Philistines,
3 *D* smote Hadarezer king of Zobah
4 *D* took from him a thousand
4 *D* also houghed all the chariot
5 *D* slew of the Syrians two and
6 *D* put garrisons in
6 Thus the Lord preserved *D*
7 *D* took the shields of gold that
8 brought *D* very much brass,
9 Tou king of Hamath heard how *D*
10 sent Hadoram his son to king *D*,
11 king *D* dedicated unto the Lord,
13 Thus the Lord preserved *D*
14 So *D* reigned over all Israel, and
17 of *D* were chief about the king.
19. 2 *D* said, I will shew kindness unto
2 *D* sent messengers to comfort
2 servants of *D* came into the land
3 Thinkest thou that *D* doth honor
5 told *D* how the men were served.
6 had made themselves odious to *D*,
8 when *D* heard of it, he sent Joab,
17 And it was told *D*; and he gathered
17 *D* had put the battle in array
18 *D* slew of the Syrians seven
19 they made peace with *D*, and
20. 1 But *D* tarried at Jerusalem. And
2 *D* took the crown of their king
3 Even so dealt *D* with all the cities
3 *D* and all the people returned to
8 and they fell by the hand of *D*, and
21. 1 and provoked *D* to number Israel.
2 *D* said to Joab, and to the rulers of
5 of the number of people unto *D*.
8 *D* said unto God, I have sinned
10 Go and tell *D*, saying, Thus saith
11 Gad came to *D*, and said unto him,
13 *D* said unto Gad, I am in a great
16 *D* lifted up his eyes, and saw the
16 Then *D* and the elders of Israel,
17 *D* said unto God, Is it not I that
18 Lord commanded Gad to say to *D*,
18 that *D* should go up, and set up
19 *D* went up at the saying of Gad,
21 as *D* came to Ornan, Ornan looked
21 and saw *D*, and went out of the
21 bowed himself to *D* with his face
22 Then *D* said to Ornan, Grant me
23 Ornan said unto *D*, Take it to thee,
24 king *D* said to Ornan, Nay; but I
25 So *D* gave to Ornan for the place
26 *D* built there an altar unto the
28 time when *D* saw that the Lord
30 *D* could not go before it to inquire
22. 1 Then *D* said, This is the house of
2 *D* commanded to gather together
3 *D* prepared iron in abundance for
4 brought much cedar wood to *D*
5 *D* said, Solomon my son is young
5 So *D* prepared abundantly before
7 *D* said to Solomon, My son, as for
17 *D* also commanded all the princes
23. 1 when *D* was old and full of days,
6 *D* divided them into courses
25 For *D* said, The Lord God of Israel
27 last words of *D* the Levites were
24. 3 *D* distributed them, both Zadok of
31 sons of Aaron in the presence of *D*
25. 1 Moreover *D* and the captains of
26.26 *D* the king, and the chief fathers,
31 the fortieth year of the reign of *D*
32 *D* made rulers over the Reubenites,
27.18 Elihu, one of the brethren of *D*:

1Ch 27.23 *D* took not the number of them
24 of the chronicles of king *D*.
28. 1 *D* assembled all the princes of
2 *D* the king stood up upon his feet,
11 Then *D* gave to Solomon his son
19 All this, said *D*, the Lord made me
20 *D* said to Solomon his son, Be
29. 1 Furthermore *D* the king said unto
9 *D* the king also rejoiced with great
10 *D* blessed the Lord before all the
10 *D* said, Blessed be thou, Lord God
20 *D* said to all the congregation,
22 the son of *D* king the second time,
23 as king instead of *D* his father, and
24 all the sons likewise of king *D*,
26 Thus *D* the son of Jesse reigned
29 acts of *D* the king, first and last,
2Ch 1. 1 And Solomon the son of *D* was
4 ark of God had *D* brought up from
4 the place which *D* had prepared
8 hast shewed great mercy unto *D*
9 let thy promise unto *D* my father
2. 3 thou didst deal with *D* my father,
7 whom *D* my father did provide.
12 hath given to *D* the king a wise son,
14 with the cunning men of my lord *D*
17 *D* his father had numbered them;
3. 1 Lord appeared unto *D* his father,
1 the place that *D* had prepared
5. 1 brought in all the things that *D* his
2 out of the city of *D*, which is Zion.
6. 4 with his mouth to my father *D*,
6 and have chosen *D* to be over my
7 it was in the heart of *D* my father
8 But the Lord said to *D* my father,
10 I am risen up in the room of *D*
15 which hast kept with thy servant *D*
16 keep with thy servant *D* my father
17 hast spoken unto thy servant *D*.
42 remember the mercies of *D* thy
7. 6 which *D* the king had made to
6 when *D* praised by their ministry;
10 that the Lord had shewed unto *D*,
17 as *D* thy father walked, and do
18 as I have covenanted with *D* thy
8.11 out of the city of *D* unto the house
11 shall not dwell in the house of *D*
14 according to the order of *D* his
14 had *D* the man of God commanded.
9.31 he was buried in the city of *D* his
10.16 What portion have we in *D*? and
16 now, *D*, see to thine own house.
19 rebelled against the house of *D*
11.17 years they walked in the way of *D*
18 daughter of Jerimoth the son of *D*
12.16 and was buried in the city of *D*:
13. 5 kingdom over Israel to *D* forever,
6 servant of Solomon the son of *D*,
8 in the hand of the sons of *D*;
14. 1 they buried him in the city of *D*:
16.14 made for himself in the city of *D*,
17. 3 in the first ways of his father *D*,
21. 1 with his fathers in the city of *D*.
7 would not destroy the house of *D*,
7 covenant that he had made with *D*,
12 saith the Lord God of *D* thy father,
20 they buried him in the city of *D*,
23. 3 Lord hath said of the sons of *D*.
18 whom *D* had distributed in the
18 singing, as it was ordained by *D*.
24.16 in the city of *D* among the kings,
25 in the city of *D*, but they buried
27. 9 they buried him in the city of *D*:
28. 1 of the Lord, like *D* his father:
29. 2 according to all that *D* his father
25 to the commandment of *D*, and of
26 stood with the instruments of *D*,
27 the instruments ordained by *D*
30 with the words of *D*, and of Asaph
30.26 the time of Solomon the son of *D*
32. 5 repaired Millo in the city of *D*,
30 to the west side of the city of *D*.
33 of the sepulchres of the sons of *D*:
33. 7 God had said to *D* and to Solomon
14 built a wall without the city of *D*,
34. 2 walked in the ways of *D* his father,
3 began to seek after the God of *D*
35. 3 house which Solomon the son of *D*
4 according to the writing of *D*
15 to the commandment of *D*, and of
Ezr 3.10 after the ordinance of *D* king of
8. 2 of the sons of *D*; Hattush.
20 of the Nethinims, whom *D* and
Neh 3.15 that go down from the city of *D*.
16 over against the sepulchres of *D*,
12.24 to the commandment of *D* the man
36 with the musical instruments of *D*
37 up by the stairs of the city of *D*,
37 above the house of *D*, even unto
45 to the commandment of *D*, and of
46 For in the days of *D* and Asaph of
Ps 18.50 to *D*, and to his seed for evermore.
72.20 The prayers of *D* the son of Jesse
78.70 He chose *D* also his servant, and
89. 3 I have sworn unto *D* my servant,
20 I have found *D* my servant; with
35 that I will not lie unto *D*.
49 which thou swearest unto *D* in
122. 5 the thrones of the house of *D*.
132. 1 Lord, remember *D*, and all his
11 Lord hath sworn in truth unto *D*;
17 There will I make the horn of *D*
144.10 who delivereth *D* his servant from
Pr 1. 1 Proverbs of Solomon, the son of *D*,
Ec 1. 1 words of the Preacher, the son of *D*,
SS 4. 4 Thy neck is like the tower of *D*
Isa 7. 2 it was told the house of *D*, saying,
13 said, Hear ye now, O house of *D*;
9. 7 upon the throne of *D*, and upon
16. 5 in truth in the tabernacle of *D*,
22. 9 the breaches of the city of *D*,
22 key of the house of *D* will I lay
29. 1 to Ariel, the city where *D* dwelt!
38. 5 the Lord, the God of *D* thy father,
55. 3 even the sure mercies of *D*.
Jer 17.25 sitting upon the throne of *D*,
21.12 O house of *D*, thus saith the Lord;
22. 2 that sittest upon the throne of *D*,
4 kings sitting upon the throne of *D*,
30 sitting upon the throne of *D*, and
23. 5 raise unto *D* a righteous Branch,
29.16 that sitteth upon the throne of *D*,
30. 9 *D* their king, whom I will raise up
33.15 righteousness to grow up unto *D*;
17 *D* shall never want a man to sit
21 my covenant be broken with *D*
22 so will I multiply the seed of *D*
26 seed of Jacob, and *D* my servant,
36.30 none to sit upon the throne of *D*:
Eze 34.23 feed them, even my servant *D*;
24 servant *D* a prince among them;
37.24 *D* my servant shall be king over
25 my servant *D* shall be their prince
Hos 3. 5 Lord their God, and *D* their king;
Am 6. 5 instruments of musick, like *D*;
9.11 will I raise up the tabernacle of *D*
Zec 12. 7 that the glory of the house of *D*
8 them at that day shall be as *D*;
8 the house of *D* shall be as God,
10 I will pour upon the house of *D*,
12 the family of the house of *D* apart,
13. 1 fountain opened to the house of *D*
Mt 1. 1 son of *D*, the son of Abraham.
6 Jesse begat *D* the king; and *D*
17 generations from Abraham to *D*
17 *D* until the carrying away into
20 Joseph, thou son of *D*, fear not to
9.27 Thou son of *D*, have mercy on us.
12. 3 have ye not read what *D* did,
23 said, Is not this the son of *D*?
15.22 Lord, thou son of *D*; my daughter
20.30, 31 on us, O Lord, thou son of *D*.
21. 9 Hosanna to the son of *D*: Blessed
15 Hosanna to the son of *D*; they
22.42 They say unto him, The son of *D*.
43 How then doth *D* in spirit call him
45 If *D* then call him Lord, how is
Mk 2.25 Have ye never read what *D* did,
10.47 Jesus, thou son of *D*, have mercy
48 Thou son of *D*, have mercy on me.
11.10 of our father *D*, that cometh in
12.35 that Christ is the son of *D*?
36 *D* himself said by the Holy Ghost,
37 *D* therefore himself calleth him
Lk 1.27 was Joseph, of the house of *D*;
32 him the throne of his father *D*:
69 in the house of his servant *D*;
2. 4 unto the city of *D*, which is called
4 was of the house and lineage of *D*:)
11 is born this day in the city of *D*
3.31 Nathan, which was the son of *D*,
6. 3 what *D* did, when himself was an
18.38 Jesus, thou son of *D*, have mercy
39 Thou son of *D*, have mercy on me.
20.42 And *D* himself saith in the book
44 *D* therefore calleth him Lord, how
Jn 7.42 Christ cometh of the seed of *D*,
42 town of Bethlehem, where *D* was?
Ac 1.16 the Holy Ghost by the mouth of *D*
2.25 For *D* speaketh concerning him,
29 speak unto you of the patriarch *D*,
34 *D* is not ascended into the heavens:
4.25 Who by the mouth of thy servant *D*
7.45 of our fathers, unto the days of *D*;
13.22 up unto them *D* to be their king;
22 I have found *D* the son of Jesse,
34 give you the sure mercies of *D*.
36 For *D*, after he had served his own
15.16 build again the tabernacle of *D*,
Ro 1. 3 which was made of the seed of *D*
4. 6 *D* also describeth the blessedness
11. 9 *D* saith, Let their table be made
2Ti 2. 8 Jesus Christ of the seed of *D*
Heb 4. 7 limiteth a certain day, saying in *D*,
11.32 *D* also, and Samuel, and of the
Rev 3. 7 he that hath the key of *D*, he that
5. 5 Root of *D*, hath prevailed to open
22.16 am the root and the offspring of *D*,

DAWN

Mt 28. 1 began to *d* toward the first day
2Pe 1.19 until the day *d*, and the day star

DAWNING

Jos 6.15 rose early about the *d* of the day,
Jdg 19.26 the woman in the *d* of the day,
Job 3. 9 neither let it see the *d* of the day:
7. 4 to and fro unto the *d* of the day.
Ps 119.147 prevented the *d* of the morning,

DAY

Gen 1. 5 God called the light *D*, and the
16 the greater light to rule the *d*,
2. 2 the seventh *d* God ended his work
2 and he rested on the seventh *d*
3 God blessed the seventh *d*, and
3. 8 the garden in the cool of the *d*:
27. 2 I know not the *d* of my death:
45 deprived also of you both in one *d*?
32.24 him until the breaking of the *d*.
26 Let me go, for the *d* breaketh.
Ex 10.28 in that *d* thou seest my face thou
12.16 in the first *d* there shall be an holy
16 the seventh *d* there shall be an
13.22 the pillar of the cloud by *d*, nor
16.30 the people rested on the seventh *d*.
20. 8 Remember the sabbath *d*, to keep
11 rested the seventh *d*: wherefore
11 the Lord blessed the sabbath *d*,
23.12 the seventh *d* thou shalt rest: that
31.15 doeth any work in the sabbath *d*,
34.21 but on the seventh *d* thou shalt
Lev 23. 8 seventh *d* is an holy convocation

27 there shall be a *d* of atonement:
28 ye shall do no work in that same *d*:
28 for it is a *d* of atonement,
Nu 9.16 alway: the cloud covered it by *d*,
14.14 by *d* time in a pillar of a cloud,
Dt 1.10 are this *d* as the stars of heaven
4.26 earth to witness against you this *d*,
32 since the *d* that God created man
5.12 Keep the sabbath *d* to sanctify it,
11.26 I set before you this *d* a blessing
26.16 This *d* the Lord thy God hath
29.12 thy God maketh with thee this *d*:
Jos 1. 8 meditate therein *d* and night,
10.12 in the *d* when the Lord delivered
14 no *d* like that before it or after it,
14.12 the Lord spake in that *d*;
23.14 this *d* I am going the way of all
24.15 choose you this *d* whom ye will
Jdg 4.14 this is the *d* in which the Lord
11.27 the Judge be judge this *d* between
1Sa 14.23 the Lord saved Israel that *d*:
24.10 the Lord had delivered thee to *d*
25. 8 we come in a good *d*: give, I pray
2Sa 13.37 David mourned for his son every *d*.
18.20 Thou shalt not bear tidings this *d*,
1Ki 8.29 toward this house night and *d*,
59 the Lord our God *d* and night,
2Ki 7. 9 this *d* is a *d* of good tidings,
19. 3 This *d* is a *d* of trouble,
1Ch 13.12 David was afraid of God that *d*,
2Ch 30.21 priests praised the Lord *d* by *d*,
Neh 1. 6 pray before thee now, *d* and night,
8.10 this *d* is holy unto our Lord:
11 Hold your peace, for the *d* is holy;
9.12 them in the *d* by a cloudy pillar;
13.17 ye do, and profane the sabbath *d*?
Job 3. 1 Job his mouth, and cursed his *d*.
3 Let the *d* perish wherein I was
4 Let that *d* be darkness; let not
17.12 They change the night into *d*: the
19.25 stand at the latter *d* upon the
Ps 1. 2 in his law doth he meditate *d* and
2. 7 Son; this *d* have I begotten thee.
19. 2 *D* unto *d* uttereth speech, and
20. 1 Lord hear thee in the *d* of trouble;
35.28 of thy praise all the *d* long.
44.22 For thy sake are we killed all the *d*
50.15 call upon me in the *d* of trouble:
59.16 and refuge in the *d* of my trouble.
73.14 all the *d* long have I been plagued,
74.16 The *d* is thine, the night also is
84.10 a *d* in thy courts is better than a
91. 5 for the arrow that flieth by *d*;
118.24 This is the *d* which the Lord hath
119.164 Seven times a *d* do I praise thee
121. 6 The sun shall not smite thee by *d*,
136. 8 The sun to rule by *d*: for his
139.12 the night shineth as the *d*: the
145. 2 Every *d* will I bless thee;
Pr 11. 4 Riches profit not in the *d* of wrath:
27. 1 for thou knowest not what a *d* may
Ec 8. 8 hath he power in the *d* of death:
SS 2.17 Until the *d* break, and the shadows
4. 6 Until the *d* break, and the shadows
Isa 3.18 In that *d* the Lord will take away
4. 1 In that *d* seven women shall take
9. 4 oppressor, as in the *d* of Midian.
19.21 shall know the Lord in that *d*,
38.12, 13 from *d* even to night wilt thou
49. 8 and in a *d* of salvation have I
58. 5 a *d* for a man to afflict his soul?
5 and an acceptable *d* to the Lord?
10 thy darkness be as the noon *d*:
59.10 We stumble at noon *d* as in the
60.11 they shall not be shut *d* nor night;
19 shall be no more thy light by *d*;
61. 2 the *d* of vengeance of our God;
63. 4 the *d* of vengeance is in mine
Jer 6. 4 the *d* goeth away, for the shadows
17.24 hallow the sabbath *d*, to do no
27 hallow the sabbath *d*, and not to

20.14 Cursed be the *d* wherein I was
31.35 giveth the sun for a light by *d*,
46.10 For this is the *d* of the Lord God
La 2.16 this is the *d* that we looked for;
Eze 7.19 in the *d* of the wrath of the Lord:
16. 5 in the *d* that thou wast born.
20. 5 In the *d* when I chose Israel,
24.27 that *d* shall thy mouth be opened
26.18 isles tremble in the *d* of thy fall;
28.13 in the *d* that thou wast created.
38.14 In that *d* when my people of Israel
39. 8 this is the *d* whereof I have spoken.
Dan 6.10 upon his knees three times a *d*,
13 maketh his petition three times a *d*.
Hos 2.18 in that *d* will I make a covenant
6. 2 in the third *d* he will raise us up,
Joel 2. 1 the *d* of the Lord cometh, for it is
2 A *d* of darkness and of gloominess,
2 *d* of clouds and of thick darkness,
11 the *d* of the Lord is great and very
31 and the terrible *d* of the Lord come.
Am 5.18 you that desire the *d* of the Lord!
18 the *d* of the Lord is darkness,
8. 9 darken the earth in the clear *d*:
Zep 1. 7 the *d* of the Lord is at hand:
14 The great *d* of the Lord is near,
15 That *d* is a *d* of wrath,
15 a *d* of trouble and distress,
15 a *d* of wasteness and desolation,
15 a *d* of darkness and gloominess,
15 a *d* of clouds and thick darkness,
16 A *d* of the trumpet and alarm
18 in the *d* of the Lord's wrath;
3.11 that *d* shalt thou not be ashamed
Hag 2.19 from this *d* will I bless you.
Zec 4.10 despised the *d* of small things?
9.16 their God shall save them in that *d*
12. 8 that *d* shall the Lord defend the
13. 1 In that *d* there shall be a fountain
14. 1 *d* of the Lord cometh, and thy
4 his feet shall stand in that *d*
9 in that *d* shall there be one Lord,
Mal 3. 2 who may abide the *d* of his coming?
17 that *d* when I make up my jewels;
4. 5 great and dreadful *d* of the Lord:
Mt 6.11 Give us this *d* our daily bread.
34 Sufficient unto the *d* is the evil
10.15 in the *d* of judgment, than for that
11.24 of Sodom in the *d* of judgment,
12. 8 is Lord even of the sabbath *d*.
11 fall into a pit on the sabbath *d*,
16.21 and be raised again the third *d*.
17.23 third *d* he shall be raised again.
20. 2 with the laborers for a penny a *d*,
12 the burden and heat of the *d*.
19 the third *d* he shall rise again.
24.36 *d* and hour knoweth no man,
25.13 know neither the *d* nor the hour
26. 5 But they said, not on the feast *d*,
17 the first *d* of the feast of unleavened
27.62 the *d* of the preparation,
Mk 1.21 on the sabbath *d* he entered into
3. 2 would heal him on the sabbath *d*;
4.27 sleep, and rise night and *d*, and
6.11 Gomorrha in the *d* of judgment,
35 And when the *d* was now far spent,
9.31 killed, he shall rise the third *d*.
10.34 the third *d* he shall rise again.
13.32 of that *d* and that hour knoweth
14. 2 But they said, Not on the feast *d*,
25 until that *d* that I drink it new
16. 2 first *d* of the week, they came unto
Lk 2.11 unto you is born this *d* in the city
4.21 This *d* is this scripture fulfilled
6.23 Rejoice ye in that *d*, and leap for
9.22 slain, and be raised the third *d*.
10.12 more tolerable in that *d* for Sodom,
11. 3 *d* by *d* our daily bread.
12.28 grass, which is to *d* in the field
13.32 the third *d* I shall be perfected
14. 3 lawful to heal on the sabbath *d*?

18.33 the third *d* he shall rise again.
19. 9 *d* is salvation come to this house,
21.34 that *d* come upon you unawares.
23.43 I say unto thee, To *d* shalt thou
24. 1 Now upon the first *d* of the week,
7 and the third *d* rise again.
29 evening, and the *d* is far spent.
46 rise from the dead the third *d*:
Jn 1.29 next *d* John seeth Jesus coming
5.10 is the sabbath *d*: it is not lawful
6.39 raise it up again at the last *d*.
40, 44, 54 raise him up at the last *d*.
8.56 Abraham rejoiced to see my *d*:
9. 4 him that sent me, while it is *d*:
11.24 in the resurrection at the last *d*.
19.31 upon the cross on the sabbath *d*,
20.19 first *d* of the week, when the doors
Ac 2. 1 the *d* of Pentecost was fully come,
20 before that great and notable *d* of
7. 8 and circumcised him the eighth *d*;
10.40 Him God raised up the third *d*,
13.33 Son, this *d* have I begotten thee.
20.16 at Jerusalem the *d* of Pentecost.
26. 7 serving God *d* and night, hope to
Ro 2. 5 the *d* of wrath and revelation
16 In the *d* when God shall judge
8.36 we are killed all the *d* long;
13.12 the *d* is at hand: let us therefore
13 Let us walk honestly, as in the *d*;
14. 5 esteemeth one *d* above another:
5 another esteemeth every *d* alike.
6 that regardeth the *d*, regardeth
6 and he that regardeth not the *d*,
1Co 1. 8 in the *d* of our Lord Jesus Christ.
15. 4 he rose again the third *d* according
2Co 1.14 ours in the *d* of the Lord Jesus.
4.16 inward man is renewed *d* by *d*.
6. 2 behold, now is the *d* of salvation.)
Eph 6.13 to withstand in the evil *d*, and
Php 1. 6 it until the *d* of Jesus Christ:
1Th 5. 2 *d* of the Lord so cometh as a thief
8 But let us, who are of the *d*,
2Th 2. 2 as that the *d* of Christ is at hand.
1Ti 5. 5 and prayers night and *d*.
2Ti 1.18 find mercy of the Lord in that *d*:
Heb 1. 5 this *d* have I begotten thee?
3.13 while it is called To *d*; lest any of
4. 4 And God did rest the seventh *d*
5. 5 my Son, to *d* have I begotten thee.
13. 8 yesterday, and to *d*, and for ever.
2Pe 1.19 in a dark place, until the *d* dawn,
3. 8 and a thousand years as one *d*.
10 But the *d* of the Lord will come
1Jn 4.17 boldness in the *d* of judgment:
Rev 1.10 I was in the Spirit on the Lord's *d*,
6.17 the great *d* of his wrath is come;
7.15 him *d* and night in his temple:
16.14 of that great *d* of God Almighty.
21.25 shall not be shut at all by *d*:

DAY'S

Nu 11.31 it were a *d* journey on this side,
31 were a *d* journey on the other side,
1Ki 19. 4 he himself went a *d* journey
1Ch 16.37 continually, as every *d* work
Est 9.13 according unto this *d* decree, and
Jon 3. 4 a *d* journey, and he cried, and said,
Lk 2.44 a *d* journey; and they sought
Ac 1.12 Jerusalem a sabbath *d* journey.
19.40 in question for this *d* uproar,

DAYS

Gen 1.14 for seasons, and for *d*, and years:
3.14 shalt thou eat all the *d* of thy life:
17 eat of it all the *d* of thy life;
6. 4 giants in the earth in those *d*;
7.12 the rain was upon the earth forty *d*
47. 9 *d* of the years of my pilgrimage
Ex 12.15 *d* shall ye eat unleavened bread;
19 Seven *d* shall there be no leaven
20. 9 Six *d* shalt thou labor, and do all

Ex 20.11 *d* the Lord made heaven and earth,
12 thy *d* may be long upon the land
23.12 Six *d* thou shalt do thy work,
31.15 Six *d* may work be done; but in
17 in six *d* the Lord made heaven and
34.21 Six *d* thou shalt work, but on the
35. 2 Six *d* shall work be done, but on
Lev 23. 3 Six *d* shall work be done: but the
42 Ye shall dwell in booths seven *d*;
Dt 5.13 Six *d* thou shalt labor, and do all
16 that thy *d* may be prolonged, and
33 that ye may prolong your *d* in the
11.21 That your *d* may be multiplied,
30.20 is thy life, and the length of thy *d*:
31.14 thy *d* approach that thou must die.
33.25 and as thy *d*, so shall thy strength
Jdg 17. 6 In those *d* there was no king in
21.25 those *d* there was no king in Israel:
1Sa 3. 1 the Lord was precious in those *d*;
Est 9.26 they called these *d* Purim after
Job 7. 1 *d* also like the *d* of an hireling?
6 My *d* are swifter than a weaver's
16 me alone; for my *d* are vanity.
8. 9 our *d* upon earth are a shadow:)
10.20 Are not my *d* few? cease then,
12.12 in length of *d* understanding.
14. 1 born of a woman is of few *d*,
17.11 My *d* are past, my purposes are
29.18 I shall multiply my *d* as the sand.
38.21 the number of thy *d* is great?
42.17 Job died, being old and full of *d*.
Ps 21. 4 length of *d* for ever and ever.
23. 6 shall follow me all the *d* of my life:
27. 4 of the Lord all the *d* of my life,
34.12 loveth many *d*, that he may see
39. 4 the measure of my *d*, what it is;
5 made my *d* as an hand breadth;
77. 5 I have considered the *d* of old,
90.10 The *d* of our years are threescore
12 So teach us to number our *d*,
14 may rejoice and be glad all our *d*.
15 *d* wherein thou hast afflicted us,
102. 3 my *d* are consumed like smoke,
11 *d* are like a shadow that declineth;
24 me not away in the midst of my *d*:
103.15 As for man, his *d* are as grass:
143. 5 I remember the *d* of old;
144. 4 his *d* are as a shadow that passeth
Pr 3.16 Length of *d* is in her right hand;
10.27 The fear of the Lord prolongeth *d*:
Ec 7.10 former *d* were better than these?
11. 1 thou shalt find it after many *d*.
12. 1 now thy Creator in the *d* of thy
1 youth, while the evil *d* come not,
Isa 38.10 I said in the cutting off of my *d*,
65.22 as the *d* of a tree are the *d* of my
Jer 7.32 behold, the *d* come, saith the Lord,
9.25 *d* come, saith the Lord, that I will
19. 6 the *d* come, saith the Lord, that
23.20 in the latter *d* ye shall consider it
30.24 in the latter *d* ye shall consider it.
La 4.18 end is near, our *d* are fulfilled;
5.21 be turned; renew our *d* as of old.
Eze 38.16 it shall be in the latter *d*, and I
46. 1 six working *d*; but on the sabbath
Dan 6. 7 of any God or man for thirty *d*,
12 of any God or man within thirty *d*,
7. 9 and the Ancient of *d* did sit,
13 and came to the Ancient of *d*,
22 Until the Ancient of *d* came, and
Hos 6. 2 After two *d* will he revive us:
9. 7 The *d* of visitation are come,
7 the *d* of recompence are come;
12. 9 as in the *d* of the solemn feast.
Joel 2.29 those *d* will I pour out my spirit.
Am 5.21 I hate, I despise your feast *d*,
9.11 I will build it as in the *d* of old:
Jon 1.17 was in the belly of the fish three *d*
Mic 4. 1 in the last *d* it shall come to pass,
Mt 2. 1 in the *d* of Herod the king,
4. 2 when he had fasted forty *d*
9.15 but the *d* will come, when the
12.10 it lawful to heal on the sabbath *d*?
12 lawful to do well on the sabbath *d*.
40 Jonas was three *d* and three
40 three *d* and three nights in the
24.22 except those *d* should be shortened,
27.40 and buildest it in three *d*, save
63 After three *d* I will rise again.
Mk 1.13 there in the wilderness forty *d*,
2.20 But the *d* will come, when the
3. 4 to do good on the sabbath *d*, or
8.31 killed, and after three *d* rise again.
13.20 had shortened those *d*, no flesh
20 chosen, he hath shortened the *d*.
15.29 temple, and buildest it in three *d*,
Lk 1.39 Mary arose in those *d*, and went
75 before him, all the *d* of our life.
2. 1 in those *d*, that there went out a
6 the *d* were accomplished that she
46 that after three *d* they found him
4. 2 forty *d* tempted of the devil. And
2 in those *d* he did eat nothing:
31 taught them on the sabbath *d*.
5.35 But the *d* will come, when the
6. 2 not lawful to do on the sabbath *d*?
9 lawful on the sabbath *d* to do good,
13.14 There are six *d* in which men
17.22 to see one of the *d* of the Son of
26 as it was in the *d* of Noe, so shall
26 be also in the *d* of the Son of man.
21.22 For these be the *d* of vengeance,
Jn 2.19 in three *d* I will raise it up.
11.17 he had lain in the grave four *d*
39 for he hath been dead four *d*.
Ac 1. 3 being seen of them forty *d*, and
5 the Holy Ghost not many *d* hence.
2.17 it shall come to pass in the last *d*,
18 pour out in those *d* of my Spirit;
12. 3 were the *d* of unleavened bread.
13.31 he was seen many *d* of them
20. 6 Philippi after the *d* of unleavened
Gal 4.10 Ye observe *d*, and months,
Eph 5.16 the time, because the *d* are evil.
Col 2.16 the new moon, or of the sabbath *d*.
2Ti 3. 1 last *d* perilous times shall come.
Heb 10.32 call to remembrance the former *d*,
12.10 they verily for a few *d* chastened
1Pe 3.10 that will love life, and see good *d*,
2Pe 3. 3 shall come in the last *d* scoffers,

DAYSMAN

Job 9.33 Neither is there any *d* betwixt us,

DAYSPRING

Job 38.12 caused the *d* to know his place;
Lk 1.78 *d* from on high hath visited us,

DAYTIME

Job 5.14 They meet with darkness in the *d*,
24.16 marked for themselves in the *d*:
Ps 22. 2 O my God, I cry in the *d*, but thou
42. 8 his lovingkindness in the *d*, and in
78.14 *d* also he led them with a cloud,
Isa 4. 6 a shadow in the *d* from the heat,
21. 8 upon the watchtower in the *d*,

DEACON

1Ti 3.10 let them use the office of a *d*,
13 that have used the office of a *d*,

DEACONS

Php 1. 1 Philippi, with the bishops and *d*:
1Ti 3. 8 Likewise must the *d* be grave,
12 the *d* be the husbands of one wife,

DEAD

Gen 20. 3 art but a *d* man, for the woman
23. 3 stood up from before his *d*,
4 that I may bury my *d* out of my
6 of our sepulchres bury thy *d*;
6 but that thou mayest bury thy *d*.
8 that I should bury my *d* out of my
11 people give I it thee: bury thy *d*.
13 and I will bury my *d* there.
15 me and thee? bury therefore thy *d*.
42.38 for his brother is *d*, and he is
44.20 and his brother is *d*, and he alone
50.15 that their father was *d*, they said,
Ex 4.19 men are *d* which sought thy life.
9. 7 one of the cattle of the Israelites *d*.
12.30 a house where there was not one *d*.
33 for they said, We be all *d* men.
14.30 Israel saw the Egyptians *d* upon
21.34 and the *d* beast shall be his.
35 the *d* ox also they shall divide.
36 and the *d* shall be his own.
Lev 11.31 when they be *d*, shall be unclean
32 when they are *d*, doth fall, it shall
19.28 cuttings in your flesh for the *d*,
21. 1 shall none be defiled for the *d*
11 shall he go in to any *d* body,
22. 4 thing that is unclean by the *d*,
Nu 5. 2 whosoever is defiled by the *d*:
6. 6 he shall come at no *d* body.
11 him, for that he sinned by the *d*,
9. 6, 7 defiled by the *d* body of a man,
10 unclean by the reason of a *d* body,
12.12 Let her not be as one *d*,
16.48 stood between the *d* and the living;
19.11 He that toucheth the *d* body of any
13 Whosoever toucheth the *d* body
13 of any man that is *d*, and
16 or a *d* body, or a bone of a man,
18 or one slain, or one *d*, or a grave:
20.29 that Aaron was *d*, they mourned
Dt 2.16 men of war were consumed and *d*
14. 1 between your eyes for the *d*.
8 flesh, nor touch their *d* carcass.
25. 5 the wife of the *d* shall not marry
6 the name of his brother which is *d*,
26.14 nor given ought thereof for the *d*:
Jos 1. 2 Moses my servant is *d*; now
Jdg 2.19 the judge was *d*, that they returned,
3.25 their lord was fallen down *d*
4. 1 of the Lord when Ehud was *d*.
22 into her tent, behold, Sisera lay *d*,
5.27 he bowed, there he fell down *d*.
8.33 as soon as Gideon was *d*, that the
9.55 Israel saw that Abimlech was *d*,
16.30 the *d* which he slew at his death
20. 5 have they forced, that she is *d*.
Ru 1. 8 as ye have dealt with the *d*,
2.20 to the living and to the *d*.
4. 5 the *d*, to raise up the name of the *d*
10 name of the *d* upon his inheritance,
10 the name of the *d* be not cut off
1Sa 4.17 Hophni and Phinehas, are *d*, and
19 in law and her husband were *d*,
17.51 saw their champion was *d*, they
24.14 after a *d* dog, after a flea.
25.39 David heard that Nabal was *d*,
28. 3 Now Samuel was *d*, and all Israel
31. 5 armorbearer saw that Saul was *d*,
7 Saul and his sons were *d*, they
2Sa 1. 4 the people also are fallen and *d*;
4 Saul and Jonathan his son are *d*
5 Saul and Jonathan his son be *d*?
2. 7 your master Saul is *d*, and also the
4. 1 Abner was *d* in Hebron, his hands
10 Saul is *d*, thinking to have brought
9. 8 such a *d* dog as I am?
11.21 Thy servant Uriah the Hittite is *d*
24 some of the king's servants be *d*,
24 Uriah the Hittite is *d* also,
26 Uriah her husband was *d*, she
12.18 to tell him that the child was *d*:
18 if we tell him that the child is *d*?
19 perceived that the child was *d*:
19 unto his servants, Is the child *d*?
19 And they said, He is *d*.
21 the child was *d*, thou didst rise
23 he is *d*, wherefore should I fast?

13.32 Amnon only is *d*: for by the
33 that all the king's sons are *d*:
33 for Amnon only is *d*.
39 Amnon, seeing he was *d*.
14. 2 a long time mourned for the *d*:
5 woman, and mine husband is *d*.
16. 9 this *d* dog curse my lord the king?
18.20 because the king's son is *d*.
19.10 we anointed over us, is *d* in battle.
28 my father's house were but *d* men
1Ki 3.20 laid her *d* child in my bosom.
21 my child suck, behold, it was *d*:
22 the *d* is thy son. And this said,
22 No, but the *d* is thy son, and
23 and thy son is the *d*: and the other
23 saith, Nay; but thy son is the *d*,
11.21 Joab the captain of the host was *d*,
13.31 When I am *d*, then bury me in the
21.14 saying, Naboth is stoned, and is *d*.
15 that Naboth was stoned, and was *d*,
15 for Naboth is not alive, but *d*.
16 Ahab heard that Naboth was *d*,
2Ki 3. 5 when Ahab was *d*, that the king
4. 1 Thy servant my husband is *d*; and
32 child was *d*, and laid upon his bed.
8. 5 he had restored a *d* body to life,
11. 1 of Ahaziah saw that her son was *d*,
19.35 morning, behold, they were all *d*
23.30 servants carried him in a chariot *d*
1Ch 1.44 when Bela was *d*, Jobab the son
45 And when Jobab was *d*, Husham
46 when Husham was *d*, Hadad
47 And when Hadad was *d*, Samlah
48 And when Samlah was *d*, Shaul
49 when Shaul was *d*, Baal-hanan
50 And when Baal-hanan was *d*,
2.19 And when Azubah was *d*, Caleb
24 after that Hezron was *d* in
10. 5 saw that Saul was *d*, he fell
7 Saul and his sons were *d*, then
2Ch 20.24 they were *d* bodies fallen to the
25 riches with the *d* bodies, and
22.10 Ahaziah saw that her son was *d*,
Est 2. 7 her father and mother were *d*,
Job 1.19 the young men, and they are *d*;
26. 5 *D* things are formed from under
Ps 31.12 I am forgotten as a *d* man
76. 6 and horse are cast into a *d* sleep.
79. 2 The *d* bodies of thy servants
88. 5 Free among the *d*, like the slain
10 Wilt thou shew wonders to the *d*?
10 shall the *d* arise and praise thee?
106.28 and ate the sacrifices of the *d*.
110. 6 fill the places with the *d* bodies;
115.17 The *d* praise not the Lord,
143. 3 as those that have been long *d*.
Pr 2.18 death, and her paths unto the *d*.
9.18 knoweth not that the *d* are there;
21.16 in the congregation of the *d*.
Ec 4. 2 praised the *d* which are already *d*
9. 3 and after that they go to the *d*.
4 a living dog is better than a *d* lion.
5 but the *d* know not any thing,
10. 1 *D* flies cause the ointment of the
Isa 8.19 their God? for the living to the *d*?
14. 9 it stirreth up the *d* for thee,
22. 2 slain with the sword, nor *d* in
26.14 They are *d*, they shall not live;
19 Thy *d* men shall live, together
19 with my *d* body shall they arise.
19 the earth shall cast out the *d*.
37.36 behold, they were all *d* corpses.
59.10 are in desolate places as *d* men
Jer 16. 7 to comfort them for the *d*;
22.10 Weep ye not for the *d*, neither
26.23 cast his *d* body into the graves
31.40 the whole valley of the *d* bodies,
33. 5 fill them with the *d* bodies of men,
34.20 their *d* bodies shall be for meat
36.30 and his *d* body shall be cast out
41. 9 cast all the *d* bodies of the men,
La 3. 6 as they that be *d* of old.
Eze 6. 5 And I will lay the *d* carcasses
24.17 make no mourning for the *d*,
44.25 they shall come at no *d* person
31 any thing that is *d* of itself, or
Am 8. 3 there shall be many *d* bodies
Hag 2.13 unclean by a *d* body touch any of
Mt 2.19 But when Herod was *d*, behold,
20 for they are *d* which sought the
8.22 me; and let the *d* bury their *d*.
9.18 My daughter is even now *d*: but
24 for the maid is not *d*, but sleepeth.
10. 8 lepers, raise the *d*, cast out
11. 5 the *d* are raised up, and the poor
14. 2 Baptist; he is risen from the *d*;
17. 9 of man be risen again from the *d*.
22.31 touching the resurrection of the *d*,
32 God is not the God of the *d*, but
23.27 within full of *d* men's bones, and
27.64 He is risen from the *d*: so the last
28. 4 did shake, and became as *d* men.
7 that he is risen from the *d*;
Mk 5.35 which said, Thy daughter is *d*:
39 the damsel is not *d*, but sleepeth.
6.14 the Baptist was risen from the *d*,
16 beheaded: he is risen from the *d*.
9. 9 Son of man were risen from the *d*.
10 what the rising from the *d* should
26 out of him: and he was as one *d*;
26 insomuch that many said, He is *d*.
12.25 when they shall rise from the *d*,
26 as touching the *d*, that they rise:
27 He is not the God of the *d*,
15.44 marvelled if he were already *d*:
44 whether he had been any while *d*.
Lk 7.12 there was a *d* man carried out,
15 And he that was *d* sat up,
22 the deaf hear, the *d* are raised,
8.49 Thy daughter is *d*; trouble not
52 not; she is not *d*, but sleepeth.
53 to scorn, knowing that she was *d*.
9. 7 that John was risen from the *d*;
60 unto him, Let the *d* bury the *d*:
10.30 and departed, leaving him half *d*.
15.24 For this my son was *d*, and is
32 for this thy brother was *d*, and is
16.30 if one went unto them from the *d*,
31 though one rose from the *d*.
20.35 and the resurrection from the *d*,
37 Now that the *d* are raised, even
38 For he is not a God of the *d*,
24. 5 seek ye the living among the *d*?
46 to rise from the *d* the third day:
Jn 2.22 therefore he was risen from the *d*,
5.21 as the Father raiseth up the *d*,
25 when the *d* shall hear the voice
6.49 in the wilderness, and are *d*.
58 fathers did eat manna, and are *d*:
8.52 Abraham is *d*, and the prophets;
53 Abraham, which is *d*?
53 and the prophets are *d*:
11.14 unto them plainly, Lazarus is *d*.
25 though he were *d*, yet shall he live:
39 the sister of him that was *d*,
39 for he hath been *d* four days.
41 the place where the *d* was laid.
44 And he that was *d* came forth,
12. 1 Lazarus was which had been *d*.
1 *d* whom he raised from the *d*,
9 whom he had raised from the *d*.
17 him from the *d*, bare record.
19.33 that he was *d* already, they brake
20. 9 he must rise again from the *d*.
21.14 after that he was risen from the *d*.
Ac 2.29 that he is both *d* and buried,
3.15 God hath raised from the *d*;
4. 2 Jesus the resurrection from the *d*.
10 whom God raised from the *d*, even
5.10 men came in and found her *d*,
7. 4 thence, when his father was *d*, he
10.41 with him after he rose from the *d*.
42 to be the Judge of quick and *d*.
13.30 But God raised him from the *d*:
34 that he raised him up from the *d*,
14.19 city, supposing he had been *d*.
17. 3 and risen again from the *d*;
31 he hath raised him from the *d*.
32 heard of the resurrection of the *d*,
20. 9 the third loft, and was taken up *d*.
23. 6 the hope and resurrection of the *d*
24.15 shall be a resurrection of the *d*,
21 Touching the resurrection of the *d*
25.19 of one Jesus, which was *d*, whom
26. 8 you, that God should raise the *d*?
23 first that should rise from the *d*,
28. 6 or fallen down *d* suddenly: but
Ro 1. 4 by the resurrection from the *d*:
4.17 God, who quickeneth the *d*,
19 not his own body now *d*,
24 Jesus our Lord from the *d*; Who
5.15 the offense of one many be *d*,
6. 2 How shall we, that are *d* to sin,
4 Christ was raised up from the *d*
7 For he that is *d* is freed from sin.
8 if we be *d* with Christ, we believe
9 raised from the *d* dieth no more:
11 to be *d* indeed unto sin, but alive
13 as those that are alive from the *d*,
7. 2 if the husband be *d*, she is loosed
3 if her husband be *d*, she is free
4 ye also are become *d* to the law
4 to him who is raised from the *d*.
6 being *d* wherein we were held;
8 For without the law sin was *d*.
8.10 the body is *d* because of sin;
11 up Jesus from the *d* dwell in you,
11 that raised up Christ from the *d*
10. 7 bring up Christ again from the *d*.
9 hath raised him from the *d*, thou
11.15 of them be, but life from the *d*?
14. 9 be Lord both of the *d* and living.
1Co 7.39 but if her husband be *d*, she is at
15.12 preached that he rose from the *d*,
12 there is no resurrection of the *d*?
13 if there be no resurrection of the *d*,
15 if so be that the *d* rise not.
16 For if the *d* rise not, then is not
20 now is Christ risen from the *d*,
21 came also the resurrection of the *d*.
29 which are baptized for the *d*,
29 if the *d* rise not at all? why are
29 they then baptized for the *d*?
32 it me, if the *d* rise not?
35 How are the *d* raised up? and with
42 also is the resurrection of the *d*.
52 the *d* shall be raised incorruptible,
2Co 1. 9 but in God which raiseth the *d*:
5.14 one died for all, then were all *d*:
Gal 1. 1 who raised him from the *d*;
2.19 I through the law am *d* to the
21 the law, then Christ is *d* in vain.
Eph 1.20 when he raised him from the *d*,
2. 1 were *d* in trespasses and sins;
5 when we were *d* in sins, hath
5.14 and arise from the *d*, and Christ
Php 3.11 unto the resurrection of the *d*.
Col 1.18 the firstborn from the *d*;
2.12 who hath raised him from the *d*.
13 And you, being *d* in your sins
20 if ye be *d* with Christ from the
3. 3 For ye are *d*, and your life is hid
1Th 1.10 whom he raised from the *d*, even
4.16 the *d* in Christ shall rise first:
1Ti 5. 6 in pleasure is *d* while she liveth.
2Ti 2. 8 of David was raised from the *d*
11 For if we be *d* with him, we shall
4. 1 shall judge the quick and the *d*
Heb 6. 1 repentance from *d* works, and of
2 and of resurrection of the *d*, and
9.14 your conscience from *d* works to
17 of force after men are *d*:
11. 4 by it he being *d* yet speaketh.

Heb 11.12 even of one, and him as good as *d*,
19 to raise him up, even from the *d*;
35 received their *d* raised to life
13.20 brought again from the *d* our Lord
Jas 2.17 hath not works, is *d*, being alone.
20 that faith without works is *d*?
26 the body without the spirit is *d*,
26 so faith without works is *d* also.
1Pe 1. 3 of Jesus Christ from the *d*,
21 that raised him up from the *d*, and
2.24 that we, being *d* to sins, should
4. 5 to judge the quick and the *d*.
6 preached also to them that are *d*,
Jude 12 without fruit, twice *d*, plucked
Rev 1. 5 the first begotten of the *d*, and
17 saw him, I fell at his feet as *d*.
18 I am he that liveth, and was *d*;
2. 8 last, which was *d*, and is alive;
3. 1 a name that thou livest, and art *d*.
11. 8 *d* bodies shall lie in the streets
9 shall see their *d* bodies three days
9 shall not suffer their *d* bodies to
18 time of the *d*, that they should
14.13 Blessed are the *d* which die in the
16. 3 became as the blood of a *d* man:
20. 5 the rest of the *d* lived not again
12 And I saw the *d*, small and great,
12 and the *d* were judged out of
13 gave up the *d* which were in it,
13 death and hell delivered up the *d*

DEADLY

1Sa 5.11 was a *d* destruction throughout
Ps 17. 9 my *d* enemies, who compass me
Eze 30.24 groanings of a *d* wounded man.
Mk 16.18 and if they drink any *d* thing,
Jas 3. 8 an unruly evil, full of *d* poison.
Rev 13. 3 *d* wound was healed: and all
12 whose *d* wound was healed.

DEADNESS

Ro 4.19 yet the *d* of Sarah's womb:

DEAF

Ex 4.11 who maketh the dumb, or *d*, or
Lev 19.14 Thou shalt not curse the *d*, nor
Ps 38.13 But I, as a *d* man, heard not;
58. 4 the *d* adder that stoppeth her ear;
Isa 29.18 in that day shall the *d* hear
35. 5 ears of the *d* shall be unstopped.
42.18 Hear, ye *d*; and look, ye blind,
19 *d*, as my messenger that I sent?
43. 8 eyes, and the *d* that have ears.
Mic 7.16 their mouth, their ears shall be *d*.
Mt 11. 5 and the *d* hear, the dead are
Mk 7.32 was *d*, and had an impediment
37 he maketh both the *d* to hear, and
9.25 Thou dumb and *d* spirit, I charge
Lk 7.22 the *d* hear, the dead are raised,

DEALETH

Jdg 18. 4 *d* Micah with me, and hath
1Sa 23.22 told me that he *d* very subtilly.
Pr 10. 4 He becometh poor that *d* with
13.16 prudent man *d* with knowledge:
14.17 He that is soon angry *d* foolishly:
21.24 his name, who *d* in proud wrath.
Isa 21. 2 treacherous dealer *d* treacherously;
Jer 6.13 the priest every one *d* falsely.
8.10 unto the priest every one *d* falsely.
Heb 12. 7 God *d* with you as with sons;

DEALINGS

1Sa 2.23 of your evil *d* by all this people
Jn 4. 9 had no *d* with the Samaritans.

DEAR

Jer 31.20 Is Ephraim my *d* son? is he a
Lk 7. 2 who was *d* unto him, was sick,
Ac 20.24 count I my life *d* unto myself,
Eph 5. 1 followers of God, as *d* children;
Col 1. 7 our *d* fellowservant, who is
13 into the kingdom of his *d* Son:
1Th 2. 8 souls, because ye were *d* unto us.

DEARLY

Jer 12. 7 the *d* beloved of my soul
Ro 12.19 *D* beloved, avenge not
1Co 10.14 Wherefore, my *d* beloved, flee
2Co 7. 1 these promises *d* beloved, let us
12.19 do all things *d* beloved for
Php 4. 1 my brethren *d* beloved and longed
1 fast in the Lord, my *d* beloved
2Ti 1. 2 To Timothy my *d* beloved son:
Phm 1. 1 unto Philemon our *d* beloved
1Pe 2.11 *D* beloved, I beseech you as

DEARTH

Gen 41.54 seven years of *d* began to come,
54 said, and the *d* was in all lands;
2Ki 4.38 and there was a *d* in the land;
2Ch 6.28 If there be *d* in the land,
Neh 5. 3 might buy corn, because of the *d*.
Jer 14. 1 to Jeremiah concerning the *d*.
Ac 7.11 there came a *d* over all the land
11.28 be great *d* throughout all the

DEATH

Gen 21.16 Let me not see the *d* of the child.
24.67 was comforted after his mother's *d*
25.11 after the *d* of Abraham, that God
26.11 his wife shall surely be put to *d*.
18 after the *d* of Abraham: and he
27. 2 I know not the day of my *d*:
7 before the Lord before my *d*.
10 he may bless thee before his *d*.
Ex 10.17 take away from me this *d* only.
19.12 mount shall be surely put to *d*:
21.12 he die shall be surely put to *d*.
15 his mother, shall be surely put to *d*.
16 hand, he shall surely be put to *d*.
17 his mother shall surely be put to *d*.
29 his owner also shall be put to *d*.
22.19 a beast shall surely be put to *d*.
31.14 defileth it shall surely be put to *d*:
15 day, he shall surely be put to *d*.
35. 2 work therein shall be put to *d*.
Lev 16. 1 after the *d* of the two sons of
19.20 they shall not be put to *d*, because
20. 2 he shall surely be put to *d*: the
9 shall be surely put to *d*: he hath
10 adulteress shall surely be put to *d*.
11, 12 them shall surely be put to *d*:
13 they shall surely be put to *d*; their
15 he shall surely be put to *d*: and ye
16 they shall surely be put to *d*; their
27 a wizard, shall surely be put to *d*:
24.16 he shall surely be put to *d*, and all
16 of the Lord, shall be put to *d*.
17 any man shall surely be put to *d*.
21 a man, he shall be put to *d*.
27.29 but shall surely be put to *d*.
Nu 1.51 that cometh nigh shall be put to *d*.
3.10, 38 cometh nigh shall be put to *d*.
15.35 The man shall be surely put to *d*:
16.29 these men die the common *d* of all
18. 7 that cometh nigh shall be put to *d*.
23.10 Let me die the *d* of the righteous,
35.16, 17, 18 murderer...be put to *d*.
21 smote him shall surely be put to *d*:
25 unto the *d* of the high priest,
28 until the *d* of the high priest:
28 but after the *d* of the high priest
35.30 the murderer shall be put to *d* by
31 a murderer, which is guilty of *d*
31 but he shall surely be put to *d*.
32 land, until the *d* of the priest.
Dt 13. 5 of dreams, shall be put to *d*;
9 be first upon him to put him to *d*,
17. 6 shall he that is worthy of *d* be
6 be put to *d*; but at the mouth of
6 witness he shall not be put to *d*.
7 upon him to put him to *d*, and
19. 6 whereas he was not worthy of *d*,
21.22 committed a sin worthy of *d*,
22 and he be to be put to *d*,
22.26 in the damsel no sin worthy of *d*:
24.16 The fathers shall not be put to *d*
16 the children be put to *d* for the
16 shall be put to *d* for his own sin.
30.15 life and good, and *d* and evil;
19 I have set before you life and *d*,
31.27 how much more after my *d*?
29 I know that after my *d* ye will
33. 1 the children of Israel before his *d*.
Jos 1. 1 after the *d* of Moses the servant of
18 he shall be put to *d*; only be
2.13 have, and deliver our lives from *d*.
20. 6 until the *d* of the high priest
Jdg 1. 1 after the *d* of Joshua it came to
5.18 jeoparded their lives unto the *d*
6.31 let him be put to *d* whilst it is yet
13. 7 the womb to the day of his *d*.
16.16 his soul was vexed unto *d*;
30 the dead which he slew at his *d*
20.13 that we may put them to *d*, and
21. 5 saying, He shall surely be put to *d*.
Ru 1.17 if ought but *d* part thee and me.
2.11 since the *d* of thine husband:
1Sa 4.20 about the time of her *d* the women
11.12 men, that we may put them to *d*.
13 There shall not a man be put to *d*
15.32 Surely the bitterness of *d* is past.
35 to see Saul until the day of his *d*:
20. 3 but a step between me and *d*.
22.22 I have occasioned the *d* of all the
2Sa 1. 1 came to pass after the *d* of Saul,
23 in their *d* they were not divided:
6.23 had no child unto the day of her *d*.
8. 2 two lines measured he to put to *d*,
15.21 whether in *d* or life, even there
19.21 shall not Shimei be put to *d* for
22 shall there any man be put to *d*
20. 3 shut up unto the day of their *d*,
21. 9 and were put to *d* in the days of
22. 5 When the waves of *d* compassed
6 the snares of *d* prevented me;
1Ki 2. 8 I will not put thee to *d* with the
24 Adonijah shall be put to *d* this day.
26 thou art worthy of *d*: but
26 not at this time put thee to *d*,
11.40 in Egypt until the *d* of Solomon.
2Ki 1. 1 against Israel after the *d* of Ahab.
2.21 thence any more *d* or barren land.
4.40 man of God, there is *d* in the pot.
14. 6 fathers shall not be put to *d* for
6 nor the children be put to *d*
6 but every man shall be put to *d*
17 after the *d* of Jehoash son of
15. 5 a leper unto the day of his *d*,
20. 1 days was Hezekiah sick unto *d*.
1Ch 22. 5 prepared abundantly before his *d*.
2Ch 15.13 God of Israel should be put to *d*,
22. 4 after the *d* of his father to his
23. 7 the house, he shall be put to *d*:
24.17 after the *d* of Jehoiada came the
25.25 after the *d* of Joash son of
26.21 a leper unto the day of his *d*,
32.24 Hezekiah was sick to the *d*, and
33 did him honor at his *d*.
Ezr 7.26 whether it be unto *d*, or to
Est 4.11 one law of his to put him to *d*,
Job 3. 5 Let darkness and the shadow of *d*
21 long for *d*, but it cometh not;
5.20 he shall redeem thee from *d*:
7.15 and *d* rather than my life.
10.21 of darkness and the shadow of *d*;
22 itself; and of the shadow of *d*,
12.22 out to light the shadow of *d*.
16.16 on my eyelids is the shadow of *d*;
18.13 firstborn of *d* shall devour his
24.17 to them even as the shadow of *d*:
17 the terrors of the shadow of *d*.

Biblical Themes

DEATH

Dust thou art, and unto dust shalt thou return. Gen 3.19

I have set before thee this day life and good, and death and evil. . . . if thine heart turn away, so that thou wilt not hear, but shall be drawn away . . . ye shall surely perish. Dt 30.15, 17-18

We must needs die, and are as water spilt on the ground, which cannot be gathered up again. 2Sa 14.14

And [David] charged Solomon his son, saying, I go the way of all the earth: be thou strong therefore, and shew thyself a man; and keep the charge of the Lord thy God, to walk in his ways . . . that thou mayest prosper in all that thou doest. 1Ki 2.1-3

There the wicked cease from troubling; and there the weary be at rest. There the prisoners rest together; they hear not the voice of the oppressor. The small and great are there; and the servant is free from his master. Job 3.17-19

Yea, though I walk through the valley of the shadow of death, I will fear no evil: for thou art with me. Ps 23.4

As for man, his days are as grass: as a flower of the field, so he flourisheth. For the wind passeth over it, and it is gone; and the place thereof shall know it no more. Ps 103.15-16

The righteous hath hope in his death. Pr 14.32

That which befalleth the sons of men befalleth beasts. . . . All go unto one place; all are of the dust, and all turn to dust again. Ec 3.19-20

He will swallow up death in victory; and the Lord God will wipe away tears from off all faces. Isa 25.8

And many of them that sleep in the dust of the earth shall awake, some to everlasting life, and some to shame and everlasting contempt. Dan 12.2

I will ransom them from the power of the grave; I will redeem them from death: O death, I will be thy plagues; O grave, I will be thy destruction. Hos 13.14

Verily I say unto you, There be some standing here, which shall not taste of death, till they see the Son of man coming in his kingdom. Mt 16.28

Lord, now lettest thou thy servant depart in peace, according to thy word: for mine eyes have seen thy salvation. Lk 2.29-30

Thou fool, this night thy soul shall be required of thee. Lk 12.20

Jesus said . . . To day shalt thou be with me in paradise. Lk 23.43

And when Jesus had cried with a loud voice, he said, Father, into thy hands I commend my spirit: and having said thus, he gave up the ghost. Lk 23.46

And as they were afraid, and bowed down their faces to the earth, they said unto them, Why seek ye the living among the dead? He is not here, but is risen. Lk 24.5-6

I am the resurrection, and the life . . . whosoever liveth and believeth in me shall never die. Jn 11.25-26

The wages of sin is death; but the gift of God is eternal life through Jesus Christ our Lord. Ro 6.23

As in Adam all die, even so in Christ shall all be made alive. 1Co 15.22

Christ . . . hath abolished death, and hath brought life and immortality to light through the gospel. 2Ti 1.10

I looked, and behold a pale horse: and his name that sat on him was Death, and Hell followed with him. Rev 6.8

There shall be no more death, neither sorrow, nor crying, neither shall there be any more pain. Rev 21.4

27.15 of him shall be buried in *d*:
28. 3 of darkness, and the shadow of *d*.
22 Destruction and *d* say, We have
30.23 thou wilt bring me to *d*, and to the
34.22 is no darkness, nor shadow of *d*,
38.17 Have the gates of *d* been opened
17 the doors of the shadow of *d*?
Ps 6. 5 in *d* there is no remembrance of
7.13 for him the instruments of *d*; he
9.13 liftest me up from the gates of *d*:
13. 3 lest I sleep the sleep of *d*;
18. 4 The sorrows of *d* compassed me,
5 the snares of *d* prevented me.
22.15 brought me into the dust of *d*.
23. 4 the valley of the shadow of *d*,
33.19 To deliver their soul from *d*, and
44.19 covered us with the shadow of *d*.
48.14 he will be our guide even unto *d*.
49.14 *d* shall feed on them; and the
55. 4 the terrors of *d* are fallen upon me.
15 Let *d* seize upon them, and
56.13 hast delivered my soul from *d*:
68.20 the Lord belong the issues from *d*.
73. 4 there are no bands in their *d*:
78.50 spared not their soul from *d*,
89.48 he that liveth, and shall not see *d*?
102.20 those that are appointed to *d*;
107.10 darkness and in the shadow of *d*,
14 of darkness and the shadow of *d*,
18 they draw near unto the gates of *d*.
116. 3 The sorrows of *d* compassed me,
8 delivered my soul from *d*, mine
15 of the Lord is the *d* of his saints.
118.18 he hath not given me over unto *d*.
Pr 2.18 her house inclineth unto *d*, and
5. 5 Her feet go down to *d*; her steps
7.27 going down to the chambers of *d*.
8.36 all they that hate me love *d*.
10. 2 righteousness delivereth from *d*.
11. 4 righteousness delivereth from *d*.
19 evil pursueth it to his own *d*.
12.28 the pathway thereof there is no *d*.
13.14 to depart from the snares of *d*.
14.12 the end thereof are the ways of *d*.
27 to depart from the snares of *d*.
32 the righteous hath hope in his *d*.
16.14 of a king is as messengers of *d*:
25 the end thereof are the ways of *d*.
18.21 *D* and life are in the power of the
21. 6 to and fro of them that seek *d*.
24.11 them that are drawn unto *d*, and
26.18 casteth firebrands, arrows, and *d*,
Ec 7. 1 day of *d* than the day of one's birth.
26 more bitter than *d* the woman,
8. 8 power in the day of *d*: and there is
SS 8. 6 love is strong as *d*; jealousy is
Isa 9. 2 the land of the shadow of *d*, upon
25. 8 He will swallow up *d* in victory;
28.15 We have made a covenant with *d*,
18 your covenant with *d* shall be
38. 1 days was Hezekiah sick unto *d*.
18 *d* can not celebrate thee: they
53. 9 wicked, and with the rich in his *d*;
12 hath poured out his soul unto *d*:
Jer 2. 6 drought, and of the shadow of *d*,
8. 3 *d* shall be chosen rather than
9.21 *d* is come up into our windows,
13.16 he turn it into the shadow of *d*,
15. 2 Such as are for *d*, to *d*; and such
18.21 let their men be put to *d*; let
21. 8 the way of life, and the way of *d*.
26.15 if ye put me to *d*, ye shall surely
19 and all Judah put him at all to *d*?
21 the king sought to put him to *d*:
24 hand of the people to put him to *d*.
38. 4 let this man be put to *d*: for thus
15 wilt thou not surely put me to *d*?
16 I will not put thee to *d*, neither
25 we will not put thee to *d*; also
43. 3 that they might put us to *d*, and
11 such as are for *d* to *d*; and such
52.11 in prison till the day of his *d*.
27 smote them, and put them to *d*
34 a portion until the day of his *d*,
La 1.20 bereaveth, at home there is as *d*.
Eze 18.32 pleasure in the *d* of him that dieth,
31.14 they are all delivered unto *d*, to the
33.11 no pleasure in the *d* of the wicked;
Hos 13.14 I will redeem them from *d*: O *d*,
Am 5. 8 turneth the shadow of *d* into the
Jon 4. 9 well to be angry, even unto *d*.
Hab 2. 5 his desire as hell, and is as *d*,
Mt 2.15 was there until the *d* of Herod:
4.16 in the region and shadow of *d*
10.21 deliver up the brother to *d*,
21 and cause them to be put to *d*.
14. 5 he would have put him to *d*,
15. 4 or mother, let him die the *d*.
16.28 shall not taste of *d*, till they see
20.18 and they shall condemn him to *d*,
26.38 exceeding sorrowful, even unto *d*:
59 against Jesus, to put him to *d*;
66 and said, He is guilty of *d*.

Mt 27. 1 against Jesus, to put him to *d*:
Mk 5.23 daughter lieth at the point of *d*:
7.10 let him die the *d*: But ye say,
9. 1 shall not taste of *d*, till they have
10.33 shall condemn him to *d*, and shall
13.12 shall betray the brother to *d*,
12 shall cause them to be put to *d*.
14. 1 him by craft, and put him to *d*.
34 is exceeding sorrowful unto *d*:
55 against Jesus to put him to *d*; and
64 condemned him to be guilty of *d*.
Lk 1.79 and in the shadow of *d*, to guide
2.26 that he should not see *d*, before
9.27 which shall not taste of *d*, till they
18.33 scourge him, and put him to *d*:
21.16 shall they cause to be put to *d*.
22.33 thee; both into prison, and to *d*.
23.15 nothing worthy of *d* is done unto
22 found no cause of *d* in him: I will
32 led with him to be put to *d*.
24.20 to be condemned to *d*, and have
Jn 4.47 for he was at the point of *d*.
5.24 but is passed from *d* unto life.
8.51 my saying, he shall never see *d*.
52 saying, he shall never taste of *d*.
11. 4 This sickness is not unto *d*, but
13 Jesus spake of his *d*: but they
53 together for to put him to *d*.
12.10 they might put Lazarus also to *d*;
33 signifying what *d* he should die.
18.31 lawful for us to put any man to *d*;
32 signifying what *d* he should die.
21.19 by what *d* he should glorify God.
Ac 2.24 up, having loosed the pains of *d*:
8. 1 Saul was consenting unto his *d*.
12.19 that they should be put to *d*.
13.28 they found no cause of *d* in him,
22. 4 I persecuted this way unto the *d*,
20 by, and consenting unto his *d*,
23.29 charge worthy of *d* or of bonds.
25.11 committed any thing worthy of *d*,
25 committed nothing worthy of *d*,
26.10 when they were put to *d*, I gave
31 nothing worthy of *d* or of bonds.
28.18 there was no cause of *d* in me.
Ro 1.32 such things are worthy of *d*,
5.10 by the *d* of his Son, much more,
12 and *d* by sin; and so *d* passed
14 *d* reigned from Adam to Moses,
17 man's offense *d* reigned by one;
21 That as sin hath reigned unto *d*,
6. 3 Christ were baptized into his *d*?
4 with him by baptism into *d*:
5 in the likeness of his *d*, we shall be
9 *d* hath no more dominion over him.
16 of sin unto *d*, or of obedience
21 the end of those things is *d*.
23 For the wages of sin is *d*; but the
7. 5 to bring forth fruit unto *d*.
10 life, I found to be unto *d*.
13 which is good made *d* unto me?
13 might appear sin, working *d* in me
24 me from the body of this *d*?
8. 2 free from the law of sin and *d*.
6 to be carnally minded is *d*;
38 neither *d*, nor life, nor angels, nor
1Co 3.22 or life, or *d*, or things present,
4. 9 last, as it were appointed to *d*:
11.26 ye do shew the Lord's *d* till he
15.21 by man came *d*, by man came
26 that shall be destroyed is *d*.
54 *D* is swallowed up in victory.
55 O *d*, where is thy sting? O grave
56 sting of *d* is sin; and the strength
2Co 1. 9 had the sentence of *d* in ourselves,
10 delivered us from so great a *d*,
2.16 one we are the savor of *d* unto *d*;
3. 7 the ministration of *d*, written and
4.11 delivered unto *d* for Jesus' sake,
12 then *d* worketh in us, but life in
7.10 the sorrow of the world worketh *d*.
Php 1.20 whether it be by life, or by *d*.
2. 8 and became obedient unto *d*,
8 even the *d* of the cross.
27 he was sick nigh unto *d*: but God
30 he was nigh unto *d*, not regarding
3.10 made comformable unto his *d*;
Col 1.22 In the body of his flesh through *d*,
2Ti 1.10 who hath abolished *d*, and
Heb 2. 9 for the suffering of *d*, crowned
9 God should taste *d* for every man.
14 through *d* he might destroy him
14 that had the power of *d*,
15 fear of *d* were all their lifetime
5. 7 to save him from *d*, and was heard
7.23 to continue by reason of *d*:
9.15 by means of *d*, for the redemption
16 must also of necessity be the *d*
11. 5 that he should not see *d*;
Jas 1.15 it is finished, bringeth forth *d*.
5.20 save a soul from *d*, and shall hide
1Pe 3.18 being put to *d* in the flesh,
1Jn 3.14 we have passed from *d* unto life,
14 not his brother abideth in *d*.
5.16 a sin which is not unto *d*, he shall
16 life for them that sin not unto *d*.
16 There is a sin unto *d*: I do not
17 and there is a sin not unto *d*.
Rev 1.18 the keys of hell and of *d*.
2.10 be thou faithful unto *d*, and I will
11 shall not be hurt of the second *d*.
23 I will kill her children with *d*;
6. 8 his name that sat on him was *D*,
8 and with hunger, and with *d*,
9. 6 men seek *d*, and shall not find it;
6 and *d* shall flee from them.
12.11 loved not their lives unto the *d*.
13. 3 as it were wounded to *d*; and his
18. 8 day, *d*, and mourning, and famine;
20. 6 the second *d* hath no power, but
13 *d* and hell delivered up the dead
14 *d* and hell were cast into the
14 lake of fire. This is the second *d*.
21. 4 be no more *d*, neither sorrow,
8 brimstone: which is the second *d*.

DEATHS

Jer 16. 4 They shall die of grievous *d*;
Eze 28. 8 the *d* of them that are slain
10 die the *d* of the uncircumcised
2Co 11.23 prisons more frequent in *d* oft.

DEBATE

Pr 25. 9 *D* thy cause with thy neighbor
Isa 27. 8 forth, thou wilt *d* with it:
58. 4 fast for strife and *d*, and to smite
Ro 1.29 murder, *d*, deceit, malignity;

DEBATES

2Co 12.20 there be *d*, envyings, wraths,

DEBORAH

Jdg 4. 4 *D*, a prophetess, the wife of
5 dwelt under the palm tree of *D*.
9 *D* arose, and went with Barak
10 and *D* went up with him.
14 *D* said unto Barak, Up; for this
5. 1 Then sang *D* and Barak the son of
7 until that I *D* arose, that I arose
12 Awake, awake, *D*: awake, awake,
15 princes of Issachar were with *D*;

DEBT

1Sa 22. 2 every one that was in *d*, and
2Ki 4. 7 sell the oil, and pay thy *d*,
Neh 10.31 and the exaction of every *d*.
Mt 18.27 him, and forgave him the *d*.
30 prison, till he should pay the *d*.
32 I forgave thee all that *d*, because
Ro 4. 4 not reckoned of grace, but of *d*.

DEBORAH

Prophet and Judge of Israel after Ehud and Shamgar, 12th century B.C. (Jdg 4.4); **her charismatic leadership inspires unity among the still-disorganized tribes of Israel; encourages Israelite commander Barak** (Jdg 4.6-9, 14; 5.12) **to victory over Sisera, commander of Canaanite forces serving Jabin, king of Hazor; foretells that Sisera himself will be killed by a woman** (Jdg 4.9, 17-22; 5.24-27); **her role in this crucial early victory celebrated in the Song of Deborah** (Jdg 5.2-31).

DEBTOR

Eze 18. 7 hath restored to the *d* his pledge,
Mt 23.16 the gold of the temple, he is a *d*!
Ro 1.14 I am *d* both to the Greeks, and
Gal 5. 3 he is a *d* to do the whole law.

DEBTORS

Mt 6.12 our debts, as we forgive our *d*.
Lk 7.41 certain creditor which had two *d*:
16. 5 called every one of his lord's *d*
Ro 8.12 we are *d*, not to the flesh,
15.27 them verily; and their *d* they are.

DEBTS

Pr 22.26 of them that are sureties for *d*.
Mt 6.12 forgive us our *d*, as we forgive

DECAPOLIS

Mt 4.25 and from *D*, and from Jerusalem,
Mk 5.20 and began to publish in *D* how
7.31 the midst of the coasts of *D*.

DECEASE

Lk 9.31 spake of his *d* which he should
2Pe 1.15 may be able after my *d* to have

DECEASED

Isa 26.14 they are *d*, they shall not rise:
Mt 22.25 when he had married a wife, *d*,

DECEIT

Job 15.35 and their belly prepareth *d*.
27. 4 nor my tongue utter *d*.
31. 5 if my foot hath hasted to *d*;
Ps 10. 7 His mouth is full of cursing and *d*
36. 3 of his mouth are iniquity and *d*:
50.19 to evil, and thy tongue frameth *d*.
55.11 *d* and guile depart not from her
72.14 shall redeem their soul from *d*
101. 7 *d* shall not dwell within my
119.118 statutes: for their *d* is falsehood.
Pr 12. 5 the counsels of the wicked are *d*.
17 but a false witness *d*.
20 *D* is in the heart of them that
14. 8 but the folly of fools is *d*.
20.17 Bread of *d* is sweet to a man;
26.24 and layeth up *d* within him;
26 Whose hatred is covered by *d*,
Isa 53. 9 neither was any *d* in his mouth.
Jer 5.27 their houses full of *d*: therefore
8. 5 hold fast *d*, they refuse to return.
9. 6 habitation is in the midst of *d*;
6 through *d* they refuse to know me,
8 it speaketh *d*: one speaketh
14.14 nought, and the *d* of their heart.
23.26 of the *d* of their own heart;
Hos 11.12 and the house of Israel with *d*:
12. 7 the balances of *d* are in his hand:
Am 8. 5 and falsifying the balances by *d*?
Zep 1. 9 houses with violence and *d*.

Mk 7.22 wickedness, *d*, lasciviousness, an
Ro 1.29 full of envy, murder, debate, *d*,
3.13 their tongues they have used *d*;
Col 2. 8 through philosophy and vain *d*,
1Th 2. 3 our exhortation was not of *d*,

DECEITFUL

Ps 5. 6 will abhor the bloody and *d* man.
35.20 devise *d* matters against them
43. 1 me from the *d* and unjust man.
52. 4 words, O thou *d* tongue.
55.23 bloody and *d* men shall not live
78.57 were turned aside like a *d* bow.
109. 2 of the *d* are opened against me:
120. 2 from lying lips, and from a *d*
Pr 11.18 The wicked worketh a *d* work:
14.25 but a *d* witness speaketh lies.
23. 3 his dainties: for they are *d* meat.
27. 6 but the kisses of an enemy are *d*.
29.13 and the *d* man meet together:
31.30 Favor is *d*, and beauty is vain:
Jer 17. 9 The heart is *d* above all things,
Hos 7.16 High: they are like a *d* bow:
Mic 6.11 and with the bag of *d* weights?
12 their tongue is *d* in their mouth.
Zep 3.13 *d* tongue be found in their mouth:
2Co 11.13 false apostles, *d* workers,
Eph 4.22 corrupt according to the *d* lusts;

DECEITFULLY

Gen 34.13 Shechem and Hamor his father *d*,
Ex 8.29 let not Pharaoh deal *d* any more
21. 8 seeing he hath dealt *d* with her.
Lev 6. 4 thing which he hath *d* gotten.
Job 6.15 brethren have dealt *d* as a brook,
13. 7 for God? and talk *d* for him?
Ps 24. 4 his soul unto vanity, nor sworn *d*.
52. 2 like a sharp razor, working *d*.
Jer 48.10 doeth the work of the Lord *d*,
Dan 11.23 he shall work *d*: for he shall
2Co 4. 2 nor handling the word of God *d*,

DECEITFULNESS

Mt 13.22 the *d* of riches, choke the word,
Mk 4.19 the *d* of riches, and the lusts of
Heb 3.13 be hardened through the *d* of sin.

DECEIVABLENESS

2Th 2.10 with all *d* of unrighteousness in

DECEIVE

2Sa 3.25 that he came to *d* thee, and to
2Ki 4.28 did I not say, Do not *d* me?
18.29 Let not Hezekiah *d* you: for he
19.10 God in whom thou trusted *d* thee,
2Ch 32.15 let not Hezekiah *d* you, nor
Pr 24.28 cause; and *d* not with thy lips.
Isa 36.14 Let not Hezekiah *d* you: for he
37.10 God, in whom thou trusted, *d* thee,
Jer 9. 5 will *d* every one his neighbor,
29. 8 that be in the midst of you *d* you,
37. 9 *D* not yourselves, saying, The
Zec 13. 4 they wear a rough garment to *d*:
Mt 24. 4 Take heed that no man *d* you.
5 I am Christ; and shall *d* many.
11 shall rise and shall *d* many.
24 they shall *d* the very elect.
Mk 13. 5 Take heed lest any man *d* you:
6 I am Christ; and shall *d* many.
Ro 16.18 speeches *d* the hearts of the
1Co 3.18 Let no man *d* himself. If any
Eph 4.14 whereby they lie in wait to *d*;
5. 6 Let no man *d* you with vain words:
2Th 2. 3 Let no man *d* you by any means:
1Jn 1. 8 we *d* ourselves, and the truth
3. 7 let no man *d* you: he that doeth
Rev 20. 3 that he should *d* the nations no
8 go out to *d* the nations which are

DECEIVED

Gen 31. 7 your father hath *d* me, and
Lev 6. 2 violence, or hath *d* his neighbor;
Dt 11.16 that your heart be not *d*,
1Sa 19.17 Why hast thou *d* me so, and sent
28.12 Why hast thou *d* me? for thou art
2Sa 19.26 my servant *d* me: for thy servant
Job 12.16 the *d* and the deceiver are his.
15.31 not him that is *d* trust in vanity:
31. 9 If mine heart have been *d* by a
Pr 20. 1 whosoever is *d* thereby is not
Isa 19.13 the princes of Noph are *d*:
44.20 a *d* heart had turned him aside,
Jer 4.10 thou hast greatly *d* this people
20. 7 thou hast *d* me, and I was *d*:
49.16 Thy terribleness hath *d* thee,
La 1.19 I called for my lovers, but they *d*
Eze 14. 9 if the prophet be *d* when he hath
9 I the Lord have *d* that prophet,
Ob 3 pride of thine heart hath *d* thee,
7 at peace with thee hath *d* thee,
Lk 21. 8 Take heed that ye be not *d*:
Jn 7.47 the Pharisees, Are ye also *d*?
Ro 7.11 *d* me, and by it slew me.
1Co 6. 9 Be not *d*: neither fornicators, nor
15.33 Be not *d*; evil communications
Gal 6. 7 Be not *d*; God is not mocked:
1Ti 2.14 Adam was not *d*, but the woman
14 being *d* was in the transgression.
2Ti 3.13 worse, deceiving, and being *d*.
Tit 3. 3 *d*, serving divers lusts and
Rev 18.23 thy sorceries were all nations *d*.
19.20 with which he *d* them that had
20.10 the devil that *d* them was cast

DECEIVER

Gen 27.12 I shall seem to him as a *d*;
Job 12.16 the deceived and the *d* are his.
Mal 1.14 cursed be the *d*, which hath in
Mt 27.63 we remember that that *d* said,
2Jn 7 This is a *d* and an antichrist.

DECEIVERS

2Co 6. 8 good report: as *d*, and yet true;
Tit 1.10 unruly and vain talkers and *d*,
2Jn 7 For many *d* are entered into the

DECEIVETH

Pr 26.19 the man that *d* his neighbor,
Jn 7.12 said, Nay; but he *d* the people.
Gal 6. 3 when he is nothing, he *d* himself.
Jas 1.26 his tongue, but *d* his own heart,
Rev 12. 9 Satan, which *d* the whole world:
13.14 *d* them that dwell on the earth

DECEIVING

2Ti 3.13 worse and worse, *d*, and being
Jas 1.22 hearers only, *d* your own selves.

DECEIVINGS

2Pe 2.13 their own *d* while they feast,

DECENTLY

1Co 14.40 all things be done *d* and in order.

DECISION

Joel 3.14 multitudes in the valley of *d*: for
14 the Lord is near in the valley of *d*

DECKED

Pr 7.16 I have *d* my bed, with coverings
Eze 16.11 I *d* thee also with ornaments,
13 wast thou *d* with gold and silver;
Hos 2.13 she *d* herself with her earrings
Rev 17. 4 *d* with gold and precious stones
18.16 *d* with gold, and precious stones,

DECKETH

Isa 61.10 as a bridegroom *d* himself with

DECLARATION

Est 10. 2 *d* of the greatness of Mordecai
Job 13.17 and my *d* with your ears.
Lk 1. 1 to set forth in order a *d* of those
2Co 8.19 and *d* of your ready mind:

DECLARE

Gen 41.24 was none that could *d* it to me.
Dt 1. 5 began Moses to *d* this law, saying,
Jos 20. 4 and shall *d* his cause in the ears
Jdg 14.12 *d* it me within the seven days of
13 if ye cannot *d* it me, then shall ye
15 that he may *d* unto us the riddle,
1Ki 22.13 prophets *d* good unto the king
1Ch 16.24 *D* his glory among the heathen;
2Ch 18.12 the words of the prophets *d* good
Est 4. 8 and to *d* unto her, and to charge
Job 12. 8 the fishes of the sea shall *d* unto
15.17 that which I have seen I will *d*;
21.31 Who shall *d* his way to his face?
28.27 Then did he see it, and *d* it;
31.37 I would *d* unto him the number
38. 4 *d*, if thou hast understanding.
18 earth? *d* if thou knowest it all.
40. 7 of thee, and *d* thou unto me.
42. 4 of thee, and *d* thou unto me.
Ps 2. 7 I will *d* the decree: the Lord
9.11 *d* among the people his doings.
19. 1 The heavens *d* the glory of God;
22.22 *d* thy name unto my brethren:
31 *d* his righteousness unto a people
30. 9 praise thee? shall it *d* thy truth?
38.18 For I will *d* mine iniquity;
40. 5 if I would *d* and speak of them,
50. 6 heavens shall *d* his righteousness:
16 hast thou to do to *d* my statutes,
64. 9 and shall *d* the work of God;
66.16 and I will *d* what he hath done
73.28 that I may *d* all thy works.
75. 1 is near thy wondrous works *d*.
9 But I will *d* for ever; I will
78. 6 and *d* them to their children:
96. 3 *D* his glory among the heathen,
97. 6 The heavens *d* his righteousness,
102.21 To *d* the name of the Lord in
107.22 and *d* his works with rejoicing.
118.17 but live, and *d* the works of the
145. 4 and shall *d* thy mighty acts.
6 acts: and I will *d* thy greatness.
Ec 9. 1 to *d* all this, that the righteous,
Isa 3. 9 they *d* their sin as Sodom, they
12. 4 *d* his doings among the people,
21. 6 let him *d* what he seeth.
41.22 or *d* us things for to come.
42. 9 new things do I *d*: before they
12 unto the Lord, and *d* his praise
43. 9 who among them can *d* this,
26 *d* thou, that thou mayest be
44. 7 as I, shall call, and shall *d* it,
45.19 I *d* things that are right.
48. 6 all this; and will not ye *d* it?
20 with a voice of singing *d* ye,
53. 8 and who shall *d* his generation?
57.12 I will *d* thy righteousness, and
66.19 and they shall *d* my glory among
Jer 4. 5 *D* ye in Judah, and publish in
5.20 *D* this in the house of Jacob,
9.12 *d* it, for what the land perisheth
31.10 and *d* it in the isles afar off,
38.15 If I *d* it unto thee, wilt thou not
25 *D* unto us now what thou hast
42. 4 I will *d* it unto you; I will keep
20 *d* unto us, and we will do it.
46.14 *D* ye in Egypt, and publish in
50. 2 *D* ye among the nations, and
28 to *d* in Zion the vengeance of the
51.10 and let us *d* in Zion the work of
Eze 12.16 they may *d* all their abominations
23.36 *d* unto them their abominations;
40. 4 *d* all that thou seest to the house
Dan 4.18 *d* the interpretation thereof,
Mic 1.10 *D* ye it not at Gath, weep ye not
3. 8 to *d* unto Jacob his transgression,
Zec 9.12 even to day do I *d* that I will
Mt 13.36 *D* unto us the parable of the
15.15 unto him, *D* unto us this parable.
Jn 17.29 them thy name, and will *d* it:

Ac 8.33 and who shall *d* his generation?
13.32 we *d* unto you glad tidings, how
41 though a man *d* it unto you.
17.23 worship, him *d* I unto you.
20.27 to *d* unto you the counsel of God.
Ro 3.25 to *d* his righteousness for the
26 To *d*, I say, at this time his
1Co 3.13 for the day shall *d* it, because
11.17 Now in this that I *d* unto you
15. 1 brethren I *d* unto you the gospel
Col 4. 7 state shall Tychicus *d* unto you,
Heb 2.12 will *d* thy name unto my brethren,
11.14 *d* plainly that they seek a
1Jn 1. 3 seen and heard *d* we unto you,
5 *d* unto you, that God is light,

DECLARED

Ex 9.16 my name may be *d* throughout
Lev 23.44 And Moses *d* unto the children
Nu 1.18 and they *d* their pedigrees after
15.34 was not *d* what should be done
Dt 4.13 And he *d* unto you his covenant
2Sa 19. 6 thou hast *d* this day, that thou
Neh 8.12 the words that were *d* unto them.
Job 26. 3 hast thou plentifully *d* the thing
Ps 40.10 I have *d* thy faithfulness and thy
71.17 have I *d* thy wondrous works.
77.14 *d* thy strength among the people.
88.11 Shall thy lovingkindness be *d*
119.13 With my lips have I *d* all the
26 I have *d* my ways, and thou
Isa 21. 2 A grievous vision is *d* unto me;
10 of Israel, have I *d* unto you.
41.26 Who hath *d* from the beginning,
43.12 I have *d*, and have saved, and I
44. 8 from that time, and have *d* it?
45.21 who hath *d* this from ancient
48. 3 I have *d* the former things from
5 from the beginning *d* it to thee;
14 among them hath *d* these things?
Jer 36.13 Then Michaiah *d* unto them all
42.21 And now I have this day *d* it
Lk 8.47 *d* unto him before all the people
Jn 1.18 the Father, he hath *d* him:
17.26 I have *d* unto them thy name,
Ac 9.27 *d* unto them how he had seen the
10. 8 when he had *d* all these things
12.17 *d* unto them how the Lord had
15. 4 *d* all things that God had done
14 Simeon hath *d* how God at the
21.19 *d* particularly what things God
25.14 *d* Paul's cause unto the king,
Ro 1. 4 *d* to be the Son of God with power,
9.17 my name might be *d* throughout
1Co 1.11 it hath been *d* unto me of you,
2Co 3. 3 manifestly *d* to be the epistle of
Col 1. 8 Who also *d* unto us your love
Rev 10. 7 *d* to his servants the prophets.

DECLARING

Isa 46.10 *D* the end from the beginning,
Ac 15. 3 *d* the conversion of the Gentiles:
12 *d* what miracles and wonders
1Co 2. 1 *d* unto you the testimony of God.

DECREASE

Ps 107.38 and suffereth not their cattle to *d*.
Jn 3.30 He must increase, but I must *d*.

DECREED

Est 2. 1 and what was *d* against her.
9.31 and as they had *d* for themselves
Job 38.10 brake up for it my *d* place
Isa 10.22 the consumption *d* shall overflow
1Co 7.37 hath so *d* in his heart that he

DECREES

Isa 10. 1 that decree unrighteous *d*, and
Ac 16. 4 delivered them the *d* for to keep,
17. 7 all do contrary to the *d* of Caesar

DEDICATED

Dt 20. 5 new house, and hath not *d* it?
Jdg 17. 3 wholly *d* the silver unto the Lord
2Sa 8.11 the silver and gold that he had *d*
1Ki 7.51 which David his father had *d*;
8.63 and all the children of Israel *d*
15.15 things which his father had *d*,
15 the things which himself had *d*,
2Ki 12. 4 money of the *d* things that is
18 kings of Judah, had *d*, and his
1Ch 18.11 king David *d* unto the Lord,
26.20 over the treasures of the *d* things
26 all the treasures of the *d* things,
26 the captains of the host, had *d*.
28 Joab the son of Jeruiah, had *d*;
28 and whosoever had *d* any thing,
28.12 of the treasuries of the *d* things:
2Ch 5. 1 things that David his father had *d*;
7. 5 and all the people *d* the house
15.18 the things that his father had *d*,
18 and that he himself had *d*,
24. 7 *d* things of the house of the Lord
31.12 and the *d* things faithfully: over
Eze 44.29 every *d* thing in Israel shall be
Heb 9.18 testament was *d* without blood.

DEDICATING

Nu 7.10 princes offered for *d* of the altar
11 on his day, for the *d* of the altar.

DEDICATION

Nu 7.84 the *d* of the altar, in the day
88 This was the *d* of the altar,
2Ch 7. 9 they kept the *d* of the altar
Ezr 6.16 kept the *d* of this house of God
17 And offered at the *d* of this house
Neh 12.27 at the *d* of the wall of Jerusalem
27 to keep the *d* with gladness,
Ps 30(T) at the *d* of the house of David.
Dan 3. 2 come to the *d* of the image
3 together unto the *d* of the image
Jn 10.22 at Jerusalem the feast of the *d*,

DEED

Gen 44.15 What *d* is this that ye have done?
Ex 9.16 And in very *d* for this cause
Jdg 19.30 There was no such *d* done nor
1Sa 25.34 For in very *d*, as the Lord God of
26. 4 that Saul was come in very *d*.
2Sa 12.14 by this *d* thou hast given great
2Ch 6.18 will God in very *d* dwell with men
Est 1.17 For this *d* of the queen shall
18 have heard of the *d* of the queen.
Lk 23.51 to the counsel and *d* of them;
24.19 mighty in *d* and word before God
Ac 4. 9 good *d* done to the impotent man,
Ro 15.18 Gentiles obedient, by word and *d*,
1Co 5. 2 hath done this *d* might be taken
3 him that hath so done this *d*,
2Co 10.11 also in *d* when we are present.
Col 3.17 ye do in word or *d*, do all in the
Jas 1.25 man shall be blessed in his *d*.
1Jn 3.18 tongue; but in *d* and in truth.

DEEDS

Gen 20. 9 thou hast done *d* unto me that
1Ch 16. 8 make known his *d* among the
2Ch 35.27 And his *d*, first and last, behold,
Ezr 9.13 for our evil *d*, and for our
Neh 6.19 reported his good *d* before him,
13.14 wipe not out my good *d* that I
Ps 28. 4 Give them according to their *d*,
105. 1 make known his *d* among the
Isa 59.18 According to their *d*,
Jer 5.28 overpass the *d* of the wicked:
25.14 them according to their *d*, and
Lk 11.48 ye allow the *d* of your fathers:
23.41 the due reward of our *d*:
Jn 3.19 because their *d* were evil.
20 lest his *d* should be reproved.
21 his *d* may be made manifest,
8.41 Ye do the *d* of your father.
Ac 7.22 was mighty in words and in *d*.
19.18 confessed, and shewed their *d*.
24. 2 and that very worthy *d* are done
Ro 2. 6 to every man according to his *d*:
3.20 by the *d* of the law there shall no
28 faith without the *d* of the law.
8.13 do mortify the *d* of the body,
2Co 12.12 and wonders, and might *d*.
Col 3. 9 put off the old man with his *d*;
2Pe 2. 8 to day with their unlawful *d*;
2Jn 11 speed is partaker of his evil *d*.
3Jn 10 his *d* which he doeth, prating
Jude 15 of all their ungodly *d* which
Rev 2. 6 hatest the *d* of the Nicolaitanes
22 except they repent of their *d*.
16.11 and repented not of their *d*.

DEEMED

Ac 27.27 shipmen *d* that they drew near

DEEP

Gen 1. 2 was upon the face of the *d*.
2.21 God caused a *d* sleep to fall upon
7.11 fountains of the great *d* broken
8. 2 The fountains also of the *d* and
15.12 down, a *d* sleep fell upon Abram;
49.25 blessings of the *d* that lieth under,
Dt 33.13 for the *d* that coucheth beneath,
1Sa 26.12 *d* sleep from the Lord was fallen
Job 4.13 when *d* sleep falleth on men,
12.22 He discovereth *d* things out of
33.15 when *d* sleep falleth upon men,
38.30 and the face of the *d* is frozen.
41.31 maketh the *d* to boil like a pot:
32 would think the *d* to be hoary.
Ps 36. 6 thy judgments are a great *d*:
42. 7 *D* calleth unto *d* at the noise of
64. 6 one of them, and the heart, is *d*.
69. 2 I sink in *d* mire, when there is no
2 I am come into *d* waters, where
14 hate me, and out of the *d* waters.
15 neither let the *d* swallow me up.
80. 9 and didst cause it to take *d* root,
92. 5 and thy thoughts are very *d*.
95. 4 In his hand are the *d* places of the
104. 6 Thou coveredst it with the *d* as
107.24 Lord, and his wonders in the *d*.
135. 6 in the seas, and all *d* places.
140.10 into the fire; into *d* pits, that
Pr 8.28 the fountains of the *d*:
18. 4 of a man's mouth are as *d* waters,
19.15 casteth into a *d* sleep: and an
20. 5 in the heart of man is like *d* water;
22.14 mouth of strange women is a *d* pit;
23.27 whore is a *d* ditch; and a strange
Ec 7.24 far off, and exceeding *d*, who can
Isa 29.10 the spirit of *d* sleep, and hath
15 Woe unto them that seek *d* to
30.33 he hath made it *d* and large:
44.27 That saith to the *d*, Be dry,
51.10 sea, the waters of the great *d*;
63.13 That led them through the *d*, as
Jer 49. 8 dwell *d*, O inhabitants of Dedan;
30 dwell *d* O ye inhabitants of Hazor,
Eze 23.32 shalt drink of thy sister's cup *d*
26.19 when I shall bring up the *d* upon
31. 4 the *d* set him up on high with her
15 I covered the *d* for him, and I
32.14 Then will I make their waters *d*,
34.18 to have drunk of the *d* waters,
Dan 2.22 revealeth the *d* and secret things:
8.18 I was in a *d* sleep on my face
10. 9 then was I in a *d* sleep on my face,
Am 7. 4 it devoured the great *d*, and did
Jon 2. 3 thou hadst cast me into the *d*,
Hab 3.10 the *d* uttered his voice, and lifted
Lk 5. 4 Launch out into the *d*, and let
6.48 built an house, and digged *d*,
8.31 them to go out into the *d*.

Jn 4.11 to draw with, and the well is *d*:
Ac 20. 9 being fallen into a *d* sleep:
Ro 10. 7 Who shall descend into the *d*?
1Co 2.10 things, yea, the *d* things of God.
2Co 8. 2 their *d* poverty abounded unto the
11.25 and a day I have been in the *d*;

DEEPLY
Isa 31. 6 children of Israel have *d* revolted
Hos 9. 9 They have *d* corrupted themselves,
Mk 8.12 he sighed *d* in his spirit, and saith,

DEEPNESS
Mt 13. 5 because they had no *d* of earth:

DEFAMED
1Co 4.13 Being *d*, we intreat: we are made

DEFENDED
2Sa 23.12 and *d* it, and slew the Philistines:
Ac 7.24 suffer wrong, he *d* him; and smote

DEFENSE
Nu 14. 9 their *d* is departed from them,
2Ch 11. 5 Jerusalem, and built cities for *d*
Job 22.25 the Almighty shall be thy *d*, and
Ps 7.10 My *d* is of God, which saveth
31. 2 for an house of *d* to save me.
59. 9 wait upon thee: for God is my *d*.
16 thou hast been my *d* and refuge
17 God is my *d*, and the God of my
62. 2 and my salvation; he is my *d*;
6 he is my *d*; I shall not be moved.
89.18 For the Lord is our *d*; and the
94.22 the Lord is my *d*; and my God
Ec 7.12 wisdom is a *d*, and money is a *d*:
Isa 4. 5 upon all the glory shall be a *d*.
19. 6 the brooks of *d* shall be emptied
33.16 place of *d* shall be the munition
Na 2. 5 and the *d* shall be prepared.
Ac 19.33 have made his *d* unto the people.
22. 1 hear ye my *d*, which I make
Php 1. 7 *d* and confirmation of the gospel,
17 I am set for the *d* of the gospel.

DEFERRED
Gen 34.19 young man *d* not to do the thing,
Pr 13.12 Hope *d* maketh the heart sick:
Ac 24.22 of that way, he *d* them, and said,

DEFILE
Lev 11.44 neither shall ye *d* yourselves
15.31 when they *d* my tabernacle that is
18.20 neighbor's wife, to *d* thyself with
23 thou lie with any beast to *d* thyself
24 *D* not ye yourselves in any of these
28 spue not you out also, when ye *d* it,
30 that ye *d* not yourselves therein:
20. 3 to *d* my sanctuary, and to profane
21. 4 shall not *d* himself, being a chief
11 nor *d* himself for his father, or for
22. 8 not eat to *d* himself therewith:
Nu 5. 3 that they *d* not their camps, in the
35.34 *D* not therefore the land which ye
2Ki 23.13 children of Ammon, did the king *d*.
SS 5. 3 my feet; how shall I *d* them?
Isa 30.22 Ye shall *d* also the covering of thy
Jer 32.34 called by my name, to *d* it.
Eze 7.22 robbers shall enter into it, and *d*
9. 7 he said unto them, *D* the house,
20. 7 *d* not yourselves with the idols of
18 nor *d* yourselves with their idols:
22. 3 maketh idols against herself to *d*
28. 7 and they shall *d* thy brightness.
33.26 ye *d* every one his neighbor's
37.23 Neither shall they *d* themselves
43. 7 shall the house of Israel no more *d*,
44.25 no dead person to *d* themselves:
25 husband, they may *d* themselves.
Dan 1. 8 he would not *d* himself with the
8 that he might not *d* himself.

Mt 15.18 the heart; and they *d* the man.
20 are the things which *d* a man:
Mk 7.15 entering into him can *d* him: but
15 him, those are they that *d* the man.
18 into the man, it cannot *d* him;
23 come from within, and *d* the man.
1Co 3.17 If any man *d* the temple of God,
1Ti 1.10 that *d* themselves with mankind,
Jude 8 these filthy dreamers *d* the flesh,

DEFILED
Gen 34. 2 and lay with her, and *d* her.
5 Jacob heard that he had *d* Dinah
13 he had *d* Dinah their sister:
27 because they had *d* their sister.
Lev 5. 3 that a man shall be *d* withal, and
11.43 them, that ye should be *d* thereby.
13.46 shall be in him he shall be *d*;
15.32 from him, and is *d* therewith;
18.24 all these the nations are *d* which
25 the land is *d*: therefore I do visit
27 before you, and the land is *d*;
19.31 wizards, to be *d* by them: I am the
21. 1 There shall none be *d* for the
3 no husband; for her may he be *d*.
Nu 5. 2 and whosoever is *d* by the dead:
13 kept close, and she be *d*, and
14 jealous of his wife, and she be *d*:
14 of his wife, and she be not *d*:
20 if thou be *d*, and some man have
27 if she be *d*, and have done trespass
28 if the woman be not *d*, but be
29 instead of her husband, and is *d*;
6. 9 and he hath *d* the head of his
12 lost, because his separation was *d*.
9. 6 men, who were *d* by the dead
7 We are *d* by the dead body of a
19.20 hath *d* the sanctuary of the Lord:
Dt 21.23 that thy land be not *d*, which the
22. 9 the fruit of thy vineyard, be *d*.
24. 4 after that she is *d*; for that is
2Ki 23. 8 and *d* the high places where the
10 And he *d* Topheth, which is in
1Ch 5. 1 forasmuch as he *d* his father's
Neh 13.29 they have *d* the priesthood,
Job 16.15 and *d* my horn in the dust.
Ps 74. 7 they have *d* by casting down the
79. 1 thy holy temple have they *d*;
106.39 Thus were they *d* with their own
Isa 24. 5 The earth also is *d* under the
59. 3 your hands are *d* with blood, and
Jer 2. 7 when ye entered, ye *d* my land,
3. 9 she *d* the land, and committed
16.18 because they have *d* my land,
19.13 be *d* as the place of Tophet,
Eze 4.13 Israel eat their *d* bread among
5.11 thou hast *d* my sanctuary with
7.24 and their holy places shall be *d*.
18. 6 hath *d* his neighbor's wife,
11 and *d* his neighbor's wife,
15 hath not *d* his neighbor's wife,
20.43 wherein ye have been *d*; and ye
22. 4 and hast *d* thyself in thine idols
11 hath lewdly *d* his daughter in law;
23. 7 with all their idols she *d* herself.
13 Then I saw that she was *d*, that
17 they *d* her with their whoredom,
38 they have *d* my sanctuary in the
28.18 Thou hast *d* thy sanctuaries by
36.17 dwelt in their own land, they *d* it
43. 8 they have even *d* my holy name
Hos 5. 3 whoredom, and Israel is *d*.
6.10 whoredom of Ephraim, Israel is *d*.
Mic 4.11 that say, Let her be *d*, and let our
Mk 7. 2 eat bread with *d*, that is to say,
Jn 18.28 lest they should be *d*; but that
1Co 8. 7 their conscience being weak is *d*.
Tit 1.15 but unto them that are *d* and
15 their mind and conscience is *d*.
Heb 12.15 you, and thereby many be *d*;

Rev 3. 4 which have not *d* their garments;
14. 4 which were not *d* with women;

DEFILETH
Ex 31.14 every one that *d* it shall surely
Nu 19.13 *d* the tabernacle of the Lord;
35.33 for blood it *d* the land: and the
Mt 15.11 into the mouth *d* a man; but that
11 out of the mouth, this *d* a man.
20 with unwashen hands *d* not a man.
Mk 7.20 of the man, that *d* the man.
Jas 3. 6 members, that it *d* the whole body,
Rev 21.27 enter into it any thing that *d*,

DEFRAUD
Lev 19.13 Thou shalt not *d* thy neighbor,
Mk 10.19 *D* not, Honor thy father and
1Co 6. 8 Nay, ye do wrong, and *d*, and that
7. 5 *D* ye not one the other, except it
1Th 4. 6 and *d* his brother in any matter:

DEFRAUDED
1Sa 12. 3 I taken? or whom have I *d*?
4 Thou hast not *d* us, nor oppressed
1Co 6. 7 rather suffer yourselves to be *d*?
2Co 7. 2 no man, we have *d* no man.

DELAY
Ex 22.29 Thou shalt not *d* to offer the
Ac 9.38 that he would not *d* to come
25.17 without any *d* on the morrow

DELAYETH
Mt 24.48 My lord *d* his coming; and shall
Lk 12.45 My lord *d* his coming; and shall

DELICACIES
Rev 18. 3 through the abundance of her *d*.

DELICATELY
1Sa 15.32 And Agag came unto him *d*.
Pr 29.21 He that *d* bringeth up his servant
La 4. 5 They that did feed *d* are desolate
Lk 7.25 and live *d*, are in kings' courts.

DELICIOUSLY
Rev 18. 7 glorified herself, and lived *d*,
9 and lived *d* with her, shall

DELIGHT
Gen 34.19 he had *d* in Jacob's daughter:
Nu 14. 8 If the Lord *d* in us, then he will
Dt 10.15 the Lord had a *d* in thy fathers
21.14 if thou have no *d* in her, then
1Sa 15.22 Hath the Lord as great *d* in burnt
18.22 the king hath *d* in thee, and all
2Sa 15.26 I have no *d* in thee; behold, here
24. 3 doth my lord the king *d* in this
Est 6. 6 To whom would the king *d* to do
Job 22.26 then shalt thou have thy *d* in the
27.10 Will he *d* himself in the Almighty?
34. 9 that he should *d* himself with God.
Ps 1. 2 But his *d* is in the law of the Lord;
16. 3 excellent, in whom is all my *d*,
37. 4 *D* thyself also in the Lord; and
11 *d* themselves in the abundance
40. 8 I *d* to do thy will, O my God:
62. 4 they *d* in lies: they bless with
68.30 thou the people that *d* in war.
94.19 me thy comforts *d* my soul.
119.16 I will *d* myself in thy statutes:
24 Thy testimonies also are my *d*
35 for therein do I *d*.
47 *d* myself in thy commandments,
70 fat as grease; but I *d* in thy law.
77 I may live: for thy law is my *d*.
174 O Lord; and thy law is my *d*.
Pr 1.22 the scorners *d* in their scorning,
2.14 and *d*, in the frowardness of the
8.30 I was daily his *d*, rejoicing always
11. 1 but a just weight is his *d*,

Pr 11.20 but such as are upright are his *d*.
12.22 but they that deal truly are his *d*.
15. 8 the prayer of the upright is his *d*.
16.13 Righteous lips are the *d* of kings;
18. 2 fool hath no *d* in understanding.
19.10 *D* is not seemly for a fool;
24.25 them that rebuke him shall be *d*,
29.17 he shall give *d* unto thy soul.
SS 2. 3 under his shadow with great *d*,
Isa 1.11 I *d* not in the blood of bullocks,
13.17 as for gold, they shall not *d* in it.
55. 2 let your soul *d* itself in fatness,
58. 2 me daily, and *d* to know my ways,
2 take *d* in approaching to God.
13 call the sabbath a *d*, the holy of
14 shalt thou *d* thyself in the Lord;
Jer 6.10 reproach; they have no *d* in it.
9.24 these things I *d*, saith the Lord.
Mal 3. 1 of the covenant, whom ye *d* in:
Ro 7.22 For I *d* in the law of God after

DELIGHTED
1Sa 19. 2 Saul's son *d* much in David:
2Sa 22.20 delivered me, because he *d* in me.
1Ki 10. 9 which *d* in thee, to set thee on the
2Ch 9. 8 which *d* in thee to set thee on his
Neh 9.25 and *d* themselves in thy great
Est 2.14 no more, except the king *d* in her,
Ps 18.19 delivered me, because he *d* in me.
22. 8 deliver him, seeing he *d* in him.
109.17 as he *d* not in blessing, so let it be
Isa 65.12 did choose that wherein I *d* not.
66. 4 and chose that in which I *d* not.
11 and be *d* with the abundance

DELIGHTEST
Ps 51.16 thou *d* not in burnt offering.

DELIGHTETH
Est 6. 6 man whom the king *d* to honor?
7 man whom the king *d* to honor,
9 withal whom the king *d* to honor
9, 11 whom the king *d* to honor.
Ps 37.23 Lord: and he *d* in his way.
112. 1 *d* greatly in his commandments.
147.10 *d* not in the strength of the horse:
Pr 3.12 a father the son in whom he *d*.
Isa 42. 1 mine elect, in whom my soul *d*;
62. 4 the Lord *d* in thee, and thy land
66. 3 their soul *d* in their abominations.
Mic 7.18 for ever, because he *d* in mercy.
Mal 2.17 and he *d* in them; or, Where is the

DELIGHTS
2Sa 1.24 you in scarlet, with other *d*,
Ps 119.92 Unless thy law had been my *d*,
143 thy commandments are my *d*.
Pr 8.31 my *d* were with the sons of men.
Ec 2. 8 and the *d* of the sons of men,
SS 7. 6 pleasant art thou, O love, for *d*!

DELILAH
Jdg 16. 4 of Sorek, whose name was *D*.
6 *D* said to Samson, Tell me, I pray
10 *D* said unto Damson, Behold, thou
12 *D* therefore took new ropes, and
13 *D* said unto Samson, Hitherto thou
18 *D* saw that he had told her all

DELIVER
Gen 32.11 *D* me, I pray thee, from the hand
37.22 to *d* him to his father again.
40.13 *d* Pharaoh's cup into his hand,
42.34 will I *d* you your brother, and ye
37 *d* him into my hand, and I will
Ex 3. 8 I am come down to *d* them
5.18 yet shall ye *d* the tale of bricks.
21.13 but God *d* him into his hand;
22. 7 a man shall *d* unto his neighbor
10 If a man *d* unto his neighbor
26 thou shalt *d* it unto him by that
23.31 *d* the inhabitants of the land into
Lev 26.26 shall *d* you your bread again
Nu 21. 2 If you wilt indeed *d* this people
35.25 congregation shall *d* the slayer
Dt 1.27 to *d* us into the hand of the
2.30 that he might *d* him into thy hand,
3. 2 *d* him, and all his people, into
7. 2 Lord thy God shall *d* them before
16 the Lord thy God shall *d* thee;
23 the Lord thy God shall *d* them unto
24 shall *d* their kings into thine hand,
19.12 *d* him into the hand of the avenger
23.14 the midst of thy camp, to *d* thee,
15 not *d* unto his master the servant
24.13 shalt *d* him the pledge again
25.11 to *d* her husband out of the hand
32.39 any that can *d* out of my hand.
Jos 2.13 have, and *d* our lives from death.
7. 7 to *d* us into the hand of the
8. 7 the Lord your God will *d* it into
11. 6 about this time will I *d* them up
20. 5 *d* the slayer up into his hand;
Jdg 4. 7 and I will *d* him into thine hand.
7. 7 I save you, and *d* the Midianites
10.11 not I *d* you from the Egyptians
13 wherefore I will *d* you no more.
14 let them *d* you in the time of
15 *d* us only, we pray thee, this day.
11. 9 and the Lord *d* them before me,
30 *d* the children of Ammon into mine
13. 5 he shall begin to *d* Israel out of
15.12 that we may *d* thee into the hand
13 fast, and *d* thee into their hand:
20.13 Now therefore *d* us the men, the
28 I will *d* them into thine hand.
1Sa 4. 8 who shall *d* us out of the hand of
7. 3 he will *d* you out of the hand of the
14 the coasts thereof did Israel *d* out
12.10 but now *d* us out of the hand of our
21 things, which cannot profit nor *d*;
14.37 *d* them into the hand of Israel?
17.37 he will *d* me out of the hand of
46 the Lord *d* thee into mine hand;
23. 4 *d* the Philistines into thine hand.
11 Will the men of Keilah *d* me up
12 Will the men of Keilah *d* me and
12 Lord said, They will *d* thee up.
20 to *d* him into the king's hand.
24. 4 I will *d* thine enemy into thine
15 and *d* me out of thine hand.
26.24 him *d* me out of all tribulation.
28.19 Lord will also *d* Israel with thee
19 the Lord also shall *d* the host into
30.15 nor *d* me into the hands of my
2Sa 3.14 *D* me my wife Michal, which I
5.19 wilt thou *d* them into mine hand?
19 will doubtless *d* the Philistines into
14. 7 *D* him that smote hs brother that
16 *d* his handmaid out of the hand
20.21 *d* him only, and I will depart
1Ki 8.46 *d* them to the enemy, so that they
18. 9 thou wouldst *d* thy servant into
20. 5 Thou shalt *d* me thy silver, and
13 I will *d* it into thine hand
28 I *d* all this great multitude into
22. 6 shall *d* it into the hand of the king.
12 Lord shall *d* it into the king's hand
15 shall *d* into the hand of the king.
2Ki 3.10, 13 *d* them into the hand of Moab!
18 he will *d* the Moabites also into
12. 7 *d* it for the breaches of the house.
17.39 he shall *d* you out of the hand of
18.23 will *d* thee two thousand horses,
29 he shall not be able to *d* you
30 The Lord will surely *d* us, and this
32 you, saying, The Lord will *d* us.
35 the Lord should *d* Jerusalem out
20. 6 I will *d* thee and this city out of the
21.14 and *d* them into the hand of their
22. 5 And let them *d* it into the hand of
1Ch 14.10 thou *d* them into mine hand?
10 for I will *d* them into thine hand.
16.35 and *d* us from the heathen, that
2Ch 6.36 angry with them, and *d* them over
18. 5 God will *d* it into the king's hand.
11 shall *d* it into the hand of the king.
25.15 could not *d* their own people
20 that he might *d* them into the
28.11 and *d* the captives again, which
32.11 The Lord our God shall *d* us out
13 *d* their lands out of mine hand?
14 *d* his people out of mine hand,
14 God should be able to *d* you out
15 able to *d* his people out of mine
15 your God *d* you out of mine hand?
17 God of Hezekiah *d* his people out
Ezr 7.19 those *d* thou before the God of
Neh 9.28 many times didst thou *d* them
Job 5. 4 neither is there any to *d* them.
19 He shall *d* thee in six troubles:
6.23 *D* me from the enemy's hand?
10. 7 there is none that can *d* out of
22.30 *d* the island of the innocent:
33.24 *D* him from going down to the
28 He will *d* his soul from going
36.18 a great ransom cannot *d* thee,
Ps 6. 4 Return, O Lord, *d* my soul: oh
7. 1 that persecute me, and *d* me:
2 in pieces, while there is none to *d*.
17.13 *d* my soul from the wicked,
22. 4 trusted, and thou didst *d* them.
8 on the Lord that he would *d* him:
8 *d* him, seeing he delighted in
20 *D* my soul from the sword; my
25.20 O keep my soul, and *d* me:
27.12 *D* me not over unto the will of
31. 1 *d* me in thy righteousness.
2 *d* me speedily: be thou my strong
15 *d* me from the hand of mine
33.17 he *d* any by his great strength.
19 To *d* their soul from death, and
37.40 *d* them: he shall *d* them from
39. 8 *D* me from all my transgressions:
40.13 Be pleased, O Lord, to *d* me:
41. 1 Lord will *d* him in time of trouble.
2 thou wilt not *d* him unto the will
43. 1 O *d* me from the deceitful and
50.15 the day of trouble: I will *d* thee,
22 in pieces, and there be none to *d*.
51.14 *D* me from bloodguiltiness, O God,
56.13 not thou *d* my foot from falling,
59. 1 *D* me from mine enemies, O my
2 *D* me from the workers of iniquity,
69.14 *D* me out of the mire, and let me
18 *d* me because of mine enemies.
70. 1 Make haste, O God, to *d* me:
71. 2 *D* me in thy righteousness, and
4 *D* me, O my God, out of the
11 for there is none to *d* him.
72.12 shall *d* the needy when he crieth;
74.19 O *d* not the soul of thy turtledove
79. 9 *d* us, and purge away our sins,
82. 4 *D* the poor and needy: rid them
89.48 shall he *d* his soul from the hand
91. 3 he shall *d* thee from the snare
14 will I *d* him: I will set him on
15 I will *d* him, and honor him
106.43 Many times did he *d* them; but
109.21 thy mercy is good, *d* thou me.
116. 4 Lord, I beseech thee, *d* my soul.
119.134 *D* me from the oppression of
153 mine affliction and *d* me: for I
154 Plead my cause, and *d* me:
170 *d* me according to thy word.
120. 2 *D* my soul, O Lord, from lying
140. 1 *D* me, O Lord, from the evil man:
142. 6 *d* me from my persecutors; for
143. 9 *D* me, O Lord, from mine enemies:
144. 7 and *d* me out of great waters,
11 and *d* me from the hand of strange
Pr 2.12 To *d* thee from the way of the evil
16 To *d* thee from the strange woman.

4. 9 a crown of glory shall she *d* to
6. 3 this now, my son, and *d* thyself,
5 *D* thyself as a roe from the hand
11. 6 of the upright shall *d* them:
12. 6 mouth of the upright shall *d* them.
19.19 if thou *d* him, yet thou must
23.14 and shall *d* his soul from hell.
24.11 If thou forbear to *d* them that are
Ec 8. 8 neither shall wickedness *d* those
Isa 5.29 away safe, and none shall *d* it.
19.20 a great one, and he shall *d* them.
29.11 men *d* to one that is learned,
31. 5 defending also he will *d* it,
36.14 he shall not be able to *d* you.
15 The Lord will surely *d* us: this city
18 you, saying, The Lord will *d* us.
20 that the Lord should *d* Jerusalem
38. 6 And I will *d* thee and this city
43.13 there is none that can *d* out of my
44.17 *D* me; for thou art my god.
20 he cannot *d* his soul, nor say,
46. 2 they could not *d* the burden, but
4 I will carry, and will *d* you.
47.14 they shall not *d* themselves from
50. 2 or have I no power to *d*?
57.13 let thy companies *d* thee; but the
Jer 1. 8 I am with thee to *d* thee, saith
19 with thee, saith the Lord, to *d* thee.
15. 9 the residue of them will I *d* to the
20 to save thee and to *d* thee,
21 And I will *d* thee out of the hand
18.21 *d* up their children to the famine,
20. 5 will *d* all the strength of the city,
21. 7 I will *d* Zedekiah king of Judah,
12 and *d* him that is spoiled out of
22. 3 and *d* the spoiled out of the hand
24. 9 And I will *d* them to be removed
29.18 and will *d* them to be removed
21 I will *d* them into the hand of
38.19 lest they *d* me into their hand.
20 They shall not *d* thee. Obey, I
39.17 But I will *d* thee in that day,
18 I will surely *d* thee, and thou
42.11 and to *d* you from his hand.
43. 3 to *d* us into the hand of the
11 and *d* such as are for death to
46.26 and I will *d* them into the hand
51. 6 and *d* every man his soul: be
45 and *d* ye every man his soul
La 5. 8 there is none that doth *d* us out
Eze 7.19 gold shall not be able to *d* them
11. 9 and *d* you into the hands of
13.21 and *d* my people out of your
23 for I will *d* my people out of your
14.14 they should *d* but their own souls
16 *d* neither sons nor daughters; they
18 *d* neither sons nor daughters, but
20 shall *d* neither son nor daughter;
20 they shall but *d* their own souls
21.31 and *d* thee into the hand of
23.28 I will *d* thee into the hand of them
25. 4 I will *d* thee to the men of the
7 and will *d* thee for a spoil to the
33. 5 taketh warning shall *d* his soul.
12 of the righteous shall not *d* him
34.10 I will *d* my flock from their mouth,
12 and will *d* them out of all places
Dan 3.15 who is that God that shall *d* you
17 is able to *d* us from the burning
17 he will *d* us out of thine hand,
29 God that can *d* after this sort.
6.14 set his heart on Daniel to *d* him:
14 going down of the sun to *d* him.
16 servest continually, he will *d* thee.
20 able to *d* thee from the lions?
8. 4 was there any that could *d* out of
7 was none that could *d* the ram
Hos 2.10 shall *d* her out of mine hand.
11. 8 how shall I *d* thee, Israel?
Am 1. 6 captivity, to *d* them up to Edom:
2.14 shall the mighty *d* himself:
15 swift of foot shall not *d* himself:
15 he that rideth the horse *d* himself.
6. 8 therefore will I *d* up the city
Jon 4. 6 head, to *d* him from his grief.
Mic 5. 6 shall he *d* us from the Assyrian,
8 teareth in peices, and none can *d*.
6.14 shalt take hold, but shalt not *d*;
Zep 1.18 shall be able to *d* them in the day
Zec 2. 7 *D* thyself, O Zion, that dwellest
11. 6 I will *d* the men every one
6 out of their hand I will not *d* them.
Mt 5.25 adversary *d* thee to the judge,
25 and the judge *d* thee to the officer,
6.13 temptation, but *d* us from evil:
10.17 will *d* you up to the councils,
19 But when they *d* you up, take
21 the brother shall *d* up the brother
20.19 And shall *d* him to the Gentiles
24. 9 Then shall they *d* you up to the
26.15 and I will *d* him unto you?
27.43 let him *d* him now, if he will have
Mk 10.33 and shall *d* him to the Gentiles:
13. 9 they shall *d* you up to councils;
11 and *d* you up, take no thought
Lk 11. 4 temptation: but *d* us from evil.
12.58 the judge *d* thee to the officer,
20.20 that so they might *d* him unto the
Ac 7.25 God by his hand would *d* them:
34 and am come down to *d* them.
21.11 and shall *d* him into the hands of
25.11 no man may *d* me unto them.
16 to *d* any man to die, before that
Ro 7.24 who shall *d* me from the body of
1Co 5. 5 To *d* such an one unto Satan
2Co 1.10 a death, and doth *d*: in whom
10 we trust that he will yet *d* us;
Gal 1. 4 that he might *d* us from this
2Ti 4.18 the Lord shall *d* me from every
Heb 2.15 and *d* them who through fear of
2Pe 2. 9 The Lord knoweth how to *d* the

DELIVERANCE

Gen 45. 7 save your lives by a great *d*.
Jdg 15.18 Thou hast given this great *d*
2Ki 5. 1 Lord had given *d* unto Syria:
13.17 The arrow of the Lord's *d*,
17 the arrow of *d* from Syria
1Ch 11.14 Lord saved them by a great *d*.
2Ch 12. 7 but I will grant them some *d*;
Ezr 9.13 hast given us such *d* as this;
Est 4.14 enlargement and *d* arise to the
Ps 18.50 Great *d* giveth he to his king;
32. 7 me about with the songs of *d*.
Isa 26.18 we have not wrought any *d* in
Joel 2.32 and in Jerusalem shall be *d*
Ob 17 upon Mount Zion shall be *d*
Lk 4.18 to preach *d* to the captives, and
Heb 11.35 were tortured, not accepting *d*;

DELIVERED

Gen 9. 2 sea; into your hand are they *d*.
14.20 hath *d* thine enemies into thy
25.24 her days to be *d* were fulfilled,
32.16 And he *d* them into the hand of
37.21 and he *d* him out of their hands;
Ex 1.19 and are *d* ere the midwives come
2.19 An Egyptian *d* us out of the hand
5.23 neither hast thou *d* thy people at
12.27 the Egyptians, and *d* our houses.
18. 4 *d* me from the sword of Pharaoh:
8 way, and how the Lord *d* them.
9 whom he had *d* out of the hand
10 who hath *d* you out of the hand of
10 of Pharaoh, who hath *d* the people
Lev 6. 2 which was *d* him to keep, or in
4 which was *d* him to keep, or the
26.25 and ye shall be *d* into the
Nu 21. 3 and *d* up the Canaanites; and they
34 I have *d* him into thy hand,
31. 5 they were *d* out of the thousands
Dt 2.33 And the Lord our God *d* him
36 the Lord our God *d* all unto us:
3. 3 So the Lord our God *d* into our
5.22 of stone, and *d* them unto me.
9.10 And the Lord *d* unto me two tables
20.13 God hath *d* it into thine hands,
21.10 the Lord thy God hath *d* them
31. 9 and *d* it unto the priests the sons
Jos 2.24 the Lord hath *d* into our hands
9.26 and *d* them out of the hand of the
10. 8 I have *d* them into thine hand;
12 the Lord *d* up the Amorites before
19 the Lord your God hath *d* them
30 And the Lord *d* it also, and the
32 And the Lord *d* Lachish into the
11. 8 *d* them into the hand of Israel,
21.44 the Lord *d* all their enemies into
22.31 ye have *d* the children of Israel
24.10 so I *d* you out of his hand.
11 and I *d* them into your hand.
Jdg 1. 2 I have *d* the land into his hand.
4 and the Lord *d* the Canaanites
2.14 and he *d* them into the hands of
16 which *d* them out of the hand of
18 and *d* them out of the hand of
23 neither *d* he them into the hand
3. 9 children of Israel who *d* them,
10 the Lord *d* Chushan-rishathaim
28 hath *d* your enemies the Moabites
31 ox-goad: and he also *d* Israel.
4.14 hath *d* Sisera into thine hand:
5.11 are *d* from the noise of archers
6. 1 *d* them into the hand of Midian
9 And I *d* you out of the hand of
13 and *d* us into the hands of the
7. 9 I have *d* it into thine hand.
14 into his hand hath God *d* Midian,
15 the Lord hath *d* into your hand
8. 3 God hath *d* into your hands the
7 when the Lord hath *d* Zebah and
22 *d* us from the hand of Midian.
34 Lord their God, who had *d* them
9.17 *d* you out of the hand of Midian:
10.12 and I *d* you out of their hand.
11.21 the Lord God of Israel *d* Sihon
32 the Lord *d* them into his hands.
12. 2 ye *d* me not out of their hands.
3 And when I saw that ye *d* me not,
3 the Lord *d* them into my hand:
13. 1 and the Lord *d* them into the hand
16.23 hath *d* Samson our enemy into our
24 hath *d* into our hands our enemy,
1Sa 4.19 was with child, near to be *d*:
10.18 and *d* you out of the hand of the
12.11 and *d* you out of the hand of your
14.10 hath *d* them into our hand:
12 *d* them into the hand of Israel.
48 *d* Israel out of the hands of them
17.35 and *d* it out of his mouth:
37 *d* me out of the paw of the lion,
23. 7 God hath *d* him into mine hand;
14 God *d* him not into his hand.
24.10 the Lord had *d* thee to day
18 Lord had *d* me into thine hand,
26. 8 *d* thine enemy into thine hand
23 the Lord *d* thee into my hand
30.23 and *d* the company that came
2Sa 3. 8 not *d* thee into the hand of David,
10.10 the rest of the people he *d*
12. 7 I *d* thee out of the hand of Saul;
16. 8 and the Lord hath *d* the kingdom
18.28 hath *d* up the men that lifted
19. 9 and he *d* us out of the hand of
21. 6 Let seven men of his sons be *d*
9 And he *d* them into the hands of
22. 1 the Lord had *d* him out of the
18 He *d* me from my strong enemy,
20 he *d* me, because he delighted in
44 *d* me from the strivings of my
49 hast *d* me from the violent man.
1Ki 3.17 *d* of a child with her in the house
18 the third day after that I was *d*,

1Ki 3.18 that this woman was *d* also:
13.26 Lord hath *d* him unto the lion,
15.18 and *d* them into the hand of his
17.23 and *d* him unto his mother: and
2Ki 12.15 they *d* the money to be bestowed
13. 3 *d* them into the hand of Hazael
17.20 *d* them into the hand of spoilers,
18.30 shall not be *d* into the hand
33 any of the gods of the nations, *d*
34 *d* Samaria out of mine hand?
35 *d* their country out of mine hand,
19.10 Jerusalem shall not be *d* into
11 utterly: and shalt thou be *d*?
12 the gods of the nation *d* them
22. 7 the money that was *d* into their
9 and have *d* it into the hand of
10 Hilkiah the priest hath *d* me a
1Ch 5.20 Hagarites were *d* into their hand,
11.14 *d* it, and slew the Philistines;
16. 7 David *d* first this psalm to thank
19.11 the rest of the people he *d* unto
2Ch 13.16 and God *d* them into their hand.
16. 8 Lord, he *d* them into thine hand.
18.14 and they shall be *d* into your hand
23. 9 Moreover Jehoiada the priest *d* to
24.24 *d* a very great host into their hand,
28. 5 Lord his God *d* him into the hand
5 he was also *d* into the hand of
9 he hath *d* them into your hand,
29. 8 and he hath *d* them to trouble,
32.17 not *d* their people out of mine
34. 9 the high priest, they *d* the money
15 Hilkiah *d* the book to Shaphan
17 *d* it into the hand of the overseers,
Ezr 5.14 and they were *d* unto one,
8.31 *d* us from the hand of the enemy,
36 they *d* the king's commissions
9. 7 our priests, been *d* into the hand
Est 6. 9 let this apparel and horse be *d*
Job 16.11 God hath *d* me to the ungodly,
22.30 *d* by the pureness of thine hands.
23. 7 I be *d* for ever from my judge
29.12 I *d* the poor that cried, and the
Ps 7. 4 have *d* him that without cause
18(T) the Lord *d* him from the hand
17 He *d* me from my strong enemy,
19 he *d* me, because be delighted in
43 hast *d* me from the strivings
48 *d* me from the violent man.
22. 5 They cried unto thee and were *d*:
33.16 a mighty man is not *d* by much
34. 4 and *d* me from all my fears.
54. 7 he hath *d* me out of all trouble:
55.18 He hath *d* my soul in peace
56.13 thou hast *d* my soul from death:
60. 5 That thy beloved may be *d*; save
69.14 me be *d* from them that hate me,
78.42 he *d* them from the enemy.
61 And *d* his strength into captivity,
81. 6 his hands were *d* from the pots.
7 calledst in trouble, and I *d* thee;
86.13 and thou hast *d* my soul from the
107. 6 he *d* them out of their distresses.
20 *d* them from their destructions.
108. 6 That thy beloved may be *d*: save
116. 8 thou hast *d* my soul from death,
Pr 11. 8 The righteous is *d* out of trouble,
9 knowledge shall the just be *d*.
21 seed of the righteous shall be *d*.
28.26 walketh wisely, he shall be *d*.
Ec 9.15 and he by his wisdom *d* the city;
Isa 20. 6 to be *d* from the king of Assyria:
29.12 And the book is *d* to him that is
34. 2 he hath *d* them to the slaughter.
36.15 this city shall not be *d* into the
18 the gods of the nations *d* his land
19 have they *d* Samaria out of my
20 that have *d* their land out of my
37.11 them utterly; and shalt thou be *d*?
12 Have the gods of the nations *d* them
38.17 hast in love to my soul *d* it from the
49.24 mighty, or the lawful captive *d*?
25 the prey of the terrible shall be *d*:
66. 7 came, she was *d* of a man child.
Jer 7.10 are *d* to do all these abominations?
20.13 he hath *d* the soul of the poor
32. 4 surely be *d* into the hand of the
16 when I had *d* the evidence of the
36 It shall be *d* into the hand of the
34. 3 shalt surely be taken, and *d* into
37.17 thou shalt be *d* into the hand of the
46.24 she shall be *d* into the hand of the
La 1.14 Lord hath *d* me into their hands,
Eze 3.19 iniquity; but thou hast *d* thy soul.
21 warned; also thou hast *d* thy soul.
14.16 they only shall be *d*, but the land
18 they only shall be *d* themselves.
16.21 and *d* them to cause them to pass
27 and *d* thee unto the will of them
17.15 he break the covenant, and be *d*?
23. 9 I have *d* her into the hand of her
31.11 I have therefore *d* him into the
14 they are all *d* unto death, to the
32.20 she is *d* to the sword: draw her
33. 9 iniquity; but thou hast *d* thy soul.
34.27 and *d* them out of the hand of those
Dan 3.28 hath sent his angel, and *d* his
6.27 who hath *d* Daniel form the power
12. 1 thy people shall be *d*, every one
Joel 2.32 the name of the Lord shall be *d*:
Am 1. 9 they *d* up the whole captivity to
9. 1 escapeth of them I shall not be *d*
Ob 14 neither shouldst thou have *d* up
Mic 4.10 there shalt thou be *d*; there the
Hab 2. 9 that he may be *d* from the power
Mal 3.15 they that tempt God are even *d*.
Mt 11.27 All things are *d* unto me of my
18.34 and *d* him to the tormentors, till
25.14 and *d* unto them his goods.
27. 2 and *d* him to Pontius Pilate the
18 that for envy they had *d* him.
26 Jesus, he *d* him to be crucified.
58 commanded the body to be *d*.
Mk 7.13 your tradition, which ye have *d*:
9.31 is *d* into the hands of men, and
10.33 the Son of man shall be *d* unto the
15. 1 him away, and *d* him to Pilate.
10 chief priests had *d* him for envy.
15 and *d* Jesus, when he had scourged
Lk 1. 2 Even as they *d* them unto us,
57 time came that she should be *d*;
74 that we being *d* out of the hand
2. 6 accomplished that she should be *d*.
4. 6 of them; for that is *d* unto me;
17 was *d* unto him the book of the
7.15 And he *d* him to his mother.
9.42 and *d* him again to his father.
44 Son of man shall be *d* into the
10.22 things are *d* to me of my Father.
12.58 that thou mayest be *d* from him;
18.32 For he shall be *d* unto the Gentiles,
19.13 *d* them ten pounds, and said unto
23.25 but he *d* Jesus to their will.
24. 7 must be *d* into the hands of sinful
20 and our rulers *d* him to be
Jn 16.21 as soon as she is *d* of the child,
18.30 we would not have *d* him up unto
35 chief priests have *d* thee unto me:
36 that I should not be *d* to the Jews:
19.11 therefore he that *d* me unto thee
16 Then *d* he him therefore unto
Ac 2.23 Him being *d* by the determinate
3.13 whom ye *d* up, and denied him
6.14 the customs which Moses *d* us.
7.10 And *d* him out of all his afflictions,
12. 4 and *d* him to four quaternions of
11 and hath *d* me out of the hand of
15.30 together, they *d* the epistle:
16. 4 *d* them the decrees for to keep
23.33 *d* the epistle to the governor,
27. 1 they *d* Paul and certain other
28.16 the centurion *d* the prisoners to
17 yet was I *d* prisoner from
Ro 4.25 Who was *d* for our offenses, and
6.17 form of doctrine which was *d* you.
7. 6 now we are *d* from the law,
8.21 shall be *d* from the bondage of
32 own Son, but *d* him up for us all,
15.31 That I may be *d* from them that
1Co 11. 2 ordinances, as I *d* them to you.
23 which also I *d* unto you, that the
15. 3 For I *d* unto you first of all that
24 when he shall have *d* up the
2Co 1.10 Who *d* us from so great a death,
4.11 are alway *d* unto death for Jesus'
Col 1.13 *d* us from the power of darkness,
1Th 1.10 Jesus which *d* us from the wrath
2Th 3. 2 we may be *d* from unreasonable
1Ti 1.20 whom I have *d* unto Satan, that
2Ti 3.11 out of them all the Lord *d* me.
4.17 was *d* out of the mouth of the lion.
Heb 11.11 and was *d* of a child when she
2Pe 2. 4 *d* them into chains of darkness,
7 And *d* just Lot, vexed with the
21 holy commandment *d* unto them.
Jude 3 faith which was once *d* unto the
Rev 12. 2 in birth, and pained to be *d*.
4 woman which was ready to be *d*,
20.13 death and hell *d* up the dead

DELIVEREDST

Neh 9.27 Therefore thou *d* them into the
Mt 25.20 Lord, thou *d* unto me five talents:
22 Lord, thou *d* unto me two talents:

DELIVERER

Jdg 3. 9 the Lord raised up a *d* to the
15 the Lord raised them up a *d*,
18.28 there was no *d*, because it was
2Sa 22. 2 rock, and my fortress, and my *d*;
Ps 18. 2 my fortress, and my *d*; my God,
40.17 thou art my help and my *d*; make
70. 5 thou art my help and my *d*; O Lord,
144. 2 my high tower, and my *d*; my
Ac 7.35 God send to be a ruler and a *d* by
Ro 11.26 shall come out of Sion the *D*,

DELIVERING

Lk 21.12 *d* you up to the synagogues, and
Ac 22. 4 and *d* into prisons both men and
26.17 *D* thee from the people, and from

DELUSION

2Th 2.11 God shall send them strong *d*.

DEMANDED

Ex 5.14 were beaten, and *d*, Wherefore
2Sa 11. 7 David *d* of him how Joab did,
Dan 2.27 The secret which the king hath *d*
Mt 2. 4 he *d* of them where Christ should
Lk 3.14 soldiers likewise *d* of him, saying,
17.20 when he was *d* of the Pharisees,
Ac 21.33 and *d* who he was, and what

DEMAS

Col 4.14 the beloved physician, and *D*,
2Ti 4.10 For *D* hath forsaken me, having
Phm 24 Marcus, Aristarchus, *D*, Lucas,

DEMETRIUS

Ac 19.24 For a certain man named *D*, a
38 Wherefore if *D*, and the craftsmen
3Jn 12 *D* hath good report of all men,

DEMONSTRATION

1Co 2. 4 in *d* of the Spirit and of power:

DEN

Ps 10. 9 in wait secretly as a lion in his *d*:
Isa 11. 8 his hand on the cockatrice' *d*.
Jer 7.11 a *d* of robbers in your eyes?
9.11 heaps, and a *d* of dragons; and I
10.22 desolate, and a *d* of dragons.

Dan 6. 7 shall be cast into the *d* of lions.
12 *d* of lions? The king answered
16 and cast him into the *d* of lions.
17 and laid upon the mouth of the *d*;
19 went in haste unto the *d* of lions.
20 when he came to the *d* he cried
23 should take Daniel up out of the *d*.
23 Daniel was taken up out of the *d*,
24 they cast them into the *d* of lions,
24 they came at the bottom of the *d*.
Am 3. 4 will a young lion cry out of his *d*,
Mt 21.13 but ye have made it a *d* of thieves.
Mk 11.17 but ye have made it a *d* of thieves.
Lk 19.46 but ye have made it a *d* of thieves.

DENIED

Gen 18.15 Sarah *d*, saying, I laughed not;
1Ki 20. 7 my gold; and I *d* him not.
Job 31.28 have *d* the God that is above.
Mt 26.70 he *d* before them all, saying,
72 again he *d* with an oath, I do not
Mk 14.68 But he *d*, saying, I know not,
70 And he *d* it again. And a little after,
Lk 8.45 When all *d*, Peter and they that
12. 9 be *d* before the angels of God.
22.57 he *d* him, saying, Woman, I know
Jn 1.20 he confessed, and *d* not; but
13.38 crow, till thou hast *d* me thrice.
18.25 He *d* it, and said, I am not.
27 Peter then *d* again: and
Ac 3.13 *d* him in the presence of Pilate,
14 ye *d* the Holy One and the Just,
1Ti 5. 8 he hath *d* the faith, and is worse
Rev 2.13 hast not *d* my faith, even in those
3. 8 word, and hast not *d* my name.

DENIETH

Lk 12. 9 he that *d* me before men shall be
1Jn 2.22 he that *d* that Jesus is the Christ?
22 that *d* the Father and the Son.
23 Whosoever *d* the Son, the same

DENS

Jdg 6. 2 of Israel made them the *d* which
Job 37. 8 Then the beasts go into *d*, and
38.40 When they couch in their *d*, and
Ps 104.22 and lay them down in their *d*.
SS 4. 8 from the lions *d*, from the
Isa 32.14 forts and towers shall be for *d*
Na 2.12 with prey, and his *d* with ravin.
Heb 11.38 and in *d* and caves of the earth
Rev 6.15 hid themselves in the *d* and in

DENY

Jos 24.27 unto you, lest ye *d* your God.
1Ki 2.16 one petition of thee, *d* me not.
Job 8.18 then it shall *d* him, saying, I have
Pr 30. 7 *d* me them not before I die:
9 be full, and *d* thee, and say, Who
Mt 10.33 whosoever shall *d* me before men,
33 him will I also *d* before my Father
16.24 come after me, let him *d* himself,
26.34 cock crow, thou shalt *d* me thrice.
35 die with thee, yet will I not *d* thee.
75 cock crow, thou shalt *d* me thrice.
Mk 8.34 let him *d* himself, and take up
14.30 crow twice, thou shalt *d* me thrice.
31 I will not *d* thee in any wise.
72 twice, thou shalt *d* me thrice.
Lk 9.23 come after me, let him *d* himself,
20.27 *d* that there is any resurrection;
22.34 thrice *d* that thou knowest me.
61 cock crow, thou shalt *d* me thrice.
Ac 4.16 Jerusalem; and we cannot *d* it.
2Ti 2.12 if we *d* him, he also will *d* us:
13 faithful: he cannot *d* himself.
Tit 1.16 but in works they *d* him, being

DENYING

2Ti 3. 5 of godliness, but *d* the power
Tit 2.12 *d* ungodliness and worldly lusts,
2Pe 2. 1 *d* the Lord that bought them,
Jude 4 *d* the only Lord God, and our Lord

DEPART

Gen 49.10 sceptre shall not *d* from Judah,
Dt 4. 9 lest they *d* from thy heart all the
Jos 1. 8 This book of the law shall not *d*
2Sa 7.15 mercy shall not *d* away from him,
22.23 statutes, I did not *d* from them.
Job 21.14 they say unto God, *D* from us;
22.17 Which said unto God, *D* from us:
28.28 to *d* from evil is understanding.
Ps 34.14 *D* from evil, and do good; seek
37.27 *D* from evil, and do good; and
119.115 *D* from me, ye evildoers: for I
Pr 3. 7 fear the Lord, and *d* from evil.
16.17 of the upright is to *d* from evil:
Isa 14.25 burden *d* from off their shoulders.
54.10 but my kindness shall not *d* from
Jer 6. 8 lest my soul *d* from thee; lest
Mt 7.23 *d* from me, ye that work iniquity.
10.14 ye *d* out of that house or city.
25.41 *D* from me, ye cursed, into
Mk 6.11 ye *d* thence, shake off the dust
Lk 2.29 lettest thou thy servant *d* in peace,
5. 8 saying, *D* from me; for I am a
13.27 *d* from me, all ye workers of
31 Get thee out, and *d* hence: for
Jn 7. 3 *D* hence, and go into Judea,
13. 1 that he should *d* out of this world
16. 7 but if I *d*, I will send him unto
Ac 1. 4 they should not *d* from Jerusalem
18. 2 all Jews to *d* from Rome:
22.21 *D*: for I will send thee far hence
1Co 7.10 not the wife *d* from her husband
11 she *d*, let her remain unmarried,
15 if the unbelieving *d*, let him *d*.
Php 1.23 having a desire to *d*, and to be
1Ti 4. 1 some shall *d* from the faith,
2Ti 2.19 name of Christ *d* from iniquity.
Jas 2.16 say unto them, *D* in peace, be ye

DEPARTED

Gen 26.31 and they *d* from him in peace.
31.40 and my sleep *d* from mine eyes.
Jdg 6.21 angel of the Lord *d* out of his
1Sa 4.21 saying, The glory is *d* from Israel:
22 is *d* from Israel: for the ark of God
16.14 the Spirit of the Lord *d* from Saul,
23 and the evil spirit *d* from him.
28.15 God is *d* from me, and answereth
16 seeing the Lord is *d* from thee,
2Ch 34.33 *d* not from following the Lord,
Neh 9.19 cloud *d* not from them by day,
Ps 119.102 have not *d* from thy judgments:
Mt 2. 9 they *d*; and, lo, the star, which
12 *d* into their own country another
13 when they were *d*, behold, the angel
14 mother by night, and *d* into Egypt:
28. 8 they *d* quickly from the sepulchre
Mk 1.42 the leprosy *d* from him, and he was
6.46 he *d* into a mountain to pray.
Lk 4.13 he *d* from him for a season.
10.30 him, *d*, leaving him half dead.
35 morrow when he *d*, he took out
Jn 6.15 *d* again into a mountain himself
Rev 6.14 the heaven *d* as a scroll when it is

DEPARTETH

Pr 14.16 A wise man feareth, and *d* from
Ec 6. 4 and *d* in darkness, and his name
Isa 59.15 and he that *d* from evil maketh
Jer 17. 5 and whose heart *d* from the Lord.
Lk 9.39 bruising him hardly *d* from him,

DEPARTING

Isa 59.13 *d* away from our God, speaking
Dan 9. 5 even by *d* from thy precepts and
11 transgressed thy law, even by *d*,
Mk 6.33 And the people saw them *d*, and
7.31 again, *d* from the coast of Tyre
Ac 13.13 John *d* from them returned to
20.29 I know this, that after my *d*
Heb 3.12 unbelief, in *d* from the living God.
11.22 the *d* of the children of Israel

DEPARTURE

Eze 26.18 the sea shall be troubled at thy *d*.
2Ti 4. 6 and the time of my *d* is at hand.

DEPTH

Job 28.14 The *d* saith, It is not in me:
38.16 walked in the search of the *d*?
Ps 33. 7 layeth up the *d* in storehouses.
Pr 8.27 compass upon the face of the *d*:
25. 3 for height, and the earth for *d*,
Isa 7.11 ask it either in the *d* or in the
Jon 2. 5 the *d* closed me round about, the
Mt 18. 6 were drowned in the *d* of the sea.
Mk 4. 5 because it had no *d* of earth:
Ro 8.39 Nor height, nor *d*, nor any other
11.33 O the *d* of the riches both of the
Eph 3.18 the breadth, and length, and *d*, and

DEPTHS

Ex 15. 5 The *d* have covered them; they
8 *d* were congealed in the heart
Dt 8. 7 of fountains and *d* that spring out
Ps 68.22 again from the *d* of the sea:
71.20 up again from the *d* of the earth.
77.16 afraid: the *d* also were troubled.
78.15 them drink as out of the great *d*.
106. 9 so he led them through the *d*,
107.26 they go down again to the *d*:
130. 1 Out of the *d* have I cried unto thee,
Pr 3.20 By his knowledge the *d* are
8.24 When there were no *d*, I was
9.18 her guests are in the *d* of hell.
Isa 51.10 that hath made the *d* of the sea
Eze 27.34 by the seas in the *d* of the waters
Mic 7.19 their sin into the *d* of the sea.
Rev 2.24 have not known the *d* of Satan,

DEPUTIES

Est 8. 9 the *d* and rulers of the provinces
9. 3 the *d* and officers of the king,
Ac 19.38 the law is open, and there are *d*:

DEPUTY

1Ki 22.47 no king in Edom: a *d* was king.
Ac 13. 7 was with the *d* of the country,
8 turn away the *d* from the faith.
12 Then the *d*, when he saw what
18.12 when Gallio was *d* of Achaia,

DERBE

Ac 14. 6 and fled unto Lystra and *D*,
20 he departed with Barnabas to *D*.
16. 1 Then came he to *D* and Lystra:
20. 4 and Secundus; and Gaius of *D*, and

DERIDED

Lu 16.14 all these things: and they *d* him.
23.35 the rulers also with them *d* him,

DERISION

Job 30. 1 are younger than I have me in *d*,
Ps 2. 4 the Lord shall have them in *d*.
44.13 a scorn and a *d* to them that are
59. 8 shalt have all the heathen in *d*.
79. 4 a scorn and *d* to them that are
119.51 proud have had me greatly in *d*:
Jer 20. 7 am in *d* daily, every one mocketh
8 a reproach unto me, and a *d*,
48.26 and he also shall be in *d*.
27 was not Israel a *d* unto thee?
39 so shall Moab be a *d* and a
La 3.14 I was a *d* to all my people;
Eze 23.32 laughed to scorn and had in *d*;
36. 4 which became a prey and *d* to the
Hos 7.16 shall be their *d* in the land of Egypt.

DESCEND
Nu 34.11 and the border shall *d*, and shall
1Sa 26.10 he shall *d* into battle, and perish.
Ps 49.17 his glory shall not *d* after him.
Isa 5.14 he that rejoiceth, shall *d* into it.
Eze 26.20 them that *d* into the pit, with the
31.16 them that *d* into the pit: and all
Mk 15.32 Let Christ the king of Israel *d*
Ac 11. 5 A certain vessel *d*, as it had been
Ro 10. 7 Or, Who shall *d* into the deep?
1Th 4.16 Lord himself shall *d* from heaven

DESCENDED
Ex 19.18 the Lord *d* upon it in fire: and
33. 9 the cloudy pillar *d*, and stood at
34. 5 And the Lord *d* in the cloud,
Dt 9.21 the brook that *d* out of the mount.
Jos 2.23 returned, and *d* from the mountain,
17. 9 And the coast *d* unto the river
18.13 the border *d* to Ataroth-adar,
16 and *d* to the valley of Hinnom,
16 south, and *d* to En-rogel,
17 and *d* to the stone of Bohan the
Ps 133. 3 *d* upon the mountains of Zion:
Pr 30. 4 ascended up into heaven, or *d*?
Mt 7.25, 27 And the rain *d*, and the floods
28. 2 for the angel of the Lord *d* from
Lk 3.22 the Holy Ghost *d* in a bodily shape
Ac 24. 1 the high priest *d* with the elders,
Eph 4. 9 but that he also *d* first into the
10 He that *d* is the same also that

DESCENDETH
Jas 3.15 This wisdom *d* not from above,

DESCENDING
Gen 28.12 angels of God ascending and *d*
Mt 3.16 Spirit of God *d* like a dove,
Mk 1.10 the Spirit like a dove *d* upon him
Jn 1.32 I saw the Spirit *d* from heaven
33 whom thou shalt see the Spirit *d*,
51 angels of God ascending and *d*
Ac 10.11 a certain vessel *d* unto him,
Rev 21.10 Jerusalem, *d* out of heaven from

DESCENT
Lk 19.37 at the *d* of the mount of Olives,
Heb 7. 3 without mother, without *d*,
6 whose *d* is not counted from

DESCRIBETH
Ro 4. 6 as David also *d* the blessedness
10. 5 Moses *d* the righteousness which

DESERT
Ex 3. 1 to the backside of the *d*, and
5. 3 three days' journey into the *d*,
19. 2 were come to the *d* of Sinai, and
23.31 and from the *d* unto the river:
Nu 20. 1 into the *d* of Zin in the first
27.14 in the *d* of Zin, in the strife of
33.16 removed from the *d* of Sinai, and
Dt 32.10 He found him in a *d* land, and
2Ch 26.10 he built towers in the *d*, and
Job 24. 5 wild asses in the *d*, go they forth
Ps 28. 4 hands; render to them their *d*.
78.40 and grieve him in the *d*!
102. 6 I am like an owl of the *d*.
106.14 and tempted God in the *d*.
Isa 13.21 beasts of the *d* shall lie there;
21. 1 burden of the *d* of the sea.
1 through; so it cometh from the *d*,
34.14 The wild beasts of the *d* shall
35. 1 the *d* shall rejoice, and blossom
6 break out, and streams in the *d*.
40. 3 make straight in the *d* a highway
41.19 I will set in the *d* the fir tree,
43.19 wilderness, and rivers in the *d*.
20 rivers in the *d*, to give drink to my
51. 3 her *d* like the garden of the Lord;
Jer 17. 6 like the heath in the *d*, and shall
25.24 people that dwell in the *d*,
50.12 wilderness, a dry land, and a *d*.
39 Therefore the wild beasts of the *d*
Eze 47. 8 go down into the *d*, and go into
Mt 14.13 by ship into a *d* place apart:
15 This is a *d* place, and the time is
24.26 Behold, he is in the *d*; go not
Mk 1.45 was without in *d* places: and they
6.31 yourselves apart into a *d* place,
32 they departed into a *d* place by
35 This is a *d* place, and now the
Lk 4.42 departed and went into a *d* place:
9.10 into a *d* place belonging to the
12 for we are here in a *d* place.
Jn 6.31 fathers did eat manna in the *d*;
Ac 8.26 Jerusalem unto Gaza, which is *d*.

DESERTS
Isa 48.21 he led them through the *d*: he
Jer 2. 6 a land of *d* and of pits,
Eze 7.27 and according to their *d* will I
13. 4 are like the foxes in the *d*.
Lk 1.80 and was in the *d* till the day of
Heb 11.38 wandered in *d*, and in mountains,

DESIRABLE
Eze 23. 6 rulers, all of them *d* young men,
12 riding upon horses, all of them *d*
23 *d* young men, captains and rulers,

DESIRE
Gen 3.16 thy *d* shall be to thy husband,
4. 7 unto thee shall be his *d*, and thou
Ex 10.11 serve the Lord; for that ye did *d*.
34.24 neither shall any man *d* thy land
Dt 5.21 shalt thou *d* thy neighbor's wife
7.25 shalt not *d* the silver or gold
18. 6 come with all the *d* of his mind
21.11 and hast a *d* unto her, that thou
Jdg 8 24 I would *d* a request of you,
1Sa 9.20 on whom is all the *d* of Israel?
23.20 according to all the *d* of thy soul
2Sa 23. 5 all my salvation, and all my *d*,
1Ki 2.20 I *d* one small petition of thee;
5. 8 I will do all thy *d* concerning
9 thou shalt accomplish my *d*, in
10 fir trees according to all his *d*.
9. 1 all Solomon's *d* which he was
11 according to all his *d*,) that then
10.13 unto the queen of Sheba all her *d*,
2Ki 4.28 Did I *d* a son of my lord?
2Ch 9.12 to the queen of Sheba all her *d*,
15.15 sought him with their whole *d*;
Neh 1.11 who *d* to fear thy name: and
Job 13. 3 and I *d* to reason with God.
14.15 thou wilt have a *d* to the work of
21.14 we *d* not the knowledge of thy
31.16 withheld the poor from their *d*.
35 my *d* is, that the Almighty would
33.32 speak, for I *d* to justify thee.
34.36 My *d* is that Job may be tried
36.20 *D* not the night, when people are
Ps 10. 3 wicked boasteth of his heart's *d*,
17 hast heard the *d* of the humble:
21. 2 Thou hast given him his heart's *d*,
38. 9 Lord, all my *d* is before thee:
40. 6 and offering thou didst not *d*;
45.11 shall the king greatly *d* thy beauty:
54. 7 mine eye hath seen his *d* upon mine
59.10 let me see my *d* upon mine enemies.
70. 2 put to confusion, that *d* my hurt.
73.25 upon earth that I *d* beside thee.
78.29 for he gave them their own *d*;
92.11 shall see my *d* upon mine enemies,
11 ears shall hear my *d* of the wicked
112. 8 he see his *d* upon his enemies.
10 the *d* of the wicked shall perish.
118. 7 therefore shall I see my *d* upon them
145.16 satisfiest the *d* of every living
19 He will fulfil the *d* of them that
Pr 3.15 all the things thou canst *d* are
10.24 but the *d* of the righteous shall
11.23 The *d* of the righteous is only good:
13.12 when the *d* cometh, it is a tree of
19 The *d* accomplished is sweet to
18. 1 Through *d* a man, having separated
19.22 The *d* of a man is his kindness:
21.25 The *d* of the slothful killeth him;
23. 6 neither *d* thou his dainty meats:
24. 1 men, neither *d* to be with them.
Ec 6. 9 than the wandering of the *d*:
12. 5 be a burden, and *d* shall fail:
SS 7.10 beloved's, and his *d* is toward me.
Isa 26. 8 the *d* of our soul is to thy name,
53. 2 no beauty that we should *d* him.
Jer 22.27 whereunto they *d* to return,
42.22 the place whither ye *d* to go
44.14 which they have a *d* to return
Eze 24.16 away from thee the *d* of thine
21 strength, the *d* of your eyes,
25 of their glory, the *d* of their eyes,
Dan 2.18 That they would *d* mercies of the
11.37 nor the *d* of women, nor regard
Hos 10.10 It is in my *d* that I should chastise
Am 5.18 Woe unto you that *d* the day of
Mic 7. 3 he uttereth his mischievous *d*:
Hab 2. 5 who enlargeth his *d* as hell, and
Hag 2. 7 the *d* of all nations shall come:
Mk 9.35 If any man *d* to be first,
10.35 do for us whatsoever we shall *d*.
11.24 What things soever ye *d*, when
15. 8 began to *d* him to do as he had
Lk 17.22 ye shall *d* to see one of the days
20.46 the scribes, which *d* to walk in
22.15 With *d* I have desired to eat this
Ac 23.20 The Jews have agreed to *d* thee
28.22 we *d* to hear of thee what thou
Ro 10. 1 Brethren, my heart's *d* and prayer
15.23 having a great *d* these many
1Co 14. 1 and *d* spiritual gifts, but rather
2Co 7. 7 he told us your earnest *d*, your
11 yea, what vehement *d*, yea, what
11.12 from them which *d* occasion;
12. 6 For though I would *d* to glory,
Gal 4. 9 ye *d* again to be in bondage?
20 I *d* to be present with you now,
21 Tell me, ye that *d* to be under the
6.12 As may as *d* to make a fair shew
13 but *d* to have you circumcised,
Eph 3.13 I *d* that ye faint not at my
Php 1.23 having a *d* to depart, and to be
4.17 Not because I *d* a gift:
17 but I *d* fruit that may abound
Col 1. 9 and to *d* that ye might be filled
1Th 2.17 to see your face with great *d*.
1Ti 3. 1 If a man *d* the office of a bishop,
Heb 6.11 And we *d* that every one of you
11.16 But now they *d* a better country,
Jas 4. 2 kill, and *d* to have, and cannot
1Pe 1.12 which things the angels *d* to look
2. 2 *d* the sincere milk of the word,
Rev 9. 6 and shall *d* to die, and death shall

DESIRED
Gen 3. 6 and a tree to be *d* to make one
1Sa 12.13 chosen, and whom ye have *d*!
1Ki 9.19 that which Solomon *d* to build in
2Ch 8. 6 all that Solomon *d* to build in
11.23 And he *d* many wives.
21.20 and departed without being *d*.
Est 2.13 whatsoever she *d* was given her
Job 20.20 shall not save of that which he *d*.
Ps 19.10 More to be *d* are they than gold,
27. 4 One thing have I *d* of the Lord,
107.30 bringeth them unto their *d* haven.
132.13 he hath *d* it for his habitation.
14 here will I dwell; for I have *d* it.
Pr 8.11 all the things that may be *d* are
21.20 There is treasure to be *d* and oil
Ec 2.10 whatsoever mine eyes *d* I kept
Isa 1.29 the oaks which ye have *d*, and ye
26. 9 With my soul have I *d* thee

Jer 17.16 neither have I *d* the woeful day;
Dan 2.16 Daniel went in, and *d* of the king
23 known unto me now what we *d*
Hos 6. 6 For I *d* mercy, and not sacrifice
Mic 7. 1 my soul *d* the first ripe fruit
Zep 2. 1 gather together, O nation not *d*;
Mt 13.17 righteous men have *d* to see those
16. 1 *d* him that he would shew them
Mk 15. 6 one prisoner, whomsoever they *d*.
Lk 7.36 And one of the Pharisees *d* him
9. 9 things? And he *d* to see him.
10.24 prophets and kings have *d* to see
22.15 With desire I have *d* to eat this
31 Satan hath *d* to have you, that
23.25 into prison, whom they had *d*;
Jo 12.21 *d* him, saying, Sir, we would see
Ac 3.14 the Just, and *d* a murderer to
7.46 *d* to find a tabernacle for the God
8.31 And he *d* Philip that he would
9. 2 *d* of him letters to Damascus to
12.20 their friend, *d* peace; because
13. 7 and *d* to hear the word of God.
21 afterward they *d* a king: and
28 yet *d* they Pilate that he should
16.39 them out, and *d* them to depart
18.20 When they *d* him to tarry longer
25. 3 *d* favor against him, that he
28.14 and were *d* to tarry with them
1Co 16.12 Apollos, I greatly *d* him to come
2Co 8. 6 Insomuch that we *d* Titus, that
12.18 I *d* Titus, and with him I sent
1Jn 5.15 the petitions that we *d* of him.

DESIREDST
Dt 18.16 According to all that thou *d* of the
Mt 18.32 all that debt, because thou *d* me:

DESIRES
Ps 37. 4 give thee the *d* of thine heart.
140. 8 Grant not, O Lord, the *d* of the
Eph 2. 3 fulfilling the *d* of the flesh and of

DESIREST
Ps 51. 6 thou *d* truth in the inward parts:
16 For thou *d* not sacrifice; else

DESIRETH
Dt 14.26 or for whatsoever thy soul *d*:
1Sa 2.16 take as much as thy soul *d*;
18.25 The king *d* not any dowry,
20. 4 Whatsoever thy soul *d*,
2Sa 3.21 reign over all that thine heart *d*.
1Ki 11.37 according to all that thy soul *d*,
Job 7. 2 As a servant earnestly *d* the
23.13 what his soul *d*, even that he
Ps 34.12 What man is he that *d* life,
68.16 the hill which God *d* to dwell in;
Pr 12.12 The wicked *d* the net of evil men:
13. 4 The soul of the sluggard *d*, and
21.10 The soul of the wicked *d* evil:
Ec 6. 2 for his soul of all that he *d*,
Lk 5.39 drunk old wine straightway *d* new:
14.32 and *d* conditions of peace.
1Ti 3. 1 of a bishop, he *d* a good work.

DESIRING
Mt 12.46 without, *d* to speak with him.
47 without, *d* to speak with thee.
20.20 and *d* a certain thing of him.
Lk 8.20 stand without, *d* to see thee.
16.21 *d* to be fed with the crumbs
Ac 9.38 *d* him that he would not delay
19.31 *d* him that he would not
25.15 *d* to have judgment against him.
2Co 5. 2 earnestly *d* to be clothed upon
1Th 3. 6 *d* greatly to see us, as we also
1Ti 1. 7 *D* to be teachers of the law;
2Ti 1. 4 Greatly *d* to see thee, being

DESIROUS
Pr 23. 3 Be not *d* of his dainties: for they
Lk 23. 8 for he was *d* to see him a long

BIBLICAL THEMES

DESIRE

When the woman saw that the tree was good for food, and that it was pleasant to the eyes, and a tree to be desired to make one wise, she took of the fruit thereof, and did eat. Gen 3.6

And they said, Go to, let us build us a city and a tower, whose top may reach unto heaven; and let us make us a name. Gen 11.4

Oh that one would hear me! behold, my desire is, that the Almighty would answer me. Job 31.35

Thou hast given him his heart's desire, and hast not withholden the request of his lips. Ps 21.2

One thing have I desired of the Lord, that will I seek after; that I may dwell in the house of the Lord all the days of my life, to behold the beauty of the Lord, and to inquire in his temple. Ps 27.4

O God, thou art my God; early will I seek thee: my soul thirsteth for thee, my flesh longeth for thee in a dry and thirsty land, where no water is. Ps 63.1

Thou openest thine hand, and satisfiest the desire of every living thing. Ps 145.16

Hope deferred maketh the heart sick: but when the desire cometh, it is a tree of life. Pr 13.12

Wisdom is before him that hath understanding; but the eyes of a fool are in the ends of the earth. Pr 17.24

How art thou fallen from heaven, O Lucifer, son of the morning! . . . For thou hast said in thine heart, I will ascend into heaven, I will exalt my throne above the stars of God. . . . I will be like the most High. Yet thou shalt be brought down to hell. Isa 14.12-15

Ask, and it shall be given you; seek, and ye shall find; knock, and it shall be opened unto you. . . . all things whatsoever ye would that men should do to you, do ye even so to them. Mt 7.7, 12

He . . . called the twelve, and saith unto them, If any man desire to be first, the same shall be last of all, and servant of all. Mk 9.35

He that glorieth, let him glory in the Lord. 1Co 1.31

Who maketh thee to differ from another? and what hast thou that thou didst not receive? 1Co 4.7

Follow after charity, and desire spiritual gifts. 1Co 14.1

There was given to me a thorn in the flesh, the messenger of Satan to buffet me, lest I should be exalted above measure. For this thing I besought the Lord thrice, that it might depart from me. And he said unto me, My grace is sufficient for thee. 2Co 12.7-9

Let us not be desirous of vain glory, provoking one another, envying one another. Gal 5.26

Brethren, I count not myself to have apprehended: but this one thing I do, forgetting those things which are behind, and reaching forth unto those things which are before, I press toward the mark for the prize of the high calling of God in Christ Jesus. Php 3.13-14

Set your affection on things above, not on things on the earth. Col 3.2

All that is in the world, the lust of the flesh, and the lust of the eyes, and the pride of life, is not of the Father, but is of the world. 1Jn 2.16

Jn 16.19 they were *d* to ask him, and said
2Co 11.32 garrison, *d* to apprehend me:
Gal 5.26 Let us not be *d* of vain glory,
1Th 2. 8 So being affectionately *d* of you,

DESOLATE
Gen 47.19 not die, that the land be not *d*.
Ex 23.29 lest the land become *d*, and the
Lev 26.22 and your high ways shall be *d*.
33 your land shall be *d*, and your
34 as long as it lieth *d*, and ye be in
35 As long as it lieth *d*, it shall rest;
43 while she lieth *d* without them:
2Sa 13.20 Tamar remained *d* in her brother
2Ch 36.21 as long as she lay *d*, she kept
Job 3.14 built *d* place for themselves;
15.28 he dwelleth in *d* cities, and in
34 of hypocrites shall be *d*, and fire
16. 7 hast made *d* all my company.
30. 3 in former time *d* and waste.
38.27 satisfy the *d* and waste ground,
Ps 25.16 upon me; for I am *d* and afflicted.
34.21 hate the righteous shall be *d*.
22 them that trust in him shall be *d*.
40.15 Let them be *d* for a reward of
69.25 Let their habitation be *d*; and
109.10 bread also out of their *d* places.
143. 4 me; my heart within me is *d*.
Isa 1. 7 Your country is *d*, your cities are
7 in your presence, and it is *d*,
3.26 being *d* shall sit upon the ground.
5. 9 many houses shall be *d*, even

Isa 6.11 and the land be utterly *d*,
7.19 all of them in the *d* valleys,
13. 9 fierce anger, to lay the land *d*:
22 shall cry in their *d* houses,
15. 6 the waters of Nimrim shall be *d*:
24. 6 they that dwell therein are *d*:
27.10 the defensed city shall be *d*,
49. 8 cause to inherit the *d* heritages;
19 thy waste and thy *d* places, and
21 children, and am *d*, a captive,
54. 1 the children of the *d* than the
3 make the *d* cities to be inhabited.
59.10 we are in *d* places as dead men.
62. 4 thy land any more be termed *D*:
Jer 2.12 be ye very *d*, saith the Lord.
4. 7 his place to make thy land *d*;
27 The whole land shall be *d*; yet
6. 8 lest I make thee *d*, a land not
7.34 bride: for the land shall be *d*.
9.11 will make the cities of Judah *d*,
10.22 to make the cities of Judah *d*,
25 and have made his habitation *d*.
12.10 pleasant portion a *d* wilderness.
11 They have made it *d*, and
11 being *d* it mourneth unto me;
11 the whole land is made *d*, because
18.16 To make their land *d*, and a
19. 8 I will make this city *d*, and an
25.38 for their land is *d* because of
26. 9 this city shall be *d* without an
32.43 It is *d* without man or beast;
33.10 which ye say shall be *d* without
10 streets of Jerusalem, that are *d*,
12 Again in this place, which is *d*
44. 6 they are wasted and *d*, as at
46.19 for Noph shall be waste and *d*
48. 9 for the cities thereof shall be *d*,
34 waters also of Nimrim shall be *d*.
49. 2 it shall be a *d* heap, and her
20 shall make their habitations *d*
50. 3 shall make her land *d*, and none
13 but it shall be wholly *d*:
45 he shall make their habitation *d*
51.26 but thou shalt be *d* for ever,
62 but that it shall be *d* for ever.
La 1. 4 feasts: all her gates are *d*: and
13 made me *d* and faint all the day.
16 my children are *d*, because the
3.11 in pieces: he hath made me *d*.
4. 5 They that did feed delicately are *d*
5.18 the mountain of Zion, which is *d*,
Eze 6. 4 And your altars shall be *d*, and
6 the high places shall be *d*; that
6 may be laid waste and made *d*,
14 and make the land *d*, yea,
14 more *d* than the wilderness
12.19 that her land may be *d* from all
20 waste, and the land shall be *d*;
14.15 spoil it, so that it be *d*,
16 delivered, but the land shall be *d*.
15. 8 I will make the land *d*, because
19. 7 he knew their *d* places, and he
7 their cities; and the land was *d*,
20.26 that I might make them *d*, to the
25. 3 land of Israel, when it was *d*;
13 I will make it *d* from Teman;
26.19 I shall make thee a *d* city,
20 of the earth, in places *d* of old,
29. 9 the land of Egypt shall be *d*
10 of Egypt utterly waste and *d*,
12 I will make the land of Egypt *d*
12 midst of the countries that are *d*,
12 laid waste shall be *d* forty years:
30. 7 they shall be *d* in the midst of
7 midst of the countries that are *d*,
14 And I will make Pathros *d*, and
32.15 I shall make the land of Egypt *d*,
33.28 For I will lay the land most *d*,
28 mountains of Israel shall be *d*,
29 when I have laid the land most *d*
35. 3 I will make thee most *d*.
4 cities waste, and thou shalt be *d*,
7 will I make mount Seir most *d*,
12 They are laid *d*, they are given
14 rejoiceth, I will make thee *d*.
15 house of Israel, because it was *d*,
15 I do unto thee: thou shalt be *d*,
36. 3 Because they have made you *d*,
4 to the valleys, to the *d* wastes,
34 And the *d* land shall be tilled,
34 whereas it lay *d* in the sight
35 This land that was *d* is become
35 waste and *d* and ruined cities
36 places, and plant that that was *d*:
38.12 thine hand upon the *d* places
Dan 9.17 upon thy sanctuary that is *d*,
27 he shall make it *d*, even until the
27 shall be poured upon the *d*.
11.31 the abomination that maketh *d*.
12.11 abomination that maketh *d* set up,
Hos 5. 9 Ephraim shall be *d* in the day
13.16 Samaria shall become *d*; for she
Joel 1.17 the garners are laid *d*, the barns
18 the flocks of sheep are made *d*.
2. 3 behind them a *d* wilderness;
20 him into a land barren and *d*,
3.19 and Edom shall be a *d* wilderness,
Am 7. 9 high places of Isaac shall be *d*,
Mic 1. 7 the idols thereof will I lay *d*:
6.13 making thee *d* because of thy sins.
7.13 land shall be *d* because of them
Zep 3. 6 their towers are *d*; I made their
Zec 7.14 the land was *d* after them, that
14 for they laid the pleasant land *d*.
Mal 1. 4 return and build the *d* places;
Mt 23.38 your house is left unto you *d*.
Lk 13.35 your house is left unto you *d*:
Ac 1.20 Let his habitation be *d*, and let
Gal 4.27 the *d* hath many more children
1Ti 5. 5 that is a widow indeed, and *d*,
Rev 17.16 shall make her *d* and naked,
18.19 for in one hour is she made *d*.

DESPAIR

1Sa 27. 1 and Saul shall *d* of me, to seek
Ec 2.20 my heart to *d* of all the labor
2Co 4. 8 we are perplexed, but not in *d*;

DESPAIRED

2Co 1. 8 insomuch that we *d* even of life:

DESPISE

Lev 26.15 if ye shall *d* my statutes, or if
1Sa 2.30 and they that *d* me shall be lightly
2Sa 19.43 why then did ye *d* us, that our
Est 1.17 that they shall *d* their husbands
Job 5.17 *d* not thou the chastening of the
9.21 my soul: I would *d* my life.
10. 3 shouldst *d* the work of thine hands,
31.13 did *d* the cause of my manservant
Ps 51.17 heart, O God, thou wilt not *d*.
73.20 awakest, thou shalt *d* their image.
102.17 destitute, and not *d* their prayer.
Pr 1. 7 fools *d* wisdom and instruction.
3.11 *d* not the chastening of the Lord;
6.30 Men do not *d* a thief, if he steal
23. 9 he will *d* the wisdom of thy words.
22 *d* not thy mother when she is old.
Isa 30.12 Because ye *d* this word, and trust
Jer 4.30 thy lovers will *d* thee, they
23.17 They say still unto them that *d*
La 1. 8 all that honored her *d* her,
Eze 16.57 of the Philistines, which *d* thee
28.26 upon all those that *d* them
Am 5.21 I hate, I *d* your feast days, and I
Mal 1. 6 you, O priests, that *d* my name.
Mt 6.24 hold to the one, and *d* the other.
18.10 ye *d* not one of these little ones;
Lk 16.13 hold to the one, and *d* the other.
Ro 14. 3 Let not him that eateth *d* him
1Co 11.22 or *d* ye the church of God,
16.11 Let no man therefore *d* him:
1Th 5.20 *D* not prophesyings. Prove all
1Ti 4.12 Let no man *d* thy youth; but be
6. 2 masters, let them not *d* them,
Tit 2.15 authority. Let no man *d* thee.
Heb 12. 5 *d* not thou the chastening of
2Pe 2.10 uncleanness, and *d* government.
Jude 8 *d* dominion, and speak evil of

DESPISED

Gen 16. 4 her mistress was *d* in her eyes.
5 conceived, I was *d* in her eyes:
25.34 way: thus Esau *d* his birthright.
Lev 26.43 because they *d* my judgments,
Nu 11.20 ye have *d* the Lord which is
14.31 know the land which ye have *d*.
15.31 he hath *d* the word of the Lord,
Jdg 9.38 this the people that thou hast *d*?
1Sa 10.27 And they *d* him, and brought him
2Sa 6.16 and she *d* him in her heart.
12. 9 *d* the commandment of the Lord,
10 because thou hast *d* me, and hast
2Ki 19.21 the daughter of Zion hath *d* thee,
1Ch 15.29 and she *d* him in her heart.
2Ch 36.16 and *d* his words, and misused his
Neh 2.19 and *d* us, and said, What is this
4. 4 Hear, O our God; for we are *d*:
Job 12. 5 a lamp *d* in the thought of him
19.18 young children *d* me; I arose,
Ps 22. 6 of men, and *d* of the people.
24 not *d* nor abhorred the afflictions
53. 5 because God hath *d* them.
106.24 Yea, they *d* the pleasant land,
119.141 I am small and *d*: yet do not I
Pr 1.30 counsel: they *d* all my reproof.
5.12 and my heart *d* reproof;
12. 8 is of a perverse heart shall be *d*.
9 He that is *d*, and hath a servant,
Ec 9.16 the poor man's wisdom is *d*,
SS 8. 1 kiss thee; yea, I should not be *d*.
Isa 5.24 *d* the word of the Holy One of
33. 8 he hath *d* the cities, he regardeth
37.22 *d* thee, and laughed thee to scorn;
53. 3 He is *d* and rejected of men; a
3 he was *d*, and we esteemed him not.
60.14 all they that *d* thee shall bow
Jer 22.28 Is this man Conaiah a *d* broken idol?
33.24 they have *d* my people, that they
49.15 the heathen, and *d* among men.
La 2. 6 *d* in the indignation of his anger
Eze 16.59 hast *d* the oath in breaking the
17.16 oath he *d*, and whose covenant
18 Seeing he *d* the oath by breaking
19 surely mine oath that he hath *d*,
20.13 they *d* my judgments, which if
16 they *d* my judgments, and walked
24 *d* my statutes, and had polluted
22. 8 Thou hast *d* mine holy things,
28.24 round about them, that *d* them;
Am 2. 4 they have *d* the law of the Lord,
Ob 2 the heathen: thou art greatly *d*.
Zec 4.10 hath *d* the day of small things?
Mal 1. 6 Wherein have we *d* thy name?
Lk 18. 9 were righteous, and *d* others:
Ac 19.27 Diana should be *d*,
1Co 1.28 things which are *d*, hath God
4.10 ye are honorable, but we are *d*.
Gal 4.14 in my flesh ye *d* not, nor rejected;
Heb 10.28 He that *d* Moses' law died without
Jas 2. 6 But ye have *d* the poor. Do not

DESPISERS

Ac 13.41 Behold, ye *d*, and wonder, and
2Ti 3. 3 fierce, *d* of those that are good,

DESPISEST

Ro 2. 4 *d* thou the riches of his goodness

DESPISETH

Job 36. 5 God is mighty, and *d* not any:
Ps 69.33 the poor, and *d* not his prisoners.
Pr 11.12 void of wisdom *d* his neighbor:

13.13 Whoso *d* the word shall be
14. 2 that is perverse in his ways *d* him.
21 He that *d* his neighbor sinneth:
15. 5 A fool *d* his father's instruction:
20 but a foolish man *d* his mother.
32 refuseth instruction *d* his own
19.16 but he that *d* his ways shall die.
30.17 father, and *d* to obey his mother,
Isa 33.15 he that *d* the gain of oppressions,
49. 7 to him whom man *d*, to him whom
Lk 10.16 he that *d* you *d* me;
16 and he that *d* me *d* him that sent
1Th 4. 8 He therefore that *d*, *d* not man,

DESPISING
Heb 12. 2 the cross, *d* the shame, and is

DESPITE
Eze 25. 6 rejoiced in heart with all thy *d*
Heb 10.29 and hath done *d* unto the Spirit

DESPITEFUL
Eze 25.15 taken vengeance with a *d* heart,
36. 5 with *d* minds, to cast it out for
Ro 1.30 Backbiters, haters of God, *d*,

DESPITEFULLY
Mt 5.44 pray for them which *d* use you,
Lk 6.28 pray for them which *d* use you.
Ac 14. 5 to use them *d*, and to stone them,

DESTITUTE
Gen 24.27 not left *d* my master of his mercy
Ps 102.17 will regard the prayer of the *d*,
141. 8 is my trust; leave not my soul *d*.
Pr 15.21 joy to him that is *d* of wisdom:
Eze 32.15 and the country shall be *d* of that
1Ti 6. 5 corrupt minds and *d* of the truth,
Heb 11.37 being *d*, afflicted, tormented;
Jas 2.15 be naked, and *d* of daily food,

DESTROY
Gen 6. 7 And the Lord said, I will *d* man
13 I will *d* them with the earth.
17 to *d* all flesh, wherein is the breath
7. 4 that I have made will I *d* from off
9.11 more be a flood to *d* the earth.
15 more become a flood to *d* all flesh.
18.23 *d* the righteous with the wicked?
24 wilt thou also *d* and not spare
28 thou *d* all the city for lack of five?
28 there forty and five, I will not *d* it.
31 I will not *d* it for twenty's sake.
32 I will not *d* it for ten's sake.
19.13 we will *d* this place, because the
13 the Lord hath sent us to *d* it.
14 place; for the Lord will *d* this city.
Ex 8. 9 to *d* the frogs from thee and thy
12.13 be upon you to *d* you, when I
15. 9 my sword, my hand shall *d* them.
23.27 *d* all the people to whom thou
34.13 But ye shall *d* their altars,
Lev 23.20 same soul will I *d* from among his
26.22 *d* your cattle, and make you few
30 And I will *d* your high places,
44 to *d* them utterly, and to break
Nu 21. 2 then I will utterly *d* their cities.
24.17 and *d* all the children of Sheth.
19 and shall *d* him that remaineth
32.15 and ye shall *d* all this people.
33.52 before you, and *d* all their pictures,
52 and *d* all their molten images,
Dt 1.27 hand of the Amorites, to *d* us.
2.15 to *d* them from among the host,
4.31 *d* thee, nor forget the covenant of
6.15 and *d* thee from off the face of
7. 2 smite them, and utterly *d* them;
4 against you, and *d* thee suddenly.
5 ye shall *d* their altars, and break
10 hate him to their face, to *d* them:
23 and shall *d* them with a mighty
24 thou shalt *d* their name from
9. 3 a consuming fire he shall *d* them,
3 thou drive them out, and *d* them
14 Let me alone, that I may *d* them,
19 was wroth against you to *d* you.
25 the Lord had said he would *d* you.
26 God, *d* not thy people and thine
10.10 and the Lord would not *d* thee.
12. 2 Ye shall utterly *d* all the places,
3 and *d* the names of them out of
20.17 But thou shalt utterly *d* them;
19 shalt not *d* the trees thereof by
20 thou shalt *d* and cut them down;
28.63 Lord will rejoice over you to *d* you,
31. 3 *d* these nations from before thee,
32.25 shall *d* both the young man and
33.27 thee; and shall say, *D* them.
Jos 7. 7 hand of the Amorites, to *d* us?
12 *d* the accursed from among you.
9.24 to *d* all the inhabitants of the land
11.20 that he might *d* them utterly,
20 favor, but that he might *d* them,
22.33 *d* the land wherein the children
Jdg 6. 5 they entered into the land to *d* it.
21.11 Ye shall utterly *d* every male,
1Sa 15. 3 smite Amalek, and utterly *d* all
6 the Amalekites, lest I *d* you with
9 and would not utterly *d* them:
18 *d* the sinners the Amalekites,
23.10 to *d* the city for my sake.
24.21 that thou wilt not *d* my name
26. 9 *D* him not; for who can stretch
15 came one of the people in to *d* the
2Sa 1.14 hand to *d* the Lord's anointed?
14. 7 and we will *d* the heir also:
11 revengers of blood to *d* any more,
11 lest they *d* my son. And he said,
16 the man that would *d* me and my
20.19 seekest to *d* a city and a mother
20 that I should swallow up or *d*.
22.41 I might *d* them that hate me.
24.16 his hand upon Jerusalem to *d* it,
1Ki 9.21 also were not able utterly to *d* it,
13.34 and to *d* it from off the face of the
16.12 did Zimri *d* all the house Baasha,
2Ki 8.19 Yet the Lord would not *d* Judah
10.19 he might *d* the worshippers of Baal
13.23 would not *d* them, neither cast
18.25 Lord against this place to *d* it?
25 Go up against this land, and *d* it.
24. 2 sent them against Judah to *d* it,
1Ch 21.15 an angel unto Jerusalem to *d* it:
2Ch 12. 7 I will not *d* them, but I will grant
12 he would not *d* him altogether:
20.23 Seir, utterly to slay and *d* them:
23 every one helped to *d* another,
21. 7 would not *d* the house of David,
25.16 God hath determined to *d* thee,
35.21 who is with me, that he *d* thee not.
Ezr 6.12 *d* all kings and people, that shall
12 to alter and to *d* this house of God
Est 3. 6 Haman sought to *d* all the Jews
13 to *d*, to kill, and to cause to perish,
4. 7 treasuries for the Jews, to *d* them.
8 was given at Shushan to *d* them,
8. 5 which he wrote to *d* the Jews which
11 *d*, to slay, and to cause to perish,
9.24 devised against the Jews to *d* them,
24 to consume them, and to *d* them;
Job 2. 3 him, to *d* him without cause.
6. 9 it would please God to *d* me;
8.18 If he *d* him from his place,
10. 8 round about; yet thou dost *d* me.
19.26 my skin worms *d* this body,
Ps 5. 6 shalt *d* them that speak leasing:
10 *D* thou them, O God; let them
18.40 I might *d* them that hate me.
21.10 fruit shalt thou *d* from the earth,
28. 5 *d* them, and not build them up.
40.14 that seek after my soul to *d* it;
52. 5 God shall likewise *d* thee for ever,
55. 9 *D*, O Lord, and divide their
63. 9 those that seek my soul, to *d* it,
69. 4 they that would *d* me, being
74. 8 Let us *d* them together: they
101. 8 early *d* all the wicked of the land;
106.23 he would *d* them, had not Moses
23 his wrath, lest he should *d* them.
34 They did not *d* the nations,
118.10, 11, 12 of the Lord will I *d* them.
119.95 wicked have waited for me to *d* me:
143.12 and *d* all them that afflict my soul:
144. 6 out thine arrows, and *d* them.
145.20 but all the wicked will he *d*.
Pr 1.32 the prosperity of fools shall *d* them.
11. 3 of transgressors shall *d* them.
15.25 will *d* the house of the proud:
21. 7 of the wicked shall *d* them;
Ec 5. 6 and *d* the work of thine hands?
7.16 why shouldest thou *d* thyself?
Isa 3.12 and *d* the way of thy paths.
10. 7 *d* and cut off nations not a few.
11. 9 shall not hurt nor *d* in all my
15 Lord shall utterly *d* the tongue of
13. 5 indignation, to *d* the whole land.
9 *d* the sinners thereof out of it.
19. 3 and I will *d* the counsel thereof:
23.11 city, to *d* the strong holds thereof.
25. 7 And he will *d* in this mountain
32. 7 wicked devices to *d* the poor with
36.10 Lord against this land to *d* it?
10 Go up against this land, and *d* it.
42.14 I will *d* and devour at once.
51.13 as if he were ready to *d*?
54.16 I have created the waster to *d*.
65. 8 *D* it not; for a blessing is in it:
8 sakes, that I may not *d* them all.
25 They shall not hurt nor *d* in all my
Jer 1.10 to pull down, and to *d*, and to
5.10 Go ye up upon her walls, and *d*;
6. 5 by night, and let us *d* her palaces.
11.19 Let us *d* the tree with the fruit
12.17 pluck up and *d* that nation,
13.14 nor have mercy, but *d* them.
15. 3 of the earth, to devour and *d*.
6 my hand against thee, and *d* thee;
7 I will *d* my people, since they return
17.18 *d* them with double destruction.
18. 7 to pull down, and to *d* it;
23. 1 Woe be unto the pastors that *d* and
25. 9 utterly *d* them, and make them
31.28 break down, and to *d*, and to afflict;
36.29 certainly come and *d* this land,
46. 8 I will *d* the city and the inhabitants
48.18 and he shall *d* thy strong holds.
49. 9 they will *d* till they have enough.
38 and will *d* from thence the king
50.21 waste and utterly *d* after them,
26 her up as heaps, and *d* her utterly:
51. 3 men, *d* ye utterly all her host.
11 device is against Babylon, to *d* it;
20 and with thee will I *d* kingdoms;
La 2. 8 Lord hath purposed to *d* the wall
3.66 Persecute and *d* them in anger
Eze 5.16 and which I will send to *d* you:
6. 3 and I will *d* your high places.
9. 8 wilt thou *d* all the residue of Israel
14. 9 and will *d* him from the midst
21.31 of brutish men, and skilful to *d*.
22.27 to shed blood, and to *d* souls,
30 the land, that I should not *d* it;
25. 7 I will *d* thee; and thou shalt know
15 heart, to *d* it for the old hatred;
16 and *d* the remnant of the sea coast.
26. 4 they shall *d* the walls of Tyrus,
12 walls, and *d* thy pleasant houses:
28.16 I will *d* thee; O covering cherub,
30.11 shall be brought to *d* the land:
13 I will also *d* the idols, and I will
32.13 I will *d* also all the beasts thereof
34.16 I will *d* the fat and the strong;
43. 3 saw when I came to *d* the city:

Dan 2.12 to *d* all the wise men of Babylon.
24 to *d* the wise men of Babylon.
24 *D* not the wise men of Babylon:
4.23 Hew the tree down, and *d* it;
7.26 consume and to *d* it unto the end.
8.24 *d* wonderfully, and shall prosper,
24 *d* the mighty and the holy people.
25 heart, and by peace shall *d* many:
9.26 shall *d* the city and the sanctuary;
11.26 portion of his meat shall *d* him,
44 shall go forth with great fury to *d*,
Hos 2.12 will *d* her vines and her fig trees,
4. 5 the night, and I will *d* thy mother
11. 9 I will not return to *d* Ephraim:
Am 9. 8 and I will *d* it from off the face of
8 I will not utterly *d* the house of
Ob 8 even *d* the wise men out of Edom,
Mic 2.10 it is polluted, it shall *d* you,
5.10 of thee, and I will *d* thy chariots:
14 of thee: so will I *d* thy cities.
Zep 2. 5 the Philistines, I will even *d* thee,
13 against the north, and *d* Assyria;
Hag 2.22 *d* the strength of the kingdoms
Zec 12. 9 seek to *d* all the nations that come
Mal 3.11 he shall not *d* the fruits of your
Mt 2.13 seek the young child to *d* him.
5.17 not that I am come to *d* the law,
17 I am not come to *d*, but to fulfil.
10.28 able to *d* both soul and body in
12.14 against him, how they might *d* him.
21.41 He will miserably *d* those wicked
26.61 said, I am able to *d* the temple
27.20 should ask Barabbas, and *d* Jesus.
Mk 1.24 art thou come to *d* us? I know thee
3. 6 against him, how they might *d* him.
9.22 and into the waters, to *d* him:
11.18 sought how they might *d* him:
12. 9 will come and *d* the husbandmen,
14.58 I will *d* this temple that is made
Lk 4.34 Nazareth? art thou come to *d* us?
6. 9 or to do evil? to save life, or to *d* it?
9.56 is not come to *d* men's lives, but
19.47 chief of the people sought to *d* him,
20.16 come and *d* these husbandmen,
Jn 2.19 *D* this temple, and in three days
10.10 for to steal, and to kill, and to *d*:
Ac 6.14 Jesus of Nazareth shall *d* this
Ro 14.15 *D* not him with thy meat, for whom
20 For meat *d* not the work of God.
1Co 1.19 I will *d* the wisdom of the wise,
3.17 temple of God, him shall God *d*;
6.13 God shall *d* both it and them.
2Th 2. 8 and shall *d* with the brightness
Heb 2.14 through death he might *d* him
Jas 4.12 who is able to save and to *d*:
1Jn 3. 8 that he might *d* the works of the
Rev 11.18 *d* them which *d* the earth.

DESTROYED

Gen 7.23 And every living substance was *d*
23 and they were *d* from the earth:
13.10 before the Lord *d* Sodom and
19.29 when God *d* the cities of the plain,
34.30 and I shall be *d*, I and my house.
Ex 10. 7 knowest thou not yet that Egypt is *d*?
22.20 Lord only, he shall be utterly *d*.
Nu 21. 3 and they utterly *d* them and their
Dt 1.44 and *d* you in Seir, even unto
2.12 them, when they had *d* them from
21 but the Lord *d* them before them;
22 in Seir, when he *d* the Horims
23 out of Caphtor, *d* them, and dwelt
34 and utterly *d* the men, and the
3. 6 And we utterly *d* them, as we did
4. 3 thy God hath *d* them from among
26 days upon it, but shall utterly be *d*.
7.20 hide themselves from thee, be *d*.
23 destruction, until they be *d*.
24 before thee, until they have *d* them.
9. 8 was angry with you to have *d* you.
20 angry with Aaron to have *d* him:
11. 4 how the Lord hath *d* them unto this
12.30 after that they be *d* from before
28.20 until thou be *d*, and until thou
24 down upon thee, until thou be *d*.
45 and overtake thee, till thou be *d*;
48 thy neck, until he have *d* thee.
51 fruit of thy land, until thou be *d*.
51 thy sheep, until he have *d* thee.
61 bring upon thee, until thou be *d*.
31. 4 the land of them, whom he *d*.
Jos 2.10 Sihon and Og, whom ye utterly *d*.
6.21 And they utterly *d* all that was in
8.26 until he had utterly *d* all the
10. 1 taken Ai, and had utterly *d* it,
28 and the king thereof he utterly *d*,
35 were therein he utterly *d* that day,
37 but *d* it utterly, and all the souls
39 and utterly *d* all the souls that
40 but utterly *d* all that breathed,
11.12 he utterly *d* them, as Moses the
14 until they had *d* them, neither left
21 Joshua *d* them utterly with their
23.15 until he have *d* you from off this
24. 8 and *d* them from before you.
Jdg 1.17 Zephath, and utterly *d* it.
4.24 until they had *d* Jabin king of
6. 4 and *d* the increase of the earth,
20.21 Gibeah, and *d* down to the ground
25 second day, and *d* down to the
35 and the children of Israel *d* of the
42 the cities they *d* in the midst of
21.16 remain, seeing the women are *d*
17 Benjamin, that a tribe be not *d*
1Sa 5. 6 Ashdod, and he *d* them, and smote
15. 8 and utterly *d* all the people with
9 and refuse, that they *d* utterly.
15 and the rest we have utterly *d*.
20. and have utterly *d* the Amalekites.
21 which should have been utterly *d*,
2Sa 11. 1 they *d* the children of Ammon,
21. 5 we should be *d* from remaining
22.38 pursued mine enemies, and *d* them;
24.16 the angel that *d* the people,
1Ki 15.13 and Asa *d* her idol, and burnt it
29 that breathed, until he had *d* him.
2Ki 10.17 in Samaria, till he had *d* him,
28 Thus Jehu *d* Baal out of Israel.
11. 1 she arose and *d* all the seed royal.
13. 7 the king of Syria had *d* them,
19.12 them which my fathers have *d*;
17 of Assyria have *d* the nations
18 stone, therefore they have *d* them.
21. 3 which Hezekiah his father had *d*;
9 nations whom the Lord *d* before
1Ch 4.41 and *d* them utterly unto this day,
5.25 land, whom God *d* before them.
20. 1 Joab smote Rabbah, and *d* it,
21.12 three months to be *d* before thy
15 and said to the angel that *d*,
2Ch 14.13 for they were *d* before the Lord,
15. 6 And nation was *d* of nation,
20.10 turned from them, and *d* them not;
22.10 she arose and *d* all the seed royal
24.23 and *d* all the princes of the people
31. 1 until they had utterly *d* them all.
32.14 nations that my fathers utterly *d*,
33. 9 whom the Lord had *d* before the
34.11 which the kings of Judah had *d*.
36.19 *d* all the goodly vessels thereof.
Ezr 4.15 for which cause was this city *d*.
5.12 who *d* this house, and carried the
Est 3. 9 it be written that they may be *d*:
4.14 and thy father's house shall be *d*:
7. 4 to be *d*, to be slain, and to perish.
9. 6 Jews slew and *d* five hundred men.
12 Jews have slain and *d* five hundred
Job 4.20 They are *d* from morning to
19.10 He hath *d* me on every side.
34.25 in the night, so that they are *d*.
Ps 9. 5 thou hast *d* the wicked, thou hast
6 hast *d* cities; their memorial
11. 3 If the foundations be *d*, what can
37.38 transgressors shall be *d* together:
73.27 thou hast *d* all them that go a
78.38 their iniquity, and *d* them not:
45 them; and frogs, which *d* them.
47 he *d* their vines with hail, and
92. 7 it is that they shall be *d* for ever:
137. 8 of Babylon, who art to be *d*;
Pr 13.13 despiseth the word shall be *d*:
13.20 a companion of fools shall be *d*.
23 there is that is *d* for want of
29. 1 shall suddenly be *d*, and that
Isa 9.16 they that are led of them are *d*.
10.27 and the yoke shall be *d* because
14.17 and *d* the cities thereof;
20 because thou hast *d* thy land,
26.14 therefore hast thou visited and *d*
34. 2 he hath utterly *d* them, he hath
37.12 them which my fathers have *d*,
19 stone: therefore they have *d* them.
48.19 not have been cut off nor *d* from
Jer 12.10 Many pastors have *d* my vineyard,
22.20 passages: for all thy lovers are *d*.
48. 4 Moab is *d*; her little ones have
8 and the plain shall be *d*, as the
42 And Moab shall be *d* from being a
51. 8 Babylon is suddenly fallen and *d*:
51.55 Babylon, and *d* out of her the great
La 2. 5 he hath *d* his strong holds, and
6 hath *d* his places of the assembly:
9 he hath *d* and broken her bars:
Eze 26.17 How art thou *d*, that wast inhabited
27.32 the *d* in the midst of the sea?
30. 8 when all her helpers shall be *d*.
32.12 the multitude thereof shall be *d*.
Dan 2.44 kingdom, which shall never be *d*:
6.26 kingdom that which shall not be *d*,
7.11 the beast was slain, and his body *d*,
14 kingdom that which shall not be *d*
11.20 but within few days he shall be *d*,
Hos 4. 6 My people are *d* for lack of
10. 8 Aven, the sin of Israel, shall be *d*:
13. 9 O Israel, thou hast *d* thyself, but
Am 2. 9 Yet *d* I the Amorite before them,
9 yet I *d* his fruit from above,
Zep 3. 6 passeth by: their cities are *d*,
Mt 22. 7 and *d* those murderers, and burned
Lk 17.27 the flood came, and *d* them all.
29 from heaven, and *d* them all.
Ac 3.23 shall be *d* from among the people.
9.21 Is not this he that *d* them which
13.19 And when he had *d* seven nations
19.27 her magnificence should be *d*,
Ro 6. 6 that the body of sin might be *d*,
1Co 10. 9 tempted and were *d* of serpents.
10 and were *d* of the destroyer.
15.26 The last enemy that shall be *d*
2Co 4. 9 forsaken; cast down, but not *d*;
Gal 1.23 the faith which once he *d*.
2.18 build again the things which I *d*,
Heb 11.28 lest he that *d* the first born
2Pe 2.12 beasts, made to be taken and *d*,
Jude 5 afterward *d* them that believed not.
Rev 8. 9 the third part of the ships were *d*.

DESTROYER

Ex 12.23 will not suffer the *d* to come in
Jdg 16.24 the *d* of our country, which slew
Job 15.21 the *d* shall come upon him.
Ps 17. 4 kept me from the paths of the *d*.
Pr 28.24 the same is the companion of a *d*.
Jer 4. 7 and the *d* of the Gentiles is on his
1Co 10.10 and were destroyed of the *d*.

DESTROYEST

Job 14.19 earth; and thou *d* the hope of man.
Jer 51.25 the Lord, which *d* all the earth:
Mt 27.40 Thou that *d* the temple, and
Mk 15.29 Ah, thou that *d* the temple, and

DESTRUCTION

Dt 7.23 destroy them with a mighty *d*,
32.24 burning heat, and with bitter *d*:
1Sa 5. 9 the city with a very great *d*:
11 there was a deadly *d* throughout
1Ki 20.42 whom I appointed to utter *d*,
2Ch 22. 4 the death of his father to his *d*.
7 the *d* of Ahaziah was of God by
26.16 his heart was lifted up to his *d*:
Est 8. 6 how can I endure to see the *d* of my
9. 5 slaughter, and *d*, and did what
Job 5.21 neither shalt thou be afraid of *d*
22 At *d* and famine thou shalt laugh:
18.12 and *d* shall be ready at his side.
21.17 oft cometh their *d* upon them!
20 His eyes shall see his *d*, and he
30 is reserved to the day of *d*?
26. 6 him, and *d* hath no covering.
28.22 *D* and death say, We have heard
30.12 against me the ways of their *d*.
24 grave, though they cry in his *d*.
31. 3 Is not *d* to the wicked?
12 it is a fire that consumeth to *d*,
23 *d* from God was a terror to me,
29 If I rejoiced at the *d* of him that
Ps 35. 8 *d* come upon him at unawares;
8 into that very *d* let him fall.
55.23 bring them down into the pit of *d*:
73.18 thou castedst them down into *d*.
88.11 grave? or thy faithfulness in *d*?
90. 3 turnest man to *d*; and sayest,
91. 6 the *d* that wasteth at noonday.
103. 4 Who redeemeth thy life from *d*;
Pr 1.27 your *d* cometh as a whirlwind;
10.14 the mouth of the foolish is near *d*.
15 the *d* of the poor is their poverty.
29 but *d* shall be to the workers of
13. 3 openeth wide his lips shall have *d*.
14.28 want of people is the *d* of the prince.
15.11 Hell and *d* are before the Lord:
16.18 Pride goeth before *d*, and an
17.19 that exalteth his gate seeketh *d*.
18. 7 A fool's mouth is his *d*, and his
12 Before *d* the heart of man is
21.15 but *d* shall be to the workers of
24. 2 their heart studieth *d*, and their
27.20 Hell and *d* are never full;
31. 8 all such as are appointed to *d*.
Isa 1.28 And the *d* of the transgressors
10.25 cease, and mine anger in their *d*.
13. 6 come as a *d* from the Almighty.
14.23 will sweep it with the besom of *d*,
15. 5 they shall raise up a cry of *d*.
19.18 one shall be called, The city of *d*.
24.12 and the gate is smitten with *d*.
49.19 the land of thy *d*, shall even now
51.19 desolation, and *d*, and the famine,
59. 7 wasting and *d* are in their paths.
60.18 wasting nor *d* within thy borders;
Jer 4. 6 evil from the north and a great *d*.
20 *D* upon *d* is cried; for the whole
6. 1 out of the north, and great *d*.
17.18 and destroy them with double *d*.
46.20 but *d* cometh; it cometh out of
48. 3 Horonaim, spoiling and great *d*.
5 the enemies have heard a cry of *d*.
50.22 battle is in the land and of great *d*.
51.54 and great *d* from the land of the
La 2.11 *d* of the daughter of my people;
3.47 come upon us, desolation and *d*.
48 *d* of the daughter of my people.
4.10 *d* of the daughter of my people.
Eze 5.16 which shall be for their *d*,
7.25 *D* cometh; and they shall seek
32. 9 bring thy *d* among the nations,
Hos 7.13 *d* unto them! because they have
9. 6 lo, they are gone because of *d*:
13.14 O grave, I will be thy *d*:
Joel 1.15 and as a *d* from the Almighty
Ob 12 of Judah in the day of their *d*;
Mic 2.10 destroy you, even with a sore *d*.
Zec 14.11 there shall be no more utter *d*;
Mt 7.13 broad is the way that leadeth to *d*,
Ro 3.16 *D* and misery are in their ways:
9.22 vessels of wrath fitted to *d*.
1Co 5. 5 unto Satan for the *d* of the flesh,
2Co 10. 8 edification, and not for your *d*,
13.10 me to edification, and not to *d*.
Php 3.19 Whose end is *d*, whose God is
1Th 5. 3 sudden *d* cometh upon them,
2Th 1. 9 be punished with everlasting *d*
1Ti 6. 9 drown men in *d* and perdition.
2Pe 2. 1 bring upon themselves swift *d*.
3.16 other scriptures, unto their own *d*.

DETERMINATE

Ac 2.23 delivered by the *d* counsel and

DETERMINED

1Sa 20. 7 be sure that evil is *d* by him.
9 evil were *d* by my father to come
33 Jonathan knew that it was *d* of his
25.17 evil is *d* against our master.
2Sa 13.32 this hath been *d* from the day
2Ch 2. 1 Solomon *d* to build an house for
25.16 know that God hath *d* to destroy
Est 7. 7 there was evil *d* against him by
Job 14. 5 Seeing his days are *d*, the number
Isa 10.23 consumption, even *d*, in the midst
19.17 hosts, which he hath *d* against it.
28.22 a consumption, even *d* upon
Dan 9.24 Seventy weeks are *d* upon thy
26 end of the war desolations are *d*.
27 that *d* shall be poured upon the
11.36 for that that is *d* shall be done.
Lk 22.22 Son of man goeth, as it was *d*:
Ac 3.13 Pilate, when he was *d* to let him
4.28 counsel *d* before to be done.
11.29 *d* to send relief unto the brethren
15. 2 they *d* that Paul and Barnabas,
37 Barnabas *d* to take with them
17.26 hath *d* the times before appointed,
19.39 shall be *d* in a lawful assembly.
20.16 Paul had *d* to sail by Ephesus,
25.25 Augustus, I have *d* to send him.
27. 1 when it was *d* that we should sail
1Co 2. 2 For I *d* not to know any thing
2Co 2. 1 But I *d* this with myself, that I
Tit 3.12 for I have *d* there to winter.

DEVICE

2Ch 2.14 to find out every *d* which shall
Est 8. 3 his *d* that he had devised against
9.25 by letters that his wicked *d*, which
Ps 21.11 they imagined a mischievous *d*,
140. 8 further not his wicked *d*; lest
Ec 9.10 for there is no work, nor *d*, nor
Jer 18.11 and devise a *d* against you:
51.11 for his *d* is against Babylon,
La 3.62 their *d* against me all the day.
Ac 17.29 stone, graven by art and man's *d*.

DEVICES

Job 5.12 He disappointeth the *d* of the
21.27 *d* which ye wrongfully imagine
Ps 10. 2 let them be taken in the *d* that
33.10 he maketh the *d* of the people
37. 7 who bringeth wicked *d* to pass.
Pr 1.31 and be filled with their own *d*.
12. 2 man of wicked *d* will he condemn.
14.17 a man of wicked *d* is hated.
19.21 are many *d* in a man's heart;
Isa 32. 7 he deviseth wicked *d* to destroy
Jer 11.19 they had devised *d* against me,
18.12 we will walk after our own *d*,
18 let us devise *d* against Jeremiah;
Dan 11.24 forecast his *d* against the strong
25 they shall forecast *d* against him.
2Co 2.11 we are not ignorant of his *d*.

DEVIL

Mt 4. 1 wilderness to be tempted of the *d*.
5 *d* taketh him up into the holy city,
8 Again the *d* taketh him up into
11 Then the *d* leaveth him, and,
9.32 a dumb man possessed with a *d*.
33 when the *d* was cast out, the
11.18 and they say, He hath a *d*.
12.22 one possessed with a *d*, blind,
13.39 enemy that sowed them is the *d*;
15.22 is grievously vexed with a *d*
17.18 Jesus rebuked the *d*; and he
25.41 prepared for the *d* and his angels:
Mk 5.15, 16 was possessed with the *d*,
18 that had been possessed with a *d*,
7.26 that he would cast forth the *d*
29 *d* is gone out of thy daughter.
30 she found the *d* gone out, and her
Lk 4. 2 Being forty days tempted of the *d*.
3 the *d* said unto him, If thou be
5 *d*, taking him up into an high
6 the *d* said unto him, All this will
13 *d* had ended all the temptation,
33 had a spirit of an unclean *d*,
35 when the *d* had thrown him in
7.33 wine; and ye say, He hath a *d*.
8.12 cometh the *d*, and taketh away
29 of the *d* into the wilderness
9.42 *d* threw him down, and tare him.
11.14 casting out a *d*, and it was dumb.
14 to pass when the *d* was gone out,
Jn 6.70 twelve, and one of you is a *d*?
7.20 and said, Thou hast a *d*:
8.44 Ye are of your father the *d*,
48 art a Samaritan, and hast a *d*?
49 Jesus answered, I have not a *d*;
52 Now we know that thou hast a *d*.
10.20 many of them said, He hath a *d*,
21 the words of him that hath a *d*.
21 a *d* open the eyes of the blind?
13. 2 *d* having now put into the heart
Ac 10.38 all that were oppressed of the *d*;
13.10 thou child of the *d*, thou enemy
Eph 4.27 Neither give place to the *d*.
6.11 stand against the wiles of the *d*.
1Ti 3. 6 into the condemnation of the *d*.
7 reproach and the snare of the *d*.
2Ti 2.26 out of the snare of the *d*, who
Heb 2.14 power of death, that is, the *d*;
Jas 4. 7 Resist the *d*, and he will flee from
1Pe 5. 8 because your adversary the *d*,
1Jn 3. 8 that committeth sin is of the *d*;
8 *d* sinneth from the beginning.
8 might destroy the works of the *d*.
10 manifest, and the children of the *d*:
Jude 9 when contending with the *d* he
Rev 2.10 the *d* shall cast some of you into
12. 9 that old serpent, called the *D*, and
12 the *d* is come down unto you,
20. 2 that old serpent, which is the *D*,
10 the *d* that deceived them was cast
(See illustration on page 222)

DEVILISH

Jas 3.15 above, but is earthly, sensual, *d*.

DEVILS

Lev 17. 7 offer their sacrifices unto *d*, after
Dt 32.17 sacrificed unto *d*, not to God;
2Ch 11.15 and for the *d*, and for the calves
Ps 106.37 sons and their daughters unto *d*,
Mt 4.24 which were possessed with *d*,
7.22 in thy name have cast out *d*?
8.16 that were possessed with *d*:
28 met him two possessed with *d*,
31 So the *d* besought him, saying, If
33 befallen to the possessed of the *d*.
9.34 Pharisees said, He casteth out *d*
34 through the prince of the *d*.
10. 8 lepers, raise the dead, cast out *d*:
12.24 This fellow doth not cast out *d*.
24 by Beelzebub the prince of the *d*.
27 if I by Beelzebub cast out *d*,
28 if I cast out *d* by the Spirit of

Mk 1.32 them that were possessed with *d*.
34 diseases, and cast out many *d*;
34 and suffered not the *d* to speak,
39 all Galilee, and cast out *d*.
3.15 sicknesses, and to cast out *d*:
22 and by the prince of the *d*
22 casteth he out *d*,
5.12 all the *d* besought him, saying,
6.13 they cast out many *d*, and
9.38 one casting out *d* in thy name,
16. 9 out of whom he had cast seven *d*.
17 my name shall they cast out *d*;
Lk 4.41 *d* also came out of many, crying
8. 2 out of whom went seven *d*,
27 a certain man, which had *d* long
30 because many *d* were entered
33 Then went the *d* out of the man,
35 of whom the *d* were departed,
36 possessed of the *d* was healed.
38 the man out of whom the *d* were
9. 1 power and authority over all *d*,
49 Master, we saw one casting out *d*
10.17 even the *d* are subject unto us
11.15 casteth out *d* through Beelzebub
15 the chief of the *d*.
18 I cast out *d* through Beelzebub.
19 if I by Beelzebub cast out *d*,
20 with the finger of God cast out *d*,
13.32 I cast out *d*, and I do cures
1Co 10.20 sacrifice to *d*, and not to God:
20 ye should have fellowship with *d*.
21 cup of the Lord, and the cup of *d*:
21 Lord's table, and of the table of *d*.
1Ti 4. 1 spirits, and doctrines of *d*;
Jas 2.19 the *d* also believe, and tremble.
Rev 9.20 that they should not worship *d*,
16.14 For they are the spirits of *d*,
18. 2 is become the habitation of *d*,

DEVISE

Ex 31. 4 To *d* cunning works, to work in
35.32 And to *d* curious works, to work in
35 and of those that *d* cunning work.
2Sa 14.14 yet doth he *d* means, that his
Ps 35. 4 to confusion that *d* my hurt.
20 *d* deceitful matters against them
41. 7 against me do they *d* my hurt.
Pr 3.29 *D* not evil against they neighbor,
14.22 Do they not err that *d* evil? but
22 shall be to them that *d* good.
16.30 shutteth his eyes to *d* froward
Jer 18.11 and *d* a device against you: return
18 let us *d* devices against Jeremiah;
Eze 11. 2 the men that *d* mischief, and give
Mic 2. 1 Woe to them that *d* iniquity, and
3 against this family do I *d* an evil,

DEVISED

2Sa 21. 5 that *d* against us that we should
1Ki 12.33 in the month which he had *d*
Est 8. 3 that he had *d* against the Jews.
5 reverse the letters *d* by Haman
9.24 had *d* against the Jews to destroy
25 which he *d* against the Jews,
Ps 31.13 they *d* to take away my life.
Jer 11.19 they had *d* devices against me,
48. 2 in Heshbon they had *d* evil
51.12 the Lord hath both *d* and done
La 2.17 hath done that which he had *d*;
2Pe 1.16 not followed cunningly *d* fables,

DEVOTIONS

Ac 17.23 I passed by, and beheld your *d*,

DEVOUT

Lk 2.25 the same man was just and *d*,
Ac 2. 5 Jews, *d* men, out of every nation
8. 2 And *d* men carried Stephen to his
10. 2 A *d* man, and one that feared God
7 a *d* soldier of them that waited on
13.50 stirred up the *d* and honorable
17. 4 of the *d* Greeks a great multitude,
17 the Jews, and with the *d* persons,
22.12 a *d* man according to the law,

DIANA

Ac 19.24 which made silver shrines for *D*
27 the temple of the great goddess *D*
28 Great is *D* of the Ephesians.
34 out, Great is *D* of the Ephesians.
35 worshipper of the great goddess *D*,

DIDYMUS

Jn 11.16 said Thomas, which is called *D*,
20.24 one of the twelve, called *D*,
21. 2 Simon Peter, and Thomas called *D*,

DIE

Gen 2.17 eatest thereof thou shalt surely *d*.
3. 3 neither shall ye touch it, lest ye *d*.
4 the woman, Ye shall not surely *d*:
6.17 thing that is in the earth shall *d*.
19.19 lest some evil take me, and I *d*:
20. 7 thou shalt surely *d*, thou, and all
25.32 Behold, I am at the point to *d*:
26. 9 Because I said, Lest I *d* for her.
27. 4 my soul may bless thee before I *d*.
30. 1 Give me children, or else I *d*.
33.13 them one day, all the flock will *d*.
38.11 Lest peradventure he *d* also, as
42. 2 thence; that we may live, and not *d*.
20 be verified, and ye shall not *d*.
43. 8 go; that we may live, and not *d*,
44. 9 it be found, both let him *d*, and we
22 leave his father, his father would *d*.
31 lad is not with us, that he will *d*:
45.28 I will go and see him before I *d*.
46.30 Now let me *d*, since I have seen
47.15 why should we *d* in thy presence?
19 Wherefore shall we *d* before thine
19 seed, that we may live, and not *d*,
29 time drew nigh that Israel must *d*:
48.21 said unto Joseph, Behold, I *d*:
50. 5 made me swear, saying, Lo, I *d*:
24 Joseph said unto his brethren, I *d*:
Ex 7.18 the fish that is in the river shall *d*,
9. 4 there shall nothing *d* of all that is
19 down upon them, and they shall *d*.
10.28 thou seest my face thou shalt *d*.
11. 5 in the land of Egypt shall *d*,
14.11 us away to *d* in the wilderness?
12 that we should *d* in the wilderness.
20.19 not God speak with us, lest we *d*.
21.12 that smiteth a man, so that he *d*,
14 from mine altar, that he may *d*.
18 or with his fist, and he *d* not,
20 a rod, and he *d* under his hand;
28 a man or a woman, that they *d*:
35 man's ox hurt another's, that he *d*;
22. 2 up, and be smitten that he *d*,
10 it *d*, or be hurt, or driven away,
14 and it be hurt, or *d*, the owner
28.35 he cometh out, that he *d* not.
43 that they bear not iniquity, and *d*:
30.20 wash with water that they *d* not;
21 and their feet, that they *d* not:
Lev 8.35 charge of the Lord, that ye *d* not;
10. 6 rend your clothes, lest ye *d*,
7 of the congregation, lest ye *d*:
9 of the congregation, lest ye *d*:
11.39 any beast of which ye may eat, *d*;
15.31 they *d* not in their uncleanness,

The Devil, depicted as a fallen angel, tempts Jesus in the wilderness in this fresco by Duccio (1255-1319).

16. 2 is upon the ark; that he *d* not:
13 the testimony, that he *d* not:
20.20 their sin: they shall *d* childless.
22. 9 lest they bear sin for it, and *d*
Nu 4.15 touch any holy thing, lest they *d*,
19 that they may live, and not *d*,
20 holy things are covered, lest they *d*.
6. 7 or for his sister, when they *d*:
9 any man *d* very suddenly by him,
14.35 consumed, and there they shall *d*.
16.29 If these men *d* the common death
17.10 from me, that they *d* not.
12 saying, Behold we *d*, we perish,
13 tabernacle of the Lord shall *d*:
18. 3 that neither they, nor ye also, *d*.
22 lest they bear sin, and *d*.
32 the children of Israel, lest ye *d*.
20. 4 that we and our cattle should *d*
26 unto his people, and shall *d* there,
21. 5 of Egypt to *d* in the wilderness?
23.10 me *d* the death of the righteous,
26.65 They shall surely *d* in the
27. 8 If a man *d*, and have no son,
35.12 that the manslayer *d* not, until he
16 instrument of iron, so that he *d*,
17, 18 wherewith he may *d*, and he *d*,
20 him by laying of wait, that he *d*;
21 him with his hand, that he *d*:
23 wherewith a man may *d*, seeing
23 cast it upon him, that he *d*,
30 any person to cause him to *d*.
Dt 4.22 I must *d* in this land, I must not
5.25 Now therefore why should we *d*?
25 our God any more, then we shall *d*.
13.10 stone him with stones, that he *d*;
17. 5 stone them with stones, till they *d*.
12 the judge, even that man shall *d*:
18.16 great fire any more that I *d* not.
20 gods, even that prophet shall *d*.
19. 5 upon his neighbor, that he *d*;
11 smite him mortally that he *d*,
12 avenger of blood, that he may *d*.
20. 5, 6, 7 lest he *d* in the battle, and
21.21 stone him with stones, that he *d*:
22.21 stone her with stones that she *d*:
22 then they shall both of them *d*,
24 stone them with stones that they *d*;
25 man only that lay with her shall *d*:
24. 3 if the latter husband *d*, which took
7 that thief shall *d*; and thou shalt
25. 5 dwell together, and one of them *d*,
31.14 days approach that thou must *d*:
32.50 And *d* in the mount whither thou
33. 6 Let Reuben live, and not *d*; and let
Jos 20. 9 not *d* by the hand of the avenger
Jdg 6.23 thee; fear not: thou shalt not *d*.
30 Bring out thy son, that he may *d*:
13.22 We shall surely *d*, because we have
15.18 and now shall I *d* for thirst, and
16.30 Let me *d* with the Philistines.
Ru 1.17 Where thou diest, will I *d*, and
1Sa 2.33 the increase of thine house shall *d*
34 in one day they shall *d* both of
12.19 the Lord thy God, that we *d* not:
14.39 my son, he shall surely *d*.
43 in mine hand, and, lo, I must *d*.
44 for thou shalt surely *d*, Jonathan.
45 Shall Jonathan *d*, who hath
20. 2 God forbid; thou shalt not *d*:
14 kindness of the Lord, that I *d* not:
31 unto me, for he shall surely *d*.
22.16 Thou shalt surely *d*, Ahimelech,
26.10 his day shall come to *d*; or he
16 ye are worthy to *d*, because ye
28. 9 for my life, to cause me to *d*?
2Sa 11.15 that he may be smitten, and *d*.
12. 5 done this thing shall surely *d*:
13 away thy sin; thou shalt not *d*.
14 is born unto thee shall surely *d*.
14.14 For we must needs *d*, and are as
18. 3 neither if half of us *d*, will they

Biblical Themes

DEVOTION

And Jacob served seven years for Rachel; and they seemed unto him but a few days, for the love he had to her.
Gen 29.20

As I was with Moses, so I will be with thee: I will not fail thee, nor forsake thee.
Jos 1.5

Intreat me not to leave thee . . . for whither thou goest, I will go; and where thou lodgest, I will lodge: thy people shall be my people, and thy God my God: where thou diest, will I die, and there will I be buried: the Lord do so to me, and more also, if ought but death part thee and me.
Ru 1.16-17

And Jonathan caused David to swear again, because he loved him: for he loved him as he loved his own soul.
1Sa 20.17

As the Lord liveth, and as my lord the king liveth, surely in what place my lord the king shall be, whether in death or life, even there also will thy servant be.
2Sa 15.21

Stablish thy word unto thy servant, who is devoted to thy fear.
Ps 119.38

Unto thee lift I up mine eyes, O thou that dwellest in the heavens. Behold, as the eyes of servants look unto the hand of their masters, and as the eyes of a maiden unto the hand of her mistress; so our eyes wait upon the Lord our God, until that he have mercy upon us.
Ps 123.1-2

Whoso keepeth the fig tree shall eat the fruit thereof: so he that waiteth on his master shall be honored.
Pr 27.18

A faithful man shall abound with blessings.
Pr 28.20

Can a woman forget her sucking child, that she should not have compassion on the son of her womb? yea, they may forget, yet will I not forget thee.
Isa 49.15

How shall I give thee up, Ephraim? how shall I deliver thee, Israel? . . . mine heart is turned within me.
Hos 11.8

How think ye? if a man have an hundred sheep, and one of them be gone astray, doth he not leave the ninety and nine, and goeth into the mountains, and seeketh that which is gone astray?
Mt 18.12

Seest thou this woman? I entered into thine house, thou gavest me no water for my feet: but she hath washed my feet with tears. . . . My head with oil thou didst not anoint: but this woman hath anointed my feet with ointment. Wherefore I say unto thee, Her sins, which are many, are forgiven; for she loved much: but to whom little is forgiven, the same loveth little.
Lk 7.44, 46-47

Then said Thomas . . . unto his fellow-disciples, Let us also go, that we may die with him.
Jn 11.16

After that he poureth water into a bason, and began to wash the disciples' feet.
Jn 13.5

Love one another, as I have loved you. Greater love hath no man than this, that a man lay down his life for his friends.
Jn 15.12-13

To the weak became I as weak, that I might gain the weak: I am made all things to all men, that I might by all means save some. And this I do for the gospel's sake, that I might be partaker thereof with you.
1Co 9.22-23

Wherefore seeing we also are compassed about with so great a cloud of witnesses, let us lay aside every weight, and the sin which doth so easily beset us, and let us run with patience the race that is set before us, looking unto Jesus the author and finisher of our faith.
Heb 12.1-2

19.23 said unto Shimei, Thou shalt not *d*.
37 that I may *d* in mine own city,
1Ki 1.52 shall be found in him, he shall *d*.
2. 1 David drew nigh that he should *d*;
30 he said, Nay; but I will *d* here.
37 certain that thou shalt surely *d*:
42 whither, that thou shalt surely *d*?
14.12 into the city, the child shall *d*.
17.12 that we may eat it, and *d*.
19. 4 for himself that he might *d*;
21.10 out, and stone him, that he may *d*.
2Ki 1. 4, 6, 16 gone up, but shalt surely *d*.
7. 3 Why sit we here until we *d*?
4 is in the city and we shall *d* there:
4 and if we sit still here, we *d* also.
4 and if they kill us, we shall but *d*.
8.10 showed me that he shall surely *d*.
18.32 that ye may live, and not *d*:
20. 1 for thou shalt *d*, and not live.
2Ch 25. 4 The fathers shall not *d* for the
4 neither shall the children *d* for the
4 but every man shall *d* for his own
32.11 to *d* by famine and by thirst,
Job 2. 9 thine integrity? curse God, and *d*.
4.21 they *d*, even without wisdom.
12. 2 and wisdom shall *d* with you.

Job 14. 8 the stock thereof *d* in the ground;
14 If a man *d*, shall he live again?
27. 5 that I should justify you: till I *d*
29.18 Then I said, I shall *d* in my nest,
34.20 In a moment shall they *d*, and the
36.12 they shall *d* without knowledge.
14 They *d* in youth, and their life is
Ps 41. 5 When shall he *d*, and his name
49.10 For he seeth that wise men *d*,
79.11 those that are appointed to *d*;
82. 7 But ye shall *d* like men, and fall
88.15 I am afflicted and ready to *d* from
104.29 they *d*, and return to their dust.
118.17 I shall not *d*, but live, and declare
Pr 5.23 He shall *d* without instruction;
10.21 but fools *d* for want of wisdom.
15.10 he that hateth reproof shall *d*.
19.16 he that despiseth his ways shall *d*.
23.13 him with the rod, he shall not *d*.
30. 7 deny me them not before I *d*:
Ec 3. 2 A time to be born, and a time to *d*;
7.17 why shouldest thou *d* before thy
9. 5 the living know that they shall *d*:
Isa 22.13 drink; for to-morrow we shall *d*.
14 not be purged from you till ye *d*,
18 there shalt thou *d*, and there the
38. 1 for thou shalt *d*, and not live.
51. 6 they that dwell therein shall *d* in
12 be afraid of a man that shall *d*,
14 that he should not *d* in the pit,
65.20 the child shall *d* an hundred years
66.24 their worm shall not *d*, neither
Jer 11.21 Lord, that thou *d* not by our hand:
22 young men shall *d* by the sword;
22 sons and their daughters shall *d*
16. 4 They shall *d* of grievous deaths;
6 the great and the small shall *d* in
20. 6 Babylon, and there thou shalt *d*,
21. 6 they shall *d* of a great pestilence.
9 He that abideth in this city shall *d*
22.12 he shall *d* in the place whither they
26 not born; and there shall ye *d*.
26. 8 him, saying, Thou shalt surely *d*.
11 This man is worthy to *d*; for he
16 This man is not worthy to *d*:
27.13 will ye *d*, thou and thy people,
28.16 this year thou shalt *d*, because
31.30 But every one shall *d* for his own
34. 4 Thou shalt not *d* by the sword:
5 Thou shalt *d* in peace: and with
37.20 Jonathan the scribe, lest I *d* there.
38. 2 that remaineth in this city shall *d*
9 and he is like to *d* for hunger
10 out of the dungeon, before he *d*.
24 these words, and thou shalt not *d*.
26 to Jonathan's house, to *d* there.
42.16 in Egypt; and there ye shall *d*.
17 they shall *d* by the sword, by the
22 know certainly that ye shall *d* by
44.12 they shall *d*, from the least even
Eze 3.18 Thou shalt surely *d*; and thou
18 the same wicked man shall *d* in
19 way, he shall *d* in his iniquity;
20 he shall *d*: because thou hast not
20 him warning, he shall *d* in his sin,
5.12 of thee shall *d* with the pestilence,
6.12 He that is far off shall *d* of the
12 remaineth and is besieged shall *d*
7.15 he that is in the field shall *d* with
12.13 not see it, though he shall *d* there.
13.19 to slay the souls that should not *d*,
17.16 in the midst of Babylon he shall *d*.
18. 4 the soul that sinneth, it shall *d*.
13 he shall surely *d*; his blood shall
17 he shall not *d* for the iniquity of
18 even he shall *d* in his iniquity.
20 The soul that sinneth, it shall *d*.
21 he shall surely live, he shall not *d*.
23 at all that the wicked should *d*?
24 hath sinned, in them shall he *d*.
26 that he hath done shall he *d*.
28 he shall surely live, he shall not *d*.
31 why will ye *d*, O house of Israel?
28. 8 and thou shalt *d* the deaths of them
10 Thou shalt *d* the deaths of the
33. 8 thou shalt surely *d*; if thou dost
8 his way, that wicked man shall *d*
9 his way he shall *d* in his iniquity;
11 why will ye *d*, O house of Israel?
13 hath committed, he shall *d* for it.
14 Thou shalt surely *d*; if he turn
15 he shall surely live, he shall not *d*.
18 iniquity, he shall even *d* thereby.
27 the caves shall *d* of the pestilence.
Am 2. 2 and Moab shall *d* with tumult,
6. 9 in one house, that they shall *d*.
7.11 Jeroboam shall *d* by the sword,
17 thou shalt *d* in a polluted land:
9.10 the sinners of my people shall *d*
Jon 4. 3 is better for me to *d* than to live.
8 wished in himself to *d*, and said,
8 It is better for me to *d* than to live.
Hab 1.12 mine Holy One? we shall not *d*.
Zec 11. 9 feed you: that that dieth, let it *d*;
13. 8 therein shall be cut off and *d*;
Mt 15. 4 or mother, let him *d* the death.
22.24 Master, Moses said, If a man *d*,
26.35 Though I should *d* with thee, yet
Mk 7.10 let him *d* the death: But ye say,
12.19 If a man's brother *d*, and leave
14.31 If I should *d* with thee, I will not
Lk 7. 2 him, was sick, and ready to *d*.
20.28 If any man's brother *d*, having a
28 wife, and he *d* without children,
36 Neither can they *d* any more: for
Jn 4.49 Sir, come down ere my child *d*.
6.50 a man may eat thereof, and not *d*.
8.21 seek me, and shall *d* in your sins:
24 that ye shall *d* in your sins: for if
24 unto you ye shall *d* in your sins.
11.16 also go, that we may *d* with him.
26 and believeth in me shall never *d*.
50 one man should *d* for the people,
51 that Jesus should *d* for that nation;
12.24 wheat fall into the ground and *d*,
24 it abideth alone: but if it *d*, it
33 signifying what death he should *d*.
18.14 one man should *d* for the people.
32 signifying what death he should *d*.
19. 7 and by our law he ought to *d*,
21.23 that disciple should not *d*: yet
23 said not unto him, He shall not *d*;
Ac 21.13 also to *d* at Jerusalem for the
25.11 worthy of death, I refuse not to *d*:
16 Romans to deliver any man to *d*,
Ro 5. 7 for a righteous man will one *d*:
7 man some would even dare to *d*.
8.13 ye live after the flesh, ye shall *d*:
14. 8 whether we *d*, we *d* unto the Lord:
8 therefore, or *d*, we are the Lord's.
1Co 9.15 better for me to *d*, than that any
15.22 For as in Adam all *d*, even so
31 in Christ Jesus our Lord, I *d* daily.
32 eat and drink; for tomorrow we *d*.
36 is not quickened, except it *d*:
2Co 7. 3 our hearts to *d* and live with you.
Php 1.21 to live is Christ, and to *d* is gain.
Heb 7. 8 here men that *d* receive tithes;
9.27 it is appointed unto men once to *d*,
Rev 3. 2 which remain, that are ready to *d*:
9. 6 not find it; and shall desire to *d*,
14.13 are the dead which *d* in the Lord

DIED

Gen 5. 5 and thirty years: and he *d*.
8 and twelve years: and he *d*.
11 hundred and five years: and he *d*.
14 hundred and ten years: and he *d*.
17 ninety and five years: and he *d*.
20 sixty and two years: and he *d*.
27 sixty and nine years: and he *d*.
31 seventy and seven years: and he *d*.
7.21 And all flesh *d* that moved upon
22 all that was in the dry land, *d*.
9.29 hundred and fifty years: and he *d*.
11.28 Haran *d* before his father Terah
32 five years: and Terah *d* in Haran,
23. 2 And Sarah *d* in Kirjath-arba; the
25. 8 *d* in a good old age, an old man,
17 and he gave up the ghost and *d*;
18 he *d* in the presence of all his
35. 8 But Deborah Rebekah's nurse *d*,
18 soul was in departing, (for she *d*)
19 And Rachel *d*, and was buried in
29 Isaac gave up the ghost, and *d*,
36.33 And Bela *d*, and Jobab the son of
34 And Jobab *d*, and Husham of the
35 And Husham *d*, and Hadad the son
36 And Hadad *d*, and Samlah of
37 Samlah *d*, and Saul of Rehoboth
38 Saul *d*, and Baal-hanan the son of
39 Baal-hanan the son of Achbor *d*,
38.12 daughter of Shuah Judah's wife *d*;
46.12 and Onan *d* in the land of Canaan.
48. 7 Rachel *d* by me in the land of
50.16 father did command before he *d*,
26 Joseph *d*, being an hundred and
Ex 1. 6 Joseph *d*, and all his brethren,
2.23 of time that the king of Egypt *d*:
7.21 the fish that was in the river *d*;
8.13 and the frogs *d* out of the houses,
9. 6 and all the cattle of Egypt *d*:
6 of the children of Israel *d* not one.
16. 3 Would to God we had *d* by the
Lev 10. 2 them, and they *d* before the Lord.
16. 1 offered before the Lord, and *d*;
17.15 soul that eateth that which *d* of
Nu 3. 4 and Abihu *d* before the Lord,
14. 2 we had *d* in the land of Egypt!
2 God we had *d* in this wilderness!
37 up the evil report upon the land, *d*
15.36 stoned him with stones, and he *d*;
16.49 they that *d* in the plague were
49 that *d* about the matter of Korah.
20. 1 Miriam *d* there, and was buried
3 Would God that we had *d* when
3 our brethren *d* before the Lord!
28 Aaron *d* there in the top of the
21. 6 and much people of Israel *d*.
25. 9 those that *d* in the plague were
26.10 when that company *d*, what time
11 the children of Korah *d* not.
19 and Onan *d* in the land of Canaan.
61 And Nadab and Abihu *d*, when
27. 3 Our father *d* in the wilderness, and
3 *d* in his own sin, and had no sons.
33.38 of the Lord, and *d* there,
39 old when he *d* in mount Hor.
Dt 10. 6 Aaron *d*, and there he was buried;
32.50 Aaron thy brother *d* in mount Hor,
34. 5 Moses the servant of the Lord *d*
7 and twenty years old when he *d*:
Jos 5. 4 *d* in the wilderness by the way,
10.11 them unto Azekah, and they *d*:
11 more which *d* with hailstones than
24.29 of Nun, the servant of the Lord, *d*.
33 Eleazar the son of Aaron *d*; and
Jdg 1. 7 him to Jerusalem, and there he *d*.
2. 8 of Nun, the servant of the Lord, *d*,
21 which Joshua left when he *d*:
3.11 And Othniel the son of Kenaz *d*.
4.21 fast asleep and weary. So he *d*.
8.32 And Gideon the son of Joash *d*
9.49 the men of the tower of Shechem *d*
54 man thrust him through, and he *d*.
10. 2 twenty and three years, and *d*,
5 And Jair *d*, and was buried in
12. 7 Then *d* Jephthah the Gileadite, and
10 Then *d* Ibzan, and was buried at
12 And Elon the Zebulonite *d*, and was
15 son of Hillel the Pirathonite *d*,
Ru 1. 3 Elimelech Naomi's husband *d*;
5 and Chilion *d* also both of them;

1Sa 4.18 and his neck brake, and he *d*:
5.12 the men that *d* not were smitten
14.45 rescued Jonathan, that he *d* not.
25. 1 Samuel *d*; and all the Israelites
37 that his heart *d* within him, and he
38 the Lord smote Nabal, that he *d*.
31. 5 upon his sword, and *d* with him.
6 So Saul *d*, and his three sons,
2Sa 1.15 And he smote him that he *d*.
2.23 and *d* in the same place: and it
23 Asahel fell down and *d* stood still.
31 hundred and threescore men *d*.
3.27 under the fifth rib, that he *d*,
33 said, *D* Abner as a fool dieth?
6. 7 and there he *d* by the ark of God.
10. 1 king of the children of Ammon *d*,
18 captain of their host, who *d* there.
11.17 and Uriah the Hittite *d* also.
21 the wall, that he *d* in Thebez?
12.18 the seventh day, that the child *d*.
17.23 and hanged himself, and *d*, and
18.33 would God I had *d* for thee,
19. 6 all we had *d* this day, then it had
20.10 struck him not again; and he *d*.
24.15 there *d* of the people from Dan
1Ki 2.25 and he fell upon him that he *d*.
46 and fell upon him, that he *d*.
3.19 woman's child *d* in the night;
12.18 stoned him with stones, that he *d*.
14.17 threshold of the door, the child *d*:
16.18 house over him with fire, and *d*,
22 so Tibni *d*, and Omri reigned.
21.13 stoned him with stones, that he *d*.
22.35 against the Syrians, and *d* at even:
37 So the king *d*, and was brought to
2Ki 1.17 So he *d* according to the word of
4.20 on her knees till noon, and then *d*.
7.17 upon him in the gate, and he *d*, as
20 upon him in the gate, and he *d*.
8.15 spread it on his face, so that he *d*:
9.27 he fled to Megiddo, and *d* there.
12.21 his servants, smote him, and he *d*;
13.14 sick of his sickness whereof he *d*.
20 And Elisha *d*, and they buried him.
24 So Hazael king of Syria *d*; and
23.34 he came to Egypt, and *d* there.
25.25 and smote Gedaliah, that he *d*,
1Ch 1.51 Hadad *d* also. And the dukes of
2.30 but Seled *d* without children.
32 and Jether *d* without children.
10. 5 fell likewise on the sword, and *d*.
6 So Saul *d*, and his three sons,
6 and all his house *d* together.
13 So Saul *d* for his transgression
13.10 and there he *d* before God.
19. 1 king of the children of Ammon *d*,
23.22 And Eleazar *d*, and had no sons,
24. 2 Nadab and Abihu *d* before their
29.28 And he *d* in a good old age,
2Ch 10.18 stoned him with stones, that he *d*.
13.20 the Lord struck him, and he *d*.
16.13 and *d* in the one and fortieth year
18.34 time of the sun going down he *d*.
21.19 sickness: so he *d* of sore diseases.
24.15 and was full of days when he *d*;
15 years old was he when he *d*.
22 And when he *d*, he said, The Lord
25 slew him on his bed, and he *d*:
35.24 him to Jerusalem, and he *d*,
Job 3.11 Why *d* I not from the womb?
42.17 Job *d*, being old and full of days.
Isa 6. 1 In the year that king Uzziah *d*
14.28 In the year that king Ahaz *d*
Jer 28.17 So Hananiah the prophet *d* the
Eze 11.13 Pelatiah the son of Benaiah *d*.
24.18 and at even my wife *d*; and I did
Hos 13. 1 when he offended in Baal, he *d*.
Mt 22.27 And last of all the woman *d* also.
Mk 12.21 the second took her, and *d*, neither
22 seed: last of all the woman *d* also.
Lk 16.22 it came to pass, that the beggar *d*,
22 rich man also *d*, and was buried;
20.29 a wife, and *d* without children.
30 her to wife, and he *d* childless.
31 and they left no children, and *d*.
32 Last of all the woman *d* also.
Jn 11.21, 32 here, my brother had not *d*.
37 even this man should not have *d*?
Ac 7.15 Egypt, and *d*, he, and our fathers,
9.37 days, that she was sick, and *d*:
Ro 5. 6 time Christ *d* for the ungodly.
8 were yet sinners, Christ *d* for us.
6.10 in that he *d*, he *d* unto sin once:
7. 9 came, sin revived, and I *d*.
8.34 It is Christ that *d*, yea rather,
14. 9 To this end Christ both *d*, and rose,
15 with thy meat, for whom Christ *d*.
1Co 8.11 brother perish, for whom Christ *d*?
15. 3 how that Christ *d* for our sins
2Co 5.14 one *d* for all, then were all dead:
15 that he *d* for all, that they which
15 but unto him which *d* for them,
1Th 4.14 that Jesus *d* and rose again, even
5.10 Who *d* for us, that, whether we
Heb 10.28 Moses' law *d* without mercy under
11.13 These all *d* in faith, not having
22 By faith Joseph when he *d*, made
Rev 8. 9 were in the sea, and had life, *d*;
11 many men *d* of the waters,
16. 3 every living soul *d* in the sea.

DIEST

Ru 1.17 Where thou *d*, will I die, and

DIET

Jer 52.34 And for his *d*, there was a
34 there was a continual *d* given

DIETH

Lev 7.24 fat of the beast that *d* of itself,
22. 8 That which *d* of itself, or is torn
Nu 19.14 when a man *d* in a tent:
Dt 14.21 eat of any thing that *d* of itself:
2Sa 3.33 said, Died Abner as a fool *d*?
1Ki 14.11 Him that *d* of Jeroboam in the
11 eat; and him that *d* in the field
16. 4 Him that *d* of Baasha in the city
4 and him that *d* of his in the fields
21.24 Him that *d* of Ahab in the city
24 eat; and him that *d* in the field
Job 14.10 But man *d*, and wasteth away:
21.23 One *d* in his full strength, being
25 *d* in the bitterness of his soul,
Ps 49.17 when he *d* he shall carry nothing
Pr 11. 7 a wicked man *d*, his expectation
Ec 2.16 And how *d* the wise man? as the
3.19 as the one *d*, so *d* the other;
Isa 50. 2 is no water, and *d* for thirst.
59. 5 he that eateth of their eggs *d*,
Eze 4.14 eaten of that which *d* of itself,
18.26 iniquity, and *d* in them:
32 pleasure in the death of him that *d*,
Zec 11. 9 feed you: that that *d*, let it die;
Mk 9.44, 46 Where their worm *d* not, and
48 Where their worm *d* not, and
Ro 6. 9 raised from the dead, *d* no more;
14. 7 himself, and no man *d* to himself.

DIFFER

1Co 4. 7 maketh thee to *d* from another?

DIFFERENCE

Ex 11. 7 the Lord doth put a *d* between
Lev 10.10 And that ye may put *d* between holy
11.47 *d* between the unclean and the
20.25 shall therefore put *d* between
Eze 22.26 they have put no *d* between the
26 have they showed *d* between
44.23 the *d* between the holy and
Ac 15. 9 no *d* between us and them,
Ro 3.22 that believe: for there is no *d*:
10.12 no *d* between the Jew and the
1Co 7.34 There is *d* also between a wife
Jude 22 have compassion, making a *d*:

DIFFERENCES

1Co 12. 5 there are *d* of administrations,

DIFFERETH

1Co 15.41 for one star *d* from another star
Gal 4. 1 a child, *d* nothing from a servant,

DIFFERING

Ro 12. 6 gifts *d* according to the grace

DIG

Ex 21.33 if a man shall *d* a pit, and not
Dt 8. 9 whose hills thou mayest *d* brass.
23.13 thou shalt *d* therewith, and shalt
Job 3.21 *d* for it more than for hid treasures:
6.27 and ye *d* a pit for your friend.
11.18 yea, thou shalt *d* about thee,
24.16 the dark they *d* through houses,
Eze 8. 8 Son of man, *d* now in the wall:
12. 5 *D* thou through the wall in their
12 *d* through the wall to carry out,
Am 9. 2 Though they *d* into hell, thence
Lk 13. 8 till I shall *d* about it, and dung it:
16. 3 I cannot *d*; to beg I am ashamed.

DIGGED

Gen 21.30 unto me, that I have *d* this well.
26.15 had *d* in the days of Abraham
18 Isaac *d* again the wells of water;
18 which they had *d* in the days of
19 Isaac's servants *d* in the valley,
21 And they *d* another well, and
22 from thence, and *d* another well;
25 there Isaac's servants *d* a well.
32 the well which they had *d*, and
49. 6 their selfwill they *d* down a wall.
50. 5 in my grave which I have *d* for
Ex 7.24 the Egyptians *d* round about the
Nu 21.18 The princes *d* the well,
18 the nobles of the people *d* it,
Dt 6.11 wells *d*, which thou diggedst not,
2Ki 19.24 *d* and drunk strange waters,
2Ch 26.10 in the desert, and *d* many wells:
Neh 9.25 houses full of all goods, wells *d*,
Ps 7.15 He made a pit, and *d* it, and is
35. 7 cause they have *d* for my soul.
57. 6 they have *d* a pit before me, into
94.13 until the pit be *d* for the wicked.
119.85 The proud have *d* pits for me,
Isa 5. 6 it shall not be pruned, nor *d*;
7.25 on all hills that shall be *d* with
37.25 I have *d*, and drunk water; and
51. 1 hole of the pit whence ye are *d*.
Jer 13. 7 Then I went to Euphrates, and *d*,
18.20 they have *d* a pit for my soul,
22 they have *d* a pit to take me,
Eze 8. 8 and when I had *d* in the wall,
12. 7 in the even I *d* through the wall
Mt 21.33 and *d* a winepress in it, and built
25.18 and *d* in the earth, and hid his
Mk 12. 1 and *d* a place for the winefat,
Lk 6.48 *d* deep, and laid the foundation
Ro 11. 3 and *d* down thine altars;

DIGNITIES

2Pe 2.10 are not afraid to speak evil of *d*.
Jude 8 dominion, and speak evil of *d*.

DIMINISHING

Ro 11.12 and the *d* of them the riches of

DIMNESS

Isa 8.22 and darkness, *d* of anguish;
9. 1 the *d* shall not be such as was

DINE

Gen 43.16 these men shall *d* with me at noon.
Lk 11.37 besought him to *d* with him:
Jn 21.12 saith unto them, Come and *d*.

DINED
Jn 21.15 So when they had *d*, Jesus saith

DINNER
Pr 15.17 is a *d* of herbs where love is,
Mt 22. 4 Behold, I have prepared my *d*:
Lk 11.38 had not first washed before *d*.
14.12 When thou makest a *d* or a supper,

DIONYSIUS
Ac 17.34 the which was *D* the Areopagite,

DIP
Ex 12.22 *d* it in the blood that is in the
Lev 4. 6 shall *d* his finger in the blood,
17 *d* his finger in some of the blood,
14. 6 shall *d* them and the living bird
16 the priest shall *d* his right finger
51 *d* them in the blood of the slain
Nu 19.18 and *d* it in the water, and sprinkle
Dt 33.24 and let him *d* his foot in oil.
Ru 2.14 and *d* thy morsel in the vinegar.
Lk 16.24 that he may *d* the tip of his finger

DIPPED
Gen 37.31 and *d* the coat in the blood;
Lev 9. 9 and he *d* his finger in the blood,
Jos 3.15 were *d* in the brim of the water,
1Sa 14.27 and *d* it in an honeycomb, and put
2Ki 5.14 *d* himself seven times in Jordan,
8.15 and *d* it in water, and spread it on
Ps 68.23 thy foot may be *d* in the blood
Jn 13.26 give a sop when I have *d* it.
26 had *d* the sop, he gave it to Judas
Rev 19.13 with a vesture *d* in blood:

DIPPETH
Mt 26.23 He that *d* his hand with me in
Mk 14.20 that *d* with me in the dish.

DIRECT
Gen 46.28 to *d* his face unto Goshen;
Ps 5. 3 will I *d* my prayer unto thee,
Pr 3. 6 him, and he shall *d* thy paths.
11. 5 of the perfect shall *d* his way:
Ec 10.10 but wisdom is profitable to *d*.
Isa 45.13 and I will *d* all his ways:
61. 8 and I will *d* their work in truth,
Jer 10.23 man that walketh to *d* his steps.
1Th 3.11 Christ, *d* our way unto you.
2Th 3. 5 *d* your hearts into the love of God,

DIRECTED
Job 32.14 hath not *d* his words against me:
Ps 119. 5 ways were *d* to keep thy statutes!
Isa 40.13 Who hath *d* the spirit of the Lord,

DIRECTETH
Job 37. 3 He *d* it under the whole heaven,
Pr 16. 9 way: but the Lord *d* his steps.
21.29 as for the upright, he *d* his way.

DISALLOWED
Nu 30. 5 her, because her father *d* her.
8 her husband *d* her on the day that
11 his peace at her, and *d* her not:
1Pe 2. 4 *d* indeed of men, but chosen of
7 the stone which the builders *d*,

DISANNUL
Job 40. 8 Wilt thou also *d* my judgment?
Isa 14.27 purposed, and who shall *d* it?
Gal 3.17 years after, cannot *d*, that it

DISANNULLETH
Gal 3.15 no man *d*, or addeth thereto.

DISANNULLING
Heb 7.18 verily a *d* of the commandment

DISCERN
Gen 31.32 *d* thou what is thine with me,
38.25 *D*, I pray thee, whose are these.
2Sa 14.17 lord the king to *d* good and bad:
19.35 can I *d* between good and evil?
1Ki 3. 9 I may *d* between good and bad:
11 understanding to *d* judgment;
Ezr 3.13 the people could not *d* the noise
Job 4.16 I could not *d* the form thereof:
6.30 cannot my taste *d* perverse things?
Eze 44.23 them to *d* between the unclean
Jon 4.11 that cannot *d* between their right
Mal 3.18 and *d* between the righteous and
Mt 16. 3 ye can *d* the face of the sky;
3 but can ye not *d* the signs of the
Lk 12.56 ye can *d* the face of the sky and
56 is it that ye do not *d* this time?
Heb 5.14 exercised to *d* both good and evil.

DISCERNED
Gen 27.23 he *d* him not, because his hands
1Ki 20.41 and the king of Israel *d* him that
Pr 7. 7 I *d* among the youths, a young
1Co 2.14 because they are spiritually *d*.

DISCERNER
Heb 4.12 and is a *d* of the thoughts and

DISCERNING
1Co 11.29 himself, not *d* the Lord's body.
12.10 to another *d* of spirits; to another

DISCHARGE
Ec 8. 8 and there is no *d* in that war;

DISCIPLE
Mt 10.24 The *d* is not above his master,
25 It is enough for the *d* that he be as
42 water only in the name of a *d*,
27.57 who also himself was Jesus' *d*:
Lk 6.40 The *d* is not above his master:
14.26 own life also, he cannot be my *d*.
27 come after me, cannot be my *d*.
33 that he hath, he cannot be my *d*,
Jn 9.28 Thou art his *d*; but we are Moses'
18.15 another *d*: that *d* was known
16 Then went out that other *d*, which
19.26 and the *d* standing by, whom he
27 Then saith he to the *d*, Behold thy
27 from that hour that *d* took her
38 of Arimathea, being a *d* of Jesus,
20. 2 to the other *d*, whom Jesus loved,
3 went forth, and that other *d*,
4 and the other *d* did outrun Peter,
8 Then went in also that other *d*,
21. 7 Therefore that *d* whom Jesus loved
20 seeth the *d* whom Jesus loved
23 that that *d* should not die;
24 This is the *d* which testifieth of
Ac 9.10 *d* at Damascus, named Ananias;
26 believed not that he was a *d*.
36 Joppa a certain *d* named Tabitha,
16. 1 *d* was there, named Timotheus,
21.16 *d*, with whom we should lodge.

DISCIPLES
Isa 8.16 seal the law among my *d*.
Mt 5. 1 he was set, his *d* came unto him:
8.21 another of his *d* said unto him,
23 into a ship, his *d* followed him.
25 his *d* came to him, and awoke
9.10 and sat down with him and his *d*.
11 they said unto his *d*, Why eateth
14 came to him the *d* of John, saying,
14 fast oft, but thy *d* fast not?
19 and followed him, and so did his *d*.
37 saith he unto his *d*, The harvest
10. 1 had called unto him his twelve *d*,
11. 1 end of commanding his twelve *d*,
2 of Christ, he sent two of his *d*,
12. 1 *d* were an hungred, and began to
2 thy *d* do that which is not lawful
49 forth his hand toward his *d*,
13.10 And the *d* came, and said unto him,
36 into the house: and his *d* came
14.12 his *d* came, and took up the body,
15 his *d* came to him, saying, This is
19 loaves to his *d*, and the *d* to the
22 constrained his *d* to get into a ship,
26 the *d* saw him walking on the sea,
15. 2 Why do thy *d* transgress the
12 Then came his *d*, and said unto him,
23 And his *d* came and besought him,
32 Jesus called his *d* unto him, and
33 his *d* say unto him, Whence
36 and brake them, and gave to his *d*,
36 and the *d* to the multitude.
16. 5 his *d* were come to the other side,
13 he asked his *d*, saying, Whom do
20 Then charged he his *d* that they
21 to shew unto his *d*, how that he
24 said Jesus unto his *d*, If any man
17. 6 when the *d* heard it, they fell
10 his *d* asked him, saying, Why then
13 Then the *d* understood that he
16 I brought him to thy *d*, and they
19 Then came the *d* to Jesus apart,
18. 1 came the *d* unto Jesus, saying,
19.10 His *d* say unto him, If the case
13 and pray: and the *d* rebuked them.
23 Then said Jesus unto his *d*, Verily
25 When his *d* heard it, they were
20.17 took the twelve *d* apart in the way,
21. 1 of Olives, then sent Jesus two *d*,
6 And the *d* went, and did as Jesus
20 when the *d* saw it, they marvelled,
22.16 sent out unto him their *d* with the
23. 1 to the multitude, and to his *d*,
24. 1 his *d* came to him for to shew him
3 the *d* came unto him privately,
26. 1 he said unto his *d*, Ye know that
8 his *d* saw it, they had indignation,
17 the *d* came to Jesus, saying unto
18 passover at thy house with my *d*.
19 the *d* did as Jesus had appointed
26 gave it to the *d*, and said, Take
35 thee. Likewise also said all the *d*.
36 and saith unto the *d*, Sit ye here
40 he cometh unto the *d*, and findeth
45 Then cometh he to his *d*, and saith
56 Then all the *d* forsook him, and
27.64 lest his *d* come by night, and steal
28. 7 *d* that he is risen from the dead;
8 and did run to bring his *d* word.
9 And as they went to tell his *d*,
13 Say ye, His *d* came by night,
16 eleven *d* went away into Galilee,
Mk 2.15 together with Jesus and his *d*:
16 they said unto his *d*, How is it
18 And the *d* of John and of the
18 Why do the *d* of John and of the
18 Pharisees fast, but thy *d* fast not?
23 his *d* began, as they went, to pluck
3. 7 himself with his *d* to the sea:
9 spake to his *d*, that a small ship
4.34 he expounded all things to his *d*.
5.31 his *d* said unto him, Thou seest
6. 1 own country; and his *d* follow him.
29 when his *d* heard of it, they came
35 his *d* came unto him, and said,
41 them to his *d* to set before them:
45 constrained his *d* to get into the
7. 2 they saw some of his *d* eat bread
5 Why walk not thy *d* according to
17 his *d* asked him concerning the
8. 1 Jesus called his *d* unto him, and
4 his *d* answered him, From whence
6 gave to his *d* to set before them;
10 entered into a ship with his *d*,
14 Now the *d* had forgotten to take
27 went out, and his *d*, into the towns
27 and by the way he asked his *d*,

33 looked on his *d*, he rebuked Peter,
34 people unto him with his *d* also,
9.14 when he came to his *d*, he saw a
18 I spake to thy *d* that they should
28 his *d* asked him privately, Why
31 taught his *d*, and said unto them,
10.10 in the house his *d* asked him
13 his *d* rebuked those that brought
23 and saith unto his *d*, How hardly
24 the *d* were astonished at his words.
46 went out of Jericho with his *d*
11. 1 he sendeth forth two of his *d*,
14 for ever. And his *d* heard it.
12.43 he called unto him his *d*, and saith
13. 1 one of his *d* saith unto him,
14.12 *d* said unto him, Where wilt thou
13 he sendeth forth two of his *d*,
14 shall eat the passover with my *d*?
16 his *d* went forth, and came into
32 and he saith to his *d*, Sit ye here,
16. 7 tell his *d* and Peter that he goeth
Lk 5.30 murmured against his *d*, saying,
33 Why do the *d* of John fast often,
33 likewise the *d* of the Pharisees
6. 1 his *d* plucked the ears of corn,
13 was day, he called unto him his *d*:
17 company of his *d*, and a great
20 And he lifted up his eyes on his *d*,
7.11 and many of his *d* went with him,
18 the *d* of John shewed him of all
19 John calling unto him two of his *d*
8. 9 his *d* asked him, saying, What
22 he went into a ship with his *d*:
9. 1 he called his twelve *d* together,
14 he said to his *d*, Make them sit
16 and gave to the *d* to set before
18 praying, his *d* were with him:
40 I besought thy *d* to cast him out;
43 said unto his *d*, Let these sayings
54 And when his *d* James and John
10.23 he turned him unto his *d*, and said
11. 1 one of his *d* said unto him, Lord,
1 as John also taught his *d*.
12. 1 he began to say unto his *d* first of
22 he said unto his *d*, Therefore I say
16. 1 he said also unto his *d*, There was
17. 1 Then said he unto the *d*, It is
22 said unto the *d*, The days will come,
18.15 his *d* saw it, they rebuked them.
19.29 of Olives, he sent two of his *d*,
37 *d* began to rejoice and praise God
39 unto him, Master, rebuke thy *d*.
20.45 unto his *d*, Beware of the scribes,
22.11 eat the passover with my *d*?
39 Olives; and his *d* also followed him.
45 was come to his *d*, he found them
Jn 1.35 John stood, and two of his *d*;
37 And the two *d* heard him speak,
2. 2 called, and his *d*, to the marriage.
11 glory; and his *d* believed on him.
12 and his brethren, and his *d*:
17 his *d* remembered that it was
22 his *d* remembered that he had said
3.22 came Jesus and his *d* into the land
25 between some of John's *d* and the
4. 1 and baptized more *d* than John,
4. 2 himself baptized not, but his *d*,)
8 (For his *d* were gone away unto
27 upon this came his *d*, and marvelled
31 the meanwhile his *d* prayed him,
33 Therefore said the *d* one to
6. 3 and there he sat with his *d*.
8 One of his *d*, Andrew, Simon
11 distributed to the *d*, and the *d* to
12 he said unto his *d*, Gather up the
16 his *d* went down unto the sea,
22 whereinto his *d* were entered,
22 Jesus went not with his *d* into the
22 that his *d* were gone away alone;
24 was not there, neither his *d*, they
60 Many therefore of his *d*, when they

The fishermen Peter and Andrew become disciples and "fishers of men" in this fresco by Duccio.

61 himself that his *d* murmured at it,
66 many of his *d* went back, and
7. 3 that thy *d* also may see the works
8.31 word, then are ye my *d* indeed;
9. 2 his *d* asked him, saying, Master,
27 it again? will ye also be his *d*?
28 his disciple; but we are Moses' *d*.
11. 7 saith he to his *d*, Let us go into
8 His *d* say unto him, Master, the
12 Then said his *d*, Lord, if he sleep,
54 and there continued with his *d*.
12. 4 Then saith one of his *d*, Judas
16 understood not his *d* at the first:
13.22 Then the *d* looked one on another.
23 one of his *d*, whom Jesus loved.
35 know that ye are my *d*, if ye have
15. 8 much fruit; so shall ye be my *d*.
16.17 Then said some of his *d* among
29 His *d* said unto him, Lo, now
18. 1 he went forth with his *d* over the
1 the which he entered, and his *d*.
2 resorted thither with his *d*.
17 not thou also one of this man's *d*?
19 priest then asked Jesus of his *d*,
25 Art not thou also one of his *d*?
20.10 Then the *d* went away unto their
18 Magdalene came and told the *d*
19 shut where the *d* were assembled
20 Then were the *d* glad, when they
25 The other *d* therefore said unto
26 his *d* were within, and Thomas
30 did Jesus in the presence of his *d*,
21. 1 himself again to the *d* at the sea
2 of Zebedee, and two other of his *d*.
4 the *d* knew not that it was Jesus.
8 And the other *d* came in a little
12 And none of the *d* durst ask him,
14 Jesus shewed himself to his *d*,

Ac 1.15 stood up in the midst of the *d*,
6. 1 number of the *d* was multiplied,
2 called the multitude of the *d* unto
7 the number of the *d* multiplied in
9. 1 against the *d* of the Lord, went
19 certain days with the *d* which
25 Then the *d* took him by night,
26 assayed to join himself to the *d*:
38 and the *d* had heard that Peter
11.26 And the *d* were called Christians
29 Then the *d*, every man according
13.52 And the *d* were filled with joy,
14.20 Howbeit, as the *d* stood round
22 Confirming the souls of the *d*, and
28 they abode long time with the *d*.
15.10 a yoke upon the neck of the *d*,
18.23 in order, strengthening all the *d*
27 exhorting the *d* to receive him:
19. 1 Ephesus; and finding certain *d*,
9 and separated the *d*, disputing
30 people, the *d* suffered him not.
20. 1 Paul called unto him the *d*, and
7 the *d* came together to break
30 things, to draw away *d* after them.
21. 4 And finding *d*, we tarried there
16 also certain of the *d* of Caesarea,

DISCIPLES'

Jn 13. 5 to wash the *d* feet, and to wipe

DISCOMFITED

Ex 17.13 And Joshua *d* Amalek and his
Nu 14.45 smote them, and *d* them, even
Jos 10.10 And the Lord *d* them before
Jdg 4.15 And the Lord *d* Sisera, and all his
8.12 And Zalmunna, and *d* all the host.
1Sa 7.10 the Philistines, and *d* them; and
2Sa 22.15 them; lightning, and *d* them.

Ps 18.14 shot out lightnings, and *d* them.
Isa 31. 8 and his young men shall be *d*.

DISCOURAGED

Nu 21. 4 the soul of the people was much *d*
32. 9 they *d* the heart of the children
Dt 1.21 thee: fear not, neither be *d*.
28 our brethren have *d* our heart,
Isa 42. 4 He shall not fail nor be *d*, till
Col 3.21 children to anger, lest they be *d*.

DISCOVERED

Ex 20.26 that thy nakedness be not *d*
Lev 20.18 he hath *d* her fountain, and she
1Sa 14.11 And both of them *d* themselves
22. 6 Saul heard that David was *d*,
2Sa 22.16 foundations of the world were *d*,
Ps 18.15 foundations of the world were *d*
Isa 22. 8 And he *d* the covering of Judah,
57. 8 thou hast *d* thyself to another
Jer 13.22 thine iniquity are thy skirts *d*,
La 2.14 they have not *d* thine iniquity,
Eze 13.14 foundation thereof shall be *d*,
16.36 thy nakedness *d* through thy
57 thy wickedness was *d*, as at the
21.24 that your transgressions are *d*,
22.10 In thee have they *d* their fathers'
23.10 These *d* her nakedness: they
18 she *d* her whoredoms, and *d* her
29 thy whoredoms shall be *d*, both
Hos 7. 1 the iniquity of Ephraim was *d*,
Ac 21. 3 when we had *d* Cyprus, we left
27.39 they *d* a certain creek with a

DISCREET

Gen 41.33 look out a man *d* and wise,
39 none so *d* and wise as thou art:
Tit 2. 5 To be *d*, chaste, keepers at home,

DISCREETLY

Mk 12.34 saw that he answered *d*, he said

DISEASE

2Ki 1. 2 whether I shall recover of this *d*.
8. 8, 9 Shall I recover of this *d*?
2Ch 16.12 until his *d* was exceeding great:
12 yet in his *d* he sought not to the
21.15 sickness by *d* of thy bowels, until
18 his bowels with an incurable *d*.
Job 30.18 By the great force of my *d* is my
Ps 38. 7 are filled with a loathsome *d*:
41. 8 An evil *d*, say they, cleaveth fast
Ec 6. 2 this is vanity, and it is an evil *d*.
Mt 4.23 all manner of *d* among the people.
9.35 and every *d* among the people.
10. 1 of sickness and all manner of *d*.
Jn 5. 4 whole of whatsoever *d* he had.

DISEASED

1Ki 15.23 his old age he was *d* in his feet.
2Ch 16.12 year of his reign was *d* in his feet,
Eze 34. 4 The *d* have ye not strengthened,
21 pushed all the *d* with your horns,
Mt 9.20 was *d* with an issue of blood
14.35 unto him all that were *d*;
Mk 1.32 unto him all that were *d*,
Jn 9. 2 which he did on them that were *d*.

DISEASES

Ex 15.26 put none of these *d* upon thee,
Dt 7.15 put none of the evil *d* of Egypt,
28.60 bring upon thee all the *d* of Egypt,
2Ch 21.19 his sickness: so he died of sore *d*.
24.25 (for they left him in great *d*,) his
Ps 103. 3 iniquities: who healeth all thy *d*;
Mt 4.24 that were taken with divers *d*
Mk 1.34 many that were sick of divers *d*,
Lk 4.40 any sick with divers *d* brought
6.17 him; and to be healed of their *d*;
9. 1 over all devils, and to cure *d*.

Ac 19.12 and the *d* departed from them,
28. 9 which had *d* in the island, came,

DISFIGURE

Mt 6.16 for they *d* their faces, that they

DISH

Jdg 5.25 brought forth butter in a lordly *d*.
2Ki 21.13 as a man wipeth a *d*, wiping it,
Mt 26.23 dippeth his hand with me in the *d*,
Mk 14.20 that dippeth with me in the *d*,

DISHONESTY

2Co 4. 2 renounced the hidden things of *d*,

DISHONOR

Ezr 4.14 meet for us to see the king's *d*,
Ps 35.26 be clothed with shame and *d* that
69.19 and my shame, and my *d*: mine
71.13 be covered with reproach and *d*
Pr 6.33 A wound and *d* shall he get;
Jn 8.49 honor my Father, and ye do *d* me.
Ro 1.24 to *d* their own bodies between
9.21 unto honor, and another unto *d*?
1Co 15.43 It is sown in *d*; it is raised in
2Co 6. 8 By honor and *d*, by evil report
2Ti 2.20 some to honor, and some to *d*.

DISHONOREST

Ro 2.23 breaking the law *d* thou God?

DISHONORETH

Mic 7. 6 son *d* the father, the daughter
1Co 11. 4 his head covered, *d* his head.
5 her head uncovered *d* her head:

DISMISSED

2Ch 23. 8 Jehoiada the priest *d* not the
Ac 15.30 So when they were *d*, they came
19.41 thus spoken, he *d* the assembly.

DISOBEDIENCE

Ro 5.19 by one man's *d* many were made
2Co 10. 6 to revenge all *d*, when your
Eph 2. 2 now worketh in the children of *d*:
5. 6 of God upon the children of *d*.
Col 3. 6 of God cometh on the children of *d*:
Heb 2. 2 transgression and *d* received a

DISOBEDIENT

1Ki 13.26 the man of God, who was *d* unto
Neh 9.26 Nevertheless they were *d*, and
Lk 1.17 the *d* to the wisdom of the just;
Ac 26.19 was not *d* unto the heavenly vision:
Ro 1.30 of evil things, *d* to parents,
10.21 unto a *d* and gainsaying people.
1Ti 1. 9 but for the lawless and *d*, for the
2Ti 3. 2 blasphemers, *d* to parents,
Tit 1.16 being abominable, and *d*, and unto
3. 3 sometimes foolish, *d*, deceived,
1Pe 2. 7 but unto them which be *d*,
8 stumble at the word, being *d*:
3.20 Which sometime were *d*, when

DISORDERLY

2Th 3. 6 every brother that walketh *d*,
7 behaved not ourselves *d* among
11 some which walk among you *d*,

DISPENSATION

1Co 9.17 a *d* of the gospel is committed
Eph 1.10 That in the *d* of the fulness of
3. 2 heard of the *d* of the grace of God
Col 1.25 according to the *d* of God which

DISPERSED

2Ch 11.23 *d* of all his children throughout
Est 3. 8 and *d* among the people in all
Ps 112. 9 He hath *d*, he hath given to the
Pr 5.16 Let thy fountains be *d* abroad,
Isa 11.12 gather together the *d* of Judah

Eze 36.19 were *d* through the countries:
Zep 3.10 the daughter of my *d*, shall bring
Jn 7.35 unto the *d* among the Gentiles?
Ac 5.37 as many as obeyed him, were *d*.
2Co 9. 9 He hath *d* abroad; he hath given

DISPLEASED

Gen 38.10 which he did *d* the Lord:
48.17 And when Joseph...it *d* him:
Nu 11. 1 complained, it *d* the Lord:
10 greatly; Moses also was *d*
1Sa 8. 6 But the thing *d* Samuel,
18. 8 and the saying *d* him; and he
2Sa 6. 8 And David was *d*, because the
11.27 thing that David had done *d*
1Ki 1. 6 his father had not *d* him at any
20.43 went to his house heavy and *d*,
21. 4 came into his house heavy and *d*
1Ch 13.11 And David was *d*, because the
21. 7 God was *d* with this thing;
Ps 60. 1 thou hast been *d*; O turn thyself
Isa 59.15 it *d* him that there was no
Dan 6.14 was sore *d* with himself, and set
Jon 4. 1 But it *d* Jonah exceedingly,
Hab 3. 8 the Lord *d* against the rivers?
Zec 1. 2 The Lord hath been sore *d* with
15 I am very sore *d* with the heathen
15 at ease: for I was but a little *d*,
Mt 21.15 son of David; they were sore *d*,
Mk 10.14 Jesus saw it, he was much *d*,
41 began to be much *d* with James
Ac 12.20 Herod was highly *d* with them of

DISPOSED

Job 34.13 who hath *d* the whole world?
37.15 thou know when God *d* them,
Ac 18.27 he was *d* to pass into Achaia,
1Co 10.27 you to a feast, and ye be *d* to go;

DISPOSITION

Ac 7.53 the law by the *d* of angels,

DISPUTATION

Ac 15. 2 no small dissension and *d* with

DISPUTATIONS

Ro 14. 1 receive ye, but not to doubtful *d*.

DISPUTED

Mk 9.33 that ye *d* among yourselves by
34 they had *d* among themselves,
Ac 9.29 and *d* against the Grecians:
17.17 *d* he in the synagogue with the
Jude 9 he *d* about the body of Moses,

DISPUTER

1Co 1.20 where is the *d* of this world?

DISPUTING

Ac 6. 9 and of Asia, *d* with Stephen.
15. 7 when there had been much *d*,
19. 8 three months, *d* and persuading
9 *d* daily in the school of one
24.12 me in the temple *d* with any man,

DISPUTINGS

Php 2.14 without murmurings and *d*:
1Ti 6. 5 Perverse *d* of men of corrupt

DISQUIETED

1Sa 28.15 Why hast thou *d* me, to bring me
Ps 39. 6 shew: surely they are *d* in vain:
42. 5 and why art thou *d* in me? hope
11 why art thou *d* within me? hope
43. 5 why art thou *d* within me? hope
Pr 30.21 For three things the earth is *d*,

DISSEMBLED

Jos 7.11 and have also stolen, and *d* also,
Jer 42.20 For ye *d* in your hearts, when ye
Gal 2.13 other Jews *d* likewise with him;

DISSENSION
Ac 15. 2 had no small *d* and disputation
23. 7 a *d* between the Pharisees and the
10 And when there arose a great *d*,

DISSIMULATION
Ro 12. 9 Let love be without *d*. Abhor
Gal 2.13 was carried away with their *d*.

DISSOLVED
Ps 75. 3 the inhabitants therefore are *d*:
Isa 14.31 thou, whole Palestina, art *d*:
24.19 the earth is clean *d*, the earth
34. 4 all the host of heaven shall be *d*,
Na 2. 6 and the palace shall be *d*.
2Co 5. 1 house of this tabernacle were *d*,
2Pe 3.11 that all these things shall be *d*.
12 heavens being on fire shall be *d*,

DISTINCTION
1Co 14. 7 they give a *d* in the sounds,

DISTRACTION
1Co 7.35 attend upon the Lord without *d*.

DISTRESS
Gen 35. 3 answered me in the day of my *d*,
42.21 therefore is this *d* come upon us.
Dt 2. 9 *D* not the Moabites, neither
19 Ammon, *d* them not, nor meddle
28.53 thine enemies shall *d* thee:
55 thine enemies shall *d* thee in all
57 enemy shall *d* thee in thy gates.
Jdg 11. 7 unto me now when ye are in *d*?
1Sa 22. 2 And every one that was in *d*,
2Sa 22. 7 In my *d* I called upon the Lord,
1Ki 1.29 redeemed my soul out of all *d*,
2Ch 28.22 And in the time of his *d* did he
Neh 2.17 Ye see the *d* that we are in,
9.37 pleasure, and we are in great *d*.
Ps 4. 1 enlarged me when I was in *d*;
18. 6 In my *d* I called upon the Lord,
118. 5 I called upon the Lord in *d*:
120. 1 In my *d* I cried unto the Lord,
Pr 1.27 *d* and anguish cometh upon you.
Isa 25. 4 a strength to the needy in his *d*,
29. 2 Yet I will *d* Ariel, and there shall
7 and her munition, and that *d* her,
Jer 10.18 and will *d* them, that they may
La 1.20 O Lord; for I am in *d*: my bowels
Ob 12 spoken proudly in the day of *d*.
14 that did remain in the day of *d*.
Zep 1.15 a day of trouble and *d*, a day of
17 And I will bring *d* upon men,
Lk 21.23 there shall be great *d* in the land,
25 and upon the earth *d* of nations,
Ro 8.35 tribulation, or *d*, or persecution,
1Co 7.26 this is good for the present *d*,
1Th 3. 7 our affliction and *d* by your faith:

DISTRESSED
Gen 32. 7 Jacob was greatly afraid and *d*:
Nu 22. 3 and Moab was *d* because of the
Jdg 2.15 them: and they were greatly *d*.
10. 9 so that Israel was sore *d*.
1Sa 13. 6 (for the people were *d*,) then the
14.24 the men of Israel were *d* that day:
28.15 And Saul answered, I am sore *d*;
30. 6 And David was greatly *d*; for the
2Sa 1.26 I am *d* for thee, my brother
2Ch 28.20 *d* him, but strengthened him not.
2Co 4. 8 troubled on every side, yet not *d*;

DISTRESSES
Ps 25.17 O bring thou me out of my *d*.
107. 6 he delivered them out of their *d*.
13 he saved them out of their *d*.
19 he saveth them out of their *d*.
28 he bringeth them out of their *d*.
Eze 30.16 and Noph shall have *d* daily.
2Co 6. 4 in afflictions, in necessities, in *d*,
12.10 persecutions, in *d* for Christ's sake:

Biblical Themes

DISHONESTY

And Rebekah took goodly raiment of her eldest son Esau . . . and put them upon Jacob her younger son: and she put the skins of the kids of the goats upon his hands. . . . And Jacob went near unto Isaac his father; and he felt him, and said, The voice is Jacob's voice, but the hands are the hands of Esau. And he discerned him not, because his hands were hairy . . . so he blessed him. Gen 27.15-16, 22-23

If a soul sin, and commit a trespass against the Lord, and lie unto his neighbor in that which was delivered him to keep . . . or have found that which was lost, and lieth concerning it . . . then it shall be, because he hath sinned, and is guilty, that he shall restore that which he took . . . and shall add the fifth part more thereto, and give it unto him to whom it appertaineth. Lev 6.2-5

Thou shalt not defraud thy neighbor, neither rob him: the wages of him that is hired shall not abide with thee all night until the morning. Lev 19.13

And Achan answered Joshua, and said, Indeed I have sinned against the Lord. . . . When I saw among the spoils a goodly Babylonish garment, and two hundred shekels of silver, and a wedge of gold of fifty shekels weight, then I coveted them, and took them. Jos 7.20-21

The inhabitants of Gibeon . . . did work wilily, and went and made as if they had been ambassadors, and took old sacks upon their asses, and wine bottles, old, and rent, and bound up. . . . And they went to Joshua . . . and said unto him . . . We be come from a far country: now therefore make ye a league with us. Jos 9.3-4, 6

The wicked borroweth, and payeth not again: but the righteous sheweth mercy, and giveth. Ps 37.21

The words of his mouth were smoother than butter, but war was in his heart. Ps 55.21

Bread of deceit is sweet to a man: but afterwards his mouth shall be filled with gravel. Pr 20.17

The getting of treasures by a lying tongue is a vanity tossed to and fro of them that seek death. Pr 21.6

We have made a covenant with death . . . we have made lies our refuge, and under falsehood have we hid ourselves. Isa 28.15

Will ye steal, murder, and commit adultery . . . And come and stand before me in this house, which is called by my name. . . ? Jer 7.9-10

Have we not all one father? hath not one God created us? why do we deal treacherously every man against his brother, by profaning the covenant of our fathers? Mal 2.10

What shall it profit a man, if he shall gain the whole world, and lose his own soul? Mk 8.36

Then came also publicans to be baptized, and said unto him, Master, what shall we do? And he said unto them, Exact no more than that which is appointed you. Lk 3.12-13

Why was not this ointment sold for three hundred pence, and given to the poor? This [Judas] said, not that he cared for the poor; but because he was a thief, and had the bag, and bare what was put therein. Jn 12.5-6

Behold, the hire of the laborers who have reaped down your fields, which is of you kept back by fraud, crieth: and the cries of them which have reaped are entered into the ears of the Lord. Jas 5.4

DISTRIBUTE
Jos 13.32 Moses did *d* for inheritance in
2Ch 31.14 to *d* the oblations of the Lord,
Neh 13.13 was to *d* unto their brethren.
Lk 18.22 *d* unto the poor, and thou shalt
1Ti 6.18 works, ready to *d*, willing to

DISTRIBUTED
Jos 14. 1 Israel, *d* for inheritance to them.
1Ch 24. 3 David *d* them, both Zadok of
2Ch 23.18 whom David had *d* in the house of
Jn 6.11 he *d* to the disciples, and the
1Co 7.17 as God hath *d* to every man,
2Co 10.13 rule which God hath *d* to us,

DISTRIBUTING
Ro 12.13 *D* to the necessity of saints;

DISTRIBUTION
Ac 4.35 feet: and *d* was made unto every
2Co 9.13 and for your liberal *d* unto them,

DITCH
Job 9.31 Yet shalt thou plunge me in the *d*,
Ps 7.15 is fallen into the *d* which he
Pr 23.27 For a whore is a deep *d*; and a
Isa 22.11 Ye made also a *d* between the
Mt 15.14 blind, both shall fall into the *d*
Lk 6.39 they not both fall into the *d*?

DIVERS
Dt 22. 9 sow thy vineyard with *d* seeds:
11 a garment of *d* sorts, as of
25.13 shalt not have in thy bag *d* weights,

Dt 25.14 not have in thine house *d* measures,
Jdg 5.30 to Sisera a prey of *d* colors,
30 a prey of *d* colors of needlework,
30 of *d* colors of needlework
2Sa 13.18 she had a garment of *d* colors
19 rent her garment of *d* colors
1Ch 29. 2 glistering stones, and of *d* colors.
2Ch 16.14 filled with sweet odors and *d* kinds
21. 4 and *d* also of the princes of Israel.
30.11 *d* of Asher and Manasseh and
Ps 78.45 sent *d* sorts of flies among them,
105.31 came *d* sorts of flies, and lice
Pr 20.10 *D* weights, and *d* measures,
23 *D* weights are an abomination
Ec 5. 7 words there are also *d* vanities:
Eze 16.16 thy high places with *d* colors,
17. 3 of feathers, which had *d* colors,
Mt 4.24 with *d* diseases and torments,
24. 7 and earthquakes, in *d* places.
Mk 1.34 many that were sick of *d* diseases.
8. 3 for *d* of them came from far.
13. 8 shall be earthquakes in *d* places,
Lk 4.40 sick with *d* diseases brought
21.11 great earthquakes shall be in *d*
Ac 19. 9 But when *d* were hardened, and
1Co 12.10 to another *d* kind of tongues;
2Ti 3. 6 with sins, led away with *d* lusts,
Tit 3. 3 serving *d* lusts and pleasures,
Heb 1. 1 times and in *d* manners spake in
2. 4 and with *d* miracles, and gifts of
9.10 meats and drinks, and *d* washings,
13. 9 with *d* and strange doctrines.
Jas 1. 2 when ye fall into *d* temptations;

DIVERSE

Lev 19.19 cattle gender with a *d* kind:
Est 1. 7 vessels being *d* one from another,)
3. 8 their laws are *d* from all people;
Dan 7. 3 the sea, *d* one from another.
7 and it was *d* from all the beasts
19 which was *d* from all the others,
23 which shall be *d* from all kingdoms,
24 and he shall be *d* from the first,

DIVERSITIES

1Co 12. 4 Now there are *d* of gifts, but the
6 there are *d* of operations, but it
28 helps, governments, *d* of tongues.

DIVIDE

Gen 1. 6 let it *d* the waters from the waters.
14 to *d* the day from the night;
18 to *d* the light from the darkness:
49. 7 will *d* them in Jacob, and scatter
27 at night he shall *d* the spoil.
Ex 14.16 thine hand over the sea, and *d* it:
15. 9 I will overtake, I will *d* the spoil;
21.35 the live ox, and *d* the money of it;
35 the dead ox also they shall *d*.
26.33 the vail shall *d* unto you between
Lev 1.17 thereof, but shall not *d* it asunder:
5. 8 neck, but shall not *d* it asunder:
11. 4 cud, or of them that *d* the hoof:
7 the swine, though he *d* the hoof,
Nu 31.27 And *d* the prey into two parts;
33.54 And ye shall *d* the land by lot for
34.17 which shall *d* the land unto you:
18 tribe, to *d* the land by inheritance.
29 Lord commanded to *d* the inheritance
Dt 14. 7 or of them that *d* the cloven hoof;
7 chew the cud, but *d* not the hoof;
19. 3 *d* the coasts...into three parts,
Jos 1. 6 shalt thou *d* for an inheritance
13. 6 *d* thou it by lot unto the Israelites
7 *d* this land for an inheritance
18. 5 And they shall *d* it into seven
22. 8 *d* the spoil of your enemies with
2Sa 19.29 said, Thou and Ziba *d* the land.
1Ki 3.25 *D* the living child in two, and
26 be neither mine nor thine, but *d* it.
Neh 9.11 thou didst *d* the sea before them,
22 and didst *d* them into corners:
Job 27.17 and the innocent shall *d* the silver.
Ps 55. 9 Destroy, O Lord, and *d* their
60. 6 I will *d* Shechem, and mete out
74.13 Thou didst *d* the sea by thy
108. 7 will rejoice, I will *d* Shechem, and
Pr 16.19 than to *d* the spoil with the proud.
Isa 9. 3 rejoice when they *d* the spoil.
53.12 Therefore will I *d* him a portion
12 he shall *d* the spoil with the strong;
Eze 5. 1 balances to weigh, and *d* the hair.
45. 1 Moreover, when ye shall *d* by lot
47.21 So shall ye *d* this land unto you
22 shall *d* it by lot for an inheritance
48.29 ye shall *d* by lot unto the tribes
Dan 11.39 and shall *d* the land for gain.
Lk 12.13 that he *d* the inheritance with me.
22.17 Take this, and *d* it among

DIVIDED

Gen 1. 4 God *d* the light from the darkness.
7 and *d* the waters which were under
10. 5 were the isles of the Gentiles *d*
25 in his days was the earth *d*;
32 by these were the nations *d* in the
14.15 And he *d* himself against them,
15.10 and *d* them in the midst, and laid
10 another: but the birds *d* he not.
32. 7 and he *d* the people that was with
33. 1 And he *d* the children unto Leah,
Ex 14.21 dry land, and the waters were *d*.
Nu 26.53 Unto these the land shall be *d*
55 the land shall be *d* by lot:
56 shall the possession thereof be *d*
31.42 which Moses *d* from the men that
Dt 4.19 which the Lord thy God hath *d*
32. 8 *d* to the nations their inheritance,
Jos 14. 5 Israel did, and they *d* the land.
18.10 there Joshua *d* the land unto the
19.51 *d* for an inheritance by lot in
23. 4 I have *d* unto you by lot
Jdg 5.30 have they not *d* the prey; to
7.16 And he *d* the three hundred men
9.43 and *d* them into three companies,
19.29 and *d* her, together with her
2Sa 1.23 in their death they were not *d*:
1Ki 16.21 Then were the people of Israel *d*
18. 6 So they *d* the land between them
2Ki 2. 8 they were *d* hither and thither,
1Ch 1.19 in his days the earth was *d*:
23. 6 And David *d* them into courses
24. 4 of Ithamar; and thus were they *d*.
5 Thus were they *d* by lot, one sort
2Ch 35.13 and *d* them speedily among all
Job 38.25 Who hath *d* a watercourse for the
Ps 68.12 that tarried at home *d* the spoil.
78.13 He *d* the sea, and caused them
55 and *d* them an inheritance by
136.13 To him which *d* the Red sea into
Isa 33.23 is the prey of a great spoil *d*;
34.17 his hand hath *d* it unto them by
51.15 the Lord thy God, that *d* the sea,
La 4.16 anger of the Lord hath *d* them;
Eze 37.22 neither shall they be *d* into two
Dan 2.41 of iron, the kingdom shall be *d*;
5.28 Thy kingdom is *d*, and given
11. 4 and shall be *d* toward the four
Hos 10. 2 Their heart is *d*; now shall they
Am 7.17 and thy land shall be *d* by line;
Mic 2. 4 away he hath *d* our fields.
Zec 14. 1 and thy spoil shall be *d* in the
Mt 12.25 Every kingdom *d* against itself is
25 city or house *d* against itself
26 Satan, he is *d* against himself;
Mk 3.24 if a kingdom be *d* against itself,
25 if a house be *d* against itself,
26 and be *d*, he cannot stand, but hath
6.41 the two fishes *d* he among them all.
Lk 11.17 Every kingdom *d* against itself is
17 house *d* against a house falleth
18 If Satan also be *d* against himself,
12.52 there shall be five in one house *d*,
53 father shall be *d* against the son,
15.12 And he *d* unto them his living.
Ac 13.19 he *d* their land to them by lot.
14. 4 the multitude of the city was *d*:
23. 7 and the multitude was *d*.
1Co 1.13 Is Christ *d*? was Paul crucified
Rev 16.19 the great city was *d* into three

DIVIDER

Lk 12.14 made me a judge or a *d* over you?

DIVIDETH

Lev 11. 4, 5 the cud; but *d* not the hoof;
6 the cud, but *d* not the hoof;
26 every beast which *d* the hoof,
Dt 14. 8 the swine, because it *d* the hoof,
Job 26.12 He *d* the sea with his power,
Ps 29. 7 the Lord *d* the flames of fire.
Jer 31.35 which *d* the sea when the waves
Mt 25.32 as a shepherd *d* his sheep from
Lk 11.22 he trusted, and *d* his spoils.

DIVIDING

Jos 19.49 end of *d* the land for inheritance
51 made an end of *d* the country.
Isa 63.12 *d* the water before them, to
Dan 7.25 a time and times and the *d* of
1Co 12.11 *d* to every man severally as he
2Ti 2.15 rightly *d* the word of truth.
Heb 4.12 even to the *d* asunder of soul and

DIVINATION

Nu 22. 7 with the rewards of *d* in their
23.23 is there any *d* against Israel:
Dt 18.10 or that useth *d*, or an observer
2Ki 17.17 used *d* and enchantments, and
Jer 14.14 a false vision and *d*, and a thing
Eze 12.24 vain vision nor flattering *d* within
13. 6 vanity and lying *d*, saying, The
7 have ye not spoken a lying *d*,
21.21 head of the two ways, to use *d*:
22 hand was the *d* for Jerusalem,
23 be unto them as a false *d* in their
Ac 16.16 possessed with a spirit of *d* met us,

DIVINE

Gen 44.15 such a man as I can certainly *d*?
1Sa 28. 8 *d* unto me by the familiar spirit,
Pr 16.10 A *d* sentence is in the lips of the
Eze 13. 9 that see vanity, and that *d* lies:
23 no more vanity, nor *d* divinations
21.29 whiles they *d* a lie unto thee,
Mic 3. 6 unto you, that ye shall not *d*;
11 the prophets thereof *d* for money:
Heb 9. 1 had also ordinances of *d* service,
2Pe 1. 3 According as his *d* power hath
4 might be partakers of the *d* nature,

DIVISION

Ex 8.23 I will put a *d* between my people
2Ch 35. 5 and after the *d* of the families
Lk 12.51 I tell you, Nay; but rather *d*:
Jn 7.43 there was a *d* among the people
9.16 there was a *d* among them.
10.19 There was a *d* therefore again

DIVISIONS

Jos 11.23 to their *d* by their tribes.
12. 7 a possession according to their *d*;
18.10 of Israel according to their *d*.
Jdg 5.15 For the *d* of Reuben...thoughts
16 the *d* of Reuben...searchings
1Ch 24. 1 are the *d* of the sons of Aaron.
26. 1 Concerning the *d* of the porters:
12 these were the *d* of the porters.
19 These are the *d* of the porters
2Ch 35. 5 according to the *d* of the families
12 according to the *d* of the families
Ezr 6.18 they set the priests in their *d*,
Neh 11.36 of the Levites were *d* in Judah,

Doctors *in Bible usage means "learned men." Above,* Jesus Amidst the Doctors *(Lk 2) by Caravaggio.*

Ro 16.17 them which cause *d* and offenses
1Co 1.10 that there be no *d* among you;
3. 3 you envying, and strife, and *d*,
11.18 hear that there be *d* among you;

DIVORCE

Jer 3. 8 away, and given her a bill of *d*;

DIVORCED

Lev 21.14 widow, or a *d* woman, or profane,
22.13 priest's daughter be a widow, or *d*,
Nu 30. 9 of a widow, and of her that is *d*,
Mt 5.32 her that is *d* committeth adultery.

DIVORCEMENT

Dt 24. 1 then let him write her a bill of *d*,
3 hate her, and write her a bill of *d*,
Isa 50. 1 Where is the bill of your mother's *d*,
Mt 5.31 let him give her a writing of *d*:
19. 7 command to give a writing of *d*,
Mk 10. 4 Moses suffered to write a bill of *d*,

DOCTOR

Ac 5.34 named Gamaliel, a *d* of the law,

DOCTORS

Lk 2.46 sitting in the midst of the *d*,
5.17 and *d* of the law sitting by,

DOCTRINE

Dt 32. 2 My *d* shall drop as the rain,
Job 11. 4 My *d* is pure, and I am clean in
Pr 4. 2 I give you good *d*, forsake ye not
Isa 28. 9 shall he make to understand *d*?
29.24 that murmured shall learn *d*.
Jer 10. 8 the stock is a *d* of vanities.
Mt 7.28 people were astonished at his *d*:
16.12 of the *d* of the Pharisees and of
22.33 they were astonished at his *d*.
Mk 1.22 they were astonished at his *d*:
27 what new *d* is this? for with
4. 2 and said unto them in his *d*,
11.18 people was astonished at his *d*.
12.38 he said unto them in his *d*,
Lk 4.32 they were astonished at his *d*:
Jn 7.16 My *d* is not mine, but his that
17 he shall know of the *d*, whether
18.19 of his disciples, and of his *d*.
Ac 2.42 in the apostles' *d* and fellowship,
5.28 filled Jerusalem with your *d*,
13.12 astonished at the *d* of the Lord.
17.19 what this new *d*, whereof thou
Ro 6.17 form of *d* which was delivered
16.17 offenses contrary to the *d* which
1Co 14. 6 or by prophesying, or by *d*?
26 of you hath a psalm, hath a *d*,
Eph 4.14 about with every wind of *d*,
1Ti 1. 3 some that they teach no other *d*,
10 that is contrary to sound *d*;
4. 6 up in words of faith and of good *d*,
13 to reading, to exhortation, to *d*.
16 unto thyself, and unto the *d*;
5.17 who labor in the word and *d*,
6. 1 God and his *d* be not blasphemed.
3 to the *d* which is according to
2Ti 3.10 thou hast fully known my *d*,
16 is profitable for *d*, for reproof,
4. 2 with all longsuffering and *d*.
3 they will not endure sound *d*;
Tit 1. 9 able by sound *d* both to exhort
2. 1 things which become sound *d*:
7 in *d* shewing uncorruptness,
10 adorn the *d* of God our Saviour
Heb 6. 1 leaving the principles of the *d*
2 Of the *d* of baptisms, and of
2Jn 9 abideth not in the *d* of Christ,
9 that abideth in the *d* of Christ,
10 bring not this *d*, receive him not
Rev 2.14 that hold the *d* of Balaam, who
15 hold the *d* of the Nicolaitanes,
24 as many as have not this *d*,

DOCTRINES

Mt 15. 9 for *d* the commandments of men.
Mk 7. 7 for *d* the commandments of men.
Col 2.22 the commandments and *d* of men?
1Ti 4. 1 seducing spirits, and *d* of devils;
Heb 13. 9 about with divers and strange *d*.

DOER

Gen 39.22 did there, he was the *d* of it.
2Sa 3.39 Lord shall reward the *d* of evil
Ps 31.23 plentifully rewardeth the proud *d*.
Pr 17. 4 wicked *d* giveth heed to false lips;
2Ti 2. 9 as an evil *d*, even unto bonds;
Jas 1.23 hearer of the word, and not a *d*,
25 hearer, but a *d* of the work,
4.11 not a *d* of the law, but a judge.

DOERS

2Ki 22. 5 the hand of the *d* of the work,
5 them give it to the *d* of the work,
Job 8.20 neither will he help the evil *d*:
Ps 26. 5 hated the congregation of evil *d*;
101. 8 that I may cut off all wicked *d*
Ro 2.13 *d* of the law shall be justified.
Jas 1.22 be ye *d* of the word, and not

DOG

Ex 11. 7 shall not *a* d move his tongue.
Dt 23.18 the price of a *d*, into the house
Jdg 7. 5 with his tongue, as a *d* lappeth,
1Sa 17.43 Am I a *d*, that thou comest to me
24.14 after a dead *d*, after a flea.
2Sa 9. 8 look upon such a dead *d* as I am?
16. 9 Why should this dead *d* curse my
2Ki 8.13 is thy servant a *d*, that he should
Ps 22.20 darling from the power of the *d*.
59. 6 they make a noise like a *d*, and go
14 let them make a noise like a *d*,
Pr 26.11 As a *d* returneth to his vomit,
17 one that taketh a *d* by the ears.
Ec 9. 4 living *d* is better than a dead lion.
2Pe 2.22 The *d* is turned to his own vomit

DOGS

Ex 22.31 the field; ye shall cast it to the *d*.
1Ki 14.11 in the city shall the *d* eat; and him
16. 4 Baasha in the city shall the *d* eat;
21.19 place where *d* licked the blood of
19 Naboth shall *d* lick thy blood,
23 The *d* shall eat Jezebel by the wall
24 Ahab in the city, the *d* shall eat;
22.38 and the *d* licked up his blood;
2Ki 9.10 the *d* shall eat Jezebel in the
36 shall *d* eat the flesh of Jezebel:
Job 30. 1 to have set with the *d* of my flock.
Ps 22.16 For *d* have compassed me: the
68.23 and the tongue of thy *d* in the
Isa 56.10 all ignorant, they are all dumb *d*,
11 Yea, they are greedy *d* which can
Jer 15. 3 and the *d* to tear, and the fowls
Mt 7. 6 not that which is holy unto the *d*,
15.26 bread, and to cast it to *d*.
27 yet the *d* eat of the crumbs which
Mk 7.27 bread, and to cast it unto the *d*.
28 yet the *d* under the table eat of the
Lk 16.21 the *d* came and licked his sores.
Php 3. 2 Beware of *d*, beware of evil
Rev 22.15 For without are *d*, and sorcerers,

DOING

Gen 31.28 hast now done foolishly in so *d*
44. 5 ye have done evil in so *d*.
Ex 15.11 fearful in praises, *d* wonders?
Nu 20.19 I will only, without *d* any thing
Dt 9.18 in *d* wickedly in the sight of the
1Ki 7.40 Hiram made an end of *d* all the
16.19 he sinned in *d* evil in the sight of
22.43 *d* that which was right in the eyes
2Ki 21.16 in *d* that which was evil in the
1Ch 22.16 Arise therefore and be *d*, and the
2Ch 20.32 and departed not from it, *d* that
Ezr 9. 1 *d* according to their abominations,
Neh 6. 3 I am *d* a great work, so that
Job 32.22 in so *d* my Maker would soon
Ps 64. 9 shall wisely consider of his *d*.
66. 5 is terrible in his *d* toward the
118.23 This is the Lord's *d*; it is
Isa 56. 2 keepeth his hand from *d* any evil.

Isa 58.13 *d* thy pleasure on my holy day;
13 honor him, not *d* thine own ways,
Mt 21.42 this is the Lord's *d*, and it is
24.46 when he cometh shall find so *d*.
Mk 12.11 This was the Lord's *d*, and it is
Lk 12.43 when he cometh shall find so *d*.
Ac 10.38 who went about *d* good, and
24.20 found any evil *d* in me, while I
Ro 2. 7 by patient continuance in well *d*
12.20 for in so *d* thou shalt heap coals
2Co 8.11 Now therefore perform the *d* of it;
Gal 6. 9 be weary in well *d*; for in due
Eph 6. 6 servants of Christ, *d* the will of
7 With good will *d* service, as to
2Th 3.13 brethren, be not weary in well *d*.
1Ti 4.16 for in *d* this thou shalt both save
5.21 one before another, *d* nothing by
1Pe 2.15 that with well *d* ye may put to
3.17 be so, that ye suffer for well *d*,
17 than for evil *d*.
4.19 of their souls to him in well *d*, as

DOINGS

Lev 18. 3 after the *d* of the land of Egypt,
3 and after the *d* of the land of
Dt 28.20 of the wickedness of thy *d*,
Jdg 2.19 they ceased not from their own *d*,
1Sa 25. 3 was churlish and evil in his *d*;
2Ch 17. 4 and not after the *d* of Israel.
Ps 9.11 declare among the people his *d*.
77.12 all thy work, and talk of thy *d*,
Pr 20.11 Even a child is known by his *d*,
Isa 1.16 put away the evil of your *d* from
3. 8 and their *d* are against the Lord,
10 they shall eat the fruit of their *d*.
12. 4 declare his *d* among the people,
Jer 4. 4 it, because of the evil of your *d*.
18 Thy way and thy *d* have procured
7. 3 Amend your ways and your *d*,
5 amend your ways and your *d*;
11.18 then thou shewedst me their *d*.
17.10 and according to the fruit of his *d*.
18.11 make your ways and your *d* good.
21.12 because of the evil of your *d*.
14 according to the fruit of your *d*,
23. 2 visit upon you the evil of your *d*,
22 way, and from the evil of their *d*.
25. 5 and from the evil of your *d*, and
26. 3 because of the evil of their *d*.
13 amend your ways and your *d*,
32.19 according to the fruit of his *d*:
35.15 his evil way, and amend your *d*,
44.22 because of the evil of your *d*, and
Eze 14.22 shall see their way and their *d*:
23 ye see their ways and their *d*:
20.43 all your *d* wherein ye have been
44 nor according to your corrupt *d*,
21.24 in all your *d*, your sins do appear;
24.14 and according to thy *d*, shall they
36.17 by their own way and by their *d*:
19 according to their *d* I judged them,
31 own evil ways, and your *d* that
Hos 4. 9 ways, and reward them their *d*.
5. 4 They will not frame their *d* to turn
7. 2 now their own *d* have beset them
9.15 for the wickedness of their *d* I
12. 2 to his *d* will he recompense him.
Mic 2. 7 are these his *d*? do not my words
3. 4 behaved themselves ill in their *d*.
7.13 therein, for the fruit of their *d*.
Zep 3. 7 early, and corrupted all their *d*.
11 thou not be ashamed for all thy *d*,
Zec 1. 4 and from your evil *d*: but they did
6 according to our *d*, so hath he

DOMINION

Gen 1.26 and let them have *d* over the fish
28 and have *d* over the fish of the sea,
27.40 pass when thou shalt have the *d*,
37. 8 shalt thou indeed have *d* over us?
Nu 24.19 shall come he that shall have *d*,
Jdg 5.13 made him that remaineth have *d*
13 made me have *d* over the mighty.
14. 4 the Philistines had *d* over Israel.
1Ki 4.24 he had *d* over all the region on
9.19 and in all the land of his *d*.
2Ki 20.13 in his house, nor in all his *d*,
1Ch 4.22 Saraph, who had the *d* in Moab,
18. 3 his *d* by the river Euphrates.
2Ch 8. 6 throughout all the land of his *d*,
21. 8 from under the *d* of Judah, and
Neh 9.28 so that they had the *d* over them:
37 also they have *d* over our bodies,
Job 25. 2 *D* and fear are with him, he
38.33 canst thou set the *d* thereof in
Ps 8. 6 Thou madest him to have *d* over
19.13 let them not have *d* over me:
49.14 and the upright shall have *d* over
72. 8 He shall have *d* also from sea to
103.22 his works in all places of his *d*:
114. 2 was his sanctuary, and Israel his *d*.
119.133 let not iniquity have *d* over me.
145.13 and thy *d* endureth throughout
Isa 26.13 beside thee have had *d* over us:
39. 2 nor in all his *d*, that Hezekiah
Jer 34. 1 the kingdoms of the earth of his *d*,
51.28 thereof, and all the land of his *d*.
Dan 4. 3 and his *d* is from generation to
22 and thy *d* to the end of the earth.
34 whose *d* is an everlasting *d*,
6.26 That in every *d* of my kingdom
26 his *d* shall be even unto the end.
7. 6 four heads; and *d* was given to it.
12 they had their *d* taken away:
14 there was given him *d*, and glory,
14 his *d* is an everlasting *d*,
26 and they shall take away his *d*,
27 And the kingdom and *d*, and the
11. 3 up, that shall rule with great *d*,
4 according to his *d* which he ruled:
5 be strong above him, and have *d*;
5 his *d* shall be a great
5 shall be a great *d*.
Mic 4. 8 shall it come, even the first *d*;
Zec 9.10 and his *d* shall be from sea to
Mt 20.25 princes of the Gentiles exercise *d*
Ro 6. 9 death hath no more *d* over him.
14 sin shall not have *d* over you:
7. 1 the law hath *d* over a man as long
2Co 1.24 that we have *d* over your faith,
Eph 1.21 might, and *d*, and every name that
1Pe 4.11 be praise and *d* for ever and ever.
5.11 To him be glory and *d* for ever
Jude 8 despise *d*, and speak evil of
25 *d* and power, both now and ever.
Rev 1. 6 to him be glory and *d* for ever

DOMINIONS

Dan 7.27 all *d* shall serve and obey him.
Col 1.16 or *d*, or principalities, or powers:

DOOR

Gen 4. 7 doest not well, sin lieth at the *d*.
6.16 and the *d* of the ark shalt thou set
18. 1 he sat in the tent *d* in the heat of
2 ran to meet them from the tent *d*,
10 Sarah heard it in the tent *d*,
19. 6 Lot went out at the *d* unto them,
6 and shut the *d* after him,
9 and came near to break the *d*.
10 house to them, and shut to the *d*.
11 the men that were at the *d*
11 wearied themselves to find the *d*.
43.19 with him at the *d* of the house,
Ex 12. 7 on the *d* post of the houses,
22 go out at the *d* of his house
23 the Lord will pass over the *d*,
21. 6 he shall also bring him to the *d*,
6 unto the *d* post; and his master
26.36 shalt make an hanging for the *d*
29. 4 bring unto the *d* of the tabernacle
11 Lord, by the *d* of the tabernacle
32 in the basket, by the *d* of the
42 at the *d* of the tabernacle of the
33. 8 and stood every man at his tent *d*,
9 stood at the *d* of the tabernacle,
10 pillar stand at the tabernacle *d*:
10 worshipped, every man in his tent *d*.
35.15 and the hanging for the *d* at the
17 hanging for the *d* of the court,
36.37 for the tabernacle *d* of blue,
38. 8 which assembled at the *d* of the
30 the sockets to the *d* of the
39.38 the hanging for the tabernacle *d*,
40. 5 and put the hanging of the *d* to the
6 before the *d* of the tabernacle of
12 and his sons unto the *d* of the
28 he set up the hanging at the *d*
29 by the *d* of the tabernacle of the
Lev 1. 3 voluntary will at the *d* of the
5 the altar that is by the *d* of the
3. 2 kill it at the *d* of the tabernacle
4. 4 unto the *d* of the tabernacle
7 which is at the *d* of the tabernacle
18 burnt offering, which is at the *d* of
8. 3 congregation together unto the *d*
4 was gathered together unto the *d*
31 the flesh at the *d* of the tabernacle
33 And ye shall not go out of the *d*
35 Therefore shall ye abide at the *d*
10. 7 And ye shall not go out from the *d*
12. 6 sin offering, unto the *d* of the
14.11 Lord, at the *d* of the tabernacle
23 the priest, unto the *d* of the
38 the house to the *d* of the house,
15.14 Lord unto the *d* of the tabernacle
29 the priest, to the *d* of the
16. 7 at the *d* of the tabernacle of the
17. 4 And bringeth it not unto the *d* of
5 unto the Lord, unto the *d* of the
6 altar of the Lord at the *d* of
9 bringeth it not unto the *d* of the
19.21 offering unto the Lord, unto the *d*
Nu 3.25 for the *d* of the tabernacle
26 the curtain for the *d* of the court,
4.25 for the *d* of the tabernacle
26 the hanging for the *d* of the gate
6.10 priest, to the *d* of the tabernacle
13 unto the *d* of the tabernacle
18 his separation at the *d* of the
10. 3 at the *d* of the tabernacle
11.10 every man in the *d* of his tent:
12. 5 stood in the *d* of the tabernacle,
16.18 stood in the *d* of the tabernacle
19 them unto the *d* of the tabernacle
27 and stood in the *d* of their tents,
50 returned unto Moses unto the *d* of
20. 6 unto the *d* of the tabernacle of the
25. 6 before the *d* of the tabernacle
27. 2 the congregation, by the *d* of the
Dt 11.20 upon the *d* posts of thine house,
15.17 it through his ear unto the *d*,
22.21 to the *d* of her father's house,
31.15 stood over the *d* of the tabernacle.
Jos 19.51 Lord, at the *d* of the tabernacle
Jdg 4.20 Stand in the *d* of the tent, and it
9.52 went hard unto the *d* of the tower
19.22 beat at the *d*, and spake to the
26 down at the *d* of the man's house
27 fallen down at the *d* of the house,
1Sa 2.22 that assembled at the *d* of the
2Sa 11. 9 Uriah slept at the *d* of the king's
13.17 from me, and bolt the *d* after her.
18 her out, and bolted the *d* after her.
1Ki 6. 8 The *d* for the middle chamber
33 made he for the *d* of the temple
34 leaves of the one *d* were folding,
34 and the two leaves of the other *d*
14. 6 her feet, as she came in at the *d*,
17 threshold of the *d*, the child died;
27 kept the *d* of the king's house.
2Ki 4. 4 thou shalt shut the *d* upon thee
5 shut the *d* upon her and upon her

15 had called her, she stood in the *d*.
21 shut the *d* upon him, and went out.
33 and shut the *d* upon them twain,
5. 9 at the *d* of the house of Elisha.
6.32 the *d*, and hold him fast at the *d*:
9. 3 Then open the *d*, and flee, and
10 And he opened the *d*, and fled.
12. 9 that kept the *d* put therein
22. 4 keepers of the *d* have gathered
23. 4 keepers of the *d*, to bring forth
25.18 and the three keepers of the *d*:
1Ch 9.21 porter of the *d* of the tabernacle
Neh 3.20 unto the *d* of the house of Eliashib
21 from the *d* of the house of Eliashib
Est 2.21 which kept the *d*, were wroth,
6. 2 the keepers of the *d*, who sought
Job 31. 9 laid wait at my neighbor's *d*;
34 silence, and went not out of the *d*?
Ps 141. 3 my mouth; keep the *d* of my lips.
Pr 5. 8 come not nigh the *d* of her house:
9.14 she sitteth at the *d* of her house,
26.14 As the *d* turneth upon his hinges,
SS 5. 4 the hole of the *d*, and my bowels
8. 9 if she be a *d*, we will enclose
Isa 6. 4 posts of the *d* moved at the voice
Jer 35. 4 of Shallum, the keeper of the *d*:
52.24 and the three keepers of the *d*:
Eze 8. 3 to the *d* of the inner gate that
7 brought me to the *d* of the court;
8 had digged in the wall, behold a *d*.
14 he brought me to the *d* of the gate
16 at the *d* of the temple of the Lord,
10.19 one stood at the *d* of the east gate
11. 1 and behold at the *d* of the gate five
40.13 and twenty cubits, *d* against *d*.
41. 2 breadth of the *d* was ten cubits;
2 the sides of the *d* were five cubits
3 and measured the post of the *d*,
3 two cubits; and the *d*, six cubits.
3 the breadth of the *d*, seven cubits
11 one *d* toward the north, and
11 another *d* toward the south:
16 The *d* posts, and the narrow
16 against the *d*, cieled with wood
17 To that above the *d*, even unto
20 From the ground unto above the *d*
24 leaves for the one *d*, and...other *d*.
42. 2 hundred cubits was the north *d*,
12 was a *d* in the head of the way,
46. 3 shall worship at the *d* of this gate
47. 1 me again unto the *d* of the house;
Hos 2.15 the valley of Achor for a *d* of hope:
Am 9. 1 he said, Smite the lintel of the *d*,
Mt 6. 6 when thou hast shut thy *d*,
25.10 marriage; and the *d* was shut.
27.60 stone to the *d* of the sepulchre,
28. 2 rolled back the stone from the *d*,
Mk 1.33 was gathered together at the *d*.
2. 2 no, not so much as about the *d*:
11. 4 colt tied by the *d* without in a place
15.46 stone unto the *d* of the sepulchre.
16. 3 stone from the *d* of the sepulchre?
Lk 11. 7 the *d* is now shut, and my children
13.25 is risen up, and hath shut to the *d*,
25 to knock at the *d*, saying, Lord,
Jn 10. 1 by the *d* into the sheepfold, but
2 the *d* is the shepherd of the sheep.
7 unto you, I am the *d* of the sheep.
9 I am the *d*: by me if any man
18.16 Peter stood at the *d* without.
16 spake unto her that kept the *d*,
17 the damsel that kept the *d*
Ac 5. 9 at the *d*, and shall carry thee out.
12. 6 before the *d* kept the prison.
13 Peter knocked at the *d* of the gate,
16 and when they had opened the *d*,
14.27 opened the *d* of faith unto the
1Co 16. 9 a great *d* and effectual is opened
2Co 2.12 and a *d* was opened unto me
Col 4. 3 open unto us a *d* of utterance,
Jas 5. 9 the judge standeth before the *d*.
Rev 3. 8 set before thee an open *d*,
20 I stand at the *d*, and knock: if any
20 man hear my voice, and open the *d*,
4. 1 a *d* was opened in heaven:

DOORKEEPER

Ps 84.10 I had rather be a *d* in the house

DOORS

Jos 2.19 shall go out of the *d* of thy house
Jdg 3.23 the *d* of the parlor upon him,
24 the *d* of the parlor were locked,
25 he opened not the *d* of the parlor;
11.31 cometh forth of the *d* of my house
16. 3 took the *d* of the gate of the city,
19.27 and opened the *d* of the house, and
1Sa 3.15 the *d* of the house of the Lord.
21.13 scrabbled on the *d* of the gate, and
1Ki 6.31 the oracle he made *d* of olive tree:
32 The two *d* also were of olive tree;
34 the two *d* were of fir tree: the two
7. 5 all the *d* and posts were square,
50 of the *d* of the inner house, the
50 place, and for the *d* of the house,
2Ki 18.16 the *d* of the temple of the Lord,
1Ch 22. 3 the nails of the *d* of the gates,
2Ch 3. 7 and the *d* thereof, with gold;
4. 9 great court and *d* for the court,
9 and overlaid the *d* of them with
22 the inner *d* thereof for the most
22 and the *d* of the house of the
23. 4 Levites, shall be porters of the *d*;
28.24 up the *d* of the house of the Lord,
29. 3 the *d* of the house of the Lord,
7 have shut up the *d* of the porch,
34. 9 the Levites that kept the *d* had
Neh 3. 1 set up the *d* of it; even unto the
3, 6, 13, 14, 15 and set up the *d* thereof,
6. 1 that time I had not set up the *d*
10 let us shut the *d* of the temple:
7. 1 I had set up the *d*, and the porters,
3 let them shut the *d* and bar them:
Job 3.10 up the *d* of my mother's womb,
31.32 but I opened my *d* to the traveller.
38. 8 Or who shut up the sea with *d*,
10 decreed place, and set bars and *d*,
17 thou seen the *d* of the shadow
41.14 Who can open the *d* of his face?
Ps 24. 7 be ye lift up, ye everlasting *d*;
9 lift them up, ye everlasting *d*;
78.23 and opened the *d* of heaven,
Pr 8. 3 city, at the coming in at the *d*.
34 waiting at the posts of my *d*.
Ec 12. 4 the *d* shall be shut in the streets,
Isa 26.20 shut thy *d* about thee: hide
57. 8 Behind the *d* also and the posts
Eze 33.30 and in the *d* of the houses,
41.11 And the *d* of the side chambers
23 and the sanctuary had two *d*.
24 the *d* had two leaves apiece,
25 on the *d* of the temple, cherubims
42. 4 and their *d* toward the north.
11 fashions, and according to their *d*.
12 according to the *d* of the chambers
Mic 7. 5 keep the *d* of my mouth from her
Zec 11. 1 Open thy *d*, O Lebanon, that the
Mal 1.10 that would shut the *d* for nought?
Mt 24.33 it is near, even at the *d*.
Mk 13.29 it is nigh, even at the *d*.
Jn 20.19 when the *d* were shut where the
26 the *d* being shut, and stood in the
Ac 5.19 opened the prison *d*, and brought
23 standing without before the *d*:
16.26 immediately all the *d* were opened,
27 seeing the prison *d* open, he drew
21.30 and forthwith the *d* were shut.

DORCAS

Ac 9.36 by interpretation is called *D*:
39 *D* made, while she was with them.

DOTED

Eze 23. 5 and she *d* on her lovers, on the
7 with all on whom she *d*; with all
9 of the Assyrians, upon whom she *d*.
12 She *d* upon the Assyrians her
16 she saw them with her eyes, she *d*
20 For she *d* upon their paramours,

DOTHAN

Gen 37.17 I heard them say, Let us go to *D*.
17 his brethren, and found them in *D*.
2Ki 6.13 him, saying, Behold, he is in *D*.

DOTING

1Ti 6. 4 but *d* about questions and strifes

DOUBLE

Gen 43.12 take *d* money in your hand;
15 they took *d* money in their hand,
Ex 22. 4 or sheep; and he shall restore *d*.
7 the thief be found, let him pay *d*.
9 shall pay *d* unto his neighbor.
26. 9 and shalt *d* the sixth curtain in
39. 9 they made the breastplate *d*: a
Dt 15.18 worth a *d* hired servant to thee,
21.17 by giving him a *d* portion of all
2Ki 2. 9 *d* portion of thy spirit be upon me.
1Ch 12.33 they were not of *d* heart.
Job 11. 6 of wisdom, that they are *d*
41.13 who can come to him with his *d*
Ps 12. 2 and with a *d* heart do they speak.
Isa 40. 2 received of the Lord's hand *d* for
61. 7 shall have *d*; and for confusion
7 they shall possess the *d*:
Jer 16.18 their iniquity and their sin *d*;
17.18 destroy them with *d* destruction.
Zec 9.12 that I will render *d* unto thee;
1Ti 5.17 be counted worthy of *d* honor,
Jas 1. 8 A *d* minded man is unstable in all
4. 8 purify your hearts, ye *d* minded.
Rev 18. 6 rewarded you, and *d* unto her
6 *d* according to her works:
6 which she hath filled fill to her *d*.

DOUBLETONGUED

1Ti 3. 8 not *d*, not given to much wine,

DOUBT

Gen 37.33 Joseph is without *d* rent in pieces.
Dt 28.66 life shall hang in *d* before thee:
Job 12. 2 No *d* but ye are the people,
Mt 14.31 faith, wherefore didst thou *d*?
21.21 If ye have faith, and *d* not, ye
Mk 11.23 shall not *d* in his heart, but shall
Lk 11.20 no *d* the kingdom of God is come
Jn 10.24 dost thou make us to *d*?
Ac 2.12 were all amazed, and were in *d*,
28. 4 No *d* this man is a murderer,
1Co 9.10 our sakes, no *d*, this is written:
Gal 4.20 voice; for I stand in *d* of you.
1Jn 2.19 they would no *d* have continued
(See box page 234)

DOUBTED

Mt 28.17 worshipped him: but some *d*.
Ac 5.24 they *d* of them whereunto this
10.17 while Peter *d* in himself what
25.20 *d* of such manner of questions,

DOUBTETH

Ro 14.23 he that *d* is damned if he eat,

DOUBTFUL

Lk 12.29 drink, neither be ye of *d* mind.
Ro 14. 1 ye, but not to *d* disputations.

DOUBTING

Jn 13.22 on another, *d* of whom we spake.
Ac 10.20 and go with them, *d* nothing:
11.12 bade me go with them, nothing *d*.
1Ti 2. 8 holy hands, without wrath and *d*.

BIBLICAL THEMES

DOUBT

And Moses said unto God, Who am I, that I should go unto Pharaoh, and that I should bring forth the children of Israel out of Egypt? Ex 3.11

And the whole congregation of the children of Israel murmured against Moses and Aaron in the wilderness. Ex 16.2

And Gideon said unto him . . . if the Lord be with us, why then is all this befallen us? and where be all his miracles which our fathers told us of . . . ? Jdg 6.13

I will say unto God . . . Is it good unto thee that thou shouldest oppress, that thou shouldest despise the work of thine hands, and shine upon the counsel of the wicked? Job 10.2-3

Why standest thou afar off, O Lord? why hidest thou thyself in times of trouble? Ps 10.1

The fool hath said in his heart, There is no God. Ps 53.1

Hast thou not known? hast thou not heard, that the everlasting God, the Lord, the Creator of the ends of the earth, fainteth not, neither is weary? Isa 40.28

For the hurt of the daughter of my people am I hurt . . . astonishment hath taken hold on me. Is there no balm in Gilead; is there no physician there? why then is not the health of the daughter of my people recovered? Jer 8.21-22

Wherefore doth the way of the wicked prosper? wherefore are all they happy that deal very treacherously? Thou hast planted them, yea, they have taken root: they grow, yea, they bring forth fruit. Jer 12.1-2

Now when John had heard in the prison the works of Christ, he sent two of his disciples, and said unto him, Art thou he that should come, or do we look for another? Mt 11.2-3

Jesus stretched forth his hand, and caught him, and said unto him, O thou of little faith, wherefore didst thou doubt? Mt 14.31

And about the ninth hour Jesus cried with a loud voice, saying, Eli, Eli, lama sabachthani? that is to say, My God, my God, why hast thou forsaken me? Mt 27.46

And he said unto them, Why are ye so fearful? how is it that ye have no faith? And they feared exceedingly, and said one to another, What manner of man is this, that even the wind and the sea obey him? Mk 4.40-41

And straightway the father of the child cried out, and said with tears, Lord, I believe; help thou mine unbelief. Mk 9.24

It was Mary Magdalene, and Joanna, and Mary the mother of James, and other women that were with them, which told these things unto the apostles. And their words seemed to them as idle tales, and they believed them not. Lk 24.10-11

O fools, and slow of heart to believe all that the prophets have spoken. Lk 24.25

Jesus answered them, I told you, and ye believed not: the works that I do in my Father's name, they bear witness of me. But ye believe not, because ye are not of my sheep. . . . My sheep hear my voice, and . . . follow me. Jn 10.25-27

The other disciples therefore said unto [Thomas], We have seen the Lord. But he said unto them, Except I shall see in his hands the print of the nails, and put my finger into the print of the nails, and thrust my hand into his side, I will not believe. . . . And Thomas answered and said unto him, My Lord and my God. Jesus saith unto him, Thomas, because thou hast seen me, thou hast believed: blessed are they that have not seen, and yet have believed. Jn 20.25, 28-29

DOUBTLESS

Nu 14.30 *D* ye shall not come into the
2Sa 5.19 I will *d* deliver the Philistines
Ps 126. 6 *d* come again with rejoicing,
Isa 63.16 *D* thou art our Father, though
1Co 9. 2 unto others, yet *d* I am to you:
2Co 12. 1 I not expedient for me *d* to glory.
Php 3. 8 Yea *d*, and I count all things

DOVE

Gen 8. 8 he sent forth a *d* from him, to
9 the *d* found no rest for the sole of
10 again he sent forth the *d* out of
11 *d* came in to him in the evening;
12 seven days; and sent forth the *d*;
Ps 55. 6 O that I had wings like a *d*! for
68.13 ye be as the wings of a *d* covered
SS 2.14 O my *d*, that art in the clefts of
5. 2 to me, my sister, my love, my *d*,
6. 9 My *d*, my undefiled is but one;
Isa 38.14 I did mourn as a *d*: mine eyes fail
Jer 48.28 be like the *d* that maketh her nest
Hos 7.11 Ephraim also is like a silly *d*
11.11 as a *d* out of the land of Assyria:
Mt 3.16 Spirit of God descending like a *d*,
Mk 1.10 and the Spirit like a *d* descending
Lk 3.22 in a bodily shape like a *d* upon
Jn 1.32 descending from heaven like a *d*,

DOVES

SS 5.12 His eyes are as the eyes of *d*
Isa 59.11 like bears, and mourn sore like *d*:
60. 8 and as the *d* to their windows?
Eze 7.16 shall be on the mountains like *d*
Na 2. 7 lead her as with the voice of *d*,
Mt 10.16 as serpents, and harmless as *d*.
21.12 the seats of them that sold *d*,
Mk 11.15 the seats of them that sold *d*;
Jn 2.14 that sold oxen and sheep and *d*,
16 said unto them that sold *d*, Take

DOVES'

SS 1.15 thou art fair; thou hast *d* eyes.
4. 1 thou hast *d* eyes within thy locks:

DOWNSITTING

Ps 139. 2 Thou knowest my *d* and mine

DRAFT

2Ki 10.27 made it *d* house unto this day.
Mt 15.17 and is cast out into the *d*?
Mk 7.19 goeth out into the *d*, purging
Lk 5. 4 and let down your nets for a *d*.
9 at the *d* of the fishes which they

DRAGGING

Jn 21. 8 cubits,) *d* the net with fishes.

DRAGON

Neh 2.13 even before the *d* well, and
Ps 91.13 the young lion and the *d* shalt
Isa 27. 1 he shall slay the *d* that is in the
51. 9 cut Rahab, and wounded the *d*?
Jer 51.34 hath swallowed me up like a *d*,
Eze 29. 3 the great *d* that lieth in the midst
Rev 12. 3 behold a great red *d*, having
4 the *d* stood before the woman
7 his angels fought against the *d*;
7 and the *d* fought and his angels,
9 the great *d* was cast out, that
13 when the *d* saw that he was cast
16 the flood which the *d* cast out
17 the *d* was wroth with the woman,
13. 2 and the *d* gave him his power,
4 they worshipped the *d* which gave
11 like a lamb, and he spake as a *d*.
16.13 out of the mouth of the *d*,
20. 2 he laid hold on the *d*, that old

DRANK

Gen 9.21 And he *d* of the wine, and was
24.46 I *d*, and she made the camels drink
27.25 he brought him wine, and he *d*.
43.34 they *d*, and were merry with him.
Nu 20.11 and the congregation *d*, and their
Dt 32.38 *d* the wine of their drink offerings?
2Sa 12. 3 and *d* of his own cup, and lay in
1Ki 13.19 bread in his house, and *d* water.
17. 6 evening; and he *d* of the brook.
Dan 1. 5 and of the wine which he *d*:
8 nor with the wine which he *d*:
5. 1 and *d* wine before the thousand.
3 his wives, and his concubines, *d*
4 They *d* wine, and praised the gods
Mk 14.23 it to them: and they all *d* of it.
Lk 17.27 They did eat, they *d*, they married
28 they did eat, they *d*, they bought,
Jn 4.12 us the well, and *d* thereof himself,
1Co 10. 4 for they *d* of that spiritual Rock

DRAVE

Ex 14.25 that they *d* them heavily: so that
Jos 16.10 they *d* not out the Canaanites
24.12 *d* them out from before you,
18 the Lord *d* out from before us

Jdg 1.19 he *d* out the inhabitants of the
6. 9 and *d* them out from before you,
1Sa 30.20 and the herds, which they *d*
2Sa 6. 3 sons of Abinadab, *d* the new cart.
2Ki 16. 6 and *d* the Jews from Elath:
17.21 *d* Israel from following the Lord,
1Ch 13. 7 and Uzza and Ahio *d* the cart.
Ac 7.45 whom God *d* out before the face
18.16 *d* them from the judgment seat.

DRAW

Gen 24.11 that women go out to *d* water.
13 of the city come out to *d* water:
19 I will *d* water for thy camels also,
20 ran unto the well to *d* water,
43 virgin cometh forth to *d* water,
44 I will also *d* for thy camels:
Ex 3. 5 *D* not nigh hither: put off thy
12.21 *D* out and take you a lamb
15. 9 I will *d* my sword, mine hand
Lev 26.33 and will *d* out a sword after you:
Jdg 3.22 he could not *d* the dagger out
4. 6 and *d* toward mount Tabor, and
7 And I will *d* unto thee to the river
9.54 *D* thy sword, and slay me, that
19.13 us *d* near to one of these places
20.32 and *d* them from the city unto
1Sa 9.11 maidens going out to *d* water,
14.36 Let us *d* near hither unto God.
38 *D* ye near hither, all the chief of
31. 4 his armorbearer, *D* thy sword,
2Sa 17.13 and we will *d* it into the river,
1Ch 10. 4 *D* thy sword, and thrust me
Job 21.33 and every man shall *d* after him.
40.23 that he can *d* up Jordan
41. 1 Canst thou *d* out leviathan with
Ps 28. 3 *D* me not away with the wicked,
35. 3 *D* out also the spear, and stop
69.18 *D* nigh unto my soul, and redeem
73.28 is good for me to *d* near to God:
85. 5 wilt thou *d* out thine anger to all
107.18 *d* near unto the gates of death.
119.150 *d* nigh that follow after mischief:
Pr 20. 5 of understanding will *d* it out.
Ec 12. 1 *d* nigh, when thou shalt say,
SS 1. 4 *D* me, we will run after thee:
Isa 5.18 *d* iniquity with cords of vanity,
19 of the Holy One of Israel *d* nigh
12. 3 Therefore with joy shall ye *d*
29.13 people *d* near me with their mouth,
45.20 *d* near together, ye that are escaped
57. 3 But *d* near hither, ye sons of the
4 mouth, and *d* out the tongue?
58.10 *d* out thy soul to the hungry,
66.19 *d* the bow, to Tubal, and Javan,
Jer 30.21 and I will cause him to *d* near,
46. 3 and shield, and *d* near to battle.
49.20 shall *d* them out; surely he shall
50.45 of the flock shall *d* them out:
La 4. 3 sea monsters *d* out the breast,
Eze 5. 2 in the wind; and I will *d* out a
12 I will *d* out a sword after them.
9. 1 charge over the city to *d* near,
12.14 will *d* out the sword after them.
21. 3 and will *d* forth my sword out of
22. 4 thy days to *d* near, and art
28. 7 *d* their swords against the beauty
30.11 *d* their swords against Egypt,
32.20 *d* her and all her multitudes.
Joel 3. 9 let all the men of war *d* near;
Na 3.14 *D* thee waters for the siege,
Hag 2.16 press at for to *d* out fifty vessels
Jn 2. 8 saith unto them, *D* out now, and
4. 7 a woman of Samaria to *d* water:
11 Sir, thou hast nothing to *d* with,
15 not, neither come hither to *d*.
6.44 Father which hath sent me *d* him:
12.32 the earth, will *d* all men unto me.
21. 6 now they were not able to *d* it for
Ac 20.30 to *d* away disciples after them.
Heb 7.19 by the which we *d* nigh unto God.
10.22 Let us *d* near with a true heart
38 but if any man *d* back, my soul
39 we are not of them who *d* back
Jas 2. 6 rich men oppress you, and *d* you
4. 8 *D* nigh to God, and he will *d* nigh

DRAWER

Dt 29.11 the hewer of thy wood unto the *d*

DRAWERS

Jos 9.21 hewers of wood and *d* of water
23 *d* of water for the house of my God.
27 *d* of water for the congregation,

DRAWETH

Dt 25.11 and the wife of the one *d* near
Jdg 19. 9 the day *d* toward evening,
Job 24.22 He *d* also the mighty with his
33.22 his soul *d* near unto the grave,
Ps 10. 9 when he *d* him into his net.
88. 3 my life *d* nigh unto the grave.
Isa 26.17 *d* near the time of her delivery,
Eze 7.12 the day *d* near: let not the
Mt 15. 8 This people *d* nigh unto me with
Lk 21. 8 the time *d* near: go ye not
28 for your redemption *d* nigh.
Jas 5. 8 the coming of the Lord *d* nigh.

DRAWING

Jdg 5.11 archers in the places of *d* water,
Jn 6.19 the sea, and *d* nigh unto the ship:

DRAWN

Nu 22.23, 31 and his sword *d* in his hand:
Dt 21. 3 which hath not *d* in the yoke;
30.17 but shall be *d* away, and worship
Jos 5.13 against him with his sword *d*
8. 6 till we have *d* them from the city;
16 and were *d* away from the city.
15. 9 And the border was *d* from the
9 and the border was *d* to Baalah,
11 and the border was *d* to Shicron,
18.14 And the border was *d* thence,
17 And was *d* from the north, and
Jdg 20.31 were *d* away from the city; and
Ru 2. 9 that which the young men have *d*,
1Ch 21.16 having a *d* sword in his hand
Job 20.25 It is *d*, and cometh out of the
Ps 37.14 The wicked have *d* out the sword,
55.21 than oil, yet were they *d* swords.
Pr 24.11 them that are *d* unto death,
Isa 21.15 the swords, from the *d* sword,
28. 9 the milk, and *d* from the breasts.
Jer 22.19 burial of an ass, *d* and cast forth
31. 3 lovingkindness have I *d* thee.
La 2. 3 he hath *d* back his right hand
Eze 21. 5 I the Lord have *d* forth my sword
28 The sword, the sword is *d*: for
Ac 11.10 all were *d* up again into heaven.
Jas 1.14 when he is *d* away of his own lust,

DREADFUL

Gen 28.17 How *d* is this place! this is none
Job 15.21 A *d* sound is in his ears:
Eze 1.18 were so high that they were *d*;
Dan 7. 7 a fourth beast, *d* and terrible,
19 from all the others, exceeding *d*,
9. 4 O Lord, the great and *d* God,
Hab 1. 7 They are terrible and *d*: their
Mal 1.14 name is *d* among the heathen.
4. 5 the great and *d* day of the Lord:

DREAM

Gen 20. 3 to Abimelech in a *d* by night,
6 And God said unto him in a *d*,
31.10 and saw in a *d*, and, behold, the
11 spake unto me in a *d*, saying,
24 came to Laban the Syrian in a *d*
37. 5 Joseph dreamed a *d*, and he told
6 you, this *d* which I have dreamed:
9 he dreamed yet another *d*, and
9 Behold, I have dreamed a *d*
10 What is this *d* that thou hast
40. 5 they dreamed a *d* both of them,
5 each man his *d* in one night,
5 to the interpretation of his *d*,
8 We have dreamed a *d*, and there
9 chief butler told his *d* to Joseph,

The archangel Michael does battle with "the great dragon" (Rev 12) in this medieval Spanish painting.

The dream of Pharaoh is interpreted by Joseph (Gen 41) in this print by Gustave Doré (1832-1883).

Gen 40. 9 In my *d*, behold, a vine was
16 I also was in my *d*, and, behold, I
41. 7 awoke, and, behold, it was a *d*.
8 Pharaoh told them his *d*; but there
11 we dreamed a *d* in one night, I and
11 to the interpretation of his *d*.
12 to each man according to his *d*
15 I have dreamed a *d*, and there is
15 that thou canst understand a *d*
17 In my *d*, behold, I stood upon the
22 I saw in my *d*, and, behold, seven
25 The *d* of Pharaoh is one: God
26 ears are seven years: the *d* is one.
32 for that the *d* was doubled unto
Nu 12. 6 and will speak unto him in a *d*.
Jdg 7.13 a man that told a *d* unto his fellow,
13 and said, Behold, I dreamed a *d*.
15 Gideon heard the telling of the *d*,
1Ki 3. 5 Lord appeared to Solomon in a *d*
15 awoke; and, behold, it was a *d*.
Job 20. 8 He shall fly away as a *d*, and shall
33.15 In a *d*, in a vision of the night,
Ps 73.20 As a *d* when one awaketh;
126. 1 Zion, we were like them that *d*.
Ec 5. 3 a *d* cometh through the multitude
Isa 29. 7 shall be as a *d* of a night vision.
Jer 23.28 The prophet that hath a *d*, let him
28 let him tell a *d*; and he that hath
Dan 2. 3 I have dreamed a *d*, and my spirit
3 was troubled to know the *d*.
4 tell thy servants the *d*, and we
5 not make known unto me the *d*,
6 But if ye shew the *d*, and the
6 honor: therefore shew me the *d*,
7 the king tell his servants the *d*,
9 not make known unto me the *d*,
9 therefore tell me the *d*, and I shall
26 able to make known unto me the *d*
28 Thy *d*, and the visions of thy head
36 This is the *d*; and we will tell the
45 and the *d* is certain, and the
4. 5 I saw a *d* which made me afraid,
6 unto me the interpretation of the *d*.
7 and I told the *d* before them;
8 and before him I told the *d*,
9 tell me the visions of my *d* that I
18 This *d* I king Nebuchadnezzar
19 let not the *d*, or the interpretation
19 the *d* be to them that hate thee,
7. 1 Daniel had a *d* and visions of his
1 then he wrote the *d*, and told the
Joel 2.28 your old men shall *d* dreams, your
Mt 1.20 Lord appeared unto him in a *d*,
2.12 being warned of God in a *d* that
13 Lord appeareth to Joseph in a *d*,
19 Lord appeareth in a *d* to Joseph
22 being warned of God in a *d*, he
27.19 this day in a *d* because of him.
Ac 2.17 and your old men shall *d* dreams:

DREAMERS

Jer 27. 9 nor to your *d*, nor to your
Jude 8 Likewise also these filthy *d* defile

DREAMS

Gen 37. 8 hated him yet the more for his *d*,
20 see what will become of his *d*.
41.12 he interpreted to us our *d*; to each
42. 9 Joseph remembered the *d* which
Dt 13. 1 or a dreamer of *d*, and giveth thee
3 that prophet, or that dreamer of *d*:
5 that prophet, or that dreamer of *d*,
1Sa 28. 6 neither by *d*, nor by Urim, nor by
15 neither by prophets, nor by *d*:
Job 7.14 Then thou scarest me with *d*, and
Ec 5. 7 in the multitude of *d* and many
Jer 23.27 to forget my name by their *d*
32 against them that prophesy false *d*,
29. 8 neither hearken to your *d* which
Dan 1.17 understanding in all visions and *d*.
2. 1 Nebuchadnezzar dreamed *d*,
2 for to shew the king his *d*.
5.12 interpreting of *d*, and shewing of
Joel 2.28 your old men shall dream *d*, your
Zec 10. 2 seen a lie, and have told false *d*;
Ac 2.17 and your old men shall dream *d*:

DRESSED

Gen 18. 8 milk, and the calf which he had *d*,
Lev 7. 9 all that is *d* in the fryingpan,
1Sa 25.18 and five sheep ready *d*, and five
2Sa 12. 4 and *d* it for the man that was come
19.24 had neither *d* his feet, nor trimmed
1Ki 18.26 which was given them, and they *d*
Heb 6. 7 for them by whom it is *d*,

DRESSER

Lk 13. 7 said he unto the *d* of his vineyard,

DREW

Gen 18.23 And Abraham *d* near, and said,
24.20 water, and *d* for all his camels.
45 down unto the well, and *d* water:
37.28 and they *d* and lifted up Joseph
38.29 to pass, as he *d* back his hand,
47.29 time *d* nigh that Israel must die:
Ex 2.10 Because I *d* him out of the water.
16 they came and *d* water, and filled
19 and also *d* water enough for us,
14.10 when Pharaoh *d* nigh, the
20.21 *d* near unto the thick darkness
Lev 9. 5 and all the congregation *d* near
Jos 8.11 went up, and *d* nigh, and came
26 Joshua *d* not his hand back,
Jdg 8.10 thousand men that *d* sword.
20 But the youth *d* not his sword:
20. 2 thousand footmen that *d* sword.
15 six thousand men that *d* sword,
17 thousand men that *d* sword:
25, 35 men; all these *d* the sword.
37 liers in wait *d* themselves along,
46 thousand men that *d* the sword;
Ru 4. 8 for thee. So he *d* off his shoe.
1Sa 7. 6 together to Mizpeh, and *d* water,
10 the Philistines *d* near to battle
9.18 Saul *d* near to Samuel in the gate,
17.16 the Philistine *d* near morning
40 and he *d* near to the Philistine.
41 Philistine came on and *d* near
48 arose, and came and *d* nigh
51 *d* it out of the sheath thereof,
2Sa 10.13 And Joab *d* nigh, and the people
18.25 And he came apace, and *d* near.
22.17 he *d* me out of many waters;
23.16 and *d* water out of the well of
24. 9 valiant men that *d* the sword;
1Ki 2. 1 Now the days of David *d* nigh
8. 8 And they *d* out the staves,
22.34 certain man *d* a bow at a venture,
2Ki 3.26 hundred men that *d* swords,
9.24 *d* a bow with his full strength,
1Ch 11.18 of the Philistines, and *d* water
19.14 people that were with him *d* nigh
16 and *d* forth the Syrians that were
21. 5 thousand men that *d* swords:
5 ten thousand men that *d* sword.
2Ch 5. 9 they *d* out the staves of the ark,
14. 8 that bare shields and *d* bows,
18.33 certain man *d* a bow at a venture
Est 5. 2 So Esther *d* near, and touched
9. 1 and his decree *d* near to be put
Ps 18.16 he *d* me out of many waters.
Isa 41. 5 the earth were afraid, *d* near,
Jer 38.13 they *d* up Jeremiah with cords,
Hos 11. 4 I *d* them with cords of a man,
Zep 3. 2 Lord; she *d* not near to her God.
Mt 13.48 they *d* to shore, and sat down,
21. 1 they *d* nigh unto Jerusalem,
34 when the time of the fruit *d* near,
26.51 and *d* his sword, and struck a
Mk 6.53 Gennesaret, and *d* to the shore.
14.47 them that stood by *d* a sword,
Lk 15. 1 Then *d* near unto him all the
25 he came and *d* nigh to the house,
22. 1 feast of unleavened bread *d* nigh,
47 *d* near unto Jesus to kiss him.
23.54 preparation, and the sabbath *d* on.
24.15 Jesus himself *d* near, and went
28 And they *d* nigh unto the village,
Jn 2. 9 servants which *d* the water knew;)
18.10 Peter having a sword *d* it, and

21.11 Peter went up, and *d* the net to
Ac 5.37 *d* away much people after him:
7.17 the time of the promise *d* nigh,
31 and as he *d* near to behold it,
10. 9 and *d* nigh unto the city, Peter
14.19 Paul, *d* him out of the city,
16.19 Paul and Silas, and *d* them into
27 he *d* out his sword, and would
17. 6 *d* Jason and certain brethren
19.33 *d* Alexander out of the multitude,
21.30 and *d* him out of the temple:
27.27 they *d* near to some country;
Rev 12. 4 *d* the third part of the stars

DRIED

Gen 8. 7 until the waters were *d* up from
13 were *d* up from off the earth:
14 of the month, was the earth *d*.
Lev 2.14 green ears of corn *d* by the fire,
Nu 6. 3 nor eat moist grapes, or *d*.
11. 6 now our soul is *d* away; there
Jos 2.10 *d* up the water of the Red sea
4.23 God *d* up the waters of Jordan
23 which he *d* up from before us,
5. 1 the Lord had *d* up the waters of
Jdg 16. 7 green withs that were never *d*,
8 green withs which had not been *d*,
1Ki 13. 4 he put forth against him, *d* up,
17. 7 that the brook *d* up, because
2Ki 19.24 with the sole of my feet have I *d*
Job 18.16 His roots shall be *d* up beneath,
28. 4 they are *d* up, they are gone
Ps 22.15 strength is *d* up like a potsherd;
69. 3 my throat is *d*: mine eyes fail
106. 9 Red sea also, and it was *d* up:
Isa 5.13 their multitude *d* up with thirst.
19. 5 river shall be wasted and *d* up.
6 shall be emptied and *d* up:
37.25 the sole of my feet have I *d*
51.10 thou not it which hath *d* the sea,
Jer 23.10 of the wilderness are *d* up.
50.38 waters; and they shall be *d* up:
Eze 17.24 have *d* up the green tree, and have
19.12 the east wind *d* up her fruit:
37.11 they say, Our bones are *d*, and
Hos 9.16 their root is *d* up, they shall bear
13.15 and his fountain shall be *d* up:
Joel 1.10 the new wine is *d* up, the oil
12 The vine is *d* up, and the fig tree
20 the rivers of waters are *d* up, and
Zec 11.17 his arm shall be clean *d* up, and
Mk 5.29 fountain of her blood was *d* up;
11.20 the fig tree *d* up from the roots.
Rev 16.12 and the water thereof was *d* up,

DRINK

Gen 19.32 let us make our father *d* wine,
33 And they made their father *d* wine
21.19 with water, and gave the lad *d*.
24.14 pitcher, I pray thee, that I may *d*;
14 and she shall say, *D*, and I will
14 I will give thy camels *d* also:
17 Let me, I pray thee, *d* a little
18 And she said, *D*, my lord: and
43 a little water of thy pitcher to *d*;
44 And she say to me, Both *d* thou,
45 unto her, Let me *d*, I pray thee.
46 from her shoulder, and said, *D*,
46 I will give thy camels *d* also:
46 and she made the camels *d* also.
25.34 he did eat and *d*, and rose up, and
26.30 a feast, and they did eat and *d*.
30.38 when the flocks came to *d*, that
35.14 poured a *d* offering thereon,
Ex 7.18 Egyptians shall lothe to *d* of the
24 about the river for water to *d*
15.24 Moses, saying, What shall we *d*?
17. 1 was no water for the people to *d*.
24.11 they saw God, and did eat and *d*.
29.40 hin of wine for a *d* offering.
32. 6 people sat down to eat and to *d*,
34.28 neither eat bread, nor *d* water.
Lev 10. 9 Do not *d* wine nor strong
Nu 5.24 cause the woman to *d* the bitter
27 he hath made her to *d* the water,
6. 3 shall he *d* any liquor of grapes
20.19 if I and my cattle *d* of thy water,
23.24 prey, and *d* the blood of the slain.
28. 7 unto the Lord for a *d* offering.
10 burnt offering, and his *d* offering.
Dt 2. 6 them for money, that ye may *d*.
9. 9 neither did eat bread, nor *d* water,
32.14 *d* the pure blood of the grape.
Jdg 4.19 I pray thee, a little water to *d*;
7. 5 boweth down upon his knees to *d*.
9.27 eat and *d*, and cursed Abimelech.
19. 4 did eat and *d*, and lodged there.
21 washed their feet, and did eat and *d*.
Ru 2. 9 and *d* of that which the young men
2Sa 11.11 to eat and to *d*, and to lie with my
16. 2 be faint in the wilderness may *d*.
19.35 taste what I eat or what I *d*?
23.15 one would give me *d* of the water
1Ki 13. 8 neither will I eat bread nor *d* water
17. 4 be, that thou shalt *d* of the brook;
10 water into a vessel, that I may *d*.
18.41 unto Ahab, Get thee up, eat and *d*;
2Ki 7. 8 into one tent, and did eat and *d*,
1Ch 11.18 David would not *d* of it, but poured
19 shall I *d* the blood of these men
29.22 did eat and *d* before the Lord
Ezr 3. 7 meat, and *d*, and oil, unto them
Neh 8.10 eat the fat, and *d* the sweet,
Est 1. 7 gave them *d* in vessels of gold,
3.15 king and Haman sat down to *d*;
4.16 neither eat nor *d* three days, night
Job 21.20 *d* of the wrath of the Almighty.
Ps 50.13 of bulls, or *d* the blood of goats?
60. 3 to *d* the wine of astonishment.
69.21 thirst they gave me vinegar to *d*.
80. 5 tears to *d* in great measure.
102. 9 and mingled my *d* with weeping,
104.11 give *d* to every beast of the field:
110. 7 shall *d* of the brook in the way:
Pr 4.17 and *d* the wine of violence.
9. 5 eat of my bread, and *d* of the wine
20. 1 is a mocker, strong *d* is raging:
23. 7 Eat and *d*, saith he to thee;
31. 4 it is not for kings to *d* wine;
5 Lest they *d*, and forget the law,
7 Let him *d*, and forget his
Ec 8.15 to eat, and to *d*, and to be merry:
9. 7 *d* thy wine with a merry heart;
Isa 5.11 that they may follow strong *d*;
22 them that are mighty to *d* wine,
21. 5 watch in the watchtower, eat, *d*:
22.13 drinking wine: let us eat and *d*;
24. 9 They shall not *d* wine with a song;
9 strong *d* shall be bitter to them
28. 7 have erred through strong *d*,
29. 9 stagger, but not with strong *d*.
32. 6 he will cause the *d* of the thirsty
43.20 desert, to give *d* to my people,
62. 8 the stranger shall not *d* thy wine,
9 *d* it in the courts of my holiness.
65.13 shall *d*, but ye shall be thirsty:
Jer 8.14 and given us water of gall to *d*,
16. 7 them the cup of consolation to *d*
22.15 did not thy father eat and *d*,
25.17 and made all the nations to *d*,
27 *D* ye, and be drunken, and spue,
28 take the cup at thine hand to *d*,
32.29 out *d* offerings unto other gods,
35. 5 I said unto them, *D* ye wine.
14 commanded his sons not to *d* wine,
14 for unto this day they *d* none,
44.19 poured out *d* offerings unto her,
Eze 4.16 they shall *d* water by measure,
12.18 and *d* thy water with trembling
19 *d* their water with astonishment,
23.32 Thou shalt *d* of thy sister's cup
25. 4 fruit, and they shall *d* thy milk.
31.14 in their height, all that *d* water:
16 all that *d* water, shall be comforted
34.19 they *d* that which ye have fouled
39.17 that ye may eat flesh, and *d* blood.
18 *d* the blood of the princes of the
19 and *d* blood till ye be drunken,
Hos 2. 5 and my flax, mine oil and my *d*,
Joel 3. 3 girl for wine, that they might *d*.
Am 2. 8 they *d* the wine of the condemned
12 ye gave the Nazarites wine to *d*;
4. 1 masters, Bring, and let us *d*.
8 unto one city, to *d* water;
5.11 but ye shall not *d* wine of them.
6. 6 That *d* wine in bowls, and anoint
9.14 vineyards, and *d* the wine thereof;
Ob 16 all the heathen *d* continually,
Jon 3. 7 let them not feed, nor *d* water:
Mic 2.11 thee of wine and of strong *d*;
6.15 and sweet wine, but shalt not *d*
Hab 2.15 him that giveth his neighbor *d*,
16 *d* thou also, and let thy foreskin
Zep 1.13 but not *d* the wine thereof.
Hag 1. 6 ye *d*, but ye are not filled
Zec 7. 6 did eat, and when ye did *d*,
9.15 they shall *d*, and make a noise
Mt 6.25 ye shall eat, or what ye shall *d*;
31 What shall we *d*? or, Wherewithal
10.42 whosoever shall give to *d* unto
20.22 to *d* of the cup that I shall *d* of,
23 Ye shall *d* indeed of my cup,
24.49 to eat and *d* with the drunken;
25.35 I was thirsty, and ye gave me *d*:
37 or thirsty, and gave thee *d*?
42 I was thirsty and ye gave me no *d*:
26.27 to them, saying, *D* ye all of it;
29 I will not *d* henceforth of this fruit
29 day when I *d* it new with you
42 except I *d* it, thy will be done.
27.34 vinegar to *d* mingled with gall:
34 tasted thereof, he would not *d*.
48 on a reed, and gave him to *d*.
Mk 9.41 shall give you a cup of water to *d*
10.38 can ye *d* of the cup that I *d* of?
39 indeed *d* of the cup that I *d* of;
14.25 I will *d* no more of the fruit of the
25 vine, until that day that I *d* it new
15.23 And they gave him to *d* wine
36 gave him to *d*, saying, Let alone;
16.18 and if they *d* any deadly thing,
Lk 1.15 shall *d* neither wine nor strong
15 neither wine nor strong *d*;
5.30 do ye eat and *d* with publicans
33 Pharisees; but thine eat and *d*?
12.19 thine ease, eat, *d*, and be merry.
29 ye shall eat, or what ye shall *d*,
45 to eat and *d*, and to be drunken;
17. 8 afterward thou shalt eat and *d*?
22.18 will not *d* of the fruit of the vine,
30 That ye may eat and *d* at my table
Jn 4. 7 Jesus saith unto her, Give me to *d*,
9 askest *d* of me, which am a woman
10 Give me to *d*; thou wouldest
6.53 and *d* his blood, ye have no life
55 and my blood is *d* indeed.
7.37 let him come unto me, and *d*.
18.11 hath given me, shall I not *d* it?
Ac 9. 9 sight, and neither did eat nor *d*
10.41 who did eat and *d* with him.
23.12 they would neither eat nor *d* till
21 they will neither eat nor *d* till
Ro 12.20 if he thirst, give him *d*: for in so
14.17 of God is not meat and *d*;
21 nor to *d* wine, nor any thing
1Co 9. 4 we not power to eat and to *d*?
10. 4 And did all *d* the same spiritual
4 same spiritual *d*: for they drank
7 The people sat down to eat and *d*,
21 Ye cannot *d* the cup of the Lord,
31 Whether therefore ye eat, or *d*, or
11.22 ye not houses to eat and to *d* in?
25 this do ye, as oft as ye *d* it,

1Co 11.26 ye eat this bread, and *d* this cup,
27 *d* this cup of the Lord, unworthily,
28 of that bread, and *d* of that cup.
12.13 all made to *d* into one Spirit.
15.32 let us eat and *d*; for to morrow
Col 2.16 judge you in meat, or in *d*,
1Ti 5.23 *D* no longer water, but use a
Rev 14. 8 because she made all nations *d*
10 The same shall *d* of the wine
16. 6 thou hast given them blood to *d*;

DRINKETH

Gen 44. 5 Is not this it in which my lord *d*,
Dt 11.11 *d* water of the rain of heaven:
Job 6. 4 poison whereof *d* up my spirit:
15.16 man, which *d* iniquity like water?
34. 7 Job, who *d* up scorning like water?
40.23 Behold, he *d* up a river, and
Pr 26. 6 cutteth off the feet, and *d* damage.
Isa 29. 8 behold, he *d*; but he awaketh,
44.12 he *d* no water, and is faint.
Mk 2.16 *d* with publicans and sinners?
Jn 4.13 *d* of this water shall thirst again:
14 But whosoever *d* of the water that
6.54 and *d* my blood, hath eternal life;
56 eateth my flesh, and *d* my blood,
1Co 11.29 For he that eateth and *d*
29 unworthily, eateth and *d* damnation
Heb 6. 7 the earth which *d* in the rain

DRINKING

Gen 24.19 also, until they have done *d*.
22 to pass, as the camels had done *d*,
Ru 3. 3 he shall have done eating and *d*.
1Sa 30.16 earth, eating and *d*, and dancing,
1Ki 4.20 eating and *d*, and making merry.
10.21 all king Solomon's *d* vessels were
16. 9 in Tirzah, *d* himself drunk in the
20.12 message, as he was *d*, he and the
16 Ben-hadad was *d* himself drunk in
1Ch 12.39 David three days, eating and *d*:
2Ch 9.20 all the *d* vessels of king Solomon
Est 1. 8 And the *d* was according to the
Job 1.13 his daughters were eating and *d*
18 thy daughters were eating and *d*
Isa 22.13 sheep, eating flesh, and *d* wine:
Mt 11.18 John came neither eating nor *d*,
19 Son of man came eating and *d*,
24.38 they were eating and *d*, marrying
Lk 7.33 neither eating bread nor *d* wine;
34 Son of man is come eating and *d*;
10. 7 eating and *d* such things as they

DRINKS

Heb 9.10 Which stood only in meats and *d*,

DRIVETH

2Ki 9.20 son of Nimshi: for he *d* furiously.
Ps 1. 4 the chaff which the wind *d* away.
Pr 25.23 The north wind *d* away rain: so
Mk 1.12 spirit *d* him into the wilderness.

DROPS

Job 36.27 he maketh small the *d* of water:
38.28 who hath begotten the *d* of dew?
SS 5. 2 my locks with the *d* of the night.
Lk 22.44 as it were great *d* of blood falling

DROPSY

Lk 14. 2 man before him which had the *d*.

DROVE

Gen 3.24 So he *d* out the man; and he
15.11 carcases, Abram *d* them away.
32.16 every *d* by themselves; and said
16 put a space betwixt *d* and *d*.
33. 8 What meanest thou by all this *d*
Ex 2.17 came and *d* them away: but
Nu 21.32 and *d* out the Amorites that were
Jos 15.14 Caleb *d* thence the three sons of
1Ch 8.13 who *d* away the inhabitants of
Ps 34(T) who *d* him away, and he
Hab 3. 6 and *d* asunder the nations; and
Jn 2.15 he *d* them all out of the temple,

DROWN

SS 8. 7 neither can the floods *d* it: if a
1Ti 6. 9 which *d* men in destruction and

DROWNED

Ex 15. 4 his chosen captains also are *d*
Am 8. 8 and it shall be cast out and *d*, as
9. 5 and shall be *d*, as by the flood of
Mt 18. 6 he were *d* in the depth of the sea.
Heb 11.29 Egyptians assaying to do were *d*.

DRUNK

Lev 11.34 all drink that may be *d* in every
Dt 29. 6 neither have ye *d* wine or strong
32.42 make mine arrows *d* with blood,
Jdg 15.19 and when he had *d*, his spirit
Ru 3. 7 when Boaz had eaten and *d*, and
1Sa 1. 9 in Shiloh, and after they had *d*.
15 I have *d* neither wine nor strong
30.12 eaten no bread, nor *d* any water,
2Sa 11.13 and he made him *d*: and at even
1Ki 13.22 and *d* water in the place, of the
23 after he had *d*, that he saddled
16. 9 drinking himself *d* in the house of
20.16 drinking himself *d* in the pavilions,
2Ki 6.23 when they had eaten and *d*, he
19.24 digged and *d* strange waters, and
SS 5. 1 I have *d* my wine with my milk:
Isa 37.25 I have digged, and *d* water; and
51.17 which hast *d* at the hand of the
63. 6 and make them *d* in my fury,
Jer 46.10 and made *d* with their blood:
51.57 And I will make *d* her princes,
Eze 34.18 to have *d* of the deep waters,
Dan 5.23 have *d* wine in them; and thou
Ob 16 have *d* upon my holy mountain,
Lk 5.39 No man also having *d* old wine
13.26 have eaten and *d* in thy presence,
Jn 2.10 when men have well *d*, then
Eph 5.18 And be not *d* with wine, wherein
Rev 17. 2 have been made *d* with the wine
18. 3 all nations have *d* of the wine

DRUNKARD

Dt 21.20 voice; he is a glutton, and a *d*.
Pr 23.21 the *d* and the glutton shall come
26. 9 goeth up into the hand of a *d*,
Isa 24.20 shall reel to and fro like a *d*,
1Co 5.11 railer, or a *d*, or an extortioner;

DRUNKARDS

Ps 69.12 and I was the song of the *d*.
Isa 28. 1 of pride, to the *d* of Ephraim,
3 crown of pride, the *d* of Ephraim.
Joel 1. 5 Awake, ye *d*, and weep; and howl,
Na 1.10 while they are drunken as *d*,
1Co 6.10 nor *d*, nor revilers, nor

DRUNKEN

Gen 9.21 he drank of the wine, and was *d*;
1Sa 1.13 Eli thought she had been *d*.
1.14 How long wilt thou be *d*? put
25.36 within him, for he was very *d*:
Job 12.25 them to stagger like a *d* man.
Ps 107.27 and stagger like a *d* man,
Isa 19.14 a *d* man staggereth in his vomit.
29. 9 they are *d*, but not with wine;
49.26 shall be *d* with their own blood,
51.17 thou hast *d* the dregs of the cup
21 and *d*, but not with wine:
Jer 23. 9 I am like a *d* man, and like a
25.27 Drink ye, and be *d*, and spue,
48.26 Make ye him *d*: for he magnified
49.12 of the cup have assuredly *d*;
51. 7 that made all the earth *d*:
7 the nations have *d* of her wine;
39 feasts, and I will make them *d*,
La 3.15 hath made me *d* with wormwood.
4.21 thou shalt be *d*, and shalt make
5. 4 We have *d* our water for money;
Eze 39.19 and drink blood till ye be *d*,
Na 1.10 while they are *d* as drunkards,
3.11 Thou also shalt be *d*: thou shalt
Hab 2.15 to him, and makest him *d* also,
Mt 24.49 and to eat and drink with the *d*;
Lk 12.45 eat and drink, and to be *d*;
17. 8 till I have eaten and *d*; and
Ac 2.15 these are not *d*, as ye suppose,
1Co 11.21 one is hungry, and another is *d*.
1Th 5. 7 they that be *d* are *d* in the night.
Rev 17. 6 *d* with the blood of the saints,

DRUNKENNESS

Dt 29.19 mine heart, to add *d* to thirst:
Ec 10.17 for strength, and not for *d*!
Jer 13.13 inhabitants of Jerusalem, with *d*.
Eze 23.33 shalt be filled with *d* and sorrow,
Lk 21.34 and *d*, and cares of this life,
Ro 13.13 rioting and *d*, not in chambering
Gal 5.21 Envyings, murders, *d*, revellings,

DRUSILLA

Ac 24.24 when Felix came with his wife *D*,

DRY

Gen 1. 9 let the *d* land appear: and it was
10 And God called the *d* land Earth;
7.22 of all that was in the *d* land, died.
8.13 the face of the ground was *d*.
Ex 4. 9 pour it upon the *d* land: and the
9 become blood upon the *d* land:
14.16 of Israel shall go on *d* ground
21 the sea *d* land, and the waters
22 of the sea upon the *d* ground:
29 of Israel walked upon *d* land
15.19 children of Israel went on *d* land
Lev 7.10 offering mingled with oil, and *d*,
13.30 it is a *d* scall, even a leprosy upon
Jos 3.17 stood firm on *d* ground in the
17 Israelites passed over on *d* ground,
4.18 were lifted up unto the *d* land,
22 came over this Jordan on *d* land.
9. 5 their provision was *d* and moldy.
12 behold, it is *d*, and it is moldy:
Jdg 6.37 be *d* upon all the earth beside,
39 it now be *d* only upon the fleece,
40 for it was *d* upon the fleece only,
2Ki 2. 8 they two went over on *d* ground.
Neh 9.11 midst of the sea on the *d* land;
Job 12.15 the waters, and they *d* up: also
13.25 wilt thou pursue the *d* stubble?
15.30 the flame shall *d* up his branches,
Ps 63. 1 for thee in a *d* and thirsty land,
66. 6 He turned the sea into *d* land:
68. 6 the rebellious dwell in a *d* land.
95. 5 and his hands formed the *d* land.
105.41 ran in the *d* places like a river.
107.33 the watersprings into *d* ground;
35 and *d* ground into watersprings,
Pr 17. 1 is a *d* morsel, and quietness
Isa 25. 5 strangers, as the heat in a *d* place;
32. 2 as rivers of water in a *d* place,
41.18 and the *d* land springs of water.
42.15 and *d* up all their herbs; and I
15 islands, and I will *d* up the pools.
44. 3 and floods upon the *d* ground:
27 saith to the deep, Be *d*,
27 and I will *d* up thy rivers.
50. 2 at my rebuke I *d* up the sea,
53. 2 as a root out of a *d* ground:
56. 3 say, Behold, I am a *d* tree.
Jer 4.11 A *d* wind of the high places
50.12 a *d* land, and a desert.
51.36 I will *d* up her sea, and make
36 and make her springs *d*.
43 a *d* land, and a wilderness,
Eze 17.24 have made the *d* tree to flourish:
19.13 in a *d* and thirsty ground.

20.47 tree in thee, and every *d* tree:
30.12 I will make the rivers *d*, and sell
37. 2 valley; and, lo, they were very *d*.
4 O ye *d* bones, hear the word of
Hos 2. 3 set her like a *d* land, and slay
9.14 miscarrying womb and *d* breasts.
13.15 and his spring shall become *d*,
Jon 1. 9 hath made the sea and the *d* land.
2.10 vomited out Jonah upon the *d* land.
Na 1. 4 rebuketh the sea, and maketh it *d*,
10 be devoured as stubble fully *d*.
Zep 2.13 desolation, and *d* like a wilderness.
Hag 2. 6 and the sea, and the *d* land;
Zec 10.11 the deeps of the river shall *d* up:
Mt 12.43 he walketh through *d* places,
Lk 11.24 he walketh through *d* places,
23.31 what shall be done in the *d*?
Heb 11.29 through the Red sea as by *d* land:

DUE

Lev 10.13 it is thy *d*, and thy sons' *d*,
14 they be thy *d*, and thy sons *d*,
26. 4 I will give thee rain in *d* season,
Nu 28. 2 offer unto me in their *d* season.
Dt 11.14 rain of your land in his *d* season,
18. 3 be the priest's *d* from the people,
32.35 their foot shall slide in *d* time:
1Ch 15.13 sought him not after the *d* order.
16.29 Give unto the Lord the glory *d*
Neh 11.23 for the singers, *d* for every day.
Ps 29. 2 Lord the glory *d* unto his name;
96. 8 the Lord the glory *d* unto his name:
104.27 give them their meat in *d* season.
145.15 them their meat in *d* season.
Pr 3.27 good from them to whom it is *d*,
15.23 a word spoken in *d* season, how
Ec 10.17 princes eat in *d* season, for strength,
Mt 18.34 pay all that was *d* unto him.
24.45 to give them meat in *d* season?
Lk 12.42 their portion of meat in *d* season?
23.41 receive the *d* reward of our deeds:
Ro 5. 6 in *d* time Christ died for the ungodly.
13. 7 dues: tribute to whom tribute is *d*;
1Co 7. 3 unto the wife *d* benevolence:
15. 8 as of one born out of *d* time.
Gal 6. 9 for in *d* season we shall reap,
1Ti 2. 6 for all, to be testified in *d* time.
Tit 1. 3 in *d* time manifested his word
1Pe 5: 6 that he may exalt you in *d* time:

DUES

Ro 13. 7 Render therefore to all their *d*:

DULL

Mt 13.15 their ears are *d* of hearing, and
Ac 28.27 their ears are *d* of hearing, and
Heb 5.11 seeing ye are *d* of hearing.

DUMB

Ex 4.11 or who maketh the *d*, or deaf,
Ps 38.13 and I was as a *d* man that openeth
39. 2 I was *d* with silence, I held my
9 I was *d*, I opened not my mouth;
Pr 31. 8 Open thy mouth for the *d* in the
Isa 35. 6 and the tongue of the *d* sing:
53. 7 a sheep before her shearers is *d*,
56.10 they are all *d* dogs, they cannot
Eze 3.26 thou shalt be *d*, and shalt not be
24.27 shalt speak, and be no more *d*:
33.22 was opened, and I was no more *d*.
Dan 10.15 toward the ground, and I became *d*.
Hab 2.18 trusteth therein, to make *d* idols?
19 Awake; to the *d* stone, Arise,
Mt 9.32 brought to him a *d* man possessed
33 devil was cast out, the *d* spake:
12.22 with a devil, blind, and *d*: and he
22 that the blind and *d* both spake
15.30 blind, *d*, maimed, and many others,
31 when they saw the *d* to speak,
Mk 7.37 deaf to hear, and the *d* to speak.
9.17 my son, which hath a *d* spirit;
25 Thou *d* and deaf spirit, I charge
Lk 1.20 shalt be *d*, and not able to speak,
11.14 casting out a devil, and it was *d*.
14 devil was gone out, the *d* spake.
Ac 8.32 like a lamb *d* before his shearer,
1Co 12. 2 carried away unto these *d* idols,
2Pe 2.16 *d* ass speaking with man's voice

DUNGHILL

1Sa 2. 8 lifted up the beggar from the *d*,
Ezr 6.11 his house be made a *d* for this.
Ps 113. 7 and lifteth the needy out of the *d*;
Isa 25.10 as straw is trodden down for the *d*.
Dan 2. 5 your houses shall be made a *d*.
3.29 their houses shall be made a *d*:
Lk 14.35 for the land, nor yet for the *d*;

DUST

Gen 2. 7 Lord God formed man of the *d* of
3.14 and *d* shalt thou eat all the days of
19 wast thou taken; for *d* thou art,
19 and unto *d* shalt thou return.
13.16 as the *d* of the earth: so that if a
16 man can number the *d* of the earth,
18.27 Lord, which am but *d* and ashes:
28.14 shall be as the *d* of the earth,
Ex 8.16 smite the *d* of the land, that it
17 and smote the *d* of the earth,
17 in beast; all the *d* of the land
9. 9 And it shall become small *d* in all
Lev 14.41 they shall pour out the *d* that
17.13 blood thereof, and cover it with *d*.
Nu 5.17 and of the *d* that is in the floor of
23.10 Who can count the *d* of Jacob,
Dt 9.21 until it was as small as *d*: and
21 I cast the *d* thereof into the brook
28.24 the rain of thy land powder and *d*:
32.24 the poison of serpents of the *d*.
Jos 7. 6 and put *d* upon their heads.
1Sa 2. 8 raiseth up the poor out of the *d*,
2Sa 16.13 threw stones at him, and cast *d*.
22.43 I beat them as small as the *d* of
1Ki 16. 2 I exalted thee out of the *d*,
18.38 the wood, and the stones, and the *d*,
20.10 if the *d* of Samaria shall suffice
2Ki 13. 7 and had made them like the *d* by
23.12 cast the *d* of them into the brook
2Ch 1. 9 people like the *d* of the earth
34. 4 and made *d* of them, and strowed
Job 2.12 sprinkled *d* upon their heads
4.19 whose foundation is in the *d*,
5. 6 affliction cometh not forth of the *d*,
7. 5 with worms and with clods of *d*;
21 now shall I sleep in the *d*; and
10. 9 wilt thou bring me into *d* again?
14.19 grow out of the *d* of the earth;
16.15 and defiled my horn in the *d*.
17.16 our rest together is in the *d*.
20.11 shall lie down with him in the *d*
21.26 They shall lie down alike in the *d*,
22.24 Then shalt thou lay up gold as *d*,
27.16 Though he heap up silver as the *d*,
28. 6 sapphires: and it hath *d* of gold.
30.19 I am become like *d* and ashes.
34.15 man shall turn again unto *d*.
38.38 When the *d* groweth into hardness,
39.14 earth, and warmeth them in *d*,
40.13 Hide them in the *d* together;
42. 6 and repent in *d* and ashes.
Ps 7. 5 and lay mine honor in the *d*.
18.42 I beat them small as the *d* before
22.15 brought me into the *d* of death.
29 they that go down to the *d* shall
30. 9 Shall the *d* praise thee? shall it
44.25 our soul is bowed down to the *d*:
72. 9 and his enemies shall lick the *d*.
78.27 rained flesh also upon them as *d*,
102.14 stones, and favor the *d* thereof.
103.14 he remembereth that we are *d*.
104.29 they die, and return to their *d*.
113. 7 raiseth up the poor out of the *d*,
119.25 My soul cleaveth unto the *d*:
Pr 8.26 highest part of the *d* of the world.
Ec 3.20 all are of the *d*, and all turn to *d*
12. 7 shall the *d* return to the earth
Isa 2.10 and hide thee in the *d*, for fear of
5.24 their blossom shall go up as *d*:
25.12 to the ground, even to the *d*.
26. 5 he bringeth it even to the *d*.
19 and sing, ye that dwell in *d*:
29. 4 speech shall be low out of the *d*,
4 speech shall whisper out of the *d*.
5 strangers shall be like small *d*,
34. 7 their *d* made fat with fatness.
9 and the *d* thereof into brimstone,
40.12 comprehended the *d* of the earth
15 as the small *d* of the balance:
41. 2 gave them as the *d* to his sword,
47. 1 Come down, and sit in the *d*,
49.23 and lick up the *d* of thy feet;
52. 2 Shake thyself from the *d*; arise,
65.25 and *d* shall be the serpent's meat.
La 2.10 have cast up *d* upon their heads;
3.29 He putteth his mouth in the *d*;
Eze 24. 7 the ground, to cover it with *d*;
26. 4 I will also scrape her *d* from her,
10 his horses their *d* shall cover thee:
12 timber and thy *d* in the midst of
27.30 shall cast up *d* upon their heads,
Dan 12. 2 many of them that sleep in the *d*
Am 2. 7 that pant after the *d* of the earth
Mic 1.10 of Aphrah roll thyself in the *d*.
7.17 shall lick the *d* like a serpent,
Na 1. 3 the clouds are the *d* of his feet.
3.18 thy nobles shall dwell in the *d*:
Hab 1.10 they shall heap *d*, and take it.
Zep 1.17 blood shall be poured out as *d*,
Zec 9. 3 heaped up silver as the *d*, and fine
Mt 10.14 city, shake off the *d* of your feet.
Mk 6.11 shake off the *d* under your feet
Lk 9. 5 shake off the very *d* from your feet
10.11 Even the very *d* of your city, which
Ac 13.51 they shook off the *d* of their feet
22.23 clothes, and threw *d* into the air,
Rev 18.19 And they cast *d* on their heads,

DUTIES

Eze 18.11 And that doeth not any of those *d*

DUTY

Ex 21.10 and her *d* of marriage, shall he not
Dt 25. 5 *d* of an husband's brother unto her.
7 the *d* of my husband's brother.
2Ch 8.14 as the *d* of every day required:
Ezr 3. 4 as the *d* of every day required;
Ec 12.13 for this is the whole *d* of man.
Lk 17.10 done that which was our *d* to do.
Ro 15.27 their *d* is also to minister unto
(See box on page 240)

DWELL

Gen 4.20 the father of such as *d* in tents,
9.27 he shall *d* in the tents of Shem;
13. 6 that they might *d* together: for
6 so that they could not *d* together,
16.12 he shall *d* in the presence of all
19.30 he feared to *d* in Zoar: and he
20.15 thee: *d* where it pleaseth thee.
24. 3 the Canaanites, among whom I *d*:
37 the Canaanites, in whose land I *d*:
26. 2 *d* in the land which I shall tell
30.20 now will my husband *d* with me,
34.10 And ye shall *d* with us: and the
10 *d* and trade ye therein, and get you
16 and we will *d* with you, and we
21 therefore let them *d* in the land,
22 consent unto us for to *d* with us,
23 unto them, and they will *d* with us.
35. 1 go up to Beth-el, and *d* there: and
36. 7 than that they might *d* together;
45.10 thou shalt *d* in the land of Goshen,
46.34 ye may *d* in the land of Goshen;
47. 4 servants *d* in the land of Goshen.

BIBLICAL THEMES

DUTY

Behold, I have taught you statutes and judgments. . . . Only take heed to thyself, and keep thy soul diligently, lest thou forget the things which thine eyes have seen . . . but teach them thy sons, and thy sons' sons.
Dt 4.5, 9

And the people said unto Joshua, Nay; but we will serve the Lord. Jos 24.21

Let us hear the conclusion of the whole matter: Fear God, and keep his commandments: for this is the whole duty of man. Ec 12.13

Is not this the fast that I have chosen? to loose the bands of wickedness, to undo the heavy burdens, and to let the oppressed go free, and that ye break every yoke? Is it not to deal thy bread to the hungry, and that thou bring the poor that are cast out to thy house? when thou seest the naked, that thou cover him. . . ? Isa 58.6-7

Seek ye first the kingdom of God, and his righteousness. Mt 6.33

Not every one that saith unto me, Lord, Lord, shall enter into the kingdom of heaven; but he that doeth the will of my Father which is in heaven. Mt 7.21

If any man will come after me, let him deny himself, and take up his cross, and follow me. Mt 16.24

Keep the commandments. . . . Thou shalt do no murder, Thou shalt not commit adultery, Thou shalt not steal, Thou shalt not bear false witness, Honor thy father and thy mother.
Mt 19.17-19

Render therefore unto Caesar the things which are Caesar's; and unto God the things that are God's.
Mt 22.21

Thou shalt love the Lord thy God with all thy heart, and with all thy soul, and with all thy mind. This is the first and great commandment. And the second is like unto it, Thou shalt love thy neighbor as thyself. Mt 22.37-39

And he said unto them, How is it that ye sought me? wist ye not that I must be about my Father's business? Lk 2.49

When ye shall have done all those things which are commanded you, say, We are unprofitable servants: we have done that which was our duty to do.
Lk 17.10

Peter and John answered and said . . . Whether it be right in the sight of God to hearken unto you more than unto God, judge ye. For we cannot but speak the things which we have seen and heard. Ac 4.19-20

We then that are strong ought to bear the infirmities of the weak, and not to please ourselves. Ro 15.1

Now we exhort you, brethren, warn them that are unruly, comfort the feebleminded, support the weak, be patient toward all men. See that none render evil for evil unto any man; but ever follow that which is good. 1Th 5.14-15

Ye are a chosen generation . . . that ye should shew forth the praises of him who hath called you out of darkness. . . . Submit yourselves to every ordinance of man for the Lord's sake. . . . For so is the will of God, that with well doing ye may put to silence the ignorance of foolish men.
1Pe 2.9, 13, 15

Love not the world, neither the things that are in the world. If any man love the world, the love of the Father is not in him. 1Jn 2.15

Gen 47. 6 make thy father and brethren to *d*;
6 in the land of Goshen let them *d*:
49.13 Zebulun shall *d* at the haven of
Ex 2.21 Moses was content to *d* with the
8.22 Goshen, in which my people *d*,
15.17 thou hast made for thee to *d* in,
23.33 They shall not *d* in thy land, lest
25. 8 that I may *d* among them.
29.45 *d* among the children of Israel,
46 that I may *d* among them: I am
Lev 13.46 he shall *d* alone; without the camp
20.22 whither I bring you to *d* therein,
23.42 Ye shall *d* in booths seven days;
42 Israelites born shall *d* in booths:
43 children of Israel to *d* in booths,
25.18 ye shall *d* in the land in safety.
19 your fill, and *d* therein in safety.
26. 5 the full, and *d* in your land safely.
32 your enemies which *d* therein
Nu 5. 3 camps, in the midst whereof I *d*.
13.19 what the land is that they *d* in,
19 that they *d* in, whether in tents,
28 people be strong that *d* in the land,
29 The Amalekites *d* in the land of
29 the Amorites, *d* in the mountains:
29 and the Canaanites *d* by the sea,
14.30 make you *d* therein, save Caleb
23. 9 the people shall *d* alone, and shall
32.17 ones shall *d* in the fenced cities
33.53 of the land, and *d* therein: for I
55 vex you in the land wherein ye *d*.
35. 2 of their possession cities to *d* in;
3 the cities shall they have to *d* in;
32 should come again to *d* in the land.
34 ye shall inhabit, wherein I *d*: for
34 *d* among the children of Israel.
Dt 2. 4 children of Esau, which *d* in Seir;
29 children of Esau which *d* in Seir,
29 and the Moabites which *d* in Ar,
11.30 which *d* in the champaign over
31 ye shall possess it, and *d* therein.
12.10 and *d* in the land which the Lord
10 round about, so that ye *d* in safety;
11 to cause his name to *d* there;
13.12 God hath given thee to *d* there,
17.14 possess it, and shalt *d* therein,
23.16 He shall *d* with thee, even among
25. 5 If brethren *d* together, and one of
28.30 and thou shalt not *d* therein:
30.20 that thou mayest *d* in the land
33.12 Lord shall *d* in safety by him;
12 he shall *d* between his shoulders.
28 Israel then shall *d* in safety
Jos 9. 7 Peradventure ye *d* among us;
22 from you; when ye *d* among us?
10. 6 *d* in the mountains are gathered
13.13 the Maachathites *d* among the
14. 4 cities to *d* in, with their suburbs
15.63 Jebusites *d* with the children
16.10 but the Canaanites *d* among the
17.12 Canaanites would *d* in that land.
16 that *d* in the land of the valley
20. 4 place, that he may *d* among them.
6 And he shall *d* in that city,
21. 2 of Moses to give us cities to *d* in,
24.13 ye built not, and ye *d* in them;
15 the Amorites, in whose land ye *d*:
Jdg 1.21 Jebusites *d* with the children
27 Canaanites would *d* in that land.
35 Amorites would *d* in mount Heres
6.10 in whose land ye *d*: but ye have
9.41 they should not *d* in Shechem.
17.10 Micah said unto him. *D* with me,
11 the Levite was content to *d* with
18. 1 sought them an inheritance to *d* in;
1Sa 12. 8 and made them *d* in this place.
27. 5 country, that I may *d* there: for
5 why should thy servant *d* in the
2Sa 7. 2 I *d* in an house of cedar, but the ark
5 build me an house for me to *d* in?
10 that they may *d* in a place of their
1Ki 2.36 house in Jerusalem, and *d* there,
3.17 I and this woman *d* in one house;
6.13 And I will *d* among the children
8.12 The Lord said that he would *d* in
13 built thee an house to *d* in, a
27 will God indeed *d* on the earth?
17. 9 belongeth to Zidon, and *d* there:
2Ki 4.13 I *d* among mine own people.
6. 1 the place where we *d* with thee
2 a place there, where we may *d*.
17.27 let them go and *d* there,
25.24 *d* in the land, and serve the king
1Ch 17. 1 I *d* in an house of cedars,
4 not build me an house to *d* in:
9 and they shall *d* in their place,
23.25 may *d* in Jerusalem for ever:
2Ch 2. 3 build him an house to *d* therein,
6. 1 he would *d* in the thick darkness.
18 will God in very deed *d* with men
8. 2 the children of Israel to *d* there.
11 shall not *d* in the house of David
19.10 brethren that *d* in their cities,
Ezr 4.17 companions that *d* in Samaria,
6.12 hath caused his name to *d* there
Neh 8.14 the children of Israel should *d* in
11. 1 to *d* in Jerusalem the holy city,
2 themselves to *d* at Jerusalem.
Job 3. 5 stain it; let a cloud *d* upon it;
4.19 in them that *d* in houses of clay,
11.14 wickedness *d* in thy tabernacles.
18.15 It shall *d* in his tabernacle,
19.15 They that *d* in mine house, and
30. 6 To *d* in the cliffs of the valleys,
Ps 4. 8 Lord, only makest me *d* in safety.

5. 4 neither shall evil *d* with thee.
15. 1 who shall *d* in thy holy hill?
23. 6 I will *d* in the house of the Lord
24. 1 world, and they that *d* therein.
25.13 His soul shall *d* at ease; and his
27. 4 I may *d* in the house of the Lord
37. 3 So shalt thou *d* in the land, and
27 and do good: and *d* for evermore.
29 inherit the land, and *d* therein for
65. 4 that he may *d* in thy courts:
8 They also that *d* in the uttermost
68. 6 but the rebellious *d* in a dry land.
16 hill which God desireth to *d* in;
16 yea, the Lord will *d* in it for ever.
18 Lord God might *d* among them
69.25 and let none *d* in their tents.
35 that they may *d* there, and have
36 they that love his name shall *d*
72. 9 that *d* in the wilderness shall bow
78.55 made the tribes of Israel to *d*
84. 4 Blessed are they that *d* in thy
10 to *d* in the tents of wickedness.
85. 9 that glory may *d* in our land.
98. 7 world, and they that *d* therein.
101. 6 the land, that they may *d* with me:
7 shall not *d* within my house:
107. 4 way; they found no city to *d* in.
34 of them that *d* therein.
36 there he maketh the hungry to *d*,
120. 5 I *d* in the tents of Kedar!
132.14 here will I *d*; for I have desired it.
133. 1 brethren to *d* together in unity!
139. 9 and *d* in the uttermost parts of the
140.13 upright shall *d* in thy presence.
143. 3 he hath made me to *d* in darkness,
Pr 1.33 hearkeneth unto me shall *d*
2.21 the upright shall *d* in the land,
8.12 I wisdom *d* with prudence, and
21. 9 to *d* in the corner of the housetop,
19 It is better to *d* in the wilderness,
25.24 to *d* in the corner of the housetop,
Isa 6. 5 I *d* in the midst of a people of
9. 2 that *d* in the land of the shadow
11. 6 wolf also shall *d* with the lamb,
13.21 owls shall *d* there, and satyrs
16. 4 Let mine outcasts *d* with thee,
23.13 them that *d* in the wilderness:
18 them that *d* before the Lord, to
24. 6 they that *d* therein are desolate:
26. 5 down them that *d* on high; the
19 and sing, ye that *d* in dust: for
30.19 For the people shall *d* in Zion at
32.16 shall *d* in the wilderness, and
18 *d* in a peaceable habitation,
33.14 shall *d* with the devouring fire?
14 shall *d* with everlasting
16 He shall *d* on high: his place of
24 the people that *d* therein shall
34.11 the raven shall *d* in it: and he
17 generation shall they *d* therein.
40.22 them out as a tent to *d* in:
49.20 give place to me that I may *d*.
51. 6 *d* therein shall die in like manner:
57.15 I *d* in the high and holy place,
58.12 The restorer of paths to *d* in.
65. 9 and my servants shall *d* there.
Jer 4.29 forsaken, and not a man *d* therein.
7. 3 I will cause you to *d* in this place.
7 will I cause you to *d* in this place,
8.16 city, and those that *d* therein.
19 of them that *d* in a far country:
9.26 corners, that *d* in the wilderness:
12. 4 wickedness of them that *d* therein?
20. 6 all that *d* in thine house shall go
23. 6 Israel shall *d* safely: and this
8 they shall *d* in their own land.
24. 8 them that *d* in the land of Egypt:
25. 5 and *d* in the land that the Lord
24 people that *d* in the desert,
27.11 they shall till it, and *d* therein.
29. 5 Build ye houses, and *d* in them;
28 build ye houses, and *d* in them;
32 a man to *d* among his people;
31.24 And there shall *d* in Judah itself,
32.27 and I will cause them to *d* safely:
33.16 and Jerusalem shall *d* safely:
35. 7 all your days ye shall *d* in tents;
9 Nor to build houses for us to *d* in:
11 Syrians: so we *d* at Jerusalem.
15 and ye shall *d* in the land which
40. 5 and *d* with him among the people:
9 *d* in the land, and serve the king
10 for me, behold, I will *d* at Mizpah,
10 and *d* in your cities that ye have
42.13 We will not *d* in this land, neither
14 of bread: and there will we *d*:
43. 4 Lord, to *d* in the land of Judah.
5 driven, to *d* in the land of Judah;
44. 1 which *d* in the land of Egypt,
1 which *d* at Migdol, and at
8 whither ye be gone to *d*, that
13 I will punish them that *d* in the
14 have a desire to return to *d* there:
26 Judah that *d* in the land of Egypt;
47. 2 the city, and them that *d* therein:
48. 9 desolate, without any to *d* therein.
28 O ye that *d* in Moab, leave the
28 cities, and *d* in the rock, and be
49. 1 and his people *d* in his cities?
8 Flee ye, turn back, *d* deep, O
18 neither shall a son of man *d* in it.
30 Flee, get you far off, *d* deep, O ye
31 gates nor bars which *d* alone.
33 nor any son of man *d* in it.
50. 3 none shall *d* therein: they shall
39 beasts of the islands shall *d* there,
39 and the owls shall *d* therein: and
40 shall any son of man *d* therein.
51. 1 against them that *d* in the midst
Eze 2. 6 thou dost *d* among scorpions:
12.19 violence of all them that *d* therein.
16.46 daughters that *d* at thy left hand:
17.23 and under it shall *d* all fowl
23 the branches thereof shall they *d*.
28.25 then shall they *d* in their land
26 And they shall *d* safely therein,
26 yea, they shall *d* with confidence,
32.15 shall smite all them that *d* therein,
34.25 and they shall *d* safely in the
28 but they shall *d* safely, and none
36.28 And ye shall *d* in the land that
33 also cause you to *d* in the cities,
37.25 And they shall *d* in the land that
25 and they shall *d* therein, even they,
38. 8 and they shall *d* safely all of them.
11 that are at rest, that *d* safely,
12 that *d* in the midst of the land.
39. 6 among them that *d* carelessly
9 they that *d* in the cities of Israel
43. 7 where I will *d* in the midst of the
9 and I will *d* in the midst of them
Dan 2.38 wheresoever the children of men *d*,
4. 1 that *d* in all the earth; Peace be
6.25 that *d* in all the earth; Peace be
Hos 9. 3 shall not *d* in the Lord's land;
12. 9 make thee to *d* in tabernacles,
14. 7 They that *d* under his shadow
Joel 3.20 Judah shall *d* for ever, and
Am 3.12 be taken out that *d* in Samaria
5.11 but ye shall not *d* in them;
9. 5 all that *d* therein shall mourn:
Mic 4.10 and thou shalt *d* in the field,
7.13 because of them that *d* therein,
14 which *d* solitarily in the wood,
Na 1. 5 the world, and all that *d* therein.
3.18 thy nobles shall *d* in the dust:
Hab 2. 8 the city, and of all that *d* therein.
17 city, and of all that *d* therein.
Zep 1.18 of all them that *d* in the land.
Hag 1. 4 to *d* in your cieled houses, and
Zec 2.10 I come, and I will *d* in the midst
11 people: and I will *d* in the midst
8. 3 will *d* in the midst of Jerusalem:
4 and old women *d* in the streets
8 shall *d* in the midst of Jerusalem:
9. 6 And a bastard shall *d* in Ashdod,
14.11 And men shall *d* in it, and there
Mt 12.45 and they enter in and *d* there:
Lk 11.26 and they enter in, and *d* there:
21.35 all them that *d* on the face of the
Ac 1.20 and let no man *d* therein:
2.14 and all ye that *d* at Jerusalem,
4.16 to all them that *d* in Jerusalem;
7. 4 into this land, wherein ye now *d*.
13.27 For they that *d* at Jerusalem, and
17.26 to *d* on all the face of the earth,
28.16 Paul was suffered to *d* by himself
Ro 8. 9 that the Spirit of God *d* in you.
11 raised up Jesus from the dead *d*
1Co 7.12 and she be pleased to *d* with him,
13 if he be pleased to *d* with her,
2Co 6.16 God hath said, I will *d* in them,
Eph 3.17 That Christ may *d* in your hearts
Col 1.19 that in him should all fulness *d*;
3.16 Let the word of Christ *d* in you
1Pe 3. 7 husbands *d* with them according
1Jn 4.13 know we that we *d* in him,
Rev 3.10 try them that *d* upon the earth.
6.10 blood on them that *d* on the earth?
7.15 the throne shall *d* among them.
11.10 they that *d* upon the earth shall
10 tormented them that *d* on the earth.
12.12 heavens, and ye that *d* in them.
13. 6 and them that *d* in heaven.
8 all that *d* upon the earth shall
12 which *d* therein to worship the
14 And deceiveth them that *d* on the
14 saying to them that *d* on the earth,
14. 6 to preach unto them that *d* on
17. 8 and they that *d* on the earth shall
21. 3 and he will *d* with them, and they

DWELLERS

Isa 18. 3 of the world, and *d* on the earth,
Ac 1.19 known unto all the *d* at Jerusalem;
2. 9 and the *d* in Mesopotamia, and in

DWELLETH

Lev 19.34 the stranger that *d* with you
25.39 And if thy brother that *d* by thee
47 and thy brother that *d* by him
Nu 13.18 people that *d* therein, whether
Dt 33.20 he *d* as a lion, and teareth the arm
Jos 6.25 and she *d* in Israel even unto
22.19 wherein the Lord's tabernacle *d*,
1Sa 4. 4 which *d* between the cherubims:
27.11 while he *d* in the country of the
2Sa 6. 2 that *d* between the cherubims.
7. 2 the ark of God *d* within curtains.
1Ch 13. 6 that *d* between the cherubims,
Job 15.28 And he *d* in desolate cities, and
38.19 Where is the way where light *d*?
39.28 She *d* and abideth on the rock,
Ps 9.11 to the Lord, which *d* in Zion:
26. 8 the place where thine honor *d*.
91. 1 He that *d* in the secret place of the
113. 5 the Lord our God, who *d* on high,
135.21 of Zion, which *d* at Jerusalem.
Pr 3.29 seeing he *d* securely by thee.
Isa 8.18 of hosts, which *d* in mount Zion.
33. 5 for he *d* on high: he hath filled
Jer 29.16 of all the people that *d* in this
44. 2 desolation, and no man *d* therein,
49.31 nation that *d* without care,
51.43 a land wherein no man *d*, neither
La 1. 3 she *d* among the heathen, she
Eze 16.46 that *d* at thy right hand, is Sodom
17.16 the place where the king *d* that
38.14 when my people of Israel *d* safely,
Dan 2.22 darkness, and the light *d* with
Hos 4. 3 every one that *d* therein shall
Joel 3.21 cleansed: for the Lord *d* in Zion.
Am 8. 8 every one mourn that *d* therein?

Mt 23.21 by it, and by him that *d* therein.
Jn 6.56 my blood, *d* in me, and I in him.
14.10 the Father that *d* in me, he doeth
17 for he *d* with you, and shall be
Ac 7.48 the most High *d* not in temples
17.24 of heaven and earth, *d* not in temples
Ro 7.17 that do it, but sin that *d* in me.
18 is, in my flesh,) *d* no good thing:
20 I that do it, but sin that *d* in me.
8.11 bodies by his Spirit that *d* in you.
1Co 3.16 and that the Spirit of God *d* in you?
Col 2. 9 in him *d* all the fulness of the
2Ti 1.14 the Holy Ghost which *d* in us.
Jas 4. 5 The spirit that *d* in us lusteth
2Pe 3.13 earth, wherein *d* righteousness.
1Jn 3.17 how *d* the love of God in him?
24 his commandments *d* in him,
4.12 God *d* in us, and his love is
15 God *d* in him, and he in God.
16 he that *d* in love *d* in God, and
2Jn 2 the truth's sake, which *d* in us,
Rev 2.13 slain among you, where Satan *d*.

DWELLING

Gen 10.30 their *d* was from Mesha, as thou
25.27 Jacob was a plain man, *d* in tents.
27.39 thy *d* shall be the fatness of the
Lev 25.29 if a man sell a *d* house in a walled
Nu 21.15 that goeth down to the *d* of Ar,
Jos 13.21 dukes of Sihon, *d* in the country.
1Ki 8.30 and hear thou in heaven thy *d*
39 Then hear thou in heaven thy *d*
43 Hear thou in heaven thy *d* place,
49 supplication in heaven thy *d* place,
21. 8 were in his city, *d* with Naboth.
2Ki 17.25 the beginning of their *d* there, that
1Ch 6.32 they ministered before the *d*
54 are their *d* places throughout
2Ch 6. 2 a place for thy *d* for ever.
21 hear thou from thy *d* place, even
30 hear thou from heaven thy *d* place,
33 even from thy *d* place, and do
39 even from thy *d* place, their prayer
30.27 came up to his holy *d* place,
36.15 his people, and on his *d* place:
Job 8.22 and the *d* place of the wicked
21.28 are the *d* places of the wicked?
Ps 49.11 their *d* places to all generations;
14 consume in the grave from their *d*.
52. 5 pluck thee out of thy *d* place,
74. 7 down the *d* place of thy name
76. 2 and his *d* place in Zion.
79. 7 Jacob, and laid waste his *d* place.
90. 1 Lord, thou hast been our *d* place
91.10 shall any plague come nigh thy *d*.
Pr 21.20 and oil in the *d* of the wise;
24.15 against the *d* of the righteous;
Isa 4. 5 every *d* place of mount Zion,
18. 4 I will consider in my *d* place
Jer 46.19 O thou daughter *d* in Egypt,
49.33 Hazor shall be a *d* for dragons,
Eze 38.11 all of them *d* without walls, and
48.15 the city, for *d*, and for suburbs:
Dan 2.11 gods, whose *d* is not with flesh.
4.25, 32 thy *d* shall be with the beasts
5.21 and his *d* was with the wild asses:
Joel 3.17 the Lord your God *d* in Zion,
Na 2.11 Where is the *d* of the lions,
Zep 3. 7 so their *d* should not be cut off,
Mk 5. 3 Who had his *d* among the tombs;
Ac 2. 5 And there were *d* at Jerusalem
19.17 Greeks also *d* at Ephesus; and
1Ti 6.16 *d* in the light which no man can
Heb 11. 9 *d* in tabernacles with Isaac and
2Pe 2. 8 righteous man *d* among them,

DWELLINGPLACE

Nu 24.21 Strong is thy *d*, and thou puttest
Jer 51.37 Babylon shall become heaps, a *d*
1Co 4.11 are buffeted, have no certain *d*;

DWELT

Gen 4.16 the Lord, and *d* in the land of Nod,
11.31 came unto Haran, and *d* there.
14.12 who *d* in Sodom, and his goods,
16. 3 after Abraham had *d* ten years in
19.29 the cities in the which Lot *d*.
21.21 he *d* in the wilderness of Paran:
22.19 and Abraham *d* at Beer-sheba.
26. 6 And Isaac *d* in Gerar:
47.27 And Israel *d* in the land of Egypt,
50.22 And Joseph *d* in Egypt, he, and his
Nu 20.15 we have *d* in Egypt a long time;
21.31 Israel *d* in the land of the Amorites.
Dt 2. 8 Esau, which *d* in Seir, through
33.16 will of him that *d* in the bush:
Jos 2.15 and she *d* upon the wall.
7. 7 and *d* on the other side Jordan!
16.10 the Canaanites that *d* in Gezer:
24. 7 in the wilderness a long season.
Jdg 1.10 Canaanites that *d* in Hebron:
32 Asherites *d* among the Canaanites,
3. 5 of Israel *d* among the Canaanites,
4. 5 *d* under the palm tree of Deborah
8.11 the way of them that *d* in tents
21.23 repaired the cities, and *d* in them.
Ru 2.23 and *d* with her mother-in-law.
1Sa 19.18 and Samuel went and *d* in Naioth.
27. 3 And David *d* with Achish at Gath,
7 *d* in the country of the Philistines
2Sa 2. 3 and they *d* in the cities of Hebron.
5. 9 David *d* in the fort, and called it
14.28 So Absalom *d* two full years in
1Ki 4.25 And Judah and Israel *d* safely,
12. 2 And Jeroboam *d* in Egypt;
13.11 there *d* an old prophet in Beth-el;
2Ki 13. 5 children of Israel *d* in their tents,
19.36 and returned, and *d* at Nineveh.
1Ch 4.40 they of Ham had *d* there of old.
5.22 *d* in their steads until the captivity.
23 tribe of Manasseh *d* in the land:
7.29 In these *d* the children of Joseph
8.32 *d* with their brethren in Jerusalem,
10. 7 Philistines came and *d* in them.
11. 7 And David *d* in the castle;
Ps 94.17 my soul and almost *d* in silence.
120. 6 My soul hath long *d* with him
Eze 3.15 that *d* by the river of Chebar, and
31. 6 and under his shadow *d* all great
Dan 4.12 the fowls of the heaven *d* in the
21 which the beasts of the field *d*,
Mt 2.23 and *d* in a city called Nazareth:
4.13 he came and *d* in Capernaum,
Ac 7. 2 Mesopotamia, before he *d* in
9.22 the Jews which *d* at Damascus,
32 to the saints which *d* at Lydda.
28.30 Paul *d* two whole years in his

DYING

Nu 17.13 shall we be consumed with *d*?
Mk 12.20 and the first took a wife, and *d*
Lk 8.42 years of age, and she lay a *d*.
2Co 4.10 bearing about in the body the *d*
6. 9 known; as *d*, and, behold, we live;
Heb 11.21 Jacob, when he was a *d*, blessed

E

EAGLE

Lev 11.13 the *e*, and the ossifrage, and the
18 and the pelican and the gier *e*,
Dt 14.12 not eat: the *e*, and the ossifrage,
17 the gier *e*, and the cormorant,
28.49 the earth, as swift as the *e* flieth;
32.11 As an *e* stirreth up her nest,
Job 9.26 as the *e* that hasteth to the prey.
39.27 Doth the *e* mount up at thy
Pr 23. 5 fly away as an *e* toward heaven.
30.19 The way of an *e* in the air;
Jer 48.40 Behold, he shall fly as an *e*,
49.16 make thy nest as high as the *e*,
22 and fly as the *e*, and spread his
Eze 1.10 they four also had the face of an *e*.
10.14 and the fourth the face of an *e*.
17. 3 A great *e* with great wings, long
7 There was also another great *e*
Hos 8. 1 He shall come as an *e* against the
Ob 4 Though thou exalt thyself as the *e*,
Mic 1.16 enlarge thy baldness as the *e*;
Hab 1. 8 they shall fly as the *e* that hasteth
Rev 4. 7 the fourth beast was like a flying *e*.
12.14 were given two wings of a great *e*,

EAGLE'S

Ps 103. 5 thy youth is renewed like the *e*.
Dan 7. 4 was like a lion, and had *e* wings;

EAGLES

2Sa 1.23 they were swifter than *e*, they
Pr 30.17 and the young *e* shall eat it.
Isa 40.31 shall mount up with wings as *e*;
Jer 4.13 his horses are swifter than *e*.
La 4.19 swifter than the *e* of the heaven:
Mt 24.28 is, there will the *e* be gathered
Lk 17.37 is, thither will the *e* be gathered

EAR

Ex 9.31 for the barley was in the *e*,
15.26 will give *e* to his commandments,
21. 6 his master shall bore his *e* through
29.20 upon the tip of the right *e* of Aaron,
20 upon the tip of the right *e* of his
Lev 8.23 upon the tip of Aaron's right *e*,
24 upon the tip of their right *e*, and
14.14, 17, 25, 28 tip of the right *e* of him
Dt 1.45 to your voice, nor give *e* unto you.
15.17 it through his *e* unto the door,
32. 1 Give *e*, O ye heavens, and I will
Jdg 5. 3 give *e*, O ye princes; I, even I, will
1Sa 8.12 and will set them to *e* his ground,
9.15 had told Samuel in his *e* a day
2Ki 19.16 Lord, bow down thine *e*, and hear:
2Ch 24.19 them: but they would not give *e*.
Neh 1. 6 Let thine *e* now be attentive, and
11 thine *e* be attentive to the prayer
9.30 yet would they not give *e*:
Job 4.12 mine *e* received a little thereof.
12.11 Doth not the *e* try words? and the
13. 1 mine *e* hath heard and understood
29.11 the *e* heard me, then it blessed me;
21 Unto me men gave *e*, and waited,
32.11 I gave *e* to your reasons, whilst
34. 2 give *e* unto me, ye that have
3 the *e* trieth words, as the mouth
36.10 openeth also their *e* to discipline,
42. 5 of thee by the hearing of the *e*:
Ps 5. 1 Give *e* to my words, O Lord,
10.17 thou wilt cause thine *e* to hear:
17. 1 my cry, give *e* unto my prayer,
6 incline thine *e* unto me, and hear
31. 2 Bow down thine *e* to me; deliver
39.12 give *e* unto my cry; hold not thy
45.10 and consider, and incline thine *e*;
49. 1 give *e*, all ye inhabitants of the
4 I will incline mine *e* to a parable:
54. 2 give *e* to the words of my mouth.
55. 1 Give *e* to my prayer, O God;
58. 4 deaf adder that stoppeth her *e*;
71. 2 incline thine *e* unto me, and save
77. 1 my voice; and he gave *e* unto me.
78. 1 Give *e*, O my people, to my law:
80. 1 Give *e*, O Shepherd of Israel,
84. 8 give *e*, O God of Jacob.
86. 1 down thine *e*, O Lord, hear me:
6 Give *e*, O Lord, unto my prayer;
88. 2 incline thine *e* unto my cry;
94. 9 planted the *e*, shall he not hear?
102. 2 trouble; incline thine *e* unto me:
116. 2 he hath inclined his *e* unto me,
141. 1 give *e* unto my voice, when I cry
143. 1 O Lord, give *e* to my supplications:
Pr 2. 2 thou incline thine *e* unto wisdom,
4.20 incline thine *e* unto my sayings.
5. 1 bow thine *e* to my understanding:
13 mine *e* to them that instructed me!
15.31 The *e* that heareth the reproof of
17. 4 liar giveth *e* to a naughty tongue.
18.15 *e* of the wise seeketh knowledge.
20.12 The hearing *e*, and the seeing eye,
22.17 Bow down thine *e*, and hear the
25.12 a wise reprover upon an obedient *e*.
28. 9 away his *e* from hearing the law,
Ec 1. 8 nor the *e* filled with hearing.
Isa 1. 2 O heavens, and give *e*, O earth:
10 give *e* unto the law of our God,
8. 9 and give *e*, all ye of far countries:
28.23 Give ye *e*, and hear my voice;
30.24 young asses that *e* the ground
32. 9 daughters; give *e* unto my speech.
37.17 Incline thine *e*, O Lord, and hear;
42.23 among you will give *e* to this?
48. 8 time that thine *e* was not opened:
50. 4 wakeneth mine *e* to hear as the
5 The Lord God hath opened mine *e*,
51. 4 give *e* unto me, O my nation:
55. 3 Incline your *e*, and come unto me:
59. 1 his *e* heavy, that it cannot hear:
64. 4 not heard, nor perceived by the *e*,
Jer 6.10 behold, their *e* is uncircumcised,
7.24 nor inclined their *e*, but walked in
26 nor inclined their *e*, but hardened
9.20 *e* receive the word of his mouth,
11. 8 nor inclined their *e*, but walked
13.15 ye, and give *e*; be not proud:
17.23 neither inclined their *e*, but made
25. 4 nor inclined your *e* to hear.
34.14 unto me, neither inclined their *e*.
35.15 but ye have not inclined your *e*,
44. 5 nor inclined their *e* to turn from
La 3.56 hide not thine *e* at my breathing,
Dan 9.18 O my God, incline thine *e*, and hear;
Hos 5. 1 give ye *e*, O house of the king;
Joel 1. 2 Hear this, ye old men, and give *e*,
Am 3.12 two legs, or a piece of an *e*;
Mt 10.27 what ye hear in the *e*, that preach
26.51 high priest's, and smote off his *e*.
Mk 4.28 first the blade, then the *e*, after
28 after that the full corn in the *e*.
14.47 high priest, and cut off his *e*.
Lk 12. 3 which ye have spoken in the *e*
22.50 high priest, and cut off his right *e*.
51 he touched his *e*, and healed him.
Jn 18.10 servant, and cut off his right *e*.
26 his kinsman whose *e* Peter cut off,
1Co 2. 9 nor *e* heard, neither have entered
12.16 And if the *e* shall say, Because I
Rev 2. 7, 11, 17, 29 He that hath an *e*, let him
3. 6, 13, 22 He that hath an *e*, let him
13. 9 If any man have an *e*, let him hear.

EARNEST

Ro 8.19 the *e* expectation of the creature
2Co 1.22 the *e* of the Spirit in our hearts.
5. 5 given unto us the *e* of the Spirit.
7. 7 he told us your *e* desire, your
8.16 put the same *e* care into the heart
Eph 1.14 Which is the *e* of our inheritance
Php 1.20 to my *e* expectation and my hope,
Heb 2. 1 we ought to give the more *e* heed

EARNESTLY

Nu 22.37 Did I not *e* send unto thee to call thee?
1Sa 20. 6 say, David *e* asked leave of me that
28 David *e* asked leave of me to go to
Neh 3.20 the son of Zabbai *e* repaired
Job 7. 2 As a servant *e* desireth the shadow,
Jer 11. 7 For I *e* protested unto your fathers
31.20 him, I do *e* remember him still:
Mic 7. 3 may do evil with both hands *e*,
Lk 22.44 in an agony he prayed more *e*:
56 and *e* looked upon him, and said,
Ac 3.12 why look ye so *e* on us,
23. 1 Paul, *e* beholding the council,
1Co 12.31 But covet *e* the best gifts:
2Co 5. 2 *e* desiring to be clothed upon
Jas 5.17 prayed *e* that it might not rain:
Jude 3 ye should *e* contend for the faith

EARS

Gen 20. 8 and told all these things in their *e*:
35. 4 earrings which were in their *e*;
41. 5 seven *e* of corn came up upon
6 seven thin *e* and blasted with the
7 And the seven thin *e* devoured the
7 devoured the seven rank and full *e*.
22 seven *e* came up in one stalk,
23 seven *e*, withered, thin, and
24 thin *e* devoured the seven good *e*:
26 the seven good *e* are seven years:
27 the seven empty *e* blasted with
44.18 speak a word in my lord's *e*,
50. 4 I pray you, in the *e* of Pharaoh,
Ex 10. 2 mayest tell in the *e* of thy son,
11. 2 Speak now in the *e* of the people,
17.14 rehearse it in the *e* of Joshua:
32. 2 which are in the *e* of your wives,
3 earrings which were in their *e*,
Lev 2.14 of thy firstfruits green *e* of corn
14 even corn beaten out of full *e*.
23.14 nor parched corn, nor green *e*,
Nu 11.18 ye have wept in the *e* of the Lord,
14.28 as ye have spoken in mine *e*, so
Dt 5. 1 which I speak in your *e* this day,
23.25 pluck the *e* with thine hand;
29. 4 eyes to see, and *e* to hear, unto this
31.28 I may speak these words in their *e*,
30 Moses spake in the *e* of all the
32.44 this song in the *e* of the people,
Jos 20. 4 his cause in the *e* of the elders
Jdg 7. 3 proclaim in the *e* of the people,
9. 2 Speak, I pray you, in the *e* of all
3 in the *e* of all the men of Shechem
17. 2 and spakest of also in mine *e*,
Ru 2. 2 and glean *e* of corn after him
1Sa 3.11 the *e* of every one that heareth
8.21 rehearse them in the *e* of the Lord.
11. 4 the tidings in the *e* of the people:
15.14 bleating of the sheep in mine *e*,
18.23 those words in the *e* of David.
2Sa 3.19 also spake in the *e* of Benjamin:
19 also to speak in the *e* of David
7.22 all that we have heard with our *e*.
22. 7 my cry did enter into his *e*.
2Ki 4.42 *e* of corn in the husk thereof.
18.26 in the *e* of the people that are on
19.28 tumult is come up into mine *e*,

2Ki 21.12 of it, both his *e* shall tingle.
23. 2 read in their *e* all the words of the
1Ch 17.20 all that we have heard with our *e*.
2Ch 6.40 and let thine *e* be attent unto the
7.15 and mine *e* attent unto the prayer
34.30 read in their *e* all the words of the
Neh 8. 3 and the *e* of all the people were
Job 13.17 and my declaration with your *e*.
15.21 A dreadful sound is in his *e*:
24.24 off as the tops of the *e* of corn.
28.22 heard the fame thereof with our *e*.
33.16 Then he openeth the *e* of men,
36.15 openeth their *e* in oppression.
Ps 18. 6 came before him, even into his *e*.
34.15 and his *e* are open unto their cry.
40. 6 mine *e* hast thou opened:
44. 1 We have heard with our *e*, O God,
78. 1 incline your *e* to the words of my
92.11 mine *e* shall hear my desire of
115. 6 They have *e*, but they hear not:
130. 2 let thine *e* be attentive to the voice
135.17 They have *e*, but they hear not;
Pr 21.13 Whoso stoppeth his *e* at the cry
23. 9 Speak not in the *e* of a fool:
12 thine *e* to the words of knowledge.
26.17 one that taketh a dog by the *e*.
Isa 5. 9 In mine *e* said the Lord of hosts,
6.10 and make their *e* heavy, and shut
10 their eyes, and hear with their *e*,
11. 3 reprove after the hearing of his *e*:
17. 5 and reapeth the *e* with his arm;
5 it shall be as he that gathereth *e*
22.14 revealed in mine *e* by the Lord
30.21 And thine *e* shall hear a word
32. 3 *e* of them that hear shall hearken.
33.15 stoppeth his *e* from hearing of
35. 5 *e* of the deaf shall be unstopped.
36.11 in the *e* of the people that are on
37.29 tumult, is come up into mine *e*,
42.20 opening the *e*, but he heareth not.
43. 8 have eyes, and the deaf that have *e*.
49.20 other, shall say again in thine *e*,
Jer 2. 2 Go and cry in the *e* of Jerusalem,
5.21 which have *e*, and hear not:
19. 3 whosoever heareth, his *e* shall
26.11 as ye have heard with your *e*.
15 speak all these words in your *e*.
28. 7 this word that I speak in thine *e*,
7 and in the *e* of all the people;
29.29 this letter in the *e* of Jeremiah
36. 6 in the *e* of the people in the Lord's
6 in the *e* of all Judah that come out
10 house, in the *e* of all the people.
13 read the book in the *e* of the people.
14 hast read in the *e* of the people,
15 down now, and read it in our *e*.
15 So Baruch read it in their *e*.
20 all the words in the *e* of the king.
21 Jehudi read it in the *e* of the king,
21 and in the *e* of all the princes
Eze 3.10 thine heart, and hear with thine *e*.
8.18 cry in mine *e* with a loud voice,
9. 1 cried also in mine *e* with a loud
12. 2 they have *e* to hear, and hear not:
16.12 and earrings in thine *e*, and a
23.25 take away thy nose and thine *e*;
24.26 cause thee to hear it with thine *e*?
40. 4 thine eyes, and hear with thine *e*,
44. 5 and hear with thine *e* all that I say
Mic 7.16 their mouth, their *e* shall be deaf.
Zec 7.11 and stopped their *e*, that they
Mt 11.15 He that hath *e* to hear, let him
12. 1 and began to pluck the *e* of corn,
13. 9 Who hath *e* to hear, let him hear.
15 and their *e* are dull of hearing,
15 their eyes, and hear with their *e*,
16 and your *e*, for they hear.
43 Who hath *e* to hear, let him hear.
28.14 if this come to the governor's *e*,
Mk 2.23 went, to pluck the *e* of corn.
4. 9 He that hath *e* to hear, let him
23 If any man have *e* to hear,
7.16 If any man have *e* to hear, let
33 and put his fingers into his *e*,
35 straightway his *e* were opened,
8.18 and having *e*, hear ye not?
Lk 1.44 thy salutation sounded in mine *e*,
4.21 this scripture fulfilled in your *e*.
6. 1 disciples plucked the *e* of corn,
8. 8 He that hath *e* to hear, let him
9.44 sayings sink down into your *e*:
14.35 He that hath *e* to hear, let him
Ac 7.51 and uncircumcised in heart and *e*,
57 and stopped their *e*, and ran upon
11.22 came unto the *e* of the church
17.20 certain strange things to our *e*:
28.27 and their *e* are dull of hearing,
27 their eyes, and hear with their *e*,
Ro 11. 8 and *e* that they should not hear:)
2Ti 4. 3 teachers, having itching *e*;
4 turn away their *e* from the truth,
Jas 5. 4 entered into the *e* of the Lord
1Pe 3.12 his *e* are open unto their prayers:

EARTH

Gen 1. 1 God created the heaven and the *e*.
2 And the *e* was without form, and
10 And God called the dry land *E*;
11 said, Let the *e* bring forth grass,
11 whose seed is in itself, upon the *e*:
12 And the *e* brought forth grass,
15 to give light upon the *e*: and it was
17 to give light upon the *e*,
20 and fowl that may fly above the *e* in
22 and let fowl multiply in the *e*.
24 Let the *e* bring forth the living
24 and beast of the *e* after his kind:
25 God made the beast of the *e* after
25 thing that creepeth upon the *e*
26 and over all the *e*, and over every
26 thing that creepeth upon the *e*.
28 multiply, and replenish the *e*, and
28 living thing that moveth upon the *e*.
29 which is upon the face of all the *e*,
30 to every beast of the *e*, and to
30 thing that creepeth upon the *e*,
2. 1 the heavens and the *e* were finished
4 of the heavens and of the *e* when
4 day that the Lord God made the *e*
5 of the field before it was in the *e*,
5 had not caused it to rain upon the *e*,
6 there went up a mist from the *e*,
4.11 now art thou cursed from the *e*,
12 vagabond shalt thou be in the *e*.
14 this day from the face of the *e*;
14 fugitive and a vagabond in the *e*;
6. 1 multiply upon the face of the *e*,
4 were giants in the *e* in those days;
5 of man was great in the *e*, and that
6 that he had made man on the *e*,
7 created from the face of the *e*;
11 *e* also was corrupt before God,
11 the *e* was filled with violence.
12 God looked upon the *e*, and, behold,
12 had corrupted his way upon the *e*,
13 for the *e* is filled with violence
13 I will destroy them with the *e*.
17 bring a flood of waters upon the *e*,
17 every thing that is in the *e* shall die.
20 of every creeping thing of the *e*
7. 3 seed alive upon the face of all the *e*.
4 I will cause it to rain upon the *e*
4 destroy from off the face of the *e*.
6 the flood of waters was upon the *e*.
8 thing that creepeth upon the *e*,
10 waters of the flood were upon the *e*.
12 the rain was upon the *e* forty days
14 creepeth upon the *e* after his kind,
17 flood was forty days upon the *e*;
17 and it was lift up above the *e*.
18 increased greatly upon the *e*;
19 prevailed exceedingly upon the *e*;
21 flesh died that moved upon the *e*,
21 thing that creepeth upon the *e*,
23 they were destroyed from the *e*:
24 the waters prevailed upon the *e*
8. 1 God made a wind to pass over the *e*,
3 the waters returned from off the *e*
7 were dried up from off the *e*:
9 were on the face of the whole *e*:
11 waters were abated from off the *e*.
13 were dried up from off the *e*:
14 day of the month, was the *e* dried.
17 thing that creepeth upon the *e*;
17 may breed abundantly in the *e*,
17 be fruitful, and multiply upon the *e*.
19 whatsoever creepeth upon the *e*,
22 While the *e* remaineth, seed time
9. 1 and multiply, and replenish the *e*.
2 shall be upon every beast of the *e*,
2 upon all that moveth upon the *e*,
7 bring forth abundantly in the *e*,
10 of every beast of the *e* with you;
10 of the ark, to every beast of the *e*.
11 more be a flood to destroy the *e*.
13 a covenant between me and the *e*.
14 when I bring a cloud over the *e*,
16 of all flesh that is upon the *e*.
17 and all flesh that is upon the *e*.
19 then was the whole *e* overspread.
10. 8 began to be a mighty one in the *e*.
25 in his days was the *e* divided;
32 were the nations divided in the *e*
11. 1 the whole *e* was of one language,
4 abroad upon the face of the whole *e*.
8 thence upon the face of all the *e*:
9 confound the language of all the *e*:
9 abroad upon the face of all the *e*.
12. 3 shall all families of the *e* be blessed.
13.16 make thy seed as the dust of the *e*:
16 a man can number the dust of the *e*,
14.19 God, possessor of heaven and *e*:
22 God, the possessor of heaven and *e*,
18.18 the nations of the *e* shall be blessed
25 not the Judge of all the *e* do right?
19.23 The sun was risen upon the *e* when
31 there is not a man in the *e* to come
31 us after the manner of all the *e*:
22.18 all the nations of the *e* be blessed;
24. 3 of heaven, and the God of the *e*,
52 the Lord, bowing himself to the *e*.
26. 4 all the nations of the *e* be blessed;
15 them, and filled them with *e*.
27.28 the fatness of the *e*, and plenty of
39 shall be the fatness of the *e*, and of
28.12 behold a ladder set up on the *e*,
14 shall be as the dust of the *e*,
14 all the families of the *e* be blessed.
37.10 down ourselves to thee to the *e*?
41.47 the *e* brought forth by handfuls.
56 was over all the face of the *e*:
42. 6 before him with their faces to the *e*.
43.26 bowed themselves to him to the *e*.
45. 7 to preserve you a posterity in the *e*,
48.12 himself with his face to the *e*,
16 a multitude in the midst of the *e*.
Ex 8.17 and smote the dust of the *e*,
22 I am the Lord in the midst of the *e*.
9.14 there is none like me in all the *e*.
15 thou shalt be cut off from the *e*.
16 be declared throughout all the *e*.
29 know how that the *e* is the Lord's.
33 the rain was not poured upon the *e*.
10. 5 they shall cover the face of the *e*,
5 that one cannot be able to see the *e*:
6 the day that they were upon the *e*
15 they covered the face of the whole *e*,
15.12 right hand, the *e* swallowed them.
19. 5 all people: for all the *e* is mine:
20. 4 or that is in the *e* beneath, or
4 that is in the water under the *e*:
11 days the Lord made heaven and *e*,
24 An altar of *e* thou shalt make unto

31.17 days the Lord made heaven and *e*,
32.12 them from the face of the *e*?
33.16 that are upon the face of the *e*.
34. 8 and bowed his head toward the *e*,
10 as have not been done in all the *e*,
Lev 11. 2 all the beasts that are on the *e*.
21 feet, to leap withal upon the *e*;
29 things that creep upon the *e*;
41 thing that creepeth upon the *e*
42 things that creep upon the *e*,
44 thing that creepeth upon the *e*.
46 creature that creepeth upon the *e*:
15.12 the vessel of *e*, that he toucheth
26.19 as iron, and your *e* as brass:
Nu 11.31 cubits high upon the face of the *e*.
12. 3 which were upon the face of the *e*.)
14.21 the *e* shall be filled with the glory
16.30 and the *e* open her mouth, and
32 And the *e* opened her mouth, and
33 and the *e* closed upon them: and
34 Lest the *e* swallow us up also.
22. 5 they cover the face of the *e*, and they
11 which covereth the face of the *e*:
26.10 And the *e* opened her mouth, and
Dt 3.24 what God is there in heaven or in *e*,
4.10 that they shall live upon the *e*,
17 of any beast that is on the *e*, the
18 that is in the waters beneath the *e*:
26 I call heaven and *e* to witness
32 that God created man upon the *e*,
36 upon *e* he shewed thee his great fire;
39 above, and upon the *e* beneath:
40 mayest prolong thy days upon the *e*
5. 8 or that is in the *e* beneath, or that
8 is in the waters beneath the *e*:
6.15 thee from off the face of the *e*.
7. 6 that are upon the face of the *e*.
10.14 the *e* also, with all that therein is.
11. 6 now the *e* opened her mouth, and
21 as the days of heaven upon the *e*.
12. 1 all the days that ye live upon the *e*.
16 ye shall pour it upon the *e* as water,
19 as long as thou livest upon the *e*.
24 thou shalt pour it upon the *e* as
13. 7 from the one end of the *e* even unto
7 even unto the other end of the *e*;
14. 2 all the nations that are upon the *e*.
26. 2 the first of all the fruit of the *e*,
28. 1 on high above all nations of the *e*:
10 all people of the *e* shall see that thou
23 and the *e* that is under thee shall be
25 into all the kingdoms of the *e*.
26 the air, and unto the beasts of the *e*,
49 from far, from the end of the *e*,
64 end of the *e* even unto the other;
30.19 call heaven and *e* to record this day
31.28 and *e* to record against them,
32. 1 hear, O *e*, the words of my mouth.
13 ride on the high places of the *e*,
22 consume the *e* with her increase,
33.16 And for the precious things of the *e*
17 people together to the ends of the *e*:
Jos 2.11 in heaven above, and in *e* beneath.
3.11 the Lord of all the *e* passeth over
13 Lord of all the *e*, shall rest in the
4.24 That all the people of the *e* might
5.14 Joshua fell on his face to the *e*, and
7. 6 and fell to the *e* upon his face before
9 cut off our name from the *e*:
21 they are hid in the *e* in the midst
23.14 I am going the way of all the *e*:
Jdg 3.25 lord was fallen down dead on the *e*.
5. 4 the *e* trembled, and the heavens
6. 4 destroyed the increase of the *e*,
37 it be dry upon all the *e* beside,
18.10 no want of anything that is in the *e*.
1Sa 2. 8 the pillars of the *e* are the Lord's,
10 Lord shall judge the ends of the *e*;
4. 5 a great shout, so that the *e* rang
12 rent, and with *e* upon his head.
5. 3 was fallen upon his face to the *e*

14.15 also trembled, and the *e* quaked:
17.46 air, and to the wild beasts of the *e*;
46 that all the *e* may know that there
49 and he fell upon his face to the *e*.
20.15 every one from the face of the *e*.
24. 8 stooped with his face to the *e*, and
25.41 bowed herself on her face to the *e*,
26. 8 the spear even to the *e* at once,
20 let not my blood fall to the *e* before
28.13 I saw gods ascending out of the *e*.
20 fell straightway all along on the *e*,
23 So he rose from the *e*, and sat upon
30.16 were spread abroad upon all the *e*,
2Sa 1. 2 clothes rent, and *e* upon his head:
2 he fell to the *e*, and did obeisance.
4.11 and take you away from the *e*?
7. 9 of the great men that are in the *e*.
23 nation in the *e* is like thy people,
12.16 in, and lay all night upon the *e*.
17 to him, to raise him up from the *e*:
20 Then David arose from the *e*, and
13.31 tare his garments, and lay on the *e*;
14. 7 name nor remainder upon the *e*.
11 not one hair of thy son fall to the *e*.
20 know all things that are in the *e*.
15.32 his coat rent, and *e* upon his head:
18. 9 up between the heaven and the *e*;
28 he fell down to the *e* upon his face
22. 8 Then the *e* shook and trembled;
43 them as small as the dust of the *e*,
23. 4 tender grass springing out of the *e*
1Ki 1.31 bowed with her face to the *e*, and
40 the *e* rent with the sound of them.
52 not an hair of him fall to the *e*:
2. 2 I go the way of all the *e*: be thou
4.34 from all kings of the *e*, which had
8.23 in heaven above, or on *e* beneath,
27 will God indeed dwell on the *e*?
43 that all people of the *e* may know
53 from among all the people of the *e*,
60 all the people of the *e* may know
10.23 exceeded all the kings of the *e* for
24 And all the *e* sought to Solomon,
13.34 destroy it from off the face of the *e*.
17.14 the Lord sendeth rain upon the *e*.
18. 1 and I will send rain upon the *e*.
42 he cast himself down upon the *e*,
2Ki 5.15 that there is no God in all the *e*,
17 servant two mules' burden of *e*?
10.10 there shall fall unto the *e* nothing
19.15 alone, of all the kingdoms of the *e*;
15 thou hast made heaven and *e*.
19 the kingdoms of the *e* may know
1Ch 1.10 he began to be mighty upon the *e*.
19 in his days the *e* was divided:
16.14 God; his judgments are in all the *e*.
23 Sing unto the Lord, all the *e*;
30 Fear before him, all the *e*: the
31 let the *e* rejoice: and let men say
33 because he cometh to judge the *e*.
17. 8 of the great men that are in the *e*.
21 what one nation in the *e* is like thy
21.16 stand between the *e* and the heaven,
22. 8 hast shed much blood upon the *e*
29.11 in the heaven and in the *e* is thine;
15 our days on the *e* are as a shadow,
2Ch 1. 9 like the dust of the *e* in multitude.
2.12 that made heaven and *e*, who hath
6.14 thee in the heaven, nor in the *e*;
18 very deed dwell with men on the *e*?
33 people of the *e* may know thy name,
9.22 passed all the kings of the *e* in
23 kings of the *e* sought the presence
16. 9 and fro throughout the whole *e*,
20.24 were dead bodies fallen to the *e*,
32.19 the gods of the people of the *e*,
36.23 All the kingdoms of the *e* hath the
Ezr 1. 2 given me all the kingdoms of the *e*;
5.11 of the God of heaven and *e*, and
Neh 9. 1 with sackclothes, and *e* upon them.
6 *e*, and all things that are therein,

Job 1. 7 From going to and fro in the *e*,
8 that there is none like him in the *e*,
2. 2 From going to and fro in the *e*,
3 that there is none like him in the *e*,
3.14 With kings and counsellors of the *e*,
5.10 Who giveth rain upon the *e*, and
22 thou be afraid of the beasts of the *e*.
25 offspring as the grass of the *e*.
7. 1 an appointed time to man upon *e*?
8. 9 our days upon *e* are a shadow:)
19 and out of the *e* shall others grow.
9. 6 shaketh the *e* out of her place, and
24 The *e* is given into the hand of the
11. 9 thereof is longer than the *e*, and
12. 8 Or speak to the *e*, and it shall
15 them out, and they overturn the *e*.
24 of the chief of the people of the *e*,
14. 8 the root thereof wax old in the *e*,
19 which grow out of the dust of the *e*;
15.19 whom alone the *e* was given,
29 the perfection thereof upon the *e*.
16.18 O *e*, cover not thou my blood,
18. 4 shall the *e* be forsaken for thee?
17 shall perish from the *e*, and he
19.25 stand at the latter day upon the *e*:
20. 4 since man was placed upon *e*,
27 and the *e* shall rise up against him.
22. 8 for the mighty man, he had the *e*;
24. 4 the poor of the *e* hide themselves
18 their portion is cursed in the *e*:
26. 7 and hangeth the *e* upon nothing.
28. 2 Iron is taken out of the *e*,
5 for the *e*, out of it cometh bread:
24 For he looketh to the ends of the *e*,
30. 6 caves of the *e*, and in the rocks.
8 men: they were viler than the *e*.
34.13 given him a charge over the *e*?
35.11 us more than the beasts of the *e*,
37. 3 his lightning unto the ends of the *e*.
6 saith to the snow, Be thou on the *e*;
12 upon the face of the world in the *e*.
17 quieteth the *e* by the south wind?
38. 4 when I laid the foundations of the *e*?
13 might take hold of the ends of the *e*,
18 perceived the breadth of the *e*?
24 scattereth the east wind upon the *e*?
26 To cause it to rain on the *e*,
33 set the dominion thereof in the *e*?
39.14 Which leaveth her eggs in the *e*,
41.33 Upon *e* there is not his like,
Ps 2. 2 The kings of the *e* set themselves,
8 parts of the *e* for thy possession.
10 be instructed, ye judges of the *e*.
7. 5 him tread down my life upon the *e*,
8. 1, 9 excellent is thy name in all the *e*!
10.18 man of the *e* may no more oppress.
12. 6 as silver tried in a furnace of *e*,
16. 3 But to the saints that are in the *e*,
17.11 their eyes bowing down to the *e*;
18. 7 Then the *e* shook and trembled;
19. 4 line is gone out through all the *e*,
21.10 fruit shalt thou destroy from the *e*,
22.29 All they that be fat upon *e* shall eat
24. 1 The *e* is the Lord's, and the
25.13 and his seed shall inherit the *e*.
33. 5 *e* is full of the goodness of the Lord.
8 Let all the *e* fear the Lord:
14 upon all the inhabitants of the *e*.
34.16 remembrance of them from the *e*.
37. 9 Lord, they shall inherit the *e*.
11 But the meek shall inherit the *e*;
22 blessed of him shall inherit the *e*;
41. 2 he shall be blessed upon the *e*:
44.25 our belly cleaveth unto the *e*.
45.16 mayest make princes in all the *e*.
46. 2 we fear, though the *e* be removed,
6 he uttered his voice, the *e* melted.
8 desolations he hath made in the *e*.
9 was to cease unto the end of the *e*;
10 am God: I will be exalted in the *e*.
47. 2 he is a great King over all the *e*.

Biblical Themes

EARTH

God called the dry land Earth; and the gathering together of the waters called he Seas: and God saw that it was good. Gen 1.10

And the Lord God formed man of the dust of the ground. Gen 2.7

Out of [the ground] wast thou taken: for dust thou art, and unto dust shalt thou return. Gen 3.19

I am come down to deliver them out of the hand of the Egyptians, and to bring them up out of that land unto a good land and a large, unto a land flowing with milk and honey. Ex 3.8

The pillars of the earth are the Lord's, and he hath set the world upon them. 1Sa 2.8

As for the earth, out of it cometh bread: and under it is turned up as it were fire. The stones of it are the place of sapphires: and it hath dust of gold. Job 28.5-6

The earth is the Lord's, and the fulness thereof; the world, and they that dwell therein. Ps 24.1

Therefore will not we fear, though the earth be removed. Ps 46.2

Thou visitest the earth, and waterest it. . . . The pastures are clothed with flocks; the valleys also are covered over with corn; they shout for joy, they also sing. Ps 65.9, 13

Before the mountains were brought forth, or ever thou hadst formed the earth and the world, even from everlasting to everlasting, thou art God. Ps 90.2

When Israel went out of Egypt . . . the mountains skipped like rams, and the little hills like lambs. Ps 114.1, 4

I will lift up mine eyes unto the hills, from whence cometh my help. My help cometh from the Lord, which made heaven and earth. Ps 121.1-2

The wilderness and the solitary place shall be glad for them; and the desert shall rejoice, and blossom as the rose. Isa 35.1

Have ye not known? have ye not heard? hath it not been told you from the beginning? have ye not understood from the foundations of the earth? It is he that sitteth upon the circle of the earth, and the inhabitants thereof are as grasshoppers; that stretcheth out the heavens as a curtain, and spreadeth them out as a tent to dwell in. Isa 40.21-22

Thus saith the Lord, The heaven is my throne, and the earth is my footstool. Isa 66.1

The mountains quake at him, and the hills melt, and the earth is burned at his presence, yea, the world, and all that dwell therein. Na 1.5

Blessed are the meek: for they shall inherit the earth. Mt 5.5

For the earth bringeth forth fruit of herself; first the blade, then the ear, after that the full corn in the ear. Mk 4.28

Glory to God in the highest, and on earth peace, good will toward men. Lk 2.14

And there shall be signs in the sun, and in the moon, and in the stars; and upon the earth distress of nations, with perplexity; the sea and the waves roaring; men's hearts failing them for fear, and for looking after those things which are coming on the earth: for the powers of heaven shall be shaken. Lk 21.25-26

The first man is of the earth, earthy: the second man is the Lord from heaven. 1Co 15.47

Set your affection on things above, not on things on the earth. Col 3.2

And I saw a new heaven and a new earth: for the first heaven and the first earth were passed away. Rev 21.1

Ps 47. 7 For God is the King of all the *e*:
9 shields of the *e* belong unto God:
48. 2 joy of the whole *e*, is mount Zion,
10 thy praise unto the ends of the *e*:
50. 1 the *e* from the rising of the sun
4 heavens from above, and to the *e*,
57. 5, 11 let thy glory be above all the *e*.
58. 2 violence of your hands in the *e*.
11 he is a God that judgeth in the *e*.
59.13 in Jacob unto the ends of the *e*.
60. 2 hast made the *e* to tremble;
61. 2 From the end of the *e* will I cry
63. 9 go into the lower parts of the *e*.
65. 5 confidence of all the ends of the *e*,
9 Thou visitest the *e*, and waterest it:
66. 4 All the *e* shall worship thee, and
67. 2 That thy way may be known upon *e*,
4 and govern the nations upon *e*.
6 Then shall the *e* yield her increase;
7 all the ends of the *e* shall fear him.
68. 8 The *e* shook, the heavens also
32 unto God, ye kingdoms of the *e*;
69.34 Let the heaven and *e* praise him,
71.20 up again from the depths of the *e*.
72. 6 grass: as showers that water the *e*.
8 the rivers unto the ends of the *e*.
16 shall be an handful of corn in the *e*
16 shall flourish like grass of the *e*.
19 the whole *e* be filled with his glory;
73. 9 their tongue walketh through the *e*.
25 there is none upon *e* that I desire
74.12 salvation in the midst of the *e*.
17 hast set all the borders of the *e*:
20 the dark places of the *e* are full of
75. 3 *e* and all the inhabitants thereof
8 wicked of the *e* shall wring them out,
76. 8 heaven; the *e* feared, and was still.
9 to save all the meek of the *e*.
12 he is terrible to the kings of the *e*.
77.18 the world: the *e* trembled and shook.
78.69 *e* which he hath established forever.
79. 2 thy saints unto the beasts of the *e*.
82. 5 all the foundations of the *e* are out
8 Arise, O God, judge the *e*: for thou
83.10 they became as dung for the *e*.
18 art the most high over all the *e*.
85.11 Truth shall spring out of the *e*;
89.11 The heavens are thine, the *e* also is
27 higher than the kings of the *e*.
90. 2 or ever thou hadst formed the *e*
94. 2 Lift up thyself, thou judge of the *e*:
95. 4 hand are the deep places of the *e*:
96. 1 sing unto the Lord, all the *e*.
9 holiness: fear before him, all the *e*.
11 rejoice, and let the *e* be glad;
13 for he cometh to judge the *e*:
97. 1 let the *e* rejoice; let the multitude
4 world: the *e* saw, and trembled.
5 presence of the Lord of the whole *e*.
9 thou, Lord, art high above all the *e*:
98. 3 all the ends of the *e* have seen the
4 noise unto the Lord, all the *e*:
9 for he cometh to judge the *e*:
99. 1 the cherubims; let the *e* be moved.
102.15 and all the kings of the *e* thy glory.
19 heaven did the Lord behold the *e*;
25 thou laid the foundation of the *e*:
103.11 the heaven is high above the *e*,
104. 5 Who laid the foundations of the *e*,
9 they turn not again to cover the *e*.
13 the *e* is satisfied with the fruit of
14 may bring forth food out of the *e*;
24 the *e* is full of thy riches.
30 thou renewest the face of the *e*.
32 looketh on the *e*, and it trembleth:
35 sinners be consumed out of the *e*,
105. 7 his judgments are in all the *e*.
106.17 *e* opened and swallowed up Dathan,
108. 5 and thy glory above all the *e*;
109.15 the memory of them from the *e*.
112. 2 His seed shall be mighty upon *e*:
113. 6 that are in heaven, and in the *e*!
114. 7 Tremble, thou *e*, at the presence
115.15 the Lord which made heaven and *e*.
16 but the *e* hath he given to the
119.19 I am a stranger in the *e*:
64 The *e*, O Lord, is full of thy mercy:
87 had almost consumed me upon *e*;
90 thou hast established the *e*, and it
119 puttest away all the wicked of the *e*
121. 2 the Lord, which made heaven and *e*.
124. 8 the Lord, who made heaven and *e*.
134. 3 The Lord that made heaven and *e*
135. 6 that did he in heaven, and in *e*,
7 to ascend from the ends of the *e*;
136. 6 To him that stretched out the *e*
138. 4 All the kings of the *e* shall praise
139.15 in the lowest parts of the *e*.
140.11 speaker be established in the *e*:
141. 7 and cleaveth wood upon the *e*.
146. 4 goeth forth, he returneth to his *e*;
6 Which made heaven, and *e*, the
147. 8 who prepareth rain for the *e*, who

15 forth his commandment upon *e*:
148. 7 Praise the Lord from the *e*,
11 Kings of the *e*, and all people;
11 princes, and all judges of the *e*:
13 his glory is above the *e* and heaven.
Pr 2.22 wicked shall be cut off from the *e*,
3.19 by wisdom hath founded the *e*;
8.16 even all the judges of the *e*.
23 the beginning, or ever the *e* was.
26 as yet he had not made the *e*,
29 appointed the foundations of the *e*:
31 in the habitable part of his *e*;
10.30 the wicked shall not inhabit the *e*.
11.31 shall be recompensed in the *e*:
17.24 of a fool are in the ends of the *e*.
25. 3 for height, and the *e* for depth,
30. 4 established all the ends of the *e*?
14 to devour the poor from off the *e*,
16 the *e* that is not filled with water;
21 For three things the *e* is disquieted,
24 things which are little upon the *e*,
Ec 1. 4 but the *e* abideth for ever.
3.21 that goeth downward to the *e*?
5. 2 God is in heaven, and thou upon *e*:
9 the profit of the *e* is for all:
7.20 there is not a just man upon *e*, that
8.14 a vanity which is done upon the *e*;
16 business that is done upon the *e*:
10. 7 walking as servants upon the *e*.
11. 2 what evil shall be upon the *e*.
3 they empty themselves upon the *e*:
12. 7 Then shall the dust return to the *e*
SS 2.12 The flowers appear on the *e*;
Isa 1. 2 Hear, O heavens, and give ear, O *e*:
2.19 rocks, and into the caves of the *e*,
19, 21 ariseth to shake terribly the *e*.
4. 2 fruit of the *e* shall be excellent
5. 8 placed alone in the midst of the *e*!
26 unto them from the end of the *e*:
6. 3 the whole *e* is full of his glory.
8.22 And they shall look unto the *e*;
10.14 are left, have I gathered all the *e*;
11. 4 with equity for the meek of the *e*:
4 and he shall smite the *e* with the rod
9 the *e* shall be full of the knowledge
12 from the four corners of the *e*.
12. 5 things: this is known in all the *e*.
13.13 and the *e* shall remove out of her
14. 7 The whole *e* is at rest, and is quiet:
9 even all the chief ones of the *e*;
16 the man that made the *e* to tremble,
26 that is purposed upon the whole *e*:
18. 3 of the world, and dwellers on the *e*,
6 and to the beasts of the *e*: and the
6 all the beasts of the *e* shall winter
23. 8 are the honorable of the *e*?
9 contempt all the honorable of the *e*.
17 the world upon the face of the *e*.
24. 1 the Lord maketh the *e* empty,
4 The *e* mourneth and fadeth away,
4 haughty people of the *e* do languish.
5 The *e* also is defiled under the
6 hath the curse devoured the *e*,
6 the inhabitants of the *e* are burned,
16 From the uttermost part of the *e*
17 upon thee, O inhabitant of the *e*.
18 the foundations of the *e* do shake.
19 The *e* is utterly broken down, the
19 *e* is clean dissolved, the *e* is moved
20 The *e* shall reel to and fro like a
21 the kings of the *e* upon the *e*.
25. 8 he take away from off all the *e*:
26. 9 when thy judgments are in the *e*,
15 it far unto all the ends of the *e*.
18 wrought any deliverance in the *e*;
19 and the *e* shall cast out the dead.
21 to punish the inhabitants of the *e*
21 the *e* also shall disclose her blood,
28. 2 shall cast down to the *e* with the
22 even determined upon the whole *e*.
30.23 bread of the increase of the *e*.
33. 9 The *e* mourneth and languisheth:
34. 1 let the *e* hear, and all that is
37.16 alone, of all the kingdoms of the *e*:
16 thou hast made heaven and *e*.
20 all the kingdoms of the *e* may know
40.12 and comprehended the dust of the *e*
21 from the foundations of the *e*?
22 that sitteth upon the circle of the *e*,
23 he maketh the judges of the *e* as
24 stock shall not take root in the *e*:
28 the Creator of the ends of the *e*,
41. 5 the ends of the *e* were afraid,
9 have taken from the ends of the *e*,
42. 4 till he have set judgment in the *e*:
5 he that spread forth the *e*, and that
10 his praise from the end of the *e*,
43. 6 daughters from the ends of the *e*;
44.23 shout, ye lower parts of the *e*:
24 that spreadeth abroad the *e* by
45. 8 let the *e* open, and let them bring
9 strive with the potsherds of the *e*.
12 I have made the *e*, and created
18 God himself that formed the *e* and
19 secret, in a dark place of the *e*:
22 be ye saved, all the ends of the *e*:
48.13 hath laid the foundation of the *e*,
20 utter it even to the end of the *e*;
49. 6 my salvation unto the end of the *e*.
8 to establish the *e*, to cause to
13 Sing, O heavens; and be joyful, O *e*;
23 with their face toward the *e*, and
51. 6 and look upon the *e* beneath: for
6 the *e* shall wax old like a garment,
13 and laid the foundations of the *e*;
16 and lay the foundations of the *e*,
52.10 all the ends of the *e* shall see the
54. 5 The God of the whole *e* shall he be
9 Noah should no more go over the *e*;
55. 9 the heavens are higher than the *e*,
10 but watereth the *e*, and maketh it
58.14 ride upon the high places of the *e*,
60. 2 the darkness shall cover the *e*,
61.11 as the *e* bringeth forth her bud,
62. 7 make Jerusalem a praise in the *e*.
63. 6 bring down their strength to the *e*.
65.16 he who blesseth himself in the *e*
16 and he that sweareth in the *e* shall
17 I create new heavens and a new *e*:
66. 1 throne, and the *e* is my footstool:
8 Shall the *e* be made to bring forth
22 as the new heavens and the new *e*,
Jer 4.23 I beheld the *e*, and, lo, it was
28 For this shall the *e* mourn, and the
6.19 Hear, O *e*: behold, I will bring evil
22 be raised from the sides of the *e*.
7.33 heaven, and for the beasts of the *e*;
8. 2 be for dung upon the face of the *e*.
9. 3 valiant for the truth upon the *e*:
24 and righteousness, in the *e*;
10.10 at his wrath the *e* shall tremble,
11 not made the heavens and the *e*,
11 even they shall perish from the *e*,
12 He hath made the *e* by his power,
13 to ascend from the ends of the *e*;
14. 4 for there was no rain in the *e*,
15. 3 and the beasts of the *e*, to devour
4 removed into all kingdoms of the *e*,
10 a man of contention to the whole *e*!
16. 4 as dung upon the face of the *e*:
4 heaven, and for the beasts of the *e*.
19 unto thee from the ends of the *e*,
17.13 from me shall be written in the *e*,
19. 7 heaven, and for the beasts of the *e*.
22.29 O *e*,*e*,*e*, hear the word of the Lord.
23. 5 judgment and justice in the *e*.
24 Do not I fill heaven and *e*? saith the
24. 9 into all the kingdoms of the *e* for
25.26 which are upon the face of the *e*:
29 upon all the inhabitants of the *e*,
30 against all the inhabitants of the *e*.
31 shall come even to the ends of the *e*;
32 be raised from the coasts of the *e*.
33 at that day from one end of the *e*
33 even unto the other end of the *e*:
26. 6 a curse to all the nations of the *e*.
27. 5 I have made the *e*, the man and the
28.16 cast thee from off the face of the *e*:
29.18 to all the kingdoms of the *e*, to be a
31. 8 them from the coasts of the *e*,
22 hath created a new thing in the *e*,
37 foundations of the *e* searched out
32.17 made the heaven and the *e* by thy
33. 9 before all the nations of the *e*, which
25 the ordinances of heaven and *e*;
34. 1 army, and all the kingdoms of the *e*
17 into all the kingdoms of the *e*.
20 heaven, and to the beasts of the *e*.
44. 8 among all the nations of the *e*?
46. 8 will go up, and will cover the *e*;
49.21 The *e* is moved at the noise of their
50.23 whole *e* cut asunder and broken!
41 raised up from the coasts of the *e*.
46 taking of Babylon the *e* is moved,
51. 7 hand, that made all the *e* drunken:
15 He hath made the *e* by his power,
16 to ascend from the ends of the *e*:
25 Lord, which destroyest all the *e*:
41 the praise of the whole *e* surprised!
48 Then the heaven and the *e*, and all
49 shall fall the slain of all the *e*.
La 2. 1 cast down from heaven unto the *e*
11 my liver is poured upon the *e*,
15 of beauty, The joy of the whole *e*?
3.34 his feet all the prisoners of the *e*,
4.12 The kings of the *e*, and all the
Eze 1.15 behold one wheel upon the *e* by the
19 creatures were lifted up from the *e*,
21 those were lifted up from the *e*,
7.21 to the wicked of the *e* for a spoil;
8. 3 up between the *e* and the heaven,
12 not; the Lord hath forsaken the *e*.
9. 9 The Lord hath forsaken the *e*, and
10.16 their wings to mount up from the *e*,
19 mounted up from the *e* in my sight:
26.20 set thee in the low parts of the *e*,
27.33 thou didst enrich the kings of the *e*
28.18 will bring thee to ashes upon the *e*
31.12 all the people of the *e* are gone
14 death, to the nether parts of the *e*,
16 in the nether parts of the *e*.
18 Eden unto the nether parts of the *e*:
32. 4 the beasts of the whole *e* with thee.
18 unto the nether parts of the *e*, with
24 into the nether parts of the *e*, which
34. 6 scattered upon all the face of the *e*,
27 and the *e* shall yield her increase,
35.14 When the whole *e* rejoiceth, I will
38.20 things that creep upon the *e*,
20 men that are upon the face of the *e*,
39.14 remain upon the face of the *e*,
18 the blood of the princes of the *e*,
43. 2 and the *e* shined with his glory.
Dan 2.10 There is not a man upon the *e*
35 mountain, and filled the whole *e*.
39 which shall bear rule over all the *e*.
4. 1 languages, that dwell in all the *e*;
10 behold a tree in the midst of the *e*,
11 sight thereof to the end of all the *e*:
15 the stump of his roots in the *e*,
15 the beasts in the grass of the *e*:
20 and the sight thereof to all the *e*;
22 thy dominion to the end of the *e*.
23 stump of the roots thereof in the *e*,
35 And all the inhabitants of the *e*
35 among the inhabitants of the *e*:
6.25 languages, that dwell in all the *e*;
27 and wonders in heaven and in *e*,
7. 4 and it was lifted up from the *e*,
17 which shall arise out of the *e*.
23 shall be the fourth kingdom upon *e*,
23 and shall devour the whole *e*, and
8. 5 west on the face of the whole *e*,

Dan 12. 2 them that sleep in the dust of the *e*
Hos 2.18 sword and the battle out of the *e*,
21 heavens, and they shall hear the *e*;
22 And the *e* shall hear the corn,
23 I will sow her unto me in the *e*;
6. 3 latter and former rain unto the *e*.
Joel 2.10 The *e* shall quake before them;
30 in the heavens and in the *e*,
3.16 the heavens and the *e* shall shake:
Am 2. 7 That pant after the dust of the *e*
3. 2 known of all the families of the *e*:
5 a bird fall in a snare upon the *e*,
5 one take up a snare from the *e*,
4.13 upon the high places of the *e*,
5. 7 leave off righteousness in the *e*,
8 them out upon the face of the *e*:
8. 9 will darken the *e* in the clear day:
9. 6 hath founded his troop in the *e*;
6 them out upon the face of the *e*:
8 destroy it from off the face of the *e*;
9 not the least grain fall upon the *e*.
Jon 2. 6 the *e* with her bars was about me
Mic 1. 2 Hear, all ye people; hearken, O *e*,
3 tread upon the high places of the *e*.
4.13 unto the Lord of the whole *e*.
5. 4 he be great unto the ends of the *e*.
6. 2 ye strong foundations of the *e*:
7. 2 good man is perished out of the *e*:
17 of their holes like worms of the *e*:
Na 1. 5 and the *e* is burned at his presence,
2.13 I will cut off thy prey from the *e*,
Hab 2.14 *e* shall be filled with the knowledge
20 let all the *e* keep silence before him.
3. 3 and the *e* was full of his praise.
6 He stood, and measured the *e*:
9 Thou didst cleave the *e* with rivers.
Zep 2. 3 ye the Lord, all ye meek of the *e*,
11 he will famish all the gods of the *e*;
3. 8 the *e* shall be devoured with the fire
20 praise among all people of the *e*,
Hag 1.10 and the *e* is stayed from her fruit.
2. 6 the heavens, and the *e*, and the sea,
21 I will shake the heavens and the *e*;
Zec 1.10 to walk to and fro through the *e*.
11 walked to and fro through the *e*,
11 all the *e* sitteth still, and is at rest.
4.10 run to and fro through the whole *e*.
14 stand by the Lord of the whole *e*.
5. 3 forth over the face of the whole *e*:
6 resemblance through all the *e*.
9 ephah between the *e* and the heaven.
6. 5 standing before the Lord of all the *e*.
7 and fro through the *e*: and he said,
7 hence, walk to and fro through the *e*.
7 walked to and fro through the *e*.
9.10 the river even to the ends of the *e*.
12. 1 and layeth the foundation of the *e*,
3 though all the people of the *e* be
14. 9 Lord shall be king over all the *e*:
17 families of the *e* unto Jerusalem
Mal 4. 6 come and smite the *e* with a curse.
Mt 5. 5 meek: for they shall inherit the *e*.
13 Ye are the salt of the *e*: but if the
18 Till heaven and *e* pass, one jot or
35 Nor by the *e*; for it is his footstool:
6.10 will be done in *e*, as it is in heaven.
19 for yourselves treasures upon *e*,
9. 6 hath power on *e* to forgive sins,
10.34 I am come to send peace on *e*:
11.25 O Father, Lord of heaven and *e*,
12.40 three nights in the heart of the *e*.
42 uttermost parts of the *e* to hear
13. 5 where they had not much *e*:
5 because they had no deepness of *e*:
16.19 whatsoever thou shalt bind on *e*
19 whatsoever thou shalt loose on *e*
17.25 whom doth the kings of the *e* take
18.18 Whatsoever ye shall bind on *e*
18 and whatsoever ye shall loose on *e*
19 if two of you shall agree on *e* as
23. 9 no man your father upon the *e*:
35 righteous blood shed upon the *e*,
24.30 shall the tribes of the *e* mourn,
35 Heaven and *e* shall pass away, but
25.18 one went and digged in the *e*,
25 went and hid thy talent in the *e*:
27.51 *e* did quake, and the rocks rent;
28.18 given unto me in heaven and in *e*.
Mk 2.10 Son of man hath power on *e* to
4. 5 ground; where it had not much *e*;
5 because it had no depth of *e*:
28 *e* bringeth forth fruit of herself;
31 it is sown in the *e*, is less than
31 all the seeds that be in the *e*:
9. 3 as no fuller on *e* can white them.
13.27 from the uttermost part of the *e*
31 Heaven and *e* shall pass away:
Lk 2.14 on *e* peace, good will toward men.
5.24 the Son of man hath power upon *e*
6.49 built an house upon the *e*;
10.21 O Father, Lord of heaven and *e*,
11. 2 be done, as in heaven, so in *e*.
31 from the utmost parts of the *e* to
12.49 I am come to send fire on the *e*;
51 that I am come to give peace on *e*?
56 the face of the sky and of the *e*;
16.17 is easier for heaven and *e* to pass,
18. 8 shall he find faith on the *e*?
21.25 and upon the *e* distress of nations,
26 which are coming on the *e*;
33 Heaven and *e* shall pass away:
35 dwell on the face of the whole *e*.
23.44 was a darkness over all the *e*
24. 5 bowed down their faces to the *e*,
Jn 3.31 he that is of the *e* is earthly,
31 and speaketh of the *e*:
12.32 if I be lifted up from the *e*,
17. 4 I have glorified thee on the *e*:
Ac 1. 8 unto the uttermost part of the *e*.
2.19 and signs in the *e* beneath; blood,
3.25 the kindreds of the *e* be blessed.
4.24 which hast made heaven, and *e*,
26 The kings of the *e* stood up,
7.49 my throne, and *e* is my footstool:
8.33 for his life is taken from the *e*.
9. 4 he fell to the *e*, and heard a voice
8 Saul arose from the *e*; and when
10.11 corners, and let down to the *e*:
12 of fourfooted beasts of the *e*, and
11. 6 and saw fourfooted beasts of the *e*,
13.47 salvation unto the ends of the *e*.
14.15 God, which made heaven, and *e*,
17.24 is Lord of heaven and *e*, dwelleth
26 to dwell on all the face of the *e*,
22.22 with such a fellow from the *e*:
26.14 when we were all fallen to the *e*,
Ro 9.17 be declared throughout all the *e*.
28 will the Lord make upon the *e*.
10.18 their sound went into all the *e*,
1Co 8. 5 gods, whether in heaven or in *e*,
10.26 For the *e* is the Lord's, and the
28 for the *e* is the Lord's, and the
15.47 The first man is of the *e*, earthy:
Eph 1.10 are in heaven, and which are on *e*;
3.15 family in heaven and *e* is named,
4. 9 into the lower parts of the *e*?
6. 3 thou mayest live long on the *e*.
Php 2.10 things in heaven, and things in *e*,
10 and things under the *e*;
Col 1.16 are in heaven, and that are in *e*,
20 whether they be things in *e*, or
3. 2 above, not on things on the *e*.
5 members which are upon the *e*;
2Ti 2.20 but also of wood and of *e*; and
Heb 1.10 hast laid the foundation of the *e*;
6. 7 the *e* which drinketh in the rain
8. 4 For if he were on *e*, he should not
11.13 strangers and pilgrims on the *e*:
38 and in dens and caves of the *e*.
12.25 who refused him that spake on *e*,
26 Whose voice then shook the *e*:
26 once more I shake not the *e* only,
Jas 5. 5 Ye have lived in pleasure on the *e*,
7 for the precious fruit of the *e*,
12 neither by heaven, neither by the *e*,
17 it rained not on the *e* by the space
18 and the *e* brought forth her fruit.
2Pe 3. 5 the *e* standing out of the water
7 heavens and the *e*, which are now,
10 the *e* also and the works that are
13 look for new heavens and a new *e*,
1Jn 5. 8 are three that bear witness in *e*,
Rev 1. 5 the prince of the kings of the *e*.
7 all kindreds of the *e* shall wail
3.10 to try them that dwell upon the *e*.
5. 3 nor in *e*, neither under the *e*,
6 of God sent forth into all the *e*.
10 and we shall reign on the *e*.
13 and on the *e*, and under the *e*,
6. 4 thereon to take peace from the *e*,
8 them over the fourth part of the *e*,
8 death, and with the beasts of the *e*.
10 blood on them that dwell on the *e*?
13 the stars of heaven fell unto the *e*,
15 kings of the *e*, and the great men,
7. 1 on the four corners of the *e*,
1 holding the four winds of the *e*,
1 the wind should not blow on the *e*,
2 to whom it was given to hurt the *e*
3 Saying, Hurt not the *e*, neither the
8. 5 altar, and cast it into the *e*:
7 and they were cast upon the *e*:
13 woe, to the inhabiters of the *e* by
9. 1 a star fall from heaven unto the *e*:
3 of the smoke locusts upon the *e*:
3 the scorpions of the *e* have power.
4 should not hurt the grass of the *e*,
10. 2 the sea, and his left foot on the *e*,
5 stand upon the sea and upon the *e*
6 *e*, and the things that therein are,
8 upon the sea and upon the *e*.
11. 4 standing before the God of the *e*.
6 to smite the *e* with all plagues,
10 that dwell upon the *e* shall rejoice
10 tormented them that dwelt on the *e*
18 destroy them which destroy the *e*.
12. 4 and did cast them to the *e*:
9 he was cast out into the *e*,
12 Woe to the inhabiters of the *e* and
13 saw that he was cast unto the *e*,
16 And the *e* helped the woman,
16 and the *e* opened her mouth.
13. 8 dwell upon the *e* shall worship
11 beast coming up out of the *e*;
12 causeth the *e* and them which
13 heaven on the *e* in the sight of men.
14 deceiveth them that dwell on the *e*
14 saying to them that dwell on the *e*,
14. 3 which were redeemed from the *e*.
6 unto them that dwell on the *e*,
7 him that made heaven, and *e*,
15 for the harvest of the *e* is ripe.
16 thrust in his sickle on the *e*;
16 and the *e* was reaped.
18 the clusters of the vine of the *e*;
19 angel thrust his sickle into the *e*,
19 and gathered the vine of the *e*,
16. 1 the wrath of God upon the *e*.
2 poured out his vial upon the *e*;
14 of the *e* and of the whole world,
18 not since men were upon the *e*,
17. 2 With whom the kings of the *e* have
2 of the *e* have been made drunk
5 harlots and abominations of the *e*
8 dwell upon the *e* shall wonder,
18 reigneth over the kings of the *e*.
18. 1 the *e* was lightened with his glory.
3 the *e* have committed fornication
3 merchants of the *e* are waxed rich
9 kings of the *e*, who have committed
11 the merchants of the *e* shall weep
23 were the great men of the *e*;
24 all that were slain upon the *e*.

19. 2 corrupt the *e* with her fornication,
19 the beast, and the kings of the *e*,
20. 8 in the four quarters of the *e*,
9 went up on the breadth of the *e*,
11 the *e* and the heaven fled away;
21. 1 I saw a new heaven and a new *e*:
1 and first *e* were passed away;
24 the kings of the *e* do bring their

EARTHEN
Lev 6.28 the *e* vessel wherein it is sodden
11.33 every *e* vessel, whereinto any of
14. 5 birds be killed in an *e* vessel
50 the one of the birds in an *e* vessel
Nu 5.17 take holy water in an *e* vessel;
2Sa 17.28 beds, and basons, and *e* vessels,
Jer 19. 1 Go and get a potter's *e* bottle,
32.14 and put them in an *e* vessel,
La 4. 2 are they esteemed as *e* pitchers,
2Co 4. 7 have this treasure in *e* vessels,

EARTHLY
Jn 3.12 If I have told you *e* things,
31 that is of the earth is *e*,
2Co 5. 1 if our *e* house of this tabernacle
Php 3.19 their shame, who mind *e* things.)
Jas 3.15 above, but is *e*, sensual, devilish.

EARTHQUAKE
1Ki 19.11 and after the wind an *e*;
11 but the Lord was not in the *e*:
12 after the *e* a fire; but the Lord
Isa 29. 6 and with *e*, and great noise,
Am 1. 1 two years before the *e*.
Zec 14. 5 the *e* in the days of Uzziah
Mt 27.54 saw the *e*, and those things that
28. 2 behold, there was a great *e*:
Ac 16.26 And suddenly there was a great *e*,
Rev 6.12 lo, there was a great *e*;
8. 5 and lightnings, and an *e*.
11.13 same hour was there a great *e*,
13 and in the *e* were slain of men
19 and an *e*, and great hail.
16.18 and there was a great *e*,
18 so mighty an *e*, and so great.

EARTHQUAKES
Mt 24. 7 and *e*, in divers places.
Mk 13. 8 there shall be *e* in divers places,
Lk 21.11 great *e* shall be in divers places,

EARTHY
1Co 15.47 The first man is of the earth, *e*:
48 As is the *e*, such are they also
48 such are they also that are *e*:
49 we have borne the image of the *e*,

EASE
Dt 23.13 when thou wilt *e* thyself abroad,
28.65 these nations shalt thou find no *e*,
Jdg 20.43 and trode them down with *e*
2Ch 10. 4 *e* thou somewhat the grievous
9 *E* somewhat the yoke that thy
Job 7.13 my couch shall *e* my complaint;
12. 5 the thought of him that is at *e*.
16.12 I was at *e*, but he hath broken
21.23 being wholly at *e* and quiet.
Ps 25.13 His soul shall dwell at *e*; and
123. 4 scorning of those that are at *e*,
Isa 1.24 will *e* me of mine adversaries,
32. 9 Rise up, ye women that are at *e*;
11 Tremble, ye women that are at *e*;
Jer 46.27 and be in rest and at *e*,
48.11 Moab hath been at *e* from his
Eze 23.42 a voice of a multitude being at *e*
Am 6. 1 Woe to them that are at *e* in Zion,
Zec 1.15 with the heathen that are at *e*:
Lk 12.19 take thine *e*, eat, drink, and be

EASED
Job 16. 6 though I forbear, what am I *e*?
2Co 8.13 I mean not that other men be *e*,

EASIER
Ex 18.22 so shall it be *e* for thyself,
Mt 9. 5 whether is *e*, to say, Thy sins be
19.24 It is *e* for a camel to go through
Mk 2. 9 Whether it is *e* to say to the sick
10.25 It is *e* for a camel to go through
Lk 5.23 Whether is *e*, to say, Thy sins be
16.17 it is *e* for heaven and earth to pass,
18.25 For it is *e* for a camel to go through

EASILY
1Co 13. 5 not *e* provoked, thinketh no evil;
Heb 12. 1 the sin which doth so *e* beset us,

EASTER
Ac 12. 4 intending after *E* to bring him

EASY
Pr 14. 6 knowledge is *e* unto him that
Mt 11.30 For my yoke is *e*, and my burden
1Co 14. 9 tongue words *e* to be understood,
Jas 3.17 *e* to be intreated, full of mercy

EAT
Gen 2.16 garden thou mayest freely *e*:
17 thou shalt not *e* of it: for in the
3.12 she gave me of the tree, and I did *e*.
13 serpent beguiled me, and I did *e*.
14 dust shalt thou *e* all the days of thy
43.32 not *e* bread with the Hebrews;
Ex 12. 8 shall *e* the flesh in that night
8 with bitter herbs they shall *e* it.
11 And thus shall ye *e* it; with your
11 and ye shall *e* it in haste:
15 days shall ye *e* unleavened bread;
16 save that which every man must *e*,
43 There shall no stranger *e* thereof:
16.35 the children of Israel did *e* manna
35 they did *e* manna, until they came
23.11 that the poor of thy people may *e*:
32. 6 people sat down to *e* and to drink,
Lev 7.23 Ye shall *e* no manner of fat,
17.12 No soul of you shall *e* blood,
21.22 He shall *e* the bread of his God,
22. 4 he shall not *e* of the holy things,
24. 9 they shall *e* it in the holy place:
25.19 shall *e* your fill, and dwell therein
26. 5 ye shall *e* your bread to the full,
26 ye shall *e*, and not be satisfied.
Dt 12.16 Only ye shall not *e* the blood;
18 thou must *e* them before the Lord
27. 7 *e* there, and rejoice before the Lord
1Sa 2.36 that I may *e* a piece of bread.
9.24 So Saul did *e* with Samuel that day.
1Ki 19. 6 did *e* and drink, and laid him down
7 Arise and *e*; because the journey is
21.23 dogs shall *e* Jezebel by the wall
2Ki 4.43 Give the people, that they may *e*:
43 shall *e*, and shall leave thereof.
6.28 thy son, that we may *e* him to day,
28 and we will *e* my son to-morrow.
29 we boiled my son, and did *e* him:
29 Give thy son, that we may *e* him:
7. 2 thine eyes, but shalt not *e* thereof.
19 thine eyes, but shalt not *e* thereof.
18.31 *e* ye every man of his own vine,
1Ch 29.22 did *e* and drink before the Lord
2Ch 30.18 did they *e* the passover otherwise
Ezr 9.12 and *e* the good of the land,
10. 6 he did *e* no bread, nor drink water:
Neh 9.25 so they did *e*, and were filled,
36 our fathers to *e* the fruit thereof
Job 31. 8 let me sow, and let another *e*;
Ps 22.26 The meek shall *e* and be satisfied:
27. 2 came upon me to *e* up my flesh,
50.13 Will I *e* the flesh of bulls, or drink
78.24 down manna upon them to *e*,
29 So they did *e*, and were well filled:
127. 2 up late, to *e* the bread of sorrows:
128. 2 shalt *e* the labor of thine hands:
Pr 23. 6 *E* thou not the bread of him that
24.13 *e* thou honey, because it is good;
25.16 *e* so much as is sufficient for thee,
27 It is not good to *e* much honey:
Isa 1.19 ye shall *e* the good of the land:
11. 7 the lion shall *e* straw like the ox.
50. 9 the moth shall *e* them up.
51. 8 For the moth shall *e* them up like
8 the worm shall *e* them like wool:
55. 1 come ye, buy, and *e*; yea, come,
2 and *e* ye that which is good,
65.25 lion shall *e* straw like the bullock:
Jer 22.22 wind shall *e* up all thy pastors,
29.28 and plant gardens, and *e* the fruit
Eze 3. 1 *e* this roll, and go speak
2 and he caused me to *e* that roll.
Mic 6.14 Thou shalt *e*, but not be satisfied;
Na 3.15 *e* thee up like the cankerworm:
Mt 6.25 what ye shall *e*, or what ye shall
31 saying, What shall we *e*? or, What
12. 1 pluck the ears of corn, and to *e*.
4 and did *e* the shewbread,
4 which was not lawful for him to *e*,
14.16 not depart; give ye them to *e*.
20 And they did all *e*, and were filled:
15. 2 wash not their hands when they *e*
20 but to *e* with unwashen hands
27 the dogs *e* of the crumbs which
32 three days, and have nothing to *e*:
37 they did all *e*, and were filled:
38 did *e* were four thousand men,
24.49 to *e* and drink with the drunken;
26.17 prepare for thee to *e* the passover?
21 as they did *e*, he said, Verily I say
26 said, Take, *e*; this is my body.
Mk 1. 6 he did *e* locusts and wild honey;
2.16 *e* with publicans and sinners,
26 and did *e* the shewbread, which is
26 not lawful to *e* but for the priests,
3.20 could not so much as *e* bread.
5.43 should be given her to *e*.
6.31 had no leisure so much as to *e*.
36 bread: for they have nothing to *e*.
37 said unto them, Give ye them to *e*.
37 of bread, and give them to *e*?
42 And they did all *e*, and were filled.
44 And they that did *e* of the loaves
7. 2 saw some of his disciples *e* bread
3 *e* not, holding the tradition of
4 except they wash, they *e* not.
5 but *e* bread with unwashen hands?
28 yet the dogs under the table *e* of
8. 1 having nothing to *e*, Jesus called
2 days, and have nothing to *e*:
8 So they did *e*, and were filled:
11.14 No man *e* fruit of thee hereafter
14.12 and prepare that thou mayest *e*
14 where I shall *e* the passover with
18 as they sat and did *e*, Jesus said,
22 as they did *e*, Jesus took bread,
22 said, Take, *e*; this is my body.
Lk 4. 2 in those days he did *e* nothing:
5.30 ye *e* and drink with publicans
33 Pharisees; but thine *e* and drink?
6. 1 and did *e*, rubbing them in their
4 did take and *e* the shewbread,
4 not lawful to *e* but for the priests
7.36 him that he would *e* with him.
9.13 unto them, Give ye them to *e*.
17 And they did *e*, and were all filled:
10. 8 *e* such things as are set before
12.19 take thine ease, *e*, drink, and be
22 for your life, what ye shall *e*;
29 seek not ye what ye shall *e*,
45 to *e* and drink, and to be drunken;
14. 1 to *e* bread on the sabbath day,
15 Blessed is he that shall *e* bread in
15.16 the husks that the swine did *e*:
23 and let us *e*, and be merry:
17. 8 afterward thou shalt *e* and drink?
27 They did *e*, they drank, they
28 they did *e*, they drank, they

Lk 22. 8 us the passover, that we may *e*,
11 where I shall *e* the passover with
15 I have desired to *e* this passover
16 I will not any more *e* thereof,
30 That ye may *e* and drink at my
24.43 he took it, and did *e* before them.
Jn 4.31 prayed him, saying, Master, *e*.
32 I have meat to *e* that ye know not
33 any man brought him ought to *e*?
6. 5 we buy bread, that these may *e*?
23 the place where they did *e* bread,
26 but because ye did *e* of the loaves,
31 Our fathers did *e* manna in the
31 gave them bread from heaven to *e*.
49 Your fathers did *e* manna in the
50 that a man may *e* thereof, and not
51 if any man *e* of this bread,
52 can this man give us his flesh to *e*?
53 Except ye *e* the flesh of the Son of
58 not as your fathers did *e* manna,
18.28 but that they might *e* the passover.
Ac 2.46 did *e* their meat with gladness
9. 9 sight, and neither did *e* nor drink.
10.13 Rise, Peter; kill, and *e*.
41 who did *e* and drink with him
11. 3 uncircumcised, and didst *e* with
7 Arise, Peter; slay and *e*.
23.12 they would neither *e* nor drink
14 we will *e* nothing until we have
21 an oath, that they will neither *e*
27.35 he had broken it, he began to *e*.
Ro 14. 2 believeth that he may *e* all things:
21 It is good neither to *e* flesh, nor to
23 that doubteth is damned if he *e*,
1Co 5.11 with such a one no not to *e*.
8. 7 *e* it as a thing offered unto an
8 neither, if we *e*, are we the better;
8 if we *e* not, are we the worse.
10 *e* those things which are offered
13 I will *e* no flesh while the world
9. 4 Have we not power to *e* and to
10. 3 did all *e* the same spiritual meat;
7 people sat down to *e* and drink,
18 are they which *e* of the sacrifices
25 is sold in the shambles, that *e*,
27 whatsoever is set before you, *e*,
28 *e* not for his sake that shewed it,
31 Whether therefore ye *e*, or drink,
11.20 this is not to *e* the Lord's supper.
22 have ye not houses to *e* and to
24 Take, *e*; this is my body, which
26 as often as ye *e* this bread,
27 whosoever shall *e* this bread, and
28 and so let him *e* of that bread,
33 when ye come together to *e*, tarry
34 man hunger, let him *e* at home;
15.32 let us *e* and drink; for to-morrow
Gal 2.12 James, he did *e* with the Gentiles:
2Th 3. 8 Neither did we *e* any man's
10 not work, neither should he *e*.
12 with quietness they work, and *e*
2Ti 2.17 word will *e* as doth a canker:
Heb 13.10 they have no right to *e* which
Jas 5. 3 and shall *e* your flesh as it were
Rev 2. 7 will I give to *e* of the tree of life,
14 to *e* things sacrificed unto idols,
17 will I give to *e* of the hidden
20 to *e* things sacrificed unto idols.
10. 9 Take it, and *e* it up; and it shall
17.16 and shall *e* her flesh, and burn her
19.18 That ye may *e* the flesh of kings,

EATEN

Gen 3.11 Hast thou *e* of the tree, whereof I
Ex 13. 7 Unleavened bread shall be *e* seven
29.34 it shall not be *e*, because it is holy.
Lev 6.23 be wholly burnt: it shall not be *e*.
26 in the holy place shall it be *e*,
7.15 shall be *e* the same day that it is
10.17 Wherefore have ye not *e* the sin
Dt 8.10 when thou hast *e* and art full,
12 Lest when thou hast *e* and art full,
1Sa 28.20 he had *e* no bread all the day,
Ps 69. 9 the zeal of thine house hath *e* me
102. 9 For I have *e* ashes like bread,
Pr 9.17 and bread *e* in secret is pleasant.
Jer 31.29 The fathers have *e* a sour grape,
Eze 18. 2 The fathers have *e* sour grapes,
Hos 10.13 ye have *e* the fruit of lies:
Joel 2.25 the years that the locust hath *e*,
Mt 14.21 And they that had *e* were about
Mk 8. 9 And they that had *e* were about
Lk 13.26 We have *e* and drunk in thy
17. 8 till I have *e* and drunken; and
Jn 2.17 zeal of thine house hath *e* me up.
6.13 and above unto them that had *e*.
Ac 10.10 very hungry, and would have *e*:
14 for I have never *e* anything that
12.23 and he was *e* of worms,
20.11 had broken bread, and *e*, and
27.38 when they had *e* enough, they
Rev 10.10 as soon as I had *e* it,

EATER

Jdg 14.14 Out of the *e* came forth meat,
Isa 55.10 to the sower, and bread to the *e*:
Na 3.12 even fall into the mouth of the *e*.

EATETH

Ex 12.15 whosoever *e* leavened bread from
19 whosoever *e* that which is leavened,
Lev 7.18 the soul that *e* of it shall bear his
20 But the soul that *e* of the flesh
25 For whosoever *e* the fat of the
25 even the soul that *e* it shall be cut
27 Whatsoever soul it be that *e* any
11.40 And he that *e* of the carcase
14.47 and he that *e* in the house shall
17.10 that *e* any manner of blood; I will
10 against that soul that *e* blood,
14 whosoever *e* it shall be cut off.
15 every soul that *e* that which died
19. 8 Therefore every one that *e* it shall
Nu 13.32 *e* up the inhabitants thereof; and
1Sa 14.24 the man that *e* any food until
28 Cursed be the man that *e* any food
Job 5. 5 the hungry *e* up, and taketh it
21.25 soul, and never *e* with pleasure.
40.15 he *e* grass as an ox.
Ps 106.20 the similitude of an ox that *e* grass.
Pr 13.25 The righteous *e* to the satisfying of
30.20 she *e*, and wipeth her mouth,
31.27 and *e* not the bread of idleness.
Ec 4. 5 together, and *e* his own flesh.
5.17 All his days also he *e* in darkness,
6. 2 but a stranger *e* it: this is vanity,
Isa 28. 4 it is yet in his hand he *e* it up.
29. 8 man dreameth, and, behold, he *e*;
44.16 with part thereof he *e* flesh;
59. 5 he that *e* of their eggs dieth,
Jer 31.10 every man that *e* the sour grape,
Mt 9.11 *e* your Master with publicans
Mk 2.16 How is it that he *e* and drinketh
14.18 you, One of you which *e* with me
Lk 15. 2 receiveth sinners, and *e* with them.
Jn 6.54 Whoso *e* my flesh, and drinketh
56 He that *e* my flesh, and drinketh
57 so he that *e* me, even he shall live
58 he that *e* of this bread shall live
13.18 He that *e* bread with me hath lifted
Ro 14. 2 another, who is weak, *e* herbs.
3 Let not him that *e* despise him that
3 *e* not; and let not him which *e* not
3 not judge him that *e*:
6 He that *e*, *e* to the Lord, for he
6 God thanks; and he that *e* not,
6 not, to the Lord he *e* not,
20 it is evil for that man who *e* with
23 because he *e* not of faith:
1Co 9. 7 and *e* not of the fruit thereof?
7 and *e* not of the milk of the flock?
11.29 he that *e* and drinketh unworthily,
29 *e* and drinketh damnation to

EATING

Ex 12. 4 every man according to his *e* shall
16.16 of it every man according to his *e*,
18 every man according to his *e*.
21 every man according to his *e*: and
Jdg 14. 9 went on *e*, and came to his father
Ru 3. 3 until he shall have done *e* and
1Sa 14.34 sin not against the Lord in *e*
30.16 *e* and drinking, and dancing,
1Ki 1.41 as they had made an end of *e*.
4.20 *e* and drinking, and making merry.
2Ki 4.40 as they were *e* of the pottage,
1Ch 12.39 David three days, *e* and drinking:
Job 1.13 his sons and his daughters were *e*
18 thy sons and thy daughters were *e*
20.23 rain it upon him while he is *e*.
Isa 22.13 killing sheep, *e* flesh, and drinking
66.17 *e* swine's flesh, and the abomination,
Am 7. 2 when they had made an end of *e*
Mt 11.18 John came neither *e* nor drinking,
19 Son of man came *e* and drinking,
24.38 were *e* and drinking, marrying
26.26 And as they were *e*, Jesus took
Lk 7.33 the Baptist came neither *e* bread
34 The Son of man is come *e* and
10. 7 remain, *e* and drinking such
1Co 8. 4 the *e* of those things that are
11.21 For in *e* every one taketh before

EBAL

Gen 36.23 Alvan and Manaheth, and *E*,
Dt 11.29 and the curse upon mount *E*.
27. 4 command you this day, in mount *E*,
13 shall stand upon mount *E* to curse;
Jos 8.30 Lord God of Israel in mount *E*,
33 half of them over against mount *E*;
1Ch 1.22 And *E*, and Abimael, and Sheba,
40 Alian, and Manahath, and *E*,

EBENEZER

1Sa 4. 1 to battle, and pitched beside *E*:
5. 1 and brought it from *E* unto Ashdod.
7.12 and called the name of it *E*,

EDEN

Gen 2. 8 planted a garden eastward in *E*;
10 went out of *E* to water the garden;
15 him into the garden of *E* to dress it
3.23 him forth from the garden of *E*,
24 east of the garden of *E* Cherubims,
4.16 the land of Nod, on the east of *E*.
2Ki 19.12 of *E* which were in Thelasar?
2Ch 29.12 of Zimnah, and *E* the son of Joah:
31.15 next him were *E*, and Miniamin,
Isa 37.12 of *E* which were in Telassar?
51. 3 will make her wilderness like *E*,
Eze 27.23 Haran, and Canneh, and *E*, the
28.13 hast been in *E* the garden of God;
31. 9 trees of *E*, that were in the garden
16 the trees of *E*, the choice and best
18 greatness among the trees of *E*?
18 brought down with the trees of *E*
36.35 is become like the garden of *E*;
Joel 2. 3 is as the garden of *E* before them,
Am 1. 5 the sceptre from the house of *E*:

EDGES

Ex 28. 7 joined at the two *e* thereof;
39. 4 two *e* was it coupled together.
Jdg 3.16 a dagger which had two *e*,
Rev 2.12 hath the sharp sword with two *e*;

EDIFICATION

Ro 15. 2 his neighbor for his good to *e*.
1Co 14. 3 speaketh unto men to *e*,
2Co 10. 8 the Lord hath given us for *e*,
13.10 the Lord hath given me to *e*,
(See box on page 252)

EDIFIED

Ac 9.31 the churches rest...and were *e*;
1Co 14.17 thanks well, but the other is not *e*.

EDIFIETH

1Co 8. 1 puffeth up, but charity *e*.
14. 4 an unknown tongue *e* himself;
4 he that propesieth *e* the church.

EDIFY

Ro 14.19 wherewith one may *e* another.
1Co 10.23 lawful for me, but all things *e* not.
1Th 5.11 together, and *e* one another,

EDIFYING

1Co 14. 5 that the church may receive *e*.
12 may excel to the *e* of the church.
26 Let all things be done unto *e*.
2Co 12.19 things, dearly beloved, for your *e*.
Eph 4.12 for the *e* of the body of Christ:
16 unto the *e* of itself in love.
29 which is good to the use of *e*,
1Ti 1. 4 than godly *e* which is in faith:

EDOM

Gen 25.30 therefore was his name called *E*.
32. 3 the land of Seir, the country of *E*.
36. 1 the generations of Esau, who is *E*.
8 Esau in mount Seir: Esau is *E*.
16 came of Eliphaz in the land of *E*;
17 came of Reuel in the land of *E*;
19 are the sons of Esau, who is *E*,
21 children of Seir in the land of *E*.
31 kings that reigned in the land of *E*,
32 Bela the son of Beor reigned in *E*:
43 these be the dukes of *E*,
Ex 15.15 the dukes of *E* shall be amazed;
Nu 20.14 from Kadesh unto the king of *E*,
18 *E* said unto him, Thou shalt not
20 *E* came out against him with much
21 *E* refused to give Israel passage
23 by the coast of the land of *E*,
21. 4 to compass the land of *E*:
24.18 And *E* shall be a possession,
33.37 in the edge of the land of *E*.
34. 3 of Zin along by the coast of *E*
Jos 15. 1 border of *E* the wilderness of Zin
21 of Judah toward the coast of *E*
Jdg 5. 4 marchedst out of the field of *E*,
11.17 sent messengers unto the king of *E*,
17 but the king of *E* would not hearken
18 and compassed the land of *E*,
1Sa 14.47 against *E*, and against the kings of
2Sa 8.14 And he put garrisons in *E*;
14 throughout all *E* put he garrisons.
14 they of *E* became David's servants.
1Ki 9.26 of the Red sea, in the land of *E*.
11.14 he was of the king's seed in *E*.
15 came to pass, when David was in *E*,
15 he had smitten every male in *E*;
16 he had cut off every male in *E*;
22.47 There was then no king in *E*:
2Ki 3. 8 way through the wilderness of *E*.
9 king of Judah, and the king of *E*:
12 the king of *E* went down to him.
20 there came water by the way of *E*,
26 through even unto the king of *E*:
8.20 *E* revolted from under the hand of
22 Yet *E* revolted from under the hand
14. 7 He slew of *E* in the valley of salt
10 Thou hast indeed smitten *E*,
1Ch 1.43 kings that reigned in the land of *E*
51 the dukes of *E* were; duke Timnah,
54 Iram. These are the dukes of *E*.
18.11 from *E*, and from Moab, and from
13 And he put garrisons in *E*; and all
2Ch 8.17 at the sea side in the land of *E*.
25.20 they sought after the gods of *E*.
Ps 60(T) smote in *E* in the valley of salt
8 over *E* will I cast out my shoe:
9 Who will lead me into *E*?
83. 6 of *E*, and the Ishmaelites;
108. 9 over *E* will I cast out my shoe;
10 who will lead me into *E*?
137. 7 the children of *E* in the day of
Isa 11.14 lay their hand upon *E* and Moab;
63. 1 Who is this that cometh from *E*,
Jer 9.26 Egypt, and Judah, and *E*, and the
25.21 *E*, and Moab, and the children of
27. 3 And send them to the king of *E*,
40.11 among the Ammonites, and in *E*,
49. 7 concerning *E*, thus saith the Lord
17 Also *E* shall be a desolation:
20 that he hath taken against *E*;
22 the heart of the mighty men of *E*
La 4.21 and be glad, O daughter of *E*,
22 thine iniquity, O daughter of *E*;
Eze 25.12 *E* hath dwelt against the house of
13 also stretch out mine hand upon *E*,
14 I will lay my vengeance upon *E*
14 do in *E* according to mine anger
32.29 There is *E*, her kings, and all her
Dan 11.41 out of his hand, even *E*, and Moab,
Joel 3.19 *E* shall be a desolate wilderness,
Am 1. 6 captivity to deliver them up to *E*:
9 up the whole captivity to *E*, and
11 For three transgressions of *E*, and
2. 1 burned the bones of the king of *E*
9.12 they may possess the remnant of *E*,
Ob 1 saith the Lord God concerning *E*;
8 even destroy the wise men out of *E*,
Mal 1. 4 *E* saith, We are impoverished,

EFFECT

Nu 30. 8 shall make her vow...of none *e*:
2Ch 34.22 and they spake to her to that *e*.
Ps 33.10 devices of the people of none *e*.
Isa 32.17 the *e* of righteousness quietness
Jer 48.30 his lies shall not so *e* it.
Eze 12.23 hand, and the *e* of every vision.
Mt 15. 6 commandment of God of none *e*
Mk 7.13 the word of God of none *e*
Ro 3. 3 make the faith of God without *e*?
4.14 and the promise made of none *e*:
9. 6 word of God hath taken none *e*.
1Co 1.17 Christ should be made of none *e*.
Gal 3.17 make the promise of none *e*.
5. 4 Christ is become of no *e* unto

EFFECTED

2Ch 7.11 own house, he prosperously *e*.

EFFECTUAL

1Co 16. 9 a great door and *e* is opened
2Co 1. 6 which is *e* in the enduring of the
Eph 3. 7 by the *e* working of his power.
4.16 the *e* working in the measure of
Phm 6 become *e* by the acknowledging
Jas 5.16 *e* fervent prayer of a righteous

EFFECTUALLY

Gal 2. 8 (For he that wrought *e* in Peter
1Th 2.13 which *e* worketh also in you

EFFEMINATE

1Co 6. 9 adulterers, nor *e*, nor abusers of

Eden, the garden of God in which Adam and Eve lived before the Fall, takes its name from a Hebrew word meaning "delight" or "place of delight." This famous Sistine Chapel fresco by Michelangelo, painted about 1510, represents two scenes in one, the eating of the fruit and the expulsion from the garden.

BIBLICAL THEMES

EDUCATION

The Lord said unto me, Gather me the people together, and I will make them hear my words, that they may learn to fear me all the days that they shall live upon the earth, and that they may teach their children. Dt 4.10

[Jehoshaphat] sent to his princes . . . to teach in the cities of Judah. And with them he sent Levites. . . . And they taught in Judah, and had the book of the law of the Lord with them, and went . . . throughout all the cities of Judah, and taught the people. 2Ch 17.7-9

I will instruct thee and teach thee in the way which thou shalt go: I will guide thee with mine eye. Be ye not as the horse, or as the mule, which have no understanding. Ps 32.8-9

But unto the wicked God saith, What hast thou to do to declare my statutes, or that thou shouldest take my covenant in thy mouth? seeing thou hatest instruction, and castest my words behind thee. Ps 50.16-17

Open thou mine eyes, that I may behold wondrous things out of thy law. Ps 119.18

When wisdom entereth into thine heart, and knowledge is pleasant unto thy soul; discretion shall preserve thee, understanding shall keep thee. Pr 2.10-11

Train up a child in the way he should go: and when he is old, he will not depart from it. Pr 22.6

I gave my heart to know wisdom. . . . I perceived that this also is vexation of spirit. For in much wisdom is much grief: and he that increaseth knowledge increaseth sorrow. . . . Of making many books there is no end; and much study is a weariness of the flesh. Ec 1.17-18; 12.12

Precept must be upon precept, precept upon precept; line upon line, line upon line. Isa 28.10

My people are destroyed for lack of knowledge. Hos 4.6

[Jesus] taught them as one having authority, and not as the scribes. Mt 7.29

And beginning at Moses and all the prophets, he expounded unto them in all the scriptures the things concerning himself. Lk 24.27

I am . . . a Jew, born in Tarsus, a city in Cilicia, yet brought up in this city at the feet of Gamaliel, and taught according to the perfect manner of the law of the fathers. Ac 22.3

For we know in part, and we prophesy in part. But when that which is perfect is come, then that which is in part shall be done away. When I was a child, I spake as a child, I understood as a child, I thought as a child: but when I became a man, I put away childish things. For now we see through a glass, darkly; but then face to face: now I know in part; but then shall I know even as also I am known. 1Co 13.9-12

The law was our schoolmaster to bring us unto Christ, that we might be justified by faith. But after that faith is come, we are no longer under a schoolmaster. For ye are all the children of God by faith in Christ Jesus. Gal 3.24-26

Study to shew thyself approved unto God . . . rightly dividing the word of truth. . . . Continue thou in the things which thou hast learned . . . knowing of whom thou hast learned them; and that from a child thou hast known the holy scriptures, which are able to make thee wise unto salvation. 2Ti 2.15; 3.14-15

EGG

Job 6. 6 any taste in the white of an *e*?
Lk 11.12 Or if he shall ask an *e*, will he

EGYPT

Gen 12.10 and Abram went down into *E*
11 was come near to enter into *E*,
14 when Abram was come into *E*,
13. 1 Abram went up out of *E*, he,
10 of the Lord, like the land of *E*,
15.18 given this land, from the river of *E*
21.21 him a wife out of the land of *E*.
25.18 *E*, as thou goest toward Assyria:
26. 2 and said, Go not down into *E*;
37.25 going to carry it down to *E*.
28 and they brought Joseph into *E*.
36 sold him into *E* unto Potiphar,
39. 1 Joseph was brought down to *E*;
40. 1 that the butler of the king of *E*
1 offended their lord the king of *E*.
5 the baker of the king of *E*, which
41. 8 the magicians of *E*, and all the
19 in all the land of *E* for badness:
29 throughout all the land of *E*:
30 be forgotten in the land of *E*;
33 and set him over the land of *E*.
34 up the fifth part of the land of *E*
36 which shall be in the land of *E*;
41 have set thee over all the land of *E*.
43 him ruler over all the land of *E*.
44 hand or foot in all the land of *E*.
45 went out over all the land of *E*.
46 he stood before Pharaoh king of *E*.
46 went throughout all the land of *E*.
48 which were in the land of *E*, and
53 that was in the land of *E*,
54 all the land of *E* there was bread.
55 all the land of *E* was famished,
56 famine waxed sore in the land of *E*.
57 And all the countries came into *E*
42. 1 saw that there was corn in *E*,
2 heard that there is corn in *E*:
3 went down to buy corn in *E*.
43. 2 which they had brought out of *E*,
15 and went down to *E*, and stood
45. 4 your brother, whom ye sold into *E*.
8 throughout all the land of *E*.
9 God hath made me lord of all *E*:
13 tell my father of all my glory in *E*,
18 give you the good of the land of *E*,
19 you wagons out of the land of *E*
20 good of all the land of *E* is yours.
23 laden with the good things of *E*,
25 they went up out of *E*, and came
26 governor over all the land of *E*.
46. 3 fear not to go down into *E*; for
4 I will go down with thee into *E*;
6 and came into *E*, Jacob, and all
7 seed brought he with him into *E*.
8 of Israel, which came into *E*,
20 unto Joseph in the land of *E* were
26 that came with Jacob into *E*,
27 Joseph, which were born him in *E*,
27 which came into *E*, were
47. 6 The land of *E* is before thee; in
11 them a possession in the land of *E*,
13 the land of *E* and all the land of
14 that was found in the land of *E*,
15 money failed in the land of *E*,
20 all the land of *E* for Pharaoh;
21 from one end of the borders of *E*
26 made it a law over the land of *E*
27 Israel dwelt in the land of *E*,
28 And Jacob lived in the land of *E*
29 bury me not, I pray thee, in *E*:
30 thou shalt carry me out of *E*,
48. 5 born unto thee in the land of *E*
5 I came unto thee into *E*, are mine;
50. 7 and all the elders of the land of *E*,
14 Joseph returned into *E*, he, and
22 Joseph dwelt in *E*, he, and his
26 and he was put in a coffin in *E*.
Ex 1. 1 of Israel, which came into E;
5 for Joseph was in *E* already.
8 there arose up a new king over *E*,
15 And the king of *E* spake to the
17 and did not as the king of *E*
18 And the king of *E* called for the
2.23 of time, that the king of *E* died:
3. 7 of my people which are in *E*, and
10 the children of Israel out of *E*,
11 the children of Israel out of *E*?
12 brought forth the people out of *E*,
16 that which is done to you in *E*:
17 you up out of the affliction of *E*
18 unto the king of *E*, and ye shall
19 the king of *E* will not let you go,
20 stretch out my hand, and smite *E*
4.18 unto my brethren which are in *E*,
19 in Midian, Go, return into *E*:
20 and he returned to the land of *E*:
21 return into *E*, see that thou do all
5. 4 the king of *E* said unto them,
12 throughout all the land of *E* to
6.11 speak unto Pharaoh king of *E*,
13 and unto Pharaoh king of *E*,
13 of Israel out of the land of *E*.
26 from the land of *E* according to
27 spake to Pharaoh king of *E*,
27 out the children of Israel from *E*:
28 spake unto Moses in the land of *E*.

29 thou unto Pharaoh king of E all
7. 3 and my wonders in the land of E.
4 lay my hand upon E, and bring
4 land of E by great judgments.
5 stretch forth mine hand upon E,
11 magicians of E, they also did in
19 thine hand upon the waters of E,
19 blood throughout all the land of E,
21 blood throughout all the land of E.
22 the magicians of E did so with
8. 5 to come up upon the land of E.
6 his hand over the waters of E;
6 came up, and covered the land of E.
7 up frogs upon the land of E.
16 become lice throughout all...of E.
17 became lice throughout all...of E.
24 houses, and into all the land of E:
9. 4 of Israel and the cattle of E:
6 and all the cattle of E died:
9 small dust in all the land of E,
9 beast, throughout all the land of E.
18 hail, such as hath not been in E
22 may be hail in all the land of E,
22 field, throughout the land of E.
23 rained hail upon the land of E.
24 none like it in all the land of E
25 smote throughout all the land of E
10. 2 what things I have wrought in E,
7 thou not yet that E is destroyed?
12 over the land of E for the locusts,
12 may come up upon the land of E,
13 forth his rod over the land of E,
14 went up over all the land of E,
14 and rested in all the coasts of E:
15 field, through all the land of E.
19 one locust in all the coasts of E.
21 be darkness over the land of E,
22 in all the land of E three days:
11. 1 more upon Pharaoh, and upon E;
3 was very great in the land of E,
4 will I go out into the midst of E:
5 firstborn in the land of E shall die,
6 cry throughout all the land of E,
9 be multiplied in the land of E.
12. 1 Moses and Aaron in the land of E,
12 through the land of E this night,
12 all the firstborn in the land of E,
12 gods of E I will execute judgment:
13 you, when I smite the land of E.
17 your armies out of the land of E:
27 of the children of Israel in E,
29 all the firstborn in the land of E,
30 and there was a great cry in E;
39 which they brought forth out of E,
39 because they were thrust out of E,
40 who dwelt in E, was four hundred
41 Lord went out from the land of E.
42 them out from the land of E:
51 of Israel out of the land of E
13. 3 day, in which ye came out from E,
8 me when I came forth out of E.
9 the Lord brought thee out of E.
14 the Lord brought us out from E,
15 in the land of E, both the firstborn
16 the Lord brought us forth out of E.
17 see war, and they return to E:
18 harnessed out of the land of E.
14. 5 the king of E that the people fled:
7 the chariots of E, and captains
8 the heart of Pharaoh king of E,
11 Because there were no graves in E,
11 us, to carry us forth out of E?
12 that we did tell thee in E, saying,
16. 1 departing out of the land of E.
3 hand of the Lord in the land of E,
6 you out from the land of E:
32 you forth from the land of E.
17. 3 thou hast brought us up out of E,
18. 1 hath brought Israel out of E;
19. 1 gone forth out of the land of E,
20. 2 brought thee out of the land of E,
22.21 ye were strangers in the land of E.
23. 9 ye were strangers in the land of E.
15 in it thou camest out from E:
29.46 out of the land of E, that I may
32. 1 us up out of the land of E,
4 thee up out of the land of E.
7 broughtest out of the land of E,
8 thee up out of the land of E.
11 brought forth out of the land of E
23 brought us up out of the land of E,
33. 1 brought up out of the land of E,
34.18 Abib thou camest out from E.
Lev 11.45 of the land of E, to be your God:
18. 3 the land of E, wherein ye dwelt,
19.34 strangers in the land of E: I am
36 brought you out of the land of E.
22.33 brought you out of the land of E,
23.43 brought them out of the land of E:
25.38 forth out of the land of E, to give
42 forth out of the land of E: they
55 forth out of the land of E: I am
26.13 forth out of the land of E, that ye
45 forth out of the land of E in the
Nu 1. 1 come out of the land of E, saying,
3.13 all the firstborn in the land of E
8.17 of E I sanctified them for myself.
9. 1 come out of the land E, saying,
11. 5 fish, which we did eat in E freely;
18 eat? for it was well with us in E:
20 Why came we forth out of E?
13.22 built seven years before Zoan in E.)
14. 2 we had died in the land of E!
3 not better for us to return into E?
4 captain, and let us return into E.
19 people, from E even until now.
22 I did in E and in the wilderness,
15.41 brought you out of the land of E,
20. 5 up out of E, to bring us in unto
15 E, and we have dwelt in E a long
16 hath brought us forth out of E:
21. 5 out of E to die in the wilderness?
22. 5 is a people come out from E:
11 out of E, which covereth the face
23.22 God brought them out of E; he
24. 8 God brought him forth out of E;
26. 4 went forth out of the land of E.
59 her mother bare to Levi in E:
32.11 of the men that came up out of E,
33. 1 went forth out of the land of E
38 the land of E, in the first day of
34. 5 from Azmon unto the river of E,
Dt 1.27 the land of E, to deliver us into
30 did for you in E before your eyes;
4.20 of the iron furnace, even out of E;
34 Lord your God did for you in E
37 with his mighty power out of E;
45 after they came forth out of E,
46 they were come forth out of E:
5. 6 brought thee out of the land of E,
15 wast a servant in the land of E,
6.12 thee forth out of the land of E,
21 We were Pharaoh's bondmen in E;
21 the Lord brought us out of E with
22 wonders, great and sore, upon E.
7. 8 the hand of Pharaoh king of E.
15 none of the evil diseases of E,
18 did unto Pharaoh, and unto all E;
8.14 thee forth out of the land of E,
9. 7 didst depart out of the land of E,
12 thou hast brought forth out of E
26 out of E with a mighty hand.
10.19 were strangers in the land of E.
22 Thy fathers went down into E with
11. 3 acts, which he did in the midst of E
3 unto Pharaoh the king of E, and
4 what he did unto the army of E,
10 it, is not as the land of E, from
13. 5 brought you out of the land of E,
10 brought thee out of the land of E,
15.15 wast a bondman in the land of E,
16. 1 God brought thee forth out of E by
3 forth out of the land of E in haste:
3 out of the land of E all the days of
6 that thou camest forth out of E.
12 that thou wast a bondman in E:
17.16 cause the people to return to E,
20. 1 brought thee up out of the land of E.
23. 4 way, when ye came forth out of E;

The might of Egypt in biblical times is reflected in these colossal temple statues from the 13th century B.C.

Dt 24. 9 that ye were come forth out of *E*.
18 that thou wast a bondman in *E*,
22 wast a bondman in the land of *E*:
25.17 when ye were come forth out of *E*;
26. 5 and he went down into *E*, and
8 the Lord brought us forth out of *E*
28.27 will smite thee with the botch of *E*,
60 upon thee all the diseases of *E*,
68 Lord shall bring thee into *E* again
29. 2 before your eyes in the land of *E*
16 we have dwelt in the land of *E*;
25 them forth out of the land of *E*:
34.11 sent him to do in the land of *E*
Jos 2.10 for you, when ye came out of *E*;
5. 4 All the people that came out of *E*,
4 the way, after they came out of *E*.
5 way as they came forth out of *E*,
6 men of war, which came out of *E*,
9 I rolled away the reproach of *E*
9. 9 of him, and all that he did in *E*,
13. 3 From Sihor, which is before *E*,
15. 4 and went out unto the river of *E*;
47 her villages, unto the river of *E*,
24. 4 his children went down into *E*.
5 and I plagued *E*, according to that
6 I brought your fathers out of *E*:
7 have seen what I have done in *E*:
14 other side of the flood, and in *E*;
17 our fathers out of the land of *E*,
32 of Israel brought up out of *E*,
Jdg 2. 1 said, I made you to go up out of *E*,
12 brought them out of the land of *E*,
6. 8 Israel, I brought you up from *E*,
13 not the Lord bring us up from *E*?
11.13 land, when they came up out of *E*,
16 When Israel came up from *E*,
19.30 came up out of the land of *E* unto
1Sa 2.27 thy father, when they were in *E*
8. 8 day that I brought them up out of *E*
10.18 I brought up Israel out of *E*, and
12. 6 fathers up out of the land of *E*.
8 When Jacob was come into *E*, and
8 brought forth your fathers out of *E*,
15. 2 the way, when he came up from *E*.
6 when they came up out of *E*.
7 to Shur, that is over against *E*.
27. 8 to Shur, even unto the land of *E*.
30.13 I am a young man of *E*, servant
2Sa 7. 6 up the children of Israel out of *E*,
23 thou redeemedst to thee from *E*,
1Ki 3. 1 affinity with Pharaoh king of *E*,
4.21 and unto the border of *E*: they
30 country, and all the wisdom of *E*.
6. 1 were come out of the land of *E*,
8. 9 they came out of the land of *E*.
16 my people Israel out of *E*, I chose
21 brought them out of the land of *E*.
51 thou broughtest forth out of *E*,
53 broughtest our fathers out of *E*,
65 in of Hamath unto the river of *E*,
9. 9 their fathers out of the land of *E*,
16 For Pharaoh king of *E* had gone
10.28 had horses brought out of *E*, and
29 and went out of *E* for six hundred
11.17 servants with him, to go into *E*;
18 came to *E*, unto Pharaoh king of *E*;
21 And when Hadad heard in *E* that
40 fled into *E*, unto Shishak king of *E*,
40 and was in *E* until the death of
12. 2 son of Nebat, who was yet in *E*,
2 Solomon, and Jeroboam dwelt in *E*;
28 brought thee up out of the land of *E*.
14.25 that Shishak king of *E* came up
2Ki 17. 4 sent messengers to So king of *E*,
7 them up out of the land of *E*,
7 the hand of Pharaoh king of *E*,
36 you up out of the land of *E* with
18.21 of this bruised reed, even upon *E*,
21 is Pharaoh king of *E* unto all that
24 put thy trust on *E* for chariots and
21.15 their fathers came forth out of *E*,
23.29 Pharaoh-nechoh king of *E* went up
34 and he came to *E*, and died there.
24. 7 And the king of *E* came not again
7 had taken from the river of *E* unto
7 all that pertained to the king of *E*.
25.26 arose, and came to *E*: for they
1Ch 13. 5 Israel together, from Shihor of *E*
17.21 whom thou hast redeemed out of *E*?
2Ch 1.16 had horses brought out of *E*, and
17 and brought forth out of *E* a
5.10 Israel, when they came out of *E*.
6. 5 forth my people out of the land of *E*
7. 8 in of Hamath unto the river of *E*.
22 them forth out of the land of *E*,
9.26 Philistines, and to the border of *E*.
28 unto Solomon horses out of *E*,
10. 2 the son of Nebat, who was in *E*,
2 that Jeroboam returned out of *E*.
12. 2 king Rehoboam, Shishak king of *E*
3 that came with him out of *E*;
9 Shishak king of *E* came up against
20.10 they came out of the land of *E*,
26. 8 abroad even to the entering in of *E*;
35.20 Necho king of *E* came up to fight
36. 3 And the king of *E* put him down at
4 the king of *E* made Eliakim his
4 his brother, and carried him to *E*.
Neh 9. 9 the affliction of our fathers in *E*,
18 that brought thee up out of *E*,
Ps 68.31 Princes shall come out of *E*;
78.12 of their fathers, in the land of *E*,
43 he had wrought his signs in *E*, and
51 And smote all the firstborn in *E*;
80. 8 Thou hast brought a vine out of *E*:
81. 5 he went out through the land of *E*:
10 brought thee out of the land of *E*:
105.23 Israel also came into *E*; and Jacob
38 *E* was glad when they departed:
106. 7 understood not thy wonders in *E*;
21 which had done great things in *E*;
114. 1 When Israel went out of *E*, the
135. 8 Who smote the firstborn of *E*, both
9 into the midst of thee, O *E*,
136.10 that smote *E* in their firstborn:
Pr 7.16 carved works, with fine linen of *E*.
Isa 7.18 uttermost part of the rivers of *E*,
10.24 against thee, after the manner of *E*.
26 he lift it up after the manner of *E*.
11.11 and from *E*, and from Pathros, and
16 he came up out of the land of *E*.
19. 1 The burden of *E*, Behold, the Lord
1 swift cloud, and shall come into *E*:
1 and the idols of *E* shall be moved
1 and the heart of *E* shall melt in
3 And the spirit of *E* shall fail in the
12 of hosts hath purposed upon *E*.
13 they have also seduced *E*, even
14 and they have caused *E* to err in
15 shall there be any work for *E*,
16 day shall *E* be like unto women:
17 of Judah shall be a terror unto *E*,
18 five cities in the land of *E* speak
19 Lord in the midst of the land of *E*,
20 the Lord of hosts in the land of *E*:
21 the Lord shall be known to *E*, and
22 And the Lord shall smite *E*: he
23 shall there be a highway out of *E*
23 the Assyrian shall come into *E*, and
24 shall Israel be the third with *E*
25 Blessed be *E* my people, and
20. 3 for a sign and wonder upon *E* and
4 uncovered, to the shame of *E*.
5 expectation, and of *E* their glory.
23. 5 As at the report concerning *E*, so
27.12 of the river unto the stream of *E*,
13 and the outcasts in the land of *E*,
30. 2 That walk to go down into *E*, and
2 and to trust in the shadow of *E*!
3 the trust in the shadow of *E* your
31. 1 that go down to *E* for help; and
36. 6 the staff of this broken reed, on *E*;
6 so is Pharaoh king of *E* to all that
9 servants, and put thy trust on *E*
43. 3 I gave *E* for thy ransom, Ethiopia
45.14 The labor of *E*, and merchandise
52. 4 people went down aforetime into *E*
Jer 2. 6 brought us up out of the land of *E*,
18 hast thou to do in the way of *E*,
36 thou also shalt be ashamed of *E*,
7.22 brought them out of the land of *E*,
25 came forth out of the land of *E*
9.26 *E*, and Judah, and Edom, and the
11. 4 them forth out of the land of *E*,
7 them up out of the land of *E*,
16.14 of Israel out of the land of *E*;
23. 7 of Israel out of the land of *E*;
24. 8 them that dwell in the land of *E*:
25.19 Pharaoh king of *E*, and his
26.21 afraid, and fled, and went into *E*;
22 the king sent men into *E*, namely,
22 and certain men with him into *E*.
23 they fetched forth Urijah out of *E*,
31.32 bring them out of the land of *E*;
32.20 signs and wonders in the land of *E*,
21 people Israel out of the land of *E*
34.13 them forth out of the land of *E*, out
37. 5 army was come forth out of *E*:
7 to help you, shall return to *E* into
41.17 Bethlehem, to go to enter into *E*,
42.14 but we will go into the land of *E*,
15 set your faces to enter into *E*,
16 overtake you there in the land of *E*,
16 follow close after you there in *E*;
17 that set their faces to go into *E*
18 you, when ye shall enter into *E*:
19 of Judah; Go ye not into *E*:
43. 2 sent thee to say, Go not into *E* to
7 they came into the land of *E*: for
11 he shall smite the land of *E*,
12 fire in the houses of the gods of *E*;
12 array himself with the land of *E*,
13 that is in the land of *E*; and the
44. 1 Jews which dwell in the land of *E*,
8 unto other gods in the land of *E*,
12 their faces to go into the land of *E*
12 consumed, and fall in the land of *E*;
13 them that dwell in the land of *E*,
14 which are gone into the land of *E*
15 people that dwelt in the land of *E*,
24 all Judah that are in the land of *E*:
26 Judah that dwell in the land of *E*;
26 man of Judah in all the land of *E*,
27 the land of *E* shall be consumed by
28 shall return out of the land of *E*
28 into the land of *E* to sojourn there,
30 give Pharaoh-hophra king of *E*
46. 2 Against *E*, against the army of
2 Pharaoh-necho king of *E*, which
8 *E* riseth up like a flood, and his
11 balm, O virgin, the daughter of *E*:
13 come and smite the land of *E*.
14 Declare ye in *E*, and publish in
17 Pharaoh king of *E* is but a noise;
19 O thou daughter dwelling in *E*,
20 *E* is like a very fair heifer, but
24 The daughter of *E* shall be
25 of No, and Pharaoh, and *E*, with
Eze 17.15 sending his ambassadors into *E*,
19. 4 him with chains into the land of *E*.
20. 5 known unto them in the land of *E*,
6 to bring them forth of the land of *E*
7 not yourselves with the idols of *E*:
8 did they forsake the idols of *E*:
8 them in the midst of the land of *E*.
9 them forth out of the land of *E*.
10 to go forth out of the land of *E*,
36 in the wilderness of the land of *E*,
23. 3 they committed whoredoms in *E*;
8 her whoredoms brought from *E*:
19 played the harlot in the land of *E*.
27 brought from the land of *E*:
27 them, nor remember *E* any more.

27. 7 linen with broidered work from *E*
29. 2 face against Pharaoh king of *E*,
2 against him, and against all *E*:
3 Pharaoh king of *E*, the great
6 *E* shall know that I am the Lord,
9 the land of *E* shall be desolate
10 make the land of *E* utterly waste
12 I will make the land of *E* desolate
14 will bring again the captivity of *E*,
19 I will give the land of *E* unto
20 given him the land of *E* for his
30. 4 And the sword shall come upon *E*,
4 when the slain shall fall in *E*,
6 They also that uphold *E* shall fall;
8 when I have set a fire in *E*, and
9 upon them, as in the day of *E*:
10 make the multitude of *E* to cease
11 shall draw their swords against *E*,
13 no more a prince of the land of *E*:
13 I will put a fear in the land of *E*.
15 fury upon Sin, the strength of *E*;
16 And I will set fire in *E*: Sin shall
18 I shall break there the yokes of *E*:
19 will I execute judgments in *E*:
21 the arm of Pharaoh king of *E*;
22 I am against Pharaoh king of *E*,
25 stretch it out upon the land of *E*.
31. 2 speak unto Pharaoh king of *E*,
32. 2 lamentation for Pharaoh king of *E*,
12 they shall spoil the pomp of *E*,
15 shall make the land of *E* desolate,
16 shall lament for her, even for *E*,
18 man, wail for the multitude of *E*,
Dan 9.15 people forth out of the land of *E*
11. 8 carry captives into *E* their gods,
42 and the land of *E* shall not escape.
43 over all the precious things of *E*:
Hos 2.15 she came up out of the land of *E*:
7.11 without heart: they call to *E*,
16 be their derision in the land of *E*.
8.13 their sins: they shall return to *E*.
9. 3 Ephraim shall return to *E*, and
6 *E* shall gather them up, Memphis
11. 1 him, and called my son out of *E*.
5 shall not return into the land of *E*,
11 shall tremble as a bird out of *E*,
12. 1 and oil is carried into *E*.
9 thy God from the land of *E* will yet
13 the Lord brought Israel out of *E*,
13. 4 Lord thy God from the land of *E*,
Joel 3.19 *E* shall be a desolation, and Edom
Am 2.10 up from the land of *E*, and led you
3. 1 up from the land of *E*, saying,
9 and in the palaces in the land of *E*,
4.10 pestilence after the manner of *E*:
8. 8 and drowned, as by the flood of *E*.
9. 5 be drowned, as by the flood of *E*.
7 up Israel out of the land of *E*?
Mic 6. 4 thee up out of the land of *E*,
7.15 of thy coming out of the land of *E*
Na 3. 9 Ethiopa and *E* were her strength,
Hag 2. 5 with you when ye came out of *E*,
Zec 10.10 them again also out of the land of *E*,
11 and the sceptre of *E* shall depart
14.18 if the family of *E* go not up, and
19 This shall be the punishment of *E*,
Mt 2.13 flee into *E*, and be thou there
14 by night, and departed into *E*:
15 Out of *E* have I called my son.
19 in a dream to Joseph in *E*,
Ac 2.10 in *E*, and in the parts of Libya
7. 9 with envy, sold Joseph into *E*:
10 the sight of Pharaoh king of *E*;
10 he made him governor over *E*
11 came a dearth over all the land of *E*
12 Jacob heard that there was corn in *E*,
15 Jacob went down into *E*, and died,
17 people grew and multiplied in *E*,
34 of my people which is in *E*,
34 now come, I will send thee into *E*.
36 wonders and signs in the land of *E*,
39 hearts turned back again into *E*,
40 brought us out of the land of *E*,
13.17 as strangers in the land of *E*,
Heb 3.16 that came out of *E* by Moses.
8. 9 to lead them out of the land of *E*;
11.26 riches than the treasures in *E*:
27 By faith he forsook *E*, not fearing
Jude 5 the people out of the land of *E*,
Rev 11. 8 spiritually is called Sodom and *E*,

EIGHT

Gen 5. 4 Seth were *e* hundred years:
7 *e* hundred and seven years, and
10 *e* hundred and fifteen years,
13 *e* hundred and forty years,
16 Jared *e* hundred and thirty years,
17 *e* hundred ninety and five years:
19 begat Enoch *e* hundred years, and
17.12 is *e* days old shall be circumcised
21. 4 his son Isaac being *e* days old, as
22.23 these *e* Milcah did bear to Nahor,
Ex 26. 2 shall be *e* and twenty cubits,
25 And they shall be *e* boards, and
36. 9 curtain was twenty and *e* cubits,
30 And there were *e* boards; and
Nu 2.24 and *e* thousand and an hundred,
3.28 *e* thousand and six hundred,
4.48 were *e* thousand and five hundred
7. 8 four wagons and *e* oxen he gave
29.29 on the sixth day *e* bullocks,
35. 7 Levites shall be forty and *e* cities:
Dt 2.14 Zered, was thirty and *e* years;
Jos 21.41 forty and *e* cities with their
Jdg 3. 8 Chushan-rishathaim *e* years.
12.14 and he judged Israel *e* years.
1Sa 4.15 Eli was ninety and *e* years old;
17.12 was Jesse; and he had *e* sons:
2Sa 23. 8 against *e* hundred, whom he slew
24. 9 *e* hundred thousand valiant men
1Ki 7.10 of ten cubits, stones of *e* cubits.
2Ki 8.17 he reigned *e* years in Jerusalem.
10.36 Samaria was twenty and *e* years.
22. 1 Josiah was *e* years old when he
1Ch 12.24 six thousand and *e* hundred,
30 twenty thousand and *e* hundred,
35 and *e* thousand and six hundred.
16.38 their brethren, three score and *e*;
23. 3 man, was thirty and *e* thousand.
24. 4 and *e* among the sons of Ithamar
25. 7 was two hundred fourscore and *e*.
2Ch 11.21 begat twenty and *e* sons, and
13. 3 *e* hundred thousand chosen men,
21. 5 he reigned *e* years in Jerusalem.
20 he reigned in Jerusalem *e* years,
29.17 the house of the Lord in *e* days;
34. 1 Josiah was *e* years old when he
36. 9 Jehoiachin was *e* years old when
Ezr 2. 6 thousand *e* hundred and twelve.
16 Ater of Hezekiah, ninety and *e*.
23 Anathoth, an hundred twenty and *e*.
41 Asaph, an hundred twenty and *e*.
8.11 and with him twenty and *e* males.
Neh 7.11 and *e* hundred and eighteen.
13 Zattu, *e* hundred forty and five.
15 Binnui, six hundred forty and *e*.
16 Bebai, six hundred twenty and *e*.
21 Ater of Hezekiah, ninety and *e*.
22 three hundred twenty and *e*.
26 an hundred fourscore and *e*.
27 an hundred twenty and *e*.
44 of Asaph, an hundred forty and *e*.
45 of Shobai, an hundred thirty and *e*.
11. 6 threescore and *e* valiant men.
8 Sallai, nine hundred twenty and *e*.
12 were *e* hundred twenty and two:
14 of valor an hundred twenty and *e*:
Ec 11. 2 a portion to seven, and also to *e*;
Jer 41.15 escaped from Johanan with *e* men,
52.29 from Jerusalem *e* hundred thirty
Eze 40. 9 he the porch of the gate, *e* cubits;
31, 34, 37 going up to it had *e* steps.
41 *e* tables, whereupon they slew
Mic 5. 5 shepherds, and *e* principal men.
Lk 2.21 when *e* days were accomplished
9.28 an *e* days after these sayings,
Jn 5. 5 an infirmity thirty and *e* years.
20.26 after *e* days again his disciples
Ac 9.33 which had kept his bed *e* years,
1Pe 3.20 is, *e* souls were saved by water.

EIGHTEEN

Gen 14.14 house, three hundred and *e*,
Jdg 3.14 the king of Moab *e* years.
10. 8 children of Israel: *e* years,
20.25 Israel again *e* thousand men;
44 Benjamin *e* thousand men;
2Sa 8.13 salt, being *e* thousand men.
1Ki 7.15 brass, *e* cubits high apiece:
2Ki 24. 8 Jehoiachin was *e* years old
25.17 of one pillar was *e* cubits,
1Ch 12.31 tribe of Manasseh *e* thousand,
18.12 the valley of salt *e* thousand.
26. 9 and brethren, strong men, *e*.
29. 7 of brass *e* thousand talents,
2Ch 11.21 for he took *e* wives, and
Ezr 8. 9 him two hundred and *e* males.
18 his sons and his brethren, *e*;
Neh 7.11 eight hundred and *e*.
Jer 52.21 of one pillar was *e* cubits;
Eze 48.35 about *e* thousand measures;
Lk 13. 4 Or those *e*, upon whom
11 spirit of infirmity *e* years,
16 lo, these *e* years, be

EIGHTH

Ex 22.30 the *e* day thou shalt give it me.
Lev 9. 1 it came to pass on the *e* day,
12. 3 the *e* day the flesh of his foreskin
14.10 *e* day he shall take two he lambs
23 he shall bring them on the *e* day
15.14 *e* day he shall take to him two
29 *e* day she shall take unto her two
22.27 from the *e* day and thenceforth
23.36 *e* day shall be a holy convocation
39 on the *e* day shall be a sabbath.
25.22 ye shall sow the *e* year, and eat
Nu 6.10 *e* day he shall bring two turtles,
7.54 the *e* day offered Gamaliel the son
29.35 On the *e* day ye shall have a
1Ki 6.38 month Bul, which is the *e* month,
8.66 the *e* day he sent the people away:
12.32 ordained a feast in the *e* month,
33 the fifteenth day of the *e* month,
16.29 in the thirty and *e* year of Asa
2Ki 15. 8 the thirty and *e* year of Azariah
24.12 took him in the *e* year of his reign.
1Ch 12.12 Johanan the *e*, Elzabad the
24.10 to Hakkoz, the *e* to Abijah,
25.15 The *e* to Jeshaiah, he, his sons
26. 5 Peulthai the *e*: for God blessed
27.11 The *e* captain for the *e* month
2Ch 7. 9 *e* day they made a solemn assembly:
29.17 and on the *e* day of the month
34. 3 For in the *e* year of his reign,
Neh 8.18 the *e* day was a solemn assembly,
Eze 43.27 upon the *e* day, and so forward,
Zec 1. 1 In the *e* month, in the second year
Lk 1.59 *e* day they came to circumcise
Ac 7. 8 and circumcised him the *e* day;
Php 3. 5 Circumcised the *e* day, of the
2Pe 2. 5 but saved Noah the *e* person,
Rev 17.11 was, and is not, even he is the *e*,
21.20 the *e*, beryl; the ninth, a topaz;

EIGHTY

Gen 5.25 an hundred *e* and seven years,
26 seven hundred *e* and two years,
28 lived an hundred *e* and two years,

EITHER

Gen 31.24 speak not to Jacob *e* good or bad.
29 speak not to Jacob *e* good or bad.

Lev 10. 1 took *e* of them his censer, and
13.49 or in the skin, *e* in the warp, or
51, 53 in the garment, *e* in the warp,
57 still in the garment, *e* in the warp,
58 And the garment, *e* warp, or woof,
59 or linen, *e* in the warp, or woof,
22.23 *E* a bullock or a lamb that hath
25.49 *E* his uncle, or his uncle's son,
Nu 6. 2 *e* man or woman shall separate
22.26 no way to turn *e* to the right hand
24.13 *e* good or bad of mine own mind;
Dt 17. 3 *e* the sun, or moon, or any of
28.51 also shall not leave thee *e* corn,
Jdg 9. 2 *e* that all the sons of Jerubbael,
1Sa 20. 2 will do nothing *e* great or small,
25.31 *e* that thou hast shed blood causeless,
30. 2 slew not any, *e* great or small,
1Ki 7.15 did compass *e* of them about.
10.19 and there were stays on *e* side
18.27 *e* he is talking, or he is pursuing,
1Ch 21.12 *E* three years' famine; or three
2Ch 18. 9 king of Judah sat *e* of them on
Ec 9. 1 man knoweth *e* love or hatred
11. 6 not whether shall prosper, *e* this
Isa 7.11 ask it *e* in the depth, or in the
17. 8 *e* the groves, or the images.
Eze 21.16 one way or other, *e* on the right
Mt 6.24 for *e* he will hate the one, and
12.33 *E* make the tree good, and his
Lk 6.42 *E* how canst thou say to thy
15. 8 *E* what woman having ten pieces
16.13 two masters: for *e* he will hate
Jn 19.18 on *e* side one, and Jesus in
Ac 17.21 but *e* to tell, or to hear some
1Co 14. 6 shall speak to you *e* by revelation,
Php 3.12 attained, *e* were already perfect:
Jas 3.12 bear olive berries? *e* a vine, figs?
Rev 22. 2 and on *e* side of the river,

ELAM

Gen 10.22 children of Shem; *E*, and Ashur,
14. 1 Chedorlaomer king of *E*, and
9 With Chedorlaomer the king of *E*,
1Ch 1.17 The sons of Shem; *E*, and Asshur,
8.24 Hananiah, and *E*, and Antothijah,
26. 3 *E* the fifth, Jehohanan the sixth,
Ezr 2. 7 The children of *E*, a thousand two
31 The children of the other *E*,
8. 7 And of the sons of *E*; Jeshaiah
10. 2 son of Jehiel, one of the sons of *E*,
26 sons of *E*; Mattaniah, Zechariah,
Neh 7.12 children of *E*, a thousand two
34 The children of the other *E*,
10.14 people; Parosh, Pahath-moab, *E*,
12.42 and Malchijah, and *E*, and Ezer.
Isa 11.11 and from Cush, and from *E*, and
21. 2 Go up, O *E*: besiege, O Media;
22. 6 *E* bare the quiver with chariots
Jer 25.25 and all the kings of *E*, and all the
49.34 Jeremiah the prophet against *E*,
35 Behold, I will break the bow of *E*,
36 upon *E* will I bring the four winds
36 the outcasts of *E* shall not come.
37 For I will cause *E* to be dismayed
38 And I will set my throne in *E*, and
39 bring again the captivity of *E*,
Eze 32.24 is *E* and all her multitude round
Dan 8. 2 which is in the province of *E*;

ELAMITES

Ezr 4. 9 the Dehavites, and the *E*,
Ac 2. 9 Parthians, and Medes, and *E*,

ELDER

Gen 10.21 the brother of Japheth the *e*,
25.23 and the *e* shall serve the younger.
27.42 these words of Esau her *e* son
29.16 the name of the *e* was Leah,
1Sa 18.17 Behold my *e* daughter Merab,
1Ki 2.22 for he is mine *e* brother;
Job 15.10 men, much *e* than thy father.
32. 4 because they were *e* than he.
Eze 16.46 thine *e* sister is Samaria, she and
61 sisters, thine *e* and thy younger:
23. 4 names of them were Aholah the *e*,
Lk 15.25 Now his *e* son was in the field:
Ro 9.12 The *e* shall serve the younger.
1Ti 5. 1 Rebuke not an *e*, but entreat him
2 *e* women as mothers; the younger
19 an *e* receive not an accusation,
1Pe 5. 1 I exhort, who am also an *e*,
5 submit yourselves unto the *e*.
2Jn 1 The *e* unto the elect lady and her
3Jn 1 The *e* unto the well beloved Gaius,

ELDERS

Gen 50. 7 of Pharaoh, the *e* of his house,
7 all the *e* of the land of Egypt,
Ex 3.16 Go, and gather the *e* of Israel
18 come, thou and the *e* of Israel,
4.29 gathered together all the *e* of the
12.21 Moses called for all the *e* of Israel,
17. 5 take with thee of the *e* of Israel;
6 did so in the sight of the *e* of
18.12 Aaron came, all the *e* of Israel,
19. 7 called for the *e* of the people,
24. 1 seventy of the *e* of Israel; and
9 and seventy of the *e* of Israel:
14 he said unto the *e*, Tarry ye here
Lev 4.15 the *e* of the congregation shall
9. 1 and his sons, and the *e* of Israel;
Nu 11.16 seventy men of the *e* of Israel,
16 knowest to be the *e* of the people,
24 seventy men of the *e* of the people,
25 and gave it unto the seventy *e*:
30 the camp, he and the *e* of Israel.
16.25 and the *e* of Israel followed him.
22. 4 Moab said unto the *e* of Midian,
7 And the *e* of Moab and the
7 and the *e* Midian departed
Dt 5.23 heads of your tribes, and your *e*;
19.12 Then the *e* of his city shall send
21. 2 thy *e* and thy judges shall come
3 *e* of that city shall take an heifer,
4 And the *e* of that city shall bring
6 And all the *e* of that city,
19 him out unto the *e* of his city,
20 shall say unto the *e* of his city,
22.15 virginity unto the *e* of the city
16 damsel's father shall say unto the *e*,
17 the cloth before the *e* of the city.
18 And the *e* of that city shall take
25. 7 go up to the gate unto the *e*,
8 the *e* of his city shall call him,
9 unto him in the presence of the *e*,
27. 1 with the *e* of Israel commanded
29.10 your *e*, and your officers, with all
31. 9 and unto all the *e* of Israel.
28 Gather unto me all the *e* of your
32. 7 thy *e*, and they will tell thee.
Jos 7. 6 eventide, he and the *e* of Israel,
8.10 he and the *e* of Israel, before the
33 all Israel, and their *e*, and officers,
9.11 our *e* and all the inhabitants
20. 4 his cause in the ears of the *e* of
23. 2 for their *e*, and for their heads,
24. 1 and called for the *e* of Israel,
31 days of the *e* that overlived Joshua,
Jdg 2. 7 days of the *e* that outlived Joshua,
8.14 and the *e* thereof, even three score
16 And he took the *e* of the city,
11. 5 the *e* of Gilead went to fetch
7 Jephthah said unto the *e* of Gilead,
8 *e* of Gilead said unto Jephthah,
9 Jephthah said unto the *e* of Gilead,
10 the *e* of Gilead said unto Jephthah,
11 Jephthah went with the *e* of Gilead,
21.16 the *e* of the congregation said,
Ru 4. 2 took ten men of the *e* of the city.
4 and before the *e* of my people.
9 And Boaz said unto the *e*,
11 and the *e*, said, We are witnesses.
1Sa 4. 3 the *e* of Israel said, Wherefore
8. 4 Then all the *e* of Israel gathered
11. 3 the *e* of Jabesh said unto him,
15.30 thee, before the *e* of my people,
16. 4 the *e* of the town trembled at his
30.26 he sent of the spoil unto the *e* of
2Sa 3.17 communication with the *e* of
5. 3 the *e* of Israel came to the king
12.17 the *e* of his house arose, and went
17. 4 Absalom well, and all the *e* of
15 Absalom and the *e* of Israel;
19.11 Speak unto the *e* of Judah, saying,
1Ki 8. 1 Solomon assembled the *e* of Israel,
3 And all the *e* of Israel came,
20. 7 king of Israel called all the *e* of
8 And all the *e* and all the people
21. 8 and sent the letters unto the *e* and
11 even the *e* and the nobles who were
2Ki 6.32 and the *e* sat with him;
32 came to him, he said to the *e*,
10. 1 unto the rulers of Jezreel, to the *e*,
5 the *e* also, and the bringers up
19. 2 and the *e* of the priests, covered
23. 1 gathered unto him all the *e* of
1Ch 11. 3 Therefore came all the *e* of Israel,
15.25 So David and the *e* of Israel,
21.16 Then David and the *e* of Israel,
2Ch 5. 2 Then Solomon assembled the *e* of
4 And all the *e* of Israel came;
34.29 gathered together all the *e* of
Ezr 5. 5 of their God was upon the *e* of
9 Then asked we those *e*, and said
6. 7 and the *e* of the Jews build this
8 what ye shall do to the *e* of these
14 And the *e* of the Jews builded,
10. 8 counsel of the princes and the *e*,
14 with them the *e* of every city,
Ps 107.32 praise him in the assembly of the *e*.
Pr 31.23 when he sitteth among the *e* of the
Isa 37. 2 and the *e* of the priests covered
Jer 26.17 Then rose up certain of the *e* of
29. 1 Jerusalem unto the residue of the *e*
La 1.19 my priests and mine *e* gave up the
2.10 The *e* of the daughter of Zion
4.16 priests, they favored not the *e*.
5.12 the faces of *e* were not honored.
14 The *e* have ceased from the gate,
Eze 8. 1 and the *e* of Judah sat before me,
14. 1 Then came certain of the *e* of
20. 1 certain of the *e* of Israel came to
3 of man speak unto the *e* of Israel,
Joel 1.14 assembly, gather the *e* and all the
2.16 congregation, assemble the *e*,
Mt 15. 2 transgress the tradition of the *e*?
16.21 suffer many things of the *e* and
21.23 and the *e* of the people came unto
26. 3 scribes, and the *e* of the people,
47 chief priests and *e* of the people.
57 scribes and the *e* were assembled.
59 the chief priests, and *e*, and all
27. 1 chief priests and *e* of the people
3 silver to the chief priests and *e*,
12 accused of the chief priests and *e*,
20 the chief priests and *e* persuaded
41 with the scribes and *e*, said,
28.12 they were assembled with the *e*,
Mk 7. 3 holding the tradition of the *e*.
5 according to the tradition of the *e*,
8.31 and be rejected of the *e*, and of the
11.27 priests, and the scribes, and the *e*,
14.43 priests and the scribes and the *e*.
53 priests and the *e* and the scribes.
15. 1 with the *e* and scribes and the
Lk 7. 3 he sent unto him the *e* of the Jews,
9.22 and be rejected of the *e* and chief
20. 1 scribes came upon him with the *e*,
22.52 captains of the temple, and the *e*,
66 the *e* of the people and the chief
Ac 4. 5 that their rulers, and *e*, and
8 of the people, and *e* of Israel,
23 chief priests and *e* had said unto

6.12 the people, and the *e*, and the
11.30 and sent it to the *e* by the hands
14.23 ordained them *e* in every church,
15. 2 unto the apostles and *e* about this
4 and of the apostles and *e*, and they
6 And the apostles and *e* came
22 Then pleased it the apostles and *e*,
23 The apostles and *e* and brethren
16. 4 were ordained of the apostles and *e*
20.17 and called the *e* of the church.
21.18 and all the *e* were present.
22. 5 and all the estate of the *e*:
23.14 came to the chief priests and *e*,
24. 1 high priest descended with the *e*,
25.15 the chief priests and the *e* of the
1Ti 5.17 Let the *e* that rule well be counted
Tit 1. 5 ordain *e* in every city, as I had
Heb 11. 2 For by it the *e* obtained a good
Jas 5.14 let him call for the *e* of the church;
1Pe 5. 1 The *e* which are among you I
Rev 4. 4 I saw four and twenty *e* sitting,
10 The four and twenty *e* fall down
5. 5 And one of the *e* saith unto me,
6 and in the midst of the *e*,
8 and four and twenty *e* fell down
11 and the beasts and the *e*:
14 the four and twenty *e* fell down
7.11 and about the *e* and the four beasts,
13 And one of the *e* answered, saying
11.16 the four and twenty *e*, which sat
14. 3 before the four beasts, and the *e*:
19. 4 the four and twenty *e* and the four

ELDEST
Gen 24. 2 Abraham said unto his *e* servant
27. 1 he called Esau his *e* son, and
15 took goodly raiment of her *e* son
44.12 began at the *e*, and left at the
Nu 1.20 children of Reuben, Israel's *e* son,
26. 5 Reuben, the *e* son of Israel: the
1Sa 17.13 And the three *e* sons of Jesse
14 and the three *e* followed Saul.
28 Eliab his *e* brother heard when he
2Ki 3.27 Then he took his *e* son that
2Ch 22. 1 of men...had slain all the *e*.
Job 1.13, 18 wine in their *e* brother's
Jn 8. 9 beginning at the *e*, even unto the

ELECT
Isa 42. 1 *e*, in whom my soul delighteth;
45. 4 sake, and Israel mine *e*,
65. 9 mine *e* shall inherit it, and my
22 mine *e* shall long enjoy the work
Mt 24.24 they shall deceive the very *e*.
31 and shall gather together his *e*
Mk 13.22 if it were possible, even the *e*.
27 and shall gather together his *e*
Lk 18. 7 shall not God avenge his own *e*,
Ro 8.33 any thing to the charge of God's *e*?
Col 3.12 Put on therefore, as the *e* of God,
1Ti 5.21 Lord Jesus Christ, and the *e* angels,
Tit 1. 1 according to the faith of God's *e*,
1Pe 1. 2 *E* according to the foreknowledge
2. 6 a chief corner stone, *e*, precious:
2Jn 1 The elder unto the *e* lady and her
13 The children of thy *e* sister greet

ELECTED
1Pe 5.13 *e* together with you, saluteth you;

ELECTION
Ro 9.11 the purpose of God according to *e*
11. 5 according to the *e* of grace.
7 the *e* hath obtained it, and the rest
28 as touching the *e*, they are beloved
1Th 1. 4 brethren beloved, your *e* of God.
2Pe 1.10 make your calling and *e* sure:

ELECT'S
Mt 24.22 for the *e* sake those days shall be
Mk 13.20 for the *e* sake, whom he hath
2Ti 2.10 endure all things for the *e* sakes,

ELEMENTS
Gal 4. 3 in bondage under the *e* of the
9 to the weak and beggarly *e*,
2Pe 3.10 the *e* shall melt with fervent heat,
12 the *e* shall melt with fervent heat?

ELEVEN
Gen 32.22 took....his *e* sons, and passed
37. 9 and the moon and the *e* stars
Ex 26. 7 *e* curtains shalt thou make.
8 *e* curtains shall be all of one
36.14 *e* curtains he made them.
15 the *e* curtains were of one
Nu 29.20 on the third day *e* bullocks,
Dt 1. 2 *e* days' journey from Horeb
Jos 15.51 *e* cities with their villages.
Jdg 16. 5 one of us *e* hundred pieces of
17. 2 *e* hundred shekels of silver
3 restored the *e* hundred shekels
2Ki 23.36 reign; and he reigned *e* years
24.18 reign, and he reigned *e* years
2Ch 36. 5, 11 and he reigned *e* years in
Jer 52. 1 reigned *e* years in Jerusalem.
Eze 40.49 and the breadth *e* cubits;
Mt 28.16 Then the *e* disciples went away
Mk 16.14 he appeared unto the *e* as they
Lk 24. 9 told all these things unto the *e*,
33 found the *e* gathered together,
Ac 1.26 was numbered with the *e* apostles.
2.14 Peter, standing up with the *e*,

ELEVENTH
Nu 7.72 the *e* day Pagiel...offered:
Dt 1. 3 in the fortieth year, in the *e*
1Ki 6.38 in the *e* year, in the month
2Ki 9.29 in the *e* year of Joram the
25. 2 the *e* year of king Zedekiah.
1Ch 12.13 the tenth, Machbanai the *e*.
24.12 The *e* to Eliashib, the twelfth
25.18 The *e* to Azareel, he, his sons,
27.14 The *e* captain for the *e* month
Jer 1. 3 of the *e* year of Zedekiah the
39. 2 in the *e* year of Zedekiah, in
52. 5 was besieged unto the *e* year
Eze 26. 1 in the *e* year, in the first day
30.20 came to pass in the *e* year,
31. 1 the *e* year, in the third month,
Zec 1. 7 twentieth day of...*e* month,
Mt 20. 6 about the *e* hour he went out,
9 that were hired about the *e* hour,
Rev 21.20 the *e*, a jacinth; the twelfth, an

ELI
1Sa 1. 3 sons of *E*, Hophni and Phinehas,
3. 6 And Samuel arose and went to *E*,
8 And *E* perceived that the Lord had
9 *E* said unto Samuel, Go, lie down:
15 Samuel feared to show *E* the vision.
Mt 27.46 *E*, *E*, lama sabachthani? that is

ELIAKIM
2Ki 18.18 there came out to them *E* the son
26 Then said *E* the son of Hilkiah,
37 Then came *E* the son of Hilkiah,
19. 2 And he sent *E*, which was over the
23.34 Pharaoh-nechoh made *E* the son of
2Ch 36. 4 of Egypt made *E* his brother king
Neh 12.41 the priests; *E*, Maaseiah, Miniamin,
Isa 22.20 I will call my servant *E* the son of
36. 3 Then came forth unto him *E*,
11 Then said *E*, and Shebna and Joah
22 Then came *E*, the son of Hilkiah,
37. 2 And he sent *E*, who was over the
Mt 1.13 Abiud begat *E*; and *E* begat Azor;
Lk 3.30 Jonan, which was the son of *E*,

ELIAS
Mt 11.14 is Elias, which was for to come.
16.14 some, *E*; and others, Jeremias,
17. 3 Moses and *E* talking with him.
4 and one for Moses, and one for *E*.
10 scribes that *E* must first come?
11 *E* truly shall first come, and
12 unto you, That *E* is come already,
27.47 This man calleth for *E*.
49 whether *E* will come to save him.
Mk 6.15 Others said, That it is *E*.
8.28 but some say, *E*; and others,
9. 4 unto them *E* with Moses:
5 and one for Moses, and one for *E*.
11 that *E* must first come?
12 *E* verily cometh first, and
13 unto you, That *E* is indeed come,
15.35 Behold, he calleth *E*.
36 whether *E* will come to take him
Lk 1.17 in the spirit and power of *E*,
4.25 were in Israel in the days of *E*,
26 But unto none of them was *E*
9. 8 of some, that *E* had appeared;
19 but some say, *E*; and others say,
30 men, which were Moses and *E*:
33 and one for Moses, and one for *E*:
54 consume them, even as *E* did?
Jn 1.21 What then? Art thou *E*? And he
25 nor *E*, neither that prophet?
Ro 11. 2 what the scripture saith of *E*?
Jas 5.17 *E* was a man subject to like

ELIJAH
1Ki 17. 1 *E* the Tishbite, who was of the
13 *E* said unto her, Fear not; go and
15 did according to the saying of *E*:
16 of the Lord, which he spake by *E*.
18 she said unto *E*, What have I to do
22 the Lord heard the voice of *E*; and
23 *E* took the child, and brought him
23 and *E* said, See thy son liveth.
24 the woman said to *E*, Now by this
18. 1 Lord came to *E* in the third year,
2 *E* went to shew himself unto Ahab.
7 was in the way, behold, *E* met him:
7 Art thou that my lord *E*?
8 go, tell thy lord, Behold, *E* is here.
11 Go, tell thy lord, Behold, *E* is here.
14 Go, tell thy lord, Behold, *E* is here:
15 *E* said, As the Lord of hosts liveth,
16 and Ahab went to meet *E*.
17 it came to pass, when Ahab saw *E*,
21 *E* came unto all the people, and
22 Then said *E* unto the people, I,
25 *E* said unto the prophets of Baal,
27 *E* mocked them, and said, Cry
30 *E* said unto all the people, Come
31 *E* took twelve stones, according to
36 *E* the prophet came near, and said,
40 And *E* said unto them, Take the
40 *E* brought them down to the brook
41 *E* said unto Ahab, Get thee up, eat
42 *E* went up to the top of Carmel;

ELI

Priest at the temple in Shiloh, 11th century B.C.; blesses Hannah, the childless wife of Elkanah, when he sees her at the temple praying for a son; she conceives, and later the child, Samuel, serves under Eli (1Sa 1); fails to discipline his sons Hophni and Phinehas for their outrageous behavior while serving as priests, and as a result doom is prophesied upon his house (1Sa 2); directs Samuel to respond to the voice of God calling him, and resigns himself to the word of divine judgment (1Sa 3); his sons accompany the ark of God into battle against the Philistines; Israel is defeated, his sons killed, and the ark captured; the news causes his death; had also judged Israel for forty years (1Sa 4).

Elijah goes to heaven in a whirlwind and a chariot of fire, witnessed by his successor, Elisha (2Ki 2).

1Ki 18.46 the hand of the Lord was on *E*;
19. 1 told Jezebel all that *E* had done,
2 Jezebel sent a messenger unto *E*,
9 unto him, What doest thou here, *E*?
13 it was so, when *E* heard it, that he
13 and said, What doest thou here, *E*?
19 and *E* passed by him, and cast his
20 he left the oxen, and ran after *E*,
21 Then he arose, and went after *E*,
21.17 the Lord came to *E* the Tishbite,
20 Ahab said to *E*, Hast thou found
28 word of the Lord came to *E* the
2Ki 1. 3 said to *E* the Tishbite, Arise, go up
4 shalt surely die. And *E* departed.
8 And he said, It is *E* the Tishbite.
10 *E* answered and said to the captain
12 *E* answered and said unto them,
13 came and fell on his knees before *E*,
15 the angel of the Lord said unto *E*,
17 of the Lord which *E* had spoken.
2. 1 Lord would take up *E* into heaven
1 *E* went with Elisha from Gilgal.
2 *E* said unto Elisha, Tarry here, I
4 *E* said unto him, Elisha, tarry here,
6 *E* said unto him, Tarry, I pray thee,
8 *E* took his mantle, and wrapped it
9 *E* said unto Elisha, Ask what I
11 *E* went up by a whirlwind into
13 He took up also the mantle of *E*
14 And he took the mantle of *E* that
14 Where is the Lord God of *E*?
15 The spirit of *E* doth rest on Elisha.
3.11 poured water on the hand of *E*.
9.36 which he spake by his servant *E* the
10.10 which he spake by his servant *E*.
17 of the Lord, which he spake to *E*.
2Ch 21.12 there came a writing to him from *E*
Ezr 10.21 Maaseiah, and *E*, and Shemaiah,
Mal 4. 5 I will send you *E* the prophet

ELIZABETH

Lk 1. 5 of Aaron, and her name was *E*.
7 child because that *E* was barren,
13 thy wife *E* shall bear thee a son,
24 those days his wife *E* conceived,
36 behold, thy cousin *E*, she hath also
40 house of Zacharias, and saluted *E*.
41 *E* heard the salutation of Mary,
41 *E* was filled with the Holy Ghost:

ELISABETH'S

Lk 1.57 Now *E* full time came that she

ELISEUS

Lk 4.27 in the time of *E* the prophet;

ELISHA

1Ki 19.16 *E* the son Shaphat of Abel-meholah
17 from the sword of Jehu shall *E* slay.
19 he departed thence, and found *E*
2Ki 2. 1 Elijah went with *E* from Gilgal.
2 Elijah said unto *E*, Tarry here,
2 *E* said unto him, As the Lord
3 were at Beth-el came forth to *E*,
4 Elijah said unto him, *E*, tarry here,
5 that were at Jericho came to *E*,
9 Elijah said unto *E*, Ask what I
9 *E* said, I pray thee, let a double
12 *E* saw it, and he cried, My father,
14 and thither: and *E* went over.
15 The spirit of Elijah doth rest on *E*.
19 the men of the city said unto *E*,
22 to the saying of *E* which he spake.
3.11 Here is *E* the son of Shaphat,
13 *E* said unto the king of Israel, What
14 *E* said, As the Lord of hosts liveth,
4. 1 of the sons of the prophets unto *E*,
2 *E* said unto her, What shall I do
8 on a day, that *E* passed to Shunem,
17 season that *E* had said unto her,
32 when *E* was come into the house,
38 *E* came again to Gilgal: and there
5. 8 when *E* the man of God had heard
9 stood at the door of the house of *E*.
10 *E* sent a messenger unto him,
20 Gehazi, the servant of *E* the man
25 *E* said unto him, Whence comest
6. 1 sons of the prophets said unto *E*,
12 but *E*, the prophet that is in Israel,
17 *E* prayed, and said, Lord, I pray
17 and chariots of fire round about *E*.
18 *E* prayed unto the Lord, and said,
18 according to the word of *E*.
19 *E* said unto them, This is not the
20 *E* said, Lord, open the eyes of these
21 the king of Israel said unto *E*,
31 the head of *E* the son of Shaphat
32 *E* sat in his house, and the elders
7. 1 *E* said, Hear ye the word of the Lord;
8. 1 Then spake *E* unto the woman,
4 the great things that *E* hath done.
5 is her son, whom *E* restored to life.
7 And *E* came to Damascus; and
10 *E* said unto him, Go, say unto him,
13 *E* answered, The Lord hath shewed
14 So he departed from *E*, and came
14 said to him, What said *E* to thee?
9. 1 *E* the prophet called one of the
13.14 *E* was fallen sick of his sickness
15 *E* said unto him, Take bow and
16 *E* put his hands upon the king's
17 Then *E* said, Shoot. And he shot.
20 And *E* died, and they buried him.
21 the man into the sepulchre of *E*:
21 down, and touched the bones of *E*,

ELOI

Mk 15.34 *E*, *E*, lama sabacthani?

ELOQUENT

Ex 4.10 O my Lord, I am not *e*,
Isa 3. 3 artificer, and the *e* orator.
Ac 18.24 an *e* man, and mighty in the

ELYMAS

Ac 13. 8 But *E* the sorcerer (for so is his

EMBALM

Gen 50. 2 the physicians to *e* his father:

EMBALMED

Gen 50. 2 and the physicians *e* Israel.
3 the days of those which are *e*:
26 and they *e* him, and he was put in

EMBOLDENED

1Co 8.10 of him which is weak be *e* to eat

EMBOLDENETH

Job 16. 3 what *e* thee that thou answerest?

EMBRACE

2Ki 4.16 time of life, thou shalt *e* a son.
Job 24. 8 *e* the rock for want of a shelter.
Pr 4. 8 to honor when thou dost *e* her.
5.20 and *e* the bosom of a stranger?
Ec 3. 5 a time to *e*, and a time to refrain
SS 2. 6 and his right hand doth *e* me.
8. 3 and his right hand should *e* me.
La 4. 5 that were brought up in scarlet *e*

EMBRACED

Gen 29.13 he ran to meet him, and *e* him,
33. 4 Esau ran to meet him, and *e* him,
48.10 he kissed them, and *e* them.
Ac 20. 1 unto him the disciples, and *e*
He 11.13 *e* them, and confessed that they

ELIJAH

A prophet from Gilead, 9th century B.C.; fierce opponent of Baal worship permitted in northern Israel by King Ahab and his wife Jezebel; appears before Ahab and predicts a long drought; is miraculously sustained by ravens at the brook Cherith and then by a widow at Zarephath, whose kindness is rewarded by a never-depleting barrel of meal and cruse of oil; restores her son to life (1Ki 17); meets Ahab and challenges the prophets of Baal to a contest on Mount Carmel; despite frenzied prayers, their offering is not consumed; his is spectacularly consumed by divine fire, and the people acknowledge that the Lord is the true God; directs the false prophets to be put to death (1Ki 18); learns that Jezebel seeks his life and flees into the wilderness, where he prays for death; sustained by an angel, he journeys to Mount Horeb (Sinai) and God appears to him in "a still small voice"; is encouraged, and on his return is joined by Elisha (1Ki 19); rebukes Ahab for letting Jezebel engineer the death of Naboth to seize his coveted vineyard, and prophesies the fall of Ahab's house (1Ki 21); calls down fire from heaven on the messengers of Ahaziah, Ahab's son, and announces that the new king will die from his illness (2Ki 1); divides the Jordan and is taken up to heaven in a whirlwind; succeeded by Elisha, who inherits his mantle of prophetic authority (2Ki 2); his return to earth predicted by later prophets as a signal of the coming Day of the Lord (Mal 4); also frequently mentioned in the Gospels (as "Elias") as a precursor of the Last Days (Mt 14, 17; Mk 9; Lk 1, 9; Jn 1).

EMBRACING
Ec 3. 5 a time to refrain from *e*;
Ac 20.10 and fell on him, and *e* him said,

EMERALD
Ex 28.18 And the second row shall be an *e*,
39.11 an *e*, a sapphire, and a diamond.
Eze 28.13 sapphire, the *e*, and the carbuncle,
Rev 4. 3 in sight like unto an *e*.
21.19 a chalcedony; the fourth, an *e*;

EMMANUEL
Mt 1.23 they shall call his name *E*,

EMMAUS
Lk 24.13 to a village called *E*, which was

EMPTY
Gen 31.42 thou hadst sent me away now *e*.
37.24 the pit was *e*; there was no water
41.27 the seven *e* ears blasted with the
Ex 3.21 when ye go, ye shall not go *e*:
23.15 and none shall appear before me *e*:)
34.20 And none shall appear before me *e*.
Lev 14.36 command that they *e* the house,
Dt 15.13 thou shalt not let him go away *e*:
16.16 shall not appear before the Lord *e*:
Jdg 7.16 *e* pitchers, and lamps within the
Ru 1.21 hath brought me home again *e*;
3.17 Go not *e* unto thy mother in law.
1Sa 6. 3 send it not *e*; but in any wise
20.18 missed because thy seat will be *e*.
25 side, and David's place was *e*.
27 that David's place was *e*: and Saul
2Sa 1.22 the sword of Saul returned not *e*.
2Ki 4. 3 borrow thee vessels...*e* vessels;
Job 22. 9 Thou hast sent widows away *e*,
26. 7 out the north over the *e* place,
Ec 11. 3 they *e* themselves upon the earth:
Isa 24. 1 the Lord maketh the earth *e*.
29. 8 he awaketh, and his soul is *e*:
32. 6 to make *e* the soul of the hungry,
Jer 14. 3 returned with their vessels *e*;
48.12 shall *e* his vessels, and break
51. 2 shall fan her, and shall *e* her land:
34 he hath made me an *e* vessel,
Eze 24.11 set it *e* upon the coals thereof.
Hos 10. 1 Israel is an *e* vine, he bringeth
Na 2.10 She is *e*, and void, and waste:
Hab 1.17 Shall they therefore *e* their net,
Zec 4.12 through the two golden pipes *e*
Mt 12.44 he findeth it *e*, swept, and
Mk 12. 3 beat him, and sent him away *e*.
Lk 1.53 the rich he hath sent *e* away.
20.10 beat him, and sent him away *e*.
11 shamefully, and sent him away *e*.

EMULATION
Ro 11.14 I may provoke to *e* them which

EMULATIONS
Gal 5.20 hatred, variance, *e*, wrath, strife,

ENABLED
1Ti 1.12 Jesus our Lord, who hath *e* me,

ENCAMP
Ex 14. 2 turn and *e* before Pi-hahiroth,
2 before it shall ye *e* by the sea.
Nu 1.50 shall minister unto it, and shall *e*
2.17 as they *e*, so shall they set forward,
27 And those that *e* by him shall be
3.38 But those that *e* before the
10.31 how we are to *e* in the wilderness,
2Sa 12.28 and *e* against the city, and take it:
Job 19.12 and *e* round about my tabernacle.
Ps 27. 3 Though an host should *e* against
Zec 9. 8 And I will *e* about mine house

ENCOUNTERED
Ac 17.18 and of the Stoicks, *e* him.

ELISHA

Prophet in the northern kingdom and successor of Elijah, 9th century B.C.; is called by Elijah and becomes his disciple (1Ki 19); like his mentor, is credited with miraculous deeds: purifies the spring waters at Jericho (2Ki 2); multiplies a widow's oil; promises a generous Shunammite woman the birth of a son; later restores the boy to life; feeds a hundred men from a small supply of bread and corn (2Ki 4); cures Naaman of his leprosy (2Ki 5); also plays a role in political and military affairs: reveals the secret counsel of the Syrians to the king of Israel; when Samaria is besieged and gripped by famine, promises liberation and a plentiful supply of food (2Ki 6–7); encourages Hazael's bloody accession to the Syrian throne and foresees his cruelty against Israel (2Ki 8); commissions the anointing of Jehu as king of Israel and encourages him to annihilate the house of Ahab (2Ki 9); predicts that Joash will enjoy three victories over Syria; after his death, Elisha's bones miraculously restore a corpse to life (2Ki 13).

END
Gen 6.13 The *e* of all flesh is come before
8. 3 after the *e* of the hundred and
6 came to pass at the *e* of forty days,
23. 9 which is in the *e* of his field;
27.30 as Isaac had made an *e* of blessing
41. 1 it came to pass at the *e* of two full
47.21 from one *e* of the borders of Egypt
21 even to the other *e* thereof.
49.33 And when Jacob had made an *e* of
Ex 8.22 to the *e* thou mayest know that I
12.41 at the *e* of the four hundred and
23.16 in the *e* of the year, when thou
25.19 one cherub on the one *e*, and the
19 the other cherub on the other *e*:
26.28 the boards shall reach from *e* to *e*.
31.18 choses, when he had made an *e* of
34.22 of ingathering at the year's *e*.
36.33 the boards from the one *e* to the
37. 8 One cherub on the *e* on this side,
8 and another cherub on the other *e*
Lev 8.33 of your consecration be at an *e*:
16.20 hath made an *e* of reconciling
17. 5 To the *e* that the children of
Nu 4.15 have made an *e* of covering
16.31 as he had made an *e* of speaking
23.10 and let my last *e* be like his!
24.20 but his latter *e* shall be that he perish
Dt 8.16 to do thee good at thy latter *e*;
9.11 at the *e* of forty days and forty
11.12 even unto the *e* of the year.
13. 7 from the one *e* of the earth even
7 even unto the other *e* of the earth;
14.28 At the *e* of three years thou shalt
15. 1 At the *e* of every seven years thou
17.16 to the *e* that he should multiply
20 to the *e* that he may prolong his
20. 9 officers have made an *e* speaking
26.12 thou hast made an *e* of tithing all
28.49 from the *e* of the earth, as swift
64 from the one *e* of the earth even
31.10 At the *e* of every seven years,
24 Moses had made an *e* of writing
32.20 I will see what their *e* shall be:
29 they would consider their latter *e*!
45 And Moses made an *e* of speaking
Jos 8.24 Israel had made an *e* of slaying
9.16 to pass at the *e* of three days
10.20 Israel had made an *e* of slaying
15. 5 sea, even unto the *e* of Jordan.
8 at the *e* of the valley of the giants
18.15 from the *e* of Kirjath-jearim,
16 down to the *e* of the mountain
19 salt sea at the south *e* of Jordan:
19.49 they had made an *e* of dividing
51 So they made an *e* of dividing the
Jdg 3.18 when he had made an *e* to offer
6.21 Lord put forth the *e* of the staff
11.39 to pass at the *e* of two months,
15.17 he had made an *e* of speaking,
19. 9 behold, the day groweth to an *e*,
Ru 2.23 unto the *e* of barley harvest and
3. 7 at the *e* of the heap of corn:
10 more kindness at the latter *e* than
1Sa 3.12 I begin, I will also make an *e*.
9.27 going down to the *e* of the city,
10.13 he had made an *e* of prophesying,
13.10 as he had made an *e* of offering
14.27 he put forth the *e* of the rod
43 a little honey with the *e* of the rod
18. 1 he had made an *e* of speaking
24.16 David had made an *e* of speaking
2Sa 2.23 Abner with the hinder *e* of the spear
26 it will be bitterness in the latter *e*?
6.18 David had made an *e* of offering
11.19 thou hast made an *e* of telling
13.36 as he had made an *e* of speaking,
14.26 every year's *e* that he polled it:
24. 8 at the *e* of nine months and twenty
1Ki 1.41 as they had made an *e* of eating.
2.39 to pass at the *e* of three years,
3. 1 he had made an *e* of building
7.40 So Hiram made an *e* of doing all
8.54 Solomon had made an *e* of praying
9.10 to pass at the *e* of twenty years,
2Ki 8. 3 came to pass at the seven years' *e*,
10.21 of Baal was full from one *e* to
25 as he had made an *e* of offering
18.10 at the *e* of three years they took it:
21.16 Jerusalem from one *e* to another;
1Ch 16. 2 David had made an *e* of offering
2Ch 4.10 sea on the right side of the east *e*,
5.12 stood at the east *e* of the altar,
7. 1 Solomon had made an *e* of praying,
8. 1 to pass at the *e* of twenty years,
20.16 find them at the *e* of the brook,
23 had made an *e* of the inhabitants
21.19 of time, after the *e* of two years,
24.10 chest, until they had made an *e*.
23 came to pass at the *e* of the year,
29.17 sixteenth day...they made an *e*.
29 they had made an *e* of offering,
Ezr 9.11 filled it from one *e* to another
10.17 they made an *e* with all the men
Neh 3.21 to the *e* of the house of Eliashib.
4. 2 will they make an *e* in a day?
Job 6.11 and what is mine *e*, that I should
8. 7 thy latter *e* should greatly increase.
16. 3 Shall vain words have an *e*?
18. 2 ere ye make an *e* of words?
26.10 the day and night come to an *e*.
28. 3 He setteth an *e* to darkness,
34.36 that Job may be tried unto the *e*
42.12 the Lord blessed the latter *e* of Job
Ps 7. 9 of the wicked come to an *e*;
9. 6 are come to a perpetual *e*:
19. 4 their words to the *e* of the world.
6 forth is from the *e* of the heaven,
30.12 To the *e* that my glory may sing
37.37 for the *e* of that man is peace.
38 *e* of the wicked shall be cut off.
39. 4 Lord, make me to know mine *e*,
46. 9 to cease unto the *e* of the earth;
61. 2 From the *e* of the earth will I cry
73.17 God; then understood I their *e*.
102.27 and thy years shall have no *e*.
107.27 man, and are at their wit's *e*.
119.33 I shall keep it unto the *e*.

Enchantments-Lev. 19:26-30
Deuteronomy 18:9-14 see also Divinations, soothsaying, observing of times.

Ps 119.96 have seen an *e* of all perfection:
112 statutes alway, even unto the *e*.
Pr 5. 4 But her *e* is bitter as wormwood,
14.12 *e* thereof are the ways of death.
13 the *e* of that mirth is heaviness.
16.25 the *e* thereof are the ways of death.
19.20 thou mayest be wise in thy latter *e*.
20.21 the *e* thereof shall not be blessed.
23.18 For surely there is an *e*; and
25. 8 what to do in the *e* thereof,
Ec 3.11 from the beginning to the *e*.
4. 8 yet is there no *e* of all his labor;
16 There is no *e* of all the people,
7. 2 for that is the *e* of all men;
8 Better is the *e* of a thing than the
14 *e* that man should find nothing
10.13 the *e* of his talk is mischievous
12.12 making many books there is no *e*;
Isa 2. 7 is there any *e* of their treasures;
7 is there any *e* of their chariots:
5.26 unto them from the *e* of the earth:
7. 3 at the *e* of the conduit of the upper
9. 7 and peace there shall be no *e*,
13. 5 far country, from the *e* of heaven,
16. 4 for the extortioner is at an *e*,
23.15 the *e* of seventy years shall Tyre
17 pass after the *e* of seventy years,
33. 1 make an *e* to deal treacherously,
38.12, 13 wilt thou make an *e* of me.
41.22 and know the latter *e* of them;
42.10 his praise from the *e* of the earth,
45.17 world without *e*.
46.10 the *e* from the beginning,
47. 7 didst remember the latter *e* of it.
48.20 it even to the *e* of the earth;
49. 6 salvation unto the *e* of the earth.
62.11 proclaimed unto the *e* of the world,
Jer 1. 3 unto the *e* of the eleventh year
3. 5 will he keep it to the *e*?
4.27 yet will I not make a full *e*.
5.10 but make not a full *e*: take away
18 I will not make a full *e* with you.
31 what will ye do in the *e* thereof?
12. 4 He shall not see our last *e*.
12 from the one *e* of the land
12 even to the other *e* of the land:
17.11 and at his *e* shall be a fool.
25.33 from one *e* of the earth even
33 unto the other *e* of the earth:
26. 8 had made an *e* of speaking all
29.11 of evil, to give you an expected *e*.
30.11 I make a full *e* of all nations
11 yet will I not make a full *e* of thee:
31.17 And there is hope in thine *e*,
34.14 At the *e* of seven years let ye go
43. 1 had made an *e* of speaking unto
44.27 until there be an *e* of them.
46.28 will make a full *e* of all the nations
28 I will not make a full *e* of thee,
51.13 thine *e* is come, and the measure
31 that his city is taken at one *e*,
63 made an *e* of reading this book,
La 1. 9 she remembereth not her last *e*;
4.18 our *e* is near, our days are fulfilled;
18 for our *e* is come.
Eze 3.16 to pass at the *e* of seven days,
7. 2 An *e*, the *e* is come upon the four
3 Now is the *e* come upon thee,
6 An *e* is come, the *e* is come:
11.13 God! wilt thou make a full *e* of
20.17 neither did I make an *e* of them
26 to the *e* that they might know
21.25 when iniquity shall have an *e*,
29 their iniquity shall have an *e*.
29.13 At the *e* of forty years will I gather
31.14 To the *e* that none of all the trees
35. 5 that their iniquity had an *e*:
39.14 after the *e* of seven months shall
41.12 at the *e* toward the west was
42.15 he had made an *e* of measuring
43.23 hast made an *e* of cleansing it,
48. 1 From the north *e* to the coast of
Dan 1. 5 at the *e* thereof they might stand
15 And at the *e* of ten days their
18 at the *e* of the days that the king
4.11 thereof to the *e* of all the earth:
22 thy dominion to the *e* of the earth.
29 the *e* of twelve months he walked
34 the *e* of the days I Nebuchadnezzar
6.26 dominion shall be even unto the *e*.
7.26 and to destroy it unto the *e*.
28 Hitherto is the *e* of the matter.
8.17 time of the *e* shall be the vision.
19 in the last *e* of the indignation:
19 the time appointed the *e* shall be.
9.24 and to make an *e* of sins,
26 the *e* thereof shall be with a flood,
26 and unto the *e* of the war
11. 6 in the *e* of years they shall join
27 the *e* shall be at the time appointed.
35 even to the time of the *e*:
40 at the time of the *e* shall the king
45 yet he shall come to his *e*,
12. 4 book, even to the time of the *e*:
6 it be to the *e* of these wonders?
8 shall be the *e* of these things?
9 and sealed till the time of the *e*.
13 go thou thy way till the *e* be:
13 stand in thy lot at the *e* of the days.
Am 3.15 the great houses shall have an *e*,
5.18 to what *e* is it for you?
7. 2 they had made an *e* of eating
8. 2 The *e* is come upon my people
10 and the *e* thereof as a bitter day.
Ob 9 to the *e* that every one of the
Na 1. 8 will make an utter *e* of the place
9 the Lord? he will make an utter *e*:
2. 9 for there is none *e* of the store
3. 3 there is none *e* of their corpses;
Hab 2. 3 but at the *e* it shall speak,
Mt 10.22 endureth to the *e* shall be saved.
11. 1 when Jesus had made an *e* of
13.39 the harvest is the *e* of the world;
40 so shall it be in the *e* of this world.
49 So shall it be at the *e* of the world:
24. 3 and of the *e* of the world?
6 come to pass, but the *e* is not yet.
13 he that shall endure unto the *e*,
14 and then shall the *e* come.
31 from one *e* of heaven to the other.
26.58 with the servants to see the *e*.
28. 1 the *e* of the sabbath, as it began
20 even unto the *e* of the world.
Mk 3.26 he cannot stand, but hath an *e*.
13. 7 but the *e* shall not be yet.
13 but he that shall endure unto the *e*,
Lk 1.33 of his kingdom there shall be no *e*.
18. 1 a parable unto them to this *e*, that men
21. 9 but the *e* is not by and by.
22.37 things concerning me have an *e*.
Jn 13. 1 world, he loved them unto the *e*.
18.37 To this *e* was I born, and for this
Ac 7.19 to the *e* they might not live.
Ro 1.11 to the *e* ye may be established;
4.16 the *e* the promise might be sure
6.21 for the *e* of those things is death.
22 and the *e* everlasting life.
10. 4 For Christ is the *e* of the law
14. 9 to this *e* Christ both died, and rose
1Co 1. 8 shall also confirm you unto the *e*,
15.24 Then cometh the *e*, when he shall
2Co 1.13 shall acknowledge even to the *e*;
2. 9 to this *e* also did I write, that I might
3.13 the *e* of that which is abolished:
11.15 *e* shall be according to their works.
Eph 3.21 ages, world without *e*.
Php 3.19 Whose *e* is destruction, whose God
1Th 3.13 To the *e* he may stablish your
1Ti 1. 5 Now the *e* of the commandment
Heb 3. 6 of the hope firm unto the *e*.
14 our confidence stedfast unto the *e*;
6. 8 cursing; whose *e* is to be burned.
11 full assurance of hope unto the *e*:
16 is to them an *e* of all strife.
7. 3 beginning of days, nor *e* of life;
9.26 *e* of the world hath he appeared
13. 7 the *e* of their conversation.
Jas 5.11 and have seen the *e* of the Lord;
1Pe 1. 9 Receiving the *e* of your faith,
13 and hope to the *e* for the grace
4. 7 But the *e* of all things is at hand:
17 what shall the *e* be of them that
2Pe 2.20 the latter *e* is worse with them
Rev 2.26 and keepeth my works unto the *e*,
21. 6 the beginning and the *e*, I will give
22.13 Omega, the beginning and the *e*,

ENDEAVOR

2Pe 1.15 I will *e* that ye may be able after

ENDEAVORED

Ac 16.10 we *e* to go to Macedonia,
1Th 2.17 *e* the more abundantly to see

ENDEAVORING

Eph 4. 4 *E* to keep the unity of the Spirit

ENDED

Gen 2. 2 And on the seventh day God *e*
41.53 years of plenteousness,...were *e*.
47.18 When that year was *e*, they came
Dt 31.30 of this song, until they were *e*.
34. 8 and mourning for Moses were *e*.
Ru 2.21 until they have *e* all my harvest.
2Sa 20.18 so they *e* the matter.
1Ki 7.51 So was *e* all the work that king
2Ch 29.34 till the work was *e*, and until the
Job 31.40 The words of Job are *e*.
Ps 72.20 of David the son of Jesse are *e*.
Isa 60.20 days of thy mourning shall be *e*.
Jer 8.20 the summer is *e*, and we are not
Eze 4. 8 till thou hast *e* the days of thy
Mt 7.28 when Jesus had *e* these sayings,
Lk 4. 2 and when they were *e*, he
13 And when the devil had *e* all the
7. 1 when he had *e* all his sayings
Jn 13. 2 supper being *e*, the devil having
Ac 19.21 After these things were *e*, Paul
21.27 the seven days were almost *e*,

ENDETH

Isa 24. 8 the noise of them that rejoice *e*,

ENDING

Rev 1. 8 Omega, the beginning and the *e*,

ENDLESS

1Ti 1. 4 to fables and *e* genealogies, which
Heb 7.16 but after the power of an *e* life.

EN-DOR

Jos 17.11 and the inhabitants of *E* and her
1Sa 28. 7 that hath a familiar spirit at *E*.
Ps 83.10 Which perished at *E*: they became

ENDS

Ex 25.18 in the two *e* of the mercy seat.
19 the cherubims on the two *e* thereof.
28.14 two chains of pure gold at the *e*;
22 the *e* of wreathen work of pure
23 on the two *e* of the breastplate.
24 are on the *e* of the breastplate
25 And the other two *e* of the two
26 upon the two *e* of the breastplate
37. 7 on the two *e* of the mercy seat;
8 cherubims on the two *e* thereof.
38. 5 four rings for the four *e* of the
39.15 the breastplate chains at the *e*,
16 in the two *e* of the breastplate.
17 rings on the *e* of the breastplate.
18 two *e* of the two wreathen chains
19 on the two *e* of the breastplate,
Dt 33.17 together to the *e* of the earth:

1Sa 2.10 Lord shall judge the *e* of the earth;
1Ki 8. 8 the *e* of the staves were seen out
2Ch 5. 9 the *e* of the staves were seen from
Job 28.24 he looketh to the *e* of the earth,
37. 3 lightning unto the *e* of the earth.
38.13 take hold of the *e* of the earth,
Ps 19. 6 and his circuit unto the *e* of it:
22.27 All the *e* of the world shall
48.10 thy praise unto the *e* of the earth:
59.13 in Jacob unto the *e* of the earth.
65. 5 confidence of all the *e* of the earth,
67. 7 all the *e* of the earth shall fear
72. 8 the river unto the *e* of the earth.
98. 3 all the *e* of the earth have seen the
135. 7 to ascend from the *e* of the earth;
Pr 17.24 of a fool are in the *e* of the earth.
30. 4 established all the *e* of the earth?
Isa 26.15 far unto all the *e* of the earth.
40.28 the Creator of the *e* of the earth,
41. 5 the *e* of the earth were afraid,
9 have taken from the *e* of the earth,
43. 6 my daughters from the *e* of the
45.22 saved, all the *e* of the earth:
52.10 all the *e* of the earth shall see the
Jer 10.13 vapours to ascend from the *e* of
16.19 shall come unto thee from the *e* of
25.31 come even to the *e* of the earth;
51.16 vapours to ascend from the *e* of the
Eze 15. 4 the fire devoureth both the *e* of it,
Mic 5. 4 be great unto the *e* of the earth.
Zec 9.10 the river even to the *e* of the earth.
Ac 13.47 salvation unto the *e* of the earth.
Ro 10.18 their words unto the *e* of the world.
1Co 10.11 upon whom the *e* of the world are

ENDUED

Gen 30.20 God hath *e* me with a good
2Ch 2.12 a wise son, *e* with prudence and
13 man, *e* with understanding,
Lk 24.49 until ye be *e* with power from on
Jas 3.13 *e* with knowledge among you?

ENDURE

Gen 33.14 me and the children be able to *e*,
Ex 18.23 then thou shalt be able to *e*,
Est 8. 6 how can I *e* to see the evil that
6 how can I *e* to see the destruction
Job 8.15 hold it fast, but it shall not *e*.
31.23 of his highness I could not *e*.
Ps 9. 7 But the Lord shall *e* for ever:
30. 5 weeping may *e* for a night, but
72. 5 as long as the sun and moon *e*,
17 His name shall *e* for ever:
89.29 His seed also will I make to *e* forever,
36 His seed shall *e* for ever, and his
102.12 thou, O Lord, shalt *e* for ever;
26 shall perish, but thou shalt *e*:
104.31 glory of the Lord shall *e* for ever:
Pr 27.24 ever: and doth the crown *e* to every
Eze 22.14 Can thine heart *e*, or can thine
Mt 24.13 But he that shall *e* unto the end,
Mk 4.17 and so *e* but for a time:
13.13 but he that shall *e* unto the end,
2Th 1. 4 and tribulations that ye *e*:
2Ti 2. 3 therefore *e* hardness, as a good
10 Therefore I *e* all things for the
4. 3 they will not *e* sound doctrine;
5 *e* afflictions, do the work of an
Heb 12. 7 If ye *e* chastening, God dealeth
20 (For they could not *e* that which
Jas 5.11 we count them happy which *e*.
1Pe 2.19 conscience toward God *e* grief,

ENDURED

Ps 81.15 their time should have *e* for ever.
Ro 9.22 *e* with much longsuffering the
2Ti 3.11 what persecutions I *e*: but out of
Heb 6.15 And so, after he had patiently *e*,
10.32 ye *e* a great fight of afflictions;
11.27 for he *e*, as seeing him who is
12. 2 *e* the cross, despising the shame,
3 him that *e* such contradiction

ENDURETH

1Ch 16.34 he is good; for his mercy *e* for ever.
41 Lord because his mercy *e* for ever;
2Ch 5.13 he is good; for his mercy *e* for ever:
7. 3 he is good; for his mercy *e* for ever.
6 Lord, because his mercy *e* for ever,
20.21 the Lord; for his mercy *e* for ever.
Ezr 3.11 his mercy *e* for ever toward Israel.
Ps 30. 5 For his anger *e* but a moment;
52. 1 the goodness of God *e* continually.
72. 7 peace so long as the moon *e*.
100. 5 and his truth *e* to all generations.
106. 1 he is good: for his mercy *e* for ever.
107. 1 he is good: for his mercy *e* for ever.
111. 3 and his righteousness *e* for ever.
10 commandments: his praise *e* for
112. 3 and his righteousness *e* for ever.
9 poor; his righteousness *e* for ever;
117. 2 and the truth of the Lord *e* for ever.
118. 1 is good: because his mercy *e* for ever.
2 Israel now say, that his mercy *e* for
3 Aaron now say, that his mercy *e* for
4 Lord say, that his mercy *e* for ever.
29 he is good: for his mercy *e* for ever.
119.160 thy righteous judgments *e* for ever.
135.13 Thy name, O Lord, *e* for ever;
138. 8 thy mercy, O Lord, *e* for ever: forsake
145.13 and thy dominion *e* throughout all
Jer 33.11 for his mercy *e* for ever: and of them
Mt 10.22 that *e* to the end shall be saved.
Jn 6.27 which *e* unto everlasting life,
1Co 13. 7 hopeth all things, *e* all things.
Jas 1.12 is the man that *e* temptation:
1Pe 1.25 the word of the Lord *e* for ever.

ENDURING

Ps 19. 9 of the Lord is clean, *e* for ever:
2Co 1. 6 is effectual in the *e* of the same
Heb 10.34 a better and an *e* substance.

ENEMIES

Gen 14.20 delivered thine *e* into thy hand.
22.17 seed shall possess the gate of his *e*;
49. 8 hand shall be in the neck of thine *e*;
Ex 1.10 they join also unto our *e*, and
23.22 I will be an enemy unto thine *e*,
27 make all thine *e* turn their backs
32.25 unto their shame among their *e*:)
Lev 26. 7 And ye shall chase your *e*,
8 and your *e* shall fall before you
16 seed in vain, for your *e* shall eat it.
17 ye shall be slain before your *e*:
32 your *e* which dwell therein shall be
36 their hearts in the lands of their *e*;
37 no power to stand before your *e*.
38 the land of your *e* shall eat you up.
41 them into the land of their *e*;
44 when they be in the land of their *e*.
Nu 10. 9 ye shall be saved from your *e*.
35 Lord, and let thine *e* be scattered;
14.42 ye be not smitten before your *e*.
23.11 I took thee to curse mine *e*,
24. 8 he shall eat up the nations his *e*,
10 I called thee to curse mine *e*,
18 also shall be a possession for his *e*;
32.21 driven out his *e* from before him,
Dt 1.42 lest ye be smitten before your *e*.
6.19 out all thine *e* from before thee,
12.10 he giveth you rest from all your *e*
20. 1 goest out to battle against thine *e*,
3 this day unto battle against your *e*:
4 to fight for you against your *e*,
14 thou shalt eat the spoil of thine *e*,
21.10 goest forth to war against thine *e*,
23. 9 host goeth forth against thine *e*,
14 to give up thine *e* before thee;
25.19 given thee rest from all thine *e*
28. 7 Lord shall cause thine *e* that rise
25 thee to be smitten before thine *e*:
31 sheep shall be given unto thine *e*,
48 Therefore shalt thou serve thine *e*
53 wherewith thine *e* shall distress
55 thine *e* shall distress thee in all
68 ye shall be sold unto your *e* for
30. 7 put all these curses upon thine *e*,
32.31 our *e* themselves being judges.
41 will render vengeance to mine *e*,
33. 7 be thou an help to him from his *e*.
29 thine *e* shall be found liars unto
Jos 7. 8 turneth their backs before their *e*!
12 Israel could not stand before their *e*,
12 turned their backs before their *e*,
13 thou canst not stand before thine *e*,
10.13 avenged themselves upon their *e*.
19 but pursue after your *e*, and smite
25 thus shall the Lord do to all your *e*
21.44 stood not a man of all their *e* before
44 delivered all their *e* into their hand.
22. 8 divide the spoil of your *e* with your
23. 1 rest unto Israel from all their *e*
Jdg 2.14 sold them into the hands of their *e*
14 any longer stand before their *e*.
18 out of the hand of their *e* all the
3.28 for the Lord hath delivered your *e*
5.31 So let all thine *e* perish,
8.34 out of the hands of all their *e* on
11.36 taken vengeance for thee of thine *e*,
1Sa 2. 1 my mouth is enlarged over mine *e*;
4. 3 save us out of the hand of our *e*.
12.10 deliver us out of the hand of our *e*,
11 out of the hand of your *e* on every
14.24 that I may be avenged on mine *e*.
30 spoil of their *e* which they found?
47 against all his *e* on every side,
18.25 to be avenged of the king's *e*.
20.15 Lord hath cut off the *e* of David
16 require it at the hand of David's *e*.
25.22 also do God unto the *e* of David,
26 let thine *e*, and they that seek evil
29 souls of thine *e*, them shall he sling
29. 8 go fight against the *e* of my lord
30.26 the spoil of the *e* of the Lord;
2Sa 3.18 out of the hand of all their *e*.
5.20 hath broken forth upon mine *e*
7. 1 rest round about from all his *e*;
9 cut off all thine *e* out of thy sight,
11 caused thee to rest from all thine *e*.
12.14 great occasion to the *e* of the Lord
18.19 the Lord hath avenged him of his *e*.
32 The *e* of my lord the king, and all
19. 6 thine *e*, and hatest thy friends.
9 saved us out of the hand of our *e*,
22. 1 him out of the hand of all his *e*, and
4 so shall I be saved from mine *e*.
38 I have pursued mine *e*, and
41 also given me the necks of mine *e*,
49 bringeth me forth from mine *e*:
24.13 flee three months before thine *e*,
1Ki 3.11 nor hast asked the life of thine *e*;
8.48 their soul, in the land of their *e*,
2Ki 17.39 you out of the hand of all your *e*.
21.14 them into the hand of their *e*;
14 a prey and a spoil to all their *e*;
1Ch 12.17 be come to betray me to mine *e*,
14.11 God hath broken in upon mine *e*
17. 8 and have cut off all thine *e* from
10 Moreover I will subdue all thine *e*.
21.12 while that the sword of thine *e*
22. 9 I will give him rest from all his *e*
2Ch 1.11 or honor, nor the life of thine *e*,
6.28 their *e* besiege them in the cities
34 go out to war against their *e* by the
36 deliver them over before their *e*,
20.27 made them to rejoice over their *e*.
29 fought against the *e* of Israel,
25.20 deliver them into the hands of their *e*,
Neh 4.15 our *e* heard that it was known
5. 9 the reproach of the heathen our *e*?
6. 1 the Arabian, and the rest of our *e*,
16 that when all our *e* heard thereof,
9.27 them into the hand of their *e*,
27 saved out of the hand of their *e*.

Neh 9.28 thou them in the hand of their *e*,
Est 8.13 to avenge themselves on their *e*.
9. 1 the day that the *e* of the Jews hoped
5 Thus the Jews smote all their *e*
16 and had rest from their *e*, and slew
22 the Jews rested from their *e*,
Job 19.11 me unto him as one of his *e*.
Ps 3. 7 thou hast smitten all mine *e*
5. 8 because of mine *e*; make thy way
6. 7 waxeth old because of all mine *e*.
10 Let all mine *e* be ashamed and
7. 6 because of the rage of mine *e*:
8. 2 strength because of thine *e*, that
9. 3 When mine *e* are turned back,
10. 5 for all his *e*, he puffeth at them.
17. 9 from my deadly *e*, who compass me
18.(T) him from the hand of all his *e*,
3 so shall I be saved from mine *e*.
37 I have pursued mine *e*, and
40 also given me the necks of mine *e*;
48 He delivereth me from mine *e*:
21. 8 Thine hand shall find out all thine *e*:
23. 5 me in the presence of mine *e*:
25. 2 let not mine *e* triumph over me.
19 consider mine *e*; for they are many;
27. 2 even mine *e* and my foes, came
6 head be lifted up above mine *e*
11 a plain path, because of mine *e*;
12 not over unto the will of mine *e*:
31.11 was a reproach among all mine *e*,
15 me from the hand of mine *e*,
35.19 Let not them that are mine *e*
37.20 and the *e* of the Lord shall be as
38.19 But mine *e* are lively, and they
41. 2 deliver him unto the will of his *e*.
5 Mine *e* speak evil of me, When
42.10 mine *e* reproach me; while they
44. 5 thee will we push down our *e*:
7 thou hast saved us from our *e*,
45. 5 in the heart of the king's *e*;
54. 5 He shall reward evil unto mine *e*:
7 hath seen his desire upon mine *e*.
56. 2 Mine *e* would daily swallow me
9 then shall mine *e* turn back:
59. 1 Deliver me from mine *e*, O my God:
10 me see my desire upon mine *e*.
60.12 it is that shall tread down our *e*.
66. 3 shall thine *e* submit themselves
68. 1 God arise, let his *e* be scattered:
21 God shall wound the head of his *e*,
23 be dipped in the blood of thine *e*,
69. 4 being mine *e* wrongfully, are mighty:
18 deliver me because of mine *e*.
71.10 For mine *e* speak against me;
72. 9 and his *e* shall lick the dust.
74. 4 Thine *e* roar in the midst of thy
23 Forget not the voice of thine *e*:
78.53 but the sea overwhelmed their *e*.
66 smote his *e* in the hinder parts:
80. 6 our *e* laugh among themselves.
81.14 I should soon have subdued their *e*,
83. 2 For, lo, thine *e* make a tumult:
89.10 scattered thine *e* with thy strong
42 thou hast made all his *e* to rejoice.
51 Wherewith thine *e* have reproached,
92. 9 For, lo, thine *e*, O Lord,
9 for, lo, thine *e* shall perish;
11 shall see my desire on mine *e*,
97. 3 burneth up his *e* round about.
102. 8 Mine *e* reproach me all the day;
105.24 made them stronger than their *e*.
106.11 And the waters covered their *e*:
42 Their *e* also oppressed them, and
108.13 it is that shall tread down our *e*.
110. 1 until I make thine *e* thy footstool.
2 rule thou in the midst of thine *e*.
112. 8 he see his desire upon his *e*.
119.98 hast made me wiser than mine *e*:
139 mine *e* have forgotten thy words.
157 are my persecutors and mine *e*;
127. 5 but they shall speak with the *e*
132.18 His *e* will I clothe with shame:
136.24 hath redeemed us from our *e*:
138. 7 hand against the wrath of mine *e*,
139.20 thine *e* take thy name in vain.
22 hatred: I count them mine *e*.
143. 9 Deliver me, O Lord, from mine *e*:
12 And of thy mercy cut off mine *e*,
Pr 16. 7 maketh even his *e* to be at peace
Isa 1.24 and avenge me of mine *e*:
9.11 and join his *e* together;
26.11 of thine *e* shall devour them.
42.13 he shall prevail against his *e*.
59.18 adversaries, recompence to his *e*;
62. 8 thy corn to be meat for thine *e*;
66. 6 rendereth recompence to his *e*.
14 and his indignation toward his *e*.
Jer 12. 7 my soul into the hand of her *e*.
15. 9 deliver to the sword before their *e*,
14 make thee to pass with thine *e*
17. 4 I will cause thee to serve thine *e*
19. 7 to fall by the sword before their *e*,
9 and straitness, wherewith their *e*,
20. 4 shall fall by the sword of their *e*,
5 I give into the hand of their *e*,
21. 7 and into the hand of their *e*,
34.20 give them into the hand of their *e*,
21 I give into the hand of their *e*,
44.30 king of Egypt into the hand of his *e*,
48. 5 *e* have heard a cry of destruction.
49.37 Elam to be dismayed before their *e*,
La 1. 2 with her, they are become her *e*.
5 are the chief, her *e* prosper;
21 mine *e* have heard of my trouble;
2.16 thine *e* have opened their mouth
3.46 All our *e* have opened their mouths
52 Mine *e* chased me sore, like a bird,
Eze 39.23 them into the hand of their *e*;
Dan 4.19 interpretation thereof to thine *e*.
Am 9. 4 go into captivity before their *e*,
Mic 4.10 thee from the hand of thine *e*.
5. 9 all thine *e* shall be cut off.
7. 6 a man's *e* are the men of his own
Na 1. 2 he reserveth wrath for his *e*.
8 and darkness shall pursue his *e*.
3.13 be set wide open unto thine *e*:
Zec 10. 5 which tread down their *e* in the
Mt 5.44 Love your *e*, bless them that curse
22.44 till I make thine *e* thy footstool?
Mk 12.36 till I make thine *e* thy footstool.
Lk 1.71 That we should be saved from our *e*,
74 delivered out of the hand of our *e*
6.27 Love your *e*, do good to them that
35 love ye your *e*, and do good,
19.27 But those mine *e*, which would not
43 thine *e* shall cast a trench about
20.43 Till I make thine *e* thy footstool.
Ro 5.10 when we were *e*, we were reconciled
11.28 they are *e* for your sakes:
1Co 15.25 till he hath put all *e* under his feet.
Php 3.18 that they are the *e* of the cross of
Col 1.21 *e* in your mind by wicked works,
Heb 1.13 until I make thine *e* thy footstool?
10.13 till his *e* be made his footstool.
Rev 11. 5 their mouth and devoureth their *e*:
12 and their *e* beheld them.

ENEMIES'

Lev 26.34 and ye be in your *e* land;
39 their iniquity in your *e* lands;
Eze 39.27 gathered them out of their *e* lands,

ENEMY

Ex 15. 6 Lord hath dashed in pieces the *e*.
9 The *e* said, I will pursue, I will
23.22 I will be an *e* unto thine enemies,
Lev 26.25 delivered into the hand of the *e*.
Nu 10. 9 the *e* that oppresseth you, then
35.23 that he die, and was not his *e*,
Dt 28.57 wherewith thine *e* shall distress
32.27 not that I feared the wrath of the *e*,
42 beginning of revenges upon the *e*.
33.27 he shall thrust out the *e* from
Jdg 16.23 hath delivered Samson our *e* into
24 hath delivered into our hands our *e*,
1Sa 2.32 shalt see an *e* in my habitation,
18.29 Saul became David's *e* continually.
19.17 and sent away mine *e*, that he is
24. 4 will deliver thine *e* into thine hand,
19 For if a man find his *e*, will he let
26. 8 hath delivered thine *e* into thine
28.16 thee, and is become thine *e*?
2Sa 4. 8 the son of Saul thine *e*, which
22.18 He delivered me from my strong *e*,
1Ki 8.33 Israel be smitten down before the *e*,
37 if their *e* besiege them in the land
44 go out to battle against their *e*,
46 them, and deliver them to the *e*,
46 captives unto the land of the *e*,
21.20 Hast thou found me, O mine *e*?
2Ch 6.24 be put to the worse before the *e*,
25. 8 shall make thee fall before the *e*:
26.13 to help the king against the *e*.
Ezr 8.22 help us against the *e* in the way:
31 delivered us from the hand of the *e*.
Est 3.10 the Agagite, the Jews' *e*.
7. 4 the *e* could not countervail the
6 and *e* is this wicked Haman,
8. 1 Haman the Jews' *e* unto Esther
9.10 Hammedatha, the *e* of the Jews,
24 the Agagite, the *e* of all the Jews,
Job 13.24 and holdest me for thine *e*?
16. 9 mine *e* sharpeneth his eyes upon
27. 7 Let mine *e* be as the wicked,
33.10 he counteth me for his *e*,
Ps 7. 4 that without cause is mine *e*:)
5 Let the *e* persecute my soul,
8. 2 that thou mightest still the *e* and
9. 6 O thou *e*, destructions are come
13. 2 how long shall mine *e* be exalted
4 Lest mine *e* say, I have prevailed
18.17 He delivered me from my strong *e*,
31. 8 shut me up into the hand of the *e*:
41.11 mine *e* doth not triumph over me.
42. 9 because of the oppression of the *e*?
43. 2 because of the oppression of the *e*?
44.10 us to turn back from the *e*:
16 by reason of the *e* and avenger.
55. 3 Because of the voice of the *e*,
12 For it was not an *e* that reproached
61. 3 and a strong tower from the *e*.
64. 1 preserve my life from fear of the *e*.
74. 3 all that the *e* hath done wickedly
10 shall the *e* blaspheme thy name
18 this, that the *e* hath reproached,
78.42 he delivered them from the *e*.
89.22 The *e* shall not exact upon him;
106.10 them from the hand of the *e*.
107. 2 redeemed from the hand of the *e*;
143. 3 the *e* hath persecuted my soul;
Pr 24.17 Rejoice not when thine *e* falleth,
25.21 If thine *e* be hungry, give him
27. 6 the kisses of an *e* are deceitful.
Isa 59.19 the *e* shall come in like a flood,
63.10 he was turned to be their *e*,
Jer 6.25 for the sword of the *e* and fear is on
15.11 I will cause the *e* to entreat thee
18.17 as with an east wind before the *e*;
30.14 thee with the wound of an *e*,
31.16 come again from the land of the *e*.
44.30 king of Babylon, his *e*, and that
La 1. 5 gone into captivity before the *e*.
7 people fell into the hand of the *e*,
9 for the *e* hath magnified himself.
16 desolate, because the *e* prevailed.
2. 3 his right hand from before the *e*,
4 He hath bent his bow like an *e*:
5 The Lord was as an *e*: he hath
7 hath given up into the hand of the *e*
17 he hath caused thine *e* to rejoice
22 brought up hath mine *e* consumed.
4.12 and the *e* should have entered into
Eze 36. 2 Because the *e* hath said against you,

Hos 8. 3 is good: the *e* shall pursue him.
Mic 2. 8 my people is risen up as an *e*:
7. 8 Rejoice not against me, O mine *e*:
10 Then she that is mine *e* shall see it,
Na 3.11 seek strength because of the *e*.
Zep 3.15 he hath cast out thine *e*:
Mt 5.43 thy neighbor, and hate thine *e*.
13.25 his *e* came and sowed tares among
28 unto them. An *e* hath done this.
39 The *e* that sowed them is the devil;
Lk 10.19 and over all the power of the *e*:
Ac 13.10 devil, thou *e* of all righteousness,
Ro 12.20 Therefore if thine *e* hunger, feed
1Co 15.26 The last *e* that shall be destroyed
Gal 4.16 Am I therefore become your *e*,
2Th 3.15 Yet count him not as an *e*,
Jas 4. 4 friend of the world is the *e* of God.

EN–GEDI
Jos 15.62 and the city of Salt, and *E*;
1Sa 23.29 and dwelt in strong holds at *E*.
24. 1 David is in the wilderness of *E*.
2Ch 20. 2 be in Hazazon-tamar, which is *E*.
SS 1.14 camphire in the vineyards of *E*.
Eze 47.10 fishers shall stand upon it from *E*

ENGRAFTED
Jas 1.21 with meekness the *e* word, which

ENGRAVEN
2Co 3. 7 written and *e* in stones, was

ENJOIN
Phm 8 much bold in Christ to *e* thee

ENJOINED
Est 9.31 and Esther the queen had *e* them,
Job 36.23 Who hath *e* him his way? who
Heb 9.20 which God hath *e* unto you.

ENJOY
Lev 26.34 shall the land *e* her sabbaths,
34 the land rest, and *e* her sabbaths.
43 shall *e* her sabbaths, while she
Nu 36. 8 children of Israel may *e* every
Dt 28.41 daughters, but thou shalt not *e*
Jos 1.15 land of your possession, and *e* it,
Ec 2. 1 with mirth, therefore *e* pleasure:
24 he should make his soul *e* good in
3.13 and *e* the good of all his labor,
5.18 eat and to drink, and to *e* the good
Isa 65.22 long *e* the work of their hands.
Ac 24. 2 Seeing that by thee we *e* great
1Ti 6.17 giveth us richly all things to *e*;
Heb 11.25 than to *e* the pleasures of sin

ENJOYED
2Ch 36.21 until the land had *e* her sabbaths:

ENLARGE
Gen 9.27 God shall *e* Japheth, and he shall
Ex 34.24 before thee, and *e* thy borders:
Dt 12.20 When the Lord thy God shall *e* thy
19. 8 if the Lord thy God *e* thy coast,
1Ch 4.10 wouldest bless...and *e* my coast,
Ps 119.32 when thou shalt *e* my heart.
Isa 54. 2 *E* the place of thy tent, and let
Am 1.13 that they might *e* their border:
Mic 1.16 *e* thy baldness as the eagle for;
Mt 23. 5 *e* the borders of their garments,

ENLARGED
1Sa 2. 1 my mouth is *e* over mine enemies;
2Sa 22.37 Thou hast *e* my steps under me;
Ps 4. 1 thou hast *e* me when I was in
18.36 Thou hast *e* my steps under me,
25.17 The troubles of my heart are *e*:
Isa 5.14 Therefore hell hath *e* herself,
57. 8 gone up; thou hast *e* thy bed,
60. 5 thine heart shall fear, and be *e*;
2Co 6.11 is open unto you, our heart is *e*.
13 unto my children,) be ye also *e*.
10.15 that we shall be *e* by you

ENLIGHTENED
1Sa 14.27 his mouth; and his eyes were *e*.
29 mine eyes have been *e*, because
Job 33.30 to be *e* with the light of the living.
Ps 97. 4 His lightnings *e* the world:
Eph 1.18 of your understanding being *e*;
Heb 6. 4 those who were once *e*, and have

ENLIGHTENING
Ps 19. 8 of the Lord is pure, *e* the eyes.

ENMITY
Gen 3.15 put *e* between thee and the woman,
Nu 35.21 Or in *e* smite him with his hand,
22 thrust him suddenly without *e*,
Lk 23.12 were at *e* between themselves.
Ro 8. 7 the carnal mind is *e* against God:
Eph 2.15 abolished in his flesh the *e*,
16 having slain the *e* thereby:

ENOCH
Gen 4.17 and she conceived, and bare *E*:
17 after the name of his son, *E*.
18 unto *E* was born Irad: and Irad
5.18 and two years, and he begat *E*:
19 Jared lived after he begat *E* eight
21 And *E* lived sixty and five years,
22 *E* walked with God after he begat
23 the days of *E* were three hundred
24 *E* walked with God: and he was not;
Lk 3.37 which was the son of *E*, which
Heb 11. 5 By faith *E* was translated that he
Jude 14 *E* also, the seventh from Adam,

ENOUGH
Gen 24.25 have both straw and provender *e*,
33. 9 Esau said, I have *e*, my brother;
11 with me, and because I have *e*.
34.21 behold, it is large *e* for them;
45.28 Israel said, It is *e*; Joseph my
Ex 2.19 and also drew water *e* for us,
9.28 Intreat the Lord (for it is *e*) that
36. 5 much more than *e* for the service
Dt 1. 6 Ye have dwelt long *e* in this mount;
2. 3 compassed this mountain long *e*:
Jos 17.16 The hill is not *e* for us:
2Sa 24.16 It is *e*: stay now thine hand. And
1Ki 19. 4 It is *e*; now, O Lord, take away
1Ch 21.15 It is *e*, stay now thine hand. And
2Ch 31.10 we have had *e* to eat, and have
Pr 27.27 have goats' milk *e* for thy food,
28.19 persons shall have poverty *e*.
30.15 yea, four things say not, It is *e*:
16 and the fire that saith not, It is *e*.
Isa 56.11 dogs which can never have *e*,
Jer 49. 9 they will destroy till they have *e*.
Hos 4.10 they shall eat, and not have *e*:
Ob 5 not have stolen till they had *e*?
Na 2.12 did tear in pieces *e* for his whelps,
Hag 1. 6 little; ye eat, but ye have not *e*;
Mal 3.10 that there shall not be room *e*
Mt 10.25 It is *e* for the disciple that he be
25. 9 lest there be not *e* for us and you:
Mk 14.41 your rest: it is *e*, the hour is come;
Lk 15.17 have bread *e* and to spare, and I
22.38 he said unto them, It is *e*.
Ac 27.38 they had eaten *e*, they lightened

ENQUIRE *see Inquire*

ENQUIRED *see Inquired*

ENQUIREST *see Inquirest*

ENQUIRY *see Inquiry*

ENRICH
1Sa 17.25 king will *e* him with great riches,
Eze 27.33 thou didst *e* the kings of the earth

ENRICHED
1Co 1. 5 in every thing ye are *e* by him,
2Co 9.11 *e* in every thing to all bountifulness,

ENSAMPLE
Php 3.17 walk as ye have us for an *e*.
2Th 3. 9 to make ourselves an *e* unto you
2Pe 2. 6 making them an *e* unto those

ENSAMPLES
1Co 10.11 things happened unto them for *e*:
1Th 1. 7 that ye were *e* to all that believe
1Pe 5. 3 but being *e* to the flock.

ENSUE
1Pe 3.11 let him seek peace, and *e* it.

ENTANGLE
Mt 22.15 how they might *e* him in his talk.

ENTANGLED
Ex 14. 3 of Israel, They are *e* in the land,
Gal 5. 1 *e* again with the yoke of bondage,
2Pe 2.20 they are again *e* therein, and

ENTANGLETH
2Ti 2. 4 *e* himself with the affairs of this

ENTER
Ex 40.35 Moses was not able to *e* into the
Nu 20.24 for he shall not *e* into the land
Dt 23. 2 A bastard shall not *e* into the
29.12 thou shouldest *e* into covenant
2Ki 11. 5 that *e* in on the sabbath shall
Est 4. 2 none might *e* into the king's gate
Ps 95.11 that they should not *e* into my rest.
100. 4 *E* into his gates with thanksgiving,
118.20 into which the righteous shall *e*.
143. 2 And *e* not into judgment with thy
Pr 18. 6 A fool's lips *e* into contention,
Isa 2.10 *E* into the rock, and hide thee in
57. 2 shall *e* into peace: they shall rest
59.14 in the street, and equity cannot *e*.
Jer 7. 2 that *e* in at these gates to worship
16. 5 *E* not into the house of mourning,
Eze 37. 5 I will cause breath to *e* into you,
44. 2 and no man shall *e* in by it;
Dan 11.41 shall *e* also into the glorious land,
Joel 2. 9 they shall *e* in at the windows
Jon 3. 4 And Jonah began to *e* into the city
Mt 5.20 *e* into the kingdom of heaven.
6. 6 thou prayest, *e* into thy closet,
7.13 *E* ye in at the strait gate:
21 Lord, shall *e* into the kingdom of
10. 5 city of the Samaritans *e* ye not:
11 whatsoever city or town ye shall *e*,
12.29 one *e* into a strong man's house,
45 and they *e* in and dwell there:
18. 3 not *e* into the kingdom of heaven.
8 thee to *e* into life halt or maimed,
9 for thee to *e* into life with one eye,
19.17 if thou wilt *e* into life, keep the
23 shall hardly *e* into the kingdom of
24 to *e* into the kingdom of God.
25.21, 23 *e* thou into the joy of thy Lord.
26.41 that ye *e* not into temptation:
Mk 1.45 no more openly *e* into the city,
3.27 can *e* into a strong man's house,
5.12 swine, that we may *e* into them.
6.10 place soever ye *e* into an house,
9.25 of him, and *e* no more into him.
43 for thee to *e* into life maimed,
45 better for thee to *e* halt into life,
47 thee to *e* into the kingdom of God
10.15 little child, he shall not *e* therein.
23 shall...*e* into the kingdom of God!
24 riches to *e* into the kingdom of God!
25 man to *e* into the kingdom of God.
13.15 neither *e* therein, to take any
14.38 pray, lest ye *e* into temptation.
Lk 7. 6 thou shouldest *e* under my roof:

Lk 8.16 they which *e* in may see the light.
32 would suffer them to *e* into them.
9. 4 house ye *e* into, there abide,
10. 5 whatsoever house ye *e*, first say,
8 into whatsoever city ye *e*, and
10 But into whatsoever city ye *e*,
11.26 and they *e* in, and dwell there:
13.24 Strive to *e* in at the strait gate:
24 seek to *e* in, and shall not be able.
18.17 child shall in no wise *e* therein.
24 riches *e* into the kingdom of God!
25 man to *e* into the kingdom of God.
21.21 are in the countries *e* thereinto.
22.40 that ye *e* not into temptation.
46 pray, lest ye *e* into temptation.
24.26 things, and to *e* into his glory?
Jn 3. 4 can he *e* the second time into his
5 cannot *e* into the kingdom of God.
10. 9 if any man *e* in, he shall be saved,
Ac 14.22 *e* into the kingdom of God.
20.29 grievous wolves *e* in among you,
Heb 3.11 They shall not *e* into my rest.)
18 that they should not *e* into his rest,
19 that they could not *e* in because
4. 3 which have believed do *e* into rest,
3 wrath, if they shall *e* into my rest:
5 again, If they shall *e* into my rest.
6 that some must *e* therein, and they
11 therefore to *e* into that rest, lest
10.19 boldness to *e* into the holiest by
Rev 15. 8 was able to *e* into the temple,
21.27 there shall in no wise *e* into it
22.14 *e* in through the gates into the city.

ENTERED

Gen 7.13 In the selfsame day *e* Noah, and
Ex 33. 9 as Moses *e* into the tabernacle,
2Ch 15.12 *e* into a covenant to seek the Lord
Neh 10.29 *e* into a curse, and into an oath,
Job 38.16 Hast thou *e* into the springs of the
22 Hast thou *e* into the treasures of
Jer 37.16 was *e* into the dungeon, and into
Eze 2. 2 the spirit *e* into me when he spake
3.24 Then the spirit *e* into me, and set
16. 8 and *e* into a covenant with thee,
44. 2 the God of Israel, hath *e* in by it,
Ob 11 and foreigners *e* into his gates,
Hab 3.16 rottenness *e* into my bones, and I
Mt 8. 5 when Jesus was *e* into Capernaum,
23 when he was *e* into a ship,
9. 1 he *e* into a ship, and passed over,
12. 4 How he *e* into the house of God,
24.38 the day that Noe *e* into the ark,
Mk 1.21 he *e* into the synagogue, and
29 they *e* into the house of Simon
2. 1 again he *e* into Capernaum after
3. 1 he *e* again into the synagogue;
4. 1 he *e* into a ship, and sat in the sea;
5.13 went out, and *e* into the swine:
6.56 whithersoever he *e*, into villages,
7.17 when he was *e* into the house
24 *e* into an house, and would have
8.10 he *e* into a ship with his disciples,
11. 2 as soon as ye be *e* into it,
11 Jesus *e* into Jerusalem, and into
Lk 1.40 And *e* into the house of Zacharias,
4.38 synagogue, and *e* into Simon's
5. 3 he *e* into one of the ships, which
6. 6 *e* into the synagogue and taught:
7. 1 people, he *e* into Capernaum.
44 I *e* into thine house, thou gavest
8.30 many devils were *e* into him.
33 *e* into the swine: and the herd ran
9.34 feared as they *e* into the cloud.
52 they went, and *e* into a village
10.38 that he *e* into a certain village:
11.52 ye *e* not in yourselves, and them
17.12 as he *e* into a certain village,
27 day that Noe *e* into the ark,
19. 1 Jesus *e* and passed through
22. 3 Then *e* Satan into Judas surnamed
10 when ye are *e* into the city, there
24. 3 they *e* in, and found not the body
Jn 4.38 and ye are *e* into their labors.
6.17 *e* into a ship, and went over the
22 whereinto his disciples were *e*,
13.27 after the sop Satan *e* into him.
18. 1 was a garden, into the which he *e*,
33 Then Pilate *e* into the judgment
21. 3 They went forth, and *e* into a ship
Ac 3. 2 ask alms of them that *e* into the
8 and *e* with them into the temple,
5.21 they *e* into the temple early in the
9.17 went his way, and *e* into the house;
10.24 And the morrow after they *e* into
11. 8 hath at any time *e* into my mouth.
12 and we *e* into the man's house:
16.40 and *e* into the house of Lydia:
18. 7 and *e* into a certain man's house,
19 *e* the synagogue, and reasoned
19.30 Paul would have *e* in unto the
21. 8 we *e* into the house of Philip
26 with them *e* into the temple, to
23.16 *e* into the castle, and told Paul.
25.23 and was *e* into the place of hearing,
28. 8 to whom Paul *e* in, and prayed,
Ro 5.12 sin *e* into the world, and death by
20 Moreover the law *e*, that the
1Co 2. 9 neither have *e* into the heart of
Heb 4. 6 *e* not in because of unbelief:
10 For he that is *e* into his rest, he
6.20 Whither the forerunner is for us *e*,
9.12 he *e* in once into the holy place,
24 For Christ is not *e* into the holy
Jas 5. 4 are *e* into the ears of the Lord
2Jn 7 deceivers are *e* into the world,
Rev 11.11 spirit of life from God *e* into them,

ENTERETH

Nu 4.30 that *e* into the service, to do the
35, 39, 43 that *e* into the service, for
2Ch 31.16 every one that *e* into the house of
Pr 2.10 When wisdom *e* into thine heart,
17.10 A reproof *e* more into a wise man
Eze 21.14 which *e* into their privy chambers.
42.12 toward the east, as one *e* into them.
46. 9 he that *e* in by the way of the north
9 he that *e* by the way of the south
Mt 15.17 whatsoever *e* in at the mouth
Mk 5.40 *e* in where the damsel was lying.
7.18 from without *e* into the man,
19 Because it *e* not into his heart,
Lk 22.10 him into the house where he *e* in.
Jn 10. 1 He that *e* not by the door into the
2 But he that *e* in by the door is
Heb 6.19 which *e* into that within the veil;
9.25 as the high priest *e* into the holy

ENTERING

1Ki 6.31 And for the *e* of the oracle he made
19.13 and stood in the *e* in of the cave.
2Ki 7. 3 leprous men at the *e* in of the gate;
10. 8 two heaps at the *e* in of the gate
23.11 at the *e* in of the house of the
1Ch 5. 9 unto the *e* in of the wilderness
2Ch 18. 9 void place at the *e* in of the gate
23. 4 part of you *e* on the sabbath
13 king stood at his pillar at the *e*
15 when she was come to the *e* of
33.14 even to the *e* in at the fish gate.
Isa 23. 1 so that there is no house, no *e* in:
Jer 17.27 *e* in at the gates of Jerusalem
Eze 44. 5 mark well the *e* in of the house,
Mt 23.13 suffer ye them that are *e* to go in.
Mk 4.19 the lusts of other things *e* in,
7.15 that *e* into him can defile him;
8.13 *e* into the ship again departed
16. 5 *e* into the sepulchre, they saw a
Lk 11.52 them that were *e* in ye hindered.
19.30 in the which at your *e* ye shall
Ac 8. 3 As for Saul...*e* into every house,
27. 2 *e* into a ship of Adramyttium,
1Th 1. 9 what manner of *e* in we had unto
Heb 4. 1 being left us of *e* into his rest,

ENTERTAIN

Heb 13. 2 Be not forgetful to *e* strangers:

ENTERTAINED

Heb 13. 2 some have *e* angels unawares.

ENTICED

Job 31.27 my heart hath been secretly *e*,
Jer 20.10 Peradventure he will be *e*, and
Jas 1.14 drawn away of his own lust, and *e*.

ENTICING

1Co 2. 4 with *e* words of man's wisdom,
Col 2. 4 should beguile you with *e* words,

ENTIRE

Jas 1. 4 that ye may be perfect and *e*,

ENTRANCE

Nu 34. 8 border unto the *e* of Hamath;
Jdg 1.24 Shew us...the *e* into the city,
25 when he shewed them the *e* into
1Ki 18.46 ran before Ahab to the *e* of Jezreel.
22.10 in the *e* of the gate of Samaria;
1Ch 4.39 they went to the *e* of Gedor,
2Ch 12.10 that kept the *e* of the king's
Ps 119.130 The *e* of thy words giveth light;
Eze 40.15 the face of the gate of the *e*
1Th 2. 1 know our *e* in unto you, that it
2Pe 1.11 an *e* shall be ministered unto you

ENTREAT

Jer 15.11 cause the enemy to *e* thee well
Ac 7. 6 and *e* them evil four hundred

ENTREATED

Gen 12.16 he *e* Abram well for her sake:
Ex 5.22 hast thou so evil *e* this people?
Dt 26. 6 And the Egyptians evil *e* us,
Mt 22. 6 *e* them spitefully, and slew them.
Lk 18.32 shall be mocked, and spitefully *e*,
20.11 *e* him shamefully, and sent him
Ac 7.19 evil *e* our fathers, so that they
27. 3 Julius courteously *e* Paul, and
1Th 2. 2 before, and were shamefully *e*.

ENVIES

1Pe 2. 1 guile, and hypocrisies, and *e*, and

ENVIETH

1Co 13. 4 charity *e* not; charity vaunteth

ENVY

Job 5. 2 and *e* slayeth the silly one.
Pr 3.31 *E* thou not the oppressor, and
14.30 but *e* the rottenness of the bones.
23.17 Let not thine heart *e* sinners: but
27. 4 who is able to stand before *e*?
Ec 9. 6 their hatred, and their *e*, is now
Isa 11.13 The *e* also of Ephraim shall depart,
13 Ephraim shall not *e* Judah, and
26.11 for their *e* at the people; yea,
Eze 35.11 according to thine *e* which thou
Mt 27.18 that for *e* they had delivered him.
Mk 15.10 priests had delivered him for *e*.
Ac 7. 9 patriarchs, moved with *e*, sold
13.45 were filled with *e*, and spake
17. 5 which believed not, moved with *e*
Ro 1.29 full of *e*, murder, debate, deceit,
Php 1.15 preach Christ even of *e* and strife;
1Ti 6. 4 whereof cometh *e*, strife, railings,
Tit 3. 3 living in malice and *e*, hateful,
Jas 4. 5 that dwelleth in us lusteth to *e*?

ENVYING

Ro 13.13 wantonness, not in strife and *e*.
1Co 3. 3 *e*, and strife, and divisions, are
Gal 5.26 one another, *e* one another.

Biblical Themes

ENVY

And Esau hated Jacob because of the blessing wherewith his father blessed him. Gen 27.41

When Rachel saw that she bare Jacob no children, Rachel envied her sister. Gen 30.1

Now Israel loved Joseph more than all his children, because he was the son of his old age: and he made him a coat of many colors. And when his brethren saw that their father loved him more than all his brethren, they hated him, and could not speak peaceably unto him. Gen 37.3-4

Thou shalt not covet thy neighbor's house, thou shalt not covet thy neighbor's wife, nor his manservant, nor his maidservant, nor his ox, nor his ass, nor any thing that is thy neighbor's. Ex 20.17

And the women answered one another as they played, and said, Saul hath slain his thousands, and David his ten thousands. And Saul was very wroth, and the saying displeased him. 1Sa 18.7-8

[Elijah] said, I have been very jealous for the Lord God of hosts: for the children of Israel have forsaken thy covenant. 1Ki 19.10

Ahab spake unto Naboth, saying, Give me thy vineyard, that I may have it for a garden of herbs, because it is near unto my house. 1Ki 21.2

I was envious at the foolish, when I saw the prosperity of the wicked. For . . . their strength is firm. They are not in trouble as other men; neither are they plagued like other men. . . . Until I went into the sanctuary of God; then understood I their end. Ps 73.3-5, 17

Jealousy is the rage of a man. Pr 6.34

A sound heart is the life of the flesh: but envy the rottenness of the bones. Pr 14.30

From the least of them even unto the greatest of them every one is given to covetousness; and from the prophet even unto the priest every one dealeth falsely. Jer 6.13

Woe to them that devise iniquity, and work evil upon their beds! when the morning is light, they practice it, because it is in the power of their hand. And they covet fields, and take them by violence; and houses, and take them away: so they oppress a man and his house, even a man and his heritage. Mic 2.1-2

And when the chief priests and scribes saw the wonderful things that he did, and the children crying in the temple, and saying, Hosanna to the son of David; they were sore displeased. Mt 21.15

Pilate said unto them, Whom will ye that I release unto you? Barabbas, or Jesus which is called Christ? For he knew that for envy they had delivered him. Mt 27.17-18

And he . . . said to his father, Lo, these many years do I serve thee, neither transgressed I at any time thy commandment: and yet thou never gavest me a kid, that I might make merry with my friends. Lk 15.29

Let us not be desirous of vain glory, provoking one another, envying one another. Gal 5.26

From whence come wars and fightings among you? come they not hence, even of your lusts that war in your members? Ye lust, and have not: ye kill, and desire to have, and cannot obtain: ye fight and war, yet ye have not, because ye ask not. Jas 4.1-2

Wherefore laying aside all malice, and all guile, and hypocrisies, and envies, and all evil speakings, as newborn babes, desire the sincere milk of the word, that ye may grow thereby. 1Pe 2.1-2

Jas 3.14 But if ye have bitter *e* and strife
16 For where *e* and strife is, there

ENVYINGS
2Co 12.20 *e*, wraths, strifes, backbitings,
Gal 5.21 *E*, murders, drunkenness,

EPAENETUS
Ro 16. 5 Salute my well beloved *E*, who

EPAPHRAS
Col 1. 7 As ye also learned of *E* our dear
4.12 *E*, who is one of you, a servant of
Phm 23 salute thee *E*, my fellowprisoner

EPAPHRODITUS
Php 2.25 it necessary to send to you *E*,
4.18 having received of *E* the things
sub. the Philippians from Rome by *E*,

EPHESIAN
Ac 21.29 him in the city Trophimus an *E*,

EPHESIANS
Ac 19.28 saying, Great is Diana of the *E*.
34 cried out, Great is Diana of the *E*.
35 the city of the *E* is a worshipper

EPHESUS
Ac 18.19 And he came to *E*, and left them
21 God will. And he sailed from *E*.
24 mighty in the scriptures, came to *E*.
19. 1 through the upper coasts came to *E*:
17 and Greeks also dwelling at *E*;
26 that not alone at *E*, but almost
35 Ye men of *E*, what man is there
20.16 Paul had determined to sail by *E*,
17 And from Miletus he sent to *E*,
1Co 15.32 I have fought with beasts at *E*,
16. 8 I will tarry at *E* until Pentecost.
Eph 1. 1 to the saints which are at *E*,
1Ti 1. 3 besought thee to abide still at *E*,
2Ti 1.18 he ministered unto me at *E*,
4.12 And Tychicus have I sent to *E*.
Rev 1.11 unto *E*, and unto Smyrna, and
2. 1 angel of the church of *E* write;
(See illustration on page 266)

EPHPHATHA
Mk 7.34 unto him, *E*, that is, Be opened.

EPICUREANS
Ac 17.18 certain philosophers of the *E*,

EPISTLE
Ac 15.30 together, they delivered the *e*:
23.33 delivered the *e* to the governor,
Ro 16.22 I Tertius, who wrote this *e*,
1Co 5. 9 I wrote unto you in an *e*
2Co 3. 2 are our *e* written in our hearts,
3 the *e* of Christ ministered by us,
7. 8 I perceive that the same *e* hath
Col 4.16 when this *e* is read among you,
16 that ye likewise read the *e* from
1Th 5.27 this *e* be read unto all the holy
2Th 2.15 whether my word, or our *e*.
3.14 our word by this *e*, note that man,
17 which is the token in every *e*:
2Pe 3. 1 second *e*, beloved, I now write

EPISTLES
2Co 3. 1 *e* of commendation to you, or
2Pe 3.16 As also in all his *e*, speaking in

EQUAL
Job 28.17 gold and the crystal cannot *e* it:
19 topaz of Ethiopia shall not *e* it,
Ps 17. 2 behold the things that are *e*.
55.13 it was thou, a man mine *e*,
Pr 26. 7 The legs of the lame are not *e*:
Isa 40.25 will ye liken me, or shall I be *e*?
46. 5 will ye liken me, and make me *e*,
La 2.13 what shall I *e* to thee, that I may
Eze 18.25 The way of the Lord is not *e*.
25 house of Israel; Is not my way *e*?
29 The way of the Lord is not *e*. O
29 of Israel, are not my ways *e*?
33.17 The way of the Lord is not *e*: but
17 as for them, their way is not *e*.
20 The way of the Lord is not *e*.
Mt 20.12 thou hast made them *e* unto us,
Lk 20.36 for they are *e* unto the angels;
Jn 5.18 making himself *e* with God.
Php 2. 6 it not robbery to be *e* with God:
Col 4. 1 servants that which is just and *e*;
Rev 21.16 breadth and the height of it are *e*.

EQUALITY
2Co 8.14 But by an *e*, that now at this time
14 your want: that there may be *e*:

EQUALS
Gal 1.14 many my *e* in mine own nation,

ERASTUS
Ac 19.22 Timotheus and *E*; but he himself

Ro 16.23 *E* the chamberlain of the city
2Ti 4.20 *E* abode at Corinth: but Trophimus

ERE

Ex 1.19 delivered *e* the midwives come
Nu 11.33 their teeth, *e* it was chewed,
14.11 how long will it be *e* they believe
1Sa 3. 3 And *e* the lamp of God went out
2Sa 2.26 it be then, *e* thou bid the people
2Ki 6.32 but *e* the messenger came to him,
Job 18. 2 How long will it be *e* ye make an
Jer 47. 6 how long will it be *e* thou be quiet?
Hos 8. 5 how long will it be *e* they attain
Jn 4.49 Sir, come down *e* my child die.

ERR

2Ch 33. 9 So Manasseh made Judah....to *e*,
Ps 95.10 is a people that do *e* in their heart,
119.21 rebuked the proud...which do *e*
118 hast trodden down all them that *e*
Pr 14.22 Do they not *e* that devise evil?
19.27 the instruction that causeth to *e*
Isa 3.12 which lead thee cause thee to *e*,
9.16 of this people cause them to *e*;
19.14 they have caused Egypt to *e* in
28. 7 they *e* in vision, they stumble in
30.28 of the people, causing them to *e*.
35. 8 men, though fools, shall not *e*
63.17 why hast thou made us to *e* from
Jer 23.13 and caused my people Israel to *e*.
32 cause my people to *e* by their lies,
Hos 4.12 whoredoms hath caused them to *e*,
Am 2. 4 and their lies caused them to *e*,
Mic 3. 5 prophets that make my people *e*,
Mt 22.29 Ye do *e*, not knowing the
Mk 12.24 Do ye not therefore *e*, because ye
27 ye therefore do greatly *e*.
Heb 3.10 They do alway *e* in their heart;
Jas 1.16 Do not *e*, my beloved brethren.
5.19 Brethren, if any of you do *e* from

ERRED

Lev 5.18 his ignorance wherein he *e* and
Nu 15.22 if ye have *e*, and not observed all
1Sa 26.21 the fool, and have *e* exceedingly.
Job 6.24 me to understand wherein I have *e*.
19. 4 And be it indeed that I have *e*,
Ps 119.110 I have *e* not from thy precepts.
Isa 28. 7 they also have *e* through wine,
7 priest and the prophet have *e*
29.24 They also that *e* in spirit shall
1Ti 6.10 they have *e* from the faith, and
21 have *e* concerning the faith.
2Ti 2.18 Who concerning the truth have *e*,

ERROR

2Sa 6. 7 God smote him there for his *e*;
Job 19. 4 mine *e* remaineth with myself.
Ec 5. 6 neither say thou...it was an *e*:
10. 5 as an *e* which proceedeth from the
Isa 32. 6 and to utter *e* against the Lord,
Dan 6. 4 neither was there any *e* or fault
Mt 27.64 so the last *e* shall be worse than
Ro 1.27 that recompence of their *e* which
Jas 5.20 the sinner from the *e* of his way
2Pe 2.18 escape from them who live in *e*.
3.17 being led away with the *e* of the
1Jn 4. 6 spirit of truth, and the spirit of *e*.
Jude 11 ran greedily after the *e* of Balaam

ERRORS

Ps 19.12 Who can understand his *e*?
Jer 10.15 are vanity, and the work of *e*:
51.18 They are vanity, the work of *e*:
Heb 9. 7 himself, and for the *e* of the people:

ESAIAS

Mt 3. 3 spoken of by the prophet *E*,
4.14 was spoken by *E* the prophet,
8.17 fulfilled which was spoken by *E*
12.17 fulfilled which was spoken by *E*

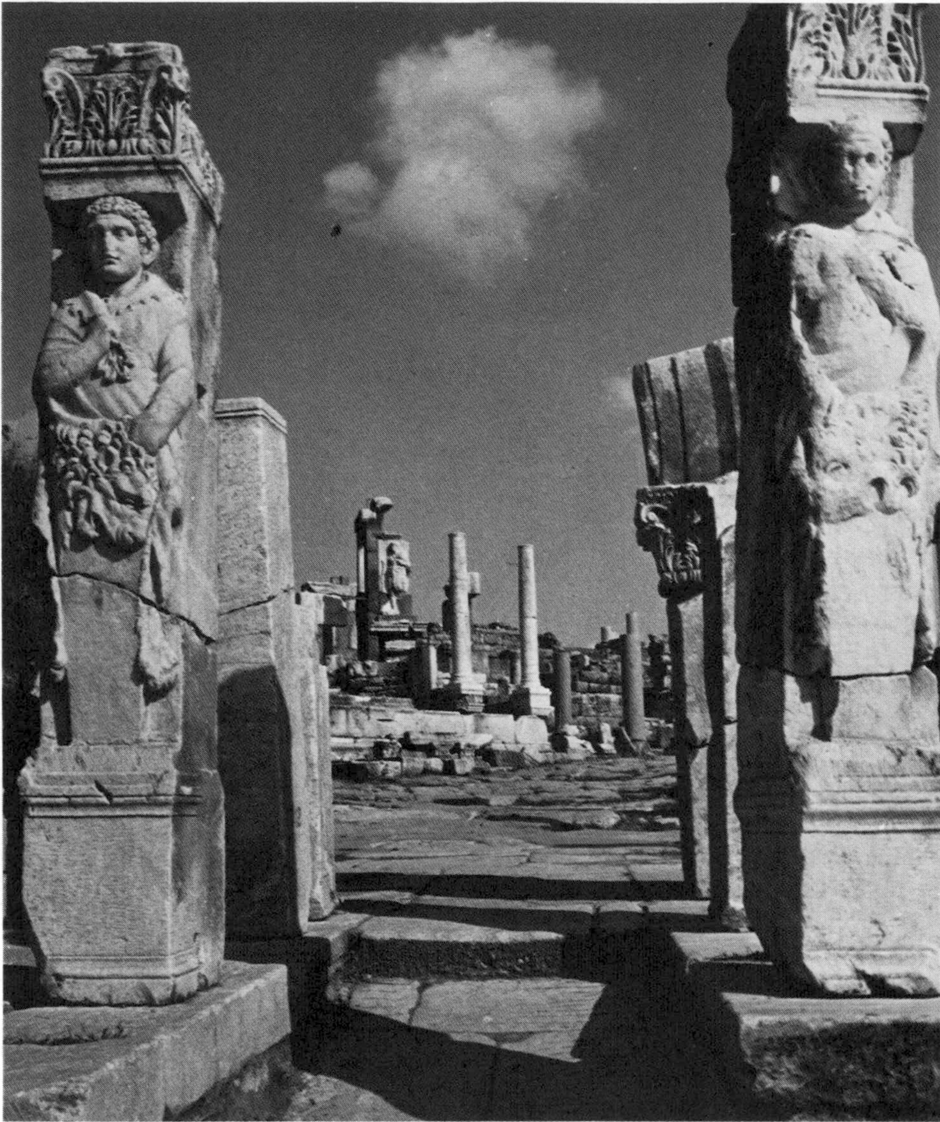

A gateway to Ephesus in Asia Minor, where Paul's preaching led to a riot by the city's silversmiths (Ac 19).

13.14 fulfilled the prophecy of *E*,
15. 7 hypocrites, well did *E* prophesy
Mk 7. 6 Well hath *E* prophesied of you
Lk 3. 4 in the book of the words of *E*
4.17 him the book of the prophet *E*.
Jn 1.23 the Lord, as said the prophet *E*.
12.38 That the saying of *E* the prophet
39 could not believe, because that *E*
41 These things said *E*, when he
Ac 8.28 sitting in his chariot read *E* the
30 heard him read the prophet *E*,
28.25 Well spake the Holy Ghost by *E*
Ro 9.27 *E* also crieth concerning Israel,
29 and as *E* said before, Except the
10.16 *E* saith, Lord, who hath believed
20 But *E* is very bold, and saith, I
15.12 And again, *E* saith, There shall

ESAU

Gen 25.25 they called his name *E*.
27 *E* was a cunning hunter, a man of
28 Isaac loved *E*, because he did eat
29 *E* came from the field, and he was
30 *E* said to Jacob, Feed me, I pray
32 *E* said, Behold, I am at the point
34 Then Jacob gave *E* bread and
34 Thus *E* despised his birthright.
26.34 And *E* was forty years old when he
27. 1 he called *E* his eldest son, and said
5 heard when Isaac spake to *E*
5 And *E* went to the field to hunt for
6 I heard thy father speak unto *E*
11 Behold, *E* my brother is a hairy
15 goodly raiment of her eldest son *E*,
19 Jacob said unto his father, I am *E*
21 whether thou be my very son *E* or
22 but the hands are the hands of *E*.
24 he said, Art thou my very son *E*?
30 that *E* his brother came in from
32 said, I am thy son, thy firstborn *E*.
34 when *E* heard the words of his
37 Isaac answered and said unto *E*,
38 *E* said unto his father, Hast thou
38 *E* lifted up his voice, and wept.
41 And *E* hated Jacob because of the
41 *E* said in his heart, The days of
42 these words of *E* her elder son
42 Behold, thy brother *E*, as touching
28. 6 When *E* saw that Isaac had blessed
8 And *E* seeing that the daughters of
9 Then went *E* unto Ishmael, and
32. 3 sent messengers before him to *E*
4 shall ye speak unto my lord *E*:
6 We came to thy brother *E*, and
8 If *E* come to the one company,
11 of my brother, from the hand of *E*:

13 hand a present for *E* his brother;
17 When *E* my brother meeteth thee,
18 sent unto my lord *E*: and, behold,
19 this manner shall ye speak unto *E*,
33. 1 and, behold, *E* came, and with him
4 And *E* ran to meet him, and
9 *E* said, I have enough, my brother;
15 And *E* said, Let me now leave
16 So *E* returned that day on his way
35. 1 from the face of *E* thy brother.
29 his sons *E* and Jacob buried him.
36. 1 generations of *E*, who is Edom.
2 *E* took his wives of the daughters
4 And Adah bare to *E* Eliphaz;
5 these are the sons of *E*, which
6 And *E* took his wives, and his sons,
8 dwelt *E* in Mount Seir: *E* is Edom.
9 of *E* the father of the Edomites in
10 the son of Adah the wife of *E*,
10 son of Bashemath the wife of *E*.
14 she bare to *E* Jeush, and Jaalam,
15 were dukes of the sons of *E*:
15 of Eliphaz, the firstborn son of *E*;
19 are the sons of *E*, who is Edom,
40 of the dukes that came of *E*,
43 he is *E* the father of the Edomites.
Dt 2. 4 children of *E*, which dwell in Seir;
5 Seir unto *E* for a possession.
8 children of *E*, which dwelt in Seir,
12 the children of *E* succeeded them,
22 As he did to the children of *E*,
29 children of *E* which dwelt in Seir,
Jos 24. 4 I gave unto Isaac Jacob and *E*:
4 and I gave unto *E* mount Seir,
1Ch 1.34 The sons of Isaac; *E* and Israel.
35 The sons of *E*; Eliphaz, Reuel,
Jer 49. 8 bring the calamity of *E* upon him,
10 But I have made *E* bare, I have
Ob 6 are the things of *E* searched out!
8 the wise men out of the mount of *E*?
9 every one of the mount of *E* may
18 and the house of *E* for stubble,
18 any remaining of the house of *E*;
19 shall possess the mount of *E*;
21 Zion to judge the mount of *E*;
Mal 1. 2 Was not *E* Jacob's brother? saith
3 I hated *E*, and laid his mountains
Ro 9.13 I loved, but *E* have I hated.
Heb 11.20 By faith Isaac blessed Jacob and *E*
12.16 fornicator, or profane person, as *E*,

ESCAPE

Gen 19.17 *E* for thy life; look not behind
1Ki 18.40 let not one of them *e*. And they
Ezr 9. 8 to leave us a remnant to *e*,
Est 4.13 thou shalt *e* in the king's house,
Job 11.20 they shall not *e*, and their hope
Ps 141.10 own nets, whilst that I withal *e*.
Pr 19. 5 he that speaketh lies shall not *e*.
Ec 7.26 pleaseth God shall *e* from her;
Jer 48. 8 no city shall *e*: the valley also
Eze 17.15 shall he *e* that doeth such things?
Mt 23.33 ye *e* the damnation of hell?
Lk 21.36 worthy to *e* all these things
Ac 27.42 of them should swim out, and *e*.
Ro 2. 3 thou shalt *e* the judgment of God?
1Co 10.13 temptation also make a way to *e*,
1Th 5. 3 with child; and they shall not *e*.
Heb 2. 3 How shall we *e*, if we neglect so
12.25 earth, much more shall not we *e*,

ESCAPED

Jdg 3.29 of valour: and there *e* not a man.
Neh 1. 2 concerning the Jews that had *e*,
Job 19.20 I am *e* with the skin of my teeth.
Ps 124. 7 Our soul is *e* as a bird out of the
Eze 33.21 one that had *e* out of Jerusalem
Jn 10.39 him: but he *e* out of their hand,
Ac 27.44 pass, that they *e* all safe to land,
28. 1 when they were *e*, then they knew
4 whom, though he hath *e* the sea,
2Co 11.33 was I let down by the wall, and *e*
Heb 11.34 of fire, *e* the edge of the sword,
12.25 For if they *e* not who refused him
2Pe 1. 4 having *e* the corruption that is in
2.18 those that were clean *e* from them
20 For if after they have *e* the

ESCHEW

1Pe 3.11 Let him *e* evil, and do good;

ESCHEWED

Job 1. 1 one that feared God, and *e* evil.

ESCHEWETH

Job 1. 8 one that feareth God and *e* evil?
2. 3 one that feareth God, and *e* evil?

ESPECIALLY

Ps 31.11 but *e* among my neighbors,
Ac 26. 3 *E* because I know thee to be
Gal 6.10 men, *e* unto them who are of the
1Ti 5.17 *e* they who labor in the word and
2Ti 4.13 the books, but *e* the parchments.

ESPOUSED

2Sa 3.14 my wife Michal, which I *e* to me
Mt 1.18 When as his mother Mary was *e*
Lk 1.27 To a virgin *e* to a man whose
2. 5 To be taxed with Mary his *e* wife,
2Co 11. 2 For I have *e* you to one husband,

ESTABLISH

Gen 6.18 with thee will I *e* my covenant;
Dt 28. 9 The Lord shall *e* thee an holy people
1Sa 1.23 only the Lord *e* his word. So the
2Ch 9. 8 loved Israel, to *e* them for ever,
Ps 48. 8 God will *e* it for ever. Selah.
90.17 and *e* thou the work of our hands
Pr 15.25 he will *e* the border of the widow.
Eze 16.60 I will *e* unto thee an everlasting
Dan 6. 8 Now, O king, *e* the decree,
Am 5.15 and *e* judgment in the gate:
Ro 3.31 God forbid: yea, we *e* the law.
10. 3 about to *e* their own righteousness,
1Th 3. 2 to *e* you, and to comfort you
Heb 10. 9 the first, that he may *e* the second.

ESTABLISHED

Gen 41.32 because the thing is *e* by God,
Dt 19.15 witnesses, shall the matter be *e*.
2Sa 7.16 thy throne shall be *e* for ever.
Ps 24. 2 and *e* it upon the floods.

ESAU

Elder of twin sons born to Isaac and Rebekah; when grown becomes a skillful hunter, and favored by Isaac because of the venison he brings him; one day returning famished from the field, sells his birthright to Jacob for a mess of pottage, thus making Jacob Isaac's prime heir (Gen 25.21-34); is further deprived of his father's blessing when Jacob deceives the old man by dressing up in Esau's clothes; vows vengeance on Jacob, who flees to Mesopotamia (Gen 27); but on Jacob's return twenty years later takes the initiative in making peace with him (Gen 33); they part amicably, and meet again briefly at their father's funeral (Gen 35.29); Jacob, settling in Canaan, becomes the traditional ancestor of the Israelites, while Esau moves south to the land of his future descendants, the Edomites (Gen 36).

40. 2 feet upon a rock, and *e* my goings.
89.37 It shall be *e* for ever as the moon,
93. 2 Thy throne is *e* of old: thou art
96.10 the world also shall be *e* that it
Pr 4.26 and let all thy ways be *e*.
12. 3 man shall not be *e* by wickedness:
19 The lip of truth shall be *e* for ever:
16.12 the throne is *e* by righteousness.
20.18 Every purpose is *e* by counsel:
24. 3 and by understanding it is *e*:
Isa 7. 9 believe, surely ye shall not be *e*.
16. 5 in mercy shall the throne be *e*:
Jer 10.12 hath *e* the world by his wisdom,
51.15 by his power, he hath *e* the world
Mt 18.16 witnesses every word may be *e*.
Ac 16. 5 were the churches *e* in the faith,
Ro 1.11 to the end ye may be *e*;
2Co 13. 1 witnesses shall every word be *e*.
Heb 8. 6 was *e* upon better promises.
13. 9 that the heart be *e* with grace;
2Pe 1.12 and be *e* in the present truth.

ESTATE

1Ch 17.17 regarded me according to the *e*
Est 1.19 give her royal *e* unto another
Ps 136.23 Who remembered us in our low *e*:
Ec 1.16 Lo, I am come to great *e*.
3.18 concerning the *e* of the sons of
Eze 16.55, 55 shall return to their former *e*,
55 shall return to your former *e*.
Dan 11. 7 shall one stand up in his *e*,
20 Then shall stand up in his *e*
21 And in his *e* shall stand up a vile
38 in his *e* shall he honor the God
Ac 22. 5 and all the *e* of the elders:
Lk 1.48 the low *e* of his handmaiden:
Ro 12.16 condescend to men of low *e*.
Col 4. 8 he might know your *e*, and
Jude 6 which kept not their first *e*,

ESTATES

Eze 36.11 I will settle you after your old *e*,
Mk 6.21 captains, and chief *e* of Galilee;

ESTEEM

Job 36.19 Will he *e* thy riches? no, not
Ps 119.128 I *e* all thy precepts...to be right;
Isa 53. 4 yet we did *e* him stricken,
Php 2. 3 *e* other better than themselves.
1Th 5.13 And to *e* them very highly in love

ESTEEMED

Dt 32.15 lightly *e* the Rock of his salvation.
1Sa 2.30 despise me shall be lightly *e*.
18.23 I am a poor man, and lightly *e*?
Job 23.12 I have *e* the words of his mouth
Pr 17.28 shutteth his lips is *e* a man of
Isa 29.16 shall be *e* as the potter's clay
17 fruitful field shall be *e* as a forest?
53. 3 was despised, and we *e* him not.
La 4. 2 are they *e* as earthen pitchers,
Lk 16.15 which is highly *e* among men
1Co 6. 4 them to judge who are least *e*

ESTEEMETH

Job 41.27 He *e* iron as straw, and brass
Ro 14. 5 One man *e* one day above another:
5 another *e* every day alike.
14 but to him that *e* any thing to be

ESTEEMING

Heb 11.26 *E* the reproach of Christ greater

ESTHER

Est 2. 7 brought up Hadassah, that is, *E*,
10 *E* had not shewed her people nor
15 *E* obtained favor in the sight of
16 *E* was taken unto king Ahasuerus
17 king loved *E* above all the women,
22 who told it unto *E* the queen;
4.13 Mordecai commanded to answer *E*,

ESTHER

Beautiful Jewish maiden living in Persia during the reign of Ahasuerus (probably Xerxes, 5th century B.C.); following the banishment of Queen Vashti, is chosen for the royal harem and so pleases the king that he makes her queen, not knowing of her Jewish identity (Est 1–2); when Persian Jews come under threat from Haman, the king's chief minister, because of Haman's hatred for Mordecai, Esther's cousin and former guardian, Mordecai persuades her to reveal her origins and plead for her people, though this involves personal risk (Est 3–4); her intercessions result in the execution of Haman, reprisals against those who had sought to destroy the Jews, and Mordecai's appointment as the king's chief minister; Esther's deliverance of her people celebrated in Feast of Purim (Est 5–9).

Est 4.17 to all that *E* had commanded
5. 1 that *E* put on her royal apparel,
2 when the king saw *E* the queen
2 held out to *E* the golden scepter
6.14 the banquet that *E* had prepared.
7. 2 What is thy petition, queen *E*?
6 *E* said, The adversary and enemy
8. 1 the Jews' enemy unto *E* the queen.
2 *E* set Mordecai over the house of
4 *E* arose, and stood before the king.
7 Ahasuerus said unto *E* the queen
7 have given *E* the house of Haman,
9.13 Then said *E*, If it please the king,
32 the decree of *E* confirmed these

ETERNAL

Dt 33.27 The *e* God is thy refuge, and
Isa 60.15 I will make thee an *e* excellency,
Mt 19.16 shall I do, that I may have *e* life?
25.46 but the righteous into life *e*.
Mk 3.29 in danger of *e* damnation:
10.17 I do that I may inherit *e* life?
30 and in the world to come *e* life,
Lk 10.25 what shall I do to inherit *e* life?
18.18 what shall I do to inherit *e* life?
Jn 3.15 should not perish, but have *e* life.
4.36 and gathereth fruit unto life *e*:
5.39 for in them ye think ye have *e* life:
6.54 and drinketh my blood, hath *e* life;
68 thou hast the words of *e* life.
10.28 And I give unto them *e* life;
12.25 this world shall keep it unto life *e*.
17. 2 he should give *e* life to as many as
3 this is life *e*, that they might know
Ac 13.48 many as were ordained to *e* life
Ro 1.20 even his *e* power and Godhead;
2. 7 and honor and immortality, *e* life:
5.21 through righteousness unto *e* life
6.23 but the gift of God is *e* life through
2Co 4.17 exceeding and *e* weight of glory;
18 the things which are not seen are *e*.
5. 1 made with hands, *e* in the heavens.
Eph 3.11 According the *e* purpose which
1Ti 1.17 Now unto the King *e*, immortal,
6.12 lay hold on *e* life, whereunto thou
6.19 that they may lay hold on *e* life.
2Ti 2.10 is in Christ Jesus with *e* glory.
Tit 1. 2 In hope of *e* life, which God, that
3. 7 according to the hope of *e* life.
Heb 5. 9 became the author of *e* salvation
6. 2 of the dead, and of *e* judgment.
9.12 having obtained *e* redemption
14 who through the *e* Spirit offered
15 the promise of *e* inheritance,
1Pe 5.10 who hath called us unto his *e* glory
1Jn 1. 2 shew unto you that *e* life, which
2.25 he hath promised us, even *e* life.
3.15 no murderer hath *e* life abiding in
5.11 that God hath given to us *e* life,
13 ye may know that ye have *e* life,
20 This is the true God, and *e* life.
Jude 7 suffering the vengeance of *e* fire.
21 of our Lord Jesus Christ unto *e* life.

ETERNITY

Isa 57.15 and lofty One that inhabiteth *e*,

EUBULUS

2Ti 4.21 *E* greeteth thee, and Pudens, and

EUNICE

2Ti 1. 5 Lois, and thy mother *E*; and I am

EUNUCH

Isa 56. 3 neither let the *e* say, Behold, I
Jer 52.25 *e*, which had the charge of the
Ac 8.27 an *e* of great authority under
34 the *e* answered Philip, and said,
36 the *e* said, See, here is water;
38 the water, both Philip and the *e*;
39 that the *e* saw him no more:

EUNUCHS

Mt 19.12 For there are some *e*, which were
12 and there are some *e*, which
12 which were made *e* of men:
12 and there be *e*, which have made
12 have made themselves *e* for the

EUODIAS

Php 4. 2 beseech *E*, and beseech Syntyche,

EUROCLYDON

Ac 27.14 a tempestuous wind, called *E*.

EUTYCHUS

Ac 20. 9 a certain young man named *E*,

EVANGELIST

Ac 21. 8 entered the house of Philip the *e*,
2Ti 4. 5 afflictions, do the work of an *e*,

EVANGELISTS

Eph 4.11 and some, *e*: and some, pastors

EVE

Gen 3.20 Adam called his wife's name *E*;
4. 1 And Adam knew *E* his wife; and
2Co 11. 3 the serpent beguiled *E* through
1Ti 2.13 Adam was first formed, then *E*.

EVENING

Gen 1. 5 *e* and the morning were the first
8.11 the dove came in to him in the *e*,
1Ch 16.40 continually morning and *e*,
Ezr 9. 4 I sat astonied until the *e* sacrifice.
Ps 65. 8 the morning and *e* to rejoice.
90. 6 the *e* it is cut down, and withereth.
104.23 forth unto his work...until the *e*.
141. 2 up of my hands as the *e* sacrifice.
Ec 11. 6 in the *e* withhold not thine hand:
Jer 6. 4 shadows of the *e* are stretched out.
Hab 1. 8 are more fierce than the *e* wolves:
Zep 3. 3 judges are *e* wolves; they gnaw
Zec 14. 7 at *e* time it shall be light.
Mt 14.15 when it was *e*, his disciples came
23 *e* was come, he was there alone.
16. 2 When it is *e*, ye say, it will be fair
Mk 14.17 in the *e* he cometh with the twelve,
Lk 24.29 toward *e*, and the day is far spent,
Jn 20.19 same day at *e*, being the first
Ac 28.23 the prophets, from morning till *e*.

EVENT

Ec 2.14 one *e* happeneth to them all.
9. 2 one *e* to the righteous, and to the
3 that there is one *e* unto all:

EVENTIDE

Gen 24.63 Isaac went out...at the *e*:
Jos 7. 6 the ark of the Lord until the *e*,
8.29 he hanged on a tree until *e*:
Mk 11.11 and now the *e* was come,
Ac 4. 3 the next day: for it was now *e*.

EVERLASTING

Gen 9.16 I may remember the *e* covenant
17. 7 an *e* covenant, to be a God unto
8 for an *e* possession; and I will be
13 be in your flesh for an *e* covenant.
19 with him for an *e* covenant,
21.33 name of the Lord, the *e* God.
48. 4 after thee for an *e* possession.
49.26 the utmost bound of the *e* hills:
Ex 40.15 an *e* priesthood throughout their
Lev 16.34 this shall be an *e* statute unto you,
24. 8 of Israel by an *e* covenant.
Nu 25.13 the covenant of an *e* priesthood;
Dt 33.27 and underneath are the *e* arms:
2Sa 23. 5 hath made with me an *e* covenant,
1Ch 16.17 and to Israel for an *e* covenant,
Ps 24. 7 be ye lift up, ye *e* doors;
9 even lift them up, ye *e* doors;
41.13 Lord God of Israel from *e*, and to *e*.
90. 2 even from *e* to *e*, thou art God.
93. 2 established of old; thou art from *e*.
100. 5 the Lord is good; his mercy is *e*;
103.17 mercy of the Lord is from *e* to *e*
105.10 and to Israel for an *e* covenant:
106.48 the Lord God of Israel from *e* to *e*:
112. 6 shall be in *e* remembrance.
119.142 Thy righteousness is an *e*
144 of thy testimonies is *e*:
139.24 and lead me in the way *e*.
145.13 Thy kingdom is an *e* kingdom,
Pr 8.23 I was set up from *e*, from the
10.25 the righteous is an *e* foundation.
Isa 9. 6 The *e* Father, The Prince of Peace.
24. 5 ordinance, broken the *e* covenant.
26. 4 in the Lord Jehovah is *e* strength:
33.14 us shall dwell with *e* burnings?
35.10 and *e* joy upon their heads:
40.28 not heard, that the *e* God, the Lord,
45.17 in the Lord with an *e* salvation:
51.11 *e* joy shall be upon their head:
54. 8 with *e* kindess will I have mercy
55. 3 I will make an *e* covenant with you,
13 an *e* sign that shall not be cut off.
56. 5 I will give them an *e* name,
60.19 Lord shall be unto thee an *e* light,
20 the Lord shall be thine *e* light,
61. 7 *e* joy shall be unto them.
8 I will make an *e* covenant with
63.12 to make himself an *e* name?
16 redeemer; thy name is from *e*.
Jer 10.10 the living God, and an *e* king:
20.11 their *e* confusion shall never be
23.40 I will bring an *e* reproach upon
31. 3 I have loved thee with an *e* love:
32.40 I will make an *e* covenant with
Eze 16.60 establish unto thee an *e* covenant.
37.26 shall be an *e* covenant with them:
Dan 4. 3 his kingdom is an *e* kingdom,
34 whose dominion is an *e* dominion,
7.14 his dominion is an *e* dominion,
27 whose kingdom is an *e* kingdom,
9.24 and to bring in *e* righteousness,
12. 2 some to *e* life, and some to shame
2 to shame and *e* contempt.
Mic 5. 2 forth have been from of old, from *e*.
Hab 1.12 Art thou not from *e*, O Lord
3. 6 the *e* mountains were scattered.
6 hills did bow: his ways are *e*.
Mt 18. 8 or two feet to be cast into *e* fire.

19.29 and shall inherit *e* life.
25.41 from me, ye cursed, into *e* fire,
46 shall go away into *e* punishment:
Lk 16. 9 receive you into *e* habitations.
18.30 and in the world to come life *e*.
Jn 3.16 should not perish, but have *e* life.
36 believeth on the Son hath *e* life;
4.14 of water springing up into *e* life.
5.24 on him that sent me, hath *e* life,
6.27 meat which endureth unto *e* life,
40 on him, may have *e* life:
47 believeth on me hath *e* life.
12.50 that his commandment is life *e*:
Ac 13.46 yourselves unworthy of *e* life, lo,
Ro 6.22 unto holiness, and the end *e* life.
16.26 the commandment of the *e* God,
Gal 6. 8 shall of the spirit reap life *e*.
2Th 1. 9 be punished with *e* destruction
2.16 and hath given us *e* consolation
1Ti 1.16 believe on him to life *e*.
6.16 to whom be honor and power *e*.
Heb 13.20 the blood of the *e* covenant,
2Pe 1.11 to the *e* kingdom of our Lord and
Jude 6 he hath reserved in *e* chains
Rev 14. 6 having the *e* gospel to preach

EVERMORE

Dt 28.29 oppressed and spoiled *e*,
2Sa 22.51 unto David, and to his seed for *e*.
2Ki 17.37 ye shall observe to do for *e*;
1Ch 17.14 throne shall be established for *e*.
Ps 16.11 hand there are pleasures for *e*.
18.50 David, and to his seed for *e*.
37.27 and do good; and dwell for *e*.
77. 8 doth his promise fail for *e*?
86.12 I will glorify thy name for *e*.
89.28 My mercy will I keep for him for *e*,
52 Blessed be the Lord for *e*. Amen,
92. 8 thou, Lord, art most high for *e*.
105. 4 and his strength: seek his face *e*.
106.31 unto all generations for *e*.
113. 2 from this time forth and for *e*.
115.18 from this time forth and for *e*.
121. 8 from this time forth, and even for *e*.
132.12 shall also sit upon thy throne for *e*.
133. 3 the blessing, even life for *e*.
Eze 37.26 in the midst of them for *e*.
28 shall be in the midst of them for *e*.
Jn 6.34 Lord, *e* give us this bread.
2Co 11.31 Christ, which is blessed for *e*,
1Th 5.16 Rejoice *e*.
Heb 7.28 Son, who is consecrated for *e*.
Rev 1.18 I am alive for *e*,

EVIDENCE

Jer 32.10 I subscribed the *e*, and sealed it,
11 So I took the *e* of the purchase,
12 And I gave the *e* of the purchase
14 this *e* of the purchase,
14 and this *e* which is open;
16 delivered the *e* of the purchase
Heb 11. 1 the *e* of things not seen.

EVIDENCES

Jer 32.14 Take these *e*, this evidence of the
44 and subscribe *e*, and seal them,

EVIDENT

Job 6.28 for it is *e* unto you if I lie.
Gal 3.11 in the sight of God, it is *e*: for,
Php 1.28 is to them an *e* token of perdition,
Heb 7.14 For it is *e* that our Lord sprang
15 And it is yet far more *e*: for that

EVIDENTLY

Ac 10. 3 He saw in a vision *e*, about the
Gal 3. 1 Jesus Christ hath been *e* set forth,

EVIL

Gen 2. 9 tree of knowledge of good and *e*.
17 of the knowledge of good and *e*,
3. 5 be as gods, knowing good and *e*.
22 as one of us, to know good and *e*:
8.21 imagination of man's heart is *e*
37.20 Some *e* beast hath devoured him:
33 an *e* beast hath devoured him;
44. 4 have ye rewarded *e* for good?
47. 9 few and *e* have the days of the
48.16 which redeemed me from all *e*,
Ex 32.12 repent of this *e* against thy people.
Nu 20. 5 to bring us in unto this *e* place?
Dt 1.39 knowledge between good and *e*,
13. 5 So shalt thou put the *e* away
29.21 Lord shall separate him unto *e*
30.15 life and good, and death and *e*;
31.29 will do *e* in the sight of the Lord,
Jdg 9.23 God sent an *e* spirit between
1Sa 16.14 an *e* spirit from the Lord troubled
15 *e* spirit from God troubleth thee.
23 the *e* spirit departed from him.
18.10 *e* spirit from God came upon Saul,
25.21 he hath requited me *e* for good.
26.18 or what *e* is in mine hand?
29. 6 I have not found *e* in thee
2Sa 19.35 I discern between good and *e*?
24.16 the Lord repented him of the *e*,
1Ki 17.20 also brought *e* upon the widow
21.20 thou hast sold thyself to work *e*
2Ki 6.33 Behold, this *e* is of the Lord;
17.13 Turn ye from your *e* ways, and
1Ch 4.10 thou wouldst keep me from *e*,
2Ch 18.17 prophesy good unto me, but *e*?
20. 9 *e* cometh upon us, as the sword,
Job 1. 1 that feared God, and eschewed *e*.
8 that feareth God, and escheweth *e*?
2. 3 that feareth God, and escheweth *e*?
28.28 depart from *e* is understanding.
Ps 15. 3 nor doeth *e* to his neighbor, nor
23. 4 I will fear no *e*: for thou art
34.13 Keep thy tongue from *e*, and thy
14 Depart from *e*, and do good; seek
16 the Lord is against them that do *e*,
35.12 They rewarded me *e* for good to
37.27 Depart from *e*, and do good; and
51. 4 and done this *e* in thy sight:
90.15 the years wherein we have seen *e*.
91.10 There shall no *e* befall thee,
97.10 Ye that love the Lord, hate *e*:
112. 7 He shall not be afraid of *e* tidings:
121. 7 Lord shall preserve thee from all *e*:
140. 1 Deliver me, O Lord, from the *e*
Pr 1.16 their feet run to *e*, and make haste
2.12 me from the way of the *e* man,
3. 7 fear the Lord, and depart from *e*.
4.14 go not in the way of *e* men.
8.13 The fear of the Lord is to hate *e*:
11.19 *e* pursueth it to his own death.
14.19 The *e* bow before the good;
15. 3 eyes of the Lord...beholding the *e*
15 All the days of the afflicted are *e*:
16.27 An ungodly man diggeth up *e*:
21.10 The soul of the wicked desireth *e*:
22. 3 A prudent man foreseeth the *e*,
23. 6 bread of him that hath an *e* eye,
24.19 Fret not thyself because of *e* men.
Ec 2.21 This also is vanity and a great *e*.
5.13 a sore *e* which I have seen
8.12 a sinner do *e* an hundred times,
9.12 sons of men snared in an *e* time,
10. 5 *e* which I have seen under the sun,
Isa 1.16 put away the *e* of your doings
16 before mine eyes, cease to do *e*;
5.20 them that call *e* good, and good *e*;
7.16 child shall know to refuse the *e*,
13.11 will punish the world for their *e*,
33.15 shutteth his eyes from seeing *e*;
45. 7 I make peace, and create *e*: I
Jer 3.17 the imagination of their *e* heart.
9. 3 they proceed from *e* to *e*, and
17.17 thou art my hope in the day of *e*.
18.20 Shall *e* be recompensed for good?
23.17 No *e* shall come upon you.
24. 8 the *e* figs, which cannot be eaten,
26.13 the Lord will repent him of the *e*
29.11 thoughts of peace, and not of *e*,
36. 3 return every man from his *e* way;
45. 5 I will bring *e* upon all flesh,
Eze 5.16 upon them the *e* arrows of famine.
33.11 turn ye from your *e* ways; for
Am 3. 6 shall there be *e* in a city,
5.14 Seek good, and not *e*, that ye may
15 Hate the *e*, and love the good,
Jon 3. 8 turn every one from his *e* way,
10 God repented of the *e*, that he had
Mic 7. 3 they may do *e* with both hands
Hab 1.13 art of purer eyes than to behold *e*,
Zep 3.15 thou shalt not see *e* any more.
Zec 1. 4 Turn ye now from your *e* ways,
7.10 none of you imagine *e* against his
Mal 1. 8 blind for the sacrifice, is it not *e*?
2.17 Every one that doeth *e* is good
Mt 5.11 and shall say all manner of *e*
37 is more than these cometh of *e*.
39 unto you, That ye resist not *e*:
45 maketh his sun to rise on the *e*
6.13 but deliver us from *e*:
23 in thine eye be *e*, thy whole body
34 Sufficient unto the day is the *e*
7.11 If ye then, being *e*, know how to
17 corrupt tree bringeth forth *e* fruit.
18 good tree cannot bring forth *e* fruit,
9. 4 Wherefore think ye *e* in your
12.34 how can ye, being *e*, speak good
35 an *e* man out of the *e* treasure
35 bringeth forth *e* things.
39 An *e* and adulterous generation
15.19 of the heart proceed *e* thoughts,
20.15 Is thine eye *e*, because I am good?
24.48 and if that *e* servant shall say
27.23 Why, what *e* hath he done?
Mk 3. 4 on the sabbath day, or to do *e*?
7.21 *e* thoughts, adulteries,
22 lasciviousness, an *e* eye,
23 these *e* things come from within,
9.39 that can lightly speak *e* of me.
15.14 Why, what *e* hath he done?
Lk 6. 9 to do good, or to do *e*?
22 and cast out your name as *e*,
35 unto the unthankful and to the *e*.
45 and an *e* man out of the *e* treasure
45 bringeth forth that which is *e*:
7.21 and plagues, and of *e* spirits;
8. 2 healed of *e* spirits and infirmities,
11. 4 but deliver us from *e*.
13 If ye then, being *e*, know how to
29 This is an *e* generation: they seek
34 when thine eye is *e*, thy body also
16.25 likewise Lazarus *e* things: but
23.22 Why, what *e* hath he done?
Jn 3.19 light, because their deeds were *e*.
20 every one that doeth *e* hateth the
5.29 they that hath done *e*, unto the
7. 7 of it, that the works thereof are *e*,
17.15 should keep them from the *e*.
18.23 answered him, If I have spoken *e*,
23 bear witness of the *e*: but if well,
Ac 7. 6 entreat them *e* four hundred
19 *e* entreated our fathers, so that
9.13 of this man, how much *e* he hath
14. 2 made their minds *e* affected
19. 9 but spake *e* of that way before the
12 the *e* spirits went out of them.
13 call over them which had *e* spirits
15 the *e* spirit answered and said,
16 the man in whom the *e* spirit was
23. 5 Thou shalt not speak *e* of the ruler
9 We find no *e* in this man:
24.20 have found any *e* doing in me,
Ro 1.30 inventors of *e* things, disobedient
2. 9 every soul of man that doeth *e*,
3. 8 that we say,) Let us do *e*, that good
7.19 but the *e* which I would not,
21 do good, *e* is present with me.

Ro 9.11 having done any good or *e*,
12. 9 Abhor that which is *e*; cleave to
17 Recompense to no man *e* for *e*.
21 Be not overcome of *e*, but
21 but overcome *e* with good.
13. 3 terror to good works, but to the *e*.
4 But if thou do that which is *e*,
4 wrath upon him that doeth *e*.
14.16 Let not then your good be *e* spoken of:
20 but it is *e* for that man who eateth
16.19 is good, and simple concerning *e*.
1Co 10. 6 we should not lust after *e* things,
30 why am I *e* spoken of for that for
13. 5 easily provoked, thinketh no *e*;
15.33 *e* communications corrupt good
2Co 6. 8 by *e* report and good report:
13. 7 I pray to God that ye do no *e*;
Gal 1. 4 deliver us from this present *e*
Eph 4.31 clamor, and *e* speaking, be put
5.16 the time, because the days are *e*.
6.13 be able to withstand in the *e* day,
Php 3. 2 of dogs, beware of *e* workers,
Co 3. 5 *e* concupiscence, and covetousness,
1Th 5.15 See that none render *e* for *e*
22 Abstain from all appearance of *e*.
2Th 3. 3 stablish you, and keep you from *e*.
1Ti 6. 4 envy, strife, railings, *e* surmisings,
10 love of money is the root of all *e*:
2Ti 2. 9 as an *e* doer, even unto bonds:
3.13 But *e* men and seducers shall wax
4.14 the coppersmith did me much *e*:
18 deliver me from every *e* work,
Tit 1.12 *e* beasts, slow bellies.
2. 8 having no *e* thing to say of you.
3. 2 speak *e* of no man, to be no
Heb 3.12 any of you an *e* heart of unbelief.
5.14 to discern both good and *e*.
10.22 sprinkled from an *e* conscience,
Jas 1.13 God cannot be tempted with *e*,
2. 4 are become judges of *e* thoughts?
3. 8 an unruly *e*, full of deadly poison.
16 is confusion and every *e* work.
4.11 Speak not *e* one of another,
11 that speaketh *e* of his brother,
11 speaketh *e* of the law, and
16 boastings: all such rejoicing is *e*.
1Pe 2. 1 and envies, and all *e* speakings,
3. 9 Not rendering *e* for *e*, or railing
10 refrain his tongue from *e*,
11 Let him eschew *e*, and do good;
12 Lord is against them that do *e*.
16 speak *e* of you, as of evildoers,
17 for well doing, than for *e* doing.
4. 4 excess of riot, speaking *e* of you:
14 on their part he is *e* spoken of,
2Pe 2. 2 of truth shall be *e* spoken of.
10 not afraid to speak *e* of dignities
12 speak *e* of the things that they
1Jn 3.12 Because his own works were *e*,
2Jn 11 is partaker of his *e* deeds.
3Jn 11 follow not that which is *e*, but
11 that doeth *e* hath not seen God.
Jude 8 despise dominion, and speak *e* of
10 these speak *e* of those things
Rev 2. 2 canst not bear them which are *e*:

EVILDOER

Isa 9.17 every one is a hypocrite and an *e*
1Pe 4.15 or as an *e*, or as a busybody

EVILDOERS

Ps 37. 1 Fret not thyself because of *e*,
9 *e* shall be cut off: but those that
94.16 will rise up for me against the *e*?
119.115 Depart from me, ye *e*: for I will
Isa 1. 4 a seed of *e*, children that are
14.20 seed of *e* shall never be renowned.
31. 2 arise against the house of the *e*,
Jer 20.13 soul of the poor from the hand of *e*.
23.14 strengthen also the hands of *e*,
1Pe 2.12 they speak against you as *e*,
14 by him for the punishment of *e*,
3.16 speak evil of you, as of *e*,

EVILS

Dt 31.17 *e* and troubles shall befall them;
17 Are not these *e* come upon us,
18 *e* which they shall have wrought,
21 *e* and troubles are befallen them,
Ps 40.12 innumerable *e* have compassed me
Jer 2.13 my people have committed two *e*;
Eze 6. 9 the *e* which they have committed
20.43 all your *e* that ye have committed.
Lk 3.19 all the *e* which Herod had done,

EWE

Gen 21.28 Abraham set seven *e* lambs of
29 What mean these seven *e* lambs
30 seven *e* lambs shalt thou take
Lev 14.10 and one *e* lamb of the first year
22.28 cow or *e*, ye shall not kill it and
Nu 6.14 and one *e* lamb of the first year
2Sa 12. 3 one little *e* lamb, which he had

EXACT

Dt 15. 2 shall not *e* it of his neighbor,
3 foreigner thou mayest *e* it again:
Neh 5. 7 Ye *e* usury, every one of his
10 and my brethren,...might *e*
11 the corn,...that ye *e* of them.
Ps 89.22 The enemy shall not *e* upon him;
Isa 58. 3 pleasure, and *e* all your labors.
Lk 3.13 *E* no more than that which is

EXALT

Ex 15. 2 my father's God, and I will *e* him.
Ps 34. 3 and let us *e* his name together.
66. 7 let not the rebellious *e* themselves.
92.10 But my horn shalt thou *e* like the
Pr 4. 8 *E* her, and she shall promote thee:
Isa 14.13 I will *e* my throne above the stars
Eze 21.26 *e* him that is low, and abase him
Mt 23.12 And whosoever shall *e* himself
2Co 11.20 a man *e* himself, if a man smite
1Pe 5. 6 that he may *e* you in due time:

EXALTED

1Ch 29.11 thou art *e* as head above all.
Job 24.24 They are *e* for a little while,
Ps 12. 8 when the vilest men are *e*.
46.10 I will be *e* among the heathen,
47. 9 belong unto God: he is greatly *e*.
97. 9 thou art *e* far above all gods.
Pr 11.11 of the upright the city is *e*:
Isa 2. 2 and shall be *e* above the hills;
40. 4 Every valley shall be *e*, and every
Mic 4. 1 and it shall be *e* above the hills;
Mt 11.23 which art *e* unto heaven, shalt be
23.12 shall humble himself, shalt be *e*.
Lk 1.52 seats, and *e* them of low degree.
10.15 which art *e* to heaven, shalt be
14.11 that humbleth himself shall be *e*.
18.14 that humbleth himself shall be *e*.
Ac 2.33 being by the right hand of God *e*,
5.31 Him that hath God *e* with his right
13.17 *e* the people when they dwelt as
2Co 11. 7 abasing myself that ye might be *e*,
12. 7 lest I should be *e* above measure
7 lest I should be *e* above measure.
Php 2. 9 God also hath highly *e* him,
Jas 1. 9 low degree rejoice in that he is *e*:

EXALTETH

Job 36.22 Behold, God *e* by his power:
Ps 148.14 also *e* the horn of his people,
Pr 14.29 he that is hasty of spirit *e* folly.
34 Righteousness *e* a nation: but sin
17.19 *e* his gate seeketh destruction.
Lk 14.11 *e* himself shall be abased;
18.14 one that *e* himself shall be abased;
2Co 10. 5 every high thing that *e* itself
2Th 2. 4 Who opposeth and *e* himself

EXAMINATION

Ac 25.26 that, after *e* had, I might have

EXAMINE

Ezr 10.16 the tenth month to *e* the matter.
Ps 26. 2 *E* me, O Lord, and prove me;
1Co 9. 3 to them that do *e* me in this,
11.28 let a man *e* himself, and so let
2Co 13. 5 *E* yourselves, whether ye be in

EXAMINED

Lk 23.14 I, having *e* him before you,
Ac 4. 9 If we this day be *e* of the good deed
12.19 found him not, he *e* the keepers,
22.24 he should be *e* by scourging;
29 him which should have *e* him:
28.18 Who, when they had *e* me,

EXAMINING

Ac 24. 8 *e* of whom thyself mayest take

EXAMPLE

Mt 1.19 make her a public *e*, was minded
Jn 13.15 For I have given you an *e*, that
1Ti 4.12 be thou an *e* of the believers,
Heb 4.11 after the same *e* of unbelief.
8. 5 serve unto the *e* and shadow
Jas 5.10 for an *e* of suffering affliction,
1Pe 2.21 leaving us an *e*, that ye should
Jude 7 for an *e*, suffering the vengeance

EXAMPLES

1Co 10. 6 Now these things were our *e*,

EXCEED

Dt 25. 3 he may give him, and not *e*:
3 lest, if he should *e*, and beat him
Mt 5.20 your righteousness shall *e* the
2Co 3. 9 of righteousness *e* in glory.

EXCEEDING

Gen 15. 1 shield, and thy *e* great reward.
27.34 with a great and *e* bitter cry,
Nu 14. 7 to search it, is an *e* good land.
1Sa 2. 3 Talk no more so *e* proudly;
2Sa 12. 2 The rich man had *e* many flocks
1Ch 22. 5 the Lord must be *e* magnifical,
Ps 43. 4 altar of God, unto God my *e* joy:
119.96 thy commandment is *e* broad.
Pr 30.24 the earth, but they are *e* wise:
Dan 3.22 and the furnace *e* hot, the flame
Jon 3. 3 Nineveh was an *e* great city
4. 6 Jonah was *e* glad of the gourd.
Mt 2.10 they rejoiced with *e* great joy.
16 of the wise men, was *e* wroth,
4. 8 him up into an *e* high mountain,
5.12 Rejoice, and be *e* glad: for great
8.28 coming out of the tombs, *e* fierce,
17.23 And they were *e* sorry.
26.22 And they were *e* sorrowful, and
38 soul is *e* sorrowful, even unto
Mk 6.26 And the king was *e* sorry; yet for
9. 3 became shining, *e* white as snow;
14.34 soul is *e* sorrowful unto death:
Lk 23. 8 Herod saw Jesus he was *e* glad:
Ac 7.20 and was *e* fair, and nourished
Ro 7.13 sin...might become *e* sinful.
2Co 4.17 a far more *e* and eternal
7. 4 am *e* joyful in all our tribulation.
9.14 for the *e* grace of God in you.
Eph 1.19 And what is the *e* greatness of
2. 7 shew the *e* riches of his grace
3.20 *e* abundantly above all that we
1Ti 1.14 Lord was *e* abundant with faith
1Pe 4.13 ye may be glad also with *e* joy.
2Pe 1. 4 us *e* great and precious promises:
Jude 24 the presence of his glory with *e* joy,
Rev 16.21 the plague thereof was *e* great.

EXCEEDINGLY

Gen 13.13 and sinners before the Lord *e*.
Ps 123. 3 for we are *e* filled with contempt.

Isa 24.19 dissolved, the earth is moved *e*.
Jon 1.10 Then were the men *e* afraid, and
Mt 19.25 they were *e* amazed, saying, Who
Mk 4.41 they feared *e*, and said one
15.14 they cried out the more *e*, Crucify
Ac 16.20 being Jews, do *e* trouble our city,
26.11 and being *e* mad against them,
27.18 we being *e* tossed with a tempest,
2Co 7.13 *e* the more joyed we for the joy of
Gal 1.14 more *e* zealous of the traditions
1Th 3.10 Night and day praying *e*
2Th 1. 3 your faith groweth *e*, and the charity
Heb 12.21 Moses said, I *e* fear and quake:)

EXCEL

Gen 49. 4 as water, thou shalt not *e*;
1Ch 15.21 with harps on the Sheminith to *e*.
Ps 103.20 that *e* in strength, that do his
Isa 10.10 whose graven images did *e* them of
1Co 14.12 that ye may *e* to the edifying of

EXCELLENCY

Gen 49. 3 *e* of dignity, and the *e* of power:
Ex 15. 7 the greatness of thine *e* thou hast
Dt 33.26 and in his *e* on the sky.
29 and who is the sword of thy *e*!
Job 4.21 Doth not their *e* which is in them
13.11 Shall not his *e* make you afraid?
20. 6 Though his *e* mount up to the
37. 4 with the voice of his *e*; and he will
40.10 thyself now with majesty and *e*;
Ps 47. 4 the *e* of Jacob whom he loved.
62. 4 to cast him down from his *e*:
68.34 his *e* is over Israel, and his
Ec 7.12 but the *e* of knowledge is, that
Isa 13.19 the beauty of the Chaldees' *e*,
35. 2 the *e* of Carmel and Sharon,
2 of the Lord, and the *e* of our God.
60.15 I will make thee an eternal *e*,
Eze 24.21 the *e* of your strength, the desire
Am 6. 8 I abhor the *e* of Jacob, and hate
8. 7 hath sworn by the *e* of Jacob,
Na 2. 2 turned away the *e* of Jacob,
2 as the *e* of Israel:
1Co 2. 1 you, came not with *e* of speech
2Co 4. 7 the *e* of the power may be of God,
Php 3. 8 the *e* of the knowledge of Christ

EXCELLENT

Est 1. 4 and the honor of his *e* majesty
Job 37.23 he is *e* in power, and in judgment,
Ps 8. 1, 9 *e* is thy name in all the earth!
16. 3 to the *e*, in whom is all my delight.
36. 7 *e* is thy loving kindness, O God!
76. 4 Thou art more glorious and *e* than
141. 5 it shall be an *e* oil, which shall
148.13 his name alone is *e*; his glory is
150. 2 him according to his *e* greatness.
Pr 8. 6 for I will speak of *e* things;
12.26 The righteous is more *e* than his
17. 7 *E* speech becometh not a fool;
27 of understanding is of an *e* spirit.
22.20 not I written to thee *e* things in
Ec 5.15 Lebanon, *e* as the cedars.
Isa 4. 2 the fruit of the earth shall be *e*
12. 5 for he hath done *e* things:
28.29 in counsel, and *e* in working.
Eze 16. 7 thou art come to *e* ornaments:
Dan 2.31 image, whose brightness was *e*,
4.36 and *e* majesty was added unto me,
5.12 Forasmuch as an *e* spirit, and
14 and *e* wisdom is found in thee.
6. 3 because an *e* spirit was in him;
Lk 1. 3 in order, most *e* Theophilus,
Ac 23.26 unto the most *e* governor Felix
Ro 2.18 the things that are more *e*, being
1Co 12.31 shew I unto you a more *e* way.
Php 1.10 ye may approve things that are *e*;
Heb 1. 4 obtained a more *e* name than they.
8. 6 hath he obtained a more *e* ministry,
11. 4 a more *e* sacrifice than Cain,
2Pe 1.17 a voice to him from the *e* glory,

EXCELLETH

Ec 2.13 Then I saw that wisdom *e* folly,
13 as far as light *e* darkness.
2Co 3.10 by reason of the glory that *e*.

EXCEPT

Gen 32.26 let thee go, *e* thou bless me.
42.15 *e* your youngest brother come
Dt 32.30 *e* their Rock had sold
2Sa 3.13 not see my face, *e* thou first
Ps 127. 1 *E* the Lord build the house,
1 *e* the Lord keep the city, the
Isa 1. 9 *E* the Lord of hosts had left unto
Dan 3.28 nor any god, *e* their own God.
Am 3. 3 walk together, *e* they be agreed?
Mt 5.20 *e* your righteousness shall exceed
12.29 *e* he first bind the strong man?
18. 3 *E* ye be converted, and become as
19. 9 *e* it be for fornication, and shall
24.22 *e* those days should be shortened,
26.42 *e* I drink it, thy will be done.
Mk 3.27 *e* he will first bind the strong man;
7. 3 *e* they wash their hands oft,
4 *e* they wash, they eat not.
13.20 *e* that the Lord had shortened
Lk 9.13 *e* we should go and buy meat for
13. 3, 5 *e* ye repent, ye shall all likewise
Jn 3. 2 that thou doest, *e* God be with him.
3 *E* a man be born again, he cannot
5 *E* a man be born of water and of
27 *e* it be given him from heaven.
4.48 *E* ye see signs and wonders, ye
6.44 *e* the Father which hath sent me
53 *E* ye eat the flesh of the Son of
65 *e* it were given unto him of my
12.24 *E* a corn of wheat fall into the
15. 4 *e* it abide in the vine; no more can
4 no more can ye, *e* ye abide in me.
19.11 *e* it were given thee from above:
20.25 *E* I shall see in his hands the print
Ac 8. 1 were all scattered...*e* the apostles.
31 How can I, *e* some man should
15. 1 *E* ye be circumcised after the
26.29 such as I am, *e* these bonds.
Ro 7. 7 *e* the law had said, Thou shalt not
9.29 *E* the Lord of Sabaoth had left us
10.15 *e* they be sent, as it is written,
1Co 7. 5 *e* it be with consent for a time,
14. 5 tongues, *e* he interpret, that
9 *e* ye utter by the tongue words
15.36 sowest is not quickened, *e* it die:
Rev 2.22 *e* they repent of their deeds.

EXCEPTED

1Co 15.27 that he is *e*, which did put

EXCESS

Mt 23.25 they are full of extortion and *e*.
Eph 5.18 drunk with wine, wherein is *e*;
1Pe 4. 3 *e* of wine, revellings,
4 *e* of riot, speaking evil of you:

EXCHANGE

Gen 47.17 them bread in *e* for horses, and
Lev 27.10 and the *e* thereof shall be holy.
Job 28.17 and the *e* of it shall not be
Eze 48.14 *e*, nor alienate the first fruits
Mt 16.26 shall a man give in *e* for his soul?
Mk 8.37 shall a man give in *e* for his soul?

EXCHANGERS

Mt 25.27 to have put my money to the *e*,

EXCLUDE

Gal 4.17 yea, they would *e* you, that ye

EXCLUDED

Ro 3.27 Where is boasting then? It is *e*.

EXCUSE

Lk 14.18 with one consent began to make *e*.
Ro 1.20 so that they are without *e*:
2Co 12.19 that we *e* ourselves unto you?

EXCUSED

Lk 14.18 and see it: I pray thee have me *e*.
19 prove them: I pray thee have me *e*.

EXCUSING

Ro 2.15 accusing or else *e* one another;

EXECUTE

Ex 12.12 will *e* judgment: I am the Lord.
Dt 10.18 *e* the judgment of the fatherless
Jer 22. 3 saith the Lord; *E* ye judgment
Jn 5.27 authority to *e* judgment also,
Ro 13. 4 a revenger to *e* wrath upon him
Jude 15 To *e* judgment upon all, and to

EXECUTED

Dt 33.21 he *e* the justice of the Lord,
1Ch 6.10 (he it is that *e* the priest's office in the
24. 2 and Ithamar *e* the priest's office,
Lk 1. 8 that while he *e* the priest's office

EXECUTETH

Ps 9.16 by the judgment which he *e*:
103. 6 The Lord *e* righteousness and
146. 7 *e* judgment for the oppressed:
Isa 46.11 the man that *e* my counsel from
Jer 5. 1 if there be any that *e* judgment,
Joel 2.11 for he is strong that *e* his word:

EXECUTIONER

Mk 6.27 king sent an *e*, and commanded

EXERCISE

Ps 131. 1 do I *e* myself in great matters,
Jer 9.24 the Lord which *e* lovingkindness,
Mt 20.25 Gentiles *e* dominion over them,
25 are great *e* authority upon them.
Mk 10.42 the Gentiles *e* lordship over them;
42 great ones *e* authority upon them.
Lk 22.25 kings of the earth *e* lordship
25 they that *e* authority upon them
Ac 24.16 herein do I *e* myself, to have alway
1Ti 4. 7 *e* thyself rather unto godliness,
8 For bodily *e* profiteth little: but

EXERCISED

Ec 1.13 sons of man to be *e* therewith.
3.10 to the sons of men to be *e* in it.
Eze 22.29 and *e* robbery, and have vexed
Heb 5.14 *e* to discern both good and evil.
12.11 unto them which are *e* thereby.
2Pe 2.14 have *e* with covetous practices;

EXERCISETH

Rev 13.12 *e* all the power of the first beast

EXHORT

Ac 2.40 did he testify and *e*, saying, Save
27.22 now I *e* you to be of good cheer:
2Co 9. 5 it necessary to *e* the brethren,
1Th 4. 1 and *e* you by the Lord Jesus,
5.14 we *e* you, brethren, warn them
2Th 3.12 and *e* by our Lord Jesus Christ,
1Ti 2. 1 I *e* therefore, that, first of all,
6. 2 These things teach and *e*.
2Ti 4. 2 rebuke, *e* with all long suffering
Tit 1. 9 to *e* and to convince the gainsayers.
2. 6 likewise *e* to be sober minded.
9 *E* servants to be obedient unto their
15 speak, and *e*, and rebuke with all
Heb 3.13 But *e* one another daily, while it
1Pe 5. 1 I *e*, who am also an elder,
Jude 3 me to write unto you, and *e* you

EXHORTATION

Lk 3.18 *e* preached he unto the people.
Ac 13.15 any word of *e* for the people,

Ac 20. 2 and had given them much *e*,
Ro 12. 8 Or he that exhorteth, on *e*:
1Co 14. 3 edification, and *e*, and comfort.
2Co 8.17 For indeed he accepted the *e*;
1Th 2. 3 For our *e* was not of deceit,
1Ti 4.13 to reading, to *e*, to doctrine.
Heb 12. 5 forgotten the *e* which speaketh
13.22 brethren, suffer the word of *e*:

EXHORTED
Ac 11.23 and *e* them all, that with purpose
15.32 *e* the brethren with many words,
1Th 2.11 As ye know how we *e* and

EXHORTETH
Ro 12. 8 Or he that *e*, on exhortation:

EXHORTING
Ac 14.22 *e* them to continue in the faith,
18.27 *e* the disciples to receive him:
Heb 10.25 but *e* one another: and so much
1Pe 5.12 written briefly, *e*, and testifying

EXORCISTS
Ac 19.13 vagabond Jews, *e*, took upon them

EXPECTATION
Ps 9.18 the *e* of the poor shall not perish
62. 5 my *e* is from him.
Pr 10.28 the *e* of the wicked shall perish.
11. 7 man dieth, his *e* shall perish:
23 the *e* of the wicked is wrath.
23.18 and thine *e* shall not be cut off.
24.14 and thy *e* shall not be cut off.
Isa 20. 5 Ethiopia their *e*, and of Egypt
6 such is our *e* whither we flee
Zec 9. 5 Ekron; for her *e* shall be ashamed;
Lk 3.15 as the people were in *e*,
Ac 12.11 all the *e* of the people of the Jews.
Ro 8.19 the earnest *e* of the creature
Php 1.20 to my earnest *e* and my hope,

EXPECTING
Ac 3. 5 *e* to receive something of them.
Heb 10.13 *e* till his enemies be made his

EXPEDIENT
Jn 11.50 Nor consider that it is *e* for us,
16. 7 It is *e* for you that I go away:
18.14 it was *e* that one man should die
1Co 6.12 unto me, but all things are not *e*:
10.23 but all things are not *e*:
2Co 8.10 this is *e* of you, who have begun
12. 1 not *e* for me doubtless to glory.

EXPELLED
Jos 13.13 of Israel *e* not the Geshurites,
Jdg 1.20 *e* thence the three sons of Anak.
2Sa 14.14 his banished be not *e* from him.
Ac 13.50 and *e* them out of their coasts.

EXPERIENCE
Gen 30.27 by *e* that the Lord hath blessed
Ec 1.16 my heart had great *e* of wisdom
Ro 5. 4 And patience, *e*; and *e*, hope:

EXPERIMENT
2Co 9.13 by the *e* of this ministration

EXPERT
1Ch 12.33 *e* in war, with all instruments of
35 of the Danites *e* in war twenty
36 battle, *e* in war, forty thousand.
SS 3. 8 being *e* in war: every man hath
Jer 50. 9 shall be as of a mighty *e* man;
Ac 26. 3 be *e* in all customs and questions

EXPIRED
Ac 7.30 And when forty years were *e*,
Rev 20. 7 when the thousand years are *e*,

EXPOUNDED
Jdg 14.19 unto them which *e* the riddle.
Mk 4.34 he *e* all things to his disciples.
Lk 24.27 he *e* unto them in all the
Ac 11. 4 *e* it by order unto them, saying,
18.26 and *e* unto him the way of God
28.23 to whom he *e* and testified the

EXPRESS
Heb 1. 3 and the *e* image of his person,

EXPRESSLY
1Sa 20.21 If I *e* say unto the lad, Behold,
Eze 1. 3 word of the Lord came *e* unto Ezekiel
1Ti 4. 1 Now the Spirit speaketh *e*,

EXTOL
Ps 30. 1 I will *e* thee, O Lord; for thou
68. 4 *e* him that rideth upon the
145. 1 I will *e* thee, my God, O King;
Dan 4.37 I Nebuchadnezzar praise and *e*

EXTORTION
Eze 22.12 gained of thy neighbors by *e*,
Mt 23.25 they are full of *e* and excess.

EXTORTIONER
Ps 109.11 Let the *e* catch all that he hath;
Isa 16. 4 the *e* is at an end, the spoiler
1Co 5.11 a railer, or a drunkard, or an *e*;

EXTORTIONERS
Lk 18.11 not as other men are, *e*, unjust,
1Co 5.10 covetous, or *e*, or with idolaters;
6.10 revilers, nor *e*, shall inherit the

EYE
Ex 21.24 *E* for *e*, tooth for tooth, hand for
Lev 24.20 *e* for *e*, tooth for tooth: as he
Dt 19.21 but life shall go for life, *e* for *e*,
32.10 he kept him as the apple of his *e*.
34. 7 his *e* was not dim, nor his natural
Ezr 5. 5 *e* of their God was upon the elders
Ps 17. 8 Keep me as the apple of the *e*,
33.18 the *e* of the Lord is upon them
Pr 20.12 The hearing ear, and the seeing *e*,
30.17 The *e* that mocketh at his father,
Isa 52. 8 they shall see *e* to *e*, when the
Mt 5.29 if thy right *e* offend thee, pluck it
38 *e* for an *e*, and a tooth for a tooth:
6.22 The light of the body is the *e*:
22 if therefore thine *e* be single,
23 But if thine *e* be evil, thy whole
7. 3 mote that is in thy brother's *e*,
3 the beam that is in thine own *e*?
4 me pull out the mote out of thine *e*;
4 behold, a beam is in thine own *e*?
5 out the beam out of thine own *e*;
5 out the mote out of thy brother's *e*.
18. 9 if thine *e* offend thee, pluck it out,
9 thee to enter into life with one *e*,
19.24 to go through the *e* of a needle,
20.15 Is thine *e* evil, because I am good?
Mk 7.22 an evil *e*, blasphemy, pride,
9.47 if thine *e* offend thee, pluck it out,
47 the kingdom of God with one *e*,
10.25 to go through the *e* of a needle,
Lk 6.41 the mote that is in thy brother's *e*,
41 the beam that is in thine own *e*?
42 out the mote that is in thine *e*,
42 the beam that is in thine own *e*?
42 first the beam out of thine own *e*,
42 the mote that is in thy brother's *e*.
11.34 The light of the body is the *e*:
34 therefore when thine *e* is single,
34 but when thine *e* is evil, thy
18.25 camel to go through a needle's *e*,
1Co 2. 9 *E* hath not seen, nor ear heard,
12.16 Because I am not the *e*, I am not
17 If the whole body were an *e*, where
21 the *e* cannot say unto the hand,
15.52 in the twinkling of an *e*, at the
Rev 1. 7 every *e* shall see him, and they

EYES
Gen 3. 7 the *e* of them both were opened,
21.19 God opened her *e*, and she saw a
27. 1 Isaac was old, and his *e* were dim,
33. 1 Jacob lifted up his *e*, and looked,
Ex 13. 9 for a memorial between thine *e*,
16 and for frontlets between thine *e*:
Nu 22.31 the Lord opened the *e* of Balaam,
Dt 3.21 Thine *e* have seen all that the Lord
6. 8 be as frontlets between thine *e*.
11. 7 your *e* have seen all the great acts
12 the *e* of the Lord thy God are
34. 4 caused thee to see it with thine *e*,
Jdg 16.21 took him, and put out his *e*,
28 of the Philistines for my two *e*.
1Ki 8.29 *e* may be open toward this house
2Ki 6.17 Lord, I pray thee, open his *e*,
17 opened the *e* of the young man;
7. 2, 19 thou shalt see it with thine *e*,
1Ch 17.17 this was a small thing in thine *e*,
Job 10. 4 Hast thou *e* of flesh? or seest the
11.20 But the *e* of the wicked shall fail,
21.20 His *e* shall see his destruction,
27.19 he openeth his *e*, and he is not.
28.21 it is hid from the *e* of all living,
29.15 I was *e* to the blind, and feet was I
32. 1 he was righteous in his own *e*.
Ps 15. 4 whose *e* a vile person is contemned;
19. 8 Lord is pure, enlightening the *e*.
25.15 Mine *e* are ever toward the Lord;
26. 3 lovingkindness is before mine *e*:
31.22 I am cut off from before thine *e*:
36. 1 there is no fear of God before his *e*.
66. 7 his *e* behold the nations: let not
115. 5 *e* have they, but they see not:
116. 8 soul from death, mine *e* from tears,
118.23 doing; it is marvellous in our *e*.
119.18 Open thou mine *e*, that I may
37 mine *e* from beholding vanity;
121. 1 I will lift up mine *e* unto the hills,
123. 1 Unto thee lift I up mine *e*, O thou
139.16 Thine *e* did see my substance, yet
145.15 The *e* of all wait upon thee:
146. 8 The Lord openeth the *e* of the blind:
Pr 3. 7 Be not wise in thine own *e*:
15.30 light of the *e* rejoiceth the heart:
17.24 but the *e* of a fool are in the ends
Ec 2.14 The wise man's *e* are in his head;
Isa 5.15 the *e* of the lofty shall be humbled:
6. 5 for mine *e* have seen the King,
10 lest they see with their *e*,
33.17 *e* shall see the King in his beauty:
40.26 Lift up your *e* on high, and behold
42. 7 To open the blind *e*, to bring out
51. 6 Lift up your *e* to the heavens,
59.10 we grope as if we had no *e*:
Eze 8. 5 Son of man, lift up thine *e* now
23.40 didst wash thyself, paintedst thy *e*,
Dan 8. 5 had a notable horn between his *e*.
Mic 7.10 mine *e* shall behold her: now shall
Hab 1.13 Thou art of purer *e* than to behold
Zec 4.10 they are the *e* of the Lord, which
Mt 9.29 Then touched he their *e*, saying,
30 their *e* were opened; and Jesus
13.15 and their *e* they have closed;
15 time they should see with their *e*,
16 blessed are your *e*, for they see:
17. 8 when they had lifted up their *e*,
18. 9 rather than having two *e* to be
20.33 Lord, that our *e* may be opened.
34 on them, and touched their *e*:
34 their *e* received sight, and they
21.42 and it is marvellous in our *e*?
26.43 for their *e* were heavy.
Mk 8.18 Having *e*, see ye not? having ears,
23 and when he had spit on his *e*,
25 put his hands again upon his *e*,
9.47 having two *e* to be cast into hell

12.11 and it is marvellous in our *e*?
14.40 (for their *e* were heavy,) neither
Lk 2.30 For mine *e* have seen thy salvation,
4.20 And the *e* of all them that were
6.20 he lifted up his *e* on his disciples,
10.23 Blessed are the *e* which see the
16.23 And in hell he lifted up his *e*,
18.13 up so much as his *e* unto heaven,
19.42 but now they are hid from thine *e*.
24.16 *e* were holden that they should
31 And their *e* were opened, and they
Jn 4.35 Lift up your *e*, and look on the
6. 5 Jesus then lifted up his *e*, and saw
9. 6 he anointed the *e* of the blind man
10 him, How were thine *e* opened?
11 and anointed mine *e*, and said
14 made the clay, and opened his *e*.
15 He put clay upon mine *e*, and I
17 him, that he hath opened thine *e*?
21 who hath opened his *e*, we know
26 thee? how opened he thine *e*?
30 and yet he hath opened mine *e*.
32 that any man opened the *e* of one
10.21 Can a devil open the *e* of the blind?
11.37 which opened the *e* of the blind,
41 Jesus lifted up his *e*, and said,
12.40 He hath blinded their *e*, and
40 they should not see with their *e*,
17. 1 and lifted up his *e* to heaven, and
Ac 3. 4 Peter, fastening his *e* upon him with
9. 8 his *e* were opened, he saw no man:
18 from his *e* as it had been scales:
40 And she opened her *e*: and when
11. 6 when I had fastened mine *e*, I
13. 9 the Holy Ghost, set his *e* on him,
26.18 To open their *e*, and to turn them
28.27 and their *e* have they closed;
27 lest they should see with their *e*,
Ro 3.18 is no fear of God before their *e*.
11. 8 *e* that they should not see, and
10 Let their *e* be darkened, that they
Gal 3. 1 before whose *e* Jesus Christ hath
4.15 have plucked out your own *e*,
Eph 1.18 The *e* of your understanding being
Heb 4.13 and opened unto the *e* of him with
1Pe 3.12 For the *e* of the Lord are over the
2Pe 2.14 Having *e* full of adultery, and that
1Jn 1. 1 which we have seen with our *e*,
2.11 that darkness hath blinded his *e*.
16 lust of the *e*, and the pride of life,
Rev 1.14 and his *e* were as a flame of fire;
2.18 hath his *e* like unto a flame of fire,
3.18 and anoint thine *e* with eyesalve,
4. 6 there four beasts full of *e* before
8 and they were full of *e* within:
5. 6 seven *e*, which are the seven spirits
7.17 wipe away all tears from their *e*.
19.12 His *e* were as a flame of fire,
21. 4 wipe away all tears from their *e*;

EYESALVE
Rev 3.18 and anoint thine eyes with *e*, that

EYESERVICE
Eph 6. 6 Not with *e*, as menpleasers; but as
Col 3.22 not with *e*, as menpleasers; but in

EYEWITNESSES
Lk 1. 2 which from the beginning were *e*,
2Pe 1.16 but were *e* of his majesty.

EZEKIEL
Eze 1. 3 the Lord came expressly unto *E*
24.24 Thus *E* is unto you a sign:

EZRA
1Ch 4.17 of *E* were, Jether, and Mered,
Ezr 7. 1 *E* the son of Seraiah, the son of
6 This *E* went up from Babylon;
10 *E* had prepared his heart to seek
11 Artaxerxes gave unto *E* the priest,
12 king of kings, Unto *E* the priest,
21 whatsoever *E* the priest, the scribe
25 *E*, after the wisdom of thy God,
10. 1 Now when *E* had prayed, and
2 said unto *E*, We have trespassed
5 Then arose *E*, and made the chief
6 *E* rose up from before the house
10 *E* the priest stood up, and said
16 And *E* the priest, with certain chief
Neh 8. 1 and they spake unto *E* the scribe
2 And *E* the priest brought the law
4 *E* the scribe stood upon a pulpit
5 *E* opened the book in the sight of
6 *E* blessed the Lord, the great God.
9 and *E* the priest the scribe, and the
13 Levites, unto *E* the scribe, even to
12. 1 Seraiah, Jeremiah, *E*,
13 Of *E*, Meshullam; of Amariah,
26 and of *E* the priest, the scribe.
33 And Azariah, *E*, Meshullam,
36 of God, and *E* the scribe before

EZRA

A Jew of priestly lineage, living in Babylonia, 5th century B.C.; described as "a scribe skilled in the law of Moses" (Ezr 7); when post-exilic community well established, goes to Jerusalem to enforce the Mosaic law, to endow the worship of the temple from the royal treasury and local taxes, and to appoint magistrates and judges (Ezr 7); accompanied by numerous exiles; particularly concerned to take Levites for the temple service (Ezr 8); first major act in Jerusalem is the dissolution of mixed marriages in a great public ceremony of repentance (Ezr 9–10); later reads law publicly (Neh 8), and joins with Nehemiah in leading triumphal procession around newly built walls (Neh 12); revered in post-biblical period as promulgator of the law.

F

FABLES
1Ti 1. 4 Neither give heed to f and endless
4. 7 refuse profane and old wives' f,
2Ti 4. 4 and shall be turned unto f.
Tit 1.14 Not giving heed to Jewish f, and
2Pe 1.16 not followed cunningly devised f,

FACE
Gen 1. 2 darkness was upon the f of the
2 Spirit of God moved upon the f of
3.19 In the sweat of thy f shalt thou eat
6. 7 destroy...from the f of the earth;
7.18 ark went upon the f of the waters.
8.13 behold, the f of the ground was dry.
17. 3 And Abram fell on his f:
32.30 for I have seen God f to f,
43. 3 Ye shall not see my f, except your
50. 1 Joseph fell upon his father's f,
Ex 3. 6 Moses hid his f; for he was afraid
10.28 thou seest my f thou shalt die.
33.11 the Lord spake unto Moses f to f,
34.33 he put a vail on his f.
35 and Moses put the vail upon his f
Nu 6.25 Lord make his f shine upon thee,
Dt 1.17 shall not be afraid of the f of man;
31.17 and I will hide my f from them,
Jdg 6.22 seen an angel of the Lord f to f.
2Sa 19. 4 But the king covered his f,
1Ki 19.13 he wrapped his f in his mantle,
2Ki 4.29 lay my staff upon the f of the child.
12.17 set his f to go up to Jerusalem.
Job 1.11 and he will curse thee to thy f.
13.24 Wherefore hidest thou thy f, and
22.26 shalt lift up thy f unto God.
38.30 and the f of the deep is frozen.
41.14 Who can open the doors of his f?
Ps 13. 1 how long wilt thou hide thy f
27. 8 Seek ye my f; my heart said unto
8 Thy f, Lord, will I seek.
9 Hide not thy f far from me;
34.16 The f of the Lord is against them
51. 9 Hide thy f from my sins,
67. 1 and cause his f to shine upon us;
80. 3 O God, and cause thy f to shine;
7 of hosts, and cause thy f to shine;
104.15 and oil to make his f to shine,
29 hidest thy f, they are troubled:
30 thou renewest the f of the earth.
Pr 8.27 compass upon the f of the depth:
21.29 A wicked man hardeneth his f:
27.19 As in water f answereth to f, so
Ec 8. 1 wisdom maketh his f to shine,
Isa 6. 2 with twain he covered his f,
50. 6 my f from shame and spitting.
7 have I set my f like a flint,
59. 2 your sins have hid his f from you,
64. 7 thou hast hid thy f from us,
Eze 1.10 the f of a man, and the f of a lion,
10 had the f of an ox on the left side;
10 four also had the f of an eagle.
10.14 the first f was the f of a cherub,
14 the second f was the f of a man,
14 and the third the f of a lion,
14 and the fourth the f of an eagle.
21. 2 man, set thy f toward Jerusalem,
38. 2 Son of man, set thy f against Gog,
39.29 Neither will I hide my f any more
Dan 11.18 shall he turn his f unto the isles,
Am 9. 8 destroy it from off the f of the earth;
Mt 6.17 anoint thine head, and wash thy f;
11.10 I send my messenger before thy f,
16. 3 ye can discern the f of the sky;
17. 2 and his f did shine as the sun,
6 on their f, and were sore afraid.
18.10 always behold the f of my Father
26.39 and fell on his f, and prayed,
67 Then did they spit in his f,
Mk 1. 2 I send my messenger before thy f,
14.65 to cover his f, and to buffet him,
Lk 1.76 shalt go before the f of the Lord
2.31 prepared before the f of all people;
5.12 who seeing Jesus fell on his f,
7.27 I send my messenger before thy f,
9.51 set his f to go to Jerusalem,
52 And sent messengers before his f:
53 because his f was as though he
10. 1 sent them two and two before his f
12.56 ye can discern the f of the sky
17.16 And fell down on his f at his feet,
21.35 dwell on the f of the whole earth.
22.64 struck him on the f, and asked
Jn 11.44 f was bound about with a napkin.
Ac 2.25 the Lord always before my f, for
6.15 saw his f as it had been the f of
7.45 out before the f of our fathers,
17.26 to dwell on all the f of the earth,
20.25 shall see my f no more.
38 that they should see his f no more.
25.16 have the accusers f to f,
1Co 13.12 a glass, darkly; but then f to f:
14.25 and so falling down on his f
2Co 3. 7 stedfastly behold the f of Moses
13 which put a vail over his f,
18 with open f beholding as in a glass
4. 6 of God in the f of Jesus Christ.
11.20 if a man smite you on the f.
Gal 1.22 unknown by f unto the churches
2.11 I withstood him to the f,
Col 2. 1 as have not seen my f in the flesh;
1Th 2.17 to see your f with great desire.
3.10 that we might see your f,
Jas 1.23 beholding his natural f in a glass:
1Pe 3.12 the f of the Lord is against them
2Jn 12 and speak f to f, that our joy may
3Jn 14 see thee, and we shall speak f to f.
Rev 4. 7 the third beast had a f as a man,
6.16 hide us from the f of him that
10. 1 and his f was as it were the sun,
12.14 a time, from the f of the serpent.
20.11 from whose f the earth and the
22. 4 And they shall see his f;

FACES
Gen 9.23 and their f were backward, and
Ex 25.20 shall the f of the cherubims be.
Nu 14. 5 Moses and Aaron fell on their f
Job 9.24 he covereth the f of the judges
Isa 3.15 and grind the f of the poor?
25. 8 wipe away tears from off all f;
53. 3 we hid as it were our f from him;
Jer 1. 8 Be not afraid of their f: for I am
17 be not dismayed at their f,
5. 3 made their f harder than a rock;
Eze 1. 6 And every one had four f,
10.14 And every one had four f:
41.18 and every cherub had two f;
Mt 6.16 for they disfigure their f, that
Lk 24. 5 bowed down their f to the earth,
Rev 7.11 fell before the throne on their f,
9. 7 and their f were as the f of men.
11.16 upon their f, and worshipped God,

FADE
2Sa 22.46 Strangers shall f away, and they
Ps 18.45 strangers shall f away, and be
Isa 64. 6 and we all do f as a leaf;
Jer 8.13 the fig tree, and the leaf shall f;
Eze 47.12 whose leaf shall not f, neither
Jas 1.11 so also shall the rich man f away

FADETH
Isa 1.30 shall be as an oak whose leaf f,
24. 4 The earth mourneth and f away,
4 the world languisheth and f away,
40. 7 the flower f: because the spirit
8 the flower f: but the word of
1Pe 1. 4 undefiled, and that f not away,
5. 4 a crown of glory that f not away.

FADING
Isa 28. 1 glorious beauty is a f flower,
4 shall be a f flower, and as the

FAIL
Dt 31. 6 he will not f thee, nor forsake
Jos 1. 5 I will not f thee, nor forsake thee.
1Sa 17.32 no man's heart f because of him;
1Ki 17.14 neither shall the cruse of oil f,
Job 11.20 the eyes of the wicked shall f,
14.11 As the waters f from the sea,
Ps 77. 8 doth his promise f for evermore?
119.82 Mine eyes f for thy word,
Ec 12. 5 and desire shall f: because man
Isa 19. 5 the waters shall f from the sea,
32.10 the vintage shall f, the gathering
51.14 nor that his bread should f.
La 3.22 because his compassions f not.
Hab 3.17 the labor of the olive shall f,
Lk 16. 9 when ye f, they may receive you
17 than one tittle of the law to f.
22.32 for thee, that thy faith f not:
1Co 13. 8 there be prophecies, they shall f;
Heb 1.12 same, and thy years shall not f.
11.32 time would f me to tell of Gedeon,
12.15 any man f of the grace of God;

FAILED
Gen 42.28 and their heart f them, and they
Jos 21.45 f not ought of any good thing
Ps 142. 4 refuge f me; no man cared for my
SS 5. 6 my soul f when he spake:

FAILETH
Ps 73.26 My flesh and my heart f:
143. 7 O Lord; my spirit f: hide not
Isa 40.26 he is strong in power; not one f.
59.15 truth f; and he that departeth
Lk 12.33 treasure in the heavens that f not,
1Co 13. 8 Charity never f: but whether

FAILING
Dt 28.65 a trembling heart, and f of eyes,
Lk 21.26 Men's hearts f them for fear,

FAIN
Job 27.22 he would f flee out of his hand.
Lk 15.16 he would f have filled his belly

FAINT
Dt 25.18 when thou wast f and weary;
1Sa 30.10 were so f that they could not go
Pr 24.10 If thou f in the day of adversity,
Isa 29. 8 he awaketh, and, behold, he is f,
40.29 He giveth power to the f;
30 Even the youths shall f and be
31 and they shall walk, and not f.
44.12 he drinketh no water, and is f.
Jer 8.18 sorrow, my heart is f in me.
La 2.19 young children, that f for hunger
Eze 21. 7 and every spirit shall f, and all
Am 8.13 the fair virgins and young men f
Mt 15.32 lest they f in the way.
Mk 8. 3 they will f by the way:
Lk 18. 1 always to pray, and not to f;
2Co 4. 1 we have received mercy, we f not;
16 For which cause we f not; but
Gal 6. 9 we shall reap, if we f not.
Eph 3.13 Wherefore I desire that ye f not
Heb 12. 3 be wearied and f in your minds.

FAINTED

Gen 45.26 Jacob's heart *f*, for he believed
47.13 all the land of Canaan *f* by reason
Ps 27.13 I had *f*, unless I had believed
107. 5 thirsty, their soul *f* in them.
Isa 51.20 Thy sons have *f*, they lie at the
Jer 45. 3 I *f* in my sighing, and I find no
Eze 31.15 the trees of the field *f* for him.
Dan 8.27 And I Daniel *f*, and was sick
Jon 2. 7 When my soul *f* within me I
4. 8 upon the head of Jonah, that he *f*,
Mt 9.36 they *f*, and were scattered
Rev 2. 3 hast labored, and hast not *f*.

FAINTETH

Ps 84. 2 My soul longeth, yea, even *f* for
119.81 My soul *f* for thy salvation:
Isa 10.18 be as when a standardbearer *f*.
40.28 of the ends of the earth, *f* not,

FAIR

Gen 6. 2 daughters of men that they were *f*;
12.11 I know that thou art a *f* woman
14 the woman that she was very *f*.
24.16 damsel was very *f* to look upon,
26. 7 because she was *f* to look upon.
1Sa 17.42 ruddy, and of a *f* countenance.
2Sa 13. 1 the son of David had a *f* sister,
14.27 was a woman of a *f* countenance.
1Ki 1. 3 So they sought for a *f* damsel
4 damsel was very *f*, and cherished
Est 1.11 for she was *f* to look on.
2. 2 *f* young virgins sought for
3 together all the *f* young virgins
7 maid was *f* and beautiful;
Job 37.22 *F* weather cometh out of the
42.15 so *f* as the daughters of Job:
Pr 7.21 With her much *f* speech she
11.22 so is a *f* woman which is without
26.25 When he speaketh *f*, believe him
SS 1.15 Behold, thou art *f*, my love;
15 behold, thou art *f*; thou hast dove's
16 Behold, thou art *f*, my beloved,
2.10 Rise up, my love, my *f* one,
13 my love, my *f* one, and come
4. 1 Behold, thou art *f*, my love;
1 behold, thou art *f*; thou hast dove's
7 Thou art all *f*, my love;
10 How *f* is thy love, my sister,
6.10 *f* as the moon, clear as the sun,
7. 6 How *f* and how pleasant art thou,
Isa 5. 9 be desolate, even great and *f*,
54.11 will lay thy stones with *f* colors,
Jer 4.30 in vain shalt thou make thyself *f*;
11.16 olive tree, *f*, and of goodly fruit:
12. 6 they speak *f* words unto thee.
46.20 Egypt is like a very *f* heifer.
Eze 16.17 Thou hast also taken thy *f* jewels
39 and shall take thy *f* jewels, and
23.26 and take away thy *f* jewels.
31. 3 cedar in Lebanon with *f* branches,
7 Thus was he *f* in his greatness,
9 made him *f* by the multitude
Dan 4.12 The leaves thereof were *f*, and
21 Whose leaves were *f*, and the fruit
Hos 10.11 passed over upon her *f* neck:
Am 8.13 In that day shall the *f* virgins
Zec 3. 5 them set a *f* miter upon his head.
5 they set a *f* miter upon his head,
Mt 16. 2 ye say, It will be *f* weather:
Ac 7.20 was born, and was exceeding *f*,
27. 8 which is called The *f* havens;
Ro 16.18 by good words and *f* speeches
Gal 6.12 to make a *f* shew in the flesh,

FAITH

Dt 32.20 children in whom is no *f*.
Hab 2. 4 but the just shall live by his *f*.
Mt 6.30 more clothe you, O ye of little *f*?
8.10 I have not found so great *f*, no, not
26 are ye fearful, O ye of little *f*?
9. 2 Jesus seeing their *f* said unto the
22 thy *f* hath made thee whole.
29 According to your *f* be it unto you.
14.31 O thou of little *f*, wherefore didst
15.28 O woman, great is thy *f*:
16. 8 O ye of little *f*, why reason ye
17.20 If ye have *f* as a grain of mustard
21.21 If ye have *f*, and doubt not,
23.23 the law, judgment, mercy, and *f*:
Mk 2. 5 When Jesus saw their *f*, he said
4.40 how is it that ye have no *f*?
5.34 Daughter, thy *f* hath made thee
10.52 way; thy *f* hath made thee whole.
11.22 saith unto them, Have *f* in God.
Lk 5.20 when he saw their *f*, he said unto
7. 9 I have not found so great *f*, no, not
50 Thy *f* hath saved thee; go in peace.
8.25 Where is your *f*? And they being
48 thy *f* hath made thee whole; go in
12.28 will he clothe you, O ye of little *f*?
17. 5 unto the Lord, Increase our *f*.
6 If ye had *f* as a grain of mustard
19 way: thy *f* hath made thee whole.
18. 8 shall he find *f* on the earth?

BIBLICAL THEMES

FAITH

And Abraham stretched forth his hand, and took the knife to slay his son. And the angel of the Lord called unto him out of heaven, and said, . . . Lay not thine hand upon the lad . . . for now I know that thou fearest God, seeing thou hast not withheld thy son, thine only son from me. Gen 22.10-12

And Moses said unto the people, Fear ye not, stand still, and see the salvation of the Lord. . . . And Moses stretched out his hand over the sea; and the Lord caused the sea to go back . . . and made the sea dry land, and the waters were divided. Ex 14.13, 21

Call ye on the name of your gods, and I will call on the name of the Lord: and the God that answereth by fire, let him be God. 1Ki 18.24

The Lord gave, and the Lord hath taken away; blessed be the name of the Lord. Job 1.21

For I know that my redeemer liveth, and that he shall stand at the latter day upon the earth. Job 19.25

They that trust in the Lord shall be as mount Zion, which cannot be removed, but abideth for ever. Ps 125.1

Behold, God is my salvation; I will trust, and not be afraid: for the Lord Jehovah is my strength and my song; he also is become my salvation. Isa 12.2

The centurion answered and said, Lord, I am not worthy that thou shouldest come under my roof: but speak the word only, and my servant shall be healed. . . .When Jesus heard it, he marvelled, and said to them that followed, Verily I say unto you, I have not found so great faith, no, not in Israel. Mt 8.8, 10

If ye have faith as a grain of mustard seed, ye shall say unto this mountain, Remove hence to yonder place; and it shall remove; and nothing shall be impossible unto you. Mt 17.20

Lord, I believe; help thou mine unbelief. Mk 9.24

We believe and are sure that thou art that Christ, the Son of the living God. Jn 6.69

She saith unto him, Yea, Lord: I believe that thou art the Christ, the Son of God, which should come into the world. Jn 11.27

Jesus saith unto him, Thomas, because thou hast seen me, thou hast believed: blessed are they that have not seen, and yet have believed. Jn 20.29

Then Peter said, Silver and gold have I none; but such as I have give I thee: In the name of Jesus Christ of Nazareth rise up and walk. Ac 3.6

By grace are ye saved through faith; and that not of yourselves: it is the gift of God: not of works, lest any man should boast. Eph 2.8-9

Stand therefore . . . taking the shield of faith, wherewith ye shall be able to quench all the fiery darts of the wicked. Eph 6.14, 16

Now faith is the substance of things hoped for, the evidence of things not seen. . . . Through faith we understand that the worlds were framed by the word of God. . . . But without faith it is impossible to please him: for he that cometh to God must believe that he is, and that he is a rewarder of them that diligently seek him. Heb 11.1, 3, 6

Wilt thou know, O vain man, that faith without works is dead? Was not Abraham our father justified by works, when he had offered Isaac his son upon the altar? . . . For as the body without the spirit is dead, so faith without works is dead also. Jas 2.20-21, 26

This is the confidence that we have in him, that, if we ask any thing according to his will, he heareth us. 1Jn 5.14

Lk 18.42 thy sight: thy *f* hath saved thee.
22.32 prayed for thee, that thy *f* fail not:
Ac 3.16 his name through *f* in his name
16 yea, the *f* which is by him
6. 5 a man full of *f* and of the Holy
7 the priests were obedient to the *f*.
8 Stephen, full of *f* and power,
11.24 full of the Holy Ghost and of *f*:
13. 8 to turn away the deputy from the *f*.
14. 9 that he had *f* to be healed,
22 exhorting them to continue in the *f*,
27 how he had opened the door of *f*
15. 9 purifying their hearts by *f*.
16. 5 the churches established in the *f*,
20.21 and *f* toward our Lord Jesus Christ.
24.24 him concerning the *f* in Christ.
26.18 are sanctified by *f* that is in me.
Ro 1. 5 for obedience to the *f* among all
8 that your *f* is spoken of throughout
12 by the mutual *f* both of you and me.
17 God revealed from *f* to *f*: as it is
17 written, The just shall live by *f*.
3. 3 make the *f* of God without effect?
22 which is by *f* of Jesus Christ unto
25 propitiation through *f* in his blood,
27 of works? Nay: but by the law of *f*.
28 a man is justified by *f* without the
30 justify the circumcision by *f*, and
30 and uncircumcision through *f*.
31 make void the law through *f*?
4. 5 his *f* is counted for righteousness.
9 for we say that *f* was reckoned to
11 seal of the righteousness of the *f*
12 walk in the steps of that *f* of our
13 through the righteousness of *f*.
14 *f* is made void, and the promise
16 Therefore it is of *f*, that it might
16 which is of the *f* of Abraham;
19 being not weak in *f*, he considered
20 but was strong in *f*, giving glory
5. 1 being justified by *f*, we have peace
2 we have access by *f* into this grace
9.30 the righteousness which is of *f*.
32 Because they sought it not by *f*,
10. 6 But the righteousness which is of *f*
8 is, the word of *f*, which we preach;
17 So then *f* cometh by hearing,
11.20 broken off, and thou standest by *f*.
12. 3 to every man the measure of *f*.
6 according to the proportion of *f*;
14. 1 Him that is weak in the *f* receive
22 Hast thou *f*? have it to thyself
23 because he eateth not of *f*: for
23 whatsoever is not of *f* is sin.
16.26 all nations for the obedience of *f*:
1Co 2. 5 That your *f* should not stand in
12. 9 To another *f* by the same Spirit;
13. 2 though I have all *f*, so that I could
13 And now abideth *f*, hope, charity.
15.14 and your *f* is also vain.
17 your *f* is vain; ye are yet in your
16.13 Watch ye, stand fast in the *f*,
2Co 1.24 that we have dominion over your *f*,
24 of your joy: for by *f* ye stand.
4.13 We having the same spirit of *f*,
5. 7 (For we walk by *f*, not by sight:)
8. 7 in *f*, and utterance, and knowledge,
10.15 hope, when your *f* is increased,
13. 5 yourselves, whether ye be in the *f*;
Gal 1.23 now preacheth the *f* which once
2.16 but by the *f* of Jesus Christ,
16 be justified by the *f* of Christ,
20 I live by the *f* of the Son of God,
3. 2, 5 the law, or by the hearing of *f*?
7 they which are of *f*, the same are
8 justify the heathen through *f*,
9 they which be of *f* are blessed
11 for, The just shall live by *f*.
12 And the law is not of *f*:
14 promise of the Spirit through *f*.
22 the promise by *f* of Jesus Christ
23 But before *f* came, we were kept
23 shut up unto the *f*, which should
24 that we might be justified by *f*.
25 But after that *f* is come,
26 children of God by *f* in Christ
5. 5 the hope of righteousness by *f*.
6 but *f* which worketh by love.
22 gentleness, goodness, *f*,
6.10 who are of the household of *f*.
Eph 1.15 after I heard of your *f* in the Lord
2. 8 by grace are ye saved through *f*;
3.12 with confidence by the *f* of him.
17 may dwell in your hearts by *f*;
4. 5 One Lord, one *f*, one baptism,
13 we all come in the unity of the *f*,
6.16 Above all, taking the shield of *f*,
23 and love with *f*, from God the
Php 1.25 for your furtherance and joy of *f*;
27 together for the *f* of the gospel;
2.17 the sacrifice and service of your *f*,
3. 9 which is through the *f* of Christ,
9 righteousness which is of God by *f*:
Col 1. 4 Since we heard of your *f* in Christ
23 If ye continue in the *f* grounded
2. 5 the stedfastness of your *f* in Christ.
7 stablished in the *f*, as ye have been
12 through the *f* of the operation of
1Th 1. 3 your work of *f*, and labor of love,
8 *f* to God-ward is spread abroad;
3. 2 to comfort you concerning your *f*:
5 forbear, I sent to know your *f*,
6 good tidings of your *f* and charity,
7 affliction and distress by your *f*:
10 that which is lacking in your *f*?
5. 8 the breastplate of *f* and love;
2Th 1. 3 your *f* groweth exceedingly, and
4 for your patience and *f* in all your
11 and the work of *f* with power:
3. 2 for all men have not *f*.
1Ti 1. 2 Timothy, my own son in the *f*:
4 than godly edifying which is in *f*:
5 conscience, and of *f* unfeigned:
14 with *f* and love which is in Christ
19 Holding *f*, and a good conscience;
19 concerning *f* have made shipwreck:
2. 7 of the Gentiles in *f* and verity.
15 if they continue in *f* and charity
3. 9 Holding the mystery of the *f* in a
13 great boldness in the *f* which is in
4. 1 some shall depart from the *f*,
6 words of *f* and of good doctrine,
12 in charity, in spirit, in *f*, in purity.
5. 8 he hath denied the *f*, and is worse
12 they have cast off their first *f*.
6.10 they have erred from the *f*,
11 godliness, *f*, love, patience,
12 Fight the good fight of *f*, lay hold
21 have erred concerning the *f*.
2Ti 1. 5 the unfeigned *f* that is in thee,
13 in *f* and love which is in Christ
2.18 and overthrow the *f* of some.
22 follow righteousness, *f*, charity,
3. 8 minds, reprobate concerning the *f*.
10 *f*, longsuffering, charity, patience,
15 through *f* which is in Christ Jesus.
4. 7 my course, I have kept the *f*:
Tit 1. 1 according to the *f* of God's elect,
4 mine own son after the common *f*;
13 that they may be sound in the *f*;
2. 2 sound in *f*, in charity, in patience.
3.15 Greet them that love us in the *f*.
Phm 5 Hearing of thy love and *f*,
6 the communication of thy *f* may
Heb 4. 2 not being mixed with *f* in them
6. 1 dead works, and of *f* toward God,
12 who through *f* and patience inherit
10.22 a true heart in full assurance of *f*,
23 hold fast the profession of our *f*
38 Now the just shall live by *f*:
11. 1 Now *f* is the substance of things
3 Through *f* we understand that the
4 By *f* Abel offerd unto God a more
5 By *f* Enoch was translated that he
6 without *f* it is impossible to please
7 By *f* Noah, being warned of God
7 of the righteousness which is by *f*.
8 By *f* Abraham, when he was called
9 By *f* he sojourned in the land of
11 Through *f*...Sara herself received
13 These all died in *f*, not having
17 By *f* Abraham, when he was tried,
20 By *f* Isaac blessed Jacob and Esau
21 By *f* Jacob, when he was a dying,
22 By *f* Joseph, when he died, made
23 by *f* Moses, when he was born,
24 by *f* Moses, when he was come to
27 By *f* he forsook Egypt, not fearing
28 Through *f* he kept the passover,
29 By *f* passed through the Red
30 By *f* the walls of Jericho fell down,
31 By *f* the harlot Rahab perished not
33 Who through *f* subdued kingdoms,
39 obtained a good report through *f*,
12. 2 the author and finisher of our *f*;
13. 7 whose *f* follow, considering the
Jas 1. 3 trying of your *f* worketh patience.
6 let him ask in *f*, nothing wavering.
2. 1 My brethren, have not the *f* of our
5 rich in *f* and heirs of the kingdom
14 though a man say he hath *f*, and
14 have not works? can *f* save him?
17 Even so *f*, if it hath not works, is
18 Thou hast *f*, and I have works:
18 shew me thy *f* without thy works,
18 I will shew thee my *f* by my works.
20 that *f* without works is dead?
22 Seest thou how *f* wrought with his
22 and by works was *f* made perfect?
24 man is justified, and not by *f* only.
26 so *f* without works is dead also.
5.15 the prayer of *f* shall save the sick,
1Pe 1. 5 through *f* unto salvation ready to
7 That the trial of your *f*, being much
9 Receiving the end of your *f*,
21 your *f* and hope might be in God.
5. 9 Whom resist stedfast in the *f*,
2Pe 1. 1 obtained like precious *f* with us
5 add to your *f* virtue: and to virtue
1Jn 5. 4 overcometh the world, even our *f*.
Jude 3 for the *f* which was once delivered
20 up yourselves on your most holy *f*,
Rev 2.13 and hast not denied my *f*,
19 and charity, and service, and *f*,
13.10 the patience and the *f* of the saints.
14.12 of God, and the *f* of Jesus.

FAITHFUL

Dt 7. 9 thy God, he is God, the *f* God,
1Sa 2.35 I will raise me up a *f* priest,
Ps 31.23 for the Lord preserveth the *f*.
89.37 and as a *f* witness in heaven.
119.86 All thy commandments are *f*:
Pr 13.17 but a *f* ambassador is health.
14. 5 A *f* witness will not lie: but a false
20. 6 but a *f* man who can find?
Isa 1.21 How is the *f* city become an harlot!
Mt 24.45 Who then is a *f* and wise servant,
25.21 done, thou good and *f* servant:
21 thou hast been *f* over a few things,
23 Well done, good and *f* servant;
23 thou hast been *f* over a few things,
Lk 12.42 then is that *f* and wise steward,
16.10 He that is *f* in that which is
10 is least is *f* also in much:
11 *f* in the unrighteous mammon,
12 And if ye have not been *f* in that
19.17 thou hast been *f* in a very little,
Ac 16.15 have judged me to be *f* to the Lord,
1Co 1. 9 God is *f*, by whom ye were called
4. 2 stewards, that a man be found *f*.
17 my beloved son, and *f* in the Lord,
7.25 mercy of the Lord to be *f*.

10.13 but God is *f*, who will not suffer
Gal 3. 9 faith are blessed with *f* Abraham.
Eph 1. 1 and to the *f* in Christ Jesus:
6.21 and *f* minister in the Lord,
Col 1. 2 saints and *f* brethren in Christ
7 is for you a *f* minister in Christ;
4. 7 a *f* minister and fellowservant in
9 Onesimus, a *f* and beloved brother,
1Th 5.24 *F* is he that calleth you,
2Th 3. 3 Lord is *f*, who shall stablish you,
1Ti 1.12 for that he counted me *f*,
15 This is a *f* saying, and worthy of all
3.11 slanderers, sober, *f* in all things.
4. 9 This is a *f* saying and worthy of all
6. 2 because they are *f* and beloved,
2Ti 2. 2 the same commit thou to *f* men,
11 It is a *f* saying: For if we be dead
13 yet he abideth *f*: he cannot deny
Tit 1. 6 having *f* children not accused
9 the *f* word as he hath been taught,
3. 8 This is a *f* saying, and these things
Heb 2.17 be a merciful and *f* high priest in
3. 2 was *f* to him that appointed him,
2 also Moses was *f* in all his house.
5 Moses verily was *f* in all his
10.23 (for he is *f* that promised;)
11.11 judged him *f* who had promised.
1Pe 4.19 in well doing, as unto a *f* Creator.
5.12 By Silvanus, a *f* brother unto you,
1Jn 1. 9 he is *f* and just to forgive us our
Rev 1. 5 Jesus Christ who is the *f* witness,
2.10 be thou *f* unto death, and I will
13 Antipas was my *f* martyr, who was
3.14 the Amen, the *f* and true witness,
17.14 him are called, and chosen, and *f*.
19.11 upon him was called *F* and True,
21. 5 for these words are true and *f*.
22. 6 These sayings are *f* and true:

FAITHFULLY

2Ki 12.15 on workmen: for they dealt *f*.
22. 7 their hand, because they dealt *f*.
2Ch 19. 9 Lord, *f*, and with a perfect heart.
31.12 tithes and the dedicated things *f*:
34.12 And the men did the work *f*:
Pr 29.14 The king that *f* judgeth the poor,
Jer 23.28 let him speak my word *f*.
3Jn 5 doest *f* whatsoever thou doest

FAITHFULNESS

1Sa 26.23 man his righteousness and his *f*:
Ps 5. 9 there is no *f* in their mouth;
36. 5 thy *f* reacheth unto the clouds.
40.10 declared thy *f* and thy salvation:
88.11 the grave? or thy *f* in destruction?
89. 1 mouth will I make known thy *f* to all
2 thy *f* shalt thou establish in the very
5 thy *f* also in the congregation of the
8 or to thy *f* round about thee?
24 But my *f* and my mercy shall be with
33 nor suffer my *f* to fail.
92. 2 and thy *f* every night,
119.75 that thou in *f* hast afflicted me,
90 Thy *f* is unto all generations:
143. 1 in thy *f* answer me, and in thy
Isa 11. 5 and *f* the girdle of his reins.
25. 1 counsels of old are *f* and truth.
La 3.23 every morning: great is thy *f*.
Hos 2.20 will even betroth thee unto me in *f*:

FAITHLESS

Mt 17.17 said, O *f* and perverse generation,
Mk 9.19 saith, O *f* generation, how long shall
Lk 9.41 said, O *f* and perverse generation,
Jn 20.27 and be not *f*, but believing.

FALL

Gen 2.21 a deep sleep to *f* upon Adam,
45.24 See that ye *f* not out by the way.
Nu 14.43 and ye shall *f* by the sword:
Jos 6. 5 the wall of the city shall *f* down
Ru 3.18 thou know how the matter will *f*:
1Sa 14.45 shall not one hair of his head *f* to
Ps 5.10 let them *f* by their own counsels;
72.11 kings shall *f* down before him:
91. 7 A thousand shall *f* at thy side,
141.10 the wicked *f* into their own nets,
145.14 The Lord upholdeth all that *f*,
Pr 11. 5 shall *f* by his own wickedness.
14 Where no counsel is, the people *f*:
28 that trusteth in his riches shall *f*:
26.27 diggeth a pit shall *f* therein:
28.10 he shall *f* himself into his own pit:
14 that hardeneth his heart shall *f*
Isa 40.30 the young men shall utterly *f*:
44.19 I *f* down to the stock of a tree?
46. 6 they *f* down, yea, they worship.
Jer 49.26 young men shall *f* in her streets,
51.44 yea, the wall of Babylon shall *f*.
La 1.14 he hath made my strength to *f*,
Eze 36.15 shalt thou cause thy nations to *f*.
Dan 3. 5 ye *f* down and worship the golden
10 shall *f* down and worship the golden
15 ye *f* down and worship the golden
Hos 10. 8 and to the hills, *F* on us.
Am 3. 5 Can a bird *f* in a snare upon the
Mt 4. 9 wilt *f* down and worship me.

BIBLICAL THEMES

FALL

The Lord God commanded the man, saying, Of every tree of the garden thou mayest freely eat: but of the tree of the knowledge of good and evil, thou shalt not eat of it: for in the day that thou eatest thereof thou shalt surely die.
Gen 2.16-17

And [God] said, . . . Hast thou eaten of the tree, whereof I commanded thee that thou shouldest not eat? And the man said, The woman whom thou gavest to be with me, she gave me of the tree, and I did eat. . . . And the woman said, The serpent beguiled me, and I did eat. And the Lord God said unto the serpent, Because thou hast done this, thou art cursed above all cattle. . . . And I will put enmity between thee and the woman, and between thy seed and her seed; it shall bruise thy head, and thou shalt bruise his heel. . . . And unto Adam he said, . . . cursed is the ground for thy sake. . . . In the sweat of thy face shalt thou eat bread, till thou return unto the ground; for out of it wast thou taken: for dust thou art, and unto dust shalt thou return. . . . Therefore the Lord God sent him forth from the garden of Eden, to till the ground from whence he was taken. So he drove out the man; and he placed at the east of the garden of Eden Cherubims, and a flaming sword which turned every way, to keep the way of the tree of life.
Gen 3.11-15, 17, 19, 23-24

And God saw that the wickedness of man was great in the earth, and that every imagination of the thoughts of his heart was only evil continually. . . . The earth also was corrupt before God, and the earth was filled with violence.
Gen 6.5, 11

What is man, that he should be clean? and he which is born of a woman, that he should be righteous? Behold, he putteth no trust in his saints; yea, the heavens are not clean in his sight. How much more abominable and filthy is man, which drinketh iniquity like water?
Job 15.14-16

There is not a just man upon earth, that doeth good, and sinneth not. . . . God hath made man upright; but they have sought out many inventions.
Ec 7.20, 29

Thy first father hath sinned, and thy teachers have transgressed against me.
Isa 43.27

Thou hast been in Eden the garden of God. . . . thou wast upon the holy mountain of God. . . . Thou wast perfect in thy ways from the day that thou wast created, till iniquity was found in thee.
Eze 28.13-15

For as by one man's disobedience many were made sinners, so by the obedience of one shall many be made righteous.
Ro 5.19

We know that the law is spiritual: but I am carnal, sold under sin. . . . For the good that I would I do not: but the evil which I would not, that I do. . . . O wretched man that I am! who shall deliver me from the body of this death?
Ro 7.14, 19, 24

For since by man came death, by man came also the resurrection of the dead. For as in Adam all die, even so in Christ shall all be made alive.
1Co 15.21-22

I fear, lest by any means, as the serpent beguiled Eve through his subtilty, so your minds should be corrupted from the simplicity that is in Christ.
2Co 11.3

And you hath he quickened, who were dead in trespasses and sins; wherein in time past ye walked according to the course of this world, according to the prince of the power of the air, the spirit that now worketh in the children of disobedience.
Eph 2.1-2

And the devil that deceived them was cast into the lake of fire and brimstone.
Rev 20.10

Mt 7.27 and great was the *f* of it.
10.29 them shall not *f* on the ground
12.11 if it *f* into the pit on the sabbath
15.14 blind, both shall *f* into the ditch.
27 which *f* from their masters' table.
21.44 whosoever shall *f* on this stone
44 on whomsoever it shall *f*, it will
24.29 and the stars shall *f* from heaven,
Mk 13.25 And the stars of heaven shall *f*,
Lk 2.34 child is set for the *f* and rising
6.39 shall they not both *f* into the ditch?
8.13 and in time of temptation *f* away.
10.18 as lightning *f* from heaven.
20.18 Whosoever shall *f* upon that
18 but on whomsoever it shall *f*,
21.24 shall *f* by the edge of the sword,
23.30 *F* on us; and to the hills, Cover us.
Jn 12.24 wheat *f* into the ground and die,
Ac 27.17 should *f* into the quicksands,
32 ropes of the boat, and let her *f* off.
34 shall not an hair *f* from the head
Ro 11.11 they stumbled that they should *f*?
11 through their *f* salvation is come
12 Now if the *f* of them be the riches
14.13 occasion to *f* in his brother's way.
1Co 10.12 he standeth take heed lest he *f*.
1Ti 3. 6 pride he *f* into the condemnation
7 he *f* into reproach and the snare
6. 9 rich *f* into temptation and a snare,
Heb 4.11 lest any man *f* after the same
6. 6 If they shall *f* away, to renew
10.31 to *f* into the hands of the living
Jas 1. 2 when ye *f* into divers temptations;
5.12 nay; lest ye *f* into condemnation.
2Pe 1.10 do these things, ye shall never *f*:
3.17 *f* from your own stedfastness,
Rev 4.10 four and twenty elders *f* down
6.16 mountains and rocks, *F* on us,
9. 1 and I saw a star *f* from heaven

FALLEN

Gen 4. 6 and why is thy countenance *f*?
Jdg 3.25 their lord was *f* down dead on the
1Sa 31. 8 found Saul and his three sons *f* in
2Sa 1.19 high places: how are the mighty *f*!
25 How are the mighty *f* in the midst
27 How are the mighty *f*, and the
1Ch 10. 8 they found Saul and his sons *f* in
Job 1.16 The fire of God is *f* from heaven,
Ps 7.15 is *f* into the ditch which he made.
16. 6 are *f* unto me in pleasant places:
36.12 There are the workers of iniquity *f*:
69. 9 reproached thee are *f* upon me.
Isa 14.12 How art thou *f* from heaven,
Am 5. 2 The virgin of Israel is *f*; she
Lk 14. 5 have an ass or an ox *f* into a pit,
Ac 8.16 yet he was *f* upon none of them:
15.16 of David, which is *f* down,
20. 9 being *f* into a deep sleep:
26.14 when we were all *f* to the earth,
27.29 lest we should have *f* upon rocks,
28. 6 should have swollen, or *f* down
1Co 15. 6 but some are *f* asleep.
18 also which are *f* asleep in Christ
Gal 5. 4 by the law; ye are *f* from grace.
Php 1.12 happened unto me have *f* out
Rev 2. 5 from whence thou art *f*,
14. 8 Babylon is *f*, is *f*, that great city,
17.10 five are *f*, and one is, and the
18. 2 Babylon the great is *f*, is *f*,

FALLETH

Ex 1.10 when there *f* out any war,
Lev 11.33 vessel, whereinto any of them *f*,
35 any part of their carcase *f* shall be
Nu 33.54 in the place where his lot *f*;
2Sa 3.29 or that *f* on the sword, or that
34 as a man *f* before wicked men,
17.12 as the dew *f* on the ground:
Job 4.13 when deep sleep *f* on men,
33.15 when deep sleep *f* upon men,
Pr 13.17 wicked messenger *f* into mischief:
17.20 that hath a perverse tongue *f* into
24.16 For a just man *f* seven times,
17 Rejoice not when thine enemy *f*,
Ec 4.10 to him that is alone when he *f*;
9.12 when it *f* suddenly upon them.
11. 3 in the place where the tree *f*,
Isa 34. 4 as the leaf *f* off from the vine,
44.15 image, and *f* down thereto.
17 he *f* down unto it, and worshippeth
Jer 21. 9 *f* to the Chaldeans that besiege
Dan 3. 6 *f* not down and worshippeth shall
11 whoso *f* not down and worshippeth,
Mt 17.15 for ofttimes he *f* into the fire,
Lk 11.17 a house divided against a house *f*.
15.12 the portion of goods that *f* to me.
Ro 14. 4 his own master he standeth or *f*.
Jas 1.11 the grass, and the flower thereof *f*,
1Pe 1.24 and the flower thereof *f* away:

FALLING

Nu 24. 4, 16 *f* into a trance, but having his
Job 4. 4 have upholden him that was *f*,
14.18 mountain *f* cometh to nought,
Ps 56.13 not thou deliver my feet from *f*,
116. 8 from tears, and my feet from *f*.
Pr 25.26 A righteous man *f* down before
Isa 34. 4 as a *f* fig from the fig tree.
Lk 8.47 trembling, and *f* down before him,
22.44 of blood *f* down to the ground.
Ac 1.18 *f* headlong, he burst asunder
27.41 And *f* into a place where two
1Co 14.25 and so *f* down on his face he will
2Th 2. 3 except there come a *f* away first,
Jude 24 that is able to keep you from *f*,

FALSE

Ex 20.16 Thou shalt not bear *f* witness
23. 1 Thou shalt not raise a *f* report:
7 Keep thee far from a *f* matter;
Dt 5.20 Neither shalt thou bear *f* witness
19.16 If a *f* witness rise up against any
18 if the witness be a *f* witness,
2Ki 9.12 they said, It is *f*: tell us now.
Job 36. 4 truly my words shall not be *f*:
Ps 27.12 *f* witnesses are risen up against
35.11 *F* witnesses did rise up: they
119.104 therefore I hate every *f* way.
128 and I hate every *f* way.
120. 3 done unto thee, thou *f* tongue?
Pr 6.19 A *f* witness that speaketh lies,
11. 1 A *f* balance is abomination to
12.17 but a *f* witness deceit.
14. 5 but a *f* witness will utter lies.
17. 4 doer giveth heed to *f* lips;
19. 5, 9 A *f* witness shall not be
20.23 and a *f* balance is not good.
21.28 A *f* witness shall perish: but the
25.14 boasteth himself of a *f* gift is
18 A man that beareth *f* witness
Jer 14.14 you a *f* vision and divination,
23.32 them that prophesy *f* dreams,
37.14 Then said Jeremiah, It is *f*;
La 2.14 have seen for thee *f* burdens and
Eze 21.23 as a *f* divination in their sight,
Zec 8.17 and love no *f* oath: for all these
10. 2 a lie, and have told *f* dreams;
Mal 3. 5 and against *f* swearers, and
Mt 7.15 Beware of *f* prophets, which come
15.19 thefts, *f* witness, blasphemies:
19.18 Thou shalt not bear *f* witness,
24.11 And many *f* prophets shall rise,
24 For there shall arise *f* Christs,
24 and *f* prophets, and shall shew
26.59 sought *f* witness against Jesus,
60 though many *f* witnesses came,
60 At the last came two *f* witnesses,
Mk 10.19 Do not bear *f* witness, Defraud
13.22 For *f* Christs...shall rise, and shall
22 and *f* prophets shall rise, and shall
14.56 For many bare *f* witness against
57 and bare *f* witness against him.
Lk 6.26 their fathers to the *f* prophets.
18.20 Do not bear *f* witness, Honor
19. 8 from any man by *f* accusation,
Ac 6.13 set up *f* witnesses, which said,
13. 6 sorcerer, a *f* prophet, a Jew,
Ro 13. 9 Thou shalt not bear *f* witness,
1Co 15.15 we are found *f* witnesses of God;
2Co 11.13 For such are *f* apostles, deceitful
26 sea, in perils among *f* brethren;
Gal 2. 4 because of *f* brethren unawares
2Ti 3. 3 trucebreakers, *f* accusers,
Tit 2. 3 not *f* accusers, not given to much
2Pe 2. 1 there were *f* prophets also among
1 there shall be *f* teachers among
1Jn 4. 1 because many *f* prophets are gone
Rev 16.13 out of the mouth of the *f* prophet.
19.20 *f* prophet that wrought miracles
20.10 the beast and the *f* prophet are,

FALSEHOOD

2Sa 18.13 wrought *f* against mine own life:
Job 21.34 your answers there remaineth *f*?
Ps 7.14 mischief, and brought forth *f*.
119.118 thy statutes: for their deceit is *f*.
144. 8 their right hand is a right hand of *f*.
11 their right hand is a right hand of *f*:
Isa 28.15 under *f* have we hid ourselves:
57. 4 of transgression, a seed of *f*,
59.13 uttering from the heart words of *f*.
Jer 10.14 for his molten image is *f*, and
13.25 hast forgotten me, and trusted in *f*.
51.17 for his molten image is *f*, and
Hos 7. 1 for they commit *f*; and the thief
Mic 2.11 walking in the spirit and *f* do lie,

FALSELY

Gen 21.23 that thou wilt not deal *f* with me,
Lev 6. 3 it, and sweareth *f*;
5 that about which he hath sworn *f*;
19.11 Ye shall not steal, neither deal *f*,
12 ye shall not swear by my name *f*,
Dt 19.18 hath testified *f* against his brother;
Ps 44.17 neither have we dealt *f* in thy
Jer 5. 2 Lord liveth; surely they swear *f*.
31 prophets prophesy *f*, and the
6.13 unto the priest every one dealeth *f*.
7. 9 and commit adultery, and swear *f*,
8.10 unto the priest every one dealeth *f*.
29. 9 prophesy *f* unto you in my name:
40.16 for thou speakest *f* of Ishmael.
43. 2 unto Jeremiah, Thou speakest *f*:
Hos 10. 4 swearing *f* in making a covenant:
Zec 5. 4 the house of him that sweareth *f*
Mt 5.11 all manner of evil against you *f*,
Lk 3.14 neither accuse any *f*; and be
1Ti 6.20 oppositions of science *f* so called:
1Pe 3.16 ashamed that *f* accuse your

FAME

Gen 45.16 *f* thereof was heard in Pharaoh's
Nu 14.15 which have heard the *f* of thee
Jos 6.27 his *f* was noised throughout all
9. 9 for we have heard the *f* of him,
1Ki 4.31 his *f* was in all nations round
10. 1 of Sheba heard of the *f* of Solomon
7 exceedeth the *f* which I heard.
1Ch 14.17 the *f* of David went out into all
22. 5 magnifical, of *f* and of glory
2Ch 9. 1 Sheba heard of the *f* of Solomon,
6 thou exceedest the *f* that I heard.
Est 9. 4 his *f* went out throughout all the
Job 28.22 We have heard the *f* thereof with
Isa 66.19 afar off, that have not heard my *f*,
Jer 6.24 We have heard the *f* thereof: our
Zep 3.19 I will get them praise and *f* in
Mt 4.24 his *f* went throughout all Syria:
9.26 the *f* hereof went abroad into all
31 spread abroad his *f* in all that
14. 1 tetrarch heard of the *f* of Jesus.
Mk 1.28 immediately his *f* spread abroad

Lk 4.14 and there went out a *f* of him
37 the *f* of him went out into every
5.15 went there a *f* abroad of him:

FAMILIAR

Lev 19.31 not them that have *f* spirits,
20. 6 turneth after such as have *f* spirits,
27 also or woman that hath a *f* spirit,
Dt 18.11 or a consulter with *f* spirits, or a
1Sa 28. 3 put away those that had *f* spirits,
7 me a woman that hath a *f* spirit,
7 woman that hath a *f* spirit at En-dor.
8 divine unto me by the *f* spirit, and
9 hath cut off those that have *f* spirits,
2Ki 21. 6 and dealt with *f* spirits and wizards:
23.24 the workers with *f* spirits, and the
1Ch 10.13 counsel of one that had a *f* spirit,
2Ch 33. 6 and dealt with a *f* spirit, and with
Job 19.14 my *f* friends have forgotten me.
Ps 41. 9 Yea, mine own *f* friend, in whom
Isa 8.19 unto them that have *f* spirits, and
19. 3 and to them that have *f* spirits, and
29. 4 as of one that hath a *f* spirit,

FAMILIARS

Jer 20.10 all my *f* watched for my halting.

FAMILIES

Gen 10. 5 after their *f*, in their nations.
18 were the *f* of the Canaanites
20 are the sons of Ham, after their *f*,
31 are the sons of Shem, after their *f*,
32 These are the *f* of the sons of Noah,
12. 3 shall all *f* of the earth be blessed.
28.14 all the *f* of the earth be blessed.
36.40 of Esau according to their *f*,
47.12 with bread, according to their *f*.
Ex 12.21 you a lamb according to your *f*,
Lev 25.45 and of their *f* that are with you,
Nu 11.10 people weep throughout their *f*,
Job 31.34 did the contempt of *f* terrify me,
Ps 68. 6 God setteth the solitary in *f*:
107.41 and maketh him *f* like a flock.
Jer 1.15 will call all the *f* of the kingdoms
2. 4 all the *f* of the house of Israel:
10.25 the *f* that call not on thy name:
25. 9 and take all the *f* of the north,
31. 1 the God of all the *f* of Israel,
33.24 two *f* which the Lord hath chosen,
Eze 20.32 as the *f* of the countries, to serve
Am 3. 2 I known of all the *f* of the earth:
Na 3. 4 and *f* through her witchcrafts.
Zec 12.14 *f* that remain, every family apart,
14.17 come up of all the *f* of the earth

FAMILY

Lev 20. 5 that man, and against his *f*,
25.10 shall return every man unto his *f*.
41 and shall return unto his own *f*,
47 or to the stock of the stranger's *f*:
49 is nigh of kin unto him of his *f*
Nu 27. 4 be done away from among is *f*,
11 that is next to him of his *f*,
36. 6 only to the *f* of the tribe of their
8 wife unto one of the *f* of the tribe
12 or the tribe of the *f* of their father.
Dt 29.18 in *f*, or tribe, whose heart turneth
Jos 7.14 the *f* which the Lord shall take
Jdg 1.25 they let go the man and all his *f*.
6.15 behold, my *f* is poor in Manasseh,
9. 1 and with all the *f* of the house of
17. 7 the *f* of Judah, who was a Levite,
18. 2 of Dan sent of their *f* five men
19 unto a tribe and a *f* in Israel?
21.24 every man to his tribe and to his *f*,
Ru 2. 1 of wealth, of the *f* of Elimelech;
1Sa 9.21 my *f* the least of all the families
10.21 the *f* of Matri was taken,
18.18 my life, or my father's *f* in Israel,
20. 6 yearly sacrifice there for all the *f*.
29 for our *f* hath a sacrifice in the city.

BIBLICAL THEMES

FAMILY

Therefore shall a man leave his father and his mother, and shall cleave unto his wife: and they shall be one flesh.
Gen 2.24

I know [Abraham], that he will command his children and his household after him, and they shall keep the way of the Lord, to do justice and judgment.
Gen 18.19

Honor thy father and thy mother: that thy days may be long upon the land which the Lord thy God giveth thee.
Ex 20.12

And Naomi had a kinsman of her husband's, a mighty man of wealth, of the family of Elimelech; and his name was Boaz. . . . And she answered, I am Ruth thine handmaid: spread therefore thy skirt over thine handmaid; for thou art a near kinsman. And he said, Blessed be thou of the Lord, my daughter. . . . I will do to thee all that thou requirest. . . . It is true that I am thy near kinsman: howbeit there is a kinsman nearer than I. . . . If he will not do the part of a kinsman to thee, then will I do the part of a kinsman to thee.
Ru 2.1; 3.9-13

God setteth the solitary in families.
Ps 68.6

He poureth contempt upon princes. . . . Yet setteth he the poor on high from affliction, and maketh him families like a flock.
Ps 107.40-41

Thy wife shall be as a fruitful vine by the sides of thine house: thy children like olive plants round about thy table. . . . Yea, thou shalt see thy children's children, and peace upon Israel.
Ps 128.3, 6

How good and how pleasant it is for brethren to dwell together in unity!
Ps 133.1

Better is a dinner of herbs where love is, than a stalled ox and hatred therewith.
Pr 15.17

A foolish son is the calamity of his father: and the contentions of a wife are a continual dropping.
Pr 19.13

Have we not all one father? hath not one God created us?
Mal 2.10

Behold, I will send you Elijah the prophet. . . . And he shall turn the heart of the fathers to the children, and the heart of the children to their fathers.
Mal 4.5-6

Who is my mother? and who are my brethren? And he stretched forth his hand toward his disciples, and said, Behold my mother and my brethren! For whosoever shall do the will of my Father which is in heaven, the same is my brother, and sister, and mother.
Mt 12.48-50

God that made the world and all things therein . . . hath made of one blood all nations of men for to dwell on all the face of the earth.
Ac 17.24, 26

Come out from among them, and be ye separate, saith the Lord, . . . and I will receive you, and will be a Father unto you, and ye shall be my sons and daughters.
2Co 6.17-18

Now therefore ye are no more strangers and foreigners, but fellowcitizens with the saints, and of the household of God.
Eph 2.19

I bow my knees unto the Father of our Lord Jesus Christ, of whom the whole family in heaven and earth is named.
Eph 3.14-15

A bishop then must be blameless. . . . one that ruleth well his own house, having his children in subjection with all gravity; (for if a man know not how to rule his own house, how shall he take care of the church of God?)
1Ti 3.2, 4-5

If any provide not for his own, and specially for those of his own house, he hath denied the faith.
1Ti 5.8

2Sa 14. 7 *f* is risen against thine handmaid,
16. 5 a man of the *f* of the house of Saul,
1Ch 4.27 neither did all their *f* multiply, like
6.61 were left of the *f* of that tribe,
70 the *f* of the remnant of the sons
71 given out of the *f* of the half tribe
13.14 ark of God remained with the *f* of
Est 9.28 every *f*, every province, and every
Jer 3.14 one of a city, and two of a *f*,
8. 3 of them that remain of this evil *f*,
Am 3. 1 the whole *f* which I brought up
Mic 2. 3 against this *f* do I devise an evil,
Zec 12.12 shall mourn, every *f* apart;
12 the *f* of the house of David apart,
12 the *f* of the house of Nathan apart,
13 The *f* of the house of Levi apart,
13 the *f* of Shimei apart, and their
14 families that remain, every *f* apart,
14.18 if the *f* of Egypt go not up,
Eph 3.15 *f* in heaven and earth is named,

FAMINE

Gen 12.10 And there was a *f* in the land:
41.27 east wind shall be seven years of *f*.

Gen 41.30 arise after them seven years of *f*;
30 and the *f* shall consume the land;
56 And the *f* was over all the face of
42.19 corn for the *f* of your houses:
47.13 Canaan fainted by reason of the *f*.
Ru 1. 1 that there was a *f* in the land.
2Ki 8. 1 the Lord hath called for a *f*;
Job 5.20 In *f* he shall redeem thee from
22 At destruction and *f* thou shalt
Ps 33.19 and to keep them alive in *f*.
37.19 days of *f* they shall be satisfied.
Jer 24.10 I will send the sword, the *f*,
42.16 and the *f*, whereof ye were afraid,
Eze 5.16 upon them the evil arrows of *f*,
14.13 and will send *f* upon it,
36.29 and lay no *f* upon you.
Am 8.11 not a *f* of bread, nor a thirst of
Lk 4.25 when great *f* was throughout all
15.14 there arose a mighty *f* in that land;
Ro 8.35 or *f*, or nakedness, or peril, or
Rev 18. 8 day, death, and mourning, and *f*;

FAMINES
Mt 24. 7 there shall be *f*, and pestilences,
Mk 13. 8 and there shall be *f* and troubles:
Lk 21.11 and *f*, and pestilences: and fearful

FAMOUS
Nu 16. 2 assembly, *f* in the congregation,
26. 9 which were *f* in the congregation,
Ru 4.11 Ephratah...*f* in Beth-lehem:
14 that his name may be *f* in Israel.
1Ch 5.24 mighty men of valour, *f* men,
12.30 *f* throughout the house of their
Ps 74. 5 A man was *f* according as he had
136.18 And slew *f* kings: for his
Eze 23.10 she became *f* among women,
32.18 the daughters of the *f* nations,

FAN
Isa 30.24 with the shovel and with the *f*.
41.16 Thou shalt *f* them, and the wind
Jer 4.11 not to *f*, nor to cleanse,
15. 7 And I will *f* them...in the gates
7 And I will...with a *f* in the gates
51. 2 Babylon fanners, that shall *f* her,
Mt 3.12 Whose *f* is in his hand, and he
Lk 3.17 Whose *f* is in his hand, and he will

FANNERS
Jer 51. 2 Babylon *f*, that shall fan her,

FAR
Gen 18.25 That be *f* from thee to do after
Jos 9. 6 We be come from a *f* country:
2Ch 26.15 And his name spread *f* abroad;
Job 13.21 Withdraw thine hand *f* from me:
21.16 counsel of the wicked is *f* from me,
34.10 *f* be it from God, that he should
Ps 22.11 Be not *f* from me; for trouble is
27. 9 Hide not thy face *f* from me;
97. 9 thou art exalted *f* above all gods.
103.12 As *f* as the east is from the west,
12 so *f* hath he removed our
119.150 they are *f* from thy law.
155 Salvation is *f* from the wicked:
Pr 15.29 The Lord is *f* from the wicked:
30. 8 Remove *f* from me vanity and
31.10 for her price is *f* above rubies.
Ec 2.13 folly, as *f* as light excelleth darkness
Isa 30.27 name of the Lord cometh from *f*,
33.13 Hear, ye that are *f* off, what I
17 behold the land that is very *f* off.
46.12 that are *f* from righteousness:
49.12 Behold, these shall come from *f*:
57.19 Peace, peace to him that is *f* off,
59. 9 Therefore is judgment *f* from us,
11 salvation, but is *f* off from us.
60. 4 thy sons shall come from *f*, and
Jer 4.16 watchers come from a *f* country,
La 3.17 thou hast removed my soul *f* off

"Famine shall consume the land," Joseph announces, interpreting Pharaoh's two dreams (Gen 41.30).

Eze 11.15 Get you *f* from the Lord:
Mt 15. 8 but their heart is *f* from me.
16.22 Be it *f* from thee, Lord:
21.33 and went into a *f* country:
25.14 man travelling into a *f* country,
Mk 6.35 when the day was now *f* spent,
35 and now the time is *f* passed:
7. 6 but their heart is *f* from me.
8. 3 for divers of them came from *f*.
12. 1 and went into a *f* country.
34 not *f* from the kingdom of God.
13.34 as a man taking a *f* journey,
Lk 7. 6 was now not *f* from the house,
15.13 his journey into a *f* country,
19.12 went into a *f* country to receive
20. 9 went into a *f* country for a long time.
22.51 and said, Suffer ye thus *f*.
24.29 and the day is *f* spent.
50 them out as *f* as to Bethany,
Jn 21. 8 for they were not *f* from land,
Ac 11.19 Stephen travelled as *f* as Phenice,
22 that he should go as *f* as Antioch.
17.27 he be not *f* from every one
22.21 I will send thee *f* hence unto the
28.15 to meet us as *f* as Appii forum,
Ro 13.12 night is *f* spent, the day is at hand:
2Co 4.17 for us a *f* more exceeding
10.14 we are come as *f* as to you also in
Eph 1.21 *F* above all principality, and
2.13 ye who sometimes were *f* off are
4.10 ascended up *f* above all heavens,
Php 1.23 Christ; which is *f* better:
Heb 7.15 And it is yet *f* more evident:

FARE
1Sa 17.18 and look how thy brethren *f*,
Jon 1. 3 he paid the *f* thereof, and went
Ac 15.29 ye shall do well. *F* ye well.

FARED
Lk 16.19 and *f* sumptuously every day:

FAREWELL
Lk 9.61 but let me first go bid them *f*,
Ac 18.21 But bade them *f*, saying, I must
23.30 what they had against him. *F*.
2Co 13.11 Finally, brethren, *f*. Be perfect,

FARM

Mt 22. 5 and went their ways, one to his *f*,

FARTHER

Ec 8.17 yea *f*; though a wise man think
Mt 26.39 And he went a little *f*, and fell
Mk 1.19 And when he had gone a little *f*
10. 1 by the *f* side of Jordan:

FARTHING

Mt 5.26 thou hast paid the uttermost *f*.
10.29 not two sparrows sold for a *f*?
Mk 12.42 in two mites, which make a *f*.

FARTHINGS

Lk 12. 6 not five sparrows sold for two *f*,

FASHION

Gen 6.15 *f* which thou shalt make it of:
Ex 26.30 according to the *f* thereof which
37.19 made after the *f* of almonds
1Ki 6.38 according to all the *f* of it.
2Ki 16.10 the *f* of the altar, and the pattern
Job 31.15 did not one *f* us in the womb?
Eze 43.11 the house, and the *f* thereof,
Mk 2.12 We never saw it on this *f*.
Lk 9.29 the *f* of his countenance was
Ac 7.44 to the *f* that he had seen.
1Co 7.31 for the *f* of this world passeth
Php 2. 8 And being found in *f* as a man,
Jas 1.11 the grace of the *f* of it perisheth:

FASHIONED

Ex 32. 4 and *f* it with a graving tool,
Job 10. 8 hands have made me and *f* me
Ps 119.73 hands have made me and *f* me:
139.16 which in continuance were *f*,
Isa 22.11 had respect unto him that *f* it
Eze 16. 7 thy breasts are *f*, and thine hair
Php 3.21 be *f* like unto his glorious body,

FASHIONETH

Ps 33.15 He *f* their hearts alike; he
Isa 44.12 the coals, and *f* it with hammers,
45. 9 Shall the clay say to him that *f* it,

FASHIONING

1Pe 1.14 not *f* yourselves according to the

FASHIONS

Eze 42.11 out were both according to their *f*,

FAST

Jdg 15.13 No, but we will bind thee *f*,
Ru 2.23 So she kept *f* by the maidens of Boaz
2Sa 12.21 didst *f* and weep for the child,
23 he is dead, wherefore should I *f*?
1Ki 21. 9 Proclaim a *f*, and set Naboth
Est 4.16 and *f* ye for me, and neither eat
Job 27. 6 My righteousness I hold *f*, and will
Ps 33. 9 be commanded, and it stood *f*.
38. 2 For thine arrows stick *f* in me,
111. 8 They stand *f* for ever and ever,
Pr 4.13 Take *f* hold of instruction; let her not
Isa 58. 4 ye *f* for strife and debate,
5 Is it such a *f* that I have chosen?
6 not this the *f* that I have chosen?
Jer 14.12 When they *f*, I will not hear their
Joel 1.14 Sanctify ye a *f*, call a solemn
Mt 6.16 Moreover when ye *f*, be not, as
16 they may appear unto men to *f*.
18 thou appear not unto men to *f*,
9.14 Why do we and the Pharisees *f* oft,
14 but thy disciples *f* not?
15 from them, and then shall they *f*.
26.48 that same is he: hold him *f*.
Mk 2.18 of the Pharisees used to *f*:
18 of John and of the Pharisees *f*,
18 but thy disciples *f* not?
19 children of the bridechamber *f*.
19 bridegroom with…,they cannot *f*.
20 then shall they *f* in those days.

BIBLICAL THEMES

FATE

Yet now, if thou wilt forgive their sin—; and if not, blot me, I pray thee, out of thy book which thou hast written.
Ex 32.32

Where are their gods, their rock in whom they trusted. . . ? let them rise up and help you, and be your protection. See now that I, even I, am he, and there is no god with me: I kill, and I make alive; I wound, and I heal: neither is there any that can deliver out of my hand.
Dt 32.37-39

Who can bring a clean thing out of an unclean? not one. Seeing his days are determined, the number of his months are with thee, thou hast appointed his bounds that he cannot pass.
Job 14.4-5

Man's goings are of the Lord; how can a man then understand his own way?
Pr 20.24

All the rivers run into the sea; yet the sea is not full; unto the place from whence the rivers come, thither they return again.
Ec 1.7

As it happeneth to the fool, so it happeneth even to me; and why was I then more wise?
Ec 2.15

All things come alike to all: there is one event to the righteous, and to the wicked; to the good and to the clean, and to the unclean; to him that sacrificeth, and to him that sacrificeth not: as is the good, so is the sinner. . . . the race is not to the swift, nor the battle to the strong, neither yet bread to the wise, nor yet riches to men of understanding, nor yet favor to men of skill; but time and chance happeneth to them all.
Ec 9.2, 11

Thus saith the Lord that created the heavens; God himself that formed the earth and made it; he hath established it, he created it not in vain, he formed it to be inhabited: I am the Lord; and there is none else. I have not spoken in secret, in a dark place of the earth: I said not unto the seed of Jacob, Seek ye me in vain: I the Lord speak righteousness, I declare things that are right.
Isa 45.18-19

If they say unto thee, Whither shall we go forth? then thou shalt tell them, Thus saith the Lord; Such as are for death, to death; and such as are for the sword, to the sword; and such as are for the famine, to the famine; and such as are for the captivity, to the captivity. . . . Thou hast forsaken me . . . therefore will I stretch out my hand against thee, and destroy thee; I am weary with repenting.
Jer 15.2, 6

Behold, as the clay is in the potter's hand, so are ye in mine hand, O house of Israel.
Jer 18.6

Blessed be the name of God for ever and ever: for wisdom and might are his: and he changeth the times and the seasons: he removeth kings, and setteth up kings: he giveth wisdom unto the wise, and knowledge to them that know understanding: he revealeth the deep and secret things: he knoweth what is in the darkness, and the light dwelleth with him.
Dan 2.20-22

Now I am no more in the world . . . and I come to thee. . . . Father, I will that they also, whom thou hast given me, be with me where I am; that they may behold my glory, which thou hast given me: for thou lovedst me before the foundation of the world.
Jn 17.11, 24

For whom he did foreknow, he also did predestinate to be conformed to the image of his Son, that he might be the firstborn among many brethren. Moreover whom he did predestinate, them he also called: and whom he called, them he also justified: and whom he justified, them he also glorified.
Ro 8.29-30

And whosoever was not found written in the book of life was cast into the lake of fire.
Rev 20.15

Lk 5.33 do the disciples of John *f* often,
34 children of the bridechamber *f*,
35 then shall they *f* in those days.
18.12 I *f* twice in the week,
Ac 16.24 made their feet *f* in the stocks.
27. 9 because the *f* was now already
41 forepart stuck *f*, and remained
1Co 16.13 Watch ye, stand *f* in the faith, quit
Gal 5. 1 Stand *f* therefore in the liberty
Php 1.27 that ye stand *f* in one spirit, with one
4. 1 so stand *f* in the Lord, my dearly
1Th 3. 8 now we live, if ye stand *f* in the Lord.
5.21 hold *f* that which is good.
2Th 2.15 brethren, stand *f*, and hold the
2Ti 1.13 Hold *f* the form of sound words,
Tit 1. 9 Holding *f* the faithful word as he
Heb 3. 6 if we hold *f* the confidence and
4.14 let us hold *f* our profession.
10.23 Let us hold *f* the profession of our
Rev 2.13 and thou holdest *f* my name,
25 ye have already, hold *f* till I come.
3. 3 and hold *f*, and repent.
11 hold that *f* which thou hast, that no

FASTED

Jdg 20.26 *f* that day until even, and offered

1Sa 7. 6 and *f* on that day, and said there,
31.13 tree at Jabesh, and *f* seven days.
2Sa 1.12 and *f* until even, for Saul,
12.16 and David *f*, and went in,
22 child was yet alive, I *f* and wept:
1Ki 21.27 and *f*, and lay in sackcloth,
1Ch 10.12 oak in Jabesh, and *f* seven days.
Ezr 8.23 So we *f* and besought our God
Neh 1. 4 and *f*, and prayed before the God of
Isa 58. 3 Wherefore have we *f*, say they,
Zec 7. 5 When ye *f* and mourned in the
Mt 4. 2 when he had *f* forty days
Ac 13. 2 they ministered to the Lord, and *f*,
3 when they had *f* and prayed,

FASTENED

Ex 39.18 chains they *f* in the two ouches,
40.18 and *f* his sockets, and set up the
Jdg 4.21 and *f* it into the ground:
16.14 And she *f* it with the pin,
1Sa 31.10 and they *f* his body to the wall of
2Sa 20. 8 with a sword *f* upon his loins in
1Ki 6. 6 beams should not be *f* in the
1Ch 10.10 and *f* his head in the temple of
2Ch 9.18 which were *f* to the throne,
Est 1. 6 *f* with cords of fine linen and purple
Job 38. 6 are the foundations thereof *f*?
Ec 12.11 *f* by the masters of assemblies,
Isa 22.25 shall the nail that is *f* in the sure
41. 7 *f* it with nails, that it should not
Eze 40.43 a hand broad, *f* round about:
Lk 4.20 in the synagogue were *f* on him.
Ac 11. 6 which when I had *f* mine eyes, I
28. 3 out of the heat, and *f* on his hand.

FASTENING

Ac 3. 4 Peter, *f* his eyes upon him with

FASTEST

Mt 6.17 when thou *f*, anoint thine head,

FASTING

Neh 9. 1 of Israel were assembled with *f*,
Est 4. 3 and *f*, and weeping, and wailing;
Ps 35.13 I humbled my soul with *f*;
69.10 and chastened my soul with *f*,
109.24 My knees are weak through *f*;
Jer 36. 6 the Lord's house upon the *f* day:
Dan 6.18 palace, and passed the night *f*:
9. 3 with *f*, and sackcloth, and ashes:
Joel 2.12 and with *f*, and with weeping, and
Mt 15.32 I will not send them away *f*, lest
17.21 not out but by prayer and *f*.
Mk 8. 3 And if I send them away *f* to their
9.29 by nothing, but by prayer and *f*.
Ac 10.30 Four days ago I was *f* until this
14.23 prayed with *f*, they commended
27.33 ye have tarried and continued *f*,
1Co 7. 5 give yourselves to *f* and prayer;

FASTINGS

Est 9.31 the matters of the *f* and their cry.
Lk 2.37 with *f* and prayers night and day.
2Co 6. 5 in labors, in watchings, in *f*;
11.27 in *f* often, in cold and nakedness.

FAT

Gen 4. 4 his flock and of the *f* thereof.
41. 4 seven well flavored and *f* kine.
20 did eat up the first seven *f* kine:
45.18 ye shall eat the *f* of the land.
2Sa 1.22 from the *f* of the mighty, the bow
1Ki 1.19 he hath slain oxen and *f* cattle
25 slain oxen and *f* cattle and sheep
4.23 Ten *f* oxen, and twenty oxen out
8.64 and the *f* of the peace offerings:
64 and the *f* of the peace offerings.
1Ch 4.40 they found *f* pasture and good,
2Ch 7. 7 and the *f* of the peace offerings,
7 the meat offerings, and the *f*.
29.35 with the *f* of the peace offerings,
35.14 offerings and the *f* until night;
Neh 8.10 eat the *f*, and drink the sweet,
9.25 took strong cities, and a *f* land,
35 and in the large and *f* land which
Job 15.27 maketh collops of *f* on his flanks.
Ps 17.10 They are inclosed in their own *f*:
22.29 All they that be *f* upon earth shall
37.20 Lord shall be as the *f* of lambs:
92.14 they shall be *f* and flourishing;
119.70 Their heart is as *f* as grease;
Pr 11.25 The liberal soul shall be made *f*:
13. 4 soul of the diligent shall be made *f*.
15.30 a good report maketh the bones *f*.
28.25 trust in the Lord shall be made *f*.
Isa 1.11 rams, and the *f* of fed beasts;
5.17 the waste places of the *f* ones
6.10 Make the heart of this people *f*,
10.16 send among his *f* ones leanness;
25. 6 unto all people a feast of *f* things,
6 of *f* things full of marrow,
28. 1 are on the head of the *f* valleys of
4 which is on the head of the *f* valley,
30.23 and it shall be *f* and plenteous:
34. 6 it is made *f* with fatness,
6 with the *f* of the kidneys of rams:
7 their dust made *f* with fatness.
43.24 hast thou filled me with the *f* of
58.11 drought, and make *f* thy bones:
Jer 5.28 They are waxen *f*, they shine:
50.11 ye are grown *f* as the heifer
Eze 34. 3 Ye eat the *f*, and ye clothe you
14 in a *f* pasture shall they feed
16 will destroy the *f* and the strong;
20 I will judge between the *f* cattle
39.19 And ye shall eat *f* till ye be full,
44. 7 my bread, the *f* and the blood,
15 offer unto me the *f* and the blood,
45.15 out of the *f* pastures of Israel:
Am 5.22 peace offerings of your *f* beasts.
Hab 1.16 by them their portion is *f*,
Zec 11.16 but he shall eat the flesh of the *f*,

FATHER

Gen 2.24 a man leave his *f* and his mother,
4.20 was the *f* of such as dwell in tents,
21 the *f* of all such as handle the harp
17. 4 thou shalt be a *f* of many nations.
19.31 Our *f* is old, and there is not a man
26.15 digged in the days of Abraham his *f*,
24 I am the God of Abraham thy *f*;
27. 9 make them savoury meat for thy *f*,
12 My *f* peradventure will feel me,
19 And Jacob said unto his *f*, I am Esau
34 and said unto his *f*, Bless me, even
28.13 am the Lord God of Abraham thy *f*,
37. 4 saw that their *f* loved him more than
35 Thus his *f* wept for him.
43. 7 Is your *f* yet alive? have ye another
44.20 my lord, We have a *f*, an old man,
22 The lad cannot leave his *f*:
45. 3 I am Joseph; doth my *f* yet live?
8 he hath made me a *f* to Pharaoh,
13 haste and bring down my *f* hither.
48. 1 told Joseph, Behold, thy *f* is sick:
50. 5 go up, I pray thee, and bury my *f*,
6 Pharaoh said, Go up, and bury thy *f*,
Ex 3. 1 the flock of Jethro his *f* in law,
20.12 Honor thy *f* and thy mother:
21.15 he that smiteth his *f*, or his mother
17 he that curseth his *f*, or his mother
Dt 5.16 Honor thy *f* and thy mother,
26. 5 A Syrian ready to perish was my *f*,
27.16 be he that setteth light by his *f*
32. 7 ask thy *f*, and he will shew thee;
Jdg 14. 3 Samson said unto his *f*, Get her for
4 But his *f* and his mother knew not
17.10 and be unto me a *f* and a priest,
18.19 and be to us a *f* and a priest:
1Sa 19. 2 Saul my *f* seeketh to kill thee:
20. 2 and why should my *f* hide this thing
6 If thy *f* at all miss me, then say,
10 what if thy *f* answer thee roughly?
2Sa 7.14 I will be his *f*, and he shall be my
16.21 that thou art abhorred of thy *f*:
1Ki 12. 4 Thy *f* made our yoke grievous:
11 whereas my *f* did lade you with
11 my *f* hath chastised you with whips,
2Ki 2.12 My *f*, my *f*, the chariot of Israel,
3. 2 image of Baal that his *f* had made.
5.13 My *f*, if the prophet had bid thee do
13.14 and said, O my *f*, my *f*, the chariot
1Ch 22.10 be my son, and I will be his *f*;
2Ch 10. 4 Thy *f* made our yoke grievous:
4 the grievous servitude of thy *f*,
11 my *f* chastised you with whips, but I
Job 17.14 said to corruption, Thou art my *f*:
29.16 I was a *f* to the poor: and the cause
38.28 Hath the rain a *f*? or who hath
42.15 and their *f* gave them inheritance
Ps 27.10 my *f* and my mother forsake me,
68. 5 A *f* of the fatherless, and a judge of
89.26 He shall cry unto me, Thou art my *f*,
103.13 Like as a *f* pitieth his children, so
Pr 1. 8 My son,hear the instruction of thy *f*,
3.12 as a *f* the son in whom he delighteth.
4. 1 ye children, the instruction of a *f*,
10. 1 A wise son maketh a glad *f*: but a
17.21 and the *f* of a fool hath no joy.
25 A foolish son is a grief to his *f*, and
19.13 foolish son is the calamity of his *f*:
24 Whoso robbeth his *f* or his mother,
Isa 9. 6 everlasting *F*, The Prince of Peace.
45.10 Woe unto him that saith unto his *f*,
63.16 Doubtless thou art our *f*, though
16 thou, O Lord, art our *f*, our
Jer 3. 4 My *f*, thou art the guide of my youth?
31. 9 for I am a *f* to Israel, and Ephraim
Eze 18.17 shall not die for the iniquity of his *f*,
19 the son bear the iniquity of the *f*?
20 shall not bear the iniquity of the *f*,
20 neither shall the *f* bear the iniquity
22. 7 have they set light by *f* and mother:
Am 2. 7 a man and his *f* will go in unto the
Mal 2.10 Have we not all one *f*? hath not one
Mt 2.22 Judea in the room of his *f* Herod,
3. 9 We have Abraham to our *f*: for I
4.21 in a ship with Zebedee their *f*,
22 left the ship and their *f*, and
5.16 glorify your *F* which is in heaven.
45 ye may be the children of your *F*
48 even as your *F* which is in heaven
6. 1 of your *F* which is in heaven.
4 and thy *F* which seeth in secret
6 pray to thy *F* which is in secret;
6 and thy *F* which seeth in secret
8 your *F* knoweth what things ye
9 *F* which art in heaven, Hallowed
14 your heavenly *F* will also forgive
15 neither will your *F* forgive your
18 but unto thy *F* which is in secret:
18 and thy *F*, which seeth in secret,
26 yet your heavenly *F* feedeth them.
32 for your heavenly *F* knoweth that
7.11 how much more shall your *F* which
21 he that doeth the will of my *F*
8.21 suffer me first to go and bury my *f*.
10.20 Spirit of your *F* which speaketh
21 the *f* the child: and the children
29 fall on the ground without your *F*.
32 will I confess also before my *F*
33 him will I also deny before my *F*
35 set a man at variance against his *f*,
37 He that loveth *f* or mother more
11.25 I thank thee, O *F*, Lord of heaven
26 Even so, *F*: for so it seemed good
27 delivered unto me of my *F*: and no
27 man knoweth the Son, but the *F*;
27 neither knoweth any man the *F*,
12.50 whosoever shall do the will of my *F*
13.43 the sun in the kingdom of their *F*.
15. 4 Honor thy *f* and mother: and,
4 He that curseth *f* or mother, let him

5 Whosoever shall say to his f or his
6 And honor not his f or his mother,
13 my heavenly F hath not planted,
16.17 but my F which is in heaven.
27 shall come in the glory of his F
18.10 do always behold the face of my F
14 Even so it is not the will of your F
19 it shall be done for them of my F
35 shall my heaven F do also unto
19. 5 shall a man leave f and mother,
19 Honor thy f and thy mother:
29 or brethren, or sisters, or f, or
20.23 for whom it is prepared of my F.
21.31 them twain did the will of his f?
23. 9 call no man your f upon the earth:
9 one is your F, which is in heaven.
24.36 angels in heaven, but my F only.
25.34 Come, ye blessed of my F, inherit
26.39 O my F, if it be possible, let this
42 O my F, if this cup may not pass
53 that I cannot now pray to my F,
28.19 baptizing them in the name of the F,
Mk 1.20 they left their f Zebedee in the ship
5.40 he taketh the f and the mother of
7.10 Honor thy f and thy mother; and
10 Whoso curseth f or mother, let him
11 If a man shall say to his f or mother,
12 him no more to do ought for his f
8.38 cometh in the glory of his F with the
9.21 he asked his f, How long is it ago
24 And straightway the f of the child
10. 7 this cause shall a man leave his f
19 not, Honor thy f and mother.
29 brethren, or sisters, or f, or mother,
11.10 be the kingdom of our f David,
25 that your F also which is in heaven
26 neither will your F which is in
13.12 and the f the son; and the children
32 neither the Son, but the F.
14.36 he said, Abba, F, all things are
15.21 f of Alexander and Rufus, to bear
Lk 1.32 unto him the throne of his f David:
59 Zacharias, after the name of his f.
62 And they made signs to his f, how
67 his f Zacharias was filled with the
73 which he sware to our f Abraham,
2.48 behold, thy f and I have sought thee
3. 8 We have Abraham to our f: for I
6.36 merciful, as your f also is merciful.
8.51 f and the mother of the maiden.
9.42 and delivered him again to his f.
59 suffer me first to go and bury my f.
10.21 I thank thee, O F, Lord of heaven
21 even so, F; for so it seemed good
22 things are delivered to me of my F:
22 but the F; and who the F is, but
11. 2 say, Our F which art in heaven,
11 bread of any of you that is a f,
13 much more shall your heavenly F
12.30 your F knoweth that ye have need
53 The f shall be divided against the
53 son, and the son against the f;
14.26 and hate not his f, and mother,
15.12 of them said to his f, F, give me
18 I will arise and go to my f, and
18 say unto him, F, I have sinned
20 And he arose, and came to his f.
20 his f saw him, and had compassion,
21 F, I have sinned against heaven,
22 But the f said to his servants.
27 and thy f hath killed the fatted calf,
28 therefore came his f out, and
29 said to his f, Lo, these many years
16.24 And he cried and said, F Abraham,
27 I pray thee therefore, f, that thou
30 And he said, Nay, f Abraham, but
18.20 Honor thy f and thy mother.
22.29 as my F appointed unto me;
42 Saying, F, if thou be willing,
23.34 F, forgive them; for they know
46 F, into thy hands I commend my
24.49 I send the promise of my F upon
Jn 1.14 as of the only begotten of the F,)
18 in the bosom of the F, he hath
3.35 The F loveth the Son, and hath
4.12 Art thou greater than our f Jacob,
21 nor yet at Jerusalem, worship the F.
23 shall worship the F in spirit and
23 in truth: for the F seeketh such to
53 So the f knew that it was at the
5.17 My F worketh hitherto, and I work.
18 but said also that God was his F,
19 but what he seeth the F do: for
20 For the F loveth the Son, and
21 For as the F raiseth up the dead,
22 For the F judgeth no man, but
23 Son, even as they honor the F.
23 honoreth not the F which hath
26 For as the F hath life in himself;
30 but the will of the F which hath
36 the works which the F hath given
36 bear witness of me, that the F hath
37 And the F himself, which hath sent
45 that I will accuse you to the F:
6.27 for him hath God the F sealed.
32 but my F giveth you the true bread
37 All that the F giveth me shall come
42 whose f and mother we know?
44 except the F which hath sent me
45 hath learned of the F, cometh unto
46 Not that any man hath seen the F,
46 which is of God, he hath seen the F.
57 As the living F hath sent me, and
57 and I live by the F: so he that
65 it were given unto him of my F.
8.16 but I and the F that sent me.
18 and the F that sent me beareth
19 they unto him, Where is thy F?
19 ye neither know me, nor my F:
19 ye should have known my F also.
27 not that he spake to them of the F.
28 as my F hath taught me, I speak
29 the F hath not left me alone;
38 which I have seen with my F:
38 which ye have seen with your f
39 said unto him, Abraham is our f.
41 Ye do the deeds of your f.
41 we have one F, even God.
42 If God were your F, ye would love
44 Ye are of your f the devil, and the
44 and the lusts of your f ye will do:
44 for he is a liar, and the f of it.
49 but I honor my F, and ye do
53 Art thou greater than our f
54 it is my F that honoreth me;
56 Your f Abraham rejoiced to see my
10.15 As the F knoweth me, even so
15 even so know I the F:
17 Therefore doth my F love me,
18 have I received of my F.
29 My F which gave them me, is
30 I and my F are one.
32 have I shewed you from my F;
36 him, whom the F hath sanctified,
37 not the works of my F, believe me
38 that the F is in me, and I in him.
11.41 F, I thank thee that thou hast
12.26 serve me, him will my F honor.
27 F, save me from this hour; but
28 F, glorify thy name. Then came
49 but the F which sent me, he gave
50 even as the F said unto me, so I
13. 1 depart out of this world unto the F,
3 that the F had given all things into
14. 6 cometh unto the F, but by me.
7 ye should have known my F also:
8 Lord, shew us the F, and it
9 hath seen the F; and how sayest
9 thou then, Shew us the F?
10 I am in the F, and the F in me?
10 but the F that dwelleth in me, he
11 Believe me that I am in the F,
11 and the F in me: or else believe
12 shall he do; because I go unto my F.
13 that the F may be glorified in the
16 And I will pray the F, and he shall
20 that I am in my F, and ye in me,
21 loveth me shall be loved of my F,
23 and my F will love him, and we
26 whom the F will send in my name,
28 because I said, I go unto the F:
28 for my F is greater than I.
31 may know that I love the F; and as
31 as the F gave me commandment,
15. 1 and my F is the husbandman.
8 Herein is my F glorified, that ye
9 As the F hath loved me, so have I
15 things that I have heard of my F
16 ye shall ask of the F in my name,
23 that hateth me hateth my F also.
24 have they hated both me and my F.
26 I will send unto you from the F,
26 which proceedeth from the F,
16. 3 they have not known the F, nor me.
10 because I go to my F, and ye see
15 things that the F hath are mine:
16 shall see me, because I go to the F.
17 and, Because I go to the F?
23 ye shall ask the F in my name,
25 shall shew you plainly of the F.
26 that I will pray the F for you:
27 For the F himself loveth you,
28 I came forth from the F, and am
28 leave the world, and go to the F.
32 alone, because the F is with me.
17. 1 F, the hour is come; glorify thy
5 And now, O F, glorify thou me
11 Holy F, keep through thine own
21 as thou, F, art in me, and I in thee,
24 F, I will that they also, whom thou
25 O righteous F, the world hath not
18.11 cup which my F hath given me,
13 for he was f in law to Caiphas,
20.17 I am not yet ascended to my F:
17 I ascend unto my F, and your F,
21 as my F hath sent me, even so
Ac 1. 4 but wait for the promise of the F,
7 the F hath put in his own power.
2.33 received of the F the promise of
7. 2 appeared unto our f Abraham,
4 when his f was dead, he removed
14 and called his f Jacob to him,
16 sons of Emmor the f of Sychem.
16. 1 but his f was a Greek:
3 knew all that his f was a Greek.
28. 8 that the f of Publius lay sick of a
Ro 1. 7 and peace from God our F, and the
4. 1 our f, as pertaining to the flesh,
11 be the f of all them that believe,
12 And the f of circumcision to them
12 of that faith of our f Abraham,
16 Abraham, who is the f of us all,
17 I have made thee a f of many
18 become the f of many nations,
6. 4 the dead by the glory of the F,
8.15 adoption, whereby we cry, Abba, F,
9.10 by one, even by our f Isaac;
15. 6 God, even the F of our Lord Jesus
1Co 1. 3 and peace, from God our F, and
8. 6 one God, the F, of whom are all
15.24 the kingdom to God, even the F;
2Co 1. 2 from God our F, and from the
3 even the F of our Lord Jesus
3 the F of mercies, and the God of
6.18 And will be a F unto you, and ye
11.31 The God and F of our Lord Jesus
Gal 1. 1 and God the F, who raised him
3 peace from God the F, and from
4 to the will of God and our F:
4. 2 until the time appointed of the f.
6 unto your hearts, crying, Abba, F.
Eph 1. 2 from God and our F, and from
3 be the God and F of our Lord

Eph 1.17 the *F* of glory, may give unto you
2.18 access by one Spirit unto the *F*.
3.14 my knees unto the *F* of our Lord
4. 6 One God and *F* of all, who is above
5.20 unto God and the *F* in the name
31 a man leave his *f* and mother,
6. 2 Honor thy *f* and mother; which
23 from God the *F* and the Lord Jesus
Php 1. 2 from God our *F*, and from the Lord
2.11 to the glory of God the *F*.
22 as a son with the *f*, he hath served
4.20 Now unto God and our *F* be glory
Col 1. 2 and peace, from God our *F* and
3 God and the *F* of our Lord Jesus
12 Giving thanks unto the *F*, which
19 For it pleased the *F* that in him
2. 2 and of the *F*, and of Christ;
3.17 thanks to God and the *F* by him.
1Th 1. 1 in God the *F* and in the Lord
1 and peace, from God our *F*, and
3 in the sight of God and our *F*;
2.11 of you, as a *f* doth his children,
3.11 Now God himself and our *F*, and
13 holiness before God, even our *F*,
2Th 1. 1 in God our *F* and the Lord Jesus
2 and peace, from God our *F* and the
2.16 and God, even our *F* which hath
1Ti 1. 2 peace, from God our *F* and Jesus
5. 1 an elder, but intreat him as a *f*;
2Ti 1. 2 peace, from God the *F* and Christ
Tit 1. 4 and peace, from God the *F* and the
Phm 3 and peace, from God our *F* and the
Heb 1. 5 And again, I will be to him a *F*,
7. 3 Without *f*, without mother,
10 he was yet in the loins of his *f*,
12. 7 for what son is he whom the *f*
9 unto the *F* of spirits, and live?
Jas 1.17 cometh down from the *F* of lights,
27 undefiled before God and the *F* is
2.21 Was not Abraham our *f* justified
3. 9 bless we God, even the *F*; and
1Pe 1. 2 the foreknowledge of God the *F*,
3 Blessed be the God and *F* of our
17 And if ye call on the *F*, who
2Pe 1.17 For he received from God the *F*
1Jo 1. 2 eternal life, which was with the *F*,
3 our fellowship is with the *F*, and
2. 1 we have an advocate with the *F*,
13 because ye have known the *F*.
15 the love of the *F* is not in him.
16 is not of the *F*, but is of the world.
22 that denieth the *F* and the Son.
23 the Son, the same hath not the *F*:
23 acknowledgeth the Son hath the *F*
24 continue in the Son, and in the *F*.
3. 1 of love the *F* hath bestowed upon
4.14 *F* sent the Son to be the Saviour
5. 7 *F*, the Word, and the Holy Ghost:
2Jo 3 and peace from God the *F*, and from
3 the Son of the *F*, in truth and love.
4 a commandment from the *F*.
9 he hath both the *F* and the Son.
Jude 1 that are sanctified by God the *F*,
Re 1. 6 and priests unto God and his *F*;
2.27 even as I received of my *F*.
3. 5 confess his name before my *F*,
21 set down with my *F* in his throne.

FATHERLESS

Ex 22.22 not afflict any widow, or *f* child.
24 be widows, and your children *f*.
Dt 10.18 the judgment of the *f* and widow,
14.29 and the stranger, and the *f*, and
16.11 and the stranger, and the *f*, and
14 the stranger, and the *f*, and the
24.17 of the stranger, nor of the *f*;
19, 20, 21 for the stranger, for the *f*,
26.12 Levite, the stranger, the *f*, and the
13 and unto the stranger, to the *f*, and
27.19 judgment of the stranger, *f*, and
Job 6.27 overwhelm the *f*, and ye dig a pit
22. 9 arms of the *f* have been broken.
24. 3 They drive away the ass of the *f*,
9 They pluck the *f* from the breast,
29.12 the poor that cried, and the *f*, and
31.17 and the *f* hath not eaten thereof;
21 lifted up my hand against the *f*,
Ps 10.14 thou art the helper of the *f*.
18 to judge the *f* and the oppressed,
68. 5 A father of the *f*, and a judge of
82. 3 Defend the poor and *f*: do justice
94. 6 the stranger, and murder the *f*.
109. 9 Let his children be *f*, and his wife
12 be any to favor his *f* children.
146. 9 he relieveth the *f* and widow: but
Pr 23.10 enter not into the fields of the *f*:
Isa 1.17 judge the *f*, plead for the widow.
23 they judge not the *f*, neither doth
9.17 neither shall have mercy on their *f*
10. 2 and that they may rob the *f*!
Jer 5.28 not the cause, the cause of the *f*,
7. 6 oppress not the stranger, the *f*, and
22. 3 no violence to the stranger, the *f*,
49.11 Leave thy *f* children, I will preserve
La 5. 3 We are orphans and *f*, our
Eze 22. 7 in thee have they vexed the *f* and
Hos 14. 3 for in thee the *f* findeth mercy.
Zec 7.10 oppress not the widow, nor the *f*,
Mal 3. 5 in his wages, the widow, and the *f*,
Jas 1.27 To visit the *f* and widows in their

FATHER'S

Gen 20.13 me to wander from my *f* house,
24.23 is there room in thy *f* house for us to
26.15 which his *f* servants had digged in
28.21 So that I come again to my *f* house
31.19 stolen the images that were her *f*.
50. 1 And Joseph fell upon his *f* face,
1Sa 17.15 to feed his *f* sheep at Beth-lehem.
34 Thy servant kept his *f* sheep,
1Ki 12.10 shall be thicker than my *f* loins.
2Ch 10.10 shall be thicker than my *f* loins.
Neh 1. 6 both I and my *f* house have sinned.
Pr 4. 3 I was my *f* son, tender and only
6.20 My son, keep thy *f* commandment,
13. 1 A wise son heareth his *f* instruction:
15. 5 A fool despiseth his *f* instruction:
Mt 26.29 new with you in my *F* kingdom.
Lk 2.49 I must be about my *F* business?
9.26 in his *F*, and of the holy angels.
12.32 it is your *F* good pleasure to give
15.17 hired servants of my *f* have bread
16.27 wouldest send him to my *f* house:
Jn 2.16 make not my *F* house an house of
5.43 I am come in my *F* name, and ye
6.39 And this is the *F* will which hath
10.25 that I do in my *F* name, they bear
29 to pluck them out of my *F* hand.
14. 2 In my *F* house are many mansions:
24 not mine, but the *F* which sent me.
15.10 I have kept my *F* commandments,
Ac 7.20 was nourished up in his *f* house
1Co 5. 1 that one should have his *f* wife.
Rev 14. 1 having his *F* name written in

FATHERS

Gen 47.30 But I will lie with my *f*, and thou
49.29 bury me with my *f* in the cave that is
Ex 3.13 The God of your *f* hath sent me unto
20. 5 visiting the iniquity of the *f* upon the
34. 7 visiting the iniquity of the *f* upon the
Nu 14.18 visiting the iniquity of the *f* upon
20.15 How our *f* went down into Egypt,
Dt 4. 1 which the Lord God of your *f* giveth
31 nor forget the covenant of thy *f* which
6.23 the land which he sware unto our *f*.
7. 8 oath, which he had sworn unto your *f*,
8.16 with manna, which thy *f* knew not,
10.15 the Lord had a delight in thy *f*
24.16 The *f* shall not be put to death for
16 children be put to death for the *f*:
Jos 4. 6 children ask their *f* in time to
22.28 altar of the Lord, which our *f* made,
24. 6 And I brought your *f* out of Egypt:
14 the gods which your *f* served on the
Jdg 2.12 they forsook the Lord God of their *f*,
6.13 his miracles which our *f* told us of,
1Ki 2.10 David slept with his *f*, and was buried
11.43 Solomon slept with his *f*, and was
15.12 all the idols that his *f* had made.
19. 4 for I am not better than my *f*.
2Ki 14. 6 The *f* shall not be put to death for
6 children be put to death for the *f*;
1Ch 29.15 and sojourners, as were all our *f*:
20 blessed the Lord God of their *f*,
2Ch 25. 4 The *f* shall not die for the children,
4 shall the children die for the *f*,
28.25 to anger the Lord God of his *f*.
29. 6 for our *f* have trespassed, and done
9 lo, our *f* have fallen by the sword,
30. 8 be ye not stiffnecked, as your *f* were,
Ezr 4.15 in the book of the records of thy *f*:
5.12 *f* had provoked the God of heaven
7.27 Blessed be the Lord God of our *f*,
Neh 9.16 But they and our *f* dealt proudly,
34 our priests, nor our *f*, kept thy law,
Ps 22. 4 Our *f* trusted in thee; they trusted,
39.12 and a sojourner, as all my *f* were.
44. 1 O God, our *f* have told us, what
45.16 Instead of thy *f* shall be thy children,
95. 9 When your *f* tempted me, proved
106. 7 Our *f* understood not thy wonders
Pr 17. 6 and the glory of children are their *f*.
Isa 49.23 And kings shall be thy nursing *f*,
Jer 7.26 they did worse than their *f*.
16.19 Surely our *f* have inherited lies,
17.22 sabbath day, as I commanded your *f*.
31.29 The *f* have eaten a sour grape,
47. 3 the *f* shall not look back to their
50. 7 even the Lord, the hope of their *f*.
La 5. 7 Our *f* have sinned, and are not;
Eze 5.10 Therefore the *f* shall eat the sons in
10 and the sons shall eat their *f*;
18. 2 saying, The *f* have eaten sour grapes,
Zec 1. 5 Your *f* where are they? and the
8.14 when your *f* provoked me to wrath.
Mal 4. 6 the heart of the *f* to the children,
6 the heart of the children to their *f*,
Mt 23.30 we had been in the days of our *f*,
32 ye up then the measure of your *f*,
Lk 1.17 to turn the hearts of the *f* to the
55 As he spake to our *f*, to Abraham,
72 the mercy promised to our *f*,
6.23 did their *f* unto the prophets.
26 so did their *f* to the false prophets.
11.47 prophets, and your *f* killed them.
48 that ye allow the deeds of your *f*:
Jn 4.20 *f* worshipped in this mountain;
6.31 Our *f* did eat manna in the desert;
49 *f* did eat manna in the wilderness,
58 not as your *f* did eat manna,
7.22 because it is of Moses, but of the *f*;
Ac 3.13 God of our *f*, hath glorified his Son
22 For Moses truly said unto the *f*,
25 which God made with our *f*,
5.30 The God of our *f* raised up Jesus,
7. 2 Men, brethren, and *f*, hearken;
11 and our *f* found no sustenance.
12 Egypt, he sent out our *f* first.
15 Egypt, and died, he, and our *f*,
19 evil entreated our *f*, so that they
32 Saying, I am the God of thy *f*,
38 the mount Sina, and with our *f*:
39 To whom our *f* would not obey,
44 *f* had the tabernacle of witness
45 Which also our *f* that came after
45 drave out before the face of our *f*,
51 as your *f* did, so do ye.
52 have not your *f* persecuted?
13.17 chose our *f*, and exalted the people
32 which was made unto the *f*,
36 and was laid unto his *f*, and saw
15.10 our *f* nor we were able to bear?

22. 1 Men, brethren, and *f*, hear ye
3 manner of the law of the *f*,
14 God of our *f* hath chosen thee,
24.14 so worship I the God of my *f*,
26. 6 promise made of God unto our *f*:
28.17 the people, or customs of our *f*,
25 Esaias the prophet unto our *f*,
Ro 9. 5 Whose are the *f*, and of whom
15. 8 the promises made unto the *f*:
1Co 4.15 yet have ye not many *f*:
10. 1 all our *f* were under the cloud,
Gal 1.14 zealous of the traditions of my *f*.
Eph 6. 4 ye *f*, provoke not your children to
Col 3.21 *F*, provoke not your children to
1Ti 1. 9 for murderers of *f* and murderers
Heb 1. 1 spake in time past unto the *f* by
3. 9 When your *f* tempted me, proved
8. 9 that I made with their *f* in the day
12. 9 Furthermore we have had *f* of our
1Pe 1.18 received by tradition from your *f*;
2Pe 3. 4 since the *f* fell asleep, all things
1Jn 2.13 I write unto you, *f*, because ye
14 I have written unto you, *f*, because

FATHERS'
Ex 10. 6 fathers, nor thy *f* fathers have seen,
Nu 32.14 ye are risen up in your *f* stead, an
Eze 20.24 their eyes were after their *f* idols.
Ro 11.28 they are beloved for the *f* sakes.

FATHOMS
Ac 27.28 sounded, and found it twenty *f*:
28 again, and found it fifteen *f*.

FATLINGS
1Sa 15. 9 and of the *f*, and the lambs,
2Sa 6.13 he sacrificed oxen and *f*.
Ps 66.15 unto thee burnt sacrifices of *f*,
Eze 39.18 bullocks, all of them *f* of Bashan.
Mt 22. 4 my oxen and my *f* are killed,

FATNESS
Gen 27.28 of heaven, and the *f* of the earth,
39 dwellng shall be the *f* of the earth,
Dt 32.15 thick, thou art covered with *f*;
Jdg 9. 9 Should I leave my *f*, wherewith
Job 15.27 he covereth his face with his *f*,
36.16 thy table should be full of *f*.
Ps 36. 8 satisfied with the *f* of thy house;
63. 5 be satisfied as with marrow and *f*;
65.11 goodness; and thy paths drop *f*.
73. 7 Their eyes stand out with *f*:
109.24 and my flesh faileth of *f*.
Isa 17. 4 the *f* of his flesh shall wax lean.
34. 6 it is made fat with *f*, and with the
7 and their dust made fat with *f*.
55. 2 let your soul delight itself in *f*.
Jer 31.14 the soul of the priests with *f*,
Ro 11.17 the root and *f* of the olive tree;

FATTED
1Ki 4.23 and fallowdeer, and *f* fowl.
Jer 46.21 the midst of her like *f* bullocks;
Lk 15.23 And bring hither the *f* calf, and
27 thy father hath killed the *f* calf,
30 thou hast killed for him the *f* calf.

FAULT
Ex 5.16 but the *f* is in thine own people.
Dt 25. 2 before his face, according to his *f*.
1Sa 29. 3 I have found no *f* in him since
2Sa 3. 8 with a *f* concerning this woman?
Ps 59. 4 prepare themselves without my *f*:
Dan 6. 4 could find none occasion nor *f*;
4 there any error or *f* found in him.
Mt 18.15 and tell him his *f* between thee
Mk 7. 2 unwashen, hands, they found *f*
Lk 23. 4 I find no *f* in this man.
14 have found no *f* in this man
Jn 18.38 I find in him no *f* at all.
19. 4 know that I find no *f* in him.
6 for I find no *f* in him.
Ro 9.19 Why doth he yet find *f*? For who
1Co 6. 7 there is utterly a *f* among you,
Gal 6. 1 if a man be overtaken in a *f*,
Heb 8. 8 For finding *f* with them, he saith,
Rev 14. 5 are without *f* before the throne

FAULTLESS
Heb 8. 7 if that first covenant had been *f*,
Jude 24 and to present you *f* before the

FAULTS
Gen 41. 9 I do remember my *f* this day:
Ps 19.12 cleanse thou me from secret *f*.
Jas 5.16 Confess your *f* one to another,
1Pe 2.20 if, when ye be buffeted for your *f*,

FAVOR
Gen 18. 3 now I have found *f* in thy sight,
39.21 him *f* in the sight of the keeper
Dt 28.50 the old, nor shew *f* to the young:
Est 2.15 Esther obtained *f* in the sight of
Job 10.12 Thou hast granted me life and *f*,
Ps 30. 5 his *f* is life: weeping may endure
102.13 for the time to *f* her, yea, the set
14 stones, and *f* the dust thereof.
Pr 3. 4 So shalt thou find *f* and good
12. 2 good man obtaineth *f* of the Lord:
13.15 Good understanding giveth *f*:
14.35 king's *f* is toward a wise servant:
16.15 *f* is as a cloud of the latter rain.
19.12 his *f* is as dew upon the grass.
31.30 *F* is deceitful, and beauty is vain:
Dan 1. 9 God had brought Daniel into *f*
Lk 1.30 for thou hast found *f* with God.
2.52 and in *f* with God and man.
Ac 2.47 and having *f* with all the people.
7.10 him *f* and wisdom in the sight of
46 Who found *f* before God, and
25. 3 And desired *f* against him, that

FAVORED
Gen 29.17 Rachel was beautiful and well *f*.
39. 6 was a goodly person, and well *f*.
41. 2 out of the river seven well *f* kine
3 seven other kine...ill *f* and
4 the ill *f*...kine did eat up the seven
4 kine did eat up the seven well *f*
18 kine, fatfleshed and well *f*;
19 poor and very ill *f* and leanfleshed,
20 the lean and the ill *f* kine did eat
21 were still ill *f*, as at the beginning.
27 And the seven thin and ill *f* kine
La 4.16 priests, they *f* not the elders.
Dan 1. 4 was no blemish, but well *f*,
Lk 1.28 Hail, thou that art highly *f*,

FEAR
Gen 15. 1 *F* not, Abram: I am thy shield,
20.11 the *f* of God is not in this place;
26.24 *f* not, for I am with thee, and will
46. 3 *f* not to go down into Egypt;
Ex 18.21 people able men, such as *f* God,
20.20 Moses said unto the people, *F* not:
Nu 14. 9 the Lord is with us; *f* them not.
21.34 Lord said unto Moses, *F* him not:
Dt 10.20 Thou shalt *f* the Lord thy God;
13. 4 the Lord your God, and *f* him,
31. 8 *f* not, neither be dismayed.
Ru 3.11 my daughter, *f* not; I will do to
1Sa 4.20 *F* not; for thou hast born a son.
1Ki 17.13 Elijah said unto her, *F* not;
2Ki 17.35 saying, Ye shall not *f* other gods,
1Ch 16.30 *F* before him, all the earth:
2Ch 14.14 the *f* of the Lord came upon them:
Neh 6.19 Tobiah sent letters to put me in *f*.
Job 1. 9 said, Doth Job *f* God for nought?
9.34 and let not his *f* terrify me:
21. 9 Their houses are safe from *f*,
39.16 her labor is in vain without *f*;
22 He mocketh at *f*, and is not
Ps 2.11 Serve the Lord with *f*, and rejoice
5. 7 and in thy *f* will I worship toward
15. 4 honoreth them that *f* the Lord,
19. 9 The *f* of the Lord is clean,
23. 4 I will *f* no evil: for thou art with
25.14 the Lord is with them that *f* him;
27. 1 whom shall I *f*? the Lord is the
3 my heart shall not *f*: though war
33. 8 Let all the earth *f* the Lord:
34. 9 O *f* the Lord, ye his saints:
36. 1 is no *f* of God before his eyes.
40. 3 many shall see it, and *f*, and shall
56. 4 I will not *f* what flesh can do unto
67. 7 the ends of the earth shall *f* him.
85. 9 salvation is nigh them that *f* him;
96. 9 *f* before him, all the earth.
103.13 the Lord pitieth them that *f* him.
111. 5 given meat unto them that *f* him:
10 The *f* of the Lord is the beginning
118. 6 Lord is on my side; I will not *f*:
Pr 1. 7 The *f* of the Lord is the beginning
2. 5 thou understand the *f* of the Lord,
3. 7 *f* the Lord, and depart from evil.
8.13 The *f* of the Lord is to hate evil:
9.10 The *f* of the Lord is the beginning
10.27 *f* of the Lord prolongeth days:
14.27 *f* of the Lord is a fountain of life,
19.23 The *f* of the Lord tendeth to life:
29.25 The *f* of man bringeth a snare:
Ec 8.12 shall be well with them that *f* God,
Isa 35. 4 Be strong, *f* not: behold, your
41.10 *F* thou not; for I am with thee:
43. 1 *F* not: for I have redeemed thee,
51. 7 *f* ye not the reproach of men,
Jer 2.19 that my *f* is not in thee,
32.40 I will put my *f* in their hearts,
La 3.47 *F* and a snare is come upon us,
Dan 6.26 and *f* before the God of Daniel:
10.19 O man greatly beloved, *f* not:
Joel 2.21 *F* not, O land; be glad and
Am 3. 8 lion hath roared, who will not *f*?
Jon 1. 9 I *f* the Lord, the God of heaven,
Mal 1. 6 if I be a master, where is my *f*?
Mt 1.20 *f* not to take unto thee Mary
10.26 *F* them not therefore: for there is
28 *f* not them which kill the body,
28 *f* him which is able to destroy both
31 *F* ye not therefore, ye are of more
14.26 a spirit; and they cried out for *f*.
21.26 we *f* the people; for all hold John
28. 4 for *f* of him the keepers did shake,
5 *F* not ye: for I know that ye seek
8 sepulchre with *f* and great joy;
Lk 1.12 was troubled, and *f* fell upon him.
13 *F* not, Zacharias: for thy prayer
30 *F* not, Mary: for thou hast found
50 his mercy is on them that *f* him
65 *f* came on all that dwelt round
74 enemies might serve him without *f*,
2.10 *F* not: for, behold, I bring you
5.10 And Jesus said unto Simon, *F* not;
26 were filled with *f*, saying, We have
7.16 came a *f* on all: and they glorified
8.37 for they were taken with great *f*:
50 *F* not: believe only, and she shall
12. 5 whom ye shall *f*: *F* him, which
5 yea, I say unto you, *F* him.
7 *F* not therefore: ye are of more
32 *F* not, little flock; for it is your
18. 4 I *f* not God, nor regard man;
21.26 Men's hearts failing them for *f*,
23.40 Dost not thou *f* God, seeing thou
Jn 7.13 openly of him for *f* of the Jews.
12.15 *F* not, daughter of Sion: behold,
19.38 but secretly for *f* of the Jews,
20.19 assembled for *f* of the Jews, came
Ac 2.43 *f* came upon every soul: and many
5. 5 great *f* came on all them that heard
11 great *f* came upon all the church,
9.31 and walking in the *f* of the Lord,
13.16 and ye that *f* God, give audience.

BIBLICAL THEMES

FEAR

A deep sleep fell upon Abram; and, lo, an horror of great darkness fell upon him. Gen 15.12

And Jacob awaked out of his sleep, and he said, Surely the Lord is in this place; and I knew it not. And he was afraid, and said, How dreadful is this place! this is none other but the house of God, and this is the gate of heaven. Gen 28.16-17

He said, I am the God of thy father, the God of Abraham, the God of Isaac, and the God of Jacob. And Moses hid his face; for he was afraid to look upon God. Ex 3.6

And when Pharaoh drew nigh, the children of Israel lifted up their eyes, and, behold, the Egyptians marched after them; and they were sore afraid: and the children of Israel cried out unto the Lord. Ex 14.10

If thou wilt not observe to do all the words of this law that are written in this book . . . thy life shall hang in doubt before thee. . . . In the morning thou shalt say, Would God it were even! and at even thou shalt say, Would God it were morning! for the fear of thine heart wherewith thou shalt fear. Dt 28.58, 66-67

For [God] is not a man, as I am, that I should answer him, and we should come together in judgment. . . . Let him take his rod away from me, and let not his fear terrify me. Job 9.32, 34

Yea, though I walk through the valley of the shadow of death, I will fear no evil: for thou art with me. Ps 23.4

Thou shalt not be afraid for the terror by night; nor for the arrow that flieth by day; nor for the pestilence that walketh in darkness. . . . Because thou hast made the Lord . . . thy habitation. Ps 91.5-6, 9

The fear of the Lord is the beginning of wisdom. Pr 9.10

Thus saith thy Lord . . . Behold, I have taken out of thine hand the cup of trembling, even the dregs of the cup of my fury; thou shalt no more drink it again. Isa 51.22

When I heard, my belly trembled; my lips quivered at the voice . . . and I trembled in myself, that I might rest in the day of trouble. Hab 3.16

Fear not them which kill the body, but are not able to kill the soul: but rather fear him which is able to destroy both soul and body in hell. Mt 10.28

But when [Peter] saw the wind boisterous, he was afraid; and beginning to sink, he cried, saying, Lord, save me. Mt 14.30

But the woman fearing and trembling, knowing what was done in her, came and fell down before him, and told him all the truth. Mk 5.33

Ye have not received the spirit of bondage again to fear; but ye have received the Spirit of adoption. Ro 8.15

God hath not given us the spirit of fear; but of power, and of love. 2Ti 1.7

Forasmuch then as the children are partakers of flesh and blood, [Jesus] . . . likewise took part of the same; that through death he might destroy him that had the power of death, that is, the devil; and deliver them who through fear of death were all their lifetime subject to bondage. Heb 2.14-15

Vengeance belongeth unto me, I will recompense, saith the Lord. . . . It is a fearful thing to fall into the hands of the living God. Heb 10.30-31

There is no fear in love; but perfect love casteth out fear. 1Jn 4.18

Ac 19.17 *f* fell on them all, and the name
27.24 *F* not, Paul; thou must be brought
Ro 3.18 There is no *f* of God before their
8.15 the spirit of bondage again to *f*;
11.20 faith. Be not highminded, but *f*:
13. 7 *f* to whom *f*; honor to whom
1Co 2. 3 and in *f*, and in much trembling.
16.10 he may be with you without *f*:
2Co 7. 1 perfecting holiness in the *f* of God.
11 what indignation, yea, what *f*, yea,
15 with *f* and trembling ye received
11. 3 But I *f*, lest by any means, as the
12.20 For I *f*, lest, when I come, I shall
Eph 5.21 one to another in the *f* of God.
6. 5 with *f* and trembling, in singleness
Php 1.14 bold to speak the word without *f*.
2.12 salvation with *f* and trembling.
1Ti 5.20 all, that others also may *f*.
2Ti 1. 7 hath not given us the spirit of *f*;
Heb 2.15 who through *f* of death were all
4. 1 Let us therefore *f*, lest, a promise
11. 7 moved with *f*, prepared an ark
12.21 I exceedingly *f* and quake:)
28 with reverence and godly *f*:
13. 6 I will not *f* what man shall do unto
1Pe 1.17 time of your sojourning here in *f*:
2.17 *F* God. Honor the king.
18 subject to your masters with all *f*;
3. 2 chaste conversation coupled with *f*.
15 is in you with meekness and *f*:
1Jn 4.18 There is no *f* in love; but perfect
18 love casteth out *f*: because *f* hath
Jude 12 feeding themselves without *f*:
23 others save with *f*, pulling them
Rev 1.17 saying unto me, *F* not; I am the
2.10 *F* none of those things which thou
11.11 great *f* fell upon them which saw
18 saints, and them that *f* thy name,
14. 7 *F* God, and give glory to him;
15. 4 Who shall not *f* thee, O Lord,
18.10, 15 afar off for the *f* of her torment,
19. 5 that *f* him, both small and great.

FEARED

Gen 26. 7 for he *f* to say, She is my wife;

FEAREST

Gen 22.12 now I know that thou *f* God,
Isa 57.11 even of old, and thou *f* me not?
Jer 22.25 hand of them whose face thou *f*,

FEARETH

1Ki 1.51 Behold, Adonijah *f* king Solomon:
Job 1. 8 an upright man, one that *f* God,
2. 3 an upright man, one that *f* God,
Ps 25.12 What man is he that *f* the Lord?
112. 1 Blessed is the man that *f* the
128. 1 is every one that *f* the Lord;
4 shall the man be blessed that *f* the
Pr 13.13 but he that *f* the commandment
14. 2 in his uprightness *f* the Lord:
16 A wise man *f*, and departeth from
28.14 Happy is the man that *f* alway:
31.30 but a woman that *f* the Lord,
Ec 7.18 he that *f* God shall come forth
8.13 because he *f* not before God.
9. 2 as he that *f* an oath.
Isa 50.10 Who is among you that *f* the Lord,
Ac 10.22 a just man, and one that *f* God,
35 But in every nation he that *f* him,
13.26 whosoever among you *f* God,
1Jn 4.18 He that *f* is not made perfect in

FEARFUL

Ex 15.11 *f* in praises, doing wonders?
Dt 20. 8 What man is there that is *f* and
28.58 fear this glorious and *f* name,
Jdg 7. 3 Whosoever is *f* and afraid, let
Isa 35. 4 Say to them that are of a *f* heart,
Mt 8.26 Why are ye *f*, O ye of little faith?
Mk 4.40 said unto them, Why are ye so *f*?
Lk 21.11 *f* sights and great signs shall
Heb 10.27 certain *f* looking for of judgment
31 It is a *f* thing to fall into the hands
Rev 21. 8 the *f*, and unbelieving, and the

FEARFULLY

Ps 139.14 I am *f* and wonderfully made:

FEARFULNESS

Ps 55. 5 *F* and trembling are come upon
Isa 21. 4 heart panted, *f* affrighted me:
33.14 *f* hath surprised the hypocrites.

FEARING

Jos 22.25 children cease from *f* the Lord.
Mk 5.33 But the woman *f* and trembling.
Ac 23.10 the chief captain, *f* lest Paul
27.17 and, *f* lest they should fall into
29 *f* lest we should have fallen upon
Gal 2.12 himself, *f* them which were of the
Col 3.22 but in singleness of heart, *f* God:
Heb 11.27 not *f* the wrath of the king:

FEARS

Ps 34. 4 and delivered me from all my *f*.
Ec 12. 5 and *f* shall be in the way,

Isa 66. 4 and will bring their *f* upon them;
2Co 7. 5 were fightings, within were *f*.

FEAST

Gen 21. 8 Abraham made a great *f* the same
Ex 10. 9 we must hold a *f* unto the Lord.
12.14 ye shall keep it a *f* to the Lord
17 observe the *f* of unleavened bread;
23.16 and the *f* of ingathering, which is
32. 5 To morrow is a *f* to the Lord.
34.22 thou shalt observe the *f* of weeks,
22 *f* of ingathering at the year's end.
Dt 16.13 shalt observe the *f* of tabernacles
Neh 8.14 should dwell in booths in the *f* of
Est 1. 9 Vashti the queen made a *f* for the
Pr 15.15 a merry heart hath a continual *f*.
Isa 25. 6 unto all people a *f* of fat things,
6 a *f* of wines on the lees,
Eze 45.21 the passover, a *f* of seven days;
Hos 2.11 her *f* days, her new moons, and
9. 5 in the day of the *f* of the Lord?
Am 5.21 I hate, I despise your *f* days,
Mt 26. 2 two days is the *f* of the passover,
5 But they said, Not on the *f* day,
17 day of the *f* of unleavened bread
27.15 at that *f* the governor was wont
Mk 14. 1 two days was the *f* of the passover,
2 But they said, Not on the *f* day,
15. 6 Now at that *f* he released unto
Lk 2.41 every year at the *f* of the passover.
42 Jerusalem after the custom of the *f*.
5.29 Levi made him a great *f* in his
14.13 when thou makest a *f*, call the
22. 1 the *f* of unleavened bread drew
23.17 release one unto them at the *f*.
Jn 2. 8 bear unto the governor of the *f*.
9 When the ruler of the *f* had tasted
9 the governor of the *f* called the
23 at the passover, in the *f* day,
4.45 that he did at Jerusalem at the *f*:
45 for they also went unto the *f*.
5. 1 After this there was a *f* of the Jews;
6. 4 a *f* of the Jews, was nigh.
7. 2 the Jews' *f* of tabernacles was at
8 Go ye up unto this *f*:
8 I go not up yet unto this *f*;
10 then went he also up unto the *f*,
11 Then the Jews sought him at the *f*,
14 Now about the midst of the *f* Jesus
37 last day, that great day of the *f*,
10.22 Jerusalem the *f* of the dedication,
11.56 that he will not come to the *f*?
12.12 people that were come to the *f*,
20 that came up to worship at the *f*:
13. 1 Now before the *f* of the passover,
29 we have need of against the *f*;
Ac 18.21 I must by all means keep this *f*
1Co 5. 8 Therefore let us keep the *f*,
10.27 them that believe not bid you to a *f*,
2Pe 2.13 deceivings while they *f* with you;
Jude 12 of charity, when they *f* with you,

FEASTS

Lev 23. 4 These are the *f* of the Lord, even
2Ch 8.13 new moons, and on the solemn *f*
Isa 1.14 your appointed *f* my soul hateth:
La 1. 4 none come to the solemn *f*:
Am 8.10 I will turn your *f* into mourning,
Mal 2. 3 even the dung of your solemn *f*;
Mt 23. 6 love the uppermost rooms at *f*,
Mk 12.39 and the uppermost rooms at *f*:
Lk 20.46 and the chief rooms at *f*;
Jude 12 are spots in your *f* of charity,

FEATHERS

Lev 1.16 pluck away his crop with his *f*,
Job 39.13 wings and *f* unto the ostrich?
Ps 68.13 and her *f* with yellow gold.
91. 4 He shall cover thee with his *f*,
Eze 17. 3 great wings, long winged, full of *f*,
7 with great wings and many *f*:
Dan 4.33 hairs were grown like eagles' *f*,

FED

Gen 30.36 Jacob *f* the rest of Laban's flocks
36.24 as he *f* the asses of Zibeon his
41. 2 fatfleshed; and they *f* in a meadow.
18 favored; and they *f* in a meadow:
47.17 and he *f* them with bread for all
48.15 the God which *f* me all my life
Ex 16.32 I have *f* you in the wilderness,
Dt 8. 3 to hunger, and *f* thee with manna,
16 Who *f* thee in the wilderness with
2Sa 20. 3 put them in ward, and *f* them,
1Ki 18. 4 and *f* them with bread and water.)
13 and *f* them with bread and water?
1Ch 27.29 over the herds that *f* in Sharon
Ps 37. 3 and verily thou shalt be *f*.
78.72 *f* them according to the integrity
81.16 He should have *f* them also with
Isa 1.11 of rams, and the fat of *f* beasts;
Jer 5. 7 when I had *f* them to the full,
8 They were as *f* horses in the
Eze 16.19 and honey, wherewith I *f* thee,
34. 3 ye kill them that are *f*: but ye
8 but the shepherds *f* themselves,
8 and *f* not my flock;
Dan 4.12 and all flesh was *f* of it.
5.21 they *f* him with grass like oxen,
Zec 11. 7 called Bands; and I *f* the flock.
Mt 25.37 thee an hungered, and *f* thee?
Mk 5.14 they that *f* the swine fled, and
Lk 8.34 they that *f* them saw what was
16.21 desiring to be *f* with the crumbs
1Co 3. 2 I have *f* you with milk, and not

FEEBLE

Gen 30.42 But when the cattle were *f*, he
Dt 25.18 even all that were *f* behind thee,
1Sa 2. 5 hath many children is waxed *f*.
2Sa 4. 1 his hands were *f*, and all the
2Ch 28.15 and carried all the *f* of them upon
Neh 4. 2 What do these *f* Jews? will they
Job 4. 4 hast strengthened the *f* knees,
Ps 38. 8 I am *f* and sore broken:
105.37 and there was not one *f* person
Pr 30.26 The conies are but a *f* folk,
Isa 16.14 the remnant shall be very *f*.
35. 3 hands, and confirm the *f* knees.
Jer 6.24 our hands wax *f*: anguish hath
49.24 Damascus is waxed *f*, and turneth
50.43 and his hands waxed *f*: anguish
Eze 7.17 All hands shall be *f*, and all knees
21. 7 and all hands shall be *f*,
Zec 12. 8 and he that is *f* among them at
1Co 12.22 which seem to be more *f*, are
Heb 12.12 hang down, and the *f* knees.

FEEBLEMINDED

1Th 5.14 comfort the *f*, support the weak,

FEED

Gen 25.30 *F* me, I pray thee, with that same
29. 7 ye the sheep, and go and *f* them.
30.31 I will again *f* and keep thy flock:
37.12 went to *f* their father's flock in
13 Do not thy brethren *f* the flock in
16 tell me, I pray thee, where they *f*
46.32 their trade hath been to *f* cattle;
Ex 22. 5 shall *f* in another man's field;
34. 3 neither let the flocks nor herds *f*
1Sa 17.15 from Saul to *f* his father's sheep
2Sa 5. 2 Thou shalt *f* my people Israel,
7. 7 to *f* my people Israel, saying,
19.33 and I will *f* thee with me in
1Ki 17. 4 commanded the ravens to *f* thee
22.27 and *f* him with bread of affliction
1Ch 11. 2 Thou shalt *f* my people Israel,
17. 6 I commanded to *f* my people,
2Ch 18.26 and *f* him with bread of affliction
Job 24. 2 take away flocks, and *f* thereof.
20 the worm shall *f* sweetly on him;
Ps 28. 9 *f* them also, and lift them up
49.14 death shall *f* on them; and the
78.71 brought him to *f* Jacob his people,
Pr 10.21 The lips of the righteous *f* many:
30. 8 *f* me with food convenient for me:
SS 1. 8 *f* thy kids beside the shepherds'
4. 5 twins, which *f* among the lilies.
6. 2 bed of spices, to *f* in the gardens,
Isa 5.17 the lambs *f* after their manner,
11. 7 And the cow and the bear shall *f*;
14.30 And the firstborn of the poor shall *f*,
27.10 there shall the calf *f*, and there
30.23 shall thy cattle *f* in large pastures.
40.11 shall *f* his flock like a shepherd:
49. 9 They shall *f* in the ways, and their
26 I will *f* them that oppress thee
58.14 *f* thee with the heritage of Jacob
61. 5 strangers shall stand and *f* your
65.25 wolf and the lamb shall *f* together,

The feast at which Jesus turns water into wine (Jn 2) is the subject of Veronese's The Wedding at Cana.

Jer 3.15 which shall f you with knowledge
6. 3 they shall f every one in his place.
9.15 I will f them, even this people,
23. 2 the pastors that f my people;
4 over them which shall f them:
15 I will f them with wormwood, and
50.19 he shall f on Carmel and Bashan,
La 4. 5 They that did f delicately are
Eze 34. 2 the shepherds of Israel that do f
2 not the shepherds f the flocks?
3 that are fed; but ye f not the flock.
10 shall the shepherds f themselves
13 and f them upon the mountains of
14 I will f them in a good pasture,
14 in a fat pasture they shall f upon
15 I will f my flock, and I will cause
16 I will f them with judgment.
23 he shall f them, even my servant
23 he shall f them, and he shall be
Dan 11.26 that f of the portion of his meat
Hos 4.16 the Lord will f them as a lamb
9. 2 and the winepress shall not f them,
Jon 3. 7 let them not f, nor drink water:
Mic 5. 4 and f in the strength of the Lord,
7.14 F thy people with thy rod, the
14 let them f in Bashan and Gilead,
Zep 2. 7 they shall f thereupon: in the
3.13 for they shall f and lie down,
Zec 11. 4 F the flock of the slaughter;
7 And I will f the flock of slaughter,
9 Then said I, I will not f you:
16 nor f that that standeth still:
Lk 15.15 him into his fields to f swine.
Jn 21.15 He saith unto him, F my lambs.
16 He saith unto him, F my sheep.
17 Jesus saith unto him, F my sheep.
Ac 20.28 overseers, to f the church of God,
Ro 12.20 if thine enemy hunger, f him; if
1Co 13. 3 bestow all my goods to f the poor,
1Pe 5. 2 F the flock of God which is
Rev 7.17 midst of the throne shall f them,
12. 6 that they should f her there a

FEEDEST
Ps 80. 5 f them with the bread of tears;
SS 1. 7 my soul loveth, where thou f,

FEEDETH
Pr 15.14 mouth of fools f on foolishness.
SS 2.16 I am his: he f among the lilies.
6. 3 is mine: he f among the lilies.
Isa 44.20 He f on ashes: a deceived heart
Hos 12. 1 Ephraim f on wind, and followeth
Mt 6.26 yet your heavenly Father f them.
Lk 12.24 and God f them: how much more
1Co 9. 7 who f a flock, and eateth not

FEEDING
Gen 37. 2 was f the flock with his brethren;
Job 1.14 oxen were plowing, and the asses f
Eze 34.10 them to cease from f the flock;
Mt 8.30 them an herd of many swine f.
Mk 5.11 mountains a great herd of swine f.
Lk 8.32 many swine f on the mountain:
17. 7 a servant plowing or f cattle,
Jude 12 you, f themselves without fear:

FEEL
Gen 27.12 will f me, and I shall seem to him
21 I pray thee, that I may f thee,
Jdg 16.26 Suffer me that I may f the pillars
Job 20.20 shall not f quietness in his belly,
Ps 58. 9 Before your pots can f the thorns,
Ec 8. 5 the commandment shall f no evil
Ac 17.27 if haply they might f after him,

FEELING
Eph 4.19 Who being past f have given
Heb 4.15 cannot be touched with the f of our

FEET
Ex 3. 5 put off thy shoes from off thy f,
Jos 3.13 of the f of the priests that bear
9. 5 old shoes and clouted upon their f,
Ru 3. 8 behold, a woman lay at his f.
2Sa 22.34 He maketh my f like hind's f:
37 so that my f did not slip.
Job 13.27 puttest my f also in the stocks,
29.15 and f was I to the lame.
Ps 8. 6 hast put all things under his f:
18.33 He maketh my f like hinds' f,
22.16 they pierced my hands and my f.
25.15 he shall pluck my f out of the net.
31. 8 thou hast set my f in a large room.
40. 2 and set my f upon a rock,
56.13 not thou deliver my f from falling,
66. 9 suffereth not our f to be moved.
73. 2 for me, my f were almost gone;
115. 7 f have they, but they walk not:
116. 8 from tears, and my f from falling.
119.105 Thy word is a lamp unto my f,
122. 2 Our f shall stand within thy gates,
Pr 4.26 Ponder the path of thy f, and let
5. 5 Her f go down to death; her steps
26. 6 the hand of a fool cutteth off the f,
Isa 6. 2 with twain he covered his f, and
52. 7 the f of him that bringeth good
59. 7 Their f run to evil, and they make
Jer 13.16 your f stumble upon the dark
Eze 2. 1 Son of man, stand upon thy f,
Dan 2.33 his f part of iron and part of clay.
34 smote the image upon his f
Hab 3. 5 burning coals went forth at his f.
Zec 14. 4 And his f shall stand in that day
Mt 7. 6 they trample them under their f,
10.14 city, shake off the dust of your f.
15.30 and cast them down at Jesus's f;
18. 8 than having two hands or two f
29 fellowservant fell down at his f,
28. 9 they came and held him by the f,
Mk 5.22 when he saw him, he fell at his f,
6.11 dust under your f for a testimony
7.25 and came and fell at his f:
9.45 having two f to be cast into hell,
Lk 1.79 guide our f into the way of peace.
7.38 stood at his f behind him weeping,
38 and began to wash his f with tears,
38 kissed his f, and anointed them
44 thou gavest me no water for my f:
44 she hath washed my f with tears,
45 hath not ceased to kiss my f.
46 hath anointed my f with ointment.
8.35 sitting at the f of Jesus, clothed,
41 fell down at Jesus' f, and besought
9. 5 off the very dust from your f for a
10.39 which also sat at Jesus's f, and
15.22 on his hand, and shoes on his f:
17.16 And fell down on his face at his f,
24.39 Behold my hands and my f,
40 shewed them his hands and his f.
Jn 11. 2 and wiped his f with her hair,
32 she fell down at his f, saying unto
12. 3 and anointed the f of Jesus,
3 and wiped his f with her hair:
13. 5 and began to wash the disciples f,
6 Lord, dost thou wash my f?
8 Thou shalt never wash my f.
9 Lord, not my f only, but also my
10 needeth not save to wash his f,
12 So after he had washed their f,
14 and Master, have washed your f;
14 also ought to wash one another's f.
20.12 at the head, and the other at the f,
Ac 3. 7 his f and ancle bones received
4.35 laid them down at the apostles' f:
37 money, and laid it at the apostles' f.
5. 2 part, and laid it at the apostles' f.
9 the f of them which have buried
10 fell she down straightway at his f,
7.33 Put off thy shoes from thy f:
58 their clothes at a young man's f,
10.25 met him, and fell down at his f,
13.25 of his f I am not worthy to loose.
51 they shook off the dust of their f
14. 8 impotent in his f, being a cripple
10 loud voice, Stand upright on thy f.
16.24 and made their f fast in the stocks.
21.11 and bound his own hands and f,
22. 3 in this city at the f of Gamaliel,
26.16 But rise, and stand upon thy f:
Ro 3.15 Their f are swift to shed blood:
10.15 How beautiful are the f of them
16.20 bruise Satan under your f shortly.
1Co 12.21 nor again the head to the f,
15.25 hath put all enemies under his f.
27 he hath put all things under his f.
Eph 1.22 And hath put all things under his f,
6.15 your f shod with the preparation
1Ti 5.10 if she have washed the saints' f,
Heb 2. 8 all things in subjection under his f.
12.13 And make straight paths for your f,
Rev 1.15 And his f like unto fine brass,
17 I saw him, I fell at his f as dead.
2.18 and his f are like fine brass;
3. 9 to come and worship before thy f,
10. 1 and his f as pillars of fire:
11.11 and they stood upon their f; and
12. 1 the sun, and the moon under her f,
13. 2 and his f were as the f of a bear,
19.10 I fell at his f to worship him.
22. 8 before the f of the angel which

FEIGN
2Sa 14. 2 thee, f thyself to be a mourner,
1Ki 14. 5 f herself to be another woman.
Lk 20.20 sent forth spies which would f

FEIGNED
1Sa 21.13 and f himself mad in their hands,
Ps 17. 1 that goeth not out of f lips.
2Pe 2. 3 with f words make merchandise

FELIX
Ac 23.24 him safe unto F the governor.
26 unto the most excellent governor F
24. 3 and in all places, most noble F,
22 And when F heard these things,
24 F came with his wife Drusilla,
25 F trembled, and answered, Go thy
27 and F, willing to shew the Jews a
25.14 a certain man left in bonds by F:

FELL
Gen 4. 5 very wroth, and his countenance f.
15.12 a deep sleep f upon Abram; and,
17. 3 And Abram f on his face: and God
33. 4 and f on his neck, and kissed him:
45.14 he f upon his brother Benjamin's
50. 1 Joseph f upon his father's face,
Nu 11. 9 in the night, the manna f upon it.
14. 5 Moses and Aaron f on their faces
Dt 9.18 And I f down before the Lord,
25 forty nights, as I f down at the first;
Jos 6.20 shout, that the wall f down flat,
1Sa 11. 7 fear of the Lord f on the people,
31. 4 Saul took a sword, and f upon it.
1Ki 18.38 Then the fire of the Lord f,
2Ki 2.13 mantle of Elijah that f from him,
6. 5 the axe head f into the water:
1Ch 10. 4 Saul took a sword, and f upon it.
Ps 27. 2 up my flesh, they stumbled and f.
Eze 11. 5 the Spirit of the Lord f upon me,
Dan 3. 7 f down and worshipped the golden
Jon 1. 7 lots, and the lot f upon Jonah.
Mt 2.11 and f down, and worshipped him:
7.25 and it f not: for it was founded
27 and it f: and great was the fall of it.
13. 4 some seeds f by the way side, and
5 Some f upon stony places, where
7 And some f among thorns; and
8 But other f into good ground, and
17. 6 they f on their face, and were sore

18.26 therefore *f* down, and worshipped
29 fellowservant *f* down at his feet.
26.39 and *f* on his face, and prayed,
Mk 3.11 they saw him, *f* down before him,
4. 4 some *f* by the way side, and the
5 And some *f* on stony ground, where
7 And some *f* among thorns, and the
8 And other *f* on good ground, and
5.22 when he saw him, he *f* at his feet,
33 came and *f* down before him, and
7.25 and came and *f* at his feet:
9.20 he *f* on the ground, and wallowed
14.35 and *f* on the ground, and prayed
Lk 1.12 troubled, and fear *f* upon him.
5. 8 he *f* down at Jesus' knees, saying,
12 *f* on his face, and besought him,
6.49 immediately it *f*; and the ruin
8. 5 he sowed, some *f* by the way side;
6 And some *f* upon a rock; and as
7 And some *f* among thorns; and the
8 And other *f* on good ground, and
14 which *f* among thorns are they,
23 as they sailed he *f* asleep: and there
28 cried out, and *f* down before him,
41 he *f* down at Jesus' feet, and
10.30 *f* among thieves, which stripped
36 him that *f* among the thieves?
13. 4 upon whom the tower in Siloam *f*,
15.20 and ran, and *f* on his neck,
16.21 which *f* from the rich man's table:
17.16 *f* down on his face at his feet,
Jn 11.32 *f* down at his feet, saying unto him,
18. 6 backward, and *f* to the ground.
Ac 1.25 from which Judas by transgression *f*,
26 and the lot *f* upon Matthias;
5. 5 *f* down, and gave up the ghost:
10 Then *f* she down straightway at
7.60 when he had said this, he *f* asleep.
9. 4 *f* to the earth, and heard a voice
18 there *f* from his eyes as it had been
10.10 made ready, he *f* into a trance,
25 and *f* down at his feet, and
44 the Holy Ghost *f* on all them which
11.15 the Holy Ghost *f* on them, as on us
12. 7 his chains *f* off from his hands.
13.11 *f* on him a mist and a darkness;
36 *f* on sleep, and was laid unto his
16.29 and *f* down before Paul and Silas,
19.17 and fear *f* on them all, and the
35 which *f* down from Jupiter?
20. 9 and *f* down from the third loft,
10 Paul went down, and *f* on him,
37 *f* on Paul's neck, and kissed him,
22. 7 I *f* unto the ground, and heard
Ro 11.22 on them which *f*, severity; but
15. 3 that reproached thee *f* on me.
1Co 10. 8 and *f* in one day three and twenty
Heb 3.17 carcasses *f* in the wilderness?
11.30 faith the walls of Jericho *f* down,
2Pe 3. 4 since the fathers *f* asleep, all things
Rev 1.17 I saw him, I *f* at his feet as dead.
5. 8 elders *f* down before the Lamb,
14 *f* down and worshipped him that
6.13 stars of heaven *f* unto the earth,
7.11 *f* before the throne on their faces,
8.10 there *f* a great star from heaven,
10 *f* upon the third part of the rivers,
11.11 fear *f* upon them which saw them.
13 and the tenth part of the city *f*,
16 *f* upon their faces, and worshipped
16. 2 *f* a noisome and grievous sore
19 and the cities of the nations *f*:
21 there *f* upon men a great hail
19. 4 and the four beasts *f* down and
10 And I *f* at his feet to worship
22. 8 I *f* down to worship before the feet

FELLOW

Ex 2.13 Wherefore smitest thou thy *f*?
Jdg 7.13 man that told a dream unto his *f*,
14 his *f* answered and said, This is
22 every man's sword against his *f*,
1Sa 14.20 man's sword was against his *f*,
21.15 have brought this *f* to play the mad
15 shall this *f* come into my house?
25.21 in vain I have kept all that this *f* hath
29. 4 Make this *f* return, that he may
2Sa 2.16 caught every one his *f* by the head,
1Ki 22.27 Put this *f* in the prison, and feed him
2Ki 9.11 wherefore came this mad *f* to thee?
2Ch 18.26 Put this *f* in the prison, and feed him
Ec 4.10 the one will lift up his *f*:
Isa 34.14 and the satyr shall cry to his *f*;
Jon 1. 7 And they said every one to his *f*,
Zec 13. 7 and against the man that is my *f*,
Mt 12.24 This *f* doth not cast out devils,
26.61 This *f* said, I am able to destroy
71 This *f* was also with Jesus of
Lk 22.59 a truth this *f* also was with him:
23. 2 We found this *f* perverting the
Jn 9.29 as for this *f*, we know not from
Ac 18.13 Saying, This *f* persuadeth men
22.22 Away with such a *f* from the
24. 5 found this man a pestilent *f*, and

FELLOWCITIZENS

Eph 2.19 but *f* with the saints, and of the

FELLOWDISCIPLES

Jn 11.16 Didymus, unto his *f*, Let us also

FELLOWLABORER

1Th 3. 2 our *f* in the gospel of Christ,
Phm 1 our dearly beloved, and *f*,

FELLOWLABORERS

Php 4. 3 also, and with other my *f*,
Phm 24 Demas, Lucas, my *f*.

FELLOWPRISONER

Col 4.10 Aristarchus my *f* saluteth you,
Phm 23 Epaphras, my *f* in Christ Jesus;

FELLOWPRISONERS

Ro 16. 7 and Junia, my kinsmen, and my *f*,

FELLOWS

Jdg 11.37 bewail my virginity, I and my *f*.
18.25 lest angry *f* run upon thee, and
2Sa 6.20 as one of the vain *f* shamelessly
Ps 45. 7 the oil of gladness above thy *f*.
Isa 44.11 Behold, all his *f* shall be ashamed:
Eze 37.19 and the tribes of Israel his *f*,
Dan 2.13 they sought Daniel and his *f*
18 that Daniel and his *f* should not
7.20 look was more stout than his *f*.
Zec 3. 8 the high priest, thou, and thy *f*
Mt 11.16 markets, and calling unto their *f*,
Ac 17. 5 certain lewd *f* of the baser sort,
Heb 1. 9 the oil of gladness above thy *f*.

FELLOWSERVANT

Mt 18.29 And his *f* fell down at his feet,
33 also have had compassion on thy *f*,
Col 1. 7 Epaphras our dear *f*, who is for
4. 7 minister and *f* in the Lord:
Rev 19.10 do it not: I am thy *f*, and of thy
22. 9 do it not: for I am thy *f*, and of thy

FELLOWSERVANTS

Mt 18.28 went out, and found one of his *f*,
31 So when his *f* saw what was done,
24.49 And shall begin to smite his *f*,
Rev 6.11 their *f* also and their brethren,

FELLOWSHIP

Lev 6. 2 or in *f*, or in a thing taken
Ps 94.20 of iniquity have *f* with thee,
Ac 2.42 and *f*, and in breaking of bread,
1Co 1. 9 were called unto the *f* of his Son
10.20 that ye should have *f* with devils.
2Co 6.14 what *f* hath righteousness with
8. 4 upon us the *f* of the ministering
Gal 2. 9 and Barnabas the right hand of *f*;
Eph 3. 9 see what is the *f* of the mystery,
5.11 And have no *f* with the unfruitful
Php 1. 5 your *f* in the gospel from the first
2. 1 of love, if any *f* of the Spirit,
3.10 and the *f* of his sufferings,
1Jn 1. 3 ye also may have *f* with us: and
3 truly our *f* is with the Father,
6 If we say that we have *f* with him,
7 light, we have *f* one with another,

FELLOWSOLDIER

Php 2.25 and companion in labor, and *f*,
Phm 2 and Archippus our *f*, and to the

FELLOWWORKERS

Col 4.11 only are my *f* unto the kingdom

FELT

Gen 27.22 and he *f* him, and said, The voice
Ex 10.21 even darkness which may be *f*.
Pr 23.35 I *f* it not: when shall I awake?
Mk 5.29 *f* in her body that she was healed
Ac 28. 5 beast into the fire, and *f* no harm.

FEMALE

Gen 1.27 him; male and *f* created he them.
5. 2 Male and *f* created he them; and
6.19 with thee; they shall be male and *f*.
7. 2 thee by sevens, the male and his *f*:
2 clean by two, the male and his *f*.
3 air by sevens, the male and the *f*;
9 into the ark, the male and the *f*,
16 went in male and *f* of all flesh,
Lev 3. 1 whether it be a male or *f*, he shall
6 flock; male or *f*, he shall offer it
4.28 of the goats, a *f* without blemish,
32 shall bring it a *f* without blemish.
5. 6 a *f* from the flock, a lamb or a kid
12. 7 her that hath born a male or a *f*.
27. 4 if it be a *f*, then thy estimation
5 and for the *f* ten shekels.
6 and for the *f* thy estimation shall
7 and for the *f* ten shekels.
Nu 5. 3 Both male and *f* shall ye put out,
Dt 4.16 the likeness of male or *f*,
7.14 there shall not be male or *f* barren
Mt 19. 4 beginning made them male and *f*,
Mk 10. 6 God made them male and *f*.
Gal 3.28 there is neither male nor *f*: for

FENCE

Ps 62. 3 shall ye be, and as a tottering *f*.

FERVENT

Ac 18.25 being *f* in the spirit, he spake
Ro 12.11 *f* in spirit; serving the Lord;
2Co 7. 7 your *f* mind toward me; so that
Jas 5.16 *f* prayer of a righteous man
1Pe 4. 8 have *f* charity among yourselves:
2Pe 3.10 the elements shall melt with *f* heat,
12 the elements shall melt with *f* heat?

FERVENTLY

Col 4.12 laboring *f* for you in prayers,
1Pe 1.22 one another with a pure heart *f*:

FESTUS

Ac 24.27 Porcius *F* came into Felix' room:
25. 1 *F* was come into the province,
4 But *F* answered, that Paul should
9 But *F*, willing to do the Jews a
12 Then *F*, when he had conferred
13 came unto Caesarea to salute *F*.
14 *F* declared Paul's cause unto the
22 Then Agrippa said unto *F*, I would
24 and *F* said, King Agrippa, and all
26.24 *F* said with a loud voice, Paul,
25 I am not mad, most noble *F*;
32 Then said Agrippa unto *F*, This

FETCH

Gen 18. 5 And I will *f* a morsel of bread,
27. 9 *f* me from thence two good kids
13 obey my voice, and go *f* me them.
45 will send, and *f* thee from thence:
42.16 and let him *f* your brother, and ye
Ex 2. 5 she sent her maid to *f* it.
Nu 20.10 we *f* you water out of this rock?
34. 5 the border shall *f* a compass
Dt 19.12 of his city shall send and *f* him
24.10 into his house to *f* his pledge.
19 thou shalt not go again to *f* it:
30. 4 and from thence will he *f* thee:
Jdg 11. 5 elders of Gilead went to *f* Jephthah
20.10 to *f* victual for the people, that
1Sa 4. 3 Let us *f* the ark of the covenant
6.21 come ye down, and *f* it up to you.
16.11 Send and *f* him: for we will not
20.31 now send and *f* him unto me, for
26.22 the young men come over and *f* it.
2Sa 5.23 but *f* a compass behind them,
14.13 the king doth not *f* home again
20 To *f* about this form of speech
1Ki 17.10 *F* me, I pray thee, a little water
11 And as she was going to *f* it,
2Ki 6.13 that I may send and *f* him.
2Ch 18. 8 *F* quickly Micaiah the son of Imla.
Neh 8.15 and *f* olive branches, and pine
Job 36. 3 I will *f* my knowledge from afar,
Isa 56.12 I will *f* wine, and we will fill
Jer 36.21 the king sent Jehudi to *f* the roll:
Ac 16.37 come themselves and *f* us out.

FETCHED

Gen 18. 4 Let a little water, I pray you, be *f*,
27.14 he went, and *f*, and brought them
Jos 15. 3 and *f* a compass to Karkaa
Jdg 18.18 *f* the carved image, the ephod,
1Sa 7. 1 and *f* up the ark of the Lord,
10.23 And they ran and *f* him thence:
2Sa 4. 6 though they would have *f* wheat;
9. 5 king David sent, and *f* him out of
11.27 sent and *f* her to his house,
14. 2 and *f* thence a wise woman, and
1Ki 7.13 king Solomon sent and *f* Hiram
9.28 to Ophir, and *f* from thence gold.
2Ki 3. 9 they *f* a compass of seven days'
11. 4 Jehoiada sent and *f* the rulers
2Ch 1.17 And they *f* up, and brought forth
12.11 the guard came and *f* them, and
Jer 26.23 they *f* forth Urijah out of Egypt,
Ac 28.13 from thence we *f* a compass, and

FETTERS

Jdg 16.21 and bound him with *f* of brass;
2Sa 3.34 not bound, nor thy feet put into *f*:
2Ki 25. 7 and bound him with *f* of brass,
2Ch 33.11 and bound him with *f*, and carried
36. 6 and bound him in *f*, to carry him
Job 36. 8 And if they be bound in *f*,
Ps 105.18 Whose feet they hurt with *f*: he
149. 8 and their nobles with *f* of iron;
Mk 5. 4 often bound with *f* and chains,
4 and the *f* broken in pieces:
Lk 8.29 kept bound with chains and in *f*;

FEVER

Dt 28.22 with a consumption, and with a *f*,
Mt 8.14 wife's mother laid, and sick of a *f*.
15 and the *f* left her: and she arose,
Mk 1.30 wife's mother lay sick of a *f*,
31 and immediately the *f* left her,
Lk 4.38 mother was taken with a great *f*;
39 and rebuked the *f*; and it left her:
Jn 4.52 at the seventh hour the *f* left him.
Ac 28. 8 lay sick of a *f* and of a bloody flux:

FEW

Gen 24.55 the damsel abide with us a *f* days
27.44 And tarry with him a *f* days,
29.20 they seemed unto him but a *f* days,
34.30 I being *f* in number, they shall
47. 9 *f* and evil have the days of the
Lev 25.52 if there remain but *f* years unto
26.22 and make you *f* in number;
Nu 9.20 when the cloud was a *f* days upon
13.18 be strong or weak, *f* or many;
26.54 and to *f* thou shalt give the less
56 be divided between many and *f*.
35. 8 but from them that have *f*
8 ye shall give *f*: every one
Dt 4.27 and ye shall be left *f* in number
26. 5 and sojourned there with a *f*, and
28.62 And ye shall be left *f* in number,
33. 6 and let not his men be *f*.
Jos 7. 3 labor thither; for they are but *f*.
1Sa 14. 6 to save by many or by *f*.
17.28 with whom hast thou left those *f*
2Ki 4. 3 empty vessels; borrow not a *f*.
1Ch 16.19 When ye were but *f*, even
19 even a *f*, and strangers in it,
2Ch 29.34 But the priests were too *f*, so
Neh 2.12 I and some *f* men with me;
7. 4 but the people were *f* therein, and
Job 10.20 Are not my days *f*? cease then,
14. 1 that is born of woman is of *f* days,
16.22 When a *f* years are come, then I
Ps 105.12 When they were but a *f* men in
12 yea, very *f*, and strangers in it.
109. 8 Let his days be *f*: and let another
Ec 5. 2 therefore let thy words be *f*.
9.14 a little city and *f* men within it;
12. 3 grinders cease because they are *f*,
Isa 10. 7 and cut off nations not a *f*.
19 the trees of his forest shall be *f*,
24. 6 earth are burned, and *f* men left.
Jer 30.19 them, and they shall not be *f*;
42. 2 we are left but a *f* of many,
Eze 5. 3 also take thereof a *f* in number,
12.16 I will leave a *f* men of them
Dan 11.20 *f* days he shall be destroyed,
Mt 7.14 and *f* there be that find it.
9.37 but the laborers are *f*;
15.34 Seven, and a *f* little fishes.
20.16 for many be called, but *f* chosen.
22.14 many are called, but *f* are chosen.
25.21, 23 thou hast been faithful over a *f*
Mk 6. 5 he laid hands upon a *f* sick folk,
8. 7 And they had a *f* small fishes:
Lk 10. 2 is great, but the laborers are *f*:
12.48 shall be beaten with *f* stripes.
13.23 Lord, are there *f* that be saved?
Ac 17. 4 and of the chief women not a *f*.
12 were Greeks, and of men, not a *f*.
24. 4 us of thy clemency a *f* words.
Eph 3. 3 (as I wrote afore in *f* words,
Heb 12.10 verily for a *f* days chastened us
13.22 a letter unto you in *f* words.
1Pe 3.20 wherein *f*, that is, eight souls
Rev 2.14 But I have a *f* things against thee,
20 I have a *f* things against thee,
3. 4 Thou hast a *f* names even in Sardis

FIDELITY

Tit 2.10 but shewing all good *f*; that they

FIELD

Gen 2.19 God formed every beast of the *f*,
23.19 the cave of the *f* of Machpelah
24.63 went out to meditate in the *f* at the
25.27 a cunning hunter, a man of the *f*;
Ex 9.25 the hail smote every herb of the *f*,
25 and brake every tree of the *f*.
Lev 25. 3 Six years thou shalt sow thy *f*,
27.21 unto the Lord, as a *f* devoted;
Dt 20.19 the tree of the *f* is man's life)
Ru 2. 2 Let me now go to the *f*, and glean
17 she gleaned in the *f* until even,
1Sa 20.24 So David hid himself in the *f*:
Job 5.23 beasts of the *f* shall be at peace
40.20 where all the beasts of the *f* play.
Ps 50.11 the wild beasts of the *f* are mine.
103.15 flower of the *f*, so he flourisheth.
Pr 31.16 She considereth a *f*, and buyeth it:
Ec 5. 9 the king himself is served by the *f*.
SS 7.11 beloved, let us go forth into the *f*;
Isa 5. 8 join house to house, that lay *f* to *f*,
29.17 and the fruitful *f* shall be esteemed
32.15 and the wilderness be a fruitful *f*,
40. 6 thereof is as the flower of the *f*:
55.12 and all the trees of the *f* shall clap
Jer 6.25 Go not forth into the *f*, nor walk
26.18 Zion shall be plowed like a *f*,
Eze 17.24 all the trees of the *f* shall know
31.15 all the trees of the *f* fainted for him.
34.27 tree of the *f* shall yield her fruit,
39.10 shall take no wood out of the *f*,
Joel 1.10 *f* is wasted, the land mourneth;
11 the harvest of the *f* is perished.
12 all the trees of the *f*, are withered:
19 hath burned all the trees of the *f*.
20 beasts of the *f* cry also unto thee:
Mic 3.12 Zion for your sake be plowed as a *f*,
Mt 6.28 Consider the lilies of the *f*, how they
30 so clothe the grass of the *f*, which
13.24 which sowed good seed in his *f*:
27 not thou sow good seed in thy *f*?
31 a man took, and sowed in his *f*:
36 us the parable of the tares of the *f*.
38 The *f* is the world; the good seed
44 is like unto treasure hid in a *f*;
44 all that he hath, and buyeth that *f*.
24.18 Neither let him which is in the *f*
40 Then shall two be in the *f*;
27. 7 bought with them the potter's *f*,
8 that *f* was called, The *f* of blood,
10 And gave them for the potter's *f*,
Mk 13.16 him that is in the *f* not turn back
Lk 2. 8 shepherds abiding in the *f*, keeping
12.28 is to day in the *f*, and to-morrow
15.25 Now his elder son was in the *f*:
17. 7 and by, when he is come from the *f*,
31 he that is in the *f*, let him likewise
36 Two men shall be in the *f*;
Ac 1.18 purchased a *f* with the reward of
19 *f* is called in their proper tongue,
19 that is to say, The *f* of blood.

FIELDS

Nu 20.17 we will not pass through the *f*,
Dt 11.15 I will send grass in thy *f*
32.13 might eat the increase of the *f*;
1Ch 16.32 let the *f* rejoice, and all that is
Job 5.10 and sendeth waters upon the *f*:
Ps 107.37 sow the *f*, and plant vineyards,
Pr 8.26 had not made the earth, nor the *f*,
Jer 32.44 Men shall buy *f* for money, and
Mk 2.23 that he went through the corn *f* on
Lk 6. 1 that he went through the corn *f*; and
15.15 sent him into his *f* to feed swine.
Jn 4.35 look on the *f*; for they are white
Jas 5. 4 who have reaped down your *f*,

FIERCE

Gen 49. 7 Cursed be their anger, for it was *f*;
Ex 32.12 Turn from thy *f* wrath, and repent
Nu 25. 4 *f* anger of the Lord may be turned
32.14 augment yet the *f* anger of the
Dt 28.50 A nation of *f* countenance, which
1Sa 20.34 arose from the table in *f* anger,
28.18 nor executedst his *f* wrath upon
2Ch 28.11 *f* wrath of the Lord is upon you.
13 and there is *f* wrath against Israel.
29.10 that his *f* wrath may turn away
Ezr 10.14 until the *f* wrath of our God for this
Job 4.10 voice of the *f* lion, and the teeth
10.16 Thou huntest me as a *f* lion:
28. 8 nor the *f* lion passed by it.
41.10 None is so *f* that dare stir him up:
Ps 88.16 Thy *f* wrath goeth over me; thy
Isa 7. 4 the *f* anger of Rezin with Syria,
13. 9 with wrath and *f* anger, to lay
13 and in the day of his *f* anger.

19. 4 and a *f* king shall rule over them,
33.19 Thou shalt not see a *f* people,
Jer 4. 8 *f* anger of the Lord is not turned
26 of the Lord, and by his *f* anger.
12.13 revenues because of the *f* anger of
25.37 cut down because of the *f* anger of
38 and because of his *f* anger.
30.24 The *f* anger of the Lord shall not
49.37 evil upon them, even my *f* anger,
51.45 man his soul from the *f* anger of
La 1.12 me in the day of his *f* anger.
2. 3 He hath cut off in his *f* anger all
4.11 he hath poured out his *f* anger,
Dan 8.23 a king of *f* countenance, and
Jon 3. 9 and turn away from his *f* anger,
Hab 1. 8 more *f* than the evening wolves:
Zep 2. 2 the *f* anger of the Lord come upon
3. 8 indignation, even all my *f* anger:
Mt 8.28 exceeding *f*, so that no man might
Lk 23. 5 they were the more *f*, saying,
2Ti 3. 3 false accusers, incontinent, *f*,
Jas 3. 4 driven of *f* winds, yet are they

FIERCENESS

Dt 13.17 turn from the *f* of his anger,
Jos 7.26 turned from the *f* of his anger.
2Ki 23.26 not from the *f* of his great wrath,
2Ch 30. 8 the *f* of his wrath may turn away
Job 39.24 He swalloweth the ground with *f*
Ps 78.49 cast upon them the *f* of his anger,
85. 3 thyself from the *f* of thine anger.
Jer 25.38 because of the *f* of the oppressor,
Hos 11. 9 not execute the *f* of mine anger,
Na 1. 6 can abide in the *f* of his anger?
Rev 16.19 of the wine of the *f* of his wrath.
19.15 the *f* and wrath of Almighty God.

FIERY

Nu 21. 6 the Lord sent *f* serpents among
8 a *f* serpent, and set it upon a pole:
Dt 8.15 were *f* serpents, and scorpions,
33. 2 right hand went a *f* law for them.
Ps 21. 9 Thou shalt make them as a *f* oven
Isa 14.29 fruit shall be a *f* flying serpent.
30. 6 the viper and *f* flying serpent,
Dan 3. 6, 11 midst of a burning *f* furnace.
15 the midst of a burning *f* furnace;
17 us from the burning *f* furnace,
20 to cast them into the burning *f*
21, 23 into the midst of the burning *f*
26 the mouth of the burning *f* furnace,
7. 9 his throne was like the *f* flame,
10 A *f* stream issued and came forth
Eph 6.16 all the *f* darts of the wicked.
Heb 10.27 and *f* indignation, which shall
1Pe 4.12 the *f* trial which is to try you,

FIFTEEN

Lev 27. 7 estimation shall be *f* shekels,
2Sa 19.17 house of Saul, and his *f* sons
2Ki 20. 6 will add unto thy days *f* years;
Isa 38. 5 will add unto thy days *f* years.
Eze 45.12 *f* shekels, shall be your
Hos 3. 2 to me for *f* pieces of silver.
Jn 11.18 unto Jerusalem, about *f* furlongs
Ac 7.14 threescore and *f* souls.
27.28 again, and found it *f* fathoms.
Gal 1.18 Peter, and abode with him *f* days.

FIFTEENTH

Ex 16. 1 *f* day of the second month
Lev 23. 6 the *f* day of the same month
34 *f* day of this seventh month
39 the *f* day of the seventh month,
Nu 28.17 in the *f* day of this month is
29.12 *f* day of the seventh month ye
33. 3 the *f* day of the first month;
1Ki 12.32 the eight month, on the *f* day
33 the *f* day of the eighth month,
2Ki 14.23 In the *f* year of Amaziah the
1Ch 24.14 The *f* to Bilgah, the sixteenth
25.22 *f* to Jeremoth, he, his sons,
2Ch 15.10 the *f* year of the reign of Asa.
Est 9.18 *f* day of the same they rested,
21 and the *f* day of the same,
Eze 32.17 in the *f* day of the month,
45.25 seventh month, in the *f* day
Lk 3. 1 Now in the *f* year of the reign

FIFTH

Gen 1.23 and the morning were the *f* day.
Neh 6. 5 the *f* time with an open letter
Jer 1. 3 Jerusalem captive in the *f* month.
Zec 7. 3 Should I weep in the *f* month,
Rev 6. 9 when he had opened the *f* seal,
9. 1 And the *f* angel sounded, and I saw
16.10 And the *f* angel poured out his vial
21.20 The *f*, sardonyx; the sixth, sardius;

FIFTIES

Ex 18.21 rulers of *f*, and rulers of tens:
25 rulers of hundreds, rulers of *f*,
Dt 1.15 captains over *f*, and captains over
1Sa 8.12 captains over *f*; and will set them
2Ki 1.14 captains of the former *f* with their
Mk 6.40 in ranks, by hundreds, and by *f*.
Lk 9.14 them sit down by *f* in a company.

FIFTIETH

Lev 25.10 And ye shall hallow the *f* year,
11 A jubile shall that *f* year be unto

FIFTY

Gen 9.28 flood three hundred and *f* years.
18.24 Peradventure there be *f* righteous
24 spare the place for the *f* righteous
26 said, If I find in Sodom *f* righteous
28 there shall lack five of the *f*
Lev 23.16 sabbath shall ye number *f* days;
27.16 be valued at *f* shekels of silver.
Nu 4. 3 even until *f* years old, all that
8.25 the age of *f* years they shall cease
Jos 7.21 and a wedge of gold of *f* shekels
2Sa 15. 1 and *f* men to run before him.
1Ki 10.29 and an horse for an hundred and *f*:
18. 4 and hid them by *f* in a cave,
19 prophets of Baal four hundred and *f*.
Est 5.14 gallows be made of *f* cubits high,
Lk 7.41 hundred pence, and the other *f*.
16. 6 and sit down quickly, and write *f*.
Jn 8.57 Thou art not yet *f* years old,
21.11 an hundred and *f* and three:
Ac 13.20 of four hundred and *f* years,
19.19 found it *f* thousand pieces of,

FIG

Gen 3. 7 and they sewed *f* leaves together,
Dt 8. 8 barley, and vines, and *f* trees,
Jdg 9.10 the trees said to the *f* tree,
11 But the *f* tree said unto them,
1Ki 4.25 his vine and under his *f* tree,
2Ki 18.31 and every one of his *f* tree,
Ps 105.33 their vines also and their *f* trees;
Pr 27.18 Whoso keepeth the *f* tree shall eat
SS 2.13 *f* tree putteth forth her green figs,
Isa 34. 4 as a falling *f* from the *f* tree
36.16 vine, and every one of his *f* tree,
Jer 5.17 eat up thy vines and thy *f* trees:
8.13 nor figs on the *f* tree, and the leaf
Hos 2.12 destroy her vines and her *f* trees,
9.10 as the firstripe in the *f* tree
Joel 1. 7 vine waste, and barked my *f* tree,
12 and the *f* tree languisheth; the
2.22 the *f* tree and the vine do yield
Am 4. 9 your vineyards and your *f* trees
Mic 4. 4 under his *f* tree; and none shall
Na 3.12 strong holds shall be like *f* trees
Hab 3.17 the *f* tree shall not blossom,
Hag 2.19 as yet the vine, and the *f* tree,
Zec 3.10 the vine and under the *f* tree.
Mt 21.19 when he saw a *f* tree in the way,
19 presently the *f* tree withered away.
20 soon is the *f* tree withered away!
21 do this which is done to the *f* tree,
24.32 learn a parable of the *f* tree;
Mk 11.13 a *f* tree afar off having leaves,
20 they saw the *f* tree dried up
21 the *f* tree which thou cursedst
13.38 learn a parable of the *f* tree;
Lk 13. 6 A certain man had a *f* tree planted
7 come seeking fruit on this *f* tree,
21.29 Behold the *f* tree, and all the trees;
Jn 1.48 when thou wast under the *f* tree,
50 I saw thee under the *f* tree,
Jas 3.12 Can the *f* tree, my brethren, bear
Rev 6.13 a *f* tree casteth her untimely figs,

FIGHT

Ex 14.14 The Lord shall *f* for you, and ye
Dt 1.42 Go not up, neither *f*; for I am
1Sa 17. 9 If he be able to *f* with me,
32 go and *f* with this Philistine.
1Ki 22.31 *F* neither with small nor great,
2Ch 13.12 *f* ye not against the Lord God
20.17 shall not need to *f* in this battle:
Neh 4.20 our God shall *f* for us.
Ps 35. 1 *f* against them that *f* against me.
56. 2 they be many that *f* against me,
Jer 21. 5 And I myself will *f* against you
Zec 10. 5 and they shall *f*, because the Lord
Jn 18.36 then would my servants *f*,
Ac 5.39 be found even to *f* against God.
23. 9 let us not *f* against God.
1Co 9.26 so *f* I, not as one that beateth
1Ti 6.12 *F* the good...of faith, lay hold on
12 the good *f* of faith, lay hold on
2Ti 4. 7 I have *f* a good..., I have finished
7 a good *f*, I have finished my course,
Heb 10.32 endured a great *f* of afflictions;
11.34 waxed valiant in *f*, turned to
Jas 4. 2 ye *f* and war, yet ye have not,
Rev 2.16 *f* against them with the sword

FIGHTETH

Ex 14.25 the Lord *f* for them against the
Jos 23.10 he it is that *f* for you, as he hath
1Sa 25.28 my lord *f* the battles of the Lord,

FIGHTINGS

2Co 7. 5 without were *f*, within were fears.
Jas 4. 1 come wars and *f* among you?

FIGS

Nu 13.23 the pomegranates, and of the *f*.
20. 5 it is no place of seed, or of *f*,
1Sa 25.18 two hundred cakes of *f*, and laid
30.12 they gave him a piece of a cake of *f*,
2Ki 20. 7 Isaiah said, Take a lump of *f*.
1Ch 12.40 oxen, and meat, meal, cakes of *f*,
Neh 13.15 also wine, grapes, and *f*,
SS 2.13 fig tree putteth forth her green *f*,
Isa 38.21 Let them take a lump of *f*,
Jer 8.13 nor *f* on the fig tree, and the leaf
24. 1 two baskets of *f* were set before
2 One basket had very good *f*,
2 even like the *f* that are first ripe:
2 other basket had very naughty *f*,
3 I said, *F*; the good *f*, very good;
5 Like these good *f*, so will I
8 the evil, *f* which cannot be eaten,
29.17 I will make them like vile *f*,
Na 3.12 like fig trees with the firstripe *f*:
Mt 7.16 grapes of thorns, or *f* of thistles?
Mk 11.13 for the time of *f* was not yet.
Lk 6. 4 of thorns men do not gather *f*,
Jas 3.12 either a vine, *f*? so can no fountain
Rev 6.13 a fig tree casteth her untimely *f*,

FIGURE

Dt 4.16 image, the similitude of any *f*,
Isa 44.13 maketh it after the *f* of a man,
Ro 5.14 is the *f* of him that was to come.
1Co 4. 6 I have in a *f* transferred to myself

Heb 9. 9 was a *f* for the time then present,
11.19 also he received him in a *f*.
1Pe 3.21 like *f* whereunto even baptism

FIGURES

1Ki 6.29 carved *f* of cherubims and palm
Ac 7.43 *f* which ye made to worship
Heb 9.24 which are the *f* of the true;

FILL

Gen 1.22 and *f* the waters in the seas,
42.25 Joseph commanded to *f* their sacks
44. 1 *F* the men's sacks with food, as
Ex 10. 6 And they shall *f* thy houses,
16.32 *F* an omer of it to be kept
Lev 25.19 eat your *f*, and dwell therein
Dt 23.24 thou mayest eat grapes thy *f* at
1Sa 16. 1 *f* thine horn with oil, and go,
1Ki 18.33 *F* four barrels with water, and
Job 8.21 Till he *f* thy mouth with laughing,
15. 2 and *f* his belly with the east wind?
20.23 When he is about to *f* his belly,
23. 4 and *f* my mouth with arguments.
38.39 *f* the appetite of the young lions,
41. 7 thou *f* his skin with barbed irons?
Ps 81.10 thy mouth wide, and I will *f* it.
83.16 *F* their faces with shame; that
110. 6 he shall *f* the places with the dead
Pr 1.13 we shall *f* our houses with spoil:
7.18 Come, let us take our *f* of love
8.21 and I will *f* their treasures.
Isa 8. 8 shall *f* the breadth of thy land,
14.21 *f* the face of the world with cities.
27. 6 *f* the face of the world with fruit.
56.12 *f* ourselves with strong drink;
Jer 13.13 I will *f* all the inhabitants of
23.24 Do not I *f* heaven and earth?
33. 5 is to *f* them with the dead bodies
51.14 Surely I will *f* thee with men,
Eze 3. 3 and *f* thy bowels with this roll
7.19 their souls, neither *f* their bowels:
9. 7 and *f* the courts with the slain:
10. 2 *f* thine hand with coals of fire
24. 4 *f* it with the choice bones.
30.11 and *f* the land with the slain.
32. 4 *f* the beasts of the whole earth
5 and *f* the valleys with thy height.
35. 8 and I will *f* his mountains with
Zep 1. 9 which *f* their masters' houses
Hag 2. 7 and I will *f* this house with glory,
Mt 9.16 which is put in to *f* it up taketh
15.33 as to *f* so great a multitude?
23.32 *F* ye up then the measure of
Jn 2. 7 *F* the water pots with water.
Ro 15.13 *f* you with all joy and peace in
Eph 4.10 that he might *f* all things.)
Col 1.24 *f* up that which is behind of the
1Th 2.16 to *f* up their sins alway: for the
Rev 18. 6 she hath filled *f* to her double.

FILLED

Gen 6.11 the earth was *f* with violence.
13 for the earth is *f* with violence
24.16 and *f* her pitcher, and came up.
Ex 28. 3 whom I have *f* with the spirit
31. 3 And I have *f* him with the spirit
35.31 And he hath *f* him with the spirit
35 hath he *f* with wisdom of heart,
40.34, 35 and the glory of the Lord *f* the
Nu 14.21 the earth shall be *f* with the glory
1Ki 7.14 and he was *f* with wisdom, and
18.35 he *f* the trench also with water.
2Ch 5.14 glory of the Lord had *f* the house
Job 3.15 who *f* their houses with silver:
22.18 *f* their houses with good things:
Ps 71. 8 Let my mouth be *f* with thy praise
72.19 the whole earth be *f* with his glory;
126. 2 was our mouth *f* with laughter,
Pr 5.10 strangers be *f* with thy wealth;
Isa 6. 1 up, and his train *f* the temple.
6. 4 and the house was *f* with smoke.
La 3.15 He hath *f* me with bitterness,
Eze 11. 6 and ye have *f* the streets thereof
36.38 the waste cities be *f* with flocks
43. 5 the glory of the Lord *f* the house.
Hab 2.14 shall be *f* with the knowledge
Mt 5. 6 righteousness: for they shall be *f*.
14.20 And they did all eat, and were *f*:
15.37 And they did all eat, and were *f*:
27.48 a spunge, and *f* it with vinegar,
Mk 2.21 the new piece that *f* it up
6.42 And they did all eat, and were *f*.
7.27 Let the children first be *f*:
8. 8 So they did eat, and were *f*:
15.36 and *f* a spunge full of vinegar,
Lk 1.15 he shall be *f* with the Holy Ghost,
41 Elisabeth was *f* with the Holy
53 He hath *f* the hungry with good
67 Zacharias was *f* with the Holy
2.40 strong in spirit, *f* with wisdom:
3. 5 Every valley shall be *f*, and every
4.28 these things, were *f* with wrath,
5. 7 they came and *f* both the ships,
26 and were *f* with fear, saying,
6.11 And they were *f* with madness;
21 hunger now: for ye shall be *f*.
8.23 and they were *f* with water,
9.17 And they did eat, and were all *f*:
14.23 come in, that my house may be *f*:
15.16 And he would fain have *f* his
Jn 2. 7 And they *f* them up to the brim.
6.12 When they were *f*, he said unto
13 and *f* twelve baskets with the
26 ye did eat the loaves, and were *f*.
12. 3 the house was *f* with the odour
16. 6 sorrow hath *f* your heart.
19.29 and they *f* a spunge with vinegar,
Ac 2. 2 *f* all the house where they were
4 were all *f* with the Holy Ghost,
3.10 and they were *f* with wonder and
4. 8 Then Peter, *f* with the Holy Ghost,
31 were all *f* with the Holy Ghost,
5. 3 hath Satan *f* thine heart to lie
17 and were *f* with indignation,
28 and, behold, ye have *f* Jerusalem
9.17 and be *f* with the Holy Ghost.
13. 9 Paul,) *f* with the Holy Ghost, set
45 they were *f* with envy, and spake
52 And the disciples were *f* with joy,
19.29 whole city was *f* with confusion:
Ro 1.29 Being *f* with all unrighteousness,
15.14 *f* with all knowledge, able also to
24 somewhat *f* with your company.
2Co 7. 4 *f* with comfort, I am exceeding
Eph 3.19 might be *f* with all the fulness of
5.18 but be *f* with the Spirit;
Php 1.11 *f* with the fruits of righteousness,
Col 1. 9 might be *f* with the knowledge
2Ti 1. 4 that I may be *f* with joy;
Jas 2.16 in peace, be ye warmed and *f*;
Rev 8. 5 *f* it with fire of the altar, and cast
15. 1 in them is *f* up the wrath of God.
8 the temple was *f* with smoke
18. 6 she hath *f* fill to her double.
19.21 the fowls were *f* with their flesh.

FILLETH

Job 9.18 but *f* me with bitterness.
Ps 84. 6 the rain also *f* the pools.
107. 9 *f* the hungry soul with goodness.
129. 7 Wherewith the mower *f* not his
147.14 *f* thee with the finest of the wheat.
Eph 1.23 the fulness of him that *f* all in all.

FILLING

Ac 14.17 *f* our hearts with food and

FILTH

Isa 4. 4 the *f* of the daughters of Zion,
Na 3. 6 I will cast abominable *f* upon thee,
1Co 4.13 are made as the *f* of the world,
1Pe 3.21 putting away of the *f* of the flesh,

FILTHINESS

2Ch 29. 5 forth the *f* out of the holy place.
Ezr 6.21 them from the *f* of the heathen of
9.11 an unclean land with the *f* of the
Pr 30.12 yet is not washed from their *f*.
Isa 28. 8 all tables are full of vomit and *f*,
La 1. 9 Her *f* is in her skirts; she
Eze 16.36 Because thy *f* was poured out,
22.15 will consume thy *f* out of thee.
24.11 that the *f* of it may be molten in it,
13 In thy *f* is lewdness: because I
13 shalt not be purged from thy *f*
36.25 ye shall be clean: from all your *f*,
2Co 7. 1 from all *f* of the flesh and spirit,
Eph 5. 4 Neither *f*, nor foolish talking, nor
Jas 1.21 lay apart all *f* and superfluity
Rev 17. 4 full of abominations and *f* of her

FILTHY

Job 15.16 more abominable and *f* is man,
Ps 14. 3 aside, they are altogether become *f*:
53. 3 back: they are altogether become *f*;
Isa 64. 6 righteousnesses are as *f* rags;
Zep 3. 1 Woe to her that is *f* and polluted,
Zec 3. 3 was clothed with *f* garments,
4 Take away the *f* garments from
Col 3. 8 *f* communication out of your
1Ti 3. 3 no striker, not greedy of *f* lucre;
8 much wine, not greedy of *f* lucre;
Tit 1. 7 no striker, not given to *f* lucre;
11 they ought not, for *f* lucre's sake.
1Pe 5. 2 not for *f* lucre, but of a ready mind;
2Pe 2. 7 vexed with the *f* conversation of
Jude 8 also these *f* dreamers defile
Rev 22.11 he which is *f*, let him be *f* still:

FINALLY

2Co 13.11 *F*, brethren, farewell. Be perfect,
Eph 6.10 *F*, my brethren, be strong in the
Php 3. 1 *F*, my brethren, rejoice in the Lord.
4. 8 *F*, brethren, whatsoever things are
2Th 3. 1 *F*, brethren, pray for us, that the
1Pe 3. 8 *F*, be ye all of one mind, having

FIND

Gen 18.26 If I *f* in Sodom fifty righteous
28 If I *f* there forty and five,
30 I will not do it, if I *f* thirty there.
32. 5 that I may *f* grace in thy sight.
Ex 5.11 get you straw where ye can *f* it:
Nu 32.23 be sure your sin will *f* you out.
Ru 2.13 Let me *f* favor in thy sight,
1Sa 20.21 saying, Go *f* out the arrows.
36 *f* out now the arrows which I shoot.
1Ki 18. 5 peradventure we may *f* grass to
Ezr 4.15 thou *f* in the book of the records,
Job 11. 7 Canst thou by searching *f* out God?
7 canst thou *f* out the Almighty
17.10 cannot *f* one wise man among you.
23. 3 that I knew where I might *f* him!
37.23 Almighty we cannot *f* him out:
Ps 17. 3 tried me, and shalt *f* nothing;
Pr 20. 6 but a faithful man who can *f*?
31.10 Who can *f* a virtuous woman?
Ec 3.11 no man can *f* out the work that God
11. 1 for thou shalt *f* it after many days.
SS 5. 8 if ye *f* my beloved, that ye tell him,
Jer 5. 1 if ye can *f* a man, if there be any
La 1. 6 like harts that *f* no pasture,
2. 9 also *f* no vision from the Lord.
Dan 6. 4 to *f* occasion against Daniel
Mt 7. 7 seek, and ye shall *f*; knock, and
14 and few there be that *f* it.
10.39 loseth his life for my sake shall *f* it.
11.29 ye shall *f* rest unto your souls.
16.25 lose his life for my sake shall *f* it.
17.27 thou shalt *f* a piece of money:
18.13 if so be that he *f* it, verily I say
21. 2 ye shall *f* an ass tied, and a colt
22. 9 as many as ye shall *f*, bid to the
24.46 when he cometh shall *f* so doing.

Mk 11. 2 ye shall *f* a colt tied, whereon
13 he might *f* any thing thereon:
13.36 coming suddenly he *f* you sleeping.
Lk 2.12 Ye shall *f* the babe wrapped in
5.19 they could not *f* by what way
6. 7 might *f* an accusation against him.
11. 9 given you; seek, and ye shall *f*;
12.37 when he cometh shall *f* watching:
38 and *f* them so, blessed are those
43 when he cometh shall *f* so doing.
13. 7 fruit on this fig tree, and *f* none:
15. 4 that which is lost, until he *f* it?
8 and seek diligently till she *f* it?
18. 8 shall he *f* faith on the earth?
19.30 your entering ye shall *f* a colt tied,
48 could not *f* what they might do:
23. 4 I *f* no fault in this man.
Jn 7.34 shall seek me, and shall not *f* me:
35 we shall not *f* him? will he go
36 and shall not *f* me: and where I
10. 9 shall go in and out, and *f* pasture.
18.38 I *f* in him no fault at all,
19. 4 may know that I *f* no fault in him.
6 for I *f* no fault in him.
21. 6 side of the ship, and ye shall *f*.
Ac 7.46 to *f* a tabernacle for the God of
17.27 might feel after him, and *f* him,
23. 9 We *f* no evil in this man:
Ro 7.18 that which is good I *f* not.
21 I *f* then a law, that, when I would
9.19 Why doth he yet *f* fault? For who
2Co 9. 4 with me, and *f* you unprepared,
12.20 I shall not *f* you such as I would,
2Ti 1.18 that he may *f* mercy of the Lord
Heb 4.16 we may obtain mercy, and *f* grace
Rev 9. 6 seek death, and shall not *f* it;
18.14 thou shalt *f* them no more at all.

FINDETH

Gen 4.14 every one that *f* me shall slay me.
Job 33.10 Behold, he *f* occasions against me,
Ps 119.162 thy word as one that *f* great spoil.
Pr 3.13 Happy is the man that *f* wisdom,
8.35 whoso *f* me, *f* life, and shall
17.20 hath a froward heart *f* no good:
18.22 Whoso *f* a wife *f* a good thing,
21.10 neighbor *f* no favor in his eyes.
21 righteousness and mercy *f* life,
Ec 9.10 Whatsoever thy hand *f* to do, do it
La 1. 3 she *f* no rest: all her persecutors
Hos 14. 3 in thee the fatherless *f* mercy.
Mt 7. 8 he that seeketh *f*; and to him
10.39 He that *f* his life shall lose it:
12.43 places, seeking rest, and *f* none.
44 is come he *f* it empty, swept, and
26.40 *f* them asleep, and saith unto
Mk 14.37 he cometh, and *f* them sleeping,
Lk 11.10 receiveth; and he that seeketh *f*;
25 he *f* it swept and garnished.
Jn 1.41 He first *f* his own brother Simon,
43 and *f* Philip, and saith unto him,
45 Philip *f* Nathanael, and saith unto
5.14 Jesus *f* him in the temple, and

FINDING

Gen 4.15 lest any *f* him should kill him.
Job 9.10 doeth great things past *f* out;
Isa 58.13 nor *f* thine own pleasure, nor
Lk 11.24 and *f* none, he saith, I will return
Ac 4.21 *f* nothing how they might punish
19. 1 and *f* certain disciples,
21. 2 And *f* a ship sailing over unto
4 *f* disciples, we tarried there seven
Ro 11.33 and his ways past *f* out!
Heb 8. 8 For *f* fault with them, he saith

FINE

Gen 41.42 and arrayed him in vestures of *f* linen,
2Ki 7. 1 measure of *f* flour be sold for a shekel,
16 So a measure of *f* flour was sold
18 a measure of *f* flour for a shekel,
1Ch 15.27 was clothed with a robe of *f* linen,
23.29 and for the *f* flour for meat offering,
2Ch 2.14 in blue, and in *f* linen, and in crimson;
3. 5 which he overlaid with *f* gold,
8 and he overlaid it with *f* gold,
14 purple, and crimson, and *f* linen,
Ezr 8.27 two vessels of *f* copper, precious
Est 1. 6 fastened with cords of *f* linen and
8.15 and with a garment of *f* linen and
Job 28. 1 place for gold where they *f* it.
17 of it shall not be for jewels of *f* gold.
31.24 or have said to the *f* gold, Thou art my
Ps 19.10 yea, than much *f* gold: sweeter also
119.127 above gold; yea, above *f* gold.
Pr 3.14 and the gain thereof than *f* gold.
7.16 works, with *f* linen of Egypt.
8.19 is better than gold, yea, than *f* gold;
25.12 and an ornament of *f* gold, so is a wise
31.24 She maketh *f* linen, and selleth
SS 5.11 His head is as the most *f* gold,
15 marble, set upon sockets of *f* gold:
Isa 3.23 The glasses, and the *f* linen, and the
13.12 a man more precious than *f* gold;
19. 9 Moreover they that work in *f* flax,
La 4. 1 how is the most *f* gold changed!
2 sons of Zion, comparable to *f* gold,
Eze 16.10 and I girded thee about with *f* linen,
13 and thy raiment was of *f* linen,
13 thou didst eat *f* flour, and honey,
19 thee, *f* flour, and oil, and honey, and
27. 7 *F* linen with broidered work from
16 and *f* linen, and coral, and agate.
46.14 of oil, to temper with the *f* flour;
Dan 2.32 This image's head was of *f* gold,
10. 5 were girded with *f* gold of Uphaz:
Zec 9. 3 and *f* gold as the mire of the streets.
Mk 15.46 And he bought *f* linen, and took
Lk 16.19 was clothed in purple and *f* linen,
Rev 1.15 And his feet like unto *f* brass,
2.18 and his feet are like *f* brass;
18.12 and of pearls, and *f* linen, and purple,
13 and *f* flour, and wheat, and
16 great city, that was clothed in *f* linen,
19. 8 that she should be arrayed in *f* linen,
8 the *f* linen is the righteousness of
14 clothed in *f* linen, white and clean.

FINEST

Ps 81.16 them also with the *f* of the wheat:
147.14 filleth thee with the *f* of the wheat.

FINGER

Ex 8.19 Pharaoh, This is the *f* of God:
29.12 the horns of the altar with thy *f*,
31.18 stone, written with the *f* of God.
Lev 4. 6 priest shall dip his *f* in the blood,
17 the priest shall dip his *f* in some
25 blood of the sin offering with his *f*,
30 take of the blood thereof with his *f*,
34 blood of the sin offering with his *f*,
8.15 of the altar round about with his *f*,
9. 9 he dipped his *f* in the blood,
14.16 the priest shall dip his right *f* in
16 sprinkle of the oil with his *f* seven
27 shall sprinkle with his right *f* some
16.14 and sprinkle it with his *f* seven
14 of the blood with his *f* seven times.
19 blood upon it with his *f* seven times,
Nu 19. 4 shall take of her blood with his *f*,
Dt 9.10 them was written with the *f* of God;
1Ki 12.10 My little *f* shall be thicker than
2Ch 10.10 My little *f* shall be thicker than
Isa 58. 9 the putting forth of the *f*, and
Lk 11.20 with the *f* of God cast out devils,
16.24 may dip the tip of his *f* in water,
Jn 8. 6 with his *f* wrote on the ground,
20.25 put my *f* into the print of the nails,
27 Reach hither thy *f*, and behold my

FINGERS

2Sa 21.20 that had on every hand six *f*,
1Ch 20. 6 *f* and toes were four and twenty,
Ps 8. 3 thy heavens, the work of thy *f*,
144. 1 my hands to war, and my *f* to fight:
Pr 6.13 his feet, he teacheth with his *f*;
7. 3 Bind them upon thy *f*, write them
SS 5. 5 my *f* with sweet smelling myrrh,
Isa 2. 8 that which their own *f* have made:
17. 8 that which his *f* have made,
59. 3 and your *f* with iniquity; your lips
Jer 52.21 the thickness thereof was four *f*:
Dan 5. 5 In the same hour came forth *f* of a
Mt 23. 4 move them with one of their *f*.
Mk 7.33 put his *f* into his ears, and he spit,
Lk 11.46 the burdens with one of your *f*.

FINISH

Gen 6.16 in a cubit shalt thou *f* it above;
Dan 9.24 to *f* the transgression, and to
Zec 4. 9 his hands shall also *f* it;
Lk 14.28 whether he have sufficient to *f* it?
29 foundation, and is not able to *f* it,
30 to build, and was not able to *f*.
Jn 4.34 that sent me, and to *f* his work.
5.36 the Father hath given me to *f*,
Ac 20.24 I might *f* my course with joy,
Ro 9.28 will *f* the work, and cut it short
2Co 8. 6 he would also *f* in you the same

FINISHED

Gen 2. 1 the heavens and the earth were *f*,
Ex 39.32 of the tent of the congregation *f*:
40.33 So Moses *f* the work.
Dt 31.24 law in a book, until they were *f*,
Jos 4.10 until every thing was *f* that the
Ru 3.18 until he have *f* the thing this day.
1Ki 6. 9 he built the house, and *f* it;
14 Solomon built the house, and *f* it.
22 until he had *f* all the house:
38 eighth month, was the house *f*
7. 1 and he *f* all his house.
22 so was the work of the pillars *f*.
9. 1 when Solomon had *f* the building
25 the Lord. So he *f* the house.
1Ch 27.24 Zeruiah began to number, but he *f*
28.20 until thou hast *f* all the work for
2Ch 4.11 Huram *f* the work that he was
5. 1 for the house of the Lord was *f*:
7.11 Solomon *f* the house of the Lord,
8.16 of the Lord, and until it was *f*.
24.14 when they had *f* it, they brought
29.28 until the burnt offering was *f*.
31. 1 Now when all this was *f*, all Israel
7 and *f* them in the seventh month.
Ezr 5.16 building, and yet it is not *f*.
6.14 And they builded, and *f* it,
15 this house was *f* on the third day
Neh 6.15 So the wall was *f* in the twenty
Dan 5.26 numbered thy kingdom, and *f* it.
12. 7 all these things shall be *f*.
Mt 13.53 when Jesus had *f* these parables,
19. 1 when Jesus had *f* these sayings,
26. 1 when Jesus had *f* all these sayings,
Jn 17. 4 I have *f* the work which thou
19.30 he said, It is *f*: and he bowed
Ac 21. 7 And when we had *f* our course
2Ti 4. 7 I have *f* my course, I have kept
Heb 4. 3 works were *f* from the foundation
Jas 1.15 sin, when it is *f*, bringeth forth
Rev 10. 7 the mystery of God should be *f*,
11. 7 they shall have *f* their testimony,
20. 5 until the thousand years were *f*.

FINISHER

Heb 12. 2 Jesus the author and *f* of our

FIR

2Sa 6. 5 of instruments made of *f* wood,
1Ki 5. 8 and concerning timber of *f*.
10 gave Solomon cedar trees and *f*
6.15 of the house with planks of *f*.
34 the two doors were of *f* tree:
9.11 with cedar trees and *f* trees, and

2Ki 19.23 and the choice *f* trees thereof:
2Ch 2. 8 Send me also cedar trees, *f* trees,
3. 5 greater house he cieled with *f* tree,
Ps 104.17 stork, the *f* trees are her house.
SS 1.17 are cedar, and our rafters of *f*.
Isa 14. 8 Yea, the *f* trees rejoice at thee,
37.24 and the choice *f* trees thereof:
41.19 I will set in the desert the *f* tree,
55.13 the thorn shall come up the *f* tree,
60.13 *f* tree, the pine tree, and the box
Eze 27. 5 thy ship boards of *f* trees of Senir:
31. 8 *f* trees were not like his boughs,
Hos 14. 8 I am like a green *f* tree.
Na 2. 3 *f* trees shall be terribly shaken.
Zec 11. 2 *f* tree; for the cedar is fallen;

FIRE

Gen 19.24 brimstone and *f* from the Lord out
22. 6 and he took the *f* in his hand, and a
7 Behold, the *f* and the wood:
Ex 3. 2 appeared unto him in a flame of *f*
2 behold, the bush burned with *f*,
13.21 and by night in a pillar of *f*,
22 nor the pillar of *f* by night,
14.24 the pillar of *f* and of the cloud,
Lev 1. 7 the priest shall put *f* upon the altar,
6.10 ashes which the *f* hath consumed
13 The *f* shall ever be burning upon
8.17 be burnt with *f* without the camp;
23. 8 ye shall offer an offering made by *f*
Nu 9.16 and the appearance of *f* by night.
Dt 4.11 the mountain burned with *f* unto
24 the Lord thy God is a consuming *f*,
5. 5 ye were afraid by reason of the *f*,
24 his voice out of the midst of the *f*:
12. 3 and burn their groves with *f*;
18.10 his daughter to pass through the *f*,
32.22 For a *f* is kindled in mine anger,
Jos 7.15 accursed thing shall be burnt with *f*,
Jdg 12. 1 burn thine house upon thee with *f*.
1Ki 18.23 lay it on wood, and put no *f* under:
24 and the God that answereth by *f*,
25 of your gods, but put no *f* under.
38 Then the *f* of the Lord fell,
19.12 a *f*; but the Lord was not in the *f*:
12 and after the *f* a still small voice.
2Ki 2.11 a chariot of *f*, and horses of *f*, and
6.17 was full of horses and chariots of *f*
16. 3 made his son to pass through the *f*,
17.17 daughters to pass through the *f*,
19.18 And have cast their gods into the *f*:
2Ch 7. 1 the *f* came down from heaven,
35.13 they roasted the passover with *f*
Neh 9.19 neither the pillar of *f* by night,
Job 1.16 The *f* of God is fallen from heaven,
Ps 18.12 passed, hail stones and coals of *f*.
46. 9 he burneth the chariot in the *f*.
68. 2 as wax melteth before the *f*, so let
89.46 shall thy wrath burn like *f*?
104. 4 spirits; his ministers a flaming *f*:
105.39 and *f* to give light in the night.
Pr 6.27 Can a man take *f* in his bosom,
16.27 in his lips there is as a burning *f*.
25.22 shalt heap coals of *f* upon his head,
Isa 9.18 For wickedness burneth as the *f*:
43. 2 when thou walkest through the *f*,
44.16 He burneth part thereof in the *f*;
16 I am warm, I have seen the *f*:
19 I have burned part of it in the *f*;
66.15 behold, the Lord will come with *f*,
Jer 19. 5 to burn their sons with *f* for burnt
23.29 Is not my word like as a *f*?
36.23 all the roll was consumed in the *f*
La 1.13 above hath he sent *f* into my bones,
4.11 and hath kindled a *f* in Zion,
Eze 1.13 was like burning coals of *f*,
10. 7 *f* that was between the cherubims,
20.47 Behold, I will kindle a *f* in thee,
Dan 3.24 bound into the midst of the *f*?
27 whose bodies the *f* had no power,
Joel 2.30 blood, and *f*, and pillars of smoke.
Am 7. 4 Lord God called to contend by *f*,
Na 1. 6 his fury is poured out like *f*.
Hab 2.13 people shall labor in the very *f*,
Zec 3. 2 this a brand plucked out of the *f*?
12. 6 and like a torch of *f* in a sheaf;
Mal 3. 2 for he is like a refiner's *f*,
Mt 3.10 is hewn down, and cast into the *f*.
11 with the Holy Ghost, and with *f*:
12 up the chaff with unquenchable *f*.
5.22 fool, shall be in danger of hell *f*.
7.19 is hewn down, and cast into the *f*.
13.40 are gathered and burned in the *f*:
42 shall cast them into a furnace of *f*:
50 cast them into the furnace of *f*:
17.15 for ofttimes he falleth into the *f*,
18. 8 feet to be cast into everlasting *f*.
9 two eyes to be cast into hell *f*.
25.41 into everlasting *f*, prepared for the
Mk 9.22 it hath cast him into the *f*,
43 the *f* that never shall be quenched:
44 not, and the *f* is not quenched.
45 the *f* that never shall be quenched;
46 not, and the *f* is not quenched.
47 two eyes to be cast into hell *f*:
48 not, and the *f* is not quenched.
49 every one shall be salted with *f*,
14.54 and warmed himself at the *f*.
Lk 3. 9 is hewn down, and cast into the *f*,
16 with the Holy Ghost and with *f*:
17 he will burn with *f* unquenchable.
9.54 that we command *f* to come down
12.49 I am come to send *f* on the earth;
17.29 it rained *f* and brimstone from
22.55 And when they had kindled a *f*
56 beheld him as he sat by the *f*.
Jn 15. 6 them, and cast them into the *f*,
18.18 had made a *f* of coals; for it was cold:
21. 9 they saw a *f* of coals there, and fish
Ac 2. 3 them cloven tongues like as of *f*,
19 blood, and *f*, and vapour of smoke:
7.30 the Lord in a flame of *f* in a bush.
28. 2 they kindled a *f*, and received us
3 of sticks, and laid them on the *f*,
5 he shook off the beast into the *f*,
Ro 12.20 shalt heap coals of *f* on his head.
1Co 3.13 shall be revealed by *f*; and the *f*
15 shall be saved; yet so as by *f*.
2Th 1. 8 In flaming *f* taking vengeance on
Heb 1. 7 and his ministers a flame of *f*.
11.34 Quenched the violence of *f*,
12.18 and that burned with *f*, nor unto
29 For our God is a consuming *f*.
Jas 3. 5 great a matter a little *f* kindleth!
6 tongue is a *f*, a world of iniquity:
6 setteth on *f* the course of nature;
6 and it is set on *f* of hell.
5. 3 shall eat your flesh as it were *f*.
1Pe 1. 7 though it be tried with *f*, might
2Pe 3. 7 reserved unto *f* against the day of
12 being on *f* shall be dissolved,
Jude 7 the vengeance of eternal *f*.
23 fear, pulling them out of the *f*;
Rev 1.14 and his eyes were as a flame of *f*;
2.18 hath his eyes like unto a flame of *f*,
3.18 to buy of me gold tried in the *f*,
4. 5 seven lamps of *f* burning before
8. 5 and filled it with *f* of the altar,
7 hail and *f* mingled with blood,
8 a great mountain burning with *f*
9.17 having breastplates of *f*, and of
17 out of their mouths issued *f* and
18 killed, by the *f*, and by the smoke,
10. 1 and his feet as pillars of *f*:
11. 5 *f* proceedeth out of their mouth,
13.13 maketh *f* come down from heaven
14.10 tormented with *f* and brimstone
18 which had power over *f*; and cried
15. 2 were a sea of glass mingled with *f*:
16. 8 unto him to scorch men with *f*.
17.16 eat her flesh, and burn her with *f*.
18. 8 she shall be utterly burned with *f*:
19.12 His eyes were as a flame of *f*,
20 lake of *f* burning with brimstone.
20. 9 and *f* came down from God out of
10 into the lake of *f* and brimstone,
14 hell were cast into the lake of *f*.
15 of life was cast into the lake of *f*.
21. 8 burneth with *f* and brimstone:

FIRM

Jos 3.17 the covenant of the Lord stood *f*
4. 3 where the priests' feet stood *f*,
Job 41.23 they are *f* in themselves; they
24 His heart is as *f* as a stone; they
Ps 73. 4 but their strength is *f*.
Dan 6. 7 and to make a *f* decree,
Heb 3. 6 rejoicing of the hope *f* unto the end.

FIRMAMENT

Gen 1. 6 Let there be a *f* in the midst of
7 God made the *f*, and divided the
7 which were under the *f* from the
7 the waters which were above the *f*:
8 And God called the *f* Heaven.
14 Let there be lights in the *f* of the
15 for lights in the *f* of heaven to give
17 God set them in the *f* of heaven to
20 earth in the open *f* of heaven.
Ps 19. 1 and the *f* sheweth his handywork.
150. 1 praise him in the *f* of his power.
Eze 1.22 the likeness of the *f* upon the heads
23 And under the *f* were their wings
25 And there was a voice from the *f*
26 And above the *f* that was over their
10. 1 in the *f* that was above the head
Dan 12. 3 shine as the brightness of the *f*;

FIRST

Gen 1. 5 and the morning were the *f* day.
8. 5 on the *f* day of the month, were
25.25 And the *f* came out red, all over
26. 1 the *f* famine that was in the days
28.19 that city was called Luz at the *f*.
38.28 saying, This came out *f*.
Ex 12.15 the *f* day ye shall put away leaven
15 from the *f* day until the seventh
16 in the *f* day there shall be an holy
23.19 The *f* of the firstfruits of thy land
34. 1 tables of stone like unto the *f*:
1 the words that were in the *f* tables,
Lev 4.21 and burn him as he burned the *f*
Nu 9. 5 *f* month at even in the wilderness
10.14 In the *f* place went the standard
28.18 *f* day shall be an holy convocation;
Dt 10. 1 two tables of stone like unto the *f*,
2 the words that were in the *f* tables
4 according to the *f* writing, the ten
11.14 the *f* rain and the latter rain,
18. 4 *f* fleece of the fleece of thy sheep,
33.21 he provided the *f* part for himself,
Jdg 20.18 Which of us shall go up *f* to the
Job 15. 7 Art thou the *f* man that was born?
Isa 1.26 will restore thy judges as at the *f*,
44. 6 I am the *f*, and I am the last; and
48.12 he; I am the *f*, I also am the last.
Eze 44.30 And the *f* of all the firstfruits
Dan 7. 4 The *f* was like a lion, and had
Hag 2. 3 saw this house in her *f* glory?
Mt 5.24 *f* be reconciled to thy brother,
6.33 But seek ye *f* the kingdom of God,
7. 5 *f* cast out the beam out of thine
8.21 suffer me *f* to go and bury my
10. 2 The *f*, Simon, who is called Peter,
12.29 except he *f* bind the strong man?
45 of that man is worse than the *f*.
13.30 Gather ye together *f* the tares,
17.10 scribes that Elias must *f* come?
11 Elias truly shall *f* come, and
27 take up the fish that *f* cometh up;
19.30 But many that are *f* shall be last;
30 shall be last; and the last shall be *f*.
20. 8 beginning from the last unto the *f*.

10 when the *f* came, they supposed
16 the last shall be *f*, and the *f* last:
21.28 and he came to the *f*, and said,
31 They say unto him, The *f*.
36 other servants more than the *f*:
22.25 and the *f*, when he had married a
38 is the *f* and great commandment.
23.26 cleanse *f* that which is within the
26.17 Now the *f* day of the feast of
27.64 last error shall be worse than the *f*.
28. 1 toward the *f* day of the week,
Mk 3.27 he will *f* bind the strong man;
4.28 *f* the blade, then the ear, after that
7.27 Let the children *f* be filled: for it
9.11 the scribes that Elias must *f* come?
12 Elias verily cometh *f*, and restoreth
35 man desire to be *f*, the same shall
10.31 But many that are *f* shall be last;
31 shall be last; and the last *f*.
12.20 *f* took a wife, and dying left no
28 Which is the *f* commandment of
29 The *f* of all the commandments is,
30 this is the *f* commandment.
13.10 the gospel must *f* be published
14.12 the *f* day of unleavened bread,
16. 2 morning the *f* day of the week,
9 early the *f* day of the week,
9 he appeared *f* to Mary Magdalene,
Lk 1. 3 of all things from the very *f*,
2. 2 taxing was *f* made when Cyrenius
6. 1 the second sabbath after the *f*,
42 hypocrite, cast out *f* the beam
9.59 suffer me *f* to go and bury my
61 but let me *f* go bid them farewell,
10. 5 *f* say, Peace be to this house.
11.26 of that man is worse than the *f*.
38 had not *f* washed before dinner.
12. 1 to say unto his disciples *f* of all,
13.30 shall be *f*, and there are *f* which
14.18 *f* said unto him, I have bought
28 sitteth not down *f*, and counteth
31 sitteth not down *f*, and consulteth
16. 5 and said unto the *f*, How much
17.25 But *f* must he suffer many things,
19.16 Then came the *f*, saying, Lord,
20.29 and the *f* took a wife, and died
21. 9 these things must *f* come to pass;
24. 1 Now upon the *f* day of the week,
Jn 1.41 *f* findeth his own brother Simon,
5. 4 then *f* after the troubling of the
8. 7 let him *f* cast a stone at her.
10.40 place where John at *f* baptized;
12.16 not his disciples at the *f*: but when
18.13 And led him away to Annas *f*; for
19.32 and brake the legs of the *f*, and of
39 at the *f* came to Jesus by night,
20. 1 *f* day of the week cometh Mary
4 Peter, and came *f* to the sepulchre.
8 which came *f* to the sepulchre, and
19 being the *f* day of the week,
Ac 3.26 Unto you *f* God, having raised up
7.12 Egypt, he sent out our fathers *f*.
11.26 were called Christians *f* in Antioch.
12.10 past the *f* and the second ward,
13.24 When John had *f* preached before his
46 should *f* have been spoken to you:
15.14 how God at the *f* did visit the
20. 7 And upon the *f* day of the week,
18 know, from the *f* day that I came
26. 4 at the *f* among mine own nation
20 shewed *f* unto them of Damascus
23 should be the *f* that should rise
27.43 cast themselves *f* into the sea,
Ro 1. 8 *F*, I thank my God through Jesus
16 to the Jew *f*, and also to the Greek.
2. 9 the Jew *f*, and also of the Gentile;
10 the Jew *f*, and also to the Gentile:
10.19 *F* Moses saith, I will provoke you
11.35 Or who hath *f* given to him,
15.24 if *f* I be somewhat filled with your
1Co 11.18 For *f* of all, when ye come
12.28 *f* apostles, secondarily prophets,
14.30 sitteth by, let the *f* hold his peace.
15. 3 I delivered unto you *f* of all
45 *f* man Adam was made a living
46 that was not *f* which is spiritual,
47 The *f* man is of the earth, earthy:
16. 2 Upon the *f* day of the week let
2Co 8. 5 *f* gave their own selves to the
12 if there be *f* a willing mind,
Gal 4.13 the gospel unto you at the *f*.
Eph 1.12 who *f* trusted in Christ.
4. 9 also descended *f* into the lower
6. 2 *f* commandment with promise;
Php 1. 5 gospel from the *f* day until now;
1Th 4.16 the dead in Christ shall rise *f*:
2Th 2. 3 except there come a falling away *f*,
1Ti 1.16 in me *f* Jesus Christ might shew
2. 1 *f* of all, supplications, prayers,
13 Adam was *f* formed, then Eve.
3.10 And let these also *f* be proved;
5. 4 let them learn *f* to shew piety
12 they have cast off their *f* faith.
2Ti 1. 5 which dwelt *f* in thy grandmother
2. 6 must be *f* partaker of the fruits.
4.16 At my *f* answer no man stood with
Tit 3.10 after the *f* and second admonition
Heb 2. 3 which at the *f* began to be spoken
4. 6 they to whom it was *f* preached
5.12 *f* principles of the oracles of God;
7. 2 *f* being by interpretation King of
27 *f* for his own sins, and then for
8. 7 that *f* covenant had been faultless,
13 covenant, he hath made the *f* old.
9. 1 Then verily the *f* covenant had
2 the *f*, wherein was the candlestick,
6 went always into the *f* tabernacle,
8 while as the *f* tabernacle was yet
15 that were under the *f* testament,
18 the *f* testament was dedicated
10. 9 He taketh away the *f*, that he may
Jas 3.17 is *f* pure, then peaceable, gentle,
1Pe 4.17 and if it *f* begin at us, what shall
2Pe 1.20 Knowing this *f*, that no prophecy
3. 3 Knowing this *f*, that there shall
1Jn 4.19 love him, because he *f* loved us.
Jude 6 which kept not their *f* estate,
Rev 1. 5 and the *f* begotten of the dead,
11 Alpha and Omega, the *f* and the
17 Fear not; I am the *f* and the last:
2. 4 because thou hast left thy *f* love.
5 and do the *f* works; or else I will
8 saith the *f* and the last, which was
19 and the last to be more than the *f*.
4. 1 and the *f* voice which I heard was
7 And the *f* beast was like a lion,
8. 7 The *f* angel sounded, and there
13.12 all the power of the *f* beast before
12 therein to worship the *f* beast,
16. 2 the *f* went, and poured out his vial
20. 5 This is the *f* resurrection.
6 hath part in the *f* resurrection:
21. 1 the *f* heaven and the *f* earth were
19 the *f* foundation was jasper; the
22.13 and the end, the *f* and the last.

FIRSTBEGOTTEN

Heb 1. 6 bringeth in the *f* into the world,

FIRSTBORN

Gen 27.19 I am Esau thy *f*; I have done
32 he said, I am thy son, thy *f* Esau.
29.26 to give the younger before the *f*.
43.33 the *f* according to his birthright,
48.18 Not so, my father: for this is the *f*;
Ex 4.22 Israel is my son, even my *f*:
23 I will slay thy son, even thy *f*.
12.12 and will smite all the *f* in the land
29 Lord smote all the *f* in the land of
29 from the *f* of Pharaoh that sat on
29 unto the *f* of the captive that was
13. 2 Sanctify unto me all the *f*,
15 all the *f* of my children I redeem.
22.29 the *f* of thy sons shalt thou give
34.20 the *f* of thy sons thou shalt redeem,
Nu 3.13 Because all the *f* are mine; for on
13 I hallowed unto me all the *f* in
40 Number all the *f* of the males of the
45 Take the Levites instead of all the *f*
Dt 21.17 strength; the right of the *f* is his.
25. 6 *f* which she beareth shall succeed
Jos 6.26 lay the foundation thereof in his *f*,
Job 18.13 the *f* of death shall devour his
Ps 78.51 And smote all the *f* in Egypt;
89.27 Also I will make him my *f*,
Isa 14.30 And the *f* of the poor shall feed,
Jer 31. 9 to Israel, and Ephraim is my *f*.
Mic 6. 7 I give my *f* for my transgression,
Mt 1.25 she had brought forth her *f* son:
Lk 2. 7 And she brought forth her *f* son,
Ro 8.29 be the *f* among many brethren.
Col 1.15 God, the *f* of every creature:
18 the beginning, the *f* from the dead;
Heb 11.28 destroyed the *f* shall touch them.
12.23 assembly and church of the *f*,

FIRSTFRUIT

Dt 18. 4 *f* also of thy corn, of thy wine,
Ro 11.16 if the *f* be holy, the lump is also

FIRSTFRUITS

Ex 23.16 the *f* of thy labors, which thou
19 The first of the *f* of thy land thou
34.22 *f* of wheat harvest, and the feast
26 first of the *f* of thy land thou shalt
Lev 2.12 the oblation of the *f*, ye shall offer
14 offer a meat offering of thy *f*
14 offer for the meat offering of thy *f*
23.10 ye shall bring a sheaf of the *f* of
17 they are the *f* unto the Lord.
20 wave them with the bread of the *f*
Nu 18.12 *f* of them which they shall offer
28.26 Also in the day of the *f*, when ye
Dt 26.10 I have brought the *f* of the land,
2Ki 4.42 bread of the *f*, twenty loaves of
2Ch 31. 5 the *f* of corn, wine, and oil, and
Neh 10.35 And to bring the *f* of our ground,
35 and the *f* of all fruit trees, yearly
37 should bring the *f* of our dough,
12.44 for the *f*, and for the tithes, to
13.31 at times appointed, and for the *f*.
Pr 3. 9 with the *f* of all thine increase:
Jer 2. 3 the Lord, and the *f* of his increase:
Eze 20.40 and the *f* of your oblations,
44.30 the first of all the *f* of all things,
48.14 nor alienate the *f* of the land:
Ro 8.23 which have the *f* of the Spirit,
16. 5 who is the *f* of Achaia unto Christ.
1Co 15.20 and become the *f* of them that slept,
23 Christ the *f*; afterward they that
16.15 Stephanas, that it is the *f* of Achaia,
Jas 1.18 be a kind of *f* of his creatures,
Rev 14. 4 the *f* unto God and to the Lamb.

FISH

Gen 1.26, 28, dominion over the *f* of the sea,
Ex 7.18 And the *f* that is in the river shall
21 And the *f* that was in the river died;
Nu 11. 5 remember the *f*, which we did eat
22 or shall all the *f* of the sea be
Dt 4.18 of any *f* that is in the waters
2Ch 33.14 the entering in at the *f* gate,
Neh 3. 3 *f* gate did the sons of Hassenaah
12.39 above the *f* gate, and the tower
13.16 which brought *f*, and all manner
Job 41. 7 irons? or his head with *f* spears?
Ps 8. 8 the *f* of the sea, and whatsoever
105.29 into blood, and slew their *f*.
Isa 19.10 make sluices and ponds for *f*.
50. 2 their *f* stinketh, because there is
Jer 16.16 and they shall *f* them; and after
Eze 29. 4 I will cause the *f* of thy rivers to
4 all the *f* of thy rivers shall stick

Eze 29. 5 thee and all the *f* of thy rivers:
47. 9 be a very great multitude of *f*,
10 *f* shall be according to their kinds,
10 as the *f* of the great sea,
Jon 1.17 the Lord had prepared a great *f*
17 Jonah was in the belly of the *f*
2.10 And the Lord spake unto the *f*,
Zep 1.10 the noise of a cry from the *f* gate,
Mt 7.10 Or if he ask a *f*, will he give him
17.27 take up the *f* that first cometh up;
Lk 11.11 or if he ask a *f*, will he for a *f* give
24.42 gave him a piece of a broiled *f*,
Jn 21. 9 and *f* laid thereon, and bread.
10 the *f* which ye have now caught.
13 and giveth them, and *f* likewise.

FISHERMEN
Lk 5. 2 but the *f* were gone out of them,

FISHER'S
Jn 21. 7 he girt his *f* coat unto him, (for

FISHERS
Isa 19. 8 The *f* also shall mourn, and all
Jer 16.16 Behold, I will send for many *f*,
Eze 47.10 that the *f* shall stand upon it
Mt 4.18 a net into the sea: for they were *f*.
19 I will make you *f* of men.
Mk 1.16 a net into the sea: for they were *f*.
17 I will make you to become *f* of men.

FISHES
Gen 9. 2 shall be upon all the *f* of the sea;
1Ki 4.33 and of creeping things, and of *f*.
Job 12. 8 the *f* of the sea shall declare unto
Ec 9.12 the *f* that are taken in an evil net,
Eze 38.20 So that the *f* of the sea, and the
Hos 4. 3 the *f* of the sea also shall be taken
Hab 1.14 makest men as the *f* of the sea,
Zep 1. 3 and the *f* of the sea, and the
Mt 14.17 here but five loaves, and two *f*.
19 took the five loaves, and the two *f*,
15.34 said, Seven, and a few little *f*.
36 took the seven loaves and the *f*,
Mk 6.38 they say, Five, and two *f*.
41 taken the five loaves and the two *f*,
41 the two *f* divided he among them
43 full of the fragments, and of the *f*.
8. 7 And they had a few small *f*:
Lk 5. 6 inclosed a great multitude of *f*;
9 draft of the *f* which they had
9.13 no more but five loaves and two *f*;
16 took the five loaves and the two *f*,
Jn 6. 9 barley loaves, and two small *f*:
11 and likewise of the *f* as much as
21. 6 to draw it for the multitude of *f*.
8 dragging the net with *f*.
11 drew the net to land full of great *f*,
1Co 15.39 another of *f*, and another of birds.

FISHING
Jn 21. 3 Peter saith unto them, I go a *f*.

FISHPOOLS
SS 7. 4 thine eyes like the *f* in Heshbon

FISH'S
Jon 2. 1 Lord his God out of the *f* belly,

FIT
Lev 16.21 by the hand of a *f* man into the
1Ch 7.11 soldiers, *f* to go out for war
12. 8 and men of war *f* for the battle,
Job 34.18 Is it *f* to say to a king, Thou art
Pr 24.27 make it *f* for thyself in the field:
Lk 9.62 back, is *f* for the kingdom of God.
14.35 It is neither *f* for the land, nor yet
Ac 22.22 it is not *f* that he should live.
Col 3.18 husbands, as it is *f* in the Lord.

FITLY
Pr 25.11 word *f* spoken is like apples,
SS 5.12 washed with milk, and *f* set.

The miraculous draft of fish (Lk 5.1-11) is depicted in a tapestry by Raphael, part of the Vatican collection.

Eph 2.21 all the building *f* framed together
4.16 the whole body *f* joined together

FITTED
1Ki 6.35 with gold *f* upon the carved work.
Pr 22.18 they shall withal be *f* in thy lips.
Ro 9.22 vessels of wrath *f* to destruction:

FITTETH
Isa 44.13 he *f* it with planes, and he

FIVE
Gen 5. 6 lived an hundred and *f* years,
21 Enoch lived sixty and *f* years,
32 Noah was *f* hundred years old:
12. 4 Abram was seventy and *f* years old
18.28 Peradventure there shall lack *f* of
28 destroy all the city for lack of *f*?
28 If I find there forty and *f*, I will
45.11 yet there are *f* years of famine;
22 silver, and *f* changes of raiment.
Ex 22. 1 he shall restore *f* oxen for an ox,
Lev 26. 8 *f* of you shall chase an hundred,
27. 5 from *f* years old even unto twenty
6 a month old even unto *f* years old,
6 of the male *f* shekels of silver,
1Sa 17.40 *f* smooth stones out of the brook,
21. 3 give me *f* loaves of bread
Isa 19.18 that day shall *f* cities in the land
30.17 at the rebuke of *f* shall ye flee:
Dan 12.12 hundred and *f* and thirty days.
Mt 14.17 here but *f* loaves, and two fishes.
19 the *f* loaves, and the two fishes,
21 were about *f* thousand men,
16. 9 neither remember the *f* loaves of
9 of the *f* thousand, and how many
25. 2 And *f* of them were wise,
2 were wise, and *f* were foolish.
15 And unto one he gave *f* talents,
16 he that had received the *f* talents
16 and made them other *f* talents.
20 so he that had received *f* talents
20 came and brought other *f* talents,
20 thou deliveredst unto me *f* talents:
20 gained beside them *f* talents more.
Mk 6.38 they say, *F*, and two fishes.
41 when he had taken the *f* loaves
44 loaves were about *f* thousand men.
8.19 When I brake the *f* loaves among
19 loaves among the *f* thousand, how
Lk 1.24 hid herself *f* months, saying,
7.41 one owed *f* hundred pence, and
9.13 more but *f* loaves and two fishes;
14 For they were about *f* thousand
16 the *f* loaves and the two fishes,
12. 6 *f* sparrows sold for two farthings,
52 there shall be *f* in one house
14.19 I have bought *f* yoke of oxen,
16.28 For I have *f* brethren; that he
19.18 thy pound hath gained *f* pounds.
19 Be thou also over *f* cities.
Jn 4.18 For thou hast had *f* husbands; and
5. 2 tongue Bethesda, having *f* porches.
6. 9 which hath *f* barley loaves, and two
10 in number about *f* thousand.
13 fragments of the *f* barley loaves,
19 rowed about *f* and twenty or thirty
Ac 4. 4 of the men was about *f* thousand.
20. 6 came unto them to Troas in *f* days;
24. 1 And after *f* days Ananias the
1Co 14.19 church I had rather speak *f* words
15. 6 seen of above *f* hundred brethren
2Co 11.24 *f* times received I forty stripes
Rev 9. 5 should be tormented *f* months:
10 power was to hurt men *f* months.
17.10 *f* are fallen, and one is, and the

FIXED
Ps 57. 7 My heart is *f*, O God, my heart
7 O God, my heart is *f*: I will sing

108. 1 O God, my heart is *f*; I will sing
112. 7 his heart is *f*, trusting in the Lord.
Lk 16.26 us and you there is a great gulf *f*:

FLAME
Ex 3. 2 the Lord appeared unto him in a *f*
Nu 21.28 a *f* from the city of Sihon:
Jdg 13.20 when the *f* went up toward heaven
20 of the Lord ascended in the *f* of
20.38 make a great *f* with smoke rise
40 But when the *f* began to rise
40 the *f* of the city ascended up
Job 15.30 the *f* shall dry up his branches,
41.21 and a *f* goeth out of his mouth.
Ps 83.14 as the *f* setteth the mountains
106.18 the *f* burned up the wicked.
SS 8. 6 which hath a most vehement *f*.
Isa 5.24 and the *f* consumeth the chaff, so
10.17 and his Holy One for a *f*:
29. 6 and the *f* of devouring fire.
30.30 and with the *f* of a devouring fire,
43. 2 neither shall the *f* kindle upon
47.14 themselves from the power of the *f*:
Jer 48.45 a *f* from the midst of Sihon,
Eze 20.47 flaming *f* shall not be quenched,
Dan 3.22 the *f* of the fire slew those men
7. 9 his throne was like the fiery *f*,
11 and given to the burning *f*.
11.33 shall fall by the sword, and by *f*,
Joel 1.19 the *f* hath burned all the trees
2. 3 and behind them a *f* burneth:
5 like the noise of a *f* of fire
Ob 18 and the house of Joseph a *f*,
Lk 16.24 for I am tormented in this *f*.
Ac 7.30 in a *f* of fire in a bush.
Heb 1. 7 and his ministers a *f* of fire.
Rev 1.14 and his eyes were as a *f* of fire;
2.18 hath his eyes like unto a *f* of fire,
19.12 His eyes were as a *f* of fire,

FLAMES
Ps 29. 7 voice of the Lord divideth the *f*
Isa 13. 8 their faces shall be as *f*.
66.15 and his rebuke with *f* of fire.

FLAMING
Gen 3.24 *f* sword which turned every way,
Ps 104. 4 and his ministers a *f* fire:
105.32 and *f* fire in their land.
Isa 4. 5 the shining of a *f* fire by night:
La 2. 3 burned against Jacob like a *f* fire,
Eze 20.47 the *f* flame shall not be quenched,
Hos 7. 6 the morning it burneth as a *f* fire,
Na 2. 3 shall be with *f* torches in the day
2Th 1. 8 In *f* fire taking vengeance on

FLASH
Eze 1.14 the appearance of a *f* of lightning.

FLAT
Lev 21.18 or he that hath a *f* nose,
Nu 22.31 bowed down his head, and fell *f*
Jos 6. 5 wall of the city shall fall down *f*,
20 that the wall fell down *f*, so that

FLATTER
Ps 5. 9 they *f* with their tongue.
78.36 Nevertheless they did *f* him with

FLATTERETH
Ps 36. 2 For he *f* himself in his own eyes,
Pr 2.16 stranger which *f* with her words;
7. 5 stranger which *f* with her words.
20.19 meddle not with him that *f*
28.23 than he that *f* with the tongue.
29. 5 A man that *f* his neighbor

FLATTERIES
Dan 11.21 and obtain the kingdom by *f*.
32 covenant shall he corrupt by *f*:
34 many shall cleave to them with *f*.

FLATTERING
Job 32.21 let me give *f* titles unto man.
22 I know not to give *f* titles;
Ps 12. 2 *f* lips and with a double heart
3 The Lord shall cut off all *f* lips,
Pr 7.21 the *f* of her lips she forced him.
26.28 and a *f* mouth worketh ruin.
Eze 12.24 any vain vision nor *f* divination
1Th 2. 5 used we *f* words, as ye know,

FLATTERY
Job 17. 5 that speaketh *f* to his friends,
Pr 6.24 from the *f* of the tongue of a

FLAX
Ex 9.31 the *f* and the barley was smitten:
31 in the ear, and the *f* was bolled
Jos 2. 6 and hid them with the stalks of *f*
Jdg 15.14 were upon his arms became of *f*
Pr 31.13 seeketh wool, and *f*, and worketh
Isa 19. 9 Moreover they that work in fine *f*,
42. 3 smoking *f* shall he not quench:
Eze 40. 3 with a line of *f* in his hand,
Hos 2. 5 my wool and my *f*, mine oil and
9 wool and my *f* given to cover her
Mt 12.20 smoking *f* shall he not quench,

FLED
Gen 35. 7 he *f* from the face of his brother.
1Sa 4.10 and they *f* every man into his tent:
17.51 their champion was dead, they *f*.
19.10 David *f*, and escaped that night.
27. 4 it was told Saul that David was *f*
2Ki 7. 7 camp as it was, and *f* for their life.
14.12 they *f* every man to their tents.
1Ch 10. 7 they forsook their cities, and *f*:
Isa 22. 3 All thy rulers are *f* together,
Jon 1.10 knew that he *f* from the presence
4. 2 I *f* before unto Tarshish:
Mt 8.33 And they that kept them *f*, and
26.56 the disciples forsook him, and *f*.
Mk 5.14 And they that fed the swine *f*, and
14.50 And they all forsook him, and *f*.
52 cloth, and *f* from them naked.
16. 8 quickly, and *f* from the sepulchre;
Lk 8.34 they *f* and went and told it in the
Ac 7.29 Then *f* Moses at this saying, and
14. 6 and *f* unto Lystra and Derbe,
16.27 that the prisoners had been *f*.
19.16 they *f* out of that house naked
Heb 6.18 who have *f* for refuge to lay hold
Rev 12. 6 the woman *f* into the wilderness,
16.20 And every island *f* away, and the
20.11 the earth and the heaven *f* away;

FLEE
Gen 19.20 now this city is near to *f* unto,
27.43 arise, *f* thou to Laban my brother
Ex 14.25 Let us *f* from the face of Israel;
Lev 26.17 and ye shall *f* when none pursueth
Dt 19. 5 he shall *f* unto one of those cities,
Neh 6.11 Should such a man as I *f*?
Job 9.25 they *f* away, they see no good.
30.10 abhor me, they *f* far from me,
Ps 11. 1 *F* as a bird to your mountain?
139. 7 shall I *f* from thy presence?
Pr 28. 1 wicked *f* when no man pursueth:
SS 2.17 and the shadows *f* away, turn, my
4. 6 and the shadows *f* away, I will
Isa 10. 3 whom will ye *f* for help? and where
35.10 sorrow and sighing shall *f* away.
51.11 sorrow and mourning shall *f*
Am 2.16 the mighty shall *f* away naked
5.19 As if a man did *f* from a lion,
Jon 1. 3 Jonah rose up to *f* unto Tarshish
Na 3.17 when the sun ariseth they *f* away,
Mt 2.13 *f* into Egypt, and be thou there
3. 7 you to *f* from the wrath to come?
10.23 *f* ye into another: for verily I say
24.16 them which be in Judea *f* into the
Mk 13.14 them that be in Judea *f* to the
Lk 3. 7 you to *f* from the wrath to come?
21.21 them which are in Judea *f* to the
Jn 10. 5 will *f* from him: for they know not
Ac 27.30 were about to *f* out of the ship,
1Co 6.18 *F* fornication. Every sin that a
10.14 my dearly beloved, *f* from idolatry.
1Ti 6.11 O man of God, *f* these things;
2Ti 2.22 *F* also youthful lusts: but follow
Jas 4. 7 the devil, and he will *f* from you.
Rev 9. 6 and death shall *f* from them.

FLEETH
Dt 19.11 and *f* into one of these cities:
Job 14. 2 he *f* also as a shadow, and
Isa 24.18 who *f* from the noise of the fear
Jer 48.19 ask him that *f*, and her that
44 he that *f* from the fear shall fall
Am 9. 1 he that *f* of them shall not flee
Na 3.16 cankerworm spoileth, and *f* away.
Jn 10.12 leaveth the sheep, and *f*: and the
13 The hireling *f*, because he is an

FLESH
Gen 2.21 closed up the *f* instead thereof;
23 bone of my bones, and *f* of my *f*:
24 and they shall be one *f*.
6.13 The end of all *f* is come before me;
7.15 two of all *f*, wherein is the breath
16 went in male and female of all *f*,
21 all *f* died that moved upon the
9.15 become a flood to destroy all *f*.
17.13 my covenant shall be in your *f* for
29.14 Surely thou art my bone and my *f*.
Ex 16. 3 when we sat by the *f* pots,
Lev 17.11 For the life of the *f* is in the blood;
26.29 And ye shall eat the *f* of your sons,
29 and the *f* of your daughters shall
Nu 11. 4 said, Who shall give us *f* to eat?
16.22 the God of the spirits of all *f*,
2Sa 19.13 thou not of my bone, and of my *f*?
1Ki 21.27 sackcloth upon his *f*, and fasted,
2Ki 9.36 shall dogs eat the *f* of Jezebel:
Job 19.26 yet in my *f* shall I see God:
Ps 16. 9 my *f* also shall rest in hope.
50.13 Will I eat the *f* of bulls, or drink
56. 4 I will not fear what *f* can do unto
63. 1 my *f* longeth for thee in a dry and
65. 2 unto thee shall all *f* come.
73.26 My *f* and my heart faileth: but
78.39 remembered that they were but *f*;
84. 2 my heart and my *f* crieth out for
136.25 Who giveth food to all *f*; for his
Pr 14.30 a sound heart is the life of the *f*:
Ec 12.12 much study is a weariness of the *f*.
Isa 40. 5 and all *f* shall see it together:
6 What shall I cry? All *f* is grass,
44.16 with part thereof he eateth *f*; he
19 I have roasted *f*, and eaten it:
58. 7 hide not thyself from thine own *f*?
66.23 all *f* come to worship before me,
Jer 32.27 I am the Lord, the God of all *f*:
45. 5 behold, I will bring evil upon all *f*,
Eze 11.19 take the stony heart out of their *f*,
19 and will give them an heart of *f*:
20.48 And all *f* shall see that I the Lord
37. 8 lo, the sinews and the *f* came up
Joel 2.28 will pour out my spirit upon all *f*:
Zec 2.13 Be silent, O all *f*, before the Lord:
Mt 16.17 *f* and blood hath not revealed it
19. 5 and they twain shall be one *f*?
6 they are no more twain, but one *f*.
24.22 there should no *f* be saved: but
26.41 indeed is willing, but the *f* is weak.
Mk 10. 8 And they twain shall be one *f*:
8 they are no more twain, but one *f*.
13.20 no *f* should be saved: but for the
14.38 truly is ready, but the *f* is weak.
Lk 3. 6 And all *f* shall see the salvation of
24.39 for a spirit hath not *f* and bones,
Jn 1.13 nor of the will of the *f*, nor of the
14 And the Word was made *f*, and

Jn 3. 6 That which is born of the *f* is *f*;
6.51 the bread that I will give is my *f*,
52 can this man give us his *f* to eat?
53 Except ye eat the *f* of the Son of
54 Whoso eateth my *f*, and drinketh
55 For my *f* is meat indeed, and my
56 He that eateth my *f*, and drinketh
63 quickeneth; the *f* profiteth nothing:
8.15 judge after the *f*; I judge no man.
17. 2 hast given him power over all *f*,
Ac 2.17 pour out of my Spirit upon all *f*:
26 also my *f* shall rest in hope:
30 fruit of his loins, according to the *f*,
31 neither his *f* did see corruption.
Ro 1. 3 seed of David according to the *f*;
2.28 which is outward in the *f*:
3.20 shall no *f* be justified in his sight:
4. 1 as pertaining to the *f*, hath found?
6.19 because of the infirmity of your *f*:
7. 5 For when we were in the *f*,
18 in me, (that is, in my *f*,)
25 but with the *f* the law of sin.
8. 1 after the *f*, but after the Spirit.
3 in that it was weak through the *f*,
3 Son in the likeness of sinful *f*, and
3 for sin, condemned sin in the *f*:
4 in us, who walk not after the *f*,
5 For they that are after the *f* do
5 do mind the things of the *f*;
8 that are in the *f* cannot please God.
9 But ye are not in the *f*, but in the
12 we are debtors, not to the *f*,
12 to live after the *f*.
13 For if ye live after the *f*, ye shall
9. 3 my kinsmen according to the *f*:
5 as concerning the *f* Christ came,
8 which are the children of the *f*,
11.14 emulation them which are my *f*,
13.14 and make not provision for the *f*,
14.21 It is good neither to eat *f*, nor to
1Co 1.26 not many wise many after the *f*,
29 no *f* should glory in his presence.
5. 5 Satan for the destruction of the *f*,
6.16 for two, saith he, shall be one *f*.
7.28 such shall have trouble in the *f*:
8.13 eat no *f* while the world standeth,
10.18 Behold Israel after the *f*: are not
15.39 All *f* is not the same *f*: but there
39 but there is one kind of *f* of men,
39 another *f* of beasts, another of
50 that *f* and blood cannot inherit the
2Co 1.17 do I purpose according to the *f*,
4.11 be made manifest in our mortal *f*.
5.16 know we no man after the *f*: yea,
16 we have known Christ after the *f*,
7. 1 all filthiness of the *f* and spirit,
5 *f* had no rest, but we were troubled
10. 2 as if we walked according to the *f*.
3 in the *f*, we do not war after the *f*:
11.18 Seeing that many glory after the *f*,
12. 7 a thorn in the *f*, the messenger of
Gal 1.16 I conferred not with *f* and blood:
2.16 of the law shall no *f* be justified.
20 the life which I now live in the *f*
3. 3 are ye now made perfect by the *f*?
4.13 infirmity of the *f* I preached
14 my temptation which was in my *f*
23 bondwoman was born after the *f*;
29 as then he that was born after the *f*
5.13 not liberty for an occasion to the *f*
16 ye shall not fulfil the lust of the *f*.
17 the *f* lusteth against the Spirit,
17 and the Spirit against the *f*:
19 the works of the *f* are manifest,
24 crucified the *f* with the affections
6. 8 soweth to his *f* shall of the *f* reap
12 desire to make a fair show in the *f*,
13 that they may glory in your *f*.
Eph 2. 3 in the lusts of our *f*, fulfilling the
3 desires of the *f* and of the mind;
11 being in time past Gentiles in the *f*,
11 is called the Circumcision in the *f*
15 Having abolished in his *f* the
5.29 no man ever yet hated his own *f*;
30 his body, of his *f*, and of his bones.
31 and they two shall be one *f*.
6. 5 your masters according to the *f*,
12 we wrestle not against *f* and blood,
Php 1.22 if I live in the *f*, this is the fruit of
24 Nevertheless to abide in the *f* is
3. 3 and have no confidence in the *f*.
4 might also have confidence in the *f*.
4 whereof he might trust in the *f*,
Col 1.22 In the body of his *f* through death,
24 in my *f* for his body's sake, which
2. 1 as have not seen my face in the *f*;
5 For though I be absent in the *f*,
11 off the body of the sins of the *f* by
13 and the uncircumcision of your *f*,
23 honor to the satisfying of the *f*.
3.22 your masters according to the *f*;
1Ti 3.16 God was manifest in the *f*, justified
Phm 16 both in the *f* and in the Lord?
Heb 2.14 the children are partakers of *f* and
5. 7 Who in the days of his *f*, when he
9.13 sanctifieth to the purifying of the *f*:
10.20 the veil, that is to say, his *f*;
12. 9 we have had fathers of our *f* which
Jas 5. 3 and shall eat your *f* as it were fire.
1Pe 1.24 For all *f* is grass, and all the glory
3.18 to death in the *f*, but quickened
21 putting away of the filth of the *f*,
4. 1 Christ hath suffered for us in the *f*,
1 he that hath suffered in the *f* hath
2 live the rest of his time in the *f* to
6 be judged according to men in the *f*,
2Pe 2.10 that walk after the *f* in the lust of
18 allure through the lusts of the *f*.
1Jn 2.16 the lust of the *f*, and the lust of the
4. 2 that Jesus Christ is come in the *f*
3 not that...Christ is come in the *f*
2Jn 7 that Jesus Christ is come in the *f*.
Jude 7 going after strange *f*, are set forth
8 these filthy dreamers defile the *f*,
23 even the garment spotted by the *f*.
Rev 17.16 and shall eat her *f*, and burn her
19.18 *f* of kings, and the *f* of captains,
18 captains, and the *f* of mighty men,
18 men, and the *f* of horses, and of
18 and the *f* of all men, both free and
21 the fowls were filled with their *f*.

FLESHLY

2Co 1.12 not with *f* wisdom, but by the
3. 3 but in *f* tables of the heart.
Col 2.18 vainly puffed up by his *f* mind,
1Pe 2.11 abstain from *f* lusts, which war

FLIES

Ex 8.21 I will send swarms of *f* upon thee, and
21 shall be full of swarms of *f*, and also
22 that no swarms of *f* shall be there;
24 there came a grievous swarm of *f* into
24 corrupted by reason of the swarm of *f*.
29 that the swarms of *f* may depart from
31 and he removed the swarms of *f* from
Ps 78.45 He sent divers sorts of *f* among
105.31 there came divers sorts of *f*, and
Ec 10. 1 Dead *f* cause the ointment of the

FLIGHT

Lev 26. 8 you shall put ten thousand to *f*:
Dt 32.30 and two put ten thousand to *f*,
1Ch 12.15 and they put to *f* all them of the
Isa 52.12 not go out with haste, nor go by *f*:
Am 2.14 the *f* shall perish from the swift,
Mt 24.20 But pray ye that your *f* be not in
Mk 13.18 And pray ye that your *f* be not in
Heb 11.34 turned to *f* the armies of the aliens.

FLOCK

Gen 33.13 them one day, all the *f* will die.
Ex 3. 1 kept the *f* of Jethro his father in
1 the *f* to the backside of the desert,
2Sa 12. 4 he spared to take of his own *f* and
Ps 77.20 Thou leddest thy people like a *f* by
78.52 them in the wilderness like a *f*.
80. 1 thou that leadest Joseph like a *f*;
107.41 and maketh him families like a *f*.
SS 1. 7 thou makest thy *f* to rest at noon:
Isa 40.11 He shall feed his *f* like a shepherd:
Jer 23. 3 I will gather the remnant of my *f*
31.10 him, as a shepherd doth his *f*.
Eze 34. 8 did my shepherds search for my *f*,
8 fed themselves, and fed not my *f*;
10 I will require my *f* at their hand,
12 As a shepherd seeketh out his *f*
Am 7.15 Lord took me as I followed the *f*,
Hab 3.17 the *f* shall be cut off from the fold,
Zec 10. 3 Lord of hosts hath visited his *f*
11.17 idol shepherd that leaveth the *f*!
Mt 26.31 sheep of the *f* shall be scattered
Lk 2. 8 watch over their *f* by night.
12.32 Fear not, little *f*; for it is your
Ac 20.28 unto yourselves, and to all the *f*,
29 in among you, not sparing the *f*.
1Co 9. 7 who feedeth a *f*, and eateth not of
7 eateth not of the milk of the *f*?
1Pe 5. 2 the *f* of God which is among you,
3 but being ensamples to the *f*.

FLOCKS

Gen 13. 5 with Abram, had *f*, and herds,
Ps 65.13 The pastures are clothed with *f*;
78.48 and their *f* to hot thunderbolts.
Isa 60. 7 the *f* of Kedar shall be gathered
61. 5 shall stand and feed your *f*, and the
Jer 5.17 shall eat up thy *f* and thine herds:
6. 3 shepherds with their *f* shall come
10.21 and all their *f* shall be scattered
33.12 shepherds causing their *f* to lie
Eze 36.38 waste cities be filled with *f* of men;
Zep 2.14 And *f* shall lie down in the midst

FLOOD

Gen 6.17 I do bring a *f* of waters upon the
7. 6 the *f* of waters was upon the earth.
7 because of the waters of the *f*.
10 waters of the *f* were upon the earth.
17 *f* was forty days upon the earth;
9.11 off any more by the waters of a *f*;
11 neither shall there any more be a *f*
15 waters shall no more become a *f*
28 And Noah lived after the *f* three
10. 1 them were sons born after the *f*.
32 divided in the earth after the *f*.
11.10 Arphaxad two years after the *f*:
Jos 24. 2 dwelt on the other side of the *f*
3 from the other side of the *f*,
14 served on the other side of the *f*,
15 were on the other side of the *f*,
Job 14.11 and the *f* decayeth and drieth up:
22.16 was overflown with a *f*:
28. 4 The *f* breaketh out from the
Ps 29.10 The Lord sitteth upon the *f*; yea,
66. 6 they went through the *f* on foot:
74.15 cleave the fountain and the *f*:
90. 5 carriest them away as with a *f*;
Isa 28. 2 *f* of mighty waters overflowing,
59.19 the enemy shall come in like a *f*,
Jer 46. 7 Who is this that cometh up as a *f*,
8 Egypt riseth up like a *f*, and his
47. 2 and shall be an overflowing *f*,
Dan 9.26 The end thereof shall be with a *f*,
11.22 with the arms of a *f* shall they be
Am 8. 8 and it shall rise up wholly as a *f*;
8 drowned, as by the *f* of Egypt.
9. 5 it shall rise up wholly like a *f*;
5 be drowned, as by the *f* of Egypt.
Na 1. 8 But with an overrunning *f* he will
Mt 24.38 *f* they were eating and drinking,
39 until the *f* came, and took them all
Lk 6.48 when the *f* arose, the stream beat
17.27 the *f* came, and destroyed them

2Pe 2. 5 bringing in the *f* upon the world
Rev 12.15 cast out of his mouth water as a *f*
15 her to be carried away of the *f*.
16 mouth, and swallowed up the *f*

FLOODS

Ex 15. 8 the *f* stood upright as an heap,
2Sa 22. 5 *f* of ungodly men made me afraid:
Job 20.17 He shall not see the rivers, the *f*,
28.11 bindeth the *f* from overflowing;
Ps 18. 4 *f* of ungodly men made me afraid.
24. 2 and established it upon the *f*.
32. 6 surely in the *f* of great waters
69. 2 waters, where the *f* overflow me.
78.44 rivers into blood; and their *f*,
93. 3 The *f* have lifted up, O Lord,
3 the *f* have lifted up their voice;
3 the *f* lift up their waves.
98. 8 the *f* clap their hands: let the hills
SS 8. 7 neither can the *f* drown it: if a
Isa 44. 3 and *f* upon the dry ground:
Eze 31.15 *f* thereof, and the great waters
Jon 2. 3 and the *f* compassed me about:
Mt 7.25, 27 and the *f* came, and the winds

FLOOR

Gen 50.11 the mourning in the *f* of Atad,
Nu 5.17 of the dust that is in the *f* of the
Dt 15.14 out of thy flock, and out of thy *f*,
Jdg 6.37 will put a fleece of wool in the *f*;
Ru 3. 3 and get thee down to the *f*:
6 And she went down unto the *f*,
14 that a woman came unto the *f*.
1Ki 6.15 the *f* of the house, and the walls
15 covered the *f* of the house with
16 the *f* and the walls with boards
30 And the *f* of the house he overlaid
7. 7 from one side of the *f* to the other.
2Ch 34.11 to *f* the houses which the kings
Isa 21.10 threshing, and the corn of my *f*:
Hos 9. 2 The *f* and the winepress shall
13. 3 with the whirlwind out of the *f*,
Mic 4.12 them as the sheaves into the *f*.
Mt 3.12 and he will throughly purge his *f*,
Lk 3.17 and he will throughly purge his *f*,

FLOUR

1Ki 4.22 was thirty measures of fine *f*,
2Ki 7. 1 a measure of fine *f* be sold for a
16 So a measure of fine *f* was sold for
18 a measure of fine *f* for a shekel,
Eze 16.13 thou didst eat fine *f*, and honey,
Rev 18.13 fine *f*, and wheat, and beasts,

FLOURISH

Ps 72. 7 In his days shall the righteous *f*;
16 and they of the city shall *f* like
92. 7 all the workers of iniquity do *f*;
12 The righteous shall *f* like the
13 shall *f* in the courts of our God.
132.18 upon himself shall his crown *f*.
Pr 11.28 the righteous shall *f* as a branch,
14.11 tabernacle of the upright shall *f*.
Ec 12. 5 and the almond tree shall *f*,
SS 7.12 let us see if the vine *f*,
Isa 17.11 shalt thou make thy seed to *f*:
66.14 your bones shall *f* like an herb:
Eze 17.24 and have made the dry tree to *f*:

FLOURISHED

SS 6.11 and to see whether the vine *f*,
Php 4.10 your care of me hath *f* again;

FLOURISHETH

Ps 90. 6 In the morning it *f*, and groweth
103.15 as a flower of the field, so he *f*.

FLOW

Job 20.28 his goods shall *f* away in the day
Ps 147.18 wind to blow, and the waters *f*.
SS 4.16 that the spices thereof may *f* out.
Isa 2. 2 and all nations shall *f* unto it.
48.21 the waters to *f* out of the rock
60. 5 thou shalt see, and *f* together,
64. 1 might *f* down at thy presence,
Jer 31.12 shall *f* together to the goodness
51.44 the nations shall not *f* together
Joel 3.18 the hills shall *f* with milk, and
18 all the rivers of Judah shall *f* with
Mic 4. 1 and people shall *f* unto it.
Jn 7.38 belly shall *f* rivers of living water.

FLOWED

Jos 4.18 and *f* over all his banks, as they
Isa 64. 3 mountains *f* down at thy presence.
La 3.54 Waters *f* over mine head; then

FLOWER

Ex 25.33 a knop and a *f* in one branch;
33 other branch, with a knop and a *f*:
37.19 in one branch, a knop and a *f*;
19 another branch, a knop and a *f*:
1Sa 2.33 shall die in the *f* of their age.
Job 14. 2 He cometh forth like a *f*, and is cut
15.33 shall cast off his *f* as the olive.
Ps 103.15 a *f* of the field, so he flourisheth.
Isa 18. 5 sour grape is ripening in the *f*,
28. 1 glorious beauty is a fading *f*,
4 shall be a fading *f*, and as the
40. 6 thereof is as the *f* of the field:
7 the *f* fadeth: because the spirit
8 *f* fadeth: but the word of our God
Na 1. 4 the *f* of Lebanon languisheth.
1Co 7.36 if she pass the *f* of her age,
Jas 1.10 because as the *f* of the grass
11 the grass, and the *f* thereof falleth,
1Pe 1.24 the glory of man as the *f* of grass.
24 and the *f* thereof falleth away:

FLOWERS

Ex 25.31 his bowls, his knops, and his *f*,
34 with their knops and their *f*.
37.17 and his *f* were of the same:
20 like almonds, his knops, and his *f*:
Lev 15.24 her *f* be upon him, he shall be
33 And of her that is sick of her *f*,
Nu 8. 4 the *f* thereof, was beaten work:
1Ki 6.18 knops and open *f*: all was cedar;
29 palm trees and open *f*, within and
32 palm trees and open *f*, and overlaid
35 palm trees and open *f*: and covered
7.26 the brim of a cup, with *f* of lilies:
49 with the *f*, and the lamps, and the
2Ch 4. 5 brim of a cup, with *f* of lilies;
21 And the *f*, and the lamps, and the
SS 2.12 The *f* appear on the earth;
5.13 as a bed of spices, as sweet *f*:

FLUX

Ac 28. 8 sick of a fever and of a bloody *f*:

FLY

Gen 1.20 fowl that may *f* above the earth
1Sa 15.19 but didst *f* upon the spoil, and
2Sa 22.11 he rode upon a cherub, and did *f*:
Job 5. 7 trouble, as the sparks *f* upward.
20. 8 He shall *f* away as a dream,
39.26 Doth the hawk *f* by thy wisdom,
Ps 18.10 rode upon a cherub, and did *f*:
10 yea, he did *f* upon the wings
55. 6 would I *f* away, and be at rest.
90.10 it is soon cut off, and we *f* away.
Pr 23. 5 they *f* away as an eagle toward
Isa 6. 2 his feet, and with twain he did *f*.
7.18 shall hiss for the *f* that is in the
11.14 they shall *f* upon the shoulders
60. 8 Who are these that *f* as a cloud,
Jer 48.40 Behold, he shall *f* as an eagle,
49.22 shall come up and *f* as the eagle,
Eze 13.20 hunt the souls to make them *f*,
20 souls that ye hunt to make them *f*.
Dan 9.21 being caused to *f* swiftly, touched
Hos 9.11 glory shall *f* away like a bird
Hab 1. 8 shall *f* as the eagle that hasteth
Rev 12.14 she might *f* into the wilderness,
14. 6 saw another angel *f* in the midst
19.17 to all the fowls that *f* in the midst

FLYING

Lev 11.21 ye eat of every *f* creeping thing
23 But all other *f* creeping things,
Ps 148.10 creeping things, and *f* fowl:
Pr 26. 2 as the swallow by *f*, so the curse
Isa 14.29 his fruit shall be a fiery *f* serpent.
30. 6 the viper and fiery *f* serpent,
31. 5 birds *f*, so will the Lord of hosts
Zec 5. 1 and looked, and behold a *f* roll.
2 And I answered, I see a *f* roll;
Rev 4. 7 fourth beast was like a *f* eagle.
8.13 *f* through the midst of heaven,

FOAL

Gen 49.11 Binding his *f* unto the vine, and
Zec 9. 9 and upon a colt the *f* of an ass.
Mt 21. 5 and a colt the *f* of an ass.

FOAMETH

Mk 9.18 he *f*, and gnasheth with his teeth,
Lk 9.39 and it teareth him that he *f* again,

FOAMING

Mk 9.20 on the ground, and wallowed *f*.
Jude 13 of the sea, *f* out their own shame;

FOES

1Ch 21.12 to be destroyed before thy *f*,
Est 9.16 their *f* seventy and five thousand,
Ps 27. 2 even mine enemies and my *f*,
30. 1 and hast not made my *f* to rejoice
89.23 beat down his *f* before his face,
Mt 10.36 And a man's *f* shall be they of his
Ac 2.35 Until I make thy *f* thy footstool.

FOLD

Isa 13.20 shall the shepherds make their *f*
65.10 And Sharon shall be a *f* of flocks,
Eze 34.14 mountains of Israel shall their *f*
14 there shall they lie in a good *f*,
Mic 2.12 the flock in the midst of their *f*:
Hab 3.17 flock shall be cut off from the *f*,
Jn 10.16 I have, which are not of this *f*:
16 shall be one *f*, and one shepherd.
Heb 1.12 as a vesture shalt thou *f* them up,

FOLK

Gen 33.15 now leave with thee some of the *f*
Pr 30.26 The conies are but a feeble *f*,
Jer 51.58 and the *f* in the fire, and they
Mk 6. 5 laid his hands upon a few sick *f*
Jn 5. 3 a great multitude of impotent *f*,

FOLKS

Ac 5.16 bring sick *f*, and them which

FOLLOW

Gen 24.39 the woman will not *f* me.
Jdg 3.28 he said unto them, *F* after me:
1Ki 18.21 God, *f* him: but if Baal, then *f*
2Ki 6.19 *f* me, and I will bring you
Ps 23. 6 goodness and mercy shall *f* me
94.15 all the upright in heart shall *f* it.
Jer 17.16 from being a pastor to *f* thee:
Hos 6. 3 if we *f* on to know the Lord:
Mt 4.19 he saith unto them, *F* me,
8.19 I will *f* thee whithersoever thou
22 And Jesus said unto him, *F* me;
9. 9 and he saith unto him, *F* me.
16.24 and take up his cross, and *f* me.
19.21 in heaven: and come and *f* me.
Mk 2.14 and said unto him, *F* me. And he
5.37 And he suffered no man to *f* him,
6. 1 country; and his disciples *f* him.
8.34 and take up his cross, and *f* me.

Mk 10.21 come, take up the cross, and *f* me.
14.13 bearing a pitcher of water: *f* him.
16.17 And these signs shall *f* them that
Lk 5.27 and he said unto him, *F* me.
9.23 take up his cross daily, and *f* me.
57 I will *f* thee whithersoever thou
59 And he said unto another, *F* me.
61 also said, Lord, I will *f* thee;
17.23 go not after them, nor *f* them.
18.22 treasure in heaven: and come, *f* me.
22.10 *f* him into the house where he
49 were about him saw what would *f*,
Jn 1.43 Philip, and saith unto him, *F* me.
10. 4 before them, and the sheep *f* him:
5 And a stranger will they not *f*,
27 and I know them, and they *f* me:
12.26 If any man serve me, let him *f* me;
13.36 not *f* me now; but thou shalt *f* me
37 why cannot I *f* thee now?
21.19 he saith unto him, *F* me.
22 what is that to thee? *f* thou me.
Ac 3.24 Samuel and those that *f* after,
12. 8 thy garment about thee, and *f* me.
Ro 14.19 therefore *f* after the things which
1Co 14. 1 *F* after charity, and desire
Php 3.12 I *f* after, if that I may apprehend
1Th 5.15 but ever *f* that which is good,
2Th 3. 7 know how ye ought to *f* us:
9 an ensample unto you to *f* us.
1Ti 5.24 and some men they *f* after.
6.11 *f* after righteousness, godliness,
2Ti 2.22 *f* righteousness, faith, charity,
Heb 12.14 *F* peace with all men, and
13. 7 whose faith *f*, considering the
1Pe 1.11 and the glory that should *f*.
2.21 example, that ye should *f* his steps:
2Pe 2. 2 And many shall *f* their pernicious
3Jn 11 Beloved, *f* not that which is evil,
Rev 14. 4 These are they which *f* the Lamb
13 and their works do *f* them.

FOLLOWED

Nu 16.25 and the elders of Israel *f* him.
32.11 because they have not wholly *f* me:
Jdg 2.12 and *f* other gods, of the gods
2Ki 5.21 So Gehazi *f* after Naaman.
Am 7.15 the Lord took me as I *f* the flock,
Mt 4.20 straightway left their nets, and *f*
22 the ship and their father, and *f* him.
25 *f* him great multitudes of people
8. 1 mountain, great multitudes *f* him.
10 and said to them that *f*, Verily I say
23 into a ship, his disciples *f* him.
9. 9 Follow me. And he arose, and *f*
19 And Jesus arose, and *f* him,
27 two blind men *f* him, crying, and
12.15 great multitudes *f* him, and he
14.13 they *f* him on foot out of the cities.
19. 2 great multitudes *f* him; and he
27 we have forsaken all, and *f* thee;
28 That ye which have *f* me, in the
20.29 Jericho, a great multitude *f* him.
34 received sight, and they *f* him.
21. 9 that went before, and that *f*,
26.58 Peter *f* him afar off unto the high
27.55 *f* Jesus from Galilee, ministering
62 day, that *f* the day of the
Mk 1.18 they forsook their nets, and *f* him.
36 they that were with him *f* after
2.14 Follow me, And he arose and *f* him.
15 there were many, and they *f* him.
3. 7 great multitude from Galilee *f* him,
5.24 with him; and much people *f* him,
10.28 have left all, and have *f* thee.
32 and as they *f*, they were afraid.
52 he received his sight, and *f* Jesus
11. 9 that went before, and they that *f*,
14.51 there *f* him a certain young man,
54 Peter *f* him afar off, even into the
15.41 when he was in Galilee, *f* him, and
Lk 5.11 they forsook all, and *f* him.
28 And he left all, rose up, and *f* him.
7. 9 and said unto the people that *f* him,
9.11 people, when they knew it, *f* him:
18.28 we have left all, and *f* thee.
43 he received his sight, and *f* him,
22.39 and his disciples also *f* him.
54 priest's house. And Peter *f* afar off.
23.27 And there *f* him a great company of
49 and the woman that *f* him from
55 *f* after, and beheld the sepulchre,
Jn 1.37 heard him speak, and they *f* Jesus.
40 which heard John speak, and *f* him,
6. 2 And a great multitude *f* him,
11.31 rose up hastily and went out, *f* her,
18.15 And Simon Peter *f* Jesus, and so did
Ac 12. 9 And he went out, and *f* him;
13.43 proselytes *f* Paul and Barnabas:
16.17 same *f* Paul and us, and cried,
21.36 the multitude of the people *f* after,
Ro 9.30 which *f* not after righteousness,
31 Israel, which *f* after the law of
1Co 10. 4 of that spiritual Rock that *f* them:
1Ti 5.10 have diligent *f* every good work.
2Pe 1.16 we have not *f* cunningly devised
Rev 6. 8 was Death, and Hell *f* with him.
8. 7 there *f* hail and fire mingled with
14. 8 and there *f* another angel, saying,
9 And the third angel *f* them, saying
19.14 armies which were in heaven *f* him

FOLLOWERS

1Co 4.16 I beseech you, be ye *f* of me.
11. 1 Be ye *f* of me, even as I also am
Eph 5. 1 Be ye therefore *f* of God,
Php 3.17 be *f* together of me, and mark
1Th 1. 6 became *f* of us, and of the Lord,
2.14 became *f* of the churches of God
Heb 6.12 but *f* of them who through faith
1Pe 3.13 if ye be *f* of that which is good?

FOLLOWETH

2Ki 11.15 that *f* her kill with the sword.
2Ch 23.14 whoso *f* her, let him be slain
Ps 63. 8 My soul *f* hard after thee:
Pr 12.11 but he that *f* vain persons is void
15. 9 him that *f* after righteousness.
21.21 He that *f* after righteousness and
28.19 but he that *f* after vain persons
Isa 1.23 loveth gifts, and *f* after rewards:
Eze 16.34 none *f* thee to commit whoredoms:
Hos 12. 1 and *f* after the east wind: he
Mt 10.38 and *f* after me, is not worthy of
Mk 9.38 in thy name, and he *f* not us:
38 we forbad him, because he *f* not
Lk 9.49 we forbad him, because he *f* not
Jn 8.12 he that *f* me shall not walk in

FOLLOWING

Gen 41.31 by reason of that famine *f*;
Dt 7. 4 will turn away thy son from *f* me,
12.30 thou be not snared by *f* them,
Jos 22.16 to turn away this day from *f* the
18 must turn away this day from *f* the
23 an altar to turn from *f* the Lord,
29 to turn this day from *f* the Lord,
Jdg 2.19 in *f* other gods to serve them,
Ru 1.16 or to return from *f* after thee:
1Sa 12.14 continue *f* the Lord your God:
20 yet turn not aside from *f* the Lord,
14.46 went up from *f* the Philistines:
15.11 for he is turned back from *f* me,
24. 1 returned from *f* the Philistines,
2Sa 2.19 hand nor to the left from *f* Abner.
21 would not turn aside from *f* of him.
22 Asahel, Turn thee aside from *f* me:
26 return from *f* their brethren?
27 up every one from *f* his brother.
30 And Joab returned from *f* Abner:
7. 8 from *f* the sheep, to be ruler over
1Ki 1. 8 and they *f* Adonijah helped him.
9. 6 if ye shall at all turn from *f* me,
21.26 very abominably in *f* idols,
2Ki 17.21 drave Israel from *f* the Lord,
18. 6 departed not from *f* him, but kept
1Ch 17. 7 sheepcote, even from *f* the sheep,
2Ch 25.27 did turn away from *f* the Lord
34.33 they departed not from *f* the Lord,
Ps 48.13 ye may tell it to the generation *f*.
78.71 From *f* the ewes great with young
109.13 in the generation *f* let their name
Mk 16.20 confirming the word with signs *f*.
Lk 13.33 and tomorrow, and the day *f*:
Jn 1.38 Jesus turned, and saw them *f*,
43 The day *f* Jesus would go forth
6.22 The day *f*, when the people
20. 6 Then cometh Simon Peter *f* him,
21.20 the disciple whom Jesus loved *f*;
Ac 21. 1 and the day *f* unto Rhodes, and
18 the day *f* Paul went in with us
23.11 And the night *f* the Lord stood
2Pe 2.15 *f* the way of Balaam the son of

FOLLY

Gen 34. 7 he had wrought *f* in Israel
Dt 22.21 she hath wrought *f* in Israel,
Jos 7.15 and because he hath wrought *f*
Jdg 19.23 come into mine house, do not this *f*.
20. 6 committed lewdness and *f* in
10 *f* that they have wrought in Israel.
1Sa 25.25 Nabal is his name, and *f* is with
2Sa 13.12 done in Israel: do not thou this *f*.
Job 4.18 his angels he charged with *f*:
24.12 yet God layeth not *f* to them.
42. 8 lest I deal with you after your *f*,
Ps 49.13 This their way is their *f*:
85. 8 but let them not turn again to *f*.
Pr 5.23 in the greatness of his *f* he shall
13.16 but a fool layeth open his *f*.
14. 8 but the *f* of fools is deceit.
18 The simple inherit *f*: but the
24 but the foolishness of fools is *f*.
29 he that is hasty of spirit exalteth *f*.
15.21 *F* is joy to him that is destitute of
16.22 but the instruction of fools is *f*.
17.12 rather than a fool in his *f*.
18.13 matter before he heareth it, it is *f*
26. 4 Answer not a fool according to his *f*,
5 Answer a fool according to his *f*,
11 so a fool returneth to his *f*.
Ec 1.17 and to know madness and *f*:
2. 3 to lay hold on *f*, till I might see
12 wisdom, and madness, and *f*:
13 I saw that wisdom excelleth *f*,
7.25 and to know the wickedness of *f*,
10. 1 so doth a little *f* him that is in
6 *F* is set in great dignity, and the
Isa 9.17 and every mouth speaketh *f*.
Jer 23.13 I have seen *f* in the prophets
2Co 11. 1 bear with me a little in my *f*:
2Ti 3. 9 their *f* shall be manifest unto all

FOOD

Gen 2. 9 to the sight, and good for *f*;
3. 6 saw that the tree was good for *f*,
6.21 unto thee of all *f* that is eaten,
21 and it shall be for *f* for thee,
41.35 And let them gather all the *f*
35 and let them keep *f* in the cities.
36 And that *f* shall be for store to the
48 And he gathered up all the *f* of the
48 laid up the *f* in the cities: the *f* of
42. 7 From the land of Canaan to buy *f*.
10 but to buy *f* are thy servants come.
33 and take *f* for the famine of your
43. 2 Go again, buy us a little *f*.
4 we will go down and buy thee *f*:
20 down at the first time to buy *f*:
22 down in our hands to buy *f*:
44. 1 Fill the men's sacks with *f*,
25 Go again, and buy us a little *f*.
47.24 seed of the field, and for your *f*,
24 and for *f* for your little ones.

Biblical Themes

FOOD AND DRINK

Every moving thing that liveth shall be meat for you; even as the green herb have I given you all things. Gen 9.3

The house of Israel called the name thereof Manna: and it was like coriander seed, white; and the taste of it was like wafers made with honey. Ex 16.31

And unleavened bread, and cakes unleavened tempered with oil, and wafers unleavened anointed with oil: of wheaten flour shalt thou make them. Ex 29.2

[David] dealt among all the people, even among the whole multitude of Israel . . . to every one a cake of bread, and a good piece of flesh, and a flagon of wine. 2Sa 6.19

One [of the prophets] went out into the field to gather herbs, and found a wild vine, and gathered thereof wild gourds his lap full, and came and shred them into the pot of pottage. 2Ki 4.39

Can that which is unsavory be eaten without salt? or is there any taste in the white of an egg? Job 6.6

The people asked, and he brought quails, and satisfied them with the bread of heaven. Ps 105.40

A man hath no better thing under the sun, than to eat, and to drink, and to be merry. Ec 8.15

Ho, every one that thirsteth, come ye to the waters, and he that hath no money; come ye, buy, and eat; yea, come, buy wine and milk without money and without price. Wherefore do ye spend money for that which is not bread? and your labor for that which satisfieth not? Isa 55.1-2

Corn shall make the young men cheerful, and new wine the maids. Zec 9.17

Blessed are they which do hunger and thirst after righteousness: for they shall be filled. Mt 5.6

Bring hither the fatted calf, and kill it; and let us eat, and be merry. Lk 15.23

And he took bread, and gave thanks, and brake it, and gave unto them, saying, This is my body which is given for you: this do in remembrance of me. Lk 22.19

Whosoever drinketh of the water that I shall give him shall never thirst. Jn 4.14

One of his disciples . . . saith unto him, There is a lad here, which hath five barley loaves, and two small fishes: but what are they among so many? And Jesus said, Make the men sit down. Now there was much grass in the place. So the men sat down, in number about five thousand. And Jesus took the loaves; and when he had given thanks, he distributed to the disciples, and the disciples to them that were set down; and likewise of the fishes as much as they would. Jn 6.8-11

Labor not for the meat which perisheth, but for that meat which endureth unto everlasting life, which the Son of man shall give unto you. Jn 6.27

Jesus said . . . I am the bread of life: he that cometh to me shall never hunger. Jn 6.35

After this, Jesus knowing that all things were now accomplished . . . saith, I thirst. Jn 19.28

I have fed you with milk, and not with meat: for hitherto ye were not able to bear it, neither yet now are ye able. For ye are yet carnal. 1Co 3.2-3

Drink no longer water, but use a little wine for thy stomach's sake and thine often infirmities. 1Ti 5.23

They shall hunger no more, neither thirst any more. . . . For the Lamb which is in the midst of the throne shall feed them, and shall lead them unto living fountains of waters. Rev 7.16-17

Ex 21.10 her *f*, her raiment, and her duty
Lev 3.11, 16 it is the *f* of the offering made
19.23 planted all manner of trees for *f*,
22. 7 holy things; because it is his *f*.
Dt 10.18 in giving him *f* and raiment.
1Sa 14.24 be the man that eateth any *f* until
24 So none of the people tasted any *f*.
28 be the man that eateth any *f* this
2Sa 9.10 master's son may have *f* to eat:
1Ki 5. 9 desire, in giving *f* for my household.
11 thousand measures of wheat for *f*
Job 23.12 mouth more than my necessary *f*.
24. 5 wilderness yieldeth *f* for them
38.41 provideth for the raven his *f*?
40.20 the mountains bring him forth *f*.
Ps 78.25 Man did eat angels *f*: he sent
104.14 bring forth *f* out of the earth;
136.25 Who giveth *f* to all flesh: for his
146. 7 which giveth *f* to the hungry.
147. 9 He giveth to the beast his *f*,
Pr 6. 8 gathereth her *f* in the harvest.
13.23 Much *f* is in the tillage of the poor:
27.27 have goats' milk enough for thy *f*,
27 for the *f* of thy household, and for
28. 3 sweeping rain which leaveth no *f*.
30. 8 feed me with *f* convenient for me:
31.14 she bringeth her *f* from afar.
Eze 16.27 and have diminished thine ordinary *f*,
48.18 *f* unto them that serve the city.
Ac 14.17 our hearts with *f* and gladness.
2Co 9.10 both minister bread for your *f*,
1Ti 6. 8 having *f* and raiment let us be
Jas 2.15 be naked, and destitute of daily *f*,

FOOL

1Sa 26.21 behold, I have played the *f*, and
2Sa 3.33 said, Died Abner as a *f* dieth?
Ps 14. 1 The *f* hath said in his heart,
49.10 the *f* and the brutish person
53. 1 The *f* hath said in his heart,
92. 6 neither doth a *f* understand this.
Pr 7.22 *f* to the correction of the stocks;
10. 8 commandments: but a prating *f*
10 sorrow: but a prating *f* shall fall.
18 he that uttereth a slander, is a *f*.
23 It is as sport to a *f* to do mischief:
11.29 *f* shall be servant to the wise
12.15 of a *f* is right in his own eyes:
13.16 but a *f* layeth open his folly.
14.16 but the *f* rageth, and is confident.
15. 5 *f* despiseth his father's instruction:
17. 7 speech becometh not a *f*:
10 than an hundred stripes into a *f*.
12 rather than a *f* in his folly.
16 in the hand of a *f* to get wisdom,
21 He that begetteth a *f* doeth it to his
21 and the father of a *f* hath no joy.
24 the eyes of a *f* are in the ends of
28 a *f*, when he holdeth his peace,
18. 2 A *f* hath no delight in
19. 1 is perverse in his lips, and is a *f*.
10 Delight is not seemly for a *f*;
20. 3 but every *f* will be meddling.
23. 9 Speak not in the ears of a *f*:
24. 7 Wisdom is too high for a *f*:
26. 1 So honor is not seemly for a *f*.
4 Answer not a *f* according to his
5 Answer a *f* according to his folly,
6 a message by the hand of a *f*
8 so is he that giveth honor to a *f*.
10 rewardeth the *f*, and rewardeth
11 so a *f* returneth to his folly.
12 is more hope of a *f* than of him.
27.22 Though thou shouldest bray a *f* in
28.26 trusteth in his own heart is a *f*:
29.11 A *f* uttereth all his mind:
20 is more hope of a *f* than of him.
30.22 a *f* when he is filled with meat;
Ec 2.14 but the *f* walketh in darkness:
15 As it happeneth to the *f*, so it
16 of the wise more than of the *f*
16 how dieth the wise man? as the *f*.
19 he shall be a wise man or a *f*?
4. 5 The *f* foldeth his hands together,
6. 8 hath the wise more than the *f*?
7. 6 so is the laughter of the *f*:
10. 3 he that is a *f* walketh by the way,
3 he saith to every one that he is a *f*.
12 but the lips of a *f* will swallow up
14 A *f* also is full of words:
Jer 17.11 and at his end shall be a *f*.
Hos 9. 7 the prophet is a *f*, the spiritual
Mt 5.22 but whosoever shall say, Thou *f*,
Lk 12.20 Thou *f*, this night thy soul shall
1Co 3.18 become a *f*, that he may be wise.
15.36 Thou *f*, that which thou sowest
2Co 11.16 Let no man think me a *f*;
16 yet as a *f* receive me,
23 (I speak as a *f*) I am more;
12. 6 I shall not be a *f*; for I will say
11 I am become a *f* in glorying;

FOOLISH

Dt 32. 6 O *f* people and unwise? is not he
21 them to anger with a *f* nation.

Job 2.10 speakest as one of the *f* women
5. 2 For wrath killeth the *f* man,
3 I have seen the *f* taking root:
Ps 5. 5 The *f* shall not stand in thy
39. 8 me not the reproach of the *f*.
73. 3 For I was envious at the *f*,
22 So *f* was I, and ignorant: I was
74.18 the *f* people have blasphemed
22 the *f* man reproacheth thee daily.
Pr 9. 6 Forsake the *f*, and live; and go
13 A *f* woman is clamorous: she is
10. 1 a *f* son is the heaviness of his
14 mouth of the *f* is near destruction.
14. 1 but the *f* plucketh it down with
3 In the mouth of the *f* is a rod of
7 Go from the presence of a *f* man,
15. 7 but the heart of the *f* doeth not so.
20 but a *f* man despiseth his mother.
17.25 A *f* son is a grief to his father,
19.13 A *f* son is the calamity of his
21.20 but a *f* man spendeth it up.
29. 9 wise man contendeth with a *f* man,
Ec 4.13 an old and *f* king, who will no
7.17 neither be thou *f*: why shouldest
10.15 The labor of the *f* wearieth
Isa 44.25 and maketh their knowledge *f*;
Jer 4.22 For my people is *f*, they have not
5. 4 they are *f*: for they know not
21 Hear now this, O *f* people,
10. 8 they are altogether brutish and *f*:
La 2.14 seen vain and *f* things for thee:
Eze 13. 3 Woe unto the *f* prophets, that
Zec 11.15 the instruments of a *f* shepherd.
Mt 7.26 shall be likened unto a *f* man,
25. 2 them were wise, and five were *f*.
3 They that were *f* took their lamps,
8 And the *f* said unto the wise,
Ro 1.21 and their *f* heart was darkened.
2.20 An instructor of the *f*, a teacher
10.19 by a *f* nation I will anger you.
1Co 1.20 hath not God made *f* the wisdom
27 God hath chosen the *f* things of
Gal 3. 1 O *f* Galatians, who hath bewitched
3 Are ye so *f*? having begun in the
Eph 5. 4 nor *f* talking, nor jesting,
1Ti 6. 9 into many *f* and hurtful lusts,
2Ti 2.23 *f* and unlearned questions avoid,
Tit 3. 3 ourselves also were sometimes *f*,
9 *f* questions, and genealogies,
1Pe 2.15 to silence the ignorance of *f* men:

FOOLISHLY

Gen 31.28 thou hast now done *f* in so doing.
Nu 12.11 wherein we have done *f*, and
1Sa 13.13 Thou hast done *f*: thou hast not
2Sa 24.10 servant; for I have done very *f*
1Ch 21. 8 thy servant; for I have done very *f*.
2Ch 16. 9 Herein thou hast done *f*:
Job 1.22 sinned not, nor charged God *f*.
Ps 75. 4 Deal not *f*: and to the wicked,
Pr 14.17 He that is soon angry dealeth *f*:
30.32 If thou hast done *f* in lifting up
2Co 11.17 but as it were *f*, in this
21 (I speak *f*,) I am bold also.

FOOLISHNESS

2Sa 15.31 the counsel of Ahithopel into *f*.
Ps 38. 5 and are corrupt because of my *f*.
69. 5 O God, thou knowest my *f*;
Pr 12.23 the heart of fools proclaimeth *f*.
14.24 but the *f* of fools is folly.
15. 2 mouth of fools poureth out *f*.
14 the mouth of fools feedeth on *f*.
19. 3 The *f* of man perverteth his way:
22.15 *F* is bound in the heart of a child;
24. 9 The thought of *f* is sin:
27.22 yet will not his *f* depart from him.
Ec 7.25 of folly, even of *f* and madness:
10.13 of the words of his mouth is *f*:
Mk 7.22 an evil eye, blasphemy, pride, *f*:
1Co 1.18 the cross is to them that perish, *f*;
21 the *f* of preaching to save them
23 and unto the Greeks *f*;
25 the *f* of God is wiser than men;
2.14 for they are *f* unto him:
3.19 wisdom of this world is *f* with God.

FOOL'S

Pr 12.16 A *f* wrath is presently known: but
18. 6 A *f* lips enter into contention,
7 A *f* mouth is his destruction,
26. 3 the ass, and a rod for the *f* back.
27. 3 a *f* wrath is heavier than them
Ec 5. 3 a *f* voice is known by multitude
10. 2 but a *f* heart at his left.

FOOLS

2Sa 13.13 shalt be as one of the *f* in Israel.
Job 12.17 amd maketh the judges *f*.
30. 8 They were children of *f*, yea,
Ps 75. 4 I said unto the *f*, Deal not
94. 8 and ye *f*, when will ye be wise?
107.17 *F*, because of their transgression,
Pr 1. 7 *f* despise wisdom and instruction.
22 and *f* hate knowledge?
32 prosperity of *f* shall destroy them.
3.35 shame shall be the promotion of *f*.
8. 5 ye *f*, be ye of an understanding
10.21 but *f* die for want of wisdom.
12.23 but the heart of *f* proclaimeth
13.19 it is abomination to *f* to depart
20 companion of *f* shall be destroyed.
14. 8 but the folly of *f* is deceit.
9 *F* make a mock at sin: but
24 but the foolishness of *f* is folly.
33 that which is in the midst of *f*
15. 2 mouth of *f* poureth out foolishness
14 mouth of *f* feedeth on foolishness.
16.22 but the instruction of *f* is folly.
19.29 and stripes for the back of *f*.
26. 7, 9 is parable in the mouth of *f*.
Ec 5. 1 than to give the sacrifice of *f*:
4 for he hath no pleasure in *f*:
7. 4 but the heart of *f* is in the house of
5 for a man to hear the song of *f*.
9 for anger resteth in the bosom of *f*.
9.17 the cry of him that ruleth among *f*.
Isa 19.11 Surely the princes of Zoan are *f*,
13 The princes of Zoan are become *f*,
35. 8 wayfaring men, though *f*, shall not
Mt 23.17 Ye *f* and blind: for whether is
19 Ye *f* and blind: for whether is
Lk 11.40 Ye *f*, did not he that made that
24.25 O *f*, and slow of heart to believe
Ro 1.22 to be wise, they became *f*,
1Co 4.10 We are *f* for Christ's sake, but ye
2Co 11.19 For ye suffer *f* gladly, seeing ye
Eph 5.15 circumspectly, not as *f*, but as

FOOT

Gen 8. 9 found no rest for the sole of her *f*,
Ex 21.24 for tooth, hand for hand, *f* for *f*,
Nu 12.25 crushed Balaam's *f* against the
Dt 25. 9 and loose his shoe from off his *f*,
Jos 5.15 Loose thy shoe from off thy *f*;
2Sa 2.18 was as light of *f* as a wild roe.
Job 23.11 My *f* hath held his steps, his way
Ps 38.16 when my *f* slippeth, they magnify
91.12 thou dash thy *f* against a stone.
121. 3 will not suffer thy *f* to be moved:
Pr 3.23 and thy *f* shall not stumble.
4.27 to the left: remove thy *f* from evil.
25.17 thy *f* from thy neighbor's house:
Isa 20. 2 and put off thy shoe from thy *f*.
Eze 29.11 No *f* of man shall pass through it,
Am 2.15 that is swift of *f* shall not deliver
Mt 4. 6 lest at any time thou dash thy *f*
5.13 and to be trodden under *f* of men.
14.13 followed him on *f* out of the cities.
18. 8 if thy hand or thy *f*, offend thee,
22.13 Bind him hand and *f*, and take him
Mk 9.45 And if thy *f* offend thee, cut it off:
Lk 4.11 thou dash thy *f* against a stone.
Jn 11.44 hand and *f* with graveclothes:
Ac 7. 5 not so much as to set his *f* on:
1Co 12.15 If the *f* shall say, Because I am not
Heb 10.29 trodden under *f* the Son of God,
Rev 1.13 with a garment down to the *f*,
10. 2 and he set his right *f* upon the
2 sea, and his left *f* on the earth,
11. 2 the holy city shall they tread under *f*

FOOTSTOOL

1Ch 28. 2 and for the *f* of our God,
2Ch 9.18 to the throne, with a *f* of gold,
Ps 99. 5 and worship at his *f*; for he
110. 1 I make thine enemies thy *f*.
132. 7 we will worship at his *f*.
Isa 66. 1 and the earth is my *f*: where
La 2. 1 remembered not his *f* in the
Mt 5.35 earth: for it is his *f*:
22.44 thine enemies thy *f*?
Mk 12.36 thine enemies thy *f*.
Lk 20.43 thine enemies thy *f*.
Ac 2.35 make thy foes thy *f*.
7.49 and earth is my *f*:
Heb 1.13 thine enemies thy *f*?
10.13 enemies be made his *f*.
Jas 2. 3 or sit here under my *f*:

FORBAD

Dt 2.37 the Lord our God *f* us.
Mt 3.14 John *f* him, saying, I have need
Mk 9.38 we *f* him, because he followeth
Lk 9.49 we *f* him, because he followeth
2Pe 2.16 *f* the madness of the prophet.

FORBEAR

Ex 23. 5 and wouldest *f* to help him,
Dt 23.22 But if thou shalt *f* to vow,
1Ki 22. 6 battle, or shall I *f*? And they said,
15 or shall we *f*? And he answered
2Ch 18. 5 or shall I *f*? And they said,
14 to battle, or shall I *f*? And he said,
25.16 *f*; why shouldest thou be smitten?
35.21 *f* thee from meddling with God,
Neh 9.30 many years didst thou *f* them,
Job 16. 6 and though I *f*, what am I eased?
Pr 24.11 If thou *f* to deliver them that are
Jer 40. 4 to come with me into Babylon, *f*:
Eze 2. 5 will hear, or whether they will *f*,
7 will hear, or whether they will *f*:
3.11 will hear, or whether they will *f*.
27 he that forbeareth, let him *f*:
24.17 *F* to cry, make no mourning
Zec 11.12 and if not, *f*. So they weighed
1Co 9. 6 have not we power to *f* working?
2Co 12. 6 I *f*, lest any man should think of
1Th 3. 1 when we could no longer *f*, we
5 when I could no longer *f*, I went

FORBEARANCE

Ro 2. 4 the riches of his goodness and *f*
3.25 that are past, through the *f* of God;

FORBEARING

Pr 25.15 by long *f* is a prince persuaded,
Jer 20. 9 I was weary with *f*, and I could
Eph 4. 2 *f* one another in love;
6. 9 things unto them, *f* threatening:
Col 3.13 *F* one another, and forgiving one

FORBID

Gen 44. 7 God *f* that thy servants should
17 God *f* that I should do so:
Nu 11.28 said, My lord Moses, *f* them.
Jos 22.29 God *f* that we should rebel
24.16 God *f* that we should forsake the
1Sa 12.23 God *f* that I should sin against
14.45 God *f*: as the Lord liveth,
20. 2 And he said unto him, God *f*;
24. 6 he said unto his men, The Lord *f*
26.11 The Lord *f* that I should stretch

1Ki 21. 3 The Lord *f* it me, that I should
1Ch 11.19 And said, My God *f* it me,
Job 27. 5 God *f* that I should justify you:
Mt 19.14 and *f* them not, to come unto me:
Mk 9.39 But Jesus said, *F* him not:
10.14 to come unto me, and *f* them not:
Lk 6.29 *f* not to take thy coat also.
9.50 *F* him not: for he that is not
18.16 and *f* them not: for of such is the
20.16 heard it, they said, God *f*.
Ac 10.47 Can any man *f* water, that these
24.23 and that he should *f* none of his
Ro 3. 4 God *f*: let God be true, but
6 God *f*; for them how shall God
31 God *f*: yea, we establish the
6. 2 God *f*. How shall we, that are
15 law, but under grace? God *f*.
7. 7 Is the law sin? God *f*. Nay, I
13 made death unto me? God *f*.
9.14 unrighteousness...God? God *f*.
11. 1 cast away his people? God *f*.
11 that they should fall? God *f*:
1Co 6.15 members of an harlot? God *f*.
14.39 and *f* not to speak with tongues.
Gal 2.17 the ministers of sin? God *f*.
3.21 the promises of God? God *f*:
6.14 God *f* that I should glory,

FORBIDDEN
Lev 5.17 things which are *f* to be done by
Dt 4.23 the Lord thy God hath *f* thee.
Ac 16. 6 *f* of the Holy Ghost to preach

FORBIDDETH
3Jn 10 *f* them that would, and casteth

FORBIDDING
Lk 23. 2 *f* to give tribute to Caesar, saying
Ac 28.31 all confidence, no man *f* him.
1Th 2.16 *F* us to speak to the Gentiles
1Ti 4. 3 *F* to marry, and commanding to

FORCE
Gen 31.31 wouldest take by *f* thy daughters
Dt 22.25 the man *f* her, and lie with her:
34. 7 not dim, nor his natural *f* abated.
1Sa 2.16 and if not, I will take it by *f*.
2Sa 13.12 Nay, my brother, do not *f* me;
Ezr 4.23 them to cease by *f* and power.
Est 7. 8 he *f* the queen also before me
Job 30.18 By the great *f* of my disease
40.16 and his *f* is in the naval of his
Jer 18.21 their blood by the *f* of the sword
23.10 is evil, and their *f* is not right.
48.45 of Heshbon because of the *f*:
Eze 34. 4 but with *f* and with cruelty have
35. 5 by the *f* of the sword in the time
Am 2.14 strong shall not strengthen his *f*,
Mt 11.12 and the violent take it by *f*.
Jn 6.15 take him by *f*, to make him a king
Ac 23.10 to take him by *f* from among them,
Heb 9.17 a testament is of *f* after men are

FOREHEAD
Ex 28.38 And it shall be upon Aaron's *f*,
38 and it shall be always upon his *f*,
Lev 13.41 he is *f* bald: yet is he clean.
42 or bald *f*, a white reddish sore;
42 in his bald head, or his bald *f*.
43 or in his bald *f*, as the leprosy
1Sa 17.49 and smote the Philistine in his *f*,
49 that the stone sunk into his *f*;
2Ch 26.19 the leprosy even rose up in his *f*
20 behold, he was leprous in his *f*,
Jer 3. 3 and thou hadst a whore's *f*,
Eze 3. 8 *f* strong against their foreheads.
9 harder than flint have I made thy *f*.
16.12 And I put a jewel on thy *f*,
Rev 14. 9 and receive his mark in his *f*,
17. 5 upon her *f* was a name written,

FOREHEADS
Eze 3. 8 forehead strong against their *f*.
9. 4 set a mark upon the *f* of the men
Rev 7. 3 servants of our God in their *f*.
9. 4 have not the seal of God in their *f*.
13.16 in their right hand, or in their *f*:
14. 1 Father's name written in their *f*.
20. 4 received his mark upon their *f*,
22. 4 and his name shall be in their *f*.

FOREIGNERS
Ob 11 and *f* entered into his gates, and
Eph 2.19 ye are no more strangers and *f*,

FOREKNEW
Ro 11. 2 cast away his people which he *f*.

FOREKNOW
Ro 8.29 For whom he did *f*, he also did

FOREKNOWLEDGE
Ac 2.23 and *f* of God, ye have taken, and
1Pe 1. 2 Elect according to the *f* of God

FOREORDAINED
1Pe 1.20 Who verily was *f* before the

FOREPART
Ex 28.27 toward the *f* thereof, over against
39.20 ephod underneath, toward the *f*
1Ki 6.20 oracle in the *f* was twenty cubits
Eze 42. 7 court on the *f* of the chambers,
Ac 27.41 the *f* stuck fast, and remained

FORERUNNER
Heb 6.20 Whither the *f* is for us entered,

FORESAW
Ac 2.25 I *f* the Lord always before my

FORESEEING
Gal 3. 8 the scripture, *f* that God would

FORESHIP
Ac 27.30 have cast anchors out of the *f*,

FOREST
Ps 50.10 For every beast of the *f* is mine,
104.20 all the beasts of the *f* do creep
Isa 21.13 In the *f* in Arabia shall ye lodge,
Jer 5. 6 a lion out of the *f* shall slay them,
10. 3 one cutteth a tree out of the *f*,
Am 3. 4 Will a lion roar in the *f*, when he
Zec 11. 2 the *f* of the vintage is come down.

FORETELL
2Co 13. 2 and *f* you, as if I were present,

FORETOLD
Mk 13.23 behold, I have *f* you all things.
Ac 3.24 have likewise *f* of these days.

FOREWARN
Lk 12. 5 I will *f* you whom ye shall fear:

FOREWARNED
1Th 4. 6 all such as we also have *f* you and

FORGAVE
Ps 78.38 *f* their iniquity, and destroyed
Mt 18.27 loosed him, and *f* him the debt.
32 I *f* thee all that debt, because thou
Lk 7.42 to pay, he frankly *f* them both.
43 that he, to whom he *f* most.
2Co 2.10 if I *f* anything, to whom I *f* it,
10 for your sakes *f* I it in the person
Col 3.13 even as Christ *f* you, so also do ye.

FORGAVEST
Ps 32. 5 and thou *f* the iniquity of my sin.
99. 8 thou wast a God that *f* them,

FORGET
Gen 41.51 hath made me *f* all my toil,
Dt 4.23 lest ye *f* the covenant of the Lord
8.11 Beware that thou *f* not the Lord
Job 8.13 So are the paths of all that *f* God;
Ps 9.17 and all the nations that *f* God.
10.12 thine hand; *f* not the humble.
13. 1 How long wilt thou *f* me, O Lord?
74.19 *f* not the congregation of thy poor
78. 7 and not *f* the works of God,
102. 4 so that I *f* to eat my bread.
103. 2 my soul, and *f* not all his benefits:
119.16 thy statutes: I will not *f* thy word.
137. 5 If I *f* thee, O Jerusalem,
5 let my right hand *f* her cunning.
Pr 3. 1 My son, *f* not my law; but let thine
4. 5 get understanding: *f* it not;
Isa 49.15 Can a woman *f* her sucking child,
15 yet will I not *f* thee.
Jer 2.32 Can a maid *f* her ornaments,
La 5.20 Wherefore dost thou *f* us for ever,
Am 8. 7 I will never *f* any of their works.
Heb 6.10 to *f* your work and labor of love,
13.16 do good and to communicate *f* not:

FORGETFUL
Heb 13. 2 Be not *f* to entertain strangers:
Jas 1.25 being not a *f* hearer, but a doer

FORGETTETH
Job 39.15 And *f* that the foot may crush
Ps 9.12 he *f* not the cry of the humble.
Pr 2.17 and *f* the covenant of her God.
Jas 1.24 *f* what manner of man he was.

FORGETTING
Php 3.13 *f* those things which are behind,

FORGIVE
Gen 50.17 *F*, I pray thee now the trespass,
17 *f* the trespass of the servants of the
Ex 10.17 Now therefore *f*, I pray thee, my
32.32 Yet now, if thou wilt *f* their sin—;
Nu 30. 5 the Lord shall *f* her, because her
8 effect: and the Lord shall *f* her.
12 void; and the Lord shall *f* her,
Jos 24.19 he will not *f* your transgressions
1Sa 25.28 I pray thee, *f* the trespass of thine
1Ki 8.30 and when thou hearest, *f*.
34 and *f* the sin of thy people Israel,
36 and *f* the sin of thy servants,
39 heaven thy dwelling place, and *f*,
50 And *f* thy people that have sinned
2Ch 6.21 heaven; and when thou hearest, *f*.
25 hear thou from the heavens, and *f*
27 hear thou from heaven, and *f*
30 heaven, thy dwelling place, and *f*,
39 and *f* thy people which have
7.14 and will *f* their sin, and will heal
Ps 25.18 my pain; and *f* all my sins.
86. 5 Lord, art good and ready to *f*;
Isa 2. 9 himself: therefore *f* them not.
Jer 18.23 *f* not their iniquity, neither blot
31.34 I will *f* their iniquity, and I will
36. 3 that I may *f* their iniquity and
Dan 9.19 O Lord, hear; O Lord, *f*;
Am 7. 2 O Lord God *f*, I beseech thee:
Mt 6.12 *f* us our debts, as we *f* our
14 For if we *f* men their trespasses,
14 your heavenly Father will also *f*
15 will your Father *f* your trespasses.
9. 6 hath power on earth to *f* sins,
18.21 my brother sin against me and I *f*
35 *f* not every one his brother their
Mk 2. 7 who can *f* sins but God only?
10 man hath power on earth to *f* sins,
11.25 *f*, if ye have ought against any:
25 may *f* you your trespasses.
26 if ye do not *f*, neither will your
26 in heaven *f* your trespasses.

BIBLICAL THEMES

FORGIVENESS

Abraham . . . said, Wilt thou also destroy the righteous with the wicked? Peradventure there be fifty righteous within the city: wilt thou also destroy and not spare the place for the fifty righteous that are therein? . . . Shall not the Judge of all the earth do right? And the Lord said, If I find in Sodom fifty righteous within the city, then I will spare all the place for their sakes.
Gen 18.23-26

And David said to Saul, . . . Behold, this day thine eyes have seen how that the Lord had delivered thee to day into mine hand in the cave: and some bade me kill thee: but mine eye spared thee; and I said, I will not put forth mine hand against my lord; for he is the Lord's anointed. 1Sa 24.9-10

Have mercy upon me, O God, according to thy lovingkindness: according unto the multitude of thy tender mercies blot out my transgressions. Wash me throughly from mine iniquity, and cleanse me from my sin. Ps 51.1-2

If thou, Lord, shouldest mark iniquities, O Lord, who shall stand? But there is forgiveness with thee, that thou mayest be feared. Ps 130.3-4

Come now, and let us reason together, saith the Lord: though your sins be as scarlet, they shall be as white as snow; though they be red like crimson, they shall be as wool. Isa 1.18

Let the wicked forsake his way, and the unrighteous man his thoughts: and let him return unto the Lord, and he will have mercy upon him; and to our God, for he will abundantly pardon.
Isa 55.7

Who is a God like unto thee, that pardoneth iniquity . . . ? he retaineth not his anger for ever, because he delighteth in mercy. . . . he will have compassion upon us; he will subdue our iniquities. Mic 7.18-19

Forgive us our debts, as we forgive our debtors. Mt 6.12

Wherefore I say unto you, All manner of sin and blasphemy shall be forgiven unto men: but the blasphemy against the Holy Ghost shall not be forgiven unto men. Mt 12.31

Then came Peter to him, and said, Lord, how oft shall my brother sin against me, and I forgive him? till seven times? Jesus saith unto him, I say not unto thee, Until seven times: but, Until seventy times seven. Mt 18.21-22

When ye stand praying, forgive, if ye have ought against any: that your Father also which is in heaven may forgive you your trespasses. Mk 11.25

And thou, child, shalt be called the prophet of the Highest: for thou shalt . . . give knowledge of salvation unto his people by the remission of their sins.
Lk 1.76-77

And he said unto her, Thy sins are forgiven. And they that sat at meat with him began to say within themselves, Who is this that forgiveth sins also? And he said to the woman, Thy faith hath saved thee; go in peace.
Lk 7.48-50

Then said Jesus, Father, forgive them; for they know not what they do.
Lk 23.34

Repent ye therefore, and be converted, that your sins may be blotted out, when the times of refreshing shall come from the presence of the Lord. Ac 3.19

Blessed are they whose iniquities are forgiven, and whose sins are covered.
Ro 4.7

Who hath delivered us from the power of darkness, and hath translated us into the kingdom of his dear Son: in whom we have redemption through his blood, even the forgiveness of sins. Col 1.13-14

Herein is love, not that we loved God, but that he loved us, and sent his Son to be the propitiation for our sins.
1Jn 4.10

Lk 5.21 Who can *f* sins, but God alone?
24 hath power upon earth to *f* sins,
6.37 *f* and ye shall be forgiven:
11. 4 *f* us our sins; for we also *f* every
17. 3 and if he repent, *f* him.
4 saying, I repent; thou shalt *f* him.
23.34 Then said Jesus, Father, *f* them;
2Co 2. 7 ought rather to *f* him, and comfort
10 To whom ye *f* anything, I *f* also:
12.13 to you? *f* me this wrong.
1Jn 1. 9 faithful and just to *f* us our sins,

FORGIVEN

Lev 4.20 for them, and it shall be *f* them.
26 concerning his sin, and it shall be *f*
31 for him, and it shall be *f* him.
35 committed, and it shall be *f* him.
5.10 hath sinned, and it shall be *f* him.
13 of these, and it shall be *f* him:
16 offering, and it shall be *f* him.
18 it not, and it shall be forgiven him.
6. 7 shall be *f* him for any thing of all
19.22 which he hath done shall be *f* him.
Nu 14.19 and as thou hast *f* this people,
15.25 and it shall be *f* them; for it is
26 it shall be *f* all the congregation
28 for him; and it shall be *f* him.
Dt 21. 8 And the blood shall be *f* them.
Ps 32. 1 is he whose transgression is *f*,
85. 2 Thou hast *f* the iniquity of thy
Isa 33.24 that dwell therein shall be *f* their
Mt 9. 2 be of good cheer; thy sins be *f*
5 to say, Thy sins be *f* thee;
12.31 and blasphemy shall be *f* unto
31 the Holy Ghost shall not be *f* unto
32 the Son of man, it shall be *f* him:
32 Holy Ghost, it shall not be *f* him,
Mk 2. 5 the palsy, Son, thy sins be *f* thee.
9 Thy sins be *f* thee; or to say, Arise,
3.28 All sins shall be *f* unto the sons of
4.12 and their sins should be *f* them.
Lk 5.20 unto him, Man, thy sins are *f* thee.
23 Thy sins be *f* thee; or to say, Rise
6.37 forgive, and ye shall be *f*:
7.47 Her sins, which are many, are *f*;
47 to whom little is *f*, the same loveth
48 he said unto her, Thy sins are *f*.
12.10 the Son of man, it shall be *f* him;
10 the Holy Ghost it shall not be *f*.
Ac 8.22 thought of thine heart may be *f* thee.
Ro 4. 7 are they whose iniquities are *f*,
Eph 4.32 God for Christ's sake hath *f* you.
Col 2.13 having *f* you all trespasses;
Jas 5.15 sins, they shall be *f* him.
1Jn 2.12 because your sins are *f* you for

FORGIVENESS

Ps 130. 4 But there is *f* with thee, that thou
Mk 3.29 the Holy Ghost hath never *f*,
Ac 5.31 repentance to Israel, and *f* of
13.38 preached unto you the *f* of sins:
26.18 that they may receive *f* of sins,
Eph 1. 7 the *f* of sins, according to the
Col 1.14 through his blood, even the *f* of sins:

FORGIVETH

Ps 103. 3 Who *f* all thine iniquities; who
Lk 7.49 Who is this that *f* sins also?

FORGIVING

Ex 34. 7 for thousands, *f* iniquity and
Nu 14.18 of great mercy, *f* iniquity and
Eph 4.32 *f* one another, even as God for
Col 3.13 and *f* one another, if any man

FORGOTTEN

Gen 41.30 and all the plenty shall be *f* in
Dt 32.18 and hast *f* God that formed thee.
Job 19.14 and my familiar friends have *f* me.
Ps 10.11 hath said in his heart, God hath *f*:
42. 9 Why hast thou *f* me? why go I
44.17 yet have we not *f* thee, neither
20 If we have *f* the name of our God,
77. 9 Hath God *f* to be gracious? hath
Isa 49.14 and my Lord hath *f* me.
Jer 3.21 they have *f* the Lord their God.
La 2. 6 solemn feasts and sabbaths to be *f*
Eze 22.12 and hast *f* me, saith the Lord God.
Hos 8.14 For Israel hath *f* his Maker,
Mt 16. 5 side, they had *f* to take bread.
Mk 8.14 disciples had *f* to take bread,
Lk 12. 6 not one of them is *f* before God?
Heb 12. 5 And ye have *f* the exhortation
2Pe 1. 9 hath *f* that he was purged

FORM

Gen 1. 2 And the earth was without *f*,
1Sa 28.14 said unto her, What *f* is he of?
2Sa 14.20 To fetch about this *f* of speech
2Ch 4. 7 of gold according to their *f*, and
Job 4.16 I could not discern the *f* thereof:
Isa 45. 7 I *f* the light, and create darkness:
52.14 his *f* more than the sons of men:
53. 2 he hath no *f* nor comeliness;

Jer 4.23 earth, and, lo, it was without *f*,
Eze 8. 3 he put forth the *f* of an hand,
10 behold every *f* of creeping things,
10. 8 the *f* of a man's hand under their
43.11 shew them the *f* of the house,
11 may keep the whole *f* thereof,
Dan 2.31 and the *f* thereof was terrible.
3.19 the *f* of his visage was changed
25 *f* of the fourth is like the Son of
Mk 16.12 he appeared in another *f* unto
Ro 2.20 which hast the *f* of knowledge
6.17 that *f* of doctrine which was
Php 2. 6 Who, being in the *f* of God,
7 took upon him the *f* of a servant,
2Ti 1.13 Hold fast the *f* of sound words,
3. 5 Having a *f* of godliness, but

FORMED

Gen 2. 7 And the Lord God *f* man of the
Dt 32.18 hast forgotten God that *f* thee.
Job 33. 6 I also am *f* out of the clay.
Ps 90. 2 or ever thou hadst *f* the earth
94. 9 that *f* the eye, shall he not see?
95. 5 and his hands *f* the dry land.
Pr 26.10 The great God that *f* all things
Isa 43. 1 and he that *f* thee, O Israel,
21 This people have I *f* for myself;
44. 2 and *f* thee from the womb,
10 Who hath *f* a god, or molten a
45.18 God himself that *f* the earth and
18 he *f* it to be inhabited: I am the
Jer 1. 5 Before I *f* thee in the belly
Ro 9.20 the thing *f* say to him that *f* it,
Gal 4.19 until Christ be *f* in you,
1Ti 2.13 Adam was first *f*, then Eve.

FORMER

Dt 24. 4 Her *f* husband, which sent her
Ps 79. 8 not against us *f* iniquities:
89.49 where are thy *f* lovingkindnesses,
Ec 7.10 the *f* days were better than these?
Isa 43.18 Remember ye not the *f* things,
65.16 the *f* troubles are forgotten,
Jer 5.24 rain, both the *f* and the latter,
51.19 for he is the *f* of all things:
Hos 6. 3 latter and *f* rain unto the earth.
Joel 2.23 given you the *f* rain moderately.
23 the *f* rain, and the latter rain
Ac 1. 1 The *f* treatise have I made, O
Eph 4.22 concerning the *f* conversation
Heb 10.32 call to remembrance the *f* days,
1Pe 1.14 according to the *f* lusts in your
Rev 21. 4 for the *f* things are passed away,

FORNICATION

2Ch 21.11 of Jerusalem to commit *f*, and
Isa 23.17 and shall commit *f* with all the
Eze 16.26 Thou hast also committed *f* with
29 hast moreover multiplied thy *f*
Mt 5.32 his wife, saving for the cause of *f*,
19. 9 away his wife, except it be for *f*,
Jn 8.41 We be not born of *f*, we have one
Ac 15.20 from *f*, and from things strangled
29 from things strangled, and from *f*:
21.25 and from strangled, and from *f*.
Ro 1.29 *f*. wickedness, covetousness,
1Co 5. 1 that there is *f* among you, and
1 such *f* as is not so much as
6.13 Now the body is not for *f*,
18 Flee *f*. Every sin that a man doeth
18 but he that committeth *f* sinneth
7. 2 to avoid *f*, let every man have
10. 8 Neither let us commit *f*, as some
2Co 12.21 and *f* and lasciviousness which
Gal 5.19 Adultery, *f*, uncleanness,
Eph 5. 3 But *f*, and all uncleanness, or
Col 3. 5 *f*, uncleanness, inordinate
1Th 4. 3 that ye should abstain from *f*:
Jude 7 giving themselves over to *f*,
Rev 2.14 unto idols, and to commit *f*.
20 to commit *f*, and to eat things
21 gave her space to repent of her *f*;
9.21 nor of their *f*, nor of their thefts.
14. 8 the wine of the wrath of her *f*.
17. 2 of the earth have committed *f*.
2 drunk with the wine of her *f*.
4 and filthiness of her *f*:
18. 3 of the wine of the wrath of her *f*,
3 have committed *f* with her, and
9 who have committed *f* and lived
19. 2 did corrupt the earth with her *f*,

FORNICATIONS

Eze 16.15 pouredst out thy *f* on every one
Mt 15.19 thoughts, murders, adulteries, *f*,
Mk 7.21 evil thoughts, adulteries, *f*,

FORNICATOR

1Co 5.11 Man that is called a brother be a *f*,
Heb 12.10 Lest there be any *f*, or profane

FORNICATORS

1Co 5. 9 an epistle not to company with *f*:
10 altogether with the *f* of this world.
6. 9 neither *f*, nor idolaters, nor

FORSAKE

Dt 4.31 he will not *f* thee, neither destroy
31.16 will *f* me, and break my covenant
17 and I will *f* them, and I will hide
Jos 1. 5 I will not fail thee, nor *f* thee.
24.20 If ye *f* the Lord, and serve strange
1Ki 8.57 let him not leave us, nor *f* us:
1Ch 28.20 he will not fail thee, nor *f* thee,
2Ch 15. 2 but if ye *f* him, he will *f* you.
Ps 27. 9 leave me not, neither *f* me, O God
10 my father and my mother *f* me,
37. 8 Cease from anger, and *f* wrath:
38.21 *F* me not, O Lord: O my God,
71. 9 *f* me not when my strength faileth.
18 O God, *f* me not; until I have
138. 8 *f* not the works of thine own
Pr 1. 8 and *f* not the law of thy mother:
3. 3 Let not mercy and truth *f* thee:
9. 6 *F* the foolish, and live; and go
Isa 55. 7 Let the wicked *f* his way, and the
65.11 But ye are they that *f* the Lord,
Jer 23.39 and I will *f* you, and the city
La 5.20 thou forget us for ever, and *f* us
Eze 20. 8 did they *f* the idols of Egypt:
Ac 21.21 among the Gentiles to *f* Moses,
Heb 13. 5 I will never leave thee, nor *f* thee.

FORSAKEN

Dt 29.25 they have *f* the covenant of the
Jdg 6.13 but now the Lord hath *f* us,
10.13 have *f* me, and served other gods:
1Ki 18.18 *f* the commandments of the Lord,
Ezr 9. 9 yet our God hath not *f* us
Neh 13.11 Why is the house of God *f*?
Job 18. 4 shall the earth be *f* for thee?
20.19 oppressed and hath *f* the poor;
Ps 22. 1 my God, why hast thou *f* me?
37.25 have I not seen the righteous *f*,
71.11 God hath *f* him: persecute and
Isa 49.14 Zion said. The Lord hath *f* me,
62. 4 Thou shalt no more be termed *F*;
12 called, Sought out, A city not *f*.
Jer 15. 6 Thou hast *f* me, saith the Lord,
16.11 fathers have *f* me, saith the Lord,
Eze 8.12 not; the Lord hath *f* the earth.
9. 9 say, The Lord hath *f* the earth.
Mt 19.27 we have *f* all, and followed thee;
29 every one that hath *f* houses,
27.46 my God, why hast thou *f* me?
Mk 15.34 God, my God, why hast thou *f* me?
2Co 4. 9 Persecuted, but not *f*; cast down,
2Ti 4.10 Demas hath *f* me, having loved
2Pe 2.15 Which have *f* the right way, and

FORSAKETH

Job 6.14 he *f* the fear of the Almighty.
Ps 37.28 judgment, and *f* not his saints;
Pr 2.17 Which *f* the guide of her youth,
15.10 is grievous unto him that *f* the way;
28.13 confesseth and *f* them shall have
Lk 14.33 of you that *f* not all that he hath,

FORSAKING

Isa 6.12 there be a great *f* in the midst
Heb 10.25 Not *f* the assembling of ourselves

FORSOMUCH

Lk 19. 9 *f* as he also is a son of Abraham.

FORSOOK

Dt 32.15 then he *f* God which made him,
Jdg 2.12 *f* the Lord God of their fathers,
13 they *f* the Lord, and served Baal
10. 6 *f* the Lord, and served not him.
1Sa 31. 7 they *f* the cities, and fled; and the
1Ki 9. 9 Because they *f* the Lord their God,
12. 8 he *f* the counsel of the old men,
13 and *f* the old men's counsel that
2Ki 21.22 he *f* the Lord God of his fathers,
1Ch 10. 7 then they *f* their cities, and fled;
2Ch 7.22 they *f* the Lord God of their fathers,
10. 8 he *f* the counsel which the old men
13 Rehoboam *f* the counsel of the old.
12. 1 he *f* the law of the Lord, and all
Ps 78.60 he *f* the tabernacle of Shiloh,
119.87 earth; but I *f* not thy precepts.
Isa 58. 2 *f* not the ordinance of their God;
Jer 14. 5 also calved in the field, and *f* it,
Mt 26.56 all the disciples *f* him, and fled.
Mk 1.18 they *f* their nets, and followed
14.50 And they all *f* him, and fled.
Lk 5.11 land, they *f* all, and followed him.
2Ti 4.16 stood with me, but all men *f* me;
Heb 11.27 By faith he *f* Egypt, not fearing

FORSWEAR

Mt 5.33 Thou shalt not *f* thyself, but shalt

FORT

2Sa 5. 9 David dwelt in the *f*, and called
Isa 25.12 fortress of the high *f* of thy walls
Eze 4. 2 and build a *f* against it, and cast
21.22 to cast a mount, and to build a *f*.
26. 8 he shall make a *f* against thee,
Dan 11.19 shall turn his face toward the *f*

FORTH

Gen 1.11 said, Let the earth bring *f* grass,
12 And the earth brought *f* grass,
20 God said, Let the waters bring *f*
24 earth bring *f* the living creature
3.16 thou shalt bring *f* children; and
23 God sent him *f* from the garden
8.16 Go *f* of the ark, thou, and thy wife,
17 Bring *f* with thee every living
18 And Noah went *f*, and his sons,
9. 7 bring *f* abundantly in the earth,
42.15 Pharaoh ye shall not go *f* hence,
Ex 7. 5 stretch *f* mine hand upon Egypt,
8. 5 Stretch *f* thine hand with thy rod over
9.23 And Moses stretched *f* his rod toward
13.16 the Lord brought us *f* out of Egypt.
16. 3 brought us *f* into this wilderness,
Nu 11.20 Why came we *f* out of Egypt?
24. 8 God brought him *f* out of Egypt;
Dt 16. 6 that thou camest *f* out of Egypt.
26. 8 Lord brought us *f* out of Egypt
Jdg 5.31 sun when he goeth *f* in his might.
14.12 I will now put *f* a riddle unto you:
13 Put *f* thy riddle, that we may hear
14 Out of the eater came *f* meat,
14 out of the strong came *f* sweetness.
16 thou hast put *f* a riddle unto the
1Sa 26. 9 for who can stretch *f* his hand against
1Ki 8.22 spread *f* his hands toward heaven:
38 spread *f* his hands toward this house:
19.11 And he said, Go *f*, and stand upon
2Ki 2.23 there came *f* little children out of

2Ki 10.26 And they brought *f* the images out
11. 7 of all you that go *f* on the sabbath,
12 And he brought *f* the king's son.
19. 3 there is no strength to bring *f*.
31 Jerusalem shall go *f* a remnant,
1Ch 14.15 for God is gone *f* before thee to
Neh 9. 7 and broughtest him *f* out of Ur of
Job 1.11 But put *f* thine hand now, and
12 went *f* from the presence of the
2. 7 went Satan *f* from the presence
14. 2 He cometh *f* like a flower, and is
28. 9 He putteth *f* his hand upon the
Ps 1. 3 that bringeth *f* his fruit in his
9. 1 I will shew *f* all thy marvellous
14 that I may shew *f* all thy praise
18.19 He brought me *f* also into a large
19. 6 His going *f* is from the end of the
37. 6 shall bring *f* thy righteousness
51.15 and my mouth shall shew *f* thy
57. 3 God shall send *f* his mercy and his
71.15 shall shew *f* thy righteousness
79.13 we will show *f* thy praise to all
80. 1 between the cherubims, shine *f*.
88. 8 am shut up, and I cannot come *f*.
90. 2 the mountains were brought *f*,
92. 2 To shew *f* thy lovingkindness
96. 2 shew *f* his salvation from day to
104.20 all the beasts of the forest do creep *f*,
23 Man goeth *f* unto his work and
30 Thou sendest *f* thy spirit, they are
106. 2 who can shew *f* all his praise?
107. 7 he led them *f* by the right way,
121. 8 thy coming in from this time *f*,
141. 2 be set *f* before thee as incense;
144. 6 Cast *f* lightning, and scatter them:
147.15 He sendeth *f* his commandment
17 He casteth *f* his ice like morsels:
Pr 8.25 before the hills was I brought *f*:
12.17 truth sheweth *f* righteousness:
27. 1 not what a day may bring *f*.
30.33 forcing of wrath bringeth *f* strife.
Isa 5. 2 that it should bring *f* grapes,
2 and it brought *f* wild grapes.
14. 7 they break *f* into singing.
42. 3 bring *f* judgment unto truth.
5 he that spread *f* the earth,
9 before they spring *f* I tell you
13 Lord shall go *f* as a mighty man,
43. 8 Bring *f* the blind people that have
21 they shall shew *f* my praise.
44.23 break *f* into singing, ye
49.13 and break *f* into singing,
51. 5 my salvation is gone *f*, and mine
52. 9 Break *f* into joy, sing together,
54. 1 break *f* into singing, and cry
55.10 and maketh it bring *f* and bud,
11 So shall my word be that goeth *f*
12 and be led *f* with peace:
58. 8 Then shall the light break *f* as
61.11 as the earth bringeth *f* her bud,
66. 7 she travailed, she brought *f*;
Jer 10.20 my children are gone *f* of me.
20 there is none to stretch *f* my tent
15. 2 Whither shall ye go *f*? then thou
23.19 the Lord is gone *f* in fury, even
30.23 the Lord goeth *f* with fury, a
Eze 8. 3 And he put *f* the form of an hand,
17. 2 Son of man, put *f* a riddle, and
47.12 it shall bring *f* new fruit according
Dan 2.13 decree went *f* that the wise men
Hos 6. 3 his going *f* is prepared as the
5 are as the light that goeth *f*.
Joel 2.16 bridegroom go *f* of his chamber
Jon 1.12 and cast me *f* into the sea: so
15 cast him *f* into the sea: and the sea
Mic 4.10 labor to bring *f*, O daughter of
10 go *f* out of the city, and thou
Hab 3. 5 burning coals went *f* at his feet.
Zec 3. 8 bring *f* my servant the Branch.
12. 1 which stretcheth *f* the heavens,
Mt 1.21 And she shall bring *f* a son, and
23 and shall bring *f* a son, and they
25 till she had brought *f* her firstborn
2.16 sent *f*, and slew all the children
3. 8 Bring *f* therefore fruits, meet for
10 which bringeth not *f* good fruit
7.17 good tree bringth *f* good fruit;
17 corrupt tree bringeth *f* evil fruit.
18 good tree cannot bring *f* evil fruit,
18 neither can a corrupt tree bring *f*
19 tree that bringeth not *f* good fruit
8. 3 And Jesus put *f* his hand,
9. 9 as Jesus passed *f* from thence
25 But when the people were put *f*,
38 that he will send *f* laborers
10. 5 These twelve Jesus sent *f*, and
16 Behold, I send you *f* as sheep
12.13 Stretch *f* thine hand.
13 And he stretched it *f*;
20 till he send *f* judgment unto
35 of the heart bringeth *f* good things:
35 treasure bringeth *f* evil things.
49 And he stretched *f* his hand
13. 3 Behold a sower went *f* to sow;
8 good ground, and brought *f* fruit,
23 beareth fruit, and bringeth *f*,
24 Another parable put he *f* unto
26 sprung up, and brought *f* fruit,
31 Another parable put he *f* unto
41 The son of man shall send *f* his
43 Then shall the righteous shine *f*
49 the angels shall come *f*,
52 bringeth *f* out of his treasure
14. 2 therefore mighty works do shew *f*
14 And Jesus went *f*, and saw
31 immediately Jesus stretched *f*
15.18 mouth come *f* from the heart;
16.21 From that time *f* began Jesus to
21.43 to a nation bringing *f* the fruits
22. 3 sent *f* his servants to call them
4 he sent *f* other servants, saying,
7 sent *f* his armies, and destroyed
46 from that day *f* ask him any more
24.26 go not *f*: behold, he is in the secret
32 and putteth *f* leaves, ye know that
25. 1 went *f* to meet the bridegroom.
Mk 1.38 there also: for therefore came I *f*.
41 put *f* his hand, and touched him,
2.12 and went *f* before them all:
13 And he went *f* again by the sea side
3. 3 he saith... Stand *f*.
5 the man, Stretch *f* thine hand.
6 And the Pharisees went *f*, and
14 he might send them *f* to preach,
4. 8 brought *f*, some thirty, and some
20 and bring *f* fruit, some thirtyfold,
28 earth bringeth *f* fruit of herself;
29 fruit is brought *f*, immediately he
6. 7 to send them *f* by two and two;
14 mighty works do shew *f*
17 Herod himself had sent *f* and laid
24 And she went *f* and said unto her
7.26 he would cast *f* the devil out of
8.11 the Pharisees came *f*, and began
9.29 This kind can come *f* by nothing,
10.17 when he was gone *f* into the way,
11. 1 sendeth *f* two of his disciples,
13.28 and putteth *f* leaves, ye know that
14.13 he sendeth *f* two of his disciples,
16 his disciples went *f*, and came
16.20 they went *f*, and preached every
Lk 1. 1 to set *f* in order a declaration
31 bring *f* a son, and shalt call his
57 be delivered; and she brought *f*
2. 7 she brought *f* her firstborn son,
3. 7 that came *f* to be baptized of
8 Bring *f* therefore fruits worthy of
9 which bringeth not *f* good fruit
5.13 he put *f* his hand, and touched
27 after these things he went *f*, and
6. 8 Rise up, and stand *f* in the midst.
8 And he arose and stood *f*.
10 unto the man, Stretch *f* thy hand.
43 bringeth not *f* corrupt fruit;
43 a corrupt tree bring *f* good fruit.
45 bringeth *f* that which is good;
45 treasure of his hearth bringeth *f*
7.17 of him went *f* throughout all
8.14 when they have heard, go *f*, and
15 and bring *f* fruit with patience.
22 of the lake. And they launched *f*.
27 And when he went *f* to land,
10. 2 that he would send *f* laborers
3 I sent you *f* as lambs among
12.16 rich man brought *f* plentifully;
37 and will come *f* and serve them,
14. 7 put *f* a parable to those which
15.22 Bring *f* the best robe, and put it
20. 9 and let it *f* to husbandmen, and
20 sent *f* spies, which should feign
21.30 When they now shoot *f*, ye see
22.53 ye stretched *f* no hands against
Jn 1.43 Jesus would go *f* into Galilee,
2.10 doth set *f* good wine; and when
11 and manifested *f* his glory;
5.29 And shall come *f*; they that have
8.42 I proceeded *f* and came from God;
10. 4 when he putteth *f* his own sheep,
11.43 a loud voice, Lazarus, come *f*.
44 he that was dead came *f*, bound
53 from that day *f* they took counsel
12.13 went *f* to meet him, and cried,
24 if it die, it bringeth *f* much fruit.
15. 2 that it may bring *f* more fruit,
5 the same bringeth *f* much fruit:
6 he is cast *f* as a branch, and is
16 should go and bring *f* fruit, and
16.28 I came *f* from the Father, and
30 that thou camest *f* from God.
18. 1 *f* with his disciples over the brook
4 went *f*, and said unto them, Whom
19. 4 Pilate therefore went *f* again,
4 unto them, Behold, I bring him *f*
5 came Jesus *f*, wearing the crown
13 he brought Jesus *f*, and sat down
17 went *f* into a place called the
20. 3 Peter therefore went *f*, and that
21. 3 went *f*, and entered into a ship
18 thou shalt stretch *f* thy hands,
Ac 1.26 And they gave *f* their lots; and
2.33 he hath shed *f* this, which ye now
4.30 By stretching *f* thine hand to heal;
5.10 and, carrying her *f*, buried her by
15 brought *f* the sick into the streets,
19 and brought them *f*, and said,
34 put the apostles *f* a little space;
7. 7 shall they come *f*, and serve me
9.30 Caesarea, and sent him *f* to Tarsus.
40 Peter put them all *f*, and kneeled
11.22 they sent *f* Barnabas, that he
12. 1 the king stretched *f* his hands to
4 Easter to bring him *f* to the people.
6 Herod would have brought him *f*,
13. 4 being sent *f* by the Holy Ghost,
16. 3 would Paul have to go *f* with him;
17.18 to be a setter *f* of strange gods:
21. 2 we went aboard, and set *f*.
23.28 brought him *f* into their council:
24. 2 he was called *f*, Tertullus began
25.17 the man to be brought *f*.
23 Paul was brought *f*.
26 have brought him *f* before you,
26. 1 Then Paul stretched *f* the hand,
25 but speak *f* the words of truth and
27.21 Paul stood *f* in the midst of them,
Ro 3.25 Whom God hath set *f* to be a
7. 4 that we should bring *f* fruit unto
5 our members to bring *f* fruit unto
10.21 I have stretched *f* my hands unto
1Co 4. 9 God hath set *f* us the apostles
16.11 but conduct him *f* in peace, that
Gal 3. 1 Christ hath been evidently set *f*,
4. 4 God sent *f* his son, made of a

6 God hath sent *f* the Spirit of his
27 *f* and cry, thou that travailest
Php 2.16 Holding *f* the word of life; that I
3.13 and reaching *f* unto those things
Col 1. 6 and bringeth *f* fruit, as it doth
1Ti 1.16 Jesus Christ might shew *f* all
Heb 6. 7 bringeth *f* herbs meet for them
13.13 Let us go *f* therefore unto him
Jas 1.15 lust hath conceived, it bringeth *f*
15 it is finished, bringeth *f* death.
3.11 Doth a fountain send *f* at the same
5.18 and the earth brought *f* her fruit.
1Pe 2. 9 that ye should shew *f* the praises
3Jn 7 for his name's sake they went *f*,
Jude 7 are set *f* for an example, suffering
Rev 5. 6 seven spirits of God sent *f* into
6. 2 went *f* conquering, and to conquer.
12. 5 And she brought *f* a man child,
13 woman which brought *f* the man
16.14 go *f* unto the kings of the earth

FORTHWITH

Ezr 6. 8 *f* expences be given unto these
Mt 13. 5 *f* they sprung up, because they
26.49 *f* he came to Jesus, and said,
Mk 1.29 *f*, when they were come out of
43 charged him, and *f* sent him away;
5.13 And *f* Jesus gave them leave.
Jn 19.34 *f* came thereout blood and water.
Ac 9.18 he received sight *f*, and arose,
12.10 *f* the angel departed from him.
21.30 and *f* the doors were shut.

FORTIETH

Nu 33.38 and died there, in the *f* year after
Dt 1. 3 and it came to pass in the *f* year,
1Ch 26.31 In the *f* year of the reign of David
2Ch 16.13 and died in the one and *f* year of

FORTRESS

2Sa 22. 2 The Lord is my rock, and my *f*,
Ps 18. 2 rock, and my *f*, and my deliverer;
31. 3 For thou art my rock and my *f*;
71. 3 for thou art my rock and my *f*.
91. 2 He is my refuge and my *f*:
144. 2 My goodness, and my *f*; my high
Isa 17. 3 *f* also shall cease from Ephraim,
25.12 And the *f* of the high fort of thy
Jer 6.27 a tower and a *f* among my people,
10.17 the land, O inhabitant of the *f*.
16.19 O Lord, my strength, and my *f*,
Dan 11. 7 shall enter into the *f* of the king
10 and be stirred up, even to his *f*.
Am 5. 9 spoiled shall come against the *f*.
Mic 7.12 and from the *f* even to the river,

FORTUNATUS

1Co 16.17 the coming of Stephanas and *F*

FORTY

Gen 7. 4 upon the earth *f* days and *f* nights;
17 flood was *f* days upon the earth;
8. 6 it came to pass at the end of *f* days,
18.28 he said, If I find there *f* and five,
29 there shall be *f* found there.
Ex 16.35 of Israel did eat manna *f* years,
24.18 in the mount *f* days and *f* nights.
34.28 with the Lord *f* days and *f* nights;
Nu 14.33 wander in the wilderness *f* years,
32.13 wander in the wilderness *f* years,
Dt 8. 2 these *f* years in the wilderness,
4 did thy foot swell, these *f* years.
9. 9 in the mount *f* days and *f* nights.
25. 3 *F* stripes he may give him, and
29. 5 led you *f* years in the wilderness:
Jdg 8.28 country was in quietness *f* years
1Ki 19. 8 of that meat *f* days and *f* nights
2Ki 2.24 tare *f* and two children of them.
Neh 9.21 Yea, *f* years didst thou sustain them
Job 42.16 lived Job an hundred and *f* years,
Ps 95.10 *F* years long was I grieved with
Eze 29.11 neither shall it be inhabited *f* years.
12 waste shall be desolate *f* years:
Am 2.10 you *f* years through the wilderness,
5.25 offerings in the wilderness *f* years,
Jon 3. 4 Yet *f* days, and Nineveh shall be
Mt 4. 2 he had fasted *f* days and *f* nights,
Mk 1.13 was there in the wilderness *f* days,
Lk 4. 2 Being *f* days tempted of the devil.
Jn 2.20 *F* and six years was this temple
Ac 1. 3 proofs, being seen of them *f* days,
4.22 For the man was above *f* years old,
7.23 And when he was full *f* years old,
30 And when *f* years were expired,
36 sea, and in the wilderness *f* years.
42 space of *f* years in the wilderness?
13.18 And about the time of *f* years
21 Benjamin, by the space of *f* years.
23.13 were more than *f* which had made
21 for him of them more than *f* men,
2Co 11.24 times received I *f* stripes save one.
Heb 3. 9 me, and saw my works *f* years.
17 with whom was he grieved *f* years?
Rev 7. 4 sealed an hundred and *f* and four
11. 2 tread under foot *f* and two months.
13. 5 him to continue *f* and two months.
14. 1 with him an hundred *f* and four
3 but the hundred and *f* and four
21.17 an hundred and *f* and four cubits,

FORTY'S

Gen 18.29 he said, I will not do it for *f* sake.

FORUM

Ac 28.15 came to meet us as far as Appii *f*,

FORWARD

Gen 26.13 the man waxed great, and went *f*,
Ex 14.15 children of Israel, that they go *f*:
Nu 4. 5 And when the camp setteth *f*,
2Ki 20. 9 shall the shadow go *f* ten degrees,
Ezr 3. 9 set *f* the workmen in the house
Job 23. 8 I go *f*, but he is not there;
Jer 7.24 and went backward, and not *f*.
Mk 14.35 And he went *f* a little, and fell on
Ac 19.33 the Jews putting him *f*.
2Co 8.10 but also to be *f* a year ago.
17 but being more *f*, of his own
Gal 2.10 the same which I also was *f* to do.
3Jn 6 if thou bring *f* on their journey

FORWARDNESS

2Co 8. 8 by occasion of the *f* of others,
9. 2 For I know the *f* of your mind,

FOUGHT

Jos 23. 3 your God is he that hath *f* for you.
Jdg 5.20 They *f* from heaven;
20 the stars in their courses *f* against
9.17 (For my father *f* for you, and
2Ch 20.29 the Lord *f* against the enemies
Ps 109. 3 and *f* against me without a cause.
Zec 14. 3 as when he *f* in the day of battle.
1Co 15.32 I have *f* with beasts at Ephesus,
2Ti 4. 7 I have *f* a good fight, I have
Rev 12. 7 his angels *f* against the dragon;
7 and the dragon *f* and his angels.

FOUL

Job 16.16 My face is *f* with weeping, and
Eze 34.18 ye must *f* the residue with your
Mt 16. 3 It will be *f* weather to day: for
Mk 9.25 he rebuked the *f* spirit, saying
Rev 18. 2 hold of every *f* spirit, and a cage

FOUND

Gen 2.20 there was not *f* an help meet
6. 8 Noah *f* grace in the eyes of the
8. 9 *f* no rest for the sole of her foot,
18.29 Peradventure there shall be forty *f*
31.35 he searched, but *f* not the images.
39. 4 And Joseph *f* grace in his sight,
44.12 the cup was *f* in Benjamin's sack.
16 God hath *f* out the iniquity of thy
Ex 15.22 in the wilderness, and *f* no water.
Lev 6. 3 Or have *f* that which was lost,
4 or the lost thing which he *f*,
Dt 24. 1 hath *f* some uncleanness in her:
Jdg 14.18 ye had not *f* out my riddle.
15.15 he *f* a new jawbone of an ass,
Ru 2.10 Why have I *f* grace in thine eyes,
1Ki 13.14 and *f* him sitting under an oak:
21.20 Hast thou *f* me, O mine enemy?
2Ki 2.17 sought three days, but *f* him not.
22. 8 I have *f* the book of the law in the
23. 2 book of the covenant which was *f*
2Ch 34.15 I have *f* the book of the law in the
Neh 8.14 And they *f* written in the law
Est 6. 2 it was *f* written, that Mordecai
Job 19.28 the root of the matter is *f* in me?
20. 8 as a dream, and shall not be *f*:
28.12 But where shall wisdom be *f*? and
32.13 should say, We have *f* out wisdom:
33.24 down to the pit: I have *f* a ransom.
42.15 were no women *f* so fair as the
Ps 32. 6 in a time when thou mayest be *f*:
107. 4 way; they *f* no city to dwell in.
116. 3 upon me: I *f* trouble and sorrow.
Pr 10.13 hath understanding wisdom is *f*:
25.16 Hast thou *f* honey? eat so much
Ec 7.29 this only have I *f*, that God hath
SS 3. 1, 2 I sought him, but I *f* him not.
Isa 51. 3 joy and gladness shall be *f* therein,
55. 6 ye the Lord while he may be *f*,
65. 1 I am *f* of them that sought me not:
Jer 2.26 the thief is ashamed when he is *f*,
34 I have not *f* it by secret search,
Eze 26.21 yet shalt thou never be *f* again,
Dan 5.11 wisdom of the gods, was *f* in him;
12 doubts, were *f* in the same Daniel,
27 in the balances, and art *f* wanting.
6.11 and *f* Daniel praying and making
23 no manner of hurt was *f* upon him,
Jon 1. 3 and he *f* a ship going to Tarshish:
Zep 3.13 shall a deceitful tongue be *f* in
Mt 1.18 she was *f* with child of the Holy
2. 8 child; and when ye have *f* him,
8.10 I have not *f* so great faith, no, not
13.44 when a man hath *f*, he hideth,
46 he had *f* one pearl of great price,
18.28 and *f* one of his fellowservants,
20. 6 and *f* others standing idle, and
21.19 *f* nothing thereon, but leaves only,
22.10 all as many as they *f*, both bad
26.43 he came and *f* them asleep again:
60 But *f* none: yea, though many
60 witnesses came, yet *f* they none.
27.32 they *f* a man of Cyrene, Simon by
Mk 1.37 And when they had *f* him, they
7. 2 unwashen, hands, they *f* fault,
30 she *f* the devil gone out, and her
11. 4 and *f* the colt tied by the door
13 to it, he *f* nothing but leaves;
14.16 and *f* as he had said unto them:
40 returned, he *f* them asleep again,
55 to put him to death; and *f* none.
Lk 1.30 Mary: for thou hast *f* favor
2.16 came with haste, and *f* Mary, and
45 And when they *f* him not, they
46 they *f* him in the temple, sitting
4.17 *f* the place where it was written,
7. 9 I have not *f* so great faith, no, not
10 *f* the servant whole that had been
8.35 and *f* the man, out of whom the
9.36 voice was past, Jesus was *f* alone.
13. 6 sought fruit thereon, and *f* none.
15. 5 when he hath *f* it, he layeth it on
6 I have *f* my sheep which was lost.
9 when she hath *f* it, she calleth
9 for I have *f* the piece which I had
24 alive again; he was lost, and is *f*.
32 alive again; and was lost, and is *f*.

Lk 17.18 There are not *f* that returned to
19.32 and *f* even as he had said unto
22.13 and *f* as he had said unto them:
45 he *f* them sleeping for sorrow,
23. 2 We *f* this fellow perverting the
14 you, have *f* no fault in this man
22 I have *f* no cause of death in him:
24. 2 And they *f* the stone rolled away
3 and *f* not the body of the Lord
23 And when they *f* not his body, they
24 and *f* it even so as the women had
33 and *f* the eleven gathered together,
Jn 1.41 We have *f* the Messias, which is,
45 saith unto him, We have *f* him,
2.14 And *f* in the temple those that sold
6.25 And when they had *f* him on the
9.35 and when he had *f* him, he said
11.17 he *f* that he had lain in the grave
12.14 he had *f* a young ass, sat thereon;
Ac 5.10 young men came in, and *f* her dead,
22 officers came, and *f* them not in
23 prison truly *f* we shut in all safety,
23 had opened, we *f* no man within.
39 ye be *f* even to fight against God.
7.11 and our fathers *f* no sustenance,
46 Who *f* favor before God, and
8.40 But Philip was *f* at Azotus:
9. 2 that if he *f* any of this way,
33 And there he *f* a certain man
10.27 *f* many that were come together.
11.26 when he had *f* him, he brought
12.19 *f* him not, he examined the keepers,
13. 6 *f* a certain sorcerer, a false prophet,
22 I have *f* David the son of Jesse,
28 though they *f* no cause of death
17. 6 when they *f* them not, they drew
23 I *f* an altar with this inscription,
18. 2 And *f* a certain Jew named Aquila,
19.19 *f* it fifty thousand pieces of silver.
24. 5 we have *f* this man a pestilent
12 they neither *f* me in the temple
18 Jews from Asia *f* me purified in
20 if they have *f* any evil doing in
25.25 when I *f* that he had committed
27. 6 And there the centurion *f* a ship
28 sounded, and *f* it twenty fathoms:
28 again, and *f* it fifteen fathoms.
28.14 Where we *f* brethren, and were
Ro 4. 1 as pertaining to the flesh, hath *f*?
7.10 to life, I *f* to be unto death.
10.20 was *f* of them that sought me not;
1Co 4. 2 stewards, that a man be *f* faithful.
15.15 Yea, and we are *f* false witnesses
2Co 2.13 because I *f* not Titus my brother:
5. 3 clothed we shall not be *f* naked.
7.14 made before Titus, is *f* a truth,
11.12 they may be *f* even as we.
12.20 and that I shall be *f* unto you such
Gal 2.17 we ourselves also are *f* sinners,
Php 2. 8 And being *f* in fashion as a man,
3. 9 And be *f* in him, not having mine
1Ti 3.10 of a deacon, being *f* blameless.
2Ti 1.17 me out very diligently, and *f* me.
Heb 11. 5 and was not *f*, because God had
12.17 for he *f* no place of repentance,
1Pe 1. 7 might be *f* unto praise and honor
2.22 neither was guile *f* in his mouth:
2Pe 3.14 that ye may be *f* of him in peace,
2Jn 4 *f* of thy children walking in truth,
Rev 2. 2 and are not, and hast *f* them liars:
3. 2 for I have not *f* thy works perfect
5. 4 no man was *f* worthy to open and
12. 8 neither was their place *f* any more
14. 5 And in their mouth was *f* no guile:
16.20 and the mountains were not *f*.
18.21 and shall be *f* no more at all.
22 he be, shall be *f* any more in thee;
24 in her was *f* the blood of prophets,
20.11 and there was *f* no place for them.
15 And whosoever was not *f* written

FOUNDATION

Ex 9.18 the *f* thereof even until now.
Ezr 3. 6 *f* of the temple of the Lord was not
12 when the *f* of the house was laid
5.16 and laid the *f* of the house of God
Job 22.16 whose *f* was overflown with a flood:
Ps 87. 1 His *f* is in the holy mountains.
102.25 Of old hast thou laid the *f* of the
Pr 10.25 the righteous is an everlasting *f*.
Isa 28.16 I lay in Zion for a *f* a stone,
16 a precious corner stone, a sure *f*:
Mt 13.35 secret from the *f* of the world.
25.34 for you from the *f* of the world:
Lk 6.48 deep, and laid the *f* on a rock:
49 without a *f* built an house upon the
11.50 shed from the *f* of the world,
14.29 after he hath laid the *f*, and is not
Jn 17.24 lovest me before the *f* of the world,
Ro 15.20 build upon another man's *f*:
1Co 3.10 I have laid the *f*, and another
11 For other *f* can no man lay than
12 upon this *f* gold, silver, precious
Eph 1. 4 in him before the *f* of the world,
2.20 built upon the *f* of the apostles
1Ti 6.19 for themselves a good *f* against
2Ti 2.19 the *f* of God standeth sure, having
Heb 1.10 hast laid the *f* of the earth;
4. 3 finished from the *f* of the world.
6. 1 laying again the *f* of repentance
9.26 suffered since the *f* of the world:
1Pe 1.20 before the *f* of the world, but was
Rev 13. 8 Lamb slain from the *f* of the world.
17. 8 of life from the *f* of the world,
21.14 The first *f* was jasper; the second,

FOUNDATIONS

Dt 32.22 on fire the *f* of the mountains.
2Sa 22. 8 the *f* of heaven moved and shook,
16 the *f* of the world were discovered,
Ezr 4.12 the wall thereof, and joined the *f*,
6. 3 let the *f* thereof be strongly laid;
Job 38. 4 thou when I laid the *f* of the earth?
6 are the *f* thereof fastened? or who
Ps 11. 3 If the *f* be destroyed, what can the
18. 7 the *f* also of the hills moved and
15 the *f* of the world were discovered
82. 5 all of the *f* of the earth are out of
104. 5 Who laid the *f* of the earth,
Pr 8.29 he appointed the *f* of the earth:
Isa 16. 7 *f* of Kir-hareseth shall ye mourn,
24.18 and the *f* of the earth do shake.
40.21 understood from the *f* of the earth?
51.13 and laid the *f* of the earth;
16 and lay the *f* of the earth,
54.11 and lay thy *f* with sapphires.
58.12 up the *f* of many generations;
Jer 31.37 and the *f* of the earth searched out
50.15 her *f* are fallen, her walls are
51.26 thee a corner, nor a stone for *f*;
La 4.11 and it hath devoured the *f* thereof.
Eze 30. 4 and her *f* shall be broken down.
41. 8 *f* of the side chambers were a full
Mic 1. 6 and I will discover the *f* thereof.
6. 2 and ye strong *f* of the earth:
Ac 16.26 the *f* of the prison were shaken:
Heb 11.10 he looked for a city which hath *f*,
Rev 21.14 the wall of the city had twelve *f*,
19 And the *f* of the wall of the city

FOUNDED

Ps 24. 2 For he hath *f* it upon the seas,
89.11 fulness thereof, thou hast *f* them.
104. 8 place which thou hast *f* for them.
119.152 that thou hast *f* them for ever.
Pr 3.19 Lord by wisdom hath *f* the earth;
Isa 14.32 the Lord hath *f* Zion, and the poor
23.13 Assyrian *f* it for them that dwell
Am 9. 6 and hath *f* his troop in the earth;
Mt 7.25 fell not: for it was *f* upon a rock.
Lk 6.48 shake it: for it was *f* upon a rock.

FOUNTAIN

Gen 16. 7 found her by a *f* of water in the
7 by the *f* in the way to Shur.
Lev 11.36 Nevertheless a *f* or pit, wherein
20.18 he hath discovered her *f*, and she
18 she hath uncovered the *f* of her
Dt 33.28 *f* of Jacob shall be upon a land
Jos 15. 9 the *f* of the water of Nephtoah,
1Sa 29. 1 Israelites pitched by a *f* which
Neh 2.14 I went on to the gate of the *f*,
3.15 the gate of the *f* repaired Shallun
12.37 And at the *f* gate, which was over
Ps 36. 9 For with thee is the *f* of life:
68.26 the Lord, from the *f* of Israel.
74.15 Thou didst cleave the *f* and the
114. 8 water, the flint into a *f* of waters.
Pr 5.18 Let thy *f* be blessed: and rejoice
13.14 The law of the wise is a *f* of life,
14.27 The fear of the Lord is a *f* of life,
25.26 troubled *f*, and a corrupt spring.
Ec 12. 6 or the pitcher be broken at the *f*,
SS 4.12 a spring shut up, a *f* sealed.
15 a *f* of gardens, a well of living
Jer 2.13 forsaken me the *f* of living waters,
6. 7 As a *f* casteth out her waters.
9. 1 waters, and mine eyes a *f* of tears,
17.13 forsaken the Lord, the *f* of living
Hos 13.15 and his *f* shall be dried up:
Joel 3.18 a *f* shall come forth of the house
Zec 13. 1 that day there shall be a *f* opened
Mk 5.29 straightway the *f* of her blood
Jas 3.11 Doth a *f* send forth at the same
12 so can no *f* both yield salt water
Rev 21. 6 that is athirst of the *f* of the water

FOUNTAINS

Gen 7.11 were all the *f* of the great deep
8. 2 *f* also of the deep and the windows
Nu 33. 9 in Elim were twelve *f* of water,
Dt 8. 7 of *f* and depths that spring out of
1Ki 18. 5 unto all of *f* of water, and unto all
2Ch 32. 3 to stop the waters of the *f* which
4 stopped all the *f*, and the brook
Pr 5.16 Let thy *f* be dispersed abroad,
8.24 when there were no *f* abounding
28 he strengthened the *f* of the deep:
Isa 41.18 and *f* in the midst of the valleys:
Rev 7.17 shall lead them unto living *f* of
8.10 rivers, and upon the *f* of waters;
14. 7 the sea, and the *f* of waters.
16. 4 upon the rivers and *f* of waters:

FOUR

Gen 2.10 parted, and because into *f* heads.
15.13 shall afflict them *f* hundred years;
Nu 25. 9 plague were twenty and *f* thousand.
Dt 22.12 upon the *f* quarters of thy vesture,
Jdg 21.12 *f* hundred young virgins, that had
1Ki 18.19 the prophets of Baal *f* hundred and
19 prophets of the groves *f* hundred,
22 Baal's prophets are *f* hundred and
33 Fill *f* barrels with water, and pour
2Ki 7. 3 And there were *f* leprous men at
1Ch 23. 5 and *f* thousand praised the Lord
2Ch 9.25 Solomon had *f* thousand stalls for
Pr 30.15 *f* things say not, It is enough:
18 yea, *f* which I know not:
Isa 11.12 from the *f* corners of the earth.
Jer 49.36 the *f* winds from the *f* quarters
Eze 1. 5 the likeness of *f* living creatures.
6 And every one had *f* faces,
6 and every one had *f* wings.
8 *f* sides; and they *f* had their faces
10 they *f* had the face of a man,
10 and they *f* had the face of an ox on
10 they *f* also had the face of an eagle.
15 living creatures, with his *f* faces.
16 they *f* had one likeness: and their
10. 9 the *f* wheels by the cherubims,
21 and every one *f* wings;
37. 9 Come from the *f* winds, O breath,

Dan 1.17 these *f* children, God gave them
3.25 Lo, I see *f* men loose, walking
7. 2 the *f* winds of the heaven strove
3 And *f* great beasts came up from
6 upon the back of it *f* wings of a
6 the beast had also *f* heads;
17 beasts, which are *f*, are *f* kings,
8. 8 and for it came up *f* notable ones
8 toward the *f* winds of heaven.
22 *f* stood up for it, *f* kingdoms shall
Zec 1.18 and saw, and behold *f* horns.
20 the Lord shewed me *f* carpenters.
2. 6 as the *f* winds of the heaven,
6. 1 there came *f* chariots out from
5 are the *f* spirits of the heavens,
Mt 15.38 *f* thousand men, beside women
16.10 the seven loaves of the *f* thousand,
24.31 together his elect from the *f*
Mk 2. 3 of the palsy, which was borne of *f*.
8. 9 eaten were about *f* thousand:
20 when the seven among *f* thousand,
13.27 his elect from the *f* winds,
Lk 2.37 of about fourscore and *f* years,
Jn 4.35 not ye, There are yet *f* months,
11.17 lain in the grave *f* days already.
39 for he hath been dead *f* days.
19.23 *f* parts, to every soldier a part;
Ac 5.36 number of men, about *f* hundred,
7. 6 entreat them evil *f* hundred years.
10.11 great sheet knit at the *f* corners,
30 *F* days ago I was fasting until
11. 5 down from heaven by *f* corners;
12. 4 and delivered him to *f* quaternions
13.20 the space of *f* hundred and fifty
21. 9 the same man had *f* daughters,
23 We have *f* men which have a vow
38 wilderness *f* thousand men that
27.29 they cast *f* anchors out of the
Gal 3.17 *f* hundred and thirty years after,
Rev 4. 4 throne were *f* and twenty seats:
4 I saw *f* and twenty elders sitting,
6 *f* beasts full of eyes before and
8 And the *f* beasts had each of them
10 The *f* and twenty elders fall down
5. 6 of the throne and of the *f* beasts,
8 *f* beasts and *f* and twenty elders
14 And the *f* beasts said, Amen.
14 *f* and twenty elders fell down
6. 1 one of the *f* beasts saying, Come
6 in the midst of the *f* beasts say,
7. 1 after these things I saw *f* angels
1 on the *f* corners of the earth,
1 holding the *f* winds of the earth,
2 with a loud voice to the *f* angels,
4 hundred and forty and *f* thousand
11 about the elders and the *f* beasts,
9.13 I heard a voice from the *f* horns
14 Loose the *f* angels which are
15 And the *f* angels were loosed,
11.16 the *f* and twenty elders, which sat
14. 1 an hundred forty and *f* thousand,
3 and before the *f* beasts, and the
3 hundred and forty and *f* thousand
15. 7 And one of the *f* beasts gave
19. 4 the *f* and twenty elders and the *f*
20. 8 are in the *f* quarters of the earth,
21.17 an hundred and forty and *f* cubits,

FOURFOLD
2Sa 12. 6 And he shall restore the lamb *f*,
Lk 19. 8 false accusation, I restore him *f*.

FOURFOOTED
Ac 10.12 manner of *f* beasts of the earth,
11. 6 and saw *f* beasts of the earth,
Ro 1.23 *f* beasts, and creeping things.

FOURSCORE
Gen 16.16 Abram was *f* and six years old,
Ex 7. 7 And Moses was *f* years old,
7 and Aaron *f* and three years old,
Jos 14.10 I am this day *f* and five years old.
2Sa 19.32 a very aged man, even *f* years old:
2Ki 6.25 an ass's head was sold for *f* pieces
Ps 90.10 if by reason of strength they be *f*
Lk 2.37 widow of about *f* and four years,
16. 7 Take thy bill, and write *f*.

FOURTEEN
Gen 31.41 I served thee *f* years for thy
46.22 Jacob: all the souls were *f*.
Nu 1.27 *f* thousand and six hundred.
2. 4 *f* thousand and six hundred.
16.49 were *f* thousand and seven
29.13 and *f* lambs of the first year;
15 to each lamb of the *f* lambs:
17, 20 *f* lambs of the first year
23, 26, 29, 32 and *f* lambs of the
Jos 15.36 *f* cities with their villages.
18.28 *f* cities with their villages.
1Ki 8.65 and seven days, even *f* days.
1Ch 25. 5 And God gave to Heman *f* sons
2Ch 13.21 mighty, and married *f* wives,
Job 42.12 for he had *f* thousand sheep,
Eze 43.17 settle shall be *f* cubits long
17 *f* broad in the four squares
Mt 1.17 Abraham to David are *f* generations
17 into Babylon are *f* generations;
17 unto Christ are *f* generations.
2Co 12. 2 a man in Christ above *f* years ago,
Gal 2. 1 *f* years after I went up again to

FOURTEENTH
Gen 14. 5 *f* year came Chedorlaomer,
Ex 12. 6 shall keep it up until the *f* day
18 on the *f* day of the month at
Lev 23. 5 In the *f* day of the first month
Nu 9. 3 In the *f* day of this month, at
5 the passover on the *f* day of
11 *f* day of the second month at
28.16 in the *f* day of the first month
Jos 5.10 the passover on the *f* day of
2Ki 18.13 in the *f* year of king Hezekiah
1Ch 24.13 Huppah, the *f* to Jeshebeab,
25.21 *f* to Mattithiah, he, his sons,
2Ch 30.15 the passover on the *f* day of
35. 1 on the *f* day of the first month.
Ezr 6.19 the passover upon the *f* day
Est 9.15 on the *f* day also of the month
17 and on the *f* day of the same
18 and on the *f* thereof;
19 the *f* day of the month Adar
21 they should keep the *f* day of
Isa 36. 1 in the *f* year of king Hezekiah,
Eze 40. 1 the *f* year after that the city
45.21 first month, in the *f* day of the
Ac 27.27 But when the *f* night was come,
33 is the *f* day that ye have tarried

FOURTH
Gen 1.19 and the morning were the *f* day.
2.14 And the *f* river is Euphrates.
15.16 the *f* generation they shall come
Ex 20. 5 unto the third and *f* generation
Dt 5. 9 unto the third and *f* generation
2Ch 20.26 And on the *f* day they assembled
Neh 9. 3 their God one *f* part of the day; of
3 and another *f* part they confessed,
Eze 10.14 and the *f* the face of an eagle.
Dan 2.40 And the *f* kingdom shall be strong
3.25 the form of the *f* is like the Son of
7. 7 and behold a *f* beast, dreadful and
19 know the truth of the *f* beast,
23 The *f* beast shall be the *f* kingdom
11. 2 *f* shall be far richer than they all:
Mt 14.25 And in the *f* watch of the night
Mk 6.48 and about the *f* watch of the night
Rev 4. 7 the *f* beast was like a flying eagle.
6. 7 And when he had opened the *f* seal,
7 I heard the voice of the *f* beast
8 them over the *f* part of the earth,
8.12 And the *f* angel sounded, and the
16. 8 And the *f* angel poured out his vial
21.19 a chalcedony; the *f*, an emerald;

FOWL
Gen 1.22 and let *f* multiply in the earth.
26 of the sea, and over the *f* of the air,
Job 28. 7 is a path which no *f* knoweth,
Ps 8. 8 The *f* of the air, and the fish of the
148.10 creeping things, and flying *f*:

FOWLER
Ps 91. 3 thee from the snare of the *f*, and
Pr 6. 5 as a bird from the hand of the *f*.
Hos 9. 8 but the prophet is a snare of a *f*

FOWLERS
Ps 124. 7 as a bird out of the snare of the *f*:

FOWLS
Ps 50.11 I know all the *f* of the mountains:
Mt 6.26 Behold, the *f* of the air: for they
13. 4 the *f* came and devoured them
Mk 4. 4 and the *f* of the air came and
32 the *f* of the air may lodge under
Lk 8. 5 and the *f* of the air devoured it.
12.24 more are ye better than the *f*?
13.19 and the *f* of the air lodged in the
Ac 10.12 creeping things, and *f* of the air.
11. 6 creeping things, and *f* of the air.
Rev 19.17 saying to all the *f* that fly in the
21 the *f* were filled with their flesh.

FOX
Neh 4. 3 if a *f* go up, he shall even break
Lk 13.32 Go ye, and tell that *f*, Behold, I

FOXES
Jdg 15. 4 went and caught three hundred *f*,
Ps 63.10 they shall be a portion for *f*.
SS 2.15 Take us the *f*, the little *f*, that
La 5.18 is desolate, the *f* walk upon it.
Eze 13. 4 are like the *f* in the deserts.
Mt 8.20 The *f* have holes, and the birds of
Lk 9.58 *F* have holes, and birds of the air

FRAGMENTS
Mt 14.20 took up of the *f* that remained
Mk 6.43 up twelve baskets full of the *f*,
8.19, 20 baskets full of *f* took ye up?
Lk 9.17 taken up of *f* that remained to
Jn 6.12 Gather up the *f* that remain,
13 filled twelve baskets with the *f*

FRAIL
Ps 39. 4 that I may know how *f* I am.

FRAME
Jdg 12. 6 could not *f* to pronounce it right.
Ps 103.14 For he knoweth our *f*; he
Jer 18.11 I *f* evil against you, and devise
Eze 40. 2 by which was as the *f* of a city on
Hos 5. 4 They will not *f* their doings to

FRAMED
Isa 29.16 or shall the thing *f* say of him
16 say of him that *f* it, He had no
Eph 2.21 In whom all the building fitly *f*
Heb 11. 3 the worlds were *f* by the word of

FRANKINCENSE
Ex 30.34 these sweet spices with pure *f*:
Lev 2. 1 oil upon it, and put *f* thereon:
2 with all the *f* thereof; and the
15 and lay *f* thereon: it is a meat
16 with all the *f* thereof: it is an
5.11 neither shall he put any *f* thereon:
6.15 all the *f* which is upon the meat
24. 7 shall put pure *f* upon each row,
Nu 5.15 put *f* thereon; for it is an offering
1Ch 9.29 the oil, and the *f*, and the spices.
Neh 13. 5 the *f*, and the vessels, and the

Neh 13. 9 with the meat offering and the *f*.
SS 3. 6 perfumed with myrrh and *f*, with
4. 6 of myrrh, and to the hill of *f*.
14 with all trees of *f*; myrrh and
Mt 2.11 gifts; gold, and *f*, and myrrh.
Rev 18.13 *f*, and wine, and oil, and fine flour,

FRANKLY

Lk 7.42 to pay. he *f* forgave them both.

FRAUD

Ps 10. 7 full of cursing and deceit and *f*:
Jas 5. 4 which is of you kept back by *f*,

FREE

Ex 21. 2 in the seventh he shall go out *f*
5 my children; I will not go out *f*:
11 shall she go out *f* without money.
26 let him go *f* for his eye's sake.
27 let him go *f* for his tooth's sake.
36. 3 brought yet unto him *f* offerings
Lev 19.20 to death, because she was not *f*.
Nu 5.19 be thou *f* from this bitter water
28 then she shall be *f*, and shall
Dt 15.12 thou shalt let him go *f* from thee.
13 thou sendest him out *f* from thee,
18 sendest him away *f* from thee;
24. 5 he shall be *f* at home one year,
1Sa 17.25 his father's house *f* in Israel.
1Ch 9.33 in the chambers were *f*: for they
2Ch 29.31 and as many as were of a *f* heart
Job 3.19 the servant is *f* from his master.
39. 5 Who hath sent out the wild ass *f*?
Ps 51.12 and uphold me with thy *f* spirit.
88. 5 *F* among the dead, like the slain
105.20 of the people, and let him go *f*.
Isa 58. 6 and to let the oppressed go *f*,
Jer 34. 9 an Hebrew or an Hebrewess, go *f*;
10 every one his maidservant, go *f*,
11 whom they had let go *f*, to return,
14 thou shalt let him go *f* from thee:
Am 4. 5 and publish the *f* offerings
Mt 15. 6 or his mother, he shall be *f*.
17.26 unto him, Then are the children *f*
Mk 7.11 be profited by me; he shall be *f*.
Jn 8.32 and the truth shall make you *f*.
33 sayest thou, Ye shall be made *f*?
36 Son therefore shall make you *f*,
36 ye shall be *f* indeed.
Ac 22.28 And Paul said, But I was *f* born.
Ro 5.15 the offense, so also is the *f* gift.
16 but the *f* gift is of many offenses
18 the *f* gift came upon all men unto
6.18 Being then made *f* from sin, ye
20 ye were *f* from righteousness.
22 But now being made *f* from sin,
7. 3 she is *f* from that law; so that
8. 2 hath made me *f* from the law of
1Co 7.21 if thou mayest be made *f*, use it
22 that is called, being *f*, is Christ's
9. 1 Am I not an apostle? am I not *f*?
19 For though I be *f* from all men,
12.13 whether we be bond or *f*; and have
Gal 3.28 Greek, there is neither bond nor *f*,
4.26 But Jerusalem which is above is *f*,
31 of the bondwoman, but of the *f*.
5. 1 wherewith Christ hath made us *f*,
Eph 6. 8 whether he be bond or *f*.
Col 3.11 Barbarian, Scythian, bond nor *f*:
2Th 3. 1 of the Lord may have *f* course,
1Pe 2.16 As *f*, and not using your liberty
Rev 6.15 every bondman, and every *f* man,
13.16 rich and poor, *f* and bond, to
19.18 all men, both *f* and bond, both

FREED

Jos 9.23 there shall none of you be *f* from
Ro 6. 7 For he that is dead is *f* from sin.

FREEDOM

Lev 19.20 at all redeemed, nor *f* given her;
Ac 22.28 a great sum obtained I this *f*.

FREELY

Gen 2.16 tree of the garden thou mayest *f* eat:
Nu 11. 5 which we did eat in Egypt *f*;
1Sa 14.30 if haply the people had eaten *f* today
Ezr 2.68 offered *f* for the house of God to
7.15 and his counsellors have *f* offered unto
Ps 54. 6 I will *f* sacrifice unto thee: I
Hos 14. 4 I will love them *f*: for mine anger
Mt 10. 8 *f* ye have received, *f* give.
Ac 2.29 let me *f* speak unto you of
26.26 before whom also I speak *f*:
Ro 3.24 Being justified *f* by his grace
8.32 shall he not with him also *f* give us
1Co 2.12 we might know the things that are *f*
2Co 11. 7 to you the gospel of God *f*?
Rev 21. 6 the fountain of the water of life *f*.
22.17 let him take the water of life *f*.

FREEMAN

1Co 7.22 being a servant, is the Lord's *f*:

FREEWOMAN

Gal 4.22 by a bondmaid, the other by a *f*.
23 but he of the *f* was by promise.
30 not be heir with the son of the *f*.

FREQUENT

2Co 11.23 in prisons more *f*, in deaths oft.

FRESH

Nu 11. 8 taste of it was as the taste of *f* oil.
Job 29.20 My glory was *f* in me, and my
Ps 92.10 I shall be anointed with *f* oil.
Jas 3.12 both yield salt water and *f*.

FRET

Ps 37. 1 *F* not thyself because of
7 *f* not thyself because of him who
8 *f* not thyself in any wise to do evil.
Pr 24.19 *F* not thyself because of evil men,

FRIEND

Gen 38.12 and his *f* Hirah the Adullamite.
20 sent the kid by the hand of his *f*
Ex 33.11 face, as a man speaketh unto his *f*.
Dt 13. 6 or the wife of thy bosom, or thy *f*,
Jdg 14.20 whom he had used as his *f*.
2Sa 13. 3 Amnon had a *f*, whose name was
15.37 Hushai David's friend came into
16.16 Hushai the Archite, David's *f*
17 Is this thy kindness to thy *f*?
17 why wentest thou not with thy *f*?
1Ki 4. 5 principal officer, and the king's *f*:
2Ch 20. 7 seed of Abraham thy *f* for ever?
Job 6.14 pity should be shewed from his *f*;
27 and ye dig a pit for your *f*.
Ps 35.14 as though he had been my *f* or
41. 9 mine own familiar *f*, in whom I trusted
88.18 Lover and *f* hast thou put far
Pr 6. 1 son, if thou be surety for thy *f*,
3 art come into the hand of thy *f*;
3 thyself, and make sure thy *f*.
17.17 A *f* loveth at all times, and a
18 surety in the presence of his *f*.
18.24 and there is a *f* that sticketh closer
19. 6 man is a *f* to him that giveth gifts.
22.11 of his lips the king shall be his *f*.
27. 6 Faithful are the wounds of a *f*;
9 doth the sweetness of a man's *f* by
10 Thine own *f*, and thy father's *f*,
14 blesseth his *f* with a loud voice.
17 a man... the countenance of his *f*.
SS 5.16 my *f*, O daughters of Jerusalem.
Isa 41. 8 chosen, the seed of Abraham my *f*.
Jer 6.21 neighbor and his *f* shall perish.
19. 9 eat every one the flesh of his *f* in
Hos 3. 1 yet, love a woman beloved of her *f*,
Mic 7. 5 Trust ye not in a *f*, put ye not
Mt 11.19 a *f* of publicans and sinners.
20.13 *F*, I do thee no wrong: didst not
22.12 *F*, how camest thou in hither not
26.50 *F*, wherefore art thou come?
Lk 7.34 a *f* of publicans and sinners!
11. 5 Which of you shall have a *f*, and
5 unto him, *F*, lend me three loaves;
6 For a *f* of mine in his journey is
8 and give him, because he is his *f*,
14.10 *F*, go up higher: then shalt thou
Jn 3.29 but the *f* of the bridegroom, which
11.11 Our *f* Lazarus sleepeth; but I go,
19.12 thou art not Caesar's *f*: whosoever
Ac 12.20 and having made Blastus their *f*,
Jas 2.23 and he was called the *F* of God.
4. 4 *f* of the world is the enemy of God.

FRIENDLY

Jdg 19. 3 to speak *f* unto her, and to bring
Ru 2.13 spoken *f* unto thine handmaid,
Pr 18.24 friends must shew himself *f*:

FRIENDS

Gen 26.26 and Ahuzzath one of his *f*, and
1Sa 30.26 to his *f*, saying, Behold a present
2Sa 3. 8 to his brethren, and to his *f*, and
19. 6 thine enemies, and hatest thy *f*.
1Ki 16.11 of his kinsfolks, nor of his *f*, and
Est 5.10 he sent and called for his *f*,
14 said Zeresh his wife and all his *f*
6.13 told Zeresh his wife and all his *f*
Job 2.11 when Job's three *f* heard of all
16.20 My *f* scorn me: but mine eye
17. 5 He that speaketh flattery to his *f*,
19.14 and my familiar *f* have forgotten me.
19 All my inward *f* abhorred me:
21 have pity upon me, O ye my *f*;
32. 3 against his three *f* was his wrath
42. 7 thee, and against thy two *f*: for ye
10 when he prayed for his *f*: also the
Ps 38.11 My lovers and my *f* stand aloof
Pr 14.20 but the rich hath many *f*.
16.28 and a whisperer separateth chief *f*.
17. 9 he that...a matter separateth very *f*.
18.24 A man that hath *f* must shew
19. 4 Wealth maketh many *f*; but the
7 more do his *f* go far from him?
SS 5. 1 eat, O *f*; drink, yea, drink
Jer 20. 4 terror to thyself, and to all thy *f*:
6 be buried there, thou, and all thy *f*,
38.22 say, Thy *f* have set thee on,
La 1. 2 her *f* have dealt treacherously
Zec 13. 6 was wounded in the house of my *f*.
Mk 3.21 when his *f* heard of it, they
5.19 Go home to thy *f*, and tell them how
Lk 7. 6 centurion sent *f* to him, saying,
12. 4 And I say unto you my *f*, Be not
14.12 call not thy *f*, nor thy brethren.
15. 6 he calleth together his *f* and
9 calleth her *f* and her neighbors
29 I might make merry with my *f*:
16. 9 to yourselves *f* of the mammon of
21.16 brethren, and kinsfolks, and *f*;
23.12 day Pilate and Herod were made *f*
Jn 15.13 a man lay down his life for his *f*.
14 Ye are my *f*, if ye do whatsoever
15 I have called you *f*; for all things
Ac 10.24 together his kinsmen and near *f*.
19.31 the chief of Asia, which were his *f*,
27. 3 to go unto his *f* to refresh himself.
3Jn 14 Our *f* salute thee.
14 Greet the *f* by name.

FRIENDSHIP

Pr 22.24 Make no *f* with an angry man;
Jas 4. 4 *f* of the world is enmity with God?

FRO

Gen 8. 7 raven, which went forth to and *f*,
2Ki 4.35 walked in the house to and *f*;
2Ch 16. 9 the eyes of the Lord run to and *f*
Job 1. 7 From going to and *f* in the earth,
2. 2 From going to and *f* in the earth,
7. 4 I am full of tossings to and *f*

13.25 break a leaf driven to and *f*?
Ps 107.27 They reel to and *f*, and stagger
Pr 21. 6 a vanity tossed to and *f* of them
Isa 24.20 shall reel to and *f* like a drunkard,
33. 4 as the running to and *f* of locusts
49.21 a captive, and removing to and *f*?
Jer 5. 1 ye to and *f* through the streets
49. 3 and run to and *f* by the hedges;
Eze 27.19 Dan also and Javan going to and *f*
Dan 12. 4 many shall run to and *f*, and
Joel 2. 9 shall run to and *f* in the city;
Am 8.12 they shall run to and *f* to seek the
Zec 1.10 to walk to and *f* through the earth.
11 We have walked to and *f* through the
4.10 of the Lord, which run to and *f*
6. 7 might walk to and *f* through the earth:
7 Get you hence, walk to and *f* through
7 So they walked to and *f* through the
Eph 4.14 tossed to and *f*, and carried about

FROGS
Ex 8. 2 will smite all thy borders with *f*:
3 And the river shall bring forth *f*
4 the *f* shall come up both on thee,
5 and cause *f* to come upon the land
6 the *f* came up, and covered the land
7 and brought up *f* upon the land of
8 that he may take away the *f* from
9 the *f* from thee and thy houses,
11 And the *f* shall depart from thee,
12 of the *f* which he had brought
13 and the *f* died out of the houses,
Ps 78.45 and *f*, which destroyed them.
105.30 land brought forth *f* in abundance,
Rev 16.13 I saw three unclean spirits like *f*

FROST
Gen 31.40 consumed me, and the *f* by night;
Ex 16.14 small as the hoar *f* on the ground.
Job 37.10 By the breath of God *f* is given:
38.29 and the hoary *f* of heaven, who
Ps 78.47 and their sycamore trees with *f*.
Jer 36.30 the heat, and in the night to the *f*.

FROWARD
Dt 32.20 for they are a very *f* generation,
2Sa 22.27 with the *f* thou wilt shew thyself
Job 5.13 counsel of the *f* is carried
Ps 18.26 and with the *f* thou wilt shew
26 with...thou wilt show thyself *f*,
101. 4 A *f* heart shall depart from me:
Pr 2.12 the man that speaketh *f* things;
15 and they *f* in their paths:
3.32 the *f* is abomination to the Lord:
4.24 Put away from thee a *f* mouth,
6.12 man, walketh with a *f* mouth,
8. 8 nothing *f* or perverse in them.
13 and the *f* mouth. do I hate.
10.31 but the *f* tongue shall be cut out.
11.20 are of a *f* heart are abomination
16.28 A *f* man soweth strife: and a
30 his eyes to devise *f* things:
17.20 hath a *f* heart findeth no good:
21. 8 way of man is *f* and strange:
22. 5 snares are in the way of the *f*:
1Pe 2.18 good and gentle, but also to the *f*.

FROZEN
Job 38.30 and the face of the deep is *f*.

FRUIT
Gen 1.11 *f* tree yielding *f* after his kind,
3. 3 *f* of the tree which is in the midst
6 took of the *f* thereof, and did eat,
4. 3 Cain brought of the *f* of the ground
Lev 27.30 the *f* of the tree, is the Lord's:
Dt 11.17 that the land yield not her *f*;
28. 4 the *f* of thy body, and the *f* of thy
30. 9 in the *f* of thy body, and in the *f* of
Ps 1. 3 bringeth forth his *f* in his season;
72.16 *f* thereof shall shake like Lebanon:
104.13 satisfied with the *f* of thy works.
Pr 11.30 The *f* of the righteous is a tree
13. 2 shall eat good by the *f* of his mouth:
SS 2. 3 and his *f* was sweet to my taste.
Isa 3.10 they shall eat the *f* of their doings.
57.19 I create the *f* of the lips;
Eze 17. 8 that it might bear *f*, that it might
34.27 tree of the field shall yield her *f*,
36.30 I will multiply the *f* of the tree,
Joel 2.22 the tree beareth her *f*, the fig tree
Am 7.14 and a gatherer of sycomore *f*:
8. 1 and behold a basket of summer *f*.
2 And I said, A basket of summer *f*.
Mic 6. 7 *f* of my body for the sin of my soul?
Zec 8.12 vine shall give her *f*, and the
Mt 3.10 which bringeth not forth good *f*
7.17 good tree bringeth forth good *f*;
17 corrupt tree bringeth forth evil *f*.
18 good tree cannot bring forth evil *f*,
18 a corrupt tree bring forth good *f*.
19 tree that bringeth not forth good *f*
12.33 the tree good, and his *f* good;
33 the tree corrupt, and his *f* corrupt:
33 for the tree is known by his *f*.
13. 8 and brought forth *f*, some an
23 also beareth *f*, and bringeth forth,
26 sprung up, and brought forth *f*,
21.19 no *f* grow on thee henceforward
34 when the time of the *f* drew near,
26.29 henceforth of this *f* of the vine,
Mk 4. 7 and choked it, and it yielded no *f*.
8 and did yield *f* that sprang up
20 and bring forth *f*, some thirtyfold,
28 earth bringeth forth *f* of herself;
29 But when the *f* is brought forth,
11.14 No man eat *f* of thee hereafter
12. 2 from the husbandmen of the *f* of
14.25 drink no more of the *f* of the vine,
Lk 1.42 blessed is the *f* of thy womb.
3. 9 bringeth forth not good *f* is hewn
6.43 tree bringeth not forth corrupt *f*;
43 a corrupt tree bring forth good *f*.
44 every tree is known by his own *f*.
8. 8 up, and bare *f* an hundredfold.
14 and bring no *f* to perfection.
15 and bring forth *f* with patience.
13. 6 he came and sought *f* thereon,
7 these three years I come seeking *f*
9 And if it bear *f*, well: and if not,
20.10 that they should give him of the *f*
22.18 will not drink of the *f* of the vine,
Jn 4.36 and gathereth *f* unto life eternal:
12.24 if it die, it bringeth forth much *f*.
15. 2 that beareth not *f* he taketh away:
2 that beareth *f*, he purgeth it,
2 that it may bring forth more *f*.
4 the branch cannot bear *f* of itself,
5 the same bringeth forth much *f*:
8 glorified, that ye bear much *f*;
16 ye should go and bring forth *f*,
16 and that your *f* should remain:
Ac 2.30 that of the *f* of his loins, he would
Ro 1.13 I might have some *f* among you
6.21 What *f* had ye then in those things
22 ye have your *f* unto holiness,
7. 4 we should bring forth *f* unto God.
5 to bring forth *f* unto death.
15.28 and have sealed to them this *f*,
1Co 9. 7 and eateth not of the *f* thereof?
Gal 5.22 But the *f* of the Spirit is love,
Eph 5. 9 *f* of the Spirit is in all goodness
Php 1.22 this is the *f* of my labor:
4.17 but I desire *f* that may abound
Col 1. 6 bringeth forth *f*, as it doth also
Heb 12.11 it yieldeth the peaceable *f* of
13.15 the *f* of our lips giving thanks
Jas 3.18 And the *f* of righteousness is sown
5. 7 for the precious *f* of the earth,
18 and the earth brought forth her *f*.
Jude 12 tree whose *f* withereth,
12 without *f*, twice dead,
Rev 22. 2 and yielded her *f* every month:

FRUITFUL
Gen 1.22 Be *f*, and multiply, and fill the
Ps 128. 3 Thy wife shall be as a *f* vine
Eze 17. 5 and planted it in a *f* field;
19.10 she was *f* and full of branches
Ac 14.17 and *f* seasons, filling our hearts
Col 1.10 being *f* in every good work,

FRUITS
Gen 43.11 take of the best *f* in the land
Ex 22.29 the first of thy ripe *f*, and of thy
23.10 shalt gather in the *f* thereof:
Lev 25.15 the *f* he shall sell unto thee:
16 the *f* doth he sell unto thee.
22 until her *f* come in ye shall eat
26.20 trees of the land yield their *f*.
Dt 33.14 for the precious *f* brought forth
2Sa 9.10 bring in the *f*, that thy master's son
16. 1 hundred of summer *f*, and a bottle
2Ki 8. 6 all the *f* of the field since the day
19.29 vineyards, and eat the *f* thereof.
Job 31.39 If I have eaten the *f* thereof
Ps 107.37 which may yield *f* of increase.
Ec 2. 5 trees in them of all kind of *f*:
SS 4.13 with pleasant *f*; camphire, with
16 his garden, and eat his pleasant *f*.
6.11 to see the *f* of the valley,
7.13 are all manner of pleasant *f*,
Isa 16. 9 for the shouting for thy summer *f*
33. 9 and Carmel shake off their *f*.
Jer 40.10 gather ye wine, and summer *f*, and
12 gathered wine and summer *f* very
48.32 spoiler is fallen upon thy summer *f*
La 4. 9 for want of the *f* of the field.
Mic 7. 1 they have gathered the summer *f*,
Mal 3.11 not destroy the *f* of your ground;
Mt 3. 8 therefore *f* meet for repentance:
7.16 Ye shall know them by their *f*.
20 by their *f* ye shall know them.
21.34 they might receive the *f* of it.
41 render him the *f* in their seasons.
43 bringeth forth the *f* thereof.
Lk 3. 8 therefore *f* worthy of repentance;
12.17 no room where to bestow my *f*?
18 I bestow all my *f* and my goods,
2Co 9.10 the *f* of your righteousness;
Php 1.11 with the *f* of righteousness,
2Ti 2. 6 must be first partaker of the *f*.
Jas 3.17 full of mercy and good *f*,
Rev 18.14 the *f* that thy soul lusted after
22. 2 which base twelve manner of *f*,

FRUSTRATE
Ezr 4. 5 to *f* their purpose, all the days
Gal 2.21 I do not *f* the grace of God:

FULFIL
Gen 29.27 *F* her week, and we will give thee
Ex 5.13 *F* your works, and your daily tasks,
23.26 the number of thy days I will *f*.
1Ki 2.27 he might *f* the word of the Lord,
1Ch 22.13 takest heed to *f* the statutes
2Ch 36.21 To *f* the word of the Lord by the
21 to *f* threescore and ten years.
Job 39. 2 number the months that they *f*?
Ps 20. 4 and *f* all thy counsel.
5 the Lord *f* all thy petitions.
145.19 He will *f* the desire of them that
Mt 3.15 us to *f* all righteousness.
5.17 I am not come to destroy, but to *f*.
Ac 13.22 heart, which shall *f* all my will.
Ro 2.27 if it *f* the law, judge thee,
13.14 provision for the flesh, to *f* the lusts
Gal 5.16 shall not *f* the lust of the flesh.
6. 2 and so *f* the law of Christ.
Php 2. 2 *F* ye my joy, that ye be
Col 1.25 for you, to *f* the word of God;
4.17 in the Lord, that thou *f* it.

2Th 1.11 and *f* all the good pleasure of his
Jas 2. 8 If ye *f* the royal law according to
Rev 17.17 to *f* his will, and to agree, and

FULFILLED

Gen 25.24 her days to be delivered were *f*,
29.21 my days are *f*, that I may go
28 Jacob did so, and *f* her week:
50. 3 And forty days were *f* for him;
3 for so are *f* the days of those
Ex 5.14 Wherefore have ye not *f* your
7.25 And seven days were *f*, after that
Lev 12. 4 until the days of her purifying be *f*.
6 the days of her purifying are *f*,
Nu 6. 5 until the days be *f*, in the which
13 the days of his separation are *f*:
2Sa 7.12 when thy days be *f*, and thou shalt
14.22 hath *f* the request of his servant.
1Ki 8.15 hath with his hand *f* it, saying,
24 and hast *f* it with thine hand,
2Ch 6. 4 who hath with his hands *f*
15 and hast *f* it with thine hand,
Ezr 1. 1 mouth of Jeremiah might be *f*,
Job 36.17 *f* the judgment of the wicked:
Jer 44.25 spoken with your mouths, and *f*
La 2.17 he hath *f* his word that he had
4.18 our end is near, our days are *f*;
Eze 5. 2 when the days of the siege are *f*:
Dan 4.33 The same hour was the thing *f*
10. 3 till three whole weeks were *f*.
Mt 1.22 this was done, that it might be *f*
2.15 it might be *f* which was spoken
17 Then was *f* that which was spoken
23 that it might be *f* which was
4.14 it might be *f* which was spoken
5.18 from the law, till all be *f*.
8.17 it might be *f* which was spoken
12.17 be *f* which was spoken by Esaias
13.14 And in them is *f* the prophecy
35 That it might be *f* which was
21. 4 it might be *f* which was spoken by
24.34 pass, till all these things be *f*.
26.54 then shall the scriptures be *f*,
56 of the prophets might be *f*.
27. 9 was *f* that which was spoken
35 it might be *f* which was spoken
Mk 1.15 The time is *f*, and the kingdom
13. 4 when all these things shall be *f*?
14.49 but the scriptures must be *f*.
15.28 the scripture was *f*, which saith,
Lk 1.20 which shall be *f* in their season.
2.43 And when they had *f* the days,
4.21 day is this scripture *f* in your ears.
21.22 things which are written may be *f*.
24 until the times of the Gentiles be *f*.
32 shall not pass away, till all be *f*,
22.16 until it be *f* in the kingdom
24.44 must be *f*, which were written
Jn 3.29 this my joy therefore is *f*.
12.38 might be *f*. which he spake, Lord.
13.18 but that the scripture may be *f*,
15.25 work might be *f* that is written
17.12 that the scripture might be *f*.
13 that they might have my joy *f*
18. 9 saying might be *f*, which he spake,
32 the saying of Jesus might be *f*,
19.24 scripture might be *f*, which saith,
28 that the scripture might be *f*,
36 the scripture should be *f*, A bone
Ac 1.16 scripture must needs have been *f*,
3.18 should suffer, he hath so *f*.
9.23 And after that many days were *f*,
12.25 when they had *f* their ministry,
13.25 as John *f* his course, he said,
27 have *f* them in condemning him.
29 *f* all that was written of him,
33 God hath *f* the same unto us
14.26 for the work which they *f*.
Ro 8. 4 of the law might be *f* in us.
13. 8 loveth another hath *f* the law.
2Co 10. 6 when your obedience is *f*.
Gal 5.14 all the law is *f* in one word,
Jas 2.23 the scripture was *f* which saith,
Rev 6.11 killed as they were, should be *f*.
15. 8 of the seven angels were *f*.
17.17 until the words of God shall be *f*.
20. 3 the thousand years should be *f*:

FULFILLING

Ps 148. 8 vapors; stormy wind *f* his word:
Ro 13.10 therefore love is the *f* of the law.
Eph 2. 3 *f* the desires of the flesh and of

FULL

Gen 35.29 old and *f* of days: and his sons
41. 7 the seven rank and *f* ears.
43.21 money in *f* weight: and we have
Ex 16. 3 when we did eat bread to the *f*;
Lev 19.29 the land become *f* of wickedness.
Dt 6.11 houses *f* of all good things,
8.12 when thou hast eaten and art *f*,
33.23 *f* with the blessing of the Lord:
34. 9 Nun was *f* of the spirit of wisdom;
Ru 1.21 went out *f*, and the Lord hath
2Ki 6.17 the mountain was *f* of horses
Job 5.26 shalt come to thy grave in a *f* age,
7. 4 and I am *f* of tossings to and fro
10.15 I am *f* of confusion; therefore see
11. 2 should a man *f* of talk be justified?
14. 1 is of few days, and *f* of trouble.
21.23 One dieth in his *f* strength, being
24 His breasts are *f* of milk, and
32.18 I am *f* of matter, the spirit within
Ps 10. 7 His mouth is *f* of cursing and
26.10 their right hand is *f* of bribes.
29. 4 voice of the Lord is *f* of majesty.
33. 5 the earth is *f* of the goodness of
65. 9 river of God, which is *f* of water:
78.25 he sent them meat to the *f*.
86.15 a God *f* of compassion, and gracious,
83. 3 For my soul is *f* of troubles:
104.16 trees of the Lord are *f* of sap;
24 the earth is *f* of thy riches.
145. 8 Lord is gracious, and *f* of compassion;
Pr 27.20 Hell and destruction are never *f*;
Ec 1. 8 All things are *f* of labor; man
9. 3 of the sons of men is *f* of evil,
10.14 A fool also is *f* of words:
Isa 1.11 I am *f* of the burnt offerings of
2. 8 Their land also is *f* of idols;
6. 3 the whole earth is *f* of his glory.
11. 9 earth shall be *f* of the knowledge
Jer 4.27 yet will I not make a *f* end.
6.11 I am *f* of the fury of the Lord;
30.11 though I make a *f* end of all nations
Eze 7.23 the land is *f* of bloody crimes,
23 and the city is *f* of violence.
28.12 *f* of wisdom, and perfect in
37. 1 the valley which was *f* of bones,
Joel 2.24 And the floors shall be *f* of wheat,
3.13 the press is *f*, the fats overflow;
Mic 3. 8 I am *f* of power by the spirit
6.12 rich men thereof are *f* of violence,
Na 3. 1 it is all *f* of lies and robbery;
Hab 3. 3 the earth was *f* of his praise.
Zec 8. 5 the city shall be *f* of boys and girls
Mt 6.22 the whole body shall be *f* of light.
23 whole body shall be *f* of darkness.
13.48 Which, when it was *f*, they drew
14.20 that remained twelve baskets *f*.
15.37 that was left seven baskets *f*.
23.25 within they are *f* of extortion
27 are within *f* of dead men's bones,
28 are *f* of hypocrisy and iniquity.
Mk 4.28 after that the *f* corn in the ear.
37 the ship, so that it was now *f*.
6.43 baskets *f* of the fragments,
7. 9 *F* well ye reject the commandment
8.19 many baskets *f* of fragments
20 how many baskets *f* of fragments
15.36 And one ran and filled a spunge *f*
Lk 1.57 Elisabeth's *f* time came that she
4. 1 Jesus being *f* of the Holy Ghost
5.12 behold a man *f* of leprosy: who
6.25 Woe unto you that are *f*! for ye
11.34 the whole body also is *f* of light;
34 thy body also is *f* of darkness.
36 whole body therefore be *f* of light,
36 the whole shall be *f* of light, as
39 your inward part is *f* of ravening
16.20 laid at his gate *f* of sores,
Jn 1.14 the Father,) *f* of grace and truth.
7. 8 my time is not yet *f* come.
15.11 and that your joy might be *f*.
16.24 receive, that your joy may be *f*.
19.29 was set a vessel *f* of vinegar:
21.11 *f* of great fishes, an hundred and
Ac 2.13 These men are *f* of new wine.
28 thou shalt make me *f* of joy with
6. 3 *f* of the Holy Ghost and wisdom,
5 *f* of faith and of the Holy Ghost,
8 Stephen, *f* of faith and power,
7.23 when he was *f* forty years old,
55 he, being *f* of the Holy Ghost,
9.36 this woman was *f* of good works
11.24 *f* of the Holy Ghost and of faith:
13.10 O *f* of all subtilty and all mischief,
19.28 they were *f* of wrath, and cried
Ro 1.29 *f* of envy, murder, debate, deceit,
3.14 is *f* of cursing and bitterness:
15.14 that ye are also *f* of goodness,
1Co 4. 8 Now ye are *f*, now ye are rich,
Php 2.26 you all, and was *f* of heaviness,
4.12 both to be *f* and to be hungry,
18 I am *f*, having received of
Col 2. 2 the *f* assurance of understanding,
2Ti 4. 5 of an evangelist, make *f* proof of
Heb 5.14 belongeth to them that are of *f*
6.11 *f* assurance of hope unto the end:
10.22 in *f* assurance of faith, having
Jas 3. 8 an unruly evil, *f* of deadly poison.
17 *f* of mercy and good fruits, without
1Pe 1. 8 with joy unspeakable and *f* of glory:
2Pe 2.14 Having eyes *f* of adultery, and that
1Jn 1. 4 you, that your joy may be *f*.
2Jn 8 but that we receive a *f* reward.
12 to face, that our joy may be *f*.
Rev 4. 6 *f* of eyes before and behind.
8 they were *f* of eyes within: and
5. 8 harps, and golden vials *f* of odors,
15. 7 *f* of the wrath of God, who liveth
16.10 his kingdom was *f* of darkness;
17. 3 *f* of names of blasphemy, having
4 cup in her hand *f* of abominations
21. 9 vials *f* of the seven last plagues,

FULLER

Mk 9. 3 as no *f* on earth can white them.

FULLERS'

Mal 3. 2 like a refiner's fire, and like *f* sope.

FULLY

Nu 7. 1 had *f* set up the tabernacle,
14.24 and hath followed me *f*, him will
Ru 2.11 It hath *f* been shewed me, all
1Ki 11. 6 went not *f* after the Lord, as did
Ec 8.11 heart of the sons of men is *f* set
Na 1.10 be devoured as stubble *f* dry.
Ac 2. 1 the day of Pentecost was *f* come,
Ro 4.21 And being *f* persuaded that, what
14. 5 Let every man be *f* persuaded
15.19 I have *f* preached the gospel of
2Ti 3.10 thou hast *f* known my doctrine,
4.17 the preaching might be *f* known,
Rev 14.18 for her grapes are *f* ripe.

FULNESS

Nu 18.27 and as the *f* of the winepress.
Dt 33.16 things of the earth and *f* thereof,
1Ch 16.32 Let the sea roar, and the *f* thereof:
Job 20.22 In the *f* of his sufficiency he shall
Ps 16.11 in thy presence is *f* of joy;

24. 1 is the Lord's, and the *f* thereof;
50.12 world is mine, and the *f* thereof.
89.11 the world and the *f* thereof, thou
96.11 let the sea roar, and the *f* thereof.
98. 7 Let the sea roar and the *f* thereof;
Eze 16.49 *f* of bread, and abundance of
19. 7 was desolate, and the *f* thereof,
Jn 1.16 of his *f* have all we received,
Ro 11.12 Gentiles; how much more their *f*?
25 the *f* of the Gentiles be come
15.29 come in the *f* of the blessing
1Co 10.26 is the Lord's, and the *f* thereof.
28 is the Lord's, and the *f* thereof:
Gal 4. 4 when the *f* of the time was come
Eph 1.10 dispensation of the *f* of times
23 the *f* of him that filleth all in all.
3.19 be filled with all the *f* of God.
4.13 the stature of the *f* of Christ:
Col 1.19 that in him should all *f* dwell;
2. 9 all the *f* of the Godhead bodily.

FURIOUSLY

2Ki 9.20 son of Nimshi; for he driveth *f*.
Eze 23.25 and they shall deal *f* with thee:

FURNACE

Dt 4.20 you forth out of the iron *f*,
1Ki 8.51 from the midst of the *f* of iron:
Ps 12. 6 as silver tried in a *f* of earth,
Pr 17. 3 and the *f* for gold: but the Lord
Dan 3. 6, 11 the midst of a burning fiery *f*.
19 heat the *f* one seven times more
20 cast them into the burning fiery *f*.
Mt 13.42 shall cast them into a *f* of fire:
50 shall cast them into the *f* of fire:
Rev 1.15 as if they burned in a *f*;
9. 2 as the smoke of a great *f*;

FURNISH

Dt 15.14 *f* him liberally out of thy flock,
Ps 78.19 God *f* a table in the wilderness?
Isa 65.11 *f* the drink offering unto that
Jer 46.19 *f* thyself to go into captivity:

FURNISHED

1Ki 9.11 Hiram the king of Tyre had *f*
Pr 9. 2 she hath also *f* her table.
Mt 22.10 the wedding was *f* with guests.
Mk 14.15 large upper room *f* and prepared:
Lk 22.12 shew you a large upper room *f*:
2Ti 3.17 throughly *f* unto all good works.

FURTHER

Nu 22.26 the angel of the Lord went *f*,
Dt 20. 8 shall speak *f* unto the people,
1Sa 10.22 inquired of the Lord *f*, if the man
Est 9.12 is thy request *f*? and it shall be
Job 38.11 shalt thou come, but no *f*:
40. 5 yea, twice; but I will proceed no *f*.
Ps 140. 8 *f* not his wicked device; lest they
Ec 12.12 And *f*, by these, my son, be
Mt 26.65 what *f* need have we of witnesses?
Mk 5.35 troublest thou the Master any *f*?
14.63 What need we any *f* witnesses?
Lk 22.71 What need we any *f* witness?
24.28 as though he would have gone *f*.
Ac 4.17 spread no *f* among the people,
21 when they had *f* threatened them,
12. 3 he proceeded *f* to take Peter also.
21.28 *f* brought Greeks also into the
24. 4 I be not *f* tedious unto thee,
27.28 when they had gone a little *f*,
2Ti 3. 9 proceed no *f*: for their folly,
Heb 7.11 *f* need was there that another

FURTHERANCE

Php 1.12 rather unto the *f* of the gospel;
25 for your *f* and joy of faith;

FURTHERMORE

Ex 4. 6 And the Lord said *f* unto him,
Dt 4.21 *F* the Lord was angry with me
9.13 *F* the Lord spake unto me,
1Sa 26.10 David said *f*, As the Lord liveth,
1Ch 17.10 *F* I tell thee that the Lord will
27.16 *F* over the tribes of Israel: the
29. 1 *F* David the king said unto
2Ch 4. 9 *F* he made the court of the
Job 34. 1 *F* Elihu answered and said,
Eze 8. 6 He said *f* unto me, Son of man,
23.40 And *f*, that ye have sent for men
2Co 2.12 *F*, when I came to Troas to
1Th 4. 1 *F* then we beseech you, brethren,
Heb 12. 9 *F* we have had fathers of our

FURY

Gen 27.44 until thy brother's *f* turn away;
Job 20.23 God shall cast the *f* of his wrath
Isa 27. 4 *F* is not in me: who would set
51.13 where is the *f* of the oppressor?
17 of the Lord the cup of his *f*;
20 they are full of the *f* of the Lord,
22 the dregs of the cup of my *f*;
Jer 6.11 I am full of the *f* of the Lord;
10.25 Pour out thy *f* upon the heathen
23.19 the Lord is gone forth in *f*,
44. 6 *f* and mine anger was poured
La 2. 4 he poured out his *f* like fire.
4.11 Lord hath accomplished his *f*;
Eze 7. 8 Now will I shortly pour out my *f*
8.18 Therefore will I also deal in *f*:
13.13 with a stormy wind in my *f*;
16.42 I make my *f* toward thee to rest,
Dan 3.19 Then was Nebuchadnezzar full of *f*,
Na 1. 6 *f* is poured out like fire, and the
Zec 8. 2 I was jealous for her with great *f*.

G

GABRIEL
Dan 8.16 *G*, make this man to understand
9.21 even the man *G*, whom I had seen
Lk 1.19 I am *G*, that stand in the
26 sixth month the angel *G* was sent

GAIN
Jdg 5.19 they took no *g* of money.
Job 22. 3 or is it *g* to him, that thou makest
Pr 1.19 every one that is greedy of *g*;
3.14 and the *g* thereof than fine gold.
15.27 He that is greedy of *g* troubleth
28. 8 by usury and unjust *g* increaseth
Isa 33.15 despiseth the *g* of oppressions,
56.11 one for his *g*, from his quarter.
Eze 22.13 mine hand at thy dishonest *g*
27 destroy souls, to get dishonest *g*.
Dan 2. 8 certainty that ye would *g* the time,
11.39 and shall divide the land for *g*.
Mic 4.13 consecrate their *g* unto the Lord,
Mt 16.26 if he shall *g* the whole world, and
Mk 8.36 if he shall *g* the whole world, and
Lk 9.25 if he *g* the whole world, and lose
Ac 16.16 brought her masters much *g* by
19.24 brought no small *g* unto the
1Co 9.19 unto all, that I might *g* the more.
20 that I might *g* the Jews;
20 that I might *g* them that are under
21 might *g* them that are without law.
22 that I might *g* the weak:
2Co 12.17 Did I make a *g* of you by any
18 Did Titus make a *g* of you?
Php 1.21 to live is Christ, and to die is *g*.
3. 7 But what things were *g* to me,
1Ti 6. 5 supposing that *g* is godliness:
6 with contentment is great *g*.
Jas 4.13 and buy and sell, and get *g*:

GAINED
Job 27. 8 though he hath *g*, when God
Eze 22.12 and thou hast greedily *g* of thy
Mt 18.15 thee, thou hast *g* thy brother.
25.17 received two, he also *g* other two.
20 I have *g* beside them five talents
22 *g* two other talents beside them.
Lk 19.15 every man had *g* by trading.
16 thy pound hath *g* ten pounds.
18 thy pound hath *g* five pounds.
Ac 27.21 to have *g* this harm and loss.

GAINS
Ac 16.19 the hope of their *g* was gone,

GAINSAY
Lk 21.15 shall not be able to *g* nor resist.

GAINSAYERS
Tit 1.19 to exhort and to convince the *g*.

GAINSAYING
Ac 10.29 came I unto you without *g*,
Ro 10.21 a disobedient and *g* people.
Jude 11 and perished in the *g* of Core.

GAIUS
Ac 19.29 caught *G* and Aristarchus,
20. 4 and *G* of Derbe, and Timotheus;
Ro 16.23 *G* mine host, and of the whole
1Co 1.14 none of you, but Crispus and *G*:
3Jn 1 The elder unto the wellbeloved *G*,

GALATIA
Ac 16. 6 Phrygia and the region of *G*,
18.23 country of *G* and Phrygia in order,
1Co 16. 1 given order to the churches of *G*,
Gal 1. 2 with me unto the churches of *G*:
2Ti 4.10 Crescens to *G*, Titus unto
1Pe 1. 1 Pontus, *G*, Cappadocia, Asia,

GALATIANS
Gal 3. 1 O foolish *G*. who hath bewitched

GALILEAN
Mk 14.70 for thou art a *G*, and thy speech
Lk 22.59 also was with him: for he is a *G*.
23. 6 asked whether the man were a *G*.

GALILEANS
Lk 13. 1 some that told him of the *G*,
2 Suppose ye that these *G* were
2 sinners above all the *G*,
Jn 4.45 the *G* received him, having seen
Ac 2. 6 are not all these which speak *G*?

GALILEE
Jos 20. 7 Kedesh in *G* in mount Naphtali,
21.32 Kedesh in *G* with her suburbs,
1Ki 9.11 twenty cities in the land of *G*.
2Ki 15.29 Hazor, and Gilead, and *G*, all the
1Ch 6.76 Kedesh in *G* with her suburbs,
Isa 9. 1 beyond Jordan, in *G* of the nations.
Mt 2.22 he turned aside in the parts of *G*:
3.13 cometh Jesus from *G* to Jordan
4.12 into prison, he departed into *G*;
15 beyond Jordan, *G* of the Gentiles;
18 Jesus, walking by the sea of *G*,
23 And Jesus went about all *G*,
25 great multitudes of people from *G*.
15.29 came nigh unto the sea of *G*;
17.22 while they abode in the *G*, Jesus said
19. 1 he departed from *G*, and came
21.11 the prophet of Nazareth of *G*.
26.32 I will go before you into *G*.
69 Thou also wast with Jesus of *G*.
27.55 which followed Jesus from *G*,
28. 7 he goeth before you into *G*;
10 that they go into *G*, and there
16 eleven disciples went away into *G*,
Mk 1. 9 Jesus came from Nazareth of *G*,
14 Jesus came into *G*, preaching the
16 Now as he walked by the sea of *G*,
28 all the region round about *G*.
39 synagogues throughout all *G*,
3. 7 multitude from *G* followed him,
6.21 captains, and chief estates of *G*;
7.31 he came unto the sea of *G*,
9.30 thence, and passed through *G*;
14.28 I will go before you into *G*.
15.41 when he was in *G*, followed him,
16. 7 that he goeth before you into *G*:
Lk 1.26 unto a city of *G*, named Nazareth,
2. 4 And Joseph also went up from *G*,
39 they returned into *G*, to their own
3. 1 and Herod being tetrarch of *G*,
4.14 in the power of the Spirit into *G*:
31 down to Capernaum, a city of *G*,
44 preached in the synagogues of *G*.
5.17 were come out of every town of *G*,
8.26 which is over against *G*.
17.11 the midst of Samaria and *G*.
23. 5 beginning from *G* to this place.
6 When Pilate heard of *G*, he asked
49 women that followed him from *G*,
55 which came with him from *G*,

The angel Gabriel tells Mary that she will be the mother of Jesus (Lk 1.26-38) in Botticelli's Annunciation.

24. 6 unto you when he was yet in *G*,
Jn 1.43 Jesus would go forth into *G*,
2. 1 there was a marriage in Cana of *G*;
11 miracles did Jesus in Cana of *G*,
4. 3 Judea, and departed again into *G*.
43 departed thence, and went into *G*.
45 Then when he was come into *G*,
46 Jesus came again into Cana of *G*,
47 was come out of Judea into *G*, he
54 he was come out of Judea into *G*.
6. 1 Jesus went over the sea of *G*,
7. 1 these things Jesus walked in *G*:
9 unto them, he abode still in *G*.
41 said, Shall Christ come out of *G*?
52 Art thou also of *G*? Search, and
52 for out of *G* ariseth no prophet.
12.21 which was of Bethsaida of *G*,
21. 2 and Nathanael of Cana in *G*,
Ac 1.11 Ye men of *G*, why stand ye gazing
5.37 After this man rose up Judas of *G*
9.31 all Judea and *G* and Samaria,
10.37 began from *G*, after the baptism
13.31 which came up with him from *G*

GALL
Dt 29.18 that beareth *g* and wormwood;
32.32 their grapes are grapes of *g*,
Job 16.13 out my *g* upon the ground.
20.14 it is the *g* of asps within him.
25 sword cometh out of his *g*:
Ps 69.21 gave me also *g* for my meat;
Jer 8.14 given us water of *g* to drink,
9.15 give them water of *g* to drink.
23.15 make them drink the water of *g*:
La 3. 5 compassed me with *g* and travel.
19 misery, the wormwood and the *g*.
Am 6.12 ye have turned judgment into *g*,
Mt 27.34 vinegar to drink mingled with *g*:
Ac 8.23 thou art in the *g* of the bitterness,

GALLIO
Ac 18.12 *G* was the deputy of Achaia,
14 *G* said unto the Jews, If it were a
17 And *G* cared for none of those

GALLOWS
Est 5.14 a *g* be made of fifty cubits high,
14 he caused the *g* to be made.
6. 4 to hang Mordecai on the *g* that he
7. 9 Behold also, the *g* fifty cubits high,
10 So they hanged Haman on the *g*
8. 7 they have hanged upon the *g*,
9.13 ten sons be hanged upon the *g*.
25 his sons should be hanged on the *g*.

GAMALIEL
Nu 1.10 Manasseh; *G* the son of Pedahzur.
2.20 of Manasseh shall be *G* the son of
7.54 offered *G* the son of Pedahzur
59 this was the offering of *G* the son
10.23 of the children of Manasseh was *G*
Ac 5.34 a Pharisee, named *G*, a doctor of
22. 3 in this city at the feet of *G*,

GAOLER *see Jailer*

GARDEN
Gen 2. 8 And the Lord God planted a *g*
15 put him into the *g* of Eden
3. 1 shall not eat of every tree of the *g*?
8 the Lord God walking in the *g*
10 I heard thy voice in the *g*,
23 sent him forth from the *g* of Eden,
Dt 11.10 with thy foot, as a *g* of herbs:
SS 4.12 A *g* inclosed is my sister, my
16 Let my beloved come into his *g*,
Isa 1. 8 as a lodge in a *g* of cucumbers,
30 and as a *g* that hath no water.
51. 3 her desert like the *g* of the Lord;
58.11 thou shalt be like a watered *g*,
Eze 28.13 been in Eden the *g* of God;
Joel 2. 3 the land is as the *g* of Eden
Lk 13.19 a man took, and cast into his *g*;

Jesus walks on the turbulent Sea of Galilee (Mt 14; Mk 6; Jn 6) in this painting by Tintoretto (1518-94).

Jn 18. 1 where was a *g*, into the which
26 Did not I see thee in the *g*
19.41 a *g*; and in the *g* a new sepulchre,

GARDENER
Jn 20.15 She, supposing him to be the *g*,

GARDENS
Nu 24. 6 forth, as *g* by the river's side,
Ec 2. 5 I made me *g* and orchards,
SS 4.15 of *g*, a well of living waters,
6. 2 in the *g*, and to gather lilies.
8.13 Thou that dwellest in the *g*,
Isa 1.29 for the *g* that ye have chosen.
65. 3 that sacrificeth in *g*, and burneth
66.17 the *g* behind one tree in the midst,
Jer 29. 5 plant *g*, and eat the fruit of them;
28 plant *g*, and eat the fruit of them.
Am 4. 9 when your *g* and your vineyards
9.14 make *g*, and eat the fruit of them.

GARLANDS
Ac 14.13 brought oxen and *g* unto the gates,

GARMENT
Gen 39.12 he left his *g* in her hand,
Dt 22. 5 shall a man put on a woman's *g*:
2Sa 13.18 she had a *g* of divers colors
19 and rent her *g* of divers colors
Ezr 9. 3 I rent my *g* and my mantle,
Job 13.28 as a *g* that is moth eaten.
41.13 Who can discover the face of his *g*?
Ps 69.11 I made sackcloth also my *g*;
73. 6 violence covereth them as a *g*.
102.26 all of them shall wax old like a *g*;
104. 2 thyself with light as with a *g*:
6 with the deep as with a *g*:
109.18 with cursing like as with his *g*,
19 Let it be unto him as the *g*
Pr 30. 4 who hath bound the waters in a *g*?
Isa 50. 9 they all shall wax old as a *g*;
51. 6 the earth shall wax old like a *g*,
61. 3 the *g* of praise for the spirit of
Jer 43.12 as a shepherd putteth on his *g*;
Mal 2.16 one covereth violence with his *g*,
Mt 9.16 piece of new cloth unto an old *g*,
16 to fill it up taketh from the *g*,
20 and touched the hem of his *g*:
21 If I may but touch his *g*,
14.36 only touch the hem of his *g*:
22.11 which had not on a wedding *g*:
12 in hither not having a wedding *g*?
Mk 2.21 piece of new cloth on an old *g*:
5.27 press behind, and touched his *g*.
6.56 it were but the border of his *g*:
10.50 And he, casting away his *g*, rose,
13.16 back again for to take up his *g*.
16. 5 clothed in a long white *g*; and
Lk 5.36 a piece of a new *g* upon an old;
8.44 and touched the border of his *g*:
22.36 let him sell his *g*, and buy one.
Ac 12. 8 Cast thy *g* about thee,
Heb 1.11 all shall wax old as doth a *g*;
Jude 23 hating even the *g* spotted by the
Rev 1.13 clothed with a *g* down to the foot,
(See illustration on page 316)

GARMENTS
Ex 28. 2 thou shalt make holy *g* for Aaron
Nu 20.28 And Moses stripped Aaron of his *g*,
2Sa 10. 4 cut off their *g* in the middle,
13.31 the king arose, and tare his *g*,
1Ch 19. 4 and cut off their *g* in the midst
Ps 22.18 They part my *g* among them,
Ec 9. 8 Let thy *g* be always white;
Isa 9. 5 noise, and *g* rolled in blood;
52. 1 on thy beautiful *g*, O Jerusalem,
17 he put on the *g* of vengeance
61.10 clothed me with the *g* of salvation,
63. 1 Edom, with dyed *g* from Bozrah?
Jer 52.33 And changed his prison *g*: and he
Joel 2.13 rend your heart, and not your *g*,
Mt 21. 8 spread their *g* in the way;
23. 5 enlarge the borders of their *g*,
27.35 and parted his *g*, casting lots:
35 They parted my *g* among them,
Mk 11. 7 and cast their *g* on him; and he
8 many spread their *g* in the way;
15.24 they parted his *g*, casting lots
Lk 19.35 they cast their *g* upon the colt,
24. 4 men stood by them in shining *g*:
Jn 13. 4 from supper, and laid aside his *g*;
12 and had taken his *g*, and was set
19.23 took his *g* and made four parts,
Ac 9.39 shewing the coats and *g* which
Jas 5. 2 and your *g* are motheaten.

Garments worn by Roman officials and their families in Jesus' time looked like those shown in this relief.

Rev 3. 4 which have not defiled their *g*:
16.15 that watcheth, and keepeth his *g*,

GARNER
Mt 3.12 and gather his wheat into the *g*;
Lk 3.17 will gather the wheat into his *g*;

GARNISH
Mt 23.29 and *g* the sepulchres of the

GARNISHED
2Ch 3. 6 And he *g* the house with precious
Job 26.13 his spirit he hath *g* the heavens;
Mt 12.44 he findeth it empty, swept, and *g*.
Lk 11.25 he findeth it swept and *g*.
Rev 21.19 of the wall of the city were *g*

GATE
Gen 19. 1 Lot sat in the *g* of Sodom:
22.17 possess the *g* of his enemies;
28.17 and this is the *g* of heaven.
Ex 32.26 Moses stood in the *g* of the camp,
Dt 22.15 unto the elders of the city in the *g*:
25. 7 go up to the *g* unto the elders,
Jos 2. 5 about the time of shutting of the *g*,
Jdg 16. 2 laid wait for him all night in the *g*
3 took the doors of the *g* of the city,
Ru 4. 1 Then went Boaz up to the *g*,
2Sa 18.33 up to the chamber over the *g*,
23.15 of Beth-lehem, which is by the *g*!
2Ki 7. 1 a shekel, in the *g* of Samaria.
17 the people trode upon him in the *g*,
1Ch 11.17 well of Beth-lehem, that is at the *g*!
2Ch 25.23 the *g* of Ephraim to the corner *g*,
26. 9 the corner *g*, and at the valley *g*,
27. 3 He built the high *g* of the house
33.14 the entering in at the fish *g*,
Neh 3. 1 they builded the sheep *g*; they
3 fish *g* did the sons of Hassenaah
6 the old *g* repaired Jehoiada
13 The valley *g* repaired Hanun,
14 the dung *g* repaired Malchiah
26 place over against the water *g*
28 the horse *g* repaired the priests,
29 the keeper of the east *g*.
31 over against the *g* Miphkad,
8.16 in the street of the *g* of Ephraim.
12.37 And at the fountain *g*, which was
39 they stood still in the prison *g*.
Est 2.19 then Mordecai sat in the king's *g*.
Ps 69.12 They that sit in the *g* speak
118.20 This *g* of the Lord, into which the
127. 5 speak with the enemies in the *g*.
Isa 14.31 Howl, O *g*; cry, O city; thou,
Jer 7. 2 Stand in the *g* of the Lord's house,
La 5.14 elders have ceased from the *g*,
Eze 46. 9 the way of the north *g* to worship
Am 5.10 hate him that rebuketh in the *g*,
12 they turn aside the poor in the *g*
15 and establish judgment in the *g*:
Mic 1. 9 he is come unto the *g* of my people,
Mt 7.13 Enter ye in at the strait *g*:
13 for wide is the *g*, and broad is the
14 Because strait is the *g*, and narrow
Lk 7.12 he came nigh to the *g* of the city,
13.24 Strive to enter in at the strait *g*:
16.20 which was laid at his *g*, full of
Ac 3. 2 the *g* of the temple which is called
10 at the Beautiful *g* of the temple:
10.17 house, and stood before the *g*,
12.10 they came unto the iron *g* that
13 knocked at the door of the *g*,
14 she opened not the *g* for gladness,
14 told how Peter stood before the *g*.
Heb 13.12 own blood, suffered without the *g*.

GATES
Ex 20.10 thy stranger that is within thy *g*:
Dt 6. 9 posts of thy house, and on thy *g*.
16. 5 the passover within any of thy *g*,
14 widow, that are within thy *g*.
Neh 1. 3 the *g* thereof are burned with fire.
Job 38.17 Have the *g* of death been opened
Ps 9.13 liftest me up from the *g* of death:
24. 7 your heads, O ye *g*; and be ye lift up
100. 4 Enter into his *g* with thanksgiving,
107.16 he hath broken the *g* of brass,
18 draw near unto the *g* of death.
118.19 Open to me the *g* of righteousness:
122. 2 Our feet shall stand within thy *g*,
Pr 14.19 wicked at the *g* of the righteous.
31.23 Her husband is known in the *g*,
31 her own works praise her in the *g*.
Isa 26. 2 Open ye the *g*, that the righteous
38.10 I shall go to the *g* of the grave:
45. 1 and the *g* shall not be shut;
60.11 thy *g* shall be open continually;
18 walls Salvation, and thy *g* Praise.
62.10 through the *g*; prepare ye the way
Jer 7. 2 that enter in at these *g* to worship
17.24 bring in no burden through the *g*
La 1. 4 *g* are desolate: her priests sigh,
2. 9 Her *g* are sunk into the ground;
Zec 8.16 truth and peace in your *g*:
Mt 16.18 the *g* of hell shall not prevail
Ac 9.24 they watched the *g* day and night
14.13 oxen and garlands unto the *g*,
Rev 21.12 and had twelve *g*,
12 and at the *g* twelve angels,
13 On the east three *g*;
13 on the north three *g*;
13 on the south three *g*;
13 and on the west three *g*.
15 and the *g* thereof, and the wall
21 the twelve *g* were twelve pearls;
25 And the *g* of it shall not be shut
22.14 enter in through the *g* into the city,

GATHER
Gen 31.46 said unto his brethren, *G* stones;
41.35 And let them *g* all the food
Ex 3.16 Go, and *g* the elders of Israel
5. 7 and *g* straw for themselves,
16.16 *G* of it every man according to his
26 Six days ye shall *g* it; but on the
27 on the seventh day for to *g*,
Lev 19.10 neither shalt thou *g* every grape
Nu 11.16 *G* unto me seventy men of the
Dt 11.14 that thou mayest *g* in thy corn,
31.28 *G* unto me all the elders of your
Ru 2. 7 me glean and *g* after the reapers
1Ki 18.19 *g* to me all Israel unto mount
2Ch 24. 5 *g* of all Israel money to repair
Job 34.14 if he *g* unto himself his spirit
Ps 26. 9 *G* not my soul with sinners,
50. 5 *G* my saints together unto me;
104.28 That thou givest them they *g*:
106.47 *g* us from among the heathen,
Pr 28. 8 *g* it for him that will pity the poor.
Ec 3. 5 and a time to *g* stones together;
Isa 11.12 *g* together the dispersed of Judah
40.11 shall *g* the lambs with his arm,
49.18 all these *g* themselves together,
54. 7 with great mercies will I *g* thee.
Jer 23. 3 I will *g* the remnant of my flock
29.14 I will *g* you from all the nations,
31. 8 *g* them from the coasts of the earth,
49. 5 shall *g* up him that wandereth.
Eze 22.20 so will I *g* you in mine anger
24. 4 *G* the pieces thereof into it,
Joel 3. 2 I will also *g* all nations, and will
Mic 2.12 surely *g* the remnant of Israel;
Hab 1. 9 shall *g* the captivity as the sand.
15 and *g* them in their drag:
Zep 2. 1 *g* together, O nation not desired;
3.18 I will *g* them that are sorrowful
19 and *g* her that was driven out;
Zec 10. 8 and *g* them; for I have redeemed
Mt 3.12 and *g* his wheat into the garner;
6.26 do they reap, nor *g* into barns;
7.16 Do men *g* grapes of thorns,
13.28 that we go and *g* them up?
29 Nay; lest while ye *g* up the tares,
30 *G* ye together first the tares,
30 but *g* the wheat into my barn.

41 they shall *g* out of his kingdom
24.31 they shall *g* together his elect
25.26 and *g* where I have not strawed:
Mk 13.27 and shall *g* together his elect
Lk 3.17 will *g* the wheat into his garner;
6.44 of thorns men do not *g* figs,
44 of a bramble bush *g* they grapes.
13.34 as a hen doth *g* her brood under
Jn 6.12 *G* up the fragments that remain,
11.52 also he should *g* together in one
15. 6 and men *g* them, and cast them
Eph 1.10 he might *g* together in one all
Rev 14.18 *g* the clusters of the vine of the
16.14 to *g* them to battle of that great
19.17 Come and *g* yourselves together
20. 8 to *g* them together to battle:

GATHERED
Gen 41.49 And Joseph *g* corn as the sand
47.14 And Joseph *g* up all the money
Ex 4.29 *g* together all the elders of Israel:
15. 8 the waters were *g* together, the
16.17 and *g*, some more, some less.
18 he that *g* much had nothing over,
18 and he that *g* little had no lack;
18 they *g* every man according to his
21 they *g* it every morning, every man
22 the sixth day they *g* twice as much
35. 1 Moses *g* all the congregation
Nu 11.24 and *g* the seventy men of the elders
Dt 16.13 after that thou hast *g* in thy corn
Jdg 1. 7 *g* their meat under my table:
1Sa 20.38 Jonathan's lad *g* up the arrows,
2Sa 6. 1 David *g* together all the chosen
2Ki 22. 9 Thy servants have *g* the money
23. 1 and they *g* unto him all the elders
Ezr 8.15 And I *g* them together to the river
Neh 12.28 the singers *g* themselves together,
Est 9. 2 The Jews *g* themselves together
Ps 59. 3 the mighty are *g* against me;
Pr 27.25 and herbs of the mountains are *g*.
30. 4 who hath *g* the winds in his fists?
Isa 10.14 are left, have I *g* all the earth;
13. 4 kingdoms of nations *g* together:
22. 9 and ye *g* together the waters
24.22 as prisoners are *g* in the pit,
34.15 there shall the vultures also be *g*,
43. 9 Let all the nations be *g* together,
60. 7 All the flocks of Kedar shall be *g*
Jer 3.17 all the nations shall be *g* unto it,
Zec 12. 3 people of the earth be *g* together
14.14 round about shall be *g* together,
Mt 2. 4 he had *g* all the chief priests
13. 2 great multitudes were *g* together
40 As therefore the tares are *g* and
47 into the sea, and *g* of every kind:
48 and *g* the good into vessels,
18.20 three are *g* together in my name,
22.10 and *g* together all as many as they
34 to silence, they were *g* together.
41 the Pharisees were *g* together,
23.37 often would I have *g* thy children
24.28 will the eagles be *g* together.
25.32 before him shall be *g* all nations:
27.17 they were *g* together, Pilate said
27 and *g* unto him the whole band
Mk 1.33 city was *g* together at the door.
2. 2 many were *g* together, insomuch
4. 1 was *g* unto him a great multitude,
5.21 much people *g* unto him: and he
6.30 the apostles *g* themselves together
Lk 8. 4 much people were *g* together,
11.29 people were *g* thick together.
12. 1 when they were *g* together an
13.34 how often would I have *g* thy
15.13 the younger son *g* all together,
17.37 will the eagles be *g* together.
24.33 and found the eleven *g* together.
Jn 6.13 Therefore they *g* them together,
11.47 Then *g* the chief priests and the
Ac 4. 6 were *g* together at Jerusalem.
26 rulers were *g* together against the
27 and the people of Israel, were *g*
12.12 many were *g* together praying.
14.27 and had *g* the church together,
15.30 had *g* the multitude together,
17. 5 *g* a company, and set all the city
20. 8 where there they were *g* together.
28. 3 And when Paul had *g* a bundle
1Co 5. 4 when ye are *g* together, and my
2Co 8.15 He that had *g* much had nothing
15 and he that had *g* little had no lack.
Rev 14.19 and *g* the vine of the earth,
16.16 And he *g* them together into a
19.19 and their armies, *g* together to

GATHERETH
Nu 19.10 he that *g* the ashes of the heifer
Ps 33. 7 he *g* the waters of the sea
41. 6 his heart *g* iniquity to itself;
147. 2 *g* together the outcasts of Israel.
Pr 6. 8 and *g* her food in the harvest.
10. 5 He that *g* in summer is a wise son:
13.11 but he that *g* by labor shall
Isa 10.14 and as one *g* eggs that are left,
17. 5 when the harvestman *g* the corn,
5 as he that *g* ears in the valley
56. 8 which *g* the outcasts of Israel
Na 3.18 mountains, and no man *g* them.
Hab 2. 5 but *g* unto him all nations,
Mt 12.30 he that *g* not with me scattereth
23.37 even as a hen *g* her chickens
Lk 11.23 he that *g* not with me scattereth.
Jn 4.36 and *g* fruit unto life eternal:

GATHERING
Gen 1.10 and the *g* together of the waters
49.10 him shall the *g* of the people be.
Nu 15.33 they that found him *g* sticks
1Ki 17.10 widow woman was there *g* of sticks:
12 and, behold, I am *g* two sticks,
2Ch 20.25 were three days in *g* of the spoil,
Isa 32.10 shall fail, the *g* shall not come.
33. 4 the gathering of the caterpiller:
Mt 25.24 *g* where thou hast not strawed:
Ac 16.10 assuredly *g* that the Lord had
2Th 2. 1 by our *g* together unto him,

GATHERINGS
1Co 16. 2 that there be no *g* when I come.

GAVE
Gen 2.20 And Adam *g* names to all cattle,
3. 6 and *g* also unto her husband
12 to be with me, she *g* me of the tree,
25. 5 And Abraham *g* all that he had
6 Abraham *g* gifts, and sent them
8 Then Abraham *g* up the ghost, and
34 Jacob *g* Esau bread and pottage
27.17 And she *g* the savory meat and
29.28 and he *g* him Rachel his daughter
35.29 And Isaac *g* up the ghost, and died,
45.21 Joseph *g* them wagons, according
21 and *g* them provision for the way.
Ex 11. 3 And the Lord *g* the people favor
14.20 but it *g* light by night to these:
36. 6 And Moses *g* commandment, and
Dt 9.11 the Lord *g* me the two tables
10. 4 and the Lord *g* them unto me.
1Sa 10. 9 Samuel, God *g* him another heart:
18.27 Saul *g* him Michal his daughter
20.40 And Jonathan *g* his artillery unto
21. 6 the priest *g* him hallowed bread:
Neh 8. 8 God distinctly, and *g* the sense,
Job 1.21 Lord *g*, and the Lord hath taken
19.16 servant, and he *g* me no answer;
32.11 I *g* ear to your reasons, whilst
42.10 also the Lord *g* Job twice as much
Ps 18.13 and the Highest *g* his voice;
69.21 in my thirst they *g* me vinegar to drink.
Ec 1.17 I *g* my heart to know wisdom,
12. 7 spirit shall return unto God who *g*
Isa 50. 6 I *g* my back to the smiters,
Jer 36.32 and *g* it to Baruch the scribe,
Eze 20.11 And I *g* them my statutes, and
12 also I *g* them my sabbaths,
Dan 1.17 God *g* them knowledge and skill
6.10 and *g* thanks before his God, as he did
Hos 13.11 I *g* thee a king in mine anger,
Am 2.12 ye *g* the Nazarites wine to drink;
Mt 8.18 he *g* commandment to depart
10. 1 *g* them power against unclean
14.19 and *g* the loaves to his disciples,
15.36 and *g* thanks, and brake them,
36 and *g* to his disciples,
21.23 who *g* thee this authority?
25.15 unto one he *g* five talents, to
35 an hungred, and ye *g* me meat:
35 was thirsty, and ye *g* me drink:
37 or thirsty, and *g* thee drink?
42 an hungred, and ye *g* me no meat:
42 thirsty, and ye *g* me no drink:
26.26 brake it, and *g* it to the disciples,
27 *g* thanks, and *g* it to them, saying,
48 that betrayed him *g* them a sign,
27.10 and *g* them for the potter's field,
34 *g* him vinegar to drink mingled
48 on a reed, and *g* him to drink.
28.12 *g* large money unto the soldiers,
Mk 2.26 also to them which were with
5.13 forthwith Jesus *g* them leave.
6. 7 and *g* them power over unclean
28 a charger, and *g* it to the damsel:
28 and the damsel *g* it to her mother.
41 *g* them to his disciples to set
8. 6 loaves and *g* thanks, and brake,
6 and *g* to his disciples to set before
11.28 who *g* thee this authority to do
13.34 and *g* authority to his servants,
14.22 brake it, and *g* to them, and said,
23 had given thanks, he *g* it to them:
15.23 And they *g* him to drink wine
36 and *g* him to drink, saying, Let
37 with a loud voice, and *g* up the ghost,
39 so cried out, and *g* up the ghost,
45 he *g* the body to Joseph.
Lk 2.38 *g* thanks likewise unto the Lord,
4.20 he *g* it again to the minister, and
6. 4 also to them that were with him;
7.21 many that were blind he *g* sight.
9. 1 *g* them power and authority over
16 *g* to the disciples to set before the
10.35 two pence, and *g* them to the host,
15.16 and no man *g* unto him.
18.43 they saw it, *g* praise unto God.
20. 2 who is he that *g* thee this authority?
22.17 *g* thanks, and said, Take this,
19 and *g* thanks, and brake it,
19 and *g* unto them, saying, This is
23.24 Pilate *g* sentence that it should be
29 and the paps which never *g* suck.
46 having said thus, he *g* up the ghost.
24.30 blessed it, and brake and *g* to them,
42 they *g* him a piece of a broiled fish,
Jn 1.12 *g* he power to become the sons
3.16 that he *g* his only begotten Son,
4. 5 that Jacob *g* to his son Joseph.
12 Father Jacob, which *g* us the well,
6.31 *g* them bread from heaven to eat.
32 Moses *g* you not that bread from
7.22 Moses...*g* unto you circumcision;
10.29 Father, which *g* them me, is
12.49 he *g* me a commandment, what I
13.26 the sop, he *g* it to Judas Iscariot,
14.31 Father *g* me commandment, even
18.14 Caiaphas was he, which *g* counsel
19. 9 thou? But Jesus *g* him no answer.
30 his head, and *g* up the ghost.
38 and Pilate *g* him leave. He came
Ac 1.26 they *g* forth their lots; and the lot
2. 4 as the Spirit *g* them utterance.
3. 5 he *g* heed unto them, expecting to
4.33 *g* the apostles witness of the

Ac 5. 5 fell down, and *g* up the ghost:
7. 5 he *g* him none inheritance in it,
8 *g* him the covenant of circumcision:
10 *g* him favor and wisdom in the
42 *g* them up to worship the host of
8. 6 *g* heed unto these things which
10 To whom they all *g* heed, from the
9.41 he *g* her his hand, and lifted her
10. 2 which *g* much alms to the people,
11.17 God *g* them the like gift as he did
12.22 And the people *g* a shout, saying,
23 because he *g* not God the glory:
23 eaten of worms, and *g* up the ghost
13.20 after he *g* unto them judges
21 God *g* unto them Saul the son of
22 to whom also he *g* testimony, and
14. 3 which *g* testimony unto the word
17 and *g* us rain from heaven, and
15.12 *g* audience to Barnabas and
24 we *g* no such commandment:
22.22 *g* him audience unto this word,
23.20 *g* commandment to his accusers
26.10 I *g* my voice against them.
27. 3 *g* him liberty to go unto his
35 *g* thanks to God in presence of them
Ro 1.24 Wherefore God also *g* them up to
26 *g* them up unto vile affections:
28 God *g* them over to a reprobate
1Co 3. 5 even as the Lord *g* to every man?
6 but God *g* the increase.
2Co 8. 5 *g* their own selves to the Lord,
Gal 1. 4 Who *g* himself for our sins, that
2. 5 whom we *g* place by subjection,
9 *g* to me and Barnabas the right
20 loved me, and *g* himself for me.
3.18 God *g* it to Abraham by promise.
Eph 1.22 *g* him to be the head over all
4. 8 captive, and *g* gifts unto men.
11 he *g* some, apostles; and some,
5.25 the church, and *g* himself for it;
1Th 4. 2 we *g* you by the Lord Jesus.
1Ti 2. 6 Who *g* himself a ransom for all,
Tit 2.14 Who *g* himself for us, that he might
Heb 7. 2 Abraham *g* a tenth part of all;
4 Abraham *g* the tenth of the spoils.
13 no man *g* attendance at the altar,
11.22 *g* commandment concerning his
12. 9 we *g* them reverence: shall we not
Jas 5.18 the heaven *g* rain, and the earth
1Pe 1.21 from the dead, and *g* him glory;
1Jn 3.23 another as he *g* us commandment.
5.10 the record that God *g* of his Son.
Jude 3 when I *g* all diligence to write
Rev 1. 1 which God *g* unto him, to shew
2.21 I *g* her space to repent of her
11.13 and *g* glory to the God of heaven.
13. 2 the dragon *g* him his power.
4 which *g* power unto the beast:
15. 7 *g* unto the seven angels seven
20.13 sea *g* up the dead which were in it;

GAVEST

Gen 3.12 woman whom thou *g* to be with
1Ki 8.34 unto the land which thou *g* unto
40 in the land which thou *g* unto our
48 their land, which thou *g* unto their
2Ch 6.25 the land which thou *g* to them
31 in the land which thou *g* unto our
38 toward their land, which thou *g*
20. 7 and *g* it to the seed of Abraham
Neh 9. 7 and *g* him the name of Abraham;
13 *g* them right judgments, and true
15 *g* them bread from heaven for
20 *g* also thy good spirit to instruct
20 and *g* them water for their thirst.
22 thou *g* them kingdoms and nations,
24 *g* them into their hands, with their
27 *g* them saviors, who saved them
30 therefore *g* thou them into the hand
35 great goodness that thou *g* them,
35 fat land which thou *g* before them.
36 land that thou *g* unto our fathers
Job 39.13 *G* thou the goodly wings unto
Ps 21. 4 life of thee, and thou *g* it him,
74.14 *g* him to be meat to the people
Lk 7.44 *g* me no water for my feet:
45 Thou *g* me no kiss: but this woman
15.29 and yet thou never *g* me a kid,
19.23 Wherefore then *g* thou not my
Jn 17. 4 the work which thou *g* me to do.
6 which thou *g* me out of the world:
6 they were, and thou *g* them me:
8 them the words which thou *g* me;
12 those that thou *g* me I have kept,
22 glory which thou *g* me I have
18. 9 which thou *g* me have I lost none.

GAY

Jas 2. 3 the *g* clothing, and say unto him,

GAZA

Gen 10.19 as thou comest to Gerar, unto *G*;
Jos 10.41 from Kadesh-barnea even unto *G*,
11.22 only in *G*, in Gath, and in Ashdod,
15.47 *G* with her towns and her villages.
Jdg 1.18 Also Judah took *G* with the coast
6. 4 till thou come unto *G*; and left no
16. 1 Then went Samson to *G*, and saw
21 and brought him down to *G*, and
1Sa 6.17 for Ashdod one, for *G* one, for
2Ki 18. 8 the Philistines, even unto *G*,
1Ch 7.28 unto *G* and the towns thereof:
Jer 47. 1 before that Pharaoh smote *G*.
5 is come upon *G*; Ashkelon is cut
Am 1. 6 transgressions of *G*, and for four,
7 will send a fire on the wall of *G*,
Zep 2. 4 For *G* shall be forsaken, and
Zec 9. 5 *G* also shall see it, and be very
5 and the king shall perish from *G*,
Ac 8.26 down from Jerusalem unto *G*,

GAZING

Ac 1.11 why stand ye *g* up into heaven?

GAZINGSTOCK

Na 3. 6 and will set thee as a *g*.
Heb 10.33 whilst ye were made a *g* both by

GENDER

Lev 19.19 Thou shalt not let thy cattle *g*
2Ti 2.23 knowing that they do *g* strifes.

GENDERETH

Job 21.10 Their bull *g*, and faileth not;
Gal 4.24 *g* to bondage, which is Agar.

GENEALOGIES

1Ch 5.17 All these were reckoned by *g* in
7. 5 reckoned in all by their *g*
7 and were reckoned by their *g*
9. 1 all Israel were reckoned by *g*;
2Ch 12.15 and of Iddo the seer concerning *g*?
31.19 to all that were reckoned by *g*
1Ti 1. 4 give heed to fables and endless *g*,
Tit 3. 9 But avoid foolish questions, and *g*,

GENERAL

1Ch 27.34 and the *g* of the king's army
Heb 12.23 To the *g* assembly and church of

GENERALLY

2Sa 17.11 that all Israel be *g* gathered
Jer 48.38 There shall be lamentation *g*

GENERATION

Dt 32. 5 they are a perverse and crooked *g*.
20 for they are a very froward *g*,
Est 9.28 kept throughout every *g*, every
Ps 12. 7 preserve them from this *g* for ever.
14. 5 God is in the *g* of the righteous.
24. 6 is the *g* of them that seek him,
71.18 shewed thy strength unto this *g*,
78. 8 a stubborn and rebellious *g*;
95.10 long was I grieved with this *g*,
112. 2 *g* of the upright shall be blessed.
145. 4 One *g* shall praise thy works to
Pr 27.24 doth the crown endure to every *g*?
30.12 a *g* that are pure in their own eyes,
14 is a *g*, whose teeth are as swords,
Ec 1. 4 One *g* passeth away, and another *g*
51. 8 my salvation from *g* to *g*.
53. 8 and who shall declare his *g*? for he
Jer 2.31 O *g*, see ye the word of the Lord.
Dan 4. 3 his dominion is from *g* to *g*.
34 his kingdom is from *g* to *g*:
Mt 1. 1 the book of the *g* of Jesus Christ,
3. 7 O *g* of vipers, who hath warned
11.16 whereunto shall I liken this *g*?
12.34 O *g* of vipers, how can ye,
39 An evil and adulterous *g* seeketh
41 shall rise in judgment with this *g*,
42 rise up in the judgment with this *g*,
45 shall it be also unto this wicked *g*.
16. 4 wicked and adulterous *g* seeketh
17.17 O faithless and perverse *g*, how
23.33 Ye serpents, ye *g* of vipers, how
36 things shall come upon this *g*.
24.34 This *g* shall not pass, till all these
Mk 8.12 Why doth this *g* seek after a sign?
12 shall no sign be given unto this *g*.
38 in this adulterous and sinful *g*;
9.19 O faithless *g*, how long shall I be
13.30 that this *g* shall not pass, till all
Lk 1.50 on them that fear him from *g* to *g*.
3. 7 O *g* of vipers, who hath warned
7.31 shall I liken the men of this *g*?
9.41 O faithless and perverse *g*, how
11.29 he began to say, This is an evil *g*:
30 also the Son of man be to this *g*.
31 the men of this *g*, and condemn
32 with this *g*, and shall condemn it:
50 may be required of this *g*;
51 It shall be required of this *g*.
16. 8 in their *g* wiser than the children
17.25 and be rejected of this *g*.
21.32 This *g* shall not pass away, till
Ac 2.40 yourselves from this untoward *g*.
8.33 who shall declare his *g*? for his
13.36 he had served his own *g* by the
Heb 3.10 I was grieved with that *g*,
1Pe 2. 9 a chosen *g*, a royal priesthood,

GENERATIONS

Gen 2. 4 These are the *g* of the heavens
5. 1 This is the book of the *g* of Adam.
6. 9 a just man and perfect in his *g*,
Ex 3.15 this is my memorial unto all *g*.
12.17 ye observe this day in your *g*
27.21 a statute for ever unto their *g*
31.16 the sabbath throughout their *g*,
Lev 6.18 a statute for ever in your *g*
Dt 7. 9 commandments to a thousand *g*;
Ps 49.11 and their dwelling places to all *g*;
72. 5 moon endure, throughout all *g*.
79.13 will shew forth thy praise to all *g*.
85. 5 draw out thine anger to all *g*?
89. 1 known thy faithfulness to all *g*.
90. 1 been our dwelling place in all *g*.
100. 5 and his truth endureth to all *g*.
102.12 and thy remembrance unto all *g*.
24 thy years are throughout all *g*.
119.90 Thy faithfulness is unto all *g*:
135.13 memorial, O Lord, throughout all *g*.
Isa 51. 9 in the ancient days, in the *g* of old.
58.12 up the foundations of many *g*;
61. 4 cities, the desolations of many *g*.
Mt 1.17 So all the *g* from Abraham to
17 Abraham to David are fourteen *g*;
17 away into Babylon are fourteen *g*;
17 Babylon unto Christ are fourteen *g*.
Lk 1.48 all *g* shall call me blessed.
Col 1.26 hid from ages and from *g*,

GENNESARET
Mt 14.34 they came into the land of *G*.
Mk 6.53 into the land of *G*, and drew to
Lk 5. 1 he stood by the lake of *G*,

GENTILE
Ro 2. 9 the Jew first, and also of the *G*;
10 the Jew first, and also to the *G*:

GENTILES
Gen 10. 5 By these were the isles of the *G*
Jdg 4. 2 dwelt in Harosheth of the *G*.
13 from Harosheth of the *G* unto the
16 the host, unto Harosheth of the *G*:
Isa 11.10 to it shall the *G* seek: and his
42. 1 bring forth judgment to the *G*.
6 of the people, for a light of the *G*;
49. 6 give thee for a light to the *G*,
22 I will lift up mine hand to the *G*,
54. 3 and thy seed shall inherit the *G*,
60. 3 the *G* shall come to thy light,
5 the forces of the *G* shall come
11 unto thee the forces of the *G*,
16 shalt also suck the milk of the *G*,
61. 6 ye shall eat the riches of the *G*,
9 shall be known among the *G*,
62. 2 *G* shall see thy righteousness,
66.12 of the *G* like a flowing stream:
19 declare my glory among the *G*.
Jer 4. 7 destroyer of the *G* is on his way;
14.22 among the vanities of the *G*
16.19 the *G* shall come unto thee
46. 1 the prophet against the *G*;
La 2. 9 her princes are among the *G*:
Eze 4.13 their defiled bread among the *G*,
Hos 8. 8 shall they be among the *G* as a
Joel 3. 9 Proclaim ye this among the *G*;
Mic 5. 8 of Jacob shall be among the *G*
Zec 1.21 to cast out the horns of the *G*.
Mal 1.11 name shall be great among the *G*;
Mt 4.15 beyond Jordan, Galilee of the *G*;
6.32 all these things do the *G* seek:)
10. 5 Go not into the way of the *G*,
18 testimony against them and the *G*.
12.18 he shall shew judgment to the *G*.
21 in his name shall the *G* trust.
20.19 they shall deliver him to the *G*
25 the princes of the *G* exercise
Mk 10.33 and shall deliver him to the *G*:
42 are accounted to rule over the *G*
Lk 2.32 A light to lighten the *G*, and the
18.32 he shall be delivered unto the *G*,
21.24 shall be trodden down of the *G*,
24 the times of the *G* be fulfilled.
22.25 kings of the *G* exercise lordship
Jn 7.35 the dispersed among the *G*,
35 and teach the *G*?
Ac 4.27 the *G*, and the people of Israel,
7.45 into the possession of the *G*,
9.15 to bear my name before the *G*,
10.45 on the *G* also was poured out
11. 1 the *G* had also received the word
18 hath God also to the *G* granted
13.42 the *G* besought that these words
46 lo, we turn to the *G*.
47 set thee to be a light of the *G*,
48 the *G* heard this, they were glad,
14. 2 Jews stirred up the *G*,
5 of the *G*, and also of the Jews
27 the door of faith unto the *G*.
15. 3 declaring the conversion of the *G*:
7 the *G* by my mouth should hear
12 wrought among the *G* by them.
14 did visit the *G*, to take out of them
17 all the *G*, upon whom my name
19 from among the *G* are turned
23 the brethren which are of the *G*
18. 6 henceforth I will go unto the *G*.
21.11 him into the hands of the *G*.
19 God had wrought among the *G*
21 the Jews which are among the *G*
25 As touching the *G* which believe,
22.21 send thee far hence unto the *G*.
26.17 from the people, and from the *G*,
20 to the *G*, that they should repent
23 light unto the people, and to the *G*.
28.28 salvation of God is sent unto the *G*,
Ro 1.13 you also, even as among other *G*.
2.14 the *G*, which have not the law,
24 God is blasphemed among the *G*
3. 9 before proved both Jews and *G*,
29 of the *G*? Yes, of the *G* also:
9.24 the Jews only, but also of the *G*?
30 That the *G*, which followed not
11.11 salvation is come unto the *G*,
12 of them the riches of the *G*;
13 For I speak to you *G*, inasmuch as
13 I am the apostle of the *G*,
25 until the fulness of the *G* be come
15. 9 And that the *G* might glorify God
9 I will confess to thee among the *G*,
10 he saith, Rejoice, ye *G*, with his
11 Praise the Lord, all ye *G*; and
12 shall rise to reign over the *G*;
12 in him shall the *G* trust.
16 minister of Jesus Christ to the *G*,
16 the offering up of the *G* might be
18 to make the *G* obedient, by word
27 if the *G* have been made partakers
16. 4 but also all the churches of the *G*.
1Co 5. 1 so much as named among the *G*,
10.20 the things which the *G* sacrifice,
32 neither to the Jews, nor to the *G*,
12. 2 Ye know that ye were *G*, carried
13 whether we be Jews or *G*,
Gal 2. 2 which I preach among the *G*,
8 was mighty in me toward the *G*:)
12 he did eat with the *G*: but when
14 livest after the manner of *G*,
14 the *G* to live as do the Jews?
15 nature, and not sinners of the *G*,
3.14 come on the *G* through Jesus
Eph 2.11 being in time past *G* in the flesh,
3. 1 prisoner of Jesus Christ for you *G*,
6 That the *G* should be fellowheirs,
8 that I should preach among the *G*
4.17 walk not as other *G* walk, in the
Col 1.27 of this mystery among the *G*;
1Th 2.16 Forbidding us to speak to the *G*
4. 5 as the *G* which know not God:
1Ti 2. 7 a teacher of the *G* in faith and
3.16 preached unto the *G*, believed
2Ti 1.11 apostle, and a teacher of the *G*.
4.17 and that all the *G* might hear:
1Pe 2.12 conversation honest among the *G*:
4. 3 to have wrought the will of the *G*,
3Jn 7 forth, taking nothing of the *G*.
Rev 11. 2 for it is given unto the *G*:

GENTLE
1Th 2. 7 But we were *g* among you, even
2Ti 2.24 not strive; but be *g* unto all men,
Tit 3. 2 to be no brawlers, but *g*, shewing
Jas 3.17 *g*, and easy to be intreated,
1Pe 2.18 not only to the good and *g*, but also

GENTLENESS
2Sa 22.36 and thy *g* hath made me great.
Ps 18.35 and thy *g* hath made me great.
2Co 10. 1 by the meekness and *g* of Christ,
Gal 5.22 longsuffering, *g*, goodness, faith,

GENTLY
2Sa 18. 5 Deal *g* for my sake with the
Isa 40.11 *g* lead those that are with young.

GERIZIM
Dt 11.29 put the blessing upon mount *G*,
27.12 upon mount *G* to bless the people,
Jos 8.33 against mount *G*, and half of them
Jdg 9. 7 in the top of mount *G*, and lifted

GET
Gen 12. 1 *G* thee out of thy county, and
19.14 said, Up, *g* you out of this place;
22. 2 *g* thee into the land of Moriah;
34. 4 saying, *G* me this damsel to wife.
44.17 *g* you up in peace unto your
Ex 5.11 *g* you straw where ye can find it:
11. 8 *G* thee out, and all the people
Dt 3.27 *G* thee up into the top of Pisgah,
5.30 *G* you into your tents again.
32.49 *G* thee up into this mountain
Jdg 14. 2 therefore *g* her for me to wife.
3 *G* her for me; for she pleaseth me
1Sa 25. 5 *G* you up to Carmel, and go to
1Ki 18.41 *G* thee up, eat and drink; for
Ps 119.104 thy precepts I *g* understanding:
Pr 4. 5 *G* wisdom, *g* understanding:
7 therefore *g* wisdom: and with all
7 thy getting *g* understanding.
16.16 better is it to *g* wisdom than gold!
Ec 3. 6 A time to *g*, and a time to lose;
40. 9 *g* thee up into the high mountain;
Jer 5. 5 I will *g* me unto the great men,
19. 1 and *g* a potter's earthen bottle,
Zec 6. 7 *G* you hence, walk to and fro
Mt 4.10 *G* thee hence, Satan: for it is
14.22 his disciples to *g* into a ship,
16.23 unto Peter, *G* thee behind me,
Mk 6.45 his disciples to *g* into the ship,
8.33 *G* thee behind me, Satan: for
Lk 4. 8 *G* thee behind me, Satan: for it
9.12 and lodge, and *g* victuals: for we
13.31 *G* thee out, and depart hence:
Ac 7. 3 *G* thee out of thy country, and
10.20 *g* thee down, and go with them,
22.18 *g* thee quickly out of Jerusalem:
27.43 first into the sea, and *g* to land:
2Co 2.11 Lest Satan should *g* an advantage
Jas 4.13 and buy and sell, and *g* gain:

GETHSEMANE
Mt 26.36 with them unto a place called *G*,
Mk 14.32 to a place which was named *G*:
(See illustration on page 320)

GETTING
Gen 31.18 the cattle of his *g*, which he had
Pr 4. 7 with all thy *g* get understanding.
21. 6 *g* of treasures by a lying tongue

GHOST
Gen 25. 8 Then Abraham gave up the *g*,
17 and he gave up the *g* and died;
35.29 And Isaac gave up the *g*, and died,
49.33 and yielded up the *g*, and was
Job 3.11 why did I not give up the *g* when
10.18 Oh that I had given up the *g*,
11.20 shall be as the giving up of the *g*.
13.19 tongue, I shall give up the *g*.
14.10 yea, man giveth up the *g*, and
Jer 15. 9 she hath given up the *g*; her sun
La 1.19 mine elders gave up the *g* in the
Mt 1.18 found with child of the Holy *G*.
20 in her is of the Holy *G*.
3.11 with the Holy *G*, and with fire:
12.31 blasphemy against the Holy *G*
32 speaketh against the Holy *G*,
27.50 yielded up the *g*.
28.19 of the Son, and of the Holy *G*:
Mk 1. 8 baptize you with the Holy *G*.
3.29 blaspheme against the Holy *G*
12.36 himself said by the Holy *G*,
13.11 ye that speak, but the Holy *G*.
15.37 a loud voice, and gave up the *g*.
39 so cried out, and gave up the *g*,
Lk 1.15 be filled with the Holy *G*,
35 Holy *G* shall come upon thee,
41 was filled with the Holy *G*:
67 was filled with the Holy *G*,
2.25 and the Holy *G* was upon him,
26 unto him by the Holy *G*,

Jesus prays at Gethsemane as his disciples sleep in this painting by Paolo Moranda (1486-1522).

Lk 3.16 baptize you with the Holy *G*
22 And the Holy *G* descended in
4. 1 Jesus being full of the Holy *G*
12.10 against the Holy *G*
12 For the Holy *G* shall teach
23.46 said thus, he gave up the *g*.
Jn 1.33 baptizeth with the Holy *G*
7.39 for the Holy *G* was not yet
14.26 Holy *G*, whom the Father
19.30 his head, and gave up the *g*.
20.22 them, Receive ye the Holy *G*:
Ac 1. 2 he through the Holy *G* had
5 be baptized with the Holy *G*
8 after that the Holy *G* is come
16 which the Holy *G* by the mouth
2. 4 were all filled with the Holy *G*.
33 the promise of the Holy *G*,
38 receive the gift of the Holy *G*.
4. 8 Peter, filled with the Holy *G*,
31 were all filled with the Holy *G*,
5. 3 to lie to the Holy *G*, and to keep
5 fell down, and gave up the *g*:
10 at his feet and yielded up the *g*:
32 and so is also the Holy *G*,
6. 3 full of the Holy *G* and wisdom,
5 of faith and of the Holy *G*,
7.51 do always resist the Holy *G*:
55 he, being full of the Holy *G*,
8.15 they might receive the Holy *G*:
17 they received the Holy *G*.
18 Holy *G* was given, he offered
19 he may receive the Holy *G*.
9.17 and be filled with the Holy *G*.
31 in the comfort of the Holy *G*,
10.38 the Holy *G* and with power:
44 the Holy *G* fell on all them
45 out the gift of the Holy *G*.
47 have received the Holy *G* as
11.15 the Holy *G* fell on them, as on
16 be baptized with the Holy *G*.
24 man, and full of the Holy *G*
12.23 of worms and gave up the *g*.
13. 2 the Holy *G* said, Separate me
4 being sent forth by the Holy *G*,
9 Paul,) filled with the Holy *G*,
52 with joy, and with the Holy *G*.
15. 8 giving them the Holy *G*, even
28 it seemed good to the Holy *G*,
16. 6 were forbidden of the Holy *G*
19. 2 Have ye received the Holy *G*
2 whether there be any Holy *G*.
6 the Holy *G* came on them; and
20.23 that the Holy *G* witnesseth
28 Holy *G* hath made you overseers,
21.11 Thus saith the Holy *G*, So
28.25 spake the Holy *G* by Esaias
Ro 5. 5 by the Holy *G* which is given
9. 1 me witness in the Holy *G*,
14.17 peace, and joy in the Holy *G*.
15.13 the power of the Holy *G*.
16 being sanctified by the Holy *G*.
1Co 2.13 the Holy *G* teacheth;
6.19 the temple of the Holy *G*
12. 3 the Lord, but by the Holy *G*.
2Co 6. 6 the Holy *G*, by love unfeigned,
13.14 the communion of the Holy *G*,
1Th 1. 5 in power, and in the Holy *G*,
6 with joy of the Holy *G*:
2Ti 1.14 by the Holy *G* which dwelleth
Tit 3. 5 and renewing of the Holy *G*;
Heb 2. 4 gifts of the Holy *G*, according
3. 7 (as the Holy *G* saith, To day if
6. 4 made partakers of the Holy *G*,
9. 8 The Holy *G* this signifying,
10.15 Holy *G* also is a witness to us:
1Pe 1.12 Holy *G* sent down from heaven;
2Pe 1.21 were moved by the Holy *G*.
1Jn 5. 7 Holy *G*: and these three are one.
Jude 20 praying in the Holy *G*,

GIANTS

Gen 6. 4 were *g* in the earth in those days;
Nu 13.33 And there we saw the *g*, the sons
Dt 2.20 accounted a land of *g*: *g* dwelt
Jos 12. 4 was of the remnants of the *g*,
15. 8 at the end of the valley of the *g*

GIDEON

Jdg 6.11 his son *G* threshed wheat by the
13 *G* said unto him, O my Lord, if the
19 *G* went in, and made ready a kid,
22 *G* perceived that he was an angel
22 *G* said, Alas, O Lord God! for
24 *G* built an altar there unto the
27 *G* took ten men of his servants,
29 *G* the son of Joash hath done this
34 Spirit of the Lord came upon *G*,
36 *G* said unto God, If thou wilt save
39 *G* said unto God, Let not thine
7. 1 who is *G*, and all the people that
2 said unto *G*, The people that are
4 said unto *G*, The people are yet
5 said unto *G*, Every one that
7 said unto *G*, By the three hundred
13 when *G* was come, behold, there
14 save the sword of *G* the son of
15 *G* heard the telling of the dream,
18 The sword of the Lord, and of *G*.
19 So *G*, and the hundred men that
20 The sword of the Lord, and of *G*.
24 *G* sent messengers throughout all
25 to *G* on the other side Jordan.
8. 4 *G* came to Jordan, and passed
7 *G* said, Therefore when the Lord
11 And *G* went up by the way of them
13 *G* the son of Joash returned from
21 *G* arose, and slew Zebah and
22 Israel said unto *G*, Rule thou over
23 *G* said unto them, I will not rule
24 *G* said unto them, I would desire
27 *G* made an ephod thereof, and put
27 thing became a snare unto *G*, and
28 forty years in the days of *G*.
30 *G* had threescore and ten sons of
32 *G* the son of Joash died in a good
33 as *G* was dead, that the children of
35 house of Jerubbaal, namely, *G*,

GIFT

Gen 34.12 me never so much dowry and *g*,
Ex 23. 8 And thou shalt take no *g*:
8 for the *g* blindeth the wise,
Nu 8.19 I have given the Levites as a *g*
18. 6 are given as a *g* for the Lord,
7 office unto you as a service of *g*:
11 the heave offering of their *g*,
Dt 16.19 neither take a *g*: for a *g* doth
2Sa 19.42 or hath he given us any *g*?
Ps 45.12 of Tyre shall be there with a *g*;
Pr 17. 8 A *g* is as a precious stone in the
23 A wicked man taketh a *g* out of
18.16 A man's *g* maketh room for him,
21.14 A *g* in secret pacifieth anger:
25.14 boasteth himself of a false *g*
Ec 3.13 of all his labor, it is the *g* of God.
5.19 in his labor; this is the *g* of God.
7. 7 a *g* destroyeth the heart.
Eze 46.16 prince give a *g* unto any of his sons,
17 if he give a *g* of his inheritance
Mt 5.23 if thou bring thy *g* to the altar,
24 Leave there thy *g* before the altar,
24 and then come and offer thy *g*.
8. 4 offer the *g* that Moses commanded,
15. 5 It is a *g*, by whatsoever thou
23.18 sweareth by the *g* that is upon it,
19 for whether is greater, the *g*, or
19 or the altar that sanctifieth the *g*?
Mk 7.11 Corban, that is to say, a *g*, by
Jn 4.10 If thou knewest the *g* of God,
Ac 2.38 receive the *g* of the Holy Ghost.

GIDEON

Deliverer of Israel from Midianite oppression, 12th–11th century B.C.; son of Joash of the tribe of Manasseh; accepts commission against Midian from emissary of the Lord, but only later recognizes his identity and builds an altar to the Lord in Ophrah; destroys his father's shrine to Baal, offering one of his bullocks on an altar rededicated to the Lord (Jdg 6.1-27); Joash insists to irate townspeople that any prosecution be brought by Baal—hence Gideon's new name, Jerubbaal: "let Baal plead" (Jdg 6.28-32); name Jerubbaal used throughout story of his son Abimelech (Jdg 9); routs Midian at night by a clever and noisy stratagem with only 300 men chosen from a much larger group by how they drank water (Jdg 7.1-23); averts Ephraimite jealousy, and harries Transjordanian Succoth and Penuel over faintheartedness in aftermath of victory over Midianites, himself executing their chieftains Zebah and Zalmunna; refuses offer of hereditary rule because the Lord alone was ruler; father of 70 sons by many wives, and of Abimelech by his concubine from Shechem; dies "in a good old age" and is buried in father's tomb (Jdg 7.24–8.32).

8.20 hast thought that the *g* of God
10.45 poured out the *g* of the Holy Ghost.
11.17 God gave them the like *g* as he did
Ro 1.11 impart unto you some spiritual *g*,
5.15 as the offense, so also is the free *g*.
15 grace of God, and the *g* by grace,
16 by one that sinned, so is the *g*:
16 the free *g* is of many offenses
17 the *g* of righteousness shall reign
18 the free *g* came upon all men unto
6.23 but the *g* of God is eternal life
1Co 1. 7 So that ye come behind in no *g*;
7. 7 every man hath his proper *g* of God,
13. 2 though I have the *g* of prophecy,
2Co 1.11 for the *g* bestowed upon us by
8. 4 that we would receive the *g*, and
9.15 unto God for his unspeakable *g*.
Eph 2. 8 of yourselves: it is the *g* of God:
3. 7 according to the *g* of the grace of
4. 7 the measure of the *g* of Christ.
Php 4.17 Not because I desire a *g*: but I
1Ti 4.14 Neglect not the *g* that is in thee,
2Ti 1. 6 stir up the *g* of God, which is in
Heb 6. 4 have tasted of the heavenly *g*,
Jas 1.17 Every good *g* and every perfect *g*
1Pe 4.10 As every man hath received the *g*,

GIFTS

Gen 25. 6 Abraham gave *g*, and sent them
Ex 28.38 Israel shall hallow all their holy *g*;
Lev 23.38 beside your *g*, and beside all your
Nu 18.29 Out of all your *g* ye shall offer
2Sa 8. 2 David's servants, and brought *g*.
6 to David, and brought *g*.
1Ch 18. 2, 6 servants and brought *g*.
2Ch 19. 7 of persons, nor taking of *g*.
21. 3 their father gave them great *g*
26. 8 Ammonites gave *g* to Uzziah:
32.23 many brought *g* unto the Lord
Est 2.18 to the provinces, and gave *g*,
9.22 portions one to another, and *g*
Ps 68.18 thou hast received *g* for men;
72.10 of Sheba and Seba shall offer *g*.
Pr 6.35 though thou givest many *g*.
15.27 but he that hateth *g* shall live.
19. 6 is a friend to him that giveth *g*.
29. 4 that receiveth *g* overthroweth it.
Isa 1.23 every one loveth *g*, and followeth
Eze 16.33 They give *g* to all whores:
33 but thou givest thy *g* to all thy
20.26 I polluted them in their own *g*,
31 when ye offer your *g*, when ye
39 holy name no more with your *g*,
22.12 have they taken *g* to shed blood;
Dan 2. 6 shall receive of me *g* and rewards
48 and gave him many great *g*, and
5.17 Let thy *g* be to thyself, and give
Mt 2.11 they presented unto him *g*; gold,
7.11 give good *g* unto your children,
Lk 11.13 give good *g* unto your children:
21. 1 casting their *g* into the treasury.
5 with goodly stones and *g*,
Ro 11.29 For the *g* and calling of God are
12. 6 Having then *g* differing according
1Co 12. 1 concerning spiritual *g*, brethren,
4 there are diversities of *g*, but the
9 to another the *g* of healing by the
28 *g* of healings, helps, governments,
30 Have all the *g* of healing? do all
31 covet earnestly the best *g*: and
14. 1 desire spiritual *g*, but rather that
12 as ye are zealous of spiritual *g*,
Eph 4. 8 captive, and gave *g* unto men.
Heb 2. 4 miracles, and *g* of the Holy Ghost,
5. 1 may offer both *g* and sacrifices
8. 3 ordained to offer *g* and sacrifices:
4 that there are priests that offer *g*
9. 9 were offered both *g* and sacrifices,
11. 4 God testifying of his *g*: and by it
Rev 11.10 shall send *g* one to another;

Biblical Themes

GENEROSITY

And when ye reap the harvest of your land, thou shalt not wholly reap the corners of thy field. . . . thou shalt leave them for the poor and stranger. Lev 19.9-10

Thou shalt open thine hand wide unto thy brother, to thy poor, and to thy needy, in thy land. Dt 15.11

Every man shall give as he is able, according to the blessing of the Lord thy God which he hath given thee. Dt 16.17

Let her glean even among the sheaves, and reproach her not. Ru 2.15

He that hath pity upon the poor lendeth unto the Lord; and that which he hath given will he pay him again. Pr 19.17

He that hath a bountiful eye shall be blessed; for he giveth of his bread to the poor. Pr 22.9

He that giveth unto the poor shall not lack. Pr 28.27

Cast thy bread upon the waters: for thou shalt find it after many days. Ec 11.1

In the morning sow thy seed, and in the evening withhold not thine hand. Ec 11.6

When thou doest thine alms, do not sound a trumpet before thee, as the hypocrites do . . . that they may have glory of men. . . . But when thou doest alms, let not thy left hand know what thy right hand doeth: that thine alms may be in secret: and thy Father which seeth in secret himself shall reward thee openly. Mt 6.2-4

All things whatsoever ye would that men should do to you, do ye even so to them. Mt 7.12

Whosoever shall give to drink unto one of these little ones a cup of cold water only in the name of a disciple, verily I say unto you, he shall in no wise lose his reward. Mt 10.42

Go and sell that thou hast, and give to the poor, and thou shalt have treasure in heaven. Mt 19.21

And Jesus sat over against the treasury, and beheld how the people cast money into the treasury: and many that were rich cast in much. And there came a certain poor widow, and she threw in two mites, which make a farthing. And he called unto him his disciples, and saith unto them, . . . this poor widow hath cast more in, than all they which have cast into the treasury: for all they did cast in of their abundance; but she of her want did cast in all that she had, even all her living. Mk 12.41-44

Give to every man that asketh of thee. . . . And as ye would that men should do to you, do ye also to them likewise. Lk 6.30-31

Thy prayers and thine alms are come up for a memorial before God. Ac 10.4

Remember the words of the Lord Jesus, how he said, It is more blessed to give than to receive. Ac 20.35

He that spared not his own Son, but delivered him up for us all, how shall he not with him also freely give us all things? Ro 8.32

We then that are strong ought to bear the infirmities of the weak, and not to please ourselves. Ro 15.1

He which soweth bountifully shall reap also bountifully. Every man according as he purposeth in his heart, so let him give; not grudgingly, or of necessity: for God loveth a cheerful giver. 2Co 9.6-7

GILBOA

1Sa 28. 4 together, and they pitched in *G*.
31. 1 and fell down slain in mount *G*.
8 his three sons fallen in mount *G*.
2Sa 1. 6 happened by chance upon mount *G*,
21 Ye mountains of *G*, let there be no
21.12 Philistines had slain Saul in *G*:
1Ch 10. 1 and fell down slain in mount *G*.
8 and his sons fallen in mount *G*.

GIRD

Ex 29. 5 and *g* him with the curious girdle
9 thou shalt *g* them with girdles,
Jdg 3.16 he did *g* it under his raiment
1Sa 25.13 *G* ye on every man his sword.
2Sa 3.31 *g* you with sackcloth, and mourn
2Ki 4.29 *G* up thy loins, and take my staff
9. 1 *G* up thy loins, and take this box
Job 38. 3 *G* up now thy loins like a man;
40. 7 *G* up thy loins now like a man:
Ps 45. 3 *G* thy sword upon thy thigh, O
Isa 8. 9, 9 *g* yourselves, and ye shall be
15. 3 *g* themselves with sackcloth:
32.11 and *g* sackcloth upon your loins.
Jer 1.17 Thou therefore *g* up thy loins,
4. 8 For this *g* you with sackcloth,
6.26 *g* thee with sackcloth, and wallow
49. 3 *g* you with sackcloth; lament, and
Eze 7.18 They shall also *g* themselves
27.31 and *g* them with sackcloth, and

Eze 44.18 they shall not *g* themselves with
Joel 1.13 *G* yourselves, and lament, ye
Lk 12.37 that he shall *g* himself, and make
17. 8 and *g* thyself, and serve me, till
Jn 21.18 another shall *g* thee, and carry
Ac 12. 8 *G* thyself, and bind on thy
1Pe 1.13 Wherefore *g* up the loins of your

GIRDED

Ex 12.11 shall ye eat it; with your loins *g*,
Lev 8. 7 and *g* him with the girdle, and
7 he *g* him with the curious girdle
13 them, and *g* them with girdles,
16. 4 and shall be *g* with a linen girdle,
Dt 1.41 And when ye had *g* on every man
1Sa 2. 4 stumbled are *g* with strength.
18 a child, *g* with a linen ephod.
17.39 And David *g* his sword upon his
25.13 they *g* on every man his sword:
13 and David also *g* on his sword:
2Sa 6.14 David was *g* with a linen ephod.
20. 8 garment that he had put on was *g*
21.16 he being *g* with a new sword,
22.40 For thou hast *g* me with strength
1Ki 18.46 and he *g* up his loins, and ran
20.32 So they *g* sackcloth on their loins,
Neh 4.18 one had his sword *g* by his side,
Ps 18.39 For thou hast *g* me with strength
30.11 sackcloth, and *g* me with gladness;
65. 6 mountains; being *g* with power:
93. 1 wherewith he hath *g* himself:
109.19 wherewith he is *g* continually.
Isa 45. 5 I *g* thee, though thou hast not
La 2.10 they have *g* themselves with
Eze 16.10 and I *g* thee about with fine linen,
23.15 *G* with girdles upon their loins,
Dan 10. 5 whose loins were *g* with fine gold
Joel 1. 8 like a virgin *g* with sackcloth
Lk 12.35 Let your loins be *g* about,
Jn 13. 4 and took a towel, and *g* himself.
5 the towel wherewith he was *g*.
Rev 15. 6 breasts *g* with golden girdles.

GIRDEDST

Jn 21.18 thou wast young, thou *g* thyself

GIRDETH

1Ki 20.11 Let not him that *g* on his harness
Job 12.18 and *g* their loins with a girdle.
Ps 18.32 It is God that *g* me with strength,
Pr 31.17 She *g* her loins with strength,

GIRDLE

2Ki 1. 8 girt with a *g* of leather about his
Ps 109.19 and for a *g* wherewith he is girded
Isa 11. 5 righteousness shall be the *g* of his
5 loins, and faithfulness the *g* of his
22.21 strengthen him with thy *g*, and I
Jer 13. 1 Go and get thee a linen *g*, and put
Mt 3. 4 and a leathern *g* about his loins;
Mk 1. 6 with a *g* of a skin about his loins;
Ac 21.11 he took Paul's *g*, and bound his
11 bind the man that owneth this *g*,
Rev 1.13 about the paps with a golden *g*.

GIRDLES

Ex 28.40 shalt make for them *g*, and bonnets
29. 9 And thou shalt gird them with *g*,
Lev 8.13 girded them with *g*, and put
Pr 31.24 delivereth *g* unto the merchant.
Eze 23.15 with *g* upon their loins, exceeding
Rev 15. 6 breasts girded with golden *g*.

GIRL

Joel 3. 3 and sold a *g* for wine, that they

GIRLS

Zec 8. 5 boys and *g* playing in the streets

GIRT

2Ki 1. 8 and *g* with a girdle of leather about
Jn 21. 7 he *g* his fisher's coat unto him,
Eph 6.14 your loins *g* about with truth,
Rev 1.13 and *g* about the paps with a golden

GIVE

Gen 1.15, 17 heaven to *g* light upon the earth,
12. 7 Unto thy seed will I *g* this land;
15. 2 what wilt thou *g* me, seeing I go
17.16 I will bless her, and *g* thee a son
23. 9 may *g* me the cave of Machpelah,
27.28 God *g* thee of the dew of heaven,
28. 4 *g* thee the blessing of Abraham,
20 and will *g* me bread to eat, and
22 I will surely *g* the tenth unto thee.
29.21 *G* me my wife, for my days are
26 *g* the younger before the firstborn.
30. 1 *G* me children, or else I die.
41.16 God shall *g* Pharaoh an answer of
43.14 God Almighty *g* you mercy before
45.18 I will *g* you the good of the land
47.15 Joseph, and said, *G* us bread:
16 And Joseph said, *G* your cattle;
Ex 5.10 Pharaoh, I will not *g* you straw.
13. 5 sware unto thy fathers to *g* thee,
21 a pillar of fire, to *g* them light;
17. 2 *G* us water that we may drink.
21.23 then thou shalt *g* life for life,
24.12 and I will *g* thee tables of stone,
Lev 26. 4 I will *g* you rain in due season,
6 And I will *g* peace in the land,
Nu 8. 2 the seven lamps shall *g* light over
11.13 *G* us flesh, that we may eat.
Dt 1.35 I sware to *g* unto your fathers,
39 unto them will I *g* it, and they shall
2.28 *g* me water for money, that I may
6.10 to *g* thee great and goodly cities,
16.10 shalt *g* unto the Lord thy God,
17 Every man shall *g* as he is able,
24. 1 her a bill of divorcement, and *g* it
25. 3 Forty stripes he may *g* him, and
Jos 15.19 *G* me a blessing; for thou hast
19 *g* me also springs of water.
Jdg 4.19 *G* me, I pray thee, a little...to drink;
1Sa 8. 6 said, *G* us a king to judge us.
14.41 *G* a perfect lot. And Saul and
18.21 *g* him her, that she may be a snare
1Ki 3. 5 God said, Ask what I shall *g* thee.
25 and *g* half to the one, and half to
26 *g* her the living child, and in no
11.13 *g* one tribe to thy son for David
31 and will *g* ten tribes to thee:
15. 4 did the Lord his God *g* him a lamp
21. 2 *G* me thy vineyard, that I may
6 *G* me thy vineyard for money; or
6 I will not *g* thee my vineyard.
2Ki 6.28 *G* thy son, that we may eat him to
1Ch 11.17 Oh that one would *g* me drink of the
16. 8 *G* thanks unto the Lord, call upon
28 *G* unto the Lord, ye kindreds of
28 *g* unto the Lord glory and strength.
29 *G* unto the Lord the glory due
34 O *g* thanks unto the Lord: for he is
35 that we may *g* thanks to thy holy
41 to *g* thanks to the Lord, because his
29.19 *g* unto Solomon my son a perfect
2Ch 1. 7 Ask what I shall *g* thee.
10 *G* me now wisdom and knowledge,
Job 2. 4 all that a man hath will he *g* for
3.11 why did I not *g* up the ghost
32.22 For I know not to *g* flattering titles;
Ps 5. 1 *G* ear to my words, O Lord,
6. 5 in the grave who shall *g* thee thanks?
18.49 Therefore will I *g* thanks unto thee,
28. 4 *G* them according to their deeds,
29. 1 *g* unto the Lord glory and strength.
2 *G* unto the Lord the glory due
51.16 not sacrifice; else would I *g* it:
55. 1 *G* ear to my prayer, O God;
72. 1 *G* the king thy judgments, O God,
75. 1 Unto thee, O God, do we *g* thanks,
78. 1 *G* ear, O my people, to my law;
80. 1 *G* ear, O Shepherd of Israel,
85.12 Lord shall *g* that which is good;
86. 6 *G* ear, O Lord, unto my prayer;
91.11 he shall *g* his angels charge over
92. 1 It is a good thing to *g* thanks
96. 7 *G* unto the Lord, O ye kindreds
7 *g* unto the Lord glory and strength.
8 *G* unto the Lord the glory due
106. 1 O *g* thanks unto the Lord; for he is
108.12 *G* us help from trouble: for vain
118. 1, 29 O *g* thanks unto the Lord; for he
119.34 *G* me understanding, and I shall keep
73 *g* me understanding, that I may learn
125 *g* me understanding, that I may know
144 *g* me understanding, and I shall live.
169 *g* me understanding according to thy
122. 4 *g* thanks unto the name of the Lord,
136. 1 O *g* thanks unto the Lord; for he is
2 O *g* thanks unto the God of gods:
3 O *g* thanks to the Lord of lords:
26 O *g* thanks unto the God of heaven:
141. 1 *g* ear unto my voice, when I cry
143. 1 *g* ear to my supplications: in thy
Pr 4. 2 I *g* you good doctrine, forsake ye
9. 9 *G* instruction to a wise man and
23.26 My son, *g* me thine heart, and let
25.21 enemy be hungry, *g* him bread to
21 if he be thirsty, *g* him water to drink:
30. 8 *g* me neither poverty nor riches;
31. 3 *G* not thy strength unto women,
6 *G* strong drink unto him that is
Isa 1. 2 Hear, O heavens, and *g* ear, O earth;
7.14 Lord himself shall *g* you a sign,
43.20 I *g* waters in the wilderness, and
48.11 I will not *g* my glory unto another.
49. 6 I will also *g* thee for a light
51. 4 *g* ear unto me, O my nation: for a
55.10 that it may *g* seed to the sower,
56. 5 I will *g* them an everlasting name,
61. 3 to *g* unto them beauty for ashes,
Jer 3.15 And I will *g* you pastors according
11. 5 to *g* them a land flowing with
13.15 Hear ye, and *g* ear; be not proud:
16 *G* glory to the Lord your God,
29. 6 *g* your daughters to husbands,
32.22 to *g* them, a land flowing with milk
37.21 *g* him daily a piece of bread out
La 2.18 *g* thyself no rest; let not the
3.65 *G* them sorrow of heart, thy
Eze 11.19 And I will *g* them one heart,
19 and will *g* them an heart of flesh:
32. 7 the moon shall not *g* her light.
36.26 A new heart also will I *g* you,
26 and I will *g* you an heart of flesh.
Hos 2. 5 *g* me my bread and my water,
11. 8 How shall I *g* thee up, Ephraim?
Mic 6. 7 shall I *g* my firstborn for my
Zec 8.12 the vine shall *g* her fruit, and the
12 ground shall *g* her increase, and
12 the heavens shall *g* their dew;
10. 1 and *g* them showers of rain, to
11.12 If ye think good, *g* me my price;
Mal 2. 2 to *g* glory unto my name, saith
Mt 4. 6 He shall *g* his angels charge
9 All these things will I *g* thee,
5.31 *g* her a writing of divorcement:
42 *G* to him that asketh thee, and
6.11 *G* us this day our daily bread.
7. 6 *G* not that which is holy unto the
9 ask bread, will he *g* him a stone?
10 a fish, will he *g* him a serpent?
11 *g* good gifts unto your children,
11 Father which is in heaven *g* good
9.24 He said unto them, *G* place: for the
10. 8 freely ye have received, freely *g*.
42 whosoever shall *g* to drink unto
11.28 heavy laden, and I will *g* you rest.
12.36 shall *g* account thereof in the day
14. 7 *g* her whatsoever she would ask.
8 *G* me here John Baptist's head in
16 need not depart; *g* ye them to eat.
16.19 I will *g* unto thee the keys of the

26 a man *g* in exchange for his soul?
17.27 and *g* unto them for me and thee.
19. 7 to *g* a writing of divorcement,
21 *g* to the poor, and thou shalt have
20. 4 whatsoever is right I will *g* you.
8 laborers, and *g* them their hire,
14 *g* unto this last, even as unto thee.
23 and on my left, is not mine to *g*,
28 to *g* his life a ransom for many.
22.17 Is it lawful to *g* tribute unto
24.19 them that *g* suck in those days!
29 the moon shall not *g* her light,
45 to *g* them meat in due season?
25. 8 *G* us of your oil; for our lamps
28 *g* it unto him which hath ten
26.15 said unto them, What will ye *g* me,
53 he shall presently *g* me more
Mk 6.22 whatsoever thou wilt, and I will *g*
23 I will *g* it thee, unto the half
25 I will that thou *g* me by and by
37 *G* ye them to eat. And they say
37 of bread, and *g* them to eat?
8.37 Or what shall a man *g* in exchange
9.41 *g* you a cup of water to drink
10.21 *g* to the poor, and thou shalt have
40 on my left hand is not mine to *g*;
45 to *g* his life a ransom for many.
12. 9 will *g* the vineyard unto others.
14 Is it lawful to *g* tribute to Caesar,
15 Shall we *g*, or shall we not *g*?
13.17 to them that *g* suck in those days!
24 the moon shall not *g* her light,
14.11 and promised to *g* him money.
Lk 1.32 the Lord God shall *g* unto him the
77 To *g* knowledge of salvation unto
79 To *g* light to them that sit in
4. 6 All this power will I *g* thee,
6 and to whomsoever I will I *g* it.
10 shall *g* his angels charge over thee,
6.30 *G* to every man that asketh of
38 *G*, and it shall be given unto you;
38 shall men *g* into your bosom.
8.55 he commanded to *g* her meat.
9.13 said unto them, *G* ye them to eat.
10. 7 drinking such things as they *g*:
19 I *g* unto you power to tread on
11. 3 *G* us day by day our daily bread.
7 I cannot rise and *g* thee.
8 Though he will not rise and *g* him.
8 he will rise and *g* him as many
11 will he *g* him a stone? or if he ask
11 will he for a fish *g* him a serpent?
13 *g* good gifts unto your children:
13 your heavenly Father *g* the Holy
36 of a candle doth *g* thee light.
41 *g* alms of such things as ye have;
12.32 Father's good pleasure to *g* you
33 Sell that ye have, and *g* alms;
42 to *g* them their portion of meat
51 I am come to *g* peace on earth?
58 *g* diligence that thou mayest be
14. 9 say to thee, *G* this man place;
15.12 Father, *g* me the portion of goods
16. 2 *g* an account of thy stewardship;
12 *g* you that which is your own?
17.18 that returned to *g* glory to God,
18.12 I *g* tithes of all that I possess.
19. 8 half of my goods I *g* to the poor;
24 *g* it to him that hath ten pounds.
20.10 they should *g* him of the fruit
16 and shall *g* the vineyard to others.
22 Is it lawful for us to *g* tribute
21.15 I will *g* you a mouth and wisdom,
23 to them that *g* suck, in those days!
22. 5 covenanted to *g* him money.
23. 2 forbidding to *g* tribute to Caesar,
Jn 1.22 *g* an answer to them that sent us.
4. 7 saith unto her, *G* me to drink.
10 saith to thee. *G* me to drink;
14 the water that I shall *g* him shall
14 water that I shall *g* him shall be in
15 *g* me this water, that I thirst not,
6.27 the Son of man shall *g* unto you:
34 Lord, evermore *g* us this bread.
51 bread that I will *g* is my flesh,
51 I will *g* for the life of the world.
52 How can this man *g* us his flesh
7.19 Did not Moses *g* you the law,
9.24 said unto him, *G* God the praise:
10.28 And I *g* unto them eternal life;
11.22 ask of God, God will *g* it thee.
13.26 to whom I shall *g* a sop, when I
29 should *g* something to the poor.
34 A new commandment I *g* unto you,
14.16 he shall *g* you another Comforter,
27 my peace I *g* unto you: not as the
27 as the world giveth, *g* I unto you.
15.16 in my name, he may *g* it you.
16.23 in my name, he will *g* it you.
17. 2 he should *g* eternal life to as many
Ac 3. 6 but such as I have *g* I thee: In the
5.31 for to *g* repentance to Israel, and
6. 4 *g* ourselves continually to prayer,
7. 5 promised that he would *g* it to
38 the lively oracles to *g* unto us:
8.19 Saying, *G* me also this power, that
10.43 *g* all the prophets witness, that
13.16 and ye that fear God, *g* audience.
34 *g* you the sure mercies of David.
19.40 *g* an account of this concourse.
20.32 to *g* you an inheritance among all
35 more blessed to *g* than to receive.
Ro 8.32 him also freely *g* us all things?
12.19 but rather *g* place unto wrath:
20 if he thirst, *g* him drink: for in so
14.12 shall *g* account of himself to God.
16. 4 I *g* thanks, but also all the churches
1Co 7. 5 ye may *g* yourselves to fasting
25 yet I *g* my judgment, as one that
10.30 for that for which I *g* thanks?
32 *G* none offense, neither to the
12. 3 I *g* you to understand, that no man
13. 3 though I *g* my body to be burned,
14. 7 they *g* a distinction in the sounds,
8 the trumpet *g* an uncertain sound,
2Co 4. 6 shined in our hearts, to *g* the light
5.12 *g* you occasion to glory on our
8.10 herein I *g* my advice: for this is
9. 7 in his heart, so let him *g*; not
Eph 1.16 Cease not to *g* thanks for you,
17 *g* unto you the spirit of wisdom
4.27 Neither *g* place to the devil.
28 have to *g* to him that needeth.
5.14 and Christ shall *g* thee light.
Col 1. 3 We *g* thanks to God and the Father
4. 1 *g* unto your servants that which
1Th 1. 2 We *g* thanks to God always for
5.18 In everything *g* thanks: for this is the
2Th 2.13 bound to *g* thanks alway to God
3.16 *g* you peace always by all means.
1Ti 1. 4 Neither *g* heed to fables and endless
4.13 I come, *g* attendance to reading, to
15 things; *g* thyself wholly to them;
5. 7 these things *g* in charge, that
14 *g* none occasion to the adversary
6.13 *g* thee charge in the sight of God,
2Ti 1.16 the Lord *g* mercy unto the house
2. 7 Lord *g* thee understanding in all
25 if God peradventure will *g* them
4. 8 judge, shall *g* me at that day:
Heb 2. 1 to *g* the more earnest heed to the
13.17 they that must *g* account, that
Jas 2.16 notwithstanding ye *g* them not
1Pe 3.15 be ready always to *g* an answer
4. 5 Who shall *g* account to him that is
2Pe 1.10 *g* diligence to make your calling
1Jn 5.16 he shall *g* him life for them that
Rev 2. 7 will I *g* to eat of the tree of life,
10 and I will *g* thee a crown of life.
17 him that overcometh will I *g* to eat
17 and will *g* him a white stone,
23 and I will *g* unto every one of you
26 to him will I *g* power over the
28 And I will *g* him the morning star.
4. 9 those beasts *g* glory and honor
10. 9 said unto him, *G* me the little book.
11. 3 will *g* power unto my two witnesses,
17 We *g* thee thanks, O Lord God
18 *g* reward unto thy servants the
13.15 *g* life unto the image of the beast,
14. 7 Fear God, and *g* glory to him;
16. 9 they repented not to *g* him glory.
19 to *g* unto her the cup of the wine
17.13 *g* their power and strength unto
17 *g* their kingdom unto the beast,
18. 7 much torment and sorrow *g* her:
19. 7 and rejoice, an *g* honor to him:
21. 6 I will *g* unto him that is athirst
22.12 *g* every man according as his work

GIVEN

Gen 1.29 *g* you every herb bearing seed,
30 I have *g* every green herb for meat:
15.18 Unto thy seed have I *g* this land,
30. 6 and hath *g* me a son: therefore
43.23 the God of your father, hath *g* you
Ex 5.18 for there shall no straw be *g* you,
16.15 bread which the Lord hath *g* you
29 the Lord hath *g* you the sabbath,
Nu 33.53 I have *g* you the land to possess it.
Dt 3.19 your cities which I have *g* you;
8.10 good land which he hath *g* thee.
Jos 1.13 Lord your God hath *g* you rest,
17.14 Why hast thou *g* me but one lot
Jdg 15.18 Thou hast *g* this great deliverance
18.10 God hath *g* it into your hands;
1Sa 1.27 the Lord hath *g* me my petition
25.44 Saul had *g* Michal his daughter,
1Ki 5. 4 the Lord my God hath *g* me rest
Ezr 6. 4 expenses be *g* out of the king's
9.13 *g* us such deliverance as this;
Neh 2. 7 letters be *g* me to the governors
10.29 God's law, which was *g* by Moses
Est 7. 3 let my life be *g* me at my petition,
Job 3.20 is light *g* to him that is in misery,
23 Why is light *g* to a man whose way
10.18 O that I had *g* up the ghost,
22. 7 not *g* water to the weary to drink,
33. 4 of the Almighty hath *g* me life.
37.10 By the breath of God frost is *g*:
38.36 *g* understanding to the heart?
39.19 Hast thou *g* the horse strength?
Ps 21. 2 hast *g* him his heart's desire,
44.11 *g* us like sheep appointed for
111. 5 *g* meat unto them that fear him:
124. 6 who hath not *g* us as a prey
Ec 6. 2 man to whom God hath *g* riches,
Isa 9. 6 a child is born, unto us a son is *g*:
50. 4 Lord God hath *g* me the tongue
55. 4 Behold, I have *g* him for a witness
Jer 3. 8 away, and *g* her a bill of divorce;
8.14 and *g* us water of gall to drink,
11.18 the Lord hath *g* me knowledge
15. 9 she hath *g* up the ghost; her sun
Eze 16.34 and no reward is *g* unto thee,
18. 8 that hath not *g* forth upon usury,
16 hath *g* his bread to the hungry,
33.24 the land is *g* us for inheritance.
Joel 3. 3 and have *g* a boy for an harlot,
Am 4. 6 have *g* you cleanness of teeth
Na 1.14 And the Lord hath *g* a commandment
Mt 7. 7 Ask, and it shall be *g* you: seek,
9. 8 glorified God, which had *g* such
10.19 it shall be *g* you in that same hour
12.39 and there shall no sign be *g* to it,
13.11 *g* unto you to know the mysteries
11 but to them it is not *g*.
12 whosoever hath, to him shall be *g*,
14. 9 he commanded it to be *g* her.
11 in a charger, and *g* to the damsel:
16. 4 there shall no sign be *g* unto it,
19.11 save they to whom it is *g*.
20.23 it shall be *g* to them for whom it

Mt 21.43 taken from you, and *g* to a nation
22.30 marry, nor are *g* in marriage,
25.29 every one that hath shall be *g*,
26. 9 sold for much, and *g* to the poor.
28.18 All power is *g* unto me in heaven
Mk 4.11 you it is *g* to know the mystery
24 you that hear shall more be *g*.
25 he that hath, to him shall be *g*:
5.43 something should be *g* her to eat.
6. 2 this which is *g* unto him, that even
8.12 no sign be *g* unto this generation.
10.40 but it shall be *g* to them for whom
12.25 neither marry, nor are *g* in marriage;
13.11 shall be *g* you in that hour,
14. 5 and have been *g* to the poor.
23 cup, and when he had *g* thanks,
44 him had *g* them a token, saying,
Lk 6.38 Give, and it shall be *g* unto you;
8.10 you it is *g* to know the mysteries
18 whosoever hath, to him shall be *g*;
11. 9 Ask, and it shall be *g* you; seek.
29 there shall no sign be *g* it, but the
12.48 unto whomsoever much is *g*, of
17.27 they were *g* in marriage, until the day
19.15 whom he had *g* the money, that
26 every one which hath shall be *g*;
20.34 marry, and are *g* in marriage; but
35 neither marry, nor are *g* in marriage:
22.19 This is my body which is *g* for you:
Jn 1.17 law was *g* by Moses, but grace
3.27 except it be *g* him from heaven.
35 hath *g* all things into his hand.
4.10 he would have *g* thee living water.
5.26 so hath he *g* to the Son to have
27 hath *g* him authority to execute
36 which the Father hath *g* me
6.11 when he had *g* thanks, he distributed
23 after that the Lord had *g* thanks:)
39 that of all which he hath *g* me
65 it were *g* unto him of my Father.
7.39 for the Holy Ghost was not yet *g*;
11.57 Pharisees had *g* a commandment,
12. 5 hundred pence, and *g* to the poor?
13. 3 the Father had *g* all things into his
15 For I have *g* you an example,
17. 2 thou hast *g* him power over all
2 to as many as thou hast *g* him.
7 whatsoever thou hast *g* me are of
8 have *g* unto them the words which
9 for them which thou hast *g* me;
11 those whom thou hast *g* me, that
14 I have *g* them thy word; and the
22 thou gavest me I have *g* them; that
24 they also, whom thou hast *g* me,
24 my glory, which thou hast *g* me:
18.11 cup which my Father hath *g* me,
19.11 except it were *g* thee from above:
Ac 1. 2 Holy Ghost had *g* commandments
3.16 hath *g* him this perfect soundness
4.12 name under heaven *g* among men,
5.32 whom God hath *g* to them that
8.18 the Holy Ghost was *g*, he offered
17.16 saw the city wholly *g* to idolatry.
31 whereof he hath *g* assurance unto
20. 2 and had *g* them much exhortation,
21.40 And when he had *g* him licence, Paul
24.26 money should have been *g* him of
27.24 God hath *g* thee all them that
Ro 5. 5 by the Holy Ghost which is *g* unto
11. 8 hath *g* them the spirit of slumber,
35 Or who hath first *g* to him, and it
12. 3 say through the grace *g* unto me,
6 the grace that is *g* to us, whether
13 necessity of saints; *g* to hospitality.
15.15 the grace that is *g* to me of God,
1Co 1. 4 the grace of God which is *g* you by
2.12 know the things that are freely *g*
3.10 the grace of God which is *g* unto
11.15 for her hair is *g* her for a covering.
24 And when he had *g* thanks, he
12. 7 manifestation of the Spirit is *g*
8 to one is *g* by the Spirit the word
24 having *g* more abundant honor
16. 1 as I have *g* order to the churches
2Co 1.11 thanks may be *g* by many on our
22 and *g* the earnest of the Spirit
5. 5 also hath *g* unto us the earnest of
18 and hath *g* to us the ministry
9. 9 *g* to the poor: his righteousness
10. 8 the Lord hath *g* us for edification,
12. 7 there was *g* to me a thorn in the
13.10 power which the Lord hath *g* me
Gal 2. 9 the grace that was *g* unto me, they
3.21 for if there had been a law *g*
21 which could have *g* life,
22 might be *g* to them that believe.
4.15 own eyes, and have *g* them to me.
Eph 3. 2 which is *g* me to you-ward:
7 the grace of God *g* unto me by the
8 is this grave *g*, that I should preach
4. 7 unto every one of us is *g* grace
19 past feeling have *g* themselves
5. 2 hath loved us, and hath *g* himself
6.19 that utterance may be *g* unto me,
Php 1.29 you it is *g* in the behalf of Christ,
2. 9 and *g* him a name which is above
Col 1.25 of God which is *g* to me for you,
1Th 4. 8 also *g* unto us his holy Spirit.
2Th 2.16 hath *g* us everlasting consolation
1Ti 3. 2 *g* to hospitality, apt to teach;
3 *g* to wine, no striker, not greedy
8 not *g* to much wine, not greedy
4.14 which was *g* thee by prophecy,
2Ti 1. 7 For God hath not *g* us the spirit
9 grace, which was *g* us in Christ
3.16 All scripture is *g* by inspiration
Tit 1. 7 not soon angry, not *g* to wine,
7 not *g* to filthy lucre;
2. 3 not *g* to much wine, teachers of
Phm 22 prayers I shall be *g* unto you.
Heb 2.13 the children which God hath *g*
4. 8 For if Jesus had *g* them rest, then
Jas 1. 5 upbraideth not; and it shall be *g*
2Pe 1. 3 power hath *g* unto us all things
4 Whereby are *g* unto us exceeding
3.15 according to the wisdom *g* unto
1Jn 3.24 by the Spirit which he hath *g* us.
4.13 because he hath *g* us of his Spirit.
5.11 that God hath *g* to us eternal life,
20 and hath *g* us an understanding,
Rev 6. 2 and a crown was *g* unto him:
4 power was *g* to him that sat thereon
4 and there was *g* unto him a great
8 power was *g* unto them over the
11 white robes were *g* unto every one
7. 2 to whom it was *g* to hurt the earth
8. 2 to them were *g* seven trumpets.
3 there was *g* unto him much incense,
9. 1 was *g* the key of the bottomless pit.
3 unto them was *g* power, as the
5 to them it was *g* that they should
10. 9 unto him, *G* me the little book.
11. 1 there was *g* me a reed like unto a
2 for it is *g* unto the Gentiles:
12.14 to the woman were *g* two wings
13. 5 there was *g* unto him a mouth
5 power was *g* unto him to continue
7 it was *g* unto him to make war
7 power was *g* him over all kindreds,
16. 6 thou hast *g* them blood to drink;
8 power was *g* unto him to scorch
20. 4 and judgment was *g* unto them:

GIVER

Isa 24. 2 so with the *g* of usury to him.
2Co 9. 7 for God loveth a cheerful *g*.

GIVEST

Ps 50.19 Thou *g* thy mouth to evil, and
80. 5 and *g* them tears to drink in great
104.28 That thou *g* them they gather:
145.15 thou *g* them their meat in due
Eze 3.18 thou *g* him not warning, nor speakest
16.33 thou *g* thy gifts to all thy lovers,
1Co 14.17 For thou verily *g* thanks well,

GIVETH

Gen 49.21 hind let loose: he *g* goodly words.
Ex 20.12 the land which the Lord thy God *g*
25. 2 every man that *g* it willingly
Lev 20. 2 *g* any of his seed unto Molech:
Nu 5.10 whatsoever any man *g* the priest,
Dt 4.21 the Lord thy God *g* thee for an
13. 1 and *g* thee a sign or a wonder,
15. 7 God *g* thee, thou shalt not harden
24. 3 a bill of divorcement, and *g* it
27. 3 thy God *g* thee, a land that floweth
Job 5.10 Who *g* rain upon the earth, and
14.10 yea, man *g* up the ghost, and
32. 8 the Almighty *g* them understanding.
35.10 who *g* songs in the night;
12 There they cry, but none *g* answer,
36. 6 but *g* right to the poor.
31 he *g* meat in abundance.
Ps 119.130 The entrance of thy words *g* light;
130 it *g* understanding unto the simple.
127. 2 for so he *g* his beloved sleep.
136.25 Who *g* food to all flesh: for his
146. 7 which *g* food to the hungry.
147. 9 He *g* to the beast his food,
Pr 2. 6 For the Lord *g* wisdom: out of his
17. 4 and a liar *g* ear to a naughty tongue.
Isa 40.29 He *g* power to the faint; and to
La 3.30 *g* his cheek to him that smiteth
Dan 2.21 he *g* wisdom unto the wise, and
Mt 5.15 and it *g* light unto all that are in
Jn 3.34 God *g* not the Spirit by measure
6.32 my Father *g* you the true bread
33 and *g* life unto the world.
37 All that the Father *g* me shall
10.11 good shepherd *g* his life for the
14.27 not as the world *g*, give I unto you.
21.13 taketh bread, and *g* them, and fish
Ac 17.25 seeing he *g* to all life, and breath,
Ro 12. 8 he that *g*, let him do it with
14. 6 for he *g* God thanks; and he that
6 eateth not, and *g* God thanks.
1Co 3. 7 but God that *g* the increase.
7.38 he that *g* her in marriage doeth well;
38 but he that *g* her not in marriage
15.38 God *g* it a body as it hath pleased
57 God which *g* us the victory through
2Co 3. 6 killeth, but the Spirit *g* life.
1Ti 6.17 *g* us richly all things to enjoy;
Jas 1. 5 ask of God, that *g* to all men
4. 6 But he *g* more grace. Wherefore
6 but *g* grace unto the humble.
1Pe 4.11 it as of the ability which God *g*:
5. 5 proud, and *g* grace to the humble.
Rev 22. 5 for the Lord God *g* them light:

GIVING

Gen 24.19 when she had done *g* him drink,
Dt 10.18 in *g* him food and raiment.
21.17 by *g* him a double portion of all
Ru 1. 6 visited his people in *g* them bread.
1Ki 5. 9 in *g* food for my household.
2Ch 6.23 by *g* him according to his
Ezr 3.11 praising and *g* thanks unto the Lord:
Job 11.20 shall be as the *g* up of the ghost.
Mt 24.38 marrying and *g* in marriage,
Lk 17.16 at his feet, *g* him thanks: and he was
Ac 8. 9 *g* out that himself was some
15. 8 *g* them the Holy Ghost, even as
Ro 4.20 strong in faith, *g* glory to God;
9. 4 covenants, and the *g* of the law,
1Co 14. 7 even things without life *g* sound,
16 say Amen at thy *g* of thanks,
2Co 6. 3 *G* no offense in any thing, that
Eph 5. 4 but rather *g* of thanks.
20 *G* thanks always for all things
Php 4.15 concerning *g* and receiving, but
Col 1.12 *G* thanks unto the Father, which

3.17 *g* thanks to God and the Father
1Ti 2. 1 intercessions, and *g* of thanks.
4. 1 *g* heed to seducing spirits, and
Tit 1.14 Not *g* heed to Jewish fables, and
Heb 13.15 of our lips *g* thanks to his name.
1Pe 3. 7 *g* honor unto the wife, as unto
2Pe 1. 5 *g* all diligence, add to your faith
Jude 7 *g* themselves over to fornication.

GLAD

Ex 4.14 thee, he will be *g* in his heart.
Jdg 18.20 And the priest's heart was *g*,
1Sa 11. 9 men of Jabesh; and they were *g*.
1Ki 8.66 joyful and *g* of heart for all the
1Ch 16.31 Let the heavens be *g*, and let
2Ch 7.10 *g* and merry in heart for the
Est 5. 9 day joyful and with a *g* heart:
8.15 of Shushan rejoiced and was *g*.
Job 3.22 rejoice exceedingly, and are *g*,
22.19 The righteous see it, and are *g*:
Ps 9. 2 I will be *g* and rejoice in thee:
14. 7 rejoice, and Israel shall be *g*.
16. 9 heart is *g*, and my glory rejoiceth:
21. 6 thou hast made him exceeding *g*
31. 7 be *g* and rejoice in thy mercy:
32.11 Be *g* in the Lord, and rejoice,
34. 2 shall hear thereof, and be *g*.
35.27 Let them shout for joy, and be *g*,
45. 8 whereby they have made thee *g*.
46. 4 shall make *g* the city of God,
48.11 let the daughters of Judah be *g*,
53. 6 rejoice, and Israel shall be *g*.
64.10 righteous shall be *g* in the Lord,
67. 4 O let the nations be *g* and sing
68. 3 But let the righteous be *g*; let
69.32 humble shall see this, and be *g*:
70. 4 seek thee rejoice and be *g* in thee:
90.14 that we may rejoice and be *g* all
15 Make us *g* according to the days
92. 4 hast made me *g* through thy work:
96.11 and let the earth be *g*; let the sea
97. 1 let the multitude of isles be *g*
8 Zion heard, and was *g*; and the
104.15 wine that maketh *g* the heart of
34 I will be *g* in the Lord.
105.38 Egypt was *g* when they departed:
107.30 Then are they *g* because they be
118.24 we will rejoice and be *g* in it.
119.74 They that fear thee will be *g*
122. 1 I was *g* when they said unto me,
126. 3 things for us; whereof we are *g*.
Pr 10. 1 A wise son maketh a *g* father:
12.25 but a good word maketh it *g*.
15.20 A wise son maketh a *g* father:
17. 5 and he that is *g* at calamities
23.25 father and thy mother shall be *g*,
24.17 let not thine heart be *g* when he
27.11 be wise, and make my heart *g*,
SS 1. 4 we will be *g* and rejoice in thee,
Isa 25. 9 we will be *g* and rejoice in his
35. 1 solitary place shall be *g* for them;
39. 2 And Hezekiah was *g* of them,
65.18 be ye *g* and rejoice for ever
66.10 and be *g* with her, all ye that love
Jer 20.15 unto thee: making him very *g*.
41.13 were with him, then they were *g*.
50.11 Because ye were *g*, because ye
La 1.21 they are *g* that thou hast done it:
4.21 Rejoice and be *g*, O daughter of
Dan 6.23 was the king exceeding *g* for him,
Hos 7. 3 They make the king *g* with their
Joel 2.21 Fear not, O land; be *g* and rejoice:
23 Be *g* then, ye children of Zion,
Jon 4. 6 So Jonah was exceeding *g* of the
Hab 1.15 therefore they rejoice and are *g*.
Zep 3.14 be *g* and rejoice with all the
Zec 10. 7 shall see it, and be *g*; their heart
Mt 5.12 Rejoice, and be exceeding *g*: for
Mk 14.11 when they heard it, they were *g*,
Lk 1.19 to shew thee these *g* tidings.
8. 1 the *g* tidings of the kingdom
15.32 we should make merry, and be *g*:
22. 5 And they were *g*, and covenanted
23. 8 saw Jesus, he was exceeding *g*:
Jn 8.56 and he saw it, and was *g*.
11.15 And I am *g* for your sakes that
20.20 Then were the disciples *g*, when
Ac 2.26 rejoice, and my tongue was *g*;
11.23 was *g*, and exhorted them all,
13.32 we declare unto you *g* tidings,
48 Gentiles heard this, they were *g*,
Ro 10.15 of peace, and bring *g* tidings
16.19 I am *g* therefore on your behalf:
1Co 16.17 am *g* of the coming of Stephanas
2Co 2. 2 who is he then that maketh me *g*,
13. 9 For we are *g*, when we are weak,
1Pe 4.13 be *g* also with exceeding joy.
Rev 19. 7 Let us be *g* and rejoice, and we

GLADLY

Mk 6.20 many things, and heard him *g*.
12.37 the common people heard him *g*.
Lk 8.40 the people *g* received him:
Ac 2.41 they that *g* received his word
21.17 the brethren received us *g*.
2Co 11.19 For ye suffer fools *g*, seeing ye
12. 9 Most *g* therefore will I rather
15 I will very *g* spend and be spent

GLADNESS

Nu 10.10 Also in the day of your *g*,
Dt 28.47 joyfulness, and with *g* of heart,
2Sa 6.12 into the city of David with *g*.
1Ch 16.27 strength and *g* are in his place.
29.22 Lord on that day with great *g*.
2Ch 29.30 they sang praises with *g*, and
30.21 bread seven days with great *g*:
23 kept other seven days with *g*.
Neh 8.17 And there was very great *g*.
12.27 to keep the dedication with *g*,
Est 8.16 The Jews had light, and *g*, and joy,
17 Jews had joy and *g*, a feast
9.17, 18 made it a day of feasting and *g*.
19 day of the month Adar a day of *g*
Ps 4. 7 Thou hast put *g* in my heart,
30.11 sackcloth, and girded me with *g*;
45. 7 anointed thee with the oil of *g*
15 With *g* and rejoicing shall they
51. 8 Make me to hear joy and *g*;
97.11 and *g* for the upright in heart.
100. 2 Serve the Lord with *g*: come
105.43 joy, and his chosen with *g*:
106. 5 rejoice in the *g* of thy nation,
Pr 10.28 hope of the righteous shall be *g*:
SS 3.11 in the day of the *g* of his heart.
Isa 16.10 And *g* is taken away, and joy out
22.13 behold joy and *g*, slaying oxen,
30.29 and *g* of heart, as when one goeth
35.10 they shall obtain joy and *g*, and
51. 3 joy and *g* shall be found therein,
11 they shall obtain *g* and joy; and
Jer 7.34 voice of mirth, and the voice of *g*,
16. 9 voice of mirth, and the voice of *g*,
25.10 voice of mirth, and the voice of *g*,
31. 7 Sing with *g* for Jacob, and shout
33.11 The voice of joy, and the voice of *g*,
48.33 And joy and *g* is taken from the
Joel 1.16 and *g* from the house of our God?
Zec 8.19 to the house of Judah joy and *g*,
Mk 4.16 immediately receive it with *g*;
Lk 1.14 And thou shalt have joy and *g*;
Ac 2.46 with *g* and singleness of heart,
12.14 she opened not the gate for *g*,
14.17 filling our hearts with food and *g*.
Php 2.29 therefore in the Lord with all *g*;
Heb 1. 9 hath anointed thee with the oil of *g*

GLASS

Job 37.18 and as a molten looking *g*?
1Co 13.12 now we see through a *g* darkly;
2Co 3.18 beholding as in a *g* the glory of
Jas 1.23 beholding his natural face in a *g*:
Rev 4. 6 was a sea of *g* like unto crystal:
15. 2 a sea of *g* mingled with fire:
2 sea of *g*, having the harps of God.
21.18 was pure gold, like unto clear *g*.
21 gold, as it were transparent *g*.

GLASSES

Isa 3.23 The *g*, and the fine linen, and

GLEAN

Lev 19.10 thou shalt not *g* thy vineyard,
Ru 2. 2 and *g* ears of corn after him
7 let me *g* and gather after the
15 Let her *g* even among the sheaves,
Jer 6. 9 shall thoroughly *g* the remnant

GLEANED

Ru 2. 3 *g* in the field after the reapers:
17 So she *g* in the field until even,
18 mother in law saw what she had *g*:

GLISTERING

1Ch 29. 2 *g* stones, and of divers colors,
Lk 9.29 his raiment was white and *g*.

GLITTER

Eze 21.10 it is furbished that it may *g*:

GLITTERING

Dt 32.41 If I whet my *g* sword, and mine
Job 20.25 yea, the *g* sword cometh out of
39.23 the *g* spear and the shield.
Eze 21.28 to consume because of the *g*:
Na 3. 3 the bright sword and the *g* spear:
Hab 3.11 at the shining of thy *g* spear.

GLORIETH

Jer 9.24 But let him that *g* glory in this,
1Co 1.31 that *g*, let him glory in the Lord.
2Co 10.17 that *g*, let him glory in the Lord.

GLORIFIED

Lev 10. 3 before all the people I will be *g*.
Isa 26.15 increased the nation: thou art *g*:
44.23 Jacob, and *g* himself in Israel.
49. 3 O Israel, in whom I will be *g*.
55. 5 One of Israel; for he hath *g* thee.
60. 9 of Israel, because he hath *g* thee.
21 of my hands, that I may be *g*.
61. 3 of the Lord, that he might be *g*.
66. 5 Let the Lord be *g*: but he shall
Eze 28.22 I will be *g* in the midst of thee:
39.13 that I shall be *g*, saith the Lord
Dan 5.23 are all thy ways, hast thou not *g*:
Hag 1. 8 and I will be *g*, saith the Lord.
Mt 9. 8 they marvelled, and *g* God, which
15.31 and they *g* the God of Israel.
Mk 2.12 then were all amazed, and *g* God,
Lk 4.15 their synagogues, being *g* of all.
5.26 were all amazed, and they *g* God,
7.16 they *g* God, saying, That a great
13.13 she was made straight, and *g* God.
17.15 and with a loud voice *g* God.
23.47 saw what was done, he *g* God,
Jn 7.39 because that Jesus was not yet *g*.)
11. 4 Son of God might be *g* thereby.
12.16 but when Jesus was *g*, then
23 that the Son of man should be *g*.
28 I have both *g* it, and will glorify
13.31 Now is the Son of man *g*,
31 and God is *g* in him.
32 If God be *g* in him, God shall
14.13 the Father may be *g* in the Son.
15. 8 Herein is my Father *g*, that ye bear
17. 4 I have *g* thee on the earth: I
10 and am *g* in them.
Ac 3.13 hath *g* his Son Jesus;
4.21 for all men *g* God for that which
11.18 they held their peace, and *g* God,
13.48 and *g* the word of the Lord: and
21.20 they *g* the Lord, and said unto him,

Ro 1.21 they *g* him not as God, neither
8.17 that we may be also *g* together.
30 whom he justified, them he also *g*.
Gal 1.24 And they *g* God in me.
2Th 1.10 shall come to be *g* in his saints,
12 of our Lord Jesus Christ may be *g*
3. 1 may have free course and be *g*,
Heb 5. 5 Christ *g* not himself to be made
1Pe 4.11 may be *g* through Jesus Christ,
14 but on your part he is *g*.
Rev 18. 7 How much she hath *g* herself,

GLORIFY

Ps 22.23 all ye the seed of Jacob, *g* him;
50.15 deliver thee, and thou shalt *g* me.
86. 9 O Lord; and shall *g* thy name.
12 I will *g* thy name for evermore.
Isa 24.15 Wherefore *g* ye the Lord in the
25. 3 shall the strong people *g* thee,
60. 7 I will *g* the house of my glory.
Jer 30.19 I will also *g* them, and they shall
Mt 5.16 see your good works, and *g* your
Jn 12.28 Father, *g* thy name. Then came
28 have both glorified it, and will *g* it
13.32 God shall also *g* him in himself,
32 and shall straightway *g* him.
16.14 He shall *g* me: for he shall receive
17. 1 *g* thy Son, that thy Son also
1 that thy Son also may *g* thee:
5 O Father, *g* thou me with thine
21.19 by what death he should *g* God.
Ro 15. 6 one mind and one mouth *g* God.
9 the Gentiles might *g* God for his
1Co 6.20 therefore *g* God in your body,
2Co 9.13 they *g* God for your professed
1Pe 2.12 *g* God in the day of visitation.
4.16 let him *g* God on this behalf.
Rev 15. 4 fear thee, O Lord, and *g* thy name?

GLORIFYING

Lk 2.20 *g* and praising God for all things
5.25 departed to his own house, *g* God.
18.43 and followed him, *g* God:

GLORIOUS

Ex 15. 6 O Lord, is become *g* in power:
11 who is like thee, *g* in holiness,
Dt 28.58 fear this *g* and fearful name,
2Sa 6.20 How *g* was the king of Israel to day,
1Ch 29.13 thank thee, and praise thy *g* name.
Neh 9. 5 blessed be thy *g* name, which is
Est 1. 4 shewed the riches of his *g* kingdom
Ps 45.13 king's daughter is all *g* within:
66. 2 of his name: make his praise *g*.
72.19 And blessed be his *g* name for ever:
76. 4 Thou art more *g* and excellent
87. 3 *G* things are spoken of thee, O
111. 3 His work is honorable and *g*:
145. 5 I will speak of the *g* honor of thy
12 and the *g* majesty of his kingdom.
Isa 4. 2 of the Lord be beautiful and *g*,
11.10 and his rest shall be *g*.
22.23 and he shall be for a *g* throne
28. 1 whose *g* beauty is a fading flower,
4 the *g* beauty, which is on the head
30.30 the Lord shall cause his *g* voice
33.21 But there the *g* Lord will be
49. 5 I be *g* in the eyes of the Lord,
60.13 I will make the place of my feet *g*.
63. 1 *g* in his apparel, travelling in the
12 with his *g* arm, dividing the water
14 people, to make thyself a *g* name.
Jer 17.12 A *g* high throne from the
Eze 27.25 wast replenished, and made very *g*
Dan 11.16 and he shall stand in the *g* land,
41 He shall enter also into the *g* land,
45 the seas in the *g* holy mountain;
Lk 13.17 *g* things that were done by him.
Ro 8.21 *g* liberty of the children of God.
2Co 3. 7 engraven in stones, was *g*,
8 of the spirit be rather *g*?
10 which was made *g* had no glory
11 which is done away was *g*,
11 that which remaineth is *g*.
4. 4 the light of the *g* gospel of Christ,
Eph 5.27 present it to himself a *g* church,
Php 3.21 fashioned like unto his *g* body,
Col 1.11 according to his *g* power, unto
1Ti 1.11 the *g* gospel of the blessed God,
Tit 2.13 the *g* appearing of the great God

GLORIOUSLY

Ex 15. 1 the Lord, for he hath triumphed *g*:
21 to the Lord, for he hath triumphed *g*:
Isa 24.23 and before his ancients *g*.

GLORY

Gen 45.13 ye shall tell my father of all my *g*
Ex 16. 7 ye shall see the *g* of the Lord;
10 *g* of the Lord appeared in a cloud.
33.18 I beseech thee, shew me thy *g*.
Lev 9. 6 *g* of the Lord shall appear unto you.
Dt 5.24 Lord our God hath shewed us his *g*
1Sa 4.21, 22 The *g* is departed from Israel:
1Ch 16.10 *G* ye in his holy name: let the
24 Declare his *g* among the heathen;
27 *G* and honor are in his presence;
28 give unto the Lord *g* and strength.
29 the Lord the *g* due unto his name:
35 holy name, and *g* in thy praise.
2Ch 5.14 *g* of the Lord had filled the house
Job 39.20 the *g* of his nostrils is terrible.
40.10 array thyself with *g* and beauty.
Ps 4. 2 long will ye turn my *g* into shame?
8. 1 hast set thy *g* above the heavens.
5 crowned him with *g* and honor.
19. 1 The heavens declare the *g* of God;
24. 7 and the King of *g* shall come in.
8 Who is this King of *g*? The Lord
9 and the King of *g* shall come in.
10 Who is this King of *g*? The Lord
10 of hosts, he is the King of *g*.
29. 1 give unto the Lord *g* and strength.
2 the Lord the *g* due unto his name:
62. 7 In God is my salvation and my *g*:
72.19 whole earth be filled with his *g*;
90.16 and thy *g* unto their children.
96. 3 Declare his *g* among the heathen,
7 give unto the Lord *g* and strength.
8 the Lord the *g* due unto his name:
104.31 *g* of the Lord shall endure for ever:
138. 5 for great is the *g* of the Lord.
148.13 *g* is above the earth and heaven.
Pr 4. 9 a crown of *g* shall she deliver
16.31 The hoary head is a crown of *g*,
20.29 *g* of young men is their strength:
Isa 3. 8 to provoke the eyes of his *g*.
6. 3 the whole earth is full of his *g*.
13.19 Babylon, the *g* of kingdoms, the
28. 5 Lord of hosts be for a crown of *g*,
42. 8 my *g* will I not give to another,
48.11 I will not give my *g* unto another.
58. 8 *g* of the...shall be thy reward.
59.19 his *g* from the rising of the sun.
60. 1 and the *g* of the Lord is risen upon
2 and his *g* shall be seen upon thee.
13 The *g* of Lebanon shall come
66.19 declare my *g* among the Gentiles.
Jer 9.23 let the mighty man *g* in his might,
23 let not the rich man *g* in his riches:
13.16 Give *g* to the Lord your God,
Eze 3.12 Blessed be the *g* of the Lord from
26.20 I shall set *g* in the land of the
Hos 9.11 their *g* shall fly away like a bird,
Hab 2.14 with the knowledge of the *g* of the
3. 3 His *g* covered the heavens, and
Mal 2. 2 give *g* unto my name, saith the
Mt 4. 8 of the world, and the *g* of them;
6. 2 that they may have *g* of men.
13 the power, and the *g*, for ever.
29 even Solomon in all his *g* was not
16.27 come in the *g* of his Father with his
19.28 also shall sit in the throne of his *g*,
24.30 with power and great *g*.
25.31 the Son of man shall come in his *g*,
31 shall he sit upon the throne of his *g*:
Mk 8.38 cometh in the *g* of his Father with
10.37 other on thy left hand, in thy *g*.
13.26 the clouds with great power and *g*.
Lk 2. 9 and the *g* of the Lord shone round
14 *G* to God in the highest, and on
32 and the *g* of thy people Israel.
4. 6 will I give thee, and the *g* of them:
9.26 when he shall come in his own *g*,
31 Who appeared in *g*, and spake of
32 they saw his *g*, and the two men
12.27 that Solomon in all his *g* was not
17.18 returned to give *g* to God, save
19.38 peace in heaven, and *g* in the
21.27 in a cloud with power and great *g*.
24.26 things, and to enter into his *g*?
Jn 1.14 we beheld his *g*, the *g* as of the
2.11 and manifested forth his *g*;
7.18 of himself seeketh his own *g*: but
18 he that seeketh his *g* that sent him,
8.50 I seek not mine own *g*: there is
11. 4 but for the *g* of God, that the Son
40 thou shouldest see the *g* of God?
12.41 said Esaias, when he saw his *g*,
17. 5 with the *g* which I had with thee
22 And the *g* which thou gavest me
24 that they may behold my *g*,
Ac 7. 2 The God of *g* appeared unto our
55 and saw the *g* of God, and Jesus
12.23 because he gave not God the *g*:
22.11 could not see for the *g* of that light,
Ro 1.23 the *g* of the uncorruptible God into
2. 7 well doing seek for *g* and honor
10 *g*, honor, and peace, to every man
3. 7 through my lie unto his *g*;
23 and come short of the *g* of God;
4. 2 he hath whereof to *g*: but not
20 strong in faith, giving *g* to God;
5. 2 and rejoice in hope of the *g* of God.
3 but we *g* in tribulations also:
6. 4 the dead by the *g* of the Father,
8.18 the *g* which shall be revealed in us.
9. 4 the adoption, and the *g*, and the
23 make known the riches of his *g* on
23 he had afore prepared unto *g*,
11.36 to whom be *g* for ever. Amen.
15. 7 also received us to the *g* of God.
17 I have therefore whereof I may *g*
16.27 To God only wise, be *g* through
1Co 1.29 no flesh should *g* in his presence.
31 that glorieth, let him *g* in the Lord.
2. 7 before the world unto our *g*:
8 not have crucified the Lord of *g*.
3.21 Therefore let no man *g* in men.
4. 7 why dost thou *g*, as if thou hadst
9.16 I have nothing to *g* of: for
10.31 ye do, do all to the *g* of God.
11. 7 as he is the image and *g* of God:
7 but the woman is the *g* of the man.
15 have long hair, it is a *g* to her:
15.40 but the *g* of the celestial is one,
40 the *g* of the terrestial is another.
41 There is one *g* of the sun, and
41 and another *g* of the moon, and
41 and another *g* of the stars: for
41 differeth from another star in *g*.
43 sown in dishonor; it is raised in *g*:
2Co 1.20 Amen, unto the *g* of God by us.
3. 7 *g* of his countenance; which *g* was
9 ministration of condemnation be *g*,
9 of righteousness exceed in *g*.
10 which was made glorious had no *g*
10 by reason of the *g* that excelleth.
18 as in a glass the *g* of the Lord,
18 into the same image from *g* to *g*,
4. 6 the knowledge of the *g* of God
15 of many redound to the *g* of God.
17 exceeding and eternal weight of *g*;

5.12 you occasion to *g* on our behalf,
12 them which *g* in appearance,
8.19 by us to the *g* of the same Lord,
23 the churches, and the *g* of Christ.
10.17 glorieth, let him *g* in the Lord.
11.12 that wherein they *g*, they may be
18 Seeing that many *g* after the flesh,
18 after the flesh, I will *g* also.
30 If I must needs *g*, I will *g* of the
12. 1 expedient for me doubtless to *g*.
5 Of such an one will I *g*:
5 yet of myself I will not *g*,
6 For though I would desire to *g*,
9 will I rather *g* in my infirmities,
Gal 1. 5 To whom be *g* for ever and ever.
5.26 Let us not be desirous of vain *g*,
6.13 that they may *g* in your flesh.
14 But God forbid that I should *g*,
Eph 1. 6 To the praise of the *g* of his grace,
12 should be to the praise of his *g*,
14 possession unto the praise of his *g*.
17 the Father of *g*, may give unto you
18 riches of the *g* of his inheritance
3.13 tribulations for you, which is your *g*.
16 according to the riches of his *g*,
21 Unto him be *g* in the church by
Php 1.11 unto the *g* and praise of God.
2.11 is Lord, to the *g* of God the Father.
3.19 and whose *g* is in their shame,
4.19 to his riches in *g* by Christ Jesus.
20 our Father be *g* for ever and ever.
Col 1.27 the riches of the *g* of this mystery
27 is Christ in you, the hope of *g*:
3. 4 shall ye also appear with him in *g*.
1Th 2. 6 Nor of men sought we *g*, neither
12 called you unto his kingdom and *g*.
20 For ye are our *g* and joy.
2Th 1. 4 So that we ourselves *g* in you
9 and from the *g* of his power;
2.14 of the *g* of our Lord Jesus Christ.
1Ti 1.17 be honor and *g* for ever and ever.
3.16 in the world, received up into *g*.
2Ti 2.10 is in Christ Jesus with eternal *g*.
4.18 to whom be *g* for ever and ever.
Heb 1. 3 Who being the brightness of his *g*,
2. 7 crownedst him with *g* and honor,
9 suffering of death, crowned with *g*
10 in bringing many sons unto *g*,
3. 3 worthy of more *g* than Moses,
9. 5 it the cherubims of *g* shadowing
13.21 to whom be *g* for ever and ever.
Jas 2. 1 Lord Jesus Christ, the Lord of *g*,
3.14 *g* not, and lie not against the
1Pe 1. 7 honor and *g* at the appearing of
8 joy unspeakable and full of *g*:
11 and the *g* that should follow.
21 up from the dead, and gave him *g*;
24 the *g* of man as the flower of grass.
2.20 For what *g* is it, if, when ye be
4.13 when his *g* shall be revealed,
14 the spirit of *g* and of God resteth
5. 1 a partaker of the *g* that shall be
4 ye shall receive a crown of *g* that
10 hath called us unto his eternal *g*
11 him be *g* and dominion for ever
2Pe 1. 3 that hath called us to *g* and virtue:
17 from God the Father honor and *g*,
17 voice to him from the excellent *g*,
3.18 To him be *g* both now and for ever.
Jude 24 before the presence of his *g* with
25 our Savior, be *g* and majesty,
Rev 1. 6 to him be *g* and dominion for ever
4. 9 those beasts give *g* and honor
11 receive *g* and honor and power:
5.12 and honor, and *g*, and blessing.
13 Blessing, and honor, and *g*, and
7.12 Saying, Amen: Blessing, and *g*,
11.13 and gave *g* to the God of heaven.
14. 7 Fear God, and give *g* to him;
15. 8 with smoke from the *g* of God,
16. 9 they repented not to give him *g*.
18. 1 the earth was lightened with his *g*.
19. 1 Salvation, and *g*, and honor, and
21.11 Having the *g* of God: and her light
23 for the *g* of God did lighten it, and
24 bring their *g* and honor into it.
26 they shall bring the *g* and honor

GLORYING

1Co 5. 6 Your *g* is not good. Know ye not
9.15 any man should make my *g* void.
2Co 7. 4 great is my *g* of you:
12.11 I am become a fool in *g*; ye have

GLUTTONOUS

Mt 11.19 a man *g*, and a winebibber, a
Lk 7.34 Behold a *g* man, and a winebibber,

GNASH

Ps 112.10 he shall *g* with his teeth, and
La 2.16 they hiss and *g* the teeth: they

GNASHED

Ps 35.16 they *g* upon me with their teeth.
Ac 7.54 they *g* on him with their teeth.

GNASHETH

Job 16. 9 he *g* upon me with his teeth;
Ps 37.12 and *g* upon him with his teeth.
Mk 9.18 foameth, and *g* with his teeth,

GNASHING

Mt 8.12 shall be weeping and *g* of teeth.
13.42, 50 shall be wailing and *g* of teeth.
22.13 shall be weeping and *g* of teeth.
24.51 shall be weeping and *g* of teeth.
25.30 shall be weeping and *g* of teeth.
Lk 13.28 shall be weeping and *g* of teeth,

GNAT

Mt 23.24 which strain at a *g*, and swallow

GNAW

Zep 3. 3 they *g* not the bones till the

GNAWED

Rev 16.10 and they *g* their tongues for pain,

GO

Gen 3.14 upon thy belly shalt thou *g*, and
11. 7 let us *g* down, and there confound
13. 9 then I will *g* to the right; or if thou
9 right hand, then I will *g* to the left.
15.15 shalt *g* to thy fathers in peace;
18.21 I will *g* down now, and see
22. 5 I and the lad will *g* yonder and
24.42 do prosper my way which I *g*:
58 Wilt thou *g* with this man?
32.26 And he said, Let me *g*, for the day
26 let thee *g*, except thou bless me.
33.12 and I will *g* before thee.
35. 1 unto Jacob, Arise, *g* up to Beth-el,
37.30 is not; and I, whither shall I *g*?
35 I will *g* down into the grave unto
45. 1 Cause every man to *g* out from
9 Haste ye, and *g* up to my father,
28 I will *g* and see him before I die.
46. 4 I will *g* down with thee into Egypt;
Ex 3.11 am I, that I should *g* unto Pharaoh,
5. 1 Let my people *g*, that they may
2 neither will I let Israel *g*.
11 *G* ye, get you straw where ye can
8. 1 Let my people *g*, that they may
20 Let my people *g*, that they may
10. 8 *G*, serve the Lord your God:
14.15 of Israel, that they *g* forward:
16 children of Israel shall *g* on dry
21 Lord caused the sea to *g* back
23.23 mine Angel shall *g* before thee,
32. 1 us gods, which shall *g* before us;
7 said unto Moses, *G*, get thee down:
23 us gods, which shall *g* before us:
33.14 My presence shall *g* with thee,
34. 9 Lord, I pray thee, *g* among us;
15 *g* a whoring after their gods,
Nu 13.30 Let us *g* up at once, and possess it;
14.42 *G* not up, for the Lord is not among
20.17 we will *g* by the king's high way,
22.35 *G* with the men: but only the word
Dt 1.28 Whither shall we *g* up? our
3.27 thou shalt not *g* over this Jordan.
28 he shall *g* over before this people,
4. 1 and *g* in and possess the land
5 the land whither ye *g* to possess it.
6.14 Ye shall not *g* after other gods,
9.23 *G* up and possess the land which
11.28 to *g* after other gods, which ye
12.10 when ye *g* over Jordan, and dwell
26 *g* unto the place which the Lord
13. 2 Let us *g* after other gods, which
19.21 life shall *g* for life, eye for eye, tooth
24.15 shall the sun *g* down upon it;
30.12 Who shall *g* up for us to heaven,
13 Who shall *g* over the sea for us,
18 over Jordan to *g* to possess it.
31. 2 I can no more *g* out and come in:
3 Joshua, he shall *g* over before thee,
34. 4 but thou shalt not *g* over thither.
Jos 2. 1 *G* view the land, even Jericho.
18. 4 rise, and *g* through the land,
Jdg 1. 1 Who shall *g* up for us against
11.35 and I cannot *g* back.
16.17 then my strength will *g* from me,
18.19 *g* with us, and be to us a father
Ru 1.11 why will ye *g* with me? are there
16 for whither thou goest, I will *g*;
2. 2 she said unto her, *G*, my daughter.
1Sa 1.17 Eli answered and said, *G* in peace:
3. 9 Eli said unto Samuel. *G*, lie down:
9. 6 shew us our way that we should *g*.
16. 2 And Samuel said, How can I *g*?
17.32 *g* and fight with this Philistine.
33 not able to *g* against this Philistine
39 he assayed to *g*; for he had not
39 I cannot *g* with these: for I have
19.17 He said unto me, Let me *g*;
20.21 saying, *G*, find out the arrows.
22 *g* thy way: for the Lord hath sent
28 asked leave of me to *g* to Bethlehem:
29 he said, Let me *g*, I pray thee;
42 Jonathan said to David, *G* in peace,
26.19 saying, *G*, serve other gods.
2Sa 7. 3 *G*, do all that is in thine heart;
24. 1 *G*, number Israel and Judah.
1Ki 2. 2 I *g* the way of all the earth;
6 let not his hoar head *g* down to
11.10 that he should not *g* after other
19.11 *G* forth, and stand upon the
21.18 Arise, *g* down to meet Ahab king
2Ki 2.23 *G* up, thou bald head; *g* up, thou
5.10 *G* and wash in Jordan seven
19 And he said unto him, *G* in peace.
20. 9 shall the shadow *g* forward ten
9 degrees, or *g* back ten degrees?
10 shadow to *g* down ten degrees:
22.13 *G* ye, inquire of the Lord for me,
1Ch 21. 2 *G*,number Israel from Beer-sheba
2Ch 34.21 *G*, inquire of the Lord for me,
Est 4.16 *G*, gather together all the Jews
Job 10.21 I *g* whence I shall not return,
20.26 it shall *g* ill with him that is left
21.13 in a moment *g* down to the grave.
24.10 They cause him to *g* naked
Ps 28. 1 them that *g* down into the pit.
30. 3 that I should not *g* down to the pit.
9 when I *g* down to the pit? shall
32. 8 the way which thou shalt *g*:
38. 6 I *g* mourning all the day long.
39.13 before I *g* hence, and be no more.
43. 4 will I *g* unto the altar of God,
55.15 let them *g* down quick into hell:
80.18 So will not we *g* back from thee:
84. 7 They *g* from strength to strength,

Ps 85.13 Righteousness shall *g* before him;
88. 4 them that *g* down into the pit:
89.14 and truth shall *g* before thy face,
104. 8 They *g* up by the mountains;
8 they *g* down by the valleys
26 There *g* the ships: there is that
107.23 They that *g* down to the sea in
26 they *g* down again to the depths:
115.17 any that *g* down into silence.
122. 1 Let us *g* into the house of the
139. 7 Whither shall I *g* from thy spirit?
143. 7 them that *g* down into the pit.
Pr 1.12 as those that *g* down into the pit:
2.19 None that *g* unto her return again,
4.14 *g* not in the way of evil men.
6. 6 *G* to the ant, thou sluggard;
Ec 3.20 All *g* unto one place; all are of
6. 6 do not all *g* to one place?
9. 3 and after that they *g* to the dead.
7 *G* thy way, eat thy bread with
12. 5 the mourners *g* about the streets:
Isa 6. 8 who will *g* for us? Then said I,
34.10 smoke thereof shall *g* up for ever:
38.10 shall *g* to the gates of the grave:
42.10 ye that *g* down to the sea, and all
52.12 for the Lord will *g* before you;
58. 8 righteousness shall *g* before thee;
60.20 Thy sun shall no more *g* down;
Eze 31.14 with them that *g* down to the pit.
32.18 with them that *g* down into the pit.
Dan 12.13 *g* thou thy way till the end be:
Hos 3. 1 *G* yet, love a woman beloved of
Joel 2.16 let the bridegroom *g* forth of his
Am 8. 9 cause the sun to *g* down at noon
Jon 1. 2 Arise *g* to Nineveh, that great city.
3. 2 Arise, *g* unto Nineveh, that great
Mic 4. 2 the law shall *g* forth of Zion,
Zec 8.21 the Lord of hosts: I will *g* also.
14. 3 Then shall the Lord *g* forth, and
8 that living waters shall *g* out from
Mt 2. 8 *G* and search diligently for the
20 and *g* into the land of Israel: for
22 he was afraid to *g* thither:
5.24 before the altar, and *g* thy way;
41 shall compel thee to *g* a mile,
41 a mile, *g* with him twain.
7.13 there be which *g* in thereat:
8. 4 but *g* thy way, shew thyself to
9 I say to this man, *G* and he goeth;
13 *G* thy way; and as thou hast
21 suffer me first to *g* and bury my
31 suffer us to *g* away into the herd
32 And he said unto them, *G*. And
9. 6 thy bed, and *g* unto thine house.
13 But *g* ye and learn what that
10. 5 *G* not into the way of the Gentiles,
6 But *g* rather to the lost sheep
7 And as ye *g*, preach, saying,
11 and there abide till ye *g* thence.
11. 4 *G* and shew John again those
13.28 that we *g* and gather them up?
14.15 that they may *g* into the villages,
22 *g* before him unto the other side,
29 on the water, to *g* to Jesus.
16.21 that he must *g* unto Jerusalem,
17.27 *g* thou to the sea, and cast an
18.15 *g* and tell him his fault between
19.21 *g* and sell that thou hast, and give
24 for a camel to *g* through the eye
20. 4 *G* ye also into the vineyard, and
7 *G* ye also into the vineyard; and
14 Take that thine is, and *g* thy way:
18 Behold, we *g* up to Jerusalem;
21. 2 *G* into the village over against
28 *g* work to day in my vineyard.
30 And he answered and said I *g*, sir:
31 *g* into the kingdom of God before
22. 9 *G* ye therefore into the highways,
23.13 ye neither *g* in yourselves,
13 ye them that are entering to *g* in.
24.26 he is in the desert; *g* not forth:

25. 6 cometh; *g* ye out to meet him.
9 but *g* ye rather to them that sell,
46 these shall *g* away into everlasting
26.18 *G* into the city to such a man,
32 I will *g* before you into Galilee.
36 here, while I *g* and pray yonder.
27.65 *g* your way, make it as sure as ye
28. 7 *g* quickly, and tell his disciples
10 Be not afraid: *g* tell my brethren
10 brethren that they *g* into Galilee,
19 *G* ye therefore, and teach all
Mk 1.38 Let us *g* into the next towns.
44 but *g* thy way, shew thyself to
2.11 and *g* thy way into thine house.
5.19 *G* home to thy friends, and tell
34 *g* in peace, and be whole of thy
6.36 that they may *g* into the country
37 Shall we *g* and buy two hundred
38 many loaves have ye? *g* and see.
45 to *g* to the other side before unto
7.29 For this saying *g* thy way; the
8.26 Neither *g* into the town, nor
9.43 having two hands to *g* into hell,
10.21 *g* thy way, sell whatsoever thou
25 to *g* through the eye of a needle,
33 Behold, we *g* up to Jerusalem;
52 *G* thy way; thy faith hath made
11. 2 *G* your way into the village over
6 commanded: and they let them *g*.
12.38 which love to *g* in long clothing,
13.15 not *g* down into the house,
14.12 wilt thou that we *g* and prepare
13 *G* ye into the city, and there
14 wheresoever he shall *g* in, say
28 I will *g* before you into Galilee.
42 Rise up, let us *g*: lo, he that
16. 7 But *g* your way, tell his disciples
15 he said unto them, *G* ye into all
Lk 1.17 shall *g* before him in the spirit
76 *g* before the face of the Lord
2.15 us now *g* even unto Bethlehem,
5.14 *g*, and shew thyself to the priest,
24 couch, and *g* unto thine house.
7. 8 I say unto one, *G*, and he goeth;
22 *G* your way, and tell John what
50 faith hath saved thee; *g* in peace.
8.14 *g* forth, and are choked with cares
22 Let us *g* over unto the other side
31 them *g* out into the deep.
48 made thee whole; *g* in peace.
51 he suffered no man to *g* in, save
9. 5 when ye *g* out of that city,
12 that they may *g* into the towns
13 except we should *g* and buy meat
51 set his face to *g* to Jerusalem,
53 though he would *g* to Jerusalem.
59 me first to *g* and bury my father.
60 *g* thou and preach the kingdom
61 let me first *g* bid them farewell,
10. 3 *G* your ways; Behold, I send you
7 *G* not from house to house.
10 *g* your ways out into the streets
37 unto him, *G*, and do thou likewise.
11. 5 and shall *g* unto him at midnight,
13.32 *G* ye, and tell that fox, Behold, I
14. 4 and healed him, and let him *g*;
10 *g* and sit down in the lowest
10 Friend, *g* up higher: then shalt
18 and I must needs *g* and see it:
19 I *g* to prove them: I pray thee
21 *G* out quickly into the streets
23 *G* out into the highways and
15. 4 and *g* after that which is lost.
18 I will arise and *g* to my father,
28 was angry, and would not *g* in:
17. 7 *G* and sit down to meat?
14 *G* shew yourselves unto the
19 Arise, *g* thy way: thy faith hath
23 *g* not after them, nor follow them.
18.25 camel to *g* through a needle's eye,
31 we *g* up to Jerusalem, and all

19.30 *G* ye into the village over against
21. 8 *g* ye not therefore after them.
22. 8 *G* and prepare us the passover,
33 am ready to *g* with thee, both
68 not answer me, nor let me *g*,
23.22 chastise him, and let him *g*.
Jn 1.43 Jesus would *g* forth into Galilee,
4. 4 must needs *g* through Samaria.
16 *G*, call thy husband, and come
50 *G* thy way; thy son liveth. And
6.67 Will ye also *g* away?
68 Lord, to whom shall we *g*? thou
7. 3 Depart hence, and *g* into Judea,
8 *G* ye up unto this feast: I *g* not up
19 Why *g* ye about to kill me?
33 then I *g* unto him that sent me.
35 Whither will he *g*, that we shall
35 will he *g* unto the dispersed
8.11 do I condemn thee: *g*, and sin no
14 whence I came, and whither I *g*;
14 whence I come, and whither I *g*.
21 I *g* my way, and ye shall seek me,
21 whither I *g*, ye cannot come.
22 Whither I *g*, ye cannot come.
9. 7 *G*, wash in the pool of Siloam,
11 *G* to the pool of Siloam, and wash:
10. 9 be saved, and shall *g* in and
11. 7 Let us *g* into Judea again.
11 but I *g*, that I may awake him
15 nevertheless let us *g* unto him.
16 Let us also *g*, that we may die with
44 them, Loose him, and let him *g*.
13.33 Whither I *g*, ye cannot come; so
36 Whither I *g*, thou canst not follow
14. 2 I *g*, to prepare a place for you.
3 if I *g* and prepare a place for you,
4 whither I *g* ye know, and the way
12 do; because I *g* unto my Father.
28 I *g* away, and come again unto
28 I said, I *g* unto the Father:
31 even so I do. Arise, let us *g* hence.
15.16 ye should *g* and bring forth fruit,
16. 5 I *g* my way to him that sent me;
7 expedient for you that I *g* away:
7 for if I *g* not away, the Comforter
10 because I *g* to my Father, and ye
16 see me, because I *g* to my Father.
17 and, Because I *g* to the Father?
28 the world, and *g* to the Father.
18. 8 ye seek me, let these *g* their way:
19.12 thou let this man *g*, thou art not
20.17 but *g* to my brethren, and say
21. 3 Peter saith unto them, I *g* a fishing.
3 unto him, We also *g* with thee.
Ac 1.11 ye have seen him *g* into heaven.
25 that he might *g* to his own place.
3. 3 Peter and John about to *g* into
13 he was determined to let him *g*.
4.15 commanded them to *g* aside out
21 they let them *g*, finding nothing
23 And being let *g*, they went to their
5.20 *G*, stand and speak in the temple
40 name of Jesus, and let them *g*.
7.40 Make us gods to *g* before us: for
8.26 Arise, and *g* toward the south
29 *G* near, and join thyself to this
9. 6 Arise, and *g* into the city, and it
11 Arise, and *g* into the street which
15 *G* thy way: for he is a chosen
10.20 get thee down, and *g* with them,
11.12 the spirit bade me *g* with them,
22 he should *g* as far as Antioch.
12.17 he said, *G* shew these things
15. 2 should *g* up to Jerusalem unto the
33 let *g* in peace from the brethren
36 *g* again and visit our brethren
16. 3 Paul have to *g* forth with him;
7 they have assayed to *g* into Bithynia:
10 endeavored to *g* into Macedonia,
35 serjeants, saying, Let those men *g*.
36 sent to let you *g*: now therefore

36 therefore depart, and *g* in peace.
17. 9 and of the other, they let them *g*.
14 Paul to *g* as it were to the sea:
18. 6 I will *g* unto the Gentiles.
19.21 to *g* to Jerusalem, saying, After I
20. 1 departed for to *g* into Macedonia.
13 appointed, minding himself to *g* afoot.
22 behold, I *g* bound in the spirit
21. 4 he should not *g* up to Jerusalem.
12 besought him not to *g* up to
22.10 Arise, and *g* into Damascus; and
23.10 commanded the soldiers to *g*
23 hundred soldiers to *g* to Caesarea,
32 left the horsemen to *g* with him,
24.25 *G* thy way for this time; when I
25. 5 *g* down with me, and accuse this
9 said, Wilt thou *g* up to Jerusalem,
12 Caesar? unto Caesar shalt thou *g*.
20 whether he would *g* to Jerusalem,
27. 3 him liberty to *g* unto his friends
28.18 would have let me *g*, because
26 *G* unto this people, and say,
Ro 15.25 now I *g* unto Jerusalem to minister
1Co 5.10 must ye needs *g* out of the world.
6. 1 another, *g* to law before the unjust,
7 ye *g* to law one with another.
10.27 ye be disposed to *g*; whatsoever
16. 4 it be meet that I *g* also, they shall *g*
6 on my journey whithersoever I *g*.
2Co 9. 5 they would *g* before unto you,
Gal 2. 9 that we should *g* unto the heathen,
Eph 4.26 let not the sun *g* down upon your
Php 2.23 I shall see how it will *g* with me.
1Th 4. 6 no man *g* beyond and defraud
Heb 6. 1 let us *g* on unto perfection; not
11. 8 he was called to *g* out into a place
13.13 Let us *g* forth therefore unto him
Jas 4.13 *G* to now, ye that say, To day or
13 we will *g* into such a city,
5. 1 *G* to now, ye rich men, weep and
Rev 3.12 and he shall *g* no more out:
10. 8 *G* and take the little book which
13.10 captivity shall *g* into captivity:
16. 1 *G* your ways and pour out the vials
14 *g* forth unto the kings of the earth
17. 8 pit, and *g* into perdition:
20. 8 shall *g* out to deceive the nations

GOAT

Gen 15. 9 and a she *g* of three years old,
Lev 3.12 if his offering be a *g*, then he shall
4.24 his hand upon the head of the *g*,
7.23 fat, of ox, or of sheep, or of *g*.
9.15 and took the *g*, which was the sin
10.16 Moses diligently sought the *g* of
16. 9 Aaron shall bring the *g* upon which
10 But the *g*, on which the lot fell to be
15 Then shall he kill the *g* of the sin
18 and of the blood of the *g*, and put it
20 he shall bring the live *g*:
21 hands upon the head of the live *g*,
21 putting them upon the head of the *g*,
22 the *g* shall bear upon him all their
22 shall let go the *g* in the wilderness.
26 that let go the *g* for the scapegoat
27 and the *g* for the sin offering,
17. 3 that killeth an ox, or lamb, or *g*,
22.27 When a bullock, or a sheep, or a *g*,
Nu 15.27 he shall bring a she *g* of the first
18.17 or the firstling of a *g*, thou shalt
28.22 And one *g* for a sin offering, to
29.22, 28, 31, 34, 38 one *g* for a sin
Dt 14. 4 eat: the ox, the sheep, and the *g*,
5 and the wild *g*, and the pygarg,
Pr 30.31 A grayhound; an he *g* also; and
Eze 43.25 every day a *g* for a sin offering:
Dan 8. 5 an he *g* came from the west
5 and the *g* had a notable horn
8 Therefore the he *g* waxed very
21 the rough *g* is the king of Grecia:

God's creation of Adam is depicted in Michelangelo's famous Sistine Chapel murals, completed in 1512.

GOATS

Gen 37.31 killed a kid of the *g*, and dipped
Lev 23.19 kid of the *g* for a sin offering,
2Ch 29.21 seven lambs, and seven he *g*,
Ezr 6.17 offering for all Israel, twelve he *g*,
8.35 twelve he *g* for a sin offering:
Job 39. 1 wild *g* of the rock bring forth?
Ps 50.13 of bulls, or drink the blood of *g*?
104.18 hills are a refuge for the wild *g*;
Isa 34. 6 and with the blood of lambs and *g*,
Eze 43.22 shall offer a kid of the *g* without
45.23 a kid of the *g* daily for a sin
Zec 10. 3 I punished the *g*: for the Lord
Mt 25.32 divideth his sheep from the *g*:
33 right hand, but the *g* on the left.
Heb 9.12 Neither by the blood of *g* and
13 For if the blood of bulls and of *g*,
19 took the blood of calves and of *g*,
10. 4 that the blood of bulls and of *g*

GOATS'

Ex 25. 4 scarlet, and fine linen, and *g* hair,
26. 7 thou shalt make curtains of *g* hair
35. 6, 23 scarlet, and fine linen, and *g* hair,
26 them up in wisdom spun *g* hair.
36.14 And he made curtains of *g* hair
Nu 31.20 all work of *g* hair, and all things
1Sa 19.13 put a pillow of *g* hair for his bolster.
16 with a pillow of *g* hair for his bolster,
Pr 27.27 thou shalt have *g* milk enough for

GOATSKINS

Heb 11.37 about in sheepskins and *g*;

GOD

Gen 1. 1 *G* created the heaven and the
2 Spirit of *G* moved upon the face
3 And *G* said, Let there be light:
4 And *G* saw the light, that it was
4 and *G* divided the light from the
5 And *G* called the light Day, and the
6 *G* said, Let there be a firmament
7 *G* made the firmament, and divided
8 *G* called the firmament Heaven.
9 *G* said, Let the waters under the
10 And *G* called the dry land Earth;
10 and *G* saw that it was good.
11 *G* said, Let the earth bring forth
12 and *G* saw that it was good.
14 And *G* said, Let there be lights
16 And *G* made two great lights; the
17 And *G* set them in the firmament
18 and *G* saw that it was good.
20 *G* said, Let the waters bring forth
21 *G* created great whales, and every
21 and *G* saw that it was good.
22 And *G* blessed them, saying, Be
24 *G* said, Let the earth bring forth
25 *G* made the beast of the earth after
25 and *G* saw that it was good.
26 And *G* said, Let us make man in
27 *G* created man in his own image,
27 in the image of *G* created he him;
28 *G* blessed them, and *G* said unto
29 And *G* said, Behold, I have given
31 And *G* saw everything that he had
2. 2 the seventh day *G* ended his work
3 And *G* blessed the seventh day, and
7 the Lord *G* formed man of the dust
8 Lord *G* planted a garden eastward
19 the Lord *G* formed every beast of
3. 1 field which the Lord *G* had made.
3 *G* hath said, Ye shall not eat of it,
9 And the Lord *G* called unto Adam,
13 the Lord *G* said unto the woman,
23 Therefore the Lord *G* sent him forth
4.25 For *G*, said she, hath appointed me
5. 1 In the day that *G* created man,
22 And Enoch walked with *G*, after he
6. 2 the sons of *G* saw the daughters
9 and Noah walked with *G*.
8. 1 And *G* remembered Noah, and every
9. 1 and *G* blessed Noah and his sons,
6 in the image of *G* made he man.
16.13 Thou *G* seest me: for she said,
17. 1 I am the Almighty *G*; walk before
3 and *G* talked with him, saying,
7 to be a *G* unto thee, and to thy seed
19.29 when *G* destroyed the cities of the
21. 2 time of which *G* had spoken to him.
19 *G* opened her eyes, and she saw
20 *G* was with the lad; and he grew,
22 *G* is with thee in all that thou doest:
22. 1 *G* did tempt Abraham, and said
8 *G* will provide himself a lamb for a
26.24 I am the *G* of Abraham thy father:
28. 3 *G* Almighty bless thee, and make
17 is none other but the house of *G*,

Biblical Themes

GOD

In the beginning God created the heaven and the earth. Gen 1.1

And God said unto Moses, I AM THAT I AM: and he said, Thus shalt thou say unto the children of Israel, I AM hath sent me unto you. Ex 3.14

I am the Lord thy God, which have brought thee out of the land of Egypt, out of the house of bondage. Thou shalt have no other gods before me. Ex 20.2-3

God is not a man, that he should lie; neither the son of man, that he should repent: hath he said, and shall he not do it? or hath he spoken, and shall he not make it good? Nu 23.19

Man doth not live by bread only, but by every word that proceedeth out of the mouth of the Lord doth man live. Dt 8.3

The Lord seeth not as man seeth; for man looketh on the outward appearance, but the Lord looketh on the heart. 1Sa 16.7

The fool hath said in his heart, There is no God. Ps 14.1

I saw also the Lord sitting upon a throne, high and lifted up, and his train filled the temple. Above it stood the seraphims: each one had six wings; with twain he covered his face, and with twain he covered his feet, and with twain he did fly. And one cried unto another, and said, Holy, holy, holy, is the Lord of hosts: the whole earth is full of his glory. Isa 6.1-3

To whom then will ye liken me, or shall I be equal? saith the Holy One. Lift up your eyes on high, and behold who hath created these things, that bringeth out their host by number: he calleth them all by names by the greatness of his might, for that he is strong in power; not one faileth. Isa 40.25-26

As the heavens are higher than the earth, so are my ways higher than your ways, and my thoughts than your thoughts. Isa 55.9

I am the Lord, I change not. Mal 3.6

Then saith Jesus unto him, Get thee hence, Satan: for it is written, Thou shalt worship the Lord thy God, and him only shalt thou serve. Mt 4.10

In the beginning was the Word, and the Word was with God, and the Word was God. . . . All things were made by him; and without him was not any thing made that was made. In him was life; and the life was the light of men. Jn 1.1, 3-4

I and my Father are one. Jn 10.30

Then Paul stood . . . and said, Ye men of Athens, I perceive that in all things ye are too superstitious. For as I passed by, and beheld your devotions, I found an altar with this inscription, TO THE UNKNOWN GOD. Whom therefore ye ignorantly worship, him declare I unto you. Ac 17.22-23

In him we live, and move, and have our being. Ac 17.28

And when all things shall be subdued unto him, then shall the Son also himself be subject unto him that put all things under him, that God may be all in all. 1Co 15.28

He that loveth not knoweth not God; for God is love. . . . No man hath seen God at any time. If we love one another, God dwelleth in us. 1Jn 4.8, 12

And I heard as it were the voice of a great multitude, and as the voice of many waters, and as the voice of mighty thunderings, saying, Alleluia: for the Lord God omnipotent reigneth. Rev 19.6

Gen 28.21 then shall the Lord be my *G*:
30. 6 Rachel said, *G* hath judged me, and
23 *G* hath taken away my reproach:
31. 5 but the *G* of my father hath been
13 I am the *G* of Beth-el, where thou
42 *G* hath seen mine affliction and the
50 *G* is witness betwixt me and thee.
32. 1 and the angels of *G* met him.
30 for I have seen *G* face to face,
33. 5 which *G* hath graciously given
11 *G* hath dealt graciously with me,
35. 1 *G* said unto Jacob, Arise, go up to
11 *G* said unto him, I am...Almighty:
40. 8 Do not interpretations belong to *G*?
41.16 *G* shall give Pharaoh an answer of
32 and *G* will shortly bring it to pass.
38 a man in whom the Spirit of *G* is?
42.18 This do, and live; for I fear *G*:
28 What is this that *G* hath done
43.14 And *G* Almighty give you mercy
29 *G* be gracious unto thee, my son.
45. 5 for *G* did send me before you to
8 not you that sent me hither, but *G*:
9 *G* hath made me lord of all Egypt:
48. 3 *G* Almighty appeared unto me at
15 *G* which fed me all my life long
Ex 1.17 But the midwives feared *G*, and did
2.23 their cry came up unto *G* by reason
24 And *G* heard their groaning, and
24 and *G* remembered his covenant
3. 1 the mountain of *G*, even to Horeb.
4 *G* called unto him out of the midst
6 I am the *G* of thy father.
6 the *G* of Abraham, the *G* of Isaac,
6 and the *G* of Jacob.
11 And Moses said unto *G*, Who am I;
12 shall serve *G* upon this mountain.
14 *G* said unto Moses, I Am that I Am:
4. 5 the Lord *G* of their fathers,
16 thou shalt be to him instead of *G*.
5. 1 Thus saith the Lord *G* of Israel,
6. 2 *G* spake unto Moses, and said
7 and I will be to you a *G*:
7 know that I am the Lord your *G*,
8.10 none like unto the Lord our *G*.
19 This is the finger of *G*: and
13.17 *G* led them not through the way
19 *G* will surely visit you; and ye
15. 2 become my salvation: he is my *G*,
16. 3 Would to *G* we had died by the hand of
17. 9 with the rod of *G* in mine hand.
18. 1 of all that *G* had done for Moses,
16 make them know the statutes of *G*,
19 mayest bring the causes unto *G*:
21 able men, such as fear *G*, men of
20. 1 *G* spake all these words, saying,
2 I am the Lord thy *G*, which have
5 serve them; for I the Lord thy *G*
5 a jealous *G*, visiting the iniquity
7 name of the Lord thy *G* in vain;
10 is the sabbath of the Lord thy *G*:
19 let not *G* speak with us, lest we die.
21 the thick darkness where *G* was.
24.10 they saw the *G* of Israel: and there
13 Moses went up into the mount of *G*.
31. 3 have filled him with the spirit of *G*,
18 stone, written with the finger of *G*.
Lev 2.13 the salt of the covenant of thy *G*
20. 7 be ye holy, for I am the Lord your *G*.
23.14 brought an offering unto your *G*:
40 rejoice before the Lord your *G*
24.15 Whosoever curseth his *G* shall
25.17 but thou shalt fear thy *G*:
36 but fear thy *G*; that thy brother
26. 1 down into it: I am the Lord your *G*.
12 among you, and will be your *G*,
Nu 6. 7 consecration of his *G* is upon his
12.13 Heal her now, O *G*, I beseech thee.
14. 2 Would *G* that we had died in
16. 9 the *G* of Israel hath separated
22 upon their faces, and said, O *G*,
22 the *G* of the spirits of all flesh,
21. 5 the people spake against *G*, and
23. 4 And *G* met Balaam: and he said
19 *G* is not a man, that he should
23 What hath *G* wrought!
24. 2 the spirit of *G* came upon him.
23 who shall live when *G* doeth this!
27.16 the *G* of the spirits of all flesh,
Dt 1. 6 The Lord our *G* spake unto us
11 Lord *G* of your fathers make you
30 Lord your *G* which goeth before
2. 7 the Lord thy *G* hath blessed thee
30 the Lord thy *G* hardened his spirit,
3. 3 So the Lord our *G* delivered into
22 Lord your *G* he shall fight for you,
24 *G* is there in heaven or in earth,
4. 1 which the Lord *G* of your fathers
7 as the Lord our *G* is in all things
24 the Lord thy *G* is a consuming fire,
31 (For the Lord...is a merciful *G*;)
35 know that the Lord he is *G*; there
39 the Lord he is *G* in heaven above,
5. 2 The Lord our *G* made a covenant
6 am the Lord thy *G*, which brought
9 for I the Lord thy *G* am a jealous
11 the name of the Lord thy *G* in vain:
24 the Lord our *G* hath shewed us his
24 that *G* doth talk with man, and he

25 we hear the voice of the Lord our *G*
6. 1 Lord your *G* commanded to teach
4 The Lord our *G* is one Lord:
5 And thou shalt love the Lord thy *G*
16 Ye shall not tempt the Lord your *G*,
7. 1 When the Lord thy *G* shall bring
6 holy people unto the Lord thy *G*:
6 the Lord thy *G* hath chosen thee
9 that the Lord thy *G*, he is *G*,
9 the faithful *G*, which keepeth
21 for the Lord thy *G* is among you,
8. 2 way which the Lord thy *G* led thee
5 so the Lord thy *G* chasteneth thee.
18 shalt remember the Lord thy *G*:
19 at all forget the Lord thy *G*, and
9. 3 Lord thy *G* is he which goeth over
10. 9 as the Lord thy *G* promised him.
12 what doth the Lord thy *G* require
12 of thee, but to fear the Lord thy *G*,
12 and to serve the Lord thy *G* with all
17 For the Lord your *G*, is *G* of gods,
17 a great *G*, and mighty, and a
11. 1 thou shalt love the Lord thy *G*, and
2 chastisement of the Lord your *G*,
12 eyes of the Lord thy *G* are always
12. 1 land which the Lord *G* of thy fathers
10 land which the Lord your *G* giveth
29 Lord thy *G* shall cut off the nations
31 shall not do so unto the Lord thy *G*:
13. 3 for the Lord your *G* proveth you,
3 whether ye love the Lord your *G*
14. 1 are the children of the Lord your *G*.
15. 4 which the Lord thy *G* giveth thee
15 and the Lord thy *G* redeemed thee:
16. 1 the passover unto the Lord thy *G*:
18. 5 the Lord thy *G* hath chosen him
23. 5 Nevertheless the Lord thy *G* would
5 but the Lord thy *G* turned the curse
5 because the Lord thy *G* loved thee.
21 vow a vow unto the Lord thy *G*,
25.15 land which the Lord thy *G* giveth
19 Lord thy *G* hath given thee rest
26. 1 land which the Lord thy *G* giveth
5 say before the Lord thy *G*, A Syrian
10 and worship before the Lord thy *G*:
19 an holy people unto the Lord thy *G*,
27. 2 Lord thy *G* giveth thee, that thou
10 obey the voice of the Lord thy *G*,
28. 1 unto the voice of the Lord thy *G*,
1 Lord thy *G* will set thee on high
67 shalt say, Would *G* it were even!
67 shalt say, Would *G* it were morning!
29. 6 know that I am the Lord your *G*.
12 covenant with the Lord thy *G*,
13 and that he may be unto thee a *G*,
29 things belong unto the Lord our *G*:
30. 1 the Lord thy *G* hath driven thee,
16 to love the Lord thy *G*, to walk in
32. 3 ascribe ye greatness unto our *G*.
4 a *G* of truth and without iniquity,
17 sacrificed unto devils, not to *G*;
18 hast forgotten *G* that formed thee.
33. 1 Moses the man of *G* blessed the
27 The eternal *G* is thy refuge, and
Jos 1. 9 for the Lord thy *G* is with thee
3. 3 the covenant of the Lord your *G*,
10 know that the living *G* is among
4. 5 before the ark of the Lord your *G*
23 Lord your *G* dried up the waters
7. 7 Joshua said, Alas, O Lord *G*,
7 would to *G* we had been content.
22. 3 commandment of the Lord your *G*.
5 love the Lord your *G*, and to walk
29 *G* forbid that we should rebel
23. 3 that the Lord your *G* hath done
5 And the Lord your *G*, he shall expel
15 the Lord your *G* promised you;
Jdg 1. 7 have done, so *G* had requited me.
3. 7 forgat the Lord their *G*, and served
20 have a message from *G* unto thee.
5. 3 sing praise to the Lord *G* of Israel.

God creates the fish of the sea and fowl of the air (Gen 1.20-22) in this 16th-century painting by Tintoretto.

6. 8 Thus saith the Lord *G* of Israel,
22 Gideon said, Alas, O Lord *G*! for
31 if he be a *g*, let him plead for
9. 7 that *G* may hearken unto you.
9 by me they honor *G* and man,
13. 5 a Nazarite unto *G* from the womb:
16.17 Nazarite unto *G* from my mother's
28 O Lord *G*, remember me, I pray
Ru 1.16 my people, and thy *G* my *G*:
1Sa 1.17 *G* of Israel grant thee thy petition
2. 2 neither is there any rock like our *G*.
3 the Lord is a *G* of knowledge,
4. 4 with the ark of the covenant of *G*.
7 they said, *G* is come into the camp.
11 And the ark of *G* was taken; and
13 his heart trembled for the ark of *G*.
5. 1, 2 the Philistines took the ark of *G*,
10 they sent the ark of *G* to Ekron.
11 hand of *G* was very heavy there.
10. 3 meet thee three men going up to *G*
9 *G* gave him another heart: and all
10 and the Spirit of *G* came upon him,
24 and said, *G* save the king.

11. 6 And the Spirit of *G* came upon Saul
16.15 evil spirit from *G* troubleth thee.
17.26 defy the armies of the living *G*?
46 know that there is a *G* in Israel.
19.20 Spirit of *G* was upon the messengers
25.22 do *G* unto the enemies of David,
29 bundle of life with the Lord thy *G*;
28.15 and *G* is departed from me, and
29. 9 good in my sight, as an angel of *G*:
30. 6 himself in the Lord his *G*.
15 Swear unto me by *G*, that thou wilt
2Sa 2.27 Joab said, As *G* liveth, unless thou
6. 2 bring up from thence the ark of *G*,
3 set the ark of *G* upon a new cart
7. 2 ark of *G* dwelleth within curtains.
20 Lord *G*, knowest thy servant.
22 thou art great, O Lord *G*: for there
22 neither is there any *G* beside thee,
14.11 king remember the Lord thy *G*,
14 neither doth *G* respect any person:
16.16 *G* save the king, *G* save the
23 had inquired at the oracle of *G*:
18.28 Blessed be the Lord thy *G*,

2Sa 18.33 would G I...died for thee, O Absalom,
22. 3 G of my rock; in him will I trust:
31 As for G, his way is perfect;
32 For who is G, save the Lord?
32 and who is a rock, save our G?
33 G is my strength and power:
47 the G of the rock of my salvation.
24. 3 Now the Lord thy G add unto the
23 The Lord thy G accept thee.
1Ki 1.17 thou swarest by the Lord thy G
4.29 And G gave Solomon wisdom and
8.15 Blessed be the Lord G of Israel,
23 And he said, Lord G of Israel.
23 there is no G like thee, in heaven
27 will G indeed dwell on the earth?
59 be nigh unto the Lord our G by day
60 earth may know that the Lord is G.
17. 1 As the Lord G of Israel liveth,
24 I know that thou art a man of G,
18.10 the Lord thy G liveth, there is no
21 If the Lord be G, follow him: but
24 and the G that answereth by fire,
27 and said, Cry aloud: for he is a g;
39 they said, The Lord, he is the G;
19. 8 nights unto Horeb the mount of G.
10, 14 jealous for the Lord G of hosts:
20.28 there came a man of G, and spake
28 said, The Lord is G of the hills,
28 but he is not G of the valleys,
2Ki 1. 3 is not a G in Israel, that ye go to
12 If I be a man of G, let fire come
12 fire of G came down from heaven,
2.14 Where is the Lord G of Elijah?
4. 7 she came and told the man of G.
27 the man of G said, Let her alone;
40 O thou man of G, there is death
5. 3 Would G my lord were with the
7 Am I G, to kill and to make alive,
8 Elisha the man of G had heard
15 now I know that there is no G in
8. 2 after the saying of the man of G:
11 and the man of G wept.
17. 7 sinned against the Lord their G,
39 But the Lord your G ye shall fear;
18. 5 He trusted in the Lord G of Israel;
22 We trust in the Lord our G:
19. 4 It may be the Lord thy G will hear
15 O Lord G of Israel, which dwellest
15 thou art the G, even thou alone,
1Ch 4.10 Jabez called on the G of Israel,
13. 2 and that it be of the Lord our G,
8 all Israel played before G with
12 David was afraid of G that day,
17. 2 thine heart; for G is with thee.
16 Who am I, O Lord G, and what is
17 a small thing in thine eyes, O G;
20 neither is there any G beside thee,
22. 1 This is the house of the Lord G,
28. 2 and for the footstool of our G,
29. 1 my son, whom alone G hath chosen,
10 Blessed be thou, Lord G of Israel
17 I know also, my G, that thou triest
2Ch 1. 1 and the Lord his G was with him,
2. 4 to the name of the Lord my G,
5 for great is our G above all gods.
6. 4 Blessed be the Lord G of Israel,
14 G of Israel, there is no G like thee
13. 5 to know that the Lord G of Israel
10 But as for us, the Lord is our G,
12 G himself is with us for our captain,
15. 1 the Spirit of G came upon Azariah
6 G did vex them with all adversity.
18. 5 for G will deliver it into the king's
31 G moved them to depart from him.
20. 6 And said, O Lord G of our fathers,
6 art not thou G in heaven?
22. 7 destruction of Ahaziah was of G by
12 was hid in the house of G six years:
31. 6 consecrated unto the Lord their G,
21 the commandments, to seek his G,
32. 8 but with us is the Lord our G to
31 G left him, to try him, that he
34. 3 began to seek after the G of David
27 thou didst humble thyself before G,
35. 3 serve now the Lord your G, and
36. 5 evil in the sight of the Lord his G.
16 they mocked the messengers of G,
19 And they burnt the house of G,
Ezr 1. 2 The Lord G of heaven hath given
4 freewill offering for the house of G
2.68 offered freely for the house of G to
4. 1 temple unto the Lord G of Israel;
2 for we seek your G, as ye do;
5. 1 in the name of the G of Israel,
5 But the eye of their G was upon
6. 3 the house of G at Jerusalem, Let
16 dedication of this house of G with
8.17 ministers for the house of our G.
22 The hand of our G is upon all them
23 fasted and besought our G for this:
9. 4 at the words of the G of Israel,
6 O my G, I am ashamed and blush
8 that our G may lighten our eyes,
9 yet our G hath not forsaken us
10 our G, what shall we say after this?
10. 1 down before the house of G, there
2 We have trespassed against our G,
9 sat in the street of the house of G,
11 make confession unto the Lord G
Neh 1. 4 and prayed before the G of heaven,
2. 4 So I prayed to the G of heaven.
8 to the good hand of my G upon me.
12 what my G had put in my heart
20 The G of heaven, he will prosper us;
4. 4 Hear, O our G; for we are despised:
5. 9 walk in the fear of our G because
19 Think upon me, my G, for good,
6. 9 therefore, O G, strengthen my hands.
8. 6 Ezra blessed the Lord, the great G.
18 he read in the book of the law of G.
9. 3 book of the law of the Lord their G
17 but thou art a G ready to pardon,
31 thou art a gracious and merciful G.
32 terrible G, who keepest covenant
13. 1 the congregation of G for ever;
11 Why is the house of G forsaken?
14 Remember me, O my G, concerning
Job 1. 1 that feared G, and eschewed evil.
5 and cursed G in their hearts.
9 said, Doth Job fear G for nought?
2. 1 a day when the sons of G came
10 we receive good at the hand of G,
4. 9 By the blast of G they perish,
17 mortal man be more just than G?
6. 4 the terrors of G do set themselves
8. 3 Doth G pervert judgment? or doth
20 G will not cast away a perfect man,
9. 2 how should man be just with G?
13 G will not withdraw his anger,
11. 5 But oh that G would speak, and
7 Canst thou by searching find out G?
13. 3 and I desire to reason with G.
8 will ye contend for G?
15. 4 and restrainest prayer before G.
8 Hast thou heard the secret of G?
16.11 G hath delivered me to the ungodly,
21 one might plead for a man with G,
19. 6 now that G hath overthrown me,
21 the hand of G hath touched me.
22 Why do ye persecute me as G,
26 yet in my flesh shall I see G:
21. 9 neither is the rod of G upon them.
17 G distributeth sorrows in his anger.
19 G layeth up his iniquity for his
22 Shall any teach G knowledge?
22. 2 Can a man be profitable unto G,
12 Is not G in the height of heaven?
13 thou sayest, How doth G know?
17 said unto G, Depart from us:
26 and shalt lift up thy face unto G.
27. 2 As G liveth, who hath taken away
3 the spirit of G is in my nostrils;
8 when G taketh away his soul?
9 Will G hear his cry when trouble
10 will he always call upon G?
11 I will teach you by the hand of G:
28.23 G understandeth the way thereof,
31. 2 portion of G is there from above?
28 have denied the G that is above.
32. 2 he justified himself rather than G.
13 G thrusteth him down, not man,
33. 4 The Spirit of G hath made me,
12 thee, that G is greater than man,
14 For G speaketh once, yea twice,
34. 5 G hath taken away my judgment.
35.10 Where is G my maker, who giveth
13 Surely G will not hear vanity,
36. 5 G is mighty, and despiseth not any:
22 Behold, G exalteth by his power:
26 G is great, and we know him not,
37. 5 G thundereth marvellously with
10 By the breath of G frost is given:
14 consider the wondrous works of G.
22 with G is terrible majesty.
38. 7 all the sons of G shouted for joy?
39.17 G hath deprived her of wisdom,
40. 2 that reproveth G, let him answer
9 Hast thou an arm like G? or canst
19 He is the chief of the ways of G:
Ps 3. 2 There is no help for him in G.
5. 2 my King, and my G: for unto thee
4 art not a G that hath pleasure in
7. 1 my G, in thee do I put my trust;
10. 4 countenance, will not seek after G:
4 G is not in all his thoughts.
14. 1 said in his heart, There is no G.
16. 1 Preserve me, O G: for in thee do
18. 2 my G, my strength, in whom I will
28 my G will enlighten my darkness.
30 As for G, his way is perfect:
31 For who is G save the Lord?
31 or who is a rock save our G?
32 G that girdeth me with strength,
46 the G of my salvation be exalted.
19. 1 heavens declare the glory of G;
22. 1 My G, my G, why hast thou
2 O my G, I cry in the daytime,
25. 2 O my G, I trust in thee: let me not
31. 5 redeemed me, O Lord G of truth.
14 I said, Thou art my G.
33.12 is the nation whose G is the Lord;
36. 1 is no fear of G before his eyes.
37.31 The law of his G is in his heart;
40. 3 even praise unto our G: many shall
8 I delight to do thy will, O my G:
42. 1 so panteth my soul after thee, O G.
2 My soul thirsteth for G,
3 say unto me, Where is thy G?
4 I went with them to the house of G,
5 hope thou in G: for I shall yet
6 O my G, my soul is cast down
44. 1 We have heard with our ears, O G,
20 have forgotten the name of our G.
21 Shall not G search this out?
45. 2 therefore G hath blessed thee for
6 Thy throne, O G, is for ever and
46. 1 G is our refuge and strength, a
5 not be moved: G shall help her,
10 and know that I am G: I will be
47. 1 unto G with the voice of triumph.
6 Sing praises to G, sing praises:
7 G is the King of all the earth:
8 G reigneth over the heathen:
48. 1 the city of our G, in the mountain
14 this G is our G for ever and ever:
51. 1 Have mercy upon me, O G,
10 Create in me a clean heart, O G;
17 sacrifices of G are a broken spirit:
17 a broken and a contrite heart, O G,
52. 1 of G endureth continually.
7 man that made not G his strength;
53. 1 said in his heart, There is no G.
2 G looked down from heaven upon

54. 1 Save me, O G, by thy name,
4 Behold, G is mine helper: the Lord
55. 1 Give ear to my prayer, O G;
16 As for me, I will call upon G;
56. 1 Be merciful unto me, O G: for man
4 in G I have put my trust;
9 this I know; for G is for me.
57. 1 Be merciful unto me, O G, be
2 I will cry unto G most high;
58. 6 Break their teeth, O G, in their
11 he is a G that judgeth in the earth.
59. 1 me from mine enemies, O my G,
9 upon thee: for G is my defense.
60. 1 O G, thou hast cast us off,
6 G hath spoke in his holiness;
62. 1 Truly my soul waiteth upon G:
7 In G is my salvation and my glory:
8 before him: G is a refuge for us.
63. 1 O G, thou art my...; early will I
1 thou art my G; early will I
66. 1 Make a joyful noise unto G, all ye
67. 1 G be merciful unto us, and bless
3, 5 Let the people praise thee, O G;
6 G, even our own G, shall bless us.
68. 1 Let G arise, let his enemies be
4 Sing unto G, sing praises to his
6 G setteth the solitary in families:
20 that is our G is the G of salvation;
20 G the Lord belong the issues
26 Bless ye G in the congregations,
34 Ascribe ye strength unto G:
35 O G, thou art terrible out of thy
69. 1 Save me, O G; for the waters are
5 O G, thou knowest my foolishness;
70. 1 Make haste, O G, to deliver me;
71. 4 Deliver me, O my G, out of the
5 thou art my hope, O Lord G:
11 Saying, G hath forsaken him:
12 O G, be not far from me: O my G,
17 O G, thou hast taught me from
19 O G, who is like unto thee!
72. 1 Give the king thy judgments, O G,
73. 1 Truly G is good to Israel,
11 they say, How doth G know?
17 I went into the sanctuary of G;
26 but G is the strength of my heart,
28 is good for me to draw near to G:
75. 1 Unto thee, O G, do we give thanks,
77. 1 G with my voice, even unto G with
3 I remembered G, and was troubled:
9 Hath G forgotten to be gracious?
13 Thy way, O G, is in the sanctuary:
13 who is so great...as our G?
14 Thou art the G that doest wonders:
78. 7 they might set their hope in G,
18 they tempted G in their heart by
19 they said, Can G furnish a table
79. 1 O G, the heathen are come into
9 Help us, O G of our salvation,
80. 3 Turn us again, O G, and cause thy
81. 1 Sing aloud unto G our strength:
1 make a joyful noise unto the G of
82. 1 G standeth in the congregation of
8 Arise, O G, judge the earth: for
83. 1 Keep not thou silence, O G:
84. 2 flesh crieth out for the living G.
3 Lord of hosts, my King, and my G.
10 doorkeeper in the house of my G,
11 For the Lord G is a sun and shield:
85. 4 Turn us, O G of our salvation,
8 I will hear what G the Lord will
86. 2 O thou my G, save thy servant
10 wondrous things: thou art G alone.
89. 7 G is greatly to be feared in the
26 Thou art my father, my G, and
90. 2 to everlasting, thou art G.
91. 2 fortress: my G; in him will I trust.
94. 1 O Lord G, to whom vengeance
1 O G, to whom vengeance belongeth,
100. 3 Know ye that the Lord he is G:
106.14 and tempted G in the desert.
108. 1 O G, my heart is fixed; I will sing
11 O G, who hast cast us off? and
113. 5 Who is like unto the Lord our G,
116. 5 yea, our G is merciful.
139.17 are thy thoughts unto me, O G!
23 Search me, O G, and know my
144. 9 sing a new song unto thee, O G:
150. 1 Praise G in his sanctuary: praise
Pr 2. 5 and find the knowledge of G.
26.10 great G that formed all things
30. 5 Every word of G is pure: he is a
Ec 1.13 this sore travail hath G given to
3.10 G hath given to the sons of men
14 whatsoever G doeth, it shall be for
15 and G requireth that which is past.
5. 1 when thou goest to the house of G,
2 utter anything before G: for G is
7.13 Consider the work of G: for who
8. 2 and that in regard of the oath of G.
17 Then I beheld all the work of G,
12. 7 shall return unto G who gave it.
13 matter: Fear G, and keep his
Isa 1.10 give ear unto the law of our G,
7. 7 Thus saith the Lord G, It shall
11 Ask thee a sign of the Lord thy G;
9. 6 The mighty G, The everlasting
12. 2 Behold, G is my salvation: I will
17. 6 thereof, saith the Lord G of Israel.
10 forgotten the G of thy salvation,
25. 1 O Lord, thou art my G; I will exalt
8 the Lord G will wipe away tears
26. 1 salvation will G appoint for
28.16 the Lord G, Behold, I lay in Zion
26 G doth instruct him to discretion,
30.15 saith the Lord G, the Holy One
18 for the Lord is a G of judgment:
31. 3 Egyptians are men, and not G;
36. 7 We trust in the Lord our G: is it
37. 4 It may be the Lord thy G will hear
40. 1 comfort ye my people, saith your G.
28 G, the Lord, the Creator
41.10 be not dismayed; for I am thy G:
44. 6 and beside me there is no G.
8 Is there a G beside me? yea,
8 there is no G; I know not any.
10 Who hath formed a g, or molten
15 he maketh a g, and worshippeth it;
17 the residue thereof he maketh a g,
45. 3 by thy name, am the G of Israel.
14 there is none else, there is no G.
15 Verily thou art a G that hidest
20 pray unto a g that cannot save.
21 there is no G else beside me;
21 a just G and a Saviour;
22 for I am G, and there is none else.
52. 4 saith the Lord G, My people
7 saith unto Zion, Thy G reigneth!
53. 4 stricken, smitten of G, and afflicted.
55. 5 because of the Lord thy G, and for
7 and to our G, for he will abundantly
59. 2 separated between you and your G,
61. 1 Spirit of the Lord G is upon me;
2 the day of vengeance of our G;
62. 3 royal diadem in the hand of thy G.
5 so shall thy G rejoice over thee.
64. 4 neither hath the eye seen, O G,
Jer 1. 6 Lord G! behold, I cannot speak:
10.10 But the Lord is the true G,
23. 2 saith the Lord G of Israel against
23 Am I a G at hand, saith the Lord,
23 and not a G afar off?
26.13 obey the voice of the Lord your G;
31. 1 will I be the G of all the families
33 and will be their G, and they shall
32.14 the Lord of hosts, the G of Israel;
18 the Great, the Mighty G, the Lord
27 I am the Lord, the G of all flesh:
Eze 1. 1 opened, and I saw visions of G.
8. 1 the hand of the Lord G fell there
4 glory of the G of Israel was there,
9. 3 glory of the G of Israel was gone
8 Ah Lord G! wilt thou destroy
11. 7 saith the Lord G; Your slain
24 in a vision by the Spirit of G
22. 3 saith the Lord G, The city
12 forgotten me, saith the Lord G.
28. 2 saith the Lord G; Because thine
2 I sit in the seat of G, in the midst
2 thou art a man, and not G, though
34. 2 the Lord G unto the shepherds;
17 saith the Lord G; Behold, I judge
24 And I the Lord will be their G,
37. 3 And I answered, O Lord G,
23 my people, and I will be their G.
Dan 1. 2 the vessels of the house of G:
17 G gave them knowledge and skill
2.18 desire mercies of the G of heaven
19 Daniel blessed the G of heaven.
28 is a G in heaven that revealeth
45 G hath made known to the king
47 that your G is a G of gods,
3.15 who is that G that shall deliver you
17 G whom we serve is able to deliver
25 the fourth is like the Son of G.
5. 3 of the temple of the house of G
23 the G in whose hand thy breath is,
26 G hath numbered thy kingdom,
6. 5 concerning the law of his G.
20 servant of the living G, is thy G,
23 him, because he believed in his G.
9. 3 And I set my face unto the Lord G,
18 O my G, incline thine ear, and hear;
Hos 1. 6 And G said unto him, Call her
2.23 they shall say, Thou art my G.
6. 6 the knowledge of G more than
9. 1 hast gone a whoring from thy G,
17 My G will cast them away, because
11. 9 for I am G, and not man;
12. 3 his strength he had power with G:
6 and wait on thy G continually.
Am 1. 8 shall perish, saith the Lord G.
4. 2 The Lord G hath sworn by his
12 prepare to meet thy G, O Israel.
5. 3 saith the Lord G; The city that
27 whose name is The G of hosts.
Jon 1. 5 cried every man unto his g,
6 call upon thy G, if so be that G
9 I fear the Lord, the G of heaven,
3. 5 the people of Nineveh believed G,
9 Who can tell if G will turn and
10 G repented of the evil, that he
Mic 1. 2 Lord G be witness against you,
6. 6 and bow myself before the high G?
8 and to walk humbly with thy G?
7. 7 will wait for the G of my salvation:
18 Who is a G like unto thee, that
Hab 1.11 imputing this his power unto his g.
3. 3 G came from Teman, and the
19 The Lord G is my strength, and
Zec 6.15 obey the voice of the Lord your G.
8. 8 I will be their G, in truth
23 we have heard that G is with you.
Mal 1. 9 beseech G that he will be gracious
2.10 hath not one G created us? why
17 Where is the G of judgment?
3. 8 Will a man rob G? Yet ye have
14 It is vain to serve G: and what
Mt 1.23 being interpreted is, G with us.
2.12 being warned of G in a dream that
22 warned of G in a dream, he turned
3. 9 G is able of these stones to raise
16 he saw the Spirit of G descending
4. 3 If thou be the Son of G, command
4 proceedeth out of the mouth of G.
6 If thou be the Son of G, cast
7 shalt not tempt the Lord thy G.
10 Thou shalt worship the Lord thy G,
5. 8 pure in heart: for they shall see G.
9 shall be called the children of G.
6.24 Ye cannot serve G and mammon.
30 G so clothe the grass of the field,
33 seek ye first the kingdom of G,

Mt 8.29 Jesus, thou Son of *G*? art thou
9. 8 and glorified *G*, which had given
12. 4 he entered into the house of *G*,
28 cast out devils by the Spirit of *G*,
28 the kingdom of *G* is come unto
14.33 Of a truth thou art the Son of *G*.
15. 3 the commandment of *G* by your
4 For *G* commanded, saying, Honor
6 the commandment of *G* of none
31 and they glorified the *G* of Israel.
16.16 Christ, the Son of the living *G*.
23 not the things that be of *G*,
19. 6 therefore *G* hath joined together,
17 none good but one, that is, *G*:
24 to enter into the kingdom of *G*.
26 but with *G* all things are possible.
21.12 into the temple of *G*, and cast out
31 into the kingdom of *G* before you.
43 The kingdom of *G* shall be taken
22.16 and teachest the way of *G* in truth,
21 and unto *G* the things that are
29 the scriptures, nor the power of *G*.
30 but are as the angels of *G* in
31 which was spoken unto you by *G*,
32 I am the *G* of Abraham,
32 the *G* of Isaac, and the *G* of Jacob?
32 *G* is not the *G* of the dead,
37 Thou shalt love the Lord thy *G*
23.22 sweareth by the throne of *G*, and
26.61 to destroy the temple of *G*, and to
63 I adjure thee by the living *G*,
63 thou be the Christ, the Son of *G*.
27.40 thou be the Son of *G*, come down
43 He trusted in *G*; let him deliver
43 for he said, I am the Son of *G*.
46 My *G*, my *G*, why hast thou
54 Truly this was the Son of *G*.
Mk 1. 1 of Jesus Christ, the Son of *G*;
14 the gospel of the kingdom of *G*,
15 the kingdom of *G* is at hand:
24 who thou art, the Holy One of *G*.
2. 7 who can forgive sins but *G* only?
12 and glorified *G*, saying, We never
26 he went into the house of *G*
3.11 saying, Thou art the Son of *G*.
35 shall do the will of *G*, the same
4.11 the mystery of the kingdom of *G*:
26 So is the kingdom of *G*, as if
30 shall we liken the kingdom of *G*?
5. 7 thou Son of the most high *G*?
7 adjure thee by *G*, that thou torment
7. 8 aside the commandment of *G*,
9 ye reject the commandment of *G*,
13 Making the word of *G* of none
8.33 not the things that be of *G*, but
9. 1 they have seen the kingdom of *G*
47 to enter into the kingdom of *G*
10. 6 *G* made them male and female.
9 therefore *G* hath joined together,
14 for of such is the kingdom of *G*.
15 shall not receive the kingdom of *G*
18 is none good but one, that is, *G*.
23 riches enter into the kingdom of *G*!
24 to enter into the kingdom of *G*!
25 to enter into the kingdom of *G*.
27 impossible, but not with *G*:
27 for with *G* all things are possible.
11.22 saith unto them, Have faith in *G*.
12.14 teachest the way of *G* in truth:
17 and to *G* the things that are God's.
24 scriptures, neither the power of *G*?
26 how in the bush, *G* spake unto him,
26 saying, I am the *G* of Abraham,
26 the *G* of Isaac, and the *G* of Jacob?
27 He is not the *G* of the dead,
27 but the *G* of the living:
29 The Lord our *G* is one Lord:
30 thou shalt love the Lord thy *G*
32 for there is one *G*; and there is
34 not far from the kingdom of *G*.
13.19 which *G* created unto this time,
14.25 drink it new in the kingdom of *G*.
15.34 My *G*, my *G*, why hast thou
39 Truly this man was the Son of *G*.
43 also waited for the kingdom of *G*,
16.19 and sat on the right hand of *G*.
Lk 1. 6 they were both righteous before *G*,
8 before *G* in the order of his course,
16 shall he turn to the Lord their *G*.
19 that stand in the presence of *G*;
26 Gabriel was sent from *G* unto a
30 for thou hast found favor with *G*.
32 the Lord *G* shall give unto him
35 of thee shall be called the Son of *G*.
37 *G* nothing shall be impossible.
47 hath rejoiced in *G* my Saviour.
64 and he spake, and praised *G*.
68 Blessed be the Lord *G* of Israel;
78 the tender mercy of our *G*;
2.13 of the heavenly host praising *G*,
14 Glory to *G* in the highest, and on
20 and praising *G* for all the things
28 arms, and blessed *G*, and said,
37 *G* with fastings and prayers
40 and the grace of *G* was upon him.
52 and in favor with *G* and man.
3. 2 the word of *G* came unto John
6 flesh shall see the salvation of *G*.
8 *G* is able of these stones to raise
38 of Adam, which was the son of *G*.
4. 3 If thou be the Son of *G*, command
4 alone, but by every word of *G*.
8 Thou shalt worship the Lord thy *G*,
9 thou be the Son of *G*, cast thyself
12 shalt not tempt the Lord thy *G*.
34 who thou art, the Holy One of *G*.
41 Thou art Christ the Son of *G*.
43 kingdom of *G* to other cities also:
5. 1 upon him to hear the word of *G*,
21 Who can forgive sins, but *G* alone?
25 to his own house, glorifying *G*.
26 and they glorified *G*, and were filled
6. 4 How he went into the house of *G*,
12 continued all night in prayer to *G*.
20 for yours is the kingdom of *G*.
7.16 and they glorified *G*, saying, That
16 *G* hath visited his people.
28 in the kingdom of *G* is greater
29 justified *G*, being baptized with
30 council of *G* against themselves,
8. 1 glad tidings of the kingdom of *G*:
10 the mysteries of the kingdom of *G*:
11 The seed is the word of *G*.
21 which hear the word of *G*, and do
28 Son of *G* most high? I beseech
39 how great things *G* hath done unto
9. 2 to preach the kingdom of *G*, and
11 unto them of the kingdom of *G*,
20 answering said, The Christ of *G*.
27 till they see the kingdom of *G*.
43 amazed at the mighty power of *G*.
60 thou and preach the kingdom of *G*.
62 back, is fit for the kingdom of *G*.
10. 9 The kingdom of *G* is come nigh
11 that the kingdom of *G* is come nigh
27 Thou shalt love the Lord thy *G*
11.20 But if I with the finger of *G* cast
20 no doubt the kingdom of *G* is come
28 are they that hear the word of *G*,
42 judgment and the love of *G*:
49 said the wisdom of *G*, I will send
12. 6 one of them is forgotten before *G*?
8 also confess before the angels of *G*:
9 be denied before the angels of *G*.
20 But *G* said unto him, Thou fool,
21 and is not rich toward *G*.
24 *G* feedeth them: how much more
28 *G* so clothed the grass, which is
31 rather seek ye the kingdom of *G*;
13.13 was made straight, and glorified *G*.
18 what is the kingdom of *G* like?
20 shall I liken the kingdom of *G*?
28 the prophets, in the kingdom of *G*,
29 shall sit down in the kingdom of *G*.
14.15 eat bread in the kingdom of *G*.
15.10 in the presence of the angels of *G*
16.13 Ye cannot serve *G* and mammon.
15 but *G* knoweth your hearts: for
15 is abomination in the sight of *G*.
16 the kingdom of *G* is preached, and
17.15 and with a loud voice glorified *G*,
18 give glory to *G*, save this stranger.
20 when the kingdom of *G* should
20 kingdom of *G* cometh not with
21 the kingdom of *G* is within you.
18. 2 feared not *G*, neither regarded
4 Though I fear not *G*, nor regard
7 And shall not *G* avenge his own
11 *G*, I thank thee, that I am not as
13 *G* be merciful to me a sinner.
16 for of such is the kingdom of *G*.
17 shall not receive the kingdom of *G*
19 None is good, save one, that is, *G*.
24 riches enter into the kingdom of *G*!
25 man to enter into the kingdom of *G*.
27 with men are possible with *G*.
43 followed him, glorifying *G*: and all
43 they saw it, gave praise unto *G*.
19.11 kingdom of *G* should immediately
37 and praise *G* with a loud voice for
20.16 heard it, they said, *G* forbid.
21 but teachest the way of *G* truly:
25 and unto *G* the things which be
36 and are the children of *G*, being
37 calleth the Lord the *G* of Abraham,
37 the *G* of Isaac, and the *G* of Jacob.
38 For he is not a *G* of the dead, but
21. 4 cast in unto the offerings of *G*:
31 the kingdom of *G* is nigh at hand.
22.16 be fulfilled in the kingdom of *G*.
18 until the kingdom of *G* shall come.
69 the right hand of the power of *G*.
70 Art thou then the Son of *G*?
23.35 if he be Christ, the chosen of *G*.
40 Dost not thou fear *G*, seeing thou
47 he glorified *G*, saying, Certainly
51 waited for the kingdom of *G*.
24.19 word before *G* and all the people:
53 temple, praising and blessing *G*.
Jn 1. 1 was with *G*, and the Word was *G*.
2 same was in the beginning with *G*.
6 There was a man sent from *G*,
12 power to become the sons of *G*,
13 nor of the will of man, but of *G*.
18 No man hath seen *G* at any time;
29 and saith, Behold the Lamb of *G*,
34 record that this is the Son of *G*.
36 he saith, Behold the Lamb of *G*!
49 Rabbi, thou art the Son of *G*;
51 and the angels of *G* ascending and
3. 2 thou art a teacher, come from *G*:
2 thou doest, except *G* be with him.
3 he cannot see the kingdom of *G*.
5 cannot enter into the kingdom of *G*.
16 *G* so loved the world, that he gave
17 *G* sent not his Son into the world
18 name of the only begotten Son of *G*.
21 that they are wrought in *G*.
33 hath set to his seal that *G* is true.
34 For he whom *G* hath sent speaketh
34 words of *G*: for *G* giveth not the
36 the wrath of *G* abideth on him.
4.10 If thou knewest the gift of *G*, and
24 *G* is a Spirit: and they that worship
5.18 said also that *G* was his Father,
18 making himself equal with *G*.
25 shall hear the voice of the Son of *G*:
42 ye have not the love of *G* in you.
44 honor that cometh from *G* only?
6.27 for him hath *G* the Father sealed.
28 we might work the works of *G*?
29 This is the work of *G*, that ye
33 For the bread of *G* is he which

45 And they shall be all taught of *G*.
46 save he which is of *G*, he hath seen
69 that Christ, the Son of the living *G*.
7.17 whether it be of *G*, or whether I
8.40 the truth which I have heard of *G*:
41 we have one Father, even *G*.
42 If *G* were your Father, ye would
42 proceeded forth, and came from *G*;
47 that is of *G* heareth God's words:
47 them not, because ye are not of *G*.
54 of whom ye say, that he is your *G*:
9. 3 that the works of *G* should be made
16 This man is not of *G*, because he
24 Give *G* the praise: we know that
29 know that *G* spake unto Moses:
31 know that *G* heareth not sinners:
31 if any man be a worshipper of *G*,
33 If this man were not of *G*, he
35 Dost thou believe on the Son of *G*?
10.33 being a man, makest thyself *G*.
35 unto whom the word of *G* came,
36 because I said, I am the Son of *G*?
11. 4 unto death, but for the glory of *G*,
4 the Son of *G* might be glorified
22 whatsoever thou wilt ask of *G*,
22 *G* will give it thee.
27 thou art the Christ, the Son of *G*,
40 thou shouldest see the glory of *G*?
52 children of *G* that were scattered
12.43 of men more than the praise of *G*.
13. 3 was come from *G*, and went to *G*;
31 glorified, and *G* is glorified in him.
32 If *G* be glorified in him,
32 *G* shall also glorify him in
14. 1 ye believe in *G*, believe also in me.
16. 2 think that he doeth *G* service.
27 believed that I came out from *G*.
30 that thou camest forth from *G*.
17. 3 might know thee the only true *G*,
19. 7 he made himself the Son of *G*.
20.17 and to my *G*, and your *G*.
28 said unto him, My Lord and my *G*,
31 Jesus is the Christ, the Son of *G*;
21.19 by what death he should glorify *G*.
Ac 1. 3 pertaining to the kingdom of *G*:
2.11 tongue the wonderful works of *G*.
32 This Jesus hath *G* raised up,
5. 4 not lied unto men, but unto *G*.
29 ought to obey *G* rather than men.
39 But if it be of *G*, ye cannot
39 be found even to fight against *G*.
10. 2 that feared *G* with all his house,
34 that *G* is no respecter of persons:
38 *G* anointed Jesus of Nazareth
15. 4 things that *G* had done with them.
7 *G* made choice among us, that the
8 And *G*, which knoweth the hearts,
18 Known unto *G* are all his works
17.13 word of *G* was preached of Paul
23 To The Unknown *G*. Whom
20.21 repentance toward *G*, and faith
26. 6 made of *G* unto our fathers:
8 that *G* should raise the dead?
Ro 1. 1 separated unto the gospel of *G*,
16 for it is the power of *G* unto
21 Because that, when they knew *G*,
21 they glorified him not as *G*,
2. 2 the judgment of *G* is according
11 is no respect of persons with *G*.
16 *G* shall judge the secrets of men
3. 2 were committed the oracles of *G*.
4 *G* forbid: yea, let
4 let *G* be true, but every man a
23 and come short of the glory of *G*;
29 Is he the *G* of the Jews only?
5. 1 we have peace with *G* through our
8 *G* commendeth his love toward us,
8. 3 *G* sending his own Son in the
31 If *G* be for us, who can be against
9. 4 the service of *G*, and the promises;
14 Is there unrighteousness with *G*?
11. 1 Hath *G* cast away his people?
2 *G* hath not cast away his people
2 how he maketh intercession to *G*
33 the wisdom and knowledge of *G*!
13. 1 For there is no power but of G:
14. 3 for *G* hath received him.
11 every tongue shall confess to *G*.
15. 5 the *G* of patience and consolation
1Co 1. 1 apostle...through the will of *G*,
9 *G* is faithful, by whom ye were
24 power of *G*, and the wisdom of *G*.
25 the foolishness of *G* is wiser than
25 men; and the weakness of *G* is
2. 1 unto you the testimony of *G*.
10 But *G* hath revealed them unto us
3. 6 watered; but *G* gave the increase.
7. 7 man hath his proper gift of *G*,
17 *G* hath distributed to every man,
8. 3 But if any man love *G*, the same
6 there is but one *G*, the Father,
10. 5 of them *G* was not well pleased:
13 *G* is faithful, who will not suffer
11. 3 and the head of Christ is *G*.
14. 2 not unto men, but unto *G*:
33 *G* is not the author of confusion,
15. 9 I persecuted the church of *G*.
10 But by the grace of *G* I am what
28 that *G* may be all in all.
34 some have not the knowledge of *G*:
2Co 1. 1 an apostle...by the will of *G*, and
3 Blessed be *G*, even the Father
3 and the *G* of all comfort;
3. 3 with the Spirit of the living *G*;
5 but our sufficiency is of *G*;
5. 1 we have a building of *G*, an house
19 To wit, that *G* was in Christ,
9. 7 for *G* loveth a cheerful giver.
8 And *G* is able to make all grace
13. 4 yet he liveth by the power of *G*.
11 and the *G* of love and peace shall
Gal 1. 1 and *G* the Father, who raised him
2. 6 *G* accepteth no man's person:)
4. 4 *G* sent forth his Son, made of a
6. 7 *G* is not mocked: for whatsoever
Eph 1. 1 an apostle...by the will of *G*, to
2. 4 But *G*, who is rich in mercy, for his
8 of yourselves: it is the gift of *G*:
10 which *G* hath before ordained that
12 hope, and without *G* in the world:
3. 2 of the grace of *G* which is given me
19 be filled with all the fulness of *G*.
4. 6 One *G* and Father of all, who is
Php 1. 2 and peace, from *G* our Father, and
2. 6 Who, being in the form of *G*,
13 For it is *G* which worketh in you
19 whose *G* is their belly, and whose
4. 6 requests be made known unto *G*.
7 And the peace of *G*, which passeth
19 my *G* shall supply all your need
Col 1. 1 an apostle...by the will of *G*, and
15 is the image of the invisible *G*,
1Th 1. 1 which is in *G* the Father and in the
9 and how ye turned to *G* from idols
9 to serve the living and true *G*;
5. 9 *G* hath not appointed us to wrath,
2Th 1. 1 church...in *G* our Father and the
8 on them that know not *G*,
2. 4 is called *G*, or that is worshipped;
4 he as *G* sitteth in the temple of *G*,
1Ti 1. 1 commandment of *G* our Saviour,
2. 3 in the sight of *G* our Saviour;
5 For there is one *G*, and one
5 one mediator between *G* and men,
3. 5 he take care of the church of *G*?)
16 *G* was manifest in the flesh,
2Ti 1. 1 an apostle...by the will of *G*,
2. 9 but the word of *G* is not bound.
19 the foundation of *G* standeth sure,
3. 4 of pleasure more than lovers of *G*;
16 is given by inspiration of *G*,
Tit 1. 1 Paul, a servant of *G*, and an
13 appearing of the great *G* and our
Heb 1. 1 *G*, who at sundry times and in
3. 4 but he that built all things is *G*.
6. 1 dead works, and of faith toward *G*,
10 For *G* is not unrighteous to forget
18 it was impossible for *G* to lie,
10. 7 written of one,) to do thy will, O *G*.
31 fall into the hands of the living *G*.
11. 3 were framed by the word of *G*,
6 he that cometh to *G* must believe
12. 2 the right hand of the throne of *G*.
29 for our *G* is a consuming fire.
Jas 1. 1 James, a servant of *G* and of the
13 he is tempted, I am tempted of *G*:
13 for *G* cannot be tempted with evil,
23 Abraham believed *G*, and it was
23 and he was called the Friend of *G*.
4. 4 of the world is enmity with *G*?
8 Draw nigh to *G*, and he will draw
1Pe 1. 2 foreknowledge of *G* the Father,
2Pe 1. 1 through the righteousness of *G*
2. 4 For if *G* spared not the angels that
1Jn 1. 5 that *G* is light, and in him is no
3. 1 should be called the sons of *G*:
20 *G* is greater than our heart, and
4. 1 the Spirits whether they are of *G*:
8 knoweth not *G*; for *G* is love.
12 No man hath seen *G* at any time.
12 *G* dwelleth in us, and his love is
16 love that *G* hath to us. *G* is love;
5. 1 Jesus is the Christ is born of *G*:
11 *G* hath given to us eternal life,
20 we know that the Son of *G* is come,
20 This is the true *G*, and eternal life.
Jude 1 that are sanctified by *G* the Father,
25 To the only wise *G* our Saviour,
Rev 1. 1 which *G* gave unto him, to shew
4. 5 which are the seven Spirits of *G*.
8 Lord *G* Almighty, which was, and
11. 1 and measure the temple of *G*, and
17 O Lord *G* Almighty, which art, and
14. 4 firstfruits unto *G* and to the Lamb.
7 Fear *G*, and give glory to him;
19. 1 and power, unto the Lord our *G*:
6 the Lord *G* omnipotent reigneth.
21. 2 coming down from *G* out of heaven,
3 the tabernacle of *G* is with men,
3 and *G* himself shall be with them,
3 be with them, and be their *G*.
4 And *G* shall wipe away all tears

GODDESS

1Ki 11. 5 went after Ashtoreth the *g*
33 Ashtoreth the *g* of the Zidonians,
Ac 19.27 the temple of the great *g* Diana
35 worshipper of the great *g* Diana,
37 nor yet blasphemers of your *g*.

GODHEAD

Ac 17.29 think that the *G* is like unto gold,
Ro 1.20 even his eternal power and *G*;
Col 2. 9 all the fulness of the *G* bodily.

GODLINESS

1Ti 2. 2 life in all *g* and honesty.
10 becometh women professing *g*)
3.16 great is the mystery of *g*: God
4. 7 and exercise thyself rather unto *g*.
8 but *g* is profitable unto all things,
6. 3 doctrine which is according to *g*;
5 supposing that gain is *g*: from such
6 *g* with contentment is great gain.
11 follow after righteousness, *g*, faith,
2Ti 3. 5 Having a form of *g*, but denying
Tit 1. 1 of the truth which is after *g*;
2Pe 1. 3 pertain unto life and *g*, through
6 patience; and to patience *g*;
7 And to *g* brotherly kindness;
3.11 in all holy conversation and *g*,

GODLY

Ps 4. 3 apart him that is *g* for himself:
12. 1 Help, Lord; for the *g* man ceaseth;
32. 6 this shall every one that is *g* pray
Mal 2.15 That he might seek a *g* seed.
2Co 1.12 simplicity and *g* sincerity, not
7. 9 made sorry after a *g* manner,
10 *g* sorrow worketh repentance
11 that ye sorrowed after a *g* sort,
11. 2 jealous over you with *g* jealousy:
1Ti 1. 4 questions, rather than *g* edifying
2Ti 3.12 all that will live *g* in Christ Jesus
Tit 2.12 live soberly, righteously, and *g*,
Heb 12.28 with reverence and *g* fear:
2Pe 2. 9 knoweth how to deliver the *g* out
3Jn 6 their journey after a *g* sort,

GOD'S

Gen 28.22 set for a pillar, shall be *G* house:
30. 2 I in *G* stead, who hath withheld
32. 2 he said, This is *G* host: and he
Nu 22.22 And *G* anger was kindled because
Dt 1.17 the judgment is *G*: and the cause
2Ch 20.15 for the battle is not your's, but *G*.
Neh 10.29 to walk in *G* law, which was given
Job 33. 6 according to thy wish in *G* stead:
35. 2 My righteousness is more than *G*?
36. 2 I have yet to speak on *G* behalf.
Mt 5.34 by heaven; for it is *G* throne:
22.21 unto God the things that are *G*.
Mk 12.17 and to God the things that are *G*.
Lk 18.29 for the kingdom of *G* sake,
20.25 unto God the things which be *G*,
Jn 8.47 that is of God heareth *G* words:
Ac 23. 4 said, Revilest thou *G* high priest?
Ro 8.33 thing to the charge of *G* elect?
10. 3 being ignorant of *G* righteousness,
13. 6 they are *G* ministers, attending
1Co 3. 9 Ye are *G* husbandry,
9 ye are *G* building.
23 ye are Christ's; and Christ is *G*.
6.20 and in your spirit, which are *G*.
Tit 1. 1 according to the faith of *G* elect,
1Pe 5. 3 as being lords over *G* heritage,

GODS

Gen 3. 5 ye shall be as *g*, knowing good
35. 2 the strange *g* that are among you,
Ex 18.11 the Lord is greater than all *g*:
20. 3 shalt have no other *g* before me.
23 not make with me *g* of silver,
23 shall ye make unto you *g* of gold.
32. 1 make us *g*, which shall go before us;
23 Make us *g*, which shall go before
Dt 5. 7 Thou shalt have none other *g* before
10.17 is God of *g*, and Lord of lords,
29.26 For they went and served other *g*,
30.17 drawn away, and worship other *g*,
Jos 24.14 put away the *g* which your fathers
Jdg 5. 8 They chose new *g*; then was war
10.13 forsaken me, and served other *g*:
17. 5 the man Micah had an house of *g*,
1Sa 7. 3 away the strange *g* and Ashtaroth
17.43 Philistine cursed David by his *g*.
28.13 saw *g* ascending out of the earth.
1Ki 12.28 behold thy *g*, O Israel, which
18.24 call ye on the name of your *g*,
20.23 Their *g* are *g* of the hills;
2Ki 17.35 Ye shall not fear other *g*, nor bow
18.34 Where are the *g* of Hamath, and of
19.12 Have the *g* of the nations delivered
18 And have cast their *g* into the fire:
18 for they were no *g*, but the work
1Ch 16.25 he also is to be feared above all *g*.
26 For all the *g* of the people are idols:
2Ch 2. 5 for great is our God above all *g*.
Ps 82. 6 I have said, Ye are *g*; and all of you
86. 8 Among the *g* there is none like unto
95. 3 and a great King above all *g*.
96. 4 he is to be feared above all *g*.
5 all the *g* of the nations are idols:
136. 2 O give thanks unto the God of *g*:
Isa 37.12 Have the *g* of the nations delivered
42.17 the molten images, Ye are our *g*.
Jer 7. 6 walk after other *g* to your hurt:
10.11 *g* that have not made the heavens
16.20 Shall a man make *g* unto himself,
Dan 2.47 your God is a God of *g*, and a Lord
3.14 do not ye serve my *g*, nor worship
18 we will not serve thy *g*, nor worship
4. 8 in whom is the spirit of the holy *g*:
Hos 14. 3 work of our hands, Ye are our *g*:
Ac 7.40 Make us *g* to go before us: for as
14.11 The *g* are come down to us in the
17.18 to be a setter forth of strange *g*:
19.26 that they be no *g*, which are made
1Co 8. 5 though there be that are called *g*,
5 (as there be *g* many, and lords
Gal 4. 8 them which by nature are no *g*.

GOD-WARD

Ex 18.19 Be thou for the people to *G*,
2Co 3. 4 have we through Christ to *G*:
1Th 1. 8 your faith to *G* is spread

GOG

1Ch 5. 4 Shemaiah his son, *G* his son,
Eze 38. 2 Son of man, set thy face against *G*,
3 I am against thee, O *G*, the chief
14 prophesy and say unto *G*, Thus
16 I shall be sanctified in thee, O *G*,
18 *G* shall come against the land
39. 1 prophesy against *G*, and say,
1 I am against thee, O *G*, the chief
11 that I will give unto *G* a place
11 and there shall they bury *G* and
Rev 20. 8 *G* and Magog, to gather them

GOLD

Gen 2.11 land of Havilah, where there is *g*;
12 And the *g* of that land is good:
41.42 put a *g* chain about his neck;
Ex 20.23 shall ye make unto you gods of *g*.
28. 6 they shall make the ephod of *g*,
35. 5 offering of the Lord; *g*, and silver,
Dt 29.17 idols, wood and stone, silver and *g*,
1Ki 10.11 that brought *g* from Ophir, brought
21 forest of Lebanon were of pure *g*;
22 the navy of Tharshish, bringing *g*,
20. 3 Thy silver and thy *g* is mine; thy
22.48 of Tharshish to go to Ophir for *g*:
2Ki 18.16 Hezekiah cut off the *g* from the
24.13 cut in pieces all the vessels of *g*
2Ch 2. 7 a man cunning to work in *g*, and in
Est 1. 6 the beds were of *g* and silver,
Job 22.24 Then shalt thou lay up *g* as dust,
23.10 tried me, I shall come forth as *g*.
28.15 It cannot be gotten for *g*,
31.24 If I have made *g* my hope,
24 or have said to the fine *g*, Thou
Ps 19.10 More to be desired are they than *g*,
10 yea, than much fine *g*:
115. 4 Their idols are silver and *g*, the
127 love thy commandments above *g*;
135.15 of the heathen are silver and *g*,
Pr 8.19 My fruit is better than *g*;
11.22 a jewel of *g* in a swine's snout,
16.16 better is it to get wisdom than *g*!
Isa 13.12 a man more precious than fine *g*;
31. 7 idols of silver, and his idols of *g*,
46. 6 They lavish *g* out of the bag,
60.17 For brass I will bring *g*, and for
La 4. 1 How is the *g* become dim!
Dan 2.32 This image's head was of fine *g*,
3. 1 the king made an image of *g*, whose
Joel 3. 5 ye have taken my silver and my *g*,
Zec 9. 3 fine *g* as the mire of the streets.
13. 9 and will try them as *g* is tried:
Mal 3. 3 and purge them as *g* and silver,
Mt 2.11 him gifts: *g*, and frankincense,
10. 9 Provide neither *g*, nor silver, nor
23.16 shall swear by the *g* of the temple,
17 whether is greater, the *g*, or the
17 temple that sanctifieth the *g*?
Ac 3. 6 said, Silver and *g* have I none;
17.29 that the Godhead is like unto *g*,
20.33 have coveted no man's silver, or *g*,
1Co 3.12 upon this foundation *g*, silver,
1Ti 2. 9 not with broidered hair, or *g*, or
2Ti 2.20 not only vessels of *g* and of silver,
Heb 9. 4 overlaid round about with *g*,
Jas 2. 2 with a *g* ring, in goodly apparel,
5. 3 Your *g* and silver is cankered;
1Pe 1. 7 much more precious than of *g*
18 corruptible things, as silver and *g*,
3. 3 the hair, and of wearing of *g*,
Rev 3.18 to buy of me *g* tried in the fire,
4. 4 had on their heads crowns of *g*.
9. 7 were as it were crowns like *g*,
20 devils, and idols of *g*, and
17. 4 decked with *g* and precious
18.12 The merchandise of *g*, and silver,
16 decked with *g*, and precious stones,
21.18 and the city was pure *g*, like unto
21 the street of the city was pure *g*,

GOLDEN

Ex 32. 2 Break off the *g* earrings, which are
2Ki 10.29 the *g* calves that were in Beth-el,
Est 4.11 king shall hold out the *g* sceptre,
5. 2 held out to Esther the *g* sceptre
Ec 12. 6 or the *g* bowl be broken, or the
Dan 3. 5 down and worship the *g* image
14 nor worship the *g* image which I
Rev 1.12 turned, I saw seven *g* candlesticks;
13 about the paps with a *g* girdle.
20 and the seven *g* candlesticks.
2. 1 midst of the seven *g* candlesticks;
5. 8 harps, and *g* vials full of odors,
8. 3 having a *g* censer; and there was
3 upon the *g* altar which was before
9.13 from the four horns of the *g* altar
14.14 having on his head a *g* crown,
15. 6 their breasts girded with *g* girdles.
7 seven *g* vials full of the wrath of
17. 4 having a *g* cup in her hand full
21.15 had a *g* reed to measure the city,

GOLGOTHA

Mt 27.33 were come unto a place called *G*,
Mk 15.22 they bring him unto the place *G*,
Jn 19.17 which is called in the Hebrew *G*:

GOLIATH

1Sa 17. 4 named *G*, of Gath, whose height
23 Gath, *G* by name, out of the armies
21. 9 sword of *G* the Philistine, whom
22.10 and gave him the sword of *G* the
2Sa 21.19 slew the brother of *G* the Gittite,
1Ch 20. 5 slew...the brother of *G* the Gittite,

GOMER

Gen 10. 2 sons of Japheth; *G*, and Magog,
3 And the sons of *G*; Ashkenaz,
1Ch 1. 5 sons of Japheth; *G*, and Magog,
6 the sons of *G*; Ashchenaz, and
Ez 38. 6 *G*, and all his bands; the house of
Hos 1. 3 went and took *G* the daughter of

GOMORRAH

Gen 10.19 thou goest, unto Sodom, and *G*,
13.10 the Lord destroyed Sodom and *G*,
14. 2 and with Birsha king of *G*, Shinab
8 and the king of *G*, and the king of
10 and the kings of Sodom and *G* fled,
11 took all the goods of Sodom and *G*,
18.20 Because the cry of Sodom and *G* is
19.24 rained upon Sodom and upon *G*,
28 he looked toward Sodom and *G*,
Dt 29.23 like the overthrow of Sodom, and *G*,
32.32 of Sodom, and of the fields of *G*:
Isa 1. 9 we should have been like unto *G*.
10 the law of our God, ye people of *G*.

13.19 when God overthrew Sodom and *G*.
Jer 23.14 and the inhabitants thereof as *G*.
49.18 in the overthrow of Sodom and *G*,
50.40 As God overthrew Sodom and *G*
Am 4.11 as God overthrew Sodom and *G*,
Zep 2. 9 and the children of Ammon as *G*,

GOMORRHA

Mt 10.15 for the land of Sodom and *G* in
Mk 6.11 more tolerable for Sodom and *G*
Ro 9.29 and been made like unto *G*.
2Pe 2. 6 turning the cities of...and *G*
Jude 7 Even as Sodom and *G*, and the

GOOD

Gen 1. 4 God saw the light, that it was *g*:
2. 9 tree of knowledge of *g* and evil.
18 not *g* that the man should be alone;
3. 5 be as gods, knowing *g* and evil.
22 to know *g* and evil: and now, lest
24.50 cannot speak unto thee bad or *g*.
27.46 what *g* shall my life do me?
40.16 that the interpretation was *g*,
44. 4 have ye rewarded evil for *g*?
45.18 I will give you the *g* of the land
Ex 3. 8 unto a *g* land and a large, unto
18.17 The thing that thou doest is not *g*.
Nu 10.29 for the Lord hath spoken *g*
13.20 And be ye of *g* courage, and bring
Dt 1.39 no knowledge between *g* and evil,
3.25 the *g* land that is beyond Jordan,
4.22 go over, and possess that *g* land.
8. 7 God bringeth thee into a *g* land,
31. 6 Be strong and of a *g* courage, fear not
7, 23 Be strong and of a *g* courage: for
Jos 1. 6 Be strong and of a *g* courage: for unto
Jdg 17.13 I that the Lord will do me *g*,
Ru 2.22 It is *g*, my daughter, that thou go
1Sa 2.24 for it is no *g* report that I hear:
12.23 teach you the *g* and the right way:
25. 8 for we come in a *g* day: give, I
21 and he hath requited me evil for *g*.
2Sa 16.12 will requite me *g* for his cursing
17. 7 Ahithophel hath given is not *g*
19.35 can I discern between *g* and evil?
1Ki 22.18 prophesy no *g* concerning me,
2Ki 7. 9 this day is a day of *g* tidings, and
20.19 *G* is the word of the Lord which
1Ch 16.34 thanks unto the Lord; for he is *g*;
2Ch 5.13 For he is *g*; for his mercy endureth
Neh 2. 8 to the *g* hand of my God upon me.
5. 9 I said, It is not *g* that ye do:
19 Think upon me, my God, for *g*,
9.20 Thou gavest also thy *g* spirit to
13.31 Remember me, O my God, for *g*.
Job 2.10 we receive *g* at the hand of God,
7. 7 mine eye shall no more see *g*.
15. 3 wherewith he can do no *g*?
22.18 filled their house with *g* things:
24.21 and doeth not *g* to the widow.
30.26 I looked for *g*, then evil came
Ps 4. 6 Who will shew us any *g*? Lord,
25. 8 *G* and upright is the Lord:
27.14 be of *g* courage, and he shall
31.24 Be of *g* courage, and he shall
34. 8 taste and see that the Lord is *g*:
10 Lord shall not want any *g* thing.
14 Depart from evil, and do *g*; seek
37. 3 Trust in the Lord, and do *g*:
23 The steps of a *g* man are ordered
27 Depart from evil, and do *g*; and
45. 1 My heart is inditing a *g* matter:
52. 3 Thou lovest evil more than *g*;
54. 6 thy name, O Lord; for it is *g*.
73. 1 Truly God is *g* to Israel,
84.11 no *g* thing will he withhold from
92. 1 It is a *g* thing to give thanks
100. 5 For the Lord is *g*; his mercy is
103. 5 thy mouth with *g* things; so that
106. 5 That I may see the *g* of thy chosen,
119.66 Teach me *g* judgment and

Biblical Themes

GOOD AND EVIL

And God saw every thing that he had made, and, behold, it was very good.
Gen 1.31

And God saw that the wickedness of man was great in the earth, and that every imagination of the thoughts of his heart was only evil continually. And it repented the Lord that he had made man on the earth, and it grieved him at his heart. Gen 6.5-6

See, I have set before thee this day life and good, and death and evil. . . . therefore choose life, that both thou and thy seed may live. Dt 30.15, 19

If I have seen any perish for want of clothing, or any poor without covering . . . if I have lifted up my hand against the fatherless . . . let mine arm fall from my shoulder blade, and mine arm be broken from the bone.
Job 31.19, 21-22

Many are the afflictions of the righteous: but the Lord delivereth him out of them all. Ps 34.19

Fret not thyself because of evildoers. . . . For they shall soon be cut down like the grass, and wither as the green herb. Trust in the Lord, and do good . . . and verily thou shalt be fed.
Ps 37.1-3

A little that a righteous man hath is better than the riches of many wicked.
Ps 37.16

I had rather be a doorkeeper in the house of my God, than to dwell in the tents of wickedness. Ps 84.10

Search me, O God, and know my heart: try me, and know my thoughts: and see if there be any wicked way in me, and lead me in the way everlasting.
Ps 139.23-24

As righteousness tendeth to life: so he that pursueth evil pursueth it to his own death. Pr 11.19

Woe unto them that call evil good, and good evil; that put darkness for light, and light for darkness. Isa 5.20

I am the Lord, and there is none else, there is no God beside me. . . . I form the light, and create darkness: I make peace, and create evil: I the Lord do all these things. Isa 45.5, 7

The heart is deceitful above all things, and desperately wicked: who can know it? I the Lord search the heart . . . to give every man according to his ways.
Jer 17.9-10

Seek good, and not evil, that ye may live: and so the Lord, the God of hosts, shall be with you. . . . Hate the evil, and love the good, and establish judgment in the gate: it may be that the Lord God of hosts will be gracious unto the remnant of Joseph. Am 5.14-15

Blessed are the pure in heart: for they shall see God. Mt 5.8

Resist not evil: but whosoever shall smite thee on thy right cheek, turn to him the other also. . . . Love your enemies, bless them that curse you, do good to them that hate you, and pray for them which despitefully use you . . . that ye may be the children of your Father which is in heaven: for he maketh his sun to rise on the evil and on the good, and sendeth rain on the just and on the unjust. Mt 5.39, 44-45

And, behold, one came and said unto him, Good Master, what good thing shall I do, that I may have eternal life? And he said unto him, Why callest thou me good? there is none good but one, that is, God. Mt 19.16-17

All things work together for good to them that love God. Ro 8.28

Eschew evil, and do good. . . . For the eyes of the Lord are over the righteous, and his ears are open unto their prayers. 1Pe 3.11-12

122. 9 the Lord our God I will seek thy *g*.
125. 4 Do *g*, O Lord, unto those that be
133. 1 how *g* and how pleasant it is for
136. 1 for he is *g*: for his mercy endureth
145. 9 The Lord is *g* to all: and his tender
147. 1 for it is *g* to sing praises unto our
Pr 3.27 Withhold not *g* from them to
4. 2 For I give you *g* doctrine,
12. 2 A *g* man obtaineth favor of the
25 but a *g* word maketh it glad.
13.15 *G* understanding giveth favor:
21 to the righteous *g* shall be repayed.
22 A *g* man leaveth an inheritance

14.19 The evil bow before the *g*; and the
17.20 hath a froward heart findeth no *g*:
26 Also to punish the just is not *g*,
18. 5 It is not *g* to accept the person of
22 findeth a wife findeth a *g* thing,
20.23 and a false balance is not *g*.
22. 1 *g* name is rather to be chosen than
24.13 eat thou honey, because it is *g*;
25.25 so is *g* news from a far country.
27 It is not *g* to eat much honey:
28.21 To have respect of persons is not *g*:
Ec 2.26 God giveth to a man that is *g* in
3.12 I know that there is no *g* in them,

Ec 5.11 what *g* is there to the owners
6. 6 yet hath he seen no *g*: do not all go
12 who knoweth what is *g* for man
7. 1 a *g* name is better than precious
11 Wisdom is *g* with an inheritance:
9. 2 as is the *g*, so is the sinner;
18 but one sinner destroyeth much *g*.
Isa 7.15 to refuse the evil, and choose the *g*.
39. 8 *G* is the word of the Lord which
40. 9 O Zion, that bringest *g* tidings, get
9 Jerusalem, that bringest *g* tidings,
41. 6 said to his brother, Be of *g* courage.
52. 7 feet of him that bringeth *g* tidings,
7 him that bringeth...tidings of *g*,
55. 2 and eat ye that which is *g*,
61. 1 preach *g* tidings unto the meek;
Jer 8.15 looked for peace, but no *g* came;
18. 4 seemed *g* to the potter to make it.
10 I will repent of the *g*, wherewith
33.11 for the Lord is *g*; for his mercy
14 I will perform that *g* thing which
39.16 this city for evil, and not for *g*;
La 3.25 The Lord is *g* unto them that wait
26 It is *g* that a man should both hope
27 It is *g* for a man that he bear the
38 High proceedeth not evil and *g*?
Am 5.15 Hate the evil, and love the *g*,
Mic 6. 8 shewed thee, O man, what is *g*;
7. 2 The *g* man is perished out of the
Na 1. 7 The Lord is *g*, a strong hold
Mal 2.17 Every one that doeth evil is *g* in
Mt 3.10 which bringeth not forth *g* fruit
5.13 it is henceforth *g* for nothing,
16 that they may see your *g* works,
44 do *g* to them that hate you, and
45 sun to rise on the evil and on the *g*,
7.11 to give *g* gifts unto your children,
11 which is in heaven give *g* things
17 Even so every *g* tree bringeth forth
17 tree bringeth forth *g* fruit; but a
18 A *g* tree cannot bring forth evil
18 a corrupt tree bring forth *g* fruit.
19 that bringeth not forth *g* fruit
8.30 there was a *g* way off from them
9. 2 be of *g* cheer; thy sins be forgiven
22 Daughter, be of *g* comfort; thy faith
11.26 for so it seemed *g* in thy sight.
12.33 make the tree *g*, and his fruit *g*;
34 can ye, being evil, speak *g* things?
35 A *g* man out of the *g* treasure of
35 the heart bringeth forth *g* things:
13. 8 fell into *g* ground, and brought,
23 received seed into the *g* ground
24 a man which sowed *g* seed in his
27 Sir, didst thou not sow *g* seed in
37 He that soweth the *g* seed is the
38 the *g* seed are the children of the
48 and gathered the *g* into vessels,
14.27 of *g* cheer; it is I; be not afraid.
17. 4 Lord, it is *g* for us to be here:
19.10 with his wife, it is not *g* to marry.
16 *G* Master, what...thing shall I do,
16 what *g* thing shall I do, that I may
17 callest thou me *g*? there is none *g*
20.15 Is thine eye evil, because I am *g*?
22.10 many as they found, both bad and *g*:
25.21 done, thou *g* and faithful servant:
23 Well done, *g* and faithful servant;
26.10 she hath wrought a *g* work upon
24 it had been *g* for that man if he had
Mk 3. 4 to do *g* on the sabbath days, or to
4. 8 And other fell on *g* ground, and
20 they which are sown on *g* ground;
6.50 Be of *g* cheer; it is I; be not afraid.
9. 5 Master, it is *g* for us to be here:
50 Salt is *g*: but if the salt have lost
10.17 *G* Master, what shall I do that I
18 callest thou me *g*? there is none *g*
49 Be of *g* comfort, rise; he calleth thee.
14. 6 hath wrought a *g* work on me.
7 ye will ye may do them *g*: but

21 *g* were it for that man if he had
Lk 1. 3 It seemed *g* to me also, having had
53 He hath filled the hungry with *g*
2.10 bring you *g* tidings of great joy,
14 earth peace, *g* will toward men.
3. 9 not forth *g* fruit is hewn down,
6. 9 on the sabbath days to do *g*, or to
27 do *g* to them which hate you,
33 ye do *g* to them which do *g* to you,
35 do *g*, and lend, hoping for nothing
38 *g* measure, pressed down, and
43 For a *g* tree bringeth not forth
43 a corrupt tree bring forth *g* fruit.
45 A *g* man out of the *g* treasure of
45 heart bringeth forth that which is *g*;
8. 8 And other fell on *g* ground, and
15 But that on the *g* ground are they
15 which in an honest and *g* heart,
48 Daughter, be of *g* comfort: thy
9.33 it is *g* for us to be here: and let
10.21 for so it seemed *g* in thy sight.
42 and Mary hath chosen that *g* part,
11.13 know how to give *g* gifts unto your
12.32 your Father's *g* pleasure to give you
14.34 Salt is *g*: but if the salt have lost
16.25 thy lifetime receivedst thy *g* things,
18.18 *G* Master, what shall I do to inherit
19 Why callest thou me *g*? none is *g*,
19.17 Well, thou *g* servant: because thou
23.50 and he was a *g* man, and a just:
Jn 1.46 Can there any *g* thing come out
2.10 doth set forth *g* wine; and when
10 but thou hast kept the *g* wine
5.29 they that have done *g*, unto the
7.12 some said, He is a *g* man: others
10.11 the *g* shepherd: the *g* shepherd
14 I am the *g* shepherd, and know
32 Many *g* works have I shewed you
33 For a *g* work we stone thee not;
16.33 but be of *g* cheer; I have overcome
Ac 4. 9 *g* deed done to the impotent man,
9.36 this woman was full of *g* works
10.22 of *g* report among all the nation
38 went about doing *g*, and healing
11.24 For he was a *g* man, and full of the
14.17 in that he did *g*, and gave us
15. 7 that a *g* while ago God made choice
25 It seemed *g* unto us, being assembled
28 For it seemed *g* to the Holy Ghost,
38 Paul thought not *g* to take him
18.18 this tarried there yet a *g* while,
22.12 having a *g* report of all the Jews
23. 1 I have lived in all *g* conscience until
11 Be of *g* cheer, Paul: for as thou hast
27.22 And now I exhort you to be of *g* cheer:
25 Wherefore, sirs, be of *g* cheer: for I
36 Then were they all of *g* cheer, and
Ro 2.10 peace to every man the worketh *g*,
3. 8 Let us do evil, that *g* may come?
12 there is none that doeth *g*, no, not
5. 7 for a *g* man some would even dare
7.12 commandment holy, and just, and *g*.
13 Was then that which is *g* made
13 death in me by that which is *g*;
16 I consent unto the law that it is *g*.
18 in my flesh,) dwelleth no *g* thing:
18 how to perform that which is *g* I
19 For the *g* that I would I do not:
21 a law, that when I would do *g*,
8.28 all things work together for *g* to
9.11 neither having done any *g* or evil,
10.15 and bring glad tidings of *g* things!
11.24 contrary to nature into a *g* olive
12. 2 that ye may prove what is that *g*,
9 is evil; cleave to that which is *g*.
21 of evil, but overcome evil with *g*.
13. 3 rulers are not a terror to *g* works,
3 do that which is *g*, and thou shalt
4 the minister of God to thee for *g*,
14.16 Let not then your *g* be evil spoken
21 It is *g* neither to eat flesh, nor to

15. 2 please his neighbor for his *g* to
16.18 by *g* words and fair speeches
19 have you wise unto that which is *g*,
1Co 5. 6 Your glorying is not *g*. Know ye
7. 1 It is *g* for a man not to touch a
8 It is *g* for them if they abide even as
26 that this is *g* for the present
26 that it is *g* for a man so to be.
15.33 evil communications corrupt *g*
2Co 5.10 hath done, whether it be *g* or bad.
6. 8 by evil report and *g* report: as
9. 8 may abound to every *g* work:
13.11 Be perfect, be of *g* comfort, be
Gal 4.18 But it is *g* to be zealously
18 affected always in a *g* thing,
6. 6 him that teacheth in all *g* things.
10 let us do *g* unto all men, especially
Eph 1. 5 according to the *g* pleasure of his
9 according to his *g* pleasure which
2.10 created in Christ Jesus unto *g*
4.28 his hands the thing which is *g*,
29 but that which is *g* to the use of
6. 7 With *g* will doing service, as to
8 whatsoever *g* thing any man doeth,
Php 1. 6 he which hath begun a *g* work in
15 and some also of *g* will:
2.13 to will and to do of his *g* pleasure.
19 that I also may be of *g* comfort,
4. 8 whatsoever things are of *g* report;
Col 1.10 being fruitful in every *g* work.
1Th 3. 1 thought it *g* to be left at Athens
6 brought us *g* tidings of your faith
6 have *g* remembrance of us always,
5.15 but ever follow that which is *g*,
21 things; hold fast that which is *g*.
2Th 1.11 the *g* pleasure of his goodness,
2.16 and *g* hope through grace,
17 you in every *g* word and work.
1Ti 1. 5 a pure heart, and of a *g* conscience,
8 But we know that the law is *g*,
18 them mightest war a *g* warfare;
19 Holding faith, and a *g* conscience;
2. 3 For this is *g* and acceptable in
10 professing godliness) with *g* works.
3. 1 of a bishop, he desireth a *g* work.
2 vigilant, sober, of *g* behavior,
7 he must have a *g* report of them
13 purchase to themselves a *g* degree,
4. 4 For every creature of God is *g*,
6 thou shalt be a *g* minister of Jesus
6 of faith and of *g* doctrine,
5. 4 for that is *g* and acceptable
10 Well reported of for *g* works;
10 diligently followed every *g* work.
25 the *g* works of some are manifest
6.12 Fight the *g* fight of faith, lay hold
12 and hast professed a *g* profession
13 Pilate witnessed a *g* confession;
18 That they do *g*, that they be
18 that they be rich in *g* works,
19 a *g* foundation against the time
2Ti 1.14 That *g* thing which was committed
2. 3 as a *g* soldier of Jesus Christ.
21 and prepared unto every *g* work.
3. 3 despisers of those that are *g*,
17 furnished unto all *g* works.
4. 7 I have fought a *g* fight, I have
Tit 1. 8 of hospitality, a lover of *g* men,
16 and unto every *g* work reprobate.
2. 3 much wine, teachers of *g* things;
5 keepers at home, *g*, obedient to
7 thyself a pattern of *g* works:
10 shewing all *g* fidelity; that they
14 peculiar people, zealous of *g*
3. 1 to be ready to every *g* work,
8 be careful to maintain *g* works.
8 These things are *g* and profitable
14 also learn to maintain *g* works for
Phm 6 the acknowledging of every *g* thing
Heb 5.14 to discern both *g* and evil,
6. 5 And have tasted the *g* word

9.11 an high priest of *g* things to come,
10. 1 a shadow of *g* things to come,
24 provoke unto love and to *g* works:
11. 2 the elders obtained a *g* report.
12 of one, and him as *g* as dead,
39 a *g* report through faith,
13. 9 it is a *g* thing that the heart be
16 But to do *g* and to communicate
18 we trust we have a *g* conscience,
21 Make you perfect in every *g* work
Jas 1.17 Every *g* gift and every perfect gift
2. 3 Sit thou here in a *g* place;
3.13 out of a *g* conversation his works
17 full of mercy and *g* fruits,
4.17 to him that knoweth to do *g*,
1Pe 2.12 they may by your *g* works, which
18 not only to the *g* and gentle, but
3.10 he that will love life, and see *g* days,
11 Let him eschew evil, and do *g*;
13 be followers of that which is *g*?
16 Having a *g* conscience; that,
16 falsely accuse your *g* conversation
21 answer of a *g* conscience toward
4.10 as *g* stewards of the manifold
1Jn 3.17 whoso hath this world's *g*, and
3Jn 11 which is evil, but that which is *g*.
11 He that doeth *g* is of God:
12 hath *g* report of all men, and of

GOODLINESS
Isa 40. 6 all the *g* thereof is as the flower

GOODLY
Gen 39. 6 Joseph was a *g* person,
Ps 16. 6 yea, I have a *g* heritage.
Zec 11.13 a *g* price that I was prised at of
Mt 13.45 merchant man, seeking *g* pearls:
Lk 21. 5 adorned with *g* stones and gifts,
Jas 2. 2 in *g* apparel, and there come
Rev 18.14 were dainty and *g* are departed

GOODMAN
Pr 7.19 For the *g* is not at home,
Mt 20.11 against the *g* of the house,
24.43 if the *g* of the house had known
Mk 14.14 say ye to the *g* of the house,
Lk 12.39 *g* of the house had known what
22.11 shall say unto the *g* of the house,

GOODNESS
Ex 18. 9 And Jethro rejoiced for all the *g*
Nu 10.32 *g* the Lord shall do unto us,
2Ch 6.41 and let thy saints rejoice in *g*.
Neh 9.25 themselves in thy great *g*.
Ps 16. 2 my *g* extendeth not to thee;
23. 6 Surely *g* and mercy shall follow me
27.13 see the *g* of the Lord in the land
31.19 how great is thy *g*, which thou
33. 5 earth is full of the *g* of the Lord.
65. 4 satisfied with the *g* of thy house,
11 crownest the year with thy *g*;
107. 8 would praise the Lord for his *g*,
9 filleth the hungry soul with *g*.
Pr 20. 6 proclaim every one his own *g*:
Jer 31.14 people shall be satisfied with my *g*,
Hos 3. 5 fear the Lord and his *g* in the
6. 4 your *g* is as a morning cloud,
Zec 9.17 For how great is his *g*, and how
Ro 2. 4 despisest thou the riches of his *g*
4 not knowing that the *g* of God
11.22 the *g* and severity of God:
22 but toward thee, *g*, if thou
22 if thou continue in his *g*:
15.14 ye also are full of *g*, filled with all
Gal 5.22 longsuffering, gentleness, *g*, faith,
Eph 5. 9 the fruit of the Spirit is in all *g*
2Th 1.11 all the good pleasure of his *g*,

GOODNESS'
Ps 25. 7 remember thou me for thy *g* sake,

GOODS
Gen 14.11 they took all the *g* of Sodom
12 Sodom, and his *g*, and departed.
16 he brought back all the *g*, and also
16 again his brother Lot, and his *g*,
21 persons, and take the *g* to thyself.
24.10 *g* of his master were in his hand:
31.18 all his *g* which he had gotten,
46. 6 they took their cattle, and their *g*,
Ex 22. 8 his hand unto his neighbor's *g*.
11 his hand unto his neighbor's *g*;
Nu 16.32 unto Korah, and all their *g*.
31. 9 all their flocks, and all their *g*.
35. 3 for their cattle, and for their *g*,
Dt 28.11 thee plenteous in *g*, in the fruit
2Ch 21.14 and thy wives, and all thy *g*:
Ezr 1. 4 silver, and with gold, and with *g*,
6 vessels of silver, with gold, with *g*,
6. 8 the king's *g*, even of the tribute
7.26 or to confiscation of *g*, or to
Neh 9.25 houses full of all *g*, wells digged,
Job 20.10 his hands shall restore their *g*.
21 shall no man look for his *g*.
28 and his *g* shall flow away in the
Ec 5.11 *g* increase, they are increased
Eze 38.12 which have gotten cattle and *g*,
13 to take away cattle and *g*, to take
Zep 1.13 their *g* shall become a booty,
Mt 12.29 and spoil his *g*, except he first
24.47 make him ruler over all his *g*.
25.14 and delivered unto them his *g*.
Mk 3.27 and spoil his *g*, except he will first
Lk 6.30 away thy *g* ask them not again.
11.21 his palace, his *g* are in peace:
12.18 I bestow all my fruits and my *g*.
19 thou hast much *g* laid up for many
15.12 me the portion of *g* that falleth
16. 1 unto him that he had wasted his *g*.
19. 8 Lord, the half of my *g* I give to the
Ac 2.45 And sold their possessions and *g*,
1Co 13. 3 though I bestow all my *g* to feed
Heb 10.34 joyfully the spoiling of your *g*,
Rev 3.17 I am rich, and increased with *g*,

GORGEOUS
Lk 23.11 arrayed him in a *g* robe, and sent

GORGEOUSLY
Eze 23.12 and rulers clothed most *g*,
Lk 7.25 they which are *g* apparelled,

GOSPEL
Mt 4.23 preaching the *g* of the kingdom,
9.35 preaching the *g* of the kingdom,
11. 5 have the *g* preached to them.
24.14 this *g* of the kingdom shall be
26.13 Wheresoever this *g* shall be
Mk 1. 1 beginning of the *g* of Jesus Christ,
14 preaching the *g* of the kingdom of
15 repent ye, and believe the *g*.
13.10 the *g* must first be published
14. 9 this *g* shall be preached throughout
16.15 preach the *g* to every creature.
Lk 4.18 to preach the *g* to the poor;
7.22 to the poor the *g* is preached.
9. 6 preaching the *g*, and healing every
20. 1 in the temple, and preached the *g*,
Ac 8.25 preached the *g* in many villages
14. 7 And there they preached the *g*,
21 And when they had preached the *g*
15. 7 should hear the word of the *g*,
16.10 to preach the *g* unto them.
20.24 testify the *g* of the grace of God.
Ro 1. 1 separated unto the *g* of God,
9 my spirit in the *g* of his Son,
15 to preach the *g* to you that are
16 For I am not ashamed of the *g*
2.16 by Jesus Christ according to my *g*.
10.15 them that preach the *g* of peace,
16 they have not all obeyed the *g*.
11.28 As concerning the *g*, they are
15.16 ministering the *g* of God, that the
19 have fully preached the *g* of Christ.
20 have I strived to preach the *g*,
29 of the blessing of the *g* of Christ.
16.25 stablish you according to my *g*,
1Co 1.17 but I preach the *g*: not with
4.15 have begotten you through the *g*.
9.12 we should hinder the *g* of Christ.
14 that they which preach the *g*
14 should live of the *g*.
16 For though I preach the *g*, I have
16 is unto me, if I preach not the *g*!
17 a dispensation of the *g* is
18 that, when I preach the *g*, I may
18 I may make the *g* of Christ of no
18 that I abuse not my power in the *g*.
15. 1 the *g* which I preached unto you,
2Co 2.12 to preach Christ's *g*, and a door
4. 3 But if our *g* be hid, it is hid to them
4 lest the light of the glorious *g* of
8.18 whose praise is in the *g*
9.13 subjection unto the *g* of Christ,
10.14 in preaching the *g* of Christ:
16 To preach the *g* in the regions
11. 4 or another *g*, which ye have not
7 have preached to you the *g* of God
Gal 1. 6 grace of Christ unto another *g*:
7 and would pervert the *g* of Christ.
8 preach any other *g* unto you than
9 if any man preach any other *g*
11 that the *g* which was preached
2. 2 communicated unto them that *g*
5 the truth of the *g* might continue
7 the *g* of the uncircumcision was
7 as the *g* of the circumcision was
14 according to the truth of the *g*,
3. 8 before the *g* unto Abraham,
4.13 I preached the *g* unto you
Eph 1.13 of truth the *g* of your salvation:
3. 6 promise in Christ by the *g*:
6.15 the preparation of the *g* of peace;
19 make known the mystery of the *g*,
Php 1. 5 For your fellowship in the *g*
7 and confirmation of the *g*, ye all
12 unto the furtherance of the *g*;
17 I am set for the defense of the *g*.
27 be as it becometh the *g* of Christ:
27 together for the faith of the *g*;
2.22 he hath served with me in the *g*.
4. 3 which labored with me in the *g*,
15 that in the beginning of the *g*,
Col 1. 5 in the word of the truth of the *g*;
23 away from the hope of the *g*,
1Th 1. 5 For our *g* came not unto you
2. 2 to speak unto you the *g* of God
4 to be put in trust with the *g*,
8 not the *g* of God only, but also our
9 we preached unto you the *g* of God.
3. 2 fellowlaborer in the *g* of Christ,
2Th 1. 8 and that obey not the *g* of our
2.14 he called you by our *g*, to the
1Ti 1.11 According to the glorious *g* of the
2Ti 1. 8 partaker of the afflictions of the *g*
10 immortality to light through the *g*:
2. 8 from the dead according to my *g*:
Phm 13 unto me in the bonds of the *g*:
Heb 4. 2 For unto us was the *g* preached,
1Pe 1.12 by them that have preached the *g*
25 by the *g* is preached unto you
4. 6 was the *g* preached also to them
17 them that obey not the *g* of God?
Rev 14. 6 the everlasting *g* to preach

GOSPEL'S
Mk 8.35 his life for my sake and the *g*,
10.29 or lands, for my sake, and the *g*,
1Co 9.23 And this I do for the *g* sake,

GOT
Gen 36. 6 which he had *g* in the land
39.12 her hand, and fled, and *g* him out.

Gen 39.15 with me, and fled, and *g* him out.
Ps 44. 3 they *g* not the land in possession
Ec 2. 7 I *g* me servants and maidens,
Jer 13. 2 So I *g* a girdle according to the
4 Take the girdle that thou hast *g*,

GOTTEN
Gen 4. 1 I have *g* a man from the Lord.
Ex 14.18 when I have *g* me honor upon
Dt 8.17 mine hand hath *g* me this
Job 28.15 It cannot be *g* for gold, neither
Ps 98. 1 arm, hath *g* him the victory.
Pr 13.11 Wealth *g* by vanity shall be
Jer 48.36 riches that he hath *g* are perished.
Ac 21. 1 after we were *g* from them,
Rev 15. 2 them that had *g* the victory

GOURD
Jon 4. 6 And the Lord God prepared a *g*,
6 Jonah was exceeding glad of the *g*.
7 it smote the *g* that it withered.
9 thou well to be angry for the *g*?
10 Thou hast had pity on the *g*,

GOVERNMENT
Isa 9. 6 the *g* shall be upon his shoulder:
7 Of the increase of his *g* and peace
22.21 and I will commit thy *g* into his
2Pe 2.10 of uncleanness, and despise *g*.

GOVERNMENTS
1Co 12.28 helps, *g*, diversities of tongues,

GOVERNOR
Gen 42. 6 Joseph was the *g* over the land,
2Ki 23. 8 gate of Joshua the *g* of the city,
Ezr 6. 7 the *g* of the Jews and the elders
Ps 22.28 he is the *g* among the nations.
Mt 2. 6 shall come a *G*, that shall rule
27. 2 him to Pontius Pilate the *g*.
11 And Jesus stood before the *g*:
11 and the *g* asked him, saying,
14 that the *g* marvelled greatly.
15 the *g* was wont to release unto
21 *g* answered and said unto them,
23 And the *g* said, Why, what evil
27 the soldiers of the *g* took Jesus
Lk 2. 2 when Cyrenius was *g* of Syria.)
3. 1 Pontius Pilate being *g* of Judea,
20.20 the power and authority of the *g*.
Jn 2. 8 And bear unto the *g* of the feast.
9 the *g* of the feast called the
Ac 7.10 and he made him *g* over Egypt
23.24 bring him safe unto Felix the *g*.
26 unto the most excellent *g* Felix
33 and delivered the epistle to the *g*,
34 when the *g* had read the letter,
24. 1 who informed the *g* against Paul.
10 after that the *g* had beckoned unto
26.30 the king rose up, and the *g*,
2Co 11.32 the *g* under Aretas the king kept
Jas 3. 4 whithersoever the *g* listeth.

GOVERNOR'S
Mt 28.14 And if this come to the *g* ears,

GOVERNORS
Jdg 5. 9 My heart is toward the *g* of Israel,
14 out of Machir came down *g*,
1Ki 10.15 and of the *g* of the country.
1Ch 24. 5 the *g* of the sanctuary, and *g* of
2Ch 9.14 *g* of the country brought gold
23.20 and the *g* of the people, and all the
Ezr 8.36 and to the *g* on this side the river:
Neh 2. 7 given me to the *g* beyond the river,
9 Then I came to the *g* beyond the
5.15 But the former *g* that had been
Est 3.12 and to the *g* that were over every
Dan 2.48 and chief of the *g* over all the
3. 2 gather together the princes, the *g*,
3 Then the princes, the *g*, and
27 And the princes, *g*, and captains,
6. 7 kingdom, the *g* and the princes, the
Zec 12. 5 And the *g* of Judah shall say in
6 day will I make the *g* of Judah
Mt 10.18 And ye shall be brought before *g*
Gal 4. 2 But is under tutors and *g* until
1Pe 2.14 Or unto *g*, as unto them that are

GRACE
Gen 6. 8 Noah found *g* in the eyes of
19.19 now, thy servant hath found *g* in
32. 5 that I may find *g* in thy sight.
33. 8 to find *g* in the sight of my lord.
10 now I have found *g* in thy sight,
15 let me find *g* in the sight of my
34.11 Let me find *g* in your eyes,
39. 4 And Joseph found *g* in his sight,
47.25 us find *g* in the sight of my lord,
29 now I have found *g* in thy sight,
50. 4 now I have found *g* in your eyes,
Ex 33.12 hast also found *g* in my sight.
13 if I have found *g* in thy sight,
13 that I may find *g* in thy sight:
16 people have found *g* in thy sight?
17 thou hast found *g* in my sight,
34. 9 now I have found *g* in thy sight,
Nu 32. 5 if we have found *g* in thy sight,
Jdg 6.17 now I have found *g* in thy sight,
Ru 2. 2 him in whose sight I shall find *g*.
10 Why have I found *g* in thine eyes,
1Sa 1.18 handmaid find *g* in thy sight.
20. 3 knoweth that I have found *g* in
27. 5 I have now found *g* in thine eyes,
2Sa 14.22 knoweth that I have found *g* in
16. 4 that I may find *g* in thy sight, my
Ezr 9. 8 a little space *g* hath been shewed
Est 2.17 she obtained *g* and favor in his
Ps 45. 2 men: *g* is poured into thy lips:
84.11 the Lord will give *g* and glory:
Pr 1. 9 an ornament of *g* unto thy head,
3.22 unto thy soul, and *g* to thy neck.
34 but he giveth *g* unto the lowly.
4. 9 to thine head an ornament of *g*:
22.11 for the *g* of his lips the king shall
Jer 31. 2 found *g* in the wilderness;
Zec 4. 7 shoutings, crying, *G*, *g* unto it.
12.10 spirit of *g* and of supplications:
Lk 2.40 and the *g* of God was upon him.
Jn 1.14 of the Father,) full of *g* and truth.
16 have all we received, and *g* for *g*.
17 *g* and truth came by Jesus Christ.
Ac 4.33 and great *g* was upon them all.
11.23 had seen the *g* of God, was glad,
13.43 them to continue in the *g* of God.
14. 3 testimony unto the word of his *g*,
26 recommended to the *g* of God for
15.11 through the *g* of the Lord Jesus
40 by the brethren unto the *g* of God.
18.27 which had believed through *g*:
20.24 testify the gospel of the *g* of God.
32 to God, and to the word of his *g*,
Ro 1. 5 By whom we have received *g* and
7 *G* to you and peace from God our
3.24 Being justified freely by his *g*
4. 4 not reckoned of *g*, but of debt.
16 of faith, that it might be by *g*;
5. 2 faith into this *g* wherein we stand,
15 the *g* of God, and the gift by *g*,
17 they which receive abundance of *g*
20 *g* did much more abound:
21 even so might *g* reign through
6. 1 continue in sin, that *g* may abound?
14 are not under the law, but under *g*.
15 not under the law, but under *g*?
11. 5 according to the election of *g*.
6 if by *g*, then is it no more of works:
6 otherwise *g* is no more *g*.
6 of works, then it is no more *g*:
12. 3 through the *g* given unto me, to
6 according to the *g* that is given to
15.15 because of the *g* that is given to
16.20 The *g* of our Lord Jesus Christ be
24 The *g* of our Lord Jesus Christ
1Co 1. 3 *G* be unto you, and peace, from
4 for the *g* of God which is given you
3.10 According to the *g* of God which
10.30 For if I by *g* be a partaker, why am
15.10 by the *g* of God I am what I am:
10 and his *g* which was bestowed upon
10 the *g* of God which was with me.
16.23 The *g* of our Lord Jesus Christ be
2Co 1. 2 *G* be to you and peace from God
12 by the *g* of God, we have had our
4.15 the abundant *g* might through the
6. 1 ye receive not the *g* of God in vain.
8. 1 you to wit of the *g* of God bestowed
6 also finish in you the same *g* also.
7 see that ye abound in this *g* also.
9 ye know the *g* of our Lord Jesus
19 to travel with us with this *g*, which
9. 8 God is able to make all *g* abound
14 for the exceeding *g* of God in you.
12. 9 My *g* is sufficient for thee: for my
13.14 The *g* of the Lord Jesus Christ,
Gal 1. 3 *G* be to you and peace from God
6 that called you into the *g* of Christ
15 womb, and called me by his *g*,
2. 9 perceived the *g* that was given unto
21 I do not frustrate the *g* of God:
5. 4 by the law; ye are fallen from *g*.
6.18 the *g* of our Lord Jesus Christ be
Eph 1. 2 *G* be to you, and peace, from God
6 To the praise of the glory of his *g*,
7 according to the riches of his *g*;
2. 5 with Christ, (by *g* ye are saved;)
7 the exceeding riches of his *g*
8 by *g* are ye saved through faith;
3. 2 the dispensation of the *g* of God
7 according to the gift of the *g* of God
8 is this *g* given, that I should preach
4. 7 unto every one of us is given *g*
29 it may minister *g* unto the hearers.
6.24 *G* be with all them that love our
Php 1. 2 *G* be unto you, and peace, from
7 ye all are partakers of my *g*.
4.23 The *g* of our Lord Jesus Christ be
Col 1. 2 *G* be unto you, and peace, from
6 and knew the *g* of God in truth:
3.16 singing with *g* in your hearts to
4. 6 your speech be always with *g*,
18 my bonds. *G* be with you. Amen.
1Th 1. 1 *G* be unto you, and peace, from
5.28 The *g* of our Lord Jesus Christ be
2Th 1. 2 *G* unto you, and peace, from God
12 according to the *g* of our God and
2.16 and good hope through *g*,
3.18 The *g* of our Lord Jesus Christ be
1Ti 1. 2 *G*, mercy, and peace, from God
14 the *g* of our Lord was exceeding
6.21 the faith. *G* be with thee. Amen.
2Ti 1. 2 *G*, mercy, and peace, from God the
9 to his own purpose and *g*,
2. 1 be strong in the *g* that is in Christ
4.22 thy spirit. *G* be with you. Amen.
Tit 1. 4 *G*, mercy, and peace, from God the
2.11 For the *g* of God that bringeth
3. 7 That being justified by his *g*, we
15 faith. *G* be with you all. Amen.
Phm 3 *G* to you, and peace, from God our
25 The *g* of our Lord Jesus Christ be
Heb 2. 9 he by the *g* of God should taste
4.16 come boldly unto the throne of *g*,
16 and find *g* to help in time of need.
10.29 done despite unto the Spirit of *g*?
12.15 lest any man fail of the *g* of God;
28 let us have *g*, whereby we may
13. 9 the heart be established with *g*;
25 *G* be with you all. Amen.
Jas 1.11 *g* of the fashion of it perisheth:
4. 6 But he giveth more *g*. Wherefore
6 but giveth *g* unto the humble.
1Pe 1. 2 *G* unto you, and peace, be

10 the *g* that should come unto you:
13 for the *g* that is to be brought
3. 7 heirs together of the *g* of life;
4.10 stewards of the manifold *g* of God.
5. 5 proud, and giveth *g* to the humble.
10 But the God of all *g*, who hath
12 true *g* of God wherein ye stand.
2Pe 1. 2 *G* and peace be multiplied unto
3.18 grow in *g*, and in the knowledge
2Jn 3 *G* be with you, mercy, and peace,
Jude 4 turning the *g* of our God into
Rev 1. 4 *G* be unto you, and peace, from
22.21 The *g* of our Lord Jesus Christ be

GRACIOUS
Gen 43.29 God be *g* unto thee, my son.
Ex 22.27 that I will hear; for I am *g*.
33.19 *g* to whom I will be *g*, and will
34. 6 The Lord God, merciful and *g*,
Nu 6.25 upon thee, and be *g* unto thee:
2Sa 12.22 God will be *g* to me, that the child
2Ki 13.23 And the Lord was *g* unto them,
2Ch 30. 9 Lord your God is *g* and merciful,
Neh 9.17 ready to pardon, *g* and merciful,
31 thou art a *g* and merciful God.
Job 33.24 Then he is *g* unto him, and saith,
Ps 77. 9 Hath God forgotten to be *g*?
86.15 a God full of compassion, and *g*,
103. 8 the Lord is merciful and *g*, slow to
111. 4 Lord is *g* and full of compassion.
112. 4 he is *g*, and full of compassion,
116. 5 *G* is the Lord, and righteous; yea,
145. 8 Lord is *g*, and full of compassion;
Pr 11.16 A *g* woman retaineth honor:
Ec 10.12 of a wise man's mouth are *g*;
Isa 30.18 that he may be *g* unto you, and
19 he will be very *g* unto thee at the
33. 2 O Lord, be *g* unto us; we have
Jer 22.23 *g* shall thou be when pangs come
Joel 2.13 is *g* and merciful, slow to anger,
Am 5.15 the Lord God of hosts will be *g*
Jon 4. 2 I knew that thou art a *g* God,
Mal 1. 9 God that he will be *g* unto us:
Lk 4.22 wondered at the *g* words which
1Pe 2. 3 ye have tasted that the Lord is *g*.

GRACIOUSLY
Gen 33. 5 God hath *g* given thy servant,
11 God hath dealt *g* with me, and
Ps 119.29 lying: and grant me thy law *g*.
Hos 14. 2 receive us *g*: so will we render

GRAIN
Am 9. 9 yet shall not the least *g* fall
Mt 13.31 like to a *g* of mustard seed, which
17.20 faith as a *g* of mustard seed, ye
Mk 4.31 It is like a *g* of mustard seed,
Lk 13.19 It is like a *g* of mustard seed,
17. 6 faith as a *g* of mustard seed, ye
1Co 15.37 body that shall be, but bare *g*,
37 of wheat, or of some other *g*:

GRANDMOTHER
2Ti 1. 5 which dwelt first in thy *g* Lois,

GRANT
Lev 25.24 shall *g* a redemption for the land.
Ru 1. 9 Lord *g* you that ye may find rest,
1Sa 1.17 God of Israel *g* thee thy petition
1Ch 21.22 *G* me the place of this
22 shalt *g* it me for the full price:
2Ch 12. 7 I will *g* them some deliverance;
Ezr 3. 7 according to the *g* that they had
Neh 1.11 and *g* him mercy in the sight of
Est 5. 8 it please the king to *g* my petition,
Job 6. 8 and that God would *g* me the thing
Ps 20. 4 *G* thee according to thine own
85. 7 O Lord, and *g* us thy salvation.
119.29 and *g* me thy law graciously.
140. 8 *G* not, O Lord, the desires of the
Mt 20.21 *G* that these my two sons may

Grape pickers harvest wine grapes in an Egyptian fresco that dates back to a period earlier than the lifetime of Moses; the Bible makes many references both to grapes and to wine, "the blood of grapes" (Gen 49.11).

Mk 10.37 *G* unto us that we may sit, one
Lk 1.74 That he would *g* unto us, that we
Ac 4.29 *g* unto thy servants, that with all
Ro 15. 5 *g* you to be likeminded one toward
Eph 3.16 That he would *g* you, according to
2Ti 1.18 Lord *g* unto him that he may find
Rev 3.21 that overcometh will I *g* to sit

GRANTED
1Ch 4.10 And God *g* him that which he
2Ch 1.12 and knowledge is *g* unto thee;
Ezr 7. 6 and the king *g* him all his request,
Neh 2. 8 And the king *g* me, according to
Est 5. 6 petition? and it shall be *g* thee:
7. 2 Esther? and it shall be *g* thee:
8.11 the king *g* the Jews which were in
9.12 petition? and it shall be *g* thee:
13 let it be *g* to the Jews which are in
Job 10.12 Thou has *g* me life and favor,
Pr 10.24 desire of the righteous shall be *g*.
Ac 3.14 a murderer to be *g* unto you;
11.18 Gentiles *g* repentance unto life.
14. 3 *g* signs and wonders to be done
Rev 19. 8 to her was *g* that she should

GRAPE
Lev 19.10 neither shalt thou gather every *g*
Dt 32.14 drink the pure blood of the *g*.
Job 15.33 He shall shake off his unripe *g*
SS 2.13 the vines with the tender *g* give
7.12 whether the tender *g* appear,
Isa 18. 5 and the sour *g* is ripening in
Jer 31.29 The fathers have eaten a sour *g*,
30 every man that eateth the sour *g*,

GRAPES
Gen 40.11 and I took the *g*, and pressed them
Nu 6. 3 shall he drink any liquor of *g*,
Dt 23.24 thou mayest eat *g* thy fill at thine
Isa 5. 2 that it should bring forth *g*, and
2 it brought forth wild *g*,
Jer 8.13 there shall be no *g* on the vine,
Mt 7.16 Do men gather *g* of thorns, or figs
Lk 6.44 of a bramble bush gather they *g*.
Rev 14.18 the earth; for her *g* are fully ripe.

GRASS
Gen 1.11 Let the earth bring forth *g*, the
1Ki 18. 5 peradventure we may find *g* to
Ps 37. 2 shall soon be cut down like the *g*,
72. 6 upon the mown *g*: as showers that
16 of the city shall flourish like *g* of
90. 5 in the morning they are like *g*
92. 7 When the wicked spring as the *g*,
102. 4 is smitten, and withered like *g*;
11 and I am withered like *g*.
103.15 As for man, his days are as *g*:
104.14 the *g* to grow for the cattle,
Pr 19.12 his favor is as dew upon the *g*.
Isa 40. 6 What shall I cry? All flesh is *g*,
7 The *g* withereth, the flower fadeth:
7 upon it: surely the people is *g*.
8 The *g* withereth, the flower fadeth:
51.12 man which shall be made as *g*;
Am 7. 2 make an end of eating the *g* of
Mic 5. 7 as the showers upon the *g*, that
Mt 6.30 God so clothe the *g* of the field,
14.19 to sit down on the *g*, and took
Mk 6.39 by companies upon the green *g*.
Lk 12.28 If then God so clothe the *g*,
Jn 6.10 there was much *g* in the place.
Jas 1.10 as the flower of the *g* he shall pass
11 it withereth the *g*, and the flower
1Pe 1.24 For all flesh is as *g*, and all the
24 glory of man as the flower of *g*.
24 The *g* withereth, and the flower
Rev 8. 7 and all green *g* was burnt up.
9. 4 should not hurt the *g* of the earth,

GRASSHOPPERS
Nu 13.33 we were in our own sight as *g*,
Jdg 6. 5 they came as *g* for multitude;
Isa 40.22 the inhabitants thereof are as *g*;

GRAVE
Gen 35.20 Jacob set a pillar upon her *g*:
20 that is the pillar of Rachel's *g*

Gen 37.35 go down into the *g* unto my son
42.38 gray hairs with sorrow to the *g*.
44.29 gray hairs with sorrow to the *g*.
31 our father with sorrow to the *g*.
50. 5 Lo, I die: in my *g* which I have
Ex 28. 9 and *g* on them the names of
36 and *g* upon it, like the engravings
Nu 19.16 a *g*, shall be unclean seven days.
18 or one slain, or one dead, or a *g*:
1Sa 2. 6 he bringeth down to the *g*, and
2Sa 3.32 and wept at the *g* of Abner;
19.37 be buried by the *g* of my father
1Ki 2. 6 head go down to the *g* in peace.
9 head bring thou down to the *g*
13.30 he laid his carcase in his own *g*:
14.13 of Jeroboam shall come to the *g*,
2Ki 22.20 thou shalt be gathered into thy *g*
2Ch 2. 7 to *g* with the cunning men that
14 also to *g* any manner of graving,
34.28 be gathered to thy *g* in peace,
Job 3.22 are glad, when they can find the *g*?
5.26 Thou shalt come to thy *g* in a full
7. 9 goeth down to the *g* shall come
10.19 carried from the womb to the *g*.
14.13 wouldest hide me in the *g*, that
17.13 *g* is mine house: I have made
21.13 in a moment go down to the *g*.
32 he be brought to the *g*, and shall
24.19 so doth the *g* those which have
30.24 stretch out his hand to the *g*,
33.22 soul draweth near unto the *g*,
Ps 6. 5 in the *g* who shall give thee
30. 3 brought up my soul from the *g*:
31.17 let them be silent in the *g*.
49.14 sheep they are laid in the *g*;
14 beauty shall consume in the *g*
15 my soul from the power of the *g*:
88. 3 my life draweth nigh unto the *g*.
5 like the slain that lie in the *g*,
11 be declared in the *g*? or thy
89.48 his soul from the hand of the *g*?
Pr 1.12 swallow them up alive as the *g*;
30.16 The *g*; and the barren womb;
Ec 9.10 knowledge, nor wisdom, in the *g*,
SS 8. 6 death; jealousy is cruel as the *g*:
Isa 14.11 pomp is brought down to the *g*,
19 thou art cast out of thy *g* like an
38.10 I shall go to the gates of the *g*:
18 the *g* cannot praise thee, death
53. 9 he made his *g* with the wicked,
Jer 20.17 my mother might have been my *g*,
Eze 31.15 when he went down to the *g* I
32.23 company is round about her *g*:
24 her multitude round about her *g*,
Hos 13.14 them from the power of the *g*;
14 O *g*, I will be thy destruction:
Na 1.14 make thy *g*; for thou art vile.
Jn 11.17 he had lain in the *g* four days
31 She goeth unto the *g* to weep
38 in himself cometh to the *g*.
12.17 he called Lazarus out of his *g*,
1Co 15.55 sting? O *g*, where is thy victory?
1Ti 3. 8 Likewise must the deacons be *g*,
11 Even so must their wives be *g*,
Tit 2. 2 aged men be sober, *g*, temperate,

GRAVEN

Ex 20. 4 not make unto thee any *g* image,
32.16 of God, *g* upon the tables.
39. 6 *g*, as signets are *g*, with the
Lev 26. 1 make you no idols nor *g* image,
Dt 4.16 and make you a *g* image,
23 you, and make you a *g* image, or
25 yourselves, and make a *g* image,
5. 8 shalt not make thee any *g* image,
7. 5 burn their *g* images with fire.
25 The *g* images of their gods shall
12. 3 ye shall hew down the *g* images
27.15 maketh any *g* or molten image,
Jdg 17. 3 to make a *g* image and a molten
4 who made thereof a *g* image and
18.14 and teraphim, and a *g* image, and
17 took the *g* image, and the ephod,
20 the teraphim, and the *g* image,
30 children of Dan set up the *g* image:
31 they set them up Micah's *g* image,
2Ki 17.41 and served their *g* images, both
21. 7 he set a *g* image of the grove
2Ch 33.19 up groves and *g* images, before
34. 7 and had beaten the *g* images into
Job 19.24 they were *g* with an iron pen
Ps 78.58 to jealousy with their *g* images.
97. 7 they that serve *g* images, that
Isa 10.10 and whose *g* images did excel
21. 9 all the *g* images of her gods
30.22 the covering of thy *g* images of
40.19 workman melteth a *g* image,
20 to prepare a *g* image, that shall
42. 8 neither my praise to *g* images.
17 that trust in *g* images, that say
44. 9 They that make a *g* image are all
10 or molten a *g* image that is
15 maketh it a *g* image, and falleth
17 maketh a god, even his *g* image:
45.20 the wood of their *g* image, and
48. 5 done them, and my *g* image, and
49.16 I have *g* thee upon the palms
Jer 8.19 me to anger with their *g* images,
10.14 is confounded by the *g* image:
17. 1 *g* upon the table of their heart,
50.38 the land of *g* images, and they
51.17 is confounded by the *g* image:
47 the *g* images of Babylon: and her
52 do judgment upon her *g* images:
Hos 11. 2 and burned incense to *g* images.
Mic 1. 7 all the *g* images thereof shall be
5.13 Thy *g* images also will I cut off,
Na 1.14 will I cut off the *g* image and the
Hab 2.18 what profiteth the *g* image that
18 the maker thereof hath *g* it;
Ac 17.29 stone, *g* by art and man's device.

GRAVES

Ex 14.11 Because there were no *g* in Egypt,
2Ki 23. 6 the powder thereof upon the *g* of
2Ch 34. 4 strowed it upon the *g* of them
Job 17. 1 extinct, the *g* are ready for me.
Isa 65. 4 Which remain among the *g*, and
Jer 8. 1 of Jerusalem, out of their *g*:
26.23 cast his dead body into the *g* of
Eze 32.22 company: his *g* are about him:
23 Whose *g* are set in the sides of the
25, 26 her *g* are round about him:
37.12 I will open your *g*, and cause you
12 you to come up out of your *g*,
13 when I have opened your *g*, O my
13 and brought you up out of your *g*,
39.11 give unto Gog a place there of *g*
Mt 27.52 the *g* were opened; and many
53 And came out of the *g* after his
Lk 11.44 for ye are as *g* which appear not,
Jn 5.28 that are in the *g* shall hear his
Rev 11. 9 their dead bodies to be put in *g*.

GREAT

Gen 1.16 And God made two *g* lights; the
21 God created *g* whales, and every
7.11 fountains of the *g* deep broken up,
12. 2 I will make of thee a *g* nation, and
15. 1 and thy exceeding *g* reward.
18 the *g* river, the river Euphrates:
18.20 cry of Sodom and Gomorrah is *g*,
29. 2 *g* stone was upon the well's mouth.
39. 9 then can I do this *g* wickedness,
Ex 3. 3 and see this *g* sight, why the bush
11. 3 the man Moses was very *g* in the
12.30 and there was a *g* cry in Egypt;
18.22 every *g* matter they shall bring
Nu 13.32 we saw in it are men of a *g* stature.
Dt 8.15 that *g* and terrible wilderness,
10.17 a *g* God, a mighty, and a terrible,
11. 7 eyes have seen all the *g* acts of the
27. 2 thou shalt set thee up *g* stones,
Jos 7.26 raised over him a *g* heap of stones
14.15 a *g* man among the Anakims.
Jdg 5.16 there were *g* searchings of heart.
16. 5 see wherein his *g* strength lieth,
23 to offer a *g* sacrifice unto Dagon
1Sa 6.18 even unto the *g* stone of Abel,
14.45 who hath wrought this *g* salvation
20. 2 will do nothing either *g* or small,
1Ki 19. 7 the journey is too *g* for thee.
11 and a *g* and strong wind rent the
2Ki 3.27 was *g* indignation against Israel:
5. 1 was a *g* man with his master, and
13 had bid thee do some *g* thing,
6.25 there was a *g* famine in Samaria:
8. 4 the *g* things that Elisha hath done.
1Ch 16.25 For *g* is the Lord, and greatly to be
21.13 Lord; for very *g* are his mercies:
2Ch 2. 5 for *g* is our God above all gods.
28.13 for our trespass is *g*, and there is
30.26 So there was *g* joy in Jerusalem:
34.21 for *g* is the wrath of the Lord
Neh 1. 5 the *g* and terrible God, that keepeth
6. 3 I am doing a *g* work, so that I
8. 6 Ezra blessed the Lord, the *g* God.
Est 2.18 the king made a *g* feast unto all
Job 2.13 saw that his grief was very *g*.
5. 9 doeth *g* things and unsearchable;
32. 9 *G* men are not always wise:
36.26 God is *g*, and we know him not,
38.21 the number of thy days is *g*?
Ps 18.50 *G* deliverance giveth he to his
19.11 keeping of them there is *g* reward.
13 innocent from the *g* transgression.
25.11 pardon mine iniquity; for it is *g*.
33.17 he deliver any by his *g* strength.
37.35 have seen the wicked in *g* power,
40.10 thy truth from the *g* congregation.
47. 2 he is a *g* king over all the earth,
48. 1 *G* is the Lord, and greatly to be
57.10 thy mercy is *g* unto the heavens,
71.19 who hast done *g* things: O God,
77.13 who is so *g* a God as our God?
92. 5 how *g* are thy works! and thy
95. 3 the Lord is a *g* God, and a *g* King
96. 4 the Lord is *g*, and greatly to be
104. 1 thou art very *g*; thou art clothed
25 So is this *g* and wide sea, wherein
107.23 that do business in *g* waters;
108. 4 thy mercy is *g* above the heavens:
119.156 *G* are thy tender mercies, O
126. 2 Lord hath done *g* things for them.
3 Lord hath done *g* things for us;
136. 7 To him that made *g* lights: for his
145. 3 *G* is the Lord, and greatly to be
8 slow to anger, and of *g* mercy.
147. 5 *G* is our Lord, and of...power:
5 is our Lord, and of *g* power: his
Pr 18. 9 brother to him that is a *g* waster.
22. 1 rather to be chosen than *g* riches,
26.10 The *g* God that formed all things
Ec 2.21 This also is vanity and a *g* evil
8. 6 the misery of man is *g* upon him.
10. 4 for yielding pacifieth *g* offenses.
6 Folly is set in *g* dignity, and the
Isa 6.12 and there be a *g* forsaking in the
8. 1 Take thee a *g* roll, and write in it
9. 2 in darkness have seen a *g* light:
32. 2 the shadow of a *g* rock in a weary
Jer 6.22 and a *g* nation shall be raised
10. 6 Lord; thou art *g*, and thy name is *g*
22. 8 Lord done thus unto this *g* city?
30. 7 Alas! for that day is *g*, so that
32.18 the *G*, the Mighty God, the Lord
19 *G* in counsel, and mighty in work:
La 3.23 morning: *g* is thy faithfulness.
Eze 17. 3 saith the Lord God; A *g* eagle
28. 5 By thy *g* wisdom and by thy
30.16 Sin shall have *g* pain, and No
Dan 2.31 and behold a *g* image.
48 the king made Daniel a *g* man,

7. 3 And four *g* beasts came up from
7 and it had *g* iron teeth:
8 and a mouth speaking *g* things.
17 These *g* beasts, which are four,
8. 8 the he goat waxed very *g*: and
9. 4 the *g* and dreadful God, keeping
10. 4 I was by the side of the *g* river,
Joel 2.21 for the Lord will do *g* things.
31 the *g* and the terrible day of the
Jon 1. 2 go to Nineveh, that *g* city, and cry
17 prepared a *g* fish to swallow up
3. 2 go unto Nineveh, that *g* city, and
Zep 1.14 The *g* day of the Lord is near,
Zec 4. 7 Who art thou, O *g* mountain?
8. 2 I was jealous for her with *g* fury.
Mal 1.11 shall be *g* among the Gentiles;
11 shall be *g* among the heathen,
14 for I am a *g* King, saith the Lord
4. 5 coming of the *g* and dreadful day
Mt 2.10 rejoiced with exceeding *g* joy.
18 and *g* mourning, Rachel weeping
4.16 which sat in darkness saw *g* light;
25 him *g* multitudes of people from
5.12 for *g* is your reward in heaven:
19 shall be called *g* in the kingdom
35 for it is the city of the *g* King.
6.23 how *g* is that darkness!
7.27 and *g* was the fall of it.
8. 1 *g* multitudes followed him.
10 I have not found so *g* faith, no,
18 Jesus saw *g* multitudes about
24 arose a *g* tempest in the sea,
26 the sea; and there was a *g* calm.
12.15 and *g* multitudes followed him,
13. 2 And *g* multitudes were gathered
46 found one pearl of *g* price, went
14.14 and saw a *g* multitude, and was
15.28 O woman, *g* is thy faith: be it
30 And *g* multitudes came unto him,
33 as to fill so *g* a multitude?
19. 2 And *g* multitudes followed him;
22 sorrowful: for he had *g* possessions.
20.25 that are *g* exercise authority
26 whosoever will be *g* among you,
29 a *g* multitude followed him.
21. 8 And a very *g* multitude spread
22.36 which is the *g* commandment in
38 is the first and *g* commandment.
24.21 then shall be *g* tribulation, such
24 shall shew *g* signs and wonders;
30 of heaven with power and *g* glory.
31 with a *g* sound of a trumpet, and
26.47 and with him a *g* multitude with
27.60 he rolled a *g* stone to the door
28. 2 there was a *g* earthquake: for the
8 with fear and *g* joy; and did run
Mk 1.35 rising up a *g* while before day,
3. 7 and a *g* multitude from Galilee
8 a *g* multitude, when they had
8 heard what *g* things he did
4. 1 gathered unto him a *g* multitude,
32 and shooteth out *g* branches; so
37 there arose a *g* storm of wind,
39 ceased; and there was a *g* calm.
5.11 a *g* herd of swine feeding.
19 tell them how *g* things the Lord
20 how *g* things Jesus had done for
42 astonished with a *g* astonishment.
7.36 so much the more a *g* deal they
8. 1 the multitude being very *g*, and
9.14 saw a *g* multitude about them,
10.22 grieved: for he had *g* possessions.
42 their *g* ones exercise authority
43 whosoever will be *g* among you,
46 his disciples and a *g* number of
48 but he cried the more a *g* deal,
13. 2 Seest thou these *g* buildings?
26 clouds with *g* power and glory.
14.43 and with him a *g* multitude
16. 4 rolled away: for it was very *g*.
Lk 1.15 For he shall be *g* in the sight of
32 He shall be *g*, and shall be called
49 hath done to me *g* things; and
58 had shewed *g* mercy upon her;
2. 5 his espoused wife, being *g* with child.
10 I bring you good tidings of *g* joy,
36 she was of a *g* age, and had lived
4.25 when *g* famine was throughout
38 was taken with a *g* fever; and
5. 6 inclosed a *g* multitude of fishes:
15 and *g* multitudes came together
29 Levi made him a *g* feast in his
29 and there was a *g* company
6.17 a *g* multitude of people out of all
23 your reward is *g* in heaven: for
35 and your reward shall be *g*, and
49 and the ruin of that house was *g*.
7. 9 I have not found so *g* faith, no,
16 That a *g* prophet is risen up
8.37 they were taken with *g* fear: and
39 how *g* things God hath done
39 how *g* things Jesus had done unto
9.48 you all, the same shall be *g*.
10. 2 The harvest truly is *g*, but the
13 they had a *g* while ago repented,
13.19 and waxed a *g* tree; and the
14.16 A certain man made a *g* supper,
25 there went *g* multitudes with him:
32 while the other is yet a *g* way off,
15.20 when he was yet a *g* way off,
16.26 there is a *g* gulf fixed: so that
21.11 *g* earthquakes shall be in divers
11 and *g* signs shall there be
23 shall be *g* distress in the land,
27 cloud with power and *g* glory.
22.44 as it were *g* drops of blood
23.27 a *g* company of people, and of
24.52 to Jerusalem with *g* joy:
Jn 5. 3 a *g* multitude of impotent folk,
6. 2 And a *g* multitude followed him,
5 saw a *g* company come unto him,
18 by reason of a *g* wind that blew.
7.37 that *g* day of the feast, Jesus
21.11 the net to land full of *g* fishes,
Ac 2.20 before that *g* and notable day of
4.33 with *g* power gave the apostles
33 and *g* grace was upon them all.
5. 5 and *g* fear came on all them that
11 And *g* fear came upon all the
6. 7 and a *g* company of the priests
8 *g* wonders and miracles among
7.11 and Chanaan, and *g* affliction: and
8. 1 there was a *g* persecution against
2 and made *g* lamentation over him.
8 And there was *g* joy in that city.
9 that himself was some *g* one:
10 This man is the *g* power of God.
27 an eunuch of *g* authority under
9.16 how *g* things he must suffer for
10.11 as it had been a *g* sheet knit at
11. 5 as it had been a *g* sheet, let down
21 and a *g* number believed, and
28 that there should be *g* dearth
14. 1 a *g* multitude both of the Jews
15. 3 they caused *g* joy unto all the
16.26 there was a *g* earthquake, so that
17. 4 devout Greeks a *g* multitude, and
19.27 of the *g* goddess Diana should be
28 *G* is Diana of the Ephesians.
34 out, *G* is Diana of the Ephesians.
35 of the *g* goddess Diana, and of the
21.40 there was made a *g* silence, he
22. 6 shone from heaven a *g* light round
28 With a *g* sum obtained I this
23. 9 And there arose a *g* cry: and the
10 there arose a *g* dissension, the
14 bound ourselves under a *g* curse,
24. 2 by thee we enjoy *g* quietness,
7 with *g* violence took him away
25.23 and Bernice, with *g* pomp, and
26.22 witnessing both to small and *g*,
28. 6 after they had looked a *g* while,
29 *g* reasoning among themselves.
Ro 9. 2 That I have *g* heaviness and
15.23 a *g* desire these many years
1Co 9.11 it is a *g* thing if we shall reap
16. 9 a *g* door and effectual is opened
2Co 1.10 delivered us from so *g* a death,
3.12 we use *g* plainness of speech:
7. 4 *G* is my boldness of speech toward
4 you, *g* is my glorying of you:
8. 2 How that in a *g* trial of affliction
22 diligent, upon the *g* confidence
11.15 it is no *g* thing if his ministers
Eph 2. 4 for his *g* love wherewith he loved
5.32 This is a *g* mystery: but I speak
Col 2. 1 ye knew what *g* conflict I have
4.13 that he hath a *g* zeal for you,
1Th 2.17 to see your face with *g* desire.
1Ti 3.13 and *g* boldness in the faith which
16 *g* is the mystery of godliness:
6. 6 with contentment is *g* gain.
2Ti 2.20 But in a *g* house there are not
Tit 2.13 glorious appearing of the *g* God
Phm 7 have *g* joy and consolation in
Heb 2. 3 if we neglect so *g* salvation;
4.14 that we have a *g* high priest,
7. 4 consider how *g* this man was,
10.32 ye endured a *g* fight of afflictions;
35 hath *g* recompence of reward.
12. 1 with so *g* a cloud of witnesses,
13.20 that *g* shepherd of the sheep,
Jas 3. 4 which though they be so *g*, and
5 member, and boasteth *g* things.
5 *g* a matter a little fire kindleth!
1Pe 3. 4 in the sight of God of *g* price.
2Pe 1. 4 *g* and precious promises:
2.18 speak *g* swelling words of vanity,
3.10 shall pass away with a *g* noise,
Jude 6 unto the judgment of the *g* day.
16 mouth speaketh *g* swelling words,
Rev 1.10 and heard behind me a *g* voice,
2.22 into *g* tribulation, except they
6. 4 was given unto him a *g* sword.
12 and, lo, there was a *g* earthquake;
15 kings of the earth, and the *g* men,
17 the *g* day of his wrath is come;
7. 9 and, lo, a *g* multitude, which no
14 which came out of *g* tribulation,
8. 8 as it were a *g* mountain burning
10 there fell a *g* star from heaven,
9. 2 as the smoke of a *g* furnace; and
14 are bound in the *g* river Euphrates.
11. 8 in the street of the *g* city, which
11 *g* fear fell upon them which saw
12 they heard a *g* voice from heaven
13 hour was there a *g* earthquake,
15 there were *g* voices in heaven,
17 hast taken to thee thy *g* power,
18 that fear thy name, small and *g*;
19 and an earthquake, and *g* hail.
12. 1 a *g* wonder in heaven; a woman
3 *g* red dragon, having seven heads
9 And the *g* dragon was cast out,
12 having *g* wrath, because he
14 two wings of a *g* eagle, that she
13. 2 and his seat, and *g* authority.
5 a mouth speaking *g* things and
13 he doeth *g* wonders, so that he
16 he causeth all, both small and *g*,
14. 2 as the voice of a *g* thunder:
8 that *g* city, because she made
19 into the *g* winepress of the wrath
15. 1 *g* and marvellous, seven angels
3 *G* and marvellous are thy works,
16. 1 I heard a *g* voice out of the temple
9 men were scorched with *g* heat,
12 vial upon the *g* river Euphrates;
14 of that *g* day of God Almighty.
17 came a *g* voice out of the temple
18 there was a *g* earthquake, such as
18 mighty an earthquake, and so *g*.
19 the *g* city was divided into three

Rev 16.19 *g* Babylon came in remembrance
21 upon men a *g* hail out of heaven,
21 plague thereof was exceeding *g*.
17. 1 judgment of the *g* whore that
5 Mystery, Babylon The *G*, The
6 I wondered with *g* admiration.
18 is that *g* city, which reigneth over
18. 1 from heaven, having *g* power;
2 Babylon the *g* is fallen, is fallen,
10 Alas, alas that *g* city Babylon, that
16 Alas, alas that *g* city, that was
17 so *g* riches is come to nought.
18 What city is like unto this *g*
19 Alas, alas that *g* city, wherein
21 took up a stone like a *g* millstone,
21 shall that *g* city Babylon be thrown
23 thy merchants were the *g* men
19. 1 I heard a *g* voice of much people
2 hath judged the *g* whore, which
5 that fear him, both small and *g*.
6 the voice of a *g* multitude, and
17 unto the supper of the *g* God;
18 free and bond, both small and *g*.
20. 1 and a *g* chain in his hand.
11 I saw a *g* white throne, and him
12 I saw the dead, small and *g*,
21. 3 I heard a *g* voice out of heaven
10 spirit to a *g* and high mountain,
10 and shewed me that *g* city,
12 had a wall *g* and high, and had

GREATER

Gen 1.16 the *g* light to rule the day, and
4.13 punishment is *g* than I can bear.
39. 9 none *g* in this house than I;
41.40 throne will I be *g* than thou.
48.19 shall be *g* than he, and his seed
Ex 18.11 the Lord is *g* than all gods:
Nu 14.12 make of thee a *g* nation and
Dt 1.28 The people is *g* and taller than
4.38 thee *g* and mightier than thou art,
7. 1 seven nations *g* and mightier
9. 1 nations *g* and mightier than
14 nation mightier and *g* than they.
11.23 ye shall possess *g* nations and
Jos 10. 2 because it was *g* than Ai, and all
1Sa 14.30 not been now a much *g* slaughter
2Sa 13.15 *g* than the love wherewith he had
16 *g* than the other that thou didst
1Ki 1.37 and make his throne *g* than thee
47 and make his throne *g* than thy
1Ch 11. 9 So David waxed *g* and...: for the
9 and *g*; for the Lord of hosts was
2Ch 3. 5 And the *g* house he cieled with
Est 9. 4 this man Mordecai waxed *g* and
4 this man Mordecai waxed...and *g*.
Job 33.12 thee, that God is *g* than man.
La 4. 6 people is *g* than the punishment
Eze 8. 6 thou shalt see *g* abominations.
13 shalt see *g* abominations that
15 shalt see *g* abominations than
43.14 lesser settle even to the *g* settle
Dan 11.13 a multitude *g* than the former,
Am 6. 2 their border *g* than your border?
Hag 2. 9 house shall be *g* than the former,
Mt 11.11 hath not risen a *g* than John the
11 kingdom of heaven is *g* than he.
12. 6 place is one *g* than the temple.
41 behold, a *g* than Jonas is here.
42 behold, a *g* than Solomon is here.
23.14 ye shall receive the *g* damnation.
17 for whether is *g*, the gold, or the
19 whether is *g*, the gift, or the
Mk 4.32 becometh *g* than all herbs, and
12.31 none other commandment *g* than
40 these shall receive *g* damnation.
Lk 7.28 there is not a *g* prophet than
28 is *g* than he.
11.31 behold, a *g* than Solomon is here.
32 and, behold, a *g* than Jonas is here.
12.18 pull down my barns, and build *g*;
20.47 same shall receive *g* damnation.
22.27 For whether is *g*, he that sitteth
Jn 1.50 thou shalt see *g* things than these.
4.12 Art thou *g* than our father Jacob,
5.20 *g* works than these, that ye may
36 But I have *g* witness than that
8.53 thou *g* than our father Abraham,
10.29 gave them me, is *g* than all; and no
13.16 The servant is not *g* than his lord;
16 neither he that is sent *g* than he
14.12 *g* works than these shall he do;
28 for my Father is *g* than I.
15.13 *G* love hath no man than this,
20 The servant is not *g* than his
19.11 me unto thee hath the *g* sin.
Ac 15.28 to lay upon you no *g* burden than
1Co 14. 5 for *g* is he that prophesieth than
15. 6 *g* part remain unto this present,
Heb 6.13 could swear by no *g*, he sware by
16 for men verily swear by the *g*:
9.11 a *g* and more perfect tabernacle,
11.26 reproach of Christ *g* riches than
Jas 3. 1 shall receive the *g* condemnation.
2Pe 2.11 which are *g* in power and might,
1Jn 3.20 God is *g* than our heart, and
4. 4 because *g* is he that is in you, than
5. 9 of men, the witness of God is *g*:
3Jn 4 I have no *g* joy than to hear that

GREATEST

1Ch 12.14 an hundred, and the *g* over a
29 the *g* part of them had kept the
Job 1. 3 was the *g* of all the men of the
Jer 6.13 the least even unto the *g* of them
8.10 the least even unto the *g* is given
31.34 least of them unto the *g* of them,
42. 1 the least even unto the *g*, came
8 people from the least even to the *g*,
44.12 the least even unto the *g*, by the
Jon 3. 5 the *g* of them even to the least of
Mt 13.32 *g* among herbs, and becometh
18. 1 Who is the *g* in the kingdom of
4 the same is *g* in the kingdom of
23.11 But he that is *g* among you shall
Mk 9.34 themselves, who should be the *g*.
Lk 9.46 which of them should be *g*.
22.24 of them should be accounted the *g*.
26 but he that is *g* among you, let
Ac 8.10 heed, from the least to the *g*,
1Co 13.13 but the *g* of these is charity.
Heb 8.11 know me, from the least to the *g*.

GREATLY

Gen 3.16 I will *g* multiply thy sorrow and
32. 7 Jacob was *g* afraid and distressed:
Ex 19.18 and the whole amount quaked *g*.
Nu 11.10 anger of the Lord was kindled *g*;
Jdg 6. 6 And Israel was *g* impoverished
2Sa 24.10 have sinned *g* in that I have done:
Ps 47. 9 belong unto God: he is *g* exalted.
48. 1 and *g* to be praised in the city
62. 2 defense; I shall not be *g* moved.
89. 7 God is *g* to be feared in the
96. 4 and *g* to be praised: he is to
112. 1 delighteth *g* in his commandments.
145. 3 the Lord, and *g* to be praised;
Isa 61.10 I will *g* rejoice in the Lord, my soul
Dan 10.19 O man *g* beloved, fear not:
Zec 9. 9 Rejoice *g*, O daughter of Zion;
Mt 27.14 that the governor marvelled *g*.
54 they feared *g*, saying, Truly this
Mk 5.23 And besought him *g*, saying, My
38 and them that wept and wailed *g*.
9.15 were *g* amazed, and running to
12.27 the living: ye therefore do *g* err.
Jn 3.29 rejoiceth *g* because of the
Ac 3.11 is called Solomon's, *g* wondering.
6. 7 multiplied in Jerusalem *g*;
1Co 16.12 *g* desired him to come unto you
Php 1. 8 how *g* I long after you all in the
4.10 I rejoiced in the Lord *g*, that now
1Th 3. 6 desiring *g* to see us, as we also
2Ti 1. 4 *G* desiring to see thee, being
4.15 he hath *g* withstood our words.
1Pe 1. 6 Wherein ye *g* rejoice, though now for
2Jn 4 I rejoice *g* that I found of thy
3Jn 3 I rejoiced *g*, when the brethren

GREATNESS

Ex 15. 7 And in the *g* of thine excellency
16 by the *g* of thine arm they
Nu 14.19 unto the *g* of thy mercy,
Dt 3.24 shew thy servant thy *g*, and thy
5.24 his glory and his *g*, and we
9.26 redeemed through thy *g*, which
11. 2 his *g*, his mighty hand, and his
32. 3 Lord: ascribe ye *g* unto our God.
1Ch 17.19 hast thou done all this *g*, in
21 a name of *g* and terribleness,
29.11 Thine, O Lord, is the *g*, and
2Ch 9. 6 the *g* of thy wisdom was not
24.27 and the *g* of the burdens laid
Neh 13.22 according to the *g* of thy mercy.
Est 10. 2 the *g* of Mordecai, whereunto the
Ps 66. 3 through the *g* of thy power shall
71.21 Thou shalt increase my *g*, and
79.11 according to the *g* of thy power
145. 3 and his *g* is unsearchable.
6 acts: and I will declare thy *g*.
150. 2 according to his excellent *g*.
Pr 5.23 and in the *g* of his folly he shall
Isa 40.26 by the *g* of his might, for that
57.10 wearied in the *g* of thy way;
63. 1 travelling in the *g* of his strength?
Jer 13.22 For the *g* of thine iniquity are
Eze 31. 2 Whom art thou like in thy *g*?
7 Thus was he fair in his *g*, in the
18 in glory and in *g* among the trees
Dan 4.22 for thy *g* is grown, and reacheth
7.27 and the *g* of the kingdom under
Eph 1.19 *g* of his power to us-ward who

GREECE

Zec 9.13 O Zion, against thy sons, O *G*,
Ac 20. 2 exhortation, he came into *G*,

GREEDILY

Pr 21.26 He coveteth *g* all the day long:
Eze 22.12 and thou hast *g* gained of thy
Jude 11 ran *g* after the error of Balaam

GREEDINESS

Eph 4.19 to work all uncleanness with *g*.

GREEDY

Ps 17.12 as a lion that is *g* of his prey,
Pr 1.19 every one that is *g* of gain;
15.27 He that is *g* of gain troubleth his
Isa 56.11 they are *g* dogs which can
1Ti 3. 3 no striker, not *g* of filthy lucre;
8 much wine, not *g* of filthy lucre;

GREEK

Mk 7.26 woman was a *G*, a Syrophenician
Lk 23.38 of *G*, and Latin, and Hebrew,
Jn 19.20 in Hebrew, and *G*, and Latin.
Ac 16. 1 believed; but his father was a *G*:
3 knew all that his father was a *G*.
21.37 Who said, Canst thou speak *G*?
Ro 1.16 the Jew first, and also to the *G*.
10.12 between the Jew and the *G*: for
Gal 2. 3 who was with me, being a *G*,
3.28 There is neither Jew nor *G*, there
Col 3.11 there is neither *G* nor Jew,
Rev 9.11 in the *G* tongue hath his name

GREEKS

Jn 12.20 there were certain *G* among
Ac 14. 1 Jews and also of the *G* believed.
17. 4 the devout *G* a great multitude,
12 women which were *G*, and of
18. 4 persuaded the Jews and the *G*.

Biblical Themes

GREED

Thou shalt not covet thy neighbor's house, thou shalt not covet thy neighbor's wife, nor his manservant, nor his maidservant, nor his ox, nor his ass, nor any thing that is thy neighbor's. Ex 20.17

Thou shalt not desire the silver or gold that is on them, nor take it unto thee, lest thou be snared therein. Dt 7.25

And when Jehoshaphat and his people came to take away the spoil of them, they found among them in abundance both riches with the dead bodies, and precious jewels, which they stripped off for themselves, more than they could carry away: and they were three days in gathering of the spoil, it was so much. 2Ch 20.25

The wicked boasteth of his heart's desire, and blesseth the covetous, whom the Lord abhorreth. Ps 10.3

My son, if sinners entice thee, consent thou not. If they say, Come with us, let us lay wait for blood, let us lurk privily for the innocent . . . walk not thou in the way with them. . . . they lay wait for their own blood; they lurk privily for their own lives. So are the ways of every one that is greedy of gain. Pr 1.10-11, 15, 18-19

He that is greedy of gain troubleth his own house; but he that hateth gifts shall live. Pr 15.27

How much better is it to get wisdom than gold! Pr 16.16

Labor not to be rich. . . . Wilt thou set thine eyes upon that which is not? for riches certainly make themselves wings; they fly away as an eagle toward heaven. Pr 23.4-5

He that loveth silver shall not be satisfied with silver; nor he that loveth abundance with increase: this is also vanity. Ec 5.10

The Lord will enter into judgment with the ancients of his people, and the princes thereof: for ye have eaten up the vineyard; the spoil of the poor is in your houses. What mean ye that ye beat my people to pieces, and grind the faces of the poor? Isa 3.14-15

Woe unto them that join house to house, that lay field to field, till there be no place, that they may be placed alone in the midst of the earth! Isa 5.8

They are waxen fat, they shine: yea, they overpass the deeds of the wicked: they judge not the cause, the cause of the fatherless, yet they prosper; and the right of the needy do they not judge. Jer 5.28

As the partridge sitteth on eggs, and hatcheth them not; so he that getteth riches, and not by right, shall leave them in the midst of his days. Jer 17.11

What is a man profited, if he shall gain the whole world, and lose his own soul? or what shall a man give in exchange for his soul? Mt 16.26

The lord of that servant was moved with compassion, and loosed him, and forgave him the debt. But the same servant went out, and found one of his fellowservants, which owed him an hundred pence: and he laid hands on him, and took him by the throat, saying, Pay me that thou owest. Mt 18.27-28

A bishop then must be blameless . . . not greedy of filthy lucre. 1Ti 3.2-3

They that will be rich fall into temptation and a snare. . . . For the love of money is the root of all evil. 1Ti 6.9-10

Be content with such things as ye have: for he hath said, I will never leave thee, nor forsake thee. Heb 13.5

17 the *G* took Sosthenes, the chief
19.10 the Lord Jesus, both Jews and *G*.
17 known to all the Jews and *G* also
20.21 to the Jews, and also to the *G*,
21.28 brought *G* also into the temple,
Ro 1.14 I am debtor both to the *G*, and to
1Co 1.22 and the *G* seek after wisdom:
23 and unto the *G* foolishness;
24 which are called, both Jews and *G*,

GREEN

Gen 1.30 have given every *g* herb for meat:
9. 3 even as the *g* herb have I given
30.37 Jacob took him rods of *g* poplar,
Ex 10.15 there remained not any *g* thing
Lev 2.14 of thy firstfruits *g* ears of corn
23.14 parched corn, nor *g* ears, until
Dt 12. 2 the hills, and under every *g* tree:
Jdg 16. 7 seven *g* withs that were never
8 seven *g* withs which had not been
1Ki 14.23 high hill, and under every *g* tree.
2Ki 16. 4 the hills, and under every *g* tree.
17.10 high hill, and under every *g* tree:
19.26 and as the *g* herb, as the grass on
2Ch 28. 4 the hills, and under every *g* tree.
Est 1. 6 white, *g*, and blue, hangings,
Job 8.16 He is *g* before the sun, and his
15.32 and his branch shall not be *g*.
39. 8 he searcheth after every *g* thing.
Ps 23. 2 me to lie down in *g* pastures:
37. 2 grass, and wither as the *g* herb.
35 himself like a *g* bay tree.
52. 8 am like a *g* olive tree in the house
SS 1.16 yea, pleasant: also our bed is *g*.
2.13 fig tree putteth forth her *g* figs,
Isa 15. 6 grass faileth, there is no *g* thing.
37.27 and as the *g* herb, as the grass
57. 5 under every *g* tree, slaying the
Jer 2.20 under every *g* tree thou wanderest,
3. 6 under every *g* tree, and there hath
13 under every *g* tree, and ye have
11.16 A *g* olive tree, fair, and of goodly
17. 2 the *g* trees upon the high hills.
8 cometh, but her leaf shall be *g*;
Eze 6.13 under every *g* tree, and under
17.24 have dried up the *g* tree, and
20.47 shall devour every *g* tree in thee,
Hos 14. 8 him: I am like a *g* fir tree.
Mk 6.39 by companies upon the *g* grass.
Lk 23.31 they do these things in a *g* tree,
Rev 8. 7 and all *g* grass was burnt up.
9. 4 neither any *g* thing, neither any

GREET

1Sa 25. 5 go to Nabal, and *g* him in
Ro 16. 3 *G* Priscilla and Aquila my
5 Likewise *g* the church that is in
6 *G* Mary; who bestowed much
8 *G* Amplias my beloved in the
11 *G* them that be of the household
1Co 16.20 All the brethren *g* you. *G* ye
2Co 13.12 *G* one another with an holy kiss.
Php 4.21 which are with me *g* you.
Col 4.14 physician, and Demas, *g* you.
1Th 5.26 *G* all the brethren with an holy
Tit 3.15 *G* them that love us in the faith.
1Pe 5.14 *G* ye one another with a kiss of
2Jn 13 of thy elect sister *g* thee.
3Jn 14 thee. *G* the friends by name.

GREETETH

2Ti 4.21 Eubulus *g* thee, and Pudens,

GREETING

Ac 15.23 send *g* unto the brethren which
23.26 excellent governor Felix sendeth *g*.
Jas 1. 1 which are scattered abroad, *g*.

GREETINGS

Mt 23. 7 And *g* in the markets, and to be
Lk 11.43 synagogues and *g* in the markets.
20.46 love *g* in the markets, and the

GREW

Gen 2. 5 herb of the field before it *g*:
19.25 that which *g* upon the ground.
21. 8 the child *g*, and was weaned:
20 God was with the lad: and he *g*,
25.27 And the boys *g*: and Esau was
26.13 *g* until he became very great:
47.27 had possession therein, and *g*,
Ex 1.12 the more they multiplied and *g*.
2.10 And the child *g*, and she brought
Jdg 11. 2 and his wife's sons *g* up, and they
13.24 and the child *g*, and the Lord
1Sa 2.21 child Samuel *g* before the Lord.
26 the child Samuel *g* on, and was
3.19 And Samuel *g*, and the Lord was
2Sa 5.10 And David went on and *g* great,
12. 3 it *g* up together with him, and
Eze 17. 6 *g*, and became a spreading vine
10 wither in the furrows where it *g*.
Dan 4.11 The tree *g*, and was strong, and
20 tree that thou sawest, which *g*,
Mk 4. 7 thorns *g* up, and choked it, and it
5.26 bettered, but rather *g* worse,
Lk 1.80 And the child *g*, and waxed strong
2.40 And the child *g*, and waxed strong
13.19 it *g*, and waxed a great tree;

Ac 7.17 people *g* and multiplied in Egypt,
12.24 the word of God *g* and multiplied.
19.20 So mightily *g* the word of God

GRIEF

Gen 26.35 Which were a *g* of mind unto Isaac
1Sa 1.16 complaint and *g* have I spoken
25.31 this shall be no *g* unto thee, nor
2Ch 6.29 his own sore and his own *g*,
Job 2.13 saw that his *g* was very great.
6. 2 my *g* were thoroughly weighed,
16. 5 of my lips should asswage your *g*.
6 I speak, my *g* is not asswaged:
Ps 6. 7 eye is consumed because of *g*;
31. 9 mine eye is consumed with *g*, yea,
10 For my life is spent with *g*,
69.26 they talk to the *g* of those whom
Pr 17.25 A foolish son is a *g* to his father,
Ec 1.18 For in much wisdom is much *g*:
2.23 days are sorrows, and his travail *g*;
Isa 17.11 shall be a heap in the day of *g*
53. 3 sorrows, and acquainted with *g*:
10 he hath put him to *g*: when thou
Jer 6. 7 before me continually is *g* and
10.19 Truly this is a *g*, and I must bear
45. 3 Lord hath added *g* to my sorrow;
La 3.32 though he cause *g*, yet will he
Jon 4. 6 head, to deliver him from his *g*.
2Co 2. 5 if any have caused *g*, he hath
Heb 13.17 do it with joy, and not with *g*:
1Pe 2.19 conscience toward God endure *g*,

GRIEFS

Isa 53. 4 hath borne our *g*, and carried our

GRIEVE

1Sa 2.33 thine eyes, and to *g* thine heart:
1Ch 4.10 from evil, that it may not *g* me!
Ps 78.40 wilderness, and *g* him in the desert!
La 3.33 willingly nor *g* the children of
Eph 4.30 And *g* not the holy spirit of God,

GRIEVED

Gen 6. 6 and it *g* him at his heart,
34. 7 and the men were *g*, and they were
45. 5 be not *g*, nor angry with yourselves,
49.23 The archers have sorely *g* him,
Ex 1.12 And they were *g* because of the
Dt 15.10 thine heart shall not be *g* when
Jdg 10.16 soul was *g* for the misery of Israel.
1Sa 1. 8 thou not? and why is thy heart *g*?
15.11 it *g* Samuel; and he cried unto
20. 3 Jonathan know this, lest he be *g*:
34 was *g* for David, because his father
30. 6 the soul of all the people was *g*,
2Sa 19. 2 the king was *g* for his son.
Neh 2.10 it *g* them exceedingly that there
8.11 the day is holy; neither be ye *g*.
13. 8 And it *g* me sore: therefore I cast
Est 4. 4 was the queen exceedingly *g*;
Job 4. 2 with thee, wilt thou be *g*?
30.25 was not my soul *g* for the poor?
Ps 73.21 Thus my heart was *g*, and I was
95.10 Forty years long was I *g* with
112.10 The wicked shall see it, and be *g*;
119.158 the transgressors, and was *g*;
139.21 am not I *g* with those that rise up
Isa 54. 6 thee as a woman forsaken and *g*
57.10 hand; therefore thou wast not *g*.
Jer 5. 3 have not *g*; thou hast consumed
Dan 7.15 I Daniel was *g* in my spirit
11.30 he shall be *g*, and return.
Am 6. 6 they are not *g* for the affliction
Mk 3. 5 *g* for the hardness of their hearts,
10.22 at that saying, and went away *g*:
Jn 21.17 Peter was *g* because he said unto
Ac 4. 2 *g* that they taught the people,
16.18 Paul, being *g*, turned and said to
Ro 14.15 if thy brother be *g* with thy meat,
2Co 2. 4 not that ye should be *g*, but that
5 he hath not *g* me, but in part:
Heb 3.10 I was *g* with that generation,
17 with whom was he *g* forty years?

GRIEVOUS

Gen 12.10 the famine was *g* in the land.
18.20 and because their sin is very *g*;
21.11 the thing was very *g* in Abraham's
12 Let it not be *g* in thy sight because
41.31 following; for it shall be very *g*.
50.11 is a *g* mourning to the Egyptians:
Ex 8.24 there came a *g* swarm of flies
9. 3 there shall be a very *g* murrain.
18 will cause it to rain a very *g* hail,
24 fire mingled with the hail, very *g*.
10.14 coasts of Egypt: very *g* were they;
1Ki 2. 8 cursed me with a *g* curse in the
12. 4 Thy father made our yoke *g*:
4 thou the *g* service of thy father,
2Ch 10. 4 Thy father made our yoke *g*: now
4 the *g* servitude of thy father,
Ps 10. 5 His ways are always *g*; thy
31.18 be put to silence; which speak *g*
Pr 15. 1 wrath: but *g* words stir up anger.
10 Correction is *g* unto him that

BIBLICAL THEMES

GRIEF

And Jacob rent his clothes, and put sackcloth upon his loins, and mourned for his son many days. Gen 37.34

Ye shall bring down my gray hairs with sorrow to the grave. Gen 44.29

[David] said, While the child was yet alive, I fasted and wept: for I said, Who can tell whether God will be gracious to me, that the child may live? But now he is dead, wherefore should I fast? can I bring him back again? I shall go to him, but he shall not return to me. 2Sa 12.22-23

And the king was much moved, and went up to the chamber over the gate, and wept: and as he went, thus he said, O my son Absalom, my son, my son Absalom! would God I had died for thee, O Absalom, my son, my son! 2Sa 18.33

The Lord gave, and the Lord hath taken away; blessed be the name of the Lord. Job 1.21

Precious in the sight of the Lord is the death of his saints. Ps 116.15

Out of the depths have I cried unto thee, O Lord. Lord, hear my voice. Ps 130.1-2

He healeth the broken in heart, and bindeth up their wounds. Ps 147.3

In much wisdom is much grief: and he that increaseth knowledge increaseth sorrow. Ec 1.18

A time to weep, and a time to laugh; a time to mourn, and a time to dance. Ec 3.4

They shall obtain gladness and joy; and sorrow and mourning shall flee away. Isa 51.11

Thy sun shall no more go down; neither shall thy moon withdraw itself: for the Lord shall be thine everlasting light, and the days of thy mourning shall be ended. Isa 60.20

Consider ye, and call for the mourning women, that they may come. . . . And let them make haste, and take up a wailing for us, that our eyes may run down with tears, and our eyelids gush out with waters. . . . For death is come up into our windows, and is entered into our palaces, to cut off the children from without, and the young men from the streets. Jer 9.17-18, 21

Blessed are they that mourn: for they shall be comforted. Mt 5.4

Let not your heart be troubled. . . . In my Father's house are many mansions: if it were not so, I would have told you. I go to prepare a place for you. And if I go and prepare a place for you, I will come again, and receive you unto myself; that where I am, there ye may be also. Jn 14.1-3

Mary stood without at the sepulcher weeping. Jn 20.11

O death, where is thy sting? O grave, where is thy victory? 1Co 15.55

Sorrow not. . . . For if we believe that Jesus died and rose again, even so them also which sleep in Jesus will God bring with him. 1Th 4.13-14

And I heard a voice from heaven saying unto me, Write, Blessed are the dead which die in the Lord from henceforth: Yea, saith the Spirit, that they may rest from their labors; and their works do follow them. Rev 14.13

God shall wipe away all tears from their eyes. Rev 21.4

Ec 2.17 under the sun is *g* unto me: for
Isa 15. 4 out; his life shall be *g* unto him.
21. 2 A *g* vision is declared unto me;
Jer 6.28 They are all *g* revolters,
10.19 for my hurt! my wound is *g*:
14.17 a great breach, with a very *g* blow.
16. 4 They shall die of *g* deaths; they
23.19 in fury, even a *g* whirlwind:
30.12 incurable, and thy wound is *g*.
Na 3.19 thy wound is *g*: all that hear
Mt 23. 4 heavy burdens and *g* to be borne,
Lk 11.46 with burdens *g* to be borne, and ye
Ac 20.29 shall *g* wolves enter in among you,
25. 7 and *g* complaints against Paul,
Php 3. 1 to me indeed is not *g*, but for
Heb 12.11 seemeth to be joyous, but *g*:
1Jn 5. 3 and his commandments are not *g*.
Rev 16. 2 noisome and *g* sore upon the men

GRIEVOUSLY
Isa 9. 1 afterward did more *g* afflict her
Jer 23.19 whirlwind: it shall fall *g* upon
La 1. 8 Jerusalem hath *g* sinned;
20 for I have *g* rebelled: abroad the
Eze 14.13 against me by trespassing *g*,
Mt 8. 6 sick of the palsy, *g* tormented.
15.22 daughter is *g* vexed with a devil.

GRIND
Jdg 16.21 and he did *g* in the prison house.
Job 31.10 Then let my wife *g* unto another,
Isa 3.15 pieces, and *g* the faces of the poor?
47. 2 Take the millstones, and *g* meal:
La 5.13 They took the young men to *g*,
Mt 21.44 shall fall, it will *g* him to powder.
Lk 20.18 shall fall, it will *g* him to powder.

GRINDERS
Ec 12. 3 the *g* cease because they are few,

GRINDING
Ec 12. 4 when the sound of the *g* is low,
Mt 24.41 Two women shall be *g* at the mill;
Lk 17.35 Two women shall be *g* together;

GROAN
Job 24.12 Men *g* from out of the city,
Jer 51.52 all her land the wounded shall *g*.
Eze 30.24 he shall *g* before him with the
Joel 1.18 How do the beasts *g*! the herds
Ro 8.23 we ourselves *g* within ourselves,
2Co 5. 2 in this we *g*, earnestly desiring to
4 we that are in this tabernacle do *g*,

GROANED
Jn 11.33 *g* in the spirit, and was troubled,

GROANETH
Ro 8.22 *g* and travaileth in pain together

GROANING
Ex 2.24 And God heard their *g*, and God
6. 5 And I have also heard the *g* of the
Job 23. 2 my stroke is heavier than my *g*.
Ps 6. 6 I am weary with my *g*; all the
38. 9 and my *g* is not hid from thee.
102. 5 By reason of the voice of my *g* my
20 To hear the *g* of the prisoner;
Jn 11.38 therefore again *g* in himself
Ac 7.34 and I have heard their *g*, and

GROANINGS
Jdg 2.18 because of their *g* by reason of
Eze 30.24 the *g* of a deadly wounded man.
Ro 8.26 with *g* which cannot be uttered.

GROUND
Gen 2. 5 there was not a man to till the *g*.
6 and watered the whole face of the *g*.
7 formed man of the dust of the *g*,
9 out of the *g* made the Lord God to
3.17 cursed is the *g* for thy sake;
4. 2 but Cain was a tiller of the *g*.
8.13 behold, the face of the *g* was dry.
21 I will not again curse the *g* any
Ex 3. 5 whereon thou standest is holy *g*.
14.16 shall go on dry *g* through the
Jos 3.17 Israelites passed over on dry *g*,
1Sa 3.19 let none of his words fall to the *g*.
14.45 one hair of his head fall to the *g*;
2Ki 2. 8 so that they two went over on dry *g*,
Neh 10.35 to bring the firstfruits of our *g*,
Job 2.13 they sat down with him upon the *g*
18.10 The snare is laid for him in the *g*,
38.27 To satisfy the desolate and waste *g*;
Ps 147. 6 casteth the wicked down to the *g*.
Isa 21. 9 her gods he hath broken unto the *g*.
29. 4 familiar spirit, out of the *g*, and
35. 7 parched *g* shall become a pool,
Jer 4. 3 Break up your fallow *g*, and sow
La 2. 9 Her gates are sunk into the *g*;
10 sit upon the *g*, and keep silence:
21 the old lie on the *g* in the streets:
Eze 19.13 wilderness, in a dry and thirsty *g*.
38.20 every wall shall fall to the *g*.
Dan 8.10 the host and of the stars to the *g*,
12 it cast down the truth to the *g*;
Hos 10.12 mercy; break up your fallow *g*:
Ob 3 shall bring me down to the *g*?
Mt 10.29 shall not fall on the *g* without
13. 8 But other fell into good *g*, and
23 received seed into the good *g* is he
15.35 multitude to sit down on the *g*.
Mk 4. 5 And some fell on stony *g*, where it
8 other fell on good *g*, and did
16 which are sown on stony *g*, who,
20 they which are sown on good *g*;
26 man should cast seed into the *g*;
8. 6 people to sit down on the *g*:
9.20 he fell on the *g*, and wallowed
14.35 fell on the *g*, and prayed that, if it
Lk 8. 8 other fell on good *g*, and sprang
15 But that on the good *g* are they,
12.16 *g* of a certain rich man brought
13. 7 down; why cumbereth it the *g*?
14.18 I have bought a piece of *g*, and I,
19.44 shall lay thee even with the *g*,
22.44 of blood falling down to the *g*.
Jn 4. 5 near to the parcel of *g* that Jacob
8. 6 with his finger wrote on the *g*,
8 stooped down, and wrote on the *g*.
9. 6 he spat on the *g*, and made clay
12.24 a corn of wheat fall into the *g*
18. 6 went backward, and fell to the *g*.
Ac 7.33 where thou standest is holy *g*.
22. 7 I fell unto the *g*, and heard
1Ti 3.15 the pillar and *g* of the truth.

GROUNDED
Isa 30.32 every place where the *g* staff
Eph 3.17 ye, being rooted and *g* in love,
Col 1.23 continue in the faith *g* and settled,

GROW
Gen 2. 9 the Lord God to *g* every tree
48.16 and let them *g* into a multitude
Nu 6. 5 locks of the hair of his head *g*.
Jdg 16.22 the hair of his head began to *g*
2Sa 23. 5 although he make it not to *g*.
2Ki 19.29 such things as *g* of themselves,
Ezr 4.22 why should damage *g* to the hurt
Job 8.11 Can the rush *g* up without mire?
11 can the flag *g* without water?
19 out of the earth shall others *g*.
14.19 washest away the things which *g*
31.40 Let thistles *g* instead of wheat,
39. 4 good liking, they *g* up with corn;
Ps 92.12 shall *g* like a cedar in Lebanon.
104.14 causeth the grass to *g* for the
147. 8 who maketh grass to *g* upon the
Ec 11. 5 how the bones do *g* in the womb of her
Isa 11. 1 Branch shall *g* out of his roots:
17.11 shalt thou make thy plant to *g*,
53. 2 For he shall *g* up before him
Jer 12. 2 they have taken root: they *g*, yea,
33.15 Branch of righteousness to *g* up
Eze 44.20 nor suffer their locks to *g* long;
47.12 this side and on that side, shall *g*
Hos 14. 5 he shall *g* as the lily, and cast
7 as the corn, and *g* as the vine:
Jon 4.10 neither madest it *g*; which came
Zec 6.12 he shall *g* up out of his place,
Mal 4. 2 and *g* up as calves of the stall.
Mt 6.28 the lilies of the field, how they *g*;
13.30 both *g* together until the harvest:
21.19 no fruit *g* on thee henceforward
Mk 4.27 the seed should spring and *g* up,
Lk 12.27 Consider the lilies how they *g*:
Ac 5.24 of them whereunto this would *g*.
Eph 4.15 may *g* up into him in all things,
1Pe 2. 2 the word, that ye may *g* thereby:
2Pe 3.18 *g* in grace, and in the knowledge

GROWETH
Ex 10. 5 every tree which *g* for you out of
Lev 13.39 freckled spot that *g* in the skin;
25. 5 That which *g* of its own accord
11 reap that which *g* of itself in it,
Dt 29.23 beareth, nor any grass *g* therein,
Jdg 19. 9 the day *g* to an end, lodge here,
Job 38.38 When the dust *g* into hardness,
Ps 90. 5 they are like grass which *g* up.
6 morning it flourisheth, and *g* up;
129. 6 which withereth afore it *g* up:
Isa 37.30 eat this year such as *g* of itself;
Mk 4.32 when it is sown, it *g* up, and
Eph 2.21 *g* unto an holy temple in the Lord:
2Th 1. 3 that your faith *g* exceedingly,

GROWN
Gen 38.11 house, till Shelah my son be *g*:
14 she saw that Shelah was *g*, and
Ex 2.11 when Moses was *g*, that he went
9.32 smitten: for they were not *g* up.
Lev 13.37 there is black hair *g* up therein;
Dt 32.15 thou art waxen fat, thou art *g* thick,
Ru 1.13 tarry for them till they were *g*?
2Sa 10. 5 until your beards be *g*, and then
1Ki 12. 8 that were *g* up with him, and
10 that were *g* up with him spake
2Ki 4.18 And when the child was *g*, it fell
19.26 as corn blasted before it be *g* up.
1Ch 19. 5 at Jericho until your beards be *g*,
Ezr 9. 6 our trespass is *g* up unto the
Ps 144.12 as plants *g* up in their youth;
Pr 24.31 it was all *g* over with thorns,
Isa 37.27 as corn blasted before it be *g* up.
Jer 50.11 are *g* fat as the heifer at grass,
Eze 16. 7 are fashioned, and thine hair is *g*,
Dan 4.22 that are *g* and become strong:
22 for thy greatness is *g*,
33 till his hairs were *g* like eagles'
Mt 13.32 when it is *g*, it is the greatest

GROWTH
Am 7. 1 the shooting up of the latter *g*;
1 and, lo, it was the latter *g* after

GRUDGE
Lev 19.18 bear any *g* against the children
Ps 59.15 and *g* if they be not satisfied.
Jas 5. 9 *G* not one against another,

GRUDGING
1Pe 4. 9 one to another without *g*.

GRUDGINGLY
2Co 9. 7 not *g*, or of necessity:

GUEST
Lk 19. 7 gone to be *g* with a man that is

GUESTCHAMBER
Mk 14.14 The Master saith, Where is the *g*,
Lk 22.11 saith unto thee, Where is the *g*,

GUESTS
1Ki 1.41 Adonijah and all the *g* that were
49 the *g* that were with Adonijah
Pr 9.18 her *g* are in the depths of hell.
Zep 1. 7 a sacrifice, he hath bid his *g*.
Mt 22.10 the wedding was furnished with *g*.
11 when the king came to see the *g*,

GUIDE
Job 38.32 canst thou *g* Arcturus with his
Ps 25. 9 The meek will he *g* in judgment:
31. 3 name's sake lead me, and *g* me.
32. 8 I will *g* thee with mine eye.
48.14 he will be our *g* even unto death.
55.13 my *g*, and mine acquaintance.
73.24 Thou shalt *g* me with thy counsel,
112. 5 will *g* his affairs with discretion.
Pr 2.17 forsaketh the *g* of her youth,
6. 7 having no *g*, overseer, or ruler,
11. 3 of the upright shall *g* them:
23.19 and *g* thine heart in the way.
Isa 49.10 springs of water shall he *g* them.
51.18 There is none to *g* her among all
58.11 And the Lord shall *g* thee
Jer 3. 4 thou art the *g* of my youth?
Mic 7. 5 put ye not confidence in a *g*:
Lk 1.79 *g* our feet into the way of peace.
Jn 16.13 he will *g* you into all truth:
Ac 1.16 was *g* to them that took Jesus.
8.31 except some man should *g* me?
Ro 2.19 art a *g* of the blind, a light of
1Ti 5.14 *g* the house, give none occasion

GUIDES
Mt 23.16 Woe unto you, ye blind *g*, which
24 Ye blind *g*, which strain at a gnat

GUILE
Ex 21.14 to slay him with *g*; thou shalt
Ps 32. 2 in whose spirit there is no *g*.
34.13 and thy lips from speaking *g*.
55.11 deceit and *g* depart not from her
Jn 1.47 Israelite indeed, in whom is no *g*!
2Co 12.16 being crafty, I caught you with *g*.
1Th 2. 3 nor of uncleanness, nor in *g*:
1Pe 2. 1 laying aside all malice, and all *g*,
22 neither was *g* found in his mouth:
3.10 his lips that they speak no *g*:
Rev 14. 5 in their mouth was found no *g*:

GUILT
Dt 19.13 shalt put away the *g* of innocent
21. 9 put away the *g* of innocent blood

GUILTLESS
Ex 20. 7 the Lord will not hold him *g*
Nu 5.31 the man be *g* from iniquity,
32.22 be *g* before the Lord, and before
Dt 5.11 the Lord will not hold him *g*
Jos 2.19 upon his head, and we will be *g*:
1Sa 26. 9 the Lord's anointed, and be *g*?
2Sa 3.28 I and my kingdom are *g*
14. 9 the king and his throne be *g*.
1Ki 2. 9 hold him not *g*: for thou art
Mt 12. 7 would not have condemned the *g*.

BIBLICAL THEMES

GUILT

And the Lord God called unto Adam, and said unto him, Where art thou? And he said, I heard thy voice in the garden, and I was afraid, because I was naked; and I hid myself. Gen 3.9-10

And they said one to another, We are verily guilty concerning our brother, in that we saw the anguish of his soul, when he besought us, and we would not hear; therefore is this distress come upon us. Gen 42.21

Be sure your sin will find you out. Nu 32.23

I have transgressed the commandment of the Lord, and thy words: because I feared the people, and obeyed their voice. 1Sa 15.24

And Nathan said to David, Thou art the man. 2Sa 12.7

O my God, I am ashamed and blush to lift up my face to thee. Ezr 9.6

If I justify myself, mine own mouth shall condemn me. Job 9.20

Mine iniquities are gone over mine head: as an heavy burden they are too heavy for me. Ps 38.4

Wash me throughly from mine iniquity, and cleanse me from my sin. For I acknowledge my transgressions: and my sin is ever before me. Ps 51.2-3

God looked down from heaven upon the children of men, to see if there were any that did understand, that did seek God. Every one of them is gone back: they are altogether become filthy; there is none that doeth good, no, not one. Ps 53.2-3

The sinners . . . are afraid; fearfulness hath surprised the hypocrites. Isa 33.14

Thou art become guilty in thy blood that thou hast shed; and hast defiled thyself in thine idols which thou hast made; and thou hast caused thy days to draw near, and art come even unto thy years: therefore have I made thee a reproach unto the heathen, and a mocking to all countries. Eze 22.4

Then the king's countenance was changed, and his thoughts troubled him. Dan 5.6

Take me up, and cast me forth into the sea . . . for I know that for my sake this great tempest is upon you. Jon 1.12

And [Judas] cast down the pieces of silver in the temple, and departed, and went and hanged himself. Mt 27.5

Then answered all the people, and said, His blood be on us, and on our children. Mt 27.25

Simon Peter . . . fell down at Jesus' knees, saying, Depart from me; for I am a sinful man, O Lord. Lk 5.8

And the Lord turned, and looked upon Peter. And Peter remembered the word of the Lord, how he had said unto him, Before the cock crow, thou shalt deny me thrice. And Peter went out, and wept bitterly. Lk 22.61-62

So when they continued asking [Jesus], he lifted up himself, and said unto them, He that is without sin among you, let him first cast a stone at her. . . . And they which heard it, being convicted by their own conscience, went out one by one. Jn 8.7, 9

I delight in the law of God . . . but I see another law in my members, warring against the law of my mind, and bringing me into captivity to the law of sin which is in my members. O wretched man that I am! who shall deliver me from the body of this death? Ro 7.22-24

Let us draw near with a true heart in full assurance of faith, having our hearts sprinkled from an evil conscience, and our bodies washed with pure water. Heb 10.22

GUILTY
Gen 42.21 verily *g* concerning our brother,
Lev 4.13 should not be done, and are *g*;
22 should not be done, and is *g*;
27 ought not to be done, and be *g*;
5. 2 he also shall be unclean, and *g*.
3 knoweth of it, then he shall be *g*.
4 then he shall be *g* in one of these.
5 he shall be *g* in one of these things,
17 he wist it not, yet is he *g*,
6. 4 he hath sinned, and is *g*, that he
Nu 5. 6 the Lord, and that person be *g*;
14.18 and by no means clearing the *g*,
35.27 he shall not be *g* of blood:
31 a murderer, which is *g* of death:
Jdg 21.22 at this time, that ye should be *g*.
Ezr 10.19 wives; and being *g*, they offered
Pr 30.10 curse thee, and thou be found *g*.
Eze 22. 4 Thou art become *g* in thy blood.
Zec 11. 5 hold themselves not *g*: and they
Mt 23.18 gift that is upon it, he is *g*.
26.66 and said, He is *g* of death.
Mk 14.64 condemned him to be *g* of death.
Ro 3.19 world may become *g* before God.
1Co 11.27 shall be *g* of the body and blood
Jas 2.10 offend in one point, he is *g* of all.

GULF
Lk 16.26 and you there is a great *g* fixed:

GUSHED
1Ki 18.28 till the blood *g* out upon them.
Ps 78.20 that the waters *g* out, and the
105.41 and the waters *g* out; they ran in
Isa 48.21 rock also, and the waters *g* out.
Ac 1.18 midst, and all his bowels *g* out.

H

HABAKKUK

Hab 1. 1 The burden which *H* the prophet
3. 1 A prayer of *H* the prophet upon

HABITATION

Ex 15. 2 and I will prepare him an *h*;
Dt 26.15 Look down from thy holy *h*,
Ez 7.15 Israel, whose *h* is in Jerusalem,
Job 8. 6 *h* of thy righteousness prosperous.
Ps 26. 8 I have loved the *h* of thy house,
68. 5 the widows, is God in his holy *h*.
69.25 Let their *h* be desolate; and let
71. 3 Be thou my strong *h*, whereunto
91. 9 refuge, even the most High, thy *h*;
132. 5 *h* for the mighty God of Jacob.
Pr 3.33 but he blesseth the *h* of the just.
Isa 33.20 eyes shall see Jerusalem a quiet *h*,
34.13 and it shall be an *h* of dragons,
35. 7 in the *h* of dragons, where each
Jer 31.23 O *h* of justice, and mountain of
Hab 3.11 and moon stood still in their *h*:
Ac 1.20 Let his *h* be desolate, and let no
17.26 and the bounds of their *h*;
Eph 2.22 for an *h* of God through the
Jude 6 but left their own *h*, he hath
Rev 18. 2 and is become the *h* of devils,

HABITATIONS

Gen 36.43 according to their *h* in the land of
49. 5 of cruelty are in their *h*.
Ex 12.20 in all your *h* shall ye eat
35. 3 kindle no fire throughout your *h*
Lev 23.17 Ye shall bring out of your *h* two
Nu 15. 2 the land of your *h*, which I give
1Ch 4.33 These were their *h*, and their
41 the *h* that were found there,
7.28 possessions and *h* were, Beth-el
Ps 74.20 are full of the *h* of cruelty.
78.28 their camp, round about their *h*.
Isa 54. 2 forth the curtains of thine *h*:
Jer 9.10 and for the *h* of the wilderness
21.13 or who shall enter into our *h*?
25.37 the peaceable *h* are cut down
49.20 he shall make their *h* desolate
La 2. 2 swallowed up all the *h* of Jacob,
Eze 6.14 toward Diblath, in all their *h*:
Am 1. 2 *h* of the shepherds shall mourn,
Lk 16. 9 receive you into everlasting *h*.

HAGGAI

Ezr 5. 1 the prophets, *H* the prophet, and
6.14 through the prophesying of *H* the
Hag 1. 1 the Lord by *H* the prophet unto
3 the Lord by *H* the prophet, saying,
12 and the words of *H* the prophet, as
13 Then spake *H* the Lord's
2. 1, 10 of the Lord by the prophet *H*,
13 Then said *H*, If one that is unclean
14 Then answered *H*, and said, So is
20 came unto *H* in the four and

HAIL

Ex 9.18 to rain a very grievous *h*, such as
19 the *h* shall come down upon them,
22 that there may be *h* in all the
23 the Lord sent thunder and *h*, and
23 rained *h* upon the land of Egypt.
24 was *h*, and fire mingled with the *h*,
25 the *h* smote throughout all the
25 the *h* smote every herb of the field,
26 of Israel were, was there no *h*.
28 more mighty thunderings and *h*;
29 neither shall there be any more *h*;
33 the thunders and *h* ceased, and
34 saw that the rain and the *h* and
10. 5 remaineth unto you from the *h*,
12 even all that the *h* hath left.
15 of the trees which the *h* had left:
Job 38.22 thou seen the treasures of the *h*,
Ps 18.12 thick clouds passed, *h* stones and
13 his voice; *h* stones and coals of
78.47 He destroyed their vines with *h*,
48 He gave up their cattle...to the *h*,
105.32 He gave them *h* for rain, and
148. 8 Fire, and *h*; snow, and vapors;
Isa 28. 2 as a tempest of *h* and a destroying
17 the *h* shall sweep away the refuge
32.19 When it shall *h*, coming down on
Hag 2.17 with mildew and with *h* in all the
Mt 26.49 and said, *H*, master; and kissed
27.29 mocked him, saying, *H*, King of the
28. 9 Jesus met them, saying, All *h*.
Mk 15.18 salute him, *H*, King of the Jews!
Lk 1.28 *H*, thou that art highly favored,
Jn 19. 3 And said, *H*, King of the Jews!
Rev 8. 7 followed *h* and fire mingled with
11.19 and an earthquake, and great *h*.
16.21 there fell upon men a great *h* out
21 because of the plague of the *h*;

HAILSTONES

Jos 10.11 more which died with *h* than
Isa 30.30 scattering, and tempest, and *h*.
Eze 13.11 ye, O great *h*, shall fall; and a
13 and great *h* in my fury to
38.22 and great *h*, fire, and brimstone.

HAIR

Lev 14. 9 he shall shave all his *h* off his head
Nu 6.19 of the Nazarite, after the *h* of his
Jdg 16.22 the *h* of his head began to grow
20.16 could sling stones at an *h* breadth,
1Sa 14.45 there shall not one *h* of his head
2Sa 14.26 because the *h* was heavy on him,
Job 4.15 the *h* of my flesh stood up:
Isa 50. 6 to them that plucked off the *h*:
Jer 7.29 Cut off thine *h*, O Jerusalem, and
Eze 5. 1 balances to weigh and divide the *h*.
Dan 3.27 nor was an *h* of their head singed,
Mt 3. 4 John had his raiment of camel's *h*,
5.36 canst not make on *h* white or
Mk 1. 6 John was clothed with camel's *h*,
21.18 But there shall not an *h* of your
Jn 11. 2 and wiped his feet with her *h*,
12. 3 wiped his feet with her *h*:
Ac 27.34 an *h* fall from the head
1Co 11.14 if a man have long *h*, it is a
15 But if a woman have long *h*, it is a
15 for her *h* is given her for a
1Ti 2. 9 not with broided *h*, or gold, or
1Pe 3. 3 of plaiting the *h*, and of wearing
Rev 6.12 black as sackcloth of *h*,
9. 8 And they had *h* as the *h* of

HAIRS

Gen 42.38 bring down my gray *h* with sorrow
44.29 bring down my gray *h* with sorrow
31 the gray *h* of thy servant our father
Lev 13.21 no white *h* therein, and if it be
Dt 32.25 suckling also with the man of gray *h*.
Ps 40.12 they are more than the *h* of mine
69. 4 cause are more than the *h* of mine
Isa 46. 4 even to hoar *h* will I carry you:
Dan 4.33 his *h* were grown like eagles'
Hos 7. 9 gray *h* are here and there upon him,
Mt 10.30 the very *h* of your head are all
Lk 7.38 wipe them with the *h* of her head,
44 wiped them with the *h* of her head.
12. 7 But even the very *h* of your head
Rev 1.14 His head and his *h* were white

HAIRY

Gen 25.25 red, all over like an *h* garment;
27.11 Esau my brother is a *h* man, and
23 because his hands were *h*, as his
2Ki 1. 8 answered him, He was an *h*
Ps 68.21 the *h* scalp of such an one as goeth

HALE

Lk 12.58 lest he *h* thee to the judge,

HALF

Lev 6.20 *h* of it in the morning, and *h*
Nu 32.33 and unto *h* the tribe of Manasseh
2Sa 10. 4 shaved off the one *h* of their beards,
1Ki 3.25 give *h* to the one, and *h* to the
10. 7 the *h* was not told me: thy wisdom
Neh 4.16 the *h* of my servants wrought in
16 and the other *h* of them held
21 *h* of them held the spears
Est 5. 3 given thee to the *h* of the kingdom.
Ps 55.23 shall not live out *h* their days;
Dan 12. 7 for a time, times, and an *h*; and
Mk 6.23 it thee, unto the *h* of my kingdom.
Lk 10.30 departed, leaving him *h* dead.
19. 8 the *h* of my goods I give to the
Rev 8. 1 about the space of *h* an hour.
11. 9 three days and an *h*, and shall not
11 three days and an *h* the Spirit of life
12.14 a time, and times, and *h* a time,

HALL

Mt 27.27 took Jesus into the common *h*,
Mk 15.16 led him away into the *h*,
Lk 22.55 a fire in the midst of the *h*, and
Jn 18.28 led...unto the *h* of judgment:
28 went not into the judgment *h*,
33 Pilate entered...the judgment *h*
19. 9 went again into the judgment *h*,
Ac 23.35 to be kept in Herod's judgment *h*.

HALLOW

Ex 28.38 the children of Israel shall *h* in
29. 1 to *h* them, to minister unto me
40. 9 and shalt *h* it, and all the vessels
Lev 16.19 cleanse it, and *h* it from the
22. 2 those things which they *h* unto me:
3 which the children of Israel *h* unto
32 I am the Lord which *h* you,
25.10 And ye shall *h* the fiftieth year,
Nu 6.11 and shall *h* his head that same day.
1Ki 8.64 same day did the king *h* the middle
Jer 17.22 but *h* ye the sabbath day, as I
24 but *h* the sabbath day, to do no
27 to *h* the sabbath day, and not to
Eze 20.20 *h* my sabbaths; and they shall be
44.24 and they shall *h* my sabbaths.

HALLOWED

Ex 20.11 blessed the sabbath day, and *h* it.
29.21 and he shall be *h*, and his garments,
Lev 12. 4 she shall touch no *h* thing, nor
19. 8 profaned the *h* thing of the Lord:
22.32 I will be *h* among the children
Nu 3.13 I *h* unto me all the firstborn
5.10 every man's *h* things shall be his:
16.37 the fire yonder; for they are *h*.
38 therefore they are *h*: and they
18. 8 all the *h* things of the children of
29 even the *h* part thereof out of it.
Dt 26.13 I have brought away the *h* things
1Sa 21. 4 there is *h* bread; if the young
6 the priest gave him *h* bread: for
1Ki 9. 3 I have *h* this house, which thou
7 which I have *h* for my name,
2Ki 12.18 all the *h* things that Jehoshaphat,
18 and his own *h* things, and all

2Ch 7. 7 Moreover Solomon *h* the middle
36.14 of the Lord which he had *h* in
Mt 6. 9 in heaven, *H* be thy name.
Lk 11. 2 in heaven, *H* be thy name.

HALT

1Ki 18.21 How long *h* ye between two
Ps 38.17 I am ready to *h*, and my sorrow
Mt 18. 8 to enter into life *h* or maimed,
Mk 9.45 better for thee to enter *h* into life,
Lk 14.21 the maimed, and the *h*, and the
Jn 5. 3 of blind, *h*, withered, waiting for

HAMMER

Jdg 4.21 took an *h* in her hand, and went
5.26 right hand to the workmen's *h*;
26 and with the *h* she smote
1Ki 6. 7 neither *h* nor axe nor any tool of
Isa 41. 7 he that smootheth with the *h*
Jer 23.29 and like a *h* that breaketh
50.23 the *h* of the whole earth

HAMMERS

Ps 74. 6 work...at once with axes and *h*.
Isa 44.12 and fashioneth it with *h*, and
Jer 10. 4 fasten it with nails and with *h*,

HAND

Gen 9. 5 require it, and at the *h* of man;
14.22 I have lift up mine *h* unto the
16.12 his *h* will be against every man,
12 and every man's *h* against him;
22.12 Lay not thine *h* upon the lad,
24. 2 Put, I pray thee, thy *h* under my
31.29 It is in the power of my *h* to do
32.11 of my brother, from the *h* of Esau:
35. 4 strange gods which were in their *h*,
38.28 put out his *h*: and the midwife
30 had the scarlet thread upon his *h*:
39. 8 committed all that he hath to my *h*;
12 left his garment in her *h*, and fled,
40.11 Pharaoh's cup was in my *h*: and I
41.42 took off his ring from his *h*, and
Ex 3.20 I will stretch out my *h*, and smite
4. 4 it became a rod in his *h*:
6 behold, his *h* was leprous as snow.
15. 6 Thy right *h*, O Lord, is become
17.11 Moses held up his *h*, that Israel
11 and when he let down his *h*,
21.24 tooth for tooth, *h* for *h*, foot
33.22 and will cover thee with my *h*
Lev 1. 4 he shall put his *h* upon the head
4.29, 33 lay his *h* upon the...sin
26.46 in mount Sinai by the *h* of Moses.
Nu 11.23 Is the Lord's *h* waxed short?
22.29 there were a sword in mine *h*,
25. 7 and took a javelin in his *h*;
Dt 3.24 thy mighty *h*: for what God
8.17 the might of mine *h* hath gotten
15. 9 the year of release, is at *h*;
16.10 a freewill offering of thine *h*,
19.21 for tooth, *h* for *h*, foot for foot.
32.27 Our *h* is high, and the Lord
Jos 8. 7 God will deliver it into your *h*.
Jdg 4. 9 Sisera into the *h* of a woman.
5.26 She put her *h* to the nail,
7. 2 Mine own *h* hath saved me.
16 put a trumpet in every man's *h*,
9.48 Abimelech took an axe in his *h*,
16.23 Samson our enemy into our *h*.
1Sa 5.11 *h* of God was very heavy there.
6. 9 we shall know that it is not his *h*
12. 3 or of whose *h* have I received any
4 taken ought of any man's *h*.
16.23 took an harp, and played with his *h*:
17.40 his sling was in his *h*:
46 the Lord deliver thee into mine *h*;
49 David put his *h* in his bag, and
19. 5 he did put his life in his *h*, and
23.16 and strengthened his *h* in God.
24.11 see the skirt of thy robe in my *h*:
18 had delivered me into thine *h*,
26.18 or what evil is in mine *h*?
28.21 I have put my life in my *h*,
2Sa 4.11 require his blood of your *h*, and
14.19 Is not the *h* of Joab with thee
24.14 let me not fall into the *h* of man.
16 It is enough: stay now thine *h*.
1Ki 13. 6 the king's *h* was restored him
17.11 a morsel of bread in thine *h*.
18.44 out of the sea, like a man's *h*.
46 the *h* of the Lord was on Elijah;
2Ki 4.29 take my staff in thine *h*, and go
5.11 strike his *h* over the place, and
1Ch 12. 2 could use both the right *h* and the
29.12 and in thine *h* is power and might;
12 and in thine *h* it is to make great,
16 cometh of thine *h*, and is all thine
Ezr 7. 6 according to the *h* of the Lord
9 according to the good *h* of his God
28 as the *h* of the Lord my God was
8.18 by the good *h* of our God upon us
Neh 2. 8 according to the good *h* of my God
6. 5 with an open letter in his *h*;
Est 8. 7 he laid his *h* upon the Jews.
Job 1.11 put forth thine *h* now, and touch
2. 6 Behold, he is in thine *h*; but save
10 we receive good at the *h* of God,
9.33 that might lay his *h* upon us both.
11.14 If iniquity be in thine *h*, put it far
12.10 In whose *h* is the soul of every
13.14 and put my life in mine *h*?
15.23 day of darkness is ready at his *h*.
25 stretcheth out his *h* against God,
19.21 the *h* of God hath touched me.
21. 5 lay your *h* upon your mouth.
27.11 I will teach you by the *h* of God:
40. 4 I will lay mine *h* upon my mouth.
14 thine own right *h* can save thee.
Ps 16. 8 he is at my right *h*, I shall not be
18.35 and thy right *h* hath holden me
21. 8 Thine *h* shall find out all thine
31. 5 Into thine *h* I commit my spirit:
15 My times are in thy *h*: deliver me
37.24 Lord upholdeth him with his *h*.
44. 3 but thy right *h*, and thine arm,
48.10 thy right *h* is full of righteousness.
74.11 Why withdrawest thou thy *h*,
77.10 the right *h* of the most High.
80.17 Let thy *h* be upon the man of thy
17 upon the man of thy right *h*,
89.48 his soul from the *h* of the grave?
95. 4 In his *h* are the deep places
7 pasture, and the sheep of his *h*.
98. 1 his right *h*, and his holy arm,
104.28 thou openest thine *h*, they are
108. 6 save with thy right *h*, and answer
110. 1 Sit thou at my right *h*, until I make
118.16 The right *h* of the Lord is exalted:
119.173 Let thine *h* help me; for I have
121. 5 Lord is thy shade upon thy right *h*.
137. 5 let my right *h* forget her cunning.
138. 7 thy right *h* shall save me.
139.10 there shall thy *h* lead me, and
10 thy right *h* shall hold me.
145.16 Thou openest thine *h*, and
Pr 3.16 Length of days is in her right *h*;
16 in her left *h* riches and honor.
12.24 The *h* of the diligent shall bear
17.16 is there a price in the *h* of a fool
19.24 A slothful man hideth his *h* in his
26. 6 a message by the *h* of a fool
9 into the *h* of a drunkard, so is a
Ec 2.24 that it was from the *h* of God.
9. 1 their works, are in the *h* of God:
10 Whatsoever thy *h* findeth to do,
10. 2 wise man's heart is at his right *h*;
11. 6 evening withhold not thine *h*:
SS 2. 6 and his right *h* doth embrace me.
Isa 1.12 who hath required this at your *h*,
5.25 but his *h* is stretched out still.
11. 8 put his *h* on the cockatrice' den.
13. 6 the day of the Lord is at *h*;
22.21 commit thy government into his *h*:
40. 2 received of the Lord's *h* double
10 Lord God will come with strong *h*,
12 the waters in the hollow of his *h*,
41.10 right *h* of my righteousness.
13 thy God will hold thy right *h*,
20 the *h* of the Lord hath done this,
42. 6 will hold thine *h*, and will keep
43.13 none that can deliver out of my *h*:
44. 5 another shall subscribe with his *h*
20 Is there not a lie in my right *h*?
49. 2 in the shadow of his *h* hath he
50. 2 Is my *h* shortened at all, that it
51.22 I have taken out of thine *h* the cup
53.10 of the Lord shall prosper in his *h*.
56. 2 keepeth his *h* from doing...evil,
59. 1 the Lord's *h* is not shortened,
Jer 18. 4 marred in the *h* of the potter:
6 as the clay is in the potter's *h*,
6 so are ye in mine *h*, O house
20.13 the poor from the *h* of evildoers.
23.23 Am I a God at *h*, saith the Lord,
25.28 take the cup at thine *h* to drink,
36.14 Take in thine *h* the roll wherein
14 took the roll in his *h*, and came
43. 9 Take great stones in thine *h*, and
La 1.10 The adversary...spread out his *h*
2. 4 stood with his right *h* as an
Eze 1. 3 the *h* of the Lord was there upon
3.14 but the *h* of the Lord was strong
8. 1 the *h* of the Lord God fell there
3 he put forth the form of an *h*,
10. 2 fill thine *h* with coals of fire
13. 9 mine *h* shall be upon the prophets
20.34 ye are scattered, with a mighty *h*,
33. 6 will I require at the watchman's *h*.
8 his blood will I require at thine *h*.
34.10 I will require my flock at their *h*,
Dan 4.35 none can stay his *h*, or say
5. 5 came forth fingers of a man's *h*,
5 saw the part of the *h* that wrote.
Hos 7. 5 stretched out his *h* with scorners.
Joel 1.15 the day of the Lord is at *h*,
Am 7. 7 with a plumbline in his *h*.
Mic 5.12 cut off witchcrafts out of thine *h*;
7.16 lay their *h* upon their mouth,
Zep 1. 7 the day of the Lord is at *h*:
Zec 2. 1 with a measuring line in his *h*.
3. 1 Satan standing at his right *h* to
8. 4 his staff in his *h* for very age.
Mal 1.10 will I accept an offering at your *h*.
13 should I accept this of your *h*?
Mt 3. 2 for the kingdom of heaven is at *h*.
12 Whose fan is in his *h*, and he will
4.17 for the kingdom of heaven is at *h*.
5.30 if thy right *h* offend thee, cut it
6. 3 doest alms, let not thy left *h*
3 know what thy right *h* doeth.
8. 3 Jesus put forth his *h*, and touched
15 he touched her *h*, and the fever
9.18 lay thy *h* upon her, and she shall
25 took her by the *h*, and the maid
10. 7 The kingdom of heaven is at *h*.
12.10 a man which had his *h* withered.
13 to the man, Stretch forth thine *h*.
49 he stretched forth his *h* toward his
14.31 Jesus stretched forth his *h*, and
18. 8 if thy *h* or thy foot offend thee,
20.21 may sit, the one on thy right *h*, and
23 to sit on my right *h*, and on my
22.13 Bind him *h* and foot, and take
44 Sit thou on my right *h*, till I make
25.33 shall set the sheep on his right *h*,
34 say unto them on his right *h*, Come
41 unto them on the left *h*, Depart
26.18 The Master saith, My time is at *h*;
23 He that dippeth his *h* with me
45 behold, the hour is at *h*, and the
46 he is at *h* that doth betray me.
51 stretched out his *h*, and drew his

64 sitting on the right *h* of power,
27.29 his head, and a reed in his right *h*:
38 one on the right *h*, and another on
Mk 1.15 the kingdom of God is at *h*:
31 and took her by the *h*, and lifted
41 put forth his *h*, and touched
3. 1 man there which had a withered *h*.
3 had the withered *h*, Stand forth.
5 Stretch forth thine *h*. And he
5 and his *h* was restored whole as the
5.41 took the damsel by the *h*, and said
7.32 beseech him to put his *h* upon
8.23 he took the blind man by the *h*,
9.27 took him by the *h*, and lifted him
43 if thy *h* offend thee, cut it off:
10.37 we may sit, one on thy right *h*, and
37 the other on thy left *h*, in thy glory.
40 to sit on my right *h* and on my left *h*,
12.36 Sit thou on my right *h*, till I make
14.42 lo, he that betrayeth me is at *h*.
62 sitting on the right *h* of power, and
15.27 the one on his right *h*, and the other
16.19 and sat on the right *h* of God.
Lk 1. 1 many have taken in *h* to set
66 And the *h* of the Lord was with
71 and from the *h* of all that hate us;
74 being delivered out of the *h* of our
3.17 Whose fan is in his *h*, and he will
5.13 he put forth his *h*, and touched
6. 6 man whose right *h* was withered.
8 which had the withered *h*, Rise up,
10 Stretch forth thy *h*. And he did so.
10 his *h* was restored whole as...other
8.54 and took her by the *h*, and called,
9.62 No man, having put his *h* to the
15.22 and put a ring on his *h*, and shoes
20.42 my Lord, Sit thou on my right *h*,
21.30 that summer is now nigh at *h*.
31 kingdom of God is nigh at *h*.
22.21 the *h* of him that betrayeth me
69 sit on the right *h* of the power of
23.33 one on the right *h*, and the other on
Jn 2.13 the Jews' passover was at *h*, and
3.35 hath given all things into his *h*.
7. 2 feast of tabernacles was at *h*.
10.28 any man pluck them out of my *h*.
29 to pluck them out of my Father's *h*.
39 him: but he escaped out of their *h*,
11.44 *h* and foot with graveclothes;
55 Jews' passover was nigh at *h*: and
18.22 struck Jesus with the palm of his *h*,
42 for the sepulchre was nigh at *h*.
20.25 and thrust my *h* into his side, I
27 and reach hither thy *h*, and thrust
Ac 2.25 for he is on my right *h*, that
33 being by the right *h* of God exalted,
34 my Lord, Sit thou on my right *h*,
3. 7 took him by the right *h*, and
4.28 whatsoever thy *h* and thy counsel
30 stretching forth thine *h* to heal;
5.31 hath God exalted with his right *h*
7.25 God by his *h* would deliver them:
35 by the *h* of the angel which
50 Hath not my *h* made all these
55 Jesus standing on the right *h* of God,
56 man standing on the right *h* of God.
9. 8 they led him by the *h*, and
12 coming in, and putting his *h* on
41 he gave her his *h*, and lifted
11.21 And the *h* of the Lord was with
12.11 delivered me out of the *h* of Herod,
17 beckoning unto them with the *h* to
13.11 behold, the *h* of the Lord is upon
11 seeking some to lead him by the *h*.
16 beckoning with his *h* said, Men of
19.33 Alexander beckoned with the *h*,
21. 3 Cyprus, we left it on the left *h*,
40 beckoned with the *h* unto the
22.11 being led by the *h* of them that
23.19 captain took him by the *h*, and
26. 1 Paul stretched forth the *h*, and
28. 3 of the heat, and fastened on his *h*.
4 beast hang on his *h*, they said
Ro 8.34 even at the right *h* of God, who also
13.12 night is far spent, the day is at *h*:
1Co 12.15 Because I am not the *h*, I am not
21 And the eye cannot say unto the *h*,
16.21 of me Paul with mine own *h*.
2Co 6. 7 on the right *h* and on the left,
10.16 of things made ready to our *h*.
Gal 3.19 by angels in the *h* of a mediator.
6.11 written unto you with mine own *h*.
Eph 1.20 set him at his own right *h* in the
Php 4. 5 unto all men. The Lord is at *h*.
Col 3. 1 Christ sitteth on the right *h* of God,
4.18 salutation by the *h* of me Paul.
2Th 2. 2 as that the day of Christ is at *h*.
3.17 of Paul with mine own *h*,
2Ti 4. 6 the time of my departure is at *h*.
Phm 19 written it with mine own *h*,
Heb 1. 3 the right *h* of the Majesty on high;
13 Sit on my right *h*, until I make
8. 1 set on the right *h* of the throne
9 when I took them by the *h* to lead
10.12 sat down on the right *h* of God;
12. 2 is set down at the right *h* of the
1Pe 3.22 is on the right *h* of God; angels, and
4. 7 the end of all things is at *h*:
5. 6 under the mighty *h* of God, that
Rev 1. 3 therein: for the time is at *h*.
16 he had in his right *h* seven stars:
17 he laid his right *h* upon me,
20 which thou sawest in my right *h*, and
2. 1 the seven stars in his right *h*,
5. 1 I saw in the right *h* of him that sat
7 took the book out of the right *h*
6. 5 him had a pair of balances in his *h*.
8. 4 up before God out of the angel's *h*.
10. 2 he had in his *h* a little book
5 the earth lifted up his *h* to heaven,
8 which is open in the *h* of the angel
10 book out of the angel's *h*, and ate
13.16 to receive a mark in their right *h*,
14. 9 mark in his forehead, or in his *h*,
14 and in his *h* a sharp sickle.
17. 4 having a golden cup in her *h* full of
19. 2 the blood of his servants at her *h*.
20. 1 pit and a great chain in his *h*.
22.10 of this book: for the time is at *h*.

HANDBREADTH

Ex 37.12 a border of an *h* round about;
2Ch 4. 5 And the thickness of it was an *h*,
Ps 39. 5 thou hast made my days as an *h*;

HANDFUL

Lev 2. 2 shall take thereout his *h* of
5.12 priest shall take his *h* of it,
6.15 shall take of it his *h*, of the flour
9.17 took an *h* thereof, and burnt
Nu 5.26 And the priest shall take an *h*
1Ki 17.12 an *h* of meal in a barrel,
Ps 72.16 There shall be an *h* of corn
Ec 4. 6 Better is an *h* with quietness,
Jer 9.22 as the *h* after the harvestman,

HANDFULS

Gen 41.47 the earth brought forth by *h*.
Ex 9. 8 Take to you *h* of ashes of
Ru 2.16 let fall also some of the *h*
1Ki 20.10 Samaria shall suffice for *h* for all
Eze 13.19 my people for *h* of barley and for

HANDKERCHIEFS

Ac 19.12 brought unto the sick *h* or aprons,

HANDLE

Gen 4.21 father of all such as *h* the harp
Jdg 5.14 they that *h* the pen of the writer.
1Ch 12. 8 that could *h* shield and buckler,
2Ch 25. 5 that could *h* spear and shield.
Ps 115. 7 They have hands, but they *h* not:
Jer 2. 8 and they that *h* the law knew
46. 9 the Libyans, that *h* the shield; and
9 the Lydians, that *h* and bend the
Eze 27.29 all that *h* the oar, the mariners,
Lk 24.39 *h* me, and see; for a spirit
Col 2.21 touch not; taste not; *h* not;

HANDLED

Eze 21.11 furbished, that it may be *h*:
Mk 12. 4 and sent him away shamefully *h*.
1Jn 1. 1 looked upon, and...hands have *h*,

HANDLING

Eze 38. 4 shields, all of them *h* swords:
2Co 4. 2 *h* the word of God deceitfully;

HANDMAID

Gen 16. 1 she had an *h*, an Egyptian,
25.12 the Egyptian, Sarah's *h*, bare unto
29.24 Leah Zilpah his maid for an *h*.
29 Bilhah his *h* to be her maid.
30. 4 she gave him Bilhah her *h* to wife
35.25 the sons of Bilhah, Rachel's *h*;
26 And the sons of Zilpah, Leah's *h*;
Ex 23.12 the son of thy *h*, and the stranger,
Jdg 19.19 also for me, and for thy *h*,
Ru 2.13 spoken friendly unto thine *h*,
3. 9 I am Ruth thine *h*: spread
9 therefore thy skirt over thine *h*;
1Sa 1.11 the affliction of thine *h*, and
11 me, and not forget thine *h*,
11 but wilt give unto thine *h*
16 Count not thine *h* for a daughter
18 Let thine *h* find grace in thy sight.
25.24 let thine *h*, I pray thee, speak in
24 and hear the words of thine *h*.
25 but I thine *h* saw not the young
27 which thine *h* hath brought unto
28 forgive the trespass of thine *h*:
31 my lord, then remember thine *h*.
41 let thine *h* be a servant
28.21 thine *h* hath obeyed thy voice,
22 also unto the voice of thine *h*,
2Sa 14. 6 And thy *h* had two sons, and they
7 family is risen against thine *h*,
12 woman said, Let thine *h*, I pray
15 and thy *h* said, I will now speak
15 perform the request of his *h*.
16 to deliver his *h* out of the hand
17 Then thine *h* said, The word of
19 words in the mouth of thine *h*:
20.17 Hear the words of thine *h*. And
1Ki 1.13 O king, swear unto thine *h*,
17 the Lord thy God unto thine *h*,
3.20 while thine *h* slept, and laid it
2Ki 4. 2 Thine *h* hath not any thing in the
16 man of God, do not lie unto thine *h*.
Ps 86.16 and save the son of thine *h*.
116.16 servant, and the son of thine *h*:
Pr 30.23 and an *h* that is heir to her
Jer 34.16 every man his *h*, whom he had
Lk 1.38 Behold the *h* of the Lord; be it

HANDMAIDEN

Lk 1.48 regarded the low estate of his *h*:

HANDMAIDENS

Gen 33. 6 Then the *h* came near, they and
Ru 2.13 like unto one of thine *h*.
Ac 2.18 on my servants and on my *h*

HANDMAIDS

Gen 33. 1 Rachel, and unto the two *h*.
2 he put the *h* and their children
2Sa 6.20 eyes of the *h* of his servants,
Isa 14. 2 them...for servants and *h*: and
Jer 34.11 the servants and the *h*, whom
11 subjection for servants and for *h*.
16 you for servants and for *h*.
Joel 2.29 upon the *h* in those days will I

HANDS

Gen 20. 5 innocency of my *h* have I done
27.22 but the *h* are the *h* of Esau.
23 him not, because his *h* were hairy
23 hairy, as his brother Esau's *h*:
48.14 guiding his *h* wittingly; for
49.24 strong by the *h* of the mighty God
Ex 17.12 But Moses' *h* were heavy; and
32.19 he cast the tables out of his *h*,
Dt 4.28 the work of men's *h*, wood and
9.15 of the covenant were in my two *h*.
21. 7 Our *h* have not shed this blood,
Jdg 7.20 held the lamps in their left *h*, and
20 the trumpets in their right *h*
12. 3 I put my life in my *h*, and
2Sa 22.35 He teacheth my *h* to war; so that
2Ki 19.18 the work of men's *h*, wood and
2Ch 15. 7 let not your *h* be weak: for your
Neh 6. 9 O God, strengthen my *h*.
13.21 ye do so again, I will lay *h* on you.
Job 5.18 woundeth, and his *h* make whole.
9.30 and make my *h* never so clean;
10. 3 despise the work of thine *h*, and
8 Thine *h* have made me and
17. 9 he that hath clean *h* shall be
27.23 Men shall clap their *h* at him,
Ps 7. 3 if there be iniquity in my *h*;
22.16 they pierced my *h* and my feet.
24. 4 He that hath clean *h*, and a pure
26. 6 I will wash mine *h* in innocency:
10 In whose *h* is mischief, and their
28. 2 when I lift up my *h* toward thy
47. 1 O clap your *h*, all ye people;
63. 4 I will lift up my *h* in thy name.
68.31 Ethiopia shall…stretch out her *h*
73.13 and washed my *h* in innocency.
90.17 the work of our *h* upon us; yea,
17 the work of our *h* establish thou
95. 5 his *h* formed the dry land.
98. 8 Let the floods clap their *h*: let
102.25 heavens are the work of thy *h*.
111. 7 The works of his *h* are verity
115. 7 They have *h*, but they handle not:
134. 2 Lift up your *h* in the sanctuary,
Pr 6.10 a little folding of the *h* to sleep:
24.33 a little folding of the *h* to sleep:
Ec 4. 5 The fool foldeth his *h* together,
SS 5. 5 and my *h* dropped with myrrh,
Isa 1.15 your *h* are full of blood.
2. 8 worship the work of their own *h*,
35. 3 Strengthen ye the weak *h*, and
37.19 the work of men's *h*, wood and
55.12 of the field shall clap their *h*.
Jer 23.14 they strengthen also the *h* of
La 2.15 All that pass by clap their *h*
4. 2 the work of the *h* of the potter!
10 The *h* of the pitiful women have
Eze 7.17 All *h* shall be feeble, and all knees
21. 7 all *h* shall be feeble, and every
22.14 can thine *h* be strong, in the days
Dan 3.15 that shall deliver you out of my *h*?
Mic 5.13 worship the work of thine *h*.
7. 3 they may do evil with both *h*
Zep 3.16 Zion, Let not thine *h* be slack.
Zec 13. 6 are these wounds in thine *h*?
Mt 4. 6 in their *h* they shall bear thee up,
15. 2 for they wash not their *h* when
20 but to eat with unwashen *h*
17.22 shall be betrayed into the *h* of
18. 8 rather than having two *h* or two
28 and he laid *h* on him, and took
19.13 should put his *h* on them, and
15 he laid his *h* on them, and
21.46 when they sought to lay *h* on
26.45 is betrayed into the *h* of sinners.
50 laid *h* on Jesus, and took him.
67 smote him with the palms of their *h*,
27.24 washed his *h* before the multitude,
Mk 5.23 come and lay thy *h* on her, that
6. 2 works are wrought by his *h*?
5 laid his *h* upon a few sick folk,
7. 2 with unwashen, *h*, they found
3 except they wash their *h* oft, eat
5 but eat bread with unwashen *h*?
8.23 his eyes, and put his *h* upon him.
25 he put his *h* again upon his eyes,
9.31 is delivered into the *h* of men,
43 than having two *h* to go into hell,
10.16 in his arms, put his *h* upon them,
14.41 is betrayed into the *h* of sinners.
46 laid their *h* on him, and took him.
58 this temple that is made with *h*,
58 will build another made without *h*.
65 strike him with the palms of their *h*.
16.18 they shall lay *h* on the sick, and
Lk 4.11 And in their *h* they shall bear thee
40 laid his *h* on every one of them,
6. 1 did eat, rubbing them in their *h*.
9.44 shall be delivered into the *h* of
13.13 And he laid his *h* on her:
20.19 hour sought to lay *h* on him;
21.12 they shall lay their *h* on you,
22.53 ye stretched forth no *h* against me:
23.46 into thy *h* I commend my spirit:
24. 7 be delivered into the *h* of sinful
39 Behold my *h* and my feet, that it
40 he shewed them his *h* and his
50 he lifted up his *h*, and blessed
Jn 7.30 but no man laid *h* on him, because
44 him; but no man laid *h* on him.
8.20 and no man laid *h* on him; for
13. 3 given all things into his *h*, and
9 but also my *h* and my head.
19. 3 and they smote him with their *h*.
20.20 shewed unto them his *h* and his
25 I shall see in his *h* the print of the
27 hither thy finger, and behold my *h*;
21.18 thou shalt stretch forth thy *h*,
Ac 2.23 by wicked *h* have crucified and
4. 3 they laid *h* on them, and put
5.12 by the *h* of the apostles were
18 laid their *h* on the apostles, and
6. 6 prayed, they laid their *h* on them.
7.41 in the works of their own *h*.
48 not in temples made with *h*;
8.17 Then laid they their *h* on them,
18 laying on of the apostles' *h*
19 that on whomsoever I lay *h*, he
9.17 and putting his *h* on him said,
11.30 by the *h* of Barnabas and Saul.
12. 1 the king stretched forth his *h* to
7 And his chains fell off from his *h*.
13. 3 prayed, and laid their *h* on them,
14. 3 and wonders to be done by their *h*.
17.24 not in temples made with *h*;
25 is worshipped with men's *h*,
19. 6 when Paul had laid his *h* upon
11 special miracles by the *h* of Paul:
26 no gods, which are made with *h*:
20.34 these *h* have ministered unto my
21.11 bound his own *h* and feet,
11 shall deliver him into the *h* of the
27 all the people, and laid *h* on him,
24. 7 took him away out of our *h*,
27.19 out with our own *h* the tackling
28. 8 laid his *h* on him, and healed him.
17 into the *h* of the Romans.
Ro 10.21 I have stretched forth my *h* unto
1Co 4.12 labor, working with our own *h*:
2Co 5. 1 an house not made with *h*, eternal
11.33 by the wall, and escaped his *h*.
Gal 2. 9 the right *h* of fellowship; that
Eph 2.11 Circumcision in…flesh made by *h*;
4.28 working with his *h* the thing
Col 2.11 the circumcision made without *h*,
1Th 4.11 and to work with your own *h*,
1Ti 2. 8 lifting up holy *h*, without wrath
4.14 with the laying on of the *h* of the
5.22 Lay *h* suddenly on no man, neither
2Ti 1. 6 in thee by the putting on of my *h*.
Heb 1.10 heavens are the works of thine *h*:
2. 7 set him over the works of thy *h*:
6. 2 of baptisms, and of laying on of *h*,
9.11 tabernacle, not made with *h*, that
24 into the holy places made with *h*,
10.31 to fall into the *h* of the living God.
12.12 lift up the *h* which hang down,
Jas 4. 8 Cleanse your *h*, ye sinners; and
1Jn 1. 1 and our *h* have handled, of the
Rev 7. 9 white robes, and palms in their *h*;
9.20 not of the works of their *h*, that
20. 4 upon their foreheads, or in their *h*;

HANDWRITING

Col 2.14 Blotting out the *h* of ordinances

HANDYWORK

Ps 19. 1 firmament sheweth his *h*.

HANG

Gen 40.19 and shall *h* thee on a tree;
Ex 26.12 shall *h* over the backside of the
13 it shall *h* over the sides of the
32 And thou shalt *h* it upon four
33 And thou shalt *h* up the vail under
40. 8 and *h* up the hanging at the
Nu 25. 4 and *h* them up before the Lord
Dt 21.22 and thou *h* him on a tree:
28.66 thy life shall *h* in doubt before
2Sa 21. 6 and we will *h* them up unto the
Est 6. 4 to *h* Mordecai on the gallows
7. 9 Then the king said, *H* him thereon.
SS 4. 4 whereon there *h* a thousand
Isa 22.24 And they shall *h* upon him all the
La 2.10 the virgins of Jerusalem *h* down
Eze 15. 3 will men take a pin of it to *h*
Mt 22.40 *h* all the law and the prophets.
Ac 28. 4 venomous beast *h* on his hand,
Heb 12.12 lift up the hands which *h* down,

HANGED

Gen 40.22 But he *h* the chief baker:
41.13 unto mine office, and him he *h*.
Dt 21.23 he that is *h* is accursed of God;
Jos 8.29 the king of Ai he *h* on a tree
10.26 them: and *h* them on five trees:
2Sa 4.12 and *h* them up over the pool
17.23 and *h* himself, and died, and was
18.10 I saw Absalom *h* in an oak.
21. 9 and they *h* them in the hill
12 where the Philistines had *h* them,
13 the bones of them that were *h*.
Ezr 6.11 let him be *h* thereon; and let his
Est 2.23 therefore they were both *h* on a
5.14 king that Mordecai may be *h*
7.10 So they *h* Haman on the gallows
8. 7 him they have *h* upon the gallows,
9.13 let Haman's ten sons be *h* upon
14 and they *h* Haman's ten sons.
25 that he and his sons should be *h*
Ps 137. 2 We *h* our harps upon the willows
La 5.12 Princes are *h* up by their hand:
Eze 27.10 they *h* the shield and helmet in
11 they *h* their shields upon thy walls
Mt 18. 6 that a millstone were *h* about his
27. 5 departed, and went and *h* himself.
Mk 9.42 that a millstone were *h* about his
Lk 17. 2 that a millstone were *h* about his
23.39 of the malefactors which were *h*
Ac 5.30 whom ye slew and *h* on a tree.
10.39 whom they slew and *h* on a tree:

HANGETH

Job 26. 7 and *h* the earth upon nothing.
Gal 3.13 Cursed is every one that *h* on a

HANNAH

1Sa 1. 2 the name of the one was *H*,
2 but *H* had no children.
5 unto *H* he gave a worthy portion;
5 for he loved *H*: but the Lord
8 *H*, why weepest thou? and why
9 So *H* rose up after they had eaten

13 Now *H*, she spake in her heart;
15 *H* answered and said, No, my lord,
19 and Elkanah knew *H* his wife;
20 about after *H* had conceived,
22 But *H* went not up; for she said
2. 1 *H* prayed, and said, My heart
21 the Lord visited *H*, so that she

HAPLY

1Sa 14.30 if *h* the people had eaten freely
Mk 11.13 if *h* he might find any thing
Lk 14.29 Lest *h*, after he hath laid the
Ac 5.39 lest *h* ye be found even to fight
17.27 if *h* they might feel after him,
2Co 9. 4 Lest *h* if they of Macedonia come

HAPPEN

1Sa 28.10 there shall no punishment *h* to
Pr 12.21 There shall no evil *h* to the just:
Isa 41.22 shew us what shall *h*: let them
Mk 10.32 what things should *h* unto him,

HAPPENED

1Sa 6. 9 it was a chance that *h* to us.
2Sa 1. 6 As I *h* by chance upon mount
20. 1 there *h* to be there a man of
Est 4. 7 all that had *h* unto him, and of
Jer 44.23 therefore this evil is *h* unto you,
Lk 24.14 of all these things which had *h*.
Ac 3.10 at that which had *h* unto him.
Ro 11.25 blindness in part is *h* to Israel,
1Co 10.11 all these things *h* unto them for
Php 1.12 that the things which *h* unto me
1Pe 4.12 as though some strange thing *h*
2Pe 2.22 But it is *h* unto them according to

HAPPENETH

Ec 2.14 that one event *h* to them all.
15 As it *h* to the fool,
15 so it *h* even to me:
8.14 men, unto whom it *h* according
14 wicked men, to whom it *h*
9.11 time and chance *h* to them all.

HAPPIER

1Co 7.40 But she is *h* if she so abide,

HAPPY

Gen 30.13 Leah said, *H* am I, for the
Dt 33.29 *H* art thou, O Israel: who is like
1Ki 10. 8 *H* are thy men, *h* are these thy
2Ch 9. 7 *H* are thy men, and *h* are these
Job 5.17 *h* is the man whom God correcteth:
Ps 127. 5 *H* is the man that hath his quiver
128. 2 *h* shalt thou be, and it shall be
137. 8 *h* shall he be, that rewardeth thee
9 *H* shall he be, that taketh and
144.15 *H* is that people, that is in such a
15 *h* is that people, whose God is the
146. 5 *H* is he that hath the God
Pr 3.13 *H* is the man that findeth wisdom,
18 *h* is every one that retaineth her.
14.21 hath mercy on the poor, *h* is he.
16.20 trusteth in the Lord, *h* is he.
28.14 *H* is the man that feareth alway:
29.18 he that keepeth the law, *h* is he.
Jer 12. 1 are all they *h* that deal very
Mal 3.15 And now we call the proud *h*;
Jn 13.17 *h* are ye if you do them.
Ac 26. 2 I think myself *h*, king Agrippa,
Ro 14.22 *H* is he that condemneth not
Jas 5.11 we count them *h* which endure.
1Pe 3.14 for righteousness' sake, *h* are ye:
4.14 for the name of Christ, *h* are ye;

HARD

Gen 18.14 Is any thing too *h* for the Lord?
35.16 travailed, and she had *h* labor.
Ex 18.26 the *h* causes they brought unto
Dt 17. 8 If there arise a matter too *h* for
1Ki 10. 1 to prove him with *h* questions.

BIBLICAL THEMES

HAPPINESS

And he fell upon his brother Benjamin's neck, and wept; and Benjamin wept upon his neck. Moreover he kissed all his brethren, and wept upon them. Gen 45.14-15

Happy art thou, O Israel: who is like unto thee, O people saved by the Lord. Dt 33.29

Let the heavens be glad, and let the earth rejoice. . . . Let the sea roar, and the fulness thereof: let the fields rejoice, and all that is therein. Then shall the trees of the wood sing out at the presence of the Lord, because he cometh to judge the earth. 1Ch 16.31-33

Go your way, eat the fat, and drink the sweet . . . for this day is holy unto our Lord: neither be ye sorry; for the joy of the Lord is your strength. Neh 8.10

Let all those that put their trust in thee rejoice: let them ever shout for joy, because thou defendest them: let them also that love thy name be joyful in thee. Ps 5.11

Weeping may endure for a night, but joy cometh in the morning. . . . Lord, be thou my helper. Thou hast turned for me my mourning into dancing: thou hast put off my sackcloth, and girded me with gladness. Ps 30.5, 10-11

O clap your hands, all ye people; shout unto God with the voice of triumph. Ps 47. 1

Make a joyful noise unto the Lord, all the earth: make a loud noise, and rejoice, and sing praise. Ps 98. 4

They that sow in tears shall reap in joy. He that goeth forth and weepeth, bearing precious seed, shall doubtless come again with rejoicing. Ps 126.5-6

A merry heart doeth good like a medicine: but a broken spirit drieth the bones. Pr 17.22

Sorrow is better than laughter: for by the sadness of the countenance the heart is made better. . . . In the day of prosperity be joyful, but in the day of adversity consider: God also hath set the one over against the other. Ec 7.3, 14

Rejoice, O young man, in thy youth; and let thy heart cheer thee in the days of thy youth. Ec 11.9

The ransomed of the Lord shall return . . . they shall obtain joy and gladness, and sorrow and sighing shall flee away. Isa 35.10

Sing, O heavens; and be joyful, O earth; and break forth into singing, O mountains: for the Lord hath comforted his people. Isa 49.13

Again there shall be heard in this place . . . the voice of joy, and the voice of gladness, the voice of the bridegroom, and the voice of the bride, the voice of them that shall say, Praise the Lord of hosts. Jer 33.10-11

And the angel said unto them, Fear not: for, behold, I bring you good tidings of great joy. Lk 2.10

Blessed are ye that weep now: for ye shall laugh. . . . Rejoice ye in that day, and leap for joy: for, behold, your reward is great in heaven. Lk 6.21, 23

There is joy in the presence of the angels of God over one sinner that repenteth. Lk 15.10

In the world ye shall have tribulation: but be of good cheer; I have overcome the world. Jn 16.33

Godliness with contentment is great gain. For we brought nothing into this world, and it is certain we can carry nothing out. And having food and raiment let us be therewith content. ITi 6.6-8

2Ki 2.10 Thou hast asked a *h* thing:
Ps 63. 8 My soul followeth *h* after thee:
88. 7 Thy wrath lieth *h* upon me, and
Pr 13.15 the way of transgressors is *h*.
Jer 32.17 and there is nothing too *h* for thee:
27 is there any thing too *h* for me?
Eze 3. 6 and of an *h* language, whose words
Jon 1.13 men rowed *h* to bring it to the land;
Mt 25.24 that thou art an *h* man, reaping
Mk 10.24 how *h* is it for them that trust
Jn 6.60 This is an *h* saying; who can
Ac 9. 5 *h* for thee to kick against the
18. 7 house joined *h* to the synagogue.
26.14 it is *h* for thee to kick against

Heb 5.11 things to say, and *h* to be uttered,
2Pe 3.16 some things *h* to be understood,
Jude 15 and of all their *h* speeches which

HARDEN

Ex 4.21 but I will *h* his heart, that he
7. 3 I will *h* Pharaoh's heart, and
14. 4 I will *h* Pharaoh's heart, that he
17 will *h* the hearts of the Egyptians,
Dt 15. 7 thou shalt not *h* thine heart, nor
Jos 11.20 was of the Lord to *h* their hearts,
1Sa 6. 6 Wherefore then do ye *h* your
Job 6.10 yea, I would *h* myself in sorrow:
Ps 95. 8 *H* not your heart, as in the

David plays the harp before Saul (1Sa 16.21-23) in this engraving by Lucas van Leyden (1494-1533).

Heb 3. 8 *H* not your hearts, as in the
15 voice, *h* not your hearts, as in the
4. 7 his voice, *h* not your hearts.

HARDENED
Ex 7.13 And he *h* Pharaoh's heart, that
14 Pharaoh's heart is *h*, he refuseth
22 Pharaoh's heart was *h*, neither
8.15 he *h* his heart, and hearkened not
19 and Pharaoh's heart was *h*, and
32 And Pharaoh *h* his heart at this
9. 7 And the heart of Pharaoh was *h*,
12 the Lord *h* the heart of Pharaoh,
34 sinned yet more, and *h* his heart,
35 And the heart of Pharaoh was *h*,
10. 1 I have *h* his heart, and the heart
20 the Lord *h* Pharaoh's heart, so
27 the Lord *h* Pharaoh's heart, and
11.10 the Lord *h* Pharaoh's heart, so
14. 8 the Lord *h* the heart of Pharaoh
Dt 2.30 the Lord thy God *h* his spirit,
1Sa 6. 6 and Pharaoh *h* their hearts?
2Ki 17.14 would not hear, but *h* their necks,
2Ch 36.13 and *h* his heart from turning
Neh 9.16 *h* their necks, and hearkened not
17 but *h* their necks, and in their
29 *h* their neck, and would not hear.
Job 9. 4 who hath *h* himself against him,
39.16 She is *h* against her young
Isa 63.17 from thy ways, and *h* our heart
Jer 7.26 but *h* their neck: they did worse
19.15 they have *h* their necks, that
Dan 5.20 up, and his mind *h* in pride,
Mk 6.52 loaves: for their heart was *h*.
8.17 have ye your heart yet *h*?
Jn 12.40 blinded their eyes, and *h* their
Ac 19. 9 But when divers were *h*, and
Heb 3.13 *h* through the deceitfulness of sin.

HARDENETH
Pr 21.29 A wicked man *h* his face: but as
28.14 but he that *h* his heart shall fall
29. 1 being often reproved *h* his neck,
Ro 9.18 mercy, and whom he will he *h*.

HARDER
Pr 18.19 A brother offended is *h* to be won
Jer 5. 3 made their faces *h* than a rock;
Eze 3. 9 As an adamant *h* than flint

HARDHEARTED
Eze 3. 7 Israel are impudent and *h*.

HARDLY
Gen 16. 6 And when Sarai dealt *h* with her,
Ex 13.15 Pharaoh would *h* let us go,
Isa 8.21 through it, *h* bestead and hungry:
Mt 19.23 a rich man shall *h* enter into
Mk 10.23 How *h* shall they that have riches
Lk 9.39 bruising him *h* departeth from
18.24 How *h* shall they that have riches
Ac 27. 8 And, *h* passing it, came unto a

HARDNESS
Job 38.38 the dust groweth into *h*, and
Mt 19. 8 because of the *h* of your hearts
Mk 3. 5 grieved for the *h* of their hearts,
10. 5 For the *h* of your heart he wrote
16.14 their unbelief and *h* of heart,
Ro 2. 5 thy *h* and impenitent heart
2Ti 2. 3 therefore endure *h*, as a good

HARLOT
Gen 34.31 with our sister as with an *h*?
38.15 he thought her to be an *h*;
21 Where is the *h*, that was openly
21 There was no *h* in this place.
22 there was no *h* in this place.
24 daughter in law hath played the *h*;
Lev 21.14 or profane, or an *h*, these shall
Jos 6.17 only Rahab the *h* shall live, she
25 Joshua saved Rahab the *h* alive,
Jdg 11. 1 he was the son of an *h*:
16. 1 saw there an *h*, and went
Pr 7.10 a woman with the attire of an *h*,
Isa 1.21 the faithful city become an *h*!
23.15 years shall Tyre sing as an *h*.
16 thou *h* that hast been forgotten;
Jer 2.20 tree thou wanderest, playing the *h*.
3. 1 played the *h* with many lovers:
6 tree, and there hath played the *h*.
8 but went and played the *h* also.
Eze 16.15 and playedst the *h* because of thy
16 and playedst the *h* thereupon:
28 yea, thou hast played the *h* with
31 hast not been as an *h*, in that thou
35 O *h*, hear the word of the Lord:
41 thee to cease from playing the *h*,
23. 5 And Aholah played the *h* when she
19 wherein she had played the *h* in
44 unto a woman that playeth the *h*:
Hos 2. 5 their mother hath played the *h*:
3. 3 thou shalt not play the *h*, and
4.15 Though thou, Israel, play the *h*,
Joel 3. 3 have given a boy for an *h*,
Am 7.17 Thy wife shall be an *h* in the city,
Mic 1. 7 she gathered it of the hire of an *h*,
7 shall return to the hire of an *h*.
Na 3. 4 of the wellfavored *h*, the mistress
1Co 6.15 make them the members of an *h*?
16 is joined to an *h* is one body?
Heb 11.31 By faith the *h* Rahab perished not
Jas 2.25 was not Rahab the *h* justified by

HARLOT'S
Jos 2. 1 came into an *h* house, named
6.22 Go into the *h* house, and bring

HARLOTS
1Ki 3.16 two women, that were *h*, unto the
Pr 29. 3 he that keepeth company with *h*
Hos 4.14 they sacrifice with *h*: therefore
Mt 21.31 and the *h* go into the kingdom
32 and the *h* believed him: and ye,
Lk 15.30 devoured thy living with *h*, thou
Rev 17. 5 mother of *h* and abominations

HARLOTS'
Jer 5. 7 by troops in the *h* houses.

HARM
Gen 31.52 and this pillar unto me, for *h*.
Lev 5.16 for the *h* that he hath done in
Nu 35.23 his enemy, neither sought his *h*:
1Sa 26.21 I will no more do thee *h*,
2Sa 20. 6 the son of Bichri do us more *h*
2Ki 4.41 there was no *h* in the pot.
1Ch 16.22 and do my prophets no *h*.
Ps 105.15 and do my prophets no *h*.
Pr 3.30 if he have done thee no *h*.
Jer 39.12 look well to him, and do him no *h*;
Ac 16.28 Do thyself no *h*: for we are all
27.21 to have gained this *h* and loss.
28. 5 into the fire, and felt no *h*.
6 saw no *h* come to him, they
21 shewed or spake any *h* of thee.
1Pe 3.13 who is he that will *h* you,

HARMLESS
Mt 10.16 wise as serpents, and *h* as doves.
Php 2.15 That ye may be blameless and *h*,
Heb 7.26 who is holy, *h*, undefiled,

HARP
Gen 4.21 such as handle the *h* and organ.
31.27 songs, with tabret, and with *h*?
1Sa 10. 5 a pipe, and a *h*, before them;
16.16 a cunning player on an *h*:
23 David took an *h*, and played
1Ch 25. 3 who prophesied with a *h*, to give
Job 21.12 They take the timbrel and *h*, and
30.31 My *h* also is turned to mourning,
Ps 33. 2 Praise the Lord with *h*: sing unto
43. 4 upon the *h* will I praise thee,
49. 4 open my dark saying upon the *h*.
57. 8 awake, psaltery and *h*: I myself
71.22 unto thee will I sing with the *h*,
81. 2 the pleasant *h* with the psaltery.
92. 3 upon the *h* with a solemn sound.
98. 5 Sing unto the Lord with the *h*;
5 with the *h*, and the voice of a
108. 2 Awake, psaltery and *h*: I myself
147. 7 sing praise upon the *h* unto our
149. 3 unto him with the timbrel and *h*.
150. 3 praise him with the psaltery and *h*.
Isa 5.12 the *h*, and the viol, the tabret, and
16.11 my bowels shall sound like an *h*
23.16 Take an *h*, go about the city,
24. 8 endeth, the joy of the *h* ceaseth.
Dan 3. 5, 7, 10, 15 flute, *h*, sackbut,
1Co 14. 7 giving sound, whether pipe or *h*,

HARPED
1Co 14. 7 be known what is piped or *h*?

HARPERS
Rev 14. 2 I heard the voice of *h* harping
18.22 And the voice of *h*, and musicians,

HARPING
Rev 14. 2 voice of harpers *h* with their

HARPS
2Sa 6. 5 even on *h*, and on psalteries, and
1Ki 10.12 *h* also and psalteries for singers:
1Ch 13. 8 and with *h*, and with psalteries,
15.16 psalteries and *h* and cymbals
21 with *h* on the Sheminith
28 a noise with psalteries and *h*.
16. 5 Jeiel with psalteries and with *h*;
25. 1 who should prophesy with *h*, with
6 with cymbals, psalteries, and *h*, for
2Ch 5.12 cymbals and psalteries and *h*,
9.11 and *h* and psalteries for singers:
20.28 with psalteries and *h* and
29.25 with psalteries, and with *h*,
Neh 12.27 cymbals, psalteries, and with *h*.
Ps 137. 2 We hanged our *h* upon the willows
Isa 30.32 it shall be with tabrets and *h*:
Eze 26.13 sound of thy *h* shall no more be
Rev 5. 8 having every one of them *h*,

14. 2 of harpers harping with their *h*:
15. 2 sea of glass, having the *h* of God.

HARVEST

Gen 8.22 seedtime and *h*, and cold and
30.14 in the days of wheat *h*, and found
45. 6 there shall neither be earing nor *h*.
Ex 23.16 the feast of *h*, the firstfruits of
34.21 in earing time and in *h* thou shalt
22 the firstfruits of wheat *h*, and the
Lev 19. 9 when ye reap the *h* of your land,
9 thou gather the gleanings of thy *h*.
23.10 shall reap the *h* thereof, then ye
10 a sheaf of the firstfruits of your *h*
22 when ye reap the *h* of your land,
22 thou gather any gleaning of thy *h*:
25. 5 groweth of its own accord of thy *h*
Dt 24.19 When thou cuttest down thine *h*
Jos 3.15 all his banks all the time of *h*,
Jdg 15. 1 in the time of wheat *h*,
Ru 1.22 in the beginning of barley *h*.
2.21 until they have ended all my *h*.
23 end of barley *h* and of wheat *h*;
1Sa 6.13 their wheat *h* in the valley:
8.12 to reap his *h*, and to make his
12.17 Is it not wheat *h* to day?
2Sa 21. 9 were put to death in the days of *h*,
9 in the beginning of barley *h*.
10 from the beginning of *h* until
23.13 came to David in the *h* time
Job 5. 5 Whose *h* the hungry eateth up,
Pr 6. 8 and gathereth her food in the *h*.
10. 5 he that sleepeth in *h* is a son
20. 4 therefore shall he beg in *h*, and
25.13 the cold of snow in the time of *h*,
26. 1 as rain in *h*, so honor is not
Isa 9. 3 according to the joy in *h*, and as
16. 9 thy summer fruits and for thy *h*
17.11 the *h* shall be a heap in the day of
18. 4 like a cloud of dew in the heat of *h*.
5 For afore the *h*, when the bud is
23. 3 the *h* of the river, is her revenue;
Jer 5.17 they shall eat up thine *h*, and thy
24 us the appointed weeks of the *h*.
8.20 The *h* is past, the summer is
50.16 the sickle in the time of *h*:
51.33 the time of her *h* shall come.
Hos 6.11 he hath set an *h* for thee,
Joel 1.11 the *h* of the field is perished.
3.13 the sickle, for the *h* is ripe:
Am 4. 7 were yet three months to the *h*:
Mt 9.37 The *h* truly is plenteous, but the
38 Lord of the *h*, that he will send
38 send forth laborers into his *h*.
13.30 both grow together until the *h*:
30 and in the time of *h* I will say
39 the *h* is the end of the world;
Mk 4.29 the sickle, because the *h* is come.
Lk 10. 2 The *h* truly is great, but the
2 ye therefore the Lord of the *h*,
2 send forth laborers into his *h*.
Jn 4.35 four months, and then cometh *h*?
35 for they are white already to *h*.
Rev 14.15 the *h* of the earth is ripe.

HASTE

Gen 19.22 *H* thee, escape thither; for I
24.46 And she made *h*, and let down her
43.30 And Joseph made *h*; for his
45. 9 *H* ye, and go up to my father,
13 and ye shall *h* and bring down
Ex 10.16 called for Moses and Aaron in *h*;
12.11 ye shall eat it in *h*: it is the
33 send them out of the land in *h*;
34. 8 And Moses made *h*, and bowed
Dt 16. 3 out of the land of Egypt in *h*:
32.35 shall come upon them make *h*.
Jdg 9.48 make *h*, and do as I have done.
13.10 And the woman made *h*, and ran,
1Sa 9.12 make *h* now, for he came to day
20.38 Make speed, *h*, stay not. And
21. 8 the king's business required *h*.
23.26 David made *h* to get away for
27 *H* thee, and come; for the
25.18 Then Abigail made *h*, and took
2Sa 4. 4 as she made *h* to flee, that he
2Ki 7.15 Syrians had cast away in their *h*.
2Ch 35.21 God commanded me to make *h*:
Ezr 4.23 they went up in *h* to Jerusalem
Est 5. 5 Cause Haman to make *h*, that
6.10 Make *h*, and take the apparel
Job 20. 2 answer, and for this I make *h*.
Ps 22.19 my strength, *h* thee to help me.
31.22 For I said in my *h*, I am cut
38.22 Make *h* to help me, O Lord
40.13 O Lord, make *h* to help me.
70. 1 Make *h*, O God, to deliver me;
1 make *h* to help me, O Lord.
5 make *h* unto me, O God: thou
71.12 my God, make *h* for my help.
116.11 I said in my *h*, All men are liars.
119.60 I made *h*, and delayed not to keep
141. 1 I cry unto thee: make *h* unto me;
Pr 1.16 evil, and make *h* to shed blood.
28.20 but he that maketh *h* to be rich
SS 8.14 Make *h*, my beloved, and be
Isa 28.16 that believeth shall not make *h*.
49.17 Thy children shall make *h*; thy
52.12 ye shall not go out with *h*,
59. 7 they make *h* to shed innocent
Jer 9.18 And let them make *h*, and take
Dan 2.25 in Daniel before the king in *h*,
3.24 was astonied, and rose up in *h*,
6.19 and went in *h* unto the den of lions.
Na 2. 5 they shall make *h* to the wall
Mk 6.25 she came in straightway with *h*
Lk 1.39 went into the hill country with *h*,
2.16 And they came with *h*, and found
19. 5 Zacchaeus, make *h*, and come
6 And he made *h*, and came down,
Ac 22.18 Make *h*, and get thee quickly out

HASTED

Gen 18. 7 young man; and he *h* to dress it.
24.18 and she *h*, and let down her
20 And she *h*, and emptied her
Ex 5.13 the taskmasters *h* them, saying,
Jos 4.10 and the people *h* and passed over.
8.14 that they *h* and rose up early,
19 and *h* and set the city on fire.
10.13 *h* not to go down about a whole
Jdg 20.37 the liers in wait *h*, and rushed
1Sa 17.48 that David *h*, and ran toward
25.23 when Abigail saw David, she *h*,
34 except thou hadst *h* and come to
42 And Abigail *h*, and arose, and
28.24 and she *h*, and killed it, and took
2Sa 19.16 was of Bahurim, *h* and came
1Ki 20.41 And he *h*, and took the ashes
2Ki 9.13 Then they *h*, and took every man
2Ch 26.20 himself *h* also to go out, because
Est 6.12 *h* to his house mourning, and
14 and *h* to bring Haman unto the
Job 31. 5 or if my foot hath *h* to deceit;
Ps 48. 5 they were troubled, and *h* away.
104. 7 voice of thy thunder they *h* away.
Ac 20.16 for he *h*, if it were possible for

HASTILY

Gen 41.14 and they brought him *h* out of
Jdg 2.23 without driving them out *h*;
9.54 he called *h* unto the young man
1Sa 4.14 And the man came in *h*, and told
1Ki 20.33 and did *h* catch it: and they said,
Pr 20.21 inheritance may be gotten *h* at
25. 8 Go not forth *h* to strive, lest thou
Jn 11.31 that she rose up *h* and went out,

HASTING

Isa 16. 5 judgment, and *h* righteousness.
2Pe 3.12 *h* unto the coming of the day of

HATE

Gen 50.15 Joseph will peradventure *h* us,
Ex 20. 5 fourth generation of them that *h*
Dt 7.10 repayeth them that *h* him to their
19.11 But if any man *h* his neighbor,
Jdg 11. 7 Did not ye *h* me, and expel me out
14.16 Thou dost but *h* me, and lovest me
2Ch 19. 2 and love them that *h* the Lord?
Ps 21. 8 shall find out those that *h* thee.
25.19 they *h* me with cruel hatred.
35.19 eye that *h* me without a cause.
41. 7 All that *h* me whisper together
69. 4 They that *h* me without a cause

At the harvest Boaz allows Ruth to gather grain (Ru 2) in this painting by Nicolas Poussin (1594-1665).

Ps 97.10 Ye that love the Lord, *h* evil:
119.113 I *h* vain thoughts: but thy law
163 I *h* and abhor lying: but thy law
139.21 I *h* them, O Lord, that *h* thee?
Pr 6.16 These six things doth the Lord *h*:
8.13 The fear of the Lord is to *h* evil:
13 and the froward mouth, do I *h*.
36 all they that *h* me love death.
9. 8 Reprove not a scorner, lest he *h*
Ec 3. 8 A time to love, and a time to *h*;
Isa 61. 8 I *h* robbery for burnt offering; and
Am 5.15 *H* the evil, and love the good,
21 I *h*, I despise your feast days,
Mic 3. 2 Who *h* the good, and love the evil;
Zec 8.17 for all these are things that I *h*,
Mt 5.43 shalt love thy neighbor, and *h*
44 do good to them that *h* you,
6.24 for either he will *h* the one,
24.10 another, and shall *h* one another.
Lk 1.71 from the hand of all that *h* us;
6.22 when men shall *h* you, and when
27 enemies, do good to them which *h*
14.26 and *h* not his father, and mother,
16.13 either he will *h* the one, and love
Jn 7. 7 cannot *h* you; but me it hateth,
15.18 If the world *h* you, ye know that
Ro 7.15 do I not; but what I *h*, that do I.
1Jn 3.13 my brethren, if the world *h* you.
Rev 2. 6 of the Nicolaitanes, which I also *h*.
15 the Nicolaitanes, which thing I *h*.
17.16 these shall *h* the whore, and shall

HATED

Gen 27.41 And Esau *h* Jacob because of the
37. 4 than all his brethren, they *h* him,
Ps 26. 5 I have *h* the congregation of evil
31. 6 I have *h* them that regard lying
44. 7 hast put them to shame that *h* us.
Pr 5.12 How have I *h* instruction, and my
14.20 The poor is *h* even of his own
Ec 2.17 Therefore I *h* life; because the
18 Yea, I *h* all my labor which I had
Mal 24. 9 and ye shall be *h* of all nations for
Mt 10.22 ye shall be *h* of all men for my
Mk 13.13 And ye shall be *h* of all men for my
Lk 19.14 But his citizens *h* him, and sent a
21.17 And ye shall be *h* of all men for my
Jn 15.18 ye know that it *h* me before it
18 me before it *h* you.
24 they both seen and *h* both me
25 They *h* me without a cause.
17.14 the world hath *h* them, because
Ro 9.13 I loved, but Esau have I *h*.
Eph 5.29 no man ever yet *h* his own flesh;
Heb 1. 9 loved righteousness, and *h* iniquity;

HATEFUL

Ps 36. 2 his iniquity be found to be *h*.
Tit 3. 3 envy, *h*, and hating one another.
Rev 18. 2 of every unclean and *h* bird.

HATERS

Ps 81.15 The *h* of the Lord should have
Ro 1.30 *h* of God, despiteful, proud,

HATEST

2Sa 19. 6 thine enemies, and *h* thy friends,
Ps 5. 5 thou *h* all workers of iniquity.
45. 7 righteousness, and *h* wickedness:
50.17 Seeing thou *h* instruction, and
Eze 23.28 the hand of them whom thou *h*,
Rev 2. 6 thou *h* the deeds of...Nicolaitanes,

HATETH

Ex 23. 5 see the ass of him that *h* thee
Dt 7.10 will not be slack to him that *h* him,
12.31 which he *h*, have they done unto
16.22 image; which the Lord thy God *h*.
22.16 unto this man to wife, and he *h* her;
Job 16. 9 teareth me in his wrath, who *h* me:
34.17 even he that *h* right govern?
Ps 11. 5 him that loveth violence his soul *h*.
120. 6 long dwelt with him that *h* peace.
Pr 11.15 and he that *h* suretiship is sure.
12. 1 but he that *h* reproof is brutish.
13. 5 A righteous man *h* lying: but a
24 He that spareth his rod *h* his son:
15.10 and he that *h* reproof shall die.
27 but he that *h* gifts shall live.
26.24 He that *h* dissembleth with his lips,
28 A lying tongue *h* those that are
28.16 he that *h* covetousness shall
29.24 partner with a thief *h* his own soul:
Isa 1.14 your appointed feasts my soul *h*:
Mal 2.16 saith that he *h* putting away:
Jn 3.20 *h* the light, neither cometh to the
7. 7 cannot hate you; but me it *h*,
12.25 he that *h* his life in this world
15.19 world, therefore the world *h* you.
23 He that *h* me *h* my Father also.
1Jn 2. 9 is in the light, and *h* his brother,
11 But he that *h* his brother is in
3.15 Whosoever *h* his brother, is a
4.20 and *h* his brother, he is a liar:

HATING

Ex 18.21 men of truth, *h* covetousness;
Tit 3. 3 envy, hateful, and *h* one another.
Jude 23 *h* even the garment spotted by the

HATRED

Nu 35.20 But if he thrust him of *h*,
2Sa 13.15 that the *h* wherewith he hated her
Ps 25.19 and they hate me with cruel *h*.
109. 3 me about also with words of *h*;
5 for good, and *h* for my love.
139.22 I hate them with perfect *h*:
Pr 10.12 *H* stirreth up strifes: but love
18 He that hideth *h* with lying lips,
15.17 than a stalled ox and *h* therewith.
26.26 Whose *h* is covered by deceit, his
Ec 9. 1 no man knoweth either love or *h*
6 Also their love, and their *h*, and
Eze 25.15 to destroy it for the old *h*;
35. 5 thou hast had a perpetual *h*, and
11 which thou hast used out of thy *h*
Hos 9. 7 thine iniquity, and the great *h*.
8 *h* in the house of his God.
Gal 5.20 *h*, variance, emulations, wrath,

HAVEN

Gen 49.13 shall dwell at the *h* of the sea
13 and he shall be for an *h* of ships;
Ps 107.30 them unto their desired *h*.
Ac 27.12 the *h* was not commodious
12 which is an *h* at Crete, and lieth

HAVENS

Ac 27. 8 place which is called The fair *h*;

HAVOCK

Ac 8. 3 Saul, he made *h* of the church,

HAWK

Lev 11.16 the owl, and the night *h*, and the
16 cuckow, and the *h* after his kind,
Dt 14.15 the owl, and the night *h*, and the
15 cuckow, and the *h* after his kind,
Job 39.26 Doth the *h* fly by thy wisdom,

HAY

Pr 27.25 The *h* appeareth, and the tender
Isa 15. 6 for the *h* is withered away, the
1Co 3.12 silver, precious stones, wood, *h*,

HAZARDED

Ac 15.26 Men that have *h* their lives for

HEAD

Gen 3.15 it shall bruise thy *h*, and thou
40.13 shall Pharaoh lift up thine *h*, and
48.14 laid it upon Ephraim's *h*, who was
Lev 4.24 his hand upon the *h* of the goat,
29, 33 upon the *h* of the sin offering,
Nu 6. 5 shall no rasor come upon his *h*:
18 Nazarite shall shave the *h* of his
Jos 2.19 his blood shall be upon his *h*,
19 his blood shall be on our *h*,
Jdg 13. 5 no rasor shall come on his *h*:
16.13 weavest the seven locks of my *h*
19 shave off the seven locks of his *h*;
1Sa 14.45 one hair of his *h* fall to the ground;
17. 5 had an helmet of brass upon his *h*,
54 David took the *h* of the Philistine,
2Ki 2. 3, 5 thy master from thy *h* to-day?
23 thou bald *h*; go up, thou bald *h*.
4.19 said unto his father, My *h*, my *h*.
9. 6 he poured the oil on his *h*,
30 painted her face, and tired her *h*,
1Ch 29.11 thou art exalted as *h* above all.
Job 1.20 rent his mantle, and shaved his *h*,
10.15 yet will I not lift up my *h*.
20. 6 and his *h* reach unto the clouds;
Ps 23. 5 thou anointest my *h* with oil;
27. 6 now shall mine *h* be lifted up
38. 4 iniquities are gone over mine *h*:
40.12 more than the hairs of mine *h*:
69. 4 more than the hairs of mine *h*:
133. 2 the precious ointment upon the *h*,
Pr 16.31 The hoary *h* is a crown of glory,
20.29 the beauty of old men is the gray *h*.
25.22 heap coals of fire upon his *h*,
Ec 2.14 The wise man's eyes are in his *h*;
SS 5.11 His *h* is as the most fine gold,
Isa 1. 5 the whole *h* is sick, and the whole
59.17 an helmet of salvation upon his *h*:
Jer 9. 1 Oh that my *h* were waters,
48.37 every *h* shall be bald, and every
La 2.15 they hiss and wag their *h* at the
3.54 Waters flowed over mine *h*; then I
5.16 The crown is fallen from our *h*:
Eze 33. 4 his blood shall be upon his own *h*.
Dan 2.32 This image's *h* was of fine gold,
38 Thou art this *h* of gold.
3.27 nor was an hair of their *h* singed,
7. 9 hair of his *h* like the pure wool:
Am 2. 7 of the earth on the *h* of the poor,
Jon 2. 5 weeds were wrapped about my *h*.
4. 6 a shadow over his *h*, to deliver
8 the sun beat upon the *h* of Jonah.
Mt 5.36 Neither shalt thou swear by thy *h*,
6.17 when thou fastest, anoint thine *h*,
8.20 hath not where to lay his *h*.
10.30 hairs of your *h* are all numbered.
14. 8 Give me here John Baptist's *h* in
11 And his *h* was brought in a
21.42 is become the *h* of the corner:
26. 7 ointment, and poured it on his *h*,
27.29 of thorns, they put it upon his *h*,
30 the reed, and smote him on the *h*.
37 set up over his *h* his accusation
Mk 6.24 she said, The *h* of John the Baptist.
25 in a charger the *h* of John the
27 commanded his *h* to be brought:
28 brought his *h* in a charger, and
12. 4 and wounded him in the *h*, and
10 is become the *h* of the corner:
14. 3 the box, and poured it on his *h*.
15.17 thorns, and put it about his *h*,
19 they smote him on the *h* with a
Lk 7.38 wipe them with the hairs of her *h*,
44 wiped them with the hairs of her *h*.
46 My *h* with oil thou didst not
9.58 hath not where to lay his *h*.
12. 7 hairs of your *h* are all numbered.
20.17 is become the *h* of the corner?
21.18 shall not an hair of your *h* perish.
Jo 13. 9 but also my hands and my *h*.
19. 2 of thorns, and put it on his *h*, and
30 and he bowed his *h*, and gave up
20. 7 the napkin, that was about his *h*,
12 the one at the *h*, and the other
Ac 4.11 is become the *h* of the corner.

18.18 having shorn his *h* in Cenchrea:
27.34 shall not an hair fall from the *h* of
Ro 12.20 shalt heap coals of fire on his *h*.
1Co 11. 3 the *h* of every man is Christ; and
3 the *h* of the woman is the man;
3 and the *h* of Christ is God.
4 prophesying, having his *h* covered,
4 covered, dishonoreth his *h*.
5 prophesieth with her *h* uncovered
5 uncovered dishonoreth her *h*:
7 indeed ought not to cover his *h*,
10 woman to have power on her *h*
12.21 nor again the *h* to the feet, I have
Eph 1.22 gave him to be *h* over all things
4.15 which is the *h*, even Christ:
5.23 the husband is the *h* of the wife,
23 as Christ is the *h* of the church:
Col 1.18 he is the *h* of the body, the church:
2.10 the *h* of all principality and power:
19 And not holding the *H*, from
1Pe 2. 7 same is made the *h* of the corner,
Rev 1.14 His *h* and his hairs were white
10. 1 and a rainbow was upon his *h*,
12. 1 her *h* a crown of twelve stars:
14.14 having on his *h* a golden crown,
19.12 and on his *h* were many crowns;

HEADLONG
Job 5.13 counsel of the froward is carried *h*.
Lk 4.29 that they might cast him down *h*.
Ac 1.18 of iniquity; and falling *h*, he burst

HEADS
Gen 2.10 parted, and became into four *h*.
Jos 7. 6 Israel, and put dust upon their *h*.
Jdg 9.57 did God render upon their *h*:
Job 2.12 sprinkled dust upon their *h*
Ps 24. 7 Lift up your *h*, O ye gates; and
9 Lift up your *h*, O ye gates; even
74.13 thou brakest the *h* of the dragons
14 Thou brakest the *h* of leviathan
109.25 upon me they shaked their *h*.
Isa 35.10 and everlasting joy upon their *h*:
Dan 7. 6 the beast had also four *h*; and
Mt 27.39 by reviled him, wagging their *h*,
Mk 15.29 railed on him, wagging their *h*,
Lk 21.28 look up, and lift up your *h*;
Ac 18. 6 Your blood be upon your own *h*;
21.24 that they may shave their *h*:
Rev 4. 4 they had on their *h* crowns of gold.
9. 7 on their *h* were as it were crowns
17 and the *h* of the horses were as the
17 horses were as the *h* of lions;
19 like unto serpents, and had *h*,
12. 3 having seven *h* and ten horns, and
3 and seven crowns upon his *h*.
13. 1 having seven *h* and ten horns,
1 upon his *h* the name of blasphemy.
3 And I saw one of his *h* as it were
17. 3 having seven *h* and ten horns.
7 hath the seven *h* and ten horns.
9 The seven *h* are seven mountains,
18.19 they cast dust on their *h*, and cried,

HEADY
2Ti 3. 4 Traitors, *h*, highminded, lovers

HEAL
Nu 12.13 *H* her now, O God, I beseech
Dt 32.39 I make alive; I wound, and I *h*:
2Ki 20. 5 I will *h* thee: on the third day
8 the sign that the Lord will *h* me,
2Ch 7.14 their sin, and will *h* their land.
Ps 6. 2 O Lord, *h* me; for my bones are
41. 4 be merciful unto me: *h* my soul;
60. 2 *h* the breaches thereof; for it
Ec 3. 3 A time to kill, and a time to *h*;
Isa 19.22 he shall smite and *h* it: and they
22 of them, and shall *h* them.
57.18 I have seen his ways, and will *h*
19 saith the Lord; and I will *h* him.
Jer 3.22 and I will *h* your backslidings.
17.14 *H* me, O Lord, and I shall be
30.17 I will *h* thee of thy wounds,
La 2.13 great like the sea: who can *h* thee?
Hos 5.13 yet could he not *h* you, nor cure
6. 1 he hath torn, and he will *h* us; he
14. 4 I will *h* their backsliding, I will
Zec 11.16 nor *h* that that is broken,
Mt 8. 7 unto him, I will come and *h* him.
10. 1 and to *h* all manner of sickness
8 *H* the sick, cleanse the lepers,
12.10 lawful to *h* on the sabbath days?
13.15 converted, and I should *h* them.
Mk 3. 2 he would *h* on the sabbath day;
15 to have power to *h* sicknesses,
Lk 4.18 sent me to *h* the brokenhearted,
23 proverb, Physician, *h* thyself:
5.17 the Lord was present to *h* them.
6. 7 he would *h* on the sabbath day;
7. 3 would come and *h* his servant.
9. 2 of God, and to *h* the sick.
10. 9 *h* the sick that are therein, and
14. 3 lawful to *h* on the sabbath day?
Jn 4.47 would come down, and *h* his son:
12.40 be converted, and I should *h* them.
Ac 4.30 stretching forth thine hand to *h*;
28.27 be converted, and I should *h* them.
(See illustration on page 358)

HEALED
Gen 20.17 and God *h* Abimelech, and his
Ex 21.19 cause him to be thoroughly *h*.
Lev 13.18 skin thereof, was a boil, and is *h*,
37 the scall is *h*, he is clean:
14. 3 if the plague of leprosy be *h* in
48 clean, because the plague is *h*.
Dt 28.27 itch, whereof thou canst not be *h*.
35 a sore botch that cannot be *h*,
1Sa 6. 3 then ye shall be *h*, and it shall be
2Ki 2.21 the Lord, I have *h* these waters;
22 So the waters were *h* unto this
8.29 king Joram went back to be *h* in
9.15 king Joram was returned to be *h*
2Ch 22. 6 he returned to be *h* in Jezreel
30.20 to Hezekiah, and *h* the people.
Ps 30. 2 cried unto thee, and thou hast *h* me.
107.20 He sent his word, and *h* them,
Isa 6.10 their heart, and convert, and be *h*.
53. 5 and with his stripes we are *h*.
Jer 6.14 They have *h* also the hurt of the
8.11 For they have *h* the hurt of the
15.18 incurable, which refuseth to be *h*?
17.14 Heal me, O Lord, and I shall be *h*;
51. 8 her pain, if so be she may be *h*.
9 We would have *h* Babylon,
9 Babylon, but she is not *h*:
Eze 30.21 not be bound up to be *h*,
34. 4 have ye *h* that which was sick,
47. 8 the sea, the waters shall be *h*.
9 for they shall be *h*; and every
11 marishes thereof shall not be *h*;
Hos 7. 1 When I would have *h* Israel, then
11. 3 they knew not that I *h* them.
Mt 4.24 had the palsy; and he *h* them.
8. 8 only, and my servant shall be *h*.
13 servant was *h* in the selfsame
16 his word, and *h* all that were sick:
12.15 followed him, and he *h* them all;
22 blind, and dumb: and he *h* him,
14.14 toward them, and he *h* their sick.
15.30 at Jesus' feet; and he *h* them:
19. 2 followed him; and he *h* them there.
21.14 him in the temple; and he *h* them.
Mk 1.34 he *h* many that were sick of
3.10 For he had *h* many; insomuch
5.23 hands on her, that she may be *h*;
29 that she was *h* of that plague.
6. 5 upon a few sick folk, and *h* them.
13 many that were sick, and *h* them.
Lk 4.40 on every one of them, and *h* them.
5.15 hear, and to be *h* by him of their
6.17 and to be *h* of their diseases;
18 unclean spirits: and they were *h*.
19 virtue out of him, and *h* them all.
7. 7 word, and my servant shall be *h*.
8. 2 women, which had been *h* of evil
36 possessed of the devils was *h*.
43 neither could be *h* of any,
47 and how she was *h* immediately.
9.11 *h* them that had need of healing.
42 and *h* the child, and delivered
13.14 Jesus had *h* on the sabbath day,
14 in them therefore come and be *h*,
14. 4 him, and *h* him, and let him go;
17.15 when he saw that he was *h*,
22.51 he touched his ear, and *h* him.
Jn 5.13 And he that was *h* wist not who
Ac 3.11 man which was *h* held Peter and
4.14 beholding the man which was *h*
5.16 and they were *h* every one.
8. 7 and that were lame, were *h*.
14. 9 that he had faith to be *h*,
28. 8 his hands on him and *h* him.
9 in the island, came, and were *h*:
Heb 12.13 the way; but let it rather be *h*.
Jas 5.16 one for another, that ye may be *h*.
1Pe 2.24 by whose stripes ye were *h*.
Rev 13. 3 his deadly wound was *h*: and all
12 beast, whose deadly wound was *h*.

HEALER
Isa 3. 7 swear, saying, I will not be an *h*;

HEALETH
Ex 15.26 for I am the Lord that *h* thee.
Ps 103. 3 iniquities; who *h* all thy diseases;
147. 3 He *h* the broken in heart, and
Isa 30.26 and *h* the stroke of their wound.

HEALING
Jer 14.19 us, and there is no *h* for us?
19 and for the time of *h*, and behold
30.13 up: thou hast no *h* medicines.
Na 3.19 There is no *h* of thy bruise;
Mal 4. 2 arise with *h* in his wings;
Mt 4.23 *h* all manner of sickness and all
9.35 *h* every sickness and every disease
Lk 9. 6 the gospel, and *h* every where.
11 healed them that had need of *h*.
Ac 4.22 this miracle of *h* was shewed.
10.38 and *h* all that were oppressed of
1Co 12. 9 gifts of *h* by the same Spirit;
30 Have all the gifts of *h*? do all
Rev 22. 2 were for the *h* of the nations.

HEALINGS
1Co 12.28 miracles, then gift of *h*, helps,

HEALTH
Gen 43.28 servant our father is in good *h*,
2Sa 20. 9 Art thou in *h*, my brother?
Ps 42.11 who is the *h* of my countenance,
43. 5 who is the *h* of my countenance,
67. 2 thy saving *h* among all nations.
Pr 3. 8 It shall be *h* to thy navel, and
4.22 find them, and *h* to all their flesh.
12.18 but the tongue of the wise is *h*.
13.17 but a faithful ambassador is *h*.
16.24 the soul, and *h* to the bones.
Isa 58. 8 and thine *h* shall spring forth
Jer 8.15 and for a time of *h*, and behold
22 the *h* of the daughter of my
30.17 For I will restore *h* unto thee,
33. 6 I will bring it *h* and cure, and I
Ac 27.34 some meat: for this is for your *h*:
3Jn 2 thou mayest prosper and be in *h*,
(See box on page 359)

HEAP
Gen 31.46 they took stones, and made an *h*:
46 they did eat there upon the *h*.
48 This *h* is a witness between me

Jesus is shown healing the multitudes (Mt 15, 19; Mk 6; Lk 6) in this 17th-century etching by Rembrandt.

Gen 31.51 Behold this *h*, and behold this
52 This *h* be witness, and this pillar
52 I will not pass over this *h* to thee,
52 thou shalt not pass over this *h* and
Ex 15. 8 the floods stood upright as an *h*,
Dt 13.16 and it shall be an *h* for ever;
32.23 I will *h* mischiefs upon them:
Jos 3.13 and they shall stand upon an *h*.
16 rose up upon an *h* very far from
7.26 over him a great *h* of stones
8.28 Ai, and made it an *h* for ever, even
29 raise thereon a great *h* of stones,
Ru 3. 7 down at the end of the *h* of corn:
2Sa 18.17 very great *h* of stones upon him:
Job 8.17 roots are wrapped about the *h*,
16. 4 I could *h* up words against you,
27.16 Though he *h* up silver as the dust,
36.13 hypocrites in heart *h* up wrath:
Ps 33. 7 waters of the seat together as an *h*:
78.13 made the waters to stand as an *h*.
Pr 25.22 shalt *h* coals of fire upon his head,
Ec 2.26 gather and to *h* up, that he may
SS 7. 2 thy belly is like an *h* of wheat
Isa 17. 1 city, and it shall be a ruinous *h*.
11 the harvest shall be a *h* in the day
25. 2 thou hast made of a city an *h*;
Jer 30.18 shall be builded on her own *h*,
49. 2 it shall be a desolate *h*, and her
Eze 24.10 *H* on wood, kindle the fire,
Mic 1. 6 make Samaria as an *h* of the field,
Hab 1.10 for they shall *h* dust, and take it.
3.15 through the *h* of great waters.
Hag 2.16 came to an *h* of twenty measures,
Ro 12.20 shalt *h* coals of fire on his head.
2Ti 4. 3 they *h* to themselves teachers,

HEAPED

Zec 9. 3 and *h* up silver as the dust, and
Jas 5. 3 Ye have *h* treasures together for

HEAR

Gen 23. 6 *H* us, my lord: thou art a mighty
37. 6 *H*, I pray you, this dream which
42.22 the child; and ye would not *h*?
Ex 6.12 how then shall Pharaoh *h* me,
20.19 Speak thou with us, and we will *h*:
Nu 9. 8 *h* what the Lord will command
Dt 1.17 ye shall *h* the small as well as the
17 bring it unto me, and I will *h* it.
4.33 Did ever people *h* the voice of God
5. 1 *H*, O Israel, the statutes and
6. 4 *H*, O Israel: The Lord our God is
9. 1 *H*, O Israel: Thou art to pass over
32. 1 and *h*, O earth, the words of my
Jdg 14.13 forth thy riddle, that we may *h* it.
1Sa 2.24 for it is no good report that I *h*:
8.18 the Lord will not *h* you in that
15.14 the lowing of the oxen which I *h*?
1Ki 8.30 and *h* thou in heaven thy dwelling
34, 36 *h* thou in heaven, and forgive
42 For they shall *h* of thy great name,
45 *h* thou in heaven their prayer
18.26 O Baal, *h* us. But there was no
2Ki 18.28 *H* the word of the great king, the
19.16 Lord, bow down thine ear, and *h*:
1Ch 14.15 thou shalt *h* a sound of going
2Ch 6.23 Then *h* thou from heaven, and
18.18 Therefore *h* the word of the Lord;
Neh 4. 4 *H*, O our God: for we are despised:
8. 2 that could *h* with understanding,
Job 5.27 *h* it, and know thou it for thy good.
13. 6 *H* now my reasoning, and hearken
17 *H* diligently my speech, and my
27. 9 Will God *h* his cry when trouble
31.35 Oh that one would *h* me! behold
34. 2 *H* my words, O ye wise men;
35.13 God will not *h* vanity, neither will
Ps 4. 1 *H* me when I call, O God of my
1 mercy upon me, and *h* my prayer.
3 the Lord will *h* when I call unto
5. 3 voice shalt thou *h* in the morning,
10.17 thou wilt cause thine ear to *h*:
20. 1 *h* thee in the day of trouble;
27. 7 *H*, O Lord, when I cry with my
28. 2 *H* the voice of my supplications,
49. 1 *H* this, all ye people; give ear,
50. 7 *H*, O my people, and I will speak;
51. 8 Make me to *h* joy and gladness;
54. 2 *H* my prayer, O God; give ear to
61. 1 *H* my cry, O God; attend unto my
64. 1 *H* my voice, O God, in my prayer:
66.16 Come and *h*, all ye that fear God,
18 in my heart, the Lord will not *h* me:
69.17 I am in trouble: *h* me speedily.
84. 8 O Lord God of hosts, *h* my prayer:
85. 8 *h* what God the Lord will speak:
86. 1 down thine ear, O Lord, *h* me:
95. 7 To day if ye will *h* his voice,
102. 1 *H* my prayer, O Lord, and let my
20 To *h* the groaning of the prisoner;
115. 6 They have ears, but they *h* not:
135.17 They have ears, but they *h* not;
143. 1 *H* my prayer, O Lord, give ear to
8 Cause me to *h* thy lovingkindness
Pr 1. 8 *h* the instruction of thy father,
8.33 *H* instruction, and be wise, and
22.17 ear, and *h* the words of the wise,
23.19 *H* thou, my son, and be wise,
Ec 5. 1 be more ready to *h*, than to give
7. 5 better to *h* the rebuke of the wise,
5 for a man to *h* the song of fools.
12.13 us *h* the conclusion of the whole
Isa 1. 2 *H*, O heavens, and give ear, O
15 make many prayers, I will not *h*:
6. 9 *H* ye indeed, but understand not;
10 *h* with their ears, and understand
29.18 And in that day shall the deaf *h* the
36.13 *H* ye the words of the great king,
37.17 Incline thine ear, O Lord, and *h*;
65.12 when I spake, ye did not *h*; but
24 while they are yet speaking, I will *h*.
Jer 5.21 *H* now this, O foolish people, and
21 which have ears, and *h* not:
6.19 *H*, O earth: behold, I will bring
7.16 to me: for I will not *h* thee.
9.20 *h* the word of the Lord, O ye women,
11. 2, 6 *H* ye the words of this covenant,
13.17 But if ye will not *h* it, my soul shall
18. 2 I will cause thee to *h* my words.
49.20 *h* the counsel of the Lord, that the
Eze 6. 3 *h* the word of the Lord God: Thus
8.18 a loud voice, yet will I not *h* them.
12. 2 they have ears to *h*, and *h* not:
16.35 O harlot, *h* the word of the Lord:
25. 3 *H* the word of the Lord God;
34. 7, 9 ye shepherds, *h* the word of the
36. 1 Ye mountains of Israel, *h* the word
37. 4 O ye dry bones, *h* the word of the
Dan 3. 5 time ye *h* the sound of the cornet,
9.18 O my God, incline thine ear, and *h*;
Hos 4. 1 *H* the word of the Lord, ye
5. 1 *H* ye this, O priests; and hearken,
Joel 1. 2 *H* this, ye old men, and give ear,
Am 4. 1 *H* this word, ye kine of Bashan,
5.23 I will not *h* the melody of thy viols,
8. 4 *H* this, O ye that swallow up the
Mic 3. 4 the Lord, but he will not *h* them:
6. 1 *H* ye now what the Lord saith;
2 *H* ye, O mountains, the Lord's
Hab 1. 2 shall I cry, and thou wilt not *h*!
Zec 7.11 their ears, that they should not *h*.
12 lest they should *h* the law, and the
10. 6 Lord their God, and will *h* them.
13. 9 call on my name, and I will *h* them:
Mal 2. 2 If ye will not *h*, and if ye will not
Mt 10.14 not receive you, nor *h* your words,
27 what ye *h* in the ear, that preach
11. 4 those things which ye do *h* and see:
5 lepers are cleansed, and the deaf *h*,
15 He that hath ears to *h*, let him *h*.
12.19 any man *h* his voice in the streets.
42 to *h* the wisdom of Solomon; and,
13. 9 Who hath ears to *h*, let him
9 Who hath ears…let him *h*.
13 see not; and hearing they *h* not,
14 By hearing ye shall *h*, and shall not
15 their eyes, and *h* with their ears,
16 they see: and your ears, for they *h*.
17 and to *h* those things which ye *h*,
18 *H* ye therefore the parable of the
43 Who hath ears to *h*, let him
43 Who hath ears…let him *h*.
15.10 said unto them, *H*, and understand:
17. 5 whom I am well pleased; *h* ye him.
18.15 if he shall *h* thee, thou hast gained

16 if he will not *h* thee, then take with
17 And if he shall neglect to *h* them,
17 but if he neglect to *h* the church,
21.33 *H* another parable: There was a
24. 6 ye shall *h* of wars and rumors of
Mk 4. 9 He that hath ears to *h*, let him *h*.
12 they may *h*, and not understand;
18 among thorns; such as *h* the word,
20 such as *h* the word, and receive it,
23 any man have ears to *h*, let him *h*.
24 Take heed what ye *h*: with what
24 you that *h* shall more be given.
33 unto them, as they were able to *h* it.
6.11 shall not receive you, nor *h* you,
7.16 any man have ears to *h*, let him *h*.
37 he maketh both the deaf to *h*, and
8.18 see ye not? having ears, *h* ye not?
9. 7 This is my beloved Son: *h* him.
12.29 *H*, O Israel; the Lord our God is one
13. 7 ye shall *h* of wars and rumors of
Lk 5. 1 upon him to *h* the word of God,
15 multitudes came together to *h*, and
6.17 came to *h* him, and to be healed of
27 I say unto you which *h*, Love your
7.22 lepers are cleansed, the deaf *h*, the
8. 8 He that hath ears to *h*, let him *h*.
12 by the way side are they that *h*;
13 they *h*, receive the word with
18 Take heed therefore how ye *h*: for
21 which *h* the word of God, and do it.
9. 9 is this, of whom I *h* such things?
35 This is my beloved Son: *h* him.
10.24 to *h* those things which ye *h*, and
11.28 blessed are they that *h* the word of
31 to *h* the wisdom of Solomon; and,
14.35 He that hath ears to *h*, let him *h*.
15. 1 publicans and sinners for to *h* him.
16. 2 him, How is it that I *h* this of thee?
29 and the prophets; let them *h* them.
31 they *h* not Moses and the prophets,
18. 6 said, *H* what the unjust judge saith.
19.48 people were very attentive to *h* him.
21. 9 ye shall *h* of wars and commotions,
38 to him in the temple, for to *h* him.
Jn 5.25 the dead shall *h* the voice of God:
25 God: and they that *h* shall live.
28 are in the graves shall *h* his voice,
30 as I *h*, I judge; and my judgment is
6.60 This is an hard saying; who can *h* it?
7.51 law judge any man, before it *h* him,
8.43 even because ye cannot *h* my word.
47 ye therefore *h* them not, because ye
9.27 told you already, and ye did not *h*:
27 wherefore would ye *h* it again?
10. 3 and the sheep *h* his voice: and he
8 but the sheep did not *h* them.
16 and they shall *h* my voice; and they
20 a devil, and is mad; why *h* ye him?
27 My sheep *h* my voice, and I know
12.47 if any man *h* my words, and believe
14.24 the word which ye *h* is not mine,
16.13 whatsoever he shall *h*, that shall he
Ac 2. 8 *h* we every man in our own tongue,
11 we do *h* them speak in our tongues,
22 Ye men of Israel, *h* these words;
33 forth this, which ye now see and *h*.
3.22 shall ye *h* in all things whatsoever
23 which will not *h* that prophet,
7.37 like unto me; him shall ye *h*.
10.22 his house, and to *h* words of thee.
33 to *h* all things that are commanded
13. 7 and desired to *h* the word of God.
44 city together, to *h* the word of God.
15. 7 should *h* the word of the gospel,
17.21 either to tell, or to *h* some new thing.
32 We will *h* thee again of this matter.
19.26 see and *h*, that not alone at Ephesus,
21.22 for they will *h* that thou art come.
22. 1 *h* ye my defense which I make
14 shouldest *h* the voice of his mouth.
23.35 I will *h* thee, said he, when thine

Biblical Themes

HEALTH AND SICKNESS

If thou wilt diligently hearken to the voice of the Lord thy God . . . I will put none of these diseases upon thee, which I have brought upon the Egyptians: for I am the Lord that healeth thee. Ex 15.26

If ye shall despise my statutes . . . I will even appoint over you terror, consumption, and the burning ague, that shall consume the eyes, and cause sorrow of heart. Lev 26.15-16

I wound, and I heal. Dt 32.39

Have pity upon me, have pity upon me, O ye my friends; for the hand of God hath touched me. Job 19.21

Bless the Lord, O my soul, and forget not all his benefits: who forgiveth all thine iniquities; who healeth all thy diseases. Ps 103.2-3

Be not wise in thine own eyes: fear the Lord, and depart from evil. It shall be health to thy navel, and marrow to thy bones. Pr 3.7-8

Say to them that are of a fearful heart, Be strong, fear not: behold, your God will come . . . and save you. Then the eyes of the blind shall be opened, and the ears of the deaf shall be unstopped. Then shall the lame man leap as an hart, and the tongue of the dumb sing. Isa 35.4-6

Is there no balm in Gilead; is there no physician there? why then is not the health of the daughter of my people recovered? Jer 8.22

Thy bruise is incurable, and thy wound is grievous. There is none to plead thy cause, that thou mayest be bound up: thou hast no healing medicines. . . . for I have wounded thee with the wound of an enemy . . . because thy sins were increased. Jer 30.12-14

Go up into Gilead, and take balm, O virgin, the daughter of Egypt: in vain shalt thou use many medicines; for thou shalt not be cured. Jer 46.11

Come, and let us return unto the Lord: for he hath torn, and he will heal us; he hath smitten, and he will bind us up. Hos 6.1

Unto you that fear my name shall the Sun of righteousness arise with healing in his wings. Mal 4.2

And they brought unto [Jesus] all sick people that were taken with divers diseases and torments, and those which were possessed with devils, and those which were lunatick, and those that had the palsy; and he healed them. Mt 4.24

The Pharisees . . . said unto his disciples, Why eateth your Master with publicans and sinners? But when Jesus heard that, he said unto them, They that be whole need not a physician, but they that are sick. Mt 9.11-12

Great multitudes came unto him, having with them those that were lame, blind, dumb, maimed, and many others . . . and he healed them: insomuch that the multitude wondered, when they saw the dumb to speak, the maimed to be whole, the lame to walk, and the blind to see: and they glorified the God of Israel. Mt 15.30-31

I was sick, and ye visited me. Mt 25.36

Lest I should be exalted . . . there was given to me a thorn in the flesh. . . . I besought the Lord thrice, that it might depart from me. And he said unto me, My grace is sufficient for thee. 2Co 12.7-9

The prayer of faith shall save the sick, and the Lord shall raise him up. Jas 5.15

24. 4 wouldest *h* us of thy clemency a
25.22 I would also *h* the man myself.
22 morrow, said he, thou shalt *h* him.
26. 3 I beseech thee to *h* me patiently.
29 thou, but also all that *h* me this day,
28.22 to *h* of thee what thou thinkest:
26 Hearing ye shall *h*, and shall not
27 their eyes, and *h* with their ears,
28 the Gentiles, and that they will *h* it.
Ro 10.14 shall they *h* without a preacher?
11. 8 see, and ears that they should not *h*;
1Co 11.18 I *h* that there be divisions among
14.21 yet for all that will they not *h* me,
Gal 4.21 under the law, do ye not *h* the law?
Php 1.27 be absent, I may *h* of your affairs,
30 saw in me, and now *h* to be in me.
2Th 3.11 *h* that there are some which walk
1Ti 4.16 save thyself, and them that *h* thee.
2Ti 4.17 and that all the Gentiles might *h*:
Heb 3. 7, 15 To day if ye will *h* his voice,
4. 7 said, To day if ye will *h* his voice,
Jas 1.19 let every man be swift to *h*, slow to
1Jn 5.15 that he *h* us, whatsoever we ask,
3Jn 4 no greater joy than to *h* that my
Rev 1. 3 that *h* the words of this prophecy,
2. 7, 11, 17, 29 that hath an ear, let him *h*
3. 6, 13 He that hath an ear, let him *h*
20 if any man *h* my voice, and open
22 He that hath an ear, let him *h*
9.20 neither can see, nor *h*, nor walk:
13. 9 If any man have an ear, let him *h*.

HEARD

Gen 3. 8 And they *h* the voice of the Lord
10 I *h* thy voice in the garden, and I
18.10 Sarah *h* it in the tent door, which
42. 2 have *h* that there is corn in Egypt:
Ex 3. 7 have *h* their cry by reason of their
16.12 I have *h* the murmurings of the
33. 4 the people *h* these evil tidings,
Nu 11.10 Then Moses *h* the people weep
Dt 1.34 the Lord *h* the voice of your words,
5.26 hath *h* the voice of the living God
26. 7 the Lord *h* our voice, and looked
Jos 2.10 we have *h* how the Lord dried up
24.27 it hath *h* all the words of the Lord
Jdg 18.25 Let not thy voice be *h* among us,
1Sa 4.19 *h* the tidings that the ark of God
22. 6 Saul *h* that David was discovered,
1Ki 2.42 The word that I have *h* is good.
9. 3 I have *h* thy prayer and thy
10. 1 the queen of Sheba *h* of the fame
17.22 the Lord *h* the voice of Elijah;
19.13 when Elijah *h* it, that he wrapped
21.16 when Ahab *h* that Naboth was dead,
2Ki 20. 5 *h* thy prayer, I have seen thy tears,
2Ch 9. 1 the queen of Sheba *h* of the fame
Neh 4. 1 when Sanballat *h* that we builded
12.43 joy of Jerusalem was *h* even afar off.
Job 4.16 there was silence, and I *h* a voice,
13. 1 mine ear hath *h* and understood it.
15. 8 Hast thou *h* the secret of God?
19. 7 I cry out of wrong, but I am not *h*:
29.11 When the ear *h* me, then it blessed
Ps 3. 4 and he *h* me out of his holy hill.
6. 9 The Lord hath *h* my supplication;
18. 6 he *h* my voice out of his temple,
19. 3 language, where their voice is not *h*,
28. 6 *h* the voice of my supplications.
34. 4 I sought the Lord, and he *h* me,
6 poor man cried, and the Lord *h*
38.13 But I, as a deaf man, *h* not;
44. 1 We have *h* with our ears, O God,
62.11 twice have I *h* this; that power
66.19 But verily God hath *h* me; he hath
78.21 the Lord *h* this, and was wroth:
81. 5 *h* a language that I understood not.
120. 1 cried unto the Lord, and he *h* me.
Ec 9.17 words of wise men are *h* in quiet
Isa 28.22 for I have *h* from the Lord of hosts
37.26 Hast thou not *h* long ago, how I
38. 5 I have *h* thy prayer, I have seen
40.21 have ye not known? have ye not *h*?
28 hast thou not *h*, that the everlasting
42. 2 cause his voice to be *h* in the street.
49. 8 In an acceptable time have I *h*
60.18 Violence shall no more be *h* in thy
65.19 voice of weeping shall be no more *h*
66. 8 Who hath *h* such a thing? who
Jer 4.31 For I have *h* a voice as of a woman
9.19 a voice of wailing is *h* out of Zion,
23.18 hath marked his word, and *h* it?
25 I have *h* what the prophets said,
31.15 voice was *h* in Ramah, lamentation,
36.11 had *h* out of the book all the words
La 1.21 mine enemies have *h* of my trouble;
3.56 Thou hast *h* my voice; hide not
61 Thou hast *h* their reproach, O Lord.
Eze 2. 2 that I *h* him that spake unto me.
3.13 I *h* also the voice of the wings of
Dan 5.14 have even *h* of thee, that the spirit
16 I have *h* of thee, that thou canst
12. 8 And I *h*, but I understood not:
Ob 1 We have *h* a rumor from the
Jon 2. 2 unto the Lord, and he *h* me;
Hab 3. 2 O Lord, I have *h* thy speech, and
Zec 8.23 for we have *h* that God is with you
Mt 2. 3 When Herod the king had *h* these
9 When they had *h* the king, they
18 In Rama was there a voice *h*,
2.22 when he *h* that Archelaus did reign
4.12 Jesus had *h* that John was cast into
5.21, 27 Ye have *h* that it was said by
33 ye have *h* that it hath been said by
38, 43 Ye have *h* that it hath been said,
6. 7 shall be *h* for their much speaking.
8.10 When Jesus *h* it, he marvelled, and
9.12 But when Jesus *h* that, he said unto
11. 2 when John had *h* in the prison the
12.24 when the Pharisees *h* it, they said,
13.17 which ye hear, and have not *h* them.
14. 1 Herod the tetrarch *h* of the fame of
13 When Jesus *h* of it, he departed
13 people had *h* thereof, they followed
15.12 offended, after they *h* this saying?
17. 6 when the disciples *h* it, they fell on
19.22 when the young man *h* that saying,
25 When his disciples *h* it, they were
20.24 when the ten *h* it, they were moved
30 when they *h* that Jesus passed by,
21.45 chief priests and Pharisees had *h*
22. 7 the king *h* thereof, he was wroth:
22 had *h* these words, they marvelled,
33 when the multitude *h* this, they were
34 had *h* that he had put the Sadducees
26.65 now ye have *h* his blasphemy.
27.47 they *h* that, said, This man calleth
Mk 2.17 When Jesus *h* it, he saith unto them,
3. 8 when they had *h* what great things
21 when his friends *h* of it, they went
4.15 when they have *h*, Satan cometh
16 who, when they have *h* the word,
5.27 When she had *h* of Jesus, came
36 As soon as Jesus *h* the word that
6.14 king Herod *h* of him; for his name
16 Herod *h* thereof, he said, It is John,
20 when he *h* him, he did many things,
20 did many things, and *h* him gladly.
29 when his disciples *h* of it, they came
55 that were sick, where they *h* he was.
7.25 had an unclean spirit, *h* of him,
10.41 when the ten *h* it, they began to be
47 when he *h* that it was Jesus of
11.14 for ever. And his disciples *h* it.
18 the scribes and chief priests *h* it,
12.28 having *h* them reasoning together,
37 the common people *h* him gladly.
14.11 And when they *h* it, they were glad,
58 We *h* him say, I will destroy this
64 Ye have *h* the blasphemy: what
15.35 *h* it, said, Behold, he calleth Elias.
16.11 when they had *h* that he was alive,
Lk 1.13 for thy prayer is *h*; and thy wife
41 when Elisabeth *h* the salutation of
58 cousins *h* how the Lord had shewed
66 *h* them laid them up in their hearts,
2.18 all they that *h* it, wondered at those
20 things that they had *h* and seen,
47 all that *h* him were astonished at his
4.23 we have *h* done in Capernaum, do
28 when they *h* these things, were filled
7. 3 when he *h* of Jesus, he sent unto
9 Jesus *h* these things, he marvelled
22 what things ye have seen and *h*;
29 all the people that *h* him, and the
8.14 which, when they have *h*, go forth,
15 having *h* the word, keep it, and bring
50 when Jesus *h* it, he answered him,
9. 7 Herod the tetrarch *h* of all that was
10.24 which ye hear, and have not *h* them.
39 sat at Jesus' feet, and *h* his word.
12. 3 in darkness shall be *h* in the light;
14.15 sat at meat with him *h* these things,
15.25 house, he *h* musick and dancing.
16.14 were covetous, *h* all these things:
18.22 when Jesus *h* these things he said
23 he *h* this, he was very sorrowful:
26 *h* it said, Who then can be saved?
19.11 as they *h* these things, he added
20.16 they *h*, they said, God forbid.
22.71 ourselves have *h* of his own mouth.
23. 6 When Pilate *h* of Galilee, he asked
8 he had *h* many things of him;
Jn 1.37 the two disciples *h* him speak, and
40 One of the two which *h* John speak,
3.32 hath seen and *h*, that he testifieth;
4. 1 Pharisees had *h* that Jesus made
42 for we have *h* him ourselves, and
47 When he *h* that Jesus was come out
5.37 Ye have neither *h* his voice at any
6.45 Every man therefore that hath *h*,
60 disciples, when they had *h* this, said,
7.32 The Pharisees *h* that the people
40 when they *h* this saying, said, Of a
8. 6 the ground, as though he *h* them not.
9 they which *h* it, being convicted by
26 those things which I have *h* of him.
40 the truth, which I have *h* of God:
9.32 world began was it not *h* that any
35 Jesus *h* that they had cast him out;
40 Pharisees which were with him *h*
11. 4 Jesus *h* that, he said, This sickness
6 had *h* therefore that he was sick,
20 soon as she *h* that Jesus was coming,
29 As soon as she *h* that, she arose
41 I thank thee that thou hast *h* me.
12.12 when they *h* that Jesus was coming
18 *h* that he had done this miracle.
29 and *h* it, said that it thundered:
34 have *h* out of the law that Christ
14.28 Ye have *h* how I said unto you, I go
15.15 things that I have *h* of my Father
18.21 ask them which *h* me, what I have
19. 8 When Pilate...*h* that saying, he was
13 Pilate...*h* that saying, he brought
21. 7 Simon Peter *h* that it was the Lord,
Ac 1. 4 which, saith he, ye have *h* of me.
2. 6 every man *h* them speak in his own
37 when they *h* this, they were pricked
4. 4 of them which *h* the word believed;
20 things which we have seen and *h*.
24 they *h* that, they lifted up their voice
5. 5 fear came on all them that *h* these
11 upon as many as *h* these things.
21 when they *h* that, they entered into
24 priests *h* these things, they doubted
33 When they *h* that, they were cut to
6.11 We have *h* him speak blasphemous
14 have *h* him say, that this Jesus
7.12 when Jacob *h* that there was corn in
34 have *h* their groaning, and am come
54 they *h* these things, they were cut
8.14 at Jerusalem *h* that Samaria had
30 and *h* him read the prophet Esaias,
9. 4 he fell to the earth, and *h* a voice
13 I have *h* by many of this man, how
21 all that *h* him were amazed, and
38 the disciples had *h* that Peter was
10.31 said, Cornelius, thy prayer is *h*,
44 fell on all them which *h* the word.
46 they *h* them speak with tongues,
11. 1 in Judea *h* that the Gentiles had
7 I *h* a voice saying unto me, Arise,
18 When they *h* these things, they held
13.48 the Gentiles *h* this, they were glad
14. 9 The same *h* Paul speak: who
14 Barnabas and Paul, *h* of, they rent
15.24 Forasmuch as we have *h*, that
16.14 which worshipped God, *h* us: whose
25 God: and the prisoners *h* them.
38 when they *h* that they were Romans.
17. 8 of the city, when they *h* these things.
32 when they *h* of the resurrection of
18.26 when Aquila and Priscilla had *h*,
19. 2 We have not so much as *h* whether
5 they *h* this, they were baptized
10 dwelt in Asia *h* the word of the Lord
28 *h* these sayings, they were full of
21.12 when we *h* these things, both we
20 when they *h* it, they glorified the
22. 2 they *h* that he spake in the Hebrew
7 *h* a voice saying unto me, Saul, Saul,
9 *h* not the voice of him that spake to
15 men of what thou hast seen and *h*.
26 When the centurion *h* that, he went

23.16 Paul's sister's son *h* of their lying
24.22 when Felix *h* these things, having
24 sent for Paul, and *h* him concerning
26.14 I *h* a voice speaking unto me, and
28.15 brethren *h* of us, they came to meet
Ro 10.14 in him of whom they have not *h*?
18 I say, Have they not *h*? Yes verily,
15.21 that have not *h* shall understand.
1Co 2. 9 Eye hath not seen, nor ear *h*,
2Co 6. 2 I have *h* thee in a time accepted,
12. 4 into paradise, and *h* unspeakable
Gal 1.13 ye have *h* of my conversation in
23 *h* only, That he which persecuted
Eph 1.13 after that ye *h* the word of truth,
15 after I *h* of your faith in the Lord
3. 2 If ye have *h* of the dispensation of
4.21 If so be that ye have *h* him, and
Php 2.26 that ye had *h* that he had been sick
4. 9 both learned, and received, and *h*,
Col 1. 4 Since we *h* of your faith in Christ
5 whereof ye *h* before in the word of
6 since the day ye *h* of it, and knew
9 since the day we *h* it, do not cease
23 the gospel, which ye have *h*, and
1Th 2.13 the word of God which ye *h* of us,
2Ti 1.13 words, which thou hast *h* of me,
2. 2 the things that thou hast *h* of me
Heb 2. 1 heed to the things which we have *h*,
3 confirmed unto us by them that *h*
3.16 when they had *h*, did provoke:
4. 2 mixed with faith in them that *h* it.
5. 7 and was *h* in that he feared;
12.19 which voice they that *h* intreated
Jas 5.11 Ye have *h* of the patience of Job,
2Pe 1.18 voice which came from heaven we *h*,
1Jn 1. 1 which we have *h*, which we have seen
3 we have seen and *h* declare we
5 message which we have *h* of him,
2. 7 the word which ye *h* heard from
18 have *h* that antichrist shall come,
24 which ye have *h* from the beginning.
24 which ye have *h* from the beginning
3.11 that ye *h* from the beginning,
4. 3 ye have *h* that it should come;
2Jn 6 as ye have *h* from the beginning,
Rev 1.10 *h* behind me a great voice, as of a
3. 3 how hast thou received and *h*, and
4. 1 first voice which I *h* was as it were
5.11 I *h* the voice of many angels round
13 and all that are in them, *h* I saying,
6. 1 I *h*, as it were, the noise of thunder,
3 I *h* the second beast say, Come
5 I *h* the third beast say, Come and
6 I *h* a voice in the midst of the four
7 I *h* the voice of the fourth beast say,
7. 4 I *h* the number of them which were
8.13 I beheld, and *h* an angel flying
9.13 I *h* a voice from the four horns of
16 and I *h* the number of them.
10. 4 I *h* a voice from heaven saying unto
8 the voice which I *h* from heaven
11.12 they *h* a great voice from heaven
12.10 I *h* a loud voice saying in heaven,
14. 2 I *h* a voice from heaven, as the voice
2 I *h* the voice of harpers harping
13 I *h* a voice from heaven saying unto
16. 1 I *h* a great voice out of the temple
5 I *h* the angel of the waters say,
7 I *h* another out of the altar say,
18. 4 I *h* another voice from heaven,
22 trumpeters, shall be *h* no more at all
22 millstone shall be *h* no more at all
23 the bride shall be *h* no more at all
19. 1 I *h* a great voice of much people
6 I *h*, as it were, the voice of a great
21. 3 I *h* a great voice out of heaven
22. 8 I John saw these things, and *h*
8 them. And when I had *h* and seen,

HEARDEST

Dt 4.36 thou *h* his words out of the midst
Jos 14.12 thou *h* in that day how the Anakims
2Ki 22.19 *h* what I spake against this place,
2Ch 34.27 thou *h* his words against this place,
Neh 9. 9 and *h* their cry by the Red sea;
27, 28 thee, thou *h* them from heaven;
Ps 31.22 thou *h* the voice of my supplications
119.26 declared my ways, and thou *h* me:
Isa 48. 7 the day when thou *h* them not;
8 Yea, thou *h* not; yea, thou knewest
Jon 2. 2 hell cried I, and thou *h* my voice.

HEARER

Jas 1.23 if any be a *h* of the word, and not
25 he being not a forgetful *h*, but

HEARERS

Ro 2.13 For not the *h* of the law are just
Eph 4.29 may minister grace unto the *h*.
2Ti 2.14 but to the subverting of the *h*.
Jas 1.22 doers of the word, and not *h* only,

HEAREST

Ru 2. 8 Boaz unto Ruth, *H* thou not, my
1Sa 24. 9 Wherefore *h* thou men's words,
2Sa 5.24 when thou *h* the sound of a going
1Ki 8.30 and when thou *h*, forgive.
2Ch 6.21 and when thou *h*, forgive.
Ps 22. 2 in the daytime, but thou *h* not;
65. 2 O thou that *h* prayer, unto thee
Mt 21.16 unto him, *H* thou what these say?
27.13 *H* thou not how many things they
Jn 3. 8 and thou *h* the sound thereof, but
11.42 I knew that thou *h* me always:

HEARETH

1Sa 3. 9 Speak, Lord; for thy servant *h*.
Job 34.28 and he *h* the cry of the afflicted.
Ps 34.17 and the Lord *h* and delivereth
69.33 for the Lord *h* the poor, and
Pr 8.34 Blessed is the man that *h* me,
13. 1 wise son *h* his father's instruction:
1 but a scorner *h* not rebuke.
8 riches: but the poor *h* not rebuke.
15.32 *h* reproof getteth understanding.
18.13 answereth a matter before he *h* it,
Isa 41.26 there is none that *h* your words.
Jer 19. 3 whosoever *h*, his ears shall tingle.
Eze 3.27 He that *h*, let him hear; and he
33. 4 Then whosoever *h* the sound of the
Mt 7.24 whosoever *h* these sayings of mine,
26 every one that *h* these sayings of
13.19 any one *h* the word of the kingdom,
20 the same is he that *h* the word,
22 the thorns is he that *h* the word;
23 good ground is he that *h* the word,
Lk 6.47 cometh to me, and *h* my sayings,
49 he that *h*, and doeth not, is like
10.16 He that *h* you *h* me; and he that
Jn 3.29 bridegroom, which standeth and *h*
5.24 He that *h* my word, and believeth
8.47 He that is of God *h* God's words:
9.31 we know that God *h* not sinners:
31 of God, and doeth his will, him he *h*.
18.37 one that is of the truth *h* my voice.
2Co 12. 6 seeth me to be, or that he *h* of me.
1Jn 4. 5 of the world, and the world *h* them.
6 he that knoweth God *h* us; he that
6 he that is not of God *h* not us.
5.14 thing according to his will, he *h* us:
Rev 22.17 And let him that *h* say, Come.
18 that *h* the words of the prophecy of

HEARING

Dt 31.11 this law before all Israel in their *h*.
2Sa 18.12 for in our *h* the king charged thee
2Ki 4.31 there was neither voice, nor *h*.
Job 33. 8 Surely thou hast spoken in mine *h*,
42. 5 heard of thee by the *h* of the ear:
Pr 20.12 The *h* ear, and the seeing eye,
28. 9 turneth away his ear from *h* the law,
Ec 1. 8 seeing, nor the ear filled with *h*.
Isa 11. 3 reprove after the *h* of his ears:
21. 3 I was bowed down at the *h* of it;
33.15 stoppeth his ears from *h* of blood,
Eze 9. 5 to the others he said in mine *h*,
10.13 it was cried unto them in my *h*,
Am 8.11 but of *h* the words of the Lord:
Mt 13.13 seeing see not; and *h* they hear not,
14 By *h* ye shall hear, and shall not
15 and their ears are dull of *h*,
Mk 4.12 and *h* they may hear, and not
6. 2 and many *h* him were astonished,
Lk 2.46 both *h* them, and asking them
8.10 and *h* they might not understand.
18.36 *h* the multitude pass by, he asked
Ac 5. 5 Ananias *h* these words fell down,
8. 6 Philip spake, *h* and seeing the
9. 7 *h* a voice, but seeing no man.
18. 8 many of the Corinthians *h* believed,
25.21 reserved unto the *h* of Augustus,
23 and was entered into the place of *h*,
28.26 *H* ye shall hear, and shall not
27 and their ears are dull of *h*,
Ro 10.17 So then faith cometh by *h*,
17 and *h* by the word of God.
1Co 12.17 body were an eye, where were the *h*?
17 whole were *h*, where...the smelling?
Gal 3. 2, 5 of the law, or by the *h* of faith?
Phm 5 *H* of thy love and faith, which thou
Heb 5.11 to be uttered, seeing ye are dull of *h*.
2Pe 2. 8 them, in seeing and *h*, vexed his

HEARKEN

Gen 49. 2 and *h* unto Israel your father.
Ex 4. 1 they will not believe me, nor *h* unto
Dt 13.18 shalt *h* to the voice of the Lord
17.12 *h* unto the priest that standeth
27. 9 Take heed, and *h*, O Israel; this day
1Ki 8.29 that thou mayest *h* unto the prayer,
30 And *h* thou to the supplication of
22.28 *H*, O people, every one of you.
Job 32.10 *H* to me; I also will shew mine
33. 1 speeches, and *h* to all my words.
31 Mark well, O Job, *h* unto me:
33 If not, *h* unto me: hold thy peace,
Ps 5. 2 *H* unto the voice of my cry,
58. 5 not *h* to the voice of charmers,
81.11 But my people would not *h* to my
Pr 29.12 If a ruler *h* to lies, all his servants
Isa 34. 1 *h*, ye people: let the earth hear,
49. 1 and *h*, ye people, from far; The
55. 2 *h* diligently unto me, and eat ye
Jer 17.27 *h* unto me to hallow the sabbath
27. 9 *h* not ye to your prophets, nor to
29.12 pray unto me, and I will *h* unto you.
44.16 of the Lord, we will not *h* unto thee.
Mic 1. 2 *h*, O earth, and all that therein is:
Mk 4. 3 *H*; Behold, there went out a sower
7.14 *H* unto me every one of you,
Ac 2.14 unto you, and *h* to my words:
4.19 right in the sight of God to *h* unto
7. 2 Men, brethren, and fathers, *h*; The
12.13 damsel came to *h*, named Rhoda,
15.13 Men and brethren, *h* unto me:
Jas 2. 5 *H*, my beloved brethren, Hath not

HEARKENED

Ex 6.12 Israel have not *h* unto me; how
18.24 So Moses *h* to the voice of his father
Nu 21. 3 the Lord *h* to the voice of Israel,
2Ki 13. 4 and the Lord *h* unto him: for he saw
Job 9.16 that he had *h* unto my voice.
Ps 81.13 Oh that my people had *h* unto me,
Jer 7.26 Yet they *h* not unto me, nor inclined
8. 6 I *h* and heard, but they spake not
34.14 but your fathers *h* not unto me,
Ac 27.21 Sirs, ye should have *h* unto me,

HEART

Gen 6. 5 thoughts of his *h* was only evil
8.21 Lord said in his *h*, I will not again
21 the imagination of man's *h* is evil

Ex 7. 3 harden Pharaoh's *h*, and multiply
25. 2 giveth it willingly with his *h* ye
28.29 breastplate of judgment upon his *h*,
35. 5 whosoever is of a willing *h*, let him
Dt 6. 5 the Lord thy God with all thine *h*,
6 thee this day, shall be in thine *h*:
8.17 And thou say in thine *h*, My power
11.18 lay up these my words in your *h*
13. 3 the Lord your God with all your *h*
24.15 he is poor,...setteth his *h* upon it:
30. 6 Lord thy God with all thine *h*, and
Jos 24.23 incline your *h* unto the Lord God
Jdg 5.16 there were great searchings of *h*.
16.17 That he told her all his *h*, and said
1Sa 2. 1 My *h* rejoiceth in the Lord, mine
4.13 his *h* trembled for the ark of God.
2Sa 6.16 and she despised him in her *h*.
1Ki 3.12 wise and an understanding *h*;
8.18 it was in thine *h* to build an house
61 Let your *h* therefore be perfect
10.24 wisdom...God had put in his *h*.
15. 3 his *h* was not perfect with the Lord
14 Asa's *h* was perfect with the Lord
2Ki 20. 3 in truth and with a perfect *h*,
1Ch 22.19 set your *h* and your soul to seek
29. 9 with perfect *h* they offered willingly
17 triest the *h*, and hast pleasure in
17 the uprightness of mine *h* I have
18 the thoughts of the *h* of thy people,
18 and prepare their *h* unto thee:
19 give...Solomon my son a perfect *h*,
2Ch 9.23 wisdom, that God had put in his *h*.
Job 9. 4 He is wise in *h*, and mighty in
15.12 Why doth thine *h* carry thee away?
22.22 and lay up his words in thine *h*.
23.16 God maketh my *h* soft, and the
31. 7 mine *h* walked after mine eyes,
38.36 given understanding to the *h*?
Ps 7.10 God, which saveth the upright in *h*.
9. 1 thee, O Lord, with my whole *h*;
10. 6 said in his *h*, I shall not be moved:
11 said in his *h*, God hath forgotten:
12. 2 and with a double *h* do they speak.
13. 5 *h* shall rejoice in thy salvation.
14. 1 The fool hath said in his *h*, There
15. 2 and speaketh the truth in his *h*.
19. 8 Lord are right, rejoicing the *h*:
22.14 my *h* is like wax: it is melted in
24. 4 hath clean hands, and a pure *h*;
26. 2 prove me; try my reins and my *h*.
27. 3 against me, my *h* shall not fear:
27.14 and he shall strengthen thine *h*:
36. 1 saith within my *h*, that there is no
37.31 The law of his God is in his *h*;
38.10 My *h* panteth, my strength faileth
44.18 Our *h* is not turned back, neither
21 he knoweth the secrets of the *h*.
45. 1 My *h* is inditing a good matter:
51.10 Create in me a clean *h*, O God;
17 a broken and a contrite *h*, O God,
53. 1 The fool hath said in his *h*, There
57. 7 My *h* is fixed, O God, my *h* is fixed:
62. 8 pour out your *h* before him:
66.18 I regard iniquity in my *h*, the Lord
73. 1 even to such as are of a clean *h*.
13 I have cleansed my *h* in vain,
26 My flesh and my *h* faileth: but God
26 but God is the strength of my *h*,
78.37 their *h* was not right with him,
84. 2 my *h* and my flesh crieth out for
5 in whose *h* are the ways of them.
86.12 O Lord my God, with all my *h*:
95. 8 Harden not your *h*, as in the
104.15 that maketh glad the *h* of man,
108. 1 O God, my *h* is fixed; I will sing
111. 1 praise the Lord with my whole *h*,
119.10 With my whole *h* have I sought
11 They word have I hid in mine *h*,
34 I shall observe it with my whole *h*.
36 Incline my *h* unto thy testimonies,
69 keep thy precepts with my whole *h*.
161 my *h* standeth in awe of thy word.
139.23 Search me...and know my *h*:
141. 4 Incline not my *h* to any evil thing,
147. 3 He healeth the broken in *h*, and
Pr 2. 2 apply thine *h* to understanding;
3. 5 Trust in the Lord with all thine *h*;
4.23 Keep thy *h* with all diligence; for
6.21 Bind them continually upon thine *h*,
8. 5 fools, be ye of an understanding *h*.
10.20 the *h* of the wicked is little worth.
12.20 Deceit is in the *h* of them that
25 Heaviness in the *h* of man maketh
13.12 Hope deferred maketh the *h* sick:
14.30 A sound *h* is the life of the flesh:
15.13 A merry *h* maketh a cheerful
28 The *h* of the righteous studieth to
30 The light of the eyes rejoiceth the *h*:
16.23 *h* of the wise teacheth his mouth,
17.22 A merry *h* doeth good like a
19. 3 his *h* fretteth against the Lord.
21 are many devices in a man's *h*;
20. 5 Counsel in the *h* of man is like
9 I have made my *h* clean, I am pure
22.17 apply thine *h* unto my knowledge.
23. 7 as he thinketh in his *h*, so is he:
17 Let not thine *h* envy sinners:
26 My son, give me thine *h*, and
25. 3 the *h* of kings is unsearchable.
28.25 He that is of a proud *h* stirreth up
26 trusteth in his own *h* is a fool:
Ec 1.16 yea, my *h* had great experience of
17 And I gave my *h* to know wisdom,
2. 1 I said in mine *h*, Go to now, I will
15 said I in my *h*, As it happeneth
23 his *h* taketh not rest in the night.
3.17 I said in mine *h*, God shall judge
7. 4 The *h* of the wise is in the house of
4 *h* of fools is in the house of mirth.
8.16 I applied mine *h* to know wisdom,
9. 7 drink thy wine with a merry *h*;
10. 2 wise man's *h* is at his right hand;
2 hand; but a fool's *h* at his left.
11.10 remove sorrow from thy *h*, and put
SS 5. 2 I sleep, but my *h* waketh: it is
8. 6 Set me as a seal upon thine *h*,
Isa 6.10 Make the *h* of this people fat,
29.13 have removed their *h* far from me,
35. 4 Say to them that are of a fearful *h*,
47. 8 that sayest in thine *h*, I am, and
51. 7 the people in whose *h* is my law;
57.15 revive the *h* of the contrite ones.
Jer 4.19 I am pained at my very *h*;
Eze 11.19 I will take the stony *h* out of their
19 and will give them an *h* of flesh:
14. 3 have set up their idols in their *h*,
18.31 and make you a new *h* and a new
22.14 Can thine *h* endure, or can thine
28. 2 thou set thine *h* as the *h* of God:
Dan 6.14 set his *h* on Daniel to deliver him:
Hos 10. 2 Their *h* is divided; now shall they
11. 8 mine *h* is turned within me, my
Joel 2.12 turn ye even to me with all your *h*,
13 And rend your *h*, and not your
Zep 1.12 that say in their *h*, The Lord will
3.14 be glad and rejoice with all the *h*,
Zec 10. 7 their *h* shall rejoice in the Lord.
Mal 4. 6 he shall turn the *h* of the fathers to
6 and the *h* of the children to their
Mt 5. 8 Blessed are the pure in *h*; for they
28 adultery with her already in his *h*.
6.21 treasure is, there will your *h* be
11.29 for I am meek and lowly in *h*:
12.34 the abundance of the *h* the mouth
35 out of the good treasure of the *h*
40 three nights in the *h* of the earth.
13.15 this people's *h* is waxed gross, and
15 should understand with their *h*,
19 away that which was sown in his *h*.
15. 8 lips; but their *h* is far from me.
18 the mouth come forth from the *h*;
19 out of the *h* proceed evil thoughts,
22.37 the Lord thy God with all thy *h*,
24.48 that evil servant shall say in his *h*,
Mk 6.52 loaves: for their *h* was hardened.
7. 6 lips, but their *h* is far from me.
19 Because it entereth not into his *h*,
21 out of the *h* of men, proceed evil
8.17 have ye your *h* yet hardened?
10. 5 the hardness of your *h* he wrote
11.23 and shall not doubt in his *h*, but
12.30 the Lord thy God with all thy *h*,
33 And to love him with all the *h*,
16.14 their unbelief and hardness of *h*,
Lk 2.19 and pondered them in her *h*.
51 kept all these sayings in her *h*.
6.45 out of the good treasure of his *h*
45 out of the evil treasure of his *h*
45 abundance of the *h* his mouth
8.15 which in an honest and good *h*,
9.47 perceiving the thought of their *h*,
10.27 the Lord thy God with all thy *h*,
12.34 treasure is, there will your *h* be
45 But and if that servant say in his *h*,
24.25 and slow of *h* to believe all that the
32 Did not our *h* burn within us, while
Jn 12.40 their eyes, and hardened their *h*;
40 eyes, nor understand with their *h*,
13. 2 having now put into the *h* of Judas
14. 1 Let not your *h* be troubled: ye
27 Let not your *h* be troubled, neither
16. 6 unto you, sorrow hath filled your *h*.
22 and your *h* shall rejoice, and your
Ac 2.26 Therefore did my *h* rejoice, and my
37 they were pricked in their *h*, and
46 with gladness and singleness of *h*,
4.32 were of one *h*, and of one soul:
5. 3 why hath Satan filled thine *h* to lie
4 conceived this thing in thine *h*?
33 heard that, they were cut to the *h*,
7.23 into his *h* to visit his brethren
51 and uncircumcised in *h* and ears,
54 they were cut to the *h*, and they
8.21 thy *h* is not right in the sight of
22 the thought of thine *h* may be
37 If thou believest with all thine *h*,
11.23 with purpose of *h* they would cleave
13.22 Jesse, a man after mine own *h*,
16.14 whose *h* the Lord opened, that she
21.13 ye to weep and to break mine *h*?
28.27 For the *h* of this people is waxed
27 understand with their *h*, and should
Ro 1.21 and their foolish *h* was darkened.
2. 5 after thy hardness and impenitent *h*
29 and circumcision is that of the *h*,
6.17 have obeyed from the *h* that form
9. 2 and continual sorrow in my *h*.
10. 6 Say not in thine *h*, Who shall ascend
8 even in thy mouth, and in thy *h*:
9 shalt believe in thine *h* that God
10 For with the *h* man believeth unto
1Co 2. 9 have entered into the *h* of man,
7.37 he that standeth stedfast in his *h*,
37 and hath so decreed in his *h* that
14.25 the secrets of his *h* made manifest;
2Co 2. 4 and anguish of *h* I wrote unto you
3. 3 stone, but in fleshy tables of the *h*.
15 is read, the vail is upon their *h*.
5.12 glory in appearance, and not in *h*.
6.11 open unto you, our *h* is enlarged.
8.16 care into the *h* of Titus for you.
9. 7 as he purposeth in his *h*, so let him
Eph 4.18 because of the blindness of their *h*:
5.19 making melody in your *h* to the
6. 5 in singleness of your *h*, as unto
6 doing the will of God from the *h*;
Php 1. 7 all, because I have you in my *h*;
Col 3.22 but in singleness of *h*, fearing God:
1Th 2.17 short time in presence, not in *h*,
1Ti 1. 5 is charity out of a pure *h*, and of a
2Ti 2.22 call on the Lord out of a pure *h*.
Heb 3.10 They do alway err in their *h*;
12 be in any of you an evil *h* of

4.12 of thoughts and intents of the *h*.
10.22 Let us draw near with a true *h* in
13. 9 thing that the *h* be established
Jas 1.26 his tongue, but deceiveth his own *h*,
1Pe 1.22 ye love one another with a pure *h*
3. 4 let it be the hidden man of the *h*,
2Pe 2.14 an *h* they have exercised with
1Jn 3.20 For if our *h* condemn us, God is
20 God is greater than our *h*, and
21 if our *h* condemn us not, then have
Rev 18. 7 for she saith in her *h*, I sit a queen,

HEARTH

Gen 18. 6 knead it and make cakes upon the *h*.
Ps 102. 3 my bones are burned as an *h*.
Isa 30.14 a sherd to take fire from the *h*, or
Jer 36.22 fire on the *h* burning before him.
23 it into the fire that was on the *h*,
23 in the fire that was on the *h*.
Zec 12. 6 like an *h* of fire among the wood,

HEARTILY

Col 3.23 whatsoever ye do, do it *h*, as to

HEART'S

Ps 10. 3 wicked boasteth of his *h* desire,
21. 2 Thou hast given him his *h* desire,
Ro 10. 1 my *h* desire and prayer to God

HEARTS

Dt 20. 3 let not your *h* faint, fear not, and
Jdg 19.22 they were making their *h* merry,
1Sa 6. 6 and Pharaoh hardened their *h*?
7. 3 and prepare your *h* unto the Lord,
10.26 men, whose *h* God had touched.
2Sa 15. 6 Absalom stole the *h* of the men of
1Ki 8.39 thou only, knowest the *h* of all
1Ch 28. 9 for the Lord searcheth all *h*, and
2Ch 11.16 such as set their *h* to seek the Lord
Job 1. 5 sinned, and cursed God in their *h*.
Ps 90.12 may apply our *h* unto wisdom.
Pr 17. 3 for gold: but the Lord trieth the *h*.
31. 6 unto those that be of heavy *h*.
Jer 32.40 but I will put my fear in their *h*,
Zec 8.17 none of you imagine evil in your *h*
Mt 9. 4 Wherefore think ye evil in your *h*?
18.35 from your *h* forgive not every one
19. 8 because of the hardness of your *h*
Mk 2. 6 there, and reasoning in their *h*,
8 reason ye these things in your *h*?
3. 5 grieved for the hardness of their *h*,
4.15 word that was sown in their *h*.
Lk 1.17 to turn the *h* of the fathers to the
51 in the imagination of their *h*.
66 laid them up in their *h*, saying,
2.35 the thoughts of many *h* may be
3.15 all men mused in their *h* of John,
5.22 them, What reason ye in your *h*?
8.12 away the word out of their *h*,
16.15 but God knoweth your *h*: for that
21.14 Settle it therefore in your *h*, not to
26 Men's *h* failing them for fear, and
34 any time your *h* be overcharged
24.38 why do thoughts arise in your *h*?
Ac 1.24 which knowest the *h* of all men,
7.39 in their *h* turned back again into
14.17 filling our *h* with food and gladness,
15. 8 And God, which knoweth the *h*,
9 them, purifying their *h* by faith.
Ro 1.24 through the lusts of their own *h*,
2.15 work of the law written in their *h*,
5. 5 love of God is shed abroad in our *h*
8.27 he that searcheth the *h* knoweth
16.18 deceive the *h* of the simple.
1Co 4. 5 manifest the counsels of the *h*:
2Co 1.22 the earnest of the Spirit in our *h*.
3. 2 written in our *h*, known and read
4. 6 hath shined in our *h*, to give the
7. 3 that ye are in our *h* to die and live
Gal 4. 6 the Spirit of his Son into your *h*,
Eph 3.17 That Christ may dwell in your *h* by
6.22 and that he might comfort your *h*.
Php 4. 7 shall keep your *h* and minds
Col 2. 2 That their *h* might be comforted,
3.15 let the peace of God rule in your *h*,
16 singing with grace in your *h* to the
4. 8 your estate, and comfort your *h*;
1Th 2. 4 men, but God, which trieth our *h*.
3.13 he may stablish your *h* unblamable
2Th 2.17 Comfort your *h*, and stablish you
3. 5 And the Lord direct your *h* into the
Heb 3. 8 Harden not your *h*, as in the
15 voice, harden not your *h*, as in the
4. 7 hear his voice, harden not your *h*.
8.10 mind, and write them in their *h*:
10.16 I will put my laws into their *h*,
22 having our *h* sprinkled from an evil
Jas 3.14 envying and strife in your *h*,
4. 8 purify your *h*, ye double minded.
5. 5 ye have nourished your *h*, as in a
8 ye also patient; stablish your *h*:
1Pe 3.15 sanctify the Lord God in your *h*:
2Pe 1.19 and the day star arise in your *h*:
1Jn 3.19 and shall assure our *h* before him.
Rev 2.23 which searcheth the reins and *h*:
17.17 God hath put in their *h* fulfil

HEAT

Gen 8.22 and cold and *h*, and summer and
18. 1 in the tent door in the *h* of the day;
Dt 29.24 meaneth the *h* of this great anger?
32.24 devoured with burning *h*, and
1Sa 11.11 Ammonites until the *h* of the day:
2Sa 4. 5 came about the *h* of the day to her
1Ki 1. 1 him with clothes, but he gat no *h*.
2 that my lord the king may get *h*.
Job 24.19 Drought and *h* consume the snow
30.30 and my bones are burned with *h*.
Ps 19. 6 nothing hid from the *h* thereof.
Ec 4.11 lie together, then they have *h*:
Isa 4. 6 shadow in the daytime from the *h*.
18. 4 like a clear *h* upon herbs, and like
4 a cloud of dew in the *h* of harvest.
25. 4 the storm, a shadow from the *h*,
5 strangers, as the *h* in a dry place;
5 the *h* with the shadow of a cloud:
49.10 neither shall the *h* nor sun smite
Jer 17. 8 and shall not see when *h* cometh,
36.30 be cast out in the day to the *h*,
51.39 their *h* I will make their feasts,
Eze 3.14 bitterness, in the *h* of my spirit;
Dan 3.19 that they should *h* the furnace
Mt 20.12 borne the burden and *h* of the
Lk 12.55 ye say, There will be *h*; and it
Ac 28. 3 there came a viper out of the *h*,
Jas 1.11 no sooner risen with a burning *h*,
2Pe 3.10 elements shall melt with fervent *h*,
12 elements shall melt with fervent *h*?
Rev 7.16 the sun light on them, nor any *h*.
16. 9 men were scorched with great *h*,

HEATHEN

Lev 26.33 I will scatter you among the *h*,
1Ch 16.24 Declare his glory among the *h*;
35 deliver us from the *h*, that we may
Neh 5. 8 Jews, which were sold unto the *h*;
Ps 2. 1 Why do the *h* rage, and the people
9.15 The *h* are sunk down in the pit
33.10 the counsel of the *h* to nought:
44.14 us a byword among the *h*, a
46. 6 The *h* raged, the kingdoms were
10 I will be exalted among the *h*,
47. 8 God reigneth over the *h*: God
59. 8 shalt have all the *h* in derision.
79. 6 Pour out thy wrath upon the *h* that
96. 3 Declare his glory among the *h*,
10 Say among the *h* that the Lord
135.15 The idols of the *h* are silver and
Jer 10. 2 Learn not the way of the *h*, and
25 Pour out thy fury upon the *h* that
49.14 an ambassador is sent unto the *h*,
Eze 20.32 say, We will be as the *h*, as the
22. 4 made thee a reproach unto the *h*,
15 will scatter thee among the *h*,
36. 6 ye have born the shame of the *h*:
23 *h* shall know that I am the Lord,
37.28 *h* shall know that I the Lord do
39. 7 *h* shall know that I am the Lord,
21 I will set my glory among the *h*
Ob 1 ambassador is sent among the *h*,
Hab 3.12 thou didst thresh the *h* in anger.
Zec 1.15 sore displeased with the *h* that
8.13 as ye were a curse among the *h*,
9.10 he shall speak peace unto the *h*:
Mal 1.11 name shall be great among the *h*,
14 name is dreadful among the *h*.
Mt 6. 7 not vain repetitions, as the *h* do:
18.17 let him be unto thee as an *h* man
Ac 4.25 Why did the *h* rage, and the
2Co 11.26 in perils by the *h*, in perils in the
Gal 1.16 I might preach him among the *h*;
2. 9 that we should go unto the *h*, and
3. 8 that God would justify the *h*

HEAVEN

Gen 1. 1 the beginning God created the *h*
8 And God called the firmament *H*.
9 waters under the *h* be gathered
14, 15 lights in the firmament of the *h*
7.11 and the windows of *h* were opened.
8. 2 the windows of *h* were stopped, and
2 the rain from *h* was restrained;
11. 4 whose top may reach unto *h*;
22.11 the Lord called unto him out of *h*,
15 Lord called unto Abraham out of *h*
26. 4 seed to multiply as the stars of *h*,
28.17 of God, and this is the gate of *h*.
Ex 9.22 Stretch forth thine hand toward *h*,
16. 4 I will rain bread from *h* for you;
31.17 days the Lord made *h* and earth,
Dt 3.24 what God is there in *h* or in earth,
4.26 I call *h* and earth to witness against
39 he is God in *h* above, and upon the
9.14 blot out their name from under *h*:
11.17 and he shut up the *h*, that there be
30.12 say, Who shall go up for us to *h*,
19 I call *h* and earth to record this day
Jos 2.11 he is God in *h* above, and in earth
10.11 Lord cast down great stones from *h*
13 the sun stood still in the midst of *h*,
Jdg 5.20 They fought from *h*; the stars in
1Sa 5.12 the cry of the city went up to *h*.
2Sa 22. 8 foundations of *h* moved and shook,
14 The Lord thundered from *h*, and
1Ki 8.23 is no God like thee, in *h* above, or
30 hear thou in *h* thy dwelling place:
34 Then hear thou in *h*, and forgive
2Ki 1.10 then let fire come down from *h*,
2.11 went up by a whirlwind into *h*.
7. 2 Lord would make windows in *h*,
17.16 and worshipped all the host of *h*,
2Ch 7.13 If I shut up *h* that there be no rain,
20. 6 our fathers, art not thou God in *h*?
28. 9 in a rage that reacheth up unto *h*.
Ezr 5.11 We are the servants of the God of *h*
Neh 2. 4 So I prayed to the God of *h*.
20 The God of *h*, he will prosper us;
9. 6 and the host of *h* worshippeth thee.
Job 1.16 The fire of God is fallen from *h*,
11. 8 It is as high as *h*; what canst thou
20.27 The *h* shall reveal his iniquity;
22.12 Is not God in the height of *h*?
Ps 14. 2 The Lord looked down from *h* upon
19. 6 forth is from the end of the *h*, and
33.13 Lord looketh from *h*; he beholdeth
53. 2 God looked down from *h* upon the
69.34 Let the *h* and earth praise him,
73.25 Whom have I in *h* but thee? and
78.23 above, and opened the doors of *h*,
85.11 righteousness shall look...from *h*.
89. 6 who in the *h* can be compared
37 and as a faithful witness in *h*.
103.11 as the *h* is high above the earth,

BIBLICAL THEMES

HEAVEN

And God said, Let there be a firmament in the midst of the waters, and let it divide the waters from the waters. . . . And God called the firmament Heaven. Gen 1.6, 8

But will God indeed dwell on the earth? behold, the heaven and heaven of heavens cannot contain thee; how much less this house that I have builded? 1Ki 8.27

When I consider thy heavens, the work of thy fingers, the moon and the stars, which thou hast ordained; what is man, that thou art mindful of him? and the son of man, that thou visitest him? Ps 8.3-4

The heavens declare the glory of God; and the firmament sheweth his handywork. . . . In them hath he set a tabernacle for the sun, which is as a bridegroom coming out of his chamber, and rejoiceth as a strong man to run a race. His going forth is from the end of the heaven, and his circuit unto the ends of it: and there is nothing hid from the heat thereof. Ps 19.1, 4-6

God is in heaven, and thou upon earth: therefore let thy words be few. Ec 5.2

The heaven is my throne, and the earth is my footstool. Isa 66.1

Thou hast been in Eden the garden of God. . . . Thou wast perfect in thy ways from the day that thou wast created, till iniquity was found in thee. Eze 28.13, 15

And Jesus, when he was baptized, went up straightway out of the water: and, lo, the heavens were opened unto him, and he saw the Spirit of God descending like a dove, and lighting upon him: and lo a voice from heaven, saying, This is my beloved Son, in whom I am well pleased. Mt 3.16-17

After this manner therefore pray ye: Our Father which art in heaven, Hallowed be thy name. Thy kingdom come. Thy will be done in earth, as it is in heaven. Mt 6.9-10

And when [Jesus] was demanded of the Pharisees, when the kingdom of God should come, he answered them and said, . . . behold, the kingdom of God is within you. Lk 17.20-21

He said unto Jesus, Lord, remember me when thou comest into thy kingdom. And Jesus said unto him, Verily I say unto thee, To day shalt thou be with me in paradise. Lk 23.42-43

Except a man be born again, he cannot see the kingdom of God. Jn 3.3

Ye men of Galilee, why stand ye gazing up into heaven? this same Jesus, which is taken up from you into heaven, shall so come in like manner as ye have seen him go. Ac 1.11

As he journeyed, he came near Damascus: and suddenly there shined round about him a light from heaven: and he fell to the earth, and heard a voice saying unto him, Saul, Saul, why persecutest thou me? Ac 9.3-4

The kingdom of God is not meat and drink; but righteousness, and peace, and joy in the Holy Ghost. Ro 14.17

We know that if our earthly house of this tabernacle were dissolved, we have a building of God, an house not made with hands, eternal in the heavens. 2Co 5.1

His servants shall serve him: and they shall see his face. . . . And there shall be no night there; and they need no candle . . . for the Lord God giveth them light: and they shall reign for ever and ever. Rev 22.3-5

Ps 107.26 They mount up to the *h*, they go
115.15 the Lord which made *h* and earth.
119.89 O Lord, thy word is settled in *h*.
136.26 O give thanks unto the God of *h*:
139. 8 If I ascend up into *h*, thou art there:
147. 8 Who covereth the *h* with clouds,
Ec 1.13 all things that are done under *h*:
3. 1 time to every purpose under the *h*;
5. 2 God is in *h*, and thou upon earth:
Isa 14.12 How art thou fallen from *h*, O
40.12 and meted out *h* with the span,
55.10 cometh down, and the snow from *h*,
63.15 Look down from *h*, and behold
Jer 7.18 to make cakes to the queen of *h*,
8. 7 Yea, the stork in the *h* knoweth her
19.13 incense unto all the host of *h*, and
23.24 Do not I fill *h* and earth? saith
31.37 If *h* above can be measured, and
51. 9 for her judgment reacheth unto *h*,
15 hath stretched out the *h* by his
La 3.50 Lord look down, and behold from *h*.
Eze 32. 8 All the bright lights of *h* will I
Dan 2.19 Then Daniel blessed the God of *h*.
28 there is a God in *h* that revealeth
4.13 and an holy one came down from *h*;
23 an holy one coming down from *h*,
31 there fell a voice from *h*, saying,
37 and extol and honor the King of *h*,
7. 2 the four winds of the *h* strove
13 of man came with the clouds of *h*,
Am 9. 2 though they climb up to *h*, thence
Jon 1. 9 the Lord, the God of *h*, which hath
Mal 3.10 will not open you the windows of *h*,
Mt 3. 2 for the kingdom of *h* is at hand.
17 And lo a voice from *h*, saying,
4.17 for the kingdom of *h* is at hand.
5. 3, 10 for theirs is the kingdom of *h*.
12 for great is your reward in *h*: for so
16 glorify your Father which is in *h*.
18 Till *h* and earth pass, one jot or one
19 called the least in the kingdom of *h*:
19 be called great in the kingdom of *h*.
20 case enter into the kingdom of *h*.
34 Swear not at all; neither by *h*; for
45 of your Father which is in *h*:
48 your Father which is in *h* is perfect.
6. 1 reward of your Father which is in *h*.
9 pray ye: Our Father which art in *h*,
10 will be done in earth, as it is in *h*.
20 up for yourselves treasures in *h*,
7.11 your Father which is in *h* give good
21 shall enter into the kingdom of *h*;
21 the will of my Father which is in *h*.
8.11 and Jacob, in the kingdom of *h*.
10. 7 saying, The kingdom of *h* is at hand.
32 also before my Father which is in *h*.
33 deny before my Father which is in *h*
11.11 he that is least in the kingdom of *h*
12 the kingdom of *h* suffereth violence,
23 which art exalted unto *h*, shalt be
25 O Father, Lord of *h* and earth,
12.50 will of my Father which is in *h*, the
13.11 the mysteries of the kingdom of *h*,
24 kingdom of *h* is likened unto a man
31 The kingdom of *h* is like to a grain
33 kingdom of *h* is like unto leaven,
44, 45 Again, the kingdom of *h* is like
47 the kingdom of *h* is like unto a net,
52 instructed unto the kingdom of *h* is
14.19 and looking up to *h*, he blessed, and
16. 1 he would shew them a sign from *h*.
17 thee, but my Father which is in *h*.
19 thee the keys of the kingdom of *h*:
19 bind on earth shall be bound in *h*:
19 loose on earth shall be loosed in *h*.
18. 1 the greatest in the kingdom of *h*?
3 not enter into the kingdom of *h*.
4 is greatest in the kingdom of *h*.
10 in *h* their angels do always behold
10 the face of my Father which is in *h*.
14 of your Father which is in *h*, that
18 bind on earth shall be bound in *h*:
18 loose on earth shall be loosed in *h*.
19 them of my Father which is in *h*.
23 the kingdom of *h* is likened unto a
19.14 me: for of such is the kingdom of *h*.
21 and thou shalt have treasure in *h*:
23 hardly enter into the kingdom of *h*.
20. 1 the kingdom of *h* is like unto a man
21.25 whence was it? from *h*, or of men?
25 If we shall say, From *h*; he will say
22. 2 The kingdom of *h* is like unto a
30 but are as the angels of God in *h*.
23. 9 one is your Father, which is in *h*.
13 shut up the kingdom of *h* against
22 that shall swear by *h*, sweareth by
24.29 the stars shall fall from *h*, and the
30 the sign of the Son of man in *h*:
30 Son of man coming in the clouds of *h*
31 from one end of *h* to the other.
35 *H* and earth shall pass away, but
36 not the angels of *h*, but my Father
25. 1 the kingdom of *h* be likened unto
14 For the kingdom of *h* is as a man
26.64 and coming in the clouds of *h*.
28. 2 of the Lord descended from *h*, and
18 is given unto me in *h* and in earth.
Mk 1.11 there came a voice from *h*, saying,
6.41 he looked up to *h*, and blessed, and
7.34 And looking up to *h*, he sighed, and
8.11 him, seeking of him a sign from *h*,
10.21 and thou shalt have treasure in *h*:
11.25 your Father also which is in *h* may

26 your Father which is in *h* forgive
30 John, was it from *h*, or of men?
31 If we shall say, From *h*; he will say,
12.25 are as the angels which are in *h*.
13.25 the stars of *h* shall fall, and the
25 the powers that are in *h* shall be
27 earth to the uttermost part of *h*.
31 *H* and earth shall pass away: but
32 no, not the angels which are in *h*,
14.62 and coming in the clouds of *h*.
16.19 he was received up into *h*, and sat
Lk 2.15 were gone away from them into *h*,
3.21 and praying, the *h* was opened, And
22 and a voice came from *h*, which
4.25 when the *h* was shut up three years
6.23 your reward is great in *h*: for in
9.16 and looking up to *h*, he blessed
54 command fire to come down from *h*,
10.15 which art exalted to *h*, shalt be
18 Satan as lightning fall from *h*.
20 your names are written in *h*.
21 O Father, Lord of *h* and earth, that
11. 2 say, Our Father which art in *h*,
2 will be done as in *h*, so in earth.
16 him, sought of him a sign from *h*.
15. 7 joy shall be in *h* over one sinner
18 I have sinned against *h*, and before
21 Father, I have sinned against *h*,
16.17 it is easier for *h* and earth to pass,
17.24 out of the one part under *h*, shineth
24 unto the other part under *h*;
29 rained fire and brimstone from *h*,
18.13 lift up so much as his eyes unto *h*,
22 and thou shalt have treasure in *h*:
19.38 peace in *h*, and glory in the highest
20. 4 baptism of John, was it from *h*, or
5 If we shall say, From *h*; he will
21.11 great signs shall there be from *h*.
26 the powers of *h* shall be shaken.
33 *H* and earth shall pass away: but
22.43 appeared an angel unto him from *h*,
24.51 from them, and carried up into *h*.
Jn 1.32 descending from *h* like a dove, and
51 Hereafter ye shall see *h* open, and
3.13 And no man hath ascended up to *h*,
13 but he that came down from *h*, even
13 even the Son of man which is in *h*.
27 except it be given him from *h*.
31 he that cometh from *h* is above all.
6.31 He gave them bread from *h* to eat.
32 gave you not that bread from *h*;
32 giveth you the true bread from *h*.
33 is he which cometh down from *h*,
38 I came down from *h*, not to do mine
41 the bread which came down from *h*.
42 that he saith, I came down from *h*?
50 bread which cometh down from *h*,
51, 58 bread which came down from *h*:
12.28 Then came there a voice from *h*,
17. 1 and lifted up his eyes to *h*, and said,
Ac 1.10 looked stedfastly toward *h* as he
11 why stand ye gazing up into *h*?
11 which is taken up from you into *h*,
11 as ye have seen him go into *h*.
2. 2 there came a sound from *h* as of a
5 men, out of every nation under *h*.
19 I will shew wonders in *h* above, and
3.21 Whom the *h* must receive until the
4.12 none other name under *h* given
24 which hast made *h*, and earth, and
7.42 them up to worship the host of *h*;
49 *H* is my throne, and earth is my
55 looked up stedfastly into *h*, and saw
9. 3 round about him a light from *h*:
10.11 And saw *h* opened, and a certain
16 vessel was received up again into *h*.
11. 5 let down from *h* by four corners;
9 voice answered me again from *h*,
14.10 and all were drawn up again into *h*.
15 which made *h*, and earth, and the
17 gave us rain from *h*, and fruitful
17.24 that he is Lord of *h* and earth,
22. 6 there shone from *h* a great light
26.13 I saw in the way a light from *h*,
Ro 1.18 wrath of God is revealed from *h*
10. 6 heart, Who shall ascend into *h*?
1Co 8. 5 gods, whether in *h* or in earth, as
15.47 the second man is the Lord from *h*.
2Co 5. 2 with our house which is from *h*:
12. 2 an one caught up to the third *h*.
Gal 1. 8 we, or an angel from *h*, preach any
Eph 1.10 both which are in *h*, and which
3.15 family in *h* and earth is named,
6. 9 your Master also is in *h*; neither
Php 2.10 of things in *h*, and things in earth
3.20 For our conversation is in *h*; from
Col 1. 5 hope which is laid up for you in *h*,
16 that are in *h*, and that are in earth,
20 be things in earth, or things in *h*.
23 every creature which is under *h*;
4. 1 knowing ye also have a Master in *h*.
1Th 1.10 And to wait for his Son from *h*,
4.16 shall descend from *h* with a shout,
2Th 1. 7 Jesus shall be revealed from *h*
Heb 9.24 but into *h* itself, now to appear in
10.34 that ye have in *h* a better and an
12.23 firstborn, which are written in *h*,
25 from him that speaketh from *h*:
26 shake not the earth only, but also *h*.
Jas 5.12 swear not neither by *h*, neither
18 and the *h* gave rain, and the earth
1Pe 1. 4 not away, reserved in *h* for you,
12 the Holy Ghost sent down from *h*;
3.22 Who is gone into *h*, and is on the
2Pe 1.18 this voice which came from *h* we
1Jn 5. 7 are three that bear record in *h*, the
Rev 3.12 cometh down out of *h* from my God:
4. 1 behold, a door was opened in *h*:
2 a throne was set in *h*, and one sat
5. 3 And no man in *h*, nor in earth,
13 every creature which is in *h*, and
6.13 the stars of *h* fell unto the earth,
14 And the *h* departed as a scroll when
8. 1 was silence in *h* about the space of
10 and there fell a great star from *h*,
13 flying through the midst of *h*,
9. 1 I saw a star fall from *h* unto the
10. 1 angel come down from *h*, clothed
4 I heard a voice from *h* saying unto
5 the earth lifted up his hand to *h*,
6 who created *h*, and the things that
8 voice which I heard from *h* spake
11. 6 These have power to shut *h*, that it
12 heard a great voice from *h* saying
12 they ascended up to *h* in a cloud;
13 and gave glory to the God of *h*.
15 were great voices in *h*, saying, The
19 the temple of God was opened in *h*,
12. 1 appeared a great wonder in *h*;
3 appeared another wonder in *h*;
4 third part of the stars of *h*, and did
7 And there was war in *h*: Michael
8 was their place found any more in *h*.
10 heard a loud voice saying in *h*, Now
13. 6 and them that dwell in *h*.
13 fire come down from *h* on the earth
14. 2 I heard a voice from *h*, as the voice
6 another angel fly in the midst of *h*,
7 that made *h*, and earth, and the
13 I heard a voice from *h* saying unto
17 out of the temple which is in *h*, he
15. 1 I saw another sign in *h*, great and
5 the tabernacle of the testimony in *h*
16.11 blasphemed the God of *h* because
17 great voice out of the temple of *h*,
21 fell upon men a great hail out of *h*,
18. 1 another angel come down from *h*,
4 and I heard another voice from *h*,
5 For her sins have reached unto *h*,
20 Rejoice over her, thou *h*, and ye
19. 1 a great voice of much people in *h*,
11 And I saw *h* opened, and behold a
14 armies which were in *h* followed
17 the fowls that fly in the midst of *h*,
20. 1 angel come down from *h*, having
9 fire came down from God out of *h*,
11 face the earth and the *h* fled away;
21. 1 I saw a new *h* and a new earth:
1 for the first *h* and the first earth
2 coming down from God out of *h*,
3 heard a great voice out of *h* saying,
10 holy Jerusalem, descending out of *h*

HEAVENLY

Mt 6.14 your *h* Father will also forgive
26 yet your *h* Father feedeth them.
32 *h* Father knoweth that ye have need
15.13 my *h* Father hath not planted,
18.35 shall my *h* Father do also unto
Lk 2.13 a multitude of the *h* host praising
11.13 your *h* Father give the Holy
Jn 3.12 believe, if I tell you of *h* things?
Ac 26.19 disobedient unto the *h* vision:
1Co 15.48 and as is the *h*, such are they also
48 such are they also that are *h*.
49 shall also bear the image of the *h*.
Eph 1. 3 spiritual blessings in *h* places in
20 own right hand in the *h* places,
2. 6 together in *h* places in Christ Jesus:
3.10 powers in *h* places might be known
2Ti 4.18 preserve me unto his *h* kingdom:
Heb 3. 1 brethren, partakers of the *h* calling,
6. 4 tasted of the *h* gift, and were made
8. 5 example and shadow of *h* things,
9.23 but the *h* things themselves with
11.16 a better country, that is, an *h*:
12.22 of the living God, the *h* Jerusalem,

HEAVEN'S

Mt 19.12 eunuchs for the kingdom of *h* sake.

HEAVENS

Gen 2. 1 the *h* and the earth were finished,
4 the generations of the *h* and of
4 God made the earth and the *h*,
Dt 32. 1 Give ear, O ye *h*, and I will speak;
1Ki 8.27 heaven of *h* cannot contain thee;
1Ch 16.26 are idols: but the Lord made the *h*.
31 Let the *h* be glad, and let the earth
2Ch 6.18 heaven of *h* cannot contain thee;
25 Then hear thou from the *h*, and
35 hear thou from the *h* their prayer
Ezr 9. 6 our trespass is grown up unto the *h*.
Job 14.12 till the *h* be no more, they shall not
26.13 his spirit he hath garnished the *h*;
Ps 2. 4 He that sitteth in the *h* shall laugh:
8. 3 When I consider thy *h*, the work of
19. 1 The *h* declare the glory of God;
33. 6 word of the Lord were the *h* made;
36. 5 Thy mercy, O Lord, is in the *h*;
57. 5 Be thou exalted, O God, above the *h*;
89. 5 And the *h* shall praise thy wonders,
96. 5 are idols: but the Lord made the *h*.
11 Let the *h* rejoice, and let the earth
102.25 and the *h* are the work of thy hands.
103.19 hath prepared his throne in the *h*;
104. 2 stretchest out the *h* like a curtain:
108. 4 For thy mercy is great above the *h*:
5 Be thou exalted, O God, above the *h*:
115. 3 our God is in the *h*: he hath done
136. 5 To him that by wisdom made the *h*:
148. 1 Praise ye the Lord from the *h*:
Pr 8.27 he prepared the *h*, I was there:
Isa 1. 2 Hear, O *h*, and give ear, O earth:
34. 4 the *h* shall be rolled together as a
44.23 Sing, O ye *h*; for the Lord hath
48.13 my right hand hath spanned the *h*:
49.13 Sing, O *h*; and be joyful, O earth;
51. 6 Lift up your eyes to the *h*, and look
6 the *h* shall vanish away like smoke,
55. 9 as the *h* are higher than the earth,
64. 1 Oh that thou wouldest rend the *h*,
65.17 I create new *h* and a new earth:

Jer 10.11 gods that have not made the *h*
La 3.41 with our hands unto God in the *h*.
Eze 1. 1 that the *h* were opened, and I saw
Joel 2.30 I will shew wonders in the *h* and in
Hab 3. 3 His glory covered the *h*, and the
Zec 6. 5 These the four spirits of the *h*,
Mt 3.16 lo, the *h* were opened unto him,
24.29 powers of the *h* shall be shaken:
Mk 1.10 he saw the *h* opened, and the Spirit
Lk 12.33 a treasure in the *h* that faileth not,
Ac 2.34 David is not ascended into the *h*:
7.56 Behold, I see the *h* opened, and the
2Co 5. 1 made with hands, eternal in the *h*.
Eph 4.10 that ascended up far above all *h*,
Heb 1.10 and the *h* are the works of thine
4.14 priest, that is passed into the *h*,
7.26 and made higher than the *h*;
8. 1 the throne of the Majesty in the *h*;
9.23 patterns of things in the *h* should
2Pe 3. 5 the word of God the *h* were of old,
7 But the *h* and the earth, which are
10 the *h* shall pass away with a great
12 *h* being on fire shall be dissolved,
13 look for new *h* and a new earth,
Rev 12.12 Therefore rejoice, ye *h*, and ye that

HEAVIER
Job 6. 3 now it would be *h* than the sand
23. 2 my stroke is *h* than my groaning.
Pr 27. 3 a fool's wrath is *h* than them both.

HEAVINESS
Ezr 9. 5 sacrifice I arose up from my *h*;
Job 9.27 I will leave off my *h*, and comfort
Ps 69.20 and I am full of *h*: and I looked
119.28 My soul melteth for *h*: strengthen
Pr 10. 1 foolish son is the *h* of his mother.
12.25 *H* in the heart of man maketh it
14.13 but the end of that mirth is *h*.
Isa 29. 2 and there shall be *h* and sorrow:
61. 3 of praise for the spirit of *h*;
Ro 9. 2 great *h* and continual sorrow
2Co 2. 1 would not come again to you in *h*.
Php 2.26 and was full of *h*, because that
Jas 4. 9 to mourning, and your joy to *h*.
1Pe 1. 6 ye are in *h* through manifold

HEAVY
Ex 17.12 Moses' hands were *h*; and they
18.18 for this thing is too *h* for thee;
Nu 11.14 alone, because it is too *h* for me.
1Sa 4.18 for he was an old man, and *h*.
5. 6 But the hand of the Lord was *h*
11 the hand of God was very *h* there.
2Sa 14.26 because the hair was *h* on him,
1Ki 12. 4 his *h* yoke which he put upon us,
10 Thy father made our yoke *h*, but
11 father did lade you with a *h* yoke,
14 My father made your yoke *h*, and
14. 6 I am sent to thee with *h* tidings.
20.43 went to his house *h* and displeased,
21. 4 Ahab came into his house *h* and
2Ch 10. 4 his *h* yoke that he put upon us,
10 Thy father made our yoke *h*, but
11 my father put a *h* yoke upon you,
14 My father made your yoke *h*, but
Neh 5.18 bondage was *h* upon this people.
Job 33. 7 neither shall my hand be *h* upon
Ps 32. 4 night thy hand was *h* upon me:
38. 4 over mine head: as an *h* burden
4 burden they are too *h* for me.
Pr 25.20 that singeth songs to an *h* heart.
27. 3 stone is *h*, and the sand weighty;
31. 6 unto those that be of *h* hearts.
Isa 6.10 make their ears *h*, and shut their
24.20 transgression thereof shall be *h*
30.27 and the burden thereof is *h*:
46. 1 your carriages were *h* loaden:
58. 6 to undo the *h* burdens, and to let
59. 1 neither his ear *h*, that it cannot
La 3. 7 get out: he hath made my chain *h*.
Mt 11.28 all ye that labor and are *h* laden,
23. 4 For they bind *h* burdens and
26.37 began to be sorrowful and very *h*.
43 asleep again: for their eyes were *h*.
Mk 14.33 be sore amazed, and to be very *h*;
40 asleep again, for their eyes were *h*,
Lk 9.32 were with him were *h* with sleep:

HEBREW
Gen 14.13 escaped, and told Abram the *H*;
39.14 he hath brought in a *H* unto us
17 The *H* servant, which thou hast
41.12 with us a young man, an *H*,
Ex 1.15 Egypt spake to the *H* midwives,
16 of a midwife to the *H* women,
19 Because the *H* women are not as
2. 7 to thee a nurse of the *H* women,
11 spied an Egyptian smiting a *H*,
21. 2 If thou buy an *H* servant, six years
Dt 15.12 an *H* man, or an *H* woman,
Jer 34. 9 being an *H* or an Hebrewess, go
14 every man his brother an *H*, which
Jon 1. 9 And he said unto them, I am a *H*:
Lk 23.38 of Greek, and Latin, and *H*,
Jn 5. 2 called in the *H* tongue Bethesda.
19.13 Pavement, but in the *H*, Gabbatha.
17 which is called in the *H* Golgotha:
20 written in *H*, and Greek, and Latin.
Ac 21.40 spake unto them in the *H* tongue,
22. 2 that he spake in the *H* tongue to
26.14 saying in the *H* tongue, Saul, Saul,
Php 3. 5 of Benjamin, an *H* of the Hebrews;
Rev 9.11 name in the *H* tongue is Abaddon,
16.16 in the *H* tongue Armageddon.

HEBREWESS
Jer 34. 9 being an Hebrew or an *H*, go free;

HEBREWS
Gen 40.15 away out of the land of the *H*:
43.32 might not eat bread with the *H*;
Ex 2.13 two men of the *H* strove together:
3.18 God of the *H* hath met with us:
5. 3 God of the *H* hath met with us:
7.16 The Lord God of the *H* hath sent
9. 1, 13 saith the Lord God of the *H*,
10. 3 Thus saith the Lord God of the *H*,
1Sa 4. 6 great shout in the camp of the *H*?
9 that ye be not servants unto the *H*
13. 3 all the land, saying, Let the *H* hear.
7 some of the *H* went over Jordan
19 the *H* make them swords or spears:
14.11 the *H* come forth out of the holes
21 *H* that were with the Philistines
29. 3 What do these *H* here? And
Ac 6. 1 of the Grecians against the *H*,
2Co 11.22 Are they *H*? so am I. Are they
Php 3. 5 of Benjamin, an Hebrew of the *H*;

HEBREWS'
Ex 2. 6 This is one of the *H* children.

HEDGE
Job 1.10 not thou made an *h* about him,
Pr 15.19 slothful man is as an *h* of thorns:
Ec 10. 8 whoso breaketh an *h*, a serpent
Isa 5. 5 I will take away the *h* thereof,
Eze 13. 5 the *h* for the house of Israel
22.30 them, that should make up the *h*,
Hos 2. 6 I will *h* up thy way with thorns,
Mic 7. 4 upright is sharper than a thorn *h*:
Mk 12. 1 and set an *h* about it, and digged

HEDGED
Job 3.23 is hid, and whom God hath *h* in?
La 3. 7 He hath *h* me about, that I cannot
Mt 21.33 a vineyard, and *h* it round

HEDGES
1Ch 4.23 that dwelt among plants and *h*:
Ps 80.12 thou then broken down her *h*,
89.40 Thou hast broken down all his *h*;
Jer 49. 3 and run to and fro by the *h*; for
Na 3.17 which camp in the *h* in the cold
Lk 14.23 Go out into the highways and *h*,

HEED
Gen 31.24 Take *h* that thou speak not to
29 Take thou *h* that thou speak not
Ex 10.28 Get thee from me, take *h* to thyself,
19.12 Take *h* to yourselves, that ye go not
34.12 Take *h* to thyself, lest thou make
Nu 23.12 Must I not take *h* to speak that
Dt 2. 4 take ye good *h* unto yourselves
4. 9 Only take *h* to thyself, and keep thy
15 Take ye therefore good *h* unto
23 Take *h* unto yourselves, lest ye
11.16 Take *h* to yourselves, that your
12.13 Take *h* to thyself that thou offer not
19 Take *h* to thyself that thou forsake
30 Take *h* to thyself that thou be not
24. 8 Take *h* in the plague of leprosy,
27. 9 Take *h*, and hearken, O Israel;
Jos 22. 5 But take diligent *h* to do the
23.11 Take good *h* therefore unto your
1Sa 19. 2 take *h* to thyself until the morning,
2Sa 20.10 Amasa took no *h* to the sword that
1Ki 2. 4 If thy children take *h* to their way,
8.25 thy children take *h* to their way,
2Ki 10.31 Jehu took no *h* to walk in the law
1Ch 22.13 prosper if thou takest *h* to fulfil
28.10 Take *h* now; for the Lord hath
2Ch 6.16 thy children take *h* to their way
19. 6 Take *h* what ye do: for ye judge
7 take *h* and do it: for there is no
33. 8 so that they will take *h* to do all
Ezr 4.22 Take *h* now that ye fail not to do
Job 36.21 Take *h*, regard not iniquity: for
Ps 39. 1 I said, I will take *h* to my ways,
119. 9 by taking *h* thereto according to
Pr 17. 4 wicked doer giveth *h* to false lips;
Ec 7.21 Also take no *h* unto all words
12. 9 he gave good *h*, and sought out,
Isa 7. 4 Take *h*, and be quiet; fear him,
21. 7 hearkened diligently with much *h*:
Jer 9. 4 Take ye *h* every one of his
17.21 Take *h* to yourselves, and bear no
18.18 us not give *h* to any of his words.
19 Give *h* to me, O Lord, and hearken
Hos 4.10 have left off to take *h* to the Lord.
Mal 2.15 Therefore take *h* to your spirit, and
16 therefore take *h* to your spirit, that
Mt 6. 1 Take *h* that ye do not your alms
16. 6 Take *h* and beware of the leaven
18.10 Take *h* that ye despise not one of
24. 4 Take *h* that no man deceive you.
Mk 4.24 Take *h* what ye hear: with what
8.15 Take *h*, beware of the leaven of
13. 5 Take *h* lest any man deceive you:
9 take *h* to yourselves: for they shall
23 take ye *h*: behold, I have foretold
33 Take ye *h*, watch and pray: for ye
Lk 8.18 Take *h* therefore how ye hear: for
11.35 Take *h* therefore that the light
12.15 Take *h*,...beware of covetousness:
17. 3 Take *h* to yourselves: If thy
21. 8 Take *h* that ye be not deceived:
34 take *h* to yourselves, lest at any
Ac 3. 5 he gave *h* unto them, expecting to
5.35 take *h* to yourselves what ye
8. 6 accord gave *h* unto those things
10 To whom they all gave *h*, from the
20.28 Take *h* therefore unto yourselves,
22.26 Take *h* what thou doest: for this
Ro 11.21 take *h* lest he also spare not thee.
1Co 3.10 every man take *h* how he buildeth
8. 9 But take *h* lest by any means this
10.12 thinketh he standeth take *h* lest he
Gal 5.15 take *h* that ye be not consumed one
Col 4.17 Take *h* to the ministry which thou
1Ti 1. 4 give *h* to fables and endless
4. 1 giving *h* to seducing spirits, and

16 Take *h* unto thyself, and unto the
Tit 1.14 Not giving *h* to Jewish fables, and
Heb 2. 1 the more earnest *h* to the things
3.12 Take *h* brethren, lest there be in
2Pe 1.19 ye do well that ye take *h*, as unto

HEEL

Gen 3.15 head, and thou shalt bruise his *h*.
25.26 his hand took hold on Esau's *h*:
Job 18. 9 The gin shall take him by the *h*.
Ps 41. 9 hath lifted up his *h* against me.
Hos 12. 3 He took his brother by the *h* in the
Jn 13.18 hath lifted up his *h* against me.

HEIFER

Gen 15. 9 Take me an *h* of three years old,
Nu 19. 2 bring thee a red *h* without spot,
5 one shall burn the *h* in his sight;
6 the midst of the burning of the *h*.
9 shall gather up the ashes of the *h*,
10 gathereth the ashes of the *h* shall
17 ashes of the burnt *h* of purification
Dt 21. 3 elders of that city shall take an *h*,
4 down the *h* unto a rough valley,
6 shall wash their hands over the *h*
Jdg 14.18 If ye had not plowed with my *h*, ye
1Sa 16. 2 Take an *h* with thee, and say, I am
Isa 15. 5 unto Zoar, an *h* of three years old;
Jer 46.20 Egypt is like a very fair *h*, but
48.34 voice,...as an *h* of three years old:
50.11 ye are grown fat as the *h* at grass,
Hos 4.16 slideth back as a backsliding *h*:
10.11 Ephraim is as an *h* that is taught,
Heb 9.13 the ashes of an *h* sprinkling the

HEIGHT

1Sa 17. 4 whose *h* was six cubits and a span.
Job 22.12 Is not God in the *h* of heaven? and
12 behold the *h* of the stars, how high
Ps 102.19 down from the *h* of his sanctuary;
Pr 25. 3 The heaven for *h*, and the earth
Isa 7.11 in the depth; or in the *h* above.
Eze 32. 5 and fill the valleys with thy *h*.
Dan 4.11 the *h* thereof reached unto heaven,
Ro 8.39 Nor *h*, nor depth, nor any other
Eph 3.18 and length, and depth, and *h*;
Rev 21.16 breadth and the *h* of it are equal.

HEIGHTS

Ps 148. 1 the heavens: praise him in the *h*.
Isa 14.14 ascend above the *h* of the clouds:

HEIR

Gen 15. 3 one born in my house is mine *h*.
4 This shall not be thine *h*; but he
4 thine own bowels shall be thine *h*.
21.10 of this bondwoman shall not be *h*
2Sa 14. 7 and we will destroy the *h* also:
Pr 30.23 handmaid that is *h* to her mistress.
Jer 49. 1 Hath Israel no sons? hath he no *h*?
2 then shall Israel be *h* unto them
Mic 1.15 Yet will I bring an *h* unto thee,
Mt 21.38 This is the *h*; come, let us kill him,
Mk 12. 7 This is the *h*; come, let us kill him,
Lk 20.14 This is the *h*: come, let us kill him,
Ro 4.13 he should be the *h* of the world,
Gal 4. 1 That the *h*, as long as he is a child,
7 then an *h* of God through Christ.
30 shall not be *h* with the son of the
Heb 1. 2 whom...appointed *h* of all things,
11. 7 and became *h* of the righteousness

HEIRS

Jer 49. 2 unto them that were his *h*, saith
Ro 4.14 if they which are of the law be *h*,
8.17 And if children, then *h*; *h* of God,
Gal 3.29 and *h* according to the promise.
Tit 3. 7 by his grace, we should be made *h*
Heb 1.14 them who shall be *h* of salvation?
6.17 to shew unto the *h* of promise
11. 9 *h* with him of the same promise:
Jas 2. 5 rich in faith, and *h* of the kingdom
1Pe 3. 7 *h* together of the grace of life;

HELD

Gen 34. 5 and Jacob *h* his peace until they
Ex 17.11 when Moses *h* up his hand, that
Jdg 7.20 *h* the lamps in their left hands,
Neh 4.16 half of them *h* both the spears,
17 with the other hand *h* a weapon.
Est 5. 2 king *h* out to Esther the golden
7. 4 I had *h* my tongue, although
Ps 39. 2 I *h* my peace, even from good;
94.18 thy mercy, O Lord, *h* me up.
SS 3. 4 I *h* him, and would not let him go,
Mt 12.14 and *h* a council against him, how
26.63 But Jesus *h* his peace. And the
28. 9 they came and *h* him by the feet,
Mk 3. 4 or to kill? But they *h* their peace.
9.34 But they *h* their peace: for by the
14.61 But he *h* his peace, and answered
15. 1 the chief priests *h* a consultation
Lk 14. 4 And they *h* their peace. And he
20.26 at his answer, and *h* their peace.
22.63 the men that *h* Jesus mocked him,
Ac 3.11 man which was healed *h* Peter
11.18 they *h* their peace, and glorified
14. 4 and part *h* with the Jews, and part
15.13 and after they had *h* their peace,
Ro 7. 6 being dead wherein we were *h*.
Rev 6. 9 for the testimony which they *h*:

HELL

Dt 32.22 shall burn unto the lowest *h*,
2Sa 22. 6 The sorrows of *h* compassed me
Job 11. 8 deeper than *h*; what canst thou
26. 6 *H* is naked before him, and
Ps 9.17 The wicked shall be turned into *h*,
16.10 thou wilt not leave my soul in *h*;
18. 5 The sorrows of *h* compassed me
55.15 let them go down quick into *h*:
86.13 my soul from the lowest *h*.
116. 3 the pains of *h* gat hold upon me:
139. 8 if I make my bed in *h*, behold,
Pr 5. 5 death; her steps take hold on *h*.
7.27 Her house is the way to *h*, going
9.18 her guests are in the depths of *h*.
15.11 *H* and destruction are before the
24 he may depart from *h* beneath.
23.14 and shalt deliver his soul from *h*.
27.20 *H* and destruction are never full;
Isa 5.14 Therefore *h* hath enlarged herself,
14. 9 *H* from beneath is moved for thee
15 thou shalt be brought down to *h*,
28.15 and with *h* are we at agreement;
18 agreement with *h* shall not stand;
57. 9 didst debase thyself even unto *h*.
Eze 31.16 I cast him down to *h* with them
17 They also went down into *h* with
32.21 speak to him out of the midst of *h*
27 gone down to *h* with their weapons
Am 9. 2 Though they dig into *h*, thence
Jon 2. 2 out of the belly of *h* cried I, and
Hab 2. 5 who enlargeth his desire as *h*, and
Mt 5.22 fool, shall be in danger of *h* fire.
29, 30 body should be cast into *h*.
10.28 to destroy both soul and body in *h*.
11.23 shalt be brought down to *h*: for if
16.18 and the gates of *h* shall not prevail
18. 9 two eyes to be cast into *h* fire.
23.15 more the child of *h* than yourselves.
33 can ye escape the damnation of *h*?
Mk 9.43 than having two hands to go into *h*,
45 having two feet to be cast into *h*,
47 having two eyes to be cast into *h* fire
Lk 10.15 heaven, shalt be thrust down to *h*.
12. 5 killed hath power to cast into *h*;
16.23 in *h* he lift up his eyes, being in
Ac 2.27 thou wilt not leave my soul in *h*,
31 that his soul was not left in *h*,
Jas 3. 6 nature; and it is set on fire of *h*.
2Pe 2. 4 sinned, but cast them down to *h*,

A Roman helmet: the Old and New Testaments both speak of guarding the righteous with a "helmet of salvation."

Rev 1.18 have the keys of *h* and of death.
6. 8 Death, and *H* followed with him.
20.13 death and *h* delivered up the dead
14 death and *h* were cast into the lake
(See box on page 368)

HELM

Jas 3. 4 turned about with a very small *h*,

HELMET

1Sa 17. 5 had an *h* of brass upon his head,
38 put an *h* of brass upon his head;
Isa 59.17 an *h* of salvation upon his head;
Eze 23.24 buckler and shield and *h* round
27.10 hanged the shield and *h* in thee;
38. 5 all of them with shield and *h*:
Eph 6.17 And take the *h* of salvation, and
1Th 5. 8 and for an *h*, the hope of salvation.

HELP

Gen 2.18 will make him an *h* meet for him.
20 was not found an *h* meet for him.
Jdg 5.23 *h* of the Lord against the mighty.
2Ch 14.11 Lord, it is nothing with thee to *h*,
11 no power: *h* us, O Lord our God;
19. 2 Shouldest thou *h* the ungodly,
25. 8 God hath power to *h*, and to cast
32. 8 with us is the Lord our God to *h* us,
Job 8.20 neither will he *h* the evil doers:
29.12 and him that had none to *h* him.
Ps 3. 2 soul, There is no *h* for him in God.
12. 1 *H*, Lord; for the godly man
20. 2 Send thee *h* from the sanctuary,
27. 9 thou hast been my *h*; leave me not,
33.20 Lord: he is our *h* and our shield.
38.22 Make haste to *h* me, O Lord my
40.17 thou art my *h* and my deliverer;
42. 5 for the *h* of his countenance.
46. 1 a very present *h* in trouble.
5 God shall *h* her, and that right
60.11 trouble: for vain is the *h* of man.
70. 1 me; make haste to *h* me, O Lord.
79. 9 *H* us, O God of our salvation, for
94.17 Unless the Lord had been my *h*,
108.12 trouble: for vain is the *h* of man.
119.173 Let thine hand *h* me; for I have
121. 1 hills, from which cometh my *h*.
2 My *h* cometh from the Lord, which
124. 8 Our *h* is in the name of the Lord,
Isa 10. 3 to whom will ye flee for *h*? and
31. 2 the *h* of them that work iniquity.

Isa 41.13 unto thee, Fear not; I will *h* thee.
50. 7 the Lord God will *h* me; therefore
9 Behold, the Lord God will *h* me;
63. 5 I looked, and there was none to *h*;
Mt 15.25 worshipped him, saying, Lord, *h* me.
Mk 9.22 have compassion on us, and *h* us.
24 I believe; *h* thou mine unbelief.
Lk 5. 7 that they should come and *h* them.
10.40 bid her therefore that she *h* me.
Ac 16. 9 over into Macedonia, and *h* us.
21.28 Crying out, Men of Israel, *h*: This
26.22 Having therefore obtained *h* of
Php 4. 3 *h* those women which labored
Heb 4.16 find grace to *h* in time of need.

HELPED

Ex 2.17 Moses stood up and *h* them, and
1Sa 7.12 Hitherto hath the Lord *h* us.
1Ch 12.19 Saul to battle: but they *h* them not:
2Ch 26. 7 God *h* him against the Philistines,
Ps 116. 6 I was brought low, and he *h* me.
Isa 49. 8 in a day of salvation have I *h* thee:
Ac 18.27 *h* them much which had believed
Rev 12.16 the earth *h* the woman, and the

HELPER

2Ki 14.26 nor any left, nor any *h* for Israel.
Job 30.13 my calamity, they have no *h*.
Ps 10.14 thou art the *h* of the fatherless.
30.10 upon me: Lord, be thou my *h*.
54. 4 Behold, God is mine *h*: the Lord is
72.12 poor also, and him that hath no *h*.
Jer 47. 4 and Zidon every *h* that remaineth:
Ro 16. 9 Salute Urbane, our *h* in Christ,
Heb 13. 6 Lord is my *h*, and I will not fear

HELPERS

1Ch 12. 1 the mighty men, *h* of the war.
18 unto thee, and peace be to thine *h*;
Job 9.13 the proud *h* do stoop under him.
Eze 30. 8 when all her *h* shall be destroyed.
Na 3. 9 Put and Lubim were thy *h*.
Ro 16. 3 and Aquila my *h* in Christ Jesus:
2Co 1.24 your faith, but are *h* of your joy:

HELPETH

1Ch 12.18 thine helpers; for thy God *h* thee.
Isa 31. 3 both he that *h* shall fall, and he
Ro 8.26 the Spirit also *h* our infirmities:
1Co 16.16 and to every one that *h* with us,

HELPING

Ezr 5. 2 were the prophets of God *h* them.
Ps 22. 1 why art thou so far from *h* me,
2Co 1.11 Ye also *h* together by prayer for us,

HELPS

Ac 27.17 they used *h*, undergirding the ship;
1Co 12.28 gifts of healings, *h*, governments,

HEM

Ex 28.33 upon the *h* of it thou shall make
33 scarlet, round about the *h* thereof;
34 upon the *h* of the robe round
39.25 upon the *h* of the robe, round
26 round about the *h* of the robe to
Mt 9.20 touched the *h* of his garment:
14.36 only touch the *h* of his garment:

HEN

Mt 23.37 even as a *h* gathereth her chickens
Lk 13.34 as a *h* doth gather her brood under

HENCEFORTH

Ps 125. 2 his people from *h* even for ever.
Mt 23.39 Ye shall not see me *h*, till ye
26.29 I will not drink *h* of this fruit of
Lk 1.48 from *h* all generations shall call me
5.10 not; from *h* thou shalt catch men.
Jn 15.15 *H* I call you not servants; for the
Ac 4.17 speak *h* to no man in this name.

Biblical Themes

HELL

Are not my days few? cease then, and let me alone, that I may take comfort a little, before I go whence I shall not return, even to the land of darkness and the shadow of death. Job 10.20-21

I am counted with them that go down into the pit: I am as a man that hath no strength: free among the dead, like the slain that lie in the grave, whom thou rememberest no more: and they are cut off from thy hand. Ps 88.4-5

If I ascend up into heaven, thou art there: if I make my bed in hell, behold, thou art there. Ps 139.8

The way of life is above to the wise, that he may depart from hell beneath. Pr 15.24

Hell hath enlarged herself, and opened her mouth without measure: and their glory, and their multitude, and their pomp, and he that rejoiceth, shall descend into it. Isa 5.14

Hell from beneath is moved for thee to meet thee at thy coming: it stirreth up the dead for thee. . . . All they shall speak and say unto thee, Art thou also become weak as we? art thou become like unto us? Isa 14.9-10

We have made a covenant with death, and with hell are we at agreement; when the overflowing scourge shall pass through, it shall not come unto us. Isa 28.15

They shall go forth, and look upon the carcases of the men that have transgressed against me: for their worm shall not die, neither shall their fire be quenched. Isa 66.24

The Son of man shall send forth his angels, and they shall gather out of his kingdom all things that offend, and them which do iniquity; and shall cast them into a furnace of fire: there shall be wailing and gnashing of teeth. Mt 13.41-43

Thou art Peter, and upon this rock I will build my church; and the gates of hell shall not prevail against it. Mt 16.18

Ye serpents, ye generation of vipers, how can ye escape the damnation of hell? Mt 23.33

Depart from me, ye cursed, into everlasting fire, prepared for the devil and his angels: for I was an hungred, and ye gave me no meat: I was thirsty, and ye gave me no drink. Mt 25.41-42

If thy foot offend thee, cut it off: it is better for thee to enter halt into life, than having two feet to be cast into hell, into the fire that never shall be quenched. Mk 9.45

Be not afraid of them that kill the body, and after that have no more that they can do. . . . Fear him, which after he hath killed hath power to cast into hell. Lk 12.4-5

In hell he lift up his eyes, being in torments, and seeth Abraham afar off, and Lazarus in his bosom. And he cried and said, Father Abraham, have mercy on me, and send Lazarus, that he may dip the tip of his finger in water, and cool my tongue; for I am tormented in this flame. But Abraham said, Son, remember that thou in thy lifetime receivedst thy good things, and likewise Lazarus evil things: but now he is comforted, and thou art tormented. And beside all this, between us and you there is a great gulf fixed. Lk 16.23-26

The Lord Jesus shall be revealed from heaven with his mighty angels, in flaming fire taking vengeance on them that know not God. 2Th 1.7-8

If any man worship the beast and his image . . . he shall be tormented with fire and brimstone . . . and the smoke of their torment ascendeth up for ever and ever: and they have no rest day nor night, who worship the beast and his image. Rev 14.9-11

Ro 6. 6 that *h* we should not serve sin.
2Co 5.16 *h* know we no man after
16 yet now *h* know we him no more.
Eph 4.14 That we *h* be no more children,
2Ti 4. 8 *H* there is laid up for me a crown
Rev 14.13 dead which die in the Lord from *h*:

HENCEFORWARD

Nu 15.23 and *h* among your generations;
Mt 21.19 no fruit grow on thee *h* for ever.

HERB

Gen 1.11 the *h* yielding seed, and the fruit
12 *h* yielding seed after his kind, and
29 I have given you every *h* bearing
30 have given every green *h* for meat:
2. 5 every *h* of the field before it grew:
3.18 and thou shalt eat the *h* of the field;
9. 3 even as the green *h* have I given
Ex 9.22 every *h* of the field, throughout
25 the hail smote every *h* of the field,
10.12 and eat every *h* of the land, even all
15 and they did eat every *h* of the land,
Dt 32. 2 the small rain upon the tender *h*,
2Ki 19.26 and as the green *h*, as the grass on
Job 8.12 it withereth before any other *h*.

38.27 the bud of the tender *h* to spring
Ps 37. 2 grass, and wither as the green *h*.
104.14 and *h* for the service of man: that
Isa 37.27 of the field, and as the green *h*, as
66.14 your bones shall flourish like an *h*:

HERBS

Ex 10.15 the trees, or in the *h* of the field,
12. 8 and with bitter *h* they shall eat it.
Nu 9.11 with unleavened bread and bitter *h*.
Dt 11.10 it with thy foot, as a garden of *h*:
1Ki 21. 2 I may have it for a garden of *h*,
2Ki 4.39 went out into the field to gather *h*,
Ps 105.35 did eat up all the *h* in their land,
Pr 15.17 Better is a dinner of *h* where love
27.25 *h* of the mountains are gathered.
Isa 18. 4 like a clear heat upon *h*, and like
26.19 thy dew is as the dew of *h*, and the
42.15 and hills, and dry up all their *h*;
Jer 12. 4 and the *h* of every field wither, for
Mt 13.32 grown, it is the greatest among *h*,
Mk 4.32 up, and becometh greater than all *h*,
Lk 11.42 mint and rue and all manner of *h*,
Ro 14. 2 another, who is weak, eateth *h*.
Heb 6. 7 and bringeth forth *h* meet for them

HERD

Gen 18. 7 And Abraham ran unto the *h*,
Lev 1. 2 even of the *h*, and of the flock.
3 offering be a burnt sacrifice of the *h*,
3. 1 peace offering, if he offer it of the *h*;
27.32 concerning the tithe of the *h*, or of
Nu 15. 3 the Lord, of the *h*, or of the flock:
Dt 12.21 shalt kill of thy *h* and of thy flock,
15.19 that come of thy *h* and of thy flock
16. 2 of the flock and the *h*, in the place
1Sa 11. 5 came after the *h* out of the field
2Sa 12. 4 of his own flock and of his own *h*,
Jer 31.12 the young of the flock and of the *h*:
Jon 3. 7 man nor beast, *h* nor flock, taste
Hab 3.17 and there shall be no *h* in the stalls:
Mt 8.30 them an *h* of many swine feeding.
31 us to go away into the *h* of swine.
32 they went into the *h* of swine: and,
32 the whole *h* of swine ran violently
Mk 5.11 mountains a great *h* of swine feeding.
13 the *h* ran violently down a steep place
Lk 8.32 an *h* of many swine feeding on the
33 the *h* ran violently down a steep place

HERE

Gen 22. 1 Abraham: and he said, Behold, *h* I am.
7 and he said, *H* am I, my son.
27. 1 and he said unto him, Behold, *h* am I.
31.11 saying, Jacob: And I said, *H* am I.
Ex 24.14 Tarry ye *h* for us, until we come
1Sa 3. 6, 8 *H* am I; for thou didst call me.
16.11 Jesse, Are *h* all thy children?
29. 3 What do these Hebrews *h*? And
1Ki 18. 8, 11 tell thy lord, Behold, Elijah is *h*.
19. 9, 13 What doest thou *h*, Elijah?
2Ki 7. 3 Why sit we *h*, until we die?
1Ch 29.17 joy thy people, which are present *h*,
Isa 6. 8 Then said I, *H* am I; send me.
28.10 line; *h* a little, and there a little:
Mt 12.41 behold, a greater then Jonas is *h*.
42 behold, a greater than Solomon is *h*.
14. 8 Give me *h* John Baptist's head in a
17 We have *h* but five loaves, and two
16.28 standing *h*, which shall not taste
17. 4 Lord, it is good for us to be *h*:
4 let us make *h* three tabernacles;
20. 6 Why stand ye *h* all the day idle?
24. 2 shall not be left *h* one stone upon
23 unto you, Lo, *h* is Christ, or there;
26.36 Sit ye *h*, while I go and pray yonder.
38 tarry ye *h*, and watch with me.
28. 6 He is not *h*: for he is risen, as
Mk 6. 3 and are not his sisters *h* with us?
8. 4 with bread *h* in the wilderness?
9. 1 there be some of them that stand *h*,
5 Master, it is good for us to be *h*:
13. 1 of stones and what buildings are *h*!
21 Lo, *h* is Christ; or, lo, he is there;
14.32 Sit ye *h*, while I shall pray.
34 unto death: tarry ye *h*, and watch.
16. 6 he is risen; he is not *h*: behold the
Lk 4.23 Capernaum, do...*h* in thy country.
9.12 for we are *h* in a desert place.
27 standing *h*, which shall not taste
33 Master, it is good for us to be *h*:
11.31 behold, a greater than Solomon is *h*.
32 behold, a greater than Jonas is *h*.
17.21 shall they say, Lo *h*! or, lo there!
23 And they shall say to you, See *h*; or
19.20 Lord, behold, *h* is thy pound, which I
22.38 Lord, behold, *h* are two swords.
24. 6 He is not *h*, but is risen: remember
41 unto them, Have ye *h* any meat?
Jn 6. 9 There is a lad *h*, which hath five
11.21, 32 if thou hadst been *h*, my brother
Ac 4.10 doth this man stand *h* before you
8.36 See, *h* is water; what doth hinder
9.10 And he said, Behold, I am *h*, Lord.
14 And *h* he hath authority from the
10.33 Now therefore are we all *h* present
16.28 thyself no harm: for we are all *h*.
24.19 ought to have been *h* before thee,
20 Or else let these same *h* say, if they
25.24 men which are *h* present with us,
24 me, both at Jerusalem, and also *h*,
Col 4. 9 you all things which are done *h*.
Heb 7. 8 And *h* men that die receive tithes;
13.14 For *h* have we no continuing city,
Jas 2. 3 unto him, Sit thou *h* in a good place:
3 there, or sit *h* under my footstool:
1Pe 1.17 the time of your sojourning *h* in fear.
Rev 13.10 *H* is the patience and the faith of
18 *H* is wisdom. Let him that hath
14.12 *H* is the patience of the saints:
12 *h* are they that keep the
17. 9 *h* is the mind which hath wisdom.

HEREAFTER

Isa 41.23 Shew the things that are to come *h*,
Eze 20.39 and *h* also, if ye will not hearken
Dan 2.29 what should come to pass *h*:
45 what shall come to pass *h*:
Mt 26.64 *H* shall ye see the Son of man
Mk 11.14 man eat fruit of thee *h* for ever.
Lk 22.69 *H* shall the Son of man sit on
Jn 1.51 *H* ye shall see heaven open,
13. 7 now; but thou shalt know *h*.

Hell in biblical times was simply a place of fiery torment; the medieval view was more vividly gruesome.

Jn 14.30 *H* I will not talk much with you:
1Ti 1.16 should *h* believe on him to life
Rev 1.19 the things which shall be *h*;
4. 1 thee things which must be *h*.
9.12 there come two woes more *h*.

HEREBY

Gen 42.15 *H* ye shall be proved: By the life
33 *H* shall I know that ye are true men;
Nu 16.28 And Moses said, *H* ye shall know
Jos 3.10 And Joshua said, *H* ye shall know
1Co 4. 4 yet am I not *h* justified: but
1Jn 2. 3 And *h* we do know that we do
5 *h* know we that we are in him.
3.16 *H* perceive we the love of God,
19 And *h* we know that we are of
24 *h* we know that he abideth in
4. 2 *H* know ye the Spirit of God:
6 *H* know we the spirit of truth,
13 *H* know we that we dwell in

HEREIN

Gen 34.22 Only *h* will the men consent unto
2Ch 16. 9 *H* thou hast done foolishly:
Jn 4.37 And *h* is that saying true, One
9.30 Why *h* is a marvellous thing,
15. 8 *H* is my Father glorified, that
Ac 24.16 And *h* do I exercise myself, to
2Co 8.10 And *h* I give my advice: for
1Jn 4.10 *H* is love, not that we loved God,
17 *H* is our love made perfect,

HERESIES

1Co 11.19 there must be also *h* among you,
Gal 5.20 wrath, strife, seditions, *h*, envyings,
2Pe 2. 1 shall bring in damnable *h*, even

HERESY

Ac 24.14 after the way which they call *h*, so

HERETICK

Tit 3.10 A man that is an *h* after the first

HERITAGE

Ex 6. 8 and I will give it you for an *h*:
Job 20.29 the *h* appointed unto him by God.
27.13 and the *h* of oppressors, which they
Ps 16. 6 places; yea, I have a goodly *h*.
61. 5 the *h* of those that fear thy name.
94. 5 people, O Lord, and afflict thine *h*.
111. 6 may give them the *h* of the heathen.
119.111 testimonies have I taken as an *h*
127. 3 Lo, children are an *h* of the Lord:
135.12 And gave their land for an *h*,
12 an *h* unto Israel his people.
136.21 And gave their land for an *h*: for his
22 Even an *h* unto Israel his servant:
Isa 54.17 the *h* of the servants of the Lord,
58.14 thee with the *h* of Jacob thy father:
Jer 2. 7 and made mine *h* an abomination.
3.19 a goodly *h* of the hosts of nations?
12. 7 I have left mine *h*; I have given the
8 Mine *h* is unto me as a lion in the
9 Mine *h* is unto me as a speckled
15 every man to his *h*, and every man
17. 4 discontinue from thine *h* that I gave
50.11 O ye destroyers of mine *h*, because
Joel 2.17 give not thine *h* to reproach, that
3. 2 for my people and for my *h* Israel,
Mic 2. 2 his house, even a man and his *h*.
7.14 the flock of thine *h*, which dwell
18 the remnant of his *h*? he retaineth
Mal 1. 3 laid his mountains and his *h* waste
1Pe 5. 3 as being lords over God's *h*, but

HERMES

Ro 16.14 *H*, and the brethren which are

HEROD

Mt 2. 1 in the days of *H* the king, behold,
3 When *H* the king had heard these

HEROD

Herod is the family name of a client dynasty that reigned in the Holy Land under Roman control from the second half of the 1st century B.C. to the end of the 1st century A.D. Three of them figure in the Bible: Herod the Great, founder of the dynasty, his son Herod Antipas, and his grandson Herod Agrippa.

With Roman support Herod the Great (c. 73 B.C.–A.D. 4) became king of Judea in 40 B.C. and proceeded to conquer in turn Idumea, Samaria, Galilee, and finally Jerusalem. The story of the massacre of the innocents (Mt 2) is not recorded elsewhere, but accords well with the character of a man who murdered his own wife, Mariamne, and many of his sons. Herod undertook the reconstruction of the temple (not finished until A.D. 62 or 64) and much other building work, including the coastal town of Caesarea and the fortress of Masada.

In his will Herod divided the kingdom among three of his sons, giving Judea and Samaria to Archelaus (Mt 2.22), the northeastern territories to Philip (Lk 3.1), and Galilee and Peraea to Antipas.

Herod Antipas (c. 22 B.C.–A.D. 39), tetrarch of Galilee (called "king" in Mk 6.14), divorced his first wife in order to marry his niece Herodias. The marriage was denounced by John the Baptist, who was consequently imprisoned and later executed (Mk 6.17-29). Antipas met Jesus, who knew him as "that fox" (Lk 13.22), when Jesus was passed on to him by Pilate on the grounds that as a Galilean he came under Herod's jurisdiction (Lk 23.7).

Herod Agrippa (10 B.C.–A.D. 44), who came to rule a territory of roughly the same extent as his grandfather's, was popular among his Jewish subjects, but attempted to suppress the new Christian movement; he executed James, the son of Zebedee, and imprisoned Peter, who escaped. Soon after this Agrippa suddenly and painfully died, an event seen by the Christian community as an act of divine judgment (Ac 12).

7 Then *H*, when he had privily
12 that they should not return to *H*,
13 for *H* will seek the young child to
15 was there until the death of *H*:
16 Then *H*, when he saw that he was
19 But when *H* was dead, behold, an
22 in the room of his father *H*, he
14. 1 At that time *H* the tetrarch heard
3 For *H* had laid hold on John, and
6 danced before them, and pleased *H*.
Mk 6.14 king *H* heard of him; for his name
16 But when *H* heard thereof, he said,
17 *H* himself had sent forth and laid
18 For John had said unto *H*, It is not
20 For *H* feared John, knowing that
21 *H* on his birthday made a supper
22 came in, and danced, and pleased *H*
8.15 Pharisees, and of the leaven of *H*.
Lk 1. 5 There was in the days of *H*, the
3. 1 and *H* being tetrarch of Galilee,
19 *H* the tetrarch, being reproved
19 for all the evils which *H* had done,
9. 7 *H* the tetrarch heard of all that was
9 And *H* said, John have I beheaded:
13.31 depart hence: for *H* will kill thee.
23. 7 he sent him to *H*, who himself also
8 And when *H* saw Jesus, he was
11 And *H* with his men of war set him
12 Pilate and *H* were made friends
15 nor yet *H*: for I sent you to him;
Ac 4.27 whom thou hast anointed, both *H*
12. 1 Now about that time *H* the king
6 *H* would have brought him forth,
11 delivered me out of the hand of *H*,
19 And when *H* had sought for him,
20 *H* was highly displeased with them
21 And upon a set day *H*, arrayed in
13. 1 brought up with *H* the tetrarch,

HERODIANS

Mt 22.16 their disciples with the *H*, saying,
Mk 3. 6 took counsel with the *H* against
12.13 of the Pharisees and of the *H*, to

HERODIAS

Mt 14. 6 the daughter of *H* danced before
Mk 6.19 Therefore *H* had a quarrel against
22 when the daughter of the said *H*
Lk 3.19 being reproved by him for *H* his

HERODIAS'

Mt 14. 3 and put him in prison for *H* sake,
Mk 6.17 bound him in prison for *H* sake,

HEROD'S

Mt 14. 6 when *H* birthday was kept, the
Lk 8. 3 the wife of Chuza *H* steward, and
23. 7 he belonged unto *H* jurisdiction,
Ac 23.35 him to be kept in *H* judgment hall.

HEW

Ex 34. 1 *H* thee two tables of stone like
Dt 10. 1 *H* thee two tables of stone like
12. 3 shall *h* down the graven images of
19. 5 with his neighbor to *h* wood, and
1Ki 5. 6 that they *h* me cedar trees out of
6 to *h* timber like unto the Sidonians.
18 and Hiram's builders did *h* them,
1Ch 22. 2 set masons to *h* wrought stones
2Ch 2. 2 thousand to *h* in the mountain,
Jer 6. 6 *H* ye down trees, and cast them
Dan 4.14 *H* down the tree, and cut off his
23 *H* the tree down, and destroy it;

HEWED

Ex 34. 4 And he *h* two tables of stone like
Dt 10. 3 and *h* two tables of stone like unto
1Sa 11. 7 of oxen, and *h* them in pieces,
15.33 And Samuel *h* Agag in pieces
1Ki 5.17 costly stones, and *h* stones, to lay
6.36 with three rows of *h* stone, and a
7. 9 to the measures of *h* stones, sawed
11 after the measures of *h* stones,
12 with three rows of *h* stones, and a
2Ki 12.12 and to buy timber and *h* stone to
Isa 22.16 thou hast *h* thee out a sepulcher
Jer 2.13 and *h* them out cisterns, broken
Hos 6. 5 have I *h* them by the prophets;

HEWER

Dt 29.11 the *h* of thy wood unto the drawer

HEWERS

Jos 9.21 let them be *h* of wood and drawers
23 bondmen, and *h* of wood and
27 make them that day *h* of wood and
1Ki 5.15 thousand *h* in the mountains;
2Ki 12.12 masons, and *h* of stone, and to buy
1Ch 22.15 *h* and workers of stone and timber,
2Ch 2.10 thy servants, the *h* that cut timber,
18 thousand to be *h* in the mountain
Jer 46.22 her with axes, as *h* of wood.

HEWN

Ex 20.25 thou shalt not build it of *h* stone:
2Ki 22. 6 timber and *h* stone to repair the
2Ch 34.11 to buy *h* stone, and timber for
Pr 9. 1 she hath *h* out her seven pillars:
Isa 9.10 but we will build with *h* stones:
10.33 ones of stature shall be *h* down,
33. 9 Lebanon is ashamed and *h* down:
51. 1 unto the rock whence ye are *h*,
La 3. 9 inclosed my ways with *h* stone,
Eze 40.42 four tables were of *h* stone for the
Am 5.11 ye have built houses of *h* stone,
Mt 3.10 is *h* down, and cast into the fire.
7.19 is *h* down, and cast into the fire.
27.60 which he had *h* out in the rock;
Mk 15.46 in a sepulchre which was *h* out of a
Lk 3. 9 is *h* down, and cast into the fire.
23.53 of a sepulchre that was *h* in stone,

HEZEKIAH

2Ki 16.20 *H* his son reigned in his stead.
18. 1 that *H* the son of Ahaz king of
14 And *H* king of Judah sent to the
14 king of Assyria appointed unto *H*
15 And *H* gave him all the silver that
22 whose altars *H* hath taken away,
29 saith the king, Let not *H* deceive
31 Hearken not to *H*: for thus saith
19. 1 when king *H* heard it, that he rent
15 And *H* prayed before the Lord,
20 Isaiah the son of Amoz sent to *H*,
20. 1 those days was *H* sick unto death.
3 in thy sight. And *H* wept sore.
5 Turn again, and tell *H* the captain
13 dominion, that *H* shewed them not.
19 Then said *H* unto Isaiah, Good is
21 And *H* slept with his fathers: and
21. 3 high places which *H* his father had
2Ch 28.27 *H* his son reigned in his stead.
29. 1 *H* began to reign when he was five
27 And *H* commanded to offer the
36 And *H* rejoiced, and all the people,
30. 1 And *H* sent to all Israel and Judah,
20 Lord hearkened to *H*, and healed
32. 2 when *H* saw that Sennacherib was
8 themselves upon the words of *H*
16 God, and against his servant *H*.
17 so shall not the God of *H* deliver
22 Lord saved *H* and the inhabitants
23 and presents to *H* king of Judah:
24 those days *H* was sick to the death,
27 *H* had exceeding much riches and
Isa 1. 1 Ahaz, and *H*, kings of Judah.
36. 1 in the fourteenth year of king *H*,
7 whose altars *H* hath taken away,
14 saith the king, Let not *H* deceive
37. 1 when king *H* heard it, that he rent
38. 1 those days was *H* sick unto death.
2 then *H* turned his face toward the
3 in thy sight. And *H* wept sore.
39. 1 sent letters and a present to *H*:
2 dominion, that *H* shewed them not
8 Then said *H* to Isaiah, Good is the
Jer 15. 4 because of Manasseh the son of *H*
26.18 prophesied in the days of *H* king
(See box on page 372)

HID

Gen 3. 8 Adam and his wife *h* themselves
10 I was naked; and I *h* myself.
Ex 2. 2 child, she *h* him three months.
3. 6 And Moses *h* his face; for he was
Jos 2. 4 took the two men, and *h* them,
6 *h* them with the stalks of flax,
1Sa 20.24 So David *h* himself in the field:
2Ki 4.27 and the Lord hath *h* it from me,
6.29 eat him: and she hath *h* her son.
Job 28.11 thing that is *h* bringeth he forth
21 Seeing it is *h* from the eyes of all
29. 8 men saw me, and *h* themselves:
38.30 The waters are *h* as with a stone,
Ps 17.14 thou fillest with thy *h* treasure:
19. 6 there is nothing *h* from the heat
32. 5 and mine iniquity have I not *h*.
69. 5 and my sins are not *h* from thee.
119.11 Thy word have I *h* in mine heart,
139.15 My substance was not *h* from
Pr 2. 4 for her as for *h* treasures;
Isa 40.27 My way is *h* from the Lord, and my
49. 2 shadow of his hand hath he *h* me,
2 in his quiver hath he *h* me;
50. 6 I *h* not my face from shame and
53. 3 and we *h* as it were our faces from
59. 2 your sins have *h* his face from you,
Jer 16.17 is their iniquity *h* from mine eyes.
33. 5 I have *h* my face from this city.
Na 3.11 thou shalt be *h*, thou also shalt
Mt 5.14 that is set on an hill cannot be *h*.
10.26 and *h*, that shall not be known.
11.25 because thou hast *h* these things
13.33 and *h* in three measures of meal,
44 is like unto treasure *h* in a field;
25.18 the earth, and *h* his lord's money.
25 went and *h* thy talent in the earth:
Mk 4.22 For there is nothing *h*, which shall
7.24 know it: but he could not be *h*.
Lk 1.24 and *h* herself five months, saying,
8.17 neither any thing *h*, that shall not
47 saw that she was not *h*, she came
9.45 and it was *h* from them, that they
10.21 that thou hast *h* these things from
12. 2 neither *h*, that shall not be known.
13.21 and *h* in three measures of meal,
18.34 and this saying was *h* from them,
19.42 now they are *h* from thine eyes.
Jn 8.59 but Jesus *h* himself, and went out
2Co 4. 3 if our gospel be *h*, it is *h* to them
Eph 3. 9 hath been *h* in God, who created
Col 1.26 which hath been *h* from ages and
2. 3 In whom are *h* all the treasures
3. 3 your life is *h* with Christ in God.
1Ti 5.25 that are otherwise cannot be *h*.
Heb 11.23 was *h* three months of his parents,
Rev 6.15 *h* themselves in the dens and in

HIDDEN

Lev 5. 2 and if it be *h* from him; he also
Dt 30.11 it is not *h* from thee, neither is
Job 3.16 Or as an *h* untimely birth I had
15.20 of years is *h* to the oppressor.
24. 1 times are not *h* from the Almighty,
Ps 51. 6 in the *h* part thou shalt make me
83. 3 and consulted against thy *h* ones.
Pr 28.12 when the wicked rise, a man is *h*.
Isa 45. 3 and *h* riches of secret places, that
48. 6 from this time, even *h* things, and
Ob 6 how are his *h* things sought up!
Ac 26.26 none of these things are *h* from
1Co 2. 7 the *h* wisdom, which God ordained
4. 5 bring to the light the *h* things of
2Co 4. 2 the *h* things of dishonesty, not
1Pe 3. 4 But let it be the *h* man of the heart,
Rev 2.17 will I give to eat of the *h* manna,

HIDE

Gen 18.17 Shall I *h* from Abraham that thing
Ex 2. 3 when she could not longer *h* him,
Lev 20. 4 ways *h* their eyes from the man,
Dt 31.17 and I will *h* my face from them,
32.20 said, I will *h* my face from them,
Jos 7.19 thou hast done; *h* it not from me.
2Sa 14.18 *H* not from me, I pray thee, the
1Ki 17. 3 *h* thyself by the brook Cherith,
Job 13.20 then will I not *h* myself from thee.
14.13 thou wouldest *h* me in the grave,
24. 4 poor of the earth *h* themselves
40.13 *H* them in the dust together;
Ps 13. 1 how long wilt thou *h* thy face
17. 8 *h* me under the shadow of thy
27. 5 the time of trouble he shall *h* me
5 of his tabernacle shall he *h* me;
9 *H* not thy face far from me; put
51. 9 *H* thy face from my sins, and blot
89.46 Lord? wilt thou *h* thyself for ever?
119.19 *h* not thy commandments from me.

Herod Antipas questions Jesus after his arrest (Lk 23) in this painting by Duccio, completed in 1311.

HEZEKIAH

King of Judah (c. 715–687 B.C.) and successor of Ahaz; reforms Judah's religious life and destroys the idolatrous high places; rebels against Assyria and campaigns against the Philistines; is later forced to surrender to the Assyrians when Sennacherib invades Judah (701 B.C.) and has to strip the temple and the royal treasury to meet the indemnity exacted (2Ki 18.1-16); is encouraged by Isaiah to stand firm when the Assyrian envoys threaten and try to demoralize the people of Jerusalem (2Ki 18.17–19.8); receives a letter from Sennacherib and spreads it out in supplication before God; his prayers are heard and Isaiah pronounces divine judgment upon the invader (2Ki 19.9-37); recovers from his deathbed and 15 years are added to his life; is succeeded by his son Manasseh (2Ki 20). The narrative in 2Ki 18–20 is repeated in Isa 36–39, with the addition of Hezekiah's lament in sickness (Isa 38.9-20). The Assyrian siege and capture of Lachish during the same campaign is depicted in vivid detail on wall reliefs from Sennacherib's palace.

Pr 28.28 wicked rise, men *h* themselves:
Isa 1.15 I will *h* mine eyes from you: yea,
3. 9 their sin as Sodom, they *h* it not.
Jer 23.24 Can any *h* himself in secret places
38.14 thee a thing; *h* nothing from me.
Eze 31. 8 the garden of God could not *h* him:
Jn 12.36 and did *h* himself from them.
Jas 5.20 and shall *h* a multitude of sins.
Rev 6.16 *h* us from the face of him that

HIDEST

Job 13.24 Wherefore *h* thou thy face, and
Ps 10. 1 why *h* thou thyself in times of
44.24 Wherefore *h* thou thy face, and
88.14 why *h* thou thy face from me?
104.29 Thou *h* thy face, they are troubled:
Isa 45.15 thou art a God that *h* thyself, O

HIDETH

1Sa 23.23 places where he *h* himself, and
Job 23. 9 he *h* himself on the right hand,
34.29 and when he *h* his face, who then
42. 3 Who is he that *h* counsel without
Ps 10.11 he *h* his face; he will never see it.
139.12 the darkness *h* not from thee;
Pr 10.18 He that *h* hatred with lying lips,
19.24 man *h* his hand in his bosom,
22. 3 foreseeth the evil, and *h* himself:
26.15 slothful *h* his hand in his bosom;
27.12 foreseeth the evil, and *h* himself;
16 Whosoever *h* her *h* the wind, and
28.27 that *h* his eyes shall have many a
Isa 8.17 that *h* his face from the house of
Mt 13.44 when a man hath found, he *h*,

HIDING

Job 31.33 by *h* mine iniquity in my bosom:
Ps 32. 7 Thou art my *h* place: thou shalt
119.114 art my *h* place and my shield:
Isa 28.17 waters shall overflow the *h* place.
32. 2 be as an *h* place from the wind,
Hab 3. 4 and there was the *h* of his power.

HIGH

Gen 14.18 was the priest of the most *h* God.
20 And blessed be the most *h* God,
Lev 26.22 and your *h* ways shall be desolate.
Nu 20.17 we will go by the king's *h* way,
Dt 28. 1 thy God will set thee on *h* above all
2Sa 1.19 Israel is slain upon thy *h* places:
22. 3 my *h* tower, and my refuge, my
14 and the most *H* uttered his voice.
1Ki 12.32 the priests of the *h* places which
21. 9 set Naboth on *h* among the people:
22.43 the *h* places were not taken away;
2Ki 18. 4 He removed the *h* places, and brake
19.22 and lifted up thine eyes on *h*?
Job 5.11 To set up on *h* those that be low;
25. 2 he maketh peace in his *h* places.
Ps 7.17 to the name of the Lord most *h*.
9. 2 praise to thy name, O thou most *H*.
46. 4 of the tabernacles of the most *H*.
57. 2 I will cry unto God most *h*; unto
68.18 Thou hast ascended on *h*, thou
83.18 art the most *h* over all the earth.
91. 1 in the secret place of the most *H*
92. 1 praises unto thy name, O most *H*:
103.11 the heaven is *h* above the earth,
104.18 The *h* hills are a refuge for the
107.41 Yet setteth he the poor on *h* from
131. 1 matters, or in things too *h* for me.
139. 6 it is *h*, I cannot attain unto it.
144. 2 my *h* tower, and my deliverer;
150. 5 him upon the *h* sounding cymbals.
Pr 24. 7 Wisdom is too *h* for a fool: he
Isa 6. 1 upon a throne, *h* and lifted up,
24.18 the windows from on *h* are open,
40. 9 get thee up into the *h* mountain;
57.15 the *h* and lofty One that inhabiteth
15 I dwell in the *h* and holy place,
Jer 4.11 A dry wind of the *h* places in the
25.30 The Lord shall roar from on *h*,
La 3.35 before the face of the most *H*,
38 Out of the mouth of the most *H*
Dan 3.26 ye servants of the most *h* God,
4.34 and I blessed the most *H*, and I
7.25 wear out the saints of the most *H*,
27 people of the saints of the most *H*,
Mic 6. 6 and bow myself before the *h* God?
Mt 4. 8 up into an exceeding *h* mountain,
17. 1 them up into an *h* mountain apart,
26. 3 the palace of the *h* priest, who was
51 struck a servant of the *h* priest's,
57 him away to Caiaphas the *h* priest,
58 afar off unto the *h* priest's palace,
62 And the *h* priest arose, and said unto
63 And the *h* priest answered and said
65 Then the *h* priest rent his clothes,
Mk 2.26 days of Abiathar the *h* priest, and
5. 7 Jesus, thou Son of the most *h* God?
6.21 supper to his lords, *h* captains, and
9. 2 them up into an *h* mountain apart
14.47 and smote a servant of the *h* priest,
53 led Jesus away to the *h* priest: and
54 into the palace of the *h* priest: and
60 the *h* priest stood up in the midst,
61 Again the *h* priest asked him, and
63 Then the *h* priest rent his clothes,
66 one of the maids of the *h* priest:
Lk 1.78 dayspring from on *h* hath visited
3. 2 and Caiaphas being the *h* priests,
4. 5 taking him up into an *h* mountain,
8.28 Jesus, thou son of God most *h*?
22.50 smote the servant of the *h* priest,
54 him into the *h* priest's house. And
24.49 be endued with power from on *h*.
Jn 11.49 being the *h* priest that same year,
51 but being *h* priest that year, he
18.10 and smote the *h* priest's servant, and
13 which was the *h* priest that same
15 was known unto the *h* priest, and
15 Jesus into the palace of the *h* priest.
16 which was known unto the *h* priest,
19 The *h* priest then asked Jesus of his
22 Answerest thou the *h* priest so?
24 bound unto Caiaphas the *h* priest.
26 of the servants of the *h* priest,
19.31 that sabbath day was an *h* day,
Ac 4. 6 Annas the *h* priest, and Caiaphas,
6 were of the kindred of the *h* priest,
5.17 the *h* priest rose up, and all they
21 But the *h* priest came, and they that
24 the *h* priest and the captain of the
27 and the *h* priest asked them,
7. 1 said the *h* priest, Are these things
48 most *H* dwelleth not in temples
9. 1 And Saul...went unto the *h* priest,
13.17 with an *h* arm brought he them
16.17 are the servants of the most *h* God,
22. 5 the *h* priest doth bear me witness,
23. 2 the *h* priest Ananias commanded
4 said, Revilest thou God's *h* priest?
5 wist not...that he was the *h* priest:
24. 1 Ananias the *h* priest descended with
25. 2 Then the *h* priest and the chief of
Ro 12.16 Mind not *h* things, but condescend
13.11 it is *h* time to awake out of sleep:
2Co 10. 5 and every *h* thing that exalteth
Eph 4. 8 When he ascended up on *h*, he led
6.12 spiritual wickedness in *h* places.
Php 3.14 the prize of the *h* calling of God in
Heb 1. 3 the right hand of the Majesty on *h*;
2.17 a merciful and faithful *h* priest in
3. 1 consider the Apostle and *H* Priest of
4.14 that we have a great *h* priest, that is
15 we have not an *h* priest which cannot
5. 1 For every *h* priest taken from among
5 not himself to be made an *h* priest;
10 of God an *h* priest after the order of
6.20 an *h* priest for ever after the order
7. 1 of Salem, priest of the most *h* God,
26 For such an *h* priest became
27 not daily, as those *h* priests, to offer
28 the law maketh men *h* priests which
8. 1 We have such an *h* priest, who is set
3 every *h* priest is ordained to offer
9. 7 went the *h* priest alone once every
11 an *h* priest of good things to come,
25 as the *h* priest entereth into the holy
10.21 having an *h* priest over the house
13.11 sanctuary by the *h* priest for sin,
Rev 21.10 spirit to a great and *h* mountain,
12 And had a wall great and *h*, and had

HIGHER

Nu 24. 7 and his king shall be *h* than Agag,
1Sa 9. 2 he was *h* than any of the people.
10.23 he was *h* than any of the people
2Ki 15.35 He built the *h* gate of the house
Neh 4.13 the wall, and on the *h* places, I
Job 35. 5 the clouds which are *h* than thou.
Ps 61. 2 me to the rock that is *h* than I.
89.27 *h* than the kings of the earth.
Ec 5. 8 for he that is *h* than the highest
8 and there be *h* than they.
Isa 55. 9 the heavens are *h* than the earth,
9 so are my ways *h* than your ways,
Jer 36.10 in the *h* court, at the entry of the
Eze 9. 2 came from the way of the *h* gate,
42. 5 the galleries were *h* than these,
43.13 shall be the *h* place of the altar.
Dan 8. 3 but one was *h* than the other, and
3 the other, and the *h* came up last.
Lk 14.10 may say unto thee, Friend, go up *h*:
Ro 13. 1 soul be subject unto the *h* powers.
Heb 7.26 and made *h* than the heavens;

HIGHEST

Ps 18.13 and the *H* gave his voice;
87. 5 the *h* himself shall establish her.
Pr 8.26 *h* part of the dust of the world.
9. 3 upon the *h* places of the city,
Ec 5. 8 for he that is higher than the *h*
Eze 17. 3 took the *h* branch of the cedar:
22 of the *h* branch of the high cedar,
41. 7 from the lowest chamber to the *h*
Mt 21. 9 of the Lord; Hosanna in the *h*.
Mk 11.10 of the Lord: Hosanna in the *h*.

The high priest Caiaphas conducts Jesus' trial (Mt 26; Mk 14; Jn 18) in a 19th-century German depiction.

Lk 1.32 shall be called the Son of the *H*:
35 power of the *H* shall overshadow
76 be called the prophet of the *H*:
2.14 Glory to God in the *h*, and on earth
6.35 ye shall be the children of the *H*:
14. 8 sit not down in the *h* room; lest
19.38 peace in heaven, and glory in the *h*.
20.46 the *h* seats in the synagogues,

HIGHLY
Lk 1.28 said, Hail, thou that art *h* favored,
16.15 which is *h* esteemed among men
Ac 12.20 Herod was *h* displeased with them
Ro 12. 3 not to think of himself more *h* than
Php 2. 9 God also hath *h* exalted him, and
1Th 5.13 to esteem them very *h* in love

HIGHMINDED
Ro 11.20 by faith. Be not *h*, but fear:
1Ti 6.17 they be not *h*, nor trust in uncertain
2Ti 3. 4 heady, *h*, lovers of pleasures more

HIGHWAY
Jdg 21.19 on the east side of the *h* that goeth
1Sa 6.12 went along the *h*, lowing as they
2Sa 20.12 in blood in the midst of the *h*. And
12 he removed Amasa out of the *h* into
13 When he was removed out of the *h*,
2Ki 18.17 which is in the *h* of the fuller's field.
Pr 16.17 The *h* of the upright is to depart
Isa 7. 3 pool in the *h* of the fuller's field;
11.16 there shall be an *h* for the remnant
19.23 day shall there be a *h* out of Egypt
35. 8 And an *h* shall be there, and a way,
36. 2 pool in the *h* of the fuller's field.
40. 3 in the desert a *h* for our God.
62.10 cast up, cast up the *h*; gather out
Jer 31.21 set thine heart toward the *h*, even
Mk 10.46 Timaeus, sat by the *h* side begging.

HIGHWAYS
Jdg 5. 6 the *h* were unoccupied, and the
20.31 in the *h*, of which one goeth up
32 draw them from the city unto the *h*.
45 they gleaned of them in the *h* five
Isa 33. 8 The *h* lie waste, the warfaring man
49.11 a way, and my *h* shall be exalted.
Am 5.16 they shall say in all the *h*, Alas!
Mt 22. 9 Go ye therefore into the *h*,
10 servants went out into the *h*, and
Lk 14.23 Go out into the *h* and hedges, and

HILL
1Sa 10. 5 thou shalt come to the *h* of God,
26.13 stood on the top of an *h* afar off;
1Ki 11. 7 in the *h* that is before Jerusalem,
2Ki 1. 9 behold, he sat on the top of an *h*.
4.27 she came to the man of God to the *h*,
Ps 3. 4 and he heard me out of his holy *h*.
24. 3 Who shall ascend into the *h* of the
42. 6 the Hermonites, from the *h* Mizar.
43. 3 let them bring me unto thy holy *h*,
68.15 *h* of God is as the *h* of Bashan;
99. 9 our God, and worship at his holy *h*;
Isa 40. 4 mountain and *h* shall be made low:
Eze 34.26 round about my *h* a blessing;
Mt 5.14 A city that is set on an *h* cannot
Lk 1.39 went into the *h* country with haste,
65 throughout all the *h* country of
3. 5 mountain and *h* shall be brought
4.29 led him unto the brow of the *h*
9.37 they were come down from the *h*,
Ac 17.22 Paul stood in the midst of Mars' *h*,

HILLS
Dt 11.11 it, is a land of *h* and valleys, and
12. 2 upon the *h*, and under every green
33.15 the precious things of the lasting *h*,
1Ki 20.23 Their gods are gods of the *h*;
28 The Lord is God of the *h*, but he is
Job 15. 7 wast thou made before the *h*?
Ps 65.12 and the little *h* rejoice on every
68.16 Why leap ye, ye high *h*? this is
95. 4 the strength of the *h* is his also.
97. 5 *h* melted like wax at the presence
98. 8 hands: let the *h* be joyful together
104.18 The high *h* are a refuge for the
32 he toucheth the *h*, and they smoke.
121. 1 I will lift up mine eyes unto the *h*,
Pr 8.25 before the *h* was I brought forth:
Isa 5.25 the *h* did tremble, and their
55.12 the mountains and the *h* shall break
Jer 3.23 salvation is hoped for from the *h*,
Hos 10. 8 Cover us; and to the *h*, Fall on us.
Joel 3.18 and the *h* shall flow with milk, and
Am 9.13 sweet wine, and all the *h* shall melt.
Mic 6. 1 and let the *h* hear thy voice.
Na 1. 5 the *h* melt, and the earth is burned
Hab 3. 6 the perpetual *h* did bow: his ways
Lk 23.30 Fall on us; and to the *h*, Cover us.

HINDER
Gen 24.56 And he said unto them, *H* me not,
Nu 22.16 thee, *h* thee from coming unto me:
2Sa 2.23 the *h* end of the spear smote him
1Ki 7.25 and all their *h* parts were inward.
2Ch 4. 4 and all their *h* parts were inward.
Neh 4. 8 against Jerusalem, and to *h*
Job 9.12 he taketh away, who can *h* him?
11.10 together, then who can *h* him?
Ps 78.66 smote his enemies in the *h* parts:
Joel 2.20 his *h* part toward the utmost sea,
Zec 14. 8 and half of them toward the *h* sea:
Mk 4.38 he was in the *h* part of the ship,
Ac 8.36 what doth *h* me to be baptized?
27.41 but the *h* part was broken with
1Co 9.12 we should *h* the gospel
Gal 5. 7 did *h* you that ye should not obey

HINDERED
Ezr 6. 8 unto these men, that they be not *h*.
Lk 11.52 them that were entering in ye *h*.
Ro 15.22 been much *h* from coming to you.
1Th 2.18 once and again; but Satan *h* us.
1Pe 3. 7 of life; that your prayers be not *h*.

HINDMOST
Nu 2.31 They shall go *h* with their standards.
Dt 25.18 and smote the *h* of thee, even all
Jos 10.19 enemies, and smite the *h* of them;

HINGES
1Ki 7.50 and the *h* of gold, both for the
Pr 26.14 As the door turneth upon its *h*, so

HIP
Jdg 15. 8 he smote them *h* and thigh with a

HIRE
Gen 30.18 God hath given me my *h*, because
32 Goats: and of such shall be my *h*.
33 shall come for my *h* before thy face:
31. 8 The ringstraked shall be thy *h*;
Ex 22.15 an hired thing, it came for his *h*.
Dt 23.18 shalt not bring the *h* of a whore,
24.15 At his day thou shalt give him his *h*.
1Ki 5. 6 thee will I give *h* for thy servants
1Ch 19. 6 to *h* them chariots and horsemen
Isa 23.17 Tyre, and she shall turn to her *h*,
18 her *h* shall be holiness to the Lord:
46. 6 the balance, and *h* a goldsmith;
Eze 16.31 an harlot, in that thou scornest *h*;
41 thou also shalt give no *h* any more.
Mic 1. 7 she gathered it of the *h* of an harlot,
7 shall return to the *h* of an harlot.
3.11 the priests thereof teach for *h*, and
Zec 8.10 no *h* for man, nor any *h* for beast;
Mt 20. 1 to *h* laborers into his vineyard.
8 give them their *h*, beginning from
Lk 10. 7 for the laborer is worthy of his *h*.
Jas 5. 4 *h* of the laborers who have reaped

HIRED
Gen 30.16 surely I have *h* thee with my son's
Ex 12.45 an *h* servant shall not eat thereof.
22.15 be an *h* thing, it came for his hire.
Lev 19.13 the wages of him that is *h* shall not

Lev 22.10 *h* servant, shall not eat of the holy
25. 6 thy *h* servant and for thy stranger
40 as an *h* servant, and as a sojourner,
50 to the time of an *h* servant shall it
53 as a yearly *h* servant shall he be
Dt 15.18 worth a double *h* servant to thee,
23. 4 *h* against thee Balaam the son of
24.14 oppress an *h* servant that is poor
Jdg 9. 4 wherewith Abimelech *h* vain and
18. 4 Micah with me, and hath *h* me, and
1Sa 2. 5 full have *h* out themselves for bread;
2Sa 10. 6 Ammon sent and *h* the Syrians of
2Ki 7. 6 Israel hath *h* against us the kings
1Ch 19. 7 So they *h* thirty and two thousand
2Ch 24.12 *h* masons and carpenters to repair
25. 6 He *h* also an hundred thousand
Ezr 4. 5 And *h* counsellers against them, to
Neh 6.12 for Tobiah and Sanballat had *h* him.
13 Therefore was he *h*, that I should
13. 2 but *h* Balaam against them, that he
Isa 7.20 Lord shave with a rasor that is *h*,
Jer 46.21 her *h* men are in the midst of her
Hos 8. 9 himself: Ephraim hath *h* lovers.
10 they have *h* among the nations,
Mt 20. 7 him, Because no man hath *h* us.
9 were *h* about the eleventh hour,
Mk 1.20 the ship with the *h* servants, and
Lk 15.17 many *h* servants of my father's
19 make me as one of thy *h* servants.
Ac 28.30 whole years in his own *h* house,

HIRELING
Job 7. 1 days also like the days of an *h*?
2 and as an *h* looketh for the reward
14. 6 shall accomplish, as an *h*, his day.
Isa 16.14 three years, as the years of an *h*,
21.16 year, according to the years of an *h*,
Mal 3. 5 that oppress the *h* in his wages,
Jn 10.12 is an *h*, and not the shepherd,
13 The *h* fleeth, because he is an
13 because he is an *h*, and careth not

HOARFROST
Ps 147.16 he scattereth the *h* like ashes.

HOLD
Gen 21.18 up the lad, and *h* him in thine hand;
25.26 his hand took *h* on Esau's heel;
Ex 14.14 for you, and ye shall *h* your peace.
15.14 sorrow shall take *h* on the
20. 7 the Lord will not *h* him guiltless
Dt 5.11 the Lord will not *h* him guiltless
Jdg 18.19 they said unto him, *H* thy peace,
2Sa 6. 6 to the ark of God, and took *h* of it;
1Ki 1.50 caught *h* on the horns of the altar.
2Ki 2. 3, 5 Yea, I know it; *h* ye your peace.
7. 9 good tidings, and we *h* our peace:
Job 6.24 Teach me, and I will *h* my tongue:
11. 3 thy lies make men *h* their peace?
13.13 *H* your peace, let me alone, that
19 for now, if I *h* my tongue, I shall
27.20 Terrors take *h* on him as waters,
Ps 39.12 *h* not thy peace at my tears: for I
40.12 iniquities have taken *h* upon me,
48. 6 Fear took *h* upon them there, and
83. 1 *h* not thy peace, and be not still,
116. 3 the pains of hell gat *h* upon me:
Isa 3. 6 a man shall take *h* of his brother
4. 1 seven women shall take *h* of one
41.13 Lord thy God will *h* thy right hand,
62. 1 Zion's sake will I not *h* my peace,
Jer 2.13 cisterns, that can *h* no water.
4.19 I cannot *h* my peace, because thou
8.21 astonishment hath taken *h* on me.
Am 6.10 Then shall he say, *H* thy tongue:
Na 1. 7 a strong *h* in the day of trouble;
Mt 6.24 or else he will *h* to the one, and
12.11 he not lay *h* on it, and lift it out?
14. 3 For Herod had laid *h* on John, and
20.31 because they should *h* their peace:
21.26 for all *h* John as a prophet.
26.48 kiss, that same is he: *h* him fast.
55 temple, and ye laid no *h* on me.
57 they that had laid *h* on Jesus led
Mk 1.25 *H* thy peace, and come out of him.
3.21 they went out to lay *h* on him:
6.17 and laid *h* upon John, and bound
7. 4 which they have received to *h*, as
8 ye *h* the tradition of men, as the
10.48 that he should *h* his peace: but
12.12 and they sought to lay *h* on him,
14.51 and the young men laid *h* on him:
Lk 4.35 *H* thy peace, and come out of him.
16.13 or else he will *h* to the one, and
18.39 him, that he should *h* his peace:
19.40 if these should *h* their peace, the
20.20 that they might take *h* of his words,
26 they could not take *h* of his words
23.26 they laid *h* upon one Simon, a
Ac 4. 3 put them in *h* unto the next day:
12.17 with the hand to *h* their peace,
18. 9 but speak, and *h* not thy peace:
Ro 1.18 *h* the truth in unrighteousness;
1Co 14.30 sitteth by, let the first *h* his peace.
Php 2.29 gladness; and *h* such in reputation.
1Th 5.21 things; *h* fast that which is good.
2Th 2.15 stand fast, and *h* the traditions
1Ti 6.12 of faith, lay *h* on eternal life,
19 that they may lay *h* on eternal life.
2Ti 1.13 *H* fast the form of sound words,
Heb 3. 6 if we *h* fast the confidence and the
14 Christ, if we *h* the beginning of our
4.14 of God, let us *h* fast our profession.
6.18 lay *h* upon the hope set before us:
10.23 Let us *h* fast the profession of our
Rev 2.14 that *h* the doctrine of Balaam,
15 *h* the doctrine of the Nicolaitanes,
25 ye have already *h* fast till I come.
3. 3 and heard, and *h* fast, and repent.
11 *h* that fast which thou hast, that
18. 2 and the *h* of every foul spirit, and
20. 2 And he laid *h* on the dragon, that

HOLDEN
2Ki 23.22 there was not *h* such a passover
23 this passover was *h* to the Lord
Job 36. 8 and be *h* in cords of affliction;
Ps 18.35 and thy right hand hath *h* me up,
71. 6 By thee have I been *h* up from the
73.23 thou hast *h* me by my right hand.
Pr 5.22 be *h* with the cords of his sins.
Isa 42.14 I have long time *h* my peace; I
45. 1 Cyrus, whose right hand I have *h*,
Lk 24.16 But their eyes were *h* that they
Ac 2.24 possible that he should be *h* of it.
Ro 14. 4 Yea, he shall be *h* up: for God is

HOLDEST
Est 4.14 if thou altogether *h* thy peace at
Job 13.24 face, and *h* me for thine enemy?
Ps 77. 4 Thou *h* mine eyes waking: I am so
Jer 49.16 rock, that *h* the height of the hill:
Hab 1.13 *h* thy tongue when the wicked
Rev 2.13 and thou *h* fast my name, and

HOLDETH
Job 2. 3 and still he *h* fast his integrity,
26. 9 He *h* back the face of his throne,
Ps 66. 9 Which *h* our soul in life, and
Pr 11.12 man of understanding *h* his peace.
17.28 a fool, when he *h* his peace,
Dan 10.21 none that *h* with me in these
Am 1. 5 that *h* the sceptre from the house
8 that *h* the sceptre from Ashkelon,
Rev 2. 1 saith he that *h* the seven stars in

HOLDING
Isa 33.15 his hands from *h* of bribes,
Jer 6.11 I am weary with *h* in: I will pour
Mk 7. 3 not, *h* the tradition of the elders.
Php 2.16 *H* forth the word of life; that I
Col 2.19 And not *h* the Head, from which
1Ti 1.19 *H* faith, and a good conscience;
3. 9 *H* the mystery of the faith in a
Tit 1. 9 *H* fast the faithful word as he
Rev 7. 1 *h* the four winds of the earth,

HOLE
Ex 28.32 there shall be an *h* in the top of it,
2Ki 12. 9 a chest, bored a *h* in the lid of it,
Isa 11. 8 shall play on the *h* of the asp,
Eze 8. 7 I looked, behold a *h* in the wall.

HOLES
1Sa 14.11 Hebrews come forth out of the *h*
Isa 2.19 shall go into the *h* of the rocks,
7.19 valleys, and in the *h* of the rocks,
42.22 all of them snared in *h*, and they
Jer 16.16 hill, and out of the *h* of the rocks.
Mic 7.17 they shall move out of their *h*
Na 2.12 filled his *h* with prey, and his dens
Hag 1. 6 wages to put it into a bag with *h*.
Zec 14.12 shall consume away in their *h*,
Mt 8.20 The foxes have *h*, and the birds
Lk 9.58 Foxes have *h*, and the birds of the

HOLIER
Isa 65. 5 near to me; for I am *h* than thou.

HOLIEST
Heb 9. 3 which is called the *H* of all;
8 the way into the *h* of all was not
10.19 into the *h* by the blood of Jesus,

HOLINESS
Ex 15.11 who is like thee, glorious in *h*,
28.36 of a signet, *H* to the Lord.
39.30 of a signet, *H* to the Lord.
1Ch 16.29 worship the Lord in the beauty of *h*.
2Ch 20.21 that should praise the beauty of *h*,
31.18 they sanctified themselves in *h*:
Ps 29. 2 worship the Lord in the beauty of *h*.
30. 4 at the remembrance of his *h*.
47. 8 sitteth upon the throne of his *h*.
48. 1 our God, in the mountain of his *h*.
60. 6 God hath spoken in his *h*; I will
89.35 Once have I sworn by my *h* that I
93. 5 *h* becometh thine house, O Lord,
96. 9 worship the Lord in the beauty of *h*:
97.12 thanks at the remembrance of his *h*.
108. 7 God hath spoken in his *h*; I will
110. 3 in the beauties of *h* from the
Isa 23.18 and her hire shall be *h* to the Lord:
35. 8 and it shall be called The way of *h*;
62. 9 shall drink it in the courts of my *h*.
63.15 behold from the habitation of thy *h*
18 people of thy *h* have possessed it
Jer 2. 3 Israel was *h* unto the Lord, and the
23. 9 and because of the words of his *h*.
31.23 of justice, and mountain of *h*.
Am 4. 2 The Lord God hath sworn by his *h*
Ob 17 deliverance, and there shall be *h*;
Zec 14.20 of the horses, *H* unto the Lord;
21 shall be *h* unto the Lord of hosts:
Mal 2.11 Judah hath profaned the *h* of the
Lk 1.75 In *h* and righteousness before him,
Ac 3.12 though by our own power or *h* we
Ro 1. 4 power, according to the spirit of *h*,
6.19 servants to righteousness unto *h*.
22 have your fruit unto *h*, and the end
2Co 7. 1 perfecting *h* in the fear of God.
Eph 4.24 in righteousness and true *h*.
1Th 3.13 hearts unblameable in *h* before God,
4. 7 us unto uncleanness, but unto *h*.
1Ti 2.15 faith...charity and *h* with sobriety.
Tit 2. 3 be in behavior as becometh *h*,
Heb 12.10 that we might be partakers of his *h*.
14 Follow peace with all men, and *h*,

HOLPEN
Ps 83. 8 they have *h* the children of Lot.
86.17 because thou, Lord, has *h* me,
Isa 31. 3 he that is *h* shall fall down, and

Dan 11.34 they shall be *h* with a little help:
Lk 1.54 He hath *h* his servant Israel, in

HOLY

Ex 3. 5 whereon thou standest is *h* ground.
16.23 of the *h* sabbath unto the Lord:
19. 6 of priests, and an *h* nation.
20. 8 the sabbath day, to keep it *h*.
Lev 5.15 in the *h* things of the Lord; then
6.17 it is most *h*, as is the sin offering,
10.10 difference between *h* and unholy,
11.44 and ye shall be *h*; for I am *h*:
45 ye shall therefore be *h*, for I am *h*.
16.16 make an atonement for the *h* place,
19. 2 for I the Lord your God am *h*.
20. 3 and to profane my *h* name.
22.32 Neither shall ye profane my *h* name;
27.28 every devoted thing is most *h* unto
32 the tenth shall be *h* unto the Lord.
Nu 4.15 they shall not touch any *h* thing,
5.17 the priest shall take *h* water in an
18.10 In the most *h* place shalt thou eat
Dt 7. 6 thou art an *h* people unto the Lord
Jos 5.15 place whereon thou standest is *h*.
2Ki 19.22 even against the *H* One of Israel.
1Ch 16.10 Glory ye in his *h* name: let the
2Ch 35. 3 Put the *h* ark in the house which
Ezr 8.28 unto them, Ye are *h* unto the Lord;
Neh 8. 9 This day is *h* unto the Lord your
11 Hold your peace, for the day is *h*;
9.14 known unto them thy *h* sabbath,
Ps 3. 4 and he heard me out of his *h* hill.
5. 7 will I worship toward thy *h* temple.
11. 4 The Lord is in his *h* temple, the
15. 1 who shall dwell in thy *h* hill?
16.10 thou suffer thine *H* One to see
20. 6 will hear him from his *h* heaven
22. 3 thou art *h*, O thou that inhabitest
24. 3 or who shall stand in his *h* place?
28. 2 up my hands toward thy *h* oracle.
33.21 we have trusted in his *h* name.
43. 3 let them bring me unto thy *h* hill,
51.11 take not thy *h* spirit from me.
68. 5 widows, is God in his *h* habitation.
86. 2 Preserve my soul; for I am *h*: O
98. 1 his right hand, and his *h* arm,
99. 9 our God, and worship at his *h* hill;
9 hill; for the Lord our God is *h*.
103. 1 is within me, bless his *h* name.
106.47 to give thanks unto thy *h* name,
138. 2 will worship toward thy *h* temple,
145.21 bless his *h* name for ever and ever.
Pr 20.25 who devoureth that which is *h*,
Isa 5.16 God that is *h* shall be sanctified
6. 3 said, *H*, *h*, *h*, is the Lord of hosts:
11. 9 nor destroy in all my *h* mountain:
27.13 worship the Lord in the *h* mount
30.15 the Lord God, the *H* One of Israel;
40.25 shall I be equal? saith the *H* One.
41.14 thy redeemer, the *H* One of Israel.
20 the *H* One of Israel hath created it.
48.17 Redeemer, the *H* One of Israel;
52.10 The Lord hath made bare his *h* arm
56. 7 will I bring to my *H* mountain,
57.15 eternity, whose name is *H*; I dwell
15 I dwell in the high and *h* place,
63.10 rebelled, and vexed his *h* Spirit:
11 he that put his *h* Spirit within him?
65.25 nor destroy in all my *h* mountain,
Eze 20.39 but pollute ye my *h* name no more
40 oblations, with all your *h* things.
39. 7 So will I make my *h* name known
25 will be jealous for my *h* name;
48.14 the land: for it is *h* unto the Lord.
Dan 4. 8 in whom is the spirit of the *h* gods:
18 the spirit of the *h* gods is in thee.
Joel 3.17 dwelling in Zion, my *h* mountain:
Hab 1.12 O Lord my God, mine *H* One?
Zep 3.11 because of my *h* mountain.
Mt 1.18 found with child of the *H* Ghost.
20 in her is of the *H* Ghost.
3.11 baptize you with the *H* Ghost,
4. 5 devil taketh him up into the *h* city,
7. 6 not that which is *h* unto the dogs,
12.31 the blasphemy against the *H* Ghost
32 speaketh against the *H* Ghost,
24.15 of desolation,...stand in the *h* place,
25.31 glory, and all the *h* angels with him,
27.53 went into the *h* city, and appeared
28.19 of the Son, and of the *H* Ghost:
Mk 1. 8 baptize you with the *H* Ghost.
24 who thou art, the *H* One of God.
3.29 blaspheme against the *H* Ghost
6.20 that he was a just man and an *h*,
8.38 of his Father with the *h* angels.
12.36 himself said by the *H* Ghost,
13.11 not ye that speak, but the *H* Ghost.
Lk 1.15 shall be filled with the *H* Ghost,
35 The *H* Ghost shall come upon
35 that *h* thing which shall be born
41 was filled with the *H* Ghost:
49 great things; and *h* is his name.
67 was filled with the *H* Ghost,
70 the mouth of his *h* prophets, which
72 and to remember his *h* covenant;
2.23 womb shall be called *h* to the Lord;
25 and the *H* Ghost was upon him.
26 unto him by the *H* Ghost, that
3.16 baptize you with the *H* Ghost
22 the *H* Ghost descended in a bodily
4. 1 Jesus being full of the *H* Ghost
34 who thou art; the *H* One of God.
9.26 in his Father's, and of the *h* angels.
11.13 give the *H* Spirit to them that ask
12.10 against the *H* Ghost it shall
12 For the *H* Ghost shall teach you
Jn 1.33 which baptizeth with the *H* Ghost.
7.39 for the *H* Ghost was not yet given;
14.26 Comforter, which is the *H* Ghost,
17.11 *H* Father, keep through thine own
20.22 them, Receive ye the *H* Ghost:
Ac 1. 2 he through the *H* Ghost had given
5 be baptized with the *H* Ghost not
8 that the *H* Ghost is come upon
16 the *H* Ghost by the mouth of David
2. 4 were all filled with the *H* Ghost,
27 thine *H* One to see corruption.
33 the promise of the *H* Ghost, he
38 receive the gift of the *H* Ghost.
3.14 ye denied the *H* One and the Just,
21 by the mouth of all his *h* prophets
4. 8 Peter, filled with the *H* Ghost, said
27 of a truth against thy *h* child Jesus,
30 by the name of thy *h* child Jesus.
31 were all filled with the *H* Ghost,
5. 3 heart to lie to the *H* Ghost, and
32 so is also the *H* Ghost, whom
6. 3 full of the *H* Ghost and wisdom,
5 full of faith and of the *H* Ghost,
13 words against this *h* place, and the
7.33 where thou standest is *h* ground.
51 do always resist the *H* Ghost:
55 he, being full of the *H* Ghost,
8.15 they might receive the *H* Ghost:
17 and they received the *H* Ghost.
18 hands the *H* Ghost was given, he
19 he may receive the *H* Ghost.
9.17 and be filled with the *H* Ghost.
31 in the comfort of the *H* Ghost,
10.22 was warned from God by an *h* angel
38 with the *H* Ghost and with power:
44 the *H* Ghost fell on all them
45 out the gift of the *H* Ghost
47 have received the *H* Ghost as well
11.15 the *H* Ghost fell on them, as on
16 shall be baptized with the *H* Ghost.
24 full of the *H* Ghost and of faith:
13. 2 the *H* Ghost said, Separate me
4 being sent forth by the *H* Ghost,
9 filled with the *H* Ghost, set his
35 thine *H* One to see corruption.
52 with joy, and with the *H* Ghost.
15. 8 giving them the *H* Ghost, even
28 it seemed good to the *H* Ghost,
16. 6 were forbidden of the *H* Ghost
19. 2 Have ye received the *H* Ghost
2 whether there be any *H* Ghost.
6 the *H* Ghost came on them;
20.23 Save that the *H* Ghost witnesseth
28 *H* Ghost hath made you overseers,
21.11 said, Thus saith the *H* Ghost, So
28 and hath polluted this *h* place.
28.25 Well spake the *H* Ghost by Esaias
Ro 1. 2 by his prophets in the *h* scriptures,
5. 5 in our hearts by the *H* Ghost
7.12 law is *h*, and the commandment *h*,
9. 1 me witness in the *H* Ghost,
11.16 For if the firstfruit be *h*, the lump is
16 the lump is also *h*: and if the lump
16 if the root be *h*, so are the branches.
12. 1 a living sacrifice, *h*, acceptable unto
14.17 peace, and joy in the *H* Ghost.
15.13 through the power of the *H* Ghost.
16 being sanctified by the *H* Ghost.
16.16 Salute one another with an *h* kiss.
1Co 2.13 which the *H* Ghost teacheth;
3.17 for the temple of God is *h*, which
6.19 is the temple of the *H* Ghost
7.14 children unclean; but now are they *h*.
34 may be *h* both in body and in spirit:
9.13 which minister about *h* things
12. 3 is the Lord, but by the *H* Ghost.
16.20 Greet ye one another with an *h* kiss.
2Co 6. 6 by kindness, by the *H* Ghost, by
13.12 Greet one another with an *h* kiss.
14 communion of the *H* Ghost, be
Eph 1. 4 we should be *h* and without blame
13 sealed with that *h* Spirit of promise,
2.21 groweth unto an *h* temple in the
3. 5 unto his *h* apostles and prophets
4.30 And grieve not the *h* Spirit of God,
5.27 it should be *h* and without blemish.
Col 1.22 to present you *h* and unblameable
3.12 as the elect of God, *h* and beloved,
1Th 1. 5 in power, and in the *H* Ghost,
6 affliction with joy of the *H* Ghost:
4. 8 hath also given unto us his *h* Spirit.
5.26 Greet all the brethren with an *h* kiss.
27 be read unto all the *h* brethren.
1Ti 2. 8 lifting up *h* hands, without wrath
2Ti 1. 9 us, and called us with an *h* calling,
14 by the *H* Ghost which dwelleth
3.15 thou hast known the *h* scriptures,
Tit 1. 8 sober, just, *h*, temperate; Holding
3. 5 and renewing of the *H* Ghost;
Heb 2. 4 miracles and gifts of the *H* Ghost,
3. 1 Wherefore, *h* brethren, partakers of
7 as the *H* Ghost saith, To day if
6. 4 made partakers of the *H* Ghost,
7.26 who is *h*, harmless, undefiled,
9. 8 The *H* Ghost this signifying,
12 he entered in once into the *h* place,
24 into the *h* places made with hands,
25 entereth into the *h* place every year
10.15 the *H* Ghost also is a witness to
1Pe 1.12 you with the *H* Ghost sent down
15 hath called you is *h*, so be ye *h* in all
16 it is written, Be ye *h*; for I am *h*.
2. 5 spiritual house, an *h* priesthood, to
9 a royal priesthood, an *h* nation, a
3. 5 in the old time the *h* women also,
2Pe 1.18 we were with him in the *h* mount.
21 *h* men of God spake as they were
21 were moved by the *H* Ghost.
2.21 from the *h* commandment delivered
3. 2 spoken before by the *h* prophets,
11 in all *h* conversation and godliness,
1Jn 2.20 ye have an unction from the *H* One,
5. 7 the Word, and the *H* Ghost:
Jude 20 yourselves in your most *h* faith,
20 faith, praying in the *H* Ghost,
Rev 3. 7 saith he that is *h*, he that is true,
4. 8 night, saying, *H*, *h*, *h*, Lord God

Biblical Themes

HOME

I have given you a land for which ye did not labor, and cities which ye built not, and ye dwell in them; of the vineyards and oliveyards which ye planted not do ye eat. Jos 24.13

Ruth said, . . . whither thou goest, I will go; and where thou lodgest, I will lodge. Ru 1.16

I pray thee . . . that I may die in mine own city, and be buried by the grave of my father and of my mother. 2Sa 19.37

And David longed, and said, Oh that one would give me drink of the water of the well of Bethlehem, which is by the gate! 2Sa 23.15

He that goeth down to the grave shall come up no more. He shall return no more to his house, neither shall his place know him any more. Job 7.9-10

I will both lay me down in peace, and sleep: for thou, Lord, only makest me dwell in safety. Ps 4.8

Yea, the sparrow hath found an house, and the swallow a nest for herself, where she may lay her young, even thine altars, O Lord of hosts. Ps 84.3

Lord, thou hast been our dwelling place in all generations. Ps 90.1

Peace be within thy walls, and prosperity within thy palaces. Ps 122.7

Except the Lord build the house, they labor in vain that build it: except the Lord keep the city, the watchman waketh but in vain. Ps 127.1

He that troubleth his own house shall inherit the wind. Pr 11.29

The wicked are overthrown . . . but the house of the righteous shall stand. Pr 12.7

Withdraw thy foot from thy neighbor's house; lest he be weary of thee. Pr 25.17

As a bird that wandereth from her nest, so is a man that wandereth from his place. Pr 27.8

They shall sit every man under his vine and under his fig tree; and none shall make them afraid. Mic 4.4

Jesus saith . . . The foxes have holes, and the birds of the air have nests; but the Son of man hath not where to lay his head. Mt 8.20

If a house be divided against itself, that house cannot stand. Mk 3.25

He came to Nazareth, where he had been brought up. . . . And they said, Is not this Joseph's son? . . . And he said, Verily I say unto you, No prophet is accepted in his own country. Lk 4.16, 22, 24

Another also said, Lord, I will follow thee; but let me first go bid them farewell, which are at home at my house. And Jesus said unto him, No man, having put his hand to the plow, and looking back, is fit for the kingdom of God. Lk 9.61-62

In my Father's house are many mansions. . . . I go to prepare a place for you. Jn 14.2

If a man love me, he will keep my words: and my Father will love him, and we will come unto him, and make our abode with him. Jn 14.23

When Jesus therefore saw his mother, and the disciple standing by, whom he loved, he saith unto his mother, Woman, behold thy son! Then saith he to the disciple, Behold thy mother! And from that hour that disciple took her unto his own home. Jn 19.26-27

Other foundation can no man lay than that is laid, which is Jesus Christ. 1Co 3.11

For here have we no continuing city, but we seek one to come. Heb 13.14

Rev 6.10 How long, O Lord, *h* and true, dost
11. 2 the *h* city shall they tread under foot
14.10 the presence of the *h* angels, and in
15. 4 for thou only art *h*: for all nations
18.20 and ye *h* apostles and prophets;
20. 6 Blessed and *h* is he that hath part
21. 2 John saw the *h* city, new Jerusalem,
10 me that great city, the *h* Jerusalem.
22. 6 God of the *h* prophets sent his angel
11 and that is *h*, let him be...still.
11 and he that is...let him be *h* still.
19 book of life, and out of the *h* city,

HOME

Gen 39.16 by her, until his lord came *h*.
43.16 Bring these men *h*, and slay, and
26 And when Joseph came *h*, they
Ex 9.19 the field, and shall not be brought *h*,
Lev 18. 9 she be born at *h*, or born abroad,
Dt 21.12 shalt bring her *h* to thine house;
24. 5 but he shall be free at *h* one year,
Jos 2.18 father's household, *h* unto thee.
Jdg 11. 9 If ye bring me *h* again to fight
19. 9 your way, that thou mayest go *h*.
Ru 1.21 hath brought me *h* again empty:
1Sa 2.20 And they went unto their own *h*.
6. 7 bring their calves *h* from them:
10 cart, and shut up their calves at *h*:
10.26 And Saul also went *h* to Gibeah;
18. 2 go no more *h* to his father's house.
24.22 And Saul went *h*; but David and
2Sa 13. 7 David sent *h* to Tamar, saying,
14.13 not fetch *h* again his banished.
17.23 and gat him *h* to his house, to his
1Ki 5.14 in Lebanon, and two months at *h*:
13. 7 Come *h* with me, and refresh thyself,
15 Come *h* with me, and eat bread.
2Ki 14.10 glory of this, and tarry at *h*: for
1Ch 13.12 shall I bring the ark of God *h* to me?
13 So David brought not the ark *h* to
2Ch 25.10 out of Ephraim, to go *h* again:
10 and they returned *h* in great anger.
19 abide now at *h*; why shouldest
Est 5.10 and when he came *h*, he sent and
Job 39.12 him, that he will bring *h* thy seed,
Ps 68.12 that tarried at *h* divided the spoil.
Pr 7.19 For the goodman is not at *h*, he is
20 will come *h* at the day appointed.
Ec 12. 5 man goeth to his long *h*, and the
Jer 39.14 that he should carry him *h*: so he
La 1.20 bereaveth, at *h* there is as death.
Hab 2. 5 proud man, neither keepeth at *h*,
Hag 1. 9 when ye brought it *h*, I did blow
Mt 8. 6 my servant lieth at *h* sick of the
Mk 5.19 Go *h* to thy friends, and tell them
Lk 9.61 bid them farewell, which are at *h* at
15. 6 And when he cometh *h*, he calleth
Jn 19.27 that disciple took her unto his own *h*.
20.10 went away again unto their own *h*.
Ac 21. 6 ship; and they returned *h* again.
1Co 11.34 any man hunger, let him eat at *h*;
14.35 let them ask their husbands at *h*:
2Co 5. 6 whilst we are at *h* in the body, we
1Ti 5. 4 learn first to shew piety at *h*, and
Tit 2. 5 be discreet, chaste, keepers at *h*,

HONEST

Lk 8.15 they, which in an *h* and good heart,
Ac 6. 3 you seven men of *h* report, full of the
Ro 12.17 things *h* in the sight of all men.
2Co 8.21 Providing for *h* things, not only in
13. 7 but ye should do that which is *h*,
Php 4. 8 are true, whatsoever things are *h*,
1Pe 2.12 your conversation *h* among the

HONESTLY

Ro 13.13 Let us walk *h*, as in the day; not
1Th 4.12 That ye may walk *h* toward them
Heb 13.18 in all things willing to live *h*.

HONESTY

1Ti 2. 2 quiet...life in all godliness and *h*.

HONEY

Ex 3. 8 a land flowing with milk and *h*;
Jdg 14. 8 was a swarm of bees and *h* in the
18 What is sweeter than *h*? and what
Ps 19.10 gold: sweeter also than *h* and the
Pr 24.13 son, eat thou *h*, because it is good;
25.16 Hast thou found *h*? eat so much as
27 It is not good to eat much *h*: so for
SS 4.11 *h* and milk are under thy tongue;
Mt 3. 4 his meat was locusts and wild *h*.
Mk 1. 6 and he did eat locusts and wild *h*;
Rev 10. 9 it shall be in thy mouth sweet as *h*.

HONEYCOMB

1Sa 14.27 and dipped it in an *h*, and put
Ps 19.10 also than honey and the *h*.
Pr 5. 3 a strange woman drop as an *h*,
16.24 Pleasant words are as an *h*,
24.13 the *h*, which is sweet to thy taste:
27. 7 The full soul loatheth an *h*; but to
SS 4.11 lips, O my spouse, drop as the *h*:
5. 1 have eaten my *h* with my honey;
Lk 24.42 a broiled fish, and of an *h*.

HONOR

Ex 20.12 *H* thy father and thy mother: that
Dt 5.16 *H* thy father and thy mother, as
Jdg 9. 9 by me they *h* God and man, and
1Ch 16.27 Glory and *h* are in his presence;
29.12 Both riches and *h* come of thee,
2Ch 1.11 hast not asked riches, wealth, or *h*,
12 give thee riches, and wealth, and *h*,
Est 6. 6 whom the king delighteth to *h*?
Ps 7. 5 earth, and lay mine *h* in the dust.
8. 5 crowned him with glory and *h*.
21. 5 *h* and majesty hast thou laid upon
26. 8 the place where thine *h* dwelleth.
66. 2 Sing forth the *h* of his name:
91.15 I will deliver him, and *h* him.
96. 6 *H* and majesty are before him:
104. 1 art clothed with *h* and majesty.
Pr 3.16 and in her left hand riches and *h*.
8.18 Riches and *h* are with me; yea,
11.16 A gracious woman retaineth *h*:
14.28 multitude of people is the king's *h*:
20. 3 It is an *h* for a man to cease from
22. 4 the Lord are riches, and *h*, and life.
26. 1 harvest, so *h* is not seemly for a fool.
8 so is he that giveth *h* to a fool.
31.25 Strength and *h* are her clothing;
Isa 29.13 with their lips do *h* me, but have
Dan 4.37 extol and *h* the King of heaven, all
Mt 13.57 A prophet is not without *h*, save in
15. 4 *H* thy father and mother: and he
6 *h* not his father or his mother, he
19.19 *H* thy father and thy mother: and,
Mk 6. 4 A prophet is not without *h*, but in
7.10 *H* thy father and thy mother;
10.19 not; *H* thy father and mother.
Lk 18.20 *h* thy father and thy mother.
Jn 4.44 hath no *h* in his own country.
5.23 that all men should *h* the Son,
23 the Son, even as they *h* the Father.
41 I receive not *h* from men.
44 which receive *h* one of another,
44 the *h* that cometh from God only?
8.49 but I *h* my Father, and ye do
54 Jesus answered, If I *h* myself,
54 If I...myself, my *h* is nothing:
12.26 serve me, him will my Father *h*.
Ro 2. 7 for glory and *h* and immortality,
10 But glory, *h*, and peace, to every
9.21 to make one vessel unto *h*, and
12.10 love; in *h* preferring one another;
13. 7 fear to whom fear; *h* to whom *h*.
1Co 12.23 these we bestow more abundant *h*;
24 given more abundant *h* to that
2Co 6. 8 *h* and dishonor, by evil report
Eph 6. 2 *H* thy father and mother; which
Col 2.23 not in any *h* to the satisfying of
1Th 4. 4 his vessel in sanctification and *h*;
1Ti 1.17 be *h* and glory for ever and ever.
5. 3 *H* widows that are widows indeed.
17 be counted worthy of double *h*,
6. 1 their own masters worthy of all *h*,
16 whom be *h* and power everlasting:
2Ti 2.20 some to *h*, and some to dishonor.
21 be a vessel unto *h*, sanctified, and
Heb 2. 7 crownedst him with glory and *h*,
9 death, crowned with glory and *h*;
3. 3 builded the house hath more *h*
5. 4 no man taketh this *h* unto himself,
1Pe 1. 7 might be found unto praise and *h*
2.17 *H* all men. Love the brotherhood.
17 Fear God. *H* the king.
3. 7 giving *h* unto the wife, as unto
2Pe 1.17 from God the Father *h* and glory,
Rev 4. 9 beasts give glory and *h* and thanks
11 to receive glory and *h* and power:
5.12 and *h*, and glory, and blessing.
13 Blessing, and *h*, and glory, and
7.12 *h*, and power, and might, be unto
19. 1 Salvation, and glory, and *h*, and
7 and rejoice, and give *h* to him:
21.24 do bring their glory and *h* into it.
26 bring the glory and *h* of the nations

HONORABLE

Gen 34.19 was more *h* than all the house of
Nu 22.15 more, and more *h* than they.
1Sa 9. 6 man of God, and he is an *h* man;
22.14 bidding, and is *h* in thine house?
2Sa 23.19 Was he not most *h* of three?
23 He was more *h* than the thirty,
2Ki 5. 1 man with his master, and *h*,
1Ch 4. 9 was more *h* than his brethren:
11.21 three, he was more *h* than the two;
25 he was *h* among the thirty, but
Job 22. 8 and the *h* man dwelt in it.
Ps 45. 9 were among thy *h* women: upon
111. 3 His work is *h* and glorious: and
Isa 3. 3 of fifty, and the *h* man, and
5 ancient, and...base against the *h*.
5.13 and their *h* men are famished, and
9.15 ancient and *h*, he is the head;
23. 8 traffickers are the *h* of the earth?
9 contempt all the *h* of the earth.
42.21 magnify the law, and make it *h*.
43. 4 thou hast been *h*, and I have loved
58.13 delight, the holy of the Lord, *h*; and
Na 3.10 and they cast lots for her *h* men,
Mk 15.43 of Arimathaea, an *h* counsellor,
Lk 14. 8 more *h* man than thou be bidden
Ac 13.50 up the devout and *h* women,
17.12 of *h* women which were Greeks,
1Co 4.10 ye are *h*, but we are despised.
12.23 body, which we think to be less *h*,
Heb 13. 4 Marriage is *h* in all, and the bed

HONORED

Ex 14. 4 and I will be *h* upon Pharaoh,
Pr 13.18 that regardeth reproof shall be *h*.
27.18 waiteth on his master shall be *h*.
Isa 43.23 hast thou *h* me with thy sacrifices.
La 1. 8 all that *h* her despise her, because
5.12 the faces of elders were not *h*.
Dan 4.34 and *h* him that liveth for ever,
Ac 28.10 also *h* us with many honors;
1Co 12.26 one member be *h*, all the members

HONOREST

1Sa 2.29 and *h* thy sons above me, to make

HONORETH

Ps 15. 4 but he *h* them that fear the Lord.
Pr 12. 9 better than he that *h* himself, and
14.31 that *h* him hath mercy on the poor.
Mal 1. 6 A son *h* his father, and a servant
Mt 15. 8 mouth, and *h* me with their lips;
Mk 7. 6 This people *h* me with their lips,
Jn 5.23 that *h* not the Son *h* not the Father
8.54 it is my Father that *h* me; of

HONORS

Ac 28.10 also honored us with many *h*;

HOOK

2Ki 19.28 I will put my *h* in thy nose,
Job 41. 1 draw out leviathan with an *h*?
2 thou put an *h* into his nose?
Isa 37.29 will I put my *h* in thy nose,
Mt 17.27 go thou to the sea, and cast an *h*,

HOPE

Ru 1.12 If I should say, I have *h*, if I
Job 6.11 is my strength, that I should *h*?
7. 6 shuttle, and are spent without *h*.
8.14 Whose *h* shall be cut off; and
11.18 be secure, because there is *h*:
17.15 And where is now my *h*? as for
15 as for my *h*, who shall see it?
31.24 If I have made gold my *h*, or have
Ps 16. 9 my flesh also shall rest in *h*.
31.24 heart, all ye that *h* in the Lord.
33.22 upon us, according as we *h* in thee.
38.15 in thee, O Lord, do I *h*: thou wilt
39. 7 what wait I for? my *h* is in thee.
42. 5 disquieted in me? *h* thou in God:
11 within me? *h* thou in God:
43. 5 disquieted within me? *h* in God:
119.81 salvation: but I *h* in thy word.
130. 5 doth wait, and in his word do I *h*.
7 Let Israel *h* in the Lord: for with
146. 5 whose *h* is in the Lord his God:
Pr 11. 7 and the *h* of unjust men perisheth.
13.12 *H* deferred maketh the heart sick:
19.18 Chasten thy son while there is *h*,
26.12 is more *h* of a fool than of him.
29.20 is more *h* of a fool than of him.
Isa 57.10 saidst thou not, There is no *h*:
Jer 2.25 but thou saidst, There is no *h*:
17.17 thou art my *h* in the day of evil.
La 3.24 soul; therefore will I *h* in him.
26 good that a man should both *h*
Eze 19. 5 had waited, and her *h* was lost,
37.11 bones are dried, and our *h* is lost:
Hos 2.15 the valley of Achor for a door of *h*:
Joel 3.16 Lord will be the *h* of his people,
Zec 9.12 the strong hold, ye prisoners of *h*:
Lk 6.34 to them of whom ye *h* to receive,
Ac 2.26 also my flesh shall rest in *h*:
16.19 that the *h* of their gains was gone,
23. 6 the *h* and resurrection of the dead
24.15 And have *h* toward God, which
26. 6 am judged for the *h* of the promise
7 God day and night, *h* to come.
27.20 all *h* that we should be saved was
28.20 that for the *h* of Israel I am bound
Ro 4.18 Who against *h* believed in *h*, that
5. 2 and rejoice in *h* of the glory of God.
4 experience; and experience, *h*:
5 And *h* maketh not ashamed:
8.20 who hath subjected the same in *h*,
24 for we are saved by *h*:
24 but *h* that is seen is not *h*:
24 man seeth, why doth he yet *h* for?
25 But if we *h* for that we see not,
12.12 Rejoicing in *h*; patient in
15. 4 of the scriptures might have *h*.
13 the God of *h* fill you with all joy and
13 that ye may abound in *h*, through
1Co 9.10 he that ploweth should plow in *h*;
10 and that he that thresheth in *h*
10 should be partaker of his *h*.
13.13 And now abideth faith, *h*, charity,
15.19 If in this life only we have *h* in
2Co 1. 7 And our *h* of you is stedfast,
3.12 Seeing then that we have such *h*,
10.15 but having *h*, when your faith is
Gal 5. 5 wait for the *h* of righteousness by
Eph 1.18 know what is the *h* of his calling,
2.12 having no *h*, and without God in
4. 4 are called in one *h* of your calling;
Php 1.20 my earnest expectation and my *h*,
2.23 Him therefore I *h* to send
Col 1. 5 the *h* which is laid up for you in
23 away from the *h* of the gospel,
27 Christ in you, the *h* of glory:
1Th 1. 3 patience of *h* in our Lord Jesus
2.19 For what is our *h*, or joy, or crown
4.13 even as others which have no *h*.
5. 8 for an helmet, the *h* of salvation.
2Th 2.16 and good *h* through grace,
1Ti 1. 1 Lord Jesus Christ, which is our *h*;
Tit 1. 2 In *h* of eternal life, which God,
2.13 Looking for that blessed *h*, and
3. 7 according to the *h* of eternal life.
Heb 3. 6 confidence and rejoicing of the *h*
6.11 full assurance of *h* unto the end:
18 lay hold upon the *h* set before us:
19 which *h* we have as an anchor of
7.19 the bringing in of a better *h* did;
1Pe 1. 3 begotten us again unto a lively *h*
13 and *h* to the end for the grace that
21 your faith and *h* might be in God.

BIBLICAL THEMES

HOPE

And the Lord said unto Abram, . . . Lift up now thine eyes, and look from the place where thou art . . . for all the land which thou seest, to thee will I give it. Gen 13.14-15

Thou shalt forget thy misery, and remember it as waters that pass away. . . . And thou shalt be secure, because there is hope. Job 11.16, 18

There is hope of a tree, if it be cut down, that it will sprout again. Job 14.7

I waited patiently for the Lord; and he inclined unto me, and heard my cry. He brought me up also out of an horrible pit, out of the miry clay, and set my feet upon a rock. Ps 40.1-2

Why art thou cast down, O my soul? and why art thou disquieted within me? hope thou in God: for I shall yet praise him, who is the health of my countenance, and my God. Ps 42.11

He is my refuge and my fortress: my God; in him will I trust. Surely he shall deliver thee from the snare of the fowler, and from the noisome pestilence. . . . his truth shall be thy shield. Ps 91.2-4

My soul fainteth for thy salvation: but I hope in thy word. . . . Uphold me according unto thy word, that I may live: and let me not be ashamed of my hope. Ps 119. 81, 116

My soul waiteth for the Lord more than they that watch for the morning: I say, more than they that watch for the morning. Let Israel hope in the Lord: for with the Lord there is mercy, and with him is plenteous redemption. Ps 130.6-7

Hope deferred maketh the heart sick: but when the desire cometh, it is a tree of life. Pr 13.12

It is of the Lord's mercies that we are not consumed, because his compassions fail not. They are new every morning. . . . therefore will I hope in him. The Lord is good unto them that wait for him. Lam 3.22-25

Turn you to the strong hold, ye prisoners of hope. Zec 9.12

My little daughter lieth at the point of death: I pray thee, come and lay thy hands on her, that she may be healed; and she shall live. Mk 5.23

And when these things begin to come to pass, then look up, and lift up your heads; for your redemption draweth nigh. Lk 21.28

These things I have spoken unto you, that in me ye might have peace. In the world ye shall have tribulation: but be of good cheer; I have overcome the world. Jn 16.33

[Abraham,] who against hope believed in hope, that he might become the father of many nations, . . . staggered not at the promise of God through unbelief; but was strong in faith, giving glory to God. Ro 4.18, 20

We are saved by hope: but hope that is seen is not hope: for what a man seeth, why doth he yet hope for? but if we hope for that we see not, then do we with patience wait for it. Ro 8.24-25

Now abideth faith, hope, charity, these three. 1Co 13.13

Which hope we have as an anchor of the soul, both sure and stedfast. Heb 6.19

Fear none of those things which thou shalt suffer . . . be thou faithful unto death, and I will give thee a crown of life. Rev 2.10

1Pe 3.15 a reason of the *h* that is in you
1Jn 3. 3 every man that hath this *h* in him

HOPED

Est 9. 1 the enemies of the Jews *h* to have
Job 6.20 confounded because they had *h*;
Ps 119.43 for I have *h* in thy judgments.
74 because I have *h* in thy word.
147 and cried: I *h* in thy word.
166 Lord, I have *h* for thy salvation,
Jer 3.23 Truly in vain is salvation *h* for from
Lk 23. 8 he *h* to have seen some miracle
Ac 24.26 He *h* also that the money should
2Co 8. 5 And this they did, not as we *h*, but
Heb 11. 1 is the substance of things *h* for,

HOPE'S

Ac 26. 7 For which *h* sake, king Agrippa, I

HOPETH

1Co 13. 7 believeth all things, *h* all things,

HOPING

Lk 6.35 and lend, *h* for nothing again;
1Ti 3.14 thee, *h* to come unto thee shortly:

HORN

Jos 6. 5 a long blast with the ram's *h*,
1Sa 2. 1 mine *h* is exalted in the Lord: my
2Sa 22. 3 shield, and the *h* of my salvation,
Ps 89.17 thy favor our *h* shall be exalted.
132.17 will I make the *h* of David to bud:
148.14 also exalteth the *h* of his people,
Dan 7. 8 up among them another little *h*,
11 great words which the *h* spake:
Lk 1.69 hath raised up an *h* of salvation

HORNS

Gen 22.13 ram caught in a thicket by his *h*:
Ex 29.12 and put it upon the *h* of the altar
30.10 an atonement upon the *h* of it once
1Ki 1.50 caught hold on the *h* of the altar.
Ps 75.10 *h* of the righteous shall be exalted.
Dan 7. 7 were before it; and it had ten *h*.
Hab 3. 4 he had *h* coming out of his hand:
Rev 5. 6 having seven *h* and seven eyes,
9.13 from the four *h* of the golden altar
12. 3 having seven heads and ten *h*,
13. 1 sea, having seven heads and ten *h*,
1 and upon his *h* ten crowns, and
11 he had two *h* like a lamb, and he
17. 3 having seven heads and ten *h*.
7 hath the seven heads and ten *h*.
12 the ten *h* which thou sawest are
16 the ten *h* which thou sawest upon

HORRIBLE

Ps 11. 6 brimstone, and an *h* tempest:
40. 2 brought me up also out of an *h* pit,
Jer 5.30 A wonderful and *h* thing is
18.13 Israel hath done a very *h* thing.
23.14 prophets of Jerusalem an *h* thing:
Hos 6.10 I have seen an *h* thing in the house

HORRIBLY

Jer 2.12 heavens, at this, and be *h* afraid,
Eze 32.10 their kings shall be *h* afraid for

HORROR

Gen 15.12 an *h* of great darkness fell upon
Ps 55. 5 and *h* hath overwhelmed me.
119.53 *H* hath taken hold upon me
Eze 7.18 *h* shall cover them; and shame

HORSE

Ex 15. 1 the *h* and his rider hath he thrown
1Ki 20.25 *h* for *h*, and chariot for chariot:
2Ch 23.15 come to the entering of the *h* gate
Job 39.19 Hast thou given the *h* strength?
Ps 32. 9 Be ye not as the *h*, or as the mule,
33.17 An *h* is a vain thing for safety:
147.10 not in the strength of the *h*:
Rev 6. 2 I saw, and behold a white *h*: and
4 went out another *h* that was red:
5 I beheld, and lo a black *h*; and he
8 And I looked, and behold a pale *h*:
14.20 winepress, even unto the *h* bridles,
19.11 opened, and behold a white *h*;
19 war against him that sat on the *h*,
21 sword of him that sat upon the *h*,

HORSEMEN

Ex 14. 9 chariots of Pharaoh, and his *h*,
2Ki 2.12 chariot of Israel, and the *h* thereof.
Hab 1. 8 and their *h* shall come from far;
Ac 23.23 and *h* threescore and ten, and
32 they left the *h* to go with him,
Rev 9.16 the number of the army of the *h*

HORSES

Ps 20. 7 trust in chariots, and some in *h*:
Isa 30.16 said, No; for we will flee upon *h*;
31. 1 stay on *h*, and trust in chariots,
Jer 4.13 his *h* are swifter than eagles.
12. 5 how canst thou contend with *h*?
Hab 1. 8 Their *h* are also swifter than the
3.15 walk through the sea with thine *h*,
Zec 6. 2 In the first chariot were red *h*;
6 The black *h* which are therein go
10. 5 riders on *h* shall be confounded.
Rev 9. 7 of the locusts were like unto *h*
9 the chariots of many *h* running to
17 And thus I saw the *h* in the vision,
17 heads of the *h* were as the heads
18.13 and *h*, and chariots, and slaves,
19.14 heaven followed him upon white *h*,
18 of mighty men, and the flesh of *h*,

HORSES'

Isa 5.28 their *h* hoofs shall be counted
Jas 3. 3 we put bits in the *h* mouths, that

HOSANNA

Mt 21. 9 *H* to the son of David: Blessed
9 name of the Lord; *H* in the highest.
15 and saying, *H* to the son of David;
Mk 11. 9 *H*; Blessed is he that cometh in
10 name of the Lord; *H* in the highest.
Jn 12.13 *H*: Blessed is the King of Israel

HOSEA

Hos 1. 1 of the Lord that came unto *H*,
2 of the word of the Lord by *H*.
2 Lord said to *H*, Go, take unto thee

HOSPITALITY

Ro 12.13 necessity of saints; given to *h*.
1Ti 3. 2 given to *h*, apt to teach;
Tit 1. 8 But a lover of *h*, a lover of good
1Pe 4. 9 Use *h* one to another without
(See box on page 380)

HOST

Gen 32. 2 them, he said, This is God's *h*:
Ex 14. 4 upon Pharaoh, and upon all his *h*;
24 troubled the *h* of the Egyptians,
Dt 4.19 stars, even all the *h* of heaven,
2Ki 5. 1 Naaman, captain of the *h* of the
21. 3 worshipped all the *h* of heaven,
1Ch 9.19 being over the *h* of the Lord,
11.18 brake through the *h* of the
2Ch 18.18 all the *h* of heaven standing on
33. 3 worshipped all the *h* of heaven,
Neh 9. 6 heaven of heavens, with all their *h*,
6 the *h* of heaven worshippeth thee.
Ps 27. 3 Though an *h* should encamp
33.16 saved by the multitude of an *h*:
Jer 8. 2 the moon, and all the *h* of heaven,
Lk 2.13 a multitude of the heavenly *h*
10.35 pence, and gave them to the *h*,
Ac 7.42 up to worship the *h* of heaven;
Ro 16.23 Gaius mine *h*, and of the whole

HOSTAGES

2Ki 14.14 house, and *h*, and returned
2Ch 25.24 house, the *h* also, and returned

HOSTS

1Sa 4. 4 of the covenant of the Lord of *h*,
15. 2 Thus saith the Lord of *h*, I
17.45 thee in the name of the Lord of *h*,
2Sa 5.10 the Lord God of *h* was with him.
6.18 in the name of the Lord of *h*.
1Ki 19.10, 14 jealous for the Lord God of *h*:
2Ki 19.31 zeal of the Lord of *h* shall do this.
1Ch 17.24 The Lord of *h* is the God of Israel,
Ps 24.10 Lord of *h*, he is the King of glory.
46. 7, 11 The Lord of *h* is with us; the
59. 5 O Lord God of *h*, the God of Israel,
80. 4 O Lord God of *h*, how long wilt
7 Turn us again, O God of *h*, and
84. 1 are thy tabernacles, O Lord of *h*!
3 O Lord of *h*, my King, and my God.
103.21 Bless ye the Lord, all ye his *h*; ye
148. 2 angels: praise ye him, all his *h*.
Isa 1. 9 Except the Lord of *h* had left unto
5. 7 For the vineyard of the Lord of *h*
6. 3 Holy, holy, holy, is the Lord of *h*:
5 have seen the King, the Lord of *h*.
9. 7 The zeal of the Lord of *h* will
19.20 for a witness unto the Lord of *h*
25 Whom the Lord of *h* shall bless,
21.10 I have heard of the Lord of *h*, the
25. 6 this mountain shall the Lord of *h*
47. 4 the Lord of *h* is his name, the
Jer 11.20 Lord of *h*,that judgest righteously,
20.12 Lord of *h*, that triest the righteous,
27.18 make intercession to the Lord of *h*,
32.18 the Mighty God, the Lord of *h*, is

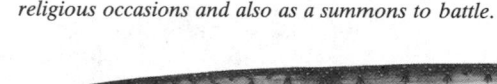

The ancient horn trumpet (or shofar), mentioned many times in the Bible, was sounded on important religious occasions and also as a summons to battle.

Am 5.15 Lord God of *h* will be gracious
Hag 2. 4 I am with you, saith the Lord of *h*:
8 gold is mine, saith the Lord of *h*.
9 I give peace, saith the Lord of *h*.
Zec 1. 3 ye unto me, saith the Lord of *h*,
3 turn unto you, saith the Lord of *h*.
12 O Lord of *h*, how long wilt thou not
4. 6 by my spirit, saith the Lord of *h*.
7.12 a great wrath from the Lord of *h*.
8. 3 the mountain of the Lord of *h* the
9.15 The Lord of *h* shall defend them;
10. 3 the Lord of *h* hath visited his flock
14.16, 17 worship the King, the Lord of *h*.
Mal 1.14 a great King, saith the Lord of *h*,
2. 7 is the messenger of the Lord of *h*.
4. 3 I shall do this, saith the Lord of *h*.

HOT

Ex 16.21 when the sun waxed *h*, it melted.
22.24 And my wrath shall wax *h*, and I
32.10 that my wrath may wax *h* against
11 why doth thy wrath wax *h* against
19 and Moses' anger waxed *h*, and he
22 not the anger of my lord wax *h*:
Lev 13.24 skin whereof there is a *h* burning,
Dt 9.19 of the anger and *h* displeasure,
19. 6 the slayer, while his heart is *h*,
Jos 9.12 This our bread we took *h* for our
Jdg 2.14, 20 the anger of the Lord was *h*
3. 8 anger of the Lord was *h* against
6.39 Let not thine anger be *h* against
10. 7 anger of the Lord was *h* against
1Sa 11. 9 by that time the sun be *h*, ye shall
21. 6 to put *h* bread in the day when it
Neh 7. 3 be opened until the sun be *h*;
Job 6.17 when it is *h*, they are consumed
Ps 6. 1 chasten me in thy *h* displeasure.
38. 1 chasten me in thy *h* displeasure.
39. 3 My heart was *h* within me, while
78.48 their flocks to *h* thunderbolts.
Pr 6.28 Can one go upon *h* coals, and his feet
Eze 24.11 that the brass of it may be *h*, and
Dan 3.22 and the furnace exceeding *h*, the
Hos 7. 7 They are all *h* as an oven, and
1Ti 4. 2 conscience seared with a *h* iron;
Rev 3.15 that thou art neither cold nor *h*:
15 I would thou wert cold or *h*.
16 lukewarm, and neither cold nor *h*,

HOUR

Dan 3. 6 the same *h* be cast into the midst
15 be cast the same *h* into the midst
4.19 was astonied for one *h*, and his
33 The same *h* was the thing fulfilled
5. 5 In the same *h* came forth fingers
Mt 8.13 was healed in the selfsame *h*.
9.22 was made whole from that *h*.
10.19 that same *h* what ye shall speak.
15.28 was made whole from that very *h*.
17.18 child was cured from that very *h*.
20. 3 he went out about the third *h*, and
5 out about the sixth and ninth *h*,
6 about the eleventh *h* he went out,
9 were hired about the eleventh *h*,
12 These last have wrought but one *h*,
24.36 of that day and *h* knoweth no man,
42 not what *h* your Lord doth come.
44 such an *h* as ye think not the Son
50 and in an *h* that he is not aware of,
25.13 ye know neither the day nor the *h*
26.40 could ye not watch with me one *h*?
45 the *h* is at hand, and the Son of
55 In that same *h* said Jesus to the
27.45 the sixth *h* there was darkness
45 over all the land unto the ninth *h*.
46 about the ninth *h* Jesus cried with
Mk 13.11 given you in that *h*, that speak ye:
32 day and that *h* knoweth no man,
14.35 possible, the *h* might pass from
37 couldest not thou watch one *h*?
41 it is enough, the *h* is come; behold,
15.25 was the third *h*, and they crucified
33 And when the sixth *h* was come,
33 the whole land until the ninth *h*.
34 the ninth *h* Jesus cried with a loud
Lk 7.21 And in that same *h* he cured many
10.21 In that *h* Jesus rejoiced in spirit,
12.12 in the same *h* what ye ought to say.
39 known what *h* the thief would
40 cometh at an *h* when ye think not.
46 at an *h* when he is not aware, and
20.19 the same *h* sought to lay hands
22.14 when the *h* was come, he sat down,
53 but this is your *h*, and the power of
59 And about the space of one *h* after
23.44 it was about the sixth *h*, and there
44 over all the earth until the ninth *h*.
24.33 rose up the same *h*, and returned
Jn 1.39 day: for it was about the tenth *h*.
2. 4 with thee? mine *h* is not yet come.
4. 6 well: and it was about the sixth *h*.
21 Woman, believe me, the *h* cometh,
23 the *h* cometh, and now is, when the
52 inquired he of them the *h* when he
52 Yesterday at the seventh *h* the
53 knew that it was at the same *h*,
5.25 The *h* is coming, and now is, when
28 the *h* is coming, in the which all
7.30 because his *h* was not yet come.
8.20 on him; for his *h* was not yet come.
12.23 The *h* is come, that the Son of man
27 I say? Father, save me from this *h*:
27 for this cause came I unto this *h*.
13. 1 when Jesus knew that his *h* was
16.21 sorrow, because her *h* is come:
32 the *h* cometh, yea, is now come,
17. 1 and said, Father, the *h* is come;
19.14 the passover, and about the sixth *h*:
27 from that *h* that disciple took her
Ac 2.15 seeing it is but the third *h* of the
3. 1 into the temple at the *h* of prayer,
1 of prayer, being the ninth *h*.
10. 3 the ninth *h* of the day an angel
9 housetop to pray about the sixth *h*:
30 days ago I was fasting until this *h*;
30 the ninth *h* I prayed in my house,
16.18 her. And he came out the same *h*.
33 took them the same *h* of the night,

BIBLICAL THEMES

HOSPITALITY

Laban ran out unto the man, unto the well. . . . And he said, Come in, thou blessed of the Lord; wherefore standest thou without? for I have prepared the house, and room for the camels.
Gen 24.29, 31

If a stranger sojourn with thee in your land, ye shall not vex him. . . . [he] shall be unto you as one born among you, and thou shalt love him as thyself; for ye were strangers in the land of Egypt. Lev 19.33-34

[God] doth execute the judgment of the fatherless and widow, and loveth the stranger, in giving him food and raiment. Dt 10.18

Now when Mephibosheth, the son of Jonathan, . . . was come unto David, he fell on his face, and did reverence. . . . And David said unto him, Fear not: for I will surely shew thee kindness for Jonathan thy father's sake . . . and thou shalt eat bread at my table continually. 2Sa 9.6-7

Elisha passed to Shunem, where was a great woman; and she constrained him to eat bread . . . And she said unto her husband, Behold now, I perceive that this is an holy man of God, which passeth by us continually. Let us make a little chamber, I pray thee, on the wall; and let us set for him there a bed, and a table, and a stool, and a candlestick.
2Ki 4.8-10

The stranger did not lodge in the street: but I opened my doors to the traveller.
Job 31.32

Eat thou not the bread of him that hath an evil eye. . . . Eat and drink, saith he to thee; but his heart is not with thee. The morsel which thou hast eaten shalt thou vomit up. Pr 23.6-8

Withdraw thy foot from thy neighbor's house; lest he be weary of thee, and so hate thee. Pr 25.17

Deal thy bread to the hungry, and . . . bring the poor that are cast out to thy house. Isa 58.7

I was an hungred, and ye gave me meat: I was thirsty, and ye gave me drink: I was a stranger, and ye took me in.
Mt 25.35

Seest thou this woman? I entered into thine house, thou gavest me no water for my feet: but she hath washed my feet with tears, and wiped them with the hairs of her head. Thou gavest me no kiss: but this woman since the time I came in hath not ceased to kiss my feet. My head with oil thou didst not anoint: but this woman hath anointed my feet with ointment. Lk 7.44-46

When thou makest a feast, call the poor, the maimed, the lame, the blind: and thou shalt be blessed; for they cannot recompense thee: for thou shalt be recompensed at the resurrection of the just. Lk 14.13-14

The chief man of the island, whose name was Publius . . . received us, and lodged us three days courteously. And it came to pass, that the father of Publius lay sick of a fever . . . to whom Paul entered in, and prayed, and laid his hands on him, and healed him.
Ac 28.7-8

Let brotherly love continue. Be not forgetful to entertain strangers: for thereby some have entertained angels unawares. Heb 13.1, 2

Use hospitality one to another without grudging. As every man hath received the gift, even so minister the same one to another. 1Pe 4.9-10

Behold, I stand at the door, and knock: if any man hear my voice, and open the door, I will come in to him, and will sup with him, and he with me. To him . . . will I grant to sit with me in my throne.
Rev 3.20-21

Ac 22.13 And the same *h* I looked up upon
23.23 hundred, at the third *h* of the night;
1Co 4.11 this present *h* we both hunger,
8. 7 of the idol unto this *h* eat it as a
15.30 stand we in jeopardy every *h*?
Gal 2. 5 by subjection, no, not for an *h*;
Rev 3. 3 shalt not know what *h* I will come
10 keep thee from the *h* of temptation,
8. 1 about the space of half an *h*.
9.15 prepared for an *h*, and a day, and
11.13 same *h* was there a great
14. 7 for the *h* of his judgment is come:
17.12 power as kings one *h* with the
18.10 for in one *h* is thy judgment come.
17 in one *h* so great riches is come
19 for in one *h* is she made desolate.

HOURS

Jn 11. 9 Are there not twelve *h* in the
Ac 5. 7 about the space of three *h* after,
19.34 about the space of two *h* cried out,

HOUSE

Gen 7. 1 thou and all thy *h* into the ark;
12.15 woman was taken into Pharaoh's *h*.
24.31 for I have prepared the *h*, and room
28.17 none other but the *h* of God, and
21 again to my father's *h* in peace;
22 set for a pillar, shall be God's *h*:
41.40 Thou shalt be over my *h*, and
Ex 12.30 there was not a *h* where there was
46 In one *h* shall it be eaten; thou
46 of the flesh abroad out of the *h*;
13. 3 Egypt, out of the *h* of bondage;
20. 2 Egypt out of the *h* of bondage.
17 shalt not covet thy neighbor's *h*,
Lev 16. 6 atonement for himself, and for his *h*.
Dt 5.21 thou covet thy neighbor's *h*, his
6. 7 when thou sittest in thine *h*, and
9 write them upon the posts of thy *h*,
11.20 upon the door posts of thine *h*,
Jdg 6.15 I am the least in my father's *h*.
9.27 and went into the *h* of their god,
12. 1 we will burn thine *h* upon thee
16.21 and he did grind in the prison *h*.
26 pillars whereupon the *h* standeth,
30 and the *h* fell upon the lords, and
19.18 am now going to the *h* of the Lord;
21. 2 the people came to the *h* of God,
1Sa 9.18 I pray thee, where the seer's *h* is.
25.35 unto her, Go up in peace to thine *h*;
2Sa 7. 5 Shalt thou build me an *h* for me
6 I have not dwelt in any *h* since
1Ki 2.36 Build thee an *h* in Jerusalem,
3. 1 the *h* of the Lord, and the wall of
2 because there was no *h* built unto
5. 5 I purpose to build an *h* unto the
8.20 built an *h* for the name of the Lord
27 how much less this *h* that I have
29 eyes may be open toward this *h*
63 Israel, dedicated the *h* of the Lord.
20.31 the *h* of Israel are merciful kings:
2Ki 4. 2 tell me, what hast thou in the *h*?
5.18 I bow myself in the *h* of Rimmon:
11. 3 hid in the *h* of the Lord six years.
12. 8 to repair the breaches of the *h*.
18 the treasures of the *h* of the Lord,
20. 1 Set thine *h* in order; for thou shalt
8 I shall go up into the *h* of the Lord
15 What have they seen in thine *h*?
22. 8 found the book of the law in the *h*
9 the oversight of the *h* of the Lord.
1Ch 17. 4 Thou shalt not build me an *h* to
5 For I have not dwelt in an *h* since
22. 1 said, This is the *h* of the Lord God,
10 He shall build an *h* for my name;
24. 5 and governors of the *h* of God,
25. 6 for song in the *h* of the Lord,
6 for the service of the *h* of God,
26.12 to minister in the *h* of the Lord.
2Ch 2. 4 build an *h* to the name of the Lord
5.13 *h* was filled with a cloud, even the *h*
6.20 eyes may be open upon this *h* day
22 come before thine altar in this *h*;
29 spread forth his hands in this *h*:
7. 1 the glory of the Lord filled the *h*.
5 the people dedicated the *h* of God.
8.16 So the *h* of the Lord was perfected.
23.17 went to the *h* of Baal, and brake it
24. 4 minded to repair the *h* of the Lord.
29.15 Lord, to cleanse the *h* of the Lord.
33. 4 he built altars in the *h* of the Lord,
34.15 book of the law in the *h* of the Lord.
17 money that was found in the *h* of
35. 3 Put the holy ark in the *h* which
36.18 all the vessels of the *h* of God,
18 the treasures of the *h* of the Lord,
Ezr 1. 4 freewill offering for the *h* of God
5 to go up to build the *h* of the Lord
2.68 offered freely for the *h* of God
6. 7 elders of the Jews build this *h* of
11 and let his *h* be made a dunghill
8.30 to Jerusalem unto the *h* of our God.
Neh 1. 6 I and my father's *h* have sinned.
10.39 will not forsake the *h* of our God.
12.40 that gave thanks in the *h* of God,
13. 7 in the courts of the *h* of God.
11 Why is the *h* of God forsaken?
14 I have done for the *h* of my God,

Est 2. 9 best place of the *h* of the women.
9. 4 Mordecai was great in the king's *h*,
Job 1.19 smote the four corners of the *h*,
17.13 If I wait, the grave is mine *h*:
21.28 say, Where is the *h* of the prince?
27.18 He buildeth his *h* as a moth, and as
30.23 to the *h* appointed for all living.
39. 6 *h* I have made the wilderness,
Ps 5. 7 as for me, I will come into thy *h* in
23. 6 dwell in the *h* of the Lord for ever.
26. 8 have loved the habitation of thy *h*,
27. 4 I may dwell in the *h* of the Lord all
36. 8 satisfied with the fatness of thy *h*;
42. 4 I went with them to the *h* of God,
65. 4 satisfied with the goodness of thy *h*,
69. 9 the zeal of thine *h* hath eaten me
84. 3 the sparrow hath found an *h*, and
4 are they that dwell in thy *h*: they
10 a doorkeeper in the *h* of my God,
92.13 be planted in the *h* of the Lord
93. 5 holiness becometh thine *h*, O Lord,
101. 2 walk within my *h* with a perfect
104.17 the stork, the fir trees are her *h*.
112. 3 Wealth and riches shall be in his *h*:
116.19 In the courts of the Lord's *h*, in
118.26 blessed you out of the *h* of the
122. 1 Let us go into the *h* of the Lord.
127. 1 Except the Lord build the *h*, they
134. 1 night stand in the *h* of the Lord.
135. 2 Ye that stand in the *h* of the Lord,
Pr 2.18 For her *h* inclineth unto death,
3.33 the Lord is in the *h* of the wicked:
7.27 Her *h* is the way to hell, going
9. 1 Wisdom hath builded her *h*, she
14 she sitteth at the door of her *h*,
12. 7 the *h* of the righteous shall stand.
14. 1 wise woman buildeth her *h*: but
15. 6 In the *h* of the righteous is much
25 will destroy the *h* of the proud:
27 greedy of gain troubleth his own *h*;
19.14 *H* and riches are the inheritance
21. 9 a brawling woman in a wide *h*.
24. 3 Through wisdom is an *h* builded;
Ec 5. 1 when thou goest to the *h* of God,
7. 2 better to go to the *h* of mourning,
2 than to go to the *h* of feasting:
4 the wise is in the *h* of mourning;
4 heart of fools is in the *h* of mirth.
12. 3 the keepers of the *h* shall tremble,
Isa 2. 3 Lord, to the *h* of the God of Jacob;
5. 8 Woe unto them that join *h* to *h*,
6. 4 and the *h* was filled with smoke.
14.17 opened not the *h* of his prisoners?
24.10 every *h* is shut up, that no man
37. 1 and went into the *h* of the Lord.
38. 1 Set thine *h* in order: for thou shalt
20 days of our life in the *h* of the Lord.
56. 7 them joyful in my *h* of prayer:
7 mine *h* shall be called an *h* of
64.11 Our holy and our beautiful *h*,
Jer 7. 2 Stand in the gate of the Lord's *h*,
30 the *h* which is called by my name,
18. 2 go down to the potter's *h*, and
6 O *h* of Israel, cannot I do with you
22.13 buildeth his *h* by unrighteousness,
14 I will build me a wide *h* and large
26. 2 Stand in the court of the Lord's *h*,
2 come to worship in the Lord's *h*,
12 to prophesy against this *h* and
36. 5 cannot go into the *h* of the Lord:
La 2. 7 made a noise in the *h* of the Lord,
Eze 2. 5 for they are a rebellious *h*, yet
3.17 a watchman unto the *h* of Israel:
8. 1 I sat in mine *h*, and the elders of
10 and all the idols of the *h* of Israel,
17 Is it a light thing to the *h* of Judah
10. 4 the *h* was filled with the cloud,
12.25 O rebellious *h*, will I say the word,
17. 2 a parable unto the *h* of Israel;
18.29 O *h* of Israel, are not my ways
30 I will judge you, O *h* of Israel,
31 for why will ye die, O *h* of Israel?
43. 5 the glory of the Lord filled the *h*.
45. 5 the Levites, the ministers of the *h*,
Dan 6.10 was signed, he went into his *h*;
Hos 9.15 I will drive them out of mine *h*,
Joel 1. 9 is cut off from the *h* of the Lord;
16 gladness from the *h* of our God?
Am 3.15 the winter *h* with the summer *h*;
5.25 forty years. O *h* of Israel?
6. 9 remain ten men in one *h*, that they
9. 9 I will sift the *h* of Israel among all
Mic 2. 2 so they oppress a man and his *h*,
Hag 1. 4 cieled houses, and this *h* lie waste?
14 work in the *h* of the Lord of hosts,
Zec 1.16 my *h* shall be built in it, saith the
4. 9 have laid the foundation of this *h*;
7. 2 they had sent unto the *h* of God
11.13 to the potter in the *h* of the Lord.
Mal 3.10 there may be meat in mine *h*, and
Mt 2.11 when they were come into the *h*,
5.15 light unto all that are in the *h*.
7.24 which built his *h* upon a rock:
25 winds blew, and beat upon that *h*;
26 which built his *h* upon the sand:
27 winds blew, and beat upon that *h*;
8.14 Jesus was come into Peter's *h*, he
9. 6 up thy bed, and go unto thine *h*.
7 he arose, and departed to his *h*.
10 as Jesus sat at meat in the *h*,
23 when Jesus came into the ruler's *h*,
28 And when he was come into the *h*,
10. 6 the lost sheep of the *h* of Israel.
12 when ye come into an *h*, salute it.
13 And if the *h* be worthy, let your
14 when ye depart out of that *h* or
25 call the master of the *h* Beelzebub,
12. 4 How he entered into the *h* of God,
25 city or *h* divided against itself
29 one enter into a strong man's *h*,
29 man? and then he will spoil his *h*.
44 return into my *h* from whence I
13. 1 same day went Jesus out of the *h*,
36 away, and went into the *h*:
57 his own country, and in his own *h*.
15.24 the lost sheep of the *h* of Israel.
17.25 And when he was come into the *h*,
20.11 against the goodman of the *h*,
21.13 My *h* shall be called the *h* of
23.38 your *h* is left unto you desolate.
24.17 to take any thing out of his *h*:
43 goodman of the *h* had known in
43 suffered his *h* to be broken up.
26. 6 in the *h* of Simon the leper,
18 I will keep the passover at thy *h*
Mk 1.29 entered into the *h* of Simon and
2. 1 was noised that he was in the *h*.
11 bed, and go thy way into thine *h*.
15 that, as Jesus sat at meat in his *h*,
26 How he went into the *h* of God in
3.19 him: and they went into an *h*.
25 And if a *h* be divided against itself,
25 itself, that *h* cannot stand.
27 can enter into a strong man's *h*,
27 man; and then he will spoil his *h*.
5.35 from the ruler of the synagogue's *h*
38 cometh to the *h* of the ruler of the
6. 4 his own kin, and in his own *h*.
10 ye enter into a *h*, there abide till ye
7.17 when he was entered into the *h*
24 and Sidon, and entered into an *h*,
30 when she was come to her *h*, she
8.26 And he sent him away to his *h*,
9.28 when he was come into the *h*, his
33 and being in the *h* he asked them,
10.10 And in the *h* his disciples asked
29 There is no man that hath left *h*, or
11.17 not written, My *h* shall be called
17 of all nations the *h* of prayer?
13.15 housetop not go down into the *h*,
15 to take anything out of his *h*:
34 taking a far journey, who left his *h*,
35 when the master of the *h* cometh,
14. 3 Bethany in the *h* of Simon the leper,
14 say ye to the goodman of the *h*,
Lk 1.23 he departed to his own *h*.
27 was Joseph, of the *h* of David;
33 reign over the *h* of Jacob for ever;
40 entered into the *h* of Zacharias,
56 months, and returned to her own *h*.
69 us in the *h* of his servant David;
2. 4 was of the *h* and lineage of David:
4.38 and entered into Simon's *h*.
5.24 up thy couch, and go into thine *h*;
25 he lay, and departed to his own *h*,
29 him a great feast in his own *h*:
6. 4 How he went into the *h* of God,
48 He is like a man which built an *h*,
48 beat vehemently upon that *h*,
49 built an *h* upon the earth; against
49 and the ruin of that *h* was great.
7. 6 he was now not far from the *h*,
10 that were sent, returning to the *h*,
36 he went into the Pharisee's *h*, and
37 sat at meat in the Pharisee's *h*,
44 I entered into thine *h*, thou gavest
8.27 neither abode in any *h*, but in the
39 Return to thine own *h*, and shew
41 him that he would come into his *h*:
49 from the ruler of the synagogue's *h*,
51 And when he came into the *h*, he
9. 4 whatsoever *h* ye enter into, there
61 which are at home at my *h*.
10. 5 into whatsoever *h* ye enter, first
5 first say, Peace be to this *h*.
7 in the same *h* remain, eating and
7 of his hire. Go not from *h* to *h*.
38 Martha received him into her *h*.
11.17 and a *h* divided against a *h* falleth.
24 I will return unto my *h* whence I
12.39 the goodman of the *h* had known
39 have suffered his *h* to be broken
52 there shall be five in one *h* divided,
13.25 the master of the *h* is risen up,
35 your *h* is left unto you desolate:
14. 1 the *h* of one of the chief Pharisees
21 the master of the *h* being angry
23 to come in, that my *h* may be filled.
15. 8 sweep the *h*, and seek diligently
25 he came and drew nigh to the *h*,
16.27 send him to my father's *h*:
17.31 housetop, and his stuff in the *h*,
18.14 man went down to his *h* justified
29 no man that hath left *h*, or parents,
19. 5 for to day I must abide at thy *h*.
9 This day is salvation come to this *h*,
46 written, My *h* is the *h* of prayer:
22.10 follow him into the *h* where he
11 say unto the goodman of the *h*,
54 him into the high priest's *h*.
Jn 2.16 Father's *h* an *h* of merchandise.
17 zeal of thine *h* hath eaten me up.
4.53 himself believed, and his whole *h*.
7.53 every man went unto his own *h*.
8.35 abideth not in the *h* for ever:
11.20 him: but Mary sat still in the *h*.
31 which were with her in the *h*,
12. 3 the *h* was filled with the odor of
14. 2 my Father's *h* are many mansions:
Ac 2. 2 all the *h* where they were sitting.
36 let all the *h* of Israel know
46 breaking bread from *h* to *h*,
5.42 in the temple, and in every *h*,
7.10 governor over Egypt and all his *h*.
20 up in his father's *h* three months:
42 O ye *h* of Israel, have ye offered to
47 But Solomon built him an *h*.
49 what *h* will ye build me? saith
8. 3 entering into every *h*, and
9.11 inquire in the *h* of Judas for one
17 his way, and entered into the *h*;
10. 2 one that feared God with all his *h*,
6 tanner, whose *h* is by the sea side:

Ac 10.17 had made inquiry for Simon's *h*,
22 angel to send for thee into his *h*,
30 ninth hour I prayed in my *h*, and,
32 he is lodged in the *h* of one Simon
11.11 three men already come unto the *h*
12 and we entered into the man's *h*:
13 how he had seen an angel in his *h*,
14 thou and all thy *h* shall be saved.
12.12 came to the *h* of Mary the mother
16.15 Lord, come into my *h*, and abide
31 and thou shalt be saved, and thy *h*.
32 Lord, and to all that were in his *h*.
34 he had brought them into his *h*,
34 believing in God with all his *h*.
40 and entered into the *h* of Lydia:
17. 5 and assaulted the *h* of Jason,
18. 7 a certain man's *h*, named Justus,
7 *h* joined hard to the synagogue.
8 believed on the Lord with all his *h*;
19.16 they fled out of that *h* naked and
20.20 you publickly, and from *h* to *h*,
21. 8 we entered into the *h* of Philip the
28.30 whole years in his own hired *h*,
Ro 16. 5 greet the church that is in their *h*.
1Co 1.11 them which are of the *h* of Chloe,
16.15 ye know the *h* of Stephanas, that
19 with the church that is in their *h*.
2Co 5. 1 we know that if our earthly *h* of
1 an *h* not made with hands, eternal
2 with our *h* which is from heaven:
Col 4.15 and the church which is in his *h*.
1Ti 3. 4 One that ruleth well his own *h*,
5 know not how to rule his own *h*,
15 to behave thyself in the *h* of God,
5. 8 specially for those of his own *h*,
13 wandering about from *h* to *h*;
14 bear children, guide the *h*, give
2Ti 1.16 mercy unto the *h* of Onesiphorus;
2.20 But in a great *h* there are not only
Phm 2 and to the church in thy *h*:
Heb 3. 2 also Moses was faithful in all his *h*.
3 as he who hath builded the *h*
3 hath more honor than the *h*.
4 every *h* is builded by some man;
5 verily was faithful in all his *h*,
6 But Christ as a son over his own *h*;
6 whose *h* are we, if we hold fast the
8. 8 *h* of Israel and with the *h* of Judah:
10 I will make with the *h* of Israel
10.21 an high priest over the *h* of God;
11. 7 an ark to the saving of his *h*;
1Pe 2. 5 stones, are built up a spiritual *h*,
4.17 must begin at the *h* of God:
2Jn 10 receive him not into your *h*,

HOUSEHOLD
Ex 12. 4 if the *h* be too little for the lamb,
Lev 16.17 for himself, and for his *h*, and for
Pr 27.27 for the food of thy *h*, and for the
31.15 giveth meat to her *h*, and a portion
21 for all her *h* are clothed with scarlet.
Mt 10.25 more shall they call them of his *h*?
36 man's foes shall be they of his own *h*.
24.45 his lord hath made ruler over his *h*,
Lk 12.42 his lord shall make ruler over his *h*,
Ac 10. 7 he called two of his *h* servants,
16.15 when she was baptized, and her *h*,
Ro 16.10 them which are of Aristobulus' *h*.
11 them that be of the *h* of Narcissus,
1Co 1.16 baptized also the *h* of Stephanas:
Gal 6.10 unto them who are of the *h* of faith.
Eph 2.19 with the saints, and of the *h* of God;
Php 4.22 chiefly they that are of Caesar's *h*.
2Ti 4.19 and the *h* of Onesiphorus.

HOUSEHOLDER
Mt 13.27 servants of the *h* came and said
52 is like unto a man that is an *h*,
20. 1 is like unto a man that is an *h*,
21.33 was a certain *h*, which planted a

HOUSEHOLDS
Gen 42.33 food for the famine of your *h*,
45.18 take your father and your *h*, and
47.24 your food, and for them of your *h*,
Nu 18.31 eat it in every place, ye and your *h*:
Dt 11. 6 swallowed them up, and their *h*,
12. 7 put your hand unto, ye and your *h*,
Jos 7.14 Lord shall take shall come by *h*;

HOUSES
Ex 1.21 feared God, that he made them *h*.
12.13 for a token upon the *h* where ye are:
Dt 6.11 and *h* full of all good things, which
8.12 and hast built goodly *h*, and dwelt
Job 21. 9 Their *h* are safe from fear, neither
22.18 he filled their *h* with good things:
24.16 In the dark they dig through *h*,
Ps 83.12 us take to ourselves the *h* of God
Isa 3.14 the spoil of the poor is in your *h*.
6.11 and the *h* without man, and the
22.10 numbered the *h* of Jerusalem,
Jer 18.22 Let a cry be heard from their *h*,
29. 5 Build ye *h*, and dwell in them; and
Eze 11. 3 say, It is not near; let us build *h*:
Dan 2. 5 your *h* shall be made a dunghill.
3.29 their *h* shall be made a dunghill:
Am 3.15 and the *h* of ivory shall perish, and
15 and the great *h* shall have an end,
Mt 11. 8 wear soft clothing are in kings' *h*.
19.29 that hath forsaken *h*, or brethren,
23.14 ye devour widows' *h*, and for a
Mk 8. 3 away, fasting to their own *h*, they
10.30 *h*, and brethren, and sisters, and
12.40 Which devour widows' *h*, and for a
Lk 16. 4 they may receive me into their *h*.
20.47 Which devour widows' *h*, and for
Ac 4.34 possessors of lands or *h* sold them,
1Co 11.22 ye not *h* to eat and to drink in?
1Ti 3.12 their children and their own *h* well.
2Ti 3. 6 sort are they which creep into *h*,
Tit 1.11 who subvert whole *h*, teaching

HOUSETOP
Pr 21. 9 better to dwell in a corner of the *h*,
25.24 better to dwell in the corner of the *h*,
Mt 24.17 Let him which is on the *h* not
Mk 13.15 let him that is on the *h* not go down
Lk 5.19 they went upon the *h*, and let him
17.31 he which shall be upon the *h*, and
Ac 10. 9 Peter went up upon the *h* to pray

HOUSETOPS
Ps 129. 6 them be as the grass upon the *h*,
Isa 22. 1 thou art wholly gone up to the *h*?
37.27 as the grass on the *h*, and as corn
Jer 48.38 upon all the *h* of Moab, and in the
Zep 1. 5 the host of heaven upon the *h*;
Mt 10.27 the ear, that preach ye upon the *h*.
Lk 12. 3 shall be proclaimed upon the *h*.

HOWL
Isa 13. 6 *H* ye; for the day of the Lord
14.31 *H*, O gate; cry, O city; thou,
15. 2 Moab shall *h* over Nebo, and
3 every one shall *h*, weeping
16. 7 *h* for Moab, every one shall *h*:
23. 1 *H*, ye ships of Tarshish; for it
6 *h*, ye inhabitants of the isle.
14 *H*, ye ships of Tarshish, for your
52. 5 rule over them make them to *h*,
65.14 and shall *h* for vexation of spirit.
Jer 4. 8 you with sackcloth, lament and *h*:
25.34 *H*, ye shepherds, and cry; and
47. 2 the inhabitants of the land shall *h*.
48.20 *h* and cry; tell ye it in Arnon,
31 Therefore will I *h* for Moab, and
39 They shall *h*, saying, How is it
49. 3 *H*, O Heshbon, for Ai is spoiled:
51. 8 fallen and destroyed: *h* for her:
Eze 21.12 Cry and *h*, son of man: for it
30. 2 Thus saith the Lord God; *H* ye,
Joel 1. 5 and *h*, all ye drinkers of wine,
11 *h*, O ye vinedressers, for the
13 *h*, ye ministers of the altar; come
Mic 1. 8 I will wail and *h*, I will go stripped
Zep 1.11 *H*, ye inhabitants of Maktesh,
Zec 11. 2 *H*, fir tree; for the cedar is fallen;
2 *h*, O ye oaks of Bashan; for the
Jas 5. 1 weep and *h* for your miseries that

HOWLED
Hos 7.14 when they *h* upon their beds:

HOWLING
Dt 32.10 and in the waste *h* wilderness; he
Isa 15. 8 Moab; the *h* thereof unto Eglaim,
8 and the *h* thereof unto Beer-elim.
Jer 25.36 an *h* of the principal of the flock,
Zep 1.10 and an *h* from the second, and
Zec 11. 3 voice of the *h* of the shepherds;

HOWLINGS
Am 8. 3 songs of the temple shall be *h*

HUMBLE
Ex 10. 3 long wilt thou refuse to *h* thyself
Dt 8. 2 to *h* thee, and to prove thee,
16 that he might *h* thee, and that he
Jdg 19.24 and *h* ye them, and do with them
2Ch 7.14 If my people,...shall *h* themselves,
34.27 thou didst *h* thyself before God,
Job 22.29 and he shall save the *h*
Ps 9.12 he forgetteth not the cry of the *h*.
10.12 up thine hand: forget not the *h*.
17 hast heard the desire of the *h*:
34. 2 the *h* shall hear thereof, and be
69.32 The *h* shall see this, and be glad
Pr 6. 3 go, *h* thyself, and make sure thy
16.19 Better it is to be of an *h* spirit
29.23 but honor shall uphold the *h* in
Isa 57.15 that is of a contrite and *h* spirit,
15 to revive the spirit of the *h*, and
Jer 13.18 the queen, *H* yourselves, sit down:
Mt 18. 4 Whosoever therefore shall *h*
23.12 and he that shall *h* himself shall
2Co 12.21 my God will *h* me among you,
Jas 4. 6 but giveth grace unto the *h*.
10 *H* yourselves in the sight of the
1Pe 5. 5 proud, and giveth grace to the *h*.
6 *H* yourselves therefore under

HUMBLED
Dt 8. 3 And he *h* thee, and suffered thee
2Ki 22.19 and thou hast *h* thyself before
2Ch 12. 7 Lord saw that they *h* themselves,
33.23 And *h* not himself before the Lord,
Ps 35.13 I *h* my soul with fasting; and
Isa 2.11 The lofty looks of man shall be *h*,
5.15 and the mighty man shall be *h*,
15 the eyes of the lofty shall be *h*:
10.33 down, and the haughty shall be *h*.
La 3.20 remembrance, and is *h* in me.
Php 2. 8 he *h* himself, and became obedient

HUMBLENESS
Col 3.12 kindness, *h* of mind, meekness,

HUMBLETH
1Ki 21.29 how Ahab *h* himself before me?
29 because he *h* himself before me,
Ps 10.10 He croucheth, and *h* himself,
113. 6 Who *h* himself to behold the
Isa 2. 9 and the great man *h* himself:
Lk 14.11 that *h* himself shall be exalted.
18.14 that *h* himself shall be exalted.

HUMBLY
2Sa 16. 4 I *h* beseech thee that I may find
Mic 6. 8 love mercy, and to walk *h* with

HUMILIATION
Ac 8.33 In his *h* his judgment was taken

HUMILITY

Pr 15.33 wisdom; and before honor is *h*.
18.12 haughty, and before honor is *h*.
22. 4 By *h* and the fear of the Lord are
Ac 20.19 Serving the Lord with all *h* of
Col 2.18 your reward in a voluntary *h* and
23 and *h*, and neglecting of the body;
1Pe 5. 5 another and be clothed with *h*:

HUNDRED

Gen 5. 3 Adam lived an *h* and thirty years,
25 Methuselah lived an *h* eighty and
30 Noah five *h* ninety and five years,
32 And Noah was five *h* years old:
7. 6 And Noah was six *h* years old
15.13 shall afflict them four *h* years;
21. 5 Abraham was an *h* years old,
50.22 Joseph lived an *h* and ten years.
Dt 34. 7 Moses was an *h* and twenty years
Jdg 7. 7 By the three *h* men that lapped will
16 he divided the three *h* men into
22 And the three *h* blew the trumpets,
1Ki 18. 4 Obadiah took an *h* prophets, and
19 prophets of Baal four *h* and fifty,
19 the prophets of the groves four *h*,
Job 42.16 this lived Job an *h* and forty years,
Pr 17.10 man than an *h* stripes into a fool.
Ec 6. 3 If a man beget an *h* children, and
8.12 Though a sinner do evil an *h* times,
Mt 18.12 if a man have an *h* sheep, and one
28 which owed him an *h* pence:
Mk 4. 8 and some sixty, and some an *h*.
20 some sixty, and some an *h*.
6.37 buy two *h* pennyworth of bread,
14. 5 sold for more than three *h* pence,
Lk 7.41 the one owed five *h* pence, and
15. 4 man of you, having an *h* sheep,
16. 6 And he said, An *h* measures of oil.
7 he said, An *h* measures of wheat.
Jn 6. 7 Two *h* pennyworth of bread is not
12. 5 ointment sold for three *h* pence,
19.39 aloes, about an *h* pound weight.
21. 8 land, but as it were two *h* cubits,
11 great fishes, an *h* and fifty and
Ac 1.15 were about an *h* and twenty,
5.36 a number of men, about four *h*,
7. 6 and entreat them evil four *h* years.
13.20 the space of four *h* and fifty years,
23.23 Make ready two *h* soldiers to go
23 and spearmen two *h*, at the third
27.37 two *h* threescore and sixteen souls.
Ro 4.19 when he was about an *h* years old,
1Co 15. 6 of above five *h* brethren at once;
Gal 3.17 was four *h* and thirty years after,
Rev 7. 4 an *h* and forty and four thousand
9.16 were two *h* thousand thousand:
11. 3 a thousand two *h* and threescore
12. 6 a thousand two *h* and threescore
13.18 number is Six *h* threescore and six.
14. 1 him an *h* forty and four thousand,
3 the *h* and forty and four thousand,
20 of a thousand and six *h* furlongs.
21.17 an *h* and forty and four cubits,

HUNGER

Ex 16. 3 to kill the whole assembly with *h*.
Dt 8. 3 thee, and suffered thee to *h*,
28.48 in *h*, and in thirst, and in
32.24 They shall be burnt with *h*, and
Neh 9.15 bread from heaven for their *h*,
Ps 34.10 young lions do lack, and suffer *h*:
Pr 19.15 sleep; an idle soul shall suffer *h*.
Isa 49.10 They shall not *h* nor thirst;
Jer 38. 9 he is like to die for *h* in the place
42.14 trumpet, nor have *h* of bread;
La 2.19 young children, that faint for *h*
4. 9 than they that be slain with *h*:
Eze 34.29 shall be no more consumed with *h*
Mt 5. 6 Blessed are they which do *h* and
Lk 6.21 Blessed are ye that *h* now: for ye
25 you that are full! for ye shall *h*.
15.17 and to spare, and I perish with *h*!
Jn 6.35 that cometh to me shall never *h*;
Ro 12.20 Therefore if thine enemy *h*, feed
1Co 4.11 we both *h*, and thirst, and are
11.34 And if any man *h*, let him eat at
2Co 11.27 often, in *h* and thirst, in fastings
Rev 6. 8 to kill with sword, and with *h*,
7.16 They shall *h* no more, neither

HUNGERED

Mt 21.18 as he returned into the city, he *h*.
Lk 4. 2 they were ended, he afterward *h*.

HUNGRED

Mt 4. 2 nights, he was afterward an *h*.
12. 1 his disciples were an *h*, and began
3 what David did, when he was an *h*,
25.35 I was an *h*, and ye gave me meat:
37 when saw we thee an *h*, and fed
42 For I was an *h*, and ye gave me no
44 Lord, when saw we thee an *h*, or
Mk 2.25 when he had need, and was an *h*,
Lk 6. 3 David did, when himself was an *h*,

HUNGRY

1Sa 2. 5 and they that were *h* ceased:
2Sa 17.29 The people is *h*, and weary, and
2Ki 7.12 They know that we be *h*; therefore
Job 5. 5 Whose harvest the *h* eateth up,
22. 7 hast withholden bread from the *h*.
24.10 take away the sheaf from the *h*;
Ps 50.12 If I were *h*, I would not tell thee:
107. 5 *H* and thirsty, their soul fainted
9 filleth the *h* soul with goodness.
36 there he maketh the *h* to dwell,
146. 7 which giveth food to the *h*.
Pr 6.30 to satisfy his soul when he is *h*;
25.21 If thine enemy be *h*, give him bread
27. 7 to the *h* soul every bitter thing is
Isa 8.21 through it, hardly bestead and *h*:
21 that when they shall be *h*, they
9.20 snatch on the right hand, and be *h*;
29. 8 be as when an *h* man dreameth,
32. 6 to make empty the soul of the *h*,
44.12 he is *h*, and his strength faileth:
58. 7 Is it not to deal thy bread to the *h*,
10 if thou draw out thy soul to the *h*,
65.13 servants shall eat, but ye shall be *h*:
Eze 18. 7, 16 hath given his bread to the *h*,
Mk 11.12 come from Bethany, he was *h*:
Lk 1.53 He hath filled the *h* with good
Ac 10.10 And he became very *h*, and would
1Co 11.21 one is *h*, and another is drunken.
Php 4.12 both to be full and to be *h*, both

HUNT

Gen 27. 5 went to the field to *h* for venison,
1Sa 26.20 *h* a partridge in the mountains.
Job 38.39 Wilt thou *h* the prey for the lion?
Ps 140.11 evil shall *h* the violent man to
Pr 6.26 adulteress will *h* for the precious
Jer 16.16 shall *h* them from every mountain,
La 4.18 They *h* our steps, that we cannot
Eze 13.18 head of every stature to *h* souls!
18 Will ye *h* the souls of my people,
20 wherewith ye there *h* the souls to
20 even the souls that ye *h* to make
Mic 7. 2 they *h* every man his brother with

HUNTER

Gen 10. 9 was a mighty *h* before the Lord:
9 Even as Nimrod the mighty *h*
25.27 Esau was a cunning *h*, a man of
Pr 6. 5 as a roe from the hand of the *h*,

HUNTEST

1Sa 24.11 thee; yet thou *h* my soul to take it.
Job 10.16 Thou *h* me as a fierce lion: and

HURT

Gen 4.23 and a young man to my *h*.
26.29 That thou wilt do us no *h*, as we
31. 7 but God suffered him not to *h* me.
29 the power of my hand to do you *h*:
Ex 21.22 strive, and *h* a woman with child,
35 if one man's ox *h* another's, that he
22.10 and it die, or be *h*, or driven away,
14 ought of his neighbor, and it be *h*,
Nu 16.15 neither have I *h* one of them.
Jos 24.20 then he will turn and do you *h*,
1Sa 20.21 there is peace to thee, and no *h*;
24. 9 Behold, David seeketh thy *h*?
25. 7 which were with us, we *h* them not,
15 good unto us, and we were not *h*,
2Sa 18.32 rise against thee to do thee *h*,
2Ki 14.10 shouldest thou meddle to thy *h*,
2Ch 25.19 shouldest thou meddle to thine *h*,
Ezr 4.22 grow to the *h* of the kings?
Est 9. 2 hand on such as sought their *h*:
Job 35. 8 Thy wickedness may *h* a man as thou
Ps 15. 4 He that sweareth to his own *h*,
35. 4 to confusion that devise my *h*.
26 together that rejoice at mine *h*:
38.12 that seek my *h* speak mischievous
41. 7 against me do they devise my *h*.
70. 2 put to confusion, that desire my *h*.
71.13 and dishonor that seek my *h*.
24 unto shame, that seek my *h*.
105.18 Whose feet they *h* with fetters:
Ec 5.13 for the owners thereof to their *h*.
8. 9 ruleth over another to his own *h*.
10. 9 Whoso removeth stones shall be *h*
Isa 11. 9 They shall not *h* nor destroy in all
27. 3 lest any *h* it, I will keep it night
65.25 They shall not *h* nor destroy in all
Jer 6.14 healed also the *h* of the daughter
7. 6 walk after other gods to your *h*:
8.11 healed the *h* of the daughter of
21 the *h* of the daughter of my people
21 the daughter of my people am I *h*;
10.19 Who is me for my *h*! my wound is
24. 9 kingdoms of the earth for their *h*,
25. 6 hands; and I will do you no *h*.
7 works of your hands to your own *h*.
38. 4 the welfare of this people, but the *h*.
Dan 3.25 of the fire, and they have no *h*;
6.22 mouths, that they have not *h* me:
22 thee, O king, have I done no *h*.
23 no manner of *h* was found upon
Mk 16.18 deadly thing, it shall not *h* them;
Lk 4.35 he came out of him, and *h* him not.
10.19 nothing shall by any means *h* you.
Ac 18.10 no man shall set on thee to *h* thee:
27.10 will be with *h* and much damage,
Rev 2.11 shall not be *h* of the second death.
6. 6 see thou *h* not the oil and the wine.
7. 2 it was given to *h* the earth and the
3 *H* not the earth, neither the sea,
9. 4 should not *h* the grass of the earth,
10 power was to *h* men five months.
19 had heads, and with them they do *h*.
11. 5 any man will *h* them, fire proceedeth
5 if any man will *h* them, he must in

HURTFUL

Ezr 4.15 rebellious city, and *h* unto kings
Ps 144.10 his servant from the *h* sword.
1Ti 6. 9 and into many foolish and *h* lusts,

HURTING

1Sa 25.34 hath kept me back from *h* thee,

HUSBAND

Gen 3. 6 and gave also unto her *h* with her;
16 and thy desire shall be to thy *h*,
16. 3 gave her to her *h* Abram to be his
29.32 now therefore my *h* will love me.
34 time will my *h* be joined unto me,
30.15 matter that thou hast taken my *h*?
18 I have given my maiden to my *h*:
20 now will my *h* dwell with me,
Ex 4.25 Surely a bloody *h* art thou to me.
26 A bloody *h* thou art, because of

Ex 21.22 as the woman's *h* will lay upon
Lev 19.20 is a bondmaid, betrothed to an *h*,
21. 3 nigh unto him, which hath had no *h*;
7 take a woman put away from her *h*:
Nu 5.13 and it be hid from the eyes of her *h*,
19 with another instead of thy *h*;
20 aside to another, instead of thy *h*,
20 have lain with thee beside thine *h*:
27 have done trespass against her *h*,
29 aside to another instead of her *h*,
30. 6 had at all an *h*, when she vowed,
7 her *h* heard it, and held his peace
8 if her *h* disallowed her on the day
11 her *h* heard it, and held his peace
12 if her *h* hath utterly made them void
12 her *h* hath made them void;
13 afflict the soul, her *h* may establish
13 it, or her *h* may make it void.
14 if her *h* altogether hold his peace
Dt 21.13 and be her *h*, and she shall be thy
22.22 with a woman married to an *h*, then
23 is a virgin be betrothed unto an *h*,
24. 3 if the latter *h* hate her, and write
3 or if the latter *h* die, which took her
4 former *h*, which sent her away,
25.11 to deliver her *h* out of the hand of
28.56 be evil toward the *h* of her bosom,
Jdg 13. 6 the woman came and told her *h*,
9 but Manoah her *h* was not with her.
10 haste, and ran, and shewed her *h*,
14.15 Entice thy *h*, that he may declare
19. 3 And her *h* arose, and went after her,
20. 4 And the Levite, the *h* of the woman
Ru 1. 3 Elimelech Naomi's *h* died; and she
5 was left of her two sons and her *h*.
9 each of you in the house of her *h*.
12 way; for I am too old to have a *h*.
12 I should have an *h* also to night,
2.11 in law since the death of thine *h*:
1Sa 1. 8 Then said Elkanah her *h* to her,
22 for she said unto her *h*, I will not
23 And Elkanah her *h* said unto her,
2.19 she came up with her *h* to offer
4.19 father in law and her *h* were dead,
21 of her father in law and her *h*.
25.19 But she told not her *h* Nabal.
2Sa 3.15 and took her from her *h*, even from
16 her *h* went with her along weeping
11.26 heard that Uriah her *h* was dead,
26 was dead, she mourned for her *h*.
14. 5 widow woman, and mine *h* is dead.
7 shall not leave to my *h* neither name
2Ki 4. 1 Thy servant my *h* is dead; and thou
9 she said unto her *h*, Behold now, I
14 she hath no child, and her *h* is old.
22 And she called unto her *h*, and said,
26 Is it well with thy *h*? is it well with
Pr 12. 4 woman is a crown to her *h*:
31.11 The heart of her *h* doth safely trust
23 Her *h* is known in the gates,
28 her *h* also, and he praiseth her.
Isa 54. 5 For thy Maker is thine *h*; the Lord
Jer 3.20 treacherously departeth from her *h*,
6.11 the *h* with the wife shall be taken,
31.32 an *h* unto them, saith the Lord:
Eze 16.32 taketh strangers instead of her *h*!
45 that lotheth her *h* and her children;
44.25 or for sister that hath had no *h*,
Hos 2. 2 is not my wife, neither am I her *h*:
7 I will go and return to my first *h*;
Joel 1. 8 sackcloth for the *h* of her youth.
Mt 1.16 begat Joseph the *h* of Mary, of
19 Then Joseph her *h*, being a just man,
Mk 10.12 a woman shall put away her *h*, and
Lk 2.36 had lived with an *h* seven years
16.18 her that is put away from her *h*
Jn 4.16 Go, call thy *h*, and come hither.
17 answered and said, I have no *h*.
17 Thou hast well said, I have no *h*:
18 whom thou now hast is not thy *h*:
Ac 5. 9 which have buried thy *h* are at the
10 her forth, buried her by her *h*.
Ro 7. 2 woman which hath an *h* is bound
2 by the law to her *h* so long as he
2 if the *h* be dead, she is loosed from
2 she is loosed from the law of her *h*.
3 while her *h* liveth, she be married
3 if her *h* be dead, she is free from
1Co 7. 2 let every woman have her own *h*.
3 Let the *h* render unto the wife due
3 likewise also the wife unto the *h*.
4 power of her own body, but the *h*:
4 likewise also the *h* hath not power
10 Let not the wife depart from her *h*:
11 or be reconciled to her *h*: and let
11 and let not the *h* put away his wife.
13 which hath an *h* that believeth not,
14 the unbelieving *h* is sanctified by
14 wife is sanctified by the *h*:
16 whether thou shalt save thy *h*? or
34 world, how she may please her *h*.
39 by the law as long as her *h* liveth;
39 if her *h* be dead, she is at liberty
2Co 11. 2 for I have espoused you to one *h*,
Gal 4.27 children than she which hath an *h*.
Eph 5.23 For the *h* is the head of the wife,
33 wife see that she reverence her *h*.
1Ti 3. 2 the *h* of one wife, vigilant, sober,
Tit 1. 6 the *h* of one wife, having faithful
Rev 21. 2 as a bride adorned for her *h*.

HUSBANDMAN

Gen 9.20 Noah began to be an *h*, and he
Jer 51.23 I break in pieces the *h* and his yoke
Am 5.16 they shall call the *h* to mourning,
Zec 13. 5 I...no prophet, I am an *h*;
Jn 15. 1 true vine, and my Father is the *h*.
2Ti 2. 6 The *h* that laboreth must be first
Jas 5. 7 the *h* waiteth for the precious fruit

HUSBANDMEN

2Ki 25.12 the land to be vinedressers and *h*.
2Ch 26.10 *h* also, and vine dressers in the
Jer 31.24 *h*, and they that go with flocks.
52.16 land for vinedressers and for *h*.
Joel 1.11 Be ye ashamed, O ye *h*; howl, O
Mt 21.33 let it out to *h*, and went into a far
34 he sent his servants to the *h*, that
35 the *h* took his servants, and beat
38 when the *h* saw the son, they said
40 what will he do unto those *h*?
41 let out his vineyard unto other *h*,
Mk 12. 1 let it out to *h*, and went into a far
2 he sent to the *h* a servant, that he
2 receive from the *h* of the fruit of
7 those *h* said among themselves,
9 will come and destroy the *h*, and
Lk 20. 9 a vineyard and let it forth to *h*,
10 sent a servant to the *h*, that they
10 the *h* beat him, and sent him away
14 when the *h* saw him, they reasoned
16 shall come and destroy these *h*,

HUSBANDRY

2Ch 26.10 and in Carmel: for he loved *h*.
1Co 3. 9 with God: ye are God's *h*, ye are

HUSBAND'S

Nu 30.10 vowed in her *h* house, or bound
Dt 25. 5 her *h* brother shall go in unto her,
5 perform the duty of an *h* brother
7 My *h* brother refuseth to raise up
7 perform the duty of my *h* brother.
Ru 2. 1 kinsman of her *h*, a mighty man

HUSBANDS

Ru 1.11 womb, that they may be your *h*?
13 ye stay for them from having *h*?
Est 1.17 they shall despise their *h* in their
20 wives shall give to their *h* honor,
Jer 29. 6 and give your daughters to *h*, that
Eze 16.45 lothed their *h* and their children:
Jn 4.18 For thou hast had five *h*; and he
1Co 14.35 let them ask their *h* at home: for it
Eph 5.22 submit yourselves unto your own *h*,
24 be to their own *h* in every thing.
25 *H*, love your wives, even as Christ
Col 3.18 submit yourselves unto your own *h*,
19 *H*, love your wives, and be not bitter
1Ti 3.12 deacons be the *h* of one wife, ruling
Tit 2. 4 love their *h*, to love their children,
5 obedient to their own *h*, that the
1Pe 3. 1 wives, in subjection to your own *h*;
5 in subjection unto their own *h*:
7 Likewise, ye *h*, dwell with them

HUSKS

Lk 15.16 filled his belly with the *h* that

HYMN

Mt 26.30 they had sung an *h*, they went out
Mk 14.26 they had sung an *h*, they went out

HYMNS

Eph 5.19 in psalms and *h* and spiritual
Col 3.16 in psalms and *h* and spiritual

HYPOCRISIES

1Pe 2. 1 and all guile, and *h*, and envies,

HYPOCRISY

Isa 32. 6 work iniquity, to practise *h*, and
Mt 23.28 within ye are full of *h* and
Mk 12.15 knowing their *h*, said unto them,
Lk 12. 1 leaven of the Pharisees, which is *h*.
1Ti 4. 2 Speaking lies in *h*; having their
Jas 3.17 without partiality, and without *h*.

HYPOCRITE

Job 13.16 for an *h* shall not come before
17. 8 stir up himself against the *h*.
20. 5 the joy of the *h* but for a moment?
27. 8 For what is the hope of the *h*,
34.30 That the *h* reign not, lest
Pr 11. 9 An *h* with his mouth destroyeth
Isa 9.17 for every one is a *h* and an
Mt 7. 5 Thou *h*, first cast out the beam
Lk 6.42 Thou *h*, cast out first the beam
13.15 Thou *h*, doth not each one of you

HYPOCRITES

Job 15.34 the congregation of *h* shall be
36.13 But the *h* in heart heap up wrath:
Isa 33.14 hath surprised the *h*.
Mt 6. 2 as the *h* do in the synagogues
5 thou shalt not be as the *h* are: for
16 when ye fast, be not, as the *h*, of
15. 7 Ye *h*, well did Esaias prophesy of
16. 3 O ye *h*, ye can discern the face
22.18 and said, Why tempt ye me, ye *h*?
23.13 scribes and Pharisees, *h*! for ye
14 scribes and Pharisees, *h*! for ye
15, 23, 25, 27 scribes and Pharisees, *h*!
29 scribes and Pharisees, *h*! because
24.51 appoint him his portion with the *h*:
Mk 7. 6 Esaias prophesied of you *h*, as it is
Lk 11.44 scribes and Pharisees, *h*! for ye
12.56 Ye *h*, ye can discern the face of the

HYSSOP

Ex 12.22 ye shall take a bunch of *h*, and dip
Lev 14. 4 cedar wood, and scarlet, and *h*:
6 wood, and the scarlet, and the *h*,
49 cedar wood, and scarlet, and *h*:
51 the cedar wood, and the *h*, and the
52 cedar wood, and with the *h*, and
Nu 19. 6 cedar wood, and *h*, and scarlet,
18 a clean person shall take *h*, and
1Ki 4.33 the *h* that springeth out of the
Ps 51. 7 Purge me with *h*, and I shall be
Jn 19.29 with vinegar, and put it upon *h*,
Heb 9.19 water, and scarlet wool, and *h*, and

I

ICONIUM
Ac 13.51 against them, and came unto *I*.
14. 1 And it came to pass in *I*, that they
19 certain Jews from Antioch and *I*.
21 to Lystra, and to *I*, and Antioch,
16. 2 brethren that were at Lystra and *I*.
2Ti 3.11 unto me at Antioch, at *I*, at Lystra;

IDLE
Ex 5. 8 for they be *i*; therefore they cry,
17 But he said, Ye are *i*, ye are *i*:
Pr 19.15 and an *i* soul shall suffer hunger.
Mt 12.36 That every *i* word that men shall
20. 3 and saw others standing *i* in the
6 found others standing *i*, and saith
6 Why stand ye here all the day *i*?
Lk 24.11 words seemed to them as *i* tales,
1Ti 5.13 And withal they learn to be *i*,
13 not only *i*, but tattlers also and

IDLENESS
Pr 31.27 and eateth not the bread of *i*.
Ec 10.18 and through *i* of the hands the
Eze 16.49 and abundance of *i* was in her

IDOL
1Ki 15.13 she had made an *i* in a grove;
13 Asa destroyed her *i*, and burnt it
2Ch 15.16 because she had made an *i* in a
16 grove: and Asa cut down her *i*,
33. 7 image, the *i* which he had made,
15 the *i* out of the house of the Lord,
Isa 48. 5 Mine *i* hath done them, and my
66. 3 incense, as if he blessed an *i*.
Jer 22.28 man Coniah a despised broken *i*?
Zec 11.17 Woe to the *i* shepherd that leaveth
Ac 7.41 and offered a sacrifice unto the *i*,
1Co 8. 4 we know that an *i* is nothing in
7 with conscience of the *i* unto this
7 eat it as a thing offered unto an *i*;
10.19 say I then? that the *i* is any thing,

IDOLATER
1Co 5.11 a fornicator, or covetous, or an *i*,
Eph 5. 5 nor covetous man, who is an *i*.

IDOLATERS
1Co 5.10 or extortioners, or with *i*;
6. 9 neither fornicators, nor *i*, nor
10. 7 Neither be *i*, as were some of
Rev 21. 8 *i*, and all liars, shall have their
22.15 and murderers, and *i*, and

IDOLATRIES
1Pe 4. 3 banquetings, and abominable *i*:

IDOLATRY
1Sa 15.23 stubbornness is as iniquity and *i*.
Ac 17.16 he saw the city wholly given to *i*.
1Co 10.14 my dearly beloved, flee from *i*.
Gal 5.20 *I*, witchcraft, hatred, variance,
Col 3. 5 and covetousness, which is *i*:
(See box on page 386)

IDOL'S
1Co 8.10 sit at meat in the *i* temple, shall

IDOLS
Lev 19. 4 Turn ye not unto *i*, nor make
26. 1 Ye shall make you no *i* nor graven
Dt 29.17 and their *i*, wood and stone, silver
1Ch 16.26 all the gods of the people are *i*:
Ps 115. 4 Their *i* are silver and gold, the
Isa 2.20 day a man shall cast his *i* of silver,
20 and his *i* of gold, which they made
31. 7 man shall cast away his *i* of silver,
7 and his *i* of gold, which your own
Eze 14. 4 that setteth up his *i* in his heart,
5 estranged from me through their *i*.
6 turn yourselves from your *i*; and
20.16 for their heart went after their *i*.
30.13 I will also destroy the *i*, and I will
Mic 1. 7 all the *i* thereof will I lay desolate:
Hab 2.18 trusteth therein, to make dumb *i*?
Zec 10. 2 For the *i* have spoken vanity,
Ac 15.20 they abstain from pollutions of *i*,
Ac 15.29 abstain from meats offered to *i*,
21.25 from things offered to *i*, and from
Ro 2.22 thou that abhorrest *i*, dost thou
1Co 8. 1 as touching things offered to *i*, we
4 that are offered in sacrifice unto *i*,
10 those things which are offered to *i*;
10.19 which is offered in sacrifice to *i* is
28 offered in sacrifice unto *i*, eat not
12. 2 carried away unto these dumb *i*,
2Co 6.16 hath the temple of God with *i*?
1Th 1. 9 ye turned to God from *i* to serve
1Jn 5.21 children, keep yourselves from *i*.
Rev 2.14 eat things sacrificed unto *i*, and
20 and to eat things sacrificed unto *i*.
9.20 *i* of gold, and silver, and brass,

IGNORANCE
Lev 4. 2 If a soul shall sin through *i*
13 of Israel sin through *i*,
22 done somewhat through *i*
27 common people sin through *i*,
5.15 a trespass, and sin through *i*,
18 his *i* wherein he erred and wist it
Nu 15.24 if ought be committed by *i*
25 shall be forgiven them; for it is *i*:
25 before the Lord, for their *i*:

The idol of the golden calf (Ex 32) epitomized the graven images forbidden by God's first commandment.

Nu 15.26 seeing all the people were in *i*.
27 if any soul sin through *i*, then he
28 he sinneth by *i* before the Lord,
29 for him that sinneth through *i*,
Ac 3.17 brethren, I wot that through *i* ye did
17.30 the times of this *i* God winked at;
Eph 4.18 God through the *i* that is in them,
1Pe 1.14 to the former lusts in your *i*:
2.15 to silence the *i* of foolish men:

IGNORANT

Ps 73.22 So foolish was I, and *i*: I was
Isa 56.10 they are all *i*, they are all
63.16 though Abraham be *i* of us,
Ac 4.13 they were unlearned and *i* men,
Ro 1.13 Now I would not have you *i*,
10. 3 For they being *i* of God's
11.25 that ye should be *i* of this mystery,
1Co 10. 1 I would not that ye should be *i*,
12. 1 brethren, I would not have you *i*.
14.38 if any man be *i*, let him be *i*.
2Co 1. 8 would not, brethren, have you *i* of
2.11 of us: for we are not *i* of his devices.
1Th 4.13 But I would not have you to be *i*,
Heb 5. 2 Who can have compassion on the *i*,
2Pe 3. 5 For this they willingly are *i* of
8 beloved, be not *i* of this one thing,

IGNORANTLY

Nu 15.28 for the soul that sinneth *i*, when
Dt 19. 4 Whoso killeth...neighbor *i*,
Ac 17.23 Whom therefore ye *i* worship, him
1Ti 1.13 mercy, because I did it *i* in unbelief.

ILL

Gen 41. 3 them out of the river, *i* favored
4 the *i* favored and leanfleshed kine
19 up after them, poor and very *i*
20 the lean and the *i* favored kine
21 they were still *i* favored, as at
27 the seven thin and *i* favored kine
43. 6 dealt so *i* with me, as to tell
Dt 15.21 blind, or have any *i* blemish,
Job 20.26 it shall go *i* with him that is left
Ps 106.32 so that it went *i* with Moses for
Isa 3.11 it shall be *i* with him: for the
Jer 40. 4 if it seem *i* unto thee to come
Joel 2.20 and his *i* savour shall come up,
Mic 3. 4 they have behaved themselves *i*
Ro 13.10 Love worketh no *i* to his

ILLUMINATED

Heb 10.32 in which, after ye were *i*, ye

ILLYRICUM

Ro 15.19 and round about unto *I*, I have

IMAGE

Gen 1.26 said, Let us make man in our *i*,
27 God created man in his own *i*,
27 in the *i* of God created he him;
5. 3 in his own likeness, after his *i*;
9. 6 for in the *i* of God made he man,
Ex 20. 4 not make unto thee any graven *i*,
1Sa 19.13 Michal took an *i*, and laid it in
16 behold, there was an *i* in the bed,
2Ki 3. 2 he put away the *i* of Baal that
Job 4.16 an *i* was before mine eyes, there
Ps 73.20 thou shalt despise their *i*.
Isa 40.19 The workman melteth a graven *i*,
44.10 formed a god, or molten a graven *i*
15 he maketh it a graven *i*, and falleth
17 he maketh a god, even his graven *i*:
Dan 2.31 king, sawest, and behold a great *i*.
3. 1 the king made an *i* of gold, whose
10 fall down and worship the golden *i*:
12 nor worship the golden *i* which
Hos 3. 4 and without an *i*, and without an
Mt 22.20 Whose is this *i* and superscription?
Mk 12.16 Whose is this *i* and superscription?
Lk 20.24 Whose *i* and superscription hath

Biblical Themes

IDOLATRY

Thou shalt have no other gods before me. Thou shalt not make unto thee any graven image . . . for I the Lord thy God am a jealous God. Ex 20.3-5

[Moses] took the calf which they had made, and burnt it in the fire, and ground it to powder, and strawed it upon the water, and made the children of Israel drink of it. Ex 32.20

They provoked [God] to jealousy with strange gods, with abominations provoked they him to anger. They sacrificed unto devils, not to God; to gods whom they knew not, to new gods that came newly up, whom your fathers feared not. Dt 32.16-17

They took the bullock . . . and they dressed it, and called on the name of Baal from morning even until noon, saying, O Baal, hear us. But there was no voice, nor any that answered. And they leaped upon the altar which was made. And it came to pass at noon, that Elijah mocked them, and said, Cry aloud: for he is a god; either he is talking, or he is pursuing, or he is in a journey, or peradventure he sleepeth, and must be awaked. 1Ki 18.26-27

Every nation made gods of their own, and put them in the houses of the high places which the Samaritans had made. 2Ki 17.29

If we have forgotten the name of our God, or stretched out our hands to a strange god; shall not God search this out? Ps 44.20-21

All the gods of the nations are idols: but the Lord made the heavens. Ps 96.5

Be astonished, O ye heavens . . . and be horribly afraid, be ye very desolate, saith the Lord. For my people have committed two evils; they have forsaken me the fountain of living waters, and hewed them out cisterns, broken cisterns, that can hold no water. Jer 2.12-13

When the people saw what Paul had done, they lifted up their voices, saying in the speech of Lycaonia, The gods are come down to us in the likeness of men. . . . Which when the apostles, Barnabas and Paul, heard of, they rent their clothes, and ran in among the people, crying out, and saying, Sirs, why do ye these things? We also are men of like passions with you, and preach unto you that ye should turn from these vanities unto the living God. Ac 14.11, 14-15

Demetrius, a silversmith, which made silver shrines for Diana . . . said, Sirs, ye know that by this craft we have our wealth. Moreover ye see and hear, that . . . this Paul hath persuaded and turned away much people, saying that they be no gods, which are made with hands: so that not only this our craft is in danger to be set at nought; but also that the temple of the great goddess Diana should be despised . . . whom all Asia and the world worshippeth. And when they heard these sayings, they were full of wrath, and cried out, saying, Great is Diana of the Ephesians. Ac 19.24-28

Professing themselves to be wise, they became fools, and changed the glory of the uncorruptible God into an image made like to corruptible man, and to birds, and fourfooted beasts, and creeping things. Ro 1.22-23

The things which the Gentiles sacrifice, they sacrifice to devils, and not to God: and I would not that ye should have fellowship with devils. Ye cannot drink the cup of the Lord, and the cup of devils. 1Co 10.20-21

What agreement hath the temple of God with idols? for ye are the temple of the living God. 2Co 6.16

If any man worship the beast and his image, and receive his mark in his forehead, or in his hand, the same shall drink of the wine of the wrath of God. Rev 14.9-10

Ac 19.35 *i* which fell down from Jupiter?
Ro 1.23 into an *i* made like to corruptible
8.29 conformed to the *i* of his Son, that
11. 4 not bowed the knee to the *i* of Baal.
1Co 11. 7 as he is the *i* and glory of God:
15.49 as we have borne the *i* of the earthy,
49 also bear the *i* of the heavenly.
2Co 3.18 changed into the same *i* from glory
4. 4 gospel of Christ, who is the *i* of God,
Col 1.15 Who is the *i* of the invisible God,
3.10 after the *i* of him that created him:
Heb 1. 3 and the express *i* of his person,
10. 1 not the very image of the things,
Rev 13.14 they should make an *i* to the beast,
15 to give life unto the *i* of the beast,
15 *i* of the beast should both speak,
15 not worship the *i* of the beast
14. 9 man worship the beast and his *i*,
11 who worship the beast and his *i*,
15. 2 victory over the beast, and over his *i*,
16. 2 upon them which worshipped his *i*.
19.20 and them that worshipped his *i*.
20. 4 worshipped the beast, neither his *i*,

IMAGERY

Eze 8.12 man in the chambers of his *i*?

IMAGE'S

Dan 2.32 This *i* head was of fine gold,

IMAGES

Gen 31.19 Rachel had stolen the *i* that were
Lev 26.30 cut down your *i*, and cast your
Dt 7. 5 and burn their graven *i* with fire.
2Ki 10.26 forth the *i* out of the house of Baal,
17.41 and served their graven *i*, both
23.24 wizards, and the *i*, and the idols,
2Ch 33.22 sacrificed unto all the carved *i*
34. 7 beaten the graven *i* into powder,
Ps 97. 7 be all they that serve graven *i*,
Isa 21. 9 and all the graven *i* of her gods
27. 9 the groves and *i* shall not stand
41.29 their molten *i* are wind and confusion.
42. 8 neither my praise to graven *i*.
17 that say to the molten *i*, Ye are our
Jer 51.47 upon the graven *i* of Babylon:
Eze 6. 4 your *i* shall be broken: and I will
16.17 and madest to thyself *i* of men, and
Hos 10. 1 his land they have made goodly *i*.
Am 5.26 Moloch and Chiun your *i*, the
Mic 5.13 Thy graven *i* also will I cut off,

IMAGINATION

Gen 6. 5 every *i* of the thoughts of his
8.21 the *i* of man's heart is evil from
Dt 29.19 I walk in the *i* of mine heart,
31.21 for I know their *i* which they go
1Ch 29.18 keep this for ever in the *i* of the
Jer 3.17 after the *i* of their evil heart.
7.24 and in the *i* of their evil heart,
9.14 the *i* of their own heart, and after
11. 8 one in the *i* of their evil heart:
13.10 walk in the *i* of their heart, and
16.12 one after the *i* of his evil heart,
18.12 every one do the *i* of his evil heart.
23.17 after the *i* of his own heart,
Lk 1.51 proud in the *i* of their hearts.

IMAGINATIONS

1Ch 28. 9 all the *i* of the thoughts: if thou
Pr 6.18 An heart that deviseth wicked *i*,
La 3.60 and all their *i* against me.
61 Lord, and all their *i* against me;
Ro 1.21 became vain in their *i*, and their
2Co 10. 5 Casting down *i*, and every high

IMAGINE

Job 6.26 Do ye *i* to reprove words, and
21.27 the devices which ye wrongfully *i*
Ps 2. 1 and the people *i* a vain thing?
38.12 and *i* deceits all the day long.
62. 3 will ye *i* mischief against a man?
140. 2 Which *i* mischiefs in their heart;
Pr 12.20 in the heart of them that *i* evil:
Hos 7.15 yet do they *i* mischief against
Na 1. 9 What do ye *i* against the Lord?
Zec 7.10 you *i* evil against his brother
8.17 none of you *i* evil in your hearts
Ac 4.25 rage, and the people *i* vain things?

IMMANUEL

Isa 7.14 a son, and shall call his name *I*
8. 8 fill the breadth of the land, O *I*.

IMMEDIATELY

Mt 4.22 And they *i* left the ship, and
8. 3 And *i* his leprosy was cleansed.
14.31 And *i* Jesus stretched forth his
20.34 *i* their eyes received sight, and
24.29 *i* after the tribulation of those
26.74 the man. And *i* the cock crew.
Mk 1.12 *i* the spirit driveth him into the
28 *i* his fame spread abroad
31 *i* the fever left her, and she
42 *i* the leprosy departed from him,
2. 8 *i* when Jesus perceived in his
12 And *i* he arose, took up the bed,
4. 5 and *i* it sprang up, because it
15 Satan cometh *i*, and taketh away
16 word, *i* receive it with gladness;
17 word's sake, *i* they are offended.
29 *i* he putteth in the sickle,
5. 2 *i* there met him out of the tombs
30 Jesus, *i* knowing in himself that
6.27 *i* the king sent an executioner,
50 *i* he talked with them, and saith
10.52 And *i* he received his sight, and
14.43 And *i*, while he yet spake,
Lk 1.64 And his mouth was opened *i*, and
4.39 *i* she arose and ministered unto
5.13 *i* the leprosy departed from him.
25 And *i* he rose up before them,
6.49 beat vehemently, and *i* it fell;
8.44 and *i* her issue of blood stanched.
47 him, and how she was healed *i*.
12.36 they may open unto him *i*.
13.13 and *i* she was made straight,
18.43 And *i* he received his sight, and
19.11 kingdom of God should *i* appear.
40 peace, the stones would *i* cry out.
22.60 And *i*, while he yet spake, the
Jn 5. 9 *i* the man was made whole, and
6.21 *i* the ship was at the land
13.30 received the sop went *i* out:
18.27 again: and *i* the cock crew
21. 3 forth, and entered into a ship *i*;
Ac 3. 7 and *i* his feet and ankle bones
9.18 *i* there fell from his eyes as it
34 make thy bed. And he arose *i*.
10.33 *I* therefore I sent to thee; and
11.11 *i* there were three men already
12.23 And *i* the angel of the Lord smote
13.11 And *i* there fell on him a mist and
16.10 *i* we endeavoured to go into
26 and *i* all the doors were opened,
17.10 the brethren *i* sent away Paul
14 *i* the brethren sent away Paul
21.32 Who *i* took soldiers and
Gal 1.16 *i* I conferred not with flesh and
Rev 4. 2 And *i* I was in the spirit: and

IMMORTAL

1Ti 1.17 Now unto the King eternal, *i*,

IMMORTALITY

Ro 2. 7 glory and honor and *i*, eternal
1Co 15.53 and this mortal must put on *i*.
54 this mortal shall have put on *i*,
1Ti 6.16 Who only hath *i*, dwelling in the
2Ti 1.10 hath brought life and *i* to light
(See box on page 389)

IMMUTABILITY

Heb 6.17 the *i* of his counsel, confirmed it

IMMUTABLE

Heb 6.18 That by two *i* things, in which it

IMPART

Lk 3.11 let him *i* to him that hath none;
Ro 1.11 *i* unto you some spiritual gift,

IMPARTED

Job 39.17 hath he *i* to her understanding.
1Th 2. 8 were willing to have *i* unto you,

IMPEDIMENT

Mk 7.32 deaf, and had an *i* in his speech;

IMPENITENT

Ro 2. 5 But, after thy hardness and *i* heart

IMPLACABLE

Ro 1.31 without natural affection, *i*,

IMPLEAD

Ac 19.38 deputies: let them *i* one another.

IMPORTUNITY

Lk 11. 8 yet because of his *i* he will rise

IMPOSED

Heb 9.10 *i* on them until the time of

IMPOSSIBLE

Mt 17.20 and nothing shall be *i* unto you.
19.26 With men this is *i*; but with God
Mk 10.27 With men it is *i*, but not with God:
Lk 1.37 with God nothing shall be *i*.
17. 1 is *i* but that offenses will come:
18.27 things which are *i* with men are
Heb 6. 4 For it is *i* for those who were once
18 in which it was *i* for God to lie,
11. 6 without faith it is *i* to please him:

IMPOTENT

Jn 5. 3 lay a great multitude of *i* folk,
7 The *i* man answered him, Sir, I
Ac 4. 9 the good deed done to the *i* man,
14. 8 certain man at Lystra, *i* in his feet,

IMPRISONED

Ac 22.19 know that I *i* and beat in every

IMPRISONMENT

Ezr 7.26 or to confiscation of goods, or to *i*.
Heb 11.36 yea, moreover of bonds and *i*:

IMPRISONMENTS

2Co 6. 5 In stripes, in *i*, in tumults, in

IMPUTE

1Sa 22.15 king *i* any thing unto his servant,
2Sa 19.19 Let not my lord *i* iniquity unto
Ro 4. 8 to whom the Lord will not *i* sin.

IMPUTED

Lev 7.18 it be *i* unto him that offereth it:
17. 4 blood shall be *i* unto that man; he
Ro 4.11 might be *i* unto them also:
22 therefore it was *i* to him for
23 sake alone, that it was *i* to him;
24 to whom it shall be *i*, if we believe
5.13 sin is not *i* when there is no law.
Jas 2.23 and it was *i* unto him for

IMPUTETH

Ps 32. 2 whom the Lord *i* not iniquity,
Ro 4. 6 unto whom God *i* righteousness

IMPUTING

Hab 1.11 offend, *i* this his power unto his God.
2Co 5.19 not *i* their trespasses unto them;

INASMUCH

Dt 19. 6 of death, *i* as he hated him not
Ru 3.10 *i* as thou followedst not young
Mt 25.40 *I* as ye have done it unto one
45 *I* as ye did it not to one of the
Ro 11.13 *i* as I am the apostle of the
Php 1. 7 *i* as both in my bonds, and in
Heb 3. 3 *i* as he who hath builded the
7.20 And *i* as not without an oath
1Pe 4.13 *i* as ye are partakers of Christ's

INCENSE

Ex 30. 8 at even, he shall burn *i* upon it,
8 a perpetual *i* before the Lord
Lev 10. 1 put fire therein, and put *i* thereon,
16.13 he shall put the *i* upon the fire
Nu 16. 7 put *i* in them before the Lord to
17 man his censer, and put *i* in them,
40 near to offer *i* before the Lord;
2Ki 12. 3 people still sacrificed and burnt *i*
18. 4 children of Israel did burn *i* to it:
23. 5 them also that burned *i* unto Baal,
2Ch 34.25 and have burned *i* unto other gods,
Ps 141. 2 prayer be set forth before thee as *i*;
Isa 1.13 *i* is an abomination unto me;
60. 6 they shall bring gold and *i*; and
Jer 18.15 they have burned *i* to vanity, and
44.18 to burn *i* to the queen of heaven,

Incense was burned daily at the temple in Jerusalem, and carried in a censer into the Holy of Holies by the high priest once a year, on the Day of Atonement; this engraving depicts him with his Levite attendants.

Eze 8.11 and a thick cloud of *i* went up.
Mal 1.11 in every place *i* shall be offered
Lk 1. 9 his lot was to burn *i* when he went
10 praying without at the time of *i*.
11 on the right side of the altar of *i*.
Rev 8. 3 there was given unto him much *i*,
4 the smoke of the *i*, which came

INCENSED

Isa 41.11 all they that were *i* against thee
45.24 and all that are *i* against him shall

INCLINE

Jos 24.23 and *i* your heart unto the Lord
1Ki 8.58 That he may *i* our hearts unto him,
Ps 17. 6 *i* thine ear unto me, and hear my
45.10 and consider, and *i* thine ear;
49. 4 I will *i* mine ear to a parable:
71. 2 escape: *i* thine ear unto me, and
78. 1 *i* your ears to the words of my
88. 2 thee: *i* thine ear unto my cry;
102. 2 *i* thine ear unto me: in the day
119.36 *I* my heart unto thy testimonies,
141. 4 *I* not my heart to any evil thing,
Pr 2. 2 thou *i* thine ear unto wisdom,
4.20 *i* thine ear unto my sayings.
Isa 37.17 *I* thine ear, O Lord, and hear;
55. 3 *I* your ear, and come unto me:
Dan 9.18 O my God, *i* thine ear, and hear;

INCLINED

Jdg 9. 3 and their hearts *i* to follow
Ps 40. 1 and he *i* unto me, and heard my
116. 2 Because he hath *i* his ear unto me,
119.112 I have *i* mine heart to perform
Pr 5.13 nor *i* mine ear to them that
Jer 7.24 hearkened not, nor *i* their ear,
26 not unto me, nor *i* their ear,
11. 8 they obeyed not, nor *i* their ear,
17.23 obeyed not, neither *i* their ear,
25. 4 hearkened, nor *i* your ear to hear.
34.14 not unto me, neither *i* their ear.
35.15 ye have not *i* your ear, nor
44. 5 nor *i* their ear to turn from their

INCLOSED

Ex 39. 6 onyx stones *i* in ouches of gold,
13 they were *i* in ouches of gold in
Jdg 20.43 Thus they *i* the Benjamites
Ps 17.10 They are *i* in their own fat: with
22.16 assembly of the wicked have *i* me:
SS 4.12 A garden *i* is my sister, my
La 3. 9 He hath *i* my ways with hewn
Lk 5. 6 they *i* a great multitude of fishes:

INCONTINENCY

1Co 7. 5 Satan tempt you not for your *i*.

INCONTINENT

2Ti 3. 3 false accusers, *i*, fierce, despisers

INCORRUPTIBLE

1Co 9.25 corruptible crown; but we an *i*.
15.52 and the dead shall be raised *i*,
1Pe 1. 4 To an inheritance *i*, and undefiled,
23 corruptible seed, but of *i*,

INCORRUPTION

1Co 15.42 in corruption; it is raised in *i*:
50 neither doth corruption inherit *i*.
53 must put on *i*, and this mortal
54 corruptible shall have put on *i*,

INCREASE

Lev 26. 4 the land shall yield her *i*, and the
Dt 16.15 God shall bless thee in all thine *i*,
Job 8. 7 thy latter end should greatly *i*.
Ps 44.12 not *i* thy wealth by their price.
62.10 if riches *i*, set not your heart upon
67. 6 Then shall the earth yield her *i*;
71.21 Thou shalt *i* my greatness, and
85.12 and our land shall yield her *i*.
Pr 9. 9 man, and he will *i* in learning.
14. 4 much *i* is by the strength of the ox.
22.16 oppresseth the poor to *i* his riches,
Isa 9. 7 Of the *i* of his government and
Eze 34.27 and the earth shall yield her *i*,
Zec 8.12 and the ground shall give her *i*,
Lk 17. 5 said unto the Lord, *I* our faith.
Jn 3.30 He must *i*, but I must decrease.
1Co 3. 6 Apollos watered; but God gave the *i*.
7 watereth; but God that giveth the *i*.
2Co 9.10 *i* the fruits of your righteousness;
Eph 4.16 *i* of the body unto the edifying
Col 2.19 increaseth with the *i* of God.
1Th 3.12 the Lord make you to *i* and abound
4.10 that ye *i* more and more;
2Ti 2.16 they will *i* unto more ungodliness.

INCREASED

Gen 7.17 and the waters *i*, and bare up the
18 and were *i* greatly upon the earth;
Ezr 9. 6 for our iniquities are *i* over our
Ps 3. 1 Lord, how are they *i* that trouble
4. 7 that their corn and their wine *i*.
Pr 9.11 and the years of thy life shall be *i*.
Isa 9. 3 the nation, and not *i* the joy:
Jer 3.16 ye be multiplied and *i* in the land,
Eze 28. 5 thy traffick hast thou *i* thy riches,
Hos 4. 7 As they were *i*, so they sinned
Mk 4. 8 yield fruit that sprang up and *i*,
Lk 2.52 Jesus *i* in wisdom and stature,
Ac 6. 7 And the word of God *i*; and the
9.22 Saul *i* the more in strength, and
16. 5 the faith, and *i* in number daily.
2Co 10.15 having hope, when your faith is *i*,
Rev 3.17 I am rich, and *i* with goods, and

INCREASETH

Job 10.16 For it *i*. Thou huntest me as a
12.23 He *i* the nations, and destroyeth
Ps 74.23 rise up against thee *i* continually.
Pr 11.24 is that scattereth, and yet *i*;
16.21 sweetness of the lips *i* learning.
23.28 *i* the transgressors among men.
24. 5 yea, a man of knowledge *i* strength.
28. 8 that by usury and unjust gain *i*
29.16 are multiplied, transgression *i*:
Ec 1.18 he that *i* knowledge, *i* sorrow.
Isa 40.29 that have no might he *i* strength.
Hos 12. 1 he daily *i* lies and desolation;
Hab 2. 6 to him that *i* that which is not his
Col 2.19 together, *i* with the increase of God.

INCREASING

Col 1.10 and *i* in the knowledge of God;

INCREDIBLE

Ac 26. 8 it be thought a thing *i* with you,

INDEBTED

Lk 11. 4 forgive every one that is *i* to us.

INDEED

Gen 17.19 thy wife shall bear thee a son *i*;
37. 8 or shalt thou *i* have dominion over us?
Dt 2.15 For *i* the hand of the Lord was
1Ki 8.27 But will God *i* dwell on the earth?
1Ch 4.10 Oh that thou wouldest bless me *i*, and
Isa 6. 9 people, Hear ye *i*, but understand not;
9 and see ye *i*, but perceive not.
Mt 3.11 I *i* baptize you with water unto
13.32 Which *i* is the least of all seeds:
20.23 them, Ye shall drink *i* of my cup,
23.27 which *i* appear beautiful outward,
26.41 the spirit *i* is willing, but the flesh
Mk 1. 8 I *i* have baptized you with water:
9.13 That Elias is *i* come, and they
10.39 Ye shall *i* drink of the cup that
11.32 John, that he was a prophet *i*.
14.21 The Son of man *i* goeth, as it is
Lk 3.16 I *i* baptize you with water; but
11.48 for they *i* killed them, and ye build
23.41 And we *i* justly; for we receive the
24.34 Saying, The Lord is risen *i*, and
Jn 1.47 Behold an Israelite *i*, in whom is
4.42 this is *i* the Christ, the Saviour of
6.55 For my flesh is meat *i*,
55 and my blood is drink *i*.

BIBLICAL THEMES

IMMORTALITY

The Lord God said, Behold, the man is become as one of us, to know good and evil: and now, lest he . . . take also of the tree of life, and eat, and live for ever: therefore the Lord God sent him forth from the garden. . . . and he placed at the east of the garden of Eden Cherubims, and a flaming sword which turned every way, to keep the way of the tree of life. Gen 3.22-24

There appeared a chariot of fire, and horses of fire . . . and Elijah went up by a whirlwind into heaven. 2Ki 2.11

I know that my redeemer liveth, and that he shall stand at the latter day upon the earth: and though after my skin worms destroy this body, yet in my flesh shall I see God. Job 19.25-26

Thou wilt not leave my soul in hell; neither wilt thou suffer thine Holy One to see corruption. Thou wilt shew me the path of life: in thy presence is fulness of joy; at thy right hand there are pleasures for evermore. Ps 16.10-11

I shall not die, but live. . . . The Lord hath chastened me sore: but he hath not given me over unto death. Open to me the gates of righteousness: I will go into them, and I will praise the Lord. Ps 118.17-19

He said unto me, Prophesy upon these bones, and say unto them, O ye dry bones, hear the word of the Lord. Thus saith the Lord God unto these bones; Behold, I will cause breath to enter into you, and ye shall live: and I will lay sinews upon you, and will bring up flesh upon you, and cover you with skin, and put breath in you, and ye shall live; and ye shall know that I am the Lord. Eze 37.4-6

And many of them that sleep in the dust of the earth shall awake, some to everlasting life, and some to shame and everlasting contempt. And they that be wise shall shine as the brightness of the firmament. Dan 12.2-3

The children of this world marry, and are given in marriage: but they which shall be accounted worthy to obtain that world, and the resurrection from the dead, neither marry, nor are given in marriage: neither can they die any more: for they are equal unto the angels; and are the children of God. . . . For he is not a God of the dead, but of the living: for all live unto him. Lk 20.34-36, 38

This is the will of him that sent me, that every one which seeth the Son, and believeth on him, may have everlasting life: and I will raise him up at the last day. Jn 6.40

I am the resurrection, and the life: he that believeth in me, though he were dead, yet shall he live: and whosoever liveth and believeth in me shall never die. Jn 11.25-26

The wages of sin is death; but the gift of God is eternal life through Jesus Christ our Lord. Ro 6.23

We look for the Saviour, the Lord Jesus Christ: who shall change our vile body, that it may be fashioned like unto his glorious body. Php 3.20-21

By faith Abel . . . obtained witness that he was righteous . . . and by it he being dead yet speaketh. By faith Enoch was translated that he should not see death . . . for before his translation he had this testimony, that he pleased God. But without faith it is impossible to please him. Heb 11.4-6

And he shewed me a pure river of water of life, clear as crystal, proceeding out of the throne of God. . . . and on either side of the river, was there the tree of life, which . . . yielded her fruit every month: and the leaves of the tree were for the healing of the nations. . . . And there shall be no night there; and they need no candle, neither light of the sun; for the Lord God giveth them light: and they shall reign for ever and ever. Rev 22.1-2, 5

7.26 know *i* that this is the very Christ?
8.31 word, then are ye my disciples *i*;
36 make you free, ye shall be free *i*.
Ac 4.16 for that *i* a noble miracle hath
11.16 John *i* baptized with water; but ye
22. 9 that were with me saw *i* the light,
Ro 6.11 to be dead *i* unto sin, but alive
8. 7 the law of God, neither *i* can be.
14.20 All things *i* are pure; but it is evil
1Co 11. 7 For a man *i* ought not to cover his
2Co 8.17 For *i* he accepted the exhortation;
11. 1 in my folly: and *i* bear with me.

Php 1.15 Some *i* preach Christ even of envy
2.27 For *i* he was sick nigh unto death:
3. 1 to me *i* is not grievous, but for you
Col 2.23 Which things have *i* a shew of
1Th 4.10 And *i* ye do it toward all the
1Ti 5. 3 Honor widows that are widows *i*.
5 Now she that is a widow *i*, and
16 relieve them that are widows *i*.
1Pe 2. 4 disallowed *i* of men, but chosen of

INDIGNATION

Dt 29.28 and in wrath, and in great *i*, and
2Ki 3.27 there was great *i* against Israel:
Neh 4. 1 was wroth, and took great *i*, and
Est 5. 9 he was full of *i* against Mordecai.
Job 10.17 and increasest thine *i* upon me;
Ps 69.24 Pour out thine *i* upon them, and
78.49 anger, wrath, and *i*, and trouble,
102.10 Because of thine *i* and thy wrath:
Isa 10. 5 the staff in their hand is mine *i*.
25 the *i* shall cease, and mine anger
13. 5 the weapons of his *i*, to destroy the
26.20 moment, until the *i* be overpast.
30.27 his lips are full of *i*, and his tongue
30 with the *i* of his anger, and with
34. 2 *i* of the Lord is upon all nations,
66.14 and his *i* toward his enemies.
Jer 10.10 shall not be able to abide his *i*.
15.17 hand: for thou hast filled me with *i*.
50.25 brought forth the weapons of his *i*:
La 2. 6 hath despised in the *i* of his anger
Eze 21.31 I will pour out mine *i* upon thee,
22.24 nor rained upon in the day of *i*.
31 I poured out mine *i* upon them;
Dan 8.19 shall be in the last end of the *i*:
11.30 have *i* against the holy covenant:
36 prosper till the *i* be accomplished:
Mic 7. 9 I will bear the *i* of the Lord,
Na 1. 6 Who can stand before his *i*? and
Hab 3.12 didst march through the land in *i*,
Zep 3. 8 to pour upon them mine *i*, even all
Zec 1.12 hast had *i* these threescore and
Mal 1. 4 whom the Lord hath *i* for ever.
Mt 20.24 were moved with *i* against the two
26. 8 they had *i*, saying, To what purpose
Mk 14. 4 some that had *i* within themselves,
Lk 13.14 of the synagogue answered with *i*,
Ac 5.17 Sadducees, and were filled with *i*,
Ro 2. 8 unrighteousness, *i*, and wrath,
2Co 7.11 yea, what *i*, yea, what fear, yea,
Heb 10.27 of judgment and fiery *i*, which
Rev 14.10 mixture into the cup of his *i*;

INDITING

Ps 45. 1 My heart is *i* a good matter: I

INEXCUSABLE

Ro 2. 1 Therefore thou art *i*, O man,

INFALLIBLE

Ac 1. 3 by many *i* proofs, being seen of them

INFANTS

Job 3.16 been; as *i* which never saw light.
Hos 13.16 their *i* shall be dashed in pieces,
Lk 18.15 they brought unto him also *i*,

INFERIOR

Job 12. 3 I am not *i* to you: yea, who
13. 2 I know also: I am not *i* unto you.
Dan 2.39 arise another kingdom *i* to thee,
2Co 12.13 you were *i* to other churches,

INFIDEL

2Co 6.15 hath he that believeth with an *i*?
1Ti 5. 8 the faith, and is worse than an *i*.

INFINITE

Job 22. 5 great? and thine iniquities *i*?
Ps 147. 5 power: his understanding is *i*.
Na 3. 9 her strength, and it was *i*;

INFIRMITIES

Mt 8.17 Himself took our *i*, and bare our
Lk 5.15 and to be healed by him of their *i*.
7.21 cured many of their *i* and plagues,
8. 2 been healed of evil spirits and *i*,
Ro 8.26 the Spirit also helpeth our *i*: for
15. 1 to bear the *i* of the weak, and not
2Co 11.30 of the things which concern my *i*.
12. 5 I will not glory, but in mine *i*.
9 will I rather glory in my *i*, that the
10 Therefore I take pleasure in *i*, in

1Ti 5.23 stomach's sake and thine often *i*.
Heb 4.15 touched with the feeling of our *i*;

INFIRMITY

Lev 12. 2 days of the separation for her *i*
Ps 77.10 And I said, This is my *i*: but I
Pr 18.14 spirit of a man will sustain his *i*;
Lk 13.11 a woman which had a spirit of *i*
12 thou art loosed from thine *i*.
Jn 5. 5 had an *i* thirty and eight years.
Ro 6.19 men because of the *i* of your flesh:
Gal 4.13 Ye know how through *i* of the flesh
Heb 5. 2 himself also is compassed with *i*.
7.28 men high priests which have *i*;

INFLICTED

2Co 2. 6 this punishment, which was *i* of many.

INFLUENCES

Job 38.31 Canst thou bind the sweet *i* of Pleiades,

INFORM

Dt 17.10 according to all that they *i* thee:

INFORMED

Dan 9.22 And he *i* me, and talked with me,
Ac 21.21 are *i* of thee, that thou teachest
24 they were *i* concerning thee,
24. 1 who *i* the governor against Paul.
25. 2 of the Jews *i* him against Paul, and
15 and the elders of the Jews *i* me,

INHABIT

Nu 35.34 the land which ye shall *i*, wherein
Pr 10.30 the wicked shall not *i* the earth.
Isa 42.11 the villages that Kedar doth *i*:
65.21 shall build houses, and *i* them;
22 shall not build and another *i*; they
Jer 17. 6 but shall *i* the parched places in
48.18 Thou daughter that dost *i* Dibon,
Eze 33.24 they that *i* those wastes of the land
Am 9.14 build the waste cities, and *i* them;
Zep 1.13 also build houses, but not *i* them;

INHABITANT

Isa 6.11 Until the cities be wasted without *i*,
Jer 2.15 his cities are burned without *i*.
4. 7 shall be laid waste, without an *i*.
21.13 I am against thee, O *i* of the valley,
51.29 Babylon a desolation without an *i*.
37 and an hissing, without an *i*.
Zep 2. 5 thee, that there shall be no *i*.
3. 6 is no man, that there is none *i*.

INHABITANTS

Ex 15.15 all the *i* of Canaan shall melt away.
23.31 I will deliver the *i* of the land into
34.15 a covenant with the *i* of the land,
Nu 33.52 ye shall drive out the *i* of the land
53 ye shall dispossess the *i* of the land,
Jos 2. 9 all the *i* of the land faint because
Jdg 2. 2 no league with the *i* of this land;
5.23 curse ye bitterly the *i* thereof;
1Ch 11. 4 Jebusites were, the *i* of the land.
2Ch 20.20 O Judah, and ye *i* of Jerusalem;
Job 26. 5 the waters, and the *i* thereof.
Ps 33. 8 all the *i* of the world stand in awe
49. 1 give ear, all ye *i* of the world:
75. 3 and all the *i* thereof are dissolved:
Isa 18. 3 All ye *i* of the world, and dwellers
23. 2 Be still, ye *i* of the isle; thou whom
40.22 the *i* thereof are as grasshoppers;
42.11 let the *i* of the rock sing, let them
Jer 10.18 I will sling out the *i* of the land
21. 6 I will smite the *i* of this city, both
46. 8 I will destroy the city and the *i*
47. 2 and all the *i* of the land shall howl.
La 4.12 the earth and all the *i* of the world,
Hos 4. 1 controversy with the *i* of the land,
Joel 1. 2 and give ear, all ye *i* of the land.
2. 1 let all the *i* of the land tremble:
Mic 6.12 and the *i* thereof have spoken lies,
16 and the *i* thereof an hissing:
Zep 2. 5 Woe unto the *i* of the sea coast,
Zec 11. 6 I will no more pity the *i* of the land,
Rev 17. 2 the *i* of the earth have been made

INHABITED

Gen 36.20 of Seir the Horite, who *i* the land;
Ex 16.35 years, until they came to a land *i*;
Lev 16.22 their iniquities unto a land not *i*:
Jdg 1.17 the Canaanites that *i* Zephath,
21 out the Jebusites that *i* Jerusalem;
1Ch 5. 9 eastward he *i* unto the entering in
Isa 13.20 It shall never be *i*, neither shall it
44.26 saith to Jerusalem, Thou shalt be *i*;
45.18 it not in vain, he formed it to be *i*:
54. 5 make the desolate cities to be *i*.
Jer 6. 8 make thee desolate, a land not *i*.
17. 6 wilderness, in a salt land and not *i*.
22. 6 and cities which are not *i*.
46.26 and afterward it shall be *i*, as in
50.13 it shall not be *i*, but it shall be
39 it shall be no more *i* for ever;
Eze 12.20 cities that are *i* shall be laid waste,
26.17 that wast *i* of seafaring men,
19 city, like the cities that are not *i*;
20 down to the pit, that thou be not *i*;
29.11 it, neither shall it be *i* forty years.
34.13 in all the *i* places of the country.
36.10 and the cities shall be *i*, and the
35 cities are become fenced, and are *i*.
38.12 the desolate places that are now *i*,
Zec 2. 4 Jerusalem shall be *i* as towns
7. 7 when Jerusalem was *i* and in
7 men *i* the south and the plain?
9. 5 Gaza, and Ashkelon shall not be *i*.
12. 6 and Jerusalem shall be *i* again in
14.10 be lifted up, and *i* in her place,
11 but Jerusalem shall be safely *i*.

INHABITERS

Rev 8.13 woe, woe, to the *i* of the earth
12.12 Woe to the *i* of the earth and of

INHABITETH

Job 15.28 and in houses which no man *i*,
Isa 57.15 high and lofty One that *i* eternity,

INHERIT

Gen 28. 4 that thou mayest *i* the land
Dt 12.10 the Lord your God giveth you to *i*,
Ps 25.13 and his seed shall *i* the earth.
37. 9 the Lord, they shall *i* the earth.
11 But the meek shall *i* the earth;
22 blessed of him shall *i* the earth;
29 The righteous shall *i* the land,
34 he shall exalt thee to *i* the land:
Pr 3.35 The wise shall *i* glory: but shame
11.29 his own house shall *i* the wind:
14.18 The simple *i* folly: but the prudent
Isa 54. 3 and thy seed shall *i* the Gentiles,
Mt 5. 5 meek: for they shall *i* the earth.
19.29 and shall *i* everlasting life.
25.34 *i* the kingdom prepared for you
Mk 10.17 shall I do that I may *i* eternal life?
Lk 10.25 what shall I do to *i* eternal life?
18.18 what shall I do to *i* eternal life?
1Co 6. 9 shall not *i* the kingdom of God?
10 shall *i* the kingdom of God.
15.50 and blood cannot *i* the kingdom
50 doth corruption *i* incorruption.
Gal 5.21 shall not *i* the kingdom of God.
Heb 6.12 faith and patience *i* the promises.
1Pe 3. 9 called, that ye should *i* a blessing.
Rev 21. 7 that overcometh shall *i* all things;

INHERITANCE

Ex 15.17 in the mountain of thine *i*, in the
Nu 18.21 Levi all the tenth in Israel for an *i*,
33.54 divide the land by lot for an *i*
34.29 Lord commanded to divide the *i*
Dt 4.20 to be unto him a people of *i*, as ye
21 Lord thy God giveth thee for an *i*:
Jos 13.14 the tribe of Levi he gave none *i*;
18. 7 priesthood of the Lord is their *i*:
Ru 4. 5 up the name of the dead upon his *i*.
2Sa 14.16 my son together out of the *i* of God.
1Ki 8.53 people of the earth to be thine *i*,
Job 31. 2 *i* of the Almighty from on high?
42.15 gave them *i* among their brethren.
Ps 16. 5 The Lord is the portion of mine *i*
28. 9 Save thy people, and bless thine *i*:
37.18 and their *i* shall be for ever.
47. 4 He shall choose our *i* for us,
74. 2 the rod of thine *i*, which thou hast
Pr 13.22 A good man leaveth an *i* to his
Ec 7.11 Wisdom is good with an *i*: and by
La 5. 2 Our *i* is turned to strangers, our
Mt 21.38 kill him, and let us seize on his *i*.
Mk 12. 7 kill him, and the *i* shall be ours.
Lk 12.13 that he divide the *i* with me.
20.14 kill him, that the *i* may be ours.
Ac 7. 5 And he gave him none *i* in it,
20.32 to give you an *i* among all them
26.18 *i* among them which are sanctified
Gal 3.18 if the *i* be of the law, it is no more
Eph 1.11 In whom...we...obtained an *i*,
14 is the earnest of our *i* until the
18 of the glory of his *i* in the saints.
5. 5 hath any *i* in the kingdom of Christ
Col 1.12 be partakers of the *i* of the saints
3.24 shall receive the reward of the *i*:
Heb 1. 4 as he hath by *i* obtained a more
9.15 receive the promise of eternal *i*.
11. 8 he should after receive for an *i*,
1Pe 1. 4 an *i* incorruptible, and undefiled,

INHERITED

Nu 32.18 have *i* every man his inheritance.
Jos 14. 1 of Israel *i* in the land of Canaan,
Ps 105.44 they *i* the labor of the people;
Jer 16.19 Surely our fathers have *i* lies,
Eze 33.24 and he *i* the land: but we are
Heb 12.17 he would have *i* the blessing,

INIQUITIES

Lev 16.21 all the *i* of the children of Israel,
22 goat shall bear upon him all their *i*
Ezr 9.13 punished us less than our *i* deserve,
Neh 9. 2 sins, and the *i* of their fathers.
Ps 38. 4 mine *i* are gone over mine head: as
40.12 mine *i* have taken hold upon me,
51. 9 my sins, and blot out all mine *i*.
65. 3 *I* prevail against me: as for
79. 8 remember not against us former *i*:
90. 8 Thou hast set our *i* before thee,
103. 3 Who forgiveth all thine *i*; who
10 rewarded us according to our *i*.
130. 3 If thou, Lord, shouldest mark *i*, O
8 shall redeem Israel from all his *i*.
Pr 5.22 His own *i* shall take the wicked
Isa 43.24 thou hast wearied me with thine *i*.
50. 1 for your *i* have ye sold yourselves,
53. 5 he was bruised for our *i*:
11 many; for he shall bear their *i*.
59. 2 But your *i* have separated between
12 and as for our *i*, we know them;
64. 6 our *i*, like the wind, have taken
7 consumed us, because of our *i*.
La 5. 7 not; and we have borne their *i*.
Eze 36.33 have cleansed you from all your *i*
43.10 they may be ashamed of their *i*:
Am 3. 2 I will punish you for all your *i*.
Ac 3.26 away every one of you from his *i*.
Ro 4. 7 are they whose *i* are forgiven,
Heb 8.12 their *i* will I remember no more.
10.17 sins and *i* will I remember no more.
Rev 18. 5 and God hath remembered her *i*.

INIQUITY

Ex 20. 5 visiting the *i* of the fathers upon
34. 9 and pardon our *i* and our sin, and

Lev 5.17 is he guilty, and shall bear his *i*.
18.25 I do visit the *i* thereof upon it,
Nu 14.19 I beseech thee, the *i* of this people
Dt 32. 4 a God of truth and without *i*,
1Sa 3.14 *i* of Eli's house shall not be purged
20. 1 have I done? what is mine *i*?
8 if there be in me *i*, slay me
2Sa 19.19 Let not my lord impute *i* unto me,
2Ch 19. 7 is no *i* with the Lord our God,
Job 6.30 Is there *i* in my tongue? cannot
11.14 If *i* be in thine hand, put it far
15.16 man, which drinketh *i* like water?
21.19 God layeth up his *i* for his children:
31. 3 punishment to the workers of *i*?
11 an *i* to be punished by the judges.
33. 9 innocent; neither is there *i* in me.
34.32 if I have done *i*, I will do no more.
Ps 5. 5 sight: thou hatest all workers of *i*.
6. 8 Depart from me, all ye workers of *i*;
14. 4 all the workers of *i* no knowledge?
25.11 O Lord, pardon mine *i*; for it is
32. 2 whom the Lord imputeth not *i*,
5 thee, and mine *i* have I not hid.
5 and thou forgavest the *i* of my sin.
51. 2 Wash me thoroughly from mine *i*,
5 I was shapen in *i*; and in sin
59. 2 Deliver me from the workers of *i*,
66.18 If I regard *i* in my heart, the Lord
85. 2 hast forgiven the *i* of thy people,
92. 7 all the workers of *i* do flourish;
106. 6 we have committed *i*, we have
107.42 and all *i* shall stop her mouth.
Pr 16. 6 By mercy and truth *i* is purged:
22. 8 that soweth *i* shall reap vanity:
Isa 6. 7 thine *i* is taken away, and thy sin
22.14 Surely this *i* shall not be purged
40. 2 her *i* is pardoned: for she hath
53. 6 hath laid on him the *i* of us all.
57.17 For the *i* of his covetousness was I
64. 9 neither remember *i* for ever:
Jer 2.22 yet thine *i* is marked before me,
31.30 every one shall die for his own *i*:
33. 8 I will cleanse them from all their *i*,
Eze 3.18 same wicked man shall die in his *i*;
7.16 mourning, every one for his *i*.
19 it is the stumblingblock of their *i*.
18.17 not die for the *i* of his father, he
19 not the son bear the *i* of the father?
20 shall not bear the *i* of the father,
20 the father bear the *i* of the son:
26 his *i* that he hath done shall he die.
21.23 he will call to remembrance the *i*,
Hos 12. 8 find none *i* in me that were sin.
14. 2 Take away all *i*, and receive us
Mic 2. 1 Woe to them that devise *i*, and
7.18 like unto thee, that pardoneth *i*,
Mal 2. 6 and *i* was not found in his lips:
6 and did turn many away from *i*.
Mt 7.23 depart from me, ye that work *i*.
13.41 that offend, and them which do *i*;
23.28 within ye are full of hypocrisy and *i*.
24.12 because *i* shall abound, the love of
Lk 13.27 depart from me, all ye workers of *i*.
Ac 1.18 a field with the reward of *i*;
8.23 of bitterness, and in the bond of *i*.
Ro 6.19 to uncleanness and to *i* unto *i*;
1Co 13. 6 Rejoiceth not in *i*, but rejoiceth in
2Th 2. 7 mystery of *i* doth already work:
2Ti 2.19 the name of Christ depart from *i*.
Tit 2.14 might redeem us from all *i*, and
Heb 1. 9 loved righteousness, and hated *i*;
Jas 3. 6 And the tongue is a fire, a world of *i*:
2Pe 2.16 But was rebuked for his *i*: the

INJURED

Gal 4.12 as ye are: ye have not *i* me at all.

INJURIOUS

1Ti 1.13 and a persecutor, and *i*: but I

INK

Jer 36.18 and I wrote them with *i* in the
2Co 3. 3 written not with *i*, but with the
2Jn 12 would not write with paper and *i*:
3Jn 13 I will not with *i* and pen write unto

INKHORN

Eze 9. 2 with a writer's *i* by his side:
3 had the writer's *i* by his side;
11 linen, which had the *i* by his side,

INN

Gen 42.27 to give his ass provender in the *i*,
43.21 when we came to the *i*, that we
Ex 4.24 came to pass by the way in the *i*,
Lk 2. 7 was no room for them in the *i*.
10.34 and brought him to an *i*, and took

INNER

1Ki 6.27 the cherubims within the *i* house:
36 he built the *i* court with three rows
7.12 for the *i* court of the house of the
50 the doors of the *i* house, the most
20.30 into the city, into an *i* chamber.
22.25 shalt go into an *i* chamber to hide
2Ki 9. 2 and carry him to an *i* chamber;
1Ch 28.11 and of the *i* parlours thereof, and
2Ch 4.22 the *i* doors thereof for the most
18.24 shalt go into an *i* chamber to hide
29.16 went into the *i* part of the house
Est 4.11 unto the king into the *i* court,
5. 1 stood in the *i* court of the king's
Eze 8. 3 the door of the *i* gate that looketh
16 he brought me into the *i* court
10. 3 and the cloud filled the *i* court.
40.15 the porch of the *i* gate were fifty
19 unto the forefront of the *i* court
23 the gate of the *i* court was over
27 a gate in the *i* court toward the
28 he brought me to the *i* court by
32 he brought me into the *i* court
44 the *i* gate were the chambers
44 of the singers in the *i* court, which
41.15 with the *i* temple, and the porches
17 the door, even unto the *i* house,
42. 3 cubits which were for the *i* court,
15 an end of measuring the *i* house,
43. 5 and brought me into the *i* court;
44.17 enter in at the gates of the *i* court,
17 minister in the gates of the *i* court,
21 when they enter into the *i* court.
27 into the sanctuary, unto the *i* court,
45.19 the posts of the gate of the *i* court.
46. 1 The gate of the *i* court that looketh
Ac 16.24 thrust them into the *i* prison, and
Eph 3.16 might by his Spirit in the *i* man;

INNOCENCY

Gen 20. 5 and *i* of my hands have I done
Ps 26. 6 I will wash mine hands in *i*: so will
73.13 in vain, and washed my hands in *i*.
Dan 6.22 as before him *i* was found in me;
Hos 8. 5 long will it be ere they attain to *i*?

INNOCENT

Ex 23. 7 the *i* and righteous slay thou not:
Dt 19.10 That *i* blood be not shed in thy
13 the guilt of *i* blood from Israel,
21. 8 and lay not *i* blood unto thy people
9 put away the guilt of *i* blood from
27.25 taketh reward to slay an *i* person.
1Sa 19. 5 then wilt thou sin against *i* blood,
1Ki 2.31 mayest take away the *i* blood,
2Ki 21.16 Manasseh shed *i* blood very much,
24. 4 also for the *i* blood that he shed:
4 he filled Jerusalem with *i* blood;
Job 4. 7 thee, who ever perished, being *i*?
9.23 he will laugh at the trial of the *i*.
28 know that thou wilt not hold me *i*.
17. 8 the *i* shall stir up himself against
22.19 and the *i* laugh them to scorn.
30 He shall deliver the island of the *i*:
27.17 on, and the *i* shall divide the silver.
33. 9 without transgression, I am *i*;
Ps 10. 8 places doth he murder the *i*:
15. 5 nor taketh reward against the *i*.
19.13 *i* from the great transgression.
94.21 and condemn the *i* blood.
106.38 And shed *i* blood, even the blood
Pr 1.11 let us lurk privily for the *i* without
6.17 and hands that shed *i* blood,
29 toucheth her shall not be *i*.
28.20 haste to be rich shall not be *i*.
Isa 59. 7 they make haste to shed *i* blood:
Jer 2.35 Yet thou sayest, Because I am *i*,
7. 6 and shed not *i* blood in this place,
22. 3 neither shed *i* blood in this place.
17 and for to shed *i* blood, and for
26.15 ye shall surely bring *i* blood upon
Joel 3.19 they have shed *i* blood in their land.
Jon 1.14 and lay not upon us *i* blood: for
Mt 27. 4 in that I have betrayed the *i* blood.
24 I am *i* of the blood of this just
(See box on page 392)

INNUMERABLE

Job 21.33 as there are *i* before him.
Ps 40.12 For *i* evils have compassed me
104.25 wherein are things creeping *i*,
Jer 46.23 the grasshoppers, and are *i*.
Lk 12. 1 an *i* multitude of people;
Heb 11.12 sand which is by the sea shore *i*.
12.22 and to an *i* company of angels,

INORDINATE

Eze 23.11 was more corrupt in her *i* love
Col 3. 5 uncleanness, *i* affection, evil

INQUIRE

Ex 18.15 people come unto me to *i* of God:
Dt 12.30 that thou *i* not after their gods,
1Sa 9. 9 when a man went to *i* of God,
1Ki 22. 8 by whom we may *i* of the Lord:
2Ki 1. 2 *i* of Baal-zebub the god of Ekron
16.15 altar shall be for me to *i* by.
1Ch 10.13 had a familiar spirit, to *i* of it;
2Ch 18. 7 by whom we may *i* of the Lord:
34.21 Go, *i* of the Lord for me, and for
Ps 27. 4 the Lord, and to *i* in his temple.
Eze 14. 7 prophet to *i* of him concerning
20. 3 Are ye come to *i* of me?
Mt 10.11 *i* who in it is worthy; and there
Lk 22.23 began to *i* among themselves,
Jn 16.19 Do ye *i* among yourselves of that
Ac 9.11 *i* in the house of Judas for one
19.39 But if ye *i* any thing concerning
23.15 as though ye would *i* something
20 as though they would *i* somewhat
2Co 8.23 Whether any do *i* of Titus, he is

INQUIRED

1Sa 30. 8 And David *i* at the Lord, saying,
2Sa 16.23 as if a man had *i* at the oracle
Ps 78.34 returned and *i* early after God.
Eze 20. 3 Lord God, I will not be *i* of by you.
Zep 1. 6 sought the Lord, nor *i* for him.
Mt 2. 7 *i* of them diligently what time the
16 had diligently *i* of the wise men.
Jn 4.52 Then *i* he of them the hour
2Co 8.23 or our brethren be *i* of, they
1Pe 1.10 have *i* and searched diligently,

INQUIRY

Pr 20.25 and after vows to make *i*
Ac 10.17 had made *i* for Simon's house,

INSCRIPTION

Ac 17.23 altar with this *i*, To The Unknown

INSPIRATION

Job 32. 8 the *i* of the Almighty giveth them
2Ti 3.16 scripture is given by *i* of God,

Biblical Themes

INNOCENCE

And they were both naked, the man and his wife, and were not ashamed. Gen 2.25

And with Absalom went two hundred men out of Jerusalem, that were called; and they went in their simplicity, and they knew not any thing. 2Sa 15.11

There was a man in the land of Uz, whose name was Job; and that man was perfect and upright, and one that feared God, and eschewed evil. Job 1.1

Naked came I out of my mother's womb, and naked shall I return thither: the Lord gave, and the Lord hath taken away; blessed be the name of the Lord. Job 1.21

Who shall ascend into the hill of the Lord? . . . He that hath clean hands, and a pure heart; who hath not lifted up his soul unto vanity, nor sworn deceitfully. Ps 24.3-4

Blessed is the man unto whom the Lord imputeth not iniquity, and in whose spirit there is no guile. Ps 32.2

Purge me with hyssop, and I shall be clean: wash me, and I shall be whiter than snow. . . . Create in me a clean heart, O God; and renew a right spirit within me. Ps 51.7, 10

Lord, my heart is not haughty, nor mine eyes lofty: neither do I exercise myself in great matters, or in things too high for me. Surely I have behaved and quieted myself, as a child that is weaned of his mother: my soul is even as a weaned child. Ps 131.1-2

Who can say, I have made my heart clean, I am pure from my sin? Pr 20.9

He was oppressed, and he was afflicted, yet he opened not his mouth: he is brought as a lamb to the slaughter, and as a sheep before her shearers is dumb, so he openeth not his mouth. Isa 53.7

Then Herod . . . was exceeding wroth, and sent forth, and slew all the children that were in Bethlehem, and in all the coasts thereof, from two years old and under, according to the time which he had diligently inquired of the wise men. Mt 2.16

Blessed are the pure in heart: for they shall see God. Mt 5.8

Whosoever therefore shall humble himself as this little child, the same is greatest in the kingdom of heaven. And whoso shall receive one such little child in my name receiveth me. Mt 18.4-5

[Judas said,] I have sinned in that I have betrayed the innocent blood. Mt 27.4

When Pilate saw that he could prevail nothing, but that rather a tumult was made, he took water, and washed his hands before the multitude, saying, I am innocent of the blood of this just person: see ye to it. Mt 27.24

Jesus called them unto him, and said, Suffer little children to come unto me, and forbid them not: for of such is the kingdom of God. Verily I say unto you, Whosoever shall not receive the kingdom of God as a little child shall in no wise enter therein. Lk 18.16-17

One of the malefactors which were hanged railed on him, saying, If thou be Christ, save thyself and us. But the other answering rebuked him, saying, Dost not thou fear God, seeing thou art in the same condemnation? and we indeed justly; for we receive the due reward of our deeds: but this man hath done nothing amiss. Lk 23.39-41

Unto the pure all things are pure: but unto them that are defiled and unbelieving is nothing pure. Tit 1.15

Christ also suffered for us, leaving us an example, that ye should follow his steps: who did no sin, neither was guile found in his mouth. 1Pe 2.21-22

INSTANT

Isa 29. 5 yea, it shall be at an *i* suddenly.
30.13 breaking cometh suddenly at an *i*.
Jer 18. 7 At what *i* I shall speak concerning
9 at what *i* I shall speak concerning
Lk 2.38 she coming in that *i* gave thanks
23.23 And they were *i* with loud voices,
Ro 12.12 continuing *i* in prayer;
2Ti 4. 2 be *i* in season, out of season;

INSTANTLY

Lk 7. 4 they besought him *i*, saying,
Ac 26. 7 *i* serving God day and night,

INSTEAD

Gen 2.21 and closed up the flesh *i* thereof;
4.25 me another seed *i* of Abel,
44.33 let thy servant abide *i* of the lad a
Ex 4.16 even he shall be to thee *i* of a mouth,
16 and thou shalt be to him *i* of God.
5.12 of Egypt to gather stubble *i* of straw.
Nu 3.12 of Israel *i* of all the firstborn
41 *i* of all the firstborn among the
41 *i* of all the firstlings among the
45 the Levites *i* of all the firstborn
45 of the Levites *i* of their cattle;
5.19 with another *i* of thy husband,
20 aside to another *i* of thy husband,
29 aside to another *i* of her husband,
8.16 *i* of such as open every womb,
16 even *i* of the firstborn of all the
10.31 thou mayest be to us *i* of eyes.
Jdg 15. 2 she? take her, I pray thee, *i* of her.
2Sa 17.25 captain of the host *i* of Joab:
1Ki 3. 7 made thy servant king *i* of David
2Ki 14.21 him king *i* of his father Amaziah.
17.24 of Samaria *i* of the children of
1Ch 29.23 as king *i* of David his father, and
2Ch 12.10 *I* of which king Rehoboam made
Est 2. 4 the king be queen *i* of Vashti.
17 and made her queen *i* of Vashti.
Job 31.40 *i* of wheat, and cockle *i* of barley.
Ps 45.16 *I* of thy fathers shall be thy
Isa 3.24 *i* of sweet smell there shall be
24 stink; and *i* of a girdle a rent;
24 and *i* of well set hair baldness;
24 and *i* of a stomacher a girding of
24 sackcloth; and burning *i* of beauty.
55.13 *I* of the thorn shall come up the fir
13 *i* of the brier shall come up the
Jer 22.11 which reigned *i* of Josiah his father,
37. 1 son of Josiah reigned *i* of Coniah
Eze 16.32 taketh strangers *i* of her husband!

INSTRUCT

Dt 4.36 his voice, that he might *i* thee:
Neh 9.20 also thy good spirit to *i* them,
Job 40. 2 with the Almighty *i* him?
Ps 16. 7 my reins also *i* me in the night
32. 8 I will *i* thee and teach thee in the
SS 8. 2 mother's house, who would *i* me:
Isa 28.26 his God doth *i* him to discretion,
Dan 11.33 among the people shall *i* many:
1Co 2.16 of the Lord, that he may *i* him?

INSTRUCTED

Dt 32.10 he *i* him, he kept him as the
2Ki 12. 2 Jehoiada the priest *i* him.
1Ch 15.22 he *i* about the song, because he
25. 7 brethren that were *i* in the songs
2Ch 3. 3 Solomon was *i* for the building
Job 4. 3 Behold, thou hast *i* many, and
Ps 2.10 be *i*, ye judges of the earth.
Pr 5.13 mine ear to them that *i* me!
21.11 when the wise is *i*, he receiveth
Isa 8.11 and *i* me that I should not walk
40.14 and who *i* him, and taught him
Jer 6. 8 Be thou *i*, O Jerusalem, lest my
31.19 and after that I was *i*, I smote
Mt 13.52 is *i* unto the kingdom of heaven
14. 8 being before *i* of her mother,
Lk 1. 4 things, wherein thou hast been *i*.
Ac 18.25 man was *i* in the way of the Lord;
Ro 2.18 excellent, being *i* out of the law;
Php 4.12 all things I am *i* both to be full

INSTRUCTERS

1Co 4.15 ye have ten thousand *i* in Christ,

INSTRUCTING

2Ti 2.25 In meekness *i* those that oppose

INSTRUCTION

Job 33.16 ears of men, and sealeth their *i*,
Ps 50.17 Seeing thou hatest *i*, and castest
Pr 1. 2 To know wisdom and *i*; to
3 To receive the *i* of wisdom,
7 but fools despise wisdom and *i*.
8 My son, hear the *i* of thy father,
4. 1 Hear, ye children, the *i* of a father,
13 Take fast hold of *i*; let her not go:
5.12 How have I hated *i*, and my heart
23 He shall die without *i*; and in the
6.23 reproofs of *i* are the way of life:
8.10 Receive my *i*, and not silver; and
33 Hear *i*, and be wise, and refuse it
9. 9 Give *i* to a wise man, and he will be
10.17 in the way of life that keepeth *i*:

12. 1 Whoso loveth *i* loveth knowledge:
13. 1 A wise son heareth his father's *i*:
18 shall be to him that refuseth *i*:
15. 5 A fool despiseth his father's *i*:
32 refuseth *i* despiseth his own soul:
33 fear of the Lord is the *i* of wisdom;
16.22 hath it: but the *i* of fools is folly.
19.20 Hear counsel, and receive *i*, that
27 to hear the *i* that causeth to err
23.12 Apply thine heart unto *i*, and
23 wisdom, and *i*, and understanding.
24.32 I looked upon it, and received *i*.
Jer 17.23 they might not hear, nor receive *i*.
32.33 have not hearkened to receive *i*.
35.13 Will ye not receive *i* to hearken to
Eze 5.15 an *i* and an astonishment unto
Zep 3. 7 wilt fear me, thou wilt receive *i*;
2Ti 3.16 correction, for *i* in righteousness:

INSTRUCTOR
Ro 2.20 An *i* of the foolish, a teacher of

INSTRUMENT
Nu 35.16 if he smite him with an *i* of iron,
Ps 33. 2 the psaltery and an *i* of ten strings.
92. 3 Upon an *i* of ten strings, and upon
144. 9 upon a psaltery and an *i* of ten strings
Isa 28.27 are not threshed with a threshing *i*,
41.15 make thee a new sharp threshing *i*
54.16 bringeth forth an *i* for his work;
Eze 33.32 voice, and can play well on an *i*:

INSTRUMENTS
Gen 49. 5 *i* of cruelty are in their
Ex 25. 9 the pattern of all the *i* thereof,
Nu 3. 8 keep all the *i* of the tabernacle
4.12 shall take all the *i* of ministry,
26 cords, and all the *i* of their service,
32 with all their *i*, and with all their
32 ye shall reckon the *i* of the charge
7. 1 sanctified it, and all the *i* thereof,
31. 6 with the holy *i*, and the trumpets
1Sa 8.12 his *i* of war, and *i* of his chariots.
18. 6 with joy, and with *i* of musick.
2Sa 6. 5 on all manner of *i* made of fir wood,
24.22 burnt sacrifice, and threshing *i*
22 and other *i* of the oxen for wood.
1Ki 19.21 their flesh with the *i* of the oxen,
1Ch 9.29 and all the *i* of the sanctuary,
12.33 with all *i* of war, fifty thousand,
37 with all manner of *i* of war for the
15.16 to be the singers with *i* of musick,
16.42 sound, and with musical *i* of God.
21.23 and the threshing *i* for wood, and the
23. 5 Lord with the *i* which I made,
28.14 for all *i* of all manner of service;
14 silver also for all *i* of silver by
14 for all *i* of every kind of service:
2Ch 4.16 and all their *i*, did Huram his
5. 1 and all the *i*, put he among the
13 and cymbals and *i* of musick, and
7. 6 also with *i* of musick of the Lord,
23.13 the singers with *i* of musick, and
29.26 Levites stood with the *i* of David,
27 with the *i* ordained by David king
30.21 singing with loud *i* unto the Lord.
34.12 all that could skill of *i* of musick.
Neh 12.36 with the musical *i* of David the
Ps 7.13 prepared for him the *i* of death;
68.25 the players on *i* followed after;
87. 7 as the players on *i* shall be there:
150. 4 him with stringed *i* and organs.
Ec 2. 8 as musical *i*, and that of all sorts.
Isa 32. 7 The *i* also of the churl are evil:
38.20 sing my songs to the stringed *i*
Eze 40.42 *i* wherewith they slew the burnt
Dan 6.18 neither were *i* of musick brought
Am 1. 3 Gilead with threshing *i* of iron:
6. 5 invent to themselves *i* of musick,
Hab 3.19 chief singer on my stringed *i*.
Zec 11.15 yet the *i* of a foolish shepherd.

Ro 6.13 as *i* of unrighteousness unto sin:
13 as *i* of righteousness unto God.

INSURRECTION
Ezr 4.19 time hath made *i* against kings,
Ps 64. 2 the *i* of the workers of iniquity:
Mk 15. 7 bound with them that had made *i*
7 had committed murder in the *i*.
Ac 18.12 the Jews made *i* with one accord

INTEGRITY
Gen 20. 5 the *i* of my heart and innocency
6 didst this in the *i* of thy heart;
1Ki 9. 4 thy father walked, in *i* of heart,
Job 2. 3 and still he holdeth fast his *i*,
9 him, Dost thou still retain thine *i*?
27. 5 till I die I will not remove mine *i*
31. 6 that God may know mine *i*.
Ps 7. 8 according to mine *i* that is in me.
25.21 Let *i* and uprightness preserve
26. 1 Lord; for I have walked in mine *i*:
11 as for me, I will walk in mine *i*:
41.12 me, thou upholdest me in mine *i*,
78.72 according to the *i* of his heart;
Pr 11. 3 The *i* of the upright shall guide
19. 1 is the poor that walketh in his *i*,
20. 7 The just man walketh in his *i*: his

INTEND
Jos 22.33 and did not *i* to go up against
2Ch 28.13 ye *i* to add more to our sins and to
Ac 5.28 and *i* to bring this man's blood
35 what ye *i* to do as touching these

INTENDING
Lk 14.28 which of you, *i* to build a tower,
Ac 12. 4 *i* after Easter to bring him forth
20.13 Assos, there *i* to take in Paul:

INTENT
2Sa 17.14 *i* that the Lord might bring evil
2Ki 10.19 to the *i* that he might destroy the
2Ch 16. 1 to the *i* that he might let none go out
Eze 40. 4 the *i* that I might shew them unto
Dan 4.17 to the *i* that the living may know
Jn 11.15 not there, to the *i* ye may believe;
13.28 for what *i* he spake this unto
Ac 9.21 and came hither for that *i*,
10.29 for what *i* ye have sent for me?
1Co 10. 6 to the *i* we should not lust after
Eph 3.10 To the *i* that now unto the

INTENTS
Jer 30.24 have performed the *i* of his heart:
Heb 4.12 of the thoughts and *i* of the heart.

INTERCESSION
Isa 53.12 and made *i* for the transgressors.
Jer 7.16 for them, neither make *i* to me:
27.18 let them now make *i* to the Lord
36.25 Gemariah had made *i* to the king
Ro 8.26 the Spirit itself maketh *i* for us
27 maketh *i* for the saints according
34 of God, who also maketh *i* for us.
11. 2 he maketh *i* to God against Israel,
Heb 7.25 he ever liveth to make *i* for them.

INTERCESSIONS
1Ti 2. 1 prayers, *i*, and giving of thanks,

INTERCESSOR
Isa 59.16 wondered that there was no *i*:

INTERPRET
Gen 41. 8 there was none that could *i* them
12 according to his dream he did *i*.
15 and there is none that can *i* it:
15 canst understand a dream to *i* it.
1Co 12.30 all speak with tongues? do all *i*?
14. 5 speaketh with tongues, except he *i*,
13 tongue pray that he may *i*.
27 and that by course; and let one *i*.

INTERPRETATION
Gen 40. 5 according to the *i* of his dream,
12 This is the *i* of it: The three
16 baker saw that the *i* was good,
18 This is the *i* thereof: The three
41.11 according to the *i* of his dream.
Jdg 7.15 of the dream, and the *i* thereof,
Pr 1. 6 understand a proverb, and the *i*;
Ec 8. 1 who knoweth the *i* of a thing?
Dan 2. 4 the dream, and we will shew the *i*.
5 me the dream, with the *i* thereof,
6 shew the dream and the *i* thereof,
6 me the dream, and the *i* thereof.
7 dream, and we will shew the *i* of it.
9 that ye can shew me the *i* thereof.
16 that he would shew the king the *i*.
24 I will shew unto the king the *i*.
25 make known unto the king the *i*.
26 I have seen, and the *i* thereof?
30 make known the *i* to the king,
36 and we will tell the *i* thereof before
45 is certain, and the *i* thereof sure.
4. 6 known unto me the *i* of the dream.
7 make known unto me the *i* thereof.
9 that I have seen, and the *i* thereof.
18 declare the *i* thereof, forasmuch
18 able to make known unto me the *i*:
19 dream, or the *i* thereof, trouble
19 and the *i* thereof to thine enemies.
24 This is the *i*, O king, and this is
5. 7 writing, and shew me the *i* thereof,
8 known to the king the *i* thereof.
12 be called, and he will shew the *i*.
15 make known unto me the *i* thereof:
15 could not shew the *i* of the thing:
16 known to me the *i* thereof, thou
17 and make known to him the *i*.
26 This is the *i* of the thing: Mene;
7.16 made me know the *i* of the things.
Jn 1.42 Cephas, which is by *i*, A stone.
9. 7 pool of Siloam, which is by *i*, Sent.
Ac 9.36 which by *i* is called Dorcas; this
13. 8 sorcerer (for so is his name by *i*)
1Co 12.10 to another the *i* of tongues:
14.26 tongue, hath a revelation, hath an *i*.
Heb 7. 2 being by *i* King of righteousness,
2Pe 1.20 the scripture is of any private *i*.

INTERPRETATIONS
Gen 40. 8 Do not *i* belong to God? tell me
Dan 5.16 that thou canst make *i*, and

INTERPRETED
Gen 40.22 baker: as Joseph had *i* to them.
41.12 him, and he *i* to us our dreams;
13 to pass, as he *i* to us, so it was;
Ezr 4. 7 and *i* in the Syrian tongue.
Mt 1.23 which being *i* is, God with us.
Mk 5.41 cumi; which is, being *i*, Damsel,
15.22 is, being *i*, The place of a skull.
34 which is, being *i*, My God, my God,
Jn 1.38 which is to say, being *i*, Master,
41 which is, being *i*, the Christ.
Ac 4.36 being *i*, The son of consolation,

INTERPRETER
Gen 40. 8 a dream, and there is no *i* of it.
42.23 for he spake unto them by an *i*.
Job 33.23 an *i*, one among a thousand, to
1Co 14.28 if there be no *i*, let him keep

INTERPRETING
Dan 5.12 understanding, *i* of dreams, and

INVENTORS
Ro 1.30 *i* of evil things, disobedient to

INVISIBLE
Ro 1.20 For the *i* things of him from the
Col 1.15 Who is the image of the *i* God,
16 and that are in earth, visible and *i*,

1Ti 1.17 unto the King eternal, immortal, *i*,
Heb 11.27 endured, as seeing him who is *i*.

INWARD

Ex 28.26 is in the side of the ephod *i*.
39.19 was on the side of the ephod *i*.
Lev 13.55 it is fret *i*, whether it be bare
2Sa 5. 9 round about from Millo and *i*.
1Ki 7.25 and all their hinder parts were *i*.
2Ch 3.13 their feet, and their faces were *i*.
4. 4 and all their hinder parts were *i*.
Job 19.19 All my *i* friends abhorred me:
38.36 hath put wisdom in the *i* parts?
Ps 5. 9 their *i* part is very wickedness;
49.11 Their *i* thought is, that their
51. 6 thou desirest truth in the *i* parts:
64. 6 *i* thought of every one of them,
Pr 20.27 all the *i* parts of the belly.
30 do stripes the *i* parts of the belly.
Isa 16.11 and mine *i* parts for Kir–haresh.
Jer 31.33 I will put my law in their *i* parts,
Eze 40. 9 and the porch of the gate was *i*.
16 and windows were round about *i*:
41. 3 Then went he *i*, and measured the
42. 4 a walk of ten cubits breadth *i*,
Lk 11.39 your *i* part is full of ravening and
Ro 7.22 the law of God after the *i* man:
2Co 4.16 the *i* man is renewed day by day.
7.15 his *i* affection is more abundant

INWARDLY

Ps 62. 4 their mouth, but they curse *i*.
Mt 7.15 but *i* they are ravening wolves.
Ro 2.29 he is a Jew, which is one *i*;

IRON

Lev 26.19 I will make your heaven as *i*, and
Dt 3.11 his bedstead was a bedstead of *i*;
28.48 shall put a yoke of *i* upon thy neck,
33.25 Thy shoes shall be *i* and brass;
1Ki 6. 7 any tool of *i* heard in the house,
2Ki 6. 6 it in thither; and the *i* did swim.
Job 19.24 they were graven with an *i* pen
28. 2 *I* is taken out of the earth, and
40.18 brass; his bones are like bars of *i*.
41.27 He esteemeth *i* as straw, and brass
Ps 2. 9 shalt break them with a rod of *i*;
107.16 and cut the bars of *i* in sunder.
Pr 27.17 *I* sharpeneth *i*; so a man
Ec 10.10 If the *i* be blunt, and he do not
Isa 45. 2 and cut in sunder the bars of *i*:
60.17 for wood brass, and for stones *i*:
Jer 17. 1 of Judah is written with a pen of *i*,
Eze 4. 3 take thou unto thee an *i* pan,
Dan 2.33 His legs of *i*, his feet part of *i* and
40 kingdom shall be strong as *i*:
41 part of potters' clay, and part of *i*,
Am 1. 3 with threshing instruments of *i*:
Mic 4.13 for I will make thine horn *i*, and I
Ac 12.10 they came unto the *i* gate that
1Ti 4. 2 conscience seared with a hot *i*;
Rev 2.27 he shall rule them with a rod of *i*;
9. 9 as it were breastplates of *i*;
12. 5 to rule all nations with a rod of *i*:
18.12 and of brass, and *i*, and marble,
19.15 he shall rule them with a rod of *i*:

ISAAC

Gen 17.19 and thou shalt call his name *I*:
21 covenant will I establish with *I*,
21. 3 him, whom Sarah bare to him, *I*.
4 Abraham circumcised his son *I*
5 when his son *I* was born unto him.
8 the same day that *I* was weaned.
10 be heir with my son, even with *I*.
12 for in *I* shall thy seed be called.
22. 2 Take now thy son, thine only son *I*
3 men with him, and *I* his son,
6 offering, and laid it upon *I* his son;
7 and *I* spake unto Abraham his
9 and bound *I* his son, and laid him

ISAAC

Son of Abraham and Sarah, promised by God (Gen 17.15-21; 18.9-15) and born to them in their old age, bringing them great joy (Gen 21.1-7); offered in sacrifice by his father in response to God's command, but saved at the last moment (Gen 22); falls in love with his cousin Rebekah and marries her (Gen 24); prays that Rebekah's barrenness be removed, and she gives birth to Esau and Jacob; favors Esau because of the venison he catches for him (Gen 25.19-28); lives among Philistines in Gerar; quarrels with local herdsmen over access to water, but eventually makes peace with king and people, settling nearby in Beersheba (Gen 26); when old, is deceived into giving blessing to Jacob rather than to Esau (Gen 27); dies in Hebron and is buried by his sons (Gen 35.28-29).

24. 4 and take a wife unto my son *I*.
14 hast appointed for thy servant *I*;
62 *I* came from the way of the well
63 *I* went out to meditate in the field
64 saw *I*, she lighted off the camel.
66 told *I* all things that he had done.
67 *I* brought her into his mother
67 *I* was comforted after his mother's
25. 5 gave all that he had unto *I*.
6 sent them away from *I* his son,
9 his sons *I* and Ishmael buried him
11 that God blessed his son *I*;
11 and *I* dwelt by the well Lahai-roi.
19 these are the generations of *I*,
19 Abraham's son: Abraham begat *I*:
20 *I* was forty years old when he took
21 *I* entreated the Lord for his wife,
26 *I* was threescore years old when
28 *I* loved Esau, because he did eat
26. 1 *I* went unto Abimelech king of
6 And *I* dwelt in Gerar:
8 *I* was sporting with Rebekah his
9 Abimelech called *I*, and said,
9 *I* said unto him, Because I said,
12 *I* sowed in that land, and received
16 Abimelech said unto *I*, Go from
17 *I* departed thence, and pitched
18 *I* digged again the wells of water,
27 *I* said unto them, Wherefore come
31 *I* sent them away, and they
35 which were a grief of mind unto *I*
27. 1 when *I* was old, and his eyes were
5 when *I* spake to Esau his son.
20 *I* said unto his son, How is it that
21 *I* said unto Jacob, Come near, I
22 Jacob went near unto *I* his father;
26 his father *I* said unto him, Come
30 *I* had made an end of blessing
30 gone out from the presence of *I*
32 *I* his father said unto him, Who
33 *I* trembled very exceedingly, and
37 *I* answered and said unto Esau,
39 *I* his father answered and said
46 Rebekah said to *I*, I am weary of
28. 1 *I* called Jacob, and blessed him,
5 *I* sent away Jacob: and he went
6 saw that *I* had blessed Jacob,
8 daughters of Canaan pleased not *I*
13 thy father, and the God of *I*:
31.18 for to go to *I* his father in the land
42 Abraham, and the fear of *I*, had
53 sware by the fear of his father *I*.
32. 9 and God of my father *I*, the Lord
35.12 land which I gave Abraham and *I*,
27 Jacob came unto *I* his father unto
27 where Abraham and *I* sojourned.
28 *I* were a hundred and fourscore
29 And *I* gave up the ghost, and died,
46. 1 unto the God of his father *I*.
48.15 fathers Abraham and *I* did walk,
16 of my fathers Abraham and *I*;
49.31 buried *I* and Rebekah his wife;
50.24 to Abraham, to *I*, and to Jacob.
Ex 2.24 Abraham, with *I*, and with Jacob.
3. 6 Abraham, the God of *I*, and the
15 the God of *I*, and the God of Jacob,
16 God of Abraham, of *I*, and of
4. 5 the God of *I*, and the God of Jacob,
6. 3 I appeared unto Abraham, unto *I*,
8 give it to Abraham, to *I*, and to
32.13 Remember Abraham, *I*, and Israel,
33. 1 swear unto Abraham, to *I*, and to
Lev 26.42 and also my covenant with *I*,
Nu 32.11 swear unto Abraham, unto *I*, and
Dt 1. 8 your fathers, Abraham, *I*, and
6.10 to Abraham, to *I*, and to Jacob,
9. 5 fathers, Abraham, *I*, and Jacob.
27 servants, Abraham, *I*, and Jacob;
29.13 to Abraham, to *I*, and to Jacob.
30.20 to Abraham, to *I*, and to Jacob,
34. 4 I sware unto Abraham, unto *I*,
Jos 24. 3 multiplied his seed, and gave him *I*.
4 I gave unto *I* Jacob and Esau:
1Ki 18.36 God of Abraham, *I*, and of Israel,
2Ki 13.23 his covenant with Abraham, *I*, and
1Ch 1.28 sons of Abraham; *I*, and Ishmael.
34 And Abraham begat *I*.
34 The sons of *I*; Esau and Israel.
16.16 Abraham, and of his oath unto *I*;
29.18 God of Abraham, *I*, and of Israel,
2Ch 30. 6 God of Abraham, *I*, and Israel,
Ps 105. 9 Abraham, and his oath unto *I*;
Jer 33.26 seed of Abraham, *I*, and Jacob:
Am 7. 9 high places of *I* shall be desolate,
16 thy word against the house of *I*.
Mt 1. 2 begat *I*; and *I* begat Jacob;
8.11 sit down with Abraham, and *I*,
22.32 God of *I*, and the God of Jacob?
Mk 12.26 God of Abraham, and the God of *I*,
Lk 3.34 which was the son of *I*, which was
13.28 see Abraham, and *I*, and Jacob,
20.37 and the God of *I*, and the God of
Ac 3.13 The God of Abraham, and of *I*,
7. 8 Abraham begat *I*, and circumcised
8 and *I* begat Jacob; and Jacob
32 God of Abraham, and the God of *I*,
Ro 9. 7 but, In *I* shall thy seed be called.
10 by one, even by our father *I*;
Gal 4.28 Now we, brethren, as *I* was, are
Heb 11. 9 dwelling in tabernacles with *I* and
17 when he was tried, offered up *I*:
18 That in *I* shall thy seed be called:
20 By faith *I* blessed Jacob and Esau
Jas 2.21 offered *I* his son upon the altar?

ISAIAH

2Ki 19. 2 to *I* the prophet the son of Amoz.
5 of king Hezekiah came to *I*.
6 And *I* said unto them, Thus shall
20 Then *I* the son of Amoz sent to
20. 1 *I* the son of Amoz came to him,
4 *I* was gone out into the middle
7 And *I* said, Take a lump of figs.
8 Hezekiah said unto *I*, What shall
9 *I* said, This sign shalt thou have of
11 *I* the prophet cried unto the Lord:
14 *I* the prophet unto king Hezekiah,
16 *I* said unto Hezekiah, Hear the
19 said Hezekiah unto *I*, Good is the
2Ch 26.22 did *I* the prophet, the son of Amoz,
32.20 *I* the son of Amoz, prayed and
32 in the vision of *I* the prophet,
Isa 1. 1 The vision of *I* the son of Amoz,
2. 1 word that *I* the son of Amoz saw
7. 3 Then said the Lord unto *I*, Go

13. 1 which *I* the son of Amoz did see.
20. 2 the same time spake the Lord by *I*
3 my servant *I* hath walked naked
37. 2 unto *I* the prophet the son of Amoz.
5 of king Hezekiah came to *I*.
6 *I* said unto them, Thus shall ye say
21 Then *I* the son of Amoz sent unto
38. 1 *I* the prophet the son of Amoz
4 came the word of the Lord to *I*,
21 *I* had said, Let them take a lump
39. 3 *I* the prophet unto king Hezekiah,
5 Then said *I* to Hezekiah, Hear the
8 Then said Hezekiah to *I*, Good is

ISCARIOT

Mt 10. 4 Judas *I*, who also betrayed him.
26.14 one of the twelve, called Judas *I*,
Mk 3.19 Judas *I*, which also betrayed him:
14.10 And Judas *I*, one of the twelve,
Lk 6.16 Judas *I*, which also was the traitor.
22. 3 Satan into Judas surnamed *I*,
Jn 6.71 spake of Judas *I* the son of Simon:
12. 4 one of his disciples, Judas *I*,
13. 3 now put it into the heart of Judas *I*,
26 the sop, he gave it to Judas *I*, the
14.22 Judas saith unto him, not *I*, Lord,
(See illustration on page 396)

ISLAND

Job 22.30 shall deliver the *i* of the innocent,
Isa 34.14 meet with the wild beasts of the *i*,
Ac 27.16 a certain *i* which is called Clauda,
26 we must be cast upon a certain *i*.
28. 1 knew that the *i* was called Melita.
7 the chief man of the *i*, whose name
9 which had diseases in the *i*, came,

ISAIAH

Great prophet of the late 8th century B.C.; active in matters concerning Judah and Jerusalem in the reigns of Uzziah, Jotham, Ahaz, and Hezekiah (Isa 1.1); vision of the Lord in his royal court in the year of Uzziah's death portrays prophet as ritually cleansed, but charged with a bleak message: "Make the heart of this people fat, and make their ears heavy, and shut their eyes" (Isa 6); prophesies divine judgment against Israel and Judah in the form of invasion by Assyria, the unwitting instrument of God's purpose (Isa 8, 10); but also foresees survival of a remnant, which will be restored as the people of God, with an anointed king of the house of David, ushering in an age of peace and revived worship of Yahweh (Isa 9, 11–12); after Assyrian assault on Philistine Ashdod, spends three years naked, without even sackcloth or sandals, to dramatize folly of expecting support from Egypt (Isa 20); trusted adviser to Hezekiah when Sennacherib invades Judah, promising that Jerusalem will not fall; announces extension to king's life, but warns him of more distant trouble from Babylon (Isa 36–39). Isa 40–66, sometimes called "Second Isaiah," is now generally recognized as the work of disciples writing in his name during and after the Babylonian Exile (6th century B.C.); these chapters preach not judgment on an apostate nation, but comfort for a suffering people and hope for the return and redemption of the Lord's "righteous servant," Israel.

Rev 6.14 every mountain and *i* were moved
16.20 And every *i* fled away, and the

ISLANDS

Isa 11.11 Hamath, and from the *i* of the sea.
13.22 the wild beasts of the *i* shall cry in
41. 1 Keep silence before me, O *i*; and
42.12 and declare his praise in the *i*.
15 I will make the rivers *i*, and I will
59.18 to the *i* he will repay recompence.
Jer 50.39 beasts of the *i* shall dwell there,

ISLE

Isa 20. 6 inhabitants of this *i* shall say in
23. 2 Be still, ye inhabitants of the *i*;
6 howl, ye inhabitants of the *i*.
Ac 13. 6 gone through the *i* unto Paphos,
28.11 which had wintered in the *i*, whose
Rev 1. 9 was in the *i* that is called Patmos,

ISLES

Gen 10. 5 were the *i* of the Gentiles divided
Est 10. 1 the land, and upon the *i* of the sea.
Ps 72.10 and of the *i* shall bring presents:
97. 1 the multitude of *i* be glad thereof.
Isa 24.15 God of Israel in the *i* of the sea.
40.15 taketh up the *i* as a very little thing.
41. 5 The *i* saw it, and feared; the ends
42. 4 and the *i* shall wait for his law.
10 the *i*, and the inhabitants thereof.
49. 1 Listen, O *i*, unto me; and hearken,
51. 5 the *i* shall wait upon me, and on
60. 9 Surely the *i* shall wait for me, and
66.19 to Tubal, and Javan, to the *i* afar off,
Jer 2.10 pass over the *i* of Chittim, and see;
25.22 the *i* which are beyond the sea,
31.10 declare it in the *i* afar off, and say,
Eze 26.15 the *i* shake at the sound of thy fall,
18 the *i* tremble in the day of thy fall;
18 the *i* that are in the sea shall be
27. 3 merchant of the people for many *i*,
6 brought out of the *i* of Chittim.
7 and purple from the *i* of Elishah
15 many *i* were the merchandise of
35 All the inhabitants of the *i* shall be
39. 6 them that dwell carelessly in the *i*:
Dan 11.18 shall he turn his face unto the *i*,
Zep 2.11 place, even all the *i* of the heathen.

ISRAEL

Gen 32.28 be called no more Jacob, but *I*:
34. 7 because he had wrought folly in *I*
35.10 Jacob, but *I* shall be thy name;
10 and he called his name *I*.
46. 1 *I* took his journey with all that he
2 God spake unto *I* in the visions of
47.27 And *I* dwelt in the land of Egypt,
31 *I* bowed himself upon the bed's
48. 2 *I* strengthened himself, and sat
20 In thee shall *I* bless, saying, God
49. 2 and hearken unto *I* your father.
7 in Jacob, and scatter them in *I*.
16 people, as one of the tribes of *I*.
24 is the shepherd, the stone of *I*:
28 these are the twelve tribes of *I*:
Ex 1. 1 are the names of the children of *I*,
4.22 Thus saith the Lord, *I* is my son,
5. 1 Thus saith the Lord God of *I*, Let
2 should obey his voice to let *I* go?
2 the Lord, neither will I let *I* go.
10.20 would not let the children of *I* go.
12. 3 ye unto all the congregation of *I*,
15 that soul shall be cut off from *I*.
50 Thus did all the children of *I*; as
14. 2 Speak unto the children of *I*, that
5 we have let *I* go from serving us?
8 of *I* went out with an high hand.
22 of *I* went into the midst of the sea
25 Let us flee from the face of *I*; for
30 the Lord saved *I* that day out of
30 *I* saw the Egyptians dead upon
15. 1 sang Moses and the children of *I*
22 Moses brought *I* from the Red sea,
17. 1 *I* journeyed from the wilderness
8 and fought with *I* in Rephidim.
11 held up his hand, that *I* prevailed:
18. 1 for Moses, and for *I* his people,
9 which the Lord had done to *I*,
25 Moses chose able men out of all *I*,
20.22 shalt say unto the children of *I*,
24. 1 and seventy of the elders of *I*;
4 according to the twelve tribes of *I*.
32. 4, 8 These be thy gods, O *I*, which
13 Remember Abraham, Isaac, and *I*,
34.23 before the Lord God, the God of *I*.
27 covenant with thee and with *I*.
Lev 1. 2 Speak unto the children of *I*, and
20. 2 shalt say to the children of *I*,
2 strangers that sojourn in *I*, that
22. 2 holy things of the children of *I*,
18 the strangers in *I*, that will offer
24. 2 Command the children of *I*, that
10 went out among the children of *I*:
Nu 1. 2 congregation of the children of *I*,
3 are able to go forth to war in *I*:
16 fathers, heads of thousands in *I*.
44 the princes of *I*, being twelve men:
45 were able to go forth to war in *I*;
54 children of *I* did according to all
3. 8 the charge of the children of *I*, to
13 unto me all the firstborn in *I*,
6. 2 Speak unto the children of *I*, and
27 my name upon the children of *I*;
10. 4 are heads of the thousands of *I*,
29 hath spoken good concerning *I*.
36 unto the many thousands of *I*.
16. 2 with certain of the children of *I*,
34 all *I* that were round about them
18. 5 any more upon the children of *I*.
14 Every thing devoted in *I* shall be
21 the tenth in *I* for an inheritance,
19. 2 Speak unto the children of *I*, that
13 that soul shall be cut off from *I*:
20. 1 Then came the children of *I*, even
14 Thus saith thy brother *I*, Thou
21. 1 *I* came by the way of the spies;
2 And *I* vowed a vow unto the Lord,
6 people; and much people of *I* died.
17 *I* sang this song, Spring up, O
23 to Jahaz, and fought against *I*.
23. 7 curse me Jacob, and come, defy *I*.
21 hath he seen perverseness in *I*:
23 it shall be said of Jacob and of *I*,
24. 1 that it pleased the Lord to bless *I*,
5 O Jacob, and thy tabernacles, O *I*!
17 a Sceptre shall rise out of *I*, and
18 enemies; and *I* shall do valiantly.
25. 1 And *I* abode in Shittim, and the
3 *I* joined himself unto Baal-peor:
3 of the Lord was kindled against *I*.
4 Lord may be turned away from *I*,
8 the man of *I*, and the woman
26. 2 congregation of the children of *I*,
2 all that are able to go to war in *I*.
31. 2 children of *I* of the Midianites:
4 throughout all the tribes of *I*, shall
36. 1 chief fathers of the children of *I*:
3 other tribes of the children of *I*,
Dt 1. 1 words which Moses spake unto all *I*
4. 1 Now therefore hearken, O *I*, unto
5. 1 Moses called all *I*, and said unto
1 Hear, O *I*, the statutes and
4 Hear, O *I*: The Lord our God is
13.11 And all *I* shall hear, and fear, and
17. 4 such abomination is wrought in *I*:
12 shalt put away the evil from *I*.
18. 1 no part nor inheritance with *I*:
21. 8 merciful, O Lord, unto thy people *I*,
21 you; and all *I* shall hear, and fear.
22.19 an evil name upon a virgin of *I*:
21 she hath wrought folly in *I*, to play
22 shalt thou put away evil from *I*.

Iscariot was the surname of the treacherous disciple, shown here in a 19th-century British illustration.

Dt 25. 6 that his name be not put out of *I*.
7 up unto his brother a name in *I*,
10 his name shall be called in *I*, The
26.15 and bless thy people *I*, and the
27. 1 elders of *I* commanded the people,
9 Take heed, and hearken, O *I*; this
29. 1 children of *I* in the land of Moab,
21 unto evil out of all the tribes of *I*,
33. 1 of God blessed the children of *I*
5 of the people and the tribes of *I*
10 thy judgments, and *I* thy law.
21 Lord, and his judgments with *I*.
28 *I* then shall dwell in safety alone:
29 Happy art thou, O *I*: who is like
34. 8 of *I* wept for Moses in the plains
10 prophet since in *I* like unto Moses,
Jos 1. 2 them, even to the children of *I*.
3. 1 Jordan, he and all the children of *I*,
12 twelve men out of the tribes of *I*,
4. 4 had prepared of the children of *I*,
5 of the tribes of the children of *I*:
8 of the tribes of the children of *I*,
6. 1 up because of the children of *I*:
18 and make the camp of *I* a curse,
23 left them without the camp of *I*.
25 and she dwelleth in *I* even unto
7. 1 children of *I* committed a trespass
8 I say, when *I* turneth their backs
11 *I* hath sinned, and they have also
13 thing in the midst of thee, O *I*:
15 because he hath wrought folly in *I*.
16 and brought *I* by their tribes;
25 And all *I* stoned him with stones,
8.10 and went up, he and the elders of *I*,
14 city went out against *I* to battle,
30 an altar unto the Lord God of *I*
33 they should bless the people of *I*.
9. 2 to fight with Joshua, and with *I*,
10. 1 of Gibeon had made peace with *I*,
14 a man: for the Lord fought for *I*.
24 Joshua called for all the men of *I*,
42 the Lord God of *I* fought for *I*.
11. 5 waters of Merom, to fight against *I*.
16 mountain of *I*, and the valley
23 gave it for an inheritance unto *I*
12. 1 which the children of *I* smote, and
7 unto the tribes of *I* for a possession
19.49 of *I* gave an inheritance to Joshua
51 of the tribes of the children of *I*,
21. 1 of the tribes of the children of *I*;
43 the Lord gave unto *I* all the land

22. 9 departed from the children of *I*
14 throughout all the tribes of *I*;
22 he knoweth, and *I* he shall know:
24. 1 all the tribes of *I* to Shechem,
9 Moab, arose and warred against *I*,
31 *I* served the Lord all the days of
Jdg 1. 1 the children of *I* asked the Lord,
28 came to pass, when *I* was strong,
2. 4 words unto all the children of *I*,
22 That through them I may prove *I*,
3. 1 the Lord left, to prove *I* by them,
4 And they were to prove *I* by them,
12 Eglon the king of Moab against *I*,
4. 1 *I* again did evil in the sight of the
5. 2 ye the Lord for the avenging of *I*,
7 arose, that I arose a mother in *I*.
8 seen among forty thousand in *I*?
9 heart is toward the governors of *I*,
6. 1 *I* did evil in the sight of the Lord:
2 of Midian prevailed against *I*:
4 left no sustenance for *I*, neither
36 said unto God, If thou wilt save *I*
7. 2 *I* vaunt themselves against me,
8.22 the men of *I* said unto Gideon,
27 *I* went thither a whoring after it:
35 which he had shewed unto *I*.
9.22 had reigned three years over *I*,
10. 1 there arose to defend *I* Tola the
9 so that *I* was sore distressed.
16 was grieved for the misery of *I*.
11. 4 of Ammon made war against *I*.
13 Because *I* took away my land,
23 from before his people *I*, and
14. 4 Philistines had dominion over *I*.
17. 6 those days there was no king in *I*,
18. 1 those days there was no king in *I*:
1 unto them among the tribes of *I*.
19 unto a tribe and a family in *I*?
19. 1 days, when there was no king in *I*,
20. 1 Then all the children of *I* went out,
2 even of all the tribes of *I*, presented
3 heard that the children of *I* were
6 committed lewdness and folly in *I*.
7 Behold, ye are all children of *I*;
10 throughout all the tribes of *I*,
10 folly that they have wrought in *I*.
11 all the men of *I* were gathered
13 death, and put away evil from *I*.
20 the men of *I* went out to battle
22 men of *I* encouraged themselves,
25 *I* again eighteen thousand men;

35 Lord smote Benjamin before *I*:
36 of *I* gave place to the Benjamites,
21. 1 men of *I* had sworn in Mizpeh,
5 all the tribes of *I* that came not up
6 one tribe cut off from *I* this day.
8 of *I* that came not up to Mizpeh to
15 made a breach in the tribes of *I*.
Ru 2.12 be given thee of the Lord God of *I*,
4. 7 the manner in former time in *I*
14 that his name may be famous in *I*.
1Sa 1.17 God of *I* grant thee thy petition
2.22 all that his sons did unto all *I*;
28 choose him out of all the tribes of *I*
29 all the offerings of *I* my people?
3.11 Behold, I will do a thing in *I*, at
20 all *I* from Dan even to Beer-sheba
4. 1 the word of Samuel came to all *I*.
2 put themselves in array against *I*:
2 *I* was smitten before the
10 fought, and *I* was smitten, and they
17 *I* is fled before the Philistines,
21, 22 The glory is departed from *I*:
7. 2 house of *I* lamented after the Lord.
7 the Philistines went up against *I*.
9 Samuel cried unto the Lord for *I*;
10 drew near to battle against *I*:
14 taken from *I* were restored to *I*,
8. 1 he made his sons judges over *I*.
9. 2 of *I* a goodlier person than he:
9 Beforetime in *I*, when a man went
16 to be captain over my people *I*,
20 on whom is all the desire of *I*? Is
21 the smallest of the tribes of *I*?
10.18 And said unto the children of *I*,
20 all the tribes of *I* to come near,
11. 2 lay it for a reproach upon all *I*.
13 Lord hath wrought salvation in *I*.
13. 1 he had reigned two years over *I*,
4 *I* heard say that Saul had smitten
5 themselves together to fight with *I*,
19 found throughout all the land of *I*:
14.12 delivered them into the hand of *I*.
23 So the Lord saved *I* that day: and
24 men of *I* were distressed that day:
45 wrought this great salvation in *I*?
15. 1 to be king over his people, over *I*:
2 that which Amalek did to *I*, how
17 not made the head of the tribes of *I*,
29 Strength of *I* will not lie nor repent:
17. 2 men of *I* were gathered together,
25 make his father's house free in *I*.
26 taketh away the reproach from *I*?
45 hosts, the God of the armies of *I*,
46 may know that there is a God in *I*.
18. 6 women came out of all cities of *I*,
16 But all *I* and Judah loved David,
18 my life, or my father's family in *I*,
26. 2 three thousand chosen men of *I*
15 man? and who is like to thee in *I*?
27. 1 me any more in any coast of *I*:
12 his people *I* utterly to abhor him;
28. 1 for warfare, to fight with *I*.
3 dead, and all *I* had lamented him,
30.25 a statute and an ordinance for *I*
31. 1 the Philistines fought against *I*:
1 *I* fled from before the Philistines,
2Sa 1. 3 Out of the camp of *I* am I escaped.
19 beauty of *I* is slain upon thy high
2. 9 and over Benjamin, and over all *I*
10 old when he began to reign over *I*
17 Abner was beaten, and the men of *I*,
3.10 set up the throne of David over *I*
12 to bring about all *I* unto thee.
18 I will save my people *I* out of the
19 Hebron all that seemed good to *I*,
37 all the people and all *I* understood
38 a great man fallen this day in *I*?
5. 1 came all the tribes of *I* to David
2 leddest out and broughtest in *I*:
2 thee, Thou shalt feed my people *I*,
2 and thou shalt be a captain over *I*.

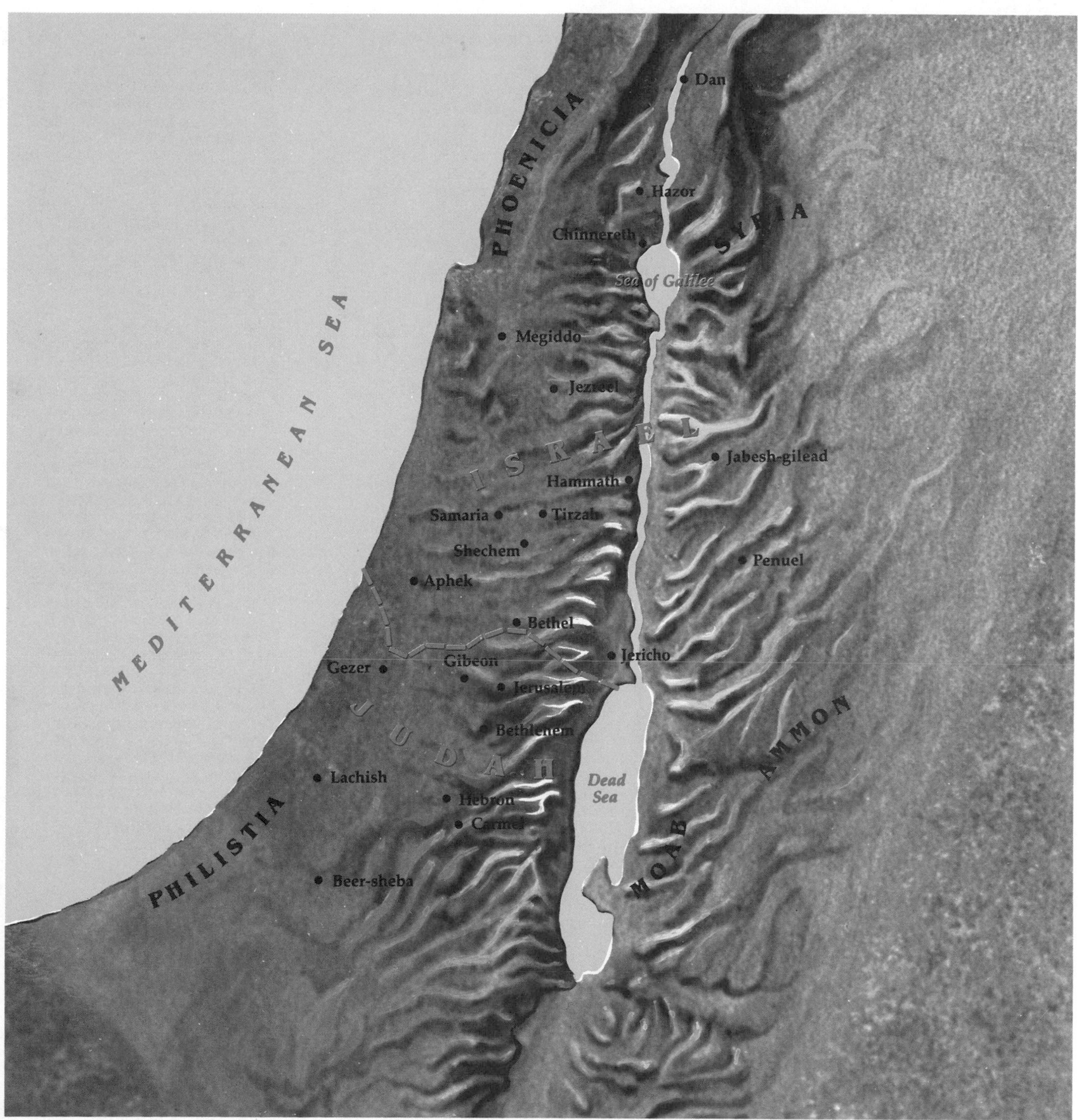

***The Divided Kingdom** came into being following Solomon's death in about 922 B.C. His son Rehoboam, rejected as king by the northern tribes, inherited only the throne of a much-reduced kingdom of Judah, which remained loyal to the house of David until Jerusalem's fall in 587 B.C. The north declared itself the independent kingdom of Israel under Jeroboam, who made his capital first in Shechem and then in Tirzah. About 875 B.C., King Omri built a splendid new capital at Samaria, which remained the center of Israel's turbulent history until its destruction by Assyria in 721 B.C.*

12 had established him king over *I*,
7. 6 up the children of *I* out of Egypt,
7 a word with any of the tribes of *I*,
7 I commanded to feed my people *I*,
23 is like thy people, even like *I*,
24 confirmed to thyself thy people *I*
26 Lord of hosts is the God over *I*:
10. 9 he chose of all the choice men of *I*,
19 they made peace with *I*, and served
11. 1 his servants with him, and all *I*;
11 The ark, and *I*, and Judah, abide
12. 7 Thus saith the Lord God of *I*,
12 I will do this thing before all *I*,
13.12 such thing ought to be done in *I*:
13 shalt be as one of the fools in *I*.
14.25 in all *I* there was none to be so
15. 2 servant is of one of the tribes of *I*.
10 spies throughout all the tribes of *I*,
13 hearts of the men of *I* are after
16. 3 house of *I* restore me the kingdom
18 this people, and all the men of *I*,
21 *I* shall hear that thou art abhorred
17. 4 well, and all the elders of *I*.
10 all *I* knoweth that thy father is a
18. 6 went out into the field against *I*:
17 all *I* fled every one to his tent.
19. 8 *I* had fled every man to his tent.
9 strife throughout all the tribes of *I*,
11 speech of all *I* is come to the king,
22 man be put to death this day in *I*?

2Sa 19.43 than the words of the men of *I*.
20. 1 Jesse: every man to his tents, O *I*.
19 destroy a city and a mother in *I*:
21. 2 were not of the children of *I*, but
4 for us shalt thou kill any man in *I*.
15 had yet war again with *I*;
23. 1 Jacob, and the sweet psalmist of *I*,
9 and the men of *I* were gone away:
24. 1 of the Lord was kindled against *I*,
2 Go now through all the tribes of *I*,
25 the plague was stayed from *I*.
1Ki 1. 3 throughout all the coast of *I*,
20 the eyes of all *I* are upon thee,
34 anoint him there king over *I*:
2. 4 (said he) a man on the throne of *I*.
15 that all *I* set their faces on me,
3.28 *I* heard of the judgment which the
4. 1 king Solomon was king over all *I*.
20 Judah and *I* were many, as the
6. 1 of *I* were come out of the land of
13 will dwell among the children of *I*,
13 and will not forsake my people *I*.
8. 1 Solomon assembled the elders of *I*,
23 Lord God of *I*, there is no God like
33 people *I* be smitten down before
38 any man, or by all thy people *I*,
43 to fear thee, as do thy people *I*;
56 hath given rest unto his people *I*,
62 And the king, and all *I* with him,
66 his servant, and for *I* his people.
9. 5 the throne of thy kingdom upon *I*
7 *I* shall be a proverb and a byword
11. 2 Lord said unto the children of *I*,
25 And he was an adversary to *I* all
25 and he abhorred *I*, and reigned
37 desireth, and shall be king over *I*.
12. 1 *I* were come to Shechem to make
16 to your tents, O *I*: now see to
18 all *I* stoned him with stones, that
19 So *I* rebelled against the house of
28 thy gods, O *I*, which brought thee
14. 7 thus saith the Lord God of *I*,
10 him that is shut up and left in *I*,
13 God of *I* in the house of Jeroboam.
14 shall raise him up a king over *I*,
15 the Lord shall smite *I*, as a reed
16 did sin, and who made *I* to sin.
15. 9 year of Jeroboam king of *I* reigned
25 and reigned over *I* two years.
16. 2 made thee prince over my people *I*;
2 hast made my people *I* to sin, to
8 Baasha to reign over *I* in Tirzah,
13 by which they made *I* to sin, in
16 wherefore all *I* made Omri, the
29 the son of Omri to reign over *I*:
18.17 him, Art thou he that troubleth *I*?
19 to me all *I* unto mount Carmel,
31 came, saying, *I* shall be thy name:
36 God of Abraham, Isaac, and of *I*,
19.10, 14 of *I* have forsaken thy covenant,
18 have left me seven thousand in *I*,
20. 2 messengers to Ahab king of *I*
26 up to Aphek, to fight against *I*.
21. 7 thou now govern the kingdom of *I*?
21 him that is shut up and left in *I*,
22 me to anger, and made *I* to sin.
22. 1 without war between Syria and *I*.
17 saw all *I* scattered upon the hills,
51 and reigned two years over *I*.
2Ki 1. 1 Moab rebelled against *I* after the
3, 6 because there is not a God in *I*,
16 not because there is no God in *I* to
3. 1 son of Ahab began to reign over *I*
24 when they came to the camp of *I*,
27 was great indignation against *I*:
5. 2 out of the land of *I* a little maid;
8 know that there is a prophet in *I*.
15 no God in all the earth, but in *I*:
6. 8 king of Syria warred against *I*,
12 Elisha, the prophet that is in *I*,
9. 3 I have anointed thee king over *I*.
8 him that is shut up and left in *I*.
10.21 And Jehu sent through all *I*: and
32 the Lord began to cut *I* short:
13. 1 son of Jehu began to reign over *I*
10 to reign over *I* in Samaria, and
14. 1 second year of Joash...king of *I*
12 was put to the worse before *I*;
26 nor any left, nor any helper for *I*.
27 he would blot out the name of *I*
15. 1 year of Jeroboam king of *I* began
8 the son of Jeroboam reigned over *I*
17 the son of Gadi to reign over *I*,
23 of Menahem began to reign over *I*
17. 1 of Elah to reign in Samaria over *I*
6 and carried *I* away into Assyria,
13 Yet the Lord testified against *I*,
18 the Lord was very angry with *I*,
34 of Jacob, whom he named *I*;
1Ch 1.34 The sons of Isaac; Esau and *I*.
6.38 the son of Levi, the son of *I*.
49 and to make an atonement for *I*,
10. 1 the Philistines fought against *I*;
11. 1 all *I* gathered themselves to David
2 leddest out and broughtest in *I*:
4 David and all *I* went to Jerusalem,
10 the word of the Lord concerning *I*.
12.32 to know what *I* ought to do;
40 for there was joy in *I*.
13. 2 unto all the congregation of *I*,
2 that are left in all the land of *I*,
8 David and all *I* played before God
14. 2 had confirmed him king over *I*,
2 on high, because of his people *I*.
15. 3 David gathered all *I* together to
28 Thus all *I* brought up the ark of
16. 3 And he dealt to every one of *I*,
13 O ye seed of *I* his servant, ye
17 to *I* for an everlasting covenant,
17. 5 since the day that I brought up *I*
6 I have walked with all *I*, spake I
7 be ruler over my people *I*:
9 will ordain a place for my people *I*,
21 in the earth is like thy people *I*,
22 thy people *I* didst thou make thine
21. 1 And Satan stood up against *I*,
3 will he be a cause of trespass to *I*?
5 And all they of *I* were a thousand
22. 1 altar of the burnt offering for *I*.
9 give peace and quietness unto *I*
17 commanded all the princes of *I* to
26.29 for the outward business over *I*,
27. 1 children of *I* after their number,
24 there fell wrath for it against *I*;
29. 6 and princes of the tribes of *I*,
23 prospered; and all *I* obeyed him.
30 that went over him, and over *I*,
2Ch 1. 2 Then Solomon spake unto all *I*,
2. 4 This is an ordinance for ever to *I*.
17 all the strangers...in the land of *I*,
6. 3 the whole congregation of *I*:
5 man to be a ruler over my people *I*:
24 thy people *I* be put to the worse
7. 3 of *I* saw how the fire came down,
10 to Solomon, and to *I* his people.
18 not fail thee a man to be ruler in *I*.
9. 8 because thy God loved *I*, to
30 in Jerusalem over all *I* forty years.
10. 1 for to Shechem were all *I* come to
16 every man to your tents, O *I*: and
11. 1 were warriors, to fight against *I*,
16 after them out of all the tribes of *I*
12. 1 law of the Lord, and all *I* with him.
6 princes of *I* and the king humbled
13. 4 me, thou Jeroboam, and all *I*;
15 God smote Jeroboam and all *I*
21. 2 the sons of Jehoshaphat king of *I*.
4 and divers also of the princes of *I*.
24. 5 gather of all *I* money to repair the
16 he had done good in *I*, both toward
25. 6 mighty men of valour out of *I*
7 let not the army of *I* go with thee;
7 for the Lord is not with *I*, to wit,
28. 2 walked in the ways of the kings of *I*,
23 were the ruin of him, and of all *I*.
30. 1 Hezekiah sent to all *I* and Judah,
25 that came out of the land of *I*,
31. 1 all *I* that were present went out to
8 blessed the Lord, and his people *I*.
34. 7 idols throughout all the land of *I*,
21 them that are left in *I* and in Judah,
33 all that were present in *I* to serve,
35. 3 unto the Levites that taught all *I*,
3 Lord your God, and his people *I*,
18 no passover like to that kept in *I*
25 and made them an ordinance to *I*:
Ezr 1. 3 the house of the Lord God of *I*,
2. 2 of the men of the people of *I*:
59 their seed, whether they were of *I*:
70 their cities, and all *I* in their cities.
3. 1 the children of *I* were in the cities,
11 mercy endureth for ever toward *I*.
6.14 the commandment of the God of *I*,
17 and for a sin offering for all *I*,
17 to the number of the tribes of *I*.
7. 6 which the Lord God of *I* had given:
11 the Lord, and of his statutes to *I*.
13 that all they of the people of *I*,
9. 1 The people of *I*, and the priests,
10. 1 assembled unto him out of *I* a
2 is hope in *I* concerning this thing.
5 all *I*, to swear that they should do
10 wives, to increase the trespass of *I*.
Neh 1. 6 for the children of *I* thy servants,
7. 7 say, of the men of the people of *I*
61 their seed, whether they were of *I*.
73 and all *I*, dwelt in their cities;
8. 1 the Lord had commanded to *I*.
10.33 to make an atonement for *I*,
12.47 all *I* in the days of Zerubbabel,
13. 2 of *I* with bread and with water,
3 separated from *I* all the mixed
Ps 14. 7 salvation of *I* were come out of
22. 3 that inhabitest the praises of *I*.
23 and fear him, all ye the seed of *I*.
25.22 Redeem *I*, O God, out of all his
50. 7 O *I*, and I will testify against thee:
53. 6 salvation of *I* were come out of
6 shall rejoice, and *I* shall be glad.
68. 8 the presence of God, the God of *I*.
26 the Lord, from the fountain of *I*.
34 his excellency is over *I*, and his
73. 1 God is good to *I*, even to such as
76. 1 God known: his name is great in *I*.
78. 5 Jacob, and appointed a law in *I*.
21 and anger also came up against *I*;
31 smote down the chosen men of *I*.
55 tribes of *I* to dwell in their tents.
59 wroth, and greatly abhorred *I*:
81. 4 For this was a statute for *I*, and
11 voice; and *I* would none of me.
13 me, and *I* had walked in my ways!
83. 4 name of *I* may be no more in
105.10 to *I* for an everlasting covenant:
114. 1 When *I* went out of Egypt, the
2 his sanctuary, and *I* his dominion.
115. 9 O *I*, trust thou in the Lord: he is
121. 4 keepeth *I* shall neither slumber
128. 6 children, and peace upon *I*.
131. 3 Let *I* hope in the Lord from
135. 4 and *I* for his peculiar treasure.
12 an heritage unto *I* his people.
136.11 brought out *I* from among them:
22 an heritage unto *I* his servant:
147. 2 together the outcasts of *I*.
19 statutes and his judgments unto *I*.
149. 2 Let *I* rejoice in him that made
Ec 1.12 was king over *I* in Jerusalem.
Isa 1. 3 *I* doth not know, my people doth
8.14 of offense to both the houses of *I*,
18 for signs and for wonders in *I*
9. 8 Jacob, and it hath lighted upon *I*.
14 Lord will cut off from *I* head and

10.17 the light of *I* shall be for a fire,
22 people *I* be as the sand of the sea,
11.12 shall assemble the outcasts of *I*,
16 like as it was to *I* in the day that
19.24 In that day shall *I* be the third
25 my hands, and *I* mine inheritance.
27. 6 *I* shall blossom and bud, and fill
40.27 thou, O Jacob, and speakest, O *I*,
41. 8 But thou, *I*, art my servant, Jacob
14 thou worm Jacob, and ye men of *I*;
42.24 for a spoil, and *I* to the robbers?
43. 1 and he that formed thee, O *I*, Fear
22 thou hast been weary of me, O *I*.
28 the curse, and *I* to reproaches.
44. 1 and *I*, whom I have chosen:
5 surname himself by the name of *I*.
23 Jacob, and glorified himself in *I*.
45. 3 thee by thy name, am the God of *I*.
4 servant's sake, and *I* mine elect,
17 But *I* shall be saved in the Lord
25 shall all the seed of *I* be justified,
46. 3 all the remnant of the house of *I*,
13 salvation in Zion for *I* my glory.
48. 1 which are called by the name of *I*,
12 Hearken unto me, O Jacob and *I*,
49. 3 Thou art my servant, O *I*, in whom
5 Though *I* be not gathered, yet
6 and to restore the preserved of *I*:
56. 8 which gathereth the outcasts of *I*
63. 7 goodness toward the house of *I*,
16 of us, and *I* acknowledge us not:
Jer 2. 3 *I* was holiness unto the Lord, and
14 Is *I* a servant? is he a homeborn
31 Have I been a wilderness unto *I*?
3. 6 which backsliding *I* hath done?
23 Lord our God is the salvation of *I*.
4. 1 wilt return, O *I*, saith the Lord,
7. 3 the Lord of hosts, the God of *I*,
12 the wickedness of my people *I*.
10. 1 speaketh unto you, O house of *I*:
16 and *I* is the rod of his inheritance:
12.14 caused my people *I* to inherit;
14. 8 the hope of *I*, the saviour thereof
17.13 O Lord, the hope of *I*, all that
23. 2 Lord God of *I* against the pastors
6 be saved, and *I* shall dwell safely:
13 and caused my people *I* to err.
29. 4 the Lord of hosts, the God of *I*,
23 they have committed villainy in *I*,
30. 2 Thus speaketh the Lord God of *I*,
10 neither be dismayed, O *I*: for, lo,
31. 1 be the God of all the families of *I*,
9 for I am a father to *I*, and Ephraim
32.14, 15 the Lord of hosts, the God of *I*;
20 and in *I*, and among other men;
36. 2 I have spoken unto thee against *I*,
46.25 The Lord of hosts, the God of *I*,
27 Jacob, and be not dismayed, O *I*:
48. 1 the Lord of hosts, the God of *I*;
27 For was not *I* a derision to thee?
49. 1 Hath *I* no sons? hath he no heir?
2 shall *I* be heir unto them that were
50. 4 the children of *I* shall come,
17 *I* is a scattered sheep; the lions
19 will bring *I* again to his habitation,
20 iniquity of *I* shall be sought for,
51. 5 For *I* hath not been forsaken, nor
La 2. 1 unto the earth the beauty of *I*,
5 enemy: he hath swallowed up *I*,
Eze 2. 3 I send thee to the children of *I*,
7. 2 the Lord God unto the land of *I*;
11. 5 Thus have ye said, O house of *I*:
10 I will judge you in the border of *I*;
13 a full end of the remnant of *I*?
17 and I will give you the land of *I*.
12. 6 thee for a sign unto the house of *I*.
19 of Jerusalem, and of the land of *I*;
23 no more use it as a proverb in *I*;
13. 2 prophesy against the prophets of *I*
4 O *I*, thy prophets are like the foxes
14. 1 certain of the elders of *I* unto me,
7 the stranger that sojourneth in *I*,
18. 2 proverb concerning the land of *I*,
3 any more to use this proverb in *I*.
19. 1 a lamentation for the princes of *I*,
20. 1 of the elders of *I* came to inquire
38 shall not enter into the land of *I*:
42 shall bring you into the land of *I*,
21. 2 prophesy against the land of *I*,
12 shall be upon all the princes of *I*:
22. 6 Behold, the princes of *I*, every one
25. 3 against the land of *I*, when it was
6 thy despite against the land of *I*;
14 Edom by the hand of my people *I*:
27.17 land of *I*, they were thy merchants:
36. 1 prophesy unto the mountains of *I*,
8 yield your fruit to my people of *I*;
12 walk upon you, even my people *I*;
37.11 bones are the whole house of *I*:
12 and bring you into the land of *I*.
19 the tribes of *I* his fellows, and will
28 know that I the Lord do sanctify *I*,
38. 8 people, against the mountains of *I*,
14 my people of *I* dwelleth safely,
16 come up against my people of *I*,
18 shall come against the land of *I*,
19 a great shaking in the land of *I*;
39. 2 thee upon the mountains of *I*:
7 I am the Lord, the Holy One in *I*.
11 Gog a place there of graves in *I*,
40. 2 brought he me into the land of *I*,
44. 2 Lord, the God of *I*, hath entered in
10 far from me, when *I* went astray,
28 shall give them no possession in *I*:
29 dedicated thing in *I* shall be theirs.
45. 6 shall be for the whole house of *I*.
8 land shall be his possession in *I*:
9 Let it suffice you, O princes of *I*:
16 this oblation for the prince in *I*.
48.11 when the children of *I* went astray,
19 serve it out of all the tribes of *I*.
Dan 1. 3 bring certain of the children of *I*,
9. 7 of Jerusalem, and unto all *I*,
11 all *I* have transgressed thy law,
20 my sin and the sin of my people *I*,
Hos 1. 1 the son of Joash, king of *I*.
4. 1 word of the Lord, ye children of *I*:
15 Though thou, *I*, play the harlot, yet
16 *I* slideth back as a backsliding
5. 1 and hearken, ye house of *I*;
3 Ephraim, and *I* is not hid from me:
5 shall *I* and Ephraim fall in their
9 tribes of *I* have I made known that
6.10 horrible thing in the house of *I*:
8. 2 *I* shall cry unto me, My God, we
3 *I* hath cast off the thing that is
6 from *I* was it also: the workman
8 *I* is swallowed up: now shall they
9. 1 Rejoice not, O *I*, for joy, as other
7 are come; *I* shall know it:
10 *I* like grapes in the wilderness;
10. 1 *I* is an empty vine, he bringeth
6 *I* shall be ashamed of his own
8 the sin of *I*, shall be destroyed:
9 *I*, thou hast sinned from the days
11. 1 When *I* was a child, then I loved
8 how shall I deliver thee, *I*? how
12.12 *I* served for a wife, and for a wife
13. 1 trembling, he exalted himself in *I*;
9 O *I*, thou hast destroyed thyself;
14. 1 O *I*, return unto the Lord thy God;
5 I will be as the dew unto *I*: he
Joel 2.27 know that I am in the midst of *I*,
3. 2 my people and for my heritage *I*,
Am 1. 1 concerning *I* in the days of Uzziah
4. 5 this liketh you, O ye children of *I*,
12 prepare to meet thy God, O *I*.
7. 8 in the midst of my people *I*:
11 *I* shall surely be led away captive
15 Go, prophesy unto my people *I*.
16 sayest, Prophesy not against *I*,
17 and *I* shall surely go into captivity
8. 2 end is come upon my people of *I*;
9. 7 unto me, O children of *I*?
14 the captivity of my people of *I*,
Mic 1. 5 and for the sins of the house of *I*.
15 come unto Adullam the glory of *I*.
3. 1 and ye princes of the house of *I*;
8 his transgression, and to *I* his sin.
5. 1 smite the judge of *I* with a rod
2 unto me that is to be ruler in *I*;
6. 2 people, and he will plead with *I*:
Zep 2. 9 the Lord of hosts, the God of *I*,
3.13 remnant of *I* shall not do iniquity,
14 O daughter of Zion; shout, O *I*; be
Zec 1.19 scattered Judah, *I*, and Jerusalem.
9. 1 of man, as of all the tribes of *I*,
12. 1 of the word of the Lord for *I*,
Mal 1. 1 word of the Lord to *I* by Malachi.
2.11 an abomination is committed in *I*
4. 4 unto him in Horeb for all *I*,
Mt 2. 6 that shall rule my people *I*.
20 mother, and go into the land of *I*:
21 and came into the land of *I*.
8.10 found so great faith, no, not in *I*.
9.33 saying, It was never so seen in *I*.
10. 6 to the lost sheep of the house of *I*.
15.24 unto the lost sheep of the house of *I*.
19.28 judging the twelve tribes of *I*.
Mk 12.29 the commandments is, Hear, O *I*;
Lk 1.16 of the children of *I* shall he turn
54 He hath holpen his servant *I*,
80 till the day of his shewing unto *I*.
2.25 waiting for the consolation of *I*:
32 and the glory of thy people *I*.
34 fall and rising again of many in *I*;
4.25 many widows were in *I* in the days
27 many lepers were in *I* in the time of
7. 9 found so great faith, no, not in *I*.
22.30 judging the twelve tribes of *I*.
Jn 1.31 he should be made manifest to *I*.
49 Son of God; thou art the King of *I*.
3.10 Art thou a master of *I*, and
12.13 King of *I* that cometh in the name
Ac 1. 6 restore again the kingdom to *I*?
2.22 Ye men of *I*, hear these words;
3.12 Ye men of *I*, why marvel ye at this?
4. 8 of the people, and elders of *I*,
27 the Gentiles, and the people of *I*,
5.21 all the senate of the children of *I*,
31 for to give repentance to *I*, and
35 Ye men of *I*, take heed to
13.16 Men of *I*, and ye that fear God,
17 The God of this people of *I* chose
23 promise raised unto *I* a Saviour,
24 repentance to all the people of *I*.
21.28 Crying out, Men of *I*, help: This
28.20 that for the hope of *I* I am bound
Ro 9. 6 they are not all *I*, which are of *I*:
27 Esaias also crieth concerning *I*.
31 But *I*, which followed after the law
10. 1 desire and prayer to God for *I* is,
21 But to *I* he saith, All day long I
11. 2 intercession to God against *I*.
7 *I* hath not obtained that which he
25 blindness in part is happened to *I*,
26 And so all *I* shall be saved: as it is
1Co 10.18 Behold *I* after the flesh: are not
Gal 6.16 and mercy, and upon the *I* of God.
Php 3. 5 of the stock of *I*, of the tribe of
Heb 8. 8 a new covenant with the house of *I*
Rev 2.14 cast a stumblingblock before...of *I*,
21.12 twelve tribes of the children of *I*:

ISRAELITE

Nu 25.14 name of the *I* that was slain,
2Sa 17.25 son, whose name was Ithra an *I*,
Jn 1.47 Behold an *I* indeed, in whom is
Ro 11. 1 For I also am an *I*, of the seed of

ISRAELITES

Ex 9. 7 not one of the cattle of the *I* dead
Lev 23.42 are *I* born shall dwell in booths:

Jos	3.17	the *I* passed over on dry ground,
	8.24	all the *I* returned unto Ai, and
	13. 6	lot unto the *I* for an inheritance,
	13	dwell among the *I* until this day.
Jdg	20.21	to the ground of the *I* that day
1Sa	2.14	in Shiloh unto all the *I* that came
	13.20	the *I* went down to the Philistines,
	14.21	be with the *I* that were with Saul
	25. 1	all the *I* were gathered together,
	29. 1	*I* pitched by a fountain which is
2Sa	4. 1	feeble, and all the *I* were troubled.
2Ki	3.24	*I* rose up and smote the Moabites.
	7.13	even as all the multitude of the *I*
1Ch	9. 2	the *I*, the priests, Levites, and
Ro	9. 4	Who are *I*; to whom pertaineth
2Co	11.22	Are they *I*? so am I. Are they

ISSUE

Gen	48. 6	And thy *i*, which thou begettest
Lev	12. 7	cleansed from the *i* of her blood.
	15. 2	When any man hath a running *i*
	2	because of his *i* he is unclean.
Nu	5. 2	leper, and every one that hath an *i*,
2Sa	3.29	house of Joab one that hath an *i*
2Ki	20.18	of thy sons that shall *i* from thee,
Isa	22.24	house, the offspring and the *i*, all
	39. 7	thy sons that shall *i* from thee,
Eze	23.20	and whose *i* is like the *i* of horses.
	47. 8	waters *i* out toward the east
Mt	9.20	with an *i* of blood twelve years,
	22.25	having no *i*, left his wife unto his
Mk	5.25	had an *i* of blood twelve years,
Lk	8.43	having an *i* of blood twelve years,
	44	and immediately her *i* of blood

ISSUED

Jos	8.22	the other *i* out of the city against
Job	38. 8	as if it had *i* out of the womb?
Eze	47. 1	waters *i* out from under the
	12	waters they *i* out of the sanctuary:
Dan	7.10	A fiery stream *i* and came forth
Rev	9.17	out of their mouths *i* fire and
	18	which *i* out of their mouths.

ISSUES

Ps	68.20	the Lord belong the *i* from death.
Pr	4.23	for out of it are the *i* of life.

ITALIAN

Ac	10. 1	of the band called the *I* band,

ITALY

Ac	18. 2	in Pontus, lately come from *I*,
	27. 1	that we should sail into *I*,
	6	ship of Alexandria sailing into *I*;
Heb	13.24	the saints. They of *I* salute you.

ITCHING

2Ti	4. 3	teachers, having *i* ears;

ITURAEA

Lk	3. 1	his brother Philip tetrarch of *I*

IVORY

1Ki	10.18	the king made a great throne of *i*,
	22	silver, *i*, and apes, and peacocks.
	22.39	and the *i* house which he made,
2Ch	9.17	the king made a great throne of *i*,
	21	silver, *i*, and apes, and peacocks.
Ps	45. 8	and cassia, out of the *i* palaces,
SS	5.14	his belly is as bright *i* overlaid
	7. 4	Thy neck is as a tower of *i*; thine
Eze	27. 6	have made thy benches of *i*,
	15	for a present horns of *i* and ebony.
Am	3.15	houses of *i* shall perish, and the
	6. 4	That lie upon beds of *i*, and stretch
Rev	18.12	wood, and all manner vessels of *i*,

This ivory figure ornamented the bed of Hazael, the king of Damascus anointed by Elijah (1Ki 19).

J

JACHIN
Gen 46.10 Jamin, and Ohad, and *J*, and
Ex 6.15 Jamin, and Ohad, and *J*, and
Nu 26.12 of *J*, the family of the Jachinites:
1Ki 7.21 and called the name thereof *J*:
1Ch 9.10 Jedaiah, and Jehoiarib, and *J*,
24.17 The one and twentieth to *J*, the
2Ch 3.17 name of that on the right hand *J*,
Neh 11.10 Jedaiah the son of Joiarib, *J*.

JACINTH
Rev 9.17 breastplates of fire, and of *j*,
21.20 the eleventh, a *j*; the twelfth, an

JACOB
Gen 25.26 heel; and his name was called *J*:
27 *J* was a plain man, dwelling in
28 venison: but Rebekah loved *J*.
29 And *J* sod pottage: and Esau came
30 Esau said to *J*, Feed me, I pray
31 and *J* said, Sell me this day thy
33 And *J* said, Swear to me this day;
33 and he sold his birthright unto *J*.
34 *J* gave Esau bread and pottage of
27. 6 Rebekah spake unto *J* her son,
11 *J* said to Rebekah his mother,
15 put them upon *J* her younger son:
17 into the hand of her son *J*.
19 *J* said unto his father, I am Esau
21 Isaac said unto *J*, Come near, I
22 *J* went near unto Isaac his father;
30 had made an end of blessing *J*,
30 *J* was yet scarce gone out from
36 said, Is not he rightly named *J*?
41 Esau hated *J* because of the
41 then will I slay my brother *J*.
42 sent and called *J* her younger son,
46 if *J* take a wife of the daughters of
28. 1 Isaac called *J*, and blessed him,
5 Isaac sent away *J*: and he went
6 Esau saw that Isaac had blessed *J*,
7 *J* obeyed his father and his mother,
10 *J* went out from Beer-sheba, and
16 *J* awaked out of his sleep, and he
18 *J* rose up early in the morning,
20 *J* vowed a vow, saying, If God will
29. 1 Then *J* went on his journey, and
4 *J* said unto them, My brethren,
10 when *J* saw Rachel the daughter
10 *J* went near, and rolled the stone
11 and *J* kissed Rachel, and lifted up
12 *J* told Rachel that he was her
13 when Laban heard the tidings of *J*
15 Laban said unto *J*, Because thou
18 *J* loved Rachel; and said, I will
20 *J* served seven years for Rachel;
21 *J* said unto Laban, Give me my
28 *J* did so, and fulfilled her week:
30. 1 saw that she bare *J* no children,
1 and said unto *J*, Give me children,
4 to wife: and *J* went in unto her.
5 Bilhah conceived, and bare *J* a son.
7 again, and bare *J* a second son.
9 her maid, and gave her *J* to wife.
10 Zilpah Leah's maid bare *J* a son.
12 Leah's maid bare *J* a second son.
16 And *J* came out of the field in the
17 conceived, and bare *J* the fifth son.
19 again, and bare *J* the sixth son.
25 *J* said unto Laban, Send me away.
31 *J* said, Thou shalt not give me any
36 journey betwixt himself and *J*:
36 *J* fed the rest of Laban's flocks.
37 *J* took him rods of green poplar,
40 *J* did separate the lambs, and set
41 that *J* laid the rods before the eyes
31. 1 *J* hath taken away all that was our
2 *J* beheld the countenance of
3 the Lord said unto *J*, Return unto
4 *J* sent and called Rachel and Leah
11 unto me in a dream, saying, *J*:
17 *J* rose up, and set his sons and his
20 *J* stole away unawares to Laban
22 on the third day that *J* was fled.
24 speak not to *J* either good or bad.
25 Then Laban overtook *J*.
25 Now *J* had pitched his tent in the
26 Laban said to *J*, What hast thou
29 speak not to *J* either good or bad.
31 *J* answered and said to Laban,
32 *J* knew not that Rachel had stolen
36 And *J* was wroth, and chode with
36 and *J* answered and said to Laban,
43 Laban answered and said unto *J*,
45 *J* took a stone, and set it up for a
46 *J* said unto his brethren, Gather
47 but *J* called it Galeed.
51 Laban said to *J*, Behold this heap,
53 *J* sware by the fear of his father
54 *J* offered sacrifice upon the mount,
32. 1 *J* went on his way, and the angels
2 when *J* saw them, he said, This is
3 *J* sent messengers before him to
4 Esau; Thy servant *J* saith thus,
6 the messengers returned to *J*,
7 Then *J* was greatly afraid and
9 And *J* said, O God of my father
20 Behold, thy servant *J* is behind us.
24 And *J* was left alone; and there
27 What is thy name? And he said, *J*.
28 name shall be called no more *J*,
29 *J* asked him, and said, Tell me,
30 And *J* called the name of the place
33. 1 *J* lifted up his eyes, and looked,
10 And *J* said, Nay, I pray thee, if
17 *J* journeyed to Succoth, and built
18 And *J* came to Shalem, a city of
34. 1 of Leah, which she bare unto *J*,
3 unto Dinah the daughter of *J*,
5 *J* heard that he had defiled Dinah
5 *J* held his peace until they were
6 out unto *J* to commune with him.
7 the sons of *J* came out of the field
13 the sons of *J* answered Shechem
25 two of the sons of *J*, Simeon and
27 The sons of *J* came upon the slain,
30 *J* said to Simeon and Levi, Ye have
35. 1 God said unto *J*, Arise, go up to
2 *J* said unto his household, and to
4 gave unto *J* all the strange gods
4 *J* hid them under the oak which
5 did not pursue after the sons of *J*.
6 *J* came to Luz, which is in the land
9 God appeared unto *J* again, when
10 said unto him, Thy name is *J*:
10 shall not be called any more *J*,
14 *J* set up a pillar in the place where
15 And *J* called the name of the place
20 And *J* set a pillar upon her grave:
22 Now the sons of *J* were twelve:
26 these are the sons of *J*, which were
27 *J* came unto Isaac his father unto
27 his sons Esau and *J* buried him.
36. 6 from the face of his brother *J*.
37. 1 *J* dwelt in the land wherein his
2 These are the generations of *J*.
34 And *J* rent his clothes, and put
42. 1 when *J* saw that there was corn in
1 *J* said unto his sons, Why do ye
4 *J* sent not with his brethren;
29 they came unto *J* their father unto
36 And *J* their father said unto them,
45.25 into the land of Canaan unto *J*
27 the spirit of *J* their father revived:
46. 2 of the night, and said, *J*, *J*.
5 And *J* rose up from Beer-sheba:
5 the sons of Israel carried *J* their
6 came into Egypt, *J*, and all his
8 came into Egypt, *J* and his sons:
15 of Leah, which she bare unto *J* in
18 and these she bare unto *J*, even
22 of Rachel, which were born to *J*:
25 and she bare these unto *J*: all the
26 souls that came with *J* into Egypt,
27 all the souls of the house of *J*,
47. 7 Joseph brought in *J* his father,
7 Pharaoh: and *J* blessed Pharaoh.
8 Pharaoh said unto *J*, How old art
9 *J* said unto Pharaoh, The days of
10 *J* blessed Pharaoh, and went out
28 And *J* lived in the land of Egypt
28 whole age of *J* was an hundred
48. 2 one told *J*, and said, Behold, thy
3 *J* said unto Joseph, God Almighty
49. 1 *J* called unto his sons, and said,
2 together, and hear, ye sons of *J*;
7 I will divide them in *J*, and scatter
24 the hands of the mighty God of *J*;
33 *J* had made an end of commanding
50.24 to Abraham, to Isaac, and to *J*.
Ex 1. 1 and his household came with *J*.
5 that came out of the loins of *J*.
2.24 Abraham, with Isaac, and with *J*,
3. 6, 15 God of Isaac, and the God of *J*.
16 of Abraham, of Isaac, and of *J*,
4. 5 the God of Isaac, and the God of *J*,
6. 3 Abraham, unto Isaac, and unto *J*,
8 to Abraham, to Isaac, and to *J*,
19. 3 shalt thou say to the house of *J*,
33. 1 to Abraham, to Isaac, and to *J*,
Lev 26.42 I remember my covenant with *J*,
Nu 23. 7 Come, curse me *J*, and come, defy
10 Who can count the dust of *J*, and
21 He hath not beheld iniquity in *J*,
23 there is no enchantment against *J*,
23 this time it shall be said of *J* and
24. 5 How goodly are thy tents, O *J*,
17 there shall come a Star out of *J*,
19 Out of *J* shall come he that shall
32.11 Abraham, unto Isaac, and unto *J*;
Dt 1. 8 fathers, Abraham, Isaac, and *J*,
6.10 to Abraham, to Isaac, and to *J*,
9. 5 fathers, Abraham, Isaac, and *J*.
27 servants, Abraham, Isaac, and *J*;
29.13 to Abraham, to Isaac, and to *J*.
30.20 to Abraham, to Isaac, and to *J*,
32. 9 *J* is the lot of his inheritance.
33. 4 inheritance of...congregation of *J*.
10 They shall teach *J* thy judgments,
28 fountain of *J* shall be upon a land
34. 4 Abraham, unto Isaac, and unto *J*,
Jos 24. 4 And I gave unto Isaac *J* and Esau:
4 but *J* and his children went down
32 parcel of ground which *J* bought
1Sa 12. 8 When *J* was come into Egypt, and
2Sa 23. 1 the anointed of the God of *J*, and
1Ki 18.31 of the tribes of the sons of *J*,
2Ki 13.23 with Abraham, Isaac, and *J*, and
17.34 Lord commanded the children of *J*,
1Ch 16.13 ye children of *J*, his chosen ones.
17 confirmed the same to *J* for a law,
Ps 14. 7 *J* shall rejoice, and Israel shall be
20. 1 name of the God of *J* defend thee;
22.23 all ye the seed of *J*, glorify him;
24. 6 seek him, that seek thy face, O *J*.
44. 4 God: command deliverances for *J*.
46. 7, 11 the God of *J* is our refuge.
47. 4 the excellency of *J* whom he loved.

JACOB

Son of Isaac and Rebekah, grandson of Abraham, and direct ancestor of the twelve tribes of Israel; younger twin brother of Esau, who foolishly sells Jacob his birthright as the elder (Gen 25); later, with Rebekah's help, impersonates Esau and tricks an aged Isaac into giving him the firstborn's blessing; flees to his mother's relatives in Mesopotamia to escape Esau's vengeance (Gen 27); on the way has dream in which he sees a ladder leading to heaven and hears God's reaffirmation of promise to Abraham; makes a vow to God and names the site Bethel, meaning "House of God" (Gen 28); arriving near Haran, meets his cousin Rachel at a well, falls in love with her, and is received by her father, Laban; agrees to work seven years for Rachel's hand but by a ruse is given her older sister Leah instead; is allowed to marry Rachel as well after pledging to serve Laban another seven years (Gen 29); eleven sons and one daughter born to him by his wives and their two handmaids; asks Laban's permission to go home but is refused; by cunning husbandry grows wealthy at his uncle's expense (Gen 30); flees when Laban turns against him but is overtaken in Gilead, where, after an argument, the two men agree to part amicably (Gen 31); is confronted by angels at Mahanaim; still afraid of Esau, prepares a series of gifts to mollify him; is again confronted by an angel of God at Peniel and wrestles with him until he wins a blessing from him; given his other name, Israel, meaning "May God strive" (Gen 32); to his relief is welcomed by his brother (Gen 33); lives for a time in Bethel and builds an altar to God there, then journeys to Hebron; on the way, near Bethlehem, his beloved Rachel dies giving birth to Benjamin, her second and Jacob's twelfth son (Gen 35); shows favoritism to Joseph and gives him coat of many colors; is shattered when Joseph, on a visit to his brothers out with their sheep, is (so they tell him) slain by a wild beast (Gen 37); now old and fearful, becomes relatively minor figure in the dramatic events played out in Egypt and Canaan between the unrecognized Joseph and his brothers (Gen 42–45); goes down into Egypt to enjoy Joseph's protection and has an emotional meeting with the son he had believed dead (Gen 46); is received graciously by Pharaoh and, contented, prepares for death (Gen 47); blesses Ephraim and Manasseh, the two sons of Joseph born in Egypt (Gen 48), and his own twelve sons; asks to be buried in Canaan beside Abraham and Isaac, and dies (Gen 49); his request carried out amid great ceremony (Gen 50).

Ps 53. 6 *J* shall rejoice, and Israel shall be
59.13 let them know that God ruleth in *J*
75. 9 I will sing praises to the God of *J*.
76. 6 At thy rebuke, O God of *J*, both
77.15 people, the sons of *J* and Joseph.
78. 5 he established a testimony in *J*,
21 so a fire was kindled against *J*,
71 brought him to feed *J* his people,
79. 7 For they have devoured *J*, and
81. 1 a joyful noise unto the God of *J*.
4 Israel, and a law of the God of *J*.
84. 8 my prayer: give ear, O God of *J*.
85. 1 brought back the captivity of *J*.
87. 2 more than all the dwellings of *J*.
94. 7 neither shall the God of *J* regard it.
99. 4 judgment and righteousness in *J*.
105. 6 ye children of *J* his chosen.
10 confirmed the same unto *J* for a
23 *J* sojourned in the land of Ham.
114. 1 house of *J* from a people of strange
7 at the presence of the God of *J*;
132. 2 vowed unto the mighty God of *J*;
5 habitation for the mighty God of *J*.
135. 4 Lord hath chosen *J* unto himself,
146. 5 that hath the God of *J* for his help,
147.19 He sheweth his word unto *J*, his
Isa 2. 3 Lord, to the house of the God of *J*;
5 O house of *J*, come ye, and let us
6 forsaken thy people the house of *J*,
8.17 his face from the house of *J*,
9. 8 The Lord sent a word into *J*, and
10.20 as are escaped of the house of *J*,
21 return, even the remnant of *J*,
14. 1 For the Lord will have mercy on *J*,
1 they shall cleave to the house of *J*.
17. 4 the glory of *J* shall be made thin,
27. 6 them that come of *J* to take root:
9 shall the iniquity of *J* be purged;
29.22 concerning the house of *J*,
22 *J* shall not now be ashamed,
23 and sanctify the Holy One of *J*,
40.27 Why sayest thou, O *J*, and
41. 8 *J* whom I have chosen, the seed
14 Fear not, thou worm *J*, and ye
21 strong reasons, saith the King of *J*.
42.24 Who gave *J* for a spoil, and Israel
43. 1 the Lord that created thee, O *J*,
22 thou hast not called upon me, O *J*:
28 and have given *J* to the curse, and
44. 1 Yet now hear, O *J* my servant;
2 Fear not, O *J*, my servant; and
5 shall call himself by the name of *J*;
21 Remember these, O *J* and Israel;
23 for the Lord hath redeemed *J*,
45. 4 For *J* my servant's sake, and
19 I said not unto the seed of *J*, Seek
46. 3 Hearken unto me, O house of *J*,
48. 1 Hear ye this, O house of *J*, which
12 Hearken unto me, O *J* and Israel,
20 Lord hath redeemed his servant *J*.
49. 5 servant, to bring *J* again to him.
6 servant to raise up the tribes of *J*,
26 thy Redeemer, the mighty One of *J*.
58. 1 and the house of *J* their sins.
14 feed thee with the heritage of *J*
59.20 that turn from transgression in *J*,
60.16 thy Redeemer, the mighty One of *J*.
65. 9 I will bring forth a seed out of *J*,
Jer 2. 4 word of the Lord, O house of *J*,
5.20 Declare this in the house of *J*, and
10.16 The portion of *J* is not like them:
25 for they have eaten up *J*, and
30.10 fear thou not, O my servant *J*,
10 and *J* shall return, and shall be in
31. 7 Sing with gladness for *J*, and
11 For the Lord hath redeemed *J*,
33.26 Then will I cast away the seed of *J*,
26 the seed of Abraham, Isaac, and *J*:
46.27 fear not thou, O my servant *J*,
27 *J* shall return, and be in rest and
28 Fear thou not, O *J* my servant,
51.19 The portion of *J* is not like them;
La 1.17 hath commanded concerning *J*,
2. 2 swallowed...the habitations of *J*,
3 burned against *J* like a flaming
Eze 20. 5 unto the seed of the house of *J*,
28.25 that I have given to my servant *J*.
37.25 the land that I have given unto *J*
39.25 I bring again the captivity of *J*,
Hos 10.11 plow, and *J* shall break his clods.
12. 2 punish *J* according to his ways;
12 *J* fled into the country of Syria,
Am 3.13 ye, and testify in the house of *J*,
6. 8 I abhor the excellency of *J*, and
7. 2, 5 thee: by whom shall *J* arise?
8. 7 hath sworn by the excellency of *J*,
9. 8 not utterly destroy the house of *J*,
Ob 10 thy violence against thy brother *J*
17 *J* shall possess their possessions.
18 And the house of *J* shall be a fire,
Mic 1. 5 the transgression of *J* is all this,
5 What is the transgression of *J*?
2. 7 that art named the house of *J*,
12 surely assemble, O *J*, all of thee;
3. 1 Hear, I pray you, O heads of *J*,
8 declare unto *J* his transgression,
9 you, ye heads of the house of *J*,
4. 2 and to the house of the God of *J*;
5. 7 remnant of *J* shall be in the midst
8 remnant of *J* shall be among the
7.20 Thou wilt perform the truth to *J*,
Na 2. 2 turned away the excellency of *J*,
Mal 1. 2 saith the Lord: yet I loved *J*,
2.12 out of the tabernacles of *J*,
3. 6 ye sons of *J* are not consumed.
Mt 1. 2 begat *J*; and *J* begat Judas
15 Matthan; and Matthan begat *J*;
16 And *J* begat Joseph the husband
8.11 with Abraham, and Isaac, and *J*,
22.32 the God of Isaac, and the God of *J*?
Mk 12.26 the God of Isaac, and the God of *J*?
Lk 1.33 he shall reign over the house of *J*
3.34 Which was the son of *J*, which was
13.28 see Abraham, and Isaac, and *J*,
20.37 the God of Isaac, and the God of *J*.
Jn 4. 5 that *J* gave to his son Joseph.
12 Art thou greater than our father *J*,
Ac 3.13 of Abraham, and of Isaac, and of *J*,
7. 8 begat *J*; and *J* begat the twelve
12 when *J* heard that there was corn
14 and called his father *J* to him,
15 *J* went down into Egypt, and died,
32 the God of Isaac, and the God of *J*.
46 find a tabernacle for the God of *J*.
Ro 9.13 *J* have I loved, but Esau have I
11.26 turn away ungodliness from *J*:
Heb 11. 9 in tabernacles with Isaac and *J*,
20 By faith, Isaac blessed *J* and Esau
21 By faith *J*, when he was a dying,

JAILOR

Ac 16.23 charging the *j* to keep them

JAIRUS

Mk 5.22 of the synagogue, *J* by name;
Lk 8.41 there came a man named *J*, and

JAMBRES

2Ti 3. 8 Jannes and *J* withstood Moses.

JAMES

Mt 4.21 *J* the son of Zebedee, and John
10. 2 *J* the son of Zebedee, and John
3 *J* the son of Alphaeus, and
13.55 brethren, *J*, and Joses, and Simon,
17. 1 Jesus taketh Peter, *J*, and John his
27.56 Mary the mother of *J* and Joses,
Mk 1.19 *J* the son of Zebedee, and John
29 and Andrew, with *J* and John.
3.17 *J*...and John the brother of *J*;
18 and *J* the son of Alphaeus, and
5.37 and *J*, and John the brother of *J*.
6. 3 the brother of *J*, and Joses, and of
9. 2 with him Peter, and *J*, and John,
10.35 *J* and John, the sons of Zebedee,
41 much displeased with *J* and John.
13. 3 Peter and *J* and John and Andrew
14.33 with him Peter and *J* and John,
15.40 Mary the mother of *J* the less and

16. 1 Mary the mother of J, and Salome,
Lk 5.10 J, and John, the sons of Zebedee,
6.14 Andrew his brother, J and John,
15 Thomas, J the son of Alphaeus,
16 And Judas the brother of J, and
8.51 go in, save Peter, and J, and John,
9.28 he took Peter and John and J, and
54 his disciples J and John saw this,
24.10 and Mary the mother of J, and
Ac 1.13 abode...Peter, and J, and John,
13 Matthew, J the son of Alphaeus,
13 and Judas the brother of J.
12. 2 he killed J the brother of John
17 Go shew these things unto J, and
15.13 J answered, saying, Men and
21.18 Paul went in with us unto J;
1Co 15. 7 After that, he was seen of J; then
Gal 1.19 I none, save J the Lord's brother.
2. 9 J, Cephas, and John, who seemed
12 before that certain came from J,
Jas 1. 1 J, a servant of God and of the
Jude 1 of Jesus Christ, and brother of J,

JANGLING
1Ti 1. 6 turned aside unto vain j; have

JANNES
2Ti 3. 8 J and Jambres withstood Moses,

JASON
Ac 17. 5 and assaulted the house of J, and
6 they drew J and certain brethren
7 Whom J hath received: and these
9 when they had taken security of J,
Ro 16.21 Lucius, and J, and Sosipater, my

JASPER
Ex 28.20 a beryl, and an onyx, and a j:
39.13 row, a beryl, an onyx, and a j:
Eze 28.13 the onyx, and the j, the sapphire,
Rev 4. 3 to look upon like a j and a sardine
21.11 even like a j stone, clear as crystal;
18 building of the wall of it was of j:
19 The first foundation was j; the

JAVELIN
Nu 25. 7 and took a j in his hand;
1Sa 18.10 and there was a j in Saul's hand.
11 And Saul cast the j; for he said, I
19. 9 in his house with his j in his hand:
10 David even to the wall with the j;
10 and he smote the j into the wall:
20.33 Saul cast a j at him to smite him:

JAW
Jdg 15.16 with the j of an ass have I slain a
19 clave an hollow place that in the j,
Job 41. 2 or bore his j through with a thorn?
Pr 30.14 their j teeth as knives, to devour

JAWS
Job 29.17 I brake the j of the wicked, and
Ps 22.15 and my tongue cleaveth to my j;
Isa 30.28 be a bridle in the j of the people,
Eze 29. 4 I will put hooks in thy j, and I will
38. 4 thee back, and put hooks into thy j,
Hos 11. 4 that take off the yoke on their j,

JEALOUS
Ex 20. 5 Lord thy God am a j God, visiting
34.14 Lord, whose name is J, is a j God:
Nu 5.14 and he be j of his wife, and she be
14 he be j of his wife, and she be not
30 and he be j over his wife, and shall
Dt 4.24 is a consuming fire, even a j God.
5. 9 for I the Lord thy God am a j God.
6.15 Lord thy God is a j God among you)
Jos 24.19 he is an holy God; he is a j God;
1Ki 19.10, 14 I have been very j for the Lord
Eze 39.25 and will be j for my holy name;
Joel 2.18 Then will the Lord be j for his land,
Na 1. 2 God is j, and the Lord revengeth;
Zec 1.14 I am j for Jerusalem and for Zion
8. 2 I was j for Zion with great jealousy,
2 and I was j for her with great fury.
2Co 11. 2 am j over you with godly jealously:

JEALOUSY
Nu 5.14 And the spirit of j come upon him,
14 or if the spirit of j come upon him,
15 for it is an offering of j, an offering
18 her hands, which is the j offering:
25 the priest shall take the j offering
30 the spirit of j cometh upon him,
25.11 not the children of Israel in my j.
Dt 29.20 his j shall smoke against that man,
32.16 provoked him to j with strange
21 They have moved me to j with that
21 I will move them to j with those
1Ki 14.22 provoked him to j with their sins
Ps 78.58 moved him to j with their graven
79. 5 for ever? shall thy j burn like fire?
Pr 6.34 For j is the rage of a man:
SS 8. 6 as death; j is cruel as the grave:
Isa 42.13 he shall stir up j like a man of war:
Eze 8. 3 was the seat of the image of j,
3 which provoketh to j.
5 altar this image of j in the entry.
16.38 I will give thee blood in fury and j.
42 and my j shall depart from thee,
23.25 And I will set my j against thee,
36. 5 in the fire of my j have I spoken
6 have spoken in my j and in my fury,
38.19 in my j and in the fire of my wrath
Zep 1.18 be devoured by the fire of his j:
3. 8 be devoured with the fire of my j.
Zec 1.14 jealous...for Zion with a great j.
8. 2 I was jealous for Zion with great j,
Ro 10.19 I will provoke you to j by them
11.11 Gentiles, for to provoke them to j.
1Co 10.22 Do we provoke the Lord to j? are we
2Co 11. 2 am jealous over you with godly j:

JEHOSHAPHAT
2Sa 8.16 J the son of Ahilud was recorder;
20.24 J the son of Ahilud was recorder:
1Ki 4. 3 J the son of Ahilud, the recorder.
17 J the son of Paruah, in Issachar:
15.24 and J his son reigned in his stead.
22. 2 J the king of Judah came down
4 he said unto J, Wilt thou go with
4 J said to the king of Israel, I am
5 And J said unto the king of Israel,
7 J said, Is there not here a prophet
8 said unto J, There is yet one man,
8 And J said, Let not the king say so.
10 and J the king of Judah sat each
18 king of Israel said unto J, Did I
29 and J the king of Judah went up
30 king of Israel said unto J, I will
32 captains of the chariots saw J, that
32 fight against him: and J cried out.
41 J the son of Asa began to reign
42 J was thirty and five years old
44 J made peace with the king of
45 the rest of the acts of J, and his
48 J made ships of Tharshish to go
49 Ahaziah the son of Ahab unto J,
49 in the ships. But J would not.
50 J slept with his fathers, and was
51 the seventeenth year of J king of
2Ki 1.17 year of Jehoram the son of J king
3. 1 the eighteenth year of J king of
7 and sent to J the king of Judah,
11 J said, Is there not here a prophet
12 J said, The word of the Lord is
12 J and the king of Edom went down
14 not that I regard the presence of J
8.16 Israel, J being then king of Judah,
16 Jehoram the son of J king of Judah
9. 2 look out there Jehu the son of J
14 Jehu the son of J...conspired
12.18 took all the hallowed things that J,
1Ch 3.10 his son, Asa his son, J his son,
15.24 Shebaniah, and J, and Nethaneel,
18.15 and J the son of Alihud, recorder.
2Ch 17. 1 And J his son reigned in his stead,
3 the Lord was with J, because he
5 all Judah brought to J presents;
10 that they made no war against J.
11 the Philistines brought J presents,
12 And J waxed great exceedingly;
18. 1 Now J had riches and honor in
3 Ahab king of Israel said unto J
4 And J said unto the king of Israel,
6 J said, Is there not here a prophet
7 And the king of Israel said unto J,
7 And J said, Let not the king say so.
9 and J king of Judah sat either
17 And the king of Israel said to J,
28 and J the king of Judah went up
29 And the king of Israel said unto J,
31 the captains of the chariot saw J,
31 J cried out, and the Lord helped
19. 1 J the king of Judah returned to
2 to meet him, and said to king J,
4 And J dwelt at Jerusalem: and he
8 Jerusalem did J set of the Levites,
20. 1 came against J to battle.
2 Then there came some that told J,
3 J feared, and set himself to seek
5 J stood in the congregation of
15 of Jerusalem, and thou king J,
18 J bowed his head with his face to
20 J stood and said, Hear me, O Judah,
25 J and his people came to take away
27 J in the forefront of them to go
30 So the realm of J was quiet: for
31 And J reigned over Judah: he was
34 Now the rest of the acts of J, first
35 did J king of Judah join himself
37 of Mareshah prophesied against J,
21. 1 J slept with his fathers, and was
2 And he had brethren the sons of J,
2 all these were the sons of J king
12 hast not walked in the ways of J
22. 9 said they, he is the son of J, who
Joel 3. 2 them down into the valley of J,
12 and come up to the valley of J:

JEHOVAH
Ex 6. 3 name J was I not known to them.
Ps 83.18 thou, whose name alone is J, art
Isa 12. 2 J is my strength and my song;
26. 4 the Lord J is everlasting strength.

JEHU

Israelite king, 9th century B.C.; anointed at the instigation of the prophet Elisha and charged to exterminate the house of Ahab (2Ki 9.1-10); pursues task vigorously: at Jezreel slays Joram, Ahab's son and successor, and Ahaziah, king of Judah (related to Ahab by marriage), and has Jezebel thrown to her death (2Ki 9.11-37); slays the entire family of Ahab and the royal courtiers at Samaria along with a company of visiting nobles from Judah (2Ki 10.1-14); demonstrates his "zeal for the Lord" by enticing the worshipers of Baal to a temple in Samaria and having them massacred there (2Ki 10.15-28); is rewarded by founding a dynasty lasting four generations, but loses his territory in Transjordan to Damascus (2Ki 10.29-36).

Israelite King Jehu appealed to the Assyrian Shalmaneser III for help against invading Syrians in 841 B.C., date of Shalmaneser's Black Obelisk (above). The inscription reads: "The tribute of Jehu, son of Omri."

JEHU

2Ki 9. 2 there *J* the son of Jehoshaphat
11 *J* came forth to the servants of his
13 with trumpets, saying, *J* is king.
16 So *J* rode in a chariot, and went to
17 spied the company of *J* as he came,
21 they went out against *J*, and met
22 it came to pass, when Joram saw *J*,
22 that he said, Is it peace, *J*?
24 And *J* drew a bow with his full
25 Then said *J* to Bidkar his captain,
30 And when *J* was come to Jezreel,
31 as *J* entered in at the gate, she
10. 1 And *J* wrote letters, and sent to
11 *J* slew all that remained of the
13 *J* met with the brethren of Ahaziah
18 *J* gathered all the people together,
18 little; but *J* shall serve him much.
19 *J* did it in subtilty, to the intent
20 And *J* said, Proclaim a solemn
21 And *J* sent through all Israel:
25 And *J* said to the guard and to the
28 *J* destroyed Baal out of Israel.
31 *J* took no heed to walk in the law
35 And *J* slept with his fathers: and
13. 1 Jehoahaz the son of *J* began to
2Ch 22. 7 went out with Jehoram against *J*
8 *J* was executing judgment upon
9 in Samaria,) and brought him to *J*:
Hos 1. 4 of Jezreel upon the house of *J*,

JEOPARDY

2Sa 23.17 the men that went in *j* of their lives?
1Ch 11.19 that have put their lives in *j*?
19 for with the *j* of their lives they brought
12.19 master Saul to the *j* of our heads.
Lk 8.23 filled with water, and were in *j*.
1Co 15.30 And why stand we in *j* every hour?

JEPHTHAH

Jdg 11. 1 Now *J* the Gileadite was a mighty
1 of an harlot: and Gilead begat *J*.
2 they thrust out *J*, and said unto
3 Then *J* fled from his brethren,
3 there were gathered vain men to *J*,
5 the elders of Gilead went to fetch *J*
6 they said unto *J*, Come, and be our
7 *J* said unto the elders of Gilead,
8 the elders of Gilead said unto *J*,
9 *J* said unto the elders of Gilead,
10 the elders of Gilead said unto *J*,
11 *J* went with the elders of Gilead,
11 *J* uttered all his words before the
12 *J* sent messengers unto the king
13 answered...the messengers of *J*,
14 *J* sent messengers again unto the
15 Thus saith *J*, Israel took not away
28 hearkened not unto the words of *J*
29 Spirit of the Lord came upon *J*,
30 *J* vowed a vow unto the Lord, and
32 *J* passed over unto the children of
34 *J* came to Mizpeh unto his house,
40 yearly to lament the daughter of *J*
12. 1 went northward, and said unto *J*,
2 *J* said unto them, I and my people
4 *J* gathered together all the men of
7 And *J* judged Israel six years.
7 Then died *J* the Gileadite, and was
1Sa 12.11 sent Jerubbaal, and Bedan, and *J*,

JEREMIAH

2Ki 23.31 the daughter of *J* of Libnah.
24.18 the daughter of *J* of Libnah.
1Ch 5.24 and Azriel, and *J*, and Hodaviah,
12. 4 and *J*, and Jahaziel, and Johanan,
10 the fourth, *J* the fifth,
13 *J* the tenth, Machbanai the
2Ch 35.25 And *J* lamented for Josiah:
36.12 and humbled not himself before *J*
21 word of the Lord by the mouth of *J*,
22 the Lord spoken by the mouth of *J*
Ezr 1. 1 word of the Lord by the mouth of *J*
Neh 10. 2 Seraiah, Azariah, *J*,
12. 1 and Jeshua: Seraiah, *J*, Ezra,
12 Seraiah, Meraiah; of *J*, Hananiah;
34 Benjamin, and Shemaiah, and *J*,
Jer 1. 1 The words of *J* the son of Hilkiah,
11 me, saying, *J* what seest thou?
7. 1 word that came to *J* from the Lord,
11. 1 word that came to *J* from the Lord,
14. 1 came to *J* concerning the dearth.
18. 1 word which came to *J* from the
18 let us devise devices against *J*;
19.14 Then came *J* from Tophet,
20. 1 heard that *J* prophesied these
2 Then Pashur smote *J* the prophet,
3 brought forth *J* out of the stocks.
3 Then said *J* unto him, The Lord
21. 1 which came unto *J* from the Lord,
3 Then said *J* unto them, Thus shall
24. 3 Lord unto me, What seest thou, *J*?
25. 1 word that came to *J* concerning
2 The which *J* the prophet spake
13 *J* hath prophesied against all the
26. 7 the people heard *J* speaking these
8 *J* had made an end of speaking all
9 people were gathered against *J* in
12 spake *J* unto all the princes and
20 according to all the words of *J*:
24 the son of Shaphan was with *J*,
27. 1 this word unto *J* from the Lord,
28. 5 *J* said unto the prophet Hananiah
6 prophet *J* said, Amen: the Lord do
11 And the prophet *J* went his way.
12 word of the Lord came unto *J* the
12 from off the neck of the prophet *J*,
15 said the prophet *J* unto Hananiah
29. 1 are the words of the letter that *J*
27 why hast thou not reproved *J* of
29 read this letter in the ears of *J*
30 came the word of the Lord unto *J*,
30. 1 word that came to *J* from the Lord,
32. 1 The word that came to *J* from the
2 *J* the prophet was shut up in the
6 *J* said, The word of the Lord came
26 came the word of the Lord unto *J*,
33. 1 Lord came unto *J* the second time,
19 the word of the Lord came unto *J*,
23 the word of the Lord came to *J*,
34. 1 which came unto *J* from the Lord,
6 Then *J* the prophet spake all these
8 that came unto *J* from the Lord,
12 the word of the Lord came to *J*
35. 1 which came unto *J* from the Lord,
3 I took Jaazaniah the son of *J*,
12 came the word of the Lord unto *J*,
18 And *J* said unto...the Rechabites,
36. 1 word came unto *J* from the Lord,
4 *J* called Baruch the son of Neriah:
4 Baruch wrote from the mouth of *J*
5 *J* commanded Baruch, saying, I
8 *J* the prophet commanded him,
10 Baruch in the book of words of *J*
19 Baruch, Go, hide thee, thou and *J*;
26 the scribe and *J* the prophet:
27 the word of the Lord came to *J*,
27 Baruch wrote at the mouth of *J*,
32 Then took *J* another roll, and gave
32 wrote therein from the mouth of *J*
37. 2 which he spake by the prophet *J*.
3 the priest to the prophet *J*, saying,
4 *J* came in and went out among
6 of the Lord unto the prophet *J*,
12 Then *J* went forth out of Jerusalem
13 and he took *J* the prophet, saying,
14 Then said *J*, It is false; I fall not
14 so Irijah took *J*, and brought him
15 the princes were wroth with *J*,
16 *J* was entered into the dungeon,
16 *J* had remained there many days;
17 And *J* said, There is: for, said he,
18 *J* said unto king Zedekiah, What
21 should commit *J* into the court of
21 *J* remained in the court of the
38. 1 heard the words that *J* had spoken
6 took they *J*, and cast him into the
6 and they let down *J* with cords.
6 but mire: so *J* sunk in the mire.
7 they had put *J* in the dungeon;
9 evil in all that they have done to *J*
10 *J* the prophet out of the dungeon,
11 by cords into the dungeon to *J*.
12 the Ethiopian said unto *J*, Put now
12 under the cords. And *J* did so.
13 So they drew up *J* with cords, and
13 *J* remained in the court of the
14 and took *J* the prophet unto him
14 the king said unto *J*, I will ask
15 *J* said unto Zedekiah, If I declare
16 the king sware secretly unto *J*,
17 said *J* unto Zedekiah, Thus saith
19 Zedekiah the king said unto *J*, I
20 *J* said, They shall not deliver thee.
24 Then said Zedekiah unto *J*, Let no
27 Then came all the princes unto *J*,
28 *J* abode in the court of the prison
39.11 Babylon gave charge concerning *J*
14 sent, and took *J* out of the court
15 the word of the Lord came unto *J*,

JEPHTHAH

Leader and "judge" of Israel from tribe of Gilead; son of a harlot, banished by his legitimate brothers; flees to the land of Tob, becoming head of a band of outcasts (Jdg 11.1-3); recalled as "head and captain" of Gilead when Ammon makes war on Israel (Jdg 11.4-11); after a first embassy to Ammon is told of the latter's territorial claims, sends a second to assert Israel's right to the disputed territory and to issue a challenge—ultimately in the name of the Lord God of Israel against the god of the Ammonites (Jdg 11.12-28); vows to offer up as sacrifice "whatsoever cometh forth of the doors of my house to meet me" on his successful return from battle; this turns out to be his daughter and only child (Jdg 11.29-40); harsh in his response to Ephraimite complaints at not being included in the campaign against Ammon (Jdg 12.1-3), in contrast to the conciliatory tone once taken by Gideon in a similar situation (Jdg 8.1-3); ensuing inter-tribal battle includes use of dialect to identify Ephraimites, who say "Sibboleth" instead of "Shibboleth" (12.4-6); rules as judge for six years before death and burial in a city of Gilead (12.7); cited in New Testament as one of early leaders made valiant by faith (Heb 11.32).

40. 1 that came to *J* from the Lord,
2 the captain of the guard took *J*,
6 Then went *J* unto Gedaliah the
42. 2 And said unto *J* the prophet, Let,
4 *J* the prophet said unto them, I
5 they said to *J*, The Lord be a true
7 the word of the Lord came unto *J*.
43. 1 *J* had made an end of speaking
2 and all proud men, saying unto *J*,
6 *J* the prophet and Baruch the son
8 came the word of the Lord unto *J*
44. 1 word that came to *J* concerning
15 in Pathros, answered *J*, saying,
20 Then *J* said unto all the people, to
24 *J* said unto all the people, and to
45. 1 word that *J* the prophet spake unto
1 words in a book at the mouth of *J*,
46. 1 word of the Lord which came to *J*
13 The word that the Lord spake to *J*
47. 1 word of the Lord that came to *J*
49.34 word of the Lord that came to *J*
50. 1 the land of the Chaldeans by *J*
51.59 which *J* the prophet commanded
60 *J* wrote in a book all the evil that
61 *J* said to Seraiah, When thou comest
64 Thus far are the words of *J*.
52. 1 the daughter of *J* of Libnah.
Dan 9. 2 the word of the Lord came to *J* the

JEREMIAS

Mt 16.14 others, *J*, or one of the prophets.

JEREMY

Mt 2.17 that which was spoken by *J* the
27. 9 that which was spoken by *J* the

JERICHO

Nu 22. 1 of Moab on this Jordan by *J*.
26. 3 plains of Moab by Jordan near *J*,
63 plains of Moab by Jordan near *J*.
31.12 Moab, which are by Jordan near *J*.
33.48 plains of Moab by Jordan near *J*.
50 plains of Moab by Jordan near *J*,
34.15 this side Jordan near *J* eastward,
35. 1 plains of Moab by Jordan near *J*,
36.13 plains of Moab by Jordan near *J*.
Dt 32.49 of Moab, that is over against *J*;
34. 1 of Pisgah, that is over against *J*.
3 and the plain of the valley of *J*, the
Jos 2. 1 saying, Go view the land, even *J*.
2 it was told the king of *J*, saying,
3 And the king of *J* sent unto Rahab,
3.16 people passed over right against *J*.
4.13 Lord unto battle, to the plains of *J*.
19 in Gilgal, in the east border of *J*.
5.10 month at even in the plains of *J*.
13 to pass, when Joshua was by *J*,
6. 1 *J* was straitly shut up because of
2 I have given into thine hand *J*,
25 which Joshua sent to spy out *J*.
26 riseth up and buildeth this city *J*:
7. 2 And Joshua sent men from *J* to Ai,
8. 2 as thou didst unto *J* and her king:
9. 3 what Joshua had done unto *J*
10. 1 as he had done to *J* and her king,
28 as he did unto the king of *J*.
30 thereof as he did unto the king of *J*.
12. 9 The king of *J*, one; the king of Ai,
13.32 Moab, on the other side Jordan, by *J*,
16. 1 of Joseph fell from Jordan by *J*,
1 unto the water of *J* on the east,
1 wilderness that goeth up from *J*
7 and to Naarath, and came to *J*,
18.12 border went up to the side of *J* on
21 according to their families were *J*,
20. 8 And on the other side Jordan by *J*
24.11 over Jordan, and came unto *J*:
11 the men of *J* fought against you,
2Sa 10. 5 Tarry at *J* until your beards be
1Ki 16.34 did Hiel the Beth-elite build *J*:
2Ki 2. 4 for the Lord hath sent me to *J*.
4 not leave thee. So they came to *J*.
5 sons of the prophets that were at *J*
15 prophets which were to view at *J*
18 again to him, (for he tarried at *J*,)
25. 5 overtook him in the plains of *J*:
1Ch 6.78 And on the other side Jordan by *J*,
19. 5 Tarry at *J* until your beards be
2Ch 28.15 upon asses, and brought them to *J*,
Ezr 2.34 The children of *J*, three hundred
Neh 3. 2 unto him builded the men of *J*.
7.36 The children of *J*, three hundred
Jer 39. 5 Zedekiah in the plains of *J*:
52. 8 Zedekiah in the plains of *J*;
Mt 20.29 And as they departed from *J*, a
Mk 10.46 came to *J*: and as he went out of *J*
Lk 10.30 went down from Jerusalem to *J*,
18.35 that as he was come nigh unto *J*,
19. 1 entered and passed through *J*.
Heb 11.30 By faith the walls of *J* fell down,

JEROBOAM

1Ki 11.26 *J* the son of Nebat, an Ephrathite
28 *J* was a mighty man of valor:
29 when *J* went out of Jerusalem,
31 And he said to *J*, Take thee ten
40 Solomon sought therefore to kill *J*.
40 And *J* arose, and fled into Egypt,
12. 2 to pass, when *J* the son of Nebat,
2 Solomon, and *J* dwelt in Egypt;)
3 And *J* and all the congregation of
12 So *J* and all the people came to
15 by Ahijah the Shilonite unto *J*
20 all Israel heard that *J* was come
25 Then *J* built Shechem in mount
26 *J* said in his heart, Now shall the
32 *J* ordained a feast in the eighth
13. 1 and *J* stood by the altar to burn
4 *J* heard the saying of the man of
33 *J* returned not from his evil way,
34 became sin unto the house of *J*,
14. 1 time Abijah the son of *J* fell sick.
2 *J* said to his wife, Arise, I pray
2 be not known to be the wife of *J*;
5 Behold, the wife of *J* cometh to ask
6 he said, Come in, thou wife of *J*;
7 Go, tell *J*, Thus saith the Lord God
10 will bring evil upon the house of *J*,
10 will cut off from *J* him that pisseth
10 the remnant of the house of *J*,
11 Him that dieth of *J* in the city
13 only of *J* shall come to the grave,
13 God of Israel in the house of *J*.
14 cut off the house of *J* that day:
16 Israel up because of the sins of *J*,
19 the rest of the acts of *J*, how he
20 *J* reigned were two and twenty
30 was war between Rehoboam and *J*
15. 1 in the eighteenth year of king *J*
6 was war between Rehoboam and *J*
7 was war between Abijam and *J*.
9 twentieth year of *J* king of Israel
25 Nadab the son of *J* began to reign
29 that he smote all the house of *J*;
29 he left not to *J* any that breathed,
30 of the sins of *J* which he sinned,
34 walked in the way of *J*, and in his
16. 2 thou hast walked in the way of *J*,
3 make thy house like the house of *J*
7 in being like the house of *J*;
19 in walking in the way of *J*, and in
26 For he walked in all the way of *J*
31 for him to walk in the sins of *J*
21.22 thine house like the house of *J*
22.52 of his mother, and in the way of *J*
2Ki 3. 3 he cleaved unto the sins of *J* the
9. 9 house of Ahab like the house of *J*
10.29 from the sins of *J* the son of Nebat.
31 he departed not from the sins of *J*,
13. 2 and followed the sins of *J* the son
6 not from the sins of the house of *J*,
11 departed not from all the sins of *J*
13 and *J* sat upon his throne:
14.16 and *J* his son reigned in his stead.

JEREMIAH

Prophet in final years of Judah's existence as independent kingdom (late 7th–early 6th centuries B.C.) and principal author of Book of Jeremiah; career possibly begun during reign of Josiah, but first records date from reign of Josiah's son Jehoiakim (609–598 B.C.); issues vivid warnings of imminent disaster resulting from Judah's moral transgressions (Jer 1; 4); highly critical of religious establishment (Jer 2; 6; 23); attacks popular confidence in Jerusalem's temple as source of divine protection (Jer 7; 26); is himself barred from the temple (Jer 36); other harassments include being put in stocks (Jer 20), imprisoned (Jer 32–33; 37–39), and threatened with death (Jer 26); sends letter to Judean captives in Babylon foretelling long exile and urging them to seek their welfare there (Jer 29); consulted for divine guidance by King Zedekiah (598–587 B.C.) after first Babylonian invasion (Jer 37), and by the remaining leadership after the destruction of Jerusalem and second deportation in 587 B.C. (Jer 42); finally taken under guard to Egypt (Jer 43); delivers several poignant laments over his unsought role as preacher of exile and doom (Jer 11; 12; 15; 17; 20); prophesies the ultimate fall of Babylon (Jer 50–51).

Jericho's walls collapse at the sound of seven trumpets (Jos 6), as depicted in a Gustave Doré engraving.

2Ki 14.23 *J* the son of Joash king of Israel
24 departed not from all the sins of *J*
27 he saved them by the hand of *J*
28 the rest of the acts of *J*, and all
29 *J* slept with his fathers, even with
15. 1 twenty and seventh year of *J* king
8 did Zachariah the son of *J* reign
9 he departed not from the sins of *J*
18 not all his days from the sins of *J*
24, 28 departed not from the sins of *J*
17.21 they made *J* the son of Nebat king:
21 *J* drave Israel from following the
22 of Israel walked in all the sins of *J*
23.15 the high place which *J* the son of
1Ch 5.17 and in the days of *J* king of Israel.
2Ch 9.29 visions of Iddo the seer against *J*
10. 2 came to pass, when *J*...heard it,
2 it, that *J* returned out of Egypt.
3 *J* and all Israel came and spake to
12 So *J* and all the people came to
15 hand of Ahijah the Shilonite to *J*
11. 4 returned from going against *J*.
14 *J* and his sons had cast them off
12.15 wars between Rehoboam and *J*
13. 1 in the eighteenth year of king *J*
2 was war between Abijah and *J*.
3 *J* also set the battle in array
4 Hear me, thou *J*, and all Israel;
6 *J* the son of Nebat, the servant of
8 calves, which *J* made you for gods.
13 *J* caused an ambushment to come
15 God smote *J* and all Israel before
19 Abijah pursued after *J*, and took
20 Neither did *J* recover strength
Hos 1. 1 in the days of *J* the son of Joash,
Am 1. 1 in the days of *J* the son of Joash
7. 9 I will rise against the house of *J*
10 the priest of Beth-el sent to *J* king
11 saith, *J* shall die by the sword,

JERUSALEM

Jos 10. 1 king of *J* had heard how Joshua
3 king of *J* sent unto Hoham king of
5, 23 king of *J*, the king of Hebron,
12.10 The king of *J*, one; the king of
15. 8 side of the Jebusite; the same is *J*:
63 the Jebusites the inhabitants of *J*,
63 with the children of Judah at *J*
18.28 Eleph, and Jebusi, which is *J*,
Jdg 1. 7 they brought him to *J*, and there
8 of Judah had fought against *J*,
21 out the Jebusites that inhabited *J*;
21 of Benjamin in *J* unto this day.
19.10 over against Jebus, which is *J*;
1Sa 17.54 the Philistine, and brought it to *J*;
2Sa 5. 5 in *J* he reigned thirty and three
6 the king and his men went to *J*
13 concubines and wives out of *J*,
14 those that were born unto him in *J*;
8. 7 Hadadezer, and brought them to *J*.
9.13 So Mephibosheth dwelt in *J*: for
10.14 children of Ammon, and came to *J*.
11. 1 But David tarried still at *J*.
12 So Uriah abode in *J* that day, and
12.31 and all the people returned unto *J*.
14.23 Geshur, and brought Absalom to *J*.
28 Absalom dwelt two full years in *J*,
15. 8 shall bring me again indeed to *J*,
11 went two hundred men out of *J*,
14 servants that were with him at *J*,
29 carried the ark of God again to *J*:
37 the city, and Absalom came into *J*.
16. 3 the king, Behold, he abideth at *J*:
15 people the men of Israel, came to *J*,
17.20 not find them, they returned to *J*.
19.19 that my lord the king went out of *J*,
25 he was come to *J* to meet the king,
33 and I will feed thee with me in *J*.
34 should go up with the king unto *J*?
20. 2 their king, from Jordan even to *J*.
3 And David came to his house at *J*;
7 and they went out of *J*, to pursue
22 Joab returned to *J* unto the king.
24. 8 they came to *J* at the end of nine
16 out his hand upon *J* to destroy it,
1Ki 2.11 and three years reigned he in *J*.
36 unto him, Build thee an house in *J*,
38 And Shimei dwelt in *J* many days.
41 Shimei had gone from *J* to Gath,
3. 1 and the wall of *J* round about.
15 he came to *J*, and stood before the
8. 1 of Israel, unto king Solomon in *J*,
9.15 and the wall of *J*, and Hazor, and
19 Solomon desired to build in *J*,
10. 2 she came to *J* with a very great
26 chariots, and with the king at *J*.
27 made silver to be in *J* as stones,
11. 7 in the hill that is before *J*, and for
29 when Jeroboam went out of *J*,
36 have a light alway before me in *J*,
42 the time that Solomon reigned in *J*
12.18 him up to his chariot, to flee to *J*.
21 when Rehoboam was come to *J*,
27 in the house of the Lord at *J*,
28 is too much for you to go up to *J*:
14.21 he reigned seventeen years in *J*,
25 king of Egypt came up against *J*:
15. 2 Three years reigned he in *J*.
4 Lord his God give him a lamp in *J*,
4 son after him, and to establish *J*:
10 forty and one years reigned he in *J*.
22.42 reigned twenty and five years in *J*.
2Ki 8.17 and he reigned eight years in *J*.
26 and he reigned one year in *J*.
9.28 carried him in a chariot to *J*,
12. 1 and forty years reigned he in *J*.
17 Hazael set his face to go up to *J*.
18 of Syria: and he went away from *J*.
14. 2 reigned twenty and nine years in *J*.
2 name was Jehoaddan of *J*.
13 at Beth-shemesh, and came to *J*,
13 and brake down the wall of *J* from
19 a conspiracy against him in *J*:
20 he was buried at *J* with his fathers
15. 2 reigned two and fifty years in *J*.
2 name was Jecholiah of *J*.
33 and he reigned sixteen years in *J*.
16. 2 and reigned sixteen years in *J*,
5 king of Israel came up to *J* to war:
18. 2 reigned twenty and nine years in *J*.
17 with a great host against *J*:
17 And they went up and came to *J*,
22 and hath said to Judah and *J*,
22 worship before this altar in *J*?
35 should deliver *J* out of mine hand?
19.10 *J* shall not be delivered into the
21 daughter of *J* hath shaken her head
31 out of *J* shall go forth a remnant,
21. 1 reigned fifty and five years in *J*.
4 Lord said, In *J* will I put my name.
7 and in *J*, which I have chosen
12 I am bringing such evil upon *J* and
13 stretch over *J* the line of Samaria,
13 wipe *J* as a man wipeth a dish,
16 filled *J* from one end to another;
19 and he reigned two years in *J*.
22. 1 reigned thirty and one years in *J*.

JEROBOAM

First ruler of northern kingdom of Israel, 10th century B.C.; becomes overseer of the levy of the northern tribes under Solomon; is designated king by the prophet Ahijah, but forced to flee to Egypt when Solomon learns of it (1Ki 11.26-40); upon Solomon's death, returns to Shechem, where the popular assembly acclaims him king after rebelling against Rehoboam, Solomon's successor in Judah (1Ki 12.1-20); to rival the Jerusalem temple, establishes national sanctuaries at Dan and Bethel equipped with calves of gold, or bull images harking back to Israel's worship in the wilderness (1Ki 12.26-33); seizes a prophet who announces the destruction of the sanctuary at Bethel and his hand withers; entreats him, and it is restored (1Ki 13.1-6); sends his wife in disguise to Ahijah and judgment is prophesied upon his house; is succeeded by his son Nadab, who reigns only a short time before being murdered and replaced by Baasha (1Ki 14.1-20; 2 Ki 15.27); in later tradition accorded much of the blame for the division of the original kingdom.

14 (now she dwelt in *J* in the college;)
23. 1 all the elders of Judah and of *J*.
2 all the inhabitants of *J* with him,
4 he burned them without *J* in the
5 and in the places round about *J*;
6 without *J*, unto the brook Kidron,
9 not up to the altar of the Lord in *J*,
13 the high places that were before *J*,
20 upon them, and returned to *J*.
23 was holden to the Lord in *J*.
24 spied in the land of Judah and in *J*,
27 off this city *J* which I have chosen,
30 brought him to *J*, and buried him
31 and he reigned three months in *J*.
33 that he might not reign in *J*;
36 and he reigned eleven years in *J*.
24. 4 for he filled *J* with innocent blood;
8 and he reigned in *J* three months.
8 the daughter of Elnathan of *J*.
10 king of Babylon came up against *J*,
14 he carried away all *J*, and all the
15 carried he into captivity from *J* to
18 and he reigned eleven years in *J*.
20 it came to pass in *J* and Judah,
25. 1 he, and all his host, against *J*,
8 of the king of Babylon, unto *J*:
9 house, and all the houses of *J*,
10 down the walls of *J* round about.
1Ch 3. 4 in *J* he reigned thirty and three
5 these were born unto him in *J*;
6.10 temple that Solomon built in *J*:)
15 Lord carried away Judah and *J*
32 built the house of the Lord in *J*:
8.28 chief men. These dwelt in *J*.
32 dwelt with their brethren in *J*,
9. 3 in *J* dwelt of the children of Judah,
34 their generations; these dwelt at *J*.
38 dwelt with their brethren at *J*,
11. 4 David and all Israel went to *J*,
14. 3 And David took more wives at *J*:
4 of his children which he had in *J*;
15. 3 gathered all Israel together to *J*,
18. 7 Hadarezer, and brought them to *J*.
19.15 into the city. Then Joab came to *J*.
20. 1 But David tarried at *J*. And Joab
3 and all the people returned to *J*.
21. 4 throughout all Israel, and came to *J*.
15 And God sent an angel unto *J* to
16 in his hand stretched out over *J*.
23.25 that they may dwell in *J* for ever:
28. 1 with all the valiant men, unto *J*.
29.27 and three years reigned he in *J*.
2Ch 1. 4 he had pitched a tent for it at *J*.
13 high place that was at Gibeon to *J*,
14 cities, and with the king at *J*.
15 silver and gold at *J* as plenteous
2. 7 are with me in Judah and in *J*,
16 and thou shalt carry it up to *J*.
3. 1 to build the house of the Lord at *J*
5. 2 unto *J*, to bring up the ark of
6. 6 But I have chosen *J*, that my name
8. 6 that Solomon desired to build in *J*,
9. 1 Solomon with hard questions at *J*,
25 cities, and with the king at *J*.
27 king made silver in *J* as stones,
30 And Solomon reigned in *J* over all
10.18 him up to his chariot, to flee to *J*.
11. 1 when Rehoboam was come to *J*,
5 Rehoboam dwelt in *J*, and built
14 and came to Judah and *J*:
16 the Lord God of Israel came to *J*,
12. 2 king of Egypt came up against *J*,
4 pertained to Judah, and came to *J*.
5 that were gathered together to *J*
7 shall not be poured out upon *J*
9 king of Egypt came up against *J*,
13 strengthened himself in *J*, and
13 he reigned seventeen years in *J*,
13. 2 He reigned three years in *J*. His
14.15 in abundance, and returned to *J*.
15.10 gathered themselves together at *J*
17.13 mighty men of valor, were in *J*.
19. 1 returned to his house in peace to *J*.
4 Jehoshaphat dwelt at *J*: and he
8 in *J* did Jehoshaphat set of the
8 when they returned to *J*.
20. 5 the congregation of Judah and *J*,
15 all Judah, and ye inhabitants of *J*,
17 the Lord with you, O Judah and *J*:
18 the inhabitants of *J* fell before the
20 O Judah, and ye inhabitants of *J*;
27 every man of Judah and *J*,
27 of them, to go again to *J* with joy;
28 they came to *J* with psalteries and
31 reigned twenty and five years in *J*.
21. 5 and he reigned eight years in *J*.
11 the inhabitants of *J* to commit
13 inhabitants of *J* to go a whoring,
20 he reigned in *J* eight years, and
22. 1 inhabitants of *J* made Ahaziah his
2 reign, and he reigned one year in *J*.
23. 2 of Israel, and they came to *J*.
24. 1 and he reigned forty years in *J*.
6 Judah and out of *J* the collection,
9 proclamation through Judah and *J*,
18 wrath came upon Judah and *J* for
23 and they came to Judah and *J*, and
25. 1 reigned twenty and nine years in *J*.
1 mother's name...Jehoaddan of *J*.
23 and brought him to *J*, and brake
23 brake down the wall of *J* from the
27 a conspiracy against him in *J*;
26. 3 he reigned fifty and two years in *J*.
3 name also was Jecoliah of *J*.
9 Moreover Uzziah built towers in *J*
15 he made in *J* engines, invented
27. 1 and he reigned sixteen years in *J*.
8 and reigned sixteen years in *J*.
28. 1 and he reigned sixteen years in *J*:
10 under the children of Judah and *J*
24 him altars in every corner of *J*.
27 buried him in the city, even in *J*:
29. 1 reigned nine and twenty years in *J*.
8 of the Lord was upon Judah and *J*,
30. 1 come to the house of the Lord at *J*,
2 and all the congregation in *J*,
3 gathered themselves together to *J*.
5 unto the Lord God of Israel at *J*:
11 themselves, and came to *J*.
13 there assembled at *J* much people
14 took away the altars that were in *J*,
21 of Israel that were present at *J*
26 So there was great joy in *J*: for
26 Israel there was not the like in *J*.
31. 4 the people that dwelt in *J* to give
32. 2 he was purposed to fight against *J*,
9 of Assyria send his servants to *J*,
9 and unto all Judah that were at *J*,
10 that ye abide in the siege in *J*?
12 and commanded Judah and *J*,
18 people of *J* that were on the wall,
19 they spake against the God of *J*,
22 Hezekiah and the inhabitants of *J*
23 brought gifts unto the Lord to *J*,
25 upon him, and upon Judah and *J*.
26 both he and the inhabitants of *J*,
33 inhabitants of *J* did him honor at
33. 1 he reigned fifty and five years in *J*:
4 In *J* shall my name be for ever.
7 and in *J*, which I have chosen
9 and the inhabitants of *J* to err,
13 him again to *J* into his kingdom.
15 in *J*, and cast them out of the city.
21 reign, and reigned two years in *J*.
34. 1 reigned in *J* one and thirty years.
3 he began to purge Judah and *J*
5 altars, and cleansed Judah and *J*.
7 land of Israel, he returned to *J*.
9 Benjamin; and they returned to *J*.
22 (now she dwelt in *J* in the college:)
29 all the elders of Judah and *J*.
30 of Judah, and the inhabitants of *J*,
32 he caused all that were present in *J*
32 the inhabitants of *J* did according
35. 1 kept a passover unto the Lord in *J*:
18 present, and the inhabitants of *J*.
24 they brought him to *J*, and he died,
24 Judah and *J* mourned for Josiah.
36. 1 him king in his father's stead in *J*.
2 and he reigned three months in *J*.
3 king of Egypt put him down at *J*,
4 his brother king over Judah and *J*,
5 and he reigned eleven years in *J*:
9 three months and ten days in *J*:
10 his brother king over Judah and *J*.
11 and reigned eleven years in *J*.
14 Lord which he had hallowed in *J*.
19 and brake down the wall of *J*,
23 me to build him an house in *J*,
Ezr 1. 2 me to build him an house at *J*,
3 with him, and let him go up to *J*,
3 (he is the God,) which is in *J*.
4 for the house of God that is in *J*.
5 house of the Lord which is in *J*.
7 had brought forth out of *J*,
11 brought up from Babylon unto *J*.
2. 1 and came again unto *J* and Judah,
68 house of the Lord which is at *J*,
3. 1 together as one man to *J*.
8 coming unto the house of God at *J*,
8 come out of the captivity unto *J*;
4. 6 the inhabitants of Judah and *J*.
8 the scribe wrote a letter against *J*
12 from thee to us are come unto *J*,
20 have been mighty kings also over *J*,
23 up in haste to *J* unto the Jews,
24 of the house of God which is at *J*.
5. 1 the Jews that were in Judah and *J*
2 the house of God which is at *J*:
14 out of the temple that was in *J*,
15 them into the temple that is in *J*,
16 of the house of God which is in *J*:
17 to build this house of God at *J*,
6. 3 concerning the house of God at *J*,
5 out of the temple which is at *J*,
5 again unto the temple which is at *J*,
9 of the priests which are at *J*,
12 this house of God which is at *J*.

1. Mount of Olives
2. Temple
3. Antonia Fortress
4. Hippodrome
5. Theater
6. Herod's Palace
7. Viaduct

***Jerusalem in Jesus' time** was dominated by the temple complex built largely by Herod the Great and completed by his successors, only to be destroyed in A.D. 70 by Roman troops sent in to crush the Jewish uprising. At the northwest corner of the complex stood Herod's palace-fortress, called the Antonia, which may have been the site of Jesus' trial before Pontius Pilate.*

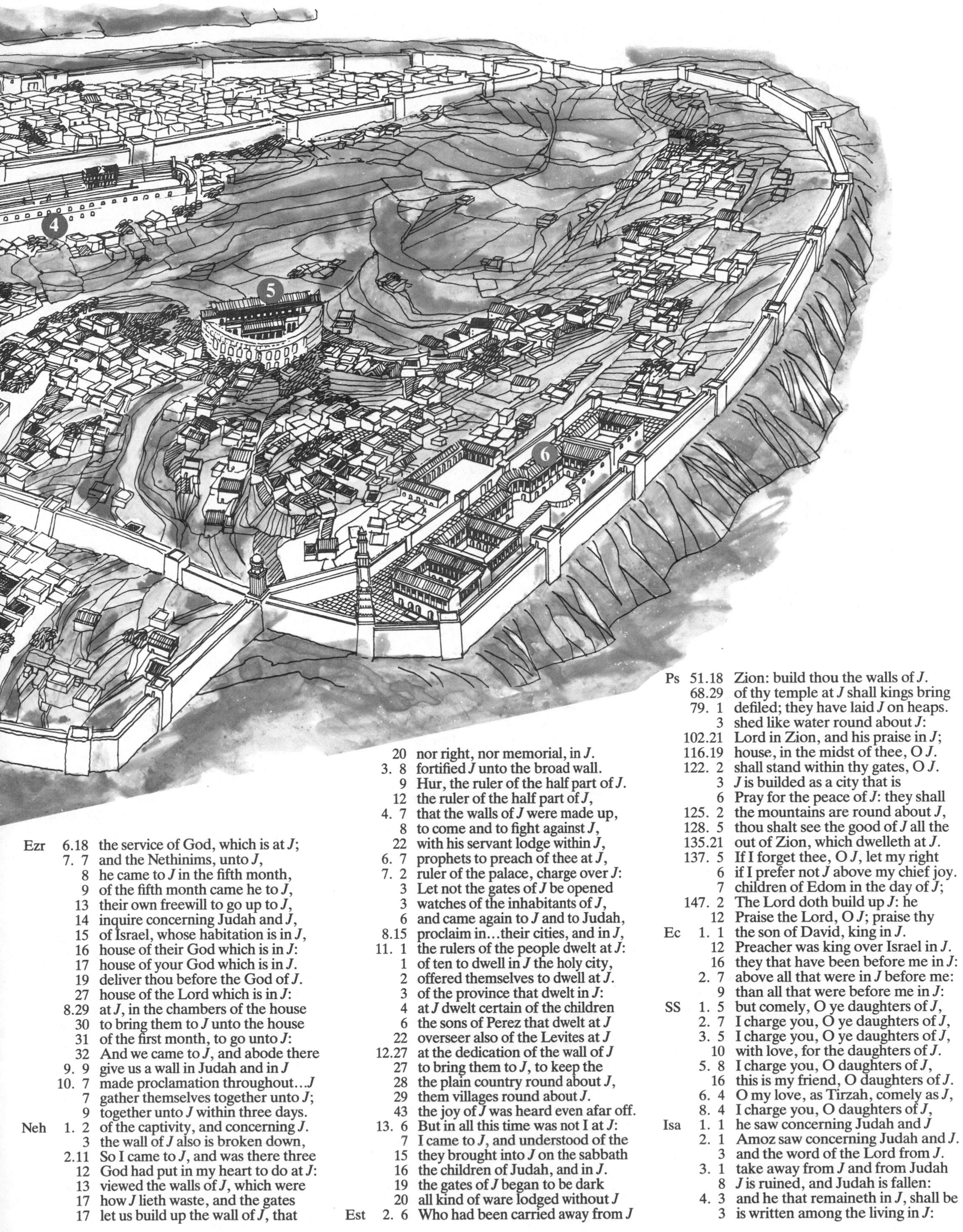

Ezr 6.18 the service of God, which is at *J*;
7. 7 and the Nethinims, unto *J*,
8 he came to *J* in the fifth month,
9 of the fifth month came he to *J*,
13 their own freewill to go up to *J*,
14 inquire concerning Judah and *J*,
15 of Israel, whose habitation is in *J*,
16 house of their God which is in *J*:
17 house of your God which is in *J*.
19 deliver thou before the God of *J*.
27 house of the Lord which is in *J*:
8.29 at *J*, in the chambers of the house
30 to bring them to *J* unto the house
31 of the first month, to go unto *J*:
32 And we came to *J*, and abode there
9. 9 give us a wall in Judah and in *J*
10. 7 made proclamation throughout...*J*
7 gather themselves together unto *J*;
9 together unto *J* within three days.
Neh 1. 2 of the captivity, and concerning *J*.
3 the wall of *J* also is broken down,
2.11 So I came to *J*, and was there three
12 God had put in my heart to do at *J*:
13 viewed the walls of *J*, which were
17 how *J* lieth waste, and the gates
17 let us build up the wall of *J*, that
20 nor right, nor memorial, in *J*.
3. 8 fortified *J* unto the broad wall.
9 Hur, the ruler of the half part of *J*.
12 the ruler of the half part of *J*,
4. 7 that the walls of *J* were made up,
8 to come and to fight against *J*,
22 with his servant lodge within *J*,
6. 7 prophets to preach of thee at *J*,
7. 2 ruler of the palace, charge over *J*:
3 Let not the gates of *J* be opened
3 watches of the inhabitants of *J*,
6 and came again to *J* and to Judah,
8.15 proclaim in...their cities, and in *J*,
11. 1 the rulers of the people dwelt at *J*:
1 of ten to dwell in *J* the holy city,
2 offered themselves to dwell at *J*.
3 of the province that dwelt in *J*:
4 at *J* dwelt certain of the children
6 the sons of Perez that dwelt at *J*
22 overseer also of the Levites at *J*
12.27 at the dedication of the wall of *J*
27 to bring them to *J*, to keep the
28 the plain country round about *J*,
29 them villages round about *J*.
43 the joy of *J* was heard even afar off.
13. 6 But in all this time was not I at *J*:
7 I came to *J*, and understood of the
15 they brought into *J* on the sabbath
16 the children of Judah, and in *J*.
19 the gates of *J* began to be dark
20 all kind of ware lodged without *J*
Est 2. 6 Who had been carried away from *J*
Ps 51.18 Zion: build thou the walls of *J*.
68.29 of thy temple at *J* shall kings bring
79. 1 defiled; they have laid *J* on heaps.
3 shed like water round about *J*:
102.21 Lord in Zion, and his praise in *J*;
116.19 house, in the midst of thee, O *J*.
122. 2 shall stand within thy gates, O *J*.
3 *J* is builded as a city that is
6 Pray for the peace of *J*: they shall
125. 2 the mountains are round about *J*,
128. 5 thou shalt see the good of *J* all the
135.21 out of Zion, which dwelleth at *J*.
137. 5 If I forget thee, O *J*, let my right
6 if I prefer not *J* above my chief joy.
7 children of Edom in the day of *J*;
147. 2 The Lord doth build up *J*: he
12 Praise the Lord, O *J*; praise thy
Ec 1. 1 the son of David, king in *J*.
12 Preacher was king over Israel in *J*.
16 they that have been before me in *J*:
2. 7 above all that were in *J* before me:
9 than all that were before me in *J*:
SS 1. 5 but comely, O ye daughters of *J*,
2. 7 I charge you, O ye daughters of *J*,
3. 5 I charge you, O ye daughters of *J*,
10 with love, for the daughters of *J*.
5. 8 I charge you, O daughters of *J*,
16 this is my friend, O daughters of *J*.
6. 4 O my love, as Tirzah, comely as *J*,
8. 4 I charge you, O daughters of *J*,
Isa 1. 1 he saw concerning Judah and *J*
2. 1 Amoz saw concerning Judah and *J*.
3 and the word of the Lord from *J*.
3. 1 take away from *J* and from Judah
8 *J* is ruined, and Judah is fallen:
4. 3 and he that remaineth in *J*, shall be
3 is written among the living in *J*:

Isa 4. 4 shall have purged the blood of *J*
5. 3 now, O inhabitants of *J*, and men of
7. 1 went up toward *J* to war against
8.14 for a snare to the inhabitants of *J*.
10.10 graven images did excel them of *J*
11 her idols, so do to *J* and her idols?
12 work upon mount Zion and on *J*,
32 the daughter of Zion, and hill of *J*.
22.10 ye have numbered the houses of *J*,
21 be a father to the inhabitants of *J*,
24.23 shall reign in mount Zion, and in *J*,
27.13 the Lord in the holy mount at *J*.
28.14 that rule this people which is in *J*.
30.19 the people shall dwell in Zion at *J*:
31. 5 so will the Lord of hosts defend *J*;
9 fire is in Zion, and his furnace in *J*.
33.20 eyes shall see *J* a quiet habitation,
36. 2 sent Rabshakeh from Lachish to *J*
7 away, and said to Judah and to *J*,
20 Lord should deliver *J* out of my
37.10 *J* shall not be given into the hand
22 the daughter of *J* hath shaken her
32 out of *J* shall go forth a remnant,
40. 2 Speak ye comfortably to *J*, and cry
9 O *J*, that bringest good tidings,
41.27 give to *J* one that bringeth good
44.26 saith to *J*, Thou shalt be inhabited;
28 saying to *J*, Thou shalt be built;
51.17 Awake, awake, stand up, O *J*,
52. 1 put on thy beautiful garments, O *J*,
2 arise, and sit down, O *J*: loose
9 sing together, ye waste places of *J*:
9 his people, he hath redeemed *J*.
62. 6 set watchmen upon thy walls, O *J*,
7 till he make *J* a praise in the earth.
64.10 Zion is a wilderness, *J* a desolation.
65.18 I create *J* a rejoicing, and her
19 I will rejoice in *J*, and joy in my
66.10 Rejoice ye with *J*, and be glad with
13 and ye shall be comforted in *J*.
20 beasts, to my holy mountain *J*,
Jer 1. 3 unto the carrying away of *J* captive
15 at the entering of the gates of *J*,
2. 2 Go and cry in the ears of *J*, saying,
3.17 shall call *J* the throne of the Lord;
17 it, to the name of the Lord, to *J*:
4. 3 Lord to the men of Judah and *J*,
4 men of Judah and inhabitants of *J*:
5 ye in Judah, and publish in *J*;
10 greatly deceived this people and *J*,
11 it be said to this people and to *J*,
14 O *J*, wash thine heart from
16 publish against *J*, that watchers
5. 1 to and fro through the streets of *J*,
6. 1 to flee out of the midst of *J*,
6 trees, and cast a mount against *J*:
8 Be thou instructed, O *J*, lest my
7.17 of Judah and in the streets of *J*?
29 Cut off thine hair, O *J*, and cast it
34 Judah, and from the streets of *J*,
8. 1 the bones of the inhabitants of *J*,
5 is this people of *J* slidden back
9.11 I will make *J* heaps, and a den of
11. 2 Judah, and to the inhabitants of *J*;
6 of Judah, and in the streets of *J*,
9 and among the inhabitants of *J*.
12 of Judah and inhabitants of *J* go,
13 to the number of streets of *J*
13. 9 of Judah, and the great pride of *J*.
13 all the inhabitants of *J*, and
27 Woe unto thee, O *J*! wilt thou not
14. 2 and the cry of *J* is gone up.
16 shall be cast out in the streets of *J*
15. 4 Judah, for that which he did in *J*.
5 shall have pity upon thee, O *J*?
17.19 go out, and in all the gates of *J*;
20 all the inhabitants of *J*, that enter
21 nor bring it in by the gates of *J*;
25 Judah, and the inhabitants of *J*:
26 Judah, and from the places about *J*,
27 even entering in at the gates of *J*
27 it shall devour the palaces of *J*,
18.11 Judah, and to the inhabitants of *J*,
19. 3 of Judah, and inhabitants of *J*;
7 void the counsel of Judah and *J*
13 the houses of *J*, and the houses of
22.19 cast forth beyond the gates of *J*.
23.14 have seen also in the prophets of *J*
15 the prophets of *J* is profaneness
24. 1 the carpenters and smiths, from *J*,
8 his princes, and the residue of *J*,
25. 2 to all the inhabitants of *J*, saying,
18 To wit, *J*, and the cities of Judah,
26.18 a field, and *J* shall become heaps,
27. 3 of the messengers which come to *J*
18 of the king of Judah, and at *J*, go
20 king of Judah from *J* to Babylon,
20 and all the nobles of Judah and *J*;
21 of the king of Judah and of *J*;
29. 1 Jeremiah the prophet sent from *J*
1 away captive from *J* to Babylon;
2 the princes of Judah and *J*, and
2 the smiths, were departed from *J*;)
4 caused to be carried away from *J*
20 I have sent from *J* to Babylon:
25 unto all the people that are at *J*,
32. 2 king of Babylon's army besieged *J*:
32 of Judah, and the inhabitants of *J*.
44 and in the places about *J*, and in
33.10 the streets of *J*, that are desolate,
13 and in the places about *J*, and in
16 be saved, and *J* shall dwell safely:
34. 1 all the people, fought against *J*,
6 unto Zedekiah king of Judah in *J*,
7 Babylon's army fought against *J*,
8 with all the people which were at *J*,
19 of Judah, and the princes of *J*,
35.11 Come, and let us go to *J* for fear
11 of the Syrians: so we dwell at *J*.
13 of Judah and the inhabitants of *J*,
17 upon all the inhabitants of *J* all
36. 9 the Lord to all the people in *J*,
9 from the cities of Judah unto *J*.
31 and upon the inhabitants of *J*,
37. 5 Chaldeans that besieged *J* heard
5 of them, they departed from *J*.
11 was broken up from *J* for fear of
12 Jeremiah went forth out of *J* to go
38.28 until the day that *J* was taken:
28 he was there when *J* was taken.
39. 1 Babylon and all his army against *J*,
8 and brake down the walls of *J*.
40. 1 away captive of *J* and Judah,
42.18 forth upon the inhabitants of *J*;
44. 2 evil that I have brought upon *J*,
6 of Judah and in the streets of *J*;
9 of Judah, and in the streets of *J*?
13 as I have punished *J*, by the sword,
17 of Judah, and in the streets of *J*:
21 of Judah, and in the streets of *J*,
51.35 inhabitants of Chaldea, shall *J* say.
50 and let *J* come into your mind.
52. 1 and he reigned eleven years in *J*.
3 it came to pass in *J* and Judah,
4 he and all his army, against *J*,
12 served the king of Babylon, into *J*,
13 and all the houses of *J*, and all the
14 brake down all the walls of *J* round
29 he carried away captive from *J*
La 1. 7 *J* remembered in the days of her
8 *J* hath grievously sinned;
17 *J* is as a menstruous woman
2.10 virgins of *J* hang down their heads
13 I liken to thee, O daughter of *J*?
15 their head at the daughter of *J*,
4.12 have entered into the gates of *J*.
Eze 4. 1 pourtray upon it the city, even *J*:
7 set thy face toward the seige of *J*,
16 I will break the staff of bread in *J*:
5. 5 saith the Lord God; This is *J*:
8. 3 me in the visions of God to *J*,
9. 4 of the city, through the midst of *J*,
8 pouring out of thy fury upon *J*?
11.15 the inhabitants of *J* have said,
12.10 burden concerneth the prince in *J*,
19 Lord God of the inhabitants of *J*,
13.16 which prophesy concerning *J*,
14.21 my four sore judgments upon *J*,
22 evil that I have brought upon *J*,
15. 6 so will I give the inhabitants of *J*.
16. 2 cause *J* to know her abominations,
3 Thus saith the Lord God unto *J*;
17.12 the king of Babylon is come to *J*,
21. 2 Son of man, set thy face toward *J*,
20 and to Judah in *J* the defensed.
22 right hand was the divination for *J*,
22.19 will gather you into the midst of *J*.
23. 4 Samaria is Aholah, and *J* Aholibah.
24. 2 of Babylon set himself against *J*
26. 2 that Tyrus hath said against *J*,
33.21 one that had escaped out of *J* came
36.38 the flock of *J* in her solemn feasts;
Dan 1. 1 came Nebuchadnezzar...unto *J*,
5. 2 out of the temple which was in *J*;
3 the house of God which was at *J*;
6.10 open in his chamber toward *J*,
9. 2 years in the desolations of *J*.
7 Judah, and to the inhabitants of *J*,
12 done as hath been done upon *J*.
16 be turned away from thy city *J*,
16 *J* and thy people are become a
25 to restore and to build *J* unto the
Joel 2.32 Zion and in *J* shall be deliverance,
3. 1 again the captivity of Judah and *J*,
6 the children of *J* have ye sold unto
16 of Zion, and utter his voice from *J*;
17 mountain: then shall *J* be holy,
20 *J* from generation to generation.
Am 1. 2 Zion, and utter his voice from *J*;
2. 5 it shall devour the palaces of *J*.
Ob 11 his gates, and cast lots upon *J*,
20 Zarephath; and the captivity of *J*,
Mic 1. 1 he saw concerning Samaria and *J*.
5 places of Judah? are they not *J*?
9 the gate of my people, even to *J*.
12 from the Lord unto the gate of *J*.
3.10 with blood, and *J* with iniquity.
12 a field, and *J* shall become heaps,
4. 2 and the word of the Lord from *J*.
8 shall come to the daughter of *J*.
Zep 1. 4 and upon all the inhabitants of *J*;
12 that I will search *J* with candles,
3.14 with all the heart, O daughter of *J*.
16 In that day it shall be said to *J*,
Zec 1.12 long wilt thou not have mercy on *J*
14 I am jealous for *J* and for Zion
16 I am returned to *J* with mercies:
16 shall be stretched forth upon *J*.
17 Zion, and shall yet choose *J*.
19 scattered Judah, Israel, and *J*.
2. 2 he said unto me, To measure *J*,
4 *J* shall be inhabited as towns
12 land, and shall choose *J* again.
3. 2 Lord that hath chosen *J* rebuke
7. 7 *J* was inhabited and in prosperity,
8. 3 and will dwell in the midst of *J*:
3 *J* shall be called a city of truth;
4 women dwell in the streets of *J*,
8 they shall dwell in the midst of *J*:
15 to do well unto *J* and to the house
22 come to seek the Lord of hosts in *J*,
9. 9 shout, O daughter of *J*: behold,
10 Ephraim, and the horse from *J*,
12. 2 I will make *J* a cup of trembling
2 both against Judah and against *J*.
3 make *J* a burdensome stone for all
5 The inhabitants of *J* shall be my
6 and *J* shall be inhabited again
6 in her own place, even in *J*.
7 the glory of the inhabitants of *J*
8 Lord defend the inhabitants of *J*;
9 the nations that come against *J*.
10 and upon the inhabitants of *J*, the

11 there be a great mourning in J,
13. 1 and to the inhabitants of J for sin
14. 2 I will gather all nations against J
4 which is before J on the east,
8 living waters shall go out from J;
10 from Geba to Rimmon south of J:
11 but J shall be safely inhabited.
12 people that have fought against J;
14 And Judah also shall fight at J;
16 the nations which came against J
17 earth unto J to worship the King,
21 every pot in J and in Judah shall
Mal 2.11 is committed in Israel and in J;
3. 4 offering of Judah and J be pleasant
Mt 2. 1 wise men from the east to J,
3 was troubled, and all J with him.
3. 5 went out to him J, and all Judea,
4.25 from J, and from Judea, and from
5.35 neither by J; for it is the city of
15. 1 and Pharisees, which were of J,
16.21 how that he must go unto J, and
20.17 And Jesus going up to J took the
18 Behold, we go up to J; and the
21. 1 And when they drew nigh unto J,
10 when he was come into J, all the
23.37 O J, J, thou that killest the
Mk 1. 5 the land of Judea, and they of J,
3. 8 And from J, and from Idumea, and
22 scribes which came down from J
7. 1 of the scribes, which came from J.
10.32 were in the way going up to J;
33 Saying, Behold, we go up to J;
11. 1 when they came nigh to J, unto
11 Jesus entered into J, and into the
15 they come to J: and Jesus went
27 And they come again to J: and as
15.41 which came up with him unto J.
Lk 2.22 they brought him to J, to present
25 there was a man in J, whose
38 that looked for redemption in J.
41 his parents went to J every year
42 went up to J after the custom
43 child Jesus tarried behind in J;
45 not, they turned back again to J,
4. 9 he brought him to J, and set him
5.17 town of Galilee, and Judea, and J:
6.17 of people out of all Judea and J,
9.31 which he should accomplish at J.
51 stedfastly set his face to go to J,
53 was as though he would go to J.
10.30 man went down from J to Jericho,
13. 4 above all men that dwelt in J?
22 teaching, and journeying toward J.
33 be that a prophet perish out of J.
34 O J, J, which killest the prophets,
17.11 it came to pass, as he went to J,
18.31 unto them, Behold, we go up to J,
19.11 parable, because he was nigh to J,
28 he went before, ascending up to J.
21.20 see J compassed with armies,
24 and J shall be trodden down of the
23. 7 himself also was at J at that
28 Daughters of J, weep not for me,
24.13 from J about threescore furlongs.
18 him, Art thou only a stranger in J,
33 the same hour, and returned to J,
47 among all nations, beginning at J.
49 tarry ye in the city of J, until ye
52 and returned to J with great joy:
Jn 1.19 sent priests and Levites from J
2.13 at hand, and Jesus went up to J,
23 when he was in J at the passover,
4.20 in J is the place where men ought
21 in this mountain, nor yet at J,
45 things that he did at J at the feast:
5. 1 the Jews; and Jesus went up to J.
2 is at J by the sheep market a pool,
7.25 Then said some of them of J, Is
10.22 was at J the feast of the dedication,
11.18 Now Bethany was nigh unto J,
55 went out of the country up to J
12.12 heard that Jesus was coming to J,
Ac 1. 4 they should not depart from J,
8 be witnesses unto me both in J,
12 Then returned they unto J from
12 is from J a sabbath day's journey.
19 known unto all the dwellers at J;
2. 5 there were dwelling at J Jews,
14 Judea, and all ye that dwell at J,
4. 6 were gathered together at J.
16 to all them that dwell in J:
5.16 of the cities round about unto J,
28 ye have filled J with your doctrine,
6. 7 disciples multiplied in J greatly;
8. 1 the church which was at J;
14 the apostles which were at J heard
25 returned to J, and preached the
26 that goeth down from J unto Gaza,
27 and had come to J for to worship,
9. 2 might bring them bound unto J.
13 evil he hath done to thy saints at J:
21 which called on this name in J,
26 And when Saul was come to J,
28 them coming in and going out at J.
10.39 in the land of the Jews, and in J;
11. 2 when Peter was come up to J,
22 ears of the church which was in J:
27 prophets from J unto Antioch.
12.25 and Saul returned from J,
13.13 John departing...returned to J.
27 for they that dwell at J, and their
31 up with him from Galilee to J,
15. 2 go up to J unto the apostles and
4 And when they were come to J,
16. 4 and elders which were at J.
18.21 keep this feast that cometh in J:
19.21 Macedonia and Achaia, to go to J,
20.16 to be at J the day of Pentecost.
22 I go bound in the spirit unto J,
21. 4 that he should not go up to J.
11 So shall the Jews at J bind the man
12 besought him not to go up to J.
13 to die at J for the name of the Lord
15 up our carriages, and went up to J.
17 And when we were come to J,
31 band, that all J was in an uproar.
22. 5 which were there bound unto J,
17 that, when I was come again to J,
18 and get thee quickly out of J:
23.11 as thou hast testified of me in J,
24.11 since I went up to J for to worship.
25. 1 he ascended from Caesarea to J.
3 that he would send for him to J,
7 Jews which came down from J
9 Wilt thou go up to J, and there be
15 About whom, when I was at J, the
20 him whether he would go to J,
24 dealt with me, both at J, and also
26. 4 first among mine own nation at J,
10 Which thing I also did in J:
20 unto them of Damascus, and at J,
28.17 yet was I delivered prisoner from J
Ro 15.19 so that from J, and round about
25 But now I go unto J to minister
26 for the poor saints which are at J.
31 that my service which I have for J
1Co 16. 3 to bring your liberality unto J.
Gal 1.17 Neither went I up to J to them
18 I went up to J to see Peter,
2. 1 went up again to J with Barnabas,
4.25 and answereth to J which now is,
26 But J which is above is free, which
Heb 12.22 of the living God, the heavenly J,
Rev 3.12 the city of my God, which is new J,
21. 2 saw the holy city, new J, coming
10 great city, the holy J, descending

JESSE

Ru 4.17 he is the father of J, the father
22 Obed begat J, and J begat David.
1Sa 16. 1 send thee to J the Bethlehemite:
3 call J to the sacrifice, and I will
5 And he sanctified J and his sons,
8 J called Abinadab, and made him
9 Then J made Shammah to pass
10 J made seven of his sons to pass
10 Samuel said unto J, The Lord hath
11 Samuel said unto J, Are here all
11 And Samuel said unto J, Send and
18 Behold, I have seen a son of J
19 Saul sent messengers unto J, and
20 J took an ass laden with bread,
22 Saul sent to J, saying, Let David, I
17.12 whose name was J, and he had
13 three eldest sons of J went and
17 J said unto David his son, Take
20 and went, as J had commanded
58 I am the son of thy servant J the
20.27 cometh not the son of J to meat,
30 chosen the son of J to thine own
31 as long as the son of J liveth upon
22. 7 the son of J give every one of you
8 made a league with the son of J,
9 I saw the son of J coming to Nob,
13 against me, thou and the son of J,
25.10 David? and who is the son of J?
2Sa 20. 1 we inheritance in the son of J:
23. 1 David the son of J said, and the
1Ki 12.16 we inheritance in the son of J:
1Ch 2.12 begat Obed, and Obed begat J,
13 And J begat his firstborn Eliab,
10.14 kingdom unto David the son of J.
12.18 and on thy side, thou son of J:
29.26 David the son of J reigned over all
2Ch 10.16 none inheritance in the son of J:
11.18 daughter of Eliab the son of J;
Ps 72.20 The prayers of David the son of J
Isa 11. 1 forth a rod out of the stem of J,
10 that day there shall be a root of J,
Mt 1. 5 Obed of Ruth; and Obed begat J;
6 And J begat David the king; and
Lk 3.32 Which was the son of J, which was
Ac 13.22 I have found David the son of J,
Ro 15.12 saith, There shall be a root of J,

JESTING

Eph 5. 4 nor foolish talking, nor j, which

JESUS

Mt 1. 1 book of the generation of J Christ,
16 of whom was born J, who is called
18 birth of J Christ was on this wise:
21 son, and thou shalt call his name J:
25 son: and he called his name J.
2. 1 when J was born in Bethlehem of
3.13 cometh J from Galilee to Jordan
15 J answering said unto him, Suffer
16 J, when he was baptized, went up
4. 1 was J led up of the spirit into the
7 J said unto him, It is written
10 saith J unto him, Get thee hence,
12 J had heard that John was cast
17 From that time J began to preach,
18 J, walking by the sea of Galilee,
23 J went about all Galilee, teaching
7.28 when J had ended these sayings,
8. 3 J put forth his hand, and touched
4 J saith unto him, See thou tell no
5 J was entered into Capernaum,
7 J saith unto him, I will come and
10 When J heard it, he marvelled,
13 J said unto the centurion, Go thy
14 J was come into Peter's house,
18 Now when J saw great multitudes
20 J saith unto him, The foxes have
22 But J said unto him, Follow me;
29 do with thee, J, thou son of God?
34 the whole city came out to meet J:
9. 2 J seeing their faith said unto the
4 And J knowing their thoughts said,
9 And as J passed forth from thence,
10 pass, as J sat at meat in the house,
12 when J heard that, he said unto

Jesus speaks to the Samaritan woman at the well (Jn 4) in this painting by Annibale Carracci (1560-1609).

Mt 9.15 *J* said unto them, Can the children
19 *J* arose, and followed him, and so
22 *J* turned him about, and when he
23 when *J* came into the ruler's house,
27 when *J* departed thence, two blind
28 *J* saith unto them, Believe ye that
30 and *J* straitly charged them,
35 And *J* went about all the cities and
10. 5 These twelve *J* sent forth, and
11. 1 *J*...made an end of commanding
4 *J* answered and said unto them,
7 *J* began to say unto the multitudes
25 *J* answered and said, I thank thee,
12. 1 *J* went on the sabbath day through
15 But when *J* knew it, he withdrew
25 *J* knew their thoughts, and said
13. 1 same day went *J* out of the house,
34 things spake *J* unto the multitudes
36 Then *J* sent the multitude away,
51 *J* saith..., Have ye understood all
53 when *J* had finished these parables,
57 But *J* said unto them, A prophet is
14. 1 tetrarch heard of the fame of *J*,
12 and buried it, and went and told *J*.
13 When *J* heard of it, he departed
14 *J* went forth, and saw a great
16 *J* said unto them, They need not
22 *J* constrained his disciples to get
25 fourth watch of the night *J* went
27 straightway *J* spake unto them,
29 he walked on the water, to go to *J*.
31 immediately *J* stretched forth his
15. 1 came to *J* scribes and Pharisees,
16 *J* said, Are ye also yet without
21 *J* went thence, and departed into
28 *J* answered and said unto her, O
29 *J* departed from thence, and came
32 *J* called his disciples unto him,
34 And *J* saith unto them, How many
16. 6 Then *J* said unto them, Take heed
8 Which when *J* perceived, he said
13 When *J* came into the coasts of
17 *J* answered and said unto him,
20 should tell no man that he was *J*
21 that time forth began *J* to shew
24 said *J* unto his disciples, If any
17. 1 And after six days *J* taketh Peter,
4 and said unto *J*, Lord, it is good
7 *J* came and touched them, and
8 they saw no man, save *J* only.
9 the mountain, *J* charged them,
11 *J* answered and said unto them,
17 *J* answered and said, O faithless
18 and *J* rebuked the devil; and he
19 Then came the disciples to *J* apart,
20 *J* said unto them, Because of your
22 abode in Galilee, *J* said unto them,
25 into the house, *J* prevented him,
26 *J* saith unto him, Then are the
18. 1 time came the disciples unto *J*,
2 *J* called a little child unto him,
22 *J* saith unto him, I say not unto
19. 1 when *J* had finished these sayings,
14 *J* said, Suffer little children, and
18 *J* said, Thou shalt do no murder,
21 *J* said unto him, If thou wilt be
23 said *J* unto his disciples, Verily I
26 *J* beheld them, and said unto them,
28 *J* said unto them, Verily I say unto
20.17 *J* going up to Jerusalem took the
22 *J* answered and said, Ye know not
25 *J* called them unto him, and said,
30 when they heard that *J* passed by,
32 *J* stood still, and called them, and
34 *J* had compassion on them, and
21. 1 Olives, then sent *J* two disciples,
6 and did as *J* commanded them.
11 This is *J* the prophet of Nazareth
12 *J* went into the temple of God, and
16 *J* said unto them, Yea; have ye
21 *J* answered and said unto them,
24 *J* answered and said unto them, I
27 they answered *J*, and said, We
31 *J* saith unto them, Verily I say
42 *J* saith unto them, Did ye never
22. 1 *J* answered and spake unto them
18 But *J* perceived their wickedness,
29 *J* answered and said unto them,
37 *J* said unto him, thou shalt love
41 gathered together, *J* asked them,
23. 1 Then spake *J* to the multitude,
24. 1 *J* went out, and departed from the
2 *J* said unto them, See ye not all
4 *J* answered and said unto them,
26. 1 when *J* had finished all these
4 that they might take *J* by subtilty,
6 *J* was in Bethany, in the house of
10 When *J* understood it, he said
17 bread the disciples came to *J*,
19 disciples did as *J* had appointed
26 *J* took bread, and blessed it,
31 saith *J* unto them, All ye shall be
34 *J* said unto him, Verily I say unto
36 cometh *J* with them unto a place
49 forthwith he came to *J*, and said
50 *J* said unto him, Friend, wherefore
50 came they, and laid hands on *J*,
51 which were with *J* stretched out
52 said *J* unto him, Put up again thy
55 In that same hour said *J* to the
57 they that had laid hold on *J* led
59 sought false witness against *J*,
63 *J* held his peace. And the high
64 *J* saith unto him, Thou hast said:
69 Thou also wast with *J* of Galilee.
71 was also with *J* of Nazareth.
75 Peter remembered the word of *J*,
27. 1 took counsel against *J* to put him
11 And *J* stood before the governor:
11 *J* said unto him, Thou sayest.
17 or *J* which is called Christ?
20 ask Barabbas, and destroy *J*.
22 then with *J* which is called Christ?
26 he had scourged *J*, he delivered
27 soldiers of the governor took *J*
37 This Is *J* The King Of The Jews.
46 ninth hour *J* cried with a loud
50 *J*, when he had cried again with a
54 watching *J*, saw the earthquake,
55 which followed *J* from Galilee,
58 Pilate, and begged the body of *J*.
28. 5 I know that ye seek *J*, which was
9 *J* met them, saying, All hail. And
10 said *J* unto them, Be not afraid:
16 into a mountain where *J* had
18 *J* came and spake unto them,
Mk 1. 1 beginning of the gospel of *J* Christ,
9 *J* came from Nazareth of Galilee,
14 *J* came into Galilee, preaching the
17 *J* said unto them, Come ye after
24 do with thee, thou *J* of Nazareth?
25 *J* rebuked him, saying, Hold thy
41 *J*, moved with compassion, put
45 insomuch that *J* could no more
2. 5 When *J* saw their faith, he said
8 when *J* perceived in his spirit
15 that, as *J* sat at meat in his house,
15 sat also together with *J* and his
17 When *J* heard it, he saith unto
19 *J* said unto them, Can the children
3. 7 *J* withdrew himself with his
5. 6 when he saw *J* afar off, he ran and
7 What have I to do with thee, *J*,
13 And forthwith *J* gave them leave.
15 they come to *J*, and see him that
19 Howbeit *J* suffered him not, but
20 great things *J* had done for him:
21 when *J* was passed over again by
24 *J* went with him; and much
27 When she had heard of *J*, came in
30 *J*, immediately knowing in
36 As soon as *J* heard the word that
6. 4 *J* said unto them, A prophet is not
30 themselves together unto *J*,
34 *J*, when he came out, saw much
7.27 *J* said unto her, Let the children
8. 1 *J* called his disciples unto him,
17 And when *J* knew it, he saith unto
27 And *J* went out, and his disciples,
9. 2 six days *J* taketh with him Peter,
4 and they were talking with *J*.

5 Peter answered and said to *J*,
8 more, save *J* only with themselves.
23 *J* said unto him, If thou canst
25 When *J* saw that the people came
27 *J* took him by the hand, and lifted
39 *J* said, Forbid him not: for there
10. 5 *J* answered and said unto them,
14 when *J* saw it, he was much
18 *J* said unto him, Why callest thou
21 Then *J* beholding him loved him,
23 *J* looked round about, and saith
24 *J* answereth again, and saith unto
27 *J* looking upon them saith, With
29 *J* answered and said, Verily I say
32 *J* went before them: and they were
38 *J* said unto them, Ye know not
39 *J* said unto them, Ye shall indeed
42 *J* called them to him, and saith
47 he heard that it was *J* of Nazareth,
47 out, and say, *J*, thou son of David,
49 *J* stood still, and commanded him
50 his garment, rose, and came to *J*.
51 *J* answered and said unto him,
52 And *J* said unto him, Go thy way;
52 sight, and followed *J* in the way.
11. 6 them even as *J* had commanded:
7 they brought the colt to *J*, and
11 *J* entered into Jerusalem, and into
14 *J* answered and said unto it, No
15 *J* went into the temple, and began
22 *J* answering saith unto them,
29 *J* answered and said unto them,
33 they answered and said unto *J*,
33 *J* answering saith unto them,
12.17 *J* answering said unto them,
24 *J* answering said unto them, Do
29 *J* answered him, The first of all
34 when *J* saw that he answered
35 *J* answered and said, while he
41 *J* sat over against the treasury,
13. 2 *J* answering said unto him, Seest
5 *J* answering them began to say,
14. 6 *J* said, Let her alone; why trouble
18 eat, *J* said, Verily I say unto you,
22 *J* took bread, and blessed, and
27 And *J* saith unto them, All ye shall
30 And *J* saith unto him, Verily I say
48 *J* answered and said unto them,
53 they led *J* away to the high priest:
55 sought for witness against *J* to put
60 and asked *J*, saying, Answerest
62 And *J* said, I am: and ye shall see
67 thou also wast with *J* of Nazareth.
72 called to mind the word that *J* said
15. 1 bound *J*, and carried him away,
5 *J* yet answered nothing; so that
15 delivered *J*, when he had scourged
34 ninth hour *J* cried with a loud
37 and *J* cried with a loud voice, and
43 Pilate, and craved the body of *J*.
16. 6 Ye seek *J* of Nazareth, which was
9 Now when *J* was risen early the
Lk 1.31 son, and shalt call his name *J*.
2.21 his name was called *J*, which was
27 the parents brought in the child *J*,
43 the child *J* tarried behind in
52 And *J* increased in wisdom and
3.21 pass, that *J* also being baptized,
23 *J* himself began to be about thirty
4. 1 And *J* being full of the Holy Ghost
4 and *J* answered him, saying, It is
8 *J* answered and said unto him,
12 *J* answering said unto him, It is
14 *J* returned in the power of the
34 *J* of Nazareth? art thou come to
35 And *J* rebuked him, saying, Hold
5.10 And *J* said unto Simon, Fear not;
12 who seeing *J* fell on his face,
19 his couch into the midst before *J*.
22 But when *J* perceived their
31 And *J* answering said unto them,
6. 3 *J* answering them said, Have ye
9 Then said *J* unto them, I will ask
11 another what they might do to *J*.
7. 3 And when he heard of *J*, he sent
4 when they came to *J*, they
6 Then *J* went with them. And
9 When *J* heard these things, he
19 two of his disciples sent them to *J*,
22 Then *J* answering said unto them,
37 when she knew that *J* sat at meat
40 And *J* answering said unto him,
8.28 When he saw *J*, he cried out, and
28 What have I to do with thee, *J*,
30 *J* asked him, saying, What is thy
35 and came to *J*, and found the man,
35 sitting at the feet of *J*, clothed,
38 be with him: but *J* sent him away.
39 great things *J* had done unto him.
40 pass, that, when *J* was returned,
45 *J* said, Who touched me? When all
46 *J* said, Somebody hath touched
50 But when *J* heard it, he answered
9.33 Peter said unto *J*, Master, it is
36 voice was past, *J* was found alone.
41 And *J* answering said, O faithless
42 And *J* rebuked the unclean spirit,
43 every one at all things which *J* did,
47 And *J*, perceiving the thought of
50 And *J* said unto him, Forbid him
58 And *J* said unto him, Foxes have
60 *J* said unto him, Let the dead bury
62 And *J* said unto him, No man,
10.21 In that hour *J* rejoiced in spirit,
29 said unto *J*, And who is my
30 And *J* answering said, A certain
37 Then said *J* unto him, Go, and do
41 And *J* answered and said unto
13. 2 And *J* answering said unto them,
12 And when *J* saw her, he called her
14 *J* had healed on the sabbath day,
14. 3 And *J* answering spake unto the
17.13 *J*, Master, have mercy on us.
17 *J* answering said, Were there not
18.16 *J* called them unto him, and said,
19 *J* said unto him, Why callest thou
22 Now when *J* heard these things, he
24 when *J* saw that he was very
37 him, that *J* of Nazareth passeth by.
38 saying, *J*, thou son of David, have
40 *J* stood, and commanded him to be
42 *J* said unto him, Receive thy sight:
19. 1 *J* entered and passed through
3 he sought to see *J* who he was;
5 And when *J* came to the place, he
9 And *J* said unto him, This day is
35 they brought him to *J*: and they
35 the colt, and they set *J* thereon.
20. 8 *J* said unto them, Neither tell I
34 And *J* answering said unto them,
22.47 and drew near unto *J* to kiss him.
48 *J* said unto him, Judas, betrayest
51 *J* answered and said, Suffer ye
52 Then *J* said unto the chief priests,
63 the men that held *J* mocked him,
23. 8 And when Herod saw *J*, he was
20 willing to release *J*, spake again
25 but he delivered *J* to their will.
26 cross, that he might bear it after *J*.
28 But *J* turning unto them said,
34 Then said *J*, Father, forgive them;
42 he said unto *J*, Lord, remember
43 *J* said unto him, Verily I say unto
46 when *J* had cried with a loud
52 Pilate, and begged the body of *J*.
24. 3 found not the body of the Lord *J*.
15 *J* himself drew near, and went
19 Concerning *J* of Nazareth, which
36 *J* himself stood in the midst of
Jn 1.17 grace and truth came by *J* Christ.
29 John seeth *J* coming unto him,
36 looking upon *J* as he walked, he
37 him speak, and they followed *J*.
38 *J* turned, and saw them following,
42 And he brought him to *J*.
42 when *J* beheld him, he said, Thou
43 The day following *J* would go
45 prophets, did write, *J* of Nazareth,
47 *J* saw Nathanael coming to him,
48, 50 *J* answered and said unto him,
2. 1 and the mother of *J* was there:
2 *J* was called, and his disciples, to
3 the mother of *J* saith unto him,
4 *J* saith unto her, Woman, what
7 *J* saith unto them, Fill the
11 This beginning of miracles did *J*
13 hand, and *J* went up to Jerusalem.
19 *J* answered and said unto them,
22 and the word which *J* had said.
24 *J* did not commit himself unto
3. 2 The same came to *J* by night, and
3 *J* answered and said unto him,
5 *J* answered, Verily, verily, I say
10 *J* answered and said unto him,
22 After these things came *J* and his
4. 1 that *J* made and baptized more
2 Though *J* himself baptized not,
6 *J* therefore, being wearied with
7 *J* saith unto her, Give me to drink.
10, 13 *J* answered and said unto her,
16 *J* saith unto her, Go, call thy
17 *J* said unto her, Thou hast well
21 *J* saith unto her, Woman, believe
26 *J* saith unto her, I that speak unto
34 *J* saith unto them, My meat is to
44 *J* himself testified, that a prophet
46 *J* came again into Cana of Galilee,
47 he heard that *J* was come out of
48 Then said *J* unto him, Except ye
50 *J* saith unto him, Go thy way;
50 man believed the word that *J* had
53 *J* said unto him, Thy son liveth:
54 the second miracle that *J* did,
5. 1 and *J* went up to Jerusalem.
6 When *J* saw him lie, and knew
8 *J* saith unto him, Rise, take up
13 for *J* had conveyed himself away,
14 Afterward *J* findeth him in the
15 told the Jews that it was *J*, which
16 therefore did the Jews persecute *J*,
17 *J* answered them, My Father
19 Then answered *J* and said unto
6. 1 *J* went over the sea of Galilee,
3 *J* went up into a mountain, and
5 When *J* then lifted up his eyes,
10 *J* said, Make the men sit down.
11 *J* took the loaves; and when he
14 had seen the miracle that *J* did,
15 When *J* therefore perceived that
17 dark, and *J* was not come to them.
19 they see *J* walking on the sea, and
22 that *J* went not with his disciples
24 therefore saw that *J* was not there,
24 came to Capernaum, seeking for *J*.
26 *J* answered them and said, Verily,
29 *J* answered and said unto them,
32 Then *J* said unto them, Verily,
35 *J* said unto them, I am the bread
42 Is not this *J*, the son of Joseph,
43 *J* therefore answered and said
53 Then *J* said unto them, Verily,
61 When *J* knew in himself that his
64 *J* knew from the beginning who
67 Then said *J* unto the twelve, Will
70 *J* answered them, Have not I
7. 1 these things *J* walked in Galilee:
6 Then *J* said unto them, My time
14 feast *J* went up into the temple,
16 *J* answered them, and said, My
21 *J* answered and said unto them,
28 Then cried *J* in the temple as he
33 Then said *J* unto them, Yet a little
37 *J* stood and cried, saying, If any

Jn 7.39 that *J* was not yet glorified.
50 (he that came to *J* by night, being
8. 1 *J* went unto the mount of Olives.
6 But *J* stooped down, and with his
9 *J* was left alone, and the woman
10 When *J* had lifted up himself, and
11 And *J* said unto her, Neither do I
12 Then spake *J* again unto them,
14 *J* answered and said unto them,
19 *J* answered, Ye neither know me
20 These words spake *J* in the
21 Then said *J* again unto them, I go
25 *J* saith unto them, Even the same
28 Then said *J* unto them, When ye
31 Then said *J* to those Jews which
34 *J* answered them, Verily, verily, I
39 *J* saith unto them, If ye were
42 *J* said unto them, If God were
49 *J* answered, I have not a devil;
54 *J* answered, If I honor myself,
58 *J* said unto them, Verily, verily, I
59 *J* hid himself, and went out of the
9. 1 And as *J* passed by, he saw a man
3 *J* answered, Neither hath this
11 A man that is called *J* made clay,
14 sabbath day when *J* made the clay,
35 *J* heard that they had cast him
37 *J* said unto him, Thou hast both
39 *J* said, For judgment I am come
41 *J* said unto them, If ye were blind,
10. 6 This parable spake *J* unto them:
7 Then said *J* unto them again,
23 *J* walked in the temple in
25 *J* answered them, I told you, and
32 *J* answered them, Many good
34 *J* answered them, Is it not written
11. 4 When *J* heard that, he said, This
5 *J* loved Martha, and her sister,
9 *J* answered, Are there not twelve
13 Howbeit *J* spake of his death: but
14 Then said *J* unto them plainly,
17 when *J* came, he found that he had
20 as soon as she heard that *J* was
21 Then said Martha unto *J*, Lord,
23 *J* saith unto her, Thy brother
25 *J* saith..., I am the resurrection,
30 Now *J* was not yet come into the
32 when Mary was come where *J* was,
33 When *J* therefore saw her weeping,
35 *J* wept.
38 *J* therefore again groaning in
39 *J* said, Take ye away the stone.
40 *J* saith unto her, Said I not unto
41 And *J* lifted up his eyes, and said,
44 *J* saith unto them, Loose him, and
45 had seen the things which *J* did,
46 told them what things *J* had done.
51 that *J* should die for that nation:
54 *J* therefore walked no more openly
56 Then sought they for *J*, and spake
12. 1 *J* six days before the passover
3 and anointed the feet of *J*, and
7 Then said *J*, Let her alone:
11 Jews went away, and believed on *J*.
12 they heard that *J* was coming to
14 And *J*, when he had found a young
16 but when *J* was glorified, then
21 him, saying, Sir, we would see *J*.
22 again Andrew and Philip tell *J*.
23 And *J* answered them, saying,
30 *J* answered and said, This voice
35 Then *J* said unto them, Yet a little
36 things spake *J*, and departed, and
44 *J* cried and said, He that believeth
13. 1 *J* knew that his hour was come
3 *J* knowing that the Father had
7 *J* answered and said unto him,
8 *J* answered him, If I wash thee
10 *J* saith to him, He that is washed
21 When *J* had thus said, he was
23 one of his disciples, whom *J* loved.
26 *J* answered, He it is, to whom I
27 Then said *J* unto him, That thou
29 *J* had said unto him, Buy those
31 *J* said, Now is the Son of man
36 *J* answered him, Whither I go,
38 *J* answered him, Wilt thou lay
14. 6 *J* saith unto him, I am the way,
9 *J* saith unto him, Have I been so
23 *J* answered and said unto him, If
16.19 *J* knew that they were desirous
31 *J* answered..., Do ye now believe?
17. 1 These words spake *J*, and lifted up
3 *J* Christ, whom thou hast sent.
18. 1 When *J* had spoken these words,
2 for *J* ofttimes resorted thither
4 *J* therefore, knowing all things
5 They answered him, *J* of Nazareth.
5 *J* saith unto them, I am he.
7 And they said, *J* of Nazareth.
8 *J* answered, I have told you that
11 Then said *J* unto Peter, Put up thy
12 and officers of the Jews took *J*,
15 Simon Peter followed *J*, and so
15 went in with *J* into the palace of
19 The high priest then asked *J* of
20 *J* answered him, I spake openly to
22 struck *J* with the palm of his hand,
23 *J* answered him, If I have spoken
28 Then led they *J* from Caiaphas
32 the saying of *J* might be fulfilled,
33 and called *J*, and said unto him,
34 *J* answered him, Sayest thou this
36 *J* answered, My kingdom is not of
37 *J* answered, Thou sayest that I
19. 1 Then Pilate therefore took *J*, and
5 came *J* forth, wearing the crown
9 saith unto *J*, Whence art thou?
9 But *J* gave him no answer.
11 *J* answered. Thou couldest have
13 he brought *J* forth, and sat down
16 they took *J*, and led him away.
18 side one, and *J* in the midst.
19 *J* of Nazareth the King of the
20 the place where *J* was crucified
23 when they had crucified *J*, took
25 stood by the cross of *J* his mother,
26 When *J* therefore saw his mother,
28 *J* knowing that all things were
30 When *J* therefore had received
33 when they came to *J*, and saw that
38 Arimathaea, being a disciple of *J*,
38 he might take away the body of *J*:
38 therefore, and took the body of *J*.
39 at the first came to *J* by night,
40 Then took they the body of *J*,
42 There laid they *J* therefore
20. 2 the other disciple, whom *J* loved,
12 where the body of *J* had lain.
14 herself back, and saw *J* standing,
14 and knew not that it was *J*.
15 *J* saith unto her, Woman, why
16 *J* saith unto her, Mary. She
17 *J* saith unto her, Touch me not;
19 came *J* and stood in the midst,
21 Then said *J* to them again, Peace
24 was not with them when *J* came.
26 then came *J*, the doors being shut,
29 *J* saith unto him, Thomas, because
30 many other signs truly did *J* in
31 might believe that *J* is the Christ,
21. 1 *J* shewed himself again to his
4 now come, *J* stood on the shore:
4 disciples knew not that it was *J*.
5 *J* saith unto them, Children, have
7 that disciple whom *J* loved saith
10 *J* saith unto them, Bring of the fish
12 *J* saith unto them, Come and dine.
13 *J* then cometh, and taketh bread,
14 third time that *J* shewed himself
15 *J* saith to Simon Peter, Simon,
17 *J* saith unto him, Feed my sheep.
20 disciple whom *J* loved following;
21 Peter seeing him saith to *J*, Lord,
22 *J* saith unto him, If I will that he
23 yet *J* said not unto him, He shall
25 many other things which *J* did,
Ac 1. 1 that *J* began both to do and teach,
11 this same *J*, which is taken up
14 Mary the mother of *J*, and with
16 was guide to them that took *J*.
21 Lord *J* went in and out among us,
2.22 *J* of Nazareth, a man approved of
32 This *J* hath God raised up,
36 God hath made that same *J*, whom
38 one of you in the name of *J* Christ
3. 6 In the name of *J* Christ of
13 fathers, hath glorified his Son *J*;
20 he shall send *J* Christ, which
26 God, having raised up his Son *J*,
4. 2 preached through *J* the
10 the name of *J* Christ of Nazareth,
13 them, that they had been with *J*.
18 at all nor teach in the name of *J*.
27 a truth against thy holy child *J*,
30 by the name of thy holy child *J*.
33 of the resurrection of the Lord *J*:
5.30 God of our fathers raised up *J*,
40 should not speak in the name of *J*
42 not to teach and preach *J* Christ.
6.14 *J* of Nazareth shall destroy this
7.45 with *J* into the possession of the
55 *J* standing on the right hand of
59 saying, Lord *J*, receive my spirit.
8.12 of God, and the name of *J* Christ,
16 baptized in the name of the Lord *J*.)
35 and preached unto him *J*.
37 that *J* Christ is the Son of God.
9. 5 I am *J* whom thou persecutest:
17 even *J*, that appeared unto thee in
27 at Damascus in the name of *J*.
29 boldly in the name of the Lord *J*,
34 *J* Christ maketh thee whole:
10.36 preaching peace by *J* Christ: (he is
38 How God anointed *J* of Nazareth
11.17 who believed on the Lord *J* Christ;
20 Grecians, preaching the Lord *J*.
13.23 raised unto Israel a Saviour, *J*:
33 in that he hath raised up *J* again;
15.11 the grace of the Lord *J* Christ we
26 for the name of our Lord *J* Christ.
16.18 in the name of *J* Christ to come out
31 Believe on the Lord *J* Christ, and
17. 3 this *J*, whom I preach unto you,
7 that there is another king, one *J*.
18 because he preached unto them *J*,
18. 5 to the Jews that *J* was Christ.
28 by the scriptures that *J* was Christ.
19. 4 come after him, that is, on Christ *J*.
5 baptized in the name of the Lord *J*.
10 Asia heard the word of the Lord *J*.
13 evil spirits the name of the Lord *J*,
13 We adjure you by *J* whom Paul
15 said, *J* I know, and Paul I know;
17 name of the Lord *J* was magnified.
20.21 and faith toward our Lord *J* Christ.
24 which I have received of the Lord *J*,
35 remember the words of the Lord *J*,
21.13 to die...for the name of the Lord *J*.
22. 8 said unto me, I am *J* of Nazareth,
25.19 and of one *J*, which was dead,
26. 9 things contrary to the name of *J* of
15 I am *J* whom thou persecutest.
28.23 persuading them concerning *J*,
31 which concern the Lord *J* Christ,
Ro 1. 1 Paul, a servant of *J* Christ, called
3 concerning his Son *J* Christ our
6 are ye also the called of *J* Christ:
7 our Father, and the Lord *J* Christ.
8 I thank my God through *J* Christ
2.16 the secrets of men by *J* Christ.
3.22 of God which is by faith of *J* Christ
24 the redemption that is in Christ *J*:

26 of him which believeth in J.
4.24 believe on him that raised up J
5. 1 God through our Lord J Christ:
11 in God through our Lord J Christ,
15 which is by one man, J Christ,
17 shall reign in life by one, J Christ.)
21 unto eternal life by J Christ our
6. 3 us as were baptized into J Christ
11 unto God through J Christ our
23 God is eternal life through J Christ
7.25 I thank God through J Christ our
8. 1 to them which are in Christ J,
2 law of the Spirit of life in Christ J
11 if the Spirit of him that raised up J
39 God, which is in Christ J our Lord.
10. 9 confess with thy mouth the Lord J,
13.14 But put ye on the Lord J Christ,
14.14 and am persuaded by the Lord J,
15. 5 another according to Christ J:
6 the Father of our Lord J Christ.
8 I say that J Christ was a minister
16 should be the minister of J Christ
17 I may glory through J Christ in
30 for the Lord J Christ's sake,
16. 3 Aquilla my helpers in Christ J:
18 such serve not our Lord J Christ,
20 grace of our Lord J Christ be with
24 grace of our Lord J Christ be with
25 and the preaching of J Christ,
27 be glory through J Christ for ever.
1Co 1. 1 called to be an apostle of J Christ
2 them that are sanctified in Christ J,
2 call upon the name of J Christ our
3 Father, and from the Lord J Christ.
4 which is given you by J Christ;
7 the coming of our Lord J Christ:
8 in the day of our Lord J Christ.
9 of his Son J Christ our Lord.
10 by the name of our Lord J Christ,
30 But of him are ye in Christ J,
2. 2 save J Christ, and him crucified.
3.11 than that is laid, which is J Christ.
4.15 for in Christ J I have begotten you
5. 4 In the name of our Lord J Christ,
4 the power of our Lord J Christ,
5 be saved in the day of the Lord J.
6.11 justified in the name of the Lord J,
8. 6 and one Lord J Christ, by whom are
9. 1 have I not seen J Christ our Lord?
11.23 the Lord J the same night in which
12. 3 Spirit of God calleth J accursed:
3 no man can say that J is the Lord,
15.31 rejoicing which I have in Christ J
57 victory through our Lord J Christ.
16.22 man love not the Lord J Christ,
23 The grace of our Lord J Christ be
24 My love be with you all in Christ J.
2Co 1. 1 Paul, an apostle of J Christ by the
2 Father, and from the Lord J Christ.
3 the Father of our Lord J Christ,
14 are ours in the day of the Lord J.
19 For the Son of God, J Christ, who
4. 5 ourselves, but Christ J the Lord;
6 glory of God in the face of J Christ.
10 the body the dying of the Lord J,
10, 11 the life also of J might be made
14 that he which raised up the Lord J
14 shall raise up us also by J, and
5.18 hath reconciled us...by J Christ,
8. 9 the grace of our Lord J Christ,
11. 4 that cometh preacheth another J,
31 and Father of our Lord J Christ,
13. 5 how that J Christ is in you, except
14 The grace of the Lord J Christ,
Gal 1. 1 neither by man, but by J Christ,
3 Father, and from our Lord J Christ,
12 but by the revelation of J Christ.
2. 4 liberty which we have in Christ J,
16 law, but by the faith of J Christ,
16 even we have believed in J Christ,
3. 1 J Christ hath been evidently set
14 on the Gentiles through J Christ;
22 that the promise by faith of J Christ
26 of God by faith in Christ J.
28 for ye are all one in Christ J.
4.14 an angel of God, even as Christ J.
5. 6 in J Christ neither circumcision
6.14 in the cross of our Lord J Christ,
15 in Christ J neither circumcision
17 my body the marks of the Lord J.
18 grace of our Lord J Christ be with
Eph 1. 1 Paul, an apostle of J Christ by the
1 and to the faithful in Christ J:
2 Father, and from the Lord J Christ.
3 and Father of our Lord J Christ,
5 adoption of children by J Christ
15 I heard of your faith in the Lord J,
17 That the God of our Lord J Christ,
2. 6 in heavenly places in Christ J:
7 toward us through Christ J.
10 created in Christ J unto good works,
13 in Christ J ye who sometimes were
20 J Christ himself being the chief
3. 1 the prisoner of J Christ for you
9 who created all things by J Christ:
11 he purposed in Christ J our Lord:
14 the Father of our Lord J Christ,
21 be glory in the church by Christ J
4.21 taught by him, as the truth is in J:
5.20 in the name of our Lord J Christ;
6.23 the Father and the Lord J Christ.
24 love our Lord J Christ in sincerity.
Php 1. 1 the servants of J Christ,
1 to all the saints in Christ J which
2 Father, and from the Lord J Christ.
6 perform it until the day of J Christ:
8 you all in the bowels of J Christ.
11 which are by J Christ, unto the
19 the supply of the Spirit of J Christ,
26 may be more abundant in J Christ
2. 5 in you, which was also in Christ J:
10 That at the name of J every knee
11 confess that J Christ is Lord,
19 But I trust in the Lord J to send
21 not the things which are J Christ's.
3. 3 the spirit, and rejoice in Christ J,
8 knowledge of Christ J my Lord:
12 also I am apprehended of Christ J.
14 the high calling of God in Christ J.
20 for the Saviour, the Lord J Christ:
4. 7 hearts and minds through Christ J.
19 to his riches in glory by Christ J,
21 Salute every saint in Christ J. The
23 grace of our Lord J Christ be with
Col 1. 1 Paul, an apostle of J Christ by the
2 our Father and the Lord J Christ.
3 the Father of our Lord J Christ,
4 we heard of your faith in Christ J,
28 every man perfect in Christ J:
2. 6 received Christ J the Lord, so walk
3.17 do all in the name of the Lord J,
4.11 And J, which is called Justus, who
1Th 1. 1 Father and in the Lord J Christ:
1 Father, and the Lord J Christ.
3 of hope in our Lord J Christ,
10 he raised from the dead, even J,
2.14 which in Judea are in Christ J:
15 Who both killed the Lord J, and
19 the presence of our Lord J Christ
3.11 Father, and our Lord J Christ,
13 at the coming of our Lord J Christ
4. 1 and exhort you by the Lord J, that
2 we gave you by the Lord J.
14 if we believe that J died and rose
14 which sleep in J will God bring
5. 9 salvation by our Lord J Christ,
18 this is the will of God in Christ J
23 the coming of our Lord J Christ.
28 grace of our Lord J Christ be with
2Th 1. 1 our Father and the Lord J Christ:
2 our Father and the Lord J Christ.
7 the Lord J shall be revealed from
8 not the gospel of our Lord J Christ:
12 name of our Lord J Christ may be
12 of our God and the Lord J Christ.
2. 1 the coming of our Lord J Christ,
14 of the glory of our Lord J Christ.
16 Now our Lord J Christ himself,
3. 6 in the name of our Lord J Christ,
12 and exhort by our Lord J Christ,
18 grace of our Lord J Christ be with
1Ti 1. 1 Paul, an apostle of J Christ by the
1 our Saviour, and Lord J Christ,
2 our Father and J Christ our Lord.
12 And I thank Christ J our Lord,
14 faith and love which is in Christ J.
15 Christ J came into the world to save
16 in me first J Christ might shew
2. 5 God and men, the man Christ J;
3.13 in the faith which is in Christ J.
4. 6 shalt be a good minister of J Christ,
5.21 before God, and the Lord J Christ,
6. 3 the words of our Lord J Christ,
13 all things, and before Christ J,
14 appearing of our Lord J Christ:
2Ti 1. 1 Paul, an apostle of J Christ by the
1 promise of life which is in Christ J,
2 the Father and Christ J our Lord.
9 was given us in Christ J before the
10 appearing of our Saviour J Christ,
13 faith and love which is in Christ J.
2. 1 in the grace that is in Christ J.
3 as a good soldier of J Christ.
8 that J Christ of the seed of David
10 the salvation which is in Christ J
3.12 all that will live godly in Christ J
15 through faith which is in Christ J.
4. 1 before God, and the Lord J Christ,
22 Lord J Christ be with thy spirit.
Tit 1. 1 of God, and an apostle of J Christ,
4 and the Lord J Christ our Saviour.
2.13 God and our Saviour J Christ;
3. 6 through J Christ our Saviour;
Phm 1 Paul, a prisoner of J Christ, and
3 our Father and the Lord J Christ.
5 which thou hast toward the Lord J,
6 thing which is in you in Christ J,
9 now also a prisoner of J Christ.
23 my fellowprisoner in Christ J;
25 grace of our Lord J Christ be with
Heb 2. 9 see J, who was made a little lower
3. 1 Priest of our profession, Christ J;
4. 8 For if J had given them rest, then
14 the heavens, J the Son of God,
6.20 even J, made an high priest for ever
7.22 was J made a surety of a better
10.10 of the body of J Christ once for all.
19 into the holiest by the blood of J
12. 2 Looking unto J the author and
24 And to J the mediator of the new
13. 8 J Christ the same yesterday, and
12 Wherefore J also, that he might
20 again from the dead our Lord J,
21 in his sight, through J Christ;
Jas 1. 1 of God and of the Lord J Christ,
2. 1 not the faith of our Lord J Christ,
1Pe 1. 1 Peter, an apostle of J Christ, to the
2 sprinkling of the blood of J Christ:
3 and Father of our Lord J Christ,
3 hope by the resurrection of J Christ
7 glory at the appearing of J Christ:
13 you at the revelation of J Christ;
2. 5 acceptable to God by J Christ.
3.21 by the resurrection of J Christ:
4.11 may be glorified through J Christ,
5.10 unto his eternal glory by Christ J,
14 be with you all that are in Christ J.
2Pe 1. 1 servant and an apostle of J Christ,
1 of God and our Saviour J Christ:
2 the knowledge...of J our Lord,
8 knowledge of our Lord J Christ.
11 of our Lord and Saviour J Christ.
14 our Lord J Christ hath shewed me.

2Pe 1.16 and coming of our Lord *J* Christ,
2.20 of the Lord and Saviour *J* Christ,
3.18 of our Lord and Saviour *J* Christ.
1Jn 1. 3 Father, and with his Son *J* Christ.
7 blood of *J* Christ his Son cleanseth
2. 1 the Father, *J* Christ the righteous:
22 that denieth that *J* is the Christ?
3.23 on the name of his Son *J* Christ,
4. 2, 3 that *J* Christ is come in the flesh
15 shall confess that *J* is the Son of
5. 1 believeth that *J* is the Christ is
5 believeth that *J* is the Son of God?
6 by water and blood, even *J* Christ;
20 is true, even in his Son *J* Christ.
2Jn 3 from the Lord *J* Christ, the Son of
7 that *J* Christ is come in the flesh.
Jude 1 Jude, the servant of *J* Christ, and
1 preserved in *J* Christ, and called:
4 Lord God, and our Lord *J* Christ.
17 the apostles of our Lord *J* Christ;
21 for the mercy of our Lord *J* Christ
Rev 1. 1 The Revelation of *J* Christ, which
2 and of the testimony of *J* Christ,
5 from *J* Christ, who is the faithful
9 kingdom and patience of *J* Christ,
9 and for the testimony of *J* Christ.
12.17 and have the testimony of *J* Christ.
14.12 of God, and the faith of *J*.
17. 6 with the blood of the martyrs of *J*:
19.10 that have the testimony of *J*:
10 the testimony of *J* is the spirit of
20. 4 were beheaded for the witness of *J*,
22.16 I *J* have sent mine angel to testify
20 Amen. Even so, come, Lord *J*.
21 grace of our Lord *J* Christ be with

JESUS'

Mt 15.30 and cast them down at *J* feet:
27.57 who also himself was *J* disciple:
Lk 5. 8 saw it, he fell down at *J* knees,
8.41 fell down at *J* feet, and besought
10.39 Mary, which also sat at *J* feet,
Jn 12. 9 they came not for *J* sake only, but
13.23 Now there was leaning on *J* bosom
25 He then lying on *J* breast saith
2Co 4. 5 ourselves your servants for *J* sake.
11 delivered unto death for *J* sake,

JEW

Est 2. 5 the palace there was a certain *J*.
3. 4 he had told them that he was a *J*.
5.13 Mordecai the *J* sitting at the king's
6.10 do even so to Mordecai the *J*, that
8. 7 the queen and to Mordecai the *J*,
9.29 of Abihail, and Mordecai the *J*,
31 Mordecai the *J* and Esther the
10. 3 Mordecai the *J* was next unto king
Jer 34. 9 them, to wit, of a *J* his brother.
Zec 8.23 hold of the skirt of him that is a *J*,
Jn 4. 9 being a *J*, askest drink of me,
18.35 Pilate answered, Am I a *J*? Thine
Ac 10.28 man that is a *J* to keep company,
13. 6 a *J*, whose name was Bar-jesus:
18. 2 found a certain *J* named Aquila,
24 certain *J* named Apollos, born at
19.14 Sceva, a *J*, and chief of the priests,
34 when they knew that he was a *J*,
21.39 a man which am a *J* of Tarsus,
22. 3 man which am a *J* born in Tarsus,
Ro 1.16 the *J* first, and also to the Greek.
2. 9 the *J* first, and also of the Gentile;
10 the *J* first, and also to the Gentile:
17 Behold, thou art called a *J*, and
28 is not a *J*, which is one outwardly;
29 he is a *J*, which is one inwardly;
3. 1 What advantage then hath the *J*?
10.12 between the *J* and the Greek:
1Co 9.20 And to the Jews I became as a *J*.
Gal 2.14 If thou, being a *J*, livest after the
3.28 There is neither *J* nor Greek,
Col 3.11 Where there is neither Greek nor *J*,

JEWEL

Pr 11.22 As a *j* of gold in a swine's snout,
20.15 lips of knowledge are a precious *j*.
Eze 16.12 I put a *j* on thy forehead, and

JEWELS

Gen 24.53 servant brought forth *j* of silver,
53 and *j* of gold, and raiment, and
Ex 3.22 sojourneth in her house, *j* of silver,
22 and *j* of gold, and raiment: and ye
11. 2 neighbor, *j* of silver, and *j* of gold.
12.35 of the Egyptians *j* of silver,
35 and *j* of gold, and raiment:
35.22 rings, and tablets, all *j* of gold:
Nu 31.50 of *j* of gold, chains, and bracelets,
51 gold of them, even all wrought *j*.
1Sa 6. 8 put the *j* of gold, which ye return
15 with it, wherein the *j* of gold were,
2Ch 20.25 precious *j*, which they stripped off
32.27 and for all manner of pleasant *j*;
Job 28.17 it shall not be for *j* of fine gold.
SS 1.10 cheeks are comely with rows of *j*,
7. 1 joints of thy thighs are like *j*, the
Isa 3.21 The rings, and nose *j*,
61.10 bride adorneth herself with her *j*.
Eze 16.17 Thou hast also taken thy fair *j* of
39 shall take thy fair *j*, and leave thee
23.26 clothes, and take away thy fair *j*.
Hos 2.13 with her earrings and her *j*,
Mal 3.17 that day when I make up my *j*;

JEWESS

Ac 16. 1 certain woman, which was a *J*,
24.24 his wife Drusilla, which was a *J*,

JEWISH

Tit 1.14 Not giving heed to *J* fables, and

JEWRY

Dan 5.13 king my father brought out of *J*?
Lk 23. 5 people, teaching throughout all *J*,
Jn 7. 1 he would not walk in *J*, because

JEWS

2Ki 16. 6 Syria, and drave the *J* from Elath:
25.25 the *J* and the Chaldees that were
Ezr 4.12 the *J* which came up from thee to
23 in haste to Jerusalem unto the *J*,
5. 1 son of Iddo, prophesied unto the *J*
5 God was upon the elders of the *J*,
6. 7 alone; let the governors of the *J*
7 and the elders of the *J* built this
8 shall do to the elders of these *J*
14 the elders of the *J* builded, and
Neh 1. 2 concerning the *J* that had escaped,
2.16 neither had I as yet told it to the *J*,
4. 1 indignation, and mocked the *J*.
2 and said, What do these feeble *J*?
12 the *J* which dwelt by them came,
5. 1 wives against their brethren the *J*.
8 have redeemed our brethren the *J*,
17 were at my table...*J* and rulers,
6. 6 that thou and the *J* think to rebel:
13.23 In those days also saw I *J* that
Est 3. 6 Haman sought to destroy all the *J*
13 kill, and to cause to perish, all *J*,
4. 3 was great mourning among the *J*,
7 to the king's treasuries for the *J*,
13 king's house, more than all the *J*.
14 and deliverance arise to the *J*
16 gather together all the *J* that are
6.13 Mordecai be of the seed of the *J*,
8. 3 that he had devised against the *J*.
5 which he wrote to destroy the *J*
7 he laid his hand upon the *J*.
8 Write ye also for the *J*, as it liketh
9 Mordecai commanded unto the *J*,
9 the *J* according to their writing,
11 Wherein the king granted the *J*
13 *J* should be ready against that day
16 The *J* had light, and gladness, and
17 the *J* had joy and gladness, a feast
17 the people of the land became *J*:
17 the fear of the *J* fell upon them.
9. 1 *J* hoped to have power over them,
1 the *J* had rule over them that
2 *J* gathered themselves together
3 officers of the king, helped the *J*;
5 the *J* smote all their enemies with
6 Shushan the palace the *J* slew and
10 the enemy of the *J*, slew they;
12 The *J* have slain and destroyed
13 king, let it be granted to the *J*
15 For the *J* that were in Shushan
16 *J* that were in the king's provinces
18 *J* that were in Shushan assembled
19 Therefore the *J* of the villages,
20 sent letters unto all the *J* that
22 the *J* rested from their enemies,
23 the *J* undertook to do as they had
24 Agagite, the enemy of all the *J*,
24 devised against the *J* to destroy
25 which he devised against the *J*,
27 *J* ordained, and took upon them,
28 should not fail from among the *J*,
30 he sent the letters unto all the *J*,
10. 3 Ahasuerus, great among the *J*,
Jer 32.12 *J* that sat in the court of the prison.
38.19 afraid of the *J* that are fallen to
40.11 when all the *J* that were in Moab,
12 all the *J* returned out of all places
15 all the *J* which are gathered unto
41. 3 Ishmael also slew all the *J* that
44. 1 concerning all the *J* which dwell
52.28 the seventh year three thousand *J*
30 carried away captive of the *J*
Dan 3. 8 came near, and accused the *J*.
12 certain *J* whom thou hast set
Mt 2. 2 is he that is born King of the *J*?
27.11 saying, Art thou the King of the *J*?
29 him, saying, Hail, King of the *J*!
37 This Is Jesus The King Of The *J*.
28.15 is commonly reported among the *J*
Mk 7. 3 For the Pharisees, and all the *J*,
15. 2 him, Art thou the King of the *J*?
9 release unto you the King of the *J*?
12 whom ye call the King of the *J*?
18 to salute him, Hail, King of the *J*!
26 written over, The King Of The *J*.
Lk 7. 3 sent unto him the elders of the *J*,
23. 3 saying, Art thou the King of the *J*?
37 If thou be the king of the *J*, save
38 This Is The King Of The *J*.
51 was of Arimathaea, a city of the *J*:
Jn 1.19 when the *J* sent priests and Levites
2. 6 manner of the purifying of the *J*,
18 Then answered the *J* and said unto
20 Then said the *J*, Forty and six
3. 1 named Nicodemus, a ruler of the *J*:
25 of John's disciples and the *J*
4. 9 the *J* have no dealings with the
22 worship: for salvation is of the *J*.
5. 1 this there was a feast of the *J*;
10 *J* therefore said unto him that was
15 and told the *J* that it was Jesus,
16 therefore did the *J* persecute Jesus,
18 the *J* sought the more to kill him,
6. 4 passover, a feast of the *J*, was nigh.
41 The *J* then murmured at him,
52 The *J* therefore strove among
7. 1 because the *J* sought to kill him.
11 Then the *J* sought him at the feast,
13 openly of him for fear of the *J*.
15 And the *J* marvelled, saying, How
35 said the *J* among themselves,
8.22 said the *J*, Will he kill himself?
31 Jesus to those *J* which believed
48 Then answered the *J*, and said
52 Then said the *J* unto him, Now we
57 Then said the *J* unto him, Thou
9.18 the *J* did not believe concerning
22 parents, because they feared the *J*:

22 for the *J* had agreed already, that
10.19 was a division…again among the *J*
24 Then came the *J* round about him,
31 Then the *J* took up stones again
33 The *J* answered him, saying, For
11. 8 the *J* of late sought to stone thee;
19 many of the *J* came to Martha
31 The *J* then which were with her
33 weeping, and the *J* also weeping
36 Then said the *J*, Behold how he
45 many of the *J* which came to Mary,
54 no more openly among the *J*;
12. 9 people of the *J* therefore knew
11 of him many of the *J* went away,
13.33 as I said unto the *J*, Whither I go,
18.12 and officers of the *J* took Jesus,
14 he, which gave counsel to the *J*,
20 whither the *J* always resort;
31 The *J* therefore said unto him, It
33 him, Art thou the King of the *J*?
36 I should not be delivered to the *J*:
38 he went out again unto the *J*, and
39 release unto you the King of the *J*?
19. 3 And said, Hail, King of the *J*! and
7 *J* answered him, We have a law,
12 but the *J* cried out, saying, If thou
14 he saith unto the *J*, Behold your
19 Of Nazareth The King Of The *J*.
20 This title then read many of the *J*;
21 Then said the chief priests of the *J*
21 Write not, The King of the *J*; but
21 that he said, I am King of the *J*.
31 The *J* therefore,…besought Pilate
38 but secretly for fear of the *J*,
40 as the manner of the *J* is to bury.
20.19 were assembled for fear of the *J*,
Ac 2. 5 were dwelling at Jerusalem *J*,
10 of Rome, *J* and proselytes,
9.22 the *J* which dwelt at Damascus,
23 the *J* took counsel to kill him:
10.22 among all the nation of the *J*,
39 he did both in the land of the *J*,
11.19 word to none but unto the *J* only.
12. 3 because he saw it pleased the *J*,
11 expectation of the people of the *J*.
13. 5 of God in the synagogues of the *J*:
42 *J* were gone out of the synagogue,
43 many of the *J* and religious
45 when the *J* saw the multitudes,
50 the *J* stirred up the devout and
14. 1 into the synagogue of the *J*,
1 great multitude both of the *J* and
2 the unbelieving *J* stirred up the
4 and part held with the *J*, and part
5 and also of the *J* with their rulers,
13 thither certain *J* from Antioch
16. 3 circumcised him because of the *J*
20 being *J*, do exceedingly trouble
17. 1 where was a synagogue of the *J*:
5 But the *J* which believed not,
10 went into the synagogue of the *J*.
13 But when the *J* of Thessalonica
17 he in the synagogue of the *J*,
18. 2 all *J* to depart from Rome:)
4 persuaded the *J* and the Greeks.
5 testified to the *J* that Jesus was
12 the *J* made insurrection with one
14 Gallio said unto the *J*, If it were
14 O ye *J*, reason would that I should
19 and reasoned with the *J*.
28 For he mightily convinced the *J*,
19.10 Lord Jesus, both *J* and Greeks.
13 Then certain of the vagabond *J*,
17 And this was known to all the *J*
33 the *J* putting him forward.
20. 3 And when the *J* laid wait for him,
19 me by the lying in wait of the *J*:
21 Testifying both to the *J*, and also
21.11 So shall the *J* at Jerusalem bind
20 how many thousands of *J* there are
21 thou teacheth all the *J* which are
27 the *J* which were of Asia, when
22.12 a good report of all the *J* which
30 wherefore he was accused of the *J*,
23.12 certain of the *J* banded together,
20 The *J* have agreed to desire thee
27 This man was taken of the *J*,
30 that the *J* laid wait for the man,
24. 5 mover of sedition among all the *J*
9 the *J* also assented, saying that
18 certain *J* from Asia found me
27 willing to shew the *J* a pleasure,
25. 2 the chief of the *J* informed him
7 the *J* which came down from
8 Neither against the law of the *J*,
9 willing to do the *J* a pleasure,
10 to the *J* have I done no wrong, as
15 the elders of the *J* informed me,
24 the multitude of the *J* have dealt
26. 2 whereof I am accused of the *J*:
3 questions which are among the *J*:
4 at Jerusalem, know all the *J*;
7 Agrippa, I am accused of the *J*.
21 the *J* caught me in the temple,
28.17 days Paul called the chief of the *J*
19 But when the *J* spake against it,
29 said these words, the *J* departed,
Ro 3. 9 before proved both *J* and Gentiles,
29 Is he the God of the *J* only?
9.24 called, not of the *J* only, but also
1Co 1.22 For the *J* require a sign, and the
23 unto the *J* a stumblingblock, and
24 are called, both *J* and Greeks,
9.20 And unto the *J* I became as a Jew,
20 that I might gain the *J*; to them
10.32 none offense, neither to the *J*, nor
12.13 whether we be *J* or Gentiles,
2Co 11.24 Of the *J* five times received I forty
Gal 2.13 the other *J* dissembled likewise
14 of Gentiles, and not as do the *J*,
14 the Gentiles to live as do the *J*?
15 We who are *J* by nature, and not
1Th 2.14 even as they have of the *J*:
Rev 2. 9 which say they are *J*, and are not,
3. 9 which say they are *J*, and are not,

JEWS'

2Ki 18.26 talk not with us in the *J* language
28 a loud voice in the *J* language,
2Ch 32.18 with a loud voice in the *J* speech
Neh 13.24 not speak in the *J* language, but
Est 3.10 the Agagite, the *J* enemy.
8. 1 the house of Haman the *J* enemy
Isa 36.11 speak not to us in the *J* language,
13 a loud voice in the *J* language,
Jn 2.13 the *J* passover was at hand, and
7. 2 the *J* feast of tabernacles was at
11.55 the *J* passover was nigh at hand:
19.42 because of the *J* preparation day;
Gal 1.13 in time past in the *J* religion,
14 profited in the *J* religion above

JEZEBEL

1Ki 16.31 he took to wife *J* the daughter of
18. 4 when *J* cut off the prophets of the
13 what I did when *J* slew the prophets
19. 1 And Ahab told *J* all that Elijah had
2 *J* sent a messenger unto Elijah,
21. 5 *J* his wife came to him, and said
7 *J* his wife said unto him, Dost thou
11 did as *J* had sent unto them, and
14 sent to *J*, saying, Naboth is stoned,
15 *J* heard that Naboth was stoned,
15 that *J* said to Ahab, Arise, take
23 And of *J* also spake the Lord,
23 The dogs shall eat *J* by the wall of
25 Lord, whom *J* his wife stirred up.
2Ki 9. 7 of the Lord, at the hand of *J*.
10 the dogs shall eat *J* in the portion
22 as the whoredoms of thy mother *J*
30 was come to Jezreel, *J* heard of it;
36 Jezreel shall dogs eat the flesh of *J*
37 the carcass of *J* shall be as dung
37 so that they shall not say, This is *J*
Rev 2.20 thou sufferest that woman *J*,

JEZEBEL

Wife of King Ahab of Israel and daughter of Ethbaal, king of Phoenicia, 9th century B.C.; has a temple for the Tyrian Baal built in Samaria and forcefully promotes the worship of her native god throughout Israel (1Ki 16.31-33); tries to extirpate God's prophets (1Ki 18.4, 13); sponsors the prophets of Baal, who gather on Mount Carmel (1Ki 18.19), and swears to slay Elijah when he has them put to death (1Ki 19.1-2); contrives to have Naboth wrongfully condemned and executed in order to procure his vineyard for Ahab (1Ki 21.5-15); later, during the bloody purge decreed by Elisha, Jehu has her thrown from a window to her death (2Ki 9.30-37); her name is symbolically applied to an unknown false prophetess in Rev 3.20.

JOAB

1Sa 26. 6 the son of Zeruiah, brother to *J*,
2Sa 2.13 *J* the son of Zeruiah, and the
14 Abner said to *J*, Let the young
14 And *J* said, Let them arise.
18 three sons of Zeruiah there, *J*, and
22 should I hold up my face to *J*
24 *J* also and Abishai pursued after
26 Abner called to *J*, and said, Shall
27 *J* said, As God liveth, unless thou
28 So *J* blew a trumpet, and all the
30 *J* returned from following Abner:
32 *J* and his men went all night, and
3.22 servants of David and *J* came
23 When *J* and all the host that was
23 they told *J*, saying, Abner the son
24 Then *J* came to the king, and
26 when *J* was come out from David,
27 *J* took him aside in the gate to
29 Let it rest on the head of *J*, and on
29 not fail from the house of *J* one
30 So *J* and Abishai his brother slew
31 David said to *J*, and to all the
8.16 *J* the son of Zeruiah was over the
10. 7 when David heard of it, he sent *J*,
9 When *J* saw that the front of the
13 *J* drew nigh, and the people that
14 So *J* returned from the children
11. 1 that David sent *J*, and his servants
6 David sent to *J*, saying, Send me
6 And *J* sent Uriah to David.
7 David demanded of him how *J* did,
11 and my lord *J*, and the servants
14 David wrote a letter to *J*, and sent
16 to pass, when *J* observed the city,
17 city went out, and fought with *J*:
18 *J* sent and told David all the
22 David all that *J* had sent him for.
25 Thus shalt thou say unto *J*, Let
12.26 *J* fought against Rabbah of the
27 *J* sent messengers to David, and
14. 1 *J* the son of Zeruiah perceived
2 *J* sent to Tekoah, and fetched
3 So *J* put the words in her mouth.
19 Is not the hand of *J* with thee in
19 for thy servant *J*, he bade me,
20 hath thy servant *J* done this thing:
21 the king said unto *J*, Behold now,
22 *J* fell to the ground on his face,
22 *J* said, To day thy servant knoweth
23 *J* arose and went to Geshur, and

2Sa 14.29 Absalom sent for *J*, to have sent
31 *J* arose, and came to Absalom
32 Absalom answered *J*, Behold, I
33 *J* came to the king, and told him:
17.25 captain of the host instead of *J*:
18. 2 of the people under the hand of *J*,
5 the king commanded *J* and
10 a certain man saw it, and told *J*,
11 *J* said unto the man that told him,
12 the man said unto *J*, Though I
14 Then said *J*, I may not tarry thus
16 *J* blew the trumpet, and the people
16 for *J* held back the people.
20 *J* said unto him, Thou shalt not
21 Then said *J* to Cushi, Go tell the
21 Cushi bowed himself unto *J*, and
22 the son of Zadok yet again to *J*,
22 *J* said, Wherefore wilt thou run,
29 When *J* sent the king's servant,
19. 1 it was told *J*, Behold, the king
5 *J* came into the house to the king,
13 me continually in the room of *J*.
20. 9 *J* said to Amasa, Art thou in
9 *J* took Amasa by the beard with
10 So *J* and Abishai his brother
11 and said, He that favoreth *J*,
11 is for David, let him go after *J*.
13 all the people went on after *J*, to
15 people that were with *J* battered
16 say, I pray you, unto *J*, Come near
17 her, the woman said, Art thou *J*?
20 *J* answered and said, Far be it,
21 the woman said unto *J*, Behold,
22 son of Bichri, and cast it out to *J*.
22 *J* returned to Jerusalem unto the
23 *J* was over all the host of Israel:
23.18 Abishai, the brother of *J*, the son

JOAB

Nephew of King David and commander of his army, 10th century B.C.; at Gibeon, after Saul's death, overcomes forces led by Saul's old general Abner; although Abner kills Joab's brother Asahel, agrees to cease hostilities to save further bloodshed (2Sa 2); remonstrates with David for subsequently accepting Abner's services; later slays Abner to avenge Asahel, for which David pronounces a curse upon him (2Sa 3); after daring capture of stronghold at Zion, is appointed David's commander in chief (2Sa 8); defeats Ammonites and their Syrian mercenaries (2Sa 10); besieges Rabbah and there complies with David's instructions to have Uriah killed in battle (2Sa 11); sends for David to lead army into Rabbah and so gain the credit (2Sa 12); devises strategy to induce David to have the exiled Absalom brought back to Jerusalem, and later presents him before the king (2Sa 14); but after Absalom's rebellion disregards David's orders and kills Absalom (2Sa 18); is replaced by Amasa (2Sa 19), but murders him and resumes command; pursues the rebel Sheba to Abel; spares the city when the rebel's head is delivered to him (2Sa 20); tries unsuccessfully to dissuade David from conducting census (2Sa 24); supports Adonijah's claim to succeed David (1Ki 1); angered by this, David on his deathbed counsels Solomon to put Joab to death; flees to the tabernacle of the Lord for sanctuary, but is slain there (1Ki 2).

24 brother of *J* was one of the thirty;
37 armorbearer to *J* the son of
24. 2 the king said to *J* the captain of
3 *J* said unto the king, Now the
4 king's word prevailed against *J*,
4 *J* and the captains of the host
9 *J* gave up the sum of the number
1Ki 1. 7 he conferred with *J* the son of
19 and *J* the captain of the host:
41 *J* heard the sound of the trumpet,
2. 5 *J* the son of Zeruiah did to me,
22 and for *J*, the son of Zeruiah.
28 Then tidings came to *J*:
28 for *J* had turned after Adonijah,
28 *J* fled unto the tabernacle of the
29 that *J* was fled unto the tabernacle
30 Thus said *J*, and thus he answered
31 the innocent blood, which *J* shed,
33 therefore return upon the head of *J*,
11.15 *J* the captain of the host was gone
16 For six months did *J* remain there
21 *J* the captain of the host was dead,
1Ch 2.16 sons of Zeruiah; Abishai and *J*,
54 Ataroth, the house of *J*, and half
4.14 Seraiah begat *J*, the father of
11. 6 So *J* the son of Zeruiah went first
8 *J* repaired the rest of the city.
20 the brother of *J*, he was chief of
26 were, Asahel the brother of *J*,
39 the armorbearer of *J* the son of
18.15 *J* the son of Zeruiah was over the
19. 8 when David heard of it, he sent *J*,
10 when *J* saw that the battle was
14 So *J* and the people that were
15 city. Then *J* came to Jerusalem.
20. 1 *J* led forth the power of the army,
1 *J* smote Rabbah, and destroyed it.
21. 2 David said to *J* and to the rulers
3 And *J* answered, The Lord make
4 king's word prevailed against *J*.
4 Wherefore *J* departed, and went
5 *J* gave the sum of the number of
6 king's word was abominable to *J*.
26.28 and *J* the son of Zeruiah, had
27. 7 month was Asahel the brother of *J*,
24 *J* the son of Zeruiah began to
34 general of the king's army was *J*.
Ezr 2. 6 of the children of Jeshua and *J*,
8. 9 Of the sons of *J*; Obadiah the son
Neh 7.11 of the children of Jeshua and *J*,
Ps 60(T) when *J* returned, and smote of

JOANNA

Lk 3.27 Which was the son of *J*, which
8. 3 And *J* the wife of Chuza Herod's
24.10 It was Mary Magdalene, and *J*,

JOB

Gen 46.13 Tola, and Phuvah, and *J*, and
Job 1. 1 land of Uz, whose name was *J*;
5 that *J* sent and sanctified them,
5 *J* said, It may be that my sons have
5 hearts. Thus did *J* continually.
8 Hast thou considered my servant *J*,
9 said, Doth *J* fear God for nought?
14 there came a messenger unto *J*,
20 Then *J* arose, and rent his mantle.
22 In all this *J* sinned not, nor charged
2. 3 Hast thou considered my servant *J*,
7 smote *J* with sore boils from the
10 In all this did not *J* sin with his
3. 1 After this opened *J* his mouth, and
2 And *J* spake, and said,
6. 1 But *J* answered, and said,
9. 1 Then *J* answered and said,
12. 1 And *J* answered and said,
16. 1 Then *J* answered and said,
19. 1 Then *J* answered and said,
21. 1 But *J* answered and said,
23. 1 Then *J* answered and said,
26. 1 But *J* answered and said,
27. 1 Moreover *J* continued his parable,
29. 1 Moreover *J* continued his parable,
31.40 barley. The words of *J* are ended.
32. 1 three men ceased to answer *J*,
2 against *J* was his wrath kindled,
3 and yet had condemned *J*.
4 Elihu had waited till *J* had spoken,
12 was none of you that convinced *J*,
33. 1 *J*, I pray thee, hear my speeches,
31 Mark well, O *J*, hearken unto me:
34. 5 For *J* hath said, I am righteous:
7 What man is like *J*, who drinketh
35 *J* hath spoken without knowledge,
36 My desire is that *J* may be tried
35.16 doth *J* open his mouth in vain;
37.14 Hearken unto this, O *J*: stand still,
38. 1 the Lord answered *J* out of the
40. 1 the Lord answered *J*, and said,
3 *J* answered the Lord, and said,
6 answered the Lord unto *J* out of
42. 1 *J* answered the Lord, and said,
7 had spoken these words unto *J*,
7 that is right, as my servant *J* hath.
8 go to my servant *J*, and offer up
8 my servant *J* shall pray for you:
8 which is right, like my servant *J*.
9 them: the Lord also accepted *J*.
10 the Lord turned the captivity of *J*,
10 gave *J* twice as much as he had
12 Lord blessed the latter end of *J*
15 found so fair as the daughter of *J*:
16 lived *J* a hundred and forty years,
17 So *J* died, being old and full of
Eze 14.14 three men, Noah, Daniel, and *J*,
20 Noah, Daniel, and *J*, were in it, as
Jas 5.11 have heard of the patience of *J*,

JOEL

1Sa 8. 2 the name of his firstborn was *J*;
1Ch 4.35 *J*, and Jehu the son of Josibiah,
5. 4 The sons of *J*; Shemaiah his son,
8 the son of *J*, who dwelt in Aroer,
12 *J* the chief, and Shapham the next,
6.33 Heman a singer, the son of *J*, the
36 Elkanah, the son of *J*, the son of
7. 3 and Obadiah, and *J*, Ishiah, five:
11.38 *J* the brother of Nathan, Mibhar
15. 7 the sons of Gershom; *J* the chief,
11 Levites, for Uriel, Asaiah, and *J*,
17 appointed Heman the son of *J*;
23. 8 Jehiel, and Zatham, and *J*, three.
26.22 Zetham, and *J* his brother, which
27.20 Manasseh, *J* the son of Pedaiah:
2Ch 29.12 Amasai, and *J* the son of Azariah,
Ezr 10.43 Zabad, Zebina, Jadau, and *J*,
Neh 11. 9 And *J* the son of Zichri was their
Joel 1. 1 word of the Lord that came to *J*
Ac 2.16 was spoken by the prophet *J*;

JOHN

Mt 3. 1 In these days came *J* the Baptist,
4 same *J* had his raiment of camel's
13 from Galilee to Jordan unto *J*,
14 *J* forbade him, saying, I have need
4.12 heard that *J* was cast into prison,
21 son of Zebedee, and *J* his brother,
9.14 came to him the disciples of *J*,
10. 2 son of Zebedee, and *J* his brother;
11. 2 when *J* had heard in the prison
4 Go and shew *J* again those things
7 unto the multitudes concerning *J*,
11 risen a greater than *J* the Baptist:
12 from the days of *J* the Baptist
13 and the law prophesied until *J*.
18 *J* came neither eating nor drinking,
14. 2 his servants, This is *J* the Baptist;
3 For Herod had laid hold on *J*,
4 *J* said unto him, It is not lawful
8 *J* the Baptist's head in a charger.
10 sent, and beheaded *J* in the prison.
16.14 say that thou art *J* the Baptist;

JOHN THE BAPTIST

Son of the priest Zecharias and Elisabeth, and cousin of Jesus; his birth and destiny predicted by the angel Gabriel, who also orders his father to give him the name John (Lk 1); in manhood emerges from the desert wearing a leather girdle and a tunic of camel's hair (Mk 1.6), an austere prophet like Elijah (Lk 1.17), "neither eating nor drinking" (Mt 11.18); castigates what he calls "this generation of vipers" and urges repentance; himself baptizing with water, he foresees the coming of one who will baptize "with the Holy Ghost and with fire" (Mt 3.1-12); when Jesus approaches him for baptism, he protests his unworthiness before acquiescing (Mt 3.13-15); afterward points Jesus out to his own disciples as "the Lamb of God" (Jn 1.29, 36); condemns the divorce of Herod Antipas and his remarriage with his sister-in-law Herodias, and is thrown in prison (Mt 14.3); from there he sends disciples to inquire of Jesus if he is the Messiah, and receives an answer pointing to the fulfillment of prophecy; Jesus praises John in glowing terms: "among them that are born of women there hath not risen a greater" (Mt 11.1-15); later, at a great feast, Herod's daughter Salome, urged on by her mother, demands John's head on a platter as a reward for her dancing; Herod reluctantly accedes, but after the execution fears that Jesus, now celebrated for his own miracles, might be John the Baptist risen from the dead (Mk 6.14-29).

17. 1 Peter, James, and *J* his brother,
13 spake unto them of *J* the Baptist.
21.25 The baptism of *J*, whence was it?
26 people; for all hold *J* as a prophet.
32 *J* came unto you in the way of
Mk 1. 4 *J* did baptize in the wilderness,
6 *J* was clothed with camel's hair,
9 and was baptized of *J* in Jordan.
14 Now after that *J* was put in prison,
19 son of Zebedee, and *J* his brother,
29 and Andrew, with James and *J*.
2.18 the disciples of *J* and of the
18 Why do the disciples of *J* and of
3.17 and *J* the brother of James;
5.37 James, and *J* the brother of James.
6.14 *J* the Baptist was risen from the
16 he said, It is *J*, whom I beheaded:
17 laid hold upon *J*, and bound him
18 *J* had said unto Herod, It is not
20 Herod feared *J*, knowing that he
24 said, The head of *J* the Baptist.
25 charger the head of *J* the Baptist.
8.28 they answered, *J* the Baptist:
9. 2 with him Peter and James, and *J*,
38 *J* answered him, saying, Master,
10.35 James and *J*, the sons of Zebedee,
41 much displeased with James and *J*.
11.30 baptism of *J*, was it from heaven,
32 all men counted *J*, that he was a
13. 3 Peter, and James, and *J*, and
14.33 with him Peter and James and *J*,
Lk 1.13 and thou shalt call his name *J*.
60 Not so; but he shall be called *J*.
63 and wrote, saying, His name is *J*.
3. 2 the word of God came unto *J* the
15 all men mused in their hearts of *J*,
16 *J* answered, saying unto them all,
20 all, that he shut up *J* in prison.
5.10 James, and *J*, the sons of Zebedee,
33 Why do the disciples of *J* fast often,
6.14 and *J*, Philip and Bartholomew,
7.18 disciples of *J* shewed him of all
19 *J* calling unto him two of his
20 *J* the Baptist hath sent us...thee,
22 tell *J* what things ye have seen
24 messengers of *J* were departed,
24 unto the people concerning *J*,
28 greater prophet than *J* the Baptist:
29 baptized with the baptism of *J*.
33 *J* the Baptist came neither eating
8.51 save Peter, and James, and *J*,
9. 7 that *J* was risen from the dead;
9 Herod said, *J* have I beheaded:
19 answering said, *J* the Baptist;
28 he took Peter and *J* and James.
49 And *J* answered and said, Master,
54 his disciples James and *J* saw this,
11. 1 as *J* also taught his disciples.
16.16 law and the prophets were until *J*:
20. 4 baptism of *J*, was it from heaven,
6 be persuaded that *J* was a prophet.
22. 8 he sent Peter and *J*, saying, Go and
Jn 1. 6 sent from God, whose name was *J*.
15 *J* bare witness of him, and cried,
19 And this is the record of *J*, when
26 *J* answered them, saying, I baptize
28 Jordan, where *J* was baptizing.
29 The next day *J* seeth Jesus coming
32 And *J* bare record, saying, I saw
35 *J* stood, and two of his disciples;
40 of the two which heard *J* speak,
3.23 And *J* also was baptizing in Aenon
24 For *J* was not yet cast into prison.
26 And they came unto *J*, and said
27 *J* answered and said, A man can
4. 1 baptized more disciples than *J*,
5.33 sent unto *J*, and he bare witness
36 have greater witness than that of *J*:
10.40 the place where *J* at first baptized;
41 him, and said, *J* did no miracle:
41 that *J* spake of this man were true.
Ac 1. 5 For *J* truly baptized with water;
13 abode both Peter, and James, and *J*,
22 Beginning from the baptism of *J*,
3. 1 Peter and *J* went up together into
3 seeing Peter and *J* about to go into
4 fastening his eyes upon him with *J*,
11 which was healed held Peter and *J*,
4. 6 Caiaphas, and *J*, and Alexander,
13 saw the boldness of Peter and *J*,
19 But Peter and *J* answered and said
8.14 they sent unto them Peter and *J*:
10.37 the baptism which *J* preached;
11.16 *J* indeed baptized with water;
12. 2 killed James the brother of *J* with
12 of *J*, whose surname was Mark;
25 them *J*, whose surname was Mark.
13. 5 they had also *J* to their minister.
13 *J* departing from them returned
24 When *J* had first preached before
25 And as *J* fulfilled his course, he
15.37 them *J*, whose surname was Mark.
18.25 knowing only the baptism of *J*.
19. 4 *J* verily baptized with the baptism
Gal 2. 9 Cephas, and *J*, who seemed to be
Rev 1. 1 it by his angel unto his servant *J*:
4 *J* to the seven churches which are
9 I *J*, who also am your brother,
21. 2 And I *J* saw the holy city, new
22. 8 And I *J* saw these things, and

JOHN'S

Jn 3.25 between some of *J* disciples and
Ac 19. 3 And they said, Unto *J* baptism.

JOIN

Ex 1.10 they *j* also unto our enemies, and
2Ch 20.35 king of Judah *j* himself with
Ezr 9.14 and *j* in affinity with the people of
Pr 11.21 Though hand *j* in hand, the wicked
16. 5 though hand *j* in hand, he shall not be
Isa 5. 8 unto them that *j* house to house,
9.11 him, and *j* his enemies together;
56. 6 that *j* themselves to the Lord, to
Jer 50. 5 let us *j* ourselves to the Lord in a
Eze 37.17 *j* them one to another into one
Dan 11. 6 they shall *j* themselves together;
Ac 5.13 durst no man *j* himself to them:
8.29 near, and *j* thyself to this chariot.
9.26 assayed to *j* himself to the disciples:

JOINED

Gen 14. 3 these were *j* together in the vale
14. 8 they *j* battle with them in the vale
29.34 will my husband be *j* unto me,
Ex 28. 7 shoulderpieces thereof *j* at the two
7 and so it shall be *j* together.
Nu 18. 2 that they may be *j* unto thee, and
4 they shall be *j* unto thee, and keep
25. 3 Israel *j* himself unto Baal-peor:
5 men that were *j* unto Baal-peor.
1Sa 4. 2 they *j* battle, Israel was smitten
1Ki 7.32 of the wheels were *j* to the base:
20.29 the seventh day the battle was *j*:
2Ch 18. 1 and *j* affinity with Ahab.
20.36 *j* himself with him to make ships
37 thou hast *j* thyself with Ahaziah,
Ezr 4.12 thereof, and *j* the foundations.
Neh 4. 6 all the wall was *j* together unto
Est 9.27 such as *j* themselves unto them,
Job 3. 6 not be *j* unto the days of the year,
41.17 They are *j* one to another, they
23 flakes of his flesh are *j* together:
Ps 83. 8 Assur also is *j* with them: they
106.28 *j* themselves also unto Baal-peor,
Ec 9. 4 to him that is *j* to all the living
Isa 13.15 every one that is *j* unto them
14. 1 strangers shall be *j* with them,
20 shalt not be *j* with them in burial,
56. 3 that hath *j* himself to the Lord,
Eze 1. 9 wings were *j* one to another;
11 two wings of every one were *j* one
46.22 there were courts *j* of forty cubits
Hos 4.17 Ephraim is *j* to idols: let him
Zec 2.11 nations shall be *j* to the Lord
Mt 19. 6 therefore God hath *j* together,
Mk 10. 9 therefore God hath *j* together,
Lk 15.15 and *j* himself to a citizen of that
Ac 5.36 about four hundred, *j* themselves:
18. 7 house *j* hard to the synagogue.
1Co 1.10 that ye be perfectly *j* together
6.16 not that he which is *j* to an harlot
17 he that is *j* unto the Lord is one
Eph 4.16 the whole body fitly *j* together
5.31 shall be *j* unto his wife, and they

JOINING

2Ch 3.12 *j* to the wing of the other cherub.

JOININGS

1Ch 22. 3 doors of the gates, and for the *j*;

JOINT

Gen 32.25 of Jacob's thigh was out of *j*,
Ps 22.14 and all my bones are out of *j*:
Pr 25.19 broken tooth, and a foot out of *j*.
Eph 4.16 by that which every *j* supplieth,

JOINT-HEIRS

Ro 8.17 heirs of God, and *j* with Christ;

JOINTS

1Ki 22.34 between the *j* of the harness:
2Ch 18.33 between the *j* of the harness:
SS 7. 1 the *j* of thy thighs are like jewels,
Dan 5. 6 that the *j* of his loins were loosed ,
Col 2.19 all the body by *j* and bands having
Heb 4.12 spirit, and of the *j* and marrow,

The story of Jonah has been a favorite subject for artists since antiquity. In this early Christian mosaic from Aquileia, Italy, Jonah is vomited up on dry land by the "great fish" (Jon 2) and subsequently enjoys his brief respite in the gourd-vine bower that shades him from the sun outside the city of Nineveh (Jon 4).

JONA

Jn 1.42 Thou art Simon the son of *J*:

JONAH

2Ki 14.25 by the hand of his servant *J*,
Jon 1. 1 the word of the Lord came unto *J*
3 *J* rose up to flee unto Tarshish
5 *J* was gone down into the sides of
7 cast lots, and the lot fell upon *J*.
15 took up *J*, and cast him forth into
17 a great fish to swallow up *J*.
17 *J* was in the belly of the fish three
2. 1 *J* prayed unto the Lord his God
10 it vomited out *J* upon the dry land.
3. 1 word of the Lord came unto *J* the
3 So *J* arose, and went unto Nineveh,
4 *J* began to enter into the city a
4. 1 But it displeased *J* exceedingly,
5 *J* went out of the city, and sat on
6 and made it to come up over *J*,
6 *J* was exceeding glad of the gourd.
8 the sun beat upon the head of *J*,
9 God said unto *J*, Doest thou well

JONAS

Mt 12.39 it, but the sign of the prophet *J*:
40 For as *J* was three days and three
41 repented at the preaching of *J*;
41 behold, a greater than *J* is here
16. 4 it, but the sign of the prophet *J*.
Lk 11.29 it, but the sign of *J* the prophet.
30 *J* was a sign unto the Ninevites,
32 repented at the preaching of *J*;
32 behold, a greater than *J* is here.
Jn 21.15, 16, 17 Simon, son of *J*, lovest thou

JONATHAN

Jdg 18.30 *J*, the son of Gershom, the son of
1Sa 13. 2 a thousand were with *J* in Gibeah
3 *J* smote the garrison of the
16 Saul, and *J* his son, and the people
22 people that were with Saul and *J*:
22 with *J* his son was there found.
14. 1 *J* the son of Saul said unto the
3 people knew not that *J* was gone.
4 which *J* sought to go over unto
6 *J* said to the young man that
8 said *J*, Behold, we will pass over
12 *J* and his armorbearer,
12 *J* said unto his armorbearer,
13 *J* climbed up upon his hands and
13 and they fell before *J*; and his
14 which *J* and his armorbearer
17 behold, *J* and his armorbearer
21 that were with Saul and *J*.
27 But *J* heard not when his father
29 said *J*, My father hath troubled
39 it be in *J* my son, he shall surely
40 I and *J* my son will be on the
41 Saul and *J* were taken: but the
42 lots between me and *J* my son.
42 And *J* was taken.
43 Then Saul said to *J*, Tell me what
43 And *J* told him, and said, I did but
44 also: for thou shalt surely die, *J*.
45 people said unto Saul, Shall *J* die,
45 So the people rescued *J*, that he
49 the sons of Saul were *J*, and Ishui,
18. 1 soul of *J* was knit with the soul of
1 and *J* loved him as his own soul.
3 *J* and David made a covenant,
4 *J* stripped himself of the robe that
19. 1 Saul spake to *J* his son, and to all
2 *J* Saul's son delighted much in
2 *J* told David, saying, Saul my
4 *J* spake good of David unto Saul
6 hearkened unto the voice of *J*:
7 *J* called David, and *J* shewed him
7 *J* brought David to Saul, and he
20. 1 said before *J*, What have I done?
3 Let not *J* know this, lest he be
4 Then said *J* unto David,
5 And David said to *J*, Behold
9 And *J* said, Far be it from thee:
10 Then said David to *J*, Who shall
11 *J* said unto David, Come, and let
12 *J* said unto David, O Lord God of
13 Lord do so and much more to *J*:
16 *J* made a covenant with the house
17 *J* caused David to swear again,
18 *J* said to David, To-morrow is the
25 *J* arose, and Abner sat by Saul's
27 Saul said unto *J* his son, Wherefore
28 *J* answered Saul, David earnestly
30 Saul's anger was kindled against *J*,
32 *J* answered Saul his father, and
33 *J* knew that it was determined
34 So *J* arose from the table in fierce
35 *J* went out into the field at the time
37 of the arrow which *J* had shot,
37 *J* cried after the lad, and said, Is
38 *J* cried after the lad, Make speed,
39 only *J* and David knew the matter.
40 *J* gave his artillery unto his lad,
42 And *J* said to David, Go in peace,
42 departed: and *J* went into the city.
23.16 *J* Saul's son arose, and went to
18 the wood, and *J* went to his house.
31. 2 Philistines slew *J*, and Abinadab,
2Sa 1. 4 Saul and *J* his son are dead also.
5 that Saul and *J* his son be dead?
12 even, for Saul, and for *J* his son,
17 lamentation over Saul and over *J*
22 the bow of *J* turned not back, and
23 Saul and *J* were lovely and
25 O *J*, thou wast slain in thine high
26 distressed for thee, my brother *J*:
4. 4 *J*, Saul's son, had a son that was
4 the tidings came of Saul and *J*
9. 3 *J* hath yet a son, which is lame
6 when Mephibosheth, the son of *J*,
7 kindness for *J* thy father's sake,
15.27 thy son, and *J* the son of Abiathar.
36 Zadok's son, and *J* Abiathar's son;
17.17 Now *J* and Ahimaaz stayed by
20 said, Where is Ahimaaz and *J*?
21. 7 spared Mephibosheth, the son of *J*
7 between David and *J* the son of
12 bones of Saul and the bones of *J*
13 Saul and the bones of *J* his son;
14 the bones of Saul and *J* his son
21 *J* the son of Shimeah the brother
23.32 of the sons of Jashen, *J*,
1Ki 1.42 *J* the son of Abiathar the priest
43 *J* answered and said to Adonijah,
1Ch 2.32 of Shammai; Jether, and *J*:
33 And the sons of *J*; Peleth, and
8.33 Saul begat *J*, and Malchi-shua,
34 And the son of *J* was Merib-baal;
9.39 Saul begat *J*, and Malchi-shua,
40 And the son of *J* was Merib-baal:
10. 2 and the Philistines slew *J*, and
11.34 *J* the son of Shage the Hararite,
20. 7 *J* the son of Shimea David's
27.32 *J* David's uncle was a counseller,
Ezr 8. 6 Ebed the son of *J*, and with him
10.15 Only *J* the son of Asahel and
Neh 12.11 And Joiada begat *J*, and *J* begat
14 Of Melicu, *J*; of Shebaniah,
35 Zechariah the son of *J*, the son of
Jer 37.15 prison in the house of *J* the scribe:
20 return to the house of *J* the scribe,
40. 8 Johanan and *J* the sons of Kareah,

JOPPA

2Ch 2.16 it to thee in floats by sea to *J*,
Ezr 3. 7 trees from Lebanon to the sea of *J*
Jon 1. 3 of the Lord, and went down to *J*;
Ac 9.36 there was at *J* a certain disciple
38 as Lydda was nigh to *J*, and the

42 it was known throughout all *J*;
43 he tarried many days in *J* with one
10. 5 now send men to *J*, and call for one
8 unto them, he sent them to *J*.
23 and certain brethren from *J*
32 Send therefore to *J*, and call
11. 5 I was in the city of *J* praying: and
13 Send men to *J*, and call for Simon,

JORDAN
Gen 13.10 and beheld all the plain of *J*,
11 Lot chose him all the plain of *J*;
32.10 with my staff I passed over this *J*;
50.10 of Atad, which is beyond *J*, and
11 Abel-mizraim, which is beyond *J*.
Nu 13.29 of the sea, and by the coast of *J*.
22. 1 in the plains of Moab on this side *J*
26. 3 them in the plains of Moab by *J*
63 Israel in the plains of Moab by *J*
31.12 the plains of Moab, which are by *J*
32. 5 possession, and bring us not over *J*.
19 inherit with them on yonder side *J*,
19 fallen to us on this side *J* eastward.
21 And will go all of you armed over *J*
29 Reuben will pass with you over *J*,
32 on this side *J* may be ours.
33.48 pitched in the plains of Moab by *J*.
49 pitched by *J*, from Beth-jesimoth
50 Moses in the plains of Moab by *J*
51 over *J* into the land of Canaan;
34.12 the border shall go down to *J*, and
15 their inheritance this side *J* near
35. 1 Moses in the plains of Moab by *J*
10 ye be come over *J* into the land of
14 give three cities on this side *J*,
36.13 Israel in the plains of Moab by *J*
Dt 1. 1 on this side *J* in the wilderness,
5 On this side *J*, in the land of Moab,
2.29 until I shall pass over *J* into the
3. 8 the land that was on this side *J*,
17 plain also, and *J*, and the coast,
20 God hath given them beyond *J*:
25 see the good land that is beyond *J*,
27 for thou shalt not go over this *J*.
4.21 sware that I should not go over *J*,
22 in this land, I must not go over *J*:
26 whereunto ye go over *J* to possess
41 severed three cities on this side *J*
46 On this side *J*, in the valley over
47 this side *J* toward the sunrising;
49 And all the plain on this side *J*
9. 1 Thou art to pass over *J* this day,
11.30 Are they not on the other side *J*,
31 For ye shall pass over *J* to go in to
12.10 But when ye go over *J*, and dwell
27. 2 when ye shall pass over *J* unto the
4 shall be when ye be gone over *J*,
12 people, when ye are come over *J*;
30.18 passest over *J* to go to possess it.
31. 2 Thou shalt not go over this *J*.
13 in the land whither ye go over *J*
32.47 whither ye go over *J* to possess it.
Jos 1. 2 go over this *J*, thou, and all this
11 days ye shall pass over this *J*,
14 Moses gave you on this side *J*;
15 this side *J* toward the sunrising.
2. 7 them the way to *J* unto the fords:
10 were on the other side *J*, Sihon
3. 1 from Shittim, and came to *J*,
8 to the brink of the water of *J*,
8 ye shall stand still in *J*.
11 passeth over before you into *J*.
13 earth, shall rest in the waters of *J*,
13 the waters of *J* shall be cut off
14 from their tents, to pass over *J*,
15 bare the ark were come unto *J*,
15 *J* overfloweth all his banks all the
17 on dry ground in the midst of *J*,
17 people were passed clean over *J*.
4. 1 people were clean passed over *J*,
3 you hence out of the midst of *J*,
5 Lord your God into the midst of *J*,
7 the waters of *J* were cut off before
7 the Lord; when it passed over *J*,
7 the waters of *J* were cut off: and
8 twelve stones out of the midst of *J*,
9 up twelve stones in the midst of *J*,
10 the ark stood in the midst of *J*,
16 that they come up out of *J*.
17 saying, Come ye up out of *J*.
18 come up out of the midst of *J*,
18 waters of *J* returned unto their
19 came up out of *J* on the tenth day
20 stones, which they took out of *J*,
22 Israel came over this *J* on dry
23 God dried up the waters of *J* from
5. 1 were on the side of *J* westward,
1 Lord had dried up the waters of *J*
7. 7 at all brought this people over *J*,
7 and dwelt on the other side *J*!
9. 1 kings which were on this side *J*,
10 the Amorites, that were beyond *J*,
12. 1 their land on the other side *J*
7 smote on this side *J* on the west,
13. 8 gave them, beyond *J* eastward,
23 And the border...of Reuben was *J*,
27 of Heshbon, *J* and his border,
27 on the other side *J* eastward.
32 plains of Moab, on the other side *J*,
14. 3 an half tribe on the other side *J*:
15. 5 salt sea, even unto the end of *J*.
5 the sea at the uttermost part of *J*:
16. 1 of Joseph fell from *J* by Jericho,
7 to Jericho, and went out at *J*.
17. 5 which were on the other side *J*;
18. 7 received their inheritance beyond *J*
12 on the north side was from *J*;
19 the salt sea at the south end of *J*:
20 *J* was the border of it on the east
19.22 outgoings of their border were at *J*:
33 the outgoings thereof were at *J*:
34 to Judah upon *J* toward the
20. 8 other side *J* by Jericho eastward,
22. 4 Lord gave you on the other side *J*.
7 brethren on this side *J* westward.
10 they came unto the borders of *J*,
10 Manasseh built there an altar by *J*,
11 in the borders of *J*, at the passage
25 the Lord hath made *J* a border
23. 4 inheritance for your tribes, from *J*,
24. 8 which dwelt on the other side *J*;
11 ye went over *J*, and came unto
Jdg 3.28 took the fords of *J* toward Moab,
5.17 Gilead abode beyond *J*: and why
7.24 waters unto Beth-barah and *J*.
25 Zeeb to Gideon on the other side *J*.
8. 4 Gideon came to *J*, and passed over,
10. 8 that were on the other side *J* in
9 children of Ammon passed over *J*
11.13 even unto Jabbok, and unto *J*:
22 from the wilderness even unto *J*.
12. 5 Gileadites took the passages of *J*
6 slew him at the passages of *J*:
1Sa 13. 7 some of the Hebrews went over *J*
31. 7 they that were on the other side *J*,
2Sa 2.29 passed over *J*, and went through
10.17 Israel together, and passed over *J*,
17.22 with him, and they passed over *J*:
22 of them that was not gone over *J*.
24 Absalom passed over *J*, he and all
19.15 the king returned, and came to *J*.
15 king, to conduct the king over *J*.
17 they went over *J* before the king.
18 the king, as he was come over *J*;
31 from Rogelim, and went over *J*
31 the king, to conduct him over *J*.
36 servant will go a little way over *J*
39 And all the people went over *J*.
41 David's men with him, over *J*?
20. 2 king from *J* even to Jerusalem.
24. 5 they passed over *J*, and pitched
1Ki 2. 8 he came down to meet me at *J*,
7.46 In the plain of *J* did the king cast
17. 3, 5 brook Cherith, that is before *J*.
2Ki 2. 6 for the Lord hath sent me to *J*.
7 afar off: and they two stood by *J*.
13 back, and stood by the bank of *J*;
5.10 Go and wash in *J* seven times,
14 dipped himself seven times in *J*,
6. 2 Let us go, we pray thee, unto *J*,
4 when they came to *J*, they cut
7.15 they went after them unto *J*: and,
10.33 From *J* eastward, all...Gilead,
1Ch 6.78 on the other side *J* by Jericho,
78 on the east side of *J*, were given
12.15 they that went over *J* in the first
37 on the other side of *J*, of the
19.17 all Israel, and passed over *J*,
26.30 among them of Israel on this side *J*
2Ch 4.17 In the plain of *J* did the king cast
Job 40.23 he can draw up *J* into his mouth.
Ps 42. 6 remember thee from the land of *J*,
114. 3 and fled: *J* was driven back.
5 thou *J*, that thou wast driven back?
Isa 9. 1 by the way of the sea, beyond *J*,
Jer 12. 5 wilt thou do in the swelling of *J*?
49.19 like a lion from the swelling of *J*
50.44 like a lion from the swelling of *J*
Eze 47.18 and from the land of Israel by *J*,
Zec 11. 3 lions; for the pride of *J* is spoiled.
Mt 3. 5 and all the region round about *J*,
6 baptized of him in *J*, confessing
13 cometh Jesus from Galilee to *J*
4.15 by the way of the sea, beyond *J*,
25 from Judea, and from beyond *J*.
19. 1 into the coasts of Judea beyond *J*;
Mk 1. 5 baptized of him in the river of *J*,
9 and was baptized of John in *J*.
3. 8 Idumea, and from beyond *J*;
10. 1 of Judea by the farther side of *J*:
Lk 3. 3 came into all the country about *J*,
4. 1 the Holy Ghost returned from *J*,
Jn 1.28 were done in Bethabara beyond *J*,
3.26 he that was with thee beyond *J*,
10.40 went away again beyond *J* into

JOSEPH
Gen 30.24 And she called his name *J*; and
25 to pass, when Rachel had borne *J*,

JONATHAN

Eldest son of King Saul, late 11th century B.C.; commands a force in Saul's army and defeats Philistine garrison at Geba; joins Saul at Gibeah (1Sa 13); his daring exploit against Philistine garrison at Michmash leads to general rout of Philistines; unwittingly violates fast imposed on army by Saul, and is spared death only through intervention of the people (1Sa 14); when David enters Saul's service, forms a deep and lasting friendship with him, sealed by a covenant (1Sa 18); warns David that Saul is jealous of his growing fame and determined to kill him; tries to placate his father (1Sa 19); later arranges with David to learn and convey to him Saul's intentions; narrowly escapes being impaled by Saul's spear, and warns David to flee (1Sa 20); has final meeting with David in wilderness of Ziph; makes new covenant before God and, despite his own position, recognizes David's destiny as Israel's next king (1Sa 23); dies with Saul on Mount Gilboa at the hands of the Philistines (1Sa 31); his death sorely lamented by David (2Sa 1).

Gen 33. 2 and Rachel and *J* hindermost.
7 and after came *J* near and Rachel,
35.24 sons of Rachel; *J*, and Benjamin:
37. 2 *J*, being seventeen years old, was
2 *J* brought unto his father...report.
3 Israel loved *J* more than all his
5 *J* dreamed a dream, and he told
13 Israel said unto *J*, Do not thy
17 *J* went after his brethren, and
23 when *J* was come unto his brethren,
23 that they stript *J* out of his coat,
28 drew and lifted up *J* out of the pit,
28 and sold *J* to the Ishmeelites for
28 and they brought *J* into Egypt.
29 behold, *J* was not in the pit; and
33 *J* is without doubt rent in pieces.
39. 1 *J* was brought down to Egypt;
2 And the Lord was with *J*, and he
4 *J* found grace in his sight, and
6 *J* was a goodly person, and well
7 master's wife cast her eyes upon *J*;
10 as she spake to *J* day by day,
11 that *J* went into the house to do
21 But the Lord was with *J*, and
40. 3 the place where *J* was bound.

JOSEPH

Eleventh son of Jacob and first by Jacob's wife Rachel (Gen 30.22-24); she later dies giving birth to his brother Benjamin (Gen 35.16-20); the favorite of his father, who gives him "a coat of many colors" (Gen 37.3); unwisely tells brothers his dreams of ruling over them; visits them as they search for pasture, and they sell him to a caravan of traders, taking his coat dipped in an animal's blood back to their father (Gen 37); the traders take him to Egypt and sell him to Potiphar, captain of Pharaoh's guard; he rejects advances of Potiphar's wife and is imprisoned (Gen 39); in prison interprets dreams of the disgraced chief butler and chief baker, and both come true (Gen 40); when Pharaoh has dream of the fat and lean kine, the butler, now released, remembers Joseph; summoned before Pharaoh, interprets his dreams as presaging a famine, and is appointed Pharaoh's vizier; marries an Egyptian woman, who bears him two sons (Gen 41); his ten older brothers come to Egypt to buy food and he, unrecognized by them, accuses them of spying, keeping Simeon in prison and demanding that Benjamin return with them (Gen 42); on their second visit engineers the arrest of Benjamin, but finally tells his brothers who he is and acknowledges God's hand in all that has happened (Gen 43.1–45.15); sends for Jacob and is reunited with the father he has not seen in 20 years; the clan of Jacob settles in Egypt (Gen 45.16–46.34); presents his father to Pharaoh; improves the Egyptian administration (Gen 47); seeks Jacob's blessing for his sons, Ephraim and Manasseh (Gen 48), and is himself blessed with his brothers (Gen 49); buries his father in Canaan and assures his brothers that he will not take revenge on them now that Jacob is dead; dies and is embalmed in Egypt (Gen 50); his bones removed by Moses for reburial in the promised land (Ex 13.19).

4 of the guard charged *J* with them,
6 And *J* came in unto them in the
8 And *J* said unto them, Do not
9 chief butler told his dream to *J*,
12 And *J* said unto him, This is the
16 he said unto *J*, I also was in my
18 *J* answered and said, This is the
22 as *J* had interpreted to them.
23 not the chief butler remember *J*,
41.14 Pharaoh sent and called *J*, and
15 And Pharaoh said unto *J*, I have
16 *J* answered Pharaoh, saying, It is
17 Pharaoh said unto *J*, In my dream,
25 *J* said unto Pharaoh, The dream
39 Pharaoh said unto *J*, Forasmuch
41 Pharaoh said unto *J*, See, I have
44 Pharaoh said unto *J*, I am
45 And *J* went out over all the land of
46 *J* was thirty years old when he
46 *J* went out from the presence of
49 *J* gathered corn as the sand of the
50 unto *J* were born two sons before
51 *J* called the name of the firstborn
54 to come, according as *J* had said:
55 unto all the Egyptians, Go unto *J*;
56 *J* opened all the storehouses, and
57 came into Egypt to *J* for to buy
42. 6 *J* was the governor over the land,
7 *J* saw his brethren, and he knew
8 *J* knew his brethren, but they knew
9 *J* remembered the dreams which
14 *J* said unto them, That is it that I
18 *J* said unto them the third day,
23 knew not that *J* understood them;
25 *J* commanded to fill their sacks
36 *J* is not, and Simeon is not, and ye
43.15 down to Egypt, and stood before *J*.
16 when *J* saw Benjamin with them,
17 And the man did as *J* bade; and
25 present against *J* came at noon:
26 when *J* came home, they brought
30 *J* made haste; for his bowels did
44. 2 to the word that *J* had spoken.
4 *J* said unto his steward, Up, follow
15 *J* said unto them, What deed is
45. 1 Then *J* could not refrain himself
1 while *J* made himself known unto
3 *J* said unto his brethren, I am *J*;
4 *J* said unto his brethren, Come
4 I am *J* your brother, whom ye sold
9 Thus saith thy son *J*, God hath
17 Pharaoh said unto *J*, Say unto thy
21 *J* gave them wagons, according to
26 told him, saying, *J* is yet alive,
27 they told him all the words of *J*,
27 saw the wagons which *J* had sent
28 It is enough; *J* my son is yet alive:
46. 4 *J* shall put his hand upon thine
19 sons of Rachel Jacob's wife; *J*, and
20 unto *J* in the land of Egypt were
27 sons of *J*, which were born him in
28 he sent Judah before him unto *J*,
29 *J* made ready his chariot, and went
30 Israel said unto *J*, Now let me die,
31 *J* said unto his brethren, and unto
47. 1 Then *J* came and told Pharaoh, and
5 And Pharaoh spake unto *J*, saying,
7 And *J* brought in Jacob his father,
11 And *J* placed his father and his
12 *J* nourished his father, and his
14 *J* gathered up all the money that
14 *J* brought the money into Pharaoh's
15 the Egyptians came unto *J*, and
16 *J* said, Give your cattle; and I will
17 they brought their cattle unto *J*:
17 *J* gave them bread in exchange for
20 *J* bought all the land of Egypt for
23 *J* said unto the people, Behold, I
26 *J* made it a law over the land of
29 and he called his son *J*, and said
48. 1 told *J*, Behold, thy father is sick:
2 thy son *J* cometh unto thee:
3 Jacob said unto *J*, God Almighty
9 *J* said unto his father, They are
11 And Israel said unto *J*, I had not
12 *J* brought them out from between
13 *J* took them both, Ephraim in his
15 he blessed *J*, and said, God, before
17 when *J* saw that his father laid his
18 *J* said unto his father, Not so, my
21 Israel said unto *J*, Behold, I die:
49.22 *J* is a fruitful bough, even a fruitful
26 shall be on the head of *J*, and on
50. 1 *J* fell upon his father's face, and
2 *J* commanded...the physicians to
4 *J* spake unto the house of Pharaoh,
7 *J* went up to bury his father: and
8 And all the house of *J*, and his
14 *J* returned into Egypt, he, and his
15 said, *J* will peradventure hate us,
16 And they sent a messenger unto *J*,
17 So shall ye say unto *J*, Forgive, I
17 *J* wept when they spake unto him.
19 *J* said unto them, Fear not: for am
22 And *J* dwelt in Egypt, he, and his
22 *J* lived an hundred and ten years.
23 *J* saw Ephraim's children of the
24 *J* said unto his brethren, I die:
25 *J* took an oath of the children of
26 *J* died, being an hundred and ten
Ex 1. 5 souls: for *J* was in Egypt already.
6 *J* died, and all his brethren, and
8 king over Egypt, which knew not *J*
13.19 Moses took the bones of *J* with
Nu 1.10 Of the children of *J*: of Ephraim;
32 Of the children of *J*, namely, of
13. 7 tribe of Issachar, Igal the son of *J*.
11 Of the tribe of *J*, namely, of the
26.28 The sons of *J* after their families
37 the sons of *J* after their families.
27. 1 families of Manasseh the son of *J*:
32.33 tribe of Manasseh the son of *J*,
34.23 prince of the children of *J*, for the
36. 1 of the families of the sons of *J*,
5 The tribe of the sons of *J* hath said
12 the sons of Manasseh the son of *J*,
Dt 27.12 Issachar, and *J*, and Benjamin:
33.13 And of *J* he said, Blessed of the
16 blessing come upon the head of *J*,
Jos 14. 4 the children of *J* were two tribes,
16. 1 the children of *J* fell from Jordan
4 So the children of *J*, Manasseh and
17. 1 for he was the firstborn of *J*;
2 children of Manasseh the son of *J*
14 children of *J* spake unto Joshua,
16 And the children of *J* said, The hill
17 Joshua spake unto the house of *J*,
18. 5 the house of *J* shall abide in their
11 of Judah and the children of *J*.
24.32 And the bones of *J*, which the
32 the inheritance of the children of *J*.
Jdg 1.22 the house of *J*, they also went up
23 house of *J* sent to descry Beth-el.
35 hand of the house of *J* prevailed,
2Sa 19.20 first this day of all the house of *J*
1Ki 11.28 all the charge of the house of *J*.
1Ch 2. 2 Dan, *J*, and Benjamin, Naphtali,
5. 1 was given unto the sons of *J*
7.29 In these dwelt the children of *J*
25. 2 the sons of Asaph; Zaccur, and *J*,
9 first lot came forth for Asaph to *J*:
Ezr 10.42 Shallum, Amariah, and *J*.
Neh 12.14 Melicu, Jonathan; of Shebaniah, *J*;
Ps 77.15 thy people, the sons of Jacob and *J*.
78.67 he refused the tabernacle of *J*,
80. 1 thou that leadest *J* like a flock;
81. 5 he ordained in *J* for a testimony,
105.17 sent a man before them, even *J*,
Eze 37.16 For *J*, the stick of Ephraim, and
19 I will take the stick of *J*, which is
47.13 Israel: *J* shall have two portions.
48.32 and one gate of *J*, one gate of

Am 5. 6 out like fire in the house of J, and
15 be gracious unto the remnant of J.
6. 6 not grieved for the affliction of J.
Ob 18 a fire, and the house of J a flame,
Zec 10. 6 and I will save the house of J, and
Mt 1.16 begat J the husband of Mary,
18 mother Mary was espoused to J,
19 Then J her husband, being a just
20 J, thou son of David, fear not to
24 J being raised from sleep did as
2.13 Lord appeareth to J in a dream,
19 Lord appeareth in a dream to J
27.57 rich man of Arimathaea, named J,
59 And when J had taken the body, he
Mk 15.43 J of Arimathaea, an honorable
45 centurion, he gave the body to J.
Lk 1.27 to a man whose name was J,
2. 4 And J also went up from Galilee,
16 found Mary, and J, and the babe
33 J and his mother marvelled at
43 J and his mother knew not of it.
3.23 (as was supposed) the son of J,
24 of Janna, which was the son of J,
26 of Semei, which was the son of J,
30 of Juda, which was the son of J,
23.50 was a man named J, a counsellor;
Jn 1.45 Jesus of Nazareth, the son of J.
4. 5 that Jacob gave to his son of J.
6.42 Is not this Jesus, the son of J,
19.38 after this J of Arimathaea, being a
Ac 1.23 J called Barsabas, who was
7. 9 with envy, sold J into Egypt:
13 J was made known to his brethren;
14 Then sent J, and called his father
18 king arose, which knew not J.
Heb 11.21 dying, blessed both the sons of J;
22 By faith J, when he died, made
Rev 7. 8 Of the tribe of J were sealed

JOSEPH'S

Gen 37.31 they took J coat, and killed a kid
42. 6 J brethren came, and bowed down
Lk 4.22 And they said, Is not this J son?
Ac 7.13 J kindred was made known unto

JOSES

Mt 13.55 James, and J, and Simon, and
27.56 Mary the mother of James and J,
Mk 6. 3 the brother of James, and J, and
15.40 mother of James the less and of J,
47 Mary the mother of J beheld where
Ac 4.36 J, who...was surnamed Barnabas,

JOSHUA

Ex 17. 9 Moses said unto J, Choose us out
10 So J did as Moses had said to him,
13 And J discomfited Amalek and his
14 and rehearse it in the ears of J:
24.13 Moses rose up, and his minister J:
32.17 And when J heard the noise of the
33.11 but his servant J, the son of Nun,
Nu 11.28 J the son of Nun, the servant of
14. 6 J the son of Nun, and Caleb the
30 Jephunneh, and J the son of Nun.
38 But J the son of Nun, and Caleb
26.65 Jephunneh, and J the son of Nun.
27.18 Take thee J the son of Nun, a man
22 and he took J, and set him before
32.12 the Kenezite, and J the son of Nun:
28 J the son of Nun, and the chief
34.17 the priest, and J the son of Nun.
Dt 1.38 J the son of Nun, which standeth
3.21 And I commanded J at that time,
28 But charge J, and encourage him,
31. 3 and J, he shall go over before thee,
7 Moses called unto J, and said unto
14 call J, and present yourselves in
14 Moses and J went, and presented
23 he gave J the son of Nun a charge,
34. 9 J the son of Nun was full of the
Jos 1. 1 Lord spake unto J the son of Nun,
10 Then J commanded the officers of
12 half the tribe of Manasseh, spake J,
16 they answered J, saying, All that
2. 1 And J the son of Nun sent out of
23 came to J the son of Nun, and told
24 said unto J, Truly the Lord hath
3. 1 J rose early in the morning; and
5 J said unto the people, Sanctify
6 J spake unto the priests, saying,
7 the Lord said unto J, This day will
9 J said unto the children of Israel,
10 J said, Hereby ye shall know that
4. 1 that the Lord spake unto J, saying,
4 Then J called the twelve men,
5 J said unto them, Pass over before
8 of Israel did so as J commanded,
8 Jordan, as the Lord spake unto J,
9 J set up twelve stones in the midst
10 Lord commanded J to speak unto
10 to all that Moses commanded J:
14 On that day the Lord magnified J
15 And the Lord spake unto J, saying,
17 J therefore commanded the priests,
20 out of Jordan, did J pitch in Gilgal.
5. 2 At that time the Lord said unto J,
3 And J made him sharp knives, and
4 the cause why J did circumcise:
7 their stead, them J circumcised:
9 Lord said unto J, This day have I
13 to pass, when J was by Jericho,
13 J went unto him, and said unto
14 J fell on his face to the earth, and
15 the Lord's host said unto J, Loose
15 standest is holy. And J did so.
6. 2 Lord said unto J, See, I have given
6 J the son of Nun called the priests,
8 when J had spoken unto the people,
10 J had commanded the people,
12 J rose early in the morning, and
16 J said unto the people, Shout; for
22 J had said unto the two men that
25 J saved Rahab the harlot alive,
25 which J sent to spy out Jericho.
26 And J adjured them at that time,
27 So the Lord was with J; and his
7. 2 J sent men from Jericho to Ai,
3 they returned to J, and said unto
6 J rent his clothes, and fell to the
7 J said, Alas, O Lord God, wherefore
10 the Lord said unto J, Get thee up;
16 So J rose up early in the morning,
19 J said unto Achan, My son, give, I
20 Achan answered J, and said, indeed
22 So J sent messengers, and they
23 brought them unto J, and unto all
24 J, and all Israel with him, took
25 J said, Why hast thou troubled us?
8. 1 Lord said unto J, Fear not, neither
3 J arose, and all the people of war,
3 J chose out thirty thousand...men
9 J therefore sent them forth; and
9 J lodged that night among the
10 J rose up early in the morning,
13 J went that night into the midst of
15 J and all Israel made as if they
16 they pursued after J, and were
18 Lord said unto J, Stretch out the
18 J stretched out the spear that he
21 when J and all Israel saw that
23 took alive, and brought him to J.
26 for J drew not his hand back,
27 the Lord which he commanded J.
28 J burnt Ai, and made it an heap for
29 J commanded that they should
30 J built an altar unto the Lord
35 which J read not before all the
9. 2 to fight with J and with Israel,
3 Gibeon heard what J had done
6 went to J unto the camp at Gilgal,
8 And they said unto J, We are thy
8 And J said unto them, Who are ye?
15 J made peace with them, and
22 J called for them, and he spake
24 they answered J, and said, Because
27 J made them that day hewers of
10. 1 had heard how J had taken Ai,
4 it hath made peace with J and
6 men of Gibeon sent unto J to the
7 So J ascended from Gilgal, he, and
8 Lord said unto J, Fear them not:
9 J therefore came unto them
12 Then spake J to the Lord in the
15 J returned, and all Israel with him,
17 it was told J, saying, the five kings
18 J said, Roll great stones upon the
20 when J and the children of Israel
21 people returned to the camp to J
22 said J, Open the mouth of the cave,
24 brought out those kings unto J,
24 J called for all the men of Israel,
25 J said unto them, Fear not, nor be
26 afterward J smote them, and slew
27 that J commanded, and they took
28 that day J took Makkedah, and
29 J passed from Makkedah, and all
31 J passed from Libnah, and all
33 J smote him and his people, until
34 from Lachish J passed unto Eglon,
36 J went up from Eglon, and all
38 J returned, and all Israel with him,
40 So J smote all the country of the
41 J smote them from Kadesh-barnea
42 their land did J take at one time,
43 J returned, and all Israel with him,
11. 6 Lord said unto J, Be not afraid
7 J came, and all the people of war
9 J did unto them as the Lord bade
10 J at that time turned back, and
12 all the kings of them, did J take,
13 save Hazor only; that did J burn.
15 Moses command J, and so did J;
16 So J took all that land, the hills,
18 J made war a long time with all
21 at that time came J, and cut off
21 J destroyed them utterly with
23 So J took the whole land, according
23 J gave it for an inheritance unto
12. 7 the kings of the country which J
7 J gave unto the tribes of Israel
13. 1 J was old and stricken in years;
14. 1 the priest, and J the son of Nun,
6 children of Judah came unto J
13 J blessed him, and gave unto Caleb
15.13 commandment of the Lord to J,
17. 4 priest, and before J the son of Nun,
14 children of Joseph spake unto J,
15 J answered them, If thou be a
17 J spake them unto the house of Joseph,
18. 3 J said unto the children of Israel,
8 J charged them that went to
9 again to J to the host at Shiloh.
10 J cast lots for them in Shiloh
10 there J divided the land unto the
19.49 of Israel gave an inheritance to J
51 J the son of Nun, and the heads of
20. 1 The Lord also spake unto J, saying,
21. 1 unto J the son of Nun, and unto
22. 1 Then J called the Reubenites, and
6 So J blessed them, and sent them
7 unto the other half thereof gave J
7 when J sent them away also unto
23. 1 J waxed old and stricken in age.
2 J called for all Israel, and for their
24. 1 J gathered all the tribes of Israel
2 J said unto all the people, Thus
19 J said unto the people, Ye cannot
21 And the people said unto J, Nay;
22 J said unto the people, Ye are
24 the people said unto J, The Lord
25 J made a covenant with the people
26 J wrote these words in the book of
27 J said unto all the people, Behold,

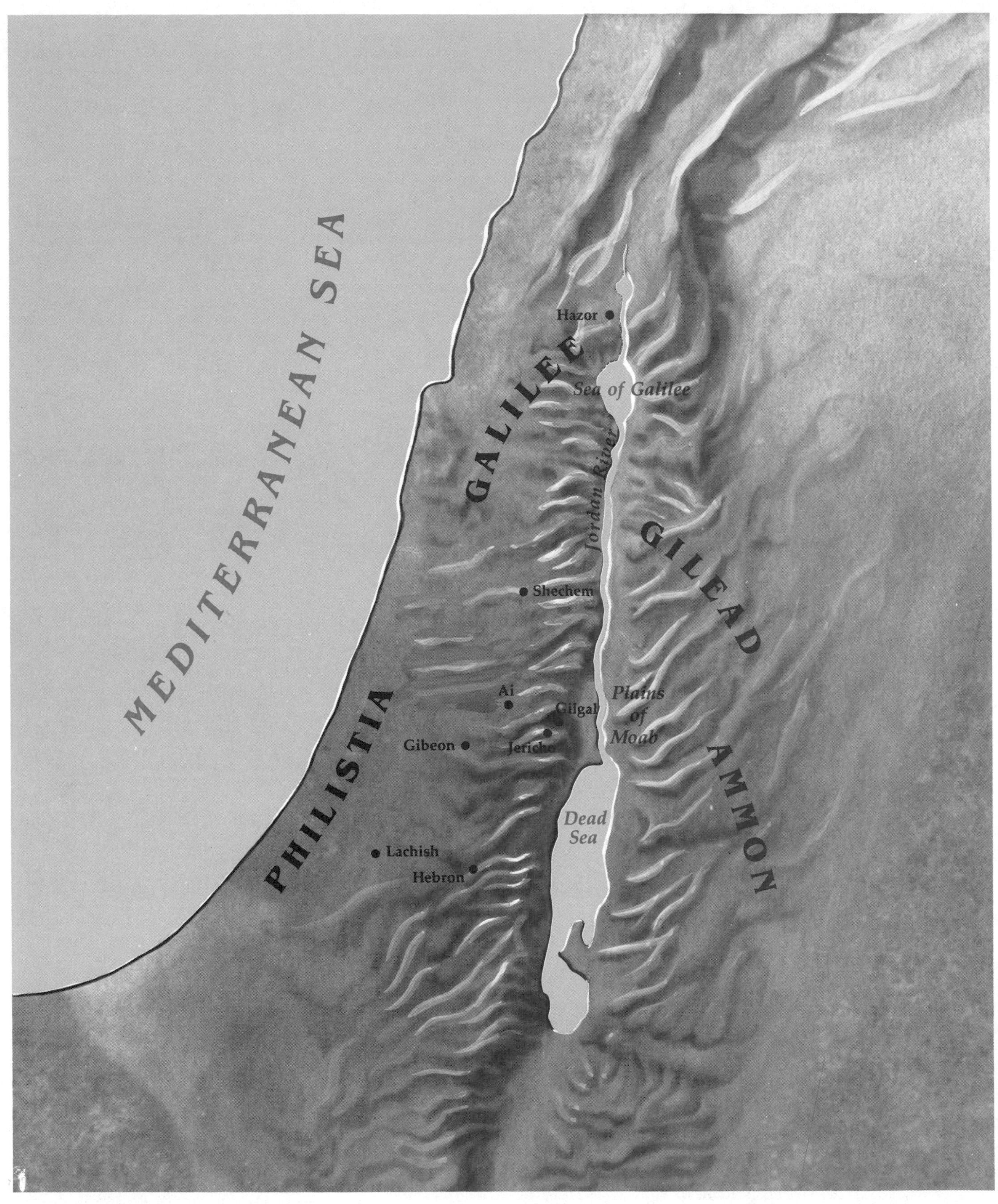

Joshua's conquest of Canaan, *one of the pivotal chapters in Old Testament history, began with the Israelites' crossing of the Jordan River from the Plains of Moab to Gilgal, where on Joshua's instructions a memorial of stones was built and all the males born during the years of wandering were circumcised. There followed the famous battle of Jericho, the destruction of Ai, and the taking of Shechem and Gibeon by peaceful means. The invaders subsequently turned south to capture a series of important strongholds, including Lachish and Hebron. The final phase of the campaign centered on Upper Galilee, well to the north, where Joshua's troops routed a large Canaanite force and then put the region's chief city, Hazor, to the torch.*

JOSHUA

Son of Nun; servant then successor to Moses; leader of Israelite conquest of Canaan, 13th century B.C.; first appears as military commander against Amalek (Ex 17); Moses' sole companion as he ascends Sinai (Ex 24.12-14); attendant in tabernacle (Ex 33.11); brings to Moses' notice both Israel's celebration of the golden calf, or bull image (Ex 32.17), and the prophesying of Eldad and Medad within the camp (Nu 11.28); Ephraim's representative among 12 spies sent to report on the land of Canaan (Nu 13.8, 16) and with Caleb one of only two to bring a favorable report (Nu 14.6-10) or indeed survive the wilderness wanderings (Nu 26.65); installed by Moses as his successor (Nu 27.18-23) and given instruction how to divide Canaan (Nu 32.28; 34.17; Dt 3.21-29); leads campaign to take control of Canaan (Jos 1–12), including the miraculous crossing of the Jordan (Jos 3–4), the successful siege of Jericho (Jos 6), and the stratagem adopted to capture Ai (Jos 8); commands the sun to stand still at Gibeon (Jos 10.12-14); supervises division of the conquered territory (Jos 13–22); renews covenant and gives farewell speech before his death and burial at Timnath-heres (Jos 23–24).

Jos 24.28 So *J* let the people depart, every
29 *J* the son of Nun, the servant of
31 served the Lord all the days of *J*,
31 days of the elders that overlived *J*,
Jdg 1. 1 after the death of *J* it came to pass,
2. 6 when *J* had let the people go, the
7 served the Lord all the days of *J*,
7 days of the elders that outlived *J*,
8 *J* the son of Nun, the servant of
21 nations which *J* left when he died:
23 he them into the hand of *J*.
1Sa 6.14 the cart came into the field of *J*,
18 unto this day in the field of *J*, the
1Ki 16.34 he spake by *J* the son of Nun.
2Ki 23. 8 in the entering in of the gate of *J*
Hag 1. 1 and to *J* the son of Josedech, the
12 *J* the son of Josedech, the high
14 the spirit of *J* the son of Josedech,
2. 2 and to *J* the son of Josedech, the
4 be strong, O *J*, son of Josedech,
Zec 3. 1 he shewed me *J* the high priest
3 Now *J* was clothed with filthy
6 angel of the Lord protested unto *J*,
8 Hear now, O *J* the high priest,
9 stone that I have laid before *J*;
6.11 and set them upon the head of *J*

JOSIAH

1Ki 13. 2 the house of David, *J* by name;
2Ki 21.24 of the land made *J* his son king
26 and *J* his son reigned in his stead.
22. 1 *J* was eight years old when he
3 in the eighteenth year of king *J*,
23.16 as *J* turned himself, he spied the
19 *J* took away, and did to them
23 in the eighteenth year of king *J*,
24 *J* put away, that he might perform
28 the rest of the acts of *J*, and all
2Ch 33.25 of the land made *J* his son king
34. 1 *J* was eight years old when he
33 *J* took away all the abominations
35. 1 *J* kept a passover unto the Lord in
7 *J* gave to the people, of the flock,
16 to the commandment of king *J*.
18 keep such a passover as *J* kept,
19 reign of *J* was this passover kept.
20 when *J* had prepared the temple,
20 and *J* went out against him.
22 would not turn his face from him,
23 the archers shot at king *J*; and
24 and Jerusalem mourned for *J*.
25 Jeremiah lamented for *J*: and all
25 spake of *J* in their lamentations
Jer 1. 2 days of *J* the son of Amon king of
3 days of Jehoiakim the son of *J* king
3 year of Zedekiah the son of *J* king
3. 6 said also unto me in the days of *J*
Zep 1. 1 days of *J* the son of Amon, king of
Zec 6.10 house of *J* the son of Zephaniah;

JOT

Mt 5.18 one *j* or one tittle shall in no wise

JOURNEY

Gen 24.21 had made his *j* prosperous or not.
29. 1 Jacob went on his *j*, and
30.36 set three days' *j* betwixt himself
31.23 pursued after him seven days' *j*;
33.12 Let us take our *j*, and let us go,
46. 1 Israel took his *j* with all that he
Ex 3.18 three days' *j* into the wilderness,
5. 3 thee, three days *j* into the desert,
8.27 three days' *j* into the wilderness,
13.20 they took their *j* from Succoth,
16. 1 And they took their *j* from Elim,
Nu 9.10 or be in a *j* afar off, yet he shall
13 man that is clean, and is not in a *j*,
10. 6 the south side shall take their *j*:
13 they first took their *j* according to
33 mount of the Lord three days' *j*:
33 before them in the three days' *j*,
11.31 as it were a day's *j* on this side,
31 it were a day's *j* on the other side,
33. 8 went three days' *j* in the wilderness
12 took their *j* out of the wilderness
Dt 1. 2 eleven days' *j* from Horeb by the way
7 Turn you, and take your *j*, and
40 take your *j* into the wilderness by
2. 1 took our *j* into the wilderness by
24 take your *j*, and pass over the river
10. 6 of Israel took their *j* from Beeroth
11 Arise, take thy *j* before the people,
Jos 9.11 Take victuals with you for the *j*,
13 old by reason of the very long *j*.
Jdg 4. 9 the *j* that thou takest shall not be
1Sa 15.18 the Lord sent thee on a *j*, and said,
2Sa 11.10 Uriah, Camest thou not from thy *j*?
1Ki 18.27 or he is pursuing, or he is in a *j*,
19. 4 went a day's *j* into the wilderness,
7 because the *j* is too great for thee.
2Ki 3. 9 fetched a compass of seven days' *j*:
2Ch 1.13 Solomon came from his *j* to the high
Neh 2. 6 For how long shall thy *j* be? and
Pr 7.19 not at home, he is gone a long *j*:
Jon 3. 3 great city of three days' *j*.
4 to enter into the city a day's *j*,
Mt 10.10 Nor scrip for your *j*, neither two
25.15 ability; and straightway took his *j*.
Mk 6. 8 should take nothing for their *j*,
13.34 of man is as a man taking a far *j*,
Lk 2.44 in the company, went a day's *j*;
9. 3 Take nothing for your *j*, neither
11. 6 a friend of mine in his *j* is come
15.13 and took his *j* into a far country,
Jn 4. 6 therefore, being wearied with his *j*,
Ac 1.12 from Jerusalem a sabbath day's *j*.
10. 9 as they went on their *j*, and drew
22. 6 as I made my *j*, and was come
Ro 1.10 I might have a prosperous *j* by
15.24 I take my *j* into Spain, I will
24 I trust to see you in my *j*, and to
1Co 16. 6 may bring me on my *j* whithersover
Tit 3.13 and Apollos on their *j* diligently,
3Jn 6 if thou bring forward on their *j*

JOURNEYED

Gen 11. 2 to pass, as they *j* from the east,
12. 9 Abram *j*, going on still toward the
13.11 and Lot *j* east: and they separated
20. 1 Abraham *j* from thence toward the
33.17 Jacob *j* to Succoth, and built him
35. 5 And they *j*: and the terror of God
16 they *j* from Beth-el; and there was
21 And Israel *j*, and spread his tent
Ex 12.37 children of Israel *j* from Rameses
17. 1 Israel *j* from the wilderness of Sin,
40.37 they *j* not till the day that it was
Nu 9.17 after that the children of Israel *j*:
18 of the Lord the children of Israel *j*,
19 the charge of the Lord, and *j* not.
20 commandment of the Lord they *j*.
21 up in the morning, then they *j*:
21 that the cloud was taken up, they *j*.
22 abode in their tents, and *j* not:
22 but when it was taken up, they *j*.
23 commandment of the Lord they *j*:
11.35 people *j* from Kibroth-hattaavah
12.15 *j* not till Miriam was brought in
20.22 whole congregation, *j* from Kadesh,
21. 4 And they *j* from mount Hor by the
11 And they *j* from Oboth, and pitched
33.22 they *j* from Rissah, and pitched in
Dt 10. 7 From thence they *j* unto Gudgodah;
Jos 9.17 children of Israel *j*, and came unto
Jdg 17. 8 the house of Micah, as he *j*.
Lk 10.33 But a certain Samaritan, as he *j*,
Ac 9. 3 as he *j*, he came near Damascus:
7 the men which *j* with him stood
26.13 me and them which *j* with me.

JOURNEYING

Nu 10. 2 and for the *j* of the camps.
29 We are *j* unto the place of which
Lk 13.22 and *j* toward Jerusalem.

JOURNEYINGS

Nu 10.28 the *j* of the children of Israel
2Co 11.26 in *j* often, in perils of waters,

JOURNEYS

Gen 13. 3 he went on his *j* from the south
Ex 17. 1 after their *j*, according to the
40.36 Israel went onward in all their *j*:

JOSIAH

of Judah and great religious reformer, 7th century B.C.; his scribe brings a law book (probably a version of our present Book of Deuteronomy) found by the high priest Hilkiah in the course of repairing the temple in Jerusalem; upon hearing its words, rends his clothes and sends a commission to Huldah the prophetess to inquire about its threat of judgment; judgment is confirmed, but Josiah is told that because he humbled himself, it will not come to pass until after his death (2Ki 22); summons the people to the temple and reads the law book; on the basis of its provisions, renews the covenant, carries out a series of sweeping religious reforms to eradicate idolatry, and celebrates the passover at the temple, which he establishes as the sole center of worship in the kingdom (2Ki 23.1-28); tries to intercept the army of Pharaoh Necho at Megiddo (609 B.C.) and is slain; succeeded by his son Jehoahaz (2Ki 23.29-30); regarded by posterity as one of Judah's greatest kings.

Ex 40.38 of Israel, throughout all their *j*.
Nu 10. 6 they shall blow an alarm for their *j*.
12 the children of Israel took their *j*
33. 1 are the *j* of the children of Israel,
2 goings out according to their *j*
2 *j* according to their goings out.

JOY

1Sa 18. 6 king Saul, with tabrets, with *j*,
1Ki 1.40 rejoiced with great *j*, so that the
1Ch 12.40 abundantly: for there was *j* in Israel.
15.16 by lifting up the voice with *j*.
25 of the house of Obed-edom with *j*.
29. 9 the king also rejoiced with great *j*.
17 now have I seen with *j* thy people,
2Ch 20.27 to go again to Jerusalem with *j*;
30.26 there was great *j* in Jerusalem: for
Ezr 3.12 and many shouted aloud for *j*:
13 discern the noise of the shout of *j*
6.16 of this house of God with *j*,
22 kept...bread seven days with *j*:
Neh 8.10 the *j* of the Lord is your strength.
12.43 made them rejoice with great *j*:
43 that the *j* of Jerusalem was heard
Est 8.16 had light, and gladness, and *j*,
17 the Jews had *j* and gladness, a
9.22 turned unto them from sorrow to *j*,
22 make them days of feasting and *j*,
Job 8.19 Behold, this is the *j* of his way,
20. 5 and the *j* of the hypocrite but for
29.13 the widow's heart to sing for *j*.
33.26 he shall see his face with *j*: for he
38. 7 all the sons of God shouted for *j*?
41.22 sorrow is turned into *j* before him.
Ps 5.11 let them ever shout for *j*, because
16.11 in thy presence is fullness of *j*;
21. 1 The king shall *j* in thy strength,
27. 6 in his tabernacle sacrifices of *j*;
30. 5 but *j* cometh in the morning.
32.11 shout for *j*, all ye that are upright
35.27 Let them shout for *j*, and be glad,
42. 4 with the voice of *j* and praise,
43. 4 God, unto God my exceeding *j*:
48. 2 the *j* of the whole earth, is mount
51. 8 Make me to hear *j* and gladness;
12 unto me the *j* of thy salvation;
65.13 corn; they shout for *j*, they also sing.
67. 4 let the nations be glad and sing for *j*:
105.43 brought forth his people with *j*,
126. 5 that sow in tears shall reap in *j*.
132. 9 and let thy saints shout for *j*.
16 her saints shall shout aloud for *j*.
137. 6 not Jerusalem above my chief *j*.
Pr 12.20 but to the counsellors of peace is *j*.
14.10 doth not intermeddle with his *j*.
15.21 Folly is *j* to him that is destitute of
23 man hath *j* by the answer of his
17.21 and the father of a fool hath no *j*.
21.15 It is *j* to the just to do judgment:
23.24 begetteth a wise child shall have *j*
Ec 2.10 withheld not my heart from any *j*;
26 wisdom, and knowledge, and *j*:
5.20 answereth him in the *j* of his heart.
9. 7 eat thy bread with *j*, and drink thy
Isa 9. 3 the nation, and not increased the *j*:
3 they *j* before thee according to
3 according to the *j* in harvest,
17 shall have no *j* in their young men,
12. 3 with *j* shall ye draw water out of
16.10 and *j* out of the plentiful field;
22.13 *j* and gladness, slaying oxen, and
24. 8 endeth, the *j* of the harp ceaseth.
11 all *j* is darkened, the mirth of the
29.19 meek also shall increase their *j*
32.13 yea, upon all the houses of *j* in the
14 a *j* of wild asses, a pasture of
35. 2 rejoice even with *j* and singing:
10 with songs and everlasting *j* upon
10 they shall obtain *j* and gladness,
51. 3 *j* and gladness shall be found
11 everlasting *j* shall be upon their
11 they shall obtain gladness and *j*;
52. 9 Break forth into *j*, sing together,
55.12 For ye shall go out with *j*, and be
60.15 a *j* of many generations.
61. 3 the oil of *j* for mourning, the
7 everlasting *j* shall be unto them.
65.14 servants shall sing for *j* of heart,
18 a rejoicing, and her people a *j*.
19 Jerusalem, and *j* in my people:
66. 5 he shall appear to your *j*, and
10 love her: rejoice for *j* with her,
Jer 15.16 the *j* and rejoicing of mine heart:
31.13 I will turn their mourning into *j*,
33. 9 And it shall be to me a name of *j*,
11 The voice of *j*, and the voice of
48.27 spakest of him, thou skippedst for *j*.
33 *j* and gladness is taken from the
49.25 of praise not left, the city of my *j*!
La 2.15 beauty, The *j* of the whole earth?
5.15 The *j* of our heart is ceased; our
Eze 24.25 the *j* of their glory, the desire of
36. 5 with the *j* of all their heart,
Hos 9. 1 Rejoice not, O Israel, for *j*, as
Joel 1.12 *j* is withered away from the sons
16 *j* and gladness from the house of
Hab 3.18 I will *j* in the God of my salvation.
Zep 3.17 he will rejoice over thee with *j*;
17 he will *j* over thee with singing.
Zec 8.19 house of Judah *j* and gladness,
Mt 2.10 rejoiced with exceeding great *j*.
13.20 word, and anon with *j* receiveth it;
44 for *j* thereof goeth and selleth all
25.21, 23 enter thou into the *j* of thy lord.
28. 8 sepulcher with fear and great *j*;
Lk 1.14 thou shalt have *j* and gladness;
44 the babe leaped in my womb for *j*.
2.10 bring you good tidings of great *j*,
6.23 ye in that day, and leap for *j*:
8.13 they hear, receive the word with *j*;
10.17 the seventy returned again with *j*,
15. 7 *j* shall be in heaven over one sinner
10 is *j* in the presence of the angels
24.41 while they yet believed not for *j*,
52 returned to Jerusalem with great *j*:
Jn 3.29 this my *j* therefore is fulfilled.
15.11 you, that my *j* might remain in you,
11 and that your *j* might be full.
16.20 your sorrow shall be turned into *j*.
21 for *j* that a man is born into the
22 your *j* no man taketh from you.
24 receive, that your *j* may be full.
17.13 have my *j* fulfilled in themselves.
Ac 2.28 thou shalt make me full of *j* with
8. 8 And there was great *j* in that city.
13.52 the disciples were filled with *j*, and
15. 3 caused great *j* unto all the brethren.
20.24 I might finish my course with *j*,
Ro 5.11 *j* in God through our Lord Jesus
14.17 peace, and *j* in the Holy Ghost.
15.13 fill you with all *j* and peace in
32 That I may come unto you with *j*
2Co 1.24 faith, but are helpers of your *j*:
2. 3 in you all, that my *j* is...of you all.
3 in you all, that...is the *j* of you all.
7.13 more joyed we for the *j* of Titus,
8. 2 abundance of their *j* and their deep
Gal 5.22 fruit of the Spirit is love, *j*, peace,
Php 1. 4 for you all making request with *j*,
25 for your furtherance and *j* of faith;
2. 2 Fulfil ye my *j*, that ye be
17 faith, I *j*, and rejoice with you all.
18 For the same cause also do ye *j*,
4. 1 and longed for, my *j* and crown,
1Th 1. 6 affliction, with *j* of the Holy Ghost:
2.19 what is our hope, or *j*, or crown of
20 For ye are our glory and *j*.
3. 9 for all the *j*...for your sakes before
9 wherewith we *j* for your sakes
2Ti 1. 4 tears, that I may be filled with *j*;
Phm 7 we have great *j* and consolation
20 let me have *j* of thee in the Lord:
Heb 12. 2 who for the *j* that was set before
13.17 that they may do it with *j*, and not
Jas 1. 2 count it all *j* when ye fall into
4. 9 mourning, and your *j* to heaviness.
1Pe 1. 8 rejoice with *j* unspeakable and full
4.13 may be glad also with exceeding *j*.
1Jn 1. 4 unto you, that your *j* may be full.
2Jn 12 face to face, that our *j* may be full.
3Jn 4 I have no greater *j* than to hear
Jude 24 of his glory with exceeding *j*,

JOYED

2Co 7.13 the more *j* we for the joy of Titus,

JOYFUL

1Ki 8.66 went unto their tents *j* and glad of
Ezr 6.22 for the Lord had made them *j*,
Est 5. 9 Haman went forth that day *j* and
Job 3. 7 let no *j* voice come therein.
Ps 5.11 them also that love thy name be *j*
35. 9 my soul shall be *j* in the Lord:
63. 5 mouth shall praise thee with *j* lips:
66. 1 Make a *j* noise unto God, all ye
81. 1 make a *j* noise unto the God of
89.15 the people that know the *j* sound:
95. 1 let us make a *j* noise to the rock
2 make a *j* noise unto him with psalms.
96.12 Let the field be *j*, and all that is
98. 4 Make a *j* noise unto the Lord, all
6 make a *j* noise before the Lord, the
8 hands: let the hills be *j* together
100. 1 Make a *j* noise unto the Lord, all
113. 9 and to be a *j* mother of children.
149. 2 children of Zion be *j* in their King.
5 Let the saints be *j* in glory: let
Ec 7.14 In the day of prosperity be *j*, but
Isa 49.13 Sing, O heavens; and be *j*, O earth;
56. 7 them *j* in my house of prayer:
61.10 my soul shall be *j* in my God;
2Co 7. 4 I am exceeding *j* in all our

JOYFULLY

Ec 9. 9 Live *j* with the wife whom thou
Lk 19. 6 came down, and received him *j*.
Heb 10.34 took *j* the spoiling of your

JOYFULNESS

Dt 28.47 not the Lord thy God with *j*,
Col 1.11 and longsuffering with *j*;

JOYING

Col 2. 5 spirit, *j* and beholding your order,

JOYOUS

Isa 22. 2 stirs, a tumultuous city, a *j* city:
23. 7 Is this your *j* city, whose antiquity
32.13 all the houses of joy in the *j* city:
Heb 12.11 for the present seemeth to be *j*,

JUDA

Mt 2. 6 thou Bethlehem, in the land of *J*.
6 the least among the princes of *J*:
Mk 6. 3 of James, and Joses, and of *J*,
Lk 1.39 with haste, into a city of J;
3.26 of Joseph, which was the son of *J*,
30 of Simeon, which was the son of *J*,
33 Phares, which was the son of *J*,
Heb 7.14 that our Lord sprang out of *J*;
Rev 5. 5 behold, the Lion of the tribe of *J*,
7. 5 Of the tribe of *J* were sealed

JUDAH

Gen 29.35 therefore she called his name *J*;
35.23 and Levi, and *J*, and Issachar, and
38. 1 *J* went down from his brethren,
15 When *J* saw her, he thought her to
26 *J* acknowledged them, and said,
43. 3 *J* spake unto him, saying, The man
8 *J* said unto Israel his father, Send
46.12 the sons of *J*; Er, and Onan, and
28 he sent *J* before him unto Joseph,

49. 8 *J*, thou art he whom thy brethren
9 *J* is a lion's whelp: from the prey,
10 sceptre shall not depart from *J*,
Ex 1. 2 Reuben, Simeon, Levi, and *J*,
31. 2 the son of Hur, of the tribe of *J*:
Nu 1. 7 *J*; Nahshon the son of Amminadab.
27 of them, even of the tribe of *J*,
2. 3 of the standard of the camp of *J*
9 numbered in the camp of *J* were an
7.12 of Amminadab, of the tribe of *J*:
26.19 The sons of *J* were Er and Onan:
34.19 Of the tribe of *J*, Caleb the son of
Dt 27.12 and Levi, and *J*, and Issachar, and
33. 7 this is the blessing of *J*: and he
34. 2 all the land of *J*, unto the utmost
Jos 7. 1 son of Zerah, of the tribe of *J*, took
16 and the tribe of *J* was taken:
17 he brought the family of *J*; and he
18 Zerah, of the tribe of *J*, was taken.
15. 1 lot of the tribe of the children of *J*
20, 21 of the tribe of the children of *J*
18. 5 *J* shall abide in their coast on the
21. 4 had by lot out of the tribe of *J*,
9 out of the tribe of the children of *J*,
Jdg 1. 2 And the Lord said, *J* shall go up:
19 Lord was with *J*; and he drave out
10. 9 over Jordan to fight also against *J*,
15. 9 Philistines went...and pitched in *J*.
10 men of *J* said, Why are ye come up
Ru 1. 7 way to return unto the land of *J*.
4.12 Pharez, whom Tamar bare unto *J*,
1Sa 11. 8 and the men of *J* thirty thousand.
18.16 But all Israel and *J* loved David,
22. 5 and get thee into the land of *J*.
23. 3 Behold, we be afraid here in *J*:
23 throughout all the thousands of *J*.
2Sa 1.18 children of *J* the use of the bow:
2. 1 I go up into any of the cities of *J*?
4 the men of *J* came, and there they
3. 8 which against *J* do shew kindness
5. 5 he reigned over *J* seven years and
11.11 and Israel, and *J*, abide in tents;
19.11 Speak unto the elders of *J*, saying,
14 bowed the heart of all the men of *J*,
15 *J* came to Gilgal, to go to meet the
43 words of the men of *J* were fiercer
20. 2 the men of *J* clave unto their king,
4 Assemble me the men of *J* within
24. 1 to say, Go, number Israel and *J*.
9 of *J* were five hundred thousand
1Ki 1. 9 the men of *J* the king's servants:
2.32 of Jether, captain of the host of *J*.
4.20 *J* and Israel were many, as the
25 *J* and Israel dwelt safely, every
12.17 which dwelt in the cities of *J*,
20 of David, but the tribe of *J* only.
32 like unto the feast that is in *J*,
14.21 the son of Solomon reigned in *J*.
22 *J* did evil in the sight of the Lord,
15. 1 of Nebat reigned Abijam over *J*.
9 king of Israel reigned Asa over *J*.
22. 2 king of *J* came down to the king
41 son of Asa began to reign over *J*
2Ki 1.17 the son of Jehoshaphat king of *J*;
8.16 Jehoshaphat being then king of *J*,
19 Lord would not destroy *J* for David
20 revolted from under the hand of *J*,
22 revolted from under the hand of *J*
9.16 of *J* was come down to see Joram.
29 began Ahaziah to reign over *J*.
14. 1 Amaziah the son of Joash king of *J*.
10 fall, even thou, and *J* with thee?
12 And *J* was put to the worse before
22 built Elath, and restored it to *J*,
15. 1 son of Amaziah king of *J* to reign.
37 the Lord began to send against *J*
17. 1 the twelfth year of Ahaz king of *J*
13 against Israel, and against *J*,
18 none left but the tribe of *J* only.
19 Also *J* kept not the commandments
21.11 Manasseh king of *J* hath done these

12 such evil upon Jerusalem and *J*,
23. 1 the elders of *J* and of Jerusalem.
17 man of God, which came from *J*,
26 his anger was kindled against *J*,
27 will remove *J* also out of my sight,
24. 2 sent them against *J* to destroy it,
3 of the Lord came this upon *J*,
25.21 *J* was carried away out of their
22 that remained in the land of *J*,
1Ch 2. 1 Simeon, Levi, and *J*, Issachar,
3 the sons of *J*; Er, and Onan, and
4. 1 The sons of *J*; Pharez, Hezron,
5. 2 *J* prevailed above his brethren,
6.15 Lord carried away *J* and Jerusalem
65 of the tribe of the children of *J*,
27.18 Of *J*, Elihu, one of the brethren of
28. 4 he hath chosen *J* to be the ruler;
2Ch 2. 7 cunning men that are with me in *J*
10.17 Israel that dwelt in the cities of *J*,
12. 4 fenced cities which pertained to *J*,
12 and also in *J* things went well.
13. 1 began Abijah to reign over *J*.
13 so they were before *J*, and the
15 Then the men of *J* gave a shout:
16 the children of Israel fled before *J*:
14. 4 commanded *J* to seek the Lord God
15. 2 me, Asa, and all *J* and Benjamin;
15 And all *J* rejoiced at the oath:
16. 1 king of Israel came up against *J*,
17. 2 forces in all the fenced cities of *J*,
6 high places and groves out of *J*.
9 they taught in *J*, and had the book
20. 3 proclaimed a fast throughout all *J*.
13 all *J* stood before the Lord, with
21. 3 things, with fenced cities in *J*:
8 from under the dominion of *J*,
10 revolted from under the hand of *J*
11 high places in the mountains of *J*,
13 hast made *J* and the inhabitants
25. 5 Amaziah gathered *J* together, and
10 was greatly kindled against *J*,
19 fall, even thou, and *J* with thee?
22 *J* was put to the worse before
26. 1 all the people of *J* took Uzziah,
2 built Eloth, and restored it to *J*,
28. 6 slew in *J* a hundred and twenty
9 of your fathers was wroth with *J*,
19 brought *J* low because of Ahaz
29. 8 the wrath of the Lord was upon *J*
21 and for the sanctuary, and for *J*.
30. 1 Hezekiah sent to all Israel and *J*,
12 in *J* the hand of God was to give
25 the congregation of *J*, with the
32. 1 entered into *J*, and encamped
25 was wrath upon him, and upon *J*
33 all *J* and the inhabitants of
33. 9 Manasseh made *J* and the
16 commanded *J* to serve the Lord
34. 3 twelfth year he began to purge *J*
5 and cleansed *J* and Jerusalem.
21 that are left in Israel and in *J*,
35.18 all *J* and Israel that was present,
24 all *J* and Jerusalem mourned for
Ezr 1. 2 house at Jerusalem, which is in *J*.
3. 9 his sons, the sons of *J*, together,
5. 1 unto the Jews that were in *J*
7.14 to inquire concerning *J* and
9. 9 to give us a wall in *J* and in
10. 7 made proclamation throughout *J*
9 men of *J* and Benjamin gathered
23 Kelita,) Pethahiah, *J*, and Eliezer.
Neh 1. 2 came, he and certain men of *J*;
2. 5 thou wouldest send me unto *J*,
7 convey me over till I come into *J*;
6. 7 saying, There is a king in *J*:
17 nobles of *J* sent many letters unto
11. 3 in the cities of *J* dwelt every one
9 *J* the son of Senuah was second
12. 8 Sherebiah, *J*, and Mattaniah,
44 *J* rejoiced for the priests and for
13.12 brought all *J* the tithe of the corn

15 days saw I in *J* some treading
Ps 48.11 let the daughters of *J* be glad,
76. 1 In *J* is God known: his name is
78.68 But chose the tribe of *J*, the
108. 8 of mine head; *J* is my lawgiver;
114. 2 *J* was his sanctuary, and Israel
Isa 1. 1 which he saw concerning *J* and
2. 1 the son of Amoz saw concerning *J*
3. 1 and from *J* the stay and the staff,
8 Jerusalem is ruined, and *J* is fallen:
5. 3 men of *J*, judge, I pray you,
7 the men of *J* his pleasant plant:
7. 1 the son of Uzziah, king of *J*,
6 Let us go up against *J*, and vex it,
17 that Ephraim departed from *J*;
8. 8 he shall pass through *J*; he shall
9.21 they together shall be against *J*.
11.12 gather together the dispersed of *J*
13 adversaries of *J* shall be cut off:
19.17 the land of *J* shall be a terror unto
22. 8 he discovered the covering of *J*,
26. 1 this song be sung in the land of *J*;
48. 1 come forth out of the waters of *J*,
65. 9 *J* an inheritor of my mountains:
Jer 1. 2 Josiah the son of Amon king of *J*,
2.28 of thy cities are thy gods, O *J*.
3. 7 her treacherous sister *J* saw it.
8 treacherous sister *J* feared not,
4. 3 saith the Lord to the men of *J*
4 Ye men of *J* and inhabitants of
5 Declare ye in *J*, and publish in
5.11 the house of *J* have dealt very
20 of Jacob, and publish it in *J*,
7. 2 the word of the Lord, all ye of *J*,
9.11 will make the cities of *J* desolate,
26 *J*, and Edom, and the children of
11. 2 speak unto the men of *J*, and to
9 is found among the men of *J*,
13. 9 manner will I mar the pride of *J*,
19 *J* shall be carried away captive all
14. 2 *J* mourneth, and the gates thereof
19 Hast thou utterly rejected *J*? hath
17. 1 sin of *J* is written with a pen of
19. 3 word of the Lord, O kings of *J*,
7 I will make void the counsel of *J*
20. 4 give all *J* into the hand of the king
22. 1 down to the house of the king of *J*,
30 David, and ruling any more in *J*.
23. 6 In his days *J* shall be saved, and
30. 3 the captivity of my people...*J*,
4 spake concerning Israel and...*J*.
31.23 use this speech in the land of *J*
32. 1 tenth year of Zedekiah king of *J*,
35 this abomination, to cause *J* to sin.
33. 4 the houses of the kings of *J*,
7 And I will cause the captivity of *J*
16 In those days shall *J* be saved, and
36. 1 Jehoiakim...of Josiah king of *J*,
2 thee against Israel, and against *J*,
31 and upon the men of *J*, all the evil
39. 1 ninth year of Zedekiah king of *J*,
10 which had nothing, in the land of *J*,
42.15 word of the Lord, ye remnant of *J*;
43. 4 the Lord, to dwell in the land of *J*.
9 in the sight of the men of *J*;
44. 2 and upon all the cities of *J*;
9 have committed in the land of *J*,
11 you for evil, and to cut off all *J*.
14 should return into the land of *J*.
26 in the mouth of any man of *J* in all
27 all man of *J* that are in the land of
50. 4 they and the children of *J* together,
20 the sins of *J*, and they shall not be
51. 5 been forsaken, nor *J* of his God,
52. 3 came to pass in Jerusalem and *J*,
27 *J* was carried away captive out of
La 1. 3 *J* is gone into captivity because of
Eze 4. 6 bear the iniquity of the house of *J*
21.20 to *J* in Jerusalem the defensed.
27.17 *J*, and the land of Israel, they were
37.16 For *J*, and for the children of Israel

Eze 48. 7 unto the west side, a portion for *J*.
31 one gate of *J*, one gate of Levi.
Dan 1. 1 of the reign of Jehoiakim king of *J*
9. 7 to the men of *J*, and to the
Hos 1. 1 Ahaz, and Hezekiah, kings of *J*,
4.15 the harlot, yet let not *J* offend;
5. 5 *J* also shall fall with them.
13 his sickness, and *J* saw his wound,
6. 4 O *J*, what shall I do unto thee?
10.11 *J* shall plow, and Jacob shall break
11.12 but *J* yet ruleth with God, and is
12. 2 hath also a controversy with *J*,
Joel 3. 1 shall bring again the captivity of *J*
20 But *J* shall dwell forever, and
Am 1. 1 in the days of Uzziah king of *J*,
2. 4 For three transgressions of *J*, and
5 I will send a fire upon *J*, and it
7.12 flee thee away into the land of *J*,
Mic 1. 1 Ahaz, and Hesekiah, kings of *J*,
9 is incurable; for it is come unto *J*;
5. 2 be little among the thousands of *J*,
Zep 1. 1 Josiah the son of Amon, king of *J*.
4 also stretch out mine hand upon *J*,
Zec 1.12 on Jerusalem and on the cities of *J*,
19, 21 horns which have scattered *J*,
21 horn over the land of *J* to scatter
2.12 the Lord shall inherit *J* his portion
9. 7 God, and he be as a governor in *J*,
13 have bent *J* for me, filled the bow
12. 2 be in the siege both against *J* and
7 also shall save the tents of *J* first,
14. 5 in the days of Uzziah king of *J*:
14 *J* also shall fight at Jerusalem;
21 every pot in Jerusalem and in *J*
Mal 2.11 *J* hath dealt treacherously, and
3. 4 shall the offering of *J*...be pleasant
Heb 8. 8 of Israel and with the house of *J*:

JUDAS

Mt 1. 2 Jacob begat *J* and his brethren;
3 And *J* begat Phares and Zara of
10. 4 *J* Iscariot, who also betrayed him.
13.55 and Joses, and Simon, and *J*?
26.14 twelve, called *J* Iscariot, went
25 *J*, which betrayed him, answered
47 lo, *J*, one of the twelve, came,
27. 3 *J*, which had betrayed him, when
Mk 3.19 *J* Iscariot, which also betrayed
14.10 *J* Iscariot, one of the twelve, went
43 cometh *J*, one of the twelve, and
Lk 6.16 And *J* the brother of James, and
16 *J* Iscariot, which...was the traitor.
22. 3 Satan into *J* surnamed Iscariot,
47 and he that was called *J*, one of
48 *J*, betrayest thou the Son of man
Jn 6.71 He spake of *J* Iscariot the son of
12. 4 disciples, *J* Iscariot, Simon's son,
13. 2 put into the heart of *J* Iscariot,
26 the sop, he gave it to *J* Iscariot,
29 thought, because *J* had the bag,
14.22 *J* saith to him, not Iscariot, Lord,
18. 2 *J* also, which betrayed him, knew
3 *J* then, having received a band of
5 *J* also, which betrayed him, stood
Ac 1.13 and *J* the brother of James.
16 David spake before concerning *J*,
25 from which *J* by transgression fell,
5.37 After this man rose up *J* of Galilee
9.11 the house of *J* for one called Saul,
15.22 *J* surnamed Barsabas, and Silas,
27 have sent therefore *J* and Silas,
32 *J* and Silas, being prophets also

JUDE

Jude 1 *J*, the servant of Jesus Christ,

JUDEA

Mt 2. 1 Jesus was born in Bethlehem of *J*
5 said unto him, In Bethlehem of *J*:
22 heard that Archelaus did reign in *J*
3. 1 preaching in the wilderness of *J*,
5 out to him Jerusalem, and all *J*,
4.25 and from Jerusalem, and from *J*,
19. 1 the coasts of *J* beyond Jordan;
24.16 be in *J* flee into the mountains:
Mk 1. 5 out unto him all the land of *J*,
3. 7 Galilee followed him, and from *J*,
10. 1 and cometh into the coasts of *J*
13.14 that be in *J* flee to the mountains:
Lk 1. 5 the days of Herod, the king of *J*,
65 all the hill country of *J*.
2. 4 out of the city of Nazareth, into *J*,
3. 1 Pontius Pilate being governor of *J*,
5.17 out of every town of Galilee, and *J*,
6.17 multitude of people out of all *J*
7.17 him went forth throughout all *J*,
21.21 are in *J* flee to the mountains;
Jn 3.22 his disciples into the land of *J*;
4. 3 He left *J*, and departed again into
47 that Jesus was come out of *J* into
54 he was come out of *J* into Galilee.
7. 3 Depart hence, and go into *J*, that
11. 7 disciples, Let us go into *J* again.
Ac 1. 8 and in all *J*, and in Samaria, and
2. 9 dwellers in Mesopotamia, and in *J*,
14 Ye men of *J*, and all ye that dwell
8. 1 the regions of *J* and Samaria,
9.31 rest throughout all *J* and Galilee
10.37 was published throughout all *J*,
11. 1 and brethren that were in *J* heard
29 unto the brethren which dwelt in *J*:
12.19 he went down from *J* to Caesarea,
15. 1 men which came down from *J*
21.10 there came down from *J* a certain
26.20 and throughout all the coasts of *J*,
28.21 neither received letters out of *J*
Ro 15.31 from them that do not believe in *J*;
2Co 1.16 be brought on my way toward *J*.
Gal 1.22 by face unto the churches of *J*
1Th 2.14 which in *J* are in Christ Jesus:

JUDGE

Gen 16. 5 the Lord *j* between me and thee.
18.25 not the *J* of all the earth do right?
Ex 2.14 thee a prince and a *j* over us?
18.22 every small matter they shall *j*:
Dt 1.16 *j* righteously between every man
17. 9 the *j* that shall be in those days,
Jdg 2.18 their enemies all the days of the *j*:
11.27 Lord the *J* be *j* this day between
1Sa 2.10 Lord shall *j* the ends of the earth;
8. 5 make us a king to *j* us like all the
6 they said, Give us a king to *j* us.
24.12 The Lord *j* between me and thee,
2Sa 15. 4 Oh that I were made *j* in the land,
1Ki 3. 9 for who is able to *j* this thy so great
2Ch 19. 6 ye *j* not for man, but for the Lord,
Job 9.15 would make supplication to my *j*.
23. 7 I be delivered for ever from my *j*.
Ps 7. 8 The Lord shall *j* the people:
8 *j* me, O Lord, according to my
9. 8 shall *j* the world in righteousness,
10.18 *j* the fatherless and the oppressed,
26. 1 *J* me, O Lord; for I have walked
43. 1 *J* me, O God, and plead my cause
50. 6 for God is *j* himself.
68. 5 a *j* of the widows, is God in his
72. 4 He shall *j* the poor of the people,
75. 7 God is the *j*: he putteth down one,
82. 2 How long will ye *j* unjustly, and
8 Arise, O God, *j* the earth: for thou
96.13 for he cometh to *j* the earth:
110. 6 He shall *j* among the heathen, he
Isa 1.17 *j* the fatherless, plead for the
5. 3 *j*, I pray you, betwixt me and
33.22 the Lord is our *j*, the Lord is our
Jer 5.28 they *j* not the cause, the cause of
28 right of the needy do they not *j*.
Eze 7.27 to their deserts will I *j* them;
18.30 Therefore I will *j* you, O house of
22. 2 Now, thou son of man, wilt thou *j*,
33.20 I will *j* you every one after his ways.
Joel 3.12 there will I sit to *j* all the heathen
Mt 5.25 adversary deliver thee to the *j*,
25 the *j* deliver thee to the officer,
7. 1 *J* not, that ye be not judged.
2 with what judgment ye *j*, ye shall
Lk 6.37 *J* not, and ye shall not be judged:
12.14 made me a *j* or a divider over you?
57 yourselves *j* ye not what is right?
58 him; lest he hale thee to the *j*,
58 and the *j* deliver thee to the officer,
18. 2 There was in a city a *j*, which
6 said, Hear what the unjust *j* saith.
19.22 of thine own mouth will I *j* thee,
Jn 5.30 as I hear, I *j*: and my judgment
7.24 *J* not according to the appearance,
24 but *j* righteous judgment.
51 Doth our law *j* any man, before it
8.15 Ye *j* after the flesh; I *j* no man.
16 And yet if I *j*, my judgment is true:
26 many things to say and to *j* of you:
12.47 words, and believe not, I *j* him not:
47 for I came not to *j* the world, but to
48 the same shall *j* him in the last day.
18.31 and *j* him according to your law.
Ac 4.19 you more than unto God, *j* ye.
7. 7 they shall be in bondage will I *j*,
27 made thee a ruler and *j* over us?
35 Who made thee a ruler and a *j*?
10.42 to be the *J* of quick and dead.
13.46 *j* yourselves unworthy of...life,
17.31 will *j* the world in righteousness
18.15 for I will be no *j* of such matters.
23. 3 sittest thou to *j* me after the law,
24.10 thou hast been of many years a *j*
Ro 2.16 God shall *j* the secrets of men
27 if it fulfil the law, *j* thee, who by
3. 6 then how shall God *j* the world?
14. 3 which eateth not *j* him that eateth:
10 But why dost thou *j* thy brother?
13 Let us not therefore *j* one another
13 but *j* this rather, that no man put
1Co 4. 3 yea, I *j* not mine own self.
5 *j* nothing before the time, until
5.12 to *j* them also that are without?
12 do not ye *j* them that are within?
6. 2 that the saints shall *j* the world?
2 are ye unworthy to *j* the smallest
3 ye not that we shall *j* angels?
4 them to *j* who are least esteemed
5 be able to *j* between his brethren?
10.15 as to wise men; *j* ye what I say.
11.13 *J* in yourselves: is it comely that
31 we would *j* ourselves, we should
14.29 two or three, and let the others *j*.
2Co 5.14 because we thus *j*, that if one
Col 2.16 Let no man therefore *j* you in
2Ti 4. 1 who shall *j* the quick and the dead
8 which the Lord, the righteous *j*,
Heb 10.30 again, The Lord shall *j* his people.
12.23 to God the *J* of all, and to the
13. 4 and adulterers God will *j*.
Jas 4.11 the law: but if thou *j* the law,
11 art not a doer of the law, but a *j*.
5. 9 the *j* standeth before the door.
1Pe 4. 5 ready to *j* the quick and the dead.
Rev 6.10 thou not *j* and avenge our blood
19.11 he doth *j* and make war.

JUDGED

Gen 30. 6 And Rachel said, God hath *j* me,
Ex 18.26 small matter they *j* themselves.
Ps 9.19 let the heathen be *j* in thy sight.
37.33 nor condemn him when he is *j*.
Jer 22.16 He *j* the cause of the poor and
Dan 9.12 and against our judges that *j* us,
Mt 7. 1 Judge not, that ye be not *j*.
2 judgment ye judge, ye shall be *j*:
Lk 6.37 Judge not, and ye shall not be *j*:
7.43 said unto him, Thou hast rightly *j*.
Jn 16.11 because the prince of this world is *j*.
Ac 16.15 If ye have *j* me to be faithful to

24. 6 would have *j* according to our law.
25. 9 be *j* of these things before me?
10 seat, where I ought to be *j*: to the
20 and there be *j* of these matters.
26. 6 now I stand and am *j* for the hope
Ro 2.12 in the law shall be *j* by the law;
3. 4 mightest overcome when thou art *j*
7 why yet am I also *j* as a sinner?
1Co 2.15 things, yet he himself is *j* of no man.
4. 3 thing that I should be *j* of you,
5. 3 present in spirit, have *j* already,
6. 2 if the world shall be *j* by you, are
10.29 why is my liberty *j* of another
11.31 ourselves, we should not be *j*.
32 when we are *j*, we are chastened
14.24 he is convinced of all, he is *j* of all:
Heb 11.11 she *j* him faithful who had
Jas 2.12 as they that shall be *j* by the law
1Pe 4. 6 they might be *j* according to men
Rev 11.18 of the dead, that they should be *j*,
16. 5 shalt be, because thou hast *j* thus.
19. 2 for he hath *j* the great whore,
20.12 the dead were *j* out of those things
13 they were *j* every man according to

JUDGES

Ex 21.22 he shall pay as the *j* determine.
22. 8 house shall be brought unto the *j*,
9 parties shall come before the *j*;
Dt 16.18 *J* and officers shalt thou make
19.18 *j* shall make diligent inquisition:
Jdg 2.16 Nevertheless the Lord raised up *j*,
2Ch 19. 6 said to the *j*, Take heed what ye do:
Job 12.17 spoiled, and maketh the *j* fools.
31.11 iniquity to be punished by the *j*.
Ps 2.10 be instructed, ye *j* of the earth.
Pr 8.16 nobles, even all the *j* of the earth.
Isa 1.26 I will restore thy *j* as at the first,
40.23 maketh the *j* of the earth as vanity.
Zep 3. 3 her *j* are evening wolves; they
Mt 12.27 therefore they shall be your *j*.
Lk 11.19 therefore shall they be your *j*.
Ac 13.20 And after that he gave unto them *j*
Jas 2. 4 And are become *j* of evil thoughts?

JUDGEST

Ps 51. 4 and be clear when thou *j*.
Jer 11.20 O Lord of hosts, that *j* righteously,
Ro 2. 1 O man, whosoever thou art that *j*:
1 for wherein thou *j* another, thou
1 thou that *j* doest the same things.
3 that *j* them which do such things,
14. 4 Who art thou that *j* another man's
Jas 4.12 who art thou that *j* another?

JUDGETH

Job 21.22 seeing he *j* those that are high.
36.31 by them *j* he the people; he giveth
Ps 7.11 God *j* the righteous, and God is
58.11 he is a God that *j* in the earth.
82. 1 the mighty; he *j* among the gods.
Pr 29.14 The king that faithfully *j* the poor,
Jn 5.22 the Father *j* no man, but hath
8.50 there is one that seeketh and *j*.
12.48 not my words, hath one that *j* him:
1Co 2.15 But he that is spiritual *j* all things,
4. 4 but he that *j* me is the Lord.
5.13 But them that are without God *j*.
Jas 4.11 evil...brother, and *j* his brother,
11 evil of the law, and *j* the law:
1Pe 1.17 *j* according to every man's work,
2.23 himself to him that *j* righteously:
Rev 18. 8 strong is the Lord God who *j* her.

JUDGING

2Ki 15. 5 house, *j* the people of the land.
2Ch 26.21 house, *j* the people of the land.
Ps 9. 4 thou satest in the throne *j* right.
Isa 16. 5 of David, *j*, and seeking judgment,
Mt 19.28 *j* the twelve tribes of Israel.
Lk 22.30 thrones *j* the twelve tribes of Israel.

The Judgment to come (Mt 25) is the theme of this painting in the Museum of San Marco, Florence.

JUDGMENT

Gen 18.19 of the Lord, to do justice and *j*;
Ex 23. 6 shalt not wrest the *j* of thy poor
28.30 thou shalt put in the breastplate of *j*
Dt 1.17 ye shall not respect persons in *j*;
17 for the *j* is God's: and the cause
16.18 shall judge the people with just *j*.
17. 8 a matter too hard for thee in *j*,
32. 4 all his ways are *j*: a God of truth
2Sa 8.15 David executed *j* and justice unto
1Ki 3.11 thyself understanding to discern *j*;
28 wisdom of God was in him, to do *j*.
2Ch 19. 8 for the *j* of the Lord, and for
Job 8. 3 Doth God pervert *j*? or doth the
9.19 and if of *j*, who shall set me a time
14. 3 and bringest me into *j* with thee?
19. 7 I cry aloud, but there is no *j*.
29 that ye may know there is a *j*.
22. 4 will he enter with thee into *j*?
27. 2 liveth, who hath taken away my *j*;
29.14 my *j* was as a robe and a diadem.
32. 9 neither do the aged understand *j*.
34.23 he should enter into *j* with God.
Ps 1. 5 ungodly shall not stand in the *j*,
9. 7 he hath prepared his throne for *j*.
25. 9 The meek will he guide in *j*: and
33. 5 He loveth righteousness and *j*: the
37. 6 the light, and thy *j* as the noonday.
28 Lord loveth *j*, and forsaketh not
76. 9 God arose to *j*, to save all the
99. 4 The king's strength also loveth *j*;
101. 1 I will sing of mercy and *j*: unto
103. 6 and *j* for all that are oppressed.
106. 3 Blessed are they that keep *j*, and
119.66 Teach me good *j* and knowledge:
149 quicken me according to thy *j*.
122. 5 For there are set thrones of *j*, the
143. 2 enter not into *j* with thy servant:
146. 7 executeth *j* for the oppressed:
149. 9 execute upon them the *j* written:
Pr 13.23 is that is destroyed for want of *j*.
19.28 An ungodly witness scorneth *j*:
21. 3 To do justice and *j* is more
15 It is joy to the just to do *j*: but
28. 5 Evil men understand not *j*: but
29. 4 king by *j* establisheth the land:
Ec 3.16 I saw under the sun the place of *j*,
8. 6 every purpose there is time and *j*,
11. 9 things God will bring thee into *j*.
Isa 5. 7 and he looked for *j*, but behold
10. 2 To turn aside the needy from *j*,
28. 6 a spirit of *j* to him that sitteth in *j*,
17 *J* also will I lay to the line, and
30.18 you: for the Lord is a God of *j*:
40.27 my *j* is passed over from my God?
42. 1 shall bring forth *j* to the Gentiles.
3 he shall bring forth *j* unto truth.
49. 4 yet surely my *j* is with the Lord,
53. 8 was taken from prison and from *j*:
59. 8 there is no *j* in their goings: they
9 Therefore is *j* far from us, neither
11 we look for *j*, but there is none;
14 *j* is turned away backward, and
61. 8 I the Lord love *j*, I hate robbery
Jer 5. 1 if there be any that executeth *j*,
8. 7 people know not the *j* of the Lord.
10.24 O Lord, correct me, but with *j*;
23. 5 execute *j* and justice in the earth.
51. 9 her *j* reacheth unto heaven, and is
47 will do *j* upon the graven images
Eze 23.24 I will set *j* before them, and they
39.21 heathen shall see my *j* that I have
Dan 4.37 works are truth, and his ways *j*:
Hos 2.19 and in *j*, and in lovingkindness,
Am 5. 7 Ye who turn *j* to wormwood, and
15 good, and establish *j* in the gate:
24 But let *j* run down as waters, and
6.12 ye have turned *j* into gall, and the
Mic 3. 9 that abhor *j*, and pervert all equity.
7. 9 my cause, and execute *j* for me:
Hab 1. 4 therefore wrong *j* proceedeth.
12 thou hast ordained them for *j*;
Zep 3. 5 morning doth he bring his *j* to light,
Zec 8.16 execute the *j* of truth and peace in
Mal 2.17 them; or, Where is the God of *j*?
Mt 5.21 kill shall be in danger of the *j*:
22 a cause shall be in danger of the *j*:
7. 2 with what *j* ye judge, ye shall be
10.15 and Gomorrha in the day of *j*,
11.22 for Tyre and Sidon at the day of *j*,
24 the land of Sodom in the day of *j*,
12.18 and he shall shew *j* to the Gentiles.
20 till he send forth *j* unto victory.
36 give account thereof in the day of *j*.
41 The men of Nineveh shall rise in *j*
42 of the south shall rise up in the *j*
23.23 of the law, *j*, mercy, and faith:
27.19 he was set down on the *j* seat,
Mk 6.11 and Gomorrah in the day of *j*,
Lk 10.14 for Tyre and Sidon at the *j*, than
11.31 of the south shall rise up in the *j*
32 of Nineve shall rise up in the *j*
42 pass over *j* and the love of God:
Jn 5.22 hath committed all *j* unto the Son:
27 him authority to execute *j* also,
30 as I hear, I judge: and my *j* is just;
7.24 appearance, but judge righteous *j*.
8.16 And yet if I judge, my *j* is true:

Biblical Themes

JUSTICE

Whoso sheddeth man's blood, by man shall his blood be shed. Gen 9.6

Thou shalt give life for life, eye for eye, tooth for tooth, hand for hand, foot for foot, burning for burning, wound for wound, stripe for stripe. Ex 21.23-25

If a thief be found breaking [in], and be smitten that he die, there shall no blood be shed for him. Ex 22.2

Judge the people with just judgment. Thou shalt not wrest judgment . . . neither take a gift: for a gift doth blind the eyes of the wise. Dt 16.18-19

Deal gently for my sake with the young man. 2Sa 18.5

Unto thee, O Lord, belongeth mercy: for thou renderest to every man according to his work. Ps 62.12

Every way of a man is right in his own eyes: but the Lord pondereth the hearts. To do justice and judgment is more acceptable to the Lord than sacrifice. Pr 21.2-3

Because sentence against an evil work is not executed speedily, therefore the heart of the sons of men is fully set in them to do evil. Ec 8.11

He that diggeth a pit shall fall into it. Ec 10.8

The Lord is our judge, the Lord is our lawgiver. Isa 33.22

I the Lord search the heart, I try the reins, even to give every man according to his ways, and according to the fruit of his doings. Jer 17.10

What doth the Lord require of thee, but to do justly, and to love mercy, and to walk humbly with thy God? Mi 6.8

Blessed are the merciful: for they shall obtain mercy. Mt 5.7

If ye forgive men their trespasses, your heavenly Father will also forgive you. Mt 6.14

Judge not, that ye be not judged. Mt 7.1

They [said] unto him, Master, this woman was taken in adultery, in the very act. Now Moses in the law commanded us, that such should be stoned: but what sayest thou? . . . he lifted up himself, and said unto them, He that is without sin among you, let him first cast a stone at her. Jn 8.4-5, 7

Woman, where are those thine accusers? hath no man condemned thee? She said, No man, Lord. And Jesus said unto her, Neither do I condemn thee: go, and sin no more. Jn 8.10-11

Let every soul be subject unto the higher powers. For there is no power but of God: the powers that be are ordained of God. Ro 13.1

Every one of us shall give account of himself to God. Ro 14.12

Ye are our epistle written in our hearts . . . not in tables of stone. . . . our sufficiency is of God; who also hath made us able ministers of the new testament; not of the letter, but of the spirit. 2Co 3.2-3, 5-6

We know that the law is good, if a man use it lawfully. 1Ti 1.8

It is better, if the will of God be so, that ye suffer for well doing, than for evil doing. For Christ also hath once suffered for sins, the just for the unjust, that he might bring us to God. 1Pe 3.17-18

If any man sin, we have an advocate with the Father, Jesus Christ. 1Jn 2.1

He that is unjust, let him be unjust still. . . . And, behold, I come quickly . . . to give every man according as his work shall be. Rev 22.11-12

Jn 9.39 For *j* I am come into this world,
12.31 Now is the *j* of this world: now
16. 8 sin, and of righteousness, and of *j*:
11 Of *j*, because the prince of this
18.28 from Caiaphas unto the hall of *j*:
28 went not into the *j* hall, lest they
33 Pilate entered into the *j* hall
19. 9 And went again into the *j* hall,
13 and sat down in the *j* seat in a
Ac 8.33 humiliation his *j* was taken away:
18.12 Paul, and brought him to the *j* seat,
16 And he drave them from the *j* seat.
17 and beat him before the *j* seat.
23.35 him to be kept in Herod's *j* hall.
24.25 temperance, and *j* to come,
25. 6 the next day sitting on the *j* seat
10 said Paul, I stand at Caesar's *j* seat,
15 desiring to have *j* against him.
17 on the morrow I sat on the *j* seat,
Ro 1.32 Who knowing the *j* of God, that
2. 2 the *j* of God is according to truth
3 that thou shalt escape the *j* of God?
5 of the righteous *j* of God;
5.16 the *j* was by one to condemnation,
18 by the offense of one *j* came upon all
14.10 all stand before the *j* seat of Christ.
1Co 1.10 the same mind and in the same *j*.
4. 3 be judged of you, or of man's *j*:
7.25 yet I give my *j*, as one that hath
40 happier if she so abide, after my *j*:
2Co 5.10 appear before the *j* seat of Christ;
Gal 5.10 that troubleth you shall bear his *j*,
Php 1. 9 more in knowledge and in all *j*;
2Th 1. 5 token of the righteous *j* of God,
1Ti 5.24 open beforehand, going before to *j*;
Heb 6. 2 of the dead, and of eternal *j*.
9.27 once to die, but after this the *j*:
10.27 certain fearful looking for of *j* and
Jas 2. 6 and draw you before the *j* seats?
13 For he shall have *j* without mercy,
13 and mercy rejoiceth against *j*.
1Pe 4.17 time is come that *j* must begin
2Pe 2. 3 *j* now of a long time lingereth
4 darkness, to be reserved unto *j*;
9 reserve the unjust unto the day of *j*
3. 7 against the day of *j* and perdition
1Jn 4.17 may have boldness in the day of *j*:
Jude 6 unto the *j* of the great day.
15 To execute *j* upon all, and to
Rev 14. 7 him; for the hour of his *j* is come:
17. 1 thee the *j* of the great whore
18.10 for in one hour is thy *j* come.
20. 4 them, and *j* was given unto them:

JUDGMENTS

Lev 18. 5 keep my statutes, and my *j*:
Dt 4.14 time to teach you statutes and *j*,
6. 1 and the *j*, which the Lord your God
12. 1 These are the statutes and *j*, which
1Ki 2. 3 and his *j*, and his testimonies,
1Ch 16.14 our God; his *j* are in all the earth.
Ps 10. 5 thy *j* are far above out of his sight:
19. 9 the *j* of the Lord are true and
72. 1 Give the king thy *j*, O God, and thy
105. 7 our God: his *j* are all in the earth.
119.13 I declared all the *j* of thy mouth.
30 truth: thy *j* have I laid before me.
39 which I fear: for thy *j* are good.
52 I remembered thy *j* of old, O Lord;
175 praise thee; and let thy *j* help me.
Pr 19.29 *J* are prepared for scorners, and
Isa 26. 9 for when thy *j* are in the earth,
Jer 1.16 And I will utter my *j* against them
Eze 5. 6 for they have refused my *j* and my
10 and I will execute *j* in thee,
20.19 walk in my statutes, and keep my *j*,
Hos 6. 5 thy *j* are as the light that goeth
Zep 3.15 the Lord hath taken away thy *j*,
Ro 11.33 how unsearchable are his *j*, and
1Co 6. 4 ye have *j* of things pertaining to
Rev 15. 4 thee; for thy *j* are made manifest.
16. 7 true and righteous are thy *j*.
19. 2 For true and righteous are his *j*:

JULIA

Ro 16.15 Salute Philologus, and *J*, Nereus,

JULIUS

Ac 27. 1 unto one named *J*, a centurion of
3 And *J* courteously entreated Paul,

JUNIA

Ro 16. 7 Salute Andronicus and *J*, my

JUNIPER

1Ki 19. 4 and sat down under a *j* tree:
5 as he lay and slept under a *j* tree,
Job 30. 4 bushes, and *j* roots for their meat.
Ps 120. 4 of the mighty, with coals of *j*.

JUPITER

Ac 14.12 And they called Barnabas, *J*;
13 Then the priest of *J*, which was
19.35 image which fell down from J?

JURISDICTION

Lk 23. 7 that he belonged unto Herod's *j*,

K

KEEP
Gen 3.24 way, to *k* the way of the tree of life.
17.10 is my covenant, which ye shall *k*,
18.19 they shall *k* the way of the Lord,
28.20 and will *k* me in this way that I go,
Ex 12.14 ye shall *k* it a feast to the Lord
48 and will *k* the passover to the Lord,
20. 6 love me, and *k* my commandments.
8 the sabbath day, to *k* it holy.
Nu 6.24 The Lord bless thee, and *k* thee:
9. 2 of Israel also *k* the passover at
Dt 5.12 *K* the sabbath day to sanctify it,
6.17 diligently *k* the commandments of
16. 1 *k* the passover unto the Lord
29. 9 *K*...the words of this covenant,
Jdg 3.19 thee, O king: who said, *K* silence.
1Sa 7. 1 his son to *k* the ark of the Lord.
2Sa 18.18 I have no son to *k* my name in
1Ki 2. 3 *k* the charge of the Lord thy God,
20.39 unto me, and said, *K* this man:
1Ch 4.10 that thou wouldest *k* me from evil,
22.12 mayest *k* the law of the Lord thy
Job 14.13 *k* me secret, until thy wrath be
Ps 12. 7 Thou shalt *k* them, O Lord, thou
17. 8 *K* me as the apple of the eye,
19.13 *K* back thy servant also from
22.29 and none can *k* alive his own soul.
25.10 such as *k* his covenant and his
20 O *k* my soul, and deliver me: let
34.13 *K* thy tongue from evil, and thy
37.34 Wait on the Lord, and *k* his way,
39. 1 I will *k* my mouth with a bridle,
50. 3 come, and shall not *k* silence:
83. 1 *K* not thou silence, O God: hold not
103. 9 neither will he *k* his anger for
18 To such as *k* his covenant, and to
119. 8 I will *k* thy statutes: O forsake
33 and I shall *k* it unto the end.
129 therefore doth my soul *k* them.
127. 1 except the Lord *k* the city, the
140. 4 *K* me, O Lord, from the hands of
141. 3 my mouth; *k* the door of my lips.
Pr 2.20 and *k* the paths of the righteous.
3.21 *k* sound wisdom and discretion:
6.20 son, *k* thy father's commandment,
24 To *k* thee from the evil woman,
7. 5 *k* thee from the strange woman,
8.32 blessed are they that *k* my ways.
Ec 3. 6 time to *k*, and a time to cast away;
7 time to *k* silence, and a time to speak;
Isa 26. 3 Thou wilt *k* him in perfect peace,
41. 1 *K* silence before me, O islands;
Jer 3.12 and I will not *k* anger for ever,
La 2.10 sit upon the ground, and *k* silence:
Am 5.13 the prudent shall *k* silence in that
Mic 7. 5 *k* the doors of thy mouth from
Hab 2.20 let all the earth *k* silence before him.
Mal 2. 7 priest's lips should *k* knowledge,
Mt 19.17 into life, *k* the commandments.
26.18 I will *k* the passover at thy house
Mk 7. 9 that ye may *k* your own tradition.
Lk 4.10 charge over thee, to *k* thee:
8.15 having heard the word, *k* it.
11.28 hear the word of God, and *k* it.
19.43 and *k* thee in on every side,
Jn 8.51, 52 If a man *k* my saying, he shall
55 but I know him, and *k* his saying.
12.25 world shall *k* it unto life eternal.
14.15 ye love me, *k* my commandments.
23 a man love me, he will *k* my words:
15.10 If ye *k* my commandments, ye
20 my saying, they will *k* yours also.
17.11 Holy Father, *k* through thine own
15 shouldest *k* them from the evil.
Ac 5. 3 to *k* back part of the price of the
10.28 man that is a Jew to *k* company,
12. 4 quaternions of soldiers to *k* him,
15. 5 them to *k* the law of Moses.
24 be circumcised, and *k* the law:
29 from which if ye *k* yourselves, ye
16. 4 deliver them the decrees for to *k*,
23 the jailor to *k* them safely:
18.21 I must by all means *k* this feast
21.25 only that they *k* themselves from
24.23 a centurion to *k* Paul, and
Ro 2.25 verily profiteth, if thou *k* the law:
26 *k* the righteousness of the law,
1Co 5. 8 Therefore let us *k* the feast, not
11 unto you not to *k* company,
7.37 heart that he will *k* his virgin,
9.27 I *k* under my body, and bring it
11. 2 *k* the ordinances, as I delivered
14.28 let him *k* silence in the church;
34 women *k* silence in the churches:
15. 2 ye *k* in memory what I preached
2Co 11. 9 unto you, and so will I *k* myself.
Gal 6.13 who are circumcised *k* the law;
Eph 4. 3 to *k* the unity of the Spirit in the
Php 4. 7 shall *k* your hearts and minds
2Th 3. 3 stablish you, and *k* you from evil.
1Ti 5.22 other men's sins: *k* thyself pure.
6.14 *k* this commandment without
20 *k* that which is committed to thy
2Ti 1.12 *k* that which I have committed
14 unto thee *k* by the Holy Ghost
Jas 1.27 to *k* himself unspotted from the
2.10 whosoever shall *k* the whole law,
1Jn 2. 3 him, if we *k* his commandments.
3.22 because we *k* his commandments,
5. 2 God, and *k* his commandments.
3 that we *k* his commandments:
21 children, *k* yourselves from idols.
Jude 21 *K* yourselves in the love of God,
24 that is able to *k* you from falling,
Rev 1. 3 *k* those things which are written
3.10 also will *k* thee from the hour of
12.17 which *k* the commandments of
14.12 that *k* the commandments of God,
22. 9 which *k* the sayings of this book:

KEEPER
Gen 4. 2 Abel was a *k* of the sheep, but
9 know not: Am I my brother's *k*?
39.21 the sight of the *k* of the prison.
22 the *k* of the prison committed to
23 The *k* of the prison looked not to
1Sa 17.20 and left the sheep with a *k*,
22 carriage in the hand of the *k* of
28. 2 make thee *k* of mine head for ever.
2Ki 22.14 son of Harhas, *k* of the wardrobe;
2Ch 34.22 son of Hasrah, *k* of the wardrobe;
Neh 2. 8 Asaph the *k* of the king's forest,
3.29 Shemaiah...the *k* of the east gate.
Est 2. 3 chamberlain, *k* of the women;
8 custody of Hegai, *k* of the women.
15 chamberlain, the *k* of the women,
Job 27.18 and as a booth that the *k* maketh.
Ps 121. 5 The Lord is thy *k*: the Lord is thy
SS 1. 6 made me *k* of the vineyards; but
Jer 35. 4 Maaseiah...the *k* of the door:
Ac 16.27 the *k* of the prison awaking out
36 the *k* of the prison told this

KEEPERS
2Ki 11. 5 even be *k* of the watch of the
22. 4 which the *k* of the door have
23. 4 the *k* of the door, to bring forth
25.18 priest, and the three *k* of the door:
1Ch 9.19 *k* of the gates of the tabernacle:
19 of the Lord, were *k* of the entry.
Est 6. 2 chamberlains, the *k* of the door,
Ec 12. 3 day when the *k* of the house shall
SS 5. 7 *k* of the walls took away any veil
8.11 he let out the vineyard unto *k*;
Jer 4.17 As *k* of a field, are they against
52.24 and the three *k* of the door:
Eze 40.45 the *k* of the charge of the house.
46 the *k* of the charge of the altar:
44. 8 ye have set *k* of my charge in my
14 them *k* of the charge of the house,
Mt 28. 4 for fear of him the *k* did shake,
Ac 5.23 *k* standing without before the
12. 6 *k* before the door kept the prison.
19 him not, he examined the *k*, and
Tit 2. 5 discreet, chaste, *k* at home, good,

KEEPEST
1Ki 8.23 who *k* convenant and mercy with
2Ch 6.14 which *k* covenant, and shewest
Neh 9.32 who *k* covenant and mercy, let not
Ac 21.24 walkest orderly, and *k* the law.

KEEPETH
Dt 7. 9 *k* covenant and mercy with them
1Sa 16.11 and, behold, he *k* the sheep.
Job 33.18 He *k* back his soul from the pit,
Ps 121. 3 he that *k* thee will not slumber.
4 he that *k* Israel shall neither
Pr 2. 8 He *k* the paths of judgment, and
21.23 Whoso *k* his mouth and his
28. 7 Whoso *k* the law is a wise son: but
29.18 he that *k* the law, happy is he.
Ec 8. 5 Whoso *k* the commandment shall
Isa 56. 2 *k* his hand from doing any evil.
La 3.28 He sitteth alone and *k* silence,
Lk 11.21 a strong man armed *k* his palace,
Jn 7.19 and yet none of you *k* the law?
9.16 because he *k* not the sabbath day.
14.21 my commandments, and *k* them,
24 loveth me not *k* not my sayings:
1Jn 2. 4 and *k* not his commandments,
5 whoso *k* his word, in him verily is
3.24 And he that *k* his commandments
5.18 that is begotten of God *k* himself,
Rev 2.26 and *k* my works unto the end,
16.15 that watcheth, and *k* his garments,
22. 7 blessed is he that *k* the sayings of

KEEPING
Ex 34. 7 *K* mercy for thousands, forgiving
Nu 3.28 *k* the charge of the sanctuary.
38 *k* the charge of the sanctuary for
Dt 8.11 God, in not *k* his commandments,
1Sa 25.16 we were with them *k* the sheep.
Neh 12.25 were porters *k* the ward at the
Ps 19.11 in *k* of them there is great reward.
Eze 17.14 by *k* of his covenant it might stand.
Dan 9. 4 *k* the covenant and mercy to them
Lk 2. 8 *k* watch over their flock by night.
1Co 7.19 *k* of the commandments of God.
1Pe 4.19 commit the *k* of their souls to him in

KEPT
Gen 39. 9 neither hath he *k* back any thing
Ex 3. 1 Moses *k* the flock of Jethro his
Nu 9. 5 *k* the passover on the fourteenth
Dt 32.10 he *k* him as the apple of his eye.
1Sa 17.34 Thy servant *k* his father's sheep,
2Sa 22.22 I have *k* the ways of the Lord, and
2Ch 7. 8 Solomon *k* the feast seven days,
35. 1 Moreover Josiah *k* a passover
18 keep such a passover as Josiah *k*,
Neh 1. 7 have not *k* the commandments,
Est 9.28 days should be remembered and *k*
Job 29.21 waited, and *k* silence at my counsel.
31.34 I *k* silence, and went not out of the
Ps 18.21 For I have *k* the ways of the Lord,
23 and I *k* myself from mine iniquity.

42. 4 with a multitude that *k* holyday.
50.21 hast thou done, and I *k* silence;
78.56 God, and *k* not his testimonies:
119.67 but now have I *k* thy word.
167 My soul hath *k* thy testimonies;
Jer 35.18 your father, and *k* all his precepts,
Eze 44.15 that *k* the charge of my sanctuary
Dan 7.28 but I *k* the matter in my heart.
Am 1.11 and he *k* his wrath for ever:
Mt 8.33 they that *k* them fled, and went
13.35 things which have been *k* secret
14. 6 But when Herod's birthday was *k*,
19.20 things have I *k* from my youth up:
Mk 4.22 neither was any thing *k* secret,
9.10 *k* that saying with themselves,
Lk 2.19 But Mary *k* all these things, and
51 his mother *k* all these sayings in
8.29 he was *k* bound with chains and
9.36 they *k* it close, and told no man
18.21 these have I *k* from my youth up.
19.20 I have *k* laid up in a napkin:
Jn 2.10 hast *k* the good wine until now.
12. 7 of my burying hath she *k* this.
15.10 even as I have *k* my Father's
20 if they have *k* my saying, they will
17. 6 me; and they have *k* thy word.
12 the world, I *k* them in thy name:
12 that thou gavest me I have *k*,
18.16 and spake unto her that *k* the door,
17 saith the damsel that *k* the door
Ac 5. 2 *k* back part of the price, his wife
7.53 of angels, and have not *k* it.
9.33 which had *k* his bed eight years,
12. 5 Peter therefore was *k* in prison:
6 before the door *k* the prison.
15.12 Then all the multitude *k* silence,
20.20 how I *k* back nothing that was
22. 2 them, they *k* the more silence:
20 *k* the raiment of them that slew
23.35 to be *k* in Herod's judgment hall.
25. 4 Paul should be *k* at Caesarea, and
21 him to be *k* till I might send him to
27.43 Paul, *k* them from their purpose;
28.16 himself with a soldier that *k* him.
Ro 16.25 *k* secret since the world began,
2Co 11. 9 *k* myself from being burdensome
32 *k* the city of the Damascenes
Gal 3.23 we were *k* under the law, shut up
2Ti 4. 7 my course, I have *k* the faith:
Heb 11.28 Through faith he *k* the passover,
Jas 5. 4 which is of you *k* back by fraud,
1Pe 1. 5 *k* by the power of God through
2Pe 3. 7 by the same word are *k* in store,
Jude 6 which *k* not their first estate,
Rev 3. 8 strength, and hast *k* my word,
10 hast *k* the word of my patience,

KEY
Jdg 3.25 they took a *k*, and opened them:
Isa 22.22 the *k* of the house of David will I
Lk 11.52 taken away the *k* of knowledge:
Rev 3. 7 true, he that hath the *k* of David,
9. 1 given the *k* of the bottomless pit.
20. 1 having the *k* of the bottomless pit

KEYS
Mt 16.19 the *k* of the kingdom of heaven:
Rev 1.18 have the *k* of hell and of death.

KICK
1Sa 2.29 Wherefore *k* ye at my sacrifice
Ac 9. 5 for thee to *k* against the pricks.
26.14 for thee to *k* against the pricks.

KID
Ex 23.19 seethe a *k* in his mother's milk.
Isa 11. 6 leopard shall lie down with the *k*;
Eze 45.23 a *k* of the goats daily for a sin
Lk 15.29 thou never gavest me a *k*, that I

KIDS
Gen 27. 9 thence two good *k* of the goats;
16 put the skins of the *k* of the goats
Lev 16. 5 two *k* of the goats for a sin
Nu 7.87 the *k* of the goats for sin offering
1Sa 10. 3 Beth-el, one carrying three *k*,
1Ki 20.27 them like two little flocks of *k*;
2Ch 35. 7 of the flock, lambs and *k*, all
SS 1. 8 feed thy *k* beside the shepherds'

KILL
Gen 4.15 any finding him should *k* him.
26. 7 place should *k* me for Rebekah;
37.21 and said, Let us not *k* him.
Ex 12.21 your families, and *k* the passover.
20.13 Thou shalt not *k*.
Nu 31.17 *k* every male among the little ones,
Dt 5.17 Thou shalt not *k*.
1Sa 16. 2 if Saul hear it, he will *k* me. And
19. 2 Saul my father seeketh to *k* thee:
2Sa 14.32 any iniquity in me, let him *k* me.
2Ki 5. 7 Am I God, to *k* and make alive,
7. 4 and if they *k* us, we shall but die.
Ec 3. 3 A time to *k*, and a time to heal;
Mt 5.21 of old time, Thou shalt not *k*;
21 shall *k* shall be in danger of the
10.28 fear not them which *k* the body,
28 but are not able to *k* the soul:
17.23 they shall *k* him, and the third day
21.38 let us *k* him, and let us seize on his
23.34 some of them ye shall *k* and crucify;
24. 9 up to be afflicted, and shall *k* you:
26. 4 take Jesus by subtilty, and *k* him.
Mk 3. 4 or to do evil? to save life, or to *k*?
9.31 hands of men, and they shall *k* him;
10.19 Do not *k*, Do not steal, Do not
34 spit upon him, and shall *k* him:
12. 7 let us *k* him, and the inheritance
Lk 12. 4 not afraid of them that *k* the body,
13.31 depart hence: for Herod will *k* thee.
15.23 hither the fatted calf, and *k* it;
18.20 Do not commit adultery, Do not *k*,
20.14 is the heir: come, let us *k* him,
22. 2 sought how they might *k* him;
Jn 5.18 the Jews sought the more to *k* him,
7. 1 because the Jews sought to *k* him.
19 the law? Why go ye about to *k* me?
20 devil: who goeth about to *k* thee?
25 Is not this he, whom they seek to *k*?
8.22 said the Jews, Will he *k* himself?
37 ye seek to *k* me, because my word
40 now ye seek to *k* me, a man that
10.10 not, but for to steal, and to *k*, and
Ac 7.28 Wilt thou *k* me, as thou didst the
9.23 the Jews took counsel to *k* him:
24 the gates day and night to *k* him.
10.13 to him, Rise, Peter; *k*, and eat.
21.31 And as they went about to *k* him,
23.15 he come near, are ready to *k* him.
25. 3 laying wait in the way to *k* him.
26.21 temple, and went about to *k* me.
27.42 counsel was to *k* the prisoners,
Ro 13. 9 Thou shalt not *k*, Thou shalt not
Jas 2.11 adultery, said also, Do not *k*.
11 yet if thou *k*, thou art become a
4. 2 ye *k*, and desire to have, and
Rev 2.23 I will *k* her children with death;
6. 4 that they should *k* one another:
8 to *k* with sword, and with hunger,
9. 5 given that they should not *k* them,
11. 7 shall overcome them, and *k* them.

KILLED
Ezr 6.20 *k* the passover for all the children
Ps 44.22 for thy sake are we *k* all the day
La 2.21 anger; thou hast *k*, and not pitied.
Mt 16.21 be *k*, and be raised again the third
21.35 beat one, and *k* another, and stoned
22. 4 my fatlings are *k*, and all things
23.31 of them which *k* the prophets.
Mk 6.19 him, and would have *k* him;
8.31 and be *k*, and after three days rise
9.31 after that he is *k*, he shall rise the
12. 5 and him they *k*, and many others;
8 they took him, and *k* him, and cast
14.12 when they *k* the passover,
Lk 11.47 prophets, and your fathers *k* them.
48 for they indeed *k* them, and ye build
12. 5 after he hath *k* hath power to cast
15.27 thy father hath *k* the fatted calf,
30 thou hast *k* for him the fatted calf.
20.15 out of the vineyard, and *k* him.
22. 7 when the passover must be *k*.
Ac 3.15 And *k* the Prince of life, whom God
12. 2 he *k* James the brother of John
16.27 sword, and would have *k* himself,
23.12 eat nor drink till they had *k* Paul.
21 eat nor drink till they have *k* him:
27 and should have been *k* of them:
Ro 8.36 For thy sake we are *k* all the day
11. 3 Lord, they have *k* thy prophets,
2Co 6. 9 we live; as chastened, and not *k*;
1Th 2.15 Who both *k* the Lord Jesus, and
Jas 5. 6 have condemned and *k* the just:
Rev 6.11 should be *k* as they were, should
9.18 three was the third part of men *k*,
20 which were not *k* by these plagues
11. 5 them, he must in this manner be *k*.
13.10 sword must be *k* with the sword.
15 the image of the beast should be *k*.

KILLEDST
Ex 2.14 kill me, as thou *k* the Egyptian?
1Sa 24.18 me into thine hand, thou *k* me not.

KILLEST
Mt 23.37 Jerusalem,...that *k* the prophets,
Lk 13.34 Jerusalem, which *k* the prophets,

KILLETH
Lev 24.17 he that *k* any man shall surely
Nu 35.30 Whoso *k* any person, the murderer
Dt 19. 4 Whoso *k* his neighbor ignorantly,
1Sa 2. 6 The Lord *k*, and maketh alive:
17.25 who *k* him, the king will enrich
Job 5. 2 For wrath *k* the foolish man, and
24.14 the light *k* the poor and needy,
Pr 21.25 The desire of the slothful *k* him;
Jn 16. 2 whosoever *k* you will think that he
2Co 3. 6 letter *k*, but the spirit giveth life.
Rev 13.10 he that *k* with the sword must be

KILLING
Jdg 9.24 him in the *k* of his brethren.
2Ch 30.17 charge of the *k* of the passovers
Isa 22.13 slaying oxen, and *k* sheep, eating
Hos 4. 2 By swearing, and lying, and *k*,
Mk 12. 5 others; beating some, and *k* some.

KIN
Lev 18. 6 any that is near of *k* to him,
20.19 for he uncovereth his near *k*:
21. 2 for his *k*, that is near unto him,
25.25 if any of his *k* come to redeem it.
49 any that is nigh of *k* unto him of
Ru 2.20 man is near of *k* unto us, one of our
2Sa 19.42 Because the king is near of *k* to us:
Mk 6. 4 country, and among his own *k*,

KIND
2Ch 10. 7 If thou be *k* to this people, and
Mt 13.47 the sea, and gathered of every *k*:
17.21 this *k* goeth not out but by prayer
Mk 9.29 This *k* can come forth by nothing,
Lk 6.35 he is *k* unto the unthankful and
1Co 13. 4 Charity suffereth long, and is *k*;
15.39 but there is one *k* of flesh of men,
Eph 4.32 And be ye *k* one to another,
Jas 1.18 a *k* of firstfruits of his creatures.

KINDLE
Ex 35. 3 shall *k* no fire throughout your
Pr 26.21 is a contentious man to *k* strife.

Isa 9.18 *k* in the thickets of the forest,
10.16 *k* a burning like the burning of a
30.33 a stream of brimstone, doth *k* it.
43. 2 shall the flame *k* upon thee.
50.11 all ye that *k* a fire, that compass
Jer 7.18 wood, and the fathers *k* the fire,
17.27 then will I *k* a fire in the gates
21.14 I will *k* a fire in the forest thereof,
33.18 and to *k* meat offerings, and to do
43.12 *k* a fire in the houses of the gods
49.27 *k* a fire in the wall of Damascus,
50.32 and I will *k* a fire in his cities,
Eze 20.47 God; Behold, I will *k* a fire in thee,
24.10 *k* the fire, consume the flesh,
Am 1.14 *k* a fire in the wall of Rabbah,
Ob 18 they shall *k* in them, and devour
Mal 1.10 neither do ye *k* fire on mine altar

KINDLED

Ex 4.14 of the Lord was *k* against Moses,
Nu 11.10 anger of the Lord was *k* greatly:
11.33 wrath of the Lord was *k* against
Dt 32.22 For a fire is *k* in mine anger, and
1Sa 20.30 Saul's anger was *k* against
2Sa 22.13 before him were coals of fire *k*.
Job 32. 3 his three friends was his wrath *k*,
42. 7 My wrath is *k* against thee, and
Jer 15.14 a fire is *k* in mine anger, which
La 4.11 hath *k* a fire in Zion, and it hath
Zec 10. 3 was *k* against the shepherds,
Lk 12.49 what will I, if it be already *k*?
22.55 they had *k* a fire in the midst of
Ac 28. 2 for they *k* a fire, and received us

KINDLETH

Job 41.21 His breath *k* coals, and a flame
Isa 44.15 yea, he *k* it; and baketh bread;
Jas 3. 5 how great a matter a little fire *k*!

KINDLY

Gen 24.49 if ye will deal *k* and truly with
34. 3 and spake *k* unto the damsel.
47.29 and deal *k* and truly with me;
50.21 and spake *k* unto them.
Jos 2.14 will deal *k* and truly with thee.
Ru 1. 8 Lord deal *k* with you, as ye have
1Sa 20. 8 shalt deal *k* with thy servant;
2Ki 25.28 he spake *k* to him, and set his
Jer 52.32 spake *k* unto him, and set his
Ro 12.10 Be *k* affectioned one to another

KINDNESS

Gen 20.13 is thy *k* which thou shalt shew
21.23 to the *k* that I have done unto thee,
Ru 3.10 shewed more *k* in the latter end
1Sa 20.14 I live shew me the *k* of the Lord,
2Sa 2. 6 will requite you this *k*, because
9. 3 may shew the *k* of God unto him?
1Ki 3. 6 hast kept for him this great *k*,
Neh 9.17 slow to anger, and of great *k*,
Ps 31.21 hath shewed me his marvellous *k*
117. 2 For his merciful *k* is great toward
119.76 thy merciful *k* be for my comfort,
141. 5 smite me; it shall be a *k*:
Joel 2.13 slow to anger, and of great *k*,
Jon 4. 2 slow to anger, and of great *k*,
Ac 28. 2 people shewed us no little *k*:
2Co 6. 6 by *k*, by the Holy Ghost, by love
Eph 2. 7 in his *k* toward us through Christ
Col 3.12 *k*, humbleness of mind, meekness,
Tit 3. 4 after that the *k* and love of God
2Pe 1. 7 to godliness brotherly *k*; and to
7 and to brotherly *k* charity.

KINDS

Gen 8.19 upon the earth, after their *k*,
2Ch 16.14 odors and divers *k* of spices
Jer 15. 3 I will appoint over them four *k*,
Eze 47.10 fish shall be according to their *k*,
Dan 3. 5 dulcimer, and all *k* of musick, ye
7 all *k* of musick, all the people, the
10 and all *k* of musick, shall fall down
15 all *k* of musick, ye fall down and
1Co 12.10 another divers *k* of tongues; to
14.10 so many *k* of voices in the world,

KING

Ex 1. 8 there arose up a new *k* over Egypt,
18 *k* of Egypt called for the midwives,
3.19 the *k* of Egypt will not let you go,
Nu 23.21 the shout of a *k* is among them.
Dt 17.14 I will set a *k* over me, like as all
15 set him *k* over thee, whom the Lord
Jdg 17. 6 days there was no *k* in Israel,
1Sa 8. 5 make us a *k* to judge us like all
6 they said, Give us a *k* to judge us.
18 your *k* which ye shall have chosen
19 Nay; but we will have a *k* over us;
24 shouted, and said, God save the *k*.
11.15 they made Saul *k* before the Lord
12.12 the Lord your God was your *k*.
17 sight of the Lord, in asking you a *k*.
19 all our sins this evil, to ask us a *k*.
20. 5 not fail to sit with the *k* at meat:
22.15 let not the *k* impute any thing unto
16 the *k* said, Thou shalt surely die,
26.14 Who art thou that criest to the *k*?
17 said, It is my voice, my lord, O *k*.
2Sa 3.31 *k* David himself followed the bier.
6.16 saw *k* David leaping and dancing
20 How glorious was the *k* of Israel
14.17 so is my lord the *k* to discern good
16. 9 this dead dog curse my lord the *k*?
16 God save the *k*, God save the *k*.
18.13 there is no matter hid from the *k*,
21 Go tell the *k* what thou hast seen.
27 the *k* said, He is a good man, and
28 and said unto the *k*, All is well.
31 Cushi said, Tidings, my lord the *k*:
33 the *k* was much moved, and went
19. 2 how the *k* was grieved for his son.
19 the *k* should take it to his heart.
27 my lord the *k* is as an angel of God:
35 yet a burden unto my lord the *k*?
24.23 Araunah, as a *k*, give unto the *k*.
1Ki 4. 1 *k* Solomon was *k* over all Israel.
10. 6 And she said to the *k*, It was a true
9 for ever, therefore made he thee *k*,
13. 8 the man of God said unto the *k*, If
19.15 anoint Hazael to be *k* over Syria:
21.13 did blaspheme God and the *k*.
22. 8 said, Let not the *k* say so.
2Ki 1. 9 Thou man of God, the *k* hath said,
5. 5 send a letter unto the *k* of Israel.
7 when the *k* of Israel had read the
6.11 which of us is for the *k* of Israel?
9.18, 19 Thus saith the *k*, Is it peace?
22.10 Shaphan the scribe shewed the *k*,
11 *k* had heard the words of the book
1Ch 14. 1 Hiram *k* of Tyre sent messengers
2 had confirmed him *k* over Israel,
27.24 account of the chronicles of *k* David.
2Ch 9. 8 throne, to be *k* for the Lord thy God:
23.11 him, and said, God save the *k*.
26.21 Uzziah the *k* was a leper unto the
34.18 Shaphan the scribe told the *k*,
Ezr 4.23 of *k* Artaxerxes' letter was read
5. 7 thus; Unto Darius the *k*, all peace.
13 first year of Cyrus the *k* of Babylon
Neh 2. 3 unto the *k*, Let the *k* live for ever:
13.26 God made him *k* over all Israel:
Est 2.17 the *k* loved Esther above all the
3.10 the *k* took his ring from his hand,
5. 2 the *k* held out to Esther the golden
3 said the *k* unto her, What wilt thou,
8 please the *k* to grant my petition,
6. 4 And the *k* said, Who is in the court?
6 whom the *k* delighteth to honor?
Job 18.14 shall bring him to the *k* of terrors.
34.18 fit to say to a *k*, Thou art wicked?
Ps 5. 2 voice of my cry, my *K*, and my God:
10.16 The Lord is *K* for ever and ever:
20. 9 let the *k* hear us when we call.
24. 7 and the *K* of glory shall come in.
8 Who is this *K* of glory? The Lord
9 and the *K* of glory shall come in.
10 Who is this *K* of glory? The Lord
10 Lord of hosts, he is the *K* of glory.
29.10 yea, the Lord sitteth *K* for ever.
33.16 no *k* saved by the multitude of an
44. 4 Thou art my *K*, O God: command
47. 2 he is a great *K* over all the earth.
6 praises unto our *K*, sing praises.
7 For God is the *K* of all the earth:
72. 1 Give the *k* thy judgments, O God,
84. 3 O Lord of hosts, my *K*, and my God.
89.18 and the Holy One of Israel is our *k*.
95. 3 God, and a great *K* above all gods.
98. 6 joyful noise before the Lord, the *K*.
145. 1 I will extol thee, my God, O *k*; and
Pr 16.10 sentence is in the lips of the *k*:
20.26 A wise *k* scattereth the wicked,
28 Mercy and truth preserve the *k*:
Ec 4.13 wise child than an old and foolish *k*,
8. 4 Where the word of a *k* is, there is
10.16 thee, O land, when thy *k* is a child,
20 Curse not the *k*, no not in thy
Isa 6. 5 eyes have seen the *K*, the Lord of
43.15 One, the creator of Israel, your *K*.
Jer 4. 9 that the heart of the *k* shall perish,
10. 7 not fear thee, O *K* of nations?
36.21 the *k* sent Jehudi to fetch the roll:
21 Jehudi read it in the ears of the *k*,
27 that the *k* had burned the roll,
42.11 Be not afraid of the *k* of Babylon,
Dan 2. 2 for to shew the *k* his dreams.
4 O *k*, live for ever: tell thy servants
10 there is no *k*, lord, nor ruler,
11 is a rare thing that the *k* requireth,
24 shew unto the *k* the interpretation.
25 brought in Daniel before the *k* in
31 Thou, O *k*, sawest, and behold a
37 Thou, O *k*, art a *k* of kings: for
48 the *k* made Daniel a great man,
3.10 Thou, O *k*, hast made a decree, that
6. 6 unto him, *K* Darius, live for ever.
9 *k* Darius signed the writing and
13 regardeth not thee, O *k*, nor the
19 Then the *k* arose very early in the
21 unto the *k*, O *k*, live for ever.
25 *k* Darius wrote unto all people,
Hos 10. 3 We have no *k*, because we feared
3 what then should a *k* do to us?
13.10 I will be thy *k*: where is any other
11 I gave thee a *k* in mine anger, and
Zec 14. 9 Lord shall be *k* over all the earth:
16 to worship the *K*, the Lord of hosts,
17 unto Jerusalem to worship the *K*,
Mal 1.14 I am a great *K*, saith the Lord of
Mt 1. 6 And Jesse begat David the *k*;
6 and David the *k* begat Solomon
2. 1 Judea in the days of Herod the *k*,
2 is he that is born *K* of the Jews?
3 When Herod the *k* had heard these
9 When they had heard the *k*, they
5.35 for it is the city of the great *K*.
14. 9 the *k* was sorry: nevertheless for
18.23 of heaven likened unto a certain *k*,
21. 5 Behold, thy *K* cometh unto thee,
22. 2 of heaven is like unto a certain *k*,
7 when the *k* heard thereof, he was
11 the *k* came in to see the guests,
13 Then said the *k* to the servants,
25.34 Then shall the *K* say unto them
40 the *K* shall answer and say unto
27.11 Art thou the *K* of the Jews?
29 him, saying, Hail, *K* of the Jews!
37 This Is Jesus The *K* Of The Jews.
42 If he be the *K* of Israel, let him
Mk 6.14 And *k* Herod heard of him; (for his
22 him, the *k* said unto the damsel,
25 straightway with haste unto the *k*,
26 the *k* was exceeding sorry; yet for

King Solomon receives the queen of Sheba in this drawing by Julius Schnorr von Carolsfeld (1794-1872).

27 the *k* sent an executioner,
15. 2 him, Art thou the *K* of the Jews?
9 release unto you the *K* of the Jews?
12 whom ye call the *K* of the Jews?
18 salute him, Hail, *K* of the Jews?
26 written over, The *K* Of The Jews.
32 Let Christ the *K* of Israel descend
Lk 1. 5 the days of Herod, the *k* of Judea,
14.31 Or what *k*, going to make war
31 against another *k*, sitteth not down
19.38 Blessed be the *K* that cometh in
23. 2 that he himself is Christ a *K*.
3 Art thou the *K* of the Jews?
37 If thou be the *K* of the Jews, save
38 This Is The *K* Of The Jews.
Jn 1.49 of God; thou art the *K* of Israel.
6.15 take him by force, to make him a *k*,
12.13 Blessed is the *K* of Israel that
15 thy *K* cometh, sitting on an ass's
18.33 him, Art thou the *K* of the Jews?
37 said unto him, Art thou a *k* then?
37 Thou sayest that I am a *k*. To this
39 unto you the *K* of the Jews?
19. 3 said, Hail, *K* of the Jews! and they
12 maketh himself a *k* speaketh
14 unto the Jews, Behold your *K*!
15 unto them, Shall I crucify your *K*?
15 answered, We have no *k* but Caesar.
19 Jesus Of Nazareth The *K* Of The
21 Write not, The *K* of the Jews;
21 that he said, I am *K* of the Jews.
Ac 7.10 the sight of Pharaoh *k* of Egypt;
18 Till another *k* arose, which knew
12. 1 Herod the *k* stretched forth his
13.21 And afterward they desired a *k*:
22 unto them David to be their *k*;
17. 7 that there is another *k*, one Jesus.
25.13 days *k* Agrippa and Bernice came
14 declared Paul's cause unto the *k*,
24 Festus said, *K* Agrippa, and all
26 specially before thee, O *k* Agrippa,
26. 2 I think myself happy, *k* Agrippa,
7 For which hope's sake, *k* Agrippa,
13 At midday, O *k*, I saw in the way a
19 O *k* Agrippa, I was not disobedient
26 For the *k* knoweth of these things,
27 *K* Agrippa, believest thou the
30 the *k* rose up, and the governor,
2Co 11.32 governor under Aretas the *k* kept
1Ti 1.17 Now unto the *K* eternal, immortal,
6.15 *K* of kings, and Lord of lords;
Heb 7. 1 Melchisedec, *k* of Salem, priest
2 interpretation *K* of righteousness,
2 *K* of Salem, which is, *K* of peace;
11.27 not fearing the wrath of the *k*: for
1Pe 2.13 whether it be to the *k*, as supreme;
17 Fear God. Honor the *k*.
Rev 9.11 they had a *k* over them, which is
15. 3 are thy ways, thou *K* of saints.
17.14 is Lord of lords, and *K* of kings:
19.16 *K* Of Kings, And Lord Of Lords.

KINGDOM

Gen 10.10 the beginning of his *k* was Babel,
Ex 19. 6 ye shall be unto me a *k* of priests,
1Ki 2.15 Thou knowest that the *k* was mine,
11.11 I will surely rend the *k* from thee,
1Ch 28. 7 I will establish his *k* for ever, if
29.11 thine is the *k*, O Lord, and thou
Ps 22.28 For the *k* is the Lord's: and he
145.11 shall speak of the glory of thy *k*,
13 Thy *k* is an everlasting *k*, and
Jer 27. 8 nation and *k* which will not serve
Dan 2.39 shall arise another *k* inferior to
39 and another third *k* of brass, which
40 fourth *k* shall be strong as iron:
44 shall the God of heaven set up a *k*,
4. 3 his *k* is an everlasting *k*, and his
17 most High ruleth in the *k* of men,
5.26 Mene; God hath numbered thy *k*,
28 Peres; Thy *k* is divided, and given
Ob 21 and the *k* shall be the Lord's.
Mic 4. 8 the *k* shall come to the daughter
Mt 3. 2 ye: for the *k* of heaven is at hand.
4.17 for the *k* of heaven is at hand.
23 and preaching the gospel of the *k*,
5. 3 spirit: for theirs is the *k* of heaven.
10 sake: for theirs is the *k* of heaven.
19 called the least in the *k* of heaven:
19 be called great in the *k* of heaven.
20 no case enter into the *k* of heaven.
6.10 Thy *k* come. Thy will be done in
13 For thine is the *k*, and the power,
33 seek ye first the *k* of God, and his
7.21 shall enter into the *k* of heaven,
8.11 Isaac, and Jacob, in the *k* of heaven:
12 children of the *k* shall be cast out
9.35 and preaching the gospel of the *k*,
10. 7 saying, The *k* of heaven is at hand.
11.11 least in the *k* of heaven is greater
12 the *k* of heaven suffereth violence,
12.25 *k* divided against itself is brought
26 how shall then his *k* stand?
28 then the *k* of God is come unto you.
13.11 the mysteries of the *k* of heaven,
19 any one heareth the word of the *k*,
24 *k* of heaven is likened unto a man
31 *k* of heaven is like to a grain of
33 *k* of heaven is like unto leaven,
38 good seed are the children of the *k*;
41 shall gather out of his *k* all things
43 as the sun in the *k* of their Father.
44 the *k* of heaven is like unto treasure
45 *k* of heaven is like unto a merchant
47 the *k* of heaven is like unto a net,
52 is instructed unto the *k* of heaven,
16.19 thee the keys of the *k* of heaven:
28 see the Son of man coming in his *k*.
18. 1 is the greatest in the *k* of heaven?
3 shall not enter into the *k* of heaven.
4 same is greatest in the *k* of heaven.
23 *k* of heaven likened unto a certain
19.12 eunuchs for the *k* of heaven's sake.
14 me; for of such is the *k* of heaven.
23 hardly enter into the *k* of heaven.
24 for a rich man to enter into the *k* of
20. 1 *k* of heaven is like unto a man that
21 and the other on the left, in thy *k*.
21.31 harlots go into the *k* of God before
43 *k* of God shall be taken from you,
22. 2 The *k* of heaven is like unto a
23.13 ye shut up the *k* of heaven against
24. 7 against nation, and *k* against *k*:
14 gospel of the *k* shall be preached
25. 1 *k* of heaven be likened unto ten
14 *k* of heaven is as a man travelling
34 inherit the *k* prepared for you from
26.29 it new with you in my Father's *k*,
Mk 1.14 preaching the gospel of the *k* of God,
15 fulfilled, and the *k* of God is at hand:
3.24 if a *k* be divided against itself,
24 that *k* cannot stand.
4.11 know the mystery of the *k* of God:
26 So is the *k* of God, as if a man
30 Whereunto shall we liken the *k* of
6.23 give it thee, unto the half of my *k*.
9. 1 have seen the *k* of God come with
47 enter into the *k* of God with one eye,
10.14 not: for of such is the *k* of God.
15 shall not receive the *k* of God as a
23 have riches enter into the *k* of God!
24 in riches to enter into the *k* of God!
25 rich man to enter into the *k* of God.
11.10 Blessed be the *k* of our father David,
12.34 Thou art not far from the *k* of God.
13. 8 against nation, and *k* against *k*:
14.25 that I drink it new in the *k* of God
15.43 which also waited for the *k* of God,
Lk 1.33 of his *k* there shall be no end.
4.43 preach the *k* of God to other cities
6.20 ye poor: for yours is the *k* of God.
7.28 he that is least in the *k* of God is
8. 1 the glad tidings of the *k* of God:
10 know the mysteries of the *k* of God:
9. 2 sent them to preach the *k* of God,

Lk 9.11 spake unto them of the *k* of God,
27 of death, till they see the *k* of God.
60 go thou and preach the *k* of God.
62 looking back, is fit for the *k* of God.
10. 9 The *k* of God is come nigh unto you.
11 the *k* of God is come nigh unto you.
11. 2 Thy *k* come. Thy will be done, as
17 Every *k* divided against itself is
18 himself, how shall his *k* stand?
20 no doubt the *k* of God is come upon
12.31 But rather seek ye the *k* of God;
32 good pleasure to give you the *k*.
13.18 he, unto what is the *k* of God like?
20 whereunto shall I liken the *k* of God?
28 all the prophets, in the *k* of God,
29 and shall sit down in the *k* of God.
14.15 that shall eat bread in the *k* of God.
16.16 that time the *k* of God is preached,
17.20 when the *k* of God should come, he
20 The *k* of God cometh not with
21 behold, the *k* of God is within you.
18.16 not: for of such is the *k* of God.
17 shall not receive the *k* of God as a
24 have riches enter into the *k* of God!
25 rich man to enter into the *k* of God.
29 or children, for the *k* of God's sake,
19.11 they thought that the *k* of God
12 to receive for himself a *k*, and to
15 was returned, having received the *k*,
21.10 against nation, and *k* against *k*:
31 ye that the *k* of God is nigh at hand.
22.16 until it be fulfilled in the *k* of God.
18 vine, until the *k* of God shall come.
29 I appoint unto you a *k*, as my
30 eat and drink at my table in my *k*,
23.42 me when thou comest into thy *k*.
51 himself waited for the *k* of God.
Jn 3. 3 again, he cannot see the *k* of God.
5 he cannot enter into the *k* of God.
18.36 answered, My *k* is not of this world:
36 if my *k* were of this world, then
36 but now is my *k* not from hence.
Ac 1. 3 things pertaining to the *k* of God:
6 time restore again the *k* to Israel?
8.12 things concerning the *k* of God,
14.22 tribulation enter into the *k* of God.
19. 8 things concerning the *k* of God.
20.25 have gone, preaching the *k* of God,
28.23 and testified the *k* of God,
31 Preaching the *k* of God, and
Ro 14.17 For the *k* of God is not meat and
1Co 4.20 the *k* of God is not in word, but in
6. 9 shall not inherit the *k* of God?
10 nor..., shall inherit the *k* of God.
15.24 have delivered up the *k* to God,
50 blood cannot inherit the *k* of God;
Gal 5.21 shall not inherit the *k* of God.
Eph 5. 5 any inheritance in the *k* of Christ
Col 1.13 us into the *k* of his dear Son:
4.11 fellow-workers unto the *k* of God,
1Th 2.12 called you unto his *k* and glory.
2Th 1. 5 be counted worthy of the *k* of God,
2Ti 4. 1 dead at his appearing and his *k*;
18 preserve me unto his heavenly *k*:
Heb 1. 8 righteousness is the scepter of thy *k*.
12.28 we receiving a *k* which cannot be
Jas 2. 5 heirs of the *k* which he hath
2Pe 1.11 into the everlasting *k* of our Lord
Rev 1. 9 in the *k* and patience of Jesus
12.10 strength, and the *k* of our God,
16.10 his *k* was full of darkness; and
17.12 which have received no *k* as yet;
17 give their *k* unto the beast, until

KINGDOMS

2Ki 19.15 thou alone, of all the *k* of the earth;
19 all the *k* of the earth may know
2Ch 20.29 the fear of God was on all the *k*
Ps 46. 6 heathen raged, the *k* were moved:
68.32 Sing unto God, ye *k* of the earth;
Isa 14.16 earth to tremble, that did shake *k*;
37.20 that all the *k* of the earth may know
47. 5 no more be called, The lady of *k*.
Eze 29.15 It shall be the basest of the *k*;
37.22 divided into two *k* any more at all:
Mt 4. 8 sheweth him all the *k* of the world,
Lk 4. 5 unto him all the *k* of the world in
Heb 11.33 Who through faith subdued *k*,
Rev 11.15 The *k* of this world are become
15 the *k* of our Lord, and of his Christ;

KING'S

Nu 20.17 we will go by the *k* high way, we
1Sa 18.23 a light thing to be a *k* son in law,
21. 8 the *k* business required haste.
1Ch 27.33 Ahithophel was the *k* counsellor:
33 the Archite was the *k* companion:
2Ch 18. 5 God will deliver it into the *k* hand.
Neh 1.11 man. For I was the *k* cupbearer.
Est 2.19 then Mordecai sat in the *k* gate.
3.12 written, and sealed with the *k* ring.
5. 9 Haman saw Mordecai in the *k* gate,
8. 8 name, and seal it with the *k* ring:
8 which is written in the *k* name,
Ps 45.13 *k* daughter is all glorious within
61. 6 Thou wilt prolong the *k* life: and
72. 1 thy righteousness unto the *k* son.
Pr 14.28 multitude of people is the *k* honor:
Dan 2.23 made known unto us the *k* matter.
5. 8 Then came in all the *k* wise men:
Ac 12.20 Blastus the *k* chamberlain their
20 was nourished by the *k* country.
Heb 11.23 afraid of the *k* commandment.

KINGS

2Ki 20.20 the chronicles of the *k* of Judah?
1Ch 9. 1 book of the *k* of Israel and Judah,
16.21 yea, he reproved *k* for their sakes,
2Ch 25.26 book of the *k* of Judah and Israel?
32. 4 Why should the *k* of Assyria come,
33.18 in the book of the *k* of Israel.
Est 10. 2 of the chronicles of the *k* of Media
Job 12.18 He looseth the bond of *k*, and
Ps 2. 2 *k* of the earth set themselves, and
68.29 shall *k* bring presents unto thee.
72.10 *k* of Tarshish and of the isles shall
10 *k* of Sheba and Seba shall offer gifts.
76.12 he is terrible to the *k* of the earth.
135.10 great nations, and slew mighty *k*;
138. 4 the *k* of the earth shall praise thee,
Pr 8.15 By me *k* reign, and princes decree
16.13 Righteous lips are the delight of *k*;
25. 3 and the heart of *k* is unsearchable.
Isa 14.18 All the *k* of the nations, even all of
Eze 27.33 thou didst enrich the *k* of the earth
32.10 *k* shall be horribly afraid for thee,
Dan 2.21 he removeth *k*, and setteth up *k*:
37 Thou, O king, art a king of *k*: for
47 is a God of gods, and a Lord of *k*,
Hos 8. 4 They have set up *k*, but not by me:
Hab 1.10 they shall scoff at the *k*, and the
Mt 10.18 governors and *k* for my sake,
17.25 of whom do the *k* of the earth take
Mk 13. 9 before rulers and *k* for my sake,
Lk 10.24 prophets and *k* have desired to see
21.12 *k* and rulers for my name's sake.
22.25 The *k* of the Gentiles exercise
Ac 4.26 The *k* of the earth stood up, and
9.15 my name before the Gentiles, and *k*,
1Co 4. 8 ye have reigned as *k* without us:
1Ti 2. 2 For *k*, and for all that are in
6.15 the King of *k*, and Lord of lords;
Heb 7. 1 returning from the slaughter of *k*,
Rev 1. 5 the prince of the *k* of the earth.
6 hath made us *k* and priests unto
5.10 us unto our God *k* and priests:
6.15 the *k* of the earth, and the great
10.11 and nations, and tongues, and *k*.
16.12 the way of the *k* of the east might
14 go forth unto the *k* of the earth
17. 2 With whom the *k* of the earth have
10 there are seven *k*: five are fallen,
12 horns which thou sawest are ten *k*,
12 receive power as *k* one hour with
14 he is Lord of lords, and King of *k*:
18 reigneth over the *k* of the earth.
18. 3 the *k* of the earth have committed
9 the *k* of the earth, who have
19.16 King Of *K*, And Lord Of Lords.
18 That ye may eat the flesh of *k*,
19 the beast, and the *k* of the earth,
21.24 the *k* of the earth do bring their

KINGS'

Mt 11. 8 wear soft clothing are in *k* houses.
Lk 7.25 and live delicately, are in *k* courts.

KINSFOLK

Job 19.14 My *k* have failed, and my familiar
Lk 2.44 they sought him among their *k*

KINSFOLKS

1Ki 16.11 neither of his *k*, nor of his
2Ki 10.11 his great men, and his *k*, and his
Lk 21.16 and brethren, and *k*, and friends

KINSMAN

Nu 5. 8 the man have no *k* to recompence
27.11 give his inheritance unto his *k*
Ru 2. 1 Naomi had a *k* of her husband's,
3. 9 handmaid; for thou art a near *k*.
12 it is true that I am thy near *k*:
12 howbeit there is a *k* nearer than I.
13 perform unto thee the part of a *k*,
13 will not do the part of a *k* to thee,
13 will I do the part of a *k* to thee,
4. 1 the *k* of whom Boaz spake came
3 he said unto the *k*, Naomi, that is
6 the *k* said, I cannot redeem it for
8 the *k* said unto Boaz, Buy it for
14 not left thee this day without a *k*,
Jn 18.26 being his *k* whose ear Peter cut
Ro 16.11 Salute Herodion my *k*. Greet them

KINSMEN

Lk 14.12 neither thy *k*, nor thy rich
Ac 10.24 together his *k* and near friends.
Ro 9. 3 my *k* according to the flesh:
16. 7 Andronicus and Junia, my *k*, and
21 and Jason, and Sosipater, my *k*,

KISS

Gen 27.26 near now, and *k* me, my son.
31.28 to *k* my sons and my daughters?
2Sa 20. 9 beard with the right hand to *k* him.
1Ki 19.20 thee, *k* my father and my mother,
Ps 2.12 *K* the Son, lest he be angry, and
Pr 24.26 shall *k* his lips that giveth a right
SS 1. 2 Let him *k* me with the kisses of his
8. 1 find thee without, I would *k* thee;
Hos 13. 2 the men that sacrifice *k* the calves.
Mt 26.48 Whomsoever I shall *k*, that same
Mk 14.44 Whomsoever I shall *k*, that same
Lk 7.45 Thou gavest me no *k*: but this
45 in hath not ceased to *k* my feet.
22.47 drew near unto Jesus to *k* him.
48 thou the Son of man with a *k*?
Ro 16.16 Salute one another with an holy *k*.
1Co 16.20 ye one another with an holy *k*.
2Co 13.12 Greet one another with an holy *k*.
1Th 5.26 all the brethren with an holy *k*.
1Pe 5.14 ye one another with a *k* of charity.

KISSED

Gen 27.27 And he came near, and *k* him:
29.11 Jacob *k* Rachel, and lifted up his
13 him, and embraced him, and *k* him,
31.55 and *k* his sons and his daughters,
33. 4 and fell on his neck, and *k* him:
45.15 Moreover he *k* all his brethren,
48.10 he *k* them, and embraced them.
50. 1 and wept upon him, and *k* him.
Ex 4.27 in the mount of God, and *k* him.

18. 7 law, and did obeisance, and *k* him;
Ru 1. 9 Then she *k* them; and they lifted up
14 and Orpah *k* her mother in law;
1Sa 10. 1 poured it upon his head, and *k* him,
20.41 they *k* one another, and wept one
2Sa 14.33 the king: and the king *k* Absalom.
15. 5 his hand, and took him, and *k* him.
19.39 the king *k* Barzillai, and blessed
1Ki 19.18 every mouth which hath not *k* him.
Job 31.27 or my mouth hath *k* my hand:
Ps 85.10 righteousness and peace have *k*
Pr 7.13 So she caught him, and *k* him, and
Mt 26.49 said, Hail, master: and *k* him.
Mk 14.45 saith, Master, master; and *k* him.
Lk 7.38 and *k* his feet, and anointed them
15.20 and fell on his neck, and *k* him.
Ac 20.37 and fell on Paul's neck, and *k* him,

KISSES
Pr 27. 6 the *k* of an enemy are deceitful.
SS 1. 2 kiss me with the *k* of his mouth:

KNEE
Gen 41.43 they cried before him, Bow the *k*:
Isa 45.23 That unto me every *k* shall bow,
Mt 27.29 they bowed the *k* before him, and
Ro 11. 4 have not bowed the *k* to the image
14.11 the Lord, every *k* shall bow to me,
Php 2.10 name of Jesus every *k* should bow,

KNEEL
Gen 24.11 he made his camels to *k* down
Ps 95. 6 let us *k* before the Lord our maker.

KNEELED
2Ch 6.13 *k* down upon his knees before
Dan 6.10 he *k* upon his knees three times
Mk 10.17 came one running, and *k* to him,
Lk 22.41 cast, and *k* down, and prayed,
Ac 7.60 he *k* down, and cried with a
9.40 forth, and *k* down, and prayed;
20.36 he *k* down, and prayed with
21. 5 we *k* down on the shore, and

KNEELING
1Ki 8.54 from *k* on his knees with his
Mt 17.14 a certain man, *k* down to him,
Mk 1.40 beseeching him, and *k* down to him,

KNEES
Gen 30. 3 she shall bear upon my *k*, that I
48.12 them out from between his *k*,
50.23 were brought up upon Joseph's *k*.
Dt 28.35 The Lord shall smite thee in the *k*,
Jdg 7. 5 boweth down upon his *k* to drink.
6 down upon their *k* to drink water.
16.19 made him sleep upon her *k*; and
1Ki 8.54 kneeling on his *k* with his hands
18.42 and put his face between his *k*,
19.18 *k* which have not bowed unto Baal,
2Ki 1.13 and fell on his *k* before Elijah,
4.20 he sat on her *k* till noon, and then
2Ch 6.13 kneeled down upon his *k* before all
Ezr 9. 5 I fell upon my *k*, and spread out
Job 3.12 Why did the *k* prevent me? or why
4. 4 hast strengthened the feeble *k*.
Ps 109.24 My *k* are weak through fasting;
Isa 35. 3 hands, and confirm the feeble *k*.
66.12 sides, and be dandled upon her *k*.
Eze 7.17 and all *k* shall be weak as water.
21. 7 and all *k* shall be weak as water:
47. 4 waters; the waters were to the *k*.
Dan 5. 6 and his *k* smote one against
6.10 kneeled upon his *k* three times a
10.10 which set me upon my *k* and upon
Na 2.10 and the *k* smite together, and
Mk 15.19 bowing their *k* worshipped him.
Lk 5. 8 he fell down at Jesus' *k*, saying,
Eph 3.14 I bow my *k* unto the Father of our
Heb 12.12 hang down, and the feeble *k*;

KNEW
Gen 3. 7 and they *k* that they were naked;
8.11 Noah *k* that the waters were abated
28.16 Lord is in this place; and I *k* it not.
37.33 he *k* it, and said, It is my son's
42. 8 Joseph *k* his brethren, but they *k*
Ex 1. 8 over Egypt, which *k* not Joseph.
Dt 8.16 manna, which thy fathers *k* not,
34.10 whom the Lord *k* face to face,
Jdg 13.21 *k* that he was an angel of the Lord.
1Sa 20.39 the lad *k* not any thing: only
39 Jonathan and David *k* the matter.
Job 23. 3 I knew where I might find him!
Pr 24.12 Behold, we *k* it not; doth not he
Jer 1. 5 formed thee in the belly I *k* thee;
2. 8 they that handle the law *k* me not:
44. 3 serve other gods, whom they *k* not,
Jon 4. 2 I *k* that thou art a gracious God,
Mt 1.25 *k* her not till she had brought
7.23 profess unto them, I never *k* you:
12.25 Jesus *k* their thoughts, and said
Mk 6.54 of the ship, straightway they *k* him,
Lk 2.43 Joseph and his mother *k* not of it.
4.41 for they *k* that he was Christ.
24.31 were opened, and they *k* him;
Jn 1.10 by him, and the world *k* him not.
31 I *k* him not: but that he should
33 I *k* him not: but he that sent me
2. 9 wine, and *k* not whence it was:
25 of man: for he *k* what was in man.
6. 6 he himself *k* what he would do.
64 For Jesus *k* from the beginning
11.42 I *k* that thou hearest me always:
13. 1 Jesus *k* that his hour was come
11 For he *k* who should betray him;
20. 9 For as yet they *k* not the scripture,
14 and *k* not that it was Jesus.
21. 4 disciples *k* not that it was Jesus.
Ac 12.14 And when she *k* Peter's voice, she
16. 3 *k* all that his father was a Greek.
19.34 when they *k* that he was a Jew,
22.29 after he *k* that he was a Roman,
Ro 1.21 when they *k* God, they glorified
1Co 1.21 the world by wisdom *k* not God,
2Co 5.21 him to be sin for us, who *k* no sin;
12. 2 *k* a man in Christ above fourteen
1Jn 3. 1 us not, because it *k* him not.
Rev 19.12 a name written, that no man *k*,

KNEWEST
Dt 8. 3 with manna, which thou *k* not,
Ru 2.11 people which thou *k* not heretofore.
Neh 9.10 for thou *k* that they dealt proudly
Ps 142. 3 within me, then thou *k* my path.
Isa 48. 8 thou heardest not; yea, thou *k* not;
Dan 5.22 heart, though thou *k* all this;
Mt 25.26 thou *k* that I reap where I sowed
Lk 19.22 Thou *k* that I was an austere man,
44 *k* not the time of thy visitation.
Jn 4.10 If thou *k* the gift of God, and who

KNIT
Jdg 20.11 the city, *k* together as one man.
1Sa 18. 1 Jonathan was *k* with the soul of
1Ch 12.17 mine heart shall be *k* unto you:
Ac 10.11 great sheet *k* at the four corners,
Col 2. 2 being *k* together in love, and unto
19 and *k* together, increaseth with the

KNOCK
Mt 7. 7 *k*, and it shall be opened unto
Lk 11. 9 *k*, and it shall be opened unto you.
13.25 stand without, and to *k* at the door,
Rev 3.20 Behold, I stand at the door, and *k*:

KNOCKED
Ac 12.13 And as Peter *k* at the door of the

KNOCKETH
SS 5. 2 is the voice of my beloved that *k*,
Mt 7. 8 to him that *k* it shall be opened.
Lk 11.10 to him that *k* it shall be opened.
12.36 that when he cometh and *k*, they

KNOCKING
Ac 12.16 But Peter continued *k*: and when

KNOW
Gen 3. 5 God doth *k* that in the day ye eat
22 as one of us, to *k* good and evil:
4. 9 I *k* not: Am I my brother's keeper?
22.12 for now I *k* that thou fearest God,
37.32 *k* now whether it be thy son's coat
42.34 then shall I *k* that ye are no spies,
Ex 3. 7 taskmasters; for I *k* their sorrows;
5. 2 I *k* not the Lord, neither will I let
7.17 thou shalt *k* that I am the Lord:
9.14 *k* that there is none like me in all
18.11 I *k* that the Lord is greater than all
33.12 I *k* thee by name, and thou hast
17 in my sight, and I *k* thee by name.
Nu 22.19 that I may *k* what the Lord will say
Dt 7. 9 *K* therefore that the Lord thy God,
13. 3 to *k* whether ye love the Lord your
31.27 I *k* thy rebellion, and thy stiff neck:
Jos 3.10 *k* that the living God is among you
Jdg 17.13 *k* I that the Lord will do me good,
1Sa 3. 7 Samuel did not yet *k* the Lord,
17.46 may *k* that there is a God in Israel.
47 *k*...the Lord saveth not with sword
21. 2 no man *k* any thing of the business
22. 3 till I *k* what God will do for me.
2Sa 14.20 *k* all things that are in the earth.
24. 2 I may *k* the number of the people.
1Ki 17.24 I *k* that thou art a man of God,
2Ki 2. 3, 5 Yea, I *k* it; hold ye your peace.
5. 8 he shall *k* that there is a prophet
19.27 I *k* thy abode, and thy going out,
1Ch 29.17 I *k* also, my God, that thou triest
2Ch 13. 5 Ought ye not to *k* that the Lord
Ezr 7.25 teach ye them that *k* them not.
Job 5.27 hear it, and *k* thou it for thy good.
7.10 shall his place *k* him any more.
8. 9 but of yesterday, and *k* nothing,
9. 2 I *k* it is so of a truth: but how
5 the mountains, and they *k* not:
21 perfect, yet would I not *k* my soul:
28 I *k* that thou wilt not hold me
10.13 heart: I *k* that this is with thee.
11. 6 *K* therefore that God exacteth of
8 than hell; what canst thou *k*?
13.18 cause; I *k* that I shall be justified.
15. 9 What knowest thou, that we *k* not?
19.25 For I *k* that my redeemer liveth,
21.19 rewardeth him, and he shall *k* it.
27 Behold, I *k* your thoughts, and
22.13 thou sayest, How doth God *k*?
30.23 I *k* that thou wilt bring...death,
31. 6 that God may *k* mine integrity.
32.22 I *k* not to give flattering titles;
34. 4 *k* among ourselves what is good.
36.26 God is great, and we *k* him not,
37.15 Dost thou *k* when God disposed
42. 2 I *k* that thou canst do every thing,
Ps 9.10 they that *k* thy name will put their
39. 4 Lord, make me to *k* mine end,
4 it is; that I may *k* how frail I am.
46.10 Be still, and *k* that I am God:
51. 6 thou shalt make me to *k* wisdom.
73.11 And they say, How doth God *k*?
16 When I thought to *k* this, it was
89.15 the people that *k* the joyful sound:
100. 3 *K* ye that the Lord he is God: it
103.16 place thereof shall *k* it no more.
139.23 me, O God, and *k* my heart:
23 heart: try me, and *k* my thoughts:
143. 8 cause me to *k* the way wherein I
Pr 1. 2 To *k* wisdom and instruction; to
10.32 righteous *k* what is acceptable:
24.12 keepeth thy soul, doth not he *k* it?
Ec 1.17 I gave my heart to *k* wisdom,
3.12 I *k* that there is no good in them,

Ec 3.14 I *k* that, whatsoever God doeth, it
9. 5 the dead *k* not any thing, neither
Isa 1. 3 Israel doth not *k*, my people doth
7.15 that he may *k* to refuse the evil,
41.23 that we may *k* that ye are gods:
44. 8 yea, there is no God; I *k* not any.
49.26 all flesh shall *k* that I the Lord
59. 8 The way of peace they *k* not;
12 as for our iniquities, we *k* them;
Jer 9. 3 and they *k* not me, saith the Lord.
10.23 I *k* that the way of man is not in
31.34 his brother, saying, *K* the Lord:
Eze 5.13 *k* that I the Lord have spoken it
17.12 *K* ye not what these things mean?
20.12 *k* that I am the Lord that sanctify
21. 5 all flesh may *k* that I the Lord have
22.22 *k* that I the Lord have poured out
Dan 4. 9 I *k* that the spirit of the holy gods
25 till thou *k* that the most High
5.23 which see not, nor hear, nor *k*:
11.32 the people that do *k* their God shall
Hos 8. 2 cry unto me, My God, we *k* thee.
13. 4 and thou shalt *k* no god but me:
5 I did *k* thee in the wilderness, in
Am 3.10 they *k* not to do right, saith the
Mic 3. 1 Is it not for you to *k* judgment?
Mt 6. 3 left hand *k* what thy right hand
7.11 *k* how to give good gifts unto your
16 Ye shall *k* them by their fruits.
20 by their fruits ye shall *k* them.
9. 6 *k* that the Son of man hath power
30 saying, See that no man *k* it.
13.11 *k* the mysteries of the kingdom of
20.22 and said, Ye *k* not what ye ask.
25 *k* that the princes of the Gentiles
22.16 Master, we *k* that thou art true,
24.32 leaves, ye *k* that summer is nigh:
33 all these things, *k* that it is near,
42 for ye *k* not what hour your Lord
43 But *k* this, that if the goodman
25.12 Verily I say unto you, I *k* you not.
13 ye *k* neither the day nor the hour
26. 2 *k* that after two days is the feast
70 saying, I *k* not what thou sayest.
72 with an oath, I do not *k* the man.
74 to swear, saying, I *k* not the man.
28. 5 I *k* that ye seek Jesus, which was
Mk 1.24 *k* thee who thou art, the Holy One
2.10 *k* that the Son of man hath power
4.11 to *k* the mystery of the kingdom
13 *K* ye not this parable? and how
13 how then will ye *k* all parables?
5.43 straitly that no man should *k* it;
7.24 house, and would have no man *k* it:
9.30 would not that any man should *k* it.
10.38 unto them, Ye *k* not what ye ask:
42 *k* that they which are accounted
12.14 Master, we *k* that thou art true,
24 because ye *k* not the scriptures,
13.28 leaves, ye *k* that summer is near:
29 come to pass, *k* that it is nigh, even
33 for ye *k* not when the time is.
35 *k* not when the master of the house
14.68 he denied, saying, I *k* not, neither
71 I *k* not this man of whom ye speak.
Lk 1. 4 mightest *k* the certainty of those
18 the angel, Whereby shall I *k* this?
34 shall this be, seeing I *k* not a man?
4.34 I *k* thee who thou art; the Holy
5.24 *k* that the Son of man hath power
8.10 *k* the mysteries of the kingdom of
9.55 Ye *k* not what manner of spirit
11.13 *k* how to give good gifts unto your
12.39 And this *k*, that if the goodman of
13.25 you, I *k* you not whence ye are:
27 you, I *k* you not whence ye are;
19.15 he might *k* how much every man
20.21 *k* that thou sayest and teachest
21.20 *k* that the desolation thereof is
30 ye see and *k* of your own selves
31 *k* ye that the kingdom of God is

22.57 him, saying, Woman, I *k* him not.
60 Man, I *k* not what thou sayest.
23.34 them; for they *k* not what they do.
24.16 that they should not *k* him.
Jn 1.26 one among you, whom ye *k* not;
3. 2 we *k* that thou art a teacher come
11 We speak that we do *k*, and testify
4.22 Ye worship ye *k* not what:
22 we *k* what we worship: for
25 unto him, I *k* that Messias cometh,
32 have meat to eat that ye *k* not of.
42 *k* that this is indeed the Christ,
5.32 and I *k* that the witness which he
42 I *k* you, that ye have not the love
6.42 whose father and mother we *k*?
7.17 his will, he shall *k* of the doctrine,
26 *k* indeed...this is the very Christ?
27 we *k* this man whence he is:
28 both *k* me, and ye *k* whence I am:
28 sent me is true, whom ye *k* not,
29 But I *k* him: for I am from him,
51 hear him, and *k* what he doeth?
8.14 I *k* whence I came, and whither I
19 Ye neither *k* me, nor my Father:
28 man, then shall ye *k* that I am he,
32 ye shall *k* the truth, and the truth
37 I *k* that ye are Abraham's seed;
52 Now we *k* that thou hast a devil.
55 have not known him; but I *k* him:
55 if I should say, I *k* him not,
55 but I *k* him, and keep his saying.
9.12 Where is he? He said, I *k* not.
20 We *k* that this is our son, and that
21 means he now seeth, we *k* not;
21 hath opened his eyes, we *k* not:
24 we *k* that this man is a sinner.
25 he be a sinner or no, I *k* not:
25 one thing I *k*, that, whereas I was
29 We *k* that God spake unto Moses:
29 fellow, we *k* not from whence he is.
30 that ye *k* not from whence he is,
31 we *k* that God heareth not sinners:
10. 4 follow him: for they *k* his voice.
5 they *k* not the voice of strangers.
14 good shepherd, and *k* my sheep,
15 me, even so *k* I the Father:
27 sheep hear my voice, and I *k* them,
38 that ye may *k*, and believe, that
11.22 I *k*, that even now, whatsoever
24 I *k* that he shall rise again in the
49 said unto them, Ye *k* nothing at all,
12.50 I *k* that his commandment is life
13. 7 now; but thou shalt *k* hereafter.
12 *K* ye what I have done to you?
17 If ye *k* these things, happy are ye
18 you all: I *k* whom I have chosen:
35 all men *k* that ye are my disciples,
14. 4 And whither I go ye *k*, and the
4 whither I go..., and the way ye *k*.
5 Lord, we *k* not whither thou goest;
5 goest; and how can we *k* the way?
7 and from henceforth ye *k* him,
17 but ye *k* him; for he dwelleth
20 ye shall *k* that I am in my Father,
31 world may *k* that I love the Father;
15.18 *k* that it hated me before it hated
21 they *k* not him that sent me.
17. 3 might *k* thee the only true God,
23 may *k* that thou hast sent me,
18.21 behold, they *k* what I said.
19. 4 may *k* that I find no fault in him.
20. 2 *k* not where they have laid him.
13 I *k* not where they have laid him.
21.24 we *k* that his testimony is true.
Ac 1. 7 not for you to *k* the times or the
2.22 you, as ye yourselves also know:
36 the house of Israel *k* assuredly,
3.16 man strong, whom ye see and *k*:
10.28 Ye *k* how that it is an unlawful
37 That word, I say, ye *k*, which was
12.11 Now I *k* of a surety, that the Lord

15. 7 ye *k* how that a good while ago
17.19 May we *k* what this new doctrine,
20 *k* therefore what these things mean.
19.15 and said, Jesus I *k*, and Paul
15 and Paul I *k*: but who are ye?
25 ye *k* that by this craft we have our
20.18 Ye *k*, from the first day that I came
25 I *k* that ye all, among whom I
29 I *k* this, that after my departing
34 ye yourselves *k*, that these hands
21.24 all may know that those things,
34 he could not *k* the certainty for the
22.14 that thou shouldest *k* his will, and
19 they *k* that I imprisoned and beat
24 *k* wherefore they cried so against
24.10 as I *k* that thou hast been of many
22 *k* the uttermost of your matter.
26. 3 I *k* thee to be expert in all customs
4 at Jerusalem, *k* all the Jews;
27 prophets? I *k* that thou believest.
28.22 we *k* that every where it is spoken
Ro 3.19 *k* that what things soever the law
6. 3 *K* ye not, that so many of us as
16 *K* ye not, that to whom ye yield
7. 1 *K* ye not, brethren, (for I speak to
1 speak to them that *k* the law,)
14 For we *k* that the law is spiritual:
18 For I *k* that in me (that is, in my
8.22 For we *k* that the whole creation
26 we *k* not what we should pray for
28 we *k* that all things work together
10.19 But I say, Did not Israel *k*? First
14.14 *k*, and am persuaded by the Lord
1Co 1.16 *k* not whether I baptized any other.
2. 2 not to *k* any thing among you, save
12 might *k* the things that are freely
14 neither can he *k* them, because
3.16 *K* ye not that ye are the temple
4. 4 For I *k* nothing by myself; yet am
19 and will *k*, not the speech of them
5. 6 *K* ye not that a little leaven
6. 2 ye not *k* that the saints shall judge
3 *K* ye not...we shall judge angels?
9 *K* ye not that the unrighteous
15 *K* ye not that your bodies are the
16 *k* ye not that he which is joined to
19 *k* ye not...your body is the temple
8. 1 we *k* that we all have knowledge.
2 nothing yet as he ought to *k*.
4 we *k* that an idol is nothing in the
9.13 ye not *k* that they which minister
24 *K* ye not that they which run in a
11. 3 I would have you *k*, that the head
12. 2 Ye *k* that ye were Gentiles, carried
13. 9 we *k* in part, and we prophesy in
12 now I *k* in part; but then shall I
12 shall I *k* even as also I am known.
14.11 I *k* not the meaning of the voice,
15.58 ye *k* that your labor is not in vain
16.15 (ye *k* the house of Stephanas, that
2Co 2. 4 ye might *k* the love which I have
9 I might *k* the proof of you, whether
5. 1 we *k* that if our earthly house of
16 *k* we no man after the flesh:
16 now henceforth *k* we him no more.
8. 9 ye *k* the grace of our Lord Jesus
9. 2 I *k* the forwardness of your mind,
13. 5 *K* ye not your own selves, how
6 *k* that we are not reprobates.
Gal 3. 7 *K* ye therefore that they which are
4.13 Ye *k* how through infirmity of the
Eph 1.18 *k* what is the hope of his calling,
3.19 And to *k* the love of Christ, which
5. 5 this ye *k*, that no whoremonger,
6.21 But that ye also may *k* my affairs,
22 that ye might *k* our affairs,
Php 1.19 For I *k* that this shall turn to my
25 I *k* that I shall abide and continue
2.19 good comfort, when I *k* your state.
22 But ye *k* the proof of him, that, as
3.10 That I may *k* him, and the power

4.12 I *k* both how to be abased, and
12 abased, and I *k* how to abound:
15 Now ye Philippians *k* also, that in
Col 4. 6 ye may *k* how ye ought to answer
8 that he might *k* your estate, and
1Th 1. 5 ye *k* what manner of men we were
2. 1 *k* our entrance in unto you, that it
2 were shamefully entreated, as ye *k*,
5 used we flattering words, as ye *k*,
11 *k* how we exhorted and comforted
3. 3 yourselves *k* that we are appointed
4 even as it came to pass, and ye *k*.
5 forbear, I sent to *k* your faith,
4. 2 *k* what commandments we gave
4 should *k* how to possess his vessel
5 as the Gentiles which *k* not God:
5. 2 yourselves *k* perfectly that the day
12 *k* them which labor among you,
2Th 1. 8 vengeance on them that *k* not God,
2. 6 now ye *k* what withholdeth that he
3. 7 *k* how ye ought to follow us:
1Ti 1. 8 But we *k* that the law is good,
3. 5 a man *k* not how to rule his own
15 *k* how thou oughtest to behave
4. 3 which believe and *k* the truth.
2Ti 1.12 for I *k* whom I have believed,
3. 1 This *k* also, that in the last days
Tit 1.16 They profess that they *k* God;
Heb 8.11 his brother, saying, *K* the Lord:
11 for all shall *k* me, from the least
10.30 *k* him that hath said, Vengeance
12.17 For ye *k* how that afterward,
13.23 *K* ye that our brother Timothy is
Jas 2.20 wilt thou *k*, O vain man, that faith
4. 4 *k* ye not that the friendship of the
14 *k* not what shall be on the morrow.
5.20 him *k*, that he which converteth
1Pe 1.18 ye *k* that ye were not redeemed
2Pe 1.12 of these things, though ye *k* them,
3.17 seeing ye *k* these things before,
1Jn 2. 3 hereby we do *k* that we *k* him,
4 He that saith, I *k* him, and keepeth
5 hereby *k* we that we are in him.
18 whereby we *k* that it is the last time.
20 the Holy One, and ye *k* all things.
21 you because ye *k* not the truth,
21 but because ye *k* it, and that no lie
29 If ye *k* that he is righteous,
29 ye *k* that every one that doeth
3. 2 we *k* that, when he shall appear,
5 *k* that he was manifested to take
14 We *k* that we have passed from
15 ye *k* that no murderer hath eternal
19 we *k* that we are of the truth,
24 hereby we *k* that he abideth in us,
4. 2 Hereby *k* ye the Spirit of God:
6 Hereby *k* we the spirit of truth,
13 Hereby *k* we that we dwell in him,
5. 2 we *k* that we love the children of
13 may *k* that ye have eternal life,
15 if we *k* that he hear us, whatsoever
15 we *k* that we have the petitions
18 We *k* that whosoever is born of God
19 we *k* that we are of God, and the
20 we *k* that the Son of God is come,
20 that we may *k* him that is true,
3Jn 12 and ye *k* that our record is true.
Jude 10 of those things which they *k* not:
10 but what they *k* naturally, as
Rev 2. 2 I *k* thy works, and thy labor,
9 I *k* thy works, and tribulation,
9 I *k* the blasphemy of them which say
13 I *k* thy works, and where thou
19 I *k* thy works, and charity, and
23 *k* that I am he which searcheth
3. 1 I *k* thy works, that thou hast a
3 shalt not *k* what hour I will come
8 I *k* thy works: behold, I have set
9 and to *k* that I have loved thee.
15 I *k* thy works, that thou art

KNOWEST

Gen 30.29 Thou *k* how I have served thee,
2Sa 7.20 for thou, Lord God, *k* thy servant.
2Ki 2. 3, 5 *k* thou that the Lord will take
Job 10. 7 Thou *k* that I am not wicked;
15. 9 What *k* thou, that we know not?
38.33 *K* thou the ordinances of heaven?
Ps 40. 9 refrained my lips, O Lord, thou *k*.
69. 5 O God, thou *k* my foolishness;
139. 2 Thou *k* my downsitting and mine
4 lo, O Lord, thou *k* it altogether.
Pr 27. 1 thou *k* not what a day may bring
Ec 11. 2 thou *k* not what evil shall be upon
Isa 55. 5 shalt call a nation that thou *k* not,
Jer 5.15 nation whose language thou *k* not,
12. 3 But thou, O Lord, *k* me: thou hast
15.15 O Lord, thou *k*: remember me,
Eze 37. 3 I answered, O Lord God, thou *k*.
Zec 4. 5 me, *K* thou not what these be?
Mt 15.12 *K* thou that the Pharisees were
Mk 10.19 Thou *k* the commandments, Do
Lk 18.20 Thou *k* the commandments, Do
22.34 shalt thrice deny that thou *k* me.
Jn 1.48 unto him, Whence *k* thou me?
3.10 of Israel, and *k* not these things?
13. 7 him, What I do thou *k* not now;
16.30 are we sure that thou *k* all things,
19.10 *k* thou not that I have power to
21.15, 16 Lord; thou *k* that I love thee.
17 unto him, Lord, thou *k* all things;
17 thou *k* that I love thee.
Ac 1.24 which *k* the hearts of all men,
25.10 no wrong, as thou very well *k*.
Ro 2.18 *k* his will, and approvest the
1Co 7.16 For what *k* thou, O wife, whether
16 or how *k* thou, O man, whether
2Ti 1.15 This thou *k*, that all they which
18 me at Ephesus, thou *k* very well.
Rev 3.17 and *k* not that thou art wretched,
7.14 And I said unto him, Sir, thou *k*.

KNOWETH

Jos 22.22 gods, the Lord God of gods, he *k*,
Job 12. 3 who *k* not such things as these?
14.21 come to honor, and he *k* it not;
15.23 he *k* that the day of darkness is
18.21 is the place of him that *k* not God.
23.10 he *k* the way that I take: when he
28.13 Man *k* not the price thereof;
Ps 1. 6 Lord *k* the way of the righteous:
44.21 for he *k* the secrets of the heart.
94.11 The Lord *k* the thoughts of man,
103.14 he *k* our frame; he remembereth
139.14 and that my soul *k* right well.
Pro 7.23 and *k* not that it is for his life.
9.18 he *k* not that the dead are there;
Ec 2.19 who *k* whether he shall be a wise
3.21 Who *k* the spirit of man that
6. 8 that *k* to walk before the living?
12 who *k* what is good for man in this
8. 7 For he *k* not that which shall be:
9.12 For man also *k* not his time: as the
Isa 1. 3 The ox *k* his owner, and the ass
29.15 Who seeth us? and who *k* us?
Jer 8. 7 the heaven *k* her appointed times;
Joel 2.14 Who *k* if he will return and repent,
Mt 6. 8 *k* what things ye have need of,
32 *k* that ye have need of all these
11.27 no man *k* the Son, but the Father;
27 neither *k* any man the Father,
24.36 of that day and hour *k* no man,
Mk 4.27 spring and grow up, he *k* not how.
13.32 that day and that hour *k* no man,
Lk 10.22 and no man *k* who the Son is,
12.30 *k* that ye have need of all these
16.15 men; but God *k* your hearts:
Jn 7.15 saying, How *k* this man letters,
27 cometh, no man *k* whence he is.
49 who *k* not the law are cursed.
10.15 As the Father *k* me, even so know
12.35 darkness *k* not whither he goeth.
14.17 it seeth him not, neither *k* him:
15.15 servant *k* not what his lord doeth:
19.35 he *k* that he saith true, that ye
Ac 15. 8 And God, which *k* the hearts, bare
19.35 there that *k* not how that the city
26.26 the king *k* of these things, before
Ro 8.27 *k* what is the mind of the Spirit,
1Co 2.11 what man *k* the things of a man,
11 the things of God *k* no man, but
3.20 Lord *k* the thoughts of the wise,
8. 2 man think that he *k* any thing,
2 he *k* nothing yet as he ought to
2Co 11.11 because I love you not? God *k*.
31 for evermore, *k* that I lie not.
12. 2, 3 of the body, I cannot tell: God *k*;)
2Ti 2.19 seal, The Lord *k* them that are his.
Jas 4.17 to him that *k* to do good, and
2Pe 2. 9 Lord *k* how to deliver the godly
1Jn 2.11 *k* not whither he goeth, because
3. 1 the world *k* us not, because it
20 than our heart, and *k* all things.
4. 6 he that *k* God heareth us; he that
7 loveth is born of God, and *k* God.
8 He that loveth not, *k* not God; for
Rev 2.17 no man *k* saving he that receiveth
12.12 he *k*...he hath but a short time.

KNOWING

Gen 3. 5 shall be as gods, *k* good and evil.
1Ki 2.32 my father David not *k* thereof,
Mt 9. 4 And Jesus *k* their thoughts said,
22.29 Ye do err, not *k* the scriptures, nor
Mk 5.30 *k* in himself that virtue had gone
33 *k* what was done in her, came
6.20 *k* that he was a just man and an
12.15 *k* their hypocrisy, said unto them,
Lk 8.53 him to scorn, *k* that she was dead.
9.33 one for Elias: not *k* what he said.
11.17 *k* their thoughts, said unto them,
Jn 13. 3 Jesus *k* that the Father had given
18. 4 *k* all things that should come upon
19.28 Jesus *k* that all things were now
21.12 art thou? *k* that it was the Lord.
Ac 2.30 *k* that God had sworn with an oath
5. 7 not *k* what was done, came in.
18.25 Lord, *k* only the baptism of John.
20.22 not *k* the things that shall befall
Ro 1.32 Who *k* the judgment of God, that
2. 4 not *k* that the goodness of God
5. 3 *k* that tribulation worketh
6. 6 *K* this, that our old man is
9 *K* that Christ being raised from
13.11 *k* the time, that now it is high time
2Co 1. 7 *k*, that as ye are partakers of the
4.14 *K* that he which raised up the Lord
5. 6 *k* that, whilst we are at home in
11 *K* therefore the terror of the Lord,
Gal 2.16 *K* that a man is not justified by
Eph 6. 8 *K* that whatsoever good thing any
9 *k* that your Master...is in heaven;
Php 1.17 *k* that I am set for the defense of
Col 3.24 *K* that of the Lord ye shall receive
4. 1 *k* that ye...have a Master in heaven.
1Th 1. 4 *K*, brethren beloved, your election
1Ti 1. 9 *K* this, that the law is not made
6. 4 *k* nothing, but doting about
2Ti 2.23 *k* that they do gender strifes.
3.14 *k* of whom thou hast learned them;
Tit 3.11 *K* that he that is such is subverted,
Phm 21 *k* that thou wilt also do more than
Heb 10.34 *k* in yourselves that ye have in
11. 8 went out, not *k* whither he went.
Jas 1. 3 *K* this, that the trying of your
3. 1 *k* that we shall receive the greater
1Pe 3. 9 *k* that ye are thereunto called,
5. 9 *k* that the same afflictions are
2Pe 1.14 *K* that shortly I must put off this
20 *K* this first, that no prophecy of
3. 3 *K* this first, that there shall come

Biblical Themes

KNOWLEDGE

The Lord God commanded the man, saying, Of every tree of the garden thou mayest freely eat: but of the tree of the knowledge of good and evil, thou shalt not eat of it: for in the day that thou eatest thereof thou shalt surely die. . . . And the serpent said unto the woman, Ye shall not surely die: for God doth know that in the day ye eat thereof, then your eyes shall be opened, and ye shall be as gods, knowing good and evil. . . . And the Lord God said, Behold, the man is become as one of us, to know good and evil. . . . Therefore the Lord God sent him forth from the garden of Eden. Gen 2.16-17; 3.4-5, 22-23

Because this was in thine heart, and thou hast not asked riches, wealth, or honor, nor the life of thine enemies, neither yet hast asked long life; but hast asked wisdom and knowledge for thyself, that thou mayest judge my people . . . wisdom and knowledge is granted unto thee; and I will give thee riches, and wealth, and honor, such as none of the kings have had that have been before thee. 2Ch 1.11-12

And all the kings of the earth sought the presence of Solomon, to hear his wisdom, that God had put in his heart. 2Ch 9.23

Lord, make me to know mine end, and the measure of my days, what it is: that I may know how frail I am. Ps 39.4

Understand, ye brutish among the people: and ye fools, when will ye be wise? . . . He that chastiseth the heathen, shall not he correct? he that teacheth man knowledge, shall not he know? Ps 94.8, 10

There is not a word in my tongue, but, lo, O Lord, thou knowest it altogether. Thou hast beset me behind and before, and laid thine hand upon me. Such knowledge is too wonderful for me; it is high, I cannot attain unto it. Ps 139.4-6

A wise man will hear, and will increase learning; and a man of understanding shall attain unto wise counsels. . . . The fear of the Lord is the beginning of knowledge: but fools despise wisdom and instruction. Pr 1.5, 7

I gave my heart to seek and search out by wisdom concerning all things that are done under heaven: this sore travail hath God given to the sons of man. . . . I have seen all the works that are done under the sun; and, behold, all is vanity and vexation of spirit. . . . For in much wisdom is much grief: and he that increaseth knowledge increaseth sorrow. Ec 1.13-14, 18

This shall be the covenant that I will make with the house of Israel; After those days, saith the Lord, I will put my law in their inward parts, and write it in their hearts. . . . And they shall teach no more every man his neighbor . . . saying, Know the Lord: for they shall all know me, from the least of them unto the greatest. Jer 31.33-34

Because thou hast rejected knowledge, I will also reject thee . . . seeing thou hast forgotten the law of thy God, I will also forget thy children. Hos 4.6

At that time Jesus answered and said, I thank thee, O Father . . . because thou hast hid these things from the wise and prudent, and hast revealed them unto babes. . . . no man knoweth the Son, but the Father; neither knoweth any man the Father, save the Son, and he to whomsoever the Son will reveal him. Mt 11.25, 27

Knowledge puffeth up, but charity edifieth. And if any man think that he knoweth any thing, he knoweth nothing yet as he ought to know. 1Co 8.1-2

If any of you lack wisdom, let him ask of God, that giveth to all men liberally . . . and it shall be given him. Jas 1.5

KNOWLEDGE

Gen 2. 9 the tree of *k* of good and evil.
Dt 1.39 had no *k* between good and evil,
1Sa 2. 3 the Lord is a God of *k*, and by
2Ch 1.10 Give me now wisdom and *k*, that
11 asked wisdom and *k* for thyself,
12 Wisdom and *k* is granted unto
30.22 taught the good *k* of the Lord:
Job 15. 2 Should a wise man utter vain *k*,
21.22 Shall any teach God *k*? seeing he
36. 3 I will fetch my *k* from afar,
4 that is perfect in *k* is with thee.
42. 3 he that hideth counsel without *k*?
Ps 19. 2 and night unto night sheweth *k*.
73.11 and is there *k* in the Most High?
119.66 Teach me good judgment and *k*:
139. 6 Such *k* is too wonderful for me;
Pr 1. 4 the young man *k* and discretion.
7 the Lord is the beginning of *k*:
2. 5 the Lord, and find the *k* of God.
6 out of his mouth cometh *k* and
3.20 By his *k* the depths are broken up,
9.10 the *k* of the holy is understanding.
10.14 Wise men lay up *k*: but the mouth
12. 1 Whoso loveth instruction loveth *k*:
23 A prudent man concealeth *k*:
15. 2 tongue of the wise useth *k* aright:
17.27 He that hath *k* spareth his words:
Ec 1.18 increaseth *k* increaseth sorrow.
2.21 labor is in wisdom, and in *k*,
26 good in his sight wisdom, and *k*,
7.12 the excellency of *k* is, that wisdom
9.10 there is no work, nor device, nor *k*,
12. 9 wise, he still taught the people *k*;
Isa 8. 4 the child shall have *k* to cry,
11. 2 the spirit of *k* and of the fear of
9 shall be full of the *k* of the Lord,
28. 9 Whom shall he teach *k*? and whom
47.10 thy *k*, it hath perverted thee;
53.11 by his *k* shall my righteous servant
58. 3 our soul, and thou takest no *k*?
Jer 10.14 Every man is brutish in his *k*:
Dan 5.12 as an excellent spirit, and *k*, and
Hos 4. 1 nor mercy, nor *k* of God in the land.
6. 6 *k* of God more than burnt offerings.
Hab 2.14 be filled with the *k* of the glory of
Mal 2. 7 the priest's lips should keep *k*,
Mt 14.35 men of that place had *k* of him,
Lk 1.77 give *k* of salvation unto his people
11.52 ye have taken away the key of *k*.
Ac 4.13 and they took *k* of them, that they
17.13 the Jews of Thessalonica had *k*
24. 8 mayest take *k* of all these things,
22 having more perfect *k* of that way,
Ro 1.28 not like to retain God in their *k*,
2.20 hast the form of *k* and of the truth
3.20 for by the law is the *k* of sin.
10. 2 zeal of God, but not according to *k*.
11.33 both of the wisdom and *k* of God!
15.14 full of goodness, filled with all *k*,
1Co 1. 5 him, in all utterance, and in all *k*;
8. 1 idols, we know that we all have *k*.
1 *K* puffeth up, but charity edifieth.
7 there is not in every man that *k*:
10 see thee which hast *k* sit at meat
11 And through thy *k* shall the weak
12. 8 the word of *k* by the same Spirit;
13. 2 understand all mysteries, and all *k*;
8 whether there be *k*, it shall vanish
14. 6 to you either by revelation, or by *k*,
15.34 for some have not the *k* of God:
2Co 2.14 manifest the savor of his *k* by us
4. 6 light of the *k* of the glory of God
6. 6 pureness, by *k*, by longsuffering,
8. 7 in faith, and utterance, and *k*, and
10. 5 exalteth itself against the *k* of God,
11. 6 I be rude in speech, yet not in *k*;
Eph 1.17 and revelation in the *k* of him:
3. 4 my *k* in the mystery of Christ)
19 love of Christ, which passeth *k*,
4.13 and of the *k* of the Son of God,
Php 1. 9 abound yet more and more in *k*
3. 8 excellency of the *k* of Christ Jesus
Col 1. 9 be filled with the *k* of his will in
10 and increasing in the *k* of God;
2. 3 all the treasures of wisdom and *k*.
3.10 is renewed in *k* after the image of
1Ti 2. 4 and to come unto the *k* of the truth.
2Ti 3. 7 able to come to the *k* of the truth.
Heb 10.26 have received the *k* of the truth,
Jas 3.13 and endued with *k* among you?
1Pe 3. 7 dwell with them according to *k*,
2Pe 1. 2 unto you through the *k* of God,
3 the *k* of him that hath called us
5 your faith virtue; and to virtue *k*;
6 And to *k*, temperance; and to
8 in the *k* of our Lord Jesus Christ.
2.20 in the *k* of the Lord and Saviour
3.18 in the *k* of our Lord and Saviour

KNOWN

Gen 45. 1 Joseph made himself *k* unto his
Nu 12. 6 Lord will make myself *k* unto him
Dt 11.28 other gods, which ye have not *k*.
1Ki 18.36 it be *k* this day that thou art God

1Ch 16. 8 make *k* his deeds among the
Ezr 4.13 Be it *k* now unto the king, that, if
Ps 9.16 The Lord is *k* by the judgment
31. 7 thou hast *k* my soul in adversities;
67. 2 That thy way may be *k* upon earth,
69.19 Thou hast *k* my reproach, and my
88.12 Shall thy wonders be *k* in the dark?
98. 2 Lord hath made *k* his salvation:
103. 7 He made *k* his ways unto Moses,
105. 1 make *k* his deeds among the people.
139. 1 thou hast searched me, and *k* me.
Pr 12.16 A fool's wrath is presently *k*: but
14.33 is in the midst of fools is made *k*.
20.11 Even a child is *k* by his doings,
31.23 Her husband is *k* in the gates,
Ec 5. 3 a fool's voice is *k* by multitude of
Isa 12. 5 things: this is *k* in all the earth.
40.21 Have ye not *k*? have ye not heard?
28 Hast thou not *k*? hast thou not
42.16 them in paths that they have not *k*:
Jer 5. 5 they have *k* the way of the Lord,
Eze 20. 5 and made myself *k* unto them in
39. 7 So will I make my holy name *k* in
Dan 2.45 God hath made *k* to the king what
3.18 be it *k* unto thee, O king, that we
Am 3. 2 You only have I *k* of all the
Zec 14. 7 day which shall be *k* to the Lord,
Mt 10.26 and hid, that shall not be *k*.
12. 7 if ye had *k* what this meaneth,
16 that they should not make him *k*:
33 for the tree is *k* by his fruit.
24.43 had *k* in what watch the thief
Mk 3.12 that they should not make him *k*.
Lk 2.15 the Lord hath made *k* unto us.
17 they made *k* abroad the saying
6.44 every tree is *k* by his own fruit.
7.39 *k* who and what manner of woman
8.17 shall not be *k* and come abroad.
12. 2 neither hid, that shall not be *k*.
39 had *k* what hour the thief would
19.42 Saying, If thou hadst *k*, even thou,
24.18 hast not *k* the things which are
35 *k* of them in breaking of bread.
Jn 7. 4 he himself seeketh to be *k* openly.
8.19 nor my Father: if ye had *k* me,
19 ye should have *k* my Father also:
55 Yet ye have not *k* him; but I
10.14 know my sheep, and am *k* of mine.
14. 7 *k* me, ye should have *k* my Father
9 yet hast thou not *k* me, Philip?
15.15 Father I have made *k* unto you.
16. 3 they have not *k* the Father, nor
17. 7 Now they have *k* that all things
8 have *k* surely that I came out from
25 Father, the world hath not *k* thee:
25 but I have *k* thee, and these
25 have *k* that thou hast sent me.
18.15 that disciple was *k* unto the high
16 which was *k* unto the high priest,
Ac 1.19 it was *k* unto all the dwellers at
2.14 be this *k* unto you, and hearken to
28 Thou hast made *k* to me the ways
4.10 Be it *k* unto you all, and to all
7.13 Joseph was made *k* to his brethren;
13 Joseph's kindred was made *k*
9.24 their laying await was *k* of Saul.
42 it was *k* throughout all Joppa;
13.38 Be it *k* unto you therefore, men
15.18 *K* unto God are all his works from
19.17 And this was *k* to all the Jews
22.30 he would have *k* the certainty
23.28 when I would have *k* the cause
28.28 Be it *k* therefore unto you, that
Ro 1.19 that which may be *k* of God is
3.17 way of peace have they not *k*:
7. 7 I had not *k* sin, but by the law:
7 I had not *k* lust, except the law
9.22 wrath, and to make his power *k*,
23 that he might make *k* the riches
11.34 who hath *k* the mind of the Lord?
16.26 made *k* to all nations for the
1Co 2. 8 for had they *k* it, they would not
16 who hath *k* the mind of the Lord,
8. 3 love God, the same is *k* of him.
13.12 shall I know even as also I am *k*.
14. 7 it be *k* what is piped or harped?
9 how shall it be *k* what is spoken?
2Co 3. 2 our hearts, *k* and read of all men:
5.16 we have *k* Christ after the flesh,
6. 9 As unknown, and yet well *k*;
Gal 4. 9 But now, after ye have *k* God,
9 rather are *k* of God, how turn ye
Eph 1. 9 made *k* unto us the mystery of his
3. 3 he made *k* unto me the mystery;
5 not made *k* unto the sons of men,
10 be *k* by the church the manifold
6.19 make *k* the mystery of the gospel,
21 shall make *k* to you all things:
Php 4. 5 moderation be *k* unto all men.
6 requests be made *k* unto God.
Col 1.27 would make *k* what is the riches
4. 9 shall make *k* unto you all things
2Ti 3.10 thou hast fully *k* my doctrine,
15 thou hast *k* the holy scriptures,
4.17 the preaching might be fully *k*,
Heb 3.10 and they have not *k* my ways.
2Pe 1.16 we made *k* unto you the power
2.21 for them not to have *k* the way
21 than, after they have *k* it, to turn
1Jn 2.13 *k* him that is from the beginning.
13 because ye have *k* the Father.
14 *k* him that is from the beginning.
3. 6 hath not seen him, neither *k* him.
4.16 have *k* and believed the love that
2Jn 1 also all they that have *k* the truth;
Rev 2.24 have not *k* the depths of Satan,

L

LABOR

Ex 20. 9 Six days shalt thou *l*, and do all
Dt 5.13 Six days thou shalt *l*, and do all
Jos 24.13 you a land for which ye did not *l*,
Job 9.29 be wicked, why then *l* I in vain?
Ps 90.10 yet is their strength *l* and sorrow;
104.23 forth unto his work and to his *l*
127. 1 house, they *l* in vain that build it:
128. 2 shalt eat the *l* of thine hands:
Pr 10.16 *l* of the righteous tendeth to life:
14.23 In all *l* there is profit: but the
23. 4 *L* not to be rich: cease from thine
Ec 1. 3 What profit hath a man of all his *l*
8 All things are full of *l*; man
2.10 for my heart rejoiced in all my *l*:
11 the *l* that I had labored to
18 I hated all my *l* which I had taken
22 For what hath man of all his *l*, and
3.13 and enjoy the good of all his *l*, it is
4. 8 yet is there no end of all his *l*;
8 For whom do I *l*, and bereave my
9 have a good reward for their *l*.
6. 7 All the *l* of man is for his mouth,
10.15 *l* of the foolish wearieth every one
Isa 55. 2 your *l* for that which satisfieth not?
65.23 They shall not *l* in vain, nor bring
Jer 51.58 and the people shall *l* in vain, and
La 5. 5 we *l*, and have no rest.
Hab 3.17 the *l* of the olive shall fail, and
Hag 1.11 and upon all the *l* of the hands.
Mt 11.28 Come unto me, all ye that *l* and
Jn 4.38 that whereon ye bestowed no *l*:
6.27 *L* not for…meat which perisheth,
Ro 16. 6 who bestowed much *l* on us.
12 and Tryphosa, who *l* in the Lord.
1Co 3. 8 reward according to his own *l*.
4.12 *l*, working with our own hands:
15.58 your *l* is not in vain in the Lord.
2Co 5. 9 Wherefore we *l*, that, whether
Gal 4.11 have bestowed upon you *l* in vain.
Eph 4.28 rather let him *l*, working with his
Php 1.22 the flesh, this is the fruit of my *l*:
2.25 my brother, and companion in *l*,
Col 1.29 Whereunto I also *l*, striving
1Th 1. 3 your work of faith, and *l* of love,
2. 9 brethren, our *l* and travail:
3. 5 tempted you, and our *l* be in vain.
5.12 to know them which *l* among you,
2Th 3. 8 wrought with *l* and travail night
1Ti 4.10 we both *l* and suffer reproach,
5.17 who *l* in the word and doctrine.
Heb 4.11 *l* therefore to enter into that rest,
6.10 to forget your work and *l* of love,
Rev 2. 2 I know thy works, and thy *l*, and

LABORED

Neh 4.21 So we *l* in the work: and half of
Job 20.18 which he *l* for shall he restore,
Ec 2.11 on the labor that I had *l* to do:
19 all my labor wherein I have *l*,
21 to a man that hath not *l* therein
22 wherein he hath *l* under the sun?
5.16 hath he that hath *l* for the wind?
Isa 47.12 thou hast *l* from thy youth;
15 with whom thou hast *l*, even thy
49. 4 Then I said, I have *l* in vain, I have
62. 8 thy wine, for the which thou hast *l*:
Dan 6.14 he *l* till the going down of the sun
Jon 4.10 for the which thou hast not *l*,
Jn 4.38 other men *l*, and ye are entered
Ro 16.12 Persis, which *l* much in the Lord.
1Co 15.10 I *l* more abundantly than they all:
Php 2.16 not run in vain, neither *l* in vain.
4. 3 which *l* with me in the gospel,
Rev 2. 3 and for my name's sake hast *l*,

LABORER

Lk 10. 7 for the *l* is worthy of his hire.
1Ti 5.18 And, The *l* is worthy of his reward.

LABORERS

Mt 9.37 is plenteous, but the *l* are few;
38 will send forth *l* into his harvest.
20. 1 morning to hire *l* into his vineyard.
2 agreed with the *l* for a penny a day,
8 Call the *l*, and give them their hire,
Lk 10. 2 truly is great, but the *l* are few:
2 that he would send forth *l* into his
1Co 3. 9 For we are *l* together with God:
Jas 5. 4 the hire of the *l* who have reaped

LABORETH

Pr 16.26 He that *l*…for himself; for
26 *l* for himself; for his mouth
Ec 3. 9 he that worketh wherein he *l*?
1Co 16.16 one that helpeth with us, and *l*.
2Ti 2. 6 husbandman that *l* must be first

LABORING

Ec 5.12 The sleep of a *l* man is sweet,
Ac 20.35 so *l* ye ought to support the weak,
Col 4.12 *l* fervently for you in prayers,
1Th 2. 9 for *l* night and day, because we

LABORS

Ex 23.16 of harvest, the firstfruits of thy *l*,
16 gathered in thy *l* out of the field.
Dt 28.33 The fruit of thy land, and all thy *l*,
Pr 5.10 *l* be in the house of a stranger;
Isa 58. 3 pleasure, and exact all your *l*.
Jer 20. 5 of this city, and all the *l* thereof,
Hos 12. 8 my *l* they shall find none iniquity
Hag 2.17 hail in all the *l* of your hands;
Jn 4.38 and ye are entered into their *l*.
2Co 6. 5 in imprisonments, in tumults, in *l*,
10.15 measure, that is, of other men's *l*;
11.23 in *l* more abundant, in stripes
Rev 14.13 that they may rest from their *l*;

LACK

Gen 18.28 there shall *l* five of the fifty
28 destroy all the city for *l* of five?
Ex 16.18 he that gathered little had no *l*;
Dt 8. 9 thou shalt not *l* any thing in it;
Job 4.11 old lion perisheth for *l* of prey,
38.41 God, they wander for *l* of meat.
Ps 34.10 The young lions do *l*, and suffer
Pr 28.27 giveth unto the poor shall not *l*:
Ec 9. 8 and let thy head *l* no ointment.
Hos 4. 6 are destroyed for *l* of knowledge:
Mt 19.20 from my youth up: what *l* I yet?
2Co 8.15 that had gathered little had no *l*.
Php 2.30 to supply your *l* of service toward
1Th 4.12 that ye may have *l* of nothing.
Jas 1. 5 If any of you *l* wisdom, let him

LACKED

Dt 2. 7 with thee; thou hast *l* nothing.
2Sa 2.30 *l* of David's servants nineteen
17.22 the morning light there *l* not one
1Ki 4.27 man in his month: they *l* nothing.
11.22 But what hast thou *l* with me,
Neh 9.21 wilderness, so that they *l* nothing;
Lk 8. 6 away, because it *l* moisture.
22.35 scrip, and shoes, *l* ye any thing?
Ac 4.34 was there any among them that *l*:
1Co 12.24 honor to that part which *l*:
Php 4.10 also careful, but ye *l* opportunity.

LACKEST

Mk 10.21 said unto him, One thing thou *l*:
Lk 18.22 unto him, Yet *l* thou one thing:

LACKETH

Nu 31.49 and there *l* not one man of us.
2Sa 3.29 on the sword, or that *l* bread.
Pr 6.32 with a woman *l* understanding:
12. 9 honoreth himself, and *l* bread.
2Pe 1. 9 that *l* these things is blind,

LACKING

Lev 2.13 to be *l* from thy meat offering:
22.23 thing superfluous or *l* in his parts,
Jdg 21. 3 be to day one tribe *l* in Israel?
1Sa 30.19 And there was nothing *l* to them,
Jer 23. 4 neither shall they be *l*, saith the
1Co 16.17 that which was *l* on your part they
2Co 11. 9 that which was *l* to me the brethren
1Th 3.10 that which is *l* in your faith?

LAD

Gen 21.20 God was with the *l*; and he grew,
22. 5 and I and the *l* will go yonder and
44.22 The *l* cannot leave his father: for
32 thy servant became surety for the *l*
1Sa 20.36 And as the *l* ran, he shot an arrow
37 when the *l* was come to the place
39 But the *l* knew not any thing: only
Jn 6. 9 There is a *l* here, which hath five

LADDER

Gen 28.12 behold a *l* set up on the earth,

LADE

Gen 45.17 *l* your beasts, and go, get you
1Ki 12.11 did *l* you with a heavy yoke,
Lk 11.46 *l* men with burdens grievous to

LADED

Gen 42.26 they *l* their asses with the corn,
44.13 and *l* every man his ass, and
Neh 4.17 bare burdens, with those that *l*,
Ac 28.10 *l* us with such things as were

LADEN

Gen 45.23 ten asses *l* with the good things
23 ten she asses *l* with corn and
1Sa 16.20 And Jesse took an ass *l* with bread,
Isa 1. 4 people *l* with iniquity, a seed of
Mt 11.28 all ye that labor and are heavy *l*,
2Ti 3. 6 captive silly women *l* with sins,

LADIES

Jdg 5.29 Her wise *l* answered her, yea, she
Est 1.18 *l* of Persia and Media say this day

LADING

Neh 13.15 bringing in sheaves, and *l* asses;
Ac 27.10 not only of the *l* and ship, but

LADY

Isa 47. 5 be called, The *l* of kingdoms.
7 thou saidst, I shall be a *l* for ever:
2Jn 1 unto the elect *l* and her children,
5 I beseech thee, *l*, not as though I

LAID

Gen 22. 6 and *l* it upon Isaac his son;
9 there, and *l* the wood in order,
9 *l* him on the altar upon the wood.
Ex 16.34 Aaron *l* it up before the Testimony,
Nu 27.23 he *l* his hands upon him, and
Dt 34. 9 Moses had *l* his hands upon him:
1Sa 3. 3 and Samuel was *l* down to sleep;
1Ki 19. 6 drink, and *l* him down again.
2Ki 9.25 the Lord *l* this burden upon him;
Ezr 3. 6 foundation of the temple…was not yet *l*.
Job 6. 2 and my calamity *l* in the balances
29. 9 and *l* their hand on their mouth.

31. 9 *l* wait at my neighbor's door;
38. 4 I *l* the foundations of the earth?
5 Who hath *l* the measures thereof,
6 or who *l* the corner stone thereof;
Ps 3. 5 I *l* me down and slept; I awaked;
88. 6 Thou hast *l* me in the lowest pit,
104. 5 Who *l* the foundations of the earth,
139. 5 before, and *l* thine hand upon me.
Isa 23.14 for your strength is *l* waste.
48.13 hath *l* the foundation of the earth,
53. 6 Lord hath *l* on him the iniquity
64.11 all our pleasant things are *l* waste.
Jer 36.20 they *l* up the roll in the chamber of
Zec 3. 9 behold the stone that I have *l*
4. 9 *l* the foundation of this house;
Mt 3.10 axe is *l* unto the root of the trees:
8.14 he saw his wife's mother *l*, and
14. 3 Herod had *l* hold on John, and bound
18.28 he *l* hands on him, and took him by
19.15 he *l* his hands on them, and
26.50 came they, and *l* hands on Jesus,
55 the temple, and ye *l* no hold on me.
57 they that had *l* hold on Jesus led him
27.60 *l* it in his own new tomb, which
Mk 6. 5 he *l* his hands upon a few sick
17 had sent forth and *l* hold upon John,
29 up his corpse, and *l* it in a tomb.
56 they *l* the sick in the streets, and
7.30 and her daughter *l* upon the bed.
14.46 they *l* their hands on him, and
51 the young men *l* hold on him: and
15.46 *l* him in a sepulcher which was
47 of Joses beheld where he was *l*.
16. 6 behold the place where they *l* him.
Lk 1.66 them *l* them up in their hearts,
2. 7 clothes, and *l* him in a manger;
3. 9 axe is *l* unto the root of the trees:
4.40 *l* his hands on every one of them,
6.48 and *l* the foundation on a rock:
12.19 much goods *l* up for many years;
13.13 he *l* his hands on her: and
14.29 he hath *l* the foundation, and is not
16.20 Lazarus, which was *l* at his gate,
19.20 which I have kept *l* up in a napkin:
22 taking up that I *l* not down, and
23.26 they *l* hold upon one Simon, a
26 on him they *l* the cross, that he
53 *l* it in a sepulcher that was hewn
53 wherein never man before was *l*.
55 and how his body was *l*.
24.12 the linen clothes *l* by themselves,
Jn 7.30 no man *l* hands on him, because
44 him; but no man *l* hands on him.
8.20 temple: and no man *l* hands on him;
11.34 Where have ye *l* him? They said
41 the place where the dead was *l*.
13. 4 supper, and *l* aside his garments:
19.41 wherein was never man yet *l*.
42 There *l* they Jesus therefore
20. 2 know not where they have *l* him.
13 I know not where they have *l* him.
15 tell me where thou hast *l* him, and
21. 9 and fish *l* thereon, and bread.
Ac 3. 2 *l* daily at the gate of the temple
4. 3 they *l* hands on them, and put
35 *l* them down at the apostles' feet:
37 and *l* it at the apostles' feet.
5. 2 part, and *l* it at the apostles' feet.
15 and *l* them on beds and couches,
18 *l* their hands on the apostles, and
6. 6 they *l* their hands on them.
7.16 *l* in the sepulcher that Abraham
58 witnesses *l* down their clothes at
8.17 Then *l* they their hands on them,
9.37 they *l* her in an upper chamber.
13. 3 and *l* their hands on them, they
29 tree, and *l* him in a sepulcher.
36 was *l* unto his fathers, and saw
16.23 had *l* many stripes upon them,
19. 6 Paul had *l* his hands upon them,
20. 3 And when the Jews *l* wait for him,
21.27 all the people, and *l* hands on him,
23.29 nothing *l* to his charge worthy of
30 that the Jews *l* wait for the man,
25. 7 *l* many and grievous complaints
16 the crime *l* against him.
27 signify the crimes *l* against him.
28. 3 of sticks, and *l* them on the fire,
8 *l* his hands on him, and healed
Ro 16. 4 my life *l* down their own necks:
1Co 3.10 I have *l* the foundation, and
11 can no man lay than that is *l*,
9.16 for necessity is *l* upon me; yea,
Col 1. 5 hope which is *l* up for you in
2Ti 4. 8 there is *l* up for me a crown of
16 it may not be *l* to their charge.
Heb 1.10 hast *l* the foundation of the earth;
1Jn 3.16 because he *l* down his life for us:
Rev 1.17 he *l* his right hand upon me,
20. 2 he *l* hold on the dragon, that old

LAIN

Nu 5.19 If no man have *l* with thee, and
20 some man have *l* with thee
Jdg 21.11 woman that hath *l* by man.
Job 3.13 I have *l* still and been quiet,
Jn 11.17 had *l* in the grave four days already.
20.12 where the body of Jesus had *l*.

LAKE

Lk 5. 1 God, stood by the *l* of Gennesaret,
2 saw two ships standing by the *l*:
8.22 over unto the other side of the *l*.
23 down a storm of wind on the *l*;
33 down a steep place into the *l*,
Rev 19.20 both were cast alive into a *l* of fire
20.10 them was cast into the *l* of fire
14 and hell were cast into the *l* of fire.
15 of life was cast into the *l* of fire.
21. 8 their part in the *l* which burneth

LAMA

Mt 27.46 saying, Eli, Eli, *l* sabachthani?
Mk 15.34 saying, Eloi, Eloi, *l* sabachthani?

LAMB

Gen 22. 8 God will provide himself a *l* for a
Ex 12. 3 shall take to them every man a *l*,
2Sa 12. 3 had nothing, save one little ewe *l*,
4 took the poor man's *l*, and dressed
6 And he shall restore the *l* fourfold,
Isa 11. 6 wolf also shall dwell with the *l*,
53. 7 is brought as a *l* to the slaughter,
65.25 wolf and the *l* shall feed together,
Jn 1.29 and saith, Behold the *L* of God,
36 he saith, Behold the *L* of God!
Ac 8.32 like a *l* dumb before his shearer, so
1Pe 1.19 of Christ, as of a *l* without blemish
Rev 5. 6 stood a *L* as it had been slain,
8 elders fell down before the *L*,
12 Worthy is the *L* that was slain to
13 the throne, and unto the *L* for ever
6. 1 when the *L* opened one of the seals,
16 and from the wrath of the *L*:
7. 9 before the throne, and before the *L*,
10 upon the throne, and unto the *L*.
14 them white in the blood of the *L*.
17 *L* which is in the midst of the throne
12.11 overcame him by the blood of the *L*,
13. 8 written in the book of life of the *L*
11 and he had two horns like a *l*, and
14. 1 lo, a *L* stood on the mount Sion, and
4 These are they which follow the *L*
4 firstfruits unto God and to the *L*.
10 angels, and in the presence of the *L*:
15. 3 of God, and the song of the *L*,
17.14 These shall make war with the *L*,
14 and the *L* shall overcome them:
19. 7 for the marriage of the *L* is come,
9 unto the marriage supper of the *L*.
21.14 of the twelve apostles of the *L*.
22 Lord God Almighty and the *L* are
23 it, and the *L* is the light thereof.
22. 1 of the throne of God and of the *L*.
3 throne of God and of the *L* shall be

LAMB'S

Rev 21. 9 shew thee the bride, the *L* wife.
27 are written in the *L* book of life.

LAMBS

Ps 114. 4 and the little hills like *l*.
6 rams; and ye little hills, like *l*?
Pr 27.26 The *l* are for thy clothing, and
Isa 5.17 the *l* feed after their manner,
40.11 shall gather the *l* with his arm,
Jer 51.40 them down like *l* to the slaughter,
Lk 10. 3 send you forth as *l* among wolves.
Jn 21.15 He saith unto him, Feed my *l*.

LAME

Lev 21.18 a blind man, or a *l*, or he that hath
Dt 15.21 as if it be *l*, or blind, or have any ill
2Sa 4. 4 had a son that was *l* of his feet.
4 to flee, that he fell, and became *l*.
5. 6 take away the blind and the *l*,
8 Jebusites, and the *l* and the blind,
8 the *l* shall not come into the house.
9. 3 yet a son, which is *l* on his feet.
13 table; and was *l* on both his feet.
19.26 the king; because thy servant is *l*.
Job 29.15 the blind, and feet was I to the *l*.
Pr 26. 7 The legs of the *l* are not equal: so
Isa 33.23 spoil divided; the *l* take the prey.
35. 6 shall the *l* man leap as an hart,
Jer 31. 8 and with them the blind and the *l*,
Mal 1. 8 offer the *l* and sick, is it not evil?
13 was torn, and the *l*, and the sick;
Mt 11. 5 *l* walk, the lepers are cleansed,
15.30 with them those that were *l*, blind,
31 the *l* to walk, and the blind to see:
21.14 the *l* came to him in the temple;
Lk 7.22 *l* walk, the lepers are cleansed,
14.13 poor, the maimed, the *l*, the blind:
Ac 3. 2 man *l* from his mother's womb
11 the *l* man which was healed held
8. 7 and that were *l*, were healed.
Heb 12.13 which is *l* be turned out of the way;

LAMENT

Jdg 11.40 to *l* the daughter of Jephthah
Isa 3.26 And her gates shall *l* and mourn;
19. 8 cast angle into the brooks shall *l*,
32.12 They shall *l* for the teats, for the
Jer 4. 8 you with sackcloth, *l* and howl:
16. 5 neither go to *l* nor bemoan them:
6 neither shall men *l* for them, nor
22.18 They shall not *l* for him, saying,
18 they shall not *l* for him, saying,
34. 5 they will *l* thee, saying, Ah lord!
49. 3 *l*, and run to and fro by the hedges;
La 2. 8 the rampart and the wall to *l*;
Eze 27.32 for thee, and *l* over thee, saying,
32.16 wherewith they shall *l* her:
16 daughters of the nations shall *l* her:
16 shall *l* for her, even for Egypt,
Joel 1. 8 *L* like a virgin girded with
13 Gird yourselves, and *l*, ye priests:
Mic 2. 4 and *l* with a doleful lamentation,
Jn 16.20 That ye shall weep and *l*, but the
Rev 18. 9 shall bewail her, and *l* for her,

LAMENTATION

Gen 50.10 with a great and very sore *l*:
2Sa 1.17 with this *l* over Saul and over
Ps 78.64 and their widows made no *l*.
Jer 6.26 as for an only son, most bitter *l*:
7.29 and take up a *l* on high places;
9.10 habitations of the wilderness a *l*,
20 and every one her neighbor *l*.
31.15 in Ramah, *l*, and bitter weeping;
48.38 There shall be *l* generally upon
La 2. 5 daughter of Judah mourning and *l*.

A lamp used by early Christians in the Roman catacombs; symbol in the halo stands for Christ.

Eze 19. 1 up a *l* for the princes of Israel,
14 This is a *l*, and shall be for a *l*.
26.17 they shall take up a *l* for thee, and
27. 2 son of man, take up a *l* for Tyrus;
32 they shall take up a *l* for thee, and
28.12 take up a *l* upon the king of Tyrus,
32. 2 up a *l* for Pharaoh king of Egypt,
16 *l* wherewith they shall lament her:
Am 5. 1 you, even a *l*, O house of Israel.
16 such as are skilful of *l* to wailing.
8.10 and all your songs into *l*;
Mic 2. 4 and lament with a doleful *l*, and
Mt 2.18 a voice heard, *l*, and weeping,
Ac 8. 2 burial, and made great *l* over him.

LAMENTATIONS

2Ch 35.25 women spake of Josiah in their *l*
25 behold, they are written in the *l*.
Eze 2.10 there was written therein *l*, and

LAMENTED

1Sa 6.19 the people *l*, because the Lord had
7. 2 house of Israel *l* after the Lord.
25. 1 and *l* him, and buried him in his
28. 3 Israel had *l* him, and buried him
2Sa 1.17 And David *l* with this lamentation
3.33 the king *l* over Abner, and said,
2Ch 35.25 And Jeremiah *l* for Josiah: and all
Jer 16. 4 they shall not be *l*; neither shall
25.33 they shall not be *l*, neither gathered,
Mt 11.17 unto you, and ye have not *l*.
Lk 23.27 which also bewailed and *l* him.

LAMP

Gen 15.17 burning *l* that passed between
Ex 27.20 to cause the *l* to burn always.
1Sa 3. 3 *l* of God went out in the temple the
2Sa 22.29 For thou art my *l*, O Lord: and the
1Ki 15. 4 his God give him a *l* in Jerusalem,
Job 12. 5 as a *l* despised in the thought of
Ps 119.105 Thy word is a *l* unto my feet,
132.17 ordained a *l* for mine anointed.
Pr 6.23 For the commandment is a *l*; and
13. 9 the *l* of the wicked shall be put out.
20.20 his *l* shall be put out in obscure
Isa 62. 1 the salvation thereof as a *l* that
Rev 8.10 heaven, burning as it were a *l*,

LAMPS

Ex 25.37 shalt make the seven *l* thereof:
37 they shall light the *l* thereof, that
30. 7 when he dresseth the *l*, he shall
8 when Aaron lighteth the *l* at even,
35.14 and his *l*, with the oil for the light,
37.23 And he made his seven *l*, and his
39.37 candlestick, with the *l* thereof,
37 even with the *l* to be set in order,
40. 4 candlestick, and light the *l* thereof,
25 he lighted the *l* before the Lord;
Lev 24. 2 to cause the *l* to burn continually.
4 the *l* upon the pure candlestick
Nu 4. 9 the light, and his *l*, and his tongs,
8. 2 unto him, When thou lightest the *l*,
2 the seven *l* shall give light over
3 lighted the *l* thereof over against
Jdg 7.16 and *l* within the pitchers.
20 and held the *l* in their left hands,
1Ki 7.49 and the *l*, and the tongs of gold,
1Ch 28.15 and for their *l* of gold, by weight
15 candlestick, and for the *l* thereof:
15 and also for the *l* thereof,
2Ch 4.20 the candlesticks with their *l*, that
21 flowers, and the *l*, and the tongs,
13.11 of gold with the *l* thereof, to burn
29. 7 put out the *l*, and have not burned
Job 41.19 Out of his mouth go burning *l*,
Eze 1.13 fire, and like the appearance of *l*:
Dan 10. 6 lightning, and his eyes as *l* of fire,
Zec 4. 2 top of it, and his seven *l* thereon,
2 and seven pipes to the seven *l*,
Mt 25. 1 ten virgins, which took their *l*,
3 foolish took their *l*, and took no oil
4 took oil in their vessels with their *l*.
7 virgins arose, and trimmed their *l*.
8 of your oil; for our *l* are gone out.
Rev 4. 5 seven *l* of fire burning before the

LAND

Gen 1. 9 place, and let the dry *l* appear:
10 and God called the dry *l* Earth; and
2.12 the gold of that *l* is good: there is
4.16 dwelt in the *l* of Nod, on the east
7.22 of all that was in the dry *l*, died.
11.31 Chaldees, to go into the *l* of Canaan;
12. 1 unto a *l* that I will shew thee:
7 said, Unto thy seed will I give this *l*:
10 was a famine in the *l*: and Abram
13. 6 the *l* was not able to bear them,
17. 8 the *l* wherein thou art a stranger,
22. 2 and get thee into the *l* of Moriah;
31. 3 Return unto the *l* of thy fathers,
37. 1 was a stranger, in the *l* of Canaan.
41.30 and the famine shall consume the *l*;
54 in all the *l* of Egypt...was bread.
42. 7 From the *l* of Canaan to buy food.
9, 12 nakedness of the *l* ye are come.
45.18 and ye shall eat the fat of the *l*.
47.13 there was no bread in all the *l*;
15 when money failed in the *l* of Egypt,
20 Joseph bought all the *l* of Egypt
20 them: so the *l* became Pharaoh's.
Ex 3. 8 them up out of that *l* unto a good *l*
8 a *l* flowing with milk and honey;
11. 3 Moses was...great in the *l* of Egypt,
5 firstborn in the *l* of Egypt shall die,
6 be a great cry throughout all the *l*
12.12 will smite all the firstborn in the *l*
13. 5 a *l* flowing with milk and honey,
14.21 made the sea dry *l*, and the waters
29 Israel walked upon dry *l* in the midst
20.12 thy days may be long upon the *l*
23.10 six years thou shalt sow thy *l*, and
19 The first of the firstfruits of thy *l*
Lev 25. 2 shall the *l* keep a sabbath unto the
4 shall be a sabbath of rest unto the *l*,
10 liberty throughout all the *l* unto
18 ye shall dwell in the *l* in safety.
19 And the *l* shall yield her fruit, and
23 The *l* shall not be sold for ever:
23 for the *l* is mine; for ye are
26. 6 And I will give peace in the *l*, and
Nu 13.17 them to spy out the *l* of Canaan,
18 see the *l*, what it is; and the people
21 they went up, and searched the *l*
32 is a *l* that eateth up the inhabitants
14. 7 to search it, is an exceeding good *l*.
35.34 Defile not therefore the *l* which ye
Dt 1. 8 Behold, I have set the *l* before you:
21 thy God hath set the *l* before thee:
25 is a good *l* which the Lord our God
8. 7 into a good *l*, a *l* of brooks of water,
11.12 A *l* which the Lord thy God careth
15. 4 Lord shall greatly bless thee in the *l*
15 wast a bondman in the *l* of Egypt.
16.20 inherit the *l* which the Lord thy God
27. 2 ye shall pass over Jordan unto the *l*
30. 5 thy God will bring thee into the *l*
Jos 4.22 Israel came over this Jordan on dry *l*.
14. 4 no part unto the Levites in the *l*,
Ru 1. 7 way to return unto the *l* of Judah.
2.11 mother, and the *l* of thy nativity,
2Sa 15. 4 Oh that I were made judge in the *l*,
2Ki 23.35 but he taxed the *l* to give the money
2Ch 19. 5 he set judges in the *l* throughout
Est 10. 1 Ahasuerus laid a tribute upon the *l*,
Job 10.22 A *l* of darkness, as darkness itself;
28.13 is it found in the *l* of the living.
39. 6 and the barren *l* his dwellings.
Ps 27.13 of the Lord in the *l* of the living.
37.29 The righteous shall inherit the *l*,
63. 1 for thee in a dry and thirsty *l*, where
85. 1 hast been favorable unto thy *l*:
9 him; that glory may dwell in our *l*.
12 and our *l* shall yield her increase.
88.12 in the *l* of forgetfulness?
137. 4 sing the Lord's song in a strange *l*?
142. 5 my portion in the *l* of the living.
143. 6 thirsteth after thee, as a thirsty *l*.
Pr 2.21 For the upright shall dwell in the *l*,
29. 4 by judgment establisheth the *l*:
31.23 he sitteth among the elders of the *l*.
Ec 10.16 Woe to thee, O *l*, when thy king is
17 Blessed art thou, O *l*, when thy king
SS 2.12 voice of the turtle is heard in our *l*;
Isa 1.19 ye shall eat the good of the *l*:
2. 8 Their *l* also is full of idols; they
24. 3 The *l* shall be utterly emptied, and
32. 2 shadow of a great rock in a weary *l*.
33.17 shall behold the *l* that is very far off.
35. 7 and the thirsty *l* springs of water:
36.17 a *l* like your own *l*, a *l* of corn and
17 wine, a *l* of bread and vineyards.
38.11 even the Lord, in the *l* of the living:
41.18 and the dry *l* springs of water.
53. 8 was cut off out of the *l* of the living:
60.18 shall no more be heard in thy *l*,
Jer 2. 6 a *l* that no man passed through,
31 a *l* of darkness? wherefore say my
7. 7 in the *l* that I gave to your fathers,
11. 5 a *l* flowing with milk and honey,
19 cut him off from the *l* of the living,
12. 4 How long shall the *l* mourn, and the
42.13 ye say, We will not dwell in this *l*,
14 but we will go into the *l* of Egypt,
44.22 therefore is your *l* a desolation,
51.47 her whole *l* shall be confounded,
52. 6 was no bread for the people of the *l*.
Eze 7.23 for the *l* is full of bloody crimes,
8.17 they have filled the *l* with violence,
14.13 when the *l* sinneth against me by
32.23 caused terror in the *l* of the living.
33. 2 When I bring the sword upon a *l*,
45. 1 the Lord, an holy portion of the *l*:
Hos 4. 1 nor knowledge of God in the *l*.

3 Therefore shall the *l* mourn, and
Joel 1. 2 give ear, all ye inhabitants of the *l*.
10 The field is wasted, the *l* mourneth;
2. 1 all the inhabitants of the *l* tremble:
3 the *l* is as the garden of Eden
18 will the Lord be jealous for his *l*,
21 Fear not, O *l*; be glad and rejoice:
Am 7. 2 an end of eating the grass of the *l*,
17 and thy *l* shall be divided by line;
Zep 1. 3 I will cut off man from off the *l*,
18 whole *l* shall be devoured by fire
Hag 2. 4 and be strong, all ye people of the *l*,
Zec 7. 5 Speak unto all the people of the *l*,
Mal 3.12 for ye shall be a delightsome *l*,
Mt 2. 6 thou Bethlehem in the *l* of Juda,
20 mother, and go into the *l* of Israel:
21 and came into the *l* of Israel.
4.15 The *l* of Zabulon, and the
15 Zabulon, and the *l* of Nephthalim,
9.26 hereof went abroad into all that *l*.
10.15 for the *l* of Sodom and Gomorrha
11.24 more tolerable for the *l* of Sodom
14.34 they came into the *l* of Gennesaret.
23.15 ye compass sea and *l* to make one
27.45 there was darkness over all the *l*
Mk 1. 5 out unto him all the *l* of Judea,
4. 1 multitude was by the sea on the *l*.
6.47 of the sea, and he alone on the *l*.
53 they came into the *l* of Gennesaret,
15.33 there was darkness over the whole *l*
Lk 4.25 famine was throughout all the *l*;
5. 3 would thrust out a little from the *l*.
11 they had brought their ships to *l*,
8.27 when he went forth to *l*, there met
14.35 It is neither fit for the *l*, nor yet for
15.14 arose a mighty famine in that *l*;
21.23 shall be great distress in the *l*,
Jn 3.22 his disciples into the *l* of Judea;
6.21 the ship was at the *l* whither they
21. 8 were not far from *l*, but as it were
9 soon then as they were come to *l*,
11 drew the net to *l* full of great fishes,
Ac 4.37 Having *l*, sold it, and brought the
5. 3 back part of the price of the *l*?
8 whether ye sold the *l* for so much?
7. 3 come into the *l* which I shall shew
4 he out of the *l* of the Chaldaeans,
4 he removed him into this *l*, wherein
6 seed should sojourn in a strange *l*;
11 dearth over all the *l* of Egypt and
29 was a stranger in the *l* of Madian,
36 and signs in the *l* of Egypt, and in
40 brought us out of the *l* of Egypt,
10.39 did both in the *l* of the Jews, and
13.17 as strangers in the *l* of Egypt,
19 seven nations in the *l* of Chanaan,
19 he divided their *l* to them by lot.
27.39 it was day, they knew not the *l*:
43 first into the sea, and get to *l*:
44 pass, that they escaped all safe to *l*.
Heb 8. 9 to lead them out of the *l* of Egypt;
11. 9 he sojourned in the *l* of promise,
29 through the Red sea as by dry *l*:
Jude 5 the people out of the *l* of Egypt,

LANDED
Ac 18.22 when he had *l* at Caesarea, and
21. 3 sailed into Syria, and *l* at Tyre:

LANDING
Ac 28.12 *l* at Syracuse, we tarried there

LANDMARK
Dt 19.14 not remove thy neighbor's *l*,
27.17 he that removeth his neighbor's *l*.
Pr 22.28 Remove not the ancient *l*, which
23.10 Remove not the old *l*; and enter

LANDMARKS
Job 24. 2 Some remove the *l*; they violently

LANDS
Ps 49.11 call their *l* after their own names.
66. 1 a joyful noise unto God, all ye *l*:
100. 1 joyful noise unto the Lord, all ye *l*.
105.44 And gave them the *l* of the heathen:
107. 3 gathered them out of the *l*, from
Isa 36.20 they among all the gods of these *l*,
Mt 19.29 children, or *l*, for my name's sake,
Mk 10.29 wife, or children, or *l*, for my sake,
30 and mothers, and children, and *l*,
Ac 4.34 as were possessors of *l* or houses

LANES
Lk 14.21 into the streets and *l* of the city,

LANGUAGE
Gen 11. 1 And the whole earth was of one *l*,
6 is one, and they have all one *l*;
7 down, and there confound their *l*,
9 confound the *l* of all the earth:
2Ki 18.26 to thy servants in the Syrian *l*;
26 and talk not with us in the Jews' *l*
28 cried with a loud voice in the Jews' *l*,
Neh 13.24 and could not speak in the Jews' *l*,
24 according to the *l* of each people.
Est 1.22 and to every people after their *l*,
22 according to the *l* of every people.
3.12 and to every people after their *l*;
8. 9 and unto every people after their *l*,
9 writing, and according to their *l*.
Ps 19. 3 There is no speech nor *l*, where
81. 5 heard a *l* that I understood not.
114. 1 Jacob from a people of strange *l*;
Isa 19.18 of Egypt speak the *l* of Canaan,
36.11 unto thy servants in the Syrian *l*;
11 and speak not to us in the Jews' *l*,
13 cried with a loud voice in the Jews' *l*,
Jer 5.15 nation whose *l* thou knowest not,
Eze 3. 5, 6 strange speech and of an hard *l*,
Dan 3.29 That every people, nation, and *l*,
Zep 3. 9 will I turn to the people a pure *l*,
Ac 2. 6 heard them speak in his own *l*.

LANGUAGES
Dan 3. 4 O people, nations, and *l*,
7 the people, the nations, and the *l*,
4. 1 unto all people, nations, and *l*, that
5.19 people, nations, and *l*, trembled
6.25 unto all people, nations, and *l*, that
7.14 that all people, nations, and *l*,
Zec 8.23 hold out of all *l* of the nations,

LANTERNS
Jn 18. 3 cometh thither with *l* and torches

LAODICEA
Col 2. 1 have for you, and for them at *L*,
4.13 for you, and them that are in *L*,
15 Salute the brethren which are in *L*,
16 ye likewise read the epistle from *L*.
Rev 1.11 unto Philadelphia, and unto *L*.

LAODICEANS
Col 4.16 read also in the church of the *L*;
Rev 3.14 angel of the church of the *L* write;

LAPPETH
Jdg 7. 5 Every one that *l* of the water with
5 water with his tongue, as a dog *l*,

LARGE
Gen 34.21 behold, it is *l* enough for them;
Ex 3. 8 that land unto a good land and a *l*,
Jdg 18.10 people secure, and to a *l* land:
2Sa 22.20 me forth also into a *l* place:
Neh 4.19 The work is great and *l*, and we
7. 4 the city was *l* and great: but
9.35 in the *l* and fat land which thou
Ps 18.19 me forth also into a *l* place;
31. 8 thou hast set my feet in a *l* room.
118. 5 me, and set me in a *l* place.
Isa 22.18 like a ball into a *l* country:
30.23 shall thy cattle feed in *l* pastures.
33 he hath made it deep and *l*:
Jer 22.14 me a wide house and *l* chambers,
Eze 23.32 of thy sister's cup deep and *l*:
Hos 4.16 feed them as a lamb in a *l* place.
Mt 28.12 gave *l* money unto the soldiers,
Mk 14.15 he will shew you a *l* upper room
Lk 22.12 he shall shew you a *l* upper room
Gal 6.11 see how *l* a letter I have written
Rev 21.16 the length is as *l* as the breadth:

LASCIVIOUSNESS
Mk 7.22 wickedness, deceit, *l*, an evil eye,
2Co 12.21 and *l* which they have committed.
Gal 5.19 fornication, uncleanness, *l*,
Eph 4.19 have given themselves over unto *l*,
1Pe 4. 3 when we walked in *l*, lusts, excess
Jude 4 turning the grace of our God into *l*,

LASEA
Ac 27. 8 nigh whereunto was the city of *L*.

LAST
Gen 49. 1 shall befall you in the *l* days.
19 but he shall overcome at the *l*
Nu 23.10 and let my *l* end be like his!
2Sa 19.11 ye the *l* to bring the king back
12 are ye the *l* to bring back the king?
23. 1 Now these be the *l* words of David.
1Ch 23.27 For by the *l* words of David the
29.29 acts of David the king, first and *l*,
2Ch 9.29 of the acts of Solomon, first and *l*,
12.15 the acts of Rehoboam, first and *l*,
16.11 behold, the acts of Asa, first and *l*,
20.34 acts of Jehoshaphat, first and *l*,
25.26 of the acts of Amaziah, first and *l*,
26.22 of the acts of Uzziah, first and *l*,
28.26 acts and of all his ways, first and *l*,
35.27 And his deeds, first and *l*, behold,
Ezr 8.13 And of the *l* sons of Adonikam,
Neh 8.18 from the first day unto the *l* day,
Pr 5.11 And thou mourn at the *l*, when
23.32 At the *l* it biteth like a serpent,
Isa 2. 2 it shall come to pass in the *l* days,
41. 4 Lord, the first, and with the *l*;
44. 6 I am the first, and I am the *l*; and
48.12 he; I am the first, I also am the *l*.
Jer 12. 4 said, He shall not see our *l* end.
50.17 and *l* this Nebuchadrezzar king of
La 1. 9 she remembereth not her *l* end;
Dan 4. 8 at the *l* Daniel came in before me,
8. 3 other, and the higher came up *l*.
19 thee know what shall be in the *l*
Am 9. 1 slay the *l* of them with the sword:
Mic 4. 1 in the *l* days it shall come to pass,
Mt 12.45 *l* state of that man is worse than
19.30 many that are first shall be *l*;
30 and the *l* shall be first.
20. 8 beginning from the *l* unto the first.
12 These *l* have wrought but one hour,
14 I will give unto this *l*, even as unto
16 So the *l* shall be first, and the first *l*:
21.37 But *l* of all he sent unto them his
22.27 And *l* of all the woman died also.
26.60 At the *l* came two false witnesses,
27.64 the *l* error shall be worse than
Mk 9.35 be first, the same shall be *l* of all,
10.31 are first shall be *l*; and the *l* first.
12. 6 he sent him also *l* unto them,
22 seed: *l* of all the woman died also.
Lk 11.26 *l* state of that man is worse than
12.59 till thou hast paid the very *l* mite.
13.30 there are *l* which shall be first,
30 there are first which shall be *l*.
20.32 *L* of all the woman died also.
Jn 6.39 raise it up again at the *l* day.
40, 44, 54 raise him up at the *l* day.
7.37 In the *l* day, that great day of the
8. 9 at the eldest, even unto the *l*:
11.24 in the resurrection at the *l* day.

Biblical Themes

LAST THINGS

Of old hast thou laid the foundation of the earth: and the heavens are the work of thy hands. They shall perish, but thou shalt endure: yea, all of them shall wax old like a garment; as a vesture shalt thou change them, and they shall be changed: but thou art the same, and thy years shall have no end.
Ps 102.25-27

There shall be a time of trouble, such as never was since there was a nation . . . and at that time thy people shall be delivered . . . . many of them that sleep in the dust of the earth shall awake, some to everlasting life, and some to shame and everlasting contempt.
Dan 12.1-2

I heard, but I understood not: then said I, O my Lord, what shall be the end of these things? And he said, Go thy way, Daniel: for the words are closed up and sealed till the time of the end.
Dan 12.8-9

The sun shall be turned into darkness, and the moon into blood, before the great and the terrible day of the Lord come. Joel 2.31

In the last days . . . the mountain of the house of the Lord shall be established in the top of the mountains, and it shall be exalted above the hills; and people shall flow unto it. And many nations shall come, and say, Come, and let us go up to the mountain of the Lord . . . and he will teach us of his ways . . . for the law shall go forth of Zion, and the word of the Lord from Jerusalem.
Mic 4.1-2

The great day of the Lord is near, it is near, and hasteth greatly, even the voice of the day of the Lord: the mighty man shall cry there bitterly. That day is a day of wrath, a day of trouble and distress, a day of wasteness and desolation, a day of darkness and gloominess, a day of clouds and thick darkness.
Zep 1.14-15

Every idle word that men shall speak, they shall give account thereof in the day of judgment. Mt 12.36

When the Son of man shall come in his glory, and all the holy angels with him, then shall he sit upon the throne of his glory: and before him shall be gathered all nations: and he shall separate them one from another, as a shepherd divideth his sheep from the goats.
Mt 25.31-32

But of that day and that hour knoweth no man, no, not the angels which are in heaven, neither the Son, but the Father. Take ye heed, watch and pray: for ye know not when the time is.
Mk 13.32-33

He that rejecteth me, and receiveth not my words, hath one that judgeth him: the word that I have spoken, the same shall judge him in the last day.
Jn 12.48

I reckon that the sufferings of this present time are not worthy to be compared with the glory which shall be revealed in us. Ro 8.18

Judge nothing before the time, until the Lord come, who both will bring to light the hidden things of darkness. 1Co 4.5

The day of the Lord will come as a thief in the night. 2Pe 3.10

To him that overcometh will I grant to sit with me in my throne, even as I also overcame, and am set down with my Father in his throne. Rev 3.21

And I saw the dead, small and great, stand before God; and the books were opened: and another book was opened, which is the book of life: and the dead were judged out of those things which were written in the books, according to their works. . . . And whosoever was not found written in the book of life was cast into the lake of fire. Rev 20.12, 15

Jn 12.48 same shall judge him in the *l* day.
Ac 2.17 it shall come to pass in the *l* days,
1Co 4. 9 hath set forth us the apostles *l*,
15. 8 And *l* of all he was seen of me also,
26 *l* enemy that shall be destroyed is
45 the *l* Adam was made a quickening
52 twinkling of an eye, at the *l* trump:
Php 4.10 at the *l* your care of me hath
2Ti 3. 1 in the *l* days perilous times shall
Heb 1. 2 Hath in the *l* days spoken unto us
Jas 5. 3 treasure together for the *l* days.
1Pe 1. 5 ready to be revealed in the *l* time.
20 manifest in these *l* times for you,
2Pe 3. 3 shall come in the *l* days scoffers,
1Jn 2.18 Little children, it is the *l* time: and
18 we know that it is the *l* time.
Jude 18 should be mockers in the *l* time,
Rev 1.11 and Omega, the first and the *l*:
17 Fear not; I am the first and the *l*,
2. 8 things saith the first and the *l*,
19 and the *l* to be more than the first.
15. 1 angels having the seven *l* plagues;
21. 9 vials full of the seven *l* plagues,
22.13 and the end, the first and the *l*.

LASTING

Dt 33.15 the precious things of the *l* hills,

LATCHET

Isa 5.27 nor the *l* of their shoes be broken:
Mk 1. 7 *l* of whose shoes I am not worthy
Lk 3.16 *l* of whose shoes I am not worthy
Jn 1.27 shoe's *l* I am not worthy to unloose.

LATE

Ps 127. 2 you to rise up early, to sit up *l*,
Mic 2. 8 of *l* my people is risen up as an
Jn 11. 8 Jews of *l* sought to stone thee;

LATELY

Ac 18. 2 *l* come from Italy, with his wife

LATIN

Lk 23.38 in letters of Greek, and *L*, and
Jn 19.20 in Hebrew, and Greek, and *L*.

LATTER

Ex 4. 8 will believe the voice of the *l* sign.
Nu 24.14 do to thy people in the *l* days.
20 but his *l* end shall be that he perish
Dt 4.30 even in the *l* days, if thou turn to
8.16 thee, to do thee good at thy *l* end;
11.14 the first rain and the *l* rain,
24. 3 if the *l* husband hate her, and
3 or if the *l* husband die, which took
31.29 evil will befall you in the *l* days;
32.29 they would consider their *l* end!
Ru 3.10 shewed more kindness in the *l* end
2Sa 2.26 it will be bitterness in the *l* end?
Job 8. 7 thy *l* end should greatly increase.
19.25 stand at the *l* day upon the earth:
29.23 their mouth wide as for the *l* rain.
42.12 the Lord blessed the *l* end of Job
Pr 16.15 favor is as a cloud of the *l* rain.
19.20 thou mayest be wise in thy *l* end.
Isa 41.22 and know the *l* end of them; or
47. 7 didst remember the *l* end of it.
Jer 3. 3 and there hath been no *l* rain;
5.24 rain, both the former and the *l*,
23.20 in the *l* days ye shall consider it
30.24 in the *l* days ye shall consider it.
48.47 the captivity of Moab in the *l* days,
49.39 it shall come to pass in the *l* days,
Eze 38. 8 in the *l* years thou shalt come into
16 the land; it shall be in the *l* days,
Dan 2.28 what shall be in the *l* days.
8.23 And in the *l* time of their kingdom,
10.14 befall thy people in the *l* days:
11.29 not be as the former, or as the *l*.
Hos 3. 5 and his goodness in the *l* days.
6. 3 as the *l* and former rain unto the
Joel 2.23 and the *l* rain in the first month.
Am 7. 1 the shooting up of the *l* growth;
1 *l* growth after the king's mowings.
Hag 2. 9 The glory of this *l* house shall be
Zec 10. 1 rain in the time of the *l* rain;
1Ti 4. 1 *l* times some shall depart from
Jas 5. 7 he receive the early and *l* rain.
2Pe 2.20 *l* end is worse with them than the

LAUD

Ro 15.11 Gentiles; and *l* him, all ye people.

LAUGH

Gen 18.13 Wherefore did Sarah *l*, saying,
15 And he said, Nay; but thou didst *l*.
21. 6 said, God hath made me to *l*,
6 that all that hear will *l* with me.
Job 5.22 and famine thou shalt *l*: neither
9.23 will *l* at the trial of the innocent.
22.19 and the innocent *l* them to scorn.
Ps 2. 4 sitteth in the heavens shall *l*:
22. 7 they that see me *l* me to scorn:
37.13 The Lord shall *l* at him: for he
52. 6 see, and fear, and shall *l* at him:
59. 8 But thou, O Lord, shalt *l* at them;
80. 6 our enemies *l* among themselves.
Pr 1.26 I also will *l* at your calamity; I
29. 9 he rage or *l*, there is no rest.

Ec 3. 4 A time to weep, and a time to *l*;
Lk 6.21 ye that weep now: for ye shall *l*.
25 Woe unto you that *l* now! for ye

LAUGHED

Gen 17.17 Abraham fell upon his face, and *l*,
18.12 Sarah *l* within herself, saying,
15 Sarah denied, saying, I *l* not; for
2Ki 19.21 despised thee, and *l* thee to scorn;
2Ch 30.10 they *l* them to scorn, and mocked
Neh 2.19 heard it, they *l* us to scorn, and
Job 12. 4 the just upright man is *l* to scorn.
29.24 If I *l* on them, they believed it not;
Isa 37.22 despised thee, and *l* thee to scorn;
Eze 23.32 be *l* to scorn and had in derision;
Mt 9.24 And they *l* him to scorn.
Mk 5.40 they *l* him to scorn. But when he
Lk 8.53 they *l* him to scorn, knowing that

LAUGHTER

Ps 126. 2 Then was our mouth filled with *l*,
Pr 14.13 Even in *l* the heart is sorrowful;
Ec 2. 2 I said of *l*, It is mad: and of mirth,
7. 3 Sorrow is better than *l*: for by the
6 under a pot, so is the *l* of the fool:
10.19 A feast is made for *l*, and wine
Jas 4. 9 let your *l* be turned to mourning,

LAUNCH

Lk 5. 4 *L* out into the deep, and let down

LAUNCHED

Lk 8.22 of the lake. And they *l* forth.
Ac 21. 1 were gotten from them, and had *l*,
27. 2 we *l*, meaning the sail by the
4 And when we *l* from thence, we

LAW

Ex 13. 9 the Lord's *l* may be in thy mouth:
16. 4 they will walk in my *l*, or no.
24.12 give thee tables of stone, and a *l*,
Nu 6.13 And this is the *l* of the Nazarite,
Dt 17.18 write him a copy of this *l* in a book
27. 8 all the words of this *l* very plainly.
28.58 do all the words of this *l* that are
31.26 Take this book of the *l*, and put it
Jos 1. 8 This book of the *l* shall not depart
8.32 the stones a copy of the *l* of Moses,
1Sa 18.23 a light thing to be a king's son in *l*,
2Ki 10.31 to walk in the *l* of the Lord God
22. 8 I have found the book of the *l* in
2Ch 12. 1 forsook the *l* of the Lord, and all
Neh 8. 2 And Ezra the priest brought the *l*
13 to understand the words of the *l*.
18 read in the book of the *l* of God.
Est 4.11 is one *l* of his to put him to death,
Ps 1. 2 his delight is in the *l* of the Lord;
2 in his *l* doth he meditate day and
19. 7 The *l* of the Lord is perfect,
37.31 The *l* of his God is in his heart;
78. 1 Give ear, O my people, to my *l*:
94.12 and teachest him out of thy *l*;
119. 1 who walk in the *l* of the Lord.
18 wondrous things out of thy *l*.
34 and I shall keep thy *l*; yea, I shall
44 So shall I keep thy *l* continually
61 but I have not forgotten thy *l*.
77 may live: for thy *l* is my delight.
97 O how love I thy *l*! it is my
142 and thy *l* is the truth.
153 me: for I do not forget thy *l*.
174 O Lord; and thy *l* is my delight.
Pr 3. 1 My son, forget not my *l*; but let
6.23 is a lamp; and the *l* is light;
7. 2 my *l* as the apple of thine eye.
13.14 *l* of the wise is a fountain of life,
28. 7 Whoso keepeth the *l* is a wise son:
29.18 he that keepeth the *l*, happy is he.
Isa 1.10 give ear unto the *l* of our God, ye
30. 9 will not hear the *l* of the Lord:
42. 4 and the isles shall wait for his *l*.
21 he will magnify the *l*, and make it
51. 7 the people in whose heart is my *l*;
Jer 8. 8 and the *l* of the Lord is with us?
9.13 they have forsaken my *l* which I
31.33 will put my *l* in their inward parts,
La 2. 9 the *l* is no more; her prophets also
Eze 7.26 the *l* shall perish from the priest,
43.12 This is the *l* of the house; upon
Dan 6. 5 him concerning the *l* of his God.
8, 12 *l* of the Medes and Persians,
Hos 4. 6 hast forgotten the *l* of thy God,
Am 2. 4 have despised the *l* of the Lord,
Mic 7. 6 daughter in *l* against her mother
6 daughter...against her mother in *l*;
Mal 2. 6 The *l* of truth was in his mouth,
Mt 5.17 that I am come to destroy the *l*,
18 shall in no wise pass from the *l*, till
40 if any man will sue thee at the *l*,
7.12 for this is the *l* and the prophets.
10.35 daughter in *l* against her mother
35 daughter...against her mother in *l*.
11.13 and the *l* prophesied until John.
12. 5 have ye not read in the *l*, how that
22.36 the great commandment in the *l*?
40 commandments hang all the *l* and
23.23 the weightier matters of the *l*,
Lk 2.22 according to the *l* of Moses were
23 it is written in the *l* of the Lord,
24 which is said in the *l* of the Lord,
27 for him after the custom of the *l*,
39 according to the *l* of the Lord,
5.17 and doctors of the *l* sitting by,
10.26 him, What is written in the *l*?
12.53 mother in *l* against her daughter
53 mother...against her daughter in *l*
53 daughter in *l* against her mother
53 daughter...against her mother in *l*.
16.16 The *l* and the prophets were until
17 pass, than one tittle of the *l* to fail.
24.44 were written in the *l* of Moses,
Jn 1.17 For the *l* was given by Moses, but
45 found him, of whom Moses in the *l*,
7.19 Did not Moses give you the *l*, and
19 and yet none of you keepeth the *l*?
23 *l* of Moses should not be broken;
49 who knoweth not the *l* are cursed.
51 Doth our *l* judge any man, before
8. 5 Now Moses in the *l* commanded us,
17 It is also written in your *l*, that
10.34 them, Is it not written in your *l*,
12.34 have heard out of the *l* that Christ
15.25 be fulfilled that is written in their *l*,
18.13 for he was father in *l* to Caiaphas,
31 judge him according to your *l*.
19. 7 a *l*, and by our *l* he ought to die,
Ac 5.34 named Gamaliel, a doctor of the *l*,
6.13 against this holy place, and the *l*:
7.53 received the *l* by the disposition
13.15 after the reading of the *l* and the
39 not be justified by the *l* of Moses.
15. 5 them to keep the *l* of Moses.
24 be circumcised, and keep the *l*:
18.13 to worship God contrary to the *l*.
15 of words and names, and of your *l*,
19.38 *l* is open, and there are deputies:
21.20 and they are all zealous of the *l*:
24 walkest orderly, and keepest the *l*.
28 against the people, and the *l*, and
22. 3 to the perfect manner of the *l* of
12 a devout man according to the *l*,
23. 3 sittest thou to judge me after the *l*,
3 to be smitten contrary to the *l*?
29 be accused of questions of their *l*,
24. 6 have judged according to our *l*.
14 all things which are written in the *l*
25. 8 Neither against the *l* of the Jews,
28.23 Jesus, both out of the *l* of Moses,
Ro 2.12 as many as have sinned without *l*
12 shall also perish without *l*:
12 as many as have sinned in the *l*
12 shall be judged by the *l*;
13 not the hearers of the *l* are just
13 the doers of the *l* shall be justified.
14 the Gentiles, which have not the *l*,
14 do...the things contained in the *l*,
14 having not the *l*, are a *l* unto
15 of the *l* written in their hearts,
17 called a Jew, and restest in the *l*,
18 being instructed out of the *l*;
20 knowledge and of the truth in the *l*.
23 that makest thy boast of the *l*,
23 through breaking the *l* dishonorest
25 verily profiteth, if thou keep the *l*:
25 but if thou be a breaker of the *l*,
26 keep the righteousness of the *l*,
27 which is by nature, if it fulfil the *l*,
27 thee, who...dost transgress the *l*?
3.19 that what things soever the *l* saith,
19 saith to them who are under the *l*:
20 by the deeds of the *l* there shall no
20 for by the *l* is the knowledge of sin.
21 of God without the *l* is manifested,
21 being witnessed by the *l* and the
27 By what *l*? of works? Nay: but by
27 Nay: but by the *l* of faith.
28 by faith without the deeds of the *l*.
31 make void the *l* through faith?
31 God forbid: yea, we establish the *l*.
4.13 or to his seed, through the *l*, but
14 if they which are of the *l* be heirs,
15 Because the *l* worketh wrath;
15 no *l* is, there is no transgression.
16 not to that only which is of the *l*,
5.13 until the *l* sin was in the world:
13 is not imputed where there is no *l*.
20 Moreover the *l* entered, that the
6.14 ye are not under the *l*, but under
15 we are not under the *l*, but under
7. 1 I speak to them that know the *l*,)
1 the *l* hath dominion over a man as
2 is bound by the *l* to her husband so
2 is loosed from the *l* of her husband.
3 be dead she is free from that *l*;
4 become dead to the *l* by the body
5 sins, which were by the *l*, did work
6 now we are delivered from the *l*,
7 say then, Is the *l* sin? God forbid.
7 I had not known sin, but by the *l*:
7 known lust, except the *l* had said,
8 For without the *l* sin was dead.
9 For I was alive without the *l* once:
12 Wherefore the *l* is holy, and the
14 For we know that the *l* is spiritual:
16 I consent unto the *l* that it is good.
21 I find then a *l*, that, when I would
22 I delight in the *l* of God after the
23 I see another *l* in my members,
23 warring against the *l* of my mind,
23 me into captivity to the *l* of sin
25 mind I myself serve the *l* of God;
25 but with the flesh the *l* of sin.
8. 2 the *l* of the Spirit of life in Christ
2 me free from the *l* of sin and death.
3 what the *l* could not do, in that it
4 the righteousness of the *l* might be
7 not subject to the *l* of God, neither
9. 4 and the giving of the *l*, and the
31 after the *l* of righteousness,
31 attained to the *l* of righteousness.
32 as it were by the works of the *l*.
10. 4 For Christ is the end of the *l* for
5 the righteousness which is of the *l*,
13. 8 loveth another hath fulfilled the *l*.
10 love is the fulfilling of the *l*.
1Co 6. 1 go to *l* before the unjust, and not
6 brother goeth to *l* with brother,
7 ye go to *l* one with another.
7.39 wife is bound by the *l* as long as
9. 8 or saith not the *l* the same also?
9 For it is written in the *l* of Moses,
20 are under the *l*, as under the *l*,
20 gain them that are under the *l*;

BIBLICAL THEMES

LAW

One law and one manner shall be for you, and for the stranger that sojourneth with you. Nu 15.16

Judges and officers shalt thou make thee in all thy gates . . . and they shall judge the people with just judgment. Thou shalt not wrest judgment . . . neither take a gift: for a gift doth blind the eyes of the wise. Dt 16.18-19

Take this book of the law, and put it in the side of the ark of the covenant of the Lord your God, that it may be there for a witness against thee. Dt 31.26

Be ye therefore very courageous to keep and to do all that is written in the book of the law of Moses, that ye turn not aside therefrom. Jos 23.6

He that ruleth over men must be just, ruling in the fear of God. 2Sa 23.3

The law of the Lord is perfect, converting the soul: the testimony of the Lord is sure, making wise the simple. The statutes of the Lord are right, rejoicing the heart: the commandment of the Lord is pure, enlightening the eyes. . . . the judgments of the Lord are true and righteous altogether. Ps 19.7-9

Thy law is within my heart. Ps 40.8

Blessed are the undefiled in the way, who walk in the law of the Lord. Blessed are they that keep his testimonies, and that seek him with the whole heart. Ps 119.1-2

To do justice and judgment is more acceptable to the Lord than sacrifice. Pr 21.3

He that hath no rule over his own spirit is like a city that is broken down, and without walls. Pr 25.28

When the righteous are in authority, the people rejoice: but when the wicked beareth rule, the people mourn. Pr 29.2

Seeing thou hast forgotten the law of thy God, I will also forget thy children. Hos 4.6

What doth the Lord require of thee, but to do justly, and to love mercy . . . ? Mic 6.8

There is none good but one, that is, God: but if thou wilt enter into life, keep the commandments. Mt 19.17

The law was given by Moses, but grace and truth came by Jesus Christ. Jn 1.17

The law worketh wrath: for where no law is, there is no transgression. Ro 4.15

I had not known sin, but by the law: for I had not known lust, except the law had said, Thou shalt not covet. But sin, taking occasion by the commandment, wrought in me all manner of concupiscence. For without the law sin was dead. . . . Wherefore the law is holy, and the commandment holy, and just, and good. Ro 7.7-8, 12

Love is the fulfilling of the law. Ro 13.10

A man is not justified by the works of the law, but by the faith of Jesus Christ. Gal 2.16

Bear ye one another's burdens, and so fulfil the law of Christ. Gal 6.2

Masters, give unto your servants that which is just and equal; knowing that ye also have a Master in heaven. Col 4.1

We know that the law is good, if a man use it lawfully . . . the law is not made for a righteous man, but for the lawless and disobedient, for the ungodly and for sinners. 1Ti 1.8, 9

So speak ye, and so do, as they that shall be judged by the law of liberty. Jas 2.12

1Co 9.21 that are without *l*, as without *l*,
21 (being not without *l* to God,
21 but under the *l* to Christ,)
21 might gain them that are without *l*.
14.21 In the *l* it is written, With men of
34 under obedience, as also saith the *l*.
15.56 sin; and the strength of sin is the *l*.
Gal 2.16 not justified by the works of the *l*,
16 and not by the works of the *l*: for
16 by the works of the *l* shall no flesh
19 I through the *l* am dead to the *l*,
21 for if righteousness come by the *l*,
3. 2 ye the Spirit by the works of the *l*,
5 doeth he it by the works of the *l*,
10 many as are of the works of the *l*
10 are written in the book of the *l* to
11 no man is justified by the *l* in the
12 And the *l* is not of faith: but, The
13 redeemed us from the curse of the *l*,
17 the *l*, which was four hundred and
18 For if the inheritance be of the *l*,
19 Wherefore then serveth the *l*?
21 Is the *l* then against the promises
21 if there had been a *l* given which
21 righteousness...have been by the *l*.
23 came, we were kept under the *l*,
24 the *l* was our schoolmaster to bring
4. 4 of a woman, made under the *l*,
5 redeem them that were under the *l*,
21 be under the *l*, do ye not hear the *l*?
5. 3 he is a debtor to do the whole *l*.
4 of you are justified by the *l*;
14 all the *l* is fulfilled in one word,
18 the Spirit, ye are not under the *l*.
23 against such there is no *l*.
6. 2 and so fulfil the *l* of Christ.
13 who are circumcised keep the *l*;
Eph 2.15 *l* of commandments contained
Php 3. 5 as touching the *l*, a Pharisee;
6 the righteousness which is in the *l*,
9 righteousness, which is of the *l*,
1Ti 1. 7 Desiring to be teachers of the *l*;
8 But we know that the *l* is good,
9 *l* is not made for a righteous man,
Tit 3. 9 and strivings about the *l*;
Heb 7. 5 of the people according to the *l*,
11 under it the people received the *l*,)
12 necessity a change also of the *l*.
16 the *l* of a carnal commandment,
19 the *l* made nothing perfect, but the
28 For the *l* maketh men high priests
28 of the oath, which was since the *l*,
8. 4 that offer gifts according to the *l*:
9.19 to all the people according to the *l*,
22 are by the *l* purged with blood;
10. 1 *l* having a shadow of good things
8 therein; which are offered by the *l*;
28 He that despised Moses' *l* died
Jas 1.25 into the perfect *l* of liberty,
2. 8 If ye fulfil the royal *l* according to
9 sin, and are convinced of the *l* as
10 whosoever shall keep the whole *l*,
11 art become a transgressor of the *l*
12 shall be judged by the *l* of liberty.
4.11 evil of the *l*, and judgeth the *l*:
11 but if thou judge the *l*, thou art
11 not a doer of the *l*, but a judge.
1Jn 3. 4 sin transgresseth also the *l*:
4 for sin is the transgression of the *l*.

LAWFUL

Ezr 7.24 it shall not be *l* to impose toll,
Isa 49.24 mighty, or the *l* captive delivered?
Eze 18. 5 and do that which is *l* and right,
19 have done that which is *l* and right,
21 and do that which is *l* and right, he
27 doeth that which is *l* and right, he
33.14 and do that which is *l* and right;
16 hath done that which is *l* and right;
19 and do that which is *l* and right, he
Mt 12. 2 is not *l* to do upon the sabbath day.
4 which was not *l* for him to eat,
10 Is it *l* to heal on the sabbath days?
12 *l* to do well on the sabbath days.
14. 4 It is not *l* for thee to have her.
19. 3 Is it *l* for a man to put away his
20.15 Is it not *l* for me to do what I will
22.17 Is it *l* to give tribute unto Caesar,
27. 6 It is not *l* for to put them into the
Mk 2.24 sabbath day that which is not *l*?
26 is not *l* to eat but for the priests,
3. 4 Is it *l* to do good on the sabbath
6.18 It is not *l*...to have thy brother's
10. 2 *l* for a man to put away his wife?
12.14 Is it *l* to give tribute to Caesar, or
Lk 6. 2 which is not *l* to do on the sabbath
4 is not *l* to eat but for the priests
9 it *l* on the sabbath days to do good,
14. 3 Is it *l* to heal on the sabbath day?
20.22 *l* for us to give tribute unto Caesar,
Jn 5.10 it is not *l* for thee to carry thy bed.
18.31 *l* for us to put any man to death:
Ac 16.21 which are not *l* for us to receive,
19.39 be determined in a *l* assembly.
22.25 *l* for you to scourge a man that is
1Co 6.12 All things are *l* unto me, but all
12 all things are *l* for me, but I will

10.23 All things are *l* for me, but all
23 all things are *l* for me, but all
2Co 12. 4 which it is not *l* for a man to utter.

LAWFULLY
1Ti 1. 8 the law is good, if a man use it *l*;
2Ti 2. 5 he not crowned, except he strive *l*.

LAWGIVER
Gen 49.10 nor a *l* from between his feet,
Nu 21.18 digged it, by the direction of the *l*,
Dt 33.21 a portion of the *l*, was he seated;
Ps 60. 7 of mine head; Judah is my *l*;
108. 8 of mine head; Judah is my *l*;
Isa 33.22 the Lord is our *l*, the Lord is our
Jas 4.12 There is one *l*, who is able to save

LAWLESS
1Ti 1. 9 man, but for the *l* and disobedient,

LAWS
Gen 26. 5 my statutes, and my *l*.
Ex 16.28 keep my commandments and my *l*?
18.16 know the statutes of God, and his *l*.
20 shalt teach them ordinances and *l*,
Lev 26.46 the statutes and judgments and *l*,
Ezr 7.25 such as know the *l* of thy God;
Neh 9.13 them right judgments, and true *l*.
14 them precepts, statutes, and *l*,
Est 1.19 *l* of the Persians and the Medes,
3. 8 their *l* are diverse from all people;
8 neither keep they the king's *l*:
Ps 105.45 observe his statutes,...keep his *l*.
Isa 24. 5 they have transgressed the *l*,
Eze 43.11 forms thereof, and all the *l* thereof:
44. 5 of the Lord, and all the *l* thereof;
24 they shall keep my *l* and my
Dan 7.25 and think to change times and *l*:
9.10 to walk in his *l*, which he set
Heb 8.10 I will put my *l* into their mind,
10.16 I will put my *l* into their hearts,

LAWYER
Mt 22.35 was a *l*, asked him a question,
Lk 10.25 a certain *l* stood up, and tempted
Tit 3.13 Bring Zenas the *l* and Apollos on

LAWYERS
Lk 7.30 and *l* rejected the counsel of God
11.45 answered one of the *l*, and said
46 he said, Woe unto you also, ye *l*!
52 Woe unto you, *l*! for ye have taken
14. 3 spake unto the *l* and Pharisees.

LAY
Gen 22.12 *L* not thine hand upon the lad,
Ex 16.33 *l* it up before the Lord, to be kept
Nu 12.11 thee, *l* not the sin upon us,
Dt 11.18 shall ye *l* up these my words in
2Ki 4.29 *l* my staff upon the face of the
34 he went up, and *l* upon the child,
Neh 13.21 do so again, I will *l* hands on you.
Job 21. 5 *l* your hand upon your mouth.
22.22 and *l* up his words in thine heart.
24 Then shalt thou *l* up gold as dust,
40. 4 I will *l* mine hand upon my mouth.
Ps 4. 8 I will both *l* me down in peace,
7. 5 and *l* mine honor in the dust.
71.10 they that *l* wait for my soul take
84. 3 where she may *l* her young,
Pr 10.14 Wise men *l* up knowledge: but the
Isa 28.16 *l* in Zion for a foundation a stone,
17 Judgment also will I *l* to the line,
35. 7 where each *l*, shall be grass with
51.16 and *l* the foundations of the earth,
Jon 1. 5 and he *l*, and was fast asleep.
Mic 1. 7 the idols thereof will I *l* desolate:
7.16 *l* their hand upon their mouth,
Mt 6.19 *L* not up for yourselves treasures
20 *l* up for yourselves treasures in
8.20 man hath not where to *l* his head.
9.18 come and *l* thy hand upon her,
12.11 will he not *l* hold on it, and lift it
21.46 they sought to *l* hands on him,
23. 4 and *l* them on men's shoulders;
28. 6 see the place where the Lord *l*.
Mk 1.30 Simon's wife's mother *l* sick of a
2. 4 bed wherein the sick of the palsy *l*.
3.21 it, they went out to *l* hold on him:
5.23 come and *l* thy hands on her, that
12.12 And they sought to *l* hold on him,
15. 7 one named Barabbas, which *l* bound
16.18 they shall *l* hands on the sick,
Lk 5.18 him in, and to *l* him before him.
25 and took up that whereon he *l*,
8.42 years of age, and she *l* a dying.
9.58 man hath not where to *l* his head.
19.44 shall *l* thee even with the ground,
20.19 hour sought to *l* hands on him;
21.12 they shall *l* their hands on you,
Jn 5. 3 *l* a great multitude of impotent
10.15 and I *l* down my life for the sheep.
17 love me, because I *l* down my life,
18 from me, but I *l* it down of myself.
18 I have power to *l* it down, and I
11.38 was a cave, and a stone *l* upon it.
13.37 I will *l* down my life for thy sake.
38 Wilt thou *l* down thy life for my
15.13 man *l* down his life for his friends.
Ac 7.60 *l* not this sin to their charge.
8.19 that on whomsoever I *l* hands,
15.28 to *l* upon you no greater burden
27.20 and no small tempest *l* on us, all
28. 8 father of Publius *l* sick of a fever
Ro 8.33 Who shall *l* any thing to the charge
9.33 I *l* in Sion a stumblingstone and
1Co 3.11 other foundation can no man *l*
16. 2 every one of you *l* by him in store,
2Co 12.14 ought not to *l* up for the parents,
1Ti 5.22 *L* hands suddenly on no man,
6.12 of faith, *l* hold on eternal life,
19 they may *l* hold on eternal life.
Heb 6.18 to *l* hold upon the hope set before us:
12. 1 let us *l* aside every weight, and the
Jas 1.21 Wherefore *l* apart all filthiness
1Pe 2. 6 I *l* in Sion a chief corner stone,
1Jn 3.16 we ought to *l* down our lives for

LAYEDST
Lk 19.21 takest up that thou *l* not down,

LAYETH
Job 21.19 God *l* up his iniquity for his
24.12 out: yet God *l* not folly to them.
41.26 sword of him that *l* at him cannot
Ps 33. 7 he *l* up the depth in storehouses.
104. 3 Who *l* the beams of his chambers
Pr 2. 7 He *l* up sound wisdom for the
13.16 but a fool *l* open his folly.
26.24 lips, and *l* up deceit within him;
31.19 She *l* her hands to the spindle,
Isa 26. 5 high; the lofty city, he *l* it low;
5 he *l* it low, even to the ground;
56. 2 the son of man that *l* hold on it;
57. 1 and no man *l* it to heart: and
Jer 9. 8 mouth, but in heart he *l* his wait.
12.11 because no man *l* it to heart.
Zec 12. 1 *l* the foundation of the earth, and
Lk 12.21 he that *l* up treasure for himself,
15. 5 found it, he *l* it on his shoulders,

LAYING
Nu 35.20 or hurl at him by *l* of wait, that
22 him any thing without *l* of wait,
Ps 64. 5 they commune of *l* snares privily;
Mk 7. 8 *l* aside the commandment of God,
Lk 11.54 *L* wait for him, and seeking to
Ac 8.18 through *l* on of the apostles' hands
9.24 their *l* await was known of Saul.
25. 3 *l* wait in the way to kill him.
1Ti 4.14 with the *l* on of the hands of the
6.19 *L* up in store for themselves a good
Heb 6. 1 not *l* again the foundation of
2 baptisms, and of *l* on of hands,
1Pe 2. 1 *l* aside all malice, and all guile,

LAZARUS
Lk 16.20 was a certain beggar named *L*,
23 afar off, and *L* in his bosom.
24 have mercy on me, and send *L*,
25 things, and likewise *L* evil things:
Jn 11. 1 a certain man was sick, named *L*,
2 her hair, whose brother *L* was sick.)
5 Martha, and her sister, and *L*.
11 unto them, Our friend *L* sleepeth;
14 unto them plainly, *L* is dead.
43 with a loud voice, *L*, come forth.
12. 1 where *L* was which had been dead,
2 *L* was one of them that sat at the
9 might see *L* also, whom he had
10 they might put *L* also to death;
17 when he called *L* out of his grave,

LEAD
Ex 13.21 of a cloud, to *l* them the way;
Dt 4.27 whither the Lord shall *l* you.
Ps 5. 8 *L* me, O Lord, in thy righteousness
25. 5 *L* me in thy truth, and teach me:
27.11 *l* me in a plain path, because of
31. 3 name's sake *l* me, and guide me.
61. 2 *l* me to the rock that is higher
139.10 Even there shall thy hand *l* me,
24 and *l* me in the way everlasting.
143.10 *l* me into the land of uprightness.
Pr 8.20 I *l* in the way of righteousness,
Isa 11. 6 and a little child shall *l* them.
40.11 shall gently *l* those that are with
42.16 *l* them in paths that they have not
Mt 6.13 And *l* us not into temptation, but
15.14 if the blind *l* the blind, both shall
Mk 13.11 when they shall *l* you, and deliver
14.44 take him, and *l* him away safely.
Lk 6.39 them, Can the blind *l* the blind?
11. 4 And *l* us not into temptation; but
13.15 stall, and *l* him away to watering?
Ac 13.11 seeking some to *l* him by the hand.
1Co 9. 5 we not power to *l* about a sister,
1Ti 2. 2 may *l* a quiet and peaceable life
2Ti 3. 6 *l* captive silly women laden with
Heb 8. 9 to *l* them out of the land of Egypt;
Rev 7.17 shall *l* them unto living fountains

LEADER
1Ch 12.27 was the *l* of the Aaronites, and
13. 1 and hundreds, and with every *l*.
Isa 55. 4 a *l* and commander to the people.

LEADERS
2Ch 32.21 the *l* and captains in the camp of
Isa 9.16 the *l* of this people cause them to
Mt 15.14 alone: they be blind *l* of the blind.

LEADEST
Ps 80. 1 thou that *l* Joseph like a flock;

LEADETH
1Sa 13.17 turned unto the way that *l* to Ophrah,
Job 12.17 He *l* counsellors away spoiled,
19 He *l* princes away spoiled, and
Ps 23. 2 he *l* me beside the still waters.
3 *l* me in...paths of righteousness
Pr 16.29 *l*...into the way that is not good.
Isa 48.17 which *l* thee by the way that thou
Mt 7.13 is the way, that *l* to destruction,
14 narrow is the way, which *l* unto life,
Mk 9. 2 *l* them up into an high mountain
Jn 10. 3 sheep by name, and *l* them out.
Ac 12.10 the iron gate that *l* unto the city;
Ro 2. 4 of God *l* thee to repentance?
Rev 13.10 He that *l* into captivity shall go

LEAF
Gen 8.11 lo, in her mouth was an olive *l*
Lev 26.36 the sound of a shaken *l* shall chase

Job 13.25 thou break a *l* driven to and fro?
Ps 1. 3 his *l* also shall not wither; and
Isa 1.30 shall be as an oak whose *l* fadeth,
34. 4 as the *l* falleth off from the vine,
64. 6 rags; and we all do fade as a *l*;
Jer 8.13 on the fig tree, and the *l* shall fade;
17. 8 cometh, but her *l* shall be green;
Eze 47.12 whose *l* shall not fade, neither shall
12 and the *l* thereof for medicine.

LEAN

Gen 41.20 *l* and the ill favored kine did eat
Nu 13.20 the land is, whether it be fat or *l*,
Jdg 16.26 standeth, that I may *l* upon them.
2Sa 13. 4 the king's son, *l* from day to day?
2Ki 18.21 on which if a man *l*, it will go into
Job 8.15 He shall *l* upon his house, but it
Pr 3. 5 *l* not unto thine...understanding.
Isa 17. 4 fatness of his flesh shall wax *l*.
36. 6 whereon if a man *l*, it will go into
Eze 34.20 fat cattle and between the *l* cattle.
Mic 3.11 yet will they *l* upon the Lord, and

LEANED

2Sa 1. 6 behold Saul *l* upon his spear;
2Ki 7. 2 a lord on whose hand the king *l*
17 the lord on whose hand he *l* to have
Eze 29. 7 and when they *l* upon thee, thou
Am 5.19 house, and *l* his hand on the wall,
Jn 21.20 also *l* on his breast at supper,

LEANING

SS 8. 5 wilderness, *l* upon her beloved?
Jn 13.23 there was *l* on Jesus' bosom one
Heb 11.21 worshipped, *l* upon the top of his staff.

LEAP

Gen 31.12 the rams which *l* upon the cattle
Lev 11.21 feet, to *l* withal upon the earth;
Dt 33.22 whelp: he shall *l* from Bashan.
Job 41.19 lamps, and sparks of fire *l* out.
Ps 68.16 Why *l* ye, ye high hills? this is
Isa 35. 6 Then shall the lame man *l* as an
Joel 2. 5 the tops of mountains shall they *l*,
Zep 1. 9 all those that *l* on the threshold,
Lk 6.23 ye in that day, and *l* for joy:

LEAPED

Gen 31.10 the rams which *l* upon the cattle
2Sa 22.30 by my God have I *l* over a wall.
1Ki 18.26 they *l* upon the altar which was
Ps 18.29 by my God have I *l* over a wall.
Lk 1.41 of Mary, the babe *l* in her womb;
44 the babe *l* in my womb for joy.
Ac 14.10 on thy feet. And he *l* and walked.
19.16 the evil spirit was *l* on them, and

LEAPING

2Sa 6.16 David *l* and dancing before the
SS 2. 8 he cometh *l* upon the mountains,
Ac 3. 8 And he *l* up stood, and walked,
8 walking, and *l*, and praising God.

LEARN

Dt 4.10 that they may *l* to fear me all the
5. 1 that ye may *l* them, and keep, and
14.23 mayest *l* to fear the Lord thy God
17.19 he may *l* to fear the Lord his God,
18. 9 not *l* to do after the abominations
31.12 that they may *l*, and fear the Lord
13 and *l* to fear the Lord your God, as
Ps 119.71 that I might *l* thy statutes.
73 that I may *l* thy commandments.
Pr 22.25 Lest thou *l* his ways, and get a
Isa 1.17 *L* to do well; seek judgment,
2. 4 neither shall they *l* war any more.
26. 9 of the world will *l* righteousness.
10 yet will he not *l* righteousness:
29.24 that murmured shall *l* doctrine.
Jer 10. 2 Lord, *L* not the way of the heathen,
12.16 diligently *l* the ways of my people,
Mic 4. 3 neither shall they *l* war any more.
Mt 9.13 go ye and *l* what that meaneth,
11.29 my yoke upon you, and *l* of me;
24.32 Now *l* a parable of the fig tree;
Mk 13.28 Now *l* a parable of the fig tree;
1Co 4. 6 might *l* in us not to think of men
14.31 one by one, that all may *l*, and all
35 And if they will *l* any thing, let
Gal 3. 2 This only would I *l* of you,
1Ti 1.20 they may *l* not to blaspheme.
2.11 Let the woman *l* in silence with
5. 4 them *l* first to shew piety at home,
13 withal they *l* to be idle, wandering
Tit 3.14 also *l* to maintain good works for
Rev 14. 3 no man could *l* that song but the

LEARNED

Gen 30.27 I have *l* by experience that the
Ps 106.35 the heathen, and *l* their works.
119. 7 have *l* thy righteous judgments.
Pr 30. 3 I neither *l* wisdom, nor have the
Isa 29.11 men deliver to one that is *l*,
12 delivered to him that is not *l*,
12 thee: and he saith, I am not *l*.
50. 4 given me the tongue of the *l*,
4 mine ear to hear as the *l*.
Eze 19. 3 lion and it *l* to catch the prey;
6 young lion, and *l* to catch the prey,
Jn 6.45 heard, and hath *l* of the Father,
7.15 this man letters, having never *l*?
Ac 7.22 Moses was *l* in all the wisdom
Ro 16.17 to the doctrine which ye have *l*;
Eph 4.20 But ye have not so *l* Christ;
Php 4. 9 things, which ye have both *l*, and
11 for I have *l*, in whatsoever state I
Col 1. 7 As ye also *l* of Epaphras our dear
2Ti 3.14 in the things which thou hast *l* and
14 knowing of whom thou hast *l* them;
Heb 5. 8 yet *l* he obedience by the things

LEARNING

Pr 1. 5 will hear, and will increase *l*;
9. 9 just man, and he will increase in *l*.
16.21 sweetness of the lips increaseth *l*.
23 his mouth, and addeth *l* to his lips.
Dan 1. 4 whom they might teach the *l* and
17 them knowledge and skill in all *l*
Ac 26.24 much *l* doth make thee mad.
Ro 15. 4 aforetime were written for our *l*,
2Ti 3. 7 Ever *l*, and never able to come to

LEASING

Ps 4. 2 ye love vanity, and seek after *l*?
5. 6 shalt destroy them that speak *l*:

LEAST

Gen 24.55 with us a few days, at the *l* ten;
32.10 worthy of the *l* of all the mercies,
Nu 11.32 gathered *l* gathered ten homers:
Jdg 3. 2 at the *l* such as before knew
6.15 I am the *l* in my father's house.
1Sa 9.21 my family the *l* of all the families
21. 4 kept themselves at *l* from women.
2Ki 18.24 of the *l* of my master's servants,
1Ch 12.14 one of the *l* was over an hundred,
Isa 36. 9 of the *l* of my master's servants,
Jer 6.13 *l* of them even unto the greatest
8.10 from the *l* even unto the greatest
31.34 the *l* of them unto the greatest
42. 1 from the *l* even unto the greatest,
8 from the *l* even to the greatest,
44.12 from the *l* even unto the greatest,
49.20 the *l* of the flock shall draw them
50.45 the *l* of the flock shall draw them
Am 9. 9 not the *l* grain fall upon the earth.
Jon 3. 5 of them even to the *l* of them.
Mt 2. 6 the *l* among the princes of Juda:
5.19 one of these *l* commandments,
19 the *l* in the kingdom of heaven:
11.11 is *l* in the kingdom of heaven is
13.32 Which indeed is the *l* of all seeds:
25.40 one of the *l* of these my brethren,
45 did it not to one of the *l* of these,
Lk 7.28 that is *l* in the kingdom of God
9.48 for he that is *l* among you all, the
12.26 not able to do that thing which is *l*,
16.10 that is faithful in that which is *l*
10 he that is unjust in the *l* is unjust
19.42 even thou, at *l* in this thy day,
Ac 5.15 that at the *l* the shadow of Peter
8.10 heed, from the *l* to the greatest,
1Co 6. 4 to judge who are *l* esteemed
15. 9 I am the *l* of the apostles, that am
Eph 3. 8 who am less than the *l* of all saints,
Heb 8.11 me, from the *l* to the greatest.

LEATHER

2Ki 1. 8 with a girdle of *l* about his loins.

LEATHERN

Mt 3. 4 and a *l* girdle about his loins;

LEAVE

Gen 2.24 man *l* his father and his mother,
28.15 I will not *l* thee, until I have done
44.22 The lad cannot *l* his father:
Ex 16.19 Let no man *l* of it till the morning.
Lev 23.22 thou shalt *l* them unto the poor,
Nu 10.31 he said, *L* us not, I pray thee;
Ru 1.16 said, Intreat me not to *l* thee, or
2Ki 2. 2, 4, 6 soul liveth, I will not *l* thee.
4.30 as thy soul liveth, I will not *l* thee.
43 They shall eat, and shall *l* thereof.
Ezr 9. 8 *l* us a remnant to escape, and to
Ps 16.10 thou wilt not *l* my soul in hell;
27. 9 *l* me not, neither forsake me, O
37.33 Lord will not *l* him in his hand,
119.121 *l* me not to mine oppressors.
Pr 2.13 Who *l* the paths of uprightness,
Jer 14. 9 are called by thy name; *l* us not.
Eze 6. 8 Yet will I *l* a remnant, that ye may
16.39 and *l* thee naked and bare.
Joel 2.14 and *l* a blessing behind him;
Am 5. 7 *l* off righteousness in the earth,
Mt 5.24 *L* there thy gift before the altar,
18.12 doth he not *l* the ninety and nine,
19. 5 shall a man *l* father and mother,
23.23 and not to *l* the other undone.
Mk 5.13 And forthwith Jesus gave them *l*.
10. 7 a man *l* his father and mother,
12.19 die, and *l* his wife behind him,
19 and *l* no children, that his brother
Lk 11.42 and not to *l* the other undone.
15. 4 doth not *l* the ninety and nine in
19.44 shall not *l* in thee one stone upon
Jn 14.18 I will not *l* you comfortless: I will
27 Peace I *l* with you, my peace I give
16.28 I *l* the world, and go to the Father.
32 to his own, and shall *l* me alone:
19.38 of Jesus: and Pilate gave him *l*.
Ac 2.27 thou wilt not *l* my soul in hell,
6. 2 that we should *l* the word of God,
18.18 then took his *l* of the brethren,
21. 6 had taken our *l* one of another,
1Co 7.13 dwell with her, let her not *l* him.
2Co 2.13 taking my *l* of them, I went from
Eph 5.31 a man *l* his father and mother,
Heb 13. 5 I will never *l* thee, nor forsake
Rev 11. 2 which is without the temple *l* out,

LEAVEN

Ex 12.15 put away *l* out of your houses:
19 be no *l* found in your houses:
13. 7 shall there be *l* seen with thee in
34.25 the blood of my sacrifice with *l*;
Lev 2.11 No...offering...shall be made with *l*:
11 for ye shall burn no *l*,
6.17 It shall not be baked with *l*. I
10.12 eat it without *l* beside the altar:
23.17 they shall be baken with *l*; they
Am 4. 5 sacrifice of thanksgiving with *l*,
Mt 13.33 kingdom of heaven is like unto *l*,

16. 6, 11 beware of the *l* of the Pharisees
12 not beware of the *l* of bread,
Mk 8.15 beware of the *l* of the Pharisees,
15 and of the *l* of Herod.
Lk 12. 1 Beware ye of the *l* of the Pharisees,
13.21 It is like *l*, which a woman took
1Co 5. 6 little *l* leaveneth the whole lump?
7 Purge out therefore the old *l*, that
8 us keep the feast, not with old *l*,
8 neither with the *l* of malice and
Gal 5. 9 little *l* leaveneth the whole lump.

LEAVENED
Ex 12.15 whosoever eateth *l* bread from
19 whosoever eateth that which is *l*,
20 Ye shall eat nothing *l*; in all your
34 took their dough before it was *l*,
39 forth out of Egypt, for it was not *l*;
13. 3 there shall no *l* bread be eaten.
7 shall no *l* bread be seen with thee,
23.18 blood of my sacrifice with *l* bread;
Lev 7.13 shall offer for his offering *l* bread
Dt 16. 3 Thou shalt eat no *l* bread with it;
4 shall be no *l* bread seen with thee
Hos 7. 4 kneaded the dough, until it be *l*.
Mt 13.33 of meal, till the whole was *l*.
Lk 13.21 of meal, till the whole was *l*.

LEAVENETH
1Co 5. 6 a little leaven *l* the whole lump?
Gal 5. 9 A little leaven *l* the whole lump.

LEAVES
Gen 3. 7 they sewed fig *l* together, and
1Ki 6.34 the two *l* of the one door were
34 the two *l* of the other door were
Isa 6.13 is in them, when they cast their *l*:
Jer 36.23 Jehudi had read three or four *l*,
Eze 17. 9 wither in all the *l* of her spring,
41.24 had two *l* apiece, two turning *l*;
24 two *l* for the one door
24 and two *l* for the other door.
Dan 4.12 The *l* thereof were fair, and the
14 off his branches, shake off his *l*,
21 Whose *l* were fair, and the fruit
Mt 21.19 found nothing thereon, but *l* only,
24.32 yet tender, and putteth forth *l*,
Mk 11.13 seeing a fig tree afar off having *l*,
13 came to it, he found nothing but *l*;
13.28 yet tender, and putteth forth *l*,
Rev 22. 2 *l* of the trees were for the healing

LEAVETH
Job 39.14 Which *l* her eggs in the earth,
Pr 13.22 A good man *l* an inheritance to his
28. 3 like a sweeping rain which *l* no food.
Zec 11.17 the idol shepherd that *l* the flock!
Mt 4.11 Then the devil *l* him, and, behold,
Jn 10.12 coming, and *l* the sheep, and fleeth:

LEAVING
Mt 4.13 *l* Nazareth, he came and dwelt
Lk 10.30 and departed, *l* him half dead.
Ro 1.27 *l* the natural use of the woman,
Heb 6. 1 *l* the principles of the doctrine of
1Pe 2.21 suffered for us, *l* us an example,

LED
Ex 13.18 God *l* the people about, through
15.13 thy mercy hast *l* forth the people
Dt 29. 5 *l* you forty years in the wilderness:
Ps 68.18 high, thou hast *l* captivity captive:
78.14 also he *l* them with a cloud,
53 And he *l* them on safely so that
106. 9 so he *l* them through the depths,
107. 7 he *l* them forth by the right way,
Pr 4.11 I have *l* thee in right paths.
Isa 48.21 he *l* them through the deserts:
55.12 joy, and be *l* forth with peace:
Jer 2. 6 that *l* us through the wilderness,
La 3. 2 He hath *l* me, and brought me

Mt 4. 1 Then was Jesus *l* up of the spirit
26.57 had laid hold on Jesus *l* him away
27. 2 had bound him, they *l* him away,
31 him, and *l* him away to crucify him.
Mk 8.23 hand, and *l* him out of the town;
14.53 And they *l* Jesus away to the high
15.16 the soldiers *l* him away into the hall,
20 him, and *l* him out to crucify him.
Lk 4. 1 *l* by the spirit into the wilderness,
29 and *l* him unto the brow of the hill
21.24 be *l* away captive into all nations:
22.54 Then they took him, and *l* him, and
66 and *l* him into their council,
23. 1 of them arose, and *l* him unto Pilate.
26 as they *l* him away, they laid hold
32 *l* with him to be put to death.
24.50 he *l* them out as far as to Bethany,
Jn 18.13 And *l* him away to Annas first; for
28 Then *l* they Jesus from Caiaphas
19.16 they took Jesus, and *l* him away.
Ac 8.32 was *l* as a sheep to the slaughter;
9. 8 *l* him by the hand, and brought
21.37 Paul was to be *l* into the castle,
22.11 being *l* by the hand of them that
Ro 8.14 many as are *l* by the Spirit of God,
1Co 12. 2 these dumb idols, even as ye were *l*.
Gal 5.18 But if ye be *l* of the Spirit, ye are not
Eph 4. 8 up on high, he *l* captivity captive,
2Ti 3. 6 with sins, *l* away with divers lusts,
2Pe 3.17 being *l* away with the error of

LEDDEST
2Sa 5. 2 wast he that *l* out and broughtest
1Ch 11. 2 wast he that *l* out and broughtest
Neh 9.12 *l* them in the day by a cloudy
Ps 77.20 Thou *l* thy people like a flock by
Ac 21.38 and *l* out into the wilderness four

LEFT
Gen 32.24 And Jacob was *l* alone; and there
Ex 34.25 passover be *l* until the morning.
Ru 1.18 then she *l* speaking unto her.
1Sa 5. 4 the stump of Dagon was *l* to him.
2Sa 9. 1 any that is *l* of the house of Saul,
2Ch 32.31 God *l* him, to try him, that he
Pr 3.16 in her *l* hand riches and honor.
29.15 a child *l* to himself bringeth his
Isa 37. 4 prayer for the remnant that is *l*.
Jer 40.11 had *l* a remnant of Judah, and
Dan 10. 8 I was *l* alone, and saw this great
Joel 1. 4 that which the locust hath *l* hath
Hag 2. 3 Who is *l* among you that saw this
Mt 4.20 they straightway *l* their nets, and
22 they immediately *l* the ship and
6. 3 let not thy *l* hand know what thy
8.15 her hand, and the fever *l* her:
15.37 broken meat that was *l* seven
16. 4 And he *l* them, and departed.
20.21 the other on the *l*, in thy kingdom.
23 sit on my right hand, and on my *l*,
21.17 he *l* them, and went out of the
22.22 and *l* him, and went their way.
25 issue, *l* his wife unto his brother:
23.38 your house is *l* unto you desolate.
24. 2 shall not be *l* here one stone upon
40, 41 shall be taken, and the other *l*.
25.33 right hand, but the goats on the *l*.
41 say also unto them on the *l* hand,
26.44 he *l* them, and went away again,
27.38 right hand, and another on the *l*.
Mk 1.20 and they *l* their father Zebedee in
31 and immediately the fever *l* her,
8. 8 meat that was *l* seven baskets.
13 he *l* them, and entering into the
10.28 we have *l* all, and have followed
29 There is no man that hath *l* house,
37 the other on thy *l* hand, in thy
40 on my *l* hand is not mine to give;
12.12 they *l* him, and went their way.
20 took a wife, and dying *l* no seed.
21 her, and died, neither *l* he any seed:

22 the seven had her, and *l* no seed:
13. 2 there shall not be *l* one stone upon
34 a far journey, who *l* his house,
14.52 he *l* the linen cloth, and fled from
15.27 right hand, and the other on his *l*.
Lk 4.39 rebuked the fever; and it *l* her:
5. 4 when he had *l* speaking, he said
28 And he *l* all, rose up, and followed
10.40 my sister hath *l* me to serve alone?
13.35 your house is *l* unto you desolate:
17.34 be taken, and the other shall be *l*.
35 shall be taken, and the other *l*.
36 shall be taken, and the other *l*.
18.28 Peter said, Lo, we have *l* all, and
29 There is no man that hath *l* house,
20.31 seven also: and they *l* no children,
21. 6 not be *l* one stone upon another,
23.33 right hand, and the other on the *l*.
Jn 4. 3 He *l* Judea, and departed again
28 woman then *l* her waterpot, and
52 at the seventh hour the fever *l* him.
8. 9 Jesus was *l* alone, and the woman
29 the Father hath not *l* me alone;
Ac 2.31 his soul was not *l* in hell, neither
14.17 he *l* not himself without witness,
18.19 to Ephesus, and *l* them there:
21. 3 we had discovered Cyprus, we *l* it
3 it on the *l* hand, and sailed into
32 soldiers, they *l* beating of Paul.
23.32 *l* the horsemen to go with him,
24.27 Jews a pleasure, *l* Paul bound.
25.14 certain man *l* in bonds by Felix:
Ro 9.29 Lord of Sabaoth had *l* us a seed,
11. 3 and I am *l* alone, and they seek
2Co 6. 7 on the right hand and on the *l*,
1Th 3. 1 thought it good to be *l* at Athens
2Ti 4.13 cloke that I *l* at Troas with Carpus,
20 Trophimus have I *l* at Miletum sick.
Tit 1. 5 For this cause *l* I thee in Crete,
Heb 2. 8 *l* nothing that is not put under him.
4. 1 a promise being *l* us of entering
Jude 6 estate, but *l* their own habitation,
Rev 2. 4 because thou hast *l* thy first love.
10. 2 sea, and his *l* foot on the earth,

LEGION
Mk 5. 9 My name is *L*: for we are many.
15 with the devil, and had the *l*,
Lk 8.30 What is thy name? And he said, *L*:

LEGIONS
Mt 26.53 me more than twelve *l* of angels?

LEGS
1Sa 17. 6 had greaves of brass upon his *l*,
Ps 147.10 not pleasure in the *l* of a man.
Pr 26. 7 The *l* of the lame are not equal: so
SS 5.15 His *l* are as pillars of marble, set
Isa 3.20 the ornaments of the *l*, and the
Dan 2.33 His *l* of iron, his feet part of iron
Am 3.12 out of the mouth of the lion two *l*,
Jn 19.31 that their *l* might be broken, and
32 and brake the *l* of the first, and of
33 dead already, they brake not his *l*:

LEISURE
Mk 6.31 they had no *l* so much as to eat.

LEND
Ex 22.25 thou *l* money to any of my people
Lev 25.37 *l* him thy victuals for increase.
Dt 15. 6 thou shalt *l* unto many nations,
8 shalt surely *l* him sufficient for his
23.19 Thou shalt not *l* upon usury to
20 thou mayest *l* upon usury;
20 thou shalt not *l* upon usury:
24.10 When thou dost *l* thy brother any
11 the man to whom thou dost *l* shall
28.12 thou shalt *l* unto many nations,
44 *l* to thee, and thou shalt not *l* to
Lk 6.34 if ye *l* to them of whom ye hope to

Lk 6.34 sinners also *l* to sinners, to receive
35 and *l*, hoping for nothing again;
11. 5 him, Friend, *l* me three loaves;

LENDER

Pr 22. 7 the borrower is servant to the *l*.
Isa 24. 2 as with the *l*, so with the borrower;

LENDETH

Dt 15. 2 Every creditor that *l* ought unto
Ps 37.26 He is ever merciful, and *l*; and
112. 5 good man sheweth favor, and *l*:
Pr 19.17 pity upon the poor *l* unto the Lord;

LENGTH

Dt 30.20 he is thy life, and the *l* of thy days:
Job 12.12 and in *l* of days understanding.
Ps 21. 4 even *l* of days for ever and ever.
Pr 3. 2 For *l* of days, and long life, and
16 *L* of days is in her right hand; and
Ro 1.10 at *l* I might have a prosperous
Eph 3.18 what is the breadth, and *l*, and
Rev 21.16 the *l* is as large as the breadth:
16 *l* and the breadth and the height

LENT

Ex 12.36 *l* unto them such things as they
Dt 23.19 of any thing that is *l* upon usury:
1Sa 1.28 also I have *l* him to the Lord;
28 he liveth he shall be *l* to the Lord.
2.20 the loan which is *l* to the Lord.
Jer 15.10 I have neither *l* on usury, nor
10 nor men have *l* to me on usury;

LEOPARD

Isa 11. 6 the *l* shall lie down with the kid;
Jer 5. 6 a *l* shall watch over their cities:
13.23 change his skin, or the *l* his spots?
Dan 7. 6 I beheld, and lo another, like a *l*,
Hos 13. 7 as a *l* by the way will I observe
Rev 13. 2 which I saw was like unto a *l*,

LEPER

Lev 13.45 And the *l* in whom the plague is,
14. 2 this shall be the law of the *l* in
3 plague of leprosy be healed in the *l*;
22. 4 soever of the seed of Aaron is a *l*,
Nu 5. 2 they put out of the camp every *l*,
2Sa 3.29 that hath an issue, or that is a *l*,
2Ki 5. 1 man in valor, but he was a *l*.
11 over the place, and recover the *l*.
27 he went out from his presence a *l*
15. 5 was a *l* unto the day of his death.
2Ch 26.21 Uzziah the king was a *l* unto the
21 dwelt in a several house, being a *l*;
23 the kings; for they said, He is a *l*:
Mt 8. 2 there came a *l* and worshipped
26. 6 in the house of Simon the *l*,
Mk 1.40 there came a *l* to him, beseeching
14. 3 in the house of Simon the *l*, as he

LEPERS

2Ki 7. 8 *l* came to the uttermost part of
Mt 10. 8 sick, cleanse the *l*, raise the dead,
11. 5 the *l* are cleansed, and the deaf
Lk 4.27 And many *l* were in Israel in the
7.22 the *l* are cleansed, the deaf hear,
17.12 there met him ten men that were *l*,

LEPROSY

Lev 13. 8 pronounce him unclean: it is a *l*.
2Ki 5. 3 for he would recover him of his *l*.
6 thou mayest recover him of his *l*.
7 unto me to recover a man of his *l*?
Mt 8. 3 immediately his *l* was cleansed.
Mk 1.42 immediately the *l* departed from
Lk 5.12 certain city, behold a man full of *l*:
13 immediately the *l* departed from

LESS

Ex 16.17 and gathered, some more, some *l*.
30.15 the poor shall not give *l* than half
Nu 22.18 the Lord my God, to do *l* or more.
26.54 thou shalt give the *l* inheritance:
33.54 ye shall give the *l* inheritance:
1Sa 22.15 nothing of all this, *l* or more.
25.36 she told him nothing, *l* or more,
1Ki 8.27 how much *l* this house that I have
2Ch 6.18 how much *l* this house which I have
32.15 how much *l* shall your God deliver
Ezr 9.13 punished us *l* than our iniquities
Job 4.19 How much *l* in them that dwell in
9.14 How much *l* shall I answer him, and
11. 6 exacteth of thee *l* than thine iniquity
25. 6 How much *l* man, that is a worm?
Pr 17. 7 a fool: much *l* do lying lips a prince.
19.10 much *l* for a servant to have rule over
Isa 40.17 are counted to him *l* than nothing,
Mk 4.31 *l* than all the seeds that be in the
15.40 Mary the mother of James the *l*
1Co 12.23 which we think to be *l* honorable,
2Co 12.15 I love you, the *l* I be loved.
Eph 3. 8 am *l* than the least of all saints,
Php 2.28 and that I may be the *l* sorrowful.
Heb 7. 7 the *l* is blessed of the better.

LESSER

Gen 1.16 and the *l* light to rule the night:
Isa 7.25 and for the treading of *l* cattle.
Eze 43.14 and from the *l* settle even to the

LET

Gen 1. 3 And God said, *L* there be light: and
6 *L* there be a firmament in the midst
9 place, and *l* the dry land appear:
24 *L* the earth bring forth the living
26.28 *L* there be now an oath betwixt us,
46.30 Now *l* me die, since I have seen thy
Ex 22. 7 the thief be found, *l* him pay double.
Nu 23.10 *L* me die the death of the righteous,
10 and *l* my last end be like his!
Dt 9.14 *L* me alone, that I may destroy
13. 2 *L* us go after other gods, which thou
1Sa 3.18 *l* him do what seemeth him good.
14.36 *L* us draw near hither unto God.
17.32 *L* no man's heart fail because of him;
2Sa 1.21 of Gilboa, *l* there be no dew,
21 neither *l* there be rain upon you, nor
16.10 so *l* him curse, because the Lord hath
11 *l* him alone, and *l* him curse; for
1Ki 17.21 *l* this child's soul come into him
18.24 that answereth by fire, *l* him be God.
20.11 *L* not him that girdeth on his harness
2Ki 1.10, 12 *l* fire come down from heaven,
5. 8 *l* him come now to me, and he shall
19.10 *L* not thy God in whom thou trustest
20.10 but *l* the shadow return backward
2Ch 6.17 God of Israel, *l* thy word be verified,
40 *l* thine ears be attent unto the prayer
36.23 his God be with him, and *l* him go up.
Ezr 5.17 *l* there be search made in the king's
Job 3. 3 *L* the day perish wherein I was born,
4 *L* that day be darkness;
4 *l* not God regard it from above,
5 *L* darkness and the shadow of death
5 *l* the blackness of the day terrify it.
6 that night, *l* darkness seize upon it;
7 *l* no joyful voice come therein.
8 *L* them curse it that curse the day,
9 *l* it look for light, but have none;
6.29 *l* it not be iniquity; yea, return again,
9.34 *L* him take his rod away from me,
34 and *l* not his fear terrify me:
10.20 and *l* me alone, that I may take
13.13 Hold your peace, *l* me alone, that I
13 speak, and *l* come on me what will.
31. 6 *L* me be weighed in an even balance,
8 Then *l* me sow, and *l* another eat;
22 *l* mine arm fall from my shoulder
40 *L* thistles grow instead of wheat, and
32.21 neither *l* me give flattering titles
34.34 *L* men of understanding tell me,
34 and *l* a wise man hearken unto me.
40. 2 reproveth God, *l* him answer it.
Ps 9.19 Arise, O Lord; *l* not man prevail:
18.46 *l* the God of my salvation be exalted.
19.13 *l* them not have dominion over me:
14 *L* the words of my...be acceptable
20. 9 *l* the king hear us when we call.
25. 3 *l* none that wait on thee be ashamed:
20 *l* me not be ashamed; for I put my
33. 8 *L* all the earth fear the Lord:
22 *L* thy mercy, O Lord, be upon us,
43. 3 light and thy truth: *l* them lead me;
48.11 *L* mount Zion rejoice,
67. 3 *L* the people praise thee, O God;
3 *l* all the people praise thee.
4 O *l* the nations be glad and sing for
5 *L* the people praise thee, O God;
5 *l* all the people praise thee.
68. 1 *L* God arise, *l* his enemies be
3 But *l* the righteous be glad;
69.14 *l* me be delivered from them that hate
28 *L* them be blotted out of the book of
34 *L* the heaven and earth praise him,
70. 4 say continually, *L* God be magnified.
71. 1 trust: *l* me never be put to confusion.
72.19 *l* the whole earth be filled with his
79.11 *L* the sighing of the prisoner come
80.17 *L* thy hand be upon the man of thy
88. 2 *L* my prayer come before thee:
90.13 *l* it repent thee concerning thy
16 *L* thy work appear unto thy servants,
17 *l* the beauty of the Lord our God be
95. 1 O come, *l* us sing unto the Lord:
1 *l* us make a joyful noise to the rock
2 *L* us come before his presence with
6 O come, *l* us worship and bow down:
6 *l* us kneel before the Lord our maker.
96.11 *L* the heavens rejoice, and *l* the earth
11 *l* the sea roar, and the fulness thereof.
12 *L* the field be joyful, and all that is
97. 1 *l* the earth rejoice; *l* the multitude
98. 8 *L* the floods clap their hands:
8 *l* the hills be joyful together.
99. 1 Lord reigneth; *l* the people tremble:
102. 1 O Lord, and *l* my cry come unto thee.
106.48 and *l* all the people say, Amen.
107. 2 *L* the redeemed of the Lord say so,
119.77 *L* thy tender mercies come unto me,
169 *L* my cry come near before thee, O
175 *L* my soul live, and it shall praise
122. 1 *L* us go into the house of the Lord,
132. 9 and *l* thy saints shout for joy.
137. 5 *l* my right hand forget her cunning.
6 *l* my tongue cleave to the roof of my
141. 2 *L* my prayer be set forth before thee
145.21 *l* all flesh bless his holy name for ever
148. 5, 13 *L* them praise the name of the Lord:
149. 3 *L* them praise his name in the dance:
5 *L* the saints be joyful in glory:
150. 6 *L* every thing that hath breath praise
Pr 1.14 among us; *l* us all have one purse:
3. 1 *l* thine heart keep my commandments:
3 *L* not mercy and truth forsake thee:
Ec 5. 2 earth: therefore *l* thy words be few.
11. 8 *l* him remember the days of darkness;
Isa 1.18 Come now, and *l* us reason together,
2. 3 *l* us go up to the mountain of the
37.10 *L* not thy God, in whom...deceive thee,
42.11 *l* the inhabitants of the rock sing,
43. 9 *L* all the nations be gathered together,
55. 2 *l* your soul delight itself in fatness.
7 *L* the wicked forsake his way, and
7 *l* him return unto the Lord, and
66. 5 *L* the Lord be glorified: but he shall
Jer 5.24 *L* us now fear the Lord our God, that
9.23 *L* not the wise man glory in his
23 *l* not the rich man glory in his riches:
31. 6 *l* us go up to Zion unto the Lord our
51.10 *l* us declare in Zion the work of the
La 2.18 *l* tears run down like a river day
18 *l* not the apple of thine eye cease.
3.40 *L* us search and try our ways, and

41 *L* us lift up our heart with our hands
Dan 2. 7 *L* the king tell his servants the dream,
Hos 6. 1 and *l* us return unto the Lord:
Am 5.24 But *l* judgment run down as waters,
Jon 1. 7 Come, and *l* us cast lots, that we may
14 *l* us not perish for this man's life, and
Zec 8.21 *L* us go speedily to pray before the
Mt 5.16 *L* your light so shine before men, that
31 his wife, *l* him give her a writing of
37 *l* your communication be, Yea,
40 thy coat, *l* him have thy cloke also.
6. 3 *l* not thy left hand know what thy
7. 4 *L* me pull out the mote out of thine
8.22 me; and *l* the dead bury their dead.
10.13 be worthy, *l* your peace come upon it:
13 worthy, *l* your peace return to you.
11.15 He that hath ears to hear, *l* him hear.
13. 9 Who hath ears to hear, *l* him hear.
30 *L* both grow together until the
43 Who hath ears to hear, *l* him hear.
15. 4 father or mother, *l* him die the death.
14 *L* them alone: they be blind
16.24 *l* him deny himself, and take up his
17. 4 *l* us make here three tabernacles;
18.17 *l* him be unto thee as an heathen
19. 6 together, *l* not man put asunder.
12 able to receive it, *l* him receive it.
20.26 you, *l* him be your minister;
27 among you, *l* him be your servant:
21.19 *L* no fruit grow on thee henceforward
33 *l* it out to husbandmen, and went
38 This is the heir; come, *l* us kill him,
41 will *l* out his vineyard unto other
24.15 (whoso readeth, *l* him understand:)
16 *l* them which be in Judea flee into the
17 *L* him which is on the housetop not
18 Neither *l* him which is in the field
26.39 be possible, *l* this cup pass from me:
46 *l* us be going: behold, he is at hand
27.22 all say unto him, *L* him be crucified.
23 the more, saying, *L* him be crucified.
42 *l* him now come down from the cross,
43 *l* him deliver him now, if he will
49 The rest said, *L* be,
49 *l* us see whether Elias will come
Mk 1.24 *L* us alone; what have we to do
38 *L* us go into the next towns, that I
2. 4 *l* down the bed wherein the sick
4. 9 He that hath ears to hear, *l* him hear.
23 man have ears to hear, *l* him hear.
35 *L* us pass over unto the other side.
7.10 father or mother, *l* him die the death:
16 man have ears to hear, *l* him hear.
27 her, *L* the children first be filled:
8.34 *l* him deny himself, and take up his
9. 5 and *l* us make three tabernacles;
10. 9 together, *l* not man put asunder.
11. 6 commanded: and they *l* them go.
12. 1 *l* it out to husbandmen, and went
7 This is the heir; come, *l* us kill him,
13.14 not, (*l* him that readeth understand,)
14 *l* them that be in Judea flee to the
15 And *l* him that is on the housetop not
16 And *l* him that is in the field not turn
14. 6 And Jesus said, *L* her alone: why
42 Rise up, *l* us go; lo, he that betrayeth
15.32 *L* Christ the King of Israel descend
36 to drink, saying, *L* alone;
36 *l* us see whether Elias will come
Lk 2.15 *L* us now go even unto Bethlehem,
3.11 *l* him impart to him that hath none;
11 he that hath meat, *l* him do likewise.
4.34 Saying, *L* us alone; what have
5. 4 *l* your nets down for a draft.
5 at thy word I will *l* down the net.
19 and *l* him down through the tiling
6.42 *l* me pull out the mote that is in
8. 8 He that hath ears to hear, *l* him hear.
22 *L* us go over unto the other side of
9.23 *l* him deny himself, and take up his
33 *l* us make three tabernacles; one for
44 *L* these sayings sink down into your
60 him, *L* the dead bury their dead:
61 *l* me first go bid them farewell,
12.35 *L* your loins be girded about, and
13. 8 Lord, *l* it alone this year also, till I
14. 4 him, and healed him, and *l* him go;
35 He that hath ears to hear, *l* him hear.
15.23 kill it; and *l* us eat, and be merry:
16.29 and the prophets; *l* them hear them.
17.31 *l* him not come down to take it away:
31 field, *l* him likewise not return back.
20. 9 and *l* it forth to husbandmen,
14 is the heir: come, *l* us kill him,
21.21 *l* them which are in Judea flee to
21 *l* them which are in the midst...depart
21 *l* not them...in the countries enter
22.26 among you, *l* him be as the younger;
36 *l* him take it, and likewise his script:
36 *l* him sell his garment, and buy one.
68 ye will not answer me, nor *l* me go.
23.22 therefore chastise him, and *l* him go.
35 *l* him save himself, if he be Christ, the
Jn 7.37 thirst, *l* him come unto me and drink.
8. 7 you, *l* him first cast a stone at her.
11. 7 disciples, *L* us go into Judea again.
15 nevertheless *l* us go unto him.
16 *L* us also go, that we may die with
44 them, Loose him, and *l* him go.
48 If we *l* him thus alone, all men will
12. 7 said Jesus, *L* her alone: against
26 any man serve me, *l* him follow me;
14. 1 *L* not your heart be troubled: ye
27 *L* not your heart be troubled,
27 neither *l* it be afraid.
31 even so I do. Arise, *l* us go hence.
18. 8 ye seek me, *l* these go their way:
19.12 If thou *l* this man go, thou art not
24 *L* us not rend it, but cast lots for it,
Ac 1.20 *L* his habitation be desolate,
20 and *l* no man dwell therein:
20 and his bishoprick *l* another take.
2.29 *l* me freely speak unto you of the
36 *l* all the house of Israel know
3.13 he was determined to *l* him go.
4.17 *l* us straitly threaten them, that they
21 threatened them, they *l* them go,
23 And being *l* go, they went to their own
5.38 these men, and *l* them alone:
40 in the name of Jesus, and *l* them go.
9.25 *l* him down by the wall in a
10.11 corners, and *l* down to the earth:
11. 5 sheet, *l* down from heaven by four
15.33 they were *l* go in peace from the
36 *L* us go again and visit our brethren
16.35 serjeants, saying, *L* those men go.
36 magistrates have sent to *l* you go:
37 *l* them come themselves and fetch us
17. 9 and of the other, they *l* them go.
19.38 deputies: *l* them implead one another.
23. 9 to him, *l* us not fight against God.
22 then *l* the young man depart,
24.20 Or else *l* these same here say, if they
23 keep Paul, and to *l* him have liberty,
25. 5 *L* them therefore...go down with me,
27.15 up into the wind, we *l* her drive.
30 had *l* down the boat into the sea,
32 ropes of the boat, and *l* her fall off.
28.18 examined me, would have *l* me go,
Ro 1.13 unto you, (but was *l* hitherto,)
3. 4 yea, *l* God be true, but every man a
8 *L* us do evil, that good may come?
6.12 *L* not sin therefore reign in your
11. 9 *L* their table be made a snare, and a
10 *L* their eyes be darkened, that they
12. 6 *l* us prophesy according to the
7 ministry, *l* us wait on our ministering:
8 giveth, *l* him do it with simplicity;
9 *L* love be without dissimulation.
13. 1 *L* every soul be subject unto the
12 *l* us therefore cast off the works of
12 and *l* us put on the armor of light.
13 *L* us walk honestly, as in the day;
14. 3 *L* not him that eateth despise him
3 *l* not him which eateth not judge him
5 *L* every man be fully persuaded in
13 *L* us not therefore judge one another
16 *L* not then your good be evil spoken
19 *L* us therefore follow after the things
15. 2 *L* every one...please his neighbor
1Co 1.31 that glorieth, *l* him glory in the Lord.
3.10 *l* every man take heed how he buildeth
18 *L* no man deceive himself. If any
18 *l* him become a fool, that he may be
21 Therefore *l* no man glory in men.
4. 1 *L* a man so account of us, as of the
5. 8 Therefore *l* us keep the feast, not
7. 2 *l* every man have his own wife, and
2 *l* every woman have her own husband.
3 *L* the husband render unto the wife
9 if they cannot contain, *l* them marry:
10 *L* not the wife depart from her
11 she depart, *l* her remain unmarried,
11 *l* not the husband put away his wife.
12 with him, *l* him not put her away.
13 to dwell with her, *l* her not leave him.
15 the unbelieving depart, *l* him depart.
17 hath called every one, so *l* him walk.
18 *l* him not become uncircumcised.
18 *l* him not be circumcised.
20 *L* every man abide in the same calling
24 *l* every man, wherein he is...abide
36 need so require, *l* him do what he will,
36 will he sinneth not: *l* them marry.
10. 8 Neither *l* us commit fornication, as
9 Neither *l* us tempt Christ, as some of
12 *l* him that...he standeth take heed
24 *L* no man seek his own, but every
11. 6 be not covered, *l* her also be shorn:
6 be shorn or shaven, *l* her be covered.
28 But *l* a man examine himself, and
28 so *l* him eat of that bread, and drink
34 any man hunger, *l* him eat at home;
14.13 *l* him that speaketh in an...pray
26 *L* all things be done unto edifying.
27 *l* it be by two, or at most by three,
27 that by course; and *l* one interpret.
28 *l* him keep silence in the church;
28 *l* him speak to himself, and to God.
29 *L* the prophets speak two or three,
29 two or three, and *l* the other judge.
30 sitteth by, *l* the first hold his peace.
34 *L* your women keep silence in the
35 *l* them ask their husbands at home:
37 *l* him acknowledge that the things
38 man be ignorant, *l* him be ignorant.
40 *L* all things be done decently and in
15.32 *l* us eat and drink, for tomorrow we
16. 2 *l* every one of you lay by him in store,
11 *L* no man therefore despise him: but
14 *L* all your things be done with charity.
22 *l* him be Anathema Maran-atha.
2Co 7. 1 *l* us cleanse ourselves from all
9. 7 purposeth in his heart, so *l* him give;
10. 7 *l* him of himself think this again, that,
11 *L* such an one think this, that, such
17 that glorieth, *l* him glory in the Lord.
11.16 say again, *L* no man think me a fool;
33 basket was I *l* down by the wall,
Gal 1. 8 unto you, *l* him be accursed.
9 have received, *l* him be accursed.
5.25 the Spirit, *l* us also walk in the Spirit.
26 *L* us not be desirous of vain glory,
6. 4 But *l* every man prove his own work,
6 *L* him that is taught...communicate
9 *l* us not be weary in well doing: for
10 *l* us do good unto all men, especially
17 henceforth *l* no man trouble me:
Eph 4.26 *l* not the sun go down upon your
28 *L* him that stole steal no more: but
28 but rather *l* him labor, working with
29 *L* no corrupt communication proceed
31 *L* all bitterness, and...be put away

Eph 5. 3 *l* it not be once named among you, as
6 *L* no man deceive you with vain
24 *l* the wives be to their own husbands
33 *l* every one of you in particular so love
Php 1.27 *l* your conversation be as it becometh
2. 3 *L* nothing be done through strife or
3 mind *l* each esteem other better than
5 *L* this mind be in you, which was also
3.15 *L* us therefore, as...be thus minded:
16 attained, *l* us walk by the same rule,
16 *l* us mind the same thing.
4. 5 *L* your moderation be known unto all
6 *l* your requests be made known unto
Col 2.16 *L* no man therefore judge you in
18 *L* no man beguile you of your reward
3.15 *l* the peace of God rule in your hearts,
16 *L* the word of Christ dwell in you
4. 6 *L* your speech be alway with grace,
1Th 5. 6 Therefore *l* us not sleep, as do others;
6 but *l* us watch and be sober.
8 But *l* us, who are of the day, be sober,
2Th 2. 3 *L* no man deceive you by any means:
7 only he who now letteth will *l*,
1Ti 2.11 *L* the woman learn in silence with all
3.10 And *l* these also first be proved; then
10 then *l* them use the office of a deacon,
12 *L* the deacons be the husbands of
4.12 *L* no man despise thy youth; but be
5. 4 *l* them learn first to show piety at
9 *L* not a widow be taken into the
16 have widows, *l* them relieve them,
16 and *l* not the church be charged; that
17 *L* the elders that rule well be counted
6. 1 *L* as many servants as are...count
2 masters, *l* them not despise them,
8 raiment *l* us be therewith content.
2Ti 2.19 *L* every one that nameth...depart
Tit 2.15 authority. *L* no man despise thee.
3.14 *l* ours also learn to maintain good
Phm 20 *l* me have joy of thee in the Lord:
Heb 1. 6 *l* all the angels of God worship him.
2. 1 at any time we should *l* them slip.
4. 1 *L* us therefore fear, lest, a promise
11 *L* us labor therefore to enter into
14 of God, *l* us hold fast our profession.
16 *L* us therefore come boldly unto the
6. 1 of Christ, *l* us go on unto perfection;
10.22 *L* us draw near with a true heart in
23 *L* us hold fast the profession of our
24 *l* us consider one another to provoke
12. 1 *l* us lay aside every weight, and the
1 *l* us run with patience the race that is
13 of the way; but *l* it rather be healed.
28 *l* us have grace, whereby we may
13. 1 *L* brotherly love continue.
5 *L* your conversation be without
13 *L* us go forth therefore unto him
15 *l* us offer the sacrifice of praise to God
Jas 1. 4 But *l* patience have her perfect work,
5 you lack wisdom, *l* him ask of God,
6 But *l* him ask in faith, nothing
7 For *l* not that man think that he shall
9 *L* the brother of low degree rejoice
13 *L* no man say when he is tempted, I
19 *l* every man be swift to hear, slow to
3.13 *l* him shew out of a good conversation
4. 9 *l* your laughter be turned to mourning,
5.12 *l* your yea be yea; and your nay, nay;
13 any among you afflicted? *l* him pray.
13 Is any merry? *l* him sing psalms.
14 *l* him call for the elders of the church;
14 *l* them pray over him, anointing him
20 *L* him know, that he which converteth
1Pe 3. 3 *l* it not be that outward adorning
4 But *l* it be the hidden man of the
10 *l* him refrain his tongue from evil,
11 *L* him eschew evil, and do good,
11 *l* him seek peace, and ensue it.
4.11 *l* him speak as the oracles of God;
11 *l* him do it as of the ability which
15 *l* none of you suffer as a murderer,
16 as a Christian, *l* him not be ashamed;
16 but *l* him glorify God on this behalf.
19 *l* them that suffer according to the
1Jn 2.24 *L* that therefore abide in you, which
3. 7 Little children, *l* no man deceive you:
18 little children, *l* us not love in word,
4. 7 *l* us love one another: for love is of
Rev 2. 7, 11, 17, 29 *l* him hear what the Spirit
3. 6, 13, 22 *l* him hear what the Spirit saith
13. 9 If any man have an ear, *l* him hear.
18 *L* him that hath understanding count
19. 7 *L* us be glad and rejoice, and give
22.11 that is unjust, *l* him be unjust still:
11 he which is filthy, *l* him be filthy still:
11 is righteous, *l* him be righteous still:
11 and he that is holy, *l* him be holy still.
17 And *l* him that heareth say, Come.
17 And *l* him that is athirst come.
17 *l* him take the water of life freely.

LETTER

2Sa 11.14 David wrote a *l* to Joab, and sent
15 And he wrote in the *l*, saying, Set
2Ki 5. 5 and I will send a *l* unto the king of
Ezr 4. 7 writing of the *l* was written in the
23 the copy of king Artaxerxes' *l* was
5. 5 returned answer by *l* concerning
Neh 6. 5 time with an open *l* in his hand;
Isa 37.14 Hezekiah received the *l* from the
Jer 29.29 the priest read this *l* in the ears of
Ac 23.25 he wrote a *l* after this manner:
34 when the governor had read the *l*,
Ro 2.27 who by the *l* and circumcision
29 heart, in the spirit, and not in the *l*;
7. 6 and not in the oldness of the *l*.
2Co 3. 6 not of the *l*, but of the spirit:
6 the *l* killeth, but the spirit giveth
7. 8 though I made you sorry with a *l*,
Gal 6.11 Ye see how large a *l* I have
2Th 2. 2 nor by word, nor by *l* as from us,
Heb 13.22 I have written a *l* unto you in few

LETTERS

1Ki 21. 8 So she wrote *l* in Ahab's name,
2Ki 20.12 sent *l* and a present unto Hezekiah:
2Ch 30. 6 the posts went with the *l* from the
32.17 He wrote also *l* to rail on the Lord
Est 3.13 the *l* were sent by posts into all
Lk 23.38 written over him in *l* of Greek,
Jn 7.15 How knoweth this man *l*, having
Ac 9. 2 And desired of him *l* to Damascus
15.23 And they wrote *l* by them after this
22. 5 I received *l* unto the brethren,
28.21 We neither received *l* out of Judea
1Co 16. 3 whomsoever...approve by your *l*,
2Co 3. 1 you, or *l* of commendation from you?
10. 9 seem as if I would terrify you by *l*.
10 For his *l*, say they, are weighty
11 in word by *l* when we are absent,

LETTEST

Job 15.13 *l* such words go out of thy mouth?
41. 1 with a cord which thou *l* down?
Lk 2.29 now *l* thou thy servant depart in

LETTETH

2Ki 10.24 he that *l* him go, his life shall be for
Pr 17.14 strife is as when one *l* out water:
2Th 2. 7 only he who now *l* will let, until

LEVI

Gen 29.34 therefore was his name called *L*.
34.25 the sons of Jacob, Simeon and *L*,
30 And Jacob said to Simeon and *L*,
35.23 firstborn, and Simeon, and *L*, and
46.11 sons of *L*; Gershon, Kohath, and
49. 5 Simeon and *L* are brethren;
Ex 1. 2 Reuben, Simeon, *L*, and Judah,
2. 1 there went a man of the house of *L*,
1 and took to wife a daughter of *L*.
6.16 are the names of the sons of *L*
16 life of *L* were an hundred thirty
19 Mushi: these are the families of *L*
32.26 the sons of *L* gathered themselves
28 of *L* did according to the word of
Nu 1.49 shalt not number the tribe of *L*,
3. 6 Bring the tribe of *L* near, and
15 Number the children of *L* after the
17 were the sons of *L* by their names;
4. 2 Kohath from among the sons of *L*,
16. 1 the son of *L*, and Dathan and
7 too much upon you, ye sons of *L*.
8 Hear, I pray you, ye sons of *L*:
10 brethren the sons of *L* with thee:
17. 3 Aaron's name upon the rod of *L*:
8 for the house of *L* was budded,
18. 2 thy brethren also of the tribe of *L*,
21 I have given the children of *L* all
26.59 was Jochebed, the daughter of *L*,
59 her mother bare to *L* in Egypt:
Dt 10. 8 the Lord separated the tribe of *L*,
9 *L* hath no part nor inheritance
18. 1 the Levites, and all the tribe of *L*,
21. 5 the sons of *L* shall come near:
27.12 Simeon, and *L*, and Judah, and
31. 9 it unto the priests the sons of *L*,
33. 8 of *L* he said, Let thy Thummim
Jos 13.14 of *L* he gave none inheritance;
33 *L* Moses gave not any inheritance:
21.10 who were of the children of *L*, had:
1Ki 12.31 which were not of the sons of *L*.
1Ch 2. 1 Reuben, Simeon, *L*, and Judah,
6. 1, 16 The sons of *L*; Gershon,
38 the son of *L*, the son of Israel.
43 the son of Gershom, the son of *L*.
47 the son of Merari, the son of *L*.
9.18 the companies of the children of *L*.
12.26 Of the children of *L* four thousand
21. 6 *L* and Benjamin counted he not
23. 6 into courses among the sons of *L*,
14 sons were named of the tribe of *L*.
24 These were the sons of *L* after the
24.20 rest of the sons of *L* were these:
Ezr 8.15 found there none of the sons of *L*.
18 the son of *L*, the son of Israel;
Neh 10.39 the children of *L* shall bring the
12.23 sons of *L*, the chief of the fathers,
Ps 135.20 Bless the Lord, O house of *L*: ye
Eze 40.46 sons of Zadok among the sons of *L*,
48.31 one gate of Judah, one gate of *L*.
Zec 12.13 The family of the house of *L* apart,
Mal 2. 4 that my covenant might be with *L*,
8 have corrupted the covenant of *L*,
3. 3 he shall purify the sons of *L*, and
Mk 2.14 he saw *L* the son of Alphaeus
Lk 3.24, 29 Matthat, which was the son of *L*,
5.27 saw a publican, named *L*, sitting
29 *L* made him a great feast in his
Heb 7. 5 they that are of the sons of *L*,
9 say, *L* also, who receiveth tithes,
Rev 7. 7 Of the tribe of *L* were sealed twelve

LEVIATHAN

Job 41. 1 Canst thou draw out *l* with an
Ps 74.14 brakest the heads of *l* in pieces,
104.26 is that *l*, whom thou hast made
Isa 27. 1 shall punish *l* the piercing serpent.
1 even *l* that crooked serpent; and he

LEVITE

Ex 4.14 Is not Aaron the *L* thy brother?
Dt 12.12 the *L* that is within your gates;
18 and the *L* that is within thy gates:
19 forsake not the *L* as long as thou
14.27 the *L* that is within thy gates;
29 the *L*, (because he hath no part
16.11 and the *L* that is within thy gates,
14 and the *L*, the stranger, and the
18. 6 if a *L* come from any of thy gates
26.11 the *L*, and the stranger that is
12 and hast given it unto the *L*,
13 also have given them unto the *L*,

Jdg 17. 7 the family of Judah, who was a *L*,
9 I am a *L* of Beth-lehem-judah,
10 and thy victuals. So the *L* went in.
11 the *L* was content to dwell with
12 Micah consecrated the *L*; and the
13 seeing I have a *L* to my priest.
18. 3 the voice of the young man the *L*:
15 the house of the young man the *L*,
19. 1 there was a certain *L* sojourning
20. 4 the *L*, the husband of the woman
2Ch 20.14 a *L* of the sons of Asaph, came the
31.12 which Cononiah the *L* was ruler,
14 And Kore the son of Imnah the *L*,
Ezr 10.15 Shabbethai the *L* helped them.
Lk 10.32 likewise a *L*, when he was at the
Ac 4.36 The son of consolation,) a *L*, and

LEVITICAL
Heb 7.11 were by the *L* priesthood,

LEWD
Eze 16.27 which are ashamed of thy *l* way.
23.44 and unto Aholibah, the *l* women.
Ac 17. 5 certain *l* fellows of the baser sort,

LEWDNESS
Ac 18.14 a matter of wrong or wicked *l*,

LIAR
Pr 17. 4 *l* giveth ear to a naughty tongue.
19.22 a poor man is better than a *l*.
Jn 8.44 for he is a *l*, and the father of it.
55 him not, I shall be a *l* like unto you:
Ro 3. 4 let God be true, but every man a *l*;
1Jn 1.10 have not sinned, we make him a *l*,
2. 4 not his commandments, is a *l*, and
22 Who is a *l* but he that denieth that
4.20 and hateth his brother, he is a *l*:
5.10 not God hath made him a *l*;

LIARS
Dt 33.29 shall be found *l* unto thee;
Ps 116.11 I said in my haste, All men are *l*.
Isa 44.25 frustrateth the tokens of the *l*, and
Jer 50.36 A sword is upon the *l*; and they
1Ti 1.10 for *l*, for perjured persons, and if
Tit 1.12 said, The Cretians are alway *l*,
Rev 2. 2 are not, and hast found them *l*:
21. 8 sorcerers, and idolaters, and all *l*,

LIBERAL
Pr 11.25 The *l* soul shall be made fat: and
Isa 32. 5 person shall be no more called *l*,
8 But the *l* deviseth *l* things; and
8 and by *l* things shall he stand.
2Co 9.13 for your *l* distribution unto them,

LIBERALITY
1Co 16. 3 to bring your *l* unto Jerusalem.
2Co 8. 2 abounded unto the riches of their *l*.

LIBERALLY
Dt 15.14 furnish him *l* out of thy flock,
Jas 1. 5 ask of God, that giveth to all men *l*,

LIBERTINES
Ac 6. 9 is called the synagogue of the *L*,

LIBERTY
Lev 25.10 proclaim *l* throughout all the land
Ps 119.45 And I will walk at *l*: for I seek thy
Isa 61. 1 to proclaim *l* to the captives, and
Jer 34. 8 to proclaim *l* unto them;
15 in proclaiming *l* every man to his
16 he had set at *l* at their pleasure,
17 in proclaiming *l*, every one to his
17 behold, I proclaim a *l* for you, saith
Eze 46.17 then it shall be his to the year of *l*;
Lk 4.18 to set at *l* them that are bruised,
Ac 24.23 to keep Paul, and to let him have *l*,
26.32 This man might have been set at *l*,
27. 3 gave him *l* to go unto his friends
Ro 8.21 glorious *l* of the children of God.
1Co 7.39 she is at *l* to be married to whom
8. 9 any means this *l* of yours become
10.29 for why is my *l* judged of another
2Co 3.17 the Spirit of the Lord is, there is *l*.
Gal 2. 4 to spy out our *l* which we have in
5. 1 the *l* wherewith Christ hath made
13 For...ye have been called unto *l*;
13 only use not *l* for an occasion to
Heb 13.23 our brother Timothy is set at *l*;
Jas 1.25 looketh into the perfect law of *l*,
2.12 that shall be judged by the law of *l*.
1Pe 2.16 and not using your *l* for a cloke of
2Pe 2.19 While they promise them *l*, they

LIBYA
Eze 30. 5 Ethiopia, and *L*, and Lydia, and
38. 5 Ethiopia, and *L* with them;
Ac 2.10 and in the parts of *L* about Cyrene,

LICE
Ex 8.16 may become *l* throughout all the
17 it became *l* in man, and in beast;
17 all the dust of the land became *l*
18 enchantments to bring forth *l*,

Biblical Themes

LIBERTY

The Lord said, I have surely seen the affliction of my people . . . and I am come down to deliver them out of the hand of the Egyptians. Ex 3.7-8

Let my people go. Ex 5.1

And [Pharaoh] called for Moses . . . and said, Rise up, and get you forth from among my people, both ye and the children of Israel; and go, serve the Lord, as ye have said. Ex 12.31

And ye shall hallow the fiftieth year, and proclaim liberty throughout all the land unto all the inhabitants thereof . . . ye shall return every man unto his possession, and ye shall return every man unto his family. Lev 25.10

If thy brother . . . be sold unto thee, and serve thee six years; then in the seventh year thou shalt let him go free from thee. And . . . thou shalt not let him go away empty: thou shalt furnish him liberally out of thy flock. Dt 15.12-14

Thus saith Cyrus king of Persia, All the kingdoms of the earth hath the Lord God of heaven given me; and he hath charged me to build him an house in Jerusalem, which is in Judah. Who is there among you of all his people? The Lord his God be with him, and let him go up. 2Ch 36.23

When the Lord turned again the captivity of Zion, we were like them that dream. Then was our mouth filled with laughter, and our tongue with singing. Ps 126.1-2

His own iniquities shall take the wicked himself, and he shall be holden with the cords of his sins. Pr 5.22

The ransomed of the Lord shall return, and come to Zion with songs and everlasting joy upon their heads. Isa 35.10

Thou mayest say to the prisoners, Go forth; to them that are in darkness, Shew yourselves. Isa 49.9

The Lord hath anointed me . . . to proclaim liberty to the captives, and the opening of the prison to them that are bound. Isa 61.1

I will turn away your captivity, and I will gather you from all the nations, and from all the places whither I have driven you. Jer 29.14

[Jesus said,] ye shall know the truth, and the truth shall make you free. They answered him, We be Abraham's seed, and were never in bondage to any man: how sayest thou, Ye shall be made free? Jesus answered them, . . . Whosoever committeth sin is the servant of sin. Jn 8.32-34

The chief captain came, and said unto [Paul], Tell me, art thou a Roman? He said, Yea. And the chief captain answered, With a great sum obtained I this freedom. And Paul said, But I was free born. Ac 22.27-28

The creature itself also shall be delivered from the bondage of corruption into the glorious liberty of the children of God. Ro 8.21

Where the Spirit of the Lord is, there is liberty. 2Co 3.17

Stand fast therefore in the liberty wherewith Christ hath made us free, and be not entangled again with the yoke of bondage. Gal 5.1

Brethren, ye have been called unto liberty; only use not liberty for an occasion to the flesh, but by love serve one another. Gal 5.13

That they may recover themselves out of the snare of the devil, who are taken captive by him at his will. 2Ti 2.26

With well doing ye may put to silence the ignorance of foolish men: as free, and not using your liberty for a cloak of maliciousness, but as the servants of God. 1Pe 2.15-16

Ex 8.18 so there were *l* upon man, and upon
Ps 105.31 of flies, and *l* in all their coasts.

LICENSE
Ac 21.40 when he had given him *l*, Paul
25.16 and have *l* to answer for himself

LICK
Nu 22. 4 Now shall this company *l* up all
1Ki 21.19 of Naboth shall dogs *l* thy blood,
Ps 72. 9 and his enemies shall *l* the dust.
Isa 49.23 and *l* up the dust of thy feet;
Mic 7.17 They shall *l* the dust like a serpent,

LICKED
1Ki 18.38 *l* up the water that was in the
21.19 where dogs *l* the blood of Naboth
22.38 and the dogs *l* up his blood;
Lk 16.21 the dogs came and *l* his sores.

LIE
Ex 21.13 if a man *l* not in wait, but God
Nu 23.19 is not a man, that he should *l*;
1Sa 3. 5 said, I called not; *l* down again.
9 Eli said unto Samuel, Go, *l* down:
Job 6.28 for it is evident unto you if I *l*.
7. 4 When I *l* down, I say, When shall
21.26 They shall *l* down alike in the dust,
34. 6 Should I *l* against my right? my
Ps 23. 2 me to *l* down in green pastures:
59. 3 For, lo, they *l* in wait for my soul:
62. 9 and men of high degree are a *l*:
Pr 14. 5 A faithful witness will not *l*: but
Ec 4.11 if two *l* together, then they have
Isa 11. 6 leopard shall *l* down with the kid;
14.30 the needy shall *l* down in safety:
43.17 they shall *l* down together, they
44.20 Is there not a *l* in my right hand?
50.11 hand; ye shall *l* down in sorrow.
Jer 27.14 for they prophesy a *l* unto you,
28.15 makest this people to trust in a *l*.
Hos 2.18 will make them to *l* down safely.
Joel 1.13 *l* all night in sackcloth,...ministers
Am 6. 4 That *l* upon beds of ivory, and
Mic 2.11 in the spirit and falsehood do *l*,
Zec 10. 2 and the diviners have seen a *l*,
Jn 5. 6 When Jesus saw him *l*, and knew
8.44 When he speaketh a *l*, he
20. 6 and seeth the linen clothes *l*,
Ac 5. 3 hath Satan filled thine heart to *l*
23.21 there *l* in wait for him of them more
Ro 1.25 changed the truth of God into a *l*,
3. 7 through my *l* unto his glory;
9. 1 I say the truth in Christ, I *l* not,
2Co 11.31 evermore, knoweth that I *l* not.
Gal 1.20 you, behold, before God, I *l* not.
Eph 4.14 whereby they *l* in wait to deceive;
Col 3. 9 *L* not one to another, seeing that
2Th 2.11 that they should believe a *l*:
1Ti 2. 7 the truth in Christ, and *l* not:)
Tit 1. 2 life, which God, that cannot *l*,
Heb 6.18 it was impossible for God to *l*,
Jas 3.14 not, and *l* not against the truth.
1Jn 1. 6 darkness, we *l*, and do not the truth:
2.21 it, and that no *l* is of the truth.
27 and is truth, and is no *l*, and even
Rev 3. 9 are Jews, and are not, but do *l*;
21.27 abomination, or maketh a *l*:
22.15 whosoever loveth and maketh a *l*.

LIED
1Ki 13.18 drink water. But he *l* unto him.
Ps 78.36 *l* unto him with their tongues.
Isa 57.11 or feared, that thou hast *l*, and
Ac 5. 4 thou hast not *l* unto men, but unto

LIES
Jdg 16.10, 13 hast mocked me, and told me *l*:
Job 11. 3 thy *l* make men hold their peace?
13. 4 But ye are forgers of *l*, ye are all
Ps 40. 4 proud, nor such as turn aside to *l*.
62. 4 they delight in *l*: they bless with
Pr 14. 5 lie: but a false witness will utter *l*.
25 but a deceitful witness speaketh *l*.
19. 5 he that speaketh *l* shall not escape.
Isa 59. 3 your lips have spoken *l*, your
Jer 23.25 said, that prophesy *l* in my name,
Hos 7.13 they have spoken *l* against me.
10.13 ye have eaten the fruit of *l*:
11.12 compasseth me about with *l*, and
Na 3. 1 city! it is all full of *l* and robbery;
Hab 2.18 molten image, and a teacher of *l*,
Zec 13. 3 speakest *l* in the name of the Lord:
1Ti 4. 2 Speaking *l* in hyprocrisy; having

LIEST
Gen 28.13 land whereon thou *l*, to thee will
Dt 6. 7 when thou *l* down, and when thou
11.19 when thou *l* down, and when thou
Jos 7.10 *l* thou thus upon thy face?
Pr 3.24 When thou *l* down, thou shalt not

LIETH
Gen 4. 7 doest not well, sin *l* at the door.
Jdg 16. 5 and see wherein his great strength *l*,
6 thee, wherein thy great strength *l*,
15 told me wherein thy great strength *l*.
Neh 2.17 Jerusalem *l* waste, and the gates
Job 14.12 So man *l* down, and riseth not:
40.21 He *l* under the shady trees, in the
Ps 10. 9 *l* in wait secretly as a lion in his
9 he *l* in wait to catch the poor: he
88. 7 Thy wrath *l* hard upon me, and
Pr 23.28 She also *l* in wait as for a prey,
34 as he that *l* upon the top of a mast.
Mt 8. 6 my servant *l* at home sick of the
Mk 5.23 daughter *l* at the point of death:
Ac 14. 6 unto the region that *l* round about:
27.12 *l* toward the south west and north
Ro 12.18 as much as *l* in you, live peaceably
1Jn 5.19 the whole world *l* in wickedness.
Rev 21.16 And the city *l* foursquare, and the

LIFE
Gen 1.20 moving creature that hath *l*,
2. 7 into his nostrils the breath of *l*;
9 the tree of *l* also in the midst of
9. 4 But flesh with the *l* thereof, which
5 brother will I require the *l* of man.
27.46 I am weary of my *l* because of the
47. 9 days of the years of my *l* been,
48.15 the God which fed me all my *l* long
Ex 4.19 men are dead which sought thy *l*.
Lev 17.11 the *l* of the flesh is in the blood:
Dt 19.21 *l* shall go for *l*, eye for eye, tooth
24. 6 for he taketh a man's *l* to pledge.
28.66 And thy *l* shall hang in doubt
30.15 set before thee this day *l* and good,
19 I have set before you *l* and death,
19 therefore choose *l*, that both thou
32.47 thing for you; because it is your *l*:
Jdg 12. 3 I put my *l* in my hands, and passed
1Sa 19. 5 For he did put his *l* in his hand,
25.29 shall be bound in the bundle of *l*
28.21 and I have put my *l* in my hand,
1Ki 19. 4 now, O Lord, take away my *l*; for
10, 14 they seek my *l*, to take it away.
20.39 then shall thy *l* be for his *l*, or else
2Ki 8. 5 he had restored a dead body to *l*,
5 her son, whom Elisha restored to *l*.
2Ch 1.11 neither yet hast asked long *l*; but
Job 2. 4 a man hath will he give for his *l*.
7. 7 O remember that my *l* is wind:
9.21 my soul: I would despise my *l*.
10. 1 My soul is weary of my *l*; I will
13.14 teeth, and put my *l* in mine hand?
24.22 riseth up, and no man is sure of *l*.
33. 4 of the Almighty hath given me *l*.
28 the pit, and his *l* shall see the light.
Ps 21. 4 He asked *l* of thee, and thou gavest
23. 6 follow me all the days of my *l*:
27. 1 the Lord is the strength of my *l*;
30. 5 but a moment; in his favor is *l*:
31.10 For my *l* is spent with grief, and
34.12 What man is he that desireth *l*,
42. 8 my prayer unto the God of my *l*.
66. 9 which holdeth our soul in *l*, and
91.16 With long *l* will I satisfy him, and
103. 4 redeemeth thy *l* from destruction;
Pr 3. 2 For length of days, and long *l*,
18 She is a tree of *l* to them that lay
4.23 for out of it are the issues of *l*.
8.35 For whoso findeth me findeth *l*,
10.11 of a righteous man is a well of *l*:
11.30 fruit of the righteous is a tree of *l*;
14.27 fear of the Lord is a fountain of *l*,
30 A sound heart is the *l* of the flesh:
15. 4 A wholesome tongue is a tree of *l*:
24 The way of *l* is above to the wise,
18.21 Death and *l* are in the power of the
19.23 The fear of the Lord tendeth to *l*:
Ec 2.17 Therefore I hated *l*; because the
6.12 what is good for man in this *l*, all
7.12 giveth *l* to them that have it.
Isa 38.12 I have cut off like a weaver my *l*:
Jer 21. 8 I set before you the way of *l*, and
Eze 32.10 every man for his own *l*, in the
Dan 12. 2 awake, some to everlasting *l*,
Jon 1.14 let us not perish for this man's *l*,
4. 3 take, I beseech thee, my *l* from me;
Mal 2. 5 My covenant was with him of *l*
Mt 2.20 which sought the young child's *l*.
6.25 Take no thought for your *l*, what
25 Is not the *l* more than meat, and
7.14 is the way, which leadeth unto *l*,
10.39 He that findeth his *l* shall lose it:
39 he that loseth his *l* for my sake
16.25 will save his *l* shall lose it:
25 will lose his *l* for my sake shall
18. 8 better for thee to enter into *l* halt
9 thee to enter into *l* with one eye,
19.16 I do, that I may have eternal *l*?
17 but if thou wilt enter into *l*, keep
29 and shall inherit everlasting *l*.
20.28 to give his *l* a ransom for many.
25.46 but the righteous into *l* eternal.
Mk 3. 4 or to do evil? to save *l*, or to kill?
8.35 will save his *l* shall lose it;
35 shall lose his *l* for my sake and the
9.43 for thee to enter into *l* maimed,
45 better for thee to enter halt into *l*,
10.17 I do that I may inherit eternal *l*?
30 and in the world to come eternal *l*.
45 to give his *l* a ransom for many.
Lk 1.75 before him, all the days of our *l*.
6. 9 evil? to save *l*, or to destroy it?
8.14 and riches and pleasures of this *l*,
9.24 will save his *l* shall lose it:
24 will lose his *l* for my sake, the
10.25 shall I do to inherit eternal *l*?
12.15 for a man's *l* consisteth not in the
22 Take no thought for your *l*, what
23 The *l* is more than meat, and the
14.26 sisters, yea, and his own *l* also,
17.33 seek to save his *l* shall lose it;
33 shall lose his *l* shall preserve it.
18.18 shall I do to inherit eternal *l*?
30 in the world to come *l* everlasting.
21.34 drunkenness, and cares of this *l*,
Jn 1. 4 In him was *l*; and the *l* was the
3.15 not perish, but have eternal *l*.
16 not perish, but have everlasting *l*.
36 on the Son hath everlasting *l*:
36 believeth not the Son shall not see *l*;
4.14 springing up into everlasting *l*.
36 gathereth fruit unto *l* eternal:
5.24 that sent me, hath everlasting *l*,
24 but is passed from death unto *l*.
26 For as the Father hath *l* in himself;
26 to the Son to have *l* in himself;
29 good, unto the resurrection of *l*;
39 in them ye think ye have eternal *l*:
40 come to me, that ye might have *l*.

6.27 which endureth unto everlasting *l*,
33 and giveth *l* unto the world.
35 unto them, I am the bread of *l*:
40 on him, may have everlasting *l*:
47 believeth on me hath everlasting *l*.
48 I am that bread of *l*.
51 I will give for the *l* of the world.
53 his blood, ye have no *l* in you.
54 drinketh my blood, hath eternal *l*;
63 you, they are spirit, and they are *l*.
68 thou hast the words of eternal *l*.
8.12 but shall have the light of *l*.
10.10 I am come that they might have *l*,
11 giveth his *l* for the sheep.
15 and I lay down my *l* for the sheep.
17 because I lay down my *l*, that I
28 I give unto them eternal *l*; and
11.25 I am the resurrection, and the *l*:
12.25 He that loveth his *l* shall lose it;
25 hateth his *l* in this world shall
25 shall keep it unto *l* eternal.
50 his commandment is *l* everlasting:
13.37 I will lay down my *l* for thy sake.
38 thou lay down thy *l* for my sake?
14. 6 am the way, the truth, and the *l*:
15.13 man lay down his *l* for his friends.
17. 2 should give eternal *l* to as many
3 this is *l* eternal, that they might
20.31 ye might have *l* through his name.
Ac 2.28 made known to me the ways of *l*;
3.15 And killed the Prince of *l*, whom
5.20 the people all the words of this *l*.
8.33 for his *l* is taken from the earth.
11.18 Gentiles granted repentance unto *l*.
13.46 unworthy of everlasting *l*, lo, we
48 many as were ordained to eternal *l*
17.25 seeing he giveth to all *l*, and breath,
20.10 not yourselves; for his *l* is in him.
24 count I my *l* dear unto myself,
26. 4 My manner of *l* from my youth,
27.22 shall be no loss of any man's *l*
Ro 2. 7 honor and immortality, eternal *l*:
5.10 we shall be saved by his *l*.
17 reign in *l* by one, Jesus Christ.)
18 upon all men unto justification of *l*.
21 righteousness unto eternal *l* by
6. 4 also should walk in newness of *l*.
22 holiness, and the end everlasting *l*.
23 but the gift of God is eternal *l*
7.10 which was ordained to *l*, I found
8. 2 the law of the Spirit of *l* in Christ
6 to be spiritually minded is *l* and
10 Spirit is *l* because of righteousness.
38 neither death, nor *l*, nor angels,
11. 3 am left alone, and they seek my *l*.
15 of them be, but *l* from the dead?
16. 4 have for my *l* laid down their own
1Co 3.22 or *l*, or death, or things present,
6. 3 more things that pertain to this *l*?
4 of things pertaining to this *l*, set
14. 7 even things without *l* giving sound,
15.19 If in this *l* only we have hope in
2Co 1. 8 that we despaired even of *l*:
2.16 the other the savor of *l* unto *l*.
3. 6 killeth, but the spirit giveth *l*.
4.10, 11 the *l* also of Jesus might be
12 death worketh in us, but *l* in you.
5. 4 might be swallowed up of *l*.
Gal 2.20 and the *l* which I now live in the flesh
3.21 given which could have given *l*,
6. 8 of the Spirit reap *l* everlasting.
Eph 4.18 being alienated from the *l* of God
Php 1.20 in my body, whether it be by *l*, or
2.16 Holding forth the word of *l*; that
30 unto death, not regarding his *l*, to
4. 3 whose names are in the book of *l*.
Col 3. 3 your *l* is hid with Christ in God.
4 When Christ, who is our *l*, shall
1Ti 1.16 believe on him to *l* everlasting.
2. 2 lead a quiet and peaceable *l* in all
4. 8 promise of the *l* that now is, and
6.12 lay hold on eternal *l*, whereunto
19 that they may lay hold on eternal *l*.
2Ti 1. 1 promise of *l* which is in Christ
10 hath brought *l* and immortality to
2. 4 himself with the affairs of this *l*;
3.10 known my doctrine, manner of *l*,
Tit 1. 2 In hope of eternal *l*, which God,
3. 7 according to the hope of eternal *l*.
Heb 7. 3 beginning of days, nor end of *l*;
16 but after the power of an endless *l*.
11.35 received their dead raised to *l* again:
Jas 1.12 he shall receive the crown of *l*.
4.14 For what is your *l*? It is even a
1Pe 3. 7 heirs together of the grace of *l*;
10 For he that will love *l*, and see good
4. 3 time past of our *l* may suffice us
2Pe 1. 3 that pertain unto *l* and godliness,
1Jn 1. 1 have handled, of the Word of *l*;
2 the *l* was manifested, and we have
2 and shew unto you that eternal *l*,
2.16 the pride of *l*, is not of the Father,
25 hath promised us, even eternal *l*.
3.14 we have passed from death unto *l*,
15 hath eternal *l* abiding in him.
16 he laid down his *l* for us: and we
5.11 God hath given to us eternal *l*,
11 and this *l* is in his Son.
12 He that hath the Son hath *l*;
12 hath not the Son of God hath not *l*.
13 may know that ye have eternal *l*,
16 shall give him *l* for them that sin
20 This is the true God, and eternal *l*.
Jude 21 Lord Jesus Christ unto eternal *l*.
Rev 2. 7 will I give to eat of the tree of *l*,
10 and I will give thee a crown of *l*.
3. 5 out his name out of the book of *l*,
8. 9 were in the sea, and had *l*, died;
11.11 Spirit of *l* from God entered into
13. 8 are not written in the book of *l*
15 power to give *l* unto the image of
17. 8 were not written in the book of *l*
20.12 was opened, which is the book of *l*:
15 not found written in the book of *l*
21. 6 fountain of the water of *l* freely.
27 written in the Lamb's book of *l*.
22. 1 me a pure river of water of *l*,
2 was there the tree of *l*, which bare
14 may have right to the tree of *l*,
17 let him take the water of *l* freely.
19 away his part out of the book of *l*,

LIFETIME

2Sa 18.18 Absalom in his *l* had taken and
Lk 16.25 thou in thy *l* receivedst thy good
Heb 2.15 all their *l* subject to bondage.

LIFT

Gen 7.17 and it was *l* up above the earth.
31.12 *L* up now thine eyes, and see, all
Nu 6.26 The Lord *l* up his countenance
2Ki 19. 4 *l* up thy prayer for the remnant
Job 22.26 and shalt *l* up thy face unto God.
Ps 4. 6 Lord, *l* thou up the light of thy
10.12 O Lord; O God, *l* up thine hand:
24. 7 *L* up your heads, O ye gates;
7 be ye *l* up, ye everlasting doors;
9 *L* up your heads, O ye gates; even
9 *l* them up, ye everlasting doors;
25. 1 thee, O Lord, do I *l* up my soul.
28. 2 I *l* up my hands toward thy holy
9 them also, and *l* them up for ever.
63. 4 I will *l* up my hands in thy name.
86. 4 thee, O Lord, do I *l* up my soul.
93. 3 voice; the floods *l* up their waves.
119.48 My hands also will I *l* up unto thy
121. 1 I will *l* up mine eyes unto the hills,
123. 1 Unto thee *l* I up mine eyes, O thou
134. 2 *L* up your hands in the sanctuary,
Isa 2. 4 nation shall not *l* up sword against
40. 9 *l* up thy voice with strength;
26 *L* up your eyes on high, and
42. 2 He shall not cry, nor *l* up, nor
49.18 *L* up thine eyes round about, and
22 will *l* up mine hand to the Gentiles,
52. 8 watchmen shall *l* up the voice;
Jer 13.20 *L* up your eyes, and behold them
La 3.41 Let us *l* up our heart with our hands
Eze 33.25 *l* up your eyes toward your idols,
Mic 4. 3 nation shall not *l* up a sword
Zec 5. 5 *L* up now thine eyes, and see what
Mt 12.11 he not lay hold on it, and *l* it out?
Lk 13.11 and could in no wise *l* up herself.
16.23 in hell he *l* up his eyes, being in
18.13 would not *l* up so much as his eyes
21.28 then look up, and *l* up your heads;
Jn 4.35 *L* up your eyes, and look on the
Heb 12.12 *l* up the hands which hang down,
Jas 4.10 of the Lord, and he shall *l* you up.

LIFTED

Gen 22. 4 third day Abraham *l* up his eyes,
37.28 and *l* up Joseph out of the pit,
Ex 7.20 *l* up the rod, and smote the waters
Jdg 2. 4 people *l* up their voice, and wept.
21. 2 *l* up their voices, and wept sore;
Ps 24. 4 hath not *l* up his soul unto vanity,
27. 6 head be *l* up above mine enemies
30. 1 for thou hast *l* me up, and hast
41. 9 hath *l* up his heel against me.
93. 3 The floods have *l* up, O Lord,
3 the floods have *l* up their voice;
Isa 6. 1 upon a throne, high and *l* up, and
37.23 voice, and *l* up thine eyes on high?
Eze 3.14 So the spirit *l* me up, and took me
8. 3 spirit *l* me up between the earth
10.15 And the cherubims were *l* up.
11. 1 the spirit *l* me up, and brought me
Hab 3.10 voice, and *l* up his hands on high.
Zec 1.18 Then *l* I up mine eyes, and saw,
Mt 17. 8 when they had *l* up their eyes,
Mk 1.31 her by the hand, and *l* her up;
9.27 him by the hand, and *l* him up;
Lk 6.20 he *l* up his eyes on his disciples,
11.27 of the company *l* up her voice,
17.13 they *l* up their voices, and said,
24.50 and he *l* up his hands, and blessed
Jn 3.14 as Moses *l* up the serpent in the
14 so must the Son of man be *l* up:
6. 5 When Jesus then *l* up his eyes,
8. 7 *l* up himself, and said unto them,
10 When Jesus had *l* up himself, and
28 When ye have *l* up the Son of man,
11.41 And Jesus *l* up his eyes, and said,
12.32 And I if I be *l* up from the earth,
34 thou The Son of man must be *l* up?
13.18 me hath *l* up his heel against me.
17. 1 Jesus, and *l* up his eyes to heaven,
Ac 2.14 But Peter,...*l* up his voice, and
3. 7 by the right hand, and *l* him up:
4.24 *l* up their voice to God with one
9.41 gave her his hand, and *l* her up,
14.11 they *l* up their voices, saying in
22.22 and then *l* up their voices, and said,
1Ti 3. 6 lest being *l* up with pride he fall
Rev 10. 5 the earth *l* up his hand to heaven,

LIGHT

Gen 1. 3 Let there be *l*: and there was *l*.
4 God saw the *l*, that it was good:
4 divided the *l* from the darkness.
5 And God called the *l* Day, and the
15 heaven to give *l* upon the earth:
Job 3.16 the greater *l* to rule the day,
16 and the lesser *l* to rule the night:
18 to divide the *l* from the darkness:
Ex 10.23 of Israel had *l* in their dwellings.
13.21 in a pillar of fire, to give them *l*;
2Ki 3.18 is but a *l* thing in the sight of the
20.10 It is a *l* thing for the shadow to
Neh 9.19 of fire by night, to shew them *l*,
Job 3. 4 neither let the *l* shine upon it.
9 let it look for *l*, but have none;

Job 3.16 been; as infants which never saw *l*.
20 is *l* given to him that is in misery,
23 why is *l* given to a man whose way is
10.22 and where the *l* is as darkness.
12.22 out to *l* the shadow of death.
25 They grope in the dark without *l*,
18. 5 the *l* of the wicked shall be put out,
22.28 the *l* shall shine upon thy ways.
24.13 of those that rebel against the *l*;
29. 3 by his *l* I walked through darkness;
36.32 With clouds he covereth the *l*;
38.19 Where is the way where *l* dwelleth?
Ps 4. 6 the *l* of thy countenance upon us.
18.28 For thou wilt *l* my candle: the Lord
27. 1 The Lord is my *l* and my salvation;
36. 9 of life: in thy *l* shall we see *l*.
37. 6 forth thy righteousness as the *l*,
43. 3 O send out thy *l* and thy truth: let
104. 2 coverest thyself with *l* as with a
119.105 my feet, and a *l* unto my path.
130 entrance of thy words giveth *l*; it
139.11 even the night shall be *l* about me.
12 darkness and the *l* are both alike
148. 3 moon: praise him, all ye stars of *l*.
Pr 4.18 path of the just is as the shining *l*,
6.23 is a lamp; and the law is *l*; and
13. 9 The *l* of the righteous rejoiceth:
Ec 11. 7 Truly the *l* is sweet, and a pleasant
Isa 2. 5 let us walk in the *l* of the Lord.
5.20 darkness for *l*, and *l* for darkness;
9. 2 in darkness have seen a great *l*:
2 death, upon them hath the *l* shined.
13.10 thereof shall not give their *l*:
10 moon shall not cause her *l* to shine.
42. 6 the people, for a *l* of the Gentiles;
16 will make darkness *l* before them,
45. 7 I form the *l*, and create darkness:
49. 6 give thee for a *l* to the Gentiles,
58. 8 Then shall thy *l* break forth as the
59. 9 we wait for *l*, but behold obscurity;
60. 1 Arise, shine; for thy *l* is come, and
3 Gentiles shall come to thy *l*, and
19 sun shall be no more thy *l* by day;
19 shall the moon give *l* unto thee:
19 shall be unto thee an everlasting *l*,
20 Lord shall be thine everlasting *l*,
Jer 31.35 which giveth the sun for a *l* by day,
35 and of the stars for a *l* by night,
La 3. 2 me into darkness, but not into *l*.
Am 5.18 the Lord is darkness, and not *l*.
20 the Lord be darkness, and not *l*?
Mic 7. 8 the Lord shall be a *l* unto me.
9 he will bring me forth to the *l*, and
Zep 3. 5 doth he bring his judgment to *l*,
Zec 14. 7 that at evening time it shall be *l*.
Mt 4.16 which sat in darkness saw great *l*;
16 shadow of death *l* is sprung up.
5.14 Ye are the *l* of the world. A city
15 Neither do men *l* a candle, and
15 giveth *l* unto all that are in the
16 Let your *l* so shine before men,
6.22 The *l* of the body is the eye: if
22 thy whole body shall be full of *l*.
23 the *l* that is in thee be darkness,
10.27 in darkness, that speak ye in *l*:
11.30 yoke is easy, and my burden is *l*.
17. 2 his raiment was white as the *l*.
22. 5 they made *l* of it, and went their
24.29 and the moon shall not give her *l*,
Mk 13.24 and the moon shall not give her *l*,
Lk 1.79 give *l* to them that sit in darkness
2.32 A *l* to lighten the Gentiles, and
8.16 they which enter in may see the *l*.
11.33 they which come in may see the *l*.
34 The *l* of the body is the eye:
34 thy whole body also is full of *l*;
35 that the *l* which is in thee be not
36 whole body therefore be full of *l*,
36 dark, the whole shall be full of *l*,
36 of a candle doth give thee *l*.
12. 3 darkness shall be heard in the *l*;

Biblical Themes

LIGHT AND DARKNESS

The earth was without form, and void; and darkness was upon the face of the deep. . . . And God said, Let there be light: and there was light. Gen 1.2-3

The Lord bless thee, and keep thee: the Lord make his face shine upon thee, and be gracious unto thee. Nu 6.24-25

Thou art my lamp, O Lord; and the Lord will lighten my darkness. 2Sa 22.29

The pillar of the cloud departed not from them by day, to lead them in the way; neither the pillar of fire by night, to shew them light, and the way wherein they should go. Neh 9.19

With thee is the fountain of life: in thy light shall we see light. Ps 36.9

Commit thy way unto the Lord. . . . And he shall bring forth thy righteousness as the light, and thy judgment as the noonday. Ps 37.5-6

Light is sown for the righteous, and gladness for the upright in heart. Ps 97.11

Thy word is a lamp unto my feet, and a light unto my path. Ps 119.105

The darkness hideth not from thee; but the night shineth as the day: the darkness and the light are both alike to thee. Ps 139.12

The people that walked in darkness have seen a great light: they that dwell in the land of the shadow of death, upon them hath the light shined. Isa 9.2

Woe unto you that desire the day of the Lord! to what end is it for you? the day of the Lord is darkness, and not light. Am 5.18

When I fall, I shall arise; when I sit in darkness, the Lord shall be a light unto me. Mi 7.8

Ye are the light of the world. A city that is set on an hill cannot be hid. Neither do men light a candle, and put it under a bushel, but on a candlestick; and it giveth light unto all that are in the house. Let your light so shine before men, that they may see your good works, and glorify your Father. Mt 5.14-16

In him was life; and the life was the light of men. And the light shineth in darkness; and the darkness comprehended it not. Jn 1.4-5

This is the condemnation, that light is come into the world, and men loved darkness rather than light, because their deeds were evil. Jn 3.19

I am the light of the world: he that followeth me shall not walk in darkness, but shall have the light of life. Jn 8.12

Whether he be a sinner or no, I know not: one thing I know, that, whereas I was blind, now I see. Jn 9.25

The night is far spent, the day is at hand: let us therefore cast off the works of darkness, and let us put on the armor of light. Ro 13.12

God, who commanded the light to shine out of darkness, hath shined in our hearts, to give the light of the knowledge of the glory of God in the face of Jesus Christ. 2Co 4.6

We wrestle not against flesh and blood, but against . . . the rulers of the darkness of this world. Eph 6.12

Take heed, as unto a light that shineth in a dark place, until the day dawn, and the day star arise in your hearts. 2Pe 1.19

And the city had no need of the sun, neither of the moon, to shine in it: for the glory of God did lighten it, and the Lamb is the light thereof. Rev 21.23

15. 8 doth not *l* a candle, and sweep the
16. 8 wiser than the children of *l*.
Jn 1. 4 and the life was the *l* of men.
5 And the *l* shineth in darkness; and
7 witness, to bear witness of the *L*,
8 He was not that *L*, but was sent
8 was sent to bear witness of that *L*.
9 That was the true *L*, which
3.19 that *l* is come into the world, and
19 men loved darkness rather than *l*,
20 one that doeth evil hateth the *l*,
20 neither cometh to the *l*, lest his
21 that doeth truth cometh to the *l*,
5.35 was a burning and a shining *l*:
35 for a season to rejoice in his *l*.
8.12 saying, I am the *l* of the world:
12 but shall have the *l* of life.
9. 5 the world, I am the *l* of the world.
11. 9 because he seeth the *l* of this world.
10 because there is no *l* in him.
12.35 Yet a little while is the *l* with you.
35 Walk while ye have the *l*, lest
36 While ye have the *l*, believe in the *l*,
36 that ye may be the children of *l*.
46 I am come a *l* into the world, that
Ac 9. 3 round about him a *l* from heaven:

12. 7 him, and a *l* shined in the prison:
13.47 set thee to be a *l* of the Gentiles,
16.29 he called for a *l*, and sprang in,
22. 6 shone from heaven a great *l* round
9 that were with me saw indeed the *l*,
11 could not see for the glory of that *l*,
26.13 I saw in the way a *l* from heaven,
18 to turn them from darkness to *l*,
23 and should shew *l* unto the people,
Ro 2.19 a *l* of them which are in darkness,
13.12 and let us put on the armor of *l*.
1Co 4. 5 will bring to *l* the hidden things
2Co 4. 4 *l* of the glorious gospel of Christ,
6 commanded the *l* to shine out of
6 to give the *l* of the knowledge of
17 our *l* affliction, which is but for a
6.14 communion hath *l* with darkness?
11.14 is transformed into an angel of *l*.
Eph 5. 8 but now are ye *l* in the Lord:
8 walk as children of *l*:
13 are made manifest by the *l*: for
13 whatsoever doth make manifest is *l*.
14 and Christ shall give thee *l*.
Col 1.12 the inheritance of the saints in *l*:
1Th 5. 5 Ye are all the children of *l*, and
1Ti 6.16 dwelling in the *l* which no man
2Ti 1.10 brought life and immortality to *l*
1Pe 2. 9 of darkness into his marvelous *l*:
2Pe 1.19 as unto a *l* that shineth in a dark
1Jn 1. 5 declare unto you, that God is *l*,
7 if we walk in the *l*, as he is in the *l*,
2. 8 past, and the true *l* now shineth.
9 He that saith he is in the *l*, and
10 loveth his brother abideth in the *l*,
Rev 7.16 neither shall the sun *l* on them,
18.23 *l* of a candle shall shine no more
21.11 her *l* was like unto a stone most
23 it, and the Lamb is the *l* thereof.
24 saved shall walk in the *l* of it:
22. 5 no candle, neither *l* of the sun;
5 for the Lord God giveth them *l*:

LIGHTED

Gen 24.64 she saw Isaac, she *l* off the camel.
28.11 And he *l* upon a certain place, and
Ex 40.25 he *l* the lamps before the Lord; as
Nu 8. 3 he *l* the lamps thereof over against
Jos 15.18 a field: and she *l* off her ass; and
Jdg 1.14 a field: and she *l* from off her ass;
4.15 that Sisera *l* down off his chariot,
1Sa 25.23 *l* off the ass, and fell before David
2Ki 5.21 he *l* down from the chariot to
10.15 *l* on Jehonadab the son of Rechab
Isa 9. 8 Jacob, and it hath *l* upon Israel.
Lk 8.16 No man, when he hath *l* a candle,
11.33 No man, when he hath *l* a candle,

LIGHTEN

1Sa 6. 5 he will *l* his hand from off you,
2Sa 22.29 and the Lord will *l* my darkness.
Ezr 9. 8 that our God may *l* our eyes, and
Ps 13. 3 *l* mine eyes, lest I sleep the sleep
Jon 1. 5 ship into the sea, to *l* it of them.
Lk 2.32 A light to *l* the Gentiles, and the
Rev 21.23 the glory of God did *l* it, and the

LIGHTENED

Ps 34. 5 looked unto him, and were *l*:
77.18 the lightnings *l* the world: the
Ac 27.18 the next day they *l* the ship;
38 they *l* the ship, and cast out the
Rev 18. 1 the earth was *l* with his glory.

LIGHTENETH

Pr 29.13 the Lord *l* both their eyes.
Lk 17.24 that *l* out of the one part under

LIGHTETH

Ex 30. 8 when Aaron *l* the lamps at even,
Dt 19. 5 and *l* upon his neighbor, that
Jn 1. 9 which *l* every man that cometh

LIGHTING

Isa 30.30 shall shew the *l* down of his arm,
Mt 3.16 like a dove, and *l* upon him:

LIGHTLY

1Sa 18.23 I am a poor man, and *l* esteemed?
Jer 4.24 trembled, and all the hills moved *l*.
Mk 9.39 that can *l* speak evil of me.

LIGHTNESS

Jer 23.32 err by their lies, and by their *l*;
2Co 1.17 was thus minded, did I use *l*?

LIGHTNING

2Sa 22.15 them; *l*, and discomfited them.
Job 28.26 a way for the *l* of the thunder:
37. 3 his *l* unto the ends of the earth.
38.25 or a way for the *l* of thunder;
Ps 144. 6 Cast forth *l*, and scatter them:
Eze 1.13 and out of the fire went forth *l*.
14 as the appearance of a flash of *l*.
Dan 10. 6 his face as the appearance of *l*.
Zec 9.14 his arrow shall go forth as the *l*:
Mt 24.27 For as the *l* cometh out of the east,
28. 3 His countenance was like *l*, and
Lk 10.18 I beheld Satan as *l* fall from heaven.
17.24 For as the *l*, that lighteneth out of

LIGHTNINGS

Ex 19.16 that there were thunders and *l*,
20.18 saw the thunderings, and the *l*,
Job 38.35 Canst thou send *l*, that they may
Ps 18.14 and he shot out *l*, and discomfited
77.18 the *l* lightened the world: the earth
97. 4 His *l* enlightened the world: the
135. 7 he maketh *l* for the rain; he
Jer 10.13 he maketh *l* with rain, and bringeth
51.16 he maketh *l* with rain, and bringeth
Na 2. 4 torches, they shall run like the *l*.
Rev 4. 5 out of the throne proceeded *l* and
8. 5 were voices, and thunderings, and *l*,
11.19 and there were *l*, and voices, and
16.18 were voices, and thunders, and *l*;

LIGHTS

Gen 1.14 Let there be *l* in the firmament of
15 let them be for *l* in the firmament
16 God made two great *l*; the greater
1Ki 6. 4 he made windows of narrow *l*.
Ps 136. 7 To him that made great *l*: for his
Eze 32. 8 bright *l* of heaven will I make
Lk 12.35 about, and your *l* burning;
Ac 20. 8 there were many *l* in the upper
Php 2.15 whom ye shine as *l* in the world;
Jas 1.17 cometh down from the Father of *l*,

LIKEMINDED

Ro 15. 5 to be *l* one toward another
Php 2. 2 Fulfil ye my joy, that ye be *l*,
20 For I have no man *l*, who will

LIKEN

Isa 40.18 To whom then will ye *l* God? or
25 To whom then will ye *l* me, or
46. 5 To whom will ye *l* me, and make
La 2.13 what thing shall I *l* to thee, O
Mt 7.24 I will *l* him unto a wise man,
11.16 whereunto shall I *l* this generation?
Mk 4.30 shall we *l* the kingdom of God?
Lk 7.31 then shall I *l* the men of this
13.20 shall I *l* the kingdom of God?

LIKENED

Ps 89. 6 mighty can be *l* unto the Lord?
Jer 6. 2 have *l* the daughter of Zion to a
Mt 7.26 shall be *l* unto a foolish man,
13.24 of heaven is *l* unto a man which
18.23 of heaven *l* unto a certain king,
25. 1 of heaven be *l* unto ten virgins,

LIKENESS

Gen 1.26 man in our image, after our *l*:
5. 1 man, in the *l* of God made he him;
3 begat a son in his own *l*, after his
Ex 20. 4 or any *l* of any thing that is in
Dt 4.16 figure, the *l* of male or female,
17 The *l* of any beast that is on the
17 the *l* of any winged fowl that flieth
18 The *l* of any thing that creepeth on
18 the *l* of any fish that is in the
23 image, or the *l* of any thing,
25 graven image, or the *l* of any thing,
5. 8 any *l* of any thing that is in heaven
Ps 17.15 satisfied, when I awake, with thy *l*.
Isa 40.18 what *l* will ye compare unto him?
Eze 1. 5 came the *l* of four living creatures.
5 they had the *l* of a man.
10 As for the *l* of their faces, they four
13 As for the *l* of the living creatures,
16 a beryl: and they four had one *l*:
22 the *l* of the firmament upon their
26 their heads was the *l* of a throne,
26 and upon the *l* of the throne was the
26 *l* as the appearance of a man above
28 of the *l* of the glory of the Lord.
8. 2 and lo a *l* as the appearance of fire:
10. 1 the appearance of the *l* of a throne.
10 appearances, they four had one *l*,
21 and the *l* of the hands of a man
22 the *l* of their faces was the same
Ac 14.11 come down to us in the *l* of men.
Ro 6. 5 together in the *l* of his death,
5 be also in the *l* of his resurrection:
8. 3 his own Son in the *l* of sinful flesh,
Php 2. 7 and was made in the *l* of men:

LILIES

1Ki 7.26 brim of a cup, with flowers of *l*:
2Ch 4. 5 brim of a cup, with flowers of *l*;
SS 2.16 I am his: he feedeth among the *l*.
4. 5 are twins, which feed among the *l*.
5.13 his lips like *l*, dropping sweet
6. 2 in the gardens, and to gather *l*.
3 is mine: he feedeth among the *l*.
7. 2 an heap of wheat set about with *l*.
Mt 6.28 Consider the *l* of the field, how
Lk 12.27 Consider the *l* how they grow:

LILY

1Ki 7.19 pillars were of *l* work in the porch,
22 the top of the pillars was *l* work:
SS 2. 1 of Sharon, and the *l* of the valleys.
2 As the *l* among thorns, so is my
Hos 14. 5 he shall grow as the *l*, and cast

LIMITETH

Heb 4. 7 he *l* a certain day, saying to David,

LINE

Jos 2.18 shalt bind this *l* of scarlet thread
21 bound the scarlet *l* in the window.
2Sa 8. 2 and measured them with a *l*,
2 and with one full *l* to keep alive.
1Ki 7.15 a *l* of twelve cubits did compass
23 a *l* of thirty cubits did compass
2Ki 21.13 over Jerusalem the *l* of Samaria,
2Ch 4. 2 a *l* of thirty cubits did compass it
Job 38. 5 who hath stretched the *l* upon it?
Ps 19. 4 Their *l* is gone out through all the
78.55 divided them an inheritance by *l*,
Isa 28.10, 13 *l* upon *l*, *l* upon *l*; here a
17 Judgment also will I lay to the *l*,
34.11 out upon it the *l* of confusion,
17 hand hath divided it unto them by *l*:
44.13 he marketh it out with a *l*; he
Jer 31.39 the measuring *l* shall yet go forth
La 2. 8 he hath stretched out a *l*, he hath
Eze 40. 3 with a *l* of flax in his hand, and
47. 3 man that had the *l* in his hand
Am 7.17 thy land shall be divided by *l*;
Zec 1.16 a *l* shall be stretched forth upon
2. 1 with a measuring *l* in his hand.
2Co 10.16 not to boast in another man's *l*

LINEAGE
Lk 2. 4 was of the house and *l* of David:)

LINEN
Lev 6.10 priest shall put on his *l* garment,
16. 4 He shall put on the holy *l* coat,
Pr 31.24 She maketh fine *l*, and selleth it;
Jer 13. 1 Go and get thee a *l* girdle, and
Eze 16.10 I girded thee about with fine *l*,
Mt 27.59 he wrapped it in a clean *l* cloth,
Mk 14.51 *l* cloth cast about his naked body;
52 And he left the *l* cloth, and fled
15.46 And he bought fine *l*, and took him
46 wrapped him in the *l*, and laid him
Lk 16.19 was clothed in purple and fine *l*,
23.53 took it down, and wrapped it in *l*,
24.12 the *l* clothes laid by themselves.
Jn 19.40 of Jesus, and wound it in *l* clothes
20. 5 looking in, saw the *l* clothes lying;
6 and seeth the *l* clothes lie,
7 not lying with the *l* clothes, but
Rev 15. 6 clothed in pure and white *l*, and
18.12 pearls, and fine *l*, and purple,
16 city, that was clothed in fine *l*,
19. 8 that she should be arrayed in fine *l*,
8 for the fine *l* is the righteousness
14 clothed in fine *l*, white and clean.

LINES
2Sa 8. 2 even with two *l* measured he to
Ps 16. 6 The *l* are fallen unto me in pleasant

LINUS
2Ti 4.21 and *L*, and Claudia, and all the

LION
Gen 49. 9 and as an old *l*; who shall rouse
Nu 24. 9 He couched, he lay down as a *l*,
Jdg 14. 5 a young *l* roared against him.
8 aside to see the carcass of the *l*:
9 honey out of the carcass of the *l*.
18 and what is stronger than a *l*?
1Sa 17.37 delivered me out of the paw of the *l*,
Job 4.11 old *l* perisheth for lack of prey,
10.16 Thou huntest me as a fierce *l*:
28. 8 it, nor the fierce *l* passed by it.
Ps 7. 2 Lest he tear my soul like a *l*,
10. 9 in wait secretly as a *l* in his den:
91.13 shalt tread upon the *l* and adder:
13 the young *l* and the dragon shalt
Pr 19.12 king's wrath is as the roaring of a *l*;
26.13 man saith, There is a *l* in the way;
13 a *l* is in the streets.
28. 1 but the righteous are bold as a *l*.
15 As a roaring *l*, and a ranging bear;
Ec 9. 4 living dog is better than a dead *l*.
Isa 11. 6 young *l* and the fatling together;
7 the *l* shall eat straw like the ox.
35. 9 No *l* shall be there, nor any
Jer 5. 6 a *l* out of the forest shall slay them,
Eze 1.10 the face of a *l*, on the right side:
Dan 7. 4 first was like a *l*, and had eagle's
Hos 11.10 the Lord: he shall roar like a *l*:
Am 3. 4 Will a *l* roar in the forest, when he
8 The *l* hath roared, who will not
12 taketh out of the mouth of the *l*
5.19 As if a man did flee from a *l*, and a
2Ti 4.17 delivered out of the mouth of the *l*.
1Pe 5. 8 adversary the devil, as a roaring *l*,
Rev 4. 7 And the first beast was like a *l*,
5. 5 behold, the *L* of the tribe of Juda,
10. 3 loud voice, as when a *l* roareth:
13. 2 and his mouth as the mouth of a *l*:

LIONS
Ps 34.10 The young *l* do lack, and suffer
Dan 6. 7 he shall be cast into the den of *l*.
19 and went in haste unto the den of *l*.
20 able to deliver thee from the *l*?
27 Daniel from the power of the *l*.
Heb 11.33 promises, stopped the mouths of *l*,

Lions leave Daniel unscathed in their den (Dan 6) in this Tunisian mosaic from the 5th–6th centuries A.D.

Rev 9. 8 their teeth were as the teeth of *l*.
17 the horses were as the heads of *l*;

LIPS
Ex 6.12 me, who am of uncircumcised *l*?
30 Behold, I am of uncircumcised *l*,
Lev 5. 4 pronouncing with his *l* to do evil
Nu 30. 6 vowed, or uttered ought out of her *l*,
8 that which she uttered with her *l*,
12 whatsoever proceeded out of her *l*
Dt 23.23 That which is gone out of thy *l*
1Sa 1.13 only her *l* moved, but her voice
2Ki 19.28 in thy nose, and my bridle in thy *l*,
Job 2.10 all this did not Job sin with his *l*.
8.21 laughing, and thy *l* with rejoicing.
11. 5 speak, and open his *l* against thee;
13. 6 hearken to the pleadings of my *l*.
15. 6 thine own *l* testify against thee.
16. 5 the moving of my *l* should asswage
23.12 from the commandment of his *l*;
27. 4 My *l* shall not speak wickedness,
32.20 I will open my *l* and answer.
33. 3 my *l* shall utter knowledge clearly.
Ps 12. 2 with flattering *l* and with a double
3 Lord shall cut off all flattering *l*,
4 our *l* are our own: who is lord over
16. 4 nor take up their names into my *l*.
17. 1 that goeth not out of feigned *l*.
4 by the word of thy *l* I have kept me
21. 2 not withholden the request of his *l*.
31.18 Let the lying *l* be put to silence;
34.13 evil, and thy *l* from speaking guile.
40. 9 I have not refrained my *l*, O Lord,
45. 2 of men: grace is poured into thy *l*:
51.15 O Lord, open thou my *l*; and my
59. 7 their mouth: swords are in their *l*:
12 the words of their *l* let them even
63. 3 than life, my *l* shall praise thee.
5 shall praise thee with joyful *l*:
66.14 Which my *l* have uttered, and my

71.23 My *l* shall greatly rejoice when I
89.34 the thing that is gone out of my *l*.
106.33 he spake unadvisedly with his *l*.
119.13 With my *l* have I declared all the
171 My *l* shall utter praise, when thou
120. 2 my soul, O Lord, from lying *l*,
140. 3 adders' poison is under their *l*.
9 mischief of their own *l* cover them.
141. 3 my mouth; keep the door of my *l*.
Pr 4.24 and perverse *l* put far from thee.
5. 2 that thy *l* may keep knowledge.
3 For the *l* of a strange woman drop
7.21 with the flattering of her *l* she
8. 6 the opening of my *l* shall be right
7 is an abomination to my *l*.
10.13 *l* of him that hath understanding
18 He that hideth hatred with lying *l*,
19 but he that refraineth his *l* is wise.
21 The *l* of the righteous feed many:
32 The *l* of the righteous know what
12.13 snared by the transgression of his *l*:
22 Lying *l* are abomination to the
13. 3 he that openeth wide his *l* shall
14. 3 but the *l* of the wise shall preserve
7 not in him the *l* of knowledge.
23 talk of the *l* tendeth only to penury.
15. 7 *l* of the wise disperse knowledge:
16.10 A divine sentence is in the *l* of the
13 Righteous *l* are the delight of kings;
21 the sweetness of the *l* increaseth
23 mouth, and addeth learning to his *l*.
27 in his *l* there is as a burning fire.
30 moving his *l* he bringeth evil to
17. 4 wicked doer giveth heed to false *l*;
7 fool: much less do lying *l* a prince.
28 he that shutteth his *l* is esteemed
18. 6 A fool's *l* enter into contention,
7 and his *l* are the snare of his soul.
20 increase of his *l* shall he be filled.
19. 1 he that is perverse in his *l*, and is a
20.15 the *l* of knowledge are a precious
19 with him that flattereth with his *l*.
22.11 the grace of his *l* the king shall be
18 they shall withal be fitted in thy *l*.
23.16 when thy *l* speak right things.
24. 2 and their *l* talk of mischief.
26 Every man shall kiss his *l* that
28 cause; and deceive not with thy *l*.
26.23 Burning *l* and a wicked heart are
24 that hateth dissembleth with his *l*,
27. 2 a stranger, and not thine own *l*.
Ec 10.12 but the *l* of a fool shall swallow up
SS 4. 3 Thy *l* are like a thread of scarlet,
11 Thy *l*, O my spouse, drop as the
5.13 his *l* like lilies, dropping sweet
7. 9 the *l* of those that are asleep to
Isa 6. 5 because I am a man of unclean *l*,
5 the midst of a people of unclean *l*:
7 said, Lo, this hath touched thy *l*;
11. 4 with the breath of his *l* shall he
28.11 with stammering *l* and another
29.13 and with their *l* do honor me,
30.27 his *l* are full of indignation, and
37.29 thy nose, and my bridle in thy *l*,
57.19 I create the fruit of the *l*; Peace,
59. 3 your *l* have spoken lies, your
Jer 17.16 which came out of my *l* was right
La 3.62 The *l* of those that rose up against
Eze 24.17 cover not thy *l*, and eat not the
22 ye shall not cover your *l*, nor eat
36. 3 are taken up in the *l* of talkers,
Dan 10.16 of the sons of men touched my *l*:
Hos 14. 2 will we render the calves of our *l*.
Mic 3. 7 yea, they shall all cover their *l*;
Hab 3.16 my *l* quivered at the voice:
Mal 2. 6 and iniquity was not found in his *l*:
7 priest's *l* should keep knowledge,
Mt 15. 8 and honoreth me with their *l*;
Mk 7. 6 people honoreth me with their *l*,
Ro 3.13 the poison of asps is under their *l*:
1Co 14.21 men of other tongues and other *l*
Heb 13.15 the fruit of our *l* giving thanks to
1Pe 3.10 and his *l* that they speak no guile:

LISTED

Mt 17.12 done unto him whatsoever they *l*.
Mk 9.13 done unto him whatsoever they *l*,

LISTEN

Isa 49. 1 *L*, O isles, unto me; and hearken,

LISTETH

Jn 3. 8 The wind bloweth where it *l*, and
Jas 3. 4 whithersoever...governor *l*.

LITTLE

Gen 18. 4 a *l* water, I pray you, be fetched,
19.20 near to flee unto, and it is a *l* one:
20 escape thither, (is it not a *l* one?)
24.17 drink a *l* water of thy pitcher.
43 a *l* water of thy pitcher to drink;
30.30 *l* which thou hadst before I came,
34.29 all their *l* ones, and their wives
35.16 but a *l* way to come to Ephrath:
43. 2 them, Go again, buy us a *l* food.
8 we, and thou, and also our *l* ones.
11 a present, a *l* balm, and a *l* honey,
44.20 and a child of his old age, a *l* one;
25 Go again, and buy us a *l* food.
45.19 the land of Egypt for your *l* ones,
46. 5 and their *l* ones, and their wives,
47.24 and for food for your *l* ones.
48. 7 a *l* way to come unto Ephrath:
50. 8 only their *l* ones, and their flocks,
21 will nourish you, and your *l* ones.
Ex 10.10 I will let you go, and your *l* ones:
24 let your *l* ones also go with you.
12. 4 household be too *l* for the lamb,
16.18 he that gathered *l* had no lack;
23.30 By *l* and *l* I will drive them out
Lev 11.17 And the *l* owl, and the cormorant,
Nu 14.31 But your *l* ones, which ye said
16.27 their sons, and their *l* children.
31. 9 Midian captives, and their *l* ones,
17 kill every male among the *l* ones,
32.16 our cattle, and cities for our *l* ones:
17 our *l* ones shall dwell in the fenced
24 Build you cities for your *l* ones,
26 Our *l* ones, our wives, our flocks,
Dt 1.39 your *l* ones, which ye said should
2.34 the women, and the *l* ones, of every
3.19 your wives, and your *l* ones, and
7.22 nations before thee by *l* and *l*:
14.16 The *l* owl, and the great owl, and
20.14 the women, and the *l* ones, and
28.38 field, and shalt gather but *l* in;
29.11 Your *l* ones, your wives, and thy
Jos 1.14 Your wives, your *l* ones, and your
8.35 the women, and the *l* ones, and the
19.47 of Dan went out too *l* for them:
22.17 Is the iniquity of Peor too *l* for us,
Jdg 4.19 I pray thee, a *l* water to drink;
18.21 put the *l* ones and the cattle and
Ru 2. 7 that she tarried a *l* in the house.
1Sa 2.19 his mother made him a *l* coat,
14.29 because I tasted a *l* of this honey.
43 I did but taste a *l* honey with the
15.17 thou wast *l* in thine own sight,
20.35 with David, and a *l* lad with him.
2Sa 12. 3 had nothing, save one *l* ewe lamb,
8 and if that had been too *l*, I would
15.22 all the *l* ones that were with him.
16. 1 was a *l* past the top of the hill,
19.36 servant will go a *l* way over Jordan
1Ki 3. 7 I am but a *l* child: I know not how
8.64 too *l* to receive the burnt offerings,
11.17 Egypt; Hadad being yet a *l* child.
12.10 My *l* finger shall be thicker than
17.10 Fetch me, I pray thee, a *l* water
12 in a barrel, and a *l* oil in a cruse:
13 but make me thereof a *l* cake first,
18.44 ariseth a *l* cloud out of the sea,
20.27 them like two *l* flocks of kids;
2Ki 2.23 forth *l* children out of the city,
4.10 Let us make a *l* chamber, I pray
5. 2 out of the land of Israel a *l* maid;
14 like unto the flesh of a *l* child, and
19 So he departed from him a *l* way.
10.18 unto them, Ahab served Baal a *l*;
2Ch 10.10 My *l* finger shall be thicker than
20.13 before the Lord, with their *l* ones,
31.18 the genealogy of all their *l* ones,
Ezr 8.21 way for us, and for our *l* ones, and
9. 8 now for a *l* space grace hath been
8 give us a *l* reviving in our bondage.
Neh 9.32 all the trouble seem *l* before thee,
Est 3.13 *l* children and women, in one day,
8.11 them, both *l* ones and women,
Job 4.12 and mine ear received a *l* thereof.
10.20 alone, that I may take comfort a *l*,
21.11 forth their *l* ones like a flock,
24.24 They are exalted for a *l* while,
26.14 how *l* a portion is heard of him?
36. 2 Suffer me a *l*, and I will shew
Ps 2.12 when his wrath is kindled but a *l*.
8. 5 made him a *l* lower than the angels,
37.10 For yet a *l* while, and the wicked
16 A *l* that a righteous man hath is
65.12 the *l* hills rejoice on every side.
68.27 There is *l* Benjamin with their
72. 3 and the *l* hills, by righteousness.
114. 4 like rams, and the *l* hills like lambs.
6 rams; and ye *l* hills, like lambs?
137. 9 dasheth thy *l* ones against the
Pr 6.10 Yet a *l* sleep, a *l* slumber,
10 a *l* folding of the hands to sleep:
10.20 the heart of the wicked is *l* worth.
15.16 is *l* with the fear of the Lord, than
16. 8 Better is a *l* with righteousness,
24.33 Yet a *l* sleep, a *l* slumber,
33 a *l* folding of the hands to sleep:
30.24 four things which are *l* upon the
Ec 5.12 sweet, whether he eat *l* or much:
9.14 There was a *l* city, and few men
10. 1 so doth a *l* folly him that is in
SS 2.15 Take us the foxes, the *l* foxes,
3. 4 but a *l* that I passed from them,
8. 8 We have a *l* sister, and she hath
Isa 10.25 For yet a very *l* while, and the
11. 6 and a *l* child shall lead them.
26.20 thyself as it were for a *l* moment,
28.10 line; here a *l*, and there a *l*:
13 upon line: here a *l*, and there a *l*;
29.17 Is it not yet a very *l* while, and
40.15 up the isles as a very *l* thing.
54. 8 In a *l* wrath I hid my face from
60.22 A *l* one shall become a thousand,
63.18 have possessed it but a *l* while:
Jer 14. 3 sent their *l* ones to the waters:
48. 4 her *l* ones have caused a cry to be
51.33 yet a *l* while, and the time of her
Eze 9. 6 maids, and *l* children, and women:
11.16 I be to them as a *l* sanctuary in
16.47 if that were a very *l* thing, thou
31. 4 out her *l* rivers unto all the trees
40. 7 every *l* chamber was one reed
7 between the *l* chambers were five
10 And the *l* chambers of the gate
12 space also before the *l* chambers
12 the *l* chambers were six cubits on
13 from the roof of one *l* chamber to
16 narrow windows to the *l* chambers,
21 the *l* chambers thereof were three
29, 33 the *l* chambers thereof, and
36 The *l* chambers thereof, the posts
Dan 7. 8 up among them another *l* horn,
8. 9 one of them came forth a *l* horn,
11.34 they shall be holpen with a *l* help:
Hos 1. 4 for yet a *l* while, and I will avenge
8.10 shall sorrow a *l* for the burden of
Am 6.11 and the *l* house with clefts.
Mic 5. 2 thou be *l* among the thousands of
Hag 1. 6 have sown much, and bring in *l*;

Hag 1. 9 for much, and, lo, it came to *l*;
2. 6 Yet once, it is a *l* while, and I will
Zec 1.15 I was but a *l* displeased, and they
13. 7 turn mine hand upon the *l* ones.
Mt 6.30 more clothe you, O ye of *l* faith?
8.26 Why are ye fearful, O ye of *l* faith?
10.42 to drink unto one of these *l* ones
14.31 O thou of *l* faith, wherefore didst
15.34 they said, Seven, and a few *l* fishes.
16. 8 O ye of *l* faith, why reason ye
18. 2 Jesus called a *l* child unto him,
3 converted, and become as *l* children,
4 humble himself as this *l* child,
5 receive one such *l* child in my
6 shall offend one of these *l* ones
10 ye despise not one of these *l* ones;
14 one of these *l* ones should perish.
19.13 brought unto him *l* children, that
14 Jesus said, Suffer *l* children, and
26.39 went a *l* farther, and fell on his
Mk 1.19 he had gone a *l* farther thence,
4.36 were also with him other *l* ships.
5.23 My *l* daughter lieth at the point
9.42 shall offend one of these *l* ones
10.14 Suffer the *l* children to come unto
15 the kingdom of God as a *l* child,
14.35 And he went forward a *l*, and fell
70 And a *l* after, they that stood by
Lk 5. 3 would thrust out a *l* from the land.
7.47 *l* is forgiven, the same loveth *l*.
12.28 will he clothe you, O ye of *l* faith?
32 Fear not, *l* flock; for it is your
17. 2 should offend one of these *l* ones.
18.16 Suffer *l* children to come unto me,
17 the kingdom of God as a *l* child
19. 3 press, because he was *l* of stature.
17 thou hast been faithful in a very *l*,
22.58 after a *l* while another saw him,
Jn 6. 7 every one of them may take a *l*.
7.33 Yet a *l* while am I with you, and
12.35 Yet a *l* while is the light with you.
13.33 *L* children, yet a...while I am with
33 children, yet a *l* while I am with
14.19 Yet a *l* while, and the world seeth
16.16 A *l* while, and ye shall not see me:
16 a *l* while, and ye shall see me:
17 A *l* while, and ye shall not see me:
17 a *l* while, and ye shall see me:
18 What is this that he saith, A *l* while?
19 A *l* while, and ye shall not see me:
19 a *l* while, and ye shall see me?
21. 8 other disciples came in a *l* ship;
Ac 5.34 to put the apostles forth a *l* space;
20.12 alive, and were not a *l* comforted.
27.28 when they had gone a *l* further,
28. 2 people shewed us no *l* kindness:
1Co 5. 6 not that a *l* leaven leaveneth the
2Co 8.15 that had gathered *l* had no lack.
11. 1 could bear with me a *l* in my folly:
16 me, that I may boast myself a *l*.
Gal 4.19 My *l* children, of whom I travail in
5. 9 A *l* leaven leaveneth the whole
1Ti 4. 8 For bodily exercise profiteth *l*:
5.23 a *l* wine for thy stomach's sake
Heb 2. 7 him a *l* lower than the angels;
9 made a *l* lower than the angels for
10.37 For yet a *l* while, and he that shall
Jas 3. 5 Even so the tongue is a *l* member,
5 great a matter a *l* fire kindleth!
4.14 vapor, that appeareth for a *l* time,
1Jn 2. 1 My *l* children, these things write
12 I write unto you, *l* children,
13 I write unto you, *l* children,
18 *L* children, it is the last time: and
28 And now, *l* children, abide in him;
3. 7 *L* children, let no man deceive you:
18 My *l* children, let us not love in
4. 4 Ye are of God, *l* children, and have
5.21 *L* children, keep yourselves from
Rev 3. 8 for thou hast a *l* strength, and
6.11 they should rest yet for a *l* season,
10. 2 he had in his hand a *l* book open:
8 take the *l* book which is open in
9 said unto him, Give me the *l* book.
10 the *l* book out of the angel's hand,
20. 3 that he must be loosed a *l* season.

LIVE

Gen 3.22 tree of life, and eat, and *l* for ever:
12.13 my soul shall *l* because of thee.
17.18 unto God, O that Ishmael might *l*
19.20 not a little one?) and my soul shall *l*.
20. 7 pray for thee, and thou shalt *l*:
27.40 by thy sword shalt thou *l*, and shalt
31.32 thou findest thy gods, let him not *l*:
42. 2 for us from thence; that we may *l*,
18 them the third day, This do, and *l*;
43. 8 that we may *l*, and not die, both we,
45. 3 am Joseph; doth my father yet *l*?
47.19 and give us seed, that we may *l*,
Ex 1.16 if it be a daughter, then she shall *l*.
19.13 it be beast or man, it shall not *l*:
21.35 they shall sell the *l* ox, and divide
22.18 Thou shalt not suffer a witch to *l*.
33.20 there shall no man see me, and *l*.
Lev 16.20 altar, he shall bring the *l* goat:
21 hands upon the head of the *l* goat,
18. 5 if a man do, he shall *l* in them:
25.35 that he may *l* with thee.
36 that thy brother may *l* with thee.
Nu 4.19 do unto them, that they may *l*,
14.21 But as truly as I *l*, all the earth
28 As truly as I *l*, saith the Lord,
21. 8 when he looketh upon it, shall *l*.
24.23 who shall *l* when God doeth this!
Dt 4. 1 ye may *l*, and go in and possess
10 all the days that they shall *l* upon
33 the fire, as thou hast heard, and *l*?
42 one of these cities he might *l*:
5.33 that ye may *l*, and that it may be
8. 1 to do, that ye may *l*, and multiply,
3 that man doth not *l* by bread only,
3 the mouth of the Lord doth man *l*.
12. 1 the days that ye *l* upon the earth.
16.20 that thou mayest *l*, and inherit
19. 4 shall flee thither, that he may *l*:
5 flee unto one of those cities, and *l*:
30. 6 all thy soul, that thou mayest *l*.
16 that thou mayest *l* and multiply:
19 that both thou and thy seed may *l*:
31.13 as long as ye *l* in the land whither
32.40 to heaven, and say, I *l* for ever.
33. 6 Let Reuben *l*, and not die; and let
Jos 6.17 only Rahab the harlot shall *l*, she
9.15 a league with them, to let them *l*:
20 we will even let them *l*, lest wrath
21 princes said unto them, Let them *l*;
1Sa 20.14 not only while yet I *l* shew me the
2Sa 1.10 not *l* after that he was fallen:
12.22 to me, that the child may *l*?
19.34 How long have I to *l*, that I should
1Ki 1.31 Let my lord king David *l* for ever.
8.40 all the days that they *l* in the land
20.32 saith, I pray thee, let me *l*. And
2Ki 4. 7 *l* thou and thy children of the rest.
7. 4 if they save us alive, we shall *l*;
10.19 shall be wanting, he shall not *l*.
18.32 honey, that ye may *l*, and not die:
20. 1 order; for thou shalt die, and not *l*.
2Ch 6.31 so long as they *l* in the land which
Neh 2. 3 the king, Let the king *l* for ever:
5. 2 for them, that we may eat, and *l*.
9.29 if a man do, he shall *l* in them;)
Est 4.11 the golden scepter, that he may *l*:
Job 7.16 I loathe it; I would not *l* alway:
14.14 If a man die, shall he *l* again?
21. 7 Wherefore do the wicked *l*, become
27. 6 not reproach me so long as I *l*.
Ps 22.26 him: your heart shall *l* for ever.
49. 9 That he should still *l* for ever,
55.23 men shall not *l* out half their days;
63. 4 I bless thee while I *l*: I will lift
69.32 your heart shall *l* that seek God.
72.15 And he shall *l*, and to him shall
104.33 sing unto the Lord as long as I *l*:
116. 2 will I call upon him as long as I *l*.
118.17 I shall not die, but *l*, and declare
119.17 that I may *l*, and keep thy word.
77 mercies come unto me, that I may *l*:
116 unto thy word, that I may *l*: and
144 me understanding, and I shall *l*.
175 Let my soul *l*, and it shall praise
146. 2 While I *l* will I praise the Lord:
Pr 4. 4 keep my commandments, and *l*.
7. 2 Keep my commandments, and *l*;
9. 6 Forsake the foolish, and *l*; and go
15.27 but he that hateth gifts shall *l*.
Ec 6. 3 children, and *l* many years, so that
6 Yea, though he *l* a thousand years
9. 3 is in their heart while they *l*, and
9 *L* joyfully with the wife whom
11. 8 But if a man *l* many years, and
Isa 6. 6 me, having a *l* coal in his hand,
26.14 They are dead, they shall not *l*;
19 Thy dead men shall *l*, together
38. 1 for thou shalt die, and not *l*.
16 O Lord, by these things men *l*,
16 thou recover me, and make me to *l*.
49.18 As I *l*, saith the Lord, thou shalt
55. 3 hear, and your soul shall *l*; and I
Jer 21. 9 that besiege you, he shall *l*, and
22.24 As I *l*, saith the Lord, though
27.12 serve him and his people, and *l*.
17 serve the king of Babylon, and *l*:
35. 7 that ye may *l* many days in the
38. 2 forth to the Chaldeans shall *l*;
2 his life for a prey, and shall *l*.
17 princes, then thy soul shall *l*,
17 and thou shalt *l*, and thine house:
20 unto thee, and thy soul shall *l*.
46.18 As I *l*, saith the King, whose name
La 4.20 said, Under his shadow we shall *l*
Eze 3.21 he doth not sin, he shalt surely *l*,
5.11 as I *l*, saith the Lord God; Surely,
13.19 the souls alive that should not *l*,
14.16 as I *l*, saith the Lord God, they
18, 20 as I *l*, saith the Lord God,
16. 6 when thou wast in thy blood, *L*;
6 when thou wast in thy blood, *L*.
48 As I *l*, saith the Lord God, Sodom
17.16 As I *l*, saith the Lord God, surely
19 As I *l*, surely mine oath that he
18. 3 As I *l*, saith the Lord God, ye shall
9 he is just, he shall surely *l*, saith
13 taken increase: shall he then *l*?
13 shall he then...he shall not *l*:
17 of his father, he shall surely *l*.
19 hath done them, he shall surely *l*.
21 he shall surely *l*, he shall not die.
22 that he hath done he shall *l*.
23 should return from his ways, and *l*?
24 the wicked man doeth, shall he *l*?
28 he shall surely *l*, he shall not die.
32 wherefore turn yourselves, and *l* ye.
20. 3 As I *l*, saith the Lord God, I will
11 man do, he shall even *l* in them.
13, 21 do, he shall even *l* in them;
25 whereby they should not *l*;
31 As I *l*, saith the Lord God, I will
33 As I *l*, saith the Lord God, surely
33.10 in them, how should we then *l*?
11 As I *l*, saith the Lord God, I have
11 wicked turn from his way and *l*:
12 shall the righteous be able to *l* for
13 righteous, that he shall surely *l*;
15 he shall surely *l*, he shall not die.
16 lawful and right; he shall surely *l*.
19 and right, he shall *l* thereby.
27 As I *l*, surely they that are in the
34. 8 As I *l*, saith the Lord God, surely
35. 6, 11 as I *l*, saith the Lord God, I will
37. 3 Son of man, can these bones *l*?
5 to enter into you, and ye shall *l*:

6 put breath in you, and ye shall l;
9 upon these slain, that they may l.
14 put my spirit in you, and ye shall l,
47. 9 the rivers shall come, shall l:
9 thing shall l whither the river
Dan 2. 4 in Syriack, O king, l for ever:
3. 9 Nebuchadnezzar, O king, l for ever.
5.10 spake and said, O king, l for ever:
6. 6 unto him, King Darius, l for ever.
21 unto the king, O king, l for ever.
Hos 6. 2 us up, and we shall l in his sight.
Am 5. 4 Israel, Seek ye me, and ye shall l:
6 Seek the Lord, and ye shall l; lest
14 good, and not evil, that ye may l:
Jon 4. 3 is better for me to die than to l.
8 It is better for me to die than to l.
Hab 2. 4 but the just shall l by his faith.
Zep 2. 9 as I l, saith the Lord of hosts,
Zec 1. 5 the prophets, do they l for ever?
10. 9 they shall l with their children,
13. 3 say unto him, Thou shalt not l;
Mt 4. 4 Man shall not l by bread alone,
9.18 thy hand upon her, and she shall l.
Mk 5.23 she may be healed; and she shall l.
Lk 4. 4 man shall not l by bread alone, but
7.25 apparelled, and l delicately, are
10.28 right: this do, and thou shalt l.
20.38 of the living: for all l unto him.
Jn 5.25 of God: and they that hear shall l.
6.51 of this bread, he shall l for ever:
57 hath sent me, and I l by the Father:
57 eateth me, even he shall l by me.
58 eateth of this bread shall l for ever.
11.25 though he were dead, yet shall he l:
14.19 see me: because I l, ye shall l also.
Ac 7.19 to the end they might not l.
17.28 For in him we l, and move, and
22.22 for it is not fit that he should l.
25.24 that he ought not to l any longer.
28. 4 yet vengeance suffereth not to l.
Ro 1.17 written, The just shall l by faith.
6. 2 dead to sin, l any longer therein?
8 that we shall also l with him:
8.12 not to the flesh, to l after the flesh.
13 For if ye l after the flesh, ye shall
13 the deeds of the body, ye shall l.
10. 5 doeth those things shall l by them.
12.18 in you, l peaceably with all men.
14. 8 whether we l, we l unto the Lord;
8 whether we l therefore, or die, we
11 As I l, saith the Lord, every knee
1Co 9.13 holy things l of the things of the
14 the gospel should l of the gospel.
2Co 4.11 For we which l are alway delivered
5.15 he died for all, that they which l
15 not henceforth l unto themselves,
6. 9 as dying, and, behold, we l; as
7. 3 our hearts to die and l with you.
13. 4 we shall l with him by the power
11 be of one mind, and l in peace;
Gal 2.14 the Gentiles to l as do the Jews?
19 the law, that I might l unto God.
20 with Christ: nevertheless I l;
20 the life which I now l in the flesh
20 I l by the faith of the Son of God,
3.11 for, The just shall l by faith.
12 that doeth them shall l in them.
5.25 If we l in the Spirit, let us also walk
Eph 6. 3 mayest l long on the earth.
Php 1.21 For to me to l is Christ, and to
22 But if I l in the flesh, this is the
1Th 3. 8 For now we l, if ye stand fast in the
5.10 we should l together with him.
2Ti 2.11 with him, we shall also l with him:
3.12 and all that will l godly in Christ
Tit 2.12 we should l soberly, righteously.
Heb 10.38 Now the just shall l by faith: but
12. 9 unto the Father of spirits, and l?
13.18 in all things willing to l honestly.
Jas 4.15 If the Lord will, we shall l, and
1Pe 2.24 sins, should l unto righteousness:
4. 2 longer should l the rest of his time
6 l according to God in the spirit.
2Pe 2. 6 those that after should l ungodly;
18 escaped from them who l in error.
1Jn 4. 9 that we might l through him.
Rev 13.14 the wound by a sword, and did l.

LIVED

Gen 5. 3 Adam l an hundred and thirty
21 Enoch l sixty and five years, and
25 Methuselah l an hundred eighty
Nu 21. 9 beheld the serpent of brass, he l.
Ps 49.18 while he l he blessed his soul:
Eze 37.10 breath came into them, and they l,
Lk 2.36 and had l with an husband seven
Ac 23. 1 I have l in all good conscience
26. 5 sect of our religion I l a Pharisee.
Col 3. 7 some time, when ye l in them.
Jas 5. 5 have l in pleasure on the earth,
Rev 18. 7 glorified herself, and l deliciously,
9 and l deliciously with her, shall
20. 4 they l and reigned with Christ a
5 rest of the dead l not again until

LIVELY

Ex 1.19 for they are l, and are delivered
Ps 38.19 But mine enemies are l, and they
Ac 7.38 the l oracles to give unto us:
1Pe 1. 3 begotten us again unto a l hope
2. 5 as l stones, are built up a spiritual

LIVER

Pr 7.23 Till a dart strike through his l;
La 2.11 my l is poured upon the earth,
Eze 21.21 with images, he looked in the l.

LIVES

Gen 9. 5 your blood of your l will I require;
45. 7 save your l by a great deliverance.
47.25 they said, Thou hast saved our l:
Ex 1.14 their l bitter with hard bondage,
Jos 2.13 and deliver our l from death.
9.24 were sore afraid of our l because
Jdg 5.18 a people that jeoparded their l
18.25 life, with the l of thy household.
2Sa 1.23 lovely and pleasant in their l,
19. 5 and the l of thy sons and of thy
5 l of thy wives, and the l of thy
23.17 that went in jeopardy of their l?
1Ch 11.19 that have put their l in jeopardy?
19 jeopardy of their l they brought it.
Est 9.16 together, and stood for their l,
Pr 1.18 they lurk privily for their own l.
Jer 19. 7 hands of them that seek their l:
9 they that seek their l, shall straiten
46.26 hand of those that seek their l,
48. 6 Flee, save your l, and be like the
La 5. 9 our bread with the peril of our l
Dan 7.12 yet their l were prolonged for a
Lk 9.56 is not come to destroy men's l,
Ac 15.26 Men that have hazarded their l
27.10 lading and ship, but also of our l.
1Jn 3.16 to lay down our l for the brethren.
Rev 12.11 loved not their l unto the death.

LIVEST

Dt 12.19 as long as thou l upon the earth.
2Sa 11.11 as thou l, and as thy soul liveth,
Gal 2.14 l after the manner of Gentiles,
Rev 3. 1 name that thou l, and art dead.

LIVETH

Gen 9. 3 Every moving thing that l shall
Dt 5.24 God doth talk with man, and he l.
Jdg 8.19 as the Lord l, if ye had saved
Ru 3.13 a kinsman to thee, as I the Lord l:
1Sa 1.26 she said, Oh my Lord, as thy soul l,
28 as long as he l he shall be lent to
14.39 For, as the Lord l, which saveth
45 as the Lord l, there shall not one
17.55 Abner said, As thy soul l, O king,
19. 6 Saul sware, As the Lord l, he shall
20. 3 as the Lord l, and as thy soul l,
21 thee, and no hurt; as the Lord l.
31 long as the son of Jesse l upon the
25. 6 ye say to him that l in prosperity,
26 as the Lord l, and as thy soul l.
34 as the Lord God of Israel l, which
26.10 As the Lord l, the Lord shall smite
16 As the Lord l, ye are worthy to die,
28.10 saying, As the Lord l, there shall no
29. 6 unto him, Surely, as the Lord l,
2Sa 2.27 Joab said, As God l, unless thou
4. 9 and said unto them, As the Lord l,
11.11 thy soul l, I will not do this thing.
12. 5 said to Nathan, As the Lord l, the
14.11 As the Lord l, there shall not one
19 answered and said, As thy soul l,
15.21 the king, and said, As the Lord l,
21 and as my lord the king l, surely
22.47 The Lord l; and blessed be my
1Ki 1.29 king sware, and said, As the Lord l,
2.24 Now therefore, as the Lord l, which
3.23 This is my son that l, and thy son
17. 1 Ahab, As the Lord God of Israel l,
12 she said, As the Lord thy God l,
23 and Elijah said, See, thy son l.
18.10 As the Lord thy God l, there is no
15 Elijah said, As the Lord of hosts l,
22.14 Micaiah said, As the Lord l, what
2Ki 2. 2, 4, 6 the Lord l, and as thy soul l,
3.14 Elisha said, As the Lord of hosts l,
4.30 As the Lord l, and as thy soul l, I
5.16 But he said, As the Lord l, before
20 As the Lord l, I will run after him,
2Ch 18.13 Micaiah said, As the Lord l, even
Job 19.25 For I know that my redeemer l,
27. 2 As God l, who hath taken away my
Ps 18.46 The Lord l; and blessed be my
89.48 What man is he that l, and shall
Jer 4. 2 The Lord l, in truth, in judgment,
5. 2 And though they say, The Lord l;
12.16 to swear by my name, The Lord l;
16.14 shall no more be said, The Lord l,
15 The Lord l, that brought up the
23. 7 they shall no more say, The Lord l,
8 But, The Lord l, which brought up
38.16 As the Lord l, that made us this
44.26 of Egypt, saying, The Lord God l.
Eze 47. 9 pass, that every thing that l,
Dan 4.34 and honored him that l for ever,
12. 7 sware by him that l for ever that it
Hos 4.15 Beth-aven, nor swear, The Lord l.
Am 8.14 and say, Thy god, O Dan, l; and
14 The manner of Beer-sheba l; even
Jn 4.50 unto him, Go thy way; thy son l.
51 and told him, saying, Thy son l.
53 Jesus said unto him, Thy son l:
11.26 whosoever l and believeth in me,
Ro 6.10 but in that he l, he l unto God.
7. 1 over a man as long as he l?
2 law to her husband so long as he l;
3 So then if, while her husband l, she
14. 7 For none of us l to himself, and no
1Co 7.39 the law as long as her husband l;
2Co 13. 4 yet he l by the power of God. For
Gal 2.20 live; yet not I, but Christ l in me:
1Ti 5. 6 l in pleasure is dead while…l.
Heb 7. 8 of whom it is witnessed that he l.
25 he ever l to make intercession
9.17 strength at all while the testator l.
1Pe 1.23 by the word of God, which l and
Rev 1.18 I am he that l, and was dead; and,
4. 9 the throne, who l for ever and ever,
10 him that l for ever and ever,
5.14 him that l for ever and ever.
10. 6 by him that l for ever and ever,
15. 7 wrath of God, who l for ever and

LIVING

Gen 1.21 and every l creature that moveth,
24 bring forth the l creature after his

Gen 1.28 over every *l* thing that moveth
2. 7 of life; and man became a *l* soul.
19 Adam called every *l* creature,
3.20 because she was the mother of all *l*.
6.19 of every *l* thing of all flesh, two of
7. 4 and every *l* substance that I have
23 And every *l* substance was destroyed
8. 1 Noah, and every *l* thing, and all
17 every *l* thing that is with thee,
21 again smite any more every thing *l*,
9.10 with every *l* creature that is with
12 and every *l* creature that is with you,
15 and every *l* creature of all flesh;
16 and every *l* creature of all flesh
Lev 11.10 any *l* thing which is in the waters,
46 every *l* creature that moveth in the
14. 6 As for the *l* bird, he shall take it,
6 the *l* bird in the blood of the bird
7 the *l* bird loose into the open field.
51 and the *l* bird, and dip them in the
52 running water, and with the *l* bird,
53 shall let go the *l* bird out of the city
20.25 any manner of *l* thing that creepeth
Nu 16.48 stood between the dead and the *l*;
Dt 5.26 hath heard the voice of the *l* God
Jos 3.10 know that the *l* God is among you,
Ru 2.20 not left off his kindness to the *l*
1Sa 17.26 defy the armies of the *l* God?
36 defied the armies of the *l* God.
2Sa 20. 3 of their death, *l* in widowhood.
1Ki 3.22 said, Nay; but the *l* is my son,
22 is thy son, and the *l* is my son.
23 is the dead, and my son is the *l*.
25 king said, Divide the *l* child in two,
26 the woman whose the *l* child was
26 said, O my lord, give her the *l* child,
27 and said, Give her the *l* child,
2Ki 19. 4 hath sent to reproach the *l* God;
16 sent him to reproach the *l* God.
Job 12.10 hand is the soul of every *l* thing,
28.13 is it found in the land of the *l*.
21 it is hid from the eyes of all *l*, and
30.23 to the house appointed for all *l*.
33.30 enlightened with the light of the *l*.
Ps 27.13 of the Lord in the land of the *l*.
42. 2 thirsteth for God, for the *l* God:
52. 5 root thee out of the land of the *l*.
56.13 walk before God in the light of the *l*?
58. 9 both *l*, and in his wrath.
69.28 be blotted out of the book of the *l*,
84. 2 my flesh crieth out for the *l* God.
116. 9 before the Lord in the land of the *l*.
142. 5 and my portion in the land of the *l*.
143. 2 sight shall no man *l* be justified,
145.16 satisfiest the desire of every *l* thing.
Ec 4. 2 than the *l* which are yet alive.
15 I considered all the *l* which walk
6. 8 that knoweth to walk before the *l*?
7. 2 and the *l* will lay it to his heart.
9. 4 For to him that is joined to all the *l*
4 a *l* dog is better than a dead lion.
5 For the *l* know that they shall die:
SS 4.15 of gardens, a well of *l* waters,
Isa 4. 3 written among the *l* in Jerusalem:
8.19 their God? for the *l* to the dead?
37. 4 hath sent to reproach the *l* God,
17 hath sent to reproach the *l* God.
38.11 even the Lord, in the land of the *l*:
19 The *l*, the *l*, he shall praise thee,
53. 8 was cut off out of the land of the *l*:
Jer 2.13 me the fountain of *l* waters,
10.10 is the true God, he is the *l* God,
11.19 cut him off from the land of the *l*,
17.13 the Lord, the fountain of *l* waters.
23.36 perverted the words of the *l* God,
La 3.39 Wherefore doth a *l* man complain,
Eze 1. 5 the likeness of four *l* creatures.
13 for the likeness of the *l* creatures,
13 and down among the *l* creatures;
14 the *l* creatures ran and returned
15 as I beheld the *l* creatures, behold
15 upon the earth by the *l* creatures,
19 And when the *l* creatures went, the
19 when the *l* creatures were lifted up
20, 21 spirit of the *l* creature was in
22 upon the heads of the *l* creature
3.13 of the wings of the *l* creatures that
10.15 This is the *l* creature that I saw by
17 the spirit of the *l* creature was in
20 This is the *l* creature that I saw
26.20 shall set glory in the land of the *l*;
32.23 caused terror in the land of the *l*.
24 their terror in the land of the *l*;
25 was caused in the land of the *l*,
26 their terror in the land of the *l*.
27 of the mighty in the land of the *l*.
32 my terror in the land of the *l*:
Dan 2.30 that I have more than any *l*,
4.17 *l* may know that the most High
6.20 Daniel, servant of the *l* God, is thy
26 God of Daniel: for he is the *l* God,
Hos 1.10 them, Ye are the sons of the *l* God.
Zec 14. 8 that *l* waters shall go out from
Mt 16.16 the Christ, the Son of the *l* God.
22.32 not the God of the dead, but of the *l*.
26.63 him, I adjure thee by the *l* God,
Mk 12.27 of the dead, but the God of the *l*:
44 in all that she had, even all her *l*.
Lk 8.43 had spent all her *l* upon physicians,
15.12 And he divided unto them his *l*.
13 his substance with riotous *l*.
30 hath devoured thy *l* with harlots,
20.38 not a God of the dead, but of the *l*:
21. 4 hath cast in all the *l* that she had.
24. 5 seek ye the *l* among the dead?
Jn 4.10 he would have given thee *l* water.
11 then hast thou that *l* water?
6.51 I am the *l* bread which came down
57 As the *l* Father hath sent me, and
69 that Christ, the Son of the *l* God.
7.38 belly shall flow rivers of *l* water.
Ac 14.15 from these vanities unto the *l* God,
Ro 9.26 be called the children of the *l* God.
12. 1 present your bodies a *l* sacrifice,
14. 9 be Lord both of the dead and *l*.
1Co 15.45 first man Adam was made a *l* soul;
2Co 3. 3 but with the Spirit of the *l* God;
6.16 for ye are the temple of the *l* God;
Col 2.20 why, as though *l* in the world, are
1Th 1. 9 idols to serve the *l* and true God;
1Ti 3.15 which is the church of the *l* God,
4.10 because we trust in the *l* God, who
6.17 uncertain riches, but in the *l* God,
Tit 3. 3 pleasures, *l* in malice and envy,
Heb 3.12 in departing from the *l* God.
9.14 dead works to serve the *l* God?
10.20 By a new and *l* way, which he hath
31 to fall into the hands of the *l* God.
12.22 and unto the city of the *l* God,
1Pe 2. 4 whom coming, as unto a *l* stone,
Rev 7. 2 east, having the seal of the *l* God:
17 them unto *l* fountains of waters:
16. 3 and every *l* soul died in the sea.

LOAF

Ex 29.23 And one *l* of bread, and one cake
1Ch 16. 3 to every one a *l* of bread, and a
Mk 8.14 ship with them more than one *l*.

LO-AMMI

Hos 1. 9 Then said God, Call his name *L*:

LOAVES

Lev 23.17 two wave *l* of two tenth deals:
Jdg 8. 5 *l* of bread unto the people that
1Sa 10. 3 another carrying three *l* of bread,
4 thee, and give thee two *l* of bread;
17.17 this parched corn, and these ten *l*,
21. 3 give me five *l* of bread in mine hand,
25.18 haste, and took two hundred *l*,
2Sa 16. 1 upon them two hundred *l* of bread,
1Ki 14. 3 take with thee ten *l*, and cracknels,
2Ki 4.42 the firstfruits, twenty *l* of barley,
Mt 14.17 We have here but five *l*, and two
19 took the five *l*, and the two fishes,
19 and gave the *l* to his disciples, and
15.34 unto them, How many *l* have ye?
36 he took the seven *l* and the fishes,
16. 9 remember the five *l* of the five
10 Neither the seven *l* of the four
Mk 6.38 unto them, How many *l* have ye?
41 when he had taken the five *l* and
41 and blessed, and brake the *l*, and
44 they that did eat of the *l* were about
52 not the miracle of the *l*: considered
8. 5 asked them, How many *l* have ye?
6 took the seven *l*, and gave thanks,
19 When I brake the five *l* among five
Lk 9.13 We have no more but five *l* and two
16 Then he took the five *l* and the two
11. 5 unto him, Friend, lend me three *l*;
Jn 6. 9 lad here, which hath five barley *l*,
11 Jesus took the *l*; and when he had
13 the fragments of the five barley *l*,
26 but because ye did eat of the *l*, and

LOCUST

Ex 10.19 not one *l* in all the coasts of Egypt.
Lev 11.22 ye may eat; the *l* after his kind,
22 and the bald *l* after his kind, and
Dt 28.38 little in; for the *l* shall consume it.
42 of thy land shall the *l* consume.
1Ki 8.37 pestilence, blasting, mildew, *l*,
Ps 78.46 and their labor unto the *l*.
109.23 I am tossed up and down as the *l*.
Joel 1. 4 hath left hath the *l* eaten; and
4 that which the *l* hath left hath the
2.25 you the years that the *l* hath eaten,

LOCUSTS

Ex 10. 4 will I bring the *l* into thy coast:
12 over the land of Egypt for the *l*,
13 the east wind brought the *l*.
14 the *l* went up over all the land of
14 them there were no such *l* as they,
19 westwind, which took away the *l*,
2Ch 6.28 there be blasting, or mildew, *l*, or
7.13 command the *l* to devour the land,
Ps 105.34 He spake, and the *l* came, and
Pr 30.27 The *l* have no king, yet go they
Isa 33. 4 as the running to and fro of *l* shall
Na 3.15 make thyself many as the *l*.
17 Thy crowned are as the *l*, and thy
Mt 3. 4 his meat was *l* and wild honey.
Mk 1. 6 and he did eat *l* and wild honey;
Rev 9. 3 there came out of the smoke *l* upon
7 of the *l* were like unto horses

LODGE

Gen 24.23 thy father's house for us to *l* in?
25 and provender...and room to *l* in.
Nu 22. 8 *L* here this night, and I will bring
Jos 4. 3 place, where ye shall *l* this night.
Jdg 19. 9 the day groweth to an end, *l* here,
11 city of the Jebusites, and *l* in it.
13 one of these places to *l* all night,
15 to go in and to *l* in Gibeah:
20 upon me; only *l* not in the street.
20. 4 Benjamin, I and my concubine, to *l*.
Ru 1.16 and where thou lodgest, I will *l*:
2Sa 17. 8 war, and will not *l* with the people.
16 *L* not this night in the plains of
Neh 4.22 Let every one with his servant *l*
13.21 unto them, Why *l* ye about the wall?
Job 24. 7 the naked to *l* without clothing,
31.32 stranger did not *l* in the street:
SS 7.11 the field; let us *l* in the villages.
Isa 1. 8 as a *l* in a garden of cucumbers,
21.13 In the forest in Arabia shall ye *l*,
65. 4 graves, and *l* in the monuments,
Jer 4.14 How long shall thy vain thoughts *l*
Zep 2.14 bittern shall *l* in the upper lintels
Mt 13.32 and *l* in the branches thereof.

Mk 4.32 of the air may *l* under the shadow
Lk 9.12 and country round about, and *l*,
Ac 21.16 disciple, with whom we should *l*.

LODGED

Gen 32.13 And he *l* there that same night;
21 himself *l* that night in the company.
Jos 2. 1 house, named Rahab, and *l* there.
3. 1 *l* there before they passed over.
4. 8 them unto the place where they *l*,
6.11 into the camp, and *l* in the camp.
8. 9 Joshua *l* that night among the
Jdg 18. 2 the house of Micah, they *l* there.
19. 4 they did eat and drink, and *l* there.
7 him: therefore he *l* there again.
1Ki 19. 9 thither unto a cave, and *l* there;
1Ch 9.27 *l* round about the house of God,
Neh 13.20 sellers of all kind of ware *l* without
Isa 1.21 Judgment; righteousness *l* in it;
Mt 21.17 city into Bethany; and he *l* there.
Lk 13.19 fowls of the air *l* in the branches
Ac 10.18 was surnamed Peter, were *l* there.
23 Then called he them in, and *l* them.
32 he is *l* in the house of one Simon
28. 7 and *l* us three days courteously.
1Ti 5.10 children, if she have *l* strangers,

LODGEST

Ru 1.16 and where thou *l*, I will lodge:

LODGETH

Ac 10. 6 He *l* with one Simon a tanner,

LODGING

Jos 4. 3 and leave them in the *l* place,
Jdg 19.15 that took them into his house to *l*.
Isa 10.29 have taken up their *l* at Geba;
Jer 9. 2 I had in the wilderness a *l* place
Ac 28.23 there came many to him into his *l*;
Phm 22 But withal prepare me also a *l*:

LOINS

Ex 12.11 with your *l* girded, your shoes on
1Ki 12.10 be thicker than my father's *l*.
Job 38. 3 Gird up now thy *l* like a man; for
40. 7 Gird up thy *l* now like a man: I
Pr 31.17 She girdeth her *l* with strength,
Isa 11. 5 righteousness...the girdle of his *l*,
20. 2 loose the sackcloth from off thy *l*,
Mt 3. 4 and a leathern girdle about his *l*;
Mk 1. 6 with a girdle of a skin about his *l*;
Lk 12.35 Let your *l* be girded about, and
Ac 2.30 to him, that of the fruit of his *l*,
Eph 6.14 having your *l* girt about with truth,
Heb 7. 5 they come out of the *l* of Abraham:
10 For he was yet in the *l* of his father,
1Pe 1.13 gird up the *l* of your mind, be sober,

LOIS

2Ti 1. 5 dwelt first in thy grandmother *L*,

LONG

Gen 26. 8 when he had been there a *l* time,
48.15 the God which fed me all my life *l*
Ex 10. 3 How *l* wilt thou refuse to humble
7 How *l* shall this man be a snare
16.28 How *l* refuse ye to keep my
19.13 when the trumpet soundeth *l*,
19 the voice of the trumpet sounded *l*,
20.12 days may be *l* upon the land which
27. 1 altar of shittim wood, five cubits *l*,
9 of an hundred cubits *l* for one side:
11 be hangings of an hundred cubits *l*,
Lev 18.19 as *l* as she is put apart for her
26.34 sabbaths, as *l* as it lieth desolate,
35 As *l* as it lieth desolate it shall rest;
Nu 9.18 as *l* as the cloud abode upon the
19 And when the cloud tarried *l* upon
14.11 How *l* will this people provoke me?
11 how *l* will it be ere they believe me,
27 How *l* shall I bear with this evil
20.15 we have dwelt in Egypt a *l* time;
Dt 1. 6 have dwelt *l* enough in this mount:
2. 3 this mountain *l* enough: turn you
4.25 shall have remained *l* in the land,
12.19 as *l* as thou livest upon the earth.
14.24 if the way be too *l* for thee, so that
19. 6 overtake him, because the way is *l*,
20.19 thou shalt besiege a city a *l* time,
28.32 longing for them all the day *l*:
59 great plagues, and of *l* continuance,
59 sicknesses, and of *l* continuance.
31.13 as *l* as ye live in the land whither
33.12 shall cover him all the day *l*, and he
Jos 6. 5 make a *l* blast with the ram's horn,
9.13 by reason of the very *l* journey.
11.18 made war a *l* time with all those
18. 3 How *l* are ye slack to go to possess
23. 1 a *l* time after that the Lord had
24. 7 dwelt in the wilderness a *l* season.
Jdg 5.28 Why is his chariot so *l* in coming?
1Sa 1.28 as *l* as he liveth he shall be lent to
7. 2 Kirjath-jearim, that...time was *l*;
16. 1 How *l* wilt thou mourn for Saul,
20.31 as *l* as the son of Jesse liveth upon
25.15 *l* as we were conversant with them,
29. 8 so *l* as I have been with thee unto
2Sa 2.26 how *l* shall it be then, ere thou bid
3. 1 Now there was *l* war between the
14. 2 be as a woman that had a *l* time
19.34 the king, How *l* have I to live,
1Ki 3.11 hast not asked for thyself *l* life;
6.17 temple before it, was forty cubits *l*.
18.21 How *l* halt ye between two
2Ki 9.22 so *l* as the whoredoms of thy
19.25 Hast thou not heard *l* ago how I
2Ch 1.11 neither yet hast asked *l* life; but
3.11 cherubims were twenty cubits *l*:
6.13 a brasen scaffold, of five cubits *l*,
31 so *l* as they live in the land which
15. 3 for a *l* season Israel hath been
26. 5 as *l* as he sought the Lord, God
30. 5 they had not done it of a *l* time
36.21 as *l* as she lay desolate she kept
Est 5.13 so *l* as I see Mordecai the Jew
Job 3.21 Which *l* for death, but it cometh
6. 8 grant me the thing that I *l* for!
7.19 How *l* wilt thou not depart from
8. 2 How *l* wilt thou speak these
2 how *l* shall the words of thy mouth
18. 2 How *l* will it be ere ye make
19. 2 How *l* will ye vex my soul, and
27. 6 not reproach me so *l* as I live.
Ps 4. 2 how *l* will ye turn my glory into
2 how *l* will ye love vanity, and seek
6. 3 vexed: but thou, O Lord, how *l*?
13. 1 How *l* wilt thou forget me, O Lord?
1 how *l* wilt thou hide thy face from
2 How *l* shall I take counsel in my soul,
2 how *l* shall mine enemy be exalted
32. 3 old through my roaring all the day *l*.
35.17 Lord, how *l* wilt thou look on?
28 and of thy praise all the day *l*.
38. 6 greatly; I go mourning all the day *l*.
12 and imagine deceits all the day *l*.
44. 8 In God we boast all the day *l*, and
22 for thy sake are we killed all the day *l*;
62. 3 How *l* will ye imagine mischief
71.24 of thy righteousness all the day *l*:
72. 5 as *l* as the sun and moon endure,
7 peace so *l* as the moon endureth.
17 be continued as *l* as the sun:
73.14 the day *l* have I been plagued,
74. 9 among us any that knoweth how *l*.
10 how *l* shall the adversary reproach?
80. 4 how *l* wilt thou be angry against the
82. 2 How *l* will ye judge unjustly, and
89.46 How *l*, Lord? wilt thou hide thyself
90.13 Return, O Lord, how *l*? and let it
91.16 With *l* life will I satisfy him, and
94. 3 Lord, how *l* shall the wicked,
3 how *l* shall the wicked triumph?
4 How *l* shall they utter and speak
95.10 Forty years *l* was I grieved with this
104.33 sing unto the Lord as *l* as I live:
116. 2 will I call upon him as *l* as I live.
120. 6 My soul hath *l* dwelt with him
129. 3 back: they made *l* their furrows.
143. 3 as those that have been *l* dead.
Pr 1.22 How *l*, ye simple ones, will ye love
3. 2 *l* life, and peace, shall they add
6. 9 How *l* wilt thou sleep, O sluggard?
7.19 at home, he is gone a *l* journey:
21.26 He coveteth greedily all the day *l*: but
23.17 in the fear of the Lord all the day *l*.
30 They that tarry *l* at the wine; they
25.15 By *l* forbearing is a prince
Ec 12. 5 because man goeth to his *l* home,
Isa 6.11 Then said I, Lord, how *l*? And he
22.11 unto him that fashioned it *l* ago.
37.26 Hast thou not heard *l* ago, how I
42.14 I have *l* time holden my peace; I
65.22 elect shall *l* enjoy the work of their
Jer 4.14 How *l* shall...vain thoughts lodge
21 How *l* shall I see the standard, and
12. 4 How *l* shall the land mourn, and
23.26 How *l* shall this be in the heart of
29.28 This captivity is *l*: build ye houses,
31.22 How *l* wilt thou go about, O thou
47. 5 valley: how *l* wilt thou cut thyself?
6 how *l* will it be ere thou be quiet?
La 2.20 their fruit, and children of a span *l*?
5.20 for ever, and forsake us so *l* time?
Eze 31. 5 his branches became *l* because of
40. 5 a measuring reed of six cubits *l* by
7 little chamber was one reed *l*,
29 it was fifty cubits *l*, and five and
30 about were five and twenty cubits *l*,
33 it was fifty cubits *l*, and five and
42 of a cubit and an half *l*, and a cubit
47 the court, an hundred cubits *l*, and
41.13 the house, a hundred cubits *l*; and
13 walls thereof, an hundred cubits *l*;
42.11 as *l* as they, and as broad as they:
20 round about, five hundred reeds *l*,
43.16 the altar shall be twelve cubits *l*,
17 the settle shall be fourteen cubits *l*
44.20 nor suffer their locks to grow *l*;
45. 6 and five and twenty thousand *l*,
46.22 courts joined of forty cubits *l* and
Dan 8.13 *l* shall be the vision concerning
10. 1 but the time appointed was *l*:
12. 6 How *l* shall it be to the end of these
Hos 8. 5 how *l* will it be ere they attain to
13.13 should not stay *l* in the place of
Hab 1. 2 O Lord, how *l* shall I cry, and thou
2. 6 that which is not his! how *l*?
Zec 1.12 how *l* wilt thou not have mercy on
Mt 9.15 mourn, as *l* as the bridegroom is
11.21 repented *l* ago in sackcloth and
17.17 how *l* shall I be with you?
17 how *l* shall I suffer you? bring
23.14 for a pretence make *l* prayer:
25.19 After a *l* time the lord of those
Mk 2.19 *l* as they have the bridegroom
9.19 how *l* shall I be with you?
19 how *l* shall I suffer you? bring
21 How *l* is it ago since this came
12.38 which love to go in *l* clothing, and
40 for a pretence make *l* prayers:
16. 5 side, clothed in a *l* white garment;
Lk 1.21 that he tarried so *l* in the temple.
8.27 man, which had devils *l* time,
9.41 how *l* shall I be with you, and
18. 7 him, though he bear *l* with them?
20. 9 into a far country for a *l* time.
46 which desire to walk in *l* robes,
47 and for a shew make *l* prayers:
23. 8 to see him of a *l* season,
Jn 5. 6 been now a *l* time in that case,
9. 5 As *l* as I am in the world, I am the
10.24 How *l* dost thou make us to
14. 9 Have I been so *l* time with you,

Ac 8.11 of *l* time he had bewitched them
14. 3 *L* time therefore abode they
28 they abode *l* time with the
20. 9 as Paul was *l* preaching, he
11 and talked a *l* while, even till
27.14 not *l* after there arose against it
21 after *l* abstinence Paul stood forth
Ro 1.11 I *l* to see you, that I may impart
7. 1 over a man as *l* as he liveth?
2 law to her husband so *l* as he liveth;
8.36 thy sake we are killed all the day *l*;
10.21 All day *l* I have stretched forth my
1Co 7.39 as *l* as her husband liveth;
11.14 if a man have *l* hair, it is a shame
15 But if a woman have *l* hair, it is a
13. 4 Charity suffereth *l*, and is kind;
2Co 9.14 *l* after you for the exceeding grace
Gal 4. 1 the heir, as *l* as he is a child,
Eph 6. 3 thou mayest live *l* on the earth.
Php 1. 8 how greatly I *l* after you all in
1Ti 3.15 But if I tarry *l*, that thou mayest
Heb 4. 7 in David, To day, after so *l* a time;
Jas 5. 7 earth, and hath *l* patience for it,
1Pe 3. 6 daughters ye are, as *l* as ye do well,
2Pe 1.13 as *l* as I am in this tabernacle, to stir
2. 3 now of a *l* time lingereth not,
Rev 6.10 How *l*, O Lord, holy and true,

LONGED

2Sa 13.39 David *l* to go forth unto Absalom:
23.15 And David *l*, and said, Oh that one
1Ch 11.17 And David *l*, and said, Oh that one
Ps 119.40 I have *l* after thy precepts:
131 for I *l* for thy commandments.
174 I have *l* for thy salvation, O Lord;
Php 2.26 For he *l* after you all, and was
4. 1 brethren dearly beloved and *l* for,

LONGER

Ex 2. 3 when she could not *l* hide him,
9.28 let you go, and ye shall stay no *l*.
Jdg 2.14 any *l* stand before their enemies.
2Sa 20. 5 he tarried *l* than the set time which
2Ki 6.33 should I wait for the Lord any *l*?
Job 11. 9 measure thereof is *l* than the earth,
Jer 44.22 So that the Lord could no *l* bear,
Lk 16. 2 for thou mayest be no *l* steward.
Ac 18.20 desired him to tarry *l* time with
25.24 that he ought not to live any *l*.
Ro 6. 2 dead to sin, live any *l* therein?
Gal 3.25 we are no *l* under a schoolmaster.
1Th 3. 1 we could no *l* forbear, we thought
5 this cause, when I could no *l* forbear,
1Ti 5.23 Drink no *l* water, but use a little
1Pe 4. 2 he no *l* should live the rest of his
Rev 10. 6 that there should be time no *l*;

LONGETH

Gen 34. 8 soul of my son Shechem *l* for your
Dt 12.20 because thy soul *l* to eat flesh;
Ps 63. 1 my flesh *l* for thee in a dry and
84. 2 My soul *l*, yea, even fainteth for

LONGING

Dt 28.32 fail with *l* for them all the day long:
Ps 107. 9 he satisfieth the *l* soul, and filleth
119.20 My soul breaketh for the *l* that it

LONGSUFFERING

Ex 34. 6 merciful and gracious, *l*, and
Nu 14.18 Lord is *l*, and of great mercy,
Ps 86.15 *l*, and plenteous in mercy and
Jer 15.15 take me not away in thy *l*:
Ro 2. 4 goodness and forbearance and *l*;
9.22 endured with much *l* the vessels
2Co 6. 6 by *l*, by kindness, by the Holy
Gal 5.22 of the Spirit is love, joy, peace, *l*,
Eph 4. 2 with *l*, forbearing one another in
Col 1.11 all patience and *l* with joyfulness;
3.12 humbleness of mind, meekness, *l*;
1Ti 1.16 Christ might shew forth all *l*,
2Ti 3.10 of life, purpose, faith, *l*, charity,
4. 2 exhort with all *l* and doctrine.
1Pe 3.20 the *l* of God waited in the days of
2Pe 3. 9 but is *l* to us-ward, not willing
3.15 the *l* of our Lord is salvation;

LOOK

Gen 9.16 and I will *l* upon it, that I may
12.11 thou art a fair woman to *l* upon:
13.14 *l* from the place where thou art
15. 5 *L* now toward heaven, and tell the
19.17 *l* not behind thee, neither stay thou
24.16 damsel was very fair to *l* upon,
26. 7 because she was fair to *l* upon.
40. 7 Wherefore *l* ye so sadly to day?
41.33 *l* out a man discreet and wise,
42. 1 Why do ye *l* one upon another?
Ex 3. 6 for he was afraid to *l* upon God.
5.21 The Lord *l* upon you, and judge;
10.10 *l* to it; for evil is before you.
25.20 their faces shall *l* one to another;
40 *l* that thou make them after their
39.43 And Moses did *l* upon all the work,
Lev 13. 3 the priest shall *l* on the plague in
3 and the priest shall *l* on him, and
5 And the priest shall *l* on him the
6 the priest shall *l* on him again the
21 But if the priest shall *l* on it, and,
25 Then the priest shall *l* upon it: and,
26 But if the priest *l* on it, and, behold,
27 And the priest shall *l* upon him the
31 priest *l* on the plague of the scall,
32 the priest shall *l* on the plague:
34 day the priest shall *l* on the scall:
36 Then the priest shall *l* on him: and,
39 Then the priest shall *l*: and,
43 Then the priest shall l upon it:
50 the priest shall *l* upon the plague,
51 And he shall *l* on the plague on the
53 if the priest shall *l*, and, behold,
55 And the priest shall *l* on the plague,
56 And if the priest *l*, and, behold,
14. 3 the priest shall *l*, and, behold, if
37 And he shall *l* on the plague, and,
39 shall *l*: and, behold, if the plague
44 Then the priest shall come and *l*,
48 priest shall come in, and *l* upon it,
Nu 15.39 for a fringe, that ye may *l* upon it,
Dt 9.27 *l* not unto the stubbornness of
26.15 *L* down from thy holy habitation,
28.32 thine eyes shall *l*, and fail with
Jdg 7.17 them, *L* on me, and do likewise:
1Sa 1.11 *l* on the affliction of thine handmaid,
16. 7 *L* not on his countenance, or on
12 countenance, and goodly to *l* to.
17.18 and *l* how thy brethren fare, and
2Sa 9. 8 *l* upon such a dead dog as I am?
11. 2 was very beautiful to *l* upon.
16.12 the Lord will *l* on mine affliction,
1Ki 18.43 Go up now, *l* toward the sea.
2Ki 3.14 I would not *l* toward thee, nor see
6.32 *l*, when the messenger cometh,
9. 2 thither, *l* out there Jehu the son of
10. 3 *L* even out the best and meetest of
23 *l* that there be here with you none
14. 8 let us *l* one another in the face.
1Ch 12.17 the God of our fathers *l* thereon,
2Ch 24.22 The Lord *l* upon it, and require
Est 1.11 for she was fair to *l* on.
Job 3. 9 let it *l* for light, but have none;
6.28 therefore be content, *l* upon me;
20.21 shall no man *l* for his goods.
35. 5 *L* unto the heavens, and see; and
40.12 *L* on every one that is proud, and
Ps 5. 3 prayer unto thee, and will *l* up.
22.17 bones: they *l* and stare upon me.
25.18 *L* upon mine affliction and my
35.17 Lord, how long wilt thou *l* on?
40.12 me, so that I am not able to *l* up;
80.14 *l* down from heaven, and behold,
84. 9 *l* upon the face of thine anointed.
85.11 righteousness shall *l* down from
101. 5 hath an high *l* and a proud heart
119.132 *L*...upon me, and be merciful
123. 2 eyes of servants *l* unto the hand of
Pr 4.25 Let thine eyes *l* right on, and let
25 thine eyelids *l* straight before thee.
6.17 A proud *l*, a lying tongue, and
21. 4 An high *l*, and a proud heart, and
23.31 *L* not thou upon the wine when it
27.23 flocks, and *l* well to thy herds.
Ec 12. 3 those that *l* out of the windows
SS 1. 6 *L* not upon me, because I am black,
4. 8 *l* from the top of Amana, from the
6.13 return, that we may *l* upon thee.
Isa 5.30 and if one *l* unto the land, behold
8.17 of Jacob, and I will *l* for him.
21 and their God, and *l* upward.
22 And they shall *l* unto the earth;
14.16 thee shall narrowly *l* upon thee,
17. 7 day shall a man *l* to his Maker,
8 And he shall not *l* to the altars,
22. 4 *L* away from me; I will weep
8 didst *l* in that day to the armour
31. 1 they *l* not unto the Holy One of
33.20 *L* upon Zion, the city of our
42.18 and *l*, ye blind, that ye may see.
45.22 *L* unto me, and be ye saved, all
51. 1 *l* unto the rock whence ye are
2 *L* unto Abraham your father, and
6 and *l* upon the earth beneath:
56.11 they all *l* to their own way, every
59.11 *l* for judgment, but there is none;
63.15 *L* down from heaven, and behold
66. 2 but to this man will I *l*, even to him
24 *l* upon the carcases of the men
Jer 13.16 while ye *l* for light, he turn it into
39.12 Take him, and *l* well to him,
40. 4 and I will *l* well unto thee:
46. 5 are fled apace, and *l* not back:
47. 3 the fathers shall not *l* back to their
La 3.50 Till the Lord *l* down, and behold
Eze 23.15 heads, all of them princes to *l* to,
29.16 when they shall *l* after them:
43.17 his stairs shall *l* toward the east.
Dan 7.20 whose *l* was more stout than his
Hos 3. 1 of Israel, who *l* to other gods,
Jon 2. 4 *l* again toward thy holy temple.
Mic 4.11 and let our eye *l* upon Zion.
7. 7 Therefore I will *l* unto the Lord;
Na 2. 8 they cry; but none shall *l* back.
3. 7 all they that *l* upon thee shall flee
Hab 1.13 evil, and canst not *l* on iniquity:
2.15 thou mayest *l* on their nakedness!
Zec 12.10 shall *l* upon me whom they have
Mt 11. 3 come, or do we *l* for another?
Mk 8.25 upon his eyes, and made him *l* up;
Lk 7.19, 20 come? or *l* we for another?
9.38 I beseech thee, *l* upon my son:
21.28 then *l* up, and lift up your heads;
Jn 4.35 up your eyes, and *l* on the fields;
7.52 Search, and *l*: for out of
19.37 shall *l* on him whom they pierced.
Ac 3. 4 upon him with John, said, *L* on us.
12 or why *l* ye so earnestly on us, as
6. 3 *l* ye out among you seven men of
18.15 names, and of your law, *l* ye to it:
1Co 16.11 for I *l* for him with the brethren.
2Co 3.13 could not stedfastly *l* to the end of
4.18 *l* not at the things which are seen,
10. 7 Do ye *l* on things after the outward
Php 2. 4 *L* not every man on his own
3.20 whence also we *l* for the Saviour,
Heb 9.28 unto them that *l* for him shall he
1Pe 1.12 things the angels desire to *l* into.
2Pe 3.13 *l* for new heavens and a new
14 seeing that ye *l* for such things,
2Jn 8 *L* to yourselves, that we lose not
Rev 4. 3 was to *l* upon like a jasper and
5. 3 open the book, neither to *l* thereon.
4 read the book, neither to *l* thereon.

LOOKED

Gen 6.12 And God *l* upon the earth, and,
8.13 the covering of the ark, and *l*, and,
16.13 here *l* after him that seeth me?
18. 2 he lift up his eyes and *l*, and, lo,
16 from thence, and *l* toward Sodom:
19.26 But his wife *l* back from behind
28 he *l* toward Sodom and Gomorrah,
22.13 Abraham lifted up his eyes, and *l*,
26. 8 the Philistines *l* out at a window,
29. 2 he *l*, and behold a well in the field,
32 Lord hath *l* upon my affliction;
33. 1 Jacob lifted up his eyes, and *l*, and,
37.25 they lifted up their eyes and *l*, and,
39.23 The keeper of the prison *l* not to
40. 6 in the morning, and *l* upon them,
Ex 2.11 brethren, and *l* on their burdens:
12 he *l* this way and that way, and
25 God *l* upon the children of Israel,
3. 2 he *l*, and, behold, the bush burned
4.31 he had *l* upon their affliction,
14.24 in the morning watch the Lord *l*
16.10 that they *l* toward the wilderness,
33. 8 *l* after Moses, until he was gone
Nu 12.10 and Aaron *l* upon Miriam, and,
16.42 *l* toward the tabernacle of the
17. 9 they *l*, and took every man his
24.20 when he *l* on Amalek, he took up
21 he *l* on the Kenites, and took up
Dt 9.16 And I *l*, and, behold, ye had sinned
26. 7 *l* on our affliction, and our labor,
Jos 5.13 that he lifted up his eyes and *l*,
8.20 And when the men of Ai *l* behind
Jdg 5.28 of Sisera *l* out at a window,
6.14 the Lord *l* upon him, and said,
9.43 and laid wait in the field, and *l*,
13.19 and Manoah and his wife *l* on.
20 and Manoah and his wife *l* on it,
20.40 the Benjamites *l* behind them,
1Sa 6.19 had *l* into the ark of the Lord,
9.16 I have *l* upon my people, because
14.16 of Saul in Gibeah of Benjamin *l*;
16. 6 they were come, that he *l* on Eliab,
17.42 And when the Philistine *l* about,
24. 8 And when Saul *l* behind him, David
2Sa 1. 7 when he *l* behind him, he saw me,
2.20 Then Abner *l* behind him, and
6.16 daughter *l* through a window,
13.34 watch lifted up his eyes, and *l*,
18.24 wall, and lifted up his eyes, and *l*,
22.42 They *l*, but there was none to
24.20 And Araunah *l*, and saw the king
1Ki 18.43 And he went up, and *l*, and said,
19. 6 And he *l*, and, behold, there was a
2Ki 2.24 he turned back, and *l* on them,
6.30 by upon the wall, and the people *l*,
9.30 her head, and *l* out at a window.
32 *l* out to him two or three eunuchs.
11.14 And when she *l*, behold, the king
14.11 of Judah *l* one another in the face
1Ch 21.21 Ornan, Ornan *l* and saw David,
2Ch 13.14 when Judah *l* back, behold, the
20.24 they *l* unto the multitude, and,
23.13 she *l*, and, behold, the king stood
26.20 and all the priests, *l* upon him,
Neh 4.14 I *l*, and rose up, and said unto the
Est 2.15 sight of all them that *l* upon her.
Job 6.19 troops of Tema *l*, the companies
30.26 When I *l* for good, then evil came
Ps 14. 2 Lord *l* down from heaven upon
34. 5 They *l* unto him, and were
53. 2 God *l* down from heaven upon
69.20 I *l* for some to take pity, but there
102.19 he hath *l* down from the height of
109.25 when they *l* upon me, they shaked
142. 4 I *l* on my right hand, and beheld,
Pr 7. 6 house I *l* through my casement,
24.32 it well: I *l* upon it, and received
Ec 2.11 Then I *l* on all the works that my
SS 1. 6 because the sun hath *l* upon me:
Isa 5. 2 he *l* that it should bring forth
4 I *l* that it should bring forth
7 and he *l* for judgment, but behold
22.11 but ye have not *l* unto the maker
63. 5 I *l*, and there was none to help;
64. 3 terrible things which we *l* not for,
Jer 8.15 We *l* for peace, but no good came;
14.19 we *l* for peace, and there is no
La 2.16 this is the day that we *l* for; we
Eze 1. 4 And I *l*, and, behold, a whirlwind
2. 9 and when I *l*, behold, an hand was
8. 7 when I *l*, behold a hole in the wall.
10. 1 I *l*, and, behold, in the firmament
9 when I *l*, behold the four wheels by
11 the head *l* they followed it; they
16. 8 I passed by thee, and *l* upon thee,
21.21 with images, he *l* in the liver.
40.20 court that *l* toward the north,
44. 4 I *l*, and, behold, the glory of the
46.19 priests, which *l* toward the north:
Dan 1.13 let our countenances be *l* upon
10. 5 Then I lifted up mine eyes, and *l*,
12. 5 I Daniel *l*, and, behold, there stood
Ob 12 shouldest not have *l* on the day
13 not have *l* on their affliction in
Hag 1. 9 Ye *l* for much, and, lo, it came to
Zec 2. 1 lifted up mine eyes again, and *l*,
4. 2 I have *l*, and behold a candlestick
5. 1 and lifted up mine eyes, and *l*,
9 Then lifted I up mine eyes, and *l*,
6. 1 and lifted up mine eyes, and *l*,
Mk 3. 5 when he had *l* round about on
34 he *l* round about on them which
5.32 he *l* round about to see her that
6.41 he *l* up to heaven, and blessed, and
8.24 he *l* up, and said, I see men as trees,
33 about and *l* on his disciples,
9. 8 when they had *l* round about, they
10.23 And Jesus *l* round about, and saith
11.11 when he had *l* round about upon
14.67 warming himself, she *l* upon him,
16. 4 And when they *l*, they saw that the
Lk 1.25 in the days wherein he *l* on me,
2.38 to all them that *l* for redemption
10.32 came and *l* on him, and passed
19. 5 to the place, he *l* up, and saw him,
21. 1 he *l* up, and saw the rich men
22.56 the fire, and earnestly *l* upon him,
61 Lord turned, and *l* upon Peter.
Jn 13.22 the disciples *l* one on another,
20.11 down, and *l* into the sepulcher,
Ac 1.10 they *l* stedfastly toward heaven
7.55 *l* up stedfastly into heaven, and
10. 4 when he *l* on him, he was afraid,
22.13 the same hour I *l* up upon him.
28. 6 they *l* when he should have
6 but after they had *l* a great while,
Heb 11.10 *l* for a city which hath foundations,
1Jn 1. 1 which we have *l* upon, and our
Rev 4. 1 After this I *l*, and, behold, a door
6. 8 And I *l*, and behold a pale horse:
14. 1 I *l*, and, lo, a Lamb stood on the
14 I *l*, and behold a white cloud, and
15. 5 And after that I *l*, and, behold, the

LOOKETH

Lev 13.12 wheresoever the priest *l*;
Nu 21. 8 when he *l* upon it, shall live.
20 Pisgah, which *l* toward Jeshimon.
23.28 of Peor, that *l* toward Jeshimon.
Jos 15. 2 from the bay that *l* southward:
1Sa 13.18 the border that *l* to the valley of
16. 7 man *l* on the outward appearance,
7 but the Lord *l* on the heart.
Job 7. 2 an hireling *l* for the reward of his
28.24 For he *l* to the ends of the earth,
33.27 He *l* upon men, and if any say,
Ps 33.13 The Lord *l* from heaven; he
14 he *l* upon all the inhabitants of
104.32 He *l* on the earth, and it trembleth:
Pr 14.15 prudent man *l* well to his going.
31.27 She *l* well to the ways of her
SS 2. 9 wall, he *l* forth at the windows,
6.10 is she that *l* forth as the morning,
7. 4 which *l* toward Damascus.
Isa 28. 4 when he that *l* upon it seeth,
Eze 8. 3 gate that *l* toward the north;
11. 1 Lord's house, which *l* eastward:
40. 6 the gate which *l* toward the east,
22 of the gate that *l* toward the east;
43. 1 the gate that *l* toward the east:
44. 1 sanctuary which *l* toward the east;
46. 1 inner court that *l* toward the east
12 the gate that *l* toward the east,
47. 2 gate by the way that *l* eastward;
Mt 5.28 *l* on a woman to lust after her
24.50 in a day when he *l* not for him,
Lk 12.46 in a day when he *l* not for him,
Jas 1.25 *l* into the perfect law of liberty,

LOOKING

Mt 14.19 and *l* up to heaven, he blessed, and
Mk 7.34 And *l* up to heaven, he sighed, and
10.27 Jesus *l* upon them saith, With men
15.40 were also women *l* on afar off:
Lk 6.10 *l* round about upon them all, he
9.16 *l* up to heaven, he blessed them,
62 his hand to the plough, and *l* back,
21.26 and for *l* after those things which
Jn 1.36 *l* upon Jesus as he walked, he
20. 5 And he stooping down, and *l* in, saw
Ac 6.15 *l* stedfastly on him, saw his face as
23.21 ready, *l* for a promise from thee.
Tit 2.13 *L* for that blessed hope, and the
Heb 10.27 a certain fearful *l* for of judgment
12. 2 *L* unto Jesus the author and
15 *L* diligently lest any man fail of
2Pe 3.12 *L* for and hasting unto the coming
Jude 21 *l* for the mercy of our Lord Jesus

LOOSE

Gen 49.21 Naphtali is a hind let *l*: he giveth
Lev 14. 7 living bird *l* into the open field.
Dt 25. 9 and *l* his shoe from off his foot,
Jos 5.15 *L* thy shoe from off thy foot; for
Job 6. 9 that he would let *l* his hand, and
30.11 also let *l* the bridle before me.
38.31 Pleiades, or *l* the bands of Orion?
Ps 102.20 *l* those that are appointed to death;
Isa 20. 2 *l* the sackcloth from off thy loins,
45. 1 I will *l* the loins of kings, to open
52. 2 *l* thyself from the bands of thy neck,
58. 6 to *l* the bands of wickedness, to
Jer 40. 4 I *l* thee this day from the chains
Dan 3.25 Lo, I see four men *l*, walking in
Mt 16.19 whatsoever thou shalt *l* on earth
18.18 whatsoever ye shall *l* on earth shall
21. 2 *l* them, and bring them unto me.
Mk 11. 2 man sat; *l* him, and bring him.
4 two ways met; and they *l* him.
Lk 13.15 on the sabbath *l* his ox or his ass
19.30 sat: *l* him, and bring him thither.
31 any man ask you, Why do ye *l* him?
33 said unto them, Why *l* ye the colt?
Jn 11.44 unto them, *L* him, and let him go.
Ac 13.25 of his feet I am not worthy to *l*.
24.26 him of Paul, that he might *l* him:
Rev 5. 2 book, and to *l* the seals thereof?
5 and to *l* the seven seals thereof.
9.14 *L* the four angels which are bound

LOOSED

Ex 28.28 the breastplate be not *l* from the
39.21 the breastplate might not be *l* from
Dt 25.10 house of him that hath his shoe *l*.
Jdg 15.14 his bands *l* from off his hands.
Job 30.11 Because he hath *l* my cord, and
39. 5 hath *l* the bands of the wild ass?
Ps 105.20 The king sent and *l* him; even
116.16 handmaid: thou hast *l* my bonds.
Ec 12. 6 Or ever the silver cord be *l*, or the
Isa 5.27 shall the girdle of their loins be *l*,
33.23 Thy tacklings are *l*; they could

Isa 51.14 exile hasteneth that he may be *l*,
Dan 5. 6 that the joints of his loins were *l*,
Mt 16.19 loose on earth shall be *l* in heaven.
18.18 loose on earth shall be *l* in heaven.
27 with compassion, and *l* him, and
Mk 7.35 and the string of his tongue was *l*,
Lk 1.64 and his tongue *l*, and he spake, and
13.12 thou art *l* from thine infirmity.
16 *l* from this bond on the sabbath
Ac 2.24 up, having *l* the pains of death:
13.13 and his company *l* from Paphos,
16.26 and every one's bands were *l*.
22.30 Jews, he *l* him from his bands,
27.21 me, and not have *l* from Crete,
40 *l* the rudder bands, and hoised up
Ro 7. 2 is *l* from the law of her husband.
1Co 7.27 unto a wife? seek not to be *l*.
27 Art thou *l* from a wife? seek not
Rev 9.15 And the four angels were *l*, which
20. 3 that he must be *l* a little season.
7 Satan shall be *l* out of his prison,

LOOSING

Mk 11. 5 unto them, What do ye, *l* the colt?
Lk 19.33 And as they were *l* the colt, the
Ac 16.11 Therefore *l* from Troas, we came
27.13 *l* thence, they sailed close by

LORD

Gen 2. 4 that the *L* God made the earth
7 *L* God formed man of the dust
8 And the *L* God planted a garden
19 the *L* God formed every beast
22 rib, which the *L* God had taken
3. 1 field which the *L* God had made.
9 *L* God called unto Adam, and
13 the *L* God said unto the woman,
14 the *L* God said unto the serpent,
22 the *L* God said, Behold, the man
23 *L* God sent him forth from the
4. 1 I have gotten a man from the *L*.
9 *L* said unto Cain, Where is Abel?
26 to call upon the name of the *L*.
5.29 ground which the *L* hath cursed.
6. 3 the *L* said, My Spirit shall not
7 the *L* said, I will destroy man
7. 1 And the *L* said unto Noah, Come
11. 5 *L* came down to see the city and
8 *L* scattered them abroad from
12. 1 Now the *L* had said unto Abram,
7 the *L* appeared unto Abram, and
13. 4 called on the name of the *L*.
10 before the *L* destroyed Sodom
15. 1 word of the *L* came unto Abram
2 said, *L* God, what wilt thou give
6 And he believed in the *L*; and he
7 *L* that brought thee out of Ur of
18 *L* made a covenant with Abram,
18. 1 the *L* appeared unto him in the
14 Is any thing too hard for the *L*?
30 Oh let not the *L* be angry, and I
19.13 great before the face of the *L*;
24 *L* rained upon Sodom and upon
24 brimstone and fire from the *L*
21. 1 *L* visited Sarah as he had said,
26. 2 the *L* appeared unto him, and
28.13 behold, the *L* stood above it, and
16 Surely the *L* is in this place; and
21 then shall the *L* be my God:
31. 3 the *L* said unto Jacob, Return
49 The *L* watch between me and
39. 2 the *L* was with Joseph, and he
23 he did, the *L* made it to prosper.
45. 8 and *l* of all his house, and a ruler
9 God hath made me *l* of all Egypt:
49.18 waited for thy salvation, O *L*.
Ex 3. 2 the angel of the *L* appeared unto
18 The *L* God of the Hebrews hath
4. 1 *L* hath not appeared unto thee.
4 the *L* said unto Moses, Put forth
10 And Moses said unto the *L*,
10 O my *L*, I am not eloquent,
22 Thus saith the *L*, Israel is my
5. 1 Thus saith the *L* God of Israel,
2 Pharaoh said, Who is the *L*, that
2 I know not the *L*, neither will I
6. 1 Then the *L* said unto Moses, Now
7 know that I am the *L* your God,
8 you for an heritage: I am the *L*.
30 Moses said before the *L*, Behold,
8. 1 the *L* spake unto Moses, Go unto
1 Thus saith the *L*, Let my people
10 is none like unto the *L* our God.
9. 1 the *L* said unto Moses, Go in
12 *L* hardened the heart of Pharaoh,
22 the *L* said unto Moses, Stretch
23 and the *L* sent thunder and hail,
23 the *L* rained hail upon the land
10. 1 And the *L* said unto Moses, Go in
8 them, Go, serve the *L* your God:
12. 1 *L* spake unto Moses and Aaron
14 ye shall keep it a feast to the *L*
23 the *L* will pass over the door,
25 land which the *L* will give you,
29 the *L* smote all the firstborn in
48 will keep the passover to the *L*,
13. 1 the *L* spake unto Moses, saying,
3 *L* brought you out from this
14. 1 And the *L* spake unto Moses,
4 may know that I am the *L*. And
8 *L* hardened the heart of Pharaoh
13 and see the salvation of the *L*,
14 The *L* shall fight for you, and ye
21 *L* caused the sea to go back by a
26 the *L* said unto Moses, Stretch
27 *L* overthrew the Egyptians in the
30 *L* saved Israel that day out of
15. 1 of Israel this song unto the *L*,
2 The *L* is my strength and song,
11 Who is like unto thee, O *L*,
18 The *L* shall reign for ever and
26 for I am the *L* that healeth thee.
16. 3 We had died by the hand of the *L*
25 to day is a sabbath unto the *L*:
17. 1 to the commandment of the *L*,
7 and because they tempted the *L*,
7 Is the *L* among us, or not?
18. 1 the *L* hath brought Israel out of
11 the *L* is greater than all gods:
19. 3 the *L* called unto him out of the
18 the *L* descended upon it in fire:
20 *L* came down upon mount Sinai,
20 *L* called Moses up to the top of
20. 2 I am the *L* thy God, which have
5 the *L* thy God am a jealous God,
7 name of the *L* thy God in vain;
7 the *L* will not hold him guiltless
10 day is the sabbath of the *L* thy
11 the *L* made heaven and earth,
11 the *L* blessed the sabbath day,
23.17 males shall appear before the *L*
25 ye shall serve the *L* your God,
29.11 kill the bullock before the *L*,
46 know that I am the *L* their God,
46 them: I am the *L* their God.
31. 1, 12 And the *L* spake unto Moses,
13 am the *L* that doth sanctify you.
32. 5 To morrow is a feast to the *L*.
14 *L* repented of the evil which he
35 And the *L* plagued the people,
33. 1 the *L* said unto Moses, Depart,
11 *L* spake unto Moses face to face,
34. 1 the *L* said unto Moses, Hew thee
6 the *L* passed by before him, and
6 The *L*, The *L* God, merciful and
40. 1 And the *L* spake unto Moses,
34, 35 the glory of the *L* filled the
Lev 1. 1 And the *L* called unto Moses,
5. 6 his trespass offering unto the *L*
19. 1 the *L* spake unto Moses, saying,
2 for I the *L* your God am holy.
27. 1 the *L* spake unto Moses, saying,
21 jubile, shall be holy unto the *L*.
32 tenth shall be holy unto the *L*.
Nu 1. 1 the *L* spake unto Moses in the
5. 1 the *L* spake unto Moses, saying,
18 shall set the woman before the *L*,
6. 1 the *L* spake unto Moses, saying,
2 separate themselves unto the *L*:
24 The *L* bless thee, and keep thee:
25 *L* make his face shine upon thee,
26 *L* lift up his countenance upon
9. 1 the *L* spake unto Moses in the
8 hear what the *L* will command
12. 2 Hath the *L* indeed spoken only
5 *L* came down in the pillar of the
8 the similitude of the *L* shall he
14. 3 wherefore hath the *L* brought us
9 Only rebel not ye against the *L*,
14 thou *L* art among this people,
18 The *L* is longsuffering, and of
16. 3 them, and the *L* is among them:
5 the *L* will shew who are his,
28 shall know that the *L* hath sent
30 if the *L* make a new thing, and
20. 3 our brethren died before the *L*!
12 *L* spake unto Moses and Aaron,
21. 2 Israel vowed a vow unto the *L*,
6 *L* sent fiery serpents among the
22. 8 as the *L* shall speak unto me:
22 angel of the *L* stood in the way
23. 3 the *L* will come to meet me;
21 the *L* his God is with him, and
32. 4 the country which the *L* smote
23 ye have sinned against the *L*:
Dt 1. 3 *L* had given him in commandment
6 *L* our God spake unto us in Horeb,
4. 1 *L* God of your fathers giveth
24 *L* thy God is a consuming fire,
31 the *L* thy God is a merciful God;)
35 know that the *L* he is God;
6. 1 *L* your God commanded to teach
4 Israel: The *L* our God is one *L*:
5 love the *L* thy God with all thine
16 shall not tempt the *L* your God,
22 *L* shewed signs and wonders,
8. 1 land which the *L* sware unto your
11 thou forget not the *L* thy God,
18 shalt remember the *L* thy God:
9. 3 *L* thy God is he which goeth over
10 *L* delivered unto me two tables of
10 *L* spake with you in the mount
10. 1 that time the *L* said unto me,
12 what doth the *L* thy God require
12 but to fear the *L* thy God, to walk
17 the *L* your God is God of gods,
17 *L* of lords, a great God, a mighty,
11. 1 love the *L* thy God, and keep his
17 good land which the *L* giveth you.
13. 3 for the *L* your God proveth you,
3 ye love the *L* your God with all
16. 1 the passover unto the *L* thy God:
10 feast of weeks unto the *L* thy God
16 not appear before the *L* empty:
18. 1 offerings of the *L* made by fire,
13 be perfect with the *L* thy God.
23. 1 into the congregation of the *L*.
5 *L* thy God turned the curse into
14 *L* thy God walketh in the midst
21 *L* thy God will surely require it
25.15 land which the *L* thy God giveth
19 *L* thy God hath given thee rest
26. 1 land which the *L* thy God giveth
7 *L* heard our voice, and looked
10 worship before the *L* thy God:
17 avouched the *L* this day to be thy
27. 2, 3 land which the *L* thy God giveth
5 build an altar unto the *L* thy God,
28. 1 unto the voice of the *L* thy God,
20 *L* shall send upon thee cursing,
21 The *L* shall make the pestilence
22 The *L* shall smite thee with a
63 *L* rejoiced over you to do you good,

29. 1 the *L* commanded Moses to make
6 know that I am the *L* your God.
20 *L* shall blot out his name from
29 belong unto the *L* our God:
30. 1 the *L* thy God hath driven thee,
3 *L* thy God will turn thy captivity,
8 and obey the voice of the *L*,
9 *L* will again rejoice over thee
16 *L* thy God shall bless thee in the
20 thou mayest love the *L* thy God,
31. 2 the *L* hath said unto me, Thou
9 the ark of the covenant of the *L*,
32. 3 will publish the name of the *L*:
36 For the *L* shall judge his people,
33. 2 he said, The *L* came from Sinai,
12 The beloved of the *L* shall dwell
21 he executed the justice of the *L*,
29 O people saved by the *L*, the
34. 1 the *L* shewed him all the land of
5 the servant of the *L* died there
Jos 1. 1 death of Moses...servant of the *L*,
1 *L* spake unto Joshua the son of
9 for the *L* thy God is with thee
3. 3 the ark of the covenant of the *L*
5 *L* will do wonders among you.
4. 1 that the *L* spake unto Joshua,
23 *L* your God dried up the waters
24 fear the *L* your God for ever.
6. 2 the *L* said unto Joshua, See, I
16 the *L* hath given you the city.
8. 1 the *L* said unto Joshua, Fear not,
30 built an altar unto the *L* God
13. 1 the *L* said unto him, Thou art old
33 the *L* God of Israel was their
14. 2 the *L* commanded by the hand of
10 behold, the *L* hath kept me alive,
18. 3 *L* God of your fathers hath given
8 cast lots for you before the *L* in
22. 2 servant of the *L* commanded you,
24 What have ye to do with the *L*
23. 1 the *L* had given rest unto Israel
8 But cleave unto the *L* your God,
10 for the *L* your God, he it is that
24. 2 Thus saith the *L* God of Israel,
15 evil unto you to serve the *L*,
15 my house, we will serve the *L*.
19 people, Ye cannot serve the *L*:
21 Nay; but we will serve the *L*.
23 incline your heart unto the *L* God
24 The *L* our God will we serve,
Jdg 1. 1 children of Israel asked the *L*,
2. 1 an angel of the *L* came up from
12 they forsook the *L* God of their
12 and provoked the *L* to anger.
15 hand of the *L* was against them
6. 1 did evil in the sight of the *L*:
6 children of Israel cried unto the *L*.
8 *L* sent a prophet unto the children
13 now the *L* hath forsaken us, and
22 seen an angel of the *L* face to
34 Spirit of the *L* came upon Gideon,
8. 7 when the *L* hath delivered Zebah
23 you: the *L* shall rule over you.
11. 9 the *L* deliver them before me,
27 the *L* the Judge be judge this day
30 Jephthah vowed a vow unto the *L*,
13. 1 evil again in the sight of the *L*;
25 the Spirit of the *L* began to move
16.20 wist not that the *L* was departed
28 O *L* God, remember me, I pray
Ru 1. 6 *L* had visited his people in giving
8 the *L* deal kindly with you, as ye
9 *L* grant you that ye may find rest,
13 the hand of the *L* is gone out
17 the *L* do so to me, and more also,
21 *L* hath brought me home again
2. 4 the reapers, The *L* be with you.
12 The *L* recompense thy work,
1Sa 1. 3 to sacrifice unto the *L* of hosts
11 O *L* of hosts, if thou wilt indeed
12 continued praying before the *L*,

15 poured out my soul before the *L*.
27 the *L* hath given me my petition
28 also I have lent him to the *L*;
2. 1 said, My heart rejoiceth in the *L*,
2 There is none holy as the *L*;
3 for the *L* is a God of knowledge,
6 The *L* killeth, and maketh alive:
7 The *L* maketh poor, and maketh
3. 1 Samuel ministered unto the *L*
1 the word of the *L* was precious
4 the *L* called Samuel: and he
9 that thou shalt say, Speak, *L*;
18 It is the *L*: let him do what
19 grew, and the *L* was with him,
7. 1 and fetched up the ark of the *L*,
3 return unto the *L* with all your
5 I will pray for you unto the *L*.
6 We have sinned against the *L*.
12. 3 witness against me before the *L*,
12 the *L* your God was your king.
13 the *L* hath set a king over you.
22 *L* will not forsake his people for
22 pleased the *L* to make you his
14. 6 be that the *L* will work for us:
35 Saul built an altar unto the *L*:
15. 1 *L* sent me to anoint thee to be
33 hewed Agag in pieces before the *L*
35 *L* repented that he had made Saul
16. 1 the *L* said unto Samuel, How long
7 *L* said unto Samuel, Look not on
7 *L* seeth not as man seeth; for
7 but the *L* looketh on the heart.
10 The *L* hath not chosen these.
17.37 *L* that delivered me out of the paw
45 in the name of the *L* of hosts,
20. 3 as the *L* liveth, and as thy soul
23 *L* be between thee and me for
24. 4 the day of which the *L* said unto
6 he is the anointed of the *L*.
18 *L* had delivered me into thine
26.10 said furthermore, As the *L* liveth,
23 The *L* render to every man his
28. 6 And when Saul inquired of the *L*,
16 the *L* is departed from thee, and
2Sa 1.10 brought them hither unto my *l*.
3. 9 as the *L* hath sworn to David,
39 *L* shall reward the doer of evil
5. 2 *L* said to thee, Thou shalt feed
10 the *L* God of hosts was with him.
6. 2 *L* of hosts that dwelleth between
14 David danced before the *L* with
7. 1 *L* had given him rest round about
18 Who am I, O *L* God? and what is
20 thou, *L* God, knowest thy servant.
12. 1 the *L* sent Nathan unto David.
5 As the *L* liveth, the man that hath
16. 4 grace in thy sight, my *l*, O king.
10 the *L* hath said unto him, Curse
22. 1 And David spake unto the *L* the
2 *L* is my rock, and my fortress,
19 but the *L* was my stay.
22 I have kept the ways of the *L*,
29 For thou art my lamp, O *L*:
29 the *L* will lighten my darkness.
32 For who is God, save the *L*? and
23. 2 The Spirit of the *L* spake by me,
16 but poured it out unto the *L*.
1Ki 1. 2 for my *l* the king a young virgin:
3. 1 house, and the house of the *L*,
3 Solomon loved the *L*, walking in
5. 3 unto the name of the *L* his God
12 the *L* gave Solomon wisdom, as
8. 1 the ark of the covenant of the *L*
12 The *L* said that he would dwell
20 *L* hath performed his word that
23 *L* God of Israel, there is no God
63 dedicated the house of the *L*.
9. 1 building of the house of the *L*,
8 Why hath the *L* done this unto
14. 5 the *L* said unto Ahijah, Behold,
21 the city which the *L* did choose

15. 3 not perfect with the *L* his God,
14 heart was perfect with the *L* all
18. 1 the word of the *L* came to Elijah
21 if the *L* be God, follow him: but
39 *L*, he is the God; the *L*, he is the
46 the hand of the *L* was on Elijah;
19. 4 now, O *L*, take away my life; for
10 jealous for the *L* God of hosts:
11 the *L* passed by, and a great and
11 but the *L* was not in the wind:
11 *L* was not in the earthquake:
12 but the *L* was not in the fire:
20. 4 Israel answered and said, My *l*,
28 said, The *L* is God of the hills,
22. 5 thee, at the word of the *L* to day.
19 I saw the *L* sitting on his throne,
2Ki 1. 3 angel of the *L* said to Elijah the
5. 1 the *L* had given deliverance unto
17 unto other gods, but unto the *L*.
6.12 servants said, None, my *l*, O king:
17 *L*, I pray thee, open his eyes,
7. 1 said, Hear ye the word of the *L*;
2 if the *L* would make windows in
19. 1 and went into the house of the *L*.
6 Thus saith the *L*, Be not afraid
16 *L*, bow down thine ear, and hear:
20. 1 Thus saith the *L*, Set thine house
9 sign shalt thou have of the *L*,
9 *L* will do the thing that he hath
19 Good is the word of the *L* which
1Ch 2. 3 was evil in the sight of the *L*;
6.15 when the *L* carried away Judah
31 of song in the house of the *L*,
16. 2 the people in the name of the *L*.
14 He is the *L* our God; his
23 Sing unto the *L*, all the earth;
25 For great is the *L*, and greatly
26 but the *L* made the heavens.
28 unto the *L* glory and strength.
29 Give unto the *L* the glory due
17. 1 the ark of the covenant of the *L*
10 the *L* will build thee an house.
20 O *L*, there is none like thee,
24 the *L* of hosts is the God of Israel,
19.13 let the *L* do that which is good in
21. 3 *L* make his people an hundred
30 the sword of the angel of the *L*.
22. 1 This is the house of the *L* God,
5 *L* must be exceeding magnifical,
11 Now, my son, the *L* be with thee;
11 build the house of the *L* thy God,
12 Only the *L* give thee wisdom and
12 keep the law of the *L* thy God.
18 Is not the *L* your God with you?
28. 2 the ark of the covenant of the *L*,
9 the *L* searcheth all hearts, and
10 *L* hath chosen thee to build an
29. 1 is not for man, but for the *L* God.
9 they offered willingly to the *L*:
10 be thou, *L* God of Israel our father,
11 Thine, O *L*, is the greatness, and
11 thine is the kingdom, O *L*, and
2Ch 1. 1 the *L* his God was with him, and
7. 1 glory of the *L* filled the house.
12 *L* appeared to Solomon by night,
13. 5 *L* God of Israel gave the kingdom
10 as for us, the *L* is our God, and
16. 2 treasures of the house of the *L*
9 the eyes of the *L* run to and fro
17. 3 And the *L* was with Jehoshaphat,
9 had the book of the law of the *L*
18. 4 I pray thee, at the word of the *L*
18 saw the *L* sitting upon his throne,
20. 3 and set himself to seek the *L*,
26. 4 was right in the sight of the *L*,
18 to burn incense unto the *L*,
30. 1 come to the house of the *L* at
18 The good *L* pardon every one
21 priests praised the *L* day by day,
22 making confession to the *L* God
31. 2 in the gates of the tents of the *L*.

2Ch 31.10 for the *L* hath blessed his people;
34. 2 was right in the sight of the *L*,
14 found a book of the law of the *L*
35. 1 Josiah kept a passover unto the *L*
3 serve now the *L* your God, and
Ezr 1. 1 word of the *L* by the mouth of
1 *L* stirred up the spirit of Cyrus
8.28 them, Ye are holy unto the *L*;
28 freewill offering unto the *L* God
10. 3 according to the counsel of my *l*,
11 make confession unto the *L* God
Neh 1. 5 O *L* God of heaven, the great and
5.13 said, Amen, and praised the *L*.
9. 3 book of the law of the *L* their
5 Stand up and bless the *L* your
6 Thou, even thou, art *L* alone;
Job 1. 6 present themselves before the *L*,
7 Satan answered the *L*, and said,
12. 9 hand of the *L* hath wrought this?
28.28 the fear of the *L*, that is wisdom;
Ps 1. 2 his delight is in the law of the *L*;
2. 2 against the *L*, and against his
4 *L* shall have them in derision.
11 Serve the *L* with fear, and rejoice
3. 1 *L*, how are they increased that
4 I cried unto the *L* with my voice,
7 Arise, O *L*; save me, O my God:
8 Salvation belongeth unto the *L*:
5. 1 Give ear to my words, O *L*,
8 Lead me, O *L*, in...righteousness
6. 1 O *L*, rebuke me not in thine
9 the *L* will receive my prayer.
8. 1 O *L*...how excellent is thy name
9. 1 I will praise thee, O *L*, with my
7 But the *L* shall endure for ever:
9 *L* also will be a refuge for the
10. 1 Why standest thou afar off, O *L*?
16 The *L* is King for ever and ever:
11. 1 In the *L* put I my trust: how say
4 The *L* is in his holy temple, the
12. 1 Help, *L*; for the godly man
6 words of the *L* are pure words:
14. 2 The *L* looked down from heaven
16. 2 soul, thou hast said unto the *L*,
2 Thou art my *L*: my goodness
8 have set the *L* always before me:
19. 7 The law of the *L* is perfect,
7 the testimony of the *L* is sure,
8 The statutes of the *L* are right,
8 commandment of the *L* is pure,
9 The fear of the *L* is clean,
9 the judgments of the *L* are true
14 be acceptable in thy sight, O *L*,
20. 1 *L* hear thee in the day of trouble;
7 will remember the name of the *L*
23. 1 The *L* is my shepherd; I shall
6 in the house of the *L* for ever.
24. 3 shall ascend into the hill of the *L*?
8 The *L* strong and mighty,
8 the *L* mighty in battle.
10 The *L* of hosts, he is the King of
25. 1 Unto thee, O *L*, do I lift up my
4 Shew me thy ways, O *L*; teach
8 Good and upright is the *L*:
27. 1 *L* is my light and my salvation;
1 the *L* is the strength of my life;
4 One thing have I desired of the *L*,
11 Teach me thy way, O *L*, and lead
14 Wait on the *L*: be of good
14 thine heart: wait, I say, on the *L*.
28. 1 thee will I cry, O *L* my rock;
7 The *L* is my strength and my
29. 1 Give unto the *L*, O ye mighty,
2 Give unto the *L* the glory due
2 worship the *L* in the beauty of
4 The voice of the *L* is powerful;
10 The *L* sitteth upon the flood;
10 yea, the *L* sitteth King for ever.
30. 1 I will extol thee, O *L*; for thou
4 Sing unto the *L*, O ye saints of his,
33. 1 Rejoice in the *L*, O ye righteous:
2 Praise the *L* with harp: sing unto
12 is the nation whose God is the *L*;
18 eye of the *L* is upon them that fear
34. 1 I will bless the *L* at all times:
3 O magnify the *L* with me, and
7 angel of the *L* encampeth round
8 taste and see that the *L* is good:
9 O fear the *L*, ye his saints: for
37. 3 Trust in the *L*, and do good; so
5 Commit thy way unto the *L*;
7 Rest in the *L*, and wait patiently
39. 4 *L*, make me to know mine end,
40. 1 I waited patiently for the *L*; and
13 O *L*, make haste to help me.
48. 1 Great is the *L*, and greatly to be
51.15 O *L*, open thou my lips; and my
55. 9 Destroy, O *L*, and divide their
22 Cast thy burden upon the *L*, and
77. 2 day of my trouble I sought the *L*:
7 Will the *L* cast off for ever? and
80. 4 O *L* God of hosts, how long wilt
19 Turn us again, O *L* God of hosts,
84. 1 thy tabernacles, O *L* of hosts!
11 the *L* God is a sun and shield:
86. 1 Bow down thine ear, O *L*, hear
4 unto thee, O *L*, do I lift up my
89. 1 I will sing of the mercies of the *L*
6 can be compared unto the *L*?
6 can be likened unto the *L*?
8 O *L* God of hosts, who is a strong
8 who is a strong *L* like unto thee?
46 How long, *L*? wilt thou hide
90. 1 *L*, thou hast been our dwelling
17 let the beauty of the *L* our God be
91. 2 will say of the *L*, He is my refuge
92. 1 thing to give thanks unto the *L*,
4 For thou, *L*, hast made me glad
5 O *L*, how great are thy works!
93. 1 The *L* reigneth, he is clothed
4 *L* on high is mightier than the
94. 1 O *L* God, to whom vengeance
11 *L* knoweth the thoughts of man,
17 Unless the *L* had been my help,
95. 1 O come, let us sing unto the *L*:
3 For the *L* is a great God, and a
96. 1 O sing unto the *L* a new song:
9 O worship the *L* in the beauty of
97. 1 The *L* reigneth; let the earth
10 Ye that love the *L*, hate evil: he
98. 1 O sing unto the *L* a new song;
2 *L* hath made known his salvation:
4 Make a joyful noise unto the *L*,
5 Sing unto the *L* with the harp;
100. 1 Make a joyful noise unto the *L*,
2 Serve the *L* with gladness: come
3 Know ye that the *L* he is God:
103. 1 Bless the *L*, O my soul: and all
2 Bless the *L*, O my soul, and forget
13 the *L* pitieth them that fear him.
104. 1 Bless the *L*, O my soul.
24 O *L*, how manifold are thy works!
106. 1 Praise ye the *L*. O give thanks
48 Blessed be the *L* God of Israel
48 say, Amen. Praise ye the *L*.
107. 1 O give thanks unto the *L*, for he
6 cried unto the *L* in their trouble,
110. 1 The *L* said...Sit thou at my right
1 said unto my *L*, Sit thou at my
111. 1 Praise ye the *L*. I will praise
10 The fear of the *L* is the beginning
113. 1 Praise ye the *L*. Praise, O ye
4 The *L* is high above all nations,
115. 1 Not unto us, O *L*, not unto us.
12 The *L* hath been mindful of us:
17 The dead praise not the *L*,
116. 1 I love the *L*, because he hath
14 I will pay my vows unto the *L*
15 Precious in the sight of the *L* is
118. 1 O give thanks unto the *L*; for he
5 I called upon the *L* in distress:
6 The *L* is on my side; I will not
8, 9 It is better to trust in the *L* than
14 The *L* is my strength and song,
18 The *L* hath chastened me sore:
24 the day which the *L* hath made;
27 God is the *L*, which hath shewed
121. 2 My help cometh from the *L*,
5 The *L* is thy keeper: the
5 *L* is thy shade upon thy right
7 *L* shall preserve thee from all
8 *L* shall preserve thy going out
126. 1 *L* turned again the captivity of
3 *L* hath done great things for us;
127. 1 Except the *L* build the house,
1 except the *L* keep the city, the
130. 1 have I cried unto thee, O *L*.
3 *L*, shouldest mark iniquities,
3 O *L*, who shall stand?
6 My soul waiteth for the *L* more
132. 1 *L*, remember David, and all his
135. 1 Praise ye the *L*. Praise ye the
5 For I know that the *L* is great,
5 and that our *L* is above all gods.
136. 1 O give thanks unto the *L*; for
3 O give thanks to the *L* of lords:
141. 1 *L*, I cry unto thee: make haste
3 watch, O *L*, before my mouth;
142. 1 cried unto the *L* with my voice;
145. 3 Great is the *L*, and greatly to be
9 The *L* is good to all: and his
14 The *L* upholdeth all that fall,
17 The *L* is righteous in all his ways,
18 *L* is nigh unto all them that call
20 *L* preserveth all them that love
146. 1 Praise ye the *L*. Praise the
8 *L* openeth the eyes of the blind:
147. 1 Praise ye the *L*: for it is good
2 *L* doth build up Jerusalem: he
6 The *L* lifteth up the meek: he
150. 1 Praise ye the *L*. Praise God in
6 that hath breath praise the *L*.
Pr 1. 7 fear of the *L* is the beginning of
3. 5 Trust in the *L* with all thine
12 whom the *L* loveth he correcteth;
19 *L* by wisdom hath founded the
6.16 These six things doth the *L* hate:
9.10 fear of the *L* is the beginning of
15. 3 eyes of the *L* are in every place,
29 The *L* is far from the wicked:
16. 1 of the tongue, is from the *L*.
3 Commit thy works unto the *L*,
9 but the *L* directeth his steps.
18.10 name of the *L* is a strong tower:
19. 3 his heart fretteth against the *L*.
14 and a prudent wife is from the *L*.
23 The fear of the *L* tendeth to life:
22. 2 the *L* is the maker of them all.
12 eyes of the *L* preserve knowledge,
Isa 1. 2 for the *L* hath spoken, I have
18 us reason together, saith the *L*:
2. 3 go up to the mountain of the *L*,
5 let us walk in the light of the *L*.
11 *L* alone shall be exalted in that
6. 1 also the *L* sitting upon a throne,
3 Holy, holy, holy, is the *L* of
9. 7 zeal of the *L* of hosts will perform
11. 2 the spirit of the *L* shall rest upon
13. 4 *L* of hosts mustereth the host of
9 Behold, the day of the *L* cometh,
21. 6 For thus hath the *L* said unto me,
10 I have heard of the *L* of hosts,
24. 1 the *L* maketh the earth empty,
25. 1 O *L*, thou art my God; I will exalt
8 *L* God will wipe away tears from
26. 4 Trust ye in the *L* forever: for
12 *L*, thou wilt ordain peace for us:
30. 1 rebellious children, saith the *L*,
18 for the *L* is a God of judgment:
20 *L* give you the bread of adversity,
33. 2 O *L*, be gracious unto us; we
6 the fear of the *L* is his treasure.
21 glorious *L* will be unto us a place

22 For the *L* is our judge,
22 the *L* is our lawgiver,
22 the *L* is our king; he will save us.
35. 2 they shall see the glory of the *L*,
10 ransomed of the *L* shall return,
37. 1 and went into the house of the *L*.
20 O *L* our God, save us from his
20 may know that thou art the *L*,
40. 3 Prepare ye the way of the *L*,
5 glory of the *L* shall be revealed,
5 mouth of the *L* hath spoken it.
27 My way is hid from the *L*, and
28 the *L*, the Creator of the ends of
31 that wait upon the *L* shall renew
41. 4 I the *L*, the first, and with the
21 Produce your cause, saith the *L*;
42. 5 saith God the *L*, he that created
8 I am the *L*: that is my name:
10 Sing unto the *L* a new song, and
13 *L* shall go forth as a mighty man,
43. 1 thus saith the *L* that created thee,
3 I am the *L* thy God, the Holy One
11 I, even I, am the *L*; and beside
15 I am the *L*, your Holy One, the
45. 1 Thus saith the *L* to his anointed,
5 I am the *L*, and there is none else,
49. 1 *L* hath called me from the womb;
14 said, The *L* hath forsaken me,
14 and my *L* hath forgotten me.
52. 3 thus saith the *L*, Ye have sold
10 *L* hath made bare his holy arm
53. 1 is the arm of the *L* revealed?
6 *L* hath laid on him the iniquity
10 it pleased the *L* to bruise him;
54. 1 of the married wife, saith the *L*.
6 *L* hath called thee as a woman
55. 5 thee because of the *L* thy God,
6 Seek ye the *L* while he may be
7 and let him return unto the *L*,
58. 5 and an acceptable day to the *L*?
11 the *L* shall guide thee continually,
60. 1 glory of the *L* is risen upon thee.
16 I the *L* am thy Saviour and thy
61. 1 Spirit of the *L* God is upon me;
1 the *L* hath anointed me to preach
2 the acceptable year of the *L*, and
3 planting of the *L*, that he might
63. 7 the lovingkindness of the *L*,
17 O *L*, why hast thou made us to err
65. 7 your fathers together, saith the *L*,
25 my holy mountain, saith the *L*.
Jer 1. 2 To whom the word of the *L* came
6 Ah, *L* God! behold, I cannot speak:
2. 1 the word of the *L* came to me,
37 *L* hath rejected thy confidences,
3. 1 return again to me, saith the *L*.
23 in the *L* our God is the salvation
7. 1 came to Jeremiah from the *L*,
4 The temple of the *L*, The temple
9. 3 they know not me, saith the *L*.
12 the mouth of the *L* hath spoken,
10. 1 the word which the *L* speaketh
10 the *L* is the true God, he is the
12. 1 Righteous art thou, O *L*, when I
3 But thou, O *L*, knowest me: thou
13. 1 saith the *L* unto me, Go and get
16 Give glory to the *L* your God,
14. 1 The word of the *L* that came to
9 thou, O *L*, art in the midst of us,
17. 5 Thus saith the *L*; Cursed be the
10 I the *L* search the heart, I try the
14 Heal me, O *L*, and I shall be
15 Where is the word of the *L*? let it
18. 1 came to Jeremiah from the *L*,
6 you as this potter? saith the *L*.
22. 1 Thus saith the *L*; Go down to
5 I swear by myself, saith the *L*,
23. 1 sheep of my pasture! saith the *L*.
6 called, The *L* Our Righteousness.
23 Am I a God at hand, saith the *L*,
33 What is the burden of the *L*?
25. 3 word of the *L* hath come unto me,
30 The *L* shall roar from on high,
31 the *L* hath a controversy with the
26. 1 Judah came this word from the *L*,
19 fear the *L*, and besought the *L*,
19 *L* repented him of the evil which
29. 4 saith the *L* of hosts, the God of
26 *L* hath made thee priest in the
31. 1 saith the *L*, will I be the God of
7 saith the *L*; Sing with gladness
7 and say, O *L*, save thy people,
22 *L* hath created a new thing in the
34 Know the *L*: for they shall all
36. 1 came unto Jeremiah from the *L*,
9 proclaimed a fast before the *L*
42. 2 pray for us unto the *L* thy God,
5 *L* be a true and faithful witness
5 *L* thy God shall send thee to us.
20 Pray for us unto the *L* our God;
49. 1 the Ammonites, thus saith the *L*;
18 saith the *L*, no man shall abide
51. 1 Thus saith the *L*; Behold, I will
10 declare in Zion the work of the *L*
19 The *L* of hosts is his name.
La 1. 5 the *L* hath afflicted her for the
20 Behold, O *L*; for I am in distress:
2. 1 hath the *L* covered the daughter
9 also find no vision from the *L*.
3.18 my hope is perished from the *L*:
24 The *L* is my portion, saith my
25 *L* is good unto them that wait
26 wait for the salvation of the *L*.
31 For the *L* will not cast off for ever:
59 O *L*, thou hast seen my wrong:
5. 1 Remember, O *L*, what is come
21 Turn thou us unto thee, O *L*,
Eze 1. 3 The word of the *L* came expressly
6. 1 the word of the *L* came unto me,
10 they shall know that I am the *L*,
7. 1 the word of the *L* came unto me,
9 that I am the *L* that smiteth.
8. 1 hand of the *L* God fell there upon
12 they say, The *L* seeth us not;
12 the *L* hath forsaken the earth.
10. 4 the glory of the *L* went up from
18 the glory of the *L* departed from
11. 5 the Spirit of the *L* fell upon me,
13. 1 the word of the *L* came unto me,
16 there is no peace, saith the *L* God.
18. 1 The word of the *L* came unto me
23 wicked should die? saith the *L* God:
25 ye say, The way of the *L* is not equal.
30. 1 word of the *L* came again unto
3 even the day of the *L* is near,
34. 1 the word of the *L* came unto me,
17 O my flock, thus saith the *L* God;
24 And I the *L* will be their God,
36. 1 of Israel, hear the word of the *L*:
4 Israel, hear the word of the *L* God;
4 saith the *L* God to the mountains,
37. 1 The hand of the *L* was upon me,
3 answered, O *L* God, thou knowest.
4 bones, hear the word of the *L*.
5 saith the *L* God unto these bones;
43. 4 glory of the *L* came into the house
5 the glory of the *L* filled the house.
48. 9 that ye shall offer unto the *L*
35 that day shall be, The *L* is there.
Dan 1. 2 *L* gave Jehoiakim king of Judah
2.10 there is no king, *l*, nor ruler, that
47 a God of gods, and a *L* of kings,
9. 2 word of the *L* came to Jeremiah
8 O *L*, to us belongeth confusion of
14 hath the *L* watched upon the evil,
15 O *L* our God, thou hast brought
19 O *L*, hear; O *L*, forgive;
19 O *L*, hearken and do; defer not,
Hos 1. 1 The word of the *L* that came
4. 1 Hear the word of the *L*, ye
16 the *L* will feed them as a lamb
8. 1 eagle against the house of the *L*,
13 but the *L* accepteth them not;
10. 3 because we feared not the *L*;
12 for it is time to seek the *L*, till
12. 2 *L* hath also a controversy with
9 I that am the *L* thy God from the
13 *L* brought Israel out of Egypt,
13. 4 yet I am the *L* thy God from the
15 the wind of the *L* shall come up
14. 1 return unto the *L* thy God; for
2 you words, and turn to the *L*:
Joel 1. 1 word of the *L* that came to Joel
15 for the day of the *L* is at hand,
19 O *L*, to thee will I cry: for the
2. 1 for the day of the *L* cometh, for
11 for the day of the *L* is great and
17 Spare thy people, O *L*, and give
21 for the *L* will do great things.
31 the terrible day of the *L* come.
3. 8 far off: for the *L* hath spoken it.
16 The *L* also shall roar out of Zion,
16 *L* will be the hope of his people,
Am 1. 2 The *L* will roar from Zion, and
3. 1 this word that the *L* hath spoken
7 Surely the *L* God will do nothing,
4. 2 *L* God hath sworn by his holiness,
5. 3 For thus saith the *L* God; The
6 Seek the *L*, and ye shall live;
8 of the earth: The *L* is his name:
18 the day of the *L* is darkness, and
7. 1 hath the *L* God shewed unto me:
2 O *L* God, forgive, I beseech thee:
15 *L* took me as I followed the flock,
15 the *L* said unto me, Go, prophesy
9. 1 saw the *L* standing upon the altar:
5 *L* God of hosts is he that toucheth
8 the eyes of the *L* God are upon the
Ob 1 Thus saith the *L* God concerning
1 have heard a rumor from the *L*,
Jon 1. 1 word of the *L* came unto Jonah
9 I am an Hebrew; and I fear the *L*,
14 thou, O *L*, hast done as it pleased
16 the men feared the *L* exceedingly,
17 the *L* had prepared a great fish to
2. 1 Jonah prayed unto the *L* his God
9 have vowed. Salvation is of the *L*.
10 the *L* spake unto the fish, and it
4. 2 he prayed unto the *L*, and said, I
3 O *L*, take, I beseech thee, my life
Mic 1. 1 The word of the *L* that came to
3 *L* cometh forth out of his place,
2. 3 Therefore thus saith the *L*;
7 is the spirit of the *L* straitened?
13 and the *L* on the head of them.
4. 1 house of the *L* shall be established
13 consecrate their gain unto the *L*,
6. 1 Hear ye now what the *L* saith;
6 shall I come before the *L*, and
7 the *L* be pleased with thousands
8 what doth the *L* require of thee,
7. 7 Therefore I will look unto the *L*;
8 the *L* shall be a light unto me.
Na 1. 2 is jealous, and the *L* revengeth;
2 the *L* revengeth, and is furious;
2 the *L* will take vengeance on his
3 The *L* is slow to anger, and great
3 *L* hath his way in the whirlwind
7 The *L* is good, a strong hold in
14 the *L* hath given a commandment
Hab 1. 2 O *L*, how long shall I cry, and
3. 2 O *L*, I have heard thy speech, and
2 O *L*, revive thy work in the midst
19 The *L* God is my strength, and he
Zep 1. 1 word of the *L* which came unto
7 for the day of the *L* is at hand:
7 the *L* hath prepared a sacrifice,
2. 2 fierce anger of the *L* come upon
3 Seek ye the *L*, all ye meek of the
5 the word of the *L* is against you;
3. 2 she trusted not in the *L*; she
5 The just *L* is in the midst thereof;
17 *L* thy God in the midst of thee is

Hag 1. 1 the word of the *L* by Haggai the
13 saying, I am with you, saith the *L*.
14 And the *L* stirred up the spirit of
2. 1 the word of the *L* by the prophet
8 gold is mine, saith the *L* of hosts.
9 I give peace, saith the *L* of hosts.
Zec 1. 1 the word of the *L* unto Zechariah,
2. 5 For I, saith the *L*, will be unto
13 silent, O all flesh, before the *L*:
3. 1 priest...before the angel of the *L*,
2 The *L* rebuke thee, O Satan;
2 *L* that hath chosen Jerusalem
9. 1 The burden of the word of the *L*
4 Behold, the *L* will cast her out,
14 the *L* shall be seen over them,
14 the *L* God shall blow the trumpet,
15 the *L* of hosts shall defend them;
16 *L* their God shall save them in
11. 4 Thus saith the *L* my God; Feed
13 the *L* said unto me, Cast it unto
14. 1 Behold, the day of the *L* cometh,
9 *L* shall be king over all the earth:
9 in that day shall there be one *L*,
20 horses. Holiness Unto The *L*;
Mal 1. 1 The burden of the word of the *L*
7 The table of the *L* is contemptible.
12 The table of the *L* is polluted;
2. 2 my name, saith the *L* of hosts,
13 the altar of the *L* with tears,
17 wearied the *L* with your words.
17 evil is good in the sight of the *L*,
3. 1 and the *L*, whom ye seek, shall
6 For I am the *L*, I change not;
16 and the *L* hearkened, and heard
Mt 1.20 angel of the *L* appeared unto him
22 spoken of the *L* by the prophet,
24 angel of the *L* had bidden him,
2.13 angel of the *L* appeareth to Joseph
15 spoken of the *L* by the prophet,
19 an angel of the *L* appeareth in a
3. 3 Prepare ye the way of the *L*, make
4. 7 shalt not tempt the *L* thy God.
10 Thou shalt worship the *L* thy God,
5.33 perform unto the *L* thine oaths:
7.21 every one that saith unto me, *L*, *L*,
22 *L*, *L*, have we not prophesied in
8. 2 *L*, if thou wilt, thou canst make
6 *L*, my servant lieth at home sick
8 said, *L*, I am not worthy that thou
21 *L*, suffer me first to go and bury
25 awoke him, saying, *L*, save us:
9.28 this? They said unto him, Yea, *L*.
38 ye therefore the *L* of the harvest,
10.24 master, nor the servant above his *l*.
25 master, and the servant as his *l*.
11.25 O Father, *L* of heaven and earth,
12. 8 man is *L* even of the sabbath day.
13.51 things? They say unto him, Yea, *L*.
14.28 *L*, if it be thou, bid me come unto
30 sink, he cried, saying, *L*, save me.
15.22 Have mercy on me, O *L*, thou son
25 worshipped him, saying, *L*, help me.
27 Truth, *L*: yet the dogs eat of the
16.22 him, saying, Be it far from thee, *L*:
17. 4 *L*, it is good for us to be here: if
15 *L*, have mercy on my son: for he
18.21 *L*, how oft shall my brother sin
25 his *l* commanded him to be sold,
26 *L*, have patience with me, and I
27 *l* of that servant was moved with
31 told unto their *l* all that was done.
32 Then his *l*, after that he had called
34 And his *l* was wroth, and delivered
20. 8 the *l* of the vineyard saith unto his
30, 31 Have mercy on us, O *L*, thou
33 *L*, that our eyes may be opened.
21. 3 say, The *L* hath need of them; and
9 that cometh in the name of the *L*;
40 *l* therefore of the vineyard cometh,
22.37 love the *L* thy God with all thy
43 then doth David in spirit call him *L*,
44 The *L* said...Sit thou on my right
44 unto my *L*, Sit thou on my right
45 If David then call him *L*, how is he
23.39 that cometh in the name of the *L*.
24.42 not what hour your *L* doth come.
45 whom his *l* hath made ruler over
46 his *l* when he cometh shall find so
48 heart, My *l* delayeth his coming;
50 *l* of that servant shall come in a
25.11 virgins, saying, *L*, *L*, open to us.
19 time the *l* of those servants cometh.
20 *L*, thou deliveredst unto me five
21 His *l* said unto him, Well done, thou
21 enter thou into the joy of thy *l*.
22 *L*, thou deliveredst unto me two
23 His *l* said unto him, Well done, good
23 enter thou into the joy of thy *l*.
24 *L*, I knew thee that thou art an
26 His *l* answered and said unto him.
37, 44 *L*, when saw we thee an hungred,
26.22 of them to say unto him, *L*, is it I?
27.10 potter's field, as the *L* appointed
28. 2 the angel of the *L* descended from
6 Come, see the place where the *L* lay.
Mk 1. 3 Prepare ye the way of the *L*, make
2.28 Son of man is *L* also of the sabbath.
5.19 how great things the *L* hath done
7.28 and said unto him, Yes, *L*: yet the
9.24 *L*, I believe; help thou mine
10.51 *L*, that I might receive my sight.
11. 3 ye that the *L* hath need of him;
9 that cometh in the name of the *L*:
10 that cometh in the name of the *L*:
12. 9 therefore the *l* of the vineyard do?
29 Israel; The *L* our God is one *L*:
30 love the *L* thy God with all thy
36 The *L* said...Sit thou on my right
36 said to my *L*, Sit thou on my right
37 therefore himself calleth him *L*;
13.20 the *L* had shortened those days,
16.19 after the *L* had spoken unto them,
20 the *L* working with them, and
Lk 1. 6 and ordinances of the *L* blameless.
9 he went into the temple of the *L*.
11 appeared unto him an angel of the *L*
15 shall be great in the sight of the *L*,
16 shall he turn to the *L* their God.
17 ready a people prepared for the *L*.
25 Thus hath the *L* dealt with me in
28 highly favored, the *L* is with thee:
32 the *L* God shall give unto him the
38 Behold the handmaid of the *L*; be
43 mother of my *L* should come to me?
45 which were told her from the *L*.
46 said, My soul doth magnify the *L*,
58 how the *L* had shewed great mercy
66 the hand of the *L* was with him.
68 Blessed be the *L* God of Israel; for
76 shalt go before the face of the *L* to
2. 9 the angel of the *L* came upon them,
9 glory of the *L* shone round about
11 a Saviour, which is Christ the *L*.
15 which the *L* hath made known unto
22 Jerusalem, to present him to the *L*;
23 (As it is written in the law of the *L*,
23 womb shall be called holy to the *L*;)
24 which is said in the law of the *L*,
29 *L*, now lettest thou thy servant
38 gave thanks likewise unto the *L*,
39 according to the law of the *L*, they
3. 4 Prepare ye the way of the *L*, make
4. 8 Thou shalt worship the *L* thy God,
12 shalt not tempt the *L* thy God.
18 Spirit of the *L* is upon me, because
19 preach the acceptable year of the *L*.
5. 8 me; for I am a sinful man, O *L*.
12 *L*, if thou wilt, thou canst make me
17 power of the *L* was present to heal
6. 5 Son of man is *L* also of the sabbath.
46 why call ye me, *L*, *L*, and do not
7. 6 unto him, *L*, trouble not thyself:
13 And when the *L* saw her, he had
31 the *L* said, Whereunto then shall
9.54 *L*, wilt thou that we command fire
57 *L*, I will follow thee whithersoever
59 *L*, suffer me first to go and bury my
61 also said, *L*, I will follow thee; but
10. 1 the *L* appointed other seventy also,
2 ye therefore the *L* of the harvest,
17 *L*, even the devils are subject unto
21 O Father, *L* of heaven and earth,
27 love the *L* thy God with all thy
40 said, *L*, dost thou not care that my
11. 1 *L*, teach us to pray, as John also
39 the *L* said unto him, Now do ye
12.36 like unto men that wait for their *l*,
37 the *l* when he cometh shall find
41 *L*, speakest thou this parable unto
42 *L* said, Who then is that faithful
42 whom his *l* shall make ruler over
43 his *l* when he cometh shall find so
45 heart, My *l* delayeth his coming;
46 *l* of that servant will come in a day
13. 8 *L*, let it alone this year also, till I
15 *L* then answered him, and said,
23 *L*, are there few that be saved?
25 *L*,...open unto us; and he shall
25 *L*, open unto us; and he shall
35 that cometh in the name of the *L*.
14.21 and shewed his *l* these things.
22 said, *L*, it is done as thou hast
23 the *l* said unto the servant, Go out
16. 3 for my *l* taketh away from me the
5 How much owest thou unto my *l*?
8 *l* commended the unjust steward,
17. 5 apostles said unto the *L*, Increase
6 *L* said, If ye had faith as a grain
37 Where, *L*? And he said unto them,
18. 6 *L* said, Hear what the unjust judge
41 *L*, that I may receive my sight.
19. 8 Zacchaeus...and said unto the *L*;
8 *L*, the half of my goods I give to
16 *L*, thy pound hath gained ten
18 *L*, thy pound hath gained five
20 *L*, behold, here is thy pound, which
25 unto him, *L*, he hath ten pounds.)
31 Because the *L* hath need of him.
34 they said, The *L* hath need of him.
38 that cometh in the name of the *L*:
20.13 said the *l* of the vineyard, What
15 *l* of the vineyard do unto them?
37 calleth the *L* the God of Abraham,
42 The *L* said...Sit thou on my right
42 unto my *L*, Sit thou on my right
44 David therefore calleth him *L*,
22.31 the *L* said, Simon, Simon, behold,
33 *L*, I am ready to go with thee,
38 *L*, behold, here are two swords.
49 *L*, shall we smite with the sword?
61 *L* turned, and looked upon Peter.
61 remembered the word of the *L*,
23.42 *L*, remember me when thou comest
24. 3 found not the body of the *L* Jesus.
34 The *L* is risen indeed, and hath
Jn 1.23 Make straight the way of the *L*, as
4. 1 the *L* knew how the Pharisees had
6.23 after that the *L* had given thanks:)
34 *L*, evermore give us this bread.
68 him, *L*, to whom shall we go?
8.11 She said, No man, *L*. And Jesus
9.36 Who is he, *L*, that I might believe
38 *L*, I believe. And he worshipped
11. 2 anointed the *L* with ointment,
3 *L*, behold, he whom thou lovest is
12 *L*, if he sleep, he shall do well.
21 Jesus, *L*, if thou hadst been here,
27 Yea, *L*: I believe that thou art the
32 *L*, if thou hadst been here, my
34 said unto him, *L*, come and see.
39 *L*, by this time he stinketh: for he
12.13 that cometh in the name of the *L*.
38 *L*, who hath believed our report?

38 the arm of the *L* been revealed?
13. 6 him, *L*, dost thou wash my feet?
9 *L*, not my feet only, but also my
13 Ye call me Master and *L*: and ye
14 If I then, your *L* and Master, have
16 servant is not greater than his *l*;
25 saith unto him, *L*, who is it?
36 unto him, *L*, whither goest thou?
37 *L*, why cannot I follow thee now?
14. 5 *L*, we know not whither thou goest;
8 him, *L*, shew us the Father, and it
22 *L*, how is it that thou wilt manifest
15.15 knoweth not what his *l* doeth: but
20 servant is not greater than his *l*.
20. 2 away the *L* out of the sepulcher,
13 they have taken away my *L*, and I
18 disciples that she had seen the *L*,
20 disciples glad, when they saw the *L*.
25 said unto him, We have seen the *L*.
28 said unto him, My *L* and my God.
21. 7 loved saith unto Peter, It is the *L*.
7 Peter heard that it was the *L*, he
12 thou? knowing that it was the *L*.
15, 16 *L*; thou knowest that I love
17 *L*, thou knowest all things; thou
20 *L*, which is he that betrayeth thee?
21 *L*, and what shall this man do?
Ac 1. 6 *L*, wilt thou at this time restore
21 time that the *L* Jesus went in and
2.20 and notable day of the *L* come:
36 have crucified, both *L* and Christ.
47 *L* added to the church daily such
4.24 *L*, thou art God, which hast made
7.30 angel of the *L* in a flame of fire in
59 saying, *L* Jesus, receive my spirit.
9. 1 against the disciples of the *L*,
5 And he said, Who art thou, *L*?
5 And the *L* said, I am Jesus whom
29 boldly in the name of the *L* Jesus,
11. 8 Not so, *L*: for nothing common or
20 Grecians, preaching the *L* Jesus.
21 the hand of the *L* was with them:
21 believed, and turned unto the *L*.
17.24 that he is *L* of heaven and earth,
27 That they should seek the *L*, if
19. 5 baptized in the name of the *L* Jesus.
17 name of the *L* Jesus was magnified.
21.13 for the name of the *L* Jesus.
14 saying, The will of the *L* be done.
22. 8 And I answered, Who art thou, *L*?
26.15 And I said, Who art thou, *L*? And
Ro 1. 3 his Son Jesus Christ our *L*, which
6.11 God through Jesus Christ our *L*.
23 life through Jesus Christ our *L*.
8.39 God, which is in Christ Jesus our *L*.
9.28 a short work will the *L* make upon
10. 9 confess with thy mouth the *L* Jesus,
12 the same *L* over all is rich unto all
14. 6 the day, regardeth it unto the *L*;
8 whether we live, we live unto the *L*;
8 whether we die, we die unto the *L*:
9 be *L* both of the dead and living.
11 As I live, saith the *L*, every knee
1Co 1. 2 the name of Jesus Christ our *L*,
31 that glorieth, let him glory in the *L*.
2. 8 not have crucified the *L* of glory.
6.11 justified in the name of the *L* Jesus,
14 God hath both raised up the *L*, and
7.10 I command, yet not I, but the *L*,
12 But to the rest speak I, not the *L*:
32 how he may please the *L*:
10.21 Ye cannot drink the cup of the *L*,
22 Do we provoke the *L* to jealousy?
11.11 woman without the man, in the *L*.
23 That the *L* Jesus the same night
27 bread, and drink this cup of the *L*,
27 of the body and blood of the *L*.
12. 3 no man can say that Jesus is the *L*,
15.31 which I have in Christ Jesus our *L*.
47 second man is the *L* from heaven.
2Co 1. 2 and from the *L* Jesus Christ.
3.16 when it shall turn to the *L*, the vail
17 Now the *L* is that Spirit: and where
17 where the Spirit of the *L* is, there
Gal 1. 3 and from our *L* Jesus Christ,
6.14 in the cross of our *L* Jesus Christ,
17 my body the marks of the *L* Jesus.
Eph 1. 2 and from the *L* Jesus Christ.
4. 1 I therefore, the prisoner of the *L*,
5 One *L*, one faith, one baptism,
6. 1 obey your parents in the *L*: for
7 good will doing service, as to the *L*,
Php 1. 2 and from the *L* Jesus Christ.
2.11 confess that Jesus Christ is *L*, to
4. 1 and crown, so stand fast in the *L*,
5 unto all men. The *L* is at hand.
Col 1. 2 our Father and the *L* Jesus Christ.
10 That ye might walk worthy of the *L*
3.16 with grace in your hearts to the *L*.
17 do all in the name of the *L* Jesus,
23 ye do, do it heartily, as to the *L*,
1Th 1. 1 Father and in the *L* Jesus Christ:
2.15 Who both killed the *L* Jesus, and
4. 1 and exhort you by the *L* Jesus,
6 the *L* is the avenger of all such,
17 the clouds, to meet the *L* in the air:
17 and so shall we ever be with the *L*.
2Th 1. 1 our Father and the *L* Jesus Christ:
7 the *L* Jesus shall be revealed from
2. 1 the coming of our *L* Jesus Christ,
3. 1 the word of the *L* may have free
3 *L* is faithful, who shall stablish
16 *L* of peace himself give you peace
1Ti 1. 1 our Saviour, and *L* Jesus Christ,
6. 3 even the words of our *L* Jesus,
15 the King of kings, and *L* of lords;
2Ti 1. 2 the Father and Christ Jesus our *L*.
2. 7 *L* give thee understanding in all
19 The *L* knoweth them that are his.
3.11 out of them all the *L* delivered me.
4. 1 before God, and the *L* Jesus Christ,
8 which the *L*, the righteous judge,
17 *L* stood with me, and strengthened
Heb 1.10 Thou, *L*, in the beginning hast
10.16 them after those days, saith the *L*;
30 me, I will recompense, saith the *L*.
13. 6 boldly say, The *L* is my helper,
Jas 1. 1 of God and of the *L* Jesus Christ,
4.10 yourselves in the sight of the *L*,
15 that ye ought to say, If the *L* will,
5. 4 into the ears of the *L* of Sabaoth.
11 that the *L* is very pitiful, and of
14 him with oil in the name of the *L*:
15 sick, and the *L* shall raise him up;
1Pe 1. 3 and Father of our *L* Jesus Christ,
25 word of the *L* endureth for ever.
2. 3 have tasted that the *L* is gracious.
2Pe 1. 2 of God, and of Jesus our *L*,
2. 1 denying the *L* that bought them,
3. 2 the apostles of the *L* and Saviour:
8 one day is with the *L* as a thousand
9 The *L* is not slack concerning his
10 day of the *L* will come as a thief
Jude 4 and denying the only *L* God,
14 the *L* cometh with ten thousands
Rev 1. 8 and the ending, saith the *L*, which
4. 8 Holy, holy, holy, *L* God Almighty,
11 Thou art worthy, O *L*, to receive
16. 5 Thou art righteous, O *L*, which
19. 1 and power, unto the *L* our God:
6 the *L* God omnipotent reigneth.
16 King Of Kings, And *L* Of Lords.
22. 5 the *L* God giveth them light: and
20 Amen. Even so, come, *L* Jesus.

LORD'S

Gen 40. 7 him in the ward of his *l* house
44. 8 we steal out of thy *l* house silver
9 and we also will be my *l* bondmen.
16 behold, we are my *l* servants, both
18 speak a word in my *l* ears, and let
Ex 9.29 know how that the earth is the *L*.
12.11 it in haste: it is the *L* passover.
27 is the sacrifice of the *L* passover,
13. 9 the *L* law may be in thy mouth:
12 hast; the male shall be the *L*.
32.26 Who is on the *L* side? let him
35.21 they brought the *L* offering to
24 and brass brought the *L* offering:
Lev 3.16 sweet savor: all the fat is the *L*.
16. 9 goat upon which the *L* lot fell,
23. 5 month at even is the *L* passover.
27.26 which should be the *L* firstling,
26 it be ox, or sheep: it is the *L*.
Nu 11.23 Is the *L* hand waxed short?
29 all the *L* people were prophets,
18.28 the *L* heave offering to Aaron
31.37 the *L* tribute of the sheep was
38, 39 the *L* tribute was three score
40 the *L* tribute was thirty and two
41 which was the *L* heave offering,
32.10 *L* anger was kindled the same
13 the *L* anger was kindled against
Dt 10.14 of heavens is the *L* thy God,
11.17 *L* wrath be kindled against you,
15. 2 because it is called the *L* release.
32. 9 For the *L* portion is his people;
Jos 1.15 Moses the *L* servant gave you
5.15 captain of the *L* host said unto
22.19 wherein the *L* tabernacle
Jdg 11.31 Ammon, shall surely be the *L*,
1Sa 2. 8 the pillars of the earth are the *L*,
24 make the *L* people to transgress.
14. 3 son of Eli, the *L* priest in Shiloh,
16. 6 the *L* anointed is before him.
17.47 for the battle is the *L*, and he will
18.17 for me, and fight the *L* battles.
22.21 that Saul had slain the *L* priests.
24. 6 unto my master, the *L* anointed,
10 lord; for he is the *L* anointed.
26. 9 his hand against the *L* anointed,
11 hand against the *L* anointed:
16 your master, the *L* anointed.
23 hand against the *L* anointed.
2Sa 1.14 hand to destroy the *L* anointed?
16 I have slain the *L* anointed.
19.21 because he cursed the *L* anointed?
20. 6 take thou thy *l* servants, and
21. 7 *L* oath that was between them,
1Ki 18.13 an hundred men of the *L* prophets
2Ki 11.17 that they should be the *L* people;
13.17 The arrow of the *L* deliverance,
1Ch 21. 3 are they not all my *l* servants?
2Ch 7. 2 glory...had filled the *L* house.
23.16 that they should be the *L* people.
Ps 11. 4 the *L* throne is in heaven: his
22.28 For the kingdom is the *L*: and
24. 1 earth is the *L*, and the fulness
113. 3 the *L* name is to be praised.
115.16 even the heavens, are the *L*:
116.19 In the courts of the *L* house, in
118.23 This is the *L* doing; it is
137. 4 How shall we sing the *L* song in
Pr 16.11 weight and balance are the *L*:
Isa 2. 2 that the mountain of the *L* house
22.18 shall be the shame of thy *l* house.
34. 8 is the day of the *L* vengeance,
40. 2 received of the *L* hand double
42.19 and blind as the *L* servant?
44. 5 One shall say, I am the *L*; and
59. 1 the *L* hand is not shortened, that
Jer 5.10 for they are not the *L*.
7. 2 Stand in the gate of the *L* house,
13.17 *L* flock is carried away captive.
19.14 stood in the court of the *L* house;
25.17 took I the cup at the *L* hand,
26. 2 Stand in the court of the *L* house,
2 come to worship in the *L* house,
10 of the new gate of the *L* house.
27.16 the vessels of the *L* house shall
28. 3 all the vessels of the *L* house,
6 again the vessels of the *L* house,
36. 6 ears of the people in the *L* house

Jer 36. 8 words of the Lord in the *L* house.
10 of the new gate of the *L* house,
51. 6 is the time of the *L* vengeance;
7 been a golden cup in the *L* hand,
51 the sanctuaries of the *L* house.
La 2.22 day of the *L* anger none escaped
3.22 of the *L* mercies that we are not
Eze 8.14 door of the gate of the *L* house
16 the inner court of the *L* house,
10. 4 of the brightness of the *L* glory.
19 of the east gate of the *L* house;
11. 1 unto the east gate of the *L* house,
Dan 9.17 that is desolate, for the *L* sake.
Hos 9. 3 shall not dwell in the *L* land;
Joel 1. 9 priests, the *L* ministers, mourn.
Ob 21 and the kingdom shall be the *L*.
Mic 6. 2 O mountains, the *L* controversy,
9 The *L* voice crieth unto the city,
Hab 2.16 the cup of the *L* right hand shall
Zep 1. 8 pass in the day of the *L* sacrifice,
18 them in the day of the *L* wrath;
2. 2 before the day of the *L* anger
3 be hid in the day of the *L* anger.
Hag 1. 2 that the *L* house should be built.
13 spake Haggai the *L* messenger
13 in the *L* message unto the people,
2.18 the foundation of the *L* temple
Zec 14.20 pots in the *L* house shall be like
Mt 21.42 this is the *L* doing, and it is
25.18 in the earth, and hid his *l* money.
Mk 12.11 This was the *L* doing, and it is
Lk 2.26 before he had seen the *L* Christ.
12.47 that servant, which knew his *l* will,
16. 5 he called every one of his *l* debtors
Ro 14. 8 live therefore, or die, we are the *L*.
1Co 7.22 being a servant, is the *L* freeman:
10.21 cannot be partakers of the *L* table,
26 the earth is the *L*, and the fulness
28 earth is the *L*, and the fulness
11.20 this is not to eat the *L* supper.
26 do shew the *L* death till he come.
29 himself, not discerning the *L* body.
Gal 1.19 none, save James the *L* brother.
1Pe 2.13 ordinance of man for the *L* sake:
Rev 1.10 I was in the Spirit on the *L* day,

LORDS

Dt 10.17 God is God of gods, and Lord of *l*,
Ps 136. 3 O give thanks to the Lord of *l*:
Mk 6.21 birthday made a supper to his *l*,
1Co 8. 5 there be gods many, and *l* many,)
1Ti 6.15 the King of kings, and Lord of *l*;
1Pe 5. 3 as being *l* over God's heritage,
Rev 17.14 is Lord of *l*, and King of kings:
19.16 King Of Kings, And Lord Of *L*.

LORDSHIP

Mk 10.42 Gentiles exercise *l* over them;
Lk 22.25 Gentiles exercise *l* over them;

LOSE

Jdg 18.25 and thou *l* thy life, with the lives
1Ki 18. 5 alive, that we *l* not all the beasts.
Job 31.39 the owners thereof to *l* their life:
Pr 23. 8 vomit up, and *l* thy sweet words.
Ec 3. 6 A time to get, and a time to *l*; a
Mt 10.39 He that findeth his life shall *l* it:
42 he shall in no wise *l* his reward.
16.25 will save his life shall *l* it:
25 will *l* his life for my sake shall find
26 whole world, and *l* his own soul?
Mk 8.35 will save his life shall *l* it;
35 shall *l* his life for my sake and
36 whole world, and *l* his own soul?
9.41 unto you, he shall not *l* his reward.
Lk 9.24 will save his life shall *l* it:
24 will *l* his life for my sake, the
25 gain the whole world, and *l* himself,
15. 4 hundred sheep, if he *l* one of them,
8 if she *l* one piece, doth not light a
17.33 shall seek to save his life shall *l* it;
33 shall *l* his life shall preserve it.
Jn 6.39 hath given me I should *l* nothing,
12.25 He that loveth his life shall *l* it;
2Jn 8 *l* not those things which we have

LOSETH

Mt 10.39 *l* his life for my sake shall find it.

LOSS

Gen 31.39 not unto thee; I bare the *l* of it;
Ex 21.19 he shall pay for the *l* of his time,
Isa 47. 8 shall I know the *l* of children:
9 in one day, the *l* of children, and
Ac 27.21 to have gained this harm and *l*.
22 be no *l* of any man's life among
1Co 3.15 shall be burned, he shall suffer *l*:
Php 3. 7 me, those I counted *l* for Christ.
8 I count all things but *l* for the
8 I have suffered the *l* of all things,

LOST

Ex 22. 9 or for any manner of *l* thing, which
Lev 6. 3 Or have found that which was *l*, and
4 keep, or the *l* thing which he found,
Nu 6.12 days that were before shall be *l*,
Dt 22. 3 with all *l* thing of thy brother's,
3 which he hath *l*, and thou hast
1Sa 9. 3 the asses of Kish Saul's father were *l*.
20 as for thine asses that were *l* three
1Ki 20.25 like the army that thou hast *l*,
Ps 119.176 I have gone astray like a *l* sheep;
Isa 49.20 have, after thou hast *l* the other,
21 seeing I have *l* my children, and
Jer 50. 6 My people hath been *l* sheep: their
Eze 19. 5 she had waited, and her hope was *l*,
34. 4 have ye sought that which was *l*;
16 I will seek that which was *l*, and
37.11 bones are dried, and our hope is *l*:
Mt 5.13 but if the salt have *l* his savor,
10. 6 the *l* sheep of the house of Israel.
15.24 the *l* sheep of the house of Israel.
18.11 is come to save that which was *l*.
Mk 9.50 if the salt have *l* his saltness,
Lk 14.34 but if the salt have *l* his savor,
15. 4 and go after that which is *l*, until
6 I have found my sheep which was *l*.
9 I have found the piece which I had *l*.
24 alive again; he was *l*, and is found.
32 alive again; and was *l*, and is found.
19.10 to seek and to save that which was *l*.
Jn 6.12 that remain, that nothing be *l*.
17.12 and none of them is *l*, but the son
18. 9 which thou gavest me have I *l* none.
2Co 4. 3 be hid, it is hid to them that are *l*:

LOT

Gen 11.27 and Haran; and Haran begat *L*.
12. 4 and *L* went with him: and Abram
13. 1 and *L* with him, into the south,
8 Abram said unto *L*, Let there be no
10 *L* lifted up his eyes, and beheld all
11 Then *L* chose him all the plain of
12 *L* dwelled in the cities of the plain,
19. 1 and *L* sat in the gate of Sodom:
1 and *L* seeing them rose up to meet
12 men said unto *L*, Hast thou here
14 *L* went…and spake unto his sons
15 then the angels hastened *L*, saying,
18 And *L* said unto them, Oh, not so,
29 the cities in the which *L* dwelt.
30 *L* went up out of Zoar, and dwelt in
36 both the daughters of *L* with child
Ps 83. 8 they have holpen the children of *L*
Lk 17.28 also as it was in the days of *L*;
29 same day that *L* went out of Sodom

LOT'S

Gen 13. 7 and the herdman of *L* cattle:
Lk 17.32 Remember *L* wife.

LOTS

Lev 16. 8 shall cast *l* upon the two goats;
Jos 18. 6 cast *l* for you here before the Lord
8 here cast *l* for you before the Lord
10 Joshua cast *l* for them in Shiloh
1Sa 14.42 Cast *l* between me and Jonathan my
1Ch 24.31 cast *l* over against their brethren
25. 8 they cast *l*, ward against ward, as
26.13 they cast *l*, as well the small as the
14 son, a wise counsellor, they cast *l*;
Neh 10.34 we cast the *l* among the priests, the
11. 1 the rest of the people also cast *l*, to
Ps 22.18 them, and cast *l* upon my vesture.
Joel 3. 3 they have cast *l* for my people; and
Ob 11 gates, and cast *l* upon Jerusalem,
Jon 1. 7 Come, and let us cast *l*, that we
7 So they cast *l*, and the lot fell upon
Na 3.10 they cast *l* for her honorable men,
Mt 27.35 parted his garments, casting *l*:
35 upon my vesture did they cast *l*.
Mk 15.24 garments, casting *l* upon them,
Lk 23.34 they parted his raiment, and cast *l*.
Jn 19.24 Let us not rend it, but cast *l* for it,
24 and for my vesture they did cast *l*.
Ac 1.26 they gave forth their *l*; and the lot

LOUD

Gen 39.14 me, and I cried with a *l* voice:
Ex 19.16 voice of the trumpet exceeding *l*;
Dt 27.14 the men of Israel with a *l* voice,
1Sa 28.12 Samuel, she cried with a *l* voice:
2Sa 15.23 all the country wept with a *l* voice,
19. 4 and the king cried with a *l* voice,
1Ki 8.55 congregation of Israel with a *l* voice,
2Ki 18.28 cried with a *l* voice in the Jews'
2Ch 15.14 sware unto the Lord with a *l* voice,
20.19 Lord God of Israel with a *l* voice
30.21 singing with *l* instruments unto
32.18 cried with a *l* voice in the Jews'
Ezr 3.12 their eyes, wept with a *l* voice;
13 the people shouted with a *l* shout,
10.12 answered and said with a *l* voice,
Neh 9. 4 cried with a *l* voice unto the Lord
12.42 the singers sang *l*, with Jezrahiah
Est 4. 1 cried with a *l* and a bitter cry;
Ps 33. 3 song: play skilfully with a *l* noise.
98. 4 make a *l* noise, and rejoice, and sing
150. 5 Praise him upon the *l* cymbals:
Pr 7.11 (She is *l* and stubborn; her feet
27.14 blesseth his friend with a *l* voice,
Isa 36.13 cried with a *l* voice in the Jews'
Eze 8.18 they cry in mine ears with a *l* voice,
9. 1 also in mine ears with a *l* voice,
11.13 my face, and cried with a *l* voice,
Mt 27.46 Jesus cried with a *l* voice, saying,
50 he had cried again with a *l* voice,
Mk 1.26 torn him, and cried with a *l* voice,
5. 7 And cried with a *l* voice, and said,
15.34 Jesus cried with a *l* voice, saying,
37 And Jesus cried with a *l* voice, and
Lk 1.42 she spake out with a *l* voice, and
4.33 devil, and cried out with a *l* voice,
8.28 and with a *l* voice said, What have
17.15 and with a *l* voice glorified God,
19.37 and praise God with a *l* voice for
23.23 they were instant with *l* voices,
46 Jesus had cried with a *l* voice,
Jn 11.43 he cried with a *l* voice, Lazarus,
Ac 7.57 Then they cried out with a *l* voice,
60 and cried with a *l* voice, Lord, lay
8. 7 unclean spirits, crying with *l* voice,
14.10 Said with a *l* voice, Stand upright
16.28 Paul cried with a *l* voice, saying,
26.24 Festus said with a *l* voice, Paul,
Rev 5. 2 angel proclaiming with a *l* voice,
12 Saying with a *l* voice, Worthy is
6.10 they cried with a *l* voice, saying,
7. 2 with a *l* voice to the four angels,
10 and cried with a *l* voice, saying,
8.13 saying with a *l* voice, Woe, woe,
10. 3 cried with a *l* voice, as when a lion

Lot flees Sodom with his family (Gen 19) in a panel from the 16th-century Raphael frescoes in the Vatican.

12.10 I heard a *l* voice saying in heaven,
14. 7 Saying with a *l* voice, Fear God,
9 saying with a *l* voice, If any man
15 crying with a *l* voice to him that
18 cried with a *l* voice to him that had
19.17 he cried with a *l* voice, saying to all

LOVE

Gen 27. 4 make me savory meat, such as I *l*,
29.20 few days, for the *l* he had to her.
32 therefore my husband will *l* me.
Ex 20. 6 unto thousands of them that *l* me,
21. 5 I *l* my master, my wife, and my
Lev 19.18 but thou shalt *l* thy neighbor as
34 and thou shalt *l* him as thyself; for
Dt 5.10 unto thousands of them that *l* me
6. 5 thou shalt *l* the Lord thy God with
7. 7 Lord did not set his *l* upon you,
9 mercy with them that *l* him and
13 he will *l* thee, and bless thee, and
10.12 walk in all his ways, and to *l* him,
15 a delight in thy fathers to *l* them,
19 *L* ye therefore the stranger: for ye
11. 1 Therefore thou shalt *l* the Lord thy
13 you this day, to *l* the Lord your God,
22 to *l* the Lord your God, to walk in
13. 3 whether ye *l* the Lord your God
19. 9 to *l* the Lord thy God, and to walk
30. 6 to *l* the Lord thy God with all thine
16 thee this day to *l* the Lord thy God,
20 thou mayest *l* the Lord thy God,
Jos 22. 5 to *l* the Lord your God, and to walk
23.11 selves, that ye *l* the Lord your God.
Jdg 5.31 let them that *l* him be as the sun
16.15 How canst thou say, I *l* thee, when
1Sa 18.22 in thee, and all his servants *l* thee:
2Sa 1.26 me: thy *l* to me was wonderful,
26 wonderful, passing the *l* of women.
13. 4 Amnon said unto him, I *l* Tamar,
15 greater than the *l* wherewith he had
1Ki 11. 2 Solomon clave unto these in *l*.
2Ch 19. 2 and *l* them that hate the Lord?
Neh 1. 5 and mercy for them that *l* him and
Ps 4. 2 how long will ye *l* vanity, and seek
5.11 let them also that *l* thy name be
18. 1 I will *l* thee, O Lord, my strength.
31.23 O *l* the Lord, all ye his saints: for
40.16 let such as *l* thy salvation say
69.36 they that *l* his name shall dwell
70. 4 and let such as *l* thy salvation say
91.14 Because he hath set his *l* upon me,
97.10 Ye that *l* the Lord, hate evil: he
109. 4 For my *l* they are my adversaries:
5 evil for good, and hatred for my *l*.
116. 1 I *l* the Lord, because he hath heard
119.97 O how *l* I thy law! it is my
113 vain thoughts: but thy law do I *l*.
119 dross: therefore I *l* thy testimonies.
127 Therefore I *l* thy commandments
132 to do unto those that *l* thy name.
159 Consider how I *l* thy precepts:
163 and abhor lying: but thy law do I *l*.
165 peace have they which *l* thy law:
167 and I *l* them exceedingly.
122. 6 they shall prosper that *l* thee.
145.20 Lord preserveth all them that *l* him:
Pr 1.22 ye simple ones, will ye *l* simplicity?
4. 6 thee: *l* her, and she shall keep thee.
5.19 thou ravished always with her *l*.
7.18 let us take our fill of *l* until the
8.17 I *l* them that *l* me; and those that
21 cause those that *l* me to inherit
36 soul: all they that hate me *l* death.
9. 8 a wise man, and he will *l* thee.
10.12 up strifes: but *l* covereth all sins.
15.17 is a dinner of herbs where *l* is, than
16.13 and they *l* him that speaketh right.
17. 9 covereth a transgression seeketh *l*;
18.21 and they that *l* it shall eat the fruit
20.13 *L* not sleep, lest thou come to
27. 5 rebuke is better than secret *l*.
Ec 3. 8 A time to *l*, and a time to hate; a
9. 1 man knoweth either *l* or hatred by
6 Also their *l*, and their hatred, and
SS 1. 2 for thy *l* is better than wine.
3 therefore do the virgins *l* thee.
4 remember thy *l* more than wine:
4 than wine: the upright *l* thee.
9 I have compared thee, O my *l*, to
15 Behold, thou art fair, my *l*; behold,
2. 2 so is my *l* among the daughters.
4 and his banner over me was *l*.
5 me with apples: for I am sick of *l*.
7 up, nor awake my *l*, till he please.
10 Rise up, my *l*, my fair one, and
13 Arise, my *l*, my fair one, and come
3. 5 up, nor awake my *l*, till he please.
10 midst thereof being paved with *l*,
4. 1 Behold, thou art fair, my *l*;
7 Thou art all fair, my *l*; there is no
10 How fair is thy *l*, my sister, my
10 how much better is thy *l* than wine!
5. 2 to me, that my sister, my *l*, my dove,
8 that ye tell him, I am sick of *l*.
6. 4 Thou art beautiful, O my *l*, as
7. 6 and how pleasant art thou, O *l*, for
8. 4 that ye stir not up, nor awake my *l*,
6 for *l* is strong as death; jealousy
7 Many waters cannot quench *l*,
7 all the substance of his house for *l*,
Isa 38.17 but thou hast in *l* to my soul
56. 6 to *l* the name of the Lord, to be
61. 8 For I the Lord *l* judgment, I hate
63. 9 in his *l* and in his pity he redeemed
66.10 be glad with her, all ye that *l* her:
Jer 2. 2 the *l* of thine espousals, when thou
33 trimmest thou thy way to seek *l*?
5.31 and my people *l* to have it so: and
31. 3 loved thee with an everlasting *l*:
Eze 16. 8 behold, thy time was the time of *l*;
23.11 more corrupt in her inordinate *l*
17 came to her into the bed of *l*, and
33.31 their mouth they shew much *l*,
Dan 1. 9 Daniel into favor and tender *l*
9. 4 and mercy to them that *l* him,
Hos 3. 1 *l* a woman beloved of her friend,
1 according to the *l* of the Lord
1 other gods, and *l* flagons of wine.
4.18 her rulers with shame do *l*, Give
9.15 mine house, I will *l* them no more:
11. 4 cords of a man, with bands of *l*:
14. 4 backsliding, I will *l* them freely:
Am 5.15 Hate the evil, and *l* the good, and
Mic 3. 2 Who hate the good, and *l* the evil;
6. 8 but to do justly, and to *l* mercy,
Zep 3.17 he will rest in his *l*, he will joy over
Zec 8.17 *l* no false oath: for all these are
19 therefore *l* the truth and peace.
Mt 5.43 Thou shalt *l* thy neighbor, and hate
44 But I say unto you, *L* your enemies,
46 For if ye *l* them which *l* you, what
6. 5 for they *l* to pray standing in the
24 he will hate the one, and *l* the other;
19.19 shalt *l* thy neighbor as thyself.
22.37 Thou shalt *l* the Lord thy God with
39 shalt *l* thy neighbor as thyself.
23. 6 *l* the uppermost rooms at feasts,
24.12 the *l* of many shall wax cold.
Mk 12.30 thou shalt *l* the Lord thy God with
31 shalt *l* thy neighbor as thyself.
33 to *l* him with all the heart, and with
33 and to *l* his neighbor as himself,
38 the scribes, which *l* to go in long
38 *l* salutations in the marketplaces,
Lk 6.27 *L* your enemies, do good to them
32 For if ye *l* them which *l* you, what
32 for sinners also *l* those that *l* them.
35 But *l* ye your enemies, and do good,
7.42 which of them will *l* him most?
10.27 Thou shalt *l* the Lord thy God with
11.42 pass over judgment and the *l* of God:
43 for ye *l* the uppermost seats in the
16.13 he will hate the one, and *l* the other;
20.46 and *l* greetings in the markets,
Jn 5.42 that ye have not the *l* of God in you.
8.42 were your Father, ye would *l* me:
10.17 Therefore doth my Father *l* me,
13.34 give unto you, That ye *l* one another;
34 loved you, that ye also *l* one another.
35 disciples, if ye have *l* one to another.
14.15 If ye *l* me, keep my commandments.
21 and I will *l* him, and will manifest
23 a man *l* me, he will keep my words:

BIBLICAL THEMES

LOVE

Love thy neighbor as thyself. Lev 19.18

Thou shalt love the Lord thy God with all thine heart, and with all thy soul, and with all thy might. Dt 6.5

Because the Lord loved you . . . the Lord brought you out with a mighty hand, and redeemed you out of the house of bondmen. . . . the faithful God, which keepeth covenant and mercy with them that love him. Dt 7.8-9

I am distressed for thee, my brother Jonathan: very pleasant hast thou been unto me: thy love to me was wonderful, passing the love of women. 2Sa 1.26

O God, thou art my God; early will I seek thee: my soul thirsteth for thee, my flesh longeth for thee in a dry and thirsty land, where no water is. . . . Because thy lovingkindness is better than life, my lips shall praise thee. Ps 63.1, 3

Hatred stirreth up strifes: but love covereth all sins. Pr 10.12

A time to love, and a time to hate. Ec 3.8

I am my beloved's, and his desire is toward me. Come, my beloved, let us go forth into the field. . . . Let us get up early to the vineyards; let us see if the vine flourish, whether the tender grape appear, and the pomegranates bud forth: there will I give thee my loves. SS 7.10-12

Love is strong as death; jealousy is cruel as the grave: the coals thereof are coals of fire, which hath a most vehement flame. Many waters cannot quench love, neither can the floods drown it. SS 8.6-7

In all their affliction he was afflicted . . . in his love and in his pity he redeemed them; and he bare them, and carried them all the days of old. Isa 63.9

I drew them with cords of a man, with bands of love. Hos 11.4

I say unto you, Love your enemies. Mt 5.44

God so loved the world, that he gave his only begotten Son, that whosoever believeth in him should not perish, but have everlasting life. Jn 3.16

When Jesus knew that his hour was come that he should depart out of this world unto the Father, having loved his own which were in the world, he loved them unto the end. . . . He riseth from supper, and laid aside his garments; and took a towel . . . and began to wash the disciples' feet. Jn 13.1, 4-5

Greater love hath no man than this, that a man lay down his life for his friends. Ye are my friends. Jn 15.13-14

Charity suffereth long, and is kind; charity envieth not; charity vaunteth not itself . . . is not easily provoked, thinketh no evil; rejoiceth not in iniquity, but rejoiceth in the truth; beareth all things, believeth all things, hopeth all things, endureth all things. Charity never faileth. 1Co 13.4-8

The life which I now live in the flesh I live by the faith of the Son of God, who loved me, and gave himself for me. Gal 2.20

For this cause I bow my knees unto the Father . . . that ye, being rooted and grounded in love, may be able . . . to know the love of Christ, which passeth knowledge. Eph 3.14, 17-19

Beloved, let us love one another: for love is of God; and every one that loveth is born of God, and knoweth God. He that loveth not knoweth not God; for God is love. 1Jn 4.7-8

Herein is love, not that we loved God, but that he loved us. 1Jn 4. 10

Jn 14.23 my Father will *l* him, and we will
31 may know that I *l* the Father; and
15. 9 I loved you: continue ye in my *l*.
10 ye shall abide in my *l*; even as I
10 commandments, and abide in his *l*.
12 That ye *l* one another, as I have
13 Greater *l* hath no man than this,
17 command you, that ye *l* one another.
19 world, the world would *l* his own:
17.26 *l* wherewith thou hast loved me
21.15, 16, 17 thou knowest that I *l* thee.
Ro 5. 5 because the *l* of God is shed abroad
8 God commendeth his *l* toward us,
8.28 together for good to them that *l* God,
35 separate us from the *l* of Christ?
39 able to separate us from the *l* of God,
12. 9 Let *l* be without dissimulation.
10 one to another with brotherly *l*;
13. 8 any thing, but to *l* one another:
9 Thou shalt *l* thy neighbor as
10 *L* worketh no ill to his neighbor:
10 therefore *l* is the fulfilling of the law.
15.30 sake, and for the *l* of the Spirit,
1Co 2. 9 hath prepared for them that *l* him.
4.21 come unto you with a rod, or in *l*;
8. 3 if any man *l* God, the same is known
16.22 If any man *l* not the Lord Jesus
24 My *l* be with you all in Christ Jesus.
2Co 2. 4 ye might know the *l* which I have
8 would confirm your *l* toward him.
5.14 For the *l* of Christ constraineth us;
6. 6 by the Holy Ghost, by *l* unfeigned,
8. 7 in all diligence, and in your *l* to us.
8 and to prove the sincerity of your *l*.
24 the churches, the proof of your *l*,
11.11 because I *l* you not? God knoweth.
12.15 though the more abundantly I *l* you,
13.11 God of *l* and peace shall be with you.
14 the *l* of God, and the communion
Gal 5. 6 but faith which worketh by *l*.
13 flesh, but by *l* serve one another.
14 shalt *l* thy neighbor as thyself.
22 the fruit of the Spirit is *l*, joy, peace,
Eph 1. 4 and without blame before him in *l*:
15 Jesus, and *l* unto all the saints.
2. 4 great *l* wherewith he loved us.
3.17 ye, being rooted and grounded in *l*,
19 And to know the *l* of Christ, which
4. 2 forbearing one another in *l*;
15 speaking the truth in *l*, may grow
16 body unto the edifying of itself in *l*.
5. 2 And walk in *l*, as Christ also hath
25 Husbands, *l* your wives, even as
28 So ought men to *l* their wives as
33 so *l* his wife even as himself; and
6.23 be to the brethren, and *l* with faith,
24 with all them that *l* our Lord Jesus
Php 1. 9 your *l* may abound yet more and
17 the other of *l*, knowing that I am
2. 1 in Christ, if any comfort of *l*, if any
2 be likeminded, having the same *l*,
Col 1. 4 and of the *l* which ye have to all the
8 Who also declared unto us your *l* in
2. 2 comforted, being knit together in *l*,
3.19 Husbands, *l* your wives, and be not
1Th 1. 3 your work of faith, and labor of *l*,
3.12 abound in *l* one toward another,
4. 9 as touching brotherly *l* ye need
9 are taught of God to *l* one another.
5. 8 on the breastplate of faith and *l*.
13 highly in *l* for their work's sake.
2Th 2.10 they received not the *l* of the truth,
3. 5 direct your hearts into the *l* of God,
1Ti 1.14 faith and *l* which is in Christ Jesus.
6.10 *l* of money is the root of all evil:
11 faith, *l*, patience, meekness.
2Ti 1. 7 and of *l*, and of a sound mind.
13 faith and *l* which is in Christ Jesus.
4. 8 all them also that *l* his appearing.
Tit 2. 4 to be sober, to *l* their husbands,
4 to be sober,...to *l* their children,
3. 4 that the kindness and *l* of God
15 Greet them that *l* us in the faith.
Phm 5 Hearing of thy *l* and faith, which
7 great joy and consolation in thy *l*,
Heb 6.10 to forget your work and labor of *l*,
10.24 to provoke unto *l* and to good works:
13. 1 Let brotherly *l* continue.
Jas 1.12 hath promised to them that *l* him.
2. 5 hath promised to them that *l* him?
8 shalt *l* thy neighbor as thyself,
1Pe 1. 8 Whom having not seen, ye *l*; in
22 unto unfeigned *l* of the brethren,
22 ye *l* one another with a pure heart
2.17 *L* the brotherhood. Fear God.
3. 8 one to another, *l* as brethren, be
10 For he that will *l* life, and see good
1Jn 2. 5 him verily is the *l* of God perfected:
15 *L* not the world, neither the things
15 If any man *l* the world,
15 the *l* of the Father is not in him.
3. 1 what manner of *l* the Father hath
11 that we should *l* one another.
14 unto life, because we *l* the brethren.
16 Hereby perceive we the *l* of God,
17 how dwelleth the *l* of God in him?
18 little children, let us not *l* in word,

23 Son Jesus Christ, and *l* one another,
4. 7 Beloved, let us *l* one another:
7 for *l* is of God; and every one that
8 not knoweth not God; for God is *l*.
9 manifested the *l* of God toward us,
10 Herein is *l*, not that we loved God,
11 us, we ought also to *l* one another.
12 If we *l* one another, God dwelleth in
12 in us, and his *l* is perfected in us.
16 believed the *l* that God hath to us.
16 God is *l*; and he that dwelleth in
16 that dwelleth in *l* dwelleth in God,
17 Herein is our *l* made perfect, that
18 There is no fear in *l*; but perfect
18 but perfect *l* casteth out fear:
18 that feareth is not made perfect in *l*.
19 We *l* him, because he first loved us.
20 If a man say, I *l* God, and hateth
20 how can he *l* God whom he hath not
21 who loveth God *l* his brother also.
5. 2 know that we *l* the children of God,
2 when we *l* God, and keep his
3 this is the *l* of God, that we keep
2Jn 1 her children, whom I *l* in the truth;
3 the Son of the Father, in truth and *l*.
5 beginning, that we *l* one another.
6 And this is *l*, that we walk after his
3Jn 1 unto...Gaius, whom I *l* in the truth.
Jude 2 Mercy unto you, and peace, and *l*,
21 Keep yourselves in the *l* of God,
Rev 2. 4 because thou hast left thy first *l*.
3.19 As many as I *l*, I rebuke and

LOVED

Gen 24.67 she became his wife; and he *l* her:
25.28 And Isaac *l* Esau, because he did
28 his venison: but Rebekah *l* Jacob.
27.14 savory meat, such as his father *l*.
29.18 Jacob *l* Rachel; and said, I will
30 he *l* also Rachel more than Leah,
34. 3 he *l* the damsel, and spake kindly
37. 3 Now Israel *l* Joseph more than all
4 saw that their father *l* him more
Dt 4.37 because he *l* thy fathers, therefore
7. 8 But because the Lord *l* you, and
23. 5 because the Lord thy God *l* thee.
33. 3 Yea, he *l* the people; all his
Jdg 16. 4 *l* a woman in the valley of Sorek,
1Sa 1. 5 he *l* Hannah: but the Lord had
16.21 before him: and he *l* him greatly;
18. 1 and Jonathan *l* him as his own soul.
3 because he *l* him as his own soul.
16 But all Israel and Judah *l* David,
20 Michal Saul's daughter *l* David:
28 that Michal Saul's daughter *l* him.
20.17 to swear again, because he *l* him:
17 for he *l* him as he...his own soul.
17 for he...him as he *l* his own soul.
2Sa 12.24 name Solomon: and the Lord *l* him.
13. 1 and Amnon the son of David *l* her.
15 the love wherewith he had *l* her.
1Ki 3. 3 And Solomon *l* the Lord, walking
10. 9 because the Lord *l* Israel for ever,
11. 1 Solomon *l* many strange women,
2Ch 2.11 Because the Lord hath *l* his people,
9. 8 thy God: because thy God *l* Israel,
11.21 And Rehoboam *l* Maachah the
26.10 and in Carmel: for he *l* husbandry.
Est 2.17 And the king *l* Esther above all the
Job 19.19 they whom I *l* are turned against
Ps 26. 8 Lord, I have *l* the habitation of thy
47. 4 the excellency of Jacob whom he *l*.
78.68 Judah, the mount Zion which he *l*.
109.17 As he *l* cursing, so let it come unto
119.47 thy commandments, which I have *l*.
48 thy commandments, which I have *l*;
Isa 43. 4 been honorable, and I have *l* thee:
48.14 The Lord hath *l* him: he will do his
Jer 2.25 I have *l* strangers, and after them
8. 2 host of heaven, whom they have *l*,
14.10 Thus have they *l* to wander, they
31. 3 I have *l* thee with an everlasting
Eze 16.37 all them that thou hast *l*, with all
Hos 9. 1 *l* a reward upon every cornfloor.
10 were according as they *l*.
11. 1 Israel was a child, then I *l* him, and
Mal 1. 2 I have *l* you, saith the Lord.
2 Yet ye say, Wherein hast thou *l* us?
2 saith the Lord: yet I *l* Jacob,
2.11 the holiness of the Lord which he *l*,
Mk 10.21 Jesus beholding him *l* him, and said
Lk 7.47 many, are forgiven; for she *l* much:
Jn 3.16 For God so *l* the world, that he
19 men *l* darkness rather than light,
11. 5 Now Jesus *l* Martha, and her sister,
36 the Jews, Behold how he *l* him!
12.43 they *l* the praise of men more than
13. 1 having *l* his own which were in the
1 the world, he *l* them unto the end.
23 one of his disciples, whom Jesus *l*.
34 as I have *l* you, that ye also love one
14.21 loveth me shall be *l* of my Father,
28 If ye *l* me, ye would rejoice, because
15. 9 As the Father hath *l* me, so have I
9 me, so have I *l* you: continue ye in
12 ye love one another, as I have *l* you.
16.27 because ye have *l* me, and have
17.23 and hast *l* them, as thou hast *l* me.
26 the love wherewith thou hast *l* me
19.26 the disciple standing by, whom he *l*,
20. 2 the other disciple, whom Jesus *l*,
21. 7 that disciple whom Jesus *l* saith
20 the disciple whom Jesus *l* following;
Ro 8.37 conquerors through him that *l* us.
9.13 As it is written, Jacob have I *l*, but
2Co 12.15 abundantly I love you, the less I be *l*.
Gal 2.20 faith of the Son of God, who *l* me,
Eph 2. 4 his great love wherewith he *l* us,
5. 2 in love, as Christ also hath *l* us,
25 even as Christ also *l* the church,
2Th 2.16 even our Father, which hath *l* us,
2Ti 4.10 me, having *l* this present world,
Heb 1. 9 hast *l* righteousness, and hated
2Pe 2.15 who *l* the wages of unrighteousness;
1Jn 4.10 Herein is love, not that we *l* God,
10 but that he *l* us, and sent his Son to
11 Beloved, if God so *l* us, we ought
19 We love him, because he first *l* us.
Rev 1. 5 Unto him that *l* us, and washed us
3. 9 feet, and to know that I have *l* thee.
12.11 they *l* not their lives unto the death.

LOVEDST

Isa 57. 8 *l* their bed where thou sawest it.
Jn 17.24 *l* me before the foundation of the

LOVELY

2Sa 1.23 and Jonathan were *l* and pleasant
SS 5.16 sweet: yea, he is altogether *l*.
Eze 33.32 art unto them as a very *l* song of
Php 4. 8 are pure, whatsoever things are *l*,

LOVER

1Ki 5. 1 for Hiram was ever a *l* of David.
Ps 88.18 *L* and friend hast thou put far from
Tit 1. 8 But a *l* of hospitality,...of good
8 a *l* of good men, sober, just, holy,

LOVERS

Ps 38.11 My *l* and my friends stand aloof
Jer 3. 1 played the harlot with many *l*;
4.30 thy *l* will despise thee, they will
22.20 for all thy *l* are destroyed.
22 and thy *l* shall go into captivity:
30.14 All thy *l* have forgotten thee; they
La 1. 2 among all her *l* she hath none to
19 I called for my *l*, but they deceived
Eze 16.33 but thou givest thy gifts to all thy *l*,
36 through thy whoredoms with thy *l*,
37 therefore I will gather all thy *l*,
23. 5 doted on her *l*, on the Assyrians
9 delivered her into the hand of her *l*,
22 I will raise up thy *l* against thee,
Hos 2. 5 I will go after my *l*, that give me my
7 she shall follow after her *l*, but she
10 her lewdness in the sight of her *l*,
12 rewards that my *l* have given me:
13 she went after her *l*, and forgat me,
8. 9 by himself: Ephraim hath hired *l*.
2Ti 3. 2 men shall be *l* of their own selves,
4 highminded, *l* of pleasures more
4 of pleasures more than *l* of God;

LOVE'S

Phm 9 for *l* sake I rather beseech thee,

LOVEST

Gen 22. 2 thine only son Isaac, whom thou *l*,
Jdg 14.16 dost but hate me, and *l* me not:
2Sa 19. 6 In that thou *l* thine enemies, and
Ps 45. 7 Thou *l* righteousness, and hatest
52. 3 Thou *l* evil more than good; and
4 Thou *l* all devouring words, O thou
Ec 9. 9 joyfully with the wife whom thou *l*
Jn 11. 3 behold, he whom thou *l* is sick.
21.15 Jonas, *l* thou me more than these?
16, 17 Simon, son of Jonas, *l* thou me?
17 him the third time, *L* thou me?

LOVETH

Gen 27. 9 meat for thy father, such as he *l*:
44.20 of his mother, and his father *l* him.
Dt 10.18 *l* the stranger, in giving him food
15.16 because he *l* thee and thine house,
Ru 4.15 thy daughter in law, which *l* thee,
Ps 11. 5 him that *l* violence his soul hateth.
7 the righteous Lord *l* righteousness;
33. 5 He *l* righteousness and judgment:
34.12 that desireth life, and *l* many days,
37.28 the Lord *l* judgment, and forsaketh
87. 2 The Lord *l* the gates of Zion more
99. 4 king's strength also *l* judgment;
119.140 pure: therefore thy servant *l* it.
146. 8 down: the Lord *l* the righteous:
Pr 3.12 for whom the Lord *l* he correcteth;
12. 1 Whoso *l* instruction *l* knowledge:
13.24 that *l* him chasteneth him betimes.
15. 9 but he *l* him that followeth after
12 A scorner *l* not one that reproveth
17.17 friend *l* at all times, and a brother
19 He *l* trangression that *l* strife:
19. 8 that getteth wisdom *l* his own soul:
21.17 that *l* pleasure shall be a poor man:
17 that *l* wine and oil shall not be rich.
22.11 He that *l* pureness of heart, for the
29. 3 Whoso *l* wisdom rejoiceth his
Ec 5.10 that *l* silver shall not be satisfied
10 he that *l* abundance with increase:
SS 1. 7 Tell me, O thou whom my soul *l*,
3. 1 bed I sought him whom my soul *l*:
2 I will seek him whom my soul *l*:
3 I said, Saw ye him whom my soul *l*?
4 but I found him whom my soul *l*:
Isa 1.23 every one *l* gifts, and followeth after
Hos 10.11 taught, and *l* to tread out the corn;
12. 7 are in his hand: he *l* to oppress.
Mt 10.37 *l* father or mother more than me
37 *l* son or daughter more than me
Lk 7. 5 he *l* our nation, and he hath built
47 little is forgiven, the same *l* little.
Jn 3.35 Father *l* the Son, and hath given
5.20 Father *l* the Son, and sheweth
12.25 He that *l* his life shall lose it; and
14.21 keepeth them, he it is that *l* me:
21 *l* me shall be loved by my Father,
24 *l* me not keepeth not my sayings:
16.27 the Father himself *l* you, because
Ro 13. 8 that *l* another hath fulfilled the law.
2Co 9. 7 necessity: for God *l* a cheerful giver.
Eph 5.28 bodies. He that *l* his wife *l* himself.
Heb 12. 6 For whom the Lord *l* he chasteneth,
1Jn 2.10 *l* his brother abideth in the light,
3.10 neither he that *l* not his brother.

1Jn 3.14 *l* not his brother abideth in death.
4. 7 and every one that *l* is born of God,
8 He that *l* not knoweth not God; for
20 *l* not his brother whom he hath seen,
21 he who *l* God love his brother also.
5. 1 and every one that *l* him that begat
1 *l* him also that is begotten of him.
3Jn 9 *l* to have the preeminence among
Rev 22.15 and whosoever *l* and maketh a lie.

LOVINGKINDNESS
Ps 17. 7 Shew thy marvellous *l*, O thou
26. 3 For thy *l* is before mine eyes: and
36. 7 How excellent is thy *l*, O God!
10 continue thy *l* unto them that know
40.10 I have not concealed thy *l* and thy
11 let thy *l* and thy truth continually
42. 8 Yet the Lord will command his *l*
48. 9 We have thought of thy *l*, O God,
51. 1 upon me, O God, according to thy *l*:
63. 3 Because thy *l* is better than life,
69.16 Hear me, O Lord; for thy *l* is good:
88.11 Shall thy *l* be declared in the grave?
89.33 my *l* will I not utterly take from
92. 2 To shew forth thy *l* in the morning,
103. 4 crowneth thee with *l* and tender
107.43 shall understand the *l* of the Lord.
119.88 Quicken me after thy *l*; so shall I
149 my voice according unto thy *l*:
159 me, O Lord, according to thy *l*.
138. 2 name for thy *l* and for thy truth:
143. 8 me to hear thy *l* in the morning;
Jer 9.24 I am the Lord which exercise *l*,
16. 5 saith the Lord, even *l* and mercies.
31. 3 therefore with *l* have I drawn thee.
32.18 Thou shewest *l* unto thousands,
Hos 2.19 judgment, and in *l*, and in mercies.

LOVINGKINDNESSES
Ps 25. 6 thy tender mercies and thy *l*;
89.49 Lord, where are thy former *l*,
Isa 63. 7 I will mention the *l* of the Lord,
7 according to the multitude of his *l*.

LOW
Jdg 11.35 thou hast brought me very *l*, and
Job 5.11 To set up on high those that be *l*;
24.24 but are gone and brought *l*; they
40.12 that is proud, and bring him *l*:
Ps 62. 9 Surely men of *l* degree are vanity,
107.39 they are minished and brought *l*
116. 6 I was brought *l*, and he helped me.
136.23 remembered us in our *l* estate:
142. 6 my cry; for I am brought very *l*:
Pr 29.23 A man's pride shall bring him *l*:
Ec 12. 4 the sound of the grinding is *l*, and
Isa 26. 5 high; the lofty city, he layeth it *l*;
5 he layeth it *l*, even to the ground;
Eze 21.26 exalt him that is *l*, and abase him
Lk 1.48 hath regarded the *l* estate of his
52 and exalted them of *l* degree.
3. 5 and hill shall be brought *l*;
Ro 12.16 but condescend to men of *l* estate.
Jas 1. 9 brother of *l* degree rejoice in that

LOWER
Gen 6.16 with *l*, second, and third stories
Ps 8. 5 him a little *l* than the angels,
63. 9 go into the *l* parts of the earth.
Eph 4. 9 descended first into the *l* parts
Heb 2. 7 madest him a little *l* than...angels;
9 was made a little *l* than the angels

LOWEST
Dt 32.22 and shall burn unto the *l* hell,
1Ki 12.31 priests of the *l* of the people,
13.33 again of the *l* of the people priests
2Ki 17.32 of the *l* of them priests of the high
Ps 86.13 delivered my soul from the *l* hell.
88. 6 Thou hast laid me in the *l* pit, in
139.15 wrought in the lowest parts of the

Eze 41. 7 increased from the *l* chamber to
42. 6 was straitened more than the *l*
Lk 114. 9 with shame to take the *l* room.
10 go and sit down in the *l* room;

LOWLINESS
Eph 4. 2 With all *l* and meekness, with
Php 2. 3 in *l* of mind let each esteem other

LOWLY
Ps 138. 6 yet hath he respect unto the *l*:
Pr 3.34 but he giveth grace unto the *l*.
11. 2 shame: but with the *l* is wisdom.
16.19 be of an humble spirit with the *l*,
Zec 9. 9 *l*, and riding upon an ass, and upon
Mt 11.29 me; for I am meek and *l* in heart:

LOWRING
Mt 16. 3 to-day: for the sky is red and *l*.

LUCIFER
Isa 14.12 O *L*, son of the morning! how

LUCIUS
Ac 13. 1 and *L* of Cyrene, and Manaen,
Ro 16.21 Timotheus my workfellow, and *L*,

LUCRE
1Sa 8. 3 but turned aside after *l*, and took
1Ti 3. 3 no striker, not greedy of filthy *l*;
8 much wine, not greedy of filthy *l*;
Tit 1. 7 no striker, not given to filthy *l*;
1Pe 5. 2 not for filthy *l*, but of a ready

LUCRE'S
Tit 1.11 they ought not, for filthy *l* sake.

LUKE
Col 4.14 *L*, the beloved physician, and
2Ti 4.11 Only *L* is with me. Take Mark,

LUKEWARM
Rev 3.16 So then because thou art *l*, and

LUMP
2Ki 20. 7 And Isaiah said, Take a *l* of figs.
Isa 38.21 had said, Let them take a *l* of figs,
Ro 9.21 same *l* to make one vessel unto
11.16 firstfruit be holy, the *l* is also holy:
1Co 5. 6 little leaven leaveneth the whole *l*?
7 old leaven, that ye may be a new *l*,
Gal 5. 9 little leaven leaveneth the whole *l*.

LUNATICK
Mt 4.24 and those which were *l*, and those
17.15 son: for he is *l*, and sore vexed:

LUST
Ex 15. 9 my *l* shall be satisfied upon them;
Ps 78.18 heart by asking meat for their *l*.
30 were not estranged from their *l*.
81.12 them up unto their own hearts' *l*:
Pr 6.25 *L* not after her beauty in thine
Mt 5.28 looketh on a woman to *l* after her
Ro 1.27 burned in their *l* one toward
7. 7 for I had not known *l*, except the
1Co 10. 6 should not *l* after evil things,
Gal 5.16 shall not fulfil the *l* of the flesh.
1Th 4. 5 Not in the *l* of concupiscence,
Jas 1.14 he is drawn away of his own *l*,
15 Then when *l* hath conceived, it
4. 2 Ye *l*, and have not: ye kill, and
2Pe 1. 4 that is in the world through *l*.
2.10 the flesh in the *l* of uncleanness,
1Jn 2.16 *l* of the flesh, and the *l* of the eyes,
17 passeth away, and the *l* thereof:

LUSTED
Nu 11.34 there they buried the people that *l*.
Ps 106.14 But *l* exceedingly in the wilderness,
1Co 10. 6 after evil things, as they also *l*.
Rev 18.14 the fruits that thy soul *l* after are

LUSTETH
Dt 12.15 eat...whatsoever thy soul *l* after,
20 flesh, whatsoever thy soul *l* after.
21 gates whatsoever thy soul *l* after.
14.26 for whatsoever thy soul *l* after,
Gal 5.17 For the flesh *l* against the Spirit,
Jas 4. 5 that dwelleth in us *l* to envy?

LUSTS
Mk 4.19 the *l* of other things entering in,
Jn 8.44 and the *l* of your father ye will do:
Ro 1.24 through the *l* of their own hearts, to
6.12 ye should obey it in the *l* thereof.
13.14 for the flesh, to fulfil the *l* thereof.
Gal 5.24 the flesh with the affections and *l*.
Eph 2. 3 in times past in the *l* of our flesh,
4.22 corrupt according to the deceitful *l*;
1Ti 6. 9 and into many foolish and hurtful *l*,
2Ti 2.22 Flee also youthful *l*: but follow
3. 6 with sins, led away with divers *l*,
4. 3 after their own *l* shall they heap
Tit 2.12 denying ungodliness and wordly *l*,
3. 3 serving divers *l* and pleasures,
Jas 4. 1 your *l* that war in your members?
3 ye may consume it upon your *l*.
1Pe 1.14 to the former *l* in your ignorance:
2.11 abstain from fleshly *l*, which war
4. 2 time in the flesh to the *l* of men,
3 walked in lasciviousness, *l*, excess
2Pe 2.18 allure through the *l* of the flesh,
3. 3 scoffers, walking after their own *l*,
Jude 16 walking after their own *l*;
18 walk after their own ungodly *l*.

LYDDA
Ac 9.32 to the saints which dwelt at *L*.
35 And all that dwelt at *L* and Saron
38 forasmuch as *L* was nigh to Joppa,

LYDIA
Eze 30. 5 Ethopia, and Libya, and *L*, and
Ac 16.14 And a certain woman named *L*,
40 and entered into the house of *L*:

LYING
1Ki 22.23 Lord hath put a *l* spirit in the mouth
Ps 31. 6 them that regard *l* vanities:
18 Let the *l* lips be put to silence;
109. 2 against me with a *l* tongue.
119.163 I hate and abhor *l*: but thy law
120. 2 Deliver my soul, O Lord, from *l* lips,
139. 3 Thou compassest...my *l* down,
Pr 6.17 proud look, a *l* tongue, and hands
12.19 but a *l* tongue is but for a moment.
22 *L* lips are abomination to the Lord:
13. 5 A righteous man hateth *l*: but
21. 6 getting of treasures by a *l* tongue
26.28 A *l* tongue hateth those that are
Jer 7. 4 Trust ye not in *l* words, saying,
8 ye trust in *l* words, that cannot
La 3.10 He was unto me as a bear *l* in wait,
Mt 9. 2 a man sick of the palsy, *l* on a bed:
Mk 5.40 entereth in where...damsel was *l*.
Lk 2.12 swaddling clothes, *l* in a manger.
16 Joseph, and the babe *l* in a manger.
Jn 13.25 He then *l* on Jesus' breast saith
20. 5 looking in, saw the linen clothes *l*;
7 not *l* with the linen clothes, but
Ac 20.19 me by the *l* in wait of the Jews:
23.16 sister's son heard of their *l* in wait,
Eph 4.25 Wherefore putting away *l*, speak
2Th 2. 9 all power and signs and *l* wonders,

LYSTRA
Ac 14. 6 fled unto *L* and Derbe, cities of
8 And there sat a certain man at *L*,
21 they returned again to *L*, and to
16. 1 Then came he to Derbe and *L*:
2 by the brethren that were at *L* and
2Ti 3.11 me at Antioch, at Iconium,at *L*;

M

MACEDONIA
Ac 16. 9 stood a man of *M*, and prayed
9 Come over into *M*, and help us.
10 we endeavored to go into *M*,
12 is the chief city of that part of *M*,
18. 5 and Timotheus were come from *M*,
19.21 when he had passed through *M* and
22 he sent into *M* two of them that
29 men of *M*, Paul's companions in
20. 1 and departed for to go into *M*.
3 he purposed to return through *M*.
Ro 15.26 it hath pleased them of *M* and
1Co 16. 5 when I shall pass through *M*:
5 for I do pass through *M*.
2Co 1.16 to pass by you into *M*, and to
16 come again out of *M* unto you,
2.13 them, I went from thence into *M*.
7. 5 when we were come into *M*, our
8. 1 bestowed on the churches of *M*;
9. 2 I boast of you to them of *M*, that
4 Lest haply if they of *M* come with
11. 9 the brethren which came from *M*
Php 4.15 when I departed from *M*, no
1Th 1. 7 ensamples to all that believe in *M*
8 word of the Lord not only in *M*
4.10 the brethren which are in all *M*:
1Ti 1. 3 at Ephesus, when I went into *M*,

MACEDONIAN
Ac 27. 2 Aristarchus,...being with a *M* of

MACHPELAH
Gen 23. 9 he may give me the cave of *M*,
17 field of Ephron, which was in *M*,
19 wife in the cave of the field of *M*
25. 9 buried him in the cave of *M*, in
49.30 In the cave that is in the field of *M*,
50.13 him in the cave of the field of *M*,

MAD
Dt 28.34 be *m* for the sight of thine eyes
1Sa 21.13 feigned himself *m* in their hands,
14 servants, Lo, ye see the man is *m*:
15 Have I need of *m* men, that ye
15 to play the *m* man in my presence?
2Ki 9.11 came this *m* fellow to thee? And
Ps 102. 8 *m* against me are sworn against
Pr 26.18 a *m* man who casteth firebrands,
Ec 2. 2 I said of laughter, It is *m*: and of
7. 7 oppression maketh a wise man *m*;
Isa 44.25 the liars, and maketh diviners *m*;
Jer 25.16 drink, and be moved, and be *m*,
29.26 every man that is *m*, and maketh
50.38 and they are *m* upon their idols.
51. 7 wine; therefore the nations are *m*.
Hos 9. 7 is a fool, the spiritual man is *m*,
Jn 10.20 said, He hath a devil, and is *m*;
Ac 12.15 they said unto her, Thou art *m*.
26.11 exceedingly *m* against them,
24 learning doth make thee *m*.
25 I am not *m*, most noble Festus;
1Co 14.23 will they not say that ye are *m*?

MADE
Gen 1. 7 And God *m* the firmament, and
16 God made two great lights; the
16 to rule the night: he *m* the stars also.
25 And God *m* the beast of the earth
31 God saw every thing that he had *m*,
2. 2 ended his work which he had *m*;
2 from all his work which he had *m*.
22 taken from man, *m* he a woman,
3. 1 beast...which the Lord God had *m*.
7 together, and *m* themselves aprons.
5. 1 in the likeness of God *m* he him;
6. 6 the Lord that he had *m* man on
7 repenteth me that I have *m* them.
7. 4 living substance that I have *m* will
8. 1 God *m* a wind to pass over the earth,
9. 6 for in the image of God *m* he man.
15.18 Lord *m* a covenant with Abram,
17. 5 of many nations have I *m* thee.
19. 3 he *m* them a feast, and did bake
33, 35 they *m* their father drink wine
21. 6 God hath *m* me to laugh, so that all
8 and Abraham *m* a great feast the
27 and both of them *m* a covenant.
24.11 And he *m* his camels to kneel down
21 had *m* his journey prosperous
37 And my master *m* me swear, saying,
46 And she *m* haste, and let down
46 and she *m* the camels drink also.
26.22 now the Lord hath *m* room for us,
30 And he *m* them a feast, and they
27.14 and his mother *m* savory meat,
30 had *m* an end of blessing Jacob,
31 And he also had *m* savory meat,
37 I have *m* him thy lord, and all his
31.46 they took stones, and *m* an heap:
33.17 house, and *m* booths for his cattle:
37. 3 he *m* him a coat of many colors.
7 and *m* obeisance to my sheaf.
39. 3 the Lord *m* all that he did to prosper
4 he *m* him overseer over his house,
41.43 he *m* him ruler over all the land
51 said he, hath *m* me forget all my toil,
45. 1 Joseph *m* himself known unto his
8 hath *m* me a father to Pharaoh,
9 God hath *m* me lord of all Egypt:
47.26 Joseph *m* it a law over the land
Ex 1.13 *m* the children of Israel to serve
14 and they *m* their lives bitter with
2.14 Who *m* thee a prince and a judge
4.11 him, Who hath *m* man's mouth?
16.31 of it was like wafers *m* with honey.
20.11 the Lord *m* heaven and earth,
29.18, 25 offering *m* by fire unto the Lord.
36 thou hast *m* an atonement for it,
31.17 the Lord *m* heaven and earth,
18 had *m* an end of communing with
32. 4 after he had *m* it a molten calf:
5 Aaron *m* proclamation, and said,
8 they have *m* them a molten calf,
25 Aaron had *m* them naked unto
31 and have *m* them gods of gold.
34. 8 And Moses *m* haste, and bowed his
27 I have *m* a covenant with thee and
35.21 every one whom his spirit *m* willing,
36. 4 man from his work which they *m*;
8 *m* ten curtains of fine twined linen,
8 of cunning work *m* he them.
19 And he *m* a covering for the tent of
20 he *m* boards for the tabernacle of
23 he *m* boards for the tabernacle;
24 forty sockets of silver he *m* under
35 cherubims *m* he it of cunning work.
37 *m* an hanging for the tabernacle
37. 1 Bezaleel *m* the ark of shittim
2 and *m* a crown of gold to it round
29 he *m* the holy anointing oil, and
38. 1 he *m* the altar of burnt offering of
22 *m* all that the Lord commanded
Lev 1. 9 an offering *m* by fire, of a sweet
2. 2 to be an offering *m* by fire, of a sweet
3 of the offerings of the Lord *m* by fire.
7 it shall be *m* of fine flour with oil.
8 offering that is *m* of these things
11 the Lord, shall be *m* with leaven:
11 in any offering of the Lord *m* by fire.
3. 3 an offering *m* by fire unto the Lord;
5 it is an offering *m* by fire, of a sweet
9 an offering *m* by fire unto the Lord;
11 it is the food of the offering *m* by fire
6.17 portion of my offerings *m* by fire;
18 the offerings of the Lord *m* by fire:
21 In a pan it shall be *m* with oil;
13.48 a skin, or in any thing *m* of skin;
14.11 the man that is to be *m* clean,
36 in the house be not *m* unclean:
16.17 have *m* an atonement for himself,
20 he hath *m* an end of reconciling
Nu 4.15 have *m* an end of covering the
26 service, and all that is *m* for them:
5. 8 an atonement shall be *m* for him.
27 he hath *m* her to drink the water,
6. 4 nothing that is *m* of the vine tree,
8. 4 Moses, so he *m* the candlestick.
21 Aaron *m* an atonement for them
11. 8 baked it in pans, and *m* cakes of
14.36 *m* all the congregation to murmur
16.31 as he had *m* an end of speaking
39 they were *m* broad plates for a
47 *m* an atonement for the people.
20. 5 ye *m* us to come up out of Egypt,
21. 9 Moses *m* a serpent of brass, and
25.13 *m* an atonement for the children
30.12 hath utterly *m* them void on the day
12 her husband hath *m* them void; and
31.20 and all that is *m* of skins, and all
20 goats' hair, and all things *m* of wood.
32.13 *m* them wander in the wilderness
Dt 1.15 and *m* them heads over you,
2.30 and *m* his heart obstinate, that he
4.23 covenant...which he *m* with you,
36 heaven he *m* thee to hear his voice,
5. 2 our God *m* a covenant with us in
12 have *m* them a molten image.
16 had *m* you a molten calf: ye had
31.16 my covenant which I have *m* with
24 Moses had *m* an end of writing
32. 6 not *m* thee, and established thee
15 he forsook God which *m* him,
Jos 2.17 oath which thou hast *m* us swear.
5. 3 And Joshua *m* him sharp knives,
9. 4 *m* as if they had been ambassadors,
15 And Joshua *m* peace with them,
27 Joshua *m* them that day hewers
10. 1 Gibeon had *m* peace with Israel,
11.18 Joshua *m* war a long time with
22.25 hath *m* Jordan a border between
24.25 *m* a covenant with the people that
Jdg 2. 1 *m* you to go up out of Egypt, and
3.16 *m* him a dagger which had two
18 had *m* an end to offer the present,
8.27 Gideon *m* an ephod thereof, and
33 and *m* Baal-berith their god.
27 and *m* merry, and went into the
11. 4 of Ammon *m* war against Israel.
13.10 the woman *m* haste, and ran, and
14.10 and Samson *m* there a feast; for
16.19 she *m* him sleep upon her knees;
25 prison house; and he *m* them sport;
27 that beheld while Samson *m* sport.
17. 4 who *m* thereof a graven image
18.24 taken away my gods which I *m*,
27 took the things which Micah had *m*,
21. 5 had *m* a great oath concerning him
15 Lord had *m* a breach in the tribes
1Sa 2.19 his mother *m* him a little coat,
3.13 his sons *m* themselves vile, and
10.13 he had *m* an end of prophesying,
11.15 they *m* Saul king before the Lord
14.14 and his armorbearer *m*, was
18. 1 he had *m* an end of speaking unto
3 and David *m* a covenant, because
20.16 So Jonathan *m* a covenant with
23.18 two *m* a covenant before the Lord:
26 David *m* haste to get away for

2Sa 2. 9 *m* him king over Gilead, and over
10.19 they *m* peace with Israel, and
11.13 before him; and he *m* him drunk:
19 thou hast *m* an end of telling
12.31 *m* them pass through the brickkiln:
13. 6 lay down, and *m* himself sick.
23. 5 he hath *m* with me an everlasting
1Ki 1.41 as they had *m* an end of eating.
43 king David hath *m* Solomon king.
8. 9 the Lord *m* a covenant with the
54 Solomon had *m* an end of praying
9.26 king Solomon *m* a navy of ships
12. 4 Thy father *m* our yoke grievous:
16.26 his sin wherewith he *m* Israel to sin,
33 Ahab *m* a grove; and Ahab did
18.26 upon the altar which was *m*.
32 he *m* a trench about the altar, as
20.34 as my father *m* in Samaria. Then
2Ki 3. 2 of Baal that his father had *m*.
3 son of Nebat, which *m* Israel to sin;
10.16 So they *m* him ride in his chariot.
31 of Jeroboam, which *m* Israel to sin.
11. 4 and *m* a covenant with them, and
17. 8 kings of Israel, which they had *m*.
15 his covenant that he *m* with their
21 the Lord, and *m* them sin a great sin.
29 every nation *m* gods of their own,
29 which the Samaritans had *m*,
18. 4 brasen serpent that Moses had *m*:
19.15 thou hast *m* heaven and earth.
20.20 how he *m* a pool, and a conduit,
21. 3 up altars for Baal, and *m* a grove,
1Ch 5.10, 19 they *m* war with the Hagarites,
19. 6 had *m* themselves odious to David,
19 they *m* peace with David, and
21.29 which Moses *m* in the wilderness,
23. 1 he *m* Solomon his son king over
28.19 the Lord *m* me understand in writing
2Ch 1. 3 the servant of the Lord had *m* in
2.11 he hath *m* thee king over them.
12 Israel, that *m* heaven and earth,
3. 8 And he *m* the most holy house, the
10 he *m* two cherubims of image work,
4. 1 Moreover he *m* an altar of brass,
18 Thus Solomon *m* all these vessels
21 lamps, and the tongs, *m* he of gold,
10. 4 Thy father *m* our yoke grievous:
10 Thy father *m* our yoke heavy, but
21. 7 covenant...he had *m* with David,
8 Judah, and *m* themselves a king.
11 *m* high places in the mountains of
26. 1 and *m* him king in the room of his
5 the Lord, God *m* him to prosper.
13 that *m* war with mighty power, to
15 And he *m* in Jerusalem engines.
Ezr 1. 1 *m* a proclamation throughout all his
5.13 Cyrus *m* a decree to build this
17 decree was *m* of Cyrus the king to
6. 1 Darius the king *m* a decree, and
1 search was *m* in the house of the
Neh 3.16 to the pool that was *m*, and unto
4. 7 walls of Jerusalem were *m* up,
9 Nevertheless we *m* our prayer
8. 4 pulpit of wood, which they had *m*
16 them, and *m* themselves booths,
Est 1. 3 he *m* a feast unto all his princes
9 Vashti the queen *m* a feast for the
2.17 *m* her queen instead of Vashti.
18 he *m* a release to the provinces,
23 inquisition was *m* of the matter,
5.14 Let a gallows be *m* of fifty cubits
7. 9 which Haman had *m* for Mordecai,
Job 1.10 not thou *m* an hedge about him,
7. 3 am I *m* to possess months of vanity,
10. 8 Thine hands have *m* me and
9 that thou hast *m* me as the clay;
16. 7 But now he hath *m* me weary:
7 hast *m* desolate all my company.
17. 6 *m* me also a byword of the people;
13 have *m* my bed in the darkness.
28.18 No mention shall be *m* of coral, or of

26 When he *m* a decree for the rain,
31. 1 I *m* a covenant with mine eyes;
15 *m* me in the womb make him?
33. 4 The Spirit of God hath *m* me, and
39. 6 house I have *m* the wilderness,
Ps 7.12 hath bent his bow, and *m* it ready.
15 He *m* a pit, and digged it, and
8. 5 thou hast *m* him a little lower
18. 4 of ungodly men *m* me afraid.
11 He *m* darkness his secret place;
35 thy gentleness hath *m* me great.
21. 6 *m* him most blessed for ever:
6 thou hast *m* him exceeding glad
33. 6 of the Lord were the heavens *m*;
39. 5 *m* my days as an handbreadth;
46. 8 he hath *m* in the earth.
49.16 thou afraid when one is *m* rich,
50. 5 that have *m* a covenant with me
52. 7 man that *m* not God his strength;
60. 2 Thou hast *m* the earth to tremble;
69.11 I *m* sackcloth also my garment;
72.15 prayer also shall be *m* for him
74.17 thou hast *m* summer and winter.
77. 6 and my spirit *m* diligent search.
86. 9 nations whom thou hast *m* shall
89. 3 *m* a covenant with my chosen,
39 Thou hast *m* void the covenant of
42 hast *m* all his enemies to rejoice.
47 hast thou *m* all men in vain?
92. 4 *m* me glad through thy work:
95. 5 The sea is his, and he *m* it: and
96. 5 idols: but the Lord *m* the heavens.
98. 2 Lord hath *m* known his salvation:
100. 3 he is God: it is he that hath *m* us,
103. 7 He *m* known his ways unto Moses,
104.24 in wisdom hast thou *m* them all:
105. 9 covenant he *m* with Abraham,
28 He sent darkness, and *m* it dark;
115.15 Lord which *m* heaven and earth.
118.24 the day which the Lord hath *m*;
119.60 I *m* haste, and delayed not to
73 Thy hands have *m* me and
121. 2 Lord, which *m* heaven and earth.
136. 5 that by wisdom *m* the heavens:
7 To him that *m* great lights: for
139.14 I am fearfully and wonderfully *m*:
15 when I was *m* in secret, and
143. 3 he hath *m* me to dwell in darkness,
146. 6 Which *m* heaven, and earth, the
Pr 8.26 as yet he had not *m* the earth, nor
11.25 The liberal soul shall be *m* fat:
13. 4 soul of the diligent shall be *m* fat.
14.33 is in the midst of fools is *m* known.
15.19 way of the righteous is *m* plain.
16. 4 hath *m* all things for himself:
20. 9 can say, I have *m* my heart clean,
12 Lord hath *m* even both of them.
21.11 is punished, the simple is *m* wise:
Ec 1.15 is crooked cannot be *m* straight:
2. 4 I *m* me great works; I builded me
3.11 He hath *m* every thing beautiful in
7. 3 countenance the heart is *m* better.
29 that God hath *m* man upright;
SS 1. 6 *m* me the keeper of the vineyards;
6.12 my soul *m* me like the chariots of
Isa 2. 8 which their own fingers have *m*:
25. 2 thou hast *m* of a city an heap;
28.15 have *m* a covenant with death,
15 for we have *m* lies our refuge,
29.16 of him that *m* it, He *m* me not?
31. 7 idols of God, own hands have *m*
37.16 thou hast *m* heaven and earth.
40. 4 mountain and hill shall be *m* low:
4 the crooked shall be *m* straight, and
45.12 have *m* the earth, and created man
18 that formed the earth and *m* it; he
51.10 hath *m* the depths of the sea a way
12 man which shall be *m* as grass;
52.10 Lord hath *m* bare his holy arm
53. 9 he *m* his grave with the wicked,
12 many, and *m* intercession for the

63.17 hast thou *m* us to err from thy ways,
66. 2 those things hath mine hand *m*,
Jer 1.18 I have *m* thee this day a defensed
2. 7 *m* mine heritage an abomination.
28 thy gods that thou hast *m* thee?
5. 3 *m* their faces harder than a rock;
10.11 gods that have not *m* the heavens
12 He hath *m* the earth by his power,
18. 4 the vessel that he *m* of clay was
4 so he *m* it again another vessel, as
29.26 The Lord hath *m* thee priest in
34. 8 king Zedekiah had *m* a covenant
13 I *m* a covenant with your fathers
38.16 the Lord liveth, that *m* us this soul,
51. 7 that *m* all the earth drunken:
15 He hath *m* the earth by his power,
La 1.13 he hath *m* me desolate and faint
14 he hath *m* my strength to fall, the
3. 4 flesh and my skin hath he *m* old;
7 out: he hath *m* my chain heavy.
9 he hath *m* my paths crooked.
11 in pieces: he hath *m* me desolate.
45 Thou hast *m* us as the offscouring
Eze 3. 8 I have *m* thy face strong against
17 *m* thee a watchman unto the house
17.13 and *m* a covenant with him, and
24 and have *m* the dry tree to flourish:
19. 5 whelps, and *m* him a young lion.
22. 4 thine idols which thou hast *m*;
4 have I *m* thee a reproach unto the
13 dishonest gain which thou hast *m*,
Dan 2. 5 houses shall be *m* a dunghill.
45 God hath *m* known to the king what
48 the king *m* Daniel a great man,
3. 1 the king *m* an image of gold,
10 Thou, O king, hast *m* a decree,
Jon 1. 9 hath *m* the sea and the dry land.
4. 5 city, and there *m* him a booth,
Mt 4. 3 that these stones be *m* bread.
9.16 garment, and the rent is *m* worse.
22 thy faith hath *m* thee whole.
22 the woman was *m* whole from that
14.36 touched were *m* perfectly whole.
19. 4 beginning *m* them male and female,
12 which were *m* eunuchs of men:
20.12 thou hast *m* them equal unto us,
21.13 but ye have *m* it a den of thieves.
23.15 when he is *m*, ye make him
25. 6 at midnight there was a cry *m*,
26.19 and they *m* ready the passover.
27.24 but that rather a tumult was *m*,
Mk 2.21 the old, and the rent is *m* worse.
27 The sabbath was *m* for man, and
8.25 upon his eyes, and *m* him look up:
10. 6 God *m* them male and female.
52 way; thy faith hath *m* thee whole.
11.17 but ye have *m* it a den of thieves.
14. 4 was this waste of the ointment *m*?
16 and they *m* ready the passover.
58 this temple that is *m* with hands,
58 build another *m* without hands.
Lk 1.62 they *m* signs to his father, how
3. 5 the crooked shall be *m* straight,
5 the rough ways shall be *m* smooth;
4. 3 this stone that it be *m* bread.
8.17 that shall not be *m* manifest;
48 thy faith hath *m* thee whole; go
50 believe only, she shall be *m* whole.
11.40 he that *m* that which is without
14.12 and a recompense be *m* thee.
17.19 way: thy faith hath *m* thee whole.
19. 6 and he *m* haste, and came down,
46 but ye have *m* it a den of thieves.
22.13 and they *m* ready the passover.
23.12 Pilate and Herod were *m* friends
19 a certain sedition *m* in the city,
Jn 1. 3 All things were *m* by him; and
3 was not anything *m* that was *m*.
10 the world was *m* by him, and the
14 the Word was *m* flesh, and dwelt
2. 9 tasted the water that was *m* wine,

3.21 that his deeds may be *m* manifest,
4. 1 that Jesus *m* and baptized more
46 Galilee, where he *m* the water wine.
5. 4 water stepped in was *m* whole of
6 unto him, Wilt thou be *m* whole?
14 him, Behold, thou art *m* whole:
8.33 sayest thou, Ye shall be *m* free?
9. 3 of God should be *m* manifest in him.
11 man that is called Jesus *m* clay,
39 they which see might be *m* blind.
12. 2 There they *m* him a supper; and
15.15 Father I have *m* known unto you.
17.23 that they may be *m* perfect in one;
19. 7 he *m* himself the Son of God.
23 his garments, and *m* four parts,
Ac 1. 1 The former treatise have I *m*, O
36 hath *m* that same Jesus...Lord
3.12 we had *m* this man to walk?
4. 9 by what means he is *m* whole;
24 which hast *m* heaven, and earth,
7.10 he *m* him governor over Egypt
48 not in temples *m* with hands; as
8. 2 *m* great lamentation over him.
3 for Saul, he *m* havock of the church,
15. 7 ago God *m* choice among us,
16.13 where prayer was wont to be *m*;
24 and *m* their feet fast in the stocks.
17.24 *m* the world and all things therein,
26 *m* of one blood all nations of men
20.28 Holy Ghost hath *m* you overseers,
Ro 1. 3 which was *m* of the seed of David
20 by the things that are *m*, even
23 an image *m* like to corruptible man,
5.19 disobedience...were *m* sinners,
19 of one shall many be *m* righteous.
8. 2 hath *m* me free from the law of
20 creature was *m* subject to vanity,
9.20 it, Why hast thou *m* me thus?
15. 8 the promises *m* unto the fathers:
27 Gentiles have been *m* partakers
16.26 now is *m* manifest, and by the
26 *m* known to all nations for the
1Co 1.17 Christ should be *m* of none effect.
20 not God *m* foolish the wisdom of
30 who of God is *m* unto us wisdom,
9.19 have I *m* myself servant unto all,
22 I am *m* all things to all men, that
12.13 been all *m* to drink into one Spirit.
15.22 so in Christ shall all be *m* alive.
2Co 2. 2 the same which is *m* sorry by me?
3. 6 Who also hath *m* us able ministers
12. 9 strength is *m* perfect in weakness.
Gal 3. 3 are ye now *m* perfect by the flesh?
4. 4 *m* of a woman, *m* under the law,
5. 1 wherewith Christ hath *m* us free,
Eph 1. 6 *m* us accepted in the beloved:
2. 6 and *m* us sit together in heavenly
13 are *m* nigh by the blood of Christ.
Php 2. 7 But *m* himself of no reputation,
7 and was *m* in the likeness of men:
Col 1.12 hath *m* us meet to be partakers of
20 having *m* peace through the blood
2.11 circumcision *m* without hands,
1Ti 1. 9 law is not *m* for a righteous man,
Heb 1. 2 by whom also he *m* the worlds;
4 Being *m* so much better than the
2. 9 *m* a little lower than the angels
7. 3 but *m* like unto the Son of God;
26 and *m* higher than the heavens;
10. 3 is a remembrance again *m* of sins
13 till his enemies be *m* his footstool.
11. 3 not *m* of things which do appear.
Rev 1. 6 *m* us kings and priests unto God
14. 7 worship him that *m* heaven, and
8 she *m* all nations drink of the wine
19. 7 his wife hath *m* herself ready.

MADEST
Neh 9. 8 *m* a covenant with him to give
14 And *m* known unto them thy holy
Ps 8. 6 Thou *m* him to have dominion over
80.15 that thou *m* strong for thyself.
17 whom thou *m* strong for thyself.
Eze 16.17 *m* to thyself images of men, and
29. 7 *m* all their loins to be at a stand.
Jon 4.10 not labored, neither *m* it grow;
Ac 21.38 before these days *m* an uproar,
Heb 2. 7 *m* him a little lower than the

MADIAN
Ac 7.29 was a stranger in the land of *M*,

MADNESS
Dt 28.28 The Lord shall smite thee with *m*,
Ec 1.17 wisdom, and to know *m* and folly:
2.12 behold wisdom, and *m*, and folly:
7.25 of folly, even of foolishness and *m*:
9. 3 *m* is in their heart while they live,
10.13 end of his talk is mischievous *m*.
Zec 12. 4 and his rider with *m*:
Lk 6.11 And they were filled with *m*; and
2Pe 2.16 voice forbad the *m* of the prophet

MAGDALA
Mt 15.39 and came into the coasts of *M*.

MAGDALENE
Mt 27.56 Among which was Mary *M*, and
61 there was Mary *M*, and the other
28. 1 came Mary *M* and the other Mary
Mk 15.40 among whom was Mary *M*, and
47 Mary *M* and Mary the mother of
16. 1 Mary *M*, and Mary the mother of
9 week, he appeared first to Mary *M*,
Lk 8. 2 Mary called *M*, out of whom went
24.10 It was Mary *M*, and Joanna, and
Jn 19.25 the wife of Cleophas, and Mary *M*.
20. 1 day of the week cometh Mary *M*
18 Mary *M* came and told...disciples

MAGICIAN
Dan 2.10 that asked such things at any *m*,

MAGICIANS
Gen 41. 8 and called for all the *m* of Egypt,
24 I told this unto the *m*; but there
Ex 7.11 now the *m* of Egypt, they also did
22 the *m* of Egypt did so with their
8. 7 *m* did so with their enchantments,
18 *m* did so with their enchantments
19 Then the *m* said unto Pharaoh,
9.11 *m* could not stand before Moses
11 the boil was upon the *m*, and upon
Dan 1.20 ten times better than all the *m* and
2. 2 the king commanded to call the *m*.
27 wise men, the astrologers, the *m*,
4. 7 came in the *m*, the astrologers,
9 O Belteshazzar, master of the *m*,
5.11 thy father, made master of the *m*,

MAGISTRATE
Jdg 18. 7 there was no *m* in the land,
Lk 12.58 with thine adversary to the *m*,

MAGISTRATES
Ezr 7.25 set *m* and judges, which may
Lk 12.11 unto the synagogues, and unto *m*,
Ac 16.20 brought them to the *m*, saying,
22 and the *m* rent off their clothes,
35 the *m* sent the serjeants, saying,
36 The *m* have sent to let you go:
38 told these words unto the *m*:
Tit 3. 1 to obey *m*, to be ready to every

MAGNIFICENCE
Ac 19.27 and her *m* should be destroyed,

MAGNIFIED
Gen 19.19 and thou hast *m* thy mercy,
Jos 4.14 *m* Joshua in the sight of all Israel;
2Sa 7.26 And let thy name be *m* for ever,
1Ch 17.24 that thy name may be *m* for ever,
29.25 the Lord *m* Solomon exceedingly
2Ch 1. 1 with him, and *m* him exceedingly.
32.23 was *m* in the sight of all nations
Ps 35.27 Let the Lord be *m*, which hath
40.16 say continually, The Lord be *m*.
70. 4 say continually, Let God be *m*.
138. 2 *m* thy word above all thy name.
Jer 48.26 for he *m* himself against the Lord:
42 hath *m* himself against the Lord.
La 1. 9 for the enemy hath *m* himself.
Dan 8.11 he *m* himself even to the prince
Zep 2. 8 *m* themselves against their border.
10 *m* themselves against the people
Mal 1. 5 Lord will be *m* from the border of
Ac 5.13 to them: but the people *m* them.
19.17 the name of the Lord Jesus was *m*.
Php 1.20 also Christ shall be *m* in my body,

MAGNIFY
Jos 3. 7 begin to *m* thee in the sight of all
Job 7.17 man, that thou shouldest *m* him?
19. 5 ye will *m* yourselves against me,
36.24 Remember that thou *m* his work,
Ps 34. 3 O *m* the Lord with me, and let us
35.26 that *m* themselves against me.
38.16 they *m* themselves against me.
55.12 me that did *m* himself against me;
69.30 and will *m* him with thanksgiving.
Isa 10.15 the saw *m* itself against him that
42.21 he will *m* the law, and make it
Eze 38.23 Thus will I *m* myself, and sanctify
Dan 8.25 he shall *m* himself in his heart,
11.36 and *m* himself above every god,
37 for he shall *m* himself above all.
Zec 12. 7 not *m* themselves against Judah.
Lk 1.46 said, My soul doth *m* the Lord,
Ac 10.46 speak with tongues, and *m* God.
Ro 11.13 of the Gentiles, I *m* mine office:

MAGOG
Eze 38. 2 face against Gog, the land of *M*,
Rev 20. 8 quarters of the earth, Gog and *M*,

MAHLON
Ru 1. 2 of his two sons *M* and Chilion,
5 *M* and Chilion died also both of
4.10 Ruth the Moabitess, the wife of *M*,

MAHLON'S
Ru 4. 9 and all that was Chilion's and *M*,

MAID
2Ki 5. 2 of the land of Israel a little *m*;
4 Thus and thus said the *m* that is of
Est 2. 7 and the *m* was fair and beautiful;
Job 31. 1 then should I think upon a *m*?
Pr 30.19 and the way of a man with a *m*.
Isa 24. 2 master; as with the *m*, so with her
Jer 2.32 Can a *m* forget her ornaments, or
Mt 9.24 the *m* is not dead, but sleepeth.
25 her by the hand, and the *m* arose.
26.71 into the porch, another *m* saw him,
Mk 14.69 a *m* saw him again, and began to
Lk 8.54 hand, and called, saying, *M*, arise.
22.56 a certain *m* beheld him as he sat

MAIDEN
Gen 30.18 have given my *m* to my husband:
Jdg 19.24 Behold, here is my daughter a *m*,
2Ch 36.17 compassion upon young man or *m*,
Est 2. 4 let the *m* which pleaseth the king
9 *m* pleased him, and she obtained
13 thus came every *m* unto the king;
Ps 123. 2 eyes of a *m* unto the hand of her
Lk 8.51 father and the mother of the *m*,

MAIDENS
Ex 2. 5 her *m* walked along by the river's
Ru 2. 8 but abide here fast by my *m*:
22 that thou go out with his *m*, that
23 So she kept fast by the *m* of Boaz

Ru 3. 2 kindred, with those *m* thou wast?
1Sa 9.11 found young *m* going out to draw
Est 2. 8 many *m* were gathered together
9 as belonged to her, and seven *m*,
4.16 I also and my *m* will fast likewise;
Job 41. 5 or wilt thou bind him for thy *m*?
Ps 78.63 *m* were not given to marriage.
148.12 Both young men, and *m*; old men,
Pr 9. 3 She hath sent forth her *m*: she
27.27 and for the maintenance for thy *m*.
31.15 household, and a portion to her *m*.
Ec 2. 7 I got me servants and *m*, and had
Eze 44.22 they shall take *m* of the seed of
Lk 12.45 to beat the menservants and *m*,

MAIDS

Ezr 2.65 Beside their servants and their *m*,
Est 2. 9 he preferred her and her *m* unto
4. 4 So Esther's *m* and...chamberlains
Job 19.15 my *m*, count me for a stranger:
La 5.11 and the *m* in the cities of Judah.
Eze 9. 6 utterly old and young, both *m*, and
Na 2. 7 her *m* shall lead her as with the
Zec 9.17 cheerful, and new wine the *m*.
Mk 14.66 one of the *m* of the high priest:

MAIL

1Sa 17. 5 he was armed with a coat of *m*;
38 also he armed him with a coat of *m*.

MAIMED

Lev 22.22 Blind, or broken, or *m*, or having
Mt 15.30 that were lame, blind, dumb, *m*,
31 dumb to speak, the *m* to be whole,
18. 8 thee to enter into life halt or *m*,
Mk 9.43 better for thee to enter into life *m*,
Lk 14.13 a feast, call the poor, the *m*, the
21 bring in hither the poor, and the *m*,

MAINSAIL

Ac 27.40 and hoised up the *m* to the wind,

MAINTAIN

1Ki 8.45 supplication, and *m* their cause.
49 dwelling place, and *m* their cause,
59 that he *m* the cause of his servant,
1Ch 26.27 to *m* the house of the Lord.
2Ch 6.35 supplication, and *m* their cause.
39 supplications, and *m* their cause,
Job 13.15 I will *m* mine own ways before
Ps 140.12 will *m* the cause of the afflicted,
Tit 3. 8 might be careful to *m* good works.
14 let ours also learn to *m* good works

MAJESTY

1Ch 29.11 glory, and the victory, and the *m*:
25 bestowed upon him such royal *m*
Est 1. 4 and the honor of his excellent *m*
Job 37.22 the north: with God is terrible *m*.
40.10 Deck thyself now with *m* and
Ps 21. 5 honor and *m* hast thou laid upon
29. 4 the voice of the Lord is full of *m*.
45. 3 mighty, with thy glory and thy *m*.
4 And in thy *m* ride prosperously
93. 1 reigneth, he is clothed with *m*;
96. 6 Honor and *m* are before him:
104. 1 thou art clothed with honor and *m*.
145. 5 of the glorious honor of thy *m*,
12 the glorious *m* of his kingdom.
Isa 2.10 Lord, and for the glory of his *m*.
19, 21 Lord, and for the glory of his *m*,
24.14 shall sing for the *m* of the Lord,
26.10 will not behold the *m* of the Lord.
Eze 7.20 of his ornament, he set it in *m*:
Dan 4.30 and for the honor of my *m*?
36 excellent *m* was added unto me.
5.18 and *m*, and glory, and honor:
19 And for the *m* that he gave him,
Mic 5. 4 in the *m* of the name of the Lord
Heb 1. 3 the right hand of the *M* on high;
8. 1 throne of the *M* in the heavens;
2Pe 1.16 but were eyewitnesses of his *m*.
Jude 25 be glory and *m*, dominion and

MAKE

Gen 1.26 said, Let us *m* man in our image,
2.18 I will *m* him an help meet for him.
3. 6 a tree to be desired to *m* one wise,
21 did the Lord *m* coats of skins,
6.14 *M* thee an ark of gopher wood;
12. 2 And I will *m* of thee a great nation,
2 bless thee, and *m* thy name great;
17. 2 will *m* my covenant between me
28. 3 bless thee, and *m* thee fruitful,
31.44 come thou, let us *m* a covenant,
34. 9 *m* ye marriages with us, and give
Ex 5. 5 ye *m* them rest from their burdens.
7 give the people straw to *m* brick,
16 and they say to us, *M* brick: and,
20. 4 *m* unto thee any graven image,
23 shall not *m* with me gods of silver,
23 shall ye *m* unto you gods of gold.
24 An altar of earth thou shalt *m*
32. 1 *m* us gods, which shall go before
10 and I will *m* of thee a great nation.
30 shall *m* an atonement for your sin.
33.19 *m* all my goodness pass before thee,
Nu 5.21 The Lord *m* thee a curse and an
6. 7 shall not *m* himself unclean for
25 the Lord *m* his face shine upon thee,
16.13 *m* thyself altogether a prince over
30 But if the Lord *m* a new thing,
21. 8 *M* thee a fiery serpent, and set it
23.19 spoken, and shall he not *m* it good?
28.22, 30 to *m* an atonement for you.
Dt 1.11 *m* you a thousand times so many
4.10 and I will *m* them hear my words,
26.19 to *m* thee high above all nations
28.11 the Lord shall *m* thee plenteous
24 The Lord shall *m* the rain of thy
32.26 *m* the remembrance of them to cease
39 I kill, and I *m* alive; I wound, and
1Sa 1. 6 her sore, for to *m* her fret, because
3.12 when I begin, I will also *m* an end.
11. 1 *M* a covenant with us, and we
20.38 cried after the lad, *M* speed, haste,
1Ki 1.37 *m* his throne greater than the throne
8.29 prayer which thy servant shall *m*
33, 47 and *m* supplication unto thee
12. 1 come to Shechem to *m* him king.
9 *M* the yoke which thy father
17.13 *m* me thereof a little cake first,
13 after *m* for thee and for thy son.
2Ki 3.16 *M* this valley full of ditches.
5. 7 Am I God, to kill and to *m* alive,
7. 2 Lord would *m* windows in heaven,
19 Lord should *m* windows in heaven,
1Ch 6.49 and to *m* an atonement for Israel,
16. 8 name, *m* known his deeds among
29.12 and in thine hand it is to *m* great,
2Ch 4.11 work that he was to *m* for king
35.21 God commanded me to *m* haste:
Ezr 5. 3 house, and to *m* up this wall?
10. 3 let us *m* a covenant with our God
11 *m* confession unto the Lord God
Neh 2. 4 me, For what dost thou *m* request?
10.33 to *m* an atonement for Israel,
Job 5.18 and his hands *m* whole.
9.15 I would *m* supplication to my judge.
30 and *m* my hands never so clean;
11. 3 thy lies *m* men hold their peace?
19 and none shall *m* thee afraid;
13.11 not his excellency *m* you afraid?
23 *m* me to know my transgression
18. 2 it be ere ye *m* an end of words?
19. 3 ye *m* yourselves strange to me.
28.25 To *m* the weight for the winds;
Ps 5. 8 *m* thy way straight before my face.
31.16 *M* thy face to shine upon thy
38.22 *M* haste to help me, O Lord my
39. 4 Lord, *m* me to know mine end,
40.13 me: O Lord, *m* haste to help me.
17 deliverer; *m* no tarrying, O my God.
45.16 mayest *m* princes in all the earth.
46. 4 shall *m* glad the city of God,
51. 6 thou shalt *m* me to know wisdom.
8 *M* me to hear joy and gladness;
66. 1 *M* a joyful noise unto God, all ye
8 *m* the voice of his praise to be heard:
70. 1 *M* haste, O God, to deliver me;
1 *m* haste to help me, O Lord.
5 needy: *m* haste unto me, O God:
5 my deliverer; O Lord, *m* no tarrying.
71.12 O my God, *m* haste for my help.
81. 1 *m* a joyful noise unto the God of
83. 2 For, lo, thine enemies *m* a tumult:
13 O my God, *m* them like a wheel; as
84. 6 the valley of Baca *m* it a well;
89. 1 will I *m* known thy faithfulness to all
90.15 *M* us glad according to the days
95. 1 us *m* a joyful noise to the rock of
2 and *m* a joyful noise unto him with
98. 4 *M* a joyful noise unto the Lord, all
4 *m* a loud noise, and rejoice, and
6 *m* a joyful noise before the Lord,
100. 1 *M* a joyful noise unto the Lord, all
104.15 oil to *m* his face to shine, and bread
17 Where the birds *m* their nests: as
105. 1 *m* known his deeds among the
106. 8 *m* his mighty power to be known.
110. 1 I *m* thine enemies thy footstool.
115. 8 that *m* them are like unto them;
119.27 *M* me to understand the way of thy
35 *M* me to go in the path of thy
135 *M* thy face to shine upon thy servant;
135.18 They that *m* them are like unto
139. 8 if I *m* my bed in hell, behold, thou
141. 1 cry unto thee: *m* haste unto me;
Pr 1.16 evil, and *m* haste to shed blood.
23 I will *m* known my words unto you.
14. 9 Fools *m* a mock at sin: but
22.21 might *m* thee know the certainty
24 *M* no friendship with an angry
27.11 be wise, and *m* my heart glad,
Ec 2.24 and that he should *m* his soul enjoy
7.13 who can *m* that straight, which
16 much; neither *m* thyself over wise:
Isa 1.15 when ye *m* many prayers, I will not
16 Wash you, *m* you clean; put away
6.10 *M* the heart of this people fat,
10 *m* their ears heavy, and shut their
27. 5 that he may *m* peace with me;
29.21 That *m* a man an offender for a
40. 3 *m*...in the desert a highway for
41.15 I will *m*...a new sharp threshing
18 *m* the wilderness a pool of water,
42.15 I will *m* waste mountains and hills,
16 will *m* darkness light before them,
44. 9 They that *m* a graven image are
19 shall I *m* the residue thereof an
45. 2 *m* the crooked places straight:
7 I *m* peace, and create evil: I the
46. 5 will ye liken me, and *m* me equal,
53.10 thou shalt *m* his soul an offering
54. 3 *m* the desolate cities to be inhabited.
55. 3 I will *m* an everlasting covenant
60.13 *m* the place of my feet glorious.
15 will *m* thee an eternal excellency,
61. 8 I will *m* an everlasting covenant
64. 2 to *m* thy name known to thine
66.22 and the new earth, which I will *m*,
Jer 4. 7 his place to *m* thy land desolate;
27 yet will I not *m* a full end.
9.11 And I will *m* Jerusalem heaps.
13.16 of death, and *m* it gross darkness.
16. 6 nor *m* themselves bald for them:
20 Shall a man *m* gods unto himself,
18. 4 seemed good to the potter to *m* it.
22. 6 surely I will *m* thee a wilderness,
Eze 3.26 *m* thy tongue cleave to the roof
12.23 I will *m* this proverb to cease, and
14. 8 will *m* him a sign and a proverb,

32. 7 and *m* the stars thereof dark; I
8 heaven will I *m* dark over thee,
Dan 1.10 shall ye *m* me endanger my head
5. 8 nor *m* known to the king the
15 *m* known unto me the interpretation
6. 7 statute, and to *m* a firm decree,
26 I *m* a decree, That in every
9.24 and to *m* an end of sins, and to
24 to *m* reconciliation for iniquity,
Am 6.10 *m* mention of the name of the Lord.
Na 1. 8 will *m* an utter end of the place
Hab 2. 2 and *m* it plain upon the tables,
Zep 1.18 he shall *m* even a speedy riddance
3.13 and none shall *m* them afraid.
20 I will *m* you a name and a praise
Zec 6.11 silver and gold, and *m* crowns,
10. 1 Lord shall *m* bright clouds, and
Mal 2.15 And did not he *m* one? Yet had he
3.17 that day when I *m* up my jewels;
Mt 1.19 to *m* her a publick example, was
3. 3 of the Lord, *m* his paths straight.
4.19 and I will *m* you fishers of men.
5.36 canst not *m* one hair white or black.
8. 2 thou wilt, thou canst *m* me clean.
12.16 they should not *m* him known:
33 Either *m* the tree good, and his
33 or else *m* the tree corrupt, and his
17. 4 let us *m* here three tabernacles;
22.44 I *m* thine enemies thy footstool?
23. 5 they *m* broad their phylacteries,
14 and for a pretense *m* long prayer:
15 sea and land to *m* one proselyte,
15 *m* him twofold more the child of
25 *m* clean the outside of the cup and
24.47 *m* him ruler over all his goods.
25.21, 23 *m* thee ruler over many things:
27.65 your way, *m* it as sure as ye can.
Mk 1. 3 of the Lord, *m* his paths straight.
17 *m* you to become fishers of men.
40 thou wilt, thou canst *m* me clean.
3.12 they should not *m* him known.
5.39 Why *m* ye this ado, and weep? the
6.39 *m* all sit down by companies upon
9. 5 let us *m* three tabernacles; one
12.36 I *m* thine enemies thy footstool.
40 for a pretense *m* long prayers:
42 in two mites, which *m* a farthing.
14.15 prepared: there *m* ready for us.
Lk 1.17 *m* ready a people prepared for the
3. 4 of the Lord, *m* his paths straight.
5.12 thou wilt, thou canst *m* me clean.
33 of John fast often, and *m* prayers,
34 *m* the children of the bridechamber
9.14 *M* them sit down by fifties in a
33 let us *m* three tabernacles; one
52 Samaritans, to *m* ready for him.
11.39 ye Pharisees *m* clean the outside
40 *m* that which is within also?
12.37 and *m* them to sit down to meat,
42 whom his lord shall *m* ruler over
44 that he will *m* him ruler over all
14.18 one consent began to *m* excuse.
31 to *m* war against another king,
15.19 *m* me as one of thy hired servants.
29 I might *m* merry with my friends:
32 was meet that we should *m* merry,
16. 9 *M* to yourself friends of the
17. 8 *M* ready wherewith I may sup,
19. 5 Zacchaeus, *m* haste, and come
20.43 I *m* thine enemies thy footstool.
47 and for a shew *m* long prayers:
22.12 room furnished: there *m* ready.
Jn 1.23 *M* straight the way of the Lord,
2.16 *m* not my Father's house an house
6.10 Jesus said, *M* the men sit down.
15 take him by force, to *m* him a king,
8.32 and the truth shall *m* you free.
36 the Son therefore shall *m* you free,
10.24 long dost thou *m* us to doubt?
14.23 him, and *m* our abode with him.
Ac 2.28 shalt *m* me full of joy with thy
35 Until I *m* thy foes thy footstool.
7.40 Aaron, *M* us gods to go before us:
44 *m* it according to the fashion
9.34 thee whole: arise, and *m* thy bed.
22. 1 my defense which I *m* now unto you.
18 *M* haste, and get thee quickly out
23.23 *M* ready two hundred soldiers to
26.16 *m* thee a minister and a witness
24 much learning doth *m* thee mad.
Ro 1. 9 *m* mention of you always in my
3. 3 *m* the faith of God without effect?
31 then *m* void the law through faith?
9.21 to *m* one vessel unto honor,
22 wrath, and to *m* his power known,
23 *m* known the riches of his glory
28 short work will the Lord *m* upon
13.14 and *m* not provision for the flesh,
14. 4 for God is able to *m* him stand.
19 the things which *m* for peace,
15.18 *m* the Gentiles obedient, by word
26 to *m* a certain contribution for the
1Co 4. 5 will *m* manifest the counsels of the
6.15 *m* them the members of an harlot?
8.13 if meat *m* my brother to offend,
13 lest I *m* my brother to offend.
9.15 man should *m* my glorying void.
18 *m* the gospel of Christ without
10.13 temptation...*m* a way to escape,
2Co 2. 2 For if I *m* you sorry, who is he
9. 5 *m* up beforehand your bounty,
8 God is able to *m* all grace abound
10.12 dare not *m* ourselves of the number,
12.17 Did I *m* a gain of you by any of
18 Did Titus *m* a gain of you? walked
Gal 2.18 I *m* myself a transgressor.
3.17 *m* the promise of none effect.
6.12 to *m* a fair shew in the flesh,
Eph 2.15 to *m* in himself of twain one new
3. 9 to *m* all men see...the fellowship
5.13 for whatsoever doth *m* manifest
6.19 to *m* known the mystery of the
21 shall *m* known to you all things:
Col 1.27 *m* known what is the riches of the
4. 4 That I may *m* it manifest, as I
9 *m* known unto you all things
1Th 3.12 *m* you to increase and abound in
2Th 3. 9 to *m* ourselves an ensample unto
2Ti 3.15 able to *m* thee wise unto salvation
4. 5 *m* full proof of thy ministry.
Heb 1.13 I *m* thine enemies thy footstool?
2.10 *m* the captain of...salvation perfect
17 to *m* reconciliation for the sins of
7.25 he ever liveth to *m* intercession
8. 5 he was about to *m* the tabernacle:
5 thou *m* all things according to the
8 *m* a new covenant with the house
10 this is the covenant that I will *m*
9. 9 *m* him that did the service perfect,
10. 1 *m* the comers thereunto perfect.
16 This is the covenant that I will *m*
12.13 *m* straight paths for your feet,
13.21 *M* you perfect in every good work
Jas 3.18 in peace of them that *m* peace.
1Pe 5.10 *m*...perfect, stablish, strengthen,
2Pe 1. 8 they *m* you that ye shall neither
10 *m* your calling and election sure:
2. 3 words *m* merchandise of you:
1Jn 1.10 have not sinned, we *m* him a liar,
Rev 3. 9 I will *m* them of the synagogue
9 will *m* them to come and worship
12 will I *m* a pillar in the temple of
10. 9 and it shall *m* thy belly bitter,
11. 7 pit shall *m* war against them,
10 rejoice over them, and *m* merry,
12.17 went to *m* war with the remnant
13. 4 who is able to *m* war with him?
7 to *m* war with the saints, and to
14 should *m* an image to the beast,
17.14 These shall *m* war with the Lamb,
16 shall *m* her desolate and naked,
19.11 he doth judge and *m* war.
19 to *m* war against him that sat on
21. 5 said, Behold, I *m* all things new.

MAKER

Job 4.17 a man be more pure than his *m*?
32.22 my *m* would soon take me away.
35.10 Where is God my *m*, who giveth
36. 3 ascribe righteousness to my *M*.
Ps 95. 6 us kneel before the Lord our *M*.
Pr 14.31 the poor reproacheth his *M*:
17. 5 the poor reproacheth his *M*:
22. 2 the Lord is the *m* of them all.
Isa 1.31 tow, and the *m* of it as a spark,
17. 7 day shall a man look to his *M*,
22.11 not looked unto the *m* thereof,
45. 9 him that striveth with his *M*!
11 the Holy One of Israel, and his *M*,
51.13 And forgettest the Lord thy *m*,
54. 5 For thy *M* is thine husband; The
Jer 33. 2 Thus saith the Lord the *m* thereof,
Hos 8.14 For Israel hath forgotten his *M*,
Hab 2.18 the *m* thereof hath graven it;
18 the *m* of his work trusteth therein,
Heb 11.10 whose builder and *m* is God.

MAKEST

Jdg 18. 3 and what *m* thou in this place?
Job 13.26 *m* me to possess the iniquities of
22. 3 him, that thou *m* thy ways perfect?
Ps 4. 8 Lord, only *m* me dwell in safety.
39.11 *m* his beauty to consume away
44.10 Thou *m* us to turn back from the
13 Thou *m* us a reproach to our
14 Thou *m* us a byword among the
65. 8 thou *m* the outgoings of...to rejoice
10 thou *m* it soft with showers:
80. 6 Thou *m* us a strife unto our
104.20 Thou *m* darkness, and it is night:
144. 3 man, that thou *m* account of him!
SS 1. 7 thou *m* thy flock to rest at noon:
Isa 45. 9 that fashioned it, What *m* thou?
Jer 22.23 that *m* thy nest in the cedars,
28.15 thou *m* this people to trust in a lie.
Eze 16.31 and *m* thine high place in every
Hab 1.14 And *m* men as the fishes of the sea,
2.15 to him, and *m* him drunken also,
Lk 14.12 When thou *m* a dinner or a supper,
13 when thou *m* a feast, call the poor,
Jn 8.53 are dead: whom *m* thou thyself?
10.33 thou, being a man, *m* thyself God.
Ro 2.17 the law, and *m* thy boast of God,
23 Thou that *m* thy boast of the law,

MAKETH

Ex 4.11 who *m* the dumb, or deaf, or the
Lev 7. 7 the priest that *m* atonement
14.11 the priest that *m* him clean shall
17.11 blood that *m* an atonement for the
Dt 18.10 *m* his son or his daughter to pass
20.20 the city that *m* war with thee,
21.16 *m* his sons to inherit that which
24. 7 and *m* merchandise of him, or
27.15 man that maketh any graven or
18 be he that *m* the blind to wander out
29.12 the Lord thy God *m* with thee this
1Sa 2. 6 The Lord killeth, and *m* alive:
7 The Lord *m* poor, and *m* rich:
2Sa 22.33 power: and he *m* my way perfect.
34 He *m* my feet like hinds' feet; and
Job 5.18 For he *m* sore, and bindeth up: he
9. 9 Which *m* Arcturus, Orion, and
12.17 spoiled, and *m* the judges fools.
25 *m* them to stagger like a drunken
15.27 *m* collops of fat on his flanks.
23.16 For God *m* my heart soft, and the
25. 2 he *m* peace in his high places.
27.18 and as a booth that the keeper *m*.
35.11 and *m* us wiser than the fowls of
36.27 he *m* small the drops of water:
41.31 He *m* the deep to boil like a pot: he
31 *m* the sea like a pot of ointment.

Job 41.32 He *m* a path to shine after him; one
Ps 9.12 When he *m* inquisition for blood,
18.32 strength, and *m* my way perfect.
33 He *m* my feet like hinds' feet, and
23. 2 He *m* me to lie down in green
29. 6 He *m* them also to skip like a calf;
9 voice of the Lord *m* the hinds to
33.10 *m* the devices of the people of none
40. 4 man that *m* the Lord his trust,
46. 9 He *m* wars to cease unto the end
104. 3 who *m* the clouds his chariot:
4 Who *m* his angels spirits; his
15 wine that *m* glad the heart of
107.29 He *m* the storm a calm, so that
36 there he *m* the hungry to dwell,
41 and *m* him families like a flock.
113. 9 He *m* the barren woman to keep
135. 7 he *m* lightnings for the rain;
147. 8 who *m* grass to grow upon the
14 He *m* peace in thy borders, and
Pr 10. 1 A wise son *m* a glad father: but a
4 the hand of the diligent *m* rich.
22 The blessing of the Lord, it *m* rich,
12. 4 she that *m* ashamed is as rottenness
25 in the heart of man *m* it stoop:
25 but a good word *m* it glad.
13. 7 There is that *m* himself rich, yet
7 there is that *m* himself poor, yet
12 Hope deferred *m* the heart sick:
15.13 A merry heart *m* a cheerful
20 A wise son *m* a glad father: but a
30 a good report *m* the bones fat.
16. 7 he *m* even his enemies to be at peace
18.16 A man's gift *m* room for him, and
19. 4 Wealth *m* many friends; but the
28.20 he that *m* haste to be rich shall not
31.22 She *m* herself coverings of
24 She *m* fine linen, and selleth it;
Ec 3.11 can find out the work that God *m*
7. 7 oppression *m* a wise man mad;
8. 1 man's wisdom *m* his face to shine,
10.19 for laughter, and wine *m* merry:
11. 5 not the works of God who *m* all.
Isa 19.17 every one that *m* mention thereof
24. 1 the Lord *m* the earth empty,
1 and *m* it waste, and turneth it upside
27. 9 he *m* all the stones of the altar
40.23 he *m* the judges of the earth as
43.16 Lord, which *m* a way in the sea,
44.13 *m* it after the figure of a man,
15 he *m* a god, and worshippeth it;
15 he *m* it a graven image, and
17 the residue thereof he *m* a god,
24 I am the Lord that *m* all things;
25 of the liars, and *m* diviners mad;
25 and *m* their knowledge foolish;
46. 6 a goldsmith; and he *m* it a god:
55.10 *m* it bring forth and bud, that it
59.15 departeth from evil *m* himself a prey:
Jer 4.19 my heart *m* a noise in me;
10.13 he *m* lightnings with rain, and
17. 5 trusteth in man, and *m* flesh his arm,
21. 2 king of Babylon *m* war against us;
29.26 that is mad, and *m* himself a prophet,
27 which *m* himself a prophet to you?
48.28 dove that *m* her nest in the sides
51.16 he *m* lightnings with rain, and
Eze 22. 3 *m* idols against herself to defile
Dan 2.28 and *m* known to the king
29 *m* known to thee what shall come
6.13 *m* his petition three times a day.
11.31 the abomination that *m* desolate.
12.11 the abomination that *m* desolate set
Am 4.13 that *m* the morning darkness,
5. 8 that *m* the seven stars and Orion,
8 and *m* the day dark with night:
Na 1. 4 He rebuketh the sea, and *m* it dry,
Mt 5.45 for he *m* his son to rise on the evil
Mk 7.37 he *m* both the deaf to hear, and
Lk 5.36 then both the new *m* a rent, and
Jn 19.12 whosoever *m* himself a king
Ac 9.34 Jesus Christ *m* thee whole:
Ro 5. 5 hope *m* not ashamed; because
8.26 Spirit itself *m* intercession for us
27 he *m* intercession for the saints
34 who also *m* intercession for us.
11. 2 he *m* intercession to God against
1Co 4. 7 For who *m* thee to differ from
2Co 2. 2 who is he then that *m* me glad,
14 and *m* manifest the savor of his
Gal 2. 6 they were, it *m* no matter to me:
Eph 4.16 *m* increase of the body unto the
Heb 1. 7 Who *m* his angels spirits, and his
7.28 law *m* men high priests which
28 *m* the Son, who is consecrated for
Rev 13.13 he *m* fire come down from heaven
21.27 worketh abomination, or *m* a lie:
22.15 and whosoever loveth and *m* a lie.

MAKING

Ex 5.14 not fulfilled your task in *m* brick
Dt 20.19 time, in *m* war against it to take it,
Jdg 19.22 they were *m* their hearts merry,
1Ki 4.20 and drinking, and *m* merry.
1Ch 15.28 *m* a noise with psalteries and
17.19 *m* known all these great things.
2Ch 30.22 *m* confession to the Lord God of
Ps 19. 7 Lord is sure, *m* wise the simple.
Ec 12.12 *m* many books there is no end;
Isa 3.16 and *m* a tinkling with their feet:
Jer 20.15 born unto thee; *m* him very glad.
Eze 27.16 multitude of the wares of thy *m*,
18 multitude of the wares of thy *m*,
Dan 6.11 and *m* supplication before his God.
Hos 10. 4 swearing falsely in *m* a covenant:
Am 8. 5 *m* the ephah small, and the shekel
Mic 6.13 in *m* thee desolate because of thy
Mt 9.23 and the people *m* a noise,
Mk 7.13 *M* the word of God of none effect
Jn 5.18 Father, *m* himself equal with God.
Ro 1.10 *M* request, if by any means now
2Co 6.10 as poor, yet *m* many rich; as
Eph 1.16 *m* mention of you in my prayers;
2.15 twain one new man, so *m* peace;
5.19 and *m* melody in you heart to the
Php 1. 4 for you all *m* request with joy,
1Th 1. 2 *m* mention of you in our prayers;
Phm 4 *m* mention of thee always in my
2Pe 2. 6 *m* them an ensample unto those
Jude 22 have compassion, *m* a difference:

MALACHI

Mal 1. 1 word of the Lord to Israel by *M*.

MALCHUS

Jn 18.10 ear. The servant's name was *M*.

MALE

Gen 1.27 *m* and female created he them.
Mt 19. 4 made them *m* and female,
Mk 10. 6 God made them *m* and female.
Lk 2.23 Every *m* that openeth the womb
Gal 3.28 free, there is neither *m* nor female:

MALEFACTOR

Jn 18.30 If he were not a *m*, we would not

MALEFACTORS

Lk 23.32 *m*, led with him to be put to death.
33 they crucified him, and the *m*,
39 one of the *m* which were hanged

MALICE

1Co 5. 8 the leaven of *m* and wickedness;
14.20 howbeit in *m* be ye children, but in
Eph 4.31 be put away from you, with all *m*:
Col 3. 8 anger, wrath, *m*, blasphemy,
Tit 3. 3 living in *m* and envy, hateful, and
1Pe 2. 1 laying aside all *m*, and all guile,

MALICIOUS

3Jn 10 prating against us with *m* words:

MALICIOUSNESS

Ro 1.29 wickedness, covetousness, *m*;
1Pe 2.16 using your liberty for a cloke of *m*,

MALIGNITY

Ro 1.29 envy, murder, debate, deceit, *m*;

MAMMON

Mt 6.24 Ye cannot serve God and *m*.
Lk 16. 9 friends of the *m* of unrighteousness;
11 been faithful in the unrighteous *m*,
13 other. Ye cannot serve God and *m*.

MAN

Gen 1.26 said, Let us make *m* in our image,
2. 7 Lord God formed *m* of the dust of
7 of life; and *m* became a living soul.
18 good that the *m* should be alone;
24 shall a *m* leave his father and his
3.22 *m* is become as one of us, to know
9. 5 I require it, and at the hand of *m*;
6 blood, by *m* shall his blood be shed:
6 for in the image of God made he *m*.
24.58 unto her, Wilt thou go with this *m*?
25.27 a cunning hunter, a *m* of the field;
27 and Jacob was a plain *m*, dwelling
27.11 is a hairy *m*, and I am a smooth *m*:
32.24 there wrestled a *m* with him until
39. 2 Joseph, and he was a prosperous *m*;
41.33 look out a *m* discreet and wise,
38 a *m* in whom the Spirit of God is?
43.14 God...give you mercy before the *m*,
45. 1 Cause every *m* to go out from me.
Ex 11. 2 every *m* borrow of his neighbor,
12. 3 shall take to them every *m* a lamb,
15. 3 The Lord is a *m* of war: the Lord
16.16 an omer for every *m*, according
19 no *m* leave of it till the morning.
21.12 He that smiteth a *m*, so that he die,
16 he that stealeth a *m*, and selleth
22.14 And if a *m* borrow ought of his
16 And if a *m* entice a maid that is not
30.12 give every *m* a ransom for his soul
33. 8 stood every *m* at his tent door, and
Lev 19. 3 Ye shall fear every *m* his mother,
32 honor the face of the old *m*, and
20. 3 I will set my face against that *m*,
27. 2 a *m* shall make a singular vow, the
14 when a *m* shall sanctify his house
Nu 9. 6 defiled by the dead body of a *m*,
12. 3 the *m* Moses was very meek, above
15.35 The *m* shall be surely put to death:
16. 7 the *m* whom the Lord doth choose,
22 shall one *m* sin, and wilt thou be
23.19 God is not a *m*, that he should lie;
19 neither the son of *m*, that he should
27.18 a *m* in whom is the spirit, and lay
Dt 4.32 the day that God created *m* upon
5.24 that God doth talk with *m*, and he
7.24 shall no *m* be able to stand before
8. 3 *m* doth not live by bread only, but
3 the mouth of the Lord doth *m* live.
5 as a *m* chasteneth his son, so the
11.25 shall no *m* be able to stand before
12. 8 every *m* whatsoever is right in his
16.17 Every *m* shall give as he is able,
21.15 If a *m* have two wives, one beloved,
24. 5 When a *m* hath taken a new wife,
25. 2 the wicked *m* be worthy to be beaten,
27.15 Cursed be the *m* that maketh any
Jos 1. 5 shall not any *m* be able to stand
4. 5 take ye up every *m* of you a stone
Jdg 3.15 Gera, a Benjamite, a *m* lefthanded:
13. 6 saying, A *m* of God came unto me,
Ru 1. 2 the name of the *m* was Elimelech,
3.16 told her all that the *m* had done to
1Sa 2.27 there came a *m* of God unto Eli,
9. 6 there is in this city a *m* of God,
6 he is an honorable *m*; all that he
10.27 said, How shall this *m* save us,
11. 3 if there be no *m* to save us, we will

BIBLICAL THEMES

MAN

And God said, Let us make man in our image, after our likeness: and let them have dominion over the fish of the sea, and over the fowl of the air, and over the cattle . . . and over every creeping thing that creepeth upon the earth. So God created man in his own image, in the image of God created he him; male and female created he them. Gen 1.26-27

And the Lord God formed man of the dust of the ground, and breathed into his nostrils the breath of life; and man became a living soul. . . . And the Lord God said, It is not good that the man should be alone; I will make him an help meet for him. Gen 2.7, 18

Behold, the man is become as one of us, to know good and evil. Gen 3.22

God is not a man, that he should lie; neither the son of man, that he should repent: hath he said, and shall he not do it? Nu 23.19

Man doth not live by bread only. Dt 8.3

Now thy kingdom shall not continue: the Lord hath sought him a man after his own heart. 1Sa 13.14

Be of good courage, and let us play the men for our people, and for the cities of our God. 2Sa 10.12

I go the way of all the earth: be thou strong therefore, and shew thyself a man. 1Ki 2.2

What is man, that thou shouldest magnify him? and that thou shouldest set thine heart upon him? . . . and try him every moment? Job 7.17-18

He is not a man, as I am, that I should answer him, and we should come together in judgment. Job 9.32

Man that is born of a woman is of few days, and full of trouble. Job 14.1

Gird up thy loins now like a man: I will demand of thee. Job 40.7

What is man, that thou art mindful of him? and the son of man, that thou visitest him? For thou hast made him a little lower than the angels, and hast crowned him with glory and honor. Ps 8.4-5

The way of an eagle in the air; the way of a serpent upon a rock; the way of a ship in the midst of the sea; and the way of a man with a maid. Pr 30.19

Therefore shall all hands be faint, and every man's heart shall melt: and they shall be afraid: pangs and sorrows shall take hold of them; they shall be in pain as a woman that travaileth. Isa 13.7-8

What manner of man is this, that even the winds and the sea obey him! Mt 8.27

What man shall there be among you, that shall have one sheep, and if it fall into a pit on the sabbath day, will he not . . . lift it out? How much then is a man better than a sheep? Mt 12.11-12

He which made them at the beginning made them male and female, and said, For this cause shall a man leave father and mother, and shall cleave to his wife. . . . Wherefore they are no more twain, but one flesh. What therefore God hath joined together, let not man put asunder. Mt 19.4-6

The sabbath was made for man, and not man for the sabbath. Mk 2.27

A man indeed ought not to cover his head, forasmuch as he is the image and glory of God. . . . Neither was the man created for the woman; but the woman for the man. 1Co 11.7, 9

Ye are all the children of God. . . . There is neither Jew nor Greek, there is neither bond nor free, there is neither male nor female: for ye are all one in Christ Jesus. Gal 3.26, 28

15.29 for he is not a *m*, that he should
16. 7 for the Lord seeth not as *m* seeth;
7 for *m* looketh on the outward
16 to seek out a *m*, who is a cunning
17. 8 choose you a *m* for you, and let him
58 Whose son art thou, thou young *m*?
18.23 am a poor *m*, and lightly esteemed?
21.14 Lo, ye see the *m* is mad: wherefore
25.17 Belial, that a *m* cannot speak to him.
25 pray thee, regard this *m* of Belial,
2Sa 12. 2 rich *m* had exceeding many flocks
3 But the poor *m* had nothing, save one
5 *m* that hath done this thing shall
7 said to David, Thou art the *m*.
18.24 and behold a *m* running alone.
29 said, Is the young *m* Absalom safe?
1Ki 2. 9 for thou art a wise *m*, and knowest
17.24 I know that thou art a *m* of God,
2Ki 1.10 If I be a *m* of God, then let fire come
13 O *m* of God, I pray thee, let my life,
4.27 the *m* of God said, Let her alone;
5. 1 was a great *m* with his master,
1 he was also a mighty *m* in valor,
7 me to recover a *m* of his leprosy?
6.17 opened the eyes of the young *m*;
2Ch 6.22 If a *m* sin against his neighbor,
10.16 every *m* to your tents, O Israel: and
18.33 certain *m* drew a bow at a venture,
25. 4 every *m* shall die for his own sin.
Neh 6.11 I said, Should such a *m* as I flee?
Job 1. 1 and that *m* was perfect and upright,
4.17 Shall mortal *m* be more just than
17 shall a *m* be more pure than his
5. 2 For wrath killeth the foolish *m*, and
7 Yet *m* is born unto trouble, as the
17 Behold, happy is the *m* whom God
7.17 What is *m*, that thou shouldest
8.20 God will not cast away a perfect *m*,
9. 2 how should *m* be just with God?
32 For he is not a *m*, as I am, that I
12. 4 just upright *m* is laughed to scorn.
25 them to stagger like a drunken *m*.
14. 1 *M* that is born of a woman is of
10 But *m* dieth, and wasteth away:
10 *m* giveth up the ghost, and where
12 So *m* lieth down, and riseth not:
14 If a *m* die, shall he live again? all
15.14 What is *m*, that he should be
20 The wicked *m* travaileth with pain
16.21 one might plead for a *m* with God,
21. 4 As for me, is my complaint to *m*?
22. 2 Can a *m* be profitable unto God,
24.22 he riseth up, and no *m* is sure of life.
25. 6 How much less *m*, that is a worm?
6 the son of *m*, which is a worm?
27.13 the portion of a wicked *m* with God,
32. 8 But there is a spirit in *m*: and the
13 God thrusteth him down, not *m*.
33.12 thee, that God is greater than *m*.
23 to shew unto *m* his uprightness:
26 render unto *m* his righteousness.
29 worketh God oftentimes with *m*,
34. 7 What *m* is like Job, who drinketh
9 It profiteth a *m* nothing that he
15 and *m* shall turn again unto dust.
38. 3 Gird up now thy loins like a *m*;
40. 7 Gird up thy loins now like a *m*:
Ps 1. 1 Blessed is the *m* that walketh not
8. 4 What is *m*, that thou art mindful
4 son of *m*, that thou visitest him?
19. 5 rejoiceth as a strong *m* to run a race.
22. 6 But I am a worm, and no *m*; a
33.16 mighty *m* is not delivered by much
34. 6 poor *m* cried, and the Lord heard
36. 6 Lord, thou preservest *m* and beast.
37.23 steps of a good *m* are ordered by
38.13 I was as a dumb *m* that openeth not
56.11 I will not be afraid what *m* can do
60.11 trouble: for vain is the help of *m*.
62.12 to every *m* according to his work.
65. 4 Blessed is the *m* whom thou
74.22 the foolish *m* reproacheth thee daily.
76.10 the wrath of *m* shall praise thee:
84. 5 Blessed is the *m* whose strength is
90. 3 Thou turnest *m* to destruction;
94.11 Lord knoweth the thoughts of *m*,
103.15 As for *m*, his days are as grass:
104.14 and herb for the service of *m*:
15 that maketh glad the heart of *m*,
23 *M* goeth forth unto his work and
107.27 fro, and stagger like a drunken *m*,
118. 8 Lord than to put confidence in *m*.
119. 9 shall a young *m* cleanse his way?
127. 5 Happy is the *m* that hath his
142. 4 failed me; no *m* cared for my soul.
143. 2 sight shall no *m* living be justified,
144. 4 *M* is like to vanity: his days are
147.10 not pleasure in the legs of a *m*.
Pr 3.13 Happy is the *m* that findeth wisdom,
30 Strive not with a *m* without cause,
6.27 Can a *m* take fire in his bosom,
7. 7 a young *m* void of understanding,
8.34 Blessed is the *m* that heareth me,
9. 9 Give instruction to a wise *m*, and he
9 teach a just *m*, and he will increase
12.16 but a prudent *m* coveteth shame.
23 prudent *m* concealeth knowledge:

Pr 13. 5 A righteous *m* hateth lying: but a
14.16 A wise *m* feareth, and departeth
17 a *m* of wicked devices is hated.
15.18 A wrathful *m* stirreth up strife: but
19 way of the slothful *m* is as an hedge
20 a foolish *m* despiseth his mother.
16.27 An ungodly *m* diggeth up evil: and
28 A froward *m* soweth strife: and a
29 A violent *m* enticeth his neighbor,
17.11 An evil *m* seeketh only rebellion:
20.27 spirit of *m* is the candle of the Lord,
21.29 A wicked *m* hardeneth his face:
22. 3 A prudent *m* foreseeth the evil, and
23.21 drowsiness shall clothe a *m* with rags.
24.12 to every *m* according to his works?
26.12 thou a *m* wise in his own conceit?
27.12 A prudent *m* foreseeth the evil, and
20 the eyes of *m* are never satisfied.
28. 1 wicked flee when no *m* pursueth:
3 poor *m* that oppresseth the poor
11 rich *m* is wise in his own conceit;
29.11 wise *m* keepeth it in till afterwards.
30.19 and the way of a *m* with a maid.
Ec 2.16 And how dieth the wise *m*? as the
19 he shall be a wise *m* or a fool? yet
22 For what hath *m* of all his labor,
3.11 no *m* can find out the work that God
21 Who knoweth the spirit of *m*
6. 3 If a *m* beget an hundred children,
7. 5 for a *m* to hear the song of fools.
7 oppression maketh a wise *m* mad;
20 there is not a just *m* upon earth,
8. 6 the misery of *m* is great upon him.
12. 5 because *m* goeth to his long home,
13 for this is the whole duty of *m*.
Isa 4. 1 women shall take hold of one *m*,
5.15 the mean *m* shall be brought down,
15 the mighty *m* shall be humbled,
6. 5 because I am a *m* of unclean lips,
11 and the houses without *m*, and the
14.16 *m* that made the earth to tremble,
17. 7 day shall a *m* look to his Maker,
19.14 drunken *m* staggereth in his vomit.
31. 7 every *m* shall cast away his idols
35. 6 shall the lame *m* leap as an hart, and
41.28 For I beheld, and there was no *m*;
42.13 Lord shall go forth as a mighty *m*,
44.13 maketh it after the figure of a *m*,
13 according to the beauty of a *m*;
15 Then shall it be for a *m* to burn: for
50. 2 when I came, was there no *m*?
52.14 was so marred more than any *m*,
53. 3 a *m* of sorrows, and acquainted with
55. 7 the unrighteous *m* his thoughts:
57. 1 and no *m* layeth it to heart:
58. 5 a day for a *m* to afflict his soul?
59.16 he saw that there was no *m*, and
62. 5 For as a young *m* marrieth a virgin,
Jer 9.23 not the wise *m* glory in his wisdom,
23 let the mighty *m* glory in his might,
23 let not the rich *m* glory in his riches:
10.14 *m* is brutish in his knowledge:
23 that the way of *m* is not in himself:
16.20 Shall a *m* make gods unto himself,
22.28 Is this *m* Coniah a despised broken
23. 9 I am like a drunken *m*, and like
9 a *m* whom wine hath overcome,
31.30 every *m* that eateth the sour grape,
34 shall teach no more every *m* his
34 neighbor, and every *m* his brother,
32.43 It is desolate without *m* or beast;
33.10 be desolate without *m* and without
La 3. 1 am the *m* that hath seen affliction
26 It is good that a *m* should both hope
27 good for a *m* that he bear the yoke
36 subvert a *m* in his cause, the Lord
Eze 1. 5 they had the likeness of a *m*.
2. 1 Son of *m*, stand upon thy feet, and
6 son of *m*, be not afraid of them,
8 son of *m*, hear what I say unto thee;
3.18 wicked *m* shall die in his iniquity;
11. 4 against them, prophesy, O son of *m*.
14. 8 I will set my face against that *m*,
17. 2 Son of *m*, put forth a riddle, and
20. 3 Son of *m*, speak unto the elders of
21.12 Cry and howl, son of *m*: for it shall
29.11 No foot of *m* shall pass through it,
33. 8 O wicked *m*, thou shalt surely die;
37. 3 Son of *m*, can these bones live?
Dan 6. 7 ask a petition of any God or *m* for
7.13 one like the Son of *m* came with the
10.18 one like the appearance of a *m*,
19 O *m* greatly beloved, fear not:
Hos 9. 7 is a fool, the spiritual *m* is mad,
11. 4 I drew them with cords of a *m*,
9 for I am God, and not *m*; the Holy
Am 5.19 As if a *m* did flee from a lion, and
Jon 1. 5 and cried every *m* unto his god, and
Mic 4. 4 shall sit every *m* under his vine and
6. 8 shewed thee, O *m*, what is good;
7. 2 The good *m* is perished out of the
2 they hunt every *m* his brother
Hab 1.13 the wicked devoureth the *m* that is
Zec 2. 1 behold a *m* with a measuring line
6.12 the *m* whose name is The Branch;
8. 4 every *m* with his staff in his hand
16 Speak ye every *m* the truth to his
12. 1 and formeth the spirit of *m* within
Mal 3. 8 Will a *m* rob God? Yet ye have
Mt 1.19 her husband, being a just *m*, and
4. 4 *M* shall not live by bread alone,
5.40 And if any *m* will sue thee at the law,
6.24 No *m* can serve two masters: for
7. 9 what *m* is there of you, whom if
24 I will liken him unto a wise *m*,
26 shall be likened unto a foolish *m*,
8. 4 See thou tell no *m*; but go thy
9 For I am a *m* under authority,
9 I say to this *m*, Go, and he goeth; and
20 the Son of *m* hath not where to lay
27 What manner of *m* is this, that even
28 that no *m* might pass by that way.
9. 2 brought to him a *m* sick of the palsy,
3 themselves, This *m* blasphemeth.
6 know that the Son of *m* hath power
9 he saw a *m*, named Matthew, sitting
16 No *m* putteth a piece of new cloth
30 saying, See that no *m* know it.
32 they brought to him a dumb *m*
10.23 of Israel, till the Son of *m* be come.
35 I am come to set a *m* at variance
41 he that receiveth a righteous *m* in
41 in the name of a righteous *m* shall
11. 8 see? A *m* clothed in soft raiment?
19 The Son of *m* came eating and
19 Behold a *m* gluttonous, and a
27 no *m* knoweth the Son, but the
27 neither knoweth any *m* the Father,
12. 8 the Son of *m* is Lord even of the
10 there was a *m* which had his hand
11 What *m* shall there be among you,
12 then is a *m* better than a sheep?
13 to the *m*, Stretch forth thine hand.
19 shall any *m* hear his voice in the
29 except he first bind the strong *m*?
32 a word against the Son of *m*,
35 A good *m* out of the good treasure
35 an evil *m* out of the evil treasure
40 so shall the Son of *m* be three days
43 unclean spirit is gone out of a *m*,
45 last state of that *m* is worse than
13.24 of heaven is likened unto a *m* which
31 of mustard seed, which a *m* took,
37 the good seed is the Son of *m*;
41 The Son of *m* shall send forth his
44 the which when a *m* hath found, he
45 of heaven is like unto a merchant *m*,
52 unto a *m* that is an householder,
54 Whence hath this *m* this wisdom,
56 then hath this *m* all these things?
15.11 goeth into the mouth defileth a *m*;
11 out of the mouth, this defileth a *m*.
18 the heart; and they defile the *m*.
20 are the things which defile a *m*:
20 unwashen hands defileth not a *m*.
16.13 do men say that I the Son of *m* am?
20 tell no *m* that he was Jesus the
24 If any *m* will come after me, let him
26 For what is a *m* profited, if he shall
26 a *m* give in exchange for his soul?
27 Son of *m* shall come in the glory of
27 shall reward every *m* according to his
28 till they see the Son of *m* coming
17. 8 they saw no *m*, save Jesus only.
9 saying, Tell the vision to no *m*,
9 until the Son of *m* be risen again
12 shall also the Son of *m* suffer of
14 came to him a certain *m* kneeling
22 The Son of *m* shall be betrayed into
18. 7 woe to that *m* by whom the offense
11 For the Son of *m* is come to save
12 if a *m* have an hundred sheep, and
17 let him be unto thee as an heathen *m*
19. 3 lawful for a *m* to put away his wife
5 this cause shall a *m* leave father
6 together, let not *m* put asunder.
10 case of the *m* be so with his wife,
20 The young *m* saith unto him, All
22 the young *m* heard that saying,
23 a rich *m* shall hardly enter into the
24 than for a rich *m* to enter into the
28 when the Son of *m* shall sit in the
20. 1 unto a *m* that is an householder,
7 him, Because no *m* hath hired us.
9 hour, they received every *m* a penny.
10 likewise received every *m* a penny.
18 Son of *m* shall be betrayed unto
28 Even as the Son of *m* came not to
21. 3 And if any *m* say ought unto you,
28 A certain *m* had two sons; and he
22.11 a *m* which had not on a wedding
16 neither carest thou for any *m*: for
24 If a *m* die, having no children, his
46 no *m* was able to answer him a
46 neither durst any *m* from that day
23. 9 And call no *m* your father upon the
24. 4 Take heed that no *m* deceive you.
23 Then if any *m* shall say unto you,
27 also the coming of the Son of *m* be.
30 the sign of the Son of *m* in heaven:
30 see the Son of *m* coming in the clouds
36 that day and hour knoweth no *m*,
37, 39 the coming of the Son of *m* be.
44 ye think not the Son of *m* cometh.
25.13 hour wherein the Son of *m* cometh.
14 as a *m* travelling into a far country,
15 every *m* according to his...ability;
24 knew thee that thou art an hard *m*,
31 Son of *m* shall come in his glory,
26. 2 and the Son of *m* is betrayed to be
18 Go into the city to such a *m*, and say
24 Son of *m* goeth as it is written of
24 but woe unto that *m* by whom the
24 by whom the Son of *m* is betrayed!
24 been good for that *m* if he had not
45 Son of *m* is betrayed into the hands
64 ye see the Son of *m* sitting on the
72 with an oath, I do not know the *m*.
74 to swear, saying, I know not the *m*.
27.19 thou nothing to do with that just *m*:
32 they found a *m* of Cyrene, Simon
47 that, said, This *m* calleth for Elias.
57 there came a rich *m* of Arimathaea,
Mk 1.23 a *m* with an unclean spirit; and
44 See thou say nothing to any *m*:
2. 7 doth this *m* thus speak blasphemies?
10 know that the Son of *m* hath power
21 No *m* also seweth a piece of new
22 no *m* putteth new wine into old
27 The sabbath was made for *m*,
27 and not *m* for the sabbath:
28 the Son of *m* is Lord also of the
3. 1 was a *m* there which had a withered

3 the *m* which had the withered hand,
5 unto the *m*, Stretch forth thine hand.
27 No *m* can enter into a strong
27 he will first bind the strong *m*;
4.23 If any *m* have ears to hear, let him
26 as if a *m* should cast seed into the
41 What manner of *m* is this, that even
5. 2 tombs a *m* with an unclean spirit,
3 no *m* could bind him, no, not with
4 neither could any *m* tame him.
8 Come out of the *m*, thou unclean
37 he suffered no *m* to follow him,
43 that no *m* should know it; and
6. 2 whence hath this *m* these things?
20 knowing that he was a just *m* and
7.11 If a *m* shall say to his father or
15 There is nothing from without a *m*,
15 those are they that defile the *m*.
16 If any *m* have ears to hear, let him
18 from without entereth into the *m*,
20 out of the *m*, that defileth the *m*.
23 come from within, and defile the *m*.
24 and would have no *m* know it:
36 them that they should tell no *m*:
8. 4 can a *m* satisfy these men with
22 and they bring a blind *m* unto him,
23 And he took the blind *m* by the hand,
25 restored, and saw every *m* clearly.
30 that they should tell no *m* of him.
31 Son of *m* must suffer many things,
36 For what shall it profit a *m*, if he
37 a *m* give in exchange for his soul?
38 also shall the Son of *m* be ashamed,
9. 8 saw no *m* any more, save Jesus
9 them that they should tell no *m*
9 till the Son of *m* were risen from
12 how it is written of the Son of *m*,
30 not that any *m* should know it.
31 The Son of *m* is delivered into the
35 If any *m* desire to be first, the same
39 is no *m* which shall do a miracle
10. 2 lawful for a *m* to put away his wife?
7 cause shall a *m* leave his father and
9 together, let not *m* put asunder.
25 for a rich *m* to enter into the kingdom
29 is no *m* that hath left house, or
33 Son of *m* shall be delivered unto
45 For even the Son of *m* came not to
49 And they call the blind *m*, saying
51 The blind *m* said unto him, Lord,
11. 2 a colt tied, whereon never *m* sat;
3 if any *m* say unto you, Why do ye
14 No *m* eat fruit of thee hereafter
16 any *m* should carry any vessel
12. 1 A certain *m* planted a vineyard,
14 thou art true, and carest for no *m*:
34 no *m* after that durst ask him any
13. 5 Take heed lest any *m* deceive you:
21 then if any *m* shall say to you, Lo,
26 shall they see the Son of *m* coming
32 day and that hour knoweth no *m*,
34 For the Son of *m* is as a...taking a
34 is as a *m* taking a far journey,
34 servants, and to every *m* his work,
14.13 meet you a *m* bearing a pitcher
21 The Son of *m* indeed goeth, as it is
21 woe to that *m* by whom the Son of
21 by whom the Son of *m* is betrayed!
21 were it for that *m* if he had never
41 Son of *m* is betrayed into the hands
51 followed him a certain young *m*,
62 ye shall see the Son of *m* sitting on
71 know not this *m* of whom ye speak.
15.24 them, what every *m* should take.
39 Truly this *m* was the Son of God.
16. 5 they saw a young *m* sitting on the
8 said they any thing to any *m*;
Lk 1.18 for I am an old *m*, and my wife well
27 to a *m* whose name was Joseph,
34 shall this be, seeing I know not a *m*?
2.25 there was a *m* in Jerusalem, whose
25 the same *m* was just and devout,
52 and in favor with God and *m*.
3.14 Do violence to no *m*, neither
4. 4 *m* shall not live by bread alone,
33 in the synagogue there was a *m*,
5. 8 me; for I am a sinful *m*, O Lord.
12 city; behold a *m* full of leprosy:
14 And he charged him to tell no *m*:
18 brought in a bed a *m* which was
20 him, *M*, thy sins are forgiven thee.
24 Son of *m* hath power upon earth to
36 No *m* putteth a piece of a new
37 no *m* putteth new wine into old
39 No *m* also having drunk old wine
6. 5 the Son of *m* is Lord also of the
6 a *m* whose right hand was withered.
8 the *m* which had the withered hand,
10 he said unto the *m*, Stretch forth
30 Give to every *m* that asketh of thee;
45 good *m* out of the good treasure
45 an evil *m* out of the evil treasure of
48 He is like a *m* which built an house,
49 like a *m* that without a foundation
7. 8 I also am a *m* set under authority,
12 there was a dead *m* carried out,
14 Young *m*, I say unto thee, Arise.
25 see? A *m* clothed in soft raiment?
34 The Son of *m* is come eating and
34 Behold a gluttonous *m*, and a
39 This *m* if he were a prophet, would
8.16 No *m*, when he hath lighted a
25 What manner of *m* is this! for he
27 a certain *m*, which had devils long
29 unclean spirit to come out of the *m*.
33 Then went the devils out of the *m*,
35 found the *m* out of whom the devils
38 the *m* out of whom the devils were
41 there came a *m* named Jairus,
51 he suffered no *m* to go in, save
56 should tell no *m* what was done.
9.21 commanded them to tell no *m* that
22 The Son of *m* must suffer many
23 If any *m* will come after me, let him
25 For what is a *m* advantaged, if he
26 him shall the Son of *m* be ashamed,
36 and told no *m* in those days any of
38 a *m* of the company cried out,
44 for the Son of *m* shall be delivered
56 Son of *m* is not come to destroy
57 a certain *m* said unto him, Lord,
58 Son of *m* hath not where to lay his
62 No *m*, having put his hand to the
10. 4 and salute no *m* by the way.
22 no *m* knoweth who the Son is,
30 *m* went down from Jerusalem to
11.21 a strong *m* armed keepeth his
24 unclean spirit is gone out of a *m*,
26 last state of that *m* is worse than
30 Son of the *m* be to this generation.
33 No *m*, when he hath lighted a
12. 8 him shall the Son of *m* also confess
10 speak a word against the Son of *m*,
14 unto him, *M*, who made me a judge
16 ground of a certain rich *m* brought
40 Son of *m* cometh at an hour when
13. 6 A certain *m* had a fig tree planted in
19 of mustard seed, which a *m* took,
14. 2 a certain *m* before him which had
8 art bidden of any *m* to a wedding,
8 lest a more honorable *m* than thou
9 and say to thee, Give this *m* place;
16 certain *m* made a great supper, and
26 If any *m* come to me, and hate not his
30 This *m* began to build, and was
15. 2 This *m* receiveth sinners, and eateth
4 What *m* of you, having an hundred
11 he said, A certain *m* had two sons:
16 did eat: and no *m* gave unto him.
16. 1 There was a certain rich *m*, which
16 preached, and every *m* presseth into
19 There was a certain rich *m*, which
22 the rich *m* also died, and was buried;
17.22 one of the days of the Son of *m*,
24 so shall also the Son of *m* be in his
26 be also in the days of the Son of *m*.
30 day when the Son of *m* is revealed.
18. 2 feared not God, neither regarded *m*:
4 I fear not God, nor regard *m*;
8 when the Son of *m* cometh, shall he
14 this *m* went down to his house
25 a rich *m* to enter into the kingdom
29 is no *m* that hath left house, or
31 prophets concerning the Son of *m*
35 blind *m* sat by the wayside begging:
19. 2 was a *m* named Zacchaeus, which
7 be guest with a *m* that is a sinner.
8 have taken any thing from any *m*
10 the Son of *m* is come to seek and
14 will not have this *m* to reign over us.
15 how much every *m* had gained by
21 because thou art an austere *m*:
22 knewest that I was an austere *m*,
30 colt tied, whereon yet never *m* sat:
31 if any *m* ask you, Why do ye loose
20. 9 A certain *m* planted a vineyard,
21.27 see the Son of *m* coming in a cloud
36 and to stand before the Son of *m*.
22.10 a *m* meet you, bearing a pitcher
22 And truly the Son of *m* goeth, as it
22 that *m* by whom he is betrayed!
48 betrayest thou the Son of *m* with a
56 and said, This *m* was also with him.
58 And Peter said, *M*, I am not.
60 *M*, I know not what thou sayest.
69 Hereafter shall the Son of *m* sit on
23. 4 the people, I find no fault in this *m*.
6 whether the *m* were a Galilean.
14 Ye have brought this *m* unto me, as
14 I,...have found no fault in this *m*
18 Away with this *m*, and release unto
41 but this *m* hath done nothing amiss.
47 Certainly this was a righteous *m*.
50 there was a *m* named Joseph, a
50 and he was a good *m*, and a just:
52 This *m* went unto Pilate, and begged
53 wherein never *m* before was laid.
24. 7 The Son of *m* must be delivered
Jn 1. 6 There was a *m* sent from God, whose
9 lighteth every *m* that cometh into
13 nor of the will of *m*, but of God.
18 No *m* hath seen God at any time;
30 me cometh a *m* which is preferred
51 and descending upon the Son of *m*.
2.10 Every *m* at the beginning doth set
25 not that any should testify of *m*:
25 for he knew what was in *m*.
3. 1 There was a *m* of the Pharisees,
2 for no *m* can do these miracles
3 Except a *m* be born again, he
4 How can a *m* be born when he is
5 Except a *m* born of water and
13 no *m* hath ascended up to heaven,
13 the Son of *m* which is in heaven.
14 so must the Son of *m* be lifted up:
27 A *m* can receive nothing, except it
32 and no *m* receiveth his testimony.
4.27 no *m* said, What seeketh thou? or,
29 Come, see a *m*, which told me all
33 any *m* brought him ought to eat?
50 the *m* believed the word that Jesus
5. 5 certain *m* was there, which had an
7 The impotent *m* answered him, Sir,
7 I have no *m*, when the water is
9 immediately the *m* was made whole,
12 What *m* is that which said unto
15 *m* departed, and told the Jews that
22 the Father judgeth no *m*, but hath
27 also, because he is the Son of *m*.
34 But I receive not testimony from *m*:
6.27 the Son of *m* shall give unto you:
44 No *m* can come to me, except the
45 Every *m* therefore that hath heard,

Jn 6.46 that any *m* hath seen the Father,
50 a *m* may eat thereof, and not die.
51 if any *m* eat of this bread, he shall
52 can this *m* give us his flesh to eat?
53 ye eat the flesh of the Son of *m*,
62 if ye shall see the Son of *m* ascend
65 no *m* can come unto me, except
7. 4 is no *m* that doeth any thing in
12 some said, He is a good *m*: others
13 no *m* spake openly of him for fear
15 How knoweth this *m* letters, having
17 If any *m* will do his will, he shall
22 on the sabbath day circumcise a *m*.
23 If a *m* on the sabbath day receive
23 made a *m* every whit whole on the
27 we know this *m* whence he is: but
27 no *m* knoweth whence he is.
30 him: but no *m* laid hands on him,
31 than these which this *m* hath done?
37 If any *m* thirst, let him come unto
44 him; but no *m* laid hands on him.
46 answered, Never *m* spake like this
46 Never...spake like this *m*.
51 Doth our law judge any *m*, before
53 every *m* went unto his own house.
8.10 hath no *m* condemned thee?
11 She said, No *m* Lord. And Jesus
15 judge after the flesh; I judge no *m*.
20 and no *m* laid hands on him; for
28 ye have lifted up the Son of *m*,
33 and were never in bondage to any *m*:
40 a *m* that hath told you the truth,
51, 52 If a *m* keep my saying, he shall
9. 1 he saw a *m* which was blind from
2 who did sin, this *m*, or his parents,
3 hath this *m* sinned, nor his parents:
4 cometh, when no *m* can work.
6 he anointed the eyes of the blind *m*
11 A *m* that is called Jesus made clay,
16 This *m* is not of God, because he
16 said, How can a *m* that is a sinner
17 say unto the blind *m* again, What
22 if any *m* did confess that he was
24 called they the *m* that was blind,
24 we know that this *m* is a sinner.
30 *m* answered and said unto them,
31 but if any *m* be a worshipper of God,
32 that any *m* opened the eyes of one
33 If this *m* were not of God, he could do
10. 9 by me if any *m* enter in, he shall be
18 No *m* taketh it from me, but I lay
28 any *m* pluck them out of my hand.
29 no *m* is able to pluck them out of
33 being a *m*, makest thyself God.
41 that John spake of this *m* were true.
11. 1 a certain *m* was sick, named Lazarus,
9 *m* walk in the day, he stumbleth
10 But if a *m* walk in the night, he
37 Could not this *m*, which opened the
37 even this *m* should not have died?
47 for this *m* doeth many miracles.
50 one *m* should die for the people,
57 if any *m* knew where he were, he
12.23 the Son of *m* should be glorified.
26 If any *m* serve me, let him follow
26 if any *m* serve me him will my
34 The Son of *m* must be lifted up?
34 who is this Son of *m*?
47 And if any *m* hear my words, and
13.28 no *m* at the table knew for what
31 said, Now is the Son of *m* glorified,
14. 6 no *m* cometh unto the Father, but
23 If a *m* love me, he will keep my
15. 6 If a *m* abide not in me, he is cast
13 Greater love hath no *m* than this,
13 that a *m* lay down his life for his
24 the works which none other *m* did,
16.21 joy that a *m* is born into the world.
22 your joy no *m* taketh from you.
30 not that any *m* should ask thee:
32 shall be scattered, every *m* to his
18.14 one *m* should die for the people.
29 accusation bring ye against this *m*?
31 lawful for us to put any *m* to death:
40 saying, not this *m*, but Barabbas.
19. 5 saith unto them, Behold the *m*!
12 If thou let this *m* go, thou are not
41 wherein was never *m* yet laid.
21.21 Lord, and what shall this *m* do?
Ac 1.18 this *m* purchased a field with the
20 desolate, and let no *m* dwell therein:
2. 6 *m* heard them speak in his own
8 we every *m* in our own tongue,
22 a *m* approved of God among you
45 to all men, as every *m* had need.
3. 2 *m* lame from his mother's womb
11 lame *m* which was healed held Peter
12 holiness we had made this *m* to walk?
16 his name hath made this *m* strong,
4. 9 good deed done to the impotent *m*,
10 doth this *m* stand here before you
14 the *m* which was healed standing
17 henceforth to no *m* in this name.
22 the *m* was above forty years old,
35 every *m* according as he had need.
5. 1 a certain *m* named Ananias, with
13 durst no *m* join himself to them:
23 had opened, we found no *m* within.
37 After this *m* rose up Judas of Galilee
6. 5 a *m* full of faith and of the Holy
13 said, This *m* ceaseth not to speak
7.56 Son of *m* standing on the right hand
8. 9 was a certain *m*, called Simon,
10 This *m* is the great power of God.
27 behold, a *m* of Ethiopia, an eunuch
31 I, except some *m* should guide me?
34 this? of himself, or of some other *m*?
9. 7 hearing a voice, but seeing no *m*.
8 eyes were opened, he saw no *m*:
12 in a vision a *m* named Ananias
13 heard by many of this *m*, how much
33 he found a certain *m* named Aeneas,
10. 1 *m* in Caesarea called Cornelius,
2 A devout *m*, and one that feared God
22 just *m*, and one that feareth God,
26 Stand up; I myself also am a *m*.
28 a *m* that is a Jew to keep company,
28 should not call any *m* common or
30 a *m* stood before me in bright
47 Can any *m* forbid water, that
11.24 he was a good *m*, and full of the
29 every *m* according to his ability,
12.22 the voice of a god, and not of a *m*.
13. 7 Sergius Paulus, a prudent *m*; who
21 of Cis, a *m* of the tribe of Benjamin,
22 of Jesse, a *m* after mine own heart,
38 through this *m* is preached unto you
41 though a *m* declare it unto you.
14. 8 there sat a certain *m* at Lystra,
16. 9 There stood a *m* of Macedonia, and
17.31 by that *m* whom he hath ordained;
18.10 and no *m* shall set on thee to hurt
24 an eloquent *m*, and mighty in the
25 This *m* was instructed in the way of
19.16 the *m* in whom the evil spirit was
24 For a certain *m* named Demetrius,
35 what *m* is there that knoweth not
38 have a matter against any *m*, the law
20. 9 sat in a window a certain young *m*
12 And they brought the young *m* alive,
21. 9 And the same *m* had four daughters,
11 bind the *m* that owneth this girdle,
28 This is the *m*, that teacheth all men
39 I am a *m* which am a Jew of Tarsus,
22. 3 I am verily a *m* which am a Jew,
12 a devout *m* according to the law,
25 to scourge a *m* that is a Roman,
26 thou doest: for this *m* is a Roman.
23. 9 saying, We find no evil in this *m*:
17 Bring this young *m* unto the chief
18 to bring this young *m* unto thee,
22 captain...let the young *m* depart,
22 tell no *m* that thou hast shewed
27 This *m* was taken of the Jews, and
30 that the Jews laid wait for the *m*,
24. 5 have found this *m* a pestilent fellow,
12 the temple disputing with any *m*,
25. 5 down with me, and accuse this *m*,
11 no *m* may deliver me unto them.
14 a certain *m* left in bonds by Felix:
16 the Romans to deliver any *m* to die,
17 commanded the *m* to be brought
22 I would also hear the *m* myself.
24 ye see this *m*, about whom all the
26.31 This *m* doeth nothing worthy of
32 This *m* might have been set at
28. 4 No doubt this *m* is a murderer,
7 possessions of the chief *m* of the
31 all confidence, no *m* forbidding him.
Ro 1.23 image made like to corruptible *m*,
2. 1 inexcusable, O *m*, whosoever thou
3 And thinkest thou this, O *m*, that
6 to every *m* according to his deeds:
9 every soul of *m* that doeth evil,
10 to every *m* that worketh good,
21 that preachest a *m* should not steal,
22 that sayest a *m* should not commit
3. 4 let God be true, but every *m* a liar;
5 taketh vengeance? (I speak as a *m*)
28 a *m* is justified by faith without the
4. 6 describeth the blessedness of the *m*,
8 Blessed is the *m* to whom the Lord
5. 7 for a righteous *m* will one die:
7 good *m* some would even dare to die.
12 as by one *m* sin entered into the
15 gift by grace, which is by one *m*,
6. 6 our old *m* is crucified with him,
7. 1 law hath dominion over a *m* as long
3 liveth, she be married to another *m*,
3 though she be married to another *m*.
22 the law of God after the inward *m*:
24 O wretched *m* that I am! who shall
8. 9 if any *m* have not the Spirit of Christ,
24 for what a *m* seeth, why doth he
9.20 O *m*, who art thou that repliest
10. 5 the *m* which doeth those things
10 For with the heart *m* believeth unto
12. 3 to every *m* that is among you, not to
3 dealt to every *m* the measure of
17 Recompense to no *m* evil for evil.
13. 8 Owe no *m* any thing, but to love
14. 5 One *m* esteemeth one day above
5 Let every *m* be fully persuaded in
7 himself, and no *m* dieth to himself.
13 that no *m* put a stumblingblock
20 for that *m* who eateth with offense.
1Co 2. 9 have entered into the heart of *m*,
11 For what *m* knoweth the things
11 knoweth the things of a *m*, save
11 the spirit of *m* which is in him?
11 the things of God knoweth no *m*,
14 natural *m* receiveth not the things
15 yet he himself is judged of no *m*.
3. 5 as the Lord gave to every *m*?
8 and every *m* shall receive his own
10 every *m* take heed how he buildeth
11 can no *m* lay than that is laid,
12 if any *m* build upon this foundation
17 If any *m* defile the temple of God,
18 Let no *m* deceive himself.
18 any *m* among you seemeth to be wise
21 Therefore let no *m* glory in men.
4. 1 Let a *m* so account of us, as of the
2 that a *m* be found faithful.
5 shall every *m* have praise of God.
5.11 if any *m* that is called a brother be
6. 5 that there is not a wise *m* among you?
18 Every sin that a *m* doeth is without
7. 1 good for a *m* not to touch a woman.
2 let every *m* have his own wife, and
7 But every *m* hath his proper gift
16 how knowest thou, O *m*, whether
17 God hath distributed to every *m*,

18 any *m* called being circumcised?
20 every *m* abide in the same calling
24 let every *m*, wherein he is called,
26 say, that is good for a *m* so to be.
36 But if any *m* think that he behaveth
8. 2 if any *m* think that he knoweth any
3 But if any *m* love God, the same is
7 not in every *m* that knowledge:
10 For if any *m* see thee which hast
9. 8 Say I these things as a *m*? or saith
15 any *m* should make my glorying
25 And every *m* that striveth for the
10.13 you but such as is common to *m*:
24 Let no *m* seek his own,
24 but every *m* another's wealth.
28 But if any *m* say unto you, This
11. 3 that the head of every *m* is Christ;
3 the head of the woman is the *m*;
4 Every *m* praying or prophesying,
7 a *m* indeed ought not to cover his
7 the woman is the glory of the *m*.
8 For the *m* is not of the woman;
8 woman; but the woman of the *m*.
9 was the *m* created for the woman;
9 woman; but the woman for the *m*.
11 neither is the *m* without the woman,
11 neither the woman without the *m*,
12 For as the woman is of the *m*, even
12 so is the *m* also by the woman;
14 if a *m* have long hair, it is a shame
16 if any *m* seem to be contentious, we
28 But let a *m* examine himself, and
34 if any *m* hunger, let him eat at home;
12. 3 no *m* speaking by the Spirit of God
3 that no *m* can say that Jesus is the
7 given to every *m* to profit withal.
11 dividing to every *m* severally as he
13.11 when I became a *m*, I put away
14. 2 for no *m* understandeth him;
27 any *m* speak in an unknown tongue,
37 any *m* think himself to be a prophet,
38 But if any *m* be ignorant, let him be
15.21 For since by *m* came death,
21 by *m* came also the resurrection of
23 But every *m* in his own order:
35 some *m* will say, How are the dead
45 first *m* Adam was made a living
47 The first *m* is of the earth, earthy:
47 second *m* is the Lord from heaven.
16.11 Let no *m* therefore despise him:
22 If any *m* love not the Lord Jesus
2Co 2. 6 Sufficient to such a *m* is this
4.16 but though our outward *m* perish,
16 the inward *m* is renewed day by day.
5.16 know we no *m* after the flesh:
17 Therefore if any *m* be in Christ, he is
7. 2 us; we have wronged no *m*,
2 we have corrupted no *m*,
2 we have defrauded no *m*.
8.12 is...according to that a *m* hath,
20 that no *m* should blame us in this
9. 7 Every *m* according as he purposeth
10. 7 If any *m* trust to himself that he is
11. 9 I was chargeable to no *m*: for
10 no *m* shall stop me of this boasting
16 again, let no *m* think me a fool; if
20 if a *m* bring you into bondage,
20 if a *m* devour you, if a *m* take of
20 a *m* exalt himself, if a *m* smite
12. 2 I knew a *m* in Christ above
3 I knew such a *m*, (whether in the
4 it is not lawful for a *m* to utter.
6 any *m* should think of me above
Gal 1. 1 men, neither by *m*, but by Jesus
9 any *m* preach any other gospel unto
11 was preached of me is not after *m*.
12 I neither received it of *m*, neither
2.16 knowing that a *m* is not justified by
3.11 no *m* is justified by the law in the
12 *m* that doeth them shall live in
15 no *m* disannulleth, or addeth

5. 3 I testify again to every *m* that is
6. 1 if a *m* be overtaken in a fault, ye
3 For if a *m* think himself to be
4 let every *m* prove his own work,
5 every *m* shall bear his own burden.
7 whatsoever a *m* soweth, that shall
17 henceforth let no *m* trouble me:
Eph 2. 9 works, lest any *m* should boast.
15 in himself of twain one new *m*,
3.16 might by his Spirit in the inner *m*;
4.13 the Son of God, unto a perfect *m*,
22 former conversation the old *m*,
24 that ye put on the new *m*, which
25 every *m* truth with his neighbor:
5. 5 nor unclean person, nor covetous *m*
6 Let no *m* deceive you with vain
29 For no *m* ever yet hated his own
31 cause shall a *m* leave his father
6. 8 whatsoever good thing any *m* doeth,
Php 2. 4 Look not every *m* on his own
4 but every *m* also on the things of
8 being found in fashion as a man,
20 I have no *m* likeminded, who will
3. 4 If any other *m* thinketh that he hath
Col 1.28 we preach, warning every *m*, and
28 teaching every *m* in all wisdom;
28 we may present every *m* perfect in
2. 4 lest any *m* should beguile you
8 Beware lest any *m* spoil you
16 Let no *m* therefore judge you in
18 Let no *m* beguile you of your
3. 9 put off the old *m* with his deeds;
10 And have put on the new *m*, which is
13 any *m* have a quarrel against any:
4. 6 how ye ought to answer every *m*.
1Th 3. 3 no *m* should be moved by these
4. 6 That no *m* go beyond and defraud his
8 despiseth not *m*, but God, who
5.15 none render evil for evil unto any *m*;
2Th 2. 3 Let no *m* deceive you by any
3 that *m* of sin be revealed, the son
3.14 if any *m* obey not our word by this
14 note that *m*, and have no company
1Ti 1. 8 is good, if a *m* use it lawfully;
9 the law is not made for a righteous *m*,
2. 5 God and men, the *m* Christ Jesus;
12 nor to usurp authority over the *m*,
3. 1 a *m* desire the office of a bishop,
5 if a *m* know now how to rule his
4.12 no *m* despise thy youth; but be
5. 9 having been the wife of one *m*,
16 If any *m* or woman that believeth
22 Lay hands suddenly on no *m*,
6. 3 If any *m* teach otherwise, and
11 O *m* of God, flee these things; and
16 the light which no *m* can approach
16 whom no *m* hath seen, nor can see:
2Ti 2. 4 No *m* that warreth entangleth
5 if a *m* also strive for masteries,
21 If a *m* therefore purge himself
3.17 That the *m* of God may be perfect,
4.16 first answer no *m* stood with me,
Tit 2.15 authority. Let no *m* despise thee.
3. 2 To speak evil of no *m*, to be no
4 our Saviour toward *m* appeared,
10 A *m* that is an heretick, after the
Heb 2. 6 What is *m*, that thou art mindful
6 son of *m*, that thou visitest him?
9 God should taste death for every *m*.
3. 3 this *m* was counted worthy of more
4 every house is builded by some *m*;
4.11 lest any *m* fall after the same example
5. 4 And no *m* taketh this honor unto
7. 4 consider how great this *m* was,
13 no *m* gave attendance at the altar.
24 But this *m*, because he continueth
8. 2 which the Lord pitched, and not *m*.
3 this *m* have somewhat also to offer.
11 shall not teach every *m* his neighbor,
11 and every *m* his brother, saying,
10.12 this *m*, after he had offered one

38 but if any *m* draw back, my soul
12.14 which no *m* shall see the Lord:
15 any *m* fail of the grace of God;
13. 6 not fear what *m* shall do unto me.
Jas 1. 7 that *m* think that he shall receive
8 double minded *m* is unstable in
11 the rich *m* fade away in his ways.
12 Blessed is the *m* that endureth
13 no *m* say when he is tempted,
13 evil, neither tempteth he any *m*:
14 every *m* is tempted, when he is
19 let every *m* be swift to hear, slow
20 For the wrath of *m* worketh not the
23 unto a *m* beholding his natural face
24 forgetteth what manner of *m* he was.
25 this *m* shall be blessed in his deed.
26 *m* among you seem to be religious,
2. 2 assembly a *m* with a gold ring,
2 come in also a poor *m* in vile raiment;
14 though a *m* say he hath faith, and
18 a *m* may say, Thou hast faith, and
20 O vain *m*, that faith without works
24 how that by works a *m* is justified,
3. 2 any *m* offend not in word, the same
2 the same is a perfect *m*, and able
8 the tongue can no *m* tame; it is an
13 Who is a wise *m* and endued with
5.16 fervent prayer of a righteous *m*
17 *m* subject to like passions as we
1Pe 1.24 glory of *m* as the flower of grass.
2.13 ordinance of *m* for the Lord's sake:
19 if a *m* for conscience toward God
3. 4 it be the hidden *m* of the heart,
15 answer to every *m* that asketh
4.10 As every *m* hath received the gift,
11 If any *m* speak, let him speak as the
11 if any *m* minister, let him do it as of
16 if any *m* suffer as a Christian, let him
2Pe 1.21 not in old time by the will of *m*:
2. 8 that righteous *m* dwelling among
19 of whom a *m* is overcome, of the
1Jn 2. 1 if any *m* sin, we have an advocate
15 If any *m* love the world, the love
27 ye need not that any *m* teach you:
3. 3 And every *m* that hath this hope
7 children, let no *m* deceive you:
4.12 No *m* hath seen God at any time.
20 If any *m* say, I love God, and
5.16 If any *m* see his brother sin a sin
Rev 1.13 one like unto the Son of *m*, clothed
2.17 which no *m* knoweth saving he
3. 7 that openeth, and no *m* shutteth;
7 and shutteth, and no *m* openeth;
8 open door, and no *m* can shut it:
11 hast, that no *m* take thy crown.
20 if any *m* hear my voice, and open
4. 7 the third beast had a face as a *m*,
5. 3 And no *m* in heaven, nor in earth,
4 no *m* was found worthy to open
6.15 every bondman, and every free *m*,
7. 9 multitude,...no *m* could number,
9. 5 a scorpion, when he striketh a *m*.
11. 5 And if any *m* will hurt them, fire
5 and if any *m* will hurt them, he must
12. 5 And she brought forth a *m* child,
13 which brought forth the *m* child.
13. 9 If any *m* have an ear, let him hear.
17 And that no *m* might buy or sell,
18 for it is the number of a *m*; and
14. 3 no *m* could learn that song but
9 If any *m* worship the beast and his
14 cloud one sat like unto the Son of *m*,
15. 8 no *m* was able to enter into the
16. 3 it became as the blood of a dead *m*:
18.11 no *m* buyeth their merchandise
19.12 a name written, that no *m* knew,
20.13 every *m* according to their works.
21.17 according to the measure of a *m*,
22.12 every *m* according as his work
18 every *m* that heareth the words

MANASSEH

King of Judah and successor of Hezekiah, 7th century B.C.; reigns for fifty-five years; restores the idolatrous high places destroyed by Hezekiah and promotes the worship of Baal; builds altars for Assyrian astral deities within the precincts of the Jerusalem temple; practices human sacrifice and divination, and sheds much innocent blood (2Ki 21.1-9, 16); for these transgressions it is prophesied that Jerusalem and Judah will fall into the hands of their enemies (2Ki 21.10-15); is taken captive by the Assyrians to Babylon, where he repents, and on returning to Jerusalem carries out some religious reforms (2Ch 33.11-17); is succeeded by his son Amon (2Ki 21.18). Despite evident prosperity of his long reign, regarded by later tradition as one of Judah's worst kings.

Rev 22.18 If any *m* shall add unto these
19 if any *m* shall take away from the

MANASSEH

2Ki 20.21 and *M* his son reigned in his stead.
21. 1 *M* was twelve years old when he
9 *M* seduced them to do more evil
11 *M* king of Judah had done these
16 *M* shed innocent blood very much,
17 the rest of the acts of *M*, and all
18 *M* slept with his fathers, and was
20 of the Lord, as his father *M* did.
23.12 the altars which *M* had made in
26 provocations that *M* had provoked
24. 3 for the sins of *M*, according to all
1Ch 3.13 son, Hezekiah his son, *M* his son,
2Ch 32.33 *M* his son reigned in his stead.
33. 1 *M* was twelve years old when he
9 So *M* made Judah and the
10 the Lord spake to *M*, and to his
11 which took *M* among the thorns,
13 *M* knew that the Lord he was God.
18 the rest of the acts of *M*, and his
20 So *M* slept with his fathers, and
22 of the Lord, as did *M* his father:
22 images which *M* his father had
23 as *M* his father had humbled
Jer 15. 4 of *M* the son of Hezekiah king of

MANASSES

Mt 1.10 And Ezekias begat *M*; and
10 *M* begat Amon; and Amon begat
Rev 7. 6 the tribe of *M* were sealed twelve

MANDRAKES

Gen 30.14 found *m* in the field, and brought
14 Give me, I pray thee, of thy son's *m*.
15 thou take away my son's *m* also?
15 with thee to night for thy son's *m*.
16 have hired thee with my son's *m*.
SS 7.13 The *m* give a smell, and our gates

MANGER

Lk 2. 7 clothes, and laid him in a *m*;
12 in swaddling clothes, lying in a *m*.
16 and the babe lying in the *m*.

MANIFEST

Ec 3.18 that God might *m* them, and that
Lk 8.17 secret, that shall not be made *m*;
Jn 1.31 he should be made *m* to Israel,
3.21 that his deeds may be made *m*,
9. 3 works of God should be made *m*
14.21 him, and will *m* myself to him.
22 that thou wilt *m* thyself unto us,
Ac 4.16 is *m* to all them that dwell in
Ro 1.19 be known of God is *m* in them;
10.20 I was made *m* unto them that
16.26 But now is made *m*, and by the
1Co 3.13 man's work shall be made *m*: for
4. 5 make *m* the counsels of the hearts:
11.19 may be made *m* among you.
14.25 the secrets of his heart made *m*;
15.27 him, it is *m* that he is excepted,
2Co 2.14 and maketh *m* the savor of his
4.10 of Jesus...be made *m* in our body.
11 of Jesus might be made *m* in our
5.11 but we are made *m* unto God; and
11 I trust also are made *m* in your
11. 6 we have been thoroughly made *m*
Gal 5.19 Now the works of the flesh are *m*,
Eph 5.13 reproved are made *m* by the light:
13 whatsoever doth make *m* is light.
Php 1.13 my bonds in Christ are *m* in all
Col 1.26 but now is made *m* to his saints:
4. 4 I may make it *m*, as I ought to
2Th 1. 5 a *m* token of the righteous judgment
1Ti 3.16 God was *m* in the flesh, justified
5.25 the good works of some are *m*
2Ti 1.10 is now made *m* by the appearing
3. 9 folly shall be *m* unto all men, as
Heb 4.13 creature that is not *m* in his sight:
9. 8 holiest of all was not yet made *m*,
1Pe 1.20 was *m* in these last times for you,
1Jn 2.19 they might be made *m* that they
3.10 In this the children of God are *m*,
Rev 15. 4 for thy judgments are made *m*.

MANIFESTATION

Ro 8.19 for the *m* of the sons of God.
1Co 12. 7 But the *m* of the Spirit is given to
2Co 4. 2 by *m* of the truth commending

MANIFESTED

Mk 4.22 nothing hid, which shall not be *m*;
Jn 2.11 of Galilee, and *m* forth his glory;
17. 6 I have *m* thy name unto the men
Ro 3.21 of God without the law is *m*, being
Tit 1. 3 But hath in due times *m* his word
1Jn 1. 2 the life was *m*, and we have seen
2 the Father, and was *m* unto us;)
3. 5 that he was *m* to take away our
8 purpose the Son of God was *m*,
4. 9 In this was *m* the love of God

MANIFESTLY

2Co 3. 3 *m* declared to be the epistle of

MANIFOLD

Neh 9.19 thou in thy *m* mercies forsookest
27 according to thy *m* mercies thou
Ps 104.24 O Lord, how *m* are thy works! in
Am 5.12 I know your *m* transgressions
Lk 18.30 Who shall not receive *m* more in
Eph 3.10 the church the *m* wisdom of God,
1Pe 1. 6 through *m* temptations:
4.10 stewards of the *m* grace of God.

MANKIND

Lev 18.22 Thou shalt not lie with *m*, as with
20.13 If a man also lie with *m*, as he
Job 12.10 thing, and the breath of all *m*,
1Co 6. 9 nor abusers of themselves with *m*,
1Ti 1.10 them that defile themselves with *m*,
Jas 3. 7 and hath been tamed of *m*:

MANNA

Ex 16.15 it, said one to another, It is *m*:
31 Israel called the name thereof *M*:
33 and put an omer full of *m* therein,
35 children of Israel did eat *m* forty
35 they did eat *m*, until they came
Nu 11. 6 is nothing at all, besides this *m*,
7 And the *m* was as coriander seed,
9 in the night, the *m* fell upon it.
Dt 8. 3 and fed thee with *m*, which thou
16 fed thee in the wilderness with *m*,
Jos 5.12 And the *m* ceased on the morrow
12 the children of Israel *m* any more;
Neh 9.20 withheldest not thy *m* from their
Ps 78.24 rained down *m* upon them to eat,
Jn 6.31 Our fathers did eat *m* in the
49 Your fathers did eat *m* in the
58 not as your fathers did eat *m*, and
Heb 9. 4 was the golden pot that had *m*,
Rev 2.17 will I give to eat of the hidden *m*,

MANNER

Gen 18.25 far from thee to do after this *m*,
19.31 us after the *m* of all the earth:
Nu 28.18 ye shall do no *m* of servile work
2Ki 11.14 stood by a pillar, as the *m* was,
17.26 not the *m* of the God of the land:
Isa 51. 6 dwell therein shall die in like *m*:
Dan 6.23 no *m* of hurt was found upon him,
Mt 4.23 and healing all *m* of sickness and
23 all *m* of disease among the people.
5.11 shall say all *m* of evil against you
6. 9 After this *m* therefore pray ye:
8.27 What *m* of man is this, that even
10. 1 and to heal all *m* of sickness and
1 of sickness and all *m* of disease.
12.31 All *m* of sin and blasphemy shall
Mk 4.41 What *m* of man is this, that
13. 1 Master, see what *m* of stones and
29 So ye in like *m*, when ye shall see
Lk 1.29 what *m* of salutation this should
66 What *m* of child shall this be!
6.23 in the like *m* did their fathers
7.39 who and what *m* of woman this is
8.25 What *m* of man is this! for he
9.55 not what *m* of spirit ye are of.
11.42 mint and rue and all *m* of herbs,
20.31 and in like *m* the seven also: and
24.17 What *m* of communications are
Jn 2. 6 the *m* of the purifying of the Jews,
7.36 What *m* of saying is this that he said,
19.40 as the *m* of the Jews is to bury.
Ac 1.11 like *m* as ye have seen him go
10.12 were all *m* of fourfooted beasts of
15. 1 circumcised after the *m* of Moses,
23 letters by them after this *m*;
17. 2 And Paul, as his *m* was, went
20.18 after what *m* I have been with you
22. 3 to the perfect *m* of the law of the
23.25 And he wrote a letter after this *m*:
25.16 It is not the *m* of the Romans to
20 doubted of such *m* of questions,
26. 4 My *m* of life from my youth, which
Ro 6.19 I speak after the *m* of men because
7. 8 in me all *m* of concupiscence.
1Co 7. 7 one after this *m*, and another
11.25 the same *m* also he took the cup,
15.32 If after the *m* of men I have fought
2Co 7. 9 ye were made sorry after a godly *m*,
Gal 2.14 livest after the *m* of Gentiles,
3.15 I speak after the *m* of men;
1Th 1. 5 ye know what *m* of men we were
9 what *m* of entering in we had
1Ti 2. 9 In like *m* also, that women adorn
2Ti 3.10 known my doctrine, *m* of life,
Heb 10.25 together, as the *m* of some is;
Jas 1.24 forgetteth what *m* of man he was.
1Pe 1.11 what *m* of time the Spirit of
15 ye holy in all *m* of conversation;
3. 5 For after this *m* in the old time
2Pe 3.11 what *m* of persons ought ye to be
1Jn 3. 1 what *m* of love the Father hath
Jude 7 cities about them in like *m*,
Rev 11. 5 them, he must in this *m* be killed.
18.12 wood, and all *m* vessels of ivory,
12 and all *m* vessels of most precious
21.19 with all *m* of precious stones.
22. 2 of life, which bare twelve *m* of fruits,

MARBLE

1Ch 29. 2 and *m* stones in abundance.
Est 1. 6 to silver rings and pillars of *m*:
6 and blue, and white, and black, *m*.
SS 5.15 His legs are as pillars of *m*, set
Rev 18.12 and of brass, and iron, and *m*,

MARCH

Ps 68. 7 didst *m* through the wilderness;
Jer 46.22 for they shall *m* with an army,
Joel 2. 7 they shall *m* every one on his ways,
Hab 1. 6 shall *m* through the breadth of
3.12 Thou didst *m* through the land in

MARCHED

Ex 14.10 the Egyptians *m* after them;

MARCUS

Col 4.10 and *M*, sister's son to Barnabas,
Phm 24 *M*, Aristarchus, Demas, Lucas,
1Pe 5.13 you; and so doth *M* my son.

MARINERS

Eze 27. 8 of Zidon and Arvad were thy *m*:
9 the ships of the sea with their *m*
27 thy *m*, and thy pilots, thy calkers,
29 the *m*, and all the pilots of the sea,
Jon 1. 5 Then the *m* were afraid, and cried

MARK

Gen 4.15 the Lord set a *m* upon Cain, lest
Ru 3. 4 *m* the place where he shall lie,
1Sa 20.20 thereof, as though I shot at a *m*.
2Sa 13.28 *M* ye now when Amnon's heart
1Ki 20. 7 *M*, I pray you, and see how this
22 and *m*, and see what thou doest:
Job 7.20 thou set me as a *m* against thee,
16.12 pieces, and set me up for his *m*.
18. 2 *m*, and afterwards we will speak.
21. 5 *M* me, and be astonished, and lay
33.31 *M* well, O Job, hearken unto me:
39. 1 thou *m* when the hinds do calve?
Ps 37.37 *M* the perfect man, and behold
48.13 *M* ye well her bulwarks, consider
56. 6 they *m* my steps, when they wait
130. 3 thou, Lord, shouldest *m* iniquities,
La 3.12 and set me as a *m* for the arrow.
Eze 9. 4 *m* upon the foreheads of the men
6 any man upon whom is the *m*;
44. 5 Son of man, *m* well, and behold
5 *m* well the entering in of the
Ro 16.17 *m* them which cause divisions and
Php 3.14 press toward the *m* for the prize
17 *m* them which walk so as ye have
Rev 13.16 to receive a *m* in their right hand,
17 save he that had the *m*, or the
14. 9 and receive his *m* in his forehead,
11 receiveth the *m* of his name.
15. 2 over his image, and over his *m*,
16. 2 upon the men which had the *m* of
19.20 had received the *m* of the beast,
20. 4 had received his *m* upon their

MARK

Ac 12.12 of John, whose surname was *M*;
25 John, whose surname was *M*.
15.37 John, whose surname was *M*.
39 and so Barnabas took *M*, and
2Ti 4.11 Take *M*, and bring him with thee:

MARKED

1Sa 1.12 the Lord, and Eli *m* her mouth.
Job 22.15 Hast thou *m* the old way which
24.16 *m* for themselves in the daytime:
Jer 2.22 yet thine iniquity is *m* before me,
23.18 who hath *m* his word, and heard
Lk 14. 7 when he *m* how they chose out

MARKEST

Job 10.14 If I sin, then thou *m* me, and

Biblical Themes

MARRIAGE

And Isaac brought her into his mother Sarah's tent, and took Rebekah, and she became his wife; and he loved her: and Isaac was comforted after his mother's death. Gen 24.67

And Jacob served seven years for Rachel; and they seemed unto him but a few days, for the love he had to her. Gen 29.20

If a man be found lying with a woman married to an husband, then they shall both of them die, both the man that lay with the woman, and the woman: so shalt thou put away evil from Israel. Dt 22.22

Whoso findeth a wife findeth a good thing, and obtaineth favor of the Lord. Pr 18.22

She looketh well to the ways of her household, and eateth not the bread of idleness. Her children arise up, and call her blessed; her husband also, and he praiseth her. Pr 31.27-28

Thou shalt no more be termed Forsaken; neither shall thy land any more be termed Desolate: but thou shalt be called Hephzibah, and thy land Beulah: for the Lord delighteth in thee, and thy land shall be married. . . . as the bridegroom rejoiceth over the bride, so shall thy God rejoice over thee. Isa 62.4-5

While he thought on these things, behold, the angel of the Lord appeared unto him in a dream, saying, Joseph, thou son of David, fear not to take unto thee Mary thy wife: for that which is conceived in her is of the Holy Ghost. Mt 1.20

The Pharisees also came unto him, tempting him, and saying . . . Is it lawful for a man to put away his wife for every cause? And he answered . . . Have ye not read, that he which made them at the beginning made them male and female, and said, For this cause shall a man leave father and mother, and shall cleave to his wife: and they twain shall be one flesh? Wherefore they are no more twain, but one flesh. What therefore God hath joined together, let not man put asunder. Mt 19.3-6

In the resurrection they neither marry, nor are given in marriage, but are as the angels of God in heaven. Mt 22.30

And the third day there was a marriage in Cana of Galilee; and the mother of Jesus was there: and both Jesus was called, and his disciples, to the marriage. Jn 2.1-2

It is good for a man not to touch a woman. Nevertheless, to avoid fornication, let every man have his own wife, and let every woman have her own husband. . . . for it is better to marry than to burn. 1Co 7.1-2, 9

The unbelieving husband is sanctified by the wife, and the unbelieving wife is sanctified by the husband. 1Co 7.14

Wives, submit yourselves unto your own husbands, as unto the Lord. . . . Husbands, love your wives, even as Christ also loved the church, and gave himself for it. Eph 5.22, 25

Ye wives, be in subjection to your own husbands; that, if any obey not the word, they also may without the word be won by the conversation of the wives . . . Likewise, ye husbands, dwell with them according to knowledge, giving honor unto the wife, as unto the weaker vessel, and as being heirs together of the grace of life. 1Pe 3.1, 7

Blessed are they which are called unto the marriage supper of the Lamb. Rev 19.9

I John saw the holy city, new Jerusalem, coming down from God out of heaven, prepared as a bride adorned for her husband. Rev 21.2

MARKET

Eze 27.13 and vessels of brass in thy *m*.
17 they traded in thy *m* wheat of
19 and calamus, were in thy *m*.
25 Tarshish did sing of thee in thy *m*:
Mk 7. 4 And when they come from the *m*,
Jn 5. 2 at Jerusalem by the sheep *m* a pool,
Ac 17.17 in the *m* daily with them that met

MARKETH

Job 33.11 in the stocks, he *m* all my paths.
Isa 44.13 *m* it out with a line; he fitteth it
13 *m* it out with the compass, and

MARKETPLACE

Mt 20. 3 saw others standing idle in the *m*,
Lk 7.32 like unto children sitting in the *m*,
Ac 16.19 them into the *m* unto the rulers,

MARKETPLACES

Mk 12.38 and love salutations in the *m*,

MARKETS

Mt 11.16 like unto children sitting in the *m*,
23. 7 greetings in the *m*, and to be called
Lk 11.43 synagogues, and greetings in the *m*.
20.46 robes, and love greetings in the *m*,

MARKS
Lev 19.28 dead, nor print any *m* upon you:
Gal 6.17 my body the *m* of the Lord Jesus.

MARRED
Isa 52.14 his visage was so *m* more than
Jer 13. 7 the girdle was *m*, it was profitable
18. 4 vessel that he made of clay was *m*
Na 2. 2 out, and *m* their vine branches.
Mk 2.22 spilled, and the bottles will be *m*:

MARRIAGE
Ex 21.10 her raiment, and her duty of *m*,
Ps 78.63 maidens were not given to *m*.
Mt 22. 2 king which made a *m* for his son,
4 are ready: come unto the *m*.
9 many as ye shall find, bid to the *m*.
30 neither marry, nor are given in *m*,
24.38 marrying and giving in *m*, until
25.10 ready went in with him to the *m*:
Mk 12.25 neither marry, nor are given in *m*;
Lk 17.27 they were given in *m*, until the
20.34 world marry, and are given in *m*:
35 neither marry, nor are given in *m*:
Jn 2. 1 there was a *m* in Cana of Galilee;
2 called, and his disciples, to the *m*.
1Co 7.38 that giveth her in *m* doeth well;
38 giveth her not in *m* doeth better.
Heb 13. 4 *M* is honorable in all, and the
Rev 19. 7 for the *m* of the Lamb is come,
9 unto the *m* supper of the Lamb.

MARRIAGES
Gen 34. 9 make ye *m* with us, and give your
Dt 7. 3 Neither shalt thou make *m* with
Jos 23.12 shall make *m* with them, and go

MARRIED
Gen 19.14 in law, which *m* his daughters,
Ex 21. 3 if he were *m*, then his wife
Lev 22.12 If the priest's daughter also be *m*
Nu 12. 1 of the...woman whom he had *m*:
1 he had *m* an Ethiopian woman.
36. 3 And if they be *m* to any of the sons
11 *m* unto their father's brother's sons:
12 were *m* into the families of the sons
Dt 22.22 with a woman *m* to an husband.
24. 1 hath taken a wife, and *m* her,
1Ch 2.21 he *m* when he was threescore
2Ch 13.21 mighty, and *m* fourteen wives,
Neh 13.23 that had *m* wives of Ashdod,
Pr 30.23 odious woman when she is *m*;
Isa 54. 1 than the children of the *m* wife,
62. 4 in thee, and thy land shall be *m*.
Jer 3.14 the Lord; for I am *m* unto you:
Mal 2.11 *m* the daughter of a strange god.
Mt 22.25 the first, when he had *m* a wife,
Mk 6.17 Philip's wife: for he had *m* her.
10.12 husband, and be *m* to another,
Lk 14.20 another said, I have *m* a wife,
17.27 did eat, they drank, they *m* wives,
Ro 7. 3 liveth, she be *m* to another man,
3 though she be *m* to another man.
4 that ye should be *m* to another,
1Co 7.10 unto the *m* I command, yet not I,
33 he that is *m* careth for the things
34 she that is *m* careth for the things
39 liberty to be *m* to whom she will;

MARRIETH
Isa 62. 5 For as a young man *m* a virgin,
Mt 19. 9 whoso *m* her which is put away
Lk 16.18 away his wife, and *m* another,
18 whosoever *m* her that is put away

MARROW
Job 21.24 his bones are moistened with *m*.
Ps 63. 5 satisfied as with *m* and fatness;
Pr 3. 8 to thy navel, and *m* to thy bones.
Isa 25. 6 of fat things full of *m*, of wines
Heb 4.12 spirit, and of the joints and *m*,

MARRY
Gen 38. 8 thy brother's wife, and *m* her,
Nu 36. 6 them *m* to whom they think best;
6 tribe of their father shall they *m*.
Dt 25. 5 not *m* without unto a stranger:
Isa 62. 5 virgin, so shall thy sons *m* thee:
Mt 5.32 shall *m* her that is divorced
19. 9 *m* another, committeth adultery:
10 with his wife, it is not good to *m*.
22.24 his brother shall *m* his wife, and
30 in the resurrection they neither *m*,
Mk 10.11 put away his wife, and *m* another,
12.25 they neither *m*, nor are given in
Lk 20.34 The children of this world *m*, and
35 the dead, neither *m*, nor are given
1Co 7. 9 they cannot contain, let them *m*:
9 for it is better to *m* than to burn.
28 if thou *m*, thou hast not sinned;
28 if a virgin *m*, she hath not sinned.
36 will, he sinneth not: let them *m*.
1Ti 4. 3 Forbidding to *m*, and commanding
5.11 wanton against Christ, they will *m*;
14 that the younger women *m*, bear

MARRYING
Neh 13.27 our God in *m* strange wives?
Mt 24.38 *m* and giving in marriage, until

MARS'
Ac 17.22 Paul stood in the midst of *M* hill,

MARTHA
Lk 10.38 and a certain woman named *M*
40 But *M* was cumbered about much
41 *M*, *M*, thou art careful and
Jn 11. 1 the town of Mary and her sister *M*.
5 Jesus loved *M*, and her sister,
19 the Jews came to *M* and Mary, to
20 Then *M*, as soon as she heard that
21 Then said *M* unto Jesus, Lord, if
24 *M* saith unto him, I know that he
30 in that place where *M* met him.
39 *M*, the sister of him that was dead,
12. 2 made him a supper; and *M* served:

MARTYR
Ac 22.20 blood, of thy *m* Stephen was shed,
Rev 2.13 Antipas was my faithful *m*, who

MARTYRS
Rev 17. 6 with the blood of the *m* of Jesus:

MARVEL
Ec 5. 8 in a province, *m* not at the matter:
Mk 5.20 done for him: and all men did *m*.
Jn 3. 7 *M* not that I said unto thee, Ye
5.20 works than these, that ye may *m*.
28 *M* not at this: for the hour is
7.21 have done one work, and ye all *m*.
Ac 3.12 men of Israel, why *m* ye at this?
2Co 11.14 And no *m*; for Satan himself is
Gal 1. 6 I *m* that ye are so soon removed
1Jn 3.13 *M* not, my brethren, if the world
Rev 17. 7 unto me, Wherefore didst thou *m*?

MARVELLED
Gen 43.33 and the men *m* one at another.
Ps 48. 5 They saw it, and so they *m*; they
Mt 8.10 When Jesus heard it, he *m*, and
27 the men *m*, saying, What manner
9. 8 when the multitudes saw it, they *m*,
33 the multitudes *m*, saying, It was
21.20 when the disciples saw it, they *m*,
22.22 had heard these words, they *m*,
27.14 that the governor *m* greatly.
Mk 6. 6 he *m* because of their unbelief.
12.17 are God's. And they *m* at him.
15. 5 answered nothing; so that Pilate *m*.
44 Pilate *m* if he were already dead:
Lk 1.21 and *m* that he tarried so long in the
63 name is John. And they *m* all.
2.33 And Joseph and his mother *m* at
7. 9 heard these things, he *m* at him,
11.38 he *m* that he had not first washed
20.26 and they *m* at his answer, and held
Jn 4.27 *m* that he talked with the woman:
7.15 the Jews *m*, saying, How knoweth
Ac 2. 7 they were all amazed and *m*,
4.13 and ignorant men, they *m*; and

MARVELLOUS
1Ch 16.12 Remember his *m* works that he
24 his *m* works among all nations.
Job 5. 9 *m* things without number:
10.16 thou shewest thyself *m* upon me.
Ps 9. 1 I will shew forth all thy *m* works.
17. 7 Shew thy *m* lovingkindness, O
31.21 hath shewed me his *m* kindness
78.12 *M* things did he in the sight of
98. 1 for he hath done *m* things: his
105. 5 Remember his *m* works that he
118.23 Lord's doing; it is *m* in our eyes.
139.14 *m* are thy works; and that my soul
Isa 29.14 I will proceed to do a *m* work
14 even a *m* work and a wonder:
Dan 11.36 speak *m* things against the God of
Mic 7.15 will I shew unto him *m* things.
Zec 8. 6 it be *m* in the eyes of the remnant
6 should it also be *m* in mine eyes?
Mt 21.42 doing, and it is *m* in our eyes?
Mk 12.11 doing, and it is *m* in our eyes?
Jn 9.30 Why herein is a *m* thing, that ye
1Pe 2. 9 out of darkness into his *m* light:
Rev 15. 1 sign in heaven, great and *m*, seven
3 Great and *m* are thy works, Lord

MARVELLOUSLY
2Ch 26.15 for he was *m* helped, till he was
Job 37. 5 God thundereth *m* with his voice;
Hab 1. 5 and regard, and wonder *m*:

MARVELS
Ex 34.10 before all thy people I will do *m*,

MARY
Mt 1.16 begat Joseph the husband of *M*,
18 mother *M* was espoused to Joseph,
20 fear not to take unto thee *M* thy
2.11 young child with *M* his mother,
13.55 son? Is not his mother called *M*?
27.56 Among which was *M* Magdalene,
56 *M* the mother of James and Joses,
61 And there was *M* Magdalene, and
61 the other *M*, sitting over against
28. 1 came *M* Magdalene and the other
1 the other *M* to see the sepulchre.
Mk 6. 3 this the carpenter, the son of *M*,

MARTHA AND MARY

The two sisters of Lazarus, whose sickness and death are the occasion of one of Jesus' greatest miracles; on Jesus' arrival Mary stays at home while Martha goes out to meet him and proclaims her faith in him as Christ, the Son of God (Jn 11). Lazarus does not figure in Luke's account of a different episode, in which Martha, when Jesus is invited to their home, is "cumbered about much serving," whereas Mary sits at his feet and hears his word (Lk 10.38-42). According to John, the sisters' home is in Bethany, near Jerusalem, and Mary is identified as the woman who anoints the feet of Jesus and wipes his feet with her hair (Jn 12.3); differing accounts of this, however, are found in the other Gospels.

The Virgin Mary is shown with the body of Christ in her arms and Mary Magdalene in the background in this Pietà by Hans Memling, a 15th-century portraitist celebrated for his many depictions of the Virgin.

Mk 15.40 among whom was *M* Magdalene,
40 *M* the mother of James the less
47 *M* Magdalene and...the mother of
47 and *M* the mother of Joses beheld
16. 1 sabbath was past, *M* Magdalene,
1 and *M* the mother of James, and
9 he appeared first to *M* Magdalene,
Lk 1.27 and the virgin's name was *M*.
30 angel said unto her, Fear not, *M*:
34 Then said *M* unto the angel, How
38 And *M* said, Behold the handmaid
39 *M* arose in those days, and went
41 heard the salutation of *M*, the
46 And *M* said, My soul doth magnify
56 And *M* abode with her about three
2. 5 be taxed with *M* his espoused wife,
16 haste, and found *M*, and Joseph,
19 But *M* kept all these things, and
34 said unto *M* his mother, Behold,
8. 2 *M* called Magdalene, out of whom
10.39 And she had a sister called *M*,
42 and *M* hath chosen that good part,
24.10 It was *M* Magdalene, and Joanna,
10 *M* the mother of James, and other
Jn 11. 1 town of *M* and her sister Martha.
2 that *M* which anointed the Lord
19 the Jews came to Martha and *M*,
20 him: but *M* sat still in the house.
28 and called *M* her sister secretly,
31 when they saw *M*, that she rose up
32 *M* was come where Jesus was,
45 of the Jews which came to *M*, and
12. 3 Then took *M* a pound of ointment
19.25 *M* the wife of Cleophas, and
25 of Cleophas, and *M* Magdalene.
20. 1 week cometh *M* Magdalene early,
11 *M* stood without at the sepulcher
16 Jesus saith unto her, *M*. She
18 *M* Magdalene came and told the
Ac 1.14 and *M* the mother of Jesus, and
12.12 house of *M* the mother of John,
Ro 16. 6 Greet *M*, who bestowed much

MASONS

2Sa 5.11 trees, and carpenters, and *m*:
2Ki 12.12 And to *m*, and hewers of stone,
22. 6 carpenters, and builders, and *m*,
1Ch 14. 1 with *m* and carpenters, to
22. 2 he set *m* to hew wrought stones
2Ch 24.12 hired *m* and carpenters to repair
Ezr 3. 7 They gave money also unto the *m*,

MAST

Pr 23.34 he that lieth upon the top of a *m*.
Isa 33.23 not well strengthen their *m*,

MASTER

2Ki 5. 1 was a great man with his *m*, and
20 my *m* hath spared Naaman this
Pr 30.10 Accuse not a servant unto his *m*,
Isa 24. 2 as with the servant, so with his *m*;
Mal 1. 6 and if I be a *m*, where is my fear?
2.12 doeth this, the *m* and the scholar,
Mt 8.19 unto him, *M*, I will follow thee
9.11 Why eateth your *M* with publicans
10.24 The disciple is not above his *m*,
25 for the disciple that he be as his *m*,
25 they have called the *m* of the house
12.38 *M*, we would see a sign from thee.
17.24 said, Doth not your *m* pay tribute?
19.16 Good *M*, what good thing shall I
22.16 *M*, we know that thou art true,
24 *M*, Moses said, If a man die,
36 *M*, which is...great commandment
23. 8 for one is your *M*, even Christ;
10 for one is your *M*, even Christ.
26.18 The *M* saith, My time is at hand;
25 answered and said, *M*, is it I?
49 and said, Hail, *m*; and kissed him.
Mk 4.38 him, *M*, carest thou not that we
5.35 troublest thou the *M* any further?
9. 5 *M*, it is good for us to be here:
17 *M*, I have brought unto thee my
38 *M*, we saw one casting out devils
10.17 Good *M*, what shall I do that I
20 *M*, all these have I observed from
35 *M*, we would that thou shouldest
11.21 *M*, behold, the fig tree which thou
12.14 *M*, we know that thou art true,
19 *M*, Moses wrote unto us, If a man's
32 Well, *M*, thou hast said the truth:
13. 1 *M*, see what manner of stones and
35 when the *m* of the house cometh,
14.14 to the goodman...The *M* saith,
45 saith, *M*, *m*; and kissed him.
Lk 3.12 unto him, *M*, what shall we do?
5. 5 *M*, we have toiled all the night,
6.40 The disciple is not above his *m*:
40 that is perfect shall be as his *m*.
7.40 thee. And he saith, *M*, say on.
8.24 him, saying, *M*, *m*, we perish.
45 *M*, the multitude throng thee and
49 is dead; trouble not the *M*.
9.33 *M*, it is good for us to be here:
38 *M*, I beseech thee, look upon my
49 *M*, we saw one casting out devils
10.25 *M*, what shall I do to inherit
11.45 *M*, thus saying thou reproachest
12.13 *M*, speak to my brother, that he
13.25 When once the *m* of the house is
14.21 *m* of the house being angry said
17.13 said, Jesus, *M*, have mercy on us.
18.18 Good *M*, what shall I do to inherit
19.39 unto him, *M*, rebuke thy disciples.
20.21 *M*, we know that thou sayest and
28 *M*, Moses wrote unto us, If any
39 said, *M*, thou hast well said.

21. 7 *M*, but when shall these things be?
22.11 The *M* saith unto thee, Where is
Jn 1.38 is to say, being interpreted, *M*,)
3.10 Art thou a *m* of Israel, and knowest
4.31 prayed him, saying, *M*, eat.
8. 4 *M*, this woman was taken in
9. 2 *M*, who did sin, this man, or his
11. 8 *M*, the Jews of late sought to stone
28 The *M* is come, and calleth for
13.13 Ye call me *M* and Lord: and ye
14 If I then, your Lord and *M*, have
20.16 him, Rabboni; which is to say, *M*.
Ac 27.11 the *m* and the owner of the ship,
Ro 14. 4 to his own *m* he standeth or
Eph 6. 9 that your *M* also is in heaven;
Col 4. 1 that ye also have a *M* in heaven.
(See box page 496)

MASTERBUILDER

1Co 3.10 is given unto me, as a wise *m*,

MASTER'S

Gen 24.27 me to the house of my *m* brethren.
36 And Sarah my *m* wife bare a son to
44 hath appointed out for my *m* son.
48 to take my *m* brother's daughter
51 and let her be thy *m* son's wife, as
39. 7 *m* wife cast her eyes upon Joseph;
8 said unto his *m* wife, Behold, my
Ex 21. 4 and her children shall be her *m*,
1Sa 29.10 thy *m* servants that are come with
2Sa 9. 9 have given unto thy *m* son all that
10 that thy *m* son may have food to
10 thy *m* son shall eat bread alway
12. 8 I gave thee thy *m* house, and thy
8 thy *m* wives into thy bosom, and
16. 3 said, And where is thy *m* son?
2Ki 6.32 the sound of his *m* feet behind him?
10. 2 seeing your *m* sons are with you,
3 best and meetest of your *m* sons,
3 throne, and fight for your *m* house.
6 the heads of the men your *m* sons,
18.24 of the least of my *m* servants,
Isa 1. 3 his owner, and the ass his *m* crib:
36. 9 of the least of my *m* servants, and
2Ti 2.21 and meet for the *m* use, and

MARY

The mother of Jesus; still a virgin when he is conceived in the course of an angelic visitation, during which, after some initial hesitation, she shows her readiness to accept God's will: "Behold the handmaid of the Lord"; visiting her cousin Elisabeth during pregnancy, she responds to her greeting with a hymn of praise: "My soul doth magnify the Lord" (Lk 1); in obedience to an imperial decree, travels to Bethlehem with her husband, Joseph, and it is there that Jesus is born; taking the child to the temple to make an offering in accordance with Jewish law, she hears a prophecy of her own pain: "a sword shall pierce through thy own soul also" (Lk 2.35); advised by the wise men who have come from the East with gifts for the newborn king, Joseph takes Mary and the child to Egypt to escape the murderous intentions of Herod (Mt 2); returning after Herod's death, they settle in Nazareth, but go up to Jerusalem annually for the passover; on one of these visits Jesus causes his mother great anxiety by staying behind to converse with some "doctors," or learned teachers (Lk 2.41-51). Outside the infancy narratives, Mary is mentioned directly only four times in the New Testament: once when she advises Jesus of the shortage of wine at the marriage feast of Cana (Jn 2.1-11); once when she joins his brethren in a request to see him, and hears him identify "my mother, my sister and my brother" as those who do the will of God (Mt 12.50); at Calvary, where she is entrusted to the care of the beloved disciple (Jn 19.27); and finally in Jerusalem after the Ascension, at prayer with the disciples, the women, and the brothers of Jesus (Ac 1.14).

MASTERS

Ps 123. 2 look unto the hand of their *m*,
Pr 25.13 for he refresheth the soul of his *m*.
Ec 12.11 fastened by the *m* of assemblies,
Jer 27. 4 command them to say unto their *m*,
4 Thus shall ye say unto your *m*;
Am 4. 1 which say to their *m*, Bring, and
Mt 6.24 No man can serve two *m*: for
23.10 Neither be ye called *m*: for one is
Lk 16.13 No servant can serve two *m*: for
Ac 16.16 which brought her *m* much gain
19 when her *m* saw that the hope of
Eph 6. 5 obedient to them that are your *m*
9 ye *m*, do the same things unto
Col 3.22 Servants, obey in all things your *m*
4. 1 *M*, give unto your servants that
1Ti 6. 1 their own *m* worthy of all honor,
2 And they that have believing *m*,
Tit 2. 9 to be obedient unto their own *m*,
Jas 3. 1 My brethren, be not many *m*,
1Pe 2.18 subject to your *m* with all fear;

MASTERS'

Zep 1. 9 fill their *m* houses with violence
Mt 15.27 which fall from their *m* table.

MASTERIES

2Ti 2. 5 And if a man also strive for *m*, yet

MASTERY

Ex 32.18 voice of them that shout for *m*,
Dan 6.24 and the lions had the *m* of them,
1Co 9.25 every man that striveth for the *m*

MATTER

Gen 30.15 Is it a small *m* that thou hast taken
Ex 18.22 every great *m* they shall bring
22 but every small *m* they shall judge:
1Sa 20.39 Jonathan and David knew the *m*.
1Ch 26.32 for every *m* pertaining to God, and
Job 19.28 the root of the *m* is found in me?
Ps 45. 1 My heart is inditing a good *m*:
Pr 11.13 a faithful spirit concealeth the *m*.
16.20 He that handleth a *m* wisely shall
17. 9 he that repeateth a *m* separateth
18.13 answereth a *m* before he heareth
25. 2 of kings is to search out a *m*.
Ec 12.13 the conclusion of the whole *m*:
Dan 2.10 earth that can shew the king's *m*:
7.28 me: but I kept the *m* in my heart.
Mk 1.45 much, and to blaze abroad the *m*,
10.10 asked him again of the same *m*.
Ac 8.21 neither part nor lot in this *m*:
11. 4 rehearsed the *m* from the beginning,
15. 6 together for to consider of this *m*.
17.32 We will hear thee again of this *m*.
18.14 a *m* of wrong or wicked lewdness,
19.38 him, have a *m* against any man,
24.22 know the uttermost of your *m*.
1Co 6. 1 you, having a *m* against another,
2Co 7.11 yourselves to be clear in this *m*.
9. 5 might be ready, as a *m* of bounty,
Gal 2. 6 they were, it maketh no *m* to me:
1Th 4. 6 and defraud his brother in any *m*:
Jas 3. 5 great a *m* a little fire kindleth!

MARY MAGDALENE

Mary Magdalene, "out of whom went seven devils," was one of a group of women similarly cured who followed Jesus and "ministered unto him of their substance" (Lk 8.2-3). She is often identified as the woman who receives Jesus' grateful praise when, anointing his feet and wiping them with her hair, she meets with the disapproval of the house owner, a Pharisee: "Her sins, which are many, are forgiven; for she loved much" (Lk 7.36-50); but Luke himself does not make this identification. (According to Matthew and Mark, this scene takes place in Bethany—Luke has it in Galilee—and it is Jesus' head that is anointed, not his feet.) Mary accompanies the other women who follow Jesus in his journey to Golgotha (Mt 27.56), and later to the sepulcher (Mt 27.61), where, along with his mother, "she beheld where he was laid" (Mk 15.47). According to John she is the first to see the empty tomb and runs to inform Peter and John; later she mistakes Jesus for the gardener, but when she tries to cling to him, she is told to go instead and tell the disciples of his ascent to his Father (Jn 20).

MATTERS

Ex 24.14 if any man have any *m* to do, let
Dt 17. 8 *m* of controversy within thy gates:
1Sa 16.18 a man of war, and prudent in *m*,
2Sa 11.19 an end of telling me the *m* of the war
15. 3 See, thy *m* are good and right;
19.29 speakest thou any more of thy *m*?
2Ch 19.11 is over you in all *m* of the Lord;
11 house of Judah, for all the king's *m*:
Neh 11.24 in all *m* concerning the people.
Est 3. 4 whether Mordecai's *m* would stand:
9.31 the *m* of the fastings and their cry.
32 confirmed these *m* of Purim;
Job 33.13 giveth not account of any of his *m*.
Ps 35.20 devise deceitful *m* against them
131. 1 do I exercise myself in great *m*,
Dan 1.20 *m* of wisdom and understanding,
7. 1 dream, and told the sum of the *m*.
Mt 23.23 omitted the weightier *m* of the law,
Ac 18.15 to it; for I will be no judge of such *m*.
19.39 any thing concerning other *m*,
25.20 and there be judged of these *m*.
1Co 6. 2 unworthy to judge the smallest *m*?
1Pe 4.15 or as a busybody in other men's *m*.

MATTHEW

Mt 9. 9 he saw a man, named *M*, sitting
10. 3 Thomas, and *M* the publican;
Mk 3.18 Bartholomew, and *M*, and Thomas,
Lk 6.15 *M* and Thomas, James the son of
Ac 1.13 Thomas, Bartholomew, and *M*,

MATTHIAS

Ac 1.23 was surnamed Justus, and *M*.
26 their lots; and the lot fell upon *M*;

MAY

Gen 3. 2 We *m* eat of the fruit of the trees of
11. 4 whose top *m* reach unto heaven;
27. 4 my soul *m* bless thee before I die.
44.26 for we *m* not see the man's face,
Ex 2. 7 that she *m* nurse the child for thee?
3.18 we *m* sacrifice to the Lord our God.
13. 9 the Lord's law *m* be in thy mouth:
16. 4 that I *m* prove them, whether they

BIBLICAL THEMES

MASTER AND SERVANT

The Lord was with Joseph, and he was a prosperous man; and he was in the house of his master the Egyptian. And his master saw . . . that the Lord made all that he did to prosper in his hand. And Joseph found grace in his sight, and he served him: and he made him overseer over his house, and all that he had he put into his hand. Gen 39.2-4

And the king of Israel answered and said, My lord, O king, according to thy saying, I am thine, and all that I have. 1Ki 20.4

Is there not an appointed time to man upon earth? are not his days also like the days of an hireling? As a servant earnestly desireth the shadow, and as an hireling looketh for the reward of his work: so am I. Job 7.1-3

I had rather be a doorkeeper in the house of my God, than to dwell in the tents of wickedness. Ps 84.10

The ox knoweth his owner, and the ass his master's crib: but Israel doth not know. Isa 1.3

Thou art my servant, O Israel, in whom I will be glorified. . . . I will also give thee for a light to the Gentiles, that thou mayest be my salvation unto the end of the earth. Isa 49.3, 6

Who is among you that feareth the Lord, that obeyeth the voice of his servant . . . ? Isa 50.10

By his knowledge shall my righteous servant justify many; for he shall bear their iniquities. Isa 53.11

No man can serve two masters. . . . Ye cannot serve God and mammon. Mt 6.24

The centurion answered and said, Lord, I am not worthy that thou shouldest come under my roof: but speak the word only, and my servant shall be healed. Mt 8.8

The disciple is not above his master, nor the servant above his lord. It is enough for the disciple that he be as his master, and the servant as his lord. Mt 10.24-25

Friend, I do thee no wrong: didst not thou agree with me for a penny? Take that thine is, and go thy way: I will give unto this last, even as unto thee. Is it not lawful for me to do what I will with mine own? Mt 20.13-15

Call no man your father upon the earth: for one is your Father, which is in heaven. Neither be ye called masters: for one is your Master, even Christ. But he that is greatest among you shall be your servant. Mt 23.9-11

Who then is a faithful and wise servant, whom his lord hath made ruler over his household, to give them meat in due season? Blessed is that servant, whom his lord when he cometh shall find so doing. Mt 24.45-46

Whosoever of you will be the chiefest, shall be servant of all. For even the Son of man came not to be ministered unto, but to minister. Mk 10.44-45

When ye shall have done all those things . . . say, We are unprofitable servants: we have done that which was our duty to do. Lk 17.10

Who art thou that judgest another man's servant? to his own master he standeth or falleth. Ro 14.4

Though I be free from all men, yet have I made myself servant unto all, that I might gain the more. 1Co 9.19

Servants, be obedient to them that are your masters according to the flesh, with fear and trembling, in singleness of your heart, as unto Christ. . . . And, ye masters, do the same things unto them, forbearing threatening: knowing that your Master also is in heaven; neither is there respect of persons with him. Eph 6.5, 9

Ex 23.11 that the poor of thy people *m* eat:
31.15 Six days *m* work be done; but in the
33.13 now thy way, that I *m* know thee,
13 that I *m* find grace in thy sight:
Dt 2.28 sell me meat for money, that I *m* eat;
28 me water for money, that I *m* drink:
4.10 they *m* learn to fear me all the days
10 and that they *m* teach their children.
40 this day, that it *m* go well with thee,
5.14 maidservant *m* rest as well as thou.
11.18 *m* be as frontlets between your eyes.
14.20 But of all clean fowls ye *m* eat.
25. 3 Forty stripes he *m* give him, and not
Jdg 14.13 Put forth thy riddle, that we *m* hear
16.26 Suffer me that I *m* feel the pillars
Ru 1. 9 Lord grant you that ye *m* find rest,
1Sa 14. 6 it *m* be that the Lord will work for us:
15.25 with me, that I *m* worship the Lord.
2Sa 24. 2 *m* know the number of the people.
1Ki 3. 9 I *m* discern between good and bad:
8.43 of the earth *m* know thy name,
60 earth *m* know that the Lord is God,
18.37 *m* know that thou art the Lord
22. 8 by whom we *m* inquire of the Lord:
2Ki 4.42 unto the people, that they *m* eat.
5.12 *m* I not wash in them, and be clean?
6.29 Give thy son, that we *m* eat him: and
2Ch 6.33 of the earth *m* know thy name,
7.16 that my name *m* be there for ever:
Ezr 9. 8 our God *m* lighten our eyes, and give
Job 10.20 alone, that I *m* take comfort a little,
13.13 peace, let me alone, that I *m* speak,
14. 6 Turn from him, that he *m* rest, till he
19.29 that ye *m* know there is a judgment.
21. 3 Suffer me that I *m* speak; and after
31. 6 that God *m* know mine integrity.
32.20 I will speak, that I *m* be refreshed:
34.36 is that Job *m* be tried unto the end
36.25 man *m* behold it afar off.
37. 7 man; that all men *m* know his work.
Ps 27. 4 I *m* dwell in the house of the Lord
30. 5 weeping *m* endure for a night, but
39. 4 it is; that I *m* know how frail I am.
51. 8 bones...thou hast broken *m* rejoice.
56.13 I *m* walk before God in the light of
61. 8 that I *m* daily perform my vows.
67. 2 That thy way *m* be known upon
73.28 God, that I *m* declare all thy works.
76. 7 and who *m* stand in thy sight when
84. 3 nest...where she *m* lay her young,
85. 9 him; that glory *m* dwell in our land.
90.12 we *m* apply our hearts unto wisdom.
14 we *m* rejoice and be glad all our
104. 9 set a bound that they *m* not pass
106. 5 That I *m* see the good of thy chosen,
5 that I *m* rejoice in the gladness of thy
5 that I *m* glory with thine inheritance.
119.18 I *m* behold wondrous things out of
77 mercies come unto me, that I *m* live:
124. 1 was on our side, now *m* Israel say;
Pr 20.21 An inheritance *m* be gotten hastily at
27. 1 knowest not what a day *m* bring
11 I *m* answer him that reproacheth
Ec 2.26 *m* give to him that is good before
Isa 10.19 be few, that a child *m* write them.
37. 4 It *m* be the Lord thy God will hear
42.18 and look, ye blind, that ye *m* see.
55. 6 Seek ye the Lord while he *m* be
10 bud, that it *m* give seed to the sower,
Jer 26. 3 that I *m* repent me of the evil, which
Eze 14.11 but that they *m* be my people, and I
11 I *m* be their God, saith the Lord
20.20 *m* know that I am the Lord your
Hos 8. 4 them idols, that they *m* be cut off.
Am 5.14 good, and not evil, that ye *m* live:
Mal 3. 2 who *m* abide the day of his coming?
Mt 2. 8 that I *m* come and worship him also.
6. 5 streets, that they *m* be seen of men.
9.21 If I *m* but touch his garment, I shall
20.21 Grant that these my two sons *m* sit,
33 Lord, that our eyes *m* be opened.
26.42 if this cup *m* not pass away from
Mk 4.12 That seeing they *m* see, and not
12 and hearing they *m* hear, and not
5.28 If I *m* touch but his clothes, I shall
10.17 shall I do that I *m* inherit eternal life?
37 Grant unto us that we *m* sit, one on
Lk 5.24 that ye *m* know that the Son of man
18.41 said, Lord, that I *m* receive my sight.
20.13 it *m* be they will reverence him
Jn 1.22 that we *m* give an answer to them
6.40 on him, *m* have everlasting life: and
50 a man *m* eat thereof, and not die.
10.38 that ye *m* know, and believe, that the
12.36 that ye *m* be the children of light.
13.18 but that the scripture *m* be fulfilled,
14. 3 that where I am, there ye *m* be also.
13 the Father *m* be glorified in the Son.
17.11 me, that they *m* be one, as we are.
21 That they all *m* be one; as thou,
21 that the world *m* believe that thou
Ac 8.19 hands, he *m* receive the Holy Ghost.
17.19 *M* we know what this new doctrine,
Ro 3. 8 Let us do evil, that good *m* come?
6. 1 in sin, that grace *m* abound?
15.13 *m* abound in hope, through the
1Co 1. 8 *m* be blameless in the day of our

3.18 become a fool, that he *m* be wise.
9.24 the prize? So run, that ye *m* obtain.
2Co 5.10 that every one *m* receive the things
12 that ye *m* have somewhat to answer
9. 8 *m* abound to every good work:
12. 9 the power of Christ *m* rest upon me.
Gal 6.13 that they *m* glory in your flesh.
Eph 3. 4 ye *m* understand my knowledge
17 Christ *m* dwell in your hearts by
18 *M* be able to comprehend with all
4.15 *m* grow up into him in all things,
6. 3 That it *m* be well with thee, and thou
11 *m* be able to stand against the wiles
19 that utterance *m* be given unto me.
20 that therein I *m* speak boldly, as I
Php 3. 8 them but dung, that I *m* win Christ,
10 That I *m* know him, and the power
Col 4. 6 ye *m* know how ye ought to answer
1Ti 6.19 that they *m* lay hold on eternal life.
2Ti 1. 4 thy tears, that I *m* be filled with joy;
2.10 *m* also obtain the salvation which is
3.17 That the man of God *m* be perfect,
Heb 4.16 we *m* obtain mercy, and find grace
12.28 whereby we *m* serve God acceptably
1Pe 2.15 with well doing ye *m* put to silence
4.11 that God in all things *m* be glorified
1Jn 4.17 that we *m* have boldness in the day
2Jn 1.12 face to face, that our joy *m* be full.
Rev 14.13 that they *m* rest from their labors;

MAYEST

Gen 2.16 tree of the garden thou *m* freely eat:
28. 4 thou *m* inherit the land wherein thou
Ex 3.10 that thou *m* bring forth my people
8.10 *m* know that there is none like unto
9.29 *m* know...the earth is the Lord's.
18.19 thou *m* bring the causes unto God:
24.12 written; that thou *m* teach them.
Lev 22.23 *m* thou offer for a free will offering;
Nu 10.31 and thou *m* be to us instead of eyes.
Dt 4.40 that thou *m* prolong thy days upon
11.15 cattle, that thou *m* eat and be full.
14.23 thou *m* learn to fear the Lord thy
16. 3 thou *m* remember the day when
23.20 a stranger thou *m* lend upon usury:
30. 6 with all thy soul, that thou *m* live.
20 That thou *m* love the Lord thy God,
Jos 1. 7 *m* prosper wheresoever thou goest.
1Ki 2. 3 *m* prosper in all that thou doest, and
8.29 *m* hearken unto the prayer which thy
2Ki 5. 6 thou *m* recover him of his leprosy.
Job 40. 8 me, that thou *m* be righteous?
Ps 94.13 That thou *m* give him rest from the
104.27 thou *m* give them their meat in due
Pr 19.20 that thou *m* be wise in thy latter end.
Isa 23.16 songs, that thou *m* be remembered.
49. 6 thou *m* be my salvation unto the end
Eze 16.54 That thou *m* bear thine own shame,
Mk 14.12 that thou *m* eat the passover?
Lk 12.58 that thou *m* be delivered from him;
16. 2 for thou *m* be no longer steward.
Ac 8.37 with all thine heart, thou *m*.
24. 8 *m* take knowledge of all these things,
11 Because that thou *m* understand,
1Co 7.21 but if thou *m* be made free, use
Eph 6. 3 and thou *m* live long on the earth.
1Ti 3.15 that thou *m* know how thou oughtest
3Jn 2 that thou *m* prosper and be in health,
Rev 3.18 tried in the fire, that thou *m* be rich;
18 that thou *m* be clothed, and that the
18 eyes with eyesalve, that thou *m* see.

MEAL

Gen 18. 6 three measures of fine *m*,
Nu 5.15 part of an ephah of barley *m*;
1Ki 4.22 and threescore measures of *m*,
17.12 but an handful of *m* in a barrel,
14 barrel of *m* shall not waste, neither
16 the barrel of *m* wasted not, neither
2Ki 4.41 But he said, Then bring *m*. And
1Ch 12.40 meat, *m*, cakes of figs, and bunches
Isa 47. 2 Take the millstones, and grind *m*:
Hos 8. 7 stalk: the bud shall yield no *m*:
Mt 13.33 and hid in three measures of *m*,
Lk 13.21 and hid in three measures of *m*,

MEAN

Ex 12.26 unto you, What *m* ye by this service?
Dt 6.20 What *m* the testimonies, and the
Jos 4. 6 saying, What *m* ye by these stones?
21 saying, What *m* these stones?
1Ki 18.45 came to pass in the *m* while,
Pr 22.29 he shall not stand before *m* men.
Isa 2. 9 the *m* man boweth down, and the
3.15 *m* ye that ye beat my people to
5.15 the *m* man shall be brought down,
31. 8 the sword, not of a *m* man, shall
Eze 17.12 Know ye not what these things *m*?
18. 2 What *m* ye, that ye use this proverb
Mk 9.10 rising from the dead should *m*.
Lk 12. 1 In the *m* time, when there were
Jn 4.31 the *m* while his disciples prayed
Ac 10.17 vision...he had seen should *m*,
17.20 know...what these things *m*.
21.13 What *m* ye to weep and to break
39 in Cilicia, a citizen of no *m* city:
Ro 2.15 thoughts the *m* while accusing
2Co 8.13 I *m* not that other men be eased, and

MEANEST

Gen 33. 8 What *m* thou by all this drove which
2Sa 16. 2 unto Ziba, What *m* thou by these?
Eze 37.18 not show us what thou *m* by these?
Jon 1. 6 unto him, What *m* thou, O sleeper?

MEANETH

Dt 29.24 what *m* the heat of this great anger?
1Sa 4. 6 What *m* the noise of this great shout
14 What *m* the noise of this tumult?
15.14 *m* then this bleating of the sheep
Isa 10. 7 Howbeit he *m* not so, neither
Mt 9.13 But go ye and learn what that *m*,
12. 7 But if ye had known what this *m*,
Ac 2.12 one to another, What *m* this?

MEANING

Dan 8.15 the vision, and sought for the *m*,
Ac 27. 2 *m* to sail by the coasts of Asia;
1Co 14.11 if I know not the *m* of the voice,

MEANS

Ex 34. 7 that will by no *m* clear the guilty;
Nu 14.18 and by no *m* clearing the guilty,
Jdg 5.22 broken by *m* of the pransings, the
16. 5 by what *m* we may prevail against
2Sa 14.14 yet doth he devise *m*, that his
1Ki 10.29 they bring them out by their *m*.
20.39 if by any *m* he be missing, then shall
2Ch 1.17 for the kings of Syria, by their *m*.
Ezr 4.16 by this *m* thou shalt have no
Ps 49. 7 can by any *m* redeem his brother,
Pr 6.26 For by *m* of a whorish woman a
Jer 5.31 the priests bear rule by their *m*;
Mal 1. 9 this hath been by your *m*: will he
Mt 5.26 Thou shalt by no *m* come out
Lk 5.18 and they sought *m* to bring him in,
8.36 by what *m* he that was possessed
10.19 nothing shall by any *m* hurt you.
Jn 9.21 But by what *m* he now seeth, we
Ac 4. 9 by what *m* he is made whole;
18.21 I must by all *m* keep this feast
27.12 if by any *m* they might attain to
Ro 1.10 if by any *m* now at length I might
11.14 If by any *m* I may provoke to
1Co 8. 9 heed lest by any *m* this liberty of
9.22 that I might by all *m* save some.
27 lest that by any *m*, when I have
2Co 1.11 upon us by the *m* of many persons
11. 3 lest by any *m*, as the serpent
Gal 2. 2 lest by any *m* I should run, or had
Php 3.11 If by any *m* I might attain unto
1Th 3. 5 lest by some *m* the tempter have
2Th 2. 3 no man deceive you by any *m*:
3.16 give you peace always by all *m*.
Heb 9.15 testament, that by *m* of death,
Rev 13.14 by the *m* of those miracles which he

MEANT

Gen 50.20 God *m* it unto good, to bring to
Lk 15.26 and asked what these things *m*.
18.36 pass by, he asked what it *m*.

MEASURE

Ex 26. 2 the curtains shall have one *m*.
8 curtains shall be all of one *m*.
Lev 19.35 in meteyard, in weight, or in *m*.
Nu 35. 5 ye shall *m* from without the city
Dt 21. 2 they shall *m* unto the cities which
25.15 and just *m* shalt thou have: that
Jos 3. 4 about two thousand cubits by *m*:
1Ki 6.25 were of one *m* and one size.
7.37 one casting, one *m*, and one size.
2Ki 7. 1 shall a *m* of fine flour be sold for
16 So a *m* of fine flour was sold for a
18 a *m* of fine flour for a shekel, shall
1Ch 23.29 and for all manner of *m* and size;
2Ch 3. 3 first *m* was threescore cubits,
Job 11. 9 The *m* thereof is longer than the
28.25 he weigheth the waters by *m*.
Ps 39. 4 and the *m* of my days, what it is;
80. 5 them tears to drink in great *m*.
Isa 5.14 opened her mouth without *m*:
27. 8 In *m*, when it shooteth forth,
40.12 the dust of the earth in a *m*, and
65. 7 I *m* their former work into their
Jer 30.11 but I will correct thee in *m*, and
46.28 end of thee, but correct thee in *m*;
51.13 and the *m* of thy covetousness.
Eze 4.11 Thou shalt drink also water by *m*,
16 and they shall drink water by *m*,
40.10 side; they three were of one *m*:
10 the posts had one *m* on this side
21 were after the *m* of the first gate:
22 were after the *m* of the gate that
41.17 about within and without, by *m*.
43.10 and let them *m* the pattern.
45. 3 of this *m* shalt thou...the length
3 of this...shalt thou *m* the length
11 and the bath shall be of one *m*,
11 the *m* thereof shall be after the
46.22 these four corners were of one *m*.
47.18 east side ye shall *m* from Hauran,
Mic 6.10 the scant *m* that is abominable?
Zec 2. 2 To *m* Jerusalem, to see what is
Mt 7. 2 and with what *m* ye mete, it shall
23.32 Fill ye up then the *m* of your
Mk 4.24 With what *m* ye mete, it shall be
6.51 in themselves beyond *m*, and
7.37 And were beyond *m* astonished,
10.26 they were astonished out of *m*,
Lk 6.38 good *m*, pressed down, and
38 For with the same *m* that ye mete
Jn 3.34 not the Spirit by *m* unto him.
Ro 12. 3 dealt to every man the *m* of faith.
2Co 1. 8 we were pressed out of *m*,
10.13 not boast of things without our *m*,
13 but according to the *m* of the rule
13 to us, a *m* to reach even unto you.
14 stretch not ourselves beyond our *m*,
15 boasting of things without our *m*,
11.23 in stripes above *m*, in prisons
12. 7 lest I should be exalted above *m*
7 lest I should be exalted above *m*.
Gal 1.13 beyond *m* I persecuted the
Eph 4. 7 to the *m* of the gift of Christ.
13 the *m* of the stature of the fulness
16 working in the *m* of every part,
Rev 6. 6 A *m* of wheat for a penny, and
11. 1 Rise, and *m* the temple of God,
2 temple leave out, and *m* it not;
21.15 had a golden reed to *m* the city,
17 according to the *m* of a man, that

MEASURED

Isa 40.12 hath *m* the waters in the hollow
Jer 31.37 If heaven above can be *m*, and the
33.22 neither the sand of the sea *m*:
Hos 1.10 which cannot be *m* nor numbered;
Hab 3. 6 He stood, and *m* the earth: he
Mt 7. 2 mete, it shall be *m* to you again.
Mk 4.24 ye mete, it shall be *m* to you:
Lk 6.38 withal it shall be *m* to you again.
Rev 21.16 and he *m* the city with the reed,
17 he *m* the wall thereof, an hundred

MEASURES

Dt 25.14 not have in thine house divers *m*,
2Ki 7.18 Two *m* of barley for a shekel, and
Job 38. 5 Who hath laid the *m* thereof, if
Pr 20.10 Divers weights, and divers *m*,
Mt 13.33 took, and hid in three *m* of meal,
Lk 13.21 took and hid in three *m* of meal,
16. 6 And he said, An hundred *m* of oil.
7 he said, An hundred *m* of wheat.
Rev 6. 6 three *m* of barley for a penny;

MEASURING

Jer 31.39 the *m* line shall yet go forth over
Eze 40. 3 of flax in his hand, and a *m* reed;
5 in the man's hand a *m* reed of six
42.15 made an end of *m* the inner house,
16 the east side with the *m* reed,
16, 17 with the *m* reed round about.
18 hundred reeds, with the *m* reed.
19 hundred reeds with the *m* reed.
Zec 2. 1 a man with a *m* line in his hand.
2Co 10.12 they *m* themselves by themselves,

MEAT

Gen 1.30 have given every green herb for *m*:
27. 4 make me savory *m*, such as I
Lev 6.14 this is the law of the *m* offering:
Dt 2. 6 Ye shall buy *m* of them for money,
20.20 that they be not trees for *m*, thou
Jdg 1. 7 gathered their *m* under my table:
14.14 Out of the eater came forth *m*,
1Sa 20.27 cometh not the son of Jesse to *m*,
2Sa 3.35 to eat *m* while it was yet day,
1Ki 19. 8 the strength of that *m* forty days
Job 20.21 There shall none of his *m* be left;
30. 4 and juniper roots for their *m*.
34. 3 words, as the mouth tasteth *m*.
38.41 God, they wander for lack of *m*.
Ps 42. 3 My tears have been my *m* day
69.21 They gave me also gall for my *m*;
74.14 gavest him to be *m* to the people
78.25 food: he sent them *m* to the full.
104.27 give them their *m* in due season.
145.15 givest them their *m* in due season.
Pr 23. 3 dainties: for they are deceitful *m*.
30.22 and a fool when he is filled with *m*;
31.15 giveth *m* to her household, and a
Isa 65.25 dust shall be the serpent's *m*.
Eze 16.19 My *m* also which I gave thee,
47.12 the fruit thereof shall be for *m*,
Dan 1. 8 with the portion of the king's *m*,
Hab 1.16 is fat, and their *m* plenteous.
3.17 and the fields shall yield no *m*;
Mal 3.10 there may be *m* in mine house,
Mt 3. 4 his *m* was locusts and wild honey.
6.25 Is not the life more than *m*, and
9.10 as Jesus sat at *m* in the house,
10.10 the workman is worthy of his *m*.
14. 9 and them which sat with him at *m*,
15.37 broken *m* that was left seven baskets
24.45 to give them *m* in due season?
25.35 an hungred, and ye gave me *m*:
42 hungred, and ye gave me no *m*:
26. 7 poured it on his head, as he sat at *m*.
Mk 2.15 as Jesus sat at *m* in his house,
8. 8 broken *m* that was left seven baskets.
14. 3 as he sat at *m*, there came a woman
16.14 unto the eleven as they sat at *m*,
Lk 3.11 and he that hath *m*, let him do
7.36 Pharisee's house, and sat down to *m*.
37 sat at *m* in the Pharisee's house,
49 they that sat at *m* with him began to
8.55 and he commanded to give her *m*.
9.13 go and buy *m* for all this people.
11.37 and he went in, and sat down to *m*.
12.23 The life is more than *m*, and the
37 and make them to sit down to *m*,
42 their portion of *m* in due season?
14.10 of them that sit at *m* with thee.
15 them that sat at *m* with him heard
17. 7 from the field, Go and sit down to *m*?
22.27 is greater, he that sitteth at *m*, or
27 serveth? is not he that sitteth at *m*?
24.30 as he sat at *m* with them, he took
41 unto them, Have ye here any *m*?
Jn 4. 8 away unto the city to buy *m*.)
32 have *m* to eat that ye know not of.
34 My *m* is to do the will of him that
6.27 not for the *m* which perisheth,
27 *m* which endureth unto everlasting
55 For my flesh is *m* indeed, and my
21. 5 them, Children, have ye any *m*?
Ac 2.46 did eat their *m* with gladness and
9.19 received *m*, he was strengthened.
16.34 set *m* before them, and rejoiced,
27.33 besought them all to take *m*,
34 I pray you to take some *m*: for
36 cheer, and they also took some *m*.
Ro 14.15 brother be grieved with thy *m*,
15 Destroy not him with thy *m*, for
17 the kingdom of God is not *m* and
20 *m* destroy not the work of God.
1Co 3. 2 fed you with milk, and not with *m*:
8. 8 But *m* commendeth us not to God:
10 sit at *m* in the idol's temple,
13 if *m* make my brother to offend,
10. 3 did all eat the same spiritual *m*;
Col 2.16 no man therefore judge you in *m*,
Heb 5.12 of milk, and not of strong *m*.
14 strong *m* belongeth to them that
12.16 morsel of *m* sold his birthright.

MEATS

Pr 23. 6 neither desire thou his dainty *m*:
Mk 7.19 into the draft, purging all *m*?
Ac 15.29 abstain from *m* offered to idols,
1Co 6.13 *M* for the belly, and the belly for
13 and the belly for *m*: but God shall
1Ti 4. 3 commanding to abstain from *m*,
Heb 9.10 Which stood only in *m* and drinks,
13. 9 not with *m*, which have not

MEDIATOR

Gal 3.19 by angels in the hand of a *m*.
20 a *m* is not...of one, but God is one.
20 is not a *m* of one, but God is one.
1Ti 2. 5 and one *m* between God and men,
Heb 8. 6 he is the *m* of a better covenant,
9.15 he is the *m* of the new testament,
12.24 Jesus the *m* of the new covenant,

MEDICINE

Pr 17.22 merry heart doeth good like a *m*:
Eze 47.12 meat, and the leaf thereof for *m*.

MEDICINES

Jer 30.13 up: thou hast no healing *m*.
46.11 in vain shalt thou use many *m*;

MEDITATE

Gen 24.63 went out to *m* in the field at the
Jos 1. 8 shalt *m* therein day and night,
Ps 1. 2 his law doth he *m* day and night.
63. 6 *m* on thee in the night watches.
77.12 I will *m* also of all thy work, and
119.15 I will *m* in thy precepts, and have
23 thy servant did *m* in thy statutes.
48 loved: and I will *m* in thy statutes.
78 cause: but I will *m* in thy precepts.
148 that I might *m* in thy word.
143. 5 I *m* on all thy works; I muse on
Isa 33.18 Thine heart shall *m* terror. Where
Lk 21.14 not to *m* before what ye shall
1Ti 4.15 *M* upon these things; give thyself

MEDITATION

Ps 5. 1 words, O Lord, consider my *m*.
19.14 the *m* of my heart, be acceptable
49. 3 *m* of my heart...be understanding.
104.34 My *m* of him shall be sweet: I will
119.97 I thy law! it is my *m* all the day.
99 for thy testimonies are my *m*.

MEEK

Nu 12. 3 man Moses was very *m*, above all
Ps 22.26 The *m* shall eat and be satisfied:
25. 9 The *m* will he guide in judgment:
9 and the *m* will he teach his way.
37.11 But the *m* shall inherit the earth;
76. 9 to save all the *m* of the earth.
147. 6 The Lord lifteth up the *m*: he
149. 4 will beautify the *m* with salvation.
Isa 11. 4 with equity for the *m* of the earth:
29.19 The *m* also shall increase their joy
61. 1 preach good tidings unto the *m*;
Am 2. 7 and turn aside the way of the *m*:
Zep 2. 3 ye the Lord, all ye *m* of the earth,
Mt 5. 5 Blessed are the *m*: for they shall
11.29 for I am *m* and lowly in heart:
21. 5 thee, *m*, and sitting upon an ass,
1Pe 3. 4 ornament of a *m* and quiet spirit,

MEEKNESS

Ps 45. 4 truth and *m* and righteousness;
Zep 2. 3 seek righteousness, seek *m*: it
1Co 4.21 or in love, and in the spirit of *m*?
2Co 10. 1 by the *m* and gentleness of Christ,
Gal 5.23 *M*, temperance: against such
6. 1 such an one in the spirit of *m*;
Eph 4. 2 With all lowliness and *m*, with
Col 3.12 of mind, *m*, longsuffering;
1Ti 6.11 godliness, faith, love, patience, *m*.
2Ti 2.25 In *m* instructing those that oppose
Tit 3. 2 gentle, shewing all *m* unto all men.
Jas 1.21 and receive with *m* the engrafted
3.13 his works with *m* of wisdom.
1Pe 3.15 that is in you with *m* and fear:

MEET

Gen 2.18 will make him an help *m* for him.
Ex 4.27 Go into the wilderness to *m* Moses.
19.17 out of the camp to *m* with God;
25.22 there I will *m* with thee, and I
Nu 23. 3 the Lord will come to *m* me: and
Jdg 11.34 came out to *m* him with timbrels
1Sa 10. 3 and there shall *m* thee three men
2Ki 4.29 if thou *m* any man, salute him not;
8. 8 hand, and go, *m* the man of God,
Neh 6.10 us *m* together in the house of God,
Pr 11.24 that withholdeth more than is *m*,
22. 2 The rich and poor *m* together: the
Isa 47. 3 and I will not *m* thee as a man.
Jer 51.31 One post shall run to *m* another,
Am 4.12 prepare to *m* thy God, O Israel.
Mt 3. 8 therefore fruits *m* for repentance:
8.34 city came out to *m* Jesus:
15.26 not *m* to take the children's bread,
25. 1 forth to *m* the bridegroom.
6 cometh; go ye out to *m* him.
Mk 7.27 not *m* to take the children's bread,
14.13 *m* you a man bearing a pitcher of
Lk 14.31 to *m* him that comest against him
15.32 *m* that we should make merry,
22.10 a man *m* you, bearing a pitcher
Jn 12.13 and went forth to *m* him,
Ac 26.20 and do works *m* for repentance.
28.15 to *m* us as far as Appii forum,
Ro 1.27 that recompence...which was *m*.
1Co 15. 9 am not *m* to be called an apostle,
16. 4 if it be *m* that I go also, they shall
Php 1. 7 is *m* for me to think this of you

Col 1.12 hath made us *m* to be partakers
1Th 4.17 to *m* the Lord in the air:
2Th 1. 3 always for you, brethren, as it is *m*,
2Ti 2.21 and *m* for the master's use, and
Heb 6. 7 forth herbs *m* for them by whom
2Pe 1.13 I think it *m*, as long as I am in

MELCHISEDEC
Heb 5. 6 for ever after the order of *M*.
10 high priest after the order of *M*.
6.20 for ever after the order of *M*.
7. 1 For this *M*, king of Salem, priest
10 of his father, when *M* met him.
11 should rise after the order of *M*,
15 for that after the similitude of *M*
17 for ever after the order of *M*.
21 for ever after the order of *M*:)

MELCHIZEDEK
Gen 14.18 *M* king of Salem brought forth
Ps 110. 4 for ever after the order of *M*.

MELITA
Ac 28. 1 that the island was called *M*.

MELODY
Isa 23.16 make sweet *m*, sing many songs,
51. 3 thanksgiving, and the voice of *m*.
Am 5.23 I will not hear the *m* of thy viols.
Eph 5.19 making *m* in your heart to the

MELT
Ex 15.15 inhabitants of Canaan shall *m*
Jos 2.11 these things, our hearts did *m*,
14. 8 made the heart of the people *m*:
2Sa 17.10 heart of a lion, shall utterly *m*:
Ps 58. 7 Let them *m* away as waters which
112.10 gnash with his teeth, and *m* away:
Isa 13. 7 and every man's heart shall *m*:
19. 1 heart of Egypt shall *m* in the midst
Jer 9. 7 I will *m* them, and try them;
Eze 21. 7 every heart shall *m*, and all hands
22.20 to blow the fire upon it, to *m* it;
20 I will leave you there, and *m* you.
Am 9. 5 toucheth the land, and it shall *m*,
13 wine, and all the hills shall *m*.
Na 1. 5 the hills *m*, and the earth is burned
2Pe 3.10 elements shall *m* with fervent
12 elements shall *m* with fervent

MELTED
Ex 16.21 when the sun waxed hot, it *m*.
Jos 5. 1 that their heart *m*, neither was
7. 5 the hearts of the people *m*, and
Jdg 5. 5 The mountains *m* from before
1Sa 14.16 the multitude *m* away, and they
Ps 22.14 is *m* in the midst of my bowels.
46. 6 he uttered his voice, the earth *m*.
97. 5 hills *m* like wax at the presence
107.26 their soul is *m* because of trouble.
Isa 34. 3 mountains...*m* with their blood.
Eze 22.21 and ye shall be *m* in the midst
22 As silver is *m* in the midst of the
22 so shall ye be *m* in the midst

MELTETH
Ps 58. 8 As a snail which *m*, let every one
68. 2 as wax *m* before the fire, so let
119.28 My soul *m* for heaviness:
147.18 out this word, and *m* them: he
Isa 40.19 The workman *m* a graven image,
Jer 6.29 the founder *m* in vain: for the
Na 2.10 and the heart *m*, and the knees

MELTING
Isa 64. 2 As when the *m* fire burneth, the

MEMBER
1Co 12.14 For the body is not one *m*, but
19 And if they were all one *m*, where
26 And whether one *m* suffer, all the
26 or one *m* be honored, all the
Jas 3. 5 Even so the tongue is a little *m*,

MEMBERS
Job 17. 7 and all my *m* are as a shadow.
Ps 139.16 in thy book all my *m* were written,
Mt 5.29, 30 one of thy *m* should perish,
Ro 6.13 Neither yield ye your *m* as
13 and your *m* as instruments of
19 as ye have yielded your *m* servants
19 so now yield your *m* servants to
7. 5 did work in our *m* to bring forth
23 But I see another law in my *m*,
23 to the law of sin which is in my *m*.
12. 4 as we have many *m* in one body,
4 all *m* have not the same office:
5 and every one *m* one of another.
1Co 6.15 your bodies are the *m* of Christ?
15 shall I then take the *m* of Christ,
15 and make them the *m* of a harlot?
12.12 the body is one, and hath many *m*,
12 and all the *m* of that one body,
18 now hath God set the *m* every one
20 But now are they many *m*, yet but
22 much more those *m* of the body,
23 And those *m* of the body, which we
25 that the *m* should have the same
26 suffer, all the *m* suffer with it;
26 honored, all the *m* rejoice with it.
27 body of Christ, and *m* in particular.
Eph 4.25 for we are *m* one of another.
5.30 For we are *m* of his body, of his
Col 3. 5 Mortify therefore your *m* which
Jas 3. 6 so is the tongue among your *m*, that
4. 1 of your lusts that war in your *m*?

MEMORIAL
Ex 3.15 is my *m* unto all generations.
12.14 day shall be unto you for a *m*;
13. 9 and for a *m* between thine eyes,
17.14 Write this for a *m* in a book, and
28.12 the ephod for stones of *m* unto the
12 upon his two shoulders for a *m*.
29 for a *m* before the Lord continually.
30.16 it may be a *m* unto the children
39. 7 stones for a *m* to the children of
Lev 2. 2 the priest shall burn the *m* of it
9 from the meat offering a *m* thereof,
16 the priest shall burn the *m* of it,
5.12 even a *m* thereof, and burn it on the
6.15 even the *m* of it, unto the Lord.
23.24 a *m* of blowing of trumpets, an
24. 7 it may be on the bread for a *m*,
Nu 5.15 an offering of *m*, bringing iniquity
18 put the offering of *m* in her hands,
26 the *m* thereof, and burn it upon
10.10 that they may be to you for a *m*
16.40 be a *m* unto the children of Israel,
31.54 for a *m* for the children of Israel
Jos 4. 7 these stones shall be for a *m* unto
Neh 2.20 nor right, nor *m*, in Jerusalem.
Est 9.28 the *m* of them perish from their
Ps 9. 6 their *m* is perished with them.
135.13 and thy *m*, O Lord, throughout all
Hos 12. 5 God of hosts; the Lord is his *m*.
Zec 6.14 for a *m* in the temple of the Lord.
Mt 26.13 hath done, be told for a *m* of her.
Mk 14. 9 shall be spoken of for a *m* of her.
Ac 10. 4 thine alms are come up for a *m*

MEMORY
Ps 109.15 cut off the *m* of them from the
145. 7 utter the *m* of thy great goodness,
Pr 10. 7 The *m* of the just is blessed: but
Ec 9. 5 for the *m* of them is forgotten.
Isa 26.14 and made all their *m* to perish.
1Co 15. 2 if ye keep in *m* what I preached unto
(See box on page 500)

MEN
Gen 6. 1 *m* began to multiply on the face
2 daughters of *m* that they were fair;
13.13 the *m* of Sodom were wicked and
32.28 thou power with God and with *m*,
41. 8 of Egypt, and all the wise *m* thereof:
42.31 him, We are true *m*; we are no spies:
Ex 4.19 *m* are dead which sought thy life.
12.33 for they said, We be all dead *m*.
18.21 the people able *m*, such as fear God,
21 *m* of truth, hating covetousness;
Nu 14.22 those *m* which have seen my glory,
Dt 1.13 you wise *m*, and understanding,
Jos 2. 4 the woman took the two *m*, and hid
Jdg 7. 7 By the three hundred *m* that lapped
Ru 4. 2 took ten *m* of the elders of the city,
1Sa 2. 4 bows of the mighty *m* are broken,
4. 9 strong, and quit yourselves like *m*,
9 quit yourselves like *m*, and fight.
21.15 Have I need of mad *m*, that ye have
2Sa 15. 6 stole the hearts of the *m* of Israel.
19.35 hear any more the voice of singing *m*
22. 5 floods of ungodly *m* made me afraid;
23. 3 that ruleth over *m* must be just,
9 of the three mighty *m* with David,
16 three mighty *m* brake through the
17 the blood of the *m* that went in
1Ki 4.31 For he was wiser than all *m*; than
12. 6 Rehoboam consulted with the old *m*,
8 he forsook the counsel of the old *m*,
8 and consulted with the young *m* that
2Ki 6.20 open the eyes of these *m*, that they
2Ch 6.18 God in very deed dwell with *m* on
34.12 And the *m* did the work faithfully:
Ezr 6. 8 expenses be given unto these *m*,
Neh 5. 5 for other *m* have our lands and
Job 4.13 night, when deep sleep falleth on *m*,
7.20 unto thee, O thou preserver of *m*?
11. 3 thy lies make *m* hold their peace?
11 For he knoweth vain *m*: he seeth
15.10 the grayheaded and very aged *m*,
18 Which wise *m* have told from their
17. 8 Upright *m* shall be astonied at this,
22.15 which wicked *m* have trodden?
20 When *m* are cast down, then thou
27.23 *M* shall clap their hands at him, and
29. 8 The young *m* saw me, and hid
21 Unto me *m* gave ear, and waited,
30. 5 were driven forth from among *m*,
32. 9 Great *m* are not always wise: neither
33.15 when deep sleep falleth upon *m*,
16 Then he openeth the ears of *m*, and
27 He looketh upon *m*, and if any say,
34. 2 Hear my words, O ye wise *m*; and
10 unto me, ye *m* of understanding:
34 Let *m* of understanding tell me,
36.24 magnify his work, which *m* behold.
37. 7 that all *m* may know his work.
21 And now *m* see not the bright light
24 *M* do therefore fear him: he
Ps 4. 2 O ye sons of *m*, how long will ye
9.20 may know themselves to be but *m*.
17.14 from *m* of the world, which have
18. 4 floods of ungodly *m* made me afraid.
33.13 he beholdeth all the sons of *m*.
49.10 For he seeth that wise *m* die,
57. 4 are set on fire, even the sons of *m*,
62. 9 *m* of low degree are vanity,
9 *m* of high degree are a lie: to be
64. 9 all *m* shall fear, and shall declare
68.18 thou hast received gifts for *m*; yea,
72.17 sun: and *m* shall be blessed in him:
82. 7 But ye shall die like *m*, and fall like
86.14 violent *m* have sought after my soul;
90. 3 and sayest, Return, ye children of *m*.
107. 8 Oh that *m* would praise the Lord for
116.11 I said in my haste, All *m* are liars.
Pr 6.30 *M* do not despise a thief, if he steal to
10.14 Wise *m* lay up knowledge: but the
11. 7 and the hope of unjust *m* perisheth.
16. 6 fear of the Lord *m* depart from evil.

Biblical Themes

MEMORY

The Lord God of your fathers, the God of Abraham, the God of Isaac, and the God of Jacob, hath sent me unto you: this is my name for ever, and this is my memorial unto all generations. Ex 3.15

Remember that thou wast a servant in the land of Egypt, and that the Lord thy God brought thee out thence through a mighty hand. Dt 5.15

Do ye thus requite the Lord, O foolish people and unwise? . . . hath he not made thee, and established thee? Remember the days of old, consider the years of many generations: ask thy father, and he will shew thee; thy elders, and they will tell thee. Dt 32.6-7

And Samson called unto the Lord, and said, O Lord God, remember me, I pray thee, and strengthen me, I pray thee, only this once. Jdg 16.28

Remember, O Lord, thy tender mercies and thy lovingkindnesses; for they have been ever of old. Remember not the sins of my youth, nor my transgressions: according to thy mercy remember thou me for thy goodness' sake, O Lord. Ps 25.6-7

I remembered thy judgments of old, O Lord; and have comforted myself. . . . Thy statutes have been my songs in the house of my pilgrimage. I have remembered thy name, O Lord, in the night, and have kept thy law. Ps 119.52, 54-55

By the rivers of Babylon, there we sat down, yea, we wept, when we remembered Zion. . . . If I forget thee, O Jerusalem, let my right hand forget her cunning. If I do not remember thee, let my tongue cleave to the roof of my mouth; if I prefer not Jerusalem above my chief joy. Ps 137.1, 5-6

The memory of the just is blessed: but the name of the wicked shall rot. Pr 10.7

The living know that they shall die: but the dead know not any thing, neither have they any more a reward; for the memory of them is forgotten. Ec 9.5

Remember ye not the former things, neither consider the things of old. Behold, I will do a new thing. Isa 43.18-19

Can a woman forget her sucking child, that she should not have compassion on the son of her womb? yea, they may forget, yet will I not forget thee. Behold, I have graven thee upon the palms of my hands; thy walls are continually before me. Isa 49.15-16

Remembering mine affliction and my misery, the wormwood and the gall. My soul hath them still in remembrance, and is humbled in me. This I recall to my mind, therefore have I hope. . . . The Lord is my portion, saith my soul; therefore will I hope in him. The Lord is good unto them that wait for him. La 3.19-21, 24-25

I have redeemed them: and they shall increase. . . . And I will sow them among the people: and they shall remember me in far countries; and they shall live with their children, and turn again. Zec 10.8-9

Verily I say . . . Wheresoever this gospel shall be preached . . . there shall also this, that this woman hath done, be told for a memorial of her. Mt 26.13

And Peter remembered the word of Jesus. . . . And he went out, and wept bitterly. Mt 26.75

Having eyes, see ye not? and having ears, hear ye not? and do ye not remember? Mk 8.18

When he had given thanks, he brake it, and said, Take, eat: this is my body, which is broken for you: this do in remembrance of me. 1Co 11.24

Pr 20.29 glory of young *m* is their strength:
29 the beauty of old *m* is the gray head.
24. 9 scorner is an abomination to *m*.
19 Fret not thyself because of evil *m*,
25. 6 and stand not in the place of great *m*:
28. 5 Evil *m* understand not judgment:
28 wicked rise, *m* hide themselves:
29. 8 snare: but wise *m* turn away wrath.
Ec 2. 8 me *m* singers and women singers,
3.10 God hath given to the sons of *m*
7. 2 for that is the end of all *m*; and the
12. 3 strong *m* shall bow themselves,
Isa 7.13 a small thing for you to weary *m*,
19.12 where are thy wise *m*? and let them
26.19 Thy dead *m* shall live, together with
29.19 the poor among *m* shall rejoice in
31. 3 the Egyptians are *m*, and not God;
35. 8 the wayfaring *m*, though fools, shall
38.16 O Lord, by these things *m* live, and
40.30 and the young *m* shall utterly fall:
46. 8 this, and shew yourselves *m*:
51. 7 fear ye not the reproach of *m*,
52.14 his form more than the sons of *m*:
53. 3 He is despised and rejected of *m*;
57. 1 merciful *m* are taken away, none
61. 6 *m* shall call you the Ministers of our
Jer 5. 5 I will get me unto the great *m*, and
32.44 *M* shall buy fields for money, and
49.26 her young *m* shall fall in her streets,
52. 7 all the *m* of war fled, and went
Eze 16.17 madest to thyself images of *m*,
22. 9 In thee are *m* that carry tales to
Dan 2.13 forth that the wise *m* should be slain;
3.12 these *m*, O king, have not
23 these three *m*, Shadrach, Meshach,
24 Did not we cast three *m* bound
25 Lo, I see four *m* loose, walking in
4.18 wise *m* of my kingdom are not able
5.15 now the wise *m*, the astrologers,
21 God ruled in the kingdom of *m*,
10.16 like the similitude of the sons of *m*
Joel 2. 7 shall run like mighty *m*; they shall
28 your old *m* shall dream dreams,
28 your young *m* shall see visions:
Am 2.11 and of your young *m* for Nazarites.
Jon 1.10 were the *m* exceedingly afraid,
16 the *m* feared the Lord exceedingly,
Mic 7. 2 there is none upright among *m*:
6 enemies are...*m* of his own house.
Hab 1.14 makest *m* as the fishes of the sea,
Zep 1.17 that they shall walk like blind *m*,
Zec 7. 2 their *m*, to pray before the Lord,
8. 4 There shall yet old *m* and old women
11. 6 I will deliver the *m* every one into
14.11 And *m* shall dwell in it, and there
Mt 2. 1 there came wise *m* from the east to
4.19 and I will make you fishers of *m*.
5.15 Neither do *m* light a candle, and put
16 Let your light so shine before *m*,
6.14 For if ye forgive *m* their trespasses,
7.16 Do *m* gather grapes of thorns, or figs
10.17 beware of *m*: for they will deliver
22 be hated of all *m* for my name's
32 shall confess me before *m*, him
33 whosoever shall deny me before *m*,
12.41 The *m* of Nineveh shall rise in
16.13 Whom do *m* say that I the Son of
19.26 With *m* this is impossible; but with
21.25 was it? from heaven, or of *m*?
41 miserably destroy those wicked *m*,
26.33 Though all *m* shall be offended
Mk 1.17 make you to become fishers of *m*.
7. 8 ye hold the tradition of *m*, as the
8.24 and said, I see *m* as trees, walking.
27 them, Whom do *m* say that I am?
33 of God, but the things that be of *m*.
10.27 With *m* it is impossible, but not with
11.30 John, was it from heaven, or of *m*?
13.13 be hated of all *m* for my name's sake:
Lk 2.14 on earth peace, good will toward *m*.
5.10 from henceforth thou shalt catch *m*.
6.22 are ye, when *m* shall hate you, and
31 ye would that *m* should do to you,
12. 8 shall confess me before *m*, him shall
9 he that denieth me before *m* shall
18. 1 that *m* ought always to pray, and not
11 thee, that I am not as other *m* are,
27 impossible with *m* are possible with
20. 4 John, was it from heaven, or of *m*?
21.17 be hated of all *m* for my name's sake.
Jn 1. 4 and the life was the light of *m*.
7 all *m* through him might believe.
2.24 unto them, because he knew all *m*,
3.19 *m* loved darkness rather than light,
4.38 other *m* labored, and ye are
12.43 For they loved the praise of *m* more
Ac 1.10 two *m* stood by them in white
11 *m* of Galilee, why stand ye gazing
16 *M* and brethren, this scripture
2.13 said, These *m* are full of new wine.
17 your young *m* shall see visions,
17 and your old *m* shall dream dreams:
4.12 under heaven given among *m*,
13 they were unlearned and ignorant *m*,
5.29 ought to obey God rather than *m*.
14.11 down to us in the likeness of *m*.
15 We also are *m* of like passions with
16.35 serjeants, saying, Let those *m* go.
17.22 Ye *m* of Athens, I perceive that in
26 made of one blood all nations of *m*
30 all *m* every where to repent:

Ro 2.16 God shall judge the secrets of *m*
12.17 things honest in the sight of all *m*.
18 in you, live peaceably with all *m*.
1Co 1.25 foolishness of God is wiser than *m*,
25 weakness of God is stronger than *m*.
26 that not many wise *m* after the flesh,
3. 3 are ye not carnal, and walk as *m*?
21 Therefore let no man glory in *m*:
7. 7 that all *m* were even as I myself.
9.22 I am made all things to all *m*, that I
13. 1 the tongues of *m* and of angels,
14.20 but in understanding be *m*.
15.19 we are of all *m* most miserable.
16.13 faith, quit you like *m*, be strong.
2Co 3. 2 hearts, known and read of all *m*:
Gal 6.10 let us do good unto all *m*, especially
Eph 4. 8 captive, and gave gifts unto *m*.
14 by the sleight of *m*, and cunning
5.28 So ought *m* to love their wives as
Php 2. 7 and was made in the likeness of *m*:
4. 5 moderation be known unto all *m*.
Col 3.23 as to the Lord, and not unto *m*;
1Th 2. 4 not as pleasing *m*, but God, which
2Th 3. 2 for all *m* have not faith.
1Ti 2. 1 of thanks, be made for all *m*;
5 one mediator between God and *m*,
8 I will...that *m* pray every where,
4.10 God, who is the Saviour of all *m*,
5. 1 and the younger *m* as brethren;
2Ti 4.16 stood with me, but all *m* forsook me:
Tit 2.11 salvation hath appeared to all *m*,
Heb 5. 1 high priest taken from among *m* is
9.27 it is appointed unto *m* once to die,
12.14 Follow peace with all *m*, and
23 the spirits of just *m* made perfect,
Jas 1. 5 that giveth to all *m* liberally, and
3. 9 Therewith curse we *m*, which are
1Pe 2. 4 disallowed indeed of *m*, but chosen
17 Honor all *m*. Love the brotherhood.
1Jn 2.13 I write unto you, young *m*,
Rev 8.11 and many *m* died of the waters,
9. 6 in those days shall *m* seek death,
7 their faces were as the faces of *m*.
14. 4 were redeemed from among *m*,
16.21 *m* blasphemed God because of the
21. 3 the tabernacle of God is with *m*,

MENDING
Mt 4.21 with...their father, *m* their nets;
Mk 1.19 also were in the ship *m* their nets.

MENE
Dan 5.25 written, *M*, *M*, Tekel, Upharsin.
26 *M*; God hath numbered thy

MENPLEASERS
Eph 6. 6 Not with eyeservice, as *m*; but as
Col 3.22 not with eyeservice, as *m*; but in

MEN'S
Gen 24.32 and the *m* feet that were with him.
44. 1 Fill the *m* sacks with food, as much
Dt 4.28 serve gods, the work of *m* hands,
1Sa 24. 9 Wherefore hearest thou *m* words,
1Ki 12.13 forsook the old *m* counsel that they
13. 2 *m* bones shall be burnt upon thee.
2Ki 19.18 no gods, but the work of *m* hands,
23.20 and burned *m* bones upon them,
Ps 115. 4 and gold, the work of *m* hands.
135.15 and gold, the work of *m* hands.
Isa 37.19 no gods, but the work of *m* hands.
Jer 48.41 the mighty *m* hearts in Moab at that
Hab 2. 8, 17 because of *m* blood, and for the
Mt 23. 4 and lay them on *m* shoulders; but
27 but are within full of dead *m* bones,
Lk 9.56 is not come to destroy *m* lives,
21.26 *M* hearts failing them for fear, and
Ac 17.25 Neither is worshiped with *m* hands,
2Co 10.15 measure, that is, of other *m* labors;
1Ti 5.22 neither be partaker of other *m* sins:
24 Some *m* sins are open beforehand,

1Pe 4.15 or as a busy body in other *m* matters.
Jude 16 having *m* persons in admiration

MENSERVANTS
Gen 12.16 and oxen, and he asses, and *m*,
20.14 took sheep, and oxen, and *m*, and
24.35 herds, and silver, and gold, and *m*,
30.43 cattle, and maidservants, and *m*,
32. 5 oxen, and asses, flocks, and *m*, and
Ex 21. 7 she shall not go out as the *m* do.
Dt 12.12 your *m*, and your maidservants,
1Sa 8.16 he will take your *m*, and your
2Ki 5.26 and sheep, and oxen, and *m*, and
Lk 12.45 shall begin to beat the *m* and

MENSTEALERS
1Ti 1.10 with mankind, for *m*, for liars,

MENTION
Gen 40.14 and make *m* of me unto Pharaoh,
Ex 23.13 make no *m* of the name of other
Jos 23. 7 make *m* of the name of their gods,
1Sa 4.18 when he made *m* of the ark of God,
Job 28.18 No *m* shall be made of coral, or of
Ps 71.16 will make *m* of thy righteousness,
87. 4 make *m* of Rahab and Babylon to
Isa 12. 4 make *m* that his name is exalted.
19.17 every one that maketh *m* thereof
26.13 only will we make *m* of thy name.
48. 1 and make *m* of the God of Israel,
49. 1 hath he made *m* of my name.
62. 6 ye that make *m* of the Lord, keep
63. 7 *m* the lovingkindness of the Lord,
Jer 4.16 Make ye *m* to the nations; behold,
20. 9 I said, I will not make *m* of him,
23.36 burden of the Lord shall ye *m* no
Am 6.10 make *m* of the name of the Lord.
Ro 1. 9 *m* of you always in my prayers;
Eph 1.16 making *m* of you in my prayers;
1Th 1. 2 making *m* of you in our prayers;
Phm 4 *m* of thee always in my prayers,
Heb 11.22 died, made *m* of the departing of

MENTIONED
Jos 21. 9 these cities which are here *m* by
1Ch 4.38 *m* by their names were princes
2Ch 20.34 who is *m* in the book of the kings
Eze 16.56 For thy sister Sodom was not *m*
18.22 they shall not be *m* unto him:
24 that he hath done shall not be *m*:
33.16 hath committed shall be *m* unto

MEPHIBOSHETH
2Sa 4. 4 lame. And his name was *M*.
9. 6 Now when *M*, the son of Jonathan,
6 And David said, *M*. And he
10 *M* thy master's son shall eat bread
11 As for *M*, said the king, he shall
12 *M* had a young son, whose name
12 of Ziba were servants unto *M*.
13 So *M* dwelt in Jerusalem: for he
16. 1 Ziba the servant of *M* met him,
4 are all that pertained unto *M*.
19.24 *M* the son of Saul came down to
25 wentest not thou with me, *M*?
30 *M* said unto the king, Yea, let him
21. 7 But the king spared *M*, the son of
8 bare unto Saul, Armoni and *M*;

MERCHANDISE
Dt 21.14 thou shalt not make *m* of her,
24. 7 maketh *m* of him, or selleth him;
Pr 3.14 For the *m* of it is better than the
14 is better than the *m* of silver,
31.18 perceiveth that her *m* is good:
Isa 23.18 *m* and her hire shall be holiness
18 her *m* shall be for them that dwell
45.14 *m* of Ethiopia and of the Sabeans,
Eze 26.12 riches, and make a prey of thy *m*:
27. 9 were in thee to occupy thy *m*.
15 isles were the *m* of thine hand:

24 and made of cedar, among thy *m*.
27 and thy fairs, thy *m*, thy mariners,
27 calkers, and the occupiers of thy *m*,
33 multitude of thy riches and of thy *m*.
34 thy *m* and all thy company in the
28.16 By the multitude of thy *m* they
Mt 22. 5 one to his farm, another to his *m*:
Jn 2.16 my Father's house an house of *m*.
2Pe 2. 3 with feigned words make *m* of you:
Rev 18.11 no man buyeth their *m* any more:
12 *m* of gold, and silver, and precious

MERCHANT
Gen 23.16 silver, current money with the *m*.
Pr 31.24 delivereth girdles unto the *m*.
SS 3. 6 with all powders of the *m*?
Isa 23.11 against the *m* city, to destroy
Eze 27. 3 a *m* of the people for many isles,
12 Tarshish was thy *m* by reason of
16 Syria was thy *m* by reason of the
18 Damascus was thy *m* in the
20 Dedan was thy *m* in precious
Hos 12. 7 He is a *m*, the balances of deceit
Zep 1.11 for all the *m* people are cut down;
Mt 13.45 of heaven is like unto a *m* man,

MERCHANTMEN
Gen 37.28 there passed by Midianites *m*;
1Ki 10.15 Besides that he had of the *m*,

MERCHANTS
1Ki 10.15 and of the traffick of the spice *m*,
28 king's *m* received the linen yarn
2Ch 1.16 king's *m* received the linen yarn at
9.14 which chapmen and *m* brought.
Neh 3.31 of the Nethinims, and of the *m*,
32 repaired the goldsmiths and the *m*.
13.20 *m* and sellers of all kind of ware
Job 41. 6 shall they part him among the *m*?
Isa 23. 2 the *m* of Zidon, that pass over
8 crowning city, whose *m* are princes,
47.15 thou hast labored, even thy *m*,
Eze 17. 4 traffick: he set it in a city of *m*.
27.13 and Mesech, they were thy *m*:
15 The men of Dedan were thy *m*;
17 land of Israel, they were thy *m*:
21 goats; in these were they thy *m*.
22 The *m* of Sheba and Raamah,
22 they were thy *m*: they occupied in
23 Canneh, and Eden, the *m* of Sheba,
23 Asshur, and Chilmad, were thy *m*.
24 were thy *m* in all sorts of things,
36 *m* among the people shall hiss at
38.13 and Dedan, and the *m* of Tarshish,
Na 3.16 multiplied thy *m* above the stars
Rev 18. 3 the *m* of the earth are waxed rich
11 the *m* of the earth shall weep and
15 The *m* of these things, which were
23 *m* were the great men of the earth;

MERCIES
Gen 32.10 worthy of the least of all the *m*,
2Sa 24.14 of the Lord, for his *m* are great:
1Ch 21.13 the Lord; for very great are his *m*:
2Ch 6.42 remember the *m* of David thy
Neh 9.19 thou in thy manifold *m* forsookest
27 according to thy manifold *m* thou
28 deliver them according to thy *m*;
Ps 25. 6 O Lord, thy tender *m* and thy
40.11 not thou thy tender *m* from me,
51. 1 unto the multitude of thy tender *m*
69.16 to the multitude of thy tender *m*.
77. 9 he in anger shut up his tender *m*?
79. 8 let thy tender *m* speedily prevent
89. 1 I will sing of the *m* of the Lord
103. 4 lovingkindness and tender *m*;
106. 7 not the multitude of thy *m*;
45 according to the multitude of his *m*.
119.41 thy *m* come also unto me, O Lord,
77 Let thy tender *m* come unto me,
156 Great are thy tender *m*, O Lord:

Ps 145. 9 his tender *m* are over all his works.
Pr 12.10 tender *m* of the wicked are cruel.
Isa 54. 7 with great *m* will I gather thee.
55. 3 you, even the sure *m* of David.
63. 7 on them according to his *m*, and
15 of thy bowels and of thy *m* toward
Jer 16. 5 Lord, even lovingkindness and *m*.
42.12 I will shew *m* unto you, that ye may
La 3.22 It is of the Lord's *m* that we are
32 according…the multitude of his *m*.
Dan 2.18 they would desire *m* of the God
9. 9 To the Lord our God belong *m*
18 righteousnesses,…for thy great *m*.
Hos 2.19 and in lovingkindness, and in *m*.
Zec 1.16 I am returned to Jerusalem with *m*:
Ac 13.34 will give you the sure *m* of David.
Ro 12. 1 by the *m* of God, that ye present
2Co 1. 3 the Father of *m*, and the God of all
Php 2. 1 of the Spirit, if any bowels and *m*,
Col 3.12 bowels of *m*, kindness, humbleness

MERCIES'

Neh 9.31 Nevertheless for thy great *m* sake
Ps 6. 4 soul: oh save me for thy *m* sake.
31.16 servant: save me for thy *m* sake.
44.26 help, and redeem us for thy *m* sake.

MERCIFUL

Gen 19.16 the Lord being *m* unto him: and
Ex 34. 6 The Lord God, *m* and gracious,
Dt 4.31 (For the Lord thy God is a *m* God;)
21. 8 Be *m*, O Lord, unto thy people
32.43 and will be *m* unto his land, and
2Sa 22.26 With the *m* thou wilt shew thyself
26 wilt shew thyself *m*, and with the
1Ki 20.31 the house of Israel are *m* kings:
2Ch 30. 9 Lord your God is gracious and *m*,
Neh 9.17 ready to pardon, gracious and *m*,
31 for thou art a gracious and *m* God.
Ps 18.25 With the *m* thou wilt shew thyself
25 shew thyself *m*; with an upright
26.11 redeem me, and be *m* unto me.
37.26 He is ever *m*, and lendeth; and his
41. 4 Lord, be *m* unto me: heal my soul;
10 But thou, O Lord, be *m* unto me,
56. 1 Be *m* unto me, O God: for man
57. 1 Be *m* unto me, O God, be *m* unto
59. 5 be not *m* to…wicked transgressors.
67. 1 God be *m* unto us, and bless us;
86. 3 Be *m* unto me, O Lord: for I cry
103. 8 the Lord is *m* and gracious, slow
116. 5 and righteous; yea, our God is *m*.
117. 2 his *m* kindness is great toward
119.58 be *m* unto me according to thy
76 *m* kindness be for my comfort,
132 be *m* unto me, as thou usest to do
Pr 11.17 The *m* man doeth good to his own
Isa 57. 1 and *m* man are taken away, none
Jer 3.12 for I am *m*, saith the Lord, and
Joel 2.13 for he is gracious and *m*, slow to
Jon 4. 2 art a gracious God, and *m*, slow to
Mt 5. 7 Blessed are the *m*: for they shall
Lk 6.36 *m*, as your Father also is *m*.
18.13 saying, God be *m* to me a sinner.
Heb 2.17 be a *m* and faithful high priest
8.12 be *m* to their unrighteousness,

MERCURIUS

Ac 14.12 Barnabas, Jupiter; and Paul, *M*,

MERCY

Gen 19.19 and thou hast magnified thy *m*,
43.14 Almighty give you *m* before the
Ex 20. 6 shewing *m* unto thousands of them
25.17 shalt make a *m* seat of pure gold:
21 put the *m* seat above upon the ark;
33.19 shew *m* on whom I will shew *m*.
34. 7 Keeping *m* for thousands,
Nu 14.18 is longsuffering, and of great *m*,
Dt 5.10 shewing *m* unto thousands of them
7. 2 with them, nor shew *m* unto them:
13.17 of his anger, and shew thee *m*,
2Sa 15.20 *m* and truth be with thee.
22.51 sheweth *m* to his anointed, unto
1Ch 16.34 good; for his *m* endureth for ever.
41 because his *m* endureth for ever;
2Ch 5.13 good; for his *m* endureth for ever:
20.21 Lord; for his *m* endureth for ever.
Ezr 7.28 hath extended *m* unto me before
Neh 1. 5 keepeth covenant and *m* for them
Ps 4. 1 have *m* upon me, and hear my
6. 2 Have *m* upon me, O Lord; for I
13. 5 But I have trusted in thy *m*; my
23. 6 goodness and *m* shall follow me
25. 7 according to thy *m* remember thou
10 paths of the Lord are *m* and truth
30.10 O Lord, and have *m* upon me:
33.18 upon them that hope in his *m*;
36. 5 Thy *m*, O Lord, is in the heavens;
52. 8 I trust in the *m* of God for ever
57.10 thy *m* is great unto the heavens,
59.16 I will sing aloud of thy *m* in the
61. 7 O prepare *m* and truth, which may
62.12 unto thee, O Lord, belongeth *m*:
69.13 in the multitude of thy *m* hear me,
77. 8 Is his *m* clean gone for ever? doth
85.10 *M* and truth are met together;
86. 5 plenteous in *m* unto all them that
13 For great is thy *m* toward me: and
89.14 *m* and truth shall go before thy
90.14 O satisfy us early with thy *m*; that
94.18 thy *m*, O Lord, held me up.
100. 5 is good; his *m* is everlasting;
101. 1 will sing of *m* and judgment: unto
103. 8 to anger, and plenteous in *m*.
11 great is his *m* toward them that
17 But the *m* of the Lord is from
106. 1 good: for his *m* endureth for ever.
108. 4 thy *m* is great above the heavens:
109.26 O save me according to thy *m*:
115. 1 for thy *m*, and for thy truth's sake.
118. 1 because his *m* endureth for ever.
29 good: for his *m* endureth for ever.
119.64 The earth, O Lord, is full of thy *m*:
130. 7 for with the Lord there is *m*, and
136. 1, 2, 3 for his *m* endureth forever.
145. 8 slow to anger, and of great *m*.
147.11 him, in those that hope in his *m*.
Pr 3. 3 Let not *m* and truth forsake thee:
14.21 but he that hath *m* on the poor,
20.28 *M* and truth preserve the king:
Isa 47. 6 thou didst shew them no *m*; upon
54.10 saith the Lord that hath *m* on thee.
60.10 in my favor have I had *m* on thee.
Jer 6.23 they are cruel, and have no *m*:
30.18 and have *m* on his dwellingplaces;
33.11 for his *m* endureth for ever: and
Dan 4.27 by shewing *m* to the poor: if it
Hos 2. 4 will not have *m* upon her children;
23 earth; and I will have *m* upon her
23 upon her that had not obtained *m*;
4. 1 because there is no truth, nor *m*,
6. 6 For I desired *m*, and not sacrifice;
10.12 in righteousness, reap in *m*; break
14. 3 in thee the fatherless findeth *m*.
Mic 6. 8 but to do justly, and to love *m*,
Zec 7. 9 and shew *m* and compassions
10. 6 for I have *m* upon them: and they
Mt 5. 7 merciful: for they shall obtain *m*.
9.13 I will have *m*, and not sacrifice:
27 Thou son of David, have *m* on us.
12. 7 I will have *m*, and not sacrifice,
15.22 Have *m* on me, O Lord, thou son
17.15 Lord, have *m* on my son: for he is
20.30, 31 Have *m* on us, O Lord, thou son
23.23 the law, judgment, *m*, and faith:
Mk 10.47, 48 son of David, have *m* on me.
Lk 1.50 his *m* is on them that fear him
54 Israel, in remembrance of his *m*;
58 Lord had shewed great *m* upon her;
72 To perform the *m* promised to our
78 Through the tender *m* of our God;
10.37 he said, He that shewed *m* on him.
16.24 Father Abraham, have *m* on me,
17.13 said, Jesus, Master, have *m* on us.
18.38, 39 thou son of Daid, have *m* on me.
Ro 9.15 have *m* on whom I will have *m*,
16 but of God that sheweth *m*.
18 Therefore hath he *m* on whom he
18 on whom he will have *m*, and on
23 of his glory on the vessels of *m*,
11.30 yet have now obtained *m* through
31 that through your *m* they also
31 they also may obtain *m*.
32 that he might have *m* upon all.
12. 8 that sheweth *m*, with cheerfulness.
15. 9 might glorify God for his *m*;
1Co 7.25 that hath obtained *m* of the Lord
2Co 4. 1 as we have received *m*, we faint not:
Gal 6.16 rule, peace be on them, and *m*,
Eph 2. 4 But God, who is rich in *m*, for his
Php 2.27 but God had *m* on him; and not on
1Ti 1. 2 Grace, *m*, and peace, from God
13 but I obtained *m*, because I did it
16 for this cause I obtained *m*, that
2Ti 1. 2 Grace, *m*, and peace, from God
16 The Lord give *m* unto the house
18 that he may find *m* of the Lord in
Tit 1. 4 Grace, *m*, and peace, from God
3. 5 but according to his *m* he saved us,
Heb 4.16 that we may obtain *m*, and find
10.28 Moses' law died without *m* under
Jas 2.13 he shall have judgment without *m*,
13 that hath shewed no *m*;
13 and *m* rejoiceth against judgment.
3.17 full of *m* and good fruits, without
5.11 is very pitiful, and of tender *m*.
1Pe 1. 3 according to his abundant *m* hath
2.10 of God: which had not obtained *m*,
10 but now have obtained *m*.
2Jn 3 Grace be with you, *m*, and peace,
Jude 2 *M* unto you, and peace, and love,
21 for the *m* of our Lord Jesus Christ

MERCYSEAT

Heb 9. 5 of glory shadowing the *m*;

MERRILY

Est 5.14 then go thou in *m* with the king

MERRY

Gen 43.34 they drank, and were *m* with him.
Jdg 9.27 trode the grapes, and made *m*,
16.25 pass, when their hearts were *m*,
19. 6 all night, and let thine heart be *m*.
9 here, that thine heart may be *m*;
22 they were making their hearts *m*,
Ru 3. 7 and drunk, and his heart was *m*,
1Sa 25.36 Nabal's heart was *m* within him,
2Sa 13.28 Amnon's heart is *m* with wine,
1Ki 4.20 and drinking, and making *m*.
21. 7 bread, and let thine heart be *m*:
2Ch 7.10 their tents, glad and *m* in heart
Est 1.10 when the heart of the king was *m*
Pr 15.13 A *m* heart maketh a cheerful
15 but he that is of a *m* heart hath a
17.22 A *m* heart doeth good like a
Ec 8.15 to eat, and to drink, and to be *m*:
9. 7 drink thy wine with a *m* heart;
10.19 for laughter, and wine maketh *m*:
Jer 30.19 the voice of them that make *m*:
31. 4 in the dances of them that make *m*.
Lk 12.19 thine ease, eat, drink, and be *m*.
15.23 and kill it; and let us eat, and be *m*:
24 is found. And they began to be *m*.
29 I might make *m* with my friends:
32 was meet that we should make *m*,
Jas 5.13 Is any *m*? let him sing psalms.
Rev 11.10 rejoice over them, and make *m*,

MESHACH

Dan 1. 7 Shadrach; and to Mishael, of *M*;
2.49 set Shadrach, *M*, and Abed-nego,

3.12 Shadrach, *M*, and Abed-nego;
13 bring Shadrach, *M*, and Abed-nego.
14 O Shadrach, *M*, and Abed-nego,
16 Shadrach, *M*, and Abed-nego,
19 was changed against Shadrach, *M*,
20 bind Shadrach, *M*, and Abed-nego,
22 men that took up Shadrach, *M*,
23 Shadrach, *M*, and Abed-nego, fell
26 spake, and said, Shadrach, *M*, and
26 Shadrach, *M*, and Abed-nego,
28 be the God of Shadrach, *M*, and
29 against the God of Shadrach, *M*,
30 the king promoted Shadrach, *M*,

MESOPOTAMIA

Gen 24.10 and he arose, and went to *M*, unto
Dt 23. 4 the son of Beor of Pethor of *M*,
Jdg 3. 8 of Chushan-rishathaim king of *M*:
10 Chushan-rishathaim king of *M*
1Ch 19. 6 chariots and horsemen out of *M*,
Ac 2. 9 the dwellers in *M*, and in Judea,
7. 2 father Abraham, when he was in *M*,

MESSAGE

Jdg 3.20 I have a *m* from God unto thee.
1Ki 20.12 when Ben-hadad heard this *m*, as
Pr 26. 6 He that sendeth a *m* by the hand
Hag 1.13 in the Lord's *m* unto the people,
Lk 19.14 him, and sent a *m* after him,
1Jn 1. 5 is the *m* which we have heard of
3.11 is the *m* that ye heard from the

MESSENGER

Gen 50.16 And they sent a *m* unto Joseph,
1Sa 4.17 the *m* answered and said, Israel
23.27 But there came a *m* unto Saul,
2Sa 11.19 And charged the *m*, saying, When
22 So the *m* went, and came and
23 the *m* said unto David, Surely the
25 David said unto the *m*, Thus shalt
15.13 there came a *m* to David, saying,
1Ki 19. 2 Jezebel sent a *m* unto Elijah,
22.13 And the *m* that was gone to call
2Ki 5.10 Elisha sent a *m* unto him, saying,
6.32 ere the *m* came to him, he said to
32 when the *m* cometh, shut the door,
33 the *m* came down unto him: and
9.18 The *m* came to them, but he
10. 8 And there came a *m*, and told him,
2Ch 18.12 the *m* that went to call Micaiah
Job 1.14 And there came a *m* unto Job, and
33.23 If there be a *m* with him, an
Pr 13.17 A wicked *m* falleth into mischief:
17.11 a cruel *m* shall be sent against
25.13 is a faithful *m* to them that send
Isa 42.19 or deaf, as my *m* that I sent?
Jer 51.31 and one *m* to meet another, to
Eze 23.40 unto whom a *m* was sent; and,
Hag 1.13 spake Haggai the Lord's *m* in the
Mal 2. 7 he is the *m* of the Lord of hosts.
3. 1 I will send my *m*, and he shall
1 even the *m* of the covenant, whom
Mt 11.10 I send my *m* before thy face, which
Mk 1. 2 I send my *m* before thy face, which
Lk 7.27 I send my *m* before thy face, which
2Co 12. 7 the *m* of Satan to buffet me, lest I
Php 2.25 your *m*, and he that ministered

MESSENGERS

Gen 32. 3 Jacob sent *m* before him to Esau
6 the *m* returned to Jacob, saying,
Jos 6.17 because he hid the *m* that we sent.
1Sa 11. 3 may send *m* unto all the coasts of
7 coasts of Israel by the hands of *m*,
19.14 when Saul sent *m* to take David,
20 Spirit of God was upon the *m* of
2Ki 19.14 the letter of the hand of the *m*, and
1Ch 19. 2 And David sent *m* to comfort him
2Ch 36.16 But they mocked the *m* of God, and
Pr 16.14 wrath of a king is as *m* of death:
Isa 37.14 the letter from the hand of the *m*,
57. 9 didst send thy *m* far off, and didst
Na 2.13 the voice of thy *m* shall no more be
Lk 7.24 when the *m* of John were departed,
9.52 And sent *m* before his face: and
2Co 8.23 they are the *m* of the churches,
Jas 2.25 she had received the *m*, and had

MESSIAH

Dan 9.25 and build Jerusalem unto the *M*
26 and two weeks shall *M* be cut off,

MESSIAS

Jn 1.41 unto him, We have found the *M*,
4.25 I know that *M* cometh, which is

MET

Gen 32. 1 and the angels of God *m* him.
33. 8 thou by all this drove which I *m*?
Ex 3.18 of the Hebrews hath *m* with us:
4.24 that the Lord *m* him, and sought
27 and *m* him in the mount of God,
5. 3 of the Hebrews hath *m* with us:
20 And they *m* Moses and Aaron,
Nu 23. 4 And God *m* Balaam: and he said
16 Lord *m* Balaam, and put a word
Dt 23. 4 they *m* you not with bread and
25.18 How he *m* thee by the way, and
Jos 11. 5 all these kings were *m* together,
17.10 *m* together in Asher on the north,
1Sa 10.10 a company of prophets *m* him;
25.20 against her; and she *m* them.
2Sa 2.13 *m* together by the pool of Gibeon:
16. 1 servant of Mephibosheth *m* him,
18. 9 Absalom *m* the servants of David.
1Ki 13.24 a lion *m* him by the way, and slew
18. 7 in the way, behold, Elijah *m* him:
2Ki 9.21 *m* him in the portion of Naboth
10.13 *m* with the brethren of Ahaziah
Neh 13. 2 *m* not the children of Israel with
Ps 85.10 Mercy and truth are *m* together
Pr 7.10 *m* him a woman with the attire
Jer 41. 6 as he *m* them, he said unto them,
Am 5.19 flee from a lion, and a bear *m* him;
Mt 8.28 *m* him two possessed with devils,
28. 9 Jesus *m* them, saying, All hail.
Mk 5. 2 there *m* him out of the tombs a man
11. 4 in a place where two ways *m*;
Lk 8.27 *m* him out of the city a certain
9.37 from the hill, much people *m* him.
17.12 *m* him ten men that were lepers,
Jn 4.51 his servants *m* him, and told him,
11.20 was coming, went and *m* him:
30 in that place where Martha *m* him.
12.18 this cause the people also *m* him,
Ac 10.25 was coming in, Cornelius *m* him,
16.16 with a spirit of divination *m* us,
17.17 daily with them that *m* with him.
20.14 when he *m* with us at Assos, we
27.41 falling into a place where two seas *m*,
Heb 7. 1 who *m* Abraham returning from
10 father, when Melchisedec *m* him.

METE

Ex 16.18 when they did *m* it with an omer,
Ps 60. 6 and *m* out the valley of Succoth.
108. 7 and *m* out the valley of Succoth.
Mt 7. 2 with what measure ye *m*, it shall
Mk 4.24 with what measure ye *m*, it shall
Lk 6.38 with the same measure that ye *m*

METED

Isa 18. 2 a nation *m* out and trodden down,
7 a nation *m* out and trodden under
40.12 and *m* out heaven with the span,

METHUSELAH

Gen 5.21 and five years, and begat *M*:
22 walked with God after he begat *M*
25 *M* lived an hundred eighty and
26 *M* lived after he begat Lamech
27 the days of *M* were nine hundred
1Ch 1. 3 Henoch, *M*, Lamech,

MICHAEL

Nu 13.13 of Asher, Sethur the son of *M*.
1Ch 5.13 house of their fathers were, *M*.
14 the son of *M*, the son of Jeshishai,
6.40 son of *M*, the son of Baaseiah, the
7. 3 *M*, and Obadiah, and Joel, Ishiah,
8.16 *M*, and Ispah, and Joha, the sons
12.20 *M*, and Jozabad, and Elihu, and
27.18 of Issachar, Omri the son of *M*:
2Ch 21. 2 Zechariah, and Azariah, and *M*,
Ezr 8. 8 Zebadiah the son of *M*, and with
Dan 10.13 *M*, one of the chief princes, came
21 in these things, but *M* your prince.
12. 1 at that time shall *M* stand up,
Jude 9 Yet *M* the archangel, when
Rev 12. 7 *M* and his angels fought against

MIDDAY

1Ki 18.29 came to pass, when *m* was past,
Neh 8. 3 from the morning until *m*,
Ac 26.13 At *m*, O king, I saw in the

MIDDLE

Ex 26.28 *m* bar in the midst of the boards
36.33 And he made the *m* bar to shoot
Jos 12. 2 from the *m* of the river, and from
Jdg 7.19 in the beginning of the *m* watch;
9.37 people down by the *m* of the land,
16.29 took hold of the two *m* pillars
1Sa 25.29 out, as out of the *m* of a sling.
2Sa 10. 4 cut off their garments in the *m*,
1Ki 6. 6 and the *m* was six cubits broad,
8 door for the *m* chamber was in the
8 winding stairs into the *m* chamber,
8 and out of the *m* into the third.
8.64 the king hallow the *m* of the court
2Ki 20. 4 was gone out into the *m* court,
2Ch 7. 7 hallowed the *m* of the court that
Jer 39. 3 came in, and sat in the *m* gate,
Eze 1.16 were a wheel in the *m* of a wheel.
Eph 2.14 hath broken down the *m* wall of

MIDNIGHT

Ex 11. 4 About *m* will I go out into
12.29 at *m* the Lord smote all the
Jdg 16. 3 lay till *m*, and arose at *m*,
Ru 3. 8 it came to pass at *m*, that the
1Ki 3.20 she arose at *m*, and took my
Job 34.20 people shall be troubled at *m*,
Ps 119.62 At *m* I will rise to give thanks
Mt 25. 6 at *m* there was a cry made,
Mk 13.35 or at *m*, or at the cockcrowing, or
Lk 11. 5 and shall go unto him at *m*, and
Ac 16.25 at *m* Paul and Silas prayed, and
20. 7 and continued his speech until *m*.
27.27 about *m* the shipmen deemed

MIDST

Gen 1. 6 firmament in the *m* of the waters,
2. 9 tree of life...in the *m* of the garden,
Ex 3. 2 of fire out of the *m* of a bush:
8.22 am the Lord in the *m* of the earth.
14.22 of Israel went into the *m* of the sea
24.18 Moses went into the *m* of the cloud,
Nu 33. 8 passed through the *m* of the sea
Dt 4.15 in Horeb out of the *m* of the fire:
5.26 speaking out of the *m* of the fire,
18.15 thee a Prophet from the *m* of thee,
Jos 3.17 on dry ground in the *m* of Jordan,
10.13 sun stood still in the *m* of heaven,
Jdg 15. 4 put a firebrand in the *m* between
2Ch 20.14 Lord in the *m* of the congregation;
Ps 22.22 in the *m* of the congregation will I
46. 5 God is in the *m* of her; she shall
48. 9 O God, in the *m* of thy temple.
55.11 Wickedness is in the *m* thereof:
74.12 salvation in the *m* of the earth.
116.19 Lord's house, in the *m* of thee, O
136.14 Israel to pass through the *m* of it:
137. 2 upon the willows in the *m* thereof.
138. 7 Though I walk in the *m* of trouble,

Pr 5.14 all evil in the *m* of the congregation
8.20 in the *m* of the paths of judgment:
23.34 he lieth down in the *m* of the sea,
30.19 way of a ship in the *m* of the sea;
SS 3.10 *m* thereof being paved with love,
Isa 6. 5 I dwell in the *m* of a people of
12. 6 Holy One of Israel in the *m* of thee.
16. 3 night in the *m* of the noonday;
19.14 a perverse spirit in the *m* thereof:
Jer 14. 9 thou, O Lord, art in the *m* of us,
46.21 her hired men are in the *m* of her
La 4.13 blood of the just in the *m* of her,
Eze 5. 5 I have set it in the *m* of the nations
10.10 wheel had been in the *m* of a wheel.
12. 2 in the *m* of a rebellious house,
28.22 I will be glorified in the *m* of thee:
32.21 speak to him out of the *m* of hell
37. 1 set me down in the *m* of the valley
26 set my sanctuary in the *m* of them
48.10 the Lord shall be in the *m* thereof.
Dan 3.24 men bound into the *m* of the fire?
25 loose, walking in the *m* of the fire,
7.15 in my spirit in the *m* of my body,
Hos 11. 9 man; the Holy One in the *m* of thee:
Am 3. 9 great tumults in the *m* thereof,
7. 8 plumbline in the *m* of my people
Mic 5.13 images out of the *m* of thee;
Hab 3. 2 thy work in the *m* of the years,
Zep 3. 5 The just Lord is in the *m* thereof;
12 leave in the *m* of thee an afflicted
15 even the Lord, is in the *m* of thee:
17 thy God in the *m* of thee is mighty;
Zec 2.10, 11 and I will dwell in the *m* of thee,
Mt 10.16 forth as sheep in the *m* of wolves:
14.24 ship was now in the *m* of the sea,
18. 2 him, and set him in the *m* of them,
20 name, there am I in the *m* of them.
Mk 6.47 the ship was in the *m* of the sea,
7.31 the *m* of the coasts of Decapolis.
9.36 child, and set him in the *m* of them:
14.60 the high priest stood up in the *m*,
Lk 2.46 sitting in the *m* of the doctors,
4.30 he passing through the *m* of them
35 the devil had thrown him in the *m*,
5.19 his couch into the *m* before Jesus.
6. 8 Rise up, and stand forth in the *m*.
17.11 passed through the *m* of Samaria
21.21 which are in the *m* of it depart out;
22.55 kindled a fire in the *m* of the hall,
23.45 of the temple was rent in the *m*.
24.36 Jesus...stood in the *m* of them,
Jn 7.14 the *m* of the feast Jesus went up
8. 3 when they had set her in the *m*,
9 and the woman standing in the *m*.
59 going through the *m* of them, and
19.18 either side one, and Jesus in the *m*.
20.19 came Jesus and stood in the *m*,
26 stood in the *m*, and said, Peace be
Ac 1.15 stood up in the *m* of the disciples,
18 he burst asunder in the *m*, and all
2.22 God did by him in the *m* of you,
4. 7 when they had set them in the *m*,
17.22 Paul stood in the *m* of Mars' hill,
27.21 Paul stood forth in the *m* of them,
Php 2.15 in the *m* of a crooked and perverse
Heb 2.12 *m* of the church will I sing praise
Rev 1.13 in the *m* of the seven candlesticks
2. 1 *m* of the seven golden candlesticks;
7 is in the *m* of the paradise of God.
4. 6 in the *m* of the throne, and round
5. 6 in the *m* of the throne and of the
6 in the *m* of the elders, stood a Lamb
6. 6 a voice in the *m* of the four beasts
7.17 which is in the *m* of the throne
8.13 flying through the *m* of heaven,
14. 6 angel fly in the *m* of heaven,
19.17 fowls that fly in the *m* of heaven,
22. 2 In the *m* of the street of it, and on

MIDWIFE

Gen 35.17 labor, that the *m* said unto her,
32.28 *m* took and bound upon his hand a
Ex 1.16 When ye do the office of a *m* to the

MIDWIVES

Ex 1.15 of Egypt spake to the Hebrew *m*,
17 the *m* feared God, and did not as
18 the king of Egypt called for the *m*,
19 the *m* said unto Pharaoh, Because
19 ere the *m* come in unto them.
20 God dealt well with the *m*: and the
21 to pass because the *m* feared God,

MIGHT

Gen 49. 3 thou art my firstborn, my *m*, and
Nu 14.13 broughtest up this people in thy *m*
Dt 3.24 works, and according to thy *m*?
4.36 his voice, that he *m* instruct thee:
6. 5 all thy soul, and with all thy *m*
8.17 the *m* of mine hand hath gotten
Jdg 5.31 sun when he goeth forth in his *m*.
6.14 Go in this thy *m*, and thou shalt
16.30 he bowed himself with all his *m*;
2Sa 6.14 before the Lord with all his *m*;
1Ki 15.23 all the acts of Asa, and all his *m*,
16. 5 what he did, and his *m*, are they
27 he did, and his *m* that he shewed,
22.45 and his *m* that he shewed, and
2Ki 7. 2 windows in heaven, *m* this thing be?
10.34 and all that he did, and all his *m*,
13. 8 and all that he did, and his *m*, are
20.20 acts of Hezekiah, and all his *m*,
23.25 all his soul, and with all his *m*,
1Ch 7. 2 men of *m* in the generations;
5 Issachar were valiant men of *m*,
12. 8 hold to the wilderness men of *m*,
13. 8 before God with all their *m*, and
29. 2 prepared with all my *m* for the
12 and in thine hand is power and *m*;
30 With all his reign and his *m*, and
2Ch 20. 6 hand is there not power and *m*,
12 no *m* against this great company
Ezr 8.21 we *m* afflict ourselves before our
Est 10. 2 the acts of his power and of his *m*,
Job 16.21 that one *m* plead for a man with
23. 3 Oh that I knew where I *m* find him!
3 that I *m* come even to his seat!
38.13 *m* take hold of the ends of the earth,
Ps 76. 5 none of the men of *m* have found
78. 7 That they *m* set their hope in God,
119.11 heart, that I *m* not sin against thee.
148 that I *m* meditate in thy word.
Ec 2. 3 I *m* see what was that good for the
9.10 findeth to do, do it with thy *m*;
Isa 11. 2 the spirit of counsel and *m*, the
40.29 have no *m* he increaseth strength.
61. 3 *m* be called trees of righteousness,
3 of the Lord, that he *m* be glorified.
Jer 9.23 let the mighty man glory in his *m*,
10. 6 great, and thy name is great in *m*.
Eze 17. 8 bear fruit, that it *m* be a goodly vine.
14 by keeping of his covenant it *m*
20.12 that they *m* know that I am the Lord
Dan 2.23 who hast given me wisdom and *m*,
4.30 kingdom by the *m* of my power,
6.17 that the purpose *m* not be changed
Joel 3. 3 a girl for wine, that they *m* drink.
Am 1.13 that they *m* enlarge their border:
Jon 4. 5 *m* see what would become of the
6 that it *m* be a shadow over his head,
Mic 3. 8 of judgment, and of *m*, to declare
Zec 4. 6 Not by *m*, nor by power, but by
11.10 *m* break my covenant which I had
Mal 2. 4 that my covenant *m* be with Levi.
Mt 1.22 it *m* be fulfilled which was spoken
2.15, 23 it *m* be fulfilled which was spoken
4.14 it *m* be fulfilled which was spoken
8.17 it *m* be fulfilled which was spoken
28 that no man *m* pass by that way.
12.10 days? that they *m* accuse him.
14 him, how they *m* destroy him.
17 it *m* be fulfilled which was spoken
13.35 it *m* be fulfilled which was spoken
14.36 they *m* only touch the hem of his
21. 4 it *m* be fulfilled which was spoken by
32 not afterward, that ye *m* believe
34 that they *m* receive the fruits of it.
22.15 how they *m* entangle him in his talk.
26. 4 that they *m* take Jesus by subtilty,
9 this ointment *m* have been sold for
56 of the prophets *m* be fulfilled.
27.35 it *m* be fulfilled which was spoken by
Mk 3. 2 day; that they *m* accuse him.
6 against him, how they *m* destroy
14 that he *m* send them forth to preach,
5.18 prayed him that he *m* be with him.
6.56 they *m* touch if it were but the border
10.51 him, Lord, that I *m* receive my sight.
11.13 if haply he *m* find any thing thereon:
18 and sought how they *m* destroy him:
12. 2 he *m* receive from the husbandmen
14. 1 scribes sought how they *m* take him
5 For it *m* have been sold for more
11 how he *m* conveniently betray him.
35 possible, the hour *m* pass from him.
16. 1 that they *m* come and anoint him.
Lk 1.74 enemies *m* serve him without fear,
4.29 that they *m* cast him down headlong.
5.19 by what way they *m* bring him in
6. 7 *m* find an accusation against him.
11 another what they *m* do to Jesus.
8. 9 saying, What *m* this parable be?
10 parables; that seeing they *m* not see,
10 and hearing they *m* not understand.
38 besought him that he *m* be with him:
11.54 of his mouth, that they *m* accuse
15.29 that I *m* make merry with my
17. 6 ye *m* say unto this sycamine tree,
19.15 *m* know how much every man had
23 I *m* have required mine own with
48 And could not find what they *m* do:
20.20 that they *m* take hold of his words,
20 *m* deliver him unto the power and
22. 2 scribes sought how they *m* kill him;
4 how he *m* betray him unto them.
23.23 requiring that he *m* be crucified.
26 cross, that he *m* bear it after Jesus.
24.45 they *m* understand the scriptures,
Jn 1. 7 that all men through him *m* believe.
3.17 the world through him *m* be saved.
5.34 things I say, that ye *m* be saved.
40 not come to me, that ye *m* have life.
6.28 that we *m* work the works of God?
8. 6 him, that they *m* have to accuse him.
9.36 is he, Lord, that I *m* believe on him?
39 world, that they which see not *m* see;
39 that they which see *m* be made blind.
10.10 I am come that they *m* have life,
10 that they *m* have it more abundantly.
17 down my life, that I *m* take it again.
11. 4 that the Son of God *m* be glorified
57 should shew it, that they *m* take him.
12. 9 that they *m* see Lazarus also, whom
10 they *m* put Lazarus also to death;
38 of Esaias the prophet *m* be fulfilled,
14.29 when it is come to pass, ye *m* believe.
15.11 you, that my joy *m* remain in you,
11 in you, and that your joy *m* be full.
25 that the word *m* be fulfilled that is
16.33 you, that in me ye *m* have peace.
17. 3 they *m* know thee the only true God,
12 that the scripture *m* be fulfilled.
13 that they *m* have my joy fulfilled in
19 that they also *m* be sanctified
18. 9 That the saying *m* be fulfilled, which
28 but that they *m* eat the passover.
32 the saying of Jesus *m* be fulfilled,
19.24, 38 that the scripture *m* be fulfilled,
31 Pilate that their legs *m* be broken,
31 and that they *m* be taken away.
35 that he saith true, that ye *m* believe.
38 he *m* take away the body of Jesus:
20.31 ye *m* believe that Jesus is the Christ,

31 ye *m* have life through his name.
Ac 1.25 fell, that he *m* go to his own place.
4.21 nothing how they *m* punish them,
5.15 Peter passing by *m* overshadow
7.19 children, to the end they *m* not live.
8.15 that they *m* receive the Holy Ghost:
9.2 *m* bring them...unto Jerusalem.
12 on him, that he *m* receive his sight.
21 that he *m* bring them bound unto
13.42 that these words *m* be preached to
15.17 of men *m* seek after the Lord,
17.27 if haply they *m* feel after him, and
20.24 so that I *m* finish my course with joy,
22.24 that he *m* know wherefore they cried
24.26 him of Paul, that he *m* loose him:
25.21 be kept till I *m* send him to Cæsar.
26 had, I *m* have somewhat to write.
26.32 man *m* have been set at liberty, if
27.12 means they *m* attain to Phenice,
Ro 1.10 I *m* have a prosperous journey
13 I *m* have some fruit among you also,
3.26 that he *m* be just, and the justifier of
4.11 that he *m* be the father of all them
11 righteousness *m* be imputed unto
16 it is of faith, that it *m* be by grace;
16 the promise *m* be sure to all the seed;
18 *m* become the father of many
5.20 entered, that the offense *m* abound.
21 *m* grace reign through righteousness
6. 6 that the body of sin *m* be destroyed,
7.13 But sin, that it *m* appear sin, working
13 sin...*m* become exceeding sinful.
8. 4 the law *m* be fulfilled in us, who walk
29 he *m* be the firstborn among many
9.11 God according to election *m* stand
17 up, that I *m* shew my power in thee,
17 my name *m* be declared throughout
23 that he *m* make known the riches of
10. 1 for Israel is, that they *m* be saved.
11.14 my flesh, and *m* save some of them.
19 broken off, that I *m* be graffed in.
32 that he *m* have mercy upon all.
14. 9 that he *m* be Lord both of the dead
15. 4 comfort of the scriptures *m* have
9 Gentiles *m* glorify God for his
16 up of the Gentiles *m* be acceptable,
1Co 2.12 that we *m* know the things that are
4. 6 ye *m* learn in us not to think of men
8 reign, that we also *m* reign with you.
5. 2 hath done this deed *m* be taken away
9.19 unto all, that I *m* gain the more.
20 as a Jew, that I *m* gain the Jews;
20 I *m* gain them that are under the
21 I *m* gain them that are without law.
22 I as weak, that I *m* gain the weak:
22 that I *m* by all means save some.
23 I *m* be partaker thereof with you.
14.19 by my voice I *m* teach others also,
2Co 1.15 that ye *m* have a second benefit;
2. 4 that ye *m* know the love which I have
9 that I *m* know the proof of you,
4.10, 11 also of Jesus *m* be made manifest
15 grace *m* through the thanksgiving of
5. 4 mortality *m* be swallowed up of life.
21 *m* be made the righteousness of God
7. 9 ye *m* receive damage by us in
12 in the sight of God *m* appear unto
8. 9 ye through his poverty *m* be rich.
9. 5 that the same *m* be ready, as a
11. 4 not accepted, ye *m* well bear with
7 abasing myself that ye *m* be exalted,
12. 8 Lord thrice, that it *m* depart from
Gal 1. 4 he *m* deliver us from this present evil
16 I *m* preach him among the heathen;
2. 4 that they *m* bring us into bondage:
5 truth of the gospel *m* continue with
16 *m* be justified by the faith of Christ,
19 to the law, that I *m* live unto God.
3.14 blessing of Abraham *m* come on the
14 we *m* receive the promise of the Spirit
22 *m* be given to them that believe.
24 Christ, that we *m* be justified by
4. 5 we *m* receive the adoption of sons.
17 exclude you, that ye *m* affect them.
Eph 1.10 he *m* gather together in one all things
21 principality, and power, and *m*,
2. 7 he *m* shew the exceeding riches of
16 *m* reconcile both unto God in one
3.10 places *m* be known by the church
16 to be strengthened with *m* by his
19 *m* be filled with all the fulness of
4.10 all heavens, that he *m* fill all things,)
5.26 he *m* sanctify and cleanse it with the
27 he *m* present it to himself a glorious
6.10 Lord, and in the power of his *m*.
22 purpose, that ye *m* know our affairs,
22 and that he *m* comfort your hearts.
Php 3. 4 I *m* also have confidence in the flesh.
4 hath whereof he *m* trust in the flesh,
11 I *m* attain unto the resurrection of
Col 1. 9 *m* be filled with the knowledge of his
10 That ye *m* walk worthy of the Lord
11 Strengthened with all *m*,
18 he *m* have the preeminence.
2. 2 their hearts *m* be comforted, being
4. 8 he *m* know your estate, and comfort
1Th 2. 6 we *m* have been burdensome, as
16 to the Gentiles that they *m* be saved,
3.10 exceedingly that we *m* see your face,
10 *m* perfect that which is lacking in
2Th 2. 6 that he *m* be revealed in his time.
10 of the truth, that they *m* be saved.
12 all *m* be damned who believed not
3. 8 *m* not be chargeable to any of you:
1Ti 1.16 *m* shew forth all longsuffering,
2Ti 4.17 me the preaching *m* be fully known,
17 and that all the Gentiles *m* hear:
Tit 2.14 *m* redeem us from all iniquity, and
3. 8 God *m* be careful to maintain good
Phm 8 though I *m* be much bold in Christ
13 stead he *m* have ministered unto me
Heb 2.14 through death he *m* destroy him that
17 he *m* be a merciful and faithful high
6.18 we *m* have a strong consolation, who
9.15 are called *m* receive the promise of
10.36 of God, ye *m* receive the promise.
11.15 they *m* have had an opportunity to
35 they *m* obtain a better resurrection:
12.10 that we *m* be partakers of his
18 unto the mount that *m* be touched,
13.12 he *m* sanctify the people with his
Jas 5.17 prayed earnestly that it *m* not rain:
1Pe 1. 7 *m* be found unto praise and honor
21 your faith and hope *m* be in God.
3.18 unjust, that he *m* bring us to God,
4. 6 that they *m* be judged according to
2Pe 1. 4 *m* be partaker of the divine nature,
2.11 which are greater in power and *m*,
1Jn 2.19 they *m* be made manifest that they
3. 8 he *m* destroy the works of the devil.
4. 9 world, that we *m* live through him.
3Jn 8 we *m* be fellowhelpers to the truth.
Rev 7.12 power, and *m*, be unto our God
12.14 that she *m* fly into the wilderness,
15 he *m* cause her to be carried away
13.17 that no man *m* buy or sell, save
16.12 the kings of the east *m* be prepared.

MIGHTEST

Dt 4.35 thou *m* know that the Lord he is
6. 2 That thou *m* fear the Lord thy God,
Jdg 16. 6 thou *m* be bound to afflict thee.
10 thee, wherewith thou *m* be bound.
13 tell me wherewith thou *m* be bound.
1Sa 17.28 down that thou *m* see the battle.
Neh 9.29 that thou *m* bring them again unto
Ps 8. 2 that thou *m* still the enemy and the
51. 4 *m* be justified when thou speakest,
Pr 22.21 thou *m* answer the words of truth
Dan 2.30 that thou *m* know the thoughts of
Mt 15. 5 whatsoever thou *m* be profited by
Mk 7.11 whatsoever thou *m* be profited by
Lk 1. 4 thou *m* know the certainty of those
Ac 9.17 that thou *m* receive thy sight, and
Ro 3. 4 thou *m* be justified in thy sayings,
4 *m* overcome when thou art judged.
1Ti 1. 3 thou *m* charge some that they teach
18 thou by them *m* war a good warfare;

MIGHTIER

Gen 26.16 for thou are much *m* than we.
Ex 1. 9 of Israel are more and *m* than we:
Nu 14.12 a greater nation and *m* than they.
Dt 4.38 thee greater and *m* than thou art,
7. 1 nations greater and *m* than thou;
9. 1 greater and *m* than thyself, cities
14 a nation *m* and greater than they.
11.23 nations and *m* than yourselves.
Ps 93. 4 Lord on high is *m* than the noise
Ec 6.10 with him that is *m* than he.
Mt 3.11 that cometh after me is *m* than I,
Mk 1. 7 cometh one *m* than I after me,
Lk 3.16 one *m* than I cometh, the lachet of

MIGHTIEST

1Ch 11.19 These things did these three *m*.

MIGHTILY

Dt 6. 3 that ye may increase *m*, as the
Jdg 4. 3 twenty years he *m* oppressed the
14. 6 Spirit of the Lord came *m* upon him,
15.14 Spirit of the Lord came *m* upon him,
Jer 25.30 he shall *m* roar upon his habitation;
Jon 3. 8 sackcloth, and cry *m* unto God:
Na 2. 1 loins strong, fortify thy power *m*.
Ac 18.28 For he *m* convinced the Jews, and
19.20 *m* grew the word of God and
Col 1.29 which worketh in me *m*.
Rev 18. 2 cried *m* with a strong voice,

MIGHTY

Gen 18.18 become a great and *m* nation,
49.24 strong by the hands of the *m* God
Ex 3.19 let you go, no, not by a *m* hand.
32.11 great power, and with a *m* hand?
Lev 19.15 nor honor the person of the *m*:
Dt 3.24 thy greatness, and thy *m* hand:
6.21 us out of Egypt with a *m* hand:
7.19 *m* hand, and the stretched out arm,
10.17 a great God, a *m*, and a terrible,
Jos 4.24 the hand of the Lord, that it is *m*:
Jdg 5.23 help of the Lord against the *m*.
1Sa 9. 1 a Benjamite, a *m* man of power.
2Sa 1.19 high places: how are the *m* fallen!
23.16 the three *m* men brake through the
Neh 9.11 as a stone into the *m* waters.
32 our God, the great, the *m*, and the
Job 6.23 me from the hand of the *m*?
9. 4 wise in heart, and *m* in strength:
12.21 weakeneth the strength of the *m*.
34.24 break in pieces *m* men without
36. 5 God is *m*, and despiseth not any:
5 he is *m* in strength and wisdom.
Ps 24. 8 strong and *m*, the Lord *m* in battle
29. 1 Give unto the Lord, O ye *m*,
33.16 a *m* man is not delivered by much
74.15 the flood: thou driedst up *m* rivers.
106. 2 can utter the *m* acts of the Lord?
120. 4 Sharp arrows of the *m*, with coals
135.10 great nations, and slew *m* kings;
145. 4 and shall declare thy *m* acts.
150. 2 Praise him for his *m* acts: praise
Pr 21.22 man scaleth the city of the *m*, and
Isa 1.24 Lord of hosts, the *m* One of Israel,
9. 6 Wonderful, Counsellor, The *m*
17.12 like the rushing of *m* waters!
42.13 Lord shall go forth as a *m* man,
49.26 thy Redeemer, the *m* One of Jacob.
Jer 9.23 let the *m* man glory in his might,
32.18 the Great, the *M* God, the Lord
19 Great in counsel, and *m* in work:
Eze 20.33, 34 with a *m* hand, and with a
Dan 8.24 the *m* and the holy people.

Joel 3.11 thy *m* ones to come down, O Lord.
Am 2.14 neither shall the *m* deliver himself:
5.24 and righteousness as a *m* stream.
Jon 1. 4 there was a *m* tempest in the sea,
Hab 1.12 O *m* God, thou hast established
Zep 3.17 thy God in the midst of thee is *m*;
Mt 11.20 most of his *m* works were done,
21 if the *m* works, which were done
23 if the *m* works, which have been
13.54 this wisdom, and these *m* works?
58 he did not many *m* works there
14. 2 *m* works do shew forth themselves
Mk 6. 2 such *m* works are wrought by his
5 he could there do no *m* work, save
14 *m* works do shew forth themselves
Lk 1.49 he that is *m* hath done to me great
52 put down the *m* from their seats,
9.43 all amazed at the *m* power of God.
10.13 if the *m* works had been done in
15.14 arose a *m* famine in that land;
19.37 the *m* works that they had seen;
24.19 was a prophet *m* in deed and word
Ac 2. 2 heaven as of a rushing *m* wind,
7.22 and was *m* in words and in deeds.
18.24 man, and *m* in the scriptures,
Ro 15.19 Through *m* signs and wonders,
1Co 1.26 not many *m*, not many noble, are
27 confound the things which are *m*;
2Co 10. 4 but *m* through God to the pulling
12.12 signs, and wonders, and *m* deeds.
13. 3 is not weak, but is *m* in you.
Gal 2. 8 *m* in me toward the Gentiles:)
Eph 1.19 to the working of his *m* power,
2Th 1. 7 from heaven with his *m* angels,
1Pe 5. 6 under the *m* hand of God, that he
Rev 6.13 when she is shaken of a *m* wind.
15 chief captains, and the *m* men,
10. 1 saw another *m* angel come down
16.18 so *m* an earthquake, and so great.
18.10 great city Babylon, that *m* city!
21 a *m* angel took up a stone like a
19. 6 and as the voice of *m* thunderings,
18 captains, and the flesh of *m* men,

MILE

Mt 5.41 shall compel thee to go to a *m*, go

MILETUS

Ac 20.15 and the next day we came to *M*.
17 from *M* he sent to Ephesus, and

MILK

Ex 3. 8 a land flowing with *m* and honey;
Lev 20.24 that floweth with *m* and honey:
Nu 13.27 it floweth with *m* and honey; and
Dt 6. 3 that floweth with *m* and honey.
Jdg 4.19 she opened a bottle of *m*, and gave
5.25 asked water, and she gave him *m*;
Job 10.10 thou not poured me out as *m*, and
SS 4.11 honey and *m* are under thy tongue;
5. 1 I have drunk my wine with my *m*:
Isa 55. 1 buy wine and *m* without money
Jer 11. 5 a land flowing with *m* and honey,
La 4. 7 than snow, they were whiter than *m*,
Eze 20. 6, 15 flowing with *m* and honey,
Joel 3.18 and the hills shall flow with *m*, and
1Co 3. 2 I have fed you with *m*, and not
9. 7 eateth not of the *m* of the flock?
Heb 5.12 become such as have need of *m*,
13 every one that useth *m* is unskilful
1Pe 2. 2 desire the sincere *m* of the word,

MILL

Ex 11. 5 maidservant that is behind the *m*;
Mt 24.41 shall be grinding at the *m*; the

MILLSTONE

Dt 24. 6 nether or the upper *m* to pledge:
Jdg 9.53 of a *m* upon Abimelech's head,
2Sa 11.21 woman cast a piece of a *m* upon him
Job 41.24 as hard as a piece of the nether *m*.

Millstones such as these were familiar and vital tools in biblical times; their grinding ranked with "the voice of gladness" (Jer 25.10) because without them there could be no daily bread. The law forbade their use as collateral for loans (Dt 24.6).

Mt 18. 6 a *m* were hanged about his
Mk 9.42 a *m* were hanged about his
Lk 17. 2 a *m* were hanged about his
Rev 18.21 took up a stone like a great *m*,
22 the sound of a *m* shall be heard no

MIND

Lev 24.12 *m* of the Lord might be shewed
Dt 30. 1 thou shalt call them to *m* among
1Ch 22. 7 was in my *m* to build an house
28. 9 heart and with a willing *m*: for
Neh 4. 6 for the people had a *m* to work.
Job 23.13 he is in one *m*, and who can turn
34.33 Should it be according to thy *m*?
Ps 31.12 forgotten as a dead man out of *m*:
Pr 29.11 A fool uttereth all his *m*: but a
Isa 26. 3 peace, whose *m* is stayed on thee:
Eze 23.17 her *m* was alienated from them.
Dan 2.29 came into thy *m* upon thy bed,
Hab 1.11 Then shall his *m* change, and he
Mt 22.37 all thy soul, and with all thy *m*.
Mk 5.15 and clothed, and in his right *m*:
12.30 all thy soul, and with all thy *m*,
14.72 Peter called to *m* the word that
Lk 1.29 and cast in her *m* what manner of
8.35 Jesus, clothed, and in his right *m*:
10.27 thy strength, and with all thy *m*;
12.29 neither be ye of doubtful *m*.
Ac 17.11 the word with all readiness of *m*,
20.19 the Lord with all humility of *m*,
Ro 1.28 gave them over to a reprobate *m*,
7.23 warring against the law of my *m*,
25 then with the *m* I myself serve the
8. 5 flesh do *m* the things of the flesh:
7 carnal *m* is enmity against God:
27 knoweth what is the *m* of the Spirit,
11.34 hath known the *m* of the Lord?
12. 2 by the renewing of your *m*, that
16 the same *m* one toward another.
16 *M* not high things, but condescend
14. 5 be fully persuaded in his own *m*.
15. 6 may with one *m* and one mouth
15 as putting you in *m*, because of
1Co 1.10 joined together in the same *m*
2.16 who hath known the *m* of the Lord,
16 him? But we have the *m* of Christ.
2Co 7. 7 mourning, your fervent *m* toward
8.12 if there be first a willing *m*, it is
19 and declaration of your ready *m*:
9. 2 I know the forwardness of your *m*,
13.11 be of one *m*, live in peace; and
Eph 2. 3 desires of the flesh and of the *m*;
4.17 walk, in the vanity of the *m*,
23 renewed in the spirit of your *m*;
Php 1.27 with one *m* striving together for
2. 2 being of one accord, of one *m*.
3 in lowliness of *m* let each esteem
5 Let this *m* be in you, which was
3.16 rule, let us *m* the same thing.
19 shame, who *m* earthly things.)
4. 2 they be of the same *m* in the Lord.
Col 1.21 enemies in your *m* by wicked
2.18 vainly puffed up by his fleshly *m*,
3.12 humbleness of *m*, meekness,
2Th 2. 2 That ye be not soon shaken in *m*,
2Ti 1. 7 and of love, and of sound *m*.
Tit 1.15 their *m* and conscience is defiled.
3. 1 Put them in *m* to be subject to
Phm 14 But without thy *m* would I do
Heb 8.10 I will put my laws into their *m*,
1Pe 1.13 gird up the loins of your *m*, be
3. 8 be ye all of one *m*, having
4. 1 likewise with the same *m*: for
5. 2 for filthy lucre, but of a ready *m*;
Rev 17. 9 here is the *m* which hath wisdom.
13 These have one *m*, and shall give

MINDED

Ru 1.18 she was steadfastly *m* to go with her.
2Ch 24. 4 was *m* to repair the house
Ezr 7.13 are *m* of their own freewill to go up
Mt 1.19 was *m* to put her away privily.
Ac 27.39 shore, into the which they were *m*,
Ro 8. 6 to be carnally *m* is death;
6 spiritually *m* is life and peace.
2Co 1.15 I was *m* to come unto you before,
17 When I therefore was thus *m*, did
Gal 5.10 that ye will be none otherwise *m*:
Php 3.15 as many as be perfect, be thus *m*:
15 if in any thing ye be otherwise *m*,
Ti 2. 6 likewise exhort to be sober *m*.

Jas 1. 8 A double *m* man is unstable in all
4. 8 purify your hearts, ye double *m*.

MINDFUL

1Ch 16.15 Be ye *m* always of his covenant;
Neh 9.17 neither were *m* of thy wonders that
Ps 8. 4 is man, that thou art *m* of him?
111. 5 he will ever be *m* of his covenant.
115.12 The Lord hath been *m* of us: he
Isa 17.10 hast not been *m* of the rock of thy
2Ti 1. 4 being *m* of thy tears, that I may
Heb 2. 6 is man, that thou art *m* of him?
11.15 they had been *m* of that country
2Pe 3. 2 That ye may be *m* of the words

MINDING

Ac 20.13 appointed, *m* himself to go afoot.

MINDS

Jdg 19.30 of it, take advice, and speak your *m*.
2Sa 17. 8 they be chafed in their *m*, as a
2Ki 9.15 If it be your *m*, then let none go
Eze 24.25 whereupon they set their *m*, their
36. 5 all their heart, with despiteful *m*,
Ac 14. 2 made their *m* evil affected against
28. 6 changed their *m*, and said that he
2Co 3.14 But their *m* were blinded: for until
4. 4 hath blinded the *m* of them which
11. 3 so your *m* should be corrupted
Php 4. 7 keep your hearts and *m* through
1Ti 6. 5 disputings of men of corrupt *m*,
2Ti 3. 8 men of corrupt *m*, reprobate
Heb 10.16 and in their *m* will I write them;
12. 3 be wearied and faint in your *m*.
2Pe 3. 1 I stir up your pure *m* by way of

MINGLED

Lev 19.19 not sow thy field with *m* seed:
19 a garment *m* of linen and woollen
Ps 102. 9 and *m* my drink with weeping,
Pr 9. 2 she hath *m* her wine; she hath
Isa 19.14 The Lord hath *m* a perverse spirit
Mt 27.34 him vinegar to drink *m* with gall:
Mk 15.23 him to drink wine *m* with myrrh:
Lk 13. 1 Pilate had *m* with their sacrifices.
Rev 8. 7 followed hail and fire *m* with blood,
15. 2 it were a sea of glass *m* with fire:

MINISHED

Ps 107.39 they are *m* and brought low

MINISTER

Ex 28. 1 may *m* unto me in the priest's office,
3, 4 *m* unto me in the priest's office.
30.20 they come near to the altar to *m*,
Lev 16.32 consecrate to *m* in the priest's office
Nu 3. 3 consecrated to *m* in the priest's
Dt 18. 5 stand to *m* in the name of the Lord,
7 he shall *m* in the name of the Lord
21. 5 God hath chosen to *m* unto him,
1Sa 2.11 And the child did *m* unto the Lord
2Ch 31. 2 to *m*, and to give thanks, and to
Ps 9. 8 shall *m* judgment to the people in
Isa 60. 7 rams of Nebaioth...*m* unto thee:
10 and their kings shall *m* unto thee:
Mt 20.26 among you, let him be your *m*;
28 to be ministered unto, but to *m*,
25.44 prison, and did not *m* unto thee?
Mk 10.43 among you, shall be your *m*:
45 to be ministered unto, but to *m*,
Lk 4.20 he gave it again to the *m*, and sat
Ac 13. 5 and they had also John to their *m*.
24.23 none...to *m* or come unto him.
26.16 to make thee a *m* and a witness
Ro 13. 4 is the *m* of God to thee for good.
4 he is the *m* of God, a revenger to
15. 8 a *m* of the circumcision for the
16 I should be the *m* of Jesus Christ
25 Jerusalem to *m* unto the saints.
27 to *m* unto them in carnal things.
1Co 9.13 they which *m* about holy things

2Co 9.10 sower both *m* bread for your food,
Gal 2.17 is therefore Christ the *m* of sin?
Eph 3. 7 Whereof I was made a *m*, according
4.29 it may *m* grace unto the hearers.
6.21 a beloved brother and faithful *m*
Col 1. 7 is for you a faithful *m* of Christ;
23 whereof I Paul am made a *m*;
25 Whereof I am made a *m*, according
4. 7 a faithful *m* and fellowservant in
1Th 3. 2 our brother, and *m* of God, and our
1Ti 1. 4 *m* questions, rather than godly
4. 6 shalt be a good *m* of Jesus Christ,
Heb 1.14 sent forth to *m* for them who shall
6.10 ministered to the saints, and do *m*.
8. 2 A *m* of the sanctuary, and of the
1Pe 1.12 but unto us they did *m* the things,
4.10 even so *m* the same one to another,
11 if any man *m*, let him do it as of

MINISTERED

1Sa 3. 1 the child Samuel *m* unto the Lord
Eze 44.19 their garments wherein they *m*,
Dan 7.10 thousand thousands *m* unto him,
Mt 4.11 angels came and *m* unto him.
8.15 and she arose, and *m* unto them.
20.28 Son of man came not to be *m* unto,
Mk 1.13 beasts; and the angels *m* unto him.
31 left her, and she *m* unto them.
10.45 Son of man came not to be *m* unto,
15.41 followed him, and *m* unto him;)
Lk 4.39 she arose and *m* unto them.
8. 3 *m* unto him of their substance.
Ac 13. 2 As they *m* to the Lord, and fasted,
19.22 two of them that *m* unto him,
20.34 hands have *m* unto my necessities,
2Co 3. 3 to be the epistle of Christ *m* by us,
Php 2.25 and he that *m* to my wants.
Col 2.19 and bands having nourishment *m*,
2Ti 1.18 things he *m* unto me at Ephesus,
Phm 13 might have *m* unto me in the bonds
Heb 6.10 *m* to the saints, and do minister.
2Pe 1.11 an entrance shall be *m* unto you

MINSTERETH

2Co 9.10 Now he that *m* seed to the sower
Gal 3. 5 therefore that *m* to you the Spirit,

MINISTERING

1Ch 9.28 had the charge of the *m* vessels,
Eze 44.11 of the house, and *m* to the house:
Mt 27.55 Jesus from Galilee, *m* unto him:
Ro 12. 7 Or ministry, let us wait on our *m*:
15.16 the Gentiles, *m* the gospel of God,
2Co 8. 4 fellowship of the *m* to the saints.
9. 1 as touching the *m* to the saints,
Heb 1.14 Are they not all *m* spirits, sent
10.11 every priest standeth daily *m* and

MINISTERS

1Ki 10. 5 attendance of his *m*, and their
2Ch 9. 4 attendance of his *m*, and their
Ezr 7.24 or *m* of this house of God,
8.17 that they should bring unto us *m*
Ps 103.21 ye *m* of his, that do his pleasure.
104. 4 angels spirits; his *m* a flaming fire:
Isa 61. 6 shall call you the *M* of our God:
Jer 33.21 with the Levites the priests, my *m*.
Eze 44.11 they shall be *m* in my sanctuary,
45. 4 the priests the *m* of the sanctuary,
5 the Levites, the *m* of the house,
46.24 with the *m* of the house shall boil
Joel 1. 9 the priests, the Lord's *m*, mourn.
13 howl, ye *m* of the altar: come, lie
13 night in sackcloth, ye *m* of my God:
2.17 Let the priests, the *m* of the Lord,
Lk 1. 2 eyewitnesses, and *m* of the word;
Ro 13. 6 for they are God's *m*, attending
1Co 3. 5 *m* by whom ye believed, even as
4. 1 account of us, as of...*m* of Christ,
2Co 3. 6 hath made us able *m* of the new
6. 4 approving ourselves as...*m* of God,

11.15 thing if his *m* also be transformed
15 as the *m* of righteousness; whose
23 Are they *m* of Christ? (I speak as a
Heb 1. 7 spirits, and his *m* a flame of fire.

MINISTRATION

Lk 1.23 days of his *m* were accomplished,
Ac 6. 1 were neglected in the daily *m*.
2Co 3. 7 But if the *m* of death, written and
8 *m* of the spirit be rather glorious?
9 if the *m* of condemnation be glory,
9 *m* of righteousness exceed in glory.
9.13 Whiles by the experiment of this *m*

MINISTRY

Nu 4.12 take all the instruments of *m*,
47 came to do the service of the *m*,
2Ch 7. 6 when David praised by their *m*;
Hos 12.10 by the *m* of the prophets.
Ac 1.17 and had obtained part of this *m*.
25 That he may take part of this *m*
6. 4 prayer, and to the *m* of the word.
12.25 when they had fulfilled their *m*,
20.24 and the *m*, which I have received
21.19 among the Gentiles by his *m*.
Ro 12. 7 Or *m*, let us wait on...ministering;
1Co 16.15 addicted...to the *m* of the saints,)
2Co 4. 1 Therefore seeing we have this *m*,
5.18 given to us the *m* of reconciliation;
6. 3 thing, that the *m* be not blamed:
Eph 4.12 for the work of the *m*, for the
Col 4.17 Take heed to the *m* which thou hast
1Ti 1.12 faithful, putting me into the *m*;
2Ti 4. 5 evangelist, make full proof of thy *m*.
11 for he is profitable to me for the *m*.
Heb 8. 6 he obtained a more excellent *m*,
9.21 and all the vessels of the *m*.
(See box on page 509)

MINSTRELS

Mt 9.23 *m* and the people making a noise,

MINT

Mt 23.23 ye pay the tithe of *m* and anise
Lk 11.42 ye tithe *m* and rue and all manner

MIRACLE

Ex 7. 9 you, saying, Shew a *m* for you:
Mk 6.52 considered not the *m* of the loaves:
9.39 which shall do a *m* in my name,
Lk 23. 8 hoped to have seen some *m* done
Jn 4.54 again the second *m* that Jesus did,
6.14 they had seen the *m* that Jesus did,
10.41 him, and said, John did no *m*:
12.18 heard that he had done this *m*.
Ac 4.16 notable *m* hath been done by them
22 this *m* of healing was shewed.

MIRACLES

Nu 14.22 and my *m*, which I did in Egypt
Dt 11. 3 his *m*, and his acts, which he did
29. 3 the signs, and those great *m*:
Jdg 6.13 and where be all his *m* which our
Jn 2.11 beginning of *m* did Jesus in Cana
23 they saw the *m* which he did.
3. 2 can do these *m* that thou doest,
6. 2 because they saw his *m* which he
26 seek me, not because ye saw the *m*,
7.31 will he do more *m* than these
9.16 man that is a sinner do such *m*?
11.47 we? for this man doeth many *m*.
12.37 though he had done so many *m*
Ac 2.22 approved of God among you by *m*
6. 8 did great wonders and *m* among
8. 6 and seeing the *m* which he did.
13 the *m* and signs which were done.
15.12 *m* and wonders God had wrought
19.11 special *m* by the hands of Paul:
1Co 12.10 To another the working of *m*; to
28 after that *m*, then gifts of healings,
29 all teachers? are all workers of *m*?

Jesus' miracles included restoring sight to the blind (Jn 9.1-16); engraving by Henry Richter (1772-1857).

Gal 3. 5 worketh *m* among you, doeth he it
Heb 2. 4 and wonders, and with divers *m*,
Rev 13.14 those *m* which he had power to do
16.14 the spirits of devils, working *m*,
19.20 the false prophet that wrought *m*

MIRE
Job 8.11 Can the rush grow up without *m*?
30.19 He hath cast me into the *m*, and
Ps 69. 2 I sink in deep *m*, where there is
14 Deliver me out of the *m*, and let
Isa 57.20 whose waters cast up *m* and dirt.
Jer 38. 6 there was no water, but *m*:
6 so Jeremiah sunk in the *m*.
2Pe 2.22 washed to her wallowing in the *m*.

MIRTH
Gen 31.27 have sent thee away with *m*, and
Neh 8.12 portions, and to make great *m*,
Ps 137. 3 that wasted us required of us *m*,
Pr 14.13 and the end of that *m* is heaviness.
Ec 2. 1 to now, I will prove thee with *m*,
2 is mad: and of *m*, What doeth it?
7. 4 heart of fools is in the house of *m*.
8.15 Then I commended *m*, because a
Isa 24. 8 The *m* of tabrets ceaseth, the
11 the *m* of the land is gone.
Jer 7.34 the voice of *m*, and the voice of
16. 9 and in your days, the voice of *m*,
25.10 will take from them the voice of *m*,
Eze 21.10 glitter: should we then make *m*?
Hos 2.11 will also cause all her *m* to cease,

MIRY
Ps 40. 2 an horrible pit, out of the *m* clay,
Eze 47.11 But the *m* places thereof and the
Dan 2.41 the iron mixed with *m* clay.
43 sawest iron mixed with *m* clay,

MISCHIEF
Gen 42. 4 Lest peradventure *m* befall him.
38 if *m* befall him by the way in the
44.29 this also from me, and *m* befall him,
Ex 21.22 from her, and yet no *m* follow:
23 if any *m* follow, then thou shalt
32.12 For *m* did he bring them out, to
22 the people, that they are set on *m*.
1Sa 23. 9 secretly practiced *m* against him;
2Sa 16. 8 thou art taken in thy *m*, because
1Ki 11.25 beside the *m* that Hadad did: and
20. 7 and see how this man seeketh *m*:
2Ki 7. 9 light, some *m* will come upon us:
Neh 6. 2 But they thought to do me *m*.
Est 8. 3 tears to put away the *m* of Haman
Job 15.35 They conceive *m*, and bring forth
Ps 7.14 iniquity, and hath conceived *m*,
16 His *m* shall return upon his own
10. 7 under his tongue is *m* and vanity.
14 for thou beholdest *m* and spite, to
26.10 In whose hands is *m*, and their
28. 3 but *m* is in their hearts.
36. 4 He deviseth *m* upon his bed; he
52. 1 Why boastest thou thyself in *m*,
55.10 *m* also and sorrow are in the midst
62. 3 will ye imagine *m* against a man?
94.20 thee, which frameth *m* by a law?
119.150 draw nigh that follow after *m*:
140. 9 *m* of their own lips cover them.
Pr 4.16 not, except they have done *m*;
6.14 he deviseth *m* continually; he
18 feet that be swift in running to *m*,
10.23 It is as sport to a fool to do *m*:
11.27 he that seeketh *m*, it shall come
12.21 the wicked shall be filled with *m*.
13.17 wicked messenger falleth into *m*:
17.20 a perverse tongue falleth into *m*.
24. 2 and their lips talk of *m*.
16 but the wicked shall fall into *m*.
28.14 his heart shall fall into *m*.
Isa 47.11 *m* shall fall upon thee; thou shalt
59. 4 they conceive *m*, and bring forth
Eze 7.26 *M* shall come upon *m*, and
11. 2 these are the men that devise *m*,
Dan 11.27 king's hearts shall be to do *m*,
Hos 7.15 do they imagine *m* against me.
Ac 13.10 O full of all subtilty and all *m*,

MISCHIEFS
Dt 32.23 I will heap *m* upon them; I will
Ps 52. 2 Thy tongue deviseth *m*; like a
140. 2 Which imagine *m* in their hearts;

MISCHIEVOUS
Ps 21.11 they imagined a *m* device, which
38.12 that seek my hurt speak *m* things,
Pr 24. 8 evil shall be called a *m* person.
Ec 10.13 the end of his talk is *m* madness.
Mic 7. 3 man, he uttereth his *m* desire:

MISERABLE
Job 16. 2 things: *m* comforters are ye all.
1Co 15.19 Christ, we are of all men most *m*.
Rev 3.17 that thou art wretched, and *m*,

MISERABLY
Mt 21.41 will *m* destroy those wicked men,

MISERIES
La 1. 7 days of her affliction and of her *m*
Jas 5. 1 weep and howl for your *m* that

MISERY
Jdg 10.16 was grieved for the *m* of Israel.
Job 3.20 is light given to him that is in *m*,
11.16 Because thou shalt forget thy *m*,
Pr 31. 7 and remember his *m* no more.
Ec 8. 6 the *m* of man is great upon him.
La 3.19 mine affliction and my *m*, the
Ro 3.16 and *m* are in their ways:

MIST
Gen 2. 6 there went up a *m* from the earth,
Ac 13.11 fell on him a *m* and a darkness;
2Pe 2.17 the *m* of darkness is reserved for

MISTRESS
Gen 16. 4 her *m* was despised in her eyes.
8 flee from the face of my *m* Sarai.
9 said unto her, Return to thy *m*,
1Ki 17.17 the *m* of the house, fell sick; and
2Ki 5. 3 And she said unto her *m*, Would
Ps 123. 2 maiden unto the hand of her *m*;
Pr 30.23 handmaid that is heir to her *m*.
Isa 24. 2 as with the maid, so with her *m*;
Na 3. 4 the *m* of witchcrafts, that selleth

MITE
Lk 12.59 till thou hast paid the very last *m*.

MITES
Mk 12.42 and she threw in two *m*, which
Lk 21. 2 widow casting in thither two *m*.

MITYLENE
Ac 20.14 we took him in, and came to *M*.

MIXED
Ex 12.38 a *m* multitude went up also with
Neh 13. 3 from Israel all the *m* multitude.
Pr 23.30 wine; they that go to seek *m* wine.
Isa 1.22 dross, thy wine *m* with water:
Dan 2.41 sawest the iron *m* with miry clay.
43 thou sawest iron *m* with miry clay,
43 even as iron is not *m* with clay.
Hos 7. 8 he hath *m* himself among the
Heb 4. 2 not being *m* with faith in them

MIXTURE
Ps 75. 8 the wine is red; it is full of *m*;
Jn 19.39 brought a *m* of myrrh and aloes,
Rev 14.10 is poured out without *m* into the

MNASON
Ac 21.16 with them one *M* of Cyprus, an

MOCK

Gen 39.14 in an Hebrew unto us to *m* us;
17 unto us, came in unto me to *m* me:
Job 13. 9 mocketh another, do ye so *m* him?
21. 3 after that I have spoken, *m* on.
Pr 1.26 I will *m* when your fear cometh;
14. 9 Fools make a *m* at sin: but among
Jer 38.19 into their hand, and they *m* me.
La 1. 7 her, and did *m* at her sabbaths.
Eze 22. 5 be far from thee, shall *m* thee,
Mt 20.19 deliver him to the Gentiles to *m*,
Mk 10.34 they shall *m* him, and shall scourge
Lk 14.29 all that behold it begin to *m* him,

MOCKED

Gen 19.14 one that *m* unto his sons in law.
Nu 22.29 the ass, Because thou hast *m* me:
Jdg 16.10, 13 hast *m* me, and told me lies:
15 thou hast *m* me these three times,
1Ki 18.27 pass at noon, that Elijah *m* them,
2Ki 2.23 children out of the city, and *m* him,
2Ch 30.10 them to scorn, and *m* them.
36.16 But they *m* the messengers of God,
Neh 4. 1 great indignation, and *m* the Jews.
Job 12. 4 I am as one *m* of his neighbor,
Mt 2.16 that he was *m* of the wise men,
27.29 the knee before him, and *m* him,
31 after that they had *m* him, they
Mk 15.20 And when they had *m* him, they
Lk 18.32 shall be *m*, and spitefully entreated,
22.63 and the men that held Jesus *m* him,
23.11 war set him at nought, and *m* him,
36 the soldiers also *m* him, coming
Ac 17.32 resurrection of the dead, some *m*:
Gal 6. 7 Be not deceived; God is not *m*: for

MOCKER

Pr 20. 1 Wine is a *m*, strong drink is

MOCKERS

Job 17. 2 Are there not *m* with me? and
Ps 35.16 With hypocritical *m* in feasts, they
Isa 28.22 therefore be ye not *m*, lest your
Jer 15.17 sat not in the assembly of the *m*,
Jude 18 there should be *m* in the last time,

MOCKETH

Job 13. 9 or as one man *m* another, do ye so
39.22 He *m* at fear, and is not affrighted;
Pr 17. 5 Whoso *m* the poor reproacheth
30.17 The eye that *m* at his father, and
Jer 20. 7 in derision daily, every one *m* me.

MOCKING

Gen 21. 9 she had born unto Abraham, *m*.
Eze 22. 4 heathen, and a *m* to all countries.
Mt 27.41 Likewise also the chief priests *m*
Mk 15.31 Likewise also the chief priests *m*
Ac 2.13 Others *m* said, These men are full

MOCKINGS

Heb 11.36 trial of cruel *m* and scourgings,

MODERATION

Php 4. 5 Let your *m* be known unto all

MODEST

1Ti 2. 9 adorn themselves in *m* apparel,

MOISTURE

Ps 32. 4 my *m* is turned into the drought of
Lk 8. 6 it withered...because it lacked *m*.

MOLOCH

Am 5.26 borne the tabernacle of your *M*
Ac 7.43 ye took up the tabernacle of *M*,

MOLTEN

Ex 32. 4 after he had made it a *m* calf:
34.17 Thou shalt make thee no *m* gods.
Lev 19. 4 nor make to yourselves *m* gods: I
Dt 9.12 they have made them a *m* image.
16 God, and had made you a *m* calf:
2Ch 28. 2 made also *m* images for Baalim.
Job 37.18 strong, and as a *m* looking glass?
Isa 41.29 *m* images are wind and confusion.
42.17 say to the *m* images, Ye are our
Hab 2.18 the *m* image, and a teacher of lies,

MOMENT

Ex 33. 5 up into the midst of thee in a *m*,
Nu 16.21 that I may consume them in a *m*.
45 I may consume them as in a *m*.
Job 7.18 morning, and try him every *m*?
20. 5 joy of the hypocrite but for a *m*?
21.13 and in a *m* go down to the grave.
34.20 In a *m* shall they die, and the
Ps 30. 5 For his anger endureth but a *m*;
73.19 brought into desolation, as in a *m*!
Pr 12.19 but a lying tongue is but for a *m*.
Isa 26.20 thyself as it were for a little *m*,
27. 3 I will water it every *m*: lest any
47. 9 things shall come to thee in a *m* in
54. 7 a small *m* have I forsaken thee;
8 I hid my face from thee for a *m*;

BIBLICAL THEMES

MINISTRY

God sent me before you to preserve you a posterity in the earth, and to save your lives by a great deliverance. . . . it was not you that sent me hither, but God.
Gen 45.7-8

The Lord came, and stood, and called . . . Samuel, Samuel. Then Samuel answered, Speak; for thy servant heareth.
1Sa 3.10

And [Josiah] set the priests in their charges, and encouraged them to the service of the house of the Lord.
2Ch 35.2

Sing unto the Lord, bless his name; shew forth his salvation. . . . Declare his glory among the heathen, his wonders among all people. . . . For all the gods of the nations are idols: but the Lord made the heavens. Ps 96.2-3, 5

I heard the voice of the Lord, saying, Whom shall I send, and who will go for us? Then said I, Here am I; send me. And he said, Go, and tell this people, Hear ye indeed, but understand not; and see ye indeed, but perceive not.
Isa 6.8-9

The earth shall be full of the knowledge of the Lord, as the waters cover the sea.
Isa 11.9

The voice of him that crieth in the wilderness, Prepare ye the way of the Lord, make straight in the desert a highway for our God. Isa 40.3

Before thou camest forth out of the womb I sanctified thee, and I ordained thee a prophet unto the nations. . . . thou shalt go to all that I shall send thee, and whatsoever I command thee thou shalt speak. . . . Then the Lord put forth his hand, and touched my mouth. And the Lord said unto me, Behold, I have put my words in thy mouth.
Jer 1.5, 7, 9

From the rising of the sun even unto the going down of the same my name shall be great among the Gentiles. Mal 1.11

Behold, I send you forth as sheep in the midst of wolves: be ye therefore wise as serpents, and harmless as doves. . . . take no thought how or what ye shall speak: for it shall be given you in that same hour what ye shall speak. For it is not ye that speak, but the Spirit of your Father. Mt 10.16, 19-20

Whosoever will be great among you, let him be your minister . . . even as the Son of man came not to be ministered unto, but to minister, and to give his life a ransom for many. Mt 20.26, 28

Go ye into all the world, and preach the gospel to every creature. Mk 16.15

Thou, child, shalt be called the prophet of the Highest: for thou shalt go before the face of the Lord to prepare his ways . . . to give light to them that sit in darkness and in the shadow of death, to guide our feet into the way of peace.
Lk 1.76, 79

I am come that they might have life. . . . I am the good shepherd: the good shepherd giveth his life for the sheep.
Jn 10.10-11

God made choice among us, that the Gentiles by my mouth should hear the word of the gospel, and believe.
Ac 15.7

I have appeared unto thee for this purpose, to make thee a minister and a witness both of these things which thou hast seen . . . delivering thee from the people, and from the Gentiles, unto whom now I send thee, to open their eyes, and to turn them from darkness to light. Ac 26.16-18

Though I preach the gospel, I have nothing to glory of: for necessity is laid upon me; yea, woe is unto me, if I preach not the gospel! 1Co 9.16

As every man hath received the gift, even so minister the same one to another, as good stewards of the manifold grace of God. 1Pe 4.10

The commonest Near Eastern form of money in New Testament times was the silver shekel, above.

Jer 4.20 spoiled, and my curtains in a *m*.
La 4. 6 that was overthrown as in a *m*, and
Eze 26.16 and shall tremble at every *m*, and
32.10 shall tremble at every *m*, and they
Lk 4. 5 kingdoms of the world in a *m* of
1Co 15.52 In a *m*, in the twinkling of an eye,
2Co 4.17 affliction, which is but for a *m*,

MONEY

Gen 17.12 or bought with *m* of any stranger,
13 he that is bought with thy *m*, must
23. 9 for as much *m* as it is worth he
13 I will give thee *m* for the field;
42.28 My *m* is restored; and, lo, it is
43.12 And take double *m* in your hand;
47.15 when *m* failed in the land of Egypt,
Ex 22.25 If thou lend *m* to any of my people
Lev 25.37 not give him thy *m* upon usury,
Dt 14.25 Then shalt thou turn it into *m*,
21.14 thou shalt not sell her at all for *m*,
1Ki 21. 2 will give thee the worth of it in *m*.
6 him, Give me thy vineyard for *m*;
2Ki 5.26 Is it a time to receive *m*, and to
12. 4 the *m* that every man is set at, and
10 there was much *m* in the chest,
23.35 but he taxed the land to give the *m*
Job 31.39 eaten the fruits thereof without *m*,
Ps 15. 5 putteth not out his *m* to usury,
Ec 7.12 is a defense, and *m* is a defense:
10.19 merry: but *m* answereth all things.
Isa 52. 3 ye shall be redeemed without *m*.
55. 1 the waters, and he that hath no *m*;
1 milk without *m* and without price.
2 do ye spend *m* for that which is not
Jer 32.44 Men shall buy fields for *m*, and
La 5. 4 We have drunken our water for *m*;
Mic 3.11 the prophets thereof divine for *m*:
Mt 17.24 that received tribute *m* came to
27 thou shalt find a piece of *m*: that
22.19 Shew me the tribute *m*. And they
25.18 in the earth, and hid his lord's *m*.
27 have put my *m* to the exchangers,
28.12 they gave large *m* unto the soldiers,
15 So they took the *m*, and did as they
Mk 6. 8 no bread, no *m* in their purse:
12.41 the people cast *m* into the treasury:
14.11 glad, and promised to give him *m*.
Lk 9. 3 nor scrip, neither bread, neither *m*;
19.15 to whom he had given the *m*, that
23 not thou my *m* into the bank, that
22. 5 glad, and covenanted to give him *m*.
Jn 2.14 and the changers of *m* sitting:
15 poured out the changers' *m*, and
Ac 4.37 land, sold it, and brought the *m*,
7.16 Abraham bought for a sum of *m* of
8.18 was given, he offered them *m*,
20 Thy *m* perish with thee, because
20 of God may be purchased with *m*.
24.26 hoped also that *m* should have
1Ti 6.10 the love of *m* is the root of all evil:

MONEYCHANGERS

Mt 21.12 and overthrew the tables of the *m*,
Mk 11.15 and overthrew the tables of the *m*,

MONTH

Ex 12. 2 be the first *m* of the year to you.
34.18 the *m* Abib thou camest out from
Nu 3.15 every male from a *m* old and
40 children of Israel from a *m* old and
43 names, from a *m* old and upward,
1Ki 6. 1 the *m* Zif, which is the second *m*,
38 Bul, which is the eighth *m*,
8. 2 Ethanim, which is the seventh *m*.
1Ch 12.15 went over Jordan in the first *m*,
2Ch 30. 2 keep the passover in the second *m*.
Ezr 6.15 on the third day of the *m* Adar,
Neh 1. 1 it came to pass in the *m* Chisleu, in
2. 1 it came to pass in the *m* Nisan, in
6.15 twenty and fifth day of the *m* Elul,
Est 2.16 tenth *m*, which is the *m* Tebeth,
3. 7 the first *m*, that is, the *m* Nisan,
7 to the twelfth *m*, that is,...Adar.
8. 9 the third *m*, that is, the *m* Sivan,
Zec 11. 8 shepherds also I cut off in one *m*;
Lk 1.26 in the sixth *m* the angel Gabriel
36 this is the sixth *m* with her, who
Rev 9.15 and a day, and a *m*, and a year, for

MONTHLY

Isa 47.13 the *m* prognosticators, stand up,

MONTHS

Ex 2. 2 child, she hid him three *m*.
Jdg 11.37 let me alone two *m*, that I may go
Job 3. 6 come into the number of the *m*.
14. 5 number of his *m* are with thee,
29. 2 Oh that I were as in *m* past, as in
39. 3 Canst thou number the *m* that they
Lk 1.24 conceived, and hid herself five *m*,
56 abode with her about three *m*,
4.25 was shut up three years and six *m*,
Jn 4.35 Say not ye, There are yet four *m*,
Ac 7.20 up in his father's house three *m*:
18.11 he continued a year and six *m*,
19. 8 boldly for the space of three *m*,
20. 3 there abode three *m*. And when
28.11 after three *m* we departed in a ship
Gal 4.10 Ye observe days, and *m*, and times,
Heb 11.23 was hid three *m* of his parents,
Jas 5.17 space of three years and six *m*.
Rev 9. 5 they should be tormented five *m*:
10 power was to hurt men five *m*.
11. 2 tread under foot forty and two *m*.
13. 5 him to continue forty and two *m*.

MOON

Gen 37. 9 sun...the *m* and the eleven stars
Dt 33.14 things put forth by the *m*,
Jos 10.13 sun stood still, and the *m* stayed,
Ps 8. 3 *m* and the stars, which thou hast
72. 5 as long as the sun and *m* endure,
7 of peace so long as the *m* endureth.
81. 3 Blow up the trumpet in the new *m*,
104.19 He appointed the *m* for seasons:
121. 6 thee by day, nor the *m* by night.
136. 9 The *m* and stars to rule by night:
148. 3 Praise ye him, sun and *m*: praise
Ec 12. 2 *m*, or the stars, be not darkened,
SS 6.10 fair as the *m*, clear as the sun,
Isa 13.10 the *m* shall not cause her light to
60.19 shall the *m* give light unto thee:
Eze 32. 7 and the *m* shall not give her light.
Joel 2.10 the sun and the *m* shall be dark,
31 darkness, and the *m* into blood,
3.15 sun and the *m* shall be darkened,
Am 8. 5 When will the new *m* be gone,
Hab 3.11 The sun and *m* stood still in their
Mt 24.29 and the *m* shall not give her light,
Mk 13.24 and the *m* shall not give her light,
Lk 21.25 be signs in the sun, and in the *m*,
Ac 2.20 darkness, and the *m* into blood,
1Co 15.41 sun, and another glory of the *m*,
Col 2.16 or of the new *m*, or of the sabbath
Rev 6.12 hair, and the *m* became as blood;
8.12 and the third part of the *m*, and the
12. 1 the sun, and the *m* under her feet,
21.23 need of the sun, neither of the *m*,

MOONS

Isa 1.14 new *m* and your appointed feasts
Hos 2.11 her feast days, her new *m*, and her

MORNING

Gen 1. 5 evening and the *m* were the first
Ex 7.15 Get thee unto Pharaoh in the *m*;
14.24 *m* watch the Lord looked unto the
27 his strength when the *m* appeared;
16.13 in the *m* the dew lay round about
19 Let no man leave of it till the *m*,
21 they gathered it every *m*, every
Lev 7.15 shall not leave any of it until the *m*.
Nu 9.15 the appearance of fire, until the *m*.
21 cloud abode from even unto the *m*,
Dt 28.67 In the *m* thou shalt say, Would God
67 shalt say, Would God it were *m*!
1Ki 18.26 of Baal from *m* even until noon,
Neh 4.21 the rising of the *m* till the stars
Job 4.20 are destroyed from *m* to evening:
7.21 thou shalt seek me in the *m*, but
11.17 shine forth, thou shalt be as the *m*.
38. 7 When the *m* stars sang together,
41.18 eyes are like the eyelids of the *m*.
Ps 5. 3 voice shalt thou hear in the *m*,
3 in the *m* will I direct my prayer
30. 5 a night, but joy cometh in the *m*.
59.16 sing aloud of thy mercy in the *m*:
65. 8 of the *m* and evening to rejoice.
90. 5 in the *m* they are like grass which
6 In the *m* it flourisheth, and groweth
92. 2 forth thy lovingkindness in the *m*,
130. 6 than they that watch for the *m*:
139. 9 If I take the wings of the *m*, and
Pr 7.18 us take our fill of love until the *m*:
Ec 11. 6 In the *m* sow thy seed, and in the
Isa 14.12 heaven, O Lucifer, son of the *m*!
17.14 and before the *m* he is not.
21.12 The *m* cometh, and also the night:
58. 8 thy light break forth as the *m*,
Jer 21.12 Execute judgment in the *m*, and
La 3.23 They are new every *m*: great is thy
Eze 12. 8 the *m* came the word of the Lord
Hos 6. 4 your goodness is as a *m* cloud,
Am 4. 4 bring your sacrifices every *m*,
5. 8 the shadow of death into the *m*,
Jon 4. 7 when the *m* rose the next day,
Zep 3. 5 every *m* doth he bring his judgment
Mt 16. 3 in the *m*, It will be foul weather
20. 1 out early in the *m* to hire laborers
21.18 Now in the *m* as he returned into
27. 1 When the *m* was come, all the chief
Mk 1.35 in the *m*, rising up a great while
11.20 And in the *m*, as they passed by,
13.35 or at the cockcrowing, or in the *m*:
15. 1 in the *m* the chief priests held
16. 2 very early in the *m*, the first day
Lk 21.38 all the people came early in the *m*
24. 1 very early in the *m*, they came unto
Jn 8. 2 early in the *m* he came again into
21. 4 But when the *m* was now come,
Ac 5.21 into the temple early in the *m*,
28.23 the prophets, from *m* till evening.
Rev 2.28 And I will give him the *m* star.
22.16 David, and the bright and *m* star.

MORROW

Ex 9. 5 To *m* the Lord shall do this thing
32. 5 said, To *m* is a feast to the Lord.
Lev 22.30 shall leave none of it until the *m*:
Nu 11.18 Sanctify yourselves against to *m*,

Jos 3. 5 for to *m* the Lord will do wonders
5.12 the manna ceased on the *m* after
1Sa 20.18 to David, To *m* is the new moon:
2Ki 6.28 day, and we will eat my son to *m*.
7. 1 To *m* about this time...a measure
Pr 27. 1 Boast not thyself of to *m*; for thou
Isa 22.13 and drink; for to *m* we shall die.
Mt 6.30 is, and to *m* is cast into the oven,
34 therefore no thought for the *m*:
34 for the *m* shall take thought for the
Mk 11.12 on the *m*, when they were come
Lk 10.35 And on the *m* when he departed,
12.28 field, and to *m* is cast into the oven;
13.32 and I do cures to day and to *m*,
33 and to *m*, and the day following:
Ac 4. 5 to pass on the *m*, that their rulers,
10. 9 On the *m*, as they went on their
23 And on the *m* Peter went away with
24 And the *m* after they entered into
20. 7 them, ready to depart on the *m*;
22.30 On the *m*, because he would have
23.15 he bring him down unto you to *m*,
20 down Paul to *m* into the council,
32 On the *m* they left the horsemen
25.17 on the *m* I sat on the judgment
22 To *m*, said he, thou shalt hear him.
23 And on the *m*, when Agrippa was
1Co 15.32 us eat and drink; for to *m* we die.
Jas 4.13 To day or to *m* we will go into such
14 ye know not what shall be on the *m*.

MORSEL

Gen 18. 5 And I will fetch a *m* of bread, and
Jdg 19. 5 thine heart with a *m* of bread, and
Ru 2.14 bread, and dip thy *m* in the vinegar.
1Sa 2.36 piece of silver and a *m* of bread,
28.22 let me set a *m* of bread before
1Ki 17.11 Bring me, I pray thee, a *m* of bread
Job 31.17 Or have eaten my *m* myself alone,
Pr 17. 1 Better is a dry *m*, and quietness
23. 8 The *m* which thou hast eaten shalt
Heb 12.16 one *m* of meat sold his birthright.

MORTAL

Job 4.17 *m* man be more just than God?
Ro 6.12 therefore reign in your *m* body,
8.11 also quicken your *m* bodies by his
1Co 15.53 this *m* must put on immortality.
54 *m* shall have put on immortality,
2Co 4.11 be made manifest in our *m* flesh.

MORTALITY

2Co 5. 4 *m* might be swallowed up of life.

MORTIFY

Ro 8.13 the Spirit do *m* the deeds of the
Col 3. 5 *M* therefore your members which

MOSES

Ex 2.10 she called his name *M*: and she
11 in those days, when *M* was grown,
14 *M* feared, and said, Surely this
15 this thing, he sought to slay *M*.
15 *M* fled from the face of Pharaoh,
17 *M* stood up and helped them, and
21 *M* was content to dwell with the
21 he gave *M* Zipporah his daughter.
3. 1 Now *M* kept the flock of Jethro his
3 *M* said, I will now turn aside, and
4 midst of the bush, and said, *M*, *M*.
6 *M* hid his face; for he was afraid to
11 *M* said unto God, Who am I, that I
13 *M* said unto God, Behold, when I
14 God said unto *M*, I Am That I Am:
15 God said moreover unto *M*, Thus
4. 1 And *M* answered and said, But,
3 serpent; and *M* fled from before it.
4 Lord said unto *M*, Put forth thine
10 *M* said unto the Lord, O my Lord,
14 the Lord was kindled against *M*,
18 *M* went and returned to Jethro his
18 And Jethro said to *M*, Go in peace.
19 Lord said unto *M* in Midian, Go,
20 *M* took his wife and his sons, and
20 *M* took the rod of God in his hand.
21 the Lord said unto *M*, When thou
27 Go into the wilderness to meet *M*.
28 *M* told Aaron all the words of the
29 *M* and Aaron went and gathered
30 the Lord had spoken unto *M*, and
5. 1 afterward *M* and Aaron went in,
4 *M* and Aaron, let the people from
20 they met *M* and Aaron, who stood
22 *M* returned unto the Lord, and
6. 1 the Lord said unto *M*, Now shalt
2 God spake unto *M*, and said unto
9 *M* spake so unto the children of
9 they hearkened not unto *M* for
10 the Lord spake unto *M*, saying,
12 *M* spake unto the Lord, saying,
13 the Lord spake unto *M* and unto
20 and she bare him Aaron and *M*:
26 These are that Aaron and *M*, to
27 these are that *M* and Aaron.
28 the Lord spake unto *M* in the land
29 the Lord spake unto *M*, saying, I
30 *M* said before the Lord, Behold, I
7. 1 The Lord said unto *M*, See, I have
6 And *M* and Aaron did as the Lord
7 *M* was fourscore years old, and
8 the Lord spake unto *M* and unto
10 *M*...Aaron went in unto Pharaoh,
14 Lord said unto *M*, Pharaoh's heart
19 the Lord spake unto *M*, Say unto
20 *M* and Aaron did so, as the Lord
8. 1 the Lord spake unto *M*, Go unto
5 the Lord spake unto *M*, Say unto
8 Pharaoh called for *M* and Aaron,
9 *M* said unto Pharaoh, Glory over
12 And *M* and Aaron went out from
12 *M* cried unto the Lord because of
13 did according to the word of *M*;
16 Lord said unto *M*, Say unto Aaron,
20 Lord said unto *M*, Rise up early
25 called for *M* and for Aaron, and
26 *M* said, It is not meet so to do; for
29 And *M* said, Behold, I go out from
30 *M* went out from Pharaoh, and
31 did according to the word of *M*;
9. 1 the Lord said unto *M*, Go in unto
8 Lord said unto *M* and unto Aaron,
8 *M* sprinkle it toward the heaven
10 *M* sprinkled it up toward heaven;
11 could not stand before *M* because
12 as the Lord had spoken unto *M*.
13 Lord said unto *M*, Rise up early
22 Lord said unto *M*, Stretch forth
23 *M* stretched forth his rod toward
27 sent, and called for *M* and Aaron,
29 *M* said unto him, As soon as I am
33 And *M* went out of the city from
35 go; as the Lord had spoken by *M*.
10. 1 the Lord said unto *M*, Go in unto
3 And *M* and Aaron came in unto
8 *M* and Aaron were brought again
9 *M* said, We will go with our young
12 the Lord said unto *M*, Stretch out
13 *M* stretched forth his rod over the
16 Pharaoh called for *M* and Aaron
21 Lord said unto *M*, Stretch out
22 *M* stretched forth his hand toward
24 Pharaoh called unto *M*, and said,
25 *M* said, Thou must give us also
29 *M* said, Thou hast spoken well, I
11. 1 Lord said unto *M*, Yet will I bring
3 *M* was very great in the land of
4 And *M* said, Thus saith the Lord,
9 Lord said unto *M*, Pharaoh shall
10 *M* and Aaron did all these wonders
12. 1 unto *M* and Aaron in the land of
21 *M* called for all the elders of Israel,
28 Lord had commanded *M*...Aaron,

MOSES

Israel's first national leader and lawgiver; preserved at birth and adopted by Pharaoh's daughter, his own mother becoming his nurse; kills an Egyptian he sees maltreating a Hebrew, and flees; stays with Jethro, priest of Midian, and marries his daughter (Ex 2); is called by God in the burning bush, and told to return and lead his enslaved people out of Egypt; raises objections, but these are met, and his brother Aaron is appointed his spokesman (Ex 3–4); asks Pharaoh to release the Israelites, but Pharaoh instead increases their labor and they rebuke Moses (Ex 5); is told the new name of God: Yahweh, or Jehovah (Ex 6.3); his commission is renewed and he is strengthened for the task ahead (Ex 6–7); has further audiences with Pharaoh and with Aaron announces the coming plagues (Ex 7.8–10); institutes the passover, and the firstborn throughout Egypt are slain; is summoned by Pharaoh and told to take the Israelites and leave (Ex 11–12); holds out his rod and the Red Sea divides before the people; holds it out again and the pursuing Egyptians are engulfed (Ex 14); joins with his sister Miriam in song of triumph (Ex 15); when the people complain of hunger, promises quails and manna (Ex 16); when they complain of thirst, strikes a rock and water gushes out (Ex 17); on Jethro's advice appoints judges to assist him (Ex 18); assembles and sanctifies the people at Mount Sinai (Ex 19); ascends and receives the 10 commandments and other laws (Ex 20–23); returns and mediates God's covenant with Israel; is alone on the mountain for 40 days to receive God's further instructions (Ex 24); on his return, breaks the stone tablets in anger and destroys the idolatrous golden calf, or bull image, built by Aaron and the people (Ex 32); speaks with God face to face; only prophet ever to do so (Ex 33); ascends once more; fresh tablets are received and the covenant is renewed; on his return, his face shines (Ex 34); receives laws concerning the tabernacle, priesthood, services, and other matters of sacred ritual (Ex 35–40; Lev; Nu 1–10); when the people's discontent grows intolerable, complains to God and 70 elders are imbued with his spirit and appointed to bear the burden with him (Nu 11); on Aaron's urging intercedes for Miriam and she is cured of leprosy (Nu 12); sends spies into Canaan (Nu 13); when on their return the people show lack of faith, announces the consequence, a 40-year sojourn in the wilderness (Nu 14); again strikes a rock to produce water, but blasphemously takes credit for the miracle; as punishment, he and Aaron are forbidden to enter Canaan; on Aaron's death appoints Eleazer to succeed his father as high priest (Nu 20); appoints Joshua as his successor (Nu 27); makes provision for the approaching settlement in Canaan (Nu 32–35); gives farewell address to Israel (Dt 1–33); ascends Mount Nebo at the top of Pisgah, views the land, and dies; is buried by God in an unknown grave (Dt 34).

Moses, *by Michelangelo, completed in 1516; the horns reflect an ancient variant translation of Ex 29.30.*

Ex 12.31 called for *M* and Aaron by night,
35 did according to the word of *M*;
43 the Lord said unto *M* and Aaron,
50 Lord commanded *M* and Aaron,
13. 1 the Lord spake unto *M*, saying,
3 *M* said unto the people, Remember
19 *M* took the bones of Joseph with
14. 1 the Lord spake unto *M*, saying,
11 they said unto *M*, Because there
13 *M* said unto the people, Fear ye
15 the Lord said unto *M*, Wherefore
21 *M* stretched out his hand over the
26 unto *M*, Stretch out thine hand
27 *M* stretched forth his hand over
31 the Lord, and his servant *M*.
15. 1 Then sang *M* and the children of
22 *M* brought Israel from the Red
24 the people murmured against *M*,
16. 2 murmured against *M* and Aaron
4 unto *M*, Behold, I will rain bread
6 *M* and Aaron said unto all the
8 *M* said, This shall be, when the
9 *M* spake unto Aaron, Say unto all
11 the Lord spake unto *M*, saying,
15 And *M* said unto them, This is the
19 *M* said, Let no man leave of it till
20 they hearkened not unto *M*; but
20 and *M* was wroth with them.
22 the congregation came and told *M*.
24 it up till the morning, as *M* bade:
25 And *M* said, Eat that to day; for
28 the Lord said unto *M*, How long
32 *M* said, This is the thing which
33 *M* said unto Aaron, Take a pot,
34 As the Lord commanded *M*, so
17. 2 the people did chide with *M*, and
2 *M* said unto them, Why chide ye
3 people murmured against *M*, and
4 *M* cried unto the Lord, saying,
5 Lord said unto *M*, Go on before
6 *M* did so in the sight of the elders
9 *M* said unto Joshua, Choose us
10 Joshua did as *M* had said to him,
10 *M*, Aaron, and Hur went up to the
11 when *M* held up his hand, that
14 the Lord said unto *M*, Write this
15 *M* built an altar, and called the
18. 1 of all that God had done for *M*,
5 wife unto *M* in the wilderness,
6 he said unto *M*, I thy father in law
7 *M* went out to meet his father in
8 *M* told his father in law all that
13 that *M* sat to judge the people:
13 stood by *M* from the morning unto
15 And *M* said unto his father in law,
24 *M* hearkened to the voice of his
25 *M* chose able men out of all Israel,
26 hard causes they brought unto *M*,
27 *M* let his father in law depart;
19. 3 And *M* went up unto God, and the
7 *M* came and called for the elders
8 And *M* returned the words of the
9 the Lord said unto *M*, Lo, I come
9 *M* told the words of the people
10 Lord said unto *M*, Go unto the
14 And *M* went down from the mount
17 *M* brought forth the people out of
19 *M* spake, and God answered him
20 Lord called *M* up to the top of the
20 top of the mount; and *M* went up.
21 the Lord said unto *M*, Go down,
23 *M* said unto the Lord, The people
25 *M* went down unto the people, and
20.19 said unto *M*, Speak thou with us,
20 *M* said unto the people, Fear not:
21 and *M* drew near unto the thick
22 the Lord said unto *M*, Thus thou
24. 1 unto *M*, Come up unto the Lord,
2 *M* alone shall come near the Lord:
3 *M* came and told the people all
4 *M* wrote all the words of the Lord,
6 *M* took half of the blood, and put
8 *M* took the blood, and sprinkled it
9 Then went up *M*, and Aaron, and
12 Lord said unto *M*, Come up to me
13 And *M* rose up, and his minister
13 *M* went up into the mount of God.
15 *M* went up into the mount, and a
16 he called unto *M* out of the midst
18 *M* went into the midst of the cloud,
18 *M* was in the mount forty days
25. 1 the Lord spake unto *M*, saying,
30.11, 17 the Lord spake unto *M*, saying,
22 the Lord spake unto *M*, saying,
34 the Lord said unto *M*, Take unto
31. 1, 12 the Lord spake unto *M*, saying,
18 And he gave unto *M*, when he had
32. 1 the people saw that *M* delayed to
1 for as for this *M*, the man that
7 Lord said unto *M*, Go, get thee
9 the Lord said unto *M*, I have seen
11 *M* besought the Lord his God, and
17 as they shouted, he said unto *M*,

21 And *M* said unto Aaron, What did
23 for as for this *M*, the man that
25 when *M* saw that the people were
26 *M* stood in the gate of the camp,
28 did according to the word of *M*:
29 *M* had said, Consecrate yourselves
30 *M* said unto the people, Ye have
31 *M* returned unto the Lord, and
33 the Lord said unto *M*, Whosoever
33. 1 Lord said unto *M*, Depart, and go
5 Lord had said unto *M*, Say unto
7 And *M* took the tabernacle, and
8 *M* went out unto the tabernacle,
8 his tent door, and looked after *M*,
9 *M* entered into the tabernacle, the
9 and the Lord talked with *M*.
11 Lord spake unto *M* face to face,
12 *M* said unto the Lord, See, thou
17 Lord said unto *M*, I will do this
34. 1 Lord said unto *M*, Hew thee two
4 *M* rose up early in the morning,
8 *M* made haste, and bowed his
27 the Lord said unto *M*, Write thou
29 *M* came down from mount Sinai
29 *M* wist not that the skin of his face
30 all the children of Israel saw *M*,
31 *M* called unto them; and Aaron
31 him: and *M* talked with them.
33 *M* had done speaking with them,
34 when *M* went in before the Lord
35 of Israel saw the face of *M*, that
35 *M* put the vail upon his face again,
35. 1 *M* gathered all the congregation
4 *M* spake unto all the congregation
20 departed from the presence of *M*.
29 to be made by the hand of *M*.
30 *M* said unto the children of Israel,
36. 2 *M* called Bezaleel and Aholiab,
3 they received of *M* all the offering,
5 they spake unto *M*, saying, The
6 *M* gave commandment, and they
38.21 to the commandment of *M*, for
22 all that the Lord commanded *M*.
39. 1, 5, 7 as the Lord commanded *M*.
32 all that the Lord commanded *M*,
33 brought the tabernacle unto *M*,
42 all that the Lord commanded *M*,
43 *M* did look upon all the work, and,
43 they done it: and *M* blessed them.
40. 1 the Lord spake unto *M*, saying,
16 Thus did *M*: according to all that
18 *M* reared up the tabernacle, and
19 it; as the Lord commanded *M*.
21 as the Lord commanded *M*.
23 as the Lord had commanded *M*.
25, 27, 29 the Lord commanded *M*.
31 *M* and Aaron and his sons washed
32 as the Lord commanded *M*.
33 gate. So *M* finished the work.
35 *M* was not able to enter into the
Lev 1. 1 the Lord called unto *M*, and spake
4. 1 the Lord spake unto *M*, saying,
5.14 the Lord spake unto *M*, saying,
6. 1, 8, 19, 24 the Lord spake unto *M*,
7.22, 28 the Lord spake unto *M*, saying,
38 Which the Lord commanded *M* in
8. 1 the Lord spake unto *M*, saying,
4 *M* did as the Lord commanded
5 *M* said unto the congregation,
6 *M* brought Aaron and his sons,
9 as the Lord commanded *M*.
10 And *M* took the anointing oil, and
13 *M* brought Aaron's sons, and put
13 them; as the Lord commanded *M*.
15 *M* took the blood, and put it upon
16 and *M* burned it upon the altar.
17 camp: as the Lord commanded *M*.
19 and *M* sprinkled the blood upon the
20 *M* burnt the head, and the pieces,
21 *M* burnt the whole ram upon the
21 Lord; as the Lord commanded *M*.
23 *M* took of the blood of it, and put
24 *M* put of the blood upon the tip of
24 and *M* sprinkled the blood upon the
28 *M* took them from off their hands,
29 *M* took the breast, and waved it
29 part; as the Lord commanded *M*.
30 *M* took of the anointing oil, and of
31 *M* said unto Aaron and to his sons,
36 Lord commanded by the hand of *M*.
9. 1 that *M* called Aaron and his sons,
5 brought that which *M* commanded
6 *M* said, This is the thing which the
7 *M* said unto Aaron, Go unto the
10 altar; as the Lord commanded *M*.
21 before the Lord; as *M* commanded.
23 And *M* and Aaron went into the
10. 3 *M* said unto Aaron, This is it that
4 *M* called Mishael and Elzaphan,
5 out of the camp; as *M* had said.
6 And *M* said unto Aaron, and unto
7 did according to the word of *M*.
11 unto them by the hand of *M*.
12 And *M* spake unto Aaron, and unto
16 *M* diligently sought the goat of the
19 Aaron said unto *M*, Behold, this
20 And when *M* heard that, he was
11. 1 Lord spake unto *M* and to Aaron,
12. 1 the Lord spake unto *M*, saying,
13. 1 the Lord spake unto *M* and Aaron,
14. 1 the Lord spake unto *M*, saying,
33 the Lord spake unto *M* and unto
15. 1 Lord spake unto *M* and to Aaron.
16. 1 Lord spake unto *M* after the death
2 And the Lord said unto *M*, Speak
34 did as the Lord commanded *M*.
17. 1 the Lord spake unto *M*, saying,
18. 1 the Lord spake unto *M*, saying,
19. 1 the Lord spake unto *M*, saying,
20. 1 the Lord spake unto *M*, saying,
21. 1 And the Lord said unto *M*, Speak
16 the Lord spake unto *M*, saying,
24 *M* told it unto Aaron, and to his
22. 1, 17, 26 Lord spake unto *M*, saying,
23. 1, 9, 23, 26, 33 spake unto *M*, saying,
44 *M* declared unto the children of
24. 1 the Lord spake unto *M*, saying,
11 they brought him unto *M*: (and his
13 the Lord spake unto *M*, saying,
23 And *M* spake unto the children of
23 did as the Lord commanded *M*,
25. 1 Lord spake unto *M* in mount Sinai,
26.46 in mount Sinai by the hand of *M*.
27. 1 the Lord spake unto *M*, saying,
34 which the Lord commanded *M* for
Nu 1. 1 And the Lord spake unto *M* in the
17 And *M* and Aaron took these men
19 As the Lord commanded *M*, so he
44 which *M* and Aaron numbered,
48 For the Lord had spoken unto *M*,
54 all that the Lord commanded *M*,
2. 1 the Lord spake unto *M* and unto
33 Israel; as the Lord commanded *M*.
34 all that the Lord commanded *M*:
3. 1 the generations of Aaron and *M*
5, 11 the Lord spake unto *M*, saying,
14 And the Lord spake unto *M* in the
16 *M* numbered them according to
38 congregation eastward, shall be *M*,
39 which *M* and Aaron numbered at
40 the Lord said unto *M*, Number all
42 And *M* numbered, as the Lord
44 the Lord spake unto *M*, saying,
49 *M* took the redemption money of
51 *M* gave the money of them that
51 Lord, as the Lord commanded *M*.
4. 1, 17 Lord spake unto *M* and unto
21 the Lord spake unto *M*, saying,
34 *M* and Aaron and the chief of the
37 which *M* and Aaron did number
37 of the Lord by the hand of *M*.
41 whom *M* and Aaron did number
45 whom *M* and Aaron numbered
45 word of the Lord by the hand of *M*.
46 whom *M* and Aaron and the chief
49 were numbered by the hand of *M*,
49 him, as the Lord commanded *M*.
5. 1 the Lord spake unto *M*, saying,
4 as the Lord spake unto *M*, so did
11 the Lord spake unto *M*, saying,
6. 1, 22 the Lord spake unto *M*, saying,
7. 1 *M* had fully set up the tabernacle,
4 the Lord spake unto *M*, saying,
6 *M* took the wagons and the oxen,
11 the Lord said unto *M*, They shall
89 *M* was gone into the tabernacle of
8. 1 the Lord spake unto *M*, saying,
3 as the Lord commanded *M*.
4 which the Lord had shewed *M*, so
5 the Lord spake unto *M*, saying,
20 And *M*, and Aaron, and all the
20 Lord commanded *M* concerning
22 had commanded *M* concerning the
23 the Lord spake unto *M*, saying,
9. 1 And the Lord spake unto *M* in the
4 And *M* spake unto the children of
5 all that the Lord commanded *M*,
6 came before *M* and before Aaron
8 *M* said unto them, Stand still, and
9 the Lord spake unto *M*, saying,
23 of the Lord by the hand of *M*.
10. 1 the Lord spake unto *M*, saying,
13 of the Lord by the hand of *M*.
29 And *M* said unto Hobab, the son of
35 that *M* said, Rise up, Lord, and let
11. 2 And the people cried unto *M*; and
2 *M* prayed unto the Lord, the fire
10 Then *M* heard the people weep
10 greatly; *M* also was displeased.
11 *M* said unto the Lord, Wherefore
16 the Lord said unto *M*, Gather unto
21 *M* said, The people, among whom
23 said unto *M*, Is the Lord's hand
24 *M* went out, and told the people the
27 ran a young man, and told *M*, and
28 the son of Nun, the servant of *M*,
28 answered and said, My lord *M*,
29 *M* said unto him, Enviest thou for
30 *M* gat him into the camp, he and
12. 1 Aaron spake against *M* because of
2 Lord indeed spoken only by *M*?
3 the man *M* was very meek, above
4 the Lord spake suddenly unto *M*,
7 My servant *M* is not so, who is
8 to speak against my servant *M*?
11 And Aaron said unto *M*, Alas, my
13 *M* cried unto the Lord, saying,
14 And the Lord said unto *M*, If her
13. 1 the Lord spake unto *M*, saying,
3 *M* by the commandment of the
16 which *M* sent to spy out the land.
16 *M* called Oshea the son of Nun
17 *M* sent them to spy out the land
26 And they went and came to *M*, and
30 Caleb stilled the people before *M*,
14. 2 Israel murmured against *M* and
5 *M* and Aaron fell on their faces
11 the Lord said unto *M*, How long
13 And *M* said unto the Lord, Then
26 the Lord spake unto *M* and unto
36 the men, which *M* sent to search
39 *M* told these sayings unto all the
41 And *M* said, Wherefore now do ye
44 *M*, departed not out of the camp.
15. 1, 17 the Lord spake unto *M*, saying,
22 the Lord hath spoken unto *M*,
23 commanded you by the hand of *M*,
23 day that the Lord commanded *M*,
33 brought him unto *M* and Aaron,
35 the Lord said unto *M*, The man
36 died; as the Lord commanded *M*.
37 the Lord spake unto *M*, saying,
16. 2 And they rose up before *M*, with

Nu 16. 3 themselves together against *M* and
4 when *M* heard it, he fell upon his
8 *M* said unto Korah, Hear, I pray
12 And *M* sent to call Dathan and
15 *M* was very wroth, and said unto
16 *M* said unto Korah, Be thou and
18 of the congregation with *M* and
20 the Lord spake unto *M* and unto
23 the Lord spake unto *M*, saying,
25 *M* rose up and went unto Dathan
28 *M* said, Hereby ye shall know that
36 the Lord spake unto *M*, saying,
40 Lord said to him by the hand of *M*.
41 murmured against *M* and against
42 gathered against *M* and against
43 And *M* and Aaron came before the
44 the Lord spake unto *M*, saying,
46 *M* said unto Aaron, Take a censer,
47 Aaron took as *M* commanded, and
50 returned unto *M* unto the door of
17. 1 the Lord spake unto *M*, saying,
6 And *M* spake unto the children of
7 *M* laid up the rods before the Lord
8 *M* went into the tabernacle of
9 *M* brought out all the rods from
10 Lord said unto *M*, Bring Aaron's
11 *M* did so: as the Lord commanded
12 children of Israel spake unto *M*,
18.25 the Lord spake unto *M*, saying,
19. 1 the Lord spake unto *M* and unto
20. 2 together against *M* and against
3 And the people chode with *M*, and
6 And *M* and Aaron went from the
7 the Lord spake unto *M*, saying,
9 *M* took the rod from before the
10 And *M* and Aaron gathered the
11 *M* lifted up his hand, and with his
12 the Lord spake unto *M* and Aaron,
14 *M* sent messengers from Kadesh
23 spake unto *M* and Aaron in mount
27 *M* did as the Lord commanded:
28 *M* stripped Aaron of his garments,
28 *M* and Eleazar came down from
21. 5 spake against God, and against *M*,
7 Therefore the people came to *M*,
7 And *M* prayed for the people.
8 the Lord said unto *M*, Make thee
9 *M* made a serpent of brass, and
16 whereof the Lord spake unto *M*,
32 *M* sent to spy out Jaazer, and they
34 Lord said unto *M*, Fear him not:
25. 4 the Lord said unto *M*, Take all the
5 *M* said unto the judges of Israel,
6 woman in the sight of *M*, and in
10, 16 the Lord spake unto *M*, saying,
26. 1 the Lord spake unto *M* and unto
3 *M* and Eleazar the priest spake
4 as the Lord commanded *M* and the
9 who strove against *M* and against
52 the Lord spake unto *M*, saying,
59 bare unto Amram Aaron and *M*,
63 they that were numbered by *M* and
64 was not a man of them whom *M*
27. 2 they stood before *M*, and before
5 *M* brought their cause before the
6 the Lord spake unto *M*, saying,
11 as the Lord commanded *M*.
12 said unto *M*, Get thee up into this
15 *M* spake unto the Lord, saying,
18 the Lord said unto *M*, Take thee
22 *M* did as the Lord commanded him:
23 commanded by the hand of *M*.
28. 1 the Lord spake unto *M*, saying,
29.40 And *M* told the children of Israel
40 all that the Lord commanded *M*.
30. 1 And *M* spake unto the heads of the
16 which the Lord commanded *M*,
31. 1 the Lord spake unto *M*, saying,
3 *M* spake unto the people, saying,
6 And *M* sent them to the war, a
7 as the Lord commanded *M*; and
12 the prey, and the spoil, unto *M*,
13 *M*, and Eleazar the priest, and all
14 *M* was wroth with the officers of
15 *M* said unto them, Have ye saved
21 which the Lord commanded *M*;
25 the Lord spake unto *M*, saying,
31 *M* and Eleazar the priest did as the
31 did as the Lord commanded *M*.
41 *M* gave the tribute, which was the
41 priest, as the Lord commanded *M*.
42 which *M* divided from the men that
47 *M* took one portion of fifty, both of
47 Lord; as the Lord commanded *M*.
48 of hundreds, came near unto *M*:
49 they said unto *M*, Thy servants
51, 54 *M* and Eleazar the priest took
32. 2 Reuben came and spake unto *M*,
6 *M* said unto the children of Gad
20 *M* said unto them, If ye will do
25 children of Reuben spake unto *M*,
28 *M* commanded Eleazar the priest,
29 *M* said unto them, If the children
33 *M* gave unto them, even to the
40 *M* gave Gilead unto Machir the son
33. 1 their armies under the hand of *M*
2 And *M* wrote their goings out
50 Lord spake unto *M* in the plains of
34. 1 the Lord spake unto *M*, saying,
13 And *M* commanded the children of
16 the Lord spake unto *M*, saying,
35. 1 Lord spake unto *M* in the plains of
9 the Lord spake unto *M*, saying,
36. 1 came near, and spake before *M*,
5 And *M* commanded the children of
10 Even as the Lord commanded *M*,
13 commanded by the hand of *M* unto
Dt 1. 1 which *M* spake unto all Israel on
3 that *M* spake unto the children
5 Moab, began *M* to declare this law,
4.41 *M* severed three cities on this side
44 *M* set before the children of Israel:
45 which *M* spake unto the children
46 *M* and the children of Israel smote,
5. 1 *M* called all Israel, and said unto
27. 1 And *M* with the elders of Israel
9 And *M* and the priests the Levites
11 *M* charged the people the same
29. 1 which the Lord commanded *M* to
2 *M* called unto all Israel, and said
31. 1 And *M* went and spake these words
7 *M* called unto Joshua, and said
9 *M* wrote this law, and delivered it
10 And *M* commanded them, saying,
14 the Lord said unto *M*, Behold, thy
14 And *M* and Joshua went, and
16 the Lord said unto *M*, Behold, thou
22 *M* therefore wrote this song the
24 *M* had made an end of writing the
25 That *M* commanded the Levites,
30 And *M* spake in the ears of all the
32.44 *M* came and spake all the words of
45 *M* made an end of speaking all
48 And the Lord spake unto *M* that
33. 1 *M* the man of God blessed the
4 *M* commanded us a law, even the
34. 1 And *M* went up from the plains of
5 So *M* the servant of the Lord died
7 *M* was an hundred and twenty
8 the children of Israel wept for *M*
8 and mourning for *M* were ended.
9 *M* had laid his hands upon him:
9 and did as the Lord commanded *M*.
10 prophet since in Israel like unto *M*,
12 terror which *M* shewed in the
Jos 1. 1 after the death of *M* the servant of
2 *M* my servant is dead; now
3 given unto you, as I said unto *M*.
5 as I was with *M*, so I will be with
7 which *M* my servant commanded
13 Remember the word which *M* the
14 in the land which *M* gave you on
15 which *M* the Lord's servant gave
17 we hearkened unto *M* in all things,
17 be with thee, as he was with *M*.
3. 7 as I was with *M*, so I will be with
4.10 to all that *M* commanded Joshua:
12 of Israel, as *M* spake unto them:
14 they feared him, as they feared *M*,
8.31 As *M* the servant of the Lord
31 written in the book of the law of *M*,
32 the stones a copy of the law of *M*,
33 as *M* the servant of the Lord had
35 a word of all that *M* commanded,
9.24 commanded his servant *M* to give
11.12 as *M* the servant of the Lord
15 As the Lord commanded *M* his
15 so did *M* command Joshua, and so
15 of all that the Lord commanded *M*.
20 them, as the Lord commanded *M*.
23 to all that the Lord said unto *M*;
12. 6 did *M* the servant of the Lord and
6 *M* the servant of the Lord gave it
13. 8 inheritance, which *M* gave them,
8 as *M* the servant of the Lord gave
12 for these did *M* smite, and cast
15 And *M* gave unto the tribe of the
21 whom *M* smote with the princes of
24 *M* gave inheritance unto the tribe
29 *M* gave inheritance unto the half
32 countries which *M* did distribute
33 Levi *M* gave not any inheritance:
14. 2 commanded by the hand of *M*, for
3 *M* had given the inheritance of two
5 As the Lord commanded *M*, so
6 the thing that the Lord said unto *M*
7 *M* the servant of the Lord sent me
9 And *M* sware on that day, saying,
10 the Lord spake this word unto *M*,
11 I was in the day that *M* sent me:
17. 4 Lord commanded *M* to give us an
18. 7 *M* the servant of the Lord gave
20. 2 spake unto you by the hand of *M*:
21. 2 commanded by the hand of *M* to
8 commanded by the hand of *M*.
22. 2 all that *M* the servant of the Lord
4 *M* the servant of the Lord gave
5 *M* the servant of the Lord charged
7 *M* had given possession in Bashan:
9 word of the Lord by the hand of *M*.
23. 6 written in the book of the law of *M*,
24. 5 I sent *M* also and Aaron, and I
Jdg 1.20 Hebron unto Caleb, as *M* said:
3. 4 their fathers by the hand of *M*.
4.11 of Hobab the father in law of *M*,
1Sa 12. 6 Lord that advanced *M* and Aaron,
8 then the Lord sent *M* and Aaron,
1Ki 2. 3 as it is written in the law of *M*,
8. 9 stone, which *M* put there at Horeb,
53 as thou spakest by the hand of *M*
56 he promised by the hand of *M* his
2Ki 14. 6 in the book of the law of *M*,
18. 4 brasen serpent that *M* had made:
6 which the Lord commanded *M*.
12 that *M* the servant of the Lord
21. 8 that my servant *M* commanded
23.25 according to all the law of *M*;
1Ch 6. 3 children of Amram; Aaron, and *M*,
49 to all that *M* the servant of God
15.15 as *M* commanded according to
21.29 which *M* made in the wilderness,
22.13 which the Lord charged *M* with
23.13 sons of Amram; Aaron and *M*:
14 concerning *M* the man of God,
15 The sons of *M* were, Gershom, and
26.24 the son of Gershom, the son of *M*,
2Ch 1. 3 *M*...servant of the Lord had made
5.10 two tables which *M* put therein
8.13 to the commandment of *M*,
23.18 as it is written in the law of *M*,
24. 6 commandment of *M* the servant of
9 that *M* the servant of God laid upon
25. 4 written in the law in the book of *M*,

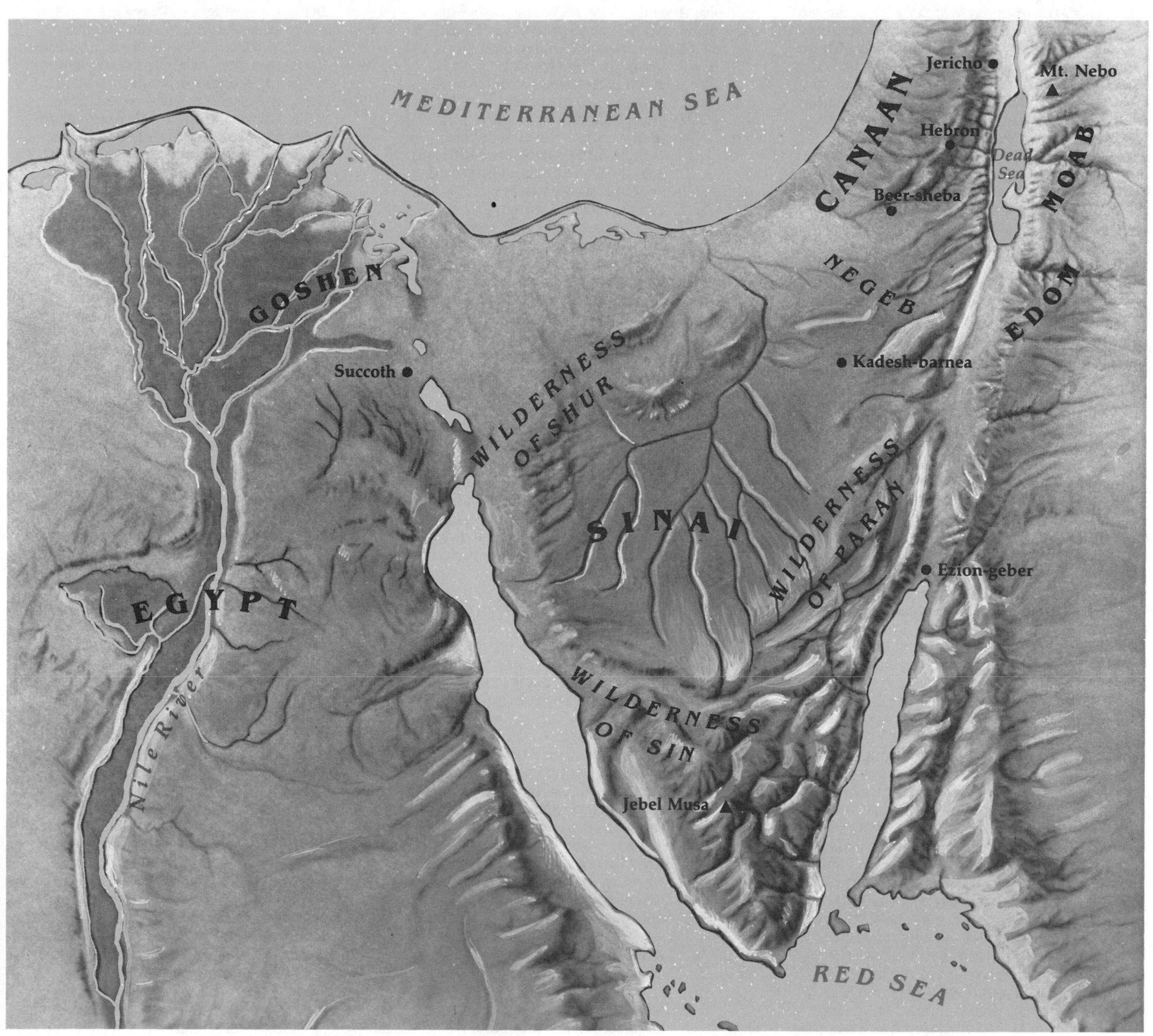

***The saga of Moses** and his followers began in the land of Goshen in the eastern Nile Delta, where the Hebrews were forced to work under harsh conditions on construction projects decreed by the Pharaoh (probably Ramses II in the 13th century* B.C.*). Although scholars disagree on the actual route of the Exodus, many support the traditional view that from Succoth the Hebrews fled Egyptian chariots across a marshy area called the Sea of Reeds (not the Red Sea, as many English-language Bibles call it) and made their way slowly down the western edge of the Sinai peninsula to Jebel Musa, long believed to be Mount Sinai. The Hebrews subsequently journeyed north to the oasis at Kadesh-barnea; from there Moses sent into Canaan the spies who returned to describe "a land flowing with milk and honey" (Ex 3.8). For nearly 40 more years the people lived a migratory existence—roughly within the triangle formed by Kadesh-barnea, Ezion-geber, and the Dead Sea. Then, preparing at last to cross the Jordan, they encamped on the Plains of Moab northwest of Mount Nebo, from atop which the aging Moses finally set eyes on the Promised Land that his people would soon enter without him.*

30.16 to the law of *M* the man of God;
33. 8 the ordinances by the hand of *M*.
34.14 of the law of the Lord given by *M*.
35. 6 word of the Lord by the hand of *M*.
12 as it is written in the book of *M*.
Ezr 3. 2 in the law of *M* the man of God.
6.18 as it is written in the book of *M*.
7. 6 a ready scribe in the law of *M*,
Neh 1. 7 thou commandest thy servant *M*.
8 thou commandest thy servant *M*,
8. 1 to bring the book of the law of *M*,
14 the Lord had commanded by *M*,
9.14 by the hand of *M* thy servant:
10.29 was given by *M* the servant of God,
13. 1 that day they read in the book of *M*
Ps 77.20 flock by the hand of *M* and Aaron.
90(T) A Prayer of *M* the man of God.
99. 6 *M* and Aaron among his priests,
103. 7 He made known his ways unto *M*,
105.26 He sent *M* his servant; and Aaron
106.16 They envied *M* also in the camp,
23 had not *M* his chosen stood before
32 it went ill with *M* for their sakes:
Isa 63.11 the days of old, *M*, and his people,
12 led them by the right hand of *M*
Jer 15. 1 *M* and Samuel stood before me,
Dan 9.11 in the law of *M* the servant of God,
13 As it is written in the law of *M*,
Mic 6. 4 I sent before thee *M*, Aaron, and
Mal 4. 4 ye the law of *M* my servant, which
Mt 8. 4 offer the gift that *M* commanded,
17. 3 appeared unto them *M* and Elias
4 one for thee, and one for *M*, and
19. 7 Why did *M* then command to give
8 *M* because of the hardness of your
22.24 *M* said, If a man die, having no

Mk 1.44 those things which *M* commanded,
7.10 *M* said, Honor thy father and thy
9. 4 appeared unto them Elias with *M*:
5 one for thee, and one for *M*, and
10. 3 them, What did *M* command you?
4 *M* suffered...a bill of divorcement,
12.19 *M* wrote...If a man's brother die,
26 have ye not read in the book of *M*,
Lk 2.22 the law of *M* were accomplished,
5.14 according as *M* commanded, for a
9.30 two men, which were *M* and Elias:
33 one for thee, and one for *M*, and
16.29 They have *M* and the prophets;
31 they hear not *M* and the prophets,
20.28 *M* wrote...If any man's brother die,
37 even *M* shewed at the bush, when
24.27 And beginning at *M* and all the
44 which were written in the law of *M*,
Jn 1.17 For the law was given by *M*, but
45 found him, of whom *M* in the law,
3.14 as *M* lifted up the serpent in the
5.45 you, even *M*, in whom ye trust.
46 For had ye believed *M*, ye would
6.32 *M* gave you not that bread from
7.19 Did not *M* give you the law, and
22 *M*...gave unto you circumcision;
22 (not because it is of *M*, but of the
23 the law of *M* should not be broken;
8. 5 *M* in the law commanded us, that
9.29 We know that God spake unto *M*:
Ac 3.22 For *M* truly said unto the fathers,
6.11 blasphemous words against *M*,
14 the customs which *M* delivered us.
7.20 In which time *M* was born, and
22 *M* was learned in all the wisdom
29 Then fled *M* at this saying, and
31 When *M* saw it, he wondered at
32 Then *M* trembled, and durst not
35 This *M* whom they refused, saying,
37 This is that *M*, which said unto the
40 for as for this *M*, which brought us
44 had appointed, speaking unto *M*,
13.39 not be justified by the law of *M*.
15. 1 circumcised after the manner of *M*,
5 command...to keep the law of *M*.
21 *M* of old time hath in every city
21.21 among the Gentiles to forsake *M*,
26.22 the prophets and *M* did say should
28.23 both out of the law of *M*, and out
Ro 5.14 death reigned from Adam to *M*,
9.15 he saith to *M*, I will have mercy
10. 5 *M* describeth the righteousness
19 First *M* saith, I will provoke you
1Co 9. 9 For it is written in the law of *M*,
10. 2 all baptized unto *M* in the cloud
2Co 3. 7 not stedfastly behold the face of *M*
13 not as *M*, which put a vail over his
15 unto this day, when *M* is read,
2Ti 3. 8 Jannes and Jambres withstood *M*,
Heb 3. 2 as also *M* was faithful in all his
3 worthy of more glory than *M*,
5 And *M* verily was faithful in all his
16 all that came out of Egypt by *M*.
7.14 of which tribe *M* spake nothing
8. 5 as *M* was admonished of God when
9.19 when *M* had spoken every precept
11.23 By faith *M*, when he was born, was
24 By faith *M*, when he was come to
12.21 that *M* said, I exceedingly fear and
Jude 9 he disputed about the body of *M*,
Rev 15. 3 sing the song of *M* the servant of

MOST

Gen 14.18 was the priest of the *m* high God.
20 blessed be the *m* high God, which
Ex 26.34 the testimony in the *m* holy place.
30.10 it is *m* holy unto the Lord.
Lev 7. 6 eaten in the holy place: it is *m* holy.
14.13 the trespass offering: it is *m* holy:
Nu 24.16 knew the knowledge of the *m* High,
Ps 7.17 to the name of the Lord *m* high.
46. 4 of the tabernacles of the *m* High.
50.14 pay thy vows unto the *m* High:
78.56 and provoked the *m* high God, and
83.18 art the *m* High over all the earth.
91. 1 in the secret place of the *m* High
92. 1 praises unto thy name, O *m* High:
La 3.38 Out of the mouth of the *m* High
Dan 3.26 ye servants of the *m* high God,
5.18 *m* high God gave Nebuchadnezzar
21 knew that the *m* high God ruled
Mt 11.20 *m* of his mighty works were done,
Mk 5. 7 thou Son of the *m* high God? I
Lk 1. 1 are *m* surely believed among us,
3 in order, *m* excellent Theophilus,
7.42 which of them will love him *m*?
43 that he, to whom he forgave *m*.
8.28 Jesus, thou Son of God *m* high?
Ac 7.48 *m* High dwelleth not in temples
16.17 the servants of the *m* high God,
20.38 Sorrowing *m* of all for the words
23.26 unto the *m* excellent governor
24. 3 and in all places, *m* noble Felix,
26. 5 that after the *m* straitest sect of our
25 I am not mad, *m* noble Festus;
1Co 14.27 let it be by two, or at the *m* by three,
15.19 we are of all men *m* miserable.
2Co 12. 9 *M* gladly therefore will I rather
Heb 7. 1 Salem, priest of the *m* high God,
Jude 20 yourselves on your *m* holy faith,
Rev 18.12 manner vessels of *m* precious wood,
21.11 was like unto a stone *m* precious,

MOTE

Mt 7. 3 the *m* that is in thy brother's eye,
4 me pull out the *m* out of thine eye;
5 out the *m* out of thy brother's eye.
Lk 6.41 the *m* that is in thy brother's eye,
42 pull out the *m* that is in thine eye,
42 the *m* that is in thy brother's eye.

MOTH

Job 4.19 which are crushed before the *m*?
13.28 as a garment that is *m* eaten.
27.18 He buildeth his house as a *m*, and
Ps 39.11 beauty to consume away like a *m*:
Isa 50. 9 garment; the *m* shall eat them up.
51. 8 For the *m* shall eat them up like a
Hos 5.12 will I be unto Ephraim as a *m*,
Mt 6.19 where *m* and rust doth corrupt,
20 where neither *m* nor rust doth
Lk 12.33 approacheth, neither *m* corrupteth.

MOTHEATEN

Jas 5. 2 and your garments are *m*.

MOTHER

Gen 2.24 a man leave his father and his *m*,
3.20 because she was the *m* of all living.
17.16 and she shall be a *m* of nations;
Ex 20.12 Honor thy father and thy *m*: that
21.17 he that curseth his father, or his *m*,
Dt 5.16 Honor thy father and thy *m*, as
27.16 setteth light by his father or his *m*.
Jdg 5. 7 arose, that I arose a *m* in Israel.
1Sa 2.19 his *m* made him a little coat, and
2Sa 20.19 to destroy a city and a *m* in Israel:
2Ki 3.13 and to the prophets of thy *m*. And
9.22 thy *m* Jezebel and her witchcrafts
2Ch 22. 3 for his *m* was his counsellor to do
Job 17.14 Thou art my *m*, and my sister.
Ps 27.10 my father and my *m* forsake me,
51. 5 and in sin did my *m* conceive me.
109.14 not the sin of his *m* be blotted out.
Pr 1. 8 and forsake not the law of thy *m*:
10. 1 foolish son is the heaviness of his *m*.
15.20 but a foolish man despiseth his *m*.
20.20 Whoso curseth his father or his *m*,
23.22 despise not thy *m* when she is old.
31. 1 prophecy that his *m* taught him.
Isa 66.13 As one whom his *m* comforteth, so
Jer 15.10 Woe is me, my *m*, that thou hast
20.17 my *m* might have been my grave,
Eze 16.44 As is the *m*, so is her daughter.
19. 2 And say, What is thy *m*? A lioness:
Mic 7. 6 daughter riseth up against her *m*,
6 in law against her *m* in law;
Mt 1.18 as his *m* Mary was espoused to
2.11 the young child with Mary his *m*,
13 take the young child and his *m*,
14 took the young child and his *m* by
20 take the young child and his *m*,
21 took the young child and his *m*,
8.14 he saw his wife's *m* laid, and sick
10.35 and the daughter against her *m*,
35 in law against her *m* in law.
37 that loveth father or *m* more than
12.46 his *m* and his brethren stood
47 thy *m* and thy brethren stand
48 Who is my *m*? and who are my
49 behold my *m* and my brethren!
50 is my brother, and sister, and *m*.
13.55 son? is not his *m* called Mary?
14. 8 being before instructed of her *m*,
11 and she brought it to her *m*.
15. 4 saying, Honor thy father and *m*:
4 that curseth father or *m*, let him
5 shall say to his father or his *m*,
6 honor not his father or his *m*,
19. 5 shall a man leave father and *m*,
19 Honor thy father and thy *m*: and,
29 father, or *m*, or wife, or children,
20.20 to him the *m* of Zebedee's children
27.56 Mary the *m* of James and Joses,
56 and the *m* of Zebedee's children.
Mk 1.30 But Simon's wife's *m* lay sick of a
3.31 then his brethren and his *m*,
32 thy *m* and thy brethren without
33 Who is my *m*, or my brethren?
34 Behold my *m* and my brethren!
35 my brother, and my sister, and *m*.
5.40 father and the *m* of the damsel,
6.24 said unto her *m*, What shall I ask?
28 and the damsel gave it to her *m*.
7.10 Honor thy father and thy *m*;
10 Whoso curseth father or *m*, let him
11 man shall say to his father or *m*,
12 do ought for his father or his *m*;
10. 7 shall a man leave his father and *m*,
19 not, Honor thy father and *m*.
29 or sisters, or father, or *m*, or wife,
15.40 Mary the *m* of James the less and
47 Mary the *m* of Joses beheld where he
16. 1 Mary the *m* of James, and Salome
Lk 1.43 the *m* of my Lord should come to
60 his *m* answered and said, Not so;
2.33 Joseph and his *m* marvelled at
34 and said unto Mary his *m*, Behold,
43 Joseph and his *m* knew not of it.
48 and his *m* said unto him, Son, why
51 his *m* kept all these sayings in her
4.38 Simon's wife's *m* was taken with
7.12 the only son of his *m*, and she
15 and he delivered him to his *m*.
8.19 Then came to him his *m* and his
20 Thy *m* and thy brethren stand
21 My *m* and my brethren are these
51 father and the *m* of the maiden.
12.53 the *m* against the daughter, and
53 and the daughter against the *m*;
53 *m* in law against the daughter
53 in law against the *m* in law.
14.26 hate not his father, and *m*, and
18.20 Honor thy father and thy *m*.
24.10 Joanna, and Mary the *m* of James,
Jn 2. 1 and the *m* of Jesus was there:
3 *m* of Jesus saith unto him, They
5 His *m* saith unto the servants,
12 and his *m*, and his brethren, and
6.42 whose father and *m* we know? how
19.25 stood by the cross of Jesus his *m*,
26 When Jesus therefore saw his *m*,
26 he saith unto his *m*, Woman,

27 he to the disciple, Behold thy *m*!
Ac 1.14 and Mary the *m* of Jesus, and with
12.12 the house of Mary the *m* of John,
Ro 16.13 in the Lord, and his *m* and mine.
Gal 4.26 is free, which is the *m* of us all.
Eph 5.31 shall a man leave his father and *m*,
6. 2 Honor thy father and *m*; which
2Ti 1. 5 Lois, and thy *m* Eunice; and I
Heb 7. 3 Without father, without *m*, without
Rev 17. 5 Great, The *M* Of Harlots And

MOTHER'S
Gen 24.67 was comforted after his *m* death.
Ex 23.19 shalt not seethe a kid in his *m* milk.
Job 1.21 Naked came I out of my *m* womb,
Ps 22. 9 when I was upon my *m* breasts.
10 thou art my God from my *m* belly.
139.13 hast covered me in my *m* womb.
Isa 50. 1 is the bill of your *m* divorcement,
Mt 19.12 were so born from their *m* womb:
Lk 1.15 Ghost, even from his *m* womb.
Jn 3. 4 the second time into his *m* womb,
19.25 And his *m* sister, Mary the wife of
Ac 3. 2 man lame from his *m* womb was
14. 8 being a cripple from his *m* womb,
Gal 1.15 separated me from my *m* womb,

MOTHERS
Isa 49.23 and their queens thy nursing *m*:
Jer 16. 3 concerning their *m* that bare them,
La 2.12 They say to their *m*, Where is corn
5. 3 fatherless, our *m* are as widows.
Mk 10.30 and sisters, and *m*, and children,
1Ti 1. 9 of fathers and murderers of *m*,
5. 2 The elder women as *m*; the

MOTIONS
Ro 7. 5 the *m* of sin, which were by the

MOUNT
Gen 22.14 in the *m* of the Lord it shall be
31.54 Jacob offered sacrifice upon the *m*,
Ex 4.27 went, and met him in the *m* of God,
18. 5 he encamped at the *m* of God:
19.11 sight of all the people upon *m* Sinai.
18 *m* Sinai was altogether on a smoke,
20 the Lord came down upon *m* Sinai,
23 people cannot come up to *m* Sinai:
24.13 Moses went up into the *m* of God.
18 Moses was in the *m* forty days and
34.32 had spoken with him in *m* Sinai.
Lev 7.38 Lord commanded Moses in *m* Sinai,
Dt 4.48 unto *m* Sion, which is Hermon,
10. 4 the Lord spake unto you in the *m*
11.29 put the blessing upon *m* Gerizim,
29 and the curse upon *m* Ebal.
32.49 unto *m* Nebo, which is in the land
1Ki 18.20 prophets together unto *m* Carmel.
19. 8 nights unto Horeb the *m* of God.
11 stand upon the *m* before the Lord.
Job 20. 6 excellency *m* up to the heavens,
39.27 the eagle *m* up at thy command,
Ps 48. 2 joy of the whole earth, is *m* Zion,
11 *m* Zion rejoice, let the daughters
107.26 They *m* up to the heaven, they go
125. 1 in the Lord shall be as *m* Zion,
Isa 9.18 *m* up like the lifting up of smoke.
14.13 upon the *m* of the congregation,
24.23 Lord of hosts shall reign in *m* Zion,
27.13 Lord in the holy *m* at Jerusalem.
40.31 shall *m* up with wings as eagles;
Zec 14. 4 in that day upon the *m* of Olives,
Mt 21. 1 Bethphage, unto the *m* of Olives,
24. 3 as he sat upon the *m* of Olives, the
26.30 they went out into the *m* of Olives.
Mk 11. 1 and Bethany, at the *m* of Olives,
13. 3 And as he sat upon the *m* of Olives
14.26 they went out into the *m* of Olives.
Lk 19.29 Bethany, at the *m* called...Olives,
29 at...the *m* of Olives, he sent two
37 at the descent of the *m* of Olives,

The site of the Sermon on the Mount, illustrated by Gustave Doré, is given only as "a mountain" (Mt 5.1).

21.37 he went out, and abode in the *m*
37 out, and abode in...the *m* of Olives.
22.39 as he was wont, to the *m* of Olives;
Jn 8. 1 Jesus went unto the *m* of Olives.
Ac 1.12 from the *m* called Olivet, which is
7.30 to him in the wilderness of *m* Sina
38 which spake to him in the *m* Sina,
Gal 4.24 the one from the *m* Sinai, which
25 For this Agar is *m* Sinai in Arabia,
Heb 8. 5 the pattern shewed to thee in the *m*.
12.18 unto the *m* that might be touched,
22 ye are come unto *m* Sion, and unto
2Pe 1.18 we were with him in the holy *m*.
Rev 14. 1 lo, a Lamb stood on the *m* Sion,

MOUNTAIN
Gen 19.19 I cannot escape to the *m*, lest some
Ex 3. 1 and came to the *m* of God, even to
12 ye shall serve God upon this *m*.
Dt 3.25 that goodly *m*, and Lebanon.
Job 14.18 the *m* falling cometh to nought,
Ps 11. 1 my soul, Flee as a bird to your *m*?
Isa 2. 2 the *m* of the Lord's house shall be
3 let us go up to the *m* of the Lord,
11. 9 hurt nor destroy in all my holy *m*:
25. 6 in this *m* shall the Lord of hosts
30.17 as a beacon, upon the top of a *m*,
40. 4 and every *m* and hill shall be made
9 get thee up into the high *m*: O
57.13 land, and shall inherit my holy *m*;
65.25 hurt nor destroy in all my holy *m*,
Eze 20.40 For in mine holy *m* in the
28.14 thou wast upon the holy *m* of God;
Mic 4. 1 that the *m* of the house of the Lord
2 let us go up to the *m* of the Lord,
Zec 4. 7 Who art thou, O great *m*? before
8. 3 *m* of the Lord of hosts the holy *m*.
Mt 4. 8 up into an exceeding high *m*,
5. 1 multitudes, he went up into a *m*:
8. 1 he was come down from the *m*,
14.23 went up into a *m* apart to pray:
15.29 went up into a *m*, and sat down
17. 1 them up into an high *m* apart,
9 as they came down from the *m*,
20 ye shall say unto this *m*, Remove
21.21 but also if ye shall say unto this *m*,
28.16 Galilee, into a *m* where Jesus had
Mk 3.13 And he goeth up into a *m*, and
6.46 he departed into a *m* to pray.
9. 2 leadeth them up into an high *m*
9 as they came down from the *m*, he
11.23 whosoever shall say unto this *m*,
Lk 3. 5 every *m* and hill shall be brought
4. 5 taking him up into an high *m*,
6.12 that he went out into a *m* to pray,
8.32 of many swine feeding on the *m*:
9.28 and went up into a *m* to pray.
Jn 4.20 Our fathers worshipped in this *m*;
21 when ye shall neither in this *m*,

Jn 6. 3 And Jesus went up into a *m*, and
15 again into a *m* himself alone.
Heb 12.20 if so much as a beast touch the *m*,
Rev 6.14 every *m* and island were moved
8. 8 as it were a great *m* burning with
21.10 in the spirit to a great and high *m*,

MOUNTAINS

Gen 8. 4 the month, upon the *m* of Ararat.
Jdg 5. 5 *m* melted from before the Lord,
2Sa 1.21 Ye *m* of Gilboa, let there be no
1Ki 19.11 great and strong wind rent the *m*,
Job 28. 9 he overturneth the *m* by the roots.
40.20 Surely the *m* bring him forth food,
Ps 46. 2 the *m* be carried into the midst
3 *m* shake with the swelling thereof.
83.14 as the flame setteth the *m* on fire;
90. 2 Before the *m* were brought forth,
104. 6 the waters stood above the *m*.
8 They go up by the *m*; they go down
114. 4 The *m* skipped like rams, and the
125. 2 the *m* are round about Jerusalem,
147. 8 maketh grass to grow upon the *m*.
Isa 18. 3 he lifteth up an ensign on the *m*;
34. 3 the *m* shall be melted with their
40.12 weighed the *m* in scales, and the
42.15 I will make waste *m* and hills, and
44.23 break forth into singing, ye *m*, O
52. 7 How beautiful upon the *m* are the
64. 3 the *m* flowed down at thy presence.
Jer 9.10 For the *m* will I take up a weeping
Eze 33.28 the *m* of Israel shall be desolate,
34.13 feed them upon the *m* of Israel
36. 4 Thus saith the Lord God to the *m*,
8 O *m* of Israel, ye shall shoot forth
Hos 10. 8 they shall say to the *m*, Cover us;
Am 4.13 For, lo, he that formeth the *m*, and
Mic 1. 4 the *m* shall be molten under him,
4. 1 be established in the top of the *m*,
Na 1. 5 The *m* quake at him, and the hills
15 Behold upon the *m* the feet of him
3.18 thy people is scattered upon the *m*,
Hab 3.10 *m* saw thee, and they trembled:
Mt 18.12 goeth into the *m*, and seeketh
24.16 which be in Judea flee into the *m*:
Mk 5. 5 night and day, he was in the *m*,
11 there nigh unto the *m* a great herd
13.14 them that be in Judea flee to the *m*:
Lk 21.21 which are in Judea flee to the *m*;
23.30 begin to say to the *m*, Fall on us;
1Co 13. 2 faith, so that I could remove *m*,
Heb 11.38 wandered in deserts, and in *m*,
Rev 6.15 dens and in the rocks of the *m*;
16 said to the *m* and rocks, Fall on us,
16.20 away, and the *m* were not found.
17. 9 The seven heads are seven *m*, on

MOURN

Gen 23. 2 Abraham came to *m* for Sarah,
1Sa 16. 1 How long wilt thou *m* for Saul,
Neh 8. 9 Lord your God; *m* not, nor weep.
Job 5.11 those which *m* may be exalted
Ps 55. 2 I *m* in my complaint, and make a
Pr 29. 2 wicked beareth rule, the people *m*.
Ec 3. 4 a time to *m*, and a time to dance;
Isa 61. 2 of our God; to comfort all that *m*;
3 To appoint unto them that *m* in
Jer 4.28 For this shall the earth *m*, and the
12. 4 How long shall the land *m*, and the
Eze 7.12 the buyer rejoice, nor the seller *m*:
Hos 4. 3 Therefore shall the land *m*, and
Am 9. 5 and all that dwell therein shall *m*:
Mt 5. 4 Blessed are they that *m*: for they
9.15 children of the bridechamber *m*,
24.30 shall all the tribes of the earth *m*,
Lk 6.25 now! for ye shall *m* and weep.
Jas 4. 9 Be afflicted, and *m*, and weep: let
Rev 18.11 earth shall weep and *m* over her;

MOURNED

Gen 37.34 loins, and *m* for his son many days.
50. 3 Egyptians *m* for him threescore
10 there they *m* with a great and
Ex 33. 4 heard these evil tidings, they *m*:
Nu 14.39 of Israel: and the people *m* greatly.
20.29 they *m* for Aaron thirty days,
1Sa 15.35 nevertheless Samuel *m* for Saul:
2Sa 1.12 And they *m*, and wept, and fasted
11.26 was dead, she *m* for her husband.
13.37 And David *m* for his son every day.
14. 2 that had a long time *m* for the dead:
1Ki 13.30 and they *m* over him, saying,
14.18 and all Israel *m* for him, according
1Ch 7.22 Ephraim their father *m* many days,
2Ch 35.24 Judah and Jerusalem *m* for Josiah.
Ezr 10. 6 he *m* because of the transgression of
Neh 1. 4 I...wept, and *m* certain days, and
Zec 7. 5 When ye fasted and *m* in the
Mt 11.17 we have *m* unto you, and ye have
Mk 16.10 with him, as they *m* and wept.
Lk 7.32 we have *m* to you, and ye have
1Co 5. 2 and have not rather *m*, that he

MOURNER

2Sa 14. 2 I pray thee, feign thyself to be a *m*,

MOURNERS

Job 29.25 army, as one that comforteth the *m*.
Ec 12. 5 and the *m* go about the streets:
Isa 57.18 comforts unto him and to his *m*.
Hos 9. 4 be unto them as the bread of *m*;

MOURNETH

2Sa 19. 1 king weepeth and *m* for Absalom.
Ps 35.14 as one that *m* for his mother.
88. 9 Mine eye *m* by reason of
Isa 24. 4 The earth *m* and fadeth away, the
7 new wine *m*, the vine languisheth,
33. 9 The earth *m* and languisheth:
Jer 12.11 and being desolate it *m* unto me;
14. 2 Judah *m*, and the gates thereof
23.10 for because of swearing the land *m*;
Joel 1.10 The field is wasted, the land *m*; for
Zec 12.10 for him, as one *m* for his only son,

MOURNFULLY

Mal 3.14 that we have walked *m* before the

MOURNING

Gen 27.41 The days of *m* for my father are at
50.10 made a *m* for his father seven days.
Job 30.28 I went *m* without the sun: I stood
31 My harp also is turned to *m*, and my
Ps 30.11 turned for me my *m* into dancing:
38. 6 greatly; I go *m* all the day long.
42. 9 go I *m* because of the oppression
Ec 7. 2 better to go to the house of *m*, than
4 of the wise is in the house of *m*;
Isa 51.11 and sorrow and *m* shall flee away.
60.20 the days of thy *m* shall be ended.
61. 3 beauty for ashes, the oil of joy for *m*,
Jer 9.17 call for the *m* women, that they
16. 5 not into the house of *m*, neither
31.13 I will turn their *m* into joy, and will
Eze 24.17 to cry, make no *m* for the dead,
Am 8.10 And I will turn your feasts into *m*,
Zec 12.11 there be a great *m* in Jerusalem,
Mt 2.18 and great *m*, Rachel weeping for
2Co 7. 7 your *m*, your fervent mind toward
Jas 4. 9 laughter be turned to *m*, and your
Rev 18. 8 day, death, and *m*, and famine;

MOUTH

Gen 8.11 in her *m* was an olive leaf pluckt
29. 2 great stone was upon the well's *m*.
43.21 money was in the *m* of his sack,
Ex 4.11 him, Who hath made man's *m*? or
12 and I will be with thy *m*, and teach
15 unto him, and put words in his *m*:
13. 9 the Lord's law may be in thy *m*:
Nu 22.28 the Lord opened the *m* of the ass,
Dt 17. 6 At the *m* of two witnesses, or three
30.14 is very nigh unto thee, in thy *m*,
32. 1 hear, O earth, the words of my *m*.
Jos 1. 8 law shall not depart out of thy *m*;
Jdg 9.38 Where is now thy *m*, wherewith
11.35 I have opened my *m* unto the Lord,
18.19 lay thine hand upon thy *m*, and go
1Ki 17.24 word of the Lord in thy *m* is truth.
19.18 every *m* which hath not kissed him.
2Ch 36.21 of the Lord by the *m* of Jeremiah,
Job 3. 1 After this opened Job his *m*, and
5.16 hope, and iniquity stoppeth her *m*.
7.11 Therefore I will not refrain my *m*;
8.21 Till he fill thy *m* with laughing,
9.20 mine own *m* shall condemn me:
15. 5 For thy *m* uttereth thine iniquity,
6 Thine own *m* condemneth thee,
13 lettest such words go out of thy *m*?
21. 5 and lay your hand upon your *m*.
23. 4 and fill my *m* with arguments.
32. 5 no answer in the *m* of these three
33. 2 Behold, now I have opened my *m*,
2 my tongue hath spoken in my *m*.
35.16 doth Job open his *m* in vain;
Ps 8. 2 Out of...*m* of babes and sucklings
19.14 Let the words of my *m*, and the
33. 6 of them by the breath of his *m*.
34. 1 shall continually be in my *m*.
39. 1 I will keep my *m* with a bridle,
40. 3 he hath put a new song in my *m*,
49. 3 My *m* shall speak of wisdom; and
51.15 my *m* shall shew forth thy praise.
55.21 The words of his *m* were smoother
62. 4 they bless with their *m*, but they
66.17 I cried unto him with my *m*, and
71.15 My *m* shall shew forth thy
78. 2 I will open my *m* in a parable: I
81.10 open thy *m* wide, and I will fill it.
103. 5 satisfieth thy *m* with good things;
107.42 and all iniquity shall stop her *m*.
109.30 greatly praise the Lord with my *m*;
119.103 yea, sweeter than honey to my *m*!
108 the freewill offerings of my *m*, O
126. 2 was our *m* filled with laughter,
137. 6 tongue cleave to the roof of my *m*;
141. 3 Set a watch, O Lord, before my *m*;
145.21 My *m* shall speak the praise of the
Pr 2. 6 out of his *m* cometh knowledge
5. 3 and her *m* is smoother than oil:
10.11 The *m* of a righteous man is a well
14 but the *m* of the foolish is near
31 The *m* of the just bringeth forth
32 but the *m* of the wicked speaketh
15. 2 but the *m* of fools poureth out
23 hath joy by the answer of his *m*:
18. 7 A fool's *m* is his destruction, and
20.17 his *m* shall be filled with gravel.
24. 7 he openeth not his *m* in the gate.
26. 7, 9 so is a parable in the *m* of fools.
31. 9 Open thy *m*, judge righteously,
26 She openeth her *m* with wisdom;
Ec 6. 7 All the labor of man is for his *m*,
10.12 The words of a wise man's *m* are
Isa 1.20 the *m* of the Lord hath spoken it.
6. 7 he laid it upon my *m*, and said, Lo,
11. 4 the earth with the rod of his *m*,
51.16 I have put my words in thy *m*,
53. 7 afflicted, yet he opened not his *m*:
7 is dumb, so he openeth not his *m*.
9 neither was any deceit in his *m*.
55.11 be that goeth forth out of my *m*:
59.21 shall not depart out of thy *m*, nor
Jer 1. 9 forth his hand, and touched my *m*.
9 I have put my words in thy *m*.
La 3.38 Out of the *m* of the most High
4. 4 cleaveth to the roof of his *m* for
Eze 3. 2 So I opened my *m*, and he caused
Hos 6. 5 slain them by the words of my *m*:
8. 1 Set the trumpet to thy *m*. He
Am 3.12 out of the *m* of the lion two legs,
Mic 4. 4 *m* of the Lord of hosts hath spoken
7. 5 keep the doors of thy *m* from her

Mal 2. 6 The law of truth was in his *m*, and
7 they should seek the law at his *m*:
Mt 4. 4 proceedeth out of the *m* of God.
5. 2 he opened his *m*, and taught them,
12.34 of the heart the *m* speaketh.
13.35 I will open my *m* in parables; I will
15. 8 draweth nigh unto me with their *m*,
11 which goeth into the *m* defileth a
11 but that which cometh out of the *m*,
17 entereth in at the *m* goeth into the
18 which proceed out of the *m* come
17.27 and when thou hast opened his *m*,
18.16 in the *m* of two or three witnesses
21.16 Out of the *m* of babes and sucklings
Lk 1.64 his *m* was opened immediately, and
70 spake by the *m* of his holy prophets,
4.22 which proceeded out of his *m*. And
6.45 of the heart his *m* speaketh.
11.54 to catch something out of his *m*,
19.22 of thine own *m* will I judge thee,
21.15 I will give you a *m* and wisdom,
22.71 ourselves have heard of his own *m*.
Jn 19.29 upon hyssop, and put it to his *m*.
Ac 1.16 the Holy Ghost by the *m* of David
3.18 by the *m* of all his prophets, that
21 by the *m* of all his holy prophets
4.25 by the *m* of thy servant David hast
8.32 shearer, so opened he not his *m*:
35 Philip opened his *m*, and began at
10.34 Then Peter opened his *m*, and said,
11. 8 hath at any time entered into my *m*.
15. 7 the Gentiles by my *m* should hear
27 tell you the same things by *m*.
18.14 was now about to open his *m*,
22.14 shouldest hear the voice of his *m*.
23. 2 by him to smite him on the *m*.
Ro 3.14 Whose *m* is full of cursing and
19 that every *m* may be stopped, and
10. 8 word is nigh thee, even in thy *m*,
9 confess with thy *m* the Lord Jesus,
10 and with the *m* confession is made
15. 6 one mind and one *m* glorify God,
1Co 9. 9 shalt not muzzle the *m* of the ox
2Co 6.11 our *m* is open unto you, our
13. 1 In the *m* of two or three witnesses
Eph 4.29 proceed out of your *m*, but that
6.19 that I may open my *m* boldly, to
Col 3. 8 communication out of your *m*.
2Th 2. 8 consume with the spirit of his *m*,
2Ti 4.17 delivered out of the *m* of the lion.
Jas 3.10 of the same *m* proceedeth blessing
1Pe 2.22 neither was guile found in his *m*:
Jude 16 *m* speaketh great swelling words,
Rev 1.16 and out of his *m* went a sharp
2.16 them with the sword of my *m*.
3.16 hot, I will spue thee out of my *m*.
9.19 For their power is in their *m*, and
10. 9 shall be in thy *m* sweet as honey.
10 it was in my *m* sweet as honey:
11. 5 fire proceedeth out of their *m*, and
12.15 cast out of his *m* water as a flood
16 earth opened her *m*, and swallowed
16 which the dragon cast out of his *m*.
13. 2 and his *m* as the *m* of a lion: and
5 him a *m* speaking great things and
6 And he opened his *m* in blasphemy
14. 5 And in their *m* was found no guile:
16.13 come out of the *m* of the dragon,
13 and out of the *m* of the beast,
13 out of the *m* of the false prophet.
19.15 out of his *m* goeth a sharp sword.
21 sword proceedeth out of his *m*:

MOUTHS

Gen 44. 8 which we found in our sacks' *m*,
Dt 31.19 put it in their *m*, that this song
21 out of the *m* of their seed: for I
Ps 22.13 They gaped upon me with their *m*,
78.30 their meat was yet in their *m*,
115. 5 They have *m*, but they speak not:
135.16 They have *m*, but they speak not;
17 is there any breath in their *m*.
Isa 52.15 the kings shall shut their *m* at him:
Jer 44.25 have both spoken with your *m*, and
La 3.46 our enemies have opened their *m*
Dan 6.22 angel, and hath shut the lions' *m*,
Mic 3. 5 he that putteth not into their *m*,
Tit 1.11 Whose *m* must be stopped, who
Heb 11.33 promises, stopped the *m* of lions,
Jas 3. 3 we put bits in the horses' *m*, that
Rev 9.17 and out of their *m* issued fire and
18 which issued out of their *m*.

MOVE

Ex 11. 7 shall not a dog *m* his tongue,
Lev 11.10 of all that *m* in the waters, and of
Dt 23.25 thou shalt not *m* a sickle unto thy
32.21 I will *m* them to jealousy with those
Jdg 13.25 Spirit of the Lord began to *m* him
2Sa 7.10 of their own, and *m* no more;
2Ki 21. 8 will I make the feet of Israel *m*
23.18 alone; let no man *m* his bones.
Jer 10. 4 and with hammers, that it *m* not.
Mic 7.17 they shall *m* out of their holes
Mt 23. 4 will not *m* them with one of their
Ac 17.28 in him we live, and *m*, and have
20.24 none of these things *m* me,

MOVED

Gen 1. 2 the Spirit of God *m* upon the face
7.21 And all flesh died that *m* upon the
2Sa 18.33 the king was much *m*, and went
2Ch 18.31 God *m* them to depart from him.
Ps 10. 6 said in his heart, I shall not be *m*:
15. 5 doeth these things shall never be *m*.
16. 8 at my right hand, I shall not be *m*.
21. 7 the most High he shall not be *m*.
46. 6 raged, the kingdoms were *m*: he
62. 2 defense; I shall not be greatly *m*.
6 he is my defense; I shall not be *m*.
66. 9 and suffereth not our feet to be *m*.
93. 1 is stablished, that it cannot be *m*.
121. 3 He will not suffer thy foot to be *m*:
Pr 12. 3 of the righteous shall not be *m*.
Isa 6. 4 posts of the door *m* at the voice
Jer 49.21 The earth is *m* at the noise of
Mt 9.36 was *m* with compassion on them,
14.14 *m* with compassion toward them,
18.27 servant was *m* with compassion,
20.24 were *m* with indignation against
21.10 all the city was *m*, saying, Who is
Mk 1.41 Jesus, *m* with compassion, put
6.34 and was *m* with compassion toward
15.11 But the chief priests *m* the people,
Ac 2.25 hand, that I should not be *m*:
7. 9 the patriarchs, *m* with envy, sold
17. 5 Jews which believed not, *m* with
21.30 And all the city was *m*, and the
Col 1.23 and be not *m* away from the hope
1Th 3. 3 no man should be *m* by these
Heb 11. 7 By faith Noah,...*m* with fear,
12.28 a kingdom which cannot be *m*,
2Pe 1.21 they were *m* by the Holy Ghost.
Rev 6.14 every mountain and island were *m*

MOVER

Ac 24. 5 and a *m* of sedition among all the

MOVING

Gen 1.20 the *m* creature that hath life,
9. 3 Every *m* thing that liveth shall be
Job 16. 5 the *m* of my lips should asswage
Pr 16.30 *m* his lips he bringeth evil to
Jn 5. 3 waiting for the *m* of the water.

MUCH

Ex 16.18 gathered *m* had nothing over, and
Nu 16. 3 Ye take too *m* upon you, seeing
Jos 11. 4 *m* people, even as the sand that is
1Sa 19. 2 Saul's son delighted *m* in David:
1Ki 8.27 how *m* less this house that I have
Ps 19.10 than gold, yea, than *m* fine gold:
33.16 is not delivered by *m* strength.
Pr 16.16 How *m* better is it to get wisdom
25.27 It is not good to eat *m* honey:
Ec 5.17 he hath *m* sorrow and wrath with
7.16 Be not righteous over *m*; neither
17 Be not over *m* wicked, neither be
9.18 but one sinner destroyeth *m* good.
12.12 and *m* study is a weariness of the
Jer 2.36 Why gaddest thou about so *m* to
Hag 1. 9 Ye looked for *m*, and lo, it came to
Mt 6. 7 be heard for their *m* speaking.
26 Are ye not *m* better than they?
30 shall he not *m* more clothe you, O
Lk 7.47 are forgiven; for she loved *m*:
12.48 given, of him shall be *m* required:
16.10 is least is faithful also in *m*:
10 in the least is unjust also in *m*.
Jn 6.10 there was *m* grass in the place.
12.24 if it die, it bringeth forth *m* fruit.
Ac 5. 8 whether ye sold the land for so *m*?
19. 2 have not so *m* as heard whether
26.24 *m* learning doth make thee mad.
Ro 1.15 So, as *m* as in me is, I am ready
5.20 grace did *m* more abound:
12.18 as *m* as lieth in you, live peaceably
2Co 8.15 had gathered *m* had nothing over;
1Th 2. 2 gospel of God with *m* contention.
1Ti 3. 8 not given to *m* wine, not greedy of
Heb 7.22 By so *m* was Jesus made a surety
Jas 5.16 of a righteous man availeth *m*.

MULBERRY

2Sa 5.23 them over against the *m* trees.
24 a going in the tops of the *m* trees,
1Ch 14.14 them over against the *m* trees.
15 of going in the tops of the *m* trees,

MULTIPLIED

Gen 47.27 and grew, and *m* exceedingly.
Ex 1. 7 *m*, and waxed exceeding mighty;
12 them, the more they *m* and grew.
20 people *m*, and waxed very mighty.
11. 9 my wonders may be *m* in the land
Dt 1.10 The Lord your God hath *m* you,
8.13 and thy silver and thy gold is *m*,
13 and all that thou hast is *m*;
11.21 That your days may be *m*, and the
Jos 24. 3 *m* his seed, and gave him Isaac.
1Ch 5. 9 their cattle were *m* in the land of
Job 27.14 If his children be *m*, it is for the
35. 6 or if thy transgressions be *m*,
Ps 16. 4 Their sorrows shall be *m* that
38.19 that hate me wrongfully are *m*.
107.38 also, so that they are *m* greatly;
Pr 9.11 For by me thy days shall be *m*,
29.16 When the wicked are *m*,
Isa 9. 3 Thou hast *m* the nation, and not
59.12 our transgressions are *m* before
Jer 3.16 when ye be *m* and increased in
Eze 5. 7 ye *m* more than the nations that
11. 6 Ye have *m* your slain in this city,
16.25 passed by, and *m* thy whoredoms.
29 hast moreover *m* thy fornication
51 thou hast *m* thine abominations
21.15 may faint, and their ruins be *m*:
23.19 she *m* her whoredoms, in calling
31. 5 boughs were *m*, and his branches
35.13 have *m* your words against me:
Dan 4. 1 the earth; Peace be *m* unto you.
6.25 the earth; Peace be *m* unto you.
Hos 2. 8 and oil, and *m* her silver and gold,
8.14 and Judah hath *m* fenced cities:
12.10 *m* visions, and used similitudes,
Na 3.16 *m* thy merchants above the stars
Ac 6. 1 number of the disciples was *m*,
7 of the disciples *m* in Jerusalem
7.17 the people grew and *m* in Egypt,
9.31 comfort of the Holy Ghost, were *m*.
12.24 But the word of God grew and *m*.
1Pe 1. 2 Grace unto you, and peace, be *m*.

2Pe 1. 2 Grace and peace be *m* unto you
Jude 2 unto you, and peace, and love, be *m*.

MULTIPLIETH

Job 9.17 and *m* my wounds without cause.
34.37 us, and *m* his words against God.
35.16 he *m* words without knowledge.

MULTIPLY

Gen 1.22 Be fruitful, and *m*, and fill the
28 Be fruitful, and *m*, and replenish
3.16 I will greatly *m* thy sorrow and thy
22.17 I will *m* thy seed as the stars of the
Eze 16. 7 I have caused thee to *m* as the bud
2Co 9.10 *m* your seed sown, and increase
Heb 6.14 and multiplying I will *m* thee.

MULTITUDE

Gen 16.10 it shall not be numbered for *m*.
Ex 23. 2 shalt not follow a *m* to do evil;
Lev 25.16 According to the *m* of years thou
Dt 28.62 were as the stars of heaven for *m*;
Jos 11. 4 that is upon the sea shore in *m*,
Jdg 6. 5 they came as grasshoppers for *m*;
1Ki 20.13 Hast thou seen all this great *m*?
Job 11. 2 not the *m* of words be answered?
32. 7 *m* of years should teach wisdom.
Ps 5.10 in the *m* of their transgressions;
33.16 no king saved by the *m* of an host:
42. 4 for I had gone with the *m*, I went
69.13 in the *m* of thy mercy hear me,
94.19 In the *m* of my thoughts within
Pr 10.19 In the *m* of words there wanteth
11.14 in the *m* of counsellors there is
24. 6 in *m* of counsellors there is safety.
Ec 5. 3 a fool's voice is known by *m* of
Eze 14. 4 according to the *m* of his idols;
Mic 2.12 noise by reason of the *m* of men.
Mt 13. 2 the whole *m* stood on the shore.
34 things spake Jesus unto the *m* in
36 Then Jesus sent the *m* away, and
14. 5 put him to death, he feared the *m*,
14 went forth, and saw a great *m*,
15 send the *m* away, that they may
19 he commanded the *m* to sit down
19 disciples, and...disciples to the *m*.
15.10 And he called the *m*, and said unto
31 Insomuch that the *m* wondered,
32 said, I have compassion on the *m*,
33 wilderness, as to fill so great a *m*?
35 he commanded the *m* to sit down
36 disciples, and...disciples to the *m*.
39 And he sent away the *m*, and took
17.14 And when they were come to the *m*,
20.29 Jericho, a great *m* followed him.
31 And the *m* rebuked them, because
21. 8 And a very great *m* spread their
11 And the *m* said, This is Jesus the
46 hands on him, they feared the *m*.
22.33 And when the *m* heard this, they
23. 1 Then spake Jesus to the *m*, and to
26.47 with him a great *m* with swords
27.20 *m* that they should ask Barabbas,
24 washed his hands before the *m*,
Mk 2.13 and all the *m* resorted unto him,
3. 7 a great *m* from Galilee followed
8 a great *m*, when they had heard
9 wait on him because of the *m*,
20 And the *m* cometh together again,
32 And the *m* sat about him, and they
4. 1 was gathered unto him a great *m*,
1 and the whole *m* was by the sea on
36 when they had sent away the *m*,
5.31 Thou seest the *m* thronging thee,
7.33 And he took him aside from the *m*,
8. 1 those days the *m* being very great,
2 I have compassion on the *m*,
9.14 he saw a great *m* about them, and
17 one of the *m* answered and said,
14.43 with him a great *m* with swords
15. 8 the *m* crying aloud began to desire

A multitude partook in the multiplication of loaves (Mt 14), shown in this medieval Book of Hours.

Lk 1.10 *m* of the people were praying
2.13 a *m* of the heavenly host praising
3. 7 *m* that came forth to be baptized
5. 6 they inclosed a great *m* of fishes:
19 bring him in because of the *m*,
6.17 and a great *m* of people out of all
19 the whole *m* sought to touch him:
8.37 Then the whole *m* of the country
45 the *m* throng thee and press thee,
9.12 Send the *m* away, that they may
16 the disciples to set before the *m*.
12. 1 an unnumerable *m* of people,
18.36 hearing the *m* pass by, he asked
19.37 whole *m* of the disciples began to
39 the Pharisees from among the *m*
22. 6 unto them in the absence of the *m*.
47 while he yet spake, behold a *m*,
23. 1 And the whole *m* of them arose,
Jn 5. 3 lay a great *m* of impotent folk,
13 away, a *m* being in that place.
6. 2 a great *m* followed him, because
21. 6 able to draw it for the *m* of fishes.
Ac 2. 6 abroad, the *m* came together, and
4.32 the *m* of them that believed were
5.16 came also a *m* out of the cities
6. 2 called the *m* of the disciples unto
5 the saying pleased the whole *m*:
14. 1 that a great *m* both of the Jews
4 But the *m* of the city was divided:
15.12 Then all the *m* kept silence, and
30 they had gathered the *m* together,
16.22 *m* rose up together against them:
17. 4 of the devout Greeks a great *m*,
19. 9 spake evil of that way before the *m*,
33 they drew Alexander out of the *m*,
21.22 the *m* must needs come together:
34 thing, some another, among...*m*:
36 the *m* of the people followed after,
23. 7 Sadducees: and the *m* was divided.
24.18 neither with *m*, nor with tumult,
25.24 about whom all the *m* of the Jews
Heb 11.12 many as the stars of the sky in *m*,
Jas 5.20 death, and shall hide a *m* of sins.
1Pe 4. 8 for charity shall cover a *m* of sins.
Rev 7. 9 a great *m*, which no man could
19. 6 as it were the voice of a great *m*,

MULTITUDES

Eze 32.20 the sword: draw her and all her *m*.
Joel 3.14 *M*, *m* in the valley of decision:
Mt 4.25 followed him great *m* of people
5. 1 And seeing the *m*, he went up into
8. 1 mountain, great *m* followed him.
18 Jesus saw great *m* about him,
9. 8 But when the *m* saw it, they
33 and the *m* marvelled, saying, It
36 But when he saw the *m*, he was
11. 7 Jesus began to say unto the *m*
12.15 and great *m* followed him, and he
13. 2 great *m* were gathered together
14.22 side, while he sent the *m* away:
23 when he had sent the *m* away, he
15.30 great *m* came unto him, having
19. 2 And great *m* followed him; and he
21. 9 And the *m* that went before, and
26.55 same hour said Jesus to the *m*,
Lk 5.15 great *m* came together to hear,
14.25 there went great *m* with him: and
Ac 5.14 Lord, *m* both of men and women.)
13.45 when the Jews saw the *m*, they
Rev 17.15 are peoples, and *m*, and nations,

MURDER

Ps 10. 8 places doth he *m* the innocent:
94. 6 stranger, and *m* the fatherless.
Jer 7. 9 Will ye steal, *m*, and commit
Hos 6. 9 company of priests *m* in the way
Mt 19.18 Jesus said, Thou shalt do no *m*,
Mk 15. 7 committed *m* in the insurrection.
Lk 23.19 and for *m*, was cast into prison.)
25 and *m* was cast into prison, whom
Ro 1.29 full of envy, *m*, debate, deceit,

MURDERER

Nu 35.16 of iron, so that he die, he is a *m*:
16 the *m* shall surely be put to death.
17 he may die, and he die, he is a *m*:
17 the *m* shall surely be put to death.
18 he may die, and he die, he is a *m*:
18 the *m* shall surely be put to death.
19 of blood himself shall slay the *m*:
21 for he is a *m*: the revenger of blood
21 shall slay the *m*, when he meeteth
30 the *m* shall be put to death by the
31 no satisfaction for the life of a *m*,
2Ki 6.32 this son of a *m* hath sent to take
Job 24.14 *m* rising with the light killeth the
Hos 9.13 bring forth his children to the *m*.
Jn 8.44 He was a *m* from the beginning,
Ac 3.14 desired a *m* to be granted unto
28. 4 No doubt this man is a *m*, whom,
1Pe 4.15 let none of you suffer as a *m*, or as
1Jn 3.15 hateth his brother is a *m*: and ye
15 know that no *m* hath eternal life

MURDERERS

2Ki 14. 6 children of the *m* he slew not:
Isa 1.21 lodged in it; but now *m*.
Jer 4.31 my soul is wearied because of *m*.
Mt 22. 7 armies, and destroyed those *m*,
Ac 7.52 been now the betrayers and *m*:
21.38 four thousand men that were *m*?
1Ti 1. 9 and profane, for *m* of fathers
9 and *m* of mothers, for manslayers,
Rev 21. 8 and the abominable, and *m*, and
22.15 and whoremongers, and *m*, and

MURDERS

Mt 15.19 heart proceed evil thoughts, *m*,
Mk 7.21 adulteries, fornications, *m*,
Gal 5.21 Envyings, *m*, drunkenness,
Rev 9.21 Neither repented they of their *m*,

MURMUR

Ex 16. 7 are we, that ye *m* against us?
8 which ye *m* against him: and
Nu 14.27 congregation which *m* against me?
27 Israel, which they *m* against me.
36 congregation to *m* against him,
16.11 is Aaron, that ye *m* against him?
17. 5 whereby they *m* against you.

Jn 6.43 them, *M* not among yourselves.
1Co 10.10 Neither *m* ye, as some of them also

MURMURED
Ex 15.24 And the people *m* against Moses,
16. 2 children of Israel *m* against Moses
17. 3 and the people *m* against Moses,
Nu 14. 2 children of Israel *m* against Moses
29 upward, which have *m* against me,
16.41 children of Israel *m* against Moses
Dt 1.27 And ye *m* in your tents, and said,
Jos 9.18 And all...*m* against the princes.
Ps 106.25 But *m* in their tents, and
Isa 29.24 they that *m* shall learn doctrine.
Mt 20.11 they *m* against the goodman of
Mk 14. 5 poor. And they *m* against her.
Lk 5.30 Pharisees *m* against his disciples,
15. 2 And the Pharisees and scribes *m*,
19. 7 And when they saw it, they all *m*,
Jn 6.41 The Jews then *m* at him, because
61 himself that his disciples *m* at it,
7.32 that the people *m* such things
1Co 10.10 as some of them also *m*, and were

MURMURERS
Jude 16 These are *m*, complainers,

MURMURING
Jn 7.12 was much *m* among the people
Ac 6. 1 there arose a *m* of the Grecians

MURMURINGS
Ex 16. 7 heareth your *m* against the Lord:
8 for that the Lord heareth your *m*
8 your *m* are not against us, but
9 Lord: for he hath heard your *m*.
12 have heard the *m* of the children of
Nu 14.27 have heard the *m* of the children of
17. 5 me the *m* of the children of Israel,
10 quite take away their *m* from me,
Php 2.14 Do all things without *m* and

MUSED
Lk 3.15 all men *m* in their hearts of John,

MUSICAL
1Ch 16.42 and with *m* instruments of God.
Neh 12.36 with the *m* instruments of David
Ec 2. 8 as *m* instruments, and that of all

MUSICIANS
Rev 18.22 of harpers, and *m*, and of pipers,

MUSICK
1Sa 18. 6 with joy, and with instruments of *m*.
1Ch 15.16 singers with instruments of *m*,
2Ch 5.13 cymbals and instruments of *m*,
7. 6 instruments of *m* of the Lord,
23.13 the singers with instruments of *m*,
34.12 could skill of instruments of *m*.
Ec 12. 4 all the daughters of *m* shall be
La 3.63 their rising up; I am their *m*.
5.14 gate, the young men from their *m*.
Dan 3. 5 dulcimer, and all kinds of *m*, ye
7 psaltery, and all kinds of *m*, all
10, 15 dulcimer, and all kinds of *m*,
6.18 neither were instruments of *m*
Am 6. 5 to themselves instruments of *m*,
Lk 15.25 house, he heard *m* and dancing.

MUSING
Ps 39. 3 while I was *m* the fire burned:

MUST
Dt 4.22 I *m* not go over Jordan: but ye
1Ki 18.27 he sleepeth, and *m* be awaked.
Jer 10. 5 they *m* needs be borne, because thy
19 Truly this is a grief, and I *m* bear it.
Mt 16.21 that he *m* go unto Jerusalem,
17.10 scribes that Elias *m* first come?
18. 7 it *m* needs be that offenses come;

BIBLICAL THEMES

MUSIC

Then sang Moses and the children of Israel this song . . . saying, I will sing unto the Lord, for he hath triumphed gloriously: the horse and his rider hath he thrown into the sea. The Lord is my strength and song. . . . And Miriam the prophetess, the sister of Aaron, took a timbrel in her hand; and all the women went out after her with timbrels and with dances. Ex 15.1-2, 20

And it came to pass, when the evil spirit from God was upon Saul, that David took an harp, and played with his hand: so Saul was refreshed, and was well, and the evil spirit departed from him. 1Sa 16.23

Thus all Israel brought up the ark of the covenant of the Lord with shouting, and with sound of the cornet, and with trumpets, and with cymbals, making a noise with psalteries and harps. 1Ch 15.28

When the builders laid the foundation of the temple of the Lord, they set the priests in their apparel with trumpets, and the Levites . . . with cymbals, to praise the Lord. . . . And they sang together by course. Ezr 3.10-11

Where wast thou when I laid the foundations of the earth? . . . when the morning stars sang together, and all the sons of God shouted for joy? Job 38.4, 7

Make a joyful noise unto the Lord, all the earth: make a loud noise, and rejoice, and sing praise. Sing unto the Lord with the harp; with the harp, and the voice of a psalm. With trumpets and sound of cornets make a joyful noise before the Lord, the King. Let the sea roar. . . . Let the floods clap their hands: let the hills be joyful together before the Lord. Ps 98.4-9

As he that taketh away a garment in cold weather . . . so is he that singeth songs to an heavy heart. Pr 25.20

Take an harp, go about the city, thou harlot that hast been forgotten; make sweet melody, sing many songs, that thou mayest be remembered. Isa 23.16

The mirth of tabrets ceaseth, the noise of them that rejoice endeth, the joy of the harp ceaseth. Isa 24.8

And the ransomed of the Lord shall return, and come to Zion with songs and everlasting joy. Isa 35.10

Lo, thou art unto them as a very lovely song of one that hath a pleasant voice, and can play well on an instrument: for they hear thy words, but they do them not. Eze 33.32

When all the people heard the sound of the cornet, flute, harp, sackbut, psaltery, and all kinds of musick, all the people . . . fell down and worshipped the golden image. Dan 3.7

We have piped unto you, and ye have not danced; we have mourned unto you, and ye have not lamented. Mt 11.17

Be filled with the Spirit; speaking to yourselves in psalms and hymns and spiritual songs, singing and making melody in your heart to the Lord. Eph 5.18-19

I heard the voice of harpers harping with their harps: and they sung as it were a new song before the throne . . . and no man could learn that song but the hundred and forty and four thousand, which were redeemed from the earth. Rev 14.2-3

24. 6 all these things *m* come to pass,
26.54 be fulfilled, that thus it *m* be?
Mk 2.22 new wine *m* be put into new bottles.
8.31 Son of man *m* suffer many things,
9.11 the scribes that Elias *m* first come?
12 man, that he *m* suffer many things,
13. 7 for such things *m* needs be; but
10 the gospel *m* first be published
14.49 but the scriptures *m* be fulfilled.
Lk 2.49 that I *m* be about my Father's
4.43 I *m* preach the kingdom of God to
5.38 new wine *m* be put into new bottles;
9.22 Son of man *m* suffer many things,
13.33 Nevertheless I *m* walk to-day, and
14.18 and I *m* needs go and see it:
17.25 first *m* he suffer many things, and
19. 5 for to day I *m* abide at thy house.
21. 9 these things *m* first come to pass;
22. 7 when the passover *m* be killed.
37 *m* yet be accomplished in me,
23.17 (he *m* release one unto them at
24. 7 Son of man *m* be delivered into
44 that all things *m* be fulfilled, which
Jn 3. 7 unto thee, Ye *m* be born again.
14 so *m* the Son of man be lifted up:
30 He *m* increase, but I...decrease.
30 He...increase, but I *m* decrease.
4. 4 he *m* needs go through Samaria.
24 *m* worship him in spirit and in
9. 4 I *m* work the works of him that
10.16 them also I *m* bring, and they
12.34 The Son of man *m* be lifted up?
20. 9 he *m* rise again from the dead.
Ac 1.16 *m* needs have been fulfilled,
22 *m* one be ordained to be a witness
3.21 Whom the heaven *m* receive until
4.12 men, whereby we *m* be saved.
9. 6 shall be told thee what thou *m* do.
16 he *m* suffer for my name's sake.
14.22 *m* through much tribulation enter

Ac 15.24 souls, saying, Ye *m* be circumcised,
16.30 Sirs, what *m* I do to be saved?
17. 3 Christ *m* needs have suffered,
18.21 I *m* by all means keep this feast
19.21 been there, I *m* also see Rome.
21.22 the multitude *m* needs come
23.11 so *m* thou bear witness also at
27.24 thou *m* be brought before Caesar:
26 *m* be cast upon a certain island.
Ro 13. 5 ye *m* needs be subject, not only
1Co 5.10 for then *m* ye needs go out of the
11.19 there *m* be also heresies among
15.25 For he *m* reign, till he hath put all
53 corruptible *m* put on incorruption,
53 this mortal *m* put on immortality.
2Co 5.10 For we *m* all appear before the
11.30 If I *m* needs glory, I will glory of
1Ti 3. 2 A bishop then *m* be blameless, the
7 Moreover he *m* have a good report
8 Likewise *m* the deacons be grave,
11 Even so *m* their wives be grave, not
2Ti 2. 6 laboreth *m* be first partaker of
24 servant of the Lord *m* not strive;
Tit 1. 7 For a bishop *m* be blameless, as
11 Whose mouths *m* be stopped, who
Heb 4. 6 remaineth that some *m* enter
9.16 there *m* also of necessity be the
26 For then *m* he often have suffered
11. 6 he that cometh to God *m* believe
13.17 as they that *m* give account, that
1Pe 4.17 judgment *m* begin at the house of
2Pe 1.14 I *m* put off this my tabernacle,
Rev 1. 1 which *m* shortly come to pass;
4. 1 thee things which *m* be hereafter.
10.11 Thou *m* prophesy again before
11. 5 he *m* in this manner be killed.
13.10 sword *m* be killed with the sword.
17.10 he *m* continue a short space.
20. 3 after that he *m* be loosed a little
22. 6 things which *m* shortly be done.

MUSTARD

Mt 13.31 heaven is like a grain of *m* seed,
17.20 ye have faith as a grain of *m* seed,
Mk 4.31 It is like a grain of *m* seed, which
Lk 13.19 It is like a grain of *m* seed, which
17. 6 ye had faith as a grain of *m* seed,

MUTUAL

Ro 1.12 *m* faith both of you and me.

MUZZLE

Dt 25. 4 not *m* the ox when he treadeth
1Co 9. 9 not *m* the mouth of the ox that
1Ti 5.18 not *m* the ox that treadeth out

MYRA

Ac 27. 5 we came to *M*, a city of Lycia.

MYRRH

Gen 37.25 bearing spicery and balm and *m*,
43.11 spices, and *m*, nuts, and almonds:
Ex 30.23 of pure *m* five hundred shekels,
Est 2.12 six months with oil of *m*, and six
Ps 45. 8 thy garments smell of *m*, and aloes,
Pr 7.17 I have perfumed my bed with *m*,
SS 1.13 A bundle of *m* is my wellbeloved
3. 6 of smoke, perfumed with *m* and
4. 6 will get me to the mountain of *m*,
14 *m* and aloes, with all the chief
5. 1 gathered my *m* with my spice; I
5 my hands dropped with *m*, and my
5 my fingers with sweet smelling *m*,
13 lilies, dropping sweet smelling *m*.
Mt 2.11 gold, and frankincense, and *m*.
Mk 15.23 to drink wine mingled with *m*:
Jn 19.39 a mixture of *m* and aloes, about

MYSIA

Ac 16. 7 After they were come to *M*, they
8 passing by *M* came down to Troas.

MYSTERIES

Mt 13.11 the *m* of the kingdom of heaven,
Lk 8.10 the *m* of the kingdom of God:
1Co 4. 1 and stewards of the *m* of God.
13. 2 and understand all *m*, and all
14. 2 in the spirit he speaketh *m*.

MYSTERY

Mk 4.11 the *m* of the kingdom of God:
Ro 11.25 ye should be ignorant of this *m*,
16.25 to the revelation of the *m*, which
1Co 2. 7 speak the wisdom of God in a *m*,
15.51 I shew you a *m*; We shall not all
Eph 1. 9 known unto us the *m* of his will,
3. 3 he made known unto me the *m*;
4 my knowledge in the *m* of Christ)
9 what is the fellowship of the *m*,
5.32 This is a great *m*: but I speak
6.19 make known the *m* of the gospel,
Col 1.26 even the *m* which hath been hid
27 glory of this *m* among the Gentiles;
2. 2 acknowledgment of the *m* of God,
4. 3 to speak the *m* of Christ, for which
2Th 2. 7 *m* of iniquity doth already work:
1Ti 3. 9 Holding the *m* of the faith in a
16 great is the *m* of godliness:
Rev 1.20 The *m* of the seven stars which
10. 7 the *m* of God should be finished,
17. 5 written, *M*, Babylon The Great,
7 will tell thee the *m* of the woman,

N

NAAMAN
2Ki 5. 1 Now *N*, captain of the host of the
11 But *N* was wroth, and went away,
Lk 4.27 cleansed, saving *N* the Syrian.

NAAMAN'S
2Ki 5. 2 maid; and she waited on *N* wife.

NAHUM
Na 1. 1 the vision of *N* the Elkoshite.

NAIL
Jdg 4.21 Heber's wife took a *n* of the tent,
21 and smote the *n* into his temples,
22 dead, and the *n* was in his temples.
5.26 She put her hand to the *n*, and her
Ezr 9. 8 to give us a *n* in his holy place,
Isa 22.23 fasten him as a *n* in a sure place;
25 *n* that is fastened in the sure place
Zec 10. 4 out of him the *n*, out of him the

NAILING
Col 2.14 out of the way, *n* it to his cross:

NAILS
Dt 21.12 shave her head, and pare her *n*;
1Ch 22. 3 iron in abundance for the *n* for
2Ch 3. 9 weight of the *n* was fifty shekels
Ec 12.11 as *n* fastened by the masters of
Isa 41. 7 and he fastened it with *n*, that it
Jer 10. 4 it with *n* and with hammers, that
Dan 4.33 and his *n* like birds' claws.
7.19 were of iron, and his *n* of brass;
Jn 20.25 in his hands the print of the *n*,
25 my finger into the print of the *n*,

NAIN
Lk 7.11 that he went into a city called *N*;

NAKED
Gen 2.25 they were both *n*, the man and
3. 7 knew that they were *n*; and they
10 I was afraid, because I was *n*;
11 Who told thee that thou wast *n*?
Ex 32.25 saw that the people were *n*,
25 had made them *n* unto their shame
1Sa 19.24 lay down *n* all that day and all
2Ch 28.15 all that were *n* among them, and
19 Israel; for he made Judah *n*,
Job 1.21 *N* came I out of my mother's
21 and *n* shall I return thither: the
22. 6 stripped the *n* of their clothing.
24. 7 the *n* to lodge without clothing,
10 him to go *n* without clothing, and
26. 6 Hell is *n* before him, and
Ec 5.15 *n* shall he return to go as he came,
Isa 20. 2 he did so, walking *n* and barefoot.
3 servant Isaiah hath walked *n* and
4 young and old, *n* and barefoot,
58. 7 when thou seest the *n*, that thou
La 4.21 and shalt make thyself *n*.
Eze 16. 7 whereas thou wast *n* and bare.
22 youth, when thou wast *n* and bare,
39 jewels, and leave these *n* and bare.
18. 7 hath covered the *n* with a garment;
16 hath covered the *n* with a garment,
23.29 and shall leave thee *n* and bare:
Hos 2. 3 Lest I strip her *n*, and set her as
Am 2.16 the mighty shall flee away *n* in
Mic 1. 8 howl, I will go stripped and *n*:
11 of Saphir, having thy shame *n*:
Hab 3. 9 Thy bow was made quite *n*,
Mt 25.36 *N*, and ye clothed me: I was sick
38 thee in? or *n*, and clothed thee?
43 *n*, and ye clothed me not: sick,
44 or *n*, or sick, or in prison, and did
Mk 14.51 linen cloth cast about his *n* body;
52 linen cloth, and fled from them *n*.
Jn 21. 7 coat unto him, (for he was *n*,) and
Ac 19.16 out of that house *n* and wounded.
1Co 4.11 hunger, and thirst, and are *n*,
2Co 5. 3 clothed we shall not be found *n*.
Heb 4.13 all things are *n* and opened unto
Jas 2.15 If a brother or sister be *n*, and
Rev 3.17 and poor, and blind, and *n*:
16.15 lest he walk *n*, and they see his
17.16 and shall make her desolate and *n*,

NAKEDNESS
Gen 42. 9, 12 to see the *n* of the land ye are
Ex 28.42 them linen breeches to cover their *n*;
Ro 8.35 famine, or *n*, or peril, or sword?
2Co 11.27 in fastings often, in cold and *n*.
Rev 3.18 the shame of thy *n* do not appear;

NAME
Gen 4.26 men to call upon the *n* of the Lord.
11. 4 and let us make us a *n*, lest we be
9 is the *n* of it called Babel; because
13. 4 Abram called on the *n* of the Lord.
17. 5 thy *n* any more be called Abram,
5 but thy *n* shall be Abraham;
28.19 called the *n* of that place Beth-el:
32.27 What is thy *n*? And he said, Jacob.
28 *n* shall be called no more Jacob,
29 said, Tell me, I pray thee, thy *n*.
30 called the *n* of the place Peniel:
35.10 Jacob, but Israel shall be thy *n*:
Ex 2.10 son. And she called his *n* Moses:
6. 3 by my *n* Jehovah was I not known
20. 7 the *n* of the Lord thy God in vain;
7 guiltless that taketh his *n* in vain.
24 in all places where I record my *n* I
33.19 proclaim the *n* of the Lord before
34.14 the Lord, whose *n* is Jealous, is a
Lev 21. 6 and not profane the *n* of their God:
Dt 5.11 the *n* of the Lord thy God in vain:
11 guiltless that taketh his *n* in vain.
12.21 God hath chosen to put his *n* there
18. 5 to minister in the *n* of the Lord,
20 presume to speak a word in my *n*,
28.58 fear this glorious and fearful *n*,
29.20 blot out his *n* from under heaven.
Jos 23. 7 make mention of the *n* of their gods,
Jdg 13.24 a son, and called his *n* Samson:
16. 4 of Sorek, whose *n* was Delilah.
Ru 1. 2 the *n* of the man was Elimelech,
2 and the *n* of his wife Naomi, and
2 the *n* of his two sons Mahlon and
4 Moab; the *n* of the one was Orpah,
4 and the *n* of the other Ruth: and
1Sa 17.23 the Philistine of Gath, Goliath by *n*,
25.25 even Nabal: for as his *n* is, so is he;
25 Nabal is his *n*, and folly is with him:
1Ki 8.20 an house for the *n* of the Lord God
29 thou hast said, My *n* shall be there:
43 people of the earth may know thy *n*,
18.24 And call ye on the *n* of your gods,
24 and I will call on the *n* of the Lord:
2Ki 21. 4 said, In Jerusalem will I put my *n*.
1Ch 16.10 Glory ye in his holy *n*: let the heart
29 the Lord the glory due unto his *n*:
35 we may give thanks to thy holy *n*,
17.24 thy *n* may be magnified for ever,
Neh 1. 9 I have chosen to set my *n* there.
9. 5 and blessed be thy glorious *n*,
10 So didst thou get thee a *n*, as it is
Job 1.21 away; blessed be the *n* of the Lord.
Ps 7.17 will sing praise to the *n* of the Lord
8. 1, 9 excellent is thy *n* in all the earth!
9. 2 I will sing praise to thy *n*, O thou
20. 5 in the *n* of our God we will set up
29. 2 the Lord the glory due unto his *n*;
34. 3 me, and let us exalt his *n* together.
44. 8 day long, and praise thy *n* for ever.
20 we have forgotten the *n* of our God,
54. 1 Save me, O God, by thy *n*, and
68. 4 upon the heavens by his *n* JAH,
69.30 will praise the *n* of God with a song,
72.17 His *n* shall endure for ever:
17 his *n* shall be continued as long as
19 blessed be his glorious *n* for ever:
79. 6 that have not called upon thy *n*.
92. 1 to sing praises unto thy *n*, O most
96. 2 Sing unto the Lord, bless his *n*;
8 the Lord the glory due unto his *n*:
100. 4 thankful unto him, and bless his *n*.
103. 1 that is within me, bless his holy *n*.
106.47 to give thanks unto thy holy *n*, and
113. 2 Blessed be the *n* of the Lord from
118.26 that cometh in the *n* of the Lord:
122. 4 give thanks unto the *n* of the Lord.
124. 8 Our help is in the *n* of the Lord,
129. 8 we bless you in the *n* of the Lord.
135.13 Thy *n*, O Lord, endureth for ever;
139.20 and thine enemies take thy *n* in vain.
145. 1 I will bless thy *n* for ever and ever.
21 let all flesh bless his holy *n* for ever
149. 3 Let them praise his *n* in the dance:
Pr 18.10 *n* of the Lord is a strong tower:
22. 1 A good *n* is rather to be chosen
Ec 7. 1 A good *n* is better than precious
Isa 9. 6 his *n* shall be called Wonderful,
26. 8 the desire of our soul is to thy *n*,
13 will we make mention of thy *n*.
42. 8 I am the Lord: that is my *n*: and
43. 1 thee, I have called thee by thy *n*;
47. 4 the Lord of hosts is his *n*, the
52. 6 my people shall know my *n*:
54. 5 the Lord of hosts is his *n*; and thy
55.13 and it shall be to the Lord for a *n*,
57.15 eternity, whose *n* is Holy; I dwell
62. 2 thou shalt be called by a new *n*,
64. 7 is none that calleth upon thy *n*,
Jer 7.12 where I set my *n* at the first, and
10.16 The Lord of hosts is his *n*.
11.21 Prophesy not in the *n* of the Lord,
14.14 prophets prophesy lies in my *n*:
31.35 roar; The Lord of hosts is his *n*:
33. 9 it shall be to me a *n* of joy, a praise
46.18 King, whose *n* is the Lord of hosts,
Eze 20.39 but pollute ye my holy *n* no more
36.23 I will sanctify my great *n*, which
Dan 2.20 Blessed be the *n* of God for ever
26 Daniel, whose *n* was Belteshazzar,
Hos 1. 6 unto him, Call her *n* Lo-ruhamah:
9 said God, Call his *n* Lo-ammi:
Joel 2.26 praise the *n* of the Lord your God,
Am 4.13 Lord, The God of hosts, is his *n*.
6.10 make mention of the *n* of the Lord.
Mic 4. 5 walk every one in the *n* of his god,
6. 9 the man of wisdom shall see thy *n*:
Zep 3.20 I will make you a *n* and a praise
Zec 6.12 the man whose *n* is The Branch;
13. 3 speakest lies in the *n* of the Lord:
9 they shall call on my *n*, and I will
14. 9 there be one Lord, and his *n* one.
Mal 1. 6 Wherein have we despised thy *n*?
11 same my *n* shall be great among
11 incense shall be offered unto my *n*,
2. 2 to heart, to give glory unto my *n*,
Mt 1.21 and thou shalt call his *n* Jesus:
23 they shall call his *n* Emmanuel,
25 son: and he called his *n* Jesus.
6. 9 art in heaven, Hallowed be thy *n*.
7.22 have we not prophesied in thy *n*?
22 and in thy *n* have cast out devils?
22 and in thy *n* done many wonderful

Mt 10.41 a prophet in the *n* of a prophet
41 man in the *n* of a righteous man
42 water only in the *n* of a disciple,
12.21 in his *n* shall the Gentiles trust.
18. 5 one such little child in my *n*
20 are gathered together in my *n*,
21. 9 that cometh in the *n* of the Lord;
23.39 that cometh in the *n* of the Lord.
24. 5 many shall come in my *n*, saying,
27.32 a man of Cyrene, Simon by *n*: him
28.19 them in the *n* of the Father, and of
Mk 5. 9 What is thy *n*? And he answered,
9 My *n* is Legion: for we are many.
22 of the synagogue, Jairus by *n*;
6.14 (for his *n* was spread abroad:) and
9.37 one of such children in my *n*,
38 saw one casting out devils in thy *n*,
39 which shall do a miracle in my *n*,
41 a cup of water to drink in my *n*,
11. 9 that cometh in the *n* of the Lord:
10 that cometh in the *n* of the Lord:
13. 6 many shall come in my *n*, saying,
16.17 In my *n* shall they cast out devils;
Lk 1. 5 of Aaron, and her *n* was Elisabeth.
13 son, and thou shalt call his *n* John.
27 to a man whose *n* was Joseph, of
27 David; and the virgin's *n* was Mary.
31 a son, and shalt call his *n* Jesus.
49 me great things; and holy is his *n*.
59 Zacharias, after the *n* of his father.
61 thy kindred that is called by this *n*.
63 and wrote, saying, His *n* is John.
2.21 the child, his *n* was called Jesus,
25 Jerusalem, whose *n* was Simeon;
6.22 and cast out your *n* as evil, for the
8.30 asked him, saying, What is thy *n*?
9.48 receive this child in my *n* receiveth
49 saw one casting out devils in thy *n*;
10.17 are subject unto us through thy *n*.
11. 2 art in heaven, Hallowed be thy *n*.
13.35 that cometh in the *n* of the Lord.
19.38 that cometh in the *n* of the Lord:
21. 8 many shall come in my *n*, saying,
24.18 one of them, whose *n* was Cleopas,
47 be preached in his *n* among all
Jn 1. 6 sent from God, whose *n* was John.
12 even to them that believe on his *n*:
2.23 feast day, many believed in his *n*,
3.18 not believed in the *n* of the only
5.43 I am come in my Father's *n*, and
43 if another shall come in his own *n*,
10. 3 he calleth his own sheep by *n*, and
25 works that I do in my Father's *n*,
12.13 that cometh in the *n* of the Lord.
28 Father, glorify thy *n*. Then came
14.13 whatsoever ye shall ask in my *n*,
14 If ye shall ask any thing in my *n*,
26 whom the Father will send in my *n*,
15.16 ye shall ask of the Father in my *n*,
16.23 ye shall ask the Father in my *n*, he
24 have ye asked nothing in my *n*:
26 At that day ye shall ask in my *n*:
17. 6 manifested thy *n* unto the men
11 keep through thine own *n* those
12 in the world, I kept them in thy *n*:
26 I have declared unto them thy *n*,
18.10 ear. The servant's *n* was Malchus.
20.31 ye might have life through his *n*.
Ac 2.21 shall call on the *n* of the Lord shall
38 one of you in the *n* of Jesus Christ
3. 6 the *n* of Jesus Christ of Nazareth
16 his *n* through faith in his *n* hath
4. 7 or by what *n*, have ye done this?
10 the *n* of Jesus Christ of Nazareth,
12 there is none other *n* under heaven
17 henceforth to no man in this *n*.
18 at all nor teach in the *n* of Jesus.
30 by the *n* of thy holy child Jesus.
5.28 that ye should not teach in this *n*?
40 should not speak in the *n* of Jesus,
41 worthy to suffer shame for his *n*.
7.58 man's feet, whose *n* was Saul.
8.12 of God, and the *n* of Jesus Christ,
16 baptized in the *n* of the Lord Jesus.)
9.14 to bind all that call on thy *n*.
15 to bear my *n* before the Gentiles,
21 called on this *n* in Jerusalem,
27 at Damascus in the *n* of Jesus.
29 boldly in the *n* of the Lord Jesus,
10.43 that through his *n* whosoever
48 to be baptized in the *n* of the Lord.
13. 6 a Jew, whose *n* was Bar-jesus:
8 (for so is his *n* by interpretation)
15.14 take out of them a people for his *n*.
17 upon whom my *n* is called, saith
26 lives for the *n* of our Lord Jesus
16.18 in the *n* of Jesus Christ to come out
19. 5 baptized in the *n* of the Lord Jesus.
13 spirits the *n* of the Lord Jesus,
17 *n* of the Lord Jesus was magnified.
21.13 Jerusalem for the *n* of the Lord
22.16 sins, calling on the *n* of the Lord.
26. 9 things contrary to the *n* of Jesus of
28. 7 the island, whose *n* was Publius;
Ro 1. 5 faith among all nations, for his *n*:
2.24 the *n* of God is blasphemed among
9.17 and that my *n* might be declared
10.13 shall call upon the *n* of the Lord
15. 9 the Gentiles, and sing unto thy *n*.
1Co 1. 2 call upon the *n* of Jesus Christ
10 by the *n* of our Lord Jesus Christ,
13 were ye baptized in the *n* of Paul?
15 that I had baptized in mine own *n*.
5. 4 In the *n* of our Lord Jesus Christ,
6.11 in the *n* of the Lord Jesus, and by
Eph 1.21 and every *n* that is named, not
5.20 in the *n* of our Lord Jesus Christ;
Php 2. 9 him a *n* which is above every *n*:
10 That at the *n* of Jesus every knee
Col 3.17 do all in the *n* of the Lord Jesus,
2Th 1.12 That the *n* of our Lord Jesus
3. 6 in the *n* of our Lord Jesus Christ,
1Ti 6. 1 that the *n* of God and his doctrine
2Ti 2.19 one that nameth the *n* of Christ
Heb 1. 4 a more excellent *n* than they.
2.12 declare thy *n* unto my brethren,
6.10 which ye have shewed toward his *n*,
13.15 of our lips giving thanks to his *n*.
Jas 2. 7 *n* by the which ye are called?
5.10 have spoken in the *n* of the Lord,
14 him with oil in the *n* of the Lord:
1Pe 4.14 be reproached for the *n* of Christ,
1Jn 3.23 believe on the *n* of his Son Jesus
5.13 believe on the *n* of the Son of God;
13 believe on the *n* of the Son of God.
3Jn 14 thee. Greet the friends by *n*.
Rev 2.13 thou holdest fast my *n*, and hast
17 and in the stone a new *n* written,
3. 1 that thou hast a *n* that thou livest,
5 not blot out his *n* out of the book
5 will confess his *n* before my Father,
8 word, and hast not denied my *n*.
12 *n* of my God, and the *n* of the city
12 I will write upon him my new *n*.
6. 8 his *n* that sat on him was Death,
8.11 *n* of the star is called Wormwood:
9.11 whose *n* in the Hebrew tongue is
11 Greek tongue hath his *n* Apollyon.
11.18 and them that fear thy *n*, small and
13. 1 upon his heads the *n* of blasphemy.
6 against God, to blaspheme his *n*,
17 had the mark, or the *n* of the beast,
17 the beast, or the number of his *n*.
14. 1 having his Father's *n* written in
11 receiveth the mark of his *n*.
15. 2 and over the number of his *n*,
4 O Lord, and glorify thy *n*? for thou
16. 9 and blasphemed the *n* of God,
17. 5 upon her forehead was a *n* written,
19.12 and he had a *n* written, that no
13 his *n* is called The Word of God.
16 and on his thigh a *n* written, King
22. 4 his *n* shall be in their foreheads.

NAMED

Gen 27.36 Is not he rightly *n* Jacob?
Jos 2. 1 into an harlot's house, *n* Rahab,
1Sa 17. 4 *n* Goliath, of Gath, whose height
2Ki 17.34 of Jacob, whom he *n* Israel;
Ec 6.10 which hath been is *n* already,
Isa 61. 6 shall be *n* the Priests of the Lord:
Jer 44.26 my name shall no more be *n* in the
Dan 5.12 whom the king *n* Belteshazzar:
Mt 9. 9 a man, *n* Matthew, sitting at the
27.57 a rich man of Arimathaea, *n* Joseph,
Mk 14.32 a place which was *n* Gethsemane:
15. 7 there was one *n* Barabbas, which
Lk 1. 5 a certain priest *n* Zacharias, of
26 unto a city of Galilee, *n* Nazareth,
2.21 which was so *n* of the angel
5.27 forth, and saw a publican, *n* Levi,
6.13 twelve, whom also he *n* apostles;
14 Simon, (whom he also *n* Peter,)
8.41 there came a man *n* Jairus, and he
10.38 woman *n* Martha received him into
16.20 was a certain beggar *n* Lazarus,
19. 2 there was a man *n* Zacchaeus,
23.50 behold, there was a man *n* Joseph,
Jn 3. 1 of the Pharisees, *n* Nicodemus,
11. 1 a certain man was sick, *n* Lazarus,
49 And one of them, *n* Caiaphas, being
Ac 5. 1 But a certain man *n* Ananias,
34 a Pharisee, *n* Gamaliel, a doctor
9.10 disciple at Damascus, *n* Ananias;
12 vision a man *n* Ananias coming in,
33 he found a certain man *n* Aeneas,
36 Joppa a certain disciple *n* Tabitha,
11.28 stood up one of them *n* Agabus,
12.13 damsel came to hearken, *n* Rhoda.
16. 1 disciple was there, *n* Timotheus,
14 woman *n* Lydia, a seller of purple,
17.34 a woman *n* Damaris, and others
18. 2 Jew *n* Aquila, born in Pontus,
7 a certain man's house, *n* Justus,
24 And a certain Jew *n* Apollos, born
19.24 man *n* Demetrius, a silversmith,
20. 9 a certain young man *n* Eutychus,
21.10 Judea a certain prophet, *n* Agabus.
24. 1 with a certain orator *n* Tertullus,
27. 1 other prisoners unto one *n* Julius,
Ro 15.20 gospel, not where Christ was *n*,
1Co 5. 1 so much as *n* among the Gentiles,
Eph 1.21 and every name that is *n*, not only
3.15 family in heaven and earth is *n*,
5. 3 let it not be once *n* among you,

NAME'S

Ps 23. 3 of righteousness for his *n* sake.
79. 9 away our sins, for thy *n* sake.
143.11 Quicken me, O Lord, for thy *n* sake:
Jer 14.21 Do not abhor us, for thy *n* sake,
Eze 20.44 wrought with you for my *n* sake,
36.22 but for mine holy *n* sake, which ye
Mt 10.22 hated of all men for my *n* sake:
19.29 children, or lands, for my *n* sake,
24. 9 hated of all nations for my *n* sake.
Mk 13.13 be hated of all men for my *n* sake:
Lk 21.12 kings and rulers for my *n* sake.
17 be hated of all men for my *n* sake.
Jn 15.21 they do unto you for my *n* sake,
Ac 9.16 he must suffer for my *n* sake.
1Jn 2.12 are forgiven you for his *n* sake,
3Jn 7 that for his *n* sake they went forth,
Rev 2. 3 and for my *n* sake hast labored,

NAMES

Ex 28.10 Six of their *n* on one stone, and the
10 six *n* of the rest on the other stone,
12 shall bear their *n* before the Lord
Ps 16. 4 nor take up their *n* into my lips.
49.11 call their lands after their own *n*.
147. 4 he calleth them all by their *n*.

Isa 40.26 he calleth them all by *n* by the
Zec 13. 2 will cut off the *n* of the idols out of
Mt 10. 2 the *n* of the twelve apostles are
Lk 10.20 your *n* are written in heaven.
Ac 1.15 (the number of the *n* together were
18.15 if it be a question of words and *n*,
Php 4. 3 whose *n* are in the book of life.
Rev 3. 4 hast a few *n* even in Sardis which
13. 8 whose *n* are not written in the
17. 3 full of *n* of blasphemy, having
8 whose *n* were not written in the
21.12 angels, and *n* written thereon,
12 are the *n* of the twelve tribes of the
14 them the *n* of the twelve apostles

NAMETH
2Ti 2.19 one that *n* the name of Christ

NAOMI
Ru 1. 2 and the name of his wife *N*, and
8 *N* said unto her two daughters in
11 *N* said, Turn again, my daughters:
19 them, and they said, Is this *N*?
20 them, Call me not *N*, call me Mara:
21 why then call ye me *N*, seeing the
22 So *N* returned, and Ruth the
2. 1 *N* had a kinsman of her husband's,
2 Ruth the Moabitess said unto *N*,
6 damsel that came back with *N*
20 *N* said unto her daughter in law,
20 *N* said unto her, The man is near
22 *N* said unto Ruth her daughter in
3. 1 *N* her mother in law said unto her,
4. 3 he said unto the kinsman, *N*, that
5 buyest the field of the hand of *N*,
9 and Mahlon's, of the hand of *N*.
14 women said unto *N*, Blessed be
16 *N* took the child, and laid it in her
17 saying, There is a son born to *N*;

NAOMI'S
Ru 1. 3 And Elimelech *N* husband died;

NAPKIN
Lk 19.20 which I have kept laid up in a *n*:
Jn 11.44 face was bound about with a *n*.
20. 7 And the *n*, that was about his head,

NARCISSUS
Ro 16.11 that be of the household of *N*,

NARROW
Nu 22.26 further, and stood in a *n* place,
Jos 17.15 mount Ephraim be too *n* for thee.
1Ki 6. 4 he made windows of *n* lights.
Pr 23.27 and a strange woman is a *n* pit.
Isa 49.19 even now be too *n* by reason of
Eze 40.16 *n* windows to the little chambers,
41.16 posts, and the *n* windows, and the
26 were *n* windows and palm trees
Mt 7.14 is the gate, and *n* is the way,

NARROWED
1Ki 6. 6 he made *n* rests round about,

NARROWER
Isa 28.20 covering *n* than that he can wrap

NARROWLY
Job 13.27 and lookest *n* unto all my paths;
Isa 14.16 that see thee shall *n* look upon thee,

NATHAN
2Sa 5.14 Shammuah, and Shobab, and *N*,
7. 2 the king said unto *N* the prophet,
3 And *N* said unto the king, Go, do
4 the word of the Lord came unto *N*,
17 vision, so did *N* speak unto David.
12. 1 And the Lord sent *N* unto David.
5 he said to *N*, As the Lord liveth,
7 And *N* said to David, Thou art the
13 David said unto *N*, I have sinned
13 *N* said unto David, The Lord also
15 And *N* departed unto his house.
25 sent by the hand of *N* the prophet;
23.36 Igal the son of *N* of Zobah, Bani
1Ki 1. 8 *N* the prophet, and Shimei, and
10 *N* the prophet, and Benaiah, and
11 *N* spake unto Bathsheba the
22 king, *N* the prophet also came in.
23 saying, Behold *N* the prophet.
24 And *N* said, My lord, O king, hast
32 the priest, and *N* the prophet, and
34 priest and *N* the prophet anoint
38, 44 the priest, and *N* the prophet,
45 *N* the prophet have anointed him
4. 5 the son of *N* was over the officers:
5 Zabud the son of *N* was principal
1Ch 2.36 Attai begat *N*, and *N* begat
3. 5 Shimea, and Shobab, and *N*, and
11.38 Joel the brother of *N*, Mibhar the
14. 4 and Shobab, *N*, and Solomon.
17. 1 that David said to *N* the prophet,
2 *N* said unto David, Do all that is
3 word of God came to *N*, saying,
15 vision, so did *N* speak unto David.
29.29 and in the book of *N* the prophet,
2Ch 9.29 in the book of *N* the prophet, and
29.25 king's seer, and *N* the prophet:
Ezr 8.16 for *N*, and for Zechariah, and for
10.39 Shelemiah, and *N*, and Adaiah,
Ps 51(T) *N* the prophet came unto him,
Zec 12.12 the family of the house of *N* a part,
Lk 3.31 which was the son of *N*, which

NATHANAEL
Jn 1.45 Philip findeth *N*, and saith unto
46 *N* said unto him, Can there any
47 Jesus saw *N* coming to him, and
48 *N* saith unto him, Whence knowest
49 *N* answered and saith unto him,
21. 2 Didymus, and *N* of Cana in Galilee,

NATION
Gen 12. 2 I will make of thee a great *n*, and
15.14 also that *n*, whom they shall serve,
17.20 and I will make him a great *n*.
18.18 become a great and might *n*, and
20. 4 wilt thou slay also a righteous *n*?
21.13 of the bondwoman will I make a *n*,
18 for I will make him a great *n*.
35.11 a *n* and a company of nations shall
46. 3 I will there make of thee a great *n*:
Ex 9.24 land of Egypt since it became a *n*.
19. 6 kingdom of priests, and an holy *n*.
21. 8 to sell her unto a strange *n* he
32.10 and I will make of thee a great *n*.
33.13 consider that this *n* is thy people.
34.10 done in all the earth, nor in any *n*:
Lev 18.26 neither any of your own *n*, nor any
20.23 not walk in the manners of the *n*,
Nu 14.12 and will make of thee a greater *n*
Dt 4. 6 Surely this great *n* is a wise and
7 what *n* is there so great, who hath
8 what *n* is there so great, that hath
34 a *n* from the midst of another *n*,
9.14 I will make of thee a *n* mightier
26. 5 with a few, and became there a *n*,
28.33 shall a *n* which thou knowest not
36 unto a *n* which neither thou nor
49 Lord shall bring a *n* against thee
49 a *n* whose tongue thou shalt not
50 A *n* of fierce countenance, which
32.21 them to anger with a foolish *n*.
28 For they are a *n* void of counsel,
2Sa 7.23 what one *n* in the earth is like thy
1Ki 18.10 there is no *n* or kingdom, whither
10 took an oath of the kingdom and *n*,
2Ki 17.29 every *n* made gods of their own,
29 every *n* in their cities wherein they
1Ch 16.20 And when they went from *n* to *n*,
17.21 what one *n* in the earth is like thy
2Ch 15. 6 *n* was destroyed of *n*, and city of
32.15 for no god of any *n* or kingdom was
Job 34.29 done against a *n*, or against a man
Ps 33.12 Blessed is the *n* whose God is the
43. 1 my cause against an ungodly *n*:
83. 4 let us cut them off from being a *n*;
105.13 they went from one *n* to another,
106. 5 rejoice in the gladness of thy *n*,
147.20 He hath not dealt so with any *n*:
Pr 14.34 Righteousness exalteth a *n*: but
Isa 1. 4 Ah sinful *n*, a people laden with
2. 4 *n* shall not lift up sword against *n*,
9. 3 Thou hast multiplied the *n*, and
10. 6 send him against an hypocritical *n*,
14.32 answer the messengers of the *n*?
18. 2 to a *n* scattered and peeled, to a
2 a *n* meted out and trodden down,
7 a *n* meted out and trodden under
26. 2 that the righteous *n* which keepeth
15 Thou hast increased the *n*, O Lord,
15 O Lord, thou hast increased the *n*:
49. 7 to him whom the *n* abhorreth, to
51. 4 and give ear unto me, O my *n*:
55. 5 shalt call a *n* that thou knowest
58. 2 as a *n* that did righteousness, and
60.12 *n* and kingdom that will not serve
22 and a small one a strong *n*; I the
65. 1 *n* that was not called by my name.
66. 8 or shall a *n* be born at once? for as
Jer 2.11 Hath a *n* changed their gods, which
5. 9 my soul be avenged on such a *n* as
15 I will bring a *n* upon you from far,
15 it is a mighty *n*, it is an ancient *n*,
15 a *n* whose language thou knowest
29 my soul be avenged on such a *n* as
6.22 a great *n* shall be raised from the
7.28 is a *n* that obeyeth not the voice of
9. 9 my soul be avenged on such a *n* as
12.17 pluck up and destroy that *n*, saith
18. 7 I shall speak concerning a *n*, and
8 If that *n*, against whom I have
9 I shall speak concerning a *n*, and
25.12 the king of Babylon, and that *n*,
32 evil shall go forth from *n* to *n*, and
27. 8 the *n* and kingdom which will not
8 that *n* will I punish, saith the Lord,
13 against the *n* that will not serve
31.36 shall cease from being a *n* before
33.24 that they should be no more a *n*
48. 2 and let us cut it off from being a *n*.
49.31 get you up unto the wealthy *n*,
36 shall be no *n* whither the outcasts
50. 3 there cometh up a *n* against her,
41 a great *n*, and many kings shall be
La 4.17 watched for a *n* that could not save
Eze 2. 3 a rebellious *n* that hath rebelled
37.22 I will make them one *n* in the land
Dan 3.29 every people, *n*, and language,
8.22 shall stand up out of the *n*,
12. 1 as never was since there was a *n*
Joel 1. 6 For a *n* is come up upon my land,
Am 6.14 I will raise up against you a *n*, O
Mic 4. 3 *n* shall not lift...sword against *n*,
7 that was cast far off a strong *n*:
Hab 1. 6 Chaldeans, that bitter and hasty *n*,
Zep 2. 1 gather together, O *n* not desired;
5 sea coast, the *n* of the Cherethites!
Hag 2.14 So is this people, and so is this *n*
Mal 3. 9 have robbed me, even this whole *n*.
Mt 21.43 to a *n* bringing forth the fruits
24. 7 For *n* shall rise against *n*, and
Mk 7.26 a Greek, a Syrophenician by *n*;
13. 8 For *n* shall rise against *n*, and
Lk 7. 5 he loveth our *n*, and he hath built
21.10 unto them, *N* shall rise against *n*,
23. 2 found this fellow perverting the *n*,
Jn 11.48 take away both our place and *n*.
50 and that the whole *n* perish not.
51 that Jesus should die for that *n*;
52 And not for that *n* only, but that
18.35 Thine own *n* and the chief priests

Biblical Themes

NATION

I will make of thee a great nation, and I will bless thee, and make thy name great. Gen. 12.2

What nation is there so great, who hath God so nigh unto them, as the Lord our God is in all things that we call upon him for? And what nation is there so great, that hath statutes and judgments so righteous as all this law, which I set before you this day? Dt 4.7-8

A Syrian ready to perish was my father, and he went down into Egypt, and sojourned there with a few, and became there a nation, great, mighty, and populous: and the Egyptians evil entreated us, and afflicted us, and laid upon us hard bondage: and when we cried . . . the Lord heard our voice . . . and the Lord brought us forth out of Egypt with a mighty hand. Dt 26.5-8

We be come from a far country: now therefore make ye a league with us. Jos 9.6

Be of good courage, and let us behave ourselves valiantly for our people, and for the cities of our God. 1Ch 19.13

Why should not my countenance be sad, when the city, the place of my fathers' sepulchers, lieth waste, and the gates thereof are consumed with fire? Neh 2.3

Blessed is the nation whose God is the Lord: and the people whom he hath chosen for his own inheritance. Ps 33.12

Except the Lord keep the city, the watchman waketh but in vain. Ps 127.1

If I forget thee, O Jerusalem, let my right hand forget her cunning. If I do not remember thee, let my tongue cleave to the roof of my mouth; if I prefer not Jerusalem above my chief joy. Ps 137.5-6

Righteousness exalteth a nation: but sin is a reproach to any people. Pr 14.34

Behold, the nations are as a drop of a bucket, and are counted as the small dust of the balance. Isa 40.15

Weep sore for him that goeth away: for he shall return no more, nor see his native country. Jer 22.10

I will make them one nation in the land upon the mountains of Israel; and one king shall be king to them all: and they shall be no more two nations. Eze 37.22

He removeth kings, and setteth up kings. Dan 2.21

Whence comest thou? what is thy country? and of what people art thou? Jon 1.8

The kingdom of God shall be taken from you, and given to a nation bringing forth the fruits thereof. Mt 21.43

Render therefore unto Caesar the things which are Caesar's; and unto God the things that are God's. Mt 22.21

O Jerusalem, Jerusalem, which killest the prophets . . . how often would I have gathered thy children together, as a hen doth gather her brood under her wings, and ye would not! Lk 13.34

[God] hath made of one blood all nations of men for to dwell on all the face of the earth. Ac 17.26

The powers that be are ordained of God. Whosoever therefore resisteth the power, resisteth the ordinance of God. . . . For rulers are not a terror to good works, but to the evil. Ro 13.1-3

Love the brotherhood. Fear God. Honor the king. 1Pe 2.17

Jesus Christ . . . the prince of the kings of the earth. Rev 1.5

Ac 2. 5 men, out of every *n* under heaven.
7. 7 *n* to whom they shall be in bondage
10.22 report among all the *n* of the Jews,
28 or come unto one of another *n*;
35 in every *n* he that feareth him,
24. 2 worthy deeds are done unto this *n*
10 of many years a judge unto this *n*,
17 I came to bring alms to my *n*, and
26. 4 among mine own *n* at Jerusalem,
28.19 that I had ought to accuse my *n* of.
Ro 10.19 and by a foolish *n* I will anger you.
Gal 1.14 many my equals in mine own *n*,
Php 2.15 of a crooked and perverse *n*,
1Pe 2. 9 an holy *n*, a peculiar people;
Rev 5. 9 and tongue, and people, and *n*;
14. 6 every *n*, and kindred, and tongue,

NATIONS

Gen 10. 5 after their families, in their *n*.
20 in their countries, and in their *n*.
31 in their lands, after their *n*.
32 after their generations, in their *n*:
32 were the *n* divided in the earth
14. 1 king of Elam, and Tidal king of *n*;
9 Elam, and with Tidal king of *n*,
17. 4 thou shalt be a father of many *n*.
5 father of many *n* have I made thee.
6 I will make *n* of thee, and kings
16 and she shall be a mother of *n*;
18.18 the *n* of the earth shall be blessed
22.18 all the *n* of the earth be blessed;
25.16 twelve princes according to their *n*.
23 Two *n* are in thy womb, and two
26. 4 all the *n* of the earth be blessed;
27.29 thee, and *n* bow down to thee:
35.11 a company of *n* shall be of thee,
48.19 seed shall become a multitude of *n*.
Ex 34.24 I will cast out the *n* before thee,
Lev 18.24 for in all these the *n* are defiled
28 spued out the *n* that were before
Nu 14.15 the *n* which have heard the fame
23. 9 shall not be reckoned among the *n*.
24. 8 he shall eat up the *n* his enemies,
20 Amalek was the first of the *n*;
Dt 2.25 the *n* that are under the whole
4. 6 understanding...the sight of the *n*,
19 unto all *n* under the whole heaven.
27 shall scatter you among the *n*,
38 To drive out *n* from before thee
7. 1 hath cast out many *n* before thee,
1 seven *n* greater and mightier than
17 These *n* are more than I; how can
22 God will put out those *n* before thee
8.20 As the *n* which the Lord destroyeth
9. 1 possess *n* greater and mightier than
4, 5 but for the wickedness of these *n*
11.23 will the Lord drive out all these *n*
23 possess greater *n* and mightier than
12. 2 the *n* which ye shall possess served
29 God shall cut off the *n* from before
30 How did these *n* serve their gods?
14. 2 all the *n* that are upon the earth.
15. 6 and thou shalt lend unto many *n*,
6 and thou shalt reign over many *n*,
17.14 like as all the *n* that are about me;
18. 9 after the abominations of those *n*.
14 these *n*, which thou shalt possess,
19. 1 Lord thy God hath cut off the *n*,
20.15 are not of the cities of these *n*.
26.19 And to make thee high above all *n*
28. 1 on high above all *n* of the earth:
12 and thou shalt lend unto many *n*,
37 all *n* whither the Lord shall lead
65 among these *n* shalt thou find no
29.16 and how we came through the *n*
18 to go and serve the gods of these *n*;
24 Even all *n* shall say, Wherefore
30. 1 call them to mind among all the *n*,
3 and gather thee from all the *n*,
31. 3 destroy these *n* from before thee,
32. 8 the Most High divided to the *n* their
43 Rejoice, O Ye *n*, with his people:
Jos 12.23 one; the king of the *n* of Gilgal,
23. 3 God hath done unto all these *n*
4 divided unto you by lot these *n* that
4 with all the *n* that I have cut off,
7 That ye come not among these *n*,
9 from before you great *n* and strong:
12 cleave unto the remnant of these *n*,
13 no more drive out any of these *n*
Jdg 2.21 *n* which Joshua left when he died:
23 Therefore the Lord left those *n*,
3. 1 these are the *n* which the Lord left,
1Sa 8. 5 a king to judge us like all the *n*.
20 That we also may be like all the *n*;
27. 8 those *n* were of old the inhabitants
2Sa 7.23 Egypt, from the *n* and their gods?
8.11 dedicated of all *n* which he subdued;
1Ki 4.31 his fame was in all *n* round about.
11. 2 *n* concerning which the Lord said
14.24 to all the abominations of the *n*
2Ki 17.26 The *n* which thou hast removed,
33 manner of the *n* whom they carried
41 So these *n* feared the Lord, and
18.33 of the gods of the *n* delivered at all
19.12 Have the gods of the *n* delivered
17 destroyed the *n* and their lands,

Rev 21.26 glory and honor of the *n* into it.
22. 2 tree were for the healing of the *n*.

NATIVE

Jer 22.10 no more, nor see his *n* country.

NATURAL

Dt 34. 7 not dim, nor his *n* force abated.
Ro 1.26 women did change the *n* use into
27 leaving the *n* use of the woman,
31 without *n* affection, implacable,
11.21 spared not the *n* branches,
24 these, which be the *n* branches,
1Co 2.14 But the *n* man receiveth not the
15.44 It is sown a *n* body; it is raised a
44 There is a *n* body, and there is a
46 is spiritual, but that which is *n*;
2Ti 3. 3 Without *n* affection, trucebreakers,
Jas 1.23 beholding his *n* face in a glass:
2Pe 2.12 But these, as *n* brute beasts, made

NATURALLY

Php 2.20 who will *n* care for your state.
Jude 10 what they know *n*, as brute beasts,

NATURE

Ro 1.26 use into that which is against *n*:
2.14 do by *n* the things contained in the
27 not uncircumcision which is by *n*,
11.24 of the olive tree which is wild by *n*,
24 and wert graffed contrary to *n* into
1Co 11.14 Doth not even *n* itself teach you,
Gal 2.15 We who are Jews by *n*, and not
4. 8 unto them which by *n* are no gods.
Eph 2. 3 were by *n* the children of wrath,
Heb 2.16 he took not on him the *n* of angels;
Jas 3. 6 and setteth on fire the course of *n*;
2Pe 1. 4 be partakers of the divine *n*,

NAUGHTINESS

1Sa 17.28 pride, and the *n* of thine heart;
Pr 11. 6 shall be taken in their own *n*.
Jas 1.21 all filthiness and superfluity of *n*,

NAY

Gen 18.15 he said, *N*; but thou didst laugh.
23.11 *N*, my lord, hear me: the field give
33.10 Jacob said, *N*, I pray thee, if now
42.10 *N*, my lord, but to buy food are
12 *N*, but to see the nakedness of
Nu 22.30 do so unto thee? And he said, *N*.
Jos 5.14 said, *N*; but as captain of the host
24.21 said unto Joshua, *N*; but we will
Jdg 12. 5 thou an Ephraimite? If he said, *N*;
19.23 *N*, my brethren,...I pray you, do
23 *n*, I pray you, do not so wickedly;
Ru 1.13 *n*, my daughters; for it grieveth me
1Sa 2.16 *N*; but thou shalt give it me now:
24 *N*, my sons; for it is no good
8.19 *N*; but we will have a king over
10.19 unto him, *N*, but set a king over us.
12.12 *N*; but a king shall reign over us:
2Sa 13.12 *N*, my brother, do not force me;
25 *N*, my son, let us not all now go,
16.18 Hushai said unto Absalom, *N*;
24.24 the king said unto Araunah, *N*;
1Ki 2.17 he will not say thee *n*,) that he give
20 I pray thee, say me not *n*. And
20 my mother: for I will not say thee *n*.
2.30 he said, *N*; but I will die here.
3.22 And the other woman said, *N*; but
23 saith, *N*; but thy son is the dead,
2Ki 3.13 king of Israel said unto him, *N*:
4.16 said, *N*, my lord, thou man of God,
20.10 *n*, but let the shadow return
1Ch 21.24 And king David said to Ornan, *N*;
Jer 6.15 *n*, they were not at all ashamed,
8.12 *n*, they were not at all ashamed,
Mt 5.37 communication be, Yea, yea; *N*, *n*:
13.29 he said, *N*; lest while ye gather
Lk 12.51 I tell you, *N*; but rather division:
13. 3, 5 tell you, *N*: but, except ye repent,
16.30 And he said, *N*, father Abraham:
Jn 7.12 *N*; but he deceiveth the people.
Ac 16.37 *n* verily; but let them come
Ro 3.27 works? *N*; but by the law of faith.
7. 7 *N*, I had not known sin, but by the
8.37 *N*, in all these things we are more
9.20 *N* but, O man, who art thou that
1Co 6. 8 *N*, ye do wrong, and defraud, and
12.22 *N*, much more those members of the
2Co 1.17 there should be yea yea, and *n n*?
18 word toward you was not yea and *n*.
19 was not yea and *n*, but in him was
Jas 5.12 your yea be yea; and your *n*, *n*;

NAZARENE

Mt 2.23 prophets, He shall be called a *N*.

NAZARENES

Ac 24. 5 a ringleader of the sect of the *N*:

NAZARETH

Mt 2.23 came and dwelt in a city called *N*:
4.13 And leaving *N*, he came and dwelt
21.11 Jesus the prophet of *N* of Galilee.
26.71 fellow was also with Jesus of *N*.
Mk 1. 9 that Jesus came from *N* of Galilee,
24 to do with thee, thou Jesus of *N*?
10.47 he heard that it was Jesus of *N*,

BIBLICAL THEMES

NATURE

In the beginning God created the heaven and the earth. . . . And God saw every thing that he had made, and, behold, it was very good. Gen 1.1, 31

And God looked upon the earth, and, behold, it was corrupt; for all flesh had corrupted his way upon the earth. Gen 6.12

The fear of you and the dread of you shall be upon every beast of the earth, and upon every fowl of the air, upon all that moveth upon the earth, and upon all the fishes of the sea; into your hand are they delivered. Gen 9.2

Blessed of the Lord be his land, for the precious things of heaven, for the dew, and for the deep that coucheth beneath, and for the precious fruits brought forth by the sun. Dt 33.13-14

Ask now the beasts, and they shall teach thee; and the fowls of the air, and they shall tell thee: or speak to the earth, and it shall teach thee: and the fishes of the sea shall declare unto thee. Who knoweth not in all these that the hand of the Lord hath wrought this? Job 12.7-9

Where wast thou when I laid the foundations of the earth? declare, if thou hast understanding. Who hath laid the measures thereof, if thou knowest? or who hath stretched the line upon it? Whereupon are the foundations thereof fastened? or who laid the corner stone thereof; when the morning stars sang together, and all the sons of God shouted for joy? Job 38.4-7

Gavest thou the goodly wings unto the peacocks? or wings and feathers unto the ostrich? which leaveth her eggs in the earth, and warmeth them in dust, and forgetteth that the foot may crush them, or that the wild beast may break them. . . . God hath deprived her of wisdom, neither hath he imparted to her understanding. Job 39.13-15, 17

The voice of the Lord maketh the hinds to calve, and discovereth the forests: and in his temple doth every one speak of his glory. Ps 29.9

O Lord, how manifold are thy works! in wisdom hast thou made them all: the earth is full of thy riches. So is this great and wide sea, wherein are things creeping innumerable, both small and great beasts. Ps 104.24-25

Lo, the winter is past, the rain is over and gone; the flowers appear on the earth; the time of the singing of birds is come, and the voice of the turtle is heard in our land. SS 2.11-12

The wolf also shall dwell with the lamb, and the leopard shall lie down with the kid. . . . They shall not hurt nor destroy in all my holy mountain: for the earth shall be full of the knowledge of the Lord, as the waters cover the sea. Isa 11.6, 9

Consider the lilies of the field, how they grow; they toil not, neither do they spin: and yet I say unto you, That even Solomon in all his glory was not arrayed like one of these. Mt 6.28-29

And they being afraid wondered, saying one to another, What manner of man is this! for he commandeth even the winds and water, and they obey him. Lk 8.25

We know that the whole creation groaneth and travaileth in pain together until now. Ro 8.22

That was not first which is spiritual, but that which is natural; and afterward that which is spiritual. . . . as we have borne the image of the earthy, we shall also bear the image of the heavenly. 1Co 15.46, 49

We, according to his promise, look for new heavens and a new earth, wherein dwelleth righteousness. 2Pe 3.13

14.67 thou also wast with Jesus of *N*.
16. 6 Ye seek Jesus of *N*, which was
Lk 1.26 unto a city of Galilee, named *N*,
2. 4 from Galilee, out of the city of *N*,
39 into Galilee, to their own city *N*.
51 down with them, and came to *N*,
4.16 he came to *N*, where he had been
34 to do with thee, thou Jesus of *N*?
18.37 told him, that Jesus of *N* passeth by.
24.19 Concerning Jesus of *N*, which was
Jn 1.45 Jesus of *N*, the son of Joseph.
46 any good thing come out of *N*?
18. 5 They answered him, Jesus of *N*.
7 seek ye? And they said, Jesus of *N*.
19.19 Jesus Of *N* The King Of The Jews.
Ac 2.22 Jesus of *N*, a man approved of God
3. 6 In the name of Jesus Christ of *N*
4.10 by the name of Jesus Christ of *N*,
6.14 this Jesus of *N* shall destroy this
10.38 How God anointed Jesus of *N* with
22. 8 me, I am Jesus of *N*, whom thou
26. 9 contrary to the name of Jesus of *N*.

NAZARITE

Nu 6. 2 themselves to vow a vow of a *N*,
13 And this is the law of the *N*, when
18 the *N* shall shave the head of his
19 put them upon the hands of the *N*,
20 after that the *N* may drink wine.
21 the law of the *N* who hath vowed,
Jdg 13. 5 the child shall be a *N* unto God
7 for the child shall be a *N* to God
16.17 I have been a *N* unto God from my

NAZARITES

La 4. 7 Her *N* were purer than snow,
Am 2.11 and of your young men for *N*.
12 But ye gave the *N* wine to drink;

NEAPOLIS

Ac 16.11 and the next day to *N*;

NEAR

Gen 12.11 was come *n* to enter into Egypt,
18.23 Abraham drew *n*, and said, Wilt
19. 9 Lot, and came *n* to break the door.
20 this city is *n* to flee unto, and it is
20. 4 Abimelech had not come *n* her:
27.21 unto Jacob, Come *n*, I pray thee,
22 Jacob went *n* unto Isaac his father;
25 Bring it *n* to me, and I will eat of
25 he brought it *n* to him, and he did
26 Come *n* now, and kiss me, my son.
27 he came *n*, and kissed him: and he
29.10 Jacob went *n*, and rolled the stone
33. 3 until he came *n* to his brother.
6 Then the handmaidens came *n*,
7 Leah also with her children came *n*,
7 after came Joseph *n* and Rachel,
37.18 even before he came *n* unto them,
43.19 came *n* to the steward of Joseph's
44.18 Then Judah came *n* unto him, and
45. 4 brethren, Come *n* to me, I pray you.
4 they came *n*. And he said, I am
10 and thou shalt be *n* unto me, thou,
48.10 And he brought them *n* unto him;
13 and brought them *n* unto him.
Ex 12.48 then let him come *n* and keep it;
13.17 Philistines, although that was *n*;
14.20 the one came not *n* the other all
16. 9 of Israel, Come *n* before the Lord:
19.22 also, which come *n* to the Lord,
20.21 drew *n* unto the thick darkness
24. 2 Moses alone shall come *n* the Lord:
28.43 come *n* unto the altar to minister
30.20 come *n* to the altar to minister,
40.32 when they came *n* unto the altar,
Lev 9. 5 all the congregation drew *n* and
10. 4 Come *n*, carry your brethren from
5 So they went *n*, and carried them
18. 6 to any that is *n* of kin to him, to
12 she is thy father's *n* kinswoman.
13 she is thy mother's *n* kinswoman.
17 for they are her *n* kinswomen:
20.19 he uncovereth his *n* kin: they
21. 2 for his kin, that is *n* unto him,
Nu 3. 6 Bring the tribe of Levi *n*, and
5.16 the priest shall bring her *n*, and
16. 5 cause him to come *n* unto him:
5 will he cause to come *n* unto him.
9 to bring you *n* to himself to do
10 he hath brought thee *n* to him,
40 come *n* to offer incense before
17.13 cometh any thing *n* unto the
26. 3 of Moab by Jordan *n* Jericho, saying,
63 plains of Moab by Jordan *n* Jericho,
31.12 which are by Jordan *n* Jericho.
48 of hundreds, came *n* unto Moses;
32.16 they came *n* unto him, and said,
33.50 plains of Moab by Jordan *n* Jericho.
34.15 this side Jordan *n* Jericho eastward,
36. 1 came *n*, and spake before Moses,
13 plains of Moab by Jordan *n* Jericho.
Dt 1.22 ye came *n* unto me every one of
4.11 ye came *n* and stood under the
5.23 that ye came *n* unto me, even all
27 Go thou *n*, and hear all that the
16.21 any trees *n* unto the altar of the
21. 5 the sons of Levi shall come *n*;
25.11 the wife of the one draweth *n* for
Jos 3. 4 come not *n* unto it, that ye may
10.24 Come *n*, put your feet upon the
24 they came *n*, and put their feet
15.46 all that lay *n* Ashdod, with their
17. 4 they came *n* before Eleazar the
18.13 *n* the hill that lieth on the south
21. 1 Then came *n* the heads of the
Jdg 18.22 were in the houses *n* to Micah's
19.13 and let us draw *n* to one of these
20.24 And the children of Israel came *n*
34 knew not that evil was *n* them.
Ru 2.20 The man is *n* of kin unto us, one
3. 9 handmaid; for thou art a *n* kinsman.
12 it is true that I am thy *n* kinsman:
1Sa 4.19 was with child, *n* to be delivered:
7.10 the Philistines drew *n* to battle
9.18 then Saul drew *n* to Samuel in the
10.20 all the tribes of Israel to come *n*,
21 the tribe of Benjamin to come *n* by
14.36 Let us draw *n* hither unto God.
38 Draw ye *n* hither, all the chief of
17.16 the Philistine drew *n* morning and
40 and he drew *n* to the Philistine.
41 Philistine came on and drew *n*
30.21 when David came *n* to the people,
2Sa 1.15 and said, Go *n*, and fall upon him.
14.30 See Joab's field is *n* mine, and he
18.25 And he came apace, and drew *n*.
19.42 the king is *n* of kin to us:
20.16 Come *n* hither, that I may speak
17 And when he was come *n* unto her,
1Ki 8.46 the land of the enemy, far or *n*;
18.30 all the people, Come *n* unto me.
30 all the people came *n* unto him.
36 Elijah the prophet came *n*, and
21. 2 because it is *n* unto my house:
22.24 the son of Chenaanah went *n*, and
2Ki 4.27 Gehazi came *n* to thrust her away.
5.13 And his servants came *n*, and
2Ch 6.36 captives unto a land far off or *n*;
18.23 the son of Chenaanah came *n*,
21.16 that were *n* the Ethiopians:
29.31 come *n* and bring sacrifices and
Est 5. 2 So Esther drew *n*, and touched
9. 1 drew *n* to be put in execution,
Job 31.37 a prince would I go *n* unto him.
33.22 his soul draweth *n* unto the grave,
41.16 One is so *n* to another, that no air
Ps 22.11 not far from me; for trouble is *n*;
32. 9 bridle, lest they come *n* unto thee.
73.28 is good for me to draw *n* to God:
75. 1 name is *n* thy wondrous works
107.18 draw *n* unto the gates of death.
119.151 Thou art *n*, O Lord; and all thy
169 Let my cry come *n* before thee,
148.14 of Israel, a people *n* unto him.
Pr 7. 8 through the street *n* her corner;
10.14 of the foolish is *n* destruction.
27.10 for better is a neighbor that is *n*
Isa 13.22 and her time is *n* to come, and her
26.17 *n* the time of her delivery, is in
29.13 draw *n* me with their mouth, and
33.13 ye that are *n*, acknowledge my
34. 1 Come *n*, ye nations, to hear; and
41. 1 let them come *n*; then let them
1 let us come *n* together to
5 of the earth were afraid, drew *n*,
45.20 draw *n* together, ye that are
21 Tell ye, and bring them *n*; yea, let
46.13 I bring *n* thy righteousness; it
48.16 Come ye *n* unto me, hear ye this;
50. 8 He is *n* that justifieth me; who
8 adversary? let him come *n* to me.
51. 5 My righteousness is *n*; my
54.14 for it shall not come *n* thee.
55. 6 call ye upon him while he is *n*:
56. 1 for my salvation is *n* to come, and
57. 3 But draw *n* hither, ye sons of the
19 is far off, and to him that is *n*,
65. 5 come not *n* to me; for I am holier
Jer 12. 2 thou art *n* in their mouth, and
25.26 the kings of the north, far and *n*,
30.21 will cause him to draw *n*, and he
42. 1 even unto the greatest, came *n*,
46. 3 and shield, and draw *n* to battle.
48.16 calamity of Moab is *n* to come,
24 cities of the land of Moab, far or *n*.
52.25 that were *n* the king's person,
La 3.57 Thou drewest *n* in the day that I
4.18 our end is *n*, our days are fulfilled;
Eze 6.12 that is *n* shall fall by the sword;
7. 7 is come, the day of trouble is *n*,
12 time is come, the day draweth *n*:
9. 1 charge over the city to draw *n*,
6 come not *n* any man upon whom
11. 3 Which say, It is not *n*; let us
18. 6 come *n* to a menstruous woman,
22. 4 hast caused thy days to draw *n*,
5 Those that be *n*, and those that
30. 3 For the day is *n*, even the day of
3 the day of the Lord is *n*, a cloudy
40.46 *n* to the Lord to minister unto
44.13 they shall not come *n* unto me,
13 come *n* to any of my holy things,
15 *n* to me to minister unto me,
16 and they shall come *n* to my table,
45. 4 come *n* to minister unto the Lord:
Dan 3. 8 time certain Chaldeans came *n*,
26 *n* to the mouth of the burning
6.12 came *n*, and spake before the king
7.13 they brought him *n* before him.
16 I came *n* unto one of them that
8.17 So he came *n* where I stood: and
9. 7 and unto all Israel, that are *n*,
Joel 3. 9 let all the men of war draw *n*;
14 the day of the Lord is *n* in the
Am 6. 3 the seat of violence to come *n*;
Ob 15 day of the Lord is *n* upon all the
Zep 1.14 great day of the Lord is *n*, it is *n*,
3. 2 Lord; she drew not *n* to her God.
Mal 3. 5 I will come *n* to you to judgment;
Mt 21.34 when the time of the fruit drew *n*,
24.33 these things, know that it is *n*,
Mk 13.28 leaves, ye know that summer is *n*:
Lk 15. 1 Then drew *n* unto him all the
18.40 when he was come *n*, he asked him,
19.41 when he was come *n*, he beheld
21. 8 the time draweth *n*: go ye not
22.47 drew *n* unto Jesus to kiss him.
24.15 Jesus himself drew *n*, and went
Jn 3.23 baptizing in Aenon *n* to Salim,
4. 5 *n* to the parcel of ground that

NEBUCHADNEZZAR

King of Babylon, late 7th–early 6th centuries B.C.; responsible for the destruction of Jerusalem and the exile of its people to Babylonia. When his father, Nabopolassar, became ill, he took command of the army and marched against Egyptian forces under Pharaoh Necho, who had established a bridgehead at Carchemish on the Upper Euphrates. In 605 B.C. a decisive battle was fought and the Egyptians were defeated. Nebuchadnezzar moved into Syria, crushing resistance and receiving tribute from the local city-states. He returned to Babylon when his father died, in order to secure the throne, but soon resumed the campaign.

It was not long before Judah was involved. With the Egyptians driven back (2Ki 24.7), Jehoiakim, the king of Judah, transferred allegiance to Nebuchadnezzar and became his vassal (2Ki 23.34-35, 24.1). In a bid to recoup his losses, Necho raised another army, and in the subsequent engagement Nebuchadnezzar suffered heavy reverses and had to return to Babylon. Therewith Jehoiakim rebelled (2Ki 24.1), but he had seriously miscalculated. After reorganizing and re-equipping his army, in 597 B.C. Nebuchadnezzar invaded and laid siege to Jerusalem, which soon surrendered. A heavy tribute was exacted; Jehoiachin (who had succeeded his father), his officials, and the leading citizens and artisans were deported to Babylon; and Zedekiah, a younger brother of Jehoiakim and uncle of Jehoiachin, was placed on the throne (2Ki 24.10-17). A weak king, Zedekiah gave in to the pro-Egyptian faction and, relying on Egypt's aid, he too eventually rebelled (2Ki 24.20). Retaliation was swift and severe. Nebuchadnezzar again besieged Jerusalem, suspending the siege temporarily to defeat an advancing Egyptian force (Jer 37.5). When the famine inside the city was at its height, Jerusalem fell (586 B.C.). Its walls were razed, the temple plundered and destroyed, and the bulk of the people taken captive to Babylon (2Ki 25). As later Isaiah spoke of Cyrus the Great, so at this time Jeremiah described Nebuchadnezzar as God's "servant" (Jer 25.9); both were in their different ways seen as serving his higher purposes.

Nebuchadnezzar also devoted much time to restoring his capital city of Babylon, site of the famed "hanging gardens," giving particular attention to building and refurbishing temples (Dan 4.30). Some of the exploits of Daniel and his companions are set within Nebuchadnezzar's court (Dan 1–4). In 567 B.C. Nebuchadnezzar invaded Egypt and brought his empire to the zenith of its power, but it did not long survive his death (562 B.C.) before falling to Cyrus in 539 B.C.

Jn 11.54 a country *n* to the wilderness,
Ac 7.31 and as he drew *n* to behold it, the
8.29 Philip, Go *n*, and join thyself to this
9. 3 journeyed, he came *n* Damascus:
10.24 together his kinsmen and *n* friends.
21.33 chief captain came *n*, and took him,
23.15 ever he come *n*, are ready to kill him.
27.27 that they drew *n* to some country;
Heb 10.22 Let us draw *n* with a true heart

NEARER

Ru 3.12 there is a kinsman *n* than I.
Ro 13.11 is our salvation *n* than when we

NEBUCHADNEZZAR

2Ki 24. 1 *N* king of Babylon came up, and
10 servants of *N* king of Babylon
11 *N* king of Babylon came against
25. 1 that *N* king of Babylon came, he,
8 is the nineteenth year of king *N*
22 whom *N* king of Babylon had left,
1Ch 6.15 and Jerusalem by the hand of *N*.
2Ch 36. 6 Against him came up *N* king of
7 *N* also carried of the vessels of the
10 king *N* sent, and brought him to
13 he also rebelled against king *N*,
Ezr 1. 7 which *N* had brought forth out of
2. 1 whom *N* the king of Babylon had
5.12 he gave them into the hand of *N*
14 which *N* took out of the temple
6. 5 *N* took forth out of the temple
Neh 7. 6 *N* the king of Babylon had carried
Est 2. 6 *N* the king of Babylon had carried
Jer 27. 6 all these lands into the hand of *N*.
8 which will not serve the same *N*
20 Which *N* king of Babylon took not,
28. 3 that *N* king of Babylon took away
11 Even so will I break the yoke of *N*
14 they may serve *N* king of Babylon:
29. 1 whom *N* had carried away captive
3 of Judah sent unto Babylon to *N*
34. 1 when *N* king of Babylon, and all
39. 5 up to *N* king of Babylon to Riblah
Dan 1. 1 came *N* king of Babylon unto
18 eunuchs brought them in before *N*.
2. 1 the second year of the reign of *N*,
1 *N* dreamed dreams, wherewith
28 maketh known to the king *N*
46 the king *N* fell upon his face, and
3. 1 *N* the king made an image of gold,
2 *N* the king sent to gather together
2 the image which *N* the king had
3 image that *N* the king had set up;
3 the image that *N* had set up.
5 image that *N* the king hath set up:
7 image that *N* the king had set up.
9 They spake and said to the king *N*,
13 *N* in his rage and fury commanded
14 *N* spake and said unto them, Is it
16 O *N*, we are not careful to answer
19 Then was *N* full of fury, and the
24 Then *N* the king was astonied,
26 *N* came near to the mouth of the
28 *N* spake, and said, Blessed be the
4. 1 *N* the king, unto all people,
4 I *N* was at rest in mine house, and
18 This dream I king *N* have seen.
28 All this came upon the king *N*.
31 O king *N*, to thee it is spoken; The
33 was the thing fulfilled upon *N*:
34 days I *N* lifted up mine eyes unto
37 I *N* praise and extol and honor
5. 2 which his father *N* had taken out
11 whom the king *N* thy father, the
18 God gave *N* thy father a kingdom,

NECESSARY

Job 23.12 his mouth more than my *n* food.
Ac 13.46 It was *n* that the word of God
15.28 burden than these *n* things;
28.10 such things as were *n*.
1Co 12.22 seem to be more feeble, are *n*:
2Co 9. 5 Therefore I thought it *n* to exhort
Php 2.25 Yet I supposed it *n* to send to you
3.14 maintain good works for *n* uses,
Heb 9.23 was therefore *n* that the patterns

NECESSITIES

Ac 20.34 hands have ministered unto my *n*,
2Co 6. 4 much patience, in affliction, in *n*,
12.10 reproaches, in *n*, in persecutions,

NECESSITY

Lk 23.17 (For of *n* he must release one
Ro 12.13 Distributing to the *n* of saints;
1Co 7.37 stedfast in his heart, having no *n*,
9.16 for *n* is laid upon me; yea, woe is
2Co 9. 7 not grudgingly, or of *n*: for God
Php 4.16 sent once and again unto my *n*.
Phm 14 not be as it were of *n*, but willingly.
Heb 7.12 there is made of *n* a change also
8. 3 wherefore it is of *n* that this man
9.16 there must also of *n* be the death

NECK

Gen 27.16 and upon the smooth of his *n*:
40 shalt break his yoke from off thy *n*.
33. 4 and fell on his *n*, and kissed him:
41.42 and put a gold chain about his *n*;
45.14 fell upon his brother Benjamin's *n*,
14 and Benjamin wept upon his *n*.
46.29 fell on his *n*, and he wept on his *n*
49. 8 shall be in the *n* of thine enemies;
Ex 13.13 it, then thou shalt break his *n*:
34.20 not, then shalt thou break his *n*.
Lev 5. 8 and wring off his head from his *n*,
Dt 21. 4 shall strike off the heifer's *n* there
28.48 put a yoke of iron upon thy *n*,
31.27 thy rebellion, and thy stiff *n*:
1Sa 4.18 and his *n* brake, and he died: for
2Ki 17.14 like to the *n* of their fathers, that
2Ch 36.13 he stiffened his *n*, and hardened
Neh 9.29 hardened their *n*, and would not
Job 15.26 runneth upon him, even on his *n*,
16.12 he hath also taken me by my *n*,
39.19 thou clothed his *n* with thunder?
41.22 In his *n* remaineth strength, and
Ps 75. 5 on high: speak not with a stiff *n*.
Pr 1. 9 thy head, and chains about thy *n*.
3. 3 bind them about thy *n*; write
22 unto thy soul, and grace to thy *n*.
6.21 heart, and tie them about thy *n*.
29. 1 often reproved hardeneth his *n*,
SS 1.10 jewels, thy *n* with chains of gold.
4. 4 Thy *n* is like the tower of David
9 eyes, with one chain of thy *n*.
7. 4 Thy *n* is as a tower of ivory;
Isa 8. 8 over, he shall reach even to the *n*;
10.27 and his yoke from off thy *n*, and
30.28 shall reach to the midst of the *n*,
48. 4 and thy *n* is an iron sinew, and
52. 2 thyself from the bands of thy *n*,
66. 3 a lamb, as if he cut off a dog's *n*;
Jer 7.26 their ear, but hardened their *n*:
17.23 their ear, but made their *n* stiff,
27. 2 yokes, and put them upon thy *n*,
8 will not put their *n* under the yoke
11 that bring their *n* under the yoke
28.10 from off the prophet Jeremiah's *n*,
11 *n* of all nations within the space
12 off the *n* of the prophet Jeremiah,
14 a yoke of iron upon the *n* of all
30. 8 will break his yoke from off thy *n*,
La 1.14 wreathed, and come up upon my *n*:
Eze 16.11 thy hands, and a chain on thy *n*.
Dan 5. 7, 16, 29 chain of gold about his *n*,
Hos 10.11 but I passed over upon her fair *n*:
Hab 3.13 the foundation unto the *n*. Selah.
Mt 18. 6 were hanged about his *n*, and that
Mk 9.42 were hanged about his *n*, and he
Lk 15.20 and fell on his *n*, and kissed him.
17. 2 were hanged about his *n*, and he
Ac 15.10 a yoke upon the *n* of the disciples,
20.37 and fell on Paul's *n*, and kissed him,

NECKS

Jos 10.24 feet upon the *n* of these kings.
24 put their feet upon the *n* of them.
Jdg 5.30 the *n* of them that take the spoil?
8.21 that were on their camels' *n*.
26 that were about their camels' *n*.
2Sa 22.41 given me the *n* of mine enemies,
2Ki 17.14 not hear, but hardened their *n*,
Neh 3. 5 put not their *n* to the work of
9.16 proudly, and hardened their *n*,
17 but hardened their *n*, and in their
Ps 18.40 given me the *n* of mine enemies;
Isa 3.16 walk with stretched forth *n* and
Jer 19.15 they have hardened their *n*, that
27.12 Bring your *n* under the yoke of
La 5. 5 Our *n* are under persecution: we
Eze 21.29 upon the *n* of them that are slain,
Mic 2. 3 which ye shall not remove your *n*;
Ro 16. 4 for my life laid down their own *n*:

NEED

Dt 15. 8 lend him sufficient for his *n*, in
1Sa 21.15 Have I *n* of mad men, that ye
Mt 3.14 I have *n* to be baptized of thee,
6. 8 knoweth what things ye have *n* of,
32 that ye have *n* of all these things.
9.12 be whole *n* not a physician,
14.16 They *n* not depart; give ye them
21. 3 shall say The Lord hath *n* of them;
26.65 further *n* have we of witnesses?
Mk 2.17 whole have no *n* of the physician,
25 what David did, when he had *n*,
11. 3 ye that the Lord hath *n* of him;
14.63 *n* we any further witnesses?
Lk 5.31 that are whole *n* not a physician;
9.11 healed them that had *n* of healing.
12.30 that ye have *n* of these things.
15. 7 which *n* no repentance.
19.31 Because the Lord hath *n* of him.
34 they said, The Lord hath *n* of him.
22.71 What *n* we any further witness?
Jn 13.29 that we have *n* of against the feast;
Ac 2.45 to all men, as every man had *n*.
4.35 every man according as he had *n*.
Ro 16. 2 business she hath *n* of you: for
1Co 7.36 and *n* so require, let him do what
12.21 the hand, I have no *n* of thee:
21 to the feet, I have no *n* of you.
24 For our comely parts have no *n*:
2Co 3. 1 or *n* we, as some others, epistles
Php 4.12 both to abound and to suffer *n*.
19 my God shall supply all your *n*
1Th 1. 8 we *n* not to speak any thing.
4. 9 love ye *n* not that I write unto you:
5. 1 ye have no *n* that I write unto you.
Heb 4.16 and find grace to help in time of *n*.
5.12 ye have *n* that one teach you
12 are become such as have *n* of milk,
7.11 further *n* was there that another
10.36 For ye have *n* of patience, that,
1Pe 1. 6 though now for a season, if *n* be,
1Jn 2.27 *n* not that any man teach you:
3.17 and seeth his brother have *n*, and
Rev 3.17 with goods, and have *n* of nothing;
21.23 And the city had no *n* of the sun,
22. 5 they *n* no candle, neither light

NEEDED

Jn 2.25 *n* not that any should testify
Ac 17.25 hands, as though he *n* any thing,

NEEDEST

Jn 16.30 *n* not that any man should ask

NEEDETH

Gen 33.15 And he said, What *n* it? let me find
Lk 11. 8 and give him as many as he *n*.
Jn 13.10 *n* not save to wash his feet,
Eph 4.28 he may have to give to him that *n*.
2Ti 2.15 workman that *n* not to be ashamed,
Heb 7.27 Who *n* not daily, as those high

NEEDFUL

Ezr 7.20 be *n* for the house of thy God,
Lk 10.42 But one thing is *n*: and Mary hath
Ac 15. 5 That it was *n* to circumcise them,
Php 1.24 abide in the flesh is more *n* for you.
Jas 2.16 things which are *n* to the body;
Jude 3 it was *n* for me to write unto you,

NEEDLE

Mt 19.24 camel to go through the eye of a *n*,
Mk 10.25 camel to go through the eye of a *n*,

NEEDLE'S

Lk 18.25 for a camel to go through a *n* eye,

NEEDS

Gen 31.30 though thou wouldest *n* be gone,
2Sa 14.14 For we must *n* die, and are as waters
Jer 10. 5 they must *n* be borne, because they
Mt 18. 7 for it must *n* be that offenses
Mk 13. 7 for such things must *n* be; but the
Lk 14.18 and I must *n* go and see it:
Jn 4. 4 he must *n* go through Samaria.
Ac 1.16 this scripture must *n* have been
17. 3 that Christ must *n* have suffered,
21.22 the multitude must *n* come
Ro 13. 5 ye must *n* be subject, not only
1Co 5.10 then must ye *n* go out of the world.
2Co 11.30 If I must *n* glory, I will glory of

NEEDY

Dt 15.11 to thy poor, and to thy *n*, in thy land.
24.14 an hired servant that is poor and *n*,
Job 24. 4 They turn the *n* out of the way:
14 with the light killeth the poor and *n*,
Ps 9.18 the *n* shall not alway be forgotten:
12. 5 of the poor, for the sighing of the *n*,
35.10 the *n* from him that spoileth him?
37.14 to cast down the poor and *n*, and to
40.17 But I am poor and *n*; yet the Lord
70. 5 I am poor and *n*: make haste unto
72. 4 he shall save the children of the *n*,
12 shall deliver the *n* when he crieth;
13 He shall spare the poor and *n*, and
13 and shall save the souls of the *n*.
74.21 let the poor and *n* praise thy name.
82. 3 do justice to the afflicted and *n*.
4 Deliver the poor and *n*: rid them
86. 1 Lord, hear me: for I am poor and *n*.
109.16 but persecuted the poor and *n* man,
22 For I am poor and *n*, and my heart
113. 7 and lifteth the *n* out of the dunghill;
Pr 30.14 earth, and the *n* from among men.
31. 9 plead the cause of the poor and *n*.
20 forth her hands to the *n*.
Isa 10. 2 turn aside the *n* from judgment,
14.30 and the *n* shall lie down in safety:
25. 4 a strength to the *n* in his distress,
26. 6 the poor, and the steps of the *n*.
32. 7 even when the *n* speaketh right.
41.17 When the poor and *n* seek water,
Jer 5.28 the right of the *n* do they not judge.
22.16 judged the cause of the poor and *n*;
Eze 16.49 the hand of the poor and *n*.
18.12 Hath oppressed the poor and *n*,
22.29 and have vexed the poor and *n*:
Am 4. 1 oppress the poor, which crush the *n*,
8. 4 this, O ye that swallow up the *n*,
6 and the *n* for a pair of shoes;

NEGLECT

Mt 18.17 And if he shall *n* to hear them,
17 but if he *n* to hear the church, let
1Ti 4.14 *N* not the gift that is in thee,
Heb 2. 3 escape, if we *n* so great salvation;

NEGLECTED

Ac 6. 1 were *n* in the daily ministration.

NEGLECTING

Col 2.23 and humility, and *n* of the body;

NEHEMIAH

Leader with Ezra of Jerusalem's revitalization, 5th century B.C.; originally living in Persepolis, capital of Persia, in the reign of Artaxerxes I (465–424 B.C.); holds position of "cupbearer to the king," which affords direct access to him; in the king's 20th year (Neh 1.1)—almost a century after the return of Jews from Babylonian exile—receives news of terrible conditions in Jerusalem; obtains commission to rebuild it, the king commanding local help (Neh 2); has 12-year tour of duty as governor (Neh 5); rebuilds the walls in 52 days (Neh 6), despite intense opposition from jealous officials in Samaria, and opposition from within the community; enrolls the people by genealogy (Neh 7); presides with Ezra over public reading of the law, with subsequent celebrations and penitence (Neh 8–9); his political role complements Ezra's religious one, yet their missions overlap; culmination of work in dedication of wall with procession and great celebration (Neh 12); after unspecified period in Persia returns to Jerusalem, to find and eradicate further abuses of temple, sabbath, and intermarriage (13.6-31).

NEGLIGENT

2Ch 29.11 My sons, be not now *n*: for the
2Pe 1.12 I will not be *n* to put you always

NEHEMIAH

Ezr 2. 2 with Zerubbabel: Jeshua, *N*,
Neh 1. 1 words of *N* the son of Hachaliah.
3.16 him repaired *N* the son of Azbuk,
7. 7 came with Zerubbabel, Jeshua, *N*,
8. 9 *N*, which is the Tirshatha, and
10. 1 that sealed were, *N*, the Tirshatha,
12.26 and in the days of *N* the governor,
47 in the days of *N*, gave the portions

NEIGHBOR

Ex 3.22 woman shall borrow of her *n*,
11. 2 let every man borrow of his *n*,
2 and every woman of her *n*, jewels
12. 4 him and his *n* next unto his house
20.16 bear false witness against thy *n*.
21.14 come presumptuously upon his *n*,
22. 7 man shall deliver unto his *n* money
9 he shall pay double unto his *n*.
10 If a man deliver unto his *n* an ass,
14 if a man borrow ought of his *n*,
32.27 companion, and every man his *n*.
Lev 6. 2 and lie unto his *n* in that which
2 violence, or hath deceived his *n*;
19.13 Thou shalt not defraud thy *n*,
15 shalt thou judge thy *n*.
16 stand against the blood of thy *n*:
17 shalt in any wise rebuke thy *n*,
18 thou shalt love thy *n* as thyself:
24.19 a man cause a blemish in his *n*;
25.14 And if thou sell ought unto thy *n*,
15 the jubile thou shalt buy of thy *n*,
Dt 4.42 which should kill his *n* unawares,
5.20 bear false witness against thy *n*.
15. 2 that lendeth ought unto his *n* shall
2 he shall not exact it of his *n*, or of
19. 4 Whoso killeth his *n* ignorantly,
5 man goeth into the wood with his *n*
5 lighteth upon his *n*, that he die;
11 But if any man hate his *n*, and lie
22.26 when a man riseth against his *n*,

Dt 23.25 into the standing corn of thy *n*,
27.24 be he that smiteth his *n* secretly.
Jos 20. 5 because he smote his *n* unwittingly,
Ru 4. 7 off his shoe, and gave it to his *n*:
1Sa 15.28 and hath given it to a *n* of thine,
28.17 given it to thy *n*, even to David:
2Sa 12.11 and give them unto thy *n*, and he
1Ki 8.31 If any man trespass against his *n*,
20.35 said unto his *n* in the word of the
2Ch 6.22 If a man sin against his *n*, and an
Job 12. 4 I am as one mocked of his *n*, who
16.21 God, as a man pleadeth for his *n*!
Ps 12. 2 speak vanity every one with his *n*:
15. 3 his tongue, nor doeth evil to his *n*,
3 up a reproach against his *n*.
101. 5 Whoso privily slandereth his *n*,
Pr 3.28 Say not unto thy *n*, Go, and come
29 Devise not evil against thy *n*,
11. 9 with his mouth destroyeth his *n*:
12 is void of wisdom despiseth his *n*:
12.26 is more excellent than his *n*:
14.20 poor is hated even of his own *n*:
21 He that despiseth his *n* sinneth:
16.29 A violent man enticeth his *n*, and
18.17 his *n* cometh and searcheth him.
19. 4 the poor is separated from his *n*.
21.10 his *n* findeth no favor in his eyes.
24.28 Be not a witness against thy *n*
25. 8 when thy *n* hath put thee to shame.
9 Debate thy cause with thy *n*
18 beareth false witness against his *n*
26.19 So is the man that deceiveth his *n*,
27.10 better is a *n* that is near than a
29. 5 that flattereth his *n* spreadeth a
Ec 4. 4 for this a man is envied of his *n*.
Isa 3. 5 by another, and every one by his *n*:
19. 2 and every one against his *n*;
41. 6 They helped every one his *n*; and
Jer 6.21 the *n* and his friend shall perish.
7. 5 between a man and his *n*;
9. 4 Take ye heed every one of his *n*,
4 every *n* will walk with slanders.
5 they will deceive every one his *n*,
8 speaketh peaceably to his *n* with
20 and every one her *n* lamentation.
22. 8 they shall say every man to his *n*,
23.27 which they tell every man to his *n*,
30 my words every one from his *n*.
35 shall ye say every one to his *n*, and
31.34 teach no more every man his *n*,
34.15 liberty every man to his *n*; and ye
17 brother, and every man to his *n*:
49.18 Gomorrah and the *n* cities thereof,
50.40 Gomorrah and the *n* cities thereof,
Hab 2.15 unto him that giveth his *n* drink,
Zec 3.10 ye call every man his *n* under the
8.10 all men every one against his *n*.
16 ye every man the truth to his *n*;
17 evil in your hearts against his *n*;
14.13 every one on the hand of his *n*, and
13 rise up against the hand of his *n*.
Mt 5.43 been said, Thou shalt love thy *n*,
19.19 Thou shalt love thy *n* as thyself.
22.39 Thou shalt love thy *n* as thyself.
Mk 12.31 Thou shalt love thy *n* as thyself.
33 and to love his *n* as himself, is
Lk 10.27 all thy mind; and thy *n* as thyself.
29 said unto Jesus, And who is my *n*?
36 was *n* unto him that fell among
Ac 7.27 he that did his *n* wrong thrust him
Ro 13. 9 Thou shalt love thy *n* as thyself.
10 Love worketh no ill to his *n*:
15. 2 Let every one of us please his *n*
Gal 5.14 Thou shalt love thy *n* as thyself.
Jas 2. 8 Thou shalt love thy *n* as thyself,
Eph 4.25 speak every man truth with his *n*:
Heb 8.11 shall not teach every man his *n*,

NEIGHBOR'S

Ex 20.17 Thou shalt not covet thy *n* house,
17 thou shalt not covet thy *n* wife,
17 his ass, nor any thing that is thy *n*.
22. 8 have put his hand unto his *n* goods.
11 not put his hand unto his *n* goods;
26 If thou at all take thy *n* raiment
Lev 18.20 not lie carnally with thy *n* wife,
20.10 adultery with his *n* wife,
25.14 or buyest ought of thy *n* hand, ye
Dt 5.21 shalt thou desire thy *n* wife,
21 shalt thou covet thy *n* house, his
21 his ass, or any thing that is thy *n*.
19.14 shalt not remove thy *n* landmark,
22.24 he hath humbled his *n* wife:
23.24 thou comest into thy *n* vineyard,
25 a sickle unto thy *n* standing corn.
27.17 he that removeth his *n* landmark.
Job 31. 9 or if I have laid wait at my *n* door;
Pr 6.29 So he that goeth in to his *n* wife;
25.17 thy foot from thy *n* house; lest he
Jer 5. 8 every one neighed after his *n* wife.
22.13 useth his *n* service without wages,
Eze 18. 6 neither hath defiled his *n* wife,
11 mountains, and defiled his *n* wife,
15 Israel, hath not defiled his *n* wife,
22.11 abomination with his *n* wife; and
33.26 and ye defile every one his *n* wife:
Zec 11. 6 the men every one into his *n* hand,

NEIGHBORS

Jos 9.16 they heard that they were their *n*,
Ru 4.17 the women her *n* gave it a name,
2Ki 4. 3 vessels abroad of all thy *n*, even
Ps 28. 3 which speak peace to their *n*, but
31.11 but especially among my *n*, and
44.13 makest us a reproach to our *n*, a
79. 4 We are become a reproach to our *n*,
12 And render unto our *n* sevenfold
80. 6 Thou makest us a strife unto our *n*:
89.41 him: he is a reproach to his *n*.
Jer 12.14 against all mine evil *n*, that touch
49.10 his brethren, and his *n*, and he is
Eze 16.26 the Egyptians thy *n*, great of flesh;
22.12 thou hast greedily gained of thy *n*
23. 5 her lovers, on the Assyrians her *n*,
12 doted upon the Assyrians her *n*,
Lk 1.58 And her *n* and her cousins heard
14.12 thy kinsmen, nor thy rich *n*; lest
15. 6 calleth together his friends and *n*,
9 she calleth her friends and her *n*
Jn 9. 8 The *n* therefore, and they which

NEPHEW

Job 18.19 neither have son nor *n* among
Isa 14.22 and son, and *n*, saith the Lord.

NEPHEWS

Jdg 12.14 he had forty sons and thirty *n*,
1Ti 5. 4 if any widow have children or *n*,

NEPHTHALIM

Mt 4.13 in the borders of Zabulon and *N*:
15 and the land of *N*, by the way of
Rev 7. 6 *N* were sealed twelve thousand.

NEREUS

Ro 16.15 Salute Philologus, and Julia, *N*,

NEST

Nu 24.21 and thou puttest thy *n* in a rock.
Dt 22. 6 If a bird's *n* chance to be before
32.11 As an eagle stirreth up her *n*,
Job 29.18 Then I said, I shall die in my *n*,
39.27 command, and make her *n* on high?
Ps 84. 3 the swallow a *n* for herself, where
Pr 27. 8 a bird that wandereth from her *n*,
Isa 10.14 as a *n* the riches of the people:
16. 2 a wandering bird cast out of the *n*,
34.15 shall the great owl make her *n*,
Jer 22.23 that makest thy *n* in the cedars,
48.28 like the dove that maketh her *n* in
49.16 make thy *n* as high as the eagle,
Ob 4 thou set thy *n* among the stars,
Hab 2. 9 that he may set his *n* on high, that

NESTS

Ps 104.17 Where the birds make their *n*: as
Eze 31. 6 heaven made their *n* in his boughs,
Mt 8.20 and the birds of the air have *n*;
Lk 9.58 holes, and birds of the air have *n*;

NET

Job 18. 8 he is cast into a *n* by his own feet,
19. 6 hath compassed me with his *n*.
Ps 25.15 he shall pluck my feet out of the *n*.
57. 6 have prepared a *n* for my steps;
Pr 1.17 *n* is spread in the sight of any bird.
12.12 wicked desireth the *n* of evil men:
29. 5 spreadeth a *n* for his feet.
Ec 9.12 fishes that are taken in an evil *n*,
La 1.13 he hath spread a *n* for my feet, he
Hab 1.16 they sacrifice unto their *n*, and
Mt 4.18 brother, casting a *n* into the sea:
13.47 the kingdom of heaven is like a *n*,
Mk 1.16 brother, casting a *n* into the sea:
Lk 5. 5 at thy word I will let down the *n*.
6 of fishes: and their *n* break.
Jn 21. 6 Cast the *n* on the right side of the
8 cubits,) dragging the *n* with fishes.
11 drew the *n* to the land full of fishes,
11 many, yet was not the *n* broken.

NETHER

Ex 19.17 stood at the *n* part of the mount.
Dt 24. 6 take the *n* or the upper millstone
Jos 15.19 upper springs, and the *n* springs.
16. 3 the coast of Beth-horon the *n*,
18.13 the south side of the *n* Beth-horon.
Jdg 1.15 upper springs and the *n* springs.
1Ki 9.17 Gezer, and Beth-horon the *n*,
1Ch 7.24 who built Beth-horon the *n*, and
2Ch 8. 5 the upper, and Beth-horon the *n*,
Job 41.24 hard as a piece of the *n* millstone.
Eze 31.14 death, to the *n* parts of the earth,
16 in the *n* parts of the earth.
18 Eden unto the *n* parts of the earth:
32.18 unto the *n* parts of the earth, with
24 into the *n* parts of the earth, which

NETS

1Ki 7.17 *n* of checker work, and wreaths
Ps 141.10 the wicked fall into their own *n*,
Ec 7.26 whose heart is snares and *n*, and
Isa 19. 8 that spread *n* upon the waters
Eze 26. 5 be a place for the spreading of *n*
14 shalt be a place to spread *n* upon;
47.10 shall be a place to spread forth *n*;
Mt 4.20 they straightway left their *n*, and
21 their father, mending their *n*; and
Mk 1.18 straightway they forsook their *n*,
19 were in the ship mending their *n*.
Lk 5. 2 them, and were washing their *n*.
4 and let down your *n* for a draft.

NETTLES

Job 30. 7 under the *n* they were gathered
Pr 24.31 *n* have covered the face thereof,
Isa 34.13 *n* and brambles in the fortresses
Hos 9. 6 their silver, *n* shall possess them:
Zep 2. 9 the breeding of *n*, and saltpits,

NEVER

Lev 6.13 upon the altar; it shall *n* go out.
Dt 15.11 poor shall *n* cease out of the land:
Jdg 16.11 new ropes that were *n* occupied,
Job 3.16 as infants which *n* saw light.
Ps 10. 6 for I shall *n* be in adversity.
11 his face; he will *n* see it.
15. 5 these things shall *n* be moved.
30. 6 I said, I shall *n* be moved.
31. 1 let me *n* be ashamed:
49.19 they shall *n* see light.
71. 1 trust: let me *n* be put to
119.93 I will *n* forget thy precepts:
Pr 10.30 righteous shall *n* be removed:
27.20 Hell and destruction are *n* full;

20 the eyes of man are *n* satisfied.
Isa 56.11 dogs which can *n* have enough,
Eze 26.21 shalt thou *n* be found again,
Am 8.14 shall fall, and *n* rise up again.
Hab 1. 4 judgment doth *n* go forth:
Mt 7.23 I *n* knew you: depart from me,
9.33 saying, It was *n* so seen in Israel.
21.16 have ye *n* read, Out of the mouth
42 Did ye *n* read in the scriptures,
26.33 of thee, yet I will *n* be offended.
27.14 answered him to *n* a word;
Mk 2.12 We *n* saw it on this fashion.
25 Have ye *n* read what David did,
3.29 hath *n* forgiveness,
9.43, 45 fire that *n* shall be quenched:
11. 2 colt tied, whereon *n* man sat;
14.21 that man if he had *n* been born.
Lk 15.29 and yet thou *n* gavest me a kid,
19.30 tied, whereon yet *n* man sat:
23.29 and the wombs that *n* bare,
29 and the paps which *n* gave suck.
53 wherein *n* man before was laid.
Jn 4.14 give...shall *n* thirst;
6.35 that cometh to me shall *n* hunger;
35 believeth on me shall *n* thirst.
7.15 man letters, having *n* learned?
46 *N* man spake like this man.
8.33 *n* in bondage to any man:
51 saying,...shall *n* see
52 shall *n* taste of death.
10.28 shall *n* perish, neither
11.26 believeth in me shall *n*
13. 8 Thou shalt *n* wash my
19.41 wherein was *n* man yet laid.
Ac 10.14 *n* eaten any thing that is common
14. 8 mother's womb, who *n* had walked:
1Co 13. 8 Charity *n* faileth: but whether
2Ti 3. 7 *n* able to come to the knowledge
Heb 10. 1 can *n* with those sacrifices which
11 which can *n* take away sins:
13. 5 I will *n* leave thee, nor forsake
2Pe 1.10 these things, ye shall *n* fall:

NEW

Ex 1. 8 arose up a *n* king over Egypt,
Lev 23.16 a *n* meat offering unto the Lord.
26.10 forth the old because of the *n*.
Nu 16.30 But if the Lord make a *n* thing,
28.26 a *n* meat offering unto the Lord,
Dt 20. 5 is there that hath built a *n* house,
22. 8 When thou buildest a *n* house,
24. 5 When a man hath taken a *n* wife,
32.17 not, to *n* gods that came newly up,
Jos 9.13 of wine, which we filled, were *n*;
Jdg 5. 8 They chose *n* gods; then was war
15.13 they bound him with two *n* cords,
15 he found a *n* jawbone of an ass,
16.11 If they bind me fast with *n* ropes
12 Delilah therefore took *n* ropes,
1Sa 6. 7 Now therefore make a *n* cart, and
20. 5 Behold, to morrow is the *n* moon,
18 To morrow is the *n* moon: and
24 and when the *n* moon was come,
2Sa 6. 3 set the ark of God upon a *n* cart,
3 sons of Abinadab, drave the *n* cart.
21.16 he being girded with a *n* sword,
1Ki 11.29 had clad himself with a *n* garment;
30 Ahijah caught the *n* garment that
2Ki 2.20 Bring me a *n* cruse, and put salt
4.23 it is neither *n* moon, nor sabbath.
1Ch 13. 7 carried the ark of God in a *n* cart
23.31 in the *n* moons, and on the set
2Ch 2. 4 on the *n* moons, and on the solemn
8.13 on the *n* moons, and on the solemn
20. 5 of the Lord, before the *n* court,
31. 3 and for the *n* moons, and for the
Ezr 3. 5 offering, both of the *n* moons, and
6. 4 stones, and a row of *n* timber:
Neh 10.33 of the sabbaths, of the *n* moons,
39 offering of the corn, of the *n* wine.
13. 5 the tithes of the corn, the *n* wine,
12 tithe of the corn and the *n* wine
Job 32.19 it is ready to burst like *n* bottles.
Ps 33. 3 Sing unto him a *n* song; play
40. 3 hath put a *n* song in my mouth,
81. 3 up the trumpet in the *n* moon,
96. 1 O sing unto the Lord a *n* song:
98. 1 O sing unto the Lord a *n* song; for
144. 9 I will sing a *n* song unto thee, O
149. 1 Sing unto the Lord a *n* song, and
Pr 3.10 presses...burst out with *n* wine.
Ec 1. 9 there is no *n* thing under the sun.
10 it may be said, See, this is *n*? it
SS 7.13 of pleasant fruits, *n* and old, which
Isa 1.13 the *n* moons and sabbaths, the
14 Your *n* moons and your appointed
24. 7 The *n* wine mourneth, the vine
41.15 a *n* sharp threshing instrument
42. 9 to pass, and *n* things do I declare:
10 Sing unto the Lord a *n* song, and
43.19 Behold, I will do a *n* thing; now it
48. 6 shewed thee *n* things from this
62. 2 thou shalt be called by a *n* name,
65. 8 the *n* wine is found in the cluster,
17 create *n* heavens and a *n* earth:
66.22 as the *n* heavens and the *n* earth,
23 that from one *n* moon to another,
Jer 26.10 down in the entry of the *n* gate
31.22 hath created a *n* thing in the earth,
31 I will make a *n* covenant with the
36.10 at the entry of the *n* gate of the
La 3.23 They are *n* every morning: great
Eze 11.19 I will put a *n* spirit within you;
18.31 make you a *n* heart and a *n* spirit:
36.26 A *n* heart also will I give you, and
26 a *n* spirit will I put within you:
45.17 in the feasts, and in the *n* moons,
46. 1 day of the *n* moon it shall be opened.
3 the sabbaths and in the *n* moons.
6 in the day of the *n* moon it shall be
47.12 shall bring forth *n* fruit according
Hos 2.11 her feast days, her *n* moons, and
4.11 and *n* wine take away the heart.
9. 2 and the *n* wine shall fail in her.
Joel 1. 5 because of the *n* wine; for it is cut
10 the *n* wine is dried up, the oil
3.18 mountains shall drop down *n* wine,
Am 8. 5 When will the *n* moon be gone,
Hag 1.11 upon the *n* wine,...upon the oil.
Zec 9.17 cheerful, and *n* wine the maids.
Mt 9.16 of *n* cloth unto an old garment, for
17 men put *n* wine into old bottles:
17 they put *n* wine into...bottles,
17 they put...wine into *n* bottles,
13.52 of his treasure things *n* and old.
26.28 this is my blood of the *n* testament,
29 that day when I drink it *n* with you
27.60 And laid it in his own *n* tomb, which
Mk 1.27 is this? What *n* doctrine is this?
2.21 piece of *n* cloth on an old garment:
21 else the *n* piece that filled it up
22 putteth *n* wine into old bottles:
22 else the *n* wine doth burst...bottles,
22 *n* wine must be put into...bottles.
22 wine must be put into *n* bottles.
14.24 is my blood of the *n* testament,
25 I drink it *n* in the kingdom of God.
16.17 they shall speak with *n* tongues;
Lk 5.36 piece of a *n* garment upon an old;
36 then both the *n* maketh a rent, and
36 of the *n* agreeth not with the old.
37 putteth *n* wine into old bottles;
37 else the *n* wine will burst...bottles,
38 *n* wine must be put into...bottles;
38 wine must be put into *n* bottles;
39 old wine straightway desireth *n*:
22.20 This cup is the *n* testament in my
Jn 13.34 A *n* commandment I give unto you,
19.41 and in the garden a *n* sepulcher,
Ac 2.13 These men are full of *n* wine.
17.19 we know what this *n* doctrine,
21 to tell, or to hear some *n* thing.)
1Co 5. 7 that ye may be a *n* lump, as ye
11.25 This cup is the *n* testament in my
2Co 3. 6 able ministers of the *n* testament;
5.17 be in Christ, he is a *n* creature:
17 behold, all things are become *n*.
Gal 6.15 uncircumcision, but a *n* creature.
Eph 2.15 in himself of twain one *n* man,
4.24 that ye put on the *n* man, which
Col 2.16 or of the *n* moon, or of the sabbath
3.10 have put on the *n* man, which is
Heb 8. 8 I will make a *n* covenant with the
13 A *n* covenant, he hath made the
9.15 the mediator of the *n* testament,
10.20 By a *n* and living way, which he
12.24 the mediator of the *n* covenant,
2Pe 3.13 look for *n* heavens and a *n* earth,
1Jn 2. 7 I write no *n* commandment unto
8 *n* commandment I write unto you,
2Jn 5 I wrote a *n* commandment unto
Rev 2.17 and in the stone a *n* name written,
3.12 city of my God,...is *n* Jerusalem,
12 I will write upon him my *n* name.
5. 9 they sung a *n* song, saying, Thou
14. 3 And they sung as it were a *n* song
21. 1 I saw a *n* heaven and a *n* earth:
2 I...saw the holy city, *n* Jerusalem,
5 said, Behold, I make all things *n*.

NEWBORN

1Pe 2. 2 As *n* babes, desire the sincere

NEWLY

Dt 32.17 new gods that came *n* up, whom
Jdg 7.19 they had but *n* set the watch:

NEWNESS

Ro 6. 4 we also should walk in *n* of life.
7. 6 that we should serve in *n* of spirit,

NEWS

Pr 25.25 so is good *n* from a far country.

NEXT

Gen 17.21 thee at this set time in the *n* year.
Ex 12. 4 his neighbor *n* unto his house
Nu 2. 5 those that do pitch *n* unto him shall
11.32 all that night, and all the *n* day,
27.11 his kinsman that is *n* to him of
Dt 21. 3 city which is *n* unto the slain man,
6 city, that are *n* unto the slain man,
Ru 2.20 of kin unto us, one of our *n* kinsmen.
1Sa 17.13 *n* unto him Abinadab, and the
23.17 Israel, I shall be *n* unto thee;
30.17 unto the evening of the *n* day:
2Ki 6.29 I said unto her on the *n* day, Give
1Ch 5.12 Joel the chief,...Shapham the *n*,
16. 5 the chief, and *n* to him Zechariah,
2Ch 17.15 And *n* to him was Jehohanan
16 *n* him was Amasiah the son of
18 And *n* him was Jehozabad, and
28. 7 Elkanah that was *n* to the king.
31.12 and Shimei his brother was the *n*.
15 and *n* him were Eden, and
Neh 3. 2 *n* unto him builded the men of
2 *n* to them builded Zaccur the
4 *n*...them repaired Meremoth
4 *n*...them repaired Meshullam
4 *n* unto them repaired Zadok
5 *n* unto them the Tekoites
7 *n* unto them repaired Melatiah
8 *N* unto him repaired Uzziel the
8 *N*...also repaired Hananiah
9 *n*...them repaired Rephaiah
10 *n* unto them repaired Jedaiah
10 *n* unto him repaired Hattush
12 *n* unto him repaired Shallum
17 *N*...him repaired Hashabiah,
19 And *n* to him repaired Ezer the
13.13 *n* to them was Hanan...son of
Est 1.14 the *n* unto him was Carshena,

NICODEMUS

A Pharisee and member of the Sanhedrin, ruling council of the Jews; also a secret follower of Jesus; mentioned only in Gospel of John; visits Jesus by night and is told of the need for spiritual regeneration, a message he at first fails to understand: "how can a man be born when he is old?" (Jn 3.4); later defends Jesus against the Pharisees: "doth our law judge any man, before it hear him?" (Jn 7.51); when Jesus is to be buried brings a hundred pounds of myrrh and aloes for the embalming (Jn 19.39).

Est 10. 3 Jew was *n* unto king Ahasuerus,
Jon 4. 7 when the morning rose the *n* day,
Mt 27.62 Now the *n* day, that followed the
Mk 1.38 Let us go into the *n* towns, that I
Lk 9.37 that on the *n* day, when they were
Jn 1.29 *n* day John seeth Jesus coming
35 the *n* day after John stood, and
12.12 On the *n* day much people that
Ac 4. 3 put them in hold unto the *n* day:
7.26 the *n* day he shewed himself unto
13.42 preached to them the *n* sabbath.
44 the *n* sabbath day came almost
14.20 *n* day he departed with Barnabas
16.11 Samothracia,...*n* day to Neapolis;
20.15 came the *n* day over against Chios;
15 the *n* day we arrived at Samos,
15 and the *n* day we came to Miletus.
21. 8 the *n* day we that were of Paul's
26 the *n* day purifying himself with
25. 6 the *n* day sitting on the judgment
27. 3 the *n* day we touched at Sidon.
18 the *n* day they lightened the ship;
28.13 we came the *n* day to Putcoli:

NICANOR
Ac 6. 5 Prochorus, and *N*, and Timon,

NICODEMUS
Jn 3. 1 a man of the Pharisees, named *N*,
4 *N* saith unto him, How can a man
9 *N* answered and said unto him,
7.50 *N* saith unto them, (he that came
19.39 And there came also *N*, which at

NICOLAITANES
Rev 2. 6 thou hatest the deeds of the *N*,
15 that hold the doctrine of the *N*,

NICOLAS
Ac 6. 5 and *N* a proselyte of Antioch:

NICOPOLIS
Tit 3.12 diligent to come unto me to *N*:

NIGER
Ac 13. 1 and Simeon that was called *N*,

NIGH
Ex 3. 5 Draw not *n* hither: put off thy
34.30 they were afraid to come *n* him.
Nu 24.17 I shall behold him, but not *n*: there
Dt 4. 7 who hath God so *n* unto them, as
30.14 But the word is very *n* unto thee,
1Ki 8.59 be *n* unto the Lord our God day and
Ps 34.18 *n* unto them that are of a broken
69.18 Draw *n* unto my soul, and
73. 2 gone; my steps had well *n* slipped.
85. 9 his salvation is *n* them that fear
88. 3 my life draweth *n* unto the grave.
91. 7 but it shall not come *n* thee.
10 any plague come *n* thy dwelling.
145.18 *n* unto all them that call upon him,
Ec 12. 1 nor the years draw *n*, when thou
Joel 2. 1 Lord cometh, for it is *n* at hand;
Mt 15. 8 draweth *n* unto me with their
24.32 ye know that summer is *n*:
Mk 2. 4 not come *n* unto him for the press,
13.29 come to pass, know that it is *n*,
Lk 10. 9, 11 kingdom of God is come *n* unto
21.20 that the desolation thereof is *n*.
28 for your redemption draweth *n*.
30 that summer is now *n* at hand.
31 the kingdom of God is *n* at hand.
Jn 11.18 Bethany was *n* unto Jerusalem,
19.20 Jesus was crucified...*n* to the city:
Ro 10. 8 The word is *n* thee, even in thy
Eph 2.13 are made *n* by the blood of Christ.
17 afar off, and to them that were *n*.
Php 2.27 indeed he was sick *n* unto death:
30 work of Christ he was *n* unto death,
Heb 7.19 by the which we draw *n* unto God.
Jas 4. 8 Draw *n* to God, and he will draw *n*
5. 8 the coming of the Lord draweth *n*.

NIGHT
Gen 1. 5 and the darkness he called *N*.
14 to divide the day from the *n*; and
16 the lesser light to rule the *n*: he
18 to rule over the day and over the *n*,
8.22 and day and *n* shall not cease.
14.15 he and his servants, by *n*, and smote
19. 2 tarry all *n*, and wash your feet, and
2 but we will abide in the street all *n*.
5 men which came in to thee this *n*?
33 made their father drink wine that *n*:
34 make him drink wine this *n* also;
35 made their father drink wine that *n*
20. 3 came to Abimelech in a dream by *n*.
24.54 that were with him, and tarried all *n*;
26.24 appeared unto him the same *n*,
28.11 tarried there all *n*, because the sun
30.15 Therefore he shall lie with thee to *n*
16 And he lay with her that *n*.
31.24 Laban the Syrian in a dream by *n*,
39 stolen by day, or stolen by *n*.
40 consumed me, and the frost by *n*;
54 bread, and tarried all *n* in the mount.
32.13 And he lodged there that same *n*;
21 lodged that *n* in the company.
22 he rose up that *n*, and took his two
40. 5 each man his dream in one *n*, each
41.11 And we dreamed a dream in one *n*,
46. 2 God spake...in the visions of the *n*,
49.27 and at *n* he shall divide the spoil.
Ex 10.13 land all that day, and all that *n*;
12. 8 they shall eat the flesh in that *n*,
12 through the land of Egypt this *n*,
30 And Pharaoh rose up in the *n*, he,
31 called for Moses and Aaron by *n*,
42 It is a *n* to be much observed unto
42 that *n* of the Lord to be observed
13.21 by *n* in a pillar of fire, to give
21 them light; to go by day and *n*:
22 by day, nor the pillar of fire by *n*,
14.20 it gave light by *n* to these: so that
20 came not near the other all the *n*.
21 by a strong east wind all that *n*,
40.38 and fire was on it by *n*, in the sight
Lev 6. 9 the burning upon the altar all *n*
20 morning, and half thereof at *n*.
8.35 day and *n* seven days, and keep
11.16 And the owl, and the *n* hawk, and
19.13 abide with thee all *n* until...morning.
Nu 9.16 and the appearance of fire by *n*.
21 whether it was by day or by *n* that
11. 9 dew fell upon the camp in the *n*,
32 up all that day, and all that *n*, and
14. 1 cried; and the people wept that *n*.
14 cloud, and in a pillar of fire by *n*.
22. 8 said unto them, Lodge here this *n*,
19 tarry ye also here this *n*, that I
20 And God came unto Balaam at *n*,
Dt 1.33 in fire by *n*, to shew you by what
14.15 the owl, and the *n* hawk, and the
16. 1 thee forth out of Egypt by *n*.
4 even, remain all *n* until the morning.
21.23 shall not remain all *n* upon the tree,
23.10 that chanceth him by *n*, then
28.66 and thou shalt fear day and *n*, and
Jos 1. 8 shalt meditate therein day and *n*,
2. 2 there came men in hither to *n* of
4. 3 place, where ye shall lodge this *n*.
8. 3 valor, and sent them away by *n*.
9 Joshua lodged that *n* among the
13 Joshua went that *n* into the midst
10. 9 and went up from Gilgal all *n*.
Jdg 6.25 And it came to pass the same *n*,
27 do it by day, that he did it by *n*.
40 And God did so that *n*: for it was
7. 9 And it came to pass the same *n*,
9.32 Now therefore up by *n*, thou and
34 people that were with him, by *n*,
16. 2 laid wait for him all *n* in the gate
2 and were quiet all the *n*, saying,
19. 6 content, I pray thee, and tarry all *n*,
9 evening, I pray you tarry all *n*:
10 But the man would not tarry that *n*,
13 to one of these places to lodge all *n*,
25 and abused her all the *n* until
20. 5 house round about upon me by *n*,
Ru 1.12 I should have an husband also to *n*,
3. 2 he winnoweth barley to *n* in the
13 Tarry this *n*, and it shall be in
1Sa 14.34 every man his ox with him that *n*,
36 go down after the Philistines by *n*,
15.11 and he cried unto the Lord all *n*.
16 the Lord hath said to me this *n*.
19.10 and David fled, and escaped that *n*.
11 If thou save not thy life to *n*, to
24 naked all that day and all that *n*.
25.16 a wall unto us both by *n* and day,
26. 7 Abishai came to the people by *n*:
28. 8 and they came to the woman by *n*:
20 no bread all the day, nor all the *n*.
25 rose up, and went away that *n*.
31.12 valiant men arose, and went all *n*,
2Sa 2.29 and his men walked all that *n*
32 And Joab and his men went all *n*,
4. 7 them away through the plain all *n*.
7. 4 And it came to pass that *n*, that
12.16 went in, and lay all *n* upon the earth.
17. 1 and pursue after David this *n*:
16 Lodge not this *n* in the plains of
19. 7 not tarry one with thee this *n*:
21.10 day, nor the beasts of the field by *n*.
1Ki 3. 5 to Solomon in a dream by *n*: and
19 this woman's child died in the *n*;
8.29 open toward this house *n* and day,
59 unto the Lord our God day and *n*,
2Ki 6.14 they came by *n*, and compassed
7.12 the king arose in the *n*, and said
8.21 and he arose by *n*, and smote the
19.35 it came to pass that *n*, that the
25. 4 all the men of war fled by *n* by the
1Ch 9.33 employed in that work day and *n*.
17. 3 it came to pass the same *n*, that
2Ch 1. 7 In that *n* did God appear unto
6.20 open upon this house day and *n*,
7.12 Lord appeared to Solomon by *n*,
21. 9 he rose up by *n*, and smote the
35.14 burnt offerings and the fat until *n*;
Neh 1. 6 I pray before thee now, day and *n*,
2.12 I arose in the *n*, I and some few
13 I went out by *n* by the gate of the
15 went I up in the *n* by the brook,
4. 9 a watch against them day and *n*,
22 in the *n* they may be a guard to us,
6.10 in the *n* will they come to slay
9.12 in the *n* by a pillar of fire, to give
19 neither the pillar of fire by *n*, to
Est 4.16 eat nor drink three days, *n* or day:
6. 1 On that *n* could not the king sleep,

Job 3. 3 the *n* in which it was said, There
6 As for that *n*, let darkness seize
7 let that *n* be solitary, let no joyful
4.13 thoughts from the visions of the *n*,
5.14 grope in the noonday as in the *n*.
7. 4 shall I arise, and the *n* be gone?
17.12 They change the *n* into day: the
20. 8 chased away as a vision of the *n*.
24.14 needy, and in the *n* is as a thief.
26.10 the day and *n* come to an end.
27.20 stealeth him away in the *n*.
29.19 the dew lay all *n* upon my branch.
30.17 bones are pierced in me in the *n*
33.15 In a dream, in a vision of the *n*,
34.25 and he overturneth them in the *n*,
35.10 maker, who giveth songs in the *n*;
36.20 Desire not the *n*, when people are
Ps 1. 2 law doth he meditate day and *n*.
6. 6 all the *n* make I my bed to swim;
16. 7 also instruct me in the *n* seasons.
17. 3 thou hast visited me in the *n*; thou
19. 2 and *n* unto *n* sheweth knowledge.
22. 2 and in the *n* season, and am not
30. 5 weeping may endure for a *n*, but
32. 4 day and *n* thy hand was heavy
42. 3 have been my meat day and *n*,
8 in the *n* his song shall be with
55.10 Day and *n* they go about it upon
63. 6 and meditate on thee in the *n*
74.16 day is thine, the *n* also is thine:
77. 2 my sore ran in the *n*, and ceased
6 to remembrance my song in the *n*:
78.14 and all the *n* with a light of fire.
88. 1 I have cried day and *n* before thee:
90. 4 is past, and as a watch in the *n*.
91. 5 not be afraid for the terror by *n*;
92. 2 and thy faithfulness every *n*,
104.20 Thou makest darkness, and it is *n*:
105.39 and fire to give light in the *n*.
119.55 O Lord, in the *n*, and have kept
148 Mine eyes prevent the *n* watches,
121. 6 thee by day, nor the moon by *n*.
134. 1 which by *n* stand in the house of
136. 9 The moon and stars to rule by *n*:
139.11 even the *n* shall be light about me.
12 thee; but the *n* shineth as the day:
Pr 7. 9 evening, in the black and dark *n*:
31.15 She riseth also while it is yet *n*,
18 her candle goeth not out by *n*.
Ec 2.23 his heart taketh not rest in the *n*.
8.16 neither day nor *n* seeth sleep with
SS 1.13 he shall lie all *n* betwixt my breasts.
3. 1 By *n* on my bed I sought him
8 his thigh because of fear in the *n*.
5. 2 my locks with the drops of the *n*.
Isa 4. 5 the shining of a flaming fire by *n*:
5.11 that continue until *n*, till wine
15. 1 in the *n* Ar of Moab is laid waste,
1 in the *n* Kir of Moab is laid waste,
16. 3 make thy shadow as the *n* in the
21. 4 the *n* of my pleasure hath he
11, 11 Watchman, what of the *n*?
12 morning cometh, and also the *n*:
26. 9 soul have I desired thee in the *n*;
27. 3 hurt it, I will keep it *n* and day.
28.19 it pass over, by day and by *n*:
29. 7 shall be as a dream of a *n* vision.
30.29 Ye shall have a song, as in the *n*
34.10 shall not be quenched *n* nor day;
38.12, 13 from day even to *n* wilt thou
59.10 stumble at noon day as in the *n*;
60.11 they shall not be shut day nor *n*;
62. 6 never hold their peace day nor *n*:
Jer 6. 5 Arise, and let us go by *n*, and let
9. 1 that I might weep day and *n* for
14. 8 that turneth aside to tarry for a *n*?
17 run down with tears *n* and day,
16.13 shall ye serve other gods day and *n*;
31.35 and of the stars for a light by *n*,
33.20 and my covenant of the *n*, and that
20 not be day and *n* in their seasons;
25 my covenant be not with day and *n*,
36.30 the heat, and in the *n* to the frost.
39. 4 and went forth out of the city by *n*,
49. 9 if thieves by *n*, they will destroy
52. 7 went forth out of the city by *n* by
La 1. 2 She weepeth sore in the *n*, and her
2.18 run down like a river day and *n*:
19 Arise, cry out in the *n*: in the
Dan 2.19 revealed unto Daniel in a *n* vision.
5.30 In that *n* was Belshazzar the king
6.18 palace, and passed the *n* fasting:
7. 2 I was in my vision by *n*, and,
7 After this I saw in the *n* visions,
13 I saw in the *n* visions, and, behold,
Hos 4. 5 also shall fall with thee in the *n*,
7. 6 their baker sleepeth all the *n*; in
Joel 1.13 lie all *n* in sackcloth, ye ministers of
Am 5. 8 and maketh the day dark with *n*:
Ob 5 thieves came to thee, if robbers by *n*,
Jon 4.10 up in a *n*, and perished in a *n*:
Mic 3. 6 Therefore *n* shall be unto you,
Zec 1. 8 I saw by *n*, and behold a man
14. 7 not day, nor *n*: but it shall come
Mt 2.14 young child and his mother by *n*,
14.25 in the fourth watch of the *n* Jesus
26.31 be offended because of me this *n*:
34 That this *n*, before the cock crow,
27.64 his disciples come by *n*, and steal
28.13 Say ye, His disciples came by *n*,
Mk 4.27 should sleep, and rise *n* and day,
5. 5 always, *n* and day, he was in the
6.48 about the fourth watch of the *n* he
14.27 be offended because of me this *n*:
30 thee, That this day, even in this *n*,
Lk 2. 8 keeping watch over their flock by *n*.
37 fastings and prayers *n* and day.
5. 5 we have toiled all the *n*, and have
6.12 continued all *n* in prayer to God.
12.20 this *n* thy soul shall be required
17.34 in that *n* there shall be two men
18. 7 which cry day and *n* unto him,
21.37 at *n* he went out, and abode in the
Jn 3. 2 same came to Jesus by *n*, and said
7.50 (he that came to Jesus by *n*, being
9. 4 the *n* cometh, when no man can
11.10 But if a man walk in the *n*, he
13.30 immediately out: and it was *n*.
19.39 at the first came to Jesus by *n*, and
21. 3 and that *n* they caught nothing.
Ac 5.19 angel...by *n* opened the prison
9.24 watched the gates day and *n* to
25 Then the disciples took him by *n*,
12. 6 the same *n* Peter was sleeping
16. 9 vision appeared to Paul in the *n*;
33 took them the same hour of the *n*,
17.10 sent away Paul and Silas by *n* unto
18. 9 spake the Lord to Paul in the *n* by
20.31 not to warn every one *n* and day
23.11 the *n* following the Lord stood by
23 hundred, at the third hour of the *n*;
31 brought him by *n* to Antipatris.
26. 7 serving God day and *n*, hope to
27.23 there stood by me this *n* the angel
27 when the fourteenth *n* was come,
Ro 13.12 The *n* is far spent, the day is at
1Co 11.23 same *n* in which he was betrayed
2Co 11.25 a *n* and a day I have been in the
1Th 2. 9 laboring *n* and day, because we
3.10 *N* and day praying exceedingly
5. 2 Lord so cometh as a thief in the *n*.
5 we are not of the *n*, nor of darkness.
7 For they that sleep sleep in the *n*;
7 be drunken are drunken in the *n*.
2Th 3. 8 with labor and travail *n* and day,
1Ti 5. 5 supplications and prayers *n* and
2Ti 1. 3 of thee in my prayers *n* and day;
2Pe 3.10 Lord will come as a thief in the *n*;
Rev 4. 8 they rest not day and *n*, saying,
7.15 serve him day and *n* in his temple:
8.12 third part of it, and the *n* likewise.
12.10 them before our God day and *n*.
14.11 they have no rest day nor *n*, who
20.10 be tormented day and *n* for ever
21.25 day: for there shall be no *n* there.
22. 5 And there shall be no *n* there; and

NIGHTS

Gen 7. 4 the earth forty days and forty *n*;
Ex 24.18 the mount forty days and forty *n*.
1Ki 19. 8 of that meat forty days and forty *n*
Job 2.13 ground seven days and seven *n*,
7. 3 wearisome *n* are appointed to me.
Jon 1.17 of the fish three days and three *n*.
Mt 4. 2 had fasted forty days and forty *n*,
12.40 and three *n* in the whale's belly;
40 three *n* in the heart of the earth.

NIMROD

Gen 10. 8 Cush begat *N*: he began to be a
9 *N* the mighty hunter before the
1Ch 1.10 Cush begat *N*: he began to be
Mic 5. 6 land of *N* in the entrances thereof:

NIMSHI

1Ki 19.16 the son of *N* shalt thou anoint
2Ki 9. 2 son of Jehoshaphat the son of *N*,
14 son of Jehoshaphat the son of *N*
20 the driving of Jehu the son of *N*;
2Ch 22. 7 against Jehu the son of *N*, whom

NINE

Mt 18.12 he not leave the ninety and *n*, and
13 and *n* which went not astray.
Lk 15. 4 ninety and *n* in the wilderness,
7 over ninety and *n* just persons,
17.17 ten cleansed? but where are the *n*?

NINETY

Gen 5.30 Noah five hundred *n* and five years,
17. 1 when Abram was *n* years old and
17 Sarah, that is *n* years old, bear?
Jer 52.23 there were *n* and six pomegranates
Mt 18.12 doth he not leave the *n* and nine,
13 *n* and nine which went not astray.
Lk 15. 4 doth not leave the *n* and nine in
7 than over *n* and nine just persons,

NINEVEH

Gen 10.11 forth Asshur, and builded *N*, and
12 And Resen between *N* and Calah:
2Ki 19.36 and returned, and dwelt at *N*.
Isa 37.37 and returned, and dwelt at *N*.
Jon 1. 2 go to *N*, that great city, and cry
3. 2 Arise, go unto *N*, that great city,
3 So Jonah arose, and went unto *N*,
3 *N* was an exceeding great city of
4 days, and *N* shall be overthrown.
5 So the people of *N* believed God,
6 word came unto the king of *N*, and
7 published through *N* by the decree
4.11 should not I spare *N*, that great
Na 1. 1 The burden of *N*. The book of the
2. 8 *N* is of old like a pool of water:
3. 7 thee, and say, *N* is laid waste:
Zep 2.13 will make *N* a desolation, and dry
Mt 12.41 men of *N* shall rise in judgment

NINEVITES

Lk 11.30 as Jonas was a sign unto the *N*,

NINTH

Lev 25.22 yet of old fruit until the *n* year;
Mt 20. 5 out about the sixth and *n* hour,
27.45 over all the land unto the *n* hour.
46 the *n* hour Jesus cried with a loud
Mk 15.33 the whole land until the *n* hour.
34 the *n* hour Jesus cried with a loud
Lk 23.44 over all the earth until the *n* hour.
Ac 3. 1 hour of prayer, being the *n* hour.
10. 3 vision evidently about the *n* hour
30 and at the *n* hour I prayed in my
Rev 21.20 the eighth, beryl; the *n*, a topaz;

NOAH

Hero of the flood story; son of Lamech and father of Shem, Ham, and Japeth, from whom the Semitic, Hamitic (African), and Euro-Asiatic races are traditionally believed to be descended; a good man who finds grace with God when God decides to destroy the earth because of mankind's corrupt ways (Gen 5.28–6.13); instructed to build an ark of gopher wood and to take into it with his own family two of every kind of animal and bird (Gen 6.14–7.10); the flood comes and all other terrestrial life is destroyed (Gen 7.11-24); as the waters begin to recede, Noah sends out birds, and when a dove returns with a leaf in its beak, he knows that the flood is over (Gen 8.1-14); leaves the ark and sacrifices to God, who pledges never again to destroy the earth by flood and enters into a covenant with Noah and his small group (representing all human beings in the future), the sign of which is the rainbow (Gen 8.15–9.17); Noah is found drunk and naked by Ham, an incident that draws God's curse on Ham's son, Canaan (Gen 9.18-27); Noah's death and vast age recorded (Gen 9.28-29), with a genealogy of the nations descended from him (Gen 10).

NISAN

Neh 2. 1 it came to pass in the month *N*,
Est 3. 7 first month, that is, the month *N*,

NOAH

Gen 5.29 he called his name *N*, saying,
30 after he begat *N* five hundred
32 And *N* was five hundred years old:
32 *N* begat Shem, Ham, and Japheth.
6. 8 *N* found grace in the eyes of the
9 These are the generations of *N*:
9 *N* was a just man and perfect in
9 and *N* walked with God.
10 *N* begat three sons, Shem, Ham,
13 And God said unto *N*, The end of
22 Thus did *N*; according to all that
7. 1 the Lord said unto *N*, Come thou
5 *N* did according unto all that the
6 *N* was six hundred years old when
7 *N* went in, and his sons, and his
9 two and two unto *N* into the ark,
9 female, as God had commanded *N*.
13 In the selfsame day entered *N*,
13 Ham, and Japheth, the sons of *N*,
15 they went in unto *N* into the ark,
23 *N* only remained alive, and they
8. 1 God remembered *N*, and every
6 *N* opened the window of the ark
11 so *N* knew that the waters were
13 *N* removed the covering of the ark,
15 And God spake unto *N*, saying,
18 *N* went forth, and his sons, and
20 *N* builded an altar unto the Lord;
9. 1 God blessed *N* and his sons, and
8 God spake unto *N*, and to his sons
17 God said unto *N*, This is the token
18 the sons of *N*, that went forth of
19 These are the three sons of *N*: and
20 *N* began to be an husbandman,
24 *N* awoke from his wine, and knew
28 And *N* lived after the flood three
29 the days of *N* were nine hundred
10. 1 the generations of the sons of *N*,
32 are the families of the sons of *N*,
Nu 26.33 Zelophehad were Mahlah, and *N*,
27. 1 of his daughters; Mahlah, *N*,
36.11 *N*, the daughters of Zelophehad,
Jos 17. 3 of his daughters, Mahlah, and *N*,
1Ch 1. 4 *N*, Shem, Ham, and Japheth.
Isa 54. 9 is as the waters of *N* unto me:
9 waters of *N* should no more go
Eze 14.14 three men, *N*, Daniel, and Job,
20 Though *N*, Daniel, and Job, were
Heb 11. 7 By faith *N*, being warned of God
1Pe 3.20 of God waited in the days of *N*,
2Pe 2. 5 but saved *N* the eighth person, a

NOBLE

Ezr 4.10 whom the great and *n* Asnapper
Est 6. 9 one of the king's most *n* princes,
Jer 2.21 Yet I had planted thee a *n* vine,
Ac 17.11 These were more *n* than those in
24. 3 and in all places, most *n* Felix,
26.25 said, I am not mad, most *n* Festus;
1Co 1.26 mighty, not many *n*, are called:

NOBLEMAN

Lk 19.12 A certain *n* went into a far
Jn 4.46 there was a certain *n*, whose son
49 The *n* saith unto him, Sir, come

NOBLES

Neh 2.16 nor to the priests, nor to the *n*,
3. 5 but their *n* put not their necks to
5. 7 I rebuked the *n*, and the rulers, and
Job 29.10 The *n* held their peace, and their
Pr 8.16 By me princes rule, and *n*, even
Isa 34.12 call the *n* thereof to the kingdom,
Jer 14. 3 their *n* have sent their little ones to
Na 3.18 thy *n* shall dwell in the dust: thy

NOD

Gen 4.16 dwelt in the land of *N*, on the

NOE

Mt 24.37 as the days of *N* were, so shall
38 day that *N* entered into the ark,
Lk 3.36 which was the son of *N*, which
17.26 as it was in the days of *N*, so shall
27 day that *N* entered into the ark,

NOISE

Ex 20.18 and the *n* of the trumpet, and the
32.17 Joshua heard the *n* of the people
17 There is a *n* of war in the camp.
18 the *n* of them that sing do I hear.
Jos 6.10 nor make any *n* with your voice,
Jdg 5.11 delivered from the *n* of archers
1Sa 4. 6 heard the *n* of the shout, they
6 meaneth the *n* of this great shout
14 when Eli heard the *n* of the crying,
14 What meaneth the *n* of this tumult?
14.19 the *n* that was in the host of the
1Ki 1.41 *n* of the city being in an uproar?
45 This is the *n* that ye have heard.
2Ki 7. 6 the Syrians to hear a *n* of chariots,
6 *n* of horses, even the *n* of a great
11.13 Athaliah heard the *n* of the guard
1Ch 15.28 making a *n* with psalteries and
2Ch 23.12 when Athaliah heard the *n* of the
Ezr 3.13 discern the *n* of the shout of joy
13 the *n* of the weeping of the people:
13 shout, and the *n* was heard afar off.
Job 36.29 or the *n* of his tabernacle?
33 *n* thereof sheweth concerning it,
37. 2 Hear attentively the *n* of his voice,
Ps 33. 3 song; play skilfully with a loud *n*.
42. 7 deep at the *n* of thy waterspouts:
55. 2 in my complaint, and make a *n*;
59. 6 they make a *n* like a dog, and go
14 let them make a *n* like a dog,
65. 7 Which stilleth the *n* of the seas,
7 *n* of their waves, and the tumult of
66. 1 Make a joyful *n* unto God, all ye
81. 1 make a joyful *n* unto the God of
93. 4 than the *n* of many waters, yea,
95. 1 let us make a joyful *n* to the rock of
2 a joyful *n* unto him with psalms.
98. 4 Make a joyful *n* unto the Lord, all
4 make a loud *n*, and rejoice, and
6 make a joyful *n* before the Lord, the
100. 1 Make a joyful *n* unto the Lord, all ye
Isa 9. 5 of the warrior is with confused *n*,
13. 4 *n* of a multitude in the mountains,
4 tumultuous *n* of the kingdoms of
14.11 the grave, and the *n* of thy viols:
17.12 make a *n* like the *n* of the seas;
24. 8 the *n* of them that rejoice endeth,
18 who fleeth from the *n* of the fear
25. 5 bring down the *n* of strangers, as
29. 6 and with earthquake, and great *n*,
31. 4 abase himself for the *n* of them:
33. 3 At the *n* of the tumult the people
66. 6 A voice of *n* from the city, a voice
Jer 4.19 my heart maketh a *n* in me; I
29 flee for the *n* of the horsemen
10.22 Behold, the *n* of the bruit is come,
11.16 with the *n* of a great tumult he
25.31 A *n* shall come even to the ends of
46.17 Pharaoh king of Egypt is but a *n*;
47. 3 the *n* of the stamping of the hoofs
49.21 is moved at the *n* of their fall;
21 at the cry the *n* thereof was heard
50.46 At the *n* of the taking of Babylon
51.55 a *n* of their voice is uttered:
La 2. 7 a *n* in the house of the Lord,
Eze 1.24 went, I heard the *n* of their wings,
24 like the *n* of great waters, as the
24 of speech, as the *n* of an host:
3.13 I heard also the *n* of the wings of
13 the *n* of the wheels over against
13 them, and a *n* of a great rushing.
19. 7 thereof, by the *n* of his roaring.
26.10 shake at the *n* of the horsemen,
13 cause the *n* of thy songs to cease;
37. 7 as I prophesied, there was a *n*,
43. 2 voice was like a *n* of many waters:
Joel 2. 5 Like the *n* of chariots on the tops of
5 like the *n* of a flame of fire that
Am 5.23 away from me the *n* of thy songs;
Mic 2.12 make a great *n* by reason of the
Na 3. 2 The *n* of a whip, and the *n* of the
Zep 1.10 the *n* of a cry from the fish gate,
Zec 9.15 and make a *n* as through wine:
Mt 9.23 minstrels and...people make a *n*,
2Pe 3.10 shall pass away with a great *n*,
Rev 6. 1 heard, as it were the *n* of thunder,

NOISED

Jos 6.27 his fame was *n* throughout all the
Mk 2. 1 it was *n* that he was in the house.
Lk 1.65 all these sayings were *n* abroad
Ac 2. 6 when this was *n* abroad, the

NOISOME

Ps 91. 3 fowler, and from the *n* pestilence.
Eze 14.15 I cause *n* beasts to pass through
21 the *n* beast, and the pestilence,
Rev 16. 2 fell a *n* and grievous sore upon the

NONE

Gen 23. 6 *n* of us shall withhold from
28.17 is *n* other but the house of God,
39. 9 is *n* greater in this house than I;
41. 8 there was *n* that could interpret
15 and there is *n* that can interpret it:
Ex 8.10 is *n* like unto the Lord our God.
Lev 18. 6 *N* of you shall approach to any
22.30 leave *n* of it until the morrow:
26. 6 down, and *n* shall make you afraid:
17 ye shall flee when *n* pursueth you.
Dt 2.34 of every city, we left *n* to remain:
3. 3 smote him until *n* was left to him
4.35 God; there is *n* else beside him.
5. 7 shalt have *n* other gods before me.

28.31 thou shalt have *n* to rescue them.
Jos 6. 1 Israel: *n* went out, and *n* came in.
8.22 let *n* of them remain or escape.
Ru 4. 4 is *n* to redeem it beside thee; and
1Sa 2. 2 There is *n* holy as the Lord: for
3.19 *n* of his words fall to the ground.
22. 8 is *n* that sheweth me that my son
8 is *n* of you that is sorry for me, or
2Sa 7.22 for there is *n* like thee, neither is
18.12 Beware that *n* touch the young man
22.42 looked, but there was *n* to save;
1Ch 15. 2 *N* ought to carry the ark of God
17.20 O Lord, there is *n* like thee,
Job 1. 8 there is *n* like him in the earth,
2. 3 there is *n* like him in the earth,
13 and *n* spake a word unto him: for
10. 7 there is *n* that can deliver out of
35.10 *n* saith, Where is God my maker,
12 they cry, but *n* giveth answer,
41.10 *N* is so fierce that dare stir him up:
Ps 7. 2 pieces, while there is *n* to deliver.
14. 1 works, there is *n* that doeth good.
22.11 is near; for there is *n* to help.
29 and *n* can keep alive his own soul.
25. 3 *n* that wait on thee be ashamed:
53. 1 iniquity: there is *n* that doeth good.
69.20 some to take pity, but there was *n*;
20 and for comforters, but I found *n*.
86. 8 the gods there is *n* like unto thee,
107.12 fell down, and there was *n* to help.
Pr 1.25 and would *n* of my reproof;
30 They would *n* of my counsel: they
Isa 1.31 together, and *n* shall quench them.
14. 6 is persecuted, and *n* hindereth.
22.22 so he shall open, and *n* shall shut;
22 and he shall shut, and *n* shall open.
34.10 *n* shall pass through it for ever and
41.17 needy seek water, and there is *n*,
26 there is *n* that heareth your words.
45. 5 I am the Lord, and there is *n* else,
50. 2 I called, was there *n* to answer?
59. 4 *n* calleth for justice, nor any
11 look for judgment, but there is *n*;
64. 7 is *n* that calleth upon thy name,
66. 4 when I called, *n* did answer;
Jer 4. 4 fire, and burn that *n* can quench it,
9.10 *n* can pass through them;
21.12 and burn that *n* can quench it,
23.14 *n* doth return from...wickedness:
30. 7 day is great, so that *n* is like it:
36.30 shall have *n* to sit upon the throne
42.17 *n* of them shall remain or escape
44. 7 Judah, to leave you *n* to remain;
La 1. 2 lovers she hath *n* to comfort her:
7 of the enemy, and *n* did help her:
21 I sigh: there is *n* to comfort me:
2.22 of the Lord's anger *n* escaped
Eze 7.11 *n* of them shall remain, nor of
16. 5 *N* eye pitied thee, to do any of
Dan 1.19 them all was found *n* like Daniel,
6. 4 could find *n* occasion nor fault;
12.10 *n* of the wicked shall understand;
Joel 2.27 the Lord your God, and *n* else:
Mic 2. 5 *n* that shall cast a cord by lot in
3.11 us? *n* evil can come upon us.
7. 2 and there is *n* upright among men:
Zep 2.15 I am, and there is *n* beside me:
Hag 1. 6 ye clothe you, but there is *n* warm;
Zec 7.10 let *n* of you imagine evil against
8.17 let *n* of you imagine evil in your
Mal 2.15 let *n* deal treacherously against
Mt 12.43 places, seeking rest, and findeth *n*.
19.17 there is *n* good but one, that is,
26.60 But found *n*: yea, though many
60 witnesses came, yet found they *n*.
Mk 7.13 Making...word of God of *n* effect
10.18 is *n* good but one, that is, God.
14.55 to put him to death; and found *n*.
Lk 1.61 is *n* of thy kindred that is called
4.26 unto *n* of them was Elias sent,
27 *n* of them was cleansed, saving
11.24 seeking rest; and finding *n*, he
13. 6 sought fruit thereon, and found *n*,
18.19 *n* is good, save one, that is, God.
Jn 6.22 that there was *n* other boat there,
7.19 *n* of you keepeth the law? Why go
16. 5 *n* of you asketh me, Whither goest
18. 9 thou gavest me have I lost *n*.
Ac 3. 6 said, Silver and gold have I *n*;
4.12 is *n* other name under heaven
18.17 Gallio cared for *n* of these things.
Ro 3.10 there is *n* righteous, no, not one:
11 There is *n* that understandeth,
11 there is *n* that seeketh after God.
12 there is *n* that doeth good, no, not
8. 9 the Spirit of Christ, he is *n* of his.
14. 7 For *n* of us liveth to himself, and
Gal 1.19 But other of the apostles saw I *n*,

Noah offers a sacrifice after the Flood (Gen 8); engraving of a painting by Nicolas Poussin (1594-1665).

1Ti 5.14 give *n* occasion to the adversary
1Pe 4.15 let *n* of you suffer as a murderer,

NOON

Gen 43.16 men shall dine with me at *n*.
25 present against Joseph came at *n*:
2Sa 4. 5 Ish-bosheth, who lay on a bed at *n*.
1Ki 18.26 Baal from morning even until *n*,
27 it came to pass at *n*, that Elijah
20.16 And they went out at *n*. But
2Ki 4.20 he sat on her knees till *n*, and then
Ps 55.17 Evening, and morning, and at *n*,
SS 1. 7 thou makest thy flock to rest at *n*:
Isa 58.10 and thy darkness be as the *n* day:
59.10 we stumble at *n* day as in the
Jer 6. 4 her; arise, and let us go up at *n*.
Am 8. 9 will cause the sun to go down at *n*,
Zep 2. 4 shall drive out Ashdod at the *n* day,
Ac 22. 6 nigh unto Damascus about *n*,

NOONDAY

Dt 28.29 And thou shalt grope at *n*, as the
Job 5.14 and grope in the *n* as in the night.
11.17 age shall be clearer than the *n*;
Ps 37. 6 light, and thy judgment as the *n*.
91. 6 the destruction that wasteth at *n*.
Isa 16. 3 as the night in the midst of the *n*;
Jer 15. 8 of the young men a spoiler at *n*:

NORTH

Job 37. 9 whirlwind: and cold out of the *n*.
22 Fair weather cometh out of the *n*:
Ps 89.12 *n* and the south thou hast created
Pr 25.23 The *n* wind driveth away rain:
SS 4.16 Awake, O *n* wind; and come, thou
Isa 14.31 shall come from the *n* a smoke,
Jer 1.14 Out of the *n* an evil shall break
47. 2 Behold, waters rise up out of the *n*,
50. 9 great nations from the *n* country:
Eze 1. 4 a whirlwind came out of the *n*,
Lk 13.29 from the *n*, and from the south,
Ac 27.12 toward the south west and *n* west.
Rev 21.13 on the *n* three gates; on the south

NOSE

Lev 21.18 or a lame, or he that hath a flat *n*,
2Ki 19.28 I will put my hook in thy *n*, and
Job 40.24 eyes: his *n* pierceth through snares.
41. 2 Canst thou put an hook into his *n*?
Pr 30.33 the wringing of the *n* bringeth forth
SS 7. 4 thy *n* is as the tower of Lebanon
8 and the smell of thy *n* like apples;
Isa 3.21 The rings, and *n* jewels,
37.29 therefore will I put my hook in thy *n*,
65. 5 These are a smoke in my *n*, a fire
Eze 8.17 lo, they put the branch to their *n*.
23.25 they shall take away thy *n* and thine

NOSES

Ps 115. 6 *n* have they, but they smell not:
Eze 39.11 it shall stop the *n* of the passengers:

NOSTRILS

Gen 2. 7 into his *n* the breath of life; and
7.22 in whose *n* was the breath of life,
Ex 15. 8 with the blast of thy *n* the waters
Nu 11.20 month, until it come out at your *n*,
2Sa 22. 9 There went up a smoke out of his *n*,
16 at the blast of the breath of his *n*.
Job 4. 9 by the breath of his *n* are they
27. 3 and the spirit of God is in my *n*;
39.20 the glory of his *n* is terrible.
41.20 Out of his *n* goeth smoke, as out
Ps 18. 8 went up a smoke out of his *n*,
15 at the blast of the breath of thy *n*.
Isa 2.22 from man, whose breath is in his *n*:
La 4.20 The breath of our *n*, the anointed
Am 4.10 your camps to come up unto your *n*:

NOTABLE

Dan 8. 5 goat had a *n* horn between his
8 and for it came up four *n* ones

Mt 27.16 a *n* prisoner, called Barabbas.
Ac 2.20 great and *n* day of the Lord come:
4.16 indeed a *n* miracle hath been done

NOTE

Isa 30. 8 in a table, and *n* it in a book,
Ro 16. 7 who are of *n* among the apostles,
2Th 3.14 *n* that man, and have no company

NOTED

Dan 10.21 is *n* in the scripture of truth:

NOTHING

Gen 11. 6 *n* will be restrained from
19. 8 only unto these men do *n*; for
26.29 have done unto thee *n* but good,
40.15 and here also have I done *n*
Ex 9. 4 *n* die of all that is the children's
12.10 ye shall let *n* of it remain until
20 Ye shall eat *n* leavened; in all your
16.18 that gathered much had *n* over,
21. 2 seventh he shall go out free for *n*.
22. 3 if he have *n*, then he shall be sold
23.26 There shall *n* cast their young,
Nu 6. 4 eat *n* that is made of the vine tree,
11. 6 is *n* at all, beside this manna,
16.26 and touch *n* of theirs, lest ye
22.16 Let *n*, I pray thee, hinder thee
Dt 2. 7 with thee; thou hast lacked *n*.
20.16 save alive *n* that breatheth:
22.26 the damsel thou shalt do *n*;
28.55 he hath *n* left him in the siege,
Jos 11.15 left *n* undone of all that the
Jdg 3. 2 such as before knew *n* thereof;
7.14 is *n* else save the sword of Gideon
14. 6 and he had *n* in his hand:
1Sa 3.18 every whit, and hid *n* from him.
20. 2 father will do *n* either great
22.15 thy servant knew *n* of all this,
25.21 so that *n* was missed of all that
36 she told him *n*, less or more,
27. 1 there is *n* better for me than that
30.19 And there was *n* lacking to them,
2Sa 12. 3 But the poor man had *n*, save
24. 4 offer...that which doth cost me *n*.
1Ki 4.27 in his month: they lacked *n*.
8. 9 There was *n* in the ark save the
10.21 *n* accounted of in the days of
11.22 country? And he answered, *N*:
18.43 looked, and said, There is *n*.
22.16 tell me *n* but that which is true
2Ki 10.10 fall unto the earth *n* of the word of
20.13 there was *n* in his house, nor
15 there is *n* among my treasures
17 *n* shall be left, saith the Lord.
2Ch 5.10 There was *n* in the ark save the
9. 2 *n* hid from Solomon which
18.15 thou say *n* but the truth to me
Neh 2. 2 this is *n* else but sorrow of heart.
5. 8 peace, and found *n* to answer.
12 them, and will require *n* of them;
8.10 unto them for whom *n* is prepared:
9.21 wilderness, so that they lacked *n*;
Est 2.15 required *n* but what Hegai
5.13 Yet all this availeth me *n*, so long
6. 3 There is *n* done for him.
10 *n* fail of all that thou hast spoken.
Job 6.18 aside; they go to *n*, and perish.
21 now ye are *n*; ye see my casting
8. 9 are but of yesterday, and know *n*,
24.25 liar, and make my speech *n* worth?
26. 7 and hangeth the earth upon *n*.
34. 9 It profiteth a man *n* that he
Ps 17. 3 hast tried me, and shalt find *n*:
19. 6 is *n* hid from the heat thereof.
39. 5 and mine age is as *n* before thee:
49.17 dieth he shall carry *n* away:
119.165 law: and *n* shall offend them.
Pr 8. 8 is *n* froward or perverse in them.
9.13 is simple, and knoweth *n*.
10. 2 Treasures of wickedness profit *n*:
13. 4 the sluggard desireth, and hath *n*:
7 himself rich, yet hath *n*:
20. 4 shall he beg in harvest and have *n*.
22.27 If thou hast *n* to pay, why should
Ec 2.24 There is *n* better for a man, than
3.14 *n* can be put to it, nor any thing
22 is *n* better, than that a man should
5.14 and there is *n* in his hand.
15 and shall take *n* of his labor,
6. 2 so that he wanteth *n* for his soul
7.14 man should find *n* after him.
Isa 34.12 and all her princes shall be *n*.
39. 2 there was *n* in his house, nor
4 is *n* among my treasures that
6 *n* shall be left, saith the Lord.
40.17 All nations before him are as *n*;
17 counted to him less than *n*,
41.11 confounded: they shall be as *n*;
12 that war against thee shall be as *n*,
24 Behold, ye are of *n*, and your work
29 are all vanity; their works are *n*:
44.10 image that is profitable for *n*?
Jer 10.24 anger, lest thou bring me to *n*.
13. 7 it was profitable for *n*.
10 girdle, which is good for *n*.
32.17 there is *n* too hard for thee:
23 *n* of all that thou commandedst
38.14 thee a thing; hide *n* from me.
39.10 of the people, which had *n*,
42. 4 I will keep *n* back from you.
50.26 her utterly: let *n* of her be left.
La 1.12 Is it *n* to you, all ye that pass by?
Eze 13. 3 their own spirit, and have seen *n*!
Dan 4.35 of the earth are reputed as *n*:
Joel 2. 3 yea, and *n* shall escape them.
Am 3. 4 out of his den, if he have taken *n*?
5 earth, and have taken *n* at all?
7 the Lord God will do *n*, but
Hag 2. 3 your eyes in comparison of it as *n*?
Mt 5.13 it is thenceforth good for *n*, but to
10.26 there is *n* covered, that shall not
15.32 three days, and have *n* to eat:
17.20 *n* shall be impossible unto you.
21.19 found *n* thereon, but leaves only,
23.16 shall swear by the temple, it is *n*;
18 shall swear by the altar, it is *n*;
26.62 said unto him, Answerest thou *n*?
27.12 priests and elders, he answered *n*.
19 thou *n* to do with that just man:
24 Pilate saw that he could prevail *n*,
Mk 1.44 See thou say *n* to any man: but
4.22 there is *n* hid, which shall not
5.26 was *n* bettered, but rather grew
6. 8 should take *n* for their journey,
36 for they have *n* to eat.
7.15 There is *n* from without a man,
8. 1 and having *n* to eat, Jesus called
2 three days, and have *n* to eat:
9.29 This kind can come forth by *n*,
11.13 came to it, he found *n* but leaves;
14.60 Jesus, saying, Answerest thou *n*?
61 he held his peace, and answered *n*.
15. 3 things: but he answered *n*.
4 again, saying, Answerest thou *n*?
5 But Jesus yet answered *n*; so that
Lk 1.37 *n* shall be impossible.
4. 2 And in those days he did eat *n*:
5. 5 all the night, and have taken *n*:
6.35 and lend, hoping for *n* again;
7.42 And when they had *n* to pay, he
8.17 *n* is secret, that shall not be made
9. 3 Take *n* for your journey, neither
10.19 *n* shall by any means hurt you.
11. 6 I have *n* to set before him?
12. 2 there is *n* covered, that shall not
22.35 ye any thing? And they said, *N*.
23. 9 words; but he answered him *n*.
15 *n* worthy of death is done unto him.
41 but this man hath done *n* amiss.
Jn 3.27 A man can receive *n*, except it be
4.11 Sir, thou hast *n* to draw with,
5.19 The Son can do *n* of himself, but
30 I can of mine own self do *n*:
6.12 that remain, that *n* be lost.
39 hath given me I should lose *n*,
63 quickeneth; the flesh profiteth *n*:
7.26 boldly, and they say *n* unto him.
8.28 I am he, and that I do *n* of myself;
54 I honor myself, my honor is *n*:
9.33 man were not of God, he could do *n*.
11.49 unto them, Ye know *n* at all,
12.19 Perceive ye how ye prevail *n*?
14.30 world cometh, and hath *n* in me.
15. 5 fruit: for without me ye can do *n*.
16.23 And in that day ye shall ask me *n*.
24 have ye asked *n* in my name:
18.20 resort; and in secret have I said *n*.
21. 3 and that night they caught *n*.
Ac 4.14 them, they could say *n* against it.
21 finding *n* how they might punish
10.20 and go with them, doubting *n*:
11. 8 *n* common or unclean hath
12 me go with them, *n* doubting.
17.21 spent their time in *n* else, but
19.36 to be quiet, and to do *n* rashly.
20.20 kept back *n* that was profitable
21.24 informed concerning thee, are *n*;
23.14 will eat *n* until we have slain Paul.
29 to have *n* laid to his charge worthy
25.25 had committed *n* worthy of death,
26.31 This man doeth *n* worthy of death
27.33 continued fasting, having taken *n*.
28.17 committed *n* against the people,
Ro 14.14 that there is *n* unclean of itself:
1Co 1.19 will bring to *n* the understanding
4. 4 For I know *n* by myself; yet am I
5 Therefore judge *n* before the time.
7.19 Circumcision is *n*, and
19 and uncircumcision is *n*, but the
8. 2 he knoweth *n* yet as he ought to
4 that an idol is *n* in the world,
9.16 the gospel, I have *n* to glory of:
13. 2 and have not charity, I am *n*.
3 not charity, it profiteth me *n*.
2Co 6.10 as having *n*, and yet possessing
7. 9 might receive damage by us in *n*.
8.15 had gathered much had *n* over;
12.11 for in *n* am I behind the very
11 chiefest apostles, though I be *n*.
13. 8 we can do *n* against the truth,
Gal 2. 6 in conference added *n* to me:
4. 1 a child, differeth *n* from a servant,
5. 2 Christ shall profit you *n*.
6. 3 to be something, when he is *n*,
Php 1.20 that in *n* I shall be ashamed,
28 in *n* terrified by your adversaries:
2. 3 Let *n* be done through strife or
4. 6 Be careful for *n*; but in every thing
1Th 4.12 and that ye may have lack of *n*.
1Ti 4. 4 God is good, and *n* to be refused,
5.21 another, doing *n* by partiality.
6. 4 He is proud, knowing *n*, but doting
7 For we brought *n* into this world,
7 certain we can carry *n* out.
Tit 1.15 defiled and unbelieving is *n* pure;
3.13 that *n* be wanting unto them.
Phm 14 without thy mind would I do *n*;
Heb 2. 8 he left *n* that is not put under him.
7.14 of which tribe Moses spake *n*
19 For the law made *n* perfect, but the
Jas 1. 4 be perfect and entire, wanting *n*.
6 let him ask in faith, *n* wavering:
3Jn 7 forth, taking *n* of the Gentiles.
Rev 3.17 with goods, and have need of *n*;

NOTICE

2Sa 3.36 all the people took *n* of it, and it
2Co 9. 5 bounty, whereof ye had *n* before,

NOUGHT

Gen 29.15 thou therefore serve me for *n*?
Dt 13.17 cleave *n* of the cursed thing

15. 9 brother, and thou givest him *n*;
28.63 destroy you, and to bring you to *n*;
Neh 4.15 had brought their counsel to *n*,
Job 1. 9 said, Doth Job fear God for *n*?
8.22 place of the wicked shall come to *n*.
14.18 the mountain falling cometh to *n*,
22. 6 a pledge from thy brother for *n*,
Ps 33.10 the counsel of the heathen to *n*:
44.12 Thou sellest thy people for *n*,
Pr 1.25 ye have set at *n* all my counsel,
Isa 8.10 together, and it shall come to *n*;
29.20 the terrible one is brought to *n*,
21 turn aside the just for a thing of *n*.
41.12 be as nothing, and as a thing of *n*.
24 of nothing, and your work of *n*:
49. 4 I have spent my strength for *n*,
52. 3 Ye have sold yourselves for *n*;
5 my people is taken away for *n*?
Jer 14.14 and a thing of *n*, and the deceit of
Am 5. 5 and Beth-el shall come to *n*.
6.13 which rejoice in a thing of *n*,
Mal 1.10 you that would shut the doors for *n*?
10 ye kindle fire on mine altar for *n*,
Mk 9.12 many things, and be set at *n*.
Lk 23.11 with his men of war set him at *n*,
Ac 4.11 is the stone which was set at *n* of
5.36 were scattered, and brought to *n*.
38 work be of men, it will come to *n*:
19.27 craft is in danger to be set at *n*;
Ro 14.10 why dost thou set at *n* thy brother?
1Co 1.28 not, to bring to *n* things that are:
2. 6 of this world, that come to *n*:
2Th 3. 8 did we eat any man's bread for *n*;
Rev 18.17 hour so great riches is come to *n*.

NOURISH
Gen 45.11 And there will I *n* thee; for yet
50.21 I will *n* you, and your little ones.
Isa 7.21 a man shall *n* a young cow, and
23. 4 neither do I *n* up young men, nor
44.14 an ash, and the rain doth *n* it.

NOURISHED
Gen 47.12 And Joseph *n* his father, and his
2Sa 12. 3 which he had bought and *n* up:
Isa 1. 2 I have *n* and brought up children,
Eze 19. 2 *n* her whelps among young lions.
Ac 7.20 *n* up in his father's house three
21 him up, and *n* him for her own son.
12.20 their country was *n* by the king's
1Ti 4. 6 *n* up in the words of faith and of
Jas 5. 5 ye have *n* your hearts, as in a day
Rev 12.14 her place, where she is *n* for a time.

NOURISHER
Ru 4.15 thy life, and a *n* of thine old age:

NOURISHETH
Eph 5.29 *n* and cherisheth it, even as the

NOURISHING
Dan 1. 5 so *n* them three years, that at the

NOURISHMENT
Col 2.19 having *n* ministered, and knit

NOVICE
1Ti 3. 6 Not a *n*, lest being lifted up with

NOW
Gen 3. 1 *N* the serpent was more subtil than
4.11 *n* art thou cursed from the earth,
18.21 I will go down *n*, and see whether
22.12 for *n* I know that thou fearest God,
31.12 Lift up *n* thine eyes, and see, all
13 *n* arise, get thee out from this
28 hast *n* done foolishly in so doing.
37. 3 *N* Israel loved Joseph more than all
46.30 *N* let me die, since I have seen
50.17 Forgive, I pray...*n*, the trespass
Ex 1. 8 *N* there arose up a new king over
3. 1 *N* Moses kept the flock of Jethro
3 I will *n* turn aside, and see this
6. 1 *N* shalt thou see what I will do to
18.11 *N* I know that the Lord is greater
32.32 *n*, if thou wilt forgive their sin–;
Nu 11. 6 But *n* our soul is dried away:
Dt 31.19 *N* therefore write ye this song for
Jos 1. 1 *N* after the death of Moses the
9. 6 *n* therefore make ye a league
25 *n*, behold, we are in thine hand:
14.12 *N* therefore give me this mountain,
22.26 Let us *n* prepare to build us an
Jdg 12. 6 they unto him, Say *n* Shibboleth:
13. 7 *n* drink no wine nor strong drink,
19. 9 *n* the day draweth toward evening,
1Sa 2.22 *N* Eli was very old, and heard all that
3. 7 *N* Samuel did not yet know the
8. 5 *n* make us a king to judge us like
10.19 *N* therefore present yourselves
16.12 *N* he was ruddy, and withal of a
17 Provide me *n* a man that can play
17.29 David said, What have I *n* done?
20.36 Run, find out *n* the arrows which I
2Sa 2. 7 *n* let your hands be strengthened,
23. 1 *N* these be the last words of David.
1Ki 19. 4 *n*, O Lord, take away my life;
21. 7 Dost thou *n* govern the kingdom
2Ki 5. 8 let him come *n* to me, and he
15 *n* I know that there is no god in
1Ch 17.26 And *n*, Lord, thou art God, and
29.20 *N* bless the Lord your God. And
2Ch 35. 3 serve *n* the Lord your God, and
Ezr 7.11 *N* this is the copy of the letter that
10.11 *N* therefore make confession unto
Est 9.12 *n* what is thy petition? and it shall
Job 1.11 But put forth thine hand *n*, and
7.21 for *n* shall I sleep in the dust; and
9.25 *N* my days are swifter than a post:
13.19 for *n*, if I hold my tongue, I shall
14.16 For *n* thou numberest my steps:
19. 6 Know *n* that God hath overthrown
23 Oh that my words were *n* written!
30. 9 And *n* am I their song, yea, I am
16 *n* my soul is poured out upon me;
37.21 And *n* men see not the bright light
38. 3 Gird up *n* thy loins like a man;
Ps 20. 6 *N* know I that the Lord saveth his
39. 7 And *n*, Lord, what wait I for? my
115. 2 say, Where is *n* their God?
116.14, 18 pay my vows unto the Lord *n* in
118.25 Save *n*, I beseech thee, O Lord: O
122. 8 I will *n* say, Peace be within thee.
124. 1 was on our side, *n* may Israel say;
Ec 3.15 That which hath been is *n*; and
9. 7 for God *n* accepteth thy works.
12. 1 Remember *n* thy Creator in the days
Isa 1.18 Come *n*, and let us reason
5. 1 *N* will I sing to my wellbeloved
38. 3 Remember *n*, O Lord, I beseech
42.14 *n* will I cry like a travailing woman;
47.13 Let *n* the astrologers, the
64. 8 *n*, O Lord, thou art our father; we
Jer 5.21 Hear *n* this, O foolish people, and
24 Let us *n* fear the Lord our God,
27.18 *n* make intercession to the Lord
Eze 8. 5 Son of man, lift up thine eyes *n*
17.12 Say *n* to the rebellious house,
26.18 *N* shall the isles tremble in the
39.25 *N* will I bring again the captivity
Dan 1. 9 *N* God had brought Daniel into
5.12 *n* let Daniel be called, and he will
6. 8 *N*, O king, establish the decree,
10 *N* when Daniel knew that the
Hos 8.13 *n* will he remember their iniquity,
10. 3 *n* they shall say, We have no king,
Am 6. 7 Therefore *n* shall they go captive
Jon 1.17 *N* the Lord...prepared a great fish
3. 3 *N* Nineveh was an exceeding great
Mt 1.18 *N* the birth of Jesus Christ was on
2. 1 *N* when Jesus was born in
3.10 *n* also the axe is laid unto the root
24.32 *N* learn a parable of the fig tree;
26.45 Sleep on *n*, and take your rest:
48 *N* he that betrayed him gave
65 *n* ye have heard his blasphemy.
27.42 him *n* come down from the cross,
43 let him deliver him *n*, if he will
Mk 13.28 *N* learn a parable of the fig tree;
14.41 Sleep on *n*, and take your rest: it
15.32 Christ...descend *n* from the cross,
Lk 2.29 *n* lettest thou thy servant depart
3. 9 *n* also the axe is laid unto the root
6.21 Blessed are ye that hunger *n*: for
21 Blessed are ye that weep *n*: for ye
25 Woe unto you that laugh *n*! for ye
8.11 *N* the parable is this: The seed is
10.36 which *n* of these three, thinkest
11. 7 the door is *n* shut, and my
14.17 Come; for all things are *n* ready.
19.42 *n* they are hid from thine eyes.
20.37 *N* that the dead are raised, even
Jn 2.10 hast kept the good wine until *n*.
4. 6 *N* Jacob's well was there. Jesus
18 he whom thou *n* hast is not thy
23 the hour cometh, and *n* is, when
8.52 *N* we know that thou hast a devil.
9.19 blind? how then doth he *n* see?
25 that, whereas I was blind, *n* I see.
31 *N* we know that God heareth not
41 *n* ye say, We see; therefore your
11. 5 *N* Jesus loved Martha, and her
12.27 *N* is my soul troubled; and what
31 *N* is the judgment of this world:
13. 2 devil having *n* put into the heart
31 *N* is the Son of man glorified,
15. 3 *N* ye are clean through the word
16. 5 *n* I go my way to him that sent me;
30 *N* are we sure that thou knowest
32 the hour cometh, yea, is *n* come,
17. 5 *n*, O Father, glorify thou me with
11 And *n* I am no more in the world,
13 And *n* come I to thee; and these
18.36 *n* is my kingdom not from hence.
40 *N* Barabbas was a robber.
19.23 *n* the coat was without seam, woven
25 *N* there stood by the cross of Jesus
28 all things were *n* accomplished,
21.14 This is *n* the third time that Jesus
Ac 4.13 *N*, when they saw the boldness of
10. 5 *n* send men to Joppa, and call for
12.11 *N* I know of a surety, that the
15.10 *N* therefore why tempt ye God, to
16.37 *n* do they thrust us out privily?
17.30 *n* commandeth all men everywhere
20.32 *n*, brethren, I commend you to God,
24.13 things whereof they *n* accuse me.
25. 1 *N* when Festus was come into
26. 6 *n* I stand and am judged for the
Ro 5. 9 being *n* justified by his blood,
11 we have *n* received the atonement.
6. 8 *N* if we be dead with Christ, we
22 But *n* being made free from sin,
7.17 *N* then it is no more I that do it,
20 *N* if I do that I would not, it is no
8. 1 therefore *n* no condemnation to
9 *N* if any man have not the Spirit
13.11 *n* it is high time to awake out of
11 for *n* is our salvation nearer than
15. 5 *N* the God of patience and
13 *N* the God of hope fill you with all
16.25 *N* to him that is of power to stablish
1Co 3. 8 *N* he that planteth and he that
4. 8 *N* ye are full, *n* ye are rich, ye
7. 1 *N* concerning the things whereof ye
10. 6 *N* these things were our examples,
12. 1 *N* concerning spiritual gifts,
4 *N* there are diversities of gifts, but
20 But *n* are they many members,
27 *N* ye are the body of Christ, and
13.12 *n* we see through a glass, darkly;
12 *N* I know in part; but then shall I

1Co 13.13 And *n* abideth faith, hope, charity,
15.20 *n* is Christ risen from the dead,
50 *N* this I say, brethren, that flesh
16. 1 *N* concerning the collection for the
2Co 3.17 *N* the Lord is that Spirit: and
6. 2 behold, *n* is the accepted time;
2 behold, *n* is the day of salvation.)
Gal 5.19 *N* the works of the flesh are
Eph 2.19 *N*...ye are no more strangers
3.20 *N* unto him that is able to do
4. 9 (*N* that he ascended, what is it but
5. 8 but *n* are ye light in the Lord:
Php 2.12 but *n* much more in my absence,
1Ti 1. 5 *N* the end of the commandment is
17 *N* unto the King eternal, immortal,
4. 1 *N* the Spirit speaketh expressly,
2Ti 4. 6 For I am *n* ready to be offered,
Heb 2. 8 *n* we see not yet all things put
8. 1 *N* of the things which we have
6 But *n* hath he obtained a more
10.18 *N* where remission of these is,
38 *N* the just shall live by faith: but
11. 1 *N* faith is the substance of things
16 *n* they desire a better country,
12.11 *N* no chastening for the present
13.20 *N* the God of peace, that brought
1Pe 1. 6 though *n* for a season, if need be,
2.10 people, but are *n* the people of God:
10 mercy, but *n* have obtained mercy.
25 are *n* returned unto the Shepherd
3.21 even baptism doth also *n* save us
2Pe 3.18 him be glory both *n* and for ever.
1Jn 2. 8 past, and the true light *n* shineth.
18 even *n* are there many antichrists;
28 *n*, little children, abide in him;
3. 2 Beloved, *n* are we the sons of God,
Jude 24 *N* unto him that is able to keep
Rev 12.10 *N* is come salvation, and strength,

NUMBER

Gen 13.16 man can *n* the dust of the earth,
15. 5 stars, if thou be able to *n* them:
41.49 numbering; for it was without *n*.
Ex 23.26 land: the *n* of thy days I will fulfil.
Nu 3.15 *N* the children of Levi after the
Dt 4.27 be left few in *n* among the heathen,
7. 7 ye were more in *n* than any people;
Jdg 7. 6 the *n* of them that lapped, putting
2Sa 24. 2 Beer-sheba, and *n* ye the people,
1Ch 21. 2 Go, *n* Israel from Beer-sheba even
2Ch 12. 3 people were without *n* that came
Job 5. 9 marvellous things without *n*:
9.10 out; yea, and wonders without *n*.
31.37 unto him the *n* of my steps; as a
36.26 can the *n* of his years be searched
38.37 Who can *n* the clouds in wisdom?
Ps 90.12 So teach us to *n* our days, that
139.18 they are more in *n* than the sand:
147. 4 He telleth the *n* of the stars; he
Jer 2.32 have forgotten me days without *n*.
Dan 9. 2 by books the *n* of the years,
Mk 10.46 disciples and a great *n* of people,
Lk 22. 3 being of the *n* of the twelve.
Jn 6.10 sat down, in *n* about five thousand.
Ac 1.15 (the *n* of names together were
4. 4 the *n* of the men was about five
5.36 to whom a *n* of men, about four
6. 1 the *n* of the disciples was multiplied,
7 the *n* of the disciples multiplied in
11.21 and a great *n* believed, and turned
16. 5 the faith, and increased in *n* daily.
Ro 9.27 the *n* of the children of Israel be
2Co 10.12 dare not make ourselves of the *n*,
1Ti 5. 9 not a widow be taken into the *n*
Rev 5.11 the *n* of them was ten thousand
7. 4 I heard the *n* of them which were
9 multitude, which no man could *n*,
9.16 the *n* of the army of the horsemen
16 and I heard the *n* of them.
13.17 of the beast, or the *n* of his name.
18 count the *n* of the beast: for it is
18 the beast: for it is the *n* of a man;
18 his *n* is Six hundred threescore
15. 2 mark, and over the *n* of his name,
20. 8 *n* of whom is as the sand of the sea.

NUMBERED

Gen 32.12 which cannot be *n* for multitude.
Nu 1.19 so he *n* them in the wilderness of
Jos 8.10 and *n* the people, and went up, he
1Ki 3. 8 be *n* nor counted for multitude.
20.15 after them he *n* all the people,
1Ch 21.17 commanded the people to be *n*?
Ps 40. 5 them, they are more than can be *n*.
Ec 1.15 which is wanting cannot be *n*.
Isa 53.12 he was *n* with the transgressors;
Jer 33.22 the host of heaven cannot be *n*,
Dan 5.26 God hath *n* thy kingdom, and
Hos 1.10 which cannot be measured nor *n*;
Mt 10.30 very hairs of your head are all *n*.
Mk 15.28 he was *n* with the transgressors.
Lk 12. 7 very hairs of your head are all *n*.
Ac 1.17 For he was *n* with us, and had
26 he was *n* with the eleven apostles.

NUMBEREST

Ex 30.12 the Lord, when thou *n* them;
12 among them, when thou *n* them.
Job 14.16 For now thou *n* my steps: dost

NURSE

Gen 24.59 Rebekah their sister, and her *n*,
35. 8 But Deborah Rebekah's *n* died, and
Ex 2. 7 to thee a *n* of the Hebrew women,
7 that she may *n* the child for thee?
9 this child away, and *n* it for me,
Ru 4.16 her bosom, and became *n* unto it.
2Sa 4. 4 and his *n* took him up, and fled:
2Ki 11. 2 they hid him, even him and his *n*,
2Ch 22.11 him and his *n* in a bed chamber.
1Th 2. 7 as a *n* cherisheth her children:

NURSED

Ex 2. 9 woman took the child, and *n* it.
Isa 60. 4 daughters shall be *n* at thy side.

NURSING

Nu 11.12 as a *n* father beareth the sucking
Isa 49.23 And kings shall be thy *n* fathers,
23 and their queens thy *n* mothers:

NURTURE

Eph 6. 4 *n* and admonition of the Lord.

NUTS

Gen 43.11 spices, and myrrh, *n*, and almonds:
SS 6.11 went down into the garden of *n* to

NYMPHAS

Col 4.15 which are in Laodicea, and *N*,

O

OAK

Gen 35. 4 Jacob hid them under the *o* which
8 buried beneath Beth-el under an *o*:
Jos 24.26 set it up there under an *o*, that was
Jdg 6.11 under an *o* which was in Ophrah,
19 brought it out unto him under the *o*,
2Sa 18. 9 under the thick boughs of a great *o*,
9 and his head caught hold of the *o*,
10 I saw Absalom hanged in an *o*.
14 was yet alive in the midst of the *o*.
1Ki 13.14 and found him sitting under an *o*:
1Ch 10.12 buried their bones under the *o* in
Isa 1.30 shall be as an *o* whose leaf fadeth,
6.13 and as an *o*, whose substance is in
44.14 taketh the cypress and the *o*, which
Eze 6.13 and under every thick *o*, the place

OAKS

Isa 1.29 be ashamed of the *o* which ye have
2.13 up, and upon all the *o* of Bashan,
Eze 27. 6 Of the *o* of Bashan have they made
Hos 4.13 hills, under *o* and poplars and elms,
Am 2. 9 and he was strong as the *o*; yet I
Zec 11. 2 howl, O ye *o* of Bashan; for the

OATH

Gen 26. 3 I will perform the *o* which I
28 Let there be now an *o* betwixt us,
Nu 5.19 priest shall charge her by an *o*,
Dt 29.12 into his *o*, which the Lord thy God
14 do I make this covenant and this *o*;
2Sa 21. 7 Lord's *o* that was between them,
1Ki 2.43 thou not kept the *o* of the Lord,
Neh 10.29 entered into a curse, and into an *o*,
Ec 8. 2 and that in regard of the *o* of God.
Eze 16.59 despised the *o* in breaking the
Zec 8.17 his neighbor; and love no false *o*:
Mt 14. 7 he promised with an *o* to give her
26.72 he denied with an *o*, I do not know
Lk 1.73 *o* which he sware to our father
Ac 2.30 God had sworn with an *o* to him,
23.21 have bound themselves with an *o*,
Heb 6.16 an *o* for confirmation is to them
17 his counsel, confirmed it by an *o*:
7.20 without an *o* he was made priest:
21 priests were made without an *o*;
21 but this with an *o* by him that said
28 the word of the *o*, which was since
Jas 5.12 the earth, neither by any other *o*:

OATH'S

Mt 14. 9 nevertheless for the *o* sake, and
Mk 6.26 yet for his *o* sake, and for their

OATHS

Eze 21.23 sight, to them that have sworn *o*:
Hab 3. 9 according to the *o* of the tribes,
Mt 5.33 perform unto the Lord thine *o*:

OBEDIENCE

Ro 1. 5 *o* to the faith among all nations,
5.19 so by the *o* of one shall many be
6.16 death, or of *o* unto righteousness?
16.19 For your *o* is come abroad unto all
26 to all nations for the *o* of faith:
1Co 14.34 are commanded to be under *o*,
2Co 7.15 he remembereth the *o* of you all,
10. 5 every thought to the *o* of Christ;
6 when your *o* is fulfilled.
Phm 21 Having confidence in thy *o* I wrote
Heb 5. 8 yet learned he *o* by the things
1Pe 1. 2 unto *o* and sprinkling of the blood

OBEDIENT

Ex 24. 7 Lord...said will we do, and be *o*.
Nu 27.20 the children of Israel may be *o*.
Dt 4.30 and shalt be *o* unto his voice;
8.20 ye would not be *o* unto the voice
2Sa 22.45 they hear, they shall be *o* unto me.
Pr 25.12 so is a wise reprover upon an *o* ear.
Isa 1.19 If ye be willing and *o*, ye shall eat
42.24 neither were they *o* unto his law.
Ac 6. 7 of the priests were *o* to the faith.
Ro 15.18 to make the Gentiles *o*, by word
2Co 2. 9 whether ye be *o* in all things.
Eph 6. 5 *o* to them that are your masters
Php 2. 8 and became *o* unto death, even
Tit 2. 5 good, *o* to their own husbands,
9 to be *o* unto their own masters,
1Pe 1.14 As *o* children, not fashioning

OBEISANCE

Gen 37. 7 about, and made *o* to my sheaf.
9 moon and the eleven stars made *o*
43.28 down their heads, and made *o*.
Ex 18. 7 meet his father in law, and did *o*,
2Sa 1. 2 that he fell to the earth, and did *o*.
14. 4 her face to the ground, and did *o*,
15. 5 man came nigh to him to do him *o*,
1Ki 1.16 Bathsheba bowed, and did *o* unto
2Ch 24.17 of Judah, and made *o* to the king.

OBEY

Gen 27. 8 my son, *o* my voice according to
13 only *o* my voice, and go fetch me
43 my son, *o* my voice; and arise, flee
Ex 5. 2 should *o* his voice to let Israel go?
19. 5 if ye will *o* my voice indeed, and
23.21 Beware of him, and *o* his voice,
22 if thou shalt indeed *o* his voice,
Dt 11.27 if ye *o* the commandments of the
28 if ye will not *o* the commandments
13. 4 commandments, and *o* his voice,
21.18 will not *o* the voice of his father,
20 rebellious, he will not *o* our voice;
27.10 *o* the voice of the Lord thy God,
28.62 wouldest not *o* the voice of the
30. 2 shalt *o* his voice according to all
8 return and *o* the voice of the Lord,
20 and that thou mayest *o* his voice,
Jos 24.24 we serve, and his voice will we *o*.
1Sa 8.19 refused to *o* the voice of Samuel;
12.14 serve him, and *o* his voice, and not
15 ye will not *o* the voice of the Lord,
15.19 didst thou not *o* the voice of the
22 to *o* is better than sacrifice, and to
Neh 9.17 refused to *o*, neither were mindful
Job 36.11 If they *o* and serve him, they shall
12 But if they *o* not, they shall perish
Ps 18.44 they hear of me, they shall *o* me:
Pr 30.17 and despiseth to *o* his mother,
Isa 11.14 children of Ammon shall *o* them.
Jer 7.23 *O* my voice, and I will be your
11. 4 *O* my voice, and do them, according
7 and protesting, saying, *O* my voice.
12.17 if they will not *o*, I will utterly
18.10 in my sight, that it *o* not my voice,
26.13 *o* the voice of the Lord your God;
35.14 but *o* their father's commandment:
38.20 *O*, I beseech thee, the voice of the
42. 6 we will *o* the voice of the Lord our
6 when we *o* the voice of the Lord
13 neither *o* the voice of the Lord your
Dan 7.27 dominions shall serve and *o* him.
9.11 that they might not *o* thy voice;
Zec 6.15 diligently *o* the voice of the Lord
Mt 8.27 even the winds and the sea *o* him!
Mk 1.27 unclean spirits, and they do *o* him.
4.41 even the wind and the sea *o* him?
Lk 8.25 winds and water, and they *o* him.
17. 6 in the sea; and it should *o* you.
Ac 5.29 ought to *o* God rather than men.
32 God hath given to them that *o* him.
7.39 our fathers would not *o*,
Ro 2. 8 and do not *o* the truth, but
8 the truth, but *o* unrighteousness,
6.12 ye should *o* it in the lusts thereof.
16 yield yourselves servants to *o*,
16 his servants ye are to whom ye *o*;
Gal 3. 1 that ye should not *o* the truth,
5. 7 that ye should not *o* the truth?
Eph 6. 1 Children, *o* your parents in the
Col 3.20 Children, *o* your parents in all
22 *o* in all things your masters
2Th 1. 8 that *o* not the gospel of our Lord
3.14 if any man *o* not our word by this
Tit 3. 1 to *o* magistrates, to be ready to
Heb 5. 9 salvation unto all them that *o*
13.17 *O* them that have the rule over
Jas 3. 3 horses' mouths, that they may *o*
1Pe 3. 1 if any *o* not the word, they also
4.17 them that *o* not the gospel of God?

OBEYED

Gen 22.18 because thou hast *o* my voice.
26. 5 Because that Abraham *o* my voice,
28. 7 Jacob *o* his father and his mother,
Jos 5. 6 they *o* not the voice of the Lord:
22. 2 *o* my voice in all that I commanded
Jdg 2. 2 but ye have not *o* my voice: why
6.10 dwell: but ye have not *o* my voice.
1Sa 15.20 Yea, I have *o* the voice of the Lord,
24 the people, and *o* their voice.
28.21 thine handmaid hath *o* thy voice,
1Ki 20.36 hast not *o* the voice of the Lord,
2Ki 18.12 they *o* not the voice of the Lord
1Ch 29.23 prospered; and all Israel *o* him.
2Ch 11. 4 they *o* the words of the Lord, and
Pr 5.13 have not *o* the voice of my teachers,
Jer 3.13 ye have not *o* my voice, saith the
25 have not *o* the voice of the Lord our
9.13 and have not *o* my voice, neither
11. 8 Yet they *o* not, nor inclined their
17.23 they *o* not, neither inclined their
32.23 but they *o* not thy voice, neither
34.10 more, then they *o*, and let them go.
35. 8 we *o* the voice of Jonadab the son
10 we have dwelt in tents, and have *o*,
18 *o* the commandment of Jonadab
40. 3 the Lord, and have not *o* his voice,
42.21 not *o* the voice of the Lord your
43. 4 *o* not the voice of the Lord, to dwell
7 they *o* not the voice of the Lord:
44.23 have not *o* the voice of the Lord,
Dan 9.10 Neither have we *o* the voice of the
14 he doeth: for we *o* not his voice.
Zep 3. 2 She *o* not the voice; she received
Hag 1.12 *o* the voice of the Lord their God,
Ac 5.36 as many as *o* him, were scattered,
37 as many as *o* him, were dispersed.
Ro 6.17 have *o* from the heart that form
10.16 they have not all *o* the gospel.
Php 2.12 my beloved, as ye have always *o*,
Heb 11. 8 By faith Abraham...*o*;
1Pe 3. 6 Even as Sara *o* Abraham, calling

OBEYEDST

1Sa 28.18 thou *o* not the voice of the Lord,
Jer 22.21 youth, that thou *o* not my voice.

OBEYETH

Isa 50.10 that *o* the voice of his servant,
Jer 7.28 a nation that *o* not the voice of the
11. 3 Cursed be the man that *o* not the

OBEYING

Jdg 2.17 *o* the commandments of the Lord;
1Sa 15.22 as in *o* the voice of the Lord?
1Pe 1.22 purified your souls in *o* the truth

OBJECT

Ac 24.19 *o*, if they had ought against me.

OBSERVATION

Lk 17.20 of God cometh not with *o*:

OBSERVE

Ex 12.17 *o* the feast of unleavened bread;
17 ye *o* this day in your generations
24 shall *o* this thing for an ordinance
31.16 *o* the sabbath throughout their
34.11 *O* thou that which I command
22 thou shalt *o* the feast of weeks,
Lev 19.26 ye use enchantment, nor *o* times.
37 shall ye *o* all my statutes, and
Nu 28. 2 shall ye *o* to offer unto me in their
Dt 5.32 shall *o* to do therefore as the Lord
6. 3 O Israel, and *o* to do it; that it
25 *o* to do all these commandments
8. 1 commandments...shall ye *o* to do,
11.32 ye shall *o* to do all the statutes
12. 1 which ye shall *o* to do in the land,
28 *O* and hear all these words which
32 soever I command you, *o* to do it:
15. 5 to *o* to do all these commandments
16. 1 *O* the mouth of Abib, and keep the
12 thou shalt *o* and do these statutes.
13 shalt *o* the feast of tabernacles
17.10 thou shalt *o* to do according to all
24. 8 of leprosy, that thou *o* diligently,
8 them, so ye shall *o* to do.
28. 1 to *o* and to do...his commandments
13 thee this day, to *o* and to do them:
15 to *o* to do all his commandments
58 wilt not *o* to do all the words of
31.12 *o* to do all the words of this law:
32.46 command your children to *o* to do,
Jos 1. 7, 8 thou mayest *o* to do according to
Jdg 13.14 all that I commanded her let her *o*.
1Ki 20.33 Now the men did diligently *o*
2Ki 17.37 ye shall *o* to do for evermore;
21. 8 only if they will *o* to do according
2Ch 7.17 and shalt *o* my statutes and my
Neh 1. 5 him and *o* his commandments:
10.29 to *o* and do all the commandments
Ps 105.45 That they might *o* his statutes,
107.43 is wise, and will *o* these things,
119.34 I shall *o* it with my whole heart.
Pr 23.26 and let thine eyes *o* my ways.
Jer 8. 7 the swallow *o* the time of their
Eze 20.18 neither *o* their judgments, nor
37.24 and *o* my statutes, and do them.
Hos 13. 7 as a leopard by the way will I *o*
Jon 2. 8 They that *o* lying vanities forsake
Mt 23. 3 whatsoever they bid you *o*, that
3 that *o* and do; but do not ye
28.20 Teaching them to *o* all things
Ac 16.21 to receive, neither to *o*, being
21.25 that they *o* no such thing, save
Gal 4.10 Ye *o* days, and months, and
1Ti 5.21 that thou *o* these things without

OBSERVED

Gen 37.11 him; but his father *o* the saying.
Ex 12.42 is a night to be much *o* unto the
42 is that night of the Lord to be *o* of
Nu 15.22 not *o* all these commandments,
Dt 33. 9 they have *o* thy word, and kept
2Sa 11.16 to pass, when Joab *o* the city,
2Ki 21. 6 through the fire, and *o* times,
2Ch 33. 6 also he *o* times, and used
Hos 14. 8 I have heard him, and *o* him: I
Mk 6.20 just man and a holy, and *o* him:
10.20 all these have I *o* from my youth.

OBSERVETH

Ec 11. 4 He that *o* the wind shall not sow;

OBTAIN

Gen 16. 2 be that I may *o* children by her.
Pr 8.35 and shall *o* favor of the Lord.
Isa 35.10 they shall *o* joy and gladness, and
51.11 they shall *o* gladness and joy; and
Dan 11.21 and *o* the kingdom by flatteries.
Mt 5. 7 merciful: for they shall *o* mercy.
Lk 20.35 accounted worthy to *o* that world,
Ro 11.31 mercy they also may *o* mercy.
1Co 9.24 the prize? So run, that ye may *o*.
25 do it to *o* a corruptible crown;
1Th 5. 9 to *o* salvation by our Lord Jesus
2Ti 2.10 that they may also *o* the salvation
Heb 4.16 that we may *o* mercy, and find
11.35 might *o* a better resurrection:
Jas 4. 2 and desire to have, and cannot *o*:

OBTAINED

Neh 13. 6 certain days *o* I leave of the king:
Est 2. 9 him, and she *o* kindness of him;
15 Esther *o* favor in the sight of all
17 she *o* grace and favor in his
5. 2 that she *o* favor in his sight:
Hos 2.23 upon her that had not *o* mercy;
Ac 1.17 and had *o* part of this ministry.
22.28 With a great sum *o* I this freedom.
26.22 Having therefore *o* help of God, I
27.13 that they had *o* their purpose,
Ro 11. 7 Israel hath not *o* that which he
7 but the election hath *o* it, and the
30 *o* mercy through their unbelief:
1Co 7.25 one that hath *o* mercy of the Lord
Eph 1.11 also we have *o* an inheritance,
1Ti 1.13 but I *o* mercy, because I did it
16 Howbeit for this cause I *o* mercy,
Heb 1. 4 by inheritance *o* a more excellent
6.15 endured, he *o* the promise.
8. 6 he *o* a more excellent ministry,
9.12 *o* eternal redemption for us.
11. 2 by it the elders *o* a good report.
4 *o* witness that he was righteous,
33 *o* promises, stopped the mouths of
39 *o* a good report through faith,
1Pe 2.10 of God: which had not *o* mercy,
10 but now have *o* mercy.
2Pe 1. 1 that have *o* like precious faith

OBTAINETH

Pr 12. 2 A good man *o* favor of the Lord:
18.22 thing, and *o* favor of the Lord.

OBTAINING

2Th 2.14 to the *o* of the glory of our Lord

OCCASION

Gen 43.18 that he may seek *o* against us, and
Jdg 9.33 do to them as thou shalt find *o*.
14. 4 sought an *o* against...Philistines:
1Sa 10. 7 thee, that thou do as *o* serve thee;
2Sa 12.14 given great *o* to the enemies of the
Ezr 7.20 which thou shalt have *o* to bestow,
Jer 2.24 in her *o* who can turn her away?
Eze 18. 3 have *o* any more to use this proverb
Dan 6. 4 sought to find *o* against Daniel
4 they could find none *o* nor fault;
5 not find any *o* against this Daniel,
Ro 7. 8, 11 taking *o* by the commandment,
14.13 or an *o* to fall in his brother's way.
2Co 5.12 give you *o* to glory on our behalf,
8. 8 by *o* of the forwardness of others,
11.12 cut off *o* from them which desire *o*;
Gal 5.13 use not liberty for an *o* to the flesh,
1Ti 5.14 give none *o* to the adversary to
1Jn 2.10 is none *o* of stumbling in him.

OCCUPATION

Gen 46.33 and shall say, What is your *o*?
47. 3 unto his brethren, What is your *o*?
Jon 1. 8 What is thine *o*? and whence
Ac 18. 3 by their *o* they were tentmakers.
19.25 together with the workmen of like *o*,

OCCUPIED

Ex 38.24 the gold that was *o* for the work
Jdg 16.11 new ropes that never were *o*,
Eze 27.16 they *o* in thy fairs with emeralds,
19 going to and fro *o* in thy fairs:
21 they *o* with thee in lambs, and
22 they *o* in thy fairs with chief of
Heb 13. 9 them that have been *o* therein.

OCCUPIETH

1Co 14.16 that *o* the room of unlearned

OCCUPY

Eze 27. 9 in thee to *o* thy merchandise.
Lk 19.13 and said unto them, *O* till I come.

ODOR

Jn 12. 3 filled with the *o* of the ointment.
Php 4.18 an *o* of a sweet smell, a sacrifice

ODORS

Lev 26.31 smell the savor of your sweet *o*.
2Ch 16.14 bed which was filled with sweet *o*
Est 2.12 and six months with sweet *o*, and
Jer 34. 5 thee, so shall they burn *o* for thee;
Dan 2.46 an oblation and sweet *o* unto him.
Rev 5. 8 golden vials full of *o*, which are
18.13 cinnamon, and *o*, and ointments,

OFFEND

Job 34.31 I will not *o* any more:
Ps 73.15 I should *o* against the generation
119.165 law: and nothing shall *o* them.
Jer 2. 3 all that devour him shall *o*; evil
50. 7 We *o* not, because they have sinned
Hos 4.15 play the harlot, yet let not Judah *o*;
Hab 1.11 he shall pass over, and *o*, imputing
Mt 5.29 if thy right eye *o* thee, pluck it
30 if thy right hand *o* thee, cut it off,
13.41 of his kingdom all things that *o*,
17.27 lest we should *o* them, go thou to
18. 6 shall *o* one of these little ones
8 if thy hand or thy foot *o* thee, cut
9 And if thine eye *o* thee, pluck it
Mk 9.42 shall *o* one of these little ones
43 And if thy hand *o* thee, cut it off:
45 And if thy foot *o* thee, cut it off:
47 And if thine eye *o* thee, pluck it
Lk 17. 2 should *o* one of these little ones.
Jn 6.61 said unto them, Doth this *o* you?
1Co 8.13 if meat make my brother to *o*,
13 lest I make my brother to *o*.
Jas 2.10 the whole law, yet *o* in one point,
3. 2 For in many things we *o* all.
2 If any man *o* not in word, the

OFFENDED

Gen 20. 9 what have I *o* thee, that thou
40. 1 baker had *o* their lord the king of
2Ki 18.14 saying, I have *o*; return from me:
2Ch 28.13 have *o* against the Lord already,
Pr 18.19 A brother *o* is harder to be won
Jer 37.18 What have I *o* against thee, or
Eze 25.12 and hath greatly *o*, and revenged
Hos 13. 1 but when he *o* in Baal, he died.
Mt 11. 6 whosoever shall not be *o* in me.
13.21 of the word, by and by he is *o*.
57 And they were *o* in him. But Jesus
15.12 thou that the Pharisees were *o*,
24.10 And then shall many be *o*, and
26.31 All ye shall be *o* because of me
33 Though all men shall be *o* because
33 of thee, yet will I never be *o*.
Mk 4.17 sake, immediately they are *o*.
6. 3 with us? And they were *o* at him.
14.27 All ye shall be *o* because of me
29 Although all shall be *o*, yet will not
Lk 7.23 whosoever shall not be *o* in me.
Jn 16. 1 unto you, that ye should not be *o*.
Ac 25. 8 Caesar, have I *o* any thing at all.
Ro 14.21 brother stumbleth, or is *o*, or
2Co 11.29 weak? who is *o*, and I burn not?

OFFENDER

Isa 29.21 That make a man an *o* for a word,
Ac 25.11 if I be an *o*, or have committed

OFFENSE

1Sa 25.31 thee, nor *o* of heart unto my lord,
Isa 8.14 a rock of *o* to both the houses of
Hos 5.15 till they acknowledge their *o*, and
Mt 16.23 Satan: thou art an *o* unto me:
18. 7 that man by whom the *o* cometh!
Ac 24.16 conscience void of *o* toward God,
Ro 5.15 not as the *o*, so also is the free
15 through...*o* of one many be dead,
17 if by one man's *o* death reigned
18 as by the *o* of one judgment came
20 entered, that the *o* might abound.
9.33 a stumblingstone and rock of *o*:
14.20 for that man who eateth with *o*.
1Co 10.32 Give none *o*, neither to the Jews,
2Co 6. 3 Giving no *o* in any thing, that the
11. 7 committed an *o* in abasing myself
Gal 5.11 then is the *o* of the cross ceased.
Php 1.10 and without *o* till the day of Christ;
1Pe 2. 8 of stumbling, and a rock of *o*,

OFFENSES

Ec 10. 4 for yielding pacifieth great *o*.
Mt 18. 7 Woe unto the world because of *o*!
7 for it must needs be that *o* come
Lk 17. 1 impossible but that *o* will come:
Ro 4.25 Who was delivered for our *o*, and
5.16 the free gift is of many *o* unto
16.17 them which cause divisions and *o*

OFFER

Gen 22. 2 *o* him there for a burnt offering
Ex 22.29 not delay to *o* the first of thy ripe
23.18 not *o* the blood of my sacrifice
29.36 thou shalt *o* every day a bullock
38 which thou shalt *o* upon the altar;
39 lamb thou shalt *o* in the morning;
39 other lamb thou shalt *o* at even:
41 other lamb thou shalt *o* at even,
30. 9 *o* no strange incense thereon,
34.25 not *o* the blood of my sacrifice
35.24 that did *o* an offering of silver
Lev 1. 3 him *o* a male without blemish:
3 shall *o* it of his own voluntary will
2. 1 when any will *o* a meat offering
12 ye shall *o* them unto the Lord:
13 thine offerings thou shalt *o* salt.
14 *o* a meat offering of thy firstfruits
14 thou shalt *o* for the meat offering
3. 1 offering, if he *o* it of the herd;
1 he shall *o* it without blemish before
3 shall *o* of the sacrifice of the peace
6 he shall *o* it without blemish.
7 If he *o* a lamb for his offering, then
7 then shall he *o* it before the Lord.
9 *o* of the sacrifice of the peace
12 then he shall *o* it before the Lord.
14 he shall *o* thereof his offering,
4.14 shall *o* a young bullock for the sin,
5. 8 who shall *o* that which is for the sin
10 *o* the second for a burnt offering,
6.14 Aaron shall *o* it before the Lord,
20 which they shall *o* unto the Lord in
21 shalt thou *o* for a sweet savor
22 is anointed in his stead shall *o* it:
7. 3 he shall *o* of it all the fat thereof;
11 which he shall *o* unto the Lord.
12 If he *o* it for a thanksgiving, then
12 *o* with the sacrifice of thanksgiving
13 *o* for his offering leavened bread
14 *o* one out of the whole oblation
25 men *o* an offering made by fire unto
38 to *o* their oblations unto the Lord,
9. 2 and *o* them before the Lord.
7 *o* thy sin offering, and thy burnt
7 *o* the offering of the people, and
12. 7 Who shall *o* it before the Lord,
14.12 *o* him for a trespass offering, and
19 the priest shall *o* the sin offering,
20 priest shall *o* the burnt offering
30 shall *o* the one of the turtledoves,
15.15 And the priest shall *o* them, the
30 shall *o* the one for a sin offering.
16. 6 *o* his bullock of the sin offering,
9 fell, and *o* him for a sin offering.
24 forth, and *o* his burnt offering,
17. 4 to *o* an offering unto the Lord
5 which they *o* in the open field,
5 *o* them for peace offerings unto
7 *o* their sacrifices unto devils,
9 to *o* it unto the Lord; even that
19. 5 ye *o* a sacrifice of peace offerings
5 Lord, ye shall *o* it at your own will.
6 be eaten the same day ye *o* it,
21. 6 bread of their God, they do *o*:
17 approach to *o* the bread of his God.
21 nigh to *o* the offerings of the Lord
21 nigh to *o* the bread of his God.
22.15 Israel, which they *o* unto the Lord;
18 that will *o* his oblation for all his
18 will *o* unto the Lord for a burnt
19 Ye shall *o* at your own will a male
20 a blemish, that shall ye not *o*:
22 ye shall not *o* these unto the Lord,
23 thou *o* for a freewill offering:
24 not *o* unto the Lord that which
25 shall ye *o* the bread of your God
29 when ye will *o* a sacrifice of
29 the Lord, *o* it at your own will.
23. 8 shall *o* an offering made by fire
12 ye shall *o* that day when ye wave
16 shall *o* a new meat offering unto
18 shall *o* with the bread seven lambs
25, 27, 36, 36, 37 *o* an offering...by fire
27.11 do not *o* a sacrifice unto the Lord,
Nu 5.25 the Lord, and *o* it upon the altar:
6.11 shall *o* the one for a sin offering,
14 shall *o* his offering unto the Lord,
16 shall *o* his sin offering, and his
17 shall *o* the ram for a sacrifice of
17 shall *o* also his meat offering, and
7.11 They shall *o* their offering, each
18 of Zuar, prince of Issachar, did *o*:
24 of the children of Zebulun, did *o*:
30 of the children of Reuben, did *o*:
36 of the children of Simeon, did *o*:
8.11 Aaron shall *o* the Levites before
12 shalt *o* the one for a sin offering,
13 *o* them for an offering unto the
15 them, and *o* them for an offering.
9. 7 not *o* an offering of the Lord in
15. 7 *o* the third part of an hin of wine,
14 will *o* an offering made by fire,
19 ye shall *o* up an heave offering
20 *o* up a cake of the first of your
24 shall *o* one young bullock for a
16.40 come near to *o* incense before
18.12 which they shall *o* unto the Lord,
19 children of Israel *o* unto the Lord,
24 they *o* as an heave offering unto
26 shall *o* up an heave offering of it
28 ye also shall *o* an heave offering
29 ye shall *o* every heave offering of
28. 2 *o* unto me in their due season.
3 which ye shall *o* unto the Lord;
4 lamb shalt thou *o* in the morning,
4 other lamb shalt thou *o* at even;
8 other lamb shalt thou *o* at even:
8 thou shalt *o* it, a sacrifice made by
11 ye shall *o* a burnt offering unto
19 ye shall *o* a sacrifice made by fire
20 tenth deals shall ye *o* for a bullock,
21 A several tenth deal shalt thou *o* for
23 *o* these beside the burnt offering
24 this manner ye shall *o* daily,
27 ye shall *o* the burnt offering for
31 shall *o* them beside the continual
29. 2 shall *o* a burnt offering for a sweet
8 shall *o* a burnt offering unto the
13 And ye shall *o* a burnt offering, a
17 shall *o* twelve young bullocks, two
36 But ye shall *o* a burnt offering,
Dt 12.13 thou *o* not thy burnt offerings in
14 thou shalt *o* thy burnt offerings,
27 thou shalt *o* thy burnt offerings,
18. 3 from them that *o* a sacrifice,
27. 6 *o* burnt offerings thereon unto
7 thou shalt *o* peace offerings, and
33.19 shall *o* sacrifices of righteousness:
Jos 22.23 *o* thereon burnt offering or meat
23 if to *o* peace offerings thereon, let
Jdg 3.18 made an end to *o* the present,
6.26 *o* a burnt sacrifice with the wood
11.31 I will *o* it up for a burnt offering.
13.16 if thou wilt *o* a burnt offering,
16 thou must *o* it unto the Lord.
16.23 *o* a great sacrifice unto Dagon
1Sa 1.21 went up to *o* unto the Lord the
2.19 husband to *o* the yearly sacrifice.
28 to *o* upon mine altar, to burn
10. 8 unto thee, to *o* burnt offerings,
2Sa 24.12 the Lord, I *o* thee three things;
22 take and *o* up what seemeth good
24 will I *o* burnt offerings unto the
1Ki 3. 4 did Solomon *o* upon that altar.
9.25 did Solomon *o* burnt offerings
13. 2 upon thee shall he *o* the priests
2Ki 5.17 *o* neither burnt offering nor
10.24 to *o* sacrifices and burnt offerings,
1Ch 16.40 *o* burnt offerings unto the Lord
21.10 the Lord, I *o* thee three things:
24 nor *o* burnt offerings without
23.31 *o* all burnt sacrifices unto the
29.14 should be able to *o* so willingly
17 here, to *o* willingly unto thee.
2Ch 23.18 *o* the burnt offerings of the Lord,
24.14 to minister, and to *o* withal, and
29.21 to *o* them on the altar of the Lord.
27 to *o* the burnt offering upon the
35.12 *o* unto the Lord, as it is written
16 *o* burnt offerings upon the altar
Ezr 3. 2 to *o* burnt offerings thereon, as it
6 *o* burnt offerings unto the Lord.
6.10 may *o* sacrifices of sweet savors
7.17 and *o* them upon the altar of the
Job 42. 8 and *o* up for yourselves a burnt
Ps 4. 5 *O* the sacrifices of righteousness,
16. 4 offerings of blood will I not *o*,
27. 6 *o* in his tabernacle sacrifices of
50.14 *O* unto God thanksgiving; and
51.19 they *o* bullocks upon thine altar.
66.15 will *o* unto thee burnt sacrifices of
15 I will *o* bullocks with goats.
72.10 Sheba and Seba shall *o* gifts.
116.17 I will *o* to thee the sacrifice of
Isa 57. 7 wentest thou up to *o* sacrifice.
Jer 11.12 gods unto whom they *o* incense:
14.12 *o* burnt offering and an oblation,
33.18 before me to *o* burnt offerings,
Eze 6.13 where they did *o* sweet savor
20.31 For when ye *o* your gifts, when
43.18 *o* burnt offerings thereon, and to
22 second day thou shalt *o* a kid
23 thou shalt *o* a young bullock
24 thou shalt *o* them before the Lord,
24 *o* them up for a burnt offering
44. 7 *o* my bread, the fat and the blood,
15 *o* unto me the fat and the blood,
27 he shall *o* his sin offering, saith
45. 1 shall *o* an oblation unto the Lord,
13 is the oblation that ye shall *o*;
14 ye shall *o* the tenth part of a bath
46. 4 offering that the prince shall *o*
48. 8 be the offering which ye shall *o*
9 oblation that ye shall *o* unto the
20 *o* the holy oblation foursquare,
Dan 2.46 *o* an oblation and sweet odors
Hos 9. 4 not *o* wine offerings to the Lord,
Am 4. 5 And *o* a sacrifice of thanksgiving
5.22 Though ye *o* me burnt offerings
Hag 2.14 which they *o* there is unclean.
Mal 1. 7 Ye *o* polluted bread upon mine
8 if ye *o* the blind for sacrifice, is it

Mal 1. 8 if ye *o* the lame and sick, is it not
8 *o* it now unto thy governor; will
3. 3 may *o* unto the Lord an offering
Mt 5.24 and then come and *o* thy gift.
8. 4 *o* the gift that Moses commanded,
Mk 1.44 *o* for thy cleansing those things
Lk 2.24 to *o* a sacrifice according to that
5.14 *o* for thy cleansing, according as
6.29 on the one cheek *o* also the other;
11.12 an egg, will he *o* him a scorpion?
Heb 5. 1 *o* both gifts and sacrifices
3 so also for himself, to *o* for sins.
7.27 to *o* up sacrifice, first for his own
8. 3 ordained to *o* gifts and sacrifices:
3 man have somewhat also to *o*.
4 that *o* gifts according to the law:
9.25 that he should *o* himself often,
13.15 let us *o* the sacrifice of praise to
1Pe 2. 5 to *o* up spiritual sacrifices,
Rev 8. 3 *o* it with the prayers of all saints

OFFERED

Gen 8.20 *o* burnt offerings on the altar.
22.13 and *o* him up for a burnt offering
31.54 *o* sacrifice upon the mount, and
46. 1 and *o* sacrifices unto the God of his
Ex 24. 5 of Israel, which *o* burnt offerings,
32. 6 *o* burnt offerings, and brought
35.22 man that *o*...an offering of gold
22 every man...*o* an offering of gold
40.29 *o* upon it the burnt offering and
Lev 7. 8 burnt offering which he hath *o*.
15 eaten the same day that it is *o*;
9.15 slew it, and *o* it for sin, as the
16 and *o* it according to the manner.
10. 1 *o* strange fire before the Lord,
19 day have they *o* their sin offering
16. 1 when they *o* before the Lord, and
Nu 3. 4 they *o* strange fire before the Lord,
7. 2 over them that were numbered, *o*:
10 *o* for dedicating of the altar in
10 *o* their offering before the altar.
12 he that *o* his offering the first day
19 He *o* for his offering one silver
42 prince of the children of Gad, *o*:
48 prince of the children of Ephraim, *o*:
54 On the eighth day *o* Gamaliel the
60 of the children of Benjamin, *o*:
66 prince of the children of Dan, *o*:
72 prince of the children of Asher, *o*:
78 prince of the children of Naphtali, *o*:
8.21 and Aaron *o* them as an offering
16.35 and fifty men that *o* incense.
38 for they *o* them before the Lord,
39 they that were burnt had *o*; and
22.40 And Balak *o* oxen and sheep,
23. 2 and Balaam *o* on every altar a
4 *o* upon every altar a bullock and
14, 30 *o* a bullock and a ram on every
26.61 *o* strange fire before the Lord.
28.15 offering unto the Lord shall be *o*,
24 *o* beside the continual burnt
31.52 gold of the offering that they *o*
Jos 8.31 they *o* thereon burnt offerings
Jdg 5. 2 the people willingly *o* themselves.
9 *o* themselves willingly among the
6.28 bullock was *o* upon the altar
13.19 *o* it upon a rock unto the Lord:
20.26 and *o* burnt offerings and peace
21. 4 and *o* burnt offerings and peace
1Sa 1. 4 the time was that Elkanah *o*,
2.13 that, when any man *o* sacrifice,
6.14 *o* the kine a burnt offering unto
15 of Beth-shemesh *o* burnt offerings
7. 9 lamb, and *o* it for a burnt offering
13. 9 And he *o* the burnt offering.
12 therefore, and *o* a burnt offering.
2Sa 6.17 David *o* burnt offerings and peace
15.12 from Giloh, while he *o* sacrifices.
24.25 and *o* burnt offerings and peace
1Ki 3.15 Lord, and *o* up burnt offerings,
15 *o* peace offerings, and made a
8.62 him, *o* sacrifice before the Lord.
63 And Solomon *o* a sacrifice of peace
63 he *o* unto the Lord, two and twenty
64 there he *o* burnt offerings, and
12.32 in Judah, and he *o* upon the altar.
33 So he *o* upon the altar which he
33 he *o* upon the altar, and burnt
22.43 the people *o* and burnt incense
2Ki 3.20 when the meat offering was *o*,
27 *o* him for a burnt offering upon
16.12 to the altar, and *o* thereon.
1Ch 6.49 his sons *o* upon the altar of the
15.26 they *o* seven bullocks and seven
16. 1 they *o* burnt sacrifices and peace
21.26 and *o* burnt offerings and peace
29. 6 of the king's work, *o* willingly,
9 rejoiced, for that they *o* willingly,
9 with perfect heart they *o* willingly
17 have willingly *o* all these things:
21 *o* burnt offerings unto the Lord,
2Ch 1. 6 *o* a thousand burnt offerings upon
4. 6 such things as they *o* for the
7. 4 *o* sacrifices before the Lord.

BIBLICAL THEMES

OFFERING

Cain brought of the fruit of the ground an offering unto the Lord. And Abel, he also brought of the firstlings of his flock and of the fat thereof. Gen 4.3-4

And the angel of the Lord called unto him out of heaven, and said, Abraham, . . . Lay not thine hand upon the lad, . . . for now I know that thou fearest God, seeing thou hast not withheld thy son, thine only son from me. Gen 22.11-12

And he shall bring his trespass offering unto the Lord, a ram without blemish . . . and the priest shall make an atonement for him before the Lord: and it shall be forgiven him for any thing of all that he hath done. Lev 6.6-7

Hath the Lord as great delight in burnt offerings and sacrifices, as in obeying the voice of the Lord? Behold, to obey is better than sacrifice, and to hearken than the fat of rams. 1Sa 15.22

Thou desirest not sacrifice; else would I give it. . . . The sacrifices of God are a broken spirit: a broken and a contrite heart, O God, thou wilt not despise. Ps 51.16-17

To do justice and judgment is more acceptable to the Lord than sacrifice. Pr 21.3

Surely he hath borne our griefs, and carried our sorrows. . . . he was wounded for our transgressions, he was bruised for our iniquities: the chastisement of our peace was upon him; and with his stripes we are healed. Isa 53.4-5

To what purpose cometh there to me incense from Sheba, and the sweet cane from a far country? your burnt offerings are not acceptable, nor your sacrifices sweet unto me. Jer 6.20

And he took the cup . . . saying, Drink ye all of it; for this is my blood of the new testament, which is shed for many for the remission of sins. Mt 26.27-28

To love him with all the heart and with all the understanding, and with all the soul, and with all the strength . . . is more than all whole burnt offerings and sacrifices. Mk 12.33

The next day John seeth Jesus . . . and saith, Behold the Lamb of God, which taketh away the sin of the world. Jn 1.29

Then took Mary a pound of ointment of spikenard, very costly, and anointed the feet of Jesus, and wiped his feet with her hair. Jn 12.3

Greater love hath no man than this, that a man lay down his life for his friends. Jn 15.13

All have sinned, and come short of the glory of God; being justified freely by his grace through the redemption that is in Christ Jesus: whom God hath set forth to be a propitiation through faith in his blood, to declare his righteousness for the remission of sins that are past, through the forbearance of God. Ro 3.23-25

I beseech you therefore, brethren, by the mercies of God, that ye present your bodies a living sacrifice, holy, acceptable unto God. Ro 12.1

If the blood of bulls and of goats . . . sanctifieth to the purifying of the flesh: how much more shall the blood of Christ, who through the eternal Spirit offered himself without spot to God, purge your conscience from dead works to serve the living God? Heb 9.13-14

Every priest standeth daily ministering and offering oftentimes the same sacrifices, which can never take away sins: but this man, after he had offered one sacrifice for sins for ever, sat down on the right hand of God. Heb 10.11-12

Who his own self bare our sins in his own body on the tree, that we, being dead to sins, should live unto righteousness. 1Pe 2.24

5 And king Solomon *o* a sacrifice of
7 there he *o* burnt offerings, and the
8.12 Solomon *o* burnt offerings unto
15.11 *o* unto the Lord the same time,
17.16 willingly *o* himself unto the Lord;
24.14 And they *o* burnt offerings in the
29. 7 incense nor *o* burnt offerings
Ezr 1. 6 beside all that was willingly *o*.
2.68 *o* freely for the house of God to
3. 3 they *o* burnt offerings thereon
4 *o* the daily burnt offerings by
5 *o* the continual burnt offering,
5 willingly *o* a freewill offering
6. 3 the place where they *o* sacrifices,
17 *o* at the dedication of this house
7.15 freely *o* unto the God of Israel,
8.25 all Israel there present, had *o*:
35 *o* burnt offerings unto the God of
10.19 they *o* a ram of the flock for their
Neh 11. 2 willingly *o* themselves to dwell at
12.43 that day they *o* great sacrifices,
Job 1. 5 *o* burnt offerings according to
Isa 57. 6 thou hast *o* a meat offering.
66. 3 oblation, as if he *o* swine's blood;
Jer 32.29 they have *o* incense unto Baal,
Eze 20.28 and they *o* there their sacrifices,
48.12 this oblation of the land that is *o*
Dan 11.18 the reproach *o* by him to cease;
Am 5.25 Have ye *o* unto me sacrifices and
Jon 1.16 *o* a sacrifice unto the Lord, and
Mal 1.11 in every place incense shall be *o*
Ac 7.41 and *o* sacrifice unto the idol, and
42 have ye *o* to me slain beasts and
8.18 was given, he *o* them money,
15.29 ye abstain from meats *o* to idols,
21.25 themselves from things *o* to idols,
26 until that an offering should be *o*
1Co 8. 1 as touching things *o* unto idols,
4 are *o* in sacrifice unto idols,
7 eat it as a thing *o* unto an idol;
10 those things which are *o* to idols;
10.19 *o* in sacrifice to idols is any thing?
28 This is *o* in sacrifice unto idols,
Php 2.17 and if I be *o* upon the sacrifice
2Ti 4. 6 For I am now ready to be *o*, and
Heb 5. 7 when he had *o* up prayers and
7.27 he did once, when he *o* up himself.
9. 7 which he *o* for himself, and for
9 were *o* both gifts and sacrifices,
14 *o* himself without spot to God,
28 once *o* to bear the sins of many;
10. 1 they *o* year by year continually
2 they not have ceased to be *o*?
8 therein; which are *o* by the law;
12 he had *o* one sacrifice for sins
11. 4 By faith Abel *o* unto God a more
17 when he was tried, *o* up Isaac:
17 *o* up his only begotten son,
Jas 2.21 when he had *o* Isaac his son upon

OFFERETH

Lev 6.26 The priest that *o* it for sin shall
7. 8 that *o* any man's burnt offering
9 shall be the priest's that *o* it.
16 same day that he *o* his sacrifice:
18 it be imputed unto him that *o* it:
29 He that *o* the sacrifice of his peace
33 *o* the blood of the peace offerings,
17. 8 that *o* a burnt offering or sacrifice,
21. 8 for he *o* the bread of thy God: he
22.21 *o* a sacrifice of peace offerings unto
Nu 15. 4 that *o* his offering unto the Lord
Ps 50.23 Whoso *o* praise glorifieth me:
Isa 66. 3 he that *o* an oblation, as if he
Jer 48.35 him that *o* in the high places, and
Mal 2.12 that *o* an offering unto the Lord

OFFERING

Gen 4. 3 the ground an *o* unto the Lord.
4 respect unto Abel and to his *o*:
5 and to his *o* he had not respect.
22. 7 where is the lamb for a burnt *o*?
8 himself a lamb for a burnt *o*: so
13 a burnt *o* in the stead of his son.
Ex 29.14 without the camp: it is a sin *o*.
35.29 of Israel brought a willing *o* unto
Lev 2.16 is an *o* made by fire unto the Lord.
5. 6 bring his trespass *o* unto the Lord
Nu 5. 9 every *o* of all the holy things of
15 thereon; for it is an *o* of jealousy,
15 *o* of memorial, bringing iniquity
1Sa 2.17 for men abhorred the *o* of the Lord.
1Ki 18.29, 36 the *o* of the evening sacrifice,
Ezr 7.16 *o* willingly for the house of their God
8.28 silver and the gold are a freewill *o*
Job 42. 8 offer up for yourselves a burnt *o*;
Ps 40. 6 and *o* thou didst not desire;
6 burnt *o*...hast thou not required.
6 and sin *o* hast thou not required.
51.16 thou delightest not in burnt *o*.
19 with burnt *o* and whole burnt *o*:
96. 8 bring an *o*, and come into his
Isa 53.10 shalt make his soul an *o* for sin,
61. 8 I hate robbery for burnt *o*;
Mal 1.10 neither will I accept an *o* at your
2.13 he regardeth not the *o* any more,
3. 3 the Lord an *o* in righteousness.
Lk 23.36 coming to him, and *o* him vinegar,
Ac 21.26 until that an *o* should be offered
Ro 15.16 the *o* up of the Gentiles might be
Eph 5. 2 hath given himself for us an *o* and
Heb 10. 5 Sacrifice and *o* thou wouldest not,
8 Sacrifice and *o* and burnt offerings
8 and *o* for sin thou wouldest not,
10 through the *o* of the body of Jesus

Making an offering on a wet altar, Elijah invokes God's fire (1Ki 18.38) in this 17th-century engraving.

Heb 10.11 *o* oftentimes the same sacrifices,
14 by one *o* he hath perfected for ever
18 these is, there is no more *o* for sin.

OFFERINGS

Ex 32. 6 and brought peace *o*; and the people
Lev 2. 3, 10 the *o* of the Lord made by fire.
13 with all thine *o*...shalt offer salt.
Nu 15. 8 a vow, or peace *o* unto the Lord:
Dt 32.38 drank the wine of their drink *o*?
Jos 8.31 the Lord, and sacrificed peace *o*.
1Ch 21.24 nor offer burnt *o* without cost.
2Ch 29.31 as were of a free heart burnt *o*.
35. 7 and kids, all for the passover *o*,
8 unto the priests for the passover *o*
Neh 10.33 for the sin *o* to make an atonement
Ps 20. 3 Remember all thy *o*, and accept
119.108 thee, the freewill *o* of my mouth,
Pr 7.14 I have peace *o* with me; this day
Isa 1.11 I am full of the burnt *o* of rams,
Jer 6.20 your burnt *o* are not acceptable,
7.18 pour out drink *o* unto other gods,
19.13 out drink *o* unto other gods.
Hos 6. 6 of God more than burnt *o*.
Am 4. 5 proclaim and publish the free *o*:
5.22 Though ye offer me burnt *o* and
22 meat *o*, I will not accept them:
Mic 6. 6 I come before him with burnt *o*,
Mal 3. 8 we robbed thee? In tithes and *o*.
Mk 12.33 all whole burnt *o* and sacrifices.
Lk 21. 4 cast in unto the *o* of God:
Ac 24.17 bring alms to my nation, and *o*.
Heb 10. 6 In burnt *o* and sacrifices for sin

OFFICE

Ex 28. 1 minister unto me in the priest's *o*,
Neh 13.13 and their *o* was to distribute unto
Ps 109. 8 few; and let another take his *o*.
Eze 44.13 to do the *o* of a priest unto me,
Lk 1. 8 while he executed the priest's *o*
9 to the custom of the priest's *o*,
Ro 11.13 of the Gentiles, I magnify mine *o*:
12. 4 all members have not the same *o*:
1Ti 3. 1 If a man desire the *o* of a bishop,
10 let them use the *o* of a deacon,
6.13 that have used the *o* of a deacon
Heb 7. 5 receive the *o* of the priesthood,

OFFICER

Gen 37.36 unto Potiphar, an *o* of Pharaoh's,
39. 1 and Potiphar, an *o* of Pharaoh,
Jdg 9.28 of Jerubbaal? and Zebul his *o*?
1Ki 4. 5 the son of Nathan was principal *o*,
19 the only *o* which was in the land.
22. 9 the king of Israel called an *o*, and
2Ki 8. 6 appointed unto her a certain *o*,
25.19 he took an *o* that was set over the
2Ch 24.11 priest's *o* came and emptied the
Mt 5.25 the judge deliver thee to the *o*,
Lk 12.58 the judge deliver thee to the *o*,
58 and the *o* cast thee into prison.

OFFICERS

Gen 41.34 let him appoint *o* over the land,
Ex 5.14 And the *o* of the children of Israel,
Dt 16.18 Judges and *o* shalt thou make thee
31.28 elders of your tribes, and your *o*,
1Ch 23. 4 six thousand were *o* and judges:
2Ch 19.11 the Levites shall be *o* before you.
Est 9. 3 *o* of the king, helped the Jews;
Jn 7.32 chief priests sent *o* to take him.
45 came the *o* of the chief priests and
46 The *o* answered, Never man spake
18. 3 received a band of men and *o* from
12 and *o* of the Jews took Jesus, and
18 the servants and *o* stood there,
22 one of the *o* which stood by struck
19. 6 priests therefore and *o* saw him,
Ac 5.22 But when the *o* came, and found
26 Then went the captain with the *o*,

OFFICES

1Sa 2.36 pray thee, into one of the priest's *o*,
1Ch 24. 3 according to their *o* in their
2Ch 7. 6 And the priests waited on their *o*:
23.18 the *o* of the house of the Lord
Neh 13.14 of my God, and for the *o* thereof.

OFFSCOURING

La 3.45 made us as the *o* and refuse in
1Co 4.13 the *o* of all things unto this day.

OFFSPRING

Job 5.25 thine *o* as the grass of the earth.
21. 8 and their *o* before their eyes.
27.14 *o* shall not be satisfied with bread.
31. 8 eat; yea, let my *o* be rooted out.
Isa 22.24 *o* and the issue, all vessels of small
44. 3 and my blessing upon thine *o*:
48.19 the *o* of thy bowels like the gravel
61. 9 and their *o* among the people:
65.23 the Lord, and their *o* with them.
Ac 17.28 have said, For we are also his *o*.
29 then as we are the *o* of God, we
Rev 22.16 I am the root and the *o* of David,

OFT

2Ki 4. 8 as *o* as he passed by, he turned
Job 21.17 *o* is the candle of...wicked put out!
17 how *o* cometh their destruction upon
Ps 78.40 How *o* did they provoke him in
Mt 9.14 do we and the Pharisees fast *o*,
17.15 into the fire, and *o* into the water.
18.21 how *o* shall my brother sin against
Mk 7. 3 they wash their hands *o*, eat not,
Ac 26.11 And I punished them *o* in every
1Co 11.25 this do ye, as *o* as ye drink it, in
2Co 11.23 more frequent, in deaths *o*.
2Ti 1.16 he *o* refreshed me, and was not
Heb 6. 7 in the rain that cometh *o* upon it,

OFTEN

Pr 29. 1 He, that being *o* reproved hardeneth
Mal 3.16 they that feared the Lord spake *o*
Mt 23.37 how *o* would I have gathered thy
Mk 5. 4 been *o* bound with fetters and
Lk 5.33 the disciples of John fast *o*, and
13.34 how *o* would I have gathered thy
1Co 11.26 For as *o* as ye eat this bread, and
2Co 11.26 In journeyings *o*, in perils of
27 watchings *o*, in hunger and thirst,
27 fastings *o*, in cold and nakedness.
Php 3.18 walk, of whom I have told you *o*,
1Ti 5.23 sake and thine *o* infirmities.
Heb 9.25 that he should offer himself *o*, as
26 For then must he *o* have suffered
Rev 11. 6 with all plagues, as *o* as they will.

OFTENER

Ac 24.26 wherefore he sent for him the *o*,

OFTENTIMES

Job 33.29 these things worketh God *o*
Ec 7.22 For *o* also thine own heart
Lk 8.29 *o* it had caught him: and he
Ro 1.13 *o* I purposed to come unto you,
2Co 8.22 *o* proved diligent in many things,
Heb 10.11 and offering *o* the same sacrifices,

OFTTIMES

Mt 17.15 for *o* he falleth into the fire, and
Mk 9.22 *o* it hath cast him into the fire,
Jn 18. 2 Jesus *o* resorted thither with his

OIL

Gen 28.18 and poured *o* upon the top of it.
35.14 thereon, and he poured *o* thereon.
Ex 25. 6 *O* for the light, spices for
6 spices for anointing *o*, and for
27.20 pure *o* olive beaten for the light,
29. 2 cakes unleavened tempered with *o*,
2 wafers unleavened anointed with *o*:
7 shalt thou take the anointing *o*,
21 the altar, and of the anointing *o*,
40 fourth part of an hin of beaten *o*;
30.24 sanctuary, and of *o* olive an hin:
25 make it an *o* of holy ointment, an
25 it shall be an holy anointing *o*.
31 be an holy anointing *o* unto me
31.11 the anointing *o*, and sweet incense
35. 8 And *o* for the light, and spices for
8 and spices for anointing *o*, and for
14 his lamps, with the *o* for the light,
15 and the anointing *o*, and the sweet
28 And spice, and *o* for the light,
28 and for the anointing *o*, and for
37.29 And he made the holy anointing *o*,
39.37 vessels thereof, and the *o* for light,
38 and the anointing *o*, and the sweet
40. 9 thou shalt take the anointing *o*,
Lev 2. 1 he shall pour *o* upon it, and put
2 and of the *o* thereof, with all the
4 cakes of fine flour mingled with *o*,
4 unleavened wafers anointed with *o*.
5 flour unleavened, mingled with *o*.
6 it in pieces, and pour *o* thereon:
7 shall be made of fine flour with *o*.
15 And thou shalt put *o* upon it, and
16 thereof, and part of the *o* thereof,
5.11 he shall put no *o* upon it, neither
6.15 meat offering, and of the *o* thereof,
21 In a pan it shall be made with *o*;
7.10 meat offering, mingled with *o*,
12 unleavened cakes mingled with *o*,
12 unleavened wafers anointed with *o*,
12 and cakes mingled with *o*, of fine
8. 2 the garments, and the anointing *o*,
10 Moses took the anointing *o*, and
12 he poured of the anointing *o* upon
30 Moses took of the anointing *o*, and
9. 4 meat offering mingled with *o*: for
10. 7 anointing *o* of the Lord is upon you.
14.10 mingled with *o*, and one log of *o*.
12 trespass offering, and the log of *o*,
15 shall take some of the log of *o*, and
16 shall dip his right finger in the *o*
16 sprinkle of the *o* with his finger
17 the rest of the *o* that is in his hand
18 the remnant of the *o* that is in the
21 deal of fine flour mingled with *o*
21 for a meat offering, and a log of *o*;
24 trespass offering, and the log of *o*,
26 priest shall pour of the *o* into the
27 some of the *o* that is in his left
28 priest shall put of the *o* that is in
29 rest of the *o* that is in the priest's
21.10 head the anointing *o* was poured,
12 the crown of the anointing *o* of his
23.13 deals of fine flour mingled with *o*,
24. 2 pure *o* olive beaten for the light,
Nu 4. 9 snuffdishes, and all the *o* vessels
16 pertaineth the *o* for the light,
16 meat offering, and the anointing *o*
5.15 he shall pour no *o* upon it, nor put
6.15 cakes of fine flour mingled with *o*,
15 unleavened bread anointed with *o*,
7.13 mingled with *o* for a meat offering:
8. 8 even fine flour mingled with *o*, and
11. 8 of it was as the taste of fresh *o*.
15. 4 with the fourth part of an hin of *o*.
6 with the third part of an hin of *o*.
9 flour mingled with half an hin of *o*.
18.12 the best of the *o*, and all the best of
28. 5 fourth part of an hin of beaten *o*.
9, 12, 12 meat offering, mingled with *o*,
13 tenth deal of flour mingled with *o*
20 shall be of flour mingled with *o*:
28 offering of flour mingled with *o*,
29. 3, 9, 14 be of flour mingled with *o*,
35.25 was anointed with the holy *o*.
Dt 7.13 corn, and thy wine, and thine *o*,
8. 8 a land of *o* olive, and honey;
11.14 corn, and thy wine, and thine *o*.

12.17 thy corn, or of thy wine, or of thy *o*,
14.23 corn, of thy wine, and of thine *o*,
18. 4 corn, of thy wine, and of thine *o*,
28.40 not anoint thyself with the *o*;
51 leave thee either corn, wine, or *o*,
32.13 rock, and *o* out of the flinty rock;
33.24 and let him dip his foot in *o*.
1Sa 10. 1 Samuel took a vial of *o*, and poured
16. 1 fill thine horn with *o*, and go, I will
13 Then Samuel took the horn of *o*,
2Sa 1.21 he had not been anointed with *o*.
14. 2 anoint not thyself with *o*, but be as
1Ki 1.39 the priest took an horn of *o* out of
5.11 and twenty measures of pure *o*:
17.12 in a barrel, and a little *o* in a cruse:
14 neither shall the cruse of *o* fail,
16 not, neither did the cruse of *o* fail,
2Ki 4. 2 thing in the house, save a pot of *o*.
6 a vessel more. And the *o* stayed.
7 Go, sell the *o*, and pay thy debt,
9. 1 take this box of *o* in thine hand,
3 Then take the box of *o*, and pour it
6 and he poured the *o* on his head,
18.32 a land of *o* olive and of honey,
1Ch 9.29 flour, and the wine, and the *o*,
12.40 bunches of raisins, and wine, and *o*,
27.28 over the cellars of *o* was Joash:
2Ch 2.10 and twenty thousand baths of *o*.
15 the barley, the *o*, and the wine,
11.11 store of victual, and of *o* and wine.
31. 5 of corn, wine, and *o*, and honey,
32.28 increase of corn, and wine, and *o*;
Ezr 3. 7 meat, and drink, and *o*, unto them
6. 9 salt, wine, and *o*, according to
7.22 to an hundred baths of *o*, and salt
Neh 5.11 the corn, the wine, and the *o*, that
10.37 of wine and of *o*, unto the priests,
39 the new wine, and the *o*, unto the
13. 5 new wine, and the *o*, which was
12 wine and the *o* unto the treasuries,
Est 2.12 wit, six months with *o* of myrrh,
Job 24.11 Which make *o* within their walls,
29. 6 rock poured me out rivers of *o*;
Ps 23. 5 thou anointest my head with *o*;
45. 7 anointed thee with...*o* of gladness
55.21 his words were softer than *o*, yet
89.20 with my holy *o* have I anointed him:
92.10 I shall be anointed with fresh *o*.
104.15 *o* to make his face to shine, and
109.18 water, and like *o* into his bones.
141. 5 it shall be an excellent *o*, which
Pr 5. 3 and her mouth is smoother than *o*:
21.17 he that loveth wine and *o* shall not
20 and *o* in the dwelling of the wise;
Isa 41.19 and the myrtle, and the *o* tree;
61. 3 ashes, the *o* of joy for mourning,
Jer 31.12 for wine, and for *o*, and for the
40.10 wine, and summer fruits, and *o*,
41. 8 of barley, and of *o*, and of honey.
Eze 16. 9 thee, and I anointed thee with *o*.
13 eat fine flour, and honey, and *o*:
18 hast set mine *o* and mine incense
19 thee, fine flour, and *o*, and honey,
23.41 hast set mine incense and mine *o*.
27.17 and honey, and *o*, and balm.
32.14 and cause their rivers to run like *o*,
45.14 the ordinance of *o*, the bath of *o*,
24 ram, and an hin of *o* for an ephah.
25 offering, and according to the *o*.
46. 5, 7, 11 and an hin of *o* to an ephah.
14 and the third part of an hin of *o*, to
15 and the meat offering, and the *o*,
Hos 2. 5 and my flax, mine *o* and my drink.
8 I gave her corn, and wine, and *o*,
22 the corn, and the wine, and the *o*;
12. 1 and *o* is carried into Egypt.
Joel 1.10 is dried up, the *o* languisheth.
2.19 send you corn, and wine, and *o*,
24 shall overflow with wine and *o*.
Mic 6. 7 with ten thousands of rivers of *o*?
15 thou shalt not anoint thee with *o*;
Hag 1.11 the new wine and upon the *o*,
2.12 bread or pottage, or wine, or *o*, or
Zec 4.12 the golden *o* out of themselves?
Mt 25. 3 lamps, and took no *o* with them:
4 wise took *o* in their vessels with
8 Give us of your *o*; for our lamps
Mk 6.13 anointed with *o* many that were
Lk 7.46 My head with *o* thou didst not
10.34 his wounds, pouring in *o* and wine,
16. 6 he said, An hundred measures of *o*.
Heb 1. 9 anointed thee with...*o* of gladness
Jas 5.14 anointing him with *o* in the name
Rev 6. 6 thou hurt not the *o* and the wine.
18.13 and wine, and *o*, and fine flour, and

OINTMENT

Ex 30.25 shalt make it an oil of holy *o*, an *o*
25 an *o* compound after the art
2Ki 20.13 the spices, and the precious *o*,
1Ch 9.30 sons of the priests made the *o* of
Job 41.31 he maketh the sea like a pot of *o*.
Ps 133. 2 like the precious *o* upon the head,
Pr 27. 9 *O* and perfume rejoice the heart:
16 and the *o* of his right hand, which
Ec 7. 1 name is better than precious *o*;
9. 8 white; and let thy head lack no *o*.
10. 1 flies cause the *o* of the apothecary
SS 1. 3 thy name is as *o* poured forth,
Isa 1. 6 bound up, neither mollified with *o*.
39. 2 and the spices, and the precious *o*,
57. 9 thou wentest to the king with *o*,
Mt 26. 7 alabaster box of very precious *o*,
9 For this *o* might have been sold for
12 she hath poured this *o* on my body,
Mk 14. 3 alabaster box of *o* of spikenard
4 Why was this waste of the *o* made?
Lk 7.37 brought an alabaster box of *o*,
38 feet, and anointed them with the *o*.
46 hath anointed my feet with *o*.
Jn 11. 2 which anointed the Lord with *o*,
12. 3 Mary a pound of *o* of spikenard,
3 was filled with the odor of the *o*.
5 Why was not this *o* sold for three

OINTMENTS

SS 1. 3 of the savor of thy good *o* thy
4.10 the smell of thine *o* than all spices!
Am 6. 6 anoint themselves with the chief *o*:
Lk 23.56 and prepared spices and *o*; and
Rev 18.13 cinnamon, and odors, and *o*, and

OLD

Gen 18.13 a surety bear a child, which am *o*?
21. 2 bare Abraham a son in his *o* age,
25. 8 an *o* man, and full of years; and
27. 2 I am *o*, I know not the day of my
35.29 people, being *o* and full of days:
47. 8 Jacob, How *o* art thou?
Lev 19.32 and honor the face of the *o* man,
Dt 2.20 giants dwelt therein in *o* time;
8. 4 raiment waxed not *o* upon thee,
28.50 not regard the person of the *o*,
32. 7 Remember the days of *o*, consider
Jos 24. 2 the other side of the flood in *o* time,
Jdg 8.32 Gideon...died in a good *o* age,
Ru 1.12 I am too *o* to have an husband.
1Sa 2.22 Now Eli was very *o*, and heard
12. 2 and I am *o* and grayheaded; and,
2Sa 20.18 They were wont to speak in *o* time,
1Ki 12. 8 forsook the counsel of the *o* men,
1Ch 23. 1 So when David was *o* and full of
29.28 And he died in a good *o* age, full
Job 4.11 *o* lion perisheth for lack of prey,
21. 7 do the wicked live, become *o*, yea,
22.15 the *o* way which wicked men have
32. 6 I am young, and ye are very *o*;
Ps 37.25 have been young, and now am *o*;
68.33 of heavens, which were of *o*;
74.12 For God is my King of *o*, working
77. 5 I have considered the days of *o*,
11 will remember thy wonders of *o*.
78. 2 I will utter dark sayings of *o*:
93. 2 Thy throne is established of *o*:
102.25 Of *o* hast thou laid the foundation
26 them shall wax *o* like a garment;
Pr 17. 6 children are the crown of *o* men;
20.29 beauty of *o* men is the gray head.
22. 6 when he is *o*, he will not depart
23.22 not thy mother when she is *o*.
Ec 4.13 child than an *o* and foolish king,
Isa 25. 1 thy counsels of *o* are faithfulness
46. 9 Remember the former things of *o*:
50. 9 all shall wax *o* as a garment:
51. 6 earth shall wax *o* like a garment,
58.12 shall build the *o* waste places:
Jer 38.11 *o* cast clouts and *o* rotten rags,
Eze 26.20 the pit, with the people of *o* time,
Joel 1. 2 Hear this, ye *o* men, and give ear,
2.28 your *o* men shall dream dreams,
Am 9.11 I will build it as in the days of *o*:
Mic 5. 2 goings forth have been from of *o*,
Zec 8. 4 yet *o* men and *o* women dwell in
Mal 3. 4 as in the days of *o*, and as in
Mt 2.16 from two years *o* and under,
5.21 that it was said by them of *o* time,
27 that it was said by them of *o* time,
33 hath been said by them of *o* time,
9.16 of new cloth unto an *o* garment,
17 men put new wine into *o* bottles:
13.52 of his treasure things new and *o*.
Mk 2.21 of new cloth on an *o* garment:
21 filled it up taketh away from the *o*,
22 putteth new wine into *o* bottles:
Lk 1.18 for I am an *o* man, and my wife
36 also conceived a son in her *o* age:
2.42 And when he was twelve years *o*,
5.36 of a new garment upon an *o*;
36 the new agreeth not with the *o*.
37 putteth new wine into *o* bottles;
39 No man also having drunk *o* wine
39 new: for he saith, The *o* is better.
9. 8 one of the *o* prophets was risen
19 one of the *o* prophets is risen again.
12.33 yourselves bags which wax not *o*,
Jn 3. 4 can a man be born when he is *o*?
8.57 Thou art not yet fifty years *o*, and
21.18 when thou shalt be *o*, thou shalt
Ac 2.17 your *o* men shall dream dreams:
4.22 For the man was above forty years *o*,
7.23 when he was full forty years *o*, it
15.21 Moses of *o* time hath in every city
21.16 Mnason of Cyprus, an *o* disciple,
Ro 4.19 he was about an hundred years *o*,
6. 6 our *o* man is crucified with him,
1Co 5. 7 Purge out therefore the *o* leaven,
8 not with *o* leaven, neither with the
2Co 3.14 in the reading of the *o* testament;
5.17 creature: *o* things are past away;
Eph 4.22 That ye put off...the *o* man, which
Col 3. 9 that ye have put off the *o* man
1Ti 4. 7 refuse profane and *o* wives' fables,
5. 9 number under threescore years *o*,
Heb 1.11 shall wax *o* as doth a garment;
8.13 covenant, he hath made the first *o*.
13 that which decayeth and waxeth *o*
1Pe 3. 5 in the *o* time the holy women
2Pe 1. 9 he was purged from his *o* sins.
21 came not in *o* time by the will of
2. 5 spared not the *o* world, but saved
3. 5 word of God the heavens were of *o*,
1Jn 2. 7 an *o* commandment which ye had
7 The *o* commandment is the word
Jude 4 who were before of *o* ordained to
Rev 12. 9 that *o* serpent, called the Devil,
20. 2 that *o* serpent, which is the Devil,

OLDNESS

Ro 7. 6 and not in the *o* of the letter.

OLIVE

Gen 8.11 in her mouth was an *o* leaf pluckt
Ex 27.20 that they bring thee pure oil *o*

Ex 30.24 the sanctuary, and of oil *o* an hin:
Lev 24. 2 they bring unto thee pure oil o
Dt 6.11 *o* trees, which thou plantedst not;
8. 8 a land of oil *o*, and honey;
24.20 When thou beatest thine *o* tree,
28.40 Thou shalt have *o* trees throughout
40 for thine *o* shall cast his fruit.
Jdg 9. 8 they said unto the *o* tree, Reign
9 But the *o* tree said unto them,
1Ki 6.23 he made two cherubims of *o* tree,
31 the oracle he made doors of *o* tree:
32 The two doors also were of *o* tree;
33 door of the temple posts of *o* tree,
2Ki 18.32 a land of oil *o* and of honey,
1Ch 27.28 over the *o* trees and the sycomore
Neh 8.15 and fetch *o* branches, and pine
Job 15.33 shall cast off his flower as the *o*.
Ps 52. 8 am like a green *o* tree in the house
128. 3 thy children like *o* plants round
Isa 17. 6 in it, as the shaking of an *o* tree,
24.13 shall be as the shaking of an *o* tree,
Jer 11.16 called thy name, A green *o* tree,
Hos 14. 6 his beauty shall be as the *o* tree,
Am 4. 9 trees and your *o* trees increased,
Hab 3.17 the labor of the *o* shall fail, and
Hag 2.19 the pomegranate, and the *o* tree,
Zec 4. 3 two *o* trees by it, one upon the right
11 What are these two *o* trees upon
12 What be these two *o* branches
Ro 11.17 and thou, being a wild *o* tree, wert
17 the root and fatness of the *o* tree;
24 if thou wert cut out of the *o* tree
24 to nature into a good *o* tree:
24 be graffed into their own *o* tree?
Jas 3.12 tree, my brethren, bear *o* berries?
Rev 11. 4 These are the two *o* trees, and the

OLIVES

Jdg 15. 5 corn, with the vineyards and *o*.
Mic 6.15 thou shalt tread the *o*, but thou
Zec 14. 4 in that day upon the mount of *O*,
4 the mount of *O* shall cleave in the
Mt 21. 1 Bethphage, unto the mount of *O*,
24. 3 And as he sat upon the mount of *O*,
26.30 they went out into the mount of *O*.
Mk 11. 1 and Bethany, at the mount of *O*,
13. 3 And as he sat upon the mount of *O*
14.26 they went out into the mount of *O*.
Lk 19.29 the mount called the mount of *O*,
37 at the descent of the mount of *O*,
21.37 that is called the mount of *O*.
22.39 as he was wont, to the mount of *O*;
Jn 8. 1 Jesus went unto the mount of *O*.

OLIVET

2Sa 15.30 up by the ascent of mount *O*,
Ac 1.12 from the mount called *O*, which

OLYMPAS

Ro 16.15 and *O*, and all the saints which

OMEGA

Rev 1. 8 I am Alpha and *O*, the beginning
11 I am Alpha and *O*, the first and
21. 6 I am Alpha and *O*, the beginning
22.13 I am Alpha and *O*, the beginning

OMITTED

Mt 23.23 *o*...weightier matters of the law,

OMNIPOTENT

Rev 19. 6 for the Lord God *o* reigneth.

OMRI

1Ki 16.16 made *O*...captain of the host, king
17 *O* went up from Gibbethon, and all
21 him king; and half followed *O*.
22 people that followed *O* prevailed
22 so Tibni died, and *O* reigned.
23 began *O* to reign over Israel, twelve
25 *O* wrought evil in the eyes of the
27 rest of the acts of *O* which he did
28 *O* slept with his fathers, and was
29 began Ahab the son of *O* to reign
29 Ahab the son of *O* reigned over
30 Ahab the son of *O* did evil in the
2Ki 8.26 Athaliah, the daughter of *O* king
1Ch 7. 8 and *O*, and Jerimoth, and Abiah,
9. 4 the son of Ammihud, the son of *O*,
27.18 of Issachar, *O* the son of Michael:
2Ch 22. 2 was Athaliah the daughter of *O*.
Mic 6.16 the statutes of *O* are kept, and all

ONCE

Gen 18.32 and I will speak yet but this *o*:
Ex 10.17 I pray thee, my sin only this *o*,
30.10 upon the horns of it *o* in a year
10 *o* in the year shall he make
Lev 16.34 of Israel for all their sins *o* a year.
Nu 13.30 Let us go up at *o*, and possess it;
Dt 7.22 mayest not consume them at *o*,
Jos 6. 3 and go round about the city *o*.
11 compassed the city, going about it *o*:
14 day they compassed the city *o*,
Jdg 6.39 me, and I will speak but this *o*:
39 prove,...but this *o* with the fleece;
16.18 Come up this *o*, for he hath shewed
28 me, I pray thee, only this *o*, O God,
28 be at *o* avenged of the Philistines
1Sa 26. 8 spear even to the earth at *o*,
1Ki 10.22 *o* in three years came the navy of
2Ki 6.10 saved himself there, not *o* nor twice.
2Ch 9.21 every three years *o* came the ships
Neh 5.18 and *o* in ten days store of all sorts
13.20 lodged without Jerusalem *o* or
Job 33.14 For God speaketh *o*, yea twice, yet
40. 5 *O* have I spoken; but I will not
Ps 62.11 God hath spoken *o*; twice have I
74. 6 carved work thereof at *o* with axes
76. 7 in thy sight when *o* thou art angry?
89.35 *O* have I sworn by my holiness that
Pr 28.18 perverse in his ways shall fall at *o*.
Isa 42.14 I will destroy and devour at *o*.
66. 8 or shall a nation be born at *o*?
Jer 10.18 inhabitants of the land at this *o*,
13.27 made clean? when shall it *o* be?
16.21 I will this *o* cause them to know,
Hag 2. 6 Yet *o*, it is a little while, and I will
Lk 13.25 When *o* the master of the house is
23.18 they cried out all at *o*, saying,
Ro 6.10 that he died, he died unto sin *o*:
7. 9 I was alive without the law *o*: but
1Co 15. 6 above five hundred brethren at *o*;
2Co 11.25 I beaten with rods, *o* was I stoned,
Gal 1.23 the faith which *o* he destroyed.
Eph 5. 3 let it not be *o* named among you,
Php 4.16 *o* and again unto my necessity.
1Th 2.18 unto you, even I Paul, *o* and again;
Heb 6. 4 for those who were *o* enlightened,
7.27 for this he did *o*, when he offered
9. 7 the high priest alone *o* every year,
12 he entered in *o* into the holy place,
26 *o* in the end of the world hath he
27 it is appointed unto men *o* to die,
28 So Christ was *o* offered to bear the
10. 2 worshippers *o* purged should have
10 the body of Jesus Christ *o* for all.
12.26 *o* more I shake not the earth only,
27 this word, Yet *o* more, signifieth the
1Pe 3.18 Christ also hath *o* suffered for sins,
20 when *o* the longsuffering of God
Jude 3 faith which was *o* delivered unto the
5 though ye *o* knew this, how that the

ONE

Gen 2.21 he took *o* of his ribs, and closed up
24 his wife: and they shall be *o* flesh.
3.22 the man is become as *o* of us, to
10. 8 began to be a mighty *o* in the earth.
11. 1 was of *o* language, and of *o* speech.
6 Lord said, Behold, the people is *o*,
6 and they have all *o* language; and
19.14 But he seemed as *o* that mocked
27.29 cursed be every *o* that curseth thee,
45 deprived also of you both in *o* day?
37.19 they said *o* to another, Behold, this
41. 5 ears of corn came up upon *o* stalk,
42.11 We are all *o* man's sons; we are
Ex 2. 6 This is *o* of the Hebrews' children.
12.49 *O* law shall be to him that is
16.15 they said *o* to another, It is manna:
Lev 20. 9 every *o* that curseth his father or
24.22 Ye shall have *o* manner of law, as
22 stranger, as for *o* of your own
25.14 ye shall not oppress *o* another:
Dt 6. 4 Israel: The Lord our God is *o* Lord:
19.15 *O* witness shall not rise up against
21.15 two wives, *o* beloved, and another
24. 5 but he shall be free at home *o* year,
Jos 17.14 Why hast thou given me but *o* lot
Jdg 7. 5 Every *o* that lappeth of the water
11.35 thou art *o* of them that trouble me:
20. 1 was gathered together as *o* man,
8 And all the people arose as *o* man,
1Sa 2.25 If *o* man sin against another, the
29. 5 they sang *o* to another in dances,
2Sa 10. 4 and shaved off *o* half of their beards,
12. 3 had nothing, save *o* little ewe lamb,
23.15 Oh that *o* would give me drink of the
1Ki 2.16 I ask *o* petition of thee, deny me
3.25 half to the *o*, and half to the other.
1Ch 11.17 *o* would give me drink of the water
2Ch 25.17 let us see *o* another in the face
32.12 Ye shall worship before *o* altar,
Ezr 3. 5 every *o* that willingly offered a
Neh 4.17 with *o* of his hands wrought in the
18 every *o* had his sword girded by
11. 1 cast lots, to bring *o* of ten to dwell
Job 1. 1 *o* that feared God, and eschewed
4 in their houses, every *o* his day;
8 *o* that feareth God, and escheweth
5. 2 man, and envy slayeth the silly *o*.
6.10 concealed the words of the Holy *O*.
26 the speeches of *o* that is desperate,
9. 3 cannot answer him *o* of a thousand.
22 This is *o* thing, therefore I said it.
12. 4 I am as *o* mocked of his neighbor,
16.21 *o* might plead for a man with God,
17.10 I cannot find *o* wise man among you.
21.23 *O* dieth in his full strength, being
29.25 as *o* that comforteth the mourners.
33.23 interpreter, *o* among a thousand,
Ps 14. 3 is none that doeth good, no, not *o*.
16.10 thine Holy *O* to see corruption.
27. 4 *O* thing have I desired of the Lord,
34.20 bones: not *o* of them is broken.
49.16 thou afraid when *o* is made rich,
50.21 I was altogether such an *o* as thyself:
53. 3 Every *o* of them is gone back: they
3 is none that doeth good, no, not *o*.
71.22 the harp, O thou Holy *O* of Israel.
73.20 As a dream when *o* awaketh; so,
75. 7 he putteth down *o* and setteth up
78.65 the Lord awaked as *o* out of sleep,
89.18 the Holy *O* of Israel is our king.
115. 8 so is every *o* that trusteth in them.
119.162 thy word, as *o* that findeth great
128. 1 Blessed is every *o* that feareth the
135.18 so is every *o* that trusteth in them.
137. 3 saying, Sing us *o* the songs of Zion.
145. 4 *O* generation shall praise thy works
Pr 1.14 among us; let us all have *o* purse:
6.28 Can *o* go upon hot coals, and his
15.12 scorner loveth not *o* that reproveth
17.14 strife is as when *o* letteth out water:
24.34 poverty come as *o* that travelleth;
26.17 like *o* that taketh a dog by the ears.
Ec 1. 4 *O* generation passeth away, and
2.14 *o* event happeneth to them all.
3.19 as the *o* dieth, so dieth the other;
19 they have all *o* breath; so that a
20 All go unto *o* place; all are of the
4. 9 Two are better than *o*; because

11 heat: but how can *o* be warm alone?
6. 6 no good: do not all go to *o* place?
7.28 *o* man among a thousand have I
9. 2 there is *o* event to the righteous,
3 that there is *o* event unto all: yea,
18 but *o* sinner destroyeth much good.
10. 3 he saith to every *o* that he is a fool.
12.11 which are given from *o* shepherd.
Isa 4. 1 women shall take hold of *o* man,
6. 2 seraphims: each *o* had six wings;
3 *o* cried unto another, and said, Holy,
6 Then flew *o* of the seraphims unto
10.14 and as *o* gathereth eggs that are left,
17 fire, and his Holy *O* for a flame:
12. 6 for great is the Holy *O* of Israel
29.20 terrible *o* is brought to nought,
40.25 shall I be equal? saith the Holy *O*.
26 is strong in power; not *o* faileth.
41. 6 They helped every *o* his neighbor;
20 the Holy *O* of Israel hath created it.
43. 3 the Holy *O* of Israel, thy Savior:
45.24 Surely, shall *o* say, in the Lord have
49. 7 Redeemer of Israel, and his Holy *O*,
53. 6 turned every *o* to his own way;
55. 1 Ho, every *o* that thirsteth, come ye
57.15 lofty *O* that inhabiteth eternity,
60.22 A little *o* shall become a thousand,
22 and a small *o* a strong nation:
66.13 As *o* whom his mother comforteth,
Jer 10. 3 for *o* cutteth a tree out of the forest,
19.11 as *o* breaketh a potter's vessel, that
20. 7 in derision daily, every *o* mocketh
31.30 But every *o* shall die for his own
32.19 give every *o* according to his ways,
39 will give them *o* heart, and *o* way,
51.31 *O* post shall run to meet another,
Eze 1. 6 And every *o* had four faces, and
6 faces, and every *o* had four wings.
28 and I heard a voice of *o* that spake.
7.16 mourning, every *o* for his iniquity.
10.14 every *o* had four faces: the first face
11.19 And I will give them *o* heart, and
16.44 Behold, every *o* that useth proverbs
20.39 Go ye, serve ye every *o* his idols,
21.16 Go thee *o* way or other, either on the
37.16 son of man, take thee *o* stick, and
17 join them *o* to another into *o* stick;
22 make them *o* nation in the land
22 *o* king shall be king to them all:
24 and they all shall have *o* shepherd:
39. 7 am the Lord, the Holy *O* in Israel.
Dan 3.19 heat the furnace *o* seven times
4.13 and an holy *o* came down from
7.13 *o* like the Son of man came with the
Hos 11. 9 and Holy *O* in the midst of thee:
Joel 2. 8 shall walk every *o* in his path:
Am 4. 7 I caused it to rain upon *o* city, and
Jon 3. 8 turn every *o* from his evil way, and
Mic 2. 4 shall *o* take up a parable against you,
4. 5 every *o* in the name of his god,
Hab 1.12 O Lord my God, mine Holy *O*?
Zep 3. 9 Lord, to serve him with *o* consent.
Zec 3. 9 upon *o* stone shall be seven eyes:
5. 3 every *o* that stealeth shall be cut off
3 every *o* that sweareth shall be cut off
12.10 as *o* mourneth for his only son, and
14. 9 there be *o* Lord, and his name *o*.
Mal 2.10 Have we not all *o* father? hath
10 hath not *o* God created us? why do
17 Every *o* that doeth evil is good in the
3.16 the Lord spake often *o* to another:
Mt 3. 3 voice of *o* crying in the wilderness,
5.18 heaven and earth pass, *o* jot or
18 *o* tittle shall in no wise pass
19 shall break *o* of these least
29, 30 should *o* of thy members perish,
36 not make *o* hair white or black.
6.24 for either he will hate the *o*, and
24 or else he will hold to the *o*, and
27 can add *o* cubit unto his stature?
29 was not arrayed like *o* of these.
7. 8 every *o* that asketh receiveth; and
21 Not every *o* that saith unto me,
26 every *o* that heareth these sayings
29 taught them as *o* having authority
10.29 and *o* of them shall not fall on the
42 *o* of these little ones a cup of cold
12. 6 place is *o* greater than the temple.
11 that shall have *o* sheep, and if it
22 unto him *o* possessed with a devil,
29 can *o* enter into a strong man's
47 Then *o* said unto him, Behold, thy
13.19 When any *o* heareth the word of
19 then cometh the wicked *o*, and
38 are the children of the wicked *o*;
46 had found *o* pearl of great price,
16.14 Jeremias, or *o* of the prophets.
17. 4 here three tabernacles, *o* for thee,
4 and *o* for Moses, and *o* for Elias.
18. 5 shall receive *o* such little child in
6 shall offend *o* of these little ones
9 for thee to enter into life with *o* eye,
10 despise not *o* of these little ones;
12 *o* of them be gone astray, doth he
14 *o* of these little ones should perish.
16 then take with thee *o* or two more,
24 *o* was brought unto him, which
28 and found *o* of his fellowservants,
35 forgive not every *o* his brother
19. 5 and they twain shall be *o* flesh?
6 they are no more twain, but *o* flesh.
16 *o* came and said unto him, Good
17 is none good but *o*, that is, God:
29 And every *o* that hath forsaken
20.12 last have wrought but *o* hour, and
13 he answered *o* of them, and said,
21 may sit, the *o* on thy right hand,
21.24 I also will ask you *o* thing, which if
35 took his servants, and beat *o*, and
22. 5 went their ways, *o* to his farm,
35 *o* of them, which was a lawyer,
23. 4 move them with *o* of their fingers
8 for *o* is your Master, even Christ;
9 for *o* is your Father, which is in
10 for *o* is your Master, even Christ.
15 sea and land to make *o* proselyte,
24. 2 be left here *o* stone upon another,
10 and shall betray *o* another,
10 another, and shall hate *o* another.
31 from *o* end of heaven to the other.
40, 41 *o* shall be taken, and the other
25.15 unto *o* he gave five talents,
15 to another two, and to another *o*;
18 he that had received *o* went and
24 he which had received the *o* talent
29 every *o* that hath shall be given,
32 separate them *o* from another, as
40 it unto *o* of the least of these my
45 did it not to *o* of the least of these,
26.14 Then *o* of the twelve, called Judas
21 you, that *o* of you shall betray me.
22 every *o* of them to say unto him,
40 ye not watch with me *o* hour?
47 lo, Judas, *o* of the twelve, came,
51 *o* of them which were with Jesus
73 Peter, Surely thou also art *o* of them;
27.38 *o* on the right hand, and another
48 And straightway *o* of them ran,
Mk 1. 3 voice of *o* crying in the wilderness,
7 cometh *o* mightier than I after me,
22 taught them as *o* that had authority,
24 who thou art, the Holy *O* of God.
2. 3 bringing *o* sick of the palsy, which
4.41 said *o* to another, What manner
5.22 *o* of the rulers of the synagogue,
6.15 prophet, or as *o* of the prophets.
7.14 Hearken unto me every *o* of you,
32 bring unto him *o* that was deaf,
8.14 ship with them more than *o* loaf.
28 and others, *O* of the prophets.
9. 5 three tabernacles; *o* for thee,
5 and *o* for Moses, and *o* for Elias.
10 questioning *o* with another what
17 *o* of the multitude answered and
26 and he was as *o* dead: insomuch
37 receive *o* of such children in my
38 *o* casting out devils in thy name,
42 shall offend *o* of these little ones
47 into the kingdom of God with *o*
49 every *o* shall be salted with fire,
50 and have peace *o* with another.
10. 8 And they twain shall be *o* flesh:
8 are no more twain, but *o* flesh.
17 came *o* running, and kneeled to
18 is none good but *o*, that is, God.
21 *O* thing thou lackest: go thy way,
37 we may sit, *o* on thy right hand,
11.29 I will also ask of you *o* question,
12. 6 Having yet therefore *o* son, his
28 *o* of the scribes came, and having
29 The Lord our God is *o* Lord:
32 there is *o* God; and there is none
13. 1 *o* of his disciples saith unto him,
2 not be left *o* stone upon another,
14.10 Judas Iscariot, *o* of the twelve,
18 *O* of you which eateth with me
19 to say unto him *o* by *o*, Is it I?
20 It is *o* of the twelve, that dippeth
37 couldest thou not watch *o* hour?
43 cometh Judas, *o* of the twelve,
47 *o* of them that stood by drew a
66 *o* of the maids of the high priest:
69 that stood by, This is *o* of them.
70 to Peter, Surely thou art *o* of them:
15. 6 he released unto them *o* prisoner,
7 And there was *o* named Barabbas,
21 they compel *o* Simon a Cyrenian,
27 the *o* on his right hand, and the
36 *o* ran and filled a sponge full of
Lk 2. 3 taxed, every *o* into his own city.
15 the shepherds said *o* to another,
36 there was *o* Anna, a prophetess,
3. 4 voice of *o* crying in the wilderness,
16 but *o* mightier than I cometh, the
4.34 who thou art; the Holy *O* of God.
40 laid his hands on every *o* of them,
5. 3 And he entered into *o* of the ships,
6. 9 unto them, I will ask you *o* thing;
11 communed *o* with another what
29 on the *o* cheek offer also the other;
40 every *o* that is perfect shall be as
7. 8 I say unto *o*, Go, and he goeth;
32 calling *o* to another, and saying,
36 *o* of the Pharisees desired him
41 the *o* owed five hundred pence,
8.25 wondered, saying *o* to another,
42 For he had *o* only daughter, about
49 cometh *o* from the ruler of the
9. 8 *o* of the old prophets was risen
19 that *o* of the old prophets is risen
33 three tabernacles; *o* for thee,
33 and *o* for Moses, and *o* for Elias:
43 wondered every *o* at all things
49 *o* casting out devils in thy name;
10.42 But *o* thing is needful: and Mary
11. 1 *o* of his disciples said unto him,
4 forgive every *o* that is indebted
10 every *o* that asketh receiveth; and
45 Then answered *o* of the lawyers,
46 burdens with *o* of your fingers.
12. 1 that they trode *o* upon another, he
6 not *o* of them is forgotten before
13 *o* of the company said unto him,
25 can add to his stature *o* cubit?
27 was not arrayed like *o* of these.
52 shall be five in *o* house divided,
13.10 teaching in *o* of the synagogues
15 not each *o* of you on the sabbath
23 Then said *o* unto him, Lord, are
14. 1 house of *o* of the chief Pharisees
15 *o* of them that sat at meat with
18 *o* consent began to make excuse.
15. 4 he lose *o* of them, doth not leave

Lk 15. 7 over *o* sinner that repenteth, more
8 if she lose *o* piece, doth not light
10 God over *o* sinner that repenteth.
19 make me as *o* of thy hired servants.
26 he called *o* of the servants, and
16. 5 called every *o* of his lord's debtors
13 either he will hate the *o*, and love
13 or else he will hold to the *o*, and
17 than *o* tittle of the law to fail.
30 if *o* went unto them from the dead,
31 though *o* rose from the dead.
17. 2 should offend *o* of these little ones.
15 And *o* of them, when he saw that
22 shall desire to see *o* of the days of
24 out of the *o* part under heaven,
34 there shall be two men in *o* bed;
34 the *o* shall be taken, and the
35 the *o* shall be taken, and the
36 the *o* shall be taken, and the
18.10 the *o* a Pharisee, and the other a
14 for every *o* that exalteth himself
19 none is good, save *o*, that is, God.
22 Yet lackest thou *o* thing: sell all
19.26 unto every *o* which hath shall be
44 leave in thee *o* stone upon another;
20. 1 on *o* of those days, as he taught
3 I will also ask you *o* thing; and
21. 6 not be left *o* stone upon another,
22.36 him sell his garment, and buy *o*.
47 was called Judas, *o* of the twelve,
50 *o* of them smote the servant of the
59 about the space of *o* hour after
23.14 as *o* that perverteth the people: and
17 release *o* unto them at the feast.)
26 away, they laid hold upon *o* Simon,
33 *o* on the right hand, and the
39 *o* of the malefactors which were
24.17 these that ye have *o* to another,
18 the *o* of them, whose name was
32 they said *o* to another, Did not our
Jn 1.23 voice of *o* crying in the wilderness,
26 there standeth *o* among you, whom
40 *O* of the two which heard John
3. 8 so is every *o* that is born of the
20 every *o* that doeth evil hateth the
4.33 said the disciples *o* to another,
37 *O* soweth, and another reapeth.
5.44 which receive honor *o* of another,
45 there is *o* that accuseth you, even
6. 7 every *o* of them may take a little.
8 *O* of his disciples, Andrew, Simon
22 save that *o* whereinto his disciples
40 every *o* which seeth the Son, and
70 you twelve, and *o* of you is a devil?
71 betray him, being *o* of the twelve.
7.21 unto them, I have done *o* work,
50 Jesus by night, being *o* of them,)
8. 9 went out *o* by *o*, beginning at the
18 am *o* that bear witness of myself,
41 we have *o* Father, even God.
50 there is *o* that seeketh and judgeth.
9.25 *o* thing I know, that, whereas I
32 the eyes of *o* that was born blind.
10.16 there shall be *o* fold, and
16 there shall be...*o* shepherd.
30 I and my Father are *o*.
11.49 *o* of them, named Caiaphas, being
50 *o* man should die for the people,
52 together in *o* the children of God
12. 2 Lazarus was *o* of them that sat at
4 *o* of his disciples, Judas Iscariot,
48 my words, hath *o* that judgeth him:
13.14 also ought to wash *o* another's feet.
21 you, that *o* of you shall betray me.
22 the disciples looked *o* on another,
23 on Jesus' bosom *o* of his disciples,
34 unto you, That ye love *o* another;
34 you, that ye also love *o* another.
35 if ye have love *o* to another.
15.12 That ye love *o* another, as I have
17 you, that ye love *o* another.
17.11 me, that they may be *o*, as we are.
21 That they all may be *o*; as thou,
21 thee, that they also may be *o* in us:
22 they may be *o*, even as we are *o*:
23 they may be made perfect in *o*;
18.14 *o* man should die for the people.
17 thou also *o* of this man's disciples?
22 *o* of the officers which stood by
25 Art not thou also *o* of his disciples?
26 *O* of the servants of the high
37 Every *o* that is of the truth
39 release unto you *o* at the passover:
19.18 on either side *o*, and Jesus in the
34 But *o* of the soldiers with a spear
20.12 the *o* at the head, and the other at
24 Thomas, *o* of the twelve, called
21.25 if they should be written every *o*,
Ac 1.14 continued with *o* accord in prayer
22 must *o* be ordained to be a witness
2. 1 they were all with *o* accord in
1 all with...accord in *o* place.
7 marvelled, saying *o* to another,
12 in doubt, saying *o* to another,
27 thine Holy *O* to see corruption.
38 and be baptized every *o* of you in
46 daily with *o* accord in the temple,
3.14 ye denied the Holy *O* and the Just,
26 turning away every *o* of you from
4.24 their voice to God with *o* accord,
32 were of *o* heart and of...soul:
32 were of...heart and of *o* soul:
5.12 with *o* accord in Solomon's porch.
16 and they were healed every *o*.
25 came *o* and told them, saying,
34 stood there up *o* in the council, a
7.24 seeing *o* of them suffer wrong, he
26 would have set them at *o* again,
26 why do ye wrong *o* to another?
52 before of the coming of the Just *O*;
57 and ran upon him with *o* accord,
8. 6 the people with *o* accord gave heed
9 that himself was some great *o*:
9.11 the house of Judas for *o* called Saul,
43 in Joppa with *o* Simon a tanner.
10. 2 *o* that feared God with all his house,
5 men to Joppa, and call for *o* Simon,
6 lodgeth with *o* Simon a tanner,
22 a just man, and *o* that feareth God,
28 or come unto *o* of another nation;
32 the house of *o* Simon a tanner by the
11.28 stood up *o* of them named Agabus,
12.10 and passed on through *o* street;
20 they came with *o* accord to him,
13.25 there cometh *o* after me, whose
35 thine Holy *O* to see corruption.
15.25 being assembled with *o* accord,
39 departed asunder *o* from the other:
17. 7 that there is another king, *o* Jesus.
26 hath made of *o* blood all nations
27 he be not far from every *o* of us:
18. 7 *o* that worshipped God, whose
12 made insurrection with *o* accord
19. 9 daily in the school of *o* Tyrannus.
14 there were seven sons of *o* Sceva, a
29 with *o* accord into the theater.
32 cried *o* thing, and some another:
34 all with *o* voice about the space of
38 let them implead *o* another.
20.31 ceased not to warn every *o* night
21. 6 had taken our leave *o* of another,
7 and abode with them *o* day.
8 evangelist, which was *o* of the seven;
16 with them *o* Mnason of Cyprus,
26 be offered for every *o* of them.
34 some cried *o* thing, and some
22.12 And *o* Ananias, a devout man
14 know his will, and see that Just *O*,
23. 6 that the *o* part were Sadducees,
17 Paul called *o* of the centurions
24.21 Except it be for this *o* voice, that
25.19 and of *o* Jesus, which was dead,
27. 1 other prisoners unto *o* named Julius,
2 *o* Aristarchus, a Macedonian of
28. 2 a fire, and received us every *o*,
13 after *o* day the south wind blew,
25 that Paul had spoken *o* word,
Ro 1.16 salvation to every *o* that believeth;
27 in their lust *o* toward another;
2.15 accusing or...excusing *o* another;)
28 is not a Jew, which is *o* outwardly;
29 But he is a Jew, which is *o* inwardly;
3.10 There is none righteous, no, not *o*:
12 is none that doeth good, no, not *o*.
30 Seeing it is *o* God, which shall
5. 7 for a righteous man will *o* die:
12 as by *o* man sin entered into the
15 the offense of *o* many be dead,
15 which is by *o* man, Jesus Christ,
16 not as it was by *o* that sinned, so
16 was by *o* to condemnation, but the
17 by *o* man's offense death reigned
17 man's offense death reigned by *o*;
17 reign in life by *o*, Jesus Christ.)
18 by the offense of *o* judgment came
18 the righteousness of *o* the free gift
19 as by *o* man's disobedience many
19 by the obedience of *o* shall many be
9.10 Rebecca also had conceived by *o*,
21 lump to make *o* vessel unto honor,
10. 4 law for righteousness to every *o*
12. 4 have many members in *o* body,
5 being many, are *o* body in Christ,
5 every *o* members...of another.
5 members *o* of another.
10 kindly affectioned *o* to another
10 in honor preferring *o* another;
16 of the same mind *o* toward another.
13. 8 any thing, but to love *o* another:
14. 2 For *o* believeth that he may eat all
5 *O* man esteemeth...day above
5 esteemeth *o* day above another:
12 every *o* of us shall give account of
13 not...judge *o* another any more:
19 wherewith *o* may edify another.
15. 2 every *o* of us please his neighbor
5 be likeminded *o* toward another
6 That ye may with *o* mind...mouth
6 with...mind and *o* mouth glorify
7 Wherefore receive ye *o* another,
14 able also to admonish *o* another.
16.16 Salute *o* another with an holy kiss.
1Co 1.12 that every *o* of you saith, I am of
3. 4 For while *o* saith, I am of Paul;
8 and he that watereth are *o*:
4. 6 no *o* of you be puffed up for *o*
5. 1 *o* should have his father's wife.
5 To deliver such an *o* unto Satan
11 with such an *o* no not to eat.
6. 5 not *o* that shall be able to judge
7 ye go to law with *o* another.
16 is joined to an harlot is *o* body?
16 two, saith he, shall be *o* flesh.
17 is joined unto the Lord is *o* spirit.
7. 5 Defraud ye not *o* the other, except
7 *o* after this manner, and
17 as the Lord hath called every *o*, so
25 as *o* that hath obtained mercy of the
8. 4 there is none other God but *o*.
6 But to us there is but *o* God, the
6 *o* Lord Jesus Christ, by whom are
9.24 run all, but *o* receiveth the prize?
26 fight I, not as *o* that beateth the air:
10. 8 and fell in *o* day three and twenty
17 many are *o* bread, and *o* body:
17 are all partakers of that *o* bread.
11. 5 is even all *o* as if she were shaven.
20 come together...into *o* place,
21 eating every *o* taketh before other
21 *o* is hungry, and another is
33 together to eat, tarry *o* for another.
12. 8 For to *o* is given by the Spirit

11 that *o* and the selfsame Spirit,
12 as the body is *o*, and hath many
12 the members of that *o* body, being
12 many, are *o* body: so also is Christ.
13 For by *o* Spirit are we all baptized
13 into *o* body, whether we be Jews or
13 been all made to drink *o* Spirit.
14 For the body is not *o* member, but
18 every *o* of them in the body, as it
19 if they were all *o* member, where
20 many members, yet but *o* body.
25 have the same care *o* for another.
26 whether *o* member suffer, all the
26 or *o* member be honored, all the
14.23 be come together into *o* place,
24 come in *o* that believeth not, or
24 or *o* unlearned, he is convinced of
26 every *o* of you hath a psalm, hath
27 by course; and let *o* interpret.
31 For ye may all prophesy *o* by
31 ye may all prophesy...by *o*,
15. 8 of me also, as of *o* born out of due
39 there is *o* kind of flesh of men,
40 the glory of the celestial is *o*, and
41 There is *o* glory of the sun, and
41 *o* star differeth from another star in
16. 2 every *o* of you lay by him in store,
16 to every *o* that helpeth with us,
20 ye *o* another with an holy kiss.
2Co 2. 7 such a *o* should be swallowed up
16 To the *o* we are the savor of
5.10 every *o* may receive the things done
14 that if *o* died for all, then were all
10.11 Let such an *o* think this, that,
11. 2 have espoused you to *o* husband,
24 received I forty stripes save *o*.
12. 2 *o* caught up to the third heaven.
5 Of such an *o* will I glory: yet of
13.11 be of *o* mind, live in peace;
12 Greet *o* another with an holy kiss.
Gal 3.10 Cursed is every *o* that continueth
13 Cursed is every *o* that hangeth on
16 as of *o*, And to thy seed, which is
20 not a mediator of *o*, but God is *o*.
28 for ye are all *o* in Christ Jesus.
4.22 *o* by a bondmaid, the other by a
24 the *o* from the mount Sinai, which
5.13 flesh, but by love serve *o* another.
14 all the law is fulfilled in *o* word,
15 if ye bite and devour *o* another,
15 ye be not consumed *o* of another.
17 are contrary the *o* to the other: so
26 *o* another, envying *o* another.
6. 1 restore such an *o* in the spirit of
2 Bear ye *o* another's burdens, and
Eph 1.10 gather together in *o* all things
2.14 who hath made both *o*, and hath
15 in himself of twain *o* new man, so
16 both unto God in *o* body by the
18 access by *o* Spirit unto the Father.
4. 2 forbearing *o* another in love;
4 There is *o* body, and *o* Spirit, even
4 called in *o* hope of your calling;
5 *O* Lord...faith, *o* baptism,
5 Lord, *o* faith,...baptism,
6 *O* God and Father of all, who is
7 unto every *o* of us is given grace
25 for we are members *o* of another.
32 And be ye kind *o* to another,
32 forgiving *o* another, even as God
5.21 Submitting yourselves *o* to another
31 wife, and they two shall be *o* flesh.
33 let every *o* of you in particular
Php 1.16 The *o* preach Christ of contention,
27 that ye stand fast in *o* spirit, with
27 with *o* mind striving together
2. 2 the same love, being of *o* accord,
2 love, being...of *o* mind.
3.13 this *o* thing I do, forgetting those
Col 3. 9 Lie not *o* to another, seeing that
13 Forbearing *o* another, and
13 forgiving *o* another, if any man
15 also ye are called in *o* body; and
16 and admonishing *o* another in
4. 9 beloved brother, who is *o* of you.
12 Epaphras, who is *o* of you, a servant
1Th 2.11 and charged every *o* of you, as a
3.12 abound in love *o* toward another,
4. 4 every *o* of you should know how
9 taught of God to love *o* another.
18 comfort *o* another with these words.
5.11 edify *o* another, even as also ye
2Th 1. 3 charity of every *o* of you all toward
1Ti 2. 5 there is *o* God, and *o* mediator
3. 2 husband of *o* wife, vigilant, sober,
4 *O* that ruleth well his own house,
12 deacons be the husbands of *o* wife,
5. 9 having been the wife of *o* man,
21 without preferring *o* before another,
2Ti 2.19 every *o* that nameth the name of
Tit 1. 6 blameless, the husband of *o* wife,
12 *O* of themselves, even a prophet
3. 3 envy, hateful, and hating *o* another.
Phm 9 being such an *o* as Paul the aged,
Heb 2. 6 But *o* in a certain place testified,
11 who are sanctified are all of *o*:
3.13 exhort *o* another daily, while it
5.12 ye have need that *o* teach you again
13 For every *o* that useth milk is
6.11 every *o* of you do shew the same
10.12 he had offered *o* sacrifice for sins
14 by *o* offering he hath perfected for
24 us consider *o* another to provoke
25 but exhorting *o* another: and so
11.12 Therefore sprang there even of *o*,
12.16 who for *o* morsel of meat sold his
13.14 continuing city,...we seek *o* to come.
Jas 2.10 yet offend in *o* point, he is guilty
16 *o* of you say unto them, Depart in
19 believest that there is *o* God; thou
4.11 Speak not evil *o* of another,
12 There is *o* lawgiver, who is able to
5. 9 Grudge not *o* against another,
16 Confess your faults *o* to another,
16 pray *o* for another, that ye may be
19 the truth, and *o* convert him;
1Pe 1.22 love *o* another with a pure heart
3. 8 Finally, be ye all of *o* mind, having
8 having compassion *o* for another,
4. 9 hospitality *o* to another without
10 minister the same *o* to another,
5. 5 all of you be subject *o* to another,
14 Greet ye *o* another with a kiss of
2Pe 3. 8 be not ignorant of this *o* thing,
8 that *o* day is with the Lord as a
8 and a thousand years as *o* day.
1Jn 1. 7 have fellowship *o* with another,
2.13 ye have overcome the wicked *o*.
14 and ye have overcome the wicked *o*.
20 ye have an unction from the Holy *O*,
29 every *o* that doeth righteousness
3.11 that we should love *o* another.
12 as Cain, who was of that wicked *o*,
23 and love *o* another, as he gave us
4. 7 Beloved, let us love *o* another: for
7 every *o* that loveth is born of God,
11 ye ought also to love *o* another.
12 If we love *o* another, God dwelleth
5. 1 every *o* that loveth him that begat
7 Ghost: and these three are *o*.
8 blood: and these three agree in *o*.
18 and that wicked *o* toucheth him not.
2Jn 5 beginning, that we love *o* another.
Rev 1.13 midst...*o* like unto the Son of man,
2.23 I will give unto every *o* of you
4. 2 in heaven, and *o* sat on the throne.
5. 5 And *o* of the elders saith unto me,
8 having every *o* of them harps, and
6. 1 the Lamb opened *o* of the seals,
1 *o* of the four beasts saying, Come
4 that they should kill *o* another:
11 robes were given unto every *o* of
7.13 *o* of the elders answered, saying
9.12 *O* woe is past; and, behold, there
11.10 and shall send gifts *o* to another;
13. 3 I saw *o* of his heads as it were
14.14 cloud *o* sat like unto the Son of man,
15. 7 *o* of the four beasts gave unto the
17. 1 there came *o* of the seven angels
10 five are fallen, and *o* is, and the
12 as kings *o* hour with the beast.
13 These have *o* mind, and shall give
18. 8 shall her plagues come in *o* day,
10 in *o* hour is thy judgment come.
17 in *o* hour so great riches is come
19 for in *o* hour is she made desolate.
21. 9 unto me *o* of the seven angels
21 every several gate was of *o* pearl:

ONE'S

Ec 7. 1 day of death than the day of *o* birth.
Ac 16.26 and every *o* bands were loosed.

ONES

Ps 137. 9 dasheth thy little *o* against the
Pr 1.22 How long, ye simple *o*, will ye love
Isa 25. 4 the blast of the terrible *o* is as a storm
Dan 4.17 demand by the word of the holy *o*
Joel 3.11 cause thy mighty *o* to come down,
Mt 10.42 of these little *o* a cup of cold water
18. 6 shall offend one of these little *o*
10 ye despise not one of these little *o*;
14 one of these little *o* should perish.
Mk 9.42 shall offend one of these little *o* that
10.42 their great *o* exercise authority upon
Lk 17. 2 he should offend one of these little *o*.

ONESIMUS

Col 4. 9 *O*, a faithful and beloved brother,
Phm 10 I beseech thee for my son *O*,

ONESIPHORUS

2Ti 1.16 give mercy unto the house of *O*;
4.19 Aquila, and the household of *O*.

ONLY

Gen 6. 5 his heart was *o* evil continually.
7.23 Noah *o* remained alive, and they
22. 2 now thy son, thine *o* son Isaac,
12 thy son, thine *o* son from me
16 withheld thy son, thine *o* son:
34.22 *O* herein will the men consent
23 *o* let us consent unto them, and
41.40 *o* in the throne will I be greater
47.22 *O* the land of the priests bought
26 except the land of the priests *o*,
50. 8 *o* their little ones, and their
Ex 8.11 they shall remain in the river *o*.
9.26 *O* in the land of Goshen, where
10.17 take away from me this death *o*.
21.19 *o* he shall pay for the loss of his
22.20 unto any god, save unto the Lord *o*,
27 For that is his covering *o*, it is his
Lev 21.23 *O* he shall not go in unto the vail,
27.26 *O* the firstling of the beasts, which
Nu 1.49 *O* thou shalt not number the tribe
12. 2 indeed spoken *o* by Moses?
14. 9 *O* rebel not ye against the Lord,
18. 3 *o* they shall not come nigh the
20.19 I will *o*, without doing any thing
22.35 *o* the word that I shall speak unto
31.22 *O* the gold, and the silver, the
36. 6 *o* to the family of the tribe of their
Dt 2.28 *o* I will pass through on my feet;
35 *O* the cattle we took for a prey
37 *O* unto the land of the children of
3.11 *o* Og king of Bashan remained of
4. 9 *O* take heed to thyself, and keep
12 similitude; *o* ye heard a voice.
8. 3 that man doth not live by bread *o*,
10.15 *O* the Lord had a delight in thy
12.16 *O* ye shall not eat the blood; ye
23 *O* be sure that thou eat not the

Dt 12.26 *O* thy holy things which thou hast,
15. 5 *O* if thou carefully hearken unto
23 *O* thou shalt not eat the blood
20.20 *O* the trees which thou knowest
22.25 man *o* that lay with her shall die:
28.13 and thou shalt be above *o*, and
29, 33 thou shalt be *o* oppressed and
29.14 with you *o* do I make this covenant
Jos 1. 7 *O* be thou strong and very
17 *o* the Lord thy God be with thee,
18 *o* be strong and of a good courage.
6.15 *o* on that day they compassed the
17 *o* Rahab the harlot shall live, she
24 *o* the silver, and the gold, and the
8. 2 *o* the spoil thereof, and the cattle
27 *O* the cattle and the spoil of that
11.13 none of them, save Hazor *o*;
22 *o* in Gaza, in Gath, and in Ashdod,
13. 6 *o* divide thou it by lot unto the
14 *O* unto the tribe of Levi he gave
17.17 thou shalt not have one lot *o*:
Jdg 3. 2 *O* that the generations of the
6.37 and if the dew be on the fleece *o*,
39 it now be dry *o* upon the fleece,
40 for it was dry upon the fleece *o*,
10.15 deliver us *o*, we pray thee, this
11.34 she was his *o* child; beside her
16.28 and strengthen me,...*o* this once,
19.20 me; *o* lodge not in the street.
1Sa 1.13 *o* her lips moved, but her voice
23 *o* the Lord establish his word.
5. 4 *o* the stump of Dagon was left to
7. 3 unto the Lord, and serve him *o*:
4 Ashtaroth, and served the Lord *o*.
12.24 *O* fear the Lord, and serve him in
18.17 *o* be thou valiant for me, and fight
20.14 shalt not *o* while yet I live shew me
39 *o* Jonathan and David knew the
2Sa 13.32 king's sons; for Ammon *o* is dead:
33 are dead: for Ammon *o* is dead.
17. 2 flee; and I will smite the king *o*:
23.10 returned after him *o* to spoil.
1Ki 3. 2 *O* the people sacrificed in high
3 *o* he sacrificed and burnt incense
4.19 *o* officer which was in the land.
8.39 (for thou, even thou *o*, knowest
12.20 David, but the tribe of Judah *o*.
14. 8 to do that *o* which was right in
13 he *o* of Jeroboam shall come to
15. 5 save *o* in the matter of Uriah the
18.22 even I *o*, remain a prophet of the
19.10, 14 and I, even I *o*, am left; and
22.31 save *o* with the king of Israel.
2Ki 3.25 *o* in Kir-haraseth left they the stones
10.23 but the worshippers of Baal *o*.
17.18 none left but the tribe of Judah *o*.
19.19 thou art the Lord God, even thou *o*.
21. 8 *o* if they will observe to do
1Ch 22.12 *O* the Lord give thee wisdom and
2Ch 2. 6 save *o* to burn sacrifice before him?
18.30 save *o* with the king of Israel.
33.17 yet unto the Lord their God *o*.
Ezr 10.15 *O* Jonathan the son of Asahel and
Est 1.16 not done wrong to the king *o*,
Job 1.12 *o* upon himself put not forth
15, 16, 17, 19 I *o* am escaped alone
13.20 *O* do not two things unto me:
34.29 a nation, or against a man *o*:
Ps 4. 8 Lord, *o* makest me dwell in safety.
51. 4 Against thee, thee *o*, have I sinned,
62. 2 He *o* is my rock and my salvation;
4 They *o* consult to cast him down
5 My soul, wait thou *o* upon God;
6 He *o* is my rock and my salvation:
71.16 thy righteousness, even of thine *o*.
72.18 who *o* doeth wonderful things.
91. 8 *O* with thine eyes shalt thou
Pr 4. 3 tender and *o* beloved in the sight
11.23 desire of the righteous is *o* good:
13.10 *O* by pride cometh contention:
14.23 of the lips tendeth *o* to penury.
17.11 An evil man seeketh *o* rebellion:
21. 5 diligent tend *o* to plenteousness;
5 every one that is hasty *o* to want.
Ec 7.29 this *o* have I found, that God hath
SS 6. 9 she is the *o* one of her mother, she
Isa 4. 1 *o* let us be called by thy name, to
26.13 by thee *o* will we make mention
28.19 *o* to understand the report.
37.20 thou art the Lord, even thou *o*.
Jer 3.13 *O* acknowledge thine iniquity,
6.26 thee mourning, as for an *o* son.
32.30 children of Judah have *o* done evil
30 have *o* provoked me to anger with
Eze 7. 5 God; An evil, an *o* evil, behold, is
14.16 they *o* shall be delivered, but the
18 *o* shall be delivered themselves.
44.20 they shall *o* poll their heads.
Am 3. 2 You *o* have I known of all the
8.10 it as the mourning of an *o* son,
Zec 12.10 one mourneth for his *o* son, and
Mt 4.10 God, and him *o* shalt thou serve.
5.47 And if ye salute your brethren *o*,
8. 8 speak the word *o*, and my servant
10.42 a cup of cold water *o* in the name
12. 4 with him, but *o* for the priests?
14.36 *o* touch the hem of his garment:
17. 8 they saw no man, save Jesus *o*.
21.19 nothing thereon, but leaves *o*,
21 not *o* do this which is done to the
24.36 of heaven, but my Father *o*.
Mk 2. 7 who can forgive sins but God *o*?
5.36 Be not afraid, *o* believe,
6. 8 for their journey, save a staff *o*;
9. 8 save Jesus *o* with themselves.
Lk 4. 8 God, and him *o* shalt thou serve.
7.12 the *o* son of his mother, and she
8.42 For he had one *o* daughter, about
50 Fear not: believe *o*, and she shall
9.38 my son: for he is mine *o* child.
24.18 thou *o* a stranger in Jerusalem,
Jn 1.14 as of the *o* begotten of the Father,)
18 the *o* begotten Son, which is in the
3.16 he gave his *o* begotten Son, that
18 name of the *o* begotten Son of God.
5.18 he not *o* had broken the sabbath,
44 honor that cometh from God *o*?
11.52 And not for that nation *o*, but
12. 9 they came not for Jesus' sake *o*,
13. 9 Lord, not my feet *o*, but also my
17. 3 might know thee the *o* true God,
Ac 8.16 *o* they were baptized in the name
11.19 word to none but unto the Jews *o*.
18.25 knowing *o* the baptism of John.
19.27 not *o* this our craft is in danger to
21.13 I am ready not to be bound *o*, but
25 save *o* that they keep themselves
26.29 not *o* thou, but also all that hear
27.10 not *o* of the lading and ship, but
Ro 1.32 not *o* do the same, but have
3.29 Is he the God of the Jews *o*? is he
4. 9 then upon the circumcision *o*, or
12 who are not of the circumcision *o*,
16 not to that *o* which is of the law,
5. 3 And not *o* so, but we glory in
11 not *o* so, but we also joy in God
8.23 And not *o* they, but ourselves also,
9.10 And not *o* this; but when Rebecca
24 not of the Jews *o*, but also of the
13. 5 needs be subject, not *o* for wrath,
16. 4 unto whom not *o* I give thanks,
27 To God *o* wise, be glory through
1Co 7.39 to whom she will; *o* in the Lord.
9. 6 Or I *o* and Barnabas, have not we
14.36 from you? or came it unto you *o*?
15.19 If in this life *o* we have hope in
2Co 7. 7 And not by his coming *o*, but by
8.10 not *o* to do, but also to be forward
19 And not that *o*, but who was also
21 not *o* in the sight of the Lord, but
9.12 not *o* supplieth the want of the
Gal 1.23 they had heard *o*, That he which
2.10 *O* they would that we should
3. 2 This *o* would I learn of you,
4.18 not *o* when I am present with you.
5.13 *o* use not liberty for an occasion to
6.12 *o* lest they...suffer persecution
Eph 1.21 not *o* in this world, but also in that
Php 1.27 *O* let your conversation be as it
29 not *o* to believe on him, but also to
2.12 obeyed, not as in my presence *o*,
27 and not on him *o*, but on me also,
4.15 giving and receiving, but ye *o*.
Col 4.11 These *o* are my fellowworkers
1Th 1. 5 came not unto you in word *o*, but
8 not *o* in Macedonia and Achaia,
2. 8 not the gospel of God *o*, but also
2Th 2. 7 *o* he who now letteth will let, until
1Ti 1.17 the *o* wise God, be honor and
5.13 not *o* idle, but tattlers also and
6.15 is the blessed and *o* Potentate,
16 Who *o* hath immortality, dwelling
2Ti 2.20 there are not *o* vessels of gold and
4. 8 and not to me *o*, but unto all them
11 *O* Luke is with me. Take Mark,
Heb 9.10 stood *o* in meats and drinks, and
11.17 offered up his *o* begotten son,
12.26 once more I shake not the earth *o*,
Jas 1.22 of the word, and not hearers *o*,
2.24 man is justified, and not by faith *o*.
1Pe 2.18 not *o* to the good and gentle, but
1Jn 2. 2 and not for ours *o*, but also for
4. 9 God sent his *o* begotten Son into
5. 6 not by water *o*, but by water and
2Jn 1. 1 and not I *o*, but also all they that
Jude 4 denying the *o* Lord God, and our
25 To the *o* wise God our Saviour, be
Rev 9. 4 *o* those men which have not the
15. 4 for thou *o* art holy: for all nations

OPEN

Gen 1.20 in the *o* firmament of heaven.
38.14 sat in an *o* place, which is by the
Ex 21.33 if a man shall *o* a pit, or if a man
Lev 14. 7 living bird loose into the *o* field.
53 bird out of the city into the *o* fields,
17. 5 which they offer in the *o* field, even
Nu 8.16 instead of such as *o* every womb,
16.30 and the earth *o* her mouth, and
19.15 And every *o* vessel, which hath no
16 slain with a sword in the *o* fields,
24. 3 man whose eyes are *o* hath said:
4 a trance, but having his eyes *o*:
15 man whose eyes are *o* hath said:
16 a trance, but having his eyes *o*:
Dt 15. 8 shalt *o* thine hand wide unto him,
11 shalt *o* thine hand wide unto thy
20.11 answer of peace, and *o* unto thee,
28.12 shall *o* unto thee his good treasure,
Jos 8.17 they left the city *o*, and pursued
10.22 *O* the mouth of the cave, and bring
1Sa 3. 1 those days; there was no *o* vision.
2Sa 11.11 lord, are encamped in the *o* fields;
1Ki 6.18 carved with knops and *o* flowers:
29 palm trees and *o* flowers, within
32 and palm trees and *o* flowers, and
35 and palm trees and *o* flowers:
8.29 thine eyes may be *o* toward this
52 That thine eyes may be *o* unto the
2Ki 6.17 Lord, I pray thee, *o* his eyes, that
20 Lord, *o* the eyes of these men,
9. 3 Then *o* the door, and flee, and
13.17 he said, *O* the window eastward.
19.16 *o*, Lord, thine eyes, and see: and
2Ch 6.20 That thine eyes may be *o* upon
40 let, I beseech thee, thine eyes be *o*,
7.15 Now mine eyes shall be *o*, and
Neh 1. 6 and thine eyes *o*, that thou mayest
6. 5 time with an *o* letter in his hand;
Job 11. 5 speak, and *o* his lips against thee;
14. 3 dost thou *o* thine eyes upon such
32.20 I will *o* my lips and answer.
34.26 men in the *o* sight of others;

35.16 doth Joab *o* his mouth in vain;
41.14 Who can *o* the doors of his face?
Ps 5. 9 their throat is an *o* sepulcher; they
34.15 and his ears are *o* unto their cry.
49. 4 I will *o* my dark saying upon the
51.15 O Lord, *o* thou my lips; and my
78. 2 I will *o* my mouth in a parable:
81.10 *o* thy mouth wide, and I will fill it.
118.19 *O*...the gates of righteousness:
119.18 *O* thou mine eyes, that I may
Pr 13.16 but a fool layeth *o* his folly.
20.13 *o* thine eyes, and thou shalt be
27. 5 *O* rebuke is better than secret
31. 8 *O* thy mouth for the dumb in the
9 *O* thy mouth, judge righteously,
SS 5. 2 *O* to me, my sister, my love, my
5 I rose up to *o* to my beloved; and
Isa 9.12 shall devour Israel with *o* mouth.
22.22 so he shall *o*, and none shall shut;
22 and he shall shut, and none shall *o*.
24.18 the windows from on high are *o*,
26. 2 *O* ye the gates, that the righteous
28.24 doth he *o* and break the clods of
37.17 *o* thine eyes, O Lord, and see: and
41.18 I will *o* rivers in high places, and
42. 7 To *o* the blind eyes, to bring out
45. 1 to *o* before him the two leaved
8 let the earth *o*, and let them bring
60.11 thy gates shall be *o* continually;
Jer 5.16 Their quiver is as an *o* sepulcher,
9.22 fall as dung upon the *o* field, and
13.19 shut up, and none shall *o* them:
32.11 custom, and that which was *o*:
14 and this evidence which is *o*; and
19 thine eyes are *o* upon all the ways
50.26 utmost border, *o* her storehouses:
Eze 2. 8 *o* thy mouth, and eat that I give
3.27 I will *o* thy mouth, and thou shalt
16. 5 thou wast cast out in the *o* field,
63 and never *o* thy mouth any more
21.22 to *o* the mouth in the slaughter,
25. 9 I will *o* the side of Moab from the
29. 5 thou shalt fall upon the *o* fields;
32. 4 cast thee forth upon the *o* field,
33.27 him that is in the *o* field will I give
37. 2 were very many in the *o* valley;
12 I will *o* your graves, and cause
39. 5 Thou shalt fall upon the *o* field:
46.12 one shall then *o* him the gate that
Dan 6.10 and his windows being *o* in his
9.18 *o* thine eyes, and behold our
Na 3.13 set wide *o* unto thine enemies:
Zec 11. 1 *O* thy doors, O Lebanon, that the
12. 4 I will *o* mine eyes upon the house
Mal 3.10 I will not *o* you the windows of
Mt 13.35 I will *o* my mouth in parables; I
25.11 virgins, saying, Lord, Lord, *o* to us.
Lk 12.36 they may *o* unto him immediately.
13.25 door, saying, Lord, Lord, *o* unto us;
Jn 1.51 Hereafter ye shall see heaven *o*,
10.21 Can a devil *o* the eyes of the blind?
Ac 16.27 sleep, and seeing the prison doors *o*,
18.14 Paul was now about to *o* his mouth,
19.38 the law is *o*, and there are deputies:
26.18 To *o* their eyes, and to turn them
Ro 3.13 Their throat is an *o* sepulcher;
2Co 3.18 with *o* face beholding as in a glass
6.11 our mouth is *o* unto you, our heart
Eph 6.19 that I may *o* my mouth boldly,
Col 4. 3 that God would *o* unto us a door of
1Ti 5.24 men's sins are *o* beforehand,
Heb 6. 6 afresh, and put him to an *o* shame.
1Pe 3.12 and his ears are *o* unto their prayers:
Rev 3. 8 I have set before thee an *o* door,
20 man hear my voice, and *o* the door,
5. 2 Who is worthy to *o* the book, and to
3 no man...was able to *o* the book,
4 worthy to *o* and to read the book,
5 hath prevailed to *o* the book, and
9 the book, and to *o* the seals thereof:
10. 2 he had in his hand a little book *o*:
8 and take the little book which is *o*

OPENED

Gen 3. 5 thereof, then your eyes shall be *o*,
7 And the eyes of them both were *o*,
4.11 which hath *o* her mouth to receive
7.11 the windows of heaven were *o*.
8. 6 that Noah *o* the window of the ark
21.19 God *o* her eyes, and she saw a
29.31 Leah was hated, he *o* her womb:
30.22 hearkened to her, and *o* her womb.
41.56 Joseph *o* all the storehouses, and
42.27 as one of them *o* his sack to give
43.21 we *o* our sacks, and, behold, every
44.11 ground, and *o* every man his sack.
Ex 2. 6 she had *o* it, she saw the child:
Nu 16.32 earth *o* her mouth, and swallowed
22.28 the Lord *o* the mouth of the ass,
31 the Lord *o* the eyes of Balaam,
26.10 earth *o* her mouth, and swallowed
Dt 11. 6 earth *o* her mouth, and swallowed
Jdg 3.25 he *o* not the doors of the parlor;
25 they took a key, and *o* them:
4.19 she *o* a bottle of milk, and gave
11.35 I have *o* my mouth unto the Lord,
36 hast *o* thy mouth unto the Lord,
19.27 *o* the doors of the house, and went
1Sa 3.15 *o* the doors of the house of the Lord.
2Ki 4.35 times, and the child *o* his eyes.
6.17 Lord *o* the eyes of the young man;
20 Lord *o* their eyes, and they saw;
9.10 And he *o* the door and fled.
13.17 window eastward. And he *o* it.
15.16 because they *o* not to him,
2Ch 29. 3 *o* the doors of the house of the Lord,
Neh 7. 3 Let not the gates of Jerusalem be *o*
8. 5 Ezra *o* the book in the sight of all
5 when he *o* it, all the people stood
13.19 that they should not be *o* till after
Job 3. 1 After this *o* Job his mouth, and
29.23 they *o* their mouth wide as for the
31.32 but I *o* my doors to the traveller.
33. 2 Behold, now I have *o* my mouth,
38.17 Have the gates of death been *o*
Ps 35.21 they *o* their mouth wide against
39. 9 I was dumb, I *o* not my mouth;
40. 6 mine ears hast thou *o*: burnt
78.23 above, and *o* the doors of heaven,
105.41 He *o* the rock, and the waters
106.17 earth *o* and swallowed up Dathan,
109. 2 the mouth of the deceitful are *o*
119.131 I *o* my mouth, and panted:
SS 5. 6 I *o* to my beloved; but my beloved
Isa 5.14 *o* her mouth without measure:
10.14 moved the wing or *o* the mouth,
14.17 *o* not the house of his prisoners?
35. 5 the eyes of the blind shall be *o*,
48. 8 time that thine ear was not *o*:
50. 5 The Lord God hath *o* mine ear,
53. 7 afflicted, yet he *o* not his mouth:
Jer 20.12 for unto thee have I *o* my cause.
50.25 The Lord hath *o* his armory,
La 2.16 enemies have *o* their mouths
3.46 our enemies have *o* their mouths
Eze 1. 1 the heavens were *o*, and I saw
3. 2 I *o* my mouth, and he caused me to
16.25 and hast *o* thy feet to every one
24.27 In that day shall thy mouth be *o*
33.22 had *o* my mouth, until he came to
22 and my mouth was *o*, and I was no
37.13 when I have *o* your graves, O my
44. 2 gate shall be shut, it shall not be *o*,
46. 1 on the sabbath it shall be *o*, and in
1 day of the new moon it shall be *o*.
Dan 7.10 was set, and the books were *o*.
10.16 then I *o* my mouth, and spake,
Na 2. 6 The gates of the rivers shall be *o*,
Zec 13. 1 shall be a fountain *o* to the house
Mt 2.11 when they had *o* their treasures,
3.16 the heavens were *o* unto him, and
5. 2 he *o* his mouth, and taught them,
7. 7 knock, and it shall be *o* unto you:
8 to him that knocketh it shall be *o*.
9.30 their eyes were *o*; and Jesus straitly
17.27 and when thou hast *o* his mouth,
20.33 him, Lord, that our eyes may be *o*.
27.52 graves were *o*; and many bodies
Mk 1.10 he saw the heavens *o*, and the
7.34 him, Ephphatha, that is, Be *o*.
35 straightway his ears were *o*, and
Lk 1.64 his mouth was *o* immediately,
3.21 and praying, the heaven was *o*,
4.17 And when he had *o* the book, he
11. 9 knock, and it shall be *o* unto you.
10 to him that knocketh it shall be *o*.
24.31 their eyes were *o*, and they knew
32 while he *o* to us the scriptures?
45 Then *o* he their understanding,
Jn 9.10 unto him, How were thine eyes *o*?
14 Jesus made the clay, and *o* his eyes.
17 of him, that he hath *o* thine eyes?
21 who hath *o* his eyes, we know not:
26 did he to thee? how *o* he thine eyes?
30 he is, and yet he hath *o* mine eyes.
32 that any man *o* the eyes of one that
11.37 man, which *o* the eyes of the blind,
Ac 5.19 Lord by night *o* the prison doors,
23 when we had *o*, we found no man
7.56 Behold, I see the heavens *o*, and
8.32 his shearer, so *o* he not his mouth:
35 Then Philip *o* his mouth, and began
9. 8 when his eyes were *o*, he saw no
40 she *o* her eyes: and when she saw
10.11 saw heaven *o*, and a certain vessel
34 Then Peter *o* his mouth, and said,
12.10 which *o* to them of his own accord:
14 she *o* not the gate for gladness, but
16 and when they had *o* the door, and
14.27 *o* the door of faith unto the Gentiles.
16.14 whose heart the Lord *o*, that she
26 immediately all the doors were *o*,
1Co 16. 9 door and effectual is *o* unto me,
2Co 2.12 a door was *o* unto me of the Lord,
Heb 4.13 all things are naked and *o* unto
Rev 4. 1 behold, a door was *o* in heaven:
6. 1 when the Lamb *o* one of the seals,
3 And when he had *o* the second seal,
5 And when he had *o* the third seal,
7 And when he had *o* the fourth seal,
9 And when he had *o* the fifth seal,
12 when he had *o* the sixth seal,
8. 1 And when he had *o* the seventh seal,
9. 2 And he *o* the bottomless pit; and
11.19 the temple of God was *o* in heaven,
12.16 earth *o* her mouth, and swallowed
13. 6 *o* his mouth in blasphemy against
15. 5 of the testimony in heaven was *o*:
19.11 And I saw heaven *o*, and behold a
20.12 before God: and the books were *o*:
12 another book was *o*, which is the

OPENEST

Ps 104.28 thou *o* thine hand, they are filled
145.16 Thou *o* thine hand, and satisfiest

OPENETH

Ex 13. 2 whatsoever *o* the womb among
12 unto the Lord all that *o* the matrix,
15 to the Lord all that *o* the matrix,
34.19 All that *o* the matrix is mine; and
Nu 3.12 all the firstborn that *o* the matrix
18.15 thing that *o* the matrix in all flesh,
Job 27.19 he *o* his eyes, and he is not.
33.16 he *o* the ears of men, and sealeth
36.10 He *o* also their ear to discipline,
15 and *o* their ears in oppression.
Ps 38.13 dumb man that *o* not his mouth.
146. 8 The Lord *o* the eyes of the blind:
Pr 13. 3 he that *o* wide his lips shall have
24. 7 he *o* not his mouth in the gate.
31.26 She *o* her mouth with wisdom;

Isa 53. 7 is dumb, so he *o* not his mouth.
Eze 20.26 the fire all that *o* the womb,
Lk 2.23 Every male that *o* the womb shall
Jn 10. 3 To him the porter *o*; and the sheep
Rev 3. 7 he that *o*, and no man shutteth;
7 and shutteth, and no man *o*;

OPENING
1Ch 9.27 and the *o* thereof every morning
Job 12.14 up a man, and there can be no *o*.
Pr 8. 6 *o* of my lips shall be right things.
Isa 42.20 *o* the ears, but he heareth not.
61. 1 *o* of the prison to them that are
Eze 29.21 will give thee the *o* of the mouth
Ac 17. 3 *O* and alleging, that Christ must

OPENLY
Gen 38.21 that was *o* by the way side?
Ps 98. 2 righteousness hath he *o* shewed in
Mt 6. 4 shall reward thee *o*.
6 secret shall reward thee *o*.
18 secret, shall reward thee *o*.
Mk 1.45 no more *o* enter into the city,
8.32 And he spake that saying *o*.
Jn 7. 4 himself seeketh to be known *o*.
10 not *o*, but as it were in secret.
13 no man spake *o* of him for fear of
11.54 walked no more *o* among the Jews;
18.20 I spake *o* to the world; I ever
Ac 10.40 the third day, and shewed him *o*;
16.37 have beaten us *o* uncondemned,
Col 2.15 he made a shew of them *o*,

OPERATION
Ps 28. 5 the Lord, nor the *o* of his hands,
Isa 5.12 neither consider the *o* of his hands.
Col 2.12 through the faith of the *o* of God,

OPERATIONS
1Co 12. 6 there are diversities of *o*, but it is

OPHIR
Gen 10.29 And *O*, and Havilah, and Jobab:
1Ki 9.28 they came to *O*, and fetched from
10.11 Hiram, that brought gold from *O*,
11 brought in from *O* great plenty of
22.48 ships of Tharshish to go to *O* for
1Ch 1.23 And *O*, and Havilah, and Jobab.
29. 4 talents of gold, of the gold of *O*,
2Ch 8.18 with the servants of Solomon to *O*,
9.10 which brought gold from *O*, brought
Job 22.24 the gold of *O* as the stones of the
28.16 cannot be valued with the gold of *O*,
Ps 45. 9 did stand the queen in gold of *O*.
Isa 13.12 man than the golden wedge of *O*.

OPINION
Job 32. 6 and durst not shew you mine *o*.
10 to me; I also will shew mine *o*.
17 my part, I also will shew mine *o*.

OPINIONS
1Ki 18.21 How long halt ye between two *o*?

OPPORTUNITY
Mt 26.16 time he sought *o* to betray him.
Lk 22. 6 sought *o* to betray him unto them
Gal 6.10 As we have therefore *o*, let us do
Php 4.10 were also careful, but ye lacked *o*.
Heb 11.15 have had *o* to have returned.

OPPOSE
2Ti 2.25 instructing those that *o* themselves;

OPPOSED
Ac 18. 6 And when they *o* themselves, and

OPPOSETH
2Th 2. 4 Who *o* and exalteth himself above

OPPOSITIONS
1Ti 6.20 and *o* of science falsely so called:

Biblical Themes

OPPRESSION

Now there arose up a new king over Egypt, which knew not Joseph. And he said unto his people, Behold, the people of the children of Israel are more and mightier than we. . . . Therefore they did set over them taskmasters to afflict them with their burdens. . . . And they made their lives bitter with hard bondage, in morter, and in brick, and in all manner of service in the field. Ex 1.8-9, 11, 14

I have surely seen the affliction of my people which are in Egypt, and have heard their cry . . . and I am come down to deliver them. Ex 3.7-8

And [David] brought forth the people that were therein, and put them under saws, and under harrows of iron, and under axes of iron, and made them pass through the brick-kiln. 2Sa 12.31

And Jeroboam and all the congregation . . . spake unto Rehoboam, saying, Thy father made our yoke grievous: now therefore make thou the grievous service of thy father, and his heavy yoke which he put upon us, lighter, and we will serve thee. 1Ki 12.3-4

Knowest thou not this of old, since man was placed upon earth, that the triumphing of the wicked is short, and the joy of the hypocrite but for a moment? . . . Because he hath oppressed and hath forsaken the poor . . . surely he shall not feel quietness in his belly, he shall not save of that which he desired. Job 20.4-5, 19-20

This is the portion of a wicked man with God, and the heritage of oppressors. . . . If his children be multiplied, it is for the sword. . . . Those that remain of him shall be buried in death: and his widows shall not weep. Job 27.13-15

He shall judge the poor of the people, he shall save the children of the needy, and shall break in pieces the oppressor. Ps 72.4

Many a time have they afflicted me from my youth. . . . The plowers plowed upon my back: they made long their furrows. Ps 129.1, 3

Envy thou not the oppressor, and choose none of his ways. . . . The curse of the Lord is in the house of the wicked: but he blesseth the habitation of the just. Pr 3.31, 33

He that oppresseth the poor reproacheth his Maker. Pr 14.31

What mean ye that ye beat my people to pieces, and grind the faces of the poor? Isa 3.15

Lo, I will bring a nation upon you from far, O house of Israel. . . . Like as ye have forsaken me, and served strange gods in your land, so shall ye serve strangers in a land that is not yours. Jer 5.15, 19

Though I have afflicted thee, I will afflict thee no more. For now will I break his yoke from off thee, and will burst thy bonds in sunder. Na 1.12-13

Blessed are they which are persecuted for righteousness' sake: for theirs is the kingdom of heaven. Mt 5.10

They bind heavy burdens and grievous to be borne, and lay them on men's shoulders; but they themselves will not move them with one of their fingers. Mt 23.4

Shall not God avenge his own elect, which cry day and night unto him, though he bear long with them? Lk 18.7

The servant is not greater than his lord. If they have persecuted me, they will also persecute you. Jn 15.20

Bless them which persecute you. . . . Be not overcome of evil, but overcome evil with good. Ro 12.14, 21

OPPRESS
Ex 3. 9 wherewith the Egyptians *o* them.
22.21 neither vex a stranger, nor *o* him:
23. 9 Also thou shalt not *o* a stranger:
Lev 25.14 hand, ye shall not *o* one another:
17 shall not therefore *o* one another;
Dt 23.16 him best: thou shalt not *o* him.
24.14 Thou shalt not *o* an hired servant
Jdg 10.12 and the Maonites, did *o* you;
Job 10. 3 unto thee that thou shouldest *o*,
Ps 10.18 man of the earth may no more *o*.
17. 9 From the wicked that *o* me, from
119.122 for good: let not the proud *o* me.
Pr 22.22 neither *o* the afflicted in the gate:
Isa 49.26 I will feed them that *o* thee with
Jer 7. 6 If ye *o* not the stranger, the
30.20 and I will punish all that *o* them.
Eze 45. 8 shall no more *o* my people; and
Hos 12. 7 are in his hand: he loveth to *o*.
Am 4. 1 which *o* the poor, which crush the
Mic 2. 2 so they *o* a man and his house,
Zec 7.10 *o* not the widow, nor the fatherless,
Mal 3. 5 that *o* the hireling in his wages,
Jas 2. 6 Do not rich men *o* you, and draw

OPPRESSED
Dt 28.29 thou shalt be only *o* and spoiled
33 thou shalt be only *o* and crushed

Jdg 2.18 by reason of them that *o* them
4. 3 mightily *o* the children of Israel.
6. 9 out of the hand of all that *o* you,
10. 8 and *o* the children of Israel:
1Sa 10.18 kingdoms, and of them that *o* you:
12. 3 whom have I *o*? or of whose hand
4 hast not defrauded us, nor *o* us,
2Ki 13. 4 because the king of Syria *o* them.
22 But Hazael king of Syria *o* Israel
2Ch 16.10 And Asa *o* some of the people
Job 20.19 *o* and hath forsaken the poor;
35. 9 they make the *o* to cry: they cry out
Ps 9. 9 also will be a refuge for the *o*,
10.18 To judge the fatherless and the *o*,
74.21 O let not the *o* return ashamed:
103. 6 and judgment for all that are *o*.
106.42 Their enemies also *o* them, and
146. 7 executeth judgment for the *o*:
Ec 4. 1 the tears of such as were *o*,
Isa 1.17 seek judgment, relieve the *o*,
3. 5 And the people shall be *o*, every
23.12 no more rejoice, O thou *o* virgin,
38.14 O Lord, I am *o*; undertake for me.
52. 4 Assyrian *o* them without cause.
53. 7 He was *o*, and he was afflicted,
58. 6 to let the *o* go free, and that ye
Jer 50.33 and the children of Judah were *o*
Eze 18. 7 hath not *o* any, but hath restored
12 Hath *o* the poor and needy, hath
16 Neither hath *o* any, hath not
18 because he cruelly *o*, spoiled his
22.29 have *o* the stranger wrongfully.
Hos 5.11 Ephraim is *o* and broken in
Am 3. 9 and the *o* in the midst thereof.
Ac 7.24 and avenged him that was *o*, and
10.38 all that were *o* of the devil;

OPPRESSION

Ex 3. 9 the *o* wherewith the Egyptians
Dt 26. 7 and our labor, and our *o*:
2Ki 13. 4 he saw the *o* of Israel, because the
Job 36.15 and openeth their ears in *o*.
Ps 12. 5 For the *o* of the poor, for the
42. 9 because of the *o* of the enemy?
43. 2 because of the *o* of the enemy?
44.24 forgettest our affliction and our *o*?
55. 3 because of the *o* of the wicked:
62.10 Trust not in *o*, and become not
73. 8 and speak wickedly concerning *o*:
107.39 brought low through *o*, affliction,
119.134 Deliver me from the *o* of man:
Ec 5. 8 If thou seest the *o* of the poor,
7. 7 Surely *o* maketh a wise man mad;
Isa 5. 7 for judgment, but behold *o*;
30.12 despise this word, and trust in *o*
54.14 thou shalt be far from *o*; for thou
59.13 speaking *o* and revolt, concerning
Jer 6. 6 she is wholly *o* in the midst of her.
22.17 and for *o*, and for violence, to do it.
Eze 22. 7 they dealt by *o* with the stranger:
29 people of the land have used *o*,
46.18 of the people's inheritance by *o*,

OPPRESSOR

Job 3.18 they hear not the voice of the *o*.
15.20 number of years is hidden to the *o*.
Ps 72. 4 and shall break in pieces the *o*.
Pr 3.31 Envy thou not the *o*, and
28.16 understanding is also a great *o*:
Isa 9. 4 of his shoulder, the rod of his *o*,
14. 4 and say, How hath the *o* ceased!
51.13 day because of the fury of the *o*,
13 and where is the fury of the *o*?
Jer 21.12 spoiled out of the hand of the *o*,
22. 3 spoiled out of the hand of the *o*:
25.38 because of the fierceness of the *o*,
Zec 9. 8 no *o* shall pass through them
10. 4 bow, out of him every *o* together.

OPPRESSORS

Job 27.13 and the heritage of *o*, which they
Ps 54. 3 and *o* seek after my soul: they
119.121 justice: leave me not to mine *o*.
Ec 4. 1 side of their *o* there was power;
Isa 3.12 children are their *o*, and women
14. 2 and they shall rule over their *o*.
16. 4 *o* are consumed out of the land.
19.20 unto the Lord because of the *o*,

ORACLE

2Sa 16.23 had inquired at the *o* of God:
Ps 28. 2 up my hands toward thy holy *o*.

ORACLES

Ac 7.38 the lively *o* to give unto us:
Ro 3. 2 were committed the *o* of God.
Heb 5.12 the first principles of the *o* of God;
1Pe 4.11 let him speak as the *o* of God;

ORATION

Ac 12.21 throne, and made an *o* unto them.

ORATOR

Isa 3. 3 artificer, and the eloquent *o*.
Ac 24. 1 with a certain *o* named Tertullus,

ORDAIN

1Ch 9.22 the seer did *o* in their set office.
17. 9 Also I will *o* a place for my people
Isa 26.12 Lord, thou wilt *o* peace for us:
1Co 7.17 walk. And so *o* I in all churches.
Ti 1. 5 and *o* elders in every city, as I

ORDAINED

Nu 28. 6 was *o* in mount Sinai for a sweet
1Ki 12.32 And Jeroboam *o* a feast in the eighth
33 *o* a feast unto the children of Israel:
2Ki 23. 5 had *o* to burn incense in the
2Ch 11.15 And he *o* him priests for the high
23.18 with singing, as it was *o* by David.
29.27 the instruments *o* by David king of
Est 9.27 The Jews *o*, and took upon them,
Ps 8. 2 thou *o* strength because of thine
3 and the stars, which thou hast *o*;
81. 5 This he *o* in Joseph for a
132.17 have *o* a lamp for mine anointed.
Isa 30.33 Tophet is *o* of old; yea, for the
Jer 1. 5 and I *o* thee a prophet unto the
Dan 2.24 Arioch, whom the king had *o*
Hab 1.12 thou hast *o* them for judgment;
Mk 3.14 *o* twelve, that they should be with
Jn 15.16 I have chosen you, and *o* you,
Ac 1.22 must one be *o* to be a witness
10.42 was *o* of God to be the Judge of
13.48 as were *o* to eternal life believed.
14.23 when they had *o* them elders in
16. 4 were *o* of the apostles and elders
17.31 by that man whom he hath *o*;
Ro 7.10 which was *o* to life, I found to be
13. 1 the powers that be are *o* of God.
1Co 2. 7 God *o* before the world unto our
9.14 Lord *o* that they which preach
Gal 3.19 was *o* by angels in the hand of a
Eph 2.10 *o* that we should walk in them.
1Ti 2. 7 Whereunto I am *o* a preacher,
Heb 5. 1 *o* for men in things pertaining to
8. 3 every high priest is *o* to offer gifts
9. 6 when these things were thus *o*,
Jude 4 who were before of old *o* to this

ORDER

Ex 26.17 set in *o* one against another:
27.21 Aaron and his sons shall *o* it from
39.37 even with the lamps to be set in *o*,
40. 4 the table, and set in *o* the things
4 that are to be set in *o* upon it;
23 And he set the bread in *o* upon it
Lev 1. 7 lay the wood in *o* upon the fire:
8 and the fat, in *o* upon the wood
12 and the priest shall lay them in *o*
6.12 lay the burnt offering in *o* upon it;
24. 3 shall Aaron *o* it from the evening
4 shall *o* the lamps upon the pure
8 every sabbath he shall set it in *o*
Jos 2. 6 she had laid in *o* upon the roof.
Jdg 13.12 How shall we *o* the child, and
2Sa 17.23 city, and put his household in *o*,
1Ki 18.33 And he put the wood in *o*, and cut
20.14 he said, Who shall *o* the battle?
2Ki 20. 1 the Lord, Set thine house in *o*;
23. 4 and the priests of the second *o*,
1Ch 6.32 their office according to their *o*.
15.13 we sought him not after the due *o*.
23.31 according to the *o* commanded
25. 2 according to the *o* of the king.
6 according to the king's *o* to Asaph,
2Ch 8.14 according to the *o* of David his
13.11 shewbread also set they in *o* upon
29.35 house of the Lord was set in *o*.
Job 10.22 shadow of death, without any *o*,
23. 4 I would *o* my cause before him,
33. 5 set thy words in *o* before me,
37.19 *o* our speech by reason of darkness.
Ps 40. 5 be reckoned up in *o* unto thee:
50.21 and set them in *o* before thine eyes.
110. 4 ever after the *o* of Melchizedek.
119.133 *O* my steps in thy word: and let
Ec 12. 9 out, and set in *o* many proverbs.
Isa 9. 7 kingdom, to *o* it, and to establish
38. 1 the Lord, Set thine house in *o*:
44. 7 declare it, and set it in *o* for me,
Jer 46. 3 *O* ye the buckler and shield, and
Eze 41. 6 over another, and thirty in *o*;
Lk 1. 1 in *o* a declaration of those things
3 to write unto thee in *o*, most
8 before God in the *o* of his course,
Ac 11. 4 and expounded it by *o* unto them,
18.23 of Galatia and Phrygia in *o*,
1Co 11.34 rest will I set in *o* when I come.
14.40 things be done decently and in *o*.
15.23 every man in his own *o*: Christ
16. 1 as I have given *o* to the churches
Col 2. 5 joying and beholding your *o*, and
Tit 1. 5 set in *o* the things that are wanting,
Heb 5. 6 ever after the *o* of Melchisedec.
10 priest after the *o* of Melchisedec.
6.20 ever after the *o* of Melchisedec.
7.11 rise after the *o* of Melchisedec,
11 not be called after the *o* of Aaron?
17 ever after the *o* of Melchisedec.
21 ever after the *o* of Melchisedec:)

ORDERED

Jdg 6.26 top of this rock, in the *o* place,
2Sa 23. 5 covenant, *o* in all things, and
Job 13.18 I have *o* my cause; I know that I
Ps 37.23 of a good man are *o* by the Lord:

ORDERLY

Ac 21.24 that thou thyself also walkest *o*,

ORDINANCE

Ex 12.43 This is the *o* of the passover:
Lev 18.30 Therefore shall ye keep mine *o*,
Nu 15.15 an *o* for ever in your generations:
2Ch 2. 4 This is an *o* for ever to Israel.
Ps 99. 7 and the *o* that he gave them.
Isa 58. 2 forsook not the *o* of their God:
Mal 3.14 is it that we have kept his *o*,
Ro 13. 2 the power, resisteth the *o* of God:
1Pe 2.13 Submit...to every *o* of man for

ORDINANCES

Lev 18. 4 and keep mine *o*, to walk therein:
Nu 9.12 all the *o* of the passover they shall
2Ch 33. 8 and the *o* by the hand of Moses.
Job 38.33 Knowest thou the *o* of heaven?
Ps 119.91 this day according to thine *o*:
Isa 58. 2 they ask of me the *o* of justice;
Jer 31.35 the *o* of the moon and of the stars
Mal 3. 7 ye are gone away from mine *o*,
Lk 1. 6 and *o* of the Lord blameless.
1Co 11. 2 keep the *o*, as I delivered them to

Eph 2.15 commandments contained in *o*;
Col 2.14 Blotting out the handwriting of *o*
20 in the world, are ye subject to *o*,
Heb 9. 1 had also *o* of divine service, and
10 divers washings, and carnal *o*,

ORGAN

Gen 4.21 such as handle the harp and *o*.
Job 21.12 and rejoice at the sound of the *o*.
30.31 and my *o* into the voice of them

ORGANS

Ps 150. 4 with stringed instruments and *o*.

ORION

Job 9. 9 Arcturus, *O*, and Pleiades, and
38.31 Pleiades, or loose the bands of *O*?
Am 5. 8 that maketh the seven stars and *O*,

ORNAMENT

Pr 1. 9 be an *o* of grace unto thy head,
4. 9 give to thine head an *o* of grace:
25.12 of gold, and an *o* of fine gold,
Isa 30.22 the *o* of thy molten images of gold:
49.18 thee with them all, as with an *o*,
Eze 7.20 As for the beauty of his *o*, he set
1Pe 3. 4 the *o* of a meek and quiet spirit,

ORNAMENTS

Ex 33. 4 and no man did put on him his *o*.
5 now put off thy *o* from thee, that
6 stripped themselves of their *o* by
Jdg 8.21 and took away the *o* that were on
26 beside *o*, and collars, and purple
2Sa 1.24 put on *o* of gold upon your apparel.
Isa 3.18 their tinkling *o* about their feet,
20 bonnets, and the *o* of the legs,
61.10 decketh himself with *o*,
Jer 2.32 Can a maid forget her *o*, or a
4.30 thou deckedst thee with *o* of gold,
Eze 16. 7 and thou art come to excellent *o*:
11 I decked thee also with *o*, and I
23.40 eyes, and deckedst thyself with *o*,

ORPAH

Ru 1. 4 the name of the one was *O*, and
14 and *O* kissed her mother in law;

ORPHANS

La 5. 3 We are *o* and fatherless, our

OSEE

Ro 9.25 As he saith also in *O*, I will call

OTHERWISE

2Sa 18.13 *O* I should have wrought
1Ki 1.21 *O* it shall come to pass, when my
2Ch 30.18 passover *o* than it was written.
Ps 38.16 lest *o* they should rejoice over me:
Mt 6. 1 *o* ye have no reward of your
Lk 5.36 if *o*, then both the new maketh a
Ro 11. 6 works: *o* grace is no more grace.
6 grace: *o* work is no more work.
22 *o* thou also shalt be cut off.
2Co 11.16 if *o*, yet as a fool receive me, that
Gal 5.10 that ye will be none *o* minded:
Php 3.15 if in any thing ye be *o* minded,
1Ti 5.25 and they that are *o* cannot be hid.
6. 3 If any man teach *o*, and consent
Heb 9.17 *o* it is of no strength at all while

OUGHT

Gen 34. 7 which thing *o* not to be done.
Ex 5.19 shall not minish *o* from your bricks
Lev 4. 2, 27 things which *o* not to be done,
Jos 21.45 failed not *o* of any good thing
Ru 1.17 if *o* but death part thee and me.
2Sa 13.12 no such thing *o* to be done in Israel:
1Ch 12.32 times, to know what Israel *o* to do;
2Ch 13. 5 *O* ye not to know that the Lord God
Neh 5. 9 *o* ye not to walk in the fear of God
Ps 76.11 unto him that *o* to be feared
Mt 5.23 thy brother hath *o* against thee;
21. 3 And if any man say *o* unto you,
23.23 these *o* ye to have done, and not
Mk 7.12 do *o* for his father or his mother;
8.23 him, he asked him if he saw *o*.
11.25 forgive, if ye have *o* against any:
13.14 prophet, standing where it *o* not,
Lk 11.42 these *o* ye to have done, and not to
12.12 in the same hour what we *o* to say.
13.14 six days in which men *o* to work:
16 *o* not this woman, being a daughter
18. 1 that men *o* always to pray, and not
24.26 *O* not Christ to have suffered
Jn 4.20 the place where men *o* to worship.
33 any man brought him *o* to eat?
13.14 also *o* to wash one another's feet.
19. 7 a law, and by our law he *o* to die,
Ac 4.32 *o* of the things which he possessed
5.29 *o* to obey God rather than men.
17.29 *o* not to think that the Godhead
19.36 ye *o* to be quiet, and to do nothing
20.35 laboring ye *o* to support the weak,
21.21 *o* not to circumcise their children,
24.19 Who *o* to have been here before
19 object, if they had *o* against me.
25.10 seat, where I *o* to be judged:
24 that he *o* not to live any longer.
26. 9 I *o* to do many things contrary to
28.19 I had *o* to accuse my nation of.
Ro 8.26 what we should pray for as we *o*:
12. 3 more highly than he *o* to think;
15. 1 strong *o* to bear the infirmities of
1Co 8. 2 nothing yet as he *o* to know.
11. 7 indeed *o* not to cover his head,
10 cause *o* the woman to have power
2Co 2. 3 from them of whom I *o* to rejoice;
7 ye *o* rather to forgive him, and
12.11 for I *o* to have been commended
14 *o* not to lay up for the parents,
Eph 5.28 So *o* men to love their wives as
6.20 may speak boldly, as I *o* to speak.
Col 4. 4 make it manifest, as I *o* to speak.
6 how ye *o* to answer every man.
1Th 4. 1 how ye *o* to walk and to please God,
2Th 3. 7 know how ye *o* to follow us:
1Ti 5.13 speaking things which they *o* not.
Tit 1.11 teaching things which they *o* not,
Phm 18 wronged thee, or oweth thee *o*,
Heb 2. 1 *o* to give the more earnest heed
5. 3 by reason hereof he *o*, as for the
12 for the time ye *o* to be teachers,
Jas 3.10 these things *o* not so to be.
4.15 For that ye *o* to say, If the Lord will
2Pe 3.11 what manner of persons *o* ye to be
1Jn 2. 6 *o* himself also so to walk, even as
3.16 we *o* to lay down our lives for the
4.11 us, we *o* also to love one another.
3Jn 8 We therefore *o* to receive such, that

OUGHTEST

1Ki 2. 9 knowest what thou *o* to do unto him;
Mt 25.27 *o* therefore to have put my money
Ac 10. 6 shall tell thee what thou *o* to do.
1Ti 3.15 know how thou *o* to behave thyself

OURS

Gen 26.20 herdmen, saying, The water is *o*:
31.16 hath taken from our father, that is *o*,
34.23 and every beast of theirs be *o*?
Nu 32.32 on this side Jordan may be *o*.
1Ki 22. 3 Know ye that Ramoth in Gilead is *o*,
Eze 36. 2 even the ancient high places are *o* in
Mk 12. 7 and the inheritance shall be *o*.
Lk 20.14 that the inheritance may be *o*.
1Co 1. 2 Christ our Lord, both theirs and *o*:
2Co 1.14 as ye also are *o* in the day of the
Tit 3.14 let *o* also learn to maintain good
1Jn 2. 2 and not for *o* only, but also for

OURSELVES

Gen 37.10 to bow down *o* to thee to the earth?
44.16 we speak? or how shall we clear *o*?
Nu 32.17 we *o* will go ready armed before
Dt 2.35 we took cattle for a prey unto *o*,
3. 7 of the cities, we took for a prey to *o*.
1Sa 14. 8 and we will discover *o* unto them.
1Ch 19.13 and let us behave *o* valiantly for our
Ezr 4. 3 but we *o* together will build unto
8.21 we might afflict *o* before our God,
Neh 10.32 to charge *o* yearly with the third
Job 34. 4 let us know among *o* what is good.
Ps 83.12 Let us take to *o* the houses of God
100. 3 that hath made us, and not we *o*;
Pr 7.18 morning: let us solace *o* with loves.
Isa 28.15 and under falsehood have we hid *o*:
56.12 and we will fill *o* with strong drink;
Jer 50. 5 Come, and let us join *o* to the Lord
Lk 22.71 we *o* have heard of his own mouth.
Jn 4.42 for we have heard him *o*, and know
Ac 6. 4 will give *o* continually to prayer,
23.14 have bound *o* under a great curse,
Ro 8.23 but *o* also, which have the first fruits
23 of the Spirit, even we *o* groan
23 groan within *o*, waiting for the
15. 1 of the weak, and not to please *o*.
1Co 11.31 For if we would judge *o*, we should
2Co 1. 4 we *o* are comforted of God.
9 we had the sentence of death in *o*,
9 that we should not trust in *o*, but
3. 1 Do we begin again to commend *o*?
5 that we are sufficient of *o* to think
5 to think any thing as of *o*; but our
4. 2 commending *o* to every man's
5 For we preach not *o*, but Christ
5 *o* your servants for Jesus' sake.
5.12 we commend not *o* again unto you,
13 whether we be beside *o*, it is to God:
6. 4 approving *o* as the ministers of
7. 1 let us cleanse *o* from all filthiness
10.12 we dare not make *o* of the number,
12 or compare *o* with some that
14 stretch not *o* beyond our measure,
12.19 think ye that we excuse *o* unto you?
Gal 2.17 if...we *o* also are found sinners, is
1Th 2.10 we behaved *o* among you that
2Th 1. 4 we *o* glory in you in the churches
3. 7 behaved not *o* disorderly among
9 to make *o* an ensample unto you
Tit 3. 3 we *o* also were sometimes foolish,
Heb 10.25 the assembling of *o* together,
1Jn 1. 8 we deceive *o*, and the truth is not

OUTCAST

Jer 30.17 they called thee an *O*, saying,

OUTCASTS

Ps 147. 2 gathereth together the *o* of Israel.
Isa 11.12 and shall assemble the *o* of Israel.
16 3 hide the *o*; bewray not him that
4 Let mine *o* dwell with thee, Moab
27.13 and the *o* in the land of Egypt,
56. 8 which gathereth the *o* of Israel
Jer 49.36 the *o* of Elam shall not come.

OUTER

Eze 10. 5 was heard even to the *o* court,
Mt 8.12 shall be cast out into *o* darkness:
22.13 and cast him into *o* darkness;
25.30 servant into *o* darkness: there

OUTRUN

Jn 20. 4 the other disciple did *o* Peter,

OUTSIDE

Jdg 7.11 unto the *o* of the armed men
17 when I come to the *o* of the camp,
19 came unto the *o* of the camp in the
1Ki 7. 9 on the *o* toward the great court.
Eze 40. 5 behold a wall on the *o* of the house
Mt 23.25 ye make clean the *o* of the cup

Mt 23.26 the *o* of them may be clean also.
Lk 11.39 make clean the *o* of the cup and

OUTSTRETCHED

Dt 26. 8 a mighty hand, and with an *o* arm,
Jer 21. 5 fight against you with an *o* hand
27. 5 by my great power by my *o* arm.

OUTWARD

Nu 35. 4 from the wall of the city and *o*
1Sa 16. 7 man looketh on the *o* appearance,
1Ch 26.29 for the *o* business over Israel,
Neh 11.16 had the oversight of the *o* business
Est 6. 4 Haman was come into the *o* court
Eze 40.17 brought he me into the *o* court,
20 the gate of the *o* court that looked
34 arches...were toward the *o* court;
44. 1 way of the gate of the *o* sanctuary
Mt 23.27 which indeed appear beautiful *o*,
Ro 2.28 which is *o* in the flesh:
2Co 4.16 though our *o* man perish, yet the
10. 7 on things after the *o* appearance?
1Pe 3. 3 *o* adorning of plaiting the hair,

OUTWARDLY

Mt 23.28 so ye also *o* appear righteous
Ro 2.28 is not a Jew, which is one *o*;

OUTWENT

Mk 6.33 out of all cities, and *o* them, and

OVEN

Lev 2. 4 of a meat offering baken in the *o*,
7. 9 offering that is baken in the *o*.
11.35 whether it be *o*, or ranges for pots,
26.26 shall bake your bread in one *o*,
Ps 21. 9 Thou shalt make them as a fiery *o*
La 5.10 skin was black like an *o* because
Hos 7. 4 as an *o* heated by the baker, who
6 made ready their heart like an *o*,
7 They are all hot as an *o*, and have
Mal 4. 1 cometh, that shall burn as an *o*;
Mt 6.30 and to morrow is cast into the *o*,
Lk 12.28 and to morrow is cast into the *o*;

OVERCAME

Ac 19.16 *o* them, and prevailed against
Rev 3.21 even as I also *o*, and am set down
12.11 *o* him by the blood of the Lamb,

OVERCHARGE

2Co 2. 5 in part: that I may not *o* you all.

OVERCHARGED

Lk 21.34 your hearts be *o* with surfeiting,

OVERCOME

Gen 49.19 Gad, a troop shall *o* him:
19 but he shall *o* at the last.
Ex 32.18 of them that cry for being *o*: but
Nu 13.30 it; for we are well able to *o* it.
22.11 I shall be able to *o* them, and
2Ki 16. 5 Ahaz, but could not *o* him.
SS 6. 5 from me, for they have *o* me:
Isa 28. 1 of them that are *o* with wine!
Jer 23. 9 like a man whom wine hath *o*,
Lk 11.22 shall come upon him, and *o* him,
Jn 16.33 of good cheer; I have *o* the world.
Ro 3. 4 mightest *o* when thou art judged.
12.21 Be not *o* of evil,
21 but *o* evil with good.
2Pe 2.19 for of whom a man is *o*, of the
20 again entangled therein, and *o*,
1Jn 2.13 because ye have *o* the wicked one.
14 and ye have *o* the wicked one.
4. 4 little children, and have *o* them:
Rev 11. 7 and shall *o* them, and kill them.
13. 7 with the saints, and to *o* them:
17.14 Lamb, and the Lamb shall *o* them:

OVERCOMETH

1Jn 5. 4 is born of God *o* the world: and
4 is the victory that *o* the world,
5 Who is he that *o* the world, but
Rev 2. 7 To him that *o* will I give to eat of
11 He that *o* shall not be hurt of the
17 To him that *o* will I give to eat of
26 he that *o*, and keepeth my works
3. 5 He that *o*, the same shall be
12 Him that *o* will I make a pillar in
21 To him that *o* will I grant to sit
21. 7 He that *o* shall inherit all things;

OVERFLOW

Dt 11. 4 water of the Red sea to *o* them
Ps 69. 2 waters, where the floods *o* me.
15 Let not the waterflood *o* me,
Isa 8. 8 he shall *o* and go over, he shall
10.22 decreed shall *o* with righteousness.
28.17 waters shall *o* the hiding place.
43. 2 the rivers, they shall not *o* thee:
Jer 47. 2 shall *o* the land, and all that is
Dan 11.10 one shall certainly come, and *o*,
26 destroy him, and his army shall *o*:
40 and shall *o* and pass over.
Joel 2.24 the fats shall *o* with wine and oil.
3.13 for the press is full, the fats *o*;

OVERLAID

Heb 9. 4 covenant *o* round about with gold,

OVERMUCH

2Co 2. 7 be swallowed up with *o* sorrow.

OVERSEER

Gen 39. 4 he made him *o* over his house,
5 he had made him *o* in his house,
Neh 11. 9 the son of Zichri was their *o*:
14 their *o* was Zabdiel, the son of one
22 *o* also of the Levites at Jerusalem
12.42 sang loud, with Jezrahiah their *o*.
Pr 6. 7 having no guide, *o*, or ruler,

OVERSEERS

2Ch 2.18 *o* to set the people a work.
34.17 it into the hand of the *o*, and to
Ac 20.28 the Holy Ghost hath made you *o*,

OVERSHADOW

Lk 1.35 power of the Highest shall *o* thee:
Ac 5.15 Peter passing by might *o* some

OVERSHADOWED

Mt 17. 5 behold, a bright cloud *o* them:
Mk 9. 7 there was a cloud that *o* them:
Lk 9.34 there came a cloud, and *o* them:

OVERSIGHT

Gen 43.12 hand; peradventure it was an *o*:
Nu 3.32 *o* of them that keep the charge of
4.16 the *o* of all the tabernacle, and of
2Ki 12.11 the *o* of the house of the Lord:
22. 5 the *o* of the house of the Lord:
9 the *o* of the house of the Lord.
1Ch 9.23 had the *o* of the gates of the house
2Ch 34.10 the *o* of the house of the Lord,
Neh 11.16 had the *o* of the outward business
13. 4 having the *o* of the chamber of
1Pe 5. 2 among you, taking the *o* thereof,

OVERSPREAD

Gen 9.19 of them was the whole earth *o*.

OVERTAKE

Gen 44. 4 when thou dost *o* them, say unto
Ex 15. 9 enemy said, I will pursue, I will *o*,
Dt 19. 6 while his heart is hot, and *o* him,
28. 2 shall come on thee, and *o* thee,
15 shall come upon thee, and *o* thee:
45 and shall pursue thee, and *o* thee,
Jos 2. 5 them quickly; for ye shall *o* them.
1Sa 30. 8 after this troop? shall I *o* them?
8 for thou shalt surely *o* them, and
2Sa 15.14 lest he *o* us suddenly, and bring
Isa 59. 9 from us, neither doth justice *o* us:
Jer 42.16 sword, which ye feared, shall *o* you
Hos 2. 7 lovers, but she shall not *o* them;
10. 9 children of iniquity did not *o* them.
Am 9.10 evil shall not *o* nor prevent us.
13 the plowman shall *o* the reaper,
1Th 5. 4 that day should *o* you as a thief.

OVERTAKEN

Ps 18.37 mine enemies, and *o* them:
Gal 6. 1 Brethren, if a man be *o* in a fault,

OVERTHREW

Gen 19.25 And he *o* those cities, and all the
29 he *o* the cities in which Lot dwelt.
Ex 14.27 and the Lord *o* the Egyptians in
Dt 29.23 which the Lord *o* in his anger,
Ps 136.15 But *o* Pharaoh and his host in the
Isa 13.19 God *o* Sodom and Gomorrah,
Jer 20.16 be as the cities which the Lord *o*,
50.40 As God *o* Sodom and Gomorrah
Am 4.11 as God *o* Sodom and Gomorrah.
Mt 21.12 *o* the tables of...moneychangers,
Mk 11.15 *o* the tables of the moneychangers,
Jn 2.15 changers' money, and *o* the tables;

OVERTHROW

Gen 19.21 also, that I will not *o* this city,
29 sent Lot out of the midst of the *o*,
Ex 23.24 but thou shalt utterly *o* them,
Dt 12. 3 ye shall *o* their altars, and break
29.23 therein, like the *o* of Sodom, and
2Sa 10. 3 and to spy it out, and to *o* it?
11.25 strong against the city, and *o* it:
1Ch 19. 3 and to *o*, and to spy out the land?
Ps 106.26 to *o* them in the wilderness:
27 To *o* their seed also among the
140. 4 have purposed to *o* my goings.
11 hunt the violent man to *o* him.
Pr 18. 5 to *o* the righteous in judgment.
Jer 49.18 in the *o* of Sodom and Gomorrah
Hag 2.22 I will *o* the throne of kingdoms,
22 I will *o* the chariots, and those
Ac 5.39 if it be of God, ye cannot *o* it;
2Ti 2.18 already; and *o* the faith of some.
2Pe 2. 6 condemned them with an *o*,

OVERTHROWETH

Job 12.19 away spoiled, and *o* the mighty.
Pr 13. 6 but wickedness *o* the sinner.
21.12 but God *o* the wicked for their
22.12 *o* the words of the transgressor.
29. 4 but he that receiveth gifts *o* it.

OVERTHROWN

Ex 15. 7 hast *o* them that rose up against
Jdg 9.40 and many were *o* and wounded,
2Sa 17. 9 some of them be *o* at the first,
2Ch 14.13 and the Ethiopians were *o*, that
Job 19. 6 Know now that God hath *o* me,
Ps 141. 6 judges are *o* in stony places,
Pr 11.11 it is *o* by the mouth of the wicked.
12. 7 The wicked are *o*, and are not:
14.11 house of the wicked shall be *o*:
Isa 1. 7 it is desolate, as *o* by strangers.
Jer 18.23 but let them be *o* before thee;
La 4. 6 that was *o* as in a moment, and
Dan 11.41 and many countries shall be *o*:
Am 4.11 I have *o* some of you, as God
Jon 3. 4 days, and Nineveh shall be *o*.
1Co 10. 5 for they were *o* in the wilderness.

OVERWHELM

Job 6.27 Yes, ye *o* the fatherless, and ye

OVERWHELMED

Ps 55. 5 upon me, and horror hath *o* me.
61. 2 unto thee, when my heart is *o*:
77. 3 and my spirit was *o*. Selah.
78.53 not: but the sea *o* their enemies.
102(T) of the afflicted, when he is *o*,

Ps 124. 4 Then the waters had *o* us, the
142. 3 When my spirit was *o* within me,
143. 4 is my spirit *o* within me; my

OWE

Ro 13. 8 *O* no man any thing, but to love

OWED

Mt 18.24 *o* him ten thousand talents.
28 which *o* him an hundred pence:
Lk 7.41 the one *o* five hundred pence, and

OWEST

Mt 18.28 saying, Pay me that thou *o*.
Lk 16. 5 How much *o* thou unto my lord?
7 another, And how much *o* thou?
Phm 19 *o* unto me even thine own self

OWETH

Phm 18 wronged thee, or *o* thee ought,

OWN

Gen 1.27 So God created man in his *o* image,
Lev 1. 3 shall offer it of his *o* voluntary will
Nu 27. 3 but died in his *o* sin, and had no sons.
32.42 and called it Nobah, after his *o*
Dt 13. 6 or thy friend, which is as thine *o* soul,
24.16 shall be put to death for his *o* sin.
Jdg 7. 2 saying, Mine *o* hand hath saved me.
17. 6 that which was right in his *o* eyes.
1Sa 15.17 thou wast little in thine *o* sight,
18. 1 Jonathan loved him as his *o* soul.
2Sa 18.18 he called the pillar after his *o* name:
1Ki 2.37 thy blood shall be upon thine *o* head.
2Ki 17.29 every nation made gods of their *o*,
21.18 buried in the garden of his *o* house,
1Ch 29.14 and of thine *o* have we given thee.
16 of thine hand, and is all thine *o*.
2Ch 9. 5 I heard in mine *o* land of thine acts,
Est 1.22 man should bear rule in his *o* house,
Job 5.13 taketh the wise in their *o* craftiness:
9.20 mine *o* mouth shall condemn me:
15. 6 Thine *o* mouth condemneth thee,
18. 7 his *o* counsel shall cast him down.
8 For he is cast into a net by his *o* feet,
40.14 that thine *o* right hand can save thee.
Ps 4. 4 commune with your *o* heart upon
9.16 is snared in the work of his *o* hands.
12. 4 our lips are our *o*: who is lord over
15. 4 He that sweareth to his *o* hurt, and
22.29 and none can keep alive his *o* soul.
44. 3 neither did their *o* arm save them:
67. 6 God, even our *o* God, shall bless us.
77. 6 I commune with mine *o* heart: and
138. 8 forsake not the works of thine *o*
140. 9 mischief of their *o* lips cover them.
141.10 the wicked fall into their *o* nets
Pr 1.18 And they lay wait for their *o* blood;
18 they lurk privily for their *o* lives.
31 they eat of the fruit of their *o* way,
3. 7 Be not wise in thine *o* eyes: fear the
8.36 that sinneth...wrongeth his *o* soul:
11.17 merciful man doeth good to his *o*
12.15 way of a fool is right in his *o* eyes:
14.20 poor is hated even of his *o* neighbor:
16. 2 ways of a man are clean in his *o* eyes;
19. 8 getteth wisdom loveth his *o* soul:
20. 6 proclaim every one his *o* goodness:
21. 2 way of a man is right in his *o* eyes:
23. 4 be rich: cease from thine *o* wisdom.
25.28 he that hath no rule over his *o* spirit
26. 5 lest he be wise in his *o* conceit.

Oxen, highly valued in biblical times, are shown in an Assyrian relief of the seventh century B.C.

28.10 he shall fall himself into his *o* pit:
11 rich man is wise in his *o* conceit;
26 that trusteth in his *o* heart is a fool:
Ec 3.22 a man should rejoice in his *o* works;
Isa 2. 8 worship the work of their *o* hands,
4. 1 saying, We will eat our *o* bread,
31. 7 which your *o* hands have made unto
56.11 all look to their *o* way, every one
58. 7 hide not thyself from thine *o* flesh?
63. 5 mine *o* arm brought salvation unto
Jer 18.12 but we will walk after our *o* devices,
31.30 every one shall die for his *o* iniquity:
Eze 33. 4 his blood shall be upon his *o* head.
Dan 3.28 worship any god, except their *o*
Mic 7. 6 enemies are the men of his *o* house.
Zec 11. 5 and their *o* shepherds pity them not.
Mal 3.17 a man spareth his *o* son that serveth
Mt 7. 3 not the beam that is in thine *o* eye?
10.36 foes shall be they of his *o* household.
16.26 whole world, and lose his *o* soul?
20.15 to do what I will with mine *o*?
Mk 8.36 whole world, and lose his *o* soul?
Lk 2. 3 be taxed, every one into his *o* city,
35 sword pierce through thy *o* soul also
4.24 is accepted in his *o* country.
6.41 the beam that is in thine *o* eye?
16.12 shall give you that which is your *o*?
Jn 1.11 He came unto his *o*, and his
4.44 hath no honor in his *o* country.
5.30 I seek not mine *o* will, but the
10. 3 he calleth his *o* sheep by name,
13. 1 loved his *o* which were in the world,
17.11 keep through thine *o* name those
Ac 2. 6 them speak in his *o* language.
17.28 also of your *o* poets have said,
18. 6 Your blood be upon your *o* heads;
20.28 hath purchased with his *o* blood.
Ro 8. 3 God sending his *o* Son in the
32 that spared not his *o* Son, but
12.16 Be not wise in your *o* conceits.
14. 5 be fully persuaded in his *o* mind.
1Co 6.19 of God, and ye are not your *o*?
9. 7 warfare any time at his *o* charges?
13. 5 seeketh not her *o*, is not easily
16.21 of me Paul with mine *o* hand.
Gal 6. 4 let every man prove his *o* work,
5 man shall bear his *o* burden.
Eph 5.28 love their wives as their *o* bodies.
29 no man ever yet hated his *o* flesh;
Php 2.21 For all seek their *o*, not the
3. 9 having mine *o* righteousness,
2Th 3.17 of Paul with mine *o* hand, which
Phm 19 have written it with mine *o* hand,
Heb 3. 6 Christ as a son over his *o* house;
9.12 but by his *o* blood he entered in
Jas 1.14 he is drawn away of his *o* lust, and
18 Of his *o* will begat he us with the
1Pe 2.24 Who his *o* self bare our sins in his
24 our sins in his *o* body on the tree,
Jude 16 walking after their *o* lusts; and
Rev 1. 5 us from our sins in his *o* blood,

OWNER

Ex 21.28 but the *o* of the ox shall be quit.
29 and it hath been testified to his *o*,
29 and his *o* also shall be put to death.
34 The *o* of the pit shall make it good,
34 give money unto the *o* of them;
36 and his *o* hath not kept him in; he
22.11 and the *o* of it shall accept thereof,
12 shall make restitution unto the *o*
14 the *o* thereof being not with it, he
15 the *o* thereof be with it, he shall not
1Ki 16.24 the name of Shemer, *o* of the hill,
Isa 1. 3 The ox knoweth his *o*, and the
Ac 27.11 the master and the *o* of the ship,

OWNERS

Job 31.39 the *o* thereof to lose their life:
Pr 1.19 taketh away the life of the *o*
Ec 5.11 good is there to the *o* thereof,
13 riches kept for the *o* thereof to
Lk 19.33 the *o* thereof said unto them,

OWNETH

Lev 14.35 And he that *o* the house shall come
Ac 21.11 bind the man that *o* this girdle,

OX

Ex 20.17 nor his *o*, nor his ass, nor any
21.36 in; he shall surely pay *o* for *o*;
22. 1 If a man shall steal an *o*, or a
Dt 5.14 thine *o*, nor thine ass, nor any of
21 his *o*, or his ass, or any thing that
22.10 not plow with an *o* and an ass
25. 4 shalt not muzzle the *o* when he
1Sa 12. 3 whose *o* have I taken? or whose ass
Job 24. 3 take the widow's *o* for a pledge.
Ps 69.31 please the Lord better than an *o*
106.20 similitude of an *o* that eateth grass.
Isa 1. 3 The *o* knoweth his owner, and the
11. 7 the lion shall eat straw like the *o*.
Eze 1.10 they four had the face of an *o* on
Lk 13.15 the sabbath loose his *o* or his ass
14. 5 an ass or an *o* fallen into a pit,
1Co 9. 9 not muzzle the mouth of the *o* that
1Ti 5.18 not muzzle the *o* that treadeth out

OXEN

Ex 22. 1 he shall restore five *o* for an ox,
24. 5 peace offerings of *o* unto the Lord.
2Ch 4. 3 under it was the similitude of *o*,
Ps 8. 7 All sheep and *o*, yea, and the beasts
Pr 14. 4 Where no *o* are, the crib is clean:
Am 6.12 rock? will one plow there with *o*?
Mt 22. 4 my *o* and my fatlings are killed,
Lk 14.19 I have bought five yoke of *o*, and
Jn 2.14 that sold *o* and sheep and doves,
15 temple, and the sheep, and the *o*;
Ac 14.13 *o* and garlands unto the gates,
1Co 9. 9 corn. Doth God take care for *o*?

P

PACIFIED
Est 7.10 Then was the king's wrath *p*.
Eze 16.63 when I am *p* toward thee for all

PACIFIETH
Pr 21.14 A gift in secret *p* anger: and a
Ec 10. 4 for yielding *p* great offenses.

PACIFY
Pr 16.14 death: but a wise man will *p* it.

PAID
Ezr 4.20 and custom, was *p* unto them.
Jon 1. 3 so he *p* the fare thereof, and went
Mt 5.26 thou hast *p* the uttermost farthing.
Lk 12.59 till thou hast *p* the very last mite.

PAIN
Job 14.22 his flesh upon him shall have *p*,
15.20 wicked man travaileth with *p* all his
33.19 He is chastened also with *p* upon
19 multitude of his bones with strong *p*:
Ps 25.18 upon mine affliction and my *p*;
48. 6 and *p*, as of a woman in travail.
Isa 13. 8 in *p* as a woman that travaileth:
21. 3 are my loins filled with *p*: pangs
26.17 the time of her delivery, is in *p*,
18 been with child, we have been in *p*,
66. 7 before her *p* came, she was
Jer 6.24 and *p*, as of a woman in travail.
12.13 they have put themselves to *p*,
15.18 Why is my *p* perpetual, and my
22.23 the *p* as of a woman in travail!
30.23 fall with *p* upon the head of the
51. 8 take balm for her *p*, if so be she
Eze 30. 4 and great *p* shall be in Ethiopia,
9 great *p* shall come upon them,
16 Sin shall have great *p*, and No
Mic 4.10 Be in *p*, and labor to bring forth
Na 2.10 and much *p* is in all loins, and the
Ro 8.22 travaileth in *p* together until now.
Rev 16.10 they gnawed their tongues for *p*,
21. 4 neither shall there be any more *p*:

PAINED
Ps 55. 4 My heart is sore *p* within me: and
Isa 23. 5 be sorely *p* at the report of Tyre.
Jer 4.19 bowels! I am *p* at my very heart;
Joel 2. 6 face the people shall be much *p*:
Rev 12. 2 in birth, and *p* to be delivered.

PAINFUL
Ps 73.16 to know this, it was too *p* for me;

PAINFULNESS
2Co 11.27 In weariness and *p*, in watchings

PAINS
1Sa 4.19 travailed; for her *p* came upon her.
Ps 116. 3 the *p* of hell gat hold upon me:
Ac 2.24 up, having loosed the *p* of death:
Rev 16.11 because of their *p* and their sores,

PAINTED
2Ki 9.30 she *p* her face, and tired her
Jer 22.14 with cedar, and *p* with vermilion.

PAINTEDST
Eze 23.40 *p* thy eyes, and deckedst thyself

PAINTING
Jer 4.30 thou rentest thy face with *p*, in

PAIR
Am 2. 6 silver, and the poor for a *p* of shoes;
8. 6 and the needy for a *p* of shoes;
Lk 2.24 A *p* of turtledoves, or two young
Rev 6. 5 had a *p* of balances in his hand.

PALACE
1Ch 29. 1 *p* is not for man, but for the Lord
Dan 8. 2 that I was at Shushan in the *p*,
Am 4. 3 and ye shall cast them into the *p*,
Na 2. 6 and the *p* shall be dissolved.
Mt 26. 3 unto the *p* of the high priest, who
58 afar off unto the high priest's *p*,
69 Now Peter sat without in the *p*:
Mk 14.54 even into the *p* of the high priest:
66 And as Peter was beneath in the *p*,
Lk 11.21 strong man armed keepeth his *p*,
Jn 18.15 Jesus into the *p* of the high priest.
Php 1.13 in Christ are manifest in all the *p*,

PALACES
Ps 48.13 well her bulwarks, consider her *p*;
122. 7 walls, and prosperity within thy *p*.
Pr 30.28 with her hands, and is in kings' *p*.
Isa 34.13 And thorns shall come up in her *p*,
La 2. 5 he hath swallowed up all her *p*:

PALE
Isa 29.22 neither shall his face now wax *p*.
Rev 6. 8 I looked, and behold a *p* horse:

PALESTINA
Ex 15.14 hold on the inhabitants of *P*.
Isa 14.29 Rejoice not thou, whole *P*, because
31 city; thou, whole *P*, art dissolved:

PALESTINE
Joel 3. 4 Zidon, and all the coasts of *P*?

PALM
Ex 15.27 and threescore and ten *p* trees:
Lev 14.15, 26 into the *p* of his own left hand:
23.40 branches of *p* trees, goodly trees,
Nu 33. 9 and threescore and ten *p* trees;
Dt 34. 3 Jericho, the city of *p* trees, unto
Jdg 1.16 went up out of the city of *p* trees
3.13 and possessed the city of *p* trees.
4. 5 under the *p* tree of Deborah
1Ki 6.29, 32 cherubims and *p* trees and open
32 cherubims, and upon the *p* trees.
35 cherubims and *p* trees and open
7.36 cherubims, lions, and *p* trees,
2Ch 3. 5 and set thereon *p* trees and chains.
28.15 to Jericho, the city of *p* trees,
Neh 8.15 myrtle branches, and *p* branches,
Ps 92.12 shall flourish like the *p* tree:
SS 7. 7 This thy stature is like to a *p* tree,
8 I said, I will go up to the *p* tree,
Jer 10. 5 They are upright as the *p* tree,

Palm branches are strewn as Christ enters Jerusalem (Jn 12.13) in this 15th-century painting by the school of Fra Angelico.

Eze 40.16 and upon each post were *p* trees.
22 and their arches, and their *p* trees,
26 and it had *p* trees, one on this side,
31, 34, 37 *p* trees were upon the posts
41.18 made with cherubims and *p* trees,
18 that a *p* tree was between a cherub
19 toward the *p* tree on the one side,
19 toward the *p* tree on the other side:
20 were cherubims and *p* trees made,
25 cherubims and *p* trees, like as were
26 were narrow windows and *p* trees
Joel 1.12 the *p* tree also, and the apple tree,
Jn 12.13 Took branches of *p* trees, and
18.22 struck Jesus with the *p* of his

PALMS

1Sa 5. 4 both the *p* of his hands were cut
2Ki 9.35 the feet, and the *p* of her hands.
Isa 49.16 graven...upon the *p* of my hands;
Dan 10.10 knees and upon the *p* of my hands.
Mt 26.67 smote him with...*p* of their hands,
Mk 14.65 smote with him...*p* of their hands.
Rev 7. 9 robes, and *p* in their hands;

PALSIES

Ac 8. 7 and many taken with *p*, and that

PALSY

Mt 4.24 lunatick, and those that had...*p*;
8. 6 servant lieth at home sick of the *p*,
9. 2 brought to him a man sick of the *p*,
2 faith said unto the sick of the *p*;
6 (then saith he to the sick of the *p*,)
Mk 2. 3 him, bringing one sick of the *p*,
4 bed wherein the sick of the *p* lay.
5 he said unto the sick of the *p*, Son,
9 easier to say to the sick of the *p*,
10 sins, (he saith to the sick of the *p*,)
Lk 5.18 a man which was taken with a *p*:
24 (he said unto the sick of the *p*,) I
Ac 9.33 eight years, and was sick of the *p*.

PAMPHYLIA

Ac 2.10 Phrygia, and *P*, in Egypt, and
13.13 Paphos, they came to Perga in *P*:
14.24 Pisidia, they came to *P*.
15.38 who departed from them from *P*,
27. 5 sailed over the sea of Cilicia and *P*,

PAN

Lev 2. 5 be a meat offering baken in a *p*,
6.21 In a *p* it shall be made with oil;
7. 9 and in the *p*, shall be the priest's
1Sa 2.14 he struck it into the *p*, or kettle,
2Sa 13. 9 she took a *p*, and poured them
1Ch 23.29 for that which is baked in the *p*,
Eze 4. 3 take thou unto thee an iron *p*,

PANGS

Isa 13. 8 *p* and sorrows shall take hold of
21. 3 *p* have taken hold upon me, as
3 the *p* of a woman that travaileth:
26.17 in pain, and crieth out in her *p*;
Jer 22.23 thou be when *p* come upon thee,
48.41 as the heart of a woman in her *p*.
49.22 as the heart of a woman in her *p*.
50.43 and *p* as of a woman in travail.
Mic 4. 9 *p* have taken thee as a woman in

PANT

Am 2. 7 That *p* after the dust of the earth

PANTED

Ps 119.131 I opened my mouth, and *p*: for I
Isa 21. 4 My heart *p*, fearfulness

PANTETH

Ps 38.10 My heart *p*, my strength faileth
42. 1 the hart *p* after the water brooks,
1 so *p* my soul after thee, O God.

PAPER

Isa 19. 7 The *p* reeds by the brooks, by the
2Jn 12 would not write with *p* and ink:

PAPHOS

Ac 13. 6 had gone through the isle unto *P*,
13 and his company loosed from *P*,

PAPS

Eze 23.21 Egyptians for the *p* of thy youth.
Lk 11.27 the *p* which thou hast sucked
23.29 and the *p* which never gave suck.
Rev 1.13 about the *p* with a golden girdle.

PARABLE

Nu 23. 7 And he took up his *p*, and said,
18 he took up his *p*, and said, Rise up,
24. 3, 15 And he took up his *p*, and said,
20 he took up his *p*, and said, Amalek
21 took up his *p*, and said, Strong is
23 he took up his *p*, and said, Alas,
Job 27. 1 Moreover Job continued his *p*,
29. 1 Moreover Job continued his *p*,
Ps 49. 4 I will incline mine ear to a *p*: I will
78. 2 I will open my mouth in a *p*: I will
Pr 26. 7, 9 so is a *p* in the mouth of fools.
Eze 17. 2 speak a *p* unto the house of Israel;
24. 3 utter a *p* unto the rebellious house,
Mic 2. 4 shall one take up a *p* against you,
Hab 2. 6 all these take up a *p* against him,
Mt 13.18 ye therefore the *p* of the sower.
24, 31 Another *p* put he forth unto
33 Another *p* spake he unto them;
34 without a *p* spake he not unto them:
36 Declare unto us the *p* of the tares
15.15 unto him, Declare unto us this *p*.
21.33 Hear another *p*: There was a
24.32 Now learn a *p* of the fig tree; When
Mk 4.10 with the twelve asked of him the *p*.
13 unto them, Know ye not this *p*?
34 without a *p* spake he not unto them:
7.17 asked him concerning the *p*.
12.12 he had spoken the *p* against them:
13.28 Now learn a *p* of the fig tree; When
Lk 5.36 And he spake also a *p* unto them;
6.39 And he spake a *p* unto them, Can
8. 4 out of every city, he spake by a *p*:
9 him, saying, What might this *p* be?
11 Now the *p* is this: The seed is the
12.16 he spake a *p* unto them, saying,
41 Lord, speakest thou this *p* unto us,
13. 6 He spake also this *p*; A certain
14. 7 he put forth a *p* to those which
15. 3 he spake this *p* unto them, saying,
18. 1 he spake a *p* unto them to this end,
9 And he spake this *p* unto certain
19.11 he added and spake a *p*, because
20. 9 he to speak to the people this *p*;
19 had spoken this *p* against them.
21.29 And he spake to them a *p*; Behold
Jn 10. 6 This *p* spake Jesus unto them:

PARABLES

Eze 20.49 say of me, Doth he not speak *p*?
Mt 13. 3 many things unto them in *p*,
10 Why speakest thou unto them in *p*?
13 Therefore speak I to them in *p*:
34 Jesus unto the multitude in *p*;
35 saying, I will open my mouth in *p*;
53 when Jesus had finished these *p*,
21.45 and Pharisees had heard his *p*,
22. 1 and spake unto them again by *p*,
Mk 3.23 and said unto them in *p*, How can
4. 2 he taught them many things by *p*,
11 all these things are done in *p*:
13 and how then will ye know all *p*?
33 many such *p* spake he the word
12. 1 he began to speak unto them by *p*.
Lk 8.10 but to others in *p*; that seeing they

PARADISE

Lk 23.43 To day shalt thou be with me in *p*.
2Co 12. 4 How that he was caught up into *p*,
Rev 2. 7 is in the midst of the *p* of God.

PARAN

Gen 21.21 he dwelt in the wilderness of *P*:
Nu 10.12 cloud rested in the wilderness of *P*.
12.16 and pitched in the wilderness of *P*.
13. 3 them from the wilderness of *P*:
26 unto the wilderness of *P*, to
Dt 1. 1 Red sea, between *P*, and Tophel,
33. 2 he shined forth from mount *P*, and
1Sa 25. 1 went down to the wilderness of *P*.
1Ki 11.18 arose out of Midian, and came to *P*:
18 they took men with them out of *P*,
Hab 3. 3 and the Holy One from mount *P*.

PARCEL

Gen 33.19 he bought a *p* of a field, where he
Jos 24.32 in a *p* of ground which Jacob bought
Ru 4. 3 selleth a *p* of land, which was our
1Ch 11.13 was a *p* of ground full of barley;
14 themselves in the midst of that *p*,
Jn 4. 5 the *p* of ground that Jacob gave

PARCHED

Lev 23.14 eat neither bread, nor *p* corn, nor
Jos 5.11 and *p* corn in the selfsame day.
Ru 2.14 he reached her *p* corn, and she
1Sa 17.17 brethren an ephah of this *p* corn,
25.18 and five measures of *p* corn, and an
2Sa 17.28 and barley, and flour, and *p* corn,
28 beans, and lentiles, and *p* pulse,
Isa 35. 7 *p* ground shall become a pool,
Jer 17. 6 shall inhabit the *p* places in the

PARCHMENTS

2Ti 4.13 the books, but especially the *p*.

PARDON

Ex 23.21 will not *p* your transgressions:
34. 9 and *p* our iniquity and our sin,
Nu 14.19 *P*, I beseech thee, the iniquity of
1Sa 15.25 I pray thee, *p* my sin, and turn
2Ki 5.18 this thing the Lord *p* thy servant,
18 Lord *p* thy servant in this thing.
24. 4 blood; which the Lord would not *p*.
2Ch 30.18 The good Lord *p* every one
Neh 9.17 but thou art a God ready to *p*,
Job 7.21 dost thou not *p* my transgression,
Ps 25.11 O Lord, *p* mine iniquity; for it is
Isa 55. 7 our God, for he will abundantly *p*.
Jer 5. 1 seeketh the truth; and I will *p* it.
7 How shall I *p* thee for this? thy
33. 8 and I will *p* all their iniquities,
50.20 for I will *p* them whom I reserve.

PARDONED

Nu 14.20 I have *p* according to thy word:
Isa 40. 2 that her iniquity is *p*: for she
La 3.42 have rebelled: thou hast not *p*.

PARDONETH

Mic 7.18 like unto thee, that *p* iniquity,

PARENTS

Mt 10.21 shall rise up against their *p*, and
Mk 13.12 shall rise up against their *p*, and
Lk 2.27 the *p* brought in the child Jesus,
41 his *p* went to Jerusalem every year
8.56 And her *p* were astonished: but he
18.29 hath left house, or *p*, or brethren,
21.16 ye shall be betrayed both by *p*,
Jn 9. 2 who did sin, this man, or his *p*,
3 hath this man sinned, nor his *p*:
18 until they called the *p* of him that
20 His *p* answered them and said, We
22 These words spake his *p*, because
23 Therefore said his *p*, He is of age;
Ro 1.30 of evil things, disobedient to *p*,

2Co 12.14 ought not to lay up for the *p*, but
14 but the *p* for the children.
Eph 6. 1 Children, obey your *p* in the Lord:
Col 3.20 obey your *p* in all things: for
1Ti 5. 4 at home, and to requite their *p*:
2Ti 3. 2 disobedient to *p*, unthankful,
Heb 11.23 was hid three months of his *p*,

PARMENAS

Ac 6. 5 and Timon, and *P*, and Nicholas a

PART

Gen 41.34 up the fifth *p* of the land of Egypt
47.24 shall give the fifth *p* unto Pharaoh,
26 that Pharaoh should have the fifth *p*;
Ex 16.36 an omer is the tenth *p* of an ephah.
19.17 stood at the nether *p* of the mount.
29.26 the Lord: and it shall be thy *p*.
40 the fourth *p* of an hin of beaten oil;
40 and the fourth *p* of an hin of wine for
Lev 1.16 cast it beside the altar on the east *p*,
2. 6 Thou shalt *p* it in pieces, and pour
16 of it, *p* of the beaten corn thereof,
16 and *p* of the oil thereof, with all the
5.11 his offering the tenth *p* of an ephah
16 and shall add the fifth *p* thereto, and
6. 5 shall add the fifth *p* more thereto,
20 the tenth *p* of an ephah of fine flour
7.33 have the right shoulder for his *p*.
8.29 of consecration it was Moses' *p*;
11.35 whereupon any *p* of their carcass
37 And if any *p* of their carcass fall
38 any *p* of their carcass fall thereon,
13.41 from the *p* of his head toward his
22.14 he shall put the fifth *p* thereof unto
23.13 be of wine, the fourth *p* of an hin.
27.13 fifth *p* thereof unto thy estimation.
15 he shall add the fifth *p* of the money
16 unto the Lord some *p* of a field of
19 he shall add the fifth *p* of the money
27 and shall add a fifth *p* of it thereto:
31 shall add thereto the fifth *p* thereof.
Nu 5. 7 and add unto it the fifth *p* thereof,
15 tenth *p* of an ephah of barley meal;
15. 4 with the fourth *p* of an hin of oil.
5 the fourth *p* of an hin of wine for
6 with the third *p* of an hin of oil.
7 offer the third *p* of an hin of wine,
18.20 thou have any *p* among them:
20 I am thy *p* and thine inheritance
26 the Lord, even a tenth *p* of the tithe.
29 even the hallowed *p* thereof out of it.
22.41 might see the utmost *p* of the people.
23.10 the number of the fourth *p* of Israel?
13 shalt see but the utmost *p* of them,
28. 5 And a tenth *p* of an ephah of flour
5 the fourth *p* of an hin of beaten oil.
7 fourth *p* of an hin for the one lamb:
14 and the third *p* of an hin unto a ram,
14 the fourth *p* of an hin unto a lamb:
Dt 10. 9 Levi hath no *p* nor inheritance
12.12 no *p* nor inheritance with you.
14.27 no *p* nor inheritance with thee.
29 no *p* nor inheritance with thee,)
18. 1 no *p* nor inheritance with Israel:
33.21 he provided the first *p* for himself,
Jos 14. 4 they gave no *p* unto the Levites
15. 1 the uttermost *p* of the south coast.
5 the sea at the uttermost *p* of Jordan:
13 a *p* among the children of Judah,
18. 7 the Levites have no *p* among you;
19. 9 for the *p* of the children of Judah
22.25 ye have no *p* in the Lord: so shall
27 to come, Ye have no *p* in the Lord.
Ru 1.17 if ought but death *p* thee and me.
2. 3 hap was to light on a *p* of the field
3.13 unto thee the *p* of a kinsman,
13 well; let him do the kinsman's *p*:
13 not do the *p* of a kinsman to thee,
13 will I do the *p* of a kinsman to thee,
1Sa 9. 8 the fourth *p* of a shekel of silver:
14. 2 tarried in the uttermost *p* of Gibeah
23.20 and our *p* shall be to deliver him into
30.24 as his *p* is that goeth down to the
24 his *p* be that tarrieth by the stuff:
24 by the stuff: they shall *p* alike.
2Sa 14. 6 there was none to *p* them, but
18. 2 sent forth a third *p* of the people
2 and a third *p* under the hand of Ittai
20. 1 We have no *p* in David, neither
1Ki 6.24 the uttermost *p* of the one wing unto
24 the uttermost *p* of the other were ten
31 side posts were a fifth *p* of the wall.
33 of olive tree, a fourth *p* of the wall.
2Ki 6.25 the fourth *p* of a cab of dove's dung
7. 5 come to the uttermost *p* of the camp
8 came to the uttermost *p* of the camp,
11. 5 A third *p* of you that enter in on the
6 a third *p* shall be at the gate of Sur;
6 and a third *p* at the gate behind the
18.23 be able on thy *p* to set riders upon
1Ch 12.29 the greatest *p* of them had kept the
2Ch 23. 4 A third *p*...entering on the sabbath,
5 And a third *p* shall be at the king's
5 and a third *p* at the gate of the
29.16 went into the inner *p* of the house
Neh 1. 9 unto the uttermost *p* of the heaven,
3. 9 ruler of the half *p* of Jerusalem.
12 ruler of the half *p* of Jerusalem,
14 the ruler of *p* of Beth-haccerem;
15 the ruler of *p* of Mizpah; he
16 the ruler of the half *p* of Beth-zur,
17 of the half *p* of Keilah, in his *p*.
18 the ruler of the half *p* of Keilah.
5.11 also the hundredth *p* of the money,
9. 3 their God one fourth *p* of the day;
3 and another fourth *p* they confessed,
10.32 yearly with the third *p* of a shekel
Job 32.17 I said, I will answer also my *p*,
41. 6 *p* him among the merchants?
Ps 5. 9 their inward *p* is very wickedness;
22.18 *p* my garments among them,
51. 6 hidden *p* thou shalt make me to
118. 7 The Lord taketh my *p* with them
Pr 8.26 highest *p* of the dust of the world.
31 in the habitable *p* of his earth;
17. 2 shall have *p* of the inheritance
Isa 7.18 uttermost *p* of the rivers of Egypt,
24.16 From the uttermost *p* of the earth
36. 8 able on thy *p* to set riders upon them.
44.16 He burneth *p* thereof in the fire;
16 with *p* thereof he eateth flesh;
19 I have burned *p* of it in the fire;
Eze 4.11 by measure, the sixth *p* of an hin:
5. 2 Thou shalt burn with fire a third *p*
2 and thou shalt take a third *p*, and
2 a third *p* thou shalt scatter in the
12 A third *p* of thee shall die with the
12 third *p* shall fall by the sword round
12 scatter a third *p* into all the winds,
39. 2 and leave but the sixth *p* of thee,
45.11 may contain the tenth *p* of an homer,
11 the ephah the tenth *p* of an homer:
13, 13 sixth *p* of an ephah of an homer
14 offer the tenth *p* of a bath out of the
17 prince's *p* to give burnt offerings,
46.14 morning, the sixth *p* of an ephah,
14 and the third *p* of an hin of oil, to
Dan 1. 2 with *p* of the vessels of the house
2.33 his feet *p* of iron and *p* of clay.
41 *p* of potters' clay, and *p* of iron,
42 the toes of the feet were *p* of iron,
42 *p* of clay, so the kingdom shall be
5. 5 the king saw the *p* of the hand
24 the *p* of the hand sent from him;
Joel 2.20 his hinder *p* toward the utmost sea,
Am 7. 4 great deep, and did eat up a *p*.
Zec 13. 9 bring the third *p* through the fire,
Mk 4.38 he was in the hinder *p* of the ship,
9.40 he that is not against us is on our *p*.
13.27 from the uttermost *p* of the earth
27 to the uttermost *p* of heaven.
Lk 10.42 Mary hath chosen that good *p*,
11.36 be full of light, having no *p* dark,
39 but your inward *p* is full of ravening
17.24 out of the one *p* under heaven,
24 unto the other *p* under heaven;
Jn 13. 8 thee not, thou hast no *p* with me.
19.23 four parts, to every soldier a *p*;
Ac 1. 8 unto the uttermost *p* of the earth.
17 had obtained *p* of this ministry.
25 he may take *p* of this ministry
5. 2 kept back *p* of the price, his wife
2 brought a certain *p*, and laid it at
3 keep back *p* of the price of the land?
8.21 neither *p* nor lot in this matter:
14. 4 and *p* held with the Jews,
4 and *p* with the apostles.
16.12 chief city of that *p* of Macedonia,
19.32 more *p* knew not wherefore they
23. 6 that the one *p* were Sadducees,
9 were of the Pharisees' *p* arose,
27.12 the more *p* advised to depart thence
41 hinder *p* was broken with the
Ro 11.25 in *p* is happened to Israel, until
1Co 12.24 honor to that *p* which lacked:
13. 9 know in *p*, and we prophesy in *p*.
10 which is in *p* shall be done away.
12 now I know in *p*; but then shall I
15. 6 the greater *p* remain unto this
16.17 lacking on your *p* they have
2Co 1.14 ye have acknowledged us in *p*,
2. 5 he hath not grieved me, but in *p*:
6.15 or what *p* hath he that believeth
Eph 4.16 in the measure of every *p*,
Tit 2. 8 is of the contrary *p* may be ashamed,
Heb 2.14 likewise took *p* of the same;
7. 2 Abraham gave a tenth *p* of all;
1Pe 4.14 on their *p* he is evil spoken of, but on
14 of, but on your *p* he is glorified.
Rev 6. 8 them over the fourth *p* of the earth,
8. 8 the third *p* of the sea became blood;
9 And the third *p* of the creatures
9 and the third *p* of the ships were
10 fell upon the third *p* of the rivers,
11 the third *p* of the waters became
12 the third *p* of the sun was smitten,
12 smitten, and the third *p* of the moon,
12 moon, and the third *p* of the stars;
12 as the third *p* of them was darkened,
12 the day shone not for a third *p* of it,
9.15 year, for to slay the third *p* of men.
18 three was the third *p* of men killed,
11.13 and the tenth *p* of the city fell, and in
12. 4 the third *p* of the stars of heaven,
20. 6 hath *p* in the first resurrection:
21. 8 liars, shall have their *p* in the lake
22.19 away his *p* out of the book of life,

PARTAKER

Ps 50.18 and hast been *p* with adulterers.
1Co 9.10 in hope should be *p* of his hope.
23 I might be *p* thereof with you.
10.30 if I by grace be a *p*, why am I evil
1Ti 5.22 neither be *p* of other men's sins:
2Ti 1. 8 be thou *p* of the afflictions of the
2. 6 must be first *p* of the fruits.
1Pe 5. 1 a *p* of the glory that shall be
2Jn 11 God speed is *p* of his evil deeds.

PARTAKERS

Mt 23.30 we would not have been *p* with
Ro 15.27 made *p* of their spiritual things,
1Co 9.12 be *p* of this power over you, are
13 at the altar are *p* with the altar?
10.17 for we are all *p* of that one bread.
18 eat of the sacrifices *p* of the altar?
21 ye cannot be *p* of the Lord's table,
2Co 1. 7 that as ye are *p* of the sufferings,
Eph 3. 6 *p* of his promise in Christ by the
5. 7 Be not ye therefore *p* with them.
Php 1. 7 gospel, ye are all *p* of my grace.
Col 1.12 us meet to be *p* of the inheritance

1Ti 6. 2 and beloved, *p* of the benefit.
Heb 2.14 as the children are *p* of flesh and
3. 1 *p* of the heavenly calling, consider
14 For we are made *p* of Christ, if we
6. 4 were made *p* of the Holy Ghost,
12. 8 whereof all are *p*, then are ye
10 we might be *p* of his holiness.
1Pe 4.13 ye are *p* of Christ's sufferings;
2Pe 1. 4 might be *p* of the divine nature,
Rev 18. 4 that ye be not *p* of her sins, and

PARTAKEST

Ro 11.17 them *p* of the root and fatness

PARTED

Gen 2.10 and from thence it was *p*, and
2Ki 2.11 of fire, and *p* them both asunder;
14 waters, they *p* hither and thither:
Job 38.24 By what way is the light *p*, which
Joel 3. 2 among the nations, and *p* my land.
Mt 27.35 and *p* his garments, casting lots:
35 They *p* my garments among them,
Mk 15.24 they *p* his garments, casting lots
Lk 23.34 they *p* his raiment, and cast lots.
24.51 he was *p* from them, and carried
Jn 19.24 They *p* my raiment among them,
Ac 2.45 *p* them to all men, as every man

PARTETH

Lev 11. 3 Whatsoever *p* the hoof, and is
Dt 14. 6 And every beast that *p* the hoof,
Pr 18.18 cease, and *p* between the mighty.

PARTHIANS

Ac 2. 9 *P*, and Medes, and Elamites, and

PARTIAL

Mal 2. 9 but have been *p* in the law,
Jas 2. 4 Are ye not then *p* in yourselves,

PARTIALITY

1Ti 5.21 another, doing nothing by *p*.
Jas 3.17 of mercy and good fruits, without *p*,

PARTICULAR

1Co 12.27 of Christ, and members in *p*.
Eph 5.33 every one of you in *p* so love

PARTICULARLY

Ac 21.19 he declared *p* what
Heb 9. 5 we cannot now speak *p*.

PARTING

Eze 21.21 Babylon stood at the *p* of the way,

PARTITION

1Ki 6.21 made a *p* by the chains of gold.
Eph 2.14 broken down the middle wall of *p*

PARTLY

Dan 2.42 shall be *p* strong, and *p* broken.
1Co 11.18 you; and I *p* believe it.
Heb 10.33 *P*, whilst ye were made a
33 *p*, whilst ye became companions

PARTNER

Pr 29.24 Whoso is *p* with a thief hateth his
2Co 8.23 he is my *p* and fellowhelper
Phm 17 If thou count me therefore a *p*,

PARTNERS

Lk 5. 7 And they beckoned unto their *p*,
10 Zebedee, which were *p* with Simon.

PARTRIDGE

1Sa 26.20 as when one doth hunt a *p* in the
Jer 17.11 the *p* sitteth on eggs, and hatcheth

PARTS

Gen 47.24 four *p* shall be your own, for seed
Ex 33.23 hand, and thou shalt see my back *p*:
Lev 1. 8 Aaron's sons, shall lay the *p*, the
22.23 thing superfluous or lacking in his *p*,
Nu 10. 5 lie on the east *p* shall go forward.
11. 1 were in the uttermost *p* of the camp.
31.27 divide the prey into two *p*; between
Dt 19. 3 giveth thee to inherit, into three *p*,
30. 4 out unto the outmost *p* of heaven,
Jos 18. 5 they shall divide it into seven *p*:
6 describe the land into seven *p*,
9 it by cities into seven *p* in a book,
1Sa 5. 9 they had emerods in their secret *p*.
2Sa 19.43 and said, We have ten *p* in the king,
1Ki 6.38 throughout all the *p* thereof, and
7.25 and all their hinder *p* were inward.
16.21 of Israel divided into two *p*:
2Ki 11. 7 two *p* of all you that go forth on
2Ch 4. 4 and all their hinder *p* were inward.
Neh 11. 1 nine *p* to dwell in other cities.
Job 26.14 these are *p* of his ways: but how
38.36 hath put wisdom in the inward *p*?
41.12 I will not conceal his *p*, nor his
Ps 2. 8 uttermost *p* of the earth for thy
51. 6 thou desirest truth in the inward *p*:
63. 9 shall go into the lower *p* of the earth.
65. 8 dwell in the uttermost *p* are afraid
78.66 he smote his enemies in the hinder *p*:
136.13 which divided the Red sea into *p*:
139. 9 dwell in the uttermost *p* of the sea;
15 wrought in the lowest *p* of the earth.
Pr 18. 8 into the innermost *p* of the belly.
20.27 searching all the inward *p* of the
30 do stripes the inward *p* of the belly.
26.22 into the innermost *p* of the belly.
Isa 3.17 the Lord will discover their secret *p*.
16.11 and mine inward *p* for Kir-haresh.
44.23 shout, ye lower *p* of the earth:
Jer 31.33 I will put my law in their inward *p*,
34.18 and passed between the *p* thereof,
19 passed between the *p* of the calf;
Eze 26.20 set thee in the low *p* of the earth,
31.14 death, to the nether *p* of the earth,
16 comforted in the nether *p* of the
18 Eden unto the nether *p* of the earth:
32.18 unto the nether *p* of the earth, with
24 into the nether *p* of the earth, which
38.15 from thy place out of the north *p*,
39. 2 thee to come up from the north *p*,
48. 8 in length as one of the other *p*,
Zec 13. 8 two *p* therein shall be cut off and
Mt 2.22 he turned aside into the *p* of Galilee:
12.42 from the uttermost *p* of the earth to
Mk 8.10 came into the *p* of Dalmanutha.
Lk 11.31 came from the utmost *p* of the earth
Jn 19.23 his garments, and made four *p*,
Ac 2.10 and in the *p* of Libya about Cyrene,
20. 2 when he had gone over those *p*,
Ro 15.23 having no more place in these *p*,
1Co 12.23 our uncomely *p* have more abundant
24 For our comely *p* have no need: but
Eph 4. 9 first into the lower *p* of the earth?
Rev 16.19 great city was divided into three *p*,

PASS

Gen 8. 1 made a wind to *p* over the earth,
31.52 I will not *p* over this heap to thee,
41.32 and God will shortly bring it to *p*.
Ex 12.12 For I will *p* through the land of
13 I see the blood, I will *p* over you,
17.11 And it came to *p* when Moses held
33.19 make all my goodness *p* before
22 thee with my hand while I *p* by:
Lev 18.21 seed *p* through the fire to Molech,
Dt 2.29 shall *p* over Jordan into the land
2Ki 7.18 came to *p* as the man of God had
1Ch 15.26 it came to *p*, when God helped the
Job 11.16 remember it as waters that *p* away:
19. 8 fenced up my way that I cannot *p*,
Ps 37. 5 him; and he shall bring it to *p*.
80.12 which *p* by the way do pluck her?
104. 9 a bound that they may not *p* over;
Pr 16.30 his lips he bringeth evil to *p*.
22. 3 but the simple *p* on...are punished.
Isa 42. 9 the former things are come to *p*,
46.11 spoken it, I will also bring it to *p*;
51.10 a way for the ransomed to *p* over?
65.24 come to *p*, that before they call,
Jer 51.43 neither doth any son of man *p*
La 1.12 it nothing to you, all ye that *p* by?
2.15 that *p* by clap their hands at thee;
Eze 32.19 Whom dost thou *p* in beauty? go
47. 5 was a river that I could not *p* over:
Dan 2.45 what shall come to *p* hereafter:
Joel 2.32 it shall come to *p*, that whosoever
Mic 4. 1 in the last days it shall come to *p*,
Zep 1.10 And it shall come to *p* in that day,
Zec 13. 2 the unclean spirit to *p* out of the
Mt 5.18 one tittle shall in no wise *p* from
24.35 Heaven and earth shall *p* away.
35 but my words shall not *p* away.
26.39 possible, let this cup *p* from me:
Mk 13.30 this generation shall not *p*, till all
31 Heaven and earth shall *p* away:
31 but my words shall not *p* away.
Lk 2.15 came to *p*, as the angels were gone
15 see this thing which is come to *p*,
11.42 *p* over judgment and the love of
16.17 easier for heaven and earth to *p*,
22 it came to *p*, that the beggar died,
21. 7 when these things shall come to *p*?
31 when ye see these things come to *p*,
32 This generation shall not *p* away,
33 Heaven and earth shall *p* away:
33 but my words shall not *p* away.
Jn 14.29 I have told you before it come to *p*,
2Pe 3.10 the heavens shall *p* away with a
Rev 1. 1 which must shortly come to *p*;

PASSED

Gen 12. 6 And Abram *p* through the land
15.17 a burning lamp that *p* between
31.21 he rose up, and *p* over the river,
32.10 with my staff I *p* over this Jordan;
22 sons, and *p* over the ford Jabbok.
31 as he *p* over Penuel the sun rose
33. 3 he *p* over before them, and bowed
37.28 *p* by Midianites merchantmen;
Ex 12.27 *p* over the houses of the children
34. 6 And the Lord *p* by before him,
Nu 14. 7 which we *p* through to search it
20.17 left, until we have *p* thy borders.
33. 8 and *p* through the midst of the sea
51 are *p* over Jordan into the land of
Dt 2. 8 when we *p* by from our brethren
8 and *p* by the way of the wilderness
27. 3 of this law, when thou art *p* over,
29.16 the nations through which ye *p* by;
Jos 2.23 *p* over, and came to Joshua the
3. 1 lodged there before they *p* over.
4 ye have not *p* this way heretofore.
16 people *p* over...against Jericho.
17 the Israelites *p* over on dry ground,
17 people were *p* clean over Jordan.
4. 1 people were clean *p* over Jordan,
7 when it *p* over Jordan, the waters
10 and the people hasted and *p* over.
11 all the people were clean *p* over,
11 the ark of the Lord *p* over, and the
12 tribe of Manasseh, *p* over armed
13 thousand prepared for war *p* over
23 until ye were *p* over, as the Lord
5. 1 until we were *p* over, that their
6. 8 priests...*p* on before the Lord,
10.29 Then Joshua *p* from Makkedah,
31 And Joshua *p* from Libnah, and
34 Lachish Joshua *p* unto Eglon,
15. 3 and *p* along to Zin, and ascended
3 and *p* along to Hezron, and went
4 From thence it *p* toward Azmon,
6 *p*...by the north of Beth-arabah;
7 the border *p* toward the waters of
10 and *p* along unto the side of mount
10 and *p* on to Timnah:

11 *p* along to mount Baalah, and went
16. 6 and *p* by it on the east to Janohah;
18. 9 men went and *p* through the land,
18 And *p* along toward the side over
19 And the border *p* along to the side
24.17 all the people through whom we *p*:
Jdg 3.26 and *p* beyond the quarries, and
8. 4 Gideon came to Jordan, and *p* over,
10. 9 children of Ammon *p* over Jordan
11.29 he *p* over Gilead, and Manasseh,
29 and *p* over Mizpeh of Gilead, and
29 *p* over unto the children of Ammon.
32 Jephthah *p* over unto the children
12. 3 and *p* over against the children of
18.13 *p* thence unto mount Ephraim,
19.14 And they *p* on and went their way;
1Sa 9. 4 And he *p* through mount Ephraim,
4 and *p* through the land of Shalisha,
4 they *p* through the land of Shalim,
4 *p* through the land of...Benjamites,
27 pass on before us, (and he *p* on,)
14.23 the battle *p* over unto Beth-aven.
15.12 and *p* on, and gone down to Gilgal.
27. 2 *p* over with the six hundred men
29. 2 the Philistines *p* on by hundreds,
2 and his men *p* on in the rereward
2Sa 2.29 the plain, and *p* over Jordan, and
10.17 Israel together, and *p* over Jordan,
15.18 all his servants *p* on beside him;
18 from Gath, *p* on before the king.
22 And Ittai the Gittite *p* over, and all
23 voice, and all the people *p* over:
23 himself *p* over the brook Kidron,
23 Kidron, and all the people *p* over,
17.22 with him, and they *p* over Jordan:
24 And Absalom *p* over Jordan, he
24. 5 they *p* over Jordan, and pitched
1Ki 13.25 And, behold, men *p* by, and saw the
19.11 And, behold, the Lord *p* by, and a
19 and Elijah *p* by him, and cast his
20.39 as the king *p* by, he cried unto the
2Ki 4. 8 on a day, that Elisha *p* to Shunem,
8 that as oft as he *p* by, he turned
31 Gehazi *p* on before them, and laid
6.30 and he *p* by upon the wall, and the
14. 9 there *p* by a wild beast that was
1Ch 19.17 all Israel, and *p* over Jordan, and
2Ch 9.22 king Solomon *p* all the kings of
25.18 and there *p* by a wild beast that
30.10 So the posts *p* from city to city
Job 4.15 Then a spirit *p* before my face;
9.26 are *p* away as the swift ships:
15.19 and no stranger *p* among them.
28. 8 it, nor the fierce lion *p* by it.
Ps 18.12 was before him his thick clouds *p*,
37.36 Yet he *p* away, and, lo, he was
48. 4 assembled, they *p* by together.
90. 9 all our days are *p* away in thy
SS 3. 4 but a little that I *p* from them,
Isa 10.28 come to Aiath, he is *p* to Migron;
40.27 judgment is *p* over from my God?
41. 3 He pursued them, and *p* safely;
Jer 2. 6 a land that no man *p* through, and
11.15 and the holy flesh is *p* from thee?
34.18 and *p* between the parts thereof,
19 *p* between the parts of the calf;
46.17 he hath *p* the time appointed.
Eze 16. 6 when I *p* by thee, and saw thee
8 Now when I *p* by thee, and looked
15 on every one that *p* by; his it
25 thy feet to every one that *p* by,
36.34 in the sight of all that *p* by.
47. 5 a river that could not be *p* over.
Dan 3.27 the smell of fire had *p* on them.
6.18 to his palace, and *p* the night fasting:
Hos 10.11 but I *p* over upon her fair neck: I
Jon 2. 3 billows and thy waves *p* over me.
Mic 2.13 up, and have *p* through the gate,
Na 3.19 not thy wickedness *p* continually?
Hab 3.10 the overflowing of the water *p* by:
Zec 7.14 no man *p* through nor returned:

Mt 9. 1 entered into a ship, and *p* over,
9 And as Jesus *p* forth from thence,
20.30 when they heard that Jesus *p* by,
27.39 And they that *p* by reviled him,
Mk 2.14 as he *p* by, he saw Levi the son
5.21 Jesus was *p* over again by ship
6.35 place, and now the time is far *p*:
48 sea, and would have *p* by them.
53 And when they had *p* over, they
9.30 thence, and *p* through Galilee;
11.20 as they *p* by, they saw the fig tree
15.21 one Simon a Cyrenian, who *p* by,
29 And they that *p* by railed on him,
Lk 10.31 saw him, he *p* by on the other side.
32 him, and *p* by on the other side.
17.11 *p* through the midst of Samaria
19. 1 entered and *p* through Jericho.
Jn 5.24 but is *p* from death unto life.
8.59 the midst of them, and so *p* by.
9. 1 and as Jesus *p* by, he saw a man
Ac 9.32 Peter *p* throughout all quarters,
12.10 out, and *p* on through one street;
14.24 they had *p* throughout Pisidia,
15. 3 *p* through Phenice and Samaria,
17. 1 they had *p* through Amphipolis
23 For as I *p* by, and beheld your
19. 1 Paul having *p* through the upper
21 when he had *p* through Macedonia
Ro 5.12 so death *p* upon all men, for that
1Co 10. 1 cloud, and all *p* through the sea;
2Co 5.17 old things are *p* away; behold, all
Heb 4.14 priest, that is *p* into the heavens,
11.29 faith they *p* through the Red sea
1Jn 3.14 we have *p* from death unto life,
Rev 21. 1 and the first earth were *p* away;
4 for the former things are *p* away.

PASSETH

Ex 30.13 them, every one that *p* among
14 Every one that *p* among them that
33.22 while my glory *p* by, that I will put
Lev 27.32 whatsoever *p* under the rod, the
Jos 3.11 *p* over before you into Jordan.
16. 2 *p* along unto the borders of Archi
19.13 from thence *p* on along on the east
1Ki 9. 8 one that *p* by it shall be astonished,
2Ki 4. 9 of God, which *p* by us continually.
12. 4 of every one that *p* the account,
2Ch 7.21 to every one that *p* by it; so that
Job 9.11 he *p* on also, but I perceive him
14.20 for ever against him, and he *p*:
30.15 my welfare *p* away as a cloud.
37.21 the wind *p*, and cleanseth them.
Ps 8. 8 *p* through the paths of the seas.
78.39 a wind that *p* away, and cometh
103.16 For the wind *p* over it, and it is
144. 4 days are as a shadow that *p* away.
Pr 10.25 As the whirlwind *p*, so is the
26.17 He that *p* by, and meddleth with
Ec 1. 4 One generation *p* away, and
Isa 29. 5 shall be as chaff that *p* away:
Jer 9.12 wilderness, that none *p* through?
13.24 scatter them as the stubble that *p*
18.16 that *p* thereby shall be astonished,
19. 8 that *p* thereby shall be astonished
Eze 35. 7 and cut off from it him that *p* out
Hos 13. 3 and as the early dew that *p* away,
Mic 7.18 and *p* by the transgression of the
Zep 2.15 every one that *p* by her shall hiss,
3. 6 their streets waste, that none *p* by:
Zec 9. 8 army, because of him that *p* by,
Lk 18.37 that Jesus of Nazareth *p* by.
1Co 7.31 the fashion of this world *p* away.
Eph 3.19 love of Christ, which *p* knowledge,
Php 4. 7 God, which *p* all understanding,
1Jn 2.17 the world *p* away, and the lust

PASSING

Jdg 19.18 We are *p* from Beth-lehem-judah
2Sa 1.26 was wonderful, *p* the love of women.
15.24 people had done *p* out of the city.

2Ki 6.26 king of Israel was *p* by upon the
Ps 84. 6 Who *p* through the valley of Baca
Pr 7. 8 *P* through the street near her
Isa 31. 5 and *p* over he will preserve it.
Eze 39.14 *p* through the land to bury with
Lk 4.30 he *p* through the midst of them
Ac 5.15 the shadow of Peter *p* by might
8.40 *p* through he preached in all the
16. 8 *p* by Mysia came down to Troas.
27. 8 hardly *p* it, came unto a place

PASSION

Ac 1. 3 shewed himself alive after his *p*

PASSIONS

Ac 14.15 We also are men of like *p* with you,
Jas 5.17 a man subject to like *p* as we are,

PASSOVER

Ex 12.11 eat it in haste: it is the Lord's *p*.
21 to your families, and kill the *p*.
27 It is the sacrifice of the Lord's *p*,
Nu 9. 6 could not keep the *p* on that day:
Dt 16. 1 keep the *p* unto the Lord thy God:
6 thou shalt sacrifice the *p* at even,
2Ch 30.15 killed the *p* on the fourteenth day
35.13 And they roasted the *p* with fire
Mt 26. 2 after two days is the feast of the *p*,
17 we prepare for thee to eat the *p*?
18 I will keep the *p* at thy house with
19 them; and they made ready the *p*.
Mk 14. 1 two days was the feast of the *p*,
12 when they killed the *p*, his disciples
12 prepare that thou mayest eat the *p*?
14 I shall eat the *p* with my disciples?
16 them: and they made ready the *p*.
Lk 2.41 every year at the feast of the *p*.
22. 1 drew nigh, which is called the *P*.
7 bread, when the *p* must be killed.
8 Go and prepare us the *p*, that we
11 I shall eat the *p* with my disciples?
13 them: and they made ready the *p*.
15 I have desired to eat this *p* with you
Jn 2.13 And the Jews' *p* was at hand, and
23 when he was in Jerusalem at the *p*,
6. 4 the *p*, a feast of the Jews, was nigh.
11.55 And the Jews' *p* was nigh at hand:
55 went...up to Jerusalem before the *p*,
12. 1 Jesus six days before the *p* came to
13. 1 Now before the feast of the *p*, when
18.28 but that they might eat the *p*.
39 release unto you one at the *p*:
19.14 And it was the preparation of the *p*,
1Co 5. 7 Christ our *p* is sacrificed for us:
Heb 11.28 Through faith he kept the *p*, and
(See illustration on page 564)

PASSOVERS

2Ch 30.17 the charge of the killing of the *p*

PAST

Dt 4.32 ask now of the days that are *p*,
1Sa 15.32 Surely the bitterness of death is *p*.
2Sa 11.27 And when the mourning was *p*,
Job 9.10 doeth great things *p* finding out;
29. 2 Oh that I were as in months *p*,
Ps 90. 4 are but as yesterday when it is *p*,
Ec 3.15 God requireth that which is *p*.
SS 2.11 the winter is *p*, the rain is over
Jer 8.20 harvest is *p*, the summer is ended,
Mt 14.15 place, and the time is now *p*;
Mk 16. 1 when the sabbath was *p*, Mary
Lk 9.36 the voice was *p*, Jesus was found
Ac 12.10 *p* the first and the second ward,
14.16 in times *p* suffered all nations
27. 9 because the fast was...already *p*,
Ro 3.25 the remission of sins that are *p*,
11.30 in times *p* have not believed God,
33 and his ways *p* finding out!
Gal 1.13 heard of my conversation in time *p*
23 he which persecuted us in times *p*

Gal 5.21 as I have also told you in time *p*,
Eph 2. 2 Wherein in time *p* ye walked
3 all had our conversation in times *p*
11 that ye, being in time *p* Gentiles
4.19 Who being *p* feeling have given
2Ti 2.18 that the resurrection is *p* already;
Phm 11 in time *p* was to thee unprofitable,
Heb 1. 1 spake in time *p* unto the fathers
11.11 of a child when she was *p* age,
1Pe 2.10 Which in time *p* were not a people,
4. 3 the time *p* of our life may suffice
1Jn 2. 8 because the darkness is *p*, and
Rev 9.12 One woe is *p*; and, behold, there
11.14 The second woe is *p*; and, behold,

PASTOR

Jer 17.16 have not hastened from being a *p*

PASTORS

Jer 2. 8 *p* also transgressed against me,
3.15 will give you *p* according to mine
10.21 *p* are become brutish, and have
12.10 Many *p*...destroyed my vineyard,
22.22 The wind shall eat up all thy *p*,
23. 1 Woe be unto the *p* that destroy
2 against the *p* that feed my people;
Eph 4.11 and some, *p* and teachers;

PASTURE

Gen 47. 4 servants have no *p* for their flocks;
1Ch 4.39 valley, to seek *p* for their flocks.
40 And they found fat *p* and good, and
41 there was *p* there for their flocks.
Job 39. 8 range of the mountains is his *p*,
Ps 74. 1 smoke against the sheep of thy *p*?
79.13 we, thy people and sheep of thy *p*
95. 7 the people of his *p*, and the sheep
100. 3 his people, and the sheep of his *p*.
Isa 32.14 a joy of wild asses, a *p* of flocks;
Jer 23. 1 and scatter the sheep of my *p*!
25.36 for the Lord hath spoiled their *p*.
La 1. 6 become like harts that find no *p*,
Eze 34.14 I will feed them in a good *p*, and
14 and in a fat *p* shall they feed upon
18 you to have eaten up the good *p*,
31 ye my flock, the flock of my *p*,
Hos 13. 6 According to their *p*, so were they
Joel 1.18 perplexed, because they have no *p*;
Jn 10. 9 shall go in and out, and find *p*.

PASTURES

1Ki 4.23 and twenty oxen out of the *p*,
Ps 23. 2 maketh me to lie down in green *p*:
65.12 drop upon the *p* of the wilderness:
13 The *p* are clothed with flocks;
Isa 30.23 day shall thy cattle feed in large *p*.
49. 9 their *p* shall be in all high places.
Eze 34.18 your feet the residue of your *p*?
45.15 hundred, out of the fat *p* of Israel;
Joel 1.19 devoured the *p* of the wilderness,
20 devoured the *p* of the wilderness.
2.22 the *p* of the wilderness do spring,

The first Passover (Ex 12) is depicted here in an illumination from a 13th-century French manuscript.

PATARA

Ac 21. 1 Rhodes, and from thence unto *P*:

PATH

Gen 49.17 an adder in the *p*, that biteth the
Nu 22.24 angel of the Lord stood in a *p* of
Job 28. 7 is a *p* which no fowl knoweth, and
30.13 They mar my *p*, they set forward
41.32 He maketh a *p* to shine after him;
Ps 16.11 Thou wilt shew me the *p* of life:
27.11 O Lord, and lead me in a plain *p*,
77.19 sea, and thy *p* in the great waters,
119.35 Make me to go in the *p* of thy
105 my feet, and a light unto my *p*.
139. 3 Thou compassest my *p* and my
142. 3 me, then thou knewest my *p*.
Pr 1.15 them; refrain thy foot from their *p*:
2. 9 and equity; yea, every good *p*.
4.14 Enter not into the *p* of the wicked,
18 the *p* of the just is as the shining
26 Ponder the *p* of thy feet, and let
5. 6 shouldest ponder the *p* of life,
Isa 26. 7 dost weigh the *p* of the just.
30.11 of the way, turn aside out of the *p*,
40.14 taught him in the *p* of judgment,
43.16 and a *p* in the mighty waters;
Joel 2. 8 shall walk every one in his *p*:

PATHS

Job 6.18 *p* of their way are turned aside;
8.13 So are the *p* of all that forget God;
13.27 lookest narrowly unto all my *p*;
19. 8 and he hath set darkness in my *p*.
24.13 thereof, nor abide in the *p* thereof.
33.11 the stocks, he marketh all my *p*.
38.20 know the *p* to the house thereof?
Ps 8. 8 passeth through the *p* of the seas.
17. 4 me from the *p* of the destroyer.
5 Hold up my goings in thy *p*, that
23. 3 me in the *p* of righteousness for
25. 4 thy ways, O Lord; teach me thy *p*.
10 All the *p* of the Lord are mercy
65.11 goodness; and thy *p* drop fatness.
Pr 2. 8 He keepeth the *p* of judgment, and
13 leave the *p* of uprightness, to walk
15 and they froward in their *p*:
18 death, and her *p* unto the dead.
19 take they hold of the *p* of life.
20 and keep the *p* of the righteous.
3. 6 him, and he shall direct thy *p*.
17 and all her *p* are peace.
4.11 wisdom; I have led thee in right *p*.
7.25 her ways, go not astray in her *p*.
8. 2 by the way in the places of the *p*.
20 in the midst of the *p* of judgment:
Isa 2. 3 his ways, and we will walk in his *p*:
3.12 err, and destroy the way of thy *p*.
42.16 in *p* that they have not known:
58.12 The restorer of *p* to dwell in.
59. 7 and destruction are in their *p*.
8 they have made them crooked *p*:
Jer 6.16 and ask for the old *p*, where is the
18.15 in their ways from the ancient *p*,
15 walk in *p*, in a way not cast up;
La 3. 9 stone, he hath made my *p* crooked.
Hos 2. 6 wall, that she shall not find her *p*.
Mic 4. 2 ways, and we will walk in his *p*:
Mt 3. 3 of the Lord, make his *p* straight.
Mk 1. 3 of the Lord, make his *p* straight.
Lk 3. 4 of the Lord, make his *p* straight.
Heb 12.13 made straight *p* for your feet, lest

PATIENCE

Mt 18.26 Lord, have *p* with me, and I will
29 Have *p* with me, and I will pay
Lk 8.15 it, and bring forth fruit with *p*.
21.19 In your *p* possess ye your souls.
Ro 5. 3 that tribulation worketh *p*;
4 And *p*, experience; and experience,
8.25 not, then do we with *p* wait for it.
15. 4 *p* and comfort of the scriptures

5 Now the God of *p* and consolation
2Co 6. 4 the ministers of God, in much *p*, in
12.12 were wrought among you in all *p*,
Col 1.11 unto all *p* and longsuffering with
1Th 1. 3 and *p* of hope in our Lord Jesus
2Th 1. 4 for your *p* and faith in all your
1Ti 6.11 godliness, faith, love, *p*, meekness.
2Ti 3.10 faith, longsuffering, charity, *p*,
Tit 2. 2 sound in faith, in charity, in *p*.
Heb 6.12 faith and *p* inherit the promises.
10.36 For ye have need of *p*, that, after
12. 1 let us run with *p* the race that is
Jas 1. 3 the trying of your faith worketh *p*.
4 But let *p* have her perfect work,
5. 7 and hath long *p* for it, until he
10 of suffering affliction, and of *p*.
11 Ye have heard of the *p* of Job,
2Pe 1. 6 temperance *p*; and to *p* godliness;
Rev 1. 9 the kingdom and *p* of Jesus Christ,
2. 2 works, and thy labor, and thy *p*,
3 hast *p*, and for my name's sake
19 faith, and thy *p*, and thy works;
3.10 thou hast kept the word of my *p*,
13.10 it the *p* and the faith of the saints.
14.12 Here is the *p* of the saints: here

PATIENT
Ec 7. 8 *p* in spirit is better than the proud
Ro 2. 7 by *p* continuance in well doing
12.12 in hope; *p* in tribulation;
1Th 5.14 the weak, be *p* toward all men.
2Th 3. 5 and into the *p* waiting for Christ.
1Ti 3. 3 *p*, not a brawler, not covetous;
2Ti 2.24 gentle unto all men, apt to teach, *p*,
Jas 5. 7 Be *p* therefore, brethren, unto the
8 Be ye also *p*; stablish your hearts:

PATIENTLY
Ps 37. 7 in the Lord, and wait *p* for him:
40. 1 I waited *p* for the Lord; and he
Ac 26. 3 I beseech thee to hear me *p*.
Heb 6.15 And so, after he had *p* endured,
1Pe 2.20 for your faults, ye shall take it *p*?
20 ye take it *p*, this as acceptable with

PATMOS
Rev 1. 9 was in the isle that is called *P*,

PATRIARCH
Ac 2.29 speak unto you of the *p* David,
Heb 7. 4 the *p* Abraham gave the tenth of

PATRIARCHS
Ac 7. 8 and Jacob begat the twelve *p*.
9 And the *p*, moved with envy, sold

PATROBAS
Ro 16.14 *P*, Hermes, and the brethren

PATTERN
Ex 25. 9 after the *p* of the tabernacle, and
9 the *p* of all the instruments thereof,
40 *p*,...shewed thee in the mount.
Nu 8. 4 the *p* which the Lord had shewed
Jos 22.28 the *p* of the altar of the Lord,
2Ki 16.10 fashion of the altar, and the *p* of it,
1Ch 28.11 *p* of the porch, and of the houses
12 the *p* of all that he had by the spirit,
18 and gold for the *p* of the chariot of
19 me, even all the works of this *p*.
Eze 43.10 and let them measure the *p*.
1Ti 1.16 *p* to them which should hereafter
Tit 2. 7 showing thyself a *p* of good works:
Heb 8. 5 the *p* shewed to thee in the mount.

PATTERNS
Heb 9.23 *p* of things in the heavens should

PAUL
Ac 13. 9 Saul, (who also is called *P*,) filled
13 when *P* and his company loosed
16 Then *P* stood up, and beckoning
43 followed *P* and Barnabas: who,
46 Then *P* and Barnabas waxed bold,
50 raised persecution against *P* and
14. 9 The same heard *P* speak: who
11 the people saw what *P* had done,
19 having stoned *P*, drew him out of
15. 2 *P* and Barnabas had no small
22 to Antioch with *P* and Barnabas;
38 *P* thought not good to take him
40 And *P* chose Silas, and departed,
16. 3 would *P* have to go forth with him;
9 vision appeared to *P* in the night;
19 they caught *P* and Silas, and drew
25 at midnight *P* and Silas prayed,
36 this saying to *P*, The magistrates
17. 2 And *P*, as his manner was, went in
16 while *P* waited for them at Athens,
22 *P* stood in the midst of Mars' hill,
19. 1 *P* having passed through the upper
4 Then said *P*, John verily baptized
6 when *P* had laid his hands upon
11 miracles by the hands of *P*:
13 you by Jesus whom *P* preacheth.
20. 1 *P* called unto him the disciples
16 *P*...determined to sail by Ephesus,
21. 4 who said to *P* through the Spirit,
30 they took *P*, and drew him out of
32 the soldiers, they left beating of *P*.
37 as *P* was to be led into the castle,
22.25 *P* said unto the centurion that
28 And *P* said, But I was free born.
23.1 *P*, earnestly beholding the council,
3 Then said *P* unto him, God shall
11 Be of good cheer, *P*: and said,
14 eat nothing until we have slain *P*.
24. 1 informed the governor against *P*.
24 he sent for *P*, and heard him
25. 2 the Jews informed him against *P*,
4 *P* should be kept at Caesarea, and
10 Then said *P*, I stand at Caesar's
19 dead, whom *P* affirmed to be alive.
21 *P* had appealed to be reserved
26. 1 Then Agrippa said unto *P*, Thou
24 *P*, thou art beside thyself; much
27. 1 they delivered *P* and certain other
24 Fear not, *P*; thou must be brought
33 *P* besought them all to take meat,
43 the centurion, willing to save *P*,
28. 3 *P* had gathered a bundle of sticks,
8 to whom *P* entered in, and prayed,
25 after that *P* had spoken one word,
30 *P* dwelt two whole years in his
1Co 1. 1 *P*, called to be an apostle of Jesus
12 every one of you saith, I am of *P*;
13 was *P* crucified for you? or were
13 were ye baptized in the name of *P*?
16.21 of me *P* with mine own hand.

PAULUS
Ac 13. 7 deputy of the country, Sergius *P*,

PAVED
Ex 24.10 were a *p* work of a sapphire stone,
SS 3.10 midst thereof being *p* with love,

PAVEMENT
2Ki 16.17 it, and put it upon a *p* of stones.
2Ch 7. 3 faces to the ground upon the *p*,
Est 1. 6 a *p* of red, and blue, and white,
Eze 40.17 *p* made for the court round about:
17 thirty chambers were upon the *p*.
18 And the *p* by the side of the gates
18 of the gates was the lower *p*.
42. 3 *p* which was for the utter court,
Jn 19.13 in a place that is called the *P*,

PAVILION
Ps 18.11 his *p* round about him were dark
27. 5 he shall hide me in his *p*: in the
31.20 shalt keep them secretly in a *p*
Jer 43.10 shall spread his royal *p* over them.

PAUL

Missionary founder of early Christian churches; author of epistles setting forth major doctrines of the new religion; called "apostle of the Gentiles" (Ro 11.13); born in Tarsus in Cilicia, a Benjamite Jew and Roman citizen (Ro 11; Php 3); at first called Saul; educated as Pharisee under Gamaliel (Ac 22); zealously joins in persecution of Christians; permits the stoning of Stephen (Ac 7); on the road to Damascus receives a vision of Jesus (Ac 9), which inspires his conversion and evangelical calling; spends time in Arabia (Gal 1) before returning to Damascus to begin preaching; three-year stay there ended by hostility of the king; escapes in basket lowered from the city walls (2Co 11); visits Jerusalem, where he is introduced to the apostles by Barnabas (Ac 9; although in Gal 1 meets only Peter and James); later summoned by Barnabas to Antioch, where he spends a year preaching (Ac 11).

Subsequent missionary career (under the name Paul) comprises three great journeys. The first (Ac 13–14) takes him and Barnabas through Cyprus to the towns of southern Galatia; there follows a visit to Jerusalem during which a council of church leaders (A.D. 49) agrees to expand Christian mission into the Gentile world; meeting with Peter in Antioch, Paul protests Peter's insistence on observance of Jewish dietary laws by Gentile converts; quarrels with and parts from Barnabas (Ac 15). Accompanied now by Silas, sets out on second journey, which leads through Syria, Cilicia, and the towns of southern Galatia; eventually crosses to Macedonia; begins preaching in Europe at Philippi, where he is imprisoned and flogged (Ac 16); goes to Athens, where mention of the Resurrection excites derision (Ac 17), and finally to Corinth, where he stays 18 months and founds a thriving Christian community; eventually returns to Antioch (Ac 18).

Main stop of third journey is at Ephesus, capital of Roman province of Asia, where he remains three years, leaving only when forced to by silversmiths' revolt (Ac 19); travels overland through Macedonia to Corinth; from Corinthian and other communities he collects contributions for the poor in Jerusalem (Ro 15.26; 1Co 16.1); crossing to Asia, he proceeds to Miletus, where he gives farewell address to the Ephesian elders (Ac 20); after return to Jerusalem, is attacked by angry Jews from Asian province and saved from death by the intervention of a Roman tribune (Ac 21–22); is transferred to Caesarea and imprisoned for two years by Felix, governor of Judea (Ac 23–24); on arrival of new governor, Festus, Paul "appeals to Caesar" and is sent for trial in Rome (Ac 25–26); sea-crossing interrupted by violent storm and shipwreck off coast of Malta (Ac 27); finally reaching Rome, is placed under house arrest but still able to continue preaching (Ac 28). The Book of Acts leaves his fate unknown; traditionally believed to have met a martyr's death.

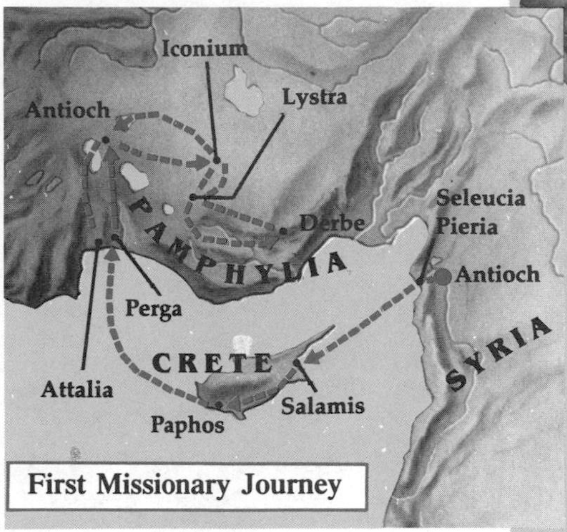

First Missionary Journey

Second Missionary Journey

Paul's three missionary journeys *took him through much of Asia Minor and across to Greece, establishing and revisiting the small, struggling Christian congregations. The first journey (Ac 13–14) began at Antioch in Syria, where church leaders selected Paul and Barnabas to carry the Gospel abroad. Sailing from Seleucia to Cyprus, they preached at Salamis and then at Paphos, where the Roman governor was converted by Paul's blinding of a false prophet. From there they sailed to Perga and then pressed on to Antioch in Pisidia, where, as was their custom, they first preached in the local synagogue. The angry reception there led Paul to cite Isaiah's words, "I have set thee to be a light of the Gentiles," heralding his future role as "apostle of the Gentiles" (Ro 11.13).*

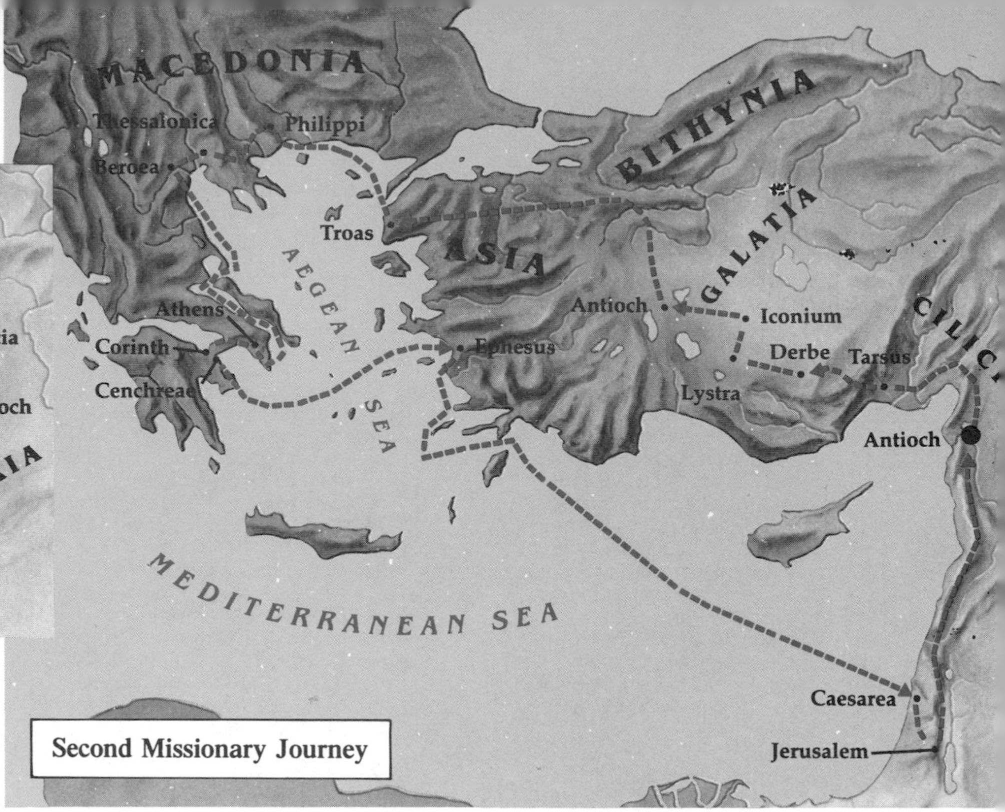

A lengthy stay in Iconium was followed by a near-fatal episode in Lystra, where Paul was stoned and left for dead by an angry mob. After a more peaceful sojourn in Derbe, he and Barnabas retraced their steps and returned by sea to Antioch. Paul's second journey (Ac 16–18), this time with Silas, began with visits to several of the Galatian churches; the two continued westward and crossed to Macedonia; at Philippi Paul won his first European convert, Lydia. He later spent 18 months in Corinth, then made his way home, stopping at Ephesus and Jerusalem. Paul's third journey (Ac 18–21) was chiefly devoted to revisiting the various churches, giving encouragement and resolving doctrinal disputes; the most dramatic event was the riot of silversmiths caused by his preaching at Ephesus. Paul's last voyage (Ac 27–28), to stand trial before Caesar, was marked by a harrowing storm and shipwreck, and capped by his triumphal progress from Puteoli into Rome.

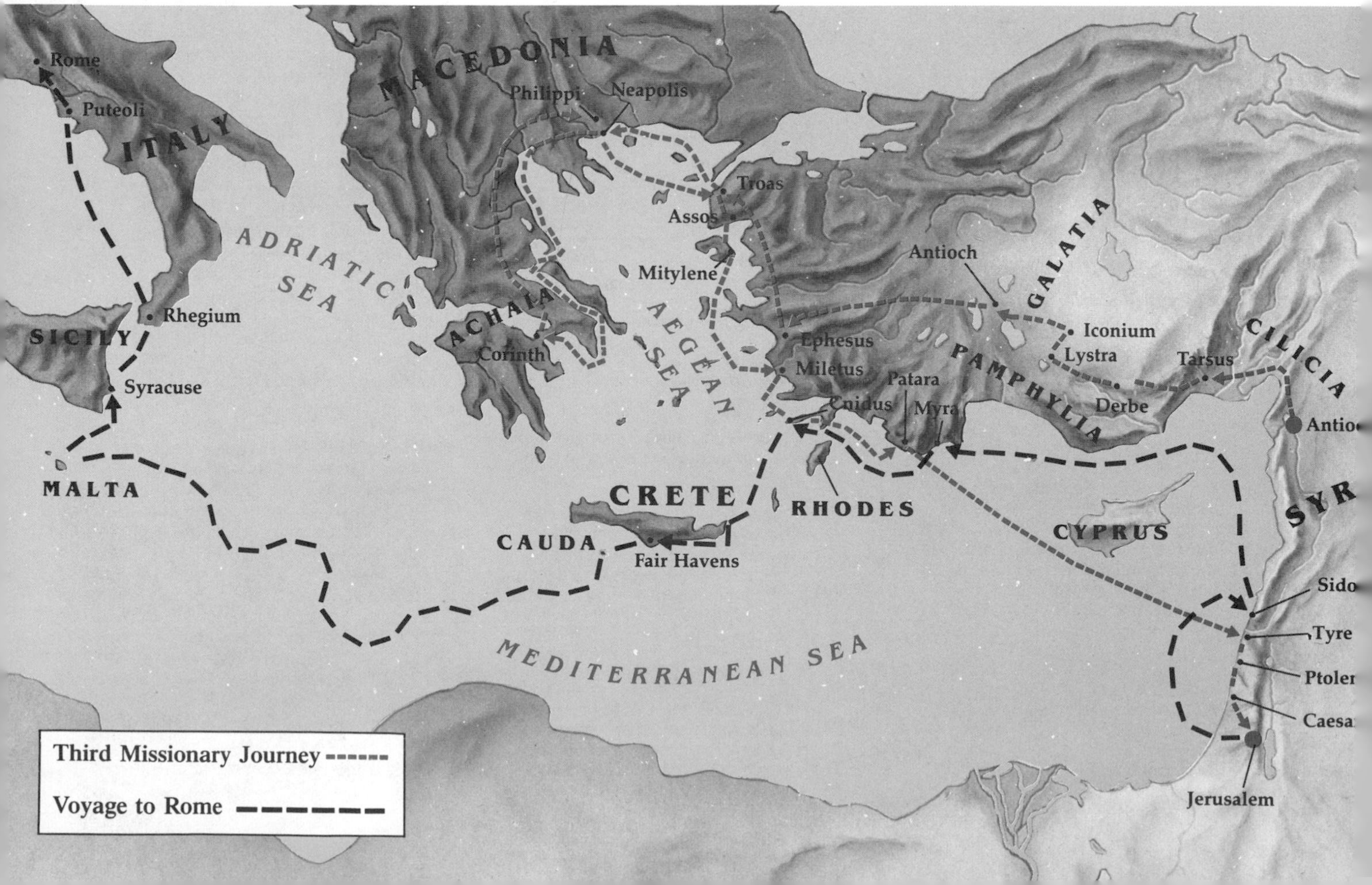

Third Missionary Journey ------

Voyage to Rome — — — — — —

PAW

1Sa 17.37 delivered me out of...*p* of the lion,
37 and out of the *p* of the bear, he will

PAY

Ex 21.19 he shall *p* for the loss of his time,
22 he shall *p* as the judges determine.
36 he shall surely *p* ox for ox; and
22. 7 thief be found, let him *p* double.
9 *p* double unto his neighbor.
17 *p* money according to the dowry
Nu 20.19 thy water, then I will *p* for it;
Dt 23.21 thou shalt not slack to *p* it: for
2Sa 15. 7 let me go and *p* my vow, which I
1Ki 20.39 else thou shalt *p* a talent of silver.
2Ki 4. 7 Go, sell the oil, and *p* thy debt,
2Ch 8. 8 make to *p* tribute until this day.
27. 5 children of Ammon *p* unto him,
Ezr 4.13 will they not *p* toll, tribute, and
Est 3. 9 will *p* ten thousand talents of silver
4. 7 that Haman had promised to *p* to
Job 22.27 thee, and thou shalt *p* thy vows.
Ps 22.25 *p* my vows before them that fear
50.14 and *p* thy vows unto the most High:
66.13 offerings: I will *p* thee my vows,
76.11 Vow, and *p* unto the Lord your God:
116.14, 18, *p* my vows unto the Lord now
Pr 19.17 he hath given will he *p* him again.
22.27 If thou hast nothing to *p*, why
Ec 5. 4 a vow unto God, defer not to *p* it;
4 *p* that which thou hast vowed.
5 thou shouldest vow and not *p*.
Jon 2. 9 I will *p* that that I have vowed.
Mt 17.24 Doth not your master *p* tribute?
18.25 forasmuch as he had not to *p*, his
26 with me, and I will *p* thee all.
28 saying, *P* me that thou owest.
29 with me, and I will *p* thee all.
30 prison, till he should *p* the debt.
34 should *p* all that was due unto him.
23.23 for ye *p* tithe of mint and anise and
Lk 7.42 when they had nothing to *p*, he
Ro 13. 6 For this cause *p* ye tribute also:

PAYED

Pr 7.14 me; this day have I *p* my vows.
Heb 7. 9 tithes, *p* tithes in Abraham.

PAYETH

Ps 37.21 borroweth, and *p* not again:

PAYMENT

Mt 18.25 that he had, and *p* to be made.

PEACE

Gen 15.15 thou shalt go to thy fathers in *p*;
24.21 man wondering at her held his *p*,
26.29 and have sent thee away in *p*:
31 and they departed from him in *p*.
28.21 again to my father's house in *p*;
34. 5 Jacob held his *p* until they were
41.16 give Pharaoh an answer of *p*.
43.23 And he said, *P* be to you, fear not:
44.17 get you up in *p* unto your father.
Ex 4.18 And Jethro said to Moses, Go in *p*.
14.14 you, and ye shall hold your *p*.
18.23 shall also go to their place in *p*.
20.24 offerings, and thy *p* offerings,
24. 5 sacrificed *p* offerings of oxen unto
29.28 of the sacrifice of their *p* offerings,
32. 6 offerings, and brought *p* offerings;
Lev 3. 1 be a sacrifice of *p* offering, if he
3 of the sacrifice of the *p* offering
6 a sacrifice of *p* offering unto the
9 of the sacrifice of the *p* offering
4.10 of the sacrifice of *p* offerings: and
26 fat of the sacrifice of *p* offerings:
31 off the sacrifice of *p* offerings: and
35 the sacrifice of the *p* offerings;
6.12 thereon the fat of the *p* offerings.
7.11 law of the sacrifice of *p* offerings,

BIBLICAL THEMES

PEACE

Let there be now an oath betwixt us, even betwixt us and thee, and let us make a covenant with thee; that thou wilt do us no hurt, as we have not touched thee, and as we have done unto thee nothing but good, and have sent thee away in peace. Gen 26.28-29

He had peace on all sides round about him. And Judah and Israel dwelt safely, every man under his vine and under his fig tree, from Dan even to Beersheba, all the days of Solomon. 1Ki 4.24-25

When he giveth quietness, who then can make trouble? Job 34.29

Great peace have they which love thy law. Ps 119.165

Pray for the peace of Jerusalem: they shall prosper that love thee. Peace be within thy walls, and prosperity within thy palaces. Ps 122.6-7

A time to love, and a time to hate; a time of war, and a time of peace. Ec 3.8

They shall beat their swords into plowshares, and their spears into pruninghooks: nation shall not lift up sword against nation, neither shall they learn war any more. Isa 2.4

For unto us a child is born . . . and his name shall be called Wonderful, Counsellor, The mighty God, The everlasting Father, The Prince of Peace. Isa 9.6

They shall not hurt nor destroy in all my holy mountain: for the earth shall be full of the knowledge of the Lord, as the waters cover the sea. Isa 11.9

Thou wilt keep him in perfect peace, whose mind is stayed on thee. Isa 26.3

The work of righteousness shall be peace; and the effect of righteousness quietness and assurance for ever. And my people shall dwell in a peaceable habitation, and in sure dwellings, and in quiet resting places. Isa 32.17-18

They have healed the hurt of the daughter of my people slightly, saying, Peace, peace; when there is no peace. Jer 8.11

There shall yet old men and old women dwell in the streets of Jerusalem, and every man with his staff in his hand for very age. And the streets of the city shall be full of boys and girls playing. Zec 8.4-5

Blessed are the peacemakers. Mt 5.9

Think not that I am come to send peace on earth: I came not to send peace, but a sword. Mt 10.34

Then said Jesus unto him, Put up again thy sword into his place: for all they that take the sword shall perish with the sword. Mt 26.52

On earth peace, good will toward men. Lk 2.14

Peace I leave with you, my peace I give unto you: not as the world giveth, give I unto you. Let not your heart be troubled, neither let it be afraid. Jn 14.27

My kingdom is not of this world: if my kingdom were of this world, then would my servants fight. Jn 18.36

How beautiful are the feet of them that preach the gospel of peace. Ro 10.15

God is not the author of confusion, but of peace. 1Co 14.33

The peace of God, which passeth all understanding, shall keep your hearts and minds through Christ Jesus. Php 4.7

It pleased the Father that in him should all fulness dwell; and, having made peace through the blood of his cross, by him to reconcile all things unto himself. Col 1.19-20

Grace be unto you, and peace, from him which is, and which was, and which is to come. Rev 1.4

13 of thanksgiving of his *p* offerings.
14 the blood of the *p* offerings.
15, 18 of the sacrifice of his *p* offerings
20, 21 of the sacrifice of *p* offerings,
29 the sacrifice of his *p* offerings unto
29 of the sacrifice of his *p* offerings.
32 the sacrifices of your *p* offerings.
33 the blood of the *p* offerings, and
34 the sacrifices of their *p* offerings,
37 of the sacrifice of the *p* offerings;
9. 4 bullock and a ram for *p* offerings,
18 ram for a sacrifice of *p* offerings,
22 the burnt offering, and *p* offerings.
10. 3 glorified. And Aaron held his *p*.
14 out of the sacrifices of *p* offerings
17. 5 them for *p* offerings unto the Lord.
19. 5 ye offer a sacrifice of *p* offerings
22.21 offereth a sacrifice of *p* offerings
23.19 year for a sacrifice of *p* offerings.
26. 6 I will give *p* in the land, and ye
Nu 6.14 without blemish for *p* offerings,
17 ram for a sacrifice of *p* offerings
18 the sacrifice of the *p* offerings.
26 upon thee, and give thee *p*.

Nu 7.17, 23, 29, 35, 41, 47, 53, 59, 65, 71, 77,
83 sacrifice of *p* offerings, two oxen,
88 for the sacrifice of the *p* offerings
10.10 the sacrifices of your *p* offerings;
15. 8 vow, or *p* offerings unto the Lord:
25.12 give unto him my covenant of *p*:
29.39 offerings, and for your *p* offerings.
30. 4 her father shall hold his *p* at her;
7 held his *p* at her in the day that
11 held his *p* at her, and disallowed her
14 hold his *p* at her from day to day;
14 he held his *p* at her in the day
Dt 2.26 king of Heshbon with words of *p*,
20.10 against it, then proclaim *p* unto it.
11 if it make thee answer of *p*, and
12 if it will make no *p* with thee, but
23. 6 Thou shalt not seek their *p* nor
27. 7 And thou shalt offer *p* offerings,
29.19 I shall have *p*, though I walk in
Jos 8.31 Lord, and sacrificed *p* offerings.
9.15 Joshua made *p* with them, and
10. 1 Gibeon had made *p* with Israel,
4 for it hath made *p* with Joshua
21 to Joshua at Makkedah in *p*:
11.19 There was not a city that made *p*
22.23 or if to offer *p* offerings thereon,
27 sacrifices, and with our *p* offerings;
Jdg 4.17 was *p* between Jabin the king of
6.23 him, *P* be unto thee; fear not:
8. 9 When I come again in *p*, I will
11.31 I return in *p* from the children of
18. 6 the priest said unto them, Go in *p*:
19 they said unto him, Hold thy *p*,
19.20 the old man said, *P* be with thee;
20.26 and *p* offerings before the Lord.
21. 4 burnt offerings and *p* offerings.
1Sa 1.17 Eli answered and said, Go in *p*:
7.14 *p* between Israel and the Amorites.
10. 8 sacrifice sacrifices of *p* offerings:
27 no presents. But he held his *p*.
11.15 sacrificed sacrifices of *p* offerings
13. 9 offering to me, and *p* offerings.
20. 7 is well: thy servant shall have *p*:
13 away, that thou mayest go in *p*:
21 for there is *p* to thee, and no hurt;
42 Jonathan said to David, Go in *p*,
25. 6 in prosperity, *P* be both to thee,
6 and *p* be to thine house,
6 and *p* be unto all that thou hast.
35 Go up in *p* to thine house; see, I
29. 7 now return, and go in *p*, that thou
2Sa 3.21 Abner away; and he went in *p*.
22 him away, and he was gone in *p*.
23 him away, and he is gone in *p*.
6.17 and *p* offerings before the Lord.
18 burnt offerings and *p* offerings,
10.19 made *p* with Israel, and served
13.20 but hold now thy *p*, my sister: he
15. 9 the king said unto him, Go in *p*.
27 return into the city in *p*, and your
17. 3 so all the people shall be in *p*.
19.24 until the day he came again in *p*.
30 again in *p* unto his own house.
24.25 burnt offerings and *p* offerings.
1Ki 2. 5 shed the blood of war in *p*, and
6 head go down to the grave in *p*.
33 there be *p* for ever from the Lord.
3.15 offered *p* offerings, and made a
4.24 and he had *p* on all sides round
5.12 *p* between Hiram and Solomon;
8.63 offered a sacrifice of *p* offerings,
64 and the fat of the *p* offerings:
64 and the fat of the *p* offerings.
9.25 *p* offerings upon the altar which
20.18 Whether they be come out for *p*,
22.17 every man to his house in *p*.
27 of affliction, until I come in *p*.
28 If thou return at all in *p*, the Lord
44 Jehoshaphat made *p* with the
2Ki 2. 3, 5 Yea, I know it; hold ye your *p*.
5.19 And he said unto him, Go in *p*.

7. 9 good tidings, and we hold our *p*:
9.17 them, and let him say, Is it *p*?
18 said, Thus saith the king, Is it *p*?
18 What hast thou to do with *p*?
19 said, Thus saith the king, Is it *p*?
19 What hast thou to do with *p*?
22 Jehu, that he said, Is it *p*, Jehu?
22 And he answered, What *p*, so long
31 Had Zimri *p*, who slew his master?
16.13 the blood of his *p* offerings,
18.36 But the people held their *p*, and
20.19 good, if *p* and truth be in my days?
22.20 be gathered into thy grave in *p*;
1Ch 12.18 son of Jesse: *p*, *p* be unto thee,
18 thee, and *p* be to thine helpers;
16. 1 offered...*p* offerings before God.
2 burnt offerings and the *p* offerings,
19.19 made *p* with David, and became
21.26 burnt offerings and *p* offerings,
22. 9 give *p* and quietness unto Israel
2Ch 7. 7 and the fat of *p* offerings,
15. 5 was no *p* to him that went out,
18.16 return...every man to his house in *p*.
26 of affliction, until I return in *p*.
27 If thou certainly return in *p*, then
19. 1 of Judah returned to his house in *p*
29.35 with the fat of the *p* offerings,
30.22 seven days, offering *p* offerings,
31. 2 burnt offerings and for *p* offerings,
33.16 *p* offerings and thank offerings,
34.28 be gathered to thy grave in *p*,
Ezr 4.17 unto the rest beyond the river, *P*,
5. 7 thus; Unto Darius the king, all *p*.
7.12 unto Ezra the priest,...perfect *p*,
9.12 nor seek their *p* or their wealth
Neh 5. 8 Then held they their *p*, and found
8.11 Hold your *p*, for the day is holy;
Est 4.14 if thou altogether holdest thy *p*
9.30 with words of *p* and truth,
10. 3 and speaking *p* to all his seed.
Job 5.23 of the field shall be at *p* with thee.
24 that thy tabernacle shall be in *p*;
11. 3 thy lies make men hold their *p*?
13. 5 ye would altogether hold your *p*!
13 Hold your *p*, let me alone, that I
22.21 now thyself with him, and be at *p*:
25. 2 he maketh *p* in his high places.
29.10 The nobles held their *p*, and their
33.31 me: hold thy *p*, and I will speak.
33 hold thy *p*, and I shall teach thee
Ps 4. 8 both lay me down in *p*, and sleep:
7. 4 unto him that was at *p* with me;
28. 3 which speak *p* to their neighbors,
29.11 Lord will bless his people with *p*.
34.14 and do good; seek *p*, and pursue it.
35.20 For they speak not *p*: but they
37.11 themselves in the abundance of *p*.
37 for the end of that man is *p*.
39. 2 dumb with silence, I held my *p*,
12 hold not thy *p* at my tears: for I
55.18 He that delivered my soul in *p*
20 against such as be at *p* with him:
72. 3 mountains...bring *p* to the people,
7 abundance of *p* so long as the moon
83. 1 hold not thy *p*, and be not still,
85. 8 he will speak *p* unto his people,
10 righteousness and *p* have kissed
109. 1 Hold not thy *p*, O God of my
119.165 Great *p* have they which love
120. 6 long dwelt with him that hateth *p*.
7 I am for *p*: but when I speak, they
122. 6 Pray for the *p* of Jerusalem: they
7 *P* be within thy walls, and
8 I will now say, *P* be within thee.
125. 5 iniquity: but *p* shall be upon Israel.
128. 6 children, and *p* upon Israel.
147.14 He maketh *p* in thy borders, and
Pr 3. 2 long life, and *p*, shall they add to
17 and all her paths are *p*.
7.14 I have *p* offerings with me; this
11.12 of understanding holdeth his *p*.

12.20 but to the counsellers of *p* is joy.
16. 7 his enemies to be at *p* with him.
17.28 Even a fool, when he holdeth his *p*,
Ec 3. 8 a time of war, and a time of *p*.
Isa 9. 6 Father, The Prince of *P*.
7 increase of his government and *p*
26. 3 wilt keep him in perfect *p*, whose
12 Lord, thou wilt ordain *p* for us:
27. 5 that he may make *p* with me;
5 me; and he shall make *p* with me.
32.17 work of righteousness shall be *p*;
33. 7 the ambassadors of *p* shall weep
36.21 they held their *p*, and answered
38.17 for *p* I had great bitterness: but
39. 8 shall be *p* and truth in my days.
42.14 I have long time holden my *p*;
45. 7 I make *p*, and create evil: I the
48.18 then had thy *p* been as a river, and
22 There is no *p*, saith the Lord, unto
52. 7 good tidings, that publisheth *p*;
53. 5 chastisement of our *p* was upon
54.10 the covenant of my *p* be removed,
13 great shall be the *p* of thy children.
55.12 with joy, and be led forth with *p*:
57. 2 He shall enter into *p*: they shall
11 have not I held my *p* even of old,
19 *P*, *p* to him that is far off, and to
21 There is no *p*, saith my God, to the
59. 8 The way of *p* they know not; and
8 goeth therein shall not know *p*.
60.17 I will also make thy officers *p*, and
62. 1 Zion's sake will I not hold my *p*,
6 never hold their *p* day nor night:
64.12 wilt thou hold thy *p*, and afflict us
66.12 I will extend *p* to her like a river,
Jer 4.10 Ye shall have *p*: whereas the sword
19 I cannot hold my *p*, because thou
6.14 saying, *P*, *p*; when there is no *p*.
8.11 saying, *P*, *p*; when there is no *p*.
15 We looked for *p*, but no good came;
12. 5 if in the land of *p*, wherein thou
12 of the land: no flesh shall have *p*.
14.13 will give you assured *p* in this place.
19 looked for *p*, and there is no good;
16. 5 taken away my *p* from this people,
23.17 Lord hath said, Ye shall have *p*;
28. 9 prophet which prophesieth of *p*,
29. 7 seek the *p* of the city whither I have
7 in the *p* thereof shall ye have *p*.
11 thoughts of *p*, and not of evil, to
30. 5 of trembling, of fear, and not of *p*.
33. 6 the abundance of *p* and truth.
34. 5 But thou shalt die in *p*: and with
43.12 he shall go forth from thence in *p*.
La 3.17 removed my soul far off from *p*:
Eze 7.25 they shall seek *p*, and there shall
13.10 saying, *P*; and there was no *p*;
16 which see visions of *p* for her, and
16 there is no *p*, saith the Lord God.
34.25 make with them a covenant of *p*,
37.26 make a covenant of *p* with them;
43.27 the altar, and your *p* offerings;
45.15 burnt offering, and for *p* offerings,
17 burnt offering, and the *p* offerings,
46. 2 burnt offering and his *p* offerings,
12 burnt offering or *p* offerings
12 burnt offering and his *p* offerings,
Dan 4. 1 earth: *P* be multiplied unto you.
6.25 earth; *P* be multiplied unto you.
8.25 and by *p* shall destroy many:
10.19 *p* be unto thee, be strong, yea, be
Am 5.22 the *p* offerings of your fat beasts.
Ob 7 men that were at *p* with thee have
Mic 3. 5 bite with their teeth, and cry, *P*;
5. 5 this man shall be the *p*, when the
Na 1.15 good tidings, that publisheth *p*!
Zep 1. 7 Hold thy *p* at the presence of the
Hag 2. 9 in this place will I give *p*, saith
Zec 6.13 the counsel of *p* shall be between
8.10 was there any *p* to him that went
16 execute...judgment of truth and *p*

19 therefore love the truth and *p*.
9.10 he shall speak *p* unto the heathen:
Mal 2. 5 covenant...with him of life and *p*;
6 he walked with me in *p* and equity,
Mt 10.13 worthy, let your *p* come upon it:
13 worthy, let your *p* return to you.
34 that I am come to send *p* on earth:
34 I came not to send *p*, but a sword.
20.31 because they should hold their *p*:
26.63 But Jesus held his *p*. And the high
Mk 1.25 Hold thy *p*, and come out of him.
3. 4 or to kill? But they held their *p*.
4.39 and said unto the sea, *P*, be still.
5.34 go in *p*, and be whole of thy plague.
9.34 But they held their *p*: for by the
50 and have *p* one with another.
10.48 him that he should hold his *p*:
14.61 held his *p*, and answered nothing.
Lk 1.79 to guide our feet into the way of *p*.
2.14 on earth *p*, good will toward men.
29 lettest thou thy servant depart in *p*,
4.35 Hold thy *p*, and come out of him.
7.50 faith hath saved thee: go in *p*.
8.48 hath made thee whole; go in *p*.
10. 5 enter, first say, *P* be to this house.
6 And if the son of *p* be there, your
6 your *p* shall rest upon it: if not, it
11.21 his palace, his goods are in *p*:
12.51 that I am come to give *p* on earth?
14. 4 And they held their *p*. And he
32 and desireth conditions of *p*.
18.39 him, that he should hold his *p*:
19.38 *p* in heaven,...glory in the highest.
40 if these should hold their *p*, the
42 things which belong unto thy *p*!
20.26 at his answer, and held their *p*.
24.36 saith unto them, *P* be unto you.
Jn 14.27 *P* I leave with you, my *p* I give
16.33 you, that in me ye might have *p*.
20.19 saith unto them, *P* be unto you.
21 Jesus to them again, *P* be unto you:
26 the midst, and said, *P* be unto you.
Ac 10.36 preaching *p* by Jesus Christ:
11.18 held their *p*, and glorified God,
12.17 with the hand to hold their *p*,
20 desired *p*; because their country
15.13 after they had held their *p*, James
33 were let go in *p* from the brethren
16.36 now therefore depart, and go in *p*.
18. 9 but speak, and hold not thy *p*:
Ro 1. 7 Grace to you and *p* from God our
2.10 But glory, honor, and *p*, to every
3.17 the way of *p* have they not known:
5. 1 we have *p* with God through our
8. 6 be spiritually minded is life and *p*.
10.15 that preach the gospel of *p*, and
14.17 but righteousness, and *p*, and joy
19 after the things which make for *p*,
15.13 you with all joy and *p* in believing,
33 Now the God of *p* be with you all.
16.20 God of *p* shall bruise Satan under
1Co 1. 3 Grace be unto you, and *p*, from God
7.15 cases: but God hath called us to *p*.
14.30 sitteth by, let the first hold his *p*.
33 the author of confusion, but of *p*,
16.11 but conduct him forth in *p*, that he
2Co 1. 2 to you and *p* from God our Father,
13.11 comfort, be of one mind, live in *p*;
11 of love and *p* shall be with you.
Gal 1. 3 Grace be to you and *p* from God
5.22 the fruit of the Spirit is love, joy, *p*,
6.16 *p* be on them, and mercy, and upon
Eph 1. 2 Grace be to you, and *p*, from God
2.14 For he is our *p*, who hath made
15 twain one new man, so making *p*;
17 preached *p* to you which were afar
4. 3 unity of the Spirit in the bond of *p*.
6.15 the preparation of the gospel of *p*;
23 *P* be to the brethren, and love
Php 1. 2 Grace be unto you, and *p*, from God
4. 7 the *p* of God, which passeth all
9 and the God of *p* shall be with you.
Col 1. 2 Grace be unto you, and *p*, from
20 made *p* through the blood of his
3.15 the *p* of God rule in your hearts,
1Th 1. 1 Grace be unto you, and *p*, from God
5. 3 when they shall say, *P* and safety;
13 And be at *p* among yourselves.
23 And the very God of *p* sanctify you
2Th 1. 2 Grace unto you, and *p*, from God
3.16 the Lord of *p* himself give you *p*
1Ti 1. 2 mercy, and *p*, from God our Father
2Ti 1. 2 mercy, and *p*, from God the Father
2.22 righteousness, faith, charity, *p*.
Tit 1. 4 mercy, and *p*, from God the Father
Phm 3 Grace to you, and *p*, from God our
Heb 7. 2 King of Salem, which is, King of *p*;
11.31 she had received the spies with *p*.
12.14 Follow *p* with all men, and
13.20 the God of *p*, that brought again
Jas 2.16 Depart in *p*, be ye warmed and
3.18 is sown in *p* of them that make *p*.
1Pe 1. 2 Christ: Grace unto you, and *p*, be
3.11 good; let him seek *p*, and ensue it.
5.14 *P* be with you all that are in Christ
2Pe 1. 2 Grace and *p* be multiplied unto
3.14 that ye may be found of him in *p*,
2Jn 3 Grace be with you, mercy, and *p*,
3Jn 14 *P* be to thee. Our friends salute
Jude 2 you, and *p*, and love, be multiplied.
Rev 1. 4 Grace be unto you, and *p*, from him
6. 4 thereon to take *p* from the earth,

PEACEABLE
Gen 34.21 These men are *p* with us;
2Sa 20.19 that are *p* and faithful in Israel:
1Ch 4.40 land was wide, and quiet, and *p*;
Isa 32.18 shall dwell in a *p* habitation, and
Jer 25.37 the *p* habitations are cut down
1Ti 2. 2 we may lead a quiet and *p* life in
Heb 12.11 the *p* fruit of righteousness unto
Jas 3.17 first pure, then *p*, gentle, and easy

PEACEABLY
Gen 37. 4 and could not speak *p* unto him.
Jdg 11.13 now...restore those lands again *p*.
21.13 Rimmon, and to call *p* unto them.
1Sa 16. 4 coming, and said, Comest thou *p*?
5 And he said, *P*: I am come to
1Ki 2.13 And she said, Comest thou *p*?
13 And he said, *P*.
1Ch 12.17 If ye be come *p* unto me to help me,
Jer 9. 8 one speaketh *p* to his neighbor
Dan 11.21 he shall come in *p*, and obtain
24 He shall enter *p* even upon the
Ro 12.18 lieth in you, live *p* with all men.

PEACEMAKERS
Mt 5. 9 Blessed are the *p*: for they shall

PEARL
Mt 13.46 he had found one *p* of great price,
Rev 21.21 every several gate was of one *p*:

PEARLS
Job 28.18 shall be made of coral, or of *p*:
Mt 7. 6 cast ye your *p* before swine,
13.45 a merchant man, seeking goodly *p*:
1Ti 2. 9 hair, or gold, or *p*, or costly array;
Rev 17. 4 gold and precious stones and *p*,
18.12 and precious stones, and of *p*, and
16 gold, and precious stones, and *p*!
21.21 the twelve gates were twelve *p*;

PECULIAR
Ex 19. 5 ye shall be a *p* treasure unto me
Dt 14. 2 thee to be a *p* people unto himself,
26.18 thee this day to be his *p* people,
Ps 135. 4 and Israel for his *p* treasure.
Ec 2. 8 and the *p* treasure of kings and of
Tit 2.14 a *p* people, zealous of good works.
1Pe 2. 9 an holy nation, a *p* people;

PEEP
Isa 8.19 and unto wizards that *p*, and that

PELICAN
Ps 102. 6 I am like a *p* of the wilderness:

PEN
Jdg 5.14 they that handle the *p* of the
Job 19.24 they were graven with an iron *p*
Ps 45. 1 tongue is the *p* of a ready writer.
Isa 8. 1 roll, and write in it with a man's *p*
Jer 8. 8 it; the *p* of the scribes is in vain.
17. 1 Judah is written with a *p* of iron,
3Jn 13 with ink and *p* write unto thee:

PENCE
Mt 18.28 which owed him an hundred *p*:
Mk 14. 5 for more than three hundred *p*,
Lk 7.41 the one owed five hundred *p*, and
10.35 he took out two *p*, and gave them
Jn 12. 5 ointment sold for three hundred *p*,

PENIEL
Gen 32.30 called the name of the place *P*:

PENKNIFE
Jer 36.23 leaves, he cut it with the *p*, and

PENNY
Mt 20. 2 with the laborers for a *p* a day,
9 hour, they received every man a *p*.
10 likewise received every man a *p*.
13 not thou agree with me for a *p*?
22.19 And they brought unto him a *p*.
Mk 12.15 bring me a *p*, that I may see it.
Lk 20.24 Shew me a *p*. Whose image and
Rev 6. 6 A measure of wheat for a *p*, and
6 three measures of barley for a *p*;

PENNYWORTH
Mk 6.37 and buy two hundred *p* of bread,
Jn 6. 7 Two hundred *p* of bread is not

PENTECOST
Ac 2. 1 the day of *P* was fully come,
20.16 to be at Jerusalem the day of *P*.
1Co 16. 8 I will tarry at Ephesus until *P*.
(See illustration on page 570)

PENURY
Pr 14.23 talk of the lips tendeth only to *p*.
Lk 21. 4 but she of her *p* hath cast in all

PEOPLE
Gen 11. 6 Lord said, Behold, the *p* is one,
27.29 Let *p* serve thee, and nations bow
41.55 the *p* cried to Pharaoh for bread:
49.29 I am to be gathered unto my *p*:
Ex 3. 7 surely seen the affliction of my *p*
10 bring forth my *p* the children of
5. 1 Let my *p* go, that they may hold a
6. 7 I will take you to me for a *p*, and I
12.31 get you forth from among my *p*,
14.13 Moses said unto the *p*, Fear ye
31 the *p* feared the Lord, and believed
15.24 the *p* murmured against Moses,
17. 2 the *p* did chide with Moses, and
3 the *p* thirsted there for water; and
3 the *p* murmured against Moses,
4 What shall I do unto this *p*? they
32. 9 unto Moses, I have seen this *p*,
12 repent of this evil against thy *p*.
31 Oh, this *p* have sinned a great sin,
33.10 all the *p* rose up and worshipped,
Lev 20.24 have separated you from other *p*.
Nu 14.11 How long will this *p* provoke me?
14 that thou Lord art among this *p*,
16.47 and made an atonement for the *p*.
21. 7 us. And Moses prayed for the *p*.
22.12 them; thou shalt not curse the *p*:
17 I pray thee, curse me this *p*.
23.24 the *p* shall rise up as a great lion,

Pentecost, or the descent of the Holy Spirit (Ac 2), is the subject of the Maestà *by Duccio (1255-1319).*

Dt 4. 6 is a wise and understanding *p*.
33 Did ever *p* hear the voice of God
7. 6 thou art an holy *p* unto the Lord
6 to be a special *p* unto himself,
14 Thou shalt be blessed above all *p*:
9.13 I have seen this *p*, and, behold, it
14. 2 hath chosen thee to be a peculiar *p*
16.18 judge the *p* with just judgment.
18. 3 be the priest's due from the *p*,
26.19 mayest be an holy *p* unto the Lord
27.15 the *p* shall answer and say, Amen.
32. 6 the Lord, O foolish *p* and unwise?
9 For the Lord's portion is his *p*;
33.29 O *p* saved by the Lord, the shield
Jos 17.14 I am a great *p*, forasmuch as the
24.19 Joshua said unto the *p*, Ye cannot
24 *p* said unto Joshua, The Lord our
25 made a covenant with the *p* that
Jdg 2. 7 the *p* served the Lord all the days
20 *p* hath transgressed my covenant
5. 2 the *p* willingly offered themselves.
14. 3 never a woman...among all my *p*,
16 a riddle unto the children of my *p*,
20. 2 in the assembly of the *p* of God,
8 all the *p* arose as one man, saying,
Ru 1. 6 the Lord had visited his *p* in giving
16 thy *p* shall be my *p*, and thy God
1Sa 9.12 there is a sacrifice of the *p* to day
10.24 the *p* shouted, and said, God save
12.20 Samuel said unto the *p*, Fear not:
22 the Lord will not forsake his *p* for
22 pleased the Lord to make you his *p*.
2Sa 3.32 grave of Abner; and all the *p* wept.
5. 2 Thou shalt feed my *p* Israel, and
7. 7 I commanded to feed my *p* Israel,
23 whom God went to redeem for a *p*
24 Israel to be a *p* unto thee for ever:
8.15 judgment and justice unto all his *p*.
14.13 such a thing against the *p* of God?
18. 1 David numbered the *p* that were
1Ki 1.39 the *p* said, God save king Solomon.
40 the *p* piped with pipes, and rejoiced
8.56 hath given rest unto his *p* Israel,
60 all the *p* of the earth may know,
9. 7 proverb and a byword among all *p*:
12.13 the king answered the *p* roughly,
21. 9 set Naboth on high among the *p*:
2Ki 4.42 Give unto the *p*, that they may eat.
6.18 Smite this *p*, I pray thee, with
7.17, 20 *p* trode upon him in the gate,
23. 3 And all the *p* stood to the covenant.
1Ch 13. 4 was right in the eyes of all the *p*.
16.26 For all the gods of the *p* are idols:
28 ye kindreds of the *p*, give unto the
36 *p* said, Amen, and praised the Lord.
29.14 But who am I, and what is my *p*,
17 and now have I seen with joy thy *p*,
18 the thoughts of the heart of thy *p*,
2Ch 1. 9 king over a *p* like the dust of the
2.11 Because the Lord hath loved his *p*,
6. 6 have chosen David to be over my *p*
18. 3 am as thou art, and my *p* as thy *p*;
23.21 And all the *p* of the land rejoiced:
29.36 that God had prepared the *p*: for
31. 8 blessed the Lord, and his *p* Israel.
Ezr 3.13 the noise of the weeping of the *p*:
9.11 the filthiness of the *p* of the lands,
Neh 8. 3 ears of all the *p* were attentive
5 the book in the sight of all the *p*;
6 And all the *p* answered, Amen,
9 and the Levites that taught the *p*,
Est 1.22 and to every *p* after their language,
3. 8 their laws are diverse from all *p*;
7. 4 For we are sold, I and my *p*, to be
Job 12. 2 No doubt but ye are the *p*, and
17. 6 made me also a byword of the *p*;
34.20 the *p* shall be troubled at midnight,
36.31 For by them judgeth he the *p*; he
Ps 2. 1 and the *p* imagine a vain thing?
7. 8 The Lord shall judge the *p*:
28. 9 Save thy *p*, and bless thine
29.11 Lord will give strength unto his *p*;
11 Lord will bless his *p* with peace.
33.10 the devices of the *p* of none effect.
44.12 Thou sellest thy *p* for nought, and
47. 1 O clap your hands, all ye *p*; shout;
49. 1 Hear this, all ye *p*; give ear, all
60. 3 hast shewed thy *p* hard things:
62. 8 ye *p*, pour out your heart before
66. 8 O bless our God, ye *p*, and make
67. 3 Let the *p* praise thee, O God; let
3 O God; let all the *p* praise thee.
4 thou shalt judge the *p* righteously,
5 Let the *p* praise thee, O God; let
5 O God; let all the *p* praise thee.
72. 2 judge thy *p* with righteousness,
3 shall bring peace to the *p*, and the
4 He shall judge the poor of the *p*,
77.15 with thine arm redeemed thy *p*.
78. 1 Give ear, O my *p*, to my law:
79.13 we thy *p* and sheep of thy pasture
85. 8 for he will speak peace unto his *p*,
89.15 the *p* that know the joyful sound:
94.14 For the Lord will not cast off his *p*,
95. 7 we are the *p* of his pasture, and
96. 7 O ye kindreds of the *p*, give unto
10 he shall judge the *p* righteously.
13 and the *p* with his truth.
97. 6 and all the *p* see his glory.
99. 1 Lord reigneth; let the *p* tremble:
100. 3 we are his *p*, and the sheep of his
105. 1 known his deeds among the *p*.
106.48 let all the *p* say, Amen. Praise ye
111. 6 He hath shewed his *p* the power of
9 He sent redemption unto his *p*: he
114. 1 from a *p* of strange language;
116.14 now in the presence of all his *p*.
18 now in the presence of all his *p*,
117. 1 ye nations: praise him, all ye *p*.
125. 2 so the Lord is round about his *p*
144.15 happy is that *p*, whose God is the
148.11 Kings of the earth, and all *p*;
149. 4 the Lord taketh pleasure in his *p*:
Pr 11.14 Where no counsel is, the *p* fall:
14.28 of *p* is the king's honor: but in
34 but sin is a reproach to any *p*.
29. 2 wicked beareth rule, the *p* mourn.
18 there is no vision, the *p* perish:
Isa 1. 3 not know, my *p* doth not consider.
3.15 What mean ye that ye beat my *p*
5.13 my *p* are gone into captivity.
6. 5 the midst of a *p* of unclean lips:
9 Go, and tell this *p*, Hear ye indeed,
10 Make the heart of this *p* fat, and
8. 6 *p* refuseth the waters of Shiloah
19 should not a *p* seek unto their God?
9. 2 The *p* that walked in darkness have
11.10 shall stand for an ensign of the *p*;
12. 4 declare his doings among the *p*,
27.11 for it is a *p* of no understanding:
29.13 *p* draw near me with their mouth,
30. 6 to a *p* that shall not profit them.
9 That this is a rebellious *p*, lying
34. 1 hearken, ye *p*: let the earth hear,
40. 1 comfort ye my *p*, saith your God.
7 upon it: surely the *p* is grass.
42. 6 give thee for a covenant of the *p*,
43. 9 and let the *p* be assembled: who
21 This *p* have I formed for myself;
49.13 for the Lord hath comforted his *p*,
51. 4 to rest for a light of the *p*.
5 and mine arms shall judge the *p*;
7 the *p* in whose heart is my law;

52. 5 my *p* is taken away for nought?
6 my *p* shall know my name:
9 for the Lord hath comforted his *p*,
53. 8 for the transgression of my *p* was
55. 4 given him for a witness to the *p*,
4 leader and commander to the *p*.
58. 1 shew my *p* their transgression,
60. 2 earth, and gross darkness the *p*:
63. 6 tread down the *p* in mine anger,
Jer 2.13 my *p* have committed two evils;
4.11 toward the daughter of my *p*, not
22 For my *p* is foolish, they have not
5.21 Hear now this, O foolish *p*, and
7.23 be your God, and ye shall be my *p*:
10. 3 For the customs of the *p* are vain:
12.16 diligently learn the ways of my *p*,
16 they taught my *p* to swear by Baal;
16. 5 taken away my peace from this *p*,
18.15 Because my *p* hath forgotten me,
23.34 prophet, and the priest, and the *p*,
26. 9 *p* were gathered against Jeremiah
27.12 and serve him and his *p*, and live.
13 Why will ye die, thou and thy *p*, by
28.15 thou makest this *p* to trust in a lie.
31. 7 Lord, save thy *p*, the remnant of
32.38 And they shall be my *p*, and I will
39. 9 the remnant of the *p* that remained
50. 6 My *p* hath been lost sheep: their
Eze 22.29 *p* of the land have used oppression,
33. 3 blow the trumpet, and warn the *p*;
37.12 O my *p*, I will open your graves,
27 their God, and they shall be my *p*,
Dan 3.29 That every *p*, nation,...language,
6.25 Darius wrote unto all *p*, nations,
11.32 but the *p* that do know their God
Hos 1. 9 for ye are not my *p*, and I will not
10 Ye are not my *p*, there it shall be
2.23 Thou art my *p*; and they shall say,
4. 6 My *p* are destroyed for lack of
8 They eat up the sin of my *p*, and
11. 7 my *p* are bent to backsliding from
Joel 2.17 Spare thy *p*, O Lord, and give not
Am 7.15 Go, prophesy unto my *p* Israel.
8. 2 end is come upon my *p* of Israel;
9.10 All the sinners of my *p* shall die
14 bring again the captivity of my *p*
Jon 1. 8 country? and of what *p* art thou?
3. 5 So the *p* of Nineveh believed God,
Mic 1. 2 Hear, all ye *p*; hearken, O earth,
2. 9 women of my *p* have ye cast out
3. 5 the prophets that make my *p* err,
4. 1 the hills; and *p* shall flow unto it.
3 he shall judge among many *p*,
5. 7 of many *p* as a dew from the Lord,
6. 2 hath a controversy with his *p*, and
3 O my *p*, what have I done unto
Hab 2.13 the *p* shall labor in the very fire,
13 and the *p* shall weary themselves
3.13 forth for the salvation of thy *p*,
Zep 2. 9 remnant of my *p* shall possess
3.20 a praise among all *p* of the earth,
Hag 1.12 and the *p* did fear before the Lord,
13 in the Lord's message unto the *p*,
14 spirit of all the remnant of the *p*;
2. 4 and be strong, all ye *p* of the land,
Zec 7. 5 Speak unto all the *p* of the land,
8. 6 the remnant of this *p* in these days,
8 shall be my *p*, and I will be their
13. 9 hear them: I will say, It is my *p*:
14. 2 residue of the *p* shall not be cut off
Mt 1.21 shall save his *p* from their sins.
2. 4 and scribes of the *p* together, he
6 Governor,...shall rule my *p* Israel.
4.16 The *p* which sat in darkness saw
23 all manner of disease among the *p*.
24 they brought unto him all sick *p*
25 great multitudes of *p* from Galilee,
7.28 *p* were astonished at his doctrine:
9.23 and the *p* making a noise,
25 when the *p* were put forth, he went
35 and every disease among the *p*.

12.23 all the *p* were amazed, and said,
46 While he yet talked to the *p*,
14.13 and when the *p* had heard thereof,
15. 8 *p* draweth nigh unto me with their
21.23 the elders of the *p* came unto him
26 shall say, Of men; we fear the *p*;
26. 3 scribes, and the elders of the *p*,
5 there be an uproar among the *p*.
47 chief priests and elders of the *p*.
27. 1 and elders of the *p* took counsel
15 to release unto the *p* a prisoner,
25 Then answered all the *p*, and said,
64 him away, and say unto the *p*,
Mk 5.21 side, much *p* gathered unto him:
24 and much *p* followed him, and
6.33 And the *p* saw them departing, and
34 saw much *p*, and was moved with
45 while he sent away the *p*.
7. 6 *p* honoreth me with their lips,
14 he had called all the *p* unto him,
17 entered into the house from the *p*,
8. 6 commanded the *p* to sit down on
6 and they did set them before the *p*.
34 he had called the *p* unto him with
9.15 And straightway all the *p*, when
25 Jesus saw that the *p* came running
10. 1 and the *p* resort unto him again;
46 disciples and a great number of *p*,
11.18 *p* was astonished at his doctrine
32 say, Of men; they feared the *p*:
12.12 lay hold on him, but feared the *p*:
37 the common *p* heard him gladly.
41 beheld how the *p* cast money into
14. 2 lest there be an uproar of the *p*.
15.11 But the chief priests moved the *p*,
15 so Pilate, willing to content the *p*,
Lk 1.10 multitude of the *p* were praying
17 ready a *p* prepared for the Lord.
21 And the *p* waited for Zacharias,
68 hath visited and redeemed his *p*,
77 knowledge of salvation unto his *p*
2.10 great joy, which shall be to all *p*.
31 prepared before the face of all *p*;
32 and the glory of thy *p* Israel.
3.10 And the *p* asked him, saying,
15 And as the *p* were in expectation,
18 preached he unto the *p*.
21 Now when all the *p* were baptized,
4.42 the *p* sought him, and came unto
5. 1 *p* pressed upon him to hear the
3 and taught the *p* out of the ship.
6.17 multitude of *p* out of all Judea
7. 1 sayings in the audience of the *p*,
9 said unto the *p* that followed
11 went with him, and much *p*.
12 much *p* of the city was with her.
16 and, That God hath visited his *p*.
24 speak unto the *p* concerning
29 And all the *p* that heard him, and
8. 4 And when much *p* were gathered
40 the *p* gladly received him: for
42 as he went the *p* thronged him.
47 declared unto him before all the *p*
9.11 And the *p*, when they knew it,
13 go and buy meat for all this *p*.
18 saying, Whom say the *p* that I
37 from the hill, much *p* met him.
11.14 dumb spake; and the *p* wondered.
29 when the *p* were gathered thick
12. 1 an innumerable multitude of *p*,
54 he said also to the *p*, When ye see
13.14 said unto the *p*, There are six days
17 the *p* rejoiced for all the glorious
18.43 all the *p*, when they saw it, gave
19.47 chief of the *p* sought to destroy
48 the *p* were very attentive to hear
20. 1 as he taught the *p* in the temple,
6 say, Of men; all the *p* will stone us:
9 he to speak to the *p* this parable;
19 and they feared the *p*: for they
26 take hold of his words before the *p*:

45 in the audience of all the *p* he said
21.23 in the land, and wrath upon this *p*.
38 all the *p* came early in the morning
22. 2 kill him; for they feared the *p*.
66 the elders of the *p* and the chief
23. 4 to the chief priests and to the *p*,
5 He stirreth up the *p*, teaching
13 priests and the rulers and the *p*,
14 me, as one that perverteth the *p*:
27 followed him a great company of *p*,
35 And the *p* stood beholding. And
48 And all the *p* that came together
24.19 and word before God and all the *p*:
Jn 6.22 *p* which stood on the other side
24 *p* therefore saw that Jesus was
7.12 much murmuring among the *p*
12 said, Nay; but he deceiveth the *p*:
20 *p* answered and said, Thou hast a
31 many of the *p* believed on him,
32 heard that the *p* murmured such
40 Many of the *p*, therefore, when
43 was a division among the *p*
49 this *p* who knoweth not the law are
8. 2 all the *p* came unto him; and he sat
11.42 because of the *p* which stand by I
50 that one man should die for the *p*,
12. 9 Much *p* of the Jews therefore knew
12 next day much *p* that were come to
17 The *p* therefore that was with him
18 For this cause the *p* also met him,
29 The *p* therefore, that stood by, and
34 *p* answered him, We have heard
18.14 that one man should die for the *p*.
Ac 2.47 and having favor with all the *p*.
3. 9 the *p* saw him walking and praising
11 all the *p* ran together unto them in
12 he answered unto the *p*, Ye men of
23 be destroyed from among the *p*.
4. 1 And as they spake unto the *p*, the
2 grieved that they taught the *p*, and
8 Ye rulers of the *p*, and elders of
10 you all, and to all the *p* of Israel,
17 it spread no further among the *p*,
21 punish them, because of the *p*: for
25 and the *p* imagine vain things?
27 *p* of Israel, were gathered together,
5.12 and wonders wrought among the *p*;
13 them: but the *p* magnified them.
20 and speak in the temple to the *p*
25 in the temple, and teaching the *p*.
26 they feared the *p*, lest they should
34 had in reputation among all the *p*,
37 and drew away much *p* after him:
6. 8 wonders and miracles among the *p*.
12 stirred up the *p*, and the elders,
7.17 the *p* grew and multiplied in Egypt,
34 seen the affliction of my *p*
8. 6 the *p* with one accord gave heed
9 and bewitched the *p* of Samaria,
10. 2 which gave much alms to the *p*,
41 Not to all the *p*, but unto witnesses
42 commanded us to preach unto the *p*,
11.24 much *p* was added unto the Lord.
26 with the church, and taught much *p*.
12. 4 Easter to bring him forth to the *p*.
11 expectation of the *p* of the Jews.
22 the *p* gave a shout, saying, It is
13.15 any word of exhortation for the *p*,
17 God of this *p* of Israel chose our
17 exalted the *p* when they dwelt as
24 of repentance to all the *p* of Israel.
31 who are his witnesses unto the *p*.
14.11 the *p* saw what Paul had done,
13 have done sacrifice with the *p*.
14 and ran in among the *p*, crying out,
18 scarce restrained they the *p*,that,
19 who persuaded the *p*, and, having
15.14 take out of them a *p* for his name.
17. 5 sought to bring them out to the *p*.
8 And they troubled the *p* and the
13 thither also, and stirred up the *p*.

Ac 18.10 thee: for I have much *p* in this city.
19. 4 saying unto the *p*, that they should
26 and turned away much *p*, saying
30 would have entered in unto the *p*,
33 have made his defense unto the *p*.
35 the townclerk had appeased the *p*,
21.27 stirred up all the *p*, and laid hands
28 against the *p*, and the law, and
30 was moved, and the *p* ran together:
35 soldiers for the violence of the *p*.
36 For the multitude of the *p* followed
39 thee, suffer me to speak unto the *p*.
40 beckoned with the hand unto the *p*.
23. 5 not speak evil of the ruler of thy *p*.
24.12 neither raising up the *p*, neither in
26.17 Delivering thee from the *p*, and
23 should shew light unto the *p*, and
28. 2 barbarous *p* shewed us no little
17 committed nothing against the *p*,
26 Go unto this *p*, and say, Hearing ye
27 the heart of this *p* is waxed gross,
Ro 9.25 also in Osee, I will call them my *p*,
25 which were not my *p*; and her
26 said unto them, Ye are not my *p*;
10.19 to jealousy by them that are no *p*,
21 a disobedient and gainsaying *p*.
11. 1 then, Hath God cast away his *p*?
2 God hath not cast away his *p* which
15.10 Rejoice, ye Gentiles, with his *p*.
11 Gentiles; and laud him, all ye *p*.
1Co 10. 7 The *p* sat down to eat and drink,
14.21 other lips will I speak unto this *p*:
2Co 6.16 their God, and they shall be my *p*.
Tit 2.14 a peculiar *p*, zealous of good works.
Heb 2.17 reconciliation for the sins of the *p*.
4. 9 therefore a rest to the *p* of God.
5. 3 as for the *p*, so also for himself, to
7. 5 to take tithes of the *p* according
11 (for under it the *p* received the law,)
8.10 God, and they shall be to me a *p*:
9. 7 himself, and for the errors of the *p*:
19 spoken every precept to all the *p*
19 sprinkled...the book, and all the *p*,
10.30 again, The Lord shall judge his *p*.
11.25 suffer affliction with the *p* of God,
13.12 sanctify the *p* with his own blood,
1Pe 2. 9 an holy nation, a peculiar *p*; that
10 Which in time past were not a *p*,
10 but are now the *p* of God: which
2Pe 2. 1 false prophets also among the *p*,
Jude 5 having saved the *p* out of...Egypt,
Rev 5. 9 and tongue, and *p*, and nation;
7. 9 and kindreds, and *p*, and tongues,
11. 9 And they of the *p* and kindreds and
14. 6 and kindred, and tongue, and *p*,
18. 4 Come out of her, my *p*, that ye be
19. 1 a great voice of much *p* in heaven,
21. 3 with them, and they shall be his *p*,

PEOPLE'S

Lev 9.15 And he brought the *p* offering,
Eze 46.18 shall not take of the *p* inheritance
Mt 13.15 For this *p* heart is waxed gross,
Heb 7.27 his own sins, and then for the *p*:

PEOPLES

Rev 10.11 prophesy again before many *p*,
17.15 where the whore sitteth, are *p*, and

PERADVENTURE

Gen 18.24 *P* there be fifty righteous within
50.15 Joseph will *p* hate us, and will
Ex 32.30 *p* I shall make an atonement for
Ro 5. 7 yet *p* for a good man some would
2Ti 2.25 if God *p* will give them repentance

PERCEIVE

Dt 29. 4 hath not given you an heart to *p*,
Jos 22.31 day we *p* that the Lord is among us,
1Sa 12.17 *p* and see that your wickedness is
2Sa 19. 6 for this day I *p*, that if Absalom
2Ki 4. 9 I *p* that this is an holy man of God,
Job 9.11 he passeth on also, but I *p* him not.
23. 8 and backward, but I cannot *p* him:
Pr 1. 2 to *p* the words of understanding;
Ec 3.22 I *p* that there is nothing better,
Isa 6. 9 not; and see ye indeed, but *p* not.
33.19 deeper speech than thou canst *p*:
Mt 13.14 seeing ye shall see, and shall not *p*:
Mk 4.12 seeing they may see, and not *p*;
7.18 Do ye not *p*, that whatsoever thing
8.17 *p* ye not yet, neither understand?
Lk 8.46 I *p* that virtue is gone out of me.
Jn 4.19 Sir, I *p* that thou art a prophet.
12.19 *P* ye how ye prevail nothing?
Ac 8.23 For I *p* that thou art in the gall of
10.34 I *p* that God is no respecter of
17.22 I *p* that in all things ye are too
27.10 I *p*...this voyage will be with hurt
28.26 and seeing ye shall see, and not *p*:
2Co 7. 8 *p* that the same epistle hath made
1Jn 3.16 Hereby *p* we the love of God,

PERCEIVED

Gen 19.33, 35 he *p* not when she lay down,
Jdg 6.22 Gideon *p* that he was an angel
1Sa 3. 8 And Eli *p* that the Lord had called
28.14 And Saul *p* that it was Samuel,
2Sa 5.12 David *p*...the Lord had established
12.19 David *p* that the child was dead:
14. 1 *p* that the king's heart was toward
1Ki 22.33 *p* that it was not the king of Israel
1Ch 14. 2 David *p*...the Lord had confirmed
2Ch 18.32 *p*...it was not the king of Israel,
Neh 6.12 I *p* that God had not sent him;
16 *p* that this work was wrought of
13.10 *p* that the portions of the Levites
Est 4. 1 Mordecai *p* all that was done,
Job 38.18 thou *p* the breadth of the earth?
Ec 1.17 I *p* that this also is vexation of
2.14 and I myself *p* also that one event
Isa 64. 4 have not heard, nor *p* by the ear,
Jer 23.18 and hath *p* and heard his word?
38.27 him; for the matter was not *p*.
Mt 16. 8 Which when Jesus *p*, he said unto
21.45 they *p* that he spake of them.
22.18 Jesus *p* their wickedness, and said
Mk 2. 8 when Jesus *p* in his spirit that
Lk 1.22 they *p* that he had seen a vision
5.22 when Jesus *p* their thoughts, he
9.45 hid from them, that they *p* it not:
20.19 *p* that he had spoken this parable
23 But he *p* their craftiness, and said
Jn 6.15 *p*...they would come and take him
Ac 4.13 *p* that they were unlearned and
23. 6 *p*...the one part were Sadducees,
29 I *p* to be accused of questions of
Gal 2. 9 *p* the grace that was given unto

PERCEIVEST

Pr 14. 7 *p* not in him the lips of knowledge
Lk 6.41 *p* not the beam that is in thine

PERCEIVING

Mk 12.28 *p* that he had answered them well,
Lk 9.47 Jesus, *p* the thought of their heart,
Ac 14. 9 *p* that he had faith to be healed,

PERDITION

Jn 17.12 of them is lost, but the son of *p*;
Php 1.28 is to them an evident token of *p*,
2Th 2. 3 of sin be revealed, the son of *p*;
1Ti 6. 9 drown men in destruction and *p*.
Heb 10.39 not of them who draw back unto *p*;
2Pe 3. 7 of judgment and *p* of ungodly men.
Rev 17. 8 of the bottomless pit, and go into *p*:
11 is of the seven, and goeth into *p*.

PERES

Dan 5.28 *P*; Thy kingdom is divided, and

PERFECT

Gen 6. 9 Noah was a just man and *p* in his
17. 1 walk before me, and be thou *p*.
Lev 22.21 sheep, it shall be *p* to be accepted;
Dt 18.13 shalt be *p* with the Lord thy God.
25.15 shalt have a *p* and just weight,
15 a *p* and just measure shalt thou
32. 4 He is the Rock, his work is *p*:
1Sa 14.41 Lord God of Israel, Give a *p* lot.
2Sa 22.31 As for God, his way is *p*; the word
33 power: and he maketh my way *p*.
1Ki 8.61 Let your heart therefore be *p*
11. 4 his heart was not *p* with the Lord
15. 3 his heart was not *p* with the Lord
14 nevertheless Asa's heart was *p*
2Ki 20. 3 thee in truth and with a *p* heart,
1Ch 12.38 came with a *p* heart to Hebron,
28. 9 serve him with a *p* heart and with
29. 9 with *p* heart they offered willingly
19 unto Solomon my son a *p* heart,
2Ch 4.21 made he of gold, and that *p* gold;
15.17 heart of Asa was *p* all his days.
16. 9 them whose heart is *p* toward him.
19. 9 faithfully, and with a *p* heart.
25. 2 of the Lord, but not with a *p* heart.
Ezr 7.12 unto Ezra the priest,...*p* peace,
Job 1. 1 and that man was *p* and upright,
8 a *p* and an upright man, one that
2. 3 a *p* and an upright man, one that
8.20 God will not cast away a *p* man,
9.20 if I say, I am *p*, it shall also prove
21 Though I were *p*, yet would I not
22 destroyeth the *p* and the wicked
22. 3 that thou makest thy ways *p*?
36. 4 he that is *p* in knowledge is with
37.16 of him which is *p* in knowledge?
Ps 18.30 As for God, his way is *p*: the
32 strength, and maketh my way *p*.
19. 7 law of the Lord is *p*, converting
37.37 Mark the *p* man, and behold the
64. 4 they may shoot in secret at the *p*:
101. 2 behave myself wisely in a *p* way.
2 within my house with a *p* heart.
6 he that walketh in a *p* way, he
138. 8 will *p* that which concerneth me:
139.22 I hate them with *p* hatred: I
Pr 2.21 land, and the *p* shall remain in it.
4.18 more and more unto the *p* day.
11. 5 righteousness of the *p* shall direct
Isa 18. 5 when the bud is *p*, and the sour
26. 3 Thou wilt keep him in *p* peace,
38. 3 thee in truth and with a *p* heart,
42.19 who is blind as he that is *p*, and
Eze 16.14 it was *p* through my comeliness,
27. 3 thou hast said, I am of *p* beauty,
11 they have made thy beauty *p*.
28.12 full of wisdom, and *p* in beauty.
15 Thou wast *p* in thy ways from the
Mt 5.48 Be ye therefore *p*, even as your
48 your Father which is in heaven is *p*.
19.21 If thou wilt be *p*, go and sell that
Lk 1. 3 having had *p* understanding of all
6.40 that is *p* shall be as his master.
Jn 17.23 that they may be made *p* in one;
Ac 3.16 hath given him this *p* soundness
22. 3 *p* manner of the law of the fathers,
24.22 more *p* knowledge of that way,
Ro 12. 2 and acceptable, and *p*, will of God.
1Co 2. 6 wisdom among them that are *p*:
13.10 But when that which is *p* is come,
2Co 12. 9 strength is made *p* in weakness.
13.11 Be *p*, be of good comfort, be of
Gal 3. 3 are ye now made *p* by the flesh?
Eph 4.13 unto a *p* man, unto the measure
Php 3.12 attained, either were already *p*:
15 Let us therefore, as many as be *p*,
Col 1.28 every man *p* in Christ Jesus:
4.12 that ye may stand *p* and complete
1Th 3.10 might *p* that which is lacking
2Ti 3.17 That the man of God may be *p*,
Heb 2.10 the captain of their salvation *p*

5. 9 And being made *p*, he became the
7.19 For the law made nothing *p*, but
9. 9 make him that did the service *p*,
11 a greater and more *p* tabernacle,
10. 1 make the comers thereunto *p*.
11.40 without us should not be made *p*.
12.23 to the spirits of just men made *p*.
13.21 Make you *p* in every good work
Jas 1. 4 But let patience have her *p* work,
4 be *p* and entire, wanting nothing.
17 and every *p* gift is from above,
25 looketh into the *p* law of liberty.
2.22 and by works was faith made *p*?
3. 2 not in word, the same is a *p* man,
1Pe 5.10 suffered a while, make you *p*,
1Jn 4.17 Herein is our love made *p*, that
18 but *p* love casteth out fear:
18 that feareth is not made *p* in love.
Rev 3. 2 have not found thy works *p*

PERFECTED

2Ch 8.16 So the house of the Lord was *p*.
24.13 and the work was *p* by them,
Eze 27. 4 thy builders have *p* thy beauty.
Mt 21.16 and sucklings thou hast *p* praise?
Lk 13.32 and the third day I shall be *p*.
Heb 10.14 by one offering he hath *p* for ever
1Jn 2. 5 in him verily is the love of God *p*:
4.12 in us, and his love is *p* in us.

PERFECTING

2Co 7. 1 *p* holiness in the fear of God.
Eph 4.12 For the *p* of the saints, for the

PERFECTION

Job 11. 7 find out the Almighty unto *p*?
15.29 shall he prolong the *p* thereof
28. 3 darkness, and searcheth out all *p*:
Ps 50. 2 Out of Zion, the *p* of beauty,
119.96 I have seen an end of all *p*:
Isa 47. 9 shall come upon thee in their *p*
La 2.15 The *p* of beauty, The joy of the
Lk 8.14 this life, and bring no fruit to *p*.
2Co 13. 9 this also we wish, even your *p*.
Heb 6. 1 of Christ, let us go on unto *p*;
7.11 *p* were by the Levitical priesthood,

PERFECTLY

Jer 23.20 latter days ye shall consider it *p*.
Mt 14.36 as touched were made *p* whole.
Ac 18.26 unto him the way of God more *p*.
23.15 would inquire something more *p*
23.20 inquire somewhat of him more *p*.
1Co 1.10 but that ye be *p* joined together
1Th 5. 2 know *p* that the day of the Lord

PERFECTNESS

Col 3.14 on charity, which is the bond of *p*.

PERFORM

Gen 26. 3 I will *p* the oath which I sware
Ex 18.18 art not able to *p* it thyself alone.
Ru 3.13 *p* unto thee the part of a kinsman,
1Ki 6.12 then will I *p* my word with thee,
2Ki 23. 3 to *p* the words of this covenant
2Ch 10.15 that the Lord might *p* his word,
Ps 21.11 device, which they are not able to *p*.
61. 8 ever, that I may daily *p* my vows.
119.106 I have sworn, and I will *p* it,
Isa 9. 7 zeal of the Lord of hosts will *p* this.
19.21 vow a vow unto the Lord, and *p* it.
Jer 29.10 and *p* my good word toward you,
Mt 5.33 shalt *p* unto the Lord thine oaths:
Lk 1.72 *p* the mercy promised to our
Ro 4.21 promised, he was able also to *p*.
7.18 how to *p* that which is good I find
2Co 8.11 Now therefore *p* the doing of it;
Php 1. 6 will *p* it until the day of Jesus

PERFORMANCE

Lk 1.45 there shall be a *p* of those things
2Co 8.11 so there may be a *p* also out of

PERFORMED

1Sa 15.11 hath not *p* my commandments.
13 *p* the commandment of the Lord.
2Sa 21.14 *p* all that the king commanded.
1Ki 8.20 And the Lord hath *p* his word
2Ch 6.10 The Lord therefore hath *p* his word
Neh 9. 8 and hast *p* thy words: for thou art
Est 1.15 she hath not *p* the commandment
5. 6 half of the kingdom it shall be *p*.
7. 2 and it shall be *p*, even to the half
Ps 65. 1 and unto thee shall the vow be *p*.
Isa 10.12 the Lord hath *p* his whole work
Jer 23.20 have *p* the thoughts of his heart:
30.24 he have *p* the intents of his heart:
34.18 not *p* the words of the covenant
35.14 The words of Jonadab...are *p*;
16 *p* the commandment of their father,
51.29 purpose of the Lord shall be *p*
Eze 37.14 the Lord have spoken it, and *p* it,
Lk 1.20 day that these things shall be *p*,
2.39 *p* all things according to the law
Ro 15.28 When therefore I have *p* this,

PERFUME

Ex 30.35 And thou shalt make it a *p*, a
37 for the *p* which thou shalt make,
Pr 27. 9 Ointment and *p* rejoice the heart:

PERFUMED

Pr 7.17 have *p* my bed with myrrh, aloes,
SS 3. 6 *p* with myrrh and frankincense,

PERFUMES

Isa 57. 9 and didst increase thy *p*, and

PERGA

Ac 13.13 they came to *P* in Pamphylia:
14 when they departed from *P*, they
14.25 they had preached the word in *P*,

PERGAMOS

Rev 1.11 and unto *P*, and unto Thyatira,
2.12 angel of the church in *P* write;

PERIL

La 5. 9 gat our bread with the *p* of our lives,
Ro 8.35 or nakedness, or *p*, or sword?

PERILOUS

2Ti 3. 1 the last days *p* times shall come.

PERILS

2Co 11.26 in *p* of waters, in *p* of robbers,
26 in *p* by mine own countrymen,
26 *p* by the heathen, in *p* in the city,
26 in the city, in *p* in the wilderness,
26 in the wilderness, in *p* in the sea,
26 the sea, in *p* among false brethren;

PERISH

Gen 41.36 land *p* not through the famine.
Ex 19.21 Lord to gaze, and many of them *p*.
21.26 or the eye of his maid, that it *p*;
Lev 26.38 And ye shall *p* among the heathen,
Nu 17.12 Behold, we die, we *p*, we all *p*.
24.20 latter end shall be that he *p* for ever.
24 Eber, and he also shall *p* for ever.
Dt 4.26 shall soon utterly *p* from off the land
8.19 you this day that ye shall surely *p*.
20 so shall ye *p*: because ye would not
11.17 ye *p* quickly from off the good land
26. 5 A Syrian ready to *p* was my father,
28.20 destroyed, and until thou *p* quickly;
22 they shall pursue thee until thou *p*.
30.18 you this day, that ye shall surely *p*,
Jos 23.13 until ye *p* from off this good land
16 shall *p* quickly from off the good
Jdg 5.31 So let all thine enemies *p*, O Lord:
1Sa 26.10 shall descend into battle, and *p*.
27. 1 *p* one day by the hand of Saul:
2Ki 9. 8 For the whole house of Ahab shall *p*:

Est 3.13 to kill, and to cause to *p*, all Jews,
4.16 according to the law: and if I *p*, I *p*.
7. 4 to be destroyed, to be slain, and to *p*.
8.11 to destroy, to slay, and to cause to *p*,
9.28 nor the memorial of them *p* from
Job 3. 3 Let the day *p* wherein I was born,
4. 9 By the blast of God they *p*, and by
20 *p* for ever without any regarding it.
6.18 aside; they go to nothing, and *p*.
8.13 and the hypocrite's hope shall *p*:
18.17 His remembrance shall *p* from the
20. 7 he shall *p* for ever like his own dung
29.13 blessing of him that was ready to *p*
31.19 have seen any *p* for want of clothing
34.15 All flesh shall *p* together, and man
36.12 they shall *p* by the sword, and
Ps 1. 6 but the way of the ungodly shall *p*.
2.12 lest he be angry, and ye *p* from the
9. 3 they shall fall and *p* at thy presence.
18 expectation of the poor shall not *p*
37.20 the wicked shall *p*, and the enemies
41. 5 When shall he die, and his name *p*?
49.10 the fool and the brutish person *p*,
12 not: he is like the beasts that *p*.
20 not, is like the beasts that *p*.
68. 2 the wicked *p* at...presence of God.
73.27 they that are far from thee shall *p*:
80.16 *p* at the rebuke of thy countenance.
83.17 let them be put to shame and *p*:
92. 9 Lord, for, lo, thine enemies shall *p*;
102.26 They shall *p*, but thou shalt endure:
112.10 the desire of the wicked shall *p*.
146. 4 in that very day his thoughts *p*.
Pr 10.28 expectation of the wicked shall *p*.
11. 7 man dieth, his expectation shall *p*:
10 the wicked *p*, there is shouting.
19. 9 and he that speaketh lies shall *p*.
21.28 A false witness shall *p*: but the man
28.28 when they *p*, the righteous increase.
29.18 there is no vision, the people *p*:
31. 6 drink unto him that is ready to *p*,
Ec 5.14 But those riches *p* by evil travail:
Isa 26.14 and made all their memory to *p*.
27.13 ready to *p* in the land of Assyria,
29.14 wisdom of their wise men shall *p*,
41.11 they that strive with thee shall *p*.
60.12 that will not serve thee shall *p*;
Jer 4. 9 that the heart of the king shall *p*,
6.21 neighbor and his friend shall *p*.
10.11 they shall *p* from the earth, and
15 time of their visitation they shall *p*.
18.18 the law shall not *p* from the priest,
27.10 drive you out, and ye should *p*.
15 drive you out, and that ye might *p*,
40.15 and the remnant in Judah *p*?
48. 8 the valley also shall *p*, and the plain
51.18 time of their visitation they shall *p*.
Eze 7.26 but the law shall *p* from the priest,
25. 7 cause thee to *p* out of the countries:
Dan 2.18 Daniel and his fellows should not *p*
Am 1. 8 the remnant of the Philistines shall *p*,
2.14 the flight shall *p* from the swift,
3.15 the houses of ivory shall *p*, and the
Jon 1. 6 will think upon us, that we *p* not.
14 let us not *p* for this man's life, and
3. 9 from his fierce anger, that we *p* not?
Zec 9. 5 and the king shall *p* from Gaza,
Mt 5.29, 30 one of thy members should *p*,
8.25 him, saying, Lord, save us: we *p*.
9.17 wine runneth out, and the bottles *p*:
18.14 one of these little ones should *p*.
26.52 the sword shall *p* with the sword.
Mk 4.38 Master, carest thou not that we *p*?
Lk 5.37 be spilled, and the bottles shall *p*.
8.24 saying, Master, master, we *p*.
13. 3, 5 repent, ye shall all likewise *p*.
33 that a prophet *p* out of Jerusalem.
15.17 and to spare, and I *p* with hunger!
21.18 shall not an hair of your head *p*.
Jn 3.15 believeth in him should not *p*,
16 believeth in him should not *p*,

Jn 10.28 and they shall never *p* neither
11.50 and that the whole nation *p* not.
Ac 8.20 Thy money *p* with thee,
13.41 ye despisers, and wonder, and *p*:
Ro 2.12 law shall also *p* without law:
1Co 1.18 cross is to them that *p* foolishness;
8.11 shall the weak brother *p*, for whom
2Co 2.15 that are saved, and in them that *p*:
4.16 but though our outward man *p*,
Col 2.22 Which all are to *p* with the using;)
2Th 2.10 unrighteousness in them that *p*;
Heb 1.11 They shall *p*; but thou remainest;
2Pe 2.12 utterly *p* in their own corruption;
3. 9 not willing that any should *p*, but

PERISHED

Nu 16.33 *p* from among the congregation.
21.30 Heshbon is *p* even unto Dibon,
Jos 22.20 man *p* not alone in his iniquity.
2Sa 1.27 fallen, and the weapons of war *p*!
Job 4. 7 thee, who ever *p*, being innocent?
30. 2 profit me, in whom old age was *p*?
Ps 9. 6 their memorial is *p* with them.
10.16 the heathen are *p* out of his land.
83.10 Which *p* at En-dor: they became
119.92 then have *p* in mine affliction.
Ec 9. 6 hatred, and their envy, is now *p*:
Jer 7.28 truth is *p*, and is cut off from their
48.36 riches that he hath gotten are *p*.
49. 7 is counsel *p* from the prudent?
La 3.18 and my hope is *p* from the Lord:
Joel 1.11 because the harvest of the field is *p*.
Jon 4.10 up in a night, and *p* in a night:
Mic 4. 9 no king in thee? is thy counsellor *p*?
7. 2 The good man is *p* out of the earth:
Mt 8.32 into the sea, and *p* in the waters.
Lk 11.51 *p* between the altar and the temple:
Ac 5.37 he also *p*; and all, even as many
1Co 15.18 are fallen asleep in Christ are *p*.
Heb 11.31 By faith the harlot Rahab *p* not
2Pe 3. 6 being overflowed with water, *p*:
Jude 11 and *p* in the gainsaying of Core.

PERISHETH

Job 4.11 The old lion *p* for lack of prey, and
Pr 11. 7 and the hope of unjust men *p*.
Ec 7.15 just man that *p* in his righteousness,
Isa 57. 1 righteous *p*, and no man layeth
Jer 9.12 for what the land *p* and is burned up
48.46 the people of Chemosh *p*: for thy
Jn 6.27 Labor not for the meat which *p*,
Jas 1.11 and the grace of the fashion of it *p*:
1Pe 1. 7 more precious than of gold that *p*,

PERJURED

1Ti 1.10 for liars, for *p* persons, and if

PERMISSION

1Co 7. 6 But I speak this by *p*, and not of

PERMIT

1Co 16. 7 a while with you, if the Lord *p*.
Heb 6. 3 And this will we do, if God *p*.

PERMITTED

Ac 26. 1 Thou art *p* to speak for thyself.
1Co 14.34 it is not *p* unto them to speak;

PERNICIOUS

2Pe 2. 2 many shall follow their *p* ways;

PERPETUAL

Gen 9.12 is with you, for *p* generations:
Ex 29. 9 shall be theirs for a *p* statute:
30. 8 a *p* incense before the Lord
31.16 generations, for a *p* covenant.
Lev 3.17 a *p* statute for your generations
6.20 fine flour for a meat offering *p*,
24. 9 Lord made by fire by a *p* statute.
25.34 sold; for it is their *p* possession.
Nu 19.21 it shall be a *p* statute unto them,
Ps 9. 6 destructions are come to a *p* end:
74. 3 thy feet unto the *p* desolations.
78.66 he put them to a *p* reproach.
Jer 5.22 bound of the sea by a *p* decree,
8. 5 slidden back by a *p* backsliding?
15.18 Why is my pain *p*, and my wound
18.16 land desolate, and a *p* hissing;
23.40 and a *p* shame, which shall not
25. 9 and an hissing, and *p* desolations.
12 and will make it *p* desolations.
49.13 the cities thereof shall be *p* wastes.
50. 5 to the Lord in a *p* covenant that
51.39 and sleep a *p* sleep, and not wake,
57 shall sleep a *p* sleep, and not wake,
Eze 35. 5 Because thou hast had a *p* hatred,
9 will make thee *p* desolations, and
46.14 by a *p* ordinance unto the Lord.
Hab 3. 6 scattered, the *p* hills did bow:
Zep 2. 9 and saltpits, and a *p* desolation:

PERPETUALLY

1Ki 9. 3 mine heart shall be there *p*.
2Ch 7.16 mine heart shall be there *p*.
Am 1.11 all pity, and his anger did tear *p*,

PERPLEXED

Est 3.15 drink; but the city Shushan was *p*.
Joel 1.18 the herds of cattle are *p*, because
Lk 9. 7 And he was *p*, because that it was
24. 4 as they were much *p* thereabout,
2Co 4. 8 we are *p*, but not in despair;

PERPLEXITY

Isa 22. 5 and of *p* by the Lord God of hosts
Mic 7. 4 cometh; now shall be their *p*.
Lk 21.25 earth distress of nations, with *p*;

PERSECUTE

Job 19.22 Why do ye *p* me as God, and are
28 Why *p* we him, seeing the root of
Ps 7. 1 save me from all them that *p* me,
5 Let the enemy *p* my soul, and
10. 2 in his pride doth *p* the poor:
31.15 enemies,...from them that *p* me.
35. 3 the way against them that *p* me:
6 let the angel of the Lord *p* them.
69.26 they *p* him whom thou hast smitten;
71.11 forsaken him: *p* and take him;
83.15 So *p* them with thy tempest, and
119.84 judgment on them that *p* me?
86 they *p* me wrongfully; help thou
Jer 17.18 them be confounded that *p* me,
29.18 I will *p* them with the sword,
La 3.66 *P* and destroy them in anger
Mt 5.11 men shall revile you, and *p* you,
44 despitefully use you, and *p* you;
10.23 when they *p* you in this city, flee
23.34 and *p* them from city to city:
Lk 11.49 of them they shall slay and *p*:
21.12 their hands on you, and *p* you,
Jn 5.16 therefore did the Jews *p* Jesus,
15.20 me, they will also *p* you;
Ro 12.14 Bless them which *p* you: bless, and

PERSECUTED

Dt 30. 7 that hate thee, which *p* thee.
Ps 109.16 but *p* the poor and needy man,
119.161 have *p* me without a cause: but
143. 3 For the enemy hath *p* my soul; he
Isa 14. 6 ruled the nations in anger, is *p*,
La 3.43 covered with anger, and *p* us:
Mt 5.10 are *p* for righteousness' sake:
12 so *p* they the prophets which were
Jn 15.20 If they have *p* me, they will also
Ac 7.52 prophets have not your fathers *p*?
22. 4 And I *p* this way unto the death,
26.11 I *p* them even unto strange cities.
1Co 4.12 we bless; being *p*, we suffer it:
15. 9 because I *p* the church of God.
2Co 4. 9 *P*, but not forsaken; cast down,
Gal 1.13 measure I *p* the church of God,
23 he which *p* us in times past now
4.29 *p* him that was born after the
1Th 2.15 own prophets, and have *p* us:
Rev 12.13 *p* the woman which brought forth

PERSECUTEST

Ac 9. 4 him, Saul, Saul, why *p* thou me?
5 said, I am Jesus whom thou *p*:
22. 7 me, Saul, Saul, why *p* thou me?
8 Jesus of Nazareth, whom thou *p*.
26.14 Saul, Saul, why *p* thou me? it is
15 he said, I am Jesus whom thou *p*.

PERSECUTING

Php 3. 6 Concerning zeal, *p* the church;

PERSECUTION

La 5. 5 Our necks are under *p*: we
Mt 13.21 or *p* ariseth because of the word,
Mk 4.17 or *p* ariseth for the word's sake,
Ac 8. 1 was a great *p* against the church
11.19 the *p* that arose about Stephen
13.50 and raised *p* against Paul and
Ro 8.35 shall tribulation, or distress, or *p*,
Gal 5.11 circumcision, why do I...suffer *p*?
6.12 suffer *p* for the cross of Christ.
2Ti 3.12 godly in Christ Jesus shall suffer *p*.

PERSECUTIONS

Mk 10.30 and children, and lands, with *p*;
2Co 12.10 *p*, in distresses for Christ's sake:
2Th 1. 4 faith in all your *p* and tribulations
2Ti 3.11 *P*, afflictions, which came unto me
11 at Lystra; what *p* I endured:

PERSECUTOR

1Ti 1.13 before a blasphemer, and a *p*,

PERSECUTORS

Neh 9.11 *p* thou threwest into the deeps,
Ps 7.13 his arrows against the *p*.
119.157 are my *p* and mine enemies;
142. 6 very low: deliver me from my *p*;
Jer 15.15 me, and revenge me of my *p*;
20.11 therefore my *p* shall stumble, and
La 1. 3 all her *p* overtook her between
4.19 Our *p* are swifter than the eagles

PERSEVERANCE

Eph 6.18 with all *p* and supplication for

PERSIS

Ro 16.12 Salute the beloved *P*, which

PERSON

Gen 39. 6 Joseph was a goodly *p*, and well
Ex 12.48 no uncircumcised *p* shall eat thereof.
Lev 19.15 not respect the *p* of the poor,
15 nor honor the *p* of the mighty:
Nu 5. 6 the Lord, and that *p* be guilty;
19.17 for an unclean *p* they shall take of
18 And a clean *p* shall take hyssop,
22 whatsoever the unclean *p* toucheth
31.19 whosoever hath killed any *p*, and
35.11 which killeth any *p* at unawares.
15 one that killeth any *p* unawares
30 Whoso killeth any *p*, the murderer
30 shall not testify against any *p* to
Dt 15.22 and the clean *p* shall eat it alike,
27.25 reward to slay an innocent *p*.
28.50 shall not regard the *p* of the old,
Jos 20. 3 that killeth any *p* unawares and
9 that whosoever killeth any *p* at
1Sa 9. 2 of Israel a goodlier *p* than he:
16.18 prudent in matters, and a comely *p*,
25.35 voice, and have accepted thy *p*.
2Sa 4.11 men have slain a righteous *p* in
14.14 neither doth God respect any *p*:
17.11 thou go to battle in thine own *p*.
Job 13. 8 Will ye accept his *p*? will ye
22.29 up; and he shall save the humble *p*.

32.21 I pray you, accept any man's *p*,
Ps 15. 4 In whose eyes a vile *p* is contemned;
49.10 the fool and the brutish *p* perish,
101. 4 from me: I will not know a wicked *p*.
105.37 not one feeble *p* among their tribes.
Pr 6.12 A naughty *p*, a wicked man,
18. 5 to accept the *p* of the wicked,
24. 8 shall be called a mischievous *p*.
28.17 violence to the blood of any *p*
Isa 32. 5 The vile *p* shall be no more called
6 the vile *p* will speak villany, and his
Jer 43. 6 every *p* that Nebuzar-adan the
52.25 them that were near the king's *p*,
Eze 16. 5 to the lothing of thy *p*, in the day
33. 6 and take any *p* from among them,
44.25 shall come at no dead *p* to defile
Dan 11.21 in his estate shall stand up a vile *p*,
Mal 1. 8 or accept thy *p*? saith the Lord
Mt 22.16 thou regardest not the *p* of men.
27.24 innocent of the blood of this just *p*:
Mk 12.14 thou regardest not the *p* of men,
Lk 20.21 neither acceptest thou the *p* of any,
1Co 5.13 among yourselves that wicked *p*.
2Co 2.10 forgave I it in the *p* of Christ;
Gal 2. 6 to me: God accepteth no man's *p*:)
Eph 5. 5 nor unclean *p*, nor covetous man,
Heb 1. 3 and the express image of his *p*,
12.16 fornicator, or profane *p*, as Esau,
2Pe 2. 5 but saved Noah the eighth *p*, a

PERSONS

Lev 27. 2 the *p* shall be for the Lord by thy
Dt 1.17 shall not respect *p* in judgment;
10.17 which regardeth not *p*, nor taketh
2Ch 19. 7 nor respect of *p*, nor taking of
Job 34.19 that accepteth not the *p* of princes,
Pr 24.23 not good to have respect of *p* in
28.21 To have respect of *p* is not good:
Mal 1. 9 means: will he regard your *p*?
Lk 15. 7 than over ninety and nine just *p*,
Ac 10.34 that God is no respecter of *p*:
17.17 with the Jews, and with the devout *p*,
Ro 2.11 there is no respect of *p* with God.
2Co 1.11 upon us by the means of many *p*
Eph 6. 9 is there respect of *p* with him.
Col 3.25 done: and there is no respect of *p*.
1Ti 1.10 for liars, for perjured *p*, and if
Jas 2. 1 Lord of glory, with respect of *p*.
9 if ye have respect to *p*, ye commit
1Pe 1.17 who without respect of *p* judgeth
2Pe 3.11 what manner of *p* ought ye to be in
Jude 16 having men's *p* in admiration

PERSUADE

1Ki 22.20 Who shall *p* Ahab, that he may
21 the Lord, and said, I will *p* him.
22 Thou shalt *p* him, and prevail
2Ch 32.11 Doth not Hezekiah *p* you to give
15 you, nor *p* you on this manner,
Isa 36.18 Beware lest Hezekiah *p* you,
Mt 28.14 we will *p* him, and secure you.
2Co 5.11 the terror of the Lord, we *p* men;
Gal 1.10 For do I now *p* men, or God? or

PERSUADED

2Ch 18. 2 and *p* him to go up with him to
Pr 25.15 By long forbearing is a prince *p*,
Mt 27.20 and elders *p* the multitude that
Lk 16.31 neither will they be *p*, though one
20. 6 they be *p* that John was a prophet.
Ac 13.43 *p* them to continue in the grace of
14.19 who *p* the people, and, having
18. 4 and *p* the Jews and the Greeks.
19.26 *p* and turned away much people,
21.14 And when he would not be *p*, we
26.26 I am *p* that none of these things
Ro 4.21 And being fully *p* that, what he
8.38 For I am *p*, that neither death,
14. 5 man be fully *p* in his own mind.
14 and am *p* by the Lord Jesus, that
15.14 also am *p* of you, my brethren,
2Ti 1. 5 and I am *p* that in thee also.
12 and am *p* that he is able to keep
Heb 6. 9 we are *p* better things of you, and
11.13 were *p* of them, and embraced

PERSUADEST

Ac 26.28 thou *p* me to be a Christian.

PERSUADETH

2Ki 18.32 unto Hezekiah, when he *p* you,
Ac 18.13 This fellow *p* men to worship God

PERSUADING

Ac 19. 8 and *p* the things concerning the
28.23 *p* them concerning Jesus, both out

PERSUASION

Gal 5. 8 *p* cometh not of him that calleth

PERTAIN

Lev 7.20 offerings, that *p* unto the Lord,
21 offerings, which *p* unto the Lord,
1Sa 25.22 if I leave of all that *p* to him by the
Ro 15.17 in those things which *p* to God.
1Co 6. 3 much more things that *p* to this life?
2Pe 1. 3 unto us all things that *p* unto life

PERTAINETH

Lev 14.32 get that which *p* to his cleansing.
Nu 4.16 the priest *p* the oil for the light,
Dt 22. 5 wear that which *p* unto a man,
1Sa 27. 6 Ziklag *p* unto the kings of Judah
2Sa 6.12 Obed-edom, and all that *p* unto him,
Ro 9. 4 to whom *p* the adoption, and the
Heb 7.13 are spoken *p* to another tribe,

PERTAINING

Jos 13.31 were *p* unto the children of Machir
1Ch 26.32 every matter *p* to God, and affairs
Ac 1. 3 things *p* to the kingdom of God:
Ro 4. 1 as *p* to the flesh, hath found?
1Co 6. 4 judgments of things *p* to this life,
Heb 2.17 high priest in things *p* to God,
5. 1 ordained for men in things *p* to God,
9. 9 perfect, as *p* to the conscience;

PERVERSE

Nu 22.32 because thy way is *p* before me:
Dt 32. 5 are a *p* and crooked generation.
1Sa 20.30 son of the *p* rebellious woman,
Job 6.30 my taste discern *p* things?
9.20 perfect, it shall also prove me *p*.
Pr 4.24 and *p* lips put far from thee.
8. 8 is nothing froward or *p* in them.
12. 8 is of a *p* heart shall be despised.
14. 2 is *p* in his ways despiseth him.
17.20 a *p* tongue falleth into mischief.
19. 1 he that is *p* in his lips, and...a fool
23.33 thine heart shall utter *p* things.
28. 6 he that is *p* in his ways, though
18 *p* in his ways shall fall at once.
Isa 19.14 The Lord hath mingled a *p* spirit
Mt 17.17 said, O faithless and *p* generation,
Lk 9.41 said, O faithless and *p* generation,
Ac 20.30 men arise, speaking *p* things, to
Php 2.15 midst of a crooked and *p* nation,
1Ti 6. 5 *P* disputings of men of corrupt

PERVERT

Dt 16.19 and *p* the words of the righteous.
24.17 *p* the judgment of the stranger,
Job 8. 3 Doth God *p* judgment?
3 or doth the Almighty *p* justice?
34.12 will the Almighty *p* judgment.
Pr 17.23 bosom to *p* the ways of judgment.
31. 5 forget...law, and *p* the judgment
Mic 3. 9 abhor judgment, and *p* all equity.
Ac 13.10 to *p* the right ways of the Lord?
Gal 1. 7 and would *p* the gospel of Christ

PERVERTETH

Ex 23. 8 and *p* the words of the righteous.
Dt 27.19 cursed be he that *p* the judgment
Pr 10. 9 that *p* his ways shall be known.
19. 3 foolishness of man *p* his way:
Lk 23.14 unto me, as one that *p* the people;

PERVERTING

Ec 5. 8 violent *p* of judgment and justice
Lk 23. 2 We found this fellow *p* the nation,

PESTILENCE

Ex 5. 3 he fall upon us with *p*, or with the
9.15 smite thee and thy people with *p*;
Lev 26.25 I will send the *p* among you; and
Nu 14.12 I will smite them with the *p*, and
Dt 28.21 shall make the *p* cleave unto thee,
2Sa 24.13 there be three days' *p* in thy land?
15 So the Lord sent a *p* upon Israel
1Ki 8.37 be in the land famine, if there be *p*,
1Ch 21.12 even the *p*, in the land, and the
14 So the Lord sent *p* upon Israel:
2Ch 6.28 if there be *p*, if there be blasting,
7.13 or if I send *p* among my people;
20. 9 sword, judgment, or *p*, or famine,
Ps 78.50 but gave their life over to the *p*;
91. 3 fowler, and from the noisome *p*.
6 for the *p* that walketh in darkness;
Jer 14.12 and by the famine, and by the *p*.
21. 6 they shall die of a great *p*.
7 as are left in this city from the *p*,
9 and by the famine, and by the *p*:
24.10 famine, and the *p*, among them,
27. 8 with the famine, and with the *p*,
13 sword, by the famine, and by the *p*,
28. 8 of war, and of evil, and of *p*.
29.17 the sword, the famine, and the *p*,
18 the famine, and with the *p*, and
32.24 famine, and of the *p*: and what
36 and by the famine, and by the *p*;
34.17 sword, to the *p*, and to the famine;
38. 2 sword, by the famine, and by the *p*:
42.17 sword, by the famine, and by the *p*:
22 sword, by the famine, and by the *p*,
44.13 sword, by the famine, and by the *p*:
Eze 5.12 A third part...shall die with the *p*,
17 *p* and blood shall pass through
6.11 sword, by the famine, and by the *p*.
12 He that is far off shall die of the *p*;
7.15 and the *p* and the famine within:
15 famine and *p* shall devour him.
12.16 from the famine, and from the *p*;
14.19 Or if I send a *p* into that land, and
21 the noisome beast, and the *p*, to
28.23 I will send into her *p*, and blood
33.27 and in the caves shall die of the *p*.
38.22 against him with *p* and with blood;
Am 4.10 I have sent among you the *p* after
Hab 3. 5 Before him went the *p*, and

PESTILENCES

Mt 24. 7 *p*, and earthquakes, in divers
Lk 21.11 divers places, and famines, and *p*;

PESTILENT

Ac 24. 5 have found this man a *p* fellow,

PETER

Mt 4.18 And Simon called *P*, and Andrew
10. 2 The first, Simon, who is called *P*,
14.28 *P* answered him and said, Lord,
29 when *P* was come down out of the
15.15 Then answered *P* and said unto
16.16 And Simon *P* answered and said,
18 That thou art *P*, and upon this
22 *P* took him, and began to rebuke
23 said unto *P*, Get thee behind me,
17. 1 Jesus taketh *P*, James, and John
4 Then answered *P*, and said unto
24 received tribute money came to *P*,
26 *P* saith unto him, Of strangers.

PETER

The most prominent of Jesus' twelve disciples, becoming their spokesman and representative; with his brother Andrew, is the first to be called to follow Jesus, either at the Sea of Galilee (Mt 4; Mk 1; Lk 5) or near the Dead Sea (Jn 1); figures in various incidents, including the cure of his mother-in-law (Mt 8.14), his attempt to walk on the water to reach Jesus (Mt 14.28-31), and his request that Jesus explain his proverbial sayings (Mt 15.15); at Caesarea Philippi declares his faith in Jesus: "Thou art the Christ, the son of the living God," and is told that he is to be entrusted with the keys of the kingdom: "upon this rock ['Peter' means stone] I will build my church" (Mt 16.16-19); protests at Jesus' prediction of his passion and receives a stinging rebuke: "Get thee behind me, Satan: thou art an offense unto me" (Mt 16.23); is a witness (with James and John) of the transfiguration (Mt 17) and later of the agony (Mt 26); after declaring unshakable loyalty to Jesus, is warned, "this night, before the cock crow, thou shalt deny me thrice" (Mt 26.34); after Jesus' arrest he does deny knowing him three times; when the crowing of the cock reminds him of Jesus' prophecy, "he went out, and wept bitterly" (Mt 26.75).

After Jesus' death, is one of the first witnesses of the Resurrection (1 Co 15.5) and receives commission to "feed my sheep" from the risen Jesus (Jn 21.17); emerges as spokesman of the apostles at Pentecost (Ac 2) and elsewhere; after curing a cripple at the Beautiful Gate of the Temple (along with John) (Ac 3), defends his actions before the Sanhedrin (Ac 4); upholding the early Christian practice of common possession of land, condemns Ananias and Sapphira (Ac 5); is the first to receive a Gentile convert (the centurion Cornelius) into the church and justifies his decision as having been decreed in a heavenly vision (Ac 10–11); apprehended by Herod Agrippa, is released from prison by an angel (Ac 12); later appears at the Council of Jerusalem (Ac 15) and in discussions with Paul (Gal 1.18). As with Paul, the Bible makes no mention of Peter's fate, although tradition holds that he went eventually to Rome and was martyred there; two epistles (1 and 2 Peter) are also attributed to him.

Mt 18.21 Then came *P* to him, and said,
19.27 answered *P* and said unto him,
26.33 *P* answered and said unto him,
35 *P* said unto him, Though I should
37 *P* and the two sons of Zebedee,
40 saith unto *P*, What, could ye not
58 *P* followed him afar off unto the
69 Now *P* sat without in the palace:
73 said to *P*, Surely thou also art one
75 *P* remembered the word of Jesus,
Mk 3.16 And Simon he surnamed *P*;
5.37 to follow him, save *P*, and James,
8.29 *P* answereth and saith unto him,
32 *P* took him, and began to rebuke
33 he rebuked *P*, saying, Get thee
9. 2 Jesus taketh with him *P*, and
5 *P* answered and said to Jesus,
10.28 *P* began to say unto him, Lo, we
11.21 *P* calling to remembrance saith
13. 3 *P* and James and John...Andrew
14.29 *P* said unto him, Although all
33 he taketh with him *P* and James
37 saith unto *P*, Simon, sleepest thou?
54 *P* followed him afar off, even into
66 *P* was beneath in the palace, there
67 when she saw *P* warming himself,
70 said again to *P*, Surely thou art
72 *P* called to mind the word that
16. 7 tell his disciples and *P* that he
Lk 5. 8 When Simon *P* saw it, he fell down
6.14 Simon, (whom he also named *P*,)
8.45 *P* and they that were with him
51 suffered no man to go in, save *P*,
9.20 *P* answering said, The Christ of
28 he took *P* and John and James,
32 But *P* and they that were with him
33 *P* said unto Jesus, Master, it is
12.41 *P* said unto him, Lord, speakest
18.28 Then *P* said, Lo, we have left all,
22. 8 And he sent *P* and John, saying,
34 I tell thee, *P*, the cock shall not
54 house. And *P* followed afar off.
55 together, *P* sat down among them.
58 them. And *P* said, Man, I am not.
60 *P* said, Man, I know not what thou
61 Lord turned, and looked upon *P*.
61 *P* remembered the word of the
62 And *P* went out, and wept bitterly.
24.12 Then arose *P*, and ran unto the
Jn 1.44 Bethsaida...city of Andrew and *P*.
6.68 Simon *P* answered him, Lord, to
13. 6 Then cometh he to Simon *P*: and
6 *P* saith unto him, Lord, dost thou
8 *P* saith unto him, Thou shalt
9 Simon *P* saith unto him, Lord, not
24 Simon *P* therefore beckoned to
36 Simon *P* said unto him, Lord,
37 *P* said unto him, Lord, why cannot
18.10 Simon *P* having a sword drew it,
11 said Jesus unto *P*, Put up thy
15 And Simon *P* followed Jesus, and
16 *P* stood at the door without. Then
16 kept the door, and brought in *P*.
17 damsel that kept the door unto *P*,
18 *P* stood with them, and warmed
25 And Simon *P* stood and warmed
26 his kinsman whose ear *P* cut off,
27 *P* then denied again: and
20. 2 runneth, and cometh to Simon *P*,
3 *P* therefore went forth, and that
4 the other disciple did outrun *P*,
6 cometh Simon *P* following him,
21. 2 together Simon *P*, and Thomas
3 Simon *P* saith unto them, I go a
7 loved saith unto *P*, It is the Lord.
7 *P* heard that it was the Lord,
11 Simon *P* went up, and drew the
15 Jesus said to Simon *P*, Simon,
17 *P* was grieved because he said
20 *P*, turning about, seeth the
21 *P* seeing him saith to Jesus, Lord,
Ac 1.13 where abode both *P*, and James,
15 *P* stood up in the midst of the
2.14 *P*, standing up with the eleven,
37 unto *P* and to the rest of the
38 Then *P* said unto them, Repent,
3. 1 *P* and John went up together into
3 seeing *P* and John about to go
4 *P*, fastening his eyes upon him
6 *P* said, Silver and gold have I
11 which was healed held *P* and John,
12 when *P* saw it he answered unto
4. 8 *P*, filled with the Holy Ghost, said
13 saw the boldness of *P* and John,
19 *P* and John answered and said
5. 3 *P* said, Ananias, why hath Satan
8 *P* answered unto her, Tell me
9 *P* said unto her, How is it that
15 the shadow of *P* passing by might
29 *P* and the other apostles answered
8.14 they sent unto him *P* and John:
20 But *P* said unto him, Thy money
9.32 *P* passed throughout all quarters,
34 *P* said unto him, Aeneas, Jesus
38 disciples had heard that *P* was
39 Then *P* arose and went with them.
40 *P* put them all forth, and kneeled
40 and when she saw *P*, she sat up.
10. 5 one Simon, whose surname is *P*:
9 *P* went up upon the housetop to
13 voice to him, Rise, *P*; kill and eat.
14 *P* said, Not so, Lord; for I have
17 *P* doubted in himself what this
18 which was surnamed *P*, were
19 While *P* thought on the vision, the
21 *P* went down to the men which
23 morrow *P* went away with them,
25 as *P* was coming in, Cornelius met
26 *P* took him up, saying, Stand up;
32 Simon, whose surname is *P*;
34 *P* opened his mouth, and said, Of
44 *P* yet spake these words, the Holy
45 as many as came with *P*,
46 magnify God. Then answered *P*,
11. 2 *P* was come up to Jerusalem,
4 *P* rehearsed the matter from the
7 unto me, Arise, *P*; slay and eat.
13 for Simon, whose surname is *P*;
12. 3 proceeded further to take *P* also.
5 *P* therefore was kept in prison:
6 *P*...sleeping between two soldiers,
7 he smote *P* on the side, and raised
11 when *P* was come to himself, he
13 as *P* knocked at the door of the
14 told how *P* stood before the gate.
16 But *P* continued knocking: and
18 soldiers, what was become of *P*.
15. 7 *P* rose up, and said unt them,
Gal 1.18 I went up to Jerusalem to see *P*,
2. 7 of the circumcision was unto *P*;
8 he that wrought effectually in *P*
11 But when *P* was come to Antioch,
14 I said unto *P* before them all,
1Pe 1. 1 *P*, an apostle of Jesus Christ,
2Pe 1. 1 Simon *P*, a servant and an apostle

PETER'S

Mt 8.14 Jesus was come into *P* house,
Jn 1.40 him, was Andrew, Simon *P* brother.
6. 8 Andrew, Simon *P* brother, saith
Ac 12.14 And when she knew *P* voice, she

PETITION

1Sa 1.17 God of Israel grant thee thy *p*
27 Lord hath given me my *p* which I
1Ki 2.16 I ask one *p* of thee, deny me not.
20 said, I desire one small *p* of thee;
Est 5. 6 What is thy *p*? and it shall be
7 and said, My *p* and my request is;
8 if it please the king to grant my *p*,
7. 2 What is thy *p*, queen Esther? and
3 let my life be given me at my *p*,
9.12 now what is thy *p*? and it shall be
Dan 6. 7 shall ask a *p* of any God or man
12 that shall ask a *p* of any God or man
13 maketh his *p* three times a day.

PETITIONS

Ps 20. 5 banners: the Lord fulfil all thy *p*.
1Jn 5.15 have the *p* that we desired of him.

PHARAOH

Gen 12.15 The princes also of *P* saw her,
15 and commended her before *P*:
17 the Lord plagued *P* and his house
18 *P* called Abram, and said, What is
20 *P* commanded his men concerning
39. 1 Potiphar, an officer of *P*, captain

40. 2 *P* was wroth against two of his
13 days shall *P* lift up thine head,
14 and make mention of me unto *P*,
17 of all manner of bakemeats for *P*;
19 three days shall *P* lift up thy head
41. 1 of full two years, that *P* dreamed:
4 favored and fat kine. So *P* awoke.
7 and *P* awoke, and, behold, it was a
8 and *P* told them his dream; but
8 that could interpret them unto *P*.
9 Then spake the chief butler unto *P*,
10 *P* was wroth with his servants,
14 Then *P* sent and called Joseph.
14 his raiment, and came in unto *P*.
15 And *P* said unto Joseph, I have
16 Joseph answered *P*, saying, It is
16 shall give *P* an answer of peace.
17 *P* said unto Joseph, In my dream,
25 And Joseph said unto *P*,
25 The dream of *P* is one: God hath
25 shewed *P* what he is about to do.
28 thing which I have spoken unto *P*:
28 is about to do he sheweth unto *P*.
32 dream was doubled unto *P* twice;
33 let *P* look out a man discreet and
34 Let *P* do this, and let him appoint
35 lay up corn under the hand of *P*,

PHARAOH

Pharaoh (meaning in Egyptian "the Great House") is a ceremonial title of the kings of ancient Egypt. Egypt played a long and complex role in the saga of ancient Israel, and various Pharaohs appear at different times in the Old Testament narrative. In the Book of Exodus at least two Pharaohs are involved: the Pharaoh of the Oppression (Ex 1–2) and the Pharaoh of the Exodus (Ex 3–15). Their identities are uncertain, however, since the events of the Exodus are not recorded in Egyptian sources. If, as many think, the Exodus took place in the 13th century B.C., the Pharaohs in question would belong to the 19th Dynasty, of which the most energetic was Rameses II (1290–1224 B.C.). He launched numerous military actions to assert Egypt's authority and concluded a treaty with the Hittite kingdom dividing Syria into separate spheres of control. Rameses also undertook massive building projects in the Nile Delta, including the city of Raamses, which became the royal capital. For these projects a source of slave labor was readily available in the many Asiatic peoples then settled in the Delta. The city of Raamses is mentioned in Ex 1.11, which makes it possible that Rameses II is the Pharaoh of the Oppression. His successor, Merneptah (1224–1214 B.C.), might then be the Pharaoh of the Exodus, but this can only be surmised. In the famous "Israel stele" erected during Merneptah's reign, Israel is referred to for the first time in Egyptian records, evidently as a people without their own territory beyond the borders of Egypt. It is also possible that Rameses III (1196–1164 B.C.) was the Pharaoh of the Exodus; the song of Moses celebrating that event (Ex 15) mentions the presence in Canaan of the Philistines (from whom the name "Palestine" derived), who were not settled there until the time of Rameses III.

37 the thing was good in the eyes of *P*,
38 *P* said unto his servants, Can we
39 *P* said unto Joseph, Forasmuch as
41 *P* said unto Joseph, See, I have set
42 *P* took off his ring from his hand,
44 And *P* said unto Joseph, I am *P*,
45 And *P* called Joseph's name
46 years old when he stood before *P*
46 went out from the presence of *P*,
55 the people cried to *P* for bread:
55 *P* said unto all the Egyptians, Go
42.15 By the life of *P* ye shall not go forth
16 by the life of *P* surely ye are spies.
44.18 servant: for thou art even as *P*.
45. 2 and the house of *P* heard.
8 he hath made me a father to *P*,
16 pleased *P* well, and his servants.
17 *P* said unto Joseph, Say unto thy
21 to the commandment of *P*,
46. 5 which *P* had sent to carry him.
31 I will go up, and shew *P*, and say
33 to pass, when *P* shall call you,
47. 1 Joseph came and told *P*, and said,
2 men, and presented them unto *P*.
3 *P* said unto his brethren, What is
3 they said unto *P*, Thy servants
4 They said moreover to *P*, For to
5 *P* spake unto Joseph, saying, Thy
7 before *P*: and Jacob blessed *P*.
8 *P* said unto Jacob, How old art
9 Jacob said unto *P*, The days of the
10 And Jacob blessed *P*, and went
10 and went out from before *P*.
11 of Rameses, as *P* had commanded.
19 our land will be servants unto *P*:
20 bought all the land of Egypt for *P*;
22 had a portion assigned them of *P*,
22 did eat their portion which *P* gave
23 have bought you this day...for *P*:
24 ye shall give the fifth part unto *P*,
26 that *P* should have the fifth part;
50. 4 Joseph spake unto the house of *P*,
4 speak, I pray you, in the ears of *P*,
6 *P* said, Go up, and bury thy father,
7 him went up all the servants of *P*,
Ex 1.11 they built for *P* treasure cities,
19 the midwives said unto *P*, Because
22 *P* charged all his people, saying,
2. 5 daughter of *P* came down to wash
15 Now when *P* heard this thing, he
15 Moses fled from the face of *P*, and
3.10 I will send thee unto *P*, that thou
11 Who am I, that I should go unto *P*,
4.21 thou do all those wonders before *P*,
22 thou shalt say unto *P*, Thus saith
5. 1 and Aaron went in, and told *P*,
2 *P* said, Who is the Lord, that I
5 *P* said, Behold, the people of the
6 And *P* commanded the same day
10 Thus saith *P*, I will not give you
15 of Israel came and cried unto *P*,
20 way, as they came forth from *P*:
21 to be abhorred in the eyes of *P*,
23 I came to *P* to speak in thy name,
6. 1 shalt thou see what I will do to *P*:
11 Go in, speak unto *P* king of Egypt,
12 how then shall *P* hear me, who am
13 Israel, and unto *P* king of Egypt,
27 which spake to *P* king of Egypt,
29 speak thou unto *P* king of Egypt
30 and how shall *P* hearken unto me?
7. 1 See, I have made thee a god to *P*:
2 thy brother shall speak unto *P*,
4 But *P* shall not hearken unto you,
7 old, when they spake unto *P*.
9 When *P* shall speak unto you,
9 Take thy rod, and cast it before *P*,
10 Moses and Aaron went in unto *P*,
10 Aaron cast down his rod before *P*,
11 Then *P* also called the wise men
15 Get thee unto *P* in the morning;

20 were in the river, in the sight of *P*,
23 *P* turned and went into his house,
8. 1 Go unto *P*, and say unto him, Thus
8 *P* called for Moses and Aaron,
9 Moses said unto *P*, Glory over me:
12 and Aaron went out from *P*:
12 which he had brought against *P*.
15 when *P* saw that there was respite,
19 Then the magicians said unto *P*,
20 the morning, and stand before *P*;
24 swarm of flies into the house of *P*,
25 *P* called for Moses and for Aaron,
28 *P* said, I will let you go, that ye
29 swarms of flies may depart from *P*,
29 let not *P* deal deceitfully any more
30 And Moses went out from *P*, and
31 the swarms of flies from *P*,
32 *P* hardened his heart at this time
9. 1 Go in unto *P*, and tell him, Thus
7 *P* sent, and, behold, there was not
7 And the heart of *P* was hardened,
8 toward...heaven in the sight of *P*,
10 of the furnace, and stood before *P*;
12 the Lord hardened the heart of *P*,
13 stand before *P*, and say unto him,
20 the Lord among the servants of *P*
27 *P* sent, and called for Moses and
33 Moses went out of the city from *P*,
34 when *P* saw that the rain and the
35 heart of *P* was hardened, neither
10. 1 said unto Moses, Go in unto *P*;
3 Moses and Aaron came in unto *P*,
6 himself, and went out from *P*.
8 Aaron were brought again unto *P*:
16 *P* called for Moses and Aaron in
18 he went out from *P*, and intreated
24 *P* called unto Moses, and said, Go
28 *P* said unto him, Get thee from
11. 1 I bring one plague more upon *P*,
5 firstborn of *P* that sitteth upon his
8 went out from *P* in a great anger.
9 *P* shall not hearken unto you;
10 did all these wonders before *P*:
12.29 the first born of *P* that sat on his
30 *P* rose up in the night, he, and all
13.15 *P* would hardly let us go, that the
17 when *P* had let the people go, that
14. 3 *P* will say of the children of Israel,
4 I will be honored upon *P*, and
5 heart of *P* and of his servants was
8 The Lord hardened the heart of *P*
9 all the horses and chariots of *P*,
10 when *P* drew nigh, the children of
17 and I will get me honor upon *P*,
18 I have gotten me honor upon *P*,
28 all the host of *P* that came into the
15.19 the horse of *P* went in with his
18. 4 delivered me from the sword of *P*:
8 all that the Lord had done unto *P*
10 and out of the hand of *P*, who hath
Dt 6.22 and sore, upon Egypt, upon *P*, and
7. 8 from the hand of *P* king of Egypt.
18 what the Lord thy God did unto *P*,
11. 3 did in the midst of Egypt unto *P*
29. 2 eyes in the land of Egypt unto *P*,
34.11 to do in the land of Egypt to *P*, and
1Sa 6. 6 and *P* hardened their hearts?
1Ki 3. 1 made affinity with *P* king of Egypt,
9.16 *P* king of Egypt had gone up, and
11. 1 together with the daughter of *P*,
18 to Egypt, unto *P* king of Egypt;
19 great favor in the sight of *P*, so
20 household among the sons of *P*.
21 Hadad said to *P*, Let me depart,
22 Then *P* said unto him, But what
2Ki 17. 7 under the hand of *P* king of Egypt,
18.21 so is *P* king of Egypt unto all that
23.35 gave the silver and the gold to *P*;
35 to the commandment of *P*:
1Ch 4.18 sons of Bithiah the daughter of *P*,
2Ch 8.11 the daughter of *P* out of the city of

Pharaoh means "great house" in Egyptian; statues of Ramses II (13th century B.C.) remain at Abu Simbel.

Neh 9.10 signs and wonders upon *P*, and
Ps 135. 9 the midst of thee, O Egypt, upon *P*,
136.15 *P* and his host in the Red sea:
Isa 19.11 wise counsellers of *P* is become
11 how say ye unto *P*, I am the son of
30. 2 themselves in the strength of *P*,
3 the strength of *P* be your shame,
36. 6 so is *P* king of Egypt to all that
Jer 25.19 *P* king of Egypt, and his servants,
46.17 *P* king of Egypt is but a noise:
25 punish the multitude of No, and *P*,
25 even *P*, and all them that trust in
47. 1 before that *P* smote Gaza.
Eze 17.17 shall *P* with his mighty army and
29. 2 thy face against *P* king of Egypt;
3 I am against thee, *P* king of Egypt,
30.21 have broken the arm of *P* king of
22 I am against *P* king of Egypt,
25 and the arms of *P* shall fall down;
31. 2 speak unto *P* king of Egypt, and
18 This is *P* and all his multitude,
32. 2 lamentation for *P* king of Egypt,
31 *P* shall see them, and shall be
31 even *P* and all his army slain by the
32 even *P* and all his multitude,
Ac 7.10 in the sight of *P* king of Egypt;
13 kindred was made known unto *P*.
Ro 9.17 For the scripture saith unto *P*,

PHARAOH'S

Ac 7.21 *P* daughter took him up, and
Heb 11.24 be called the son of *P* daughter;

PHARISEE

Mt 23.26 Thou blind *P*, cleanse first that
Lk 7.39 the *P* which had bidden him saw it,
11.37 *P* besought him to dine with him:
38 when the *P* saw it, he marveled
18.10 one a *P*, and the other a publican.
11 The *P* stood and prayed thus with
Ac 5.34 a *P*, named Gamaliel, a doctor of
23. 6 Men and brethren, I am a *P*,
6 the son of a *P*: of the hope and
26. 5 sect of our religion I lived a *P*.
Php 3. 5 as touching the law, a *P*;

PHARISEE'S

Lk 7.36 he went into the *P* house, and sat
37 Jesus sat at meat in the *P* house,

PHARISEES

Mt 3. 7 saw many of the *P* and Sadducees
5.20 righteousness of the scribes and *P*,
9.11 when the *P* saw it, they said unto
14 Why do we and the *P* fast oft, but
34 the *P* said, He casteth out devils
12. 2 But when the *P* saw it, they said,
14 the *P* went out, and held a council
24 when the *P* heard it, they said,
38 certain of the scribes and of the *P*
15. 1 Then came to Jesus scribes and *P*,
12 thou that the *P* were offended,
16. 1 *P* also with the Sadducees came,
6, 11 beware of the leaven of the *P*
12 but of the doctrine of the *P* and of
19. 3 *P* also came unto him, tempting
21.45 and *P* had heard his parables,
22.15 Then went the *P*, and took counsel
34 the *P* had heard that he had put
41 the *P* were gathered together,
23. 2 scribes and the *P* sit in Moses'
13, 14, 15, 23, 25, 27, 29 *P*, hypocrites!
27.62 chief priests and *P* came together
Mk 2.16 the scribes and *P* saw him eat with
18 of John and of the *P* used to fast:
18 disciples of John and of the *P* fast,
24 *P* said unto him, Behold, why do
3. 6 the *P* went forth, and straightway
7. 1 came together unto him the *P*,
3 For the *P*, and all the Jews, except
5 Then the *P* and scribes asked him,
8.11 *P* came...and began to question
15 beware of the leaven of the *P*,
10. 2 the *P* came to him, and asked him,
12.13 send unto him certain of the *P*
Lk 5.17 were *P* and doctors of the law
21 scribes and the *P* began to reason,
30 their scribes and *P* murmured
33 likewise the disciples of the *P*;
6. 2 certain of the *P* said unto them,
7 the scribes and *P* watched him,
7.30 *P* and lawyers rejected the counsel
36 one of the *P* desired him that he
11.39 do ye *P* make clean the outside of
42 woe unto you, *P*! for ye tithe mint
43 Woe unto you, *P*! for ye love the
44 Woe unto you, scribes and *P*,
53 *P* began to urge him vehemently,
12. 1 Beware ye of the leaven of the *P*,
13.31 day there came certain of the *P*,
14. 1 house of one of the chief *P* to eat
3 spake unto the lawyers and *P*,
15. 2 And the *P* and scribes murmured,
16.14 *P* also, who were covetous, heard
17.20 when he was demanded of the *P*,
19.39 the *P* from among the multitude
Jn 1.24 which were sent were of the *P*.
3. 1 man of the *P*, named Nicodemus,
4. 1 Lord knew how the *P* had heard
7.32 *P* heard that the people murmured
32 *P* and...chief priests sent officers
45 officers to the chief priests and *P*;
47 answered them the *P*, Are ye also
48 rulers or of the *P* believed on him?
8. 3 and *P* brought unto him a woman
13 The *P* therefore said unto him,
9.13 They brought to the *P* him that
15 the *P* also asked him how he had
16 said some of the *P*, This man is not
40 some of the *P* which were with him
11.46 went their ways to the *P*, and told
47 gathered the chief priests and...*P*
57 the *P* had given a commandment,
12.19 The *P* therefore said among
42 of the *P* they did not confess him,
18. 3 officers from the...priests and *P*,
Ac 15. 5 of the sect of the *P* which believed,
23. 6 were Sadducees, and the other *P*,
7 a dissension between the *P* and
8 nor spirit: but the *P* confess both.

PHARISEES'

Ac 23. 9 scribes that were of the *P* part

PHARPAR

2Ki 5.12 and *P*, rivers of Damascus,

PHEBE

Ro 16. 1 I commend unto you *P* our sister,

PHENICE

Ac 11.19 Stephen travelled as far as *P*,
15. 3 passed through *P* and Samaria,
27.12 means they might attain to *P*,

PHENICIA

Ac 21. 2 finding a ship sailing...unto *P*,

PHILADELPHIA

Rev 1.11 and unto Sardis, and unto *P*, and
3. 7 angel of the church in *P* write;

PHILEMON

Phm 1 unto *P* our dearly beloved, and

PHILETUS

2Ti 2.17 of whom is Hymenaeus and *P*;

PHILIP

Mt 10. 3 *P*, and Bartholomew; Thomas,
Mk 3.18 Andrew, and *P*, and Bartholomew,
Lk 3. 1 his brother *P* tetrarch of Ituraea
6.14 and John, *P* and Bartholomew,
Jn 1.43 findeth *P*, and saith unto him,
44 Now *P* was of Bethsaida, the city
45 *P* findeth Nathanael, and saith
46 *P* saith unto him, Come and see.
48 Before that *P* called thee, when
6. 5 he saith unto *P*, Whence shall we
7 *P* answered him, Two hundred
12.21 same came therefore to *P*, which
22 *P* cometh and telleth Andrew: and
22 again Andrew and *P* tell Jesus.
14. 8 *P* saith unto him, Lord, shew us
9 yet hast thou not known me, *P*?
Ac 1.13 *P*, and Thomas, Bartholomew,
6. 5 *P*, and Prochorus, and Nicanor,
8. 5 *P* went down to...city of Samaria,
6 unto those things which *P* spake,
12 when they believed *P* preaching
13 baptized, he continued with *P*,
26 angel of the Lord spake unto *P*,
29 Then the Spirit said unto *P*, Go
30 *P* ran thither to him, and heard
31 he desired *P* that he would come
34 And the eunuch answered *P*, and
35 *P* opened his mouth, and began
37 *P* said, If thou believest with all
38 the water, both *P* and the eunuch;
39 Spirit of the Lord caught away *P*,
40 But *P* was found at Azotus: and
21. 8 into the house of *P* the evangelist,

PHILIPPI

Mt 16.13 into the coasts of Caesarea *P*,
Mk 8.27 into the towns of Caesarea *P*:
Ac 16.12 And from thence to *P*, which is
20. 6 And we sailed away from *P* after
Php 1. 1 in Christ Jesus which are at *P*,
1Th 2. 2 as ye know, at *P*, we were bold in

PHILIPPIANS

Php 4.15 Now ye *P* know also, that in the

PHILIP'S

Mt 14. 3 Herodias' sake, his brother *P* wife.
Mk 6.17 Herodias' sake, his brother *P* wife:
Lk 3.19 for Herodias his brother *P* wife,

PHILISTINE

1Sa 17. 8 am not I a *P*, and ye servants to
10 *P* said, I defy the armies of Israel
16 *P* drew near morning and evening,
23 up the champion, the *P* of Gath,
26 done to the man that killeth this *P*,
26 for who is this uncircumcised *P*,
32 will go and fight with his *P*,
41 *P* came on and drew near unto
42 *P* looked about, and saw David,
43 the *P* said unto David, Am I a dog,
43 the *P* cursed David by his gods.
48 the *P* arose, and came and drew
48 toward the army to meet the *P*.
49 and smote the *P* in his forehead,
50 prevailed over the *P* with a sling,
50 and smote the *P*, and slew him;
54 And David took the head of the *P*,
57 before Saul with the head of the *P*
21. 9 The sword of Goliath the *P*, whom

PHILISTINES

Gen 21.32 returned into the land of the *P*.
26. 1 unto Abimelech king of the *P*
8 Abimelech king of the *P* looked
14 servants: and the *P* envied him.
15 *P* had stopped them, and filled
18 the *P* had stopped them after the
Ex 13.17 the way of the land of the *P*,
23.31 sea even unto the sea of the *P*,
Jos 13. 2 all the borders of the *P*, and all
3 five lords of the *P*; the
Jdg 3. 3 Namely, five lords of the *P*, and
31 slew of the *P* six hundred men
10. 6 the gods of the *P*, and forsook the
7 sold them into the hands of the *P*,
11 of Ammon, and from the *P*?
13. 1 into the hand of the *P* forty years.
5 Israel out of the hand of the *P*.
14. 1 Timnath of the daughters of the *P*.
2 Timnath of the daughters of the *P*:
3 a wife of the uncircumcised *P*?
4 sought an occasion against the *P*:
4 the *P* had dominion over Israel.
15. 3 I be more blameless than the *P*,
5 go into the standing corn of the *P*,
6 the *P* said, Who hath done this?
6 the *P* came up, and burnt her and
9 *P* went up, and pitched in Judah,
11 not that the *P* are rulers over us?
12 deliver thee into the hand of the *P*.
14 Lehi,the *P* shouted against him:
20 judged Israel in the days of the *P*
16. 5 lords of the *P* came up unto her,
8 lords of the *P* brought up to her
9, 12, 14 The *P* be upon thee, Samson.
18 and called for the lords of the *P*,
18 lords of the *P* came up unto her,
20 The *P* be upon thee, Samson.
21 *P* took him, and put out his eyes,
23 the lords of the *P* gathered them
27 all the lords of the *P* were there;
28 may be at once avenged of the *P*
30 Samson said, Let me die with the *P*.
1Sa 4. 1 went out against the *P* to battle,
1 and the *P* pitched in Aphek.
2 *P* put themselves in array against
2 Israel was smitten before the *P*:
3 smitten us to day before the *P*?
6 when the *P* heard the noise of the
7 the *P* were afraid, for they said,
9 quit yourselves like men, O ye *P*,
10 *P* fought, and Israel was smitten,
17 and said, Israel is fled before the *P*,
5. 1 And the *P* took the ark of God, and
2 When the *P* took the ark of God,
8 and gathered all the lords of the *P*
11 together all the lords of the *P*, and
6. 1 the country of the *P* seven months.
2 the *P* called for the priests and
4 the number of the lords of the *P*:
12 the lords of the *P* went after them
16 the five lords of the *P* had seen it,
17 emerods which the *P* returned for
18 the number of all the cities of the *P*
21 *P* have brought again the ark of
7. 3 deliver you out of the hand of the *P*.
7 *P* heard that the children of Israel
7 the lords of the *P* went up against
7 heard it, they were afraid of the *P*.
8 save us out of the hand of the *P*.
10 the *P* drew near to battle against
10 thunder on that day upon the *P*,
11 pursued the *P*, and smote them,
13 So the *P* were subdued, and they
13 hand of the Lord was against the *P*
14 which the *P* had taken from Israel
14 deliver out of the hand of the *P*.
9.16 my people out of the hand of the *P*:
10. 5 where is the garrison of the *P*:
12. 9 Hazor, and into the hand of the *P*,
13. 3 smote the garrison of the *P* that
3 was in Geba, and the *P* heard of it.
4 had smitten a garrison of the *P*,
4 had in abomination with the *P*.
5, 11 the *P* gathered themselves
12 *P* will come down now upon me to
16 but the *P* encamped in Michmash.
17 camp of the *P* in three companies:

Pharisees are rebuked by Jesus (Mt 23); engraving from a painting by Friedrich Overbeck (1789-1869).

1Sa 13.19 for the *P* said, Lest the Hebrews
20 the Israelites went down to the *P*,
23 the garrison of the *P* went out to
14.11 unto the garrison of the *P*: and
11 the *P* said, Behold, the Hebrews
19 of the *P* went on and increased:
21 Hebrews that were with the *P*
22 when they heard that the *P* fled,
30 greater slaughter among the *P*?
31 they smote the *P* that day from
36 us go down after the *P* by night,
37 God, Shall I go down after the *P*?
46 went up from following the *P*:
46 and the *P* went to their own place.
47 kings of Zobah, and against the *P*:
52 war against the *P* all the days of
17. 1 *P* gathered together their armies
2 the battle in array against the *P*.
3 *P* stood on a mountain on the one
4 champion out of the camp of the *P*,
19 valley of Elah, fighting with the *P*.
21 the *P* had put the battle in array,
23 name, out of the armies of the *P*,
46 carcases of the hosts of the *P* this
51 *P* saw their champion was dead,
52 and shouted, and pursued the *P*,
52 the wounded of the *P* fell down by
53 returned from chasing after the *P*,
18.17 let the hand of the *P* be upon him.
21 hand of the *P* may be against him.
25 but an hundred foreskins of the *P*,
25 David fall by the hand of the *P*.
27 slew of the *P* two hundred men;
30 the princes of the *P* went forth:
19. 8 fought with the *P*, and slew them
23. 1 Behold, the *P* fight against Keilah,
2 Shall I go and smite these *P*?
2 Go, and smite the *P*, and save
3 against the armies of the *P*?
4 will deliver the *P* into thine hand.
5 to Keilah, and fought with the *P*,
27 for the *P* have invaded the land.
28 David, and went against the *P*:
24. 1 was returned from following the *P*,
27. 1 escape into the land of the *P*; and
7 David dwelt in the country of the *P*
11 dwelleth in the country of the *P*.
28. 1 *P* gathered their armies together
4 *P* gathered themselves together,
5 when Saul saw the host of the *P*,
15 for the *P* make war against me,
19 with thee into the hand of the *P*:
19 of Israel into the hand of the *P*.
29. 1 the *P* gathered together all their
2 the lords of the *P* passed on by
3 Then said the princes of the *P*,
3 said unto the princes of the *P*, Is
4 of the *P* were wroth with him;
4 the princes of the *P* said unto him,
7 displease not the lords of the *P*.
9 the princes of the *P* have said, He
11 to return into the land of the *P*.
11 And the *P* went up to Jezreel.
30.16 had taken out of the land of the *P*,
31. 1 Now the *P* fought against Israel:
1 of Israel fled from before the *P*,
2 the *P* followed hard upon Saul and
2 *P* slew Jonathan, and Abinadab,
7 and the *P* came and dwelt in them.
8 when the *P* came to strip the slain,
9 into the land of the *P* round about,
11 that which the *P* had done to Saul:
2Sa 1.20 lest the daughters of the *P* rejoice,
3.14 for an hundred foreskins of the *P*.
18 Israel out of the hand of the *P*, and
5.17 *P* heard that they had anointed
17 all the *P* came up to seek David;
18 The *P* also came and spread
19 saying, Shall I go up to the *P*?
19 deliver the *P* into thine hand.
22 And the *P* came up yet again, and
24 thee, to smite the host of the *P*.
25 smote the *P* from Geba until thou
8. 1 smote the *P*, and subdued them:
1 out of the hand of the *P*.
12 children of Ammon, and of the *P*,
19. 9 us out of the hand of the *P*;
21.12 where the *P* had hanged them,
12 the *P* had slain Saul in Gilboa:
15 *P* had yet war again with Israel;
15 him, and fought against the *P*:
18 again a battle with the *P* at Gob:
19 again a battle in Gob with the *P*,
23. 9 with David, when they defied the *P*
10 smote the *P* until his hand was
11 *P*...gathered together into a troop,
11 and the people fled from the *P*.
12 and defended it, and slew the *P*:
13 of the *P* pitched in the valley
14 of the *P* was then in Bethlehem.
16 brake through the host of the *P*,
1Ki 4.21 the river unto the land of the *P*,
15.27 which belonged to the *P*;
16.15 which belonged to the *P*.
2Ki 8. 2 sojourned in the land of the *P*
3 returned out of the land of the *P*:
18. 8 He smote the *P*, even unto Gaza,
1Ch 1.12 Casluhim, (of whom came the *P*,)
10. 1 Now the *P* fought against Israel;
1 of Israel fled from before the *P*,
2 the *P* followed hard after Saul,
2 *P* slew Jonathan, and Abinadab,
7 and the *P* came and dwelt in them.
8 the *P* came to strip the slain,
9 and sent into the land of the *P*.
11 all that the *P* had done to Saul,
11.13 the *P* were gathered together
13 the people fled from before the *P*.
14 and delivered it, and slew the *P*;
15 host of the *P* encamped in the
18 brake through the host of the *P*,
12.19 with the *P* against Saul to battle:
19 lords of the *P* upon advisement
14. 8 *P* heard that David was anointed
8 all the *P* went up to seek David.
9 the *P* came and spread themselves
10 Shall I go up against the *P*?
13 the *P* yet again spread themselves
15 thee to smite the host of the *P*.
16 smote the host of the *P* from
18. 1 David smote the *P*, and subdued
1 towns out of the hand of the *P*.
11 Ammon, and from the *P*, and from
20. 4 arose war at Gezer with the *P*:
5 there was war again with the *P*;
2Ch 9.26 river even unto the land of the *P*,
17.11 *P* brought Jehoshaphat presents,
21.16 Jehoram the spirit of the *P*,
26. 6 warred against the *P*, and brake
6 about Ashdod, and among the *P*.
7 God helped him against the *P*,
28.18 The *P* also had invaded the cities
Ps 56(T) when the *P* took him in Gath.
83. 7 *P* with the inhabitants of Tyre;
Isa 2. 6 and are soothsayers like the *P*,
9.12 Syrians before, and the *P* behind;
11.14 shoulders of the *P* toward the west;
Jer 25.20 all the kings of the land of the *P*,
47. 1 the prophet against the *P*,
4 day that cometh to spoil all the *P*,
4 the Lord will spoil the *P*, the
Eze 16.27 the daughters of the *P*, which are
57 the daughters of the *P*, which
25.15 the *P* have dealt by revenge,
16 stretch out mine hand upon the *P*,
Am 1. 8 remnant of the *P* shall perish,
6. 2 then go down to Gath of the *P*:
9. 7 *P* from Caphtor, and the Syrians
Ob 19 and they of the plain the *P*: and
Zep 2. 5 O Canaan, the land of the *P*, I will
Zec 9. 6 I will cut off the pride of the *P*.

PHILISTINES'
Gen 21.34 Abraham sojourned in...*P* land
1Sa 14. 1 us go over to the *P* garrison
4 to go over unto the *P* garrison
1Ch 11.16 *P* garrison was then at Bethlehem

PHILOLOGUS
Ro 16.15 Salute *P*, and Julia, Nereus, and

PHILOSOPHERS
Ac 17.18 Then certain *p* of the Epicureans,

PHILOSOPHY
Col 2. 8 spoil you through *p* and...deceit

PHLEGON
Ro 16.14 Salute Asyncritus, *P*, Hermas,

PHRYGIA
Ac 2.10 *P*, and Pamphylia, in Egypt, and
16. 6 when they had gone throughout *P*
18.23 all the country of Galatia and *P*

PHYGELLUS
2Ti 1.15 of whom are *P* and Hermogenes.

PHYLACTERIES
Mt 23. 5 they make broad their *p*, and

PHYSICIAN
Jer 8.22 in Gilead; is there no *p* there?
Mt 9.12 They that be whole need not a *p*,
Mk 2.17 are whole have no need of the *p*,
Lk 4.23 me this proverb, *P*, heal thyself:
5.31 They that are whole need not a *P*;
Col 4.14 Luke, the beloved *p*, and Demas,

PHYSICIANS
Gen 50. 2 commanded his servants the *p*
2 and the *p* embalmed Israel.
2Ch 16.12 sought not to the Lord, but to the *p*.
Job 13. 4 of lies, ye are all *p* of no value.
Mk 5.26 suffered many things of many *p*,
Lk 8.43 had spent all her living upon *p*,

PICTURES
Nu 33.52 destroy all their *p*, and destroy
Pr 25.11 is like apples of gold in *p* of silver.
Isa 2.16 Tarshish,...upon all pleasant *p*.

PIECE
Gen 15.10 laid each *p* one against another:
Ex 37. 7 of gold, beaten out of one *p* made
Nu 10. 2 of a whole *p* shalt thou make them:
Jdg 9.53 woman cast a *p* of a millstone
1Sa 2.36 crouch to him for a *p* of silver and
36 that I may eat a *p* of bread.
30.12 gave him a *p* of a cake of figs,
2Sa 6.19 of bread, and a good *p* of flesh,
11.21 a woman cast a *p* of a millstone
23.11 a *p* of ground full of lentiles:
2Ki 3.19 and mar every good *p* of land with
25 on every good *p* of land cast every
1Ch 16. 3 of bread, and a good *p* of flesh,
Neh 3.11 repaired the other *p*, and the
19 another *p* over against the going
20 earnestly repaired the other *p*,
21 Urijah the son of Koz another *p*,
24 the son of Henadad another *p*,
27 the Tekoites repaired another *p*,
30 the sixth son of Zalaph, another *p*.
Job 41.24 as a *p* of the nether millstone.
42.11 man also gave him a *p* of money,
Pr 6.26 a man is brought to a *p* of bread:
28.21 for a *p* of bread that man will
SS 4. 3 are like a *p* of a pomegranate
6. 7 As a *p* of a pomegranate are thy
Jer 37.21 give him daily a *p* of bread out
Eze 24. 4 thereof into it, even every good *p*,
6 bring it out *p* by *p*; let no lot fall
Am 3.12 the lion two legs, or a *p* of an ear;

4. 7 one *p* was rained upon, and the
7 *p* whereupon it rained not withered.
Mt 9.16 putteth a *p* of new cloth unto an
17.27 mouth, thou shalt find a *p* of money:
Mk 2.21 seweth a *p* of new cloth on an old
21 the new *p* that filled it up taketh
Lk 5.36 putteth a *p* of a new garment upon
36 the *p* that was taken out of the
14.18 I have bought a *p* of ground, and
15. 8 if she lose one *p*, doth not light a
9 have found the *p* which I had lost.
24.42 gave him a *p* of a broiled fish,

PIECES

Gen 15.17 that passed between those *p*.
20.16 thy brother a thousand *p* of silver:
33.19 father, for an hundred *p* of money.
37.28 Ishmeelites for twenty *p* of silver:
33 Joseph is without doubt rent in *p*.
44.28 and I said, Surely he is torn in *p*;
45.22 he gave three hundred *p* of silver,
Ex 15. 6 Lord, hath dashed in *p* the enemy.
22.13 If it be torn in *p*, then let him bring
29.17 And thou shalt cut the ram in *p*,
17 put them unto his *p*, and unto his
Lev 1. 6 burnt offering, and cut it into his *p*.
12 he shall cut it into his *p*, with his
2. 6 Thou shalt part it in *p*, and pour
6.21 the baken *p* of the meat offering
8.20 he cut the ram into *p*; and Moses
20 the head, and the *p*, and the fat.
9.13 with the *p* thereof, and the head:
Jos 24.32 Shechem for an hundred *p* of silver:
Jdg 9. 4 him threescore and ten *p* of silver
16. 5 of us eleven hundred *p* of silver.
19.29 with her bones, into twelve *p*,
20. 6 my concubine, and cut her in *p*,
1Sa 2.10 of the Lord shall be broken to *p*;
11. 7 yoke of oxen, and hewed them in *p*,
15.33 Samuel hewed Agag in *p* before the
1Ki 11.30 on him, and rent it in twelve *p*:
31 to Jeroboam, Take thee ten *p*:
18.23 and cut it in *p*, and lay it on wood,
33 and cut the bullock in *p*, and laid
19.11 brake in *p* the rocks before the Lord;
2Ki 2.12 clothes, and rent them in two *p*.
5. 5 silver, and six thousand *p* of gold,
6.25 was sold for fourscore *p* of silver,
25 of dove's dung for five *p* of silver.
11.18 and his images brake they in *p*
18. 4 brake in *p* the brasen serpent that
23.14 he brake in *p* the images, and cut
24.13 cut in *p* all the vessels of gold which
25.13 did the Chaldees break in *p*, and
2Ch 23.17 brake his altars and his images in *p*,
25.12 that they all were broken in *p*.
28.24 cut in *p* the vessels of the house of
31. 1 brake the images in *p*, and cut
34. 4 the molten images, he brake in *p*,
Job 16.12 me by my neck, and shaken me to *p*,
19. 2 soul, and brake me in *p* with words?
34.24 brake in *p* mighty men without
40.18 His bones are as strong *p* of brass;
Ps 2. 9 dash them in *p* like a potter's vessel.
7. 2 my soul like a lion, rending it in *p*,
50.22 that forget God, lest I tear you in *p*,
58. 7 his arrows, let them be as cut in *p*.
68.30 submit himself with *p* of silver:
72. 4 and shall break in *p* the oppressor.
74.14 breakest the heads of leviathan in *p*,
89.10 Thou hast broken Rahab in *p*, as one
94. 5 They break in *p* thy people, O Lord,
SS 8.11 was to bring a thousand *p* of silver.
Isa 3.15 mean ye that ye beat my people to *p*,
8. 9 ye shall be broken in *p*: and give ear,
9 and ye shall be broken in *p*; gird
9 yourselves,...ye shall be broken in *p*.
13.16 children also shall be dashed to *p*
18 also shall dash the young men to *p*;
30.14 potter's vessel that is broken in *p*;
45. 2 I will break in *p* the gates of brass,
Jer 5. 6 goeth out thence shall be torn in *p*:
23.29 hammer that breaketh the rock in *p*?
50. 2 Merodach is broken in *p*; her idols
2 her images are broken in *p*.
51.20 thee will I break in *p* the nations,
21 break in *p* the horse and his rider;
21 break in *p* the chariot and his rider;
22 will I break in *p* man and woman;
22 will I break in *p* old and young;
22 break in *p* the young man and the
23 break in *p* with thee the shepherd
23 will I break in *p* the husbandman
23 I break in *p* captains and rulers.
La 3.11 aside my ways, and pulled me in *p*:
Eze 4.14 that dieth of itself, or is torn in *p*;
13.19 of barley and for *p* of bread,
24. 4 Gather the *p* thereof into it, even
Dan 2. 5 ye shall be cut in *p*, and your
34 iron and clay, and brake them to *p*.
35 and the gold, broken to *p* together,
40 forasmuch as iron breaketh in *p* and
40 these, shall it break in *p* and bruise.
44 it shall break in *p* and consume all
45 and that it break in *p* the iron, the
3.29 and Abed-nego, shall be cut in *p*,
6.24 and brake all their bones in *p* or
7. 7 it devoured and brake in *p*, and
19 which devoured, brake in *p*, and
23 shall tread it down, and break it in *p*.
Hos 3. 2 her to me for fifteen *p* of silver,
8. 6 of Samaria shall be broken in *p*.
10.14 mother was dashed in *p* upon her
13.16 their infants shall be dashed in *p*,
Mic 1. 7 images thereof shall be beaten to *p*,
3. 3 their bones, and chop them in *p*,
4.13 thou shalt beat in *p* many people:
5. 8 treadeth down, and teareth in *p*,
Na 2. 1 He that dasheth in *p* is come up
12 The lion did tear in *p* enough for his
3.10 young children also were dashed in *p*
Zec 11.12 for my price thirty *p* of silver.
13 And I took the thirty *p* of silver, and
16 the fat, and tear their claws in *p*.
12. 3 themselves with it shall be cut in *p*,
Mt 26.15 with him for thirty *p* of silver.
27. 3 brought again the thirty *p* of silver
5 cast down the *p* of silver in the
6 the chief priests took the silver *p*,
9 And they took the thirty *p* of silver,
Mk 5. 4 by him, and the fetters broken in *p*:
Lk 15. 8 what woman having ten *p* of silver
Ac 19.19 found it fifty thousand *p* of silver
23.10 should have been pulled in *p* of
27.44 some on broken *p* of the ship

PIERCE

Nu 24. 8 *p* them through with his arrows.
2Ki 18.21 it will go into his hand, and *p* it:
Isa 36. 6 it will go into his hand, and *p* it:
Lk 2.35 shall *p* through thy own soul also,)

PIERCED

Jdg 5.26 had *p* and stricken through his
Job 30.17 My bones are *p* in me in the night
Ps 22.16 me: they *p* my hands and my feet.
Zec 12.10 look upon me whom they have *p*,
Jn 19.34 soldiers with a spear *p* his side,
37 shall look on him whom they *p*.
1Ti 6.10 *p* themselves through with many
Rev 1. 7 him, and they also which *p* him:

PIERCING

Isa 27. 1 punish leviathan the *p* serpent,
Heb 4.12 *p* even to the dividing asunder of

PIERCINGS

Pr 12.18 speaketh like the *p* of a sword:

PIETY

1Ti 5. 4 them learn first to show *p* at

PILATE

Pontius Pilate, Roman governor of Judea (c. A.D. 25–35); when Jesus is brought before him on charges of sedition, Pilate sends him first to Herod Antipas (who, as tetrarch of Galilee, would have jurisdiction over Galilean prisoners), a gesture that reconciles the two (Lk 23.1-12); when he is returned, Pilate finds no substance in the charges and proposes to "chastise him and release him" (Lk 23.16); he then invokes a custom of releasing at the Passover feast a prisoner of the people's choice, but the people choose Barabbas, a common criminal, instead of Jesus; thereupon Pilate, despite his wife's urging that Jesus not be punished (Mt 27.19), pronounces sentence of crucifixion, after washing his hands in an effort to symbolize his own innocence (Mt 27.24). In the Gospel of John, Pilate questions Jesus concerning his kingship and is told, "My kingdom is not of this world" (Jn 18.36); after authorizing crucifixion, writes inscription on the cross ("King of the Jews") and refuses to change it in spite of protests from chief priests (Jn 19.19-22).

PIGEON

Gen 15. 9 and a turtledove, and a young *p*.
Lev 12. 6 and a young *p*, or a turtledove,

PIGEONS

Lev 5. 7, 11 two turtledoves, or two young *p*,
Lk 2.24 of turtledoves, or two young *p*.

PILATE

Mt 27. 2 him to Pontius *P* the governor.
13 said *P* unto him, Hearest thou not
17 *P* said unto them, Whom will ye
22 *P* saith unto them, What shall I do
24 When *P* saw that he could prevail
58 went to *P*, and begged the body of
58 Then *P* commanded the body to be
62 Pharisees came together unto *P*,
65 *P* said unto them, Ye have a
Mk 15. 1 him away, and delivered him to *P*.
2 *P* asked him, Art thou the King of
4 And *P* asked him again, saying,
5 nothing; so that *P* marvelled.
9 *P* answered them, saying, Will ye
12 *P* answered and said again unto
14 *P* said unto them, Why, what evil
15 And so *P*, willing to content the
43 went in boldly unto *P*, and craved
44 *P* marvelled if he were already
Lk 3. 1 Pontius *P* being governor of
13. 1 blood *P* had mingled with their
23. 1 of them arose, and led him unto *P*.
3 And *P* asked him, saying, Art thou
4 said *P* to the chief priests and to
6 When *P* heard of Galilee, he asked
11 robe, and sent him again to *P*.
12 *P* and Herod were made friends
13 *P*, when he had called together
20 *P* therefore, willing to release
24 *P* gave sentence that it should be
52 This man went unto *P*, and begged
Jn 18.29 *P* then went out unto them, and
31 Then said *P* unto them, Take ye
33 *P* entered into the judgment hall
35 *P* answered, Am I a Jew? Thine
37 *P* therefore said unto him, Art thou
38 *P* saith unto him, What is truth?

Christ before Pilate *(Mt 27; Mk 15; Lk 23; Jn 18–19) by Rembrandt (1606-1669).*

Jn 19. 1 Then *P* therefore took Jesus, and
4 *P* therefore went forth again, and
5 *P* saith unto them, Behold the man!
6 *P* saith unto them, Take ye him,
8 *P* therefore heard that saying,
10 Then saith *P* unto him, Speakest
12 thenceforth *P* sought to release
13 *P* therefore heard that saying,
15 *P* saith unto them, Shall I crucify
19 *P* wrote a title, and put it on the
21 the chief priests of the Jews to *P*,
22 *P* answered, What I have written
31 besought *P* that their legs might
38 besought *P* that he might take
38 of Jesus: and *P* gave him leave.
Ac 3.13 denied him in the presence of *P*,
4.27 both Herod, and Pontius *P*, with
13.28 they *P* that he should be slain.
1Ti 6.13 before Pontius *P* witnessed a good

PILGRIMAGE

Gen 47. 9 The days of the years of my *p* are
9 my fathers in the days of their *p*.
Ex 6. 4 land of Canaan, the land of their *p*,
Ps 119.54 my songs in the house of my *p*.

PILGRIMS

Heb 11.13 strangers and *p* on the earth.
1Pe 2.11 I beseech you as strangers and *p*,

PILLAR

Gen 19.26 him, and she became a *p* of salt.
28.18 his pillows, and set it up for a *p*,
22 this stone, which I have set for a *p*,
31.52 this *p* be witness, that I will not
35.14 And Jacob set up a *p* in the place
20 that is the *p* of Rachel's grave
Ex 13.21 them by day in a *p* of a cloud, to
21 by night in a *p* of fire, to give them
33. 9 the cloudy *p* descended, and stood
2Sa 18.18 he called the *p* after his own name:
Ps 99. 7 spake unto them in the cloudy *p*:
1Ti 3.15 the *p* and ground of the truth.
Rev 3.12 a *p* in the temple of my God,

PILLARS

Ex 24. 4 *p*, according to the twelve tribes
Dt 12. 3 break their *p*, burn their groves
Jdg 16.25 and they set him between the *p*.
26 Suffer me that I may feel the *p*
29 took hold of the two middle *p*
1Sa 2. 8 the *p* of the earth are the Lord's,
Job 26.11 The *p* of heaven tremble and are
Ps 75. 3 are dissolved: I bear up the *p* of it.
SS 3. 6 of the wilderness like *p* of smoke,
Joel 2.30 blood, and fire, and *p* of smoke.
Gal 2. 9 and John, who seemed to be *p*,
Rev 10. 1 the sun, and his feet as *p* of fire:

PILLOW

1Sa 19.13 a *p* of goats' hair for his bolster,
16 a *p* of goats' hair for his bolster.
Mk 4.38 part of the ship, asleep on a *p*:

PILLOWS

Gen 28.11 that place, and put them for his *p*,
18 the stone that he had put for his *p*,
Eze 13.18 women that sew *p* in all armholes,
20 I am against your *p*, wherewith ye

PILOTS

Eze 27. 8 that were in thee, were thy *p*.
27 thy mariners, and thy *p*, thy
28 at the sound of the cry of thy *p*.
29 all the *p* of the sea, shall come

PINE

Lev 26.39 that are left of you shall *p* away
39 shall they *p* away with them.
Neh 8.15 fetch olive branches, and *p*
Isa 41.19 the desert the fire tree, and the *p*,
60.13 unto thee, the fire tree, the *p* tree,
La 4. 9 these *p* away, stricken through
Eze 24.23 shall *p* away for your iniquities,
33.10 upon us, and we *p* away in them,

PINETH

Mk 9.18 with his teeth, and *p* away:

PINNACLE

Mt 4. 5 setteth him on a *p* of the temple,
Lk 4. 9 and set him on a *p* of the temple,

PIPE

1Sa 10. 5 with a tabret, and a *p*, and a harp,
Isa 5.12 viol, the tabret, and *p*, and wine,
30.29 one goeth with a *p* to come into the
1Co 14. 7 giving sound, whether *p* or harp,

PIPED

1Ki 1.40 and the people *p* with pipes, and
Mt 11.17 We have *p* unto you, and ye have
Lk 7.32 We have *p* unto you, and ye have
1Co 14. 7 it be known what is *p* or harped?

PIPERS

Rev 18.22 harpers, and musicians, and of *p*,

PISIDIA

Ac 13.14 they came to Antioch in *P*, and
14.24 they had passed throughout *P*,

PIT

Gen 37.20 him, and cast him into some *p*,
22 but cast him into this *p* that is in
24 took him, and cast him into a *p*:
24 *p* was empty, there was no water
28 and lifted up Joseph out of the *p*,
29 And Reuben returned unto the *p*;
29 behold, Joseph was not in the *p*;
Ex 21.33 And if a man shall open a *p*, or
33 if a man shall dig a *p*, and not cover
34 owner of the *p* shall make it good,
Lev 11.36 Nevertheless a fountain or *p*,
Nu 16.30 they go down quick into the *p*;
33 went down alive into the *p*, and

2Sa 17. 9 he is hid now in some *p*, or in
18.17 cast him into a great *p* in the wood,
23.20 and slew a lion in the midst of a *p*
2Ki 10.14 slew them at the *p* of the shearing
1Ch 11.22 slew a lion in a *p* in a snowy day.
Job 6.27 and ye dig a *p* for your friend.
17.16 go down to the bars of the *p*,
33.18 keepeth back his soul from the *p*,
24 him from going down to the *p*:
28 his soul from going into the *p*,
30 To bring back his soul from the *p*,
Ps 7.15 He made a *p*, and digged it, and
9.15 heathen are sunk down in the *p*
28. 1 like them that go down into the *p*.
30. 3 that I should not go down to the *p*.
9 blood, when I go down to the *p*?
35. 7 they hid for me their net in a *p*,
40. 2 me up also out of an horrible *p*,
55.23 down into the *p* of destruction:
57. 6 they have digged a *p* before me,
69.15 let not the *p* shut her mouth upon
88. 4 with them that go down into the *p*:
6 Thou hast laid me in the lowest *p*,
94.13 the *p* be digged for the wicked.
143. 7 unto them that go down into the *p*.
Pr 1.12 as those that go down into the *p*:
22.14 of strange woman is a deep *p*:
23.27 a strange woman is a narrow *p*.
26.27 Whoso diggeth a *p* shall fall
28.10 shall fall himself into his own *p*:
17 doeth violence...shall flee to the *p*;
Ec 10. 8 He that diggeth a *p* shall fall into
Isa 14.15 down to hell, to the sides of the *p*.
19 that go down to the stones of the *p*;
24.17 Fear, and the *p*, and the snare,
18 noise of...fear shall fall into the *p*;
18 cometh up out of the midst of the *p*
22 as prisoners are gathered in the *p*,
30.14 to take water withal out of the *p*.
38.17 it from the *p* of corruption:
18 that go down into the *p* cannot hope
51. 1 hole of the *p* whence ye are digged.
14 that he should not die in the *p*,
Jer 18.20 they have digged a *p* for my soul.
22 have digged a *p* to take me,
41. 7 cast them into the midst of the *p*,
9 the *p* wherein Ishmael had cast all
48.43 Fear, and the *p*, and the snare,
44 from the fear shall fall into the *p*;
44 and he that getteth up out of the *p*
Eze 19. 4 he was taken in their *p*, and
8 over him: he was taken in their *p*.
26.20 with them that descend into the *p*,
20 with them that go down to the *p*,
28. 8 shall bring thee down to the *p*,
31.14 with them that go down to the *p*,
16 with them that descend into the *p*:
32.18 with them that go down into the *p*.
23 graves are set in the sides of the *p*,
24 with them that go down to the *p*.
25 with them that go down to the *p*:
29, 30 with them that go down to the *p*.
Zec 9.11 out of the *p* wherein is no water.
Mt 12.11 it fall into a *p* on the sabbath day,
Lk 14. 5 an ass or an ox fallen into a *p*,
Rev 9. 1 given the key of the bottomless *p*.
2 And he opened the bottomless *p*;
2 there arose a smoke out of the *p*,
2 by reason of the smoke of the *p*.
11 is the angel of the bottomless *p*,
11. 7 ascendeth out of the bottomless *p*
17. 8 ascend out of the bottomless *p*, and
20. 1 having the key of the bottomless *p*
3 And cast him into the bottomless *p*,

PITCH

Gen 6.14 shalt *p* it within and without
14 it within and without with *p*.
Ex 2. 3 daubed it with slime and with *p*,
Nu 1.52 of Israel shall *p* their tents,
53 the Levites shall *p* round about
2. 2 shall *p* by his own standard,
2 of the congregation shall they *p*.
3 Judah *p* throughout their armies:
5 And those that do *p* next unto him
12 And those which *p* by him shall be
3.23 shall *p* behind the tabernacle
29, 35 *p* on the side of the tabernacle
Dt 1.33 you out a place to *p* your tents in,
Jos 4.20 of Jordan, did Joshua *p* in Gilgal.
Isa 13.20 neither shall the Arabian *p* tent
34. 9 thereof shall be turned into *p*,
9 thereof shall become burning *p*.
Jer 6. 3 shall *p* their tents against her

PITCHER

Gen 24.14 Let down thy *p*, I pray thee, that
15 with her *p* upon her shoulder.
16 well, and filled her *p*, and came up.
17 thee, drink a little water of thy *p*.
18 and let down her *p* upon her hand,
20 and emptied her *p* into the trough,
43 a little water of thy *p* to drink;
45 forth with her *p* on her shoulder;
46 let down her *p* from her shoulder,
Ec 12. 6 or the *p* be broken at the fountain,
Mk 14.13 you a man bearing a *p* of water:
Lk 22.10 meet you, bearing a *p* of water;

PITIETH

Ps 103.13 Like as a father *p* his children,
13 so the Lord *p* them that fear him.
Eze 24.21 eyes, and that which your soul *p*;

PITIFUL

La 4.10 The hands of the *p* women have
Jas 5.11 the Lord is very *p*, and of tender
1Pe 3. 8 love as brethren, be *p*, be

PITS

1Sa 13. 6 rocks, and in high places, and in *p*.
Ps 119.85 The proud have digged *p* for me,
140.10 be cast into the fire: into deep *p*,
Jer 2. 6 through a land of deserts and...*p*,
14. 3 they came to the *p*, and found no
La 4.20 the Lord, was taken in their *p*,

PITY

Dt 7.16 eye shall have no *p* upon them:
13. 8 neither shall thine eye *p* him,
19.13 Thine eye shall not *p* him, but thou
21 thine eye shall not *p*; but life shall
25.12 her hand, thine eye shall not *p* her.
2Sa 12. 6 thing, and because he had no *p*.
Job 6.14 is afflicted *p* should be shewed
19.21 Have *p* upon me, have *p* upon me,
Ps 69.20 I looked for some to take *p*, but
Pr 19.17 He that hath *p* upon the poor
28. 8 it for him that will *p* the poor.
Isa 13.18 no *p* on the fruit of the womb;
63. 9 and in his *p* he redeemed them;
Jer 13.14 I will not *p*, nor spare, nor have
15. 5 For who shall have *p* upon thee, O
21. 7 neither have *p*, nor have mercy.
Eze 5.11 spare, neither will I have any *p*.
7. 4 spare thee, neither will I have *p*:
9 not spare, neither will I have *p*:
8.18 not spare, neither will I have *p*:
9. 5 your eye spare, neither have ye *p*:
10 not spare, neither will I have *p*,
36.21 But I had *p* for mine holy name,
Joel 2.18 for his land, and *p* his people.
Am 1.11 the sword, and did cast off all *p*,
Jon 4.10 Thou hast had *p* on the gourd,
Zec 11. 5 their own shepherds *p* them not.
6 no more *p* the inhabitants of the
Mt 18.33 fellowservant,...I had *p* on thee?

PLACE

Gen 18.24 spare the *p* for the fifty righteous
19.14 and said, Up, get you out of this *p*;
20.11 the fear of God is not in this *p*;
22. 4 up his eyes, and saw the *p* afar off.
28.16 Surely the Lord is in this *p*; and I
17 and said, How dreadful is this *p*!
19 called the name of that *p* Beth-el:
30.25 that I may go unto mine own *p*,
35.15 the *p* where God spake with him,
50.19 Fear not: for am I in the *p* of God?
Ex 3. 5 *p* whereon thou standest is holy
13. 3 Lord brought you out from this *p*:
29.30 to minister in the holy *p*.
Dt 12. 5 *p* which the Lord your God shall
14 the *p* which the Lord shall choose
14.23 choose to *p* his name there,
Jdg 18.10 *p* where there is no want of any
1Sa 3. 2 Eli was laid down in his *p*, and his
9 Samuel went and lay down in his *p*.
20.25 side, and David's *p* was empty.
2Sa 18.18 called unto this day, Absalom's *p*.
1Ki 8.30 when they shall pray toward this *p*:
30 hear thou in heaven thy dwelling *p*:
2Ki 5.11 and strike his hand over the *p*, and
6. 1 *p* where we dwell with thee is too
1Ch 15. 1 and prepared a *p* for the ark of God,
2Ch 6.20 thy servant prayeth toward this *p*.
26 yet if they pray toward this *p*, and
Job 7.10 shall his *p* know him any more.
8.18 If he destroy him from his *p*, then
22 the dwelling *p* of the wicked shall
14.18 and the rock is removed out of his *p*.
18.21 the *p* of him that knoweth not God.
20. 9 shall his *p* any more behold him.
28.12, 20 is the *p* of understanding?
Ps 18.11 He made darkness his secret *p*; his
24. 3 or who shall stand in his holy *p*?
26. 8 *p* where thine honor dwelleth.
32. 7 Thou art my hiding *p*; thou shalt
90. 1 Lord, thou hast been our dwelling *p*
91. 1 He that dwelleth in the secret *p* of
103.16 *p* thereof shall know it no more.
119.114 Thou art my hiding *p* and my
132. 5 until I find out a *p* for the Lord,
Pr 15. 3 eyes of the Lord are in every *p*,
25. 6 stand not in the *p* of great men:
Ec 3.20 All go unto one *p*; all are of the
6. 6 no good: do not all go to one *p*?
Isa 32. 2 as rivers of water in a dry *p*, as the
35. 1 solitary *p* shall be glad for them;
49.20 ears, The *p* is too straight for me:
57.15 I dwell in the high and holy *p*, with
60.13 beautify the *p* of my sanctuary;
Jer 4. 7 he is gone forth from his *p* to
17.12 is the *p* of our sanctuary.
Eze 41. 4 unto me, This is the most holy *p*.
Dan 2.35 no *p* was found for them: and the
Mic 1. 3 the Lord cometh forth out of his *p*,
Zep 2.11 worship him every one from his *p*,
Hag 2. 9 and in this *p* will I give peace,
Mal 1.11 in every *p* incense shall be offered
Mt 8.32 violently down a steep *p* into the sea,
9.24 He said unto them, Give *p*: for the
12. 6 in this *p* is one...than the temple.
14.13 by ship into a desert *p* apart:
15 This is a desert *p*, and the time is
35 the men of that *p* had knowledge
17.20 Remove hence to yonder *p*; and it
24.15 the prophet, stand in the holy *p*,
26.36 them unto a *p* called Gethsemane,
52 Put up again thy sword into his *p*:
27.33 come unto a *p* called Golgotha,
33 that is to say, a *p* of a skull,
28. 6 Come see the *p* where the Lord lay.
Mk 1.35 departed into a solitary *p*, and
5.13 violently down a steep *p* into the sea,
6.10 *p* soever ye enter into an house,
10 abide till ye depart from that *p*.
31 yourselves apart into a desert *p*,
32 they departed into a desert *p* by
35 This is a desert *p*, and now the
11. 4 without in a *p* where two ways met;
12. 1 and digged a *p* for the winefat, and
14.32 to a *p* which...named Gethsemane:

Mk 15.22 bring him unto the *p* Golgotha,
22 being interpreted, The *p* of a skull.
16. 6 behold the *p* where they laid him.
Lk 4.17 found the *p* where it was written,
37 went out into every *p* of the country
42 departed and went into a desert *p*;
8.33 violently down a steep *p* into the
9.10 aside privately into a desert *p*
12 for we are here in a desert *p*.
10. 1 his face into every city and *p*,
32 a Levite, when he was at the *p*,
11. 1 as he was praying in a certain *p*,
33 a candle, putteth it in a secret *p*,
14. 9 and say to thee, Give this man *p*;
16.28 also come into this *p* of torment.
19. 5 And when Jesus came to the *p*, he
22.40 when he was at the *p*, he said unto
23. 5 beginning from Galilee to this *p*
33 And when they were come to the *p*,
Jn 4.20 in Jerusalem is the *p* where men
5.13 away, a multitude being in that *p*.
6.10 there was much grass in the *p*.
23 unto the *p* where they did eat
8.37 my word hath no *p* in you.
10.40 *p* where John at first baptized;
11. 6 still in the same *p* where he was.
30 in that *p* where Martha met him.
41 from the *p* where the dead was laid.
48 take away both our *p* and nation.
14. 2 you. I go to prepare a *p* for you.
3 if I go and prepare a *p* for you,
18. 2 which betrayed him, knew the *p*:
19.13 in a *p* that is called the Pavement,
17 his cross went forth into a *p*
17 called the *p* of a skull, which is
20 the *p* where Jesus was crucified
41 the *p* where he was crucified there
20. 7 wrapped together in a *p* by itself.
Ac 1.25 fell, that he might go to his own *p*.
2. 1 were all with one accord in one *p*.
4.31 the *p* was shaken where they
6.13 words against this holy *p*, and the
14 of Nazareth shall destroy this *p*,
7. 7 come forth, and serve me in this *p*.
33 the *p* where thou standest is holy
49 Lord: or what is the *p* of my rest?
8.32 *p* of the scripture which he read
12.17 departed, and went into another *p*.
21.12 and they of that *p*, besought him
28 people, and the law, and this *p*:
28 and hath polluted this holy *p*.
25.23 was entered into the *p* of hearing,
27. 8 a *p* which is called The fair havens;
41 into a *p* where two seas met,
Ro 9.26 *p* where it was said unto them,
12.19 but rather give *p* unto wrath:
15.23 having no more *p* in these parts,
1Co 1. 2 that in every *p* call upon the name
11.20 come together therefore into one *p*,
14.23 church be come together into one *p*,
2Co 2.14 his knowledge by us in every *p*.
Gal 2. 5 whom we gave *p* by subjection,
Eph 4.27 Neither give *p* to the devil.
1Th 1. 8 in every *p* your faith to God-ward
Heb 2. 6 But one in a certain *p* testified,
4. 4 spake in a certain *p* of the seventh
5 And in this *p* again, If they shall
5. 6 As he saith also in another *p*, Thou
8. 7 no *p* have been sought for the
9.12 he entered in once into the holy *p*,
25 high priest entereth into the holy *p*
11. 8 he was called to go out into a *p*
12.17 for he found no *p* of repentance,
Jas 2. 3 Sit thou here in a good *p*; and
3.11 at the same *p* sweet water and
2Pe 1.19 a light that shineth in a dark *p*,
Rev 2. 5 thy candlestick out of this *p*,
12. 6 she hath a *p* prepared of God,
8 was their *p* found any more
14 into her *p*, where she is nourished
16.16 a *p* called in the Hebrew tongue
20.11 and there was found no *p* for them.

PLACED

Gen 3.24 he *p* at the east of the garden of
47.11 And Joseph *p* his father and his
1Ki 12.32 and he *p* in Beth-el the priests of
2Ki 17. 6 *p* them in Halah and in Habor by
24 *p* them in the cities of Samaria
26 *p* in the cities of Samaria, know
2Ch 1.14 which he *p* in the chariot cities.
4. 8 *p* them in the temple, five on the
17. 2 he *p* forces in all the fenced cities
Job 20. 4 old, since man was *p* upon earth,
Ps 78.60 the tent which he *p* among men;
Isa 5. 8 they may be *p* alone in the midst
Jer 5.22 have *p* the sand for the bound of
Eze 17. 5 he *p* it by great waters, and set

PLACES

Gen 28.15 keep thee in all *p* whither thou goest,
Ex 20.24 *p* where I record my name I will
2Sa 1.19 of Israel is slain upon thy high *p*:
1Ki 22.43 the high *p* were not taken away;
2Ki 18. 4 He removed the high *p*, and brake
Job 3.14 built desolate *p* for themselves;
20.26 darkness shall be hid in his secret *p*:
21.28 are the dwelling *p* of the wicked?
25. 2 him, he maketh peace in his high *p*.
Ps 16. 6 are fallen unto me in pleasant *p*;
73.18 thou didst set them in slippery *p*:
Isa 40. 4 made straight, and the rough *p* plain:
45. 2 and make the crooked *p* straight:
49.19 For thy waste and thy desolate *p*,
51. 3 he will comfort all her waste *p*; and
52. 9 together, ye waste *p* of Jerusalem:
58.12 be of thee shall build the old waste *p*:
Jer 3. 2 Lift up thine eyes unto the high *p*,
23.24 Can any hide himself in secret *p* that
Mic 1. 5 and what are the high *p* of Judah?
Hab 3.19 make me to walk upon mine high *p*.
Mal 1. 4 will return and build the desolate *p*;
Mt 12.43 he walketh through dry *p*, seeking
13. 5 Some fell upon stony *p*, where they
20 that received the seed into stony *p*,
24. 7 and earthquakes, in divers *p*.
Mk 1.45 city, but was without in desert *p*:
13. 8 shall be earthquakes in divers *p*,
Lk 11.24 he walketh through dry *p*, seeking
21.11 earthquakes shall be in divers *p*,
Ac 24. 3 We accept it always, and in all *p*,
Eph 1. 3 blessings in heavenly *p* in Christ:
20 his own right hand in the heavenly *p*,
2. 6 in heavenly *p* in Christ Jesus:
3.10 in heavenly *p* might be known by
6.12 spiritual wickedness in high *p*.
Php 1.13 all the palace, and in all other *p*;
Heb 9.24 into the holy *p* made with hands,
Rev 6.14 island were moved out of their *p*.

PLAGUE

Ex 11. 1 bring one *p* more upon Pharaoh,
Nu 16.46 from the Lord; the *p* is begun.
48 the living; and the *p* was stayed.
1Ki 8.38 every man the *p* of his own heart,
Ps 91.10 neither shall any *p* come nigh thy
106.30 judgment: and so the *p* was stayed.
Mk 5.29 that she was healed of that *p*.
34 go in peace, and be whole of thy *p*.
Rev 16.21 God because of the *p* of the hail;
21 the *p* thereof was exceeding great.

PLAGUED

Gen 12.17 Lord *p* Pharaoh and his house
Ex 32.35 the Lord *p* the people, because
Jos 24. 5 I *p* Egypt, according to that which
1Ch 21.17 thy people, that they should be *p*.
Ps 73. 5 neither are they *p* like other men.
14 all the day long have I been *p*,

PLAGUES

Gen 12.17 plagued Pharaoh...with great *p*
Ex 9.14 at this time send all my *p* upon
Lev 26.21 seven times more *p* upon you
Dt 28.59 Lord will make thy *p* wonderful,
59 and the *p* of thy seed, even great *p*,
29.22 when they see the *p* of that land,
1Sa 4. 8 smote the Egyptians with all the *p*
Jer 19. 8 hiss because of all the *p* thereof.
49.17 and shall hiss at all the *p* thereof.
50.13 be astonished, and hiss at all her *p*.
Hos 13.14 O death, I will be thy *p*; O grave,
Mk 3.10 to touch him, as many as had *p*.
Lk 7.21 many of their infirmities and *p*,
Rev 9.20 which were not killed by these *p*
11. 6 and to smite the earth with all *p*,
15. 1 angels having the seven last *p*;
6 of the temple, having the seven *p*,
8 seven *p* of the seven angels were
16. 9 which hath power over these *p*:
18. 4 and that ye receive not of her *p*.
8 shall her *p* come in one day, death,
21. 9 seven vials full of the seven last *p*,
22.18 God shall add unto him the *p* that

PLAIN

Gen 13.11 Lot chose him all the *p* of Jordan;
12 Lot dwelled in the cities of the *p*,
19.29 God destroyed the cities of the *p*,
25.27 Jacob was a *p* man, dwelling in
Ps 27.11 lead me in a *p* path, because of
Pr 8. 9 all *p* to him that understandeth,
15.19 way of the righteous is made *p*.
Isa 40. 4 straight, and the rough places *p*:
Mk 7.35 tongue was loosed, and he spake *p*.
Lk 6.17 and stood in the *p*, and the

PLAINLY

Ex 21. 5 if the servant shall *p* say, I love
Dt 27. 8 all the words of this law very *p*.
1Sa 2.27 *p* appear unto the house of thy
10.16 He told us *p* that the asses were
Ezr 4.18 sent unto us hath been *p* read
Isa 32. 4 shall be ready to speak *p*.
Jn 10.24 If thou be the Christ, tell us *p*.
11.14 Then said Jesus unto them *p*,
16.25 I shall shew you *p* of the Father.
29 him, Lo, now speakest thou *p*,
Heb 11.14 declare *p* that they seek a country.

PLAINNESS

2Co 3.12 hope, we use great *p* of speech:

PLAITING

1Pe 3. 3 outward adorning of *p* the hair,

PLANT

Dt 28.30 thou shalt *p* a vineyard, and shalt
Ec 3. 2 a time to *p*, and a time to pluck up
Isa 53. 2 grow up before him as a tender *p*,
65.22 they shall not *p*, and another eat:
Jer 1.10 to throw down, to build, and to *p*.
18. 9 a kingdom, to build and to *p* it;
24. 6 and I will *p* them, and not pluck
31. 5 yet *p* vines upon the mountains
Am 9.15 and I will *p* them upon their land,
Mt 15.13 *p*, which my heavenly Father

PLANTATION

Eze 17. 7 water it by the furrows of her *p*.

PLANTED

Gen 2. 8 Lord God *p* a garden eastward
9.20 husbandman, and he *p* a vineyard:
Ps 1. 3 shall be like a tree *p* by the rivers
Ec 2. 4 me houses; I *p* me vineyards:
5 and I *p* trees in them of all kinds of
Jer 11.17 the Lord of hosts, that *p* thee, hath
Am 5.11 ye have *p* pleasant vineyards, but
Mt 15.13 my heavenly Father hath not *p*,
21.33 which *p* a vineyard, and hedged it

Mk 12. 1 A certain man *p* a vineyard, and
Lk 13. 6 had a fig tree *p* in his vineyard;
17. 6 the root, and be thou *p* in the sea;
28 they sold, they *p*, they builded;
20. 9 A certain man *p* a vineyard, and
Ro 6. 5 *p* together in the likeness of his
1Co 3. 6 I have *p*, Apollos watered; but

PLANTETH

Pr 31.16 of her hands she *p* a vineyard.
Isa 44.14 he *p* an ash, and the rain doth
1Co 3. 7 neither is he that *p* any thing,
8 Now he that *p* and he that watereth
9. 7 who *p* a vineyard, and eateth not

PLANTING

Isa 60.21 the branch of my *p*, the work of
61. 3 the *p* of the Lord, that he might

PLANTS

1Ch 4.23 that dwelt among *p* and hedges:
Ps 128. 3 children like olive *p* round about
144.12 our sons may be as *p* grown up
SS 4.13 *p* are...orchard of pomegranates,
Isa 16. 8 broken down the principal *p*
17.10 shalt thou plant pleasant *p*, and
Jer 48.32 thy *p* are gone over the sea, they
Eze 31. 4 rivers running round about...*p*,

PLATTED

Mt 27.29 they had *p* a crown of thorns,
Mk 15.17 *p* a crown of thorns, and put it
Jn 19. 2 the soldiers *p* a crown of thorns,

PLATTER

Mt 23.25 outside of the cup and of the *p*,
26 that which is within the cup and *p*,
Lk 11.39 the outside of the cup and the *p*;

PLAY

Ex 32. 6 and to drink, and rose up to *p*.
Dt 22.21 to *p* the whore in her father's house:
1Sa 16.16 he shall *p* with his hand, and
17 me now a man that can *p* well,
21.15 to *p* the mad man in my presence?
2Sa 2.14 men now arise, and *p* before us.
6.21 therefore will I *p* before the Lord.
10.12 and let us *p* the men for our people,
Job 40.20 where all the beasts of the field *p*.
41. 5 thou *p* with him as with a bird?
Ps 33. 3 *p* skillfully with a loud noise.
104.26 thou hast made to *p* therein.
Isa 11. 8 shall *p* on the hole of the asp,
Eze 33.32 and can *p* well on an instrument:
Hos 3. 3 thou shalt not *p* the harlot, and thou
4.15 *p* the harlot, yet let not Judah
1Co 10. 7 eat and drink, and rose up to *p*.

PLAYED

Gen 38.24 daughter in law hath *p* the harlot;
Jdg 19. 2 concubine *p* the whore against him,
1Sa 16.23 an harp, and *p* with his hand:
18. 7 answered one another as they *p*,
10 David *p* with his hand, as at other
19. 9 and David *p* with his hand.
26.21 I have *p* the fool, and have erred
2Sa 6. 5 house of Israel *p* before the Lord
2Ki 3.15 came to pass, when the minstrel *p*,
1Ch 13. 8 David and all Israel *p* before God
Jer 3. 1 thou hast *p* the harlot with many
6 tree, and there hath *p* the harlot.
8 not, but went and *p* the harlot also.
Eze 16.28 Thou hast *p* the whore also with the
28 yea, thou hast *p* the harlot with
23. 5 Aholah *p* the harlot when she was
19 had *p* the harlot in the land of Egypt.
Hos 2. 5 For their mother hath *p* the harlot:

PLAYER

1Sa 16.16 who is a cunning *p* on a harp:

BIBLICAL THEMES

PLANTS

And God said, Let the earth bring forth grass, the herb yielding seed, and the fruit tree yielding fruit after his kind, whose seed is in itself, upon the earth: and it was so. Gen 1.11

And the Lord God planted a garden eastward in Eden. . . . And out of the ground made the Lord God to grow every tree that is pleasant to the sight, and good for food; the tree of life also in the midst of the garden, and the tree of knowledge of good and evil. Gen 2.8-9

And the dove came in to him in the evening; and, lo, in her mouth was an olive leaf pluckt off: so Noah knew that the waters were abated from off the earth. Gen 8.11

And when she could not longer hide him, she took for him an ark of bulrushes, and daubed it with slime and with pitch, and put the child therein; and she laid it in the flags by the river's brink. Ex 2.3

We remember the fish, which we did eat in Egypt freely; the cucumbers, and the melons, and the leeks, and the onions, and the garlick: but now our soul is dried away: there is nothing at all, beside this manna, before our eyes. And the manna was as coriander seed. Nu 11.5-7

Then said all the trees unto the bramble, Come thou, and reign over us. Jdg 9.14

I went by the field of the slothful, and by the vineyard of the man void of understanding; and, lo, it was all grown over with thorns, and nettles had covered the face thereof. Pr 24.30-31

A time to plant, and a time to pluck up that which is planted. Ec 3.2

I am the rose of Sharon, and the lily of the valleys. As the lily among thorns, so is my love among the daughters. SS 2.1-2

What could have been done more to my vineyard, that I have not done in it? wherefore, when I looked that it should bring forth grapes, brought it forth wild grapes? Isa 5.4

Instead of the thorn shall come up the fir tree, and instead of the brier shall come up the myrtle tree. Isa 55.13

And the desolate land shall be tilled. . . . And they shall say, This land that was desolate is become like the garden of Eden. Eze 36.34-35

Consider the lilies of the field, how they grow. . . . even Solomon in all his glory was not arrayed like one of these. Mt 6.28-29

The kingdom of heaven is like to a grain of mustard seed, which a man took, and sowed in his field: which indeed is the least of all seeds: but when it is grown, it is the greatest among herbs, and becometh a tree, so that the birds of the air come and lodge in the branches thereof. Mt 13.31-32

So is the kingdom of God, as if a man should cast seed into the ground . . . and the seed should spring and grow up, he knoweth not how. For the earth bringeth forth fruit of herself; first the blade, then the ear, after that the full corn in the ear. Mk 4.26-28

And seeing a fig tree afar off having leaves, he came, if haply he might find anything thereon: and when he came to it, he found nothing but leaves; for the time of figs was not yet. Mk 11.13

I am the true vine, and my Father is the husbandman. Every branch in me that beareth not fruit he taketh away: and every branch that beareth fruit, he purgeth it, that it may bring forth more fruit. Jn 15.1-2

The grass withereth, and the flower thereof falleth away: but the word of the Lord endureth for ever. 1Pe 1.24-25

PLAYING

Lev 21. 9 she profane herself by *p* the whore,
1Sa 16.18 Bethlehemite that is cunning in *p*,
1Ch 15.29 saw king David dancing and *p*:
Ps 68.25 were the damsels *p* with timbrels.
Jer 2.20 tree thou wanderest, *p* the harlot.
Eze 16.41 thee to cease from *p* the harlot,
Zec 8. 5 boys and girls *p* in the streets

PLEAD

Jdg 6.31 Will ye *p* for Baal? will ye save
31 he that will *p* for him, let him be
31 let him *p* for himself, because one
32 Let Baal *p* against him, because
1Sa 24.15 and *p* my cause, and deliver me
Job 9.19 who shall set me a time to *p*?
13.19 Who is he that will *p* with me?
16.21 one might *p* for a man with God,
19. 5 and *p* against me my reproach:
23. 6 Will he *p* against me with his
Ps 35. 1 *P* my cause, O Lord, with them
Pr 43. 1 Judge me, O God, and *p* my cause
74.22 Arise, O God, *p* thine own cause:
119.154 *P* my cause, and deliver me:
22.23 the Lord will *p* their cause, and
23.11 he shall *p* their cause with thee.

Pr 31. 9 *p* the cause of the poor and needy.
Isa 1.17 the fatherless, *p* for the widow.
3.13 The Lord standeth up to *p*, and
43.26 remembrance: let us *p* together:
66.16 will the Lord *p* with all flesh:
Jer 2. 9 I will yet *p* with you, saith the
9 your children's children will I *p*.
29 Wherefore will ye *p* with me? ye
35 I will *p* with thee, because thou
12. 1 thou, O Lord, when I *p* with thee:
25.31 he will *p* with all flesh; he will
30.13 There none to *p* thy cause, that
50.34 he shall thoroughly *p* their cause,
51.36 Behold, I will *p* thy cause, and take
Eze 17.20 and will *p* with him there for his
20.35 will I *p* with you face to face.
36 so will I *p* with you, saith the Lord
38.22 will *p* against him with pestilence
Hos 2. 2 *P* with your mother, *p*: for she is
Joel 3. 2 *p* with them there for my people
Mic 6. 2 people, and he will *p* with Israel.
7. 9 until he *p* my cause, and execute

PLEADED

1Sa 25.39 the Lord that hath *p* the cause
La 3.58 thou hast *p* the causes of my soul;
Eze 20.36 Like as I *p* with your fathers in

PLEADETH

Job 16.21 as a man *p* for his neighbor!
Isa 51.22 that *p* the cause of his people,
59. 4 for justice, nor any *p* for truth:

PLEADINGS

Job 13. 6 and hearken to the *p* of my lips.

PLEASANT

Gen 2. 9 every tree that is *p* to the sight,
3. 6 it was *p* to the eyes, and a tree
49.15 good, and the land that it was *p*;
2Sa 1.23 and Jonathan were lovely and *p*
26 very *p* hast thou been unto me:
1Ki 20. 6 whatsoever is *p* in thine eyes,
2Ki 2.19 situation of this city is *p*, as my
2Ch 32.27 and for all manner of *p* jewels;
Ps 16. 6 are fallen unto me in *p* places;
81. 2 the *p* harp with the psaltery.
106.24 they despised the *p* land, they
133. 1 how *p* it is for brethren to dwell
135. 3 praises unto his name; for it is *p*.
147. 1 praises unto our God; for it is *p*:
Pr 2.10 and knowledge is *p* to thy soul;
5.19 be as the loving hind and *p* roe;
9.17 and bread eaten in secret is *p*.
15.26 the words of the pure are *p* words.
16.24 *P* words are as an honeycomb,
22.18 *p* thing if thou keep them within
24. 4 with all precious and *p* riches.
Ec 11. 7 a *p* thing it is for the eyes to
SS 1.16 thou art fair, my beloved, yea, *p*:
4.13 of pomegranates, with *p* fruits;
16 his garden, and eat his *p* fruits.
7. 6 How fair and how *p* art thou, O
13 gates are all manner of *p* fruits,
Isa 2.16 Tarshish, and upon all *p* pictures.
5. 7 the men of Judah his *p* plant:
13.22 and dragons in their *p* palaces:
17.10 shalt thou plant *p* plants, and
32.12 for the teats, for the *p* fields,
54.12 and all thy borders of *p* stones.
64.11 all our *p* things are laid waste.
Jer 3.19 and give thee a *p* land, a goodly
12.10 *p* portion a desolate wilderness.
23.10 *p* places of the wilderness are
25.34 and ye shall fall like a *p* vessel.
31.20 my dear son? is he a *p* child?
La 1. 7 all her *p* things that she had in
10 his hand upon all her *p* things:
11 have given their *p* things for meat
2. 4 slew all that were *p* to the eye
Eze 26.12 walls, and destroy thy *p* houses:
33.32 song of one that hath a *p* voice,
Dan 8. 9 the east, and toward the *p* land.
10. 3 I ate no *p* bread, neither came
11.38 precious stones, and *p* things.
Hos 9. 6 *p* places for their silver, nettles
13 Tyrus, is planted in a *p* place:
13.15 the treasure of all *p* vessels.
Joel 3. 5 temples my goodly *p* things:
Am 5.11 ye have planted *p* vineyards, but
Mic 2. 9 ye cast out from their *p* houses;
Na 2. 9 glory out of all the *p* furniture.
Zec 7.14 for they laid the *p* land desolate.
Mal 3. 4 of Judah and Jerusalem be *p*

PLEASANTNESS

Pr 3.17 Her ways are ways of *p*, and all

PLEASE

Ex 21. 8 If she *p* not her master, who
Nu 23.27 peradventure it will *p* God
1Sa 20.13 if it *p* my father to do thee evil,
2Sa 7.29 *p* thee to bless the house of thy
1Ki 21. 6 else, if it *p* thee, I will give thee
1Ch 17.27 *p* thee to bless the house of thy
2Ch 10. 7 kind to this people, and *p* them,
Neh 2. 5 If it *p* the king, and if thy servant
7 If it *p* the king, let letters be
Est 1.19 it *p* the king, let there go a royal
3. 9 If it *p* the king, let it be written
5. 8 it *p* the king to grant my petition,
7. 3 if it *p* the king, let my life be given
8. 5 it *p* the king, and if I have found
9.13 If it *p* the king, let it be granted
Job 6. 9 it would *p* God to destroy me;
20.10 children shall seek to *p* the poor,
Ps 69.31 shall *p* the Lord better than an ox
Pr 16. 7 When a man's ways *p* the Lord,
SS 2. 7 up, nor awake my love, till he *p*.
3. 5 up, nor awake my love, till he *p*.
8. 4 up, nor awake my love, until he *p*.
Isa 2. 6 *p* themselves in the children of
55.11 shall accomplish that which I *p*,
56. 4 and choose the things that *p* me,
Jn 8.29 do always those things that *p* him.
Ro 8. 8 that are in the flesh cannot *p* God.
15. 1 the weak, and not to *p* ourselves.
2 Let every one of us *p* his neighbor
1Co 7.32 the Lord, how he may *p* the Lord:
33 the world, how he may *p* his wife.
34 world, how she may *p* her husband.
10.33 Even as I *p* all men in all things,
Gal 1.10 men, or God? or do I seek to *p* men?
1Th 2.15 they *p* not God, and are contrary
4. 1 how ye ought to walk and to *p* God,
2Ti 2. 4 he may *p* him who hath chosen him
Tit 2. 9 to *p* them well in all things;
Heb 11. 6 faith it is impossible to *p* him:

PLEASED

Gen 28. 8 daughters of Canaan *p* not
33.10 of God, and thou wast *p* with me.
34.18 And their words *p* Hamor,
45.16 and it *p* Pharaoh well, and his
Nu 24. 1 Balaam saw that it *p* the Lord
Dt 1.23 And the saying *p* me well:
Jos 22.30 of Manasseh spake, it *p* them.
33 thing *p* the children of Israel;
Jdg 13.23 If the Lord was *p* to kill us, he
14. 7 and she *p* Samson well.
1Sa 12.22 hath *p* the Lord to make you his
18.20 Saul, and the thing *p* him.
26 it *p* David well to be the king's
2Sa 3.36 notice of it, and it *p* them:
36 whatsoever the king did *p* all
17. 4 the saying *p* Absalom well,
19. 6 day, then it had *p* thee well.
1Ki 3.10 the speech *p* the Lord, that
9. 1 desire which he was *p* to do,
12 him; and they *p* him not.
2Ch 30. 4 the thing *p* the king and all
Neh 2. 6 So it *p* the king to send me; and I
Est 1.21 *p* the king and the princes;
2. 4 And the thing *p* the king;
9 And the maiden *p* him, and
5.14 And the thing *p* Haman; and he
Ps 40.13 Be *p*, O Lord, to deliver me: O
51.19 shalt thou be *p* with the sacrifices
115. 3 hath done whatsoever he hath *p*.
135. 6 Whatsoever the Lord *p*, that did
Isa 42.21 Lord is well *p* for his righteousness
53.10 Yet it *p* the Lord to bruise him;
Dan 6. 1 It *p* Darius to set over the
Jon 1.14 O Lord, hast done as it *p* thee.
Mic 6. 7 Lord be *p* with thousands of rams,
Mal 1. 8 will he be *p* with thee, or accept
Mt 3.17 beloved Son, in whom I am well *p*.
12.18 beloved, in whom my soul is well *p*:
14. 6 danced before them, and *p* Herod.
17. 5 beloved Son, in whom I am well *p*;
Mk 1.11 beloved Son, in whom I am well *p*.
6.22 came in, and danced, and *p* Herod
Lk 3.22 beloved Son; in thee I am well *p*.
Ac 6. 5 the saying *p* the whole multitude:
12. 3 And because he saw it *p* the Jews,
15.22 Then *p* it the apostles and elders,
34 it *p* Silas to abide there still.
Ro 15. 3 For even Christ *p* not himself;
26 For it hath *p* them of Macedonia
27 It hath *p* them verily; and their
1Co 1.21 it *p* God by the foolishness of
7.12 and she be *p* to dwell with him,
13 if he be *p* to dwell with her, let
10. 5 many of them God was not well *p*:
12.18 in the body, as it hath *p* him.
15.38 giveth it a body as it hath *p* him,
Gal 1.10 for if I yet *p* men, I should not be
15 But when it *p* God, who separated
Col 1.19 it *p* the Father that in him should
Heb 11. 5 had this testimony, that he *p* God.
13.16 with such sacrifices God is well *p*.
2Pe 1.17 beloved son, in whom I am well *p*.

PLEASETH

Gen 16. 6 hand; do to her as it *p* thee.
20.15 thee: dwell where it *p* thee.
Jdg 14. 3 for me; for she *p* me well.
Est 2. 4 the maiden which *p* the king
Ec 7.26 whoso *p* God shall escape
8. 3 for he doeth whatsoever *p* him.

PLEASING

Est 8. 5 the king, and I be *p* in his eyes,
Hos 9. 4 neither shall they be *p* unto him:
Col 1.10 walk worthy of the Lord unto all *p*,
3.20 this is well *p* unto the Lord.
1Th 2. 4 not as *p* men, but God, which trieth
1Jn 3.22 those things that are *p* in his sight.

PLEASURE

Gen 18.12 I am waxed old shall I have *p*,
Ezr 10.11 God of your fathers, and do his *p*:
Job 21.21 For what *p* hath he in his house
25 soul, and never eateth with *p*.
22. 3 Is it any *p* to the Almighty, that
Ps 5. 4 God that hath *p* in wickedness:
102.14 thy servants take *p* in her stones,
103.21 ye ministers of his, that do his *p*.
147.10 taketh not *p* in the legs of a man.
11 Lord taketh *p* in them that fear
149. 4 the Lord taketh *p* in his people:
Pr 21.17 that loveth *p* shall be a poor man;
Ec 5. 4 pay it; for he hath no *p* in fools:
12. 1 thou shalt say, I have no *p* in them;
Eze 18.23 Have I any *p* at all that the wicked
32 no *p* in the death of him that dieth,
33.11 no *p* in the death of the wicked;
Mal 1.10 I have no *p* in you, saith the Lord
Lk 12.32 your Father's good *p* to give you
Ac 24.27 willing to shew the Jews a *p*,
25. 9 Festus, willing to do the Jews a *p*,
Ro 1.32 but have *p* in them that do them.
2Co 12.10 Therefore I take *p* in infirmities,

Eph 1. 5 according to the good *p* of his will,
9 according to his good *p* which he
Php 2.13 both to will and to do of his good *p*.
2Th 1.11 all the good *p* of his goodness,
2.12 but had *p* in unrighteousness.
1Ti 5. 6 But she that liveth in *p* is dead
Heb 10. 6 sacrifices...thou hast had no *p*.
8 not, neither hadst *p* therein;
38 my soul shall have no *p* in him.
12.10 chastened...after their own *p*;
Jas 5. 5 Ye have lived in *p* on the earth,
2Pe 2.13 count it *p* to riot in the day time.
Rev 4.11 and for thy *p* they are and were

PLEASURES

Job 36.11 in prosperity, and their years in *p*.
Ps 16.11 hand there are *p* for evermore.
36. 8 them drink of the river of thy *p*.
Isa 47. 8 thou that art given to *p*, that
Lk 8.14 cares and riches and *p* of this life,
2Ti 3. 4 lovers of *p* more than lovers of
Tit 3. 3 serving divers lusts and *p*, living
Heb 11.25 to enjoy the *p* of sin for a season;

PLEDGE

Gen 38.17 Wilt thou give me a *p*, till thou
18 he said, What *p* shall I give thee?
20 his *p* from the woman's hand:
Ex 22.26 thy neighbor's raiment to *p*,
Dt 24. 6 nether or the upper millstone to *p*:
6 for he taketh a man's life to *p*.
10 go into his house to fetch his *p*.
11 bring out the *p* abroad unto thee.
12 thou shalt not sleep with his *p*:
13 shalt deliver him the *p* again when
17 take the widow's raiment to *p*:
1Sa 17.18 brethren fare, and take their *p*.
Job 22. 6 taken a *p* from thy brother for
24. 3 they take the widow's ox for a *p*.
9 breast, and take a *p* of the poor.
Pr 20.16 a *p* of him for a strange woman.
27.13 a *p* of him for a strange woman.
Eze 18. 7 hath restored to the debtor his *p*,
12 hath not restored the *p*, and hath
16 hath not withholden the *p*, neither
33.15 If the wicked restore the *p*, give
Am 2. 8 clothes laid to *p* by every altar.

PLEIADES

Job 9. 9 maketh Arcturus, Orion, and *P*,
38.31 bind the sweet influences of *P*,

PLENTEOUS

Gen 41.34 of Egypt in the seven *p* years.
47 And in the seven *p* years the earth
Dt 28.11 Lord shall make thee *p* in goods,
30. 9 make thee *p* in every work of thine
2Ch 1.15 gold at Jerusalem as *p* as stones,
Ps 86. 5 *p* in mercy unto all them that call
15 and *p* in mercy and truth.
103. 8 slow to anger, and *p* in mercy.
130. 7 and with him is *p* redemption.
Isa 30.23 earth, and it shall be fat and *p*:
Hab 1.16 portion is fat, and their meat *p*.
Mt 9.37 The harvest truly is *p*, but the

PLENTEOUSNESS

Gen 41.53 the seven years of *p*, that was in
Pr 21. 5 of the diligent tend only to *p*;

PLENTIFUL

Ps 68. 9 Thou, O God, didst send a *p* rain,
Isa 16.10 away, and joy out of the *p* field;
Jer 2. 7 I brought you into a *p* country,
48.33 gladness is taken from the *p* field,

PLENTIFULLY

Job 26. 3 hast thou *p* declared the thing
Ps 31.23 and *p* rewardeth the proud doer.
Lk 12.16 certain rich man brought forth *p*:

PLENTY

Gen 27.28 the earth, and *p* of corn and wine:
41.29 come seven years of great *p*
30 the *p* shall be forgotten in the land
31 *p* shall not be known in the land
Lev 11.36 pit, wherein there is *p* of water,
1Ki 10.11 Ophir great *p* of almug trees,
2Ch 31.10 enough to eat, and have left *p*:
Job 22.25 and thou shalt have *p* of silver.
37.23 in judgment, and in *p* of justice:
Pr 3.10 So shall thy barns be filled with *p*,
28.19 his land shall have *p* of bread:
Jer 44.17 for then had we *p* of victuals, and
Joel 2.26 And ye shall eat in *p*, and be

PLOTTETH

Ps 37.12 The wicked *p* against the just,

PLOW

Dt 22.10 Thou shalt not *p* with an ox and
1Sa 14.14 land, which a yoke of oxen might *p*.
Job 4. 8 I have seen, they that *p* iniquity,
Pr 20. 4 sluggard will not *p* by reason of
Isa 28.24 the plowman *p* all day to sow?
Hos 10.11 Judah shall *p*, and Jacob shall
Am 6.12 rock? will one *p* there with oxen?
Lk 9.62 man, having put his hand to the *p*,
1Co 9.10 he that ploweth should *p* in hope;

PLOWED

Jdg 14.18 If ye had not *p* with my heifer,
Ps 129. 3 The plowers *p* upon my back:
Jer 26.18 Zion shall be *p* like a field, and
Hos 10.13 Ye have *p* wickedness, ye have
Mic 3.12 Zion for your sake be *p* as a field,

PLOWERS

Ps 129. 3 The *p* plowed upon my back: they

PLOWING

1Ki 19.19 was *p* with twelve yoke of oxen
Job 1.14 The oxen were *p*, and the asses
Pr 21. 4 and the *p* of the wicked, is sin.
Lk 17. 7 having a servant *p* or feeding

PLOWMAN

Isa 28.24 Doth the *p* plow all day to sow?
Am 9.13 the *p* shall overtake the reaper,

PLOWMEN

Isa 61. 5 sons of the alien shall be your *p*
Jer 14. 4 *p* were ashamed, they covered their

PLOWSHARES

Isa 2. 4 shall beat their swords into *p*, and
Joel 3.10 Beat your *p* into swords, and your
Mic 4. 3 shall beat their swords into *p*, and

PLUCK

Lev 1.16 *p* away his crop with his feathers,
Nu 33.52 *p* down all their high places:
Dt 23.25 thou mayest *p* the ears with thine
2Ch 7.20 will I *p* them up by the roots out
Job 24. 9 *p* the fatherless from the breast,
Ps 25.15 he shall *p* my feet out of the net.
52. 5 *p* thee out of thy dwelling place,
74.11 right hand? *p* it out of thy bosom.
80.12 which pass by the way do *p* her?
Ec 3. 2 time to *p* up that which is planted;
Jer 12.14 I will *p* them out of their land,
14 and *p* out the house of Judah from
17 *p* up and destroy that nation,
18. 7 to *p* up, and to pull down, and to
22.24 hand, yet would I *p* thee thence;
24. 6 plant them, and not *p* them up.
31.28 to *p* up, and to break down, and to
42.10 will plant you, and not *p* you up:
45. 4 which I have planted I will *p* up,
Eze 17. 9 to *p* it up by the roots thereof.
23.34 *p* off thine own breasts: and
Mic 3. 2 *p* off their skin from off them,
5.14 And I will *p* up thy groves out of
Mt 5.29 right eye offend thee, *p* it out,
12. 1 and began to *p* the ears of corn,
18. 9 thine eye offend thee, *p* it out,
Mk 2.23 they went, to *p* the ears of corn.
9.47 if thine eye offend thee, *p* it out:
Jn 10.28 any man *p* them out of my hand.
29 to *p* them out of my Father's hand.

PLUCKED

Ex 4. 7 *p* it out of his bosom, and, behold,
Dt 28.63 ye shall be *p* from off the land
Ru 4. 7 a man *p* of his shoe, and gave it
2Sa 23.21 *p* the spear out of the Egyptian's
1Ch 11.23 *p* the spear out of the Egyptian's
Ezr 9. 3 *p* off the hair of my head and of
Neh 13.25 *p* off their hair, and made them
Job 29.17 and *p* the spoil out of his teeth.
Isa 50. 6 cheeks to them that *p* off the hair:
Jer 6.29 for the wicked are not *p* away.
12.15 I have *p* them out I will return,
31.40 it shall not be *p* up, nor thrown
Eze 19.12 she was *p* up in fury, she was cast
Dan 7. 4 till the wings thereof were *p*,
8 the first horns *p* up by the roots:
11. 4 for his kingdom shall be *p* up,
Am 4.11 a firebrand *p* out of the burning:
Zec 3. 2 not this a brand *p* out of the fire?
Mk 5. 4 had been *p* asunder by him, and
Lk 6. 1 his disciples *p* the ears of corn,
17. 6 Be thou *p* up by the root, and be
Gal 4.15 would have *p* out your own eyes,
Jude 12 twice dead, *p* up by the roots;

PLUMBLINE

Am 7. 7 made by a *p*, with a *p* in his hand.
8 what seest thou? And I said, A *p*.
8 I will set a *p* in the midst of my

POETS

Ac 17.28 also of your own *p* have said,

POINT

Gen 25.32 said, Behold, I am at the *p* to die:
Nu 34. 7 ye shall *p* out for you mount Hor:
8 mount Hor ye shall *p* out your
10 ye shall *p* out your east border
Jer 17. 1 and with the *p* of a diamond:
Eze 21.15 have set the *p* of the sword against
Mk 5.23 daughter lieth at the *p* of death:
Jn 4.47 son: for he was at the *p* of death.
Jas 2.10 yet offend in one *p*, he is guilty of all.

POINTS

Ec 5.16 in all *p* as he came, so shall he
Heb 4.15 was in all *p* tempted like as we are,

POISON

Dt 32.24 with the *p* of serpents of the dust.
33 Their wine is the *p* of dragons, and
Job 6. 4 *p* whereof drinketh up my spirit:
20.16 He shall suck the *p* of asps: the
Ps 58. 4 Their *p* is like the *p* of a serpent:
140. 3 adders' *p* is under their lips.
Ro 3.13 the *p* of asps is under their lips:
Jas 3. 8 an unruly evil, full of deadly *p*.

POLE

Nu 21. 8 fiery serpent, and set it upon a *p*:
9 of brass, and put it upon a *p*,

POLLUTE

Nu 18.32 neither shall ye *p* the holy things
35.33 So ye shall not *p* the land wherein
Jer 7.30 is called by my name, to *p* it.
Eze 7.21 for a spoil; and they shall *p* it.
22 and they shall *p* my secret place:
13.19 And will ye *p* me among my people
20.31 ye *p* yourselves with all your idols,
39 *p* ye my holy name no more with
39. 7 I will not let them *p* my holy name

Eze 44. 7 to *p* it, even my house, when ye
Dan 11.31 shall *p* the sanctuary of strength,

POLLUTED

Ex 20.25 thy tool upon it, thou hast *p* it.
2Ki 23.16 burned...upon the altar, and *p* it,
2Ch 36.14 *p* the house of the Lord, which he
Ezr 2.62 as *p*, put from the priesthood.
Neh 7.64 as *p*, put from the priesthood.
Ps 106.38 and the land was *p* with blood.
Isa 47. 6 I have *p* mine inheritance, and
48.11 how should my name be *p*? and I
Jer 2.23 How canst thou say, I am not *p*, I
3. 1 shall not that land be greatly *p*?
2 and thou hast *p* the land with thy
34.16 But ye turned and *p* my name,
La 2. 2 he hath *p* the kingdom and the
4.14 have *p* themselves with blood, so
Eze 4.14 soul hath not been *p*; for, from
14.11 neither be *p* any more with all
16. 6 saw thee *p* in thine own blood,
22 naked and bare,...*p* in thy blood.
20. 9 should not be *p* before...heathen,
13 and my sabbaths they greatly *p*:
14 should not be *p* before...heathen,
16 my statutes, but *p* my sabbaths:
21 they *p* my sabbaths: then I said,
22 be *p* in the sight of the heathen,
24 had *p* my sabbaths, and their eyes
26 I *p* them in their own gifts, in
30 Are ye *p* after the manner of your
23.17 she was *p* with them, and her mind
30 because thou art *p* with their idols.
36.18 idols wherewith they had *p* it:
Hos 6. 8 iniquity, and is *p* with blood.
9. 4 all that eat thereof shall be *p*:
Am 7.17 and thou shalt die in a *p* land:
Mic 2.10 because it is *p*, it shall destroy
Zep 3. 1 Woe to her that is filthy and *p*, to
4 her priests have *p* the sanctuary,
Mal 1. 7 Ye offer *p* bread upon mine altar;
7 ye say, Wherein have we *p* thee?
12 The table of the Lord is *p*; and the
Ac 21.28 temple,...hath *p* this holy place.

POLLUTING

Isa 56. 2, 6 keepeth the sabbath from *p* it,

POLLUTIONS

Ac 15.20 that they abstain from *p* of idols,
2Pe 2.20 have escaped the *p* of the world

POLLUX

Ac 28.11 whose sign was Castor and *P*.

POMEGRANATE

Ex 28.34 bell and a *p*, a golden bell and a *p*,
39.26 A bell and a *p*, a bell and a *p*,
1Sa 14. 2 under a *p* tree which is in Migron:
SS 4. 3 thy temples are like a piece of a *p*
6. 7 As a piece of a *p* are thy temples
8. 2 spiced wine of the juice of my *p*.
Joel 1.12 the *p* tree, the palm tree also, and
Hag 2.19 the *p*, and the olive tree, hath not

POMP

Isa 5.14 and their multitude, and their *p*,
14.11 Thy *p* is brought down to the
Eze 7.24 make the *p* of the strong to cease;
30.18 the *p* of her strength shall cease
32.12 they shall spoil the *p* of Egypt,
33.28 the *p* of her strength shall cease;
Ac 25.23 come, and Bernice, with great *p*,

PONDER

Pr 4.26 *P* the path of thy feet, and let all
5. 6 thou shouldest *p* the path of life,

PONDERED

Lk 2.19 things, and *p* them in her heart.

PONDERETH

Pr 5.21 the Lord, and he *p* all his goings.
21. 2 eyes: but the Lord *p* the hearts.
24.12 not he that *p* the heart consider it?

PONTIUS

Mt 27. 2 him to *P* Pilate the governor.
Lk 3. 1 *P* Pilate being governor of Judea,
Ac 4.27 both Herod, and *P* Pilate, with the
1Ti 6.13 before *P* Pilate witnessed a good

PONTUS

Ac 2. 9 and Cappadocia, in *P*, and Asia,
18. 2 Jew named Aquila, born in *P*,
1Pe 1. 1 strangers scattered throughout *P*,

POOL

2Sa 2.13 met together by the *p* of Gibeon:
13 the one on the one side of the *p*,
13 other on the other side of the *p*.
4.12 them up over the *p* in Hebron.
1Ki 22.38 the chariot in the *p* of Samaria;
2Ki 18.17 by the conduit of the upper *p*,
20.20 how he made a *p*, and a conduit,
Neh 2.14 the fountain, and to the king's *p*:
3.15 *p* of Siloah by the king's garden,
16 and to the *p* that was made, and
Isa 7. 3 end of the conduit of the upper *p*
22. 9 together the waters of the lower *p*.
11 two walls for the water of the old *p*:
35. 7 parched ground shall become a *p*,
36. 2 by the conduit of the upper *p*
41.18 make the wilderness a *p* of water,
Na 2. 8 Nineveh is...like a *p* of water:
Jn 5. 2 there is...by the sheep market a *p*,
4 down at a certain season into the *p*,
7 is troubled, to put me into th *p*:
9. 7 him, Go, wash in the *p* of Siloam,
11 Go to the *p* of Siloam, and wash:

POOLS

Ex 7.19 and upon all their *p* of water,
Ps 84. 6 a well; the rain also filleth the *p*.
Ec 2. 6 I made me *p* of water, to water
Isa 14.23 for the bittern, and *p* of water:
42.15 islands, and I will dry up the *p*.

POOR

Ex 22.25 lend...to any of my people that is *p*
30.15 more, and the *p* shall not give less
Lev 19.15 not respect the person of the *p*,
Dt 15. 4 there shall be no *p* among you;
11 *p* shall never cease out of the land:
1Sa 2. 7 The Lord maketh *p*, and maketh
8 raiseth up the *p* out of the dust,
2Sa 12. 3 But the *p* man had nothing, save
4 took the *p* man's lamb, and dressed
Job 24. 4 *p* of the earth hide themselves
29.16 I was a father to the *p*: and the
30.25 was not my soul grieved for the *p*?
31.19 clothing, or any *p* without covering;
Ps 10. 8 eyes are privily set against the *p*.
9 he lieth in wait to catch the *p*:
14 *p* committeth himself unto thee;
34. 6 This *p* man cried, and the Lord
37.14 bow, to cast down the *p* and needy,
40.17 I am *p* and needy; yet the Lord
41. 1 is he that considereth the *p*:
69.29 But I am *p* and sorrowful: let thy
33 For the Lord heareth the *p*, and
72. 4 He shall judge the *p* of the people,
12 *p* also, and him that had no helper.
82. 3 Defend the *p* and fatherless: do
86. 1 hear me: for I am *p* and needy.
109.22 For I am *p* and needy, and my
132.15 I will satisfy her *p* with bread.
Pr 10. 4 He becometh *p* that dealeth with
13. 7 there is that maketh himself *p*,
23 Much food is in the tillage of the *p*:
14.20 The *p* is hated even of his own
18.23 The *p* useth intreaties; but the
21.17 loveth pleasure shall be a *p* man:
22. 2 The rich and *p* meet together:
7 The rich ruleth over the *p*, and the
9 he giveth of his bread to the *p*.
22 Rob not the *p*, because he is *p*:
30. 9 or lest I be *p*, and steal, and take
31.20 She stretched out her hand to the *p*;
Ec 4.13 Better is a *p* and a wise child
5. 8 thou seest the oppression of the *p*,
Isa 3.15 pieces, and grind the faces of the *p*?
11. 4 righteousness shall he judge the *p*,
66. 2 that is *p* and of a contrite spirit,
Jer 20.13 delivered the soul of the *p* from the
22.16 He judged the cause of the *p* and
Am 2. 6 silver, and the *p* for a pair of shoes;
5.12 turn aside the *p* in the gate from
8. 4 the *p* of the land to fail,
6 That we may buy the *p* for silver,
Mt 5. 3 Blessed are the *p* in spirit: for
11. 5 the *p* have the gospel preached to
19.21 that thou hast, and give to the *p*,
26. 9 sold for much, and given to the *p*.
11 For ye have the *p* always with you;
Mk 10.21 thou hast, and give to the *p*, and
12.42 there came a certain *p* widow, and
43 this *p* widow hath cast more in,
14. 5 and have been given to the *p*.
7 ye have the *p* with you always, and
Lk 4.18 me to preach the gospel to the *p*;
6.20 Blessed be ye *p*: for yours is the
7.22 to the *p* the gospel is preached.
14.13 thou makest a feast, call the *p*, the
21 and bring in hither the *p*, and the
18.22 hast, and distribute unto the *p*,
19. 8 half of my goods I give to the *p*;
21. 2 *p* widow casting in thither two
3 *p* widow hath cast in more than
Jn 12. 5 hundred pence, and given to the *p*?
6 he said, not that he cared for the *p*;
8 the *p* always ye have with you; but
13.29 he should give something to the *p*.
Ro 15.26 *p* saints which are at Jerusalem.
1Co 13. 3 I bestow all my goods to feed the *p*,
2Co 6.10 as *p*, yet making many rich; as
8. 9 yet for your sakes he became *p*,
9. 9 abroad: he hath given to the *p*:
Gal 2.10 that we should remember the *p*;
Jas 2. 2 in also a *p* man in vile raiment;
3 say to the *p*, Stand thou there, or
5 not God chosen the *p* of this world
6 But ye have despised the *p*. Do
Re 3.17 miserable, and *p*, and blind, and
13.16 great, rich and *p*, free and bond,

POORER

Lev 27. 8 if he be *p* than thy estimation,

POOREST

2Ki 24.14 *p* sort of the people of the land.

POPLAR

Gen 30.37 Jacob took him rods of green *p*,

POPLARS

Hos 4.13 hills, under oaks and *p* and elms,

POPULOUS

Dt 26. 5 a nation, great, mighty, and *p*:
Na 3. 8 Art thou better than *p* No, that

PORCH

1Ch 28.11 to Solomon...the pattern of the *p*,
2Ch 15. 8 that was before the *p* of the Lord.
29. 7 have shut up the doors of the *p*, and
17 came they to the *p* of the Lord:
Joel 2.17 weep between the *p* and the altar,
Mt 26.71 when he was gone out into the *p*,
Mk 14.68 And he went out into the *p*; and
Jn 10.23 in the temple in Solomon's *p*.
Ac 3.11 in the *p* that is called Solomon's,
5.12 all with one accord in Solomon's *p*.

PORCHES
Eze 41.15 temple, and the *p* of the court;
Jn 5. 2 tongue Bethesda, having five *p*.

PORCIUS
Ac 24.27 after two years *P* Festus came

PORT
Neh 2.13 dragon well, and to the dung *p*,

PORTER
2Sa 18.26 the watchman called unto the *p*,
2Ki 7.10 and called unto the *p* of the city:
1Ch 9.21 was *p* of the door of the tabernacle
2Ch 31.14 the *p* toward the east, was over the
Mk 13.34 and commanded the *p* to watch.
Jn 10. 3 To him the *p* openeth; and the

PORTION
Gen 47.22 the priests had a *p* assigned them
Dt 21.17 a double *p* of all that he hath:
32. 9 For the Lord's *p* is his people;
2Ki 2. 9 double *p* of thy spirit be upon me.
Neh 11.23 a certain *p* should be for the singers,
Job 20.29 the *p* of a wicked man from God,
24.18 their *p* is cursed in the earth: he
26.14 but how little a *p* is heard of him?
27.13 the *p* of a wicked man with God,
31. 2 what *p* of God is there from above?
Ps 17.14 which have their *p* in this life,
73.26 of my heart, and my *p* for ever.
119.57 Thou art my *p*, O Lord: I have
142. 5 and my *p* in the land of the living.
Ec 5.18 God giveth him: for it is his *p*.
Isa 53.12 I divide him a *p* with the great,
Jer 12.10 pleasant *p* a desolate wilderness.
La 3.24 The Lord is my *p*, saith my soul;
Mic 2. 4 hath changed the *p* of my people:
Zec 2.12 Lord shall inherit Judah his *p* in
Mt 24.51 him his *p* with the hypocrites:
Lk 12.42 their *p* of meat in due season?
46 him his *p* with the unbelievers.
15.12 give me the *p* of goods that falleth

PORTIONS
Dt 18. 8 shall have like *p* to eat, besides
Jos 17. 5 fell ten *p* to Manasseh, besides
1Sa 1. 4 her sons and her daughters, *p*:
2Ch 31.19 give *p* to all the males among the
Neh 8.10 and send *p* unto them for whom
12 and to send *p*, and to make great
12.44 *p* of the law for the priests and
47 gave the *p* of the singers and the
13.10 the *p* of the Levites had not been
Est 9.19 and of sending *p* one to another.
22 and of sending *p* one to another,
Eze 45. 7 shall be over against one of the *p*,
47.13 Israel: Joseph shall have two *p*.
48.21 over against the *p* for the prince:
29 these are their *p*, saith the Lord
Hos 5. 7 month devour them with their *p*.

POSSESS
Nu 33.53 I have given you the land to *p* it.
Dt 1. 8 *p* the land which the Lord sware
4.26 ye go over Jordan to *p* it; ye shall
9. 1 *p* nations greater and mightier
19. 2, 14 Lord thy God giveth thee to *p* it.
Jos 18. 3 long are ye slack to go to *p* the land,
Job 13.26 to *p* the iniquities of my youth.
Zep 2. 9 remnant of my people shall *p*
Lk 18.12 I give tithes of all that I *p*.
21.19 In your patience *p* ye your souls.
1Th 4. 4 *p* his vessels in sanctification and

POSSESSED
Nu 21.24 and *p* his land from Arnon unto
35 them alive: and they *p* his land.
Dt 3.12 this land which we *p* at that time,
4.47 they *p* his land, and the land of Og
30. 5 the land which thy fathers *p*,
Jos 1.15 they also have *p* the land which
12. 1 *p* their land on the other side
13. 1 yet very much land to be *p*.
19.47 the edge of the sword, and *p* it,
21.43 and they *p* it, and dwelt therein.
22. 9 possession, whereof they were *p*,
Jdg 3.13 and *p* the city of palm trees.
11.21 *p* all the land of the Amorites,
22 *p* all the coasts of the Amorites,
2Ki 17.24 *p* Samaria, and dwelt in the cities
Neh 9.22 so they *p* the land of Sihon, and
24 children went in and *p* the land,
25 *p* houses full of all goods, wells
Ps 139.13 For thou hast *p* my reins: thou
Pr 8.22 Lord *p* me in the beginning of
Isa 63.18 people of thy holiness have *p* it
Jer 32.15 shall be *p* again in this land.
23 And they came in, and *p* it; but
Dan 7.22 that the saints *p* the kingdom.
Mt 4.24 those which were *p* with devils,
8.16 many that were *p* with devils:
28 there met him two *p* with devils,
33 befallen to the *p* of the devils.
9.32 him a dumb man *p* with a devil.
12.22 one *p* with a devil, blind, and
Mk 1.32 and them that were *p* with devils.
5.15 see him that was *p* with the devil,
16 to him that was *p* with the devil,
18 had been *p* with the devil prayed
Lk 8.36 was *p* of the devils was healed.
Ac 4.32 aught of the things which he *p*
8. 7 of many that were *p* with them:
16.16 damsel *p* with a spirit of divination
1Co 7.30 that buy, as though they *p* not;

POSSESSETH
Nu 36. 8 daughter, that *p* an inheritance
Lk 12.15 abundance of...things which he *p*.

POSSESSING
2Co 6.10 nothing, and yet *p* all things.

POSSESSION
Gen 23.20 Abraham for a *p* of a buryingplace
48. 4 seed after thee for an everlasting *p*.
Lev 25.34 be sold; for it is their perpetual *p*.
1Ki 21.15 *p* of the vineyard of Naboth the
16 the Jezreelite, to take *p* of it.
19 Hast thou killed, and also taken *p*?
Ps 2. 8 parts of the earth for thy *p*.
83.12 ourselves the houses of God in *p*.
Ac 5. 1 with Sapphira his wife, sold a *p*,
7. 5 he would give it to him for a *p*,
45 Jesus into the *p* of the Gentiles,
Eph 1.14 redemption of the purchased *p*,

POSSESSIONS
Gen 34.10 therein, and get you *p* therein.
47.27 and they had *p* therein, and grew,
Nu 32.30 have *p* among you in the land
1Sa 25. 2 Maon, whose *p* were in Carmel;
1Ch 7.28 And their *p* and habitations were,
9. 2 that dwelt in their *p* in their cities
2Ch 32.29 cities, and *p* of flocks and herds in
Ec 2. 7 great *p* of great and small cattle
Ob 17 of Jacob shall possess their *p*.
Mt 19.22 sorrowful: for he had great *p*.
Mk 10.22 grieved: for he had great *p*.
Ac 2.45 And sold their *p* and goods, and
28. 7 quarters were *p* of the chief man

POSSESSOR
Gen 14.19 high God, *p* of heaven and earth:
22 God, the *p* of heaven and earth,

POSSESSORS
Zec 11. 5 Whose *p* slay them, and hold
Ac 4.34 *p* of lands or houses sold them,

POSSIBLE
Mt 19.26 but with God all things are *p*.
24.24 if it were *p*, they shall deceive
26.39 if it be *p*, let this cup pass from me:
Mk 9.23 things are *p* to him that believeth.
10.27 God: for with God all things are *p*.
13.22 seduce, if it were *p*, even the elect.
14.35 if it were *p*, the hour might pass
36 Father, all things are *p* unto thee;
Lk 18.27 impossible with men are *p* with God.
Ac 2.24 not *p* that he should be holden of it.
20.16 it were *p* for him, to be at Jerusalem
27.39 if it were *p*, to thrust in the ship.
Ro 12.18 If it be *p*, as much as lieth in you,
Gal 4.15 if it had been *p*, ye would have
Heb 10. 4 it is not *p* that the blood of bulls

POSTERITY
Gen 45. 7 to preserve you a *p* in the earth,
Nu 9.10 you or of your *p* shall be unclean
1Ki 16. 3 I will take away the *p* of Baasha,
3 and the *p* of his house; and will
21.21 will take away thy *p*, and will cut
Ps 49.13 yet their *p* approve their sayings.
109.13 Let his *p* be cut off; and in the
Dan 11. 4 and not to his *p*, nor according to
Am 4. 2 hooks, and your *p* with fishhooks.

POSTS
Dt 6. 9 write them upon the *p* of thy house,
2Ch 30. 6 *p* went with the letters from the
Isa 6. 4 the *p* of the door moved at the
Eze 45.19 and put it upon the *p* of the house,
Am 9. 1 the door, that the *p* may shake:

POT
Ex 16.33 Take a *p*, and put an omer full of
Lev 6.28 if it be sodden in a brasen *p*, it
Jdg 6.19 and he put the broth in a *p*, and
1Sa 2.14 pan, or kettle, or caldron, or *p*;
2Ki 4. 2 thing in the house, save a *p* of oil.
38 his servant, Set on the great *p*,
39 shred them into the *p* of pottage:
40 man of God, there is death in the *p*.
41 meal. And he cast it into the *p*;
41 And there was no harm in the *p*.
Job 41.20 as out of a seething *p* or caldron.
31 maketh the deep to boil like a *p*:
31 the sea like a *p* of ointment.
Pr 17. 3 The fining *p* is for silver, and the
27.21 As the fining *p* for silver, and the
Ec 7. 6 the crackling of thorns under a *p*,
Jer 1.13 I said, I see a seething *p*; and the
Eze 24. 3 Set on a *p*, set it on, and also
6 to the *p* whose scum is therein,
Mic 3. 3 chop them in pieces, as for the *p*,
Zec 14.21 every *p* in Jerusalem and in Judah
Heb 9. 4 was the golden *p* that had manna,

POTENTATE
1Ti 6.15 who is the blessed and only *P*, the

POTIPHAR
Gen 37.36 sold him into Egypt unto *P*, an
39. 1 *P*, an officer of Pharaoh, captain

POTS
Ex 16. 3 when we sat by the flesh *p*, and
38. 3 *p*, and the shovels, and the basons,
Lev 11.35 whether it be oven, or ranges for *p*,
1Ki 7.45 the *p*, and the shovels, and the
2Ki 25.14 the *p*, and the shovels, and the
2Ch 4.11 And Huram made the *p*, and the
16 The *p* also, and the shovels, and the
35.13 other holy offerings sod they in *p*,
Ps 58. 9 Before your *p* can feel the thorns,
68.13 Though ye have lien among the *p*,
81. 6 hands were delivered from the *p*.
Jer 35. 5 of the Rechabites *p* full of wine,
Zec 14.20 *p* in the Lord's house shall be like
Mk 7. 4 *p*, brasen vessels, and of tables.
8 men, as the washing of *p* and cups:

POTSHERD

Job 2. 8 he took him a *p* to scrape himself
Ps 22.15 My strength is dried up like a *p*;
Pr 26.23 and a wicked heart are like a *p*
Isa 45. 9 Let the *p* strive with the potsherds

POTSHERDS

Isa 45. 9 Let the potsherd strive with the *p*

POTTAGE

Gen 25.29 And Jacob sod *p*: and Esau came
30 I pray thee, with that same red *p*;
34 gave Esau bread and *p* of lentiles;
2Ki 4.38 and seethe *p* for the sons of the
39 and shred them into the pot of *p*:
40 pass, as they were eating of the *p*,
Hag 2.12 with his skirt do touch bread, or *p*,

POTTER

Isa 41.25 morter, and as the *p* treadeth clay.
64. 8 we are the clay, and thou our *p*;
Jer 18. 4 was marred in the hand of the *p*:
4 as seemed good to the *p* to make it.
6 cannot I do with you as this *p*?
La 4. 2 the work of the hands of the *p*!
Zec 11.13 said unto me, Cast it unto the *p*:
13 cast them to the *p* in the house of
Ro 9.21 not the *p* power over the clay,
Rev 2.27 as the vessels of a *p* shall they be

POTTER'S

Ps 2. 9 them in pieces like a *p* vessel.
Isa 29.16 shall be esteemed as the *p* clay:
Jer 18. 2 Arise, and go down to the *p* house,
3 I went down to the *p* house, and,
6 Behold, as the clay is in the *p* hand,
19. 1 Go and get a *p* earthen bottle, and
11 city, as one breaketh a *p* vessel,
Dan 2.41 part of *p* clay, and part of iron,
Mt 27. 7 bought with them the *p* field, to
10 And gave them for the *p* field, as

POTTERS'

Isa 30.14 *p* vessel that is broken in pieces;

POUND

1Ki 10.17 three *p* of gold went to one shield:
Ezr 2.69 five thousand *p* of silver, and one
Neh 7.71 and two hundred *p* of silver.
72 gold, and two thousand *p* of silver,
Lk 19.16 thy *p* hath gained ten pounds.
18 thy *p* hath gained five pounds.
20 here is thy *p*, which I have kept
24 Take from him the *p*, and give it to
Jn 12. 3 a *p* of ointment of spikenard,
19.39 aloes, about a hundred *p* weight.

POUNDS

Lk 19.13 servants, and delivered them ten *p*,
16 Lord, thy pound hath gained ten *p*.
18 Lord, thy pound hath gained five *p*.
24 and give it to him that hath ten *p*.
25 said unto him, Lord, he hath ten *p*.

POUR

Ex 29. 7 and *p* it upon his head, and anoint
Ps 42. 4 things, I *p* out my soul in me:
62. 8 *p* out your heart before him: God
69.24 *P* out thine indignation upon them,
Pr 1.23 I will *p* out my spirit unto you, I
Isa 44. 3 I will *p* my spirit upon thy seed,
45. 8 the skies *p* down righteousness:
Jer 10.25 *P* out thy fury upon the heathen
La 2.19 *p* out thine heart like water
Eze 20. 8 I will *p* out my fury upon them,
21.31 *p* out mine indignation upon thee,
Hos 5.10 *p* out my wrath upon them like
Joel 2.28 will *p* out my spirit upon all flesh;
29 those days will I *p* out my spirit.
Mal 3.10 heaven, and *p* you out a blessing,
Ac 2.17 *p* out of my Spirit upon all flesh:
18 *p* out in those days of my Spirit;
Rev 16. 1 *p* out the vials of the wrath of God

POURED

1Sa 1.15 *p* out my soul before the Lord.
1Ch 11.18 drink of it, but *p* it out to the Lord,
2Ch 34.21 wrath of the Lord that is *p* out upon
Job 10.10 Hast thou not *p* me out as milk,
29. 6 the rock *p* me out rivers of oil;
30.16 now my soul is *p* out upon me;
Ps 22.14 I am *p* out like water, and all my
142. 2 *p* out my complaint before him;
Isa 29.10 hath *p* out upon you the spirit
42.25 *p* upon him the fury of his anger,
53.12 hath *p* out his soul unto death:
Jer 42.18 and my fury hath been *p* forth
La 2. 4 Zion: he *p* out his fury like fire.
Eze 22.22 Lord have *p* out my fury upon you.
39.29 *p* out my spirit upon the house
Na 1. 6 his fury is *p* out like fire, and the
Mt 26. 7 ointment, and *p* it on his head,
12 hath *p* this ointment on my body,
Mk 14. 3 the box, and *p* it on his head.
Jn 2.15 and *p* out the changers' money,
Ac 10.45 *p* out the gift of the Holy Ghost.
Rev 14.10 *p* out without mixture into the
16. 2 *p* out his vial upon the earth;
3 angel *p* out his vial upon the sea;
4 *p* out his vial upon the rivers and
8 angel *p* out his vial upon the sun;
10 angel *p* out his vial upon the seat
12 *p* out his vial upon the great river
17 angel *p* out his vial into the air;

POURETH

Job 12.21 He *p* contempt upon princes, and
16.13 *p* out my gall upon the ground.
20 mine eye *p* out tears unto God.
Ps 75. 8 *p* out of the same: but the dregs
102(T) *p* out his complaint before the
107.40 He *p* contempt upon princes, and
Pr 15. 2 mouth of fools *p* out foolishness.
28 of the wicked *p* out evil things.
Am 5. 8 *p* them out upon the face of the
9. 6 *p* them out upon the face of the
Jn 13. 5 After that he *p* water into a bason,

POURING

Eze 9. 8 *p* out of thy fury upon Jerusalem?
Lk 10.34 *p* in oil and wine, and set him on his

POVERTY

Gen 45.11 and all that thou hast, come to *p*.
Pr 6.11 thy *p* come as one that travelleth,
10.15 destruction of the *p* is their *p*.
11.24 than is meet, but it tendeth to *p*.
13.18 *P* and shame shall be to him that
20.13 not sleep, lest thou come to *p*;
23.21 and the glutton shall come to *p*:
24.34 thy *p* come as one that travelleth;
28.19 vain persons shall have *p* enough.
22 not that *p* shall come upon him.
30. 8 give me neither *p* nor riches;
31. 7 Let him drink, and forget his *p*,
2Co 8. 2 deep *p* abounded unto the riches
9 ye through his *p* might be rich.
Rev 2. 9 thy works, and tribulation, and *p*,

POWDER

Ex 32.20 it in the fire, and ground it to *p*,
Dt 28.24 the rain of thy land *p* and dust:
2Ki 23. 6 and stamped it small to *p*, and
6 the *p* thereof upon the graves of
15 stamped it small to *p*, and burned
2Ch 34. 7 beaten the graven images into *p*,
Mt 21.44 shall fall, it will grind him to *p*.
Lk 20.18 shall fall, it will grind him to *p*.

POWDERS

SS 3. 6 with all *p* of the merchant?

POWER

Gen 31. 6 with all my *p* I have served your
29 the *p* of my hand to do you hurt:
32.28 prince hast *p* with God and with
49. 3 dignity, and the excellency of *p*:
Ex 9.16 up, for to shew in thee my *p*;
15. 6 O Lord, is become glorious in *p*:
21. 8 strange nation he shall have no *p*,
32.11 the land of Egypt with great *p*,
Lev 26.19 will break the pride of your *p*;
37 *p* to stand before your enemies.
Nu 14.17 let the *p* of my lord be great,
22.38 now any *p* at all to say any thing?
Dt 4.37 with his mighty *p* out of Egypt;
8.17 My *p* and the might of mine hand
18 that giveth thee *p* to get wealth,
9.29 broughtest out by thy mighty *p*
32.36 he seeth that their *p* is gone, and
Jos 8.20 *p* to flee this way or that way:
17.17 a great people, and hast great *p*:
1Sa 9. 1 a Benjamite, a mighty man of *p*.
30. 4 until they had no more *p* to weep.
2Sa 22.33 God is my strength and *p*: and
2Ki 17.36 the land of Egypt with great *p*
19.26 their inhabitants were of small *p*,
1Ch 20. 1 Joab led forth the *p* of the army,
29.11 and the *p*, and the glory, and the
12 in thine hand is *p* and might;
2Ch 14.11 or with them that have no *p*:
20. 6 in thine hand is there not *p* and
22. 9 no *p* to keep still the kingdom.
25. 8 God hath *p* to help, and to cast
26.13 that made war with mighty *p*, to
32. 9 Lachish, and all his *p* with him,)
Ezr 4.23 them to cease by force and *p*.
8.22 his *p* and his wrath is against all
Neh 1.10 hast redeemed by thy great *p*,
5. 5 is it in our *p* to redeem them;
Est 1. 3 *p* of Persia and Media, the nobles
8.11 *p* of the people and province that
9. 1 Jews hoped to have *p* over them,
10. 2 the acts of his *p* and of his might,
Job 1.12 all that he hath is in thy *p*; only
5.20 in war from the *p* of the sword.
21. 7 old, yea, are mighty in *p*?
23. 6 against me with his great *p*?
24.22 draweth also the mighty with his *p*:
26. 2 thou helped him that is without *p*?
12 He divideth the sea with his *p*,
14 but the thunder of his *p* who can
36.22 Behold, God exalteth by his *p*:
37.23 he is excellent in *p*, and in
41.12 not conceal his parts, nor his *p*,
Ps 21.13 so will we sing and praise thy *p*.
22.20 my darling from the *p* of the dog.
37.35 I have seen the wicked in great *p*,
49.15 my soul from the *p* of the grave:
59.11 scatter them by thy *p*; and bring
16 But I will sing of thy *p*; yea, I
62.11 this; that *p* belongeth unto God.
63. 2 To see thy *p* and thy glory, so as I
65. 6 mountains; being girded with *p*:
66. 3 through the greatness of thy *p*
7 He ruleth by his *p* for ever; his
68.35 giveth strength and *p* unto his
71.18 thy *p* to every one that is to come.
78.26 by his *p* he brought in the south
79.11 according to the greatness of thy *p*
90.11 knoweth the *p* of thine anger?
106. 8 make his mighty *p* to be known.
110. 3 shall be willing in the day of thy *p*,
111. 6 his people the *p* of his works,
145.11 thy kingdom, and talk of thy *p*;
147. 5 Great is our Lord, and of great *p*:
150. 1 him in the firmament of his *p*.
Pr 3.27 it is in the *p* of thine hand to do it.
18.21 and life are in the *p* of the tongue:
Ec 4. 1 of their oppressors there was *p*;
5.19 hath given him *p* to eat thereof,
6. 2 God giveth him not *p* to eat thereof,
8. 4 the word of a king is, there is *p*:

8 no man that hath *p* over the spirit
8 hath he *p* in the day of death:
Isa 37.27 their inhabitants were of small *p*,
40.26 might, for that he is strong in *p*;
29 He giveth *p* to the faint; and to
43.17 and horse, the army and the *p*;
47.14 deliver...from the *p* of the flame:
50. 2 redeem? or have I no *p* to deliver?
Jer 10.12 He hath made the earth by his *p*,
27. 5 my great *p* and by my outstretched
32.17 by thy great *p* and stretched out
51.15 He hath made the earth by his *p*,
Eze 17. 9 without great *p* or many people
22. 6 in thee to their *p* to shed blood.
30. 6 pride of her *p* shall come down:
Dan 2.37 given thee a kingdom, *p*, and
3.27 whose bodies the fire had no *p*,
4.30 kingdom by the might of my *p*,
6.27 Daniel from the *p* of the lions.
8. 6 ran unto him in the fury of his *p*.
7 there was no *p* in the ram to stand
22 out of the nation, but not in his *p*.
24 And his *p* shall be mighty, but not
24 be mighty, but not by his own *p*:
11. 6 shall not retain the *p* of the arm;
25 shall stir up his *p* and his courage
43 have *p* over the treasures of gold
12. 7 to scatter the *p* of the holy people,
Hos 12. 3 his strength he had *p* with God:
4 Yea, he had *p* over the angel, and
13.14 ransom...from the *p* of the grave;
Mic 2. 1 because it is in the *p* of their hand.
3. 8 I am full of *p* by the spirit of the
Na 1. 3 is slow to anger, and great in *p*,
2. 1 loins, strong, fortify thy *p* mightily.
Hab 1.11 imputing this his *p* unto his god.
2. 9 be delivered from the *p* of evil!
3. 4 and there was the hiding of his *p*.
Zec 4. 6 Not by might, nor by *p*, but by my
9. 4 he will smite her *p* in the sea;
Mt 6.13 kingdom, and the *p*, and the glory,
9. 6 Son of man hath *p* on earth to
8 which had given such *p* unto men.
10. 1 he gave them *p* against unclean
22.29 the scriptures, nor the *p* of God.
24.30 of heaven with *p* and great glory.
26.64 man sitting on the right hand of *p*,
28.18 All *p* is given unto me in heaven
Mk 2.10 Son of man hath *p* on earth to
3.15 And to have *p* to heal sicknesses,
6. 7 gave them *p* over unclean spirits;
9. 1 the kingdom of God come with *p*.
12.24 scriptures, neither the *p* of God?
13.26 the clouds with great *p* and glory.
14.62 man sitting on the right hand of *p*,
Lk 1.17 him in the spirit and *p* of Elias, to
35 *p* of the Highest shall overshadow
4. 6 All this *p* will I give thee, and the
14 returned in the *p* of the Spirit into
32 doctrine: for his word was with *p*.
36 authority and *p* he commandeth
5.17 *p* of the Lord was present to heal
24 Son of man hath *p* upon earth to
9. 1 *p* and authority over all devils,
43 amazed at the mighty *p* of God.
10.19 unto you *p* to tread on serpents
19 and over all the *p* of the enemy:
12. 5 hath killed hath *p* to cast into hell;
20.20 *p* and authority of the governor.
21.27 of man coming in a cloud with *p*
22.53 your hour, and the *p* of darkness.
69 on the right hand of the *p* of God.
24.49 be endued with *p* from on high.
Jn 1.12 he *p* to become the sons of God,
10.18 I have *p* to lay it down, and I
18 and I have *p* to take it again.
17. 2 hast given him *p* over all flesh,
19.10 not that I have *p* to crucify thee,
10 thee, and have *p* to release thee?
11 have no *p* at all against me,
Ac 1. 7 the Father hath put in his own *p*.
8 But ye shall receive *p*, after that
3.12 by our own *p* or holiness we had
4. 7 By what *p*, or by what name, have
33 great *p* gave the apostles witness
5. 4 sold, was it not in thine own *p*?
6. 8 Stephen, full of faith and *p*, did
8.10 This man is the great *p* of God.
19 Saying, Give me also this *p*, that
10.38 with the Holy Ghost and with *p*:
26.18 and from the *p* of Satan unto God,
Ro 1. 4 to be the Son of God with *p*,
16 it is the *p* of God unto salvation
20 even his eternal *p* and Godhead;
9.17 that I might shew my *p* in thee,
21 not the potter *p* over the clay,
22 wrath, and to make his *p* known,
13. 1 For there is no *p* but of God: the
2 therefore resisteth the *p*,
3 thou then not be afraid of the *p*?
15.13 through the *p* of the Holy Ghost.
19 by the *p* of the Spirit of God; so
16.25 to him that is of *p* to stablish you
1Co 1.18 which are saved it is the *p* of God.
24 Christ the *p* of God, and the
2. 4 demonstration of...Spirit and of *p*:
5 of men, but in the *p* of God.
4.19 which are puffed up, but the *p*.
20 of God is not in word, but in *p*.
5. 4 with the *p* of our Lord Jesus Christ,
6.12 not be brought under the *p* of any.
14 will also raise up us by his own *p*.
7. 4 wife hath not *p* of her own body,
4 hath not *p* of his own body, but
37 but hath *p* over his own will, and
9. 4 Have we not *p* to eat and to drink?
5 Have we not *p* to lead...a sister,
6 have not we *p* to forbear working?
12 be partakers of this *p* over you,
12 we have not used this *p*; but
18 I abuse not my *p* in the gospel.
11.10 the woman to have *p* on her head
15.24 all rule and all authority and *p*.
43 in weakness; it is raised in *p*:
2Co 4. 7 excellency of the *p* may be of God,
6. 7 the word of truth, by the *p* of God,
8. 3 For to their *p*, I bear record, yea,
3 beyond their *p* they were willing
12. 9 the *p* of Christ may rest upon me.
13. 4 yet he liveth by the *p* of God.
4 him by the *p* of God toward you.
10 according to the *p* which the Lord
Eph 1.19 the exceeding greatness of his *p*
19 to the working of his mighty *p*,
21 all principality, and *p*, and might,
2. 2 to the prince of the *p* of the air,
3. 7 by the effectual working of his *p*.
20 to the *p* that worketh in us,
6.10 Lord, and in the *p* of his might.
Php 3.10 him, and the *p* of his resurrection,
Col 1.11 according to his glorious *p*, unto
13 us from the *p* of darkness, and
2.10 the head of all principality and *p*:
1Th 1. 5 but also in *p*, and in the Holy
2Th 1. 9 Lord, and from the glory of his *p*;
11 and the work of faith with *p*:
2. 9 all *p* and signs and lying wonders,
3. 9 Not because we have not *p*, but to
1Ti 6.16 be honor and *p* everlasting.
2Ti 1. 7 of *p*, and of love, and of a sound
8 gospel according to the *p* of God;
3. 5 but denying the *p* thereof: from
Heb 1. 3 all things by the word of his *p*,
2.14 him that had the *p* of death, that
7.16 but after the *p* of an endless life.
1Pe 1. 5 kept by the *p* of God through faith
2Pe 1. 3 as his divine *p* hath given unto us
16 you the *p* and coming of our Lord
2.11 are greater in *p* and might, bring
Jude 25 and majesty, dominion and *p*,
Rev 2.26 will I give *p* over the nations:
4.11 to receive glory and honor and *p*:
5.12 Lamb that was slain to receive *p*,
13 and honor, and glory, and *p*, be
6. 4 *p* was given to him that sat thereon
8 *p* was given unto them over the
7.12 *p*, and might, be unto our God
9. 3 and unto them was given *p*, as
3 the scorpions of the earth have *p*.
10 *p* was to hurt men five months.
19 their *p* is in their mouth, and in
11. 3 I will give *p* unto my two witnesses,
6 have *p* to shut heaven, that it
6 have *p* over waters to turn them to
17 hast taken to thee thy great *p*,
12.10 our God, and the *p* of his Christ:
13. 2 the dragon gave him his *p*, and
4 which gave *p* unto the beast: and
5 *p* was given unto him to continue
7 and *p* was given him over all
12 he exerciseth all the *p* of the first
14 miracles which he had *p* to do in
15 And he had *p* to give life unto the
14.18 the altar, which had *p* over fire;
15. 8 the glory of God, and from his *p*;
16. 8 *p* was given unto him to scorch men
9 which hath *p* over these plagues:
17.12 receive *p* as kings one hour with
13 *p* and strength unto the beast.
18. 1 from heaven, having great *p*;
19. 1 honor, and *p*, unto the Lord our
20. 6 such the second death hath no *p*,

POWERFUL

Ps 29. 4 The voice of the Lord is *p*; the
2Co 10.10 his letters,. . .are weighty and *p*;
Heb 4.12 the word of God is quick, and *p*,

POWERS

Mt 24.29 *p* of the heavens shall be shaken:
Mk 13.25 the *p* that are in heaven shall be
Lk 12.11 unto magistrates, and *p*, take ye
21.26 the *p* of heaven shall be shaken.
Ro 8.38 angels, nor principalities, nor *p*,
13. 1 soul be subject unto the higher *p*.
1 the *p* that be are ordained of God.
Eph 3.10 and *p* in heavenly places might be
6.12 against principalities, against *p*,
Col 1.16 dominions, or principalities, or *p*:
2.15 having spoiled principalities and *p*,
Tit 3. 1 be subject to principalities and *p*,
Heb 6. 5 and the *p* of the world to come,
1Pe 3.22 *p* being made subject unto him.

PRACTICE

Ps 141. 4 to *p* wicked works with men that
Isa 32. 6 to *p* hypocrisy, and to utter error
Dan 8.24 and shall prosper, and *p*, and shall
Mic 2. 1 when the morning is light, they *p* it,

PRACTICED

1Sa 23. 9 Saul secretly *p* mischief against
Dan 8.12 ground; and it *p*, and prospered.

PRACTICES

2Pe 2.14 they have exercised with covetous *p*;

PRAETORIUM

Mk 15.16 him away into the hall, called *P*;

PRAISE

Gen 29.35 she said, Now will I *p* the Lord:
49. 8 art he whom thy brethren shall *p*:
Lev 19.24 shall be holy to *p* the Lord withal.
Dt 10.21 He is thy *p*, and he is thy God,
26.19 in *p*, and in name, and in honor;
Jdg 5. 2 *P* ye the Lord for the avenging
3 will sing *p* to the Lord God of Israel.
1Ch 16. 4 and *p* the Lord God of Israel:
35 thy holy name, and glory in thy *p*.
23. 5 made, said David, to *p* therewith.
30 morning to thank and *p* the Lord,
25. 3 to give thanks and to *p* the Lord.

1Ch 29.13 thee, and *p* thy glorious name.
2Ch 7. 6 the king had made to *p* the Lord,
8.14 *p* and minister before the priests,
20.19 stood up to *p* the Lord God of
21 should *p* the beauty of holiness,
21 the army, and to say, *P* the Lord;
22 when they began to sing and to *p*,
23.13 and such as taught to sing *p*.
29.30 Levites to sing *p* unto the Lord
31. 2 to *p* in the gates of the tents of the
Ezr 3.10 *p* the Lord, after the ordinance of
Neh 9. 5 exalted above all blessing and *p*.
12.24 to *p* and to give thanks, according
46 songs of *p* and thanksgiving unto
Ps 7.17 I will *p* the Lord according to his
17 sing *p* to the name of the Lord
9. 1 I will *p* thee, O Lord, with my
2 I will sing *p* to thy name, O thou
14 I may shew forth all thy *p* in the
21.13 so will we sing and *p* thy power.
22.22 of the congregation will I *p* thee.
23 Ye that fear the Lord, *p* him; all
25 My *p* shall be of thee in the great
26 shall *p* the Lord that seek him:
28. 7 and with my son will I *p* him.
30. 9 Shall the dust *p* thee? shall it
12 that my glory may sing *p* to thee,
33. 1 for *p* is comely for the upright.
2 *P* the Lord with harp: sing unto
34. 1 his *p* shall continually be in my
35.18 I will *p* thee among much people.
28 and of thy *p* all the day long.
40. 3 my mouth, even *p* unto our God:
42. 4 with the voice of joy and *p*, with
5 shall yet *p* him for the help of
11 for I shall yet *p* him, who is the
43. 4 upon the harp will I *p* thee, O God
5 for I shall yet *p* him, who is the
44. 8 day long, and *p* thy name for ever.
45.17 shall the people *p* thee for ever
48.10 thy *p* unto the ends of the earth:
49.18 and men will *p* thee, when thou
50.23 Whoso offereth *p* glorifieth me:
51.15 my mouth shall shew forth thy *p*.
52. 9 I will *p* thee for ever, because
54. 6 I will *p* thy name, O Lord; for it is
56. 4 In God I will *p* his word, in God I
10 In God will I *p* his word: in the
10 in the Lord will I *p* his word.
57. 7 is fixed: I will sing and give *p*.
9 I will *p* thee, O Lord, among the
61. 8 I sing *p* unto thy name for ever,
63. 3 than life, my lips shall *p* thee.
5 shall *p* thee with joyful lips:
65. 1 *P* waiteth for thee, O God, in
66. 2 of his name: make his *p* glorious.
8 make the voice of his *p* to be heard:
67. 3 Let the people *p* thee, O God; let
3 O God; let all the people *p* thee.
5 Let the people *p* thee, O God; let
5 O God; let all the people *p* thee.
69.30 *p* the name of God with a song,
34 Let the heaven and earth *p* him,
71. 6 my *p* shall be continually of thee.
8 Let my mouth be filled with thy *p*
14 will yet *p* thee more and more.
22 will also *p* thee with the psaltery,
74.21 the poor and needy *p* thy name.
76.10 the wrath of man shall *p* thee:
79.13 forth thy *p* to all generations.
86.12 I will *p* thee, O Lord my God, with
88.10 shall the dead arise and *p* thee?
89. 5 the heavens shall *p* thy wonders,
98. 4 noise, and rejoice, and sing *p*.
99. 3 *p* thy great and terrible name;
100(T) A Psalm of *p*.
4 and into his courts with *p*:
102.18 shall be created shall *p* the Lord.
21 in Zion, and his *p* in Jerusalem;
104.33 I will sing *p* to my God while I
35 Lord, O my soul. *P* ye the Lord.
105.45 and keep his laws. *P* ye the Lord.
106. 1 *P* ye the Lord. O give thanks
2 who can shew forth all his *p*?
12 they his words; they sang his *p*.
47 holy name, and to triumph in thy *p*.
48 people say, Amen. *P* ye the Lord.
107. 8, 15, 21, 31 Oh that men would *p*
32 and *p* him in the assembly of the
108. 1 I will sing and give *p*, even with
3 I will *p* thee, O Lord, among the
109. 1 not thy peace, O God of thy *p*;
30 *p* the Lord with my mouth;
30 will *p* him among the multitude.
111. 1 *P* ye the Lord, I will
1 *p* the Lord with my whole heart,
10 his *p* endureth for ever.
112. 1 *P* ye the Lord. Blessed is the
113. 1 *P* ye the Lord. *P*, O ye servants
1 the Lord, *p* the name of the Lord.
9 mother of children. *P* ye the Lord.
115.17 The dead *p* not the Lord, neither
18 forth...for evermore. *P* the Lord.
116.19 thee, O Jerusalem. *P* ye the Lord.
117. 1 O *p* the Lord, all ye nations:
1 ye nations: *p* him, all ye people.
2 endureth for ever. *P* ye the Lord.
118.19 into them, and I will *p* the Lord:
21 I will *p* thee: for thou hast heard
28 Thou art my God, and I will *p* thee:
119. 7 *p* thee with uprightness of heart,
164 Seven times a day do I *p* thee
171 My lips shall utter *p*, when thou
175 my soul live, and it shall *p* thee;
135. 1 *P* ye the Lord. *P* ye the name
1 *p* him, O ye servants of the Lord.
3 *P* the Lord; for the Lord is good:
21 at Jerusalem. *P* ye the Lord.
138. 1 will *p* thee with my whole heart:
1 the gods will I sing *p* unto thee.
2 *p* thy name for...lovingkindness
4 the kings of the earth shall *p* thee,
139.14 I will *p* thee; for I am fearfully
142. 7 of prison, that I may *p* thy name:
145(T) David's Psalm of *p*.
2 I will *p* thy name for ever and
4 generation shall *p* thy works to
10 All thy works shall *p* thee, O
21 shall speak the *p* of the Lord:
146. 1 *P* ye the Lord. *P* the Lord, O
2 While I live I will *p* the Lord: I will
10 all generations. *P* ye the Lord.
147. 1 *P* ye the Lord: for it is good to
1 it is pleasant; and *p* is comely.
7 sing *p* upon the harp unto our
12 *P* the Lord, O Jerusalem;
12 Jerusalem; *p* thy God, O Zion.
20 not known them. *P* ye the Lord.
148. 1 *P* ye the Lord. *P* ye the Lord.
1 the heavens: *p* him in the heights.
2 *P* ye him, all his angels:
2 his angels: *p* ye him, all his hosts.
3 *P* ye him, sun and moon:
3 moon: *p* him, all ye stars of light:
4 *P* him, ye heavens of heavens, and
5 Let them *p* the name of the Lord:
7 *P* the Lord from the earth, ye
13 Let them *p* the name of the Lord:
14 people, the *p* of all his saints;
14 near unto him. *P* ye the Lord.
149. 1 *P* ye the Lord. Sing unto the Lord
1 and his *p* in the congregation of
3 Let them *p* his name in the
9 have all his saints. *P* ye the Lord.
150. 1 *P* ye the Lord.
1 *P* God in his sanctuary:
1 *p* him in the firmament of his
2 *P* him for his mighty acts;
2 *p* him according to his excellent
3 *P* him with the sound of the
3 *p* him with the psaltery and harp.
4 *P* him with the timbrel and dance:
4 *p* him with stringed instruments
5 *P* him upon the loud cymbals:
5 *p* him upon the high sounding
6 that hath breath *p* the Lord.
6 the Lord. *P* ye the Lord.
Pr 27. 2 Let another man *p* thee, and not
21 for gold; so is a man to his *p*.
28. 4 that forsake the law *p* the wicked:
31.31 her own works *p* her in the gates.
Isa 12. 1 O Lord, I will *p* thee: though
4 *P* the Lord, call upon his name,
25. 1 I will *p* thy name; for thou hast
38.18 For the grave cannot *p* thee, death
19 living, the living, he shall *p* thee,
42. 8 neither my *p* to graven images.
10 his *p* from the end of the earth,
12 and declare his *p* in the islands.
43.21 myself; they shall shew forth my *p*.
48. 9 and for my *p* will I refrain for thee,
60.18 walls Salvation, and thy gates *P*.
61. 3 garment of *p* for the spirit of
11 *p* to spring forth before all the
62. 7 make Jerusalem a *p* in the earth.
9 it shall eat it, and *p* the Lord;
Jer 13.11 and for a *p*, and for a glory:
17.14 I shall be saved: for thou art my *p*.
26 sacrifices of *p* unto the house of
20.13 *p* ye the Lord: for he hath
31. 7 *p* ye, and say, O Lord, save thy
33. 9 a *p* and an honor before all the
11 *P* the Lord of hosts: for the Lord
11 shall bring the sacrifice of *p* into
48. 2 shall be no more *p* of Moab:
49.25 is the city of *p* not left, the city of
51.41 how is the *p* of the whole earth
Dan 2.23 I thank thee, and *p* thee, O thou
4.37 Now I Nebuchadnezzar *p* and extol
Joel 2.26 *p* the name of the Lord your God,
Hab 3. 3 and the earth was full of his *p*.
Zep 3.19 get them *p* and fame in every land
20 and a *p* among all people of the
Mt 21.16 sucklings thou hast perfected *p*?
Lk 18.43 when they saw it, gave *p* unto God.
19.37 rejoice and *p* God with a loud voice
Jn 9.24 said unto him, Give God the *p*: we
12.43 For they loved the *p* of men more
43 of men more than the *p* of God.
Ro 2.29 whose *p* is not of men, but of God.
13. 3 and thou shalt have *p* of the same:
15.11 again, *P* the Lord, all ye Gentiles;
1Co 4. 5 shall every man have *p* of God.
11. 2 Now I *p* you, brethren, that ye
17 I *p* you, not that ye come together
22 shall I *p* you in this? I *p* you not.
2Co 8.18 brother, whose *p* is in the gospel
Eph 1. 6 To the *p* of the glory of his grace,
12 to the *p* of this glory, who first
14 possession, unto the *p* of his glory.
Php 1.11 Christ, unto the glory and *p* of God.
4. 8 if there be any *p*, think on these
Heb 2.12 the church will I sing *p* unto thee.
13.15 let us offer the sacrifice of *p* to God
1Pe 1. 7 be found unto *p* and honor and
2.14 and for the *p* of them that do well.
4.11 whom be *p* and dominion for ever
Rev 19. 5 *P* our God, all ye his servants,

PRAISED

Jdg 16.24 people saw him, they *p* their god:
2Sa 14.25 none to be so much *p* as Absalom
22. 4 on the Lord, who is worthy to be *p*:
1Ch 16.25 is the Lord, and greatly to be *p*:
36 people said, Amen, and *p* the Lord.
23. 5 four thousand *p* the Lord with the
2Ch 5.13 *p* the Lord, saying, For he is good;
7. 3 and worshipped, and *p* the Lord,
6 when David *p* by their ministry;
30.21 Levites and the priests *p* the Lord
Ezr 3.11 great shout, when they *p* the Lord,
Neh 5.13 said, Amen, and *p* the Lord.
Ps 18. 3 the Lord, who is worthy to be *p*:

48. 1 greatly to be *p* in the city of our
72.15 continually;...daily shall he be *p*.
96. 4 Lord is great, and greatly to be *p*:
113. 3 same the Lord's name is to be *p*.
145. 3 is the Lord, and greatly to be *p*;
Pr 31.30 feareth the Lord, she shall be *p*.
Ec 4. 2 I *p* the dead which are already
SS 6. 9 the concubines, and they *p* her.
Isa 64.11 house, where our fathers *p* thee, is
Dan 4.34 I *p* and honored him that liveth
5. 4 drank wine, and *p* the gods of gold,
23 thou hast *p* the gods of silver, and
Lk 1.64 loosed, and he spake, and *p* God.

PRAISES
Ex 15.11 fearful in *p*, doing wonders?
2Sa 22.50 and I will sing *p* unto thy name.
2Ch 29.30 And they sang *p* with gladness,
Ps 9.11 Sing *p* to the Lord, which
18.49 heathen,...sing *p* unto thy name,
22. 3 that inhabitest the *p* of Israel.
27. 6 yea, I will sing *p* unto the Lord.
47. 6 Sing *p* to God, sing *p*:
6 sing *p* unto our King, sing *p*.
7 sing ye *p* with understanding.
56.12 O God: I will render *p* unto thee.
68. 4 unto God, sing *p* to his name:
32 the earth; O sing *p* unto the Lord;
75. 9 I will sing *p* to the God of Jacob.
78. 4 *p* of the Lord, and his strength,
92. 1 to sing *p* unto thy name, O most
108. 3 I will sing *p* unto thee among the
135. 3 Lord is good: sing *p* unto his name;
144. 9 ten strings will I sing *p* unto thee.
146. 2 I will sing *p* unto my God while I
147. 1 it is good to sing *p* unto our God;
149. 3 sing *p* unto him with the timbrel
6 the high *p* of God be in their mouth,
Isa 60. 6 shew forth the *p* of the Lord.
63. 7 and the *p* of the Lord, according
Ac 16.25 prayed, and sang *p* unto God:
1Pe 2. 9 shew forth the *p* of him who hath

PRAISETH
Pr 31.28 her husband also, and he *p* her.

PRAISING
2Ch 5.13 heard in *p* and thanking the Lord;
23.12 the people running and *p* the king,
Ezr 3.11 *p* and giving thanks unto the Lord;
Ps 84. 4 thy house: they will be still *p* thee.
Lk 2.13 heavenly host *p* God, and saying,
20 glorifying and *p* God for all the
24.53 in the temple, *p* and blessing God.
Ac 2.47 *P* God, and having favor with all
3. 8 walking, and leaping, and *p* God.
9 people saw him walking and *p* God:

PRATING
Pr 10. 8 but a *p* fool shall fall.
10 sorrow: but a *p* fool shall fall.
3Jn 10 *p* against us with malicious

PRAY
Gen 12.13 Say, I *p* thee, thou art my sister:
20. 7 he shall *p* for thee, and thou shalt
33.11 Take, I *p* thee, my blessing that is
40.14 shew kindness, I *p* thee, unto me,
Ex 4.13 O my Lord, send, I *p* thee, by
10.17 forgive, I *p* thee, my sin only this
32.32 blot me, I *p* thee, out of thy book
Jos 7.19 give, I *p* thee, glory to the Lord
Jdg 16. 6 Tell me, I *p* thee, wherein thy great
28 Lord God, remember me, I *p* thee,
18. 5 Ask counsel, we *p* thee, of God,
Ru 2. 7 I *p* you, let me glean and gather
1Sa 7. 5 I will *p* for you unto the Lord.
12.23 the Lord in ceasing to *p* for you:
1Ki 17.10 Fetch me, I *p* thee, a little water in
21 I *p* thee, let this child's soul come
2Ki 1.13 O man of God, I *p* thee, let my life,
6.17 said, Lord, I *p* thee, open his eyes,
2Ch 6.26 *p* toward this place, and confess
7.14 humble themselves, and *p*, and seek
Ezr 6.10 *p* for the life of the king, and of
Neh 5.10 I *p* you, let us leave off this usury.
Job 8. 8 inquire, I *p* thee, of the former age,
33.26 He shall *p* unto God, and he will
42. 8 my servant Job shall *p* for you:
Ps 32. 6 this shall every one that is godly *p*
55.17 and morning, and at noon will I *p*
122. 6 *P* for the peace of Jerusalem: they
Isa 29.11 Read this, I *p* thee: and he saith,
Jer 21. 2 Inquire, I *p* thee, of the Lord for
37. 3 *P* now unto the Lord our God for
Zec 7. 2 their men, to *p* before the Lord,
8.21 us go speedily to *p* before the Lord,
Mal 1. 9 now, I *p* you, beseech God that
Mt 5.44 *p* for them which despitefully use
6. 5 to *p* standing in the synagogues
6 *p* to thy Father which is in secret;
7 when ye *p*, use not vain repetitions,
9 After this manner therefore *p* ye:
9.38 *P* ye therefore the Lord of the
14.23 up into a mountain apart to *p*:
19.13 put his hands on them and *p*:
24.20 *p* ye that your flight be not in the
26.36 ye here, while I go and *p* yonder.
41 Watch and *p*, that ye enter not into
53 that I cannot now *p* to my Father,
Mk 5.17 they began to *p* him to depart out
23 I *p* thee, come and lay thy hands on
6.46 he departed into a mountain to *p*.
11.24 things ye desire, when ye *p*, believe
13.18 *p* ye that your flight be not in the
33 watch and *p*: for ye know not
14.32 disciples, Sit ye here, while I shall *p*.
38 Watch ye and *p*, lest ye enter into
Lk 6.12 he went out into a mountain to *p*,
28 *p* for them which despitefully use
9.28 and went up into a mountain to *p*.
10. 2 *p* ye therefore the Lord of the
11. 1 unto him, Lord, teach us to *p*,
2 When ye *p*, say, Our Father which
14.18 see it: I *p* thee have me excused.
19 them: I *p* thee have me excused.
16.27 I *p* thee therefore, father, that thou
18. 1 men ought always to *p*, and not
10 went up into the temple to *p*;
21.36 ye therefore, and *p* always, that
22.40 *P* that ye enter not into
46 and *p*, lest ye enter into temptation.
Jn 14.16 I will *p* the Father, and he shall
16.26 that I will *p* the Father for you:
17. 9 I *p* for them: I *p* not for the
15 I *p* not that thou shouldest take
20 Neither *p* I for these alone, but
Ac 8.22 this thy wickedness, and *p* God,
24 *P* ye to the Lord for me, that
34 I *p* thee, of whom speaketh the
10. 9 went up upon the housetop to *p*
24. 4 I *p* thee that thou wouldest hear
27.34 I *p* you to take some meat: for
Ro 8.26 we should *p* for as we ought:
1Co 11.13 comely that a woman *p* unto God
14.13 tongue *p* that he may interpret.
14 if I *p* in an unknown tongue, my
15 it then? I will *p* with the spirit,
15 will *p* with the understanding also:
2Co 5.20 we *p* you in Christ's stead, be ye
13. 7 Now *p* to God that ye do no evil;
Php 1. 9 And this I *p*, that your love may
Col 1. 9 do not cease to *p* for you, and to
1Th 5.17 *P* without ceasing.
23 I *p* God your whole spirit and soul
25 Brethren, *p* for us.
2Th 1.11 we *p* always for you, that our God
3. 1 brethren, *p* for us, that the word
1Ti 2. 8 therefore that men *p* every where,
2Ti 4.16 I *p* God that it may not be laid to
Heb 13.18 *P* for us: for we trust we have
Jas 5.13 among you afflicted? let him *p*.
14 let them *p* over him, anointing
16 *p* one for another, that ye may
1Jn 5.16 I do not say that he shall *p* for it.

PRAYED
Gen 20.17 So Abraham *p* unto God: and
Nu 11. 2 when Moses *p* unto the Lord,
21. 7 us. And Moses *p* for the people.
Dt 9.20 I *p* for Aaron also the same time.
26 I *p* therefore unto the Lord, and
1Sa 1.10 *p* unto the Lord, and wept sore.
2. 1 Hannah *p*, and said, My heart
2Ki 6.17 Elisha *p*, and said, Lord, I pray
Neh 1. 4 and *p* before the God of heaven.
2. 4 So I *p* to the God of heaven.
Job 42.10 Job, when he *p* for his friends:
Dan 6.10 *p*, and gave thanks before his
9. 4 And I *p* unto the Lord my God,
Jon 2. 1 Jonah *p* unto the Lord his God
4. 2 And he *p* unto the Lord, and said,
Mt 26.39 fell on his face, and *p*, saying, O
42 away the second time, and *p*,
44 *p* the third time, saying the same
Mk 1.35 a solitary place, and there *p*.
5.18 *p* him that he might be with him.
14.35 and *p* that, if it were possible,
39 went away, and *p*, and spake the
Lk 5. 3 *p* him that he would thrust out a
16 himself into the wilderness, and *p*.
9.29 And as he *p*, the fashion of his
18.11 stood and *p* thus with himself,
22.32 *p* for thee, that thy faith fail not:
41 cast, and kneeled down and *p*,
44 in an agony he *p* more earnestly:
Jn 4.31 his disciples *p* him, saying,
Ac 1.24 And they *p*, and said, Thou, Lord,
4.31 And when they had *p*, the place
6. 6 when they had *p*, they laid their
8.15 *p* for them, that they might receive
9.40 forth, and kneeled down, and *p*;
10. 2 to the people, and *p* to God alway.
30 the ninth hour I *p* in my house,
48 *p* they him to tarry certain days.
13. 3 when they had fasted and *p*, and
14.23 *p* with fasting, they commended
16. 9 man of Macedonia, and *p* him,
25 Paul and Silas *p*, and sang
20.36 kneeled down, and *p* with them all.
21. 5 kneeled down on the shore, and *p*.
22.17 while I *p* in the temple, I was in a
23.18 *p* me to bring this young man
28. 8 Paul entered in, and *p*, and laid
Jas 5.17 he *p* earnestly that it might not
18 he *p* again, and the heaven gave

PRAYER
2Sa 7.27 heart to pray this *p* unto thee.
1Ki 8.28 thou respect unto the *p* of thy
28 hearken unto the cry and to the *p*,
29 *p* which thy servant shall make
38 *p* and supplication soever be made
45 hear thou in heaven their *p* and
49 Then hear thou their *p* and their
54 made an end of praying all this *p*
9. 3 him, I have heard thy *p* and thy
2Ki 19. 4 lift up thy *p* for the remnant that
20. 5 I have heard thy *p*, I have seen
2Ch 6.19 Have respect therefore to the *p*
19 to the *p* which thy servant prayeth
20 to hearken unto the *p* which thy
29 *p* or what supplication soever
35 hear thou from the heavens their *p*
39 their *p* and their supplications,
40 attent unto the *p* that is made in
7.12 I have heard thy *p*, and have
15 unto the *p* that is made in this
30.27 and their *p* came up to his holy
33.18 Manasseh, and his *p* unto his God,
19 His *p* also, and how God was
Neh 1. 6 hear the *p* of thy servant, which
11 attentive to the *p* of thy servant,

Biblical Themes

PRAYER

There was no day like that before it or after it, that the Lord hearkened unto the voice of a man. Jos 10.14

Let thine ear now be attentive, and thine eyes open, that thou mayest hear the prayer of thy servant. Neh 1.6

In the time of their trouble, when they cried unto thee, thou heardest them. Neh 9.27

Let the words of my mouth, and the meditation of my heart, be acceptable in thy sight, O Lord, my strength, and my redeemer. Ps 19.14

Be merciful unto me, O God . . . for my soul trusteth in thee: yea, in the shadow of thy wings will I make my refuge. Ps 57.1

I have cried day and night before thee: let my prayer come before thee: incline thine ear unto my cry. Ps 88.1-2

They called upon the Lord. . . . Thou answeredst them, O Lord our God: thou wast a God that forgavest them. Ps 99.6, 8

The preparations of the heart in man, and the answer of the tongue, is from the Lord. Pr 16.1

When ye spread forth your hands, I will hide mine eyes from you: yea, when ye make many prayers, I will not hear: your hands are full of blood. Isa 1.15

Before they call, I will answer; and while they are yet speaking, I will hear. Isa 65.24

Ye shall seek me, and find me, when ye shall search for me with all your heart. Jer 29.13

Whosoever shall call on the name of the Lord shall be delivered. Joel 2.32

When thou prayest, enter into thy closet, and when thou hast shut thy door, pray to thy Father which is in secret; and thy Father which seeth in secret shall reward thee openly. Mt 6.6

Your Father knoweth what things ye have need of, before ye ask him. After this manner therefore pray ye: Our Father which art in heaven, Hallowed be thy name. Mt 6.8-9

Ask, and it shall be given you; seek, and ye shall find; knock, and it shall be opened unto you. Mt 7.7

Where two or three are gathered together in my name, there am I in the midst of them. Mt 18.20

When ye stand praying, forgive, if ye have ought against any: that your Father also which is in heaven may forgive you your trespasses. Mk 11.25

As he prayed, the fashion of his countenance was altered, and his raiment was white and glistering. Lk 9.29

Shall not God avenge his own elect, which cry day and night unto him, though he bear long with them? Lk 18.7

And he was withdrawn from them about a stone's cast, and kneeled down, and prayed. . . . And there appeared an angel unto him from heaven, strengthening him. Lk 22.41, 43

Father, forgive them; for they know not what they do. Lk 23.34

If ye abide in me, and my words abide in you, ye shall ask what ye will, and it shall be done unto you. Jn 15.7

Ask in faith, nothing wavering. Jas 1.6

Draw nigh to God, and he will draw nigh to you. Jas 4.8

Neh 1.11 and to the *p* of thy servants, who
4. 9 Nevertheless we made our *p* unto
11.17 begin the thanksgiving in *p*: and
Job 15. 4 and restrainest *p* before God.
16.17 mine hands: also my *p* is pure.
22.27 Thou shalt make thy *p* unto him,
Ps 4. 1 mercy upon me, and hear my *p*.
5. 3 will I direct my *p* unto thee, and
6. 9 the Lord will receive my *p*.
17(T) A *p* of David.
1 give ear unto my *p*, that goeth
35.13 *p* returned into mine own bosom.
39.12 Hear my *p*, O Lord, and give ear
42. 8 *p* unto the God of my life.
54. 2 Hear my *p*, O God; give ear to the
55. 1 Give ear to my *p*, O God; and hide
61. 1 my cry, O God; attend unto my *p*.
64. 1 Hear my voice, O God, in my *p*:
65. 2 O thou that hearest *p*, unto thee
66.19 attended to the voice of my *p*.
20 which hath not turned away my *p*,
69.13 for me, my *p* is unto thee, O Lord,
72.15 *p* also shall be made for him
80. 4 against the *p* of thy people?
84. 8 O Lord God of hosts, hear my *p*:
86(T) A *p* of David.
6 Give ear, O Lord, unto my *p*;
88. 2 Let my *p* come before thee: incline
13 morning shall my *p* prevent thee.
90(T) A *p* of Moses the man of God.
102(T) A *p* of the afflicted, when he is
1 Hear my *p*, O Lord, and let my
17 will regard the *p* of the destitute,
17 and not despise their *p*.
109. 4 but I give myself unto *p*.
7 and let his *p* become sin.
141. 2 Let my *p* be set forth before thee
5 yet my *p* also shall be in their
142(T) David; A *P* when he was in
143. 1 Hear my *p*, O Lord, give ear to my
Pr 15. 8 the *p* of the upright is his delight.
29 he heareth the *p* of the righteous.
28. 9 his *p* shall be an abomination.
Isa 26.16 poured out a *p* when...chastening
37. 4 thy *p* for the remnant that is left.
38. 5 I have heard thy *p*, I have seen
56. 7 them joyful in my house of *p*:
7 house shall be called an house of *p*
Jer 7.16 neither lift up cry nor *p* for them,
11.14 neither lift up a cry or *p* for them:
La 3. 8 and shout, he shutteth out my *p*.
44 that our *p* should not pass through.
Dan 9. 3 seek by *p* and supplications with
13 we not our *p* before the Lord our
17 God, hear the *p* of thy servant,
21 whiles I was speaking in *p*, even
Jon 2. 7 my *p* came in unto thee, into thine
Hab 3. 1 A *p* of Habakkuk the prophet
Mt 17.21 not out but by *p* and fasting.
21.13 shall be called the house of *p*; but
22 whatsoever ye shall ask in *p*,
23.14 and for a pretence make long *p*:
Mk 9.29 by nothing, but by *p* and fasting.
11.17 called of all nations the house of *p*?
Lk 1.13 not, Zacharias: for thy *p* is heard;
6.12 continued all night in *p* to God.
19.46 My house is the house of *p*: but ye
22.45 when he rose up from *p*, and was
Ac 1.14 one accord in *p* and supplication,
3. 1 the hour of *p*, being the ninth hour.
6. 4 will give ourselves continually to *p*,
10.31 And said, Cornelius, thy *p* is heard,
12. 5 but *p* was made without ceasing of
16.13 where *p* was wont to be made;
16 as we went to *p*, a certain damsel
Ro 10. 1 desire and *p* to God for Israel is,
12.12 continuing instant in *p*;
1Co 7. 5 give yourselves to fasting and *p*;
2Co 1.11 also helping together by *p* for us,
9.14 by their *p* for you, which long after
Eph 6.18 Praying always with all *p* and
Php 1. 4 Always in every *p* of mine for you
19 to my salvation through your *p*,
4. 6 every thing by *p* and supplication
Col 4. 2 Continue in *p*, and watch in the
1Ti 4. 5 sanctified by...word of God and *p*.
Jas 5.15 the *p* of faith shall save the sick,
16 fervent *p* of a righteous man
1Pe 4. 7 therefore sober, and watch unto *p*.

PRAYERS

Ps 72.20 *p* of David the son of Jesse are
Isa 1.15 when ye make many *p*, I will not
Mk 12.40 and for a pretence make long *p*:
Lk 2.37 with fastings and *p* night and day.
5.33 of John fast often, and make *p*,
20.47 and for a shew make long *p*:
Ac 2.42 and in breaking of bread, and in *p*.
10. 4 Thy *p* and thine alms are come up
Ro 1. 9 mention of you always in my *p*;
15.30 with me in your *p* to God for me;
Eph 1.16 making mention of you in my *p*;
Col 4.12 laboring fervently for you in *p*,
1Th 1. 2 making mention of you in our *p*;
1Ti 2. 1 supplications, *p*, intercessions, and
5. 5 continueth in supplications and *p*
2Ti 1. 3 have remembrance of thee in my *p*
Phm 4 mention of thee always in my *p*,
22 through your *p* I shall be given
Heb 5. 7 he had offered up *p*...supplications
1Pe 3. 7 life; that your *p* be not hindered.
12 and his ears are open unto their *p*:
Rev 5. 8 odors, which are the *p* of saints.

8. 3 offer it with the *p* of all saints upon
4 came with the *p* of the saints,

PRAYEST

Mt 6. 5 when thou *p*, thou shalt not be as
6 when thou *p*, enter into thy closet,

PRAYETH

1Ki 8.28 thy servant *p* before thee to day:
2Ch 6.19 which thy servant *p* before thee:
20 thy servant *p* toward this place.
Isa 44.17 and worshippeth it, and *p* unto it,
Ac 9.11 Saul, of Tarsus: for, behold, he *p*,
1Co 11. 5 every woman that *p* or prophesieth
14.14 my spirit *p*, but my understanding

PRAYING

1Sa 1.12 she continued *p* before the Lord,
26 stood by thee here, *p* unto the Lord.
1Ki 8.54 Solomon had made an end of *p* all
2Ch 7. 1 Solomon had made an end of *p*,
Dan 6.11 and found Daniel *p* and making
9.20 And whiles I was speaking, and *p*,
Mk 11.25 And when ye stand *p*, forgive, if ye
Lk 1.10 people were *p* without at the time
3.21 Jesus also being baptized, and *p*,
9.18 it came to pass, as he was alone *p*,
11. 1 as he was *p* in a certain place,
Ac 11. 5 I was in the city of Joppa *p*: and in
12.12 many were gathered together *p*.
1Co 11. 4 Every man *p* or prophesying,
2Co 8. 4 *P* us with much intreaty that we
Eph 6.18 *P* always with all prayer and
Col 1. 3 Lord Jesus Christ, *p* always for you,
4. 3 *p* also for us, that God would open
1Th 3.10 Night and day *p* exceedingly that
Jude 20 holy faith, *p* in the Holy Ghost,

PREACH

Neh 6. 7 prophets to *p* of thee at Jerusalem,
Isa 61. 1 anointed me to *p* good tidings
Jon 3. 2 *p* unto it the preaching that I bid
Mt 4.17 From that time Jesus began to *p*,
10. 7 as ye go, *p*, saying, The kingdom of
27 ear, that *p* ye upon the housetops.
11. 1 to teach and to *p* in their cities.
Mk 1. 4 *p* the baptism of repentance for the
38 next towns, that I may *p* there also:
3.14 that he might send them forth to *p*,
16.15 and *p* the gospel to every creature.
Lk 4.18 me to *p* the gospel to the poor;
18 to *p* deliverance to the captives,
19 *p* the acceptable year of the Lord.
43 I must *p* the kingdom of God to
9. 2 he sent them to *p* the kingdom of
60 thou and *p* the kingdom of God.
Ac 5.42 not to teach and *p* Jesus Christ.
10.42 he commanded us to *p* unto the
14.15 and *p* unto you that ye should turn
15.21 hath in every city them that *p* him,
16. 6 Holy Ghost to *p* the word in Asia,
10 us for to *p* the gospel unto them.
17. 3 this Jesus, whom I *p* unto you, is
Ro 1.15 I am ready to *p* the gospel to you
10. 8 is, the word of faith, which we *p*;
15 shall they *p*, except they be sent?
15 of them that *p* the gospel of peace,
15.20 so have I strived to *p* the gospel,
1Co 1.17 not to baptize, but to *p* the gospel:
23 But we *p* Christ crucified, unto the
9.14 they which *p* the gospel should
16 For though I *p* the gospel, I have
16 woe is unto me, if I *p* not the gospel!
18 when I *p* the gospel, I may make
15.11 they, so we *p*, and so ye believed.
2Co 2.12 I came to Troas to *p* Christ's gospel,
4. 5 For we *p* not ourselves, but Christ
10.16 *p* the gospel in the regions beyond
Gal 1. 8 *p* any other gospel unto you than
9 man *p* any other gospel unto you
16 I might *p* him among the heathen;
2. 2 which I *p* among the Gentiles,
5.11 if I yet *p* circumcision, why do I
Eph 3. 8 I should *p* among the Gentiles the
Php 1.15 Some indeed *p* Christ even of envy
16 The one *p* Christ of contention,
Col 1.28 we *p*, warning every man, Whom
2Ti 4. 2 *P* the word; be instant in season,
Rev 14. 6 to *p* unto them that dwell on the

PREACHED

Ps 40. 9 have *p* righteousness in the great
Mt 11. 5 the poor have the gospel *p* to them.
24.14 be *p* in all the world for a witness
26.13 this gospel shall be *p* in the whole
Mk 1. 7 And *p*, saying, There cometh one
39 And he *p* in their synagogues
2. 2 and he *p* the word unto them.
6.12 and *p* that men should repent.
14. 9 this gospel shall be *p* throughout
16.20 they went forth, and *p* every where,
Lk 3.18 exhortation *p* he unto the people.
4.44 And he *p* in the synagogues of
7.22 raised, to the poor the gospel is *p*.
16.16 that time the kingdom of God is *p*,
20. 1 in the temple, and *p* the gospel,
24.47 should be *p* in his name among all
Ac 3.20 which before was *p* unto you:
4. 2 *p* through Jesus the resurrection
8. 5 Samaria, and *p* Christ unto them.
25 testified and *p* the word of the
25 *p* the gospel in many villages of
35 scripture, and *p* unto him Jesus.

Jesus at prayer in the garden of Gethsemane (Mt 27); carved oak panel from Normandy, about 1500.

Ac 8.40 he *p* in all the cities, till he came
9.20 he *p* Christ in the synagogues,
27 how he had *p* boldly at Damascus
10.37 after the baptism which John *p*;
13. 5 they *p* the word of God in the
24 John had first *p* before his coming
38 *p* unto you the forgiveness of sins:
42 be *p* to them the next sabbath.
14. 7 And there they *p* the gospel.
21 they had *p* the gospel to that city,
25 they had *p* the word in Perga,
15.36 where we have *p* the word of the
17.13 that the word of God was *p* of Paul
18 because he *p* unto them Jesus,
20. 7 Paul *p* unto them, ready to depart
Ro 15.19 have fully *p* the gospel of Christ.
1Co 9.27 when I have *p* to others, I myself
15. 1 you the gospel which I *p* unto you,
2 keep in memory what I *p* unto you,
12 if Christ be *p* that he rose from the
2Co 1.19 who was *p* among you by us, even
11. 4 Jesus, whom we have not *p*,
7 I have *p* to you the gospel of God
Gal 1. 8 that which we have *p* unto you,
11 the gospel which was *p* of me is not
3. 8 *p* before the gospel unto Abraham,
4.13 I *p* the gospel unto you at the
Eph 2.17 came and *p* peace to you which
Php 1.18 pretence, or in truth, Christ is *p*;
Col 1.23 which was *p* to every creature
1Th 2. 9 we *p* unto you the gospel of God.
1Ti 3.16 *p* unto the Gentiles, believed on in
Heb 4. 2 For unto us was the gospel *p*, as
2 but the word *p* did not profit them,
6 and they to whom it was first *p*.
1Pe 1.12 them that have *p* the gospel unto
25 which by the gospel is *p* unto you.
3.19 and *p* unto the spirits in prison;
4. 6 for this cause was the gospel *p*

PREACHER

Ec 1. 1 words of the *P*, the son of David,
2 Vanity of vanities, saith the *P*,
12 I the *P* was king over Israel in
7.27 this have I found, saith the *p*,
12. 8 Vanity of vanities, saith the *p*; all
9 because the *p* was wise, he still
10 *p* sought to find out acceptable
Ro 10.14 how shall they hear without a *p*?
1Ti 2. 7 I am ordained a *p*, and an apostle,
2Ti 1.11 I am appointed a *p*, and an apostle,
2Pe 2. 5 eighth person, a *p* of righteousness,

PREACHEST

Ro 2.21 that *p* a man should not steal,

PREACHETH

Ac 19.13 you by Jesus whom Paul *p*.
2Co 11. 4 if he that cometh *p* another Jesus,
Gal 1.23 now *p* the faith which once he

PREACHING

Jon 3. 2 unto it the *p* that I bid thee.
Mt 3. 1 *p* in the wilderness of Judea,
4.23 and *p* the gospel of the kingdom,
9.35 and *p* the gospel of the kingdom,
12.41 they repented at the *p* of Jonas;
Mk 1.14 *p* the gospel of the kingdom of
Lk 3. 3 *p* the baptism of repentance for
8. 1 *p* and shewing the glad tidings of
9. 6 *p* the gospel, and healing every
11.32 they repented at the *p* of Jonas;
Ac 8. 4 went every where *p* the word.
12 believed Philip *p* the things
10.36 Israel, *p* peace by Jesus Christ:
11.19 *p* the word to none but unto the
20 the Grecians, *p* the Lord Jesus.
15.35 and *p* the word of the Lord, with
20. 9 as Paul was long *p*, he sunk down
25 have gone *p* the kingdom of God,
28.31 *P* the kingdom of God, and

Jesus preaching from a boat at the shore of the Sea of Galilee; engraving by Gustave Doré (1832-1883).

Ro 16.25 gospel, and the *p* of Jesus Christ,
1Co 1.18 For the *p* of the cross is to them
21 by the foolishness of *p* to save
2. 4 my *p* was not with enticing words
15.14 be not risen, then is our *p* vain,
2Co 10.14 to you also in *p* the gospel of Christ:
2Ti 4.17 me the *p* might be fully known,
Tit 1. 3 manifested his word through *p*,

PRECEPT

Isa 28.10 *p* must be upon *p*, *p* upon *p*;
13 unto them *p* upon *p*, *p* upon *p*;
29.13 me is taught by the *p* of men:
Mk 10. 5 your heart he wrote you this *p*.
Heb 9.19 Moses had spoken every *p* to all

PRECEPTS

Neh 9.14 and commandedst them *p*,
Ps 119. 4 commanded us to keep thy *p*
15 I will meditate in thy *p*, and have
27 to understand the way of thy *p*:
40 I have longed after thy *p*: quicken
45 walk at liberty: for I seek thy *p*.
56 This I had, because I kept thy *p*.
63 thee, and of them that keep thy *p*.
69 keep thy *p* with my whole heart.
78 cause: but I will meditate in thy *p*.
87 earth; but I forsook not thy *p*.
93 I will never forget thy *p*: for with
94 save me; for I have sought thy *p*.
100 the ancients, because I keep thy *p*.
104 thy *p* I get understanding:
110 for me: yet I erred not from thy *p*.
128 I esteem all thy *p* concerning all
134 of man: so will I keep thy *p*.
141 despised: yet do not I forget thy *p*.
159 Consider how I love thy *p*:
168 kept thy *p* and thy testimonies:
173 help me; for I have chosen thy *p*.
Jer 35.18 and kept all his *p*, and done
Dan 9. 5 even by departing from thy *p* and

PRECIOUS

Dt 33.14 *p* things put forth by the moon,
15 for the *p* things of the lasting hills,
1Sa 3. 1 of the Lord was *p* in those days;
26.21 my soul was *p* in thine eyes this
2Ki 1.14 let my life now be *p* in thy sight.
1Ch 20. 2 and there were *p* stones in it;
Ezr 8.27 vessels of fine copper, *p* as gold.
Job 28.10 and his eyes seeth every *p* thing.
Ps 49. 8 the redemption of their soul is *p*,

72.14 and *p* shall their blood be in his
116.15 *P* in the sight of the Lord is the
126. 6 and weepeth, bearing *p* seed,
139.17 How *p* also are thy thoughts
Pr 3.15 She is more *p* than rubies: and all
17. 8 A gift is as a *p* stone in the eyes
20.15 lips of knowledge are a *p* jewel.
Ec 7. 1 name is better than *p* ointment;
Isa 43. 4 Since thou wast *p* in my sight,
Mt 26. 7 alabaster box of very *p* ointment,
Mk 14. 3 of ointment of spikenard very *p*;
1Co 3.12 silver, *p* stones, wood, hay,
Jas 5. 7 waiteth for the *p* fruit of the earth,
1Pe 1. 7 more *p* than of gold that perisheth,
19 But with the *p* blood of Christ, as
2. 4 of men, but chosen of God, and *p*,
6 Sion a chief corner stone, elect, *p*:
7 therefore which believe he is *p*:
2Pe 1. 1 that have obtained like *p* faith
4 exceeding great and *p* promises:
Rev 17. 4 decked with gold and *p* stones and
18.12 silver, and *p* stones, and of pearls,
12 all manner vessels of most *p* wood,
16 decked with gold, and *p* stones, and
21.11 light was like unto a stone most *p*,
19 with all manner of *p* stones.

PREDESTINATE

Ro 8.29 also did *p* to be conformed to the
30 whom he did *p*, them he also

PREDESTINATED

Eph 1. 5 Having *p* us unto the adoption
11 being *p* according to the purpose

PREEMINENCE

Ec 3.19 a man hath no *p* above a beast:
Col 1.18 all things he might have the *p*.
3Jn 9 loveth to have the *p* among them,

PREFER

Ps 137. 6 If I *p* not Jerusalem above my

PREFERRED

Est 2. 9 he *p* her and her maids unto the
Dan 6. 3 this Daniel was *p* above the
Jn 1.15 cometh after me is *p* before me:
27 coming after me is *p* before me,
30 a man which is *p* before me:

PREFERRING

Ro 12.10 love; in honor *p* one another;
1Ti 5.21 without *p* one before another,

PREMEDITATE

Mk 13.11 ye shall speak, neither do ye *p*:

PREPARATION

1Ch 22. 5 will therefore now make *p* for it.
Na 2. 3 flaming torches in the day of his *p*,
Mt 27.62 that followed the day of the *p*,
Mk 15.42 was come, because it was the *p*,
Lk 23.54 And that day was the *p*, and the
Jn 19.14 And it was the *p* of the passover,
31 because it was the *p*, that the
42 because of the Jews' *p* day;
Eph 6.15 with the *p* of the gospel of peace;

PREPARATIONS

Pr 16. 1 The *p* of the heart in man, and

PREPARE

Ex 15. 2 God, and I will *p* him an habitation;
1Sa 7. 3 *p* your hearts unto the Lord, and
Job 11.13 If thou *p* thine heart, and stretch
Ps 10.17 thou wilt *p* their heart, thou wilt
61. 7 O *p* mercy and truth, which may
Isa 40. 3 *P* ye the way of the Lord, make
Eze 45.23 *p* a burnt offering to the Lord,
Joel 3. 9 *P* war, wake up the mighty men,
Am 4.12 thee, *p* to meet thy God, O Israel.
Mal 3. 1 and he shall *p* the way before me:
Mt 3. 3 *P* ye the way of the Lord, make
11.10 which shall *p* thy way before thee.
26.17 *p* for thee to eat the passover?
Mk 1. 2 which shall *p* thy way before thee.
3 *P* ye the way of the Lord, make
14.12 Where wilt thou that we go and *p*
Lk 1.76 face of the Lord to *p* his ways;
3. 4 *P* ye the way of the Lord, make
7.27 which shall *p* thy way before thee.
22. 8 Go and *p* us the passover, that we
9 him, Where wilt thou that we *p*?
Jn 14. 2 told you. I go to *p* a place for you.
3 And if I go and *p* a place for you,
1Co 14. 8 who shall *p* himself to the battle?
Phm 22 *p* me also a lodging: for I trust

PREPARED

Ex 12.39 neither had they *p* for themselves
1Ch 15. 1 and *p* a place for the ark of God,
29. 2 Now I have *p* with all my might for
3 all that I have *p* for the holy house,
16 we have *p* to build thee an house
2Ch 12.14 he *p* not his heart to seek the Lord.
16.14 spices *p* by the apothecaries' art:
19. 3 hast *p* thine heart to seek God.
27. 6 *p* his ways before the Lord his God.
29.36 people, that God had *p* the people:
Job 28.27 it; he *p* it, yea, and searched it out.
29. 7 city, when I *p* my seat in the street!
Ps 9. 7 he hath *p* his throne for judgment.
57. 6 They have *p* a net for my steps;
74.16 thou hast *p* the light and the sun.
103.19 hath *p* his throne in the heavens:
Pr 8.27 When he *p* the heavens, I was
19.29 Judgments are *p* for scorners, and
Eze 38. 7 Be thou *p*, and prepare for thyself,
Hos 6. 3 going forth is *p* as the morning;
Jon 1.17 *p* a great fish to swallow up
4. 6 And the Lord God *p* a gourd, and
7 God *p* a worm when the morning
8 that God *p* a vehement east wind;
Zep 1. 7 the Lord hath *p* a sacrifice, he hath
Mt 20.23 for whom it is *p* of my Father.
22. 4 Behold, I have *p* my dinner: my
25.34 inherit the kingdom *p* for you from
41 fire, *p* for the devil and his angels:
Mk 10.40 be given to them for whom it is *p*.
14.15 upper room furnished and *p*:
Lk 1.17 ready a people *p* for the Lord.
2.31 *p* before the face of all people;
12.47 his lord's will, and *p* not himself,
23.56 and *p* spices and ointments;
24. 1 the spices which they had *p*, and
Ro 9.23 which he had afore *p* unto glory,
1Co 2. 9 hath *p* for them that love him.
2Ti 2.21 use, and *p* unto every good work.
Heb 10. 5 not, but a body hast thou *p* me:
11. 7 *p* an ark to the saving of his house;
16 God: for he hath *p* for them a city.
Rev 8. 6 trumpets *p* themselves to sound.
9. 7 like unto horses *p* unto battle;
15 which were *p* for an hour, and a
12. 6 where she hath a place *p* of God,
16.12 the kings of the east might be *p*.
21. 2 *p* as a bride adorned for her

PREPAREST

Nu 15. 8 thou *p* a bullock for a burnt
Ps 23. 5 Thou *p* a table before me in the
65. 9 thou *p* them corn, when thou

PREPARING

Neh 13. 7 in *p* him a chamber in the courts
1Pe 3.20 while the ark was a *p*, wherein

PRESBYTERY

1Ti 4.14 laying on of the hands of the *p*.

PRESENCE

Gen 3. 8 from the *p* of the Lord God
4.16 Cain went out from the *p* of the
16.12 dwell in the *p* of all his brethren.
23.11 in the *p* of the sons of my people
18 in the *p* of the children of Heth,
25.18 died in the *p* of all his brethren.
27.30 out from the *p* of Isaac his father,
41.46 went out from the *p* of Pharaoh,
45. 3 for they were troubled at his *p*.
47.15 for why should we die in thy *p*?
Ex 10.11 driven out from Pharaoh's *p*.
33.14 My *p* shall go with thee, and I
15 If thy *p* go not with me, carry us
35.20 departed from the *p* of Moses.
Lev 22. 3 soul shall be cut off from my *p*:
Nu 20. 6 Moses and Aaron went from the *p*
Dt 25. 9 unto him in the *p* of the elders,
Jos 4.11 the priests, in the *p* of the people.
8.32 in the *p* of the children of Israel.
1Sa 18.11 David avoided out of his *p* twice.
19. 7 he was in his *p*, as in times past.
10 he slipped away out of Saul's *p*,
21.15 to play the mad man in my *p*?
2Sa 16.19 I not serve in the *p* of his son?
19 as I have served in thy father's *p*,
19 so will I be in thy *p*.
24. 4 went out from the *p* of the king, to
1Ki 1.28 And she came into the king's *p*,
8.22 in the *p* of all the congregation
12. 2 fled from the *p* of king Solomon,
21.13 against Naboth in the *p* of the
2Ki 3.14 that I regard the *p* of Jehoshaphat
5.27 his *p* a leper as white as snow.
13.23 cast he them from his *p* as yet.
24.20 he had cast them out from his *p*,
25.19 of them that were in the king's *p*,
1Ch 16.27 Glory and honor are in his *p*;
33 wood sing out at the *p* of the Lord,
24.31 Aaron in the *p* of David the king,
2Ch 6.12 the *p* of all the congregation of
9.23 earth sought the *p* of Solomon,
10. 2 from the *p* of Solomon the king,
20. 9 and in thy *p*, (for thy name is in
34. 4 down the altars of Baalim in his *p*;
Neh 2. 1 not been beforetime sad in his *p*.
Est 1.10 in the *p* of Ahasuerus the king,
8.15 went out from the *p* of the king
Job 1.12 went forth from the *p* of the Lord.
2. 7 Satan forth from the *p* of the Lord.
23.15 Therefore am I troubled at his *p*:
Ps 9. 3 they shall fall and perish at thy *p*.
16.11 of life: in thy *p* is fulness of joy;
17. 2 sentence come forth from thy *p*;
23. 5 me in the *p* of mine enemies:
31.20 hide them in the secret of thy *p*
51.11 Cast me not away from thy *p*; and
68. 2 the wicked perish at the *p* of God.
8 also dropped at the *p* of God:
8 itself was moved at the *p* of God,
95. 2 before his *p* with thanksgiving,
97. 5 like wax at the *p* of the Lord,
5 *p* of the Lord of the whole earth.
100. 2 come before his *p* with singing.
114. 7 thou earth, at the *p* of the Lord,
7 at the *p* of the God of Jacob;
116.14 Lord now in the *p* of all his people.
139. 7 whither shall I flee from thy *p*?
140.13 the upright shall dwell in thy *p*.
Pr 14. 7 Go from the *p* of a foolish man,
17.18 surety in the *p* of his friend.
25. 6 forth thyself in the *p* of the king,
7 be put lower in the *p* of the prince
Isa 1. 7 strangers devour it in your *p*, and
19. 1 of Egypt shall be moved at his *p*,
63. 9 and the angel of his *p* saved them:
64. 1 mountains might flow...at thy *p*,
2 the nations may tremble at thy *p*!
3 mountains flowed down at thy *p*.
Jer 4.26 broken down at the *p* of the Lord,
5.22 will ye not tremble at my *p*, which
23.39 fathers, and cast you out of my *p*:
28. 1 the *p* of the priests and of all the
5 Hananiah in the *p* of the priests,

Jer 28. 5 and in the *p* of all the people that
11 spake in the *p* of all the people,
32.12 and in the *p* of the witnesses that
52. 3 he had cast them out from his *p*,
Eze 38.20 of the earth, shall shake at my *p*,
Dan 2.27 answered in the *p* of the king,
Jon 1. 3 Tarshish from the *p* of the Lord,
3 Tarshish from the *p* of the Lord.
10 he fled from the *p* of the Lord,
Na 1. 5 and the earth is burned at his *p*,
Zep 1. 7 thy peace at the *p* of the Lord God:
Lk 1.19 that stand in the *p* of God;
13.26 We have eaten and drunk in thy *p*,
14.10 in the *p* of them that sit at meat
15.10 there is joy in the *p* of the angels
Jn 20.30 did Jesus in the *p* of his disciples,
Ac 3.13 and denied him in the *p* of Pilate,
16 soundness in the *p* of you all.
19 come from the *p* of the Lord;
5.41 departed from the *p* of the council,
27.35 thanks to God in the *p* of them
1Co 1.29 That no flesh should glory in his *p*.
2Co 10. 1 who in *p* am base among you,
10 but his bodily *p* is weak, and his
Php 2.12 always obeyed, not as in my *p* only,
1Th 2.17 from you for a short time in *p*,
19 in the *p* of our Lord Jesus Christ
2Th 1. 9 from the *p* of the Lord, and from
Heb 9.24 to appear in the *p* of God for us:
Jude 24 faultless before the *p* of his glory
Rev 14.10 in the *p* of the holy angels, and in
10 angels, and in the *p* of the Lamb:

PRESENT

Gen 32.13 came to his hand a *p* for Esau
18 it is a *p* sent unto my lord Esau:
20 I will appease him with the *p* that
21 So went the *p* over before him: and
33.10 then receive my *p* at my hand: for
43.11 carry down the man a *p*, a little
15 the men took that *p*, and they took
25 made ready the *p* against Joseph
26 brought him the *p* which was in
Ex 34. 2 Sinai, and *p* thyself there to me
Lev 14.11 *p* the man that is to be made
16. 7 goats, and *p* them before the Lord
27. 8 shall *p* himself before the priest,
11 shall *p* the beast before the priest:
Nu 3. 6 *p* them before Aaron the priest,
Dt 31.14 *p* yourselves in the tabernacle of
Jdg 3.15 sent a *p* unto Eglon the king of
17 he brought the *p* unto Eglon king
18 he had made an end to offer the *p*,
18 away the people that bare the *p*.
6.18 bring forth my *p*, and set it before
1Sa 9. 7 is not a *p* to bring to the man of
10.19 *p* yourselves before the Lord by
13.15 the people that were *p* with him,
16 the people that were *p* with them,
21. 3 in mine hand, or what there is *p*.
30.26 a *p* for you of the spoil of the
2Sa 20. 4 three days, and be thou here *p*.
1Ki 9.16 a *p* unto his daughter, Solomon's
10.25 they brought every man his *p*,
15.19 unto thee a *p* of silver and gold;
20.27 were numbered, and were all *p*,
2Ki 8. 8 Take a *p* in thine hand, and go,
9 took a *p* with him, even of every
16. 8 it for a *p* to the king of Assyria.
17. 4 no *p* to the king of Assyria, as he
18.31 an agreement with me by a *p*,
20.12 letters and a *p* unto Hezekiah:
1Ch 29.17 joy thy people, which are *p* here,
2Ch 5.11 all the priests...*p* were sanctified,
9.24 they brought every man his *p*,
29.29 all that were *p* with him bowed
30.21 that were *p* at Jerusalem kept the
31. 1 all Israel that were *p* went out to
34.32 all that were *p* in Jerusalem and
33 all that were *p* in Israel to serve,
35. 7 for all that were *p*, to the number
17 that were *p* kept the passover at
18 all Judah and Israel that were *p*,
Ezr 8.25 all Israel there *p*, had offered:
Est 1. 5 the people that were *p* in Shushan
4.16 all the Jews that are *p* in Shushan,
Job 1. 6 to *p* themselves before the Lord,
2. 1 to *p* themselves before the Lord,
1 them to *p* himself before the Lord.
Ps 46. 1 strength, a very *p* help in trouble.
Isa 18. 7 the *p* be brought unto the Lord of
36.16 an agreement with me by a *p*,
39. 1 sent letters and a *p* to Hezekiah:
Jer 36. 7 *p* their supplication before the
42. 9 ye sent me to *p* your supplication
Eze 27.15 for a *p* horns of ivory and ebony.
Dan 9.18 *p* our supplications before thee
Hos 10. 6 Assyria for a *p* to king Jareb:
Lk 2.22 Jerusalem, to *p* him to the Lord;
5.17 of the Lord was *p* to heal them.
13. 1 There were *p* at that season some
18.30 receive manifold more in this *p* time,
Jn 14.25 unto you, being yet *p* with you.
Ac 10.33 are we all here *p* before God, to
21.18 James; and all the elders were *p*.
25.24 all men which are here *p* with us,
28. 2 because of the *p* rain, and because
Ro 7.18 for to will is *p* with me; but how
21 would do good, evil is *p* with me.
8.18 sufferings of this *p* time are not
38 nor things *p*, nor things to come,
11. 5 then at this *p* time also there is a
12. 1 ye *p* your bodies a living sacrifice,
1Co 3.22 or things *p*, or things to come;
4.11 unto this *p* hour we both hunger,
5. 3 as absent in body, but *p* in spirit,
3 have judged...as though I were *p*,
7.26 that this is good for the *p* distress,
15. 6 greater part remain unto this *p*,
2Co 4.14 by Jesus, and shall *p* us with you.
5. 8 body, and to be *p* with the Lord.
9 that, whether *p* or absent, we may
10. 2 when I am *p* with that confidence,
11 we be also in deed when we are *p*.
11. 2 I may *p* you as a chaste virgin to
9 And when I was *p* with you, and
13. 2 as if I were *p*, the second time;
10 being *p* I should use sharpness,
Gal 1. 4 deliver us from this *p* evil world,
4.18 not only when I am *p* with you.
20 I desire to be *p* with you now, and
Eph 5.27 *p* it to himself a glorious church,
Col 1.22 *p* you holy and unblameable and
28 may *p* every man perfect in Christ
2Ti 4.10 me, having loved this *p* world,
Tit 2.12 and godly, in this *p* world;
Heb 9. 9 was a figure for the time then *p*,
12.11 no chastening for the *p* seemeth
2Pe 1.12 and be established in the *p* truth.
Jude 24 and to *p* you faultless before the

PRESENTED

Gen 46.29 Goshen, and *p* himself unto him;
47. 2 men, and *p* them unto Pharaoh.
Lev 2. 8 when it is *p* unto the priest, he
7.35 *p* them to minister unto the Lord
9.12 sons *p* unto him the blood,
13 they *p* the burnt offering unto him,
18 sons *p* unto him the blood,
16.10 be the scapegoat, shall be *p* alive
Dt 31.14 *p* themselves in the tabernacle of
Jos 24. 1 and they *p* themselves before God.
Jdg 6.19 unto him under the oak, and *p* it.
20. 2 *p* themselves in the assembly of
1Sa 17.16 evening, and *p* himself forty days.
Jer 38.26 I *p* my supplication before the
Eze 20.28 they *p* the provocation of their
Mt 2.11 treasures, they *p* unto him gifts;
Ac 9.41 saints and widows, *p* her alive.
23.33 governor, *p* Paul also before him.

PRESENTLY

1Sa 2.16 Let them not fail to burn the fat *p*,
Pr 12.16 A fool's wrath is *p* known: but a
Mt 21.19 And *p* the fig tree withered away.
26.53 shall *p* give me more than twelve
Php 2.23 Him therefore I hope to send *p*,

PRESERVE

Gen 19.32, 34 we may *p* seed of our father.
45. 5 did send me before you to *p* life.
7 to *p* you a posterity in the earth,
Dt 6.24 that he might *p* us alive, as it is
Ps 12. 7 *p* them from this generation for
16. 1 *P* me, O God: for in thee do I put
25.21 integrity and uprightness *p* me;
32. 7 thou shalt *p* me from trouble;
40.11 and thy truth continually *p* me.
41. 2 The Lord will *p* him, and keep
61. 7 and truth, which may *p* him.
64. 1 *p* my life from fear of the enemy.
79.11 *p* thou those that are appointed to
86. 2 *P* my soul; for I am holy: O thou
121. 7 The Lord shall *p* thee from all evil:
7 he shall *p* thy soul.
8 Lord shall *p* thy going out and thy
140. 1 man: *p* me from the violent man;
4 wicked; *p* me from the violent man;
Pr 2.11 Discretion shall *p* thee,
4. 6 her not, and she shall *p* thee:
14. 3 the lips of the wise shall *p* them.
20.28 Mercy and truth *p* the king: and
22.12 The eyes of the Lord *p* knowledge,
Isa 31. 5 it; and passing over he will *p* it.
49. 8 and I will *p* thee, and give thee
Jer 49.11 children, I will *p* them alive;
Lk 17.33 shall lose his life shall *p* it.
2Ti 4.18 *p* me unto his heavenly kingdom:

PRESERVED

Gen 32.30 God face to face, and my life is *p*.
Jos 24.17 *p* us in all the way wherein we
1Sa 30.23 who hath *p* us, and delivered the
2Sa 8. 6, 14 *p* David whithersoever he
1Ch 18. 6, 13 *p* David whithersoever he went.
Job 10.12 thy visitation hath *p* my spirit.
29. 2 as in the days when God *p* me;
Ps 37.28 they are *p* for ever: but the seed
Isa 49. 6 and to restore the *p* of Israel:
Hos 12.13 Egypt, and by a prophet was he *p*.
Mt 9.17 into new bottles, and both are *p*.
Lk 5.38 into new bottles; and both are *p*.
1Th 5.23 be *p* blameless unto the coming
Jude 1 and *p* in Jesus Christ, and called:

PRESERVER

Job 7.20 I do unto thee, O thou *p* of men?

PRESERVEST

Neh 9. 6 is therein, and thou *p* them all;
Ps 36. 6 O Lord, thou *p* man and beast.

PRESERVETH

Job 36. 6 He *p* not the life of the wicked:
Ps 31.23 for the Lord *p* the faithful, and
97.10 he *p* the souls of his saints; he
116. 6 The Lord *p* the simple: I was
145.20 The Lord *p* all them that love him:
146. 9 The Lord *p* the strangers; he
Pr 2. 8 and *p* the way of his saints.
16.17 he that keepeth his way *p* his soul.

PRESS

Joel 3.13 for the *p* is full, the fats overflow;
Hag 2.16 draw out fifty vessels out of the *p*,
Mk 2. 4 not come nigh unto him for the *p*,
5.27 came in the *p* behind, and touched
30 him, turned him about in the *p*,
Lk 8.19 could not come at him for the *p*.
45 multitude throng thee and *p* thee,
19. 3 could not for the *p*, because he
Php 3.14 I *p* toward the mark for the prize

PRESSED

Gen 19. 3 And he *p* upon them greatly; and
9 they *p* sore upon the man, even
40.11 and *p* them into Pharaoh's cup,
Jdg 16.16 she *p* him daily with her words,
2Sa 13.25 he *p* him: howbeit he would not
27 But Absalom *p* him, that he let
Est 8.14 *p* on by the king's commandment.
Eze 23. 3 there were their breasts *p*, and
Am 2.13 Behold, I am *p* under you, as a
13 as a cart is *p* that is full of sheaves.
Mk 3.10 they *p* upon him for to touch him,
Lk 5. 1 people *p* upon him to hear the
6.38 good measure, *p* down, and shaken
Ac 18. 5 Paul was *p* in the spirit, and
2Co 1. 8 that we were *p* out of measure,

PRESSETH

Ps 38. 2 in me, and thy hand *p* me sore.
Lk 16.16 preached, and every man *p* into it.

PRESUMPTUOUS

Ps 19.13 thy servant also from *p* sins;
2Pe 2.10 *P* are they, selfwilled, they are

PRETENSE

Mt 23.14 and for a *p* make long prayer:
Mk 12.40 for a *p* make long prayers: these
Php 1.18 whether in *p*, or in truth, Christ is

PREVAIL

Gen 7.20 cubits upward did the waters *p*;
2Ch 14.11 God; let not man *p* against thee.
18.21 entice him, and thou shalt also *p*:
Ps 9.19 Arise, O Lord; let not man *p*: let
12. 4 With our tongue will we *p*; our
65. 3 Iniquities *p* against me: as for our
Ec 4.12 if one *p* against him, two shall
Isa 16.12 to pray; but he shall not *p*.
Jer 5.22 themselves, yet can they not *p*;
Mt 16.18 gates of hell shall not *p* against it.
27.24 Pilate saw...he could *p* nothing,
Jn 12.19 Perceive ye how ye *p* nothing?

PREVAILED

Gen 7.18 the waters *p*, and were increased
32.28 with God and with men, and has *p*.
Ex 17.11 held up his hand, that Israel *p*:
11 he let down his hand, Amalek *p*.
1Sa 17.50 So David *p* over the Philistine
Ps 13. 4 enemy say, I have *p* against him;
129. 2 yet they have not *p* against me.
Jer 20. 7 art stronger than I, and hast *p*:
La 1.16 desolate, because the enemy *p*.
Dan 7.21 the saints, and *p* against them;
Hos 12. 4 had power over the angel, and *p*:
Ob 7 deceived thee, and *p* against thee;
Lk 23.23 them and of the chief priests *p*.
Ac 19.16 *p* against them, so that they fled
20 grew the word of God, and *p*.
Rev 5. 5 David hath *p* to open the book,
12. 8 *p* not; neither was their place

PREVAILEST

Job 14.20 Thou *p* for ever against him,

PREVENT

Job 3.12 Why did the knees *p* me? or why
Ps 59.10 The God of my mercy shall *p* me:
79. 8 thy tender mercies speedily *p* us;
88.13 morning shall my prayer *p* thee.
119.148 Mine eyes *p* the night watches,
Am 9.10 evil shall not overtake nor *p* us.
1Th 4.15 shall not *p* them which are asleep.

PREVENTED

2Sa 22. 6 about; the snares of death *p* me;
19 *p* me in the day of my calamity:
Job 30.27 not: the days of affliction *p* me.
41.11 Who hath *p* me, that I should
Ps 18. 5 about: the snares of death *p* me.
18 They *p* me in the day of my
119.147 I *p* the dawning of the morning,
Isa 21.14 *p* with their bread him that fled.
Mt 17.25 come into the house, Jesus *p* him,

PREY

Gen 49. 9 from the *p*, my son, thou art gone
27 morning he shall devour the *p*,
Nu 14. 3 and our children should be a *p*?
Dt 1.39 ones, which ye said should be a *p*,
2Ki 21.14 they shall become a *p* and a spoil
Neh 4. 4 for a *p* in the land of captivity:
Job 4.11 old lion perisheth for lack of *p*,
9.26 as the eagle that hasteth to the *p*.
24. 5 work; rising betimes for a *p*:
38.39 Wilt thou hunt the *p* for the lion?
39.29 thence she seeketh the *p*, and her
Ps 17.12 as a lion that is greedy of his *p*,
104.21 The young lions roar after their *p*,
124. 6 not given us as a *p* to their teeth.
Pr 23.28 She also lieth in wait as for a *p*,
Isa 10. 2 that widows may be their *p*, and
31. 4 the young lion roaring on his *p*,
33.23 spoil divided; the lame take the *p*.
49.24 the *p* be taken from the mighty,
Jer 21. 9 his life shall be unto him for a *p*.
38. 2 he shall have his life for a *p*, and
39.18 thy life shall be for a *p* unto thee:
Eze 19. 3 and it learned to catch the *p*;
34.22 and they shall no more be a *p*;
36. 4 became a *p* and derision to the
Am 3. 4 in the forest, when he hath no *p*?
Na 3. 1 robbery; the *p* departeth not;
Zep 3. 8 the day that I rise up to the *p*:

PRICE

Lev 25.16 thou shalt increase the *p* thereof.
16 thou shalt diminish the *p* of it:
50 *p* of his sale shall be according
51 give again the *p* of his redemption
52 him again the *p* of his redemption.
Dt 23.18 then *p* of a dog, into the house of
2Sa 24.24 I will surely buy it of thee at a *p*:
1Ki 10.28 received the linen yarn at a *p*.
1Ch 21.22 shalt grant it me for the full *p*:
24 I will verily buy it for the full *p*:
2Ch 1.16 received the linen yarn at a *p*.
Job 28.13 Man knoweth not the *p* thereof;
15 be weighed for the *p* thereof.
18 the *p* of wisdom is above rubies.
Ps 44.12 increase thy wealth by their *p*.
Pr 17.16 a *p* in the hand of a fool to get
27.26 the goats are the *p* of the field.
31.10 for her *p* is far above rubies.
Isa 45.13 my captives, not for *p* nor reward,
55. 1 without money and without *p*.
Jer 15.13 will I give to the spoil without *p*,
Zec 11.12 If you think good, give me my *p*;
12 for my *p* thirty pieces of silver.
13 a goodly *p* that I was prised at of
Mt 13.46 had found one pearl of great *p*,
27. 6 because it is the *p* of blood.
9 the *p* of him that was valued,
Ac 5. 2 kept back part of the *p*, his wife
3 keep back part of the *p* of the land?
19.19 and they counted the *p* of them,
1Co 6.20 For ye are bought with a *p*:
7.23 Ye are bought with a *p*; be not ye
1Pe 3. 4 is in the sight of God of great *p*.

PRICES

Ac 4.34 *p* of the things that were sold,

PRICKED

Ps 73.21 grieved, and I was *p* in my reins.
Ac 2.37 they were *p* in their heart, and

PRICKS

Nu 33.55 be *p* in your eyes, and thorns
Ac 9. 5 for thee to kick against the *p*.
26.14 for thee to kick against the *p*.

PRIDE

Lev 26.19 I will break the *p* of your power;
1Sa 17.28 I know thy *p*, and the
2Ch 32.26 humbled himself for the *p* of his
Job 33.17 purpose, and hide *p* from man.
35.12 because of the *p* of evil men.
41.15 His scales are his *p*, shut up
34 a king over all the children of *p*.
Ps 10. 2 wicked in his *p* doth persecute
4 through the *p* of his countenance,
31.20 thy presence from the *p* of man:
36.11 the foot of *p* come against me,
59.12 them even be taken in their *p*:
73. 6 *p* compasseth them about as a
Pr 8.13 *p*, and arrogancy, and the evil
11. 2 *p* cometh, then cometh shame:
13.10 Only by *p* cometh contention: but
14. 3 mouth of the foolish is a rod of *p*:
16.18 *P* goeth before destruction, and
29.23 man's *p* shall bring him low: but
Isa 9. 9 in the *p* and stoutness of heart,
16. 6 We have heard of the *p* of Moab;
6 even of his haughtiness, and his *p*,
23. 9 it, to stain the *p* of all glory,
25.11 he shall bring down their *p*
28. 1 Woe to the crown of *p*, to the
3 The crown of *p*, the drunkards of
Jer 13. 9 will I mar the *p* of Judah,
9 and the great *p* of Jerusalem.
17 weep in secret places for your *p*;
48.29 We have heard the *p* of Moab, (he
29 and his arrogancy, and his *p*,
49.16 thee, and the *p* of thine heart,
Eze 7.10 hath blossomed, *p* hath budded.
16.49 Sodom, *p*, fulness of bread, and
56 thy mouth in the day of thy *p*,
30. 6 and the *p* of her power shall come
Dan 4.37 those that walk in *p* he is able
5.20 his mind hardened in *p*, he was
Hos 5. 5 the *p* of Israel doth testify to his
7.10 the *p* of Israel testifieth to his
Ob 3 *p* of thine heart hath deceived
Zep 2.10 This shall they have for their *p*,
3.11 them that rejoice in thy *p*, and
Zec 9. 6 cut off the *p* of the Philistines.
10.11 the *p* of Assyria shall be brought
11. 3 for the *p* of Jordan is spoiled.
Mk 7.22 eye, blasphemy, *p*, foolishness:
1Ti 3. 6 being lifted up with *p* he fall into
1Jn 2.16 lust of the eyes, and the *p* of life,

PRIEST

Gen 14.18 was the *p* of the most high God.
Ex 2.16 *p* of Midian had seven daughters:
18. 1 Jethro, the *p* of Midian, Moses'
31.10 holy garments for Aaron the *p*,
Lev 4.20 the *p* shall make an atonement for
5.18 for a trespass offering, unto the *p*:
7. 8 *p* that offereth any man's burnt
13. 6 the *p* shall pronounce him clean:
11 *p* shall pronounce him unclean,
14. 3 *p* shall go forth out of the camp;
19 *p* shall offer the sin offering, and
24 the *p* shall wave them for a wave
23.10 first fruits of...harvest unto the *p*:
20 shall be holy to the Lord for the *p*.
27. 8 shall present himself before the *p*,
8 the *p* shall value him; according
Nu 5.17 the *p* shall take holy water in an
35.28 until the death of the high *p*:
Dt 17.12 will not hearken unto the *p* that
Jdg 17.12 the young man became his *p*, and
13 seeing I have a Levite to my *p*.
18. 4 and hath hired me, and I am his *p*.
6 *p* said unto them, Go in peace:
1Sa 2.35 And I will raise me up a faithful *p*,
14.19 Saul said unto the *p*, Withdraw
21. 6 So the *p* gave him hallowed bread:
23. 9 he said to Abiathar the *p*, Bring
1Ki 1. 8 But Zadok the *p*, and Benaiah the
2Ki 22. 8 And Hilkiah the high *p* said unto

BIBLICAL THEMES

PRIDE AND HUMILITY

And they said, Go to, let us build us a city and a tower, whose top may reach unto heaven. Gen 11.4

Who is the Lord, that I should obey his voice to let Israel go? Ex 5.2

Now the man Moses was very meek, above all the men which were upon the face of the earth. Nu 12.3

When men are cast down, then thou shalt say, There is lifting up; and he shall save the humble person. Job 22.29

Though the Lord be high, yet hath he respect unto the lowly: but the proud he knoweth afar off. Ps 138.6

Be not wise in thine own eyes. Pr 3.7

Pride goeth before destruction, and an haughty spirit before a fall. Pr 16.18

I will cause the arrogancy of the proud to cease, and will lay low the haughtiness of the terrible. Isa 13.11

Woe to the crown of pride . . . whose glorious beauty is a fading flower. Isa 28.1

The most high God gave Nebuchadnezzar thy father a kingdom. . . . But when his heart was lifted up, and his mind hardened in pride, he was deposed from his kingly throne, and they took his glory from him: and he was driven from the sons of men; and his heart was made like the beasts . . . till he knew that the most high God ruled in the kingdom of men, and that he appointeth over it whomsoever he will. Dan 5.18, 20-21

Though thou exalt thyself as the eagle, and though thou set thy nest among the stars, thence will I bring thee down. Ob 1.4

Blessed are the meek: for they shall inherit the earth. Mt 5.5

Ye know that the princes of the Gentiles exercise dominion over them, and they that are great exercise authority upon them. But it shall not be so among you: but whosoever will be great among you, let him be your minister; and whosoever will be chief among you, let him be your servant. Mt 20.25-27

Behold, thy King cometh unto thee, meek, and sitting upon an ass, and a colt the foal of an ass. Mt 21.5

My soul doth magnify the Lord. . . . he hath regarded the low estate of his handmaiden: for, behold, from henceforth all generations shall call me blessed. . . . he hath scattered the proud in the imagination of their hearts. He hath put down the mighty from their seats, and exalted them of low degree. Lk 1.46, 48, 51-52

The Pharisee stood and prayed thus with himself, God, I thank thee, that I am not as other men are. . . . And the publican, standing afar off, would not lift up so much as his eyes unto heaven, but smote upon his breast, saying, God be merciful to me a sinner. I tell you, this man went down to his house justified rather than the other: for every one that exalteth himself shall be abased; and he that humbleth himself shall be exalted. Lk 18.11, 13-14

Charity suffereth long, and is kind . . . charity vaunteth not itself, is not puffed up. 1Co 13.4

I am the least of the apostles, that am not meet to be called an apostle, because I persecuted the church of God. 1Co 15.9

He humbled himself, and became obedient unto death, even the death of the cross. Php 2.8

Humble yourselves therefore under the mighty hand of God, that he may exalt you in due time. 1Pe 5.6

2Ch 13. 9 be a *p* of them that are no gods.
15. 3 without a teaching *p*, and without
23. 8 Jehoiada the *p* had commanded,
34.14 Hilkiah the *p* found a book of the
18 the *p* hath given me a book.
Ezr 2.63 till there stood up a *p* with Urim
10.10 Ezra the *p* stood up, and said unto
Neh 8. 9 and Ezra the *p* the scribe, and the
Ps 110. 4 art a *p* for ever after the order of
Isa 24. 2 as with the people, so with the *p*;
28. 7 the *p* and the prophet have erred
Jer 6.13 from the prophet even unto the *p*
14.18 and the *p* go about into a land
18.18 the law shall not perish from the *p*,
23.11 both prophet and *p* are profane;
29.26 The Lord hath made thee *p* in the
Eze 7.26 the law shall perish from the *p*,
44.21 Neither shall any *p* drink wine,
Hos 4. 4 are as they that strive with the *p*.
6 that thou shalt be no *p* to me:
9 there shall be, like people, like *p*:
Zec 3. 1 he shewed me Joshua the high *p*
6.13 he shall be a *p* upon his throne:
Mt 8. 4 shew thyself to the *p*, and offer
26. 3 unto the palace of the high *p*, who
57 him away to Caiaphas the high *p*,
62 And the high *p* arose, and said unto
63 the high *p* answered and said unto
65 Then the high *p* rent his clothes,
Mk 1.44 shew thyself to the *p*, and offer for
2.26 in the days of Abiathar the high *p*,
14.47 smote a servant of the high *p*, and
53 they led Jesus away to the high *p*:
54 even into the palace of the high *p*:
60 the high *p* stood up in the midst,
61 Again the high *p* asked him, and
63 Then the high *p* rent his clothes,
66 one of the maids of the high *p*:
Lk 1. 5 a certain *p* named Zacharias, of
5.14 and shew thyself to the *p*, and offer
10.31 there came down a certain *p* that
22.50 smote the servant of the high *p*,
Jn 11.49 being the high *p* that same year,
51 but being high *p* that year, he
18.13 was the high *p* that same year.
15 disciple was known unto the high *p*,
15 Jesus into the palace of the high *p*.
16 which was known unto the high *p*,
19 The high *p* then asked Jesus of his
22 Answerest thou the high *p* so?
24 him bound unto Caiaphas the high *p*.
26 One of the servants of the high *p*,
Ac 4. 6 Annas the high *p*, and Caiaphas.
6 were of the kindred of the high *p*,
5.17 Then the high *p* rose up, and all
21 But the high *p* came, and they that
24 the high *p* and the captain of the
27 council: and the high *p* asked them,
7. 1 Then said the high *p*, Are these
9. 1 of the Lord, went unto the high *p*,
14.13 Then the *p* of Jupiter, Which was
22. 5 the high *p* doth bear me witness,
23. 2 the high *p* Ananias commanded
4 said, Revilest thou God's high *p*?
5 brethren, that he was the high *p*:
24. 1 Ananias the high *p* descended with
25. 2 high *p* and the chief of the Jews
Heb 2.17 a merciful and faithful high *p* in
3. 1 and High *P* of our profession,
4.14 then that we have a great high *p*,
15 For we have not an high *p* which
5. 1 every high *p* taken from among
5 not himself to be made an high *p*;
6 Thou art a *p* forever after the
10 of God an high *p* after the order of
6.20 made an high *p* for ever after the
7. 1 *p* of the most high God, who met
3 of God; abideth a *p* continually.
11 *p* should rise after the order of
15 of Melchisedec...ariseth another *p*,
17 Thou art a *p* for ever after the
20 not without an oath he was made *p*:
21 Thou art a *p* for ever after the
26 such an high *p* became us, who is
8. 1 We have such an high *p*, who is set
3 For every high *p* is ordained to
4 on earth, he should not be a *p*,
9. 7 went the high *p* alone once every
11 But Christ being come an high *p* of
25 high *p* entereth into the holy place
10.11 *p* standeth daily ministering and
21 an high *p* over the house of God;
13.11 sanctuary by the high *p* for sin,

PRIESTHOOD

Ex 40.15 shall surely be an everlasting *p*
Nu 16.10 with thee: and seek ye the *p* also?
18. 1 shall bear the iniquity of your *p*.
25.13 the covenant of an everlasting *p*;
Jos 18. 7 *p* of the Lord is their inheritance:
Ezr 2.62 they, as polluted, put from the *p*.
Neh 7.64 they, as polluted, put from the *p*.
13.29 because they have defiled the *p*,
29 and the covenant of the *p*, and of
Heb 7. 5 who receive the office of the *p*,
11 perfection were by the Levitical *p*,
12 For the *p* being changed, there is
14 Moses spake nothing concerning *p*.
24 ever, hath an unchangeable *p*.

1Pe 2. 5 up a spiritual house, an holy *p*,
9 a chosen generation, a royal *p*,

PRIEST'S

Ex 28. 1 minister unto me in the *p* office,
Lev 14.13 for as the sin offering is the *p*, so
22.12 the *p* daughter also be married
13 if the *p* daughter be a widow, or
Nu 18. 7 I have given your *p* office unto you
Dt 18. 3 be the *p* due from the people,
Mal 2. 7 the *p* lips should keep knowledge,
Mt 26.51 struck a servant of the high *p*,
58 him afar off unto the high *p* palace,
Lk 1. 8 executed the *p* office before God
9 to the custom of the *p* office,
22.54 brought him into the high *p* house.
Jn 18.10 it, and smote the high *p* servant,

PRIESTS

Gen 47.22 the *p* had a portion assigned them
Ex 19. 6 shall be unto me a kingdom of *p*,
Lev 6.29 the males among the *p* shall eat
16.33 shall make an atonement for the *p*,
Dt 17. 9 shalt come unto the *p* the Levites,
19.17 before the *p* and the judges, which
Jos 3. 8 command the *p* that bear the ark
6. 4 the *p* shall blow with the trumpets.
12 the *p* took up the ark of the Lord.
1Sa 1. 3 the *p* of the Lord, were there.
5. 5 neither the *p* of Dagon, nor any
22.17 Turn, and slay the *p* of the Lord;
21 that Saul had slain the Lord's *p*,
2Sa 15.35 thee Zadok and Abiathar the *p*?
1Ki 8.11 the *p* could not stand to minister
12.31 made *p* of the lowest of the people,
32 in Beth-el the *p* of the high places
2Ki 23. 4 *p* of the second order, and the
5 put down the idolatrous *p*, whom
2Ch 4. 6 the sea was for the *p* to wash in.
6.41 thy *p*, O Lord God, be clothed with
13. 9 ye not cast out the *p* of the Lord,
Ezr 7.16 of the *p*, offering willingly for the
8.15 I viewed the people, and the *p*,
Ps 132. 9 *p* be clothed with righteousness;
16 also clothe her *p* with salvation:
Isa 61. 6 shall be named the *P* of the Lord:
Jer 2. 8 The *p* said not, Where is the Lord?
4. 9 the *p* shall be astonished, and the
5.31 the *p* bear rule by their means;
La 1.19 my *p* and mine elders gave up the
4.13 the iniquities of her *p*, that have
16 respected not the persons of the *p*,
Eze 22.26 Her *p* have violated my law, and
42.13 the *p* that approach unto the Lord
Hos 5. 1 Hear ye this, O *p*; and hearken, ye
6. 9 so the company of *p* murder in the
10. 5 the *p* thereof that rejoiced on it,
Joel 1. 9 the *p*, the Lord's ministers, mourn.
13 yourselves, and lament, ye *p*:
Mic 3.11 *p* thereof teach for hire, and the
Zep 3. 4 her *p* have polluted the sanctuary,
Hag 2.11 Ask now the *p* concerning the law,
12 And the *p* answered and said, No.
Mal 1. 6 you, O *p*, that despise my name.
Mt 2. 4 gathered all the chief *p* and scribes
12. 4 were with him, but only for the *p*?
5 the *p* in the temple profane the
16.21 the elders and chief *p* and scribes,
20.18 shall be betrayed unto the chief *p*
21.15 when the chief *p* and scribes saw
23 chief *p* and the elders of the people
45 chief *p* and Pharisees had heard
26. 3 assembled together the chief *p*,
14 Iscariot, went unto the chief *p*,
47 the chief *p* and elders of the people.
59 Now the chief *p*, and elders, and
27. 1 the chief *p* and elders of the people
3 of silver to the chief *p* and elders,
6 the chief *p* took the silver pieces,
12 accused of the chief *p* and elders,
20 chief *p* and elders persuaded the
41 also the chief *p* mocking him, with
62 the chief *p* and Pharisees came
28.11 and shewed unto the chief *p* all the
Mk 2.26 is not lawful to eat but for the *p*,
8.31 of the chief *p*, and scribes, and be
10.33 shall be delivered unto the chief *p*,
11.18 the scribes and chief *p* heard it,
27 there come to him the chief *p*, and
14. 1 the chief *p* and the scribes sought
10 went unto the chief *p* to betray
43 from the chief *p* and the scribes
53 him were assembled all the chief *p*
55 And the chief *p* and all the council
15. 1 the chief *p* held a consultation with
3 the chief *p* accused him of many
10 the chief *p* had delivered him for
11 But the chief *p* moved the people,
31 also the chief *p* mocking said
Lk 3. 2 and Caiaphas being the high *p*, the
6. 4 lawful to eat but for the *p* alone?
9.22 rejected of the elders and chief *p*
17.14 Go shew yourselves unto the *p*.
19.47 But the chief *p* and the scribes
20. 1 the chief *p* and the scribes came
19 the chief *p* and the scribes the same
22. 2 the chief *p* and scribes sought how
4 with the chief *p* and captains, how
52 Then Jesus said unto the chief *p*,
66 the chief *p* and the scribes came
23. 4 Then said Pilate to the chief *p* and
10 the chief *p* and scribes stood and
13 together the chief *p* and the rulers
23 voices...of the chief *p* prevailed.
24.20 chief *p* and our rulers delivered
Jn 1.19 the Jews sent *p* and Levites from
7.32 the Pharisees and the chief *p* sent
45 came the officers to the chief *p* and
11.47 Then gathered the chief *p* and the
57 both the chief *p* and the Pharisees
12.10 But the chief *p* consulted that they
18. 3 from the chief *p* and Pharisees,
35 Thine own nation and the chief *p*
19. 6 the chief *p* therefore and officers
15 The chief *p* answered, We have no
21 the chief *p* of the Jews to Pilate,
Ac 4. 1 spake unto the people, the *p*, and
23 the chief *p* and elders had said
5.24 and the chief *p* heard these things,
6. 7 the *p* were obedient to the faith.
9.14 authority from the chief *p* to bind
21 bring them bound unto the chief *p*?
19.14 a Jew, and chief of the *p*, which did
22.30 and commanded the chief *p* and all
23.14 they came to the chief *p* and elders,
25.15 chief *p* and the elders of the Jews
26.10 received authority from the chief *p*;
12 and commission from the chief *p*,
Heb 7.21 *p* were made without an oath;
23 they truly were many *p*, because
27 needeth not daily, as those high *p*,
28 men high *p* which have infirmity;
8. 4 that there are *p* that offer gifts
9. 6 the *p* went always into the first
Rev 1. 6 made us kings and *p* unto God
5.10 us unto our God kings and *p*: and
20. 6 they shall be *p* of God and of

PRINCE

Gen 23. 6 thou art a mighty *p* among us:
32.28 as a *p* hast thou power with God and
Ex 2.14 thee a *p* and a judge over us?
Nu 16.13 thou make thyself altogether a *p*
Job 21.28 say, Where is the house of the *p*?
31.37 as a *p* would I go near unto him.
Pr 14.28 people is the destruction of the *p*.
17. 7 fool: much less do lying lips a *p*.
25.15 forbearing is a *p* persuaded,
28.16 *p* that wanteth understanding
Isa 9. 6 everlasting Father,...*P* of Peace.
Eze 45. 7 a portion shall be for the *p* on the
22 shall the *p* prepare for himself and
46.18 the *p* shalt not take of the people's
48.21 And the residue shall be for the *p*,
Dan 10.21 these things, but Michael your *p*.
11.18 a *p* for his own behalf shall cause
22 yea, also the *p* of the covenant.
12. 1 *p* which standeth for the children
Hos 3. 4 without a king, and without a *p*,
Mic 7. 3 *p* asketh, and the judge asketh for
Mt 9.34 devils through the *p* of the devils.
12.24 by Beelzebub the *p* of the devils.
Mk 3.22 by the *p* of the devils casteth he out
Jn 12.31 shall the *p* of this world be cast out.
14.30 the *p* of this world cometh, and hath
16.11 the *p* of this world is judged.
Ac 3.15 killed the *P* of life, whom God hath
5.31 right hand to be a *P* and a Saviour,
Eph 2. 2 to the *p* of the power of the air,
Rev 1. 5 and the *p* of the kings of the earth.

PRINCES

Nu 21.18 The *p* digged the well, the nobles
Jos 9.18 murmured against their *p*.
21 *p* said unto them, Let them live;
22.30 *p* of the congregation and heads of
Jdg 5. 3 O ye kings; give ear, O ye *p*; I,
1Sa 2. 8 to set them among *p*, and to make
2Sa 19. 6 regardest neither *p* nor servants:
1Ch 28. 1 David assembled all the *p* of Israel,
1 *p* of the tribes, and the captains of
2Ch 32. 3 He took counsel with his *p* and his
35. 8 *p* gave willingly unto the people,
Neh 9.38 our *p*, Levites, and priests, seal
Est 1. 3 made a feast unto all his *p* and his
3. 1 set his seat above all the *p* that
Job 12.19 He leadeth *p* away spoiled, and
21 poureth contempt upon *p*, and
34.18 wicked? and to *p*, Ye are ungodly?
19 accepteth not the persons of *p*,
Ps 45.16 mayest make *p* in all the earth.
47. 9 The *p* of the people are gathered
76.12 He shall cut off the spirit of *p*:
107.40 He poureth contempt upon *p*,
118. 9 than to put confidence in *p*.
119.161 *P* have persecuted me without a
146. 3 Put not your trust in *p*, nor in the
148.11 *p*, and all judges of the earth:
Pr 8.15 kings reign, and *p* decree justice.
16 By me *p* rule, and nobles, even
19.10 for a servant to have rule over *p*.
31. 4 wine; nor for *p* strong drink:
Isa 1.23 Thy *p* are rebellious, and
10. 8 Are not my *p* altogether kings?
32. 1 and *p* shall rule in judgment.
Jer 37.15 the *p* were wroth with Jeremiah,
44.17 our fathers, our kings, and our *p*,
51.57 And I will make drunk her *p*, and
La 1. 6 her *p* are become like harts that
Eze 45. 8 my *p* shall no more oppress my
Dan 6. 2 *p* might give accounts unto them,
3 above the presidents and *p*,
8.25 stand up against the Prince of *p*;
10.13 Michael, one of the chief *p*, came
Hos 7. 3 and the *p* with their lies.
8. 4 have made *p*, and I knew it not:
9.15 no more: all their *p* are revolters.
13.10 thou saidst, Give me a king and *p*?
Mic 3. 1 and ye *p* of the house of Israel;
Hab 1.10 the *p* shall be a scorn unto them:
Zep 1. 8 will punish the *p*, and the king's
3. 3 *p* within her are roaring lions;
Mt 2. 6 not the least among the *p* of Juda:
20.25 that the *p* of the Gentiles exercise
1Co 2. 6 nor of the *p* of this world, that
8 none of the *p* of this world knew:

PRINCESS

La 1. 1 and *p* among the provinces, how

PRINCIPAL

Ex 30.23 thou also unto thee *p* spices,
Lev 6. 5 restore it in the *p*, and shall add

Nu 5. 7 his trespass with the *p* thereof,
1Ki 4. 5 the son of Nathan was *p* officer,
2Ki 25.19 the *p* scribe of the host, which
1Ch 24. 6 one *p* household being taken for
31 the *p* fathers over against their
Neh 11.17 *p* to begin the thanksgiving in
Pr 4. 7 Wisdom is the *p* thing; therefore
Isa 16. 8 have broken down the *p* plants
28.25 and cast in the *p* wheat and the
Jer 25.34 in the ashes, ye *p* of the flock:
35 nor the *p* of the flock to escape.
36 an howling of the *p* of the flock,
52.25 and the *p* scribe of the host who
Mic 5. 5 shepherds, and eight *p* men.
Ac 25.23 and *p* men of the city,

PRINCIPALITIES

Jer 13.18 your *p* shall come down, even
Ro 8.38 nor *p*, nor powers, nor things
Eph 3.10 now unto the *p* and powers in
6.12 but against *p*, against powers,
Col 1.16 or dominions, or *p*, or powers:
2.15 And having spoiled *p* and powers,
Tit 3. 1 mind to be subject to *p* and powers,

PRINCIPALITY

Eph 1.21 Far above all *p*, and power, and
Col 2.10 is the head of all *p* and power:

PRINCIPLES

Heb 5.12 the first *p* of the oracles of God;
6. 1 leaving the *p* of the doctrine of

PRINT

Lev 19.28 dead, nor *p* any marks upon you:
Job 13.27 a *p* upon the heels of my feet.
Jn 20.25 in his hands the *p* of the nails,
25 my finger into the *p* of the nails,

PRINTED

Job 19.23 oh that they were *p* in a book!

PRISCA

2Ti 4.19 Salute *P* and Aquila, and the

PRISCILLA

Ac 18. 2 come from Italy, with his wife *P*;
18 and with him *P* and Aquila;
26 when Aquila and *P* had heard,
Ro 16. 3 Greet *P* and Aquila my helpers
1Co 16.19 Aquila and *P* salute you much

PRISON

Gen 39.20 and put him into the *p*, a
20 and he was there in the *p*.
21 sight of the keeper of the *p*.
22 the keeper of the *p* committed
22 prisoners that were in the *p*;
23 keeper of the *p* looked not to
40. 3 into the *p*, the place where
5 which were bound in the *p*.
42.16 ye shall be kept in *p*, that your
19 be bound in the house of your *p*:
Jdg 16.21 and he did grind in the *p* house.
25 for Samson out of the *p* house;
1Ki 22.27 Put this fellow in the *p*, and
2Ki 17. 4 him up, and bound him in *p*.
25.27 king of Judah out of *p*;
29 And changed his *p* garments:
2Ch 16.10 seer, and put him in a *p* house;
18.26 Put this fellow in the *p*, and
Neh 3.25 that was by the court of the *p*
12.39 and they stood still in the *p* gate.
Ps 142. 7 Bring my soul out of *p*, that I
Ec 4.14 out of *p* he cometh to reign,
Isa 24.22 and shall be shut up in the *p*,
42. 7 bring out the prisoners from the *p*,
7 in darkness out of the *p* house.
22 and they are hid in *p* houses:
53. 8 He was taken from *p* and from
61. 1 opening of the *p* to them that are
Jer 29.26 thou shouldest put him in *p* and
32. 2 was shut up in the court of the *p*,
8 came to me in the court of the *p*
12 Jews that sat in the court of the *p*.
33. 1 yet shut up in the court of the *p*,
37. 4 they had not put him into *p*.
15 in *p* in the house of Jonathan
15 for they had made that the *p*.
18 that ye have put me in *p*?
21 Jeremiah into the court of the *p*,
21 remained in the court of the *p*.
38. 6 that was in the court of the *p*: and
13 remained in the court of the *p*.
28 abode in the court of the *p* until
39.14 Jeremiah out of the court of the *p*,
15 was shut up in the court of the *p*,
52.11 in *p* till the day of his death.
31 brought him forth out of *p*,
33 And changed his *p* garments:
Mt 4.12 heard that John was cast into *p*,
5.25 officer, and thou be cast into *p*.
11. 2 John had heard in the *p* the works
14. 3 put him in *p* for Herodias' sake,
10 sent, and beheaded John in the *p*.
18.30 went and cast him into *p*, till he
25.36 I was in *p*, and ye came unto me.
39 when saw we thee sick, or in *p*,
43 sick, and in *p*, and ye visited me
44 or sick, or in *p*, and did not
Mk 1.14 after that John was put in *p*,
6.17 bound him in *p* for Herodias' sake,
27 went and beheaded him in the *p*,
Lk 3.20 all, that he shut up John in *p*.
12.58 and the officer cast thee into *p*.
22.33 ready to go with thee, both into *p*,
23.19 and for murder, was cast into *p*.)
25 and murder was cast into *p*,
Jn 3.24 For John was not yet cast into *p*.
Ac 5.18 and put them in the common *p*.
19 Lord by night opened the *p* doors,
21 to the *p* to have them brought.
22 and found them not in the *p*,
23 The *p* truly found we shut with
25 the men whom ye put in *p* are
8. 3 women committed them to *p*.
12. 4 he put him in *p*, and delivered
5 Peter therefore was kept in *p*:
6 keepers before the door kept the *p*,
7 and a light shined in the *p*: and he
17 had brought him out of the *p*.
16.23 they cast them into *p*, charging
24 thrust them into the inner *p*, and
26 foundations...the *p* were shaken:
27 keeper of the *p* awaking out of
27 and seeing the *p* doors open, he
36 keeper of the *p* told this saying to
37 Romans, and have cast us into *p*;
40 And they went out of the *p*, and
26.10 of the saints did I shut up in *p*,
1Pe 3.19 preached unto the spirits in *p*;
Rev 2.10 devil shall cast some of you into *p*,
20. 7 Satan shall be loosed out of his *p*,

PRISONER

Ps 79.11 the sighing of the *p* come before
102.20 To hear the groaning of the *p*:
Mt 27.15 to release unto the people a *p*,
16 they had then a notable *p*, called
Mk 15. 6 he released unto them one *p*,
Ac 23.18 Paul the *p* called me unto him, and
25.27 to me unreasonable to send a *p*,
28.17 was I delivered *p* from Jerusalem
Eph 3. 1 Paul, the *p* of Jesus Christ for you
4. 1 I therefore, the *p* of the Lord,
2Ti 1. 8 of our Lord, nor of me his *p*:
Phm 1 Paul, a *p* of Jesus Christ, and
9 and now also *p* of Jesus Christ.

PRISONERS

Gen 39.20 where the king's *p* were bound:
22 all the *p* that were in the prison;
Nu 21. 1 Israel, and took some of them *p*.
Job 3.18 There the *p* rest together; they
Ps 69.33 the poor, and despiseth not his *p*.
146. 7 hungry. The Lord looseth the *p*:
Isa 10. 4 they shall bow down under the *p*,
14.17 that opened not the house of his *p*?
20. 4 Assyria lead away...Egyptians *p*,
24.22 as *p* are gathered in the pit, and
42. 7 to bring out the *p* from the prison.
49. 9 That thou mayest say to the *p*, Go
La 3.34 his feet all the *p* of the earth,
Zec 9.11 have sent forth thy *p* out of the pit
12 to the strong hold, ye *p* of hope:
Ac 16.25 unto God: and the *p* heard them.
27 supposing that the *p* had been fled.
27. 1 delivered Paul and certain other *p*
42 soldiers' counsel was to kill the *p*,
28.16 delivered the *p* to the captain of

PRISONS

Lk 21.12 up to the synagogues, and into *p*,
Ac 22. 4 delivering into *p* both men and
2Co 11.23 in *p* more frequent, in deaths oft.

PRIVATE

2Pe 1.20 is of any *p* interpretation.

PRIVATELY

Mt 24. 3 disciples came unto him *p*,
Mk 6.32 into a desert place by ship *p*.
9.28 his disciples asked him *p*, Why
13. 3 John and Andrew asked him *p*,
Lk 9.10 aside *p* into a desert place
10.23 and said *p*, Blessed are the eyes
Ac 23.19 and went with him aside *p*, and
Gal 2. 2 but *p* to them which were of

PRIVILY

Jdg 9.31 messengers unto Abimelech *p*,
1Sa 24. 4 cut off the skirt of Saul's robe *p*.
Ps 10. 8 his eyes are *p* set against the poor.
11. 2 *p* shoot at the upright in heart.
31. 4 net that they have laid *p* for me:
64. 5 they commune of laying snares *p*;
101. 5 Whose *p* slandereth his neighbor,
142. 3 have they *p* laid a snare for me.
Pr 1.11 let us lurk *p* for the innocent without
18 they lurk *p* for their own lives.
Mt 1.19 was minded to put her away *p*.
2. 7 when he had *p* called the wise men,
Ac 16.37 and now do they thrust us out *p*?
Gal 2. 4 came in *p* to spy out our liberty
2Pe 2. 1 who *p* shall bring in damnable

PRIVY

Eze 21.14 entereth into their *p* chambers.
Ac 5. 2 price, his wife also being *p* to it,

PRIZE

1Co 9.24 run all, but one receiveth the *p*?
Php 3.14 mark for the *p* of the high calling

PROCEED

Ex 25.35 that *p* out of the candlestick.
Jos 6.10 any word *p* out of your mouth,
2Sa 7.12 which shall *p* out of thy bowels,
Job 40. 5 yea, twice; but I will *p* no further.
Isa 29.14 I will *p* to do a marvellous work
51. 4 for a law shall *p* from me, and I
Jer 9. 3 for they *p* from evil to evil, and
30.19 out of them shall *p* thanksgiving
21 shall *p* from the midst of them;
Hab 1. 7 their dignity shall *p* of themselves.
Mt 15.18 things which *p* out of the mouth
19 out of the heart *p* evil thoughts,
Mk 7.21 the heart of men, *p* evil thoughts,
Eph 4.29 communication *p* out...your mouth,
3. 9 they shall *p* no further: for their

PROCEEDED

Nu 30.12 then whatsoever *p* out of her lips
32.24 which hath *p* out of your mouth.

Jdg 11.36 which hath *p* out of thy mouth;
Job 36. 1 Elihu also *p*, and said,
Lk 4.22 words which *p* out of his mouth.
Jn 8.42 for I *p* forth and came from God;
Ac 12. 3 he *p* further to take Peter also.
Rev 4. 5 out of the throne *p* lightnings
19.21 which sword *p* out of his mouth:

PROCEEDETH

Gen 24.50 The thing *p* from the Lord: we
Nu 30. 2 to all that *p* out of his mouth.
Dt 8. 3 word that *p* out of the mouth of
1Sa 24.13 Wickedness *p* from the wicked:
Ec 10. 5 as an error which *p* from the ruler:
La 3.38 most High *p* not evil and good?
Hab 1. 4 therefore wrong judgment *p*.
Mt 4. 4 word that *p* out of the mouth of
Jn 15.26 truth, which *p* from the Father,
Jas 3.10 mouth *p* blessing and cursing.
Rev 11. 5 fire *p* out of their mouth, and

PROCEEDING

Rev 22. 1 crystal, *p* out of the throne of God

PROCHORUS

Ac 6. 5 Philip, and *P*, and Nicanor, and

PROCLAIM

Ex 33.19 and I will *p* the name of the Lord
Lev 23. 2 ye shall *p* to be holy convocations,
4 which ye shall *p* in their seasons.
21 And ye shall *p* on the selfsame day,
37 ye shall *p* to be holy convocations,
25.10 *p* liberty throughout all the land
Dt 20.10 against it, then *p* peace unto it.
Jdg 7. 3 *p* in the ears of the people, saying,
1Ki 21. 9 *P* a fast, and set Naboth on high
2Ki 10.20 *P* a solemn assembly for Baal.
Neh 8.15 publish and *p* in all their cities,
Est 6. 9 of the city, and *p* before him,
Pr 20. 6 will *p* every one his own goodness:
Isa 61. 1 to *p* liberty to the captives, and
2 *p* the acceptable year of the Lord,
Jer 3.12 Go and *p* these words toward the
7. 2 *p* there this word, and say, Hear
11. 6 *P* all these words in the cities of
19. 2 *p* there the words that I shall tell
34. 8 Jerusalem, to *p* liberty unto them;
17 I *p* a liberty for you, saith the Lord,
Joel 3. 9 *P* ye this among the Gentiles;
Am 4. 5 *p* and publish the free offerings:

PROCLAIMED

Ex 34. 5 there, and *p* the name of the Lord.
6 Lord passed by before him, and *p*,
36. 6 it to be *p* throughout the camp,
1Ki 21.12 They *p* a fast, and set Naboth on
2Ki 10.20 assembly for Baal. And they *p* it.
23.16 man of God *p*, who *p* these words.
17 *p* these things that thou hast done
2Ch 20. 3 and *p* a fast throughout all Judah.
Ezr 8.21 Then I *p* a fast there, at the river
Est 6.11 *p* before him, Thus shall it be done
Isa 62.11 the Lord hath *p* unto the end of
Jer 36. 9 that they *p* a fast before the Lord
Jon 3. 5 and *p* a fast, and put on sackcloth,
7 he caused it to be *p* and published
Lk 12. 3 shall be *p* upon the housetops.

PROCLAIMING

Jer 34.15 in *p* liberty every man to his
17 *p* liberty, every one to his brother,
Rev 5. 2 strong angel *p* with a loud voice,

PROCLAMATION

Ex 32. 5 and Aaron made *p*, and said, To
1Ki 15.22 king Asa made a *p* throughout
22.36 went a *p* throughout the host
2Ch 24. 9 they made a *p* through Judah
30. 5 make *p* throughout all
36.22 he made a *p* throughout all
Ezr 1. 1 he made a *p* throughout all his
10. 7 they made *p* throughout
Dan 5.29 and made a *p* concerning him,

PROCURE

Jer 26.19 we *p* great evil against our souls.
33. 9 all the prosperity that I *p* unto it.

PROFANE

Lev 18.21 shalt thou *p* the name of thy God:
19.12 shalt thou *p* the name of thy God:
20. 3 sanctuary, and to *p* my holy name.
21. 4 among his people, to *p* himself.
6 and not *p* the name of their God:
7 take a wife that is a whore, or *p*;
9 *p* herself by playing the whore,
12 nor *p* the sanctuary of his God;
14 widow, or a divorced woman, or *p*,
15 he *p* his seed among his people:
23 that he *p* not my sanctuaries: for
22. 2 that they *p* not my holy name in
9 it, and die therefore, if they *p* it:
15 they shall not *p* the holy things of
32 Neither shall ye *p* my holy name:
Neh 13.17 that ye do, and *p* the sabbath day?
Jer 23.11 both prophet and priest are *p*;
Eze 21.25 thou, *p* wicked prince of Israel,
22.26 between the holy and *p*, neither
23.39 day into my sanctuary to *p* it;
24.21 Behold, I will *p* my sanctuary,
28.16 cast thee as *p* out of the mountain
42.20 the sanctuary and the *p* place.
44.23 difference between the holy and *p*,
48.15 shall be a *p* place for the city, for
Am 2. 7 same maid, to *p* my holy name:
Mt 12. 5 priests in the temple *p* the sabbath,
Ac 24. 6 hath gone about to *p* the temple:
1Ti 1. 9 and for sinners, for unholy and *p*,
4. 7 But refuse *p* and old wives' fables,
6.20 avoiding *p* and vain babblings, and
2Ti 2.16 But shun *p* and vain babblings:
Heb 12.16 be any fornicator, or *p* person,

PROFANED

Lev 19. 8 hath *p* the hallowed thing of the
Ps 89.39 thou hast *p* his crown by casting
Eze 22. 8 things, and hast *p* my sabbaths.
26 law, and have *p* mine holy things:
26 sabbaths, and I am *p* among them.
23.38 day, and have *p* my sabbaths.
25. 3 my sanctuary, when it was *p*;
36.20 they went, they *p* my holy name,
21 Israel had *p* among the heathen,
22 ye have *p* among the heathen,
23 ye have *p* in the midst of them;
Mal 1.12 But ye have *p* it, in that ye say,
2.11 hath *p* the holiness of the Lord

PROFESS

Dt 26. 3 him, I *p* this day unto the Lord
Mt 7.23 then will I *p* unto them, I never
Tit 1.16 They *p* that they know God; but

PROFESSED

2Co 9.13 for your *p* subjection unto the
1Ti 6.12 hast *p* a good profession before

PROFESSING

Ro 1.22 *P* themselves to be wise, they
1Ti 2.10 becometh women *p* godliness)
6.21 some *p* have erred concerning the

PROFESSION

1Ti 6.12 good *p* before many witnesses.
Heb 3. 1 Apostle and High Priest of our *p*,
4.14 Son of God, let us hold fast our *p*.
10.23 Let us hold fast the *p* of our faith

PROFIT

Gen 25.32 what *p* shall this birthright do to me?
37.26 What *p* is it if we slay our brother,
1Sa 12.21 which cannot *p* nor deliver; for
Est 3. 8 for the king's *p* to suffer them.
Job 21.15 what *p* should we have, if we
30. 2 the strength of their hands *p* me,
35. 3 and, What *p* shall I have, if I be
8 righteousness may *p* the son of man.
Ps 30. 9 What *p* is there in my blood, when
Pr 10. 2 of wickedness *p* nothing: but
11. 4 Riches *p* not in the day of wrath:
14.23 In all labor there is *p*: but the
Ec 1. 3 What *p* hath a man of all his
2.11 and there was no *p* under the sun.
3. 9 What *p* hath he that worketh in
5. 9 the *p* of the earth is for all: the
16 and what *p* hath he that hath
7.11 is *p* to them that see the sun.
Isa 30. 5 a people that could not *p* them,
5 nor be an help nor *p*, but a shame,
6 to a people that shall not *p* them.
44. 9 their delectable things shall not *p*;
47.12 if so be thou shalt be able to *p*, if
48.17 thy God which teacheth thee to *p*,
57.12 works; for they shall not *p* thee.
Jer 2. 8 walked after things that do not *p*.
11 glory for that which doth not *p*.
7. 8 trust in lying words, that cannot *p*.
12.13 themselves to pain, but shall not *p*:
16.19 and things wherein there is no *p*.
23.32 they shall not *p* this people at all,
Mal 3.14 what *p* is it that we have kept his
Mk 8.36 For what shall it *p* a man, if he
Ro 3. 1 what *p* is there of circumcision?
1Co 7.35 And this I speak for your own *p*;
10.33 things, not seeking mine own *p*,
33 *p* of many, that they may be saved.
12. 7 is given to every man to *p* withal.
14. 6 what shall I *p* you, except I shall
Gal 5. 2 Christ shall *p* you nothing.
2Ti 2.14 strive not about words to no *p*,
Heb 4. 2 word preached did not *p* them,
12.10 he for our *p*, that we might be
Jas 2.14 What doth it *p*, my brethren,
16 to the body; what doth it *p*?

PROFITABLE

Job 22. 2 Can a man be *p* unto God, as he
2 is wise may be *p* unto himself?
Ec 10.10 but wisdom is *p* to direct.
Isa 44.10 image that is *p* for nothing?
Jer 13. 7 was marred, it was *p* for nothing.
Mt 5.29, 30 it is *p* for thee that one of thy
Ac 20.20 back nothing that was *p* unto you,
1Ti 4. 8 godliness is *p* unto all things,
2Ti 3.16 and is *p* for doctrine, for reproof,
4.11 for he is *p* to me for the ministry.
Tit 3. 8 things are good and *p* unto men.
Phm 11 but now *p* to thee and to me:

PROFITED

Job 33.27 which was right, and it *p* me not;
Mt 15. 5 thou mightest be *p* by me;
16.26 For what is a man *p*, if he shall
Mk 7.11 thou mightest be *p* by me; he
Gal 1.14 And *p* in the Jews' religion above
Heb 13. 9 *p* them that have been occupied

PROFITETH

Job 34. 9 It *p* a man nothing that he
Hab 2.18 What *p* the graven image that the
Jn 6.63 the flesh *p* nothing: the words
Ro 2.25 circumcision verily *p*, if thou keep
1Co 13. 3 have not charity, it *p* me nothing.
1Ti 4. 8 For bodily exercise *p* little:

PROFITING

1Ti 4.15 that thy *p* may appear to all.

PROLONG

Dt 4.26 shall not *p* your days upon it, but
40 mayest *p* thy days upon the earth,
5.33 ye may *p* your days in the land

Dt 11. 9 ye may *p* your days in the land,
17.20 he may *p* his days in his kingdom,
22. 7 and that thou mayest *p* thy days.
30.18 shall not *p* your days upon the land,
32.47 ye shall *p* your days in the land,
Job 6.11 mine end, that I should *p* my life?
15.29 neither shall he *p* the perfection
Ps 61. 6 Thou wilt *p* the king's life: and
Pr 28.16 covetousness shall *p* his days.
Ec 8.13 neither shall he *p* his days, which
Isa 53.10 seed, he shall *p* his days, and the

PROLONGETH

Pr 10.27 The fear of the Lord *p* days: but
Ec 7.15 a wicked man that *p* his life in

PROMISE

Nu 14.34 and ye shall know my breach of *p*.
1Ki 8.56 failed one word of all his good *p*,
2Ch 1. 9 let thy *p* unto David my father be
Neh 5.12 should do according to this *p*.
13 performeth not this *p*, even thus
13 the people did according to this *p*.
Ps 77. 8 doth his *p* fail for evermore?
105.42 he remembered his holy *p*, and
Lk 24.49 the *p* of my Father upon you:
Ac 1. 4 but wait for the *p* of the Father,
2.33 Father, the *p* of the Holy Ghost,
39 For the *p* is unto you, and to your
7.17 when the time of the *p* drew nigh,
13.23 according to his *p*, raised unto
32 *p* which was made unto the fathers,
23.21 ready, looking for a *p* from thee.
26. 6 for the hope of the *p* made of God
7 Unto which *p* our twelve tribes,
Ro 4.13 For the *p*, that he should be the
14 and the *p* made of none effect:
16 the end the *p* might be sure to all
20 He staggered not at the *p* of God
9. 8 children of the *p* are counted for
9 this is the word of *p*, At this time
Gal 3.14 the *p* of the Spirit through faith.
17 should make the *p* of none effect.
18 be of the law, it is no more of *p*:
18 but God gave it to Abraham by *p*.
19 come to whom the *p* was made;
22 that the *p* by faith of Jesus Christ
29 and heirs according to the *p*.
4.23 he of the freewoman was by *p*.
28 as Isaac was, are the children of *p*.
Eph 1.13 sealed with that holy Spirit of *p*,
2.12 from the covenants of *p*, having
3. 6 partakers of his *p* in Christ by the
6. 2 is the first commandment with *p*;
1Ti 4. 8 having *p* of the life that now is,
2Ti 1. 1 the *p* of life which is in Christ
Heb 4. 1 a *p* being left us of entering into
6.13 when God made *p* to Abraham,
15 endured, he obtained the *p*.
17 to shew unto the heirs of *p* the
9.15 the *p* of eternal inheritance.
10.36 of God, ye might receive the *p*.
11. 9 faith he sojourned in the land of *p*,
9 the heirs with him of the same *p*:
39 through faith, received not the *p*:
2Pe 2.19 While they *p* them liberty, they
3. 4 Where is the *p* of his coming?
9 is not slack concerning his *p*,
13 according to his *p*, look for new
1Jn 2.25 the *p* that he hath promised us,

PROMISED

Ex 12.25 according as he hath *p*, that ye
Nu 14.40 place which the Lord hath *p*:
Dt 1.11 and bless you, as he hath *p* you!)
6. 3 Lord God of thy fathers hath *p*
9.28 into the land which he *p* them,
10. 9 as the Lord thy God *p* him.
12.20 thy border, as he hath *p* thee, and
15. 6 God blesseth thee, as he *p* thee:
19. 8 land which he *p* to give unto thy
23.23 thou hast *p* with thy mouth.
26.18 peculiar people, as he hath *p* thee,
27. 3 God of thy fathers hath *p* thee.
Jos 9.21 as the princes had *p* them.
22. 4 unto your brethren, as he *p* them:
23. 5 Lord your God hath *p* unto you.
10 fighteth for you, as he hath *p* you.
15 the Lord your God *p* you; which
2Sa 7.28 *p* this goodness unto thy servant:
1Ki 2.24 hath made me an house, as he *p*,
5.12 Solomon wisdom, as he *p* him:
8.20 throne of Israel, as the Lord *p*,
56 Israel, according to all that he *p*:
56 which he *p* by the hand of Moses
9. 5 as I *p* to David thy father, saying,
2Ki 8.19 as he *p* him to give him alway a
1Ch 17.26 *p* this goodness unto thy servant:
2Ch 6.10 throne of Israel, as the Lord *p*,
15 that which thou hast *p* him; and
16 which thou hast *p* him, saying,
21. 7 as he *p* to give a light to him and
Neh 9.23 which thou hadst *p* to their fathers,
Est 4. 7 money that Haman had *p* to pay
Jer 32.42 all the good that I have *p* them.
33.14 that good thing which I have *p*
Mt 14. 7 he *p* with an oath to give her
Mk 14.11 glad, and *p* to give him money.
Lk 1.72 perform the mercy *p* to our fathers,
22. 6 he *p*, and sought opportunity to
Ac 7. 5 yet he *p* that he would give it…him
Ro 1. 2 he had *p* afore by his prophets
4.21 what he had *p*, he was able also
Tit 1. 2 God, that cannot lie, *p* before the
Heb 10.23 wavering; (…he is faithful that *p*;)
11.11 judged him faithful who had *p*.
12.26 now he hath *p*, saying, Yet once
Jas 1.12 Lord hath *p* to them that love him.
2. 5 kingdom which he hath *p* to them
1Jn 2.25 promise that he hath *p* us, even

PROMISES

Ro 9. 4 and the service of God, and the *p*;
15. 8 the *p* made unto the fathers:
2Co 1.20 For all the *p* of God in him are yea,
7. 1 Having therefore these *p*, dearly
Gal 3.16 and his seed were the *p* made.
21 the law then against the *p* of God?
Heb 6.12 faith and patience inherit the *p*.
7. 6 and blessed him that had the *p*.
8. 6 was established upon better *p*.
11.13 faith, not having received the *p*,
17 he that had received the *p* offered
33 obtained *p*, stopped the mouths of
2Pe 1. 4 exceeding great and precious *p*:

PROMOTE

Nu 22.17 I will *p* thee unto very great
37 able indeed to *p* thee to honor?
24.11 to *p* thee unto great honor; but
Est 3. 1 did king Ahasuerus *p* Haman
Pr 4. 8 Exalt her, and she shall *p* thee:

PROMOTION

Ps 75. 6 *p* cometh neither from the east,
Pr 3.35 but shame shall be the *p* of fools.

PRONOUNCE

Lev 14.48 the priest shall *p* the house clean,
Jdg 12. 6 he could not frame to *p* it right.

PROOF

2Co 2. 9 that I might know the *p* of you,
8.24 *p* of your love, and of our boasting
13. 3 a *p* of Christ speaking in me,
Php 2.22 But ye know thee *p* of him, that,
2Ti 4. 5 make full *p* of thy ministry.

PROOFS

Ac 1. 3 his passion by many infallible *p*,

PROPER

1Ch 29. 3 I have of mine own *p* good, of
Ac 1.19 field is called in their *p* tongue,
1Co 7. 7 every man hath his *p* gift of God,
Heb 11.23 they saw he was a *p* child;

PROPHECIES

1Co 13. 8 whether there be *p*, they shall
1Ti 1.18 the *p* which went before on thee,

PROPHECY

2Ch 9.29 in the *p* of Ahijah the Shilonite,
15. 8 and the *p* of Oded the prophet,
Neh 6.12 he pronounced this *p* against me:
Pr 30. 1 the son of Jakeh, even the *p*:
31. 1 the *p* that his mother taught him.
Dan 9.24 to seal up the vision and *p*, and
Mt 13.14 them is fulfilled the *p* of Esaias,
Ro 12. 6 that is given to us, whether *p*,
1Co 12.10 working of miracles; to another *p*;
13. 2 though I have the gift of *p*, and
1Ti 4.14 in thee, which was given thee by *p*,
2Pe 1.19 have also a more sure word of *p*;
20 that no *p* of the scripture is of any
21 For the *p* came not in old time by
Rev 1. 3 they that hear the words of this *p*,
11. 6 it rain not in the days of their *p*:
19.10 testimony of Jesus is the spirit of *p*.
22. 7 the sayings of the *p* of this book.
10 the sayings of the *p* of this book:
18 the words of the *p* of this book,
19 the words of the book of this *p*,

PROPHESIED

Nu 11.25 spirit rested upon them, they *p*,
26 tabernacle: and they *p* in the camp.
1Sa 10.10 upon him, and he *p* among them.
11 he *p* among the prophets, that the
18.10 and he *p* in the midst of the house:
19.20 of Saul, and they also *p*,
21 messengers, and they *p* likewise.
21 the third time, and they *p* also.
23 he went on, and *p*, until he came
24 *p* before Samuel in like manner,
1Ki 18.29 and they *p* until the time of the
22.10 all the prophets *p* before them.
12 all the prophets *p* so, saying, Go
1Ch 25. 2 *p* according to the order of the
3 also *p* with a harp, to give thanks
2Ch 18. 7 for he never *p* good unto me, but
9 all the prophets *p* before them.
11 And all the prophets *p* so, saying,
20.37 *p* Eliezer…against Jehoshaphat,
Ezr 5. 1 *p* unto the Jews that were in
Jer 2. 8 and the prophets *p* by Baal, and
20. 1 that Jeremiah *p* these things.
6 friends, to whom thou hast *p* lies.
23.13 they *p* in Baal, and caused my
21 not spoken to them, yet they *p*.
25.13 hath *p* against all the nations.
26. 9 thou *p* in the name of the Lord,
11 for he hath *p* against this city, as
18 Micah the Morasthite *p* in the days
20 man that *p* in the name of the Lord,
20 who *p* against this city and against
28. 6 thy words which thou hast *p*,
8 old *p* both against many countries,
29.31 that Shemaiah hath *p* unto you,
37.19 your prophets which *p* unto you,
Eze 11.13 to pass, when I *p*, that Pelatiah
37. 7 So I *p* as I was commanded:
7 and as I *p*, there was a noise, and
10 So I *p* as he commanded me, and
38.17 which *p* in those days many years
Zec 13. 4 one of his vision, when he hath *p*;
Mt 7.22 Lord, have we not *p* in thy name?
11.13 prophets and the law *p* until John.
Mk 7. 6 Well hath Esaias *p* of you
Lk 1.67 the Holy Ghost, and *p*, saying,
Jn 11.51 he *p* that Jesus should die for that
Ac 19. 6 and they spake with tongues, and *p*.

1Co 14. 5 with tongues, but rather that ye *p*:
1Pe 1.10 who *p* of the grace that should
Jude 14 Adam, *p* of these, saying, Behold,

PROPHESIETH

Jer 28. 9 The prophet which *p* of peace,
Eze 12.27 he *p* of the times that are far off.
Zec 13. 3 thrust him through when he *p*.
1Co 11. 5 or *p* with her head uncovered
14. 3 But he that *p* speaketh unto men
4 but he that *p* edifieth the church.
5 greater is he that *p* than he that

PROPHESY

Nu 11.27 and Medad do *p* in the camp.
1Sa 10. 5 before them; and they shall *p*:
6 thou shalt *p* with them, and shalt
1Ki 22. 8 he doth not *p* good concerning me,
18 would *p* no good concerning me,
1Ch 25. 1 who should *p* with harps, with
2Ch 18.17 he would not *p* good unto me, but
Isa 30.10 *P* not unto us right things, speak
10 unto us smooth things, *p* deceits:
Jer 5.31 The prophets *p* falsely, and the
11.21 *P* not in the name of the Lord,
14.14 The prophets *p* lies in my name:
14 they *p* unto you a false vision and
15 the prophets that *p* in my name,
16 the people to whom they *p* shall be
19.14 whither the Lord had sent him to *p*;
23.16 words of the prophets that *p* unto
25 said, that *p* lies in my name,
26 heart of the prophets that *p* lies?
32 against them that *p* false dreams,
25.30 *p* thou against them all these
26.12 sent me to *p* against this house
27.10 For they *p* a lie unto you, to remove
14 Babylon: for they *p* a lie unto you.
15 Lord, yet they *p* a lie in my name;
15 and the prophets that *p* unto you.
16 of your prophets that *p* unto you,
16 Babylon: for they *p* a lie unto you.
29. 9 *p* falsely unto you in my name:
21 *p* a lie unto you in my name;
32. 3 Wherefore dost thou *p*, and say,
Eze 4. 7 and thou shalt *p* against it.
6. 2 of Israel, and *p* against them,
11. 4 *p* against them, *p*, O son of man.
13. 2 *p* against the prophets of Israel
2 the prophets of Israel that *p*,
2 unto them that *p* out of their own
16 the prophets of Israel which *p*
17 daughters of thy people, which *p*
17 heart; and *p* thou against them,
20.46 *p* against the forest of the south
21. 2 and *p* against the land of Israel,
9 Son of man, *p*, and say, Thus saith
14 son of man, *p*, and smite thine
28 son of man, *p* and say, Thus saith
25. 2 Ammonites, and *p* against them;
28.21 against Zidon, and *p* against it,
29. 2 king of Egypt, and *p* against him,
30. 2 Son of man, *p* and say, Thus saith
34. 2 *p* against the shepherds of Israel,
2 *p*, and say unto them, Thus saith
35. 2 mount Seir, and *p* against it,
36. 1 *p* unto the mountains of Israel,
3 Therefore *p* and say, Thus saith
6 *P* therefore concerning the land of
37. 4 *P* upon these bones, and say unto
9 *P* unto the wind, *p*, son of man,
12 Therefore *p* and say unto them,
38. 2 and Tubal, and *p* against him,
14 son of man, *p* and say unto Gog,
39. 1 thou son of man, *p* against Gog,
Joel 2.28 sons and your daughters shall *p*,
Am 2.12 the prophets, saying, *P* not.
3. 8 God hath spoken, who can but *p*?
7.12 and there eat bread, and *p* there:
13 *p* not again any more at Beth-el:
15 me, Go, *p* unto my people Israel.
16 Thou sayest, *P* not against Israel,
Mic 2. 6 *P* ye not, say they to them that
6 say they to them that *p*: they shall
6 they shall not *p* to them, that they
11 I will *p* unto thee of wine and of
Zec 13. 3 that when any shall yet *p*, then
Mt 15. 7 well did Esaias *p* of you, saying,
26.68 *P* unto us, thou Christ, Who is he
Mk 14.65 him, and to say unto him, *P*:
Lk 22.64 *P*, who is it that smote thee?
Ac 2.17 sons and your daughters shall *p*,
18 of my Spirit; and they shall *p*:
21. 9 daughters, virgins, which did *p*.
Ro 12. 6 let us *p* according to the proportion
1Co 13. 9 we know in part, and we *p* in part.
14. 1 gifts, but rather that ye may *p*.
24 if all *p*, and there come in one that
31 For ye may all *p* one by one, that
39 covet to *p*, and forbid not to speak
Rev 10.11 Thou must *p* again before many
11. 3 shall *p* a thousand two hundred

PROPHESYING

1Sa 10.13 when he had made an end of *p*,
19.20 the company of the prophets *p*,
Ezr 6.14 prospered through the *p* of Haggai
1Co 11. 4 Every man praying or *p*, having
14. 6 or by knowledge, or by *p*, or by
22 but *p* serveth not for them that

PROPHESYINGS

1Th 5.20 Despise not *p*.

PROPHET

Gen 20. 7 for he is a *p*, and he shall pray for
Ex 7. 1 Aaron thy brother shall be thy *p*.
Nu 12. 6 If there be a *p* among you, I the
Dt 13. 1 If there arise among you a *p*, or a
3 hearken unto the words of that *p*,
5 that *p*, or that dreamer of dreams,
18.15 thy God will raise up unto thee a *P*
18 I will raise them up a *P* from
20 But the *p*, which shall presume to
20 of other gods, even that *p* shall die.
22 When a *p* speaketh in the name of
22 *p* hath spoken it presumptuously:
34.10 arose not a *p* since in Israel like
Jdg 6. 8 Lord sent a *p* unto the children of
1Sa 3.20 established to be a *p* of the Lord.
9. 9 a *P* was before time called a Seer.)
22. 5 *p* Gad said unto David, Abide not
2Sa 7. 2 the king said unto Nathan the *p*,
12.25 sent by the hand of Nathan the *p*:
24.11 of the Lord came unto the *p* Gad,
1Ki 1. 8 Nathan the *p*, and Shimei, and Rei,
10 Nathan the *p*, and Benaiah, and
22 the king, Nathan the *p* also came
23 king, saying, Behold Nathan the *p*.
32 the priest, and Nathan the *p*, and
34 Nathan the *p* anoint him there
38, 44 and Nathan the *p*, and Benaiah
45 Nathan the *p* have anointed him
11.29 *p* Ahijah the Shilonite found him
13.11 there dwelt an old *p* in Beth-el;
18 him, I am a *p* also as thou art;
20 unto the *p* that brought him back:
23 the *p* whom he had brought back.
25 in the city where the old *p* dwelt.
26 when the *p* that brought him back
29 the *p* took up the carcase of the
29 and the old *p* came to the city, to
14. 2 there is Ahijah the *p*, which told
18 hand of his servant Ahijah the *p*.
16. 7 by the hand of the *p* Jehu the son
12 against Baasha by Jehu the *p*,
18.22 I only, remain a *p* of the Lord;
36 Elijah the *p* came near, and said,
19.16 thou anoint to be *p* in thy room.
20.13 there came a *p* unto Ahab king of
22 the *p* came to the king of Israel,
38 So the *p* departed, and waited for
22. 7 Is there not here a *p* of the Lord
2Ki 3.11 Is there not here a *p* of the Lord,
5. 3 were with the *p* that is in Samaria!
8 know that there is a *p* in Israel.
13 if the *p* had bid thee do some great
6.12 but Elisha, the *p* that is in Israel,
9. 1 the *p* called one of the children of
4 even the young man the *p*, went to
14.25 Jonah the son of Amittai, the *p*,
19. 2 to Isaiah the *p* the son of Amoz.
20. 1 the *p* Isaiah the son of Amoz came
11 Isaiah the *p* cried unto the Lord:
14 Then came Isaiah the *p* unto king
23.18 of the *p* that came out of Samaria.
1Ch 17. 1 David said to Nathan the *p*, Lo, I
29.29 and in the book of Nathan the *p*,
2Ch 9.29 in the book of Nathan the *p*, and
12. 5 came Shemaiah the *p* to Rehoboam,
15 in the book of Shemaiah the *p*, and
13.22 written in the story of the *p* Iddo.
15. 8 and the prophecy of Oded the *p*,
18. 6 Is there not here a *p* of the Lord
21.12 a writing to him from Elijah the *p*,
25.15 he sent unto him a *p*, which said
16 Then the *p* forbare, and said, I
26.22 did Isaiah the *p*, the son of Amoz,
28. 9 a *p* of the Lord was there, whose
29.25 the king's seer, and Nathan the *p*:
32.20 *p* Isaiah the son of Amoz, prayed
32 written in the vision of Isaiah the *p*,
35.18 from the days of Samuel the *p*;
36.12 Jeremiah the *p* speaking from the
Ezr 5. 1 Haggai the *p*, and Zechariah the
6.14 the prophesying of Haggai the *p*
Ps 51(T) Nathan the *p* came unto him,
74. 9 there is no more any *p*: neither is
Isa 3. 2 man of war, the judge, and the *p*,
9.15 the *p* that teacheth lies, he is the
28. 7 the priest and the *p* have erred
37. 2 unto Isaiah the *p* the son of Amoz.
38. 1 Isaiah the *p* the son of Amoz came
39. 3 Isaiah the *p* unto king Hezekiah,
Jer 1. 5 ordained thee a *p* unto the nations.
6.13 from the *p* even unto the priest
8.10 from the *p* even unto the priest
14.18 both the *p* and the priest go about
18.18 the wise, nor the word from the *p*.
20. 2 Pashur smote Jeremiah the *p*, and
23.11 both *p* and priest are profane; yea,
28 The *p* that hath a dream, let him
33 or the *p*, or a priest shall ask thee,
34 And as for the *p*, and the priest,
37 Thus shalt thou say to the *p*, What
25. 2 Jeremiah the *p* spake unto all the
28. 1 Hananiah the son of Azar the *p*,
5 *p* Jeremiah said unto...*p* Hananiah
6 Even the *p* Jeremiah said, Amen:
9 The *p* which prophesieth of peace,
9 the word of the *p* shall come to
9 then shall the *p* be known, that
10 Hananiah the *p* took the yoke
10 from off the *p* Jeremiah's neck,
11 And the *p* Jeremiah went his way.
12 Lord came unto Jeremiah the *p*,
12 the *p* had broken the yoke
12 off the neck of the *p* Jeremiah,
15 *p* Jeremiah unto Hananiah the *p*,
17 So Hananiah the *p* died the same
29. 1 that Jeremiah the *p* sent from
26 is mad, and maketh himself a *p*,
27 which maketh himself a *p* to you?
29 in the ears of Jeremiah the *p*.
32. 2 Jeremiah the *p* was shut up in the
34. 6 Jeremiah the *p* spake all these
36. 8 Jeremiah the *p* commanded him,
26 the scribe and Jeremiah the *p*:
37. 2 which he spake by the *p* Jeremiah.
3 the priest to the *p* Jeremiah,
6 of the Lord unto the *p* Jeremiah,
13 he took Jeremiah the *p*, saying,
38. 9 they have done to Jeremiah the *p*,

Jer 38.10 take up Jeremiah the *p* out of the
14 took Jeremiah the *p* unto him into
42. 2 And said unto Jeremiah the *p*, Let,
4 Jeremiah the *p* said unto them, I
43. 6 and Jeremiah the *p*, and Baruch
45. 1 that Jeremiah the *p* spake unto
46. 1 Lord which came to Jeremiah the *p*
13 the Lord spake to Jeremiah the *p*,
47. 1 Lord that came to Jeremiah the *p*
49.34 came to Jeremiah the *p* against
50. 1 the Chaldeans by Jeremiah the *p*.
51.59 which Jeremiah the *p* commanded
La 2.20 the priest and the *p* be slain in the
Eze 2. 5 there hath been a *p* among them.
7.26 shall they seek a vision of the *p*;
14. 4 his face, and cometh to the *p*;
7 cometh to a *p* to inquire of him
9 And if the *p* be deceived when he
9 I the Lord have deceived that *p*,
10 the punishment of the *p* shall be
33.33 that a *p* hath been among them.
Dan 9. 2 the Lord came to Jeremiah the *p*,
Hos 4. 5 *p* also shall fall with thee in the
9. 7 the *p* is a fool, the spiritual man
8 the *p* is a snare of a fowler in all
12.13 by a *p* the Lord brought Israel out
13 and by a *p* was he preserved.
Am 7.14 I was no *p*, neither was I a
Mic 2.11 shall even be the *p* of his people.
Hab 1. 1 which Habakkuk the *p* did see.
3. 1 A prayer of Habakkuk the *p* upon
Hag 1. 1 word of the Lord by Haggai the *p*
3 word of the Lord by Haggai the *p*,
12 and the words of Haggai the *p*,
2. 1 word of the Lord by the *p* Haggai,
10 word of the Lord by Haggai the *p*,
Zec 1. 1, 7 Berechiah, the son of Iddo the *p*,
13. 5 shall say, I am no *p*, I am an
Mal 4. 5 Behold, I will send you Elijah the *p*
Mt 1.22 was spoken of the Lord by the *p*,
2. 5 for thus it is written by the *p*,
15 was spoken of the Lord by the *p*,
17 which was spoken by Jeremy the *p*,
3. 3 that was spoken of by the *p* Esaias,
4.14 spoken by Esaias the *p*, saying,
8.17 which was spoken by Esaias the *p*,
10.41 a *p* in the name of a *p* shall receive
11. 9 what went ye out for to see? A *p*?
9 I say unto you, and more than a *p*.
12.17 which was spoken by Esaias the *p*,
39 to it, but the sign of the *p* Jonas:
13.35 which was spoken by the *p*,
57 A *p* is not without honor, save in
14. 5 because they counted him as a *p*.
16. 4 unto it, but the sign of the *p* Jonas.
21. 4 which was spoken by the *p*,
11 This is Jesus the *p* of Nazareth of
26 people; for all hold John as a *p*.
46 because they took him for a *p*.
24.15 spoken of by Daniel the *p*, stand in
27. 9 which was spoken by Jeremy the *p*,
35 which was spoken by the *p*, They
Mk 6. 4 A *p* is not without honor, but in
15 others said, That it is a *p*, or as one
11.32 John, that he was a *p* indeed.
13.14 spoken of by Daniel the *p*,
Lk 1.76 be called the *p* of the Highest:
3. 4 book of the words of Esaias the *p*,
4.17 unto him the book of the *p* Esaias.
24 No *p* is accepted in his own
27 Israel in the time of Eliseus the *p*;
7.16 a great *p* is risen up among us;
26 what went ye out for to see? A *p*?
26 unto you, and much more than a *p*.
28 a greater *p* than John the Baptist:
39 This man, if he were a *p*, would
11.29 it, but the sign of Jonas the *p*.
13.33 that a *p* perish out of Jerusalem.
20. 6 be persuaded that John was a *p*.
24.19 which was a *p* mighty in deed and
Jn 1.21 Art thou that *p*? And he answered,
23 of the Lord, as said the *p* Esaias.
25 Christ, nor Elias, neither that *p*?
4.19 Sir, I perceive that thou art a *p*.
44 that a *p* hath no honor in his own
6.14 *p* that should come into the world.
7.40 said, Of a truth this is the *P*.
52 look: for out of Galilee ariseth no *p*.
9.17 thine eyes? He said, He is a *p*.
12.38 of Esaias the *p* might be fulfilled,
Ac 2.16 which was spoken by the *p* Joel;
30 being a *p*, and knowing that God
3.22 A *p* shall the Lord your God raise
23 soul, which will not hear that *p*,
7.37 A *p* shall the Lord your God raise
48 made with hands; as saith the *p*,
8.28 in his chariot read Esaias the *p*.
30 and heard him read the *p* Esaias,
34 of whom speaketh the *p* this? of
13. 6 sorcerer, a false *p*, a Jew, whose
20 fifty years, until Samuel the *p*.
21.10 Judea a certain *p*, named Agabus.
28.25 the Holy Ghost by Esaias the *p*
1Co 14.37 If any man think himself to be a *p*,
Tit 1.12 even a *p* of their own, said, The
2Pe 2.16 voice forbad the madness of the *p*.
Rev 16.13 out of the mouth of the false *p*.
19.20 the false *p* that wrought miracles
20.10 where the beast and the false *p* are,

PROPHETESS

Ex 15.20 Miriam the *p*, the sister of Aaron,
Jdg 4. 4 Deborah, a *p*, the wife of Lapidoth,
2Ki 22.14 went unto Huldah the *p*, the wife
2Ch 34.22 appointed, went to Huldah the *p*,
Neh 6.14 and on the *p* Noadiah, and the rest
Isa 8. 3 And I went unto the *p*; and she
Lk 2.36 was one Anna, a *p*, the daughter
Rev 2.20 Jezebel, which calleth herself a *p*,

PROPHET'S

Am 7.14 neither was I a *p* son; but I was a
Mt 10.41 prophet shall receive a *p* reward;

PROPHETS

Nu 11.29 that all the Lord's people were *p*,
1Sa 10. 5 meet a company of *p* coming down
10 behold, a company of *p* met him;
11 he prophesied among the *p*, then
11 Kish? Is Saul also among the *p*?
12 proverb, Is Saul also among the *p*?
19.20 they saw the company of the *p*
24 they say, Is Saul also among the *p*?
28. 6 by dreams, nor by Urim, nor by *p*.
15 more, neither by *p*, nor by dreams:
1Ki 18. 4 Jezebel cut off the *p* of the Lord,
4 Obadiah took an hundred *p*, and
13 Jezebel slew the *p* of the Lord,
13 an hundred men of the Lord's *p*
19 *p* of Baal four hundred and fifty,
19 the *p* of the groves four hundred,
20 gathered the *p* together unto
22 Baal's *p* are four hundred and fifty
25 said unto the *p* of Baal, Choose
40 unto them, Take the *p* of Baal; let
19. 1 how he had slain all the *p* with the
10, 14 and slain thy *p* with the sword;
20.35 man of the sons of the *p* said unto
41 discerned him that he was of the *p*.
22. 6 of Israel gathered the *p* together,
10 all the *p* prophesied before them.
12 all the *p* prophesied so, saying, Go
13 the *p* declare good unto the king
22 lying spirit in...mouth of all his *p*.
23 in the mouth of all these thy *p*,
2Ki 2. 3 sons of the *p* that were at Beth-el
5 sons of the *p* that were at Jericho
7 fifty men of the sons of the *p* went,
15 And when the sons of the *p* which
3.13 get thee to the *p* of thy father,
13 to the *p* of thy mother. And the
4. 1 of the wives of the sons of the *p*
38 sons of the *p* were sitting before
38 seethe pottage for the sons of the *p*.
5.22 young men of the sons of the *p*:
6. 1 the sons of the *p* said unto Elisha,
9. 1 called one of the children of the *p*,
7 the blood of my servants the *p*,
10.19 call unto me all the *p* of Baal, all
17.13 against Judah, by all the *p*, and
13 I sent to you by my servants the *p*.
23 had said by all his servants the *p*.
21.10 Lord spake by his servants the *p*,
23. 2 the priests, and the *p*, and all the
24. 2 he spake by his servants the *p*.
1Ch 16.22 anointed, and do my *p* no harm.
2Ch 18. 5 together of *p* four hundred men,
9 all the *p* prophesied before them.
11 all the *p* prophesied so, saying, Go
12 the *p* declare good to the king
21 lying spirit in...mouth of all his *p*.
22 spirit in the mouth of these thy *p*,
20.20 believe his *p*, so shall ye prosper.
24.19 Yet he sent *p* to them, to bring
29.25 commandment of the Lord by...*p*.
36.16 his words, and misused his *p*,
Ezr 5. 1 Then the *p*, Haggai the prophet,
2 were the *p* of God helping them,
9.11 commanded by thy servants the *p*,
Neh 6. 7 hast also appointed *p* to preach
14 the rest of the *p*, that would have
9.26 slew thy *p* which testified against
30 against them by thy spirit in thy *p*:
32 and on our priests, and on our *p*,
Ps 105.15 anointed, and do my *p* no harm.
Isa 29.10 the *p* and your rulers, the seers
30.10 to the *p*, Prophesy not unto us
Jer 2. 8 the *p* prophesied by Baal, and
26 and their priests, and their *p*,
30 own sword hath devoured your *p*,
4. 9 astonished, and the *p* shall wonder.
5.13 And the *p* shall become wind, and
31 The *p* prophesy falsely, and the
7.25 unto you all my servants the *p*,
8. 1 the bones of the *p*, and the bones
13.13 the priests, and the *p*, and all the
14.13 the *p* say unto them, Ye shall not
14 The *p* prophesy lies in my name:
15 *p* that prophesy in my name, and
15 famine shall those *p* be consumed.
23. 9 me is broken because of the *p*;
13 seen folly in the *p* of Samaria;
14 seen also in the *p* of Jerusalem
15 Lord of hosts concerning the *p*;
15 the *p* of Jerusalem is profaneness
16 not unto the words of the *p* that
21 I have not sent these *p*, yet they
25 I have heard what the *p* said, that
26 this be in the heart of the *p* that
26 *p* of the deceit of their own heart;
30, 31 I am against the *p*, saith the
25. 4 unto you all his servants the *p*,
26. 5 the words of my servants the *p*,
7, 8 So the priests and the *p* and all
11 Then spake the priests and the *p*
16 people unto the priests and to the *p*;
27. 9 hearken not ye to your *p*, nor to
14 not unto the words of the *p* that
15 and the *p* that prophesy unto you.
16 of your *p* that prophesy unto you,
18 But if they be *p*, and if the word
28. 8 The *p* that have been before me
29. 1 and to the priests, and to the *p*, and
8 Let not your *p* and your diviners,
15 hath raised us up *p* in Babylon;
19 unto them by my servants the *p*,
32.32 and their *p*, and the men of Judah,
35.15 unto you all my servants the *p*,
37.19 Where are now your *p* which
44. 4 unto you all my servants the *p*,
La 2. 9 her *p* also find no vision from the
14 Thy *p* have seen vain and foolish
4.13 For the sins of her *p*, and the

Eze 13. 2 prophesy against the *p* of Israel
3 Woe unto the foolish *p*, that follow
4 *p* are like the foxes in the deserts.
9 be upon the *p* that see vanity,
16 the *p* of Israel which prophesy
22.25 conspiracy of her *p* in the midst
28 her *p* have daubed them with
38.17 time by my servants the *p* of Israel,
Dan 9. 6 hearkened unto thy servants the *p*,
10 set before us by his servants the *p*.
Hos 6. 5 have I hewed them by the *p*;
12.10 I have also spoken by the *p*, and I
10 by the ministry of the *p*.
Am 2.11 And I raised up of your sons for *p*,
12 and commanded the *p*, saying,
3. 7 his secret unto his servants the *p*.
Mic 3. 5 the *p* that make my people err,
6 the sun shall go down over the *p*,
11 the *p* thereof divine for money:
Zep 3. 4 Her *p* are light and treacherous
Zec 1. 4 whom the former *p* have cried,
5 and the *p*, do they live for ever?
6 I commanded my servants the *p*,
7. 3 and to the *p*, saying, Should I weep
7 Lord hath cried by the former *p*,
12 sent in his spirit by the former *p*:
8. 9 these words by the mouth of the *p*,
13. 2 cause the *p* and the unclean spirit
4 the *p* shall be ashamed every one
Mt 2.23 which was spoken by the *p*,
5.12 so persecuted they the *p* which
17 come to destroy the law, or the *p*:
7.12 them: for this is the law and the *p*.
15 Beware of false *p*, which come to
11.13 For all the *p* and the law
13.17 that many *p* and righteous men
16.14 others, Jeremias, or one of the *p*.
22.40 hang all the law and the *p*.
23.29 ye build the tombs of the *p*, and
30 with them in the blood of the *p*.
31 children of them which killed the *p*.
34 behold, I send unto you *p*, and
37 thou that killest the *p*, and stonest
24.11 And many false *p* shall rise, and
24 and false *p*, and shall shew great
26.56 of the *p* might be fulfilled.
Mk 1. 2 As it is written in the *p*, Behold,
6.15 it is a prophet, or as one of the *p*.
8.28 Elias; and others, One of the *p*.
13.22 false Christs and false *p* shall rise,
Lk 1.70 spake by the mouth of his holy *p*,
6.23 did their fathers unto the *p*.
26 so did their fathers to the false *p*.
9. 8 one of the old *p* was risen again.
19 one of the old *p* is risen again.
10.24 many *p* and kings have desired
11.47 ye build the sepulchers of the *p*,
49 I will send them *p* and apostles,
50 That the blood of all the *p*, which
13.28 all the *p*, in the kingdom of God,
34 Jerusalem, which killeth the *p*,
16.16 The law and the *p* were until John:
29 him, They have Moses and the *p*;
31 If they hear not Moses and the *p*,
18.31 all things that are written by the *p*
24.25 believe all that the *p* have spoken;
27 beginning at Moses and all the *p*,
44 in the law of Moses, and in the *p*,
Jn 1.45 law, and the *p*, did write, Jesus of
6.45 It is written in the *p*, And they
8.52 Abraham is dead, and the *p*; and
53 and the *p* are dead: whom makest
Ac 3.18 shewed by the mouth of all his *p*,
21 by the mouth of all his holy *p*
24 and all the *p* from Samuel and
25 Ye are the children of the *p*, and of
7.42 it is written in the book of the *p*,
52 Which of the *p* have not your
10.43 To him give all the *p* witness, that
11.27 days came *p* from Jerusalem unto
13. 1 Antioch certain *p* and teachers;
15 the reading of the law and the *p*
27 nor yet the voices of the *p* which
40 you, which is spoken of in the *p*;
15.15 to this agree the words of the *p*;
32 being *p* also themselves, exhorted
24.14 written in the law and in the *p*:
26.22 which the *p* and Moses did say
27 Agrippa, believest thou the *p*?
28.23 and out of the *p*, from morning till
Ro 1. 2 by his *p* in the holy scriptures,)
3.21 witnessed by the law and the *p*;
11. 3 Lord, they have killed thy *p*, and
16.26 the scriptures of the *p*, according
1Co 12.28 apostles, secondarily *p*, thirdly
29 are all *p*? are all teachers? are all
14.29 Let the *p* speak two or three, and
32 spirits of the *p* are subject to the *p*.
Eph 2.20 foundation of the apostles and *p*,
3. 5 holy apostles and *p* by the Spirit;
4.11 gave some, apostles; and some, *p*:
1Th 2.15 the Lord Jesus, and their own *p*,
Heb 1. 1 past unto the fathers by the *p*,
11.32 also, and Samuel, and of the *p*:
Jas 5.10 the *p*, who have spoken in the
1Pe 1.10 salvation the *p* have inquired
2Pe 2. 1 there were false *p* also among
3. 2 were spoken before by the holy *p*,
1Jn 4. 1 many false *p* are gone out into
Rev 10. 7 declared to his servants the *p*.
11.10 these two *p* tormented them that
18 reward unto thy servants the *p*,
16. 6 shed the blood of saints and *p*, and
18.20 heaven, and ye holy apostles and *p*;
24 was found the blood of *p*, and of
22. 6 Lord God of the holy *p*, sent his
9 and of thy brethren the *p*, and

PROPITIATION
Ro 3.25 a *p* through faith in his blood,
1Jn 2. 2 he is the *p* for our sins: and not
4.10 his Son to be the *p* for our sins.

PROPORTION
1Ki 7.36 according to the *p* of every one,
Job 41.12 nor his power, nor his comely *p*.
Ro 12. 6 according to the *p* of faith;

PROSELYTE
Mt 23.15 sea and land to make one *p*, and
Ac 6. 5 and Nicolas a *p* of Antioch:

PROSELYTES
Ac 2.10 strangers of Rome, Jews and *p*,
13.43 and religious *p* followed Paul and

PROSPER
Gen 24.40 angel with thee, and *p* thy way:
42 if now thou do *p* my way which I
39. 3 made all that he did to *p* in his
23 he did, the Lord made it to *p*.
Nu 14.41 of the Lord? but it shall not *p*.
Dt 28.29 and thou shalt not *p* in thy ways:
29. 9 that ye may *p* in all that ye do.
Jos 1. 7 *p* whithersoever thou goest.
1Ki 2. 3 mayest *p* in all that thou doest,
22.12 Go up to Ramoth-gilead, and *p*:
15 Go, and *p*, for the Lord shall
1Ch 22.11 *p* thou, and build the house of the
13 Then shalt thou *p*, if thou takest
2Ch 13.12 of your fathers; for ye shall not *p*.
18.11 Go up to Ramoth-gilead, and *p*:
14 Go ye up, and *p*, and they shall be
20.20 believe his prophets, so shall ye *p*.
24.20 that ye cannot *p*? because ye have
26. 5 the Lord, God made him to *p*.
Neh 1.11 and *p*, I pray thee, thy servant this
2.20 The God of heaven, he will *p* us;
Job 12. 6 The tabernacles of robbers *p*, and
Ps 1. 3 and whatsoever he doeth shall *p*.
73.12 the ungodly, who *p* in the world;
122. 6 they shall *p* that love thee.
Pr 28.13 covereth his sins shall not *p*.:
Ec 11. 6 knowest not whether shall *p*,
Isa 53.10 of the Lord shall *p* in his hand.
54.17 that is formed against thee shall *p*;
55.11 *p* in the thing whereto I sent it.
Jer 2.37 and thou shalt not *p* in them.
5.28 cause of the fatherless, yet they *p*;
10.21 therefore they shall not *p*, and all
12. 1 doth the way of the wicked *p*?
20.11 for they shall not *p*: their
22.30 man that shall not *p* in his days:
30 for no man of his seed shall *p*,
23. 5 a King shall reign and *p*, and
32. 5 the Chaldeans, ye shall not *p*.
La 1. 5 are the chief, her enemies *p*;
Eze 16.13 and thou didst *p* into a kingdom.
17. 9 Shall it *p*? shall he not pull up
10 being planted, shall it *p*? shall it
15 Shall he *p*? shall he escape that
Dan 8.24 shall *p*, and practise, and shall
25 shall cause craft to *p* in his hands;
11.27 it shall not *p*: for yet the end shall
36 shall *p* till the indignation be
3Jn 2 thou mayest *p* and be in health,

PROSPERED
Gen 24.56 seeing the Lord hath *p* my way;
Jdg 4.24 hand of the children of Israel *p*,
2Sa 11. 7 people did, and how the war *p*.
2Ki 18. 7 and he *p* whithersoever he went
1Ch 29.23 of David his father, and *p*:
2Ch 14. 7 every side. So they built and *p*.
31.21 he did it with all his heart, and *p*.
32.30 And Hezekiah *p* in all his works.
Ezr 6.14 they *p* through the prophesying
Job 9. 4 himself against him, and hath *p*?
Dan 6.28 Daniel *p* in the reign of Darius,
8.12 ground; and it practised, and *p*.
1Co 16. 2 him in store, as God hath *p* him,

PROSPERETH
Ezr 5. 8 fast on, and *p* in their hands.
Ps 37. 7 because of him who *p* in his way,
Pr 17. 8 whithersoever it turneth, it *p*.
3Jn 2 be in health, even as thy soul *p*.

PROSPERITY
Dt 23. 6 not seek their peace nor their *p*
1Sa 25. 6 shall ye say to him that liveth in *p*,
1Ki 10. 7 and *p* exceedeth the fame which
Job 15.21 in *p* the destroyer shall come
36.11 they shall spend their days in *p*,
Ps 30. 6 in my *p* I said, I shall never be
35.27 pleasure in the *p* of his servant.
73. 3 when I saw the *p* of the wicked.
118.25 Lord, I beseech thee, send now *p*.
122. 7 walls, and *p* within thy palaces.
Pr 1.32 the *p* of fools shall destroy them.
Ec 7.14 In the day of *p* be joyful, but in
Jer 22.21 I spake unto theee in thy *p*; but
33. 9 all the *p* that I procure unto it.
La 3.17 far off from peace: I forgat *p*.
Zec 1.17 My cities through *p* shall yet be
7. 7 was inhabited and in *p*, and
(See box on page 608)

PROSPEROUS
Gen 24.21 had made his journey *p* or not.
39. 2 Joseph, and he was a *p* man;
Jos 1. 8 then thou shalt make thy way *p*,
Jdg 18. 5 our way which we go shall be *p*.
Job 8. 6 habitation of thy righteousness *p*.
Isa 48.15 him, and he shall make his way *p*.
Zec 8.12 For the seed shall be *p*; the vine
Ro 1.10 I might have a *p* journey by the

PROTEST
Gen 43. 3 The man did solemnly *p* unto us,
1Sa 8. 9 howbeit yet *p* solemnly unto them,
1Co 15.31 I *p* by your rejoicing which I have

Biblical Themes

PROSPERITY

And Abram was very rich in cattle, in silver, and in gold. Gen 13.2

Thou say in thine heart, My power and the might of mine hand hath gotten me this wealth. But thou shalt remember the Lord thy God: for it is he that giveth thee power to get wealth. Dt 8.17-18

The Lord thy God will make thee plenteous in every work of thine hand, in the fruit of thy body, and in the fruit of thy cattle, and in the fruit of thy land, for good. Dt 30.9

Observe to do according to all the law, which Moses my servant commanded thee . . . that thou mayest prosper whithersoever thou goest. Jos 1.7

The Lord maketh poor, and maketh rich. 1Sa 2.7

Then Satan answered the Lord, and said, Doth Job fear God for nought? Hast not thou made an hedge about him, and about his house, and about all that he hath on every side? thou hast blessed the work of his hands, and his substance is increased in the land. But put forth thine hand now, and touch all that he hath, and he will curse thee to thy face. Job 1.9-11

Will [God] esteem thy riches? no, not gold, nor all the forces of strength. Job 36.19

Fret not thyself because of him who prospereth in his way. Ps 37.7

I was envious at the foolish, when I saw the prosperity of the wicked. . . . the ungodly, who prosper in the world; they increase in riches. . . . it was too painful for me; until I went into the sanctuary of God; then understood I their end. Surely thou didst set them in slippery places. . . . How are they brought into desolation, as in a moment! Ps 73.3, 12, 16-19

The righteous shall flourish like the palm tree: he shall grow like a cedar in Lebanon. Those that be planted in the house of the Lord . . . shall still bring forth fruit in old age; they shall be fat and flourishing. Ps 92.12-14

The sleep of a laboring man is sweet, whether he eat little or much: but the abundance of the rich will not suffer him to sleep. Ec 5.12

In the day of prosperity be joyful, but in the day of adversity consider: God also hath set the one over against the other. Ec 7.14

The floors shall be full of wheat, and the fats shall overflow with wine and oil. And I will restore to you the years that the locust hath eaten. . . . ye shall eat in plenty, and be satisfied, and praise the name of the Lord. Joel 2.24-26

What shall it profit a man, if he shall gain the whole world, and lose his own soul? Mk 8.36

A man's life consisteth not in the abundance of the things which he possesseth. Lk 12.15

Upon the first day of the week let every one of you lay by him in store, as God hath prospered him. 1Co 16.2

I mean not that other men be eased, and ye burdened: but by an equality, that now at this time your abundance may be a supply for their want, that their abundance also may be a supply for your want. 2Co 8.13-14

What things were gain to me, those I counted loss for Christ. Php 3.7

Thou sayest, I am rich, and increased with goods, and have need of nothing; and knowest not that thou art wretched, and miserable, and poor, and blind, and naked. Rev 3.17

PROUD

Job 9.13 the *p* helpers do stoop under him.
26.12 he smiteth through the *p*.
38.11 here shall thy *p* waves be stayed?
40.11 and behold every one that is *p*,
12 Look on every one that is *p*, and
Ps 12. 3 tongue that speaketh *p* things:
31.23 plentifully rewarded the *p* doer.
40. 4 respecteth not the *p*, nor such as
86.14 the *p* are risen against me, and
94. 2 earth: render a reward to the *p*.
101. 5 look and a *p* heart will not I suffer.
119.21 rebuked the *p* that are cursed,
51 *p* have had me greatly in derision:
69 *p* have forged a lie against me: but
78 Let the *p* be ashamed; for they
85 The *p* have digged pits for me,
122 good: let not the *p* oppress me.
123. 4 and with the contempt of the *p*.
124. 5 *p* waters had gone over our soul.
138. 6 but the *p* he knoweth afar off.
140. 5 *p* have hid a snare for me, and
Pr 6.17 A *p* look, a lying tongue, and
15.25 will destroy the house of the *p*:
16. 5 Every one that is *p* in heart is an
19 to divide the spoil with the *p*.
21. 4 high look, and a *p* heart, and the
24 *P* and haughty scorner is his
24 name, who dealeth in *p* wrath.
28.25 He that is of a *p* heart stirreth up
Ec 7. 8 is better than the *p* in spirit.
Isa 2.12 upon every one that is *p* and lofty,
13.11 the arrogancy of the *p* to cease,
16. 6 the pride of Moab; he is very *p*:
Jer 13.15 hear me, and give ear; be not *p*:
43. 2 and all the *p* men, saying unto
49.29 of Moab, (he is exceeding *p*)
50.29 hath been *p* against the Lord,
31 am against thee, O thou most *p*,
32 the most *p* shall stumble and fall,
Hab 2. 5 he is a *p* man, neither keepeth
Mal 3.15 now we call the *p* happy; yea,
4. 1 all the *p*, yea, and all that do
Lk 1.51 the *p* in the imagination of their
Ro 1.30 of God, despiteful, *p*, boasters,
1Ti 6. 4 He is *p*, knowing nothing, but
2Ti 3. 2 *p*, blasphemers, disobedient to
Jas 4. 6 God resisteth the *p*, but giveth
1Pe 5. 5 God resisteth the *p*, and giveth

PROUDLY

Ex 18.11 the thing wherein they dealt *p*
1Sa 2. 3 Talk no more so exceeding *p*; let
Neh 9.10 that they dealt *p* against them.
16 But they and our fathers dealt *p*,
29 yet they dealt *p*, and hearkened
Ps 17.10 with their mouth they speak *p*.
31.18 which speak grievous things *p*
Isa 3. 5 the child shall behave himself *p*
Ob 12 spoken *p* in the day of distress.

PROVE

Ex 16. 4 that I may *p* them, whether they
20.20 Fear not: for God is come to *p* you,
Dt 8. 2 to humble thee, and to *p* thee, to
16 thee, and that he might *p* thee,
33. 8 whom thou didst *p* at Massah,
Jdg 2.22 through them I may *p* Israel,
3. 1 to *p* Israel by them, even as many
4 they were to *p* Israel by them, to
6.39 let me *p*, I pray thee, but this once
1Ki 10. 1 came to *p* him with hard questions.
2Ch 9. 1 to *p* Solomon with hard questions
Job 9.20 perfect, it shall also *p* me perverse.
Ps 26. 2 Examine me, O Lord, and *p* me;
Ec 2. 1 Go to now, I will *p* thee with mirth,
Dan 1.12 *P* thy servants, I beseech thee, ten
Mal 3.10 *p* me now herewith, saith the Lord
Lk 14.19 yoke of oxen, and I go to *p* them:
Jn 6. 6 And this he said to *p* him: for he
Ac 24.13 Neither can they *p* the things
25. 7 Paul, which they could not *p*.
Ro 12. 2 that ye may *p* what is that good,
2Co 8. 8 and to *p* the sincerity of your love.
13. 5 be in the faith; *p* your own selves.
Gal 6. 4 But let every man *p* his own work,
1Th 5.21 *P* all things; hold fast that which

PROVED

Gen 42.15 Hereby ye shall be *p*: By the life
16 prison, that your words may be *p*,
Ex 15.25 ordinance, and there he *p* them,
1Sa 17.39 assayed to go; for he had not *p* it.
39 with these; for I have not *p* them.
Ps 17. 3 Thou hast *p* mine heart; thou hast
66.10 thou, O God, hast *p* us: thou hast
81. 7 I *p* thee at the waters of Meribah.
95. 9 me, *p* me, and saw my work.
Ec 7.23 All this have I *p* by wisdom: I
Dan 1.14 this matter, and *p* them ten days.
Ro 3. 9 we have before *p* both Jews and
2Co 8.22 *p* diligent in many things, but
1Ti 3.10 let these also first be *p*; then let
Heb 3. 9 your fathers tempted me, *p* me,

PROVENDER

Gen 24.25 have both straw and *p* enough,
32 gave straw and *p* for the camels,
42.27 opened his sack to give his ass *p* in
43.24 feet; and he gave their asses *p*.
Jdg 19.19 is both straw and *p* for our asses;

21 house, and gave *p* unto the asses:
Isa 30.24 ear the ground shall eat clean *p*,

PROVERB
Dt 28.37 become an astonishment, a *p*,
1Sa 10.12 Therefore it became a *p*, Is Saul
24.13 As saith the *p* of the ancients,
1Ki 9. 7 Israel shall be a *p* and a byword
2Ch 7.20 to be a *p* and a byword among all
Ps 69.11 and I became a *p* to them.
Pr 1. 6 To understand a *p*, and the
Isa 14. 4 take up this *p* against the king of
Jer 24. 9 to be a reproach and a *p*, a taunt
Eze 12.22 that *p* that ye have in the land of
23 I will make this *p* to cease, and they
23 no more use it as a *p* in Israel;
14. 8 and will make him a sign and a *p*,
16.44 shall use this *p* against thee,
18. 2 ye use this *p* concerning the land
3 any more to use this *p* in Israel.
Hab 2. 6 and a taunting *p* against him,
Lk 4.23 Ye will surely say unto me this *p*,
Jn 16.29 thou plainly, and speakest no *p*.
2Pe 2.22 unto them according to the true *p*,

PROVERBS
Nu 21.27 Wherefore they that speak in *p*
1Ki 4.32 And he spake three thousand *p*:
Pr 1. 1 The *p* of Solomon the son of David,
10. 1 The *p* of Solomon. A wise son
25. 1 These are also *p* of Solomon, which
Ec 12. 9 out, and set in order many *p*.
Eze 16.44 every one that useth *p* shall use
Jn 16.25 have I spoken unto you in *p*:
25 shall no more speak unto you in *p*,

PROVIDE
Gen 22. 8 God will *p* himself a lamb for a
30.30 shall I *p* for mine own house also?
Ex 18.21 *p* out of all the people able men,
1Sa 16.17 *P* me now a man that can play
2Ch 2. 7 whom David my father did *p*.
Ps 78.20 can he *p* flesh for his people?
Mt 10. 9 *P* neither gold, nor silver, nor
Lk 12.33 *p* yourselves bags which wax not
Ac 23.24 And *p* them beasts, that they may
Ro 12.17 *P* things honest in the sight of
1Ti 5. 8 But if any *p* not for his own, and

PROVIDED
Dt 33.21 And he *p* the first part for himself,
1Sa 16. 1 have *p* me a king among his sons.
2Sa 19.32 he had *p* the king of sustenance
1Ki 4. 7 which *p* victuals for the king and his
27 *p* victual for king Solomon, and
2Ch 32.29 he *p* him cities, and possessions
Ps 65. 9 corn, when thou hast so *p* for it.
Lk 12.20 things be, which thou hast *p*?
Heb 11.40 God having *p* some better thing

PROVIDENCE
Ac 24. 2 done unto this nation by thy *p*,

PROVIDING
2Co 8.21 *P* for honest things, not only in

PROVINCE
Ezr 2. 1 the children of the *p* that went up
5. 8 that we went into the *p* of Judea,
6. 2 that is in the *p* of the Medes,
7.16 canst find in all the *p* of Babylon,
Neh 1. 3 The remnant that are left...in the *p*
7. 6 These are the children of the *p*,
11. 3 are the chief of the *p* that dwelt in
Est 1.22 into every *p* according to the
3.12 governors that were over every *p*,
Ec 5. 8 of judgment and justice in a *p*,
Dan 2.48 ruler over the whole *p* of Babylon,
49 over the affairs of the *p* of Babylon:
3. 1 plain of Dura, in the *p* of Babylon.
12 over the affairs of the *p* of Babylon,

Biblical Themes

PROVIDENCE

Unto Adam also and to his wife did the Lord God make coats of skins, and clothed them. Gen 3.21

I am Joseph your brother, whom ye sold into Egypt. Now therefore be not grieved, nor angry with yourselves, that ye sold me hither: for God . . . sent me before you to preserve you a posterity in the earth, and to save your lives by a great deliverance. So now it was not you that sent me hither, but God. Gen 45.4-5, 7-8

My presence shall go with thee, and I will give thee rest. Ex 33.14

Beware that thou forget not the Lord thy God . . . which brought thee forth out of the land of Egypt, from the house of bondage; who led thee through that great and terrible wilderness . . . that he might prove thee, to do thee good at thy latter end; and thou say in thine heart, My power and the might of mine hand hath gotten me this wealth. But thou shalt remember . . . it is he that giveth thee power to get wealth. Dt 8.11, 14-18

The land, whither ye go to possess it, is a land of hills and valleys, and drinketh water of the rain of heaven: a land which the Lord thy God careth for. Dt 11.11-12

Then said David to the Philistine, Thou comest to me with a sword, and with a spear . . . but I come to thee in the name of the Lord of hosts. . . . And all this assembly shall know that the Lord saveth not with sword and spear: for the battle is the Lord's, and he will give you into our hands. 1Sa 17.45, 47

Thou . . . withheldest not thy manna from their mouth, and gavest them water for their thirst. Yea, forty years didst thou sustain them in the wilderness, so that they lacked nothing. Neh 9.20-21

The Lord gave, and the Lord hath taken away; blessed be the name of the Lord. Job 1.21

Despise not thou the chastening of the Almighty: for he maketh sore, and bindeth up: he woundeth, and his hands make whole. Job 5.17-18

The Lord is my shepherd; I shall not want. Ps 23.1

The steps of a good man are ordered by the Lord. . . . Though he fall, he shall not be utterly cast down: for the Lord upholdeth him with his hand. I have been young, and now am old; yet have I not seen the righteous forsaken, nor his seed begging bread. Ps 37.23-25

These wait all upon thee; that thou mayest give them their meat in due season. That thou givest them they gather: thou openest thine hand, they are filled with good. Thou hidest thy face, they are troubled: thou takest away their breath, they die, and return to their dust. Thou sendest forth thy spirit, they are created: and thou renewest the face of the earth. Ps 104.27-30

Behold the fowls of the air: for they sow not, neither do they reap, nor gather into barns; yet your heavenly Father feedeth them. Are ye not much better than they? Mt 6.26

He hath abounded toward us in all wisdom and prudence. . . . we have obtained an inheritance, being predestinated according to the purpose of him who worketh all things after the counsel of his own will. Eph 1.8, 11

Humble yourselves therefore under the mighty hand of God . . . casting all your care upon him; for he careth for you. 1Pe 5.6-7

To him that overcometh will I give to eat of the hidden manna. Rev 2.17

30 Abed-nego, in the *p* of Babylon.
8. 2 the palace, which is the *p* of Elam;
11.24 upon the fattest places of the *p*;
Ac 23.34 letter, he asked of what *p* he was.
25. 1 when Festus was come into the *p*,

PROVING
Ac 9.22 *p* that this is very Christ.
Eph 5.10 *P* what is acceptable unto...Lord.

PROVISION
Gen 42.25 and to give them *p* for the way:
45.21 and gave them *p* for the way.
Jos 9. 5 of their *p* was dry and moldy.
12 our bread we took hot for our *p*
1Ki 4. 7 man his month in a year made *p*.
22 Solomon's *p* for one day was
2Ki 6.23 he prepared great *p* for them:
1Ch 29.19 for the which I have made *p*.
Ps 132.15 I will abundantly bless her *p*: I
Dan 1. 5 them a daily *p* of the king's meat,
Ro 13.14 and make not *p* for the flesh, to

PROVOCATION
1Ki 15.30 Israel sin, by his *p*, wherewith he
21.22 for the *p* wherewith thou hast
Job 17. 2 not mine eye continue in their *p*?
Ps 95. 8 not your heart, as in the *p*, and
Jer 32.31 For this city hath been to me as a *p*
Eze 20.28 presented the *p* of their offering:

BIBLICAL THEMES

PRUDENCE

Forasmuch as God hath shewed thee all this, there is none so discreet and wise as thou art. Gen 41.39

Thou shalt not follow a multitude to do evil. Ex 23.2

And God said to Solomon, Because this was in thine heart, and thou hast not asked riches, wealth, or honor . . . but hast asked wisdom and knowledge for thyself . . . wisdom and knowledge is granted unto thee; and I will give thee riches, and wealth, and honor, such as none of the kings have had that have been before thee. 2Ch 1.11-12

Set a watch, O Lord, before my mouth; keep the door of my lips. Ps 141.3

To give subtilty to the simple, to the young man knowledge and discretion. Pr 1.4

Happy is the man that findeth wisdom. . . . all her paths are peace. She is a tree of life to them that lay hold upon her. Pr 3.13, 17-18

He that is slow to anger is better than the mighty; and he that ruleth his spirit than he that taketh a city. Pr 16.32

A prudent man forseeth the evil, and hideth himself: but the simple pass on, and are punished. Pr 22.3

Answer not a fool according to his folly, lest thou also be like unto him. Answer a fool according to his folly, lest he be wise in his own conceit. Pr 26.4-5

Wisdom is better than weapons of war: but one sinner destroyeth much good Ec 9.18

Let not the wise man glory in his wisdom. . . . But let him that glorieth glory in this, that he understandeth and knoweth me, that I am the Lord which exercise lovingkindness, judgment, and righteousness. Jer 9.23-24

O generation of vipers, who hath warned you to flee from the wrath to come? Mt 3.7

Strait is the gate, and narrow is the way, which leadeth unto life, and few there be that find it. Mt 7.14

Whosoever heareth these sayings of mine, and doeth them, I will liken him unto a wise man, which built his house upon a rock: and the rain descended, and the floods came, and the winds blew, and beat upon that house; and it fell not: for it was founded upon a rock. And every one that heareth these sayings of mine, and doeth them not, shall be likened unto a foolish man, which built his house upon the sand: and the rain descended, and the floods came, and the winds blew, and beat upon that house; and it fell: and great was the fall of it. Mt 7.24-27

Behold, I send you forth as sheep in the midst of wolves: be ye therefore wise as serpents, and harmless as doves. Mt 10.16

I thank thee, O Father, . . . that thou hast hid these things from the wise and prudent, and hast revealed them unto babes. Lk 10.21

The lord commended the unjust steward, because he had done wisely: for the children of this world are in their generation wiser than the children of light. Lk 16.8

Every man that striveth for the mastery is temperate in all things. 1Co 9.25

See then that ye walk circumspectly, not as fools, but as wise, redeeming the time, because the days are evil. Eph 5.15-16

By faith Noah, being warned of God of things not seen as yet, moved with fear, prepared an ark to the saving of his house. Heb 11.7

Heb 3. 8 not your hearts, as in the *p*, in
15 harden not your hearts, as in the *p*,

PROVOKE

Ex 23.21 and obey his voice, *p* him not;
Nu 14.11 How long will this people *p* me?
Dt 4.25 Lord thy God, to *p* him to anger:
9.18 of the Lord, to *p* him to anger.
31.20 gods, and serve them, and *p* me,
29 to *p* him to anger through the
32.21 I will *p* them to anger with a
1Ki 14. 9 molten images, to *p* me to anger,
16. 2 to *p* me to anger with their sins;
26 to *p* the Lord God of Israel to anger
33 to *p* the Lord God of Israel to anger
2Ki 17.11 things to *p* the Lord to anger:
17 of the Lord, to *p* him to anger.
21. 6 of the Lord, to *p* him to anger.
22.17 they might *p* me to anger with all
23.19 had made to *p* the Lord to anger,
2Ch 33. 6 of the Lord, to *p* him to anger.
34.25 that they might *p* me to anger
Job 12. 6 and they that *p* God are secure;
Ps 78.40 did they *p* him in the wilderness,
Isa 3. 8 Lord, to *p* the eyes of his glory.
Jer 7.18 that they may *p* me to anger.
19 Do they *p* me to anger? saith the
19 not *p* themselves to the confusion of
11.17 *p* me to anger in offering incense
25. 6 *p* me not to anger with the works
7 ye might *p* me to anger with the
32.29 unto other gods, to *p* me to anger.
32 they have done to *p* me to anger.
44. 3 have committed to *p* me to anger,
8 *p* me unto wrath with the works
Eze 8.17 have returned to *p* me to anger:
16.26 thy whoredoms, to *p* me to anger.
Lk 11.53 to *p* him to speak of many things:
Ro 10.19 saith, I will *p* you to jealousy by
11.11 Gentiles, for to *p* them to jealousy.
14 any means I may *p* to emulation
1Co 10.22 Do we *p* the Lord to jealousy? are
Eph 6. 4 *p* not your children to wrath:
Col 3.21 *p* not your children to anger,
Heb 3.16 when they had heard, did *p*:
10.24 to *p* unto love and to good works:

PROVOKED

Nu 14.23 any of them that *p* me see it:
16.30 that these men have *p* the Lord.
Dt 9. 8 in Horeb ye *p* the Lord to wrath,
22 ye *p* the Lord to wrath.
32.16 *p* him to jealousy with strange
16 abominations *p* they him to anger.
21 *p* me to anger with their vanities:
Jdg 2.12 them, and *p* the Lord to anger.
1Sa 1. 6 And her adversary also *p* her sore,
7 so she *p* her; therefore she wept;
1Ki 14.22 they *p* him to jealousy with their sins
15.30 *p* the Lord God of Israel to anger.
21.22 thou hast *p* me to anger,
22.53 *p* to anger the Lord God of Israel,
2Ki 21.15 have *p* me to anger, since the day
23.26 that Manasseh had *p* him withal.
1Ch 21. 1 and *p* David to number Israel.
2Ch 28.25 and *p* to anger the Lord God of his
Ezr 5.12 *p* the God of heaven unto wrath,
Neh 4. 5 have *p* thee to anger before the
Ps 78.56 tempted and *p* the most high
58 *p* him to anger with their high
106. 7 but *p* him at the sea, even at the
29 they *p* him to anger with their
33 Because they *p* his spirit, so that
43 but they *p* him with their counsel,
Isa 1. 4 have *p* the Holy One of Israel
Jer 8.19 *p* me to anger with their graven
32.30 Israel have only *p* me to anger
Hos 12.14 Ephraim *p* him to anger most
Zec 8.14 when your fathers *p* me to wrath,
1Co 13. 5 is not easily *p*, thinketh no evil;
2Co 9. 2 and your zeal hath *p* very many.

PROVOKING

Dt 32.19 because of the *p* of his sons, and
1Ki 14.15 their groves, *p* the Lord to anger.
16. 7 in *p* him to anger with the work of
13 *p* the Lord God of Israel to anger
Ps 78.17 by *p* the most High in the
Gal 5.26 *p* one another, envying one

PRUDENCE

2Ch 2.12 a wise son, endued with *p* and
Pr 8.12 I wisdom dwell with *p*, and find
Eph 1. 8 toward us in all wisdom and *p*;

PRUDENT

1Sa 16.18 a man of war, and *p* in matters,
Pr 12.16 but a *p* man covereth shame.
23 A *p* man concealeth knowledge:
13.16 *p* man dealeth with knowledge:
14. 8 wisdom of the *p* is to understand
15 but the *p* man looketh well to his
18 the *p* are crowned with knowledge.
15. 5 he that regardeth reproof is *p*.
16.21 wise in heart shall be called *p*:
18.15 heart of the *p* getteth knowledge;
19.14 and a *p* wife is from the Lord.
22. 3 A *p* man foreseeth the evil, and
27.12 A *p* man foreseeth the evil, and

Isa 3. 2 and the *p*, and the ancient,
5.21 eyes, and *p* in their own sight!
10.13 for I am *p*: and I have removed
29.14 the understanding of their *p* men
Jer 49. 7 is counsel perished from the *p*? is
Hos 14. 9 *p*, and he shall know them? for the
Am 5.13 *p* shall keep silence in that time;
Mt 11.25 these things from the wise and *p*,
Lk 10.21 these things from the wise and *p*,
Ac 13. 7 country, Sergius Paulus, a *p* man:
1Co 1.19 the understanding of the *p*.

PRUDENTLY
Isa 52.13 my servant shall deal *p*, he shall

PRUNINGHOOKS
Isa 2. 4 and their spears into *p*:
Joel 3.10 swords, and your *p* into spears:
Mic 4. 3 and their spears into *p*:

PSALM
1Ch 16. 7 David delivered first this *p* to thank
Ps 81. 2 Take a *P*, and bring hither the
98. 5 the harp, and the voice of a *p*.
Ac 13.33 it is also written in the second *p*,
35 he saith also in another *p*,
1Co 14.26 every one of you hath a *p*, hath a

PSALMIST
2Sa 23. 1 Jacob, and the sweet *p* of Israel,

PSALMS
1Ch 16. 9 Sing unto him, sing *p* unto him,
Ps 95. 2 a joyful noise unto him with *p*.
105. 2 Sing unto him, sing *p* unto him:
Lk 20.42 himself saith in the book of *P*,
24.44 and in the *p*, concerning me.
Ac 1.20 it is written in the book of *P*, Let
Eph 5.19 Speaking to yourselves in *p* and
Col 3.16 admonishing one another in *p* and
Jas 5.13 Is any merry? let him sing *p*.

PSALTERIES
2Sa 6. 5 even on harps, and on *p*, and on
1Ki 10.12 harps also and *p* for singers: there
1Ch 13. 8 and with harps, and with *p*, and
15.16 musick, *p* and harp and cymbals,
20 and Benaiah, with *p* on Alamoth;
28 making a noise with *p* and harps.
16. 5 and Jeiel with *p* and with harps;
25. 1 prophesy with harps, with *p*,
6 with cymbals, *p*, and harps, for
2Ch 5.12 having cymbals and *p* and harps,
9.11 and harps and *p* for singers: and
20.28 they came to Jerusalem with *p* and
29.25 with *p*, and with harps, according
Neh 12.27 with cymbals, *p*, and with harps.

PSALTERY
1Sa 10. 5 from the high place with a *p*,
Ps 33. 2 sing unto him with the *p* and an
57. 8 awake, *p* and harp: I myself will
71.22 also praise thee with the *p*, even
81. 2 the pleasant harp with the *p*.
92. 3 of ten strings, and upon the *p*;
108. 2 Awake, *p* and harp: I myself will
144. 9 upon a *p* and an instrument of ten
150. 3 praise him with the *p* and harp.
Dan 3. 5 *p*, dulcimer, and all kings of
7 *p*, and all kinds of musick,
10, 15 *p*, and dulcimer, and all kinds

PTOLEMAIS
Ac 21. 7 from Tyre, we came to *P*, and

PUBLICAN
Mt 10. 3 Thomas, and Matthew the *p*;
18.17 thee as an heathen man and a *p*.
Lk 5.27 and saw a *p*, named Levi, sitting
18.10 one a Pharisee, and the other a *p*.
11 adulterers, or even as this *p*.
13 And the *p*, standing afar off, would

PUBLICANS
Mt 5.46 ye? do not even the *p* the same?
47 others? do not even the *p* so?
9.10 many *p* and sinners came and sat
11 Why eateth your Master with *p* and
11.19 a friend of *p* and sinners.
21.31 That the *p* and the harlots go into
32 the *p* and the harlots believed him:
Mk 2.15 house, many *p* and sinners sat also
16 saw him eat with *p* and sinners,
16 and drinketh with *p* and sinners?
Lk 3.12 Then came also *p* to be baptized,
5.29 there was a great company of *p*
30 eat and drink with *p* and sinners?
7.29 the *p*, justified God, being baptized
34 a friend of *p* and sinners!
15. 1 Then drew near unto him all the *p*
19. 2 which was the chief among the *p*,

PUBLICK
Mt 1.19 willing to make her a *p* example,

PUBLICKLY
Ac 18.28 convinced the Jews, and that *p*,
20.20 shewed you, and have taught you *p*,

PUBLISH
Dt 32. 3 I will *p* the name of the Lord:
1Sa 31. 9 to *p* it in the house of their idols,
2Sa 1.20 *p* it not in the streets of Askelon;
Neh 8.15 *p* and proclaim in all their cities,
Ps 26. 7 That I may *p* with the voice of
Jer 4. 5 and *p* in Jerusalem; and say, Blow
16 behold, *p* against Jerusalem, that
5.20 house of Jacob, and *p* it in Judah,
31. 7 *p* ye, praise ye, and say, O Lord,
46.14 Declare ye in Egypt,...*p* in Migdol,
14 and *p* in Noph and in Tahpanhes:
50. 2 ye among the nations, and *p*,
2 up a standard; *p*, and conceal not:
Am 3. 9 *P* in the palaces at Ashdod, and in
4. 5 proclaim and *p* the free offerings:
Mk 1.45 went out, and began to *p* it much,
5.20 began to *p* in Decapolis how great

PUBLISHED
Est 1.20 be *p* throughout all his empire,
22 that it should be *p* according to
3.14 province was *p* unto all people,
8.13 province was *p* unto all people,
Ps 68.11 the company of those that *p* it.
Jon 3. 7 *p* through Nineveh by the decree
Mk 7.36 the more a great deal they *p* it;
13.10 must first be *p* among all nations.
Lk 8.39 and *p* throughout the whole city
Ac 10.37 which was *p* throughout all Judea,
13.49 And the word of the Lord was *p*

PUBLISHETH
Isa 52. 7 good tidings, that *p* peace;
7 tidings of good, that *p* salvation;
Jer 4.15 *p* affliction from mount Ephraim.
Na 1.15 good tidngs, that *p* peace!

PUBLIUS
Ac 28. 7 of the island, whose name was *P*;
8 the father of *P* lay sick of a fever

PUDENS
2Ti 4.21 Eubulus greeteth thee, and *P*,

PUFFED
1Co 4. 6 that no one of you be *p* up for one
18 Now some are *p* up, as though I
19 the speech of them which are *p* up,
5. 2 ye are *p* up, and have not rather
13. 4 vaunteth not itself, is not *p* up,
Col 2.18 vainly *p* up by his fleshly mind,

PUFFETH
Ps 10. 5 for all his enemies, he *p* at them.
12. 5 in safety from him that *p* at him.
1Co 8. 1 Knowledge *p* up, but charity

PULL
1Ki 13. 4 he could not *p* it in again to him.
Ps 31. 4 *P* me out of the net that they
Isa 22.19 thy state shall he *p* thee down.
Jer 1.10 to root out, and to *p* down, and to
12. 3 *p* them out like sheep for the
18. 7 and to *p* down, and to destroy it;
24. 6 them, and not *p* them down;
42.10 build you, and not *p* you down,
Eze 17. 9 shall he not *p* up the roots
Mic 2. 8 *p* off the robe with the garment
Mt 7. 4 *p* out the mote out of thine eye;
Lk 6.42 *p* out the mote that is in thine eye.
42 to *p* out the mote that is in thy
12.18 I will *p* down my barns, and build
14. 5 *p* him out on the sabbath day?

PULLED
Gen 8. 9 *p* her in unto him into the ark.
19.10 and *p* Lot into the house to them,
Ezr 6.11 timber be *p* down from his house,
La 3.11 my ways, and *p* me in pieces:
Am 9.15 no more be *p* up out of their land
Zec 7.11 and *p* away the shoulder, and
Ac 23.10 Paul should have been *p* in pieces

PULLING
2Co 10. 4 to the *p* down of strong holds;)
Jude 23 with fear, *p* them out of the fire;

PULPIT
Neh 8. 4 the scribe stood upon a *p* of wood,

PUNISH
Lev 26.18 I will *p* you seven times more for
24 *p* you yet seven times for your
Pr 17.26 Also to *p* the just is not good, nor
Isa 10.12 will *p* the fruit of the stout heart
13.11 I will *p* the world for their evil, and
24.21 shall *p* the host of the high ones
26.21 to *p* the inhabitants of the earth
27. 1 *p* leviathan the piercing serpent,
Jer 9.25 that I will *p* all them which are
11.22 of hosts, Behold, I will *p* them:
13.21 thou say when he shall *p* thee?
21.14 I will *p* you according to the fruit
23.34 I will even *p* that man and his
25.12 that I will *p* the king of Babylon,
27. 8 that nation will I *p*, saith the Lord,
29.32 I will *p* Shemaiah the Nehelamite,
30.20 and I will *p* all that oppress them.
36.31 I will *p* him and his seed and his
44.13 I will *p* them that dwell in the land
29 I will *p* you in this place, that ye
46.25 I will *p* the multitude of No, and
50.18 I will *p* the king of Babylon and
51.44 And I will *p* Bel in Babylon, and
Hos 4. 9 I will *p* them for their ways, and
14 I will not *p* your daughters when
12. 2 will *p* Jacob according to his ways;
Am 3. 2 I will *p* you for all your iniquities.
Zep 1. 8 I will *p* the princes, and the king's
9 day also will I *p* all those that leap
12 *p* the men that are settled on their
Zec 8.14 As I thought to *p* you, when your
Ac 4.21 how they might *p* them, because

PUNISHED
Ex 21.20 his hand; he shall be surely *p*.
21 a day or two, he shall not be *p*:
22 he shall be surely *p*, according as
Ezr 9.13 hast *p* us less than our iniquities
Job 31.11 it is an iniquity to be *p* by the judges.
28 were an iniquity to be *p* by the judge:
Pr 21.11 When the scorner is *p*, the simple
22. 3 but the simple pass on, and are *p*.
27.12 but the simple pass on, and are *p*.

Jer 44.13 as I have *p* Jerusalem, by the
50.18 as I have *p* the king of Assyria.
Zep 3. 7 not be cut off, howsoever I *p* them:
Zec 10. 3 the shepherds, and I *p* the goats:
Ac 22. 5 unto Jerusalem, for to be *p*,
26.11 I *p* them oft in every synagogue,
2Th 1. 9 *p*...everlasting destruction
2Pe 2. 9 unto the day of judgment to be *p*:

PUNISHMENT

Gen 4.13 My *p* is greater than I can bear.
Lev 26.41, 43 accept of the *p* of their iniquity:
1Sa 28.10 there shall no *p* happen to thee for
Job 31. 3 strange *p* to the workers of iniquity?
Pr 19.19 man of great wrath shall suffer *p*:
La 3.39 a man for the *p* of his sins?
4. 6 *p* of the iniquity of the daughter
6 than the *p* of the sin of Sodom,
22 *p* of thine iniquity...accomplished,
Eze 14.10 shall bear the *p* of their iniquity:
10 the *p* of the prophet shall be even
10 as the *p* of him that seeketh unto
Am 1. 3, 6, 9, 11, 13 I will not turn away the *p*
2. 1, 4, 6 will not turn away the *p* thereof;
Zec 14.19 This shall be the *p* of Egypt, and
19 the *p* of all nations that come not
Mt 25.46 shall go away into everlasting *p*:
2Co 2. 6 Sufficient to such a man is this *p*,
Heb 10.29 Of how much sorer *p*, suppose ye,
1Pe 2.14 sent by him for the *p* of evildoers,

PUNISHMENTS

Job 19.29 bringeth the *p* of the sword,
Ps 149. 7 upon the heathen, and *p* upon the

PURCHASE

Gen 49.32 The *p* of the field and of the cave
Lev 25.33 if a man *p* of the Levites, then the
Jer 32.11 So I took the evidence of the *p*,
12 I gave the evidence of the *p* unto
12 that subscribed the book of the *p*,
14 evidences, this evidence of the *p*,
16 the evidence of the *p* unto Baruch
1Ti 3.13 *p* to themselves a good degree,

PURCHASED

Gen 25.10 Abraham *p* of the sons of Heth:
Ex 15.16 pass over, which thou hast *p*.
Ru 4.10 of Mahlon, have I *p* to be my wife,
Ps 74. 2 which thou hast *p* of old; the rod of
78.54 which his right hand had *p*.
Ac 1.18 man *p* a field with the reward of
8.20 gift of God may be *p* with money.
20.28 he hath *p* with his own blood.
Eph 1.14 redemption of the *p* possession,

PURE

Ex 25.11 thou shalt overlay it with *p* gold,
17 shalt make a mercy seat of *p* gold:
24 thou shalt overlay it with *p* gold,
29 of *p* gold shalt thou make them.
31 shalt make a candlestick of *p* gold:
36 shall be one beaten work of *p* gold.
38 thereof, shall be of *p* gold.
39 a talent of *p* gold shall he make it,
27.20 *p* oil olive beaten for the light,
28.14 two chains of *p* gold at the ends;
22 ends of wreathen work of *p* gold.
36 thou shalt make a plate of *p* gold,
30. 3 shalt overlay it with *p* gold, the top
23 of *p* myrrh five hundred shekels,
34 sweet spices with *p* frankincense:
35 tempered together, *p* and holy:
31. 8 and the *p* candlestick with all his
37. 2 he overlaid it with *p* gold within
6 he made the mercy seat of *p* gold:
11 And he overlaid it with *p* gold, and
16 covers to cover withal, of *p* gold.
17 made the candlestick of *p* gold: of
22 it was one beaten work of *p* gold.
23 and his snuffdishes, of *p* gold.
24 Of a talent of *p* gold made he it,
26 he overlaid it with *p* gold, both the
29 and the *p* incense of sweet spices,
39.15 ends, of wreathen work of *p* gold.
25 they made bells of *p* gold, and put
30 plate of the holy crown of *p* gold.
37 The *p* candlestick, with the lamps
Lev 24. 2 bring unto thee *p* oil olive beaten
4 the lamps upon the *p* candlestick
6 upon the *p* table before the Lord.
7 *p* frankincense upon each row,
Dt 32.14 drink the *p* blood of the grape.
2Sa 22.27 the *p* thou wilt shew thyself *p*;
1Ki 5.11 and twenty measures of *p* oil:
6.20 he overlaid it with *p* gold; and so
21 the house within with *p* gold;
7.49 candlesticks of *p* gold, five on the
50 spoons, and the censers of *p* gold;
10.21 forest of Lebanon were of *p* gold;
1Ch 28.17 Also *p* gold for the fleshhooks,
2Ch 3. 4 he overlaid it within with *p* gold.
4.20 before the oracle, of *p* gold;
22 spoons, and the censers, of *p* gold:
9.17 ivory, and overlaid it with *p* gold.
20 forest of Lebanon were of *p* gold:
13.11 they in order upon the *p* table;
Ezr 6.20 all of them were *p*, and killed the
Job 4.17 a man be more *p* than his Maker?
8. 6 If thou wert *p* and upright; surely
11. 4 thou hast said, My doctrine is *p*,
16.17 in mine hands: also my prayer is *p*.
25. 5 the stars are not *p* in his sight.
28.19 shall it be valued with *p* gold.
Ps 12. 6 words of the Lord are *p* words:
18.26 the *p* thou wilt shew thyself *p*;
19. 8 commandment of the Lord is *p*,
21. 3 settest a crown of *p* gold on his
24. 4 hath clean hands, and a *p* heart;
119.140 Thy word is very *p*: therefore
Pr 15.26 the words of the *p* are pleasant
20. 9 heart clean. I am *p* from my sin?
11 whether his work be *p*, and
21. 8 but as for the *p*, his work is right.
30. 5 Every word of God is *p*: he is a
12 a generation that are *p* in their
Dan 7. 9 hair of his head like the *p* wool:
Mic 6.11 Shall I count them *p* with the
Zep 3. 9 turn to the people a *p* language,
Mal 1.11 unto my name, and a *p* offering:
Mt 5. 8 Blessed are the *p* in heart: for
Ac 20.26 I am *p* from the blood of all men.
Ro 14.20 All things indeed are *p*; but it is
Php 4. 8 are just, whatsoever things are *p*,
1Ti 1. 5 is charity out of a *p* heart, and of
3. 9 of the faith in a *p* conscience.
5.22 of other men's sins: keep thyself *p*.
2Ti 1. 3 my forefathers with *p* conscience,
2.22 call on the Lord out of a *p* heart.
Tit 1.15 Unto the *p* all things are *p*: but
15 and unbelieving is nothing *p*;
Heb 10.22 our bodies washed with *p* water.
Jas 1.27 *P* religion and undefiled before
3.17 wisdom that is from above is first *p*,
1Pe 1.22 love one another with a *p* heart
2Pe 3. 1 I stir up your *p* minds by way
1Jn 3. 3 purifieth himself, even as he is *p*.
Rev 15. 6 clothed in *p* and white linen, and
21.18 and the city was *p* gold, like unto
21 street of the city was *p* gold, as it
22. 1 he shewed me a *p* river of water

PURELY

Isa 1.25 and *p* purge away the dross,

PURENESS

Job 22.30 delivered by the *p* of thine hands.
Pr 22.11 He that loveth *p* of heart, for the
2Co 6. 6 By *p*, by knowledge, by

PURER

La 4. 7 Her Nazarites were *p* than snow,
Hab 1.13 art of *p* eyes than to behold evil,

PURGE

2Ch 34. 3 year he began to *p* Judah and
Ps 51. 7 *P* me with hyssop, and I shall be
65. 3 thou shalt *p* them away.
79. 9 deliver us, and *p* away our sins,
Isa 1.25 and purely *p* away thy dross, and
Eze 20.38 *p* out from among you the rebels,
43.20 thus shalt thou cleanse and *p* it.
26 Seven days shall they *p* the altar
Dan 11.35 to *p*, and to make them white,
Mal 3. 3 and *p* them as gold and silver,
Mt 3.12 he will thoroughly *p* his floor,
Lk 3.17 he will thoroughly *p* his floor,
1Co 5. 7 *P* out therefore the old leaven,
2Ti 2.21 If a man therefore *p* himself from
Heb 9.14 *p* your conscience from dead

PURGED

1Sa 3.14 shall not be *p* with sacrifice nor
2Ch 34. 8 when he had *p* the land, and the
Pr 16. 6 mercy and truth iniquity is *p*:
Isa 4. 4 have *p* the blood of Jerusalem
6. 7 is taken away, and thy sin *p*.
22.14 iniquity shall not be *p* from you
27. 9 shall the iniquity of Jacob be *p*;
Eze 24.13 lewdness: because I have *p* thee,
13 not *p*, thou shalt not be *p* from
Heb 1. 3 had by himself *p* our sins,
9.22 are by the law *p* with blood;
10. 2 worshippers once *p* should have
2Pe 1. 9 that he was *p* from his old sins.

PURGETH

Jn 15. 2 he *p* it, that it may bring forth

PURGING

Mk 7.19 into the draft, *p* all meats?

PURIFICATION

Nu 19. 9 of separation: it is a *p* for sin.
17 of the burnt heifer of *p* for sin,
2Ch 30.19 to the *p* of the sanctuary.
Neh 12.45 their God, and the ward of the *p*,
Est 2. 3 their things for *p* be given them:
9 speedily gave her her things for *p*,
Lk 2.22 And when the days of her *p*
Ac 21.26 accomplishment of the days of *p*,

PURIFICATIONS

Est 2.12 days of their *p* accomplished,

PURIFIED

Lev 8.15 with his finger, and *p* the altar,
Nu 8.21 And the Levites were *p*, and they
31.23 nevertheless it shall be *p* with the
2Sa 11. 4 she was *p* from her uncleanness:
Ezr 6.20 priests and the Levites were *p*
Neh 12.30 and the Levites *p* themselves,
30 *p* the people, and the gates, and
Ps 12. 6 furnace of earth, *p* seven times.
Dan 12.10 Many shall be *p*, and made
Ac 24.18 Asia found me *p* in the temple,
Heb 9.23 heavens should be *p* with these;
1Pe 1.22 ye have *p* your souls in obeying

PURIFIER

Mal 3. 3 sit as a refiner and *p* of silver:

PURIFIETH

Nu 19.13 and *p* not himself, defileth the
1Jn 3. 3 hath this hope in him *p* himself,

PURIFY

Nu 19.12 *p* himself with it on the third day,
12 if he *p* not himself the third day,
19 the seventh day he shall *p* himself,
20 unclean, and shall not *p* himself,
31.19 *p* both yourselves and your
20 *p* all your raiment, and all that is
Job 41.25 of breakings they *p* themselves.
Isa 66.17 and *p* themselves in the gardens

Eze 43.26 shall they purge the altar and *p* it;
Mal 3. 3 and he shall *p* the sons of Levi,
Jn 11.55 the passover, to *p* themselves.
Ac 21.24 take, and *p* thyself with them,
Tit 2.14 *p* unto himself a peculiar people,
Jas 4. 8 *p* your hearts, ye double minded.

PURIFYING

Lev 12. 4 blood of her *p* three and thirty
4 the days of her *p* be fulfilled.
5 blood of her *p* three score and
6 the days of her *p* are fulfilled,
Nu 8. 7 Sprinkle water of *p* upon them,
1Ch 23.28 and in the *p* of all holy things,
Est 2.12 things for the *p* of the women;)
Jn 2. 6 manner of the *p* of the Jews,
3.25 disciples and the Jews about *p*.
Ac 15. 9 them, *p* their hearts by faith.
21.26 the next day *p* himself with them
Heb 9.13 sanctifieth to the *p* of the flesh:

PURIM

Est 9.26 called these days *P* after the
28 these days of *P* should not fail
29 confirm this second letter of *P*.
31 To confirm these days of *P* in
32 confirmed these matters of *P*;

PURITY

1Ti 4.12 charity, in spirit, in faith, in *p*.
5. 2 the younger as sisters, with all *p*.

PURLOINING

Tit 2.10 Not *p*, but shewing all good

PURPLE

Jdg 8.26 *p* raiment that was on the kings of
Pr 31.22 tapestry; her clothing is silk and *p*.
Jer 10. 9 blue and *p* is their clothing: they
Eze 27. 7 blue and *p* from the isles of Elishah
Mk 15.17 they clothed him with *p*, and
20 they took off the *p* from him, and
Lk 16.19 was clothed in *p* and fine linen,
Jn 19. 2 and they put on him a *p* robe,
5 crown of thorns, and the *p* robe.
Ac 16.14 Lydia, a seller of *p*, of the city of
Rev 17. 4 arrayed in *p* and scarlet color,
18.12 and fine linen, and *p*, and silk,
16 was clothed in fine linen, and *p*,

PURPOSE

Ru 2.16 of the handfuls of *p* for her, and
1Ki 5. 5 I *p* to build an house unto the
2Ch 28.10 ye *p* to keep under the children
Ezr 4. 5 against them, to frustrate their *p*,
Neh 8. 4 which they had made for the *p*;
Job 33.17 may withdraw man from his *p*,
Pr 20.18 *p* is established by counsel: and
Ec 3. 1 to every *p* under the heaven:
17 a time there for every *p* and for
8. 6 Because to every *p* there is time
Isa 1.11 To what *p* is the multitude of your
14.26 is the *p* that is purposed upon
30. 7 shall help in vain, and to no *p*:
Jer 6.20 To what *p* cometh there to me
26. 3 which I *p* to do unto them because
36. 3 evil which I *p* to do unto them;
49.30 hath conceived a *p* against you.
51.29 *p* of the Lord shall be performed
Dan 6.17 that the *p* might not be changed
Mt 26. 8 saying, To what *p* is this waste?
Ac 11.23 with *p* of heart they would cleave
26.16 I have appeared unto thee for this *p*,
27.13 that they had obtained their *p*,
43 Paul, kept them from their *p*;
Ro 8.28 are the called according to his *p*.
9.11 the *p* of God according to election
17 Even for this same *p* have I raised
2Co 1.17 lightness? or the things that I *p*,
17 do I *p* according to the flesh, that
Eph 1.11 *p* of him who worketh all things
3.11 the eternal *p* which he purposed
6.22 I have sent unto you for the same *p*,
Col 4. 8 I have sent unto you for the same *p*,
2Ti 1. 9 but according to his own *p* and
3.10 doctrine, manner of life, *p*, faith,
1Jn 3. 8 For this *p* the Son...was manifested,

PURPOSED

2Ch 32. 2 that he was *p* to fight against
Ps 17. 3 I am *p* that my mouth shall not
140. 4 have *p* to overthrow my goings.
Isa 14.24 as I have *p*, so shall it stand:
26 that is *p* upon the whole earth:
27 For the Lord of hosts hath *p*, and
19.12 Lord of hosts hath *p* upon Egypt.
23. 9 The Lord of hosts hath *p* it, to
46.11 pass; I have *p* it, I will also do it.
Jer 4.28 I have *p* it, and will not repent,
49.20 hath *p* against the inhabitants
50.45 that he hath *p* against the land of
La 2. 8 The Lord hath *p* to destroy the
Dan 1. 8 Daniel *p* in his heart that he
Ac 19.21 Paul *p* in the spirit, when he had
20. 3 he *p* to return through
Ro 1.13 oftentimes I *p* to come unto you,
Eph 1. 9 which he hath *p* in himself:
3.11 which he *p* in Christ Jesus our

PURPOSETH

2Co 9. 7 according as he *p* in his heart,

PURSE

Pr 1.14 among us; let us all have one *p*:
Mk 6. 8 no bread, no money in their *p*:
Lk 10. 4 Carry neither *p*; nor scrip, nor
22.35 I sent you without *p*, and scrip,
36 he that hath a *p*, let him take it,

PURSES

Mt 10. 9 nor silver, nor brass in your *p*,

PURSUE

Gen 35. 5 did not *p* after the sons of Jacob.
Ex 15. 9 The enemy said, I will *p*, I will
Dt 19. 6 avenger of the blood *p* the slayer,
28.22 they shall *p* thee until thou perish.
45 shall *p* thee, and overtake thee,
Jos 2. 5 *p* after them quickly; for ye shall
8.16 called together to *p* after them:
10.19 *p* after your enemies, and smite
20. 5 the avenger of blood *p* after him,
1Sa 24.14 after whom dost thou *p*? after a
25.29 Yet a man is risen to *p* thee, and
26.18 my lord thus *p* after his servant?
30. 8 Shall I *p* after this troop? shall I
8 *P*: for thou shalt surely overtake
2Sa 17. 1 I will arise and *p* after David this
20. 6 lord's servants, and *p* after him,
7, 13 *p* after Sheba the son of Bichri.
24.13 thine enemies, while they *p* thee?
Job 13.25 and wilt thou *p* the dry stubble?
30.15 they *p* my soul as the wind: and
Ps 34.14 and do good; seek peace, and *p* it.
Isa 30.16 shall they that *p* you be swift.
Jer 48. 2 Madmen; the sword shall *p* thee.
Eze 35. 6 blood, and blood shall *p* thee:
6 blood, even blood shall *p* thee:
Hos 8. 3 is good: the enemy shall *p* him.
Am 1.11 did *p* his brother with the sword,
Na 1. 8 and darkness shall *p* his enemies.

PURSUETH

Lev 26.17 ye shall flee when none *p* you.
36 and they shall fall when none *p*.
37 were before a sword, when none *p*:
Pr 11.19 tendeth to life: so he that *p* evil
19 *p* it to his own death.
13.21 Evil *p* sinners: but to the
19. 7 he *p* them with words, yet they
28. 1 The wicked flee when no man *p*:

PUT

Gen 2. 8 there he *p* the man whom he had
15 *p* him into the garden of Eden to
3.15 I will *p* enmity between thee and
22 lest he *p* forth his hand, and take
8. 9 he *p* forth his hand, and took her,
19.10 But the men *p* forth their hand,
24. 2 *P*, I pray thee, thy hand under
9 the servant *p* his hand under the
47 I *p* the earring upon her face, and
26.11 his wife shall surely be *p* to death.
27.15 *p* them upon Jacob her younger
16 she *p* the skins of the kids of the
28.11 and *p* them for his pillows, and
18 stone that he had *p* for his pillows,
20 bread to eat, and raiment to *p* on,
29. 3 *p* the stone again upon the well's
30.40 he *p* his own flocks by themselves,
40 *p* them not unto Laban's cattle.
42 were feeble, he *p* them not in:
31.34 *p* them in the camel's furniture,
32.16 *p* a space betwixt drove and drove.
33. 2 And he *p* the handmaids and their
35. 2 *P* away the strange gods that are
37.34 *p* sackcloth upon his loins, and
38.14 she *p* her widow's garments off
19 and *p* on the garments of her
28 that the one *p* out his hand: and
39. 4 all that he had he *p* into his hand.
20 him, and *p* him into the prison,
40. 3 he *p* them in ward in the house of
15 should *p* me into the dungeon.
41.10 *p* me in ward in the captain of the
42 and *p* it upon Joseph's hand, and
42 and *p* a gold chain about his neck;
42.17 he *p* them altogether into ward
43.22 who *p* our money in our sacks.
44. 1 *p* every man's money in his sack's
2 *p* my cup, the silver cup, in the
46. 4 shall *p* his hand upon thine eyes.
47.29 *p*, I pray thee, thy hand under my
48.18 *p* thy right hand upon his head.
50.26 and he was *p* in a coffin in Egypt.
Ex 2. 3 pitch, and *p* the child therein;
3. 5 *p* off thy shoes from off thy feet,
22 ye shall *p* them upon your sons,
4. 4 *P* forth thine hand, and take it by
4 he *p* forth his hand, and caught it,
6 *P* now thine hand into thy bosom.
6 he *p* his hand into his bosom: and
7 *P* thine hand into thy bosom
7 *p* his hand into his bosom again;
15 him, and *p* words in his mouth:
21 which I have *p* in thine hand:
5.21 to *p* a sword in their hand to slay
8.23 *p* a division between my people
11. 7 doth *p* a difference between the
12.15 shall *p* away leaven out of your
15.26 I will *p* none of these diseases
16.33 and *p* an omer full of manna
17.12 took a stone, and *p* it under him,
14 utterly *p* out the remembrance
19.12 the mount shall be surely *p* to death:
21.12 he die, shall be surely *p* to death.
15 mother, shall be surely *p* to death.
16 hand, he shall surely be *p* to death.
17 mother, shall surely be *p* to death.
29 his owner also shall be *p* to death.
22. 5 and shall *p* his beast, and shall
8 whether he have *p* his hand unto
11 not *p* his hand unto his neighbor's
19 a beast shall surely be *p* to death.
23. 1 *p* not thine hand with the wicked
24. 6 of the blood, and *p* it in basons;
25.12 and *p* them in the four corners
14 shalt *p* the staves into the rings
16 shalt *p* into the ark the testimony
21 *p* the mercy seat above upon the
21 the ark thou shalt *p* the testimony
26 *p* the rings in the four corners that
26.11 and *p* the taches into the loops,

Ex 26.34 *p* the mercy seat upon the ark of
35 shalt *p* the table on the north side.
27. 5 *p* it under the compass of the altar
7 the staves shall be *p* into the rings,
28.12 shalt *p* the two stones upon the
23 *p* the two rings on the two ends
24 shalt *p* the two wreathen chains
25 *p* them on the shoulderpieces of the
26 shalt *p* them upon the two ends
27 *p* them on the two sides of the
30 *p* in the breastplate of judgment
37 thou shalt *p* it on a blue lace, that
41 *p* them upon Aaron thy brother,
29. 3 shalt *p* them into one basket,
5 *p* upon Aaron the coat, and the
6 shalt *p* the miter upon his head,
6 *p* the holy crown upon the miter.
8 his sons, and *p* coats upon them.
9 sons, and *p* the bonnets on them:
10 *p* their hands upon the head of
12 *p* it upon the horns of the altar
15 *p* their hands upon the head of
17 *p* them unto his pieces, and unto
19 *p* their hands upon the head of
20 *p* it upon the tip of the right ear
24 shalt *p* all in the hands of Aaron,
30 stead shall *p* them on seven days,
30. 6 *p* it before the vail that is by the
18 *p* it between the tabernacle of the
18 and thou shalt *p* water therein.
36 *p* of it before the testimony in the
31. 6 are wise hearted I have *p* wisdom,
14 defileth it shall surely be *p* to death:
15 day, he shall surely be *p* to death.
32.27 *P* every man his sword by his
33. 4 man did *p* on him his ornaments.
5 now *p* off thy ornaments from
22 I will *p* thee in a clift of the rock,
34.33 with them, he *p* a vail on his face.
35 and Moses *p* the vail upon his face
35. 2 work therein shall be *p* to death.
34 hath *p* in his heart that he may
36. 1 in whom the Lord *p* wisdom and
2 heart the Lord had *p* wisdom,
37. 5 he *p* the staves into the rings by
13 *p* the rings upon the four corners
38. 7 he *p* the staves into the rings on
39. 7 he *p* them on the shoulders of the
16 *p* the two rings in the two ends of
17 they *p* the two wreathen chains of
18 *p* them on the shoulderpieces of
19 *p* them on the two ends of the
20 and *p* them on the two sides of the
25 gold, and *p* the bells between the
40. 3 *p* therein the ark of the testimony,
5 *p* the hanging of the door to the
7 altar, and shalt *p* water therein.
13 *p* upon Aaron the holy garments,
18 *p* in the bars thereof, and reared
19 *p* the covering of the tent above
20 and *p* the testimony into the ark,
20 and *p* the mercy seat above upon
22 he *p* the table in the tent of the
24 he *p* the candlestick in the tent of
26 *p* the golden altar in the tent of the
29 he *p* the altar of burnt offering by
30 *p* water there, to wash withal.
Lev 1. 4 he shall *p* his hand upon the head
7 priest shall *p* fire upon the altar,
2. 1 it, and *p* frankincense thereon:
15 thou shalt *p* oil upon it, and lay
4. 7, 18 *p* some of the blood upon the
25, 30, 34 *p* it upon the horns of the
5.11 offering; he shall *p* no oil upon it,
11 he *p* any frankincense thereon:
6.10 shall *p* on his linen garment,
10 breeches shall he *p* upon his
10 he shall *p* them beside the altar.
11 And he shall *p* off his garments,
11 and *p* on other garments, and
12 in it; it shall not be *p* out: and
8. 7 And he *p* upon him the coat, and
7 and *p* the ephod upon him, and he
8 he *p* the breastplate upon him:
8 *p* in the breastplate the Urim and
9 he *p* the miter upon his head;
9 forefront, did he *p* the golden
13 sons, and *p* coats upon them, and
13 girdles,...*p* bonnets upon them;
15 *p* it upon the horns of the altar
23 *p* it upon the tip of Aaron's right
24 *p* of the blood upon the tip of
26 one wafer, and *p* them on the fat,
27 And he *p* all upon Aaron's hands,
9. 9 *p* it upon the horns of the altar,
20 *p* the fat upon the beasts, and he
10. 1 his censer, and *p* fire therein,
1 and *p* incense thereon, and
10 *p* difference between holy and
11.32 it must be *p* into water, and it
38 if any water be *p* upon the seed,
13.45 *p* a covering upon his upper lip,
14.14 *p* it upon the tip of the right ear
17 *p* upon the tip of the right ear
25 *p* it upon the tip of the right ear
28 shall *p* of the oil that is in his
29 shall *p* upon the head of him that
34 *p* the plague of leprosy in a house
42 *p* them in the place of those stones;
15.19 she shall be *p* apart seven days:
16. 4 He shall *p* on the holy linen coat,
4 flesh in water, and so *p* them on.
13 shall *p* the incense upon the fire
18 *p* it upon the horns of the altar
23 shall *p* off the linen garments,
23 which he *p* on when he went into
24 and *p* on his garments, and come
32 and shall *p* on the linen clothes,
18.19 is *p* apart for her uncleanness.
19.14 *p* a stumblingblock before the
20 they shall not be *p* to death,
20. 2 he shall surely be *p* to death: the
9 shall be surely *p* to death: he hath
10 adulteress shall surely be *p* to death.
11 of them shall surely be *p* to death;
12 of them shall surely be *p* to death:
13 they shall surely be *p* to death;
15 beast, he shall surely be *p* to death:
16 they shall surely be *p* to death; their
25 *p* difference between clean beasts
27 is a wizard, shall surely be *p* to death:
21. 7 woman *p* away from her husband:
10 consecrated to *p* on the garments,
22.14 *p* the fifth part thereof unto it,
24. 7 *p* pure frankincense upon each
12 And they *p* him in ward, that the
16 he shall surely be *p* to death, and all
16 of the Lord, shall be *p* to death.
17 any man shall surely be *p* to death.
21 killeth a man, he shall be *p* to death.
26. 8 of you shall *p* ten thousand to flight:
27.29 redeemed; but shall surely be *p* to
Nu 1.51 that cometh nigh shall be *p* to death.
3.10, 38 cometh nigh shall be *p* to death.
4. 6 shall *p* thereon the covering of
6 and shall *p* in the staves thereof.
7 *p* thereon the dishes, and the
8 and shall *p* in the staves thereof.
10 they shall *p* it, and all the vessels
10 skins, and shall *p* it upon a bar.
11 and shall *p* to the staves thereof:
12 *p* them in a cloth of blue, and
12 skins, and shall *p* them on a bar:
14 they shall *p* upon it all the vessels
14 skins, and *p* to the staves of it.
5. 2 *p* out of the camp every leper,
3 male and female shall ye *p* out,
3 without the camp shall ye *p* them;
4 and *p* them out without the camp:
15 it, nor *p* frankincense thereon;
17 take, and *p* it into the water:
18 *p* the offering of memorial in her
6.18 *p* it in the fire which is under the
19 *p* them upon the hands of the
27 they shall *p* my name upon the
8.10 *p* their hands upon the Levites:
11.17 thee, and will *p* it upon them;
29 the Lord would *p* his spirit upon
15.34 they *p* him in ward, because it
35 The man shall be surely *p* to death:
38 *p* upon the fringe of the borders
16. 7 And *p* fire therein,
7 *p* incense in them before the
14 thou *p* out the eyes of these men?
17 his censer, and *p* incense in them,
18 his censer, and *p* fire in them,
46 Take a censer, and *p* fire therein
46 off the altar, and *p* on incense,
47 and he *p* on incense, and made an
18. 7 that cometh nigh shall be *p* to death.
19.17 running water shall be *p* thereto
20.26, 28 and *p* them upon Eleazar his
21. 9 of brass, and *p* it upon a pole, and
23. 5 Lord *p* a word in Baalam's mouth,
12 the Lord hath *p* in my mouth?
16 and *p* a word in his mouth, and
27.20 shalt *p* some of thine honor upon
35.16, 17, 18 shall surely be *p* to death.
21 smote him shall surely be *p* to death;
30 shall be *p* to death by the mouth of
31 but he shall be surely *p* to death.
36. 3 shall be *p* to the inheritance of
4 their inheritance be *p* unto the
Dt 2.25 I begin to *p* the dread of thee
7.15 will *p* none of the evil diseases of
22 thy God will *p* out those nations
10. 2 and thou shalt *p* them in the ark.
5 *p* the tables in the ark which I had
11.29 shalt *p* the blessing upon mount
12. 5 your tribes to *p* his name there,
7 in all that ye *p* your hand unto,
21 hath chosen to *p* his name there
13. 5 of dreams shall be *p* to death;
5 *p* the evil away from the midst of
9 be first upon him to *p* him to death,
16. 9 beginnest to *p* the sickle to the corn.
17. 6 that is worthy of death be *p* to death;
6 witness he shall not be *p* to death,
7 be first upon him to *p* him to death,
7 *p* the evil away from among you.
12 shalt *p* away the evil from Israel.
18.18 will *p* my words in his mouth;
19.13 *p* away the guilt of innocent
19 *p* the evil away from among you.
21. 9 *p* away the guilt of innocent blood
13 *p* the raiment of her captivity
21 *p* evil away from among you;
22 he be to be *p* to death, and thou hang
22. 5 a man *p* on a woman's garment:
19 may not *p* her away all his days.
21 *p* evil away from among you.
22 thou *p* away evil from Israel.
24 shalt *p* away evil from among you.
29 may not *p* her away all his days.
23.24 thou shalt not *p* any in thy vessel.
24. 7 *p* evil away from among you.
16 fathers shall not be *p* to death for the
16 children be *p* to death for the
16 shall be *p* to death for his own sin.
25. 6 his name be not *p* out of Israel.
26. 2 shalt *p* it in a basket, and shalt
28.14 *p* a yoke of iron upon the neck
30. 7 thy God will *p* all these curses
31.19 *p* it in the mouths, that this
26 law, and *p* it in the side of the ark
32.30 two *p* ten thousand to flight, except
33.10 they shall *p* incense before thee,
14 precious things *p* forth by the
Jos 1.18 him, he shall be *p* to death:
6.24 they *p* into the treasury of the
7. 6 and *p* dust upon their heads.
11 *p* it even among their own stuff.
10.24 *p* your feet upon the necks of

24 *p* their feet upon the necks of
17.13 they *p* the Canaanites to tribute;
24. 7 he *p* darkness between you and
14 and *p* away the gods which your
23 *p* away, said he, the strange gods
Jdg 1.28 they *p* the Canaanites to tribute,
3.21 And Ehud *p* forth his left hand,
5.26 She *p* her hand to the nail, and her
6.19 flour: the flesh he *p* in a basket,
19 he *p* the broth in a pot, and
21 angel of the Lord *p* forth the end
31 be *p* to death whilst it is yet morning:
37 *p* a fleece of wool in the floor; and
7.16 *p* a trumpet in every man's hand,
8.27 *p* it in his city, even in Ophrah:
9.15 and *p* your trust in my shadow;
26 of Shechem *p* their confidence in
49 and *p* them to the hold, and set
10.16 *p* away the strange gods from
12. 3 I *p* my life in my hands, and
14.12 I will now *p* forth a riddle unto
13 *P* forth thy riddle, that we may
16 *p* forth a riddle unto the children
15. 4 and *p* a firebrand in the midst
15 and *p* forth his hand, and took it,
16. 3 *p* them upon his shoulders, and
21 took him, and *p* out his eyes, and
18. 7 *p* them to shame in any thing;
21 *p* the little ones and the cattle
20.13 Gibeah, that we may *p* them to
13 and *p* away evil from Israel.
20 Israel *p* themselves in array to fight
22 *p* themselves in array the first day.
30 *p* themselves in array against
33 *p* themselves in array at Baal-tamar:
21. 5 saying, He shall surely be *p* to death.
Ru 3. 3 and *p* thy raiment upon thee,
1Sa 1.14 *p* away thy wine from thee.
2.36 *P* me, I pray thee, into one of the
4. 2 Philistines *p* themselves in array,
6. 8 *p* the jewels of gold, which ye
15 and *p* them on the great stone:
7. 3 then *p* away the strange gods and
4 did *p* away Baalim and Ashtaroth,
8.16 asses, and *p* them to his work.
11.11 *p* the people in three companies;
12 men, that we may *p* them to death.
13 not a man be *p* to death this day:
14.26 no man *p* his hand to his mouth:
27 he *p* forth the end of the rod that
27 and *p* his hand to his mouth; and
17.21 Philistines had *p* the battle in array,
38 *p* an helmet of brass upon his
39 them. And David *p* them off him.
40 *p* them in a shepherd's bag which
49 And David *p* his hand in his bag,
54 but he *p* his armor in his tent.
19. 5 For he did *p* his life in his hand,
13 *p* a pillow of goat's hair for his
21. 6 to *p* hot bread in the day when it
22.17 king would not *p* forth their hand
24.10 will not *p* forth mine hand against
28. 3 *p* away those that had familiar
8 himself, and *p* on other raiment,
21 I have *p* my life in my hand, and
31.10 they *p* his armor in the house of
2Sa 1.24 who *p* on ornaments of gold upon
3.34 bound, nor thy feet *p* into fetters,
6. 6 Uzzah *p* forth his hand to the ark
7.15 Saul, whom I *p* away before thee.
8. 2 two lines measured he to *p* to death,
6 David *p* garrisons in Syria of
14 And he *p* garrisons in Edom;
14 all Edom *p* he garrisons, and all
10. 8 *p* the battle in array at the entering
9 *p* them in array against the Syrians:
10 that he might *p* them in array
12.13 Lord also hath *p* away thy sin;
31 therein, and *p* them under saws,
13.17 *P* now this woman out from me,
19 Tamar *p* ashes on her head, and

14. 2 and *p* on now mourning apparel,
3 Joab *p* the words in her mouth.
19 he *p* all these words in the mouth
15. 5 he *p* forth his hand, and took him,
17.23 *p* his household in order, and hanged
18.12 would I not *p* forth mine hand
19.21 not Shimei be *p* to death for this,
22 there any man be *p* to death this day
20. 3 *p* them in ward, and fed them,
21. 9 *p* to death in the days of harvest,
1Ki 2. 5 *p* the blood of war upon his girdle
8 not *p* thee to death with the sword.
24 Adonijah shall be *p* to death this
26 will not at this time *p* thee to death,
35 the king *p* Benaiah the son of
35 priest did the king *p* in the room of
5. 3 *p* them under the soles of his feet.
7.39 he *p* five bases on the right side
51 *p* among the treasures of the house
8. 9 which Moses *p* there at Horeb,
9. 3 built, to *p* my name there for ever;
10.17 *p* them in the house of the forest
24 which God had *p* in his heart.
11.36 chosen me to *p* my name there.
12. 4 heavy yoke which he *p* upon us,
9 thy father did *p* upon us lighter?
29 Beth-el, and the other *p* he in Dan.
13. 4 *p* forth his hand from the altar,
4 hand, which he *p* forth against
14.21 of Israel, to *p* his name there.
18.23, 23 on wood, and *p* no fire under:
25 of your gods, but *p* no fire under.
33 And he *p* the wood in order, and
42 and *p* his face between his knees,
20. 6 they shall *p* it in their hand, and
24 and *p* captains in their rooms:
31 pray thee, *p* sackcloth on our loins,
32 loins, and *p* ropes on their heads,
21.27 and *p* sackcloth upon his flesh,
22.10 throne, having *p* on their robes,
23 hath *p* a lying spirit in the mouth
27 *P* this fellow in the prison, and
30 battle; but *p* thou on thy robes.
2Ki 2.20 a new cruse, and *p* salt therein.
3. 2 he *p* away the image of Baal that
21 all that were able to *p* on armor,
4.34 and *p* his mouth upon his mouth,
6. 7 he *p* out his hand, and took it.
9.13 and *p* it under him on the top of
10. 7 and *p* their heads in baskets, and
11.12 king's son, and *p* the crown upon
12. 9 *p* therein all the money that was
10 *p* up in bags, and told the money
13.16 *P* thine hand upon the bow.
16 And he *p* his hand upon it: and
16 Elisha *p* his hands upon the king's
14. 6 not be *p* to death for the children,
6 be *p* to death for the fathers;
6 shall be *p* to death for his own sin:
12 was *p* to the worse before Israel;
16.14 *p* it on the north side of the altar.
17 *p* it upon a pavement of stones.
17.29 *p* them in the houses of the high
18.11 *p* them in Halah and in Habor
24 *p* thy trust on Egypt for chariots and
19.28 I will *p* my hook in thy nose, and
21. 4 In Jerusalem will I *p* my name.
7 Israel, will I *p* my name for ever:
23. 5 he *p* down the idolatrous priests,
24 did Josiah *p* away, that he might
33 *p* him in bands at Riblah in the
33 *p* the land to a tribute of an hundred
25. 7 *p* out the eyes of Zedekiah, and
1Ch 5.20 because they *p* their trust in him.
10.10 *p* his armor in the house of their
11.19 that have *p* their lives in jeopardy?
12.15 and they *p* to flight all them of the
13. 9 Uzza *p* forth his hand to hold the
10 because he *p* his hand to the ark:
18. 6 *p* garrisons in Syria-damascus;
13 And he *p* garrisons in Edom; and

19. 9 and *p* the battle in array before the
10 *p* them in array against the Syrians.
16 were *p* to the worse before Israel,
17 when David had *p* the battle in array
19 saw that they were *p* to the worse
21.27 and he *p* up his sword again into
27.24 was the number *p* in the account
2Ch 1. 5 he *p* before the tabernacle of the
2.14 device which shall be *p* to him,
3.16 *p* them on the heads of the pillars;
16 and *p* them on the chains.
4. 6 and *p* five on the right hand, and
5. 1 *p* he among the treasures of the
10 two tables which Moses *p* therein
6.11 in it have I *p* the ark, wherein is
20 thou wouldest *p* thy name there;
24 thy people Israel be *p* to the worse
9.16 And the king *p* them in the house
23 wisdom,...God had *p* in his heart.
10. 4 his heavy yoke that he *p* upon us,
9 yoke that thy father did *p* upon us?
11 father *p* a heavy yoke upon you,
11 you, I will *p* more to your yoke:
11.11 holds, and *p* captains in them,
12 several city he *p* shields and spears,
12.13 of Israel, to *p* his name there.
15. 8 *p* away the abominable idols out
13 God of Israel should be *p* to death,
16.10 and *p* him in a prison house; for
17.19 whom the king *p* in the fenced
18.22 hath *p* a lying spirit in the mouth
26 *P* this fellow in the prison, and
29 battle; but *p* thou on thy robes.
22.11 and *p* him and his nurse in a
23. 7 the house, he shall be *p* to death:
11 son, and *p* upon him the crown,
25.22 was *p* to the worse before Israel,
29. 7 and *p* out the lamps, and have not
33. 7 Israel, will I *p* my name for ever:
14 *p* captains of war in all the fenced
34.10 *p* it in the hand of the workmen
35. 3 *P* the holy ark in the house which
24 *p* him in the second chariot that
36. 3 Egypt *p* him down at Jerusalem,
7 *p* them in his temple at Babylon.
22 his kingdom, and *p* it also in writing,
Ezr 1. 1 his kingdom, and *p* it also in writing,
7 *p* them in the house of his gods;
2.62 as polluted, *p* from the priesthood.
6.12 shall *p* to their hand to alter and
7.27 *p* such a thing as this in the king's
10. 3 our God to *p* away all the wives,
19 they would *p* away their wives;
Neh 2.12 *p* in my heart to do at Jerusalem:
3. 5 *p* not their necks to the work of
4.23 me, none of us *p* off our clothes,
23 every one *p* them off for washing.
6.14 that would have *p* me in fear.
19 Tobiah sent letters to *p* me in fear.
7. 5 And my God *p* into mine heart to
64 as polluted, *p* from the priesthood.
Est 4. 1 and *p* on sackcloth with ashes,
11 is one law of his to *p* him to death,
5. 1 Esther *p* on her royal apparel,
8. 3 to *p* away the mischief of Haman
9. 1 drew near to be *p* in execution,
Job 1.11 But *p* forth thine hand now, and
12 himself *p* not forth thine hand.
2. 5 But *p* forth thine hand now, and
4.18 Behold, he *p* no trust in his servants;
11.14 be in thine hand, *p* it far away,
13.14 and *p* my life in mine hand?
17. 3 now, *p* me in a surety with thee;
18. 5 light of the wicked shall be *p* out,
6 his candle shall be *p* out with him.
19.13 hath *p* my brethren far from me,
21.17 is the candle of the wicked *p* out!
22.23 *p* away iniquity far from thy
23. 6 but he would *p* strength in me.
27.17 but the just shall *p* it on, and the
29.14 I *p* on righteousness, and it

Job 38.36 *p* wisdom in the inward parts?
41. 2 thou *p* an hook into his nose?
Ps 2.12 are all they that *p* their trust in him.
4. 5 and *p* your trust in the Lord.
7 Thou hast *p* gladness in my heart,
5.11 that *p* their trust in thee rejoice:
7. 1 my God in thee did I *p* my trust:
8. 6 hast *p* all things under his feet:
9. 5 thou hast *p* out their name for
10 thy name will *p* their trust in thee:
20 *P* them in fear, O Lord: that the
11. 1 In the Lord *p* I my trust: how say ye
16. 1 O God: for in thee do I *p* my trust.
17. 7 them which *p* their trust in thee from
18.22 not *p* away his statutes from me.
25.20 be ashamed; for I *p* my trust in thee.
27. 9 *p* not thy servant away in anger:
30.11 thou hast *p* off my sackcloth, and
31. 1 In thee, O Lord, do I *p* my trust; let
18 Let the lying lips be *p* to silence;
35. 4 and *p* to shame that seek after my
36. 7 *p* their trust under the shadow of thy
40. 3 hath *p* a new song in my mouth,
14 and *p* to shame that wish me evil.
44. 7 hast *p* them to shame that hated us.
9 thou hast cast off, and *p* us to shame;
53. 5 thou hast *p* them to shame, because
55.20 He hath *p* forth his hands against
56. 4 his word, in God I have *p* my trust;
8 *p* thou my tears into thy bottle:
11 In God have I *p* my trust: I will not
70. 2 backward, and *p* to confusion,
71. 1 In thee, O Lord, do I *p* my trust:
1 trust: let me never be *p* to confusion.
73.28 I have *p* my trust in the Lord God,
78.66 *p* them to a perpetual reproach.
83.17 yea, let them be *p* to shame, and
88. 8 hast *p* away mine acquaintance
18 and friend hast thou *p* far from me,
118. 8 Lord than to *p* confidence in man.
9 Lord than to *p* confidence in princes.
119.31 O Lord, *p* me not to shame.
125. 3 the righteous *p* forth their hands
146. 3 *P* not your trust in princes, nor in
Pr 4.24 *P* away from thee a froward
24 and perverse lips *p* far from thee.
8. 1 understanding *p* forth her voice?
13. 9 lamp of the wicked shall be *p* out.
20.20 shall be *p* out in obscure darkness.
23. 2 And *p* a knife to thy throat, if thou
24.20 of the wicked shall be *p* out.
25. 6 *P* not forth thyself in the
7 shouldest be *p* lower in the presence
8 thy neighbor hath *p* thee to shame.
10 he that heareth it *p* thee to shame,
30. 5 unto them that *p* their trust in him.
Ec 3.14 nothing can be *p* to it, nor any
10.10 then must he *p* to more strength:
11.10 and *p* away evil from thy flesh:
SS 5. 3 I have *p* off my coat; how shall I
3 my coat; how shall I *p* it on?
4 beloved *p* in his hand by the hole
Isa 1.16 *p* away the evil of your doings
5.20 *p* darkness for light, and light for
20 that *p* bitter for sweet, and sweet
10.13 *p* down the inhabitants like a
11. 8 *p* his hand on the cockatrice' den.
20. 2 and *p* off thy shoe from thy foot.
36. 9 *p* thy trust on Egypt for chariots and
37.29 will I *p* my hook in thy nose, and
42. 1 I have *p* my spirit upon him: he
43.26 *P* me in remembrance; let us plead
47.11 thou shalt not be able to *p* it off:
50. 1 divorcement, whom I have *p* away?
1 transgressions is your mother *p*
51. 9 *p* on strength, O arm of the Lord;
16 I have *p* my words in thy mouth,
23 *p* it into the hand of them that
52. 1 awake; *p* on thy strength, O Zion;
1 *p* on thy beautiful garments, O
53.10 he hath *p* him to grief: when thou
54. 4 for thou shalt not be *p* to shame:
59.17 For he *p* on righteousness as a
17 he *p* on the garments of vengeance
21 which I have *p* in thy mouth,
63.11 that *p* his holy Spirit within him?
Jer 1. 9 Then the Lord *p* forth his hand,
9 I have *p* my words in thy mouth.
3. 1 If a man *p* away his wife, and she
8 I had *p* her away, and given her
19 How shall I *p* thee among the
4. 1 *p* away thine abominations out of
7.21 *P* your burnt offerings unto your
8.14 our God hath *p* us to silence,
12.13 they have *p* themselves to pain, but
13. 1 girdle, and *p* it upon thy loins,
1 thy loins, and *p* it not in water.
2 of the Lord, and *p* it on my loins.
18.21 and let their men be *p* to death;
20. 2 and *p* him in the stocks that were
26.15 that if ye *p* me to death, ye shall
19 and all Judah *p* him at all to death?
21 the king sought to *p* him to death:
24 hand of the people to *p* him to death.
27. 2 yokes, and *p* them upon thy neck,
8 not *p* their neck under the yoke of
28.14 *p* a yoke of iron upon the neck of
29.26 thou shouldest *p* him in prison,
31.33 will *p* my law in their inward parts,
32.14 *p* them in an earthen vessel, that
40 I will *p* my fear in their hearts,
37. 4 for they had not *p* him into prison.
15 *p* him in prison in the house of
18 that ye have *p* me in prison?
38. 4 thee, let this man be *p* to death:
7 had *p* Jeremiah in the dungeon;
12 *P* now these old cast clouts and
15 wilt thou not surely *p* me to death?
16 I will not *p* thee to death, neither will
25 us, and we will not *p* thee to death;
39. 7 Moreover he *p* out Zedekiah's
18 because thou hast *p* thy trust in me,
40.10 and *p* them in your vessels, and
43. 3 that they might *p* us to death, and
46. 4 spears, and *p* on the brigandines.
47. 6 *p* up thyself into thy scabbard,
50.14 *P* yourselves in array against
42 every one *p* in array, like a man to
52.11 he *p* out the eyes of Zedekiah;
11 *p* him in prison till the day of his
27 *p* them to death in Riblah in the land
Eze 3.25 they shall *p* bands upon thee,
4. 9 and *p* them in one vessel, and
8. 3 *p* forth the form of an hand, and
17 they *p* the branch to their nose.
10. 7 *p* it into the hands of him that
11.19 I will *p* a new spirit within you;
14. 3 and *p* the stumblingblock of their
16.11 I *p* bracelets upon thy hands, and
12 I *p* a jewel on thy forehead, and
14 which I had *p* upon thee,
17. 2 Son of man, *p* forth a riddle, and
19. 9 they *p* him in ward in chains, and
22.26 *p* no difference between the holy and
23.42 *p* bracelets upon their hands, and
24.17 *p* on thy shoes upon thy feet, and
26.16 *p* off their broidered garments:
29. 4 I will *p* hooks in thy jaws, and I
30.13 will *p* a fear in the land of Egypt.
21 to *p* a roller to bind it, to make it
24 and *p* my sword in his hand: but
25 *p* my sword into the hand of the
32. 7 when I shall *p* thee out, I will
25 *p* in the midst of them that be
36.26 a new spirit will I *p* within you:
27 I will *p* my spirit within you, and
37. 6 *p* breath in you, and ye shall live;
14 shall *p* my spirit in you,and ye
19 and will *p* them with him, even
38. 4 back, and *p* hooks into thy jaws,
42.14 and shall *p* on other garments,
43. 9 let them *p* away their whoredom,
20 and *p* it on the four horns of it,
44.19 they shall *p* off their garments
19 they shall *p* on other garments;
22 a widow, nor her that is *p* away:
45.19 *p* it upon the posts of the house,
Dan 5.19 and whom he would he *p* down.
29 and *p* a chain of gold about his neck,
Hos 2. 2 therefore *p* away her whoredoms
Joel 3.13 *P* ye in the sickle, for the harvest
Am 6. 3 Ye that *p* far away the evil day, and
Jon 3. 5 a fast, and *p* on sackcloth, from
Mic 2.12 will *p* them together as the sheep
7. 5 *p* ye not confidence in a guide:
Zep 3.19 where they have been *p* to shame.
Hag 1. 6 wages to *p* it into a bag with holes.
Mt 1.19 was minded to *p* her away privily.
5.15 candle, and *p* it under a bushel,
31 Whosoever shall *p* away his wife,
32 whosoever shall *p* away his wife,
6.25 for your body, what ye shall *p* on.
8. 3 And Jesus *p* forth his hand, and
9.16 that which is *p* in to fill it up taketh
17 do men *p* new wine into old bottles:
17 they *p* new wine into new bottles,
25 when the people were *p* forth, he
10.21 and cause them to be *p* to death.
12.18 I will *p* my spirit upon him, and
13.24, 31 parable *p* he forth unto them,
14. 3 *p* him in prison for Herodias' sake,
5 he would have *p* him to death,
19. 3 for a man to *p* away his wife for
6 together, let not man *p* asunder.
7 divorcement, and to *p* her away?
8 suffered you to *p* away your wives:
9 Whosoever shall *p* away his wife,
9 marrieth her which is *p* away doth
13 he should *p* his hands on them,
21. 7 and *p* on them their clothes, and
22.34 had *p* the Sadducees to silence,
25.27 *p* my money to the exchangers,
26.52 *P* up again thy sword into his
59 against Jesus, to *p* him to death;
27. 1 against Jesus, to *p* him to death:
6 for to *p* them into the treasury,
28 him, and *p* on him a scarlet robe.
29 thorns, they *p* it upon his head,
31 and *p* his own raiment on him,
48 *p* it on a reed, and gave him to
Mk 1.14 after that John was *p* in prison,
41 compassion, *p* forth his hand,
2.22 wine must be *p* into new bottles.
4.21 brought to be *p* under a bushel,
5.40 But when he had *p* them all out,
6. 9 sandals; and not *p* on two coats.
7.32 beseech him to *p* his hand upon
33 *p* his fingers into his ears, and he
8.23 *p* his hands upon him, he asked
25 *p* his hands again upon his eyes,
10. 2 for a man to *p* away his wife?
4 divorcement, and to *p* her away.
9 together, let not man *p* asunder.
11 shall *p* away his wife, and marry
12 woman shall *p* away her husband,
16 *p* his hands upon them, and
13.12 shall cause them to be *p* to death.
14. 1 him by craft, and *p* him to death.
55 against Jesus to *p* him to death;
15.17 thorns, and *p* it about his head,
20 *p* his own clothes on him, and led
36 full of vinegar, and *p* it on a reed,
Lk 1.52 He hath *p* down the mighty from
5.13 he *p* forth his hand, and touched
38 new wine must be *p* into new
8.54 *p* them all out, and took her by
9.62 having *p* his hand to the plow,
12.22 for the body, what ye shall *p* on.
14. 7 And he *p* forth a parable to those
15.22 the best robe, and *p* it on him;
22 *p* a ring on his hand, and shoes on
16. 4 I am *p* out of the stewardship,
18 that is *p* away from her husband

18.33 scourge him, and *p* him to death:
21.16 shall they cause to be *p* to death.
23.32 led with him to be *p* to death.
Jn 5. 7 troubled, to *p* me into the pool:
9.15 He *p* clay upon mine eyes, and I
22 he should be *p* out of the synagogue.
11.53 together for to *p* him to death.
12. 6 bag, and bare what was *p* therein.
10 might *p* Lazarus also to death;
42 should be *p* out of the synagogue:
13. 2 now *p* into the heart of Judas
16. 2 shall *p* you out of the synagogues:
18.11 *P* up thy sword into the sheath:
31 for us to *p* any man to death:
19. 2 of thorns, and *p* it on his head,
2 and they *p* on him a purple robe,
19 a title, and *p* it on the cross.
29 vinegar, and *p* it upon hyssop,
29 and *p* it to his mouth.
20.25 *p* my finger into the print of the
Ac 1. 7 Father hath *p* in his own power.
4. 3 *p* them in hold unto the next day:
5.18 and *p* them in the common prison.
25 the men whom ye *p* in prison are
34 *p* the apostles forth a little space;
7.33 *P* off thy shoes from thy feet:
9.40 But Peter *p* them all forth, and
12. 4 him, he *p* him in prison,
19 that they should be *p* to death.
13.46 seeing ye *p* it from you, and judge
15. 9 *p* no difference between us and
10 to *p* a yoke upon the neck of the
26.10 when they were *p* to death, I gave
27. 6 into Italy; and he *p* us therein.
Ro 13.12 let us *p* on the armor of light.
14 But *p* ye on the Lord Jesus Christ,
14.13 that no man *p* a stumblingblock
1Co 5.13 *p* away from among yourselves
7.11 not the husband *p* away his wife.
12 with him, let him not *p* her away.
13.11 a man, I *p* away childish things.
15.24 he shall have *p* down all rule and
25 hath *p* all enemies under his feet.
27 hath *p* all things under his feet.
27 saith all things are *p* under him,
27 which did *p* all things under him.
28 subject unto him that *p* all things
53 corruptible must *p*...incorruption,
53 this mortal must *p* on immortality.
54 shall have *p* on incorruption, and
54 mortal shall have *p* on immortality,
2Co 3.13 which *p* a vail over his face, that
8.16 which *p* the same earnest care
Gal 3.27 into Christ have *p* on Christ.
Eph 1.22 hath *p* all things under his feet,
4.22 That ye *p* off concerning the former
24 that ye *p* on the new man, which
31 evil speaking, be *p* away from you,
6.11 *P* on the whole armor of God,
Col 3. 8 also *p* off all these; anger, wrath,
9 *p* off the old man with his deeds;
10 have *p* on the new man, which is
12 *P* on therefore, as the elect of God,
14 above all these things *p* on charity,
1Th 2. 4 to be *p* in trust with the gospel,
1Ti 1.19 having *p* away concerning faith
4. 6 *p* the brethren in remembrance
2Ti 1. 6 I *p* thee in remembrance that
2.14 things *p* them in remembrance,
Tit 3. 1 *P* them in mind to be subject to
Phm 18 ought, *p* that on mine account;
Heb 2. 5 *p* in subjection the world to come,
8 *p* all things in subjection under his
8 he *p* all in subjection under him,
8 nothing that is not *p* under him.
8 not yet all things *p* under him.
13 again, I will *p* my trust in him.
6. 6 and *p* him to an open shame.
8.10 I will *p* my laws into their mind,
9.26 to *p* away sin by the sacrifice of
10.16 I will *p* my laws into their hearts,
Jas 3. 3 we *p* bits in the horses' mouths,
1Pe 2.15 may *p* to silence the ignorance of
3.18 being *p* to death in the flesh, but
2Pe 1.12 to *p* you always in remembrance
14 I must *p* off this my tabernacle,
Jude 5 therefore *p* you in remembrance,
Rev 2.24 *p* upon you none other burden:
11. 9 dead bodies to be *p* in graves.
17.17 *p* in their hearts to fulfil his will,

PUTEOLI

Ac 28.13 we came the next day to *P*:

PUTTETH

Ex 30.33 *p* any of it upon a stranger, shall
Nu 22.38 word that God *p* in my mouth,
Dt 25.11 and *p* forth her hand, and taketh
27.15 and *p* it in a secret place.
1Ki 20.11 boast himself as he that *p* it off.
Job 15.15 Behold, he *p* no trust in his saints;
28. 9 *p* forth his hand upon the rock;
33.11 He *p* my feet in the stocks, he
Ps 15. 5 He that *p* not out his money to
75.7 he *p* down one, and setteth up
Pr 28.25 he that *p* his trust in the Lord shall be
29.25 whoso *p* his trust in the Lord shall be
SS 2.13 fig tree *p* forth her green figs,
Isa 57.13 he that *p* his trust in me shall
Jer 43.12 as a shepherd *p* on his garment;
La 3.29 He *p* his mouth in the dust; if so
Eze 14. 4, 7 *p* the stumblingblock of his
Mic 3. 5 he that *p* not into their mouths,
Mt 9.16 *p* a piece of new cloth unto an old
24.32 is yet tender, and *p* forth leaves,
Mk 2.22 no man *p* new wine into old bottles:
4.29 immediately he *p* in the sickle,
13.28 is yet tender, and *p* forth leaves,
Lk 5.36 *p* a piece of a new garment upon
37 man *p* new wine into old bottles;
8.16 with a vessel, or *p* it under a bed;
11.33 a candle, *p* it in a secret place,
16.18 Whosoever *p* away his wife, and
Jn 10. 4 when he *p* forth his own sheep,

PUTTING

Gen 21.14 *p* it on her shoulder, and the
Lev 16.21 *p* them...the head of the goat,
Jdg 7. 6 lapped, *p* their hand to their mouth,
Isa 58. 9 *p* forth of the finger, and speaking
Mal 2.16 Israel, saith that he hateth *p* away:
Ac 9.12 coming in,...*p* his hand on him,
17 *p* his hands on him said, Brother
19.33 the Jews *p* him forward. And
Ro 15.15 as *p* you in mind, because of the
Eph 4.25 Wherefore *p* away lying, speak
Col 2.11 *p* off the body of the sins of the
1Th 5. 8 *p* on the breastplate of faith and
1Ti 1.12 faithful, *p* me into the ministry;
2Ti 1. 6 in thee by the *p* on of my hands.
1Pe 3. 3 of gold, or of *p* on of apparel;
21 the *p* away of the filth of the flesh,
2Pe 1.13 you up by *p* you in remembrance;

QUAILS
Ex 16.13 pass, that at even the *q* came up,
Nu 11.31 brought *q* from the sea, and let
32 next day, and they gathered the *q*:
Ps 105.40 people asked, and he brought *q*,

QUAKE
Joel 2.10 The earth shall *q* before them;
Na 1. 5 The mountains *q* at him, and the
Mt 27.51 and the earth did *q*, and the rocks
Heb 12.21 said, I exceedingly fear and *q*:)

QUAKED
Ex 19.18 and the whole mount *q* greatly.
1Sa 14.15 also trembled, and the earth *q*:

QUAKING
Eze 12.18 Son of man, eat thy bread with *q*,
Dan 10. 7 but a great *q* fell upon them, so

QUARREL
Lev 26.25 avenge the *q* of my covenant:
2Ki 5. 7 see how he seeketh a *q* against me.
Mk 6.19 Herodias had a *q* against him,
Col 3.13 if any man have a *q* against any:

QUARTER
Gen 19. 4 all the people from every *q*:
Nu 34. 3 *q* shall be from the wilderness
Jos 15. 5 north *q* was from the bay of the sea
18.14 of Judah: this was the west *q*.
15 the south *q* was from the end of
Isa 47.15 shall wander every one to his *q*;
56.11 every one for his gain, from his *q*.
Mk 1.45 they came to him from every *q*.

QUARTERS
Ex 13. 7 leaven seen with thee in all thy *q*.
Dt 22.12 upon the four *q* of thy vesture,
1Ch 9.24 In four *q* were the porters,
Jer 49.36 winds from the four *q* of heaven,
Eze 38. 6 of Togarmah of the north *q*,
Ac 9.32 as Peter passed throughout all *q*,
16. 3 the Jews which were in those *q*:
28. 7 In the same *q* were possessions
Rev 20. 8 are in the four *q* of the earth,

QUARTUS
Ro 16.23 saluteth you, and *Q* a brother.

QUATERNIONS
Ac 12. 4 delivered him to four *q* of soldiers

QUEEN
1Ki 10. 1 the *q* of Sheba heard of the fame
4 when the *q* of Sheba had seen all
10 which the *q* of Sheba gave to king
13 unto the *q* of Sheba all her desire,
11.19 wife, the sister of Tahpenes the *q*.
15.13 even her he removed from being *q*,
2Ki 10.13 the king and the children of the *q*.
2Ch 9. 1 *q* of Sheba heard of the fame of
3 *q* of Sheba had seen the wisdom of
9 the *q* of Sheba gave king Solomon.
12 Solomon gave to the *q* of Sheba all
15.16 he removed her from being *q*,
Neh 2. 6 me, (the *q* also sitting by him,)
Est 1. 9 Vashti the *q* made a feast for the
11 bring Vashti the *q* before the king
12 the *q* Vashti refused to come at the
15 do unto the *q* Vashti according to
16 Vashti the *q* hath not done wrong
17 deed of the *q* shall come abroad
17 Vashti the *q* to be brought in
18 have heard of the deed of the *q*.
2. 4 which pleaseth the king be *q*
17 and made her *q* instead of Vashti.
22 who told it unto Esther the *q*;
4. 4 was the *q* exceedingly grieved;
5. 2 Esther the *q* standing in the court,
3 her, What wilt thou, *q* Esther?
12 the *q* did let no man come in with
7. 1 came to banquet with Esther the *q*.
2 What is thy petition, *q* Esther?
3 Esther the *q* answered and said,
5 said unto Esther the *q*, Who is he,
6 afraid before the king and the *q*.
7 request for his life to Esther the *q*;
8 Will he force the *q* also before me
8. 1 Jews' enemy unto Esther the *q*.
7 Ahasuerus said unto Esther the *q*,
9.12 the king said unto Esther the *q*,
29 Then Esther the *q*, the daughter of
31 Esther the *q* had enjoined them,
Ps 45. 9 right hand did stand the *q* in gold
Jer 7.18 to make cakes to the *q* of heaven,
13.18 Say unto the king and to the *q*,
29. 2 king, and the *q*, and the eunuchs,
44.17 incense unto the *q* of heaven,
18 to burn incense to the *q* of heaven,
19 burned incense to the *q* of heaven,
25 to burn incense to the *q* of heaven,
Dan 5.10 the *q* by reason of the words of
10 the *q* spake and said, O king, live
Mt 12.42 The *q* of the south shall rise up in
Lk 11.31 The *q* of the south shall rise up in
Ac 8.27 under Candace *q* of the Ethiopians,
Rev 18. 7 for she saith in her heart, I sit a *q*,

QUEENS
SS 6. 8 are threescore *q*, and fourscore
9 yea, the *q* and the concubines, and
Isa 49.23 and their *q* thy nursing mothers:

QUENCH
2Sa 14. 7 they shall *q* my coal which is left,
21.17 that thou *q* not the light of Israel.
Ps 104.11 the wild asses *q* their thirst.
SS 8. 7 Many waters cannot *q* love,
Isa 1.31 together, and none shall *q* them.
42. 3 the smoking flax shall he not *q*:
Jer 4. 4 fire, and burn that none can *q* it,
21.12 fire, and burn that none can *q* it,
Am 5. 6 there be none to *q* it in Beth-el.
Mt 12.20 and smoking flax shall he not *q*,
Eph 6.16 *q* all the fiery darts of the wicked.
1Th 5.19 *Q* not the Spirit.

QUENCHED
Nu 11. 2 unto the Lord, the fire was *q*.
2Ki 22.17 this place, and shall not be *q*.
2Ch 34.25 this place, and shall not be *q*.
Ps 118.12 they are *q* as the fire of thorns:
Isa 34.10 It shall not be *q* night nor day;
43.17 they are extinct, they are *q* as tow.
66.24 die, neither shall their fire be *q*;
Jer 7.20 it shall burn, and shall not be *q*.
17.27 of Jerusalem, and it shall not be *q*.
Eze 20.47 the flaming flame shall not be *q*,
48 have kindled it: it shall not be *q*.
Mk 9.43 into the fire that never shall be *q*:
44 dieth not, and the fire is not *q*.
45 into the fire that never shall be *q*:
46 dieth not, and the fire is not *q*.
48 dieth not, and the fire is not *q*.
Heb 11.34 *Q* the violence of fire, escaped the

QUESTION
Mt 22.35 which was a lawyer, asked him a *q*,
Mk 8.11 began to *q* with him, seeking of

The Queen of Sheba's visit to Solomon presages the church's coming to Christ, as depicted by Rubens.

9.16 the scribes, What *q* ye with them?
11.29 I will also ask of you one *q*, and
12.34 man after that durst ask him any *q*:
Lk 20.40 they durst not ask him any *q* at all.
Jn 3.25 there arose a *q* between some of
Ac 15. 2 apostles and elders about this *q*.
18.15 if it be a *q* of words and names,
19.40 we are in danger to be called in *q*
23. 6 of the dead I am called in *q*.
24.21 I am called in *q* by you this day.
1Co 10.25 asking no *q* for conscience sake:
27 asking no *q* for conscience sake.

QUESTIONED
2Ch 31. 9 Hezekiah *q* with the priests and
Mk 1.27 that they *q* among themselves,
Lk 23. 9 he *q* with him in many words;

QUESTIONING
Mk 9.10 *q* one with another what the
14 them, and the scribes *q* with them.

QUESTIONS
1Ki 10. 1 came to prove him with hard *q*.
3 And Solomon told her all her *q*:
2Ch 9. 1 to prove Solomon with hard *q* at
2 And Solomon told her all her *q*:
Mt 22.46 that day forth ask him any more *q*.
Lk 2.46 hearing them, and asking them *q*.
Ac 23.29 to be accused of *q* of their law,
25.19 But had certain *q* against him of
20 I doubted of such manner of *q*,
26. 3 to be expert in all customs and *q*
1Ti 1. 4 genealogies, which minister *q*,
6. 4 about *q* and strifes of words,
2Ti 2.23 But foolish and unlearned *q* avoid,
Tit 3. 9 avoid foolish *q*, and genealogies,

QUICK
Lev 13.10 there be *q* raw flesh in the rising;
24 *q* flesh that burneth have a white
Nu 16.30 and they go down *q* into the pit;
Ps 55.15 and let them go down *q* into hell:
124. 3 they had swallowed us up *q*, when
Isa 11. 3 shall make him of *q* understanding
Ac 10.42 to be the Judge of *q* and dead.
2Ti 4. 1 shall judge the *q* and the dead at
Heb 4.12 the word of God is *q*, and powerful,
1Pe 4. 5 ready to judge the *q* and the dead.

QUICKEN
Ps 71.20 sore troubles, shalt *q* me again,
80.18 *q* us, and we will call upon thy
119.25 *q* thou me according to thy word.
37 vanity; and *q* thou me in thy way.
40 *q* me in thy righteousness.
88 *Q* me after thy lovingkindness; so
107 *q* me, O Lord, according unto thy
149 *q* me according to thy judgment.
154 me: *q* me according to thy word.
156 *q* me according to thy judgments.
159 *q* me, O Lord, according to thy
143.11 *Q* me, O Lord, for thy name's sake;
Ro 8.11 also *q* your mortal bodies by his

QUICKENED
Ps 119.50 affliction: for thy word hath *q* me.
93 for with them thou hast *q* me.
1Co 15.36 that which thou sowest is not *q*,
Eph 2. 1 you hath he *q*, who were dead
5 hath *q* us together with Christ,
Col 2.13 flesh, hath he *q* together with him,
1Pe 3.18 in the flesh, but *q* by the Spirit:

QUICKENETH
Jn 5.21 raiseth up the dead, and *q* them;
21 even so the Son *q* whom he will.
6.63 It is the spirit that *q*; the flesh
Ro 4.17 even God, who *q* the dead, and
1Ti 6.13 the sight of God, who *q* all things,

QUICKENING
1Co 15.45 last Adam was made a *q* spirit.

QUICKLY
Gen 18. 6 Make ready *q* three measures of
27.20 is it that thou hast found it so *q*,
Ex 32. 8 turned aside *q* out of the way
Nu 16.46 go *q* unto the congregation, and
Dt 9. 3 them out, and destroy them *q*,
12 get thee down *q* from hence;
12 they are *q* turned aside out of the
16 had turned aside *q* out of the way
11.17 lest ye perish *q* from off the good
28.20 and until thou perish *q*; because
Jos 2. 5 pursue after them *q*; for ye shall
8.19 the ambush arose *q* out of their
10. 6 come up to us *q*, and save us, and
23.16 ye shall perish *q* from off the good
Jdg 2.17 they turned *q* out of the way
1Sa 20.19 then thou shalt go down *q*, and
2Sa 17.16 Now therefore send *q*, and tell
18 they went both of them away *q*,
21 Arise, and pass *q* over the water:
2Ki 1.11 hath the king said, Come down *q*.
2Ch 18. 8 Fetch *q* Micaiah the Son of Imla.
Ec 4.12 a threefold cord is not *q* broken.
Mt 5.25 Agree with thine adversary *q*,
28. 7 And go *q*, and tell his disciples
8 departed *q* from the sepulchre
Mk 16. 8 they went out *q*, and fled from the
Lk 14.21 Go out *q* into the streets and
16. 6 and sit down *q*, and write fifty.
Jn 11.29 she arose *q*, and came unto him.
13.27 unto him, That thou doest, do *q*.
Ac 12. 7 him up, saying, Arise up *q*.
22.18 get thee *q* out of Jerusalem:
Rev 2. 5 or else I will come unto thee *q*,
16 or else I will come unto thee *q*,
3.11 Behold, I come *q*: hold that fast
11.14 behold, the third woe cometh *q*.
22. 7 Behold, I come *q*: blessed is he
12 I come *q*; and my reward is with
20 saith, Surely I come *q*. Amen.

QUICKSANDS
Ac 27.17 lest they should fall into the *q*,

QUIET
Jdg 16. 2 were *q* all the night, saying, In
18. 7 of the Zidonians, *q* and secure;
27 a people that were at *q* and secure:
2Ki 11.20 rejoiced, and the city was in *q*:
1Ch 4.40 the land was wide, and *q*, and
2Ch 14. 1 his days the land was *q* ten years.
5 the kingdom was *q* before him.
20.30 the realm of Jehoshaphat was *q*:
23.21 the city was *q*, after that they had
Job 3.13 should I have lain still and been *q*,
26 had I rest, neither was I *q*;
21.23 being wholly at ease and *q*.
Ps 35.20 them that are *q* in the land.
107.30 are they glad because they be *q*;
Pr 1.33 and shall be *q* from fear of evil.
Ec 9.17 of wise men are heard in *q* more
Isa 7. 4 Take heed, and be *q*; fear not,
14. 7 whole earth is at rest, and is *q*:
32.18 dwellings, and in *q* resting places;
33.20 shall see Jerusalem a *q* habitation,
Jer 30.10 shall be in rest, and be *q*, and
47. 6 how long will it be ere thou be *q*?
7 How can it be *q*, seeing the Lord
49.23 sorrow on the sea; it cannot be *q*.
51.59 And this Seraiah was a *q* prince.
Eze 16.42 be *q*, and will be no more angry.
Na 1.12 Though they be *q*, and likewise
Ac 19.36 ye ought to be *q*, and to do
1Th 4.11 that ye study to be *q*, and to do
1Ti 2. 2 may lead a *q* and peaceable life
1Pe 3. 4 ornament of a meek and *q* spirit,

QUIETED
Ps 131. 2 I have behaved and *q* myself,
Zec 6. 8 have *q* my spirit in the north

QUIETETH
Job 37.17 he *q* the earth by the south wind?

QUIETLY
2Sa 3.27 in the gate to speak with him *q*,
La 3.26 *q* wait for the salvation of the Lord.

QUIETNESS
Jdg 8.28 the country was in *q* forty years
1Ch 22. 9 will give peace and *q* unto Israel
Job 20.20 he shall not feel *q* in his belly,
34.29 When he giveth *q*, who then can
Pr 17. 1 is a dry morsel, and *q* therewith,
Ec 4. 6 Better is an handful with *q*, than
Isa 30.15 in *q* and in confidence shall be
32.17 *q* and assurance for ever.
Ac 24. 2 that by thee we enjoy great *q*,
2Th 3.12 that with *q* they work, and eat

QUIT
Ex 21.19 shall he that smote him be *q*:
28 the owner of the ox shall be *q*.
Jos 2.20 then we will be *q* of thine oath
1Sa 4. 9 and *q* yourselves like men,
9 *q* yourselves like men, and fight.
1Co 16.13 faith, *q* you like men, be strong.

QUITE
Gen 31.15 hath *q* devoured also our money.
Ex 23.24 and *q* break down their images.
Nu 17.10 *q* take away their murmurings
33.52 *q* plucked down all their high places:
2Sa 3.24 sent him away, and he is *q* gone?
Job 6.13 and is wisdom driven *q* from me?
Hab 3. 9 Thy bow was made *q* naked,

QUIVER
Gen 27. 3 thy weapons, thy *q* and thy bow,
Job 39.23 The *q* rattleth against him, the
Ps 127. 5 Happy is the man that hath his *q*
Isa 22. 6 Elam bare the *q* with chariots of
49. 2 shaft; in his *q* hath he hid me;
Jer 5.16 Their *q* is as an open sepulchre,
La 3.13 of his *q* to enter into my reins.

QUIVERED
Hab 3.16 trembled; my lips *q* at the voice:

R

RABBI

Mt 23. 7 and to be called of men, *R*, *R*.
8 But be not ye called *R*: for one is
Jn 1.38 They said unto him, *R*, (which is
49 him, *R*, thou art the Son of God;
3. 2 *R*, we know...thou art a teacher
26 *R*, he that was with thee beyond
6.25 *R*, when camest thou hither?

RABBONI

Jn 20.16 herself, and saith unto him, *R*;

RACA

Mt 5.22 shall say to his brother, *R*, shall

RACE

Ps 19. 5 as a strong man to run a *r*.
Ec 9.11 the *r* is not to the swift, nor the
1Co 9.24 they which run in a *r* run all, but
Heb 12. 1 patience the *r* that is set before us,

RACHEL

Gen 29. 6 *R* his daughter cometh with the
9 *R* came with her father's sheep:
10 Jacob saw *R* the daughter of Laban
11 Jacob kissed *R*, and lifted up his
12 And Jacob told *R* that he was her
16 the name of the younger was *R*.
17 *R* was beautiful and well favored.
18 And Jacob loved *R*; and said, I
18 will serve thee seven years for *R*
20 Jacob served seven years for *R*;
25 did I not serve with thee for *R*?
28 gave him *R* his daughter to wife
29 And Laban gave to *R* his daughter
30 he went in also unto *R*, and he
30 he loved also *R* more than Leah,
31 her womb: but *R* was barren.
30. 1 when *R* saw that she bare Jacob
1 *R* envied her sister; and said unto
2 Jacob's anger...kindled against *R*:
6 *R* said, God hath judged me, and
8 And *R* said, With great wrestlings
14 *R* said to Leah, Give me, I pray
15 And *R* said, Therefore he shall lie
22 And God remembered *R*, and God
25 pass, when *R* had borne Joseph,
31. 4 Jacob sent and called *R* and Leah
14 *R* and Leah answered and said
19 and *R* had stolen the images that
32 knew not that *R* had stolen them.
34 Now *R* had taken the images, and
33. 1 children unto Leah, and unto *R*,
2 and *R* and Joseph hindermost.
7 after came Joseph near and *R*,
35.16 and *R* travailed, and she had hard
19 *R* died, and was buried in the way
24 sons of *R*; Joseph, and Benjamin:
46.19 The sons of *R*, Jacob's wife;
22 These are the sons of *R*, which
25 Laban gave unto *R* his daughter,
48. 7 *R* died by me in the land of Canaan
Ru 4.11 thine house like *R* and like Leah,
Mt 2.18 *R* weeping for her children, and

RACHEL

Daughter of Laban, wife of Jacob, and mother of Joseph and Benjamin; is first encountered at a well near her home in Haran by Jacob, who has fled to Mesopotamia to escape Esau's vengeance; discovering they are cousins, she runs to tell her father; Jacob falls in love with her and offers to serve Laban seven years for her; when, at the end of that time, he is instead given her older sister Leah, he agrees to serve a further seven years and is allowed to marry her (Gen 29); is rebuked by her husband when she complains of her barrenness; desperate for a child, requests Leah to give her some of Reuben's mandrakes (a fruit believed to have fertilizing properties); at last gives birth to Joseph (Gen 30); with Leah supports Jacob's decision to flee; steals her father's images and, when he pursues, hides them under her on her camel (Gen 31); dies giving birth to a second son, whom she calls Benoni ("son of my sorrow") but whom Jacob, though heartbroken, renames Benjamin ("son of the right hand"); is buried near Bethlehem (Gen 35).

RAGE

2Ki 5.12 he turned and went away in a *r*.
19.27 coming in, and thy *r* against me.
28 Because thy *r* against me and thy
2Ch 16.10 for he was in a *r* with him because
28. 9 slain them in a *r* that reacheth
Job 39.24 the ground with fierceness and *r*:
40.11 Cast abroad the *r* of thy wrath:
Ps 2. 1 Why do the heathen *r*, and the
7. 6 because of the *r* of mine enemies:
Pr 6.34 For jealousy is the *r* of a man:
29. 9 whether he *r* or laugh, there is
Isa 37.28 coming in, and thy *r* against me.
29 Because thy *r* against me, and thy
Jer 46. 9 ye horses; and *r*, ye chariots;
Dan 3.13 Nebuchadnezzar in his *r* and
Hos 7.16 sword for the *r* of their tongue:
Na 2. 4 The chariots shall *r* in the streets,
Ac 4.25 Why did the heathen *r*, and the

RAGED

Ps 46. 6 The heathen *r*, the kingdoms

RAGETH

Pr 14.16 but the fool *r*, and is confident.

RAGING

Ps 89. 9 Thou rulest the *r* of the sea:
Pr 20. 1 is a mocker, strong drink is *r*:
Jon 1.15 and the sea ceased from her *r*.
Lk 8.24 the wind and the *r* of the water:
Jude 13 *R* waves of the sea, foaming out

RAGS

Pr 23.21 shall clothe a man with *r*.
Isa 64. 6 righteousnesses are as filthy *r*;
Jer 38.11 old cast clouts and old rotten *r*,
12 and rotten *r* under thine armholes

RAHAB

Jos 2. 1 into an harlot's house, named *R*,
3 the king of Jericho sent unto *R*,
6.17 only *R* the harlot shall live, she
23 spies went in, and brought out *R*,
25 Joshua saved *R* the harlot alive,
Ps 87. 4 make mention of *R* and Babylon
89.10 Thou hast broken *R* in pieces, as
Isa 51. 9 Art thou not it that hath cut *R*,
Heb 11.31 By faith the harlot *R* perished
Jas 2.25 was not *R* the harlot justified by

RAHEL

Jer 31.15 *R* weeping for her children

RAILED

1Sa 25.14 our master; and he *r* on them.
Mk 15.29 And they that passed by *r* on him,
Lk 23.39 which were hanged *r* on him,

RAILER

1Co 5.11 idolater, or a *r*, or a drunkard,

RAILING

1Pe 3. 9 rendering evil for evil, or *r* for *r*:
2Pe 2.11 bring not *r* accusation against
Jude 9 bring against him a *r* accusation,

RAILINGS

1Ti 6. 4 whereof cometh envy, strife, *r*, evil

RAIMENT

Gen 24.53 of gold, and *r*, and gave them to
27.15 goodly *r* of her eldest son Esau,
27 and he smelled the smell of his *r*,
28.20 me bread to eat, and *r* to put on,
41.14 changed his *r*, and came in unto
45.22 he gave each man changes of *r*;
22 of silver, and five changes of *r*.
Ex 3.22 of silver, and jewels of gold, and *r*:
12.35 of silver, and jewels of gold, and *r*:
21.10 her food, her *r*, and her duty of
22. 9 for ass, for sheep, for *r*, or for any
26 take thy neighbor's *r* to pledge,
27 only, it is his *r* for his skin:
Lev 11.32 it be any vessel of wood, or *r*, or
Nu 31.20 purify all your *r*, and all that is
Dt 8. 4 Thy *r* waxed not old upon thee,
10.18 stranger, in giving him food and *r*.
21.13 the *r* of her captivity from off her,
22. 3 and so shalt thou do with his *r*;
24.13 that he may sleep in his own *r*,
17 nor take a widow's *r* to pledge:
Jos 22. 8 with iron, and with very much *r*:
Jdg 3.16 under his *r* upon his right thigh.
8.26 purple *r* that was on the kings of
Ru 3. 3 thee, and put thy *r* upon thee,
1Sa 28. 8 and put on other *r*, and he went,
2Ki 5. 5 pieces of gold, and ten changes of *r*.
7. 8 gold, and *r*, and went and hid it;
2Ch 9.24 vessels of gold, and *r*, harness,
Est 4. 4 and she sent *r* to clothe Mordecai,
Job 27.16 dust, and prepare *r* as the clay;
Ps 45.14 unto the king in *r* of needlework:
Isa 14.19 as the *r* of those that are slain,
63. 3 and I will stain all my *r*.
Eze 16.13 thy *r* was of fine linen, and silk,
Zec 3. 4 will clothe thee with change of *r*.
Mt 3. 4 John had his *r* of camel's hair,
6.25 than meat, and the body than *r*?
28 And why take ye thought for *r*?
11. 8 for to see? A man clothed in soft *r*?
17. 2 and his *r* was white as the light.
27.31 put his own *r* on him, and led him
28. 3 and his *r* white as snow:
Mk 9. 3 his *r* became shining, exceeding
Lk 7.25 to see? A man clothed in soft *r*?
9.29 his *r* was white and glistering.
10.30 thieves, which stripped him of his *r*,
12.23 meat, and the body is more than *r*.
23.34 they parted his *r*, and cast lots.
Jn 19.24 They parted my *r* among them,
Ac 18. 6 he shook his *r*, and said unto them,
22.20 kept the *r* of them that slew him.
1Ti 6. 8 And having food and *r* let us be
Jas 2. 2 come in also a poor man in vile *r*;
Rev 3. 5 same shall be clothed in white *r*;
18 and white *r*, that thou mayest be
4. 4 elders sitting, clothed in white *r*;

Rachel meets Jacob (Gen 29) in this fresco from the Raphael Logge at the Vatican, completed in 1519.

RAIN

Gen 2. 5 not caused it to *r* upon the earth,
7. 4 I will cause it to *r* upon the earth
12 the *r* was upon the earth forty
8. 2 the *r* from heaven was restrained;
Ex 9.18 cause it to *r* a very grievous hail,
33 *r* was not poured upon the earth.
34 when Pharaoh saw that the *r* and
16. 4 will *r* bread from heaven for you;
Lev 26. 4 I will give you *r* in due season,
Dt 11.11 drinketh water of the *r* of heaven:
14 I will give you the *r* of your land
14 in his due season, the first *r* and
14 and the latter *r*, that thou mayest
17 up the heaven, that there be no *r*,
28.12 the *r* unto thy land in his season,
24 make the *r* of thy land powder and
32. 2 My doctrine shall drop as the *r*, my
2 the small *r* upon the tender herb,
1Sa 12.17 and he shall send thunder and *r*;
18 the Lord sent thunder and *r* that
2Sa 1.21 neither let there be *r*, upon you,
23. 4 the earth by clear shining after *r*.
1Ki 8.35 is shut up, and there is no *r*,
36 and give *r* upon thy land, which
17. 1 shall not be dew nor *r* these years,
7 there had been no *r* in the land.
14 the Lord sendeth *r* upon the earth.
18. 1 and I will send *r* upon the earth.
41 is a sound of abundance of *r*,
44 thee down, that the *r* stop thee not.
45 and wind, and there was a great *r*.
2Ki 3.17 see wind, neither shall ye see *r*;
2Ch 6.26 is shut up, and there is no *r*,
27 send *r* upon thy land, which thou
7.13 shut up heaven that there be no *r*,
Ezr 10. 9 of this matter, and for the great *r*.
13 it is a time of much *r*, and we are
Job 5.10 Who giveth *r* upon the earth, and
20.23 *r* it upon him while he is eating.
28.26 When he made a decree for the *r*,
29.23 they waited for me as for the *r*;
23 mouth wide as for the latter *r*.
36.27 they pour down *r* according to the
37. 6 to the small *r*, and to the great *r*
38.26 To cause it to *r* on the earth,
28 Hath the *r* a father? or who hath
Ps 11. 6 Upon the wicked he shall *r* snares,
68. 9 didst send a plentiful *r*, whereby
72. 6 come down like *r* upon the mown
84. 6 a well; the *r* also filleth the pools.
105.32 He gave them hail for *r*, and
135. 7 he maketh lightnings for the *r*;
147. 8 who prepareth *r* for the earth,
Pr 16.15 favor is as a cloud of the latter *r*.
25.14 is like clouds and wind without *r*.
23 The north wind driveth away *r*: so
26. 1 and as *r* in harvest, so honor is
28. 3 sweeping *r* which leaveth no food.
Ec 11. 3 If the clouds be full of *r*, they
12. 2 nor the clouds return after the *r*:
SS 2.11 is past, the *r* is over and gone;
Isa 4. 6 a covert from storm and from *r*.
5. 6 the clouds that they *r* no
6 clouds that they...no *r* upon it.
30.23 shall he give the *r* of thy seed,
44.14 an ash, and the *r* doth nourish it.
55.10 For as the *r* cometh down, and the
Jer 3. 3 and there hath been no latter *r*;
5.24 the Lord our God, that giveth *r*,
10.13 he maketh lightnings with *r*, and
14. 4 for there was no *r* in the earth,
22 of the Gentiles that can cause *r*?
51.16 he maketh lightnings with *r*, and
Eze 1.28 is in the cloud in the day of *r*,
38.22 I will *r* upon him, and upon his
22 an overflowing *r*, and great
Hos 6. 3 and he shall come unto us as the *r*,
3 as the latter and former *r* unto the
10.12 and *r* righteousness upon you.
Joel 2.23 you the former *r* moderately,
23 cause to come down for you the *r*,
23 down for you...the former *r*,
23 the latter *r* in the first month.
Am 4. 7 have withholden the *r* from you,
7 I caused it to *r* upon one city,
7 it not to *r* upon another city:
Zec 10. 1 Ask ye of the Lord *r* in the time of
1 of the latter *r*; so the Lord shall
1 and give them showers of *r*, to
14.17 even upon them shall be no *r*.
18 not up, and come not, that have no *r*;
Mt 5.45 sendeth *r* on the just and on the
7.25, 27 And the *r* descended, and the
Ac 14.17 and gave us *r* from heaven, and
28. 2 because of the present *r*, and
Heb 6. 7 the earth which drinketh in the *r*
Jas 5. 7 he receive the early and latter *r*.
17 earnestly that it might not *r*:
18 again, and the heaven gave *r*,
Rev 11. 6 it *r* not in the days of their

RAINBOW

Rev 4. 3 was a *r* round about the throne,
10. 1 a *r* was upon his head, and his

RAINED

Gen 19.24 *r* upon Sodom and Gomorrah
Ex 9.23 *r* hail upon the land of Egypt.
Ps 78.24 *r* down manna upon them to eat,
27 He *r* flesh also upon them as dust,
Eze 22.24 *r* upon in the day of indignation.
Am 4. 7 one piece was *r* upon, and the
7 whereupon it *r* not withered.
Lk 17.29 *r* fire and brimstone from heaven,
Jas 5.17 *r* not on the earth for the space of

RAINY

Pr 27.15 *r* day and contentious woman are

RAISE

Gen 38. 8 her, and *r* up seed to thy brother.
Ex 23. 1 Thou shalt not *r* a false report:
Dt 18.15 God will *r* up unto thee a Prophet
18 I will *r* them up a Prophet from
25. 7 to *r* up unto his brother a name
Jos 8.29 *r* thereon a great heap of stones,
Ru 4. 5, 10 *r* up the name of the dead upon
1Sa 2.35 will *r* me up a faithful priest, that
2Sa 12.11 I will *r* up evil against thee out of
17 him, to *r* him up from the earth:
1Ki 14.14 Lord shall *r* him up a king over
1Ch 17.11 that I will *r* up thy seed after thee,
Job 3. 8 ready to *r* up their mourning.
19.12 and *r* up their way against me,
30.12 they *r* up against me the ways of
Ps 41.10 merciful unto me, and *r* me up,
Isa 15. 5 shall *r* up a cry of destruction.
29. 3 and I will *r* forts against thee.
44.26 and I will *r* up the decayed places
49. 6 servant to *r* up the tribes of Jacob,
58.12 thou shalt *r* up the foundation
61. 4 shall *r* up the former desolations,
Jer 23. 5 *r* unto David a righteous Branch,
30. 9 king, whom I will *r* up unto them.
50. 9 I will *r* and cause to come up
32 fall, and none shall *r* him up:
51. 1 I will *r* up against Babylon, and
Eze 23.22 will *r* up thy lovers against thee,
34.29 I will *r* up for them a plant of
Hos 6. 2 in the third day he will *r* us up, and
Joel 3. 7 I will *r* them out of the place
Am 5. 2 land; there is none to *r* her up.
6.14 I will *r* up against you a nation,
9.11 day will I *r* up the tabernacle of
11 I will *r* up his ruins, and I will
Mic 5. 5 we *r* against him seven shepherds,
Hab 1. 3 that *r* up strife and contention.
6 lo, I *r* up the Chaldeans, that
Zec 11.16 will *r* up a shepherd in the land,
Mt 3. 9 to *r* up children unto Abraham.
10. 8 sick, cleanse the lepers, *r* the dead,
22.24 and *r* up seed unto his brother.
Mk 12.19 and *r* up seed unto his brother.
Lk 3. 8 to *r* up children unto Abraham.
20.28 and *r* up seed unto his brother.
Jn 2.19 and in three days I will *r* it up.
6.39 *r* it up again at the last day.
40, 44, 54 will *r* him up at the last day.
Ac 2.30 *r* up Christ to sit on his throne;
3.22 shall the Lord your God *r* up unto
7.37 shall the Lord your God *r* up unto
26. 8 you, that God should *r* the dead?
1Co 6.14 will also *r* up us by his own power.
2Co 4.14 Jesus shall *r* up us also by Jesus,
Heb 11.19 that God was able to *r* him up,
Jas 5.15 sick, and the Lord shall *r* him up;

RAISED

Ex 9.16 for this cause have I *r* thee up,
Jdg 2.16 Nevertheless the Lord *r* up judges,
Ezr 1. 5 all them whose spirit God had *r*,
Isa 41. 2 Who *r* up the righteous man from

Isa 45.13 I have *r* him up in righteousness,
Jer 29.15 The Lord hath *r* us up prophets
51.11 the Lord hath *r* up the spirit of
Am 2.11 I *r* up of your sons for prophets,
Mt 1.24 Joseph being *r* from sleep did as
11. 5 the deaf hear, the dead are *r* up,
16.21 and be *r* again the third day.
17.23 the third day he shall be *r* again.
Lk 1.69 *r* up an horn of salvation for us
7.22 the deaf hear, the dead are *r*, to
9.22 be slain, and be *r* the third day.
20.37 Now that the dead are *r*, even
Jn 12. 1 dead, whom he *r* from the dead.
9 whom he had *r* from the dead.
17 *r* him from the dead, bare record.
Ac 2.24 Whom God hath *r* up, having
32 This Jesus hath God *r* up, whereof
3.15 whom God hath *r* from the dead;
26 God, having *r* up his Son Jesus,
4.10 whom God *r* from the dead, even
5.30 God of our fathers *r* up Jesus,
10.40 Him God *r* up the third day, and
12. 7 *r* him up, saying, Arise up quickly.
13.22 he *r* up unto them David to be
23 *r* unto Israel a Saviour, Jesus:
30 But God *r* him from the dead:
33 in that he hath *r* up Jesus again;
34 that he *r* him up from the dead,
37 he, whom God *r* again, saw no
50 *r* persecution against Paul and
17.31 that he hath *r* him from the dead.
Ro 4.24 believe on him that *r* up Jesus
25 was *r* again for our justification.
6. 4 as Christ was *r* up from the dead
9 Christ being *r* from the dead dieth
7. 4 to him who is *r* from the dead,
8.11 him that *r* up Jesus from the dead
11 he that *r* up Christ from the dead
9.17 same purpose have I *r* thee up,
10. 9 God hath *r* him from the dead,
1Co 6.14 God hath both *r* up the Lord, and
15.15 of God that he *r* up Christ:
15 whom he *r* not up, if so be that the
16 dead rise not, then is not Christ *r*:
17 Christ be not *r*, your faith is vain;
35 will say, How are the dead *r* up?
42 corruption, it is *r* in incorruption:
43 sown in dishonor; it is *r* in glory:
43 sown in weakness; it is *r* in power:
44 body; it is *r* a spiritual body.
52 dead shall be *r* incorruptible, and
2Co 4.14 that he which *r* up the Lord
Gal 1. 1 Father, who *r* him from the dead;)
Eph 1.20 when he *r* him from the dead, and
2. 6 hath *r* us up together, and made
Col 2.12 who hath *r* him from the dead.
1Th 1.10 whom he *r* from the dead, even
2Ti 2. 8 seed of David was *r* from the dead
Heb 11.35 received their dead *r* to life again:
1Pe 1.21 God, that *r* him up from the dead,

RAISETH

1Sa 2. 8 He *r* up the poor out of the dust,
Job 41.25 When he *r* up himself, the
Ps 107.25 and *r* the stormy wind, which
113. 7 *r* up the poor out of the dust,
145.14 *r* up all those that be bowed down.
146. 8 *r* them that are bowed down:
Jn 5.21 For as the Father *r* up the dead,
2Co 1. 9 but in God which *r* the dead:

RAISING

Hos 7. 4 from *r* after he hath kneaded
Ac 24.12 neither *r* up the people,

RAM

Gen 15. 9 and a *r* of three years old, and a
22.13 *r* caught in a thicket by his horns:
13 Abraham went and took the *r*, and
Ex 29.15 Thou shalt also take one *r*; and
16 And thou shalt slay the *r*, and thou

A ram is provided for Abraham to sacrifice instead of Isaac (Gen 22); by Julius Schnorr von Carolsfeld.

18 burn the whole *r* upon the altar:
22 for it is a *r* of consecration:
32 his sons shall eat the flesh of the *r*,
Lev 5.15 unto the Lord a *r* without blemish
8.18 the *r* for the burnt offering:
29 the *r* of consecration it was Moses'
Ezr 10.19 a *r* of the flock for their trespass.
Dan 8. 3 the river a *r* which had two horns:
4 I saw the *r* pushing westward, and
7 I saw him come close unto the *r*,
7 and smote the *r*, and brake his two
7 and there was no power in the *r* to
7 could deliver the *r* out of his hand.

RAMA

Mt 2.18 In *R* was there a voice heard,

RAMS

1Sa 15.22 and to hearken than the fat of *r*.
Ps 114. 4 The mountains skipped like *r*, and
6 mountains, that ye skipped like *r*;
Isa 1.11 am full of the burnt offerings of *r*,
60. 7 the *r* of Nebaioth shall minister
Mic 6. 7 be pleased with thousands of *r*,

RAN

Gen 18. 2 he *r* to meet them from the tent
7 Abraham *r* unto the herd, and
24.17 And the servants *r* to meet her,
20 and *r* again unto the well to draw
28 the damsel *r*, and told them of her
29 Laban *r* out unto the man, unto
29.12 son: and she *r* and told her father.
13 son, that he *r* to meet him, and
33. 4 Esau *r* to meet him, and embraced
Ex 9.23 the fire *r* along upon the ground;
Nu 11.27 there *r* a young man, and told
16.47 and *r* into the midst of the
Jos 7.22 and they *r* unto the tent; and,
8.19 they *r* as soon as he had stretched
Jdg 7.21 and all the host *r*, and cried, and
9.44 other companies *r* upon all the
13.10 the woman made haste, and *r*,
1Sa 3. 5 And he *r* unto Eli, and said, Here
4.12 And there *r* a man of Benjamin
10.23 they *r* and fetched him thence: and
17.22 and *r* into the army, and came and
48 and *r* toward the army to meet the
51 Therefore David *r*, and stood upon
20.36 And as the lad *r*, he shot an arrow
2Sa 18.21 bowed himself unto Joab, and *r*.
23 Ahimaaz *r* by the way of the plain,
1Ki 2.39 of the servants of Shimei *r* away
18.35 the water *r* round about the altar;
46 *r* before Ahab to the entrance of
19.20 left the oxen, and *r* after Elijah,
22.35 the blood *r* out of the wound into
2Ch 32. 4 the brook that *r* through the
Ps 77. 2 my sore *r* in the night, and
105.41 *r* in the dry places like a river.
133. 2 that *r* down upon the beard, even
Jer 23.21 sent these prophets, yet they *r*:
Eze 1.14 living creatures *r* and returned
47. 2 *r* out waters on the right side.
Dan 8. 6 *r* unto him in the fury of his
Mt 8.32 swine *r* violently down a steep
27.48 straightway one of them *r*, and
Mk 5. 6 afar off, he *r* and worshipped him,
13 *r* violently down a steep place
6.33 *r* afoot thither out of all cities,
55 And *r* through that whole region
15.36 one *r* and filled a spunge full of
Lk 8.33 herd *r* violently down a steep
15.20 *r*, and fell on his neck, and kissed
19. 4 he *r* before, and climbed up into
24.12 Peter, and *r* unto the sepulchre;
Jn 20. 4 So they *r* both together: and the
Ac 3.11 people *r* together unto them in
7.57 and *r* upon him with one accord,
8.30 And Philip *r* thither to him, and
12.14 the gate for gladness, but *r* in,
14.14 *r* in among the people, crying out,
21.30 and the people *r* together: and
32 centurions, and *r* down unto them:

27.41 they *r* the ship aground; and the
Jude 11 and *r* greedily after the error of

RANG
1Sa 4. 5 shout, so that the earth *r* again.
1Ki 1.45 rejoicing, so that the city *r* again.

RANGE
Job 39. 8 The *r* of the mountains is his

RANGING
Pr 28.15 As a roaring lion, and a *r* bear;

RANKS
1Ki 7. 4, 5 was against light in three *r*.
Joel 2. 7 and they shall not break their *r*:
Mk 6.40 And they sat down in *r*, by

RANSOM
Ex 21.30 the *r* of his life whatsoever is
30.12 give every man a *r* for his soul
Job 33.24 down to the pit: I have found a *r*.
36.18 then a great *r* cannot deliver thee.
Ps 49. 7 nor give to God a *r* for him:
Pr 6.35 He will not regard any *r*; neither
13. 8 The *r* of a man's life are his riches:
21.18 The wicked shall be a *r* for the
Isa 43. 3 I gave Egypt for thy *r*, Ethiopia
Hos 13.14 I will *r* them from the power of
Mt 20.28 and to give his life a *r* for many.
Mk 10.45 and to give his life a *r* for many.
1Ti 2. 6 Who gave himself a *r* for all, to be

RANSOMED
Isa 35.10 the *r* of the Lord shall return,
51.10 sea a way for the *r* to pass over?
Jer 31.11 *r* him from the hand of him that

RASH
Ec 5. 2 Be not *r* with thy mouth, and let
Isa 32. 4 *r* shall understand knowledge,

RASHLY
Ac 19.36 to be quiet, and to do nothing *r*.

RATHER
2Ki 5.13 how much *r* then, when he saith to
Job 7.15 strangling, and death *r* than my life,
32. 2 he justified himself *r* than God.
Ps 84.10 I had *r* be a doorkeeper in the
Pr 8.10 and knowledge *r* than choice gold.
16.16 understanding *r* to be chosen than
17.12 a man, *r* than a fool in his folly.
22. 1 A good name is *r* to be chosen than
Jer 8. 3 And death shall be chosen *r* than life
Mt 10. 6 But go *r* to the lost sheep of the
28 *r* fear him which is able to destroy
18. 8 *r* than having two hands or two
9 *r* than having two eyes to be cast
25. 9 go ye *r* to them that sell, and buy
27.24 but that *r* a tumult was made, he
Mk 5.26 nothing bettered, but *r* grew worse,
15.11 should *r* release Barabbas unto
Lk 10.20 but *r* rejoice, because your names
11.28 Yea *r*, blessed are they that hear
41 *r* give alms of such things as ye
12.31 But *r* seek ye the kingdom of God;
51 I tell you, Nay; but *r* division:
17. 8 And will not *r* say unto him, Make
18.14 his house justified *r* than the other:
Jn 3.19 men loved darkness *r* than light,
Ac 5.29 We ought to obey God *r* than men.
Ro 3. 8 And not *r*, (as we be slanderously
8.34 died, yea *r*, that is risen again,
11.11 *r* through their fall salvation is come
12.19 but *r* give place unto wrath: for
14.13 but judge this *r*, that no man put
1Co 5. 2 puffed up, and have not *r* mourned,
6. 7 Why do ye not *r* take wrong? why
7 *r* suffer yourselves to be defrauded?
7.21 thou mayest be made free, use it *r*.
9.12 this power over you, are not we *r*?
14. 1 gifts, but *r* that ye may prophesy.
5 tongues, but *r* that ye prophesied:
19 I had *r* speak five words with my
2Co 2. 7 ye ought *r* to forgive him, and
3. 8 of the spirit be *r* glorious?
5. 8 *r* to be absent from the body, and
12. 9 will I *r* glory in my infirmities,
Gal 4. 9 known God, or *r* are known of God,
Eph 4.28 but *r* let him labor, working with
5. 4 convenient: but *r* giving of thanks.
11 of darkness, but *r* reprove them.
Php 1.12 fallen out *r* unto the furtherance of
1Ti 1. 4 *r* than godly edifying which is in
4. 7 exercise thyself *r* unto godliness.
6. 2 but *r* do them service, because
Phm 9 Yet for love's sake I *r* beseech thee,
Heb 11.25 Choosing *r* to suffer affliction with
12. 9 *r* be in subjection unto the Father
13 of the way; but let it *r* be healed.
13.19 But I beseech you the *r* to do this,
2Pe 1.10 Wherefore the *r*, brethren, give

RAVEN
Gen 8. 7 And he sent forth a *r*, which went
Lev 11.15 Every *r* after his kind;
Dt 14.14 And every *r* after his kind,
Job 38.41 Who provideth for the *r* his food?
SS 5.11 locks are bushy, and black as a *r*.
Isa 34.11 owl also and the *r* shall dwell in it:

RAVENING
Ps 22.13 mouths, as a *r* and a roaring lion.
Eze 22.25 like a roaring lion *r* the prey; they
27 are like wolves *r* the prey, to shed
Mt 7.15 but inwardly they are *r* wolves.
Lk 11.39 part is full of *r* and wickedness.

RAVENS
1Ki 17. 4 the *r* to feed thee there.
6 the *r* brought him bread and flesh
Ps 147. 9 food, and to the young *r* which cry.
Pr 30.17 the *r* of the valley shall pick it out,
Lk 12.24 Consider the *r*: for they neither

RAZOR
Nu 6. 5 shall no *r* come upon his head:
Jdg 13. 5 and no *r* shall come on his head:
16.17 hath not come a *r* upon mine head;
1Sa 1.11 shall no *r* come upon his head.
Ps 52. 2 like a sharp *r*, working deceitfully.
Isa 7.20 Lord shave with a *r* that is hired,
Eze 5. 1 take thee a barber's *r*, and cause it

REACH
Gen 11. 4 whose top may *r* unto heaven;
Ex 26.28 boards shall *r* from end to end.
28.42 even unto the thighs shall they *r*:
Lev 26. 5 threshing shall *r* unto the vintage,
5 vintage shall *r* unto...sowing time:
Nu 34.11 shall *r* unto the side of the sea of
35. 4 shall *r* from the wall of the city and
Job 20. 6 and his head *r* unto the clouds;
Isa 8. 8 over, he shall *r* even to the neck;
Jer 48.32 they *r* even to the sea of Jazer: the
Zec 14. 5 the mountains shall *r* unto Azal:
Jn 20.27 *R* hither thy finger, and behold
27 *r* hither thy hand, and thrust it
2Co 10.13 us, a measure to *r* even unto you.

REACHED
Gen 28.12 and the top of it *r* to heaven: and
Jos 19.11 Maralah, and *r* to Dabbasheth,
11 *r* to the river...before Jokneam;
Ru 2.14 and he *r* her parched corn, and
Dan 4.11 the height thereof *r* unto heaven,
20 whose height *r* unto the heaven,
2Co 10.14 as though we *r* not unto you: for
Rev 18. 5 For her sins have *r* unto heaven,

REACHETH
Nu 21.30 unto Nophah, which *r* unto Medeba.
Jos 19.22 And the coast *r* to Tabor, and
26 and *r* to Carmel westward, and to
27 and *r* to Zebulun, and to the valley
34 and *r* to Zebulun on the south side,
34 and *r* to Asher on the west side,
2Ch 28. 9 in a rage that *r* up unto heaven.
Ps 36. 5 thy faithfulness *r* unto the clouds.
108. 4 and thy truth *r* unto the clouds.
Pr 31.20 *r* forth her hands to the needy.
Jer 4.10 the sword *r* unto the soul.
18 because it *r* unto thine heart.
51. 9 for her judgment *r* unto heaven,
Dan 4.22 is grown, and *r* unto heaven,

REACHING
2Ch 3.11 cubits, *r* to the wall of the house:
11 *r* to the wing of the other cherub.
12 cubits, *r* to the wall of the house:
Php 3.13 *r* forth unto those things which

READ
Ex 24. 7 *r* in the audience of the people:
Dt 17.19 *r* therein all the days of his life:
31.11 shalt *r* this law before all Israel
Jos 8.34 he *r* all the words of the law,
35 which Joshua *r* not before all the
2Ki 5. 7 the king of Israel had *r* the letter,
19.14 hand of the messengers, and *r* it:
22. 8 the book to Shaphan, and he *r* it.
10 And Shaphan *r* it before the king.
16 which the king of Judah hath *r*:
23. 2 he *r* in their ears all the words of
2Ch 34.18 And Shaphan *r* it before the king.
24 have *r* before the king of Judah:
30 he *r* in their ears all the words of
Ezr 4.18 hath been plainly *r* before me.
23 Artaxerxes' letter was *r* before
Neh 8. 3 And he *r* therein before the street
8 they *r* in the book in the law of God
18 he *r* in the book of the law of God.
9. 3 *r* in the book of the law of the Lord
13. 1 day they *r* in the book of Moses
Est 6. 1 and they were *r* before the king.
Isa 29.11, 12 *R* this, I pray thee: and he saith,
34.16 out of the book of the Lord, and *r*:
37.14 hand of the messengers, and *r* it:
Jer 29.29 Zephaniah the priest *r* this letter
36. 6 Therefore go thou, and *r* in the roll,
6 shalt *r* them in the ears of all Judah
10 *r* Baruch in the book the words of
13 when Baruch *r* the book in the ears
14 roll wherein thou hast *r* in the ears
15 Sit down now, and *r* it in our ears.
15 ears. So Baruch *r* it in their ears.
21 Jehudi *r* it in the ears of the king,
23 Jehudi had *r* three or four leaves,
51.61 see, and shalt *r* all these words;
Dan 5. 7 Whosoever shall *r* this writing,
8 but they could not *r* the writing,
15 that they should *r* this writing,
16 now if thou canst *r* the writing, and
17 I will *r* the writing unto the king,
Mt 12. 3 Have ye not *r* what David did,
5 Or have ye not *r* in the law, how
19. 4 Have ye not *r*, that he which made
21.16 have ye never *r*, Out of the mouth
42 Did ye never *r* in the scriptures,
22.31 have ye not *r* that which was spoken
Mk 2.25 Have ye never *r* what David did,
12.10 And have ye not *r* this scripture;
26 have ye not *r* in the book of Moses,
Lk 4.16 sabbath day, and stood up for to *r*.
6. 3 Have ye not *r* so much as this, what
Jn 19.20 This title then *r* many of the Jews:
Ac 8.28 in his chariot *r* Esaias the prophet.
30 heard him *r* the prophet Esaias,
32 the scripture which he *r* was this,
13.27 prophets which are *r* every sabbath
15.21 being *r* in the synagogues every

Ac 15.31 when they had *r*, they rejoiced
23.34 when the governor had *r* the letter,
2Co 1.13 than what ye *r* or acknowledge;
3. 2 our hearts, known and *r* of all men:
15 even unto this day, when Moses is *r*,
Eph 3. 4 when ye *r*, ye may understand my
Col 4.16 when this epistle is *r* among you,
16 that it be *r* also in the church of the
16 *r* the epistle from Laodicea.
1Th 5.27 be *r* unto all the holy brethren.
Rev 5. 4 worthy to open and to *r* the book,

READEST

Lk 10.26 is written in the law? how *r* thou?
Ac 8.30 Understandest thou what thou *r*?

READETH

Hab 2. 2 tables, that he may run that *r* it.
Mt 24.15 (whoso *r*, let him understand:)
Mk 13.14 (let him that *r* understand,) then
Rev 1. 3 Blessed is he that *r*, and they that

READINESS

Ac 17.11 received the word with all *r* of
2Co 8.11 that as there was a *r* to will, so
10. 6 a *r* to revenge all disobedience,

READING

Neh 8. 8 caused them to understand the *r*.
Jer 36. 8 *r* in the book...words of the Lord
51.63 hast made an end of *r* this book,
Ac 13.15 the *r* of the law and the prophets
2Co 3.14 away in the *r* of the old testament;
1Ti 4.13 Till I come, give attendance to *r*,

READY

Gen 18. 6 Make *r* quickly three measures
43.16 men home, and slay, and make *r*;
25 made *r* the present against Joseph
46.29 And Joseph made *r* his chariot,
Ex 14. 6 he made *r* his chariot, and took
17. 4 they be almost *r* to stone me.
19.11 And be *r* against the third day:
15 people. Be *r* against the third day:
34. 2 And be *r* in the morning, and come
Nu 32.17 But we ourselves will go *r* armed
Dt 1.41 ye were *r* to go up into the hill.
26. 5 Syrian *r* to perish was my father,
Jos 8. 4 far from the city, but be ye all *r*:
Jdg 6.19 Gideon went in, and made *r* a kid,
13.15 we shall have made *r* a kid for thee.
1Sa 25.18 and five sheep *r* dressed, and five
2Sa 15.15 thy servants are *r* to do whatsoever
18.22 that thou hast no tidings *r*?
1Ki 6. 7 was built of stone made *r* before
2Ki 9.21 And Joram said, Make *r*.
21 And his chariot was made *r*.
1Ch 12.23 bands that were *r* armed to the war,
24 eight hundred, *r* armed to the war.
28. 2 and had made *r* for the building:
2Ch 17.18 thousand *r* prepared for the war.
35.14 they made *r* for themselves,
Ezr 7. 6 a *r* scribe in the law of Moses,
Neh 9.17 but thou art a God *r* to pardon,
Est 3.14 they should be *r* against that day.
8.13 Jews should be *r* against that day
Job 3. 8 are *r* to raise up their mourning.
12. 5 He that is *r* to slip with his feet
15.23 day of darkness is *r* at his hand.
24 him, as a king *r* to the battle.
28 which are *r* to become heaps.
17. 1 are extinct, the graves are *r* for me.
18.12 destruction shall be *r* at his side.
29.13 blessing of him that was *r* to perish
32.19 it is *r* to burst like new bottles.
Ps 7.12 hath bent his bow, and made it *r*.
11. 2 make *r* their arrow upon the string,
21.12 thou shalt make *r* thine arrows
38.17 I am *r* to halt, and my sorrow is
45. 1 tongue is the pen of a *r* writer.
86. 5 Lord, art good, and *r* to forgive;
88.15 and *r* to die from my youth up:
Pr 24.11 and those that are *r* to be slain;
31. 6 drink unto him that is *r* to perish,
Ec 5. 1 be more *r* to hear, than to give
Isa 27.13 *r* to perish in the land of Assyria,
30.13 shall be to you as a breach *r* to fall,
32. 4 shall be *r* to speak plainly.
38.20 The Lord was *r* to save me: therefore
41. 7 saying, It is *r* for the sodering:
51.13 as if he were *r* to destroy? and
Eze 7.14 the trumpet, even to make all *r*;
Dan 3.15 if ye be *r* that at what time ye
Hos 7. 6 made *r* their heart like an oven,
Mt 22. 4 are killed, and all things are *r*:
8 The wedding is *r*, but they which
24.44 Therefore be ye also *r*: for in such
25.10 they that were *r* went in with him
26.19 and they made *r* the passover.
Mk 14.15 prepared: there make *r* for us.
16 and they made *r* the passover.
38 The spirit truly is *r*, but the flesh
Lk 1.17 *r* a people prepared for the Lord.
7. 2 unto him, was sick, and *r* to die.
9.52 Samaritans, to make *r* for him.
12.40 Be ye therefore *r* also: for the
14.17 Come; for all things are now *r*.
17. 8 Make *r* wherewith I may sup,
22.12 room furnished: there make *r*.
13 and they made *r* the passover.
33 Lord, I am *r* to go with thee, both
Jn 7. 6 come: but your time is alway *r*.
Ac 10.10 they made *r*, he fell into a trance.
20. 7 *r* to depart on the morrow; and
21.13 I am *r* not to be bound only, but
23.15 he come near, are *r* to kill him.
21 now are they *r*, looking for a
23 Make *r* two hundred soldiers to
Ro 1.15 am *r* to preach the gospel to you
2Co 8.19 and declaration of your *r* mind:
9. 2 Achaia was *r* a year ago; and
3 that, as I said, ye may be *r*:
5 that the same might be *r*, as a
10.16 line of things made *r* to our hand.
12.14 third time I am *r* to come to you;
1Ti 6.18 in good works, *r* to distribute,
2Ti 4. 6 For I am now *r* to be offered, and
Tit 3. 1 to be *r* to every good work,
Heb 8.13 waxeth old is *r* to vanish away.
1Pe 1. 5 *r* to be revealed in the last time.
3.15 and be *r* always to give an answer
4. 5 *r* to judge the quick and the dead.
5. 2 for filthy lucre, but of a *r* mind;
Rev 3. 2 which remain, that are *r* to die:
12. 4 the woman...*r* to be delivered,
19. 7 and his wife hath made herself *r*.

REAP

Lev 19. 9 ye *r* the harvest of your land,
9 shalt not wholly *r* the corners of
23.10 and shall *r* the harvest thereof,
22 ye *r* the harvest of your land,
25. 5 of thy harvest thou shalt not *r*,
11 neither *r* that which groweth of
Ru 2. 9 eyes be on the field that they do *r*,
1Sa 8.12 his ground, and to *r* his harvest,
2Ki 19.29 in the third year sow ye, and *r*,
Job 4. 8 and sow wickedness, *r* the same.
24. 6 *r* every one his corn in the field:
Ps 126. 5 that sow in tears shall *r* in joy.
Pr 22. 8 soweth iniquity shall *r* vanity:
Ec 11. 4 regardeth the clouds shall not *r*.
Isa 37.30 in the third year sow ye, and *r*,
Jer 12.13 sown wheat, but shall *r* thorns:
Hos 8. 7 and they shall *r* the whirlwind:
10.12 in righteousness, *r* in mercy;
Mic 6.15 shalt sow, but thou shalt not *r*;
Mt 6.26 neither do they *r*, nor gather
25.26 I *r* where I sowed not, and gather
Lk 12.24 ravens: for they neither sow nor *r*;
Jn 4.38 to *r* that whereon ye bestowed no
1Co 9.11 if we shall *r* your carnal things?
2Co 9. 6 sparingly shall *r* also sparingly;
6 bountifully shall *r*...bountifully.
Gal 6. 7 man soweth, that shall he also *r*.
8 shall of the flesh *r* corruption;
8 of the Spirit *r* life everlasting.
9 for in due season we shall *r*, if we
Rev 14.15 Thrust in thy sickle, and *r*: for
15 for the time is come for thee to *r*;

REAPED

Hos 10.13 wickedness, ye have *r* iniquity;
Jas 5. 4 who have *r* down your fields,
4 the cries of them which have *r*
Rev 14.16 the earth; and the earth was *r*.

REAPER

Am 9.13 the plowman shall overtake the *r*,

REAPERS

Ru 2. 3 gleaned in the field after the *r*:
4 said unto the *r*, the Lord be with
5 his servant that was set over the *r*,
6 the servant that was set over the *r*,
7 after the *r* among the sheaves:
14 And she sat beside the *r*: and he
2Ki 4.18 he went out to his father to the *r*.
Mt 13.30 I will say to the *r*, Gather ye
39 world; and the *r* are the angels.

REAPEST

Lev 23.22 corners of thy field when thou *r*,
Lk 19.21 and *r* that thou didst not sow.

REAPETH

Isa 17. 5 and *r* the ears with his arm;
Jn 4.36 he that *r* receiveth wages, and
36 he that *r* may rejoice together.
37 true, One soweth, and another *r*.

REAPING

1Sa 6.13 were *r* their wheat harvest in the
Mt 25.24 *r* where thou hast not sown, and
Lk 19.22 down, and *r* that I do not sow:

REAR

Ex 26.30 thou shalt *r* up the tabernacle
Lev 26. 1 neither *r* you up a standing image,
2Sa 24.18 Go up, *r* an altar unto the Lord in
Jn 2.20 wilt thou *r* it up in three days?

REARED

Ex 40.17 that the tabernacle was *r* up.
18 Moses *r* up the tabernacle, and
18 bars thereof, and *r* up his pillars.
33 And he *r* up the court round about
Nu 9.15 day that the tabernacle was *r* up
2Sa 18.18 and *r* up for himself a pillar,
1Ki 16.32 And he *r* up an altar for Baal in
2Ki 21. 3 and he *r* up altars for Baal, and
2Ch 3.17 And he *r* up the pillars before the
33. 3 and he *r* up altars for Baalim, and

REASON

Gen 41.31 in the land by *r* of that famine
47.13 Canaan fainted by *r* of the famine.
Ex 2.23 Israel sighed by *r* of the bondage,
23 up unto God by *r* of the bondage,
3. 7 cry by *r* of their taskmasters;
8.24 corrupted by *r* of the swarm of flies.
Nu 9.10 shall be unclean by *r* of a dead body,
18. 8 I given them by *r* of the anointing,
32 And ye shall bear no sin by *r* of
Dt 5. 5 for ye were afraid by *r* of the fire,
23.10 that is not clean by *r* of uncleanness
Jos 9.13 old by *r* of the very long journey.
Jdg 2.18 by *r* of them that oppressed them
1Sa 12. 7 may *r* with you before the Lord
1Ki 9.15 this is the *r* of the levy which
2Ch 5.14 stand to minister by *r* of the
20.15 by *r* of this great multitude;
21.15 fall out by *r* of the sickness day

REBEKAH

Niece of Abraham, wife of Isaac, and mother of Esau and Jacob; her betrothal to Isaac, her cousin, is arranged by Abraham's servant, sent to Mesopotamia to find him a wife; he meets her at a well and after negotiations with her brother, Laban, and with her willing consent, returns with her to Canaan; Isaac falls in love and marries her (Gen 24)**; after a long period of barrenness, bears the twins Esau and Jacob; Jacob becomes her favorite** (Gen 25)**; because of her beauty, is at first presented by Isaac as his sister when they settle in Gerar ("lest, said he, the men of the place should kill me for Rebekah")** (Gen 26.7)**; shares Isaac's disappointment when Esau takes two foreign wives** (Gen 26.34-35)**; devises plan to deceive the aged Isaac and get Esau's blessing as firstborn for her favorite, and helps Jacob to carry the plan through** (Gen 27.1-17)**; when Esau vows vengeance, advises Jacob to flee to her brother in Mesopotamia, and suggests to Isaac that Jacob find himself a wife there** (Gen 27.41-46)**; she never sees Jacob again and her death is not recorded, though it is later noted that she was buried beside her husband in the cave at Machpelah in Canaan** (Gen 49.31).

19 fell out by *r* of his sickness:
Job 6.16 which are blackish by *r* of the ice,
9.14 choose out my words to *r* with him?
13. 3 and I desire to *r* with God.
15. 3 Should he *r* with unprofitable talk?
17. 7 Mine eye also is dim by *r* of sorrow,
31.23 and by *r* of his highness I could not
35. 9 By *r* of the multitude of oppressions
9 cry out by *r* of the arm of the mighty.
37.19 our speech by *r* of darkness.
Ps 38. 8 have roared by *r* of the disquietness
44.16 by *r* of the enemy and avenger.
78.65 man that shouteth by *r* of wine.
88. 9 eye mourneth by *r* of affliction:
90.10 if by *r* of strength they be fourscore
102. 5 By *r* of the voice of my groaning my
Pr 20. 4 will not plow by *r* of the cold;
26.16 seven men that can render a *r*.
Ec 7.25 out wisdom, and the *r* of things,
Isa 1.18 Come now, and let us *r* together,
49.19 too narrow by *r* of the inhabitants,
Eze 19.10 full of branches by *r* of many waters.
21.12 terrors by *r* of the sword shall be
26.10 By *r* of the abundance of his horses
27.12, 16 thy merchant by *r* of the multitude
28.17 wisdom by *r* of thy brightness:
Dan 4.36 time my *r* returned unto me;
5.10 by *r* of the words of the king and
8.12 daily sacrifice by *r* of transgression,
Jon 2. 2 I cried by *r* of mine affliction unto
Mic 2.12 noise by *r* of the multitude of men.
Mt 16. 8 why *r* ye among yourselves,
Mk 2. 8 Why *r* ye these things in your
8.17 Why *r* ye, because ye have no
Lk 5.21 and the Pharisees began to *r*,
22 them, What *r* ye in your hearts?
Jn 6.18 sea arose by *r* of a great wind that
12.11 by *r* of him many of the Jews
Ac 6. 2 It is not *r* that we should leave the
18.14 *r* would that I should bear with
Ro 8.20 by *r* of him who hath subjected
2Co 3.10 by *r* of the glory that excelleth.
Heb 5. 3 by *r* hereof he ought, as for the
14 who by *r* of use have their senses
7.23 suffered to continue by *r* of death:
1Pe 3.15 a *r* of the hope that is in you with
2Pe 2. 2 by *r* of whom the way of truth
Rev 8.13 earth by *r* of the other voices of
9. 2 by *r* of the smoke of the pit.
18.19 in the sea by *r* of her costliness!

REASONABLE

Ro 12. 1 unto God, which is your *r* service.

REASONED

Mt 16. 7 they *r* among themselves, saying,
21.25 they *r* among themselves, saying,
Mk 2. 8 that they so *r* among themselves,
8.16 they *r* among themselves, saying,
11.31 they *r* with themselves, saying, If
Lk 20. 5 they *r* with themselves, saying, If
14 they *r* among themselves, saying,
24.15 they communed together and *r*,
Ac 17. 2 *r* with them out of the scriptures,
18. 4 *r* in the synagogue every sabbath,
19 synagogue, and *r* with the Jews.
24.25 And as he *r* of righteousness,

REASONING

Job 13. 6 Hear now my *r*, and hearken to
Mk 2. 6 sitting there, and *r* in their hearts,
12.28 having heard them *r* together,
Lk 9.46 Then there arose a *r* among them,
Ac 28.29 had great *r* among themselves.

REASONS

Job 32.11 I gave ear to your *r*, whilst ye
Isa 41.21 bring forth your strong *r*, saith the

REBECCA

Ro 9.10 *R* also had conceived by one, even

REBEKAH

Gen 22.23 Bethuel begat *R*: these eight
24.15 *R* came out, who was born to
29 *R* had a brother, and his name was
30 he heard the words of *R* his sister,
59 they sent away *R* their sister, and
61 *R* arose, and her damsels, and they
61 servant took *R*, and went his way.
64 *R* lifted up her eyes, and when she
67 took *R*, and she became his wife;
25.20 years old when he took *R* to wife,
21 of him, and *R* his wife conceived.
28 of his venison: but *R* loved Jacob.
26. 7 of the place should kill me for *R*;
8 was sporting with *R* his wife.
35 grief of mind unto Isaac and to *R*.
27. 5 *R* heard when Isaac spake to Esau
6 And *R* spake unto Jacob her son,
42 Esau her elder son were told to *R*:
46 *R* said to Isaac, I am weary of my
49.31 they buried Isaac and *R* his wife;

REBEL

Nu 14. 9 Only *r* not ye against the Lord,
Jos 1.18 doth *r* against thy commandment,
22.16 *r* this day against the Lord?
18 seeing ye *r* to day against the Lord,
19 but *r* not against the Lord, nor
19 against the Lord, nor *r* against us,
29 God forbid that we should *r* against
1Sa 12.14 not *r* against the commandment
15 but *r* against the commandment
Neh 2.19 ye do? will ye *r* against the king?
6. 6 that thou and the Jews think to *r*:
Job 24.13 of those that *r* against the light;
Isa 1.20 But if ye refuse and *r*, ye shall be
Hos 7.14 and wine, and they *r* against me.

REBELLED

Gen 14. 4 and in the thirteenth year they *r*.
Nu 20.24 because ye *r* against my word at
27.14 ye *r* against my commandment in
Dt 1.26, 43 but *r* against the commandment
9.23 ye *r* against the commandment of
1Ki 12.19 So Israel *r* against the house of
2Ki 1. 1 Then Moab *r* against Israel after
3. 5 Moab *r* against the king of Israel.
7 king of Moab hath *r* against me:
18. 7 he *r* against the king of Assyria,
24. 1 then he turned and *r* against him.
20 Zedekiah *r* against the king of
2Ch 10.19 And Israel *r* against the house of
13. 6 up, and hath *r* against his lord.
36.13 *r* against king Nebuchadnezzar,
Neh 9.26 disobedient, and *r* against thee,
Ps 5.10 for they have *r* against thee.
105.28 and they *r* not against his word.
107.11 they *r* against the words of God,
Isa 1. 2 and they have *r* against me.
63.10 they *r*, and vexed his holy Spirit:
Jer 52. 3 Zedekiah *r* against the king of
La 1.18 *r* against his commandment:
20 for I have grievously *r*: abroad
3.42 We have transgressed and have *r*:
Eze 2. 3 nation that hath *r* against me:
17.15 he *r* against him in sending his
20. 8 they *r* against me, and would not
13 *r* against me in the wilderness:
21 the children *r* against me: they
Dan 9. 5 have *r*, even by departing from
9 though we have *r* against him;
Hos 13.16 for she hath *r* against her God:

Rebekah meets the servant sent for her by Abraham (Gen 24) in this 1648 painting by Nicolas Poussin.

REBELLION
Dt 31.27 I know thy *r*, and thy stiff neck:
Jos 22.22 if it be in *r*, or if in transgression
1Sa 15.23 For *r* is as the sin of witchcraft,
Ezr 4.19 *r* and sedition have been made
Neh 9.17 in their *r* appointed a captain to
Job 34.37 For he addeth *r* unto his sin, he
Pr 17.11 An evil man seeketh only *r*:
Jer 28.16 hast taught *r* against the Lord.
29.32 he hath taught *r* against the Lord.

REBELLIOUS
Dt 9. 7 ye have been *r* against the Lord.
24 Ye have been *r* against the Lord
21.18 a man have a stubborn and *r* son,
20 This our son is stubborn and *r*, he
31.27 ye have been *r* against the Lord;
1Sa 20.30 son of the perverse *r* woman, do
Ezr 4.12 building the *r* and the bad city,
15 and know that this city is a *r* city,
Ps 66. 7 let not the *r* exalt themselves.
68. 6 but the *r* dwell in a dry land.
18 yea, for the *r* also, that the Lord
78. 8 a stubborn and *r* generation; a
Isa 1.23 princes are *r*, and companions of
30. 1 Woe to the *r* children, saith the
9 this is a *r* people, lying children,
50. 5 I was not *r*, neither turned away
65. 2 hands all the day unto a *r* people,
Jer 4.17 she hath been *r* against me, saith
5.23 hath a revolting and a *r* heart;
Eze 2. 3 to a *r* nation that hath rebelled
5 (for they are a *r* house,) yet shall
6 looks, though they be a *r* house.
7 will forbear: for they are most *r*.
8 Be not thou *r* like that *r* house:
3. 9 looks, though they be a *r* house.
26 a reprover: for they are a *r* house.
27 forbear: for they are a *r* house.
12. 2 dwellest in the midst of a *r* house,
2 hear not: for they are a *r* house.
3 consider, though they be a *r* house.
9 the house of Israel, the *r* house,
25 O *r* house, will I say the word, and
17.12 Say now to the *r* house, Know ye
24. 3 utter a parable unto the *r* house,
44. 6 thou shalt say to the *r*, even to the

REBUKE
Lev 19.17 in any wise *r* thy neighbor, and
Dt 28.20 upon thee cursing, vexation and *r*,
Ru 2.16 may glean them, and *r* her not.
2Ki 19. 3 day is a day of trouble, and of *r*,
1Ch 12.17 our fathers look thereon, and *r* it.
Ps 6. 1 O Lord, *r* me not in thine anger,
18.15 were discovered at thy *r*, O Lord,
38. 1 O Lord, *r* me not in thy wrath:
68.30 *R* the company of spearmen, the
76. 6 At thy *r*, O God of Jacob, both the
80.16 perish at the *r* of thy countenance.
104. 7 At thy *r* they fled; at the voice of
Pr 9. 8 *r* a wise man, and he will love
13. 1 but a scorner heareth not *r*.
8 riches: but the poor heareth not *r*.
24.25 them that *r* him shall be delight,
27. 5 Open *r* is better than secret love.
Ec 7. 5 is better to hear the *r* of the wise,
Isa 2. 4 and shall *r* many people:
17.13 God shall *r* them, and they shall
25. 8 *r* of his people shall he take away
30.17 shall flee at the *r* of one; at the
17 at the *r* of five shall ye flee: till ye
37. 3 day is a day of trouble, and of *r*,
50. 2 behold, at my *r* I dry up the sea, I
51.20 fury of the Lord, the *r* of thy God.
54. 9 be wroth with thee, nor *r* thee.
66.15 fury, and his *r* with flames of fire.
Jer 15.15 for thy sake I have suffered *r*.
Hos 5. 9 shall be desolate in the day of *r*:
Mic 4. 3 and *r* strong nations afar off;
Zec 3. 2 The Lord *r* thee, O Satan; even
2 hath chosen Jerusalem *r* thee:
Mal 3.11 *r* the devourer for your sakes, and
Mt 16.22 took him, and began to *r* him,
Mk 8.32 took him, and began to *r* him.
Lk 17. 3 trespass against thee, *r* him; and
19.39 unto him, Master, *r* thy disciples.
Php 2.15 the sons of God, without *r*, in the
1Ti 5. 1 *R* not an elder, but intreat him as
20 Them that sin *r* before all, that
2Ti 4. 2 *r*, exhort with all longsuffering
Tit 1.13 Wherefore *r* them sharply, that
2.15 exhort, and *r* with all authority.
Jude 9 but said, The Lord *r* thee.
Rev 3.19 many as I love, I *r* and chasten:

REBUKED
Gen 31.42 my hands, and *r* thee yesternight.
37.10 and his father *r* him, and said
Neh 5. 7 and I *r* the nobles, and the rulers,
Ps 9. 5 Thou hast *r* the heathen, thou
106. 9 He *r* the Red sea also, and it was
119.21 hast *r* the proud that are cursed,
Mt 8.26 and *r* the winds and the sea; and
17.18 And Jesus *r* the devil; and he
19.13 pray: and the disciples *r* them.
20.31 the multitude *r* them, because they
Mk 1.25 And Jesus *r* him, saying, Hold thy
4.39 he arose, and *r* the wind, and said
8.33 he *r* Peter, saying, Get thee behind
9.25 he *r* the foul spirit, saying unto
10.13 his disciples *r* those that brought
Lk 4.35 And Jesus *r* him, saying, Hold thy
39 and *r* the fever; and it left her:
8.24 he arose, and *r* the wind and the
9.42 Jesus *r* the unclean spirit, and
55 he turned, and *r* them, and said,
18.15 his disciples saw it, they *r* them.
39 they which went before *r* him,
23.40 But the other answering *r* him,
Heb 12. 5 nor faint when thou art *r* of him:
2Pe 2.16 But was *r* for his iniquity: the

REBUKETH
Pr 9. 7 he that *r* a wicked man getteth
28.23 He that *r* a man afterwards shall
Am 5.10 They hate him that *r* in the gate,
Na 1. 4 He *r* the sea, and maketh it dry,

REBUKING
2Sa 22.16 discovered, at the *r* of the Lord,
Lk 4.41 he *r* them suffered them not to

RECEIPT
Mt 9. 9 Matthew, sitting at...*r* of custom:
Mk 2.14 Alphaeus sitting at the *r* of custom,
Lk 5.27 Levi, sitting at the *r* of custom:

RECEIVE
Gen 4.11 mouth to *r* thy brother's blood
33.10 then *r* my present at my hand:
38.20 to *r* his pledge from the woman's
Ex 27. 3 make his pans to *r* his ashes,
29.25 thou shalt *r* them of their hands,
Nu 18.28 ye *r* of the children of Israel;
Dt 9. 9 the mount to *r* the tables of stone,
33. 3 every one shall *r* of thy words.
1Sa 10. 4 which thou shalt *r* of their hands.
2Sa 18.12 *r* a thousand shekels of silver in
1Ki 5. 9 there, and thou shalt *r* them:
8.64 too little to *r* the burnt offerings,
2Ki 5.16 whom I stand, I will *r* none.
26 to *r* money, and to *r* garments,
12. 7 *r* no more money of your
8 to *r* no more money of the people.
2Ch 7. 7 not able to *r* the burnt offerings,
Job 2.10 we *r* good at the hand of God,
10 of God, and shall we not *r* evil?
22.22 *R*, I pray thee, the law from his
27.13 they shall *r* of the Almighty.
Ps 6. 9 the Lord will *r* my prayer.
24. 5 *r* the blessing from the Lord,
49.15 of the grave: for he shall *r* me.
73.24 and afterward *r* me to glory.
75. 2 When I shall *r* the congregation I
Pr 1. 3 To *r* the instruction of wisdom,
2. 1 My son, if thou wilt *r* my words,
4.10 Hear, O my son, and *r* my sayings;
8.10 *R* my instruction, and not silver;
10. 8 The wise...will *r* commandments:
19.20 Hear counsel, and *r* instruction,
Isa 57. 6 Should I *r* comfort in these?
Jer 5. 3 they have refused to *r* correction:
9.20 your ear *r* the word of his mouth,
17.23 might not hear, nor *r* instruction.
32.33 have not hearkened to *r* instruction.
35.13 Will ye not *r* instruction to hearken
Eze 3.10 speak unto thee *r* in thine heart,
16.61 when thou shalt *r* thy sisters, thine
36.30 shall *r* no more reproach of famine
Dan 2. 6 ye shall *r* of me gifts and rewards
Hos 10. 6 Ephraim shall *r* shame, and
14. 2 all iniquity, and *r* us graciously:
Mic 1.11 he shall *r* of you his standing.
Zep 3. 7 fear me, thou wilt *r* instruction;
Mal 3.10 shall not be room enough to *r* it.
Mt 10.14 whosoever shall not *r* you, nor
41 shall *r* a prophet's reward; and
41 shall *r* a righteous man's reward.
11. 5 blind *r* their sight, and the lame
14 if ye will *r* it, this is Elias, which
18. 5 whoso shall *r* one such little child
19.11 All men cannot *r* this saying, save
12 that is able to *r* it, let him *r* it.
29 shall *r* an hundredfold, and shall
20. 7 is right, that shall ye *r*.
21.22 ask in prayer, believing, ye shall *r*.
34 that they might *r* the fruits of it.
23.14 ye shall *r* the greater damnation.
Mk 2. 2 there was no room to *r* them,
4.16 immediately *r* it with gladness;
20 such as hear the word, and *r* it,
6.11 whosoever shall not *r* you, nor
9.37 shall *r* one of such children in
37 whosoever shall *r* me, receiveth not
10.15 shall not *r* the kingdom of God as
30 he shall *r* an hundredfold now in
51 Lord, that I might *r* my sight.
11.24 ye pray, believe that ye *r* them,
12. 2 he might *r* from the husbandmen
40 these shall *r* greater damnation.
Lk 6.34 to them of whom ye hope to *r*,
34 lend to sinners, to *r* as much again.
8.13 they hear, *r* the word with joy;
9. 5 whosoever will not *r* you, when ye
48 shall *r* this child in my name
48 whosoever shall *r* me receiveth
53 they did not *r* him, because his
10. 8 city ye enter, and they *r* you, eat
10 they *r* you not, go your ways out
16. 4 they may *r* me into their houses.
9 they may *r* you into everlasting
18.17 shall not *r* the kingdom of God as
30 not *r* manifold more in this present
41 said, Lord, that I may *r* my sight.
42 Jesus said unto him, *R* thy sight:
19.12 to *r* for himself a kingdom, and
20.47 same shall *r* greater damnation.
23.41 for we *r* the due reward of our
Jn 3.11 seen; and ye *r* not our witness.
27 A man can *r* nothing, except it be
5.34 But I *r* not testimony from man:
41 I *r* not honor from men.
43 Father's name, and ye *r* me not:
43 in his own name, him ye will *r*.
44 which *r* honor one of another,
7.23 the sabbath day *r* circumcision,
39 they that believe on him should *r*:
14. 3 again, and *r* you unto myself;
17 whom the world cannot *r*, because
16.14 for he shall *r* of mine, and shall
24 ask, and ye shall *r*, that your joy
20.22 unto them, *R* ye the Holy Ghost:

Ac 1. 8 But ye shall *r* power, after that the
2.38 shall *r* the gift of the Holy Ghost.
3. 5 expecting to *r* something of them.
21 Whom the heaven must *r* until
7.59 and saying, Lord Jesus, *r* my spirit.
8.15 that they might *r* the Holy Ghost:
19 hands, he may *r* the Holy Ghost.
9.12 on him, that he might *r* his sight.
17 that thou mightest *r* thy sight, and
10.43 in him shall *r* remission of sins.
16.21 which are not lawful for us to *r*,
18.27 exhorting the disciples to *r* him:
20.35 is more blessed to give than to *r*.
22.13 unto me, Brother Saul, *r* thy sight.
18 *r* thy testimony concerning me.
26.18 they may *r* forgiveness of sins,
Ro 5.17 they which *r* abundance of grace
13. 2 shall *r* to themselves damnation.
14. 1 that is weak in the faith *r* ye,
15. 7 *r* ye one another, as Christ also
16. 2 That ye *r* her in the Lord, as
1Co 3. 8 man shall *r* his own reward
14 thereupon, he shall *r* a reward.
4. 7 hast thou that thou didst not *r*?
7 thou didst *r* it, why dost thou glory,
14. 5 that the church may *r* edifying.
2Co 5.10 *r* the things done in his body,
6. 1 ye *r* not the grace of God in vain.
17 unclean thing; and I will *r* you,
7. 2 *R* us; we have wronged no man,
9 might *r* damage by us in nothing.
8. 4 intreaty that we would *r* the gift,
11. 4 or if ye *r* another spirit, which ye
16 as a fool *r* me, that I may boast
Gal 3.14 might *r* the promise of the Spirit
4. 5 we might *r* the adoption of sons.
Eph 6. 8 the same shall he *r* of the Lord,
Php 2.29 *R* him therefore in the Lord with
Col 3.24 *r* the reward of the inheritance:
25 *r* for the wrong which he hath
4.10 if he come unto you, *r* him;)
1Ti 5.19 an elder *r* not an accusation, but
Phm 12 thou therefore *r* him, that is,
15 that thou shouldest *r* him for ever;
17 a partner, *r* him as myself.
Heb 7. 5 who *r* the office of the priesthood,
8 And here men that die *r* tithes;
9.15 might *r* the promise of eternal
10.36 of God, ye might *r* the promise.
11. 8 should after *r* for an inheritance,
Jas 1. 7 he shall *r* any thing of the Lord.
12 is tried, he shall *r* the crown of life,
21 *r* with meekness the engrafted
3. 1 shall *r* the greater condemnation.
4. 3 Ye ask, and *r* not, because ye ask
5. 7 until he *r* the early and latter rain.
1Pe 5. 4 *r* a crown of glory that fadeth not
2Pe 2.13 *r* the reward of unrighteousness,
1Jn 3.22 whatsoever we ask, we *r* of him,
5. 9 If we *r* the witness of men, the
2Jn 8 but that we *r* a full reward.
10 *r* him not into your house, neither
3Jn 8 We therefore ought to *r* such, that
10 doth he himself *r* the brethren,
Rev 4.11 to *r* glory and honor and power:
5.12 Lamb that was slain to *r* power,
13.16 to *r* a mark in their right hand,
14. 9 *r* his mark in his forehead, or in
17.12 but *r* power as kings one hour with
18. 4 and that ye *r* not of her plagues.

RECEIVED

Gen 26.12 land, and *r* in the same year an
Ex 32. 4 And he *r* them at their hand, and
36. 3 they *r* of Moses all the offering,
Nu 12.14 after that let her be *r* in again.
23.20 I have *r* commandment to bless:
34.14 fathers, have *r* their inheritance;
14 have *r* their inheritance:
15 half tribe have *r* their inheritance
36. 3, 4 the tribe whereunto they are *r*:
Jos 13. 8 Gadites have *r* their inheritance,
18. 2 had not yet *r* their inheritance.
7 have *r* their inheritance beyond
Jdg 13.23 would not have *r* a burnt offering
1Sa 12. 3 of whose hand have I *r* any bribe
25.35 So David *r* of her hand that which
1Ki 10.28 merchants *r* the linen yarn at a
2Ki 19.14 Hezekiah *r* the letter of the hand
1Ch 12.18 David *r* them, and made them
2Ch 1.16 merchants *r* the linen yarn at a
4. 5 *r* and held three thousand baths.
29.22 and the priests *r* the blood, and
30.16 they *r* at the hand of the Levites.
Est 4. 4 from him: but he *r* it not.
Job 4.12 and mine ear *r* a little thereof.
Ps 68.18 thou hast *r* gifts for men; yea, for
Pr 24.32 looked upon it, and *r* instruction.
Isa 37.14 And Hezekiah *r* the letter from the
40. 2 for she hath *r* of the Lord's hand
Jer 2.30 children; they *r* no correction:
Eze 18.17 hath not *r* usury nor increase,
Zep 3. 2 she *r* not correction; she trusted
Mt 10. 8 freely ye have *r*, freely give.
13.19 he which *r* seed by the way side.
20 that *r* the seed into stony places,
22 also that *r* seed among the thorns
23 that *r* seed into the good ground
17.24 they that *r* tribute money came to
20. 9 hour, they *r* every man a penny.
10 that they should have *r* more;
10 they likewise *r* every man a penny.
11 And when they had *r* it, they
34 and immediately their eyes *r* sight,
25.16 he that had *r* the five talents went
17 And likewise he that had *r* two,
18 But he that had *r* one went and
20 so he that had *r* five talents came
22 also that had *r* two talents came
24 which had *r* the one talent came
27 have *r* mine own with usury.
Mk 7. 4 which they have *r* to hold, as the
10.52 And immediately he *r* his sight,
15.23 with myrrh: but he *r* it not.
16.19 he was *r* up into heaven, and sat on
Lk 6.24 for ye have *r* your consolation.
8.40 returned, the people gladly *r* him:
9.11 he *r* them, and spake unto them
51 was come that he should be *r* up,
10.38 Martha *r* him into her house.
15.27 he hath *r* him safe and sound.
18.43 And immediately he *r* his sight,
19. 6 came down, and *r* him joyfully.
15 returned, having *r* the kingdom,
Jn 1.11 his own, and his own *r* him not.
12 as many as *r* him, to them gave
16 And of his fulness have all we *r*,
3.33 He that hath *r* his testimony hath
4.45 the Galilaeans *r* him, having seen
6.21 they willingly *r* him into the ship:
9.11 I went and washed, and I *r* sight.
15 asked him how he had *r* his sight.
18 he had been blind, and *r* his sight,
18 parents of him that had *r* his sight.
10.18 This commandment have I *r* of
13.30 He then having *r* the sop went
17. 8 they have *r* them, and have known
18. 3 then, having *r* a band of men and
19.30 Jesus therefore had *r* the vinegar,
Ac 1. 9 a cloud *r* him out of their sight.
2.33 and having *r* of the Father the
41 gladly *r* his word were baptized:
3. 7 feet and ankle bones *r* strength.
7.38 *r* the lively oracles to give unto us:
53 *r* the law by the disposition of
8.14 Samaria had *r* the word of God,
17 them, and they *r* the Holy Ghost.
9.18 he *r* sight forthwith, and arose,
19 And when he had *r* meat, he was
10.16 vessel was *r* up again into heaven.
47 *r* the Holy Ghost as well as we?
11. 1 Gentiles had also *r* the word of
15. 4 they were *r* of the church, and of
16.24 Who, having *r* such a charge,
17. 7 Whom Jason hath *r*: and these
11 they *r* the word with all readiness
19. 2 Have ye *r* the Holy Ghost since ye
20.24 which I have *r* of the Lord Jesus,
21.17 the brethren *r* us gladly.
22. 5 from whom also I *r* letters unto
26.10 *r* authority from the chief priests;
28. 2 fire, and *r* us every one, because
7 who *r* us, and lodged us three days
21 We neither *r* letters out of Judea
30 and *r* all that came in unto him,
Ro 1. 5 we have *r* grace and apostleship,
4.11 And he *r* the sign of circumcision,
5.11 we have now *r* the atonement.
8.15 ye have not *r* the spirit of bondage
15 ye have *r* the Spirit of adoption,
14. 3 that eateth: for God hath *r* him.
15. 7 as Christ also *r* us to the glory of
1Co 2.12 Now we have *r*, not the spirit of
4. 7 glory, as if thou hadst not *r* it?
11.23 I have *r* of the Lord that which
15. 1 which also ye have *r*, and wherein
3 you first of all that which I also *r*,
2Co 4. 1 as we have *r* mercy, we faint not;
7.15 with fear and trembling ye *r* him.
11. 4 which ye have not *r*, or another
24 times *r* I forty stripes save one.
Gal 1. 9 unto you than that ye have *r*,
12 For I neither *r* it of man, neither
3. 2 *R* ye the Spirit by the works of
4.14 but *r* me as an angel of God, even
Php 4. 9 ye have both learned, and *r*, and
18 having *r* of Epaphroditus the
Col 2. 6 ye have therefore *r* Christ Jesus
4.10 whom ye *r* commandments: if
17 which thou hast *r* in the Lord,
1Th 1. 6 *r* the word in much affliction,
2.13 when ye *r* the word of God which
13 ye *r* it not as the word of men,
4. 1 as ye have *r* of us how ye ought
2Th 2.10 they *r* not the love of the truth,
3. 6 the tradition which he *r* of us.
1Ti 3.16 on in the world, *r* up into glory.
4. 3 which God hath created to be *r*
4 if it be *r* with thanksgiving:
Heb 2. 2 *r* a just recompense of reward;
7. 6 from them *r* tithes of Abraham,
11 (for under it the people *r* the law,)
10.26 *r* the knowledge of the truth,
11.11 Sara herself *r* strength to conceive
13 not having *r* the promises, but
17 he that had *r* the promises offered
19 whence also he *r* him in a figure.
31 she had *r* the spies with peace.
35 Women *r* their dead raised to life
39 through faith, *r* not the promise:
Jas 2.25 when she had *r* the messengers,
1Pe 1.18 vain conversation *r* by tradition
4.10 As every man hath *r* the gift, even
2Pe 1.17 he *r* from God the Father honor
1Jn 2.27 anointing which ye have *r* of him
2Jn 4 we have *r* a commandment from
Rev 2.27 shivers: even as I *r* of my Father.
3. 3 how thou hast *r* and heard, and
17.12 which have *r* no kingdom as yet;
19.20 that had *r* the mark of the beast,
20. 4 *r* his mark upon their foreheads,

RECEIVEDST

Lk 16.25 in thy lifetime *r* thy good things,

RECEIVETH

Jdg 19.18 is no man that *r* me to house.
Job 35. 7 him? or what *r* he of thine hand?
Pr 21.11 wise is instructed, he *r* knowledge.
29. 4 but he that *r* gifts overthroweth it.
Jer 7.28 Lord their God, nor *r* correction:
Mal 2.13 or *r* it with good will at your hand.
Mt 7. 8 For every one that asketh *r*; and

Mt 10.40 He that *r* you *r* me, and he
40 that *r* me *r* him that sent me.
41 He that *r* a prophet in the name
41 he that *r* a righteous man in the
13.20 the word, and anon with joy *r* it;
18. 5 such little child in my name *r* me.
Mk 9.37 little children in my name, *r* me:
37 shall receive me, *r* not me, but
Lk 9.48 receive this child in my name *r* me:
48 receive me *r* him that sent me:
11.10 every one that asketh *r*; and he
15. 2 This man *r* sinners, and eateth
Jn 3.32 and no man *r* his testimony.
4.36 And he that reapeth *r* wages, and
12.48 and *r* not my words, hath one that
13.20 that *r* whomsoever I send *r* me;
20 he that *r* me *r* him that sent me.
1Co 2.14 the natural man *r* not the things
9.24 race run all, but one *r* the prize?
Heb 6. 7 it is dressed, *r* blessing from God:
7. 8 but there he *r* them, of whom it is
9 Levi also, who *r* tithes, payed
12. 6 scourgeth every son whom he *r*.
3Jn 9 among them, *r* us not.
Rev 2.17 man knoweth saving he that *r* it.
14.11 whosoever *r* the mark of his name.

RECEIVING

2Ki 5.20 not *r* at his hands that which he
Ac 17.15 *r* a commandment unto Silas and
Ro 1.27 *r* in themselves that recompence
11.15 what shall the *r* of them be, but
Php 4.15 me as concerning giving and *r*,
Heb 12.28 Wherefore we *r* a kingdom which
1Pe 1. 9 *R* the end of your faith, even the

RECHABITES

Jer 35. 2 Go unto the house of the *R*, and
3 and the whole house of the *R*;
5 house of the *R* pots full of wine,
18 said unto the house of the *R*,

RECKON

Lev 25.50 he shall *r* with him that bought
27.18 priest shall *r* unto him the money
23 priest shall *r* unto him the worth
Nu 4.32 name ye shall *r* the instruments
Eze 44.26 they shall *r* unto him seven days.
Mt 18.24 And when he had begun to *r*, one
Ro 6.11 *r* ye also yourselves to be dead
8.18 For I *r* that the sufferings of this

RECKONED

Nu 18.27 offering shall be *r* unto you,
23. 9 shall not be *r* among the nations.
1Ch 9. 1 all Israel were *r* by genealogies;
Ps 40. 5 cannot be *r* up in order unto thee:
Lk 22.37 was *r* among the transgressors:
Ro 4. 4 is the reward not *r* of grace, but
9 say that faith was *r* to Abraham
10 How was it then *r*? when he was

RECKONETH

Mt 25.19 cometh, and *r* with them.

RECOMMENDED

Ac 14.26 had been *r* to the grace of God
15.40 being *r* by the brethren unto the

RECOMPENCE

Dt 32.35 me belongeth vengeance, and *r*;
Job 15.31 vanity: for vanity shall be his *r*.
Pr 12.14 the *r* of a man's hands shall be
Isa 35. 4 vengeance, even God with a *r*; he
59.18 his adversaries, *r* to his enemies;
18 to the islands he will repay *r*.
66. 6 that rendereth *r* to his enemies.
Jer 51. 6 he will render unto her a *r*.
La 3.64 Render unto them a *r*, O Lord,
Hos 9. 7 the days of *r* are come; Israel
Joel 3. 4 will ye render me a *r*? and if ye
4, 7 return...*r* upon your own head;
Lk 14.12 thee again, and a *r* be made thee.
Ro 1.27 *r* of their error which was meet.
11. 9 stumblingblock,...a *r* unto them:
2Co 6.13 Now for a *r* in the same, (I speak
Heb 2. 2 received a just *r* of reward;
10.35 which hath great *r* of reward.
11.26 respect unto the *r* of the reward.

RECOMPENSE

Nu 5. 7 he shall *r* his trespass with the
8 if the man have no kinsman to *r*
Ru 2.12 The Lord *r* thy work, and a full
2Sa 19.36 king *r* it me with such a reward?
Job 34.33 he will *r* it, whether thou refuse,
Pr 20.22 Say not thou, I will *r* evil; but
Isa 65. 6 but will *r*, even *r* into their bosom,
Jer 16.18 And first I will *r* their iniquity
25.14 *r* them according to their deeds,
50.29 *r* her according to her work;
Eze 7. 3 and will *r* upon thee all thine
4 I will *r* thy ways upon thee, and
8 and will *r* thee for all thine
9 I will *r* thee according to thy ways
9.10 will *r* their way upon their head.
11.21 *r* their way upon their own heads,
16.43 will *r* thy way upon thine head,
17.19 even it will I *r* upon his own head.
23.49 they shall *r* your lewdness upon
Hos 12. 2 to his doings will he *r* him.
Joel 3. 4 if ye *r* me, swiftly and speedily
Lk 14.14 they cannot *r* thee: for thou shalt
Ro 12.17 *R* to no man evil for evil. Provide
2Th 1. 6 with God to *r* tribulation to them
Heb 10.30 unto me, I will *r*, saith the Lord.

RECOMPENSED

Nu 5. 8 the trespass be *r* unto the Lord,
2Sa 22.21 of my hands hath he *r* me.
25 Lord hath *r* me according to my
Ps 18.20 of my hands hath he *r* me.
24 the Lord *r* me according to my
Pr 11.31 righteous shall be *r* in the earth:
Jer 18.20 Shall evil be *r* for good? for they
Eze 22.31 way have I *r* upon their heads,
Lk 14.14 thou shalt be *r* at the resurrection
Ro 11.35 and it shall be *r* unto him again?

RECONCILE

Lev 6.30 to *r* withal in the holy place,
1Sa 29. 4 he *r* himself unto his master?
Eze 45.20 simple: so shall ye *r* the house.
Eph 2.16 *r* both unto God in one body by the
Col 1.20 him to *r* all things unto himself;

RECONCILED

Mt 5.24 first be *r* to thy brother, and then
Ro 5.10 *r* to God by the death of his Son,
10 much more, being *r*, we shall be
1Co 7.11 unmarried, or be *r* to her husband:
2Co 5.18 of God, who hath *r* us to himself by
20 in Christ's stead, be ye *r* to God.
Col 1.21 wicked works, yet now hath he *r*

RECONCILIATION

Lev 8.15 sanctified it, to make *r* upon it.
2Ch 29.24 made *r* with their blood upon
Eze 45.15 offerings, to make *r* for them,
17 to make *r* for the house of Israel.
Dan 9.24 and to make *r* for iniquity, and to
2Co 5.18 hath given to us the ministry of *r*;
19 committed unto us the word of *r*.
Heb 2.17 make *r* for the sins of the people.

RECONCILING

Lev 16.20 made an end of *r* the holy place,
Ro 11.15 of them be the *r* of the world,
2Co 5.19 Christ, *r* the world unto himself,

RECORD

Ex 20.24 where I *r* my name I will come
Dt 30.19 heaven and earth to *r* this day
31.28 heaven and earth to *r* against
1Ch 16. 4 and to *r*, and to thank and praise
Ezr 6. 2 and therein was a *r* thus written:
Job 16.19 in heaven, and my *r* is on high.
Isa 8. 2 unto me faithful witnesses to *r*,
Jn 1.19 And this is the *r* of John, when
32 John bare *r*, saying, I saw the
34 bare *r* that this is the Son of God.
8.13 him, Thou bearest *r* of thyself;
13 of thyself; thy *r* is not true.
14 Though I bear *r* of myself, yet
14 of myself, yet my *r* is true: for
12.17 raised him from the dead, bare *r*.
19.35 And he that saw it bare *r*, and
35 his *r* is true: and he knoweth
Ac 20.26 I take you to *r* this day, that I am
Ro 10. 2 bear them *r* that they have a zeal
2Co 1.23 I call God for a *r* upon my soul,
8. 3 I bear *r*, yea, and beyond their
Gal 4.15 for I bear you *r*, that, if it had
Php 1. 8 For God is my *r*, how greatly I
Col 4.13 For I bear him *r*, that he hath a
1Jn 5. 7 are three that bear *r* in heaven,
10 the *r* that God gave of his Son.
11 this is the *r*, that God hath given
3Jn 12 itself: yea, and we also bear *r*;
12 and ye know that our *r* is true.
Rev 1. 2 Who bare *r* of the word of God,

RECOUNT

Na 2. 5 He shall *r* his worthies: they

RECOVER

Jdg 11.26 did ye not *r* them within that
1Sa 30. 8 them, and without fail *r* all.
2Sa 8. 3 went to *r* his border at the river
2Ki 1. 2 whether I shall *r* of this disease.
5. 3 for he would *r* him of his leprosy.
6 thou mayest *r* him of his leprosy.
7 unto me to *r* a man of his leprosy?
11 hand over the place, and *r* the leper.
8. 8, 9 saying, Shall I *r* of this disease?
10 him, Thou mayest certainly *r*:
14 me that thou shouldest surely *r*.
2Ch 13.20 Neither did Jeroboam *r* strength
14.13 that they could not *r* themselves;
Ps 39.13 spare me, that I may *r* strength,
Isa 11.11 to *r* the remnant of his people,
38.16 so wilt thou *r* me, and make me to
21 upon the boil, and he shall *r*.
Hos 2. 9 will *r* my wool and my flax given
Mk 16.18 on the sick, and they shall *r*.
2Ti 2.26 may *r* themselves out of the snare

RECOVERED

1Sa 30.18 *r* all that the Amalekites had
19 had taken to them: David *r* all.
22 ought of the spoil that we have *r*,
2Ki 13.25 him, and *r* the cities of Israel.
14.28 how he *r* Damascus, and Hamath,
16. 6 time Rezin king of Syria *r* Elath
20. 7 and laid it on the boil, and he *r*.
Isa 38. 9 sick, and was *r* of his sickness:
39. 1 that he had been sick, and was *r*.
Jer 8.22 of the daughter of my people *r*?
41.16 whom he had *r* from Ishmael the

RECOVERING

Lk 4.18 *r* of sight to the blind, to set at

RED

Gen 25.25 And the first came out *r*, all over
30 thee, with that same *r* pottage;
49.12 His eyes shall be *r* with wine, and
Ex 25. 5 rams' skins dyed *r*, and badgers'
26.14 for the tent of rams' skins dyed *r*,
35. 7 rams' skins dyed *r*, and badgers'
23 *r* skins of rams, and badgers' skins,
36.19 for the tent of rams' skins dyed *r*,
39.34 the covering of rams' skins dyed *r*,
Nu 19. 2 bring thee a *r* heifer without spot,

2Ki 3.22 on the other side as *r* as blood:
Est 1. 6 upon a pavement of *r*, and blue,
Ps 75. 8 there is a cup, and the wine is *r*;
Pr 23.31 thou upon the wine when it is *r*,
Isa 1.18 though they be *r* like crimson,
27. 2 unto her, A vineyard of *r* wine.
63. 2 art thou *r* in thine apparel, and
Na 2. 3 of his mighty men is made *r*,
Zec 1. 8 behold a man riding upon a *r* horse,
8 behind him were there *r* horses,
6. 2 In the first chariot were *r* horses;
Mt 16. 2 be fair weather: for the sky is *r*.
3 to day: for the sky is *r* and lowring.
Rev 6. 4 out another horse that was *r*:
12. 3 behold a great *r* dragon, having

The crossing of the Red Sea (Ex 14), as depicted in the Raphael Logge at the Vatican, completed in 1519.

RED SEA

Ex 10.19 and cast them into the *R* sea;
13.18 way the wilderness of the *R* sea:
15. 4 also are drowned in the *R* sea.
22 brought Israel from the *R* sea,
23.31 will set thy bounds from the *R* sea
Nu 14.25 wilderness by the way of the *R* sea.
21. 4 mount Hor by the way of the *R* sea,
14 What he did in the *R* sea, and
33.10 Elim, and encamped by the *R* sea.
11 And they removed from the *R* sea.
Dt 1. 1 the plain over against the *R* sea,
40 wilderness by...way of the *R* sea.
2. 1 wilderness by the way of the *R* sea,
11. 4 the water of the *R* sea to overflow
Jos 2.10 dried up the water of the *R* sea
4.23 Lord your God did to the *R* sea,
24. 6 and horsemen unto the *R* sea.
Jdg 11.16 the wilderness unto the *R* sea,
1Ki 9.26 on the shore of the *R* sea, in the
Neh 9. 9 heardest their cry by the *R* sea;
Ps 106. 7 him at the sea, even at the *R* sea,
9 He rebuked the *R* sea also, and it
22 and terrible things by the *R* sea.
136.13 which divided the *R* sea into parts:
15 Pharaoh and his host in the *R* sea:
Jer 49.21 noise...was heard in the *R* sea.
Ac 7.36 land of Egypt, and in the *R* sea,
Heb 11.29 passed through the *R* sea as by dry

REDEEM

Ex 6. 6 *r* you with a stretched out arm,
13.13 firstling of an ass thou shalt *r*
13 if thou wilt not *r* it, then thou shalt
13 firstborn of man...shalt thou *r*.
15 all the firstborn of my children I *r*.
34.20 firstling of an ass thou shalt *r*
20 if thou *r* him not, then shalt thou
20 firstborn of thy sons thou shalt *r*.
Lev 25.25 and if any of his kin come to *r* it,
25 he *r* that which his brother sold.
26 And if the man have none to *r* it,
26 and himself be able to *r* it;
29 he may *r* it within a whole year
29 within a full year may he *r* it.
32 may the Levites *r* at any time.
48 one of his brethren may *r* him:
49 or his uncle's son, may *r* him,
49 unto him of his family may *r* him;
49 or if he be able, he may *r* himself.
27.13 But if he will at all *r* it, then he
15 that sanctified it will *r* his house,
19 that sanctified the field will...*r* it,
20 And if he will not *r* the field, or if
27 he shall *r* it according to thine
31 will at all *r* ought of his tithes,
Nu 18.15 firstborn of man shalt thou...*r*,
15 of unclean beasts shalt thou *r*.
16 from a month old shalt thou *r*,
17 firstling of a goat, thou shalt not *r*;
Ru 4. 4 If thou wilt *r* it, *r* it: but
4 if thou wilt not *r* it, then tell me,
4 there is none to *r* it beside thee;
4 after thee. And he said, I will *r* it.
6 I cannot *r* it for myself, lest I mar
6 *r* thou my right to thyself;
6 for I cannot *r* it.
2Sa 7.23 whom God went to *r* for a people
1Ch 17.21 God went to *r* to be his own people,
Neh 5. 5 neither is it in our power to *r* them;
Job 5.20 famine he shall *r* thee from death:
6.23 *R* me from the hand of the mighty?
Ps 25.22 *R* Israel, O God, out of all his
26.11 *r* me, and be merciful unto me.
44.26 and *r* us for thy mercies' sake.
49. 7 can by any means *r* his brother,
15 God will *r* my soul from the power
69.18 Draw nigh unto my soul, and *r* it:
72.14 He shall *r* their soul from deceit
130. 8 *r* Israel from all his iniquities.
Isa 50. 2 shortened at all, that it cannot *r*?
Jer 15.21 I will *r* thee out of the hand of
Hos 13.14 grave; I will *r* them from death:
Mic 4.10 shall *r* thee from the hand of thine
Gal 4. 5 To *r* them that were under the
Tit 2.14 he might *r* us from all iniquity

REDEEMED

Gen 48.16 Angel which *r* me from all evil,
Ex 15.13 led forth the people...thou hast *r*:
21. 8 then shall he let her be *r*:
Lev 19.20 not at all *r*, nor freedom given her;
25.30 *r* within the space of a full year,
31 they may be *r*, and they shall go
48 After that he is sold he may be *r*
54 And if he be not *r* in these years,
27.20 man, it shall not be *r* any more.
27 if it be not *r*, then it shall be sold
28 devoted thing,...shall be sold or *r*:
29 None devoted,...shall be *r*;
33 shall be holy; it shall not be *r*.
Nu 3.46 And for those that are to be *r* of
48 the odd number of them is to be *r*,
49 them that were *r* by the Levites:
51 the money of them that were *r*
18.16 that are to be *r* from a month old
Dt 7. 8 *r* you out of the house of bondmen,
9.26 thou hast *r* through thy greatness,
13. 5 *r* you out of the house of bondage,
15.15 and the Lord thy God *r* thee:
21. 8 people Israel, whom thou hast *r*,
24.18 the Lord thy God *r* thee thence:
2Sa 4. 9 hath *r* my soul out of all adversity,
1Ki 1.29 hath *r* my soul out of all distress,
1Ch 17.21 whom thou hast *r* out of Egypt?
Neh 1.10 thou hast *r* by thy great power,
5. 8 have *r* our brethren the Jews,
Ps 31. 5 hast *r* me, O Lord God of truth.
71.23 and my soul, which thou hast *r*.
74. 2 inheritance, which thou hast *r*;
77.15 hast with thine arm *r* thy people,
106.10 *r* them from the hand of the enemy.
107. 2 Let the *r* of the Lord say so, whom
2 hath *r* from the hand of the enemy;
136.24 And hath *r* us from our enemies:
Isa 1.27 Zion shall be *r* with judgment,
29.22 saith the Lord, who *r* Abraham,
35. 9 there; but the *r* shall walk there:
43. 1 Fear not: for I have *r* thee, I have
44.22 return unto me; for I have *r* thee.
23 for the Lord hath *r* Jacob, and
48.20 The Lord hath *r* his servant Jacob.
51.11 the *r* of the Lord shall return,
52. 3 and ye shall be *r* without money.
9 his people, he hath *r* Jerusalem.
62.12 The holy people, The *r* of the Lord:
63. 4 and the year of my *r* is come.
9 his love and in his pity he *r* them;
Jer 31.11 For the Lord hath *r* Jacob, and
La 3.58 of my soul; thou hast *r* my life.
Hos 7.13 though I have *r* them, yet they
Mic 6. 4 *r* thee out of the house of servants;
Zec 10. 8 for I have *r* them: and they shall
Lk 1.68 hath visited and *r* his people,
24.21 he which should have *r* Israel:
Gal 3.13 Christ hath *r* us from the curse
1Pe 1.18 not *r* with corruptible things,
Rev 5. 9 and hast *r* us to God by thy blood
14. 3 which were *r* from the earth.
4 These were *r* from among men,

REDEEMER

Job 19.25 I know that my *r* liveth, and that
Ps 19.14 O Lord, my strength, and my *r*.
78.35 rock, and the high God their *r*.
Pr 23.11 For their *r* is mighty; he shall
Isa 41.14 saith the Lord, and thy *r*, the Holy

Biblical Themes

REDEMPTION

Then shall they give every man a ransom for his soul unto the Lord, when thou numberest them. Ex 30.12

The land shall not be sold for ever: for the land is mine. . . . If thy brother be waxen poor, and hath sold away some of his possession, and if any of his kin come to redeem it, then shall he redeem that which his brother sold. Lev 25.23, 25

Thou shalt remember that thou wast a bondman in the land of Egypt, and the Lord thy God redeemed thee. Dt 15.15

I know that my redeemer liveth. Job 19.25

They that trust in their wealth . . . none of them can by any means redeem his brother, nor give to God a ransom for him. . . . But God will redeem my soul from the power of the grave. Ps 49.6-7, 15

Fear not: for I have redeemed thee, I have called thee by thy name; thou art mine. Isa 43.1

Which of my creditors is it to whom I have sold you? Behold, for your iniquities have ye sold yourselves. . . . Is my hand shortened at all, that it cannot redeem? or have I no power to deliver? Isa 50.1-2

He hath poured out his soul unto death: and he was numbered with the transgressors; and he bare the sin of many, and made intercession for the transgressors. Isa 53.12

The Son of man came . . . to give his life a ransom for many. Mt 20.28

What man of you, having an hundred sheep, if he lose one of them, doth not leave . . . and go after that which is lost, until he find it? Lk 15.4

Except a man be born again, he cannot see the kingdom of God. Jn 3.3

Take heed therefore unto yourselves, and to all the flock . . . to feed the church of God, which he hath purchased with his own blood. Ac 20.28

In due time Christ died for the ungodly. . . . scarcely for a righteous man will one die. . . . But God commendeth his love toward us, in that, while we were yet sinners, Christ died for us. Ro 5.6-8

Know ye not that . . . ye are not your own? For ye are bought with a price. 1Co 6.19-20

All things are of God, who hath reconciled us to himself by Jesus Christ. . . . we pray you in Christ's stead, be ye reconciled to God. For he hath made him to be sin for us, who knew no sin; that we might be made the righteousness of God in him. 2Co 5.18, 20-21

When the fulness of the time was come, God sent forth his Son . . . to redeem them that were under the law, that we might receive the adoption of sons. Gal 4.4-5

You, being dead in your sins . . . hath he quickened together with him, having forgiven you all trespasses; blotting out the handwriting of ordinances that was against us, which was contrary to us, and took it out of the way, nailing it to his cross. Col 2. 13-14

Our Saviour Jesus Christ; who gave himself for us, that he might redeem us from all iniquity, and purify unto himself a peculiar people. Tit 2.13-14

Ye know that ye were not redeemed with corruptible things, as silver and gold . . . but with the precious blood of Christ, as of a lamb without blemish. 1Pe 1.18-19

Thou art worthy to take the book, and to open the seals thereof: for thou wast slain, and hast redeemed us to God by thy blood. Rev 5.9

Isa 43.14 Thus saith the Lord, your *r*, the
44. 6 Israel, and his *r* the Lord of hosts;
24 Thus saith the Lord, thy *r*, and he
47. 4 As for our *r*, the Lord of hosts is his
48.17 Thus saith the Lord, thy *R*, the
49. 7 the *R* of Israel, and his Holy One,
26 Lord am thy Saviour and thy *R*,
54. 5 and thy *R* the Holy One of Israel;
8 on thee, saith the Lord thy *R*.
59.20 And the *R* shall come to Zion, and
60.16 Lord am thy Saviour and thy *R*,
63.16 thou, O Lord, art our father, our *r*;
Jer 50.34 Their *R* is strong; The Lord of

REDEEMETH

Ps 34.22 Lord *r* the soul of his servants:
103. 4 Who *r* thy life from destruction;

REDEEMING

Ru 4. 7 concerning *r* and concerning
Eph 5.16 *R* the time, because the days are
Col 4. 5 them that are without, *r* the time.

REDEMPTION

Lev 25.24 ye shall grant a *r* for the land.
51 shall give again the price of his *r*
52 give him again the price of his *r*.
Nu 3.49 Moses took the *r* money of them
Ps 49. 8 (For the *r* of their soul is precious,
111. 9 He sent *r* unto his people: he
130. 7 mercy, and with him is plenteous *r*.
Jer 32. 7 the right of *r* is thine to buy it.
8 the *r* is thine; buy it for thyself.
Lk 2.38 that looked for *r* in Jerusalem.
21.28 heads; for your *r* draweth nigh.
Ro 3.24 through the *r* that is in Christ Jesus:
8.23 adoption, to wit, the *r* of our body.
1Co 1.30 and sanctification, and *r*:
Eph 1. 7 whom we have *r* through his blood,
14 the *r* of the purchased possession,
4.30 ye are sealed unto the day of *r*.
Col 1.14 whom we have *r* through his body,
Heb 9.12 having obtained eternal *r* for us.
15 for the *r* of the transgressions that

REDOUND

2Co 4.15 of many *r* to the glory of God.

REED

1Ki 14.15 as a *r* is shaken in the water,
Isa 42. 3 A bruised *r* shall he not break, and
Mt 11. 7 to see? A *r* shaken with the wind?
12.20 A bruised *r* shall he not break, and
27.29 head, and a *r* in his right hand:
30 took the *r*, and smote him on the
48 it with vinegar, and put it on a *r*,
Mk 15.19 smote him on the head with a *r*,
36 full of vinegar, and put it on a *r*,
Lk 7.24 to see? A *r* shaken with the wind?
Rev 11. 1 was given me a *r* like unto a rod:
21.15 talked with me had a golden *r* to
16 he measured the city with the *r*,

REEL

Ps 107.27 They *r* to and fro, and stagger
Isa 24.20 earth shall *r* to and fro like a

REFINE

Zec 13. 9 will *r* them as silver is refined,

REFINER

Mal 3. 3 he shall sit as a *r* and purifier of

REFINER'S

Mal 3. 2 for he is like a *r* fire, and like

REFORMATION

Heb 9.10 on them until the time of *r*.

REFRAIN

Gen 45. 1 Joseph could not *r* himself before
Job 7.11 I will not *r* my mouth; I will
Pr 1.15 them; *r* thy foot from their path:
Ec 3. 5 and a time to *r* from embracing;
Isa 48. 9 for my praise will I *r* for thee,
64.12 Wilt thou *r* thyself for these things,
Jer 31.16 *R* thy voice from weeping, and
Ac 5.38 *R* from these men, and let them
1Pe 3.10 let him *r* his tongue from evil,

REFRAINED

Gen 43.31 *r* himself, and said, Set on bread.
Est 5.10 Nevertheless Haman *r* himself:
Job 29. 9 The princes *r* talking, and laid
Ps 40. 9 I have not *r* my lips, O Lord, thou
119.101 *r* my feet from every evil way,
Isa 42.14 I have been still, and *r* myself:
Jer 14.10 they have not *r* their feet,

REFRAINETH

Pr 10.19 sin: but he that *r* his lips is wise.

REFRESH

1Ki 13. 7 home with me, and *r* thyself,
Ac 27. 3 unto his friends to *r* himself.
Phm 20 the Lord: *r* my bowels in the Lord.

REFRESHED

Ex 23.12 and the stranger, may be *r*.
31.17 seventh day he rested, and was *r*.

1Sa 16.23 so Saul was *r*, and was well, and
2Sa 16.14 weary, and *r* themselves there.
Job 32.20 I will speak, that I may be *r*:
Ro 15.32 of God, and may with you be *r*.
1Co 16.18 they have *r* my spirit and yours:
2Co 7.13 because his spirit was *r* by you all.
2Ti 1.16 he oft *r* me, and was not ashamed
Phm 7 bowels of the saints are *r* by thee,

REFRESHETH

Pr 25.13 for he *r* the soul of his masters.

REFRESHING

Isa 28.12 weary to rest; and this is the *r*:
Ac 3.19 the times of *r* shall come from

REFUGE

Nu 35. 6 there shall be six cities for *r*,
11 you cities to be cities of *r* for you:
12 shall be unto you cities for *r* from
13 give six cities shall ye have for *r*.
14 Canaan, which shall be cities of *r*.
15 These six cities shall be a *r*, both
25 shall restore him to the city of his *r*,
26 out the border of the city of his *r*,
27 the borders of the city of his *r*,
28 remained in the city of his *r* until
32 him that is fled to the city of his *r*,
Dt 33.27 The eternal God is thy *r*, and
Jos 20. 2 Appoint out for you cities of *r*,
3 your *r* from the avenger of blood.
21.13, 21, 27, 32, 38 city of *r* for the slayer;
2Sa 22. 3 my high tower, and my *r*, my
1Ch 6.57 Hebron, the city of *r*, and Libnah
67 gave unto them, of the cities of *r*,
Ps 9. 9 also will be a *r* for the oppressed,
9 oppressed, a *r* in times of trouble.
14. 6 poor, because the Lord is his *r*.
46. 1 God is our *r* and strength, a very
7, 11 us; the God of Jacob is our *r*.
48. 3 is known in her palaces for a *r*.
57. 1 of thy wings will I make my *r*,
59.16 and *r* in the day of my trouble.
62. 7 my strength, and my *r*, is in God.
8 before him: God is a *r* for us.
71. 7 many; but thou art my strong *r*.
91. 2 Lord, He is my *r* and my fortress:
9 hast made the Lord, which is my *r*,
94.22 and my God is the rock of my *r*.
104.18 high hills are a *r* for the wild goats;
142. 4 *r* failed me; no man cared for
5 Thou art my *r* and my portion in
Pr 14.26 his children shall have a place of *r*.
Isa 4. 6 for a place of *r*, and for a covert
25. 4 a *r* from the storm, a shadow from
28.15 for we have made lies our *r*, and
17 hail shall sweep away the *r* of lies,
Jer 16.19 and my *r* in the day of affliction,
Heb 6.18 have fled for *r* to lay hold upon the

REFUSE

Ex 4.23 if thou *r* to let him go, behold, I
8. 2 if thou *r* to let them go, behold, I
9. 2 if thou *r* to let them go, and wilt
10. 3 long wilt thou *r* to humble thyself
4 if thou *r* to let my people go,
16.28 *r* ye to keep my commandments
22.17 utterly *r* to give her unto him,
1Sa 15. 9 every thing that was vile and *r*,
Job 34.33 whether thou *r*, or whether thou
Pr 8.33 and be wise, and *r* it not.
21. 7 because they *r* to do judgment.
25 him; for his hands *r* to labor.
Isa 1.20 But if ye *r* and rebel, ye shall be
7.15 that he may know to *r* the evil,
16 the child shall know to *r* the evil,
Jer 8. 5 hold fast deceit, they *r* to return.
9. 6 through deceit they *r* to know me,
13.10 people, which *r* to hear my words,
25.28 *r* to take the cup at thine hand to
38.21 But if thou *r* to go forth, this is

La 3.45 and *r* in the midst of the people.
Am 8. 6 yea, and sell the *r* of the wheat?
Ac 25.11 worthy of death, I *r* not to die:
1Ti 4. 7 *r* profane and old wives' fables,
5.11 But the younger widows *r*: for
Heb 12.25 that ye *r* not him that speaketh.

REFUSED

Gen 37.35 but he *r* to be comforted; and he
39. 8 he *r*, and said unto his master's
48.19 his father *r*, and said, I know it,
Nu 20.21 Edom *r* to give Israel passage
1Sa 8.19 the people *r* to obey the voice of
16. 7 stature; because I have *r* him:
28.23 But he *r*, and said, I will not eat.
2Sa 2.23 Howbeit he *r* to turn aside:
13. 9 out before him; but he *r* to eat.
1Ki 20.35 thee. And the man *r* to smite him.
21.15 which he *r* to give thee for money:
2Ki 5.16 he urged him to take it; but he *r*.
Neh 9.17 *r* to obey, neither were mindful of
Est 1.12 Vashti *r* to come at the king's
Job 6. 7 things that my soul *r* to touch are
Ps 77. 2 not: my soul *r* to be comforted.
78.10 of God, and *r* to walk in his law;
67 he *r* the tabernacle of Joseph,
118.22 The stone which the builders *r* is
Pr 1.24 Because I have called, and ye *r*;
Isa 54. 6 wife of youth, when thou wast *r*,
Jer 5. 3 they have *r* to receive correction:
3 a rock; they have *r* to return.
11.10 which *r* to hear my words; and
31.15 *r* to be comforted for her children,
50.33 them fast; they *r* to let them go.
Eze 5. 6 they have *r* my judgments and
Hos 11. 5 king, because they *r* to return.
Zec 7.11 But they *r* to hearken, and pulled
Ac 7.35 Moses whom they *r*, saying, Who
1Ti 4. 4 God is good, and nothing to be *r*,
Heb 11.24 *r* to be called the son of Pharaoh's
12.25 escaped not who *r* him that spake

REFUSEDST

Jer 3. 3 forehead, thou *r* to be ashamed.

REFUSETH

Ex 7.14 hardened, he *r* to let the people go.
Nu 22.13 the Lord *r* to give me leave to go
14 said, Baalam *r* to come with us.
Dt 25. 7 My husband's brother *r* to raise up
Pr 10.17 but he that *r* reproof erreth.
13.18 shall be to him that *r* instruction:
15.32 He that *r* instruction despiseth
Isa 8. 6 people *r* the waters of Shiloah
Jer 15.18 incurable, which *r* to be healed?

REGARD

Gen 45.20 Also *r* not your stuff;
Ex 5. 9 and let them not *r* vain words.
Lev 19.31 *R* not them that have familiar
Dt 28.50 shall not *r* the person of the old,
1Sa 4.20 answered not, neither did she *r* it.
25.25 I pray thee, *r* this man of Belial,
2Sa 13.20 is thy brother; *r* not this thing.
2Ki 3.14 I *r* the presence of Jehoshaphat
Job 3. 4 let not God *r* it from above,
35.13 neither will the Almighty *r* it.
36.21 Take heed, *r* not iniquity: for
Ps 28. 5 they *r* not the works of the Lord,
31. 6 hated them that *r* lying vanities:
66.18 If I *r* iniquity in my heart, the
94. 7 neither shall the God of Jacob *r* it.
102.17 will *r* the prayer of the destitute,
Pr 5. 2 That thou mayest *r* discretion,
6.35 He will not *r* any ransom;
Ec 8. 2 that in *r* of the oath of God.
Isa 5.12 they *r* not the work of the Lord,
13.17 which shall not *r* silver; and as
La 4.16 he will no more *r* them: they
Dan 11.37 shall he *r* the God of his fathers,
37 desire of women, nor *r* any god:

Am 5.22 will I *r* the peace offerings of
Hab 1. 5 and *r*, and wonder marvellously:
Mal 1. 9 means: will he *r* your persons?
Lk 18. 4 I fear not God, nor *r* man;
Ac 8.11 to him they had *r*, because that
Ro 14. 6 day, to the Lord he doth not *r* it.

REGARDED

Ex 9.21 that *r* not the word of the Lord
1Ki 18.29 nor any to answer, nor any that *r*.
1Ch 17.17 *r* me according to the estate of a
Ps 106.44 Nevertheless he *r* their affliction,
Pr 1.24 out my hand, and no man *r*;
Dan 3.12 men, O king, have not *r* thee:
Lk 1.48 he hath *r* the low estate of his
18. 2 feared not God, neither *r* man:
Heb 8. 9 and I *r* them not, saith the Lord.

REGARDEST

2Sa 19. 6 thou *r* neither princes nor servants:
Job 30.20 I stand up, and thou *r* me not.
Mt 22.16 for thou *r* not the person of men.
Mk 12.14 for thou *r* not the person of men,

REGARDETH

Dt 10.17 *r* not persons, nor taketh reward:
Job 34.19 nor *r* the rich more than the poor?
39. 7 *r* he the crying of the driver.
Pr 12.10 man *r* the life of his beast:
13.18 that *r* reproof shall be honored.
15. 5 but he that *r* reproof is prudent.
29. 7 but the wicked *r* not to know it.
Ec 5. 8 that is higher than the highest *r*;
11. 4 that *r* the clouds shall not reap.
Isa 33. 8 despised the cities, he *r* no man.
Dan 6.13 of Judah, *r* not thee, O king,
Mal 2.13 he *r* not the offering any more,
Ro 14. 6 *r* the day, *r* it unto the Lord;
6 he that *r* not the day, to the Lord

REGARDING

Job 4.20 perish for ever without any *r* it.
Php 2.30 nigh unto death, not *r* his life,

REGENERATION

Mt 19.28 the *r* when the Son of man shall
Tit 3. 5 he saved us, by the washing of *r*,

REGION

Dt 3. 4 all the *r* of Argob, the kingdom of
13 the *r* of Argob, with all Bashan,
1Ki 4.11 of Abinadab, in all the *r* of Dor;
13 *r* of Argob, which is in Bashan,
24 over all the *r* on this side the river,
Mt 3. 5 and all the *r* round about Jordan,
4.16 sat in the *r* and shadow of death
Mk 1.28 all the *r* round about Galilee.
6.55 through that whole *r* round about,
Lk 3. 1 and of the *r* of Trachonitis, and
4.14 through all the *r* round about.
7.17 throughout all the *r* round about.
Ac 13.49 published throughout all the *r*.
14. 6 unto the *r* that lieth round about:
16. 6 Phrygia and the *r* of Galatia, and

REGIONS

Ac 8. 1 throughout the *r* of Judea and
2Co 10.16 preach the gospel in the *r* beyond
11.10 this boasting in the *r* of Achaia.
Gal 1.21 I came into the *r* of Syria and

REHEARSED

1Sa 8.21 he *r* them in the ears of the Lord.
17.31 spake, they *r* them before Saul:
Ac 11. 4 But Peter *r* the matter from the
14.27 they *r* all that God had done with

REHOBOAM

1Ki 11.43 *R* his son reigned in his stead.
12. 1 *R* went to Shechem: for all Israel
3 of Israel came, and spake unto *R*,

REHOBOAM

Son and successor of Solomon, 10th century B.C. (1Ki 11.43); having been accepted as king by Judah, attends an assembly at Shechem for acceptance by northern Israel; when they express readiness on condition that he treat them less harshly than Solomon, rejects the advice of the elders and threatens even harsher treatment, thereby causing them to revolt; flees for his life back to Jerusalem; raises an army to attack Israel and compel submission but is dissuaded by the prophet Shemaiah (1Ki 12); in his reduced domain of Judah, allows the idolatrous high places to flourish unchecked; is invaded by the Egyptian force of Shishak and the temple is plundered; maintains hostilities with Jeroboam of Israel; dies and is succeeded by his son Abijam (1Ki 14).

1Ki 12. 6 king *R* consulted with the old men,
12 the people came to *R* the third day,
17 of Judah, *R* reigned over them.
18 king *R* sent Adoram, who was over
18 king *R* made speed to get him up
21 when *R* was come to Jerusalem,
21 to bring the kingdom again to *R*
23 Speak unto *R*, the son of Solomon,
27 lord, even unto *R* king of Judah,
27 and go again to *R* king of Judah.
14.21 *R* the son of Solomon reigned in
21 *R* was forty and one years old when
25 to pass in the fifth year of king *R*,
27 king *R* made in their stead brasen
29 Now the rest of the acts of *R*, and
30 was war between *R* and Jeroboam
31 And *R* slept with his fathers, and
15. 6 was war between *R* and Jeroboam
1Ch 3.10 Solomon's son was *R*, Abia his son,
2Ch 9.31 and *R* his son reigned in his stead.
10. 1 And *R* went to Shechem: for to
3 all Israel came and spake to *R*,
6 *R* took counsel with the old men
12 and all the people came to *R* on
13 *R* forsook the counsel of the old
17 of Judah, *R* reigned over them.
18 *R* sent Hadoram that was over the
18 *R* made speed to get him up to his
11. 1 when *R* was come to Jerusalem,
1 bring the kingdom again to *R*.
3 Speak unto *R* the son of Solomon,
5 *R* dwelt in Jerusalem, and built
17 made *R* the son of Solomon strong,
18 *R* took him Mahalath the daughter
21 *R* loved Maachah the daughter of
22 *R* made Abijah the son of Maachah
12. 1 *R* had established the kingdom,
2 that in the fifth year of king *R*
5 came Shemaiah the prophet to *R*,
10 king *R* made shields of brass, and
13 So king *R* strengthened himself in
13 for *R* was one and forty years old
15 Now the acts of *R*, first and last,
15 wars between *R* and Jeroboam
16 *R* slept with his fathers, and was
13. 7 strengthened themselves against *R*
7 *R* was young and tenderhearted,

REIGN

Gen 37. 8 him, Shalt thou indeed *r* over us?
Ex 15.18 The Lord shall *r* for ever and ever.
Jdg 9. 8 the olive tree, *R* thou over us.
1Sa 11.12 that said, Shall Saul *r* over us?
12.12 Nay; but a king shall *r* over us:
1Ki 1.30 Solomon thy son shall *r* after me,
Job 34.30 That the hypocrite *r* not, lest the
Ps 146.10 The Lord shall *r* for ever, even thy
Pr 8.15 By me kings *r*, and princes decree
Ec 4.14 For out of prison he cometh to *r*;
Isa 24.23 the Lord of hosts shall *r* in mount
32. 1 a king shall *r* in righteousness,
Jer 23. 5 and a King shall *r* and prosper,
Dan 6.28 this Daniel prospered in the *r* of
Mt 2.22 that Archelaus did *r* in Judea in
Lk 1.33 *r* over the house of Jacob for ever;
3. 1 year of the *r* of Tiberius Caesar,
19.14 not have this man to *r* over us.
27 would not that I should *r* over them,
Ro 5.17 shall *r* in life by one, Jesus Christ.)
21 grace *r* through righteousness unto
6.12 Let not sin...*r* in your mortal body,
15.12 shall rise to *r* over the Gentiles;
1Co 4. 8 us: and I would to God ye did *r*,
8 that we also might *r* with you.
15.25 For he must *r*, till he hath put all
2Ti 2.12 suffer, we shall also *r* with him:
Rev 5.10 and we shall *r* on the earth.
11.15 and he shall *r* for ever and ever.
20. 6 shall *r* with him a thousand years.
22. 5 and they shall *r* for ever and ever.

REIGNED

Gen 36.31 kings that *r* in the land of Edom,
37 died, and Saul...*r* in his stead.
2Sa 8.15 And David *r* over all Israel; and
Ro 5.14 death *r* from Adam to Moses, even
17 one man's offense death *r* by one;
21 as sin hath *r* unto death, even so
1Co 4. 8 ye have *r* as kings without us:
Rev 11.17 thee thy great power, and hast *r*.
20. 4 and *r* with Christ a thousand years.

REIGNEST

1Ch 29.12 come of thee, and thou *r* over all;

REIGNETH

1Sa 12.14 and also the king that *r* over you
2Sa 15.10 shall say, Absalom *r* in Hebron.
1Ki 1.18 now, behold, Adonijah *r*; and now,
1Ch 16.31 among the nations, The Lord *r*.
Ps 47. 8 God *r* over the heathen: God
93. 1 The Lord *r*, he is clothed with
96.10 the heathen that the Lord *r*:
97. 1 The Lord *r*; let the earth rejoice;
99. 1 The Lord *r*; let the people
Pr 30.22 For a servant when he *r*; and a
Isa 52. 7 that saith unto Zion, Thy God *r*!
Rev 17.18 which *r* over the kings of the
19. 6 for the Lord God omnipotent *r*.

REINS

Job 16.13 he cleaveth my *r* asunder, and
19.27 my *r* be consumed within me.
Ps 7. 9 God trieth the hearts and *r*.
16. 7 my *r* also instruct me in the night
26. 2 prove me; try my *r* and my heart.
73.21 grieved, and I was pricked in my *r*.
139.13 For thou hast possessed my *r*:
Pr 23.16 my *r* shall rejoice, when thy lips
Isa 11. 5 faithfulness the girdle of his *r*.
Jer 11.20 that triest the *r* and the heart,
12. 2 their mouth, and far from their *r*.
17.10 Lord search the heart, I try the *r*,
20.12 and seest the *r* and the heart, let
La 3.13 of his quiver to enter into my *r*.
Rev 2.23 which searcheth the *r* and hearts:

REJECT

Hos 4. 6 I will also *r* thee, and thou shalt
Mk 6.26 sat with him, he would not *r* her.
7. 9 well ye *r* the commandment of God,
Tit 3.10 first and second admonition *r*;

REJECTED

1Sa 8. 7 they have not *r* thee, but they
7 they have *r* me, that I should not
10.19 And ye have this day *r* your God,
15.23 thou hast *r* the word of the Lord,
23 hath also *r* thee from being king.
26 thou hast *r* the word of the Lord,
26 Lord hath *r* thee from being king
16. 1 *r* him from reigning over Israel?
2Ki 17.15 And they *r* his statutes, and his
20 the Lord *r* all the seed of Israel,
Isa 53. 3 He is despised and *r* of men; a
Jer 2.37 the Lord hath *r* thy confidences,
6.19 my words, nor to my law, but *r* it.
30 because the Lord hath *r* them.
7.29 the Lord hath *r* and forsaken the
8. 9 they have *r* the word of the Lord;
14.19 Hast thou utterly *r* Judah? hath
La 5.22 thou hast utterly *r* us; thou art
Hos 4. 6 because thou hast *r* knowledge, I
Mt 21.42 The stone which the builders *r*,
Mk 8.31 and be *r* of the elders, and of the
12.10 The stone which the builders *r* is
Lk 7.30 and lawyers *r* the counsel of God
9.22 be *r* of the elders and chief priests
17.25 things, and be *r* of this generation.
20.17 The stone which the builders *r*,
Gal 4.14 in my flesh ye despised not, nor *r*;
Heb 6. 8 beareth thorns and briers is *r*,
12.17 inherited the blessing, he was *r*:

REJECTETH

Jn 12.48 He that *r* me, and receiveth not

REJOICE

Lev 23.40 shall *r* before the Lord your God
Dt 12. 7 shall *r* in all that ye put your hand
12 shall *r* before the Lord your God,
18 shalt *r* before the Lord your God
14.26 and thou shalt *r*, thou, and thine
16.11 shalt *r* before the Lord thy God,
14 thou shalt *r* in thy feast, thou, and
15 therefore thou shalt surely *r*.
26.11 thou shalt *r* in every good thing
27. 7 and *r* before the Lord thy God.
28.63 Lord will *r* over you to destroy
30. 9 will again *r* over thee for good,
32.43 *R*, O ye nations, with his people:
33.18 *R*, Zebulun, in thy going out;
Jdg 9.19 this day, then *r* ye in Abimelech,
19 and let him also *r* in you:
16.23 unto Dagon their god, and to *r*:
1Sa 2. 1 because I *r* in thy salvation.
19. 5 thou sawest it, and didst *r*:
2Sa 1.20 the daughters of the Philistines *r*,
1Ch 16.10 heart of them *r* that seek the Lord.
31 be glad, and let the earth *r*:
32 let the fields *r*, and all that is
2Ch 6.41 and let thy saints *r* in goodness.
20.27 made them to *r* over their enemies.
Neh 12.43 had made them *r* with great joy:
Job 3.22 Which *r* exceedingly, and are glad,
20.18 be,and he shall not *r* therein.
21.12 and *r* at the sound of the organ.
Ps 2.11 with fear, and *r* with trembling.
5.11 that put their trust in thee *r*:
9. 2 I will be glad and *r* in thee: I will
14 of Zion: I will *r* in thy salvation.
13. 4 trouble me *r* when I am moved.
5 my heart shall *r* in thy salvation.
14. 7 Jacob shall *r*, and Israel shall be
20. 5 We will *r* in thy salvation, and in
21. 1 salvation how greatly shall he *r*!
30. 1 not made my foes to *r* over me.
31. 7 I will be glad and *r* in thy mercy:
32.11 Be glad in the Lord, and *r*, ye
33. 1 *R* in the Lord, O ye righteous:
21 For our heart shall *r* in him,
35. 9 Lord: it shall *r* in his salvation.
19 enemies wrongfully *r* over me:
24 and let them not *r* over me.
26 together that *r* at mine hurt:
38.16 otherwise they should *r* over me:
40.16 Let all those that seek thee *r*

RELIEF

Ac 11.29 to send *r* unto the brethren

RELIEVE

Lev 25.35 then thou shalt *r* him: yea,
Isa 1.17 seek judgment, *r* the oppressed,
La 1.11 things for meat to *r* the soul:
16 comforter that should *r* my soul is
19 sought their meat to *r* their souls.
1Ti 5.16 let them *r* them, and let not the
16 that it may *r* them that are widows

RELIEVED

1Ti 5.10 feet, if she have *r* the afflicted,

RELIGION

Ac 26. 5 sect of our *r* I lived a Pharisee.
Gal 1.13 in time past in the Jews' *r*, how
14 profited in the Jews' *r* above many
Jas 1.26 own heart, this man's *r* is vain.
27 Pure *r* and undefiled before God

RELIGIOUS

Ac 13.43 many of the Jews and *r* proselytes
Jas 1.26 any man among you seem to be *r*,

REMAIN

Gen 38.11 *R* a widow at thy father's house,
Ex 8. 9 that they may *r* in the river only?
11 they shall *r* in the river only.
12.10 nothing of it *r* until the morning;
23.18 shall the fat of my sacrifice *r*
29.34 of the bread, *r* unto the morning,
Lev 19. 6 ought *r* until the third day, it shall
25.28 *r* in the hand of him that...bought
52 *r* but few years unto the year of
27.18 according to the years that *r*,
Nu 33.55 those which ye let *r* of them shall
Dt 2.34 of every city, we left none to *r*:
16. 4 *r* all night until the morning.
19.20 which *r* shall hear, and fear, and
21.13 and shall *r* in thine house, and
23 His body shall not *r* all night
Jos 1.14 shall *r* in the land which Moses
2.11 *r* any more courage in any man,
8.22 they let none of them *r* or escape.
10.27 mouth, which *r* until this very day.
28 that were therein: he let none *r*:
30 were therein; he let none *r* in it;
23. 4 you by lot these nations that *r*,
7 nations, these that *r* among you;
12 even these that *r* among you, and
Jdg 5.17 and why did Dan *r* in ships?
21. 7, 16 do for wives for them that *r*,
1Sa 20.19 hand, and shalt *r* by the stone Ezel.
1Ki 11.16 (For six months did Joab *r* there
18.22 I only, *r* a prophet of the Lord;
2Ki 7.13 thee, five of the horses that *r*,
Ezr 9.15 for we *r* yet escaped, as it is this
Job 21.32 grave, and shall *r* in the tomb.
27.15 that *r* of him shall be buried in
37. 8 go into dens, and *r* in their places.
Ps 55. 7 far off, and *r* in the wilderness.
Pr 2.21 land, and the perfect shall *r* in it.
21.16 *r* in the congregation of the dead.
Isa 10.32 yet shall he *r* at Nob that day: he
32.16 righteousness *r* in the fruitful
44.13 man; that it may *r* in the house.
65. 4 Which *r* among the graves, and
66.22 I will make, shall *r* before me,
22 shall your seed and your name *r*.
Jer 8. 3 residue...that *r* of this evil family,
3 *r* in all the places whither I have
17.25 and this city shall *r* for ever.
24. 8 of Jerusalem, that *r* in this land,
27.11 will I let *r* still in their own land,
19 of the vessels that *r* in this city,
21 the vessels that *r* in the house of
30.18 palace shall *r* after the manner
38. 4 the men of war that *r* in this city,
42.17 none of them shall *r* or escape
44. 7 Judah, to leave you none to *r*;
14 shall escape or *r*, that they should
51.62 that none shall *r* in it, neither
Eze 7.11 none of them shall *r*, nor of their
17.21 and they that *r* shall be scattered
31.13 all the fowls of the heaven *r*,
32. 4 all the fowls of the heaven to *r*
39.14 that *r* upon the face of the earth,
Am 6. 9 if there *r* ten men in one house,
Ob 14 that did *r* in the day of distress.
Zec 5. 4 shall *r* in the midst of his house,
12.14 All the families that *r*, every
Lk 10. 7 And in the same house *r*, eating
Jn 6.12 Gather up the fragments that *r*,
15.11 that my joy might *r* in you, and
16 fruit, and that your fruit should *r*:
19.31 bodies should not *r* upon the cross
1Co 7.11 if she depart, let her *r* unmarried,
15. 6 the greater part *r* unto this present,
1Th 4.15 and *r* unto the coming of the Lord
17 are alive and *r* shall be caught up
Heb 12.27 which cannot be shaken may *r*.
1Jn 2.24 from the beginning shall *r* in you,
Rev 3. 2 strengthen the things which *r*,

REMAINDER

Ex 29.34 thou shalt burn the *r* with fire:
Lev 6.16 the *r* thereof shall Aaron and his
7.16 also the *r* of it shall be eaten:
17 the *r* of the flesh of the sacrifice
2Sa 14. 7 name nor *r* upon the earth.
Ps 76.10 the *r* of wrath shalt thou restrain.

REMAINED

Gen 7.23 Noah only *r* alive, and they that
14.10 they that *r* fled to the mountain.
Ex 8.31 from his people; there *r* not one.
10.15 there *r* not any green thing in
19 *r* not one locust in all the coasts
14.28 there *r* not so much as one of them.
Nu 11.26 *r* two of the men in the camp,
35.28 have *r* in the city of his refuge
36.12 their inheritance *r* in the tribe
Dt 3.11 only Og king of Bashan *r* of the
4.25 ye shall have *r* long in the land,
Jos 10.20 the rest which *r* of them entered
11.22 in Gath, and in Ashdod, there *r*.
13.12 who *r* of the remnant of the giants:
18. 2 *r* among the children of Israel
21.20 which *r* of the children of Kohath,
26 of the children of Kohath that *r*.
Jdg 7. 3 and there *r* ten thousand.
1Sa 11.11 they which *r* were scattered, so that
23.14 *r* in a mountain in the wilderness
24. 3 his men *r* in the sides of the cave.
2Sa 13.20 Tamar *r* desolate in her brother
1Ki 22.46 which *r* in the days of his father
2Ki 10.11 Jehu slew all that *r* of the house of
17 he slew all that *r* unto Ahab in
13. 6 there *r* the grove also in Samaria.)
24.14 none *r*, save the poorest sort of
25.22 as for the people that *r* in the land
1Ch 13.14 ark of God *r* with the family of
Ec 2. 9 also my wisdom *r* with me.
Jer 34. 7 cities *r* of the cities of Judah.
37.10 there *r* but wounded men among
16 Jeremiah had *r* there many days;
21 Thus Jeremiah *r* in the court of the
38.13 and Jeremiah *r* in the court of the
39. 9 of the people that *r* in the city,
9 with the rest of the people that *r*.
41.10 all the people that *r* in Mizpah,
48.11 therefore his taste *r* in him, and
51.30 flight, they have *r* in their holds:
52.15 of the people that *r* in the city,
La 2.22 Lord's anger none escaped nor *r*:
Eze 3.15 *r* there astonished among them
Dan 10. 8 and there *r* no strength in me:
13 I *r* there with the kings of Persia.
17 there *r* no strength in me,
Mt 11.23 it would have *r* until this day.
14.20 fragments that *r* twelve baskets
Lk 1.22 unto them, and *r* speechless.
9.17 that *r* to them twelve baskets.
Jn 6.13 which *r* over and above unto them
Ac 5. 4 Whiles it *r*, was it not thine own?
27.41 stuck fast, and *r* unmovable, but

REMAINEST

La 5.19 Thou, O Lord, *r* for ever; thy
Heb 1.11 They shall perish; but thou *r*;

REMAINETH

Gen 8.22 While the earth *r*, seedtime and
Ex 12.10 which *r* of it until the morning
Jos 8.29 heap of stones, that *r* unto this day.
1Ch 17. 1 the covenant of the Lord *r* under
Job 19. 4 erred, mine error *r* with myself.
Jer 38. 2 He that *r* in this city shall die
Hag 2. 5 so my spirit *r* among you: fear ye
Jn 9.41 say, We see; therefore your sin *r*.
1Co 7.29 it *r*, that both they that have
2Co 3.11 more that which *r* is glorious.
14 for until this day *r* the same vail
9. 9 poor: his righteousness *r* for ever.
Heb 4. 6 it *r* that some must enter therein,
9 *r* therefore a rest to the people of
10.26 there *r* no more sacrifice for sins,
1Jn 3. 9 his seed *r* in him: and he cannot

REMAINING

Nu 9.22 upon the tabernacle, *r* thereon,
Dt 3. 3 him until none was left to him *r*.
Jos 10.33 until he had left him none *r*.
37 he left none *r*, according to all that
39 he left none *r*: as he had done to
40 left none *r*, but utterly destroyed
11. 8 them, until they left them none *r*.
21.40 *r* of the families of the Levites,
2Sa 21. 5 *r* in any of the coasts of Israel,
2Ki 10.11 priests, until he left him none *r*.
1Ch 9.33 who *r* in the chambers were free:
Job 18.19 people, nor any *r* in his dwellings.
Ob 18 not be any *r* of the house of Esau;
Jn 1.33 Spirit descending, and *r* on him,

REMEDY

2Ch 36.16 his people, till there was no *r*.
Pr 6.15 shall he be broken without *r*.
29. 1 be destroyed, and that without *r*.

REMEMBER

Gen 9.15 And I will *r* my covenant, which
16 I may *r* the everlasting covenant
40.23 did not the chief butler *r* Joseph,
41. 9 saying, I do *r* my faults this day:
Ex 13. 3 *R* this day, in which ye came out
20. 8 *R* the sabbath day, to keep it holy.
32.13 *R* Abraham, Isaac, and Israel, thy
Lev 26.42 will I *r* my covenant with Jacob,
42 covenant with Abraham will I *r*;
42 and I will *r* the land.
45 will for their sakes *r* the covenant
Nu 11. 5 We *r* the fish, which we did eat in
15.39 and *r* all the commandments of the
40 That ye may *r*, and do all my
Dt 5.15 And *r* that thou wast a servant in
7.18 but shalt well *r* what the Lord thy
8. 2 And thou shalt *r* all the way which
18 thou shalt *r* the Lord thy God: for
9. 7 *R*, and forget not, how thou
27 *R* thy servants, Abraham, Isaac,
15.15 shalt *r* that thou wast a bondman
16. 3 thou mayest *r* the day when thou
12 shalt *r* that thou wast a bondman
24. 9 *R* what the Lord thy God did unto
18, 22 shalt *r*...thou wast a bondman
25.17 *R* what Amalek did unto thee by
32. 7 *R* the days of old, consider the
Jos 1.13 *R* the word which Moses the
Jdg 9. 2 *r* also that I am your bone and
16.28 *r* me, I pray thee, and strengthen

1Sa 1.11 and *r* me, and not forget thine
15. 2 I *r* that which Amalek did to
25.31 my lord, then *r* thine handmaid.
2Sa 14.11 let the king *r* the Lord thy God,
19.19 neither do thou *r* that which thy
2Ki 9.25 *r* how that, when I and thou rode
20. 3 *r* now how I have walked before
1Ch 16.12 *R* his marvellous works that he
2Ch 6.42 *r* the mercies of David thy servant.
Neh 1. 8 *R*, I beseech thee, the word that
4.14 *r* the Lord, which is great and
13.14 *R* me, O my God, concerning this,
22 *R* me, O my God, concerning this
29 *R* them, O my God, because they
31 *R* me, O my God, for good.
Job 4. 7 *R*, I pray thee, who ever perished,
7. 7 O *r* that my life is wind: mine eye
10. 9 *R*, I beseech thee, that thou hast
11.16 and *r* it as waters that pass away:
14.13 appoint me a set time, and *r* me!
21. 6 Even when I *r* I am afraid, and
36.24 *R* that thou magnify his work,
41. 8 upon him, *r* the battle, do no more.
Ps 20. 3 *R* all thy offerings, and accept thy
7 *r* the name of the Lord our God.
22.27 All the ends of the world shall *r*
25. 6 *R*, O Lord, thy tender mercies and
7 *R* not the sins of my youth, nor
7 *r* thou me for thy goodness' sake,
42. 4 When I *r* these things, I pour out
6 I *r* thee from the land of Jordan,
63. 6 When I *r* thee upon my bed, and
74. 2 *R* thy congregation, which thou
18 *R* this, that the enemy hath
22 *r* how the foolish man reproacheth
77.10 I will *r* the years of the right hand
11 I will *r* the works of the Lord:
11 surely I will *r* thy wonders of old.
79. 8 *r* not against us former iniquities:
89.47 *R* how short my time is: wherefore
50 *R*, Lord, the reproach of thy
103.18 to those that *r* his commandments
105. 5 *R* his marvellous works that he
106. 4 *R* me, O Lord, with the favor that
119.49 *R* the word unto thy servant, upon
132. 1 *r* David, and all his afflictions:
137. 6 If I do not *r* thee, let my tongue
7 *R*, O Lord, the children of Edom
143. 5 I *r* the days of old; I meditate on
Pr 31. 7 poverty, and *r* his misery no more.
Ec 5.20 not much *r* the days of his life;
11. 8 yet let him *r* the days of darkness;
12. 1 *R* now thy Creator in the days of
SS 1. 4 we will *r* thy love more than wine:
Isa 38. 3 *R* now, O Lord, I beseech thee,
43.18 *R* ye not the former things, neither
25 own sake, and will not *r* thy sins.
44.21 *R* these, O Jacob and Israel; for
46. 8 *R* this, and shew yourselves men:
9 *R* the former things of old: for I
47. 7 neither didst *r* the latter end of it.
54. 4 and shalt not *r* the reproach of thy
64. 5 those that *r* thee in thy ways:
9 O Lord, neither *r* iniquity for ever:
Jer 2. 2 I *r* thee, the kindness of thy
3.16 to mind: neither shall they *r* it;
14.10 he will now *r* their iniquity, and
21 *r*, break not thy covenant with us.
15.15 *r* me, and visit me, and revenge
17. 2 Whilst their children *r* their altars
18.20 *R* that I stood before thee to speak
31.20 him, I do earnestly *r* him still:
34 and I will *r* their sin no more.
44.21 did not the Lord *r* them, and came
51.50 *r* the Lord afar off, and let
La 5. 1 *R*, O Lord, what is come upon us:
Eze 6. 9 you shall *r* me among the nations
16.60 Nevertheless I will *r* my covenant
61 shalt *r* thy ways, and be ashamed,
63 thou mayest *r*, and be confounded,
20.43 And there shall ye *r* your ways,
23.27 unto them, nor *r* Egypt any more.
36.31 Then shall ye *r* your own evil ways,
Hos 7. 2 that I *r* all their wickedness:
8.13 now will he *r* their iniquity, and
9. 9 therefore he will *r* their iniquity,
Mic 6. 5 *r* now what Balak king of Moab
Hab 3. 2 make known; in wrath *r* mercy.
Zec 10. 9 they shall *r* me in far countries;
Mal 4. 4 *R* ye the law of Moses my servant,
Mt 16. 9 neither *r* the five loaves of the
27.63 Sir, we *r* that that deceiver said,
Mk 8.18 hear ye not? and do ye not *r*?
Lk 1.72 and to *r* his holy covenant;
16.25 Son, *r* that thou in thy lifetime
17.32 *R* Lot's wife.
23.42 *r* me when thou comest into thy
24. 6 *r* how he spake unto you when he
Jn 15.20 *R* the word that I said unto you,
16. 4 ye may *r* that I told you of them.
Ac 20.31 *r*, that by the space of three years
35 to *r* the words of the Lord Jesus,
1Co 11. 2 that ye *r* me in all things, and
Gal 2.10 would that we should *r* the poor;
Eph 2.11 Wherefore *r*, that ye being in time
Col 4.18 *R* my bonds. Grace be with you.
1Th 2. 9 For ye *r*, brethren, our labor and
2Th 2. 5 *R* ye not, that, when I was yet with
2Ti 2. 8 *R* that Jesus Christ of the seed of
Heb 8.12 their iniquities will I *r* no more.
10.17 sins and iniquities will I *r* no more.
13. 3 *R* them that are in bonds, as
7 *R* them which have the rule over
3Jn 10 will *r* his deeds which he doeth,
Jude 17 *r* ye the words which were spoken
Rev 2. 5 *R* therefore from whence thou art
3. 3 *R* therefore how thou hast received

REMEMBERED

Gen 8. 1 And God *r* Noah, and every living
19.29 that God *r* Abraham, and sent Lot
30.22 And God *r* Rachel, and God
42. 9 And Joseph *r* the dreams which he
Ex 2.24 God *r* his covenant with Abraham,
6. 5 and I have *r* my covenant.
Nu 10. 9 shall be *r* before the Lord your God,
Jdg 8.34 children of Israel *r* not the Lord
1Sa 1.19 Hannah his wife; and the Lord *r*
2Ch 24.22 Joash the king *r* not the kindness
Est 2. 1 *r* Vashti, and what she had done,
9.28 these days should be *r* and kept
Job 24.20 he shall be no more *r*; and
Ps 45.17 name to be *r* in all generations:
77. 3 I *r* God, and was troubled: I
78.35 they *r* that God was their rock,
39 For he *r* that they were but flesh;
42 They *r* not his hand, nor the day
98. 3 He hath *r* his mercy and his truth
105. 8 He hath *r* his covenant for ever,
42 For he *r* his holy promise, and
106. 7 *r* not the multitude of thy mercies;
45 And he *r* for them his covenant,
109.14 Let the iniquity of his fathers be *r*
16 that he *r* not to shew mercy, but
111. 4 made his wonderful works to be *r*:
119.52 I *r* thy judgments of old, O Lord;
55 I have *r* thy name, O Lord, in the
136.23 Who *r* us in our low estate: for his
137. 1 yea, we wept, when we *r* Zion.
Ec 9.15 yet no man *r* that same poor man.
Isa 23.16 many songs, that thou mayest be *r*.
57.11 thou hast lied, and hast not *r* me,
63.11 Then he *r* the days of old, Moses,
65.17 and the former shall not be *r*, nor
Jer 11.19 that his name may be no more *r*.
La 1. 7 Jerusalem *r* in the days of her
2. 1 *r* not his footstool in the day of his
Eze 3.20 which he hath done shall not be *r*;
16.22, 43 hast not *r* the days of thy youth,
21.24 ye have made your iniquity to be *r*,
32 thou shalt be no more *r*: for I the
25.10 that the Ammonites may not be *r*
33.13 his righteousnesses shall not be *r*;
Hos 2.17 shall no more be *r* by their name.
Am 1. 9 and *r* not the brotherly covenant:
Jon 2. 7 soul fainted within me I *r* the Lord:
Zec 13. 2 land, and they shall no more be *r*:
Mt 26.75 And Peter *r* the word of Jesus,
Lk 22.61 And Peter *r* the word of the Lord,
24. 8 And they *r* his words,
Jn 2.17 his disciples *r* that it was written,
22 his disciples *r* that he had said this
12.16 then *r* they that these things were
Ac 11.16 Then *r* I the word of the Lord, how
Rev 18. 5 and God hath *r* her iniquities.

REMEMBEREST

Ps 88. 5 the grave, whom thou *r* no more:
Mt 5.23 and there *r* that thy brother hath

REMEMBERETH

Ps 9.12 inquisition for blood, he *r* them:
103.14 our frame; he *r* that we are dust.
La 1. 9 she *r* not her last end; therefore
Jn 16.21 child, she *r* no more the anguish,
2Co 7.15 he *r* the obedience of you all, how

REMEMBERING

La 3.19 *R* mine affliction and my misery,
1Th 1. 3 *R* without ceasing your work of

REMEMBRANCE

Ex 17.14 utterly put out the *r* of Amalek
Nu 5.15 memorial, bringing iniquity to *r*.
Dt 25.19 shalt blot out the *r* of Amalek
32.26 I would make the *r* of them to cease
2Sa 18.18 have no son to keep my name in *r*:
1Ki 17.18 come unto me to call my sin to *r*,
Job 18.17 His *r* shall perish from the earth,
Ps 6. 5 For in death there is no *r* of thee:
30. 4 thanks at the *r* of his holiness.
34.16 to cut off the *r* of them from the
38(T) A Psalm of David, to bring to *r*
70(T) A Psalm of David, to bring to *r*.
77. 6 I call to *r* my song in the night:
83. 4 name of Israel may be no more in *r*.
97.12 thanks at the *r* of his holiness.
102.12 and thy *r* unto all generations.
112. 6 righteous shall be in everlasting *r*.
Ec 1.11 There is no *r* of former things;
11 any *r* of things that are to come
2.16 there is no *r* of the wise more than
Isa 26. 8 thy name, and to the *r* of thee.
43.26 Put me in *r*: let us plead together:
57. 8 the posts hast thou set up thy *r*:
La 3.20 My soul hath them still in *r*,
Eze 21.23 but he will call to *r* the iniquity,
24 because,...that ye are come to *r*,
23.19 calling to *r* the days of her youth,
21 thou calledst to *r* the lewdness of
29.16 which bringeth their iniquity to *r*,
Mal 3.16 a book of *r* was written before
Mk 11.21 Peter calling to *r* saith unto him,
Lk 1.54 servant Israel, in *r* of his mercy;
22.19 given for you: this do in *r* of me.
Jn 14.26 and bring all things to your *r*,
Ac 10.31 and thine alms are had in *r* in the
1Co 4.17 shall bring you into *r* of my ways
11.24 broken for you: this do in *r* of me.
25 do ye, as oft as ye drink it, in *r* of me.
Php 1. 3 thank...God upon every *r* of you,
1Th 3. 6 that ye have good *r* of us always,
1Ti 4. 6 the brethren in *r* of these things,
2Ti 1. 3 I have *r* of thee in my prayers
5 I call to *r* the unfeigned faith
6 I put thee in *r* that thou stir up
2.14 Of these things put them in *r*,
Heb 10. 3 there is a *r* again made of sins
32 But call to *r* the former days, in
2Pe 1.12 you always in *r* of these things,
13 stir you up by putting you in *r*;
15 to have these things always in *r*.
3. 1 up your pure minds by way of *r*:

Jude 5 I will therefore put you in *r*,
Rev 16.19 Babylon came in *r* before God,

REMEMBRANCES

Job 13.12 Your *r* are like unto ashes, your

REMISSION

Mt 26.28 is shed for many for the *r* of sins.
Mk 1. 4 of repentance for the *r* of sins.
Lk 1.77 his people by the *r* of their sins,
3. 3 of repentance for the *r* of sins;
24.47 and *r* of sins should be preached
Ac 2.38 of Jesus Christ for the *r* of sins,
10.43 in him shall receive *r* of sins.
Ro 3.25 for the *r* of sins that are past,
Heb 9.22 without shedding of blood is no *r*.
10.18 Now where *r* of these is, there is no

REMIT

Jn 20.23 Whose soever sins ye *r*, they are

REMITTED

Jn 20.23 ye remit, they are *r* unto them;

REMNANT

Ex 26.12 *r* that remaineth of the curtains
Lev 2. 3 *r* of the meat offering shall be
5.13 the *r* shall be the priest's, as a meat
14.18 *r* of the oil that is in the priest's
Dt 3.11 remained of the *r* of giants;
28.54 *r* of his children which he shall
Jos 12. 4 which was of the *r* of the giants,
13.12 remained of the *r* of the giants:
23.12 cleave unto the *r* of these nations,
2Sa 21. 2 but of the *r* of the Amorites; and
1Ki 12.23 to the *r* of the people, saying,
14.10 the *r* of the house of Jeroboam,
22.46 the *r* of the sodomites, which
2Ki 19. 4 lift up thy prayer for the *r* that
30 *r* that is escaped of the house of
31 of Jerusalem shall go forth a *r*,
21.14 forsake the *r* of mine inheritance,
25.11 with the *r* of the multitude, did
1Ch 6.70 of the *r* of the sons of Kohath.
2Ch 30. 6 and he will return to the *r* of you,
34. 9 and of all the *r* of Israel, and of
Ezr 3. 8 *r* of their brethren the priests
9. 8 our God, to leave us a *r* to escape,
14 should be no *r* nor escaping?
Neh 1. 3 *r* that are left of the captivity
Job 22.20 the *r* of them the fire consumeth.
Isa 1. 9 had left unto us a very small *r*,
10.20 in that day, that the *r* of Israel,
21 The *r* shall return, even the *r* of
22 sea, yet a *r* of them shall return:
11.11 time to recover the *r* of his people,
16 an highway for the *r* of his people,
14.22 the name, and *r*, and son, and
30 famine, and he shall slay thy *r*.
15. 9 Moab, and upon the *r* of the land.
16.14 *r* shall be very small and feeble.
17. 3 from Damascus, and the *r* of Syria:
37. 4 lift up thy prayer for the *r* that is
31 *r* that is escaped of the house of
32 of Jerusalem shall go forth a *r*,
46. 3 and all the *r* of the house of Israel,
Jer 6. 9 glean the *r* of Israel as a vine:
11.23 there shall be no *r* of them: for
15.11 Verily it shall be well with thy *r*;
23. 3 will gather the *r* of my flock out
25.20 and Ekron, and the *r* of Ashdod,
31. 7 save thy people, the *r* of Israel.
39. 9 captive...the *r* of the people that
40.11 of Babylon had left a *r* of Judah,
15 and the *r* in Judah perish?
41.16 the *r* of the people whom he had
42. 2 Lord thy God, even for all this *r*;
15 word of the Lord, ye *r* of Judah;
19 concerning you, O ye *r* of Judah;
43. 5 took all the *r* of Judah, that were
44.12 I will take the *r* of Judah, that
14 none of the *r* of Judah, which are
28 all the *r* of Judah, that are gone
47. 4 the *r* of the country of Caphtor.
5 cut off with the *r* of their valley:
Eze 5.10 whole *r* of thee will I scatter into
6. 8 Yet will I leave a *r*, that ye may
11.13 make a full end of the *r* of Israel?
14.22 therein shall be left a *r* that shall
23.25 thy *r* shall fall by the sword: they
25.16 and destroy the *r* of the sea coast.
Joel 2.32 in the *r* whom the Lord shall call.
Am 1. 8 *r* of the Philistines shall perish,
5.15 be gracious unto the *r* of Joseph.
9.12 they may possess the *r* of Edom,
Mic 2.12 will surely gather the *r* of Israel;
4. 7 I will make her that halted a *r*,
5. 3 *r* of his brethren shall return
7 *r* of Jacob shall be in the midst
8 the *r* of Jacob shall be among the
7.18 of the *r* of his heritage?
Hab 2. 8 all the *r* of the people shall spoil
Zep 1. 4 I will cut off the *r* of Baal from
2. 7 for the *r* of the house of Judah;
9 the *r* of my people shall possess
3.13 *r* of Israel shall not do iniquity,
Hag 1.12 with all the *r* of the people, obeyed
14 spirit of all the *r* of the people;
Zec 8. 6 in the eyes of the *r* of this people
12 the *r* of this people to possess all
Mt 22. 6 And the *r* took his servants, and
Ro 9.27 of the sea, a *r* shall be saved:
11. 5 is a *r* according to the election of
Rev 11.13 the *r* were affrighted, and gave
12.17 make war with the *r* of her seed,
19.21 the *r* were slain with the sword of

REMOVE

Gen 48.17 to *r* it from Ephraim's head unto
Nu 36. 7 of Israel *r* from tribe to tribe:
9 the inheritance *r* from one tribe
Dt 19.14 not *r* thy neighbor's landmark,
Jos 3. 3 then ye shall *r* from your place,
Jdg 9.29 hand! then would I *r* Abimelech.
2Sa 6.10 So David would not *r* the ark of
2Ki 23.27 will *r* Judah also out of my sight,
24. 3 to *r* them out of his sight, for the
2Ch 33. 8 will I any more *r* the foot of Israel
Job 24. 2 Some *r* the landmarks; they
27. 5 not *r* mine integrity from me.
Ps 36.11 not the hand of the wicked *r* me.
39.10 *R* thy stroke away from me: I
119.22 *R* from me reproach...contempt;
29 *R* from me the way of lying: and
Pr 4.27 nor to the left: *r* thy foot from evil.
5. 8 *R* thy way far from her, and come
22.28 *R* not the ancient landmark,
23.10 *R* not the old landmark; and
30. 8 *R* far from me vanity and lies:
Ec 11.10 *r* sorrow from thy heart, and put
Isa 13.13 the earth shall *r* out of her place,
46. 7 from his place shall he not *r*:
Jer 4. 1 my sight, then shalt thou not *r*.
27.10 you, to *r* you far from your land;
32.31 should *r* it from before my face,
50. 3 they shall *r*, they shall depart,
8 *R* out of the midst of Babylon, and
Eze 12. 3 *r* by day in their sight; and thou
3 *r* from thy place to another place
21.26 *R* the diadem, and take off the
45. 9 *r* violence and spoil, and execute
Hos 5.10 were like them that *r* the bound:
Joel 2.20 *r* far off from you the northern
3. 6 *r* them far from their border.
Mic 2. 3 which ye shall not *r* your necks;
Zec 3. 9 I will *r* the iniquity of that land in
14. 4 mountain shall *r* toward the north,
Mt 17.20 *R* hence to yonder place; and it
20 to yonder place; and it shall *r*;
Lk 22.42 be willing, *r* this cup from me:
1Co 13. 2 faith, so that I could *r* mountains,
Rev 2. 5 *r* thy candlestick out of his place,

REMOVED

Gen 8.13 Noah *r* the covering of the ark,
12. 8 he *r* from thence unto a mountain
13.18 Then Abram *r* his tent, and came
26.22 he *r* from thence, and digged
30.35 he *r* that day the he goats that
47.21 he *r* them to cities from one end
Ex 8.31 and he *r* the swarms of flies from
14.19 angel *r*...and went behind them;
20.18 when the people saw it, they *r*,
Nu 12.16 the people *r* from Hazeroth, and
21.12, 13 From thence they *r*, and pitched
33. 5 children of Israel *r* from Rameses,
7 they *r* from Etham, and turned
9 they *r* from Marah, and came unto
10 they *r* from Elim, and encamped
11 And they *r* from the Red sea, and
14 they *r* from Alush, and encamped
16 they *r* from the desert of Sinai,
21 they *r* from Libnah, and pitched
24 they *r* from mount Shapher, and
25 they *r* from Haradah, and pitched
26 And they *r* from Makheloth, and
28 they *r* from Tarah, and pitched in
32 And they *r* from Bene-jaakan, and
34 And they *r* from Jotbathah, and
36 And they *r* from Ezion-gaber, and
37 they *r* from Kadesh, and pitched
46 And they *r* from Dibon-gad, and
47 they *r* from Almon-diblathaim,
Dt 28.25 be *r* into all the kingdoms of the
Jos 3. 1 they *r* from Shittim, and came to
14 when the people *r* from their tents,
1Sa 6. 3 why his hand is not *r* from you.
18.13 Saul *r* him from him, and made
2Sa 20.12 he *r* Amasa out of the highway
13 he was *r* out of the highway,
1Ki 15.12 *r* all the idols that his fathers
13 even her he *r* from being queen,
14 But the high places were not *r*:
2Ki 15. 4 Save that...high places were not *r*:
35 Howbeit...high places were not *r*:
16.17 and *r* the laver from off them;
17.18 and *r* them out of his sight: there
23 the Lord *r* Israel out of his sight,
26 The nations which thou hast *r*,
18. 4 He *r* the high places, and brake
23.27 as I have *r* Israel, and will cast off
1Ch 8. 6 and they *r* them to Manahath:
7 and Ahiah, and Gera, he *r* them,
2Ch 15.16 king, he *r* her from being queen,
35.12 And they *r* the burnt offerings,
Job 14.18 and the rock is *r* out of his place.
18. 4 shall the rock be *r* out of his place?
19.10 mine hope hath he *r* like a tree.
36.16 would he have *r* thee out of the
Ps 46. 2 we fear, though the earth be *r*,
81. 6 I *r* his shoulder from the burden:
103.12 far hath he *r* our transgressions
104. 5 that it should not be *r* for ever.
125. 1 as mount Zion, which cannot be *r*,
Pr 10.30 The righteous shall never be *r*:
Isa 6.12 the Lord have *r* men far away,
10.13 I have *r* the bounds of the people,
31 Madmenah is *r*; the inhabitants
22.25 fastened in the sure place be *r*,
24.20 and shall be *r* like a cottage; and
26.15 *r* it far unto all the ends of the
29.13 but have *r* their heart far from me,
30.20 yet shall not thy teachers be *r*
33.20 the stakes thereof shall ever be *r*,
38.12 *r* from me as a shepherd's tent:
54.10 shall depart, and the hills be *r*;
10 the covenant of my peace be *r*,
Jer 15. 4 them to be *r* into all kingdoms of
24. 9 them to be *r* into all the kingdoms
29.18 them to be *r* to all the kingdoms
34.17 you to be *r* into all the kingdoms
La 1. 8 sinned; therefore she is *r*:
3.17 hast *r* my soul far off from peace:
Eze 7.19 streets, and their gold shall be *r*:

23.46 give them to be *r* and spoiled.
36.17 the uncleanness of a *r* woman.
Am 6. 7 stretched themselves shall be *r*.
Mic 2. 4 how hath he *r* it from me!
7.11 in that day shall the decree be far *r*.
Mt 21.21 Be thou *r*, and be thou cast into
Mk 11.23 Be thou *r*, and be thou cast into
Ac 7. 4 was dead, he *r* him into this land,
13.22 when he had *r* him, he raised up
Gal 1. 6 I marvel that ye are so soon *r*

REMOVETH
Dt 27.17 that *r* his neighbor's landmark.
Job 9. 5 *r* the mountains, and they know
12.20 *r* away the speech of the trusty,
Ec 10. 9 Whoso *r* stones shall be hurt
Dan 2.21 he *r* kings, and setteth up kings:

REMPHAN
Ac 7.43 the star of your god *R*, figures

REND
Lev 10. 6 neither *r* your clothes; lest ye
Ec 3. 7 A time to *r*, and a time to sew; a
Isa 64. 1 that thou wouldest *r* the heavens,
Eze 13.13 *r* it with a stormy wind in my fury;
Joel 2.13 And *r* your heart, and not your
Mt 7. 6 feet, and turn again and *r* you.
Jn 19.24 Let us not *r* it, but cast lots for it,

RENDER
Nu 18. 9 which they shall *r* unto me, shall
Dt 32.41 will *r* vengeance to mine enemies,
43 *r* vengeance to his adversaries,
Jdg 9.57 did God *r* upon their heads: and
1Sa 26.23 *r* to every man his righteousness
2Ch 6.30 *r* unto every man according unto
Job 33.26 *r* unto man his righteousness.
34.11 work of a man shall he *r* unto him,
Ps 28. 4 hands; *r* to them their desert.
38.20 They also that *r* evil for good are
56.12 God: I will *r* praises unto thee.
79.12 *r* unto our neighbors sevenfold
94. 2 earth: *r* a reward to the proud.
116.12 What shall I *r* unto the Lord for
Pr 24.12 not he *r* to every man according to
29 *r* to the man according to his work.
26.16 seven men that can *r* a reason.
Isa 66.15 to *r* his anger with fury, and his
Jer 51. 6 he will *r* unto her a recompence.
24 I will *r* unto Babylon and to all
La 3.64 *R* unto them a recompence, O
Hos 14. 2 so will we *r* the calves of our lips.
Joel 3. 4 will ye *r* me a recompence? and if
Zec 9.12 that I will *r* double unto thee;
Mt 21.41 *r* him the fruits in their seasons.
22.21 *R* therefore unto Caesar the things
Mk 12.17 *R* to Caesar the things that are
Lk 20.25 *R* therefore unto Caesar the things
Ro 2. 6 will *r* to every man according to his
13. 7 *R* therefore to all their dues:
1Co 7. 3 Let the husband *r* unto the wife due
1Th 3. 9 what thanks can we *r* to God again
5.15 that none *r* evil for evil unto any

RENDEREST
Ps 62.12 *r* to every man according to his

RENDERING
1Pe 3. 9 Not *r* evil for evil, or railing for

RENEW
1Sa 11.14 Gilgal, and *r* the kingdom there.
Ps 51.10 and *r* a right spirit within me.
Isa 40.31 the Lord shall *r* their strength;
41. 1 and let the people *r* their strength:
La 5.21 be turned; *r* our days as of old.
Heb 6. 6 to *r* them again unto repentance;

RENEWED
2Ch 15. 8 and *r* the altar of the Lord, that
Job 29.20 and my bow was *r* in my hand.
Ps 103. 5 thy youth is *r* like the eagle's.
2Co 4.16 the inward man is *r* day by day.
Eph 4.23 be *r* in the spirit of your mind;
Col 3.10 which is *r* in knowledge after the

RENEWEST
Job 10.17 Thou *r* thy witnesses against me,
Ps 104.30 and thou *r* the face of the earth.

RENEWING
Ro 12. 2 transformed by the *r* of your mind,
Tit 3. 5 regeneration,...*r* of the Holy Ghost;

RENOUNCED
2Co 4. 2 But have *r* the hidden things of

RENOWN
Gen 6. 4 men which were of old, men of *r*.
Nu 16. 2 in the congregation, men of *r*:
Eze 16.14 thy *r* went forth among...heathen
15 the harlot because of thy *r*, and
34.29 I will raise up for them a plant of *r*,
39.13 it shall be to them a *r* the day that
Dan 9.15 hast gotten thee *r*, as at this day;

RENOWNED
Nu 1.16 were the *r* of the congregation,
Isa 14.20 seed of evildoers shall never be *r*.
Eze 23.23 and rulers great lords and *r*, all
26.17 the *r* city, which wast strong in

RENT
Gen 37.34 And Jacob *r* his clothes, and put
Jos 9. 4 and wine bottles, old, and *r*, and
13 were new; and behold, they be *r*:
1Ki 13. 3 the altar shall be *r*, and the ashes
19.11 and strong wind *r* the mountains,
2Ki 5. 7 the letter, that he *r* his clothes,
8 Wherefore hast thou *r* thy clothes?
6.30 the woman, that he *r* his clothes;
Ezr 9. 3 I *r* my garment and my mantle,
Job 1.20 Then Job arose, and *r* his mantle,
Mt 9.16 garment, and the *r* is made worse.
26.65 Then the high priest *r* his clothes,
27.51 veil of the temple was *r* in twain
51 earth did quake, and the rocks *r*;
Mk 2.21 the old, and the *r* is made worse.
9.26 the spirit cried, and *r* him sore,
14.63 Then the high priest *r* his clothes,
15.38 veil of the temple was *r* in twain
Lk 5.36 then both the new maketh a *r*, and
23.45 the veil of the temple was *r* in the
Ac 14.14 they *r* their clothes, and ran in
16.22 the magistrates *r* off their clothes,

REPAIR
2Ki 12. 5 them *r* the breaches of the house,
Ezr 9. 9 and to *r* the desolations thereof,
Isa 61. 4 and they shall *r* the waste cities,

REPAIRED
Jdg 21.23 *r* the cities, and dwelt in them.
1Ki 18.30 *r* the altar of the Lord that was
2Ki 12.14 *r* therewith the house of the Lord.
2Ch 33.16 he *r* the altar of the Lord, and

REPAY
Dt 7.10 him, he will *r* him to his face.
Job 21.31 shall *r* him what he hath done?
41.11 prevented me, that I should *r* him?
Isa 59.18 accordingly he will *r*, fury to his
18 the islands he will *r* recompence.
Lk 10.35 when I come again, I will *r* thee.
Ro 12.19 is mine; I will *r*, saith the Lord.
Phm 19 with mine own hand, I will *r* it:

REPENT
Ex 13.17 the people *r* when they see war,
32.12 *r* of this evil against thy people.
Nu 23.19 the son of man, that he should *r*:
Dt 32.36 and *r* himself for his servants,
1Sa 15.29 Strength of Israel will not lie nor *r*:
29 he is not a man, that he should *r*.
1Ki 8.47 and *r*, and make supplication
Job 42. 6 myself, and *r* in dust and ashes.
Ps 90.13 it *r* thee concerning thy servants.
110. 4 Lord hath sworn, and will not *r*,
135.14 *r* himself concerning his servants.
Jer 4.28 I have purposed it, and will not *r*,
18. 8 *r* of the evil that I thought to do
10 my voice, then I will *r* of the good,
26. 3 that I may *r* me of the evil, which
13 and the Lord will *r* him of the evil
42.10 I *r* me of the evil that I have done
Eze 14. 6 *R*, and turn...from your idols;
18.30 *R*, and turn yourselves from all
24.14 will I spare, neither will I *r*;
Joel 2.14 knoweth if he will return and *r*,
Jon 3. 9 Who can tell if God will turn and *r*,
Mt 3. 2 *R* ye: for the kingdom of heaven
4.17 *R*: for the kingdom of heaven is at
Mk 1.15 hand: *r* ye, and believe the gospel.
6.12 and preached that men should *r*.
Lk 13. 3, 5 except ye *r*, ye shall all likewise
16.30 them from the dead, they will *r*.
17. 3 him; and if he *r*, forgive him.
4 saying, I *r*; thou shalt forgive him.
Ac 2.38 *R*, and be baptized every one of you
3.19 *R* ye therefore, and be converted,
8.22 *R* therefore of this thy wickedness,
17.30 all men every where to *r*:
26.20 that they should *r* and turn to God,
2Co 7. 8 I do not *r*, though I did *r*: for I
Heb 7.21 The Lord sware and will not *r*,
Rev 2. 5 whence thou art fallen, and *r*, and
5 out of his place, except thou *r*.
16 *R*; or else I will come unto thee
21 her space to *r* of her fornication;
22 except they *r* of their deeds.
3. 3 and heard, and hold fast, and *r*.
19 be zealous therefore, and *r*.

REPENTANCE
Hos 13.14 *r* shall be hid from mine eyes.
Mt 3. 8 Bring forth...fruits meet for *r*:
11 baptize you with water unto *r*:
9.13 the righteous, but sinners to *r*.
Mk 1. 4 and preach the baptism of *r* for the
2.17 the righteous, but sinners to *r*.
Lk 3. 3 preaching the baptism of *r* for the
8 Bring forth...fruits worthy of *r*,
5.32 call the righteous, but sinners to *r*.
15. 7 nine just persons, which need no *r*.
24.47 And that *r* and remission of sins
Ac 5.31 to give *r* to Israel, and forgiveness
11.18 to the Gentiles granted *r* unto life.
13.24 the baptism of *r* to all the people
19. 4 baptized with the baptism of *r*,
20.21 *r* toward God, and faith toward
26.20 to God, and do works meet for *r*.
Ro 2. 4 goodness of God leadeth thee to *r*?
11.29 and calling of God are without *r*.
2Co 7. 9 sorry, but that ye sorrowed to *r*:
10 For goodly sorrow worketh *r* to
2Ti 2.25 God peradventure will give them *r*
Heb 6. 1 laying again the foundation of *r*
6 to renew them again unto *r*;
12.17 for he found no place of *r*, though
2Pe 3. 9 but that all should come to *r*.

REPENTED
Gen 6. 6 *r* the Lord that he had made man
Ex 32.14 Lord *r* of the evil which he thought
Jdg 2.18 for it *r* the Lord because of their
21. 6 children of Israel *r*...for Benjamin
15 the people *r* them for Benjamin,
1Sa 15.35 Lord *r* that he had made Saul king
2Sa 24.16 the Lord *r* him of the evil, and said
1Ch 21.15 beheld, and he *r* him of the evil,
Ps 106.45 *r* according to the multitude of his
Jer 8. 6 no man *r* him of his wickedness,
20.16 the Lord overthrew, and *r* not:

Jer 26.19 the Lord *r* him of the evil which
31.19 Surely after that I was turned, I *r*;
Am 7. 3 Lord *r* for this: It shall not be,
6 Lord *r* for this: This also shall not
Jon 3.10 God *r* of the evil, that he had said
Zec 8.14 saith the Lord of hosts, and I *r* not:
Mt 11.20 were done, because they *r* not:
21 would have *r* long ago in sackcloth
12.41 they *r* at the preaching of Jonas;
21.29 not: but afterward he *r*, and went.
32 ye had seen it, *r* not afterward,
27. 3 that he was condemned, *r* himself,
Lk 10.13 they had a great while ago *r*,
11.32 they *r* at the preaching of Jonas;
2Co 7.10 worketh repentance...not to be *r* of:
12.21 and have not *r* of the uncleanness
Rev 2.21 of her fornication; and she *r* not.
9.20 *r* not of the works of their hands,
21 Neither *r* they of their murders
16. 9 and they *r* not to give him glory.
11 sores, and *r* not of their deeds.

REPENTEST

Jon 4. 2 kindness, and *r* thee of the evil.

REPENTETH

Gen 6. 7 it *r* me that I have made them.
1Sa 15.11 It *r* me that I have set up Saul to
Joel 2.13 kindness, and *r* him of the evil.
Lk 15. 7 in heaven over one sinner that *r*,
10 angels...over one sinner that *r*.

REPETITIONS

Mt 6. 7 But when ye pray, use not vain *r*,

REPLENISH

Gen 1.28 and multiply, and *r* the earth, and
9. 1 and multiply, and *r* the earth.

REPLENISHED

Jer 31.25 and I have *r* every sorrowful soul.
Eze 26. 2 I shall be *r*, now she is laid waste:

REPLIEST

Ro 9.20 who art thou that *r* against God?

REPORT

Gen 37. 2 brought unto his father their evil *r*.
Ex 23. 1 Thou shalt not raise a false *r*:
Nu 13.32 brought up an evil *r* of the land
14.37 bring up the evil *r* upon the land,
Dt 2.25 who shall hear *r* of thee, and shall
1Sa 2.24 for it is no good *r* that I hear:
1Ki 10. 6 was a true *r* that I heard in mine
2Ch 9. 5 was a true *r* which I heard in mine
Neh 6.13 might have matter for an evil *r*,
Pr 15.30 a good *r* maketh the bones fat.
Isa 23. 5 As at the *r* concerning Egypt,
5 be sorely pained at the *r* of Tyre.
28.19 a vexation...to understand the *r*.
53. 1 Who hath believed our *r*? and to
Jer 20.10 *R*, say they, and we will *r* it. All
50.43 king of Babylon hath heard the *r*
Jn 12.38 Lord, who hath believed our *r*?
Ac 6. 3 among you seven men of honest *r*,
10.22 and of good *r* among all the nation
22.12 having a good *r* of all the Jews
Ro 10.16 Lord, who hath believed our *r*?
1Co 14.25 and *r* that God is in you of a truth.
2Co 6. 8 By honor and dishonor, by evil *r*
8 and good *r*: as deceivers, and yet
Php 4. 8 whatsoever things are of good *r*;
1Ti 3. 7 he must have a good *r* of them
Heb 11. 2 it the elders obtained a good *r*.
39 obtained a good *r* through faith,
3Jn 12 Demetrius hath good *r* of all men,

REPORTED

Neh 6. 6 It is *r* among the heathen, and
7 and now shall it be *r* to the king
19 they *r* his good deeds before me,
Est 1.17 in their eyes, when it shall be *r*,
Eze 9.11 inkhorn by his side, *r* the matter,
Mt 28.15 commonly *r* among the Jews is
Ac 4.23 and *r* all that the chief priests and
16. 2 was well *r* of by the brethren
Ro 3. 8 (as we be slanderously *r*, and as
1Co 5. 1 It is *r* commonly that there is
1Ti 5.10 Well *r* of for good works; if she
1Pe 1.12 which are now *r* unto you by them

REPROACH

Gen 30.23 said, God hath taken away my *r*:
34.14 for that were a *r* unto us:
Jos 5. 9 have I rolled away the *r* of Egypt
Ru 2.15 among the sheaves, and *r* her not:
1Sa 11. 2 and lay it for a *r* upon all Israel.
17.26 and taketh away the *r* from Israel?
25.39 hath pleaded the cause of my *r*
2Ki 19. 4 hath sent to *r* the living God;
16 hath sent him to *r* the living God.
Neh 1. 3 are in great affliction and *r*:
2.17 Jerusalem, that we be no more a *r*.
4. 4 turn their *r* upon their own head,
5. 9 the *r* of the heathen our enemies?
6.13 evil report, that they might *r* me.
Job 19. 5 me, and plead against me my *r*:
20. 3 I have heard the check of my *r*,
27. 6 my heart shall not *r* me so long
Ps 15. 3 up a *r* against his neighbor.
22. 6 a *r* of men, and despised of the
31.11 I was a *r* among all mine enemies,
39. 8 make me not the *r* of the foolish.
42.10 in my bones, mine enemies *r* me;
44.13 makest us a *r* to our neighbors,
57. 3 and save me from the *r* of him
69. 7 for thy sake I have borne *r*;
10 soul with fasting, that was to my *r*.
19 Thou hast known my *r*, and my
20 *R* hath broken my heart; and I
71.13 be covered with *r* and dishonor
74.10 how long shall the adversary *r*?
78.66 he put them to a perpetual *r*.
79. 4 are become a *r* to our neighbors,
12 sevenfold into their bosom their *r*,
89.41 him: he is a *r* to his neighbors.
50 Remember,...the *r* of thy servants;
50 bosom the *r* of all the mighty people;
102. 8 Mine enemies *r* me all the day;
109.25 I became also a *r* unto them:
119.22 Remove from me *r* and contempt;
39 Turn away my *r* which I fear: for
Pr 6.33 his *r* shall not be wiped away.
14.34 but sin is a *r* to any people.
18. 3 contempt, and with ignominy *r*.
19.26 causeth shame, and bringeth *r*.
22.10 yea, strife and *r* shall cease.
Isa 4. 1 by thy name, to take away our *r*.
30. 5 profit, but a shame, and also a *r*.
37. 4 hath sent to *r* the living God, and
17 hath sent to *r* the living God.
51. 7 fear ye not the *r* of men, neither
54. 4 remember the *r* of thy widowhood
Jer 6.10 word of the Lord is unto them a *r*;
20. 8 the word of the Lord was made a *r*
23.40 bring an everlasting *r* upon you,
24. 9 be a *r* and a proverb, a taunt and
29.18 an hissing, and a *r*, among all the
31.19 I did bear the *r* of my youth.
42.18 astonishment, and a curse, and a *r*;
44. 8 a *r* among all the nations of the
12 astonishment, and a curse, and a *r*.
49:13 shall become a desolation, a *r*, a
51.51 because we have heard *r*: shame
La 3.30 smiteth him: he is filled full with *r*.
61 Thou hast heard their *r*, O Lord,
5. 1 us: consider, and behold our *r*.
Eze 5.14 a *r* among the nations that are
15 So it shall be a *r* and a taunt, an
16.57 of thy *r* of the daughters of Syria,
21.28 Ammonites, and concerning their *r*;
22. 4 I made thee a *r* unto the heathen,
36.15 bear the *r* of the people any more,
30 shall receive no more *r* of famine
Dan 9.16 become a *r* to all that are about us.
11.18 cause the *r* offered by him to cease;
18 without his own *r* he shall cause it
Hos 12.14 his *r* shall his Lord return unto
Joel 2.17 give not thine heritage to *r*, that
19 make you a *r* among the heathen:
Mic 6.16 ye shall bear the *r* of my people.
Zep 2. 8 I have heard the *r* of Moab, and
3.18 to whom the *r* of it was a burden.
Lk 1.25 to take away my *r* among men.
6.22 and shall *r* you, and cast out your
2Co 11.21 I speak as concerning *r*, as though
1Ti 3. 7 fall into *r* and...snare of the devil.
4.10 we both labor and suffer *r*,
Heb 11.26 Esteeming the *r* of Christ greater
13.13 without the camp, bearing his *r*.

REPROACHED

2Ki 19.22 hast thou *r* and blasphemed?
23 messengers thou hast *r* the Lord,
Job 19. 3 These ten times have ye *r* me: ye
Ps 55.12 it was not an enemy that *r* me;
69. 9 reproaches of them that *r* thee are
74.18 this, that the enemy hath *r*, O Lord,
79.12 wherewith they have *r* thee, O Lord.
89.51 Wherewith thine enemies have *r*,
51 they have *r* the footsteps of thine
Isa 37.23 hast thou *r* and blasphemed?
24 thy servants hast thou *r* the Lord,
Zep 2. 8 whereby they have *r* my people,
10 have *r* and magnified themselves
Ro 15. 3 reproaches of them that *r* thee
1Pe 4.14 If ye be *r* for the name of Christ,

REPROACHES

Ps 69. 9 the *r* of them that reproached thee
Isa 43.28 Jacob to the curse, and Israel to *r*.
Ro 15. 3 The *r* of them that reproached thee
2Co 12.10 take pleasure in infirmities, in *r*,
Heb 10.33 both by *r* and afflictions; and

REPROACHEST

Lk 11.45 Master, thus saying thou *r* us also.

REPROACHETH

Nu 15.30 a stranger, the same *r* the Lord;
Ps 44.16 For the voice of him that *r* and
74.22 how the foolish man *r* thee daily.
119.42 to answer him that *r* me: for
Pr 14.31 oppresseth the poor *r* his Maker:
17. 5 mocketh the poor *r* his Maker:
27.11 that I may answer him that *r* me.

REPROACHFULLY

Job 16.10 smitten me upon the cheek *r*;
1Ti 5.14 to the adversary to speak *r*.

REPROBATE

Jer 6.30 *R* silver shall men call them,
Ro 1.28 God gave them over to a *r* mind,
2Ti 3. 8 minds, *r* concerning the faith.
Tit 1.16 and unto every good work *r*.

REPROBATES

2Co 13. 5 Christ is in you, except ye be *r*?
6 ye shall know that we are not *r*.
7 which is honest, though we be as *r*.

REPROOF

Job 26.11 and are astonished at his *r*.
Pr 1.23 Turn you at my *r*: behold, I will
25 counsel, and would none of my *r*:
30 my counsel: they despised all my *r*.
5.12 and my heart despised *r*;
10.17 but he that refuseth *r* erreth.
12. 1 but he that hateth *r* is brutish.
13.18 that regardeth *r* shall be honored.
15. 5 but he that regardeth *r* is prudent.

10 way: and he that hateth *r* shall die.
31 The ear that heareth the *r* of life
32 heareth *r* getteth understanding.
17.10 A *r* entereth more into a wise
29.15 The rod and *r* give wisdom: but
2Ti 3.16 for doctrine, for *r*, for correction,

REPROOFS

Ps 38.14 and in whose mouth are no *r*.
Pr 6.23 *r* of instruction are the way of life:

REPROVE

2Ki 19. 4 will *r* the words which the Lord
Job 6.25 but what doth your arguing *r*?
26 Do ye imagine to *r* words, and the
13.10 He will surely *r* you, if ye do
22. 4 Will he *r* thee for fear of thee? will
Ps 50. 8 I will not *r* thee for thy sacrifices
21 I will *r* thee, and set them in order
141. 5 and let him *r* me; it shall be an
Pr 9. 8 *R* not a scorner, lest he hate thee:
19.25 and *r* one that hath understanding,
30. 6 lest he *r* thee, and thou be found a
Isa 11. 3 *r* after the hearing of his ears:
4 *r* with equity for the meek of the
37. 4 will *r* the words which the Lord
Jer 2.19 and thy backslidings shall *r* thee:
Hos 4. 4 let no man strive, nor *r* another:
Jn 16. 8 is come, he will *r* the world of sin,
Eph 5.11 of darkness, but rather *r* them.
2Ti 4. 2 *r*, rebuke, exhort with all

REPROVED

Gen 20.16 with all other: thus she was *r*.
21.25 Abraham *r* Abimelech because
1Ch 16.21 yea, he *r* kings for their sakes,
Ps 105.14 yea, he *r* kings for their sakes;
Pr 29. 1 being often *r* hardeneth his neck,
Jer 29.27 why hast thou not *r* Jeremiah
Hab 2. 1 what I shall answer when I am *r*.
Lk 3.19 being *r* by him for Herodias his
Jn 3.20 light, lest his deeds should be *r*.
Eph 5.13 that are *r* are made manifest by

REPROVETH

Job 40. 2 he that *r* God, let him answer it,
Pr 9. 7 He that *r* a scorner getteth to
15.12 scorner loveth not one that *r* him:
Isa 29.21 a snare for him that *r* in the gate,

REPUTATION

Ec 10. 1 is in *r* for wisdom and honor.
Ac 5.34 had in *r* among all the people,
Gal 2. 2 privately to them which were of *r*,
Php 2. 7 But made himself of no *r*, and
29 gladness; and hold such in *r*:

REQUEST

Jdg 8.24 them, I would desire a *r* of you,
2Sa 14.15 perform the *r* of his handmaid.
22 hath fulfilled the *r* of his servant.
Ezr 7. 6 the king granted him all his *r*,
Neh 2. 4 me, For what dost thou make *r*?
Est 4. 8 make *r* before him for her people.
5. 3 queen Esther? and what is thy *r*?
6 and what is thy *r*? even to the half
7 and said, My petition and my *r* is;
8 my petition, and to perform my *r*,
7. 2 and what is thy *r*? and it shall be
3 petition, and my people at my *r*:
7 Haman stood up to make *r* for his
9.12 what is thy *r* further? and it shall
Job 6. 8 Oh that I might have my *r*; and
Ps 21. 2 not withholden the *r* of his lips.
106.15 he gave them their *r*; but sent
Ro 1.10 Making *r*, if by any means now at
Php 1. 4 for you all making *r* with joy,

REQUESTED

Jdg 8.26 of the golden earrings that he *r*
1Ki 19. 4 he *r* for himself that he might die;

BIBLICAL THEMES

REPUTATION

Saul said to David, Thou art not able to go against this Philistine to fight with him: for thou art but a youth, and he a man of war from his youth. 1Sa 17.33

And [David] was accepted in the sight of all the people, and. . . . the women came out of all cities of Israel, singing and dancing, to meet king Saul . . . and said, Saul hath slain his thousands, and David his ten thousands. 1Sa 18.5-7

Solomon's wisdom excelled the wisdom of all the children of the east country, and all the wisdom of Egypt. . . . and his fame was in all nations round about. 1Ki 4.30-31

She said to the king, It was a true report that I heard in mine own land of thy acts and of thy wisdom. Howbeit I believed not the words, until I came, and mine eyes had seen it: and, behold, the half was not told me: thy wisdom and prosperity exceedeth the fame which I heard. 1Ki 10.6-7

Oh that I were as in months past. . . . When I went out to the gate through the city. . . . The young men saw me, and hid themselves: and the aged arose, and stood up. . . . Unto me men gave ear, and waited, and kept silence at my counsel. Job 29.2, 7-8, 21

As for me, I will walk in mine integrity. Ps 26.11

Be not thou afraid when one is made rich, when the glory of his house is increased; for when he dieth he shall carry nothing away: his glory shall not descend after him. . . . Man that is in honor, and understandeth not, is like the beasts that perish. Ps 49.16-17, 20

Not unto us, O Lord, not unto us, but unto thy name give glory. Ps 115.1

A good name is rather to be chosen than great riches. Pr 22.1

For men to search their own glory is not glory. Pr 25.27

His fame went throughout all Syria: and they brought unto him all sick people that were taken with divers diseases and torments. Mt 4.24

Then touched he their eyes. . . . And their eyes were opened; and Jesus straitly charged them, saying, See that no man know it. But they, when they were departed, spread abroad his fame in all that country. Mt 9.29-31

At that time Herod the tetrarch heard of the fame of Jesus, and said unto his servants, This is John the Baptist; he is risen from the dead. Mt 14.1-2

There cometh one mightier than I . . . the latchet of whose shoes I am not worthy to stoop down and unloose. Mk 1.7

Whosoever exalteth himself shall be abased. Lk 14.11

A prophet hath no honor in his own country. Jn 4.44

We know that God spake unto Moses: as for this fellow, we know not from whence he is. Jn 9.29

Your faith is spoken of throughout the whole world. Ro 1.8

[Jesus] made himself of no reputation, and . . . humbled himself, and became obedient unto death. . . . Wherefore God also hath highly exalted him, and given him a name which is above every name: that at the name of Jesus every knee should bow . . . and that every tongue should confess that Jesus Christ is Lord. Php 2.7-11

1Ch 4.10 God granted him that which he *r*.
Dan 1. 8 he *r* the prince of the eunuchs
2.49 Then Daniel *r* of the king, and he

REQUESTS

Php 4. 6 let your *r* be made known unto God.

REQUIRE

Gen 9. 5 your blood of your lives will I *r*;
5 the hand of every beast will I *r* it,
5 brother will I *r* the life of man.
31.39 of it; of my hand didst thou *r* it,
43. 9 of my hand shalt thou *r* him: if I
Dt 10.12 doth the Lord thy God *r* of thee,
18.19 in my name, I will *r* it of him.
23.21 thy God will surely *r* it of thee;
Jos 22.23 thereon, let the Lord himself *r* it;
1Sa 20.16 the Lord even *r* it at the hand of
2Sa 3.13 but one thing I *r* of thee, that is,
4.11 now *r* his blood of your hand, and
19.38 whatsoever thou shalt *r* of me,
1Ki 8.59 at all times, as the matter shall *r*:
1Ch 21. 3 then doth my lord *r* this thing?
2Ch 24.22 The Lord look upon it, and *r* it.
Ezr 7.21 the God of heaven, shall *r* of you,
8.22 ashamed to *r* of the king a band
Neh 5.12 them, and will *r* nothing of them;
Ps 10.13 in his heart, Thou wilt not *r* it.
Eze 3.18, 20 blood will I *r* at thine hand.
20.40 there will I *r* your offerings, and
33. 6 blood will I *r* at the watchman's
8 his blood will I *r* at thine hand.
34.10 I will *r* my flock at their hand,
Mic 6. 8 and what doth the Lord *r* of thee,

1Co 1.22 the Jews *r* a sign, and the Greeks
7.36 and need so *r*, let him do what he

REQUIRED
Gen 42.22 behold, also his blood is *r*.
Ex 12.36 lent unto them such things as they *r*.
1Sa 21. 8 the king's business *r* haste.
2Sa 12.20 when he *r*, they set bread before
1Ch 16.37 continually, as every day's work *r*:
2Ch 8.14 priests, as the duty of every day *r*:
24. 6 hast thou not *r* of the Levites to
Ezr 3. 4 as the duty of every day *r*;
Neh 5.18 *r* not I the bread of the governor,
Est 2.15 she *r* nothing but what Hegai the
Ps 40. 6 and sin offering hast thou not *r*.
137. 3 us away captive *r* of us a song;
3 they that wasted us *r* of us mirth,
Pr 30. 7 Two things have I *r* of thee; deny
Isa 1.12 who hath *r* this at your hand, to
Lk 11.50 world, may be *r* of this generation;
51 It shall be *r* of this generation.
12.20 night thy soul shall be *r* of thee:
48 is given, of him shall be much *r*:
19.23 have *r* mine own with usury?
23.24 that it should be as they *r*.
1Co 4. 2 Moreover it is *r* in stewards, that

REQUIREST
Ru 3.11 I will do to thee all that thou *r*:

REQUIRETH
Ec 3.15 and God *r* that which is past.
Dan 2.11 it is a rare thing that the king *r*,

REQUIRING
Lk 23.23 voice, *r* that he might be crucified.

REQUITE
Gen 50.15 and will certainly *r* us all the evil
Dt 32. 6 Do ye thus *r* the Lord, O foolish
2Sa 2. 6 and I will also *r* you this kindness,
16.12 the Lord will *r* me good for his
2Ki 9.26 I will *r* thee in this plat, saith the
Ps 10.14 and spite, to *r* it with thy hand:
41.10 raise me up, that I may *r* them.
Jer 51.56 God of recompences shall surely *r*.
1Ti 5. 4 at home, and to *r* their parents:

REQUITED
Jdg 1. 7 as I have done, so God hath *r* me.
1Sa 25.21 and he hath *r* me evil for good.

REREWARD
Isa 52.12 the God of Israel will be your *r*.
58. 8 the glory of the Lord shall be thy *r*.

RESCUE
Dt 28.31 thou shalt have none to *r* them.
Ps 35.17 look on? *r* my soul from their
Hos 5.14 take away, and none shall *r* him.

RESCUED
1Sa 14.45 So the people *r* Jonathan, that he
30.18 away: and David *r* his two wives.
Ac 23.27 came I with an army, and *r* him,

RESCUETH
Dan 6.27 He delivereth and *r*, and he

RESEMBLE
Lk 13.18 like? and whereunto shall I *r* it?

RESERVE
Jer 3. 5 Will he *r* his anger for ever? will
50.20 for I will pardon them whom I *r*.
2Pe 2. 9 to *r* the unjust unto the day of

RESERVED
Gen 27.36 thou not *r* a blessing for me?
Nu 18. 9 most holy things, *r* from the fire:
Jdg 21.22 we *r* not to each man his wife
Ru 2.18 gave to her that she had *r* after
2Sa 8. 4 *r* of them for an hundred chariots.
1Ch 18. 4 but *r* of them an hundred chariots.
Job 21.30 is *r* to the day of destruction?
38.23 Which I have *r* against the time of
Ac 25.21 be *r* unto the hearing of Augustus,
Ro 11. 4 I have *r* to myself seven thousand
1Pe 1. 4 not away, *r* in heaven for you,
2Pe 2. 4 darkness, to be *r* unto judgment;
17 the mist of darkness is *r* for ever.
3. 7 *r* unto fire against the day of
Jude 6 hath *r* in everlasting chains under
13 to whom is *r* the blackness of

RESIDUE
Isa 38.10 am deprived of the *r* of my years.
44.17 the *r* thereof he maketh a god,
19 the *r* thereof an abomination?
Jer 24. 8 the *r* of Jerusalem, that remain in
29. 1 Jerusalem unto the *r* of the elders
Eze 9. 8 wilt thou destroy all the *r* of Israel
48.21 And the *r* shall be for the prince,
Dan 7. 7 stamped the *r* with the feet of it:
Hag 2. 2 and to the *r* of the people, saying,
Zec 14. 2 *r* of the people shall not be cut off
Mal 2.15 Yet had he the *r* of the spirit.
Mk 16.13 they went and told it unto the *r*:
Ac 15.17 *r* of the men might seek after the

RESIST
Zec 3. 1 at his right hand to *r* him.
Mt 5.39 I say unto you, that ye *r* not evil:
Lk 21.15 shall not be able to gainsay nor *r*.
Ac 6.10 were not able to *r* the wisdom and
7.51 ears, ye do always *r* the Holy Ghost:
Ro 13. 2 and they that *r* shall receive to
2Ti 3. 8 Moses, so do these also *r* the truth:
Jas 4. 7 *R* the devil, and he will flee from
5. 6 the just; and he doth not *r* you.
1Pe 5. 9 Whom *r* stedfast in the faith,

RESISTED
Ro 9.19 find fault? For who hath *r* his will?
Heb 12. 4 Ye have not yet *r* unto blood,

RESISTETH
Ro 13. 2 Whosoever therefore *r* the power,
2 *r* the ordinance of God: and they
Jas 4. 6 God *r* the proud, but giveth grace
1Pe 5. 5 God *r* the proud, and giveth grace

RESOLVED
Lk 16. 4 I am *r* what to do, that, when I

RESORT
Neh 4.20 trumpet, *r* ye thither unto us:
Ps 71. 3 whereunto I may continually *r*:
Mk 10. 1 and the people *r* unto him again;
Jn 18.20 whither the Jews always *r*;

RESORTED
2Ch 11.13 *r* to him out of all their coasts.
Mk 2.13 and all the multitude *r* unto him,
Jn 10.41 many *r* unto him, and said, John
18. 2 Jesus ofttimes *r* thither with his
Ac 16.13 unto the women which *r* thither.

RESPECT
Gen 4. 4 And the Lord had *r* unto Abel
5 and to his offering he had not *r*.
Ex 2.25 Israel, and God had *r* unto them.
Lev 19.15 not *r* the person of the poor,
Nu 16.15 Lord, *R* not thou their offering:
Dt 16.19 thou shalt not *r* persons, neither
2Sa 14.14 neither doth God *r* any person:
1Ki 8.28 have thou *r* unto the prayer of
2Ch 6.19 Have *r* therefore to the prayer of
19. 7 Lord our God, nor *r* of persons,
Ps 74.20 Have *r* unto the covenant: for
119. 6 have *r* unto all thy commandments.
138. 6 yet hath he *r* unto the lowly:
Pr 24.23 have *r* of persons in judgment.
28.21 To have *r* of persons is not good:
Isa 17. 7 have *r* to the Holy One of Israel.
Ro 2.11 there is no *r* of persons with God.
2Co 3.10 glorious had no glory in this *r*,
Eph 6. 9 is there *r* of persons with him.
Php 4.11 Not that I speak in *r* of want: for
Col 2.16 or in *r* of an holyday, or of the
3.25 and there is no *r* of persons.
Heb 11.26 had *r* unto the recompence of the
Jas 2. 1 Lord of glory, with *r* of persons.
3 *r* to him that weareth the gay
9 But if ye have *r* to persons, ye
1Pe 1.17 who without *r* of persons judgeth

RESPECTER
Ac 10.34 that God is no *r* of persons:

RESPECTETH
Job 37.24 *r* not any that are wise of heart.
Ps 40. 4 and *r* not the proud, nor such as

RESPITE
Ex 8.15 Pharaoh saw that there was *r*,
1Sa 11. 3 Give us seven days' *r*, that we

REST
Gen 8. 9 dove found no *r* for the sole of her
49.15 he saw that *r* was good, and the
Ex 5. 5 make them *r* from their burdens.
23.12 on the seventh day thou shalt *r*:
31.15 the seventh is the sabbath of *r*,
33.14 with thee, and I will give thee *r*.
Lev 16.31 shall be a sabbath of *r* unto you,
25. 5 for it is a year of *r* unto the land.
Dt 5.14 maidservant may *r* as well as thou.
12. 9 ye are not as yet come to the *r*
10 he giveth you *r* from all your
Jdg 3.30 the land had *r* fourscore years.
Ru 1. 9 grant you that ye may find *r*,
3. 1 shall I not seek *r* for thee, that
1Ki 5. 4 the Lord my God hath given me *r*
2Ki 2.15 spirit of Elijah doth *r* on Elisha.
1Ch 22. 9 to thee, who shall be a man of *r*;
9 give him *r* from all his enemies,
18 he not given you *r* on every side?
28. 2 build an house of *r* for the ark of
2Ch 14.11 for we *r* on thee, and in thy
Neh 9.28 But after they had *r*, they did evil
Est 9.16 and had *r* from their enemies,
Job 3.13 have slept: then had I been at *r*,
17 and there the weary be at *r*.
26 was not in safety, neither had I *r*,
11.18 thou shalt take thy *r* in safety.
17.16 when our *r* together is in the dust.
Ps 16. 9 my flesh also shall *r* in hope.
37. 7 *R* in the Lord, and wait patiently
55. 6 then would I fly away, and be at *r*.
95.11 they should not enter into my *r*.
116. 7 Return unto thy *r*, O my soul; for
125. 3 the rod of the wicked shall not *r*
132. 8 Arise, O Lord, into thy *r*; thou,
14 This is my *r* for ever: here will I
Ec 2.23 his heart taketh not *r* in the night.
Isa 11. 2 spirit of the Lord shall *r* upon
10 seek: and his *r* shall be glorious.
14. 7 whole earth is at *r*, and is quiet:
18. 4 I will take my *r*, and I will
28.12 ye may cause the weary to *r*;
30.15 returning and *r* shall ye be saved;
57.20 troubled sea, when it cannot *r*,
62. 1 for Jerusalem's sake I will not *r*,
63.14 Spirit of the Lord caused him to *r*:
66. 1 and where is the place of my *r*?
Jer 6.16 and ye shall find *r* for your souls.
47. 6 into thy scabbard, *r*, and be still.
La 2.18 day and night: give thyself no *r*;
5. 5 we labor, and have no *r*.
Eze 5.13 cause my fury to *r* upon them,
38.11 I will go to them that are at *r*,
44.30 the blessing to *r* in thine house.

Dan 12.13 thou shalt *r*, and stand in thy lot
Mic 2.10 depart; for this is not your *r*:
Hab 3.16 I might *r* in the day of trouble:
Zec 1.11 the earth sitteth still, and is at *r*.
Mt 11.28 heavy laden, and I will give you *r*.
29 and ye shall find *r* unto your souls.
12.43 places, seeking *r*, and finding none.
26.45 Sleep on now, and take your *r*:
27.49 The *r* said, Let be, let us see
Mk 6.31 into a desert place, and *r* a while:
14.41 Sleep on now, and take your *r*:
Lk 10. 6 there, your peace shall *r* upon it:
11.24 through dry places, seeking *r*;
12.26 why take ye thought for the *r*?
24. 9 unto the eleven, and to all the *r*.
Jn 11.13 had spoken of taking of *r* in sleep.
Ac 2.26 also my flesh shall *r* in hope:
37 Peter and to the *r* of the apostles,
5.13 of the *r* durst no man join himself
7.49 or what is the place of my *r*?
9.31 had the churches *r* throughout
27.44 And the *r*, some on boards, and
Ro 11. 7 obtained it, and the *r* were blinded
1Co 7.12 But to the *r* speak I, not the Lord:
11.34 *r* will I set in order when I come.
2Co 2.13 I had no *r* in my spirit, because I
7. 5 Macedonia, our flesh had no *r*,
12. 9 power of Christ may *r* upon me.
2Th 1. 7 to you who are troubled *r* with us,
Heb 3.11 They shall not enter into my *r*.)
18 they should not enter into his *r*,
4. 1 being left us of entering into his *r*,
3 which have believed do enter into *r*,
3 if they shall enter into my *r*:
4 God did *r* the seventh day from
5 If they shall enter into my *r*.
8 For if Jesus had given them *r*,
9 therefore a *r* to the people of God.
10 For he that is entered into his *r*,
11 labor therefore to enter into that *r*,
1Pe 4. 2 live the *r* of his time in the flesh
Rev 2.24 I say, and unto the *r* in Thyatira,
4. 8 and they *r* not day and night,
6.11 should *r* yet for a little season,
9.20 *r* of the men which were not killed
14.11 and they have no *r* day nor night,
13 that they may *r* from their labors;
20. 5 the *r* of the dead lived not again

RESTED

Gen 2. 2 he *r* on the seventh day from all
3 that in it he had *r* from all his work
8. 4 the ark *r* in the seventh month,
Ex 10.14 and *r* in all the coasts of Egypt:
16.30 the prople *r* on the seventh day.
20.11 in them is, and *r* the seventh day:
31.17 and on the seventh day he *r*, and
Nu 9.18 tabernacle they *r* in their tents.
23 of the Lord they *r* in the tents,
10.12 the cloud *r* in the wilderness of
36 when it *r*, he said, Return, O Lord,
11.25 when the spirit *r* upon them, they
26 Medad: and the spirit *r* upon them;
Jos 11.23 tribes. And the land *r* from war.
1Ki 6.10 they *r* on the house with timber of
2Ch 32. 8 *r* themselves upon the words of
Est 9.17 fourteenth day of the same *r* they,
18 fifteenth day of the same they *r*,
22 the Jews *r* from their enemies,
Job 30.27 My bowels boiled, and *r* not: the
Lk 23.56 and *r* the sabbath day according

RESTEST

Ro 2.17 art called a Jew, and *r* in the law,

RESTETH

Job 24.23 him to be in safety, whereon he *r*;
Pr 14.33 Wisdom *r* in the heart of him that
Ec 7. 9 for anger *r* in the bosom of fools.
1Pe 4.14 spirit of glory and of God *r* upon

RESTING

Nu 10.33 to search out a *r* place for them.
2Ch 6.41 O Lord God, into thy *r* place, thou,
Pr 24.15 righteous; spoil not his *r* place:
Isa 32.18 dwellings, and in quiet *r* places;

RESTITUTION

Ex 22. 3 he should make full *r*; if he have
5 his own vineyard, shall he make *r*.
6 kindled...fire shall surely make *r*.
12 he shall make *r* unto the owner
Job 20.18 to his substance shall the *r* be,
Ac 3.21 until the times of *r* of all things,

RESTORE

Gen 20. 7 *r* the man his wife; for he is a
7 if thou *r* her not, know thou that
40.13 head, and *r* thee unto thy place:
42.25 *r* every man's money into his sack,
Ex 22. 1 he shall *r* five oxen for an ox, and
4 ass, or sheep; he shall *r* double,
Lev 6. 4 *r* that which he took violently
5 he shall even *r* it in the principal,
24.21 that killeth a beast, he shall *r* it:
25.27 *r* the overplus unto the man to
28 But if he be not able to *r* it to him,
Nu 35.25 *r* him to the city of his refuge,
Dt 22. 2 and thou shalt *r* it to him again.
Jdg 11.13 *r* those lands again peaceably.
17. 3 now therefore I will *r* it unto thee.
1Sa 12. 3 eyes therewith? and I will *r* it you.
2Sa 9. 7 will *r* thee all the land of Saul thy
12. 6 And he shall *r* the lamb fourfold,
16. 3 *r* me the kingdom of my father.
1Ki 20.34 took from thy father, I will *r*;
2Ki 8. 6 *R* all that was hers, and all the
Neh 5.11 *R*, I pray you, to them, even this
12 Then said they, We will *r* them,
Job 20.10 and his hands shall *r* their goods.
18 which he labored for shall he *r*,
Ps 51.12 *R* unto me the joy of thy
Pr 6.31 he be found, he shall *r* sevenfold;
Isa 1.26 I will *r* thy judges as at the first,
42.22 for a spoil, and none saith, *R*.
49. 6 and to *r* the preserved of Israel:
57.18 *r* comforts unto him and to his
Jer 27.22 them up, and *r* them to this place.
30.17 For I will *r* health unto thee, and
Eze 33.15 If the wicked *r* the pledge, give
Dan 9.25 to *r* and to build Jerusalem unto
Joel 2.25 I will *r* to you the years that the
Mt 17.11 shall first come, and *r* all things.
Lk 19. 8 false accusation, I *r* him fourfold.
Ac 1. 6 *r* again the kingdom to Israel?
Gal 6. 1 *r* such an one in the spirit of

RESTORED

Gen 20.14 and *r* him Sarah his wife.
40.21 And he *r* the chief butler unto his
41.13 me he *r* unto mine office, and him
42.28 My money is *r*; and, lo, it is even
Dt 28.31 and shall not be *r* to thee: thy
Jdg 17. 3 had *r* the eleven hundred shekels
4 he *r* the money unto his mother;
1Sa 7.14 taken from Israel were *r* to Israel,
1Ki 13. 6 that my hand may be *r* me again.
6 the king's hand was *r* him again,
2Ki 8. 1 whose son he had *r* to life,
5 how he had *r* a dead body to life,
5 woman, whose son he had *r* to life,
5 is her son, whom Elisha *r* to life.
14.22 He built Elath, and *r* it to Judah,
25 He *r* the coast of Israel from the
2Ch 8. 2 which Huram had *r* to Solomon,
26. 2 He built Eloth, and *r* it to Judah,
Ezr 6. 5 be *r*, and brought again unto the
Ps 69. 4 I *r* that which I took not away.
Eze 18. 7 but hath *r* to the debtor his pledge,
12 hath not *r* the pledge, and hath
Mt 12.13 it was *r* whole, like as the other.
Mk 3. 5 his hand was *r* whole as the other.
8.25 and he was *r*, and saw every man
Lk 6.10 his hand was *r* whole as the other.
Heb 13.19 that I may be *r* to you the sooner.

RESTORETH

Ps 23. 3 He *r* my soul: he leadeth me in
Mk 9.12 cometh first, and *r* all things;

RESTRAIN

Job 15. 8 dost thou *r* wisdom to thyself?
Ps 76.10 remainder of wrath shalt thou *r*.

RESTRAINED

Gen 8. 2 and the rain from heaven was *r*;
11. 6 now nothing will be *r* from them,
16. 2 the Lord hath *r* me from bearing:
Ex 36. 6 the people were *r* from bringing.
1Sa 3.13 vile, and he *r* them not.
Isa 63.15 mercies toward me? are they *r*?
Eze 31.15 and I *r* the floods thereof, and
Ac 14.18 sayings scarce *r* they the people,

RESURRECTION

Mt 22.23 which say that there is no *r*, and
28 in the *r* whose wife shall she be of
30 For in the *r* they neither marry,
31 But as touching the *r* of the dead,
27.53 came out the graves after his *r*,
Mk 12.18 Sadducees, which say there is no *r*;
23 In the *r* therefore, when they shall
Lk 14.14 be recompensed at the *r* of the just.
20.27 which deny that there is any *r*;
33 in the *r* whose wife of them is she?
35 that world, and the *r* from the dead,
36 of God, being the children of the *r*.
Jn 5.29 have done good, unto the *r* of life;
29 done evil, unto the *r* of damnation.
11.24 rise again in the *r* at the last day.
25 unto her, I am the *r*, and the life:
Ac 1.22 to be a witness with us of his *r*.
2.31 this before spake of the *r* of Christ,
4. 2 through Jesus the *r* from the dead.
33 witness of the *r* of the Lord Jesus:
17.18 preached unto them Jesus, and...*r*.
32 when they heard of the *r* of the dead,
23. 6 of the hope and *r* of the dead I am
8 Sadducees say that there is no *r*,
24.15 that there shall be a *r* of the dead,
21 Touching the *r* of the dead I am
Ro 1. 4 of holiness, by the *r* from the dead:
6. 5 be also in the likeness of his *r*:
1Co 15.12 you that there is no *r* of the dead?
13 But if there be no *r* of the dead, then
21 by man came also the *r* of the dead.
42 So also is the *r* of the dead. It is
Php 3.10 know him, and the power of his *r*,
11 attain unto the *r* of the dead.
2Ti 2.18 saying that the *r* is past already;
Heb 6. 2 of *r* of the dead, and of eternal
11.35 that they might obtain a better *r*:
1Pe 1. 3 lively hope by the *r* of Jesus Christ
3.21 God,) by the *r* of Jesus Christ:
Rev 20. 5 were finished. This is the first *r*.
6 is he that hath part in the first *r*:

RETAIN

Job 2. 9 Dost thou still *r* thine integrity?
Pr 4. 4 Let thine heart *r* my words: keep
11.16 honor: and strong men *r* riches,
Ec 8. 8 over the spirit to *r* the spirit;
Dan 11. 6 shall not *r* the power of the arm;
Jn 20.23 whose soever sins ye *r*, they are
Ro 1.28 like to *r* God in their knowledge,

RETAINED

Jdg 7. 8 and *r* those three hundred men:
19. 4 the damsel's father, *r* him; and
Dan 10. 8 corruption, and I *r* no strength.
16 upon me, and I have *r* no strength.
Jn 20.23 soever sins ye retain, they are *r*.
Phm 13 Whom I would have *r* with me,

RETAINETH
Pr 3.18 and happy is every one that *r* her.
11.16 A gracious woman *r* honor: and
Mic 7.18 he *r* not his anger for ever,

RETURN
Gen 3.19 art, and unto dust shalt thou *r*.
32. 9 *R* unto thy country, and to thy
Nu 10.36 said, *R*, O Lord, unto the many
Dt 17.16 henceforth *r* no more that way.
Jdg 7. 3 let him *r* and depart early from
Ru 1. 8 Go, *r* each to her mother's house:
16 or to *r* from following after thee:
1Sa 9. 5 with him, Come, and let us *r*;
29. 7 Wherefore now *r*, and go in peace,
2Sa 12.23 him, but he shall not *r* to me.
1Ki 12.26 kingdom *r* to the house of David:
22.17 *r* every man to his house in peace.
2Ki 20.10 shadow *r* backward ten degrees.
2Ch 10. 6 give ye me to *r* answer to this
Job 1.21 and naked shall I *r* thither: the
6.29 yea, *r* again, my righteousness is
7.10 He shall *r* no more to his house,
10.21 Before I go whence I shall not *r*,
15.22 believeth not that he shall *r* out of
16.22 go the way whence I shall not *r*.
22.23 If thou *r* to the Almighty, thou
33.25 shall *r* to the days of his youth:
Ps 6. 4 *R*, O Lord, deliver my soul: oh
73.10 Therefore his people *r* hither:
80.14 *R*, we beseech thee, O God of
90. 3 and sayest, *R*, ye children of men.
13 *R*, O Lord, how long? and let it
104.29 they die, and *r* to their dust.
116. 7 *R* unto thy rest, O my soul; for
Pr 2.19 None that go unto her *r* again,
26.27 rolleth a stone, it will *r* upon him.
Ec 1. 7 rivers come, thither they *r* again.
5.15 shall he *r* to go as he came, and
12. 2 nor the clouds *r* after the rain:
7 the dust *r* to the earth as it was:
7 shall *r* unto God who gave it.
Isa 10.21 The remnant shall *r*, even the
21.12 will inquire, inquire ye: *r*, come.
35.10 the ransomed of the Lord shall *r*,
44.22 *r* unto me; for I have redeemed
45.23 in righteousness, and shall not *r*,
51.11 the redeemed of the Lord shall *r*,
55. 7 and let him *r* unto the Lord, and
11 it shall not *r* unto me void, but it
Jer 3.22 *R*, ye backsliding children, and I
4. 1 If thou wilt *r*, O Israel, saith the
15.19 If thou *r*, then will I bring thee
18.11 *r* ye now every one from his evil
23.20 The anger of the Lord shall not *r*,
24. 7 *r* unto me with their whole heart.
31. 8 a great company shall *r* thither.
33.11 cause to *r* the captivity of the land,
35.15 *R* ye now every man from his evil
36. 3 may *r* every man from his evil way;
7 will *r* every one from his evil way,
50. 9 expert man; none shall *r* in vain.
Eze 18.23 not that he should *r* from his ways,
46. 9 shall not *r* by the way of the gate
Hos 2. 7 I will go and *r* to my first husband;
5.15 I will go and *r* to my place, till they
6. 1 Come, and let us *r* unto the Lord:
7.16 They *r*, but not to the most High:
14. 1 O Israel, *r* unto the Lord thy God;
7 dwell under his shadow shall *r*;
Joel 2.14 knoweth if he will *r* and repent,
Ob 15 thy reward shall *r* upon thine own
Mal 1. 4 *r* and build the desolate places;
3. 7 *R* unto me, and I will *r* unto you,
7 But ye said, Wherein shall we *r*?
18 Then shall ye *r*, and discern
Mt 2.12 that they should not *r* to Herod,
10.13 not worthy, let your peace *r* to you.
12.44 will *r* into my house from whence
24.18 let him which is in the field *r* back
Lk 8.39 *R* to thine own house, and shew
11.24 *r* unto my house whence I came
12.36 when he will *r* from the wedding;
17.31 field, let him likewise not *r* back.
19.12 to receive...a kingdom, and to *r*.
Ac 13.34 now no more to *r* to corruption,
15.16 After this I will *r*, and will build
18.21 but I will *r* again unto you, if God
20. 3 purposed to *r* through Macedonia.

RETURNED
Gen 8. 3 the waters *r* from off the earth
9 and she *r* unto him into the ark,
12 dove; which *r* not again unto him
14. 7 they *r*, and came to En-mishpat,
18.33 and Abraham *r* unto his place.
21.32 *r* into the land of the Philistines.
22.19 So Abraham *r* unto his young men,
31.55 departed, and *r* unto his place.
32. 6 the messengers *r* to Jacob, saying,
33.16 So Esau *r* that day on his way unto
37.29 And Reuben *r* unto the pit; and,
30 he *r* unto his brethren, and said,
38.22 he *r* to Judah, and said, I cannot
42.24 *r* to them again, and communed
43.10 now we had *r* this second time.
18 the money that was *r* in our sacks
44.13 every man his ass, and *r* to the city.
50.14 And Joseph *r* into Egypt, he, and
Ex 4.18 And Moses went and *r* to Jethro his
20 ass, and he *r* to the land of Egypt:
5.22 And Moses *r* unto the Lord, and
14.27 and the sea *r* to his strength when
28 And the waters *r*, and covered the
19. 8 Moses *r* the words of the people
32.31 And Moses *r* unto the Lord, and
34.31 all the rulers of the congregation *r*
Lev 22.13 and is *r* unto her father's house, as
Nu 13.25 they *r* from searching of the land
14.36 sent to search the land, who *r*,
16.50 Aaron *r* unto Moses unto the door
23. 6 he *r* unto him, and, lo, he stood
24.25 up, and went and *r* to his place:
Dt 1.45 And ye *r* and wept before the Lord;
Jos 2.16 three days, until the pursuers be *r*:
22 days, until the pursuers were *r*:
23 So the two men *r*, and descended
4.18 waters of Jordan *r* unto their place
6.14 the city once, and *r* into the camp:
7. 3 And they *r* to Joshua, and said
8.24 that all the Israelites *r* unto Ai,
10.15 And Joshua *r*, and all Israel with
21 And all the people *r* to the camp
38, 43 Joshua *r*, and all Israel with
22. 9 and the half tribe of Manasseh *r*,
32 *r* from the children of Reuben, and
Jdg 2.19 they *r*, and corrupted themselves
5.29 her, yea, she *r* answer to herself,
7. 3 *r* of the people twenty and two
15 *r* into the host of Israel, and said,
8.13 the son of Joash *r* from battle
11.39 that she *r* unto her father, who did
14. 8 And after a time he *r* to take her,
21.23 went and *r* unto their inheritance,
Ru 1.22 So Naomi *r*,...Ruth the Moabitess,
22 *r* out of the country of Moab:
1Sa 1.19 worshipped before the Lord, and *r*,
6.16 it, they *r* to Ekron the same day.
17 Philistines *r* for a trespass offering
17.15 David went and *r* from Saul to feed
53 *r* from chasing after...Philistines,
57 *r* from the slaughter of...Philistine,
18. 6 *r* from the slaughter of...Philistine,
23.28 Saul *r* from pursuing after David,
24. 1 *r* from following the Philistines,
25.39 hath *r* the wickedness of Nabal
26.25 on his way, and Saul *r* to his place.
27. 9 apparel, and *r*, and came to Achish.
2Sa 1. 1 David was *r* from the slaughter of
22 and the sword of Saul *r* not empty.
2.30 And Joab *r* from following Abner:
3.16 unto him, Go, return. And he *r*.
27 when Abner was *r* to Hebron, Joab
6.20 David *r* to bless his household.
8.13 he *r* from smiting of the Syrians
10.14 So Joab *r* from the children of
11. 4 and she *r* unto her house.
12.31 all the people *r* unto Jerusalem.
14.24 So Absalom *r* to his own house,
16. 8 hath *r* upon thee all the blood of
17. 3 whom thou seekest is as if all *r*:
20 not find them, they *r* to Jerusalem.
18.16 the people *r* from pursuing after
19.15 So the king *r*, and came to Jordan.
39 him; and he *r* unto his own place.
20.22 Joab *r* to Jerusalem unto the king.
23.10 people *r* after him only to spoil.
1Ki 12.24 *r* to depart, according to the word
13.10 *r* not by the way that he came to
33 Jeroboam *r* not from his evil way,
19.21 And he *r* back from him, and took
2Ki 2.25 and from thence he *r* to Samaria.
3.27 from him, and *r* to their own land.
4.35 he *r*, and walked in the house
5.15 And he *r* to the man of God, he and
7.15 And the messengers *r*, and told the
8. 3 that the woman *r* out of the land
9.15 king Joram was *r* to be healed in
14.14 and hostages, and *r* to Samaria.
19. 8 Rab-shakeh *r*, and found the king
36 and went and *r*, and dwelt at
23.20 upon them, and *r* to Jerusalem.
1Ch 16.43 and David *r* to bless his house.
20. 3 and all the people *r* to Jerusalem.
2Ch 10. 2 it, that Jeroboam *r* out of Egypt.
11. 4 *r* from going against Jeroboam.
14.15 in abundance, and *r* to Jerusalem.
19. 1 Jehoshaphat the king of Judah *r*
8 when they *r* to Jerusalem.
20.27 Then they *r*, every man of Judah
22. 6 And he *r* to be healed in Jezreel
25.10 and they *r* home in great anger.
24 hostages also, and *r* to Samaria.
28.15 brethren: then they *r* to Samaria.
31. 1 Then all the children of Israel *r*,
32.21 he *r* with shame of face to his own
34. 7 land of Israel, he *r* to Jerusalem.
9 Benjamin;...they *r* to Jerusalem.
Ezr 5. 5 and then they *r* answer by letter
11 thus they *r* us answer, saying, We
Neh 2.15 the gate of the valley, and so *r*.
4.15 we *r* all of us to the wall, every one
9.28 yet when they *r*, and cried unto
Est 2.14 the morrow she *r* into the second
7. 8 the king *r* out of the palace garden
Ps 35.13 my prayer *r* into mine own bosom.
60(T) when Joab *r*, and smote of Edom
78.34 *r* and inquired early after God.
Ec 4. 1 So I *r*, and considered all the
7 Then I *r*, and I saw vanity under
9.11 I *r*, and saw under the sun, that
Isa 37. 8 So Rabshakeh *r*, and found the
37 went and *r*, and dwelt at Nineveh.
38. 8 So the sun *r* ten degrees, by which
Jer 3. 7 Turn thou unto me. But she *r* not.
14. 3 they *r* with their vessels empty;
40.12 Even all the Jews *r* out of all places
41.14 from Mizpah cast about and *r*,
43. 5 that were *r* from all nations,
Eze 1.14 And the living creatures ran and *r*
8.17 have *r* to provoke me to anger:
47. 7 Now when I had *r*, behold, at the
Dan 4.34 mine understanding *r* unto me,
36 same time my reason *r* unto me;
36 honor and brightness *r* unto me;
Hos 6.11 I *r* the captivity of my people.
Am 4. 6, 8, 9, 10, 11 have ye not *r* unto me,
Zec 1. 6 and they *r* and said, Like as the
16 I am *r* to Jerusalem with mercies:
7.14 that no man passed through nor *r*:
8. 3 I am *r* unto Zion, and will dwell in
Mt 21.18 as he *r* into the city, he hungered.
Mk 14.40 when he *r*, he found them asleep

BIBLICAL THEMES

REVELATION

And the Lord appeared unto Abram, and said, Unto thy seed will I give this land: and there builded he an altar unto the Lord, who appeared unto him.
Gen 12.7

[Moses] came to the mountain of God. . . . And the angel of the Lord appeared unto him in a flame of fire out of the midst of a bush: and he looked, and, behold, the bush burned with fire, and the bush was not consumed. Ex 3.1-2

All the people saw the cloudy pillar stand at the tabernacle door: and all the people rose up and worshipped. . . . And the Lord spake unto Moses face to face, as a man speaketh unto his friend. Ex 33.10-11

I will raise them up a Prophet from among their brethren, like unto thee, and will put my words in his mouth.
Dt 18.18

And, behold, the Lord passed by, and a great and strong wind rent the mountains, and brake in pieces the rocks before the Lord; but the Lord was not in the wind: and after the wind an earthquake; but the Lord was not in the earthquake: and after the earthquake a fire; but the Lord was not in the fire: and after the fire a still small voice.
1Ki 19.11-12

Elisha prayed, and said, Lord, I pray thee, open his eyes, that he may see. And the Lord opened the eyes of the young man; and he saw: and, behold, the mountain was full of horses and chariots of fire round about Elisha.
2Ki 6.17

The heavens declare the glory of God; and the firmament sheweth his handywork. Day unto day uttereth speech, and night unto night sheweth knowledge. There is no speech nor language, where their voice is not heard. Their line is gone out through all the earth, and their words to the end of the world. Ps 19.1-4

Thus saith the Lord, Keep ye judgment, and do justice: for my salvation is near to come, and my righteousness to be revealed. Isa 56.1

The lion hath roared, who will not fear? the Lord God hath spoken, who can but prophesy? Am 3.8

Behold, I will send my messenger, and he shall prepare the way before me: and the Lord, whom ye seek, shall suddenly come to his temple. Mal 3.1

Then took [Simeon] him up in his arms, and blessed God, and said, Lord, now lettest thou thy servant depart in peace, according to thy word: for mine eyes have seen thy salvation, which thou hast prepared before the face of all people. Lk 2.28-31

What I do thou knowest not now; but thou shalt know hereafter. Jn 13.7

These are written, that ye might believe that Jesus is the Christ, the Son of God; and that believing ye might have life through his name. Jn 20.31

The wrath of God is revealed from heaven against all ungodliness and unrighteousness of men . . . because that which may be known of God is manifest in them; for God hath shewed it unto them. For the invisible things of him from the creation of the world are clearly seen, being understood by the things that are made. Ro 1.18-20

How then shall they call on him in whom they have not believed? and how shall they believe in him of whom they have not heard? and how shall they hear without a preacher? Ro 10.14

We all, with open face beholding as in a glass the glory of the Lord, are changed into the same image from glory to glory.
2Co 3.18

All scripture is given by inspiration of God. 2Ti 3.16

Lk 1.56 months, and *r* to her own house.
2.20 the shepherds *r*, glorifying and
39 they *r* into Galilee, to their own
43 as they *r*, the child Jesus tarried
4. 1 of the Holy Ghost *r* from Jordan,
14 Jesus *r* in the power of the Spirit
8.37 up into the ship, and *r* back again.
40 to pass, that, when Jesus was *r*,
9.10 the apostles, when they were *r*,
10.17 And the seventy *r* again with joy,
17.18 found that *r* to give glory to God,
19.15 came to pass, that when he was *r*,
23.48 done, smote their breasts, and *r*.
56 And they *r*, and prepared spices
24. 9 *r* from the sepulcher, and told all
33 the same hour, and *r* to Jerusalem,
52 and *r* to Jerusalem with great joy:
Ac 1.12 Then *r* they unto Jerusalem from
5.22 not in the prison, they *r*, and told,
8.25 *r* to Jerusalem, and preached the
12.25 and Saul *r* from Jerusalem, when
13.13 John departing from them *r* to
14.21 they *r* again to Lystra, and to
21. 6 took ship; and they *r* home again.
23.32 to go with him, and *r* to the castle:
Gal 1.17 and *r* again unto Damascus.
Heb 11.15 have had opportunity to have *r*.
1Pe 2.25 but are now *r* unto the Shepherd

RETURNETH

Ps 146. 4 goeth forth, he *r* to his earth;
Pr 26.11 As a dog *r* to his vomit,
11 so a fool *r* to his folly.
Ec 1. 6 the wind *r* again according to his
Isa 55.10 from heaven, and *r* not thither,
Eze 35. 7 that passeth out and him that *r*.
Zec 9. 8 by, and because of him that *r*:

RETURNING

Isa 30.15 In *r* and rest shall ye be saved;
Lk 7.10 *r* to the house, found the servant
Ac 8.28 Was *r*, and sitting in his chariot
Heb 7. 1 *r* from the slaughter of the kings,

REVEAL

Job 20.27 The heaven shall *r* his iniquity;
Jer 33. 6 will *r* unto them the abundance of
Dan 2.47 seeing thou couldest *r* this secret.
Mt 11.27 to whomsoever the Son will *r* him.
Lk 10.22 and he to whom the Son will *r* him.
Gal 1.16 To *r* his Son in me, that I might
Php 3.15 God shall *r* even this unto you.

REVEALED

Dt 29.29 those things which are *r* belong
1Sa 3. 7 word of the Lord yet *r* unto him.
21 for the Lord *r* himself to Samuel
Isa 22.14 it was *r* in mine ears by the Lord
40. 5 the glory of the Lord shall be *r*,
53. 1 to whom is the arm of the Lord *r*?
56. 1 and my righteousness to be *r*.
Jer 11.20 for unto thee have I *r* my cause.
Mt 10.26 covered, that shall not be *r*; and
11.25 and hast *r* them unto babes.
16.17 and blood hath not *r* it unto thee,
Lk 2.26 *r* unto him by the Holy Ghost,
35 thoughts of many hearts may be *r*.
10.21 and hast *r* them unto babes:
12. 2 nothing covered, that shall not be *r*;
17.30 the day when the Son of man is *r*.
Jn 12.38 hath the arm of the Lord been *r*?
Ro 1.17 righteousness of God *r* from faith
18 the wrath of God is *r* from heaven
8.18 the glory which shall be *r* in us.
1Co 2.10 hath *r* them unto us by his Spirit:
3.13 it, because it shall be *r* by fire;
14.30 If any thing be *r* to another that
Gal 3.23 faith which should afterwards be *r*.
Eph 3. 5 as it is now *r* unto his holy apostles
2Th 1. 7 the Lord Jesus shall be *r* from
2. 3 and that man of sin be *r*, the son
6 that he might be *r* in his time.
8 then shall that Wicked be *r*, whom
1Pe 1. 5 ready to be *r* in the last time.
12 Unto whom it was *r*, that not unto
4.13 when his glory shall be *r*, ye may
5. 1 of the glory that shall be *r*:

REVEALETH

Pr 11.13 A talebearer *r* secrets: but he
20.19 about as a talebearer *r* secrets:
Dan 2.22 He *r* the deep and secret things:
28 is a God in heaven that *r* secrets,
29 he that *r* secrets maketh known to
Am 3. 7 he *r* his secret unto his servants

REVELATION

Ro 2. 5 and *r* of the righteous judgment of
16.25 according to the *r* of the mystery,
1Co 14. 6 I shall speak to you either by *r*, or
26 doctrine, hath a tongue, hath a *r*,
Gal 1.12 it, but by the *r* of Jesus Christ.
2. 2 And I went up by *r*, and
Eph 1.17 unto you the spirit of wisdom and *r*
3. 3 How that by *r* he made known unto
1Pe 1.13 unto you at the *r* of Jesus Christ;
Rev 1. 1 The *R* of Jesus Christ, which God

REVELATIONS

2Co 12. 1 come to visions and *r* of the Lord.
7 through the abundance of the *r*,

REVELLINGS

Gal 5.21 drunkenness, *r*, and such like:
1Pe 4. 3 *r*, banquetings, and abominable

REVENGE

Jer 15.15 me, and *r* me of my persecutors;
20.10 and we shall take our *r* on him.
Eze 25.15 the Philistines hath dealt by *r*,
2Co 7.11 desire, yea, what zeal, yea, what *r*!
10. 6 readiness to *r* all disobedience,

REVENGED

Eze 25.12 and *r* himself upon them;

REVENGER

Ro 13. 4 a *r* to execute wrath upon him

REVENUE

Ezr 4.13 shalt endamage the *r* of the kings.
Pr 8.19 gold; and my *r* than choice silver.
Isa 23. 3 the harvest of the river, is her *r*;

REVERENCE

Lev 19.30 sabbaths, and *r* my sanctuary:
26. 2 my sabbaths, and *r* my sanctuary:
2Sa 9. 6 he fell on his face, and did *r*.
1Ki 1.31 and did *r* to the king, and said,
Est 3. 2 Mordecai bowed not, nor did him *r*.
5 Mordecai bowed not, nor did him *r*,
Ps 89. 7 to be had in *r* of all them that
Mt 21.37 son, saying, They will *r* my son.
Mk 12. 6 them, saying, They will *r* my son.
Lk 20.13 they will *r* him when they see him.
Eph 5.33 wife see that she *r* her husband.
Heb 12. 9 us, and we gave them *r*:
28 acceptably with *r* and godly fear:

REVILE

Ex 22.28 Thou shalt not *r* the gods, nor
Mt 5.11 are ye, when men shall *r* you,

REVILED

Mt 27.39 And they that passed by *r* him,
Mk 15.32 were crucified with him *r* him.
Jn 9.28 Then they *r* him, and said, Thou
1Co 4.12 being *r*, we bless; being
1Pe 2.23 Who, when he was *r*,...not again;
29 Who when he was..., *r* not again;

REVILERS

1Co 6.10 nor *r*, nor extortioners, shall

REVILEST

Ac 23. 4 said, *R* thou God's high priest?

REVIVE

Neh 4. 2 *r* the stones out of the heaps of
Ps 85. 6 Wilt thou not *r* us again: that thy
138. 7 midst of trouble, thou wilt *r* me:
Isa 57.15 to *r* the spirit of the humble, and
15 *r* the heart of the contrite ones.
Hos 6. 2 after two days will he *r* us: in the
14. 7 They shall *r* as the corn, and grow
Hab 3. 2 *r* thy work in the midst of the

REVIVED

Gen 45.27 the spirit of Jacob their father *r*:
Jdg 15.19 his spirit came again, and he *r*.
1Ki 17.22 came into him again, and he *r*.
2Ki 13.21 touched the bones of Elisha, he *r*,
Ro 7. 9 the commandment came, sin *r*,
14. 9 Christ both died, and rose, and *r*,

REWARD

Gen 15. 1 shield, and thy exceeding great *r*.
Nu 18.31 *r* for your service in the tabernacle
Dt 10.17 not persons, nor taketh *r*:
27.25 *r* to slay an innocent person:
32.41 and will *r* them that hate me.
Ru 2.12 a full *r* be given thee of the Lord
1Sa 24.19 Lord *r* thee good for that thou
2Sa 3.39 the Lord shall *r* the doer of evil
4.10 have given him a *r* for his tidings:
19.36 recompense it me with such a *r*?
1Ki 13. 7 thyself, and I will give thee a *r*.
2Ch 20.11 Behold, I say, how they *r* us, to
Job 6.22 a *r* for me of your substance?
7. 2 hireling looketh for the *r* of his work:
Ps 15. 5 taketh *r* against the innocent.
19.11 keeping of them there is great *r*.
40.15 them be desolate for a *r* of their
54. 5 shall *r* evil unto mine enemies:
58.11 there is a *r* for the righteous:
70. 3 for a *r* of their shame that say,
91. 8 and see the *r* of the wicked.
94. 2 earth: render a *r* to the proud.
109.20 this be the *r* of mine adversaries
127. 3 the fruit of the womb is his *r*.
Pr 11.18 righteousness shall be a sure *r*.

BIBLICAL THEMES

REWARD AND PUNISHMENT

All these blessings shall come on thee, and overtake thee, if thou shalt hearken unto the voice of the Lord thy God. Dt 28.2

They have moved me to jealousy with that which is not God; they have provoked me to anger with their vanities. . . . a fire is kindled in mine anger, and shall burn unto the lowest hell, and shall consume the earth with her increase, and set on fire the foundations of the mountains. . . . To me belongeth vengeance, and recompence. Dt 32.21-22, 35

The wicked have drawn out the sword, and have bent their bow, to cast down the poor and needy, and to slay such as be of upright conversation. Their sword shall enter into their own heart, and their bows shall be broken. Ps 37.14-15

Blessed is the man whom thou chastenest, O Lord. Ps 94.12

The turning away of the simple shall slay them, and the prosperity of fools shall destroy them. But whoso hearkeneth unto me shall dwell safely, and shall be quiet from fear of evil. Pr 1.32-33

Whom the Lord loveth he correcteth; even as a father the son in whom he delighteth. Pr 3.12

Cast thy bread upon the waters: for thou shalt find it after many days. Ec 11.1

Behold, the Lord God will come with strong hand, and his arm shall rule for him: behold, his reward is with him, and his work before him. He shall feed his flock like a shepherd. Isa 40.10-11

I will do unto them after their way, and according to their deserts will I judge them; and they shall know that I am the Lord. Eze 7.27

Though they dig into hell, thence shall mine hand take them; though they climb up to heaven, thence will I bring them down. Am 9.2

Blessed are ye, when men shall revile you, and persecute you . . . for my sake. Rejoice, and be exceeding glad: for great is your reward in heaven. Mt 5.11-12

If ye love them which love you, what reward have ye? do not even the publicans the same? Mt 5.46

Whosoever shall give you a cup of water to drink in my name . . . verily I say unto you, he shall not lose his reward. Mk 9.41

But love ye your enemies, and do good, and lend, hoping for nothing again; and your reward shall be great, and ye shall be the children of the Highest. Lk 6.35

And, behold, there are last which shall be first, and there are first which shall be last. Lk 13.30

The wages of sin is death; but the gift of God is eternal life through Jesus Christ our Lord. Ro 6.23

Vengeance is mine; I will repay, saith the Lord. Therefore if thine enemy hunger, feed him; if he thirst, give him drink: for in so doing thou shalt heap coals of fire on his head. Ro 12.19-20

Be not deceived; God is not mocked: for whatsoever a man soweth, that shall he also reap. . . . And let us not be weary in well doing: for in due season we shall reap, if we faint not. Gal 6.7, 9

Whatsoever ye do, do it heartily, as to the Lord, and not unto men; knowing that of the Lord ye shall receive the reward of the inheritance: for ye serve the Lord Christ. But he that doeth wrong shall receive for the wrong which he hath done. Col 3.23-25

It is a fearful thing to fall into the hands of the living God. Heb 10.31

I am he which searcheth the reins and hearts: and I will give unto every one of you according to your works. Rev 2.23

21.14 a *r* in the bosom strong wrath.
24.14 then there shall be a *r*, and thy
20 shall be no *r* to the evil man;
25.22 head, and the Lord shall *r* thee.
Ec 4. 9 have a good *r* for their labor.
9. 5 neither have they any more a *r*;
Isa 3.11 *r* of his hands shall be given him.
5.23 Which justify the wicked for *r*,
40.10 behold, his *r* is with him, and his
45.13 not for price nor *r*, saith the Lord
62.11 his *r* is with him, and his work
Jer 40. 5 guard gave him victuals and a *r*,
Eze 16.34 and in that thou givest a *r*,
34 and no *r* is given unto thee,
Hos 4. 9 ways, and *r* them their doings.
9. 1 loved a *r* upon every cornfloor.
Ob 15 thy *r* shall return upon thine own
Mic 3.11 heads thereof judge for *r*, and
7. 3 and the judge asketh for a *r*;
Mt 5.12 for great is your *r* in heaven: for
46 which love you, what *r* have ye?
6. 1 ye have no *r* of your Father which
2 I say unto you, They have their *r*.
4 secret himself shall *r* thee openly.
5 say unto you, They have their *r*.
6 seeth in secret shall *r* thee openly.
16 I say unto you. They have their *r*.
18 seeth in secret, shall *r* thee openly.
10.41 shall receive a prophet's *r*; and
41 shall receive a righteous man's *r*.
42 you, he shall in no wise lose his *r*.
16.27 he shall *r* every man according
Mk 9.41 unto you, he shall not lose his *r*.
Lk 6.23 behold your *r* is great in heaven:
35 your *r* shall be great, and ye shall
23.41 we receive the due *r* of our deeds:
Ac 1.18 a field with the *r* of iniquity;
Ro 4. 4 worketh is the *r* not reckoned of
1Co 3. 8 every man shall receive his own *r*
14 thereupon, he shall receive a *r*.
9.17 do this thing willingly, I have a *r*:
18 What is my *r* then? Verily that,
Col 2.18 Let no man beguile you of your *r*
3.24 receive the *r* of the inheritance:
1Ti 5.18 The laborer is worthy of his *r*.
2Ti 4.14 the Lord *r* him according to his
Heb 2. 2 received a just recompence of *r*;
10.35 hath a great recompence of *r*.
11.26 unto the recompence of the *r*.
2Pe 2.13 receive the *r* of unrighteousness,
2Jn 8 but that we receive a full *r*.
Jude 11 after the error of Balaam for *r*,
Rev 11.18 shouldest give *r* unto thy servants
18. 6 *R* her even as she rewarded you,
22.12 my *r* is with me, to give every

REWARDED

Gen 44. 4 Wherefore have ye *r* evil for good?
1Sa 24.17 thou hast *r* me good, whereas
17 whereas I have *r* thee evil.
2Sa 22.21 The Lord *r* me according to my
2Ch 15. 7 weak: for your work shall be *r*.
Ps 7. 4 I have *r* evil unto him that was
18.20 The Lord *r* me according to my
35.12 They *r* me evil for good to the
103.10 *r* us according to our iniquities.
109. 5 And they have *r* me evil for good,
Pr 13.13 the commandment shall be *r*.
Isa 3. 9 they have *r* evil unto themselves.
Jer 31.16 for thy work shall be *r*, saith the
Rev 18. 6 Reward her even as she *r* you,

REWARDER

Heb 11. 6 a *r* of them that diligently seek

REWARDETH

Job 21.19 he *r* him, and he shall know it.
Ps 31.23 and plentifully *r* the proud doer.
137. 8 *r* thee as thou hast served us.
Pr 17.13 Whoso *r* evil for good, evil shall

26.10 formed all things both *r* the fool,
10 the fool, and *r* transgressors.

REWARDS

Nu 22. 7 the *r* of divination in their hand;
Isa 1.23 gifts, and followeth after *r*:
Dan 2. 6 ye shall receive of me gifts and *r*
5.17 thyself, and give thy *r* to another;
Hos 2.12 These are my *r* that my lovers

RHODA

Ac 12.13 damsel came to hearken, named *R*.

RHODES

Ac 21. 1 and the day following unto *R*,

RIB

Gen 2.22 And the *r*,...made he a woman,
2Sa 2.23 spear smote him under the fifth *r*,

RIBS

Gen 2.21 took one of his *r*, and closed up
Dan 7. 5 it had three *r* in the mouth of it

RICH

Gen 13. 2 And Abram was very *r* in cattle,
14.23 shouldest say, I...made Abram *r*:
Ex 30.15 The *r* shall not give more, and
Lev 25.47 a sojourner or stranger wax *r*
Ru 3.10 young men, whether poor or *r*.
1Sa 2. 7 Lord maketh poor, and maketh *r*:
2Sa 12. 1 the one *r*, and the other poor.
2 *r* man had exceeding many flocks
4 came a traveller unto the *r* man,
Job 15.29 He shall not be *r*, neither shall
27.19 The *r* man shall lie down, but he
34.19 nor regardeth the *r* more than
Ps 45.12 *r* among the people shall intreat
49. 2 low and high, *r* and poor, together.
16 thou afraid when one is made *r*,
Pr 10. 4 the hand of the diligent maketh *r*.
15 *r* man's wealth is his strong city:
22 blessing of the Lord, it maketh *r*,
13. 7 There is that maketh himself *r*,
14.20 but the *r* hath many friends.
18.11 *r* man's wealth is his strong city,
23 but the *r* answereth roughly.
21.17 loveth wine and oil shall not be *r*.
22. 2 The *r* and poor meet together:
7 The *r* ruleth over the poor, and
16 he that giveth to the *r*, shall surely
23. 4 Labor not to be *r*: cease from
28. 6 is perverse...though he be *r*.
11 *r* man is wise in his own conceit;
20 he that maketh haste to be *r* shall
22 hasteth to be *r* hath an evil eye,
Ec 5.12 abundance of the *r* will not suffer
10. 6 dignity, and the *r* sit in low place.
20 curse not the *r* in thy bedchamber:
Isa 53. 9 wicked, and with the *r* in his death;
Jer 5.27 are become great, and waxen *r*.
9.23 not the *r* man glory in his riches:
Eze 27.24 in chests of *r* apparel, bound with
Hos 12. 8 Ephraim said, Yet I am become *r*,
Mic 6.12 the *r* men...are full of violence,
Zec 11. 5 Blessed be the Lord; for I am *r*:
Mt 19.23 a *r* man shall hardly enter into
24 than for a *r* man to enter into the
27.57 there came a *r* man of Arimathaea,
Mk 10.25 than for a *r* man to enter into the
12.41 many that were *r* cast in much.
Lk 1.53 the *r* he hath sent empty away.
6.24 But woe unto you that are *r*!
12.16 The ground of a certain *r* man
21 himself, and is not *r* toward God.
14.12 kinsmen, nor thy *r* neighbors;
16. 1, 19 There was a certain *r* man,
21 which fell from the *r* man's table:
22 *r* man also died, and was buried;
18.23 very sorrowful: for he was very *r*.
25 than for a *r* man to enter into the

19. 2 among the publicans, and he was *r*.
21. 1 saw the *r* men casting their gifts
Ro 10.12 is *r* unto all that call upon him.
1Co 4. 8 Now ye are full, now ye are *r*, ye
2Co 6.10 as poor, yet making many *r*;
8. 9 though he was *r*, yet for your
9 through his poverty might be *r*.
Eph 2. 4 God, who is *r* in mercy, for his
1Ti 6. 9 that will be *r* fall into temptation
17 Charge them that are *r* in this
18 that they be *r* in good works,
Jas 1.10 But the *r*, in that he is made low:
11 So also shall the *r* man fade away
2. 5 the poor of this world *r* in faith,
6 Do not *r* men oppress you, and
5. 1 Go to now, ye *r* men, weep and
Rev 2. 9 and poverty, (but thou art *r*)
3.17 Because thou sayest, I am *r*, and
18 in the fire, that thou mayest be *r*;
6.15 the *r* men, and the chief captains,
13.16 great, *r* and poor, free and bond,
18. 3 merchants of the earth...waxed *r*
15 things, which were made *r* by her,
19 were made *r* all that had ships

RICHER

Dan 11. 2 fourth shall be far *r* than they all:

RICHES

Gen 31.16 the *r* which God hath taken from
36. 7 their *r* were more than that they
Jos 22. 8 Return with much *r* unto your
1Sa 17.25 king will enrich him with great *r*,
1Ki 3.11 neither hast asked *r* for thyself,
13 hast not asked, both *r*, and honor:
10.23 exceeded...kings of the earth for *r*
1Ch 29.12 Both *r* and honor come of thee,
28 old age, full of days, *r*, and honor:
2Ch 1.11 not asked *r*, wealth, or honor.
12 I will give thee *r*, and wealth, and
9.22 passed...the kings of the earth in *r*
17. 5 he had *r* and honor in abundance.
18. 1 Jehoshaphat had *r* and honor in
20.25 both *r* with the dead bodies, and
32.27 Hezekiah had exceeding much *r*
Est 1. 4 the *r* of his glorious kingdom and
5.11 told them of the glory of his *r*, and
Job 20.15 He hath swallowed down *r*, and
36.19 Will he esteem thy *r*? no, not gold,
Ps 37.16 better than the *r* of many wicked.
39. 6 he heapeth up *r*, and knoweth not
49. 6 boast...in the multitude of their *r*;
52. 7 trusted in the abundance of his *r*,
62.10 if *r* increase, set not your heart
73.12 in the world; they increase in *r*.
104.24 them all: the earth is full of thy *r*.
112. 3 and *r* shall be in his house:
119.14 testimonies, as much as in all *r*.
Pr 3.16 in her left hand *r* and honor.
8.18 *R* and honor are with me; yea,
18 yea, durable *r* and righteousness.
11. 4 *R* profit not in the day of wrath:
16 honor: and strong men retain *r*.
28 He that trusteth in his *r* shall fall:
13. 7 himself poor, yet hath great *r*.
8 ransom of a man's life are his *r*:
14.24 The crown of the wise is their *r*:
19.14 House and *r* are the inheritance
22. 1 rather to be chosen than great *r*,
4 and the fear of the Lord are *r*, and
16 oppresseth the poor to increase his *r*,
23. 5 *r* certainly make themselves wings;
24. 4 with all precious and pleasant *r*.
27.24 For *r* are not for ever: and doth
30. 8 give me neither poverty nor *r*;
Ec 4. 8 neither is his eye satisfied with *r*;
5.13 *r* kept for the owners thereof to
14 But those *r* perish by evil travail:
19 whom God hath given *r* and wealth,
6. 2 A man to whom God hath given *r*,
9.11 nor yet *r* to men of understanding,

Isa 8. 4 *r* of Damascus and the spoil of
10.14 found as a nest the *r* of the people:
30. 6 carry their *r* upon the shoulders of
45. 3 and hidden *r* of secret places,
61. 6 ye shall eat the *r* of the Gentiles,
Jer 9.23 not the rich man glory in his *r*:
17.11 he that getteth *r*, and not by right,
48.36 *r*...he hath gotten are perished.
Eze 26.12 they shall make a spoil of thy *r*,
27.12 of the multitude of all kind of *r*;
18 making, for the multitude of all *r*;
27 *r*, and thy fairs, thy merchandise,
33 earth with the multitude of thy *r*
28. 4 thou hast gotten thee *r*, and hast
5 traffick hast thou increased thy *r*,
5 heart is lifted up because of thy *r*:
Dan 11. 2 through his *r* he shall stir up all
13 a great army and with much *r*.
24 them the prey, and spoil, and *r*:
28 return into his land with great *r*;
Mt 13.22 world, and the deceitfulness of *r*,
Mk 4.19 world, and the deceitfulness of *r*,
10.23 they that have *r* enter into the
24 that trust in *r* to enter into the
Lk 8.14 are choked with cares and *r* and
16.11 will commit to your trust the true *r*?
18.24 they that have *r* enter into the
Ro 2. 4 Or despisest thou the *r* of his
9.23 make known the *r* of his glory on
11.12 fall of them be the *r* of the world,
12 diminishing of them the *r* of the
33 depth of the *r* both of the wisdom
2Co 8. 2 unto the *r* of their liberality.
Eph 1. 7 according to the *r* of his grace;
18 *r* of the glory of his inheritance in
2. 7 shew the exceeding *r* of his grace
3. 8 the unsearchable *r* of Christ;
16 according to the *r* of his glory, to
Php 4.19 to his *r* in glory by Christ Jesus.
Col 1.27 the *r* of the glory of this mystery
2. 2 unto all *r* of the full assurance of
1Ti 6.17 nor trust in uncertain *r*, but in the
Heb 11.26 reproach of Christ greater *r*
Jas 5. 2 Your *r* are corrupted, and your
Rev 5.12 was slain to receive power, and *r*,
18.17 hour so great *r* is come to nought.

RICHLY

Col 3.16 the word of Christ dwell in you *r*
1Ti 6.17 who giveth us *r* all things to enjoy;

RIDDLE

Jdg 14.12 I will now put forth a *r* unto you:
13 Put forth thy *r*, that we may hear
14 not in three days expound the *r*.
15 that he may declare unto us the *r*,
16 thou hast put forth a *r* unto the
17 she told the *r* to the children of her
18 heifer, ye had not found out my *r*.
19 unto them which expounded the *r*.
Eze 17. 2 Son of man, put forth a *r*, and

RIDE

Gen 41.43 he made him to *r* in the second
Dt 32.13 He made him *r* on the high places
Jdg 5.10 Speak, ye that *r* on white asses, ye
2Sa 16. 2 be for the king's household to *r* on;
19.26 me an ass, that I may *r* thereon,
1Ki 1.33 cause Solomon my son to *r* upon
38 Solomon to *r* upon king David's
44 caused him to *r* upon the king's
2Ki 10.16 So they made him *r* in his chariot.
Job 30.22 thou causest me to *r* upon it, and
Ps 45. 4 And in thy majesty *r* prosperously
66.12 caused men to *r* over our heads;
Isa 30.16 We will *r* upon the swift; therefore
58.14 and I will cause thee to *r* upon the
Jer 6.23 they *r* upon horses, set in array
50.42 they shall *r* upon horses, every one
Hos 10.11 I will make Ephraim to *r*; Judah
14. 3 save us: we will not *r* upon horses:
Hab 3. 8 thou didst *r* upon thine horses and
Hag 2.22 chariots, and those that *r* in them;

RIDER

Gen 49.17 so that this *r* shall fall backward.
Ex 15. 1, 21 horse and his *r* hath he thrown
Job 39.18 she scorneth the horse and his *r*.
Jer 51.21 break in pieces the horse and his *r*;
21 in pieces the chariot and his *r*;
Zec 12. 4 and his *r* with madness: and I

RIDING

Nu 22.22 Now he was *r* upon his ass, and
2Ki 4.24 slack not thy *r* for me, except I bid
Jer 17.25 *r* in chariots and on horses, they,
22. 4 *r* in chariots and on horses, he, and
Eze 23. 6 men, horsemen *r* upon horses.
12 horsemen *r* upon horses, all of them
23 all of them *r* upon horses.
38.15 all of them *r* upon horses, a great
Zec 1. 8 behold a man *r* upon a red horse,
9. 9 lowly, and *r* upon an ass, and

RIGHT

Gen 13. 9 left hand, then I will go to the *r*;
9 if thou depart to the *r* hand, then
18.25 the Judge of all the earth do *r*?
24.48 which had led me in the *r* way to
49 that I may turn to the *r* hand, or
48.13 Ephraim in his *r* hand toward
13 left hand toward Israel's *r* hand,
14 Israel stretched out his *r* hand,
17 *r* hand upon the head of Ephraim,
18 put thy *r* hand upon his head.
Ex 14.22, 29 wall unto them on their *r* hand,
15. 6 Thy *r* hand, O Lord, is become
6 thy *r* hand, O Lord, hath dashed
12 Thou stretchedst out thy *r* hand,
26 do that which is *r* in his sight,
29.20 upon the tip of the *r* ear of Aaron,
20 the tip of the *r* ear of his sons,
20 upon the thumb of their *r* hand,
20 upon the great toe of their *r* foot,
22 is upon them, and the *r* shoulder;
Lev 7.32 *r* shoulder shall ye give unto the
33 have the *r* shoulder for his part.
8.23 it upon the tip of Aaron's *r* ear,
23 upon the thumb of his *r* hand,
23 upon the great toe of his *r* foot.
24 blood upon the tip of their *r* ear,
24 upon the thumbs of their *r* hands,
24 upon the great toes of their *r* feet:
25 and their fat, and the *r* shoulder:
26 the fat, and upon the *r* shoulder:
9.21 the *r* shoulder Aaron waved for
14.14 put it upon the tip of the *r* ear
14 and upon the thumb of his *r* hand,
14 and upon the great toe of his *r* foot:
16 dip his *r* finger in the oil that is in
17 priest put upon the tip of the *r* ear
17 and upon the thumb of his *r* hand,
17 and upon the great toe of his *r* foot,
25 it upon the tip of the *r* ear of him
25 and upon the thumb of the *r* hand,
25 and upon the great toe of his *r* foot:
27 shall sprinkle with his *r* finger
28 upon the tip of the *r* ear of him
28 and upon the thumb of his *r* hand,
28 and upon the great toe of his *r* foot,
Nu 18.18 and as the *r* shoulder are thine.
20.17 will not turn to the *r* hand nor to
22.26 either to the *r* hand or to the left.
27. 7 daughters of Zelophehad speak *r*:
Dt 2.27 neither turn unto the *r* hand nor
5.32 aside to the *r* hand or to the left.
6.18 do that which is *r* and good in the
12. 8 whatsoever is *r* in his own eyes.
25 do that which is *r* in the sight of
28 that which is good and *r* in the
13.18 to do that which is *r* in the eyes of
17.11 thee, to the *r* hand, nor to the left.
20 to the *r* hand, or to the left:
21. 9 which is *r* in the sight of the Lord.
17 the *r* of the firstborn is his.
28.14 day, to the *r* hand, or to the left,
32. 4 without iniquity, just and *r* is he.
33. 2 from his *r* hand went a fiery law
Jos 1. 7 turn not from it to the *r* hand or to
3.16 people passed over *r* against Jericho.
9.25 seemeth good and *r* unto thee to
17. 7 border went along on the *r* hand
23. 6 not aside therefrom to the *r* hand
Jdg 3.16 under his raiment upon his *r* thigh.
21 took the dagger from his *r* thigh,
5.26 *r* hand to the workmen's hammer;
7.20 trumpets in their *r* hands to blow
12. 6 could not frame to pronounce it *r*.
16.29 one with his *r* hand, and of the
17. 6 every man did that which was *r*
21.25 every man did that which was *r* in
Ru 4. 6 redeem thou my *r* to thyself; for I
1Sa 6.12 turned not aside to the *r* hand or
11. 2 I may thrust out all your *r* eyes,
12.23 teach you the good and the *r* way:
2Sa 2.19 he turned not to the *r* hand nor
21 Turn thee aside to thy *r* hand or to
14.19 none can turn to the *r* hand or to
15. 3 See, thy matters are good and *r*;
16. 6 mighty men were on his *r* hand
19.28 What *r* therefore have I yet to cry
43 we have also more *r* in David than
20. 9 beard with the *r* hand to kiss him.
24. 5 *r* side of the city that lieth in the
1Ki 2.19 mother; and she sat on his *r* hand.
6. 8 was in the *r* side of the house:
7.21 he set up the *r* pillar, and called
49 five on the *r* side, and five on the
11.33 do that which is *r* in mine eyes,
38 and do that is *r* in my sight, to
14. 8 to do that only which is *r* in mine
15. 5 David did that which was *r* in the
11 Asa did that which was *r* in the
2Ki 10.15 Is thine heart *r*, as my heart is
30 executing that which is *r* in mine
11.11 from the *r* corner of the temple to
12. 2 Jehoash did that which was *r* in
9 it beside the altar, on the *r* side
14. 3 did that which was *r* in the sight
16. 2 did not that which was *r* in the
22. 2 And that which was *r* in the sight
2 turned not aside to the *r* hand or
23.13 were on the *r* hand of the mount
1Ch 6.39 Asaph, who stood on his *r* hand,
12. 2 could use both the *r* hand and
13. 4 the thing was *r* in the eyes of all
2Ch 3.17 one on the *r* hand, and the other
17 of that on the *r* hand Jachin,
4. 6 lavers, and put five on the *r* hand,
7 five on the *r* hand, and five on the
8 five on the *r* side, and five on the
10 set the sea on the *r* side of the
14. 2 did that which was good and *r* in
18.18 of heaven standing on his *r* hand
20.32 that which was *r* in the sight of
23.10 from the *r* side of the temple to
24. 2 Joash did that which was *r* in the
34. 2 did that which was *r* in the sight of
2 declined neither to the *r* hand,
Ezr 8.21 God, to seek of him a *r* way for us,
Neh 2.20 but ye have no portion, nor *r*, nor
9.13 and gavest them *r* judgments,
33 for thou hast done *r*, but we have
12.31 one went on the *r* hand upon the
Est 8. 5 the thing seem *r* before the king,
Job 6.25 How forcible are *r* words! but
23. 9 he hideth himself on the *r* hand,
30.12 Upon my *r* hand rise the youth;
33.27 and perverted that which was *r*,
34. 6 Should I lie against my *r*? my
17 Shall even he that hateth *r* govern?
23 will not lay upon man more than *r*;
35. 2 Thinkest thou this to be *r*, that

36. 6 wicked: but giveth *r* to the poor.
40.14 thine own *r* hand can save thee.
42. 7 spoken of me the thing that is *r*,
8 spoken of me the thing which is *r*,
Ps 9. 4 maintained my *r* and my cause;
4 satest in the throne judging *r*.
16. 8 he is at my *r* hand, I shall not
11 at thy *r* hand there are pleasures
17. 1 Hear the *r*, O Lord, attend unto
7 O thou that savest by thy *r* hand
18.35 and thy *r* hand hath holden me up,
20. 6 the saving strength of his *r* hand.
21. 8 thy *r* hand shall find out those that
26.10 and their *r* hand is full of bribes.
44. 3 but thy *r* hand, and thine arm,
45. 4 thy *r* hand shall teach thee terrible
6 of thy kingdom is a *r* scepter.
9 thy *r* hand did stand the queen
48.10 *r* hand is full of righteousness.
60. 5 save with thy *r* hand, and hear
63. 8 thee: thy *r* hand upholdeth me.
77.10 of the *r* hand of the most High.
78.37 their heart was not *r* with him,
54 which his *r* hand had purchased.
80.15 which thy *r* hand hath planted,
17 be upon the man of thy *r* hand,
89.13 thy hand, and high is thy *r* hand.
25 sea, and his *r* hand in the rivers.
42 up the *r* hand of his adversaries;
91. 7 and ten thousand at thy *r* hand;
98. 1 his *r* hand, and his holy arm, hath
107. 7 he led them forth by the *r* way,
109. 6 and let Satan stand at his *r* hand.
31 stand at the *r* hand of the poor,
110. 1 Sit thou at my *r* hand, until I make
5 The Lord at thy *r* hand shall strike
118.15 *r* hand of the Lord doeth valiantly.
16 The *r* hand of the Lord is exalted:
16 *r* hand of the Lord doeth valiantly.
121. 5 Lord is thy shade upon thy *r* hand.
137. 5 let my *r* hand forget her cunning.
138. 7 and thy *r* hand shall save me.
140.12 the afflicted, and the *r* of the poor.
Pr 3.16 Length of days is in her *r* hand;
4.11 I have led thee in *r* paths.
25 Let thine eyes look *r* on, and let
27 Turn not to the *r* hand nor to the
8. 6 opening of my lips...be *r* things.
9 *r* to them that find knowledge.
9.15 passengers...go *r* on their ways:
12. 5 thoughts of the righteous are *r*:
15 way of a fool is *r* in his own eyes:
14.12 There is a way which seemeth *r*
16. 8 than great revenues without *r*.
13 they love him that speaketh *r*.
25 There is a way that seemeth *r*
20.11 work be pure, and whether it be *r*.
21. 2 Every way of a man is *r* in his own
8 but as for the pure, his work is *r*.
23.16 when thy lips speak *r* things.
24.26 his lips that giveth a *r* answer.
27.16 and the ointment of his *r* hand,
Ec 4. 4 all travail, and every *r* work,
10. 2 wise man's heart is at his *r* hand;
SS 2. 6 and his *r* hand doth embrace me.
8. 3 and his *r* hand should embrace me.
Isa 9.20 And he shall snatch on the *r* hand,
10. 2 to take away the *r* from the poor
30.10 Prophesy not unto us *r* things,
21 when ye turn to the *r* hand, and
32. 7 even when the needy speaketh *r*.
41.10 the *r* hand of my righteousness.
13 Lord thy God will hold thy *r* hand,
44.20 Is there not a lie in my *r* hand?
45. 1 Cyrus, whose *r* hand I have holden,
19 I declare things that are *r*.
48.13 *r* hand...spanned the heavens:
54. 3 shalt break forth on the *r* hand
62. 8 Lord hath sworn by his *r* hand,
63.12 led them by the *r* hand of Moses
Jer 2.21 thee a noble vine, wholly a *r* seed:

5.28 *r* of the needy do they not judge.
17.11 he that getteth riches, and not by *r*,
16 which came out of my lips was *r*
22.24 were the signet upon my *r* hand,
23.10 is evil, and their force is not *r*.
32. 7 *r* of redemption is thine to buy it.
8 for the *r* of inheritance is thine,
34.15 and had done *r* in my sight, in
49. 5 be driven out every man *r* forth;
La 2. 3 he hath drawn back his *r* hand
4 with his *r* hand as an adversary,
3.35 To turn aside the *r* of a man
Eze 1.10 the face of a lion, on the *r* side:
4. 6 them, lie again on thy *r* side,
10. 3 the cherubims stood on the *r* side
16.46 sister, that dwelleth at thy *r* hand,
18. 5 and do that which is lawful and *r*,
19 done that which is lawful and *r*,
21 and do that which is lawful and *r*,
27 doeth that which is lawful and *r*,
21.16 way or other, either on the *r* hand,
22 At his *r* hand was the divination
27 until he come whose *r* it is;
33.14 and do that which is lawful and *r*;
16 done that which is lawful and *r*;
19 and do that which is lawful and *r*,
39. 3 arrows to fall out of thy *r* hand.
47. 1 from the *r* side of the house,
2 there ran out waters on the *r* side.
Dan 12. 7 held up his *r* hand and his left
Hos 14. 9 for the ways of the Lord are *r*,
Am 3.10 they know not to do *r*, saith the
5.12 the poor in the gate from their *r*,
Jon 4.11 discern between their *r* hand and
Hab 2.16 cup of the Lord's *r* hand shall be
Zec 3. 1 and Satan standing at his *r* hand
4. 3 one upon the *r* side of the bowl,
11 upon the *r* side of the candlestick
11.17 upon his arm, and upon his *r* eye:
17 his *r* eye shall be utterly darkened.
12. 6 on the *r* hand and on the left:
Mal 3. 5 turn aside the stranger from his *r*,
Mt 5.29 if thy *r* eye offend thee, pluck it
30 if thy *r* hand offend thee, cut it off,
39 shall smite thee on thy *r* cheek,
6. 3 hand know what thy *r* hand doeth.
20. 4 whatsoever is *r* I will give you.
7 and whatsoever is *r*, that shall ye
21 may sit, the one on thy *r* hand,
23 but to sit on my *r* hand, and on my
22.44 Sit thou on my *r* hand, till I make
25.33 shall set the sheep on his *r* hand,
34 King say unto them on his *r* hand,
26.64 man sitting on the *r* hand of power,
27.29 his head, and a reed in his *r* hand:
38 one on the *r* hand, and another on
Mk 5.15 and clothed, and in his *r* mind:
10.37 we may sit, one on thy *r* hand,
40 But to sit on my *r* hand and on my
12.36 Sit thou on my *r* hand, till I make
14.62 man sitting on the *r* hand of power,
15.27 one on his *r* hand, and the other
16. 5 a young man sitting on the *r* side,
19 and sat on the *r* hand of God.
Lk 1.11 standing on the *r* side of the altar
6. 6 a man whose *r* hand was withered.
8.35 Jesus, clothed, and in his *r* mind:
10.28 unto him, Thou hast answered *r*:
12.57 yourselves judge ye not what is *r*?
20.42 my Lord, Sit thou on my *r* hand,
22.50 high priest, and cut off his *r* ear.
69 on the *r* hand of the power of God.
23.33 one on the *r* hand, and the other
Jn 18.10 servant, and cut off his *r* ear.
21. 6 the net on the *r* side of the ship,
Ac 2.25 my face, for he is on my *r* hand,
33 being by the *r* hand of God exalted,
34 my Lord, Sit thou on my *r* hand,
3. 7 And he took him by the *r* hand,
4.19 Whether it be *r* in the sight of
5.31 hath God exalted with his *r* hand

7.55 standing on the *r* hand of God,
56 standing on the *r* hand of God.
8.21 thy heart is not *r* in the sight of
13.10 to pervert the *r* ways of the Lord?
Ro 8.34 who is even at the *r* hand of God,
2Co 6. 7 righteousness on the *r* hand and on
Gal 2. 9 gave...the *r* hands of fellowship;
Eph 1.20 and set him at his own *r* hand in
6. 1 parents in the Lord: for this is *r*.
Col 3. 1 sitteth on the *r* hand of God.
Heb 1. 3 the *r* hand of the Majesty on high;
13 he at any time, Sit on my *r* hand,
8. 1 is set on the *r* hand of the throne of
10.12 sat down on the *r* hand of God;
12. 2 at the *r* hand of the throne of God.
13.10 whereof they have no *r* to eat
1Pe 3.22 and is on the *r* hand of God;
2Pe 2.15 Which have forsaken the *r* way,
Rev 1.16 he had in his *r* hand seven stars:
17 And he laid his *r* hand upon me,
20 which thou sawest in my *r* hand,
2. 1 the seven stars in his *r* hand,
5. 1 I saw in the *r* hand of him that sat
7 took the book out of the *r* hand of
10. 2 and he set his *r* foot upon the sea,
13.16 to receive a mark in their *r* hand,
22.14 they may have *r* to the tree of life,

RIGHTEOUS

Gen 7. 1 thee have I seen *r* before me in
18.23 Wilt thou also destroy the *r* with
24 Peradventure there be fifty *r*
24 place for the fifty *r* that are therein?
25 to slay the *r* with the wicked: and
25 that the *r* should be as the wicked,
26 If I find in Sodom fifty *r* within the
28 there shall lack five of the fifty *r*:
20. 4 Lord, wilt thou slay also a *r* nation?
38.26 She hath been more *r* than I;
Ex 9.27 Lord is *r*, and I and my people
23. 7 the innocent and *r* slay thou not:
8 and perverteth the words of the *r*.
Nu 23.10 Let me die the death of the *r*, and
Dt 4. 8 judgments so *r* as all this law,
16.19 wise, and pervert the words of the *r*.
25. 1 then they shall justify the *r*, and
Jdg 5.11 rehearse the *r* acts of the Lord,
11 the *r* acts toward the inhabitants
1Sa 12. 7 all the *r* acts of the Lord, which he
24.17 to David, Thou art more *r* than I:
2Sa 4.11 wicked men have slain a *r* person
1Ki 2.32 who fell upon two men more *r* and
8.32 and justifying the *r*, to give him
2Ki 10. 9 and said to all the people, Ye be *r*:
2Ch 6.23 and by justifying the *r*, by giving
12. 6 and they said, The Lord is *r*.
Ezr 9.15 O Lord God of Israel, thou art *r*:
Neh 9. 8 performed thy words; for thou art *r*:
Job 4. 7 or where were the *r* cut off?
9.15 though I were *r*, yet would I not
10.15 if I be *r*, yet will I not lift up my
15.14 of a woman, that he should be *r*?
17. 9 The *r* also shall hold on his way,
22. 3 to the Almighty, that thou art *r*?
19 The *r* see it, and are glad: and
23. 7 the *r* might dispute with him;
32. 1 because he was *r* in his own eyes.
34. 5 For Job hath said, I am *r*: and
35. 7 If thou be *r*, what givest thou him?
36. 7 withdraweth not...eyes from the *r*:
40. 8 me, that thou mayest be *r*?
Ps 1. 5 in the congregation of the *r*.
6 the Lord knoweth the way of the *r*:
5.12 For thou, Lord, wilt bless the *r*;
7. 9 for the *r* God trieth the hearts and
11 God judgeth the *r*, and God is
11. 3 be destroyed, what can the *r* do?
5 The Lord trieth the *r*: but the
7 the *r* Lord loveth righteousness;
14. 5 God is in the generation of the *r*.

Ps 19. 9 Lord are true and *r* altogether.
31.18 and contemptuously against the *r*.
32.11 glad in the Lord, and rejoice, ye *r*:
33. 1 Rejoice in the Lord, O ye *r*: for
34.15 eyes of the Lord are upon the *r*,
17 The *r* cry, and the Lord heareth,
19 Many are the afflictions of the *r*:
21 that hate the *r* shall be desolate.
35.27 be glad, that favor my *r* cause:
37.16 little that a *r* man hath is better
17 but the Lord upholdeth the *r*.
21 the *r* sheweth mercy, and giveth.
25 yet have I not seen the *r* forsaken,
29 The *r* shall inherit the land, and
30 mouth of the *r* speaketh wisdom,
32 The wicked watcheth the *r*, and
39 But the salvation of the *r* is of the
52. 6 The *r* also shall see, and fear, and
55.22 never suffer the *r* to be moved.
58.10 The *r* shall rejoice when he seeth
11 Verily there is a reward for the *r*:
64.10 The *r* shall be glad in the Lord,
68. 3 let the *r* be glad; let them rejoice
69.28 and not be written with the *r*.
72. 7 In his days shall the *r* flourish;
75.10 horns of the *r* shall be exalted.
92.12 The *r* shall flourish like the palm
94.21 together against the soul of the *r*,
97.11 Light is sown for the *r*, and
12 Rejoice in the Lord, ye *r*; and give
107.42 The *r* shall see it, and rejoice:
112. 4 and full of compassion, and *r*.
6 the *r* shall be in everlasting
116. 5 Gracious is the Lord, and *r*; yea,
118.15 is in the tabernacles of the *r*:
20 Lord, into which the *r* shall enter.
119. 7 have learned thy *r* judgments.
62 thee because of thy *r* judgments.
106 that I will keep thy *r* judgments.
137 *R* art thou, O Lord, and upright
138 that thou hast commanded are *r*
160 thy *r* judgments endureth for ever.
164 thee because of thy *r* judgments.
125. 3 not rest upon the lot of the *r*;
3 lest the *r* put forth their hands
129. 4 Lord is *r*: he hath cut asunder
140.13 *r* shall give thanks unto thy name:
141. 5 Let the *r* smite me; it shall be a
142. 7 the *r* shall compass me about; for
145.17 The Lord is *r* in all his ways, and
146. 8 bowed down: the Lord loveth the *r*:
Pr 2. 7 layeth up sound wisdom for the *r*:
20 men, and keep the paths of the *r*.
3.32 Lord: but his secret is with the *r*.
10. 3 suffer the soul of the *r* to famish:
11 mouth of a *r* man is a well of life:
16 labor of the *r* tendeth to life:
21 The lips of the *r* feed many: but
24 the desire of the *r* shall be granted.
25 the *r* is an everlasting foundation.
28 hope of the *r* shall be gladness:
30 The *r* shall never be removed: but
32 The lips of the *r* know what is
11. 8 The *r* is delivered out of trouble,
10 When it goeth well with the *r*, the
21 seed of the *r* shall be delivered.
23 The desire of the *r* is only good:
28 the *r* shall flourish as a branch.
30 The fruit of the *r* is a tree of life;
31 the *r* shall be recompensed in the
12. 3 root of the *r* shall not be moved.
5 The thoughts of the *r* are right:
7 but the house of the *r* shall stand.
10 A *r* man regardeth the life of his
12 but the root of the *r* yieldeth fruit.
26 The *r* is more excellent than his
13. 5 A *r* man hateth lying: but a
9 The light of the *r* rejoiceth: but
21 but to the *r* good shall be repayed.
25 The *r* eateth to the satisfying of
14. 9 but among the *r* there is favor.
19 the wicked at the gates of her *r*.
32 but the *r* hath hope in his death.
15. 6 house of the *r* is much treasure:
19 the way of the *r* is made plain.
28 heart of the *r* studieth to answer:
29 but he heareth the prayer of the *r*
16.13 *R* lips are the delight of kings;
18. 5 to overthrow the *r* in judgment.
10 the *r* runneth into it, and is safe.
21.12 The *r* man wisely considereth the
18 wicked shall be a ransom for the *r*,
26 but the *r* giveth and spareth not.
23.24 The father of the *r* shall greatly
24.15 man, against the dwelling of the *r*;
24 saith unto the wicked, Thou art *r*;
25.26 A *r* man falling down before the
28. 1 but the *r* are bold as a lion.
10 Whoso causeth the *r* to go astray
12 When *r* men do rejoice, there is
28 when they perish, the *r* increase.
29. 2 When the *r* are in authority, the
6 but the *r* doth sing and rejoice.
7 *r* considereth the cause of the poor:
16 but the *r* shall see their fall.
Ec 3.17 God shall judge the *r* and the
7.16 Be not *r* over much; neither make
8.14 according to the work of the *r*:
9. 1 that the *r*, and the wise, and their
2 there is one event to the *r*, and to
Isa 3.10 Say ye to the *r*, that it shall be well
5.23 away the righteousness of the *r*
24.16 we heard songs, even glory to the *r*.
26. 2 *r* nation which keepeth the truth
41. 2 Who raised up the *r* man from
26 that we may say, He is *r*? yea,
53.11 shall my *r* servant justify many;
57. 1 *r* perisheth, and no man layeth
1 the *r* is taken away from the evil
60.21 Thy people also shall be all *r*: they
Jer 12. 1 *R* art thou, O Lord, when I plead
20.12 O Lord of hosts, that triest the *r*,
23. 5 will raise unto David a *r* Branch,
La 1.18 Lord is *r*; for I have rebelled
Eze 3.20 When a *r* man doth turn from his
21 if thou warn the *r* man, that the
21 that the *r* sin not, and he doth not
13.22 have made the heart of the *r* sad,
16.52 they are more *r* than thou: yea,
18.20 the righteousness of the *r* shall be
24 when the *r* turneth away from his
26 When a *r* man turneth away from
21. 3 off from thee the *r* and the wicked.
4 off from thee the *r* and the wicked,
23.45 the *r* men, they shall judge them
33.12 righteousness of the *r* shall not
12 neither shall the *r* be able to live
13 When I shall say to the *r*, that he
18 *r* turneth from his righteousness,
Dan 9.14 Lord our God is *r* in all his works
Am 2. 6 because they sold the *r* for silver,
Hab 1. 4 wicked doth compass about the *r*;
13 the man that is more *r* than he?
Mal 3.18 between the *r* and the wicked,
Mt 9.13 for I am not come to call the *r*, but
10.41 a *r* man in the name of a *r* man
41 shall receive a *r* man's reward.
13.17 *r* men have desired to see those
43 shall the *r* shine forth as the sun
23.28 also outwardly appear *r* unto men,
29 and garnish the sepulchers of the *r*,
35 all the *r* blood shed upon the earth,
35 blood of *r* Abel unto the blood of
25.37 Then shall the *r* answer him,
46 but the *r* into life eternal.
Mk 2.17 I came not to call the *r*, but sinners
Lk 1. 6 And they were both *r* before God,
5.32 I came not to call the *r*, but sinners
18. 9 in themselves that they were *r*,
23.47 saying, Certainly this was a *r* man.
Jn 7.24 appearance, but judge *r* judgment.
17.25 O *r* Father, the world hath not
Ro 2. 5 and revelation of the *r* judgment of
3.10 There is none *r*, no, not one:
5. 7 scarcely for a *r* man will one die:
19 of one shall many be made *r*.
2Th 1. 5 token of the *r* judgment of God,
6 Seeing it is a *r* thing with God to
1Ti 1. 9 the law is not made for a *r* man,
2Ti 4. 8 which the Lord, the *r* judge, shall
Heb 11. 4 he obtained witness that he was *r*,
Jas 5.16 prayer of a *r* man availeth much.
1Pe 3.12 the eyes of the Lord are over the *r*,
4.18 if the *r* scarcely be saved, where
2Pe 2. 8 that *r* man dwelleth among them,
8 vexed his *r* soul from day to day
1Jn 2. 1 the Father, Jesus Christ the *r*:
29 If ye know that he is *r*, ye know
3. 7 righteousness is *r*, even as he is *r*.
12 were evil, and his brother's *r*.
Rev 16. 5 Thou art *r*, O Lord, which art, and
7 true and *r* are thy judgments.
19. 2 For true and *r* are his judgments:
22.11 be filthy still: and he that is *r*,
11 let him be *r* still: and he that is

RIGHTEOUSLY

Dt 1.16 judge *r* between every man and
Ps 67. 4 for thou shalt judge the people *r*,
96.10 he shall judge the people *r*.
Pr 31. 9 Open thy mouth, judge *r*, and
Isa 33.15 He that walketh *r*, and speaketh
Jer 11.20 O Lord of hosts, that judgest *r*,
Tit 2.12 we should live soberly, *r*, and
1Pe 2.23 himself to him that judgeth *r*:

RIGHTEOUSNESS

Gen 15. 6 and he counted it to him for *r*.
30.33 shall my *r* answer for me in time
Lev 19.15 but in *r* shalt thou judge thy
Dt 6.25 it shall be our *r*, if we observe
9. 4 For my *r* the Lord hath brought
5 Not for thy *r*, or for the
6 good land to possess it for thy *r*;
24.13 it shall be *r* unto thee before the
33.19 they shall offer sacrifices of *r*:
1Sa 26.23 Lord render to every man his *r*
2Sa 22.21 rewarded me according to my *r*:
25 recompensed me according to my *r*;
1Ki 3. 6 before thee in truth, and in *r*, and
8.32 to give him according to his *r*.
2Ch 6.23 by giving him according to his *r*.
Job 6.29 yea, return again, my *r* is in it.
8. 6 the habitation of thy *r* prosperous.
27. 6 My *r* I hold fast, and will not let it
29.14 I put on *r*, and it clothed me: my
33.26 for he will render unto man his *r*.
35. 2 saidst, My *r* is more than God's?
8 thy *r* may profit the son of man.
36. 3 and will ascribe *r* to my Maker.
Ps 4. 1 me when I call, O God of my *r*:
5 Offer the sacrifices of *r*, and put
5. 8 Lead me, O Lord, in thy *r* because
7. 8 me, O Lord, according to my *r*,
17 praise the Lord according to his *r*:
9. 8 And he shall judge the world in *r*,
11. 7 For the righteous Lord loveth *r*;
15. 2 walketh uprightly, and worketh *r*,
17.15 for me, I will behold thy face in *r*:
18.20 rewarded me according to my *r*;
24 recompensed me according to my *r*,
22.31 shall declare his *r* unto a people
23. 3 he leadeth me in the paths of *r*
24. 5 *r* from the God of his salvation.
31. 1 be ashamed: deliver me in thy *r*.
33. 5 He loveth *r* and judgment: the
35.24 my God, according to thy *r*;
28 my tongue shall speak of thy *r*
36. 6 Thy *r* is like the great mountains;
10 and thy *r* to the upright in heart.
37. 6 bring forth thy *r* as the light,
40. 9 I have preached *r* in the great
10 not hid thy *r* within my heart;

45. 4 of truth and meekness and *r*;
7 lovest *r*, and hatest wickedness:
48.10 earth: thy right hand is full of *r*.
50. 6 the heavens shall declare his *r*:
51.14 tongue shall sing aloud of thy *r*.
19 pleased with the sacrifices of *r*,
52. 3 and lying rather than to speak *r*.
58. 1 Do ye...speak *r*, O congregation?
65. 5 things in *r* wilt thou answer us,
69.27 and let them not come into thy *r*.
71. 2 Deliver me in thy *r*, and cause me
15 My mouth shall shew forth thy *r*
16 I will make mention of thy *r*, even
19 Thy *r* also, O God, is very high,
24 My tongue also shall talk of thy *r*
72. 1 and thy *r* unto the king's son.
2 He shall judge thy people with *r*,
3 people, and the little hills, by *r*.
85.10 *r* and peace have kissed each
11 *r* shall look down from heaven.
13 *R* shall go before him; and shall
88.12 thy *r* in the land of forgetfulness?
89.16 and in thy *r* shall they be exalted.
94.15 But judgment shall return unto *r*:
96.13 he shall judge the world with *r*,
97. 2 *r* and judgment are the habitation
6 The heavens declare his *r*, and
98. 2 his *r* hath he openly shewed in
9 with *r* shall he judge the world,
99. 4 thou executest judgment and *r* in
103. 6 Lord executeth *r* and judgment
17 and his *r* unto children's children;
106. 3 and he that doeth *r* at all times.
31 counted unto him for *r* unto all
111. 3 and his *r* endureth for ever.
112. 3 house: and his *r* endureth for ever.
9 the poor; his *r* endureth for ever;
118.19 Open to me the gates of *r*: but
119.40 precepts: quicken me in thy *r*.
123 and for the word of thy *r*.
142 Thy *r* is an everlasting
142 is an evelasting *r*, and thy law
144 *r* of my testimonies is everlasting:
172 for all thy commandments are *r*.
132. 9 let thy priests be clothed with *r*;
143. 1 answer me, and in thy *r*.
145. 7 goodness, and shall sing of thy *r*.
Pr 2. 9 Then shalt thou understand *r*,
8. 8 the words of my mouth are in *r*;
18 me; yea, durable riches and *r*.
20 I lead in the way of *r*, in the
10. 2 but *r* delivereth from death.
11. 4 but *r* delivereth from death.
5 *r* of the perfect shall direct his
6 *r* of the upright shall deliver them:
18 to him that soweth *r* shall be a
19 As *r* tendeth to life: so he that
12.17 speaketh truth sheweth forth *r*:
28 In the way of *r* is life; and in the
13. 6 *R* keepeth him that is upright in
14.34 *R* exalteth a nation: but sin is a
15. 9 loveth him that followeth after *r*.
16. 8 Better is a little with *r* than great
12 for the throne is established by *r*.
31 if it be found in the way of *r*.
21.21 that followeth after *r* and mercy
21 mercy findeth life, *r*, and honor.
25. 5 throne shall be established in *r*.
Ec 3.16 the place of *r*, that iniquity was
7.15 just man that perisheth in his *r*,
Isa 1.21 *r* lodged in it; but now murderers.
26 The city of *r*, the faithful city.
27 judgment,...her converts with *r*.
5. 7 oppression; for *r*, but behold a cry.
16 is holy shall be sanctified in *r*.
23 take away the *r* of the righteous.
10.22 decreed shall overflow with *r*.
11. 4 with *r* shall he judge the poor,
5 *r* shall be the girdle of his loins,
16. 5 seeking judgment, and hasting *r*.
26. 9 inhabitants of the world...learn *r*.
10 wicked, yet will he not learn *r*:
28.17 to the line, and *r* to the plummet:
32. 1 Behold, a king shall reign in *r*,
16 and *r* remain in the fruitful field.
17 And the work of *r* shall be peace:
17 and the effect of *r* quietness and
33. 5 filled Zion with judgment and *r*.
41.10 thee with the right hand of my *r*.
42. 6 I the Lord have called thee in *r*,
45. 8 and let the skies pour down *r*:
8 and let *r* spring up together;
13 I have raised him up in *r*, and I
19 I the Lord speak *r*, I declare
23 word...gone out of my mouth in *r*,
24 in the Lord have I *r* and strength:
46.12 stouthearted, that are far from *r*:
13 I bring near my *r*; it shall not be
48. 1 Israel, but not in truth, nor in *r*.
18 and thy *r* as the waves of the sea:
51. 1 ye that follow after *r*, ye that
5 My *r* is near; my salvation is
6 and my *r* shall not be abolished.
7 Hearken unto me, ye that know *r*,
8 but my *r* shall be for ever, and
54.14 In *r* shalt thou be established:
17 their *r* is of me, saith the Lord.
56. 1 to come, and my *r* to be revealed.
57.12 I will declare thy *r*, and thy works;
58. 2 my ways, as a nation that did *r*,
8 and thy *r* shall go before thee;
59.16 him; and his *r*, it sustained him.
17 For he put on *r* as a breastplate,
60.17 officers peace, and thine exactors *r*.
61. 3 they might be called trees of *r*,
10 covered me with the robe of *r*,
11 so the Lord God will cause *r* and
62. 1 *r* thereof go forth as brightness,
2 And the Gentiles shall see thy *r*,
63. 1 I that speak in *r*, mighty to save.
64. 5 him that rejoiceth and worketh *r*,
Jer 4. 2 in truth, in judgment, and in *r*;
9.24 lovingkindness, judgment, and *r*,
22. 3 Execute ye judgment and *r*, and
23. 6 he shall be called, The Lord Our *R*.
33.15 Branch of *r* to grow up unto David;
15 execute judgment and *r* in the
16 shall be called, The Lord our *r*.
51.10 Lord hath brought forth our *r*:
Eze 3.20 man doth turn from his *r*, and
20 his *r* which he hath done shall
14.14 but their own souls by their *r*,
20 deliver their own souls by their *r*.
18.20 the *r* of the righteous shall be upon
22 in his *r*...he hath done he shall live.
24 righteous turneth away from his *r*,
24 All his *r* that he hath done shall
26 righteous man turneth...from his *r*,
33.12 *r* of the righteous shall not deliver
12 righteous be able to live for his *r* in
13 if he trust to his own *r*, and
18 the righteous turneth from his *r*,
Dan 4.27 and break off thy sins by *r*, and
9. 7 O Lord, *r* belongeth unto thee,
16 O Lord, according to all thy *r*, I
24 to bring in everlasting *r*, and to
12. 3 that turn many to *r* as the stars
Hos 2.19 I will betroth thee unto me in *r*,
10.12 Sow to yourselves in *r*, reap in
12 till he come and reign *r* upon you.
Am 5. 7 and leave off *r* in the earth,
24 waters, and *r* as a mighty stream.
6.12 and the fruit of *r* into hemlock:
Mic 6. 5 ye may know the *r* of the Lord.
7. 9 the light, and I shall behold his *r*.
Zep 2. 3 seek *r*, seek meekness: it may be
Zec 8. 8 be their God, in truth and in *r*.
Mal 3. 3 offer unto the Lord and offering in *r*.
4. 2 Sun of *r* arise with healing in his
Mt 3.15 thus it becometh us to fulfil all *r*.
5. 6 which do hunger and thirst after *r*:
20 I say unto you, That except your *r*
20 shall exceed the *r* of the scribes
6.33 the kingdom of God, and his *r*;
21.32 John came unto you in the way of *r*,
Lk 1.75 In holiness and *r* before him, all
Jn 16. 8 reprove the world of sin, and of *r*,
10 Of *r*, because I go to my Father,
Ac 10.35 he feareth him, and worketh *r*, is
13.10 of the devil, thou enemy of all *r*,
17.31 which he will judge the world in *r*
24.25 as he reasoned of *r*, temperance,
Ro 1.17 therein is the *r* of God revealed
2.26 keep the *r* of the law, shall not
3. 5 commend the *r* of God, what shall
21 But now *r* of God without the law
22 Even the *r* of God which is by faith
25 to declare his *r* for the remission
26 To declare, I say, at this time his *r*:
4. 3 and it was counted unto him for *r*.
5 ungodly, his faith is counted for *r*.
6 man, unto whom God imputeth *r*
9 was reckoned to Abraham for *r*.
11 a seal of the *r* of the faith which
11 that *r* might be imputed unto them
13 the law, but through the *r* of faith.
22 it was imputed to him for *r*.
5.17 receive abundance...of the gift of *r*
18 by the *r* of one the free gift came
21 so might grace reign through *r*
6.13 as instruments of *r* unto God.
16 unto death, or of obedience unto *r*?
18 sin, ye became the servants of *r*.
19 yield your members servants to *r*
20 servants of sin, ye were free from *r*.
8. 4 the *r* of the law might be fulfilled
10 but the Spirit is life because of *r*.
9.28 the work, and cut it short in *r*:
30 followed not after *r*,...attained to *r*,
30 even the *r* which is of faith.
31 which followed after the law of *r*,
31 hath not attained to the law of *r*.
10. 3 For they being ignorant of God's *r*,
3 going about to establish her own *r*,
3 not submitted...unto the *r* of God.
4 Christ is the end of the law for *r*
5 describeth the *r* which is of the law,
6 But the *r* which is of faith speaketh
10 the heart man believeth unto *r*;
14.17 *r*, and peace, and joy in the Holy
1Co 1.30 is made unto us wisdom, and *r*,
15.34 Awake to *r*, and sin not; for
2Co 3. 9 ministration of *r* exceed in glory.
5.21 might be made the *r* of God in him.
6. 7 the armor of *r* on the right hand
14 for what fellowship hath *r* with
9. 9 the poor: his *r* remaineth for ever.
10 and increase the fruits of your *r*;)
11.15 transformed as the ministers of *r*;
Gal 2.21 if *r* come by the law, then Christ
3. 6 and it was accounted to him for *r*.
21 *r* should have been by the law.
5. 5 wait for the hope of *r* by faith.
Eph 4.24 is created in *r* and true holiness.
5. 9 is in all goodness and *r* and truth;)
6.14 and having on the breastplate of *r*:
Php 1.11 Being filled with the fruits of *r*,
3. 6 touching the *r* which is in the law,
9 not having mine own *r*, which is of
9 the *r* which is of God by faith:
1Ti 6.11 and follow after *r*, godliness, faith,
2Ti 2.22 but follow *r*, faith, charity, peace,
3.16 for correction, for instruction in *r*:
4. 8 there is laid up for me a crown of *r*.
Tit 3. 5 Not by works of *r* which we have
Heb 1. 8 a scepter of *r* is the scepter of thy
9 hast loved *r*, and hated iniquity;
5.13 milk is unskilful in the word of *r*:
7. 2 being by interpretation King of *r*,
11. 7 heir of the *r* which is by faith.
33 wrought *r*, obtained promises,
12.11 it yieldeth the peaceable fruit of *r*
Jas 1.20 of man worketh not the *r* of God.

Jas 2.23 and it was imputed unto him for *r*:
3.18 And the fruit of *r* is sown in peace
1Pe 2.24 dead to sins, should live unto *r*:
2Pe 1. 1 the *r* of God and our Saviour Jesus
2. 5 the eighth person, a preacher of *r*,
21 not to have known the way of *r*,
3.13 a new earth, wherein dwelleth *r*.
1Jn 2.29 every one that doeth *r* is born of
3. 7 he that doeth *r* is righteous, even
10 whosoever doeth not *r* is not of God,
Rev 19. 8 for the fine linen is the *r* of saints.
11 in *r* he doth judge and make war.

RIGHTEOUSNESS'

Ps 143.11 for thy *r* sake bring my soul out
Isa 42.21 is well pleased for his *r* sake;
Mt 5.10 which are persecuted for *r* sake:
1Pe 3.14 But and if ye suffer for *r* sake,

RIGHTEOUSNESSES

Isa 64. 6 and all our *r* are as filthy rags;
Eze 33.13 all his *r* shall not be remembered;
Dan 9.18 supplications before thee for our *r*,

RIGHTLY

Gen 27.36 he said, Is not he *r* named Jacob?
Lk 7.43 said unto him, Thou hast *r* judged
20.21 that thou sayest and teachest *r*,
2Ti 2.15 ashamed, *r* dividing the word of truth.

RING

Gen 41.42 Pharaoh took off his *r* from his
Ex 26.24 above the head of it unto one *r*:
36.29 at the head thereof, to one *r*:
Est 3.10 the king took his *r* from his hand,
12 and sealed with the king's *r*.
8. 2 And the king took off his *r*, which
8. name, and seal it with the king's *r*:
8 name, and sealed with the king's *r*,
10 and sealed it with the king's *r*, and
Lk 15.22 put a *r* on his hand, and shoes on
Jas 2. 2 assembly a man with a gold *r*,

RINGLEADER

Ac 24. 5 a *r* of the sect of the Nazarenes:

RIOT

Tit 1. 6 faithful children not accused of *r*
1Pe 4. 4 with them to the same excess of *r*,
2Pe 2.13 count it pleasure to *r* in the day

RIOTING

Ro 13.13 not in *r* and drunkenness, not in

RIOTOUS

Pr 23.20 among *r* eaters of flesh:
28. 7 is a companion of *r* men shameth
Lk 15.13 wasted his substance with *r* living.

RIPE

Gen 40.10 clusters...brought forth *r* grapes:
Ex 22.29 delay to offer the first of thy *r* fruits,
Jer 24. 2 figs, even like the figs that are first *r*:
Joel 3.13 in the sickle, for the harvest is *r*:
Rev 14.15 for the harvest of the earth is *r*.
18 earth; for her grapes are fully *r*.

RISE

Gen 19. 2 and ye shall *r* up early, and go on
31.35 that I cannot *r* up before thee;
Ex 8.20 *R* up early in the morning, and
9.13 *R* up early in the morning, and
12.31 *R* up, and get you forth from
21.19 If he *r* again, and walk abroad
Lev 19.32 shalt *r* up before the hoary head,
Nu 10.35 *R* up, Lord, and let thine enemies
22.20 call thee, *r* up, and go with them;
23.18 *R* up, Balak, and hear; hearken
24 people shall *r* up as a great lion,
24.17 a Scepter shall *r* out of Israel, and
Dt 2.13 Now *r* up, said I, and get you over
24 *R* ye up, take your journey, and
19.11 wait for him, and *r* up against him,
15 One witness shall not *r* up against
16 false witness *r* up against any man
28. 7 thine enemies that *r* up against
29.22 your children that shall *r* up after
31.16 and this people will *r* up, and go a
32.38 let them *r* up and help you, and be
33.11 loins of them that *r* against him,
11 hate him, that they *r* not again.
Jos 8. 7 ye shall *r* up from the ambush, and
18. 4 they shall *r*, and go through the
Jdg 8.21 said, *R* thou, and fall upon us:
9.33 *r* early, and set upon the city:
20.38 make a great flame with smoke *r*.
1Sa 22.13 he should *r* against me, to lie in
24. 7 suffered them not to *r* against Saul.
29.10 *r* up early in the morning with thy
2Sa 12.21 dead, thou didst *r* and eat bread.
18.32 that *r* against thee to do thee hurt,
2Ki 16. 7 of Israel, which *r* up against me.
Neh 2.18 they said, Let us *r* up and build.
Job 20.27 the earth shall *r* up against him.
30.12 Upon my right hand *r* the youth;
Ps 3. 1 many are they that *r* up against me.
17. 7 from those that *r* up against them.
18.38 them that they were not able to *r*:
48 above those that *r* up against me:
27. 3 though war should *r* against me,
35.11 False witnesses did *r* up; they laid
36.12 down, and shall not be able to *r*,
41. 8 that he lieth he shall *r* up no more.
44. 5 them under that *r* up against us.
59. 1 from them that *r* up against me.
74.23 tumult of those that *r* up against
92.11 of the wicked that *r* up against me.
94.16 *r* up for me against the evildoers?
119.62 At midnight I will *r* to give thanks
127. 2 It is vain for you to *r* up early, to
139.21 not I grieved with those that *r* up
140.10 pits, that they *r* not up again.
Pr 24.22 their calamity shall *r* suddenly;
28.12 but when the wicked *r*, a man is
28 When the wicked *r*, men hide
Ec 10. 4 spirit of the ruler *r* up against
12. 4 shall *r* up at the voice of the bird,
SS 2.10 *R* up, my love, my fair one, and
3. 2 I will *r* now, and go about the city
Isa 5.11 Woe unto them that *r* up early in
14.21 that they do not *r*, nor possess the
22 I will *r* up against them, saith the
24.20 and it shall fall, and not *r* again.
26.14 they are deceased, they shall not *r*:
28.21 the Lord shall *r* up as in mount
32. 9 *R* up, ye women that are at ease;
33.10 Now will I *r*, saith the Lord; now
43.17 lie down together, they shall not *r*:
54.17 tongue that shall *r* against thee in
58.10 then shall thy light *r* in obscurity,
Jer 25.27 and spue, and fall, and *r* no more,
37.10 they *r* up every man in his tent,
47. 2 waters *r* up out of the north, and
49.14 against her, and *r* up to the battle.
51. 1 of them that *r* up against me,
64 shall not *r* from the evil that I will
La 1.14 from whom I am not able to *r* up.
Dan 7.24 another shall *r* after them; and
Am 5. 2 is fallen; she shall no more *r*: she
7. 9 *r* against the house of Jeroboam
8. 8 and it shall *r* up wholly as a flood;
14 shall fall, and never *r* up again.
9. 5 it shall *r* up wholly like a flood;
Ob 1 let us *r* up against her in battle.
Na 1. 9 affliction shall not *r* up the second
Hab 2. 7 Shall they not *r* up suddenly that
Zep 3. 8 the day that I *r* up to the prey: for
Zec 14.13 shall *r* up against the hand of his
Mt 5.45 he maketh his sun to *r* on the evil
10.21 and the children shall *r* up against
12.41 men of Nineveh shall *r* in judgment
42 south shall *r* up in the judgment
20.19 and the third day he shall *r* again.
24. 7 For nation shall *r* against nation,
11 And many false prophets shall *r*,
26.46 *R*, let us be going: behold, he is at
27.63 After three days I will *r* again.
Mk 3.26 And if Satan *r* up against himself,
4.27 should sleep, and *r* night and day,
8.31 and after three days *r* again.
9.31 be killed, he shall *r* the third day.
10.34 and the third day he shall *r* again.
49 Be of good comfort, *r*; he calleth
12.23 when they shall *r*, whose wife
25 when they shall *r* from the dead,
26 as touching the dead, that they *r*:
13. 8 For nation shall *r* against nation,
12 shall *r* up against their parents,
22 Christs and false prophets shall *r*,
14.42 *R* up, let us go; lo, he that
Lk 5.23 thee; or to say, *R* up and walk?
6. 8 *R* up, and stand forth in the midst.
11. 7 in bed; I cannot *r* and give thee.
8 Though he will not *r* and give
8 he will *r* and give him as many as
31 queen of the south shall *r* up in
32 Nineve shall *r* up in the judgment
12.54 ye see a cloud *r* out of the west,
18.33 and the third day he shall *r* again.
21.10 Nation shall *r* against nation,
22.46 *r* and pray, lest ye enter into
24. 7 crucified, and the third day *r* again.
46 to *r* from the dead the third day:
Jn 5. 8 unto him, *R*, take up thy bed, and
11.23 her, Thy brother shall *r* again.
24 I know that he shall *r* again in the
20. 9 he must *r* again from the dead.
Ac 3. 6 name of Jesus...of Nazareth *r* up
10.13 to him, *R*, Peter; kill, and eat.
26.16 *r*, and stand upon thy feet: for I
23 first that should *r* from the dead,
Ro 15.12 shall *r* to reign over the Gentiles;
1Co 15.15 up, if so be that the dead *r* not.
16 if the dead *r* not,...is not Christ
29 the dead, if the dead *r* not at all?
32 advantageth it me, if the dead *r*
1Th 4.16 the dead in Christ shall *r* first:
Heb 7.11 that another priest should *r* after
Rev 11. 1 *R*, and measure the temple of
13. 1 saw a beast *r* up out of the sea,

RISEN

Gen 19.23 The sun was *r* upon the earth
Nu 32.14 ye are *r* up in your fathers' stead,
1Ki 8.20 I am *r* up in the room of David my
Isa 60. 1 glory of the Lord is *r* upon thee.
Mic 2. 8 my people is *r* up as an enemy:
Mt 11.11 hath not *r* a greater than John
14. 2 Baptist; he is *r* from the dead;
17. 9 the Son of man be *r* again from
26.32 But after I am *r* again, I will go
27.64 the people, He is *r* from the dead:
28. 6 He is not here: for he is *r*, as he
7 his disciples that he is *r* from the
Mk 6.14 John the Baptist was *r* from the
16 beheaded: he is *r* from the dead.
9. 9 Son of man were *r* from the dead.
14.28 after that I am *r*, I will go before
16. 6 he is *r*; he is not here: behold the
9 Jesus was *r* early the first day of
14 had seen him after he was *r*.
Lk 7.16 a great prophet is *r* up among us;
9. 7 that John was *r* from the dead;
8 of the old prophets was *r* again.
19 one of the old prophets is *r* again.
13.25 the master of the house is *r* up,
24. 6 He is not here, but is *r*: remember
34 The Lord is *r* indeed, and hath
Jn 2.22 therefore he was *r* from the dead,
21.14 after that he was *r* from the dead.
Ac 17. 3 suffered,...*r* again from the dead;
Ro 8.34 died, yea rather, that is *r* again,

1Co 15.13 of the dead, then is Christ not *r*:
14 And if Christ be not *r*, then is our
20 But now is Christ *r* from the dead,
Col 2.12 *r* with him through the faith of
3. 1 If ye then be *r* with Christ, seek
Jas 1.11 sun is...*r* with a burning heat,

RISEST
Dt 6. 7 liest down, and when thou *r* up.
11.19 liest down, and when thou *r* up.

RISETH
Dt 22.26 a man *r* against his neighbor,
Jos 6.26 *r* up and buildeth this city Jericho:
2Sa 23. 4 when the sun *r*, even a morning
Job 9. 7 commandeth the sun, and it *r* not;
14.12 So man lieth down, and *r* not:
24.22 he *r* up, and no man is sure of life.
27. 7 he that *r* up against me as the
31.14 then shall I do when God *r* up?
Pr 24.16 falleth seven times, and *r* up again:
31.15 She *r* also while it is yet night, and
Isa 47.11 shalt not know from whence it *r*:
Jer 46. 8 Egypt *r* up like a flood, and his
Mic 7. 6 daughter *r* up against her mother,
Jn 13. 4 He *r* from supper, and laid aside

RISING
Nu 2. 3 east side toward the *r* of the sun
Neh 4.21 spears from the *r* of the morning
Job 24.14 murderer *r* with the light killeth
Ps 113. 3 From the *r* of the sun unto the
Pr 30.31 against whom there is no *r* up.
Isa 59.19 and his glory from the *r* of the sun.
60. 3 kings to the brightness of thy *r*.
Jer 7.13 *r* up early and speaking, but ye
11. 7 *r* early and protesting, saying,
25. 4 the prophets, *r* early and sending
44. 4 the prophets, *r* early and sending
La 3.63 sitting down, and their *r* up;
Mal 1.11 from the *r* of the sun even unto
Mk 1.35 *r* up a great while before day, he
9.10 the *r* from the dead should mean.
16. 2 the sepulcher at the *r* of the sun.
Lk 2.34 and *r* again of many in Israel;

RIVER
Gen 2.10 a *r* went out of Eden to water the
13 the name of the second *r* is Gihon:
14 name of the third *r* is Hiddekel:
14 And the fourth *r* is Euphrates.
41. 2 came up out of the *r* seven...kine
Ex 1.22 Every son...ye shall cast into the *r*,
2. 5 came down to wash herself at the *r*;
7.18 the fish that is in the *r* shall die,
21 could not drink...the water of the *r*;
Dt 2.24 and pass over the *r* Arnon:
37 nor unto any place of the *r* Jabbok,
2Sa 10.16 Syrians that were beyond the *r*:
17.13 city, and...will draw it unto the *r*,
24. 5 lieth in the midst of the *r* of Gad,
2Ki 17. 6 and in Habor by the *r* of Gozan,
Ezr 4.10 rest that are on this side the *r*,
16 have no portion on this side the *r*.
8.15 to the *r* that runneth to Ahava;
Job 40.23 drinketh up a *r*, and hasteth not:
Ps 36. 8 drink of the *r* of thy pleasures.
46. 4 There is a *r*, the streams whereof
65. 9 enrichest it with the *r* of God,
72. 8 and from the *r* unto the ends of
Isa 23.10 Pass through thy land as a *r*, O
48.18 then had thy peace been as a *r*,
66.12 I will extend peace to her like a *r*,
La 2.18 let tears run down like a *r* day
Eze 10.15 that I saw by the *r* of Chebar.
29. 9 The *r* is mine, and I have made it.
47. 5 was a *r* that I could not pass over:
9 shall live whither the *r* cometh.
Am 6.14 unto the *r* of the wilderness.
Mic 7.12 from the fortress even to the *r*,
Zec 9.10 from the *r* even to the ends of the
Mk 1. 5 baptized of him in the *r* of Jordan,
Ac 16.13 we went out of the city by a *r* side,
Rev 9.14 bound in the great *r* Euphrates.
16.12 vial upon the great *r* Euphrates;

RIVERS
Ex 7.19 upon their streams, upon their *r*,
2Ki 5.12 and Pharpar, *r* of Damascus,
Job 20.17 He shall not see the *r*, the floods,
28.10 cutteth out *r* among the rocks;
29. 6 the rock poured me out *r* of oil;
Ps 1. 3 a tree planted by the *r* of water,
107.33 He turneth *r* into a wilderness,
137. 1 By the *r* of Babylon, there we sat
Pr 21. 1 hand of the Lord, as the *r* of water:
Ec 1. 7 All the *r* run into the sea; yet the
Isa 32. 2 as rivers of water in a dry place,
43. 2 and through the *r*, they shall not
19 the wilderness, and *r* in the desert.
La 3.48 runneth down with *r* of water
Eze 31. 4 *r* running round about his plants,
Mic 6. 7 or with ten thousands of *r* of oil?
Na 2. 6 The gates of the *r* shall be opened,
Hab 3. 8 the Lord displeased against the *r*?
Jn 7.38 belly shall flow *r* of living water.
Rev 8.10 it fell upon the third part of the *r*,
16. 4 poured out his vial upon the *r* and

ROAD
1Sa 27.10 Whither have ye made a *r* to day?

ROAR
1Ch 16.32 Let the sea *r*, and the fulness
Ps 46. 3 waters thereof *r* and be troubled,
104.21 The young lions *r* after their prey,
Isa 59.11 We *r* all like bears, and mourn
Jer 25.30 The Lord shall *r* from on high,
31.35 the sea when the waves thereof *r*;
50.42 their voice shall *r* like the sea, and
51.38 They shall *r* together like lions:
Am 1. 2 he said, The Lord will *r* from Zion,
3. 4 Will a lion *r* in the forest, when he

ROARED
Jdg 14. 5 a young lion *r* against him.
Ps 38. 8 *r* by reason of the disquietness of
Isa 51.15 divided the sea, whose waves *r*:
Jer 2.15 The young lions *r* upon him, and
Am 3. 8 The lion hath *r*, who will not fear?

ROARETH
Job 37. 4 After it a voice *r*: he thundereth
Jer 6.23 mercy; their voice *r* like the sea;
Rev 10. 3 a loud voice, as when a lion *r*:

ROARING
Job 4.10 The *r* of the lion, and the voice of
Ps 22. 1 me, and from the words of my *r*?
13 as a ravening and a *r* lion.
32. 3 my bones waxed old through my *r*
Pr 19.12 king's wrath is as the *r* of a lion;
20. 2 fear of a king is as the *r* of a lion:
28.15 As a *r* lion, and a ranging bear;
Isa 5.29 Their *r* shall be like a lion, they
30 shall roar...like the *r* of the sea:
31. 4 and the young lion *r* on his prey,
Eze 19. 7 thereof, by the noise of his *r*.
22.25 like a *r* lion ravening the prey;
Zep 3. 3 princes within her are *r* lions;
Zec 11. 3 a voice of the *r* of young lions;
Lk 21.25 the sea and the waves *r*;
1Pe 5. 8 devil, as a *r* lion, walketh about,

ROARINGS
Job 3.24 *r* are poured out like the waters.

ROB
Lev 19.13 thy neighbor, neither *r* him:
26.22 which shall *r* you of your children,
1Sa 23. 1 and they *r* the threshingfloors.
Pr 22.22 *R* not the poor, because he is
Isa 10. 2 that they may *r* the fatherless!
17.14 us, and the lot of them that *r* us.
Eze 39.10 and *r* those that robbed them, saith
Mal 3. 8 Will a man *r* God? Yet ye have

ROBBED
Jdg 9.25 they *r* all that came along that
2Sa 17. 8 as a bear *r* of her whelps in the
Ps 119.61 bands of the wicked have *r* me:
Pr 17.12 Let a bear *r* of her whelps meet a
Isa 10.13 and have *r* their treasures, and I
42.22 But this is a people *r* and spoiled;
Jer 50.37 her treasures; and they shall be *r*,
Eze 33.15 pledge, give again that he had *r*,
39.10 rob those that *r* them, saith the
Mal 3. 8 man rob God? Yet ye have *r* me.
8 ye say, Wherein have we *r* thee?
9 for ye have *r* me, even this whole
2Co 11. 8 I *r* other churches, taking wages

ROBBER
Job 5. 5 *r* swalloweth up their substance.
18. 9 the *r* shall prevail against him.
Eze 18.10 If he beget a son that is a *r*, a
Jn 10. 1 way, the same is a thief and a *r*.
18.40 Barabbas. Now Barabbas was a *r*.

ROBBERS
Job 12. 6 The tabernacles of *r* prosper, and
Isa 42.24 for a spoil, and Israel to the *r*?
Jer 7.11 become a den of *r* in your eyes?
Eze 7.22 for the *r* shall enter into it, and
Dan 11.14 the *r* of thy people shall exalt
Hos 6. 9 And as troops of *r* wait for a man,
7. 1 and the troop of *r* spoileth without.
Ob 5 thieves came to thee, if *r* by night,
Jn 10. 8 came before me are thieves and *r*:
Ac 19.37 which are neither *r* of churches,
2Co 11.26 in perils of waters, in perils of *r*,

ROBBERY
Ps 62.10 and become not vain in *r*: if
Pr 21. 7 The *r* of the wicked shall destroy
Isa 61. 8 I hate *r* for burnt offering; and
Eze 22.29 used oppression, and exercised *r*,
Am 3.10 violence and *r* in their palaces.
Na 3. 1 city! it is all full of lies and *r*; the
Php 2. 6 it not *r* to be equal with God:

ROBBETH
Pr 28.24 Whoso *r* his father or his mother,

ROBE
1Sa 24. 4 cut off the skirt of Saul's *r* privily.
11 see the skirt of thy *r* in my hand:
Job 29.14 my judgment was as a *r* and a
Isa 61.10 me with the *r* of righteousness,
Mic 2. 8 ye pull off the *r* with the garment
Mt 27.28 him, and put on him a scarlet *r*.
31 they took the *r* off from him, and
Lk 15.22 Bring forth the best *r*, and put it
23.11 and arrayed him in a gorgeous *r*,
Jn 19. 2 and they put on him a purple *r*,
5 crown of thorns, and the purple *r*.

ROBES
2Sa 13.18 for with such *r* were the king's
1Ki 22.10 his throne, having put on their *r*.
30 the battle; but put thou on thy *r*.
2Ch 18. 9 on his throne, clothed in their *r*,
29 the battle; but put thou on thy *r*.
Eze 26.16 thrones, and lay away their *r*,
Lk 20.46 which desire to walk in long *r*,
Rev 6.11 white *r* were given unto every one
7. 9 clothed with white *r*, and palms in
13 these which are arrayed in white *r*?
14 have washed their *r*, and made

ROCK
Ex 17. 6 thee there upon the *r* in Horeb;
6 and thou shall smite the *r*, and

Ex 33.21 me, and thou shalt stand upon a *r*:
22 I will put thee in a clift of a *r*, and
Nu 20.10 we fetch you water out of this *r*?
11 with his rod he smote the *r* twice:
Dt 32. 4 He is the *R*, his work is perfect:
13 and oil out of the flinty *r*;
15 esteemed the *R* of his salvation.
18 Of the *R* that begat thee thou art
31 For their *r* is not as our *R*, even
37 gods, their *r* in whom they trusted,
Jdg 6.26 thy God upon the top of this *r*,
1Sa 2. 2 is there any *r* like our God.
2Sa 22. 2 said, The Lord is my *r*, and my
3 The God of my *r*; in him will I
32 and who is a *r*, save our God?
47 the God of the *r* of my salvation.
Job 14.18 the *r* is removed out of his place.
24. 8 embrace the *r* for want of a shelter.
29. 6 the *r* poured me out rivers of oil;
Ps 18. 2 The Lord is my *r*, and my fortress,
27. 5 me; he shall set me up upon a *r*.
28. 1 Unto thee will I cry, O Lord my *r*;
31. 2 be thou my strong *r*, for an house
40. 2 clay, and set my feet upon a *r*,
61. 2 lead me to the *r* that is higher
62. 2 He only is my *r* and my salvation;
81.16 with honey out of the *r* should I
94.22 And my God is the *r* of my refuge.
95. 1 noise to the *r* of our salvation.
Pr 30.19 the way of a serpent upon a *r*;
Isa 32. 2 shadow of a great *r* in a weary land.
42.11 let the inhabitants of the *r* sing,
51. 1 unto the *r* whence ye are hewn,
Jer 5. 3 made their faces harder than a *r*;
23.29 hammer that breaketh the *r* in
Eze 26.14 will make thee like the top of a *r*:
Mt 7.24 which built his house upon a *r*:
25 not: for it was founded upon a *r*.
16.18 upon this *r* I will build my church;
27.60 which he had hewn out in the *r*:
Mk 15.46 sepulcher...was hewn out of a *r*,
Lk 6.48 and laid the foundation on a *r*:
48 it: for it was founded upon a *r*.
8. 6 And some fell upon a *r*; and as
13 They on the *r* are they, which,
Ro 9.33 a stumblingstone and *r* of offense:
1Co 10. 4 they drank of that spiritual *R* that
4 them: and that *R* was Christ.
1Pe 2. 8 a *r* of offense, even to them which

ROCKS

1Ki 19.11 brake in pieces the *r* before the
Job 28.10 cutteth out rivers among the *r*;
Ps 78.15 He clave the *r* in the wilderness,
104.18 goats; and the *r* for the conies.
Na 1. 6 the *r* are thrown down by him.
Mt 27.51 earth did quake, and the *r* rent;
Ac 27.29 we should have fallen upon *r*,
Rev 6.15 and in the *r* of the mountains;
16 And said to the mountains and *r*,

ROD

Ex 4.20 and Moses took the *r* of God in his
7.12 Aaron's *r* swallowed up their rods.
19 Say unto Aaron, Take thy *r*, and
10.13 stretched forth his *r* over the land
Nu 20.11 with his *r* he smote the rock twice:
2Sa 7.14 chasten him with the *r* of man,
Job 9.34 Let him take his *r* away from me,
21. 9 neither is the *r* of God upon them.
Ps 2. 9 shalt break them with a *r* of iron;
23. 4 *r* and thy staff they comfort me.
Pr 10.13 a *r* is for the back of him that is
13.24 that spareth his *r* hateth his son:
22. 8 and the *r* of his anger shall fail.
26. 3 the ass, and a *r* for the fool's back.
29.15 The *r* and reproof give wisdom:
Isa 9. 4 shoulder, the *r* of his oppressor,
10.26 and as his *r* was upon the sea, so
11. 1 forth a *r* out of the stem of Jesse,
4 smite the earth with the *r* of his

With his rod Moses smites a rock to bring forth water (Nu 20); painting by Nicolas Poussin (1594-1665).

Jer 10.16 Israel is the *r* of his inheritance:
Eze 7.10 the *r* hath blossomed, pride hath
20.37 cause you to pass under the *r*,
Mic 5. 1 smite the judge of Israel with a *r*
1Co 4.21 shall I come unto you with a *r*, or
Heb 9. 4 Aaron's *r* that budded, and the
Rev 2.27 shall rule them with a *r* of iron;
11. 1 was given me a reed like unto a *r*:
12. 5 to rule all nations with a *r* of iron:
19.15 he shall rule them with a *r* of iron:

RODS

Gen 30.37 Jacob took him *r* of green poplar,
39 the flocks conceived before the *r*,
Ex 7.12 Aaron's rod swallowed up their *r*.
Eze 19.11 strong *r* for the scepters of them
2Co 11.25 Thrice was I beaten with *r*, once

ROES

1Ch 12. 8 were as swift as the *r* upon the
SS 2. 7 by the *r*, and by the hinds of the
3. 5 by the *r*, and by the hinds of the
4. 5 like two young *r* that are twins,
7. 3 like two young *r* that are twins.

ROLL

Gen 29. 8 and till they *r* the stone from the
Jos 10.18 *R* great stones upon the mouth of
1Sa 14.33 *r* a great stone unto me this day.
Ezr 6. 2 in the province of the Medes, a *r*,
Isa 8. 1 Take thee a great *r*, and write in
Jer 36. 2 Take thee a *r* of a book, and write
4 unto him, upon a *r* of a book,
6 and read in the *r*, which thou hast
14 Take in thine hand the *r* wherein
14 Baruch...took the *r* in his hand,
20 they laid up the *r* in the chamber
21 king sent Jehudi to fetch the *r*:
23 until all the *r* was consumed in
25 king that he would not burn the *r*:
27 that the king had burned the *r*,
28 Take thee again another *r*, and
28 words that were in the first *r*,
29 Thou hast burned this *r*, saying,
32 Then took Jeremiah another *r*,
51.25 and *r* thee down from the rocks,
Eze 2. 9 and, lo, a *r* of a book was therein;
3. 1 eat this *r*, and go speak unto the
2 and he caused me to eat that *r*.
3 fill thy bowels with this *r* that I
Mic 1.10 of Aphrah *r* thyself in the dust.
Zec 5. 1 and looked, and behold a flying *r*.
2 I see a flying *r*: the length thereof
Mk 16. 3 Who shall *r* us away the stone

ROLLED

Gen 29. 3 they *r* the stone from the well's
10 *r* the stone from the well's mouth,
Jos 5. 9 I *r* away the reproach of Egypt
Job 30.14 they *r* themselves upon me.
Isa 9. 5 noise, and garments *r* in blood;
34. 4 the heavens shall be *r* together as
Mt 27.60 and he *r* a great stone to the door
28. 2 came and *r* back the stone from
Mk 15.46 and *r* a stone unto the door of the
16. 4 saw that the stone was *r* away:
Lk 24. 2 stone *r* away from the sepulcher.
Rev 6.14 as a scroll when it is *r* together;

ROLLETH

Pr 26.27 he that *r* a stone, it will return

ROMAN

Ac 22.25 you to scourge a man that is a *R*,
26 thou doest: for this man is a *R*.
27 Tell me, art thou a *R*? He said,
29 after he knew that he was a *R*, and
23.27 having understood that he was a *R*.

ROMANS

Jn 11.48 *R* shall come and take away both
Ac 16.21 neither to observe, being *R*.
37 us openly uncondemned, being *R*,
38 when they heard that they were *R*.
25.16 not the manner of the *R* to deliver
28.17 Jerusalem into the hands of the *R*.

ROME

Ac 2.10 and strangers of *R*, Jews and
18. 2 all Jews to depart from *R*:) and
19.21 have been there, I must also see *R*.
23.11 must thou bear witness also at *R*.
28.14 days: and so we went toward *R*.
16 And when we came to *R*, the
Ro 1. 7 To all that be in *R*, beloved of God,
15 gospel to you that are at *R* also.
2Ti 1.17 when he was in *R*, he sought me

ROOF

Gen 19. 8 they under the shadow of my *r*.
Dt 22. 8 shalt make a battlement for thy *r*,

Jos 2. 6 them up to the *r* of the house, and
6 she had laid in order upon the *r*.
8 she came up unto them upon the *r*;
Jdg 16.27 upon the *r* about three thousand
2Sa 11. 2 upon the *r* of the king's house:
2 and from the *r* he saw a woman
18.24 the watchman went up to the *r*
Neh 8.16 every one upon the *r* of his house,
Job 29.10 cleaved to the *r* of their mouth.
Ps 137. 6 cleave to the *r* of my mouth; if I
SS 7. 9 *r* of thy mouth like the best wine
La 4. 4 cleaveth to the *r* of his mouth for
Eze 3.26 cleave to the *r* of thy mouth,
40.13 *r* of one little chamber to the *r* of
Mt 8. 8 thou shouldest come under my *r*:
Mk 2. 4 uncovered the *r* where he was:
Lk 7. 6 thou shouldest enter under my *r*:

ROOFS

Jer 19.13 upon whose *r* they have burned
32.29 upon whose *r* they have offered

ROOM

Gen 24.23 is there *r* in thy father's house
25 straw...enough, and *r* to lodge in.
31 the house, and *r* for the camels.
26.22 now the Lord hath made *r* for us,
1Ki 5. 5 I will set upon thy throne in thy *r*,
Ps 31. 8 thou hast set my feet in a large *r*.
80. 9 Thou preparedst *r* before it, and
Pr 18.16 A man's gift maketh *r* for him,
Mal 3.10 shall not be *r* enough to receive it.
Mt 2.22 Judea in the *r* of his father Herod,
Mk 2. 2 there was no *r* to receive them,
14.15 shew you a large upper *r* furnished
Lk 2. 7 there was no *r* for them in the
12.17 have no *r* where to bestow my fruits?
14. 8 sit not down in the highest *r*; lest
9 with shame to take the lowest *r*.
10 go sit down in the lowest *r*; that
22 commanded, and yet there is *r*.
22.12 shew you a large upper *r* furnished:
Ac 1.13 in, they went up into an upper *r*,
24.27 Porcius Festus came into Felix' *r*:
1Co 14.16 occupieth the *r* of the unlearned

ROOMS

Gen 6.14 *r* shalt thou make in the ark, and
Mt 23. 6 love the uppermost *r* at feasts,
Mk 12.39 and the uppermost *r* at feasts:
Lk 14. 7 how they chose out the chief *r*;
20.46 synagogues,...the chief *r* at feasts;

ROOT

Dt 29.18 among you a *r* that beareth gall
2Ki 19.30 of Judah shall yet again take *r*
Job 5. 3 I have seen the foolish taking *r*:
14. 8 the *r* thereof wax old in the earth,
19.28 the *r* of the matter is found in me?
29.19 *r* was spread out by the waters,
Pr 12. 3 *r* of the righteous shall not be
12 *r* of the righteous yieldeth fruit.
Isa 5.24 so their *r* shall be as rottenness,
11.10 that day there shall be a *r* of Jesse,
27. 6 that come of Jacob to take *r*:
53. 2 and as a *r* out of a dry ground:
Jer 1.10 to *r* out, and to pull down, and to
Eze 31. 7 for his *r* was by great waters.
Mal 4. 1 leave them neither *r* nor branch.
Mt 3.10 ax is laid unto the *r* of the trees:
13. 6 and because they had no *r*, they
21 Yet hath he not *r* in himself, but
29 ye *r* up also the wheat with them.
Mk 4. 6 because it had no *r*, it withered
17 And have no *r* in themselves, and
Lk 3. 9 axe is laid unto the *r* of the trees:
8.13 these have no *r*, which for a while
17. 6 Be thou plucked up by the *r*, and
Ro 11.16 and if the *r* be holy, so are the
17 of the *r* and fatness of the olive
18 bearest not the *r*, but the *r* thee.
15.12 There shall be a *r* of Jesse, and he
1Ti 6.10 love of money is the *r* of all evil:
Heb 12.15 lest any *r* of bitterness springing
Rev 5. 5 the tribe of Juda, the *R* of David,
22.16 the *r* and the offspring of David,

ROOTED

Dt 29.28 the Lord *r* them out of their land
Job 18.14 His confidence shall be *r* out of his
31. 8 eat; yea, let my offspring be *r* out.
Pr 2.22 transgressors shall be *r* out of it.
Zep 2. 4 day, and Ekron shall be *r* up.
Mt 15.13 hath not planted, shall be *r* up.
Eph 3.17 ye, being *r* and grounded in love,
Col 2. 7 *R* and built up in him, and

ROOTS

2Ch 7.20 will I pluck them up by the *r* out
Job 8.17 His *r* are wrapped about the heap,
18.16 His *r* shall be dried up beneath,
28. 9 overturneth the mountains by the *r*.
30. 4 and juniper *r* for their meat.
Isa 11. 1 a Branch shall grow out of his *r*:
Jer 17. 8 spreadeth out her *r* by the river,
Eze 17. 6 and the *r* thereof were under him:
7 vine did bend her *r* toward him,
9 shall he not pull up the *r* thereof,
9 to pluck it up by the *r* thereof.
Dan 4.15 the stump of his *r* in the earth,
23 leave the stump of the *r* thereof in

The center of Rome as it appeared when the first small Christian community was established there.

Dan 4.26 to leave the stump of the tree *r*;
7. 8 first horns plucked up by the *r*:
11. 7 out of a branch of her *r* shall one
Hos 14. 5 and cast forth his *r* as Lebanon.
Am 2. 9 from above, and his *r* from beneath.
Mk 11.20 the fig tree dried up from the *r*.
Jude 12 twice dead, plucked up by the *r*;

ROPE

Isa 5.18 and sin as it were with a cart *r*:

ROPES

Jdg 16.11 If they bind me fast with new *r*
12 Delilah therefore took new *r*, and
2Sa 17.13 shall all Israel bring *r* to that city,
1Ki 20.31 on our loins, and *r* upon our heads,
32 loins, and put *r* on their heads,
Ac 27.32 soldiers cut off the *r* of the boat,

ROSE

Gen 4. 8 *r* up against Abel his brother,
32.31 over Penuel the sun *r* upon him,
Jos 3.16 the waters...*r* up upon an heap
Job 1. 5 and *r* up early in the morning,
Ps 124. 2 our side, when men *r* up against us:
SS 2. 1 I am the *r* of Sharon, and the lily
Isa 35. 1 rejoice, and blossom as the *r*.
Jon 1. 3 Jonah *r* up to flee unto Tarshish
Mk 10.50 garment, *r*, and came to Jesus.
Lk 4.29 *r* up, and thrust him out of the city,
5.25 immediately he *r* up before them,
28 he left all, *r* up, and followed him.
16.31 though one *r* from the dead.
22.45 And when he *r* up from prayer, and
24.33 And they *r* up the same hour, and
11.31 that she *r* up hastily and went out,
Ac 5.17 Then the high priest *r* up, and all
36 For before these days *r* up Theudas,
37 After this man *r* up Judas of
10.41 with him after he *r* from the dead.
14.20 him, he *r* up, and came into the city:
15. 5 *r* up certain of the sect of the
7 Peter *r* up, and said unto them,
16.22 *r* up together against them: and
26.30 the king *r* up, and the governor,
Ro 14. 9 this end Christ both died, and *r*,
1Co 10. 7 to eat and drink, and *r* up to play.
15. 4 and that he *r* again the third day
12 preached that he *r* from the dead,
2Co 5.15 which died for them, and *r* again.
1Th 4.14 that Jesus died and *r* again, even
Rev 19. 3 her smoke *r* up for ever and ever.

ROUGH

Dt 21. 4 down the heifer unto a *r* valley,
Isa 27. 8 he stayeth his *r* wind in the day
40. 4 straight, and the *r* places plain:
Jer 51.27 to come up as the *r* caterpillers.
Dan 8.21 the *r* goat is the king of Grecia:
Zec 13. 4 wear a *r* garment to deceive;
Lk 3. 5 the *r* ways shall be made smooth;

ROUGHLY

Gen 42. 7 them, and spake *r* unto them;
30 spake *r* to us, and took us for spies
1Sa 20.10 what if thy father answer thee *r*?
1Ki 12.13 the king answered the people *r*,
2Ch 10.13 And the king answered them *r*;
Pr 18.23 but the rich answereth *r*.

ROUND

Gen 37. 7 your sheaves stood *r* about, and
Ex 16.14 there lay a small *r* thing, as
Lev 25.44 the heathen that are *r* about you;
1Ki 4.24 had peace on all sides *r* about him.
31 fame was in all nations *r* about.
18.35 the water ran *r* about the altar;
2Ki 6.17 and chariots of fire *r* about Elisha.
1Ch 9.27 lodged *r* about the house of God,
Job 10. 8 fashioned me together *r* about;
22.10 snares are *r* about thee, and
37.12 turned *r* about by his counsels:
Ps 34. 7 encampeth *r* about them that fear
79. 3 like water *r* about Jerusalem;
97. 2 and darkness are *r* about him:
125. 2 mountains are *r* about Jerusalem,
2 so the Lord is *r* about his people
Isa 49.18 Lift up thine eyes *r* about, and
60. 4 Lift up thine eyes *r* about, and see:
Jer 12. 9 the birds *r* about are against her;
Eze 1.18 full of eyes *r* about them four.
10.12 wheels, were full of eyes *r* about,
31. 4 rivers running *r* about his plants,
32.23 her company is *r* about her grave:
Joel 3.12 to judge all the heathen *r* about.
Jon 2. 5 the depth closed me *r* about, the
Zec 2. 5 be unto her a wall of fire *r* about,
Mk 3.34 he looked *r* about on them which
5.32 he looked *r* about to see her that
10.23 Jesus looked *r* about, and saith
Lk 2. 9 glory of the Lord shone *r* about
19.43 compass thee *r*, and keep thee in
Ac 9. 3 there shined *r* about him a light
22. 6 heaven a great light *r* about me.
Rev 4. 3 was a rainbow *r* about the throne,
7.11 angels stood *r* about the throne,

ROW

Ex 28.17 the first *r* shall be a sardius, a
17 carbuncle: this shall be the first *r*.
18 the second *r* shall be an emerald,
19 the third *r* a ligure, an agate, and
20 the fourth *r* a beryl, and an onyx,
39.10 the first *r* was a sardius, a topaz,
10 a carbuncle: this was the first *r*.
11 second, *r*, an emerald, a sapphire,
12 the third *r*, a ligure, an agate, and
13 the fourth *r*, a beryl, an onyx, and
Lev 24. 6 set them in two rows, six on a *r*,
7 put pure frankincense upon each *r*,
1Ki 6.36 stone, and a *r* of cedar beams.
7. 3 on forty five pillars, fifteen in a *r*.
12 stones, and a *r* of cedar beams,
Ezr 6. 4 stones, and a *r* of good timber:
Eze 46.23 there was a *r* of building round

ROWED

Jon 1.13 men *r* hard to bring it to the land;
Jn 6.19 they had *r* about five and twenty

ROWING

Mk 6.48 And he saw them toiling in *r*; for

ROYAL

Gen 49.20 fat, and he shall yield *r* dainties.
Jos 10. 2 great city, as one of the *r* cities,
1Sa 27. 5 thy servant dwell in the *r* city with
2Sa 12.26 of Ammon, and took the *r* city.
1Ki 10.13 Solomon gave her of his *r* bounty.
2Ki 11. 1 arose and destroyed all the seed *r*.
25.25 the son of Elishama, the seed *r*,
1Ch 29.25 such *r* majesty as had not been
2Ch 22.10 the seed *r* of the house of Judah.
Est 1. 7 *r* wine in abundance, according
9 feast for the women in the *r* house
11 before the king with the crown *r*,
19 go a *r* commandment from him,
19 king give her *r* estate unto another
2.16 king Ahasuerus into his house *r*
17 he set the *r* crown upon her head,
5. 1 Esther put on her *r* apparel, and
1 upon his *r* throne in the *r* house,
6. 8 Let the *r* apparel be brought
8 crown *r* which is set upon his head:
8.15 in *r* apparel of blue and white,
Isa 62. 3 *r* diadem in the hand of thy God.
Jer 41. 1 the son of Elishama, of the seed *r*,
43.10 spread his *r* pavilion over them.
Dan 6. 7 together to establish a *r* statute,
Ac 12.21 Herod, arrayed in *r* apparel, sat
Jas 2. 8 If ye fulfill the *r* law according to
1Pe 2. 9 a *r* priesthood, an holy nation, a

RUBBING

Lk 6. 1 did eat, *r* them in their hands.

RUBIES

Job 28.18 the price of wisdom is above *r*.
Pr 3.15 She is more precious than *r*: and
8.11 For wisdom is better than *r*; and
20.15 There is gold, and a multitude of *r*:
31.10 woman? for her price is far above *r*.
La 4. 7 were more ruddy in body than *r*,

RUDDER

Ac 27.40 the sea, and loosed the *r* bands,

RUDE

2Co 11. 6 But though I be *r* in speech, yet

RUDIMENTS

Col 2. 8 after the *r* of the world, and not
20 be dead...from the *r* of the world,

RUE

Lk 11.42 for ye tithe mint and *r* and all

RUFUS

Mk 15.21 the father of Alexander and *R*,
Ro 16.13 Salute *R* chosen in the Lord, and

RUIN

2Ch 28.23 But they were the *r* of him, and
Ps 89.40 hast brought his strong holds to *r*.
Pr 24.22 who knoweth the *r* of them both?
26.28 and a flattering mouth worketh *r*.
Isa 3. 6 and let this *r* be under thy hand:
23.13 thereof; and he brought it to *r*.
25. 2 city an heap; of a defensed city a *r*:
Eze 18.30 so iniquity shall not be your *r*.
27.27 midst of the seas in...day of thy *r*.
31.13 Upon his *r* shall all the fowls of the
Lk 6.49 and the *r* of that house was great.

RUINS

Eze 21.15 faint, and their *r* be multiplied:
Am 9.11 and I will raise up his *r*, and I will
Ac 15.16 I will build again the *r* thereof,

RULE

Gen 1.16 the greater light to *r* the day,
16 and the lesser light to *r* the night:
3.16 husband, and he shall *r* over thee.
4. 7 desire, and thou shalt *r* over him.
Ps 136. 8 The sun to *r* by day: for his
9 The moon and stars to *r* by night:
Pr 8.16 By me princes *r*, and nobles,
19.10 a servant to have *r* over princes.
25.28 hath no *r* over his own spirit is
29. 2 but when the wicked beareth *r*,
Isa 3. 4 and babes shall *r* over them.
12 oppressors,...women *r* over them.
40.10 and his arm shall *r* for him:
44.13 carpenter stretcheth out his *r*;
Dan 2.39 shall bare *r* over all the earth.
Joel 2.17 the heathen should *r* over them:
Zec 6.13 shall sit and *r* upon his throne;
Mt 2. 6 that shall *r* my people Israel.
Mk 10.42 accounted to *r* over the Gentiles
1Co 15.24 he shall have put down all *r* and
2Co 10.13 the *r* which God hath distributed
15 you according to our *r* abundantly,
Gal 6.16 many as walk according to this *r*,
Php 3.16 let us walk by the same *r*, let us
Col 3.15 the peace of God *r* in your hearts,
1Ti 3. 5 know not how to *r* his own house,
5.17 the elders that *r* well be counted
Heb 13. 7 them which have the *r* over you,
17 Obey them that have...*r* over you,
24 Salute all...that have...*r* over you,
Rev 2.27 shall *r* them with a rod of iron;
12. 5 *r* all nations with a rod of iron:
19.15 he shall *r* them with a rod of iron:

RUTH

Heroine of the Book of Ruth; young Moabite woman married to one of the two sons of the widow Naomi, who with her husband and family earlier took refuge in Moab from famine at home in Judah; when both sons die, insists on leaving her own homeland to accompany Naomi back to Bethlehem (Ru 1); gleaning in the harvest field, is protected by Boaz, a relative of Naomi's late husband, Elimelech, who praises her loyalty to Naomi (Ru 2); at the harvest celebration, following Naomi's instructions, lies at the feet of Boaz as he sleeps in the field; startled but pleased by her devotion, he commits himself to her protection and sends her with a gift of barley to Naomi (Ru 3); before a quorum of elders, in accordance with tradition, Boaz negotiates with a closer relative and arranges to redeem Elimelech's land and marry Ruth, thus preserving the property and family line of her deceased husband; she bears him a son, Obed, whose own son will be Jesse, father of David (Ru 4).

S

SABACHTHANI

Mt 27.46 loud voice, saying, Eli, Eli, lama *s*?
Mk 15.34 voice, saying, Eloi, Eloi, lama *s*?

SABAOTH

Ro 9.29 Except the Lord of *S* had left us a
Jas 5. 4 into the ears of the Lord of *S*.

SABBATH

Ex 16.23 rest of the holy *s* unto the Lord:
25 for to day is a *s* unto the Lord:
29 that the Lord hath given you the *s*,
20. 8 Remember the *s* day, to keep it holy.
11 the Lord blessed the *s* day, and
31.15 whosoever doeth any work in the *s*
35. 3 kindle no fire...upon the *s* day.
Lev 25. 4 shall be a *s* of rest unto the land,
Dt 5.14 seventh day is the *s* of the Lord
2Ki 4.23 it is neither new moon, nor *s*.
1Ch 9.32 shewbread, to prepare it every *s*.
Neh 10.31 would not buy it of them on the *s*,
13.17 that ye do, and profane the *s* day?
Isa 56. 2, 6 keepeth the *s* from polluting it,
58.13 and call the *s* a delight, the holy of
Jer 17.21 and bear no burden on the *s* day,
24 but hallow the *s* day, to do no work
Am 8. 5 and the *s*, that we may set forth
Mt 12. 1 Jesus went on the *s* day through
2 is not lawful to do upon the *s* day:
5 how that on the *s* days the priests
5 in the temple profane the *s*, and are
8 of man is Lord even of the *s* day.
10 Is it lawful to heal on the *s* days?
11 and if it fall into a pit on the *s* day,
12 is lawful to do well on the *s* days.
24.20 in the winter, neither on the *s* day:
28. 1 In the end of the *s*, as it began to
Mk 1.21 *s* day he entered...the synagogue,
2.23 through the corn fields on the *s*
24 on the *s*...that which is not lawful?
27 The *s* was made for man, and not
27 for man, and not man for the *s*:
28 Son of man is Lord also of the *s*.
3. 2 he would heal him on the *s* day;
4 it lawful to do good on the *s* days,
6. 2 And when the *s* day was come,
15.42 that is, the day before the *s*,
16. 1 And when the *s* was past, Mary
Lk 4.16 into the synagogue on the *s* day,
31 and taught them on the *s* days.
6. 1 pass on the second *s* after the first,
2 is not lawful to do on the *s* days?
5 Son of man is Lord also of the *s*.
6 it came to pass also on another *s*,
7 whether he would heal on the *s*
9 lawful on the *s* days to do good, or
13.10 in one of the synagogues on the *s*.
14 that Jesus had healed on the *s* day,
14 and be healed, and not on the *s* day.
15 one of you on the *s* loose his ox or
16 loosed from this bond on the *s* day?
14. 1 Pharisees to eat bread on the *s* day,
3 Is it lawful to heal on the *s* day?
5 straightway pull him out on the *s*
23.54 the preparation, and the *s* drew on.
56 and rested the *s* day according to
Jn 5. 9 and on the same day was the *s*.
10 It is the *s* day: it is not lawful for
16 had done these things on the *s* day.
18 he not only had broken the *s*, but
7.22 ye on the *s* day circumcise a man.
23 on the *s* day receive circumcision,
23 man every whit whole on the *s* day?
9.14 *s* day when Jesus made the clay,
16 because he keepeth not the *s* day.
19.31 remain upon the cross on the *s* day,
31 (for that *s* day was an high day,)
Ac 1.12 from Jerusalem a *s* day's journey.
13.14 into the synagogue on the *s* day,
27 prophets which are read every *s*
42 be preached to them the next *s*.
44 next *s* day came almost the whole
15.21 read in the synagogues every *s* day.
16.13 on the *s* we went out of the city by
17. 2 three *s* days reasoned with them
18. 4 reasoned in the synagogue every *s*,
Col 2.16 of the new moon, or of the *s* days:

SABBATHS

Ex 31.13 Verily my *s* ye shall keep: for it
Lev 25. 8 thou shalt number seven *s* of years
26.34 shall the land rest, and enjoy her *s*.
Eze 20.12 Moreover also I gave them my *s*,
16 in my statutes, but polluted my *s*:
20 And hallow my *s*; and they shall be
45.17 and in the new moons, and in the *s*,
Hos 2.11 her new moons, and her *s*, and all

SACK

Gen 42.25 every man's money into his *s*,
27 as one of them opened his *s* to give
28 restored; and, lo, it is even in my *s*:
35 bundle of money was in his *s*:
43.21 money was in the mouth of his *s*,
44.11 down every man his *s* to the ground,
11 and opened every man his *s*.
12 the cup was found in Benjamin's *s*.
Lev 11.32 of wood, or raiment, or skin, or *s*,

SACKBUT

Dan 3. 5, 7, 10, 15 of the cornet, flute, harp, *s*,

SACKCLOTH

2Sa 3.31 your clothes, and gird you with *s*,
2Ki 6.30 he had *s* within upon his flesh.
Est 4. 1 clothes, and put on *s* with ashes,
3 and many lay in *s* and ashes.
Job 16.15 I have sewed *s* upon my skin, and
Ps 69.11 I made *s* also my garment; and I
Isa 20. 2 and loose the *s* from off thy loins,
37. 2 elders of the priests covered with *s*,
La 2.10 they have girded themselves with *s*:
Dan 9. 3 with fasting, and *s*, and ashes:
Joel 1. 8 Lament like a virgin girded with *s*
13 come, lie all night in *s*, ye ministers
Am 8.10 and I will bring up *s* upon all loins,
Jon 3. 6 and covered him with *s*, and sat in
Mt 11.21 repented long ago in *s* and ashes.
Lk 10.13 repented, sitting in *s* and ashes.
Rev 6.12 the sun became black as *s* of hair,
11. 3 and threescore days, clothed in *s*.

SACKS

Gen 42.25 Joseph commanded to fill their *s*
35 to pass as they emptied their *s*,
43.12 the money...in the mouth of your *s*,
18 money that was returned in our *s*
21 that we opened our *s*, and, behold,
22 tell who put our money in our *s*.
23 hath given you treasure in your *s*:
44. 1 saying, Fill the men's *s* with food,
Jos 9. 4 and took old *s* upon their asses,

SACRIFICE

Ex 3.18 we may *s* to the Lord our God.
8.29 the people go to *s* to the Lord.
12.27 It is the *s* of the Lord's passover,
13.15 I *s* to the Lord all that openeth
20.24 *s* thereon thy burnt offerings,
29.28 of the *s* of their peace offerings,
Lev 7.12 offer with the *s* of thanksgiving
27.11 they do not offer a *s* unto the Lord,
Nu 28.13 a *s* made by fire unto the Lord.
Dt 16. 6 thou shalt *s* the passover at even,
Jdg 16.23 a great *s* unto Dagon their god,
1Sa 2.29 Wherefore kick ye at my *s* and at
16. 2 say, I am come to *s* to the Lord.
1Ki 18.29 the offering of the evening *s*,
38 fell, and consumed the burnt *s*,
2Ch 33.17 people did *s*...in the high places,
Ps 40. 6 *S* and offering thou didst not
51.16 For thou desirest not *s*; else
116.17 offer to thee...*s* of thanksgiving,
141. 2 up of my hands as the evening *s*.
Pr 15. 8 *s* of the wicked is an abomination
Ec 5. 1 hear, than to give the *s* of fools:
Jer 33.11 that shall bring the *s* of praise
Dan 8.11 by him the daily *s* was taken away,
Hos 4.13 *s* upon the tops of the mountains,
6. 6 For I desired mercy, and not *s*;
Jon 1.16 and offered a *s* unto the Lord,
Zep 1. 8 pass in the day of the Lord's *s*,
Mal 1. 8 And if ye offer the blind for *s*, is it
Mt 9.13 I will have mercy, and not *s*: for
12. 7 I will have mercy, and not *s*, ye
Mk 9.49 every *s* shall be salted with salt.
Lk 2.24 And to offer a *s* according to that
Ac 7.41 and offered *s* unto the idol, and
14.13 and would have done *s* with the
18 they had not done *s* unto them.
Ro 12. 1 ye present your bodies a living *s*,
1Co 8. 4 that are offered in *s* unto idols,
10.19 is offered in *s* to idols is any thing?
20 the things which the Gentiles *s*,
20 they *s* to devils, and not to God:
28 This is offered in *s* unto idols, eat
Eph 5. 2 for us an offering and a *s* to God
Php 2.17 the *s* and service of your faith,
4.18 *s* acceptable, wellpleasing to God.
Heb 7.27 to offer up *s*, first for his own sins,
9.26 to put away sin by the *s* of himself.
10. 5 *S* and offering thou wouldest not,
8 *S* and offering and burnt offerings
12 after he had offered one *s* for sins
26 remaineth no more *s* for sins,
11. 4 God a more excellent *s* than Cain,
13.15 let us offer the *s* of praise to God

SACRIFICED

Dt 32.17 They *s* unto devils, not to God; to
Jdg 2. 5 and they *s* there unto the Lord.
2Ch 28.23 he *s* unto the gods of Damascus,
33.22 Amon *s* unto all the carved images
Ps 106.37 *s* their sons and their daughters
38 they *s* unto the idols of Canaan:
1Co 5. 7 Christ our passover is *s* for us:
Rev 2.14 to eat things *s* unto idols, and to
20 and to eat things *s* unto idols.

SACRIFICES

Gen 46. 1 and offered *s* unto the God of his
Ex 18.12 a burnt offering and *s* for God:
Lev 7.34 off the *s* of their peace offerings,
17. 5 children of Israel may bring their *s*,
7 no more offer their *s* unto devils,
1Ch 29.21 and *s* in abundance for all Israel:
Neh 12.43 that day they offered great *s*,
Ps 4. 5 Offer the *s* of righteousness, and
27. 6 I offer in his tabernacle *s* of joy;
51.17 The *s* of God are a broken spirit:
106.28 and ate the *s* of the dead.
Pr 17. 1 than an house full of *s* with strife.
Isa 1.11 the multitude of your *s* unto me?
Jer 6.20 nor your *s* sweet unto me.
Hos 4.19 be ashamed because of their *s*.
Am 4. 4 and bring your *s* every morning,
5.25 ye offered unto me *s* and offerings
Mk 12.33 all whole burnt offerings and *s*.

Lk 13. 1 Pilate had mingled with their *s*.
Ac 7.42 offered to me slain beasts and *s*
1Co 10.18 which eat of the *s* partakers of the
Heb 5. 1 may offer both gifts and *s* for sins:
8. 3 is ordained to offer gifts and *s*:
9. 9 were offered both gifts and *s*, that
23 with better *s* than these.
10. 1 can never with those *s* which they
3 in those *s* there is a remembrance
6 In burnt offerings and *s* for sin thou
11 offering oftentimes the same *s*,
13.16 with such *s* God is well pleased.
1Pe 2. 5 to offer up spiritual *s*, acceptable

SACRIFICETH

Ex 22.20 He that *s* unto any god, save unto
Ec 9. 2 him that *s*, and to him that *s* not:
Isa 65. 3 *s* in gardens, and burneth incense
66. 3 he that *s* a lamb, as if he cut off a
Mal 1.14 *s* unto the Lord a corrupt thing:

SACRILEGE

Ro 2.22 idols, dost thou commit *s*?

SAD

Gen 40. 6 them, and, behold, they were *s*.
1Sa 1.18 and her countenance was no more *s*.
1Ki 21. 5 Why is thy spirit so *s*, that thou
Neh 2. 1 been beforetime *s* in his presence.
2 Why is thy countenance *s*, seeing
3 should not my countenance be *s*,
Eze 13.22 made the heart of the righteous *s*,
22 whom I have made *s*; and
Mt 6.16 hypocrites, of a *s* countenance:
Mk 10.22 he was *s* at that saying, and went
Lk 24.17 to another, as ye walk, and are *s*?

SADDUCEES

Mt 3. 7 saw many of the Pharisees and *S*
16. 1 Pharisees also with the *S* came,
6 leaven of the Pharisees and...*S*.
11 leaven of the Pharisees and...*S*?
12 doctrine of the Pharisees and...*S*.
22.23 The same day came to him the *S*,
34 that he had put the *S* to silence,
Mk 12.18 Then come unto him the *S*, which
Lk 20.27 Then came to him certain of the *S*,
Ac 4. 1 captain of the temple, and the *S*,
5.17 (which is the sect of the *S*,) and
23. 6 perceived that the one part were *S*,
7 between the Pharisees and the *S*:
8 *S* say that there is no resurrection,

SAFE

1Sa 12.11 on every side, and ye dwelled *s*.
2Sa 18.29, 32 Is the young man Absalom *s*?
Job 21. 9 Their houses are *s* from fear,
Ps 119.117 Hold...me up, and I shall be *s*:
Pr 18.10 runneth into it, and is safe.
29.25 his trust in the Lord shall be *s*.
Isa 5.29 prey, and shall carry it away *s*,
Eze 34.27 and they shall be *s* in their land,
Lk 15.27 he hath received him *s* and sound.
Ac 23.24 and bring him *s* unto Felix the
27.44 pass, that they escaped all *s* to land.
Php 3. 1 is not grievous, but for you it is *s*.

SAFELY

Lev 26. 5 the full, and dwell in your land *s*.
1Ki 4.25 And Judah and Israel dwelt *s*, every
Ps 78.53 he led them on *s* so that they feared
Pr 1.33 hearkeneth unto me shall dwell *s*,
3.23 Then shalt thou walk in thy way *s*,
31.11 of her husband doth *s* trust in her,
Isa 41. 3 He pursued them, and passed *s*;
Jer 23. 6 be saved, and Israel shall dwell *s*:
32.37 and I will cause them to dwell *s*:
33.16 saved, and Jerusalem shall dwell *s*:
Eze 28.26 And they shall dwell *s* therein, and
34.25 they shall dwell *s* in the wilderness,
28 they shall dwell *s*, and none shall
38. 8 and they shall dwell *s* all of them.
11 them that are at rest, that dwell *s*,
14 my people of Israel dwelleth *s*,
39.26 when they dwelt *s* in their land,
Hos 2.18 and will make them to lie down *s*.
Zec 14.11 but Jerusalem shall be *s* inhabited.
Mk 14.44 take him, and lead him away *s*:
Ac 16.23 charging the jailor to keep them *s*:

SAFETY

Lev 25.18 and ye shall dwell in the land in *s*.
19 eat your fill, and dwell therein in *s*.
Dt 12.10 round about, so that ye dwell in *s*;
33.12 beloved of the Lord shall dwell in *s*
28 Israel then shall dwell in *s* alone:
Job 3.26 I was not in *s*, neither had I rest,
5. 4 His children are far from *s*, and
11 which mourn may be exalted to *s*.
11.18 and thou shalt take thy rest in *s*.
24.23 Though it be given him to be in *s*,
Ps 4. 8 Lord, only makest me dwell in *s*.
12. 5 set him in *s* from him that puffeth
33.17 An horse is a vain thing for *s*:
Pr 11.14 multitude of counsellers there is *s*.
21.31 day of battle: but *s* is of the Lord.
24. 6 multitude of counsellers there is *s*.
Isa 14.30 and the needy shall lie down in *s*:
Ac 5.23 prison...found we shut with all *s*,
1Th 5. 3 when they shall say, Peace and *s*;

SAIL

Isa 33.23 they could not spread the *s*:
Eze 27. 7 thou spreadest forth to be thy *s*;
Ac 20. 3 as he was about to *s* into Syria,
16 For Paul had determined to *s* by
27. 1 that we should *s* into Italy, they
2 to *s* by the coasts of Asia; one
17 strake *s*, and so were driven.
24 thee all them that *s* with thee.

SAILED

Lk 8.23 But as they *s* he fell asleep: and
Ac 13. 4 and from thence they *s* to Cyprus.
14.26 thence *s* to Antioch, from whence
15.39 took Mark, and *s* unto Cyprus;
18.18 brethren, and *s* thence into Syria,
21 God will. And he *s* from Ephesus.
20. 6 we *s* away from Philippi after the
13 before to ship, and *s* unto Assos,
15 we *s* thence, and came the next
21. 3 on the left hand, and *s* into Syria,
27. 4 we *s* under Cyprus, because the
5 we had *s* over the sea of Cilicia
7 when we had *s* slowly many days,
7 we *s* under Crete, over against
13 thence, they *s* close by Crete.

SAILING

Ac 21. 2 a ship *s* over unto Phenicia, we
27. 6 a ship of Alexandria *s* into Italy;
9 and when *s* was now dangerous,

SAILORS

Rev 18.17 *s*, and as many as trade by sea,

SAINT

Ps 106.16 and Aaron the *s* of the Lord.
Dan 8.13 Then I heard one *s* speaking,
13 and another *s* said unto that
13 said unto that certain *s* which spake,
Php 4.21 Salute every *s* in Christ Jesus.

SAINTS

Dt 33. 2 came with ten thousands of *s*:
3 all his *s* are in thy hand: and
1Sa 2. 9 He will keep the feet of his *s*,
2Ch 6.41 and let thy *s* rejoice in goodness.
Job 5. 1 to which of the *s* wilt thou turn?
15.15 he putteth no trust in his *s*; yea,
Ps 16. 3 But to the *s* that are in the earth,
30. 4 Sing unto the Lord, O ye *s* of his,
31.23 O love the Lord, all ye his *s*: for
34. 9 O fear the Lord, ye his *s*: for
37.28 and forsaketh not his *s*; they are
50. 5 Gather my *s* together unto me;
52. 9 name; for it is good before thy *s*.
79. 2 the flesh of thy *s* unto the beasts
85. 8 peace unto his people, and to his *s*:
89. 5 also in the congregation of the *s*.
7 be feared in the assembly of the *s*,
97.10 he preserveth the souls of his *s*;
116.15 of the Lord is the death of his *s*.
132. 9 and let thy *s* shout for joy.
16 and her *s* shall shout aloud for joy.
145.10 Lord; and thy *s* shall bless thee.
148.14 his people, the praise of all his *s*;
149. 1 praise in the congregation of *s*.
5 Let the *s* be joyful in glory: let
9 this honor have all his *s*. Praise
Pr 2. 8 and preserveth the way of his *s*.
Dan 7.18 the *s* of the most High shall take
21 same horn made war with the *s*,
22 judgment was given to the *s* of the
22 that the *s* possessed the kingdom.
25 wear out the *s* of the most High,
27 people of the *s* of the most High,
Hos 11.12 God, and is faithful with the *s*.
Zec 14. 5 shall come, and all the *s* with thee.
Mt 27.52 bodies of the *s* which slept arose,
Ac 9.13 much evil he hath done to thy *s* at
32 also to the *s* which dwelt at Lydda.
41 he had called the *s* and widows,
26.10 many of the *s* did I shut up in prison,
Ro 1. 7 beloved of God, called to be *s*:
8.27 he maketh intercession for the *s*
12.13 Distributing to the necessity of *s*;
15.25 Jerusalem to minister unto the *s*.
26 the poor *s* which are at Jerusalem.
31 Jerusalem may be accepted of the *s*;
16. 2 her in the Lord, as becometh *s*,
15 and all the *s* which are with them.
1Co 1. 2 in Christ Jesus, called to be *s*,
6. 1 the unjust, and not before the *s*?
2 that the *s* shall judge the world?
14.33 of peace, as in all churches of the *s*.
16. 1 concerning the collection for the *s*,
15 addicted...to the ministry of the *s*,)
2Co 1. 1 all the *s* which are in all Achaia:
8. 4 fellowship of...ministering to the *s*.
9. 1 as touching the ministering to the *s*,
12 not only supplieth the want of the *s*,
13.13 All the *s* salute you.
Eph 1. 1 to the *s* which are at Ephesus, and
15 Lord Jesus, and love unto all the *s*,
18 the glory of his inheritance in the *s*,
2.19 fellowcitizens with the *s*, and of the
3. 8 who am less than the least of all *s*,
18 to comprehend with all *s* what is the
4.12 For the perfecting of the *s*, for the
5. 3 named among you, as becometh *s*;
6.18 and supplication for all *s*;
Php 1. 1 to all the *s* in Christ Jesus which are
4.22 All the *s* salute you, chiefly they
Col 1. 2 To the *s* and faithful brethren in
4 the love which ye have to all the *s*,
12 of the inheritance of the *s* in light:
26 but now is made manifest to his *s*:
1Th 3.13 the coming of...Christ with all his *s*.
2Th 1.10 he shall come to be glorified in his *s*,
Phm 5 the Lord Jesus, and toward all *s*;
7 the bowels of the *s* are refreshed by
Heb 6.10 in that ye have ministered to the *s*,
13.24 have the rule over you, and all the *s*.
Jude 3 faith...once delivered unto the *s*.
14 cometh with ten thousands of his *s*,
Rev 5. 8 odors, which are the prayers of *s*.
8. 3 offer it with the prayers of all *s*
4 came with the prayers of the *s*,
11.18 servants the prophets, and to the *s*,
13. 7 unto him to make war with the *s*,
10 the patience and the faith of the *s*.
14.12 Here is the patience of the *s*: here

Rev 15. 3 true are thy ways, thou King of *s*.
16. 6 shed the blood of *s* and prophets,
17. 6 drunken with the blood of the *s*,
18.24 the blood of prophets, and of *s*, and
19. 8 fine linen is the righteousness of *s*.
20. 9 and compassed the camp of the *s*

SAINTS'
1Ti 5.10 if she have washed the *s* feet, if she

SAKE
Gen 3.17 cursed is the ground for thy *s*;
18.32 I will not destroy it for ten's *s*.
30.27 Lord hath blessed me for thy *s*.
2Sa 5.12 kingdom for his people Israel's *s*.
18. 5 gently for my *s* with the young man,
1Ki 15. 4 for David's *s* did the Lord his God
Neh 9.31 for thy great mercies' *s* thou didst
Job 19.17 for the children's *s* of my own body.
Ps 6. 4 oh save me for thy mercies' *s*,
23. 3 of righteousness for his name's *s*.
25. 7 me for thy goodness *s*, O Lord.
31.16 servant: save me for thy mercies' *s*.
44.22 for thy *s* are we killed all the day
26 redeem us for thy mercies' *s*.
79. 9 away our sins, for thy name's *s*
115. 1 for thy mercy, and for thy truth's *s*.
143.11 me, O Lord, for thy name's *s*:
Isa 42.21 pleased for his righteousness' *s*;
62. 1 and for Jerusalem's *s* I will not
63.17 Return for thy servants' *s*, the
Jer 14.21 Do not abhor us, for thy name's *s*,
Eze 36.22 but for mine holy name's *s*, which
Dan 9.19 not, for thine own *s*, O my God:
Jon 1.12 for my *s* this great tempest is
Mic 3.12 shall Zion for your *s* be plowed as
Mt 5.10 persecuted for righteousness' *s*:
11 evil against you falsely, for my *s*.
10.18 governors and kings for my *s*, for
22 hated of all men for my name's *s*:
39 that loseth his life for my *s* shall
14. 3 put him in prison for Herodias' *s*,
9 nevertheless for the oath's *s*, and
16.25 will lose his life for my *s* shall
19.12 for the kingdom of heaven's *s*.
29 or lands, for my name's *s*, shall
24. 9 of all nations for my name's *s*.
22 the elect's *s* those days shall be
Mk 4.17 persecution ariseth for the word's *s*,
6.17 him in prison for Herodias' *s*,
26 yet for his oath's *s*, and for their
8.35 shall lose his life for my *s* and
10.29 lands, for my *s*, and the gospel's,
13. 9 before rulers and kings for my *s*,
13 hated of all men for my name's *s*:
20 for the elect's *s*, whom he hath
Lk 6.22 as evil, for the Son of man's *s*.
9.24 will lose his life for my *s*, the
18.29 for the kingdom of God's *s*.
21.12 kings and rulers for my name's *s*.
17 hated of all men for my name's *s*.
Jn 12. 9 they came not for Jesus' *s* only,
13.37 I will lay down my life for thy *s*.
38 thou lay down thy life for my *s*?
14.11 believe me for the very works' *s*.
15.21 they do unto you for my name's *s*,
Ac 9.16 he must suffer for my name's *s*.
26. 7 For which hope's *s*, king Agrippa,
Ro 4.23 was not written for his *s* alone,
8.36 For thy *s* we are killed all the day
13. 5 wrath, but also for conscience *s*.
15.30 for the Lord Jesus Christ's *s*, and
1Co 4.10 We are fools for Christ's *s*, but ye
9.23 this I do for the gospel's *s*, that I
10.25, 27 no question for conscience *s*:
28 eat not for his *s* that shewed it,
28 for conscience *s*: for the earth
2Co 4. 5 your servants for Jesus' *s*.
11 delivered unto death for Jesus' *s*,
12.10 in distresses for Christ's *s*: for
Eph 4.32 for Christ's *s* hath forgiven you.
Php 1.29 him, but also to suffer for his *s*;
Col 1.24 Christ in my flesh for his body's *s*,
3. 6 For which things' *s* the wrath of
1Th 1. 5 we were among you for your *s*.
5.13 highly in love for their work's *s*.
1Ti 5.23 a little wine for thy stomach's *s*
Tit 1.11 they ought not, for filthy lucre's *s*.
Phm 9 Yet for love's *s* I rather beseech
1Pe 2.13 ordinance of man for the Lord's *s*:
3.14 if ye suffer for righteousness' *s*,
1Jn 2.12 are forgiven you for his name's *s*.
2Jn 2 For the truth's *s*, which dwelleth
3Jn 7 for his name's *s* they went forth,
Rev 2. 3 and for my name's *s* hast labored,

SAKES
Gen 18.26 will spare all the place for their *s*.
Lev 26.45 for their *s* remember the covenant
Dt 1.37 was angry with me for your *s*,
Ru 1.13 it grieveth me much for your *s* that
Ps 122. 8 my brethren and companions' *s*,
Eze 36.32 Not for your *s* do I this, saith the
Mal 3.11 I will rebuke the devourer for your *s*,
Mk 6.26 and for their *s* which sat with him,
Jn 11.15 glad for your *s* that I was not there,
12.30 because of me, but for your *s*.
17.19 And for their *s* I sanctify myself,
Ro 11.28 they are enemies for your *s*:
28 are beloved for the fathers' *s*.
1Co 4. 6 and to Apollos for your *s*;
9.10 saith he it altogether for our *s*?
10 For our *s*, no doubt, this is
2Co 2.10 for your *s* forgave I it in the
4.15 all things are for your *s*, that
8. 9 yet for your *s* he became poor,
1Th 3. 9 joy for your *s* before our God;
2Ti 2.10 endure all things for the elect's *s*,

SALEM
Gen 14.18 Melchizedek king of *S* brought
Ps 76. 2 In *S* also is his tabernacle, and his
Heb 7. 1 For this Melchisedec king of *S*,
2 after that also King of *S*, which is,

SALOME
Mk 15.40 the less and of Joses, and *S*;
16. 1 Mary the mother of James, and *S*,

SALT
Gen 14. 3 vale of Siddim, which is the *s* sea.
19.26 him, and she became a pillar of *s*.
Lev 2.13 offering shalt thou season with *s*
13 the *s* of the covenant of thy God
13 thine offerings thou shalt offer *s*.
Jdg 9.45 down the city, and sowed it with *s*.
2Ki 2.20 Bring me a new cruse, and put *s*
Job 6. 6 is unsavory be eaten without *s*?
Jer 17. 6 in a *s* land and not inhabited.
Mt 5.13 Ye are the *s* of the earth: but if the
13 but if the *s* have lost his savor,
Mk 9.49 sacrifice shall be salted with *s*.
50 *S* is good: but if the *s* have lost
50 Have *s* in yourselves, and have
Lk 14.34 *S* is good: but if the *s* have lost
Col 4: 6 alway with grace, seasoned with *s*,
Jas 3.12 both yield *s* water and fresh.

SALTED
Eze 16. 4 not *s* at all, nor swaddled at all.
Mt 5.13 savor, wherewith shall it be *s*?
Mk 9.49 For every one shall be *s* with fire,
49 every sacrifice shall be *s* with salt.

SALTNESS
Mk 9.50 but if the salt have lost his *s*,

SALUTATION
Lk 1.29 what manner of *s* this should be.
41 when Elisabeth heard the *s* of Mary,
44 voice of thy *s* sounded in mine ears,
1Co 16.21 *s* of me Paul with mine own hand.
Col 4.18 The *s* by the hand of me Paul.
2Th 3.17 The *s* of Paul with mine own hand,

SALUTATIONS
Mk 12.38 and love *s* in the marketplaces,

SALUTE
1Sa 10. 4 And they will *s* thee, and give
13.10 to meet him, that he might *s* him.
25.14 of the wilderness to *s* our master;
2Sa 8.10 son unto king David, to *s* him,
2Ki 4.29 if thou meet any man, *s* him not;
29 and if any *s* thee, answer him not
10.13 to *s* the children of the king and
Mt 5.47 And if ye *s* your brethren only,
10.12 when ye come into an house, *s* it.
Mk 15.18 began to *s* him, Hail, King of the
Lk 10. 4 shoes: and *s* no man by the way.
Ac 25.13 came unto Caearea to *s* Festus.
Ro 16. 5 *S* my wellbeloved Epaenetus, who
7 *S* Andronicus and Junia, my
9 *S* Urbane, our helper in Christ,
10 *S* Apelles approved in Christ.
10 *S* them which are of Aristobulus'
11 *S* Herodion my kinsman. Greet
12 *S* Tryphena and Tryphosa, who
12 *S* the beloved Persis, which
13 *S* Rufus chosen in the Lord, and
14 *S* Asyncritus, Phlegon, Hermas,
15 *S* Philologus, and Julia, Nereus,
16 *S* one another with an holy kiss.
16 The churches of Christ *s* you.
21 and Sosipater, my kinsmen, *s* you.
22 who wrote this epistle, *s* you in the
1Co 16.19 The churches of Asia *s* you.
19 Aquila and Priscilla *s* you much in
2Co 13.13 All the saints *s* you.
Php 4.21 *S* every saint in Christ Jesus.
22 All the saints *s* you, chiefly they
Col 4.15 *S* the brethren...in Laodicea,
2Ti 4.19 *S* Prisca and Aquila, and the
Tit 3.15 All that are with me *s* thee. Greet
Phm 23 There *s* thee Epaphras, my
Heb 13.24 *S* all them that have the rule over
24 all the saints. They of Italy *s* you.
3Jn 14 Peace be to thee. Our friends *s* thee.

SALUTED
Jdg 18.15 house of Micah, and *s* him.
1Sa 17.22 and came and *s* his brethren.
30.21 near to the people, he *s* them.
2Ki 10.15 he *s* him, and said to him, Is thine
Mk 9.15 amazed, and running to him *s* him.
Lk 1.40 house of Zacharias, and *s* Elisabeth.
Ac 18.22 and gone up, and *s* the church, he
21. 7 and *s* the brethren, and abode with
19 when he had *s* them, he declared

SALUTETH
Ro 16.23 and of the whole church, *s* you.
23 the chamberlain of the city *s* you,
Col 4.10 Aristarchus...*s* you, and Marcus,
12 Epaphras, who is one of you,...*s*
1Pe 5.13 church that is at Babylon, *s*...you;

SALVATION
Gen 49.18 I have waited for thy *s*, O Lord.
Ex 14.13 still, and see the *s* of the Lord,
15. 2 and song, and he is become my *s*:
Dt 32.15 lightly esteemed the Rock of his *s*.
1Sa 11.13 Lord hath wrought *s* in Israel.
19. 5 Lord wrought a great *s* for all
2Sa 22.47 be the God of the rock of my *s*.
51 He is the tower of *s* for his king:
23. 5 this is all my *s*, and all my desire,
1Ch 16.35 Save us, O God of our *s*, and
Job 13.16 He also shall be my *s*: for an
Ps 3. 8 *S* belongeth unto the Lord: thy
14. 7 Oh that the *s* of Israel were come
18.46 and let the God of my *s* be exalted.
21. 5 His glory is great in thy *s*: honor

Biblical Themes

SALVATION

The Lord's portion is his people; Jacob is the lot of his inheritance. He found him in a desert land, and in the waste howling wilderness; he led him about, he instructed him, he kept him as the apple of his eye. As an eagle stirreth up her nest, fluttereth over her young, spreadeth abroad her wings, taketh them, beareth them on her wings: so the Lord alone did lead him, and there was no strange god with him. Dt 32.9-12

Thus saith the Lord concerning the king of Assyria, He shall not come into this city, nor shoot an arrow there, nor come before it with shield, nor cast a bank against it. By the way that he came, by the same shall he return. . . . For I will defend this city, to save it, for mine own sake, and for my servant David's sake. 2Ki 19.32-34

Blessed is the man whom thou choosest, and causest to approach unto thee, that he may dwell in thy courts. Ps 65.4

Their soul is melted because of trouble. They reel to and fro, and stagger like a drunken man, and are at their wit's end. Then they cry unto the Lord in their trouble, and he bringeth them out of their distresses. He maketh the storm a calm, so that the waves thereof are still. Ps 107.26-29

With joy shall ye draw water out of the wells of salvation. Isa 12.3

In that day shall the deaf hear the words of the book, and the eyes of the blind shall see out of obscurity. . . . The meek also shall increase their joy in the Lord, and the poor among men shall rejoice in the Holy One of Israel. . . . They also that erred in spirit shall come to understanding. Isa 29.18-19, 24

As I live, saith the Lord God, I have no pleasure in the death of the wicked; but that the wicked turn from his way and live. Eze 33.11

Many are called, but few are chosen. Mt 22.14

They that are whole have no need of the physician, but they that are sick: I came not to call the righteous, but sinners to repentance. Mk 2.17

I say unto you, that . . . joy shall be in heaven over one sinner that repenteth, more than over ninety and nine just persons, which need no repentance. Lk 15.7

As Moses lifted up the serpent in the wilderness, even so must the Son of man be lifted up: that whosoever believeth in him should not perish, but have eternal life. . . . For God sent not his Son into the world to condemn the world; but that the world through him might be saved. Jn 3.14-15, 17

Then he called for a light, and sprang in, and came trembling, and fell down before Paul and Silas, and brought them out, and said, Sirs, what must I do to be saved? And they said, Believe on the Lord Jesus Christ, and thou shalt be saved, and thy house. Ac 16.29-31

God commendeth his love toward us, in that, while we were yet sinners, Christ died for us. Much more then, being now justified by his blood, we shall be saved from wrath through him. Ro 5.8-9

If God be for us, who can be against us? He that spared not his own Son, but delivered him up for us all, how shall he not with him also freely give us all things? Ro 8.31-32

It is high time to awake out of sleep: for now is our salvation nearer than when we believed. Ro 13.11

The Lord is not slack concerning his promise . . . but is longsuffering . . . not willing that any should perish, but that all should come to repentance. 2Pe 3.9

24. 5 righteousness from...God of his *s*.
27. 1 Lord is my light and my *s*; whom
9 neither forsake me, O God of my *s*.
37.39 *s* of the righteous is of the Lord:
51.12 Restore unto me the joy of thy *s*;
14 O God, thou God of my *s*:
62. 2, 6 He only is my rock and my *s*; he
7 In God is my *s* and my glory:
68.19 benefits, even the God of our *s*.
79. 9 Help us, O God of our *s*, for the
85. 9 his *s* is nigh them that fear him;
89.26 my God, and the rock of my *s*.
95. 1 joyful noise to the rock of our *s*.
96. 2 shew forth his *s* from day to day.
98. 2 The Lord hath made known his *s*:
3 earth have seen the *s* of our God.
106. 4 thy people: O visit me with thy *s*;
116.13 I will take the cup of *s*, and call
118.14 and song, and is become my *s*.
119.81 My soul fainteth for thy *s*: but I
155 *S* is far from the wicked: for they
132.16 also clothe her priests with *s*:
Isa 12. 2 Behold, God is my *s*; I will trust,
33. 2 our *s* also in the time of trouble.
45.17 in the Lord with an everlasting *s*:
49. 8 in a day of *s* have I helped thee:
52. 7 tidings of good, that publisheth *s*;
10 earth shall see the *s* of our God.
59.17 and an helmet of *s* upon his head;
62. 1 *s* thereof as a lamp that burneth.
63. 5 mine own arm brought *s* unto me;
Jer 3.23 Lord our God is the *s* of Israel.
La 3.26 quietly wait for the *s* of the Lord.
Jon 2. 9 I have vowed. *S* is of the Lord.
Mic 7. 7 I will wait for the God of my *s*:
Hab 3.18 Lord, I will joy in the God of my *s*.
Zec 9. 9 he is just, and having *s*; lowly,
Lk 1.69 hath raised up an horn of *s* for us
77 knowledge of *s* unto his people by
2.30 For mine eyes have seen thy *s*,
3. 6 And all flesh shall see the *s* of God.
19. 9 This day is *s* come to this house,
Jn 4.22 we worship: for *s* is of the Jews.
Ac 4.12 Neither is there *s* in any other: for
13.26 to you is the word of this *s* sent.
47 be for *s* unto the ends of the earth.
16.17 which shew unto us the way of *s*.
28.28 *s* of God is sent unto the Gentiles,
Ro 1.16 power of God unto *s* to every one
10.10 mouth confession is made unto *s*.
11.11 fall *s* is come unto the Gentiles,
13.11 *s* nearer than when we believed.
2Co 1. 6 it is for your consolation and *s*,
6 it is for your consolation and *s*.
6. 2 in the day of *s* have I succored
2 time; behold, now is the day of *s*.)
7.10 sorrow worketh repentance to *s*
Eph 1.13 of truth, the gospel of your *s*:
6.17 And take the helmet of *s*, and the
Php 1.19 turn to my *s* through your prayer,
28 but to you of *s*, and that of God.
2.12 work out your own *s* with fear and
1Th 5. 8 and for an helmet, the hope of *s*.
9 but to obtain *s* by our Lord Jesus
2Th 2.13 you to *s* through sanctification of
2Ti 2.10 also obtain the *s* which is in Christ
3.15 are able to make thee wise unto *s*
Tit 2.11 the grace of God that bringeth *s*
Heb 1.14 for them who shall be heirs of *s*?
2. 3 we escape, if we neglect so great *s*;
10 make the captain of their *s* perfect
5. 9 author of eternal *s* unto all them
6. 9 you, and things that accompany *s*,
9.28 the second time without sin unto *s*.
1Pe 1. 5 power of God through faith unto *s*
9 your faith, even the *s* of your souls.
10 Of which *s* the prophets have
2Pe 3.15 the longsuffering of our Lord is *s*;
Jude 3 to write unto you of the common *s*,
Rev 7.10 *S* to our God which sitteth upon
12.10 Now is come *s*, and strength, and
19. 1 saying, Alleluia; *S*, and glory,

SAMARIA

1Ki 13.32 places which are in the cities of *S*,
16.24 he bought the hill *S* of Shemer for
24 of Shemer, owner of the hill, *S*.
28 his fathers, and was buried in *S*:
29 Ahab...reigned over Israel in *S*
32 of Baal, which he had built in *S*.
18. 2 And there was a sore famine in *S*.
20. 1 and he went up and besieged *S*,
10 if the dust of *S* shall suffice for
17 There are men come out of *S*.
34 Damascus, as my father made in *S*.
43 and displeased, and came to *S*.
21. 1 by the palace of Ahab king of *S*.
18 Ahab king of Israel, which is in *S*:
22.10 in the entrance of the gate of *S*;
37 king died, and was brought to *S*;
37 and they buried the king in *S*.
38 washed the chariot in the pool of *S*;
51 began to reign over Israel in *S* the
2Ki 1. 2 his upper chamber that was in *S*,
3 the messengers of the king of *S*,
2.25 and from thence he returned to *S*.
3. 1 began to reign over Israel in *S* the
6 king Jehoram went out of *S* the
5. 3 were with the prophet that is in *S*!

2Ki 6.19 ye seek. But he led them to *S*.
20 pass, when they were come into *S*,
20 behold, they were in the midst of *S*.
24 host, and went up, and besieged *S*.
25 And there was a great famine in *S*:
7. 1 barley for a shekel, in the gate of *S*.
18 about this time in the gate of *S*:
10. 1 And Ahab had seventy sons in *S*.
1 Jehu wrote letters and sent to *S*,
12 arose and departed, and came to *S*.
17 And when he came to *S*, he slew
17 all that remained unto Ahab in *S*,
35 fathers: and they buried him in *S*.
36 that Jehu reigned over Israel in *S*
13. 1 began to reign over Israel in *S*,
6 there remained the grove also in *S*.)
9 fathers; and they buried him in *S*:
10 Jehoahaz to reign over Israel in *S*,
13 Joash was buried in *S* with the
14.14 and hostages, and returned to *S*.
16 was buried in *S* with the kings of
23 king of Israel began to reign in *S*,
15. 8 of Jeroboam reign over Israel in *S*
13 and he reigned a full month in *S*.
14 up from Tirzah, and came to *S*,
14 Shallum the son of Jabesh in *S*,
17 Israel, and reigned ten years in *S*.
23 began to reign over Israel in *S*,
25 smote him in *S*, in the palace
27 began to reign over Israel in *S*,
17. 1 the son of Elah to reign in *S* over
5 and went up to *S*, and besieged it
6 the king of Assyria took *S*, and
24 and placed them in the cities of *S*
24 and they possessed *S*, and dwelt in
26 and placed in the cities of *S*, know
28 whom they had carried...from *S*
18. 9 king of Assyria came up against *S*,
10 king of Israel, *S* was taken.
34 they delivered *S* out of mine hand?
21.13 over Jerusalem the line of *S*, and
23.18 of the prophet that came out of *S*.
19 places that were in the cities of *S*,
2Ch 18. 2 years he went down to Ahab to *S*.
9 at the entering in of the gate of *S*;
22. 9 caught him, (for he was hid in *S*,)
25.13 Judah, from *S*...unto Beth-horon,
24 hostages also, and returned to *S*.
28. 8 them, and brought the spoil to *S*.
9 out before the host that came to *S*,
15 brethren: then they returned to *S*.
Ezr 4.10 and set in the cities of *S*, and the
17 their companions that dwell in *S*,
Neh 4. 2 his brethren and the army of *S*,
Isa 7. 9 And the head of Ephraim is *S*, and
9 the head of *S* is Remaliah's son.
8. 4 the spoil of *S* shall be taken away
9. 9 Ephraim and the inhabitant of *S*,
10. 9 as Arpad? is not *S* as Damascus?
10 excel them of Jerusalem and of *S*;
11 I have done unto *S* and her idols,
36.19 they delivered *S* out of my hand?
Jer 23.13 seen folly in the prophets of *S*;
31. 5 vines upon the mountains of *S*:
41. 5 and from *S*, even fourscore men,
Eze 16.46 thine elder sister is *S*, she and her
51 Neither hath *S* committed half of
53 captivity of *S* and her daughters,
55 *S* and her daughters shall return
23. 4 *S* is Aholah, and Jerusalem
33 with the cup of thy sister *S*.
Hos 7. 1 and the wickedness of *S*: for they
8. 5 Thy calf, O *S*, hath cast thee off;
6 calf of *S* shall be broken in pieces.
10. 5 inhabitants of *S* shall fear because
7 As for *S*, her king is cut off as the
13.16 *S* shall become desolate; for she
Am 3. 9 upon the mountains of *S*, and
12 Israel be taken out that dwell in *S*
4. 1 that are in the mountain of *S*,
6. 1 and trust in the mountain of *S*,
8.14 that sware by the sin of *S*, and say,
Ob 19 of Ephraim, and the fields of *S*:
Mic 1. 1 saw concerning *S* and Jerusalem.
5 transgression of Jacob? is it not *S*?
6 will make *S* as an heap of the field,
Lk 17.11 he passed through the midst of *S*
Jn 4. 4 And he must needs go through *S*.
5 cometh he to a city of *S*, which
7 a woman of *S* to draw water:
9 saith the woman of *S* unto him,
9 of me, which am a woman of *S*?
Ac 1. 8 and in *S*, and unto the uttermost
8. 1 the regions of Judea and *S*, except
5 Philip went down to the city of *S*,
9 and bewitched the people of *S*,
14 *S* had received the word of God,
9.31 all Judea and Galilee and *S*, and
15. 3 passed through Phenice and *S*,

SAMARITAN

Lk 10.33 But a certain *S*, as he journeyed,
17.16 him thanks: and he was a *S*.
Jn 8.48 Say we not well that thou art a *S*,

SAMARITANS

2Ki 17.29 places which the *S* had made,
Mt 10. 5 into any city of the *S* enter...not:
Lk 9.52 and entered into a village of the *S*,
Jn 4. 9 Jews have no dealings with the *S*.)
39 many of the *S* of that city believed
40 when the *S* were come unto him,
Ac 8.25 gospel in many villages of the *S*.

SAME

Gen 15.18 *s* day the Lord made a covenant
Lev 23.28 ye shall do no work in that *s* day:
1Ki 8.64 The *s* day did the king hallow the
2Ch 35.16 service...was prepared the *s* day,
Job 4. 8 and sow wickedness, reap the *s*.
13. 2 What ye know, the *s* do I know also:
Ps 102.27 But thou art the *s*, and thy years
113. 3 the sun unto the going down of the *s*
Ec 9.15 man remembered that *s* poor man.
Eze 3.18 the *s* wicked man shall die in his
Mal 1.11 even unto the going down of the *s*
Mt 5.19 the *s* shall be called great in the
10.19 that *s* hour what ye shall speak.
12.50 the *s* is my brother, and sister, and
18. 4 the *s* is greatest in the kingdom
21.42 *s* is become the head of the corner:
26.48 Whomsoever I...kiss, that *s* is he:
Mk 3.35 the *s* is my brother, and my sister,
8.35 the gospel's, the *s* shall save it.
9.35 to be first, the *s* shall be last of all.
14.44 Whomsoever I...kiss, that *s* is he;
Lk 6.33 ye? for sinners also do even the *s*.
38 *s* measure that ye mete withal it
7.47 little is forgiven, the *s* loveth little.
9.24 for my sake, the *s* shall save it.
48 among you all, the *s* shall be great.
12.12 in the *s* hour what ye ought to say.
20.17 *s* is become...head of the corner?
23.12 And the *s* day Pilate and Herod
40 thou art in the *s* condemnation?
Jn 1. 2 *s* was in the beginning with God.
7 The *s* came for a witness, to bear
3. 2 The *s* came to Jesus by night, and
7.18 *s* is true, and no unrighteousness
10. 1 way, the *s* is a thief and a robber.
Ac 1.11 *s* Jesus, which is taken up from
2.36 that God hath made that *s* Jesus,
7.35 *s* did God send to be a ruler and a
Ro 1.32 not only do the *s*, but have pleasure
2. 1 that judgest doest the *s* things.
3 and doest the *s*, that thou shalt
10.12 for the *s* Lord over all is rich unto
12.16 Be of the *s* mind one toward
1Co 1.10 that ye all speak the *s* thing, and
10. 3 did all eat the *s* spiritual meat;
4 did all drink the *s* spiritual drink:
11.25 *s* manner also he took the cup,
12. 4 diversities of gifts, but the *s* Spirit.
5 of administrations, but the *s* Lord.
6 it is the *s* God which worketh all
8 word of knowledge by the *s* Spirit;
15.39 All flesh is not the *s* flesh: but
2Co 4.13 We having the *s* spirit of faith,
12.18 walked we not in the *s* spirit?
Php 3. 1 To write the *s* things to you, to me
16 let us walk by the *s* rule, let us
16 rule, let us mind the *s* thing.
Heb 1.12 but thou art the *s*, and thy years
13. 8 Jesus Christ the *s* yesterday, and
Jas 3.10 Out of the *s* mouth proceedeth
11 the *s* place sweet water and bitter?
1Pe 2. 7 *s* is made the head of the corner,
1Jn 2.23 Son, the *s* hath not the Father:
Rev 3. 5 the *s* shall be clothed in white

SAMSON

Jdg 13.24 a son, and called his name *S*:
14. 1 And *S* went down to Timnath, and
3 *S* said unto his father, Get her for
5 Then went *S* down, and his father
7 woman; and she pleased *S* well,
10 and *S* made there a feast; for so
12 *S* said unto them, I will now put
15. 1 that *S* visited his wife with a kid;
3 And *S* said concerning them,
4 *S* went and caught three hundred
6 *S*, the son in law of the Timnite,
7 *S* said unto them, Though ye have
10 To bind *S* are we come up, to do
11 said to *S*, Knowest thou not that
12 *S* said unto them, Swear unto me,

SAMSON

Judge of Israel, 12th–11th centuries B.C.; endowed with superhuman strength; born to Manoah and his previously barren wife, of the tribe of Dan, after meetings with an angel who stipulates that their son be a Nazarite, devoted to God from the womb (Jdg 13); to his parents' dismay, courts a Philistine woman from nearby Timnah; kills a lion with his bare hands, and later finds a swarm of bees and honey in its carcass; at the wedding feast, makes a wager with 30 Philistine guests about a riddle, "Out of the eater came forth meat, and out of the strong came forth sweetness"; they force his bride to learn the solution and tell them; angrily pays the wager, 30 sets of garments, taken from 30 men whom he slays in Ashkelon (Jdg 14); after an absence, discovers his wife has been given to another man and retaliates by burning the Philistines' grain; they in turn burn his wife and her father, and are themselves slaughtered by Samson; his own people, fearing reprisal, leave him bound for the Philistines to capture, but he bursts his bonds and kills a thousand men with the jawbone of an ass (Jdg 15); besieged in Gaza at a harlot's house, he carries the city gates to Hebron; takes another Philistine woman, Delilah, who is bribed by his enemies to discover the source of his strength; after three attempts, she learns it is in his hair, uncut in accordance with Nazarite vow; shorn in his sleep, is blinded and taken captive to Gaza; gains final revenge by pulling down on himself a temple filled with thousands of Philistines gathered for a religious celebration (Jdg 16).

16 *S* said, With the jawbone of an ass,
16. 1 Then went *S* to Gaza, and saw
2 Gazites, saying, *S* is come hither.
3 And *S* lay till midnight, and arose
6 And Delilah said to *S*, Tell me, I
7 *S* said unto her, If they bind me
9 The Philistines be upon thee, *S*.
10 And Delilah said unto *S*, Behold,
12 The Philistines be upon thee, *S*.
13 And Delilah said unto *S*, Hitherto
14, 20 The Philistines be upon thee, *S*.
23 delivered *S* our enemy into our
25 Call for *S*, that he may make us
25 they called for *S* out of the prison
26 *S* said unto the lad that held him
27 that beheld while *S* made sport.
28 *S* called unto the Lord, and said,
29 And *S* took hold of the two middle
30 And *S* said, Let me die with the
Heb 11.32 Barak, and of *S*, and of Jephthae;

SAMUEL

1Sa 1.20 a son, and called his name *S*,
2.18 But *S* ministered before the Lord,
21 the child *S* grew before the Lord.
26 the child *S* grew on, and was in
3. 1 child *S* ministered unto the Lord
3 was, and *S* was laid down to sleep:
4 That the Lord called *S*: and he
6 And the Lord called yet again, *S*.
6 *S* arose and went to Eli, and said,
7 Now *S* did not yet know the Lord,
8 the Lord called *S* again the third
9 Eli said unto *S*, Go, lie down: and
9 *S* went and lay down in his place.
10 and called as at other times, *S*, *S*.
10 Then *S* answered, Speak; for thy
11 the Lord said to *S*, Behold, I will
15 And *S* lay until the morning, and
15 *S* feared to show Eli the vision.
16 Eli called *S*, and said, *S*, my son.
18 *S* told him every whit, and hid
19 *S* grew, and the Lord was with
20 knew that *S* was established to be
21 for the Lord revealed himself to *S*
4. 1 the word of *S* came to all Israel.
7. 3 *S* spake unto all the house of
5 And *S* said, Gather all Israel to
6 *S* judged the children of Israel in
8 the children of Israel said to *S*,
9 And *S* took a sucking lamb, and
9 *S* cried unto the Lord for Israel;
10 as *S* was offering up the burnt
12 Then *S* took a stone, and set it
13 the Philistines all the days of *S*.
15 *S* judged Israel all the days of his
8. 1 when *S* was old, that he made his
4 and came to *S* unto Ramah,
6 But the thing displeased *S*, when
6 us. And *S* prayed unto the Lord.
7 the Lord said unto *S*, Hearken
10 *S* told all the words of the Lord
19 refused to obey the voice of *S*;
21 And *S* heard all the words of the
22 the Lord said to *S*, Hearken unto
22 And *S* said unto the men of Israel,
9.14 behold, *S* came out against them;
15 Now the Lord had told *S* in his ear
17 when *S* saw Saul, the Lord said
18 Saul drew near to *S* in the gate,
19 *S* answered Saul,...I am the seer:
22 And *S* took Saul and his servant,
23 And *S* said unto the cook, Bring
24 *S* said, Behold that which is left!
24 So Saul did eat with *S* that day.
25 *S* communed with Saul upon the top
26 *S* called Saul to the top of the
26 went out both of them, he and *S*,
27 *S* said to Saul, Bid the servant pass
10. 1 *S* took a vial of oil, and poured it
9 had turned his back to go from *S*,

Samson pulls the Philistine temple down on himself and 3,000 worshipers of Dagon (Jdg 16.23-30).

14 they were no where, we came to *S*.
15 Tell me,...what *S* said unto you.
16 of the kingdom, whereof *S* spake,
17 And *S* called the people together
20 when *S* had caused all the tribes of
24 *S* said to all the people, See ye him
25 *S* told the people the manner of
25 And *S* sent all the people away,
11. 7 not forth after Saul and after *S*,
12 the people said unto *S*, Who is he
14 Then said *S* to the people, Come,
12. 1 And *S* said unto all Israel, Behold,
6 *S* said unto...people, It is the Lord
11 Lord sent...Jephthah, and *S*, and
18 So *S* called unto the Lord; and the
18 greatly feared the Lord and *S*.

19 people said unto *S*, Pray for thy
20 *S* said unto the people, Fear not:
13. 8 the set time that *S* had appointed:
8 but *S* came not to Gilgal; and the
10 *S* came; and Saul went out to meet
11 And *S* said, What hast thou done?
13 And *S* said to Saul, Thou hast done
15 And *S* arose, and gat him up from
15. 1 *S*...said unto Saul, The Lord sent
10 came the word of the Lord unto *S*,
11 And it grieved *S*; and he cried unto
12 when *S* rose early to meet Saul in
12 it was told *S*, saying, Saul came
13 And *S* came to Saul: and Saul said
14 *S* said, What meaneth then this
16 *S* said unto Saul, Stay, and I will

SAMUEL

Prophet and last of Israel's Judges, 11th century B.C.; prayed for by Hannah and presented as a child to the priest Eli for the service of God in the shrine at Shiloh (1Sa 1); is called in his sleep by God, who reveals the judgment decreed upon Eli's house; reluctantly recounts his vision to Eli; as he grows older, reputation as a prophet spreads throughout Israel (1Sa 3); after long period of Philistine encroachment assembles the Israelites at Mizpeh and exhorts them to repentance and supplication; when the Philistines threaten, invokes God's help; erects a stone to commemorate the ensuing victory; makes a yearly circuit judging Israel (1Sa 7); appoints his sons as judges, but they prove worthless; is angered by Israel's request for a king, but is told by God to grant it; warns of the consequences (1Sa 8); secretly anoints Saul as God instructed, and predicts signs to confirm his choice (1Sa 9.1–10.8); gathers the Israelites at Mizpeh and, after chiding them for rebellion, conducts the sacred lot and announces the selection of Saul as king (1Sa 10.17-27); addresses Israel at Gilgal, defending his integrity and exhorting king and people to fear and serve God (1Sa 12); rebukes Saul for offering sacrifice in his absence and announces God's rejection of his kingship (1Sa 13); later rebukes Saul for failing to completely destroy the Amalekites and again announces his rejection as king; slays Agag, the Amalekite king (1Sa 15); obeying God's instructions, anoints David to replace Saul (1Sa 16); dies and is buried in his house at Ramah (1Sa 25.1).

1Sa 15.17 And *S* said, When thou wast little
20 And Saul said unto *S*, Yea, I have
22 And *S* said, Hath the Lord as great
24 Saul said unto *S*, I have sinned:
26 *S* said unto Saul, I will not return
27 And as *S* turned about to go away,
28 And *S* said...The Lord hath rent
31 So *S* turned again after Saul; and
32 Then said *S*, Bring ye hither to me
33 *S* said, As thy sword hath made
33 *S* hewed Agag in pieces before the
34 Then *S* went to Ramah; and Saul
35 *S* came no more to see Saul until
35 nevertheless *S* mourned for Saul:
16. 1 the Lord said unto *S*, How long
2 And *S* said, How can I go? if Saul
4 *S* did that which the Lord spake,
7 Lord said unto *S*, Look not on his
8 and made him pass before *S*.
10 seven of his sons to pass before *S*.
10 *S* said unto Jesse, The Lord hath
11 *S* said unto Jesse, Are here all thy
11 *S* said unto Jesse, Send and fetch
13 Then *S* took the horn of oil, and
13 So *S* rose up, and went to Ramah.
19.18 escaped, and came to *S* to Ramah,
18 he and *S* went and dwelt in Naioth.
20 *S* standing as appointed over them,
22 and said, Where are *S* and David?
24 and prophesied before *S* in like
25. 1 And *S* died; and all the Israelites
28. 3 Now *S* was dead, and all Israel had
11 thee? And he said, Bring me up *S*.
12 when the woman saw *S*, she cried
14 And Saul perceived that it was *S*,
15 And *S* said to Saul, Why hast thou
16 Then said *S*, Wherefore then dost
20 afraid, because of the words of *S*:
1Ch 6.28 the sons of *S*; the firstborn Vashni,
9.22 David and *S* the seer did ordain
11. 3 to the word of the Lord by *S*.
26.28 And all that *S* the seer, and Saul
29.29 written in the book of *S* the seer,
2Ch 35.18 from the days of *S* the prophet;
Ps 99. 6 and *S* among them that call upon
Jer 15. 1 Though Moses and *S* stood before
Ac 3.24 Yea, and all the prophets from *S*
13.20 and fifty years, until *S* the prophet.
Heb 11.32 of David also, and *S*, and of the

SANCTIFICATION

1Co 1.30 righteousness,...*s*, and redemption:
1Th 4. 3 this is the will of God, even your *s*,
4 possess his vessel in *s* and honor;
2Th 2.13 to salvation through *s* of the Spirit
1Pe 1. 2 Father, through *s* of the Spirit, unto

SANCTIFIED

Gen 2. 3 blessed the seventh day, and *s* it:
Lev 8.30 and *s* Aaron, and his garments,
10. 3 I will be *s* in them that come nigh
27.15 if he that *s* it will redeem his house,
1Sa 16. 5 And he *s* Jesse and his sons, and
2Ch 7.16 have I chosen and *s* this house,
20 house, which I have *s* for my name,
30. 3 had not *s* themselves sufficiently,
8 sanctuary, which he hath *s* for ever:
Isa 5.16 is holy shall be *s* in righteousness.
Jer 1. 5 camest...out of the womb I *s* thee,
Eze 36.23 shall be *s* in you before their eyes.
Jn 10.36 whom the Father hath *s*, and sent
17.19 also might be *s* through the truth.
Ac 20.32 among all them which are *s*.
26.18 among them which are *s* by faith
Ro 15.16 being *s* by the Holy Ghost.
1Co 1. 2 to them that are *s* in Christ Jesus,
6.11 but ye are washed, but ye are *s*, but
7.14 unbelieving husband is *s* by the wife,
14 unbelieving wife is *s* by the husband:
1Ti 4. 5 For it is *s* by the word of God and
2Ti 2.21 *s*, and meet for the master's use, and
Heb 2.11 that sanctifieth and they who are *s*
10.10 By the which will we are *s* through
14 perfected for ever them that are *s*.
29 of the covenant, wherewith he was *s*,
Jude 1 them that are *s* by God the Father,

SANCTIFIETH

Mt 23.17 gold, or the temple that *s* the gold?
19 the gift, or the altar that *s* the gift?
Heb 2.11 that *s* and they who are sanctified
9.13 *s* to the purifying of the flesh:

SANCTIFY

Ex 13. 2 *S* unto me all the firstborn,
28.41 and consecrate them, and *s* them,
29.44 And I will *s* the tabernacle of the
31.13 that I am the Lord that doth *s* you.
Lev 20. 7 *S* yourselves therefore, and be ye
8 them: I am the Lord which *s* you.
27.14 when a man shall *s* his house to
Dt 5.12 Keep the sabbath day to *s* it, as the
15.19 shalt *s* unto the Lord thy God:
2Ch 29. 5 me, ye Levites, *s* now yourselves,
5 and *s* the house of the Lord God of
35. 6 kill the passover, and *s* yourselves,
Isa 8.13 *S* the Lord of hosts himself; and
29.23 of him, they shall *s* my name,
23 and *s* the Holy One of Jacob, and
Eze 37.28 know that I the Lord do *s* Israel,
Joel 1.14 *S* ye a fast, call a solemn assembly,
2.15 *s* a fast, call a solemn assembly:
16 *s* the congregation, assemble the
Jn 17.17 *S* them through thy truth: thy
19 for their sakes I *s* myself, that they
Eph 5.26 he might *s* and cleanse it with the
1Th 5.23 the very God of peace *s* you wholly;
Heb 13.12 he might *s* the people with his own
1Pe 3.15 But *s* the Lord God in your hearts:

SANCTUARIES

Lev 21.23 that he profane not my *s*: for I
26.31 and bring your *s* unto desolation,
Jer 51.51 strangers are come into the *s* of
Eze 28.18 Thou hast defiled thy *s* by the
Am 7. 9 the *s* of Israel shall be laid waste;

SANCTUARY

Ex 15.17 *S*, O Lord, which thy hands have
36. 1 of work for the service of the *s*,
Lev 16.33 make an atonement for the holy *s*,
19.30 my sabbaths, and reverence my *s*:
21.12 nor profane the *s* of his God; for
Nu 18. 1 shall bear the iniquity of the *s*:
1Ch 22.19 build ye the *s* of the Lord God,
2Ch 30.19 to the purification of the *s*.
Ps 20. 2 Send thee help from the *s*, and
73.17 Until I went into the *s* of God;
77.13 Thy way, O God, is in the *s*: who is
96. 6 strength and beauty are in his *s*.
134. 2 Lift up your hands in the *s*, and
150. 1 Praise God in his *s*: praise him
Isa 16.12 that he shall come to his *s* to pray;
60.13 to beautify the place of my *s*;
La 2. 7 he hath abhorred his *s*, he hath
20 prophet be slain in...*s* of the Lord?
Eze 8. 6 that I should go far off from my *s*?
9. 6 is the mark; and begin at my *s*.
11.16 yet will I be to them as a little *s* in
25. 3 thou saidst, Aha, against my *s*,
37.26 will set my *s* in the midst of them
44. 7 have brought into my *s* strangers,
8 set keepers of my charge in my *s*
11 they shall be ministers in my *s*,
48.10 *s* of the Lord shall be in the midst
Dan 9.17 cause thy face to shine upon thy *s*
Zep 3. 4 her priests have polluted the *s*,
Heb 8. 2 A minister of the *s*, and of the true
9. 1 of divine service, and a worldly *s*.
2 shewbread; which is called the *s*.
13.11 whose blood is brought into the *s*

SAND

Gen 22.17 *s* which is upon the sea shore;
32.12 make thy seed as the *s* of the sea,
Ex 2.12 the Egyptian, and hid him in the *s*.
Dt 33.19 seas, and of treasures hid in the *s*.
Jos 11. 4 as the *s* that is upon the sea shore
Jdg 7.12 the *s* by the sea side for multitude.
Job 29.18 I shall multiply my days as the *s*.
Ps 139.18 are more in number than the *s*:
Jer 33.22 neither the *s* of the sea measured:
Hos 1.10 Israel shall be as the *s* of the sea,
Mt 7.26 which built his house upon the *s*:
Ro 9.27 of Israel be as the *s* of the sea,
Heb 11.12 as the *s* which is by the sea shore
Rev 13. 1 And I stood upon the *s* of the sea,
20. 8 the number...is as the *s* of the sea.

SANDALS

Mk 6. 9 But be shod with *s*; and not put
Ac 12. 8 Gird thyself, and bind on thy *s*.

SANG

Ex 15. 1 Then *s* Moses and the children of
Nu 21.17 Then Israel *s* this song, Spring up,
Jdg 5. 1 Then *s* Deborah and Barak the
1Sa 29. 5 Is not this David, of whom they *s*
2Ch 29.28 the singers *s*, and the trumpeters
30 they *s* praises with gladness, and
Ezr 3.11 And they *s* together by course in
Neh 12.42 the singers *s* loud, with Jezrahiah
Job 38. 7 the morning stars *s* together, and
Ps 106.12 they his words; they *s* his praise.
Ac 16.25 prayed, and *s* praises unto God:

SANK
Ex 15. 5 they *s* into the bottom as a stone.
10 *s* as lead in the mighty waters.

SAP
Ps104. 16 The trees of the Lord are full of *s*;

SAPPHIRA
Ac 5. 1 named Ananias, with *S* his wife,

SAPPHIRE
Ex 24.10 were a paved work of a *s* stone,
28.18 row shall be an emerald, a *s*, and
39.11 the second row, an emerald, a *s*,
Job 28.16 with the precious onyx, or the *s*.
La 4. 7 rubies, their polishing was of *s*:
Eze 1.26 as the appearance of a *s* stone:
10. 1 over them as it were a *s* stone, as
28.13 and the jasper, the *s*, the emerald,
Rev 21.19 was jasper; the second, *s*; the

SAPPHIRES
Job 28. 6 stones of it are the place of *s*: and
SS 5.14 is as bright ivory overlaid with *s*.
Isa 54.11 and lay thy foundations with *s*.

SARAH
Gen 17.15 Sarai, but *S* shall her name be.
17 shall *S*, that is ninety years old,
19 *S* thy wife shall bear thee a son
21 which *S* shall bear unto thee at
18. 6 hastened into the tent unto *S*, and
9 unto him, Where is *S* thy wife?
10 lo, *S* thy wife shall have a son.
10 *S* heard it in the tent door, which
11 Abraham and *S* were old and well
11 with *S* after the manner of women.
12 *S* laughed within herself, saying,
13 Wherefore did *S* laugh, saying,
14 of life, and *S* shall have a son.
15 *S* denied, saying, I laughed not;
20. 2 Abraham said of *S* his wife, She is
2 king of Gerar sent, and took *S*.
14 and restored him *S* his wife.
16 And unto *S* he said, Behold, I have
18 because of *S* Abraham's wife.
21. 1 the Lord visited *S* as he had said,
1 Lord did unto *S* as he had spoken.
2 *S* conceived, and bare Abraham a
3 him, whom *S* bare to him, Isaac.
6 And *S* said, God hath made me to
7 *S* should have given children suck?
9 And *S* saw the son of Hagar the
12 in all that *S* hath said unto thee,
23. 1 *S* was an hundred and seven and
1 were the years of the life of *S*.
2 *S* died in Kirjath-arba; the same
2 and Abraham came to mourn for *S*,
19 Abraham buried *S* his wife in the
24.36 *S* my master's wife bare a son to
25.10 Abraham buried, and *S* his wife.
49.31 buried Abraham and *S* his wife;
Nu 26.46 of the daughter of Asher was *S*.
Isa 51. 2 father, and unto *S* that bare you:
Ro 9. 9 I come, and *S* shall have a son.

SARAH

Wife of Abraham and mother of Isaac; at first called Sarai; childless when she accompanies Abraham from Mesopotamia to Canaan (Gen 11.29–12.5) and remains so for many years; on a visit to Egypt her beauty attracts the Egyptians, and Abraham, thinking to save himself, pretends that she is his sister; Pharaoh, after taking her into his harem, learns of the deception and sends them both away (Gen 12); distressed over barrenness, gives her maid, Hagar, to Abraham; but when Hagar becomes pregnant with Ishmael, grows jealous and urges Abraham to reject her (Gen 16); God tells Abraham that Sarai herself will have a son and that her name should be changed to Sarah (Gen 17); overhearing visitors confirming the news, she laughs, being now old, and is chided for lack of faith (Gen 18); in Gerar, Abraham pretends a second time that she is his sister, and a second time trouble ensues (Gen 20); gives birth to Isaac and again laughs, this time in joy; grows jealous once more and has Hagar and Ishmael banished (Gen 21); dies and is buried in cave at Machpelah bought by Abraham (Gen 23).

SARDINE
Rev 4. 3 upon like a jasper and a *s* stone:

SARDIS
Rev 1.11 and unto Thyatira, and unto *S*,
3. 1 the angel of the church in *S* write;
4 Thou hast a few names even in *S*

SARDIUS
Ex 28.17 the first row shall be a *s*, a topaz,
39.10 the first row was a *s*, a topaz, and
Eze 28.13 covering, the *s*, and the diamond,
Rev 21.20 The fifth, sardonyx; the sixth, *s*;

SAT
Gen 18. 1 he *s* in the tent door in the heat
19. 1 and Lot *s* in the gate of Sodom:
Ex 16. 3 when we *s* by the flesh pots, and
32. 6 people *s* down to eat and to drink,
Jdg 20.26 wept, and *s* there before the Lord.
Ru 2.14 And she *s* beside the reapers: and
1Ki 19. 4 and *s* down under a juniper tree:
2Ki 6.32 But Elisha *s* in his house, and the
32 house, and the elders *s* with him;
Ezr 9. 3 of my beard, and *s* down astonied.
4 and I *s* astonied until the evening
10. 9 *s* in the street of the house of God,
Neh 1. 4 I *s* down and wept, and mourned
Job 2. 8 and he *s* down among the ashes.
29.25 I chose out their way, and *s* chief,
Ps 26. 4 I have not *s* with vain persons,
137. 1 rivers of Babylon, there we *s* down,
Jer 15.17 I *s* not in the assembly of the
17 I *s* alone because of thy hand: for
Eze 3.15 of Chebar, and I *s* where they *s*,
Jon 3. 6 with sackcloth, and *s* in ashes.
4. 5 booth, and *s* under it in the shadow,
Mt 4.16 The people which *s* in darkness
16 which *s* in the region and shadow
9.10 as Jesus *s* at meat in the house,
10 and *s* down with him and his
13. 1 the house, and *s* by the sea side.
2 that he went into a ship, and *s*;
48 they drew to shore, and *s* down,
14. 9 them which *s* with him at meat,
15.29 a mountain, and *s* down there.
24. 3 as he *s* upon the mount of Olives,
26. 7 it on his head, as he *s* at meat.
20 come, he *s* down with the twelve.
55 I *s* daily with you teaching in the
58 went in, and *s* with the servants,
69 Now Peter *s* without in the palace:
28. 2 stone from the door, and *s* upon it.
Mk 2.15 as Jesus *s* at meat in his house,
15 sinners *s* also together with Jesus
3.32 And the multitude *s* about him,
34 looked...on them which *s* about him,
4. 1 into a ship, and *s* in the sea;
6.22 Herod and them that *s* with him,
26 for their sakes which *s* with him,
40 they *s* down in ranks, by hundreds,
9.35 he *s* down, and called the twelve,
10.46 *s* by the highway side begging.
11. 2 colt tied, whereon never man *s*;
7 on him; and he *s* upon him.
12.41 Jesus *s* over against the treasury,
13. 3 as he *s* upon the mount of Olives
14. 3 as he *s* at meat,...came a woman
18 as they *s* and did eat, Jesus said,
54 and he *s* with the servants, and
16.14 unto the eleven as they *s* at meat,
19 and *s* on the right hand of God.
Lk 4.20 again to the minister, and *s* down.
5. 3 *s* down, and taught the people out
29 of others that *s* down with them.
7.15 he that was dead *s* up, and began
36 house, and *s* down to meat.
37 knew that Jesus *s* at meat in the
49 And they that *s* at meat with him
10.39 Mary which also *s* at Jesus' feet,
11.37 he went in, and *s* down to meat.
14.15 one of them that *s* at meat with
18.35 blind man *s* by the way side
19.30 tied, whereon never yet man *s*:
22.14 the hour was come, he *s* down, and
55 Peter *s* down among them.
56 maid beheld him as he *s* by the
24.30 as he *s* at meat with them, he took
Jn 4. 6 his journey, *s* thus on the well:
6. 3 and there he *s* with his disciples.
10 So the men *s* down, in number
8. 2 and he *s* down, and taught them.
9. 8 Is not this he that *s* and begged?
11.20 him: but Mary *s* still in the house.
12. 2 them that *s* at the table with him.
14 had found a young ass, *s* thereon;
19.13 *s* down in the judgment seat in a
Ac 2. 3 of fire, and it *s* upon each of them.
3.10 it was he which *s* for alms at the
6.15 all that *s* in the council, looking
9.40 and when she saw Peter, she *s* up.
12.21 *s* upon his throne, and made an
13.14 on the sabbath day, and *s* down.
14. 8 there *s* a certain man at Lystra,
16.13 and we *s* down, and spake unto
20. 9 And there *s* in a window a certain
25.17 I *s* on the judgment seat, and
26.30 Bernice,...they that *s* with them:
1Co 10. 7 people *s* down to eat and drink,
Heb 1. 3 *s* down on the right hand of the
10.12 *s* down on the right hand of God;
Rev 4. 2 heaven, and one *s* on the throne.
3 he that *s* was to look upon like a
9 thanks to him that *s* on the throne,
10 before him that *s* on the throne,
5. 1 hand of him that *s* on the throne
7 hand of him that *s* upon the throne.
6. 2 he that *s* on him had a bow; and a
4 was given to him that *s* thereon to
5 *s* on him had a pair of balances
8 his name that *s* on him was Death,
9.17 and them that *s* on them, having
11.16 which *s* before God on their seats,
14.14 one *s* like unto the Son of man,
15 voice to him that *s* on the cloud,
16 *s* on the cloud thrust in his sickle
19. 4 God that *s* on the throne, saying,
11 *s* upon him was called Faithful
19 against him that *s* on the horse,
21 sword of him that *s* upon the horse,
20. 4 thrones, and they *s* upon them,
11 white throne, and him that *s* on
21. 5 he that *s* upon the throne said,

SATAN
1Ch 21. 1 *S* stood up against Israel, and
Job 1. 6 and *S* came also among them.
7 Lord said unto *S*, Whence comest
7 *S* answered the Lord, and said,
8 the Lord said unto *S*, Hast thou
9 *S* answered the Lord, and said,

BIBLICAL THEMES

SATAN

Now the serpent was more subtil than any beast of the field which the Lord God had made. Gen 3.1

And the Lord God said unto the serpent, Because thou hast done this, thou art cursed above all cattle, and above every beast of the field; upon thy belly shalt thou go, and dust shalt thou eat all the days of thy life. Gen 3.14

Now there was a day when the sons of God came to present themselves before the Lord, and Satan came also among them. And the Lord said unto Satan, Whence comest thou? Then Satan answered the Lord, and said, From going to and fro in the earth, and from walking up and down in it. Job 1.6-7

How art thou fallen from heaven, O Lucifer, son of the morning! Isa 14.12

In that day the Lord with his sore and great and strong sword shall punish leviathan . . . that crooked serpent; and he shall slay the dragon that is in the sea. Isa 27.1

And he shewed me Joshua the high priest standing before the angel of the Lord, and Satan standing at his right hand to resist him. And the Lord said unto Satan, . . . the Lord that hath chosen Jerusalem rebuke thee: is not this a brand plucked out of the fire? Zec 3.1-2

Again, the devil taketh him up into an exceeding high mountain, and sheweth him all the kingdoms of the world, and the glory of them; and saith unto him, All these things will I give thee, if thou wilt fall down and worship me. Then saith Jesus unto him, Get thee hence, Satan. Mt 4.8-10

The scribes . . . said, He hath Beelzebub, and by the prince of the devils casteth he out devils. And he called them unto him, and said . . . How can Satan cast out Satan? Mk 3.22-23

And the seventy returned again with joy, saying, Lord, even the devils are subject unto us through thy name. And he said unto them, I beheld Satan as lightning fall from heaven. Lk 10.17-18

Then entered Satan into Judas surnamed Iscariot, being of the number of the twelve. And he went his way, and communed with the chief priests and captains, how he might betray [Jesus] unto them. Lk 22.3, 6

The god of this world hath blinded the minds of them which believe not, lest the light of the glorious gospel of Christ . . . should shine unto them. 2Co 4.4

What communion hath light with darkness? And what concord hath Christ with Belial? 2Co 6.14-15

Put on the whole armor of God, that ye may be able to stand against the wiles of the devil. For we wrestle not against flesh and blood, but against principalities, against powers, against the rulers of the darkness of this world, against spiritual wickedness in high places. Eph 6.11-12

Forasmuch . . . as the children are partakers of flesh and blood, he also himself likewise took part of the same; that through death he might destroy him that had the power of death, that is, the devil; and deliver them who through fear of death were all their lifetime subject to bondage. Heb 2.14-15

Be sober, be vigilant; because your adversary the devil, as a roaring lion, walketh about, seeking whom he may devour. 1Pe 5.8

And there was war in heaven. . . . And the great dragon . . . that old serpent, called the Devil, and Satan, which deceiveth the whole world: he was cast out into the earth. Rev 12.7, 9

Job 1.12 Lord said unto *S*, Behold, all that
12 *S* went forth from the presence of
2. 1 and *S* came also among them to
2 Lord said unto *S*, From whence
2 *S* answered the Lord, and said,
3 the Lord said unto *S*, Hast thou
4 *S* answered the Lord, and said,
6 Lord said unto *S*, Behold, he is in
7 went *S* forth from the presence of
Ps 109. 6 and let *S* stand at his right hand.
Zec 3. 1 *S* standing at his right hand to
2 the Lord said unto *S*, The Lord
2 Lord rebuke thee, O *S*; even the
Mt 4.10 unto him, Get thee hence, *S*:
12.26 And if *S* cast out *S*, he is divided
16.23 Get thee behind me, *S*: thou art
Mk 1.13 forty days, tempted of *S*; and was
3.23 parables, How can *S* cast out *S*?
26 *S* rise up against himself, and be
4.15 *S* cometh immediately, and taketh
8.33 saying, Get thee behind me, *S*:
Lk 4. 8 unto him, Get thee behind me, *S*:
10.18 I beheld *S* as lightning fall from
11.18 *S* also be divided against himself,
13.16 of Abraham, whom *S* hath bound,
22. 3 Then entered *S* into Judas
31 *S* hath desired to have you, that
Jn 13.27 after the sop *S* entered into him.
Ac 5. 3 why hath *S* filled thine heart to lie
26.18 from the power of *S* unto God, that
Ro 16.20 bruise *S* under your feet shortly.
1Co 5. 5 To deliver such an one unto *S*
7. 5 that *S* tempt you not for your
2Co 2.11 *S* should get an advantage of us:
11.14 *S* himself is transformed into an
12. 7 the messenger of *S* to buffet me,
1Th 2.18 and again; but *S* hindered us.
2Th 2. 9 is after the working of *S* with all
1Ti 1.20 whom I have delivered unto *S*,
5.15 are already turned aside after *S*.
Rev 2. 9 not, but are the synagogue of *S*.
13 slain among you, where *S* dwelleth.
24 have not known the depths of *S*,
3. 9 make them of the synagogue of *S*,
12. 9 serpent, called the Devil, and *S*,
20. 2 serpent, which is the Devil, and *S*,
7 *S* shall be loosed out of his prison,

SATAN'S

Rev 2.13 dwellest, even where *S* seat is:

SATEST

Ps 9. 4 *s* in the throne judging right.
Eze 23.41 *s* upon a stately bed, and a table

SATIATE

Jer 31.14 And I will *s* the soul of the priests
46.10 and it shall be *s* and made drunk

SATIATED

Jer 31.25 I have *s* the weary soul, and I

SATISFACTION

Nu 35.31 no *s* for the life of a murderer,
32 no *s* for him that is fled to the city

SATISFIED

Lev 26.26 and ye shall eat, and not be *s*.
Dt 14.29 shall come, and shall eat and be *s*;
Job 27.14 offspring shall not be *s* with bread.
Ps 22.26 The meek shall eat and be *s*: they
36. 8 They shall be abundantly *s* with
65. 4 we shall be *s* with the goodness of
105.40 *s* them with the bread of heaven.
Pr 12.11 He that tilleth his land shall be *s*
14.14 a good man shall be *s* from himself.
27.20 so the eyes of man are never *s*.
30.15 are three things that are never *s*,
Ec 1. 8 the eye is not *s* with seeing, nor
4. 8 neither is his eye *s* with riches;
5.10 He that loveth silver shall not be *s*
Isa 44.16 flesh; he roasteth roast, and is *s*:
53.11 travail of his soul, and shall be *s*:
La 5. 6 the Assyrians, to be *s* with bread.
Joel 2.26 ye shall eat in plenty, and be *s*,
Am 4. 8 drink water; but they were not *s*:
Mic 6.14 Thou shalt eat, but not be *s*; and
Hab 2. 5 and is as death, and cannot be *s*,

SATISFIEST

Ps 145.16 *s* the desire of every living thing.

SATISFIETH

Ps 103. 5 *s* thy mouth with good things;
107. 9 he *s* the longing soul, and filleth
Isa 55. 2 your labor for that which *s* not?

SATISFY

Job 38.27 *s* the desolate and waste ground;
Ps 90.14 *s* us early with thy mercy; that
91.16 With long life will I *s* him, and
132.15 I will *s* her poor with bread.
Pr 5.19 let her breasts *s* thee at all times;
6.30 if he steal to *s* his soul when he
Isa 58.10 hungry, and *s* the afflicted soul;
11 *s* thy soul in drought, and make
Eze 7.19 they shall not *s* their souls,
Mk 8. 4 can a man *s* these men with bread

SATISFYING

Pr 13.25 eateth to the *s* of his soul: but
Col 2.23 any honor to the *s* of the flesh.

SAUL

1Sa 9. 2 he had a son, whose name was *S*,
3 Kish said to *S* his son, Take now
17 when Samuel saw *S*, the Lord said
18 *S* drew near to Samuel in the gate,
22 Samuel took *S* and his servant,
24 So *S* did eat with Samuel that day.
25 communed with *S* upon the top of
10.11, 12 Is *S* also among the prophets?
11. 4 the messengers to Gibeah of *S*,
6 And the Spirit of God came upon *S*
12 he that said, Shall *S* reign over us?
15 made *S* king before the Lord in
13. 1 *S* reigned one year; and when he
13 Samuel said to *S*, Thou hast done
15 *S* numbered the people that were
16 *S*, and Jonathan his son, and the
14. 1 that Jonathan the son of *S* said
35 *S* built an altar unto the Lord: the
41 *S* and Jonathan were taken: but
42 And *S* said, Cast lots between me
15. 1 Samuel also said unto *S*, The Lord
7 And *S* smote the Amalekites from
9 *S* and the people spared Agag, and
24 *S* said unto Samuel, I have sinned:
31 So Samuel turned again after *S*;
31 and *S* worshipped the Lord.
35 And Samuel came no more to see *S*
35 repented that he had made *S* king
23 so *S* was refreshed and was well,
17. 2 And *S* and the men of Israel were
8 a Philistine, and ye servants to *S*?
38 *S* armed David with his armor,
39 And David said unto *S*, I cannot go
18. 1 made an end of speaking unto *S*,
5 David went...whithersoever *S* sent
5 *S* set him over the men of war,
7 said, *S* has slain his thousands,
8 *S* was very wroth, and the saying
9 *S* eyed David from that day and
10 evil spirit from God came upon *S*,
11 *S* cast the javelin; for he said, I
27 *S* gave him Michal his daughter to
29 *S* was yet the more afraid of David;
29 and *S* became David's enemy
19. 1 *S* spake to Jonathan his son, and
2 *S* my father seeketh to kill thee:
7 Jonathan brought David to *S*, and
10 *S* sought to smite David even to
22. 6 *S* heard that David was discovered,
21 that *S* had slain the Lord's priests.
24. 1 *S* was returned from following the
7 But *S* rose up out of the cave, and
9 And David said to *S*, Wherefore
16 *S* lifted up his voice, and wept.
26. 1 Ziphites came unto *S* to Gibeah,
5 and David beheld...where *S* lay,
21 Then said *S*, I have sinned:
25 *S* said to David, Blessed be thou,
28. 3 And *S* had put away those that had
5 *S* saw the host of the Philistines,
6 *S* inquired of the Lord, the Lord
13 woman said unto *S*, I saw gods
15 Samuel said to *S*, Why hast thou
31. 2 Philistines followed hard upon *S*
4 *S* took a sword, and fell upon it.
6 So *S* died, and his three sons, and
2Sa 1. 1 came to pass after the death of *S*,
4 *S* and Jonathan his son are dead
17 with this lamentation over *S* and
21 is vilely cast away, the shield of *S*,
23 *S* and Jonathan were lovely and
24 daughters of Israel, weep over *S*,
21. 1 It is for *S*, and for his bloody house
12 David went and took the bones of *S*
14 bones of *S* and Jonathan his son
1Ch 5.10 in the days of *S* they made war
10. 2 Philistines followed hard after *S*,
13 So *S* died for his transgression
Ac 7.58 man's feet, whose name was *S*.
8. 1 *S* was consenting unto his death.
3 As for *S*, he made havock of the
9. 1 *S*, yet breathing out threatenings
4 *S*, *S*, why persecutest thou me?
8 And *S* arose from the earth; and
17 Brother *S*, the Lord, even Jesus,
22 *S* increased the more in strength,
26 when *S* was come to Jerusalem,
11.25 Barnabas to Tarsus, for to seek *S*:
13. 1 up with Herod the tetrarch, and *S*.
2 Separate me Barnabas and *S* for
9 Then *S*, (who also is called Paul,)
26.14 *S*, *S*, why persecutest thou me?
(See box on page 666)

SAVE

Gen 12.12 kill me, but they will *s* thee alive.
45. 7 and to *s* your lives by a great
50.20 is this day, to *s* much people alive.
Ex 22.20 any god, *s* unto the Lord only,
Dt 28.29 evermore, and no man shall *s* thee.
Jos 10. 6 come up to us quickly, and *s* us,
Jdg 6.15 Lord, wherewith shall I *s* Israel?
31 ye plead for Baal? will ye *s* him?
1Sa 4. 3 it may *s* us out of the hand of our
10.24 shouted, and said, God *s* the king
27 said, How shall this man *s* us?
11. 3 and then, if there be no man to *s* us,
14. 6 is no restraint to the Lord to *s* by
2Sa 12. 3 nothing, *s* one little ewe lamb,
16.16 God *s* the king, God *s* the king.
22.32 For who is God, *s* the Lord? and
42 looked, but there was none to *s*;
1Ki 8. 9 the ark *s* the two tables of stone,
1Ch 16.35 ye, *S* us, O God of our salvation,
2Ch 23.11 him, and said, God *s* the king.
Neh 6.11 go into the temple to *s* his life?
Job 2. 6 he is in thine hand; but *s* his life.
22.29 and he shall *s* the humble person.
40.14 thine own right hand can *s* thee.
Ps 3. 7 *s* me, O my God: for thou hast
6. 4 soul: oh *s* me for thy mercies' sake.
18.31 For who is God *s* the Lord?
20. 9 *S*, Lord: let the king hear us when
31.16 *s* me for thy mercies' sake.
69. 1 *S* me, O God; for the waters are
72.13 and shall *s* the souls of the needy.
86. 2 *s* thy servant that trusteth in
106.47 *S* us, O Lord our God, and gather
109.26 O *s* me according to thy mercy:
138. 7 and thy right hand shall *s* me.
Pr 20.22 on the Lord, and he shall *s* thee.
Isa 33.22 the Lord is our king; he will *s* us.
35. 4 your God...will come and *s* you.
45.20 and pray unto a god that cannot *s*.
59. 1 is not shortened, that it cannot *s*;
Jer 2.28 *s* thee in the time of thy trouble:
15.20 for I am with thee to *s* thee and to
30.10 for, lo, I will *s* thee from afar, and
31. 7 *s* thy people, the remnant of Israel.
Hos 1. 7 will *s* them by the Lord their God,
7 and will not *s* them by bow, nor by
Zep 3.17 he will *s*, he will rejoice over thee
19 and I will *s* her that halteth, and
Zec 8.13 so will I *s* you, and ye shall be a
9.16 the Lord their God shall *s* them in
Mt 1.21 shall *s* his people from their sins.
8.25 him, saying, Lord, *s* us: we perish.
11.27 any man the Father, *s* the Son,
13.57 honor, *s* in his own country, and
14.30 sink, he cried, saying, Lord, *s* me.
16.25 whosoever will *s* his life shall lose
17. 8 they saw no man, *s* Jesus only.
18.11 is come to *s* that which was lost.
19.11 saying, *s* they to whom it is given.
27.40 buildest it in three days, *s* thyself.
42 saved others; himself he cannot *s*.
49 whether Elias will come to *s* him.
Mk 3. 4 or to do evil? to *s* life, or to kill?
5.37 no man to follow him, *s* Peter, and
6. 5 *s* that he laid his hands upon a few
8 for their journey, *s* a staff only;
8.35 whosoever will *s* his life shall lose
35 the gospel's, the same shall *s* it.
9. 8 saw no man any more, *s* Jesus only

Satan contends with the archangel Michael, protector of the righteous dead, in this medieval painting.

SAUL

First king of Israel, 11th century B.C.; son of Kish, a Benjamite; while on errand for his father, is secretly anointed by Samuel; predicted signs are fulfilled and, possessed by God's Spirit, he prophesies; is chosen king by sacred lot at Mizpeh (1Sa 9–10); rallies Israelites and proves own worth by gaining victory against Ammonites; is confirmed as king at Gilgal (1Sa 11); when Samuel's coming is delayed, makes burnt offering himself; is rebuked by Samuel and told that God has rejected his kingship (1Sa 13); obliges the people not to eat until Philistines are fully defeated; learns that son Jonathan has transgressed and resolves his death, sparing him only when the people insist; wins victories on all sides (1Sa 14); disobeys Samuel's instructions by failing to kill Agag, the Amalekite king, and the best livestock; again is rebuked and rejected as king; repents and pleads for forgiveness, but to no avail (1Sa 15); troubled by an "evil spirit" sent from God, takes servants' advice and appoints David his minstrel to soothe him (1Sa 16); reluctantly allows David to fight Goliath (1Sa 17); later becomes jealous of David's popularity and sees him as rival for the throne; tries to impale him with spear as David plays to him; then devises plan to have him killed by the Philistines; when it fails, has to give daughter Michal in marriage to him (1Sa 18); though reconciled for a time, again throws spear at David; is deceived by Michal, who helps David escape; pursues him to Ramah, and once more finds himself prophesying (1Sa 19); angered by Jonathan's support of David, also casts spear at him (1Sa 20); has Ahimelech and his house put to death for aiding David, and destroys Nob and its people (1Sa 22); while pursuing David, learns Philistines have invaded and is forced to return (1Sa 23); resuming pursuit, is twice spared when David has opportunities to kill him (1Sa 24, 26); when David flees to Gath, finally abandons pursuit (1Sa 27); as Philistines mass against Israel, is denied divine oracle and seeks guidance from witch of Endor; spirit of Samuel appears to his troubled conscience, foretelling defeat and death at their hands (1Sa 28); after Philistine victory and death of Jonathan, falls on own sword and dies on Mount Gilboa (1Sa 31); his passing mourned by David (2Sa 1).

Mk 15.30 *S* thyself, and come down from
31 saved others; himself he cannot *s*.
Lk 4.26 *s* unto Sarepta, a city of Sidon,
6. 9 do evil? to *s* life, or to destroy it?
8.51 suffered no man to go in, *s* Peter,
9.24 whosoever will *s* his life shall lose
24 for my sake, the same shall *s* it.
56 destroy men's lives, but to *s* them.
17.18 give glory to God, *s* this stranger.
33 shall seek to *s* his life shall lose it;
18.19 none is good, *s* one, that is, God.
19.10 seek and to *s* that which was lost.
23.35 let him *s* himself, if he be Christ,
37 be the king of the Jews, *s* thyself.
39 If thou be Christ, *s* thyself and us.
Jn 6.22 *s* that one whereinto his disciples
46 *s* he which is of God, he hath seen
12.27 Father, *s* me from this hour: but
47 judge the world, but to *s* the world.
13.10 needeth not *s* to wash his feet, but
Ac 2.40 *S* yourselves from this untoward
20.23 *S* that the Holy Ghost witnesseth
21.25 *s* only that they keep themselves
27.43 the centurion, willing to *s* Paul,
Ro 11.14 flesh, and might *s* some of them.
1Co 1.21 preaching to *s* them that believe.
2. 2 *s* Jesus Christ, and him crucified.
11 *s* the spirit of man which is in him?
7.16 whether thou shalt *s* thy husband?
16 whether thou shalt *s* thy wife?
9.22 that I might by all means *s* some.
2Co 11.24 received I forty stripes *s* one.
Gal 1.19 none, *s* James the Lord's brother.
6.14 *s* in the cross of our Lord Jesus
1Ti 1.15 came into the world to *s* sinners;
4.16 thou shalt both *s* thyself, and them
Heb 5. 7 that was able to *s* him from death,
7.25 also to *s* them to the uttermost
Jas 1.21 word, which is able to *s* your souls.
2.14 have not works? can faith *s* him?
4.12 who is able to *s* and to destroy: who
5.15 the prayer of faith shall *s* the sick,
20 his way shall *s* a soul from death,
1Pe 3.21 even baptism doth also now *s* us
Jude 23 others *s* with fear, pulling them
Rev 13.17 or sell, *s* he that had the mark,

SAVED

Ex 14.30 the Lord *s* Israel that day out of
Jdg 7. 2 saying, Mine own hand hath *s* me.
2Ki 6.10 and *s* himself there, not once nor
1Ch 11.14 *s* them by a great deliverance.
Ps 33.16 is no king *s* by the multitude of
34. 6 and *s* him out of all his troubles.
80. 3 face to shine; and we shall be *s*.
106. 8 he *s* them for his name's sake,
107.13 he *s* them out of their distresses.
Pr 28.18 walketh uprightly shall be *s*: but
Isa 30.15 returning and rest shall ye be *s*;
45.22 Look unto me, and be ye *s*, all the
Jer 8.20 summer is ended, and we are not *s*.
17.14 save me, and I shall be *s*: for thou
Mt 10.22 endureth to the end shall be *s*.
19.25 amazed, saying, Who then can be *s*?
24.13 unto the end, the same shall be *s*.
22 there should no flesh be *s*: but for
27.42 He *s* others; himself he cannot
Mk 10.26 themselves, Who then can be *s*?
13.13 unto the end, the same shall be *s*.
20 those days, no flesh should be *s*:
15.31 He *s* others; himself he cannot
16.16 believeth and is baptized shall be *s*;
Lk 1.71 we should be *s* from our enemies,
7.50 Thy faith hath *s* thee; go in peace.
8.12 lest they should believe and be *s*.
13.23 him, Lord, are there few that be *s*?
18.26 heard it said, Who then can be *s*?
42 thy sight: thy faith hath *s* thee.
23.35 He *s* others; let him save himself,
Jn 3.17 the world through him might be *s*.
5.34 things I say, that ye might be *s*.
10. 9 if any man enter in, he shall be *s*,
Ac 2.21 on the name of the Lord shall be *s*.
47 church daily such as should be *s*.
4.12 among men, whereby we must be *s*.
11.14 thou and all thy house shall be *s*.
15. 1 manner of Moses, ye cannot be *s*.
11 the grace of...Christ we shall be *s*,
16.30 said, Sirs, what must I do to be *s*?
31 thou shalt be *s*, and thy house.
27.20 all hope that we should be *s* was
31 abide in the ship, ye cannot be *s*.
Ro 5. 9 shall be *s* from wrath through him.
10 reconciled, we shall be *s* by his life.
8.24 For we are *s* by hope: but hope
9.27 of the sea, a remnant shall be *s*:
10. 1 Israel is, that they might be *s*.
9 from the dead, thou shalt be *s*.
13 the name of the Lord shall be *s*.
11.26 And so all Israel shall be *s*: as it
1Co 1.18 unto us which are *s* it is the power
3.15 but he himself shall be *s*; yet so
5. 5 the spirit may be *s* in the day of
10.33 profit of many, that they may be *s*.
15. 2 By which also ye are *s*, if ye keep
2Co 2.15 in them that are *s*, and in them
Eph 2. 5 with Christ, (by grace ye are *s*;)
8 by grace are ye *s* through faith;
1Th 2.16 the Gentiles that they might be *s*,
2Th 2.10 of the truth, that they might be *s*.
1Ti 2. 4 Who will have all men to be *s*, and
15 she shall be *s* in childbearing, if
2Ti 1. 9 Who hath *s* us, and called us with
Tit 3. 5 but according to his mercy he *s* us,
1Pe 3.20 is, eight souls were *s* by water.
4.18 And if the righteous scarcely be *s*,
2Pe 2. 5 but *s* Noah the eighth person, a
Jude 5 *s* the people out of the land of
Rev 21.24 which are *s* shall walk in the light

SAVEST

2Sa 22. 3 saviour; thou *s* me from violence.
Job 26. 2 how *s* thou the arm that hath no
Ps 17. 7 O thou that *s* by thy right hand

SAVETH

1Sa 14.39 the Lord liveth, which *s* Israel,
17.47 Lord *s* not with sword and spear:
Job 5.15 he *s* the poor from the sword, from
Ps 7.10 God, which *s* the upright in heart.
20. 6 I that the Lord *s* his anointed;
34.18 *s* such as be of a contrite spirit.
107.19 he *s* them out of their distresses.

SAVING

Gen 19.19 hast shewed unto me in *s* my life;
Neh 4.23 *s* that every one put them off for
Ps 20. 6 the *s* strength of his right hand.
28. 8 the *s* strength of his anointed.
67. 2 the *s* health among all nations.
Ec 5.11 *s* the beholding of them with their
Am 9. 8 *s* that I will not utterly destroy
Mt 5.32 *s* for the cause of fornication,
Lk 4.27 cleansed, *s* Naaman the Syrian.
Heb 10.39 that believe to the *s* of the soul.
11. 7 an ark to the *s* of his house; by
Rev 2.17 knoweth *s* he that receiveth it.

SAVIOUR

2Sa 22. 3 tower, and my refuge, my *s*;
2Ki 13. 5 (And the Lord gave Israel a *s*, so
Ps 106.21 They forgat God their *s*, which had
Isa 19.20 he shall send them a *s*, and a great
43. 3 God, the Holy One of Israel, thy *S*:
11 Lord; and beside me there is no *s*.
45.15 thyself, O God of Israel, the *S*.
21 a just God and a *S*; there is none
49.26 know that I the Lord am thy *S* and
60.16 know that I the Lord am thy *S* and
63. 8 that will not lie: so he was their *S*.
Jer 14. 8 the *s* thereof in time of trouble,
Hos 13. 4 me: for there is no *s* beside me.
Lk 1.47 spirit hath rejoiced in God my *S*.
2.11 this day in the city of David a *S*,
Jn 4.42 the Christ, the *S* of the world.
Ac 5.31 right hand to be a Prince and a *S*,
13.23 his promise raised unto Israel a *S*,
Eph 5.23 church: and he is the *s* of the body.
Php 3.20 we look for the *S*, the Lord Jesus
1Ti 1. 1 the commandment of God our *S*,
2. 3 acceptable in the sight of...our *S*;
4.10 God, who is the *S* of all men,
2Ti 1.10 appearing of our *S* Jesus Christ,
Tit 1. 3 the commandment of God our *S*;
4 and the Lord Jesus Christ our *S*.
2.10 the doctrine of God our *S* in all

13 great God and our S Jesus Christ,
3. 4 and love of God our S toward man
6 through Jesus Christ our S;
2Pe 1. 1 righteousness of God and our S
11 kingdom of our Lord and S Jesus
2.20 the knowledge of the Lord and S
3. 2 us the apostles of the Lord and S:
18 the knowledge of our Lord and S
1Jn 4.14 Father sent the Son to be the S of
Jude 25 To the only wise God our S, be

SAVIOURS

Neh 9.27 mercies thou gavest them s, who
Ob 21 s shall come up on mount Zion to

SAVOR

Gen 8.21 And the Lord smelled a sweet s;
Ex 5.21 ye have made our s to be abhorred
Lev 6.15 burn it upon the altar for a sweet s,
Nu 28. 6 in mount Sinai for a sweet s,
Ec 10. 1 apothecary to send...a stinking s:
Eze 6.13 did offer sweet s to all their idols.
20.41 I will accept you with your sweet s,
Joel 2.20 and his ill s shall come up,
Mt 5.13 but if the salt have lost his s,
Lk 14.34 but if the salt have lost his s,
2Co 2.14 manifest the s of his knowledge
15 are unto God a sweet s of Christ,
16 we are the s of death unto death;
16 to the other the s of life unto life.
Eph 5. 2 to God for a sweetsmelling s.

SAVOREST

Mt 16.23 s not the things that be of God,
Mk 8.33 s not the things that be of God,

SAW

Gen 1. 4 God s the light, that it was good:
31 God s everything that he had made,
3. 6 woman s that the tree was good
22. 4 up his eyes, and s the place afar off.
26.28 We s certainly...the Lord was with
31.10 up mine eyes, and s in a dream,
39. 3 his master s that the Lord was with
42. 1 when Jacob s that there was corn
49.15 And he s that rest was good, and
Ex 2. 5 when she s the ark among the flags,
6 she had opened it, she s the child:
3. 4 Lord s that he turned aside to see,
10.23 They s not one another, neither
24.10 And they s the God of Israel: and
32. 1 the people s that Moses delayed
19 that he s the calf, and the dancing:
33.10 all the people s the cloudy pillar
Nu 22.23 And the ass s the angel of the Lord
Dt 4.12 of the words, but s no similitude;
32.19 when the Lord s it, he abhorred
Jdg 16.18 when Delilah s that he had told all
1Sa 6.13 lifted up their eyes, and s the ark,
9.17 And when Samuel s Saul, the Lord
28.13 I s gods ascending out of the
2Sa 6.16 s king David leaping and dancing
18.26 watchman s another man running:
1Ki 22.19 I s the Lord sitting on his throne,
2Ki 2.12 And Elisha s it, and he cried, My
12 he s him no more: and he took
6.17 eyes of the young man; and he s:
13. 4 for he s the oppression of Israel,
2Ch 25.21 they s one another in the face,
Job 3.16 as infants which never s light.
20. 9 eye...which s him shall see him
29.11 when the eye s me, it gave witness
31.21 when I s my help in the gate:
Ps 73. 3 I s the prosperity of the wicked.
95. 9 me, proved me, and s my work.
97. 4 world: the earth s, and trembled.
Pr 24.32 Then I s, and considered it well:
Ec 2.13 I s that wisdom excelleth folly, as
24 This also I s, that it was from the
4. 7 and I s vanity under the sun.
SS 3. 3 S ye him whom my soul loveth?
Isa 6. 1 I s also the Lord sitting upon a
41. 5 The isles s it, and feared; the ends
59.16 And he s that there was no man,
Eze 1. 1 opened, and I s visions of God.
3.23 which I s by the river of Chebar:
Dan 4. 5 I s a dream which made me afraid,
5. 5 s the part of the hand that wrote.
8. 2 And I s in a vision: and it came to
10. 7 And I Daniel alone s the vision:
Am 1. 1 which he s concerning Israel in
9. 1 I s the Lord standing upon the
Jon 3.10 And God s their works, that they
Hab 3. 7 I s...tents of Cushan in affliction:
10 The mountains s thee, and they
Hag 2. 3 that s this house in her first glory?
Zec 1.18 Then lifted I up mine eyes, and s,
Mt 2. 9 the star, which they s in the east,
10 When they s the star, they rejoiced
11 s the young child with Mary his
3. 7 when he s many of the Pharisees
16 he s the Spirit of God descending
4.16 which sat in darkness s great light;
18 s two brethren, Simon called Peter,
9. 8 But when the multitudes s it, they
9 he s a man, named Matthew,
22 when he s her, he said, Daughter,
36 But when he s the multitudes, he
12. 2 But when the Pharisees s it, they
22 blind and dumb both spake and s.
14.14 forth, and s a great multitude,
26 disciples s him walking on the sea,
30 when he s the wind boisterous, he
17. 8 they s no man, save Jesus only.
21.15 scribes s the wonderful things that
19 when he s a fig tree in the way, he
25.37 Lord, when s we thee an hungred,
38 When s we thee a stranger, and
39 when s we thee sick, or in prison,
27. 3 when he s that he was condemned,
24 When Pilate s that he could prevail
54 s the earthquake, and those
28.17 when they s him, they worshipped
Mk 1.10 he s the heavens opened, and the
16 he s Simon and Andrew his brother
2. 5 When Jesus s their faith, he said
16 Pharisees s him eat with publicans
3.11 unclean spirits, when they s him,
5. 6 when he s Jesus afar off, he ran
22 when he s him, he fell at his feet,
6.33 And the people s them departing,
48 And he s them toiling in rowing;
49 they s him walking upon the sea,
8.23 him, he asked him if he s ought.
25 restored, and s every man clearly.
9. 8 s no man any more, save Jesus
14 he s a great multitude about them,
38 we s one casting out devils in thy
11.20 they s the fig tree dried up from the
16. 4 s that the stone was rolled away:
5 s a young man sitting on the right
Lk 1.12 And when Zacharias s him, he was
5. 2 s two ships standing by the lake:
8 When Simon Peter s it, he fell down
20 when he s their faith, he said unto
9.32 they were awake, they s his glory,
49 we s one casting out devils in thy
13.12 when Jesus s her, he called her to
19. 5 he looked up, and s him, and said
7 when they s it, they all murmured,
21. 1 s the rich men casting their gifts
2 s also a certain poor widow casting
23. 8 And when Herod s Jesus, he was
24.24 had said: but him they s not.
Jn 1.32 I s the Spirit descending from
38 turned, and s them following, and
47 Jesus s Nathanael coming to him,
48 wast under the fig tree, I s thee.
2.23 they s the miracles which he did.
8.10 and s none but the woman, he
9. 1 s a man which was blind from his
11.31 when they s Mary, that she rose up,
33 Jesus therefore s her weeping,
19. 6 chief priests...and officers s him,
33 and s that he was dead already,
20. 5 in, s the linen clothes lying, yet
8 sepulcher, and he s, and believed.
14 s Jesus standing, and knew not
20 glad, when they s the Lord.
Ac 3. 9 all the people s him walking and
12 when Peter s it, he answered unto
6.15 s his face as it had been the face
7.31 When Moses s it, he wondered at
55 and s the glory of God, and Jesus
9. 8 eyes were opened, he s no man:
11. 5 in a trance I s a vision, A certain
6 s fourfooted beasts of the earth,
14.11 the people s what Paul had done,
22. 9 were with me s indeed the light,
26.13 I s in the way a light from heaven,
28. 4 barbarians s the venomous beast
6 and s no harm come to him, they
Rev 1. 2 Christ, and of all things that he s.
12 I s seven golden candlesticks;
4. 4 I s four and twenty elders sitting,
6. 1 I s when the Lamb opened one of
2 And I s, and behold a white horse:
8. 2 I s the seven angels which stood
9. 1 I s a star fall from heaven unto the
12.13 dragon s that he was cast unto
13. 1 and s a beast rise up out of the sea,
14. 6 s another angel fly in the midst of
16.13 I s three unclean spirits like frogs
17. 3 and I s a woman sit upon a scarlet
19.11 I s heaven opened, and behold a
17 I s an angel standing in the sun;
21. 1 I s a new heaven and a new earth:
22. 8 I John s these things, and heard

SAWED

1Ki 7. 9 s with saws, within and without,

SAWEST

Gen 20.10 What s thou, that thou hast done
1Sa 19. 5 Israel: thou s it, and didst rejoice:
28.13 Be not afraid: for what s thou?
2Sa 18.11 behold, thou s him, and why didst
Ps 50.18 When thou s a thief, then thou
Isa 57. 8 lovedst their bed where thou s it.
Dan 2.31 king, s, and behold a great image.
34 Thou s till that a stone was cut out
41 whereas thou s the feet and toes,
41 as thou s the iron mixed with miry
43 thou s iron mixed with miry clay,
45 thou s that the stone was cut of the
4.20 The tree that thou s, which grew,
8.20 The ram which thou s having two
Rev 1.20 of the seven stars which thou s in
20 candlesticks which thou s are the
17. 8 The beast that thou s was, and is
12 the ten horns which thou s are ten
15 The waters which thou s, where
16 the ten horns which thou s upon
18 woman which thou s is that great

SAWN

Heb 11.37 were stoned, they were s asunder,

SAWS

2Sa 12.31 and put them under s, and under
1Ki 7. 9 sawed with s, within and without,
1Ch 20. 3 cut them with s, and with harrows

SAYINGS

2Ch 33.19 written among the s of the seers.
Ps 78. 2 parable: I will utter dark s of old:
Pr 1. 6 words of the wise, and their dark s.
4.20 words; incline thine ear unto my s.
Mt 7.24 whosoever heareth these s of
26 one that heareth these s of mine,
28 when Jesus had ended these s, the
19. 1 when Jesus had finished these s,
26. 1 when Jesus...finished all these s,

Lk 1.65 all these *s* were noised abroad
2.51 but his mother kept all these *s* in
6.47 heareth my *s*, and doeth them,
7. 1 ended all his *s* in the audience of
9.28 about an eight days after these *s*,
44 Let these *s* sink...into your ears:
Jn 10.19 again among the Jews for these *s*.
14.24 loveth me not keepeth not my *s*:
Ac 14.18 with these *s* scarce restrained
19.28 when they heard these *s*, they were
Ro 3. 4 mightest be justified in thy *s*,
Rev 19. 9 me, These are the true *s* of God.
22. 6 me, These *s* are faithful and true:
7 that keepeth the *s* of the prophecy
9 them which keep the *s* of this book:
10 Seal not the *s* of the prophecy of

SCABBARD
Jer 47. 6 put up thyself into thy *s*, rest, and

SCALES
Lev 11. 9 whatsoever hath fins and *s* in the
10 that have not fins and *s* in the seas,
12 Whatsoever hath no fins nor *s* in
Dt 14. 9 all that have fins and *s* shall ye eat:
10 hath not fins and *s* ye may not eat;
Job 41.15 His *s* are his pride, shut up
Isa 40.12 and weighed the mountains in *s*,
Eze 29. 4 cause the fish...to stick unto thy *s*,
4 all the fish...shall stick unto thy *s*.
Ac 9.18 fell from his eyes as it had been *s*:

SCANT
Mic 6.10 the *s* measure that is abominable?

SCAPEGOAT
Lev 16. 8 Lord, and the other lot for the *s*.
10 on which the lot fell to be the *s*,
10 him go for a *s* into the wilderness.
26 goat for the *s* shall wash his

SCARCE
Gen 27.30 Jacob was yet *s* gone out from the
Ac 14.18 *s* restrained they the people,
27. 7 *s* were come over against Cnidus,

SCARCELY
Ro 5. 7 *s* for a righteous man will one die:
1Pe 4.18 if the righteous *s* be saved, where

SCARLET
Gen 38.28 bound upon his hand a *s* thread,
Ex 25. 4 purple, and *s*, and fine linen,
Jos 2.18 shalt bind this line of *s* thread in
21 bound the *s* line in the window.
Isa 1.18 though your sins be as *s*, they
La 4. 5 they that were brought up in *s*
Na 2. 3 red, the valiant men are in *s*:
Mt 27.28 him, and put on him a *s* robe.
Heb 9.19 water, and *s* wool, and hyssop,
Rev 17. 3 woman sit upon a *s* colored beast,
4 arrayed in purple and *s* color,
18.12 and purple, and silk, and *s*, and all
16 in fine linen, and purple, and *s*,

SCATTER
Gen 11. 9 did the Lord *s* them abroad upon
Lev 26.33 I will *s* you among the heathen,
Ps 59.11 *s* them by thy power; and bring
68.30 *s* thou the people that delight in
Isa 41.16 and the whirlwind shall *s* them:
Jer 13.24 will I *s* them as the stubble that
18.17 I will *s* them as with an east wind
23. 1 that destroy and *s* the sheep of my
Eze 12.15 shall *s* them among the nations,
Dan 12. 7 to *s* the power of the holy people,
Hab 3.14 came out as a whirlwind to *s* me:
Zec 1.21 over the land of Judah to *s* it.

SCATTERED
Gen 11. 4 we be *s* abroad upon the face of
Nu 10.35 Lord, and let thine enemies be *s*;
Job 18.15 brimstone shall be *s* upon his
68. 1 God arise, let his enemies be *s*:
92. 9 the workers of iniquity shall be *s*.
Jer 10.21 and all their flocks shall be *s*.
31.10 He that *s* Israel will gather him,
50.17 Israel is a *s* sheep; the lions have
Eze 34. 5 And they were *s*, because there is
Joel 3. 2 they have *s* among the nations,
Na 3.18 people is *s* upon the mountains,
Hab 3. 6 the everlasting mountains were *s*,
Zec 7.14 I *s* them with a whirlwind among
13. 7 and the sheep shall be *s*: and I
Mt 9.36 were *s* abroad, as sheep having
26.31 of the flock shall be *s* abroad.
Mk 14.27 shepherd, and the sheep shall be *s*.
Lk 1.51 *s* the proud in the imagination of
Jn 11.52 children of God that were *s* abroad.
16.32 is now come, that ye shall be *s*,
Ac 5.36 were *s*, and brought to nought.
8. 1 they were all *s* abroad throughout
4 they that were *s* abroad went
11.19 they which were *s* abroad upon the
Jas 1. 1 twelve tribes which are *s* abroad,
1Pe 1. 1 strangers *s* throughout Pontus,

SCATTERETH
Job 37.11 cloud: he *s* his bright cloud:
38.24 *s* the east wind upon the earth?
Ps 147.16 he *s* the hoarfrost like ashes.
Pr 11.24 There is that *s*, and yet increaseth;
20. 8 *s* away all evil with his eyes.
26 A wise king *s* the wicked, and
Isa 24. 1 *s* abroad the inhabitants thereof.
Mt 12.30 gathereth not with me *s* abroad.
Lk 11.23 he that gathereth not with me *s*.
Jn 10.12 catcheth them, and *s* the sheep.

SCENT
Job 14. 9 through the *s* of water it will bud,
Jer 48.11 in him, and his *s* is not changed.
Hos 14. 7 *s* thereof shall be as the wine of

SCEPTER
Gen 49.10 *s* shall not depart from Judah,
Nu 24.17 and a *S* shall rise out of Israel,
Est 4.11 king shall hold out the golden *s*,
5. 2 held out to Esther the golden *s*
2 near, and touched the top of the *s*.
8. 4 out the golden *s* toward Esther.
Ps 45. 6 and ever: the *s* of thy kingdom
6 of thy kingdom is a right *s*.
Isa 14. 5 the wicked, and the *s* of the rulers.
Eze 19.14 she hath no strong rod to be a *s* to
Am 1. 5 him that holdeth the *s* from the
8 that holdeth the *s* from Ashkelon,
Zec 10.11 the *s* of Egypt shall depart away.
Heb 1. 8 a *s* of righteousness is the *s* of

SCEVA
Ac 19.14 there were seven sons of one *S*,

SCHISM
1Co 12.25 there should be no *s* in the body;

SCHOLAR
1Ch 25. 8 the great, the teacher as the *s*.
Mal 2.12 the master and the *s*, out of the

SCHOOL
Ac 19. 9 daily in the *s* of one Tyrannus.

SCHOOLMASTER
Gal 3.24 law was our *s* to bring us unto
25 we are no longer under a *s*.

SCIENCE
Dan 1. 4 knowledge, and understanding *s*,
1Ti 6.20 oppositions of *s* falsely so called:

SCOFFERS
2Pe 3. 3 shall come in the last days *s*,

SCORCH
Rev 16. 8 unto him to *s* men with fire.

SCORCHED
Mt 13. 6 the sun was up, they were *s*;
Mk 4. 6 when the sun was up, it was *s*;
Rev 16. 9 And men were *s* with great heat,

SCORN
2Ki 19.21 thee, and laughed thee to *s*;
2Ch 30.10 but they laughed them to *s*, and
Neh 2.19 heard it, they laughed us to *s*,
Est 3. 6 *s* to lay hands on Mordecai alone;
Job 12. 4 the just upright man is laughed to *s*.
16.20 My friends *s* me: but mine eye
22.19 and the innocent laugh them to *s*.
Ps 22. 7 they that see me laugh me to *s*:
44.13 a *s* and a derision to them that
79. 4 a *s* and derision to them that are
Isa 37.22 thee, and laughed thee to *s*;
Eze 23.32 thou shalt be laughed to *s* and
Hab 1.10 princes shall be a *s* unto them:
Mt 9.24 sleepeth...they laughed him to *s*.
Mk 5.40 And they laughed him to *s*. But
Lk 8.53 they laughed him to *s*, knowing

SCORNER
Pr 9. 7 He that reproveth a *s* getteth to
8 Reprove not a *s*, lest he hate thee:
13. 1 but a *s* heareth not rebuke.
14. 6 A *s* seeketh wisdom, and findeth
15.12 A *s* loveth not one that reproveth
19.25 Smite a *s*, and the simple will
21.11 When the *s* is punished, the simple
24 Proud and haughty *s* is his name,
22.10 Cast out the *s*, and contention
24. 9 the *s* is an abomination to men.
Isa 29.20 the *s* is consumed, and all that

SCORNERS
Pr 1.22 the *s* delight in their scorning,
3.34 Surely he scorneth the *s*: but he
19.29 Judgments are prepared for *s*,
Hos 7. 5 he stretched out his hand with *s*.

SCORNFUL
Ps 1. 1 nor sitteth in the seat of the *s*.
Pr 29. 8 *S* men bring a city into a snare:
Isa 28.14 the word of the Lord, ye *s* men,

SCORNING
Job 34. 7 who drinketh up *s* like water?
Ps 123. 4 the *s* of those that are at ease,
Pr 1.22 the scorners delight in their *s*,

SCORPION
Lk 11.12 ask an egg, will he offer him a *s*?
Rev 9. 5 torment was as the torment of a *s*,

SCORPIONS
Dt 8.15 were fiery serpents, and *s*, and
1Ki 12.11, 14 but I will chastise you with *s*.
2Ch 10.11, 14 but I will chastise you with *s*.
Eze 2. 6 thee, and thou dost dwell among *s*:
Lk 10.19 power to tread on serpents and *s*,
Rev 9. 3 as the *s* of the earth have power.
10 And they had tails like unto *s*, and

SCOURGE
Job 5.21 be hid from the *s* of the tongue:
9.23 If the *s* slay suddenly, he will
Isa 10.26 the Lord of hosts shall stir up a *s*
28.15 overflowing *s* shall pass through,
18 overflowing *s* shall pass through,
Mt 10.17 will *s* you in their synagogues:
20.19 to mock, and to *s*, and to crucify
23.34 some of them shall ye *s* in your
Mk 10.34 shall *s* him, and shall spit upon
Lk 18.33 they shall *s* him, and put him to
Jn 2.15 he had made a *s* of small cords,
Ac 22.25 Is it lawful for you to *s* a man

SCOURGED
Lev 19.20 she shall be *s*; they shall not be
Mt 27.26 and when he had *s* Jesus, he
Mk 15.15 when he had *s* him, to be crucified.
Jn 19. 1 therefore took Jesus, and *s* him.

SCOURGETH
Heb 12. 6 *s* every son whom he receiveth.

SCOURGING
Ac 22.24 that he should be examined by *s*;

SCOURGINGS
Heb 11.36 trial of cruel mockings and *s*,

SCRAPE
Lev 14.41 the dust that they *s* off without
Job 2. 8 a potsherd to *s* himself withal;
Eze 26. 4 I will also *s* her dust from her,

SCRIBE
2Ki 25.19 and the principal *s* of the host,
1Ch 27.32 a counsellor, a wise man, and a *s*:
Ezr 4. 8 and Shimshai the *s* wrote a letter
7.11 gave unto Ezra the priest, the *s*,
12, 21 *s* of the law of...God of heaven,
Isa 33.18 Where is the *s*? where is the
Jer 36.26 to take Baruch the *s* and Jeremiah
32 roll, and gave it to Baruch the *s*,
Mt 8.19 And a certain *s* came, and said
13.52 every *s* which is instructed unto
Mk 12.32 the *s* said unto him, Well, Master,
1Co 1.20 Where is the wise? where is the *s*?

SCRIBE'S
Jer 36.12 king's house, into the *s* chamber:
21 it out of Elishama the *s* chamber.

SCRIBES
2Ch 34.13 and of the Levites there were *s*,
Jer 8. 8 he it; the pen of the *s* is in vain.
Mt 2. 4 chief priests and *s* of the people
5.20 exceed the righteousness of the *s*
7.29 having authority, and not as the *s*.
9. 3 behold, certain of the *s* said within
12.38 certain of the *s* and of the Pharisees
15. 1 came to Jesus *s* and Pharisees,
16.21 the elders and chief priests and *s*,
17.10 Why then say the *s* that Elias must
20.18 the chief priests and unto the *s*,
21.15 when the chief priests and *s* saw
23. 2 *s* and the Pharisees sit in Moses'
13 But woe unto you, *s* and Pharisees,
14 Woe unto you, *s* and Pharisees,
15, 23, 25, 27, 29 Woe unto you, *s* and
34 prophets, and wise men, and *s*:
26. 3 the chief priests, and the *s*, and the
57 *s* and the elders were assembled.
27.41 mocking him, with the *s* and elders,
Mk 1.22 had authority, and not as the *s*.
2. 6 were certain of the *s* sitting there,
16 the *s* and Pharisees saw him eat
3.22 *s* which came down from Jerusalem
7. 1 Pharisees, and certain of the *s*,
5 the Pharisees and *s* asked him,
8.31 and of the chief priests, and *s*,
9.11 Why say the *s* that Elias must first
14 and the *s* questioning with them.
16 he asked the *s*, What question ye
10.33 the chief priests, and unto the *s*;
11.18 And the *s* and chief priests heard it,
27 the chief priests, and the *s*, and the
12.28 And one of the *s* came, and having
35 How say the *s* that Christ is the son
38 Beware of the *s*, which love to go
14. 1 chief priests and the *s* sought how
43 from the chief priests and the *s* and
53 priests and the elders and the *s*.
15. 1 consultation with the elders and *s*
31 said among themselves with the *s*,
Lk 5.21 *s* and...Pharisees began to reason,
30 their *s* and Pharisees murmured
6. 7 the *s* and Pharisees watched him,
9.22 the elders and chief priests and *s*,
11.44 Woe unto you, *s* and Pharisees,
53 *s* and the Pharisees began to urge
15. 2 Pharisees and *s* murmured, saying,
19.47 the chief priests and the *s* and the
20. 1 priests and the *s* came upon him
19 chief priests and...*s* the same hour
39 certain of the *s* answering said,
46 Beware of the *s*, which desire to
22. 2 the chief priests and *s* sought how
66 priests and the *s* came together,
23.10 And the chief priests and *s* stood
Jn 8. 3 *s* and Pharisees brought unto him
Ac 4. 5 that their rulers, and elders, and *s*,
6.12 the people, and the elders, and the *s*,
23. 9 *s* that were of the Pharisees' part

SCRIP
1Sa 17.40 bag which he had, even in a *s*;
Mt 10.10 Nor *s* for your journey, neither
Mk 6. 8 no *s*, no bread, no money in their
Lk 9. 3 neither staves, nor *s*, neither
10. 4 Carry neither purse, nor *s*, nor
22.35 sent you without purse, and *s*, and
36 let him take it, and likewise his *s*:

SCRIPTURE
Dan 10.21 which is noted in the *s* of truth:
Mk 12.10 have ye not read this *s*: The stone
15.28 the *s* was fulfilled, which saith,
Lk 4.21 This day is this *s* fulfilled in your
Jn 2.22 they believed the *s*, and the word
7.38 as the *s* hath said, out of his belly
42 Hath not the *s* said, That Christ
10.35 came, and the *s* cannot be broken;
13.18 that the *s* may be fulfilled, He that
17.12 that the *s* might be fulfilled.
19.24 that the *s* might be fulfilled, which
28 that the *s* might be fulfilled, saith,
36 *s* should be fulfilled, A bone of him
37 again another *s* saith, They shall
20. 9 For as yet they knew not the *s*,
Ac 1.16 *s* must needs have been fulfilled,
8.32 The place of the *s* which he read
35 began at the same *s*, and preached
Ro 4. 3 For what saith the *s*? Abraham
9.17 the *s* saith unto Pharaoh, Even for
10.11 the *s* saith, Whosoever believeth
11. 2 Wot ye not what the *s* saith of Elias?
Gal 3. 8 the *s*, forseeing that God would
22 the *s* hath concluded all under sin,
4.30 Nevertheless what saith the *s*?
1Ti 5.18 the *s* saith, Thou shalt not muzzle
2Ti 3.16 All *s* is given by inspiration of God,
Jas 2. 8 the royal law according to the *s*,
23 And the *s* was fulfilled which saith,
4. 5 ye think that the *s* saith in vain,
1Pe 2. 6 Wherefore...it is contained in the *s*,
2Pe 1.20 no prophecy of the *s* is of...private

SCRIPTURES
Mt 21.42 Did ye never read in the *s*, The
22.29 Ye do err, not knowing the *s*, nor
26.54 how then shall the *s* be fulfilled,
56 *s* of the prophets might be fulfilled,
Mk 12.24 err, because ye know not the *s*,
14.49 me not: but the *s* must be fulfilled.
Lk 24.27 expounded unto them in all the *s*
32 and while he opened to us the *s*?
45 that they might understand the *s*,
Jn 5.39 Search the *s*; for in them ye think
Ac 17. 2 reasoned with them out of the *s*,
11 and searched the *s* daily, whether
18.24 eloquent man, and mighty in the *s*,
28 shewing by the *s* that Jesus was
Ro 1. 2 afore by his prophets in the holy *s*,)
15. 4 patience and comfort of the *s* we
16.26 by the *s* of the prophets, according
1Co 15. 3 died for our sins according to the *s*;
4 the third day according to the *s*:
2Ti 3.15 child thou hast known the holy *s*,
2Pe 3.16 wrest, as they do also the other *s*,

SCROLL
Isa 34. 4 shall be rolled together as a *s*:
Rev 6.14 And the heaven departed as a *s*

SEA
Gen 1.26, 28 dominion over the fish of the *s*,
14. 3 vale of Siddim, which is the salt *s*.
22.17 sand which is upon the *s* shore;
Ex 14.21 *s* to go back by a strong east wind
21 and made the *s* dry land, and the
27 and the *s* returned to his strength
15. 1 rider hath he thrown into the *s*.
4 his host hath he cast into the *s*:
10 with thy wind, the *s* covered them:
21 rider hath he thrown into the *s*.
Nu 14.25 wilderness by the way of the Red *s*:
Dt 30.13 Neither is it beyond the *s*, that
13 Who shall go over the *s* for us, and
Jos 4.23 Lord your God did to the Red *s*,
1Ki 5. 9 I will convey them by *s* in floats
7.23 And he made a molten *s*, ten cubits
18.44 ariseth a little cloud out of the *s*,
1Ch 16.32 Let the *s* roar, and the fulness
18. 8 Solomon made the brasen *s*, and
Neh 9.11 And thou didst divide the *s* before
11 through the midst of the *s* on...dry
Est 10. 1 land, and upon the isles of the *s*.
Job 6. 3 be heavier than the sand of the *s*:
7.12 Am I a *s*, or a whale, that thou
9. 8 treadeth upon the waves of the *s*.
26.12 He divideth the *s* with his power,
28.14 and the *s* saith, It is not with me.
36.30 and covereth the bottom of the *s*.
38. 8 Or who shut up the *s* with doors,
16 entered into the springs of the *s*?
Ps 8. 8 the fish of the *s*, and whatsoever
72. 8 have dominion also from *s* to *s*,
74.13 didst divide the *s* by thy strength:
96.11 let the *s* roar, and the fulness
104.25 So is this great and wide *s*, wherein
107.23 that go down to the *s* in ships, that
114. 3 The *s* saw it, and fled: Jordan was
139. 9 in the uttermost parts of the *s*;
146. 6 the *s*, and all that therein is:
Pr 30.19 way of a ship in the midst of the *s*;
Ec 1. 7 into the *s*; yet the *s* is not full;
Isa 10.22 Israel be as the sand of the *s*,
19. 5 the waters shall fail from the *s*,
24.15 God of Israel in the isles of the *s*.
27. 1 slay the dragon that is in the *s*.
42.10 ye that go down to the *s*, and all
48.18 righteousness as the waves of the *s*.
51.10 made the depths of the *s* a way for
57.20 the wicked are like the troubled *s*,
63.11 that brought them up out of the *s*
Jer 33.22 the sand of the *s* measured: so
49.23 there is sorrow on the *s*; it cannot
51.36 I will dry up her *s*, and make her
Eze 26.18 that are in the *s* shall be troubled
27. 9 ships of the *s* with their mariners
29 all the pilots of the *s*, shall come
39.11 the passengers on the east of the *s*:
Dan 7. 2 heaven strove upon the great *s*.
3 great beasts came up from the *s*,
Am 5. 8 that calleth for the waters of the *s*,
8.12 And they shall wander from *s* to *s*,
9. 6 that calleth for the waters of the *s*,
Jon 1. 4 sent out a great wind into the *s*,
4 was a mighty tempest in the *s*, so
11 that the *s* may be calm unto us?
11 unto us? for the *s* wrought and was
15 Jonah, and cast him forth into the *s*:
15 and the *s* ceased from her raging.
Mic 7.19 their sins into the depths of the *s*.
Na 1. 4 He rebuketh the *s*, and maketh it
3. 8 and her wall was from the *s*?
Hab 1.14 makest men as the fishes of the *s*,

BIBLICAL THEMES

SEA

God said, Let the waters under the heaven be gathered together unto one place, and let the dry land appear: and it was so. And God called the dry land Earth; and the gathering together of the waters called he Seas. Gen 1.9-10

Moses stretched out his hand over the sea; and the Lord caused the sea to go back by a strong east wind all that night, and made the sea dry land, and the waters were divided. And the children of Israel went into the midst of the sea upon the dry ground: and the waters were a wall unto them on their right hand, and on their left. Ex 14.21-22

Save me, O God; for the waters are come in unto my soul. I sink in deep mire, where there is no standing. Ps 69.1-2

The Lord on high is mightier than the noise of many waters. Ps 93.4

The earth is full of thy riches. So is this great and wide sea. . . . There go the ships: there is that leviathan, whom thou hast made to play therein. Ps 104.24-26

They that go down to the sea in ships, that do business in great waters; these see the works of the Lord, and his wonders in the deep. Ps 107.23-24

All the rivers run into the sea; yet the sea is not full; unto the place from whence the rivers come, thither they return again. Ec 1.7

The fishers also shall mourn, and all they that cast angle into the brooks shall lament, and they that spread nets upon the waters shall languish. Isa 19.8

Sing unto the Lord a new song, and his praise from the end of the earth, ye that go down to the sea, and all that is therein; the isles, and the inhabitants thereof. Isa 42.10

Now shall the isles tremble in the day of thy fall. . . . I shall bring up the deep upon thee, and great waters shall cover thee. Eze 26.18-19

So they took up Jonah, and cast him forth into the sea: and the sea ceased from her raging. Then the men feared the Lord exceedingly, and offered a sacrifice unto the Lord, and made vows. Now the Lord had prepared a great fish to swallow up Jonah. And Jonah was in the belly of the fish three days and three nights. Jon 1.15-17

Then he arose, and rebuked the winds and the sea; and there was a great calm. But the men marvelled, saying, What manner of man is this, that even the winds and the sea obey him! Mt. 8.26-27

About the fourth watch of the night he cometh unto them, walking upon the sea. . . . But when they saw him . . . they supposed it had been a spirit, and cried out: for they all saw him, and were troubled. And immediately he talked with them, and saith unto them, Be of good cheer: it is I; be not afraid. Mk 6.48-50

When Simon Peter saw it, he fell down at Jesus' knees, saying, Depart from me; for I am a sinful man, O Lord. For he was astonished, and all that were with him, at the draft of the fishes which they had taken. . . . And Jesus said unto Simon, Fear not; from henceforth thou shalt catch men. Lk 5.8-10

Fearing lest we should have fallen upon rocks, they cast four anchors out of the stern, and wished for the day. Ac 27.29

He that wavereth is like a wave of the sea driven with the wind and tossed. Jas 1.6

The first heaven and the first earth were passed away; and there was no more sea. Rev 21.1

Hab 2.14 the Lord, as the waters cover the *s*.
3.15 walk through the *s* with thine
Hag 2. 6 heavens, and the earth, and the *s*,
Zec 9.10 dominion shall be from *s* even to *s*,
10.11 and shall smite the waves in the *s*,
Mt 4.13 which is upon the *s* coast, in the
15 by the way of the *s*, beyond Jordan,
18 Jesus, walking by the *s* of Galilee,
18 brother, casting a net into the *s*:
8.24 arose a great tempest in the *s*,
26 and rebuked the winds and the *s*;
27 even the winds and the *s* obey him!
32 down a steep place into the *s*, and
13. 1 of the house, and sat by the *s* side.
47 unto a net, that was cast into the *s*,
14.24 ship was now in the midst of the *s*,
25 went unto them, walking on the *s*.
26 disciples saw him walking on the *s*,
15.29 came nigh unto the *s* of Galilee;
17.27 go thou to the *s*, and cast an hook,
18. 6 were drowned in the depth of the *s*.
21.21 and be thou cast into the *s*;
23.15 ye compass *s* and land to make one
Mk 1.16 as he walked by the *s* of Galilee, he
16 brother casting a net into the *s*:
2.13 he went forth again by the *s* side;
3. 7 himself with his disciples to the *s*:
4. 1 began again to teach by the *s* side:
1 entered into a ship, and sat in the *s*;
1 whole multitude was by the *s* on
39 and said unto the *s*, Peace, be still.
41 even the wind and the *s* obey him?
5. 1 over unto the other side of the *s*,
13 down a steep place into the *s*,
13 thousand;) and...choked in the *s*.
21 him: and he was nigh unto the *s*.
6.47 the ship was in the midst of the *s*,
48 unto them, walking upon the *s*,
49 they saw him walking upon the *s*,
7.31 he came unto the *s* of Galilee,
9.42 neck, and he were cast into the *s*.
11.23 and be thou cast into the *s*;
Lk 6.17 from the *s* coast of Tyre and Sidon,
17. 2 his neck, and he cast into the *s*,
6 root, and be thou planted in the *s*;
21.25 the *s* and the waves roaring;
Jn 6. 1 Jesus went over the *s* of Galilee,
1 Galilee, which is the *s* of Tiberias.
16 his disciples went down unto the *s*,
17 went over the *s* toward Capernaum.
18 *s* arose by reason of a great wind
19 they see Jesus walking on the *s*,
22 stood on the other side of the *s* saw
25 him on the other side of the *s*,
21. 1 the disciples at the *s* of Tiberias;
7 and did cast himself into the *s*.
Ac 4.24 made heaven, and earth, and the *s*,
7.36 in the Red *s*, and in the wilderness
10. 6 whose house is by the *s* side:
32 one Simon a tanner by the *s* side:
14.15 made heaven, and earth, and the *s*,
17.14 away Paul to go as it were to the *s*:
27. 5 we had sailed over the *s* of Cilicia
30 had let down the boat into the *s*,
38 and cast out the wheat into the *s*.
40 committed themselves unto the *s*,
43 cast themselves first into the *s*,
28. 4 though he hath escaped the *s*, yet
Ro 9.27 of Israel be as the sand of the *s*,
1Co 10. 1 cloud, and all passed through the *s*;
2 Moses in the cloud and in the *s*;
2Co 11.26 in perils in the *s*, in perils among
Heb 11.12 is by the *s* shore innumerable.
29 passed through the Red *s* as by dry
Jas 1. 6 that wavereth is like a wave of the *s*
3. 7 and of things in the *s*, is tamed,
Jude 13 Raging waves of the *s*, foaming
Rev 4. 6 was a *s* of glass like unto crystal:
5.13 such as are in the *s*, and all that
7. 1 not blow on the earth, nor on the *s*,
2 given to hurt the earth and the *s*,
3 Hurt not the earth, neither the *s*,
8. 8 with fire was cast into the *s*: and
8 third part of the *s* became blood;
9 the creatures which were in the *s*,
10. 2 and he set his right foot upon the *s*,
5 angel which I saw stand upon the *s*
6 *s*, and the things which are therein,
8 the angel which standeth upon the *s*
12.12 inhabiters of the earth and of the *s*!
13. 1 And I stood upon the sand of the *s*,
1 and saw a beast rise up out of the *s*,
14. 7 the *s*, and the fountains of waters.
15. 2 were a *s* of glass mingled with fire:
2 stand on the *s* of glass, having the
16. 3 poured out his vial upon the *s*; and
3 and every living soul died in the *s*.
18.17 sailors, and as many as trade by *s*,
19 made rich all that had ships in the *s*
21 millstone, and cast it into the *s*,
20. 8 of whom is as the sand of the *s*.
13 *s* gave up the dead which were in it;
21. 1 away; and there was no more *s*.

SEAFARING

Eze 26.17 that wast inhabited of *s* men, the

SEAL

1Ki 21. 8 name, and sealed them with his *s*,
Neh 9.38 Levites, and priests, *s* unto it.
Est 8. 8 name, and *s* it with the king's ring:

Job 38.14 It is turned as clay to the *s*; and
41.15 shut up together as with a close *s*.
SS 8. 6 Set me as a *s* upon thine heart,
6 as a *s* upon thine arm: for love is
Isa 8.16 *s* the law among my disciples.
Jer 32.44 subscribe evidences, and *s* them,
Dan 9.24 to *s* up the vision and prophecy,
12. 4 shut up the words, and *s* the book,
Jn 3.33 hath set to his *s* that God is true.
Ro 4.11 *s* of the righteousness of the faith
1Co 9. 2 *s* of mine apostleship are ye in the
2Ti 2.19 of God standeth sure, having this *s*,
Rev 6. 3 when he had opened the second *s*,
5 when he had opened the third *s*,
7 when he had opened the fourth *s*,
9 And when he had opened the fifth *s*,
12 when he had opened the sixth *s*,
7. 2 east, having the *s* of the living God:
8. 1 when he had opened the seventh *s*,
9. 4 not the *s* of God in their foreheads.
10. 4 *S* up those things which the seven
20. 3 shut him up, and set a *s* upon him,
22.10 *S* not the sayings of the prophecy

SEALED

Dt 32.34 and *s* up among my treasures?
1Ki 21. 8 name, and *s* them with his seal,
Neh 10. 1 Now those that *s* were, Nehemiah,
Est 3.12 written, and *s* with the king's ring.
8. 8 name, and *s* with the king's ring,
10 *s* it with the king's ring, and sent
Job 14.17 My transgression is *s* up in a bag,
SS 4.12 a spring shut up, a fountain *s*.
Isa 29.11 as the words of a book that is *s*,
11 and he saith, I cannot; for it is *s*:
Jer 32.10 subscribed the evidence, and *s* it,
11 which was *s* according to the law
14 both which is *s*, and this evidence
Dan 6.17 the king *s* it with his own signet,
12. 9 up and *s* till the time of the end.
Jn 6.27 for him hath God the Father *s*.
Ro 15.28 this, and have *s* to them this fruit,
2Co 1.22 Who hath also *s* us, and given the
Eph 1.13 *s* with that holy Spirit of promise,
4.30 are *s* unto the day of redemption.
Rev 5. 1 the backside, *s* with seven seals.
7. 3 we have *s* the servants of our God
4 the number of them which were *s*:
4 there were *s* an hundred and forty
5 of Juda were *s* twelve thousand.
5 Reuben were *s* twelve thousand.
5 of Gad were *s* twelve thousand.
6 of Aser were *s* twelve thousand.
6 Nepthalim were *s* twelve thousand.
6 Manasses were *s* twelve thousand.
7 of Simeon were *s* twelve thousand.
7 of Levi were *s* twelve thousand.
7 Issachar were *s* twelve thousand.
8 Zabulon were *s* twelve thousand.
8 Joseph were *s* twelve thousand.
8 Benjamin were *s* twelve thousand.

SEALING

Mt 27.66 *s* the stone, and setting a watch.

SEALS

Rev 5. 1 the backside, sealed with seven *s*.
2 book, and to loose the *s* thereof?
5 and to loose the seven *s* thereof.
9 the book, and to open the *s* thereof:
6. 1 when the Lamb opened one of the *s*,

SEAM

Jn 19.23 now the coat was without *s*, woven

SEARCH

Lev 27.33 He shall not *s* whether it be good
Jdg 18. 2 to spy out the land, and to *s* it;
1Ki 20. 6 and they shall *s* thine house, and
Ezr 4.15 *s* may be made in the book of the
6. 1 *s* was made in the house of the
Job 13. 9 Is it good that he should *s* you
Ps 44.21 Shall not God *s* this out? for he
139.23 *S* me,...and know my heart:
Pr 25. 2 of kings is to *s* out a matter.
Ec 1.13 to seek and *s* out by wisdom
7.25 and to *s*, and to seek out wisdom,
Jer 17.10 I the Lord *s* the heart, I try the
La 3.40 Let us *s* and try our ways, and
Eze 34. 8 did my shepherds *s* for my flock,
Zep 1.12 I will *s* Jerusalem with candles,
Mt 2. 8 *s* diligently for the young child;
Jn 5.39 *S* the scriptures; for in them ye
7.52 *S*, and look: for out of Galilee

SEARCHED

Gen 31.34 Laban *s* all the tent, but found
35 he *s*, but found not the images.
37 whereas thou hast *s* all my stuff,
44.12 he *s*, and began at the eldest,
Nu 13.21 *s* the land from the wilderness
32 of the land which they had *s* unto
14. 6 were of them that *s* the land, rent
34 of the days in which ye *s* the land,
Dt 1.24 the valley of Eshcol, and *s* it out.
Job 5.27 Lo this, we have *s* it, so it is;
28.27 it; he prepared it, yea, and *s* it out.
29.16 the cause which I knew not I *s* out.
32.11 whilst ye *s* out what to say.
36.26 the number of his years be *s* out.
Ps 139. 1 O Lord, thou hast *s* me, and
Jer 31.37 the foundations of the earth *s* out
46.23 though it cannot be *s*; because
Ob 6 How are the things of Esau *s* out!
Ac 17.11 *s* the scriptures daily, whether
1Pe 1.10 have inquired and *s* diligently,

SEARCHEST

Job 10. 6 mine iniquity, and *s* after my sin?
Pr 2. 4 and *s* for her as for hid treasures;

SEARCHETH

1Ch 28. 9 for the Lord *s* all hearts, and
Job 28. 3 and *s* out all perfection: the
39. 8 and he *s* after every green thing.
Pr 18.17 his neighbor cometh and *s* him.
28.11 hath understanding *s* him out.
Ro 8.27 And he that *s* the hearts knoweth
1Co 2.10 for the Spirit *s* all things, yea, the
Rev 2.23 he which *s* the reins and hearts:

SEARCHING

Nu 13.25 they returned from *s* of the land
Job 11. 7 Canst thou by *s* find out God?
Pr 20.27 *s* all the inward parts of the belly.
Isa 40.28 is no *s* of his understanding.
1Pe 1.11 *S* what, or what manner of time

SEARCHINGS

Jdg 5.16 there were great *s* of heart.

SEARED

1Ti 4. 2 conscience *s* with a hot iron;

SEAS

Gen 1.10 of the waters called he *S*: and
Neh 9. 6 the *s*, and all that is therein, and
Ps 8. 8 passeth through the paths of the *s*.
24. 2 For he hath founded it upon the *s*,
65. 7 Which stilleth the noise of the *s*,
69.34 the *s*, and every thing that moveth
135. 6 earth, in the *s*, and all deep places.
Jer 15. 8 to me above the sand of the *s*:
Eze 28. 2 seat of God, in the midst of the *s*;
Jon 2. 3 the deep, in the midst of the *s*;
Ac 27.41 into a place where two *s* met,

SEASON

Gen 40. 4 and they continued a *s* in ward.
Ex 13.10 keep this ordinance in his *s* from
Lev 2.13 offering shalt thou *s* with salt;
26. 4 I will give you rain in due *s*, and
Nu 9. 2 the passover at his appointed *s*.
3 ye shall keep it in his appointed *s*:
7 of the Lord in his appointed *s*
13 of the Lord in his appointed *s*,
28. 2 to offer unto me in their due *s*.
Dt 11.14 the rain of your land in his due *s*,
16. 6 the *s* that thou camest forth out
28.12 the rain unto thy land in his *s*,
Jos 24. 7 dwelt in the wilderness a long *s*.
2Ki 4.16 About this *s*, according to the
17 bare a son at that *s* that Elisha had
2Ch 15. 3 a long *s* Israel hath been without
Job 5.26 shock of corn cometh in in his *s*.
30.17 are pierced in me in the night *s*:
38.32 bring forth Mazzaroth in his *s*?
Ps 1. 3 bringeth forth his fruit in his *s*;
22. 2 in the night *s*, and am not silent.
104.27 give them their meat in due *s*.
145.15 givest them their meat in due *s*.
Pr 15.23 a word spoken in due *s*, how good
Ec 3. 1 To every thing there is a *s*, and a
10.17 and thy princes eat in due *s*, for
Isa 50. 4 know how to speak a word in *s* to
Jer 5.24 the former and the latter, in his *s*:
33.20 not be day and night in their *s*;
Eze 34.26 the shower to come down in his *s*;
Dan 7.12 their lives were prolonged for a *s*
Hos 2. 9 and my wine in the *s* thereof, and
Mt 24.45 to give them meat in due *s*?
Mk 9.50 saltness, wherewith will ye *s* it?
12. 2 the *s* he sent to the husbandmen
Lk 1.20 which shall be fulfilled in their *s*.
4.13 he departed from him for a *s*.
12.42 them their portion of meat in due *s*?
13. 1 were present at that *s* some that
20.10 at the *s* he sent a servant to the
23. 8 was desirous to see him of a long *s*,
Jn 5. 4 down at a certain *s* into the pool,
35 ye were willing for a *s* to rejoice
Ac 13.11 blind, not seeing the sun for a *s*.
19.22 he himself stayed in Asia for a *s*.
24.25 when I have a convenient *s*, I will
2Co 7. 8 sorry, though it were but for a *s*.
Gal 6. 9 for in due *s* we shall reap, if we
2Ti 4. 2 Preach the word; be instant in *s*,
2 be instant...out of *s*; reprove,
Phm 15 he therefore departed for a *s*, that
Heb 11.25 enjoy the pleasures of sin for a *s*;
1Pe 1. 6 rejoice, though now for a *s*, if
Rev 6.11 they should rest yet for a little *s*,
20. 3 that he must be loosed a little *s*.

SEASONED

Lk 14.34 his savor, wherewith shall it be *s*?
Col 4. 6 be alway with grace, *s* with salt,

SEASONS

Gen 1.14 let them be for signs, and for *s*,
Ex 18.22 them judge the people at all *s*:
26 they judged the people at all *s*:
Lev 23. 4 which ye shall proclaim in their *s*.
Ps 16. 7 reins also instruct me in the night *s*.
104.19 He appointed the moon for *s*:
Dan 2.21 he changeth the times and the *s*:
Mt 21.41 render him the fruits in their *s*.
Ac 1. 7 for you to know the times or the *s*,
14.17 us rain from heaven, and fruitful *s*,
20.18 I have been with you at all *s*,
1Th 5. 1 of the times and the *s*, brethren,

SEAT

Ex 25.17 shalt make a mercy *s* of pure gold:
21 put the mercy *s* above upon the ark;
1Sa 20.18 because thy *s* will be empty.
Est 3. 1 and set his *s* above all the princes
Job 23. 3 that I might come even to his *s*!
29. 7 I prepared my *s* in the street!
Ps 1. 1 nor sitteth in the *s* of the scornful.
Pr 9.14 on a *s* in the high places of the
Eze 8. 3 the *s* of the image of jealousy,
28. 2 I am a God, I sit in the *s* of God,

Mt 23. 2 and the Pharisees sit in Moses' *s*:
27.19 he was set down on the judgment *s*,
Jn 19.13 and sat down in the judgment *s* in a
Ac 18.12 and brought him to the judgment *s*,
16 he drave them from the judgment *s*.
17 and beat him before the judgment *s*.
25. 6 next day sitting on the judgment *s*
10 Paul, I stand at Caesar's judgment *s*,
17 the morrow I sat on the judgment *s*,
Ro 14.10 before the judgment *s* of Christ.
2Co 5.10 before the judgment *s* of Christ;
Rev 2.13 dwellest, even where Satan's *s* is:
13. 2 and his *s*, and great authority.
16.10 out his vial upon the *s* of the beast;

SEATS

Mt 21.12 and the *s* of them that sold doves,
23. 6 and the chief *s* in the synagogues,
Mk 11.15 and the *s* of them that sold doves;
12.39 the chief *s* in the synagogues, and
Lk 1.52 put down the mighty from their *s*,
11.43 uppermost *s* in the synagogues,
20.46 the highest *s* in the synagogues,
Jas 2. 6 draw you before the judgment *s*?
Rev 4. 4 throne were four and twenty *s*:
4 upon the *s* I saw four and twenty
11.16 which sat before God on their *s*,

SECOND

Gen 1. 8 and the morning were the *s* day.
2.13 the name of the *s* river is Gihon:
6.16 with lower, *s*, and third stories
22.15 Abraham out of heaven the *s* time,
Nu 10. 6 When ye blow an alarm the *s* time,
Jos 5. 2 circumcise...of Israel the *s* time.
2Ch 30. 2 keep the passover in the *s* month.
Eze 10.14 the *s* face was the face of a man,
Jon 3. 1 Lord came unto Jonah the *s* time,
Mt 22.39 *s* is like unto it, Thou shalt love
Mk 12.31 the *s* is like,...Thou shalt love
14.72 And the *s* time the cock crew.
Jn 3. 4 the *s* time into his mother's womb,
4.54 again the *s* miracle that Jesus did,
Ac 7.13 the *s* time Joseph was made known
1Co 15.47 the *s* man is the Lord from heaven.
Tit 3.10 after the first and *s* admonition
Heb 9.28 he appear the *s* time without sin
10. 9 first, that he may establish the *s*.
2Pe 3. 1 This *s* epistle, beloved, I now write
Rev 2.11 shall not be hurt of the *s* death.
11.14 The *s* woe is past; and, behold, the
20. 6 on such the *s* death hath no power,
14 lake of fire. This is the *s* death.
21. 8 brimstone: which is the *s* death.

SECONDARILY

1Co 12.28 first apostles, *s* prophets, thirdly

SECRET

Dt 29.29 *s* things belong unto the Lord
Job 15. 8 Hast thou heard the *s* of God?
11 is there any *s* thing with thee?
20.26 darkness...be hid in his *s* places:
29. 4 *s* of God was upon my tabernacle;
Ps 19.12 cleanse thou me from *s* faults.
27. 5 in the *s* of his tabernacle shall he
90. 8 thee, our *s* sins in the light of thy
91. 1 dwelleth in the *s* place of the most
139.15 from thee, when I was made in *s*,
Pr 3.32 but his *s* is with the righteous.
9.17 and bread eaten in *s* is pleasant.
27. 5 rebuke is better than *s* love.
Isa 45.19 I have not spoken in *s*, in a dark
Jer 2.34 I have not found it by *s* search, but
23.24 Can any hide himself in *s* places
Dan 2.18 God of heaven concerning this *s*;
22 revealeth the deep and *s* things:
Am 3. 7 revealeth his *s* unto his servants
Mt 6. 4 That thine alms may be in *s*: and
4 and thy Father which seeth in *s*
6 pray to thy Father which is in *s*;
6 thy Father which seeth in *s* shall
18 but unto thy Father which is in *s*:
18 thy Father, which seeth in *s*, shall
13.35 things which have been kept *s*
24.26 behold, he is in the *s* chambers;
Mk 4.22 neither was any thing kept *s*, but
Lk 8.17 For nothing is *s*, that shall not
11.33 a candle, putteth it in a *s* place,
Jn 7. 4 no man that doeth any thing in *s*,
10 not openly, but as it were in *s*.
18.20 and in *s* have I said nothing.
Ro 16.25 was kept *s* since the world began,
Eph 5.12 which are done of them in *s*.

SECRETLY

Gen 31.27 didst thou flee away *s*, and steal
Jos 2. 1 out of Shittim two men to spy *s*,
2Sa 12.12 For thou didst it *s*: but I will do
Job 4.12 a thing was *s* brought to me,
13.10 you, if ye do *s* accept persons.
31.27 my heart hath been *s* enticed, or
Hab 3.14 was as to devour the poor *s*.
Jn 11.28 way, and called Mary her sister *s*,
19.38 Jesus, but *s* for fear of the Jews,

SECRETS

Dt 25.11 hand, and taketh him by the *s*:
Job 11. 6 shew thee the *s* of wisdom, that
Ps 44.21 for he knoweth the *s* of the heart.
Pr 11.13 A talebearer revealeth *s*: but he
20.19 about as a talebearer revealeth *s*:
Dan 2.28 a God in heaven that revealeth *s*,
29 and he that revealeth *s* maketh
47 lord of kings, and a revealer of *s*,
Ro 2.16 God shall judge the *s* of men
1Co 14.25 the *s* of his heart made manifest;

SECT

Ac 5.17 (which is the *s* of the Sadducees,)
15. 5 up certain of the *s* of the Pharisees
24. 5 ringleader of the *s* of the Nazarenes;
26. 5 the most straitest *s* of our religion
28.22 for as concerning this *s*, we know

SECUNDUS

Ac 20. 4 Aristarchus and *S*; and Gaius

SECURE

Jdg 8.11 the host: for the host was *s*.
18. 7 of the Zidonians, quiet and *s*;
10 ye shall come unto a people *s*, and
27 a people that were at quiet and *s*:
Job 11.18 thou shalt be *s*, because there is
12. 6 and they that provoke God are *s*;
Mt 28.14 will persuade him, and *s* you.

SECURELY

Pr 3.29 seeing he dwelleth *s* by thee.
Mic 2. 8 pass by *s* as men averse from war.

SECURITY

Ac 17. 9 when they had taken *s* of Jason,

SEDITION

Ezr 4.15 that they have moved *s* within
19 rebellion and *s* have been made
Lk 23.19 for a certain *s* made in the city,
25 for *s* and murder was cast into
Ac 24. 5 a mover of *s* among all the Jews

SEDITIONS

Gal 5.20 emulations, wrath, strife, *s*,

SEDUCE

Mk 13.22 to *s*, if it were possible, even the
1Jn 2.26 you, concerning them that *s* you.
Rev 2.20 to teach and to *s* my servants to

SEDUCED

2Ki 21. 9 Manasseh *s* them to do more evil
Isa 19.13 they have also *s* Egypt, even they
Eze 13.10 they have *s* my people, saying,

SEDUCERS

2Ti 3.13 and *s* shall wax worse and worse,

SEDUCETH

Pr 12.26 the way of the wicked *s* them.

SEDUCING

1Ti 4. 1 giving heed to *s* spirits, and

SEE

Gen 8. 8 to *s* if the waters were abated
27. 1 were dim, so that he could not *s*,
42. 9, 12 to *s* the nakedness of the land
43. 3, 5 Ye shall not *s* my face, except
44.23 you, ye shall *s* my face no more.
Ex 3. 3 turn aside, and *s* this great sight,
4 Lord saw that he turned aside to *s*,
7. 1 *S*, I have made thee a god to
12.13 when I *s* the blood, I will pass over
16. 7 ye shall *s* the glory of the Lord; for
33.20 he said, Thou canst not *s* my face:
20 there shall no man *s* me, and live.
Nu 24.17 I shall *s* him, but not now: I shall
Dt 3.25 and *s* the good land that is beyond
4.28 which neither *s*, nor hear, nor eat,
29. 4 eyes to *s*, and ears to hear, unto
30.15 *S*, I have set before thee this day
34. 4 caused thee to *s* it with thine eyes,
Jos 3. 3 ye *s* the ark of the covenant of the
Jdg 16. 5 *s* wherein his great strength lieth,
1Sa 12.17 and *s* that your wickedness is great,
1Ki 17.23 and Elijah said, *S*, thy son liveth.
2Ki 2.10 *s* me when I am taken from thee,
6.17 thee, open his eyes, that he may *s*.
10.16 me, and *s* my zeal for the Lord.
19.16 open, Lord, thine eyes, and *s*: and
23.17 he said, What title is that that I *s*?
Est 5.13 as I *s* Mordecai the Jew sitting at
Job 3. 9 let it *s* the dawning of the day:
7. 7 mine eye shall no more *s* good.
8 seen me shall *s* me no more:
9.11 he goeth by me, and I *s* him not:
25 they flee away, they *s* no good.
17.15 as for my hope, who shall *s* it?
19.26 body, yet in my flesh shall I *s* God:
21.20 His eyes shall *s* his destruction,
22.19 The righteous *s* it, and are glad:
24.15 saying. No eye shall *s* me:
31. 4 Doth not he *s* my ways, and count
34.32 That which I *s* not teach thou me:
35. 5 Look unto the heavens, and *s*;
14 thou sayest thou shalt not *s* him,
Ps 10.11 hideth his face; he will never *s* it.
16.10 thine Holy One to *s* corruption.
27.13 to *s* the goodness of the Lord in the
34. 8 taste and *s* that the Lord is good:
40. 3 many shall *s* it, and fear, and shall
52. 6 The righteous also shall *s*, and fear,
63. 2 To *s* thy power and thy glory, so as
66. 5 Come and *s* the works of God: he
74. 9 We *s* not our signs: there is no
89.48 that liveth, and shall not *s* death?
91. 8 and *s* the reward of the wicked.
106. 5 That I may *s* the good of thy chosen,
115. 5 eyes have they, but they *s* not:
119.74 thee will be glad when they *s* me;
135.16 eyes have they, but they *s* not;
139.16 Thine eyes did *s* my substance,
24 *s* if there be any wicked way in me,
Pr 29.16 but the righteous shall *s* their fall.
Ec 1.10 it may be said, *S*, this is new?
3.22 him to *s* what shall be after him?
7.11 is profit to them that *s* the sun.
Isa 6. 9 and *s* ye indeed, but perceive not.
10 lest they *s* with their eyes, and hear
29.18 the blind shall *s* out of obscurity,
30.10 Which say to the seers, *S* not:
20 but thine eyes shall *s* thy teachers:
33.17 eyes shall *s* the king in his beauty:
35. 2 they shall *s* the glory of the Lord,
40. 5 and all flesh shall *s* it together:

42.18 and look, ye blind, that ye may *s*.
52. 8 for they shall *s* eye to eye, when
10 shall *s* the salvation of our God.
53. 2 when we…*s* him, there is no beauty
10 he shall *s* his seed, he shall prolong
11 He shall *s* of the travail of his soul,
60. 4 up thine eyes round about, and *s*:
62. 2 Gentiles shall *s* thy righteousness.
66.18 they shall come, and *s* my glory.
Jer 1.11 I said, I *s* a rod of an almond tree.
2.19 *s* that it is an evil thing and bitter,
31 O generation, *s* ye the word of the
5.12 shall we *s* sword nor famine:
21 which have eyes, and *s* not; which
22.10 no more, nor *s* his native country.
La 1.11 *s*, O Lord, and consider; for I am
12 *s* if there be any sorrow like unto
Eze 12. 2 which have eyes to *s*, and *s* not;
13.16 which *s* visions of peace for her,
33. 6 the watchman *s* the sword come,
Dan 3.25 Lo, I *s* four men loose, walking in
Joel 2.28 your young men shall *s* visions:
Jon 4. 5 *s* what would become of the city.
Mic 6. 9 man of wisdom shall *s* thy name:
7.16 nations shall *s* and be confounded
Hab 2. 1 to *s* what he will say unto me,
Zep 3.15 thou shalt not *s* evil any more.
Zec 4.10 shall *s* the plummet in the hand of
5. 2 And I answered, I *s* a flying roll;
Mal 1. 5 your eyes shall *s*, and ye shall say,
Mt 5. 8 in heart: for they shall *s* God.
16 that they may *s* your good works,
7. 5 then shalt thou *s* clearly to cast
11. 8, 9 But what went ye out for to *s*?
12.38 we would *s* a sign from thee.
13.13 because they seeing *s* not; and
16 blessed are your eyes, for they *s*:
15.31 lame to walk, and the blind to *s*:
16.28 till they *s* the Son of man coming
24.15 *s* the abomination of desolation,
30 shall *s* the Son of man coming in
33 when ye shall *s* all these things,
27. 4 What is that to us? *s* thou to that.
28. 6 *s* the place where the Lord lay.
7 there shall ye *s* him: lo, I have
10 Galilee, and there shall they *s* me.
Mk 1.44 *S* thou say nothing to any man:
4.12 That seeing they may *s*, and not
8.18 Having eyes, *s* ye not? and having
24 and said, I *s* men as trees, walking.
13.26 shall they *s*…Son of man coming
14.62 *s* the Son of man sitting on the
15.32 cross, that we may *s* and believe.
36 *s* whether Elias will come to take
16. 7 there shall ye *s* him, as he said
Lk 2.15 and *s* this thing which is come to
3. 6 flesh shall *s* the salvation of God.
6.42 thou *s* clearly to pull out the mote
7.22 that the blind *s*, the lame walk,
8.16 they which enter in may *s* the light.
9.27 till they *s* the kingdom of God.
10.23 eyes which *s* the things that ye *s*:
13.35 Ye shall not *s* me, until the time
17.23 they shall say to you, *S* here; or,
19. 4 up into a sycomore tree to *s* him:
21.27 shall they *s*…Son of man coming
23. 8 desirous to *s* him of a long season,
Jn 1.33 thou shalt *s* the Spirit descending,
39 He saith unto them, Come and *s*.
50 shalt *s* greater things than these.
51 Hereafter ye shall *s* heaven open,
3. 3 he cannot *s* the kingdom of God.
4.29 *s* a man, which told me all things
48 Except ye *s* signs and wonders, ye
6.30 that we may *s*, and believe thee?
8.51 my saying, he shall never *s* death.
56 Abraham rejoiced to *s* my day:
9.25 that, whereas I was blind, now I *s*.
41 but now ye say, We *s*; therefore
12.21 him, saying, Sir, we would *s* Jesus.
14.19 seeth me no more; but ye *s* me:
16.10 my Father, and ye *s* me no more;
18.26 Did not I *s* thee in the garden with
20.25 I shall *s* in his hands the print of
Ac 2.17 your young men shall *s* visions,
27 thine Holy One to *s* corruption.
7.56 I *s* the heavens opened, and the
19.21 been there, I must also *s* Rome.
23.22 *S* thou tell no man that thou hast
28.26 and seeing ye shall *s*, and not
Ro 7.23 I *s* another law in my members,
1Co 1.26 For ye *s* your calling, brethren,
13.12 now we *s* through a glass, darkly;
Gal 6.11 Ye *s* how large a letter I have
Eph 5.33 and the wife *s* that she reverence her
1Th 3. 6 always, desiring greatly to *s* us,
Heb 2. 8 *s* not yet all things put under him.
9 we *s* Jesus, who was made a little
1Pe 1. 8 in whom, though now ye *s* him not,
1Jn 3. 2 him; for we shall *s* him as he is.
Rev 1. 7 and every eye shall *s* him, and
3.18 with eyesalve, that thou mayest *s*.
9.20 which neither can *s*, nor hear, nor
19.10 he said unto me, *S* thou do it not:
22. 9 saith he unto me, *S* thou do it not:

SEED

Gen 1.11 after his kind, whose *s* is in itself,
12. 7 Unto thy *s* will I give this land:
13.16 I will make thy *s* as the dust of the
17. 7 between me and thee and thy *s*
12 any stranger, which is not of thy *s*.
22.17 I will multiply thy *s* as the stars of
28.14 and in thy *s* shall all the families
47.19 give us *s*, that we may live, and not
Ex 16.31 and it was like coriander *s*, white;
Lev 19.19 not sow thy field with mingled *s*:
20. 2 giveth any of his *s* unto Molech;
26.16 and ye shall sow your *s* in vain, for
Nu 11. 7 And the manna was as coriander *s*,
Dt 22. 9 fruit of thy *s* which thou hast sown,
28.38 carry much *s* out into the field.
Neh 9. 2 *s* of Israel separated themselves
Est 10. 3 and speaking peace to all his *s*.
Ps 22.23 and fear him, all ye the *s* of Israel.
25.13 and his *s* shall inherit the earth.
37.25 forsaken, nor his *s* begging bread.
26 and lendeth; and his *s* is blessed.
28 the *s* of the wicked shall be cut off.
126. 6 and weepeth, bearing precious *s*,
Pr 11.21 but the *s* of the righteous shall be
Ec 11. 6 In the morning sow thy *s*, and in
Isa 30.23 shall he give the rain of thy *s*, that
44. 3 I will pour my spirit upon thy *s*,
45.25 If the Lord shall all the *s* of Israel
53.10 he shall see his *s*, he shall prolong
54. 3 thy *s* shall inherit the Gentiles,
55.10 that it may give *s* to the sower,
65. 9 I will bring forth a *s* out of Jacob,
Jer 22.30 for no man of his *s* shall prosper,
Joel 1.17 The *s* is rotten under their clods,
Hag 2.19 Is the *s* yet in the barn? yea, as
Zec 8.12 For the *s* shall be prosperous; the
Mal 2. 3 I will corrupt your *s*, and spread
Mt 13.19 which received *s* by the way side.
20 received the *s* into stony places,
22 that received *s* among the thorns
23 received *s* into the good ground
24 which sowed good *s* in his field:
27 not thou sow good *s* in thy field?
31 heaven is like to a grain of mustard *s*,
37 the good *s* is the Son of man;
38 the good *s* are the children of the
17.20 ye have faith as a grain of mustard *s*,
22.24 and raise up *s* unto his brother.
Mk 4.26 should cast *s* into the ground;
27 the *s* should spring and grow up,
31 It is like a grain of mustard *s*,
12.19 and raise up *s* unto his brother.
20 took a wife, and dying left no *s*.
21 her, and died, neither left he any *s*:
22 the seven had her, and left no *s*:
Lk 1.55 to Abraham, and to his *s* for ever.
8. 5 A sower went out to sow his *s*:
11 is this: The *s* is the word of God.
13.19 It is like a grain of mustard *s*, which
17. 6 ye had faith as a grain of mustard *s*,
20.28 and raise up *s* unto his brother.
Jn 7.42 Christ cometh of the *s* of David,
8.33 We be Abraham's *s*, and were
37 I know that ye are Abraham's *s*;
Ac 3.25 in thy *s* shall all the kindreds of
7. 5 possession, and to his *s* after him,
6 his *s* should sojourn in a strange
13.23 Of this man's *s* hath God according
Ro 1. 3 which was made of the *s* of David
4.13 was not to Abraham, or to his *s*,
16 promise might be sure to all the *s*
18 was spoken, So shall thy *s* be.
9. 7 because they are the *s* of Abraham,
7 but, In Isaac shall thy *s* be called.
8 the promise are counted for the *s*.
29 the Lord of Sabaoth had left us a *s*,
11. 1 an Israelite, of the *s* of Abraham,
1Co 15.38 him, and to every *s* his own body.
2Co 9.10 he that ministereth *s* to the sower
10 food, and multiply your *s* sown,
11.22 Are they the *s* of Abraham? so am
Gal 3.16 and his *s* were the promises made.
16 one, And to thy *s*, which is Christ.
19 till the *s* should come to whom the
29 Christ's, then are ye Abraham's *s*,
2Ti 2. 8 Jesus Christ of the *s* of David was
Heb 2.16 he took on him the *s* of Abraham.
11.11 received strength to conceive *s*,
18 That in Isaac shall thy *s* be called:
1Pe 1.23 born again, not of corruptible *s*,
1Jn 3. 9 for his *s* remaineth in him: and
Rev 12.17 war with the remnant of her *s*,

SEEDS

Dt 22. 9 not sow thy vineyard with divers *s*:
Mt 13. 4 some *s* fell by the way side, and the
32 which indeed is the least of all *s*:
Mk 4.31 is less than all the *s* that be in the
Gal 3.16 He saith not, And to *s*, as of many;

SEEDTIME

Gen 8.22 *s* and harvest, and cold and heat,

SEEING

Gen 22.12 *s* thou hast not withheld thy son.
24.56 *s* the Lord hath prospered my way;
Lev 10.17 in the holy place, *s* it is most holy,
Nu 16. 3 you, *s* all the congregation are holy,
Jos 22.18 *s* ye rebel to day against the Lord,
Jdg 17.13 *s* I have a Levite to my priest.
Ru 2.10 knowledge of me, *s* I am a stranger?
1Sa 18.23 *s* that I am a poor man, and lightly
2Ch 2. 6 *s* the heaven and heaven of heavens
Job 14. 5 *S* his days are determined, the
19.28 *s* the root of the matter is found in
21.22 *s* he judgeth those that are high.
28.21 *S* it is hid from the eyes of all living,
Ps 50.17 *S* thou hatest instruction, and castest
Pr 20.12 The hearing ear, and the *s* eye,
Ec 1. 8 the eye is not satisfied with *s*, nor
6.11 *S* there be many things that
Isa 33.15 and shutteth his eyes from *s* evil;
Eze 22.28 *s* vanity, and divining lies unto
Dan 2.47 *s* thou couldest reveal this secret.
Hos 4. 6 *s* thou hast forgotten the law of thy
Mt 5. 1 *s* the multitudes, he went up into
9. 2 Jesus *s* their faith said unto the
13.13 parables: because they *s* see not;
14 *s* ye shall see, and shall not perceive:
Mk 4.12 *s* they may see, and not perceive;
11.13 *s* a fig tree afar off having leaves,
Lk 1.34 shall this be, *s* I know not a man?
5.12 who *s* Jesus fell on his face, and
8.10 *s* they might not see, and hearing
23.40 *s* thou art in the…condemnation?
Jn 2.18 us, *s* that thou doest these things?

Jn 9. 7 therefore, and washed, and came *s*.
21.21 Peter *s* him saith to Jesus, Lord,
Ac 2.15 *s* it is but the third hour of the day.
31 He *s* this before spake of the
3. 3 Who *s* Peter and John about to go
7.24 And *s* one of them suffer wrong, he
8. 6 and *s* the miracles which he did.
9. 7 hearing a voice, but *s* no man.
13.11 blind, not *s* the sun for a season.
46 but *s* ye put it from you, and judge
16.27 *s* the prison doors open, he drew
17.24 *s* that he is Lord of heaven and
25 *s* he giveth to all life, and breath,
19.36 *S* then that these things cannot be
24. 2 *S* that by thee we enjoy great
28.26 and *s* ye shall see, and not perceive:
Ro 3.30 *S* it is one God, which shall justify
1Co 14.16 *s* he understandeth not what thou
2Co 3.12 *S* then that we have such hope, we
4. 1 *s* we have this ministry, as we have
11.18 *S* that many glory after the flesh,
19 gladly, *s* ye yourselves are wise.
Col 3. 9 *s* that ye have put off the old man
2Th 1. 6 *S* it is a righteous thing with God
Heb 4. 6 *S* therefore it remaineth that some
14 *S* then that we have a great high
5.11 uttered, *s* ye are dull of hearing.
6. 6 *s* they crucify to themselves the Son
7.25 *s* he ever liveth to make intercession
8. 4 *s* that there are priests that offer
11.27 endured, as *s* him who is invisible.
12. 1 *s* we also are compassed about
1Pe 1.22 *S* ye have purified your souls in
2Pe 2. 8 among them, in *s* and hearing,
3.11 *S* then that all these things shall be
14 *s* that ye look for such things, be
17 *s* ye know these things before,

SEEK

Gen 37.16 I *s* my brethren: tell me, I pray
43.18 that he may *s* occasion against us,
Lev 19.31 neither *s* after wizards, to be
Nu 16.10 thee: and *s* ye the priesthood also?
Dt 4.29 thou shalt *s* the Lord thy God,
1Sa 16.16 to *s* out a man, who is a cunning
1Ki 19.10, 14 they *s* my life, to take it away.
1Ch 16.11 *S* the Lord and his strength,
11 strength, *s* his face continually.
22.19 your soul to *s* the Lord your God;
28. 9 if thou *s* him, he will be found of
2Ch 11.16 set their hearts to *s* the Lord God
15. 2 if ye *s* him, he will be found of you;
12 into a covenant to *s* the Lord God
Ezr 4. 2 for we *s* your God, as ye do; and we
7.10 his heart to *s* the law of the Lord,
8.21 to *s* of him a right way for us, and
Job 5. 8 I would *s* unto God, and unto God
7.21 thou shalt *s* me in the morning,
8. 5 If thou wouldest *s* unto God
20.10 children shall *s* to please the poor,
Ps 4. 2 love vanity, and *s* after leasing?
9.10 not forsaken them that *s* thee.
24. 6 the generation of them that *s* him,
6 him, that *s* thy face, O Jacob.
27. 4 of the Lord, that will I *s* after;
8 When thou saidst, *S* ye my face;
8 unto thee, Thy face, Lord, will I *s*.
34.10 that *s* the Lord shall not want
14 do good; *s* peace, and pursue it.
40.16 Let all those that *s* thee rejoice
63. 1 art my God; early will I *s* thee:
69.32 your heart shall live that *s* God.
83.16 that they may *s* thy name, O Lord.
104.21 prey, and *s* their meat from God.
105. 4 *S* the Lord, and his strength:
119.176 *s* thy servant; for I do not forget
122. 9 the Lord our God I will *s* thy good.
Pr 1.28 they shall *s* me early, but they
8.17 those that *s* me early shall find me.
23.35 shall I awake? I will *s* it yet again.
29.10 the upright: but the just *s* his soul.
26 Many *s* the ruler's favor; but
Ec 7.25 to search, and to *s* out wisdom,
8.17 though a man labor to *s* it out,
Isa 8.19 *S* unto them that have familiar
9.13 them, neither do they *s* the Lord
11.10 to it shall the Gentiles *s*: and his
41.12 Thou shalt *s* them, and shalt not
17 When the poor and needy *s* water,
55. 6 *S* ye the Lord while he may be
Jer 30.14 forgotten thee; they *s* thee not;
50. 4 shall go, and *s* the Lord their God.
La 1.11 All her people sigh, they *s* bread;
Eze 7.26 shall they *s* a vision of the prophet;
34.11 search my sheep, and *s* them out.
12 so will I *s* out my sheep, and will
16 I will *s* that which was lost, and
Hos 2. 7 she shall *s* them, but shall not
5.15 their offense, and *s* my face: in
10.12 for it is time to *s* the Lord, till he
Am 5. 4 Israel, *S* ye me, and ye shall live:
6 *S* the Lord, and ye shall live; lest
14 *S* good, and not evil, that ye may
Na 3. 7 shall I *s* comforters for thee?
Zep 2. 3 *S* ye the Lord, all ye meek of the
3 *s* righteousness, *s* meekness: it
Mal 2. 7 should *s* the law at his mouth:
3. 1 and the Lord, whom ye *s*, shall
Mt 2.13 *s* the young child to destroy him.
6.32 all these things do the Gentiles *s*:)
33 But *s* ye first the kingdom of God,
7. 7 *s*, and ye shall find: knock, and it
28. 5 ye *s* Jesus, which was crucified.
Mk 1.37 said unto him, All men *s* for thee.
3.32 thy brethren without *s* for thee.
8.12 this generation *s* after a sign?
16. 6 Ye *s* Jesus of Nazareth, which was
Lk 11. 9 *s*, and ye shall find: knock, and it
29 they *s* a sign; and there shall no
12.29 And *s* not ye what ye shall eat, or
30 the nations of the world *s* after:
31 rather *s* ye the kingdom of God;
13.24 for many,...will *s* to enter in, and
15. 8 and *s* diligently till she find it?
17.33 shall *s* to save his life shall lose it;
19.10 *s* and to save that which was lost.
24. 5 *s* ye the living among the dead?
Jn 1.38 and saith unto them, What *s* ye?
5.30 because I *s* not mine own will, but
44 *s* not the honor that cometh
6.26 Ye *s* me, not because ye saw the
7.25 not this he, whom they *s* to kill?
34, 36 Ye shall *s* me, and shall not
8.21 ye shall *s* me, and shall die in your
37 ye *s* to kill me, because my word
40 But now ye *s* to kill me, a man
50 And I *s* not mine own glory: there
13.33 Ye shall *s* me: and as I said unto
18. 4 and said unto them, Whom *s* ye?
7 asked he them again, Whom *s* ye?
8 if therefore ye *s* me, let these go
Ac 10.19 him, Behold, three men *s* thee.
21 said, Behold, I am he whom ye *s*:
11.25 Barnabas to Tarsus, for to *s* Saul:
15.17 of men might *s* after the Lord,
17.27 That they should *s* the Lord, if
Ro 2. 7 in well doing *s* for glory and
11. 3 am left alone, and they *s* my life.
1Co 1.22 and the Greeks *s* after wisdom:
7.27 unto a wife? *s* not to be loosed.
27 loosed from a wife? *s* not a wife.
10.24 Let no man *s* his own, but every
14.12 *s* that ye may excel to the edifying
2Co 12.14 for I *s* not yours, but you: for the
13. 3 ye *s* a proof of Christ speaking in
Gal 1.10 or do I *s* to please men? for if I
2.17 while we *s* to be justified by Christ,
Php 2.21 For all *s* their own, not the things
Col 3. 1 *s* those things which are above,
Heb 11. 6 of them that diligently *s* him.
14 plainly that they *s* a country.
13.14 city, but we *s* one to come.
1Pe 3.11 let him *s* peace, and ensue it.
Rev 9. 6 in those days shall men *s* death,

SEEKEST

Gen 37.15 asked him, saying, What *s* thou?
Jdg 4.22 shew thee the man whom thou *s*.
2Sa 17. 3 the man whom thou *s* is as if all
20.19 thou *s* to destroy a city and a
1Ki 11.22 thou *s* to go to thine own country?
Pr 2. 4 If thou *s* her as silver, and
Jer 45. 5 *s* thou great things for thyself?
Jn 4.27 yet no man said, What *s* thou?
20.15 why weepest thou? whom *s* thou?

SEEKETH

1Sa 19. 2 Saul my father *s* to kill thee: now
22.23 for he that *s* my life *s* thy life:
2Ki 5. 7 see how he *s* a quarrel against me.
Pr 14. 6 A scorner *s* wisdom, and findeth
15.14 hath understanding *s* knowledge:
17.11 an evil man *s* only rebellion:
18.15 the ear of the wise *s* knowledge.
Jer 5. 1 executeth judgment,...*s* the truth;
Eze 34.12 As a shepherd *s* out his flock in
Mt 7. 8 receiveth; and he that *s* findeth;
12.39 evil...generation *s* after a sign;
16. 4 wicked...generation *s* after a sign;
18.12 and *s* that which is gone astray?
Lk 11.10 receiveth; and he that *s* findeth;
Jn 4.23 the Father *s* such to worship him.
7. 4 he himself *s* to be known openly.
18 speaketh of himself *s* his own glory:
18 he that *s* his glory that sent him,
8.50 there is one that *s* and judgeth.
Ro 3.11 there is none that *s* after God.
11. 7 not obtained that which he *s* for;
1Co 13. 5 itself unseemly, *s* not her own,

SEEKING

Est 10. 3 *s* the wealth of his people, and
Isa 16. 5 judging, and *s* judgment, and
Mt 12.43 places, *s* rest, and findeth none.
13.45 a merchant man, *s* goodly pearls:
Mk 8.11 him, *s* of him a sign from heaven,
Lk 2.45 back again to Jerusalem, *s* him.
11.24 walketh through dry places, *s* rest;
54 and *s* to catch something out of his
13. 7 three years I come *s* fruit on this
Jn 6.24 came to Capernaum, *s* for Jesus.
Ac 13. 8 *s* to turn away the deputy from the
11 *s* some to lead him by the hand.
1Co 10.33 not *s* mine own profit, but the
1Pe 5. 8 about, *s* whom he may devour:

SEEM

Gen 27.12 shall *s* to him as a deceiver;
Dt 15.18 It shall not *s* hard unto thee,
25. 3 brother should *s* vile unto thee.
Jos 24.15 *s* evil unto you to serve the
1Sa 24. 4 as it shall *s* good unto thee.
2Sa 19.37 what shall *s* good unto thee.
38 which shall *s* good unto thee:
1Ki 21. 2 if it *s* good to thee, I will give
1Ch 13. 2 If it *s* good unto you, and that it
Ezr 5.17 if it *s* good to the king, let there be
7.18 whatsoever shall *s* good to thee,
Neh 9.32 let not all the trouble *s* little
Est 5. 4 If it *s* good unto the king, let the
8. 5 the thing *s* right before the king,
Jer 40. 4 If it *s* good unto thee to come
4 but if it *s* ill unto thee to come
Na 2. 4 they shall *s* like torches, they
1Co 11.16 if any man *s* to be contentious,
12.22 body, which *s* to be more feeble,
2Co 10. 9 I may not *s* as if I would terrify
Heb 4. 1 of you should *s* to come short of it.
Jas 1.26 man among you *s* to be religious,

SEEMED

Gen 19.14 he *s* as one that mocked unto
29.20 *s* unto him but a few days,

2Sa 3.19 all that *s* good to Israel, and
19 that *s* good to the whole house of
Ec 9.13 the sun, and it *s* great unto me:
Jer 18. 4 as *s* good to the potter to make it.
27. 5 have given it unto whom it *s* meet
Mt 11.26 for so it *s* good in thy sight.
Lk 1. 3 It *s* good to me also, having had
10.21 for so it *s* good in thy sight.
24.11 words *s* to them as idle tales, and
Ac 15.25 *s* good unto us, being assembled
28 For it *s* good to the Holy Ghost,
Gal 2. 6 But of these who *s* to be somewhat,
6 *s* to be somewhat in conference
9 and John, who *s* to be pillars

SEEMETH

Lev 14.35 It *s* to me there is as it were a
Nu 16. 9 *S* it but a small thing unto you,
Jos 9.25 as it *s* good and right unto thee
Jdg 10.15 us whatsoever *s* good unto thee;
19.24 unto them what *s* good unto you:
1Sa 1.23 Do what *s* thee good; tarry until
3.18 let him do what *s* him good.
11.10 with us all that *s* good unto you.
14.36 Do whatsoever *s* good unto thee.
40 Do what *s* good unto thee.
18.23 *S* it to you a light thing to be a
2Sa 10.12 Lord do that which *s* him good.
15.26 him do to me as *s* good unto him.
18. 4 What *s* you best I will do.
24.22 offer up what *s* good unto him:
Est 3.11 with them as it *s* good to thee.
Pr 14.12 a way which *s* right unto a man,
16.25 is a way that *s* right unto a man,
18.17 that is first in his own cause *s* just;
Jer 26.14 do with me as *s* good and meet
40. 4 it *s* good and convenient for thee
5 wheresoever it *s* convenient unto
Eze 34.18 *S* it a small thing unto you to have
Lk 8.18 even that which he *s* to have.
Ac 17.18 He *s* to be a setter forth of strange
25.27 it *s* to me unreasonable to send a
1Co 3.18 you *s* to be wise in this world,
Heb 12.11 for the present *s* to be joyous, but

SEEMLY

Pr 19.10 Delight is not *s* for a fool; much
26. 1 so honor is not *s* for a fool.

SEEN

Gen 9.14 the bow shall be *s* in the cloud:
22.14 the mount of the Lord it shall be *s*.
31.42 God hath *s* mine affliction and the
32.30 I have *s* God face to face, and my
33.10 as though I had *s* the face of God,
Ex 3. 7 I have surely *s* the affliction of my
33.23 parts: but my face shall not be *s*.
Nu 14.14 that thou Lord art *s* face to face,
Dt 3.21 eyes have *s* all that the Lord your
11. 7 your eyes have *s* all the great acts
Jos 24. 7 your eyes have *s* what I have done
Jdg 6.22 I have *s* an angel of the Lord face
14. 2 I have *s* a woman in Timnath of the
1Ki 10. 4 when the queen of Sheba had *s* all
2Ki 20. 5 thy prayer, I have *s* thy tears:
1Ch 29.17 now have I *s* with joy thy people,
Job 5. 3 I have *s* the foolish taking root:
8.18 him, saying, I have not *s* thee.
10.18 up the ghost, and no eye had *s* me!
13. 1 mine eye hath *s* all this, mine ear
15.17 that which I have *s* I will declare;
38.17 *s* the doors of the shadow of death?
Ps 35.22 This thou hast *s*, O Lord: keep not
37.25 have I not *s* the righteous forsaken,
35 I have *s* the wicked in great power,
90.15 the years wherein we have *s* evil.
98. 3 have *s* the salvation of our God.
Ec 3.10 I have *s* the travail, which God hath
5.13 evil which I have *s* under the sun,
18 Behold that which I have *s*: it is
8. 9 All this have I *s*, and applied my
9.13 This wisdom have I *s* also under
Isa 6. 5 for mine eyes have *s* the King, the
9. 2 in darkness have *s* a great light:
38. 5 heard thy prayer, I have *s* thy tears:
44.16 Aha, I am warm, I have *s* the fire:
60. 2 and his glory shall be *s* upon thee.
64. 4 by the ear, neither hath the eye *s*,
Jer 7.11 even I have *s* it, saith the Lord.
La 3. 1 I am the man that hath *s* affliction
59 O Lord, thou hath *s* my wrong:
Eze 8.15, 17 Hast thou *s* this, O son of man?
13. 3 own spirit, and have *s* nothing!
8 ye have spoken vanity, and *s* lies,
47. 6 me, Son of man, hast thou *s* this?
Dan 8.15 I, even I Daniel, had *s* the vision,
9.21 Gabriel, whom I had *s* in the vision
Hos 6.10 I have *s* an horrible thing in the
Zec 9. 8 for now have I *s* with mine eyes.
14 And the Lord shall be *s* over them,
Mt 2. 2 for we have *s* his star in the east,
6. 1 alms before men, to be *s* of them:
5 that they may be *s* of men.
9.33 saying, It was never so *s* in Israel.
13.17 ye see, and have not *s* them;
21.32 ye, when ye had *s* it, repented not
23. 5 works they do for to be *s* of men:
Mk 9. 1 they have *s* the kingdom of God
9 no man what things they had *s*,
16.11 was alive, and had been *s* of her,
14 believed not them which had *s* him
Lk 1.22 perceived that he had *s* a vision in
2.17 they had *s* it, they made known
20 things that they had heard and *s*,
26 before he had *s* the Lord's Christ.
30 For mine eyes have *s* thy salvation,
5.26 We have *s* strange things to day.
7.22 tell John what things ye have *s* and
9.36 of those things which they had *s*.
10.24 ye see, and have not *s* them;
19.37 the mighty works that they had *s*;
23. 8 he hoped to have *s* some miracle
24.23 they had also *s* a vision of angels,
37 supposed that they had *s* a spirit.
Jn 1.18 No man hath *s* God at any time;
3.11 know, and testify that we have *s*;
32 what he hath *s* and heard, that he
4.45 having *s* all the things that he did
5.37 voice at any time, nor *s* his shape.
6.14 had *s* the miracle that Jesus did,
36 ye also have *s* me, and believe
46 that any man hath *s* the Father,
46 is of God, he hath *s* the Father.
8.38 which I have *s* with my Father:
38 which ye have *s* with your father.
57 old, and hast thou *s* Abraham?
9. 8 had *s* him that he was blind,
37 Thou hast both *s* him, and it is he
11.45 had *s* the things which Jesus did,
14. 7 ye know him, and have *s* him.
9 that hath *s* me hath *s* the Father;
15.24 now have they both *s* and hated me
20.18 disciples that she had *s* the Lord,
25 said unto him, We have *s* the Lord.
29 because thou hast *s* me, thou hast
29 blessed are they that have not *s*,
Ac 1. 3 being *s* of them forty days, and
11 as ye have *s* him go into heaven.
4.20 which we have *s* and heard.
7.34 I have *s*,...the affliction of my
34 I have *s* the affliction of my people,
44 to the fashion that he had *s*.
9.12 hath *s* in a vision a man named
27 how he had *s* the Lord in the way,
10.17 vision which he had *s* should mean,
11.13 how he had *s* an angel in his house,
23 came, and had *s* the grace of God,
13.31 And he was *s* many days of them
16.10 And after he had *s* the vision,
40 and when they had *s* the brethren,
21.29 (For they had *s* before with him
22.15 of what thou hast *s* and heard.
26.16 of these things which thou hast *s*,
Ro 1.20 creation of the world are clearly *s*,
8.24 but hope that is *s* is not hope: for
1Co 2. 9 Eye hath not *s*, nor ear heard,
9. 1 have I not *s* Jesus Christ our
15. 5 And that he was *s* of Cephas,
6 he was *s* of above five hundred
7 After that, he was *s* of James;
8 And last of all he was *s* of me also,
2Co 4.18 look not at the things which are *s*,
18 but at the things which are not *s*:
18 things which are *s* are temporal;
18 things which are not *s* are eternal.
Php 4. 9 and heard, and *s* in me, do;
Col 2. 1 as have not *s* my face in the flesh;
18 those things which he hath not *s*,
1Ti 3.16 justified in the Spirit, *s* of angels,
6.16 whom no man hath *s*, nor can see:
Heb 11. 1 for, the evidence of things not *s*.
3 things which are *s* were not made
7 warned of God of things not *s* as yet,
13 but having *s* them afar off, and
Jas 5.11 and have *s* the end of the Lord;
1Pe 1. 8 Whom having not *s*, ye love; in
1Jn 1. 1 which we have *s* with our eyes,
2 and we have *s* it, and bear witness,
3 That which we have *s* and heard
3. 6 whosoever sinneth hath not *s* him,
4.12 No man hath *s* God at any time.
14 And we have *s* and do testify that
20 not his brother whom he hath *s*,
20 he love God whom he hath not *s*?
3Jn 11 he that doeth evil hath not *s* God.
Rev 1.19 Write the things...thou hast *s*,
11.19 there was *s* in his temple the ark
22. 8 And when I had heard and *s*, I fell

SEER

1Sa 9. 9 Come, and let us go to the *s*: for
9 Prophet was beforetime called a *S*.)
11 and said unto them, Is the *s* here?
19 answered Saul, and said, I am the *s*:
2Sa 15.27 Zadok the priest, Art not thou a *s*?
24.11 unto the prophet Gad, David's *s*,
1Ch 9.22 David and Samuel the *s* did ordain
21. 9 Lord spake unto Gad, David's *s*,
25. 5 the sons of Heman the king's *s* in
26.28 all that Samuel the *s*, and Saul
29.29 in the book of Samuel the *s*,
29 and in the book of Gad the *s*,
2Ch 9.29 and in the visions Iddo the *s*
12.15 Iddo the *s* concerning genealogies?
16. 7 Hanani the *s* came to Asa king
10 Then Asa was wroth with the *s*,
19. 2 of Hanani the *s* went out to meet
29.25 of David, and of Gad the king's *s*,
30 of David, and of Asaph the *s*.
35.15 Heman, and Jeduthun the king's *s*;
Am 7.12 O thou *s*, go, flee thee away into

SEER'S

1Sa 9.18 Tell me,..where the *s* house is.

SEERS

2Ki 17.13 all the prophets, and by all the *s*,
2Ch 33.18 words of the *s* that spake to him
19 written among the sayings of the *s*.
Isa 29.10 your rulers, the *s* hath he covered.
30.10 Which say to the *s*, See not; and
Mic 3. 7 Then shall the *s* be ashamed, and

SEEST

Gen 16.13 spake unto her, Thou God *s* me;
31.43 and all that thou *s* is mine: and
Ex 10.28 day thou *s* my face thou shalt die,
Jdg 9.36 *s* the shadow of the mountains as
Job 10. 4 of flesh? of *s* thou as man seeth?
Pr 26.12 *S* thou a man wise in his own
29.20 *S* thou a man that is hasty in his
Ec 5. 8 thou *s* the oppression of the poor,
Jer 1.11 saying, Jeremiah, what *s* thou?

Eze 8. 6 Son of man, *s* thou what they do?
Am 7. 8 said unto me, Amos, what *s* thou?
Zec 4. 2 And said unto me, What *s* thou?
Mk 5.31 *s* the multitude thronging thee,
13. 2 him, *S* thou these great buildings?
Lk 7.44 unto Simon, *S* thou this woman?
Ac 21.20 him, Thou *s*, brother, how many
Jas 2.22 *S* thou how faith wrought with his
Rev 1.11 What thou *s*, write in a book, and

SEETH

Ex 12.23 he *s* the blood upon the lintel, and
1Sa 16. 7 him: for the Lord *s* not as man
7 not as man *s*; for man looketh
Job 10. 4 of flesh? or seest thou as man *s*?
11.11 he *s* wickedness also; will he not
22.14 a covering to him, that he *s* not;
28.10 his eye *s* every precious thing.
34.21 of man, and he *s* all his goings.
42. 5 the ear: but now mine eye *s* thee.
Ps 49.10 he *s* that wise men die, likewise
Isa 29.15 the dark, and they say, Who *s* us?
47.10 thou hast said, None *s* me. Thy
Eze 8.12 The Lord *s* us not: the Lord hath
Mt 6. 4 and thy Father which *s* in secret
6 thy Father which *s* in secret shall
18 which *s* in secret, shall reward thee
Mk 5.38 *s* the tumult, and them that wept
Lk 16.23 *s* Abraham afar off, and Lazarus
Jn 1.29 John *s* Jesus coming unto him,
5.19 but what he *s* the Father do: for
6.40 that every one which *s* the Son,
9.21 means he now *s*, we know not; or
10.12 *s* the wolf coming, and leaveth
11. 9 he *s* the light of this world.
12.45 that *s* me *s* him that sent me.
14.17 it *s* him not, neither knoweth him:
19 and the world *s* me no more; but
20. 1 *s* the stone taken away from the
6 sepulcher, and *s* the linen clothes
12 *s* two angels in white sitting, the
21.20 *s* the disciple whom Jesus loved
Ro 8.24 for what a man *s*, why doth he
2Co 12. 6 me above that which he *s* me to be,
1Jn 3.17 and *s* his brother have need.

SEIZE

Jos 8. 7 the ambush, and *s* upon the city:
Job 3. 6 that night, let darkness *s* upon it:
Ps 55.15 Let death *s* upon them, and let
Mt 21.38 and let us *s* on his inheritance.

SELEUCIA

Ac 13. 4 the Holy Ghost, departed unto *S*;

SELF

Ex 32.13 whom thou swarest by thine own *s*,
Jn 5.30 I can of mine own *s* do nothing:
17. 5 glorify thou me with thine own *s*
1Co 4. 3 yea, I judge not mine own *s*.
Phm 19 owest unto me even thine own *s*
1Pe 2.24 Who his own *s* bare our sins in his

SELFWILLED

Tit 1. 7 not *s*, not soon angry, not given to
2Pe 2.10 Presumptuous are they, *s*, they

SELL

Gen 25.31 said, *S* me this day thy birthright.
37.27 and let us *s* him to the Ishmeelites,
Ex 21. 7 *s* his daughter to be a maidservant,
8 to *s* her unto a strange nation he
35 then they shall *s* the live ox, and
22. 1 ox, or a sheep, and kill it, or *s* it;
25.14 thou *s* ought unto thy neighbor,
15 of the fruits he shall *s* unto thee:
16 of the fruits doth he *s* unto thee.
29 *s* a dwelling house in a walled city,
47 and *s* himself unto the stranger or
Dt 2.28 Thou shalt *s* me meat for money,
14.21 thou mayest *s* it unto an alien:
21.14 shalt not *s* her at all for money,
Jdg 4. 9 the Lord shall *s* Sisera into the
1Ki 21.25 did *s* himself to work wickedness
2Ki 4. 7 Go, *s* the oil, and pay thy debt, and
Neh 5. 8 and will ye even *s* your brethren?
10.31 victuals on the sabbath day to *s*,
Pr 23.23 Buy the truth, and *s* it not; also
Eze 30.12 *s* the land into the hand of the
48.14 And they shall not *s* of it, neither
Joel 3. 8 And I will *s* your sons and your
8 they shall *s* them to the Sabeans,
Am 8. 5 be gone, that we may *s* corn?
6 yea, and *s* the refuse of the wheat?
Zec 11. 5 they that *s* them say, Blessed be
Mt 19.21 go and *s* that thou hast, and give
25. 9 go ye rather to them that *s*, and
Mk 10.21 *s* whatsoever thou hast, and give
Lk 12.33 *S* that ye have, and give alms;
18.22 *s* all that thou hast, and distribute
22.36 no sword, let him *s* his garment,
Jas 4.13 and buy and *s*, and get gain:
Rev 13.17 that no man might buy of *s*, save

SELLER

Isa 24. 2 as with the buyer, so with the *s*;
Eze 7.12 buyer rejoice, nor the *s* mourn:
13 For the *s* shall not return to that
Ac 16.14 named Lydia, a *s* of purple,

SELLEST

Ps 44.12 Thou *s* thy people for nought,

SELLETH

Ex 21.16 that stealeth a man, and *s* him,
Dt 24. 7 merchandise of him, or *s* him;
Ru 4. 3 *s* a parcel of land, which was our
Pr 11.26 upon the head of him that *s* it.
31.24 She maketh fine linen, and *s* it;
Na 3. 4 *s* nations through her whoredoms,
Mt 13.44 goeth and *s* all that he hath, and

SELVES

Lk 21.30 own *s* that summer is now nigh
Ac 20.30 Also of your own *s* shall men arise,
2Co 8. 5 first gave their own *s* to the Lord,
13. 5 be in the faith; prove your own *s*.
5 Know ye not your own *s*, how that
2Ti 3. 2 men shall be lovers of their own *s*,
Jas 1.22 hearers only, deceiving...own *s*.

SENATE

Ac 5.21 all the *s* of the children of Israel,

SENATORS

Ps 105.22 pleasure; and teach his *s* wisdom.

SEND

Gen 24. 7 he shall *s* his angel before thee,
12 thee, *s* me good speed this day,
45. 5 For God did *s* me before you to
Ex 4.13 he said, O my Lord, *s*, I pray thee,
23.20 I *s* an Angel before thee, to keep
1Sa 5.11 *S* away the ark of the God of Israel,
16.19 *S* me David thy son, which is with
20.21 I will *s* a lad, saying, Go, find out
2Sa 11. 6 saying, *S* me Uriah the Hittite.
2Ki 5. 5 *s* a letter unto the king of Israel.
7 doth *s* unto me to recover a man
2Ch 2. 7 *S* me now therefore a man cunning
8 *S* me also cedar trees, fir trees,
Neh 2. 6 So it pleased the king to *s* me;
Job 38.35 Canst thou *s* lightnings, that they
Ps 20. 2 *S* thee help from the sanctuary,
43. 3 O *s* out thy light and thy truth:
57. 3 God shall *s* forth his mercy and his
118.25 I beseech thee, *s* now prosperity.
Pr 10.26 is the sluggard to them that *s* him.
Isa 6. 8 Whom shall I *s*, and who will go
8 Then said I, Here am I; *s* me.
Jer 42. 5 the Lord thy God shall *s* thee to us.
Eze 2. 3 I *s* thee to the children of Israel,
Joel 2.19 I will *s* you corn, and wine, and oil,
Am 8.11 that I will *s* a famine in the land,
Mal 3. 1 Behold, I will *s* my messenger,
4. 5 I will *s* you Elijah the prophet
Mt 9.38 *s* forth laborers into his harvest.
10.16 I *s* you forth as sheep in the midst
34 I am come to *s* peace on earth:
34 I come not to *s* peace, but a sword.
11.10 I *s* my messenger before thy face,
12.20 he *s* forth judgment unto victory.
13.41 Son of man shall *s* forth his angels,
14.15 *s* the multitude away, that they
15.23 *S* her away; for she crieth after us.
32 I will not *s* them away fasting, lest
21. 3 and straightway he will *s* them.
23.34 behold, I *s* unto you prophets, and
24.31 he shall *s* his angels with a great
Mk 1. 2 I *s* my messenger before thy face,
3.14 he might *s* them forth to preach,
5.10 that he would not *s* them away out
12 *S* us into the swine, that we may
6. 7 to *s* them forth by two and two;
36 *S* them away, that they may go
8. 3 if I *s* them away fasting to their
11. 3 straightway he will *s* him hither.
12.13 *s* unto him certain of the Pharisees
13.27 then shall he *s* his angels, and shall
Lk 7.27 I *s* my messenger before thy face,
9.12 *S* the multitude away, that they
10. 2 *s* forth laborers into his harvest.
3 *s* you forth as lambs among wolves.
11.49 I will *s* them prophets and apostles,
12.49 I am come to *s* fire on the earth;
16.24 *s* Lazarus, that he may dip the tip
27 *s* him to my father's house:
20.13 I will *s* my beloved son: it may be
24.49 I *s* the promise of my Father upon
Jn 13.20 whomsoever I *s* receiveth me;
14.26 whom the Father will *s* in my name,
15.26 I will *s* unto you from the Father,
16. 7 but if I depart, I will *s* him unto you.
17. 8 have believed that thou didst *s* me.
20.21 hath sent me, even so *s* I you.
Ac 3.20 And he shall *s* Jesus Christ, which
7.34 now come, I will *s* thee into Egypt.
35 the same did God *s* to be a ruler
10. 5 *s* men to Joppa, and call for one
22 angel to *s* for thee into his house,
32 *S* therefore to Joppa, and call
11.13 *S* men to Joppa, and call for Simon,
29 *s* relief unto the brethren which
15.22 *s* chosen men of their own company
23 and elders and brethren *s* greeting
25 to *s* chosen men unto you with our
22.21 for I will *s* thee far hence unto the
25. 3 he would *s* for him to Jerusalem,
21 be kept till I might *s* him to Cæsar.
25 Augustus, I...determined to *s* him.
27 to me unreasonable to *s* a prisoner,
26.17 Gentiles, unto whom now I *s* thee,
1Co 16. 3 will I *s* to bring your liberality
Php 2.19 to *s* Timotheus shortly unto you,
23 Him...I hope to *s* presently, so
25 necessary to *s* to you Epaphroditus,
2Th 2.11 God shall *s* them strong delusion,
Tit 3.12 When I shall *s* Artemas unto thee,
Jas 3.11 fountain *s* forth at the same time
Rev 1.11 *s* it unto the seven churches
11.10 and shall *s* gifts one to another;

SENDEST

Dt 1 5.13 thou *s* him out free from thee,
18 thou *s* him away free from thee;
Jos 1.16 whithersoever thou *s* us, we will
2Ki 1. 6 thou *s* to inquire of Baal-zebub
Job 14.20 his continuance, and *s* him away.
Ps 104.30 Thou *s* forth thy spirit, they are

SENDETH

Dt 24. 3 hand, and *s* her out of his house;
1Ki 17.14 until the day that the Lord *s* rain

Job 5.10 and *s* waters upon the fields:
12.15 he *s* them out, and they overturn
Ps 104.10 He *s* the springs into the valleys,
147.15 He *s* forth his commandment upon
18 He *s* out his word, and melteth
Pr 26. 6 *s* a message by the hand of a fool
SS 1.12 my spikenard *s* forth the smell
Isa 18. 2 That *s* ambassadors by the sea,
Mt 5.45 and *s* rain on the just and on the
Mk 11. 1 he *s* forth two of his disciples,
14.13 And he *s* forth two of his disciples,
Lk 14.32 he *s* an ambassage, and desireth
Ac 23.26 excellent governor Felix *s* greeting.

SENDING

2Sa 13.16 this evil in *s* me away is greater
2Ch 36.15 rising up betimes, and *s*; because
Est 9.19 and of *s* portions zone to another.
22 and of *s* portions one to another,
Ps 78.49 by *s* evil angels among them.
Isa 7.25 it shall be for the *s* forth of oxen,
Jer 7.25 daily rising up early and *s* them:
25. 4 prophets, rising early and *s* them;
26. 5 both rising up early, and *s* them,
29.19 rising up early and *s* them;
35.15 rising up early and *s* them,
44. 4 prophets, rising early and *s* them,
Eze 17.15 in *s* his ambassadors into Egypt,
Ro 8. 3 God *s* his own Son in the likeness

SENNACHERIB

2Ki 18.13 did *S* king of Assyria come up
19.16 and hear the words of *S*, which
20 thou hast prayed to me against *S*
36 So *S* king of Assyria departed,
2Ch 32. 1 *S* king of Assyria came, and
2 Hezekiah saw that *S* was come,
9 this did *S* king of Assyria send his
10 Thus saith *S* king of Assyria,
22 the hand of *S* the king of Assyria,
Isa 36. 1 that *S* king of Assyria came up
37.17 and hear all the words of *S*, which
21 thou hast prayed to me against *S*
37 So *S* king of Assyria departed,

SENSE

Neh 8. 8 of God distinctly, and gave the *s*,

SENSES

Heb 5.14 have their *s* exercised to discern

SENSUAL

Jas 3.15 above, but is earthly, *s*, devilish.
Jude 19 *s*, having not the Spirit.

SENT

Gen 8. 7 And he *s* forth a raven, which went
8 And he *s* forth a dove from him, to
37.32 they *s* the coat of many colors,
41. 8 *s* and called for all the magicians
14 then Pharaoh *s* and called Joseph,
45. 7 God *s* me before you to preserve
Ex 2. 5 flags, she *s* her maid to fetch it.
3.13 God of your fathers hath *s* me
14 of Israel, I Am hath *s* me unto you.
15 God of Jacob, hath *s* me unto you:
9.27 Pharaoh *s*, and called for Moses
Nu 13.17 Moses *s* them to spy out the land
21. 6 Lord *s* fiery serpents among the
Jdg 6. 8 Lord *s* a prophet unto the children
9.23 Then God *s* an evil spirit between
1Sa 5.10 they *s* the ark of God to Ekron.
16.22 Saul *s* to Jesse, saying, Let David,
2Sa 12. 1 the Lord *s* Nathan unto David.
2Ki 2. 2 for the Lord hath *s* me to Beth-el.
5.10 Elisha *s* a messenger unto him,
19.16 *s* him to reproach the living God.
2Ch 25.15 he *s* unto him a prophet, which
32.21 the Lord *s* an angel, which cut off
Ezr 4.11 copy of the letter that they *s* unto
Neh 6. 2 Sanballat and Geshem *s* unto me,
Est 3.13 letters were *s* by posts into all the
Job 22. 9 Thou hast *s* widows away empty,
Ps 18.14 Yea, he *s* out his arrows, and
105.26 He *s* Moses his servant; and Aaron
28 He *s* darkness, and made it dark;
106.15 but *s* leanness into their soul.
107.20 He *s* his word, and healed them,
111. 9 He *s* redemption unto his people:
Isa 48.16 God, and his Spirit, hath *s* me.
55.11 prosper in the thing whereto I *s* it.
Jer 26.12 The Lord *s* me to prophesy against
42.20 ye *s* me unto the Lord your God,
43. 2 Lord our God hath not *s* thee to
Eze 3. 5 For thou art not *s* to a people of a
Dan 3.28 the God...who hath *s* his angel,
6.22 My God hath *s* his angel, and hath
Jon 1. 4 the Lord *s* out a great wind into
Mic 6. 4 I *s* before thee Moses, Aaron, and
Zec 2. 8 he *s* me unto the nations which
9 that the Lord of hosts hath *s* me.
7.12 Lord of hosts hath *s* in his spirit
Mt 2. 8 And he *s* them to Bethlehem, and
16 *s* forth, and slew all the children
10. 5 These twelve Jesus *s* forth, and
40 receive me receiveth him that *s* me.
11. 2 of Christ, he *s* two of his disciples,
13.36 Then Jesus *s* the multitude away,
14.10 he *s*, and beheaded John in the
22 while he *s* the multitudes away.
23 when he had *s* the multitudes away,
35 they *s* out into all that country
15.24 I am not *s* but unto the lost sheep
39 he *s* away the multitude, and took
20. 2 a day, he *s* them into his vineyard.
21. 1 of Olives, then *s* Jesus two disciples,
34 *s* his servants to the husbandmen,
36 he *s* other servants more than the
37 last of all he *s* unto them his son,
22. 3 *s* forth his servants to call them
4 he *s* forth other servants, saying,
7 *s* forth his armies, and destroyed
16 they *s* out unto him their disciples
23.37 stonest them which are *s* unto thee,
27.19 his wife *s* unto him, saying, Have
Mk 1.43 him, and forthwith *s* him away;
3.31 standing without, *s* unto him,
4.36 they had *s* away the multitude,
6.17 *s* forth and laid hold upon John,
27 the king *s* an executioner, and
45 while he *s* away the people.
46 And when he had *s* them away, he
8. 9 thousand: and he *s* them away.
26 he *s* him away to his house, saying,
9.37 receiveth not me, but him that *s* me.
12. 2 he *s* to the husbandmen a servant,
3 beat him, and *s* him away empty.
4 he *s* unto them another servant;
4 *s* him away shamefully handled.
5 again he *s* another; and him they
6 he *s* him also last unto them,
Lk 1.19 am *s* to speak unto thee, and to
26 the angel Gabriel was *s* from God
53 the rich he hath *s* empty away.
4.18 *s* me to heal the brokenhearted, to
26 But unto none of them was Elias *s*,
43 cities also: for therefore am I *s*.
7. 3 *s* unto him the elders of the Jews,
6 the centurion *s* friends to him,
10 they that were *s*, returning to the
19 of his disciples, *s* them to Jesus,
20 John Baptist hath *s* us unto thee,
8.38 with him: but Jesus *s* him away,
9. 2 he *s* them to preach the kingdom
48 receive me receiveth him that *s* me:
52 And *s* messengers before his face:
10. 1 *s* them two and two before his face
16 me, despiseth him that *s* me.
13.34 stonest them that are *s* unto thee;
14.17 *s* his servant at supper time to say
15.15 *s* him into his fields to feed swine.
19.14 and *s* a message after him, saying,
29 of Olives, he *s* two of his disciples,
32 they that were *s* went their way,
20.10 he *s* a servant to the husbandmen.
10 beat him, and *s* him away empty.
11 And again he *s* another servant:
11 shamefully...*s* him away empty.
12 And again he *s* a third: and they
20 *s* forth spies, which should feign
22. 8 he *s* Peter and John, saying, Go and
35 When I *s* you without purse, and
23. 7 he *s* him to Herod, who himself
11 robe, and *s* him again to Pilate.
15 nor yet Herod: for I *s* you to him;
Jn 1. 6 There was a man *s* from God,
8 was *s* to bear witness of that Light.
19 Jews *s* priests and Levites from
22 give an answer to them that *s* us.
24 which were *s* were of the Pharisees.
33 that *s* me to baptize with water,
3.17 God *s* not his Son into the world
28 Christ, but that I am *s* before him.
34 God hath *s* speaketh the words of
4.34 is to do the will of him that *s* me,
38 I *s* you to reap that whereon ye
5.23 not the Father which hath *s* him.
24 believeth on him that *s* me, hath
30 will of the Father which hath *s* me.
33 Ye *s* unto John, and he bare
36 of me, that the Father hath *s* me.
37 Father himself, which hath *s* me,
38 for whom he hath *s*, him ye believe
6.29 ye believe on him whom he hath *s*.
38 will, but the will of him that *s* me.
39 the Father's will which hath *s* me,
40 this is the will of him that *s* me,
44 Father which hath *s* me draw him:
57 As the living Father hath *s* me,
7.16 is not mine, but his that *s* me.
18 that seeketh his glory that *s* him,
28 he that *s* me is true, whom ye know
29 am from him, and he hath *s* me.
32 chief priests *s* officers to take him.
33 and then I go unto him that *s* me.
8.16 but I and the Father that *s* me.
18 Father that *s* me beareth witness of
26 he that *s* me is true; and I speak
29 he that *s* me is with me: the Father
42 came I of myself, but he *s* me.
9. 4 work the works of him that *s* me,
7 (which is by interpretation, *S*.)
10.36 sanctified, and *s* into the world,
11. 3 Therefore his sisters *s* unto him,
42 may believe that thou hast *s* me.
12.44 not on me, but on him that *s* me.
45 that seeth me seeth him that *s* me.
49 but the Father which *s* me, he gave
13.16 is *s* greater than he that *s* him.
20 me receiveth him that *s* me.
14.24 mine, but the Father's which *s* me.
15.21 they know not him that *s* me.
16. 5 now I go my way to him that *s* me;
17. 3 Jesus Christ, whom thou hast *s*.
18 As thou hast *s* me into the world,
18 have I also *s* them into the world.
21 may believe that thou hast *s* me.
23 may know that thou hast *s* me,
25 have known that thou hast *s* me.
18.24 had *s* him bound unto Caiaphas
20.21 as my Father hath *s* me, even so
Ac 3.26 his Son Jesus, *s* him to bless you,
5.21 and *s* to the prison to have them
7.12 Egypt, he *s* out our fathers first.
14 Then *s* Joseph,...called his father
8.14 they *s* unto them Peter and John:
9.17 hath *s* me, that thou mightest
30 and *s* him forth to Tarsus.
38 they *s* unto him two men, desiring
10. 8 unto them, he *s* them to Joppa.
17 the men which were *s* from
20 doubting nothing:...I have *s* them.
21 to the men which were *s* unto him

In the sepulcher after the Resurrection, an angel sits where Jesus' body had been; engraving by Doré.

Ac 10.29 gainsaying, as soon as I was *s* for:
29 for what intent ye have *s* for me?
33 Immediately therefore I *s* to thee;
36 God *s* unto the children of Israel,
11.11 I was, *s* from Caesarea unto me.
22 and they *s* forth Barnabas, that he
30 *s* it to the elders by the hands of
12.11 that the Lord hath *s* his angel,
13. 3 hands on them, they *s* them away.
4 being *s* forth by the Holy Ghost,
15 of the synagogue *s* unto them,
26 you is the word of this salvation *s*.
15.27 *s* therefore Judas and Silas, who
16.35 magistrates *s* the serjeants, saying,
36 magistrates have *s* to let you go:
17.10 *s* away Paul and Silas by night
14 the brethren *s* away Paul to go as
19.22 he *s* into Macedonia two of them
31 *s* unto him, desiring him that he
20.17 *s* to Ephesus, and called the elders
23.30 I *s* straightway to thee, and gave
24.24 he *s* for Paul, and heard him
26 wherefore he *s* for him the oftener,
28.28 salvation...is *s* unto the Gentiles,
Ro 10.15 shall they preach, except they be *s*?
1Co 1.17 For Christ *s* me not to baptize, but
4.17 cause have I *s* unto you Timotheus,
2Co 8.18 we have *s* with him the brother,
22 we have *s* with them our brother,
9. 3 Yet have I *s* the brethren, lest our
12.17 any of them whom I *s* unto you?
18 Titus, and with him I *s* a brother.
Gal 4. 4 God *s* forth his Son, made of a
6 God hath *s* forth the Spirit of his
Eph 6.22 Whom I have *s* unto you for the
Php 2.28 *s* him therefore the more carefully,
4.16 ye *s* once and again unto my
18 the things which were *s* from you,
Col 4. 8 Whom I have *s* unto you for the
1Th 3. 2 And *s* Timotheus, our brother, and
5 I *s* to know your faith, lest by some
2Ti 4.12 And Tychicus have I *s* to Ephesus.
Phm 12 Whom I have *s* again: thou
Heb 1.14 *s* forth to minister for them who
Jas 2.25 and had *s* them out another way?
1Pe 1.12 Holy Ghost *s* down from heaven;
2.14 unto them that are *s* by him for
1Jn 4. 9 God *s* his only begotten Son into
10 and *s* his Son to be the propitiation
14 Father *s* the Son to be the Saviour
Rev 1. 1 he *s* and signified it by his angel
5. 6 of God *s* forth into all the earth.
22. 6 God of the holy prophets *s* his angel
16 Jesus have *s* mine angel to testify

SENTENCE

Dt 17. 9 shall shew thee the *s* of judgment:
10 thou shalt do according to the *s*,
11 According to the *s* of the law
11 from the *s* which they shall shew
Ps 17. 2 Let my *s* come forth from thy
Pr 16.10 divine *s* is in the lips of the king:
Ec 8.11 *s* against an evil work is not
Jer 4.12 also will I give *s* against them.
Lk 23.24 Pilate gave *s* that it should be
Ac 15.19 my *s* is, that we trouble not them,
2Co 1. 9 we had the *s* of death in ourselves,

SEPARATE

Gen 13. 9 *s* thyself, I pray thee, from me:
30.40 And Jacob did *s* the lambs, and
49.26 him that was *s* from his brethren.
Lev 15.31 shall ye *s* the children of Israel
22. 2 *s* themselves from the holy things
Nu 6. 2 *s* themselves to vow a vow of a
2 to *s* themselves unto the Lord:
3 He shall *s* himself from wine and
8.14 thou *s* the Levites from among the
16.21 *S* yourselves from among this
Dt 19. 2 Thou shalt *s* three cities for thee
7 Thou shalt *s* three cities for thee.
29.21 *s* him unto evil out of all the tribes
Jos 16. 9 the *s* cities for the children of
1Ki 8.53 *s* them from among all the people
Ezr 10.11 *s* yourselves from the people of the
Jer 37.12 to *s* himself thence in the midst
Eze 41.12 was before the *s* place at the end
13 the *s* place, and the building, with
14 and of the *s* place toward the east,
15 the *s* place which was behind it,
42. 1 that was over against the *s* place,
10 the east, over against the *s* place,
13 which are before the *s* place, they
Mt 25.32 he shall *s* them one from another,
Lk 6.22 shall *s* you from their company,
Ac 13. 2 *S* me Barnabas and Saul for the
Ro 8.35 shall *s* us from the love of Christ?
39 able to *s* us from the love of God,
2Co 6.17 them, and be ye *s*, saith the Lord,
Heb 7.26 undefiled, *s* from sinners, and
Jude 19 These be they who *s* themselves.

SEPARATED

Gen 13.11 they *s* themselves the one from
14 after that Lot was *s* from him,
25.23 two manner of people shall be *s*
Ex 33.16 so shall we be *s*, I and thy people,
Lev 20.24 have *s* you from other people.
25 I have *s* from you as unclean.
Nu 16. 9 God of Israel hath *s* you from the
Dt 10. 8 time the Lord *s* the tribe of Levi,
32. 8 when he *s* the sons of Adam, he
33.16 him that was *s* from his brethren.
1Ch 12. 8 there *s* themselves unto David into
23.13 and Aaron was *s*, that he should
25. 1 *s* to the service of the sons of Asaph,
2Ch 25.10 Then Amaziah *s* them, to wit, the
Ezr 6.21 *s* themselves unto them from the
8.24 Then I *s* twelve of the chief of the
9. 1 not *s* themselves from the people of
10. 8 himself *s* from the congregation of
16 all of them by their names, were *s*,
Neh 4.19 we are *s* upon the wall, one far

9. 2 seed of Israel *s* themselves from
10.28 all they that had *s* themselves from
13. 3 they *s* from Israel all the mixed
Pr 18. 1 desire a man, having *s* himself,
19. 4 the poor is *s* from his neighbor.
Isa 56. 3 Lord hath utterly *s* me from his
59. 2 your iniquities have *s* between you
Hos 4.14 themselves are *s* with whores,
9.10 *s* themselves unto that shame;
Ac 19. 9 from them, and *s* the disciples,
Ro 1. 1 apostle, *s* unto the gospel of God,
Gal 1.15 who *s* me from my mother's womb,
2.12 he withdrew and *s* himself, fearing

SEPULCHER
Dt 34. 6 but no man knoweth of his *s*
1Ki 13.31 *s* wherein the man of God is buried;
2Ki 23.17 It is the *s* of the man of God,
Ps 5. 9 their throat is an open *s*; they
Jer 5.16 Their quiver is as an open *s*, they
Mt 27.60 a great stone to the door of the *s*,
61 Mary, sitting over against the *s*.
64 *s* be made sure until the third day,
66 So they went, and made the *s* sure,
28. 1 and the other Mary to see the *s*.
8 they departed quickly from the *s*
Mk 15.46 laid him in a *s* which was hewn
46 a stone unto the door of the *s*.
16. 2 they came unto the *s* at the rising
3 the stone from the door of the *s*?
5 And entering into the *s*, they saw
8 out quickly, and fled from the *s*;
Lk 23.53 and laid it in a *s* that was hewn
55 beheld the *s*, and how his body
24. 1 morning, they came unto the *s*,
2 the stone rolled away from the *s*.
9 returned from the *s*, and told all
12 arose Peter, and ran unto the *s*;
22 which were early at the *s*;
24 which were with us went to the *s*,
Jn 19.41 in the garden a new *s*, wherein
42 day; for the *s* was nigh at hand.
20. 1 when it was yet dark, unto the *s*,
1 the stone taken away from the *s*.
2 taken away the Lord out of the *s*,
3 other disciple, and came to the *s*.
4 outrun Peter, and came...to the *s*.
6 and went into the *s*, and seeth the
8 disciple, which came first to the *s*,
11 But Mary stood without at the *s*
11 stooped down, and looked in the *s*,
Ac 2.29 his *s* is with us unto this day.
7.16 and laid in the *s* that Abraham
13.29 from the tree, and laid him in a *s*.
Ro 3.13 Their throat is an open *s*; with

SEPULCHERS
2Ch 16.14 And they buried him in his own *s*,
21.20 David, but not in the *s* of the kings.
Neh 2. 3 the city, the place of my fathers' *s*,
Mt 23.27 ye are like unto whited *s*, which
29 garnish the *s* of the righteous,
Lk 11.47 for ye build the *s* of the prophets,
48 killed them, and ye build their *s*.

SERAPHIMS
Isa 6. 2 Above it stood the *s*: each one
6 Then flew one of the *s* unto me,

SERGIUS
Ac 13. 7 *S* Paulus, a prudent man; who

SERJEANTS
Ac 16.35 the magistrates sent the *s*, saying,
38 the *s* told these words unto the

SERPENT
Gen 3. 1 *s* was more subtil than any beast
2 woman said unto the *s*, We may eat
4 *s* said unto the woman, Ye shall not
13 The *s* beguiled me, and I did eat.
14 Lord God said unto the *s*, Because
49.17 Dan shall be a *s* by the way, an
Ex 4. 3 on the ground, and it became a *s*:
7. 9 Pharaoh, and it shall become a *s*.
10 his servants, and it became a *s*.
15 the rod which was turned to a *s*
Nu 21. 8 Make thee a fiery *s*, and set it
9 Moses made a *s* of brass, and put
9 that if a *s* had bitten any man,
9 when he beheld the *s* of brass, he
2Ki 18. 4 the brasen *s* that Moses had made:
Job 26.13 hand hath formed the crooked *s*.
Ps 58. 4 poison is like the poison of a *s*:
140. 3 sharpened their tongues like a *s*;
Pr 23.32 At the last it biteth like a *s*, and
30.19 the way of a *s* upon a rock; the way
Ec 10. 8 breaketh an hedge, a *s* shall bite
11 *s* will bite without enchantment;
Isa 14.29 his fruit shall be a fiery flying *s*.
27. 1 punish leviathan the piercing *s*,
1 even leviathan that crooked *s*; and
30. 6 lion, the viper and fiery flying *s*,
Jer 46.22 voice thereof shall go like a *s*;
Am 5.19 hand on the wall, and a *s* bit him.
9. 3 sea, thence will I command the *s*,
Mic 7.17 They shall lick the dust like a *s*,
Mt 7.10 ask a fish, will he give him a *s*?
Lk 11.11 fish, will he for a fish give him a *s*?
Jn 3.14 And as Moses lifted up the *s* in the
2Co 11. 3 as the *s* beguiled Eve through his
Rev 12. 9 old *s*, called the Devil, and Satan,
14 half a time, from the face of the *s*.
15 the *s* cast out of his mouth water
20. 2 old *s*, which is the Devil, and Satan,

SERPENT'S
Isa 14.29 out of the *s* root shall come forth
65.25 and dust shall be the *s* meat.

SERPENTS
Ex 7.12 man his rod, and they became *s*:
Nu 21. 6 the Lord sent fiery *s* among the
7 that he take away the *s* from us.
Dt 8.15 wilderness, wherein were fiery *s*,
32.24 with the poison of *s* of the dust.
Jer 8.17 I will send *s*, cockatrices, among
Mt 10.16 be ye therefore wise as *s*, and
23.33 Ye *s*, ye generation of vipers, how
Mk 16.18 They shall take up *s*; and if they
Lk 10.19 power to tread on *s* and scorpions,
1Co 10. 9 tempted, and were destroyed of *s*.
Jas 3. 7 of *s*, and of things in the sea, is
Rev 9.19 for their tails were like unto *s*,

SERVANT
Gen 9.25 a *s* of servants shall he be unto
19.19 thy *s* hath found grace in thy sight,
24. 9 the *s* put his hand under the thigh
44.10 whom it is found shall be my *s*;
31 bring down the gray hairs of thy *s*
Ex 21. 2 If thou buy an Hebrew *s*, six years
Nu 12. 7 My *s* Moses is not so, who is
Dt 5.15 thou wast a *s* in the land of Egypt,
Jos 1. 2 Moses my *s* is dead; now therefore
Ru 2. 6 the *s* that was set over the reapers
1Sa 3.10 answered, Speak: for thy *s* heareth.
17.36 Thy *s* slew both the lion and the
22. 8 hath stirred up my *s* against me,
15 king impute any thing unto his *s*,
2Sa 7.20 for thou, Lord God, knowest thy *s*.
29 thee to bless the house of thy *s*,
24.10 take away the iniquity of thy *s*;
1Ki 8.28 respect unto the prayer of thy *s*,
28 which thy *s* prayeth before thee
29 the prayer which thy *s* shall make
30 thou to the supplication of thy *s*,
52 unto the supplication of thy *s*,
12. 7 If thou wilt be a *s* unto this people
2Ki 5. 6 sent Naaman my *s* to thee, that
18 the Lord pardon thy *s* in this thing.
8. 4 Gehazi the *s* of the man of God,
13 said, But what, is thy *s* a dog,
1Ch 17.26 promised this goodness unto thy *s*:
Job 1. 8 Hast thou considered my *s* Job,
3.19 and the *s* is free from his master.
7. 2 a *s* earnestly desireth the shadow,
19.16 I called my *s*, and he gave me no
41. 4 wilt thou take him for a *s* for ever?
42. 7 that is right, as my *s* Job hath.
8 and go to my *s* Job, and offer up
8 and my *s* Job shall pray for you:
8 thing which is right, like my *s* Job.
Ps 19.11 by them is thy *s* warned: and in
13 thy *s* also from presumptuous
31.16 Make thy face to shine upon thy *s*:
86. 2 save thy *s* that trusteth in thee.
4 Rejoice the soul of thy *s*: for unto
116.16 O Lord, truly I am thy *s*;
16 I am thy *s*, and the son of thine
119.38 Stablish thy word unto thy *s*, who
135 Make thy face to shine upon thy *s*;
176 astray like a lost sheep; seek thy *s*;
143. 2 enter not into judgment with thy *s*
Pr 11.29 and the fool shall be *s* to the wise
14.35 king's favor is toward a wise *s*:
17. 2 A wise *s* shall have rule over a son
22. 7 and the borrower is *s* to the lender.
29.19 A *s* will not be corrected by words:
30.10 Accuse not a *s* unto his master,
Ec 7.21 lest thou hear thy *s* curse thee:
Isa 24. 2 as with the *s*, so with his master;
42. 1 Behold my *s*, whom I uphold; mine
19 Who is blind, but my *s*? or deaf, as
44.21 for thou art my *s*: I have formed
49. 5 me from the womb to be his *s*,
7 nation abhorreth, to a *s* of rulers,
52.13 Behold, my *s* shall deal prudently,
53.11 shall my righteous *s* justify many;
Jer 2.14 Is Israel a *s*? is he a homeborn
Dan 9.17 O our God, hear the prayer of thy *s*,
Zec 3. 8 I will bring forth my *s* the Branch.
Mal 1. 6 son...his father, and a *s* his master:
4. 4 Remember...law of Moses my *s*,
Mt 8. 6 *s* lieth at home sick of the palsy,
8 only, and my *s* shall be healed.
9 to my *s*, Do this, and he doeth it.
13 his *s* was healed in the selfsame
10.24 master, nor the *s* above his lord.
25 as his master, and the *s* as his lord.
12.18 Behold my *s*, whom I have chosen;
18.26 The *s* therefore fell down, and
27 the lord of that *s* was moved with
28 But the same *s* went out, and found
32 O thou wicked *s*, I forgave thee all
20.27 chief among you, let him be your *s*:
23.11 greatest among you shall be your *s*.
24.45 Who then is a faithful and wise *s*,
46 Blessed is that *s*, whom his lord
48 if that evil *s* shall say in his heart,
50 lord of that *s* shall come in a day
25.21 Well done, thou good and faithful *s*:
23 Well done, good and faithful *s*;
26 Thou wicked and slothful *s*, thou
30 unprofitable *s* into outer darkness:
26.51 and struck a *s* of the high priest's,
Mk 9.35 shall be last of all, and *s* of all.
10.44 be the chiefest, shall be *s* of all.
12. 2 he sent to the husbandmen a *s*,
4 again he sent unto them another *s*:
14.47 and smote a *s* of the high priest,
Lk 1.54 He hath holpen his *s* Israel, in
69 for us in the house of his *s* David;
2.29 lettest thou thy *s* depart in peace,
7. 2 a certain centurion's *s*, who was
3 that he would come and heal his *s*.
7 a word, and my *s* shall be healed.
8 to my *s*, Do this, and he doeth it.
10 the *s* whole that had been sick.
12.43 Blessed is that *s*, whom his lord
45 But and if that *s* say in his heart,
46 lord of that *s* will come in a day
47 that *s*, which knew his lord's will,

Lk 14.17 And sent his *s* at supper time to say
21 So that *s* came, and shewed his lord
21 angry said to his *s*, Go out quickly
22 the *s* said, Lord, it is done as thou
23 lord said unto his *s*, Go out into
16.13 No *s* can serve two masters: for
17. 7 having a *s* plowing or feeding
9 Doth he thank that *s* because he
19.17 said unto him, Well, thou good *s*:
22 will I judge thee, thou wicked *s*.
20.10 he sent a *s* to the husbandmen,
11 And again he sent another *s*: and
22.50 them smote the *s* of the high priest,
Jn 8.34 committeth sin is the *s* of sin.
35 the *s* abideth not in the house for
12.26 I am, there shall also my *s* be:
13.16 The *s* is not greater than his lord;
15.15 *s* knoweth not what his lord doeth:
20 The *s* is not greater than his lord.
18.10 and smote the high priest's *s*, and
Ac 4.25 Who by the mouth of thy *s* David
Ro 1. 1 Paul, a *s* of Jesus Christ, called
14. 4 that judgest another man's *s*?
16. 1 sister, which is a *s* of the church
1Co 7.21 Art thou called being a *s*? care
22 being a *s*, is the Lord's freeman:
22 is called, being free, is Christ's *s*.
9.19 yet have I made myself *s* unto all,
Gal 1.10 I should not be the *s* of Christ.
4. 1 a child, differeth nothing from a *s*,
7 Wherefore thou art no more a *s*,
Php 2. 7 and took upon him the form of a *s*,
Col 4.12 who is one of you, a *s* of Christ,
2Ti 2.24 the *s* of the Lord must not strive;
Tit 1. 1 Paul, a *s* of God, and an apostle of
Phm 16 Not now as a *s*, but above a *s*,
Heb 3. 5 faithful in all his house, as a *s*,
Jas 1. 1 James, a *s* of God and of the Lord
2Pe 1. 1 Simon Peter, a *s* and an apostle of
Jude 1 Jude, the *s* of Jesus Christ, and
Rev 1. 1 it by his angel unto his *s* John:
15. 3 sing the song of Moses the *s* of God,

SERVANT'S

Gen 19. 2 in, I pray you, into your *s* house,
2Ki 8.19 destroy Judah for David his *s* sake,
1Ch 17.17 hast also spoken of thy *s* house
19 Lord, for thy *s* sake, and according
Isa 45. 4 For Jacob my *s* sake, and Israel
Jn 18.10 ear. The *s* name was Malchus.

SERVANTS

Gen 9.25 a servant of *s* shall he be unto his
40.20 that he made a feast unto all his *s*:
41.10 Pharaoh was wroth with his *s*, and
42.11 we are true men, thy *s* are no spies.
47. 3 Thy *s* are shepherds, both we, and
Ex 5.16 There is no straw given unto thy *s*,
1Sa 4. 9 ye be not *s* unto the Hebrews, as
12.19 Pray for thy *s* unto the Lord thy
25.10 be many *s* now a days that break
41 wash the feet of the *s* of my lord.
2Sa 8. 2 so the Moabites became David's *s*,
6 the Syrians became *s* to David,
14.30 Absalom's *s* set the field on fire.
1Ki 9.27 And Hiram sent in the navy his *s*,
11.17 certain Edomites of his father's *s*
2Ki 18.26 Speak,...to thy *s* in the Syrian
21.10 Lord spake by his *s* the prophets,
2Ch 6.27 forgive the sin of thy *s*, and of thy
24.25 his own *s* conspired against him
Ezr 5.11 We are the *s* of the God of heaven
Job 1.15 have slain the *s* with the edge of the
4.18 Behold, he put no trust in his *s*;
Ps 34.22 Lord redeemeth the soul of his *s*:
90.13 let it repent thee concerning thy *s*.
16 Let thy work appear unto thy *s*,
102.14 thy *s* take pleasure in her stones,
113. 1 Praise, O ye *s* of the Lord, praise
134. 1 ye the Lord, all ye *s* of the Lord,
Pr 29.12 to lies, all his *s* are wicked.
Ec 10. 7 I have seen *s* upon horses, and
7 and princes walking as *s* upon the
Isa 36. 9 of the least of my master's *s*,
65.13 *s* shall eat, but ye shall be hungry:
66.14 Lord shall be known toward his *s*,
Jer 29.19 unto them by my *s* the prophets,
44. 4 Howbeit I sent unto you all my *s*
La 5. 8 *S* have ruled over us: there is none
Eze 38.17 I have spoken in old time by my *s*
Dan 2. 4 tell thy *s* the dream, and we will
3.26 ye *s* of the most high God, come
Am 3. 7 revealeth his secret unto his *s* the
Zec 1. 6 I commanded my *s* the prophets,
2. 9 they shall be a spoil to their *s*:
Mt 13.27 the *s* of the householder came and
28 *s* said unto him, Wilt thou then
14. 2 And said unto his *s*, This is John
18.23 which would take account of his *s*.
21.34 he sent his *s* to the husbandmen,
35 husbandmen took his *s*, and beat
36 he sent other *s* more than the first:
22. 3 sent forth his *s* to call them that
4 he sent forth other *s*, saying, Tell
6 And the remnant took his *s*, and
8 saith he to his *s*, The wedding is
10 *s* went out into the highways, and
13 said the king to the *s*, Bind him
25.14 who called his own *s*, and delivered
19 time the lord of those *s* cometh,
26.58 and sat with the *s*, to see the end.
Mk 1.20 in the ship with the hired *s*,
13.34 and gave authority to his *s*, and to
14.54 he sat with the *s*, and warmed
65 *s* did strike him with the palms of
Lk 12.37 Blessed are those *s*, whom the
38 find them so, blessed are those *s*.
15.17 many hired *s* of my father's have
19 son: make me as one of thy hired *s*.
22 But the father said to his *s*, Bring
26 he called one of the *s*, and asked
17.10 say, We are unprofitable *s*: we
19.13 he called his ten *s*, and delivered
15 he commanded these *s* to be called
Jn 2. 5 His mother saith unto the *s*,
9 the *s* which drew the water knew;)
4.51 going down, his *s* met him, and
15.15 Henceforth I call you not *s*;
18.18 the *s* and officers stood there, who
26 One of the *s* of the high priest,
36 this world, then would my *s* fight,
Ac 2.18 on my *s* and on my handmaidens
4.29 and grant unto thy *s*, that with all
10. 7 he called two of his household *s*, and
16.17 are the *s* of the most high God,
Ro 6.16 whom ye yield yourselves *s* to obey,
16 his *s* ye are to whom ye obey;
17 thanked, that ye were the *s* of sin,
18 ye became the *s* of righteousness.
19 your members *s* to uncleanness
19 your members *s* to righteousness
20 when ye were the *s* of sin, ye were
22 and become *s* to God, ye have your
1Co 7.23 a price; be not ye the *s* of men.
2Co 4. 5 ourselves your *s* for Jesus' sake.
Eph 6. 5 *S*, be obedient to them that are
6 but as the *s* of Christ, doing the
Php 1. 1 *s* of Jesus Christ, to all the saints
Col 3.22 *S*, obey in all things your masters
4. 1 give unto your *s* that which is just
1Ti 6. 1 as many *s* as are under the yoke
Tit 2. 9 Exhort *s* to be obedient unto their
1Pe 2.16 maliciousness, but as the *s* of God.
18 *S*, be subject to your masters
2Pe 2.19 they...are the *s* of corruption:
Rev 1. 1 to shew unto his *s* things which
2.20 to teach and to seduce my *s* to
7. 3 we have sealed the *s* of our God in
10. 7 hath declared to his *s* the prophets.
11.18 reward unto thy *s* the prophets,
19. 2 hath avenged the blood of his *s* at
5 Praise our God, all ye his *s*, and ye
22. 3 in it; and his *s* shall serve him:
6 sent his angel to shew unto his *s*

SERVE

Gen 15.13 is not theirs, and shall *s* them;
14 that nation, whom they shall *s* also,
25.23 and the elder shall *s* the younger.
27.29 Let people *s* thee, and nations bow
40 thou live, and shalt *s* thy brother;
29.15 thou therefore *s* me for nought?
18 I will *s* thee seven years for Rachel
25 did not I *s* with thee for Rachel?
27 *s* with me yet seven other years.
Ex 1.13 children of Israel to *s* with rigor:
14 they made them *s*, was with rigor.
3.12 ye shall *s* God upon this mountain.
4.23 Let my son go, that he may *s* me:
7.16 they may *s* me in the wilderness:
8. 1, 20 people go, that they may *s* me.
9. 1 my people go, that they may *s* me.
10. 3 my people go, that they may *s* me.
8 them, Go, *s* the Lord your God:
11 ye that are men, and *s* the Lord;
24 Moses, and said, Go ye, *s* the Lord;
26 we take to *s* the Lord our God;
26 not with what we must *s* the Lord,
12.31 and go, *s* the Lord, as ye have said.
14.12 that we may *s* the Egyptians?
12 better for us to *s* the Egyptians,
20. 5 down thyself to them, nor *s* them:
21. 2 servant, six years he shall *s*: and
6 aul; and he shall *s* him for ever.
23.24 down to their gods, nor *s* them,
25 And ye shall *s* the Lord your God,
33 if thou *s* their gods, it will surely
Lev 25.39 compel him to *s* as a bondservant:
40 and shall *s* thee unto the year of
Nu 4.24 families of the Gershonites, to *s*,
26 is made for them: so shall they *s*.
8.25 thereof, and shall *s* no more:
18. 7 and within the vail; and ye shall *s*:
21 for their service which they *s*, even
Dt 4.19 to worship them, and *s* them, for
28 there ye shall *s* gods, the work of
5. 9 thyself unto them, nor *s* them:
6.13 fear the Lord thy God, and *s* him,
7. 4 me, that they may *s* other gods:
16 neither shalt thou *s* their gods;
8.19 walk after other gods, and *s* them,
10.12 to *s* the Lord thy God with all thy
20 him shalt thou *s*, and to him shalt
11.13 and to *s* him with all your heart
16 ye turn aside, and *s* other gods,
12.30 How did these nations *s* their gods?
13. 2 hast not known, and let us *s* them;
4 and ye shall *s* him, and cleave unto
6, 13 Let us go and *s* other gods,
15.12 unto thee, and *s* thee six years;
20.11 unto thee, and they shall *s* thee.
28.14 to go after other gods to *s* them.
36 and there shalt thou *s* other gods,
48 shalt thou *s* thine enemies which
64 and there thou shalt *s* other gods,
29.18 and *s* the gods of these nations;
30.17 worship other gods, and *s* them;
31.20 turn unto other gods, and *s* them,
Jos 16.10 unto this day, and *s* under tribute.
22. 5 and to *s* him with all your heart
23. 7 neither *s* them, nor bow yourselves
24.14 and *s* him in sincerity and in truth:
14 and in Egypt; and *s* ye the Lord.
15 it seem evil unto you to *s* the Lord,
15 choose you this day whom ye will *s*;
15 and my house, we will *s* the Lord.
16 forsake the Lord, to *s* other gods;
18 therefore will we also *s* the Lord;
19 Ye cannot *s* the Lord: for he is an
20 the Lord, and *s* strange gods, then
21 Nay; but we will *s* the Lord.
22 have chosen you the Lord, to *s* him.
24 The Lord our God will we *s*, and

Jdg 2.19 in following other gods to *s* them,
9.28 is Shechem, that we should *s* him?
28 *s* the men of Hamor the father of
28 Shechem: for why should we *s* him?
38 Abimelech, that we should *s* him?
1Sa 7. 3 unto the Lord, and *s* him only:
10. 7 that thou do as occasion *s* thee;
11. 1 covenant with us,...we will *s* thee.
12.10 of our enemies, and we will *s* thee.
14 If ye will fear the Lord, and *s* him,
20 but *s* the Lord with all your heart;
24 *s* him in truth with all your heart:
17. 9 shall ye be our servants, and *s* us.
26.19 the Lord, saying, Go, *s* other gods.
2Sa 15. 8 Jerusalem, then I will *s* the Lord.
16.19 And again, whom should I *s*?
19 should I not *s* in the presence of
22.44 which I knew not shall *s* me.
1Ki 9. 6 go and *s* other gods, and worship
12. 4 upon us, lighter,...we will *s* thee.
7 and wilt *s* them, and answer them,
2Ki 10.18 little; but Jehu shall *s* him much.
17.35 nor *s* them, nor sacrifice to them:
25.24 land, and *s* the king of Babylon;
1Ch 28. 9 *s* him with a perfect heart and with
2Ch 7.19 and shall go and *s* other gods, and
10. 4 he put upon us, and we will *s* thee.
29.11 to stand before him, to *s* him,
30. 8 and *s* the Lord your God, that the
33.16 commanded Judah to *s* the Lord
34.33 all that were present in Israel to *s*,
33 even to *s* the Lord their God. And
35. 3 *s* now the Lord your God, and his
Job 21.15 Almighty, that we should *s* him?
36.11 If they obey and *s* him, they shall
39. 9 the unicorn be willing to *s* thee,
Ps 2.11 *S* the Lord with fear, and rejoice
18.43 whom I have not known shall *s* me.
22.30 A seed shall *s* him; it shall be
72.11 before him: all nations shall *s* him.
97. 7 be all they that *s* graven images,
100. 2 *S* the Lord with gladness: come
101. 6 in a perfect way, he shall *s* me.
102.22 and the kingdoms, to *s* the Lord.
Isa 14. 3 wherein thou wast made to *s*,
19.23 and the Egyptians shall *s* with the
43.23 caused thee to *s* with an offering,
24 hast made me to *s* with thy sins,
56. 6 themselves to the Lord, to *s* him,
60.12 that will not *s* thee shall perish;
Jer 5.19 so shall ye *s* strangers in a land
11.10 went after other gods to *s* them:
13.10 walk after other gods, to *s* them,
16.13 ye *s* other gods day and night;
17. 4 will cause thee to *s* thine enemies
25. 6 go not after other gods to *s* them,
11 nations shall *s* the king of Babylon
14 kings shall *s* themselves of them
27. 6 have I given him also to *s* him.
7 And all nations shall *s* him, and
7 kings shall *s* themselves of him.
8 not *s* the same Nebuchadnezzar
9 Ye shall not *s* the king of Babylon:
11 of the king of Babylon, and *s* him,
12 and *s* him and his people, and live.
13 that will not *s* the king of Babylon?
14 Ye shall not *s* the king of Babylon:
17 *s* the king of Babylon, and live:
28.14 that they may *s* Nebuchadnezzar
14 and they shall *s* him: and I have
30. 8 shall no more *s* themselves of him:
9 they shall *s* the Lord their God,
34. 9 none should *s* himself of them, to
10 none should *s* themselves of them
35.15 go not after other gods to *s* them,
40. 9 Fear not to *s* the Chaldeans: dwell
9 land, and *s* the king of Babylon,
10 *s* the Chaldeans, which will
44. 3 to *s* other gods, whom they knew
Eze 20.32 countries, to *s* wood and stone.
39 Go ye, *s* ye every one his idols,
40 all of them in the land, *s* me:
29.18 caused his army to *s* a great service
48.18 for food unto them that *s* the city.
19 And they that *s* the city shall *s*
19 *s* it out of all the tribes of Israel.
Dan 3.12 they *s* not thy gods, nor worship
14 do not ye *s* my gods, nor worship
17 God whom we *s* is able to deliver
18 we will not *s* thy gods, nor worship
28 might not *s* nor worship any god,
7.14 and languages, should *s* him:
27 dominions shall *s* and obey him.
Zep 3. 9 Lord, to *s* him with one consent.
Mal 3.14 Ye have said, It is vain to *s* God:
Mt 4.10 God, and him only shalt thou *s*.
6.24 No man can *s* two masters: for
24 Ye cannot *s* God and mammon.
Lk 1.74 might *s* him without fear,
4. 8 thy God, and him only shalt thou *s*.
10.40 my sister hath left me to *s* alone?
12.37 and will come forth and *s* them.
15.29 Lo, these many years do I *s* thee,
16.13 No servant can *s* two masters: for
13 Ye cannot *s* God and mammon.
17. 8 sup, and gird thyself, and *s* me.
22.26 he that is chief, as he that doth *s*.
Jn 12.26 If any man *s* me, let him follow
26 if any man *s* me, him will my
Ac 6. 2 leave the word of God, and *s* tables.
7. 7 come forth, and *s* me in this place.
27.23 of God, whose I am, and whom I *s*,
Ro 1. 9 whom I *s* with my spirit in the
6. 6 henceforth we should not *s* sin.
7. 6 we should *s* in newness of spirit,
25 mind I myself *s* the law of God;
9.12 her, The elder shall *s* the younger.
16.18 such *s* not our Lord Jesus Christ,
Gal 5.13 flesh, but by love *s* one another.
Col 3.24 for ye *s* the Lord Christ.
1Th 1. 9 idols to *s* the living and true God;
2Ti 1. 3 whom I *s* from my forefathers
Heb 8. 5 Who *s* unto the example and
9.14 dead works to *s* the living God?
12.28 we may *s* God acceptably with
13.10 right to eat which *s* the tabernacle.
Rev 7.15 *s* him day and night in his temple:
22. 3 it; and his servants shall *s* him:

SERVED

Gen 14. 4 years they *s* Chedorlaomer, and
29.20 Jacob *s* seven years for Rachel;
30 *s* with him yet seven other years.
30.26 children, for whom I have *s* thee,
29 Thou knowest how I have *s* thee,
31. 6 all my power have I *s* your father.
41 I *s* thee fourteen years for thy two
39. 4 grace in his sight, and he *s* him:
40. 4 Joseph with them, and he *s* them:
Dt 12. 2 ye shall possess *s* their gods,
17. 3 And hath gone and *s* other gods,
29.26 For they went and *s* other gods,
Jos 23.16 and have gone and *s* other gods,
24. 2 of Nachor: and they *s* other gods.
14, 15 the gods which your fathers *s*
31 Israel *s* the Lord all the days of
Jdg 2. 7 people *s* the Lord all the days of
11 sight of the Lord, and *s* Baalim:
13 Lord, and *s* Baal and Ashtaroth.
3. 6 to their sons, and *s* their gods.
7 God, and *s* Baalim and the groves.
8 Israel *s* Cushan-rishathaim eight
14 Israel *s* Eglon the king of Moab
8. 1 him, Why hast thou *s* us thus,
10. 6 and *s* Baalim, and Ashtaroth, and
6 forsook the Lord, and *s* not him.
10 forsaken our God, and...*s* Baalim.
13 forsaken me, and *s* other gods:
16 from among them, and *s* the Lord:
1Sa 7. 4 and Ashtaroth, and *s* the Lord only.
8. 8 forsaken me, and *s* other gods,
12.10 and have *s* Baalim and Ashtaroth:
2Sa 10.19 made peace with Israel, and *s* them.
16.19 as I have *s* in thy father's presence,
1Ki 4.21 *s* Solomon all the days of his life.
9. 9 have worshipped them, and *s* them:
16.31 went and *s* Baal, and worshipped
22.53 For he *s* Baal, and worshipped him,
2Ki 10.18 unto them, Ahab *s* Baal a little;
17.12 For they *s* idols, whereof the Lord
16 all the host of heaven, and *s* Baal.
33 the Lord, and *s* their own gods,
41 Lord, and *s* their graven images,
18. 7 the king of Assyria, and *s* him not.
21. 3 all the host of heaven, and *s* them.
21 and *s* the idols that his father *s*,
1Ch 27. 1 and their officers that *s* the king
2Ch 7.22 worshipped them, and *s* them:
24.18 fathers, and *s* groves and idols:
33. 3 all the host of heaven, and *s* them.
22 his father had made, and *s* them;
Neh 9.35 have not *s* thee in their kingdom,
Est 1.10 *s* in the presence of Ahasuerus
Ps 106.36 And they *s* their idols: which
137. 8 rewardeth thee as thou hast *s* us.
Ec 5. 9 the king himself is *s* by the field.
Jer 5.19 and *s* strange gods in your land, so
8. 2 have loved, and whom they have *s*,
16.11 after other gods, and have *s* them,
22. 9 worshipped other gods, and *s* them.
34.14 and when he hath *s* thee six years,
52.12 which *s* the king of Babylon,
Eze 29.18 service that he had *s* against it:
20 labor wherewith he *s* against it,
34.27 of those that *s* themselves of them.
Hos 12.12 Israel *s* for a wife, and for a wife
Lk 2.37 *s* God with fastings and prayers
Jn 12. 2 made him a supper; and Martha *s*:
Ac 13.36 after he had *s* his own generation
Ro 1.25 and *s* the creature more than the
Php 2.22 he hath *s* with me in the gospel.

SERVEST

Dan 6.16 Thy God whom thou *s* continually,
20 thy God, whom thou *s* continually,

SERVETH

Nu 3.36 thereof, and all that *s* thereto,
Mal 3.17 spareth his own son that *s* him.
18 that *s* God and him that *s* him not.
Lk 22.27 that sitteth at meat, or he that *s*?
27 but I am among you as he that *s*.
Ro 14.18 he that in these things *s* Christ is
1Co 14.22 but prophesying *s*, not for them that
Gal 3.19 Wherefore then *s* the law? It was

SERVICE

Gen 29.27 for the *s* which thou shalt serve
30.26 knowest my *s* which I have done
Ex 1.14 and in all manner of *s* in the field:
14 all their *s*,...was with rigor.
12.25 promised, that ye shall keep this *s*.
26 unto you, What mean ye by this *s*?
13. 5 thou shalt keep this *s* in this month.
27.19 the tabernacle in all the *s* thereof,
30.16 it for the *s* of the tabernacle of the
31.10 And the cloths of *s*, and the holy
35.19 The cloths of *s*, to do
19 to do *s* in the holy place,
21 and for all his *s*, and for the holy
24 shittim wood for any work of the *s*,
36. 1 of work for the *s* of the sanctuary,
3 the work of the *s* of the sanctuary,
5 than enough for the *s* of the work,
38.21 for the *s* of the Levites, by the hand
39. 1 scarlet, they made cloths of *s*,
1 do *s* in the holy place, and made
40 vessels of the *s* of the tabernacle,
41 The cloths of *s* to do
41 to do *s* in the holy place,
Nu 3. 7, 8 to do the *s* of the tabernacle.
26 the cords of it for all the *s* thereof.
31 the hanging, and all the *s* thereof.

Nu 4. 4 shall be the *s* of the sons of Kohath
19 and appoint them every one to his *s*
23 all that enter in to perform the *s*,
24 *s* of the families of the Gershonites,
26 and all the instruments of their *s*,
27 *s* of the sons of the Gershonites,
27 their burdens, and in all their *s*:
28 is the *s* of the families...of Gershon
30 every one that entereth into the *s*,
31 according to all their *s* in the
32 instruments, and with all their *s*:
33 *s* of the families...of Merari,
33 according to all their *s*, in the
35 every one that entereth into the *s*,
37 that might do *s* in the tabernacle
39 every one that entereth into the *s*.
41 that might do *s* in the tabernacle
43 every one that entereth into the *s*,
47 came to do the *s* of the ministry,
47 *s* of the burden in the tabernacle
49 every one according to his *s*, and
7. 5 may be to do the *s* of the tabernacle
5 to every man according to his *s*.
7 of Gershon, according to their *s*:
8 of Merari, according unto their *s*,
9 *s* of the sanctuary belonging unto
8.11 they may execute the *s* of the Lord.
15 go in to do the *s* of the tabernacle
19 do the *s* of the children of Israel
22 went the Levites in to do their *s*
24 wait upon the *s* of the tabernacle
25 cease waiting upon the *s* thereof,
26 keep the charge, and shall do no *s*.
16. 9 to do the *s* of the tabernacle of the
18. 4 for all the *s* of the tabernacle:
6 to do the *s* of the tabernacle of the
7 priest's office unto you as a *s* of gift:
21 for their *s* which they serve,
21 even the *s* of the tabernacle of the
23 shall do the *s* of the tabernacle of
31 reward for your *s* in the tabernacle
Jos 22.27 that we might do the *s* of the Lord
1Ki 12. 4 thou the grievous *s* of thy father,
1Ch 6.31 whom David set over the *s* of song
48 all manner of *s* of the tabernacle
9.13 work of the *s* of the house of God.
19 were over the work of the *s*, keepers
23.24 work for the *s* of the house of the
26 any vessels of it for the *s* thereof.
28 for the *s* of the house of the Lord,
28 work of the *s* of the house of God;
32 in the *s* of the house of the Lord.
24. 3 according to their offices in their *s*.
19 the orderings of them in their *s*
25. 1 separated to the *s* of the sons of
1 workmen according to their *s* was:
6 harps, for the *s* of the house of God,
26. 8 able men for strength for the *s*,
30 the Lord, and in the *s* of the king.
28.13 work of the *s* of the house of the
13 the vessels of *s* in the house of the
14 all instruments of all manner of *s*;
14 all instruments of every kind of *s*:
20 finished all the work for the *s* of the
21 for all the *s* of the house of God:
21 skilful man, for any manner of *s*:
29. 5 is willing to consecrate his *s*
7 gave for the *s* of the house of God
2Ch 8.14 the courses of the priests to their *s*,
12. 8 that they may know my *s*, and
8 *s* of the kingdoms of the countries.
24.12 to such as did the work of the *s* of
29.35 So the *s* of the house of the Lord
31. 2 every man according to his *s*, the
16 daily portion for their *s* in their
21 began in the *s* of the house of God,
34.13 the work in any manner of *s*:
35. 2 and encouraged them to the *s* of the
10 So the *s* was prepared, and the
15 they might not depart from their *s*;
16 all the *s* of the Lord was prepared
Ezr 6.18 their courses, for the *s* of God,
7.19 given thee for the *s* of the house
8.20 had appointed for the *s* of the
Neh 10.32 the third part of a shekel for the *s*
Ps 104.14 cattle, and herb for the *s* of man:
Jer 22.13 useth his neighbor's *s* without
Eze 29.18 caused his army to serve a great *s*
18 the *s* that he had served against it:
44.14 of the house, for all the *s* thereof,
Jn 16. 2 will think that he doeth God *s*.
Ro 9. 4 and the *s* of God, and the promises:
12. 1 God, which is your reasonable *s*.
15.31 *s* which I have for Jerusalem may
2Co 9.12 administration of this *s* not only
11. 8 taking wages of them, to do you *s*.
Gal 4. 8 did *s* unto them which by nature
Eph 6. 7 With good will doing *s*, as to the
Php 2.17 the sacrifice and *s* of your faith,
30 to supply your lack of *s* toward me
1Ti 6. 2 but rather do them *s*, because
Heb 9. 1 had also ordinances of divine *s*,
6 accomplishing the *s* of God.
9 make him that did the *s* perfect,
Rev 2.19 thy works, and charity, and *s*,

SERVILE

Lev 23. 7, 8 ye shall do no *s* work therein.
21 ye shall do no *s* work therein: it
25 Ye shall do no *s* work therein: but
35, 36 ye shall do no *s* work therein.
Nu 28.18 do no manner of *s* work therein:
25 convocation; ye shall do no *s* work.

SERVING

Ex 14. 5 we have let Israel go from *s* us?
Dt 15.18 to thee, in *s* thee six years:
Lk 10.40 was cumbered about much *s*, and
Ac 20.19 *S* the Lord with all humility of
26. 7 instantly *s* God day and night,
Ro 12.11 fervent in spirit: *s* the Lord;
Tit 3. 3 *s* divers lusts and pleasures, living

SET

Gen 1.17 God *s* them in the firmament of
4.15 And the Lord *s* a mark upon Cain,
6.16 of the ark shalt thou *s* in the side
9.13 I do *s* my bow in the cloud, and it
28.11 all night, because the sun was *s*;
12 behold a ladder *s* up on the earth,
18 pillows, and *s* it up for a pillar,
41.33 and *s* him over the land of Egypt.
44.21 that I may *s* mine eyes upon him.
Ex 1.11 they did *s* over them taskmasters
4.20 his sons, and *s* them upon an ass,
7.23 did he *s* his heart to this also.
13.12 thou shalt *s* apart unto the Lord all
19.12 thou shalt *s* bounds unto the people
Lev 17.10 even *s* my face against that soul
20. 3 I will *s* my face against that man,
26. 1 neither shall ye *s* up any image
11 I will *s* my tabernacle among you:
Nu 1.51 pitched, the Levites shall *s* it up:
21. 8 fiery serpent, and *s* it upon a pole:
10 the children of Israel *s* forward,
24. 1 *s* his face toward the wilderness.
Dt 1. 8 I have *s* the land before you: go
21 God hath *s* the land before thee:
4. 8 law, which I *s* before you this day?
11.26 I *s* before you this day a blessing
16.22 shalt thou *s* thee up any image;
17.14 I will *s* a king over me, like as all
19.14 time have *s* in thine inheritance,
26. 4 *s* it down before the altar of the
27. 2 thou shalt *s* thee up great stones,
28. 1 God will *s* thee on high above all
36 king which thou shalt *s* over thee,
30. 1 curse, which I have *s* before thee,
19 I have *s* before you life and death,
32. 8 he *s* the bounds of the people
Jos 4. 9 Joshua *s* up twelve stones in the
18. 1 and *s* up the tabernacle of the
24.25 *s* them a statute and an ordinance
26 and *s* it up there under an oak,
1Sa 2. 8 to *s* them among princes, and to
6.18 they *s* down the ark of the Lord:
10.19 him, Nay, but *s* a king over us.
12.13 the Lord hath *s* a king over you.
13. 8 *s* time that Samuel had appointed:
15.11 that I have *s* up Saul to be king:
2Sa 3.10 to *s* up the throne of David over
7.12 I will *s* up thy seed after thee,
11.15 *S* ye Uriah in the forefront of the
14.30 barley there; go and *s* it on fire.
31 thy servants *s* my field on fire?
23.23 And David *s* him over his guard.
1Ki 2.15 that all Israel *s* their faces on me,
24 *s* me on the throne of David my
5. 5 whom I will *s* upon thy throne in
6.19 to *s* there the ark of the covenant
27 And he *s* the cherubims within the
Est 2.17 *s* the royal crown upon her head,
8. 2 Esther *s* Mordecai over the house
Job 5.11 To *s* up on high those that be low;
7.17 shouldest *s* thine heart upon him?
19. 8 he hath *s* darkness in my paths.
30. 1 have *s* with the dogs of my flock.
34.14 If he *s* his heart upon man, if he
Ps 2. 2 kings of the earth *s* themselves,
16. 8 have *s* the Lord always before me:
20. 5 of our God we will *s* up our banners:
40. 2 clay, and *s* my feet upon a rock,
62.10 *s* not your heart upon them.
69.29 salvation, O God, *s* me up on high.
73. 9 They *s* their mouth against the
18 didst *s* them in slippery places:
109. 6 *S* thou a wicked man over him:
Pr 1.25 have *s* at nought all my counsel,
27 he *s* a compass upon the face of
SS 5.12 washed with milk, and fitly *s*.
8. 6 *S* me as a seal upon thine heart,
Isa 3.24 and instead of well *s* hair baldness;
9.11 Lord shall *s* up the adversaries
21. 6 Go, *s* a watchman, let him declare
38. 1 *S* thine house in order: for thou
50. 7 have I *s* my face like a flint, and
62. 6 *s* watchmen upon thy walls, O
66.19 I will *s* a sign among them, and I
Jer 1.10 this day *s* thee over the nations
9.13 my law which I *s* before them,
31.21 *S* thee up waymarks, make thee
29 the children's teeth are *s* on edge.
30 grape, his teeth shall be *s* on edge.
51.12 *S* up the standard upon the walls
La 2.17 he hath *s* up the horn of thine
3. 6 He hath *s* me in dark places, as
Am 7. 8 *s* a plumbline in the midst of my
Ob 4 thou *s* thy nest among the stars,
Na 3. 6 and will *s* thee as a gazingstock.
Mt 5. 1 and when he was *s*, his disciples
14 that is *s* on an hill cannot be hid.
18. 2 and *s* him in the midst of them,
21. 7 clothes, and they *s* him thereon.
27.19 was *s* down on the judgment seat,
Mk 1.32 at even, when the sun did *s*, they
4.21 and not to be *s* on a candlestick?
9.12 many things, and be *s* at nought.
36 and *s* him in the midst of them:
12. 1 *s* an hedge about it, and digged a
Lk 1. 1 to *s* forth in order a declaration of
4. 9 *s* him on a pinnacle of the temple,
18 *s* at liberty them that are bruised,
7. 8 also am a man *s* under authority,
9.16 disciples to *s* before the multitude.
51 *s* his face to go to Jerusalem,
19.35 the colt, and they *s* Jesus thereon.
22.55 and were *s* down together, Peter
23.11 his men of war *s* him at nought,
Jn 2. 6 there were *s* there six waterpots
3.33 hath *s* to his seal that God is true.
8. 3 when they had *s* her in the midst,
13.12 garments, and was *s* down again,
19.29 was *s* a vessel full of vinegar:

Ac 4. 7 when they had *s* them in the midst,
6. 6 Whom they *s* before the apostles:
13 And *s* up false witnesses, which
7. 5 not so much as to *s* his foot on:
12.21 upon a *s* day Herod, arrayed in
13. 9 the Holy Ghost, *s* his eyes on him,
47 I have *s* thee to be a light of the
Ro 3.25 hath *s* forth to be a propitiation
14.10 dost thou *s* at nought thy brother?
1Co 4. 9 God hath *s* forth us the apostles
10.27 whatsoever is *s* before you, eat,
Gal 3. 1 Christ hath been evidently *s* forth,
Col 3. 2 *S* your affection on things above,
Rev 3. 8 I have *s* before thee an open door,
21 am *s* down with my Father in his
4. 2 behold, a throne was *s* in heaven,
10. 2 he *s* his right foot upon the sea,

SETTER
Ac 17.18 to be a *s* forth of strange gods:

SETTEST
Dt 23.20 in all that thou *s* thine hand to
28. 8 in all that thou *s* thine hand unto;
20 in all that thou *s* thine hand unto
Job 7.12 that thou *s* a watch over me?
13.27 *s* a print upon the heels of my feet.
Ps 21. 3 thou *s* a crown of pure gold on
41.12 and *s* me before thy face for ever.

SETTETH
Nu 1.51 when the tabernacle *s* forward,
4. 5 And when the camp *s* forward,
Dt 24.15 is poor, and *s* his heart upon it:
27.16 that *s* light by his father or his
2Sa 22.34 and *s* me upon my high places.
Job 28. 3 He *s* an end to darkness, and
Ps 18.33 and *s* me upon my high places.
36. 4 he *s* himself in a way that is not
65. 6 his strength *s* fast the mountains;
68. 6 God *s* the solitary in families: he
75. 7 down one, and *s* up another.
83.14 flame *s* the mountains on fire;
107.41 *s* he the poor on high from affliction,
Jer 5.26 they lay wait, as he that *s* snares;
43. 3 of Neriah *s* thee on against us,
Eze 14. 4 that *s* up his idols in his heart,
7 and *s* up his idols in his heart,
Dan 2.21 removeth kings, and *s* up kings:
4.17 and *s* up over it the basest of men.
Mt 4. 5 and *s* him on the pinnacle of the
Lk 8.16 *s* it on a candlestick, that they
Jas 3. 6 *s* on fire the course of nature;

SETTING
Eze 43. 8 In their *s* of their threshold by
Mt 27.66 sealing the stone, and *s* a watch.
Lk 4.40 Now when the sun was *s*, all they

SETTLE
1Ch 17.14 I will *s* him in mine house and
Eze 36.11 will *s* you after your old estates,
43.14 the lower *s* shall be two cubits,
14 the lesser *s* even to the greater
14 greater *s* shall be four cubits,
17 the *s* shall be fourteen cubits long
20 and on the four corners of the *s*,
45.19 upon the four corners of the *s* of
Lk 21.14 *S* it therefore in your hearts, not
1Pe 5.10 stablish, strengthen, *s* you.

SETTLED
1Ki 8.13 a *s* place for thee to abide in for
2Ki 8.11 he *s* his countenance stedfastly,
Ps 119.89 O Lord, thy word is *s* in heaven.
Pr 8.25 Before the mountains were *s*,
Jer 48.11 he hath *s* on his lees, and hath
Zep 1.12 the men that are *s* on their lees:
Col 1.23 in the faith grounded and *s*, and

SEVEN
Gen 7. 4 *s* days, and I will cause it to rain
29.20 Jacob served *s* years for Rachel;
41. 2 of the river *s* well favored kine
5 *s* ears of corn came up upon one
Ex 13. 6 *S* days thou shalt eat unleavened
Lev 23.42 Ye shall dwell in booths *s* days; all
25. 8 shalt number *s* sabbaths of years
26.28 chastise you *s* times for your sins.
Nu 12.14 be shut out from the camp *s* days,
29.12 keep a feast unto the Lord *s* days:
Dt 16.13 the feast of tabernacles *s* days,
Jdg 16. 7 If they bind me with *s* green withs
13 weavest the *s* locks of my head
1Ki 18.43 And he said, Go again *s* times.
19.18 I have left me *s* thousand in Israel,
2Ki 4.35 the child sneezed *s* times, and the
5.10 Go and wash in Jordan *s* times,
2Ch 7. 8 Solomon kept the feast *s* days,
9 the dedication of the altar *s* days,
Job 1. 2 there were born unto him *s* sons
2.13 the ground *s* days and *s* nights,
5.19 in *s* there shall no evil touch thee.
42.13 also *s* sons and three daughters.
Ps 119.164 *S* times a day do I praise thee
Pr 24.16 For a just man falleth *s* times, and
26.25 are *s* abominations in his heart.
Ec 11. 2 Give a portion to *s*, and also to
Isa 4. 1 *s* women shall take hold of one
Eze 45.21 the passover, a feast of *s* days;
Dan 3.19 the furnace one *s* times more
Am 5. 8 Seek him that maketh the *s* stars
Mic 5. 5 we raise against him *s* shepherds,
Mt 12.45 *s* other spirits more wicked than
15.34 they said, *S*, and a few little fishes.
36 And he took the *s* loaves and the
37 meat that was left *s* baskets full.
16.10 Neither the *s* loaves of the four
18.21 and I forgive him? till *s* times?
22 say not unto thee, Until *s* times:
22 but, Until seventy times *s*.
22.25 Now there were with us *s* brethren:
28 whose wife shall she be of the *s*?
Mk 8. 5 loaves have ye? And they said, *S*.
6 and he took the *s* loaves, and gave
8 meat that was left *s* baskets.
20 when the *s* among four thousand,
20 took ye up? And they said, *S*.
12.20 Now there were *s* brethren: and
22 And the *s* had her, and left no seed.
23 them? for the *s* had her to wife.
16. 9 out of whom he had cast *s* devils.
Lk 2.36 had lived with an husband *s* years
8. 2 out of whom went *s* devils,
11.26 him *s* other spirits more wicked
17. 4 against thee *s* times in a day,
4 and *s* times in a day turn again to
20.29 There were therefore *s* brethren:
31 and in like manner the *s* also: and
33 them is she? for *s* had her to wife.
Ac 6. 3 among you *s* men of honest report,
13.19 destroyed *s* nations in the land of
19.14 there were *s* sons of one Sceva, a
20. 6 five days; where we abode *s* days.
21. 4 disciples, we tarried there *s* days:
8 which was one of the *s*; and abode
27 And when the *s* days were almost
28.14 desired to tarry with them *s* days:
Ro 11. 4 to myself *s* thousand men, who
Heb 11.30 were compassed about *s* days.
Rev 1. 4 John to the *s* churches which are
4 and from the *s* Spirits which are
11 the *s* churches which are in Asia;
12 I saw *s* golden candlesticks;
13 in the midst of the *s* candlesticks
16 he had in his right hand *s* stars:
20 The mystery of the *s* stars which
20 and the *s* golden candlesticks.
20 The *s* stars are the angels of the *s*
20 and the *s* candlesticks which thou
20 thou sawest are the *s* churches.
2. 1 he that holdeth the *s* stars in his
1 midst of the *s* golden candlesticks;
3. 1 *s* Spirits of God, and the *s* stars;
4. 5 there were *s* lamps of fire burning
5 which are the *s* Spirits of God.
5. 1 the backside, sealed with *s* seals.
5 and to loose the *s* seals thereof.
6 slain, having *s* horns and *s* eyes,
6 which are the *s* Spirits of God
8. 2 And I saw the *s* angels which stood
2 to them were given *s* trumpets.
6 *s* angels which had the *s* trumpets
10. 3 *s* thunders uttered their voices.
4 *s* thunders had uttered their voices,
4 which the *s* thunders uttered, and
11.13 were slain of men *s* thousand: and
12. 3 having *s* heads and ten horns, and
3 and *s* crowns upon his heads.
13. 1 having *s* heads and ten horns, and
15. 1 *s* angels having the *s* last plagues;
6 *s* angels came out of the temple,
6 having the *s* plagues, clothed in
7 unto the *s* angels *s* golden vials
8 the *s* plagues of the *s* angels were
16. 1 saying to the *s* angels, Go your
17. 1 the *s* angels which had the *s* vials,
3 having *s* heads and ten horns.
7 hath the *s* heads and ten horns.
9 The *s* heads are *s* mountains, on
10 there are *s* kings: five are fallen,
11 and is of the *s*, and goeth into
21. 9 came unto me one of the *s* angels
9 *s* vials full of the *s* last plagues,

SEVENFOLD
Gen 4.15 vengeance...be taken on him *s*.
24 If Cain shall be avenged *s*, truly
24 truly Lamech seventy and *s*.
Ps 79.12 render unto our neighbors *s* into
Pr 6.31 if he be found, he shall restore *s*;
Isa 30.26 and the light of the sun shall be *s*.

SEVENTH
Gen 2. 2 *s* day God ended his work which
2 rested on the *s* day from all his
3 And God blessed the *s* day, and
8. 4 the ark rested in the *s* month, on
Ex 16.30 So the people rested on the *s* day.
20.10 *s* day is the sabbath of the Lord
Lev 23. 8 the *s* day is an holy convocation:
Jdg 14.17 on the *s* day, that he told her,
Mt 22.26 also, and the third, unto the *s*.
Jn 4.52 at the *s* hour the fever left him.
Heb 4. 4 spake...of the *s* day on this wise,
4 rest the *s* day from all his works.
Jude 14 And Enoch also, the *s* from Adam,
Rev 8. 1 when he had opened the *s* seal,
10. 7 the days of the voice of the *s* angel,
11.15 And the *s* angel sounded; and
16.17 And the *s* angel poured out his vial
21.20 the *s*, chrysolite; the eighth, beryl;

SEVENTY
Nu 11.16 me *s* men of the elders of Israel.
Mt 18.22 times: but, Until *s* times seven.
Lk 10. 1 the Lord appointed other *s* also,
17 And the *s* returned again with joy,

SEVER
Ex 8.22 *s* in that day the land of Goshen,
9. 4 shall *s* between the cattle of Israel
Eze 39.14 they shall *s* out men of continual
Mt 13.49 *s* the wicked from among the just,

SEVERAL
Mt 25.15 man according to his *s* ability;
Rev 21.21 every *s* gate was of one pearl:

SEVERALLY
1Co 12.11 dividing to every man *s* as he will.

SEVERITY
Ro 11.22 Behold...the goodness and *s* of God:
22 on them which fell, *s*; but toward

SEW
Ec 3. 7 A time to rend, and a time to *s*;
Eze 13.18 Woe to the women that *s* pillows

SEWED
Gen 3. 7 they *s* fig leaves together, and
Job 16.15 I have *s* sackcloth upon my skin,

SEWEST
Job 14.17 and thou *s* up mine iniquity.

SEWETH
Mk 2.21 No man...*s* a piece of new cloth

SHADE
Ps 121. 5 Lord is thy *s* upon thy right hand.

SHADOW
Gen 19. 8 come they under the *s* of my roof.
Jdg 9.15 come and put your trust in my *s*:
36 Thou seest the *s* of the mountains
2Ki 20. 9 shall the *s* go forward ten degrees,
10 for the *s* to go down ten degrees:
10 the *s* return backward ten degrees.
11 the *s* ten degrees backward, by
1Ch 29.15 our days on the earth are as a *s*,
Job 3. 5 and the *s* of death stain it; let a
7. 2 servant earnestly desireth the *s*,
8. 9 our days upon earth are a *s*:)
10.21 of darkness and the *s* of death;
22 and of the *s* of death, without any
12.22 bringeth out to light the *s* of death.
14. 2 is cut down: he fleeth also as a *s*,
16.16 on my eyelids is the *s* of death;
17. 7 and all my members are as a *s*.
24.17 is to them even as the *s* of death:
17 are in the terrors of the *s* of death.
28. 3 of darkness, and the *s* of death.
34.22 is no darkness, nor *s* of death,
38.17 seen the doors of the *s* of death?
40.22 trees cover him with their *s*; the
Ps 17. 8 hide me under the *s* of thy wings,
23. 4 the valley of the *s* of death,
36. 7 trust under the *s* of thy wings.
44.19 and covered us with the *s* of death.
57. 1 in the *s* of thy wings will I make
63. 7 in the *s* of thy wings will I rejoice.
80.10 hills were covered with the *s* of it,
91. 1 abide under the *s* of the Almighty.
102.11 days are like a *s* that declineth;
107.10 in darkness and in the *s* of death,
14 out of darkness and the *s* of death,
109.23 I am gone like the *s* when it
144. 4 days are as a *s* that passeth away.
Ec 6.12 vain life which he spendeth as a *s*?
8.13 prolong his days, which are as a *s*;
SS 2. 3 I sat down under his *s* with great
Isa 4. 6 tabernacle for a *s* in the daytime
9. 2 dwell in the land of the *s* of death,
16. 3 make thy *s* as the night in the
25. 4 a *s* from the heat, when the blast
5 even the heat with the *s* of a cloud:
30. 2 and to trust in the *s* of Egypt!
3 the trust in the *s* of Egypt your
32. 2 *s* of a great rock in a weary land.
34.15 and hatch, and gather under her *s*:
38. 8 bring again the *s* of the degrees,
49. 2 in the *s* of his hand hath he hid me,
51.16 thee in the *s* of mine hand,
Jer 2. 6 of drought, and of the *s* of death,
13.16 light, he turn it into the *s* of death,
48.45 fled stood under the *s* of Heshbon
La 4.20 Under his *s* we shall live among
Eze 17.23 the *s* of the branches thereof shall
31. 6 under his *s* dwelt all great nations.
12 the earth are gone down from his *s*,
17 dwelt under his *s* in the midst of
Dan 4.12 beasts of the field had *s* under it,
Hos 4.13 because the *s* thereof is good:
14. 7 dwell under his *s* shall return;
Am 5. 8 the *s* of death into the morning,
Jon 4. 5 sat under it in the *s*, till he might
6 that it might be a *s* over his head,
Mt 4.16 sat in the region and *s* of death
Mk 4.32 the air may lodge under the *s* of it.
Lk 1.79 in darkness and in the *s* of death,
Ac 5.15 the *s* of Peter passing by might
Col 2.17 Which are a *s* of things to come;
Heb 8. 5 example and *s* of heavenly things,
10. 1 the law having a *s* of good things
Jas 1.17 variableness, neither *s* of turning.

SHADOWING
Isa 18. 1 Woe to the land *s* with wings,
Eze 31. 3 with a *s* shroud, and of an high
Heb 9. 5 of glory *s* the mercyseat;

SHADOWS
SS 2.17 day break, and the *s* flee away,
4. 6 the day break, and the *s* flee away,
Jer 6. 4 *s* of the evening are stretched out.

SHADRACH
Dan 1. 7 and to Hananiah, of *S*; and to
2.49 set *S*, Meshach, and Abed-nego,
3.12 of the province of Babylon, *S*,
13 and fury commanded to bring *S*,
14 them, Is it true, O *S*, Meshach, and
16 *S*, Meshach, and Abed-nego,
19 his visage was changed against *S*,
20 that were in his army to bind *S*,
22 slew those men that took up *S*,
23 *S*, Meshach, Abed-nego, fell down
26 said, *S*, Meshach, and Abed-nego,
26 Then *S*, Meshach, and Abed-nego,
28 Blessed be the God of *S*, Meshach,
29 thing amiss against the God of *S*,
30 the king promoted *S*, Meshach, and

SHAKE
Jdg 16.20 times before, and *s* myself.
Neh 5.13 So God *s* out every man from his
Job 4.14 which made all my bones to *s*.
15.33 *s* off his unripe grape as the vine,
16. 4 you, and *s* mine head at you.
Ps 22. 7 shoot out the lip, they *s* the head,
46. 3 mountains *s* with the swelling
69.23 make their loins continually to *s*.
72.16 fruit thereof shall *s* like Lebanon:
Isa 2.19, 21 ariseth to *s* terribly the earth.
10.15 if the rod should *s* itself against
32 he shall *s* his hand against the
11.15 shall he *s* his hand over the river,
13. 2 *s* the hand, that they may go into
13 I will *s* the heavens, and the
14.16 to tremble, that did *s* kingdoms;
24.18 the foundations of the earth do *s*.
33. 9 and Carmel *s* off their fruits.
52. 2 *S* thyself from the dust; arise, and
Jer 23. 9 all my bones *s*; I am like a
Eze 26.10 thy walls shall *s* at the noise of
15 the isles *s* at the sound of thy fall,
27.28 suburbs shall *s* at the sound of the
31.16 nations to *s* at the sound of his fall,
38.20 of the earth, shall *s* at my presence,
Dan 4.14 *s* off his leaves, and scatter his
Joel 3.16 the heavens and the earth shall *s*:
Am 9. 1 of the door, that the posts may *s*:
Hag 2. 6 while, and I will *s* the heavens,
7 I will *s* all nations, and the desire
21 I will *s* the heavens and the earth;
Zec 2. 9 I will *s* mine hand upon them, and
Mt 10.14 or city, *s* off the dust of your feet.
28. 4 for fear of him the keepers did *s*,
Mk 6.11 *s* off the dust under your feet for
Lk 6.48 that house, and could not *s* it: for
9. 5 *s* off the very dust from your feet
Heb 12.26 once more I *s* not the earth only,

SHAKEN
Lev 26.36 the sound of a *s* leaf chase them;
1Ki 14.15 Israel, as a reed is *s* in the water,
2Ki 19.21 of Jerusalem hath *s* her head at
Neh 5.13 even thus be he *s* out, and
Job 16.12 by my neck, and *s* me to pieces,
38.13 the wicked might be *s* out of it?
Ps 18. 7 of the hills moved and were *s*,
Isa 37.22 of Jerusalem hath *s* her head at
Na 2. 3 the fir trees shall be terribly *s*.
3.12 if they be *s*, they shall even fall
Mt 11. 7 to see? A reed *s* with the wind?
24.29 powers of the heavens shall be *s*:
Mk 13.25 that are in heaven shall be *s*.
Lk 6.38 measure, pressed down, *s* together,
7.24 to see? A reed *s* with the wind?
21.26 the powers of heaven shall be *s*.
Ac 4.31 the place was *s* where they were
16.26 foundations of the prison were *s*:
2Th 2. 2 That ye be not soon *s* in mind, or
Heb 12.27 removing of those things that are *s*,
27 which cannot be *s* may remain.
Rev 6.13 when she is *s* of a mighty wind.

SHAMBLES
1Co 10.25 Whatsoever is sold in the *s*, that

SHAME
Ex 32.25 made them naked unto their *s*
Jdg 18. 7 that might put them to *s* in any
1Sa 20.34 because his father had done him *s*.
2Sa 13.13 whither shall I cause my *s* to go?
2Ch 32.21 with *s* of face to his own land.
Job 8.22 hate thee shall be clothed with *s*;
Ps 4. 2 long will ye turn my glory into *s*?
35. 4 put to *s* that seek after my soul:
26 let them be clothed with *s* and
40.14 and put to *s* that wish me evil.
15 for a reward of their *s* that say
44. 7 hast put them to *s* that hated us.
9 hast cast off, and put us to *s*;
15 the *s* of my face hath covered me,
53. 5 thou hast put them to *s*, because
69. 7 reproach; *s* hath covered my face.
19 known my reproach, and my *s*,
70. 3 for a reward of their *s* that say,
71.24 for they are brought unto *s*, that
83.16 Fill their faces with *s*; that they
17 let them be put to *s*, and perish:
89.45 thou hast covered him with *s*.
109.29 adversaries be clothed with *s*,
119.31 O Lord, put me not to *s*.
132.18 His enemies will I clothe with *s*:
Pr 3.35 *s* shall be the promotion of fools.
9. 7 a scorner getteth to himself *s*:
10. 5 in harvest is a son that causeth *s*.
11. 2 pride cometh, then cometh *s*: but
12.16 but a prudent man covereth *s*.
13. 5 is loathsome, and cometh to *s*.
18 Poverty and *s* shall be to him
14.35 is against him that causeth *s*.
17. 2 have rule over a son that causeth *s*,
18.13 it, it is folly and *s* unto him.
19.26 mother, is a son that causeth *s*,
25. 8 thy neighbor hath put thee to *s*.
10 he that heareth it put thee to *s*,
29.15 himself bringeth his mother to *s*.
Isa 20. 4 uncovered, to the *s* of Egypt.
22.18 shall be the *s* of thy lord's house.
30. 3 strength of Pharaoh be your *s*,
5 profit, but a *s*, and also a reproach.
47. 3 yea, thy *s* shall be seen:
50. 6 not my face from *s* and spitting.
54. 4 for thou shalt not be put to *s*:
4 shalt forget the *s* of thy youth,
61. 7 For your *s* ye shall have double;
Jer 3.24 *s* hath devoured the labor of our
25 We lie down in our *s*, and our
13.26 thy face, that thy *s* may appear.
20.18 days should be consumed with *s*?
23.40 a perpetual *s*, which shall not be
46.12 The nations have heard of thy *s*,
48.39 hath Moab turned the back with *s*!
51.51 *s* hath covered our faces: for

Eze 7.18 and *s* shall be upon all faces, and
16.52 bear thine own *s* for thy sins that
52 confounded also, and bear thy *s*,
54 That thou mayest bear thine own *s*,
63 mouth any more because of thy *s*,
32.24, 25 yet have they borne their *s*
30 and bear their *s* with them that go
34.29 neither bear the *s* of the heathen
36. 6 yet have borne the *s* of the heathen:
7 about you, they shall bear their *s*.
15 bear in thee the *s* of the heathen
39.26 After that they have borne their *s*,
44.13 but they shall bear their *s*, and
Dan 12. 2 to *s* and everlasting contempt.
Hos 4. 7 will I change their glory into *s*.
18 her rulers with *s* do love, Give ye.
9.10 separated themselves...that *s*;
10. 6 Ephraim shall receive *s*, and
Ob 10 brother Jacob *s* shall cover thee,
Mic 1.11 of Saphir, having thy *s* naked:
2. 6 them, that they shall not take *s*.
7.10 *s* shall cover her which said unto
Na 3. 5 and the kingdoms thy *s*.
Hab 2.10 hast consulted *s* to thy house by
16 Thou art filled with *s* for glory:
Zep 3. 5 but the unjust knoweth no *s*.
19 land where they have been put to *s*.
Lk 14. 9 begin with *s* to take the lowest
Ac 5.41 worthy to suffer *s* for his name.
1Co 4.14 I write not these things to *s* you,
6. 5 I speak to your *s*. Is it so, that
11. 6 it be a *s* for a woman to be shorn
14 have long hair, it is a *s* unto him?
22 of God, and *s* them who have not?
14.35 *s* for women to speak in...church.
15.34 of God: I speak this to your *s*.
Eph 5.12 a *s* even to speak of those things
Php 3.19 and whose glory is in their *s*, who
Heb 6. 6 afresh, and put him to an open *s*.
12. 2 endured the cross, despising the *s*,
Jude 13 the sea, foaming out their own *s*;
Rev 3.18 *s* of thy nakedness do not appear;
16.15 he walk naked, and they see his *s*.

SHAMED

Gen 38.23 Let her take it to her, lest we be *s*:
2Sa 19. 5 hast *s* this day the faces of all thy
Ps 14. 6 Ye have *s* the counsel of the poor,

SHAMEFACEDNESS

1Ti 2. 9 apparel, with *s* and sobriety;

SHAMEFUL

Jer 11.13 have ye...altars to that *s* thing,
Hab 2.16 *s* spewing shall be on thy glory.

SHAMEFULLY

Hos 2. 5 that conceived them hath done *s*:
Mk 12. 4 head, and sent him away *s* handled.
Lk 20.11 beat him also, and entreated him *s*,
1Th 2. 2 and were *s* entreated, as ye know,

SHAPE

Lk 3.22 a bodily *s* like a dove upon him,
Jn 5.37 voice at any time, nor seen his *s*.

SHAPEN

Ps 51. 5 I was *s* in iniquity; and in sin

SHAPES

Rev 9. 7 *s* of the locusts were like unto

SHARON

1Ch 5.16 and in all the suburbs of *S*, upon
27.29 over the herds that fed in *S* was
SS 2. 1 I am the rose of *S*, and the lily of
Isa 33. 9 *S* is like a wilderness; and Bashan
35. 2 the excellency of Carmel and *S*,
65.10 And *S* shall be a fold of flocks, and

SHARP

Ex 4.25 Then Zipporah took a *s* stone,
Jos 5. 2 unto Joshua, Make thee *s* knives,
3 Joshua made him *s* knives, and
1Sa 14. 4 was a *s* rock on the one side,
4 and a *s* rock on the other side:
Job 41.30 *S* stones are under him: he
30 *s* pointed things upon the mire.
Ps 45. 5 Thine arrows are *s* in the heart
52. 2 mischiefs; like a *s* rasor, working
57. 4 and their tongue a *s* sword.
120. 4 *S* arrows of the mighty, with
Pr 5. 4 *s* as a twoedged sword.
25.18 maul, and a sword, and a *s* arrow.
Isa 5.28 Whose arrows are *s*, and all their
41.15 a new *s* threshing instrument
49. 2 made my mouth like a *s* sword;
Eze 5. 1 take thee a *s* knife, take thee a
Ac 15.39 contention was so *s* between them,
Rev 1.16 mouth went a *s* twoedged sword:
2.12 hath the *s* sword with two edges;
14.14 crown, and in his hand a *s* sickle.
17 heaven, he also having a *s* sickle.
18 cry to him that had the *s* sickle,
18 Thrust in thy *s* sickle, and gather
19.15 out of his mouth goeth a *s* sword,

SHARPEN

1Sa 13.20 to *s* every man his share, and his
21 for the axes, and to *s* the goads.

SHARPENED

Ps 140. 3 They have *s* their tongues like a
Eze 21. 9 A sword, a sword is *s*, and also
10 It is *s* to make a sore slaughter;
11 this sword is *s*, and it is furbished,

SHARPENETH

Job 16. 9 mine enemy *s* his eyes upon me.
Pr 27.17 Iron *s* iron; so a man *s* the

SHARPER

Mic 7. 4 the most upright is *s* than a thorn
Heb 4.12 and *s* than any twoedged sword,

SHARPLY

Jdg 8. 1 And they did chide with him *s*.
Tit 1.13 Wherefore rebuke them *s*, that

SHARPNESS

2Co 13.10 lest being present I should use *s*.

SHAVE

Lev 13.33 but the scall shall he not *s*;
14. 8 *s* off all his hair, and wash himself
9 *s* all his hair off his head and his
9 even all his hair he shall *s* off: and
21. 5 they *s* off the corner of their beard,
Nu 6. 9 shall *s* his head in the day of his
9 on the seventh day shall he *s* it.
18 shall *s* the head of his separation
8. 7 let them *s* all their flesh, and
Dt 21.12 she shall *s* her head, and pare
Jdg 16.19 to *s* off the seven locks of his head;
Isa 7.20 Lord *s* with a rasor that is hired,
Eze 44.20 Neither shall they *s* their heads,
Ac 21.24 them, that they may *s* their heads:

SHAVED

Gen 41.14 and he *s* himself, and changed his
2Sa 10. 4 *s* off the one half of their beards,
1Ch 19. 4 *s* them, and cut off their garments
Job 1.20 *s* his head, and fell down upon

SHAVEN

Lev 13.33 He shall be *s*, but the scall shall
Nu 6.19 the hair of his separation is *s*:
Jdg 16.17 if I be *s*, then my strength will go
22 hair...grow again after he was *s*.
Jer 41. 5 men, having their beards *s*, and
1Co 11. 5 is even all one as if she were *s*.
6 for a woman to be shorn or *s*, let

SHEAF

Gen 37. 7 and, lo, my *s* arose, and also stood
7 about, and made obeisance to my *s*.
Lev 23.10 shall bring a *s* of the firstfruits
11 shall wave the *s* before the Lord,
12 ye wave the *s* an he lamb without
15 brought the *s* of the wave offering;
Dt 24.19 and hast forgot a *s* in the field,
Job 24.10 take away the *s* from the hungry,
Zec 12. 6 and like a torch of fire in a *s*;

SHEAR

Gen 31.19 And Laban went to *s* his sheep:
38.13 up to Timnath to *s* his sheep.
Dt 15.19 nor *s* the firstling of thy sheep.
1Sa 25. 4 that Nabal did *s* his sheep.

SHEARER

Ac 8.23 like a lamb dumb before his *s*,

SHEARERS

1Sa 25. 7 I have heard that thou hast *s*:
11 flesh that I have killed for my *s*,
Isa 53. 7 as a sheep before her *s* is dumb, so

SHEATH

1Sa 17.51 and drew it out of his *s* thereof,
2Sa 20. 8 upon his loins in the *s* thereof;
1Ch 21.27 put his sword again into the *s*
Eze 21. 3 forth my sword out of his *s*,
4 my sword go forth out of his *s*
5 drew forth my sword out of his *s*:
30 cause it to return into his *s*? I will
Jn 18.11 Put up thy sword into the *s*;

SHEAVES

Gen 37. 7 we were binding *s* in the fields,
7 behold, your *s* stood round about,
Ru 2. 7 after the reapers among the *s*:
15 Let her glean even among the *s*,
Neh 13.15 bringing in *s*, and lading asses;
Ps 126. 6 rejoicing, bringing his *s* with him.
129. 7 nor he that bindeth *s* his bosom.
Am 2.13 a cart is pressed that is full of *s*.
Mic 4.12 gather them as the *s* into the floor.

SHEBA

1Ki 10. 1 queen of *S* heard of the fame of
4 queen of *S* had seen all Solomon's
10 queen of *S* gave to king Solomon.
13 unto the queen of *S* all her desire,
2Ch 9. 1 queen of *S* heard of the fame of
3 queen of *S* had seen the wisdom
9 spice as the queen of *S* gave king
12 to the queen of *S* all her desire,
Job 6.19 companies of *S* waited for them.
Ps 72.10 kings of *S* and Seba shall offer
15 shall be given of the gold of *S*:
Isa 60. 6 all they from *S* shall come: they
Jer 6.20 there to me incense from *S*, and

SHED

Gen 9. 6 by man shall his blood be *s*: for
37.22 *S* no blood, but cast him into
Ex 22. 2 die, there shall no blood be *s* for him.
3 him, there shall be blood *s* for him;
Lev 17. 4 he hath *s* blood; and that man
Nu 35.33 be cleansed of the blood that is *s*
33 but by the blood of him that *s* it.
Dt 19.10 That innocent blood be not *s* in
21. 7 Our hands have not *s* this blood,
1Sa 25.26 thee from coming to *s* blood,
31 thou hast *s* blood causeless, or
33 me this day from coming to *s* blood,
2Sa 20.10 *s* out his bowels to the ground,
1Ki 2. 5 and *s* the blood of war in peace,
31 the innocent blood, which Joab *s*,
2Ki 21.16 Manasseh *s* innocent blood very
24. 4 for the innocent blood that he *s*:
1Ch 22. 8 Thou hast *s* blood abundantly, and
8 thou hast *s* much blood upon the
28. 3 a man of war, and hast *s* blood.
Ps 79. 3 Their blood have they *s* like water
10 blood of thy servants which is *s*.

Ps 106.38 *s* innocent blood, even the blood
Pr 1.16 to evil, and make haste to *s* blood.
6.17 and hands that *s* innocent blood,
Isa 59. 7 make haste to *s* innocent blood:
Jer 7. 6 *s* not innocent blood in this place,
22. 3 *s* innocent blood in this place.
17 and for to *s* innocent blood, and
La 4.13 *s* the blood of the just in the midst
Eze 16.38 wedlock and *s* blood are judged;
22. 4 in thy blood that thou hast *s*: and
6 in thee to their power to *s* blood.
9 are men that carry tales to *s* blood:
12 have they taken gifts to *s* blood;
27 ravening the prey, to *s* blood, and
23.45 manner of women that *s* blood;
33.25 toward your idols, and *s* blood:
35. 5 hast *s* the blood of the children
36.18 that they had *s* upon the land,
Joel 3.19 *s* innocent blood in their land.
Mt 23.35 righteous blood *s* upon the earth,
26.28 *s* for many for the remission of sins.
Mk 14.24 testament, which is *s* for many.
Lk 11.50 which was *s* from the foundation
22.20 in my blood, which is *s* for you.
Ac 2.33 he hath *s* forth this, which ye now
22.20 blood of thy martyr Stephen was *s*,
Ro 3.15 Their feet are swift to *s* blood:
5. 5 the love of God is *s* abroad in our
Tit 3. 6 *s* on us abundantly through Jesus
Rev 16. 6 For they have *s* the blood of saints

SHEDDETH
Gen 9. 6 Whoso *s* man's blood, by man
Eze 22. 3 The city *s* blood in the midst of it,

SHEDDING
Heb 9.22 and without *s* of blood is no

SHEEP
Gen 4. 2 Abel was a keeper of *s*, but Cain
29. 6 his daughter cometh with the *s*.
9 Rachel came with her father's *s*:
30.32 all the brown cattle among the *s*,
Nu 27.17 not as *s* which have no shepherd.
1Sa 15.14 meaneth then this bleating of the *s*
15 the people spared the best of the *s*
16.11 and, behold, he keepeth the *s*.
2Sa 24.17 but these *s*, what have they done?
Neh 3. 1 priests, and they builded the *s* gate;
32 corner unto the *s* gate repaired
Ps 8. 7 All *s* and oxen, yea, and the
44.22 are counted as *s* for the slaughter.
78.52 his own people to go forth like *s*,
79.13 we thy people and *s* of thy pasture
95. 7 his pasture, and the *s* of his hand.
119.176 I have gone astray like a lost *s*;
Isa 53. 6 All we like *s* have gone astray; we
7 and as a *s* before her shearers is
Jer 12. 3 them out like *s* for the slaughter,
23. 1 and scatter the *s* of my pasture!
Eze 34.12 so will I seek out my *s*, and will
Joel 1.18 the flocks of *s* are made desolate.
Mic 5. 8 a young lion among the flocks of *s*:
Zec 13. 7 and the *s* shall be scattered: and I
Mt 9.36 abroad, as *s* having no shepherd.
10. 6 go rather to the lost *s* of the house
16 I send you forth as *s* in the midst
12.11 that shall have one *s*, and if it fall
12 then is a man better than a *s*?
15.24 but unto the lost *s* of the house of
18.12 if a man have an hundred *s*, and
13 he rejoiceth more of that *s*, than of
25.32 divideth his *s* from the goats:
33 he shall set the *s* on his right hand,
26.31 the *s* of the flock shall be scattered
Mk 6.34 were as *s* not having a shepherd:
14.27 and the *s* shall be scattered.
Lk 15. 4 man of you, having an hundred *s*,
6 I have found my *s* which was lost.
Jn 2.14 that sold oxen and *s* and doves,
15 temple, and the *s*, and the oxen;

Sheep are symbolically separated from goats (Mt 25.31-33) in this sixth-century mosaic from Ravenna.

5. 2 Jerusalem by the *s* market a pool,
10. 2 the door is the shepherd of the *s*.
3 openeth; and the *s* hear his voice:
3 and he calleth his own *s* by name,
4 when he putteth forth his own *s*,
4 before them, and the *s* follow him:
7 unto you, I am the door of the *s*.
8 but the *s* did not hear them.
11 shepherd giveth his life for the *s*.
12 shepherd, whose own the *s* are not,
12 and leaveth the *s*, and fleeth: and
12 them, and scattereth the *s*.
13 hireling, and careth not for the *s*.
14 know my *s*, and am known of mine.
15 and I lay down my life for the *s*.
16 And other *s* I have, which are not
26 ye are not of my *s*, as I said unto
27 My *s* hear my voice, and I know
21.16 He saith unto him, Feed my *s*.
17 Jesus saith unto him, Feed my *s*.
Ac 8.32 He was led as a *s* to the slaughter;
Ro 8.36 accounted as *s* for the slaughter.
Heb 13.20 Jesus, that great shepherd of the *s*,
1Pe 2.25 For ye were as *s* going astray; but
Rev 18.13 and beasts, and *s*, and horses, and

SHEEPFOLD
Jn 10. 1 not by the door into the *s*, but

SHEEP'S
Mt 7.15 which come to you in *s* clothing,

SHEEPSKINS
Heb 11.37 they wandered about in *s* and

SHEET
Ac 10.11 great *s* knit at the four corners,
11. 5 as it had been a great *s*, let down

SHELTER
Job 24. 8 embrace the rock for want of a *s*.
Ps 61. 3 thou hast been a *s* for me, and a

SHEPHERD
Gen 46.34 every *s* is an abomination
Nu 27.17 be not as sheep which have no *s*.
1Ki 12.17 hills, as sheep that have not a *s*:
2Ch 18.16 as sheep that have no *s*; and the
Ps 23. 1 The Lord is my *s*; I shall not want.
Ec 12.11 which are given from one *s*.
Isa 40.11 He shall feed his flock like a *s*: he
Jer 31.10 and keep him, as a *s* doth his flock.
49.19 and who is that *s* that will stand
Eze 34. 5 scattered, because there is no *s*:
23 And I will set up one *s* over them,
Am 3.12 As the *s* taketh out of the mouth of
Zec 10. 2 troubled, because there was no *s*.
11.16 lo, I will raise up a *s* in the land,
17 Woe to the idol *s* that leaveth the
13. 7 smite the *s*, and the sheep shall be
Mt 9.36 abroad, as sheep having no *s*.
25.32 as a *s* divideth his sheep from the
26.31 I will smite the *s*, and the sheep of
Mk 6.34 they were as sheep not having a *s*:
14.27 I will smite the *s*, and the sheep
Jn 10. 2 in by the door is the *s* of the sheep.
11 I am the good *s*: the good *s* giveth
12 that is an hireling, and not the *s*,
14 I am the good *s*, and know my
16 there shall be one fold, and one *s*.
Heb 13.20 Jesus, that great *s* of the sheep,
1Pe 2.25 returned unto the *S* and Bishop of
5. 4 And when the chief *S* shall appear,

SHEPHERD'S
1Sa 17.40 put them in a *s* bag which he had,
Isa 38.12 is removed from me as a *s* tent:

SHEPHERDS
Gen 47. 3 Thy servants are *s*, both we,
Isa 13.20 neither shall the *s* make their fold
56.11 they are *s* that cannot understand:
Jer 23. 4 And I will set up *s* over them which
25.34 Howl, ye *s*, and cry; and wallow
35 And the *s* shall have no way to flee,
50. 6 their *s* have caused them to go
Eze 34. 2 prophesy against the *s* of Israel,
2 Woe be to the *s* of Israel that do
7 ye *s*, hear the word of the Lord;
10 Behold, I am against the *s*; and I
Zec 11. 3 is a voice of the howling of the *s*;
5 and their own *s* pity them not.

Lk 2. 8 country *s* abiding in the field,
15 the *s* said one to another, Let us
18 which were told them by the *s*.
20 And the *s* returned, glorifying and

SHEW
Gen 12. 1 unto a land that I will *s* thee:
20.13 thy kindness which thou shalt *s*
24.12 and *s* kindness unto my master
40.14 *s* kindness, I pray thee, unto me,
46.31 I will go up, and *s* Pharaoh, and
Ex 7. 9 you, saying, *S* a miracle for you:
9.16 up, for to *s* in thee my power;
10. 1 that I might *s* these my signs
13. 8 thou shalt *s* thy son in that day,
14.13 which he will *s* to you to day: for
18.20 shalt *s* them the way wherein
25. 9 According to all that I *s* thee,
33.13 *s* me now thy way, that I may
18 I beseech thee, *s* me thy glory.
19 will *s* mercy on whom I will *s* mercy.
Nu 16. 5 the Lord will *s* who are his, and
Dt 1.33 to *s* you by what way ye should go,
3.24 to *s* thy servants thy greatness,
5. 5 to *s* you the word of the Lord:
7. 2 with them, nor *s* mercy unto them:
13.17 of his anger, and *s* thee mercy,
17. 9 they shall *s* thee the sentence of
10 the Lord shall choose shall *s* thee;
11 sentence which they shall *s* thee,
28.50 of the old, nor *s* favor to the young:
32. 7 ask thy father, and he will *s* thee;
Jos 2.12 ye will also *s* kindness unto my
5. 6 he would not *s* them the land,
Jdg 1.24 *S* us, we pray thee, the entrance
24 the city, and we will *s* thee mercy.
4.22 will *s* thee the man…thou seekest.
6.17 *s* me a sign that thou talkest with
1Sa 3.15 Samuel feared to *s* Eli the vision.
8. 9 and *s* them the manner of the king
9. 6 peradventure he can *s* us our way
27 I may *s* thee the word of God.
10. 8 and *s* thee what thou shalt do.
14.12 up to us, and we will *s* you a thing.
16. 3 I will *s* thee what thou shalt do:
20. 2 or small, but that he will *s* it me:
12 send not unto thee, and *s* it thee;
13 then I will *s* it thee, and send thee
14 *s* me the kindness of the Lord,
22.17 he fled, and did not *s* it to me.
25. 8 young men, and they will *s* thee.
2Sa 2. 6 *s* kindness and truth unto you:
3. 8 *s* kindness this day unto the house
9. 1 may *s* him kindness for Jonathan's
3 that I may *s* the kindness of God
7 surely *s* thee kindness for Jonathan
10. 2 I will *s* kindness unto Hanun the
15.25 *s* me both it, and his habitation:
22.26 merciful thou wilt *s* thyself merciful,
26 man thou wilt *s* thyself upright.
27 the pure thou wilt *s* thyself pure;
27 thou wilt *s* thyself unsavory.
1Ki 1.52 If he will *s* himself a worthy man,
2. 2 therefore, and *s* thyself a man;
7 *s* kindness unto…sons of Barzillai
18. 1 saying, Go, *s* thyself unto Ahab;
2 Elijah went to *s* himself unto Ahab.
15 I will surely *s* myself unto him
2Ki 6.11 *s* me which of us is for the king
7.12 *s* you what the Syrians have done
1Ch 16.23 *s*…from day to day his salvation.
19. 2 I will *s* kindness unto Hanun the
2Ch 16. 9 to *s* himself strong in the behalf of
Ezr 2.59 could not *s* their father's house,
Neh 7.61 could not *s* their father's house,
9.19 of fire by night, to *s* them light,
Est 1.11 to *s* the people…her beauty:
2.10 charged her…she should not *s* it.
4. 8 to *s* it unto Esther, and to declare
Job 10. 2 *s* me wherefore thou contendest
11. 6 *s* thee the secrets of wisdom,
15.17 I will *s* thee, hear me; and that
32. 6 and durst not *s* you mine opinion.
10 to me; I also will *s* mine opinion.
17 my part, I also will *s* mine opinion.
33.23 to *s* unto man his uprightness:
36. 2 Suffer me a little, and I will *s*
Ps 4. 6 that say, Who will *s* us any good?
9. 1 *s* forth all thy marvellous works.
14 That I may *s* forth all thy praise
16.11 Thou wilt *s* me the path of life:
17. 7 *S* thy marvellous lovingkindness,
18.25 merciful thou wilt *s* thyself merciful;
25 man thou wilt *s* thyself upright;
26 the pure thou wilt *s* thyself pure;
26 froward thou wilt *s* thyself froward.
25. 4 *S* me thy ways, O Lord; teach me
14 and he will *s* them his covenant.
39. 6 every man walketh in a vain *s*:
50.23 will I *s* the salvation of God.
51.15 my mouth shall *s* forth thy praise.
71.15 shall *s* forth thy righteousness
79.13 *s* forth thy praise to all generations.
85. 7 *S* us thy mercy, O Lord, and
86.17 *S* me a token for good; that they
88.10 Wilt thou *s* wonders to the dead?
91.16 him, and *s* him my salvation.
92. 2 To *s* forth thy lovingkindness in
15 To *s* that the Lord is upright: he
94. 1 vengeance belongeth, *s* thyself.
96. 2 *s*…his salvation from day to day.
106. 2 who can *s* forth all his praise?
109.16 he remembered not to *s* mercy,
Pr 18.24 hath friends must *s* himself friendly:
Isa 3. 9 The *s* of their countenance doth
27.11 formed them will *s* them no favor.
30.30 *s* the lighting down of his arm,
41.22 and *s* us what shall happen:
22 let them *s* the former things, what
23 *S* the things that are to come
43. 9 this, and *s* us former things?
21 they shall *s* forth my praise.
44. 7 shall come, let them *s* unto them.
46. 8 Remember this, and *s* yourselves
47. 6 thou didst *s* them no mercy;
49. 9 are in darkness, *S* yourselves.
58. 1 *s* my people their transgression,
60. 6 *s* forth the praises of the Lord.
Jer 16.10 shalt *s* this people all these words,
13 where I will not *s* you favor.
18.17 I will *s* them the back, and not
33. 3 *s* thee great and mighty things,
42. 3 the Lord thy God may *s* us the way
12 And I will *s* mercies unto you,
50.42 they are cruel, and will not *s* mercy:
51.31 to *s* the king of Babylon…his city
Eze 22. 2 shalt *s* her all her abominations.
33.31 their mouth they *s* much love,
37.18 thou not *s* us what thou meanest
40. 4 heart upon all that I shall *s* thee;
4 that I might *s* them unto thee art
43.10 *s* the house to the house of Israel,
11 *s* them the form of the house,
Dan 2. 2 for to *s* the king his dreams.
4 and we will *s* the interpretation.
6 But if ye *s* the dream, and the
6 therefore *s* me the dream, and the
7 we will *s* the interpretation of it.
9 that ye can *s* me the interpretation
10 earth that can *s* the king's matter:
11 there is none other that can *s* it
16 *s* the king the interpretation.
24 *s* unto the king the interpretation.
27 the soothsayers, *s* unto the king;
4. 2 I thought it good to *s* the signs
5. 7 *s* me the interpretation thereof,
12 and he will *s* the interpretation.
15 they could not *s* the interpretation
9.23 forth, and I am come to *s* thee;
10.21 I will *s* thee that which is noted
11. 2 And now will I *s* thee the truth.
Joel 2.30 I will *s* wonders in the heavens
Mic 7.15 I *s* unto him marvellous things.
Na 3. 5 I will *s* the nations thy nakedness,
Hab 1. 3 Why dost thou *s* me iniquity, and
Zec 1. 9 unto me, I will *s* thee what these be.
7. 9 and *s* mercy and compassions
Mt 8. 4 thy way, *s* thyself to the priest,
11. 4 Go and *s* John again those things
12.18 shall *s* judgment to the Gentiles.
14. 2 mighty works do *s*…themselves
16. 1 would *s* them a sign from heaven.
21 began Jesus to *s* unto his disciples,
22.19 *S* me the tribute money. And
24. 1 *s* him the buildings of the temple.
24 shall *s* great signs and wonders;
Mk 1.44 thy way, *s* thyself to the priest,
6.14 mighty works do *s*…themselves
13.22 and shall *s* signs and wonders, to
14.15 he will *s* you a large upper room
Lk 1.19 and to *s* thee these glad tidings.
5.14 but go, and *s* thyself to the priest,
6.47 I will *s* you to whom he is like:
8.39 *s* how great things God hath done
17.14 Go *s* yourselves unto the priests.
20.24 *S* me a penny. Whose image and
47 and for a *s* make long prayers:
22.12 he shall *s* you a large upper room
Jn 5.20 *s* him greater works than these,
7. 4 things, *s* thyself to the world.
11.57 knew where he was, he should *s* it,
14. 8 *s* us the Father, and it sufficeth
9 sayest thou then, *S* us the Father?
16.13 and he will *s* you things to come.
14, 15 of mine, and shall *s* it unto you.
25 I shall *s* you plainly of the Father.
Ac 1.24 *s* whether of these two thou hast
2.19 I will *s* wonders in heaven above,
7. 3 into the land which I shall *s* thee.
9.16 For I will *s* him how great things
12.17 Go *s* these things unto James, and
16.17 *s* unto us the way of salvation.
24.27 willing to *s* the Jews a pleasure,
26.23 should *s* light unto the people,
Ro 2.15 *s* the work of the law written in
9.17 that I might *s* my power in thee,
22 What if God, willing to *s* his wrath,
1Co 11.26 ye do *s* the Lord's death till he
12.31 *s* I unto you a more excellent way.
15.51 I *s* you a mystery; We shall not
2Co 8.24 Wherefore *s* ye to them, and before
Gal 6.12 desire to make a fair *s* in the flesh,
Eph 2. 7 he might *s* the exceeding riches
Col 2.15 he made a *s* of them openly,
23 things have indeed a *s* of wisdom
1Th 1. 9 *s* of us what manner of entering
1Ti 1.16 might *s* forth all longsuffering,
5. 4 learn first to *s* piety at home, and
6.15 Which in his times he shall *s*,
2Ti 2.15 Study to *s* thyself approved unto
Heb 6.11 one of you do *s* the same diligence
17 to *s* unto the heirs of promise the
Jas 2.18 *s* me thy faith without thy works,
18 I will *s* thee my faith by my works.
3.13 let him *s* out of a good conversation
1Pe 2. 9 should *s* forth the praises of him
1Jn 1. 2 and *s* unto you that eternal life,
Rev 1. 1 to *s* unto his servants things which
4. 1 I will *s* thee things which must be
17. 1 I will *s* unto thee the judgment of
21. 9 I will *s* thee the bride, the Lamb's
22. 6 to *s* unto his servants the things

SHEWBREAD
Ex 25.30 shalt set upon the table *s*
35.13 and all his vessels, and the *s*,
39.36 the vessels thereof, and the *s*;
Nu 4. 7 upon the table of *s* they shall spread
1Sa 21. 6 was no bread there but the *s*,
1Ki 7.48 of gold, whereupon the *s* was,
1Ch 9.32 were over the *s*, to prepare it
23.29 Both for the *s*, and for the fine
28.16 he gave gold for the tables of *s*,

2Ch 2. 4 incense, and for the continual *s*,
4.19 tables whereon the *s* was set;
13.11 the *s* also set they in order
29.18 and the *s* table, with all the vessels
Neh 10.33 For the *s*, and...the continual
Mt 12. 4 eat the *s*, which was not lawful
Mk 2.26 eat the *s*, which is not lawful
Lk 6. 4 and did take and eat the *s*, and
Heb 9. 2 and the table, and the *s*;

SHEWED

Gen 41.25 God hath *s* Pharaoh what he is
Ex 15.25 and the Lord *s* him a tree, which
Nu 8. 4 pattern...the Lord had *s* Moses,
Dt 5.24 Lord our God hath *s* us his glory
6.22 the Lord *s* signs and wonders,
Jdg 16.18 for he hath *s* me all his heart.
Ru 2.11 It hath fully been *s* me, all that thou
2Ki 8.10 Lord hath *s* me that he shall...die.
13 Lord hath *s* me thou shalt be king
Ps 60. 3 Thou hast *s* thy people hard things:
78.11 his wonders that he had *s* them.
98. 2 righteousness hath he openly *s* in
Ec 2.19 I have *s* myself wise under the sun.
Isa 40.14 *s*...him the way of understanding?
48. 5 before it came to pass I *s* it thee:
Jer 38.21 the word that the Lord hath *s* me:
Am 7. 1 hath the Lord God *s* unto me;
4 Thus hath the Lord God *s* unto me:
Mic 6. 8 He hath *s* thee, O man, what is
Mt 28.11 and *s* unto the chief priests all the
Lk 1.51 He hath *s* strength with his arm:
58 Lord had *s* great mercy upon her;
4. 5 *s* unto him all the kingdoms of the
7.18 of John *s* him of all these things.
10.37 he said, He that *s* mercy on him.
14.21 came, and *s* his lord these things.
20.37 even Moses *s* at the bush, when
24.40 he *s* them his hands and his
Jn 10.32 good works have I *s* you from my
20.20 he *s* unto them his hands and his
21. 1 Jesus *s* himself again to the
1 and on this wise *s* he himself.
14 third time that Jesus *s* himself to
Ac 1. 3 To whom also he *s* himself alive
3.18 *s* by...mouth of all his prophets,
4.22 this miracle of healing was *s*.
7.26 he *s* himself unto them as they
36 *s* wonders and signs in the land
52 slain them which *s* before of the
10.28 God hath *s* me that I should not
40 day, and *s* him openly;
11.13 he *s* us how he had seen an angel
19.18 and confessed, and *s* their deeds.
20.20 but have *s* you, and have taught
35 I have *s* you all things, how that
23.22 thou hast *s* these things to me.
26.20 *s* first unto them of Damascus, and
28. 2 people *s* us no little kindness:
21 came *s* or spake any harm of thee.
Ro 1.19 for God hath *s* it unto them.
1Co 10.28 eat not for his sake that *s* it, and
Heb 6.10 which ye have *s* toward his name,
8. 5 the pattern *s* to thee in the mount.
Jas 2.13 mercy, that hath *s* no mercy;
2Pe 1.14 our Lord Jesus Christ hath *s* me.
Rev 21.10 and *s* me that great city, the holy
22. 1 he *s* me a pure river of water of
8 the angel which *s* me these things.

SHEWEST

2Ch 6.14 *s* mercy unto thy servants, that walk
Job 10.16 thou *s* thyself marvellous upon me.
Jer 32.18 Thou *s* lovingkindness unto
Jn 2.18 What sign *s* thou unto us, seeing
6.30 What sign *s* thou then, that we

SHEWETH

Gen 41.28 about to do he *s* unto Pharaoh.
Nu 23. 3 and whatsoever he *s* me I will tell
1Sa 22. 8 is none that *s* me that my son
8 or *s* unto me that my son hath
2Sa 22.51 and *s* mercy to his anointed, unto
Job 36. 9 Then he *s* them their work, and
33 The noise thereof *s* concerning it,
Ps 18.50 and *s* mercy to his anointed, to
19. 1 the firmament *s* his handywork.
2 night unto night *s* knowledge.
37.21 righteous *s* mercy, and giveth.
112. 5 A good man *s* favor, and lendeth:
147.19 He *s* his word unto Jacob, his
Pr 12.17 He that speaketh truth *s* forth
27.25 tender grass *s* itself, and herbs
Isa 41.26 there is none that *s*, yea, there is
Mt 4. 8 and *s* him all the kingdoms of the
Jn 5.20 *s* him all things that himself doeth:
Ro 9.16 runneth, but of God that *s* mercy.
12. 8 he that *s* mercy, with cheerfulness.

SHEWING

Ex 20. 6 *s* mercy unto thousands of them
Dt 5.10 *s* mercy unto thousands of them
Ps 78. 4 *s* to the generation to come the
SS 2. 9 *s* himself through the lattice.
Dan 4.27 iniquities by *s* mercy to the poor;
5.12 *s* of hard sentences, and dissolving
Lk 1.80 till the day of his *s* unto Israel.
8. 1 preaching and *s* the glad tidings
Ac 9.39 *s* the coats and garments which
18.28 *s* by the scriptures that Jesus was
2Th 2. 4 of God, *s* himself that he is God.
Tit 2. 7 *s* thyself a pattern of good works:
7 in doctrine *s* uncorruptness, gravity,
10 but *s* all good fidelity; that
3. 2 gentle, *s* all meekness unto all men.

SHIBBOLETH

Jdg 12. 6 said they unto him, Say now *S*:

SHIELD

Gen 15. 1 Fear not, Abram: I am thy *s*, and
Dt 33.29 by the Lord, the *s* of thy help,
Jdg 5. 8 was there a *s* or spear seen among
2Sa 1.21 *s* of the mighty is vilely cast away,
22. 3 he is my *s*, and the horn of my
36 given me the *s* of thy salvation:
2Ch 17.17 him armed men with bow and *s*
Ps 3. 3 But thou, O Lord, art a *s* for me;
5.12 thou compass him as with a *s*.
28. 7 The Lord is my strength and my *s*;
33.20 the Lord: he is our help and our *s*.
84. 9 Behold, O God our *s*, and look
11 For the Lord God is a sun and *s*:
91. 4 his truth shall be thy *s* and
119.114 art my hiding place and my *s*:
Pr 30. 5 he is a *s* unto them that put their
Isa 21. 5 arise, ye princes, and anoint the *s*.
Na 2. 3 *s* of his mighty men is made red,
Eph 6.16 taking the *s* of faith, wherewith

SHIELDS

Ps 47. 9 the *s* of the earth belong unto God:
Isa 37.33 nor come before it with *s*, nor
Jer 51.11 bright the arrows; gather the *s*:
Eze 27.11 hanged their *s* upon thy walls

SHILOAH

Isa 8. 6 people refuseth the waters of *S*

SHINE

Nu 6.25 Lord make his face *s* upon thee,
Job 3. 4 neither let the light *s* upon it.
10. 3 *s* upon the counsel of the wicked?
11.17 thou shalt *s* forth, thou shalt be
18. 5 the spark of his fire shall not *s*.
22.28 the light shall *s* upon thy ways.
36.32 commandeth it not to *s* by the cloud
37.15 caused the light of his cloud to *s*?
41.18 By his neesings a light doth *s*,
32 He maketh a path to *s* after him;
Ps 31.16 thy face to *s* upon thy servant:
67. 1 and cause his face to *s* upon us.
80. 1 between the cherubims, *s* forth.
3 and cause thy face to *s*; and we
7, 19 cause thy face to *s*; and we
104.15 oil to make his face to *s*, and
119.135 thy face to *s* upon thy servant;
Ec 8. 1 man's wisdom maketh his face to *s*,
Isa 13.10 shall not cause her light to *s*.
60. 1 Arise, *s*; for thy light is come,
Jer 5.28 They are waxen fat, they *s*: yea,
Dan 9.17 thy face to *s* upon thy sanctuary
12. 3 they that be wise shall *s* as the
Mt 5.16 Let your light so *s* before men,
13.43 Then shall the righteous *s* forth
17. 2 his face did *s* as the sun, and his
2Co 4. 4 image of God, should *s* unto them.
6 who commanded the light to *s*
Php 2.15 among whom ye *s* as lights in
Rev 18.23 light of a candle shall *s* no more
21.23 neither of the moon, to *s* in it:

SHINED

Dt 33. 2 he *s* forth from mount Paran, and
Job 29. 3 When his candle *s* upon my head,
31.26 If I beheld the sun when it *s*, or
Ps 50. 2 perfection of beauty, God hath *s*.
Isa 9. 2 upon them hath the light *s*.
Eze 43. 2 and the earth *s* with his glory.
Ac 9. 3 *s* round about him a light from
12. 7 him, and a light *s* in the prison:
2Co 4. 6 of darkness, hath *s* in our hearts,

SHINETH

Job 25. 5 even to the moon, and it *s* not;
Ps 139.12 but the night *s* as the day: the
Pr 4.18 *s* more and more unto the perfect
Mt 24.27 east, and *s* even unto the west;
Lk 17.24 *s* unto the other part under
Jn 1. 5 And the light *s* in darkness; and
2Pe 1.19 unto a light that *s* in a dark place,
1Jn 2. 8 is past, and the true light now *s*.
Rev 1.16 was as the sun *s* in his strength.

SHINING

2Sa 23. 4 of the earth by clear *s* after rain.
Pr 4.18 path of the just is as the *s* light,
Isa 4. 5 the *s* of a flaming fire by night:
Joel 2.10 the stars shall withdraw their *s*:
3.15 the stars shall withdraw their *s*.
Hab 3.11 at the *s* of thy glittering spear.
Mk 9. 3 And his raiment became *s*,
Lk 11.36 bright *s* of a candle doth give thee
24. 4 men stood by them in *s* garments:
Jn 5.35 He was a burning and a *s* light:
Ac 26.13 *s* round about me and them

SHIP

Pr 30.19 way of a *s* in the midst of the sea;
Isa 33.21 oars, neither shall gallant *s* pass
Eze 27. 5 made all thy *s* boards of fir trees
Jon 1. 3 he found a *s* going to Tarshish:
4 that the *s* was like to be broken.
5 the wares that were in the *s* into
5 gone down into the sides of the *s*;
Mt 4.21 in a *s* with Zebedee their father,
22 they immediately left the *s* and
8.23 when he was entered into a *s*, his
24 the *s* was covered with the waves:
9. 1 he entered into a *s*, and passed
13. 2 so that he went into a *s*, and sat;
14.13 he departed thence by *s* into a
22 his disciples to get into a *s*, and
24 *s* was now in the midst of the sea,
29 Peter was come down out of the *s*,
32 when they were come into the *s*,
33 they that were in the *s* came and
15.39 took *s*, and came into the coasts
Mk 1.19 were in the *s* mending their nets.
20 left their father Zebedee in the *s*
3. 9 that a small *s* should wait on him
4. 1 so that he entered into a *s*, and
36 took him even as he was in the *s*.

37 and the waves beat into the *s*, so
38 he was in the hinder part of the *s*.
5. 2 when he was come out of the *s*,
18 And when he was come into the *s*,
21 again by *s* unto the other side,
6.32 into a desert place by *s* privately.
45 his disciples to get into the *s*,
47 the *s* was in the midst of the sea,
51 he went up unto them into the *s*;
54 when they were come out of the *s*,
8.10 straightway he entered into a *s*
13 and entering into the *s* again
14 had they in the *s* with them more
Lk 5. 3 and taught the people out of the *s*,
7 which were in the other *s*, that
8.22 that he went into a *s* with his
37 and he went up into the *s*, and
Jn 6.17 entered into a *s*, and went over the
19 sea, and drawing nigh unto the *s*:
21 willingly received him into the *s*:
21 and immediately the *s* was at the
21. 3 and entered into a *s* immediately;
6 the net on the right side of the *s*,
8 other disciples came in a little *s*;
Ac 20.13 we went before to *s*, and sailed
38 they accompanied him unto the *s*.
21. 2 And finding a *s* sailing over unto
3 the *s* was to unlade her burden.
6 leave one of another, we took *s*;
27. 2 entering into a *s* of Adramyttium,
6 centurion found a *s* of Alexandria
10 not only of the lading and *s*, but
11 the master and the owner of the *s*,
15 And when the *s* was caught, and
17 used helps, undergirding the *s*;
18 the next day they lightened the *s*;
19 own hands the tackling of the *s*.
22 man's life among you, but of the *s*.
30 were about to flee out of the *s*,
31 Except these abide in the *s*, ye
37 were in all in the *s* two hundred
38 they lightened the *s*, and cast out
39 it were possible, to thrust in the *s*.
41 seas met, they ran the *s* aground
44 some on broken pieces of the *s*.
28.11 we departed in a *s* of Alexandria,

SHIPMASTER

Jon 1. 6 So the *s* came to him, and
Rev 18.17 every *s*, and all the company in

SHIPMEN

1Ki 9.27 *s* that had knowledge of the
Ac 27.27 *s* deemed that they drew near to
30 the *s* were about to flee out of the

SHIPPING

Jn 6.24 they also took *s*, and came to

SHIPS

Gen 49.13 and he shall be for an haven of *s*;
Nu 24.24 *s* shall come from the coast of
Dt 28.68 bring thee into Egypt again with *s*,
Jdg 5.17 and why did Dan remain in *s*?
1Ki 9.26 made a navy of *s* in Ezion-geber,
22.48 Jehoshaphat made *s* of Tharshish
48 the *s* were broken at Ezion-geber.
49 go with thy servants in the *s*.
2Ch 8.18 him by the hands of his servants *s*,
9.21 the king's *s* went to Tarshish with
21 the *s* of Tarshish bringing gold,
20.36 him to make *s* to go to Tarshish:
36 they made the *s* in Ezion-gaber.
37 the *s* were broken, that they were
Job 9.26 are passed away as the swift *s*:
Ps 48. 7 Thou breakest the *s* of Tarshish
104.26 There go the *s*: there is that
107.23 They that go down to the sea in *s*,
Pr 31.14 She is like the merchants' *s*; she
Isa 2.16 And upon all the *s* of Tarshish,
23. 1 Howl, ye *s* of Tarshish; for it is
14 Howl, ye *s* of Tarshish: for your
43.14 Chaldeans, whose cry is in the *s*.
60. 9 for me, and the *s* of Tarshish first,
Eze 27. 9 *s* of the sea with their mariners
25 The *s* of Tarshish did sing of thee
29 shall come down from their *s*,
30. 9 messengers go forth from me in *s*
Dan 11.30 *s* of Chittim shall come against
40 with horsemen, and with many *s*;
Mk 4.36 were also with him other little *s*.
Lk 5. 2 saw two *s* standing by the lake:
3 And he entered into one of the *s*,
7 they came, and filled both the *s*,
11 they had brought their *s* to land,
Jas 3. 4 Behold also the *s*, which though
Rev 8. 9 third part of the *s* were destroyed.
18.17 all the company in *s*, and sailors,
19 made rich all that had *s* in the sea

SHIPWRECK

2Co 11.25 thrice I suffered *s*, a night and a
1Ti 1.19 concerning faith have made *s*:

SHIVERS

Rev 2.27 potter shall they be broken to *s*:

SHOD

2Ch 28.15 arrayed them, and *s* them, and
Eze 16.10 and *s* thee with badgers' skin, and
Mk 6. 9 But be *s* with sandals; and not
Eph 6.15 your feet *s* with the preparation

SHOE

Dt 25. 9 and loose his *s* from off his foot,
10 of him that hath his *s* loosed.
29. 5 *s* is not waxen old upon thy foot.
Jos 5.15 Loose thy *s* from off thy foot; for
Ru 4. 7 a man plucked off his *s*, and gave
8 it for thee. So he drew off his *s*.
Ps 60. 8 over Edom will I cast out my *s*:
108. 9 over Edom will I cast out my *s*;
Isa 20. 2 and put off thy *s* from thy foot.

SHOE'S

Jn 1.27 *s* latchet I am not worthy to

SHOES

Ex 3. 5 put off thy *s* from off thy feet,
12.11 your *s* on your feet, and your staff
Am 2. 6 and the poor for a pair of *s*;
8. 6 and the needy for a pair of *s*;
Mt 3.11 whose *s* I am not worthy to bear:
10.10 neither two coats, neither *s*, nor
Mk 1. 7 the latchet of whose *s* I am not
Lk 3.16 the latchet of whose *s* I am not
10. 4 neither purse, nor scrip, nor *s*;
15.22 on his hand, and *s* on his feet:
22.35 without purse, and scrip, and *s*,
Ac 7.33 Put off thy *s* from thy feet: for the
13.25 *s* of his feet I am not worthy to

SHONE

Ex 34.29 wist not that the skin of his face *s*
30 behold, the skin of his face *s*; and
35 that the skin of Moses' face *s*: and
2Ki 3.22 and the sun *s* upon the water, and
Lk 2. 9 and the glory of the Lord *s* round
Ac 22. 6 *s* from heaven a great light round
Rev 8.12 the day *s* not for a third part of it,

SHOOK

2Sa 6. 6 took hold of it; for the oxen *s* it.
22. 8 Then the earth *s* and trembled;
8 foundations of heaven moved and *s*,
Neh 5.13 Also I *s* my lap, and said, So God
Ps 18. 7 Then the earth *s* and trembled;
68. 8 The earth *s*, the heavens also
77.18 world: the earth trembled and *s*.
Isa 23.11 over the sea, he *s* the kingdoms:
Ac 13.51 *s* off the dust of their feet against
18. 6 he *s* his raiment, and said unto
28. 5 he *s* off the beast into the fire, and
Heb 12.26 Whose voice then *s* the earth: but

SHOOT

Ex 36.33 the middle bar to *s* through the
1Sa 20.20 *s* three arrows on the side thereof,
36 find out now the arrows which I *s*.
2Sa 11.20 that they would *s* from the wall?
2Ki 13.17 Then Elisha said, *S*. And he shot.
19.32 into this city, nor *s* an arrow there,
1Ch 5.18 and sword, and to *s* with bow,
2Ch 26.15 *s* arrows and great stones withal.
Ps 11. 2 privily *s* at the upright in heart.
22. 7 they *s* out the lip, they shake the
58. 7 he bendeth his bow to *s* his arrows,
64. 3 bend their bows to *s* their arrows,
4 may *s* in secret at the perfect:
4 suddenly do they *s* at him, and
7 God shall *s* at them with an arrow;
144. 6 *s* out thine arrows, and destroy
Isa 37.33 into this city, nor *s* an arrow there,
Jer 50.14 bow, *s* at her, spare no arrows:
Eze 31.14 *s* up their top among the thick
36. 8 ye shall *s* forth your branches, and
Lk 21.30 When they now *s* forth, ye see

SHOOTETH

Job 8.16 his branch *s* forth in his garden.
Isa 27. 8 In measure, when it *s* forth, thou
Mk 4.32 *s* out great branches; so that

SHORE

Gen 22.17 the sand which is upon the sea *s*;
Ex 14.30 the Egyptians dead upon the sea *s*.
Jos 11. 4 that is upon the sea *s* in multitude,
15. 2 was from the *s* of the salt sea,
Jdg 5.17 Asher continued on the sea *s*,
1Sa 13. 5 as the sand which is on the sea *s*
1Ki 4.29 as the sand that is on the sea *s*.
9.26 on the *s* of the Red sea, in the
Jer 47. 7 Ashkelon, and against the sea *s*?
Mt 13. 2 whole multitude stood on the *s*.
48 when it was full, they drew to *s*,
Mk 6.53 of Gennesaret, and drew to the *s*.
Jn 21. 4 now come, Jesus stood on the *s*:
Ac 21. 5 and we kneeled down on the *s*, and
27.39 discovered a certain creek with a *s*,
40 to the wind, and made toward *s*.
Heb 11.12 as the sand which is by the sea *s*

SHORN

SS 4. 2 a flock of sheep that are even *s*,
Ac 18.18 having *s* his head in Cenchrea:
1Co 11. 6 be not covered, let her also be *s*:
6 it be a shame for a woman to be *s*

SHORT

Nu 11.23 Is the Lord's hand waxed *s*?
2Ki 10.32 days the Lord began to cut Israel *s*:
Job 17.12 the light is *s* because of darkness.
20. 5 the triumphing of the wicked is *s*,
Ps 89.47 Remember how *s* my time is:
Ro 3.23 and come *s* of the glory of God;
9.28 and cut it *s* in righteousness:
28 a *s* work will the Lord make upon
1Co 7.29 this I say, brethren, the time is *s*:
1Th 2.17 being taken from you for a *s* time
Heb 4. 1 of you should seem to come *s* of it.
Rev 12.12 knoweth that he hath but a *s* time.
17.10 he must continue a *s* space.

SHORTENED

Ps 89.45 The days of his youth hast thou *s*:
102.23 strength in the way; he *s* my days.
Pr 10.27 the years of the wicked shall be *s*.
Isa 50. 2 Is my hand *s* at all, that it cannot
59. 1 Behold, the Lord's hand is not *s*,
Mt 24.22 except those days should be *s*,
22 elect's sake those days shall be *s*,
Mk 13.20 that the Lord had *s* those days,
20 he hath chosen, he hath *s* the days.

SHORTER

Isa 28.20 the bed is *s* than that a man can
Eze 42. 5 Now the upper chambers were *s*:

SHORTLY

Gen 41.32 and God will *s* bring it to pass.
Jer 27.16 *s* be brought again from Babylon:
Eze 7. 8 I *s* pour out my fury upon thee,
Ac 25. 4 himself...depart *s* thither.
Ro 16.20 bruise Satan under your feet *s*.
1Co 4.19 I will come to you *s*, if the Lord
Php 2.19 to send Timotheus *s* unto you,
24 that I also myself shall come *s*.
1Ti 3.14 thee, hoping to come unto thee *s*:
2Ti 4. 9 thy diligence to come *s* unto me:
Heb 13.23 with whom, if he come *s*, I will see
2Pe 1.14 that *s* I must put off this my
3Jn 14 But I trust I shall *s* see thee, and
Rev 1. 1 which must *s* come to pass;
22. 6 things which must *s* be done.

SHOT

Gen 40.10 budded, and her blossoms *s* forth;
1Sa 20.20 thereof, as though I *s* at a mark.
36 ran, he *s* an arrow beyond him.
Ps 18.14 and he *s* out lightnings, and
Jer 9. 8 tongue is as an arrow *s* out; it

SHOULDER

Job 31.22 mine arm fall from my *s* blade,
Ps 81. 6 I removed his *s* from the burden:
Isa 9. 4 and the staff of his *s*, the rod of his
6 government shall be upon his *s*:

SHOULDERS

1Sa 9. 2 from his *s* and upward he was
1Ch 15.15 bare the ark of God upon their *s*
Isa 14.25 burden depart from off their *s*.
Eze 12. 6 sight shalt thou bear it upon thy *s*,
Mt 23. 4 borne, and lay them on men's *s*;
Lk 15. 5 hath found it, he layeth it on his *s*,

SHOUT

Ex 32.18 voice of them that *s* for mastery,
Jos 6. 5 with a great *s*; and the wall of
16 Joshua said unto the people, *S*; for
Ps 5.11 let them ever *s* for joy, because
32.11 *s* for joy, all ye that are upright in
35.27 Let them *s* for joy, and be glad,
47. 1 *s* unto God with the voice of
5 God is gone up with a *s*, the Lord
65.13 they *s* for joy, they also sing.
Isa 42.11 *s* from the top of the mountains.
44.23 *s*, ye lower parts of the earth:
La 3. 8 when I cry and *s*, he shutteth out
Zep 3.14 *s*, O Israel; be glad and rejoice
Zec 9. 9 Zion; *s*, O daughter of Jerusalem:
Ac 12.22 And the people gave a *s*, saying,
1Th 4.16 descend from heaven with a *s*,

SHOUTED

Ex 32.17 the noise of the people as they *s*,
Lev 9.24 when all the people saw, they *s*,
Jos 6.20 people *s* when the priests blew
20 the people *s* with a great shout,
Jdg 15.14 Lehi, the Philistines *s* against him:
1Sa 4. 5 all Israel *s* with a great shout, so
10.24 the people *s*, and said, God save the
17.20 to the fight, and *s* for the battle.
52 of Israel and of Judah arose, and *s*,
2Ch 13.15 as the men of Judah *s*, it came to
Ezr 3.11 all the people *s* with a great shout,
12 voice; and many *s* aloud for joy:
13 for the people *s* with a loud shout,
Job 38. 7 and all the sons of God *s* for joy?

SHOUTETH

Ps 78.65 man that *s* by reason of wine.

SHOWER

Eze 13.11 there shall be an overflowing *s*;
13 and there shall be an overflowing *s*
34.26 I will cause the *s* to come down in
Lk 12.54 ye say, There cometh a *s*; and so

SHOWERS

Dt 32. 2 and as the *s* upon the grass:
Job 24. 8 wet with the *s* of the mountains,
Ps 65.10 thou makest it soft with *s*: thou
72. 6 grass: as *s* that water the earth.
Jer 3. 3 the *s* have been withholden, and
14.22 rain? or can the heavens give *s*?
Eze 34.26 there shall be *s* of blessing.
Mic 5. 7 the Lord, as the *s* upon the grass,
Zec 10. 1 clouds, and give them *s* of rain,

SHRANK

Gen 32.32 eat not of the sinew which *s*,
32 Jacob's thigh in the sinew that *s*.

SHRINES

Ac 19.24 which made silver *s* for Diana,

SHUT

Gen 7.16 him: and the Lord *s* him in.
19. 6 unto them, and *s* the door after him,
10 house to them, and *s* to the door.
Ex 14. 3 the wilderness hath *s* them in.
Lev 13. 4 priest shall *s* up him that hath the
5 priest shall *s* him up seven days
11 unclean, and shall not *s* him up:
21, 26 priest shall *s* him up seven days:
31, 33 priest shall *s* up him that hath
50 *s* up it that hath the plague seven
54 he shall *s* it up seven days more:
14.38 and *s* up the house seven days:
46 into the house...while that it is *s*
Nu 12.14 let her be *s* out from the camp
15 Miriam was *s* out from the camp
Dt 11.17 *s* up the heaven, that there be no
15. 7 nor *s* thine hand from thy poor
32.30 and the Lord had *s* them up?
36 and there is none *s* up, or left.
Jos 2. 7 were gone out, they *s* the gate.
6. 1 Jericho was straitly *s* up because
Jdg 3.23 and *s* the doors of the parlor upon
9.51 they of the city, and *s* it to them,
1Sa 1. 5 but the Lord had *s* up her womb.
6 the Lord had *s* up her womb.
6.10 and *s* up their calves at home:
23. 7 for he is *s* in, by entering into a
2Sa 20. 3 *s* up unto the day of their death,
1Ki 8.35 When heaven is *s* up, and there is
14.10 him that is *s* up and left in Israel.
21.21 him that is *s* up and left in Israel,
2Ki 4. 4 thou shalt *s* the door upon thee
5 and *s* the door upon her and upon
21 *s* the door upon him, and went out.
33 and *s* the door upon them twain,
6.32 *s* the door, and hold him fast at the
9. 8 him that is *s* up and left in Israel.
14.26 for there was not any *s* up, nor any
17. 4 the king of Assyria *s* him up, and
2Ch 6.26 When the heaven is *s* up, and there
7.13 I *s* up heaven that there be no rain,
28.24 *s* up the doors of the house of the
29. 7 have *s* up the doors of the porch,
Neh 6.10 son of Mehetabeel, who was *s* up;
10 let us *s* the doors of the temple:
7. 3 let them *s* the doors, and bar them:
13.19 that the gates should be *s*, and
Job 3.10 *s* not up the doors of my mother's
11.10 If he cut off, and *s* up, or gather
38. 8 Or who *s* up the sea with doors,
41.15 *s* up together as with a close seal.
Ps 31. 8 *s* me up into the hand of the enemy;
69.15 not the pit *s* her mouth upon me.
77. 9 in anger *s* up his tender mercies?
88. 8 I am *s* up, and I cannot come
Ec 12. 4 the doors shall be *s* in the streets,
SS 4.12 a spring *s* up, a fountain sealed.
Isa 6.10 their ears heavy, and *s* their eyes;
22.22 he shall open, and none shall *s*;
22 and he shall *s*, and none shall open.
24.10 every house is *s* up, that no man
22 and shall be *s* up in the prison,
26.20 and *s* thy doors about thee:
44.18 for he hath *s* their eyes, that they
45. 1 and the gates shall not be *s*;
52.15 kings shall *s* their mouths at him:
60.11 they shall not be *s* day nor night;
66. 9 to bring forth, and *s* the womb?
Jer 13.19 cities of the south shall be *s* up,
20. 9 a burning fire *s* up in my bones,
32. 2 Jeremiah...was *s* up in the court
3 For Zedekiah...had *s* him up,
33. 1 while he was yet *s* up in the court
36. 5 saying, I am *s* up; I cannot go
39.15 while he was *s* up in the court of
Eze 3.24 Go, *s* thyself within thine house.
44. 1 toward the east; and it was *s*.
2 This gate shall be *s*, it shall not be
2 entered in...therefore it shall be *s*.
46. 1 shall be *s* the six working days;
2 gate shall not be *s* until...evening.
12 going forth one shall *s* the gate.
Dan 6.22 and hath *s* the lions' mouths, that
8.26 wherefore *s* thou up the vision;
12. 4 But thou, O Daniel, *s* up the words,
Mal 1.10 would *s* the doors for nought?
Mt 6. 6 and when thou hast *s* thy door,
23.13 for ye *s* up the kingdom of heaven
25.10 the marriage: and the door was *s*.
Lk 3.20 all, that he *s* up John in prison.
4.25 heaven was *s* up three years and
11. 7 the door is now *s*, and my children
13.25 is risen up, and hath *s* to the door,
Jn 20.19 doors were *s* where the disciples
26 then came Jesus, the doors being *s*,
Ac 5.23 The prison truly found we *s* with
21.30 and forthwith the doors were *s*.
26.10 of the saints did I *s* up in prison,
Gal 3.23 *s* up unto the faith which should
Rev 3. 8 open door, and no man can *s* it:
11. 6 These have power to *s* heaven, that
20. 3 the bottomless pit, and *s* him up,
21.25 the gates of it shall not be *s* at all

SHUTTETH

Job 12.14 he *s* up a man, and there can be
Pr 16.30 He *s* his eyes to devise froward
17.28 that *s* his lips is esteemed a man
Isa 33.15 and *s* his eyes from seeing evil;
La 3. 8 and shout, he *s* out my prayer.
1Jn 3.17 *s* up his bowels of compassion
Rev 3. 7 he that openeth, and no man *s*;
7 and *s*, and no man openeth;

SHUTTLE

Job 7. 6 days are swifter than a weaver's *s*,

SIBBOLETH

Jdg 12. 6 and he said *S*: for he could not

SICK

Pr 13.12 Hope deferred maketh the heart *s*:
SS 2. 5 me with apples: for I am *s* of love.
5. 8 that ye tell him, I am *s* of love.
Eze 34.16 will strengthen that which was *s*:
Hos 7. 5 king the princes have made him *s*
Mal 1. 8 if ye offer the lame and *s*, is it not
Mt 4.24 brought unto him all *s* people
8. 6 servant...at home *s* of the palsy,
14 wife's mother laid,...*s* of a fever.
16 and healed all that were *s*:
9. 2 brought...a man *s* of the palsy,
2 faith said unto the *s* of the palsy;
6 (then saith he to the *s* of the palsy,)
12 physician, but they that are *s*.
10. 8 Heal the *s*, cleanse the lepers,
14.14 toward them, and he healed their *s*.
25.36 I was *s*, and ye visited me: I was
39 when saw we thee *s*, or in prison,
43 *s*, and in prison, and ye visited me

44 naked, or *s*, or in prison, and did
Mk 1.30 Simon's wife's mother lay *s* of a
34 he healed many that were *s*
2. 3 him, bringing one *s* of the palsy,
4 bed wherein the *s* of the palsy lay.
5 he said unto the *s* of the palsy, Son,
9 it easier to say to the *s* of the palsy,
10 sins, (he saith to the *s* of the palsy,)
17 physician, but they that are *s*:
6. 5 laid his hands upon a few *s* folks,
13 anointed with oil many that were *s*,
55 in beds those that were *s*,
56 they laid the *s* in the streets, and
16.18 they shall lay hands on the *s*, and
Lk 4.40 all they that had any *s* with divers
5.24 (he said unto the *s* of the palsy,)
31 physician; but they that are *s*.
7. 2 him, was *s*, and ready to die.
10 the servant whole that had been *s*.
9. 2 kingdom of God, and to heal the *s*.
10. 9 And heal the *s* that are therein,
Jn 4.46 whose son was *s* at Capernaum.
11. 1 Now a certain man was *s*, named
2 hair, whose brother Lazarus was *s*.)
3 behold, he whom thou lovest is *s*.
6 had heard therefore that he was *s*,
Ac 5.15 they brought forth the *s* into the
16 bringing *s* folks, and them which
9.33 years, and was *s* of the palsy.
37 days, that she was *s*, and died:
19.12 brought unto the *s* handkerchiefs
28. 8 father of Publius lay *s* of a fever and
Php 2.26 ye had heard that he had been *s*.
27 indeed he was *s* nigh unto death:
2Ti 4.20 Trophimus have I left at Miletum *s*.
Jas 5.14 Is any *s* among you? let him call
15 prayer of faith shall save the *s*,

SICKLE
Dt 16. 9 beginnest to put the *s* to the corn.
23.25 not move a *s* unto thy neighbor's
Jer 50.16 that handleth the *s* in the time of
Joel 3.13 Put ye in the *s*, for the harvest is
Mk 4.29 immediately he putteth in the *s*,
Rev 14.14 crown, and in his hand a sharp *s*.
15 cloud, Thrust in thy *s*, and reap:
16 cloud thrust in his *s* on the earth;
17 heaven, he also having a sharp *s*.
18 cry to him that had the sharp *s*,
18 Thrust in thy sharp *s*, and gather
19 angel thrust in his *s* into the earth,

SICKLY
1Co 11.30 many are weak and *s* among you,

SICKNESS
Ex 23.25 I will take *s* away from the midst
Lev 20.18 lie with a woman having her *s*,
Dt 7.15 will take away from thee all *s*,
28.61 Also every *s*, and every plague,
1Ki 8.37 plague, whatsoever *s* there be;
17.17 his *s* was so sore, that there was
2Ki 13.14 Now Elisha was fallen sick of his *s*
2Ch 6.28 sore or whatsoever *s* there be:
21.15 shalt have great *s* by disease of
15 bowels fall out by reason of the *s*
19 bowels fell out by reason of his *s*:
Ps 41. 3 wilt make all his bed in his *s*.
Ec 5.17 sorrow and wrath with his *s*.
Isa 38. 9 sick, and was recovered of his *s*:
12 he will cut me off with pining *s*,
Hos 5.13 When Ephraim saw his *s*, and
Mt 4.23 healing all manner of *s* and all
9.35 healing every *s* and every disease
10. 1 to heal all manner of *s* and all
Jn 11. 4 This *s* is not unto death, but for

SICKNESSES
Dt 28.59 sore *s*, and of long continuance.
29.22 *s* which the Lord hath laid upon
Mt 8.17 our infirmities, and bare our *s*.
Mk 3.15 to have power to heal *s*, and to

SIDE
Ex 32.26 said, Who is on the Lord's *s*? let him
27 Put every man his sword by his *s*,
Nu 32.19 not inherit...on yonder *s* Jordan,
19 is fallen to us on this *s* Jordan
Dt 4.32 one *s* of heaven unto the other,
Jos 1.14 Moses gave you on this *s* Jordan;
Jdg 7.12 sand by the sea *s* for multitude.
1Sa 20.20 I will shoot three arrows on the *s*
21 the arrows are on this *s* of thee,
1Ch 12.18 Thine are we, David, and on thy *s*,
22.18 he not given you rest on every *s*?
2Ch 9.19 lions stood there on the one *s*, and
Ezr 4.16 have no portion on this *s* the river.
Job 19.10 He hath destroyed me on every *s*,
Ps 12. 8 The wicked walk on every *s*, when
65.12 the little hills rejoice on every *s*.
91. 7 A thousand shall fall at thy *s*, and
118. 6 Lord is on my *s*; I will not fear:
124. 1, 2 been the Lord who was on our *s*,
Isa 60. 4 daughters...be nursed at thy *s*.
Jer 49.29 cry unto them, Fear is on every *s*.
Eze 1.10 the face of a lion, on the right *s*:
10 had the face of an ox on the left *s*;
9. 2 with a writer's inkhorn by his *s*:
Dan 10. 4 I was by the *s* of the great river,
Mt 8.18 to depart unto the other *s*.
28 when he was come to the other *s*
13. 1 of the house, and sat by the sea *s*.
4 some seeds fell by the way *s*, and
19 which received seed by the way *s*.
14.22 to go before him unto the other *s*,
16. 5 disciples were come to the other *s*,
20.30 blind men sitting by the way *s*,
Mk 2.13 he went forth again by the sea *s*;
4. 1 began again to teach by the sea *s*:
4 as he sowed, some fell by the way *s*,
15 And these are they by the way *s*,
35 Let us pass over unto the other *s*.
5. 1 over unto the other *s* of the sea,
21 again by ship unto the other *s*,
6.45 the other *s* before unto Bethsaida,
8.13 ship again departed to the other *s*.
10. 1 Judea by the farther *s* of Jordan:
46 sat by the highway *s* begging.
16. 5 young man sitting on the right *s*,
Lk 1.11 standing on the right *s* of the altar
8. 5 he sowed, some fell by the way *s*;
12 Those by the way *s* are they that
22 over unto the other *s* of the lake.
10.31 him, he passed by on the other *s*.
32 him, and passed by on the other *s*.
18.35 man sat by the way *s* begging:
19.43 round, and keep thee in on every *s*,
Jn 6.22 stood on the other *s* of the sea
25 found him on the other *s* of the
19.18 other with him, on either *s* one,
34 with a spear pierced his *s*, and
20.20 unto them his hands and his *s*.
25 and thrust my hand into his *s*, I
27 thy hand, and thrust it into my *s*:
21. 6 Cast the net on the right *s* of the
Ac 10. 6 he whose house is by the sea *s*:
32 one Simon a tanner by the sea *s*:
12. 7 smote Peter on the *s*, and raised
16.13 went out of the city by a river *s*,
2Co 4. 8 We are troubled on every *s*, yet not
7. 5 but we were troubled on every *s*;
Rev 22. 2 on either *s* of the river, was there

SIDES
Nu 33.55 your eyes, and thorns in your *s*,
Jdg 2. 3 they shall be as thorns in your *s*,
Ps 128. 3 vine by the *s* of thine house:
Isa 14.15 down to hell, to the *s* of the pit.
Eze 32.23 graves are set in the *s* of the pit,
42.20 He measured it by the four *s*: it
Am 6.10 him that is by the *s* of the house,
Jon 1. 5 gone down into the *s* of the ship;

SIDON
Gen 10.15 And Canaan begat *S* his firstborn,
19 of the Canaanites was from *S*,
Mt 11.21 had been done in Tyre and *S*,
22 be more tolerable for Tyre and *S*
15.21 into the coasts of Tyre and *S*.
Mk 3. 8 and they about Tyre and *S*, a great
7.24 into the borders of Tyre and *S*,
31 from the coasts of Tyre and *S*,
Lk 4.26 save unto Sarepta, a city of *S*, unto
6.17 from the sea coast of Tyre and *S*,
10.13 had been done in Tyre and *S*,
14 be more tolerable for Tyre and *S*
Ac 12.20 displeased with them of Tyre and *S*:
27. 3 And the next day we touched at *S*.

SIEGE
Dt 20.19 down...to employ them in the *s*:
28.53 in the *s*, and in the straitness,
55 he hath nothing left in the *s*, and
57 secretly in the *s* and straitness,
1Ki 15.27 and all Israel laid *s* to Gibbethon.
2Ch 32. 9 but he himself laid *s* against Lachish,
10 ye abide in the *s* in Jerusalem?
Isa 29. 3 and will lay *s* against thee with a
Jer 19. 9 eat the flesh of his friend in the *s*
Eze 4. 2 And lay *s* against it, and build a
3 and thou shalt lay *s* against it.
7 face toward the *s* of Jerusalem,
8 thou hast ended the days of thy *s*.
5. 2 when the days of the *s* are fulfilled:
Mic 5. 1 troops: he hath laid *s* against us:
Na 3.14 Draw thee waters for the *s*, fortify
Zec 12. 2 shall be in the *s* both against Judah

SIEVE
Isa 30.28 the nations with the *s* of vanity:
Am 9. 9 nations, like as corn is sifted in a *s*,

SIFT
Isa 30.28 to *s* the nations with the sieve of
Am 9. 9 I will *s* the house of Israel among
Lk 22.31 you, that he may *s* you as wheat:

SIGH
Isa 24. 7 all the merryhearted do *s*.
La 1. 4 priests *s*, her virgins are afflicted,
11 All her people *s*, they seek bread;
21 They have heard that I *s*: there is
Eze 9. 4 upon the foreheads of the men that *s*
21. 6 *S* therefore, thou son of man, with
6 with bitterness *s* before their eyes.

SIGHED
Ex 2.23 children of Israel *s* by reason of
Mk 7.34 And looking up to heaven, he *s*,
8.12 he *s* deeply in his spirit, and saith,

SIGHING
Job 3.24 For my *s* cometh before I eat, and
Ps 12. 5 of the poor, for the *s* of the needy,
31.10 with grief, and my years with *s*:
79.11 the *s* of the prisoner come before
Isa 21. 2 the *s* thereof have I made to cease.
35.10 and sorrow and *s* shall flee away.
Jer 45. 3 fainted in my *s*, and I find no rest.

SIGHT
Gen 2. 9 every tree that is pleasant to the *s*,
18. 3 now I have found favor in thy *s*,
19.19 servant hath found grace in thy *s*,
21.11 was very grievous in Abraham's *s*
32. 5 lord,...I may find grace in thy *s*.
Ex 3. 3 turn aside, and see this great *s*,
15.26 wilt do that which is right in his *s*,
Lev 10.19 been accepted in the *s* of the Lord?
Nu 3. 4 in the *s* of Aaron their father.
13.33 were in our own *s* as grasshoppers,
Dt 4. 6 wisdom...in the *s* of the nations.
25 shall do evil in the *s* of the Lord
12.25 which is right in the *s* of the Lord.
21. 9 which is right in the *s* of the Lord.

Dt 28.34 mad for the *s* of thine eyes which
31. 7 unto him in the *s* of all Israel,
29 ye will do evil in the *s* of the Lord,
Jos 3. 7 magnify thee in the *s* of all Israel,
24.17 did those great signs in our *s*, and
Jdg 2.11 Israel did evil in the *s* of the Lord,
6. 1 Israel did evil in the *s* of the Lord:
17 If now I have found grace in thy *s*,
1Sa 1.18 handmaid find grace in thy *s*.
15.17 thou wast little in thine own *s*,
29. 6 me in the host is good in my *s*:
9 know that thou art good in my *s*,
2Sa 6.22 and will be base in mine own *s*:
7. 9 off all thine enemies out of thy *s*,
19 was yet a small thing in thy *s*,
1Ki 8.25 shall not fail thee a man in my *s*
2Ki 1.13 thy servants, be precious in thy *s*.
14 my life now be precious in thy *s*.
23.27 remove Judah also out of my *s*,
Neh 1.11 him mercy in the *s* of this man.
8. 5 book in the *s* of all the people;
Est 2.15 in the *s* of all them that looked
5. 2 that she obtained favor in his *s*:
7. 3 have found favor in thy *s*, O king,
Job 15.15 the heavens are not clean in his *s*.
18. 3 beasts, and reputed vile in your *s*?
19.15 stranger: I am an alien in their *s*.
25. 5 the stars are not pure in his *s*.
41. 9 be cast down even at the *s* of him?
Ps 5. 5 foolish shall not stand in thy *s*:
9.19 the heathen be judged in thy *s*.
19.14 be acceptable in thy *s*, O Lord,
51. 4 sinned and done this evil in thy *s*:
72.14 precious...their blood be in his *s*.
90. 4 For a thousand years in thy *s* are
Pr 1.17 net is spread in the *s* of any bird.
3. 4 understanding in the *s* of God and
Ec 2.26 man that is good in his *s* wisdom,
6. 9 Better is the *s* of the eyes than
Isa 5.21 eyes, and prudent in their own *s*!
11. 3 not judge after the *s* of his eyes,
43. 4 Since thou wast precious in my *s*,
Jer 4. 1 thine abominations out of my *s*,
Eze 4.12 that cometh out of man, in their *s*.
12. 3 and remove by day in their *s*;
5 Dig...through the wall in their *s*,
20. 9 in whose *s* I made myself known
36.31 lothe yourselves in your own *s*
43.11 and write it in their *s*, that they
Dan 4.11 and the *s* thereof to the end of all
Hos 2. 2 her whoredoms out of her *s*,
6. 2 us up, and we shall live in his *s*.
Mal 2.17 evil is good in the *s* of the Lord,
Mt 11. 5 The blind receive their *s*, and the
20.34 immediately their eyes received *s*,
Mk 10.51 Lord, that I might receive my *s*.
52 And immediately he received his *s*,
Lk 1.15 shall be great in the *s* of the Lord,
4.18 and recovering of *s* to the blind,
7.21 many that were blind he gave *s*.
18.41 Lord, that I may receive my *s*.
42 Jesus said unto him, Receive thy *s*:
43 And immediately he received his *s*,
24.31 him; and he vanished out of their *s*.
Jn 9.11 went and washed, and I received *s*.
18 had been blind, and received his *s*,
Ac 1. 9 cloud received him out of their *s*.
9. 9 And he was three days without *s*,
Ro 3.20 shall no flesh be justified in his *s*:
2Co 2.17 the *s* of God speak we in Christ.
4. 2 man's conscience in the *s* of God.
5. 7 (For we walk by faith, not by *s*:)
8.21 not only in the *s* of the Lord, but
21 Lord, but also in the *s* of men.
Heb 4.13 that is not manifest in his *s*:
12.21 And so terrible was the *s*, that
1Jn 3.22 things that are pleasing in his *s*.
Rev 4. 3 throne, in *s* like unto an emerald.

SIGHTS

Lk 21.11 fearful *s* and great signs shall

SIGN

Ex 4. 8 hearken to the voice of the first *s*,
8 will believe the voice of the latter *s*.
8.23 people: to morrow shall this *s* be.
13. 9 for a *s* unto thee upon thine hand,
31.13 for it is a *s* between me and you
17 a *s* between me and the children of
Nu 16.38 they shall be a *s* unto the children
26.10 fifty men: and they became a *s*.
Dt 6. 8 bind them for a *s* upon thine hand,
11.18 bind them for a *s* upon your hand,
13. 1 and giveth thee a *s* or a wonder,
2 the *s* or the wonder come to pass,
28.46 they shall be upon thee for a *s* and
Jos 4. 6 That this may be a *s* among you,
Jdg 6.17 me a *s* that thou talkest with me.
20.38 there was an appointed *s* between
1Sa 2.34 this shall be a *s* unto thee, that
14.10 hand: and this shall be a *s* unto us.
1Ki 13. 3 he gave a *s* the same day, saying,
3 the *s* which the Lord hath spoken;
5 according to the *s* which the man of
2Ki 19.29 And this shall be a *s* unto thee, Ye
20. 8 What shall be the *s* that the Lord
9 This *s* shalt thou have of the Lord,
2Ch 32.24 unto him, and he gave him a *s*.
Isa 7.11 Ask thee a *s* of the Lord thy God;
14 the Lord himself shall give you a *s*;
19.20 it shall be for a *s* and for a witness
20. 3 *s* and wonder upon Egypt and upon
37.30 this shall be a *s* unto thee, Ye shall
38. 7 this shall be a *s* unto thee from the
22 What is the *s* that I shall go up to
55.13 for an everlasting *s* that shall not be
66.19 I will set a *s* among them, and I
Jer 6. 1 up a *s* of fire in Beth-haccerem:
44.29 And this shall be a *s* unto you,
Eze 4. 3 shall be a *s* to the house of Israel.
12. 6 for a *s* unto the house of Israel.
11 Say, I am your *s*: like as I have
14. 8 will make him a *s* and a proverb,
20.12 to be a *s* between me and them,
20 shall be a *s* between me and you,
24.24 Thus Ezekiel is unto you a *s*:
27 and thou shalt be a *s* unto them;
39.15 then shall he set up a *s* by it, till
Dan 6. 8 and *s* the writing, that it be not
Mt 12.38 we would see a *s* from thee.
39 generation seeketh after a *s*;
39 and there shall no *s* be given to it,
39 but the *s* of the prophet Jonas:
16. 1 would shew them a *s* from heaven.
4 generation seeketh after a *s*;
4 and there...no *s* be given unto it,
4 but the *s* of the prophet Jonas.
24. 3 what shall be the *s* of thy coming,
30 appear the *s* of the Son of man in
26.48 that betrayed him gave them a *s*,
Mk 8.11 seeking of him a *s* from heaven,
12 doth this generation seek after a *s*?
12 no *s* be given unto this generation.
13. 4 what shall be the *s* when all these
Lk 2.12 And this shall be a *s* unto you; Ye
34 and for a *s* which shall be spoken
11.16 sought of him a *s* from heaven.
29 an evil generation: they seek a *s*;
29 and there shall no *s* be given it,
29 but the *s* of Jonas the prophet.
30 Jonas was a *s* unto the Ninevites,
21. 7 what *s* will there be when these
Jn 2.18 him, What *s* shewest thou unto us,
6.30 What *s* shewest thou then, that we
Ac 28.11 whose *s* was Castor and Pollux.
Ro 4.11 he received the *s* of circumcision,
1Co 1.22 For the Jews require a *s*, and the
14.22 Wherefore tongues are for a *s*,
Rev 15. 1 I saw another *s* in heaven, great

SIGNED

Dan 6. 9 king Darius *s* the writing and the
10 Daniel knew that the writing was *s*,
12 Hast thou not *s* a decree, that
13 nor the decree that thou hast *s*, but

SIGNIFICATION

1Co 14.10 and none of them is without *s*.

SIGNIFIED

Ac 11.28 *s* by the spirit that there should be
Rev 1. 1 *s* it by his angel unto his servant

SIGNIFIETH

Heb 12.27 *s* the removing of those things

SIGNIFY

Ac 21.26 to *s* the accomplishment of the
23.15 the council *s* to the chief captain
25.27 to *s* the crimes laid against him.
1Pe 1.11 of Christ which was in them did *s*,

SIGNIFYING

Jn 12.33 said, *s* what death he should die.
18.32 spake, *s* what death he should die.
21.19 *s* by what death he should glorify
Heb 9. 8 The Holy Ghost this *s*, that the

SIGNS

Gen 1.14 let them be for *s*, and for seasons,
Ex 4. 9 will not believe also these two *s*,
17 hand, wherewith thou shalt do *s*.
28 all the *s* which he had commanded
30 did the *s* in the sight of the people.
7. 3 my *s* and my wonders in the land of
10. 1 might shew these my *s* before him:
2 and my *s* which I have done among
Nu 14.11 for all the *s* which I have shewed
Dt 4.34 by *s*, and by wonders, and by war,
6.22 the Lord shewed *s* and wonders,
7.19 and the *s*, and the wonders, and the
26. 8 and with *s*, and with wonders:
29. 3 the *s*, and those great miracles:
34.11 In all the *s* and the wonders, which
Jos 24.17 which did those great *s* in our sight,
1Sa 10. 7 when these *s* are come unto thee,
9 all those *s* came to pass that day.
Neh 9.10 *s* and wonders upon Pharaoh, and
Ps 74. 4 they set up their ensigns for *s*.
9 We see not our *s*: there is no more
78.43 How he had wrought his *s* in Egypt,
105.27 shewed his *s* among them,
Isa 8.18 are for *s* and for wonders in Israel
Jer 10. 2 not dismayed at the *s* of heaven;
32.20 hast set *s* and wonders in the land
21 out of the land of Egypt with *s*, and
Dan 4. 2 I thought it good to shew the *s* and
3 How great are his *s*! and how
6.27 and he worketh *s* and wonders in
Mt 16. 3 ye not discern the *s* of the times?
24.24 shall shew great *s* and wonders;
Mk 13.22 and shall shew *s* and wonders, to
16.17 And these *s* shall follow them that
20 and confirming the word with *s*
Lk 1.62 they made *s* to his father, how he
21.11 *s* shall there be from heaven.
25 And there shall be *s* in the sun,
Jn 4.48 Except ye see *s* and wonders, ye
20.30 many other *s* truly did Jesus in the
Ac 2.19 above, and *s* in the earth beneath;
22 by miracles and wonders and *s*,
43 wonders and *s* were done by the
4.30 that *s* and wonders may be done by
5.12 were many *s* and wonders wrought
7.36 shewed wonders and *s* in the land
8.13 miracles and *s* which were done.
14. 3 granted *s* and wonders to be done
Ro 15.19 Through mighty *s* and wonders, by
2Co 12.12 Truly the *s* of an apostle were
12 in *s*, and wonders, and mighty
2Th 2. 9 of Satan with all power and *s* and
Heb 2. 4 witness, both with *s* and wonders,

SILAS

Important figure in early Christian community of Jerusalem; appointed along with Judas to transmit the decisions of the Council of Jerusalem to Antioch (Ac 15.27); does not return to Jerusalem, but is chosen by Paul to accompany him on second missionary journey (Ac 15.40); imprisoned with Paul at Philippi and also caught up in riot at Thessalonica (Ac 16–17); on reaching Berea, stays there with Timothy (Ac 17.13), but rejoins Paul later in Corinth (Ac 18.5); probably the same person as the Silvanus who helps Paul preach at Corinth (2Co 1.19) and who figures in superscriptions of epistles to the Thessalonians (1Th 1; 2Th 1).

SILAS

Ac 15.22 Barsabas,...*S*, chief men among
27 have sent therefore Judas and *S*,
32 Judas and *S*, being prophets also
34 it pleased *S* to abide there still.
40 And Paul chose *S*, and departed,
16.19 they caught Paul and *S*, and drew
25 at midnight Paul and *S* prayed,
29 and fell down before Paul and *S*,
17. 4 and consorted with Paul and *S*;
10 sent away Paul and *S* by night
14 but *S* and Timotheus abode there
15 receiving a commandment unto *S*
18. 5 when *S* and Timotheus were come

SILENCE

Jdg 3.19 thee, O king: who said, Keep *s*.
Job 4.16 there was *s*, and I heard a voice,
29.21 waited, and kept *s* at my counsel.
31.34 that I kept *s*, and went not out of
Ps 31.18 Let the lying lips be put to *s*;
32. 3 When I kept *s*, my bones waxed
35.22 keep not *s*: O Lord, be not far
39. 2 I was dumb with *s*, I held my
50. 3 shall come, and shall not keep *s*:
21 hast thou done, and I kept *s*;
83. 1 Keep not thou *s*, O God: hold not
94.17 my soul had almost dwelt in *s*.
115.17 neither any that go down into *s*.
Ec 3. 7 a time to keep *s*, and a time to
Isa 15. 1 is laid waste, and brought to *s*;
41. 1 Keep *s* before me, O islands; and
62. 6 mention of the Lord, keep not *s*,
65. 6 I will not keep *s*, but will
Jer 8.14 the Lord our God hath put us to *s*,
La 2.10 sit upon the ground, and keep *s*:
3.28 He sitteth alone and keepeth *s*,
Am 5.13 Therefore the prudent shall keep *s*
8. 3 shall cast them forth with *s*.
Hab 2.20 temple: let all the earth keep *s*
Mt 22.34 he had put the Sadducees to *s*,
Ac 15.12 Then all the multitude kept *s*,
21.40 when there was made a great *s*,
22. 2 to them, they kept the more *s*:
1Co 14.28 let him keep *s* in the church; and
34 Let your women keep *s* in the
1Ti 2.11 Let the woman learn in *s* with all
12 over the man, but to be in *s*.
1Pe 2.15 put to *s* the ignorance of foolish
Rev 8. 1 there was *s* in heaven about the

SILENT

1Sa 2. 9 the wicked shall be *s* in darkness;
Ps 22. 2 in the night season, and am not *s*.
28. 1 O Lord my rock; be not *s* to me:
1 lest, if thou be *s* to me, I become
30.12 sing praise to thee, and not be *s*.
31.17 and let them be *s* in the grave.
Isa 47. 5 Sit thou *s*, and get thee into
Jer 8.14 cities, and let us be *s* there: for
Zec 2.13 Be *s*, O all flesh, before the Lord:

SILK

Pr 31.22 her clothing is *s* and purple.
Eze 16.10 linen, and I covered thee with *s*.
13 raiment was of fine linen, and *s*,
Rev 18.12 and purple, and *s*, and scarlet,

SILLY

Job 5. 2 man, and envy slayeth the *s* one.
Hos 7.11 Ephraim also is like a *s* dove
2Ti 3. 6 lead captive *s* women laden with

SILOAM

Lk 13. 4 upon whom the tower in *S* fell,
Jn 9. 7 him, Go, wash in the pool of *S*,
11 said unto me, Go to the pool of *S*,

SILVANUS

2Co 1.19 even by me and *S* and Timotheus,
1Th 1. 1 Paul, and *S*, and Timotheus, unto
2Th 1. 1 Paul, and *S*, and Timotheus, unto
1Pe 5.12 By *S*, a faithful brother unto you,

SILVER

Gen 13. 2 was very rich in cattle, in *s*, and
23.16 Abraham weighed to Ephron the *s*,
44. 2 the *s* cup, in the sack's mouth of
Ex 20.23 shall not make with me gods of *s*,
Jdg 17. 2 mine ears, behold, the *s* is with me;
3 dedicated the *s* unto the Lord
1Sa 2.36 and crouch to him for a piece of *s*
2Sa 21. 4 We will have no *s* nor gold of Saul,
1Ki 10.25 vessels of *s*, and vessels of gold,
27 *s* to be in Jerusalem as stones,
20. 3 Thy *s* and thy gold is mine; thy
2Ki 22. 4 may sum the *s* which is brought
23.35 he exacted the *s* and the gold of the
2Ch 2. 7 cunning to work in gold, and in *s*,
9.14 brought gold and *s* to Solomon.
20 were of pure gold: none were of *s*;
21. 3 father gave them great gifts of *s*,
Est 1. 6 the beds were of gold and *s*, upon
Job 3.15 who filled their houses with *s*:
22.25 and thou shalt have plenty of *s*.
27.16 Though he heap up *s* as the dust,
28. 1 Surely there is a vein for the *s*,
15 *s* be weighed for the price thereof.
Ps 12. 6 as *s* tried in a furnace of earth,
66.10 thou hast tried us, as *s* is tried.
115. 4 Their idols are *s* and gold, the work
135.15 idols of the heathen are *s* and gold,
Pr 3.14 is better than the merchandise of *s*,
8.10 Receive my instruction, and not *s*;
16.16 rather to be chosen than *s*!
25.11 like apples of gold in pictures of *s*.
Ec 5.10 He that loveth *s* shall not be
10 shall not be satisfied with *s*;
12. 6 Or ever the *s* cord be loosed, or the
Isa 1.22 Thy *s* is become dross, thy wine
2.20 day a man shall cast his idols of *s*,
48.10 I have refined thee, but not with *s*;
Jer 6.30 Reprobate *s* shall men call them,
Eze 16.17 fair jewels of my gold and of my *s*,
22.22 As *s* is melted in the midst of the
Hos 3. 2 her to me for fifteen pieces of *s*,
9. 6 pleasant places for their *s*, nettles
Am 2. 6 they sold the righteous for *s*, and
8. 6 That we may buy the poor for *s*,
Hag 2. 8 *s* is mine, and the gold is mine,
Zec 11.12 for my price thirty pieces of *s*.
13 I took the thirty pieces of *s*, and
13. 9 and will refine them as *s* is refined,
Mal 3. 3 sit as a refiner and purifier of *s*:
3 and purge them as gold and *s*,
Mt 10. 9 neither gold, nor *s*, nor brass in
26.15 with him for thirty pieces of *s*.
27. 3 the thirty pieces of *s* to the chief
5 he cast down the pieces of *s* in the
6 the chief priests took the *s* pieces,
9 took the thirty pieces of *s*, the price
Lk 15. 8 what woman having ten pieces...*s*,
Ac 3. 6 said, *S* and gold have I none; but
17.29 the Godhead is like unto gold, or *s*,
19.19 found it fifty thousand pieces of *s*.
24 which make *s* shrines for Diana,
20.33 I have coveted no man's *s*, or gold,
1Co 3.12 this foundation gold, *s*, precious
2Ti 2.20 not only vessels of gold and of *s*,
Jas 5. 3 Your gold and *s* is cankered; and
1Pe 1.18 corruptible things, as *s* and gold,
Rev 9.20 devils, and idols of gold, and *s*, and
18.12 The merchandise of gold, and *s*,

SILVERSMITH

Ac 19.24 certain man named Demetrius, a *s*,

SIMEON

Lk 2.25 Jerusalem, whose name was *S*;
34 And *S* blessed them, and said unto
3.30 Which was the son of *S*, which was
Ac 13. 1 and *S* that was called Niger, and
15.14 *S* hath declared how God at the
Rev 7. 7 the tribe of *S* were sealed twelve

SIMILITUDE

Nu 12. 8 the *s* of the Lord shall he behold:
Dt 4.12 voice of the words, but saw no *s*;
15 ye saw no manner of *s* on the day
16 the *s* of any figure, the likeness of
2Ch 4. 3 under it was the *s* of oxen, which
Ps 106.20 their glory into the *s* of an ox
144.12 polished after the *s* of a palace:
Dan 10.16 *s* of the sons of men touched my
Ro 5.14 the *s* of Adam's transgression,
Heb 7.15 the *s* of Melchisedec there ariseth
Jas 3. 9 are made after the *s* of God.

SIMILITUDES

Hos 12.10 and used *s*, by the ministry of the

SIMON

Mt 4.18 *S* called Peter, and Andrew his
10. 2 The first, *S*, who is called Peter,
4 *S* the Canaanite, and Judas
13.55 and Joses, and *S*, and Judas?
16.16 *S* Peter answered and said, Thou
17 Blessed art thou, *S* Bar-jona: for
17.25 What thinkest thou, *S*? of whom
26. 6 in the house of *S* the leper,
27.32 a man of Cyrene, *S* by name: him
Mk 1.16 he saw *S* and Andrew his brother
29 entered into the house of *S* and
36 *S* and they that were with him
3.16 And *S* he surnamed Peter;
18 Thaddaeus, and *S* the Canaanite,
6. 3 and Joses, and of Juda, and *S*?
14. 3 in the house of *S* the leper, as he
37 saith unto Peter, *S*, sleepest thou?
15.21 they compel one *S* a Cyrenian, who
Lk 5. 4 he said unto *S*, Launch out into
5 And *S* answering said unto him,
8 When *S* Peter saw it, he fell down
10 which were partners with *S*.
10 Jesus said unto *S*, Fear not; from
6.14 *S*, (whom he also named Peter,)
15 of Alphaeus, and *S* called Zelotes,
7.40 *S*, I have somewhat to say unto
43 *S* answered and said, I suppose
44 unto *S*, Seest thou this woman?
22.31 *S*, *S*, behold, Satan hath desired
23.26 away, they laid hold upon one *S*,
24.34 indeed, and hath appeared to *S*.
Jn 1.40 was Andrew, *S* Peter's brother.
41 He first findeth his own brother *S*,
42 Thou art *S* the son of Jona: thou
6. 8 Andrew, *S* Peter's brother, saith
68 Then *S* Peter answered him, Lord,
71 of Judas Iscariot the son of *S*: for

Jn 13. 6 Then cometh he to *S* Peter: and
9 *S* Peter saith unto him, Lord, not
24 *S* Peter therefore beckoned to him,
26 it to Judas Iscariot, the son of *S*.
36 *S* Peter said unto him, Lord,
18.10 *S* Peter having a sword drew it,
15 *S* Peter followed Jesus, and so did
25 *S* Peter stood and warmed himself.
20. 2 runneth, and cometh to *S* Peter,
6 cometh *S* Peter following him, and
21. 2 There were together *S* Peter, and
3 *S* Peter saith unto them, I go a
7 when *S* Peter heard that it was
11 *S* Peter went up, and drew the net
15 Jesus saith to *S* Peter, *S*, son of
16, 17 *S*, son of Jonas, lovest thou me?
Ac 1.13 *S* Zelotes, and Judas the brother
8. 9 there was a certain man, called *S*,
13 Then *S* himself believed also: and
18 when *S* saw that through laying
24 Then answered *S*, and said, Pray
9.43 days in Joppa with one *S* a tanner.
10. 5 for one *S*, whose surname is Peter:
6 He lodgeth with one *S* a tanner,
18 *S*, which was surnamed Peter,
32 call hither *S*, whose surname is
32 in the house of one *S* a tanner by
11.13 call for *S*, whose surname is Peter;
2Pe 1. 1 *S* Peter, a servant and an apostle

SIMON'S

Mk 1.30 But *S* wife's mother lay sick of a
Lk 4.38 and entered into *S* house. And
38 *S* wife's mother was taken with a
5. 3 into one of the ships, which was *S*,
Jn 12. 4 disciples, Judas Iscariot, *S* son,
13. 2 the heart of Judas Iscariot, *S* son,
Ac 10.17 had made inquiry for *S* house,

SIMPLE

Ps 19. 7 Lord is sure, making wise the *s*.
116. 6 The Lord preserveth the *s*: I was
119.130 giveth understanding unto the *s*.
Pr 1. 4 To give subtilty to the *s*, to the
22 How long, ye *s* ones, will ye love
32 the turning away of the *s* shall
7. 7 And beheld among the *s* ones, I
8. 5 O ye *s*, understand wisdom: and,
9. 4 Whoso is *s*, let him turn in hither:
13 she is *s*, and knoweth nothing.
16 Whoso is *s*, let him turn in hither:
14.15 The *s* believeth every word: but
18 *s* inherit folly: but the prudent
19.25 a scorner, and the *s* will beware:
21.11 is punished, the *s* is made wise:
22. 3 the *s* pass on, and are punished.
27.12 the *s* pass on, and are punished.
Eze 45.20 that erreth, and for him that is *s*;
Ro 16.18 deceive the hearts of the *s*.
19 is good, and *s* concerning evil.

SIMPLICITY

2Sa 15.11 and they went in their *s*, and they
Pr 1.22 ye simple ones, will ye love *s*?
Ro 12. 8 that giveth, let him do it with *s*;
2Co 1.12 that in *s* and godly sincerity, not
11. 3 from the *s* that is in Christ.

BIBLICAL THEMES

SIN

Hast thou eaten of the tree, whereof I commanded thee that thou shouldest not eat? Gen 3.11

And God saw that the wickedness of man was great in the earth, and that every imagination of the thoughts of his heart was only evil continually. Gen 6.5

Remember, and forget not, how thou provokedst the Lord thy God to wrath in the wilderness: from the day that thou didst depart out of the land of Egypt, until ye came unto this place, ye have been rebellious against the Lord. Dt 9.7

I have sinned . . . I have played the fool, and have erred exceedingly. 1Sa 26.21

And he said to Nathan, As the Lord liveth, the man that hath done this thing shall surely die. . . . And Nathan said to David, Thou art the man. 2Sa 12.5, 7

I acknowledge my transgressions: and my sin is ever before me. Against thee, thee only, have I sinned. Ps 51.3-4

If thou, Lord, shouldest mark iniquities, O Lord, who shall stand? Ps 130.3

There is not a just man upon earth, that doeth good, and sinneth not. Ec 7.20

One sinner destroyeth much good. Ec 9.18

Though your sins be as scarlet, they shall be as white as snow. . . . If ye be willing and obedient, ye shall eat the good of the land. Isa 1.18-19

How is the faithful city become an harlot! it was full of judgment; righteousness lodged in it; but now murderers. . . . and companions of thieves: every one loveth gifts, and followeth after rewards: they judge not the fatherless, neither doth the cause of the widow come unto them. Isa 1.21, 23

Out of the heart proceed evil thoughts, murders, adulteries, fornications, thefts, false witness, blasphemies: these are the things which defile a man: but to eat with unwashen hands defileth not a man. Mt 15.19-20

He that is without sin among you, let him first cast a stone. Jn 8.7

What then? are we better than they? No, in no wise. . . . as it is written, There is none righteous, no, not one. Ro 3.9-10

We know that the law is spiritual: but I am carnal, sold under sin. . . . what I would, that do I not; but what I hate, that do I. . . . it is no more I that do it, but sin that dwelleth in me. Ro 7.14-15, 17

As in Adam all die, even so in Christ shall all be made alive. 1Co 15.22

We pray you in Christ's stead, be ye reconciled to God. For he hath made him to be sin for us, who knew no sin; that we might be made the righteousness of God in him. 2Co 5.20-21

You hath he quickened, who were dead in trespasses and sins. Eph 2.1

He that committeth sin is of the devil; for the devil sinneth from the beginning. For this purpose the Son of God was manifested, that he might destroy the works of the devil. 1Jn 3.8

There are certain men crept in unawares. . . . These are spots in your feasts of charity, when they feast with you, feeding themselves without fear: clouds they are without water, carried about of winds . . . raging waves of the sea, foaming out their own shame; wandering stars, to whom is reserved the blackness of darkness for ever. Jude 4, 12-13

The great day of his wrath is come; and who shall be able to stand? Rev 6.17

SIN

Gen 4. 7 doest not well, *s* lieth at the door.
18.20 because their *s* is very grievous;
20. 9 me and on my kingdom a great *s*?
31.36 what is my *s*, that thou hast so
Ex 10.17 forgive,...my *s* only this once,
32.30 people, Ye have sinned a great *s*:
30 make an atonement for your *s*.
34. 9 pardon our iniquity and our *s*,
Lev 4. 2 a soul shall *s* through ignorance
29 upon the head of the *s* offering,
35 make an atonement for his *s* that
5. 1 if a soul *s*, and hear the voice of
6.25 This is the law of the *s* offering:
24.15 curseth his God shall bear his *s*.
Nu 9.13 that man shall bear his *s*.
32.23 be sure your *s* will find you out.
Dt 9.21 I took your *s*, the calf which ye had
24.16 shall be put to death for his own *s*.
1Sa 2.25 but if a man *s* against the Lord,
12.23 God forbid that I should *s* against
1Ki 17.18 me to call my *s* to remembrance,
2Ch 6.25 forgive the *s* of thy people Israel,
25. 4 every man shall die for his own *s*.
Neh 13.26 did outlandish women cause to *s*.
Job 2.10 all this did not Job *s* with his lips.
13.23 know my transgression and my *s*.
14.16 dost thou not watch over my *s*?
35. 3 I have, if I be cleansed from my *s*?
Ps 4. 4 Stand in awe, and *s* not: commune
32. 1 is forgiven, whose *s* is covered.
5 I acknowledged my *s* unto thee,
39. 1 ways, that I *s* not with my tongue:
40. 6 *s* offering hast thou not required.
51. 2 and cleanse me from my *s*.
3 and my *s* is ever before me.
5 in *s* did my mother conceive me.
59. 3 my transgression, nor for my *s*,
Pr 14. 9 Fools make a mock at *s*: but

34 but *s* is a reproach to any people.
Isa 6. 7 is taken away, and thy *s* purged.
30. 1 spirit, that they may add *s* to *s*:
53.10 make his soul an offering for *s*,
12 he bare the *s* of many, and made
Jer 16.18 their iniquity and their *s* double;
17. 1 *s* of Judah is written with a pen of
31.34 I will remember their *s* no more.
51. 5 was filled with *s* against the Holy
Dan 9.20 my *s* and the *s* of my people Israel
Hos 4. 8 They eat up the *s* of my people,
13. 2 And now they *s* more and more,
Mic 6. 7 of my body for the *s* of my soul?
Mt 12.31 All manner of *s* and blasphemy
18.21 oft shall my brother *s* against me,
Jn 1.29 taketh away the *s* of the world.
5.14 *s* no more, lest a worse thing
8. 7 He that is without *s* among you,
11 condemn thee: go, and *s* no more.
34 committeth *s* is the servant of *s*.
46 Which of you convinceth me of *s*?
9. 2 Master, who did *s*, this man, or his
41 ye were blind, ye should have no *s*:
41 We see; therefore your *s* remaineth.
15.22 unto them, they had not had *s*: but
22 now they have no cloke for their *s*.
24 other man did, they had not had *s*:
16. 8 he will reprove the world of *s*, and
9 Of *s*, because they believe not on
19.11 delivered me...hath the greater *s*.
Ac 7.60 Lord, lay not this *s* to their charge.
Ro 3. 9 Gentiles, that they are all under *s*;
20 for by the law is the knowledge of *s*.
4. 8 whom the Lord will not impute *s*.
5.12 by one man *s* entered into the world,
12 into the world, and death by *s*;
13 until the law *s* was in the world:
13 *s* is not imputed when there is no
20 But where *s* abounded, grace did
21 That as *s* hath reigned unto death,
6. 1 Shall we continue in *s*, that grace
2 How shall we that are dead to *s*, live
6 the body of *s* might be destroyed,
6 henceforth we should not serve *s*.
7 For he that is dead is freed from *s*.
10 in that he died, he died unto *s* once:
11 ye also...to be dead indeed unto *s*,
12 Let not *s* therefore reign in your
13 of unrighteousness unto *s*:
14 *s* shall not have dominion over you:
15 shall we *s*, because we are not under
16 whether of *s* unto death, or of
17 that ye were the servants of *s*, but
18 Being then made free from *s*, ye
20 For when we were the servants of *s*,
22 But now being made free from *s*,
23 For the wages of *s* is death: but the
7. 7 Is the law *s*? God forbid. Nay,
7 I had not known *s*, but by the law:
8 But *s*, taking occasion by the
8 For without the law *s* was dead.
9 the commandment came, *s* revived,
11 For *s*, taking occasion by the
13 But *s*, that it might appear *s*,
13 that *s* by the commandment might
14 but I am carnal, sold under *s*.
17, 20 it, but *s* that dwelleth in me.
23 me into captivity to the law of *s*
25 God; but with the flesh the law of *s*.
8. 2 me free from the law of *s* and death.
3 likeness for sinful flesh, and for *s*,
3 condemned *s* in the flesh:
10 you, the body is dead because of *s*;
14.23 for whatsoever is not of faith is *s*.
1Co 6.18 Every *s* that a man doeth is without
8.12 when ye *s* so against the brethren,
12 weak conscience, ye *s* against Christ.
15.34 Awake to righteousness, and *s* not:
56 The sting of death is *s*; and the
56 and the strength of *s* is the law.
2Co 5.21 him to be *s* for us, who knew no *s*;
Gal 2.17 is therefore Christ the minister of *s*?
3.22 hath concluded all under *s*, that
Eph 4.26 Be ye angry, and *s* not: let not the
2Th 2. 3 that man of *s* be revealed, the son
1Ti 5.20 Them that *s* rebuke before all,
Heb 3.13 through the deceitfulness of *s*.
4.15 like as we are, yet without *s*.
9.26 hath he appeared to put away *s*
28 appear...without *s* unto salvation.
10. 6 burnt offerings and sacrifices for *s*
8 burnt offerings and offering for *s*
18 is, there is no more offering for *s*.
26 if we *s* wilfully after that we have
11.25 than to enjoy the pleasures of *s* for
12. 1 *s* which doth so easily beset us,
4 unto blood, striving against *s*.
13.11 sanctuary by the high priest for *s*,
Jas 1.15 it bringeth forth *s*: and *s*, when it
2. 9 respect of persons, ye commit *s*,
4.17 and doeth it not, to him it is *s*.
1Pe 2.22 Who did no *s*, neither was guile
4. 1 in the flesh hath ceased from *s*;
2Pe 2.14 and that cannot cease from *s*;
1Jn 1. 7 his Son cleanseth us from all *s*.
8 If we say that we have no *s*, we
2. 1 write I unto you, that ye *s* not.
1 if any man *s*, we have an advocate
3. 4 committeth *s* transgresseth also
4 for *s* is the transgression of the law.
5 away our sins; and in him is no *s*.
8 He that committeth *s* is of the devil;
9 is born of God doth not commit *s*;
9 he cannot *s*, because he is born of
5.16 If any man see his brother *s*
16 a *s* which is not unto death, he
16 for them that *s* not unto death.
16 There is a *s* unto death: I do not
17 All unrighteousness is *s*: and there
17 and there is a *s* not unto death.

SINA

Ac 7.30 him in the wilderness of mount *S*
38 which spake to him in the mount *S*,

SINAI

Ex 16. 1 which is between Elim and *S*, on
19. 1 came they into the wilderness of *S*
2 were come to the desert of *S*, and
11 of all the people upon mount *S*.
18 And mount *S* was altogether on a
20 Lord came down upon mount *S*,
23 cannot come up to mount *S*: for
24.16 of the Lord abode upon mount *S*.
31.18 him upon mount *S*, two tables
34. 2 up in the morning unto mount *S*,
4 and went up unto mount *S*, as the
29 Moses came down from mount *S*
32 had spoken with him in mount *S*.
Lev 7.38 commanded Moses in mount *S*, in
38 the Lord, in the wilderness of *S*.
25. 1 spake unto Moses in mount *S*,
26.46 children of Israel in mount *S* by
27.34 the children of Israel in mount *S*,
Nu 1. 1 unto Moses in the wilderness of *S*,
19 them in the wilderness of *S*.
3. 1 spake with Moses in mount *S*.
4 the Lord, in the wilderness of *S*,
9. 1 unto Moses in the wilderness of *S*,
5 at even in the wilderness of *S*:
28. 6 which was ordained in mount *S*
33.15 and pitched in the wilderness of *S*
16 removed from the desert of *S*,
Ps 68. 8 even *S* itself was moved at the
17 the Lord is among them, as in *S*,
Gal 4.24 the one from the mount *S*, which
25 this Agar is mount *S* in Arabia,

SINCE

Gen 46.30 let me die, *s* I have seen thy face,
Dt 4.32 *s* the day that God created man
Jos 14.10 *s* the Lord spake this word unto
1Sa 29. 6 *s* the day of thy coming unto me
1Ch 17.10 *s* the time that I commanded judges
Job 20. 4 *s* man was placed upon earth,
Isa 14. 8 *S* thou art laid down, no feller is
43. 4 *S* thou wast precious in my sight,
64. 4 *s* the beginning of the world men
Jer 23.38 *s* ye say, The burden of the Lord;
Mt 24.21 not *s* the beginning of the world to
Lk 1.70 have been *s* the world began:
24.21 third day *s* these things were done.
1Co 15.21 For *s* by man came death, by man
Col 1. 4 *S* we heard of your faith in Christ
Heb 9.26 *s* the foundation of the world:
Rev 16.18 such as was not *s* men were

SINCERE

Php 1.10 ye may be *s* and without offense
1Pe 2. 2 desire the *s* milk of the word, that

SINCERELY

Jdg 9.16 if ye have done truly and *s*, in
19 If ye then have dealt truly and *s*
Php 1.16 preach Christ of contention, not *s*,

SINCERITY

Jos 24.14 and serve him in *s* and in truth:
1Co 5. 8 with the unleavened bread of *s* and
2Co 1.12 that in simplicity and godly *s*, not
2.17 but as of *s*, but as of God, in the
8. 8 and to prove the *s* of your love.
Eph 6.24 love our Lord Jesus Christ in *s*.
Tit 2. 7 shewing uncorruptness, gravity, *s*,

SINEW

Gen 32.32 eat not of the *s* which shrank,
32 Jacob's thigh in the *s* that shrank.
Isa 48. 4 and thy neck is an iron *s*, and thy

SINEWS

Job 10.11 hast fenced me with bones and *s*.
30.17 season: and my *s* take no rest.
40.17 the *s* of his stones are wrapped
Eze 37. 6 And I will lay *s* upon you, and will
8 *s* and the flesh came up upon them,

SINFUL

Nu 32.14 an increase of *s* men, to augment
Isa 1. 4 Ah *s* nation, a people laden with
Am 9. 8 Lord God are upon the *s* kingdom,
Mk 8.38 this adulterous and *s* generation;
Lk 5. 8 from me; for I am a *s* man, O Lord.
24. 7 delivered into the hands of *s* men,
Ro 7.13 sin...might become exceeding *s*.
8. 3 own Son in the likeness of *s* flesh,

SING

Ex 15. 1 I will *s* unto the Lord, for he hath
21 *S* ye to the Lord, for he hath
32.18 the noise of them that *s* do I hear.
Nu 21.17 Spring up, O well; *s* ye unto it:
Jdg 5. 3 I, even I, will *s* unto the Lord;
3 will *s* praise to the Lord of Israel.
1Sa 21.11 *s* one to another of him in dances,
2Sa 22.50 I will *s* praises unto thy name.
1Ch 16. 9 *S* unto him,...talk ye of all his
9 *s* psalms unto him, talk ye of all
23 *S* unto the Lord, all the earth;
33 shall the trees of the wood *s* out
2Ch 20.22 they began to *s* and to praise,
23.13 and such as taught to *s* praise.
29.30 to *s* praise unto the Lord with the
Job 29.13 the widow's heart to *s* for joy.
Ps 7.17 will *s* praise to the name of the Lord
9. 2 I will *s* praise to thy name, O thou
11 *S* praises to the Lord, which
13. 6 I will *s* unto the Lord, because he
18.49 and *s* praises unto thy name.
21.13 so will we *s* and praise thy power.
27. 6 sacrifice of joy; I will *s*, yea,
6 I will *s* praises unto the Lord.
30. 4 *S* unto the Lord, O ye saints of his,

Ps 30.12 that my glory may *s* praise to thee,
33. 2 *s* unto him with the psaltery and
3 *S* unto him a new song; play
47. 6 *S* praises to God, *s* praises:
6 *s* praises unto our King, *s* praises.
7 *s* ye praises with understanding.
51.14 shall *s* aloud of thy righteousness.
57. 7 is fixed: I will *s* and give praise.
9 *s* unto thee among the nations.
59.16 But I will *s* of thy power; yea, I
16 I will *s* aloud of thy mercy in the
17 Unto thee, O my strength, will I *s*:
61. 8 So will I *s* praise unto thy name for
65.13 they shout for joy, they also *s*.
66. 2 *S* forth the honor of his name:
4 worship thee, and...*s* unto thee;
4 they shall *s* to thy name. Selah.
67. 4 the nations be glad and *s* for joy:
68. 4 *S* unto God,...extol him that rideth
4 *s* praises to his name: extol him
32 *S* unto God, ye kingdoms of the
32 O *s* praises unto the Lord; Selah:
71.22 unto thee will I *s* with the harp,
23 greatly rejoice when I *s* unto thee;
75. 9 I will *s* praises to the God of Jacob.
81. 1 *S* aloud unto God our strength:
89. 1 I will *s* of the mercies of the Lord
92. 1 and to *s* praises unto thy name, O
95. 1 O come, let us *s* unto the Lord:
96. 1 O *s* unto the Lord a new song:
1 *s* unto the Lord, all the earth.
2 *S* unto the Lord, bless his name;
98. 1 O *s* unto the Lord a new song; for
4 noise, and rejoice, and *s* praise.
5 *S* unto the Lord with the harp;
101. 1 I will *s* of mercy and judgment:
1 unto thee, O Lord, will I *s*.
104.12 which *s* among the branches.
33 *s* unto the Lord as long as I live:
33 *s* praise to my God while I have
105. 2 *S* unto him,...talk ye of all his
2 *s* psalms unto him: talk ye of
108. 1 I will *s* and give praise, even with
3 I will *s* praises unto thee among
135. 3 *s* praises unto his name; for it is
137. 3 *S* us one of the songs of Zion.
4 *s* the Lord's song in a strange
138. 1 the gods will I *s* praise unto thee.
5 shall *s* in the ways of the Lord:
144. 9 I will *s* a new song unto thee, O
9 ten strings will I *s* praises unto
145. 7 and shall *s* of thy righteousness.
146. 2 I will *s* praises unto...God while I
147. 1 is good to *s* praises unto our God;
7 *S* unto...Lord with thanksgiving;
7 *s* praise upon the harp unto our
149. 1 *S* unto the Lord a new song, and
3 *s* praises unto him with...timbrel
5 let them *s* aloud upon their beds.
Pr 29. 6 the righteous doth *s* and rejoice.
Isa 5. 1 will I *s* to my wellbeloved a song
12. 5 *S* unto the Lord; for he hath
23.15 years shall Tyre *s* as an harlot.
16 make sweet melody, *s* many songs,
24.14 shall *s* for the majesty of the
26.19 Awake and *s*, ye that dwell in
27. 2 In that day *s* ye unto her, A
35. 6 and the tongue of the dumb *s*:
38.20 therefore will we *s* my songs to
42.10 *S* unto the Lord a new song, and
11 let the inhabitants of the rock *s*,
44.23 *S*, O ye heavens; for the Lord
49.13 *S*, O heavens; and be joyful, O
52. 8 the voice together shall they *s*:
9 joy, *s* together, ye waste places of
54. 1 *S*, O barren, thou that didst not
65.14 servants shall *s* for joy of heart,
Jer 20.13 *S* unto the Lord, praise ye the
31. 7 *S* with gladness for Jacob, and
12 come and *s* in the height of Zion,
51.48 that is therein, shall *s* for Babylon:
Eze 27.25 ships of Tarshish did *s* of thee in
Hos 2.15 she shall *s* there, as in the days
Zep 2.14 voice shall *s* in the windows;
3.14 *S*, O daughter of Zion; shout, O
Zec 2.10 *S* and rejoice, O daughter of Zion:
Ro 15. 9 Gentiles, and *s* unto thy name.
1Co 14.15 also: I will *s* with the spirit, and
15 will *s* with the understanding also.
Heb 2.12 the church will I *s* praise unto thee.
Jas 5.13 is any merry? let him *s* psalms.
Rev 15. 3 And they *s* the song of Moses the

SINGED

Dan 3.27 nor was an hair of their head *s*,

SINGER

1Ch 6.33 Heman a *s*, the son of Joel, the
Hab 3.19 To the chief *s* on my stringed

SINGERS

1Ki 10.12 harps also and psalteries for *s*:
1Ch 9.33 these are the *s*, chief of the fathers
15.16 the *s* with instruments of musick,
19 So the *s*, Heman, Asaph, and
27 that bare the ark and the *s*, and
27 the master of the song with the *s*:
2Ch 5.12 the Levites which were the *s*, all of
13 the trumpeters and *s* were as one,
9.11 and harps and psalteries for *s*:
20.21 he appointed *s* unto the Lord, and
23.13 the *s* with instruments of musick,
29.28 and the *s* sang, and the trumpets
35.15 And the *s* the sons of Asaph were
Ezr 2.41 The *s*: the children of Asaph, an
70 people, and the *s*, and the porters,
24 Levites, *s*, porters, Nethinims,
10.24 Of the *s* also; Eliashib: and of
Neh 7. 1 and the *s* and the Levites were
44 The *s*: the children of Asaph, an
73 Levites, and the porters, and the *s*,
10.28 the Levites, the porters, the *s*, the
39 minister,...the porters, and the *s*:
11.22 the *s* were over the business of the
23 certain portion should be for the *s*,
12.28 And the sons of the *s* gathered
29 *s* had builded them villages round
42 the *s* sang loud, with Jezrahiah
45 both the *s* and the porters kept
46 of old thou were chief of the *s*,
47 gave the portions of the *s* and the
13. 5 be given to the Levites, and the *s*,
10 the Levites, and the *s*, that did the
Ps 68.25 The *s* went before, the players on
87. 7 As well the *s* as the players on
Ec 2. 8 I gat me men *s* and women *s*, and
Eze 40.44 the chambers of the *s* in the inner

SINGETH

Pr 25.20 so is he that *s* songs to an heavy

SINGING

1Sa 18. 6 cities of Israel, *s* and dancing,
2Sa 19.35 the voice of *s* men and *s* women?
Neh 12.27 with thanksgivings, and with *s*,
Ps 100. 2 come before his presence with *s*.
126. 2 laughter, and our tongue with *s*:
SS 2.12 time of the *s* of birds is come,
Isa 35. 2 and rejoice even with joy and *s*:
44.23 break forth into *s*, ye mountains,
Zep 3.17 love, he will joy over thee with *s*.
Eph 5.19 *s* and making melody in your
Col 3.16 *s* with grace in your hearts to the

SINGLE

Mt 6.22 if therefore thine eye be *s*, thy
Lk 11.34 therefore when thine eye is *s*, thy

SINGLENESS

Ac 2.46 with gladness and *s* of heart,
Eph 6. 5 in *s* of your heart, as unto Christ;
Col 3.22 but in *s* of heart, fearing God:

SINK

Ps 69. 2 I *s* in deep mire, where there is
14 out of the mire, and let me not *s*:
Jer 51.64 Thus shall Babylon *s*, and shall
Mt 14.30 beginning to *s*, he cried, saying,
Lk 5. 7 the ships, so that they began to *s*.
9.44 sayings *s* down into your ears:

SINNED

Ex 10.16 I have *s* against the Lord your God,
32.30 the people, Ye have *s* a great sin:
Lev 4.22 When a ruler hath *s*, and done
Nu 21. 7 We have *s*, for we have spoken
32.23 behold, ye have *s* against the Lord:
1Sa 15.24 Saul said unto Samuel, I have *s*:
1Ki 18. 9 What have I *s*, that thou wouldest
1Ch 21. 8 said unto God, I have *s* greatly,
2Ch 6.37 We have *s*, we have done amiss,
Job 1.22 In all this Job *s* not, nor charged
7.20 I have *s*; what shall I do unto thee,
Ps 51. 4 Against thee, thee only, have I *s*,
Jer 3.25 for we have *s* against the Lord our
La 5. 7 Our fathers have *s*, and are not;
Hab 2.10 people, and hath *s* against thy soul.
Mt 27. 4 I have *s* in that I have betrayed
Lk 15.18, 21 Father, I have *s* against heaven,
Jn 9. 3 Neither hath this man *s*, nor his
Ro 2.12 For as many as have *s* without law
12 and as many as have *s* in the law
3.23 For all have *s*, and come short of
5.12 upon all men, for that all have *s*:
14 that had not *s* after the similitude
16 And not as it was by one that *s*, so
1Co 7.28 and if thou marry, thou hast not *s*;
28 if a virgin marry, she hath not *s*.
2Co 12.21 many which have *s* already,
13. 2 to them which heretofore have *s*,
Heb 3.17 was it not with them that had *s*,
2Pe 2. 4 God spared not the angels that *s*,
1Jn 1.10 If we say that we have not *s*, we

SINNER

Pr 11.31 much more the wicked and the *s*.
13. 6 wickedness overthroweth the *s*.
22 the wealth of the *s* is laid up for
Ec 2.26 but to the *s* he giveth travail, to
7.26 but the *s* shall be taken by her.
8.12 Though a *s* do evil an hundred
9. 2 as is the good, so is the *s*; and he
18 but one *s* destroyeth much good.
Isa 65.20 the *s* being an hundred years old
Lk 7.37 woman in the city, which was a *s*,
39 that toucheth him: for she is a *s*.
15. 7 heaven over one *s* that repenteth,
10 of God over one *s* that repenteth.
18.13 saying, God be merciful to me a *s*.
19. 7 to be guest with a man that is a *s*.
Jn 9.16 man that is a *s* do such miracles?
24 we know that this man is a *s*.
25 Whether he be a *s* or no, I know not:
Ro 3. 7 why yet am I also judged as a *s*?
Jas 5.20 converteth the *s* from the error of
1Pe 4.18 shall the ungodly and the *s* appear?

SINNERS

Gen 13.13 men of Sodom were wicked and *s*
Nu 16.38 The censers of these *s* against
1Sa 15.18 destroy the *s* the Amalekites,
Ps 1. 1 nor standeth in the way of *s*, nor
5 nor *s* in the congregation of the
25. 8 therefore will he teach *s* in the way.
26. 9 Gather not my soul with *s*, nor my
51.13 *s* shall be converted unto thee.
104.35 *s* be consumed out of the earth,
Pr 1.10 if *s* entice thee, consent thou not.
13.21 Evil pursueth *s*: but to the
23.17 Let not thine heart envy *s*: but be
Isa 1.28 of the transgressors and of the *s*
13. 9 and he shall destroy the *s* thereof
33.14 The *s* in Zion are afraid; fearfulness
Am 9.10 All the *s* of my people shall die by

Mt	9.10	many publicans and *s* came and
	11	your Master with publicans and *s*?
	13	the righteous, but *s* to repentance.
	11.19	a friend of publicans and *s*.
	26.45	is betrayed into the hands of *s*.
Mk	2.15	publicans and *s* sat also together
	16	saw him eat with publicans and *s*,
	16	and drinketh with publicans and *s*?
	17	the righteous, but *s* to repentance.
	14.41	is betrayed into the hands of *s*.
Lk	5.30	eat and drink with publicans and *s*?
	32	the righteous, but *s* to repentance.
	6.32	for *s* also love those that love them.
	33	ye? for *s* also do even the same.
	34	*s* also lend to *s*, to receive as much
	7.34	a friend of publicans and *s*!
	13. 2	were *s* above all the Galileans,
	4	were *s* above all men that dwelt
	15. 1	publicans and *s* for to hear him.
	2	This man receiveth *s*, and eateth
Jn	9.31	we know that God heareth not *s*:
Ro	5. 8	while we were yet *s*, Christ died for
	19	disobedience many were made *s*,
Gal	2.15	by nature, and not *s* of the Gentiles,
	17	we ourselves also are found *s*, is
1Ti	1. 9	for the ungodly and for *s*, for unholy
	15	Jesus came into the world to save *s*;
Heb	7.26	undefiled, separate from *s*, and
	12. 3	contradiction of *s* against himself,
Jas	4. 8	Cleanse your hands, ye *s*; and
Jude	15	ungodly *s* have spoken against him.

SINNEST

Job	35. 6	If thou *s*, what doest thou against

SINNETH

Nu	15.28	for the soul that *s* ignorantly,
	28	*s* by ignorance before the Lord,
	29	for him that *s* through ignorance,
Dt	19.15	for any sin, in any sin that he *s*:
1Ki	8.46	(for there is no man that *s* not,)
2Ch	6.36	(for there is no man which *s* not,)
Pr	8.36	*s* against me wrongeth his own
	14.21	He that despiseth his neighbor *s*:
	19. 2	and he that hasteth with his feet *s*.
	20. 2	whoso provoketh him to anger *s*
Ec	7.20	earth, that doeth good, and *s* not.
Eze	14.13	when the land *s* against me by
	18. 4	mine: the soul that *s*, it shall die.
	20	The soul that *s*, it shall die. The
	33.12	righteousness in the day that he *s*.
1Co	6.18	fornication *s* against his own body.
	7.36	let him do what he will, he *s* not:
Tit	3.11	he that is such is subverted, and *s*,
1Jn	3. 6	Whosoever abideth in him *s* not:
	6	whosoever *s* hath not seen him,
	8	for the devil *s* from the beginning.
	5.18	whosoever is born of God *s* not;

SINNING

Gen	20. 6	for I also withheld thee from *s*
Lev	6. 3	these that a man doeth, *s* therein:

SINS

Lev	16.16	their transgressions in all their *s*:
	21	their transgressions in all their *s*,
	30	from all your *s* before the Lord.
	34	of Israel for all their *s* once a year.
	26.18	you seven times more for your *s*.
	21	upon you according to your *s*.
	24	you yet seven times for your *s*.
	28	chastise you seven times for your *s*.
Nu	16.26	lest ye be consumed in all their *s*.
Dt	9.18	because of all your *s* which ye
Jos	24.19	your transgressions nor your *s*.
1Sa	12.19	added unto all our *s* this evil,
1Ki	14.16	up because of the *s* of Jeroboam,
	22	their *s* which they had committed,
	15. 3	he walked in all the *s* of his father,
	30	the *s* of Jeroboam which he sinned,
	16. 2	provoke me to anger with their *s*;
	13	For all the *s* of Baasha, and the
	13	and the *s* of Elah his son, by which
	19	his *s* which he sinned in doing evil
	31	him to walk in the *s* of Jeroboam
2Ki	3. 3	he cleaved unto the *s* of Jeroboam
	10.29	*s* of Jeroboam the son of Nebat,
	31	not from the *s* of Jeroboam,
	13. 2	and followed the *s* of Jeroboam
	6	the *s* of the house of Jeroboam,
	11	from all the *s* of Jeroboam the son
	14.24	from all the *s* of Jeroboam the son
	15. 9, 18, 24, 28	*s* of Jeroboam the son of
	17.22	walked in all the *s* of Jeroboam
	24. 3	for the *s* of Manasseh, according to
2Ch	28.10	you, *s* against the Lord your God?
	13	ye intend to add more to our *s*
	33.19	and all his *s*, and his trespass, and
Neh	1. 6	and confess the *s* of the children of
	9. 2	and stood and confessed their *s*,
	37	hast set over us because of our *s*:
Job	13.23	many are mine iniquities and *s*?
Ps	19.13	servant also from presumptuous *s*;
	25. 7	Remember not the *s* of my youth,
	18	and my pain; and forgive all my *s*.
	51. 9	Hide thy face from my *s*, and blot
	69. 5	and my *s* are not hid from thee.
	79. 9	deliver us, and purge away our *s*,
	90. 8	our secret *s* in the light of thy
	103.10	hath not dealt with us after our *s*;
Pr	5.22	be holden with the cords of his *s*.
	10.12	up strifes: but love covereth all *s*.
	28.13	covereth his *s* shall not prosper:
Isa	1.18	though your *s* be as scarlet, they
	38.17	hast cast all my *s* behind thy back.
	40. 2	Lord's hand double for all her *s*.
	43.24	hast made me to serve with thy *s*,
	25	sake, and will not remember thy *s*.
	44.22	as a cloud, thy *s*: return unto me;
	58. 1	and the house of Jacob their *s*.
	59. 2	your *s* have hid his face from you,
	12	thee, and our *s* testify against us:
Jer	5.25	and your *s* have withholden good
	14.10	their iniquity, and visit their *s*.
	15.13	and that for all thy *s*, even in all
	30.14	because thy *s* were increased.
	15	because thy *s* were increased, I
	50.20	the *s* of Judah, and they shall not
La	3.39	man for the punishment of his *s*?
	4.13	For the *s* of her prophets, and the
	22	of Edom; he will discover thy *s*.
Eze	16.51	Samaria committed half of thy *s*;
	52	for thy *s* that thou hast committed
	18.14	that seeth all his father's *s* which
	21	all his *s* that he hath committed,
	21.24	all your doings your *s* do appear;
	23.49	ye shall bear the *s* of your idols:
	33.10	If our transgressions and our *s* be
	16	of his *s* that he hath committed
Dan	4.27	break off thy *s* by righteousness,
	9.16	for our *s*, and for the iniquities
	24	to make an end of *s*, and to make
Hos	8.13	their iniquity, and visit their *s*:
	9. 9	their iniquity, he will visit their *s*.
Am	5.12	transgressions and your mighty *s*:
Mic	1. 5	and for the *s* of the house of Israel.
	6.13	thee desolate because of thy *s*.
	7.19	their *s* into the depths of the sea.
Mt	1.21	shall save his people from their *s*.
	3. 6	of him in Jordan, confessing their *s*.
	9. 2	good cheer; thy *s* be forgiven thee.
	5	to say, Thy *s* be forgiven thee; or
	6	hath power on earth to forgive *s*,
	26.28	shed for many for the remission of *s*.
Mk	1. 4	of repentance for the remission of *s*.
	5	river of Jordan, confessing their *s*.
	2. 5	palsy, Son, thy *s* be forgiven thee.
	7	who can forgive *s* but God only?
	9	the palsy, Thy *s* be forgiven thee;
	10	hath power on earth to forgive *s*,
	3.28	*s* shall be forgiven unto the sons of
	4.12	their *s* should be forgiven them.
Lk	1.77	people by the remission of their *s*,
	3. 3	repentance for the remission of *s*;
	5.20	him, Man, thy *s* are forgiven thee.
	21	Who can forgive *s*, but God alone?
	23	to say, Thy *s* be forgiven thee; or to
	24	hath power upon earth to forgive *s*,
	7.47	Her *s*, which are many, are forgiven;
	48	he said unto her, Thy *s* are forgiven.
	49	Who is this that forgiveth *s* also?
	11. 4	forgive us our *s*; for we also forgive
	24.47	remission of *s* should be preached
Jn	8.21	seek me, and shall die in your *s*:
	24	unto you, that ye shall die in your *s*:
	24	that I am he, ye shall die in your *s*.
	9.34	Thou wast altogether born in *s*,
	20.23	Whose soever *s* ye remit, they are
	23	whose soever *s* ye retain, they are
Ac	2.38	Jesus Christ for the remission of *s*,
	3.19	that your *s* may be blotted out,
	5.31	to Israel, and forgiveness of *s*.
	10.43	in him receive shall remission of *s*.
	13.38	unto you the forgiveness of *s*:
	22.16	be baptized, and wash away thy *s*,
	26.18	they may receive forgiveness of *s*,
Ro	3.25	for the remission of *s* that are past,
	4. 7	forgiven, and whose *s* are covered.
	7. 5	the motions of *s*, which were by the
	11.27	when I shall take away their *s*.
1Co	15. 3	how that Christ died for our *s*
	17	faith is vain; ye are yet in your *s*.
Gal	1. 4	Who gave himself for our *s*, that he
Eph	1. 7	the forgiveness of *s*, according to
	2. 1	who were dead in trespasses and *s*,
	5	Even when we were dead in *s*,
Col	1.14	blood, even the forgiveness of *s*:
	2.11	off the body of the *s* of the flesh by
	13	And you, being dead in your *s*
1Th	2.16	be saved, to fill up their *s* alway:
1Ti	5.22	be partaker of other men's *s*:
	24	Some men's *s* are open beforehand,
2Ti	3. 6	captive silly women laden with *s*,
Heb	1. 3	he had by himself purged our *s*, sat
	2.17	reconciliation for the *s* of the people.
	5. 1	offer both gifts and sacrifices for *s*:
	3	so also for himself, to offer for *s*.
	7.27	first for his own *s*, and then for the
	8.12	and their *s* and their iniquities will I
	9.28	once offered to bear the *s* of many;
	10. 2	have had no more conscience of *s*.
	3	is a remembrance again made of *s*
	4	and of goats should take away *s*.
	11	which can never take away *s*:
	12	he had offered one sacrifice for *s*
	17	*s* and iniquities will I remember
	26	remaineth no more sacrifice for *s*,
Jas	5.15	if he have committed *s*, they shall
	20	and shall hide a multitude of *s*.
1Pe	2.24	own self bare our *s* in his own body
	24	that we, being dead to *s*, should live
	3.18	Christ also hath once suffered for *s*,
	4. 8	shall cover the multitude of *s*.
2Pe	1. 9	that he was purged from his old *s*.
1Jn	1. 9	If we confess our *s*, he is faithful and
	9	faithful and just to forgive us our *s*,
	2. 2	And he is the propitiation for our *s*:
	2	but also for the *s* of the whole world.
	12	because your *s* are forgiven you for
	3. 5	was manifested to take away our *s*;
	4.10	Son to be the propitiation for our *s*.
Rev	1. 5	and washed us from our *s* in his own
	18. 4	that ye be not partakers of her *s*,
	5	her *s* have reached unto heaven,

SION

Dt	4.48	unto mount *S*, which is Hermon.
Ps	65. 1	waiteth for thee, O God, in *S*:
Mt	21. 5	Tell ye the daughter of *S*, Behold,
Jn	12.15	Fear not, daughter of *S*: behold,
Ro	9.33	I lay in *S* a stumblingstone and
	11.26	shall come out of *S* the Deliverer,
Heb	12.22	But ye are come unto mount *S*,

1Pe 2. 6 I lay in *S* a chief corner stone,
Rev 14. 1 lo, a Lamb stood on the mount *S*,

SIR
Gen 43.20 O *s*, we came indeed down at the
Mt 13.27 *S*, didst not thou sow good seed in
21.30 and said, I go, *s*; and went not.
27.63 *S*, we remember that that deceiver
Jn 4.11 *S*, thou hast nothing to draw with,
15 *S*, give me this water, that I thirst
19 *S*, I perceive…thou art a prophet.
49 *S*, come down ere my child die.
5. 7 *S*, I have no man, when the water
12.21 saying, *S*, we would see Jesus.
20.15 *S*, if thou have borne him hence,
Rev 7.14 I said unto him, *S*, thou knowest.

SIRS
Ac 7.26 *S*, ye are brethren; why do ye
14.15 saying, *S*, why do ye these things?
16.30 *S*, what must I do to be saved?
19.25 *S*, ye know that by this craft we
27.10 *S*, I perceive that this voyage will
21 *S*, ye should have hearkened unto
25 Wherefore, *s*, be of good cheer: for

SISERA
Jdg 4. 2 the captain of whose host was *S*,
7 *S* the captain of Jabin's army, with
9 the Lord shall sell *S* into the hand
12 And they shewed *S* that Barak the
13 And *S* gathered together all his
14 Lord hath delivered *S* into thine
15 And the Lord discomfited *S*, and
15 that *S* lighted down off his chariot,
16 host of *S* fell upon the edge of the
17 *S* fled away on his feet to the tent
18 And Jael went out to meet *S*, and
22 as Barak pursued *S*, Jael came out
22 *S* lay dead, and the nail was in his
5.20 in their courses fought against *S*.
26 and with the hammer she smote *S*,
28 The mother of *S* looked out at a
30 to *S* a prey of divers colors, a
1Sa 12. 9 he sold them into the hand of *S*,
Ezr 2.53 the children of *S*, the children of
Neh 7.55 the chldren of *S*, the children of
Ps 83. 9 as to *S*, as to Jabin, at the brook

SISTER
Gen 12.19 Why saidst thou, She is my *s*? so I
20. 2 said of Sarah his wife, She is my *s*:
Ru 1.15 thy *s* in law is gone back unto her
15 gods: return thou after thy *s* in law.
Job 17.14 Thou art my mother, and my *s*.
Pr 7. 4 Say unto wisdom, Thou art my *s*;
SS 4.10 How fair is thy love, my *s*, my
Eze 16.46 And thine elder *s* is Samaria, she
48 Sodom thy *s* hath not done, she nor
Mt 12.50 the same is my brother, and *s*, and
Mk 3.35 the same is my brother, and my *s*,
Lk 10.39 And she had a *s* called Mary, which
40 not care that my *s* hath left me to
Jn 11. 1 the town of Mary and her *s* Martha.
5 Now Jesus loved Martha, and her *s*,
28 called Mary her *s* secretly, saying,
39 Martha, the *s* of him that was dead,
19.25 his mother, and his mother's *s*,
Ro 16. 1 I commend unto you Phebe our *s*,
15 and Julia, Nereus, and his *s*, and
1Co 7.15 A brother or a *s* is not under
9. 5 we not power to lead about a *s*, a
Jas 2.15 If a brother or *s* be naked, and
2Jn 13 The children of thy elect *s* greet

SISTER'S
Gen 24.30 and bracelets upon his *s* hands,
29.13 heard the tidings of Jacob his *s* son,
Lev 20.17 he hath uncovered his *s* nakedness;
1Ch 7.15 whose *s* name was Maachah;) and
Eze 23.32 shalt drink of thy *s* cup deep and
Ac 23.16 when Paul's *s* son heard of their
Col 4.10 and Marcus, *s* son to Barnabas,

SISTERS
Jos 2.13 and my brethren, and my *s*, and all
1Ch 2.16 Whose *s* were Zeruiah, and Abigail.
Job 1. 4 called for their three *s* to eat and to
42.11 him all his brethren, and all his *s*,
Eze 16.45 thou art the sister of thy *s*, which
51 hast justified thy *s* in all thine
52 Thou also, which hast judged thy *s*,
52 in that thou hast justified thy *s*.
55 thy *s*, Sodom and her daughters,
61 when thou shalt receive thy *s*, thine
Hos 2. 1 Ammi; and to your *s*, Ruhamah.
Mt 13.56 And his *s*, are they not all with us?
19.29 forsaken houses, or brethren, or *s*,
Mk 6. 3 and are not his *s* here with us?
10.29 hath left house, or brethren, or *s*,
30 houses, and brethren, and *s*, and
Lk 14.26 and children, and brethren, and *s*,
Jn 11. 3 Therefore his *s* sent unto him,
1Ti 5. 2 the younger as *s*, with all purity.

SIT
Jdg 5.10 ye that *s* in judgment, and walk by
1Sa 9.22 made them *s* in the chiefest place
20. 5 fail to *s* with the king at meat:
1Ki 3. 6 him a son to *s* on his throne, as it
2Ki 7. 3 Why *s* we here until we die?
Ps 26. 5 and will not *s* with the wicked.
69.12 They that *s* in the gate speak
107.10 Such as *s* in darkness and in the
110. 1 *S* thou at my right hand, until I
127. 2 you to rise up early, to *s* up late,
Isa 3.26 desolate shall *s* upon the ground.
30. 7 this, Their strength is to *s* still.
47. 1 Come down, and *s* in the dust, O
Jer 8.14 Why do we *s* still? assemble
Eze 28. 2 I *s* in the seat of God, in the midst
33.31 they *s* before thee as my people,
Dan 7. 9 the Ancient of days did *s*, whose
Joel 3.12 will I *s* to judge all the heathen
Mic 4. 4 shall *s* every man under his vine
Mal 3. 3 he shall *s* as a refiner and purifier
Mt 8.11 shall *s* down with Abraham, and
14.19 multitude to *s* down on the grass,
15.35 multitude to *s* down on the ground.
19.28 Son of man shall *s* in the throne
28 ye also shall *s* upon twelve thrones,
20.21 that these my two sons may *s*, the
23 to *s* on my right hand, and on my
22.44 *S* thou on my right hand, till I
23. 2 the Pharisees *s* at Moses' seat:
25.31 then shall he *s* upon the throne of
26.36 *S* ye here, while I go and pray
Mk 6.39 to make all *s* down by companies
8. 6 people to *s* down on the ground:
10.37 Grant unto us that we may *s*, one
40 But to *s* on my right hand and on
12.36 *S* thou on my right hand, till I
14.32 *S* ye here, while I shall pray.
Lk 1.79 light to them that *s* in darkness
9.14 Make them *s* down by fifties in a
15 did so, and made then all *s* down.
12.37 and make them to *s* down to meat,
13.29 *s* down in the kingdom of God.
14. 8 *s* not down in the highest room;
10 go and *s* down in the lowest room;
10 of them that *s* at meat with thee.
16. 6 *s* down quickly, and write fifty.
17. 7 the field, Go and *s* down to meat?
20.42 Lord, *S* thou on my right hand,
22.30 *s* on thrones judging the twelve
69 Son of man *s* on the right hand
Jn 6.10 Jesus said, Make the men *s* down.
Ac 2.30 raise up Christ to *s* on his throne;
34 Lord, *S* thou on my right hand,
8.31 he would come up and *s* with him.
1Co 8.10 *s* at meat in the idol's temple,
Eph 2. 6 made us *s* together in heavenly
Heb 1.13 *S* on my right hand, until I make
Jas 2. 3 him, *S* thou here in a good place;
3 or *s* here under my footstool:
Rev 3.21 grant to *s* with me in my throne,
17. 3 woman *s* upon a scarlet colored
18. 7 I *s* a queen, and am no widow, and
19.18 of them that *s* on them, and the

SITTEST
Ex 18.14 why *s* thou thyself alone, and all
Dt 6. 7 them when thou *s* in thine house,
11.19 them when thou *s* in thine house,
Ps 50.20 Thou *s* and speakest against thy
Pr 23. 1 When thou *s* to eat with a ruler,
Jer 22. 2 that *s* upon the throne of David,
Ac 23. 3 *s* thou to judge me after the law,

SITTETH
Ex 11. 5 Pharaoh that *s* upon his throne,
Est 6.10 the Jew, that *s* at the king's gate:
Ps 1. 1 nor *s* in the seat of the scornful.
2. 4 that *s* in the heavens shall laugh:
29.10 The Lord *s* upon the flood;
99. 1 he *s* between the cherubims; let
Pr 20. 8 that *s* in the throne of judgment
31.23 when he *s* among the elders of the
Isa 40.22 that *s* upon the circle of the earth,
Jer 17.11 As the partridge *s* on eggs, and
La 3.28 He *s* alone and keepeth silence,
Mt 23.22 of God, and by him that *s* thereon.
Lk 14.28 *s* not down first, and counteth
31 *s* not down first, and consulteth
22.27 is greater, he that *s* at meat, or he
27 is not he that *s* at meat? but I am
1Co 14.30 be revealed to another that *s* by,
Col 3. 1 Christ *s* on the right hand of God.
2Th 2. 4 he as God *s* in the temple of God,
Rev 5.13 unto him that *s* upon the throne,
6.16 face of him that *s* on the throne,
7.10 our God which *s* upon the throne,
15 he that *s* on the throne shall dwell
17. 1 whore that *s* upon many waters:
9 mountains, on which the woman *s*.
15 where the whore *s*, are peoples,

SITTING
Dt 22. 6 and the dam *s* upon the young, or
Jdg 3.20 and he was *s* in a summer parlor,
1Ki 10. 5 table, and the *s* of his servants,
13.14 and found him *s* under an oak:
22.19 I saw the Lord *s* on his throne, and
2Ki 4.38 of the prophets were *s* before him:
9. 5 the captains of the host were *s*;
2Ch 9. 4 table, and the *s* of his servants,
18 stays on each side of the *s* place,
18.18 I saw the Lord *s* upon his throne,
Neh 2. 6 unto me, (the queen also *s* by him,)
Est 5.13 Mordecai…*s* at the king's gate.
Isa 6. 1 saw also the Lord *s* upon a throne,
Jer 17.25 princes *s* upon the throne of David,
22. 4 kings *s* upon the throne of David,
30 *s* upon the throne of David, and
38. 7 then *s* in the gate of Benjamin;
La 3.63 Behold their *s* down, and their
Mt 9. 9 *s* at the receipt of custom:
11.16 unto children *s* in the markets,
20.30 two blind men *s* by the way side,
21. 5 thee, meek, and *s* upon an ass,
26.64 Son of man *s* on the right hand
27.36 *s* down they watched him there;
61 Mary, *s* over against the sepulcher.
Mk 2. 6 were certain of the scribes *s* there,
14 Alphaeus *s* at the receipt of custom,
5.15 had the legion, *s*, and clothed, and
14.62 Son of man *s* on the right hand of
16. 5 a young man *s* on the right side,
Lk 2.46 *s* in the midst of the doctors, both
5.17 and doctors of the law *s* by, which
27 Levi, *s* at the receipt of custom:
7.32 unto children *s* in the marketplace,
8.35 *s* at the feet of Jesus, clothed, and

10.13 repented, *s* in sackcloth and ashes.
Jn 2.14 and the changers of money *s*:
12.15 King cometh, *s* on an ass's colt.
20.12 And seeth two angels in white *s*,
Ac 2. 2 all the house where they were *s*.
8.28 *s* in his chariot read Esaias the
25. 6 next day *s* on the judgment seat
Rev 4. 4 I saw four and twenty elders *s*,

SITUATION
2Ki 2.19 the *s* of this city is pleasant, as
Ps 48. 2 Beautiful for *s*, the joy of the

SIX
Gen 7. 6 Noah was *s* hundred years old
Ex 16.26 *S* days ye shall gather it; but on
20. 9 *S* days shalt thou labor, and do
11 *s* days the Lord made heaven and
28.10 *S* of their names on one stone, and
31.15 *S* days may work be done; but in
Nu 35. 6 there shall be *s* cities for refuge,
Dt 5.13 *S* days thou shalt labor, and do
16. 8 *S* days thou shalt eat unleavened
2Sa 21.20 that had on every hand *s* fingers,
20 and on every foot *s* toes, four and
2Ch 9.18 there were *s* steps to the throne,
22.12 hid in the house of God *s* years:
Job 5.19 He shall deliver thee in *s* troubles:
Pr 6.16 These *s* things doth the Lord hate:
Isa 6. 2 seraphims: each one had *s* wings;
Mt 17. 1 after *s* days Jesus taketh Peter,
Mk 9. 2 after *s* days Jesus taketh with him
Lk 4.25 shut up three years and *s* months,
13.14 are *s* days in which men ought to
Jn 2. 6 were set there *s* waterpots of stone,
20 Forty and *s* years was this temple
12. 1 *s* days before the passover came to
Ac 11.12 these *s* brethren accompanied me,
18.11 there a year and *s* months,
Jas 5.17 space of three years and *s* months.
Rev 4. 8 each of them *s* wings about him;
13.18 is *S* hundred threescore and *s*.
14.20 thousand and *s* hundred furlongs.

SIXTH
Gen 1.31 and the morning were the *s* day.
Ex 16.22 on the *s* day they gathered twice
29 on the *s* day the bread of two days;
Lev 25.21 blessing upon you in the *s* year,
Mt 20. 5 out about the *s* and ninth hour,
27.45 the *s* hour there was darkness
Mk 15.33 when the *s* hour was come, there
Lk 1.26 the *s* month the angel Gabriel was
36 this is the *s* month with her, who
23.44 it was about the *s* hour, and there
Jn 4. 6 well: and it was about the *s* hour.
19.14 passover, and about the *s* hour:
Ac 10. 9 housetop to pray about the *s* hour:
Rev 6.12 when he had opened the *s* seal,
9.13 the *s* angel sounded, and I heard a
14 Saying to the *s* angel which had
16.12 And the *s* angel poured out his vial
21.20 The fifth, sardonyx; the *s*, sardius;

SIXTY
Mt 13.23 some an hundredfold, some *s*,
Mk 4. 8 some thirty, and some *s*, and some
20 some thirtyfold, some *s*, and some

SIXTYFOLD
Mt 13. 8 some *s*, some thirtyfold.

SKIES
2Sa 22.12 waters, and thick clouds of the *s*.
Ps 18.11 waters and thick clouds of the *s*.
77.17 out water: the *s* sent out a sound:
Isa 45. 8 let the *s* pour down righteousness:
Jer 51. 9 and is lifted up even to the *s*.

SKILFUL
1Ch 5.18 and *s* in war, were four and forty
15.22 about the song, because he was *s*.
28.21 every willing *s* man, for any
2Ch 2.14 *s* to work in gold, and in silver, in
Eze 21.31 of brutish men, and *s* to destroy.
Dan 1. 4 favored, and *s* in all wisdom,
Am 5.16 such as are *s* of lamentation to

SKILFULLY
Ps 33. 3 song; play *s* with a loud noise.

SKILL
1Ki 5. 6 can *s* to hew timber like unto the
2Ch 2. 7 *s* to grave with the cunning men
8 thy servants can *s* to cut timber
34.12 could *s* of instruments of musick.
Ec 9.11 nor yet favor to men of *s*; but
Dan 1.17 and *s* in all learning and wisdom:
9.22 to give thee *s* and understanding.

SKIN
Ex 34.29 wist not that the *s* of his face shone
35 that the *s* of Moses' face shone:
Job 2. 4 *S* for *s*, yea, all that a man
10.11 hast clothed me with *s* and flesh,
16.15 have sewed sackcloth upon my *s*,
19.20 My bone cleaveth to my *s* and to
20 and I am escaped with the *s* of my
26 though after my *s* worms destroy
30.30 My *s* is black upon me, and my
41. 7 thou fill his *s* with barbed irons?
Ps 102. 5 my bones cleave to my *s*.
Jer 13.23 Can the Ethiopian change his *s*,
La 5.10 Our *s* was black like an oven
Eze 37. 6 upon you, and cover you with *s*,
Mic 3. 2 pluck off their *s* from off them,
Mk 1. 6 a girdle of a *s* about his loins;

SKINS
Gen 3.21 did the Lord God make coats of *s*,
Ex 26.14 for the tent of rams' *s* dyed red,
14 and a covering above of badgers' *s*.

SKIP
Ps 29. 6 them also to *s* like a calf;

SKIPPED
Ps 114. 4 The mountains *s* like rams, and
6 mountains, that ye *s* like rams;

SKIRT
Dt 22.30 wife, nor discover his father's *s*.
27.20 he uncovereth his father's *s*.
Ru 3. 9 spread therefore thy *s* over thine
1Sa 15.27 laid hold upon the *s* of his mantle,
24. 4 cut off the *s* of Saul's robe privily.
5 because he had cut off Saul's *s*.
11 see the *s* of thy robe in my hand:
11 in that I cut off the *s* of thy robe,
Eze 16. 8 and I spread my *s* over thee, and
Hag 2.12 holy flesh in the *s* of his garment,
12 and with his *s* do touch bread, or
Zec 8.23 hold of the *s* of him that is a Jew,

SKIRTS
Ps 133. 2 down to the *s* of his garments;
Jer 2.34 Also in thy *s* is found the blood of
13.22 iniquity are thy *s* discovered, and
26 I discover thy *s* upon thy face,
La 1. 9 Her filthiness is in her *s*; she
Eze 5. 3 number, and bind them in thy *s*.
Na 3. 5 will discover thy *s* upon thy face,

SKULL
Jdg 9.53 head, and all to brake his *s*.
2Ki 9.35 found no more of her than the *s*,
Mt 27.33 that is to say, a place of a *s*,
Mk 15.22 being interpreted, The place of a *s*.
Jn 19.17 into a place called the place of a *s*,

SKY
Dt 33.26 and in his excellency on the *s*.
Job 37.18 thou with him spread out the *s*,
Mt 16. 2 be fair weather: for the *s* is red.
3 day: for the *s* is red and lowering.
3 ye can discern the face of the *s*;
Lk 12.56 ye can discern the face of the *s*
Heb 11.12 so many as the stars of the *s* in

SLACK
Dt 7.10 not be *s* to him that hateth him,
23.21 thy God, thou shalt not *s* to pay it:
Jos 10. 6 *S* not thy hand from thy servants;
18. 3 How long are ye *s* to go to possess
2Ki 4.24 *s* not thy riding for me, except I
Pr 10. 4 poor that dealeth with a *s* hand:
Zep 3.16 Zion, Let not thine hands be *s*.
2Pe 3. 9 The Lord is not *s* concerning his

SLACKED
Hab 1. 4 the law is *s*, and judgment doth

SLACKNESS
2Pe 3. 9 promise, as some men count *s*;

SLAIN
Gen 4.23 I have *s* a man to my wounding,
Nu 23.24 and drink the blood of the *s*.
Jdg 15.16 an ass have I *s* a thousand men.
1Sa 18. 7 Saul hath *s* his thousands, and
2Sa 1.16 I have *s* the Lord's anointed.
19 The beauty of Israel is *s* upon thy
1Ki 19.10, 14 *s* thy prophets with the sword;
1Ch 10. 8 the Philistines came to strip the *s*,
Job 39.30 and where the *s* are, there is she.
Ps 88. 5 like the *s* that lie in the grave,
Pr 7.26 strong men have been *s* by her.
22.13 without, I shall be *s* in the streets.
24.11 and those that are ready to be *s*;
Isa 22. 2 *s* men are not *s* with the sword,
26.21 and shall no more cover her *s*.
66.16 the *s* of the Lord shall be many.
Jer 9. 1 the *s* of the daughter of my people!
La 2.20 the priest and the prophet be *s* in
3.43 thou hast *s*, thou hast not pitied.
4. 9 They that be *s* with the sword are
Eze 31.17 them that be *s* with the sword;
37. 9 breathe upon these *s*, that they
Dan 2.13 that the wise men should be *s*;
13 Daniel and his fellows to be *s*.
Hos 6. 5 *s* them by the words of my mouth:
Lk 9.22 be *s*, and be raised the third day.
Ac 2.23 wicked hands have crucified and *s*:
5.36 who was *s*; and all, as many as
7.42 have ye offered to me *s* beasts and
52 they have *s* them which shewed
13.28 they Pilate that he should be *s*.
23.14 eat nothing until we have *s* Paul.
Eph 2.16 cross, having *s* the enmity thereby:
Heb 11.37 were *s* with the sword:
Rev 2.13 martyr, who was *s* among you,
5. 6 stood a Lamb as it had been *s*,
9 thou wast *s*, and hast redeemed
12 Worthy is the Lamb that was *s* to
6. 9 that were *s* for the word of God,
11.13 were *s* of men seven thousand:
13. 8 the Lamb *s* from the foundation
18.24 of all that were *s* upon the earth.
19.21 remnant were *s* with the sword of

SLANDER
Nu 14.36 by bringing up a *s* upon the land,
Ps 31.13 For I have heard the *s* of many:
Pr 10.18 and he that uttereth a *s*, is a fool.

SLANDERERS
1Ti 3.11 must their wives be grave, not *s*,

SLANDEREST
Ps 50.20 *s* thine own mother's son.

SLANDERETH
Ps 101. 5 Whoso privily *s* his neighbor,

SLANDEROUSLY
Ro 3. 8 (as we be *s* reported, and as some

SLANDERS
Jer 6.28 revolters, walking with *s*:
9. 4 every neighbor will walk with *s*.

SLAUGHTER
1Sa 14.30 not been now a much greater *s*
Ps 44.22 we are counted as sheep for the *s*.
Pr 7.22 as an ox goeth to the *s*, or as a
Isa 53. 7 he is brought as a lamb to the *s*,
Jer 11.19 or an ox that is brought to the *s*;
12. 3 pull them out like sheep for the *s*,
Eze 9. 2 every man a *s* weapon in his hand;
Hos 5. 2 revolters are profound to make *s*,
Zec 11. 4 my God; Feed the flock of the *s*;
Ac 8.32 He was led as a sheep to the *s*;
9. 1 *s* against the disciples of the Lord,
Ro 8.36 are accounted as sheep for the *s*.
Heb 7. 1 returning from the *s* of the kings,
Jas 5. 5 your hearts, as in a day of *s*.

SLAVE
Jer 2.14 Israel a servant? is he a homeborn *s*?

SLAVES
Rev 18.13 chariots, and *s*, and souls of men.

SLAY
Gen 4.14 one that findeth me shall *s* me.
18.25 *s* the righteous with the wicked:
20. 4 thou *s* also a righteous nation?
11 they will *s* me for my wife's sake.
22.10 and took the knife to *s* his son.
27.41 then will I *s* my brother Jacob.
34.30 together against me, and *s* me;
37.18 conspired against him to *s* him.
20 let us *s* him, and cast him into
26 What profit is it if we *s* our brother,
42.37 *S* my two sons, if I bring him not
43.16 Bring these men home, and *s*,
Ex 2.15 this thing, he sought to *s* Moses.
4.23 I will *s* thy son, even thy firstborn.
5.21 put a sword in their hand to *s* us.
21.14 his neighbor, to *s* him with guile;
23. 7 innocent and righteous *s* thou not:
29.16 And thou shalt *s* the ram, and
32.12 out, to *s* them in the mountains,
27 *s* every man his brother, and every
Lev 4.29 *s* the sin offering in the place of
33 *s* it for a sin offering in the place
14.13 he shall *s* the lamb in the place
20.15 death: and ye shall *s* the beast.
Nu 19. 3 one shall *s* her before his face:
25. 5 *S* ye every one his men that were
35.19 himself shall *s* the murderer:
19 he meeteth him, he shall *s* him.
21 of blood shall *s* the murderer,
Dt 9.28 out to *s* them in the wilderness.
19. 6 the way is long, and *s* him;
27.25 reward to *s* an innocent person:
Jos 13.22 children of Israel *s* with the sword
Jdg 8.19 saved them alive, I would not *s* you.
20 his firstborn, Up, and *s* them.
9.54 Draw thy sword, and *s* me, that
1Sa 2.25 because the Lord would *s* them.
5.10 ark...to us, to *s* us and our people.
11 that it *s* us not, and our people:
14.34 sheep, and *s* them here, and eat;
15. 3 but *s* both man and woman,
19. 5 blood, to *s* David without a cause?
11 him, and to *s* him in the morning:
15 to me in the bed, that I may *s* him.
20. 8 be in me iniquity, *s* me thyself;
33 determined of his father to *s* David.
22.17 Turn, and *s* the priests of the Lord;
2Sa 1. 9 Stand...upon me, and *s* me: for
3.37 it was not of the king to *s* Abner
21. 2 Saul sought to *s* them in his zeal
1Ki 1.51 not *s* his servant with the sword.
3.26 the living child, and in no wise *s* it.
27 the living child, and in no wise *s* it:
15.28 did Baasha *s* him, and reigned in
17.18 to remembrance, and to *s* my son?
18. 9 into the hand of Ahab, to *s* me?
12 he cannot find thee, he shall *s* me:
14 Elijah is here: and he shall *s* me.
19.17 the sword of Hazael shall Jehu *s*:
17 the sword of Jehu shall Elisha *s*.
20.36 from me, a lion shall *s* thee.
2Ki 8.12 young men wilt thou *s* with the
10.25 the captains, Go in, and *s* them;
17.26 *s* them, because they know not
2Ch 20.23 utterly to *s* and destroy them:
23.14 *S* her not in the house of the Lord,
Neh 4.11 and *s* them, and cause the work to
6.10 for they will come to *s* thee;
10 the night will they come to *s* thee.
Est 8.11 to *s*, and to cause to perish, all the
Job 9.23 If the scourge *s* suddenly, he will
13.15 Though he *s* me, yet will I trust
20.16 the viper's tongue shall *s* him.
Ps 34.21 Evil shall *s* the wicked: and they
37.14 and to *s* such as be of upright
32 righteous, and seeketh to *s* him.
59.11 *S* them not, lest my people forget:
94. 6 *s* the widow and the stranger, and
109.16 might even *s* the broken in heart.
139.19 Surely thou wilt *s* the wicked,
Pr 1.32 away of the simple shall *s* them
Isa 11. 4 of his lips shall he *s* the wicked.
14.30 and he shall *s* thy remnant.
27. 1 he shall *s* the dragon that is in the
65.15 for the Lord God shall *s* thee, and
Jer 5. 6 lion out of the forest shall *s* them,
15. 3 sword to *s*, and the dogs to tear,
18.23 their counsel against me to *s* me:
20. 4 and shall *s* them with the sword.
29.21 he shall *s* them before your eyes;
40.14 son of Nethaniah to *s* thee?
15 and I will *s* Ishmael the son of
15 wherefore should he *s* thee, that
41. 8 that said unto Ishmael, *S* us not:
50.27 *S* all her bullocks; let them go
Eze 9. 6 *S* utterly old and young, both
13.19 to *s* the souls that should not die,
23.47 they shall *s* their sons and their
26. 8 *s* with the sword thy daughters in
11 he shall *s* thy people by the sword,
40.39 to *s* thereon the burnt offering
44.11 they shall *s* the burnt offering and
Dan 2.14 was gone forth to *s* the wise men
Hos 2. 3 a dry land, and *s* her with thirst.
9.16 I *s* even the beloved fruit of their
Am 2. 3 will *s* all the princes thereof with
9. 1 *s* the last of them with the sword:
4 the sword, and it shall *s* them:
Hab 1.17 spare continually to *s* the nations?
Zec 11. 5 Whose possessors *s* them, and hold
Lk 11.49 and some of them they shall *s* and
19.27 hither, and *s* them before me.
Jn 5.16 Jesus, and sought to *s* him,
Ac 5.33 heart, and took counsel to *s* them.
9.29 but they went about to *s* him.
11. 7 unto me, Arise, Peter; *s* and eat.
Rev 9.15 year, for to *s* the third part of men.

SLAYETH
Gen 4.15 him, Therefore whosoever *s* Cain,
Dt 22.26 his neighbor, and *s* him,
Job 5. 2 man, and envy *s* the silly one.
Eze 28. 9 before him that *s* thee, I am God?
9 in the hand of him that *s* thee.

SLAYING
Jos 8.24 end of *s* all the inhabitants of Ai
10.20 had made an end of *s* them with
Jdg 9.56 father, in *s* his seventy brethren:
1Ki 17.20 whom I sojourn, by *s* her son?
Isa 22.13 *s* oxen, and killing sheep, eating
57. 5 *s* the children in the valleys
Eze 9. 8 to pass, while they were *s* them,

SLEEP
Gen 2.21 a deep *s* to fall upon Adam, and
28.16 And Jacob awaked out of his *s*,
1Sa 3. 3 was, and Samuel was laid down to *s*;
Job 7.21 for now shall I *s* in the dust; and
Ps 4. 8 both lay me down in peace, and *s*:
78.65 the Lord awaked as one out of *s*,
90. 5 as with a flood; they are as a *s*:
121. 4 Israel shall neither slumber nor *s*.
127. 2 for so he giveth his beloved *s*.
132. 4 I will not give *s* to mine eyes, or
Pr 4.16 and their *s* is taken away, unless
6. 9 How long wilt thou *s*, O sluggard?
10 Yet a little *s*, a little slumber, a
10 a little folding of the hands to *s*:
19.15 Slothfulness casteth into a deep *s*;
20.13 Love not *s*, lest thou come to
Ec 5.12 *s* of a laboring man is sweet,
SS 5. 2 I *s*, but my heart waketh: it is the
Jer 31.26 and my *s* was sweet unto me.
51.39 a perpetual *s*, and not wake,
Dan 12. 2 many of them that *s* in the dust
Zec 4. 1 man that is wakened out of his *s*,
Mt 1.24 Joseph being raised from *s* did as
26.45 *S* on now, and take your rest:
Mk 4.27 And should *s*, and rise night and
14.41 *S* on now, and take your rest:
Lk 9.32 were with him were heavy with *s*:
22.46 Why *s* ye? rise and pray, lest ye
Jn 11.11 that I may awake him out of *s*.
12 Lord, if he *s*, he shall do well.
13 had spoken of taking of rest in *s*.
Ac 13.36 fell on *s*, and was laid unto his
16.27 of the prison awaking out of his *s*,
20. 9 being fallen into a deep *s*:
9 he sunk down with *s*, and fell
Ro 13.11 it is high time to awake out of *s*:
1Co 11.30 sickly among you, and many *s*.
15.51 We shall not all *s*, but we shall all
1Th 4.14 so them also which *s* in Jesus
5. 6 let us not *s*, as do others; but let
7 For they that *s* *s* in the night;
10 for us, that, whether we wake or *s*,

SLEEPER
Jon 1. 6 What meanest thou, O *s*? arise,

SLEEPEST
Ps 44.23 why *s* thou, O Lord? arise, cast
Pr 6.22 when thou *s*, it shall keep thee;
Mk 14.37 saith unto Peter, Simon, *s* thou?
Eph 5.14 Awake thou that *s*, and arise from

SLEEPETH
1Ki 18.27 peradventure he *s*, and must be
Pr 10. 5 *s* in harvest is a son that causeth
Hos 7. 6 wait: their baker *s* all the night;
Mt 9.24 for the maid is not dead, but *s*.
Mk 5.39 the damsel is not dead, but *s*.
Lk 8.52 Weep not; she is not dead, but *s*.
Jn 11.11 unto them, Our friend Lazarus *s*;

SLEEPING
1Sa 26. 7 Saul lay *s* within the trench, and
Isa 56.10 *s*, lying down, loving to slumber.
Mk 13.36 coming suddenly he find you *s*.
14.37 he cometh, and findeth them *s*,
Lk 22.45 he found them *s* for sorrow,
Ac 12. 6 Peter was *s* between two soldiers,

SLEIGHT
Eph 4.14 by the *s* of men, and cunning

SLEPT
Job 3.13 and been quiet, I should have *s*:
Ps 3. 5 I laid me down and *s*; I awaked;
Mt 13.25 But while men *s*, his enemy came
25. 5 tarried, they all slumbered and *s*.
27.52 bodies of the saints which *s* arose,
28.13 and stole him away while we *s*.
1Co 15.20 the firstfruits of them that *s*.

SLEW

Gen 4. 8 Abel his brother, and *s* him.
25 seed instead of Abel, whom Cain *s*.
34.25 the city boldly, and *s* all the males.
26 they *s* Hamor and Shechem his son
38. 7 of the Lord; and the Lord *s* him.
10 the Lord: wherefore he *s* him also.
49. 6 for in their anger they *s* a man,
Ex 2.12 he *s* the Egyptian, and hid him in
13.15 the Lord *s* all the firstborn in the
Lev 8.15 And he *s* it; and Moses took the
23 And he *s* it; and Moses took of the
9. 8 *s* the calf of the sin offering, which
12 And he *s* the burnt offering; and
15 *s* it, and offered it for sin, as the
18 He *s* also the bullock and the ram
Nu 31. 7 Moses; and they *s* all the males.
8 they *s* the kings of Midian, beside
8 son of Beor they *s* with the sword.
Jos 8.21 again, and *s* the men of Ai.
9.26 of Israel, that they *s* them not.
10.10 *s* them with a great slaughter at
11 children of Israel *s* with...sword.
26 Joshua smote them, and *s* them,
11.17 took, and smote them, and *s* them.
Jdg 1. 4 *s* of them in Bezek ten thousand
5 and they *s* the Canaanites and the
10 and they *s* Sheshai, and Ahiman,
17 *s* the Canaanites that inhabited
3.29 they *s* of Moab at that time about
31 *s* of the Philistines six hundred
7.25 they *s* Oreb upon the rock Oreb,
25 and Zeeb they *s* at the winepress of
8.17 Penuel, and *s* the men of the city.
18 were they whom ye *s* at Tabor?
21 arose, and *s* Zebah and Zalmunna,
9. 5 *s* his brethren...sons of Jerubbaal,
24 their brother, which *s* them; and
44 were in the fields, and *s* them.
45 *s* the people that was therein,
54 say not of me, A woman *s* him.
12. 6 *s* him at the passages of Jordan:
14.19 *s* thirty men of them, and took
15.15 and *s* a thousand men therewith.
16.24 our country, which *s* many of us.
30 the dead which he *s* at his death
30 than they which he *s* in his life.
20.45 and *s* two thousand men of them.
1Sa 1.25 they *s* a bullock, and brought the
4. 2 and they *s* of the army in the field
11.11 *s* the Ammonites until the heat of
14.13 and his armorbearer *s* after him.
32 calves, and *s* them on the ground:
34 him that night, and *s* them there.
17.35 beard, and smote him, and *s* him.
36 Thy servant *s* both the lion and
50 smote the Philistine, and *s* him;
51 and *s* him, and cut off his head
18.27 *s* of the Philistines two hundred
19. 5 in his hand, and *s* the Philistine,
8 and *s* them with a great slaughter;
22.18 *s* on that day fourscore and five
29. 5 Saul *s* his thousands, and David
30. 2 they *s* not any, either great or
31. 2 and the Philistines *s* Jonathan,
2Sa 1.10 So I stood upon him, and *s* him,
3.30 and Abishai his brother *s* Abner,
4. 7 and they smote him, and *s* him,
10 hold of him, and *s* him in Ziklag,
12 and they *s* them, and cut off their
8. 5 David *s* of the Syrians two and
10.18 David *s* the men of seven hundred
14. 6 one smote the other, and *s* him.
7 the life of his brother whom he *s*;
18.15 and smote Absalom, and *s* him.
21. 1 house, because he *s* the Gibeonites,
18 Sibbechai the Hushathite *s* Saph,
19 *s* the brother of Goliath the Gittite,
21 the brother of David *s* him.
23. 8 hundred, whom he *s* at one time.
12 defended it, and *s* the Philistines:
18 three hundred, and *s* them, and
20 he *s* two lionlike men of Moab:
20 and *s* a lion in the midst of a pit
21 And he *s* an Egyptian, a goodly
21 and *s* him with his own spear.
1Ki 1. 9 Adonijah *s* sheep and oxen and
2. 5 and unto Amasa...whom he *s*,
32 than he, and *s* them with the sword,
34 up, and fell upon him, and *s* him:
11.24 when David *s* them of Zobah:
13.24 met him by the way, and *s* him:
16.11 that he *s* all the house of Baasha:
18.13 I did when Jezebel *s* the prophets
40 brook Kishon, and *s* them there.
19.21 took a yoke of oxen, and *s* them,
20.20 And they *s* every one his man:
21 and *s* the Syrians with a great
29 Israel *s* of the Syrians an hundred
36 him, a lion found him, and *s* him.
2Ki 9.31 Zimri peace, who *s* his master?
10. 7 king's sons, and *s* seventy persons,
9 against my master, and *s* him:
9 but who *s* all these?
11 So Jehu *s* all that remained of the
14 *s* them at the pit of the shearing
17 he *s* all that remained unto Ahab
11.18 and *s* Mattan the priest of Baal
20 they *s* Athaliah with the sword
12.20 and *s* Joash in the house of Millo,
14. 5 *s* his servants which had slain the
6 children of...murderers he *s* not:
7 *s* of Edom in the valley of salt ten
19 him to Lachish, and *s* him there.
15.10, 14 *s* him, and reigned in his stead.
30 *s* him, and reigned in his stead,
16. 9 of it captive to Kir, and *s* Rezin.
17.25 them, which *s* some of them.
21.23 and *s* the king in his own house.
24 *s* all them that had conspired
23.20 he *s* all the priests of the high
29 he *s* him at Megiddo, when he had
25. 7 And they *s* the sons of Zedekiah
21 *s* them at Riblah in the land
1Ch 2. 3 sight of the Lord; and he *s* him.
7.21 that were born in that land *s*,
10. 2 and the Philistines *s* Jonathan,
14 *s* him, and turned the kingdom
11.14 delivered it, and *s* the Philistines;
20 against three hundred, he *s* them,
22 he *s* two lionlike men of Moab:
22 *s* a lion in a pit in a snowy day.
23 he *s* an Egyptian, a man of great
23 and *s* him with his own spear.
18. 5 David *s* of the Syrians two and
12 *s* of the Edomites in the valley of
19.18 and David *s* of the Syrians seven
20. 4 Sibbechai the Hushathite *s* Sippai,
5 Elhanan the son of Jair *s* Lahmi
7 of Shimea David's brother *s* him.
2Ch 13.17 And Abijah and his people *s* them
21. 4 *s* all his brethren with the sword,
22. 8 ministered to Ahaziah, he *s* them.
11 Athaliah, so that she *s* him not.
23.15 the king's house, they *s* her there.
17 and *s* Mattan the priest of Baal
24.22 not the kindness...but *s* his son.
25 and *s* him on his bed, and he died:
25. 3 he *s* his servants that had killed
4 But he *s* not their children, but
27 to Lachish after him, and *s* him
28. 6 *s* in Judah an hundred and
7 *s* Maaseiah the king's son, and
32.21 *s* him there with the sword.
33.24 and *s* him in his own house.
25 *s* all them that had conspired
36.17 who *s* their young men with the
Neh 9.26 and *s* thy prophets which testified
Est 9. 6 Jews *s* and destroyed five hundred
10 the enemy of the Jews, *s* they;
15 *s* three hundred men at Shushan;
16 and *s* of their foes seventy and five
Ps 78.31 *s* the fattest of them, and smote
34 When he *s* them, then they sought
105.29 waters into blood, and *s* their fish.
135.10 great nations, and *s* mighty kings;
136.18 And *s* famous kings; for his mercy
Isa 66. 3 killeth an ox as if he *s* a man;
Jer 20.17 he *s* me not from the womb; or
26.23 king; who *s* him with the sword,
39. 6 Babylon *s* the sons of Zedekiah
6 Babylon *s* all the nobles of Judah.
41. 2 *s* him, whom the king of Babylon
3 Ishmael also *s* all the Jews that
7 the son of Nethaniah *s* them, and
8 *s* them not among their brethren.
52.10 Babylon *s* the sons of Zedekiah
10 he *s* also all the princes of Judah
La 2. 4 *s* all that were pleasant to the eye
Eze 9. 7 they went forth, and *s* in the city.
23.10 daughters, and *s* her with the sword:
40.41 whereupon they *s*...sacrifices.
42 they *s* the burnt offering and the
Dan 3.22 the flame of the fire *s* those men
5.19 whom he would he *s*; and whom he
Mt 2.16 *s* all the children...in Bethlehem,
21.39 out of the vineyard, and *s* him.
22. 6 them spitefully, and *s* them.
23.35 *s* between the temple and...altar.
Lk 13. 4 tower in Siloam fell, and *s* them,
Ac 5.30 raised up Jesus, whom ye *s* and
10.39 whom they *s* and hanged on a tree:
22.20 kept the raiment of them that *s* him.
Ro 7.11 deceived me, and by it *s* me.
1Jn 3.12 wicked one, and *s* his brother.
12 And wherefore *s* he him? Because

SLIDE

Dt 32.35 their foot shall *s* in due time:
Ps 26. 1 the Lord; therefore I shall not *s*.
37.31 his heart; none of his steps shall *s*.

SLIGHTLY

Jer 6.14 of the daughter of my people *s*,
8.11 of the daughter of my people *s*,

SLIME

Gen 11. 3 stone, and *s* had they for morter.
Ex 2. 3 daubed it with *s* and with pitch,

SLING

Jdg 20.16 could *s* stones at an hair breadth,
1Sa 17.40 and his *s* was in his hand: and he
50 with a *s* and with a stone,
25.29 enemies, them shall he *s* out, as
29 as out of the middle of a *s*.
Pr 26. 8 As he that bindeth a stone in a *s*,
Jer 10.18 *s* out the inhabitants of the land
Zec 9.15 devour, and subdue with *s* stones;

SLINGS

2Ch 26.14 and bows, and *s* to cast stones.

SLINGSTONES

Job 41.28 *s* are turned with him into

SLIP

2Sa 22.37 me; so that my feet did not *s*.
Job 12. 5 He that is ready to *s* with his feet
Ps 17. 5 thy paths, that my footsteps *s* not.
18.36 under me, that my feet did not *s*.
Heb 2. 1 at any time we should let them *s*.

SLIPPED

1Sa 19.10 he *s* away out of Saul's presence,
Ps 73. 2 gone; my steps had well nigh *s*.

SLIPPERY

Ps 35. 6 Let their way be dark and *s*: and
73.18 thou didst set them in *s* places:
Jer 23.12 way shall be unto them as *s* ways

SLIPPETH
Dt 19. 5 and the head *s* from the helve,
Ps 38.16 when my foot *s*, they magnify
94.18 When I said, My foot *s*; thy mercy,

SLOTHFUL
Jdg 18. 9 be not *s* to go, and to enter to
Pr 12.24 but the *s* shall be under tribute.
27 The *s* man roasteth not that which
15.19 way of the *s* man is as an hedge
18. 9 He also that is *s* in his work is
19.24 A *s* man hideth his hand in his
21.25 The desire of the *s* killeth him;
22.13 The *s* man saith, There is a lion
24.30 I went by the field of the *s*, and by
26.13 The *s* man saith, There is a lion in
14 hinges, so doth the *s* upon his bed.
15 *s* hideth his hand in his bosom;
Mt 25.26 Thou wicked and *s* servant, thou
Ro 12.11 Not *s* in business; fervent in spirit;
Heb 6.12 That ye be not *s*, but followers of

SLOTHFULNESS
Pr 19.15 *S* casteth into a deep sleep; and
Ec 10.18 By much *s* the building decayeth;

SLOW
Ex 4.10 *s* of speech, and of a *s* tongue.
Neh 9.17 *s* to anger, and of great kindness,
Ps 103. 8 *s* to anger, and plenteous in mercy,
145. 8 *s* to anger, and of great mercy.
Pr 14.29 He that is *s* to wrath is of great
15.18 that is *s* to anger appeaseth strife.
16.32 He that is *s* to anger is better than
Joel 2.13 *s* to anger, and of great kindness,
Jon 4. 2 *s* to anger, and of great kindness,
Na 1. 3 The Lord is *s* to anger, and great in
Lk 24.25 O fools, and *s* of heart to believe
Tit 1.12 alway liars, evil beasts, *s* bellies.
Jas 1.19 to hear, *s* to speak, *s* to wrath:

SLOWLY
Ac 27. 7 when we had sailed *s* many days,

SLUGGARD
Pr 6. 6 Go to the ant, thou *s*; consider
9 How long wilt thou sleep, O *s*?
10.26 so is the *s* to them that send him.
13. 4 The soul of the *s* desireth, and
20. 4 The *s* will not plow by reason of
26.16 The *s* is wiser in his own conceit

SLUMBER
Ps 121. 3 he that keepeth thee will not *s*.
4 Israel shall neither *s* nor sleep.
132. 4 to my eyes, or *s* to mine eyelids,
Pr 6. 4 thine eyes, nor *s* to thine eyelids.
10 Yet a little sleep, a little *s*, a little
24.33 Yet a little sleep, a little *s*, a little
Isa 5.27 none shall *s* nor sleep; neither
56.10 sleeping, lying down, loving to *s*.
Na 3.18 Thy shepherds *s*, O king of
Ro 11. 8 hath given them the spirit of *s*,

SLUMBERED
Mt 25. 5 tarried, they all *s* and slept.

SLUMBERETH
2Pe 2. 3 not, and their damnation *s* not.

SLUMBERINGS
Job 33.15 upon men, in *s* upon the bed;

SMALL
Gen 19.11 with blindness, both *s* and great:
30.15 a *s* matter that thou hast taken
Ex 9. 9 shall become *s* dust in all the land
16.14 wilderness...lay a *s* round thing,
14 as *s* as the hoar frost on the ground.
18.22 every *s* matter they shall judge:
26 *s* matter they judged themselves.
30.36 thou shalt beat some of it very *s*,
Lev 16.12 full of sweet incense beaten *s*,
Nu 16. 9 it but a *s* thing unto you, that
13 *s* thing that thou has brought us
32.41 and took the *s* towns thereof,
Dt 1.17 hear the *s* as well as the great;
9.21 stamped it, and ground it very *s*,
21 even until it was as *s* as dust:
25.13 divers weights, a great and a *s*.
14 divers measures, a great and a *s*.
32. 2 as the *s* rain upon the tender herb,
1Sa 5. 9 men of the city, both *s* and great,
20. 2 will do nothing either great or *s*,
30. 2 slew not any, either great or *s*,
19 to them, neither *s* nor great,
2Sa 7.19 this was yet a *s* thing in thy sight,
17.13 be not one *s* stone found there.
22.43 I beat them as *s* as the dust of the
1Ki 2.20 I desire one *s* petition of thee;
19.12 and after the fire a still *s* voice.
22.31 Fight neither with *s* nor great,
2Ki 19.26 their inhabitants were of *s* power,
23. 2 all the people, both *s* and great:
6, 15 and stamped it *s* to powder,
25.26 all the people, both *s* and great,
1Ch 17.17 this was a *s* thing in thine eyes,
25. 8 ward, as well the *s* as the great,
26.13 lots, as well the *s* as the great,
2Ch 15.13 put to death, whether *s* or great,
18.30 Fight ye not with *s* or great, save
24.24 came with a *s* company of men,
31.15 as well to the great as to the *s*:
34.30 and all the people, great and *s*:
35. 8 thousand and six hundred *s* cattle,
9 offerings five thousand *s* cattle,
36.18 of the house of God, great and *s*,
Est 1. 5 both unto great and *s*, seven days,
20 honor, both to great and *s*.
Job 3.19 The *s* and great are there; and the
8. 7 Though thy beginning was *s*, yet
15.11 consolations of God *s* with thee?
36.27 he maketh *s* the drops of water:
37. 6 likewise to the *s* rain, and to the
Ps 18.42 did I beat them *s* as the dust before
104.25 both *s* and great beasts.
115.13 fear the Lord, both *s* and great.
119.141 I am *s* and despised: yet do not
Pr 24.10 day of adversity, thy strength is *s*.
Ec 2. 7 possessions of great and *s* cattle
Isa 1. 9 left unto us a very *s* remnant,
7.13 Is it a *s* thing for you to weary men,
16.14 the remnant shall be very *s* and
22.24 all vessels of *s* quantity, from the
29. 5 thy strangers shall be like *s* dust,
37.27 their inhabitants were of *s* power,
40.15 counted as the *s* dust of the balance:
41.15 the mountains, and beat them *s*,
43.23 me the *s* cattle of thy burnt offerings;
54. 7 For a *s* moment have I forsaken
60.22 and a *s* one a strong nation:
Jer 16. 6 Both the great and the *s* shall die
30.19 them, and they shall not be *s*.
44.28 Yet a *s* number that escape the
49.15 I will make thee *s* among the
Eze 16.20 of thy whoredoms a *s* matter,
34.18 Seemeth it a *s* thing unto you to
Dan 11.23 become strong with a *s* people.
Am 7. 2, 5 shall Jacob arise? for he is *s*.
8. 5 forth wheat, making the ephah *s*,
Ob 2 made thee *s* among the heathen:
Zec 4.10 hath despised the day of *s* things?
Mk 3. 9 that a *s* ship should wait on him
8. 7 And they had a few *s* fishes: and
Jn 2.15 he had made a scourge of *s* cords,
6. 9 five barley loaves,...two *s* fishes:
Ac 12.18 was no *s* stir among the soldiers,
15. 2 no *s* dissension and disputation
19.23 arose no *s* stir about that way.
24 no *s* gain unto the craftsman;
26.22 witnessing both to *s* and great,
27.20 and no *s* tempest lay on us, all
1Co 4. 3 with me it is a very *s* thing that
Jas 3. 4 turned about with a very *s* helm,
Rev 11.18 that fear thy name, *s* and great;
13.16 both *s* and great, rich and poor,
19. 5 that fear him, both *s* and great.
18 free and bond, both *s* and great.
20.12 And I saw the dead, *s* and great,

SMALLEST
1Sa 9.21 of the *s* of the tribes of Israel?
1Co 6. 2 unworthy to judge the *s* matters?

SMELL
Gen 27.27 *s* of my son is as the *s* of a field
Lev 26.31 will not *s* the savor of your sweet
Dt 4.28 see, nor hear, nor eat, nor *s*.
Ps 45. 8 All thy garments *s* of myrrh, and
115. 6 noses have they, but they *s* not:
SS 1.12 my spikenard sendeth forth the *s*
2.13 the tender grape give a good *s*.
4.10 and the *s* of thine ointments than
7. 8 and the *s* of thy nose like apples;
Isa 3.24 instead of sweet *s* there shall be
Dan 3.27 nor the *s* of fire had passed on
Am 5.21 not *s* in your solemn assemblies.
Php 4.18 an odor of a sweet *s*, a sacrifice

SMELLED
Gen 8.21 And the Lord *s* a sweet savor;
27.27 and he *s* the smell of his raiment,

SMELLETH
Job 39.25 and he *s* the battle afar off, the

SMELLING
SS 5. 5 my fingers with sweet *s* myrrh,
13 lilies, dropping sweet *s* myrrh.
1Co 12.17 were hearing, where were the *s*?

SMITE
Gen 8.21 neither will I again *s* any more
32. 8 come to the one company, and *s* it,
11 him, lest he will come and *s* me,
Ex 3.20 *s* Egypt with all my wonders which
7.17 I will *s* with the rod that is in mine
8. 2 I will *s* all thy borders with frogs:
16 and *s* the dust of the land, that it
9.15 I may *s* thee and thy people with
12.12 will *s* all the firstborn in the land of
13 you, when I *s* the land of Egypt.
23 pass through to *s* the Egyptians;
23 come in unto your houses to *s* you.
17. 6 thou shalt *s* the rock, and there
21.18 and one *s* another with a stone, or
20 And if a man *s* his servant, or his
26 if a man *s* the eye of his servant,
27 he *s* out his manservant's tooth,
Nu 14.12 I will *s* them with the pestilence,
22. 6 that we may *s* them, and that I may
24.17 and shall *s* the corners of Moab,
25.17 Vex the Midianites, and *s* them:
35.16 if he *s* him with an instrument of
17 if he *s* him with throwing a stone,
18 if he *s* him with an hand weapon
21 Or in enmity *s* him with his hand,
Dt 7. 2 thou shalt *s* them, and utterly
13.15 Thou shalt surely *s* the inhabitants
19.11 and *s* him mortally that he die, and
20.13 thou shalt *s* every male thereof
28.22 shall *s* thee with a consumption,
27 *s* thee with the botch of Egypt,
28 Lord shall *s* thee with madness,
35 The Lord shall *s* thee in the knees,
33.11 *s* through the loins of them that
Jos 7. 3 thousand men go up and *s* Ai;
10. 4 help me, that we may *s* Gibeon:
19 and *s* the hindmost of them;
12. 6 Lord and the children of Israel *s*:
13.12 these did Moses *s*, and cast them
Jdg 6.16 shalt *s* the Midianites as one man.
20.31 and they began to *s* of the people,

39 Benjamin began to *s* and kill of the
21.10 saying, Go and *s* the inhabitants of
1Sa 15. 3 Now go and *s* Amalek, and utterly
17.46 I will *s* thee, and take thine head
18.11 I will *s* David even to the wall with
19.10 Saul sought to *s* David even to the
20.33 Saul cast a javelin at him to *s* him:
23. 2 Shall I go and *s* these Philistines?
2 Go, and *s* the Philistines, and save
26. 8 therefore let me *s* him, I pray thee,
8 and I will not *s* him the second time.
10 Lord liveth, the Lord shall *s* him;
2Sa 2.22 should I *s* thee to the ground?
5.24 to *s* the host of the Philistines.
13.28 when I say unto you, *S* Amnon;
15.14 and *s* the city with the edge of the
17. 2 flee; and I will *s* the king only:
18.11 thou not *s* him there to the ground?
1Ki 14.15 the Lord shall *s* Israel, as a reed
20.35 word of the Lord, *S* me, I pray thee.
35 And the man refused to *s* him.
37 man, and said, *S* me, I pray thee.
2Ki 3.19 And ye shall *s* every fenced city,
6.18 *S* this people, I pray thee, with
21 shall I *s* them? shall I *s* them?
22 answered, Thou shalt not *s* them:
22 thou *s* those whom thou hast taken
9. 7 thou shalt *s* the house of Ahab thy
27 and said, *S* him also in the chariot.
13.17 thou shalt *s* the Syrians in Aphek.
18 king of Israel, *S* upon the ground.
19 now thou shalt *s* Syria but thrice.
1Ch 14.15 to *s* the host of the Philistines.
2Ch 21.14 plague will the Lord *s* thy people,
Ps 121. 6 The sun shall not *s* thee by day,
141. 5 Let the righteous *s* me; it shall be
Pr 19.25 *S* a scorner, and the simple will
Isa 3.17 Lord will *s* with a scab the crown
10.24 he shall *s* thee with a rod, and
11. 4 he shall *s* the earth with the rod of
15 and shall *s* it in the seven streams,
19.22 And the Lord shall *s* Egypt: he
22 he shall *s* and heal it: and they
49.10 shall the heat nor sun *s* them:
58. 4 and to *s* with the fist of wickedness:
Jer 18.18 and let us *s* him with the tongue,
21. 6 And I will *s* the inhabitants of this
7 he shall *s* them with the edge of the
43.11 he shall *s* the land of Egypt, and
46.13 come and *s* the land of Egypt.
49.28 which Nebuchadrezzar...shall *s*,
Eze 5. 2 part, and *s* about it with a knife:
6.11 *S* with thine hand, and stamp with
9. 5 after him through the city, and *s*:
21.12 *s* therefore upon thy thigh.
14 and *s* thine hands together, and
17 I will also *s* mine hands together,
32.15 when I shall *s* all them that dwell
39. 3 And I will *s* thy bow out of thy left
Am 3.15 I will *s* the winter house with the
6.11 and he will *s* the great house with
9. 1 *S* the lintel of the door, that the
Mic 5. 1 *s* the judge of Israel with a rod
Na 2.10 the knees *s* together, and much
Zec 9. 4 and he will *s* her power in the sea;
10.11 and shall *s* the waves in the sea,
11. 6 they shall *s* the land, and out of
12. 4 *s* every horse with astonishment,
4 *s* every horse of the people with
13. 7 *s* the shepherd, and the sheep shall
14.12 the Lord will *s* all the people that
18 the Lord will *s* the heathen that
Mal 4. 6 come and *s* the earth with a curse.
Mt 5.39 shall *s* thee on thy right cheek,
24.49 begin to *s* his fellowservants,
26.31 I will *s* the shepherd, and the
Mk 14.27 I will *s* the shepherd, and the
Lk 22.49 Lord, shall we *s* with the sword?
Ac 23. 2 by him to *s* him on the mouth.
3 God shall *s* thee, thou whited wall:
2Co 11.20 if a man *s* you on the face.
Rev 11. 6 to *s* the earth with all plagues,
19.15 with it he should *s* the nations:

SMITERS

Isa 50. 6 I gave my back to the *s*, and my

SMITEST

Ex 2.13 Wherefore *s* thou thy fellow?
Jn 18.23 evil: but if well, why *s* thou me?

SMITETH

Ex 21.12 He that *s* a man, so that he die,
15 he that *s* his father, or his mother,
Dt 25.11 out of the hand of him that *s* him,
27.24 he that *s* his neighbor secretly.
Jos 15.16 He that *s* Kirjath-sepher, and
Jdg 1.12 He that *s* Kirjath-sepher, and
2Sa 5. 8 and *s* the Jebusites, and the lame
1Ch 11. 6 Whosoever *s* the Jebusites first
Job 26.12 he *s* through the proud.
Isa 9.13 turneth not unto him that *s* them,
La 3.30 giveth his cheek to him that *s* him:
Eze 7. 9 know that I am the Lord that *s*.
Lk 6.29 him that *s* thee on the one cheek

SMITH

1Sa 13.19 no *s* found throughout all the
Isa 44.12 The *s* with the tongs both
54.16 created the *s* that bloweth the

SMITHS

2Ki 24.14 and all the craftsmen and *s*:
16 craftsmen and *s* a thousand, all
Jer 24. 1 with the carpenters and *s*, from
29. 2 and the carpenters, and the *s*, were

SMITING

Ex 2.11 he spied an Egyptian *s* an Hebrew,
2Sa 8.13 he returned from *s* of the Syrians
1Ki 20.37 him, so that in *s* he wounded him.
2Ki 3.24 they went forward *s* the Moabites,
Mic 6.13 will I make thee sick in *s* thee,

SMITTEN

Nu 22.32 thou *s* thine ass these three times?
1Sa 4. 3 Wherefore hath the Lord *s* us to
Isa 24.12 and the gate is *s* with destruction.
53. 4 stricken, *s* of God, and afflicted.
Hos 6. 1 he hath *s*, and he will bind us up.
Ac 23. 3 me to be *s* contrary to the law?
Rev 8.12 the third part of the sun was *s*,

SMOKE

Ex 19.18 Sinai was altogether on a *s*,
Jdg 20.40 up out of the city with a pillar of *s*,
Job 41.20 Out of his nostrils goeth *s*, as out
Ps 37.20 into *s* shall they consume away.
68. 2 As *s* is driven away, so drive them
102. 3 my days are consumed like *s*, and
104.32 toucheth the hills, and they *s*.
Pr 10.26 to the teeth, and as *s* to the eyes,
Isa 6. 4 and the house was filled with *s*.
51. 6 heavens shall vanish away like *s*,
Hos 13. 3 and as the *s* out of the chimney.
Joel 2.30 blood, and fire, and pillars of *s*.
Ac 2.19 blood, and fire, and vapor of *s*:
Rev 8. 4 And the *s* of the incense, which
9. 2 and there arose a *s* out of the pit,
2 as the *s* of a great furnace; and the
2 was darkened by reason of the *s*
3 there came out of the *s* locusts
17 issued fire and *s* and brimstone.
18 killed, by the fire, and by the *s*,
14.11 the *s* of their torment ascendeth
15. 8 filled with *s* from the glory of God,
18. 9 they shall see the *s* of her burning,
18 when they saw the *s* of her burning,
19. 3 And her *s* rose up for ever and ever.

SMOKING

Gen 15.17 behold a *s* furnace, and a burning
Ex 20.18 the trumpet, and the mountain *s*:
Isa 7. 4 the two tails of these *s* firebrands,
42. 3 the *s* flax shall he not quench:
Mt 12.20 and *s* flax shall he not quench,

SMOOTH

Gen 27.11 a hairy man, and I am a *s* man:
16 hands, and upon the *s* of his neck:
1Sa 17.40 chose him five *s* stones out of the
Isa 30.10 speak unto us *s* things, prophesy
57. 6 Among the *s* stones of the stream
Lk 3. 5 the rough ways shall be made *s*;

SMOOTHER

Ps 55.21 of his mouth were *s* than butter,
Pr 5. 3 and her mouth is *s* than oil:

SMOTE

Gen 14. 5 and *s* the Rephaims in Ashteroth
7 *s* all the country of the Amalekites,
36.35 who *s* Midian in the field of Moab,
Ex 7.20 *s* the waters that were in the river,
8.17 his rod, and *s* the dust of the earth,
12.27 Egypt, when he *s* the Egyptians,
29 the Lord *s* all the firstborn in the
Nu 3.13 that I *s* all the firstborn in the land
14.45 and *s* them, and discomfited them,
20.11 with his rod he *s* the rock twice:
32. 4 the country which the Lord *s*
Jos 7. 5 men of Ai *s* of them about thirty
9.18 the children of Israel *s* them not,
10.10 and *s* them to Azekah, and unto
26 afterward Joshua *s* them, and slew
28 and *s* it with the edge of the sword,
11. 8 who *s* them, and chased them unto
8 *s* them, until they left them none
10 *s* the king thereof with the sword:
11 *s* all the souls that were therein
20. 5 he *s* his neighbor unwittingly,
Jdg 1.25 they *s* the city with the edge of the
3.13 and Amalek, and went and *s* Israel,
4.21 and *s* the nail into his temples,
5.26 with the hammer she *s* Sisera,
8.11 Gideon went up...and *s* the host:
12. 4 and the men of Gilead *s* Ephraim,
15. 8 *s* them hip and thigh with a great
20.35 Lord *s* Benjamin before Israel:
1Sa 4. 8 are the Gods that *s* the Egyptians
7.11 pursued the Philistines, and *s* them,
13. 3 *s* the garrison of the Philistines
15. 7 And Saul *s* the Amalekites from
17.35 I went out after him, and *s* him,
49 and *s* the Philistine in his forehead,
50 with a stone, and *s* the Philistine,
19.10 and he *s* the javelin into the wall:
23. 5 and *s* them with a great slaughter.
24. 5 afterward, that David's heart *s* him,
25.38 the Lord *s* Nabal, that he died.
27. 9 David *s* the land, and left neither
2Sa 1.15 him. And he *s* him that he died.
2.23 spear *s* him under the fifth rib,
6. 7 and God *s* him there for his error;
8. 1 that David *s* the Philistines, and
18.15 and *s* Absalom, and slew him.
2Ki 2. 8 his mantle,...and *s* the waters,
15. 5 And the Lord *s* the king, so that he
25 against him, and *s* him in Samaria,
25.21 And the king of Babylon *s* them,
1Ch 1.46 which *s* Midian in the field of Moab,
14.11 and David *s* them there.
2Ch 13.15 God *s* Jeroboam and all Israel
14.12 Lord *s* the Ethiopians before Asa,
18.23 and *s* Micaiah upon the cheek, and
33 *s* the king of Israel between the
21. 9 up by night, and *s* the Edomites
18 the Lord *s* him in his bowels with
28. 5 and they *s* him, and carried away
23 gods of Damascus, which *s* him:
Est 9. 5 the Jews *s* all their enemies with
Job 1.19 *s* the four corners of the house,
2. 7 *s* Job with sore boils from the
Ps 60(T) and *s* of Edom in the valley of

Ps 78.20 he *s* the rock, that the waters
51 And *s* all the firstborn in Egypt;
105.33 He *s* their vines also and their fig
SS 5. 7 me, they *s* me, they wounded me;
Isa 10.20 again stay upon him that *s* them;
14. 6 He who *s* the people in wrath with
29 rod of him that *s* thee is broken:
41. 7 the hammer him that *s* the anvil,
60.10 for in my wrath I *s* thee, but in my
Dan 2.34 *s* the image upon his feet that were
5. 6 his knees *s* one against another.
8. 7 and *s* the ram, and brake his two
Mt 26.51 the high priest's, and *s* off his ear.
67 others *s* him with the palms of
68 thou Christ, Who is he that *s* thee?
Mk 14.47 and *s* a servant of the high priest,
Lk 18.13 *s* upon his breast, saying, God be
22.50 *s* the servant of the high priest,
63 held Jesus mocked him,...*s* him.
64 Prophesy, who is it that *s* thee?
Jn 18.10 and *s* the high priest's servant,
19. 3 they *s* him with their hands.
Ac 7.24 oppressed, and *s* the Egyptian:
12. 7 he *s* Peter on the side, and raised
23 angel of the Lord *s* him, because

SMOTEST

Ex 17. 5 rod, wherewith thou *s* the river,

SMYRNA

Rev 1.11 unto *S*, and unto Pergamos, and
2. 8 unto the angel of the church in *S*

SNAIL

Lev 11.30 and the lizard, and the *s*, and the
Ps 58. 8 As a *s* which melteth, let every

SNARE

Ex 10. 7 shall this man be a *s* unto us?
23.33 it will surely be a *s* unto thee.
34.12 it be for a *s* in the midst of thee:
Dt 7.16 for that will be a *s* unto thee.
Jdg 2. 3 their gods shall be a *s* unto you.
8.27 thing became a *s* unto Gideon,
1Sa 18.21 that she may be a *s* to him, and
28. 9 then layest thou a *s* for my life,
Job 18. 8 feet, and he walketh upon a *s*.
10 *s* is laid for him in the ground,
Ps 69.22 Let their table become a *s* before
91. 3 thee from the *s* of the fowler, and
106.36 idols: which were a *s* unto them.
119.110 The wicked have laid a *s* for me:
124. 7 bird out of the *s* of the fowlers:
7 *s* is broken, and we are escaped.
140. 5 The proud have hid a *s* for me, and
142. 3 have they privily laid a *s* for me.
Pr 7.23 as a bird hasteth to the *s*, and
18. 7 and his lips are the *s* of his soul.
20.25 It is a *s* to the man who devoureth
22.25 his ways, and get a *s* to thy soul.
29. 6 of an evil man there is a *s*: but the
8 Scornful men bring a city into a *s*:
25 The fear of man bringeth a *s*:
Ec 9.12 birds that are caught in the *s*;
Isa 8.14 and for a *s* to the inhabitants of
24.17 the pit, and the *s*, are upon thee,
18 of the pit shall be taken in the *s*:
29.21 lay a *s* for him that reproveth in
Jer 48.43 the pit, and the *s*, shall be upon
44 of the pit shall be taken in the *s*:
50.24 I have laid a *s* for thee, and thou
La 3.47 Fear and a *s* is come upon us,
Eze 12.13 and he shall be taken in my *s*:
17.20 him, and he shall be taken in my *s*,
Hos 5. 1 ye have been a *s* on Mizpah, and
9. 8 the prophet is a *s* of a fowler in all
Am 3. 5 a bird fall in a *s* upon the earth,
5 shall one take up a *s* from the
Lk 21.35 as a *s* shall it come on all them
Ro 11. 9 Let their table be made a *s*, and a
1Co 7.35 not that I may cast a *s* upon you,
1Ti 3. 7 reproach and the *s* of the devil.
6. 9 rich fall into temptation and a *s*,
2Ti 2.26 themselves out of the *s* of the devil,

SNARED

Dt 7.25 unto thee, lest thou be *s* therein:
12.30 thou be not *s* by following them,
Ps 9.16 wicked is *s* in the work of his own
Pr 6. 2 *s* with the words of thy mouth,
12.13 wicked is *s* by the transgression
Ec 9.12 the sons of men *s* in an evil time,
Isa 8.15 be broken, and be *s*, and be taken.
28.13 and be broken, and *s*, and taken.
42.22 they are all of them *s* in holes,

SNARES

Jos 23.13 shall be *s* and traps unto you,
2Sa 22. 6 the *s* of death prevented me;
Job 22.10 Therefore *s* are round about thee,
40.24 eyes: his nose pierceth through *s*.
Ps 11. 6 Upon the wicked he shall rain *s*,
18. 5 the *s* of death prevented me.
38.12 seek after my life lay *s* for me:
64. 5 they commune of laying *s* privily;
141. 9 me from the *s* which they have
Pr 13.14 life, to depart from the *s* of death.
14.27 life, to depart from the *s* of death.
22. 5 Thorns and *s* are in the way of
Ec 7.26 whose heart is *s* and nets, and
Jer 5.26 lay wait, as he that setteth *s*;
18.22 to take me, and hid *s* for my feet.

SNOUT

Pr 11.22 As a jewel of gold in a swine's *s*,

SNOW

Ex 4. 6 behold, his hand was leprous as *s*.
Nu 12.10 became leprous, white as *s*: and
2Sa 23.20 in the midst of a pit in time of *s*:
2Ki 5.27 his presence a leper as white as *s*.
Job 6.16 the ice, and wherein the *s* is hid:
9.30 If I wash myself with *s* water, and
24.19 and heat consume the *s* waters:
37. 6 For he saith to the *s*, Be thou on
38.22 entered into the treasures of the *s*?
Ps 51. 7 me, and I shall be whiter than *s*.
68.14 in it, it was white as *s* in Salmon.
147.16 He giveth *s* like wool: he
148. 8 Fire, and hail; *s*, and vapors;
Pr 25.13 As the cold of *s* in the time of
26. 1 As *s* in summer, and as rain in
31.21 She is not afraid of the *s* for her
Isa 1.18 scarlet, they shall be as white as *s*;
55.10 down, and the *s* from heaven, and
Jer 18.14 Will a man leave the *s* of Lebanon
La 4. 7 Her Nazarites were purer than *s*,
Dan 7. 9 whose garment was white as *s*,
Mt 28. 3 and his raiment white as *s*:
Mk 9. 3 shining, exceeding white as *s*;
Rev 1.14 were white like wool, as white as *s*;

SNOWY

1Ch 11.22 slew a lion in a pit in a *s* day.

SNUFFED

Jer 14. 6 they *s* up the winds like dragons;
Mal 1.13 ye have *s* at it, saith the Lord of

SOBER

2Co 5.13 or whether we be *s*, it is for your
1Th 5. 6 others; but let us watch and be *s*.
8 But let us, who are of the day, be *s*,
1Ti 3. 2 husband of one wife, vigilant, *s*,
11 wives be grave, not slanderers, *s*,
Tit 1. 8 a lover of good men, *s*, just,
2. 2 That the aged men be *s*, grave,
4 teach the young women to be *s*,
6 likewise exhort to be *s* minded.
1Pe 1.13 be *s*, and hope to the end for the
4. 7 be ye therefore *s*, and watch unto
5. 8 Be *s*, be vigilant; because your

SOBERLY

Ro 12. 3 but to think *s*, according as
Tit 2.12 we should live *s*, righteously, and

SOBERNESS

Ac 26.25 forth the words of truth and *s*.

SOBRIETY

1Ti 2. 9 with shamefacedness and *s*; not
15 and charity and holiness with *s*.

SODOM

Gen 10.19 goest, unto *S*, and Gomorrah,
13.10 before the Lord destroyed *S* and
12 and pitched his tent toward *S*.
13 men of *S* were wicked and sinners
18.20 cry of *S* and Gomorrah is great,
26 said, If I find in *S* fifty righteous
19.24 rained upon *S* and upon Gomorrah
Isa 1. 9 we should have been as *S*, and we
Jer 23.14 they are all of them unto me as *S*,
50.40 As God overthrew *S* and Gomorrah
Eze 16.46 right hand, is *S* and her daughters.
49 this was the iniquity of thy sister *S*,
Am 4.11 God overthrew *S* and Gomorrah,
Mt 10.15 more tolerable for the land of *S*
11.23 done in thee, had been done in *S*,
24 more tolerable for the land of *S*
Mk 6.11 shall be more tolerable for *S* and
Lk 10.12 more tolerable in that day for *S*,
17.29 same day that Lot went out of *S*
2Pe 2. 6 And turning the cities of *S* and
Jude 7 Even as *S* and Gomorrha, and the
Rev 11. 8 city, which spiritually is called *S*

SODOMA

Ro 9.29 we had been as *S*, and been made

SODOMITES

1Ki 14.24 there were also *s* in the land:
15.12 took away the *s* out of the land,
22.46 And the remnant of the *s*, which
2Ki 23. 7 he brake down the houses of the *s*,

SOFT

Job 23.16 For God maketh my heart *s*, and
41. 3 will he speak *s* words unto thee?
Ps 65.10 thou makest it *s* with showers:
Pr 15. 1 A *s* answer turneth away wrath:
25.15 and a *s* tongue breaketh the bone.
Mt 11. 8 A man clothed in *s* raiment?
8 behold, they that wear *s* clothing
Lk 7.25 A man clothed in *s* raiment?

SOFTER

Ps 55.21 his words were *s* than oil, yet

SOFTLY

Gen 33.14 I will lead on *s*, according as the
Jdg 4.21 and went *s* unto him, and smote
Ru 3. 7 came *s* and uncovered his feet,
1Ki 21.27 and lay in sackcloth, and went *s*.
Isa 8. 6 the waters of Shiloah that go *s*,
38.15 I shall go *s* all my years in the
Ac 27.13 And when the south wind blew *s*,

SOIL

Eze 17. 8 It was planted in a good *s* by

SOJOURN

Gen 12.10 went down into Egypt to *s* there;
19. 9 This one fellow came in to *s*, and
26. 3 *S* in this land, and I will be with
47. 4 For to *s* in the land are we come;
Ex 12.48 when a stranger shall *s* with thee,
Lev 17. 8 the strangers which *s* among you,
10, 13 the strangers that *s* among you,
19.33 And if a stranger *s* with thee in
20. 2 or of the strangers that *s* in Israel,
25.45 the strangers that do *s* among you,
Nu 9.14 if a stranger shall *s* among you,

15.14 And if a stranger *s* with you, or
Jdg 17. 8 to *s* where he could find a place:
9 I go to *s* where I may find a place.
Ru 1. 1 went to *s* in the country of Moab,
1Ki 17.20 evil upon the widow with whom I *s*,
2Ki 8. 1 and *s* wheresoever thou canst *s*:
Ps 120. 5 Woe is me, that I *s* in Mesech, that
Isa 23. 7 feet shall carry her afar off to *s*.
52. 4 aforetime into Egypt to *s* there;
Jer 42.15 enter into Egypt, and go to *s* there;
17 faces to go into Egypt to *s* there;
22 whither ye desire to go and to *s*.
43. 2 say, Go not into Egypt to *s* there:
44.12, 14, 28 the land of Egypt to *s* there,
La 4.15 They shall no more *s* there.
Eze 20.38 out of the country where they *s*,
47.22 to the strangers that *s* among you,
Ac 7. 6 should *s* in a strange land;

SOJOURNED

Gen 20. 1 Kadesh and Shur, and *s* in Gerar.
21.23 to the land wherein thou hast *s*.
34 And Abraham *s* in the Philistines'
32. 4 I have *s* with Laban, and stayed
35.27 where Abraham and Isaac *s*.
Dt 18. 6 gates out of all Israel, where he *s*,
26. 5 Egypt, and *s* there with a few,
Jdg 17. 7 who was a Levite, and he *s* there.
19.16 and he *s* in Gibeah: but the men
2Ki 8. 2 and *s* in the land of the Philistines
Ps 105.23 and Jacob *s* in the land of Ham.
Heb 11. 9 faith he *s* in the land of promise,

SOJOURNER

Gen 23. 4 I am a stranger and a *s* with you:
Lev 22.10 a *s* of the priest, or an hired
25.35 though he be a stranger, or a *s*;
40 But as an hired servant, and as a *s*,
47 a *s* or stranger wax rich by thee,
47 sell himself unto the stranger or *s*
Nu 35.15 and for the *s* among them: that
Ps 39.12 and a *s*, as all my fathers were.

SOJOURNERS

Lev 25.23 ye are strangers and *s* with me.
2Sa 4. 3 and were *s* there until this day.)
1Ch 29.15 are strangers before thee, and *s*,

SOJOURNING

Ex 12.40 the *s* of the children of Israel,
Jdg 19. 1 a certain Levite *s* on the side of
1Pe 1.17 the time of your *s* here in fear:

SOLACE

Pr 7.18 let us *s* ourselves with loves.

SOLD

Gen 25.33 he *s* his birthright unto Jacob.
31.15 for he hath *s* us, and hath quite
37.28 and *s* Joseph to the Ishmeelites for
36 Midianites *s* him into Egypt unto
41.56 and *s* unto the Egyptians; and
42. 6 he it was that *s* to all the people
45. 4 brother, whom ye *s* into Egypt.
5 yourselves, that ye *s* me hither:
47.20 Egyptians *s* every man his field,
22 wherefore they *s* not their lands.
Ex 22. 3 then he shall be *s* for his theft.
Lev 25.23 The land shall not be *s* for ever:
25 hath *s* away...of his possession,
25 redeem that which his brother *s*.
27 unto the man to whom he *s* it;
28 that which is *s* shall remain in
29 within a whole year after it is *s*;
33 then the house that was *s*, and the
34 of their cities may not be *s*;
39 waxen poor, and be *s* unto thee;
42 they shall not be *s* as bondmen.
48 After...he is *s* he may be redeemed
50 from the year that he was *s* to him
27.20 he have *s* the field to another man,
27 be *s* according to thy estimation.
28 possession, shall be *s* or redeemed:
Dt 15.12 Hebrew woman, be *s* unto thee,
28.68 ye shall be *s* unto your enemies
32.30 except their Rock had *s* them, and
Jdg 2.14 he *s* them into the hands of their
3. 8 and he *s* them into the hand of
4. 2 Lord *s* them into the hand of Jabin
10. 7 and he *s* them into the hands of the
1Sa 12. 9 he *s* them into the hand of Sisera,
1Ki 21.20 hast *s* thyself to work evil in the
2Ki 6.25 ass's head was *s* for fourscore pieces
7. 1 of fine flour be *s* for a shekel,
16 of fine flour was *s* for a shekel,
17.17 and *s* themselves to do evil in the
Neh 5. 8 which were *s* unto the heathen;
8 or shall they be *s* unto us?
13.15 in the day wherein they *s* victuals.
16 *s* on the sabbath unto the children
Est 7. 4 For we are *s*, I and my people, to
4 if we had been *s* for bondmen and
Ps 105.17 Joseph, who was *s* for a servant:
Isa 50. 1 creditors is it to whom I have *s* you?
1 iniquities have ye *s* yourselves,
52. 3 Ye have *s* yourselves for nought;
Jer 34.14 which hath been *s* unto thee;
La 5. 4 money; our wood is *s* unto us.
Eze 7.13 shall not return to that which is *s*,
Joel 3. 3 *s* a girl for wine, that they might
6 have ye *s* unto the Grecians,
7 the place whither ye have *s* them,
Am 2. 6 they *s* the righteous for silver, and
Mt 10.29 not two sparrows *s* for a farthing?
13.46 went and *s* all that he had, and
18.25 his lord commanded him to be *s*,
21.12 that *s* and bought in the temple,
12 the seats of them that *s* doves,
26. 9 ointment might have been *s* for
Mk 11.15 that *s* and bought in the temple,
15 and the seats of them that *s* doves;
14. 5 *s* for more than three hundred
Lk 12. 6 five sparrows *s* for two farthings,
17.28 they bought, they *s*, they planted,
19.45 to cast out them that *s* therein, and
Jn 2.14 in the temple those that *s* oxen and
16 said unto them that *s* doves, Take
12. 5 this ointment *s* for three hundred
Ac 2.45 And *s* their possessions and goods,
4.34 of lands or houses *s* them, and
34 prices of the things that were *s*,
37 Having land, *s* it, and brought the
5. 1 Sapphira his wife, *s* a possession,
4 and after it was *s*, was it not in
8 whether ye *s* the land for so much?
7. 9 with envy, *s* Joseph into Egypt:
Ro 7.14 but I am carnal, *s* under sin.
1Co 10.25 Whatsoever is *s* in the shambles,
Heb 12.16 morsel of meat *s* his birthright.

SOLDIER

Jn 19.23 made four parts, to every *s* a part;
Ac 10. 7 a devout *s* of them that waited on
28.16 by himself with a *s* that kept him.
2Ti 2. 3 as a good *s* of Jesus Christ.
4 who hath chosen him to be a *s*.

SOLDIERS

1Ch 7. 4 fathers, were bands of *s* for war,
11 thousand and two hundred *s*,
2Ch 25.13 the *s* of the army which Amaziah
Ezr 8.22 to require of the king a band of *s*
Isa 15. 4 the armed *s* of Moab...cry out;
Mt 8. 9 authority, having *s* under me:
27.27 the *s* of the governor took Jesus
27 unto him the whole band of *s*.
28.12 they gave large money unto the *s*,
Mk 15.16 the *s* led him away into the hall,
Lk 3.14 the *s* likewise demanded of him,
7. 8 authority, having under me *s*,
23.36 the *s* also mocked him, coming to
Jn 19. 2 the *s* platted a crown of thorns,
23 *s*, when they had crucified Jesus,
24 These things therefore the *s* did.
32 Then came the *s*, and brake the
34 one of the *s* with a spear pierced
Ac 12. 4 him to four quaternions of *s* to
6 Peter was sleeping between two *s*,
18 was no small stir among the *s*,
21.32 Who immediately took *s* and
32 saw the chief captain and the *s*,
35 that he was borne of the *s* for the
23.10 commanded the *s* to go down, and
23 Make ready two hundred *s* to go to
31 the *s*, as it was commanded them,
27.31 said to the centurion and to the *s*,
32 Then the *s* cut off the ropes of the

SOLDIERS'

Ac 27.42 And the *s* counsel was to kill the

SOLE

Gen 8. 9 no rest for the *s* of her foot,
Dt 28.35 from the *s* of thy foot unto the top
56 to set the *s* of her foot upon the
65 shall the *s* of thy foot have rest:
Jos 1. 3 the *s* of your foot shall tread upon,
2Sa 14.25 from the *s* of his foot even to the
2Ki 19.24 with the *s* of my feet have I dried
Job 2. 7 the *s* of his foot unto his crown.
Isa 1. 6 *s* of the foot even unto the head
37.25 with the *s* of my feet have I dried
Eze 1. 7 *s* of their feet was like the *s* of a

SOLEMN

Lev 23.36 it is a *s* assembly; and ye shall
Nu 10.10 gladness, and in your *s* days,
15. 3 in your *s* feasts, to make a sweet
29.35 day ye shall have a *s* assembly:
Dt 16. 8 seventh day shall be a *s* assembly
15 thou keep a *s* feast unto the Lord
2Ki 10.20 Proclaim a *s* assembly for Baal.
2Ch 2. 4 on the *s* feasts of the Lord your
7. 9 day they made a *s* assembly:
8.13 new moons, and on the *s* feasts,
Neh 8.18 the eighth day was a *s* assembly,
Ps 81. 3 appointed, on our *s* feast day.
92. 3 upon the harp with a *s* sound.
Isa 1.13 it is iniquity, even the *s* meeting.
La 1. 4 because none come to the *s* feasts:
2. 6 Lord hath caused the *s* feasts and
7 Lord, as in the day of a *s* feast.
22 called as in a *s* day my terrors
Eze 36.38 of Jerusalem in her *s* feasts; so
46. 9 before the Lord in the *s* feasts,
Hos 2.11 her sabbaths, and all her *s* feasts.
9. 5 What will ye do in the *s* day, and
12. 9 as in the days of the *s* feast.
Joel 1.14 ye a fast, call a *s* assembly,
2.15 sanctify a fast, call a *s* assembly:
Am 5.21 not smell in your *s* assemblies.
Na 1.15 keep thy *s* feasts, perform thy
Zep 3.18 are sorrowful for the *s* assembly,
Mal 2. 3 even the dung of your *s* feasts;

SOLEMNLY

Gen 43. 3 The man did *s* protest unto us,
1Sa 8. 9 howbeit yet protest *s* unto them,

SOLES

Dt 11.24 *s* of your feet shall tread shall be
Jos 3.13 the *s* of the feet of the priests that
4.18 *s* of the priests' feet were lifted
1Ki 5. 3 put them under the *s* of his feet.
Isa 60.14 down at the *s* of thy feet; and
Eze 43. 7 and the place of the *s* of my feet,
Mal 4. 3 be ashes under the *s* of your feet

SOLITARY

Job 3. 7 Lo, let that night be *s*, let no
30. 3 For want and famine they were *s*;
Ps 68. 6 God setteth the *s* in families: he
107. 4 in the wilderness in a *s* way;

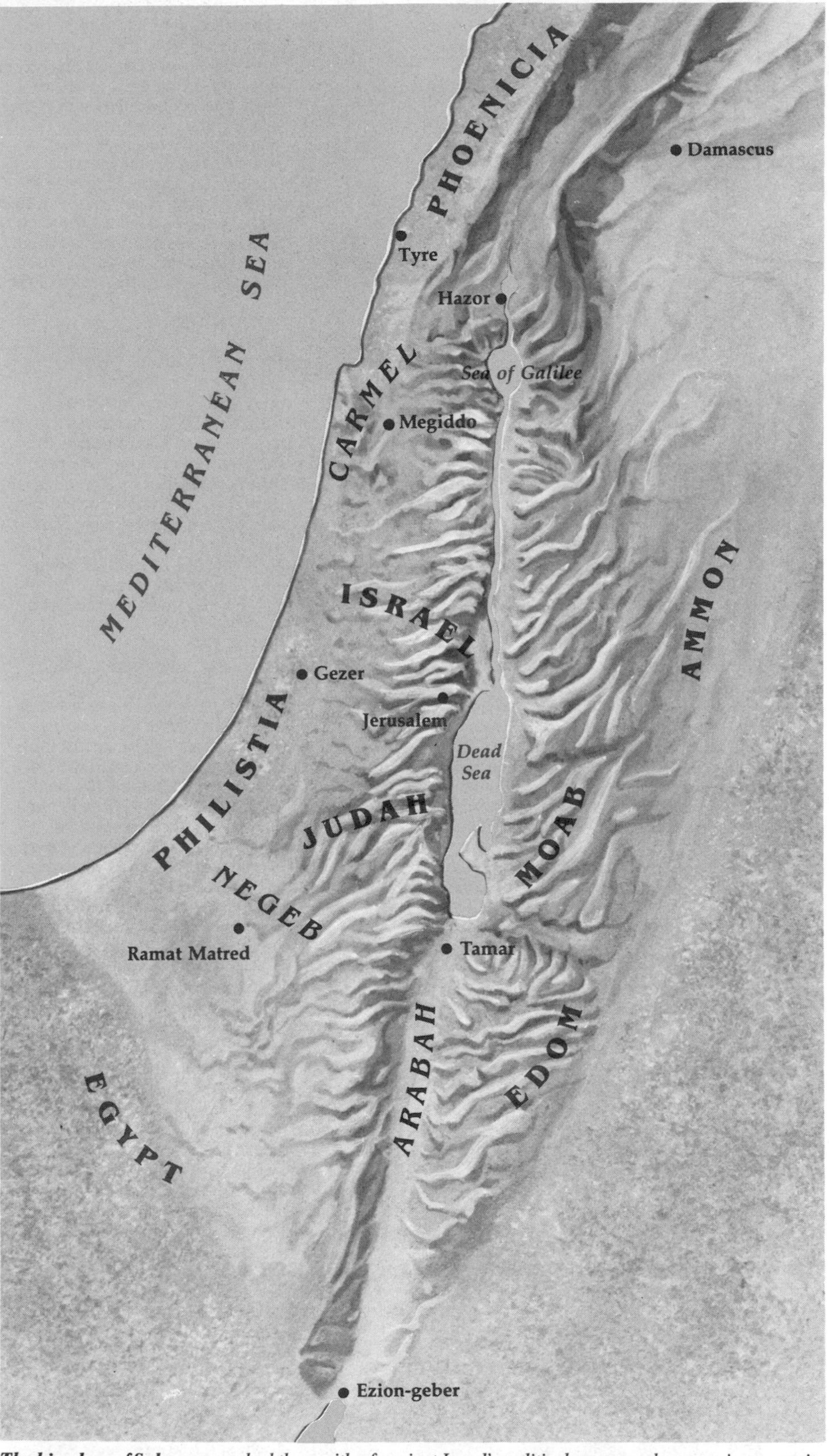

***The kingdom of Solomon** marked the zenith of ancient Israel's political power and economic prosperity. Assuming the throne of David in about 961 B.C., Solomon inherited a realm extending from the southern port of Ezion-geber as far north as Kadesh. Moving decisively to consolidate this domain, he strengthened his foreign alliances with numerous marriages and commercial pacts, established important farming centers at Ramat Matred and elsewhere, and guarded vital trade routes with fortified garrisons at Hazor, Megiddo, Gezer, and Tamar. Thus Solomon, by securing his control over the crossroads through which caravans from Egypt, Arabia, Mesopotamia, and Asia Minor passed in endless succession, emerged as the Middle East's most powerful monarch and remained so until his death about 922 B.C.*

Isa 35. 1 *s* place shall be glad for them;
La 1. 1 How doth the city sit *s*, that was
Mk 1.35 out, and departed into a *s* place,

SOLOMON

2Sa 5.14 Shobab, and Nathan, and *S*,
12.24 a son, and he called his name *S*:
1Ki 1.10 and *S* his brother, he called not.
11 unto Bathsheba the mother of *S*,
13, 17 *S* thy son shall reign after me,
21 I and my son *S* shall be counted
30 *S* thy son shall reign after me,
33 *S* my son to ride upon mine own
34 and say, God save king *S*.
39 of the tabernacle, and anointed *S*.
39 the people said, God save king *S*.
43 king David hath made *S* king.
50 And Adonijah feared because of *S*,
51 Let king *S* swear unto me to day
2. 1 and he charged *S* his son, saying,
12 sat *S* upon the throne of David
17 Speak, I pray thee, unto *S* the king,
19 Bathsheba...went unto king *S*,
23 Then king *S* sware by the Lord,
27 *S* thrust out Abiathar from being
3. 1 And *S* made affinity with Pharaoh
3 *S* loved the Lord, walking in the
5 Lord appeared to *S* in a dream by
10 Lord, that *S* had asked this thing.
15 And *S* awoke, and behold, it was a
4. 1 king *S* was king over all Israel.
21 *S* reigned over all kingdoms from
25 to Beer-sheba, all the days of *S*.
29 *S* wisdom and understanding
34 all people to hear the wisdom of *S*,
5. 1 of Tyre sent his servants unto *S*;
10 So Hiram gave *S* cedar trees and
12 the Lord gave *S* wisdom, as he
12 was peace between Hiram and *S*;
6. 2 house which king *S* built for the
11 the word of the Lord came to *S*,
14 So *S* built the house, and finished
8. 1 *S* assembled the elders of Israel,
9. 1 when *S* had finished the building
2 appeared to *S* the second time,
10. 1 of Sheba heard of the fame of *S*
3 *S* told her all her questions: there
10 the queen of Sheba gave to king *S*.
23 So king *S* exceeded all the kings
24 all the earth sought to *S*, to hear
11. 1 king *S* loved many strange women,
2 gods: *S* clave unto these in love.
5 *S* went after Ashtoreth the goddess
6 *S* did evil in the sight of the Lord,
9 Lord was angry with *S*, because
27 *S* built Millo, and repaired the
40 *S* sought...to kill Jeroboam. And
40 was in Egypt until the death of *S*.
43 *S* slept with his fathers, and was
12. 2 fled from the presence of king *S*,
1Ch 3. 5 Shobab, and Nathan, and *S*, four,
22. 5 *S* my son is young and tender, and
7 David said to *S*, My son, as for me,
23. 1 made *S* his son king over Israel.
28. 5 chosen *S* my son to sit upon the
20 David said to *S* his son, Be strong
29. 1 *S* my son, whom alone God hath
19 give unto *S* my son a perfect heart,
23 *S* sat on the throne of the Lord as
25 the Lord magnified *S* exceedingly
2Ch 1. 1 And *S*...was strengthened in his
7 that night did God appear unto *S*,
2. 1 *S* determined to build an house for
8. 1 wherein *S* had built the house of
6 and all the store cities that *S* had,
8 them did *S* make to pay tribute
11 And *S* brought up the daughter of
17 Then went *S* to Ezion-geber, and
18 with the servants of *S* to Ophir,
18 gold, and brought them to king *S*.
9. 1 of Sheba heard of the fame of *S*,

1 she came to prove *S* with hard
2 And *S* told her all her questions:
3 of Sheba had seen the wisdom of *S*,
22 *S* passed all the kings of the earth
23 kings...sought the presence of *S*,
31 And *S* slept with his fathers, and
Pr 1. 1 The proverbs of *S* the son of David,
10. 1 proverbs of *S*. A wise son maketh
SS 1. 5 of Kedar, as the curtains of *S*.
3. 9 King *S* made himself a chariot of
11 and behold king *S* with the crown
Mt 1. 6 and David the king begat *S* of her
6.29 *S* in all his glory was not arrayed
12.42 the earth to hear the wisdom of *S*;
42 behold, a greater than *S* is here.
Lk 11.31 the earth to hear the wisdom of *S*;
31 behold, a greater than *S* is here.
12.27 *S* in all his glory was not arrayed
Ac 7.47 But *S* built him an house.
(See box on page 708)

SOLOMON'S
Jn 10.23 walked in the temple in *S* porch.
Ac 3.11 them in the porch that is called *S*,
5.12 all with one accord in *S* porch.

SOME
Gen 37.20 *S* evil beast hath devoured him:
Ex 16.17 did so, and gathered, *s* more, *s* less.
Jdg 21.13 whole congregation sent *s* to speak
Ru 2.16 let fall also *s* of the handfuls of
2Sa 17. 9 he is hid now in *s* pit, or in *s* other
1Ki 14.13 in him there is found *s* good thing
2Ki 2.16 and cast him upon *s* mountain,
5.13 had bid thee do *s* great thing,
Neh 13.19 *s* of my servants set I at the gates,
Job 24. 2 *S* remove the landmarks; they
Ps 20. 7 *S* trust in chariots, and *s* in
69.20 and I looked for *s* to take pity, but
Jer 49. 9 they not leave *s* gleaning grapes?
Dan 12. 2 shall awake, *s* to everlasting life,
2 *s* to shame...everlasting contempt.
Mt 13. 4 *s* seeds fell by the way side,
8 forth fruit, *s* an hundredfold,
16.14 *S* say...thou art John the Baptist:
28 There be *s* standing here, which
27.47 *S* of them that stood there, when
28.17 worshipped him: but *s* doubted.
Mk 4. 4 he sowed, *s* fell by...way side,
8 and brought forth, *s* thirty,
8.28 *s* say, Elias; and others, One of
9. 1 be *s* of them that stand here,
12. 5 many others; beating *s*, and
Lk 8. 5 sowed, *s* fell by the way side;
9.19 but *s* say, Elias; and others say,
27 there be *s* standing here, which
23. 8 have seen *s* miracle done by him.
Jn 6.64 are *s* of you that believe not.
7.12 for *s* said, He is a good man:
41 *s* said, Shall Christ come out of
9. 9 *S* said, This is he: others said, He
10. 1 but climbeth up *s* other way, the
Ac 8. 9 out that himself was *s* great one:
31 I, except *s* man should guide me?
34 this? of himself, or of *s* other man?
17.18 *s* said, What will this babbler say?
21 to tell, or to hear *s* new thing.)
19.32 *S*...cried one thing, and *s* another:
28.24 *s* believed the things which
24 were spoken, and *s* believed not.
Ro 3. 3 For what if *s* did not believe? shall
5. 7 good man *s* would even dare to die.
1Co 6.11 And such were *s* of you: but ye are
10. 7 be ye idolaters, as were *s* of them;
15. 6 present, but *s* are fallen asleep.
12 say *s* among you that there is no
34 *s* have not the knowledge of God:
35 *s* man will say, How are the dead
Gal 1. 7 but there be *s* that trouble you,
Eph 4.11 And he gave *s*, apostles;
Php 1.15 *S* indeed preach Christ even of

Solomon in Judgment, *from the Raphael Logge in the Vatican, represents the story found in 1Ki 3.16-28.*

1Ti 1. 6 *s* having swerved have turned
19 *s* having put away concerning faith
5.24 *S* men's sins are open beforehand,
2Ti 2.18 and overthrow the faith of *s*.
20 to honor, and *s* to dishonor.
Heb 3. 4 For every house is builded by *s*
4. 6 it remaineth that *s* must enter
10.25 together, as the manner of *s* is;
11.40 provided *s* better thing for us,
13. 2 thereby *s* have entertained angels
2Pe 3. 9 as *s* men count slackness; but
16 *s* things hard to be understood,
Jude 22 *s* have compassion, making

SOMEBODY
Lk 8.46 Jesus said, *S* hath touched me:
Ac 5.36 Theudas, boasting himself to be *s*;

SOMETHING
1Sa 20.26 *S* hath befallen him, he is not
Mk 5.43 that *s* should be given her to eat.
Lk 11.54 to catch *s* out of his mouth, that
Jn 13.29 that he should give *s* to the poor.
Ac 3. 5 expecting to receive *s* of them.
23.15 *s* more perfectly concerning him:
18 thee, who hath *s* to say unto thee.
Gal 6. 3 a man think himself to be *s*, when

SOMETIME
Col 1.21 you, that were *s* alienated and
1Pe 3.20 Which *s* were disobedient, when

SOMETIMES
Eph 2.13 ye who *s* were far off are made
5. 8 For ye were *s* darkness, but now
Tit 3. 3 we ourselves also were *s* foolish,

SOMEWHAT
Lev 4.13 they have done *s* against any of the
22 done *s* through ignorance against
27 while he doeth *s* against any of the
1Ki 2.14 I have *s* to say unto thee. And
2Ki 5.20 run after him, and take *s* of him.
2Ch 10. 4 ease thou *s* the grievous servitude
9 Ease *s* the yoke that thy father did
10 but make thou it *s* lighter for us;
Lk 7.40 Simon, I have *s* to say unto thee.
Ac 23.20 inquire *s* of him more perfectly.
25.26 had, I might have *s* to write.
Ro 15.24 I be *s* filled with your company.
2Co 5.12 that ye may have *s* to answer them
10. 8 boast *s* more of our authority,
Gal 2. 6 But of these who seemed to be *s*,
6 who seemed to be *s* in conference
Heb 8. 3 that this man have *s* also to offer.
Rev 2. 4 Nevertheless I have *s* against thee,

SON
Gen 5. 3 begat a *s* in his own likeness, after
16.11 art with child, and shalt bear a *s*,
18.10 lo, Sarah thy wife shall have a *s*.
21. 2 bare Abraham a *s* in his old age.
4 Abraham circumcised his *s* Isaac
10 for the *s* of this bondwoman shall
22. 2 And he said, Take now thy *s*,
8 My *s*, God will provide himself a
10 and took the knife to slay his *s*.
12 seeing thou hast not withheld thy *s*,
24. 7 thou shalt take a wife unto my *s*
27.13 Upon me be thy curse, my *s*: only
24 he said, Art thou my very *s* Esau?
45.28 enough; Joseph my *s* is yet alive:
Nu 11.28 Joshua the *s* of Nun, the servant of
Dt 5.14 not do any work, thou, nor thy *s*,
6.20 when thy *s* asketh thee in time to
8. 5 as a man chasteneth his *s*, so the
21.20 our *s* is stubborn and rebellious,
1Sa 3. 6 I called not, my *s*; lie down again.
20.30 thou hast chosen the *s* of Jesse
2Sa 9. 6 Mephibosheth, the *s* of Jonathan,
13.37 David mourned for his *s* every day.
18.18 said, I have no *s* to keep my name
33 said, O my *s* Absalom, my *s*, my *s*
33 for thee, O Absalom, my *s*, my *s*!
1Ki 3.22 living is my *s*,...the dead is thy *s*.
22 dead is thy *s*,...the living is my *s*.

SOLOMON

Son of David by Bathsheba (2Sa 12.24) and, as his successor, ruler of Israel at the peak of its power, 10th century B.C.; when half brother Adonijah claims throne, Solomon receives David's designation; is anointed king by the priest Zadok and ceremonially enters Jerusalem to popular acclaim; accepts Adonijah's obeisance (1Ki 1); later has Adonijah put to death when the latter requests Abishag (a concubine of David's and thus a symbol of royal authority); expels the priest Abiathar and has Joab and Shimei killed (1Ki 2); marries Pharaoh's daughter; when God appears to him in a dream, asks for wisdom to rule justly and is promised great riches and honor as well; displays his wisdom in the matter of the disputed child (1Ki 3); provides for the administration of his kingdom; his wisdom reputed to excel that of the wise men of the east and of Egypt (1Ki 4); negotiates with Hiram for wood and skilled craftsmen and raises a levy to quarry stone (1Ki 5); builds the temple (1Ki 6) and his own palace (1Ki 7); has the Ark brought into the temple and offers dedicatory prayer and sacrifices (1Ki 8); God confirms with him the covenant with David; builds supply and garrison cities and a navy for trade ventures (1Ki 9); is visited by the queen of Sheba and impresses her with his wisdom and the glory of his kingdom; his riches reputed to excel all the kings of the earth (1Ki 10); his foreign wives seduce him into idolatry, and he is told by God his son will lose the kingdom except for Judah and one other tribe (originally Simeon; later interpreted to mean Benjamin); learns that Jeroboam has been chosen king of northern Israel and seeks to kill him, but he flees; dies and is succeeded by his son Rehoboam (1Ki 11).

1Ki 3.23 my *s*...liveth, and thy *s* is the dead:
17.18 to remembrance, and to slay my *s*?
2Ki 6.28 Give thy *s*, that we may eat him
9.20 driving of Jehu the *s* of Nimshi;
16. 3 made his *s* to pass through the fire,
1Ch 20. 5 Elhanan the *s* of Jair slew Lahmi
6 he also was the *s* of the giant.
22.11 Now, my *s*, the Lord be with thee;
28. 9 Solomon my *s*, know thou the God
Job 25. 6 the *s* of man, which is a worm?
35. 8 may profit the *s* of man.
Ps 2. 7 hath said unto me, Thou art my *S*;
12 Kiss the *S*, lest he be angry, and
8. 4 *s* of man, that thou visitest him?
80.17 upon the *s* of man whom thou
Pr 1. 8 My *s*, hear the instruction of thy
3. 1 My *s*, forget not my law; but let
11 My *s*, despise not the chastening
12 even as a father the *s* in whom he
4.20 My *s*, attend to my words; incline
7. 1 My *s*, keep my words, and lay up
10. 1 A wise *s* maketh a glad father:
1 but a foolish *s* is the heaviness of
5 gathereth in summer is a wise *s*:
13. 1 A wise *s* heareth his father's
24 that spareth his rod hateth his *s*:
17.25 A foolish *s* is a grief to his father,
19.13 A foolish *s* is the calamity of his
18 Chasten thy *s* while there is hope,
24.21 My *s*, fear thou the Lord and the
29.17 Correct thy *s*, and he shall give
Ec 5.14 and he begetteth a *s*, and there is
Isa 9. 6 child is born, unto us a *s* is given:
51.12 and of the *s* of man which shall be
Jer 6.26 thee mourning, as for an only *s*,
Eze 2. 1 *S* of man, stand upon thy feet, and
6 *s* of man, be not afraid of them,
8.15, 17 Hast thou seen this, O *s* of man?
12.22 *S* of man, what is that proverb that
17. 2 *S* of man, put forth a riddle, and
18.20 *s* shall not bear the iniquity of the
20 father bear the iniquity of the *s*:
21. 9 *S* of man, prophesy, and say, Thus
37. 3 me, *S* of man, can these bones live?
Dan 3.25 of the fourth is like the *S* of God.
7.13 one like the *S* of man came with
Am 7.14 neither was I a prophet's *s*;
8.10 make it as the mourning of an only *s*,
Zec 12.10 as one mourneth for his only *s*,
Mal 1. 6 A *s* honoreth his father, and a
3.17 as a man spareth his own *s* that
Mt 1. 1 of Jesus Christ, the *s* of David,
20 Joseph, thou *s* of David, fear not to
21 she shall bring forth a *s*, and thou
2.15 Out of Egypt have I called my *s*.
3.17 This is my beloved *S*, in whom I
7. 9 if his *s* ask bread, will he give him
9. 2 *S*, be of good cheer; thy sins be
27 Thou *s* of David, have mercy on us.
10. 2 James the *s* of Zebedee, and John
23 Israel, till the *S* of man be come.
37 loveth *s* or daughter more than me
11.19 The *S* of man came eating and
27 and no man knoweth the *S*, but the
27 any man the Father, save the *S*,
12. 8 *S* of man is Lord...of the sabbath
23 and said, Is not this the *s* of David?
13.37 the good seed is the *S* of man;
55 Is not this the carpenter's *s*? is not
16.13 men say that I the *S* of man am?
16 the Christ, the *S* of the living God.
17. 5 This is my beloved *S*, in whom I
20.18 *S* of man shall be betrayed unto
28 *S* of man came not to be ministered
21. 9 saying, Hosanna to the *s* of David:
37 last of all he sent unto them his *s*,
22. 2 which made a marriage for his *s*,
42 They say unto him, The *s* of David.
45 call him Lord, how is he his *s*?
27.40 If thou be the *S* of God, come down
54 Truly this was the *S* of God.
28.19 name of the Father, and of the *S*,
Mk 1. 1 of Jesus Christ, the *S* of God;
11 Thou art my beloved *S*, in whom I
5. 7 thou *S* of the most high God?
6. 3 this the carpenter, the *s* of Mary,
9. 7 This is my beloved *S*: hear him.
12. 6 Having yet therefore one *s*, his
37 Lord; and whence is he then his *s*?
14.21 *S* of man indeed goeth, as it is
61 the Christ, the *S* of the Blessed?
Lk 1.13 wife Elisabeth shall bear thee a *s*,
32 shall be called the *S* of the Highest;
3. 2 came unto John the *s* of Zacharias
38 which was the *s* of Adam,
38 which was the *s* of God.
7.12 the only *s* of his mother, and she
10. 6 and if the *s* of peace be there, your
12. 8 shall the *S* of man also confess
53 shall be divided against the *s*,
53 and the *s* against the father; the
15.13 younger *s* gathered all together,
19 no more worthy to be called thy *s*:
24 For this my *s* was dead, and is
19. 9 as he also is a *s* of Abraham.
Jn 1.18 the only begotten *S*, which is in
3.13 the *S* of man which is in heaven.
16 that he gave his only begotten *S*,
17 God sent not his *S* into the world
35 The Father loveth the *S*, and hath
36 He that believeth on the *S* hath
4. 5 that Jacob gave to his *s* Joseph.
50 unto him, Go thy way; thy *s* liveth.
5.19 The *S* can do nothing of himself,
20 For the Father loveth the *S*, and
22 committed all judgment unto the *S*:
23 that all men should honor the *S*,
26 hath he given to the *S* to have life
6.27 which the *S* of man shall give unto
40 that every one which seeth the *S*,
8.28 ye have lifted up the *S* of man,
35 for ever: but the *S* abideth ever.
36 *S* therefore shall make you free, ye
14.13 Father may be glorified in the *S*.
17. 1 the hour is come; glorify thy *S*,
1 that thy *S* also may glorify thee:
12 them is lost, but the *s* of perdition;
19. 7 he made himself the *S* of God.
26 his mother, Woman, behold thy *s*!
Ac 1.13 James the *s* of Alphaeus, and Simon
3.13 fathers,...glorified his *S* Jesus;
26 having raised up his *S* Jesus, sent
8.37 that Jesus Christ is the *S* of God.
Ro 1. 3 his *S* Jesus Christ our Lord,
5.10 reconciled...by the death of his *S*,
8. 3 sending his own *S* in the likeness
29 be conformed to the image of his *S*,
32 He that spared not his own *S*, but
1Co 1. 9 of his *S* Jesus Christ our Lord.
15.28 the *S* also himself be subject unto
Gal 1.16 To reveal his *S* in me, that I might
4. 4 God sent forth his *S*, made of a
6 the Spirit of his *S* into your hearts,
7 art no more a servant, but a *s*;
Eph 4.13 of the knowledge of the *S* of God,
Php 2.22 him, that, as a *s* with the father,
Col 1.13 into the kingdom of his dear *S*:
1Th 1.10 to wait for his *S* from heaven,
2Th 2. 3 be revealed, the *s* of perdition;
1Ti 1. 2 Timothy, my own *s* in the faith:
Heb 1. 2 last days spoken unto us by his *S*,
3. 6 Christ as a *s* over his own house;
5. 5 him, Thou art my *S*, to day have I
8 Though he were a *S*, yet learned he
7. 3 but made like unto the *S* of God;
28 maketh the *S*, who is consecrated
11.17 offered up his only begotten *s*,
12. 5 My *s*, despise not...the chastening
6 and scourgeth every *s* whom he
7 *s* is he whom the father chasteneth
1Jn 1. 3 and with his *S* Jesus Christ.
2.22 that denieth the Father and the *S*.
3. 8 For this purpose the *S* of God was
23 believe on the name of his *S* Jesus
4. 9 God sent his only begotten *S* into
10 his *S* to be the propitiation for our
14 *S* to be the Saviour of the world.
5. 5 believeth that Jesus is the *S* of God?
12 He that hath the *S* hath life; and
12 hath not the *S* of God hath not life.
Rev 1.13 one like unto the *S* of man,
21. 7 be his God, and he shall be my *s*.

SONG

Ex 15. 2 The Lord is my strength and *s*,
Dt 31.22 Moses therefore wrote this *s* the
Jdg 5.12 Deborah: awake, awake, utter a *s*:
Job 30. 9 And now am I their *s*, yea, I am
Ps 33. 3 Sing unto him a new *s*; play
40. 3 he hath put a new *s* in my mouth,
69.12 and I was the *s* of the drunkards.
96. 1 O sing unto the Lord a new *s*:
98. 1 O sing unto the Lord a new *s*; for
118.14 The Lord is my strength and *s*,
137. 4 How shall we sing the Lord's *s* in a
144. 9 I will sing a new *s* unto thee, O
149. 1 Sing unto the Lord a new *s*, and
Ec 7. 5 for a man to hear the *s* of fools.
SS 1. 1 The *s* of songs, which is Solomon's.
Isa 42.10 Sing unto the Lord a new *s*, and
Eze 33.32 art unto them as a very lovely *s*

Rev 5. 9 And they sung a new *s*, saying,
14. 3 And they sung as it were a new *s*
3 no man could learn that *s* but the
15. 3 And they sing the *s* of Moses the
3 and the *s* of the Lamb, saying,

SONGS

Gen 31.27 thee away with mirth, and with *s*,
1Ki 4.32 and his *s* were a thousand and five.
1Ch 25. 7 instructed in the *s* of the Lord,
Neh 12.46 *s* of praise and thanksgiving unto
Job 35.10 maker, who giveth *s* in the night;
Ps 32. 7 me about with *s* of deliverance.
119.54 Thy statutes have been my *s* in
137. 3 Sing us one of the *s* of Zion.
Pr 25.20 he that singeth *s* to an heavy heart.
SS 1. 1 The song of *s*, which is Solomon's.
Isa 23.16 make sweet melody, sing many *s*,
24.16 part of the earth have we heard *s*,
35.10 to Zion with *s* and everlasting
38.20 we will sing my *s* to the stringed
Eze 26.13 cause the noise of thy *s* to cease;
Am 5.23 away from me the noise of thy *s*;
8. 3 And the *s* of the temple shall be
10 and all your *s* into lamentation;
Eph 5.19 psalms and hymns and spiritual *s*,
Col 3.16 psalms and hymns and spiritual *s*,

SONS

Gen 6. 2 the *s* of God saw the daughters of
10 Noah begat three *s*, Shem, Ham,
7. 7 Noah went in, and his *s*, and his
42.11 We are all one man's *s*; we are
46. 5 *s* of Israel carried Jacob their
Ex 22.29 firstborn of thy *s* shalt thou give
27.21 Aaron and his *s* shall order it
29.44 sanctify also both Aaron and his *s*,
Dt 4. 9 teach them thy *s*, and thy sons' *s*;
1Sa 16. 1 provided me a king among his *s*.
Job 1. 5 It may be that my *s* have sinned,
6 when the *s* of God came to present
2. 1 when the *s* of God came to present
38. 7 all the *s* of God shouted for joy?
32 thou guide Arcturus with his *s*?
Ps 4. 2 O ye *s* of men, how long will ye
145.12 To make known to the *s* of men
Pr 8. 4 and my voice is to the *s* of man.
Ec 1.13 hath God given to the *s* of man to
2. 3 was that good for the *s* of men,
8 and the delights of the *s* of men,
3.19 that which befalleth the *s* of men
9. 3 heart of the *s* of men is full of evil,
12 so are the *s* of men snared in an
Isa 43. 6 bring my *s* from far, and my
52.14 his form more than the *s* of men:
60. 4 thy *s* shall come from far, and thy
10 the *s* of strangers shall build up
14 *s* also of them that afflicted thee
61. 5 the *s* of the alien shall be your
Jer 19. 9 them to eat the flesh of their *s* and
35.14 commanded his *s* not to drink wine,
49. 1 Hath Israel no *s*? hath he no heir?
Eze 5.10 the fathers shall eat the *s* in the
10 and the *s* shall eat their fathers;
Dan 10.16 like the similitude of the *s* of men
Hos 1.10 Ye are the *s* of the living God.
Joel 2.28 your *s* and your daughters shall
Am 2.11 I raised up of your *s* for prophets,
7.17 thy *s* and thy daughters shall fall
Mal 3. 3 and he shall purify the *s* of Levi,
Mt 20.20 of Zebedee's children with her *s*,
21 Grant that these my two *s* may sit,
21.28 A certain man had two *s*; and he
26.37 Peter and the two *s* of Zebedee,
Mk 3.17 which is, The *s* of thunder:
28 shall be forgiven unto the *s* of men,
10.35 James and John, the *s* of Zebedee,
Lk 5.10 James, and John, the *s* of Zebedee,
11.19 by whom do your *s* cast them out?
15.11 he said, A certain man had two *s*:
Jn 1.12 he power to become the *s* of God,
21. 2 the *s* of Zebedee, and two other
Ac 2.17 your *s* and your daughters shall
7.16 sum of money of the *s* of Emmor
29 of Madian, where he begat two *s*.
19.14 there were seven *s* of one Sceva,
Ro 8.14 Spirit of God, they are the *s* of God.
19 the manifestation of the *s* of God.
1Co 4.14 but as my beloved *s* I warn you.
2Co 6.18 ye shall be my *s* and daughters,
Gal 4. 5 might receive the adoption of *s*.
6 because ye are *s*, God hath sent
22 Abraham had two *s*, the one by a
Eph 3. 5 not made known unto the *s* of men,
Php 2.15 the *s* of God, without rebuke,
Heb 2.10 in bringing many *s* unto glory,
7. 5 they that are of the *s* of Levi, who
11.21 blessed both the *s* of Joseph; and
12. 7 God dealeth with you as with *s*;
8 then are ye bastards, and not *s*.
1Jn 3. 1 we should be called the *s* of God:
2 Beloved, now are we the *s* of God,

SOON

Gen 44. 3 As *s* as the morning was light, the
Ex 2.18 How is it that ye are come so *s*
Jos 8.29 and as *s* as the sun was down, Joshua
Job 32.22 my maker would *s* take me away.
Ps 37. 2 shall *s* be cut down like the grass,
58. 3 go astray as *s* as they be born,
68.31 Ethiopia shall *s* stretch out her
90.10 for it is *s* cut off, and we fly away.
106.13 They *s* forgat his works; they
Pr 14.17 that is *s* angry dealeth foolishly:
Mt 21.20 How *s* is the fig tree withered
Lk 8. 6 *s* as it was sprung up, it withered
15.30 as *s* as this thy son was come,
Gal 1. 6 ye are so *s* removed from him
2Th 2. 2 That ye be not *s* shaken in mind,
Tit 1. 7 not *s* angry, not given to wine, no

SOONER

Heb 13.19 I may be restored to you the *s*.
Jas 1.11 sun is no *s* risen with a burning heat,

SOOTHSAYERS

Isa 2. 6 and are *s* like the Philistines, and
Dan 2.27 the *s*, shew unto the king;
4. 7 the Chaldeans, and the *s*: and I
5. 7 the Chaldeans, and the *s*.
11 astrologers, Chaldeans, and *s*;
Mic 5.12 and thou shalt have no more *s*:

SOOTHSAYING

Ac 16.16 her masters much gain by *s*:

SOP

Jn 13.26 He it is, to whom I shall give a *s*,
26 when he had dipped the *s*, he gave
27 after the *s* Satan entered into him.
30 He then having received the *s*

SOPATER

Ac 20. 4 accompanied him into Asia *S* of

SOPE

Jer 2.22 and take thee much *s*, yet thine
Mal 3. 2 refiner's fire, and like fullers' *s*:

SORCERER

Ac 13. 6 they found a certain *s*, a false
8 But Elymas the *s* (for so is his

SORCERERS

Ex 7.11 called the wise men and the *s*:
Jer 27. 9 nor to your *s*, which speak unto
Dan 2. 2 and the *s*, and the Chaldeans, for
Mal 3. 5 be a swift witness against the *s*,
Rev 21. 8 and whoremongers, and *s*, and
22.15 For without are dogs, and *s*, and

SORCERESS

Isa 57. 3 near hither, ye sons of the *s*,

SORCERIES

Isa 47. 9 for the multitude of thy *s*, and
12 and with the multitude of thy *s*,
Ac 8.11 he had bewitched them with *s*.
Rev 9.21 of their murders, nor of their *s*,
18.23 by thy *s* were all nations deceived.

SORCERY

Ac 8. 9 beforetime in the same city used *s*,

SORE

Gen 19. 9 And they pressed *s* upon the man,
20. 8 ears: and the men were *s* afraid.
31.30 thou *s* longest after thy father's
34.25 when they were *s*, that two of
41.56 the famine waxed *s* in the land of
57 the famine was so *s* in all lands.
43. 1 And the famine was *s* in the land.
47. 4 famine is *s* in the land of Canaan:
13 the famine was very *s*, so that the
50.10 a great and very *s* lamentation:
Ex 14.10 them; and they were *s* afraid:
Lev 13.42 bald forehead, a white reddish *s*;
43 rising of the *s* be white reddish
Nu 22. 3 Moab was *s* afraid of the people,
Dt 6.22 signs and wonders, great and *s*,
28.35 a *s* botch that cannot be healed,
59 and *s* sicknesses, and of long
Jos 9.24 we were *s* afraid of our lives
Jdg 10. 9 so that Israel was *s* distressed.
14.17 her, because she lay *s* upon him:
15.18 And he was *s* athirst, and called
20.34 all Israel, and the battle was *s*:
21. 2 up their voices, and wept *s*;
1Sa 1. 6 adversary also provoked her *s*,
10 prayed unto the Lord, and wept *s*.
5. 7 his hand is *s* upon us, and upon
14.52 was *s* war against the Philistines
17.24 fled from him, and were *s* afraid.
21.12 was *s* afraid of Achish the king of
28.15 Saul answered, I am *s* distressed;
20 on the earth, and was *s* afraid,
21 and saw that he was *s* troubled,
31. 3 the battle went *s* against Saul,
3 he was *s* wounded of the archers.
4 would not; for he was *s* afraid.
2Sa 2.17 there was a very *s* battle that day;
13.36 and all his servants wept very *s*.
1Ki 17.17 and his sickness was so *s*, that
18. 2 there was a *s* famine in Samaria.
2Ki 3.26 that the battle was too *s* for him,
6.11 king of Syria was *s* troubled for this
20. 3 thy sight. And Hezekiah wept *s*.
1Ch 10. 3 the battle went *s* against Saul,
4 would not; for he was *s* afraid.
2Ch 6.28 whatsoever *s* or whatsoever
29 one shall know his own *s* and his
21.19 so he died of *s* diseases. And his
28.19 and transgressed *s* against the Lord.
35.23 me away; for I am *s* wounded.
Ezr 10. 1 for the people wept very *s*.
Neh 2. 2 of heart. Then I was very *s* afraid,
13. 8 it grieved me *s*: therefore I cast
Job 2. 7 smote Job with *s* boils from the
5.18 For he maketh *s*, and bindeth up:
Ps 2. 5 and vex them in his *s* displeasure.
6. 3 My soul is also *s* vexed: but thou,
10 enemies be ashamed and *s* vexed:
38. 2 in me, and thy hand presseth me *s*.
8 I am feeble and *s* broken: I
11 friends stand aloof from my *s*;
44.19 *s* broken us in the place of dragons,
55. 4 My heart is *s* pained within me: and
71.20 shewed me great and *s* troubles,
77. 2 my *s* ran in the night, and ceased
118.13 Thou hast thrust *s* at me that I might
18 The Lord hath chastened me *s*: but
Ec 1.13 this *s* travail hath God given to
4. 8 is also vanity, yea, it is a *s* travail.
5.13 a *s* evil which I have seen under
16 this also is a *s* evil, that in all

Isa 27. 1 his *s* and great and strong sword
38. 3 sight. And Hezekiah wept *s*.
59.11 like bears, and mourn *s* like doves:
64. 9 Be not wroth very *s*, O Lord,
12 thy peace, and afflict us very *s*?
Jer 13.17 and mine eye shall weep *s*, and run
22.10 but weep *s* for him that goeth away:
50.12 mother shall be *s* confounded;
52. 6 the famine was *s* in the city, so
La 1. 2 She weepeth *s* in the night, and her
3.52 Mine enemies chased me *s*, like a
Eze 14.21 I send my four *s* judgments upon
21.10 sharpened to make a *s* slaughter;
27.35 and their kings shall be *s* afraid,
Dan 6.14 was *s* displeased with himself,
Mic 2.10 you, even with a *s* destruction.
Zec 1. 2 *s* displeased with your fathers.
15 very *s* displeased with the heathen
Mt 17. 6 on their face, and were *s* afraid.
15 for he is lunatick, and *s* vexed:
21.15 of David; they were *s* displeased,
Mk 6.51 were *s* amazed in themselves
9. 6 to say; for they were *s* afraid.
26 the spirit cried, and rent him *s*,
14.33 began to be *s* amazed, and to be
Lk 2. 9 them: and they were *s* afraid.
Ac 20.37 they all wept *s*, and fell on Paul's
Rev 16. 2 fell a noisome and grievous *s* upon

SOREK

Jdg 16. 4 loved a woman in the valley of *S*,

SORER

Heb 10.29 Of how much *s* punishment,

SORES

Isa 1. 6 and bruises, and putrifying *s*:
Lk 16.20 was laid at his gate, full of *s*,
21 the dogs came and licked his *s*.
Rev 16.11 because of their pains and their *s*,

SORROW

Gen 3.16 said, I will greatly multiply thy *s*
16 in *s* shalt thou bring forth
17 in *s* shalt thou eat of it all the
42.38 my gray hairs with *s* to the grave.
44.29 my gray hairs with *s* to the grave.
31 our father with *s* to the grave.
Ex 15.14 *s*...take hold on the inhabitants
Lev 26.16 the eyes, and cause *s* of heart:
Dt 28.65 failing of eyes, and *s* of mind:
1Ch 4. 9 Because I bare him with *s*.
Neh 2. 2 this is nothing else but *s* of heart.
Est 9.22 turned unto them from *s* to joy,
Job 3.10 womb, nor hid *s* from mine eyes.
6.10 yea, I would harden myself in *s*:
17. 7 eye also is dim by reason of *s*,
41.22 *s* is turned into joy before him.
Ps 13. 2 soul, having *s* in my heart daily?
38.17 my *s* is continually before me.
39. 2 from good; and my *s* was stirred.
55.10 mischief...and *s* are in the midst
90.10 yet is their strength labor and *s*;
107.39 oppression, affliction, and *s*.
116. 3 upon me: I found trouble and *s*.
Pr 10.10 winketh with the eye causeth *s*:
22 rich, and he addeth no *s* with it.
15.13 but by *s* of the heart the spirit is
17.21 begetteth a fool doeth it to his *s*:
23.29 Who hath woe? who hath *s*? who
Ec 1.18 knowledge increaseth *s*.
5.17 *s* and wrath with his sickness.
7. 3 *S* is better than laughter: for by
11.10 Therefore remove *s* from thy heart,
Isa 5.30 the land, behold darkness and *s*,
14. 3 shall give thee rest from thy *s*,
17.11 day of grief and of desperate *s*.
29. 2 there shall be heaviness and *s*:
35.10 and *s* and sighing shall flee away.
50.11 mine hand; ye shall lie down in *s*.
51.11 *s* and mourning shall flee away.
65.14 but ye shall cry for *s* of heart, and
Jer 8.18 I would comfort myself against *s*,
20.18 of the womb to see labor and *s*,
30.15 *s* is incurable for the multitude
31.12 they shall not *s* any more at all.
13 make them rejoice from their *s*.
45. 3 Lord hath added grief to my *s*;
49.23 there is *s* on the sea; it cannot be
51.29 And the land shall tremble and *s*:
La 1.12 if there be any *s* like unto my *s*,
18 you, all people, and behold my *s*:
3.65 Give them *s* of heart, thy curse
Eze 23.33 be filled with drunkenness and *s*,
Hos 8.10 they shall *s* a little for the burden
Lk 22.45 he found them sleeping for *s*,
Jn 16. 6 unto you, *s* hath filled your heart.
20 but your *s* shall be turned into joy.
21 when she is in travail hath *s*,
22 And ye now therefore have *s*: but I
Ro 9. 2 and continual *s* in my heart.
2Co 2. 3 *s* from them of whom I ought to
7 be swallowed up with overmuch *s*.
7.10 For godly *s* worketh repentance to
10 the *s* of the world worketh death.
Php 2.27 also, lest I should have *s* upon *s*.
1Th 4.13 that ye *s* not, even as others which
Rev 18. 7 so much torment and *s* give her:
7 am no widow, and shall see no *s*.
21. 4 neither *s*, nor crying, neither shall

SORROWED

2Co 7. 9 sorry, but that ye *s* to repentance:
11 thing, that ye *s* after a godly sort,

SORROWFUL

1Sa 1.15 lord, I am a woman of a *s* spirit:
Job 6. 7 refused to touch are as my *s* meat.
Ps 69.29 But I am poor and *s*: let thy
Pr 14.13 Even in laughter the heart is *s*;
Jer 31.25 I have replenished every *s* soul.
Zep 3.18 are *s* for the solemn assembly,
Zec 9. 5 also shall see it, and be very *s*,
Mt 19.22 that saying, he went away *s*: for
26.22 they were exceeding *s*, and began
37 and began to be *s* and very heavy.
38 My soul is exceeding *s*, even unto
Mk 14.19 And they began to be *s*, and to say
34 My soul is exceeding *s* unto death:
Lk 18.23 when he heard this, he was very *s*:
24 when Jesus saw that he was very *s*,
Jn 16.20 and ye shall be *s*, but your sorrow
2Co 6.10 As *s*, yet alway rejoicing; as poor,
Php 2.28 and that I may be the less *s*.

SORROWING

Lk 2.48 father and I have sought thee *s*.
Ac 20.38 *S* most of all for the words which

SORROWS

Ex 3. 7 taskmasters; for I know their *s*;
2Sa 22. 6 *s* of hell compassed me about;
Job 9.28 I am afraid of all my *s*, I know
21.17 God distributeth *s* in his anger.
39. 3 young ones, they cast out their *s*.
Ps 16. 4 Their *s* shall be multiplied that
18. 4 The *s* of death compassed me,
5 *s* of hell compassed me about:
32.10 Many *s* shall be to the wicked: but
116. 3 The *s* of death compassed me,
127. 2 sit up late, to eat the bread of *s*:
Ec 2.23 all his days are *s*, and his travail
Isa 13. 8 and *s* shall take hold of them;
53. 3 a man of *s*, and acquainted with
4 our griefs, and carried our *s*:
Jer 13.21 shall not *s* take thee, as a woman
49.24 anguish and *s* have taken her, as a
Dan 10.16 vision my *s* are turned upon me,
Hos 13.13 The *s* of a travailing woman shall
Mt 24. 8 All these are the beginning of *s*.
Mk 13. 8 these are the beginning of *s*.
1Ti 6.10 themselves through with many *s*.

SORRY

1Sa 22. 8 is none of you that is *s* for me,
Neh 8.10 neither be ye *s*; for the joy of the
Ps 38.18 iniquity; I will be *s* for my sin.
Isa 51.19 thee: who shall be *s* for thee?
Mt 14. 9 And the king was *s*: nevertheless
17.23 again. And they were exceeding *s*.
18.31 what was done, they were very *s*,
Mk 6.26 And the king was exceeding *s*;
2Co 2. 2 For if I make you *s*, who is he
2 the same which is made *s* by me?
7. 8 though I made you *s* with a letter,
8 the same epistle hath made you *s*,
9 rejoice, not that ye were made *s*,
9 were made *s* after a godly manner,

SORT

Gen 6.19 two of every *s* shalt thou bring into
20 two of every *s* shall come unto thee,
7.14 his kind, every bird of every *s*.
2Ki 24.14 save the poorest *s* of the people
1Ch 24. 5 divided by lot, one *s* with another;
29.14 able to offer so willingly after this *s*?
2Ch 30. 5 long time in such *s* as it was written.
Ezr 1.10 silver basons of a second *s* four
4. 8 to Artaxerxes the king in this *s*:
Neh 6. 4 unto me four times after this *s*;
Eze 23.42 men of the common *s* were brought
39. 4 unto the ravenous birds of every *s*,
44.30 of every *s* of your oblations, shall be
Dan 1.10 children which are of your *s*?
3.29 God that can deliver after this *s*.
Ac 17. 5 certain lewd fellows of the baser *s*,
Ro 15.15 more boldly unto you in some *s*,
1Co 3.13 every man's work of what *s* it is.
2Co 7.11 that ye sorrowed after a godly *s*,
2Ti 3. 6 For of this *s* are they which creep
3Jn 6 on their journey after a godly *s*,

SORTS

Dt 22.11 shalt not wear a garment of divers *s*,
Neh 5.18 in ten days store of all *s* of wine:
Ps 78.45 He sent divers *s* of flies among them,
105.31 and there came divers *s* of flies,
Ec 2. 8 instruments, and that of all *s*.
Eze 27.24 thy merchants in all *s* of things,
38. 4 clothed with all *s* of armor,

SOSTHENES

Ac 18.17 Greeks took *S*, the chief ruler
1Co 1. 1 will of God, and *S* our brother,

SOUGHT

Gen 43.30 and he *s* where to weep; and he
Ex 2.15 this thing, he *s* to slay Moses.
4.24 Lord met him, and *s* to kill him.
1Sa 10.21 when they *s* him, he could not be
13.14 Lord hath *s* him a man after his
2Ki 2.17 *s* three days, but found him not.
2Ch 15. 4 and *s* him, he was found of them.
15 and *s* him with their whole desire;
16.12 his disease he *s* not to the Lord,
22. 9 who *s* the Lord with all his heart.
26. 5 as long as he *s* the Lord, God made
Ps 34. 4 I *s* the Lord, and he heard me,
37.36 I *s* him, but he could not be found.
77. 2 day of my trouble I *s* the Lord:
111. 2 *s* out of all...that have pleasure
119.10 my whole heart have I *s* thee:
94 save me; for I have *s* thy precepts.
Ec 7.29 they have *s* out many inventions.
12.10 *s* to find out acceptable words:
Isa 62.12 called, *S* out, A city not forsaken.
65. 1 am found of them that *s* me not:
Jer 10.21 brutish, and have not *s* the Lord:
La 1.19 while they *s* their meat to relieve
Eze 22.30 And I *s* for a man among them,
34. 4 neither have ye *s* that which was
Dan 6. 4 *s* to find occasion against Daniel
8.15 the vision, and *s* for the meaning,
Ob 6 how are his hidden things *s* up!

Zep 1. 6 those that have not *s* the Lord,
Mt 2.20 which *s* the young child's life.
21.46 when they *s* to lay hands on him,
26.16 he *s* opportunity to betray him.
59 *s* false witness against Jesus, to
Mk 11.18 and *s* how they might destroy him:
12.12 And they *s* to lay hold on him, but
14. 1 scribes *s* how they might take him
11 he *s* how he might conveniently
55 council *s* for witness against Jesus
Lk 2.44 they *s* him among their kinsfolk
48 and I have *s* thee sorrowing.
49 unto them, How is it that ye *s* me?
4.42 the people *s* him, and came unto
5.18 and they *s* means to bring him in,
6.19 whole multitude *s* to touch him:
11.16 him, *s* of him a sign from heaven.
13. 6 and he came and *s* fruit thereon,
19. 3 And he *s* to see Jesus who he was;
47 of the people *s* to destroy him,
20.19 same hour *s* to lay hands on him;
22. 2 scribes *s* how they might kill him;
6 *s* opportunity to betray him unto
Jn 5.16 persecute Jesus, and *s* to slay him,
18 the Jews *s* the more to kill him,
7. 1 because the Jews *s* to kill him.
11 Then the Jews *s* him at the feast,
30 Then they *s* to take him: but no
10.39 they *s* again to take him: but he
11. 8 the Jews of late *s* to stone thee;
56 Then *s* they for Jesus, and spake
19.12 thenceforth Pilate *s* to release him:
Ac 12.19 And when Herod had *s* for him,
17. 5 *s* to bring them out to the people.
Ro 9.32 Because they *s* it not by faith, but
10.20 I was found of them that *s* me not;
1Th 2. 6 Nor of men *s* we glory, neither of
2Ti 1.17 he *s* me out very diligently, and
Heb 8. 7 then should no place have been *s*
12.17 though he *s* it carefully with tears.

SOUL

Gen 2. 7 life; and man became a living *s*.
12.13 and my *s* shall live because of thee.
27. 4 my *s* may bless thee before I die.
Ex 12.15 that *s* shall be cut off from Israel.
30.12 give every man a ransom for his *s*
Lev 4. 2 If a *s* shall sin through ignorance
7.18 the *s* that eateth of it shall bear his
17.10 will even set my face against that *s*
11 maketh an atonement for the *s*.
12 No *s* of you shall eat blood, neither
Nu 9.13 same *s* shall be cut off from among
11. 6 But now our *s* is dried away: there
15.27 if any *s* sin through ignorance,
28 make an atonement for the *s* that
21. 4 and the *s* of the people was much
5 and our *s* loatheth this light bread.
Dt 4. 9 and keep thy *s* diligently, lest thou
29 with all thy heart and with all thy *s*.
12.15 whatsoever thy *s* lusteth after,
Jos 22. 5 all your heart and with all your *s*.
Jdg 5.21 O my *s*, thou hast trodden down
16.16 so that his *s* was vexed unto death;
1Sa 1.10 And she was in bitterness of *s*, and
15 poured out my *s* before the Lord.
18. 1 that the *s* of Jonathan was knit
1 was knit with the *s* of David,
24.11 yet thou huntest my *s* to take it.
26.21 my *s* was precious in thine eyes
30. 6 the *s* of all the people was grieved,
2Sa 4. 9 who hath redeemed my *s* out of all
13.39 the *s* of king David longed to go forth
1Ki 1.29 redeemed my *s* out of all distress,
2Ki 2. 2, 4, 6 Lord liveth, and as thy *s* liveth,
Job 3.20 and life unto the bitter in *s*;
7.11 complain in the bitterness of my *s*.
15 So that my *s* chooseth strangling,
10. 1 My *s* is weary of my life; I will
1 speak in the bitterness of my *s*.
12.10 hand is the *s* of every living thing,

30.15 they pursue my *s* as the wind:
16 now my *s* is poured out upon me;
33.18 keepeth back his *s* from the pit,
Ps 3. 2 Many there be which say of my *s*,
6. 3 My *s* is also sore vexed: but thou,
4 Return, O Lord, deliver my *s*: O
16. 2 O my *s*, thou hast said unto the
10 thou wilt not leave my *s* in hell;
19. 7 Lord is perfect, converting the *s*:
23. 3 He restoreth my *s*: he leadeth me
24. 4 not lifted up his *s* unto vanity,
25. 1 thee, O Lord, do I lift up my *s*.
33.19 To deliver their *s* from death, and
20 Our *s* waiteth for the Lord: he is
42. 1 so panteth my *s* after thee, O God.
2 My *s* thirsteth for God, for the
5 Why art thou cast down, O my *s*?
62. 1 Truly my *s* waiteth upon God:
63. 1 my *s* thirsteth for thee, my flesh
8 My *s* followeth hard after thee:
66. 9 Which holdeth our *s* in life, and
69. 1 the waters are come in unto my *s*.
86. 2 Preserve my *s*; for I am holy: O
4 unto thee, O Lord, do I lift up my *s*.
103. 1 Bless the Lord, O my *s*: and all
107. 5 and thirsty, their *s* fainted in them.
9 For he satisfieth the longing *s*, and
116. 4 Lord, I beseech thee, deliver my *s*.
7 Return unto thy rest, O my *s*; for
119.20 My *s* breaketh for the longing that
25 My *s* cleaveth unto the dust:
121. 7 all evil: he shall preserve thy *s*.
124. 4 us, the stream had gone over our *s*:
5 proud waters had gone over our *s*.
7 Our *s* is escaped as a bird out of
130. 5 I wait for the Lord, my *s* doth wait,
6 My *s* waiteth for the Lord more
139.14 and that my *s* knoweth right well.
142. 4 failed me; no man cared for my *s*.
7 Bring my *s* out of prison, that I
143. 3 the enemy hath persecuted my *s*;
6 my *s* thirsteth after thee, as a
146. 1 Lord. Praise the Lord, O my *s*.
Pr 2.10 knowledge is pleasant unto thy *s*;
19. 2 that the *s* be without knowledge,
15 and an idle *s* shall suffer hunger.
20. 2 anger sinneth against his own *s*.
21.10 The *s* of the wicked desireth evil:
23.14 and shalt deliver his *s* from hell.
25.13 he refresheth the *s* of his masters.
25 As cold waters to a thirsty *s*, so is
27. 7 The full *s* loatheth an honeycomb;
29.10 upright: but the just seek his *s*.
24 with a thief hateth his own *s*:
Isa 1.14 your appointed feasts my *s* hateth:
26. 8 the desire of our *s* is to thy name,
32. 6 to make empty the *s* of the hungry.
42. 1 elect, in whom my *s* delighteth;
53.10 thou shalt make his *s* an offering
11 He shall see of the travail of his *s*,
12 hath poured out his *s* unto death:
55. 2 let your *s* delight itself in fatness.
3 me: hear, and your *s* shall live;
58. 3 wherefore have we afflicted our *s*,
5 a day for a man to afflict his *s*? is it
10 hungry, and satisfy the afflicted *s*;
61.10 my *s* shall be joyful in my God;
Jer 4.10 the sword reacheth unto the *s*.
19 O my *s*, the sound of the trumpet,
31 *s* is wearied because of murderers.
18.20 for they have digged a pit for my *s*.
La 1.11 things for meat to relieve the *s*:
3.17 thou hast removed my *s* far off
24 Lord is my portion, saith my *s*;
Eze 3.19 but thou hast delivered thy *s*.
18. 4 are mine; as the *s* of thine father,
4 the *s* that sinneth, it shall die.
20 The *s* that sinneth, it shall die.
Jon 2. 5 me about, even to the *s*: the
7 When my *s* fainted within me I
Mic 6. 7 of my body for the sin of my *s*?

Hab 2. 4 his *s* which is lifted up is not
10 and hast sinned against thy *s*.
Mt 10.28 but are not able to kill the *s*:
28 to destroy both *s* and body in hell.
12.18 in whom my *s* is well pleased:
16.26 whole world, and lose his own *s*?
26 a man give in exchange for his *s*?
22.37 all thy heart, and with all thy *s*,
26.38 My *s* is exceeding sorrowful, even
Mk 8.36 whole world, and lose his own *s*?
37 a man give in exchange for his *s*?
12.30 all thy heart, and with all thy *s*,
33 understanding, and with all the *s*,
14.34 My *s* is exceeding sorrowful unto
Lk 1.46 said, My *s* doth magnify the Lord,
2.35 shall pierce through thy own *s*
10.27 all thy heart, and with all thy *s*,
12.19 say to my *s*, *S*, thou hast much
20 this night thy *s* shall be required
Jn 12.27 Now is my *s* troubled; and what
Ac 2.27 thou wilt not leave my *s* in hell,
31 that his *s* was not left in hell,
43 And fear came upon every *s*: and
3.23 every *s*, which will not hear that
4.32 were of one heart and of one *s*:
Ro 2. 9 every *s* of man that doeth evil;
13. 1 Let every *s* be subject unto the
1Co 15.45 man Adam was made a living *s*;
2Co 1.23 call God for a record upon my *s*,
1Th 5.23 your whole spirit and *s* and body
Heb 4.12 dividing asunder of *s* and spirit,
6.19 we have as an anchor of the *s*,
10.38 my *s* shall have no pleasure in
39 that believe to the saving of the *s*.
Jas 5.20 his way shall save a *s* from death,
1Pe 2.11 lusts, which war against the *s*;
2Pe 2. 8 vexed his righteous *s* from day to
3Jn 2 in health, even as thy *s* prospereth.
Rev 16. 3 and every living *s* died in the sea.
18.14 fruits that thy *s* lusted after are

SOULS

Ex 30.15, 16 make an atonement for your *s*.
Lev 16.29 ye shall afflict your *s*, and do no
Nu 16.38 these sinners against their own *s*,
Ps 72.13 and shall save the *s* of the needy.
97.10 preserveth the *s* of his saints; he
Pr 11.30 life; and he that winneth *s* is wise.
14.25 A true witness delivereth *s*: but a
Jer 26.19 procure great evil against our *s*.
La 1.19 sought their meat to relieve their *s*.
Eze 13.18 Will ye hunt the *s* of my people,
18. 4 Behold, all *s* are mine; as the soul
Mt 11.29 and ye shall find rest unto your *s*.
Lk 21.19 your patience possess ye your *s*.
Ac 2.41 unto them about three thousand *s*.
7.14 kindred, threescore and fifteen *s*.
14.22 Confirming the *s* of the disciples,
15.24 with words, subverting your *s*,
27.37 hundred threescore and sixteen *s*.
1Th 2. 8 of God only, but also our own *s*,
Heb 13.17 for they watch for your *s*, as they
Jas 1.21 word, which is able to save your *s*.
1Pe 1. 9 faith, even the salvation of your *s*.
22 have purified your *s* in obeying the
2.25 Shepherd and Bishop of your *s*.
3.20 is, eight *s* were saved by water.
4.19 commit the keeping of their *s* to
2Pe 2.14 from sin; beguiling unstable *s*:
Rev 6. 9 under the altar the *s* of them that
18.13 chariots, and slaves, and *s* of men.
20. 4 the *s* of them that were beheaded

SOUND

Ex 28.35 and his *s* shall be heard when he
Lev 25. 9 trumpet of the jubile to *s* on the
26.36 the *s* of a shaken leaf shall chase
1Ki 18.41 there is a *s* of abundance of rain.
2Ki 6.32 *s* of his master's feet behind him?
Job 15.21 A dreadful *s* is in his ears: in
21.12 and rejoice at the *s* of the organ.

Ps 77.17 out water: the skies sent out a *s*:
89.15 the people that know the joyful *s*:
92. 3 upon the harp with a solemn *s*.
119.80 Let my heart be *s* in thy statutes;
Pr 2. 7 He layeth up *s* wisdom for the
8.14 Counsel is mine, and *s* wisdom: I
14.30 A *s* heart is the life of the flesh:
Ec 12. 4 when the *s* of the grinding is low,
Jer 50.22 A *s* of battle is in the land, and of
Eze 26.13 the *s* of thy harps shall be no more
15 the isles shake at the *s* of thy fall,
Dan 3. 5 ye hear the *s* of the cornet, flute,
Joel 2. 1 *s* an alarm in my holy mountain:
Mt 6. 2 do not *s* a trumpet before thee, as
24.31 angels with a great *s* of a trumpet,
Lk 15.27 he hath received him safe and *s*.
Jn 3. 8 thou hearest the *s* thereof, but
Ac 2. 2 there came a *s* from heaven as of
Ro 10.18 their *s* went into all the earth,
1Co 14. 7 even things without life giving *s*,
8 if the trumpet give an uncertain *s*,
15.52 the trumpet shall *s*, and the dead
1Ti 1.10 that is contrary to *s* doctrine;
2Ti 1. 7 and of love, and of a *s* mind.
13 Hold fast the form of *s* words,
4. 3 they will not endure *s* doctrine;
Tit 1. 9 he may be able by *s* doctrine both
13 that they may be *s* in the faith;
2. 1 things which become *s* doctrine:
2 *s* in faith, in charity, in patience.
8 *S* speech, that cannot be
Heb 12.19 And the *s* of a trumpet, and the
Rev 1.15 his voice as the *s* of many waters.
8. 6 angels...prepared themselves to *s*.
13 the three angels, which are yet to *s*!
9. 9 and the *s* of their wings was as the
9 as the *s* of chariots of many horses
10. 7 angel, when he shall begin to *s*,
18.22 *s* of a millstone shall be heard no

SOUNDED
1Sa 20.12 when I have *s* my father about
2Ch 7. 6 priests *s* trumpets before them,
13.14 the priests *s* with the trumpets.
23.13 rejoiced, and *s* with trumpets,
29.28 sang, and the trumpeters *s*:
Neh 4.18 he that *s* the trumpet was by me.
Lk 1.44 of thy salutation *s* in mine ears,
Ac 27.28 *s*, and found it twenty fathoms:
28 they *s* again, and found it fifteen
1Th 1. 8 you *s* out the word of the Lord
Rev 8. 7 The first angel *s*, and there
8 the second angel *s*, and as it were
10 the third angel *s*, and there fell a
12 the fourth angel *s*, and the third
9. 1 the fifth angel *s*, and I saw a star
13 the sixth angel *s*, and I heard a
11.15 And the seventh angel *s*; and there

SOUNDING
1Ch 15.16 harps and cymbals, *s*, by lifting
2Ch 5.12 twenty priests *s* with trumpets:)
13.12 with *s* trumpets to cry alarm
Ps 150. 5 him upon the high *s* cymbals.
Isa 63.15 the *s* of thy bowels and of thy
Eze 7. 7 not the *s* again of the mountains.
1Co 13. 1 I am become as *s* brass, or a

SOUNDNESS
Ps 38. 3 no *s* in my flesh because of thine
7 and there is no *s* in my flesh.
Isa 1. 6 unto the head there is no *s* in it;
Ac 3.16 him hath given him this perfect *s*

SOUNDS
1Co 14. 7 they give a distinction in the *s*,

SOUR
Isa 18. 5 and the *s* grape is ripening in the
Jer 31.29 The fathers have eaten a *s* grape,
30 every man that eateth the *s* grape,
Eze 18. 2 The fathers have eaten *s* grapes,
Hos 4.18 Their drink is *s*: they have

SOUTH
Gen 12. 9 going on still toward the *s*.
24.62 for he dwelt in the *s* country.
Jdg 1.15 for thou hast given me a *s* land;
Job 37. 9 Out of the *s* cometh...whirlwind:
17 quieteth the earth by the *s* wind?
Ps 126. 4 O Lord, as the streams in the *s*.
Ec 1. 6 The wind goeth toward the *s*,
Eze 20.46 man, set thy face toward the *s*,
Mt 12.42 queen of the *s* shall rise up in the
Lk 11.31 queen of the *s* shall rise up in the
12.55 And when ye see the *s* wind blow,
13.29 and from the *s*, and shall sit down
Ac 8.26 Arise, and go toward the *s* unto
27.12 toward the *s* west and north west.
13 And when the *s* wind blew softly,
28.13 and after one day the *s* wind blew,
Rev 21.13 three gates; on the *s* three gates;

SOW
Ex 23.10 six years thou shalt *s* thy land,
Lev 19.19 shalt not *s* thy field with mingled
25. 3 Six years thou shalt *s* thy field,
26.16 and ye shall *s* your seed in vain,
Job 4. 8 plow iniquity, and *s* wickedness,
31. 8 Then let me *s*, and let another eat;
Ps 126. 5 that *s* in tears shall reap in joy.
Ec 11. 4 observeth the wind shall not *s*;
6 In the morning *s* thy seed, and in
Isa 32.20 Blessed are ye that *s* beside all
Jer 4. 3 ground, and *s* not among thorns.
Hos 10.12 *S* to yourselves in righteousness,
Mic 6.15 Thou shalt *s*, but thou shalt not
Mt 6.26 the fowls of the air: for they *s* not,
13. 3 Behold, a sower went forth to *s*;
27 Sir, didst thou not *s* good seed in
Mk 4. 3 there went out a sower to *s*:
Lk 8. 5 A sower went out to *s* his seed:
12.24 for they neither *s* nor reap; which
19.21 and reapest that thou didst not *s*
22 down, and reaping that I did not *s*:
2Pe 2.22 and the *s* that was washed to her

SOWED
Gen 26.12 Then Isaac *s* in that land, and
Jdg 9.45 down the city, and *s* it with salt.
Mt 13. 4 when he *s*, some seeds fell by the
24 unto a man which *s* good seed in
25 came and *s* tares among the wheat,
31 which a man took, and *s* in his field:
39 The enemy that *s* them is the devil;
25.26 knewest that I reap where I *s* not,
Mk 4. 4 as he *s*, some fell by the way side,
Lk 8. 5 as he *s*, some fell by the way side;

SOWER
Isa 55.10 that it may give seed to the *s*,
Jer 50.16 Cut off the *s* from Babylon, and
Mt 13. 3 Behold, a *s* went forth to sow;
18 Hear ye...the parable of the *s*.
Mk 4. 3 Behold, there went out a *s* to sow:
14 The *s* soweth the word.
Lk 8. 5 A *s* went out to sow his seed: and
2Co 9.10 he that ministereth seed to the *s*

SOWEST
1Co 15.36 which thou *s* is not quickened,
37 And that which thou *s*,
37 thou *s* not that body that shall be

SOWETH
Pr 6.14 continually; he *s* discord.
19 that *s* discord among brethren.
11.18 but to him that *s* righteousness
16.28 A froward man *s* strife: and a
22. 8 He that *s* iniquity shall reap
Am 9.13 treader of grapes him that *s* seed;
Mt 13.37 He that *s* the good seed is the Son
Mk 4.14 The sower *s* the word.
Jn 4.36 that both he that *s* and he that
37 true, One *s*, and another reapeth.
2Co 9. 6 He which *s* sparingly shall reap
6 he which *s* bountifully shall reap
Gal 6. 7 whatsoever a man *s*, that shall he
8 For he that *s* to his flesh shall of
8 but he that *s* to the Spirit shall of

SOWN
Ex 23.16 which thou hast *s* in the field:
Lev 11.37 any sowing seed which is to be *s*,
Dt 21. 4 which is neither eared nor *s*,
22. 9 fruit of thy seed which thou hast *s*,
29.23 and burning, that it is not *s*, nor
Jdg 6. 3 And so it was when Israel had *s*,
Ps 97.11 Light is *s* for the righteous, and
Isa 19. 7 every thing *s* by the brooks, shall
40.24 yea, they shall not be *s*: yea,
61.11 things that are *s* in it to spring
Jer 2. 2 in a land that was not *s*.
12.13 They have *s* wheat, but shall reap
Eze 36. 9 you, and ye shall be tilled and *s*:
Hos 8. 7 For they have *s* the wind, and they
Na 1.14 that no more of thy name be *s*:
Hag 1. 6 Ye have *s* much, and bring in
Mt 13.19 that which was *s* in his heart.
25.24 reaping where thou hast not *s*,
Mk 4.15 the way side, where the word is *s*;
15 the word that was *s* in their hearts.
16 which are *s* on stony ground; who,
18 they which are *s* among thorns;
20 they which are *s* on good ground;
31 when it is *s* in the earth, is less
32 But when it is *s*, it groweth up, and
1Co 9.11 have *s* unto you spiritual things,
15.42 It is *s* in corruption; it is raised in
43 It is *s* in dishonor; it is raised in
43 it is *s* in wickedness; it is raised in
44 It is *s* a natural body; it is raised
2Co 9.10 multiply your seed *s*, and increase
Jas 3.18 fruit of righteousness is *s* in peace

SPACE
Gen 29.14 abode with him the *s* of a month.
32.16 put a *s* betwixt drove and drove.
Lev 25. 8 the *s* of the seven sabbaths of
30 within the *s* of a full year, then
Dt 2.14 And the *s* in which we came from
Jos 3. 4 shall be a *s* between you and it,
1Sa 26.13 a great *s* being between them:
Ezr 9. 8 a little *s* grace hath been shewed
Jer 28.11 within the *s* of two full years.
Eze 40.12 *s* also before the little chambers
12 the *s* was one cubit on that side:
Lk 22.59 And about the *s* of one hour after
Ac 5. 7 it was about the *s* of three hours
34 to put the apostles forth a little *s*;
7.42 by the *s* of forty years in the
13.20 the *s* of four hundred and fifty years,
21 of Benjamin, but the *s* of forty years.
15.33 after they had tarried there a *s*,
19. 8 boldly for the *s* of three months,
10 continued by the *s* of two years;
34 about the *s* of two hours cried out,
20.31 the *s* of three years I ceased not
Jas 5.17 the *s* of three years and six months.
Rev 2.21 And I gave her *s* to repent of her
8. 1 in heaven about the *s* of half an hour.
14.20 *s* of a thousand and six hundred
17.10 cometh, he must continue a short *s*.

SPAIN
Ro 15.24 I take my journey into *S*, I will
28 fruit, I will come by you into *S*.

SPAKE
Gen 8.15 And God *s* unto Noah, saying,
31.11 angel of God *s* unto me in a dream
34. 3 and *s* kindly unto the damsel.
42.23 he *s* unto them by an interpreter.

46. 2 God *s* unto Israel in the visions of
Nu 16.20 Lord *s* unto Moses and unto Aaron,
21. 5 And the people *s* against God,
Dt 1. 6 Lord our God *s* unto us in Horeb,
Jdg 2. 4 the angel of the Lord *s* these words
2Sa 23. 2 The Spirit of the Lord *s* by me, and
3 the Rock of Israel *s* to me, He that
1Ki 4.32 he *s* three thousand proverbs:
2Ki 24. 2 he *s* by his servants the prophets.
Ps 33. 9 For he *s*, and it was done; he
99. 7 He *s* unto them in the cloudy pillar:
106.33 so that he *s* unadvisedly with his
Isa 65.12 when I *s*, ye did not hear; but did
Jer 7.13 I *s* unto you, rising up early and
8. 6 and heard, but they *s* not aright:
25. 2 the prophet *s* unto all the people of
Eze 3.24 me upon my feet, and *s* with me,
Dan 7.11 the great words which the horn *s*:
Jon 2.10 And the Lord *s* unto the fish, and
Mal 3.16 the Lord *s* often one to another:
Mt 9.33 the devil was cast out, the dumb *s*:
13. 3 he *s* many things...in parables,
34 and without a parable *s* he not
17.13 *s* unto them of John the Baptist.
Mk 4.33 many such parables *s* he the word
7.35 tongue was loosed, and he *s* plain.
12.26 how in the bush God *s* unto him,
Lk 1.64 and his tongue loosed, and he *s*,
70 As he *s* by the mouth of his holy
5.36 he *s* also a parable unto them;
7.39 he *s* within himself, saying, This
9.31 *s* of his decease which he should
22.60 while he yet *s*, the cock crew.
Jn 2.21 he *s* of the temple of his body.
7.39 (But this *s* he of the Spirit, which
46 Never man *s* like this man.
9.29 We know that God *s* unto Moses:
10. 6 This parable *s* Jesus unto them:
11.13 Howbeit Jesus *s* of his death:
12.29 others said, An angel *s* to him.
18.16 and *s* unto her that kept the door,
32 he *s*, signifying what death he
Ac 6.10 wisdom and...spirit by which he *s*.
22. 2 he *s* in the Hebrew tongue to them,
9 heard not the voice of him that *s*
28.25 Well *s* the Holy Ghost by Esaias
1Co 13.11 When I was a child, I *s* as a child,
Heb 1. 1 *s* in time past unto the fathers
Rev 10. 8 from heaven *s* unto me again,

SPARE

Gen 18.24 also destroy and not *s* the place
26 will *s* all the place for their sakes.
Dt 13. 8 eye pity him, neither shalt thou *s*,
29.20 The Lord will not *s* him, but then
1Sa 15. 3 that they have, and *s* them not;
Neh 13.22 *s* me according to the greatness
Job 6.10 let him not *s*; for I have not
16.13 my reins asunder, and doth not *s*;
20.13 Though he *s* it, and forsake it not;
27.22 shall cast upon him, and not *s*:
30.10 me, and *s* not to spit in my face.
Ps 39.13 O *s* me, that I may recover
72.13 He shall *s* the poor and needy,
Pr 6.34 will not *s* in the day of vengeance.
19.18 let not thy soul *s* for his crying.
Isa 9.19 fire: no man shall *s* his brother.
13.18 their eye shall not *s* children.
30.14 broken in pieces; he shall not *s*:
54. 2 *s* not, lengthen thy cords, and
58. 1 Cry aloud, *s* not, lift up thy voice
Jer 13.14 I will not pity, nor *s*, nor have
21. 7 he shall not *s* them, neither have
50.14 bow, shoot at her, *s* no arrows:
51. 3 *s* ye not her young men; destroy
Eze 5.11 neither shall mine eye *s*, neither
7. 4 mine eye shall not *s* thee, neither
9 And mine eye shall not *s*, neither
8.18 mine eye shall not *s*, neither will I
9. 5 let not your eye *s*, neither have ye
10 mine eye shall not *s*, neither will I
24.14 I will not go back, neither will I *s*,
Joel 2.17 *S* thy people, O Lord, and give not
Jon 4.11 should not I *s* Nineveh, that great
Hab 1.17 and not *s* continually to slay the
Mal 3.17 I will *s* them, as a man spareth
Lk 15.17 have bread enough and to *s*,
Ro 11.21 take heed lest he also *s* not thee.
1Co 7.28 trouble in the flesh: but I *s* you.
2Co 1.23 to *s* you I came not as yet unto
13. 2 that, if I come again, I will not *s*:

SPARED

1Sa 15. 9 But Saul and the people *s* Agag,
15 people *s* the best of the sheep and
24.10 but mine eye *s* thee; and I said,
2Sa 12. 4 he *s* to take of his own flock and
21. 7 But the king *s* Mephibosheth, the
2Ki 5.20 my master hath *s* Naaman this
Ps 78.50 he *s* not their soul from death,
Eze 20.17 mine eye *s* them from destroying
Ro 8.32 He that *s* not his own Son, but
11.21 if God *s* not the natural branches,
2Pe 2. 4 if God *s* not the angels that sinned,
5 And *s* not the old world, but saved

SPARETH

Pr 13.24 He that *s* his rod hateth his son:
17.27 that hath knowledge *s* his words:
21.26 but the righteous giveth and *s* not.
Mal 3.17 man *s* his own son that serveth

SPARING

Ac 20.29 wolves enter...not *s* the flock.

SPARINGLY

2Co 9. 6 which soweth *s* shall reap also *s*;

SPARK

Job 18. 5 the *s* of his fire shall not shine.
Isa 1.31 as tow, and the maker of it as a *s*,

SPARKS

Job 5. 7 trouble, as the *s* fly upward.
41.19 lamps, and *s* of fire leap out.
Isa 50.11 compass yourselves about with *s*:
11 and in the *s* that ye have kindled.

SPARROW

Ps 84. 3 Yea, the *s* hath found an house,
102. 7 am as a *s* alone upon the house

SPARROWS

Mt 10.29 Are not two *s* sold for a farthing?
31 ye are of more value than many *s*.
Lk 12. 6 not five *s* sold for two farthings,
7 ye are of more value than many *s*.

SPAT

Jn 9. 6 he *s* on the ground, and made

SPEAK

Gen 18.27 taken upon me to *s* unto the Lord,
32 and I will *s* yet but this once:
Ex 14. 2 *S* unto the children of Israel, that
20.19 let not God *s* with us, lest we die.
Nu 20. 8 *s* ye unto the rock before their eyes;
21.27 they that *s* in proverbs say, Come
Dt 5.27 the Lord our God shall *s* unto thee;
Jdg 19.30 it, take advice, and *s* your minds.
1Sa 3. 9 *S*, Lord; for thy servant heareth.
10 *S*; for thy servant heareth.
2Ch 18.23 Spirit...from me to *s* unto thee?
Neh 13.24 could not *s* in the Jews' language,
Job 7.11 will *s* in the anguish of my spirit;
9.19 If I *s* of strength, lo, he is strong: and
35 Then would I *s*, and not fear him;
10. 1 I will *s* in the bitterness of my soul.
13. 3 Surely I would *s* to the Almighty,
7 Will ye *s* wickedly for God? and
27. 4 My lips shall not *s* wickedness, nor
36. 2 I have yet to *s* on God's behalf.
41. 3 will he *s* soft words unto thee?
Ps 5. 6 shalt destroy them that *s* leasing:
12. 2 and with a double heart do they *s*.
28. 3 which *s* peace to their neighbors,
50. 7 Hear, O my people, and I will *s*; O
85. 8 will hear what God the Lord will *s*:
8 he will *s* peace unto his people,
94. 4 shall they utter and *s* hard things?
109.20 them that *s* evil against my soul.
115. 5 They have mouths, but they *s* not:
119.172 My tongue shall *s* of thy word:
120. 7 but when I *s*, they are for war.
135.16 They have mouths, but they *s* not;
Pr 8. 6 for I will *s* of excellent things;
23. 9 *S* not in the ears of a fool: for he
Ec 3. 7 to keep silence, and a time to *s*;
SS 7. 9 lips of those that are asleep to *s*.
Isa 32. 4 the stammerers shall be ready to *s*
40. 2 *S* ye comfortably to Jerusalem,
45.19 I the Lord *s* righteousness, I
50. 4 know how to *s* a word in season
59. 4 they trust in vanity, and *s* lies;
Jer 1. 6 Ah, Lord God! behold, I cannot *s*:
9. 5 neighbor, and will not *s* the truth:
5 have taught their tongue to *s* lies,
Eze 12.25 For I am the Lord: I will *s*, and
17. 2 and *s* a parable unto the house of
20. 3 man, *s* unto the elders of Israel,
49 of me, Doth he not *s* parables?
33. 8 dost not *s* to warn the wicked from
Hos 2.14 and *s* comfortably unto her.
Zep 3.13 shall not do iniquity, nor *s* lies;
Zec 8.16 *S* ye every man the truth to his
9.10 he shall *s* peace unto the heathen:
Mt 8. 8 *s* the word only, and my servant
10.19 thought how or what ye shall *s*:
12.34 can ye, being evil, *s* good things?
36 every idle word that men shall *s*,
13.13 Therefore *s* I to them in parables:
Mk 1.34 and suffered not the devils to *s*,
7.37 the deaf to hear, and the dumb to *s*.
16.17 they shall *s* with new tongues;
Lk 1.19 and am sent to *s* unto thee, and to
4.41 them suffered them not to *s*:
6.26 when all men shall *s* well of you!
7.15 was dead sat up, and began to *s*.
12.10 *s* a word against the Son of man,
Jn 1.37 the two disciples heard him *s*, and
3.11 We *s* that we do know, and testify
16.13 for he shall not *s* of himself; but
25 no more *s* unto you in proverbs,
17.13 these things I *s* in the world, that
Ac 2. 4 they began to *s* with other tongues,
6 heard them *s* in his own language.
4.17 they *s* henceforth to no man in
20 *s* the things which we have seen
5.20 Go, stand and *s* in the temple to the
40 should not *s* in the name of Jesus,
11.15 as I began to *s*, the Holy Ghost fell
18. 9 Be not afraid, but *s*, and hold not
26 began to *s* boldly in the synagogue:
23. 5 shalt not *s* evil of the ruler of thy
1Co 1.10 that ye all *s* the same thing, and
2. 6 we *s* wisdom among them that
3. 1 not *s* unto you as unto spiritual,
7. 6 I *s* this by permission, and not of
2Co 2.17 in the sight of God *s* we in Christ.
8. 8 I *s* not by commandment, but by
Col 4. 3 to *s* the mystery of Christ, for
Tit 2. 1 *s* thou the things which become
3. 2 To *s* evil of no man, to be no
Heb 2. 5 the world to come, whereof we *s*.
Jas 1.19 to hear, slow to *s*, slow to wrath:
4.11 *S* not evil one of another,
1Pe 2.12 they *s* against you as evildoers,
3.10 and his lips that they *s* no guile:
2Pe 2.10 are not afraid to *s* evil of dignities.
2Jn 12 *s* face to face, that our joy may be
Jude 8 dominion, and *s* evil of dignities.
Rev 2.24 the depths of Satan, as they *s*;

SPEAKER
Ps 140.11 not an evil *s* be established
Ac 14.12 because he was the chief *s*.

SPEAKEST
1Sa 9.21 wherefore then *s* thou so to me?
2Sa 19.29 him, Why *s* thou any more of thy
2Ki 6.12 words...thou *s* in thy bedchamber.
Job 2.10 Thou *s* as one of the foolish women
Ps 50.20 sittest and *s* against thy brother;
51. 4 mightest be justified when thou *s*,
Isa 40.27 Why sayest thou, O Jacob, and *s*, O
Jer 40.16 for thou *s* falsely of Ishmael.
43. 2 unto Jeremiah, Thou *s* falsely:
Eze 3.18 nor *s* to warn the wicked from his
Zec 13. 3 thou *s* lies in the name of the Lord:
Mt 13.10 Why *s*...unto them in parables?
Lk 12.41 Lord, *s* thou this parable unto us,
Jn 16.29 unto him, Lo, now *s* thou plainly,
29 thou plainly, and *s* no proverb.
19.10 unto him, *S* thou not unto me?
Ac 17.19 new doctrine, whereof thou *s*, is?

SPEAKETH
Gen 45.12 it is my mouth that *s* unto you,
Ex 33.11 to face, as a man *s* unto his friend.
Nu 23.26 All that the Lord *s*, that I must do?
Job 2.10 as one of the foolish women *s*.
17. 5 He that *s* flattery to his friends,
33.14 God *s* once, yea twice, yet man
Ps 15. 2 and *s* the truth in his heart.
144. 8 Whose mouth *s* vanity, and their
Pr 6.13 he *s* with his feet, he teacheth
19 A false witness that *s* lies, and he
14.25 but a deceitful witness *s* lies.
16.13 and they love him that *s* right.
19. 5 he that *s* lies shall not escape.
26.25 When he *s* fair, believe him not:
Isa 9.17 and every mouth *s* folly.
Eze 10. 5 of the Almighty God when he *s*.
Am 5.10 they abhor him that *s* uprightly.
Mt 10.20 of your Father which *s* in you.
12.32 whosoever *s* a word against the
32 whosoever *s* against the Holy
34 out...of the heart the mouth *s*.
Lk 5.21 Who is this which *s* blasphemies?
6.45 of the heart his mouth *s*.
Jn 3.31 earth is earthly, and *s* of the earth:
34 God hath sent *s* the words of God:
7.18 He that *s* of himself seeketh his
26 But, lo, he *s* boldly, and they say
8.44 When he *s* a lie, he *s* of his own:
19.12 himself a king *s* against Cæsar.
Ac 2.25 For David *s* concerning him, I
8.34 thee, of whom *s* the prophet this?
Ro 10. 6 which is of faith *s* on this wise,
1Co 14. 2 he that *s* in an unknown tongue
2 *s* not unto men, but unto God: for
2 in the spirit he *s* mysteries.
3 he that prophesieth *s* unto men
4 *s* in an unknown tongue edifieth
5 than he that *s* with tongues,
11 be unto him that *s* a barbarian,
11 and he that *s* shall be a barbarian
13 let him that *s* in an unknown
1Ti 4. 1 the Spirit *s* expressly, that in the
Heb 11. 4 and by it he being dead yet *s*.
12. 5 which *s* unto you as unto children,
24 that *s* better things than that of
25 See that ye refuse not him that *s*.
25 away from him that *s* from heaven:
Jas 4.11 He that *s* evil of his brother, and
11 *s* evil of the law, and judgeth the
Jude 16 mouth *s* great swelling words,

SPEAKING
Dt 4.33 God *s* out of the midst of the fire,
11.19 *s* of them when thou sittest in
2Ch 36.12 the prophet *s* from the mouth of the
Job 4. 2 who can withhold himself from *s*?
Ps 34.13 evil, and thy lips from *s* guile.
58. 3 as soon as they be born, *s* lies.
Isa 65.24 while they are yet *s*, I will hear.
Dan 9.21 whiles I was *s* in prayer, even the
Mt 6. 7 shall be heard for their much *s*.
Lk 5. 4 Now when he had left *s*, he said
Ac 1. 3 *s* of the things pertaining to the
7.44 *s* unto Moses, that he should
13.43 who, *s* to them, persuaded them
14. 3 abode thy *s* boldly in the Lord,
20.30 *s* perverse things, to draw away
26.14 I heard a voice *s* unto me, and
1Co 12. 3 that no man *s* by the Spirit of God
14. 6 I come unto you *s* with tongues,
2Co 13. 3 ye seek a proof of Christ *s* in me,
Eph 4.15 *s* the truth in love, may grow up
31 and evil *s*, be put away from you,
5.19 *S* to yourselves in psalms and
1Ti 4. 2 *S* lies in hypocrisy; having their
5.13 *s* things which they ought not.
1Pe 4. 4 same excess of riot, *s* evil of you:
2Pe 2.16 the dumb ass *s* with man's voice
3.16 epistles, *s* in them of these things;
Rev 13. 5 him a mouth *s* great things and

SPEAKINGS
1Pe 2. 1 and envies, and all evil *s*,

SPEAR
1Sa 13.22 neither sword nor *s* found in the
17. 7 staff of his *s* was like a weaver's
45 to me with a sword, and with a *s*,
47 Lord saveth not with sword and *s*:
2Sa 21.19 of whose *s* was like a weaver's
1Ch 11.23 was a *s* like a weaver's beam; and
Ps 46. 9 bow, and cutteth the *s* in sunder;
Jn 19.34 soldiers with a *s* pierced his side,

SPEARMEN
Ps 68.30 Rebuke the company of *s*, the
Ac 23.23 *s* two hundred, at the third hour

SPEARS
1Sa 13.19 Hebrews make them swords or *s*:
Neh 4.16 half of them held both the *s*, and
21 half of them held the *s* from the
Ps 57. 4 whose teeth are *s* and arrows,
Isa 2. 4 and their *s* into pruninghooks:
Joel 3.10 and your pruninghooks into *s*:
Mic 4. 3 and their *s* into pruninghooks:

SPECIAL
Dt 7. 6 to be a *s* people unto himself,
Ac 19.11 God wrought *s* miracles

SPECIALLY
Dt 4.10 *S* the day that thou stoodest before
Ac 25.26 and *s* before thee, O king Agrippa,
1Ti 4.10 of all men, *s* of those that believe.
5. 8 and *s* for those of his own house,
Tit 1.10 *s* they of the circumcision:
Phm 16 servant, a brother beloved, *s* to me,

SPECTACLE
1Co 4. 9 we are made a *s* unto the world,

SPEECH
Gen 11. 1 was of one language, and of one *s*.
7 not understand one another's *s*.
Ex 4.10 but I am slow of *s*, and of a slow
Dt 32. 2 my *s* shall distil as the dew, as the
2Ch 32.18 with a loud voice in the Jews' *s*,
Job 12.20 removeth away the *s* of the trusty,
13.17 Hear diligently my *s*, and my
24.25 and make my *s* nothing worth?
Ps 17. 6 thine ear to me, and hear my *s*.
19. 2 Day unto day uttereth *s*, and night
3 There is no *s* nor language, where
Pr 17. 7 Excellent *s* becometh not a fool:
Isa 29. 4 thy *s* shall be low out of the dust,
4 thy *s* shall whisper out of the dust.
Eze 1.24 the voice of *s*, as the noise of an
Hab 3. 2 O Lord, I have heard thy *s*, and
Mt 26.73 them; for thy *s* bewrayeth thee.
Mk 7.32 and had an impediment in his *s*;
14.70 and thy *s* agreeth thereto.
Jn 8.43 Why do ye not understand my *s*?
Ac 14.11 saying in the *s* of Lycaonia,
20. 7 continued his *s* until midnight.
1Co 2. 1 with excellency of *s* or of wisdom,
4 my *s* and my preaching was not
4.19 not the *s* of them which are puffed
2Co 3.12 hope, we use great plainness of *s*:
7. 4 Great is my boldness of *s* toward
10.10 is weak, and his *s* contemptible.
11. 6 But though I be rude in *s*, yet not
Col 4. 6 Let your *s* be always with grace,
Tit 2. 8 Sound *s*, that cannot be condemned;

SPEECHES
Nu 12. 8 apparently, and not in dark *s*;
Job 6.26 and the *s* of one that is desperate,
15. 3 *s* wherewith he can do no good?
32.14 will I answer him with your *s*.
33. 1 Job, I pray thee, hear my *s*, and
Ro 16.18 fair *s* deceive the hearts of the
Jude 15 hard *s* which ungodly sinners have

SPEECHLESS
Mt 22.12 wedding garment? And he was *s*.
Lk 1.22 unto them, and remained *s*.
Ac 9. 7 which journeyed with him stood *s*,

SPEED
Gen 24.12 send me good *s* this day, and shew
1Sa 20.38 the lad, Make *s*, haste, stay not.
2Sa 15.14 make *s* to depart, lest he overtake
1Ki 12.18 Rehoboam made *s* to get him up to
2Ch 10.18 Rehoboam made *s* to get him up to
Ezr 6.12 a decree; let it be done with *s*.
Isa 5.19 Let him make *s*, and hasten his
26 they shall come with *s* swiftly:
Ac 17.15 for to come to him with all *s*,
2Jn 10 house, neither bid him God *s*:
11 For he that biddeth him God *s* is

SPEEDILY
Gen 44.11 they *s* took down every man his
1Sa 27. 1 I should *s* escape into the land of
2Sa 17.16 the wilderness, but *s* pass over;
2Ch 35.13 divided them *s* among all the people.
Ezr 6.13 the king had sent, so they did *s*.
7.17 thou mayest buy *s* with this money
21 shall require of you, it be done *s*,
26 judgment be executed *s* upon him,
Est 2. 9 and he *s* gave her her things for
Ps 31. 2 thine ear to me: deliver me *s*:
69.17 for I am in trouble: hear me *s*.
79. 8 thy tender mercies *s* prevent us:
102. 2 in the day when I call answer me *s*.
143. 7 Hear me *s*, O Lord: my spirit
Ec 8.11 an evil work is not executed *s*,
Isa 58. 8 thine health shall spring forth *s*:
Joel 3. 4 *s* will I return your recompense
Zec 8.21 us go *s* to pray before the Lord,
Lk 18. 8 that he will avenge them *s*.

SPEND
Dt 32.23 I will *s* mine arrows upon them.
Job 21.13 They *s* their days in wealth,
36.11 shall *s* their days in prosperity,
Ps 90. 9 we *s* our years as a tale that is told.
Isa 55. 2 do ye *s* money for that which is
Ac 20.16 he would not *s* the time in Asia:
2Co 12.15 I will very gladly *s* and be spent

SPENDEST
Lk 10.35 whatsoever thou *s* more, when I

SPENDETH
Pr 21.20 wise; but a foolish man *s* it up.
29. 3 with harlots *s* his substance.
Ec 6.12 vain life which he *s* as a shadow?

SPENT
Gen 21.15 And the water was *s* in the bottle,
47.18 my lord, how that our money is *s*;
Lev 26.20 your strength shall be *s* in vain:
Jdg 19.11 were by Jebus, the day was far *s*;
1Sa 9. 7 for the bread is *s* in our vessels,
Job 7. 6 shuttle, and are *s* without hope.
Ps 31.10 For my life is *s* with grief, and
Isa 49. 4 I have *s* my strength for nought,
Jer 37.21 all the bread in the city were *s*.
Mk 5.26 had *s* all that she had, and was
6.35 when the day was now far *s*, his
Lk 8.43 which had *s* all her living upon
15.14 when he had *s* all, there arose a
24.29 evening, and the day is far *s*.
Ac 17.21 there *s* their time in nothing else,
18.23 after he had *s* some time there,
27. 9 Now when much time was *s*, and
Ro 13.12 The night is far *s*, the day is at
2Co 12.15 gladly spend and be *s* for you;

SPICE
Ex 35.28 *s*, and oil for the light, and for
1Ki 10.15 of the traffick of the *s* merchants,
2Ch 9. 9 there any such *s* as the queen of
SS 5. 1 gathered my myrrh with my *s*;
Eze 24.10 consume the flesh, and *s* it well,

SPICES
Gen 43.11 *s*, and myrrh, nuts, and almonds:
Ex 25. 6 *s* for anointing oil, and for sweet
30.23 also unto thee principal *s*, of pure
34 Take unto thee sweet *s*, stacte,
34 sweet *s* with pure frankincense:
35. 8 *s* for anointing oil, and for the
37.29 and the pure incense of sweet *s*,
1Ki 10. 2 with camels that bare *s*, and very
10 of gold, and of *s* very great store,
10 no more such abundance of *s* as
25 garments, and armor, and *s*, and
2Ki 20.13 gold, and the *s*, and the precious
1Ch 9.29 and the frankincense, and the *s*.
30 priests made the ointment of the *s*.
2Ch 9. 1 and camels that bare *s*, and gold in
9 of gold, and of *s* great abundance,
24 raiment, harness, and *s*, horses,
16.14 sweet odors and divers kinds of *s*
32.27 precious stones, and for *s*, and
SS 4.10 smell of thine ointments than all *s*!
14 and aloes, with all the chief *s*:
16 that the *s* thereof may flow out.
5.13 His cheeks are as a bed of *s*, as
6. 2 into his garden, to the beds of *s*,
8.14 hart upon the mountains of *s*.
Isa 39. 2 and the gold, and the *s*, and the
Eze 27.22 in thy fairs with chief of all *s*,
Mk 16. 1 and Salome, had bought sweet *s*,
Lk 23.56 and prepared *s* and ointments;
24. 1 bringing the *s* which they had
Jn 19.40 wound it in linen clothes with the *s*,

SPIED
Ex 2.11 And he *s* an Egyptian smiting an
Jos 6.22 men that had *s* out the country,
2Ki 9.17 he *s* the company of Jehu as he
13.21 that, behold, they *s* a band of men;
23.16 he *s* the sepulchers that were there
24 abominations that were *s* in the

SPIES
Gen 42. 9 and said unto them, Ye are *s*;
11 true men, thy servants are no *s*.
14 spake unto you, saying, Ye are *s*:
16 the life of Pharaoh surely ye are *s*.
30 and took us for *s* of the country.
31 We are true men; we are no *s*:
34 I know that ye are no *s*, but that
Nu 21. 1 Israel came by the way of the *s*;
Jos 6.23 young men that were *s* went in,
Jdg 1.24 the *s* saw a man come forth out
1Sa 26. 4 David therefore sent out *s*, and
2Sa 15.10 Absalom sent *s* throughout all the
Lk 20.20 watched him, and sent forth *s*,
Heb 11.31 when she had received the *s* with

SPIKENARD
SS 1.12 my *s* sendeth forth the smell
4.13 pleasant fruits; camphire, with *s*,
14 *S* and saffron; calamus and
Mk 14. 3 box of ointment of *s* very
Jn 12. 3 Mary a pound of ointment of *s*

SPILLED
Gen 38. 9 that he *s* it on the ground, lest
Mk 2.22 the bottles, and the wine is *s*,
Lk 5.37 will burst the bottles, and be *s*,

SPIN
Ex 35.25 that were wise hearted did *s*
Mt 6.28 they toil not, neither do they *s*:
Lk 12.27 grow: they toil not, they *s* not;

SPINDLE
Pr 31.19 She layeth her hands to the *s*,

SPIRIT
Gen 1. 2 *S* of God moved upon the face of
41. 8 morning that his *s* was troubled;
38 is, a man in whom the *S* of God is?
Ex 28. 3 I have filled with the *s* of wisdom,
31. 3 I have filled him with the *s* of God,
Nu 11.25 when the *s* rested upon them, they
29 Lord would put his *s* upon them!
24. 2 and the *s* of God came upon him.
Dt 2.30 the Lord thy God hardened his *s*,
Jdg 9.23 Then God sent an evil *s* between
14. 6 *S* of the Lord came mightily upon
1Sa 16.13 *S* of the Lord came upon David
14 *S* of the Lord departed from Saul,
28. 7 a woman that hath a familiar *s*,
1Ki 18.12 the *S* of the Lord shall carry thee
22.22 I will be a lying *s* in the mouth of
24 Which way went the *S* of the Lord
2Ki 2. 9 double portion of thy *s* be upon me.
15 The *s* of Elijah doth rest on Elisha.
Neh 9.20 gavest also thy good *s* to instruct
Job 4.15 Then a *s* passed before my face;
7.11 I will speak in the anguish of my *s*;
15.13 that turnest thy *s* against God,
21. 4 why should not my *s* be troubled?
27. 3 and the *s* of God is in my nostrils;
32. 8 But there is a *s* in man: and the
33. 4 The *S* of God hath made me, and
Ps 31. 5 Into thine hand I commit my *s*:
32. 2 and in whose *s* there is no guile.
51.10 and renew a right *s* within me.
11 and take not thy holy *s* from me.
12 and uphold me with thy free *s*.
17 sacrifices of God are a broken *s*:
77. 6 and my *s* made diligent search.
104.30 Thou sendest forth thy *s*, they are
139. 7 Whither shall I go from thy *s*? or
143.10 thou art my God: thy *s* is good;
Pr 14.29 he that is hasty of *s* exalteth folly.
15.13 sorrow of the heart the *s* is broken.
16.18 and an haughty *s* before a fall.
17.22 but a broken *s* drieth the bones.
18.14 but a wounded *s* who can bear?
20.27 The *s* of man is the candle of the
Ec 1.14 all is vanity and vexation of *s*.
7. 8 and the patient in *s* is better
9 Be not hasty in thy *s* to be angry:
11. 5 knowest not...the way of the *s*,
12. 7 and the *s* shall return unto God
Isa 11. 2 *s* of the Lord shall rest upon him,
2 the *s* of wisdom and understanding,
2 the *s* of counsel and might,
2 the *s* of knowledge and of the fear
40. 7 the *s* of the Lord bloweth upon it:
61. 1 The *S* of the Lord God is upon me;
3 of praise for the *s* of heaviness;
63.11 he that put his holy *S* within him?
66. 2 him that is poor and of a contrite *s*,
Eze 1.20, 21 *s* of the living creature was in
3.12 Then the *s* took me up, and I heard
24 Then the *s* entered into me, and
11. 5 the *S* of the Lord fell upon me,
19 and I will put a new *s* within you;
36.27 And I will put my *s* within you,
Dan 4. 8 in whom is the *s* of the holy gods:
5.12 Forasmuch as an excellent *s*, and
Joel 2.28 I will pour out my *s* upon all flesh;
29 in those days will I pour out my *s*.
Mic 3. 8 full of power by the *s* of the Lord,
Zec 4. 6 might, nor by power, but by my *s*,
7.12 the Lord of hosts hath sent in his *s*
Mal 2.15 Therefore take heed to your *s*.
Mt 3.16 he saw the *S* of God descending
4. 1 led up of the *s* into the wilderness
5. 3 Blessed are the poor in *s*: for
10.20 *S* of your Father which speaketh
12.18 I will put my *s* upon him, and he
28 I cast out devils by the *S* of God,
22.43 doth David in *s* call him Lord,
26.41 the *s* indeed is willing, but the
Mk 1.10 and the *S* like a dove descending
23 a man with an unclean *s*; and he
2. 8 Jesus perceived in his *s* that they
5. 2 tombs a man with an unclean *s*,
8 out of the man, thou unclean *s*.
6.49 they supposed it had been a *s*,
14.38 The *s* truly is ready, but the flesh
Lk 1.17 him in the *s* and power of Elias,
80 child grew, and waxed strong in *s*,
2.27 came by the *S* into the temple:
4. 1 led by the *S* into the wilderness,
14 in the power of the *S* into Galilee:
8.29 unclean *s* to come out of the man.
9.39 And, lo, a *s* taketh him, and he
55 not what manner of *s* ye are of.
10.21 In that hour Jesus rejoiced in *s*,
23.46 into thy hands I commend my *s*:
24.37 supposed that they had seen a *s*.
39 for a *s* hath not flesh and bones, as
Jn 1.32 I saw the *S* descending from
3. 5 be born of water and of the *S*,
6 that which is born of the *S* is *s*.
4.23 shall worship the Father in *s* and
24 God is a *S*: and they that worship
6.63 It is the *s* that quickeneth; the
63 you, they are *s*, and they are life.
15.26 the *S* of truth, which proceedeth
16.13 when he, the *S* of truth, is come,
Ac 2. 4 as the *S* gave them utterance.
5. 9 to tempt the *S* of the Lord?
6.10 the wisdom and the *s* by which he
10.19 *S* said unto him, Behold, three
16. 7 but the *S* suffered them not.
17.16 his *s* was stirred in him, when he
18. 5 Paul was pressed in the *s*, and
19.15 And the evil *s* answered and said,
20.22 go bound in the *s* unto Jerusalem,
Ro 1. 4 according to the *s* of holiness, by
2.29 in the *s*, and not in the letter:
8. 1 not after the flesh, but after the *S*.
2 the law of the *S* of life in Christ
9 any man have not the *S* of Christ,
13 if ye through the *S* do mortify the
15 have not received the *s* of bondage
15 have received the *S* of adoption,
16 *S* itself beareth witness with our
26 *S* itself maketh intercession for us
27 knoweth what is the mind of the *S*,
1Co 2. 4 but in demonstration of the *S* and
10 for the *S* searcheth all things, yea,
5. 3 absent in body, but present in *s*,
6.11 Jesus, and by the *S* of our God.
17 is joined unto the Lord is one *s*.
7.34 may be holy both in body and in *s*:
12. 3 no man speaking by the *S* of God
4 diversities of gifts, but the same *S*.
8 word of knowledge by the same *S*:
9 To another faith by the same *S*;

BIBLICAL THEMES

SPIRIT

And the Spirit of God moved upon the face of the waters. Gen 1.2

And the Lord came down in a cloud, and spake unto [Moses], and took of the spirit that was upon him, and gave it unto the seventy elders: and . . . when the spirit rested upon them, they prophesied, and did not cease. Nu 11.25

Man doth not live by bread only, but by every word that proceedeth out of the mouth of the Lord. Dt 8.3

The spirit of God hath made me, and the breath of the Almighty hath given me life. Job 33.4

The spirit of man is the candle of the Lord. Pr 20.27

He put forth the form of an hand, and took me by a lock of mine head; and the spirit lifted me up between the earth and the heaven, and brought me in the visions of God to Jerusalem. Eze 8.3

Joseph, thou son of David, fear not to take unto thee Mary thy wife: for that which is conceived in her is of the Holy Ghost. And she shall bring forth a son, and thou shalt call his name JESUS: for he shall save his people from their sins. Mt 1.20-21

I indeed baptize you with water unto repentance . . . he shall baptize you with the Holy Ghost, and with fire. Mt 3.11

Jesus, when he was baptized, . . . saw the Spirit of God descending like a dove, and lighting upon him: and lo a voice from heaven, saying, This is my beloved Son. Mt 3.16-17

The spirit indeed is willing, but the flesh is weak. Mt 26.41

A man with an unclean spirit . . . cried out, . . . Let us alone; what have we to do with thee, thou Jesus of Nazareth? art thou come to destroy us? I know thee who thou art, the Holy One of God. Mk 1.23-24

The wind bloweth where it listeth, and thou hearest the sound thereof, but canst not tell whence it cometh, and whither it goeth: so is every one that is born of the Spirit. Jn 3.8

It is the spirit that quickeneth; the flesh profiteth nothing. Jn 6.63

I will pray the Father, and he shall give you another Comforter, that he may abide with you for ever; even the Spirit of truth. Jn 14.16-17

I have yet many things to say unto you, but ye cannot bear them now. Howbeit when he, the Spirit of truth, is come, he will guide you into all truth. Jn 16.12-13

And when the day of Pentecost was fully come, they were all with one accord in one place. And suddenly there came a sound from heaven as of a rushing mighty wind, and it filled all the house where they were sitting. And there appeared unto them cloven tongues like as of fire, and it sat upon each of them. And they were all filled with the Holy Ghost, and began to speak with other tongues, as the Spirit gave them utterance. Ac 2.1-4

The Spirit itself beareth witness with our spirit, that we are the children of God. . . . the Spirit also helpeth our infirmities . . . maketh intercession for us with groanings which cannot be uttered. Ro 8.16, 26

The Spirit searcheth all things, yea, the deep things of God. . . . But the natural man receiveth not the things of the Spirit of God. 1Co 2.10, 14

The flesh lusteth against the Spirit, and the Spirit against the flesh. . . . But the fruit of the Spirit is love, joy, peace, longsuffering, gentleness, goodness, faith, meekness, temperance. Gal 5.17, 22-23

It is the Spirit that beareth witness, because the Spirit is truth. 1Jn 5.6

1Co 12. 9 the gifts of healing by the same *S*;
13 by one *S* are we all baptized into
2Co 1.22 and given the earnest of the *S* in
3. 3 but with the *S* of the living God;
6 not of the letter, but of the *s*: for
6 letter killeth, but the *s* giveth life.
17 where the *S* of the Lord is, there is
7. 1 all filthiness of the flesh and *s*,
Gal 3. 2 Received ye the *S* by the works of
3 having begun in the *S*, are ye now
4. 6 sent forth the *S* of his Son into
5. 5 we through the *S* wait for the hope
17 For the flesh lusteth against the *S*,
18 But if ye be led of the *S*, ye are not
22 fruit of the *S* is love, joy, peace,
25 If we live in the *S*, let us also walk
Eph 1.13 sealed with that holy *S* of promise,
4. 3 to keep the unity of the *S* in the
4 There is one body, and one *S*,
23 be renewed in the *s* of your mind;
5. 9 (For the fruit of the *S* is in all
18 excess; but be filled with the *S*
6.17 the sword of the *S*, which is the
Col 1. 8 unto us your love in the *S*.
2. 5 yet am I with you in the *s*, joying
1Th 4. 8 hath also I given unto us his holy *S*.
5.19 Quench not the *S*.
23 your whole *s* and soul and body be
1Ti 3.16 justified in the *S*, seen of angels,
4. 1 Now the *S* speaketh expressly,
12 in charity, in *s*, in faith, in purity.
2Ti 1. 7 hath not given us the *s* of fear;
4.22 Lord Jesus Christ be with thy *s*.
Heb 4.12 the dividing asunder of soul and *s*,
9.14 who through the eternal *s* offered
Jas 2.26 as the body without the *s* is dead,
4. 5 The *s* that dwelleth in us lusteth
1Pe 1. 2 through sanctification of the *S*,
3. 4 ornament of a meek and quiet *s*,
18 the flesh, but quickened by the *S*:
1Jn 3.24 by the *S* which he hath given us.
4. 1 Beloved, believe not every *s*, but
Jude 19 sensual, having not the *S*.
Rev 1.10 I was in the *S* on the Lord's day,
11.11 the *S* of life from God entered into
14.13 Yea, saith the *S*, that they may
22.17 the *S* and the bride say, Come.

SPIRITS

Lev 19.31 Regard not...that have familiar *s*,
Nu 16.22 God, the God of the *s* of all flesh,
1Sa 28. 3 put away those that had familiar *s*,
2Ki 21. 6 dealt with familiar *s* and wizards:
Ps 104. 4 Who maketh his angels *s*; his
Pr 16. 2 eyes; but the Lord weigheth the *s*.
Zec 6. 5 are the four *s* of the heavens,
Mt 8.16 he cast out the *s* with his word,
10. 1 gave them power against unclean *s*,
12.45 seven other *s* more wicked than
Mk 1.27 commandeth he even the unclean *s*,
3.11 unclean *s*, when they saw him, fell
5.13 And the unclean *s* went out, and
6. 7 gave them power over unclean *s*;
Lk 4.36 he commandeth the unclean *s*,
6.18 that were vexed with unclean *s*:
7.21 and plagues, and of evil *s*; and
8. 2 which had been healed of evil *s*
10.20 that the *s* are subject unto you;
11.26 seven other *s* more wicked than
Ac 5.16 which were vexed with unclean *s*:
8. 7 unclean *s*, crying with loud voice,
19.12 and the evil *s* went out of them.
13 call over them which had evil *s*
1Co 12.10 to another discerning of *s*; to
14.32 *s* of the prophets are subject to the
1Ti 4. 1 giving heed to seducing *s*, and
Heb 1. 7 Who maketh his angels *s*, and his
14 Are they not all ministering *s*, sent
12. 9 in subjection unto the Father of *s*,
23 to the *s* of just men made perfect,
1Pe 3.19 and preached unto the *s* in prison;
1Jn 4. 1 try the *s* whether they are of God:
Rev 1. 4 the seven *S* which are before his
3. 1 he that hath the seven *S* of God,
4. 5 which are the seven *S* of God.
5. 6 which are the seven *S* of God sent
16.13 three unclean *s* like frogs come out
14 they are the *s* of devils, working

SPIRITUAL

Hos 9. 7 is a fool, the *s* man is mad.
Ro 1.11 may impart unto you some *s* gift,
7.14 For we know that the law is *s*: but
15.27 made partakers of their *s* things,
1Co 2.13 comparing *s* things with *s*.
15 But he that is *s* judgeth all things,
3. 1 not speak unto you as unto *s*,
9.11 If we have sown unto you *s* things,
10. 3 And did all eat the same *s* meat;
4 And did all drink the same *s* drink:
4 drank of that *s* Rock that followed
12. 1 Now concerning *s* gifts, brethren, I
14. 1 after charity, and desire *s* gifts,
12 as ye are zealous of *s* gifts, seek
37 himself to be a prophet, or *s*,

15.44 natural body; it is raised a *s* body.
44 natural body, and there is a *s* body.
46 that was not first which is *s*, but
46 and afterward that which is *s*.
Gal 6. 1 ye which are *s*, restore such an one
Eph 1. 3 blessed us with all *s* blessings in
5.19 in psalms and hymns and *s* songs,
6.12 against *s* wickedness in high
Col 1. 9 all wisdom and *s* understanding;
3.16 in psalms and hymns and *s* songs,
1Pe 2. 5 stones, are built up a *s* house,
5 priesthood, to offer up *s* sacrifices,

SPIRITUALLY
Ro 8. 6 but to be *s* minded is life and
1Co 2.14 because they are *s* discerned.
Rev 11. 8 which *s* is called Sodom and Egypt,

SPIT
Lev 15. 8 he that hath the issue *s* upon him
Nu 12.14 her father had but *s* in her face,
Dt 25. 9 and *s* in his face, and shall answer
Job 30.10 me, and spare not to *s* in my face.
Mt 26.67 Then did they *s* in his face, and
27.30 And they *s* upon him, and took the
Mk 7.33 and he *s*, and touched his tongue;
8.23 when he had *s* on his eyes, and put
10.34 and shall *s* upon him, and shall
14.65 And some began to *s* on him, and to
15.19 did *s* upon him, and bowing their

SPITE
Ps 10.14 thou beholdest mischief and *s*, to

SPITEFULLY
Mt 22. 6 servants, and entreated them *s*,
Lk 18.32 shall be mocked, and *s* entreated,

SPITTED
Lk 18.32 spitefully entreated, and *s* on:

SPITTING
Isa 50. 6 hid not my face from shame and *s*.

SPITTLE
1Sa 21.13 let his *s* fall down upon his beard.
Job 7.19 alone till I swallow down my *s*?
Jn 9. 6 ground, and made clay of the *s*,

SPOIL
Ex 3.22 and ye shall *s* the Egyptians.
Jos 11.14 the *s* of these cities, and the cattle,
1Sa 14.32 And the people flew upon the *s*,
15.19 but didst fly upon the *s*, and didst
2Ch 20.25 three days in gathering of the *s*,
Ps 68.12 that tarried at home divided the *s*.
89.41 All that pass by the way *s* him:
119.162 word, as one that findeth great *s*.
Isa 3.14 the *s* of the poor is in your houses.
9. 3 men rejoice when they divide the *s*.
53.12 divide the *s* with the strong;
Zec 2. 9 shall be a *s* to their servants:
Mt 12.29 man's house, and *s* his goods,
29 man? and then he will *s* his house.
Mk 3.27 man's house, and *s* his goods,
27 man; and then he will *s* his house.
Col 2. 8 Beware lest any man *s* you

SPOILED
Job 12.17 He leadeth counsellers away *s*,
19 He leadeth princes away *s*, and
Jer 4.13 Woe unto us! for we are *s*.
10.20 My tabernacle is *s*, and all my
Eze 39.10 they shall spoil those that *s* them,
Am 3.11 thee, and thy palaces shall be *s*.
Mic 2. 4 and say, We be utterly *s*: he hath
Hab 2. 8 thou hast *s* many nations, all the
Zec 11. 2 fallen; because the mighty are *s*:
3 for their glory is *s*: a voice of the
Col 2.15 having *s* principalities...powers,

SPOILER
Isa 16. 4 to them from the face of the *s*:
4 the *s* ceaseth, the oppressors are
21. 2 treacherously, and the *s* spoileth.
Jer 6.26 the *s* shall suddenly come upon us.
15. 8 of the young men a *s* at noonday:
48. 8 the *s* shall come upon every city,
18 *s* of Moab shall come upon thee,
32 *s* is fallen upon thy summer fruits
51.56 Because the *s* is come upon her,

SPOILERS
Jdg 2.14 the hands of *s* that spoiled them,
1Sa 13.17 the *s* came out of the camp of the
14.15 and the *s*, they also trembled, and
2Ki 17.20 them into the hand of *s*, until
Jer 12.12 *s* are come upon all high places
51.48 the *s* shall come unto her from the
53 yet from me shall *s* come unto her,

SPOILING
Ps 35.12 evil for good to the *s* of my soul.
Isa 22. 4 because of the *s* of the daughter
Jer 48. 3 *s* and great destruction.
Hab 1. 3 for *s* and violence are before me:
Heb 10.34 took joyfully the *s* of your goods,

SPOILS
Jos 7.21 among the *s* a goodly Babylonish
1Ch 26.27 Out of the *s* won in battles did
Isa 25.11 together with the *s* of their hands.
Lk 11.22 he trusted, and divideth his *s*.
Heb 7. 4 Abraham gave the tenth of the *s*.

SPOKEN
Gen 12. 4 as the Lord had *s* unto him;
21. 1 Lord did unto Sarah as he had *s*.
Ex 19. 8 All that the Lord hath *s* we will do.
32.34 place of which I have *s* unto thee:
33.17 do this thing also that thou hast *s*:
Dt 1.14 thing which thou hast *s* is good for
18.22 prophet hath *s* it presumptuously:
2Ch 18.22 the Lord hath *s* evil against thee.
Est 7. 9 who had *s* good for the king,
Job 33. 2 my tongue hath *s* in my mouth.
34.35 Job hath *s* without knowledge,
40. 5 Once have I *s*; but I will not
Ps 50. 1 God, even the Lord, hath *s*, and
87. 3 Glorious things are *s* of thee, O
108. 7 God hath *s* in his holiness; I will
116.10 believed, therefore have I *s*: I was
Pr 15.23 a word *s* in due season, how good
25.11 word fitly *s* is like apples of gold
Isa 1. 2 ear, O earth: for the Lord hath *s*,
20 for the mouth of the Lord hath *s* it.
39. 8 is the word...which thou hast *s*.
40. 5 for the mouth of the Lord hath *s* it.
45.19 I have not *s* in secret, in a dark
46.11 I have *s* it, I will also bring it to
58.14 for the mouth of the Lord hath *s* it.
59. 3 your lips have *s* lies, your tongue
Jer 29.23 have *s* lying words in my name,
Eze 17.24 I the Lord have *s* and have done it.
22.28 God, when the Lord hath not *s*.
Hos 7.13 yet they have *s* lies against me.
12.10 I have also *s* by the prophets, and
Joel 3. 8 far off: for the Lord hath *s* it.
Am 3. 8 the Lord hath *s*, who can but
Mic 4. 4 mouth of the Lord of hosts hath *s*
6.12 the inhabitants thereof have *s* lies,
Mt 2.17 which was *s* by Jeremy the prophet,
3. 3 that was *s* of by the prophet Esaias,
26.65 saying, He hath *s* blasphemy;
Mk 12.12 had *s* the parable against them:
Lk 2.34 for a sign which shall be *s* against;
12. 3 whatsoever ye have *s* in darkness
3 ye have *s* in the ear in closets
Jn 11.13 had *s* of taking of rest in sleep.
12.49 For I have not *s* of myself; but
14.25 These things have I *s* unto you,

Spoils from the sack of Jerusalem in A.D. 70 included the seven-branched candlestick from the temple, shown being carried away by victorious troops in this relief on the commemorative Arch of Titus in Rome.

Jn 16.25 have I *s* unto you in proverbs:
18.23 If I have *s* evil, bear witness of
Ac 23. 9 a spirit or an angel hath *s* to him,
27.35 he had thus *s*, he took bread,
Ro 1. 8 that your faith is *s* of throughout
14.16 Let not then your good be evil *s* of:
1Co 10.30 why am I evil *s* of for that for
2Co 4.13 believed, and therefore have I *s*;
Heb 1. 2 last days *s* unto us by his Son,
2Pe 2. 2 the way of truth shall be evil *s* of.
3. 2 *s* before by the holy prophets,
Jude 17 were *s* before of the apostles

SPOKESMAN
Ex 4.16 he shall be thy *s* unto the people:

SPORT
Jdg 16.25 Samson, that he may make us *s*.
25 house; and he made them *s*:
27 that beheld while Samson made *s*.
Pr 10.23 It is as *s* to a fool to do mischief:
26.19 neighbor, and saith, Am...I in *s*?
Isa 57. 4 Against whom do ye *s* yourselves?

SPORTING
Gen 26. 8 behold, Isaac was *s* with Rebekah
2Pe 2.13 *s* themselves with their own

SPOT
Job 11.15 thou lift up thy face without *s*;
Eph 5.27 not having *s*, or wrinkle, or any
1Ti 6.14 keep this commandment without *s*,
Heb 9.14 offered himself without *s* to God,
1Pe 1.19 without blemish and without *s*:
2Pe 3.14 found of him in peace, without *s*,

SPOTS
Jer 13.23 his skin, or the leopard his *s*?
2Pe 2.13 *S* they are and blemishes,
Jude 12 These are *s* in your feasts of

SPOTTED
Gen 30.32 all the speckled and *s* cattle, and
Jude 23 even the garment *s* by the flesh.

SPOUSE
SS 4. 8 with me from Lebanon, my *s*,
9 my heart, my sister, my *s*; thou
10 fair is thy love, my sister, my *s*!
11 Thy lips, O my *s*, drop as the
12 garden inclosed is my sister, my *s*;
5. 1 into my garden, my sister, my *s*:

SPOUSES
Hos 4.13 and your *s* shall commit adultery.
14 your *s* when they commit adultery:

SPRANG
Mk 4. 5 and immediately it *s* up, because
8 yield fruit that *s* up and increased,
Lk 8. 7 and the thorns *s* up with it, and
8 fell on good ground, and *s* up,
Ac 16.29 he called for a light, and *s* in, and
Heb 7.14 that our Lord *s* out of Juda; of
11.12 Therefore *s* there even of one, and

SPREAD
Ex 9.29 I will *s* abroad my hands unto the
37. 9 the cherubims *s* out their wings on
Jdg 8.25 And they *s* a garment, and did cast
Ru 3. 9 *s* therefore thy skirt over thine
1Sa 30.16 were *s* abroad upon all the earth,
2Ch 6.13 *s* forth his hands toward heaven,
29 *s* forth his hands in this house:
Ezr 9. 5 *s* out my hands unto the Lord my
Job 29.19 My root was *s* out by the waters,
37.18 thou with him *s* out the sky,
Ps 105.39 He *s* a cloud for a covering; and
140. 5 they have *s* a net by the wayside;
Pr 1.17 Surely in vain the net is *s* in the
Isa 19. 8 they that *s* nets upon the waters
25. 7 the vail that is *s* over all nations.
58. 5 to *s* sackcloth and ashes under
65. 2 I have *s* out my hands all the day
La 1.13 he hath *s* a net for my feet, he hath
Eze 12.13 My net also will I *s* upon him, and
16. 8 I *s* my skirt over thee, and covered
Hos 14. 6 His branches shall *s*, and his
Joel 2. 2 morning *s* upon the mountains:
Zec 2. 6 *s* you abroad as the four winds
Mt 9.31 *s* abroad his fame in all that
21. 8 *s* their garments in the way;
Mk 1.28 immediately his fame *s* abroad
6.14 (for his name was *s* abroad:) and
11. 8 many *s* their garments in the way:
Lk 19.36 they *s* their clothes in the way.
Ac 4.17 it *s* no further among the people,
1Th 1. 8 faith to God-ward is *s* abroad;

SPREADETH
Lev 13. 8 the scab *s* in the skin,then the
Dt 32.11 As an eagle...*s* abroad her wings,
Job 9. 8 Which alone *s* out the heavens,
26. 9 throne, and *s* his cloud upon it.
36.30 Behold, he *s* his light upon it,
41.30 he *s* sharp pointed things upon
Pr 29. 5 his neighbor *s* a net for his feet.
Isa 25.11 that swimmeth *s* forth his hands
40.19 the goldsmith *s* it over with gold,
22 *s* them out as a tent to dwell in:
44.24 *s* abroad the earth by myself;
Jer 4.31 that *s* her hands, saying, Woe is
17. 8 that *s* out her roots by the river,
La 1.17 Zion *s* forth her hands, and there

SPREADING
Ps 37.35 *s* himself like a green bay tree.

SPRING
Nu 21.17 sang this song, *S* up, O well;
Dt 8. 7 and depths that *s* out of valleys
Jdg 19.25 when the day began to *s*, they let
1Sa 9.26 to pass about the *s* of the day,
2Ki 2.21 forth unto the *s* of the waters,
Job 5. 6 neither doth trouble *s* out of the
38.27 bud of the tender herb to *s* forth?
Ps 85.11 Truth shall *s* out of the earth; and
92. 7 When the wicked *s* as the grass,
Pr 25.26 fountain, and a corrupt *s*.
SS 4.12 a *s* shut up, a fountain sealed.
Isa 42. 9 before they *s* forth I tell you of
43.19 now it shall *s* forth; shall ye not
44. 4 they shall *s* up as among the grass,
45. 8 let righteousness *s* up together;
58. 8 thine health shall *s* forth speedily:
11 like a *s* of water, whose waters
61.11 that are sown in it to *s* forth;
11 and praise to *s* forth before all the
Eze 17. 9 wither in all the leaves of her *s*,
Hos 13.15 and his *s* shall become dry, and
Joel 2.22 pastures of the wilderness do *s*,
Mk 4.27 and the seed should *s* and grow up,

SPRINGING
Gen 26.19 and found there a well of *s* water.
2Sa 23. 4 as the tender grass *s* out of the earth
Ps 65.10 thou blessest the *s* thereof.
Jn 4.14 of water *s* up into everlasting life.
Heb 12.15 lest any root of bitterness *s* up

SPRINGS
Dt 4.49 the plain, under the *s* of Pisgah.
Jos 10.40 and of the *s*, and all their kings;
12. 8 and in the *s*, and in the wilderness,
15.19 land; give me also *s* of water.
19 her the upper *s*, and the nether *s*.
Jdg 1.15 land; give me also *s* of water.
15 her the upper *s* and the nether *s*.
Job 38.16 entered into the *s* of the sea?
Ps 87. 7 be there: all my *s* are in thee.
104.10 He sendeth the *s* into the valleys,
Isa 35. 7 and the thirsty land *s* of water:
41.18 and the dry land *s* of water.
49.10 *s* of water shall he guide them.
Jer 51.36 up her sea, and make her *s* dry.

SPRINKLE
Nu 8. 7 *S* water of purifying upon them,
Isa 52.15 So shall he *s* many nations; the
Eze 36.25 will I *s* clean water upon you, and

SPRINKLED
Ex 9.10 Moses *s* it up toward heaven;
24. 8 the blood, and *s* it on the people,
Job 2.12 *s* dust upon their heads toward
Isa 63. 3 blood...be *s* upon my garments,
Heb 9.19 and *s* both the book, and all the
21 *s* with blood both the tabernacle,
10.22 hearts *s* from an evil conscience,

SPRINKLING
Heb 9.13 ashes of an heifer *s* the unclean,
11.28 the passover, and the *s* of blood,
12.24 to the blood of *s*, that speaketh
1Pe 1. 2 and *s* of the blood of Jesus Christ:

SPROUT
Job 14. 7 be cut down, that it will *s* again,

SPRUNG
Gen 41. 6 the east wind *s* up after them.
23 the east wind, *s* up after them:
Lev 13.42 a leprosy *s* up in his bald head,
Mt 4.16 and shadow of death light is *s* up.
13. 5 and forthwith they *s* up, because
7 the thorns *s* up, and choked them:
26 But when the blade was *s* up, and
Lk 8. 6 soon as it was *s* up, it withered

SPUE
Lev 18.28 That the land *s* not you out also,
20.22 to dwell therein, *s* you not out.
Jer 25.27 be drunken, and *s*, and fall, and
Rev 3.16 I will *s* thee out of my mouth.

SPUNGE
Mt 27.48 a *s*, and filled it with vinegar,
Mk 15.36 ran and filled a *s* full of vinegar.
Jn 19.29 and they filled a *s* with vinegar,

SPY
Nu 13.16 Moses sent to *s* out the land.
17 Moses sent them to *s* out the land
21.32 And Moses sent to *s* out Jaazer,
Jos 2. 1 of Shittim two men to *s* secretly,
6.25 Joshua sent to *s* out Jericho.
Jdg 18. 2 to *s* out the land, and to search it;
14 went to *s* out the country of Laish,
17 men that went to *s* out the land
2Sa 10. 3 to search the city, and to *s* it out,
2Ki 6.13 Go and *s* where he is, that I may
1Ch 19. 3 overthrow, and to *s* out the land?
Gal 2. 4 came in privily to *s* out our liberty

SQUARE
1Ki 7. 5 all the doors and posts were *s*,
Eze 43.16 *s* in the four squares thereof.
45. 2 hundred in breadth, *s* round about;

STABLE
1Ch 16.30 the world also shall be *s*, that it

STABLISH
2Sa 7.13 I will *s* the throne of his kingdom
1Ch 17.12 and I will *s* his throne for ever.
18. 3 to *s* his dominion by the river
2Ch 7.18 Then will I *s* the throne of thy
Est 9.21 To *s* this among them, that they
Ps 119.38 *S* thy word unto thy servant, who
Ro 16.25 to *s* you according to my gospel,
1Th 3.13 To the end he may *s* your hearts
2Th 2.17 and *s* you in every good word and
3. 3 who shall *s* you, and keep you
Jas 5. 8 Be ye also patient; *s* your hearts:
1Pe 5.10 make you perfect, *s*, strengthen,

STABLISHED
2Ch 17. 5 the Lord *s* the kingdom in his
Ps 93. 1 the world also is *s*, that it cannot
148. 6 He hath also *s* them for ever and
Col 2. 7 and *s* in the faith, as ye have been

STABLISHETH
Hab 2.12 blood, and *s* a city by iniquity!
2Co 1.21 he which *s* us with you in Chirst,

STAFF
Gen 38.18 and thy *s* that is in thine hand.
25 the signet, and bracelets, and *s*.
Ex 12.11 feet, and your *s* in your hand;
1Sa 17. 7 And the *s* of his spear was like a
2Sa 21.19 the *s* of whose spear was like a
2Ki 4.29 lay my *s* upon the face of the child.
1Ch 20. 5 spear *s* was like a weaver's beam.
Ps 23. 4 rod and thy *s* they comfort me.
Isa 9. 4 the *s* of his shoulder, the rod of
14. 5 hath broken the *s* of the wicked,
Zec 8. 4 every man with his *s* in his hand
11.10 And I took my *s*, even Beauty,
14 Then I cut asunder mine other *s*,
Mk 6. 8 for their journey, save a *s* only;
Heb 11.21 leaning upon the top of his *s*.

STAGGER
Job 12.25 them to *s* like a drunken man.
Ps 107.27 fro, and *s* like a drunken man,
Isa 29. 9 they *s*, but not with strong drink.

STAGGERED
Ro 4.20 He *s* not at the promise of God

STAIN
Job 3. 5 and the shadow of death *s* it;
Isa 23. 9 to *s* the pride of all glory, and to
63. 3 and I will *s* all my raiment.

STAIRS
1Ki 6. 8 with winding *s* into the middle
2Ki 9.13 it under him on the top of the *s*,
Ne 3.15 the *s* that go down from the city
9. 4 up upon the *s*, of the Levites,
12.37 up by the *s* of the city of David,
SS 2.14 rock, in the secret places of the *s*,
Eze 40. 6 east, and went up the *s* thereof,
43.17 his *s* shall look toward the east.
Ac 21.35 And when he came upon the *s*, so
40 Paul stood on the *s*, and beckoned

STALK
Gen 41. 5 ears of corn came up upon one *s*,
22 seven ears came up in one *s*, full
Hos 8. 7 reap the whirlwind: it hath no *s*:

STALL
Am 6. 4 calves out of the midst of the *s*;
Mal 4. 2 and grow up as calves of the *s*.
Lk 13.15 loose his ox or his ass from the *s*,

STALLS
1Ki 4.26 had forty thousand *s* of horses
2Ch 9.25 had four thousand *s* for horses
32.28 and *s* for all manner of beasts, and
Hab 3.17 there shall be no herd in the *s*;

STAMMERING
Isa 28.11 with *s* lips and another tongue
33.19 of a *s* tongue, that thou canst not

STAMP
2Sa 22.43 I did *s* them as the mire of the
Eze 6.11 thine hand, and *s* with thy foot,

STAMPED
Dt 9.21 and burnt it with fire, and *s* it,
2Ki 23. 6 *s* it small to powder, and cast the
15 *s* it small to powder, and burned
2Ch 15.16 Asa cut down her idol, and *s* it,
Eze 25. 6 and *s* with the feet, and rejoiced
Dan 7. 7 *s* the residue with the feet of it:
19 and *s* the residue with his feet;
8. 7 to the ground, and *s* upon him:
10 to the ground, and *s* upon them.

STANCHED
Lk 8.44 immediately her issue of blood *s*.

STAND
Gen 24.13 I *s* here by the well of water; and
Ex 14.13 Fear ye not, *s* still, and see the
Nu 9. 8 *S* still, and I will hear what the
Dt 7.24 no man be able to *s* before thee,
10. 8 to *s* before the Lord to minister
Jos 10.12 Sun, *s* thou still upon Gibeon;
1Sa 6.20 Who is able to *s* before this holy
12.16 Now...*s* and see this great thing,
2Ki 10. 4 before him: how then shall we *s*?
1Ch 21.16 angel of the Lord *s* between the
23.30 to *s* every morning to thank and
Neh 9. 5 *S* up and bless the Lord your God
Job 19.25 he shall *s* at the latter day upon
30.20 I *s* up, and thou regardest me
33. 5 thy words in order before me, *s* up.
Ps 1. 5 the ungodly shall not *s* in the
4. 4 *S* in awe, and sin not: commune
5. 5 foolish shall not *s* in thy sight:
24. 3 or who shall *s* in his holy place?
33. 8 inhabitants of the world *s* in awe
94.16 who will *s* up for me against the
109. 6 and let Satan *s* at his right hand.
122. 2 Our feet shall *s* within thy gates,
130. 3 iniquities, O Lord, who shall *s*?
134. 1 which by night *s* in the house of the
Pr 25. 6 *s* not in the place of great men:
27. 4 but who is able to *s* before envy?
Ec 8. 3 of his sight: *s* not in an evil thing;
Isa 21. 8 I *s*...upon the watchtower
40. 8 word of our God shall *s* for ever.
50. 8 let us *s* together: who is mine
Jer 7. 2 *S* in the gate of the Lord's house,
46.14 *S* fast, and prepare thee; for the
Eze 2. 1 Son of man, *s* upon thy feet, and I
44.24 they shall *s* in judgment; and
Dan 7. 4 and made *s* upon the feet as a man,
8. 7 there was no power in the ram to *s*
11.20 *s* up in his estate a raiser of taxes
12. 1 And at that time shall Michael *s* up,
Na 1. 6 Who can *s* before his indignation?
Hab 2. 1 I will *s* upon my watch, and set me
Zec 4.14 *s* by the Lord of the whole earth.
14. 4 his feet shall *s* in that day upon
Mal 3. 2 who shall *s* when he appeareth?
Mt 12.25 divided against itself shall not *s*:
26 how shall then his kingdom *s*?
47 mother and thy brethren *s* without,
20. 6 them, Why *s* ye here all the day idle?
24.15 the prophet, *s* in the holy place,
Mk 3. 3 had the withered hand, *S* forth.
24 itself, that kingdom cannot *s*.
25 against itself, that house cannot *s*.
26 and be divided, he cannot *s*, but
9. 1 there be some of them that *s* here,
11.25 And when ye *s* praying, forgive,
Lk 1.19 that *s* in the presence of God;
6. 8 Rise up, and *s* forth in the midst.
8.20 mother and thy brethren *s* without,
11.18 himself, how shall his kingdom *s*?
13.25 and ye begin to *s* without, and to
21.36 and to *s* before the Son of man.
Jn 11.42 of the people which *s* by I said it,
Ac 1.11 why *s* ye gazing up into heaven?
4.10 this man *s* here before you whole.
5.20 Go, *s* and speak in the temple to
8.38 commanded the chariot to *s* still:
10.26 *S* up; I myself also am a man.
14.10 loud voice, *S* upright on thy feet.
25.10 I *s* at Caesar's judgment seat,
26. 6 I *s* and am judged for the hope of
16 But rise, and *s* upon thy feet: for
Ro 5. 2 faith into this grace wherein we *s*,
9.11 God according to election might *s*,
14. 4 up: for God is able to make him *s*.
10 we shall all *s* before the judgment
1Co 2. 5 should not *s* in the wisdom of men,
15. 1 have received, and wherein ye *s*;
30 why *s* we in jeopardy every hour?
16.13 *s* fast in the faith, quit you like
2Co 1.24 of your joy: for by faith ye *s*.
Gal 4.20 my voice; for I *s* in doubt of you.
5. 1 *S* fast therefore in the liberty
Eph 6.11 may be able to *s* against the wiles
13 evil day, and having done all, to *s*.
14 *S* therefore, having your loins girt
Php 1.27 that ye *s* fast in one spirit, with
4. 1 so *s* fast in the Lord, my dearly
Col 4.12 ye may *s* perfect and complete in
1Th 3. 8 we live, if ye *s* fast in the Lord.
2Th 2.15 *s* fast, and hold the traditions
Jas 2. 3 *S* thou there, or sit here under
1Pe 5.12 the true grace of God wherein ye *s*.
Rev 3.20 Behold, I *s* at the door, and knock:
6.17 come; and who shall be able to *s*?
10. 5 angel which I saw *s* upon the sea
15. 2 *s* on the sea of glass, having the
18.15 shall *s* afar off for the fear of her
20.12 I saw the dead...*s* before God;

STANDARD
Nu 1.52 and every man by his own *s*,
2. 2 of Israel shall pitch by his own *s*,
3 they of the *s* of the camp of Judah
10 be the *s* of the camp of Reuben
18 be the *s* of the camp of Ephraim
25 The *s* of the camp of Dan shall be
10.14 went the *s* of the camp...of Judah
18 And the *s* of the camp of Reuben
22 the *s* of the camp...of Ephraim
25 And the *s* of the camp...of Dan
Isa 49.22 and set up my *s* to the people:
59.19 Spirit of the Lord shall lift up a *s*
62.10 stones; lift up a *s* for the people.
Jer 4. 6 Set up the *s* toward Zion: retire
21 How long shall I see the *s*, and
50. 2 and publish, and set up a *s*;
51.12 Set...*s* upon the walls of Babylon,
27 Set ye up a *s* in the land, blow the

STANDEST
Gen 24.31 wherefore *s* thou without? for I
Ex 3. 5 the place whereon thou *s* is holy
Jos 5.15 the place whereon thou *s* is holy.
Ps 10. 1 Why *s* thou afar off, O Lord? why
Ac 7.33 for the place where thou *s* is holy
Ro 11.20 broken off, and thou *s* by faith.

STANDETH
Nu 14.14 and that thy cloud *s* over them,
Dt 1.38 son of Nun, which *s* before thee,
17.12 that *s* to minister there before the
29.15 him that *s* here with us this day
Jdg 16.26 pillars whereupon the house *s*,
Est 6. 5 Behold, Haman *s* in the court.
7. 9 gallows...*s* in the house of Haman.
Ps 1. 1 nor *s* in the way of sinners, nor
26.12 My foot *s* in an even place: in the
33.11 The counsel of the Lord *s* for ever,
82. 1 God *s* in the congregation of the
119.161 but my heart *s* in awe of thy word.
Pr 8. 2 She *s* in the top of high places, by
SS 2. 9 he *s* behind our wall, he looketh
Isa 3.13 The Lord *s* up to plead,
13 and *s* to judge the people.
46. 7 and set him in his place, and he *s*;
59.14 backward, and justice *s* afar off:
Dan 12. 1 prince which *s* for the children of
Zec 11.16 broken, nor feed that that *s* still:
Jn 1.26 but there *s* one among you, whom
3.29 which *s* and heareth him,
Ro 14. 4 to his own master he *s* or falleth.
1Co 7.37 he that *s* stedfast in his heart,
8.13 I will eat no flesh while the world *s*,
10.12 let him that thinketh he *s* take

2Ti 2.19 the foundation of God *s* sure,
Heb 10.11 every priest *s* daily ministering
Jas 5. 9 behold, the judge *s* before the door.
Rev 10. 8 the angel which *s* upon the sea and

STANDING

Ex 22. 6 stacks of corn, or the *s* corn,
26.15 tabernacle of shittim wood *s* up.
36.20 tabernacle of shittim wood, *s* up.
Lev 26. 1 neither rear you up a *s* image,
Nu 22.23, 31 angel of the Lord *s* in the way,
Dt 23.25 When thou comest into the *s* corn
25 sickle unto thy neighbor's *s* corn.
Jdg 15. 5 into the *s* corn of the Philistines,
5 the shocks, and also the *s* corn,
1Sa 19.20 Samuel *s* as appointed over them,
22. 6 his servants were *s* about him;)
1Ki 13.25 and the lion *s* by the carcass:
28 ass and the lion *s* by the carcass:
22.19 and all the host of heaven *s* by him
2Ch 9.18 place, and two lions *s* by the stays:
18.18 the host of heaven *s* on his right
Est 5. 2 Esther the queen *s* in the court,
Ps 69. 2 deep mire, where there is no *s*:
107.35 the wilderness into a *s* water,
114. 8 turned the rock into a *s* water,
Dan 8. 6 I had seen *s* before the river,
Am 9. 1 I saw the Lord *s* upon the altar:
Mic 1.11 he shall receive of you his *s*.
5.13 thy *s* images out of the midst of
Zec 3. 1 the high priest *s* before the angel
1 Satan *s* at his right hand to resist
6. 5 from *s* before the Lord of all the
Mt 6. 5 to pray *s* in the synagogues
16.28 There be some *s* here, which shall
20. 3 others *s* idle in the marketplace,
6 went out, and found others *s* idle,
Mk 3.31 and, *s* without, sent unto him,
13.14 desolation,...*s* where it ought not,
Lk 1.11 *s* on the right side of the altar of
5. 2 And saw two ships *s* by the lake:
9.27 there be some *s* here, which shall
18.13 publican, *s* afar off, would not lift
Jn 8. 9 and the woman *s* in the midst.
19.26 disciple *s* by, whom he loved,
20.14 herself back, and saw Jesus *s*,
Ac 2.14 Peter, *s* up with the eleven, lifted
4.14 the man which was healed *s* with
5.23 keepers *s* without before the doors:
25 put in prison are *s* in the temple,
7.55 Jesus *s* on the right hand of God.
56 Son of man *s* on the right hand of
22.20 I also was *s* by, and consenting
24.21 voice, that I cried *s* among them,
Heb 9. 8 the first tabernacle was yet *s*:
2Pe 3. 5 earth *s* out of the water and in
Rev 7. 1 four angels *s* on the four corners
11. 4 two candlesticks *s* before the God
18.10 *S* afar off for...fear of her torment,
19.17 And I saw an angel *s* in the sun;

STAR

Nu 24.17 shall come a *S* out of Jacob, and
Am 5.26 your images, the *s* of your god,
Mt 2. 2 for we have seen his *s* in the east,
7 what time the *s* appeared.
9 the *s*, which they saw in the east,
10 When they saw the *s*, they rejoiced
Ac 7.43 and the *s* of your god Remphan,
1Co 15.41 for one *s* differeth from another
41 differeth from another *s* in glory.
2Pe 1.19 the day *s* arise in your hearts:
Rev 2.28 And I will give him the morning *s*.
8.10 there fell a great *s* from heaven,
11 name of the *s* is called Wormwood:
9. 1 I saw a *s* fall from heaven unto the
22.16 and the bright and morning *s*.

STARS

Gen 1.16 the night: he made the *s* also.
15. 5 now toward heaven, and tell the *s*,
22.17 thy seed as the *s* of the heaven,
26. 4 seed to multiply as the *s* of heaven,
37. 9 eleven *s* made obeisance to me.
Ex 32.13 your seed as the *s* of heaven, and
Dt 1.10 as the *s* of heaven for multitude.
4.19 the sun, and the moon, and the *s*,
10.22 made thee as the *s* of heaven for
28.62 ye were as the *s* of heaven for
Jdg 5.20 the *s* in their courses fought
1Ch 27.23 Israel like to the *s* of the heavens.
Neh 4.21 the morning till the *s* appeared.
9.23 thou as the *s* of heaven, and
Job 3. 9 Let the *s* of the twilight...be dark;
9. 7 it riseth not; and sealeth up the *s*.
22.12 and behold the height of the *s*, how
25. 5 yea, the *s* are not pure in his sight,
38. 7 When the morning *s* sang together,
Ps 8. 3 the moon and the *s*, which thou
136. 9 The moon and *s* to rule by night:
147. 4 He telleth the number of the *s*;
148. 3 moon: praise him, all ye *s* of light.
Ec 12. 2 moon, or the *s*, be not darkened,
Isa 13.10 For the *s* of heaven and the
14.13 will exalt my throne above the *s*
Jer 31.35 and of the *s* for a light by night,
Eze 32. 7 and make the *s* thereof dark;
Dan 8.10 host and of the *s* to the ground,
12. 3 as the *s* for ever and ever.
Joel 2.10 the *s* shall withdraw their shining:
3.15 the *s* shall withdraw their shining.
Am 5. 8 Seek him that maketh the seven *s*
Ob 4 thou set thy nest among the *s*,
Na 3.16 merchants above the *s* of heaven:
Mt 24.29 and the *s* shall fall from heaven,
Mk 13.25 And the *s* of heaven shall fall, and
Lk 21.25 sun, and in the moon, and in the *s*;
Ac 27.20 sun nor *s* in many days appeared,
1Co 15.41 moon, and another glory of the *s*:
Heb 11.12 as the *s* of the sky in multitude,
Jude 13 wandering *s*, to whom is reserved
Rev 1.16 he had in his right hand seven *s*:
20 The mystery of the seven *s* which
20 seven *s* are the angels of the seven
2. 1 he that holdeth the seven *s* in his
3. 1 Spirits of God, and the seven *s*;
6.13 the *s* of heaven fell unto the earth,
8.12 moon, and the third part of the *s*;
12. 1 upon her head a crown of twelve *s*:
4 the third part of the *s* of heaven,

STATE

Gen 43. 7 The man asked us straitly of our *s*,
2Ch 24.13 they set the house of God in his *s*,
Est 1. 7 according to the *s* of the king.
2.18 according to the *s* of the king.
Ps 39. 5 at his best *s* is altogether vanity.
Pr 27.23 to know the *s* of thy flocks, and
28. 2 the *s* thereof shall be prolonged.
Isa 22.19 and from thy *s* shall he pull thee
Mt 12.45 the last *s* of that man is worse than
Lk 11.26 the last *s* of that man is worse than
Php 2.19 comfort, when I know your *s*.
20 will naturally care for your *s*.
4.11 in whatsoever *s* I am, therewith to
Col 4. 7 my *s* shall Tychicus declare

STATURE

Nu 13.32 we saw in it are men of a great *s*.
1Sa 16. 7 or on the height of his *s*; because
2Sa 21.20 where was a man of great *s*, that
1Ch 11.23 an Egyptian, a man of great *s*,
20. 6 Gath, where was a man of great *s*,
SS 7. 7 This thy *s* is like to a palm tree,
Isa 10.33 high ones of *s* shall be hewn down,
45.14 and of the Sabeans, men of *s*,
Eze 13.18 the head of every *s* to hunt souls!
17. 6 became a spreading vine of low *s*,
19.11 her *s* was exalted among the thick
31. 3 shadowing shroud...of an high *s*;
Mt 6.27 can add one cubit unto his *s*?
Lk 2.52 Jesus increased in wisdom and *s*,
12.25 thought can add to his *s* one cubit?
19. 3 press, because he was little of *s*.
Eph 4.13 unto the measure of the *s* of the

STATUTE

Ex 15.25 there he made for them a *s* and
28.43 it shall be a *s* for ever unto him
29. 9 shall be theirs for a perpetual *s*:
Lev 16.31 afflict your souls, by a *s* for ever.
34 shall be an everlasting *s* unto you,
Jos 24.25 set them a *s* and an ordinance in
Ps 81. 4 For this was a *s* for Israel, and a
Dan 6. 7 together to establish a royal *s*,

STATUTES

Gen 26. 5 my commandments, my *s*, and my
Ex 15.26 commandments, and keep...his *s*,
Lev 10.11 all the *s* which the Lord hath
26.43 because their soul abhorred my *s*.
Dt 4.40 Thou shalt keep therefore his *s*,
1Ki 2. 3 to walk in his ways, to keep his *s*,
11.33 to keep my *s* and my judgments,
2Ki 17. 8 And walked in the *s* of the heathen,
23. 3 his testimonies and his *s* with all
Ps 19. 8 The *s* of the Lord are right,
119. 8 I will keep thy *s*: O forsake me not
12 art thou, O Lord: teach me thy *s*.
33 me, O Lord, the way of thy *s*; and
54 Thy *s* have been my songs in the
Eze 11.12 for ye have not walked in my *s*,
20.18 Walk...not in the *s* of your fathers,
33.15 walk in the *s* of life, without
Mal 4. 4 Israel, with the *s* and judgments.

STAVES

Nu 21.18 of the lawgiver, with their *s*.
1Sa 17.43 that thou comest to me with *s*?
Hab 3.14 didst strike through with his *s*
Zec 11. 7 I took unto me two *s*; the one I
Mt 10.10 coats, neither shoes, nor yet *s*:
26.47 great multitude with swords and *s*,
55 against a thief with swords and *s*
Mk 14.43 great multitude with swords and *s*,
48 with swords and with *s* to take me?
Lk 9. 3 your journey, neither *s*, nor scrip,
22.52 against a thief, with swords and *s*?

STAY

Gen 19.17 neither *s* thou in all the plain;
Ex 9.28 let you go, and ye shall *s* no longer.
1Sa 20.38 the lad, Make speed, haste, *s* not.
2Sa 22.19 calamity: but the Lord was my *s*.
24.16 It is enough: *s* now thine hand.
1Ch 21.15 It is enough, *s* now thine hand.
Job 37. 4 will not *s* them when his voice
38.37 who can *s* the bottles of heaven,
Ps 18.18 calamity: but the Lord was my *s*.
Pr 28.17 flee to the pit; let no man *s* him.
SS 2. 5 *S* me with flagons, comfort me
Isa 3. 1 from Judah the *s* and the staff,
19.13 are the *s* of the tribes thereof.
29. 9 *S* yourselves, and wonder; cry
30.12 and perverseness, and *s* thereon:
50.10 of the Lord, and *s* upon his God.
Dan 4.35 none can *s* his hand, or say unto

STAYED

Nu 16.48, 50 and the plague was *s*.
Dt 10.10 I *s* in the mount, according to the
Jos 10.13 the sun stood still, and the moon *s*,
2Sa 24.21 plague may be *s* from the people.
Job 38.11 here shall thy proud waves be *s*?
Ps 106.30 and so the plague was *s*.
Isa 26. 3 peace, whose mind is *s* on thee:
Eze 31.15 and the great waters were *s*:
Hag 1.10 the heaven over you is *s* from dew,
10 and the earth is *s* from her fruit.
Lk 4.42 *s* him, that he should not depart
Ac 19.22 he himself *s* in Asia for a season.

STEAD

Gen 22.13 burnt offering in the *s* of his son.
30. 2 Am I in God's *s*, who hath withheld
Nu 32.14 ye are risen up in your fathers' *s*,
Job 16. 4 if your soul were in my soul's *s*, I
33. 6 according to thy wish in God's *s*:
34.24 number, and set others in their *s*.
Pr 11. 8 and the wicked cometh in his *s*.
2Co 5.20 we pray you in Christ's *s*, be ye
Phm 13 in thy *s* he might have ministered

STEAL

Gen 31.27 secretly, and *s* away from me;
44. 8 should we *s* out of thy lord's house
Ex 20.15 Thou shalt not *s*.
22. 1 If a man shall *s* an ox, or a sheep,
Lev 19.11 Ye shall not *s*, neither deal falsely,
Dt 5.19 Neither shalt thou *s*.
2Sa 19. 3 as people being ashamed *s* away
Pr 6.30 if he *s* to satisfy his soul when he
30. 9 or lest I be poor, and *s*, and take
Jer 7. 9 Will ye *s*, murder, and commit
23.30 that *s* my words every one from his
Mt 6.19 thieves break through and *s*:
20 thieves do not break through nor *s*:
19.18 Thou shalt not *s*, Thou shalt not
27.64 come by night, and *s* him away,
Mk 10.19 Do not kill, Do not *s*, Do not bear
Lk 18.20 Do not kill, Do not *s*, Do not bear
Jn 10.10 The thief cometh not, but for to *s*,
Ro 2.21 a man should not *s*, dost thou *s*?
13. 9 shalt not kill, Thou shalt not *s*,
Eph 4.28 Let him that stole *s* no more: but

STEALETH

Ex 21.16 he that *s* a man, and selleth him,
Job 27.20 tempest *s* him away in the night.
Zec 5. 3 for every one that *s* shall be cut off

STEALING

Dt 24. 7 If a man be found *s* any of his
Hos 4. 2 and lying, and killing, and *s*, and

STEDFAST

Job 11.15 yea, thou shalt be *s*, and shalt not
Ps 78. 8 whose spirit was not *s* with God.
37 neither were they *s* in his covenant,
Dan 6.26 is the living God, and *s* for ever,
1Co 7.37 he that standeth *s* in his heart,
15.58 my beloved brethren, be ye *s*,
2Co 1. 7 And our hope of you is *s*, knowing,
Heb 2. 2 if the word spoken by angels was *s*,
3.14 of our confidence *s* unto the end;
6.19 anchor of the soul, both sure and *s*,
1Pe 5. 9 Whom resist *s* in the faith,

STEDFASTLY

Ru 1.18 she was *s* minded to go with her,
2Ki 8.11 he settled his countenance *s*,
Lk 9.51 *s* set his face to go to Jerusalem,
Ac 1.10 they looked *s* toward heaven as
2.42 they continued *s* in the apostles'
6.15 looking *s* on him, saw his face as
7.55 looked up *s* into heaven, and saw
14. 9 Paul speak: who *s* beholding him,
2Co 3. 7 could not *s* behold the face of
13 could not *s* look to the end of that

STEDFASTNESS

Col 2. 5 and the *s* of your faith in Christ.
2Pe 3.17 the wicked, fall from your own *s*.

STEEL

2Sa 22.35 bow of *s* is broken by mine arms.
Job 20.24 and the bow of *s* shall strike him
Ps 18.34 bow of *s* is broken by mine arms.
Jer 15.12 the northern iron and the *s*?

STEEP

Eze 38.20 *s* places shall fall, and every wall
Mic 1. 4 that are poured down a *s* place.

STEPHEN

First Christian martyr; one of seven deacons in Jerusalem chosen to assist in administering relief to the poor in the growing Christian community (Ac 6); "a man full of faith and of the Holy Ghost" (Ac 6.5), attracts special enmity of certain synagogue members who have him summoned before the Sanhedrin, where he is charged with blasphemy against the temple and the law (Ac 6.13-14); at conclusion of speech in his own defense, is stoned to death; while dying, has vision of Jesus as Son of Man "standing on the right hand of God"; last words are a prayer that his enemies be forgiven (Ac 7).

Mt 8.32 ran violently down a *s* place into
Mk 5.13 herd ran violently down a *s* place
Lk 8.33 herd ran violently down a *s* place

STEM

Isa 11. 1 forth a rod out of the *s* of Jesse,

STEP

1Sa 20. 3 is but a *s* between me and death.
Job 31. 7 If my *s* hath turned out of the way,

STEPHEN

Ac 6. 5 they chose *S*, a man full of faith
8 And *S*, full of faith and power, did
9 and of Asia, disputing with *S*.
7.59 they stoned *S*, calling upon God,
8. 2 devout men carried *S* to his burial,
11.19 the persecution that arose about *S*
22.20 blood of thy martyr *S* was shed,

STEPPED

Jn 5. 4 the troubling of the water *s* in

STEPPETH

Jn 5. 7 coming, another *s* down before

STEPS

Ex 20.26 thou go up by *s* unto mine altar,
2Sa 22.37 hast enlarged my *s* under me;
Job 14.16 For now thou numberest my *s*:
23.11 My foot hath held his *s*, his way
29. 6 When I washed my *s* with butter,
31. 4 see my ways, and count all my *s*?
Ps 37.23 The *s* of a good man are ordered
31 his heart; none of his *s* shall slide.
44.18 have our *s* declined from thy way;
56. 6 they mark my *s*, when they wait
73. 2 gone; my *s* had well nigh slipped.
85.13 shall set us in the way of his *s*.
119.133 Order my *s* in thy word: and let
Pr 4.12 thy *s* shall not be straitened;
5. 5 to death; her *s* take hold on hell.
16. 9 way: but the Lord directeth his *s*.
Isa 26. 6 the poor, and the *s* of the needy.
Jer 10.23 man that walketh to direct his *s*.
Ro 4.12 walk in the *s* of that faith of our
2Co 12.18 spirit? walked we not in the same *s*?
1Pe 2.21 that ye should follow his *s*:

STERN

Ac 27.29 cast four anchors out of the *s*,

STEWARD

Gen 15. 2 the *s* of my house is this
43.19 to the *s* of Joseph's house,
44. 1 commanded the *s* of his house,
4 far off, Joseph said unto his *s*,
1Ki 16. 9 Arza *s* of his house in Tirzah.
Mt 20. 8 of the vineyard saith unto his *s*,
Lk 8. 3 the wife of Chuza Herod's *s*, and
12.42 then is that faithful and wise *s*,
16. 1 a certain rich man, which had a *s*;
2 for thou mayest be no longer *s*.
3 Then the *s* said within himself,
8 the lord commended the unjust *s*,
Tit 1. 7 must be blameless, as the *s* of God;

STEWARDS

1Ch 28. 1 the *s* over all the substance and
1Co 4. 1 and *s* of the mysteries of God.
2 Moreover it is required in *s*, that a
1Pe 4.10 *s* of the manifold grace of God.

STEWARDSHIP

Lk 16. 2 give an account of thy *s*; for thou
3 lord taketh away from me the *s*:
4 when I am put out of the *s*, they

STICK

2Ki 6. 6 And he cut down a *s*, and cast it
Job 33.21 bones that were not seen *s* out.
41.17 they *s* together, that they cannot
Ps 38. 2 For thine arrows *s* fast in me, and
La 4. 8 is withered, it is become like a *s*.
Eze 29. 4 the fish of thy rivers to *s* unto thy
4 the fish of thy rivers shall *s* unto
37.16 thou son of man, take thee one *s*,
16 then take another *s*, and write upon
16 For Joseph, the *s* of Ephraim, and
17 them one to another into one *s*;
19 Behold, I will take the *s* of Joseph,
19 with him, even with the *s* of Judah,
19 and make them one *s*, and they

STICKETH

Pr 18.24 is a friend that *s* closer than a

STICKS

Nu 15.32 they found a man that gathered *s*
33 they that found him gathering *s*
1Ki 17.10 woman was there gathering of *s*:
12 behold, I am gathering two *s*, that
Eze 37.20 the *s* whereon thou writest shall
Ac 28. 3 Paul had gathered a bundle of *s*,

STIFFNECKED

Ex 32. 9 and, behold, it is a *s* people:
33. 3 thee; for thou art a *s* people:
5 Ye are a *s* people: I will come
34. 9 among us; for it is a *s* people;
Dt 9. 6 for thou art a *s* people.
13 and, behold, it is a *s* people:
10.16 your heart, and be no more *s*.
2Ch 30. 8 be ye not *s*, as your fathers
Ac 7.51 Ye *s* and uncircumcised in heart

STILL

Ex 14.13 not stand *s*, and see the salvation of
15.16 arm they shall be as *s* as a stone;
Nu 14.38 that went to search the land, lived *s*.
Jos 10.12 Sun, stand thou *s* upon Gibeon;
13 And the sun stood *s*, and the moon
24.10 Balaam: therefore he blessed you *s*:
Jdg 18. 9 it is very good: and are ye *s*?
1Ki 19.12 and after the fire a *s* small voice.
2Ki 7. 4 and if we sit *s* here, we die also.
2Ch 20.17 stand ye *s*, and see the salvation of
Job 2. 9 Dost thou *s* retain thine integrity?
4.16 It stood *s*, but I could not discern
37.14 stand *s*, and consider the wondrous
Ps 4. 4 heart upon your bed, and be *s*.
8. 2 thou mightest *s* the enemy and
23. 2 leadeth me beside the *s* waters.
46.10 Be *s*, and know that I am God: I
76. 8 the earth feared, and was *s*,
83. 1 thy peace, and be not *s*, O God.
84. 4 they will be *s* praising thee.
107.29 so that the waves thereof are *s*.
139.18 when I awake, I am *s* with thee.

Ec 12. 9 he *s* taught the people knowledge;
Isa 5.25 but his hand is stretched out *s*.
23. 2 Be *s*, ye inhabitants of the isle;
30. 7 this, Their strength is to sit *s*.
42.14 I have been *s*, and refrained
Jer 8.14 Why do we sit *s*? assemble
Eze 33.30 thy people *s* are talking against thee
Hab 3.11 The sun and moon stood *s* in
Zec 1.11 all the earth sitteth *s*, and is at
Mt 20.32 Jesus stood *s*, and called them,
Mk 4.39 said unto the sea, Peace, be *s*.
10.49 Jesus stood *s*, and commanded
Lk 7.14 and they that bare him stood *s*.
Jn 7. 9 unto them, he abode *s* in Galilee.
11. 6 abode two days *s* in the same place
20 him: but Mary sat *s* in the house.
Ac 8.38 commanded the chariot to stand *s*:
15.34 it pleased Silas to abide there *s*.
17.14 Silas and Timotheus abode there *s*.
Ro 11.23 also, if they abide not *s* in unbelief,
1Ti 1. 3 thee to abide *s* at Ephesus, when
Rev 22.11 is unjust, let him be unjust *s*:
11 which is filthy, let him be filthy *s*:
11 righteous, let him be righteous *s*:
11 he that is holy, let him be holy *s*.

STILLETH

Ps 65. 7 Which *s* the noise of the seas,

STING

1Co 15.55 O death, where is thy *s*? O grave,
56 The *s* of death is sin; and the

STINGS

Rev 9.10 and there were *s* in their tails:

STINK

Gen 34.30 have troubled me to make me to *s*
Ex 7.18 shall die, and the river shall *s*;
16.24 it did not *s*, neither was there any
Ps 38. 5 My wounds *s* and are corrupt
Isa 3.24 of sweet smell there shall be *s*;
34. 3 their *s* shall come up out of their
Joel 2.20 his *s* shall come up, and his ill
Am 4.10 made the *s* of your camps to come

STINKETH

Isa 50. 2 their fish *s*, because there is no
Jn 11.39 him, Lord, by this time he *s*:

STIR

Nu 24. 9 a great lion: who shall *s* him up?
Job 17. 8 the innocent shall *s* up himself
41.10 is so fierce that dare *s* him up:
Ps 35.23 *S* up thyself, and awake to my
78.38 and did not *s* up all his wrath.
80. 2 and Manasseh *s* up thy strength,
Pr 15. 1 but grievous words *s* up anger.
SS 2. 7 ye *s* not up, nor awake my love,
3. 5 ye *s* not up, nor awake my love,
8. 4 ye *s* not up, nor awake my love,
Isa 10.26 Lord of hosts shall *s* up a scourge
13.17 I will *s* up the Medes against them,
42.13 he shall *s* up jealousy like a man
Dan 11. 2 shall *s* up all against the realm of
25 And he shall *s* up his power and
Ac 12.18 no small *s* among the soldiers,
19.23 there arose no small *s* about that
2Ti 1. 6 that thou *s* up the gift of God,
2Pe 1.13 to *s* you up by putting you in
3.11 I *s* up your pure minds by way of

STIRRED

Ex 35.21 every one whose heart *s* him up,
26 women whose heart *s* them up in
36. 2 one whose heart *s* him up to come
1Sa 22. 8 son hath *s* up my servant against
26.19 Lord have *s* thee up against me,
1Ki 11.14 the Lord *s* up an adversary unto
23 God *s* him up another adversary,
21.25 whom Jezebel his wife *s* up.
1Ch 5.26 the God of Israel *s* up the spirit
2Ch 21.16 the Lord *s* up against Jehoram the
36.22 Lord *s* up the spirit of Cyrus king
Ezr 1. 1 Lord *s* up the spirit of Cyrus king
Ps 39. 2 good; and my sorrow was *s*.
Dan 11.10 But his sons shall be *s* up, and
10 then shall he return, and be *s* up,
25 king of the south shall be *s* up to
Hag 1.14 And the Lord *s* up the spirit of
Ac 6.12 And they *s* up the people, and the
13.50 the Jews *s* up the devout and
14. 2 Jews *s* up the Gentiles, and
17.13 thither also, and *s* up the people.
16 his spirit was *s* in him, when
21.27 *s* up all the people, and laid

STIRRETH

Dt 32.11 As an eagle *s* up her nest,
Pr 10.12 Hatred *s* up strifes: but love
15.18 A wrathful man *s* up strife: but
28.25 is of a proud heart *s* up strife:
29.22 An angry man *s* up strife, and a
Isa 14. 9 it *s* up the dead for thee, even all
64. 7 that *s* up himself to take hold of
Lk 23. 5 He *s* up the people, teaching

STOCK

Lev 25.47 to the *s* of the stranger's family:
Job 14. 8 the *s* thereof die in the ground;
Isa 40.24 their *s* shall not take root in the
44.19 shall I fall down to the *s* of a tree?
Jer 2.27 Saying to a *s*, Thou art my father;
10. 8 the *s* is a doctrine of vanities.
Ac 13.26 children of the *s* of Abraham, and
Php 3. 5 the eighth day, of the *s* of Israel,

STOCKS

Job 13.27 puttest my feet also in the *s*, and
33.11 He putteth my feet in the *s*, he
Pr 7.22 a fool to the correction of the *s*;
Jer 3. 9 adultery with stones and with *s*.
20. 2 put him in the *s* that were in the
3 forth Jeremiah out of the *s*.
29.26 put him in prison, and in the *s*.
Hos 4.12 My people ask counsel at their *s*,
Ac 16.24 and made their feet fast in the *s*.

STOICKS

Ac 17.18 and of the *S*, encountered him.

STOLE

Gen 31.20 Jacob *s* away unawares to Laban
2Sa 15. 6 Absalom *s* the hearts of the men
2Ki 11. 2 *s* him from among the king's sons
2Ch 22.11 *s* him from among the king's sons
Mt 28.13 and *s* him away while we slept.
Eph 4.28 Let him that *s* steal no more: but

STOLEN

Gen 30.33 that shall be counted *s* with me.
31.19 Rachel had *s* the images that were
26 thou hast *s* away unawares to me,
30 wherefore hast thou *s* my gods?
32 knew not that Rachel had *s* them.
39 whether *s* by day,or *s* by night.
40.15 I was *s* away out of the land of the
Ex 22. 7 and it be *s* out of the man's house;
12 if it be *s* from him, he shall make
Jos 7.11 have also *s*, and dissembled also,
2Sa 19.41 the men of Judah *s* thee away,
21.12 had *s* them from the street of
Pr 9.17 *S* waters are sweet, and bread
Ob 5 not have *s* till they have enough?

STOMACH'S

1Ti 5.23 a little wine for thy *s* sake and

STONE

Gen 11. 3 And they had brick for *s*, and slime
28.18 the *s* that he had put for his pillows,
22 this *s*, which I have set for a pillar,
31.45 And Jacob took a *s*, and set it up for
Ex 15. 5 they sank into the bottom as a *s*.
24.12 and I will give thee tables of *s*, and
31.18 two tables of testimony, tables of *s*,
34. 1 Hew thee two tables of *s* like unto
Lev 24.14 and let all the congregation *s* him.
26. 1 neither shall ye set up any image of *s*
Dt 9.11 Lord gave me the two tables of *s*,
28.36 thou serve other gods, wood and *s*.
Jos 24.27 this *s* shall be a witness unto us;
1Sa 17.49 that the *s* sunk into his forehead;
50 Philistine with a sling and with a *s*,
20.19 and shalt remain by the *s* Ezel.
2Sa 17.13 be not one small *s* found there.
20. 8 at the great *s* which is in Gibeon,
1Ki 6.18 all was cedar; there was no *s* seen.
2Ki 3.25 piece of land cast every man his *s*,
Job 38.30 The waters are hid as with a *s*, and
41.24 His heart is as firm as a *s*; yea, as
Ps 91.12 lest thou dash thy foot against a *s*.
118.22 The *s* which the builders refused
22 is become the head *s* of the corner.
Pr 26.27 and he that rolleth a *s*, it will return
27. 3 A *s* is heavy, and the sand weighty:
Isa 8.14 but for a *s* of stumbling and for a
28.16 Zion for a foundation a *s*, a tried *s*,
16 a precious corner *s*, a sure
Jer 2.27 and to a *s*, Thou hast brought me
La 3. 9 inclosed my ways with hewn *s*,
Dan 2.34 that a *s* was cut out without hands,
Am 5.11 ye have built houses of hewn *s*,
Hab 2.11 For the *s* shall cry out of the wall,
19 to the dumb *s*, Arise, it shall teach!
Hag 2.15 a *s* was laid upon a *s* in the temple
Zec 3. 9 upon on *s* shall be seven eyes:
7.12 their hearts as an adamant *s*,
Mt 4. 6 thou dash thy foot against a *s*.
7. 9 ask bread, will he give him a *s*?
21.42 The *s* which the builders rejected,
44 shall fall on this *s* shall be broken:
24. 2 not be left here one *s* upon another,
27.60 rolled a great *s* to the door of the
66 sealing the *s*, and setting a watch.
28. 2 came and rolled back the *s* from
Mk 12.10 The *s* which the builders rejected
13. 2 not be left one *s* upon another,
15.46 and rolled a *s* unto the door of the
16. 3 roll us away the *s* from the door
4 they saw that the *s* was rolled
Lk 4. 3 command this *s* that it be made
11 thou dash thy foot against a *s*.
11.11 is a father, will he give him a *s*?
19.44 leave in thee one *s* upon another;
20. 6 all the people will *s* us: for they
17 The *s* which the builders rejected,
18 shall fall upon that *s* be broken;
21. 6 not be left one *s* upon another,
23.53 in a sepulcher that was hewn in *s*,
24. 2 they found the *s* rolled away from
Jn 1.42 which is by interpretation, A *s*.
2. 6 were set there six waterpots of *s*,
8. 7 you, let him first cast a *s* at her.
10.31 Jews took…stones again to *s* him.
32 which of those works do ye *s* me?
33 For a good work we *s* thee not;
11. 8 the Jews of late sought to *s* thee;
38 It was a cave, and a *s* lay upon it.
39 Jesus said, Take ye away the *s*.
41 they took away the *s* from the
20. 1 seeth the *s* taken away from the
Ac 4.11 This is the *s* which was set at
14. 5 them despitefully, and to *s* them,
17.29 is like unto gold, or silver, or *s*,
2Co 3. 3 not in tables of *s*, but in fleshy
Eph 2.20 himself being the chief corner *s*;
1Pe 2. 4 whom coming, as unto a living *s*,
6 I lay in Sion a chief corner *s*, elect,
7 *s* which the builders disallowed,
8 And a *s* of stumbling, and a rock of
Rev 2.17 and will give him a white *s*,
17 and in the *s* a new name written,

4. 3 like a jasper and a sardine *s*:
9.20 gold, and silver, and brass, and *s*,
16.21 every *s* about the weight of a talent:
18.21 mighty angel took up a *s* like a
21.11 was like unto a *s* most precious,
11 like a jasper *s*, clear as crystal;

STONED

Ex 19.13 but he shall surely be *s*, or shot
21.28 then the ox shall be surely *s*, and
29 the ox shall be *s*, and his owner
32 of silver, and the ox shall be *s*.
Nu 15.36 *s* him with stones, and he died;
Jos 7.25 And all Israel *s* him with stones,
25 after they had *s* them with stones.
1Ki 12.18 and all Israel *s* him with stones,
21.13 *s* him with stones, that he died.
14 saying, Naboth is *s*, and is dead.
15 Jezebel heard that Naboth was *s*,
2Ch 10.18 children of Israel *s* him with
24.21 and *s* him with stones at the
Mt 21.35 and killed another, and *s* another.
Jn 8. 5 commanded us, that such...be *s*:
Ac 5.26 lest they should have been *s*.
7.58 him out of the city, and *s* him:
59 they *s* Stephen, calling upon God,
14.19 having *s* Paul, drew him out of
2Co 11.25 once was I *s*, thrice I suffered
Heb 11.37 They were *s*, they were sawn
12.20 it shall be *s*, or thrust through

STONE'S

Lk 22.41 from them about a *s* cast,

STONES

Ex 28.12 for *s* of memorial unto the children
39. 7 be *s* for a memorial to the children
Dt 8. 9 a land whose *s* are iron, and out of
13.10 thou shalt stone him with *s*, that he
27. 5 unto the Lord thy God, an altar of *s*:
Jos 4. 6 saying, What mean ye by these *s*?
8.32 he wrote there upon the *s* a copy of
10.11 Lord cast down great *s* from heaven
1Sa 17.40 chose him five smooth *s* out of the
1Ki 15.22 and they took away the *s* of Ramah,
18.31 Elijah took twelve *s*, according to
1Ch 22. 2 he set masons to hew wrought *s* to
2Ch 1.15 gold at Jerusalem as plenteous as *s*,
9.27 king made silver in Jerusalem as *s*,
Job 6.12 Is my strength the strength of *s*? or
14.19 waters wear the *s*: thou washest
28. 3 the *s* of darkness, and the shadow of
Ps 18.13 gave his voice; hail *s* and coals of fire.
102.14 thy servants take pleasure in her *s*,
Ec 3. 5 A time to cast away *s*, and a time to
5 a time to gather *s* together; a time
Isa 54.11 I will lay thy *s* with fair colors, and
60.17 and for wood brass, and for *s* iron:
62.10 up the highway; gather out the *s*;
La 3.16 broken my teeth with gravel *s*,
Mt 3. 9 able of these *s* to raise up children
4. 3 that these *s* be made bread.
Mk 5. 5 crying, and cutting himself with *s*.
12. 4 and at him they cast *s*, and
13. 1 see what manner of *s* and what
Lk 3. 8 able of these *s* to raise up children
19.40 the *s* would immediately cry out.
21. 5 adorned with goodly *s* and gifts,
Jn 8.59 Then took they up *s* to cast at him:
10.31 the Jews took up *s* again to stone
1Co 3.12 gold, silver, precious *s*, wood, hay,
2Co 3. 7 death, written and engraven in *s*,
1Pe 2. 5 Ye also, as lively *s*, are built up a
Rev 17. 4 decked with gold and precious *s*
18.12 gold, and silver, and precious *s*,
16 decked with gold, and precious *s*,
21.19 with all manner of precious *s*.

STONEST

Mt 23.37 *s* them which are sent unto thee,
Lk 13.34 *s* them that are sent unto thee;

STONY

Ps 141. 6 are overthrown in *s* places,
Eze 11.19 take the *s* heart out of their flesh,
36.26 away the *s* heart out of your flesh,
Mt 13. 5 Some fell upon *s* places, where
20 received the seed into *s* places,
Mk 4. 5 And some fell on *s* ground, where
16 which are sown on *s* ground;

STOOD

Gen 18.22 Abraham *s* yet before the Lord.
28.13 And, behold, the Lord *s* above it,
37. 7 my sheaf arose, and also *s* upright;
Ex 2. 4 his sister *s* afar off, to wit what
Lev 9. 5 drew near and *s* before the Lord.
Nu 22.22 angel of the Lord *s* in the way
Dt 31.15 pillar of the cloud *s* over the door
Jos 3.16 waters which came...from above *s*
5.13 these *s* a man over against him with
10.13 So the sun *s* still in he midst of
1Ki 3.15 *s* before the ark of the covenant of
19.13 and *s* in the entering in of the cave.
22.21 a spirit, and *s* before the Lord,
2Ki 5. 9 *s* at the door of the house of Elisha.
23. 3 all the people *s* to the covenant.
1Ch 21. 1 And Satan *s* up against Israel,
2Ch 20.13 And all Judah *s* before the Lord,
19 *s* up to praise the Lord God of
Neh 8. 4 Ezra the scribe *s* upon a pulpit of
9. 2 and *s* and confessed their sins,
Est 8. 4 Esther arose, and *s* before the king,
Isa 6. 2 Above it *s* the seraphims: each one
36. 2 he *s* by the conduit of the upper
Jer 15. 1 Moses and Samuel *s* before me, yet
18.20 I *s* before thee to speak good for
19.14 and he *s* in the court of the Lord's
Hab 3. 6 He *s*, and measured the earth: he
11 The sun and moon *s* still in their
Mt 2. 9 over where the young child was.
12.46 mother and his brethren *s* without,
13. 2 the whole multitude *s* on the shore.
20.32 And Jesus *s* still, and called them,
26.73 while came unto him they that *s* by,
27.11 And Jesus *s* before the governor:
47 Some of them that *s* there, when
Mk 10.49 Jesus *s* still, and commanded him
11. 5 certain of them that *s* there said
14.47 of them that *s* by drew a sword,
60 the high priest *s* up in the midst,
69 began to say to them that *s* by,
70 they that *s* by said again to Peter,
15.35 And some of them that *s* by, when
39 centurion, which *s* over against
Lk 4.16 sabbath day, and *s* up for to read.
39 And he *s* over her, and rebuked
5. 1 he *s* by the lake of Gennesaret,
6. 8 midst. And he arose and *s* forth.
17 down with them, and *s* in the plain,
7.14 and they that bare him *s* still.
38 *s* at his feet behind him weeping,
9.32 and the two men that *s* with him.
10.25 behold, a certain lawyer *s* up, and
17.12 that were lepers, which *s* afar off:
18.11 Pharisee *s* and prayed thus with
40 And Jesus *s*, and commanded him
19. 8 And Zacchaeus *s*, and said unto the
24 And he said unto them that *s* by,
23.10 scribes *s* and vehemently accused
35 And the people *s* beholding. And
49 *s* afar off, beholding these things.
24. 4 two men *s* by them in shining
36 Jesus...*s* in the midst of them,
Jn 1.35 Again the next day after John *s*,
6.22 people which *s* on the other side of
7.37 Jesus *s* and cried, saying, If any
11.56 themselves, as they *s* in the temple,
12.29 The people therefore, that *s* by,
18. 5 which betrayed him, *s* with them.
16 But Peter *s* at the door without.
18 the servants and officers *s* there,
18 Peter *s* with them, and warmed
22 officers which *s* by struck Jesus
25 Peter *s* and warmed himself.
19.25 *s* by the cross of Jesus his mother,
20.11 Mary *s* without at the sepulcher
19 came Jesus and *s* in the midst, and
26 *s* in the midst, and said, Peace be
21. 4 now come, Jesus *s* on the shore:
Ac 1.10 men *s* by them in white apparel;
15 days Peter *s* up in the midst of the
3. 8 And he leaping up *s*, and walked,
4.26 The kings of the earth *s* up, and
5.34 Then *s* there up one in the council,
9. 7 journeyed with him *s* speechless,
39 all the widows *s* by him weeping,
10.17 house, and *s* before the gate,
30 *s* before me in bright clothing,
11.13 which *s* and said unto him, Send
28 And there *s* up one of them named
12.14 told how Peter *s* before the gate.
13.16 Then Paul *s* up, and beckoning
14.20 the disciples *s* round about him,
16. 9 There *s* a man of Macedonia, and
17.22 Paul *s* in the midst of Mars' hill,
21.40 Paul *s* on the stairs, and beckoned
22.13 Came unto me, and *s*, and said
25 said unto the centurion that *s* by,
23. 2 them that *s* by him to smite him
4 And they that *s* by said, Revilest
11 night following the Lord *s* by him,
24.20 in me, while I *s* before the council,
25. 7 Jews...from Jerusalem *s* round
18 whom when the accusers *s* up, they
27.21 Paul *s* forth in the midst of them,
23 For there *s* by me this night the
2Ti 4.16 first answer no man *s* with me,
17 Lord *s* with me, and strengthened
Heb 9.10 Which *s* only in meats and drinks,
Rev 5. 6 *s* a Lamb as it had been slain,
7. 9 *s* before the throne, and before the
11 angels *s* round about the throne,
8. 2 seven angels which *s* before God;
3 angel came and *s* at the altar,
11. 1 and the angel *s*, saying, Rise, and
11 them, and they *s* upon their feet;
12. 4 and the dragon *s* before the woman
13. 1 And I *s* upon the sand of the sea,
14. 1 lo, a Lamb *s* on the mount Sion,
18.17 as many as trade by sea, *s* afar off,

STOOP

Job 9.13 proud helpers do *s* under him.
Pr 12.25 in the heart of man maketh it *s*:
Isa 46. 2 They *s*, they bow down together;
Mk 1. 7 I am not worthy to *s* down and

STOOPED

Gen 49. 9 he *s* down, he couched as a lion,
1Sa 24. 8 David *s* with his face to the earth,
28.14 he *s* with his face to the ground,
2Ch 36.17 old man, or him that *s* for age:
Jn 8. 6 But Jesus *s* down, and with his
8 again he *s* down, and wrote on the
20.11 she *s* down, and looked into the

STOOPETH

Isa 46. 1 Bel bowed down, Nebo *s*, their

STOOPING

Lk 24.12 and *s* down, he beheld the linen
Jn 20. 5 And he *s* down, and looking in, saw

STOP

1Ki 18.44 down, that the rain *s* thee not.
2Ki 3.19 *s* all wells of water, and mar every
2Ch 32. 3 to *s* the waters of the fountains
Ps 35. 3 and *s* the way against them that
107.42 and all iniquity shall *s* her mouth.
Eze 39.11 and it shall *s* the noses of the
2Co 11.10 no man shall *s* me of this boasting

STOPPED

Gen 8. 2 the windows of heaven were *s*,
26.15 the Philistines had *s* them, and
18 for the Philistines had *s* them after
Lev 15. 3 or his flesh be *s* from his issue, it
2Ki 3.25 and they *s* all the wells of water,
2Ch 32. 4 who *s* all the fountains, and the
30 *s* the upper watercourse of Gihon,
Neh 4. 7 that the breaches began to be *s*,
Ps 63.11 of them that speak lies shall be *s*.
Jer 51.32 that the passages are *s*, and the
Zec 7.11 *s* their ears, that they should not
Ac 7.57 *s* their ears, and ran upon him
Ro 3.19 that every mouth may be *s*, and all
Tit 1.11 Whose mouths must be *s*, who
Heb 11.33 promises, *s* the mouths of lions,

STOPPETH

Job 5.16 hope, and iniquity *s* her mouth.
Ps 58. 4 like the deaf adder that *s* her ear;
Pr 2 21.13 Whoso *s* his ears at the cry of the
Isa 33.15 that *s* his ears from hearing of blood,

STORE

Gen 26.14 of herds, and great *s* of servants:
41.36 that food shall be for *s* to the land
Lev 25.22 come in ye shall eat of the old *s*.
26.10 And ye shall eat old *s*, and bring
Dt 28. 5, 17 shall be thy basket and thy *s*.
32.34 Is not this laid up in *s* with me, and
1Ki 9.19 the cities of *s* that Solomon had,
10.10 and of spices very great *s*, and
2Ki 20.17 which thy fathers have laid up in *s*
1Ch 29.16 all this *s* that we have prepared
2Ch 8. 4 all the *s* cities, which he built in
6 all the *s* cities that Solomon had,
11.11 *s* of victual, and of oil and wine.
16. 4 and all the *s* cities of Naphtali.
17.12 in Judah castles, and cities of *s*.
31.10 that which is left is this great *s*.
Neh 5.18 in ten days *s* of all sorts of wine:
Ps 144.13 be full, affording all manner of *s*:
Isa 39. 6 which thy fathers have laid up in *s*
Am 3.10 who *s* up violence and robbery in
Na 2. 9 for there is none end of the *s* and
1Co 16. 2 every one of you lay by him in *s*,
1Ti 6.19 Laying up in *s* for themselves a
2Pe 3. 7 by the same word are kept in *s*,

STOREHOUSE

Mal 3.10 Bring ye all the tithes into the *s*,
Lk 1 2.24 which neither have *s* nor barn;

STORIES

Gen 6.16 second, and third *s* shalt thou make it.
Eze 42. 3 was gallery against gallery in three *s*.
6 For they were in three *s*, but had not
Am 9. 6 that buildeth his *s* in the heaven,

STORK

Lev 11.19 the *s*, the heron after her kind,
Dt 14.18 And the *s*, and the heron after her
Ps 104.17 as for the *s*, the fir trees are her
Jer 8. 7 the *s* in the heaven knoweth her
Zec 5. 9 had wings like the wings of a *s*:

STORM

Job 21.18 chaff that the *s* carrieth away.
27.21 as a *s* hurleth him out of his place.
Ps 55. 8 my escape from the windy *s* and
83.15 and make them afraid with thy *s*.
107.29 He maketh the *s* a calm, so that
Isa 4. 6 for a covert from *s* and from rain,
25. 4 a refuge from the *s*, a shadow from
4 blast...is as a *s* against the wall.
28. 2 tempest of hail and a destroying *s*,
29. 6 great noise, with *s* and tempest,
Eze 38. 9 shalt ascend and come like a *s*,
Na 1. 3 in the whirlwind and in the *s*,
Mk 4.37 there arose a great *s* of wind, and
Lk 8.23 there came down a *s* of wind on

STORMY

Ps 107.25 raiseth the *s* wind, which lifteth
148. 8 vapors; *s* wind fulfilling his word:
Eze 13.11 fall; and a *s* wind shall rend it.
13 even rend it with a *s* wind in my

STORY

2Ch 13.22 in the *s* of the prophet of Iddo.
24.27 in the *s* of the book of the kings.

STOUT

Job 4.11 the *s* lion's whelps are scattered
Isa 10.12 punish the fruit of the *s* heart of
Dan 7.20 look was more *s* than his fellows.
Mal 3.13 words have been *s* against me,

STRAIGHT

Jos 6. 5 ascend up every man *s* before him.
20 the city, every man *s* before him,
1Sa 6.12 the kine took the *s* way to the
2Ch 32.30 brought it *s* down to the west side
Ps 5. 8 make thy way *s* before my face.
Pr 4.25 let thine eyelids look *s* before thee.
Ec 1.15 is crooked cannot be made *s*:
7.13 for who can make that *s*, which he
Isa 40. 3 make *s* in the desert a highway
4 the crooked shall be made *s*, and
42.16 before them, and crooked things *s*.
45. 2 and make the crooked places *s*:
Jer 31. 9 by the river of waters in a *s* way,
Eze 1. 7 their feet were *s* feet; and the sole
9 they went every one *s* forward.
12 they went every one *s* forward:
23 the firmament were their wings *s*,
10.22 they went every one *s* forward.
Mt 3. 3 of the Lord, make his paths *s*.
Mk 1. 3 way of the Lord, make his paths *s*.
Lk 3. 4 way of the Lord, make his paths *s*.
5 and the crooked shall be made *s*,
13.13 and immediately she was made *s*,
Jn 1.23 Make *s* the way of the Lord, as
Ac 9.11 into the street which is called *S*,
16.11 with a *s* course to Samothracia,
21. 1 came with a *s* course unto Coos,
Heb 12.13 And make *s* paths for your feet,

STRAIGHTWAY

Pr 7.22 He goeth after her *s*, as an ox
Mt 3.16 went up *s* out of the water: and,
4.20 they *s* left their nets, and followed
21. 3 of them; and *s* he will send them.
Mk 1.18 And *s* they forsook their nets, and
5.29 *s* the fountain of her blood was
42 *s* the damsel arose, and walked;
6.54 out of the ship, *s* they knew him,
9.20 he saw him, *s* the spirit tare him;
11. 3 and *s* he will send him hither.
15. 1 *s* in the morning the chief priests
Lk 5.39 drunk old wine *s* desireth new:
14. 5 not *s* pull him out on the sabbath
Ac 5.10 Then fell she down *s* at his feet,
9.20 And *s* he preached Christ in the
16.33 was baptized, he and all his, *s*.
23.30 man, I sent *s* to thee, and gave
Jas 1.24 *s* forgotteth what manner of man

STRAIN

Mt 23.24 blind guides, which *s* at a gnat,

STRAIT

1Sa 13. 6 Israel saw that they were in a *s*,
2Sa 24.14 said unto Gad, I am in a great *s*:
2Ki 6. 1 dwell with thee is too *s* for us.
1Ch 21.13 said unto Gad, I am in a great *s*:
Job 36.16 remove thee out of the *s* into a
Isa 49.20 ears, The place is too *s* for me:
Mt 7.13 Enter ye in at the *s* gate: for wide
14 *s* is the gate, and narrow is the
Lk 13.24 Strive to enter in at the *s* gate:
Php 1.23 For I am in a *s* betwixt two,

STRAITEN

Jer 19. 9 that seek their lives, shall *s* them.

STRAITENED

Job 18. 7 steps of his strength shall be *s*,
37.10 the breadth of the waters is *s*.
Pr 4.12 goest, thy steps shall not be *s*;
Eze 42. 6 the building was *s* more than the
Mic 2. 7 Jacob, is the spirit of the Lord *s*?
Lk 12.50 am I *s* till it be accomplished!
2Co 6.12 Ye are not *s* in us, but ye are
12 but ye are *s* in your own bowels.

STRAITEST

Ac 26. 5 that after the most *s* sect of our

STRAITLY

Gen 43. 7 The man asked us *s* of our state,
Ex 13.19 had *s* sworn the children of Israel,
Jos 6. 1 Jericho was *s* shut up because
1Sa 14.28 Thy father *s* charged the people
Mt 9.30 Jesus *s* charged them, saying, See
Mk 1.43 he *s* charged him, and forthwith sent
3.12 And he *s* charged them that they
5.43 he charged them *s* that no man
Lk 9.21 he *s* charged them, and commanded
Ac 4.17 let us *s* threaten them, that they
5.28 Did not we *s* command you that ye

STRANGE

Gen 35. 2 Put away the *s* gods...among you,
42. 7 but made himself *s* unto them,
Ex 2.22 I have been a stranger in a *s* land.
Lev 10. 1 and offered *s* fire before the Lord,
Dt 32.16 him to jealousy with *s* gods,
Jdg 10.16 put away the *s* gods from among
1Ki 11. 1 Solomon loved many *s* women,
Ezr 10. 2 have taken *s* wives of the people
Neh 13.27 transgress...in marrying *s* wives?
Job 19. 3 that ye make yourselves *s* to me.
17 My breath is *s* to my wife,
31. 3 a *s* punishment to the workers
Ps 81. 9 shalt thou worship any *s* god.
114. 1 Jacob from a people of *s* language;
137. 4 sing the Lord's song in a *s* land?
Pr 7. 5 keep thee from the *s* woman,
21. 8 way of man is froward and *s*:
Isa 28.21 he may do his work, his *s* work;
21 bring to pass his act, his *s* act.
Eze 3. 5 not sent to a people of a *s* speech
Hos 5. 7 they have begotten *s* children:
Zep 1. 8 as are clothed with *s* apparel.
Mal 2.11 married the daughter of a *s* god.
Lk 5.26 We have seen *s* things to day.
Ac 7. 6 seed should sojourn in a *s* land;
17.18 to be a setter forth of *s* gods:
20 certain *s* things to our ears:
26.11 I persecuted them...unto *s* cities.
Heb 11. 9 land of promise, as in a *s* country,
13. 9 about the divers and *s* doctrines.
1Pe 4. 4 think it *s*...ye run not with them
12 think it not *s* concerning the fiery
12 some *s* thing happened unto you:
Jude 7 and going after *s* flesh, are set

STRANGER

Gen 15.13 be a *s* in a land that is not theirs,
17.12 bought with money of any *s*,
23. 4 I am a *s* and a sojourner with you:
Ex 20.10 nor thy *s* that is within thy gates:
23. 9 for ye know the heart of a *s*, seeing
29.33 but a *s* shall not eat thereof,
Nu 18. 4 a *s* shall not come nigh unto you.
Dt 10.18 and loveth the *s*, in giving him food
19 Love ye therefore the *s*: for ye
23.20 Unto a *s* thou mayest lend upon
24.17 not pervert the judgment of the *s*,
26.12 *s*, the fatherless, and the widow,
2Sa 15.19 thou art a *s*, and also an exile.
Job 19.15 and my maids, count me for a *s*:
31.32 The *s* did not lodge in the street:

Ps 39.12 I am a *s* with thee, and a sojourner
119.19 I am a *s* in the earth: hide not thy
Pr 20.16 his garment that is surety for a *s*:
Isa 62. 8 the sons of the *s* shall not drink
Ob 12 in the day that he became a *s*;
Zec 7.10 widow, nor the fatherless, the *s*,
Mal 3. 5 turn aside the *s* from his right,
Mt 25.35 I was a *s*, and ye took me in:
38 When saw we thee a *s*, and took
43 I was a *s*, and ye took me not in:
44 or a *s*, or naked, or sick, or in
Lk 17.18 to give glory to God, save this *s*.
24.18 Art thou only a *s* in Jerusalem,
Jn 10. 5 And a *s* will they not follow, but
Ac 7.29 was a *s* in the land of Madian,

STRANGERS

Gen 31.15 Are we not counted of him *s*? for
Dt 10.19 ye were *s* in the land of Egypt.
31.16 after the gods of the *s* of the land,
2Ch 2.17 Solomon numbered all the *s*
Ps 54. 3 For *s* are risen up against me,
Isa 25. 2 a palace of *s* to be no city; it
60.10 sons of *s* shall build up thy walls,
61. 5 *s* shall stand and feed your flocks,
Jer 2.25 for I have loved *s*, and after them
La 5. 2 Our inheritance is turned to *s*, our
Eze 11. 9 and deliver you into the hands of *s*,
Hos 8. 7 it yield, the *s* shall swallow it up.
Mt 17.25 of their own children, or of *s*?
26 Peter saith unto him, Of *s*. Jesus
27. 7 the potter's field, to bury *s* in.
Jn 10. 5 for they know not the voice of *s*
Ac 2.10 *s* of Rome, Jews and proselytes,
13.17 dwelt as *s* in...land of Egypt,
17.21 *s* which were there spent their
Eph 2.12 *s* from the covenants of promise,
19 ye are no more *s* and foreigners,
1Ti 5.10 up children, if she have lodged *s*,
Heb 11.13 confessed that they were *s* and
13. 2 Be not forgetful to entertain *s*:
1Pe 1. 1 to the *s* scattered throughout
2.11 I beseech you as *s* and pilgrims,
3Jn 5 doest to the brethren, and to *s*;

STRANGLED

Na 2.12 whelps, and *s* for his lionesses,
Ac 15.20 fornication, and from things *s*,
29 and from blood, and from things *s*,
21.25 and from *s*, and from fornication.

STRAW

Gen 24.25 We have both *s* and provender
32 *s* and provender for the camels,
Ex 5. 7 give the people *s* to make brick,
7 go and gather *s* for themselves.
10 Pharaoh, I will not give you *s*.
11 get you *s* where ye can find it: yet
12 to gather stubble instead of *s*.
13 daily tasks, as when there was *s*.
16 is no *s* given unto thy servants,
18 for there shall no *s* be given you,
Jdg 19.19 Yet there is both *s* and provender
1Ki 4.28 Barley also and *s* for the horses
Job 41.27 He esteemeth iron as *s*, and brass
Isa 11. 7 and the lion shall eat *s* like the ox.
25.10 even as *s* is trodden down for the
65.25 lion shall eat *s* like the bullock:

STRAWED

Ex 32.20 powder, and *s* it upon the water,
Mt 21. 8 the trees, and *s* them in the way.
25.24 gathering where thou hast not *s*:
26 and gather where I have not *s*:
Mk 11. 8 the trees, and *s* them in the way.

STREAM

Nu 21.15 at the *s* of the brooks that goeth
Job 6.15 as the *s* of brooks they pass away;
Ps 124. 4 us, the *s* had gone over our soul:
Isa 27.12 of the river unto the *s* of Egypt,
30.28 his breath, as an overflowing *s*,
33 like a *s* of brimstone, doth kindle
57. 6 Among the smooth stones of the *s*
66.12 of the Gentiles like a flowing *s*:
Dan 7.10 A fiery *s* issued and came forth
Am 5.24 and righteousness as a mighty *s*.
Lk 6.48 the *s* beat vehemently upon that
49 against which the *s* did beat

STREAMS

Ex 7.19 the waters of Egypt, upon their *s*,
8. 5 thine hand with thy rod over the *s*,
Ps 46. 4 the *s* whereof shall make glad the
78.16 He brought *s* also out of the rock,
20 gushed out, and the *s* overflowed;
126. 4 O Lord, as the *s* in the south.
SS 4.15 waters, and *s* from Lebanon.
Isa 11.15 and shall smite it in the seven *s*,
30.25 rivers and *s* of waters in the day
33.21 us a place of broad rivers and *s*;
34. 9 the *s* thereof shall be turned into
35. 6 break out, and *s* in the desert.

STREET

Jdg 19.15 he sat him down in a *s* of the city:
Ezr 10. 9 sat in the *s* of the house of God,
Neh 8. 1 *s* that was before the water gate;
16 in the *s* of the gate of Ephraim.
Job 18.17 shall have no name in the *s*.
29. 7 when I prepared my seat in the *s*!
Isa 42. 2 his voice to be heard in the *s*.
59.14 truth is fallen in the *s*, and equity
La 4. 1 poured out in the top of every *s*.
Eze 16.24 thee an high place in every *s*.
Ac 9.11 the *s* which is called Straight,
12.10 out, and passed on through one *s*;
Rev 11. 8 dead bodies shall lie in the *s* of
21.21 the *s* of the city was pure gold, as it
22. 2 In the midst of the *s* of it, and on

STREETS

2Sa 1.20 publish it not in the *s* of Askelon;
Ps 18.42 cast them out as the dirt in the *s*.
144.14 there be no complaining in our *s*.
Pr 7.12 Now is she without, now in the *s*,
22.13 without, I shall be slain in the *s*.
26.13 a lion in the way; a lion is in the *s*.
Ec 12. 5 and the mourners go about the *s*:
Isa 24.11 is a crying for wine in the *s*; all
Jer 49.26 her young men shall fall in her *s*,
La 2.21 the old lie on the ground in the *s*:
4. 8 they are not known in the *s*:
14 wandered as blind men in the *s*,
Eze 7.19 shall cast their silver in the *s*,
Am 5.16 Wailing shall be in all the *s*;
Zep 3. 6 I made their *s* waste, that none
Zec 8. 5 *s* of the city shall be full of boys
5 and girls playing in the *s* thereof.
Mt 6. 2 in the synagogues and in the *s*,
5 and in the corners of the *s*,
12.19 any man hear his voice in the *s*.
Mk 6.56 they laid the sick in the *s*, and
Lk 10.10 go your ways out into the *s* of
13.26 and thou hast taught in our *s*.
14.21 Go out quickly into the *s* and lanes
Ac 5.15 brought forth the sick into the *s*,

STRENGTH

Ex 13. 3 by *s* of hand the Lord brought you
14.27 sea returned to his *s* when the
15. 2 The Lord is my *s* and song, and
Nu 24. 8 hath as it were the *s* of an unicorn:
Dt 33.25 and as thy days, so shall thy *s* be.
Jos 14.11 *s* was then, even so is my *s* now,
Jdg 8.21 for as the man is, so is his *s*.
16. 5 and see wherein his great *s* lieth,
19 him, and his *s* went from him.
1Sa 15.29 the *S* of Israel will not lie nor
2Sa 22.33 God is my *s* and power: and he
2Ki 19. 3 and there is not *s* to bring forth.
1Ch 16.28 give unto the Lord glory and *s*,
Neh 8.10 for the joy of the Lord is your *s*.
Job 6.11 What is my *s*, that I should hope?
12 Is my *s* the *s* of stones? or is my
9. 4 is wise in heart, and mighty in *s*:
19 If I speak of *s*, lo, he is strong:
12.13 With him is wisdom and *s*, he
16 With him is *s* and wisdom: the
21.23 One dieth in his full *s*, being
39.19 Hast thou given the horse *s*?
Ps 8. 2 sucklings hast thou ordained *s*
18. 2 my God, my *s*, in whom I will
19.14 O Lord, my *s*, and my redeemer.
21. 1 king shall joy in thy *s*, O Lord;
22.15 My *s* is dried up like a potsherd;
27. 1 Lord is the *s* of my life; of whom
28. 7 The Lord is my *s* and my shield;
33.16 man is not delivered by much *s*.
43. 2 For thou art the God of my *s*:
46. 1 God is our refuge and *s*, a very
59.17 Unto thee, O my *s*, will I sing: for
62. 7 the rock of my *s*, and my refuge,
68.34 Ascribe ye *s* unto God: his
71. 9 forsake me not when my *s* faileth.
73.26 but God is the *s* of my heart, and
81. 1 Sing aloud unto God our *s*: make
84. 5 is the man whose *s* is in thee;
7 They go from *s* to *s*, every one of
90.10 by reason of *s* they be fourscore
10 yet is their *s* labor and sorrow;
95. 4 the *s* of the hills is his also.
96. 6 *s* and beauty are in his sanctuary.
7 give unto the Lord glory and *s*.
103.20 ye his angels, that excel in *s*, that
118.14 The Lord is my *s* and song, and is
147.10 delighteth not in...*s* of the horse:
Pr 20.29 glory of young men is their *s*:
31.25 *S* and honor are her clothing;
Ec 9.16 said I, Wisdom is better than *s*:
Isa 10.13 By the *s* of my hand I have done
12. 2 Jehovah is my *s* and my song;
25. 4 For thou hast been a *s* to the poor,
30. 7 I cried...Their *s* is to sit still.
15 and in confidence shall be your *s*:
37. 3 and there is not *s* to bring forth.
40.29 have no might he increaseth *s*.
41. 1 and let the people renew their *s*:
44.12 yea, he is hungry, and his *s* faileth:
49. 4 I have spent my *s* for nought, and
51. 9 awake, put on *s*, O arm of the Lord;
52. 1 awake; put on thy *s*, O Zion;
Jer 16.19 O Lord, my *s*, and my fortress,
La 3.18 My *s* and my hope is perished
Dan 10. 8 and there remained no *s* in me:
Hos 12. 3 by his *s* he had power with God:
Am 6.13 taken to us horns by our own *s*?
Mic 5. 4 and feed in the *s* of the Lord,
Hab 3.19 The Lord God is my *s*, and he will
Zec 12. 5 shall be my *s* in the Lord of hosts
Mk 12.30 all thy mind, and with all thy *s*:
33 all the soul, and with all the *s*,
Lk 1.51 He hath shewed *s* with his arm;
10.27 all thy soul, and with all thy *s*,
Ac 3. 7 feet and ancle bones received *s*.
9.22 But Saul increased the more in *s*,
Ro 5. 6 For when we were yet without *s*,
1Co 15.56 is sin; and the *s* of sin is the law.
2Co 1. 8 pressed out of measure, above *s*,
12. 9 *s* is made perfect in weakness.
Heb 9.17 of no *s* at all while the testator
11.11 Sara...received *s* to conceive seed,
Rev 1.16 was as the sun shineth in his *s*.
3. 8 thou hast a little *s*, and hast kept
5.12 and riches and wisdom, and *s*,
12.10 Now is come salvation, and *s*, and
17.13 their power and *s* unto the beast.

STRENGTHEN

Jdg 16.28 *s* me, I pray thee, only this once,
Neh 6. 9 therefore, O God, *s* my hands.
Ps 31.24 courage, and he shall *s* your heart,
Isa 35. 3 *S* ye the weak hands, and confirm

Isa 41.10 I will *s* thee; yea, I will help thee;
Eze 7.13 *s* himself in the iniquity of his life.
16.49 *s* the hand of the poor and needy.
Lk 22.32 art converted, *s* thy brethren.
1Pe 5.10 perfect, stablish, *s*, settle you.
Rev 3. 2 and *s* the things which remain,

STRENGTHENED

Ezr 7.28 I was *s* as the hand of the Lord my
Neh 2.18 *s* their hands for this good work.
Job 4. 3 and thou hast *s* the weak hands.
4 and thou hast *s* the feeble knees.
Ps 52. 7 and *s* himself in his wickedness.
Pr 8.28 he *s* the fountains of the deep:
Dan 10.19 my lord speak; for thou hast *s* me.
Ac 9.19 he had received meat, he was *s*.
Eph 3.16 to be *s* with might by his Spirit
Col 1.11 *S* with all might, according to his
2Ti 4.17 Lord stood with me, and *s* me;

STRENGTHENETH

Job 15.25 *s* himself against the Almighty.
Ps 104.15 and bread which *s* man's heart.
Pr 31.17 with strength, and *s* her arms.
Ec 7.19 Wisdom *s* the wise more than ten
Isa 44.14 the oak, which he *s* for himself
Am 5. 9 *s* the spoiled against the strong,
Php 4.13 things through Christ which *s* me.

STRENGTHENING

Lk 22.43 an angel...from heaven, *s* him.
Ac 18.23 in order, *s* all the disciples.

STRETCH

Ex 7. 5 I *s* forth mine hand upon Egypt,
8. 5 *S* forth thine hand with thy rod
25.20 cherubims...*s* forth their wings
Ps 68.31 Ethiopia shall soon *s* out her
143. 6 I *s* forth my hands unto thee:
Isa 28.20 than that a man can *s* himself
31. 3 the Lord shall *s* out his hand,
Jer 51.25 I will *s* out mine hand upon thee,
Mt 12.13 he to the man, *S* forth thine hand.
Mk 3. 5 unto the man, *S* forth thine hand.
Lk 6.10 unto the man, *S* forth thy hand.
Jn 21.18 old, thou shalt *s* forth thy hands,
2Co 10.14 we *s* not ourselves beyond our

STRETCHED

Ex 6. 6 will redeem you with a *s* out arm,
8. 6 Aaron *s*...his hand over the waters
14.27 Moses *s* forth his hand over the sea,
Dt 4.34 a mighty hand, and by a *s* out arm,
9.29 mighty power and by thy *s* out arm.
Job 38. 5 or who hath *s* the line upon it?
Ps 44.20 *s*...our hands to a strange god;
88. 9 I have *s* out my hands unto thee.
136. 6 To him that *s* out the earth above
Pr 1.24 I have *s* out my hand, and no man
Isa 42. 5 the heavens, and *s* them out;
Jer 6. 4 shadows of the evening are *s* out.
32.17 by thy great power and *s* out arm,
Eze 16.27 I have *s* out my hand over thee,
Mt 12.13 he *s* it forth; and it was restored
49 And he *s* forth his hand toward his
14.31 Jesus *s* forth his hand, and caught
26.51 *s* out his hand, and drew his sword,
Mk 3. 5 And he *s* it out: and his hand was
Lk 22.53 ye *s* forth no hands against me:
Ac 12. 1 Herod the king *s* forth his hands
26. 1 Then Paul *s* forth the hand, and
Ro 10.21 I have *s* forth my hands unto a

STRETCHEST

Ps 104. 2 *s* out the heavens like a curtain:

STRETCHETH

Job 15.25 he *s* out his hand against God,
26. 7 He *s* out the north over the empty
Pr 31.20 She *s* out her hand to the poor;
Isa 40.22 *s* out the heavens as a curtain,
44.13 The carpenter *s* out his rule; he
24 that *s* forth the heavens alone;
Zec 12. 1 Lord, which *s* forth the heavens,

STRETCHING

Isa 8. 8 the *s* out of his wings shall fill the
Ac 4.30 By *s* forth thine hand to heal; and

STRICKEN

Gen 18.11 Sarah were old and well *s* in age;
24. 1 Abraham was old, and well *s* in age:
Jos 13. 1 Now Joshua was old and *s* in years;
1 Thou art old and *s* in years, and
23. 1 that Joshua waxed old and *s* in age.
2 unto them, I am old and *s* in age:
Jdg 5.26 and *s* through his temples.
1Ki 1. 1 king David was old and *s* in years;
Pr 6. 1 hast *s* thy hand with a stranger,
23.35 They have *s* me, shalt thou say,
Isa 1. 5 Why should ye be *s* any more?
16. 7 shall ye mourn; surely they are *s*.
53. 4 yet we did esteem him *s*, smitten
8 transgression of my people...he *s*.
Jer 5. 3 thou hast *s* them, but they have
La 4. 9 *s* through for want of the fruits of
Lk 1. 7 both were now well *s* in years.
18 man, and my wife well *s* in years.

STRIFE

Dt 1.12 and your burden, and your *s*?
Ps 31.20 a pavilion from the *s* of tongues.
80. 6 us a *s* unto our neighbors:
Pr 15.18 A wrathful man stirreth up *s*:
18 that is slow to anger appeaseth *s*.
16.28 A froward man soweth *s*: and a
17.14 The beginning of *s* is as when one
26.17 meddleth with *s* belonging not
20 is no talebearer, the *s* ceaseth.
21 is a contentious man to kindle *s*.
29.22 An angry man stirreth up *s*, and a
Jer 15.10 a man of *s* and a man of contention
Hab 1. 3 and there are that raise up *s* and
Lk 22.24 there was also a *s* among them,
Ro 13.13 wantonness, not in *s* and envying.
1Co 3. 3 you envying, and *s*, and divisions,
Gal 5.20 emulations, wrath, *s*, seditions,
Php 1.15 preach Christ even of envy and *s*;
2. 3 Let nothing be done through *s* or
1Ti 6. 4 whereof cometh envy, *s*, railings,
Heb 6.16 oath...is to them an end of all *s*.
Jas 3.14 envying and *s* in your hearts,
16 For where envying and *s* is, there

STRIFES

Pr 10.12 Hatred stirreth up *s*: but love
2Co 12.20 envyings, wraths, *s*, backbitings,
1Ti 6. 4 about questions and *s* of words,
2Ti 2.23 knowing that they do gender *s*.

STRIKE

Ex 12. 7 and *s* it on the two side posts
2Ki 5.11 and *s* his hand over the place,
Job 17. 3 is he that will *s* hands with me?
Pr 22.26 Be not...one of them that *s* hands,
Mk 14.65 did *s* him with the palms of their

STRIKER

1Ti 3. 3 Not given to wine, no *s*, not greedy
Tit 1. 7 not given to wine, no *s*, not given to

STRIKETH

Job 34.26 He *s* them as wicked men in the
Pr 17.18 void of understanding *s* hands,
Rev 9. 5 a scorpion, when he *s* a man.

STRING

Ps 11. 2 ready their arrow upon the *s*,
Mk 7.35 the *s* of his tongue was loosed,

STRINGED

Ps 150. 4 praise him with *s* instruments
Isa 38.20 my songs to the *s* instrument
Hab 3.19 chief singer on my *s* instruments.

STRINGS

Ps 21.12 arrows upon thy *s* against the
33. 2 and an instrument of ten *s*.
92. 3 Upon an instrument of ten *s*, and
144. 9 and an instrument of ten *s* will I

STRIP

Nu 20.26 *s* Aaron of his garments, and put
1Sa 31. 8 the Philistines came to *s* the slain,
1Ch 10. 8 the Philistines came to *s* the slain,
Isa 32.11 *s* you, and make you bare, and
Eze 16.39 shall *s* thee also of thy clothes,
23.26 shall also *s* thee out of thy clothes,
Hos 2. 3 Lest I *s* her naked, and set her as

STRIPE

Ex 21.25 wound for wound, *s* for *s*.

STRIPES

Dt 25. 3 Forty *s* he may give him, and
3 him above these with many *s*,
2Sa 7.14 with the *s* of the children of men:
Ps 89.32 rod, and their iniquity with *s*.
Pr 17.10 than an hundred *s* into a fool.
19.29 and *s* for the back of fools.
20.30 so do *s* the inward parts of the
Isa 53. 5 and with his *s* we are healed.
Lk 12.47 will, shall be beaten with many *s*.
48 commit things worthy of *s*, shall
48 shall be beaten with few *s*. For
Ac 16.23 they had laid many *s* upon them,
33 of the night, and washed their *s*;
2Co 6. 5 In *s*, in imprisonments, in tumults,
11.23 in *s* above measure, in prisons
24 times received I forty *s* save one.
1Pe 2.24 by whose *s* ye were healed.

STRIPPED

Ex 33. 6 children of Israel *s* themselves
Nu 20.28 Moses *s* Aaron of his garments,
1Sa 18. 4 Jonathan *s* himself of the robe
19.24 And he *s* off his clothes also, and
31. 9 off his head, and *s* off his armor,
1Ch 10. 9 when they had *s* him, they took
2Ch 20.25 which they *s* off for themselves,
Job 19. 9 He hath *s* me of my glory, and
22. 6 and *s* the naked of their clothing.
Mic 1. 8 and howl, I will go *s* and naked:
Mt 27.28 And they *s* him, and put on him a
Lk 10.30 which *s* him of his raiment, and

STRIPT

Gen 37.23 they *s* Joseph out of his coat, his

STRIVE

Gen 6. 3 My spirit shall not...*s* with man,
Dt 33. 8 whom thou didst *s* at the waters
Job 33.13 Why dost thou *s* against him? for
Pr 3.30 *S* not with a man without cause,
Isa 45. 9 the potsherd *s* with the potsherds
Hos 4. 4 are as they that *s* with the priest.
Mt 12.19 He shall not *s*, nor cry; neither
Lk 13.24 *S* to enter in at the strait gate:
Ro 15.30 ye *s* together with me in your
2Ti 2. 5 if a man also *s* for masteries, yet
5 not crowned, except he *s* lawfully.
14 *s* not about words to no profit,
24 servant of the Lord must not *s*;

STRIVED

Ro 15.20 so have I *s* to preach the gospel,

STRIVETH

Isa 45. 9 unto him that *s* with his Maker!
1Co 9.25 every man that *s* for the mastery

STRIVING

Php 1.27 one mind *s* together for the faith
Col 1.29 *s* according to his working, which
Heb 12. 4 resisted unto blood, *s* against sin.

STRIVINGS

2Sa 22.44 delivered me from the *s* of my
Ps 18.43 delivered me from the *s* of the
Tit 3. 9 contentions, and *s* about the law;

STROKE

Dt 17. 8 between *s* and *s*, being matters
19. 5 his hand fetcheth a *s* with the axe
21. 5 controversy and every *s* be tried:
Est 9. 5 enemies with the *s* of the sword,
Job 23. 2 *s* is heavier than my groaning.
36.18 he take thee away with his *s*:
Ps 39.10 Remove thy *s* away from me: I
Isa 14. 6 the people...with a continual *s*,
30.26 and healeth the *s* of their wound.
Eze 24.16 the desire of thine eyes with a *s*:

STRONG

Ex 6. 1 a *s* hand shall he let them go,
1 a *s* hand shall he drive them out
10.19 Lord turned a mighty *s* west wind,
Lev 10. 9 Do not drink wine nor *s* drink, thou,
Nu 6. 3 himself from wine and *s* drink, and
13.28 people be *s* that dwell in the land,
Dt 31. 6 Be *s* and of a good courage, fear
Jos 1. 6 Be *s* and of a good courage: for
Jdg 6. 2 mountains,...caves, and *s* holds.
14.14 out of the *s* came forth sweetness.
1Sa 4. 9 Be *s*, and quit yourselves like
1Ki 19.11 and *s* wind rent the mountains,
1Ch 28.10 the sanctuary: be *s*, and do it.
20 his son, be *s* and of good courage,
Job 8. 2 of thy mouth be like a *s* wind?
9.19 If I speak of strength, lo, he is *s*:
37.18 spread out the sky, which is *s*,
Ps 18.17 me: for they were too *s* for me.
19. 5 and rejoiceth as a *s* man to run a
24. 8 The Lord *s* and mighty, the Lord
31. 2 be thou my *s* rock, for an house
61. 3 and a *s* tower from the enemy.
71. 7 many; but thou art my *s* refuge.
80.15 that thou madest *s* for thyself.
Pr 10.15 rich man's wealth is his *s* city:
14.26 fear of the Lord is *s* confidence:
18.10 The name of the Lord is a *s* tower:
24. 5 A wise man is *s*; yea, a man of
30.25 The ants are a people not *s*, yet
Ec 9.11 nor the battle to the *s*, neither yet
SS 8. 6 for love is *s* as death; jealousy is
Isa 26. 1 We have a *s* city; salvation will
29. 9 they stagger, but not with *s* drink.
40.10 Lord God will come with *s* hand,
26 might, for that he is *s* in power;
41.21 bring forth your *s* reasons, saith
53.12 shall divide the spoil with the *s*;
60.22 and a small one a *s* nation:
Jer 21. 5 outstretched hand and...a *s* arm,
50.34 Their Redeemer is *s*; the Lord of
51.12 make the watch *s*, set up the
Eze 3.14 hand of the Lord was *s* upon me.
7.24 make the pomp of the *s* to cease;
Dan 11.32 that do know their God shall be *s*.
Joel 3.10 spears: let the weak say, I am *s*.
Am 2. 9 cedars, and he was *s* as the oaks;
Mic 4. 7 her that was cast far off a *s* nation:
Na 1. 7 a *s* hold in the day of trouble;
Zec 8. 9 Let your hands be *s*, ye that hear
13 fear not, but let your hands be *s*.
Mt 12.29 one enter into a *s* man's house,
29 except he first bind the *s* man?
Mk 3.27 can enter into a *s* man's house,
27 except he will first bind the *s* man;
Lk 1.15 drink neither wine nor *s* drink;
80 child grew, and waxed *s* in spirit,
2.40 child grew, and waxed *s* in spirit,
11.21 *s* man armed keepeth his palace,
Ac 3.16 his name hath made this man *s*,
Ro 4.20 was *s* in faith, giving glory to God;
15. 1 We...that are *s* ought to bear the
1Co 4.10 we are weak, but ye are *s*;
16.13 the faith, quit you like men, be *s*.
2Co 10. 4 to the pulling down of *s* holds;)
12.10 for when I am weak, then am I *s*.
13. 9 when we are weak, and ye are *s*:
Eph 6.10 my brethren, be *s* in the Lord,
2Th 2.11 God shall send them *s* delusion,
2Ti 2. 1 my son, be *s* in the grace that is
Heb 5. 7 with *s* crying and tears unto him
12 need of milk, and not of *s* meat.
14 But *s* meat belongeth to them that
6.18 we might have a *s* consolation,
11.34 out of weakness were made *s*,
1Jn 2.14 young men, because ye are *s*, and
Rev 5. 2 I saw a *s* angel proclaiming with
18. 2 he cried mightily with a *s* voice,
8 *s* is the Lord God who judgeth

STRONGER

Jdg 14.18 honey? and what is *s* than a lion?
2Sa 1.23 eagles, they were *s* than lions.
Job 17. 9 that hath clean hands shall be *s*
Lk 11.22 when a *s* than he shall come upon
1Co 1.25 the weakness of God is *s* than men.
10.22 to jealousy? are we *s* than he?

STRONGEST

Pr 30.30 A lion which is *s* among beasts,

STROVE

Gen 26.20 Esek; because they *s* with him.
21 another well, and *s* for that also:
22 another well,...for that they *s* not:
Ex 2.13 men of the Hebrews *s* together:
Lev 24.10 of Israel *s* together in the camp;
Nu 20.13 children of Israel *s* with the Lord,
26. 9 who *s* against Moses and against
9 when they *s* against the Lord:
2Sa 14. 6 they two *s* together in the field,
Ps 60(T) when he *s* with Aram-naharaim
Dan 7. 2 four winds of the heaven *s* upon
Jn 6.52 Jews...*s* among themselves,
Ac 7.26 he shewed himself...as they *s*,
23. 9 the Pharisees' part arose, and *s*,

STRUCK

1Sa 2.14 And he *s* it into the pan, or kettle,
2Sa 12.15 the Lord *s* the child that Uriah's
20.10 the ground, and *s* him not again:
2Ch 13.20 and the Lord *s* him, and he died.
Mt 26.51 *s* a servant of the high priest's,
Lk 22.64 him, they *s* him on the face,
Jn 18.22 *s* Jesus with the palm of his

STUBBLE

Ex 5.12 to gather *s* instead of straw.
15. 7 wrath, which consumed them as *s*.
Job 13.25 and wilt thou pursue the dry *s*?
21.18 They are as *s* before the wind,
41.28 slingstones are turned...into *s*.
29 Darts are counted as *s*: he
Ps 83.13 wheel; as the *s* before the wind.
Isa 5.24 as the fire devoureth the *s*, and
33.11 chaff, ye shall bring forth *s*:
40.24 shall take them away as *s*.
41. 2 sword, and as driven *s* to his bow.
47.14 Behold, they shall be as *s*; the fire
Jer 13.24 scatter them as the *s* that passeth
Joel 2. 5 flame of fire that devoureth the *s*,
Ob 18 flame, and the house of Esau for *s*,
Na 1.10 they shall be devoured as *s*
Mal 4. 1 all that do wickedly, shall be *s*:
1Co 3.12 precious stones, wood, hay, *s*;

STUBBORN

Dt 21.18 man have a *s* and rebellious son,
20 This our son is *s* and rebellious,
Jdg 2.19 doings, nor from their *s* way.
Ps 78. 8 a *s* and rebellious generation;
Pr 7.11 (She is loud and *s*; her feet abide

STUCK

1Sa 26. 7 his spear *s* in the ground at his
Ps 119.31 I have *s* unto thy testimonies:
Ac 27.41 the forepart *s* fast, and remained

STUDIETH

Pr 15.28 of the righteous *s* to answer:
24. 2 For their heart *s* destruction, and

STUDY

Ec 12.12 much *s* is a weariness of the flesh.
1Th 4.11 that ye *s* to be quiet, and to do
2Ti 2.15 *S* to shew thyself approved unto

STUFF

Gen 31.37 thou hast searched all my *s*,
37 thou found of all thy household *s*?
45.20 Also regard not your *s*; for the
Ex 22. 7 his neighbor money or *s* to keep,
36. 7 *s* they had was sufficient for all
Jos 7.11 put it even among their own *s*.
1Sa 10.22 he hath hid himself among the *s*.
25.13 and two hundred abode by the *s*.
30.24 his part be that tarrieth by the *s*:
Neh 13. 8 forth all the household *s* of Tobiah
Eze 12. 3 prepare thee *s* for removing,
4 shalt thou bring forth thy *s* by day
4 in their sight, as *s* for removing:
7 I brought forth my *s* by day,
7 as *s* for captivity, and in the even
Lk 17.31 housetop, and his *s* in the house,

STUMBLE

Pr 3.23 safely, and thy foot shall not *s*.
4.12 thou runnest, thou shalt not *s*.
19 they know not at what they *s*.
Isa 5.27 shall be weary nor *s* among them;
8.15 And many among them shall *s*,
28. 7 err in vision, they *s* in judgment.
59.10 we *s* at noon day as in the night;
63.13 wilderness, that they should not *s*?
Jer 13.16 feet *s* upon the dark mountains,
18.15 caused them to *s* in their ways
20.11 therefore my persecutors shall *s*,
31. 9 way, wherein they shall not *s*:
46. 6 shall *s*, and fall toward the north
50.32 the most proud shall *s* and fall,
Dan 11.19 shall *s* and fall, and not be found
Na 2. 5 they shall *s* in their walk; they
3. 3 corpses; they *s* upon their corpses:
Mal 2. 8 have caused many to *s* at the law;
1Pe 2. 8 even to them which *s* at the word,

STUMBLED

1Sa 2. 4 that *s* are girded with strength.
1Ch 13. 9 to hold the ark; for the oxen *s*.
Ps 27. 2 eat up my flesh, they *s* and fell.
Jer 46.12 man hath *s* against the mighty,
Ro 9.32 they *s* at that stumblingstone;
11.11 Have they *s* that they should fall?

STUMBLETH

Pr 24.17 thine heart be glad when he *s*:
Jn 11. 9 man walk in the day, he *s* not,
10 if a man walk in the night, he *s*,
Ro 14.21 any thing whereby thy brother *s*,

STUMBLING

Isa 8.14 for a stone of *s* and for a rock of
57.14 take up the *s* block out of the way
1Pe 2. 8 And a stone of *s*, and a rock of
1Jn 2.10 there is none occasion of *s* in him.

STUMBLINGBLOCK

Lev 19.14 deaf, nor put a *s* before the blind,
Isa 57.14 *s* out of the way of my people
Eze 3.20 iniquity, and I lay a *s* before him,
7.19 because it is the *s* of their iniquity.
14. 3 put the *s* of their iniquity before
4, 7 and putteth the *s* of his iniquity
Ro 11. 9 made a snare, and a trap, and a *s*,
14.13 no man put a *s* or an occasion to
1Co 1.23 unto the Jews a *s*, and unto the
8. 9 become a *s* to them that are weak.
Rev 2.14 to cast a *s* before the children of

STUMBLINGBLOCKS
Jer 6.21 I will lay *s* before this people,
Zep 1. 3 sea, and the *s* with the wicked;

STUMBLINGSTONE
Ro 9.32 For they stumbled at that *s*;
33 I lay in Zion a *s* and rock of

STUMP
1Sa 5. 4 only the *s* of Dagon was left to him.
Dan 4.15 leave the *s* of his roots in the
23 yet leave the *s* of the roots thereof
26 to leave the *s* of the tree roots;

SUBDUE
Gen 1.28 and replenish the earth, and *s* it:
1Ch 17.10 Moreover I will *s*...thine enemies.
Ps 47. 3 He shall *s* the people under us,
Isa 45. 1 holden, to *s* nations before him;
Dan 7.24 first, and he shall *s* three kings.
Mic 7.19 he will *s* our iniquities; and thou
Zec 9.15 devour, and *s* with sling stones;
Php 3.21 to *s* all things unto himself.

SUBDUED
Nu 32.22 the land be *s* before the Lord:
29 and the land shall be *s* before you;
Dt 20.20 war with thee, until it be *s*.
Jos 18. 1 And the land was *s* before them.
Jdg 3.30 So Moab was *s* that day under the
4.23 So God *s* on that day Jabin the
8.28 was Midian *s* before the children
11.33 the children of Ammon were *s*
1Sa 7.13 So the Philistines were *s*, and they
2Sa 8. 1 smote the Philistines, and *s* them:
11 of all nations which he *s*;
22.40 against me hast thou *s* under me.
1Ch 18. 1 smote the Philistines, and *s* them,
20. 4 of the giant: and they were *s*.
22.18 and the land is *s* before the Lord,
Ps 18.39 thou hast *s* under me those that
81.14 should soon have *s* their enemies,
1Co 15.28 all things shall be *s* unto him,
Heb 11.33 Who through faith *s* kingdoms,

SUBDUETH
Ps 18.47 me, and *s* the people under me.
144. 2 trust; who *s* my people under me.
Dan 2.40 in pieces and *s* all things: and as

SUBJECT
Lk 2.51 Nazareth, and was *s* unto them:
10.17 devils are *s* unto us through thy
20 not, that the spirits are *s* unto you;
Ro 8. 7 for it is not *s* to the law of God,
20 the creature was made *s* to vanity,
13. 1 every soul be *s* unto the higher
5 Wherefore ye must needs be *s*, not
1Co 14.32 the prophets are *s* to the prophets.
15.28 the Son also himself be *s* unto him
Eph 5.24 as the church is *s* unto Christ,
Col 2.20 the world, are ye *s* to ordinances,
Tit 3. 1 in mind to be *s* to principalities
Heb 2.15 all their lifetime *s* to bondage.
Jas 5.17 Elias...a man *s* to like passions
1Pe 2.18 Servants, be *s* to your masters
3.22 powers being made *s* unto him.
5. 5 all of you be *s* one to another, and

SUBJECTED
Ro 8.20 who hath *s* the same in hope,

SUBJECTION
Ps 106.42 brought into *s* under their hand.
Jer 34.11 brought them into *s* for servants
16 to return, and brought them into *s*,
1Co 9.27 my body, and bring it into *s*:
2Co 9.13 your professed *s* unto the gospel
Gal 2. 5 To whom we gave place by *s*, no,
1Ti 2.11 woman learn in silence with all *s*.
3. 4 his children in *s* with all gravity;
Heb 2. 5 not put in *s* the world to come,
8 Thou hast put all things in *s* under
8 in that he put all in *s* under him,
12. 9 rather be in *s* unto the Father of
1Pe 3. 1 be in *s* to your own husbands;
5 in *s* unto their own husbands:

SUBMIT
Gen 16. 9 and *s* thyself under her hands.
2Sa 22.45 Strangers shall *s* themselves unto
Ps 18.44 strangers shall *s* themselves unto
66. 3 shall thine enemies *s* themselves
68.30 *s* himself with pieces of silver:
1Co 16.16 That ye *s* yourselves unto such,
Eph 5.22 Wives, *s* yourselves unto your own
Col 3.18 Wives, *s* yourselves unto your own
Heb 13.17 rule over you, and *s* yourselves:
Jas 4. 7 *S* yourselves therefore to God.
1Pe 2.13 *S* yourselves to every ordinance
5. 5 *s* yourselves unto the elder.

SUBMITTED
1Ch 29.24 *s* themselves unto Solomon
Ps 81.15 should have *s* themselves unto
Ro 10. 3 have not *s* themselves unto the

SUBMITTING
Eph 5.21 *S* yourselves one to another in

SUBSCRIBE
Isa 44. 5 *s* with his hand unto the Lord,
Jer 32.44 and *s* evidences, and seal them,

SUBSCRIBED
Jer 32.10 I *s* the evidence, and sealed it,
12 witnesses that *s* the book of the

SUBSTANCE
Gen 13. 6 for their *s* was great, so that they
2Ch 32.29 God had given him *s* very much.
Job 5. 5 the robber swalloweth up their *s*.
22.20 Whereas our *s* is not cut down,
30.22 upon it, and dissolvest my *s*.
Ps 17.14 the rest of their *s* to their babes.
139.15 My *s* was not hid from thee,
16 Thine eyes did see my *s*, yet
Pr 3. 9 Honor the Lord with thy *s*, and
28. 8 and unjust gain increaseth his *s*,
29. 3 with harlots spendeth his *s*.
SS 8. 7 give all the *s* of his house for love,
Jer 15.13 Thy *s* and thy treasures will I
Hos 12. 8 rich, I have found me out *s*:
Mic 4.13 their *s* unto the Lord of the whole
Lk 8. 3 ministered unto him of their *s*.
15.13 wasted his *s* with riotous living.
Heb 10.34 a better and an enduring *s*.
11. 1 faith is the *s* of things hoped for,

SUBTIL
Gen 3. 1 the serpent was more *s* than any
2Sa 13. 3 and Jonadab was a very *s* man.
Pr 7.10 attire of an harlot, and *s* of heart.

SUBTILLY
1Sa 23.22 told me that he dealeth very *s*.
Ps 105.25 to deal *s* with his servants.
Ac 7.19 The same dealt *s* with our kindred,

SUBTILTY
Gen 27.35 The brother came with *s*, and
2Ki 10.19 But Jehu did it in *s*, to the intent
Pr 1. 4 To give *s* to the simple, to the
Mt 26. 4 that they might take Jesus by *s*,
Ac 13.10 O full of all *s* and all mischief,
2Co 11. 3 beguiled Eve through his *s*,

SUBVERT
La 3.36 To *s* a man in his cause, the Lord
Tit 1.11 who *s* whole houses, teaching

SUBVERTED
Tit 3.11 Knowing that he that is such is *s*,

SUBVERTING
Ac 15.24 you with words, *s* your souls,
2Ti 2.14 profit, but to the *s* of the hearers.

SUCCEED
Dt 25. 6 shall *s* in the name of his brother

SUCCEEDED
Dt 2.12 but the children of Esau *s* them,
21, 22 they *s* them, and dwelt in their

SUCCESS
Jos 1. 8 and then thou shalt have good *s*.

SUCCOR
2Sa 8. 5 Syrians of Damascus came to *s*
18. 3 that thou *s* us out of the city.
Heb 2.18 is able to *s* them that are tempted.

SUCCORED
2Sa 21.17 Abishai the son of Zeruiah *s* him,
2Co 6. 2 the day of salvation have I *s* thee:

SUCCORER
Ro 16. 2 for she hath been a *s* of many.

SUCCOTH
Gen 33.17 Jacob journeyed to *S*, and built
17 the name of the place is called *S*.
Ex 12.37 journeyed from Rameses to *S*,
13.20 they took their journey from *S*.
Nu 33. 5 from Rameses, and pitched in *S*.
6 they departed from *S*, and pitched

SUCH
Gen 41.38 Can we find *s* a one as this is, a
Ex 18.21 *s* as fear God, men of truth, hating
Dt 5.29 O that there were *s* an heart in
25.16 For all that do *s* things, and all
1Sa 4. 7 not been *s* a thing heretofore.
2Sa 13.12 no *s* thing ought to be done in
2Ch 11.16 *s* as set their hearts to seek the Lord
23.13 and *s* as taught to sing praise.
Ezr 4.17 the river, Peace, and at *s* a time.
Neh 6.11 I said, Should *s* a man as I flee?
Job 15.13 lettest *s* words go out of thy mouth?
Ps 34.18 saveth *s* as be of a contrite spirit.
40. 4 proud, nor *s* as turn aside to lies.
103.18 To *s* as keep his covenant, and to
107.10 *S* as sit in darkness and in the
139. 6 *S* knowledge is too wonderful for
Isa 58. 5 Is it *s* a fast that I have chosen?
Mt 9. 8 had given *s* power unto men.
19.14 for of *s* is the kingdom of heaven.
24.21 *s* as was not since the beginning
Mk 7. 8 many other *s* like things ye do.
10.14 not; for of *s* is the kingdom of God.
13. 7 for *s* things must needs be; but the
19 *s* as was not from the beginning
Lk 10. 8 eat *s* things as are set before you:
18.16 not: for of *s* is the kingdom of God.
Jn 4.23 Father seeketh *s* to worship him.
8. 5 us, that *s* should be stoned:
Ac 3. 6 I none; but *s* as I have give I thee:
18.15 I will be no judge of *s* matters.
26.29 and altogether *s* as I am, except
Ro 1.32 *s* things are worthy of death,
1Co 5. 5 To deliver *s* an one unto Satan for
11 with *s* an one no not to eat.
6.11 And *s* were some of you: but ye
11.16 we have no *s* custom, neither the
2Co 10.11 *s* as we are in word by letters
12. 3 And I knew *s* a man, (whether in
20 I shall not find you *s* as I would,
Gal 5.23 against *s* there is no law.
Phm 9 being *s* an one as Paul the aged,
Heb 8. 1 We have *s* an high priest, who is
3Jn 8 We therefore ought to receive *s*,
Rev 16.18 *s* as was not since men were upon
20. 6 on *s* the second death hath no

SUCK
Gen 21. 7 should have given children *s*?
Dt 32.13 him to *s* honey out of the rock,
33.19 *s* of the abundance of the seas,
1Sa 1.23 gave her son *s* until she weaned
1Ki 3.21 in the morning to give my child *s*,
Job 3.12 why the breasts that I should *s*?
20.16 He shall *s* the poison of asps:
39.30 Her young ones also *s* up blood:
Isa 60.16 also *s* the milk of the Gentiles,
16 and shalt *s* the breast of kings:
66.11 That ye may *s*, and be satisfied
12 then shall ye *s*, ye shall be borne
La 4. 3 they give *s* to their young ones:
Eze 23.34 shalt even drink it and *s* it out,
Joel 2.16 and those that *s* the breasts:
Mt 24.19 and to them that give *s* in those
Mk 13.17 to them that give *s* in those days!
Lk 21.23 to them that give *s*, in those days!
23.29 and the paps which never gave *s*.

SUCKED
SS 8. 1 that *s* the breasts of my mother!
Lk 11.27 and the paps which thou hast *s*.

SUCKING
Nu 11.12 nursing father beareth the *s* child,
1Sa 7. 9 Samuel took a *s* lamb, and offered
Isa 11. 8 the *s* child shall play on the hole
49.15 Can a woman forget her *s* child,
La 4. 4 The tongue of the *s* child cleaveth

SUCKLING
Dt 32.25 the *s* also with the man of gray
1Sa 15. 3 infant and *s*, ox and sheep, camel
Jer 44. 7 you man and woman, child and *s*,

SUCKLINGS
1Sa 22.19 men and woman, children and *s*,
Ps 8. 2 Out of the mouth of babes and *s*
La 2.11 and the *s* swoon in the streets
Mt 21.16 Out of the mouth of babes and *s*

SUDDEN
Job 22.10 thee, and *s* fear troubleth thee;
Pr 3.25 Be not afraid of *s* fear, neither of
1Th 5. 3 then *s* destruction cometh upon

SUDDENLY
Nu 12. 4 And the Lord spake *s* unto Moses,
Pr 22.22 For their calamity shall rise *s*;
Isa 30.13 breaking cometh *s* at an instant.
47.11 desolation shall come upon thee *s*,
Jer 4.20 *s* are my tents spoiled, and my
6.26 the spoiler shall *s* come upon us.
Hab 2. 7 Shall they not rise up *s* that shall
Mal 3. 1 seek, shall *s* come to his temple,
Mk 9. 8 *s*, when they had looked round
13.36 coming *s* he find you sleeping.
Lk 2.13 And *s* there was with the angel a
9.39 taketh him, and he *s* crieth out;
Ac 2. 2 *s* there came a sound from heaven
9. 3 *s* there shined round about him a
16.26 *s* there was a great earthquake,
22. 6 *s* there shone from heaven a great
28. 6 swollen, or fallen down dead *s*:
1Ti 5.22 Lay hands *s* on no man, neither

SUE
Mt 5.40 If any man will *s* thee at the law,

SUFFER
Ex 22.18 Thou shalt not *s* a witch to live.
Jdg 15. 1 father would not *s* him to go in.
16.26 *S* me that I may feel the pillars
Job 21. 3 *S* me that I may speak; and after
36. 2 *S* me a little, and I will shew thee
Ps 16.10 wilt thou *s* thine Holy One to see
34.10 young lions do lack, and *s* hunger:
55.22 he shall never *s* the righteous to
89.33 him, nor *s* my faithfulness to fail.
121. 3 will not *s* thy foot to be moved:
Pr 19.15 sleep; and an idle soul shall *s* hunger.
Ec 5.12 the rich will not *s* him to sleep.
Eze 44.20 heads, nor *s* their locks to grow long;
Mt 3.15 said unto him, *S* it to be so now:
8.21 *s* me first to go and bury my
31 *s* us to go away into the herd of
16.21 *s* many things of the elders and
17.12 also the Son of man *s* of them,
17 with you? how long shall I *s* you?
19.14 *S* little children, and forbid them
23.13 neither *s* ye them that are entering
Mk 7.12 ye *s* him no more to do ought for
8.31 Son of man must *s* many things,
9.12 man, that he must *s* many things,
19 with you? how long shall I *s* you?
10.14 *S* the little children to come unto
11.16 would not *s* that any man should
Lk 8.32 would *s* them to enter into them.
9.22 Son of man must *s* many things,
41 shall I be with you, and *s* you?
59 Lord, *s* me first to go and bury my
17.25 But first must he *s* many things,
18.16 *S* little children to come unto me,
22.15 this passover with you before I *s*:
51 answered and said, *S* ye thus far.
24.46 and thus it behoved Christ to *s*,
Ac 2.27 wilt thou *s* thine Holy One to see
3.18 prophets, that Christ should *s*,
5.41 counted worthy to *s* shame for his
7.24 seeing one of them *s* wrong, he
9.16 him how great things he must *s*
13.35 shalt not *s* thine Holy One to see
21.39 *s* me to speak unto the people.
26.23 That Christ should *s*, and that he
Ro 8.17 If so be that we *s* with him, that
1Co 3.15 shall be burned, he shall *s* loss:
4.12 bless; being persecuted, we *s* it:
6. 7 rather *s* yourselves to be defrauded?
9.12 but *s* all things, lest we should
10.13 will not *s* you to be tempted above
12.26 whether one member *s*, all the
26 all the members *s* with it; or one
2Co 1. 6 same sufferings which we also *s*:
11.19 For ye *s* fools gladly, seeing ye
20 For ye *s*, if a man bring you into
Gal 5.11 why do I yet *s* persecution? then
6.12 should *s* persecution for the cross
Php 1.29 on him, but also to *s* for his sake;
4.12 both to abound and to *s* need.
1Th 3. 4 before that we should *s* tribulation:
2Th 1. 5 kingdom of God, for which ye also *s*:
1Ti 2.12 I *s* not a woman to teach, nor to
4.10 we both labor and *s* reproach,
2Ti 1.12 which cause I also *s* these things:
2. 9 Wherein I *s* trouble, as an evil doer,
12 If we *s*, we shall also reign with
3.12 Christ Jesus shall *s* persecution.
Heb 11.25 Choosing rather to *s* affliction
13. 3 and them which *s* adversity, as
22 *s* the word of exhortation: for
1Pe 2.20 when ye do well, and *s* for it, ye
3.14 if ye *s* for righteousness' sake,
17 that ye *s* for well doing, than for
4.15 let none of you *s* as a murderer, or
16 if any man *s* as a Christian, let him
19 let them that *s* according to the
Rev 2.10 of those things which thou shalt *s*:
11. 9 not *s* their dead bodies to be put in

SUFFERED
Dt 18.14 thy God hath not *s* thee so to do.
1Ch 16.21 He *s* no man to do them wrong:
Job 31.30 Neither have I *s* my mouth to sin
Ps 105.14 He *s* no man to do them wrong:
Jer 15.15 that for thy sake I have *s* rebuke.
Mt 3.15 all righteousness. Then he *s* him.
19. 8 *s* you to put away your wives:
24.43 have *s* his house to be broken up.
27.19 for I have *s* many things this day
Mk 1.34 and *s* not the devils to speak,
5.19 Howbeit Jesus *s* him not, but saith
26 *s* many things of many physicians,
37 And he *s* no man to follow him,
10. 4 *s* to write a bill of divorcement,
Lk 4.41 rebuking...*s* them not to speak:
8.32 enter into them. And he *s* them.
51 he *s* no man to go in, save Peter,
12.39 *s* his house to be broken through.
13. 2 because they *s* such things?
24.26 not Christ to have *s* these things,
Ac 13.18 *s* he their manners in the
14.16 *s* all nations to walk in their own
16. 7 but the Spirit *s* them not.
17. 3 that Christ must needs have *s*,
19.30 people, the disciples *s* him not.
28.16 Paul was *s* to dwell by himself
2Co 7.12 nor for his cause that *s* wrong, but
11.25 was I stoned, thrice I *s* shipwreck,
Gal 3. 4 Have ye *s* so many things in vain?
Php 3. 8 I have *s* the loss of all things,
1Th 2. 2 even after that we had *s* before,
14 *s* like things of your...countrymen,
Heb 2.18 he himself hath *s* being tempted,
5. 8 he obedience by the things...he *s*;
7.23 were not *s* to continue by reason
9.26 For then must he often have *s*
13.12 his own blood, *s* without the gate.
1Pe 2.21 because Christ also *s* for us,
23 when he *s*, he threatened not; but
3.18 Christ also hath once *s* for sins,
4. 1 as Christ hath *s* for us in the flesh
1 for he that hath *s* in the flesh hath
5.10 after that ye have *s* a while, make

SUFFEREST
Rev 2.20 thou *s* that woman Jezebel,

SUFFERETH
Ps 66. 9 and *s* not our feet to be moved.
107.38 and *s* not their cattle to decrease.
Mt 11.12 the kingdom of heaven *s* violence,
Ac 28. 4 sea, yet vengeance *s* not to live.
1Co 13. 4 Charity *s* long, and is kind;

SUFFERING
Ac 27. 7 the wind not *s* us, we sailed under
Heb 2. 9 than the angels for the *s* of death,
Jas 5.10 for an example of *s* affliction.
1Pe 2.19 God endure grief, *s* wrongfully.
Jude 7 *s* the vengeance of eternal fire.
(See box on page 729)

SUFFERINGS
Ro 8.18 I reckon that the *s* of this present
2Co 1. 5 as the *s* of Christ abound in us,
6 enduring of the same *s* which we
7 that as ye are partakers of the *s*,
Php 3.10 and the fellowship of his *s*,
Col 1.24 Who now rejoice in my *s* for you,
Heb 2.10 their salvation perfect through *s*.
1Pe 1.11 testified beforehand the *s* of Christ,
4.13 as ye are partakers of Christ's *s*;
5. 1 and a witness of the *s* of Christ,

SUFFICE
Nu 11.22 herds be slain for them, to *s* them?
22 gathered...for them, to *s* them?
Dt 3.26 Lord said unto me, Let it *s* thee;
1Ki 20.10 dust of Samaria...*s* for handfuls
Eze 44. 6 it *s* you of all your abominations,
45. 9 Let it *s* you, O princes of Israel:
1Pe 4. 3 the time past of our life may *s* us

SUFFICED
Jdg 21.14 and yet so they *s* them not.
Ru 2.14 corn, and she did eat, and was *s*,
18 she had reserved after she was *s*.

SUFFICETH
Jn 14. 8 shew us the Father, and it *s* us.

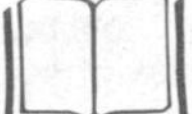

Biblical Themes

SUFFERING

There was a great cry in Egypt; for there was not a house where there was not one dead. Ex 12.30

Wherefore is light given to him that is in misery, and life unto the bitter in soul; which long for death, but it cometh not; and dig for it more than for hid treasures . . . ? Job 3.20-21

God hath delivered me to the ungodly, and turned me over into the hands of the wicked. I was at ease, but he hath broken me asunder. . . . My friends scorn me: but mine eye poureth out tears unto God. Job 16.11-12, 20

He was oppressed, and he was afflicted. . . . he was cut off out of the land of the living: for the transgression of my people was he stricken. . . . Yet it pleased the Lord to bruise him; he hath put him to grief. Isa 53.7-8, 10

The king of Babylon slew the sons of Zedekiah before his eyes. . . . Then he put out the eyes of Zedekiah; and the king of Babylon bound him in chains, and carried him to Babylon, and put him in prison till the day of his death. Jer 52.10-11

How doth the city sit solitary, that was full of people! how is she become as a widow! . . . She weepeth sore in the night, and her tears are on her cheeks. La 1.1-2

Nation shall rise against nation, and kingdom against kingdom: and there shall be famines, and pestilences, and earthquakes, in divers places. All these are the beginning of sorrows. Mt 24.7-8

And being in an agony he prayed more earnestly: and his sweat was as it were great drops of blood falling down to the ground. Lk 22.44

Thus it is written, and thus it behoved Christ to suffer, and to rise from the dead the third day. Lk 24.46

They took Jesus, and led him away. And he bearing his cross went forth into a place called the place of a skull, which is called in the Hebrew Golgotha: where they crucified him, and two other with him, on either side one, and Jesus in the midst. Jn 19.16-18

I reckon that the sufferings of this present time are not worthy to be compared with the glory which shall be revealed in us. Ro 8.18

Out of much affliction and anguish of heart I wrote unto you with many tears; not that ye should be grieved, but that ye might know the love which I have more abundantly unto you. 2Co 2.4

Our light affliction, which is but for a moment, worketh for us a far more exceeding and eternal weight of glory. 2Co 4.17

If we suffer, we shall also reign with him. 2Ti 2.12

Moses . . . refused to be called the son of Pharaoh's daughter; choosing rather to suffer affliction with the people of God, than to enjoy the pleasures of sin for a season. Heb 11.24-25

Others had trial of cruel mockings and scourgings, yea, moreover of bonds and imprisonment: they were stoned, they were sawn asunder, were tempted, were slain with the sword: they wandered about in sheepskins and goatskins; being destitute, afflicted, tormented; (of whom the world was not worthy:) they wandered in deserts, and in mountains, and in dens and caves of the earth. Heb 11.36-38

Christ also suffered for us, leaving us an example, that ye should follow his steps. . . . Who, when he was reviled, reviled not again; when he suffered, he threatened not; but committed himself to him that judgeth righteously. 1Pe 2.21, 23

SUFFICIENCY

Job 20.22 In the fulness of his *s* he shall be
2Co 3. 5 of ourselves; but our *s* is of God;
9. 8 always having all *s* in all things,

SUFFICIENT

Ex 36. 7 stuff they had was *s* for all the
Dt 15. 8 surely lend him *s* for his need,
33. 7 let his hands be *s* for him; and
Pr 25.16 eat so much as is *s* for thee, lest
Isa 40.16 And Lebanon is not *s* to burn, nor
16 the beasts thereof *s* for a burnt
Mt 6.34 *S* unto the day is the evil thereof.
Lk 14.28 cost, whether he have *s* to finish it?
Jn 6. 7 pennyworth of bread is not *s* for
2Co 2. 6 *S* to such...is this punishment,
16 And who is *s* for these things?
3. 5 Not that we are *s* of ourselves to
12. 9 unto me, My grace is *s* for thee:

SUFFICIENTLY

2Ch 30. 3 had not sanctified themselves *s*,
Isa 23.18 eat *s*, and for durable clothing.

SUM

Nu 1. 2 Take ye the *s* of the congregation
2Sa 24. 9 the *s* of the number of the people
Ps 139.17 God! how great is the *s* of them!
Ac 7.16 Abraham bought for a *s* of money
22.28 a great *s* obtained I this freedom.
Heb 8. 1 we have spoken this is the *s*:

SUMMER

Gen 8.22 cold and heat, and *s* and winter,
Ps 32. 4 is turned into the drought of *s*.
74.17 thou hast made *s* and winter.
Pr 6. 8 Provideth her meat in the *s*, and
10. 5 that gathereth in *s* is a wise son:
26. 1 As snow in *s*, and as rain in
Jer 8.20 The harvest is past, the *s* is ended,
Am 8. 1 me: and behold a basket of *s* fruit.
Mic 7. 1 they have gathered the *s* fruits,
Zec 14. 8 sea: in *s* and in winter shall it be.
Mt 24.32 leaves, ye know that *s* is nigh:
Mk 13.28 leaves, ye know that *s* is near:
Lk 21.30 selves that *s* is now nigh at hand.

SUMPTUOUSLY

Lk 16.19 fine linen, and fared *s* every day:

SUN

Gen 32.31 as he passed over Penuel the *s* rose
37. 9 the *s* and the moon and the eleven
Ex 17.12 until the going down of the *s*.
Jos 10.12 *S*, stand thou still upon Gibeon;
Jdg 5.31 as the *s* when he goeth forth in his
2Ki 3.22 and the *s* shone upon the water,
23. 5 burned incense unto Baal, to the *s*,
11 and burned the chariots of the *s*
Job 8.16 He is green before the *s*, and his
Ps 19. 4 hath he set a tabernacle for the *s*,
58. 8 that they may not see the *s*.
72. 5 as long as the *s* and moon endure,
84.11 For the Lord God is a *s* and shield:
113. 3 From the rising of the *s* unto the
121. 6 The *s* shall not smite thee by day,
136. 8 The *s* to rule by day: for his mercy
148. 3 Praise ye him, *s* and moon: praise
Ec 1. 9 there is no new thing under the *s*.
2.11 and there was no profit under the *s*.
6. 5 Moreover he hath not seen the *s*,
8.15 hath no better thing under the *s*,
11. 7 it is for the eyes to behold the *s*:
12. 2 While the *s*, or the light, or the
SS 1. 6 because the *s* hath looked upon me:
6.10 fair as the moon, clear as the *s*,
Isa 38. 8 So the *s* returned ten degrees, by
60.19 The *s* shall be no more thy light by
20 Thy *s* shall no more go down;
Jer 15. 9 her *s* is gone down while it was yet
31.35 giveth the *s* for a light by day,
Dan 6.14 labored till...going down of the *s*
Joel 2.10 the *s* and the moon shall be dark,
31 *s* shall be turned into darkness,
Am 8. 9 cause the *s* to go down at noon,
Jon 4. 8 the *s* beat upon the head of Jonah,
Hab 3.11 The *s* and moon stood still in their
Mal 4. 2 the *S* of righteousness arise with
Mt 5.45 for he maketh his *s* to rise on the
13. 6 And when the *s* was up, they were
43 the righteous shine forth as the *s*
17. 2 his face did shine as the *s*, and his
24.29 days shall the *s* be darkened,
Mk 1.32 when the *s* did set, they brought
4. 6 But when the *s* was up, it was
13.24 the *s* shall be darkened, and the
16. 2 the sepulcher at the rising of the *s*.
Lk 4.40 Now when the *s* was setting, all they
21.25 And there shall be signs in the *s*,
23.45 And the *s* was darkened, and the
Ac 2.20 *s* shall be turned into darkness,
13.11 blind, not seeing the *s* for a season.
26.13 above the brightness of the *s*,
27.20 when neither *s* nor stars in many
1Co 15.41 There is one glory of the *s*, and
Eph 4.26 not the *s* go down upon your wrath:
Jas 1.11 For the *s* is no sooner risen with a
Rev 1.16 as the *s* shineth in his strength.
6.12 the *s* became black as sackcloth of

7.16 neither shall the *s* light on them,
8.12 the third part of the *s* was smitten,
9. 2 the *s* and the air were darkened by
10. 1 and his face was as it were the *s*,
12. 1 a woman clothed with the *s*, and
16. 8 poured out his vial upon the *s*;
19.17 I saw an angel standing in the *s*;
21.23 And the city had no need of the *s*,
22. 5 no candle, neither light of the *s*;

SUNDER

Ps 46. 9 bow, and cutteth the spear in *s*;
107.14 death, and break their bands in *s*.
16 of brass, and cut the bars of iron in *s*.
Isa 27. 9 as chalkstones that are beaten in *s*,
45. 2 and cut in *s* the bars of iron:
Na 1.13 thee, and will burst thy bonds in *s*.
Lk 12.46 he is not aware, and will cut him in *s*,

SUNDRY

Heb 1. 1 at *s* times and in divers manners

SUNG

Isa 26. 1 In that day shall this song be *s* in
Mt 26.30 when they had *s* an hymn, they
Mk 14.26 when they had *s* an hymn, they
Rev 5. 9 they *s* a new song, saying, Thou
14. 3 *s* as it were a new song before the

SUNK

1Sa 17.49 the stone *s* into his forehead;
2Ki 9.24 and he *s* down in his chariot.
Ps 9.15 heathen are *s* down in the pit
Jer 38. 6 mire: so Jeremiah *s* in the mire.
22 thy feet are *s* in the mire, and they
La 2. 9 Her gates are *s* into the ground;
Ac 20. 9 preaching, he *s* down with sleep,

SUP

Hab 1. 9 faces shall *s* up as the east wind,
Lk 17. 8 Make ready wherewith I may *s*,
Rev 3.20 in to him, and will *s* with him,

SUPERSCRIPTION

Mt 22.20 them, Whose is this image and *s*?
Mk 12.16 them, Whose is this image and *s*?
15.26 the *s* of his accusation was written
Lk 20.24 Whose image and *s* hath it? They
23.38 And a *s* also was written over him

SUPERSTITION

Ac 25.19 against him of their own *s*, and

SUPERSTITIOUS

Ac 17.22 that in all things ye are too *s*.

SUPPED

1Co 11.25 he took the cup, when he had *s*,

SUPPER

Mk 6.21 birthday made a *s* to his lords,
Lk 14.12 When thou makest a dinner or a *s*,
16 A certain man made a great *s*, and
17 sent his servant at *s* time to say to
24 were bidden shall taste of my *s*.
22.20 Likewise also the cup after *s*,
Jn 12. 2 There they made him a *s*; and
13. 2 *s* being ended, the devil having
4 He riseth from *s*, and laid aside
21.20 also leaned on his breast at *s*, and
1Co 11.20 this is not to eat the Lord's *s*.
21 one taketh before other his own *s*:
Rev 19. 9 unto the marriage *s* of the Lamb.
17 unto the *s* of the great God;

SUPPLICATION

1Sa 13.12 I have not made *s* unto the Lord:
1Ki 8.28 prayer of thy servant, and to his *s*,
30 And hearken thou to the *s* of thy
33 make *s* unto thee in this house:
38 prayer and *s* soever be made by
45 in heaven their prayer and their *s*,
47 and make *s* unto thee in the land
49 their prayer and their *s* in heaven
52 be open unto the *s* of thy servant,
52 and unto the *s* of thy people Israel,
54 all this prayer and *s* unto the Lord,
59 I have made *s* before the Lord,
9. 3 have heard thy prayer and thy *s*,
2Ch 6.19 prayer of thy servant, and to his *s*,
24 make *s* before thee in this house;
29 what *s* soever shall be made of
35 heavens their prayer and their *s*,
33.13 and heard his *s*, and brought him
Est 4. 8 the king, to make *s* unto him,
Job 8. 5 and make thy *s* to the Almighty:
9.15 but I would make *s* to my judge.
Ps 6. 9 The Lord hath heard my *s*; the
30. 8 and unto the Lord I made *s*.
55. 1 and hide not thyself from my *s*.
119.170 Let my *s* come before thee:
142. 1 unto the Lord did I make my *s*.
Isa 45.14 they shall make *s* unto thee,
Jer 36. 7 present their *s* before the Lord,
37.20 let my *s*, I pray thee, be accepted
38.26 I presented my *s* before the king,
42. 2 our *s* be accepted before thee, and
9 me to present your *s* before him;
Dan 6.11 and making *s* before his God.
9.20 presenting my *s* before the Lord
Hos 12. 4 he wept, and made *s* unto him:
Ac 1.14 with one accord in prayer and *s*,
Eph 6.18 with all prayer and *s* in the Spirit,
18 perseverance and *s* for all saints;
Php 4. 6 by prayer and *s* with thanksgiving

SUPPLICATIONS

2Ch 6.21 unto the *s* of thy servant, and
39 their prayer and their *s*, and
Job 41. 3 Will he make many *s* unto thee?

Leonardo da Vinci's The Last Supper, *completed in 1497, memorializes the solemn meal shared by Jesus and his disciples on the eve of the Crucifixion.*

Ps 28. 2 Hear the voice of my *s*, when I cry
6 he hath heard the voice of my *s*.
31.22 heardest the voice of my *s* when I
86. 6 and attend to the voice of my *s*.
116. 1 he hath heard my voice and my *s*.
130. 2 be attentive to the voice of my *s*.
140. 6 hear the voice of my *s*, O Lord.
143. 1 prayer, O Lord, give ear to my *s*:
Jer 3.21 weeping and *s* of the children of
31. 9 and with *s* will I lead them:
Dan 9. 3 Lord God, to seek by prayer and *s*,
17 prayer of thy servant, and his *s*,
18 for we do not present our *s* before
23 At the beginning of thy *s* the
Zec 12.10 the spirit of grace and of *s*: and
1Ti 2. 1 that, first of all, *s*, prayers,
5. 5 continueth in *s* and prayers night
Heb 5. 7 he had offered up prayers and *s*

SUPPLIED

1Co 16.17 lacking on your part they have *s*.
2Co 11. 9 which came from Macedonia *s*:

SUPPLIETH

2Co 9.12 not only *s* the want of the saints,
Eph 4.16 by that which every joint *s*,

SUPPLY

2Co 8.14 abundance...be a *s* for their want,
14 also may be a *s* for your want:
Php 1.19 the *s* of the Spirit of Jesus Christ,
2.30 to *s* your lack of service toward
4.19 But my God shall *s* all your need

SUPPORT

Ac 20.35 laboring ye ought to *s* the weak,
1Th 5.14 *s* the weak, be patient toward all

SUPPOSE

2Sa 13.32 not my lord *s* that they have slain
Lk 7.43 I *s* that he, to whom he forgave
12.51 *S* ye that I am come to give peace
13. 2 *S* ye that these Galileans were
Jn 21.25 I *s* that even the world itself
Ac 2.15 these are not drunken, as ye *s*,
1Co 7.26 I *s* therefore that this is good for
2Co 11. 5 I *s* I was not a whit behind the
Heb 10.29 much sorer punishment, *s* ye,
1Pe 5.12 a faithful brother...as I *s*,

SUPPOSED

Mt 20.10 *s* that they should have received
Mk 6.49 sea, they *s* it had been a spirit,
Lk 3.23 being (as was *s*) the son of Joseph,
24.37 and *s* that they had seen a spirit.
Ac 7.25 For he *s* his brethren would have
21.29 whom they *s*...Paul had brought
25.18 accusation of such things as I *s*:
Php 2.25 I *s* it necessary to send to you

SUPPOSING

Lk 2.44 they, *s* him...in the company,
Jn 20.15 She, *s* him to be the gardener,
Ac 14.19 out of the city, *s* he had been dead.
16.27 *s* that the prisoners had been fled.
27.13 *s* that they had obtained their
Php 1.16 *s* to add affliction to my bonds:
1Ti 6. 5 truth, *s* that gain is godliness:

SUPREME

1Pe 2.13 whether it be to the king, as *s*;

SURE

Nu 32.23 and be *s* your sin will find you out.
Job 24.22 riseth up, and no man is *s* of life.
Ps 19. 7 the testimony of the Lord is *s*,
93. 5 Thy testimonies are very *s*:
111. 7 all his commandments are *s*.
Pr 6. 3 thyself, and make *s* thy friend.
11.15 and he that hateth suretiship is *s*.
18 righteousness shall be a *s* reward.
Isa 28.16 corner stone, a *s* foundation:
33.16 given him; his waters shall be *s*.
55. 3 you, even the *s* mercies of David.
Dan 2.45 and the interpretation thereof *s*.
4.26 thy kingdom shall be *s* unto thee,
Mt 27.64 sepulcher be made *s* until the third
65 your way, make it as *s* as ye can.
66 went, and made the sepulcher *s*,
Lk 10.11 be ye *s* of this, that the kingdom
Jn 6.69 are *s* that thou art that Christ,
16.30 Now are we *s* that thou knowest
Ac 13.34 give you the *s* mercies of David.
Ro 2. 2 we are *s* that the judgment of God
4.16 might be *s* to all the seed;
15.29 And I am *s* that, when I come
2Ti 2.19 the foundation of God standeth *s*,
Heb 6.19 of the soul, both *s* and stedfast,
2Pe 1.10 make your calling and election *s*:
19 also a more *s* word of prophecy;

SURELY

Gen 20.11 *S* the fear of God is not in this
28.16 said, *S* the Lord is in this place:
32.12 I will *s* do thee good, and make thy
44.28 *S* he is torn in pieces; and I saw
Ex 3. 7 I have *s* seen the affliction of my
Lev 20.27 a wizard, shall *s* be put to death:
Dt 23.21 thy God will *s* require it of thee;
Jdg 6.16 *S* I will be with thee, and thou
13.22 We shall *s* die, because we have seen
2Sa 24.24 will *s* buy it of thee at a price:
2Ki 5.11 He will *s* come out to me, and stand,
Job 13. 3 *S* I would speak to the Almighty,
34.12 Yea, *s* God will not do wickedly,
35.13 *S* God will not hear vanity, neither
Ps 23. 6 *S* goodness and mercy shall
62. 9 *S* men of low degree are vanity,
85. 9 *S* his salvation is nigh them that
139.11 *S* the darkness shall cover me;
Ec 7. 7 *S* oppression maketh a wise man
Isa 45.14 *S* God is in thee; and there is none
49. 4 *s* my judgment is with the Lord,
53. 4 *S* he hath borne our griefs, and
60. 9 *S* the isles shall wait for me, and
63. 8 For he said, *S* they are my people,
Jer 44.25 We will *s* perform our vows that we
Eze 33. 8 O wicked man, thou shalt *s* die;
Hos 12.11 *s* they are vanity: they sacrifice
Am 3. 7 *S* the Lord God will do nothing,
Mt 26.73 *S* thou also art one of them;
Mk 14.70 to Peter, *S* thou art one of them:
Lk 1. 1 things which are most *s* believed
4.23 will *s* say unto me this proverb,
Jn 17. 8 known *s* that I came out from
Heb 6.14 *S* blessing I will bless thee, and
Rev 22.20 things saith, *S* I come quickly.

SURETY

Gen 15.13 Know of a *s* that thy seed shall be
18.13 Shall I of a *s* bear a child, which
26. 9 said, Behold, of a *s* she is thy wife:
43. 9 I will be *s* for him: of my hand
44.32 servant became *s* for the lad unto
Job 17. 3 down now, put me in a *s* with thee;
Ps 119.122 Be *s* for thy servant for good: let
Pr 6. 1 My son, if thou be *s* for thy friend,
11.15 He that is *s* for a stranger shall
17.18 becometh *s* in the presence of his
20.16 garment that is *s* for a stranger:
27.13 garment that is *s* for a stranger,
Ac 12.11 Now I know of a *s*, that the Lord
Heb 7.22 made a *s* of a better testament.

SURNAME

Isa 44. 5 *s* himself by the name of Israel.
Mt 10. 3 whose *s* was Thaddaeus;
Ac 10. 5 for one Simon, whose *s* is Peter:
32 hither Simon, whose *s* is Peter;
11.13 call for Simon, whose *s* is Peter;
12.12 of John, whose *s* was Mark;
25 them John, whose *s* was Mark.
15.37 them John, whose *s* was Mark.

SURNAMED

Isa 45. 4 I have *s* thee, though thou hast
Mk 3.16 And Simon he *s* Peter;
17 he *s* them Boanerges, which
Lk 22. 3 Satan into Judas *s* Iscariot,
Ac 1.23 Barsabas, who was *s* Justus, and
4.36 by the apostles was *s* Barnabas,
10.18 whether Simon, which was *s* Peter,
15.22 Judas *s* Barsabas, and Silas, chief

SURPRISED

Isa 33.14 fearfulness hath *s* the hypocrites.
Jer 48.41 taken, and the strong holds are *s*,
51.41 is the praise of the whole earth *s*!

SUSANNA

Lk 8. 3 wife of...Herod's steward, and *S*,

SUSTAIN

1Ki 17. 9 a widow woman there to *s* thee.
Neh 9.21 Yea, forty years didst thou *s* them
Ps 55.22 upon the Lord, and he shall *s* thee:
Pr 18.14 spirit of a man will *s* his infirmity;

SUSTAINED

Gen 27.37 with corn and wine have I *s* him:
Ps 3. 5 I awaked; for the Lord *s* me.
Isa 59.16 and his righteousness, it *s* him.

SUSTENANCE

Jdg 6. 4 left no *s* for Israel, neither sheep,
2Sa 19.32 and he had provided the king of *s*
Ac 7.11 and our fathers found no *s*.

SWADDLING

Lk 2. 7 and wrapped him in *s* clothes,
12 find the babe wrapped in *s* clothes,

SWALLOW

Nu 16.30 open her mouth, and *s* them up,
34 said, Lest the earth *s* us up also.
2Sa 20.19 why wilt thou *s* up the inheritance
20 me, that I should *s* up or destroy.
Job 7.19 me alone till I *s* down my spittle?
20.18 he restore, and shall not *s* it down:
Ps 21. 9 Lord shall *s* them up in his wrath,
56. 1 O God: for man would *s* me up;
2 Mine enemies would daily *s* me up:
57. 3 reproach of him that would *s* me
69.15 neither let the deep *s* me up, and
84. 3 house, and the *s* a nest for herself,
Pr 1.12 us *s* them up alive as the grave;
26. 2 by wandering, as the *s* by flying,
Ec 10.12 the lips of a fool will *s* up himself.
Isa 25. 8 He will *s* up death in victory; and
38.14 Like a crane or a *s*, so did I
Jer 8. 7 *s* observe the time of their coming;
Hos 8. 7 yield, the strangers shall *s* it up.
Am 8. 4 this, O ye that *s* up the needy,
Ob 16 drink, and they shall *s* down,
Jon 1.17 a great fish to *s* up Jonah.
Mt 23.24 strain at a gnat, and *s* a camel.

SWALLOWED

Ex 7.12 but Aaron's rod *s* up their rods.
15.12 thy right hand, the earth *s* them.
Nu 16.32 and *s* them up, and their houses,
26.10 and *s* them up together with Korah,
Dt 11. 6 *s* them up, and their households,
2Sa 17.16 lest the king be *s* up, and all the
Job 6. 3 sea: therefore my words are *s* up.
20.15 He hath *s* down riches, and he
37.20 man speak, surely he shall be *s* up.
Ps 35.25 them not say, We have *s* him up.
106.17 The earth opened and *s* up Dathan,
124. 3 Then they had *s* us up quick, when
Isa 28. 7 they are *s* up of wine, they are out
49.19 that *s* thee up shall be far away.
Jer 51.34 he hath *s* me up like a dragon, he
44 mouth that which he hath *s* up:
La 2. 2 Lord hath *s* up all the habitations

5 as an enemy: he hath *s* up Israel,
5 he hath *s* up all her palaces: he
16 We have *s* her up: certainly this is
Eze 36. 3 and *s* you up on every side, that
Hos 8. 8 Israel is *s* up: now shall they be
1Co 15.54 written, Death is *s* up in victory.
2Co 2. 7 be *s* up with overmuch sorrow.
5. 4 that mortality might be *s* up of life.
Rev 12.16 *s* up the flood which the dragon

SWARE
Gen 26. 3 oath which I *s* unto Abraham thy
31.53 Jacob *s* by the fear of his father
Dt 4.21 *s* that I should not go over Jordan,
31 covenant...which he *s* unto them.
31.23 into the land which I *s* unto them:
Ps 95.11 Unto whom I *s* in my wrath that
Dan 12. 7 and *s* by him that liveth for ever
Mk 6.23 he *s* unto her, Whatsoever thou
Lk 1.73 The oath which he *s* to our father
Heb 3.11 So I *s* in my wrath, They shall not
18 to whom *s* he that they should not
6.13 by no greater, he *s* by himself,
7.21 The Lord *s* and will not repent,
Rev 10. 6 *s* by him that liveth for ever and

SWAREST
Ex 32.13 to whom thou *s* by thine own self,
Nu 11.12 the land which thou *s* unto their
Dt 26.15 as thou *s* unto our fathers, a land
1Ki 1.17 thou *s* by the Lord thy God unto
Ps 89.49 thou *s* unto David in thy truth?

SWEAR
Gen 21.24 And Abraham said, I will *s*.
Lev 19.12 ye shall not *s* by my name falsely,
1Sa 20.17 Jonathan caused David to *s* again,
Isa 45.23 shall bow, every tongue shall *s*.
65.16 earth shall *s* by the God of truth;
Jer 4. 2 And thou shalt *s*, The Lord liveth,
22. 5 I *s* by myself, saith the Lord, that
Mt 5.34 *S* not at all; neither by heaven;
36 Neither shalt thou *s* by thy head,
23.16 Whosoever shall *s* by the temple,
16 shall *s* by the gold of the temple,
18 Whosoever shall *s* by the altar, it
20 therefore shall *s* by the altar,
21 And whoso shall *s* by the temple,
22 And he that shall *s* by heaven,
26.74 Then began he to curse and to *s*,
Mk 14.71 But he began to curse and to *s*,
Heb 6.13 because he could *s* by no greater,
16 For men verily *s* by the greater:
Jas 5.12 all things, my brethren, *s* not,

SWEARETH
Lev 6. 3 lieth concerning it, and *s* falsely;
Ps 15. 4 He that *s* to his own hurt, and
63.11 one that *s* by him shall glory:
Ec 9. 2 he that *s*, as he that feareth an
Isa 65.16 he that *s* in the earth shall swear
Zec 5. 3 every one that *s* shall be cut off as
4 of him that *s* falsely by my name:
Mt 23.18 whosoever *s* by the gift that is
20 *s* by it, and by all things thereon.
21 *s* by it, and by him that dwelleth
22 by heaven, *s* by the throne of God,

SWEARING
Lev 5. 1 soul sin, and hear the voice of *s*,
Jer 23.10 because of *s* the land mourneth;
Hos 4. 2 By *s*, and lying, and killing, and
10. 4 *s* falsely in making a covenant:

SWEAT
Gen 3.19 In the *s* of thy face shalt thou eat
Eze 44.18 with any thing that causeth *s*.
Lk 22.44 his *s* was as it were great drops of

SWEEP
Isa 14.23 and I will *s* it with the besom of
28.17 hail shall *s* away the refuge of lies,
Lk 15. 8 light a candle, and *s* the house,

SWEET
Gen 8.21 And the Lord smelled a *s* savor;
Ex 15.25 waters, the waters were made *s*:
2Sa 23. 1 and the *s* psalmist of Israel, said,
Job 20.12 wickedness be *s* in his mouth,
38.31 bind the *s* influences of Pleiades,
Ps 55.14 We took *s* counsel together, and
104.34 My meditation of him shall be *s*:
119.103 How *s* are thy words unto my
Pr 3.24 lie down, and thy sleep shall be *s*.
9.17 Stolen waters are *s*, and bread
13.19 desire accomplished is *s* to the
16.24 as an honeycomb, *s* to the soul,
20.17 Bread of deceit is *s* to a man; but
27. 7 hungry soul every bitter thing is *s*.
Ec 5.12 The sleep of a laboring man is *s*,
11. 7 Truly the light is *s*, and a pleasant
SS 2. 3 and his fruit was *s* to my taste.
Isa 5.20 put bitter for *s*, and *s* for bitter!
23.16 make *s* melody, sing many songs,
Jer 31.26 and my sleep was *s* unto me.
Am 9.13 the mountains shall drop *s* wine,
Mic 6.15 and *s* wine, but shalt not drink
Mk 16. 1 and Salome, had bought *s* spices,
2Co 2.15 are unto God a *s* savor of Christ,
Php 4.18 an odor of a *s* smell, a sacrifice
Jas 3.11 same place *s* water and bitter?
Rev 10. 9 it shall be in thy mouth *s* as honey.
10 and it was in my mouth *s* as honey:

SWEETER
Jdg 14.18 What is *s* than honey? and what
Ps 19.10 *s*...than honey and the honeycomb.
119.103 yea, *s* than honey to my mouth!

SWEETNESS
Jdg 9.11 Should I forsake my *s*, and my
14.14 and out of the strong came forth *s*.
Pr 16.21 *s* of the lips increaseth learning.
27. 9 so doth the *s* of a man's friend by
Eze 3. 3 was in my mouth as honey for *s*.

SWELL
Nu 5.21 thigh to rot, and thy belly to *s*;
22 to make thy belly to *s*, and thy
27 and her belly shall *s*, and her thigh
Dt 8. 4 neither did thy foot *s*, these forty

SWELLED
Neh 9.21 waxed not old, and their feet *s* not.

SWELLING
Ps 46. 3 the mountains shake with the *s*
Isa 30.13 *s* out in a high wall, whose
Jer 12. 5 wilt thou do in the *s* of Jordan?
49.19 up like a lion from the *s* of Jordan
50.44 up like a lion from the *s* of Jordan
2Pe 2.18 speak great *s* words of vanity,
Jude 16 mouth speaketh great *s* words,

SWELLINGS
2Co 12.20 backbitings, whisperings, *s*,

SWEPT
Jdg 5.21 The river of Kishon *s* them away,
Jer 46.15 Why are thy valiant men *s* away?
Mt 12.44 findeth it empty, *s*, and garnished.
Lk 11.25 he findeth it *s* and garnished.

SWERVED
1Ti 1. 6 From which some having *s* have

SWIFT
Dt 28.49 of the earth, as *s* as the eagle flieth;
1Ch 12. 8 were as *s* as the roes upon the
Job 9.26 are passed away as the *s* ships:
24.18 He is *s* as the waters; their
Pr 6.18 feet...be *s* in running to mischief,
Ec 9.11 that the race is not to the *s*, nor
Isa 18. 2 Go, ye *s* messengers, to a nation
19. 1 the Lord rideth upon a *s* cloud,
30.16 flee: and, We will ride upon the *s*;
16 shall they that pursue you be *s*.
66.20 upon mules, and upon *s* beasts,
Jer 2.23 thou art a *s* dromedary traversing
46. 6 Let not the *s* flee away, nor the
Am 2.14 the flight shall perish from the *s*,
15 and he that is *s* of foot shall not
Mic 1.13 bind the chariot to the *s* beast:
Mal 3. 5 I will be a *s* witness against the
Ro 3.15 Their feet are *s* to shed blood:
Jas 1.19 let every man be *s* to hear, slow
2Pe 2. 1 upon themselves *s* destruction.

SWIFTER
2Sa 1.23 they were *s* than eagles, they
Job 7. 6 My days are *s* than a weaver's
9.25 Now my days are *s* than a post:
Jer 4.13 his horses are *s* than eagles.
La 4.19 persecutors are *s* than the eagles
Hab 1. 8 horses...are *s* than the leopards,

SWIFTLY
Ps 147.15 earth: his word runneth very *s*.
Isa 5.26 they shall come with speed *s*:
Dan 9.21 being caused to fly *s*, touched me
Joel 3. 4 *s* and speedily will I return your

SWIM
2Ki 6. 6 it in thither; and the iron did *s*.
Ps 6. 6 all the night make I my bed to *s*;
Isa 25.11 spreadeth forth his hands to *s*:
Eze 47. 5 waters were risen, waters to *s* in,
Ac 27.42 lest any of them should *s* out,
43 they which could *s* should cast

SWINE
Lev 11. 7 the *s*, though he divide the hoof,
Dt 14. 8 the *s*, because it divideth the hoof,
Mt 7. 6 neither cast ye...pearls before *s*,
8.30 them an herd of many *s* feeding.
31 us to go away into the herd of *s*.
32 out, they went into the herd of *s*:
32 whole herd of *s* ran violently down
Mk 5.11 a great herd of *s* feeding.
12 Send us into the *s*, that we may
13 went out, and entered into the *s*:
14 they that fed the *s* fled, and told
16 the devil, and also concerning the *s*.
Lk 8.32 an herd of many *s* feeding on the
33 of the man, and entered into the *s*:
15.15 he sent him into his fields to feed *s*.
16 with the husks that the *s* did eat:

SWINE'S
Pr 11.22 As a jewel of gold in a *s* snout, so
Isa 65. 4 which eat *s* flesh, and broth of
66. 3 oblation, as if he offered *s* blood;
17 tree in the midst, eating *s* flesh,

SWOLLEN
Ac 28. 6 looked when he should have *s*,

SWORD
Gen 3.24 a flaming *s* which turned every
Ex 5.21 to put a *s* in their hand to slay us.
32.27 Put every man his *s* by his side,
Lev 26. 6 shall the *s* go through your land.
Jdg 7.18 The *s* of the Lord, and of Gideon.
1Sa 17.47 that the Lord saveth not with *s* and
2Sa 12. 9 killed Uriah the Hittite with the *s*,
10 the *s* shall never depart from thine
1Ki 19.10, 14 slain thy prophets with the *s*;
1Ch 21.30 afraid because of the *s* of the angel
Job 5.15 But he saveth the poor from the *s*,
Ps 22.20 Deliver my soul from the *s*; my
37.15 *s* shall enter into their own heart,
57. 4 arrows, and their tongue a sharp *s*.
149. 6 and a twoedged *s* in their hand;

Pr 5. 4 wormwood, sharp as a twoedged *s*.
Isa 2. 4 shall not lift up *s* against nation,
49. 2 made my mouth like a sharp *s*;
Jer 47. 6 O thou *s* of the Lord, how long will
Eze 7.15 The *s* is without, and the pestilence
11. 8 bring a *s* upon you, saith the Lord
21.13 what if the *s* contemn even the rod?
Hos 2.18 and I will break the bow and the *s*
Mic 4. 3 shall not lift up a *s* against nation,
Zec 13. 7 Awake, O *s*, against my shepherd,
Mt 10.34 I came not to send peace, but a *s*.
26.51 drew his *s*, and struck a servant
52 Put up again thy *s* into his place:
52 for all they that take the *s*
52 shall perish with the *s*.
Mk 14.47 one of them that stood by drew a *s*,
Lk 2.35 a *s*...pierce through thy own soul
21.24 they shall fall by the edge of the *s*,
22.36 he that hath no *s*, let him sell his
49 Lord, shall we smite with the *s*?
Jn 18.10 Simon Peter having a *s* drew it,
11 Peter, Put up thy *s* into the sheath:
Ac 12. 2 And he killed James...with the *s*.
16.27 doors open, he drew out his *s*, and
Ro 8.35 or nakedness, or peril, or *s*?
13. 4 for he beareth not the *s* in vain:
Eph 6.17 *s* of the Spirit, which is the word
Heb 4.12 and sharper than any twoedged *s*,
11.34 escaped the edge of the *s*, out of
37 tempted, were slain with the *s*:
Rev 1.16 mouth went a sharp twoedged *s*:
2.12 hath the sharp *s* with two edges;
16 them with the *s* of my mouth.
6. 4 was given unto him a great *s*.
8 to kill with *s*, and with hunger,
13.10 he that killeth with the *s*
10 must be killed with the *s*.
14 beast, which had the wound by a *s*,
19.15 out of his mouth goeth a sharp *s*,
21 the remnant were slain with the *s*
21 which *s* proceeded out of his mouth:

SWORDS

Ps 59. 7 their mouths: *s* are in their lips:
Pr 30.14 a generation, whose teeth are as *s*,
Isa 2. 4 shall beat their *s* into plowshares,
Joel 3.10 Beat your plowshares into *s*, and
Mic 4. 3 shall beat their *s* into plowshares,
Mt 26.47 with him a great multitude with *s*
55 come out as against a thief with *s*
Mk 14.43 with him a great multitude with *s*
48 come out, as against a thief, with *s*
Lk 22.38 said, Lord, behold, here are two *s*.
52 come out, as against a thief, with *s*

SWORN

Ps 24. 4 unto vanity, nor *s* deceitfully.
110. 4 Lord hath *s*, and will not repent,
119.106 I have *s*, and I will perform it,
Jer 5. 7 and *s* by them that are no gods:
44.26 I have *s* by my great name, saith
49.13 I have *s* by myself, saith the Lord,
Am 6. 8 The Lord God hath *s* by himself,
Mic 7.20 which thou hast *s* unto our fathers
Ac 2.30 God had *s* with an oath to him,
7.17 which God had *s* to Abraham, the
Heb 4. 3 As I have *s* in my wrath, if they

SYCOMORE

1Ki 10.27 as the *s* trees that are in the vale,
1Ch 27.28 *s* trees that were in the low plains
2Ch 1.15 cedar trees made he as the *s* trees
9.27 cedar trees made he as the *s* trees
Ps 78.47 hail, and their *s* trees with frost.
Am 7.14 herdman, and a gatherer of *s* fruit:
Lk 19. 4 climbed up into a *s* tree to see

SYNAGOGUE

Mt 12. 9 thence, he went into their *s*:
13.54 country, he taught them in their *s*,
Mk 1.21 sabbath day he entered into the *s*,
23 in their *s* a man with an unclean
29 when they were come out of the *s*,
3. 1 And he entered again into the *s*;
5.22 cometh one of the rulers of the *s*.
36 unto the ruler of the *s*, Be not
38 to the house of the ruler of the *s*,
6. 2 come, he began to teach in the *s*:
Lk 4.16 he went into the *s* on the sabbath
20 eyes of all them that were in the *s*
28 And all they in the *s*, when they
33 in the *s* there was a man, which
38 he arose out of the *s*, and entered
6. 6 he entered into the *s* and taught:
7. 5 nation, and he hath built us a *s*.
8.41 and he was a ruler of the *s*: and
13.14 the ruler of the *s* answered with
Jn 6.59 These things said he in the *s*, as
9.22 he should be put out of the *s*.
12.42 lest they should be put out of the *s*:
18.20 I ever taught in the *s*, and in the
Ac 6. 9 Then there arose certain of the *s*,
9 is called the *s* of the Libertines,
13.14 and went into the *s* on the sabbath
15 the rulers of the *s* sent unto them,
42 the Jews were gone out of the *s*,
14. 1 both together into the *s* of the
17. 1 where was a *s* of the Jews:
10 thither went into the *s* of the Jews.
17 disputed he in the *s* with the Jews,
18. 4 reasoned in the *s* every sabbath,
7 whose house joined hard to the *s*.
8 Crispus, the chief ruler of the *s*,
17 Sosthenes, the chief ruler of the *s*,
19 but he himself entered into the *s*,
26 he began to speak boldly in the *s*:
19. 8 And he went into the *s*, and spake
22.19 and beat in every *s* them that
26.11 I punished them oft in every *s*,
Rev 2. 9 and are not, but are the *s* of Satan.
3. 9 I will make them of the *s* of Satan.

SYNAGOGUES

Ps 74. 8 have burned up all the *s* of God
Mt 4.23 teaching in their *s*, and preaching
6. 2 as the hypocrites do in the *s* and
5 they love to pray standing in the *s*
9.35 teaching in their *s*, and preaching
10.17 they will scourge you in their *s*;
23. 6 feasts, and the chief seats in the *s*,
34 of them shall ye scourge in your *s*,
Mk 1.39 he preached in their *s* throughout
12.39 And the chief seats in the *s*, and
13. 9 and in the *s* ye shall be beaten:
Lk 4.15 And he taught in their *s*, being
44 he preached in the *s* of Galilee.
11.43 love the uppermost seats in the *s*,
12.11 when they bring you unto the *s*,
13.10 he was teaching in one of the *s*
20.46 and the highest seats in the *s*, and
21.12 delivering you up to the *s*, and into
Jn 16. 2 They shall put you out of the *s*:
Ac 9. 2 him letters to Damascus to the *s*,
20 he preached Christ in the *s*, that
13. 5 preached the word of God in the *s*
15.21 being read in the *s* every sabbath
24.12 neither in the *s*, nor in the city:

SYNTYCHE

Php 4. 2 I beseech Euodias, and beseech *S*,

SYRACUSE

Ac 28.12 landing at *S*, we tarried there

SYRIA

Jdg 10. 6 and the gods of *S*, and the gods of
2Sa 8. 6 put garrisons in *S* of Damascus:
12 Of *S*, and of Moab, and of the
15. 8 vow while I abode at Geshur in *S*,
1Ki 10.29 Hittites, and for the kings of *S*,
11.25 Israel, and reigned over *S*.
15.18 the son of Hezion, king of *S* that
19.15 anoint Hazael to be king over *S*:
20. 1 Ben-hadad the king of *S* gathered
20 the king of *S* escaped on an horse
22 king of *S* will come up against thee.
23 servants of the king of *S* said unto
22. 1 without war between *S* and Israel.
3 not out of the hand of the king of *S*?
31 king of *S* commanded his thirty
2Ki 5. 1 captain of the host of the king of *S*,
1 Lord had given deliverance unto *S*:
5 the king of *S* said, Go to, go, and I
6. 8 king of *S* warred against Israel,
11 the heart of the king of *S* was sore
23 the bands of *S* came no more into
24 Ben-hadad king of *S* gathered all
7. 5 uttermost part of the camp of *S*,
8. 7 Ben-hadad the king of *S* was sick;
9 Ben-hadad king of *S* hath sent me
13 that thou shalt be king over *S*.
28 the war against Hazael king of *S*
29 he fought against Hazael king of *S*.
9.14 Israel, because of Hazael king of *S*.
15 he fought with Hazael king of *S*.)
12.17 Then Hazael king of *S* went up, and
18 and sent it to Hazael king of *S*:
13. 3 into the hand of Hazael king of *S*,
4 the king of *S* oppressed them.
7 the king of *S* had destroyed them,
17 the arrow of deliverance from *S*:
19 then hadst thou smitten *S* till thou
19 now thou shalt smite *S* but thrice.
22 Hazael king of *S* oppressed Israel
24 So Hazael king of *S* died; and
15.37 against Judah Rezin the king of *S*,
16. 5 Then Rezin king of *S* and Pekah
6 Rezin king of *S* recovered Elath
6 recovered Elath to *S*, and drave the
7 me out of the hand of the king of *S*,
2Ch 1.17 for the kings of *S*, by their means.
16. 2 and sent to Ben-hadad king of *S*,
7 thou hast relied on the king of *S*,
7 king of *S* escaped out of thine hand.
18.10 With these thou shalt push *S* until
30 the king of *S* had commanded the
20. 2 from beyond the sea on this side *S*;
22. 5 to war against Hazael king of *S* at
6 he fought with Hazael king of *S*.
24.23 the host of *S* came up against him:
28. 5 him into the hand of the king of *S*;
23 gods of the kings of *S* help them,
Isa 7. 1 Rezin the king of *S*, and Pekah the
2 *S* is confederate with Ephraim.
4 for the fierce anger of Rezin with *S*,
5 Because *S*, Ephraim, and the son
8 For the head of *S* is Damascus, and
17. 3 Damascus, and the remnant of *S*:
Eze 16.57 thy reproach of the daughters of *S*,
27.16 *S* was thy merchant by reason of
Hos 12.12 Jacob fled into the country of *S*,
Am 1. 5 people of *S* shall go into captivity
Mt 4.24 his fame went throughout all *S*:
Lk 2. 2 when Cyrenius was governor of *S*.)
Ac 15.23 of the Gentiles in Antioch and *S*
41 he went through *S* and Cilicia,
18.18 brethren, and sailed thence into *S*,
20. 3 as he was about to sail into *S*, he
21. 3 sailed into *S*, and landed at Tyre:
Gal 1.21 I came into the regions of *S* and

SYRIAN

Gen 31.24 And God came to Laban the *S* in a
Dt 26. 5 A *S* ready to perish was my father,
2Ki 5.20 master hath spared Naaman this *S*.
18.26 to thy servants in the *S* language;
Ezr 4. 7 letter was written in the *S* tongue,
7 and interpreted in the *S* tongue.
Isa 36.11 thy servant in the *S* language;
Lk 4.27 cleansed, saving Naaman the *S*.

SYROPHENICIAN

Mk 7.26 The woman was a Greek, a *S* by

T

TABERNACLE
Ex 25. 9 thee, after the pattern of the *t*,
27. 9 thou shalt make the court of the *t*:
29.44 sanctify the *t* of the congregation,
30.16 service of the *t* of the congregation;
33. 7 And Moses took the *t*, and pitched it
10 cloudy pillar stand at the *t* door:
40.34, 35 the glory of the Lord filled the *t*.
38 cloud of the Lord was upon the *t*
Lev 16.33 atonement for...*t* of...congregation,
26.11 And I will set my *t* among you:
Nu 4.41 service in the *t* of the congregation,
43 work in the *t* of the congregation,
47 burden in the *t* of the congregation,
9.15 reared up the cloud covered the *t*,
17. 8 Moses went into the *t* of witness;
Job 5.24 know that thy *t* shall be in peace;
18. 6 The light shall be dark in his *t*, and
19.12 me, and encamp round about my *t*.
29. 4 the secret of God was upon my *t*;
Ps 15. 1 Lord, who shall abide in thy *t*?
19. 4 In them hath he set a *t* for the sun,
27. 5 In the secret of his *t* shall he hide
Pr 14.11 the *t* of the upright shall flourish.
Isa 4. 6 a *t* for a shadow in the daytime
Jer 10.20 My *t* is spoiled, and all my cords
Eze 37.27 My *t* also shall be with them:
Ac 7.43 ye took up the *t* of Moloch, and
44 Our fathers had the *t* of witness in
46 to find a *t* for the God of Jacob.
15.16 will build again the *t* of David,
2Co 5. 1 our earthly house of this *t* were
4 For we that are in this *t* do groan,
Heb 8. 2 and of the true *t*, which the Lord
5 when he was about to make the *t*.
9. 2 For there was a *t* made; the first,
3 *t* which is called the Holiest of all;
6 priests went always into the first *t*,
8 as the first *t* was yet standing:
11 by a greater and more perfect *t*,
21 he sprinkled with blood both the *t*,
13.10 no right to eat which serve the *t*.
2Pe 1.13 as long as I am in this *t*, to stir
14 shortly I must put off this my *t*,
Rev 13. 6 to blaspheme his name, and his *t*,
15. 5 temple of the *t* of the testimony
21. 3 the *t* of God is with men, and he

TABERNACLES
Lev 23.34 be the feast of *t* for seven days
Nu 24. 5 tents, O Jacob, and thy *t*, O Israel!
Dt 16.13 observe the feast of *t* seven days,
16 feast of weeks, and in the feast of *t*:
31.10 the year of release, in the feast of *t*,
2Ch 8.13 feast of weeks, and in the feast of *t*.
Ezr 3. 4 They kept also the feast of *t*, as it is
Job 11.14 let not wickedness dwell in thy *t*.
12. 6 The *t* of robbers prosper, and they
15.34 fire shall consume the *t* of bribery.
22.23 put away iniquity far from thy *t*.
Ps 43. 3 me unto thy holy hill, and to thy *t*.
46. 4 place of the *t* of the most High.
78.51 of their strength in the *t* of Ham:
83. 6 *t* of Edom, and the Ishmaelites;
84. 1 How amiable are thy *t*, O Lord of
118.15 is in the *t* of the righteous:
132. 7 We will go into his *t*: we will
Dan 11.45 he shall plant the *t* of his palace
Hos 9. 6 them: thorns shall be in their *t*.
12. 9 will yet make thee to dwell in *t*,
Zec 14.16 of hosts, and to keep the feast of *t*.
18, 19 not up to keep the feast of *t*.
Mal 2.12 the scholar, out of the *t* of Jacob,
Mt 17. 4 let us make here three *t*; one for
Mk 9. 5 let us make three *t*; one for thee,
Lk 9.33 let us make three *t*; one for thee,
Jn 7. 2 the Jews' feast of *t* was at hand.
Heb 11. 9 dwelling in *t* with Isaac...Jacob,

TABITHA
Ac 9.36 a certain disciple named *T*,
40 him to the body said, *T*, arise.

TABLE
2Sa 9. 7 and thou shalt eat bread at my *t*
1Ki 18.19 hundred, which eat at Jezebel's *t*.
2Ki 4.10 us set for him there a bed, and a *t*,
Ps 23. 5 Thou preparest a *t* before me in the
69.22 Let their *t* become a snare before
78.19 God furnish a *t* in the wilderness?
128. 3 like olive plants round about thy *t*.
Pr 3. 3 them upon the *t* of thine heart:
7. 3 write them upon the *t* of thine heart.
9. 2 she hath also furnished her *t*.
Jer 17. 1 graven upon the *t* of their heart,
Eze 41.22 This is the *t* that is before the Lord.
Mal 1. 7 The *t* of the Lord is contemptible.
12 say, The *t* of the Lord is polluted;
Mt 15.27 which fall from their masters' *t*,
Mk 7.28 yet the dogs under the *t* eat of the
Lk 1.63 And he asked for a writing *t*, and
16.21 which fell from the rich man's *t*:
22.21 betrayeth me is with me on the *t*.
30 ye may eat and drink at my *t* in my
Jn 12. 2 of them that sat at the *t* with him.
13.28 Now no man at the *t* knew for what
Ro 11. 9 saith, Let their *t* be made a snare,
1Co 10.21 cannot be partakers of the Lord's *t*,
21 and of the *t* of devils.
Heb 9. 2 and the *t*, and the shewbread;

TABLES
Ex 24.12 and I will give thee *t* of stone,
32.15 *t* were written on both their sides;
16 And the *t* were the work of God,
34. 1 two *t* of stone like unto the first:
Dt 9. 9 *t* of the covenant which the Lord
1Ki 8. 9 in the ark save the two *t* of stone,
2Ch 4.19 *t* whereon the shewbread was set;
Hab 2. 2 vision, and make it plain upon *t*,
Mt 21.12 the *t* of the moneychangers, and
Mk 7. 4 and pots, brasen vessels, and of *t*.
11.15 the *t* of the moneychangers,
Jn 2.15 money, and overthrew the *t*;
Ac 6. 2 leave the word of God, and serve *t*.
2Co 3. 3 living God; not in *t* of stone,
3 but in fleshy *t* of the heart.
Heb 9. 4 budded, and the *t* of the covenant;

TABLETS
Ex 35.22 and earrings, and rings, and *t*, all
Nu 31.50 bracelets, rings, earrings, and *t*,
Isa 3.20 headbands, and the *t*, and

TABRET
Gen 31.27 with songs, with *t*, and with harp?
1Sa 10. 5 and a *t*, and a pipe, and a harp,
Job 17. 6 and aforetime I was as a *t*.
Isa 5.12 the *t*, and pipe, and wine, are in

TABRETS
1Sa 18. 6 to meet king Saul, with *t*, with
Isa 24. 8 The mirth of *t* ceaseth, the noise of
30.32 him, it shall be with *t* and harps:
Jer 31. 4 shalt again be adorned with thy *t*,
Eze 28.13 the workmanship of thy *t* and of

TACKLING
Ac 27.19 our own hands the *t* of the ship.

TAIL
Ex 4. 4 thine hand, and take it by the *t*.
Dt 28.13 thee the head, and not the *t*;
44 the head, and thou shalt be the *t*.

Tables of testimony are received by Moses (Ex 31.18); engraving by Julius Schnorr von Carolsfeld.

Jdg 15. 4 turned *t* to *t*, and put a firebrand
Job 40.17 He moveth his *t* like a cedar: the
Isa 9.14 cut off from Israel head and *t*,
15 that teacheth lies, he is the *t*.
19.15 which the head or *t*, branch or
Rev 12. 4 his *t* drew the third part of the

TAILS

Jdg 15. 4 in the midst between two *t*.
Isa 7. 4 two *t* of these smoking firebrands,
Rev 9.10 they had *t* like unto scorpions,
10 and there were stings in their *t*:
19 is in their mouth, and in their *t*:
19 their *t* were like unto serpents,

TAKE

Gen 3.22 *t* also of the tree of life, and eat,
22. 2 *T* now thy son, thine only son
24. 4 and *t* a wife unto my son Isaac.
33.11 *T*, I pray thee, my blessing that is
Ex 2. 9 *T* this child away, and nurse it
4.17 shalt *t* this rod in thine hand,
6. 7 I will *t* you to me for a people, and
34. 9 sin, and *t* us for thine inheritance.
12 *T* heed to thyself, lest thou make
35. 5 *T* ye from among you an offering
Lev 25.36 *T* thou no usury of him, or
Nu 11.17 *t* of the spirit which is upon thee,
Dt 1.13 *T* you wise men, and
40 *t* your journey into the wilderness
16.19 respect persons, neither *t* a gift:
24.17 *t* a widow's raiment to pledge:
Jos 3. 6 *T* up the ark of the covenant, and
7.13 *t* away the accursed thing from
Jdg 19.30 consider of it, *t* advice, and speak
1Sa 24.11 yet thou huntest my soul to *t* it.
2Sa 5. 6 *t* away the blind and the lame,
12. 4 he spared to *t* of his own flock
1Ki 19. 4 now, O Lord, *t* away my life; for
10, 14 they seek my life, to *t* it away.
2Ki 2. 3, 5 Lord will *t* away thy master
4.36 unto him, he said, *T* up thy son.
8. 8 *T* a present in thine hand, and go,
1Ch 28.10 *T* heed now; for the Lord hath
2Ch 19. 6 to the judges, *T* heed what ye do:
Est 4. 4 to *t* away his sackcloth from him:
Job 7.21 and *t* away mine iniquity?
9.18 He will not suffer me to *t* my breath,
34 Let him *t* his rod away from me,
11.18 and thou shalt *t* thy rest in safety.
13.14 do I *t* my flesh in my teeth, and
23.10 But he knoweth the way that I *t*:
24. 3 they *t* the widow's ox for a pledge.
9 breast, and *t* a pledge of the poor.
27.20 Terrors *t* hold on him as waters,
32.22 my maker would soon *t* me away.
36.18 he *t* thee away with his stroke:
Ps 2. 2 and the rulers *t* counsel together,
27.10 me, then the Lord will *t* me up.
39. 1 I will *t* heed to my ways, that I
51.11 and *t* not thy holy spirit from me.
58. 9 *t* them away as with a whirlwind,
81. 2 *T* a psalm, and bring hither the
102.14 thy servants *t* pleasure in her stones,
24 *t* me not away in the midst of my
109. 8 few; and let another *t* his office.
116.13 I will *t* the cup of salvation, and
139. 9 If I *t* the wings of the morning,
20 thine enemies *t* thy name in vain.
Pr 2.19 *t* they hold of the paths of life.
4.13 *T* fast hold of instruction; let her
5. 5 to death; her steps *t* hold on hell.
6.27 Can a man *t* fire in his bosom, and
7.18 let us *t* our fill of love until the
22.27 why should he *t* away thy bed
30. 9 and *t* the name of my God in vain.
SS 2.15 *T* us the foxes, the little foxes,
Isa 3. 6 a man shall *t* hold of his brother
4. 1 seven women shall *t* hold of one
8. 1 *T* thee a great roll, and write in
13. 8 and sorrows shall *t* hold of them;
14. 4 shalt *t* up this proverb against
18. 4 I will *t* my rest, and I will consider
33.23 spoil divided; the lame *t* the prey.
58. 2 they *t* delight in approaching to God.
Jer 16. 2 Thou shalt not *t* thee a wife,
36. 2 *T* thee a roll of a book, and write
39.12 *T* him, and look well to him, and
Eze 10. 6 *T* fire from between the wheels,
11.19 *t* the stony heart out of their flesh,
Dan 7.18 most High shall *t* the kingdom,
Hos 1. 2 to Hosea, Go, *t* unto thee a wife of
4.10 have left off to *t* heed to the Lord.
11. 4 as they that *t* off the yoke on their
14. 2 *T* with you words, and turn to the
Am 5.12 they afflict the just, they *t* a bribe,
Jon 1.12 *T* me up, and cast me forth into
4. 3 O Lord, *t*, I beseech thee, my life
Mic 2. 4 one *t* up a parable against you,
Hab 2. 6 not all these *t* up a parable against
Zec 8.23 *t* hold of the skirt of him that is a
Mal 2.15 Therefore *t* heed to your spirit,
16 therefore *t* heed to your spirit,
Mt 1.20 fear not to *t* unto thee Mary thy
2.13, 20 *t* the young child and his mother,
6. 1 *T* heed that ye do not your alms
25 *T* no thought for your life, what
28 And why *t* ye thought for raiment?
34 *T* therefore no thought for the
9. 6 *t* up thy bed, and go unto thine
11.12 and the violent *t* it by force.
29 *T* my yoke upon you, and learn of
16. 5 side, they had forgotten to *t* bread.
24 and *t* up his cross, and follow me.
17.25 do the kings of the earth *t* custom
27 *t* up the fish that first cometh up;
24. 4 *T* heed that no man deceive you.
25.28 *T* therefore the talent from him,
26. 4 they might *t* Jesus by subtilty,
26 and said, *T*, eat; this is my body.
52 they that *t* the sword shall perish
55 swords and staves for to *t* me?
Mk 2. 9 or to say, Arise, and *t* up thy bed,
6. 8 should *t* nothing for their journey,
7.27 not meet to *t* the children's bread,
8.14 disciples had forgotten to *t* bread,
15 *T* heed, beware of the leaven of
34 deny himself, and *t* up his cross,
10.21 come, *t* up the cross, and follow me.
14. 1 how they might *t* him by craft,
22 and said, *T*, eat: this is my body.
48 swords and with staves to *t* me?
15.24 them, what every man should *t*.
36 Elias will come to *t* him down.
Lk 1.25 to *t* away my reproach among men.
5.24 *t* up thy couch, and go into thine
6. 4 and did *t* and eat the shewbread,
29 thy cloke forbid not to *t* thy coat also.
12.11 *t* ye no thought how or what thing
19 *t* thine ease, eat, drink, and be
22 *T* no thought for your life, what
Jn 2.16 sold doves, *T* these things hence;
5. 8 him, Rise, *t* up thy bed, and walk.
7.30 Then they sought to *t* him: but no
32 chief priests sent officers to *t* him.
11.39 Jesus said, *T* ye away the stone.
18.31 said Pilate unto them, *T* ye him,
19. 6 them, *T* ye him, and crucify him:
38 he might *t* away the body of Jesus:
Ac 1.20 and his bishoprick let another *t*.
12. 3 he proceeded further to *t* Peter
15.14 to *t* out of them a people for his
21.24 Them *t*, and purify thyself with
27.33 Paul besought them all to *t* meat,
Ro 11.21 *t* heed lest he also spare not thee.
27 when I shall *t* away their sins.
1Co 3.10 let every man *t* heed how he buildeth
11.24 *T*, eat: this is my body, which is
2Co 8. 4 *t* upon us the fellowship of the
12.10 I *t* pleasure in infirmities, in
Eph 6.13 *t* unto you the whole armor of
17 *t* the helmet of salvation, and the
1Jn 3. 5 manifested to *t* away our sins;
Rev 3.11 hast, that no man *t* thy crown.
5. 9 Thou art worthy to *t* the book, and
6. 4 thereon to *t* peace from the earth,
22.17 let him *t* the water of life freely.

TAKEN

Gen 2.22 rib,...the Lord God had *t* from man,
23 because she was *t* out of Man.
3.19 ground; for out of it wast thou *t*:
Ex 14.11 hast thou *t* us away to die in the
Nu 9.21 the cloud was *t* up in the morning,
Dt 24. 1 When a man hath *t* a wife, and
5 When a man hath *t* a new wife, he
Jdg 14. 9 had *t* the honey out of the carcase
18.24 Ye have *t* away my gods which I
1Sa 4.11 the ark of God was *t*; and the two
12. 3 his anointed: whose ox have I *t*?
3 or whose ass have I *t*? or whom
2Ki 2.10 thou see me when I am *t* from thee,
16 Spirit of the Lord hath *t* him up,
Ezr 10. 2 *t* strange wives of the people of
Job 1.21 gave, and the Lord hath *t* away;
19. 9 and *t* the crown from my head.
24.24 are *t* out of the way as all other,
27. 2 who hath *t* away my judgment;
30.16 of affliction have *t* hold upon me.
Ps 40.12 iniquities have *t* hold upon me,
Pr 3.26 shall keep thy foot from being *t*.
4.16 and their sleep is *t* away, unless
Isa 6. 6 he had *t* with the tongs from off
7 thine iniquity is *t* away, and thy
16.10 And gladness is *t* away, and joy out
52. 5 my people is *t* away for nought?
53. 8 He was *t* from prison and from
64. 6 like the wind, have *t* us away.
Eze 36. 3 ye are *t* up in the lips of talkers,
Dan 6.23 So Daniel was *t* up out of the den,
8.11 the daily sacrifice was *t* away,
Joel 3. 5 ye have *t* my silver and my gold,
Am 3. 5 earth, and have *t* nothing at all?
Mic 2. 9 have ye *t* away my glory for ever.
Zep 3.15 Lord hath *t* away thy judgments,
Mt 4.24 that were *t* with divers diseases
9.15 bridegroom shall be *t* from them,
13.12 from him shall be *t* away even that
16. 7 It is because we have *t* no bread.
21.43 kingdom of God shall be *t* from you,
24.40, 41 one shall be *t*, and the other
25.29 be *t* away even that which he hath.
27.59 And when Joseph had *t* the body,
28.12 with the elders, and had *t* counsel,
Mk 2.20 bridegroom shall be *t* away from
4.25 shall be *t* even that which he hath.
6.41 when he had *t* the five loaves and
9.36 when he had *t* him in his arms, he
Lk 1. 1 as many have *t* in hand to set
4.38 mother was *t* with a great fever;
5. 5 all the night, and have *t* nothing:
9 of the fishes which they had *t*:
18 bed a man which was *t* with a palsy:
35 bridegroom shall be *t* away from
36 the piece that was *t* out of the new
8.18 from him shall be *t* even that which
37 for they were *t* with great fear:
9.17 there was *t* up of fragments that
10.42 which shall not be *t* away from her.
11.52 have *t* away the key of knowledge:
17.34, 35 the one shall be *t*, and the other
36 one shall be *t*, and the other left.
19. 8 *t* any thing...by false accusation,
26 he hath shall be *t* away from him.
Jn 7.44 some of them would have *t* him;
8. 3 unto him a woman *t* in adultery;
4 this woman was *t* in adultery, in
13.12 had *t* his garments, and was set
19.31 and that they might be *t* away.
20. 1 and seeth the stone *t* away from the
2 They have *t* away the Lord out of
13 they have *t* away my Lord, and I
Ac 1. 2 Until the day in which he was *t* up,

9 while they beheld, he was *t* up;
11 Jesus, which is *t* up from you into
22 same day that he was *t* up from us,
2.23 ye have *t*, and by wicked hands
8. 7 and many *t* with palsies, and that
33 his judgment was *t* away:
33 for his life is *t* from the earth.
17. 9 when they had *t* security of Jason,
20. 9 the third loft, and was *t* up dead.
21. 6 And when we had *t* our leave one of
23.27 This man was *t* of the Jews, and
27.17 Which when they had *t* up, they
20 should be saved was then *t* away.
33 fasting, having *t* nothing.
40 when they had *t* up the anchors,
Ro 9. 6 the word of God hath *t* none effect.
1Co 5. 2 done this deed might be *t* away
10.13 There hath no temptation *t* you
2Co 3.16 the Lord, the vail shall be *t* away.
1Th 2.17 being *t* from you for a short time
2Th 2. 7 let, until he be *t* out of the way.
1Ti 5. 9 not a widow be *t* into the number
2Ti 2.26 who are *t* captive by him at his will.
Heb 5. 1 every high priest *t* from among
2Pe 2.12 beasts, made to be *t* and destroyed,
Rev 5. 8 when he had *t* the book, the four
11.17 thou hast *t* to thee thy great power,
19.20 the beast was *t*, and with him the

TAKER

Isa 24. 2 as with the *t* of usury, so with the

TAKEST

Ex 4. 9 the water which thou *t* out of the
30.12 thou *t* the sum of the children
Jdg 4. 9 the journey that thou *t* shall not be
1Ch 22.13 if thou *t* heed to fulfil the statutes
Ps 104.29 thou *t* away their breath, they die,
144. 3 is man, that thou *t* knowledge of
Ec 9. 9 labor...thou *t* under the sun.
Isa 58. 3 our soul, and thou *t* no knowledge?
Lk 19.21 *t* up that thou layedst not down,

TAKETH

Ex 20. 7 guiltless that *t* his name in vain.
Dt 10.17 not persons, nor *t* reward:
Job 5.13 He *t* the wise in their...craftiness:
9.12 he *t* away, who can hinder him?
27. 8 gained, when God *t* away his soul?
Ps 15. 5 nor *t* reward against the innocent.
147.10 *t* not pleasure in the legs of a man.
149. 4 the Lord *t* pleasure in his people:
Pr 26.17 like one that *t* a dog by the ears.
Ec 2.23 yea, his heart *t* not rest in the night.
5.18 his labor that he *t* under the sun
Isa 40.15 he *t* up the isles as a very little
Eze 33. 5 that *t* warning shall deliver his soul.
Am 3.12 *t* out of the mouth of the lion
Mt 4. 5 devil *t* him up into the holy city,
8 devil *t* him up into an exceeding
9.16 in to fill it up *t* from the garment,
10.38 And he that *t* not his cross, and
12.45 *t* with himself seven other spirits
17. 1 after six days Jesus *t* Peter, James,
Mk 2.21 that filled it up *t* away from the old,
4.15 and *t* away the word that was sown
5.40 he *t* the father and the mother of
9. 2 six days Jesus *t* with him Peter,
18 wheresoever he *t* him, he teareth
14.33 he *t* with him Peter and James and
Lk 6.29 him that *t* away thy cloke forbid
30 of him that *t* away thy goods ask
8.12 *t* away the word out of their hearts,
9.39 lo, a spirit *t* him, and he suddenly
11.22 he *t* from him all his armor
26 and *t* to him seven other spirits
16. 3 *t* away from me the stewardship:
Jn 1.29 which *t* away the sin of the world.
10.18 No man *t* it from me, but I lay it
15. 2 me that beareth not fruit he *t* away:
16.22 and your joy no man *t* from you.
21.13 and *t* bread, and giveth them,
Ro 3. 5 unrighteous who *t* vengeance?
1Co 3.19 *t* the wise in their own craftiness.
11.21 *t* before other his own supper:
Heb 5. 4 no man *t* this honor unto himself,
10. 9 He *t* away the first, that he may

TAKING

2Ch 19. 7 respect of persons, nor *t* of gifts.
Job 5. 3 I have seen the foolish *t* root: but
Ps 119. 9 by *t* heed thereto according to thy
Jer 50.46 At the noise of the *t* of Babylon the
Eze 25.12 the house of Judah by *t* vengeance,
Hos 11. 3 also to go, *t* them by their arms;
Mt 6.27 Which of you by *t* thought can
Mk 13.34 of man is as a man *t* a far journey,
Lk 4. 5 *t* him up into an high mountain,
12.25 And which of you with *t* thought
19.22 man, *t* up that I laid not down.
Jn 11.13 he had spoken of *t* of rest in sleep.
Ro 7. 8 But sin, *t* occasion by the
11 For sin, *t* occasion by the
2Co 2.13 *t* my leave of them, I went from
11. 8 other churches, *t* wages of them,
Eph 6.16 Above all, *t* the shield of faith,
2Th 1. 8 *t* vengeance on them that know
1Pe 5. 2 flock...*t* the oversight thereof, not by
3Jn 7 forth, *t* nothing of the Gentiles.

TALE

Ex 5. 8 And the *t* of the bricks, which
18 yet shall ye deliver the *t* of bricks.
1Sa 18.27 they gave them in full *t* to the king,
1Ch 9.28 bring them in and out by *t*.
Ps 90. 9 spend our years as a *t* that is told.

TALEBEARER

Lev 19.16 down as a *t* among thy people:
Pr 11.13 A *t* revealeth secrets: but he
18. 8 The words of a *t* are as wounds,
20.19 about as a *t* revealeth secrets:
26.20 there is no *t*, the strife ceaseth.
22 The words of a *t* are as wounds,

TALENT

Mt 25.24 he which had received the one *t*
25 went and hid thy *t* in the earth:
28 Take therefore the *t* from him, and
Rev 16.21 stone about the weight of a *t*:

TALENTS

Mt 18.24 which owed him ten thousand *t*.
25.15 And unto one he gave five *t*, and to
16 he that had received the five *t* went
16 same, and made them other five *t*.
20 And so he that had received five *t*
20 came and brought other five *t*,
20 thou deliveredst unto me five *t*:
20 gained beside them five *t* more.
22 He also that had received two *t*
22 thou deliveredst unto me two *t*:
22 gained two other *t* beside them.
28 give it unto him which hath ten *t*.

TALES

Eze 22. 9 men that carry *t* to shed blood:
Lk 24.11 words seemed to them as idle *t*,

TALITHA

Mk 5.41 hand, and said unto her, *T* cumi;

TALK

Nu 11.17 come down and *t* with thee there:
Dt 5.24 this day that God doth *t* with man,
6. 7 *t* of them when thou sittest in thine
1Sa 2. 3 *T* no more so exceeding proudly;
2Ki 18.26 and *t* not...in the Jews' language
1Ch 16. 9 *t* ye of all his wondrous works.
Job 11. 2 should a man full of *t* be justified?
13. 7 God? and *t* deceitfully for him?
15. 3 he reason with unprofitable *t*?
Ps 69.26 they *t* to the grief of those whom
71.24 also shall *t* of thy righteousness
77.12 all thy work, and *t* of thy doings.
105. 2 *t* ye of all his wondrous works.
119.27 so shall I *t* of thy wondrous works:
145.11 thy kingdom, and *t* of thy power;
Pr 6.22 thou awakest, it shall *t* with thee.
14.23 but the *t* of the lips tendeth only
24. 2 and their lips *t* of mischief.
Ec 10.13 the end of his *t* is mischievous
Jer 12. 1 *t* with thee of thy judgments:
Eze 3.22 plain, and I will there *t* with thee.
Dan 10.17 the servant...*t* with this my lord?
Mt 22.15 they might entangle him in his *t*.
Jn 14.30 Hereafter I will not *t* much with

TALKED

Gen 4. 8 And Cain *t* with Abel his brother:
17. 3 on his face: and God *t* with him,
Ex 20.22 that I have *t* with you from heaven.
33. 9 and the Lord *t* with Moses.
34.29 his face shone while he *t* with him.
Dt 5. 4 The Lord *t* with you face to face
Zec 1. 9 And the angel that *t* with me said
4. 1 angel that *t* with me came again,
6. 4 said unto the angel that *t* with me,
Mt 12.46 While he yet *t* to the people,
Mk 6.50 And immediately *t* with them,
Lk 9.30 there *t* with him two men, which
24.14 they *t* together of all these things
32 while he *t* with us by the way,
Jn 4.27 marvelled...he *t* with the woman:
Ac 10.27 as he *t* with him, he went in, and
20.11 and *t* a long while, even till break
26.31 aside, they *t* between themselves,
Rev 17. 1 *t* with me, saying unto me, Come
21. 9 *t* with me, saying, Come hither,
15 that *t* with me had a golden reed

TALKERS

Eze 36. 3 ye are taken up in the lips of *t*,
Tit 1.10 unruly and vain *t* and deceivers,

TALKEST

Jdg 6.17 me a sign that thou *t* with me.
1Ki 1.14 while thou...*t* there with the king,
Jn 4.27 thou? or, Why *t* thou with her?

TALKETH

Ps 37.30 and his tongue *t* of judgment.
Jn 9.37 him, and it is he that *t* with thee.

TALKING

Gen 17.22 And he left off *t* with him, and
1Ki 18.27 either he is *t*, or he is pursuing,
Est 6.14 while they were yet *t* with him,
Job 29. 9 The princes refrained *t*, and laid
Eze 33.30 people still are *t* against thee
Mt 17. 3 them Moses and Elias *t* with him.
Mk 9. 4 Moses: and they were *t* with Jesus.
Eph 5. 4 nor foolish *t*, nor jesting,
Rev 4. 1 it were of a trumpet *t* with me;

TALL

Dt 2.10 a people great, and many, and *t*,
21 A people great, and many, and *t*,
9. 2 A people great and *t*, the children
2Ki 19.23 will cut down the *t* cedar trees
Isa 37.24 I will cut down the *t* cedars thereof,

TAMAR

Gen 38. 6 his firstborn, whose name was *T*.
11 Judah to *T* his daughter in law,
11 *T* went and dwelt in her father's
13 And it was told *T*, saying, Behold
24 *T* thy daughter in law hath played
Ru 4.12 Pharez, whom *T* bare unto Judah,
2Sa 13. 1 a fair sister, whose name was *T*;
2 that he fell sick for his sister *T*;
4 I love *T*, my brother Absalom's
7 David sent home to *T*, saying, Go

TAMAR

Name of two of the most ill-used women in the Old Testament: (1) Canaanite wife of Er, oldest son of Judah, Jacob's son; when Er dies she is given to his brother Onan, who refuses to consummate union and is slain by God (Gen 38.6-10); **she is then promised to a third brother, Shelah, still a minor; when Judah later refuses to keep the promise, she disguises herself and encounters him, lets him think she is a prostitute, and becomes pregnant** (Gen 38.11-18); **when Judah, unaware of his responsibility for her condition, sentences her to death, she shows him some personal belongings he had given her; he acknowledges his guilt and her claim to justice, and accepts the twin sons she bears as his own** (Gen 38.19-30); **she is later cited as ancestress of tribe of Judah** (Ru 4.12). **(2) Daughter of David and sister of Absalom; her beauty obsesses Amnon, her half-brother, who lures her to his house on a pretext and rapes her** (2Sa 13.1-14); **his desire thereupon turns to loathing and he has her thrown out by a servant; weeping and distraught, she tells Absalom, who takes her into his home and quietly plans revenge, culminating in Amnon's murder two years later** (2Sa 13.15-29).

2Sa 13. 8 So *T* went to her brother Amnon's
10 And Amnon said unto *T*, Bring the
10 *T* took the cakes which she had
19 *T* put ashes on her head, and rent
20 So *T* remained desolate in her
22 because he had forced his sister *T*.

TAME

Mk 5. 4 neither could any man *t* him.
Jas 3. 8 But the tongue can no man *t*; it is

TAMED

Jas 3. 7 and of things in the sea, is *t*,
7 and hath been *t* of mankind:

TANNER

Ac 9.43 days in Joppa with one Simon a *t*.
10. 6 He lodgeth with one Simon a *t*,
32 in the house of one Simon a *t* by the

TARE

2Sa 13.31 king arose, and *t* his garments,
2Ki 2.24 *t* forty and two children of them.
Mk 9.20 him, straightway the spirit *t* him;
Lk 9.42 devil threw him down, and *t* him.

TARES

Mt 13.25 and sowed *t* among the wheat,
26 fruit, then appeared the *t* also.
27 field? from whence then hath it *t*?
29 Nay; lest while ye gather up the *t*,
30 Gather ye together first the *t*, and
36 us the parable of the *t* of the field.
38 the *t* are the children of the wicked
40 the *t* are gathered and burned in the

TARRIED

Nu 9.19 cloud *t* long upon the tabernacle
Ps 68.12 and she that *t* at home divided the
Mt 25. 5 While the bridegroom *t*, they all
Lk 1.21 that he *t* so long in the temple.
2.43 child Jesus *t* behind in Jerusalem;
Jn 3.22 and there he *t* with them, and
Ac 9.43 he *t* many days in Joppa with one
15.33 after they had *t* there a space,
18.18 Paul after this *t* there yet a good
20. 5 These going before *t*...at Troas.
15 at Samos, and *t* at Trogyllium;
21. 4 disciples, we *t* there seven days:
10 And as we *t* there many days,
25. 6 he had *t* among them more than
27.33 the fourteenth day that ye have *t*
28.12 at Syracuse, we *t* there three days.

TARRIEST

Ac 22.16 And now why *t* thou? arise, and be

TARRIETH

1Sa 30.24 his part be that *t* by the stuff;
Mic 5. 7 upon the grass, that *t* not for man,

TARRY

Gen 27.44 And *t* with him a few days, until
Ru 1.13 *t* for them till they were grown?
2Ki 2. 2 unto Elisha, *T* here, I pray thee;
7. 9 if we *t* till the morning light, some
9. 3 open the door, and flee, and *t* not.
1Ch 19. 5 *T* at Jericho until your beards be
Ps 101. 7 he that telleth lies shall not *t* in
Pr 23.30 They that *t* long at the wine; they
Hab 2. 3 not lie: though it *t*, wait for it;
Mt 26.38 *t* ye here, and watch with me.
Mk 14.34 unto death: *t* ye here, and watch.
Lk 24.29 And he went in to *t* with them.
49 but *t* ye in the city of Jerusalem,
Jn 4.40 him that he would *t* with them:
21.22, 23 If I will that he *t* till I come,
Ac 10.48 prayed they him to *t* certain days.
18.20 they desired him to *t* longer time
28.14 desired to *t* with them seven days:
1Co 11.33 together to eat, *t* one for another.
16. 7 I trust to *t* a while with you, if the
8 will *t* at Ephesus until Pentecost.
1Ti 3.15 But if I *t* long, that thou mayest
Heb 10.37 come will come, and will not *t*.

TARRYING

Ps 40.17 deliverer; make no *t*, O my God.
70. 5 my deliverer; O Lord, make no *t*.

TARSUS

Ac 9.11 Judas for one called Saul, of *T*:
30 Caesarea, and sent him forth to *T*.
11.25 Then departed Barnabas to *T*,
21.39 I am a man which am a Jew of *T*,
22. 3 man which am a Jew, born in *T*,

TASK

Ex 5.14 fulfilled your *t* in making brick
19 from your bricks of your daily *t*.

TASKMASTERS

Ex 1.11 they did set over them *t*
3. 7 their cry by reason of their *t*;
5. 6 And Pharaoh commanded...the *t*
10 And the *t* of the people went out,
13 And the *t* hasted them, saying,
14 Pharaoh's *t* had set over them,

TASTE

Ex 16.31 *t* of it was like wafers made with
Nu 11. 8 the *t* of it was as the *t* of fresh oil.
1Sa 14.43 I did but *t* a little honey with the
2Sa 3.35 to me, and more also, if I *t* bread,
19.35 *t* what I eat or what I drink?
Job 6. 6 there any *t* in the white of an egg?
30 my *t* discern perverse things?
12.11 and the mouth *t* his meat?
Ps 34. 8 O *t* and see that the Lord is good:
119.103 sweet are thy words unto my *t*!
Pr 24.13 honeycomb, which is sweet to thy *t*:
SS 2. 3 and his fruit was sweet to my *t*.
Jer 48.11 therefore his *t* remained in him,
Jon 3. 7 beast, herd nor flock, *t* any thing:
Mt 16.28 here, which shall not *t* of death,
Mk 9. 1 here, which shall not *t* of death,
Lk 9.27 here, which shall not *t* of death,
14.24 were bidden shall *t* of my supper.
Jn 8.52 saying, he shall never *t* of death.
Col 2.21 (Touch not; *t* not; handle not;
Heb 2. 9 should *t* death for every man.

TASTED

1Sa 14.24 So none of the people *t* any food.
29 because I *t* a little of this honey.
Dan 5. 2 Belshazzar, whiles he *t* the wine,
Mt 27.34 had *t* thereof, he would not drink.
Jn 2. 9 *t* the water that was made wine,
Heb 6. 4 and have *t* of the heavenly gift, and
5 And have *t* the good word of God,
1Pe 2. 3 ye have *t* that the Lord is gracious.

TATTLERS

1Ti 5.13 idle, but *t* also and busybodies,

TAUGHT

Jdg 8.16 them he *t* the men of Succoth.
2Ch 6.27 thou hast *t* them the good way,
23.13 and such as *t* to sing praise.
30.22 *t* the good knowledge of the Lord:
Ps 71.17 thou hast *t* me from my youth:
119.102 judgments: for thou hast *t* me.
171 when thou hast *t* me thy statutes.
Pr 4. 4 He *t* me also, and said unto me,
11 I have *t* thee in the way of wisdom:
Ec 12. 9 he still *t* the people knowledge;
Isa 40.13 being his counsellor hath *t* him?
14 *t* him in the path of judgment,
Jer 32.33 though I *t* them, rising up early
Hos 11. 3 I *t* Ephraim also to go, taking
Mt 5. 2 he opened his mouth, and *t* them,
7.29 he *t* them as one having
13.54 he *t* them in their synagogue,
28.15 the money, and did as they were *t*:
Mk 1.21 entered into the synagogue, and *t*.
22 for he *t* them as one that had
2.13 resorted unto him, and he *t* them.
4. 2 he *t* them many things by parables,
6.30 they had done, and what they had *t*.
9.31 For he *t* his disciples, and said unto
10. 1 as he was wont, he *t* them again.
11.17 he *t*, saying unto them, Is it not
12.35 and said, while he *t* in the temple,
Lk 4.15 And he *t* in their synagogues, being
31 *t* them on the sabbath days.
5. 3 and *t* the people out of the ship.
6. 6 entered into the synagogue and *t*:
11. 1 pray, as John also *t* his disciples.
13.26 and thou hast *t* in our streets.
19.47 And he *t* daily in the temple.
20. 1 as he *t* the people in the temple.
Jn 6.45 And they shall be all *t* of God.
59 synagogue, as he *t* in Capernaum.
7.14 went up into the temple, and *t*.
28 cried Jesus in the temple as he *t*,
8. 2 and he sat down, and *t* them.
20 treasury, as he *t* in the temple:
28 as my Father hath *t* me, I speak
18.20 I ever *t* in the synagogue, and in
Ac 4. 2 grieved that they *t* the people,
5.21 temple early in the morning, and *t*.
11.26 the church, and *t* much people.
14.21 to that city, and had *t* many,
15. 1 down from Judea *t* the brethren,
18.25 *t* diligently the things of the Lord,
20.20 you, and have *t* you publickly,
22. 3 *t* according to the perfect manner
Gal 1.12 it of man, neither was I *t* it,
6. 6 Let him that is *t* in the word
Eph 4.21 heard him, and...been *t* by him,
Col 2. 7 in the faith, as ye have been *t*,
1Th 4. 9 are *t* of God to love one another.
2Th 2.15 traditions which ye have been *t*,
Tit 1. 9 faithful word as he hath been *t*,
1Jn 2.27 no lie, and even as it hath *t* you,
Rev 2.14 *t* Balac to cast a stumblingblock

TAVERNS
Ac 28.15 far as Appii forum,...The three *t*:

TAXED
2Ki 23.35 he *t* the land to give the money
Lk 2. 1 that all the world should be *t*.
3 all went to be *t*, every one into his
5 be *t* with Mary his espoused wife,

TAXING
Lk 2. 2 And this *t* was first made when
Ac 5.37 Judas of Galilee in the days of the *t*,

TEACH
Ex 4.12 and *t* thee what thou shalt say.
15 and will *t* you what ye shall do.
Dt 4. 1 the judgments, which I *t* you, for
9 but *t* them thy sons, and thy sons'
6. 7 shalt *t* them diligently unto thy
24. 8 the priests the Levites shall *t* you:
1Sa 12.23 I will *t* you the good and the right
1Ki 8.36 that thou *t* them the good way
2Ki 17.27 *t* them the manner of the God of
Ezr 7.25 and *t* ye them that know them not.
Job 6.24 *T* me, and I will hold my tongue:
12. 8 to the earth, and it shall *t* thee:
27.11 I will *t* you by the hand of God:
34.32 That which I see not *t* thou me:
Ps 25. 4 thy ways, O Lord; *t* me thy paths.
5 Lead me in thy truth, and *t* me:
8 will he *t* sinners in the way.
9 and the meek will he *t* his way.
27.11 *T* me thy way, O Lord, and lead
34.11 I will *t* you the fear of the Lord.
51.13 will I *t* transgressors thy ways;
86.11 *T* me thy way, O Lord; I will
90.12 *t* us to number our days, that we
119.12 thou, O Lord: *t* me thy statutes.
143.10 *T* me to do thy will; for thou art
Pr 9. 9 *t* a just man, and he will increase
Isa 2. 3 he will *t* us of his ways, and we
Mic 3.11 and the priests thereof *t* for hire,
4. 2 and he will *t* us of his ways, and we
Mt 5.19 and shall *t* men so, he shall be
19 but whosoever shall do and *t* them,
11. 1 to *t* and to preach in their cities.
28.19 Go ye therefore, and *t* all nations,
Mk 4. 1 began again to *t* by the sea side:
6. 2 he began to *t* in the synagogue:
34 he began to *t* them many things.
8.31 he began to *t* them, that the Son of
Lk 11. 1 said unto him, Lord, *t* us to pray,
12.12 Holy Ghost shall *t* you in the same
Jn 7.35 the Gentiles, and *t* the Gentiles?
9.34 born in sins, and dost thou *t* us?
14.26 he shall *t* you all things, and bring
Ac 1. 1 that Jesus began both to do and *t*,
4.18 at all nor *t* in the name of Jesus.
5.28 that ye should not *t* in this name?
42 ceased not to *t* and preach Jesus
16.21 *t* customs, which are not lawful
1Co 4.17 I *t* every where in every church.
11.14 Doth not even nature itself *t* you,
14.19 by my voice I might *t* others also,
1Ti 1. 3 some that they *t* no other doctrine,
2.12 But I suffer not a woman to *t*, nor
3. 2 given to hospitality, apt to *t*;
4.11 These things command and *t*.
6. 2 benefit. These things *t* and exhort.
3 If any man *t* otherwise, and
2Ti 2. 2 who shall be able to *t* others also.
24 but be gentle unto all men, apt to *t*,
Tit 2. 4 *t* the young women to be sober,
Heb 5.12 ye have need that one *t* you again
8.11 not *t* every man his neighbor,
1Jn 2.27 ye need not that any man *t* you:
Rev 2.20 to *t* and to seduce my servants to

TEACHER
1Ch 25. 8 as the great, the *t* as the scholar.
Hab 2.18 the molten image, and a *t* of lies,
Jn 3. 2 that thou art a *t* come from God:
Ro 2.20 a *t* of babes, which hast the form
1Ti 2. 7 a *t* of the Gentiles in faith and
2Ti 1.11 an apostle, and a *t* of the Gentiles.

TEACHERS
Ps 119.99 understanding than all my *t*:
Pr 5.13 have not obeyed the voice of my *t*,
Isa 30.20 not thy *t* be removed into a corner
20 but thine eyes shall see thy *t*:
43.27 *t* have transgressed against me.
Ac 13. 1 at Antioch certain prophets and *t*;
1Co 12.28 secondarily prophets, thirdly *t*,
29 are all prophets? are all *t*? are all
Eph 4.11 and some, pastors and *t*;
1Ti 1. 7 Desiring to be *t* of the law;
2Ti 4. 3 shall they heap to themselves *t*,
Tit 2. 3 to much wine, *t* of good things;
Heb 5.12 when for the time ye ought to be *t*,
2Pe 2. 1 there shall be false *t* among you,

TEACHEST
Ps 94.12 O Lord, and *t* him out of thy law;
Mt 22.16 true, and *t* the way of God in truth,
Mk 12.14 men, but *t* the way of God in truth:
Lk 20.21 know that thou sayest and *t* rightly,
21 of any, but *t* the way of God truly:
Ac 21.21 that thou *t* all the Jews which are
Ro 2.21 Thou therefore which *t* another,
21 *t* thou not thyself? thou that

TEACHETH
2Sa 22.35 He *t* my hands to war; so that a
Job 35.11 Who *t* us more than the beasts of
36.22 by his power: who *t* like him?
Ps 18.34 He *t* my hands to war, so that a
94.10 he that *t* man knowledge, shall not
144. 1 which *t* my hands to war, and my
Pr 6.13 his feet, he *t* with his fingers;
16.23 The heart of the wise *t* his mouth,
Isa 9.15 prophet that *t* lies, he is the tail.
48.17 thy God which *t* thee to profit,
Ac 21.28 man, that *t* all men every where
Ro 12. 7 or he that *t*, on teaching;
1Co 2.13 the words which man's wisdom *t*,
13 but which the Holy Ghost *t*;
Gal 6. 6 unto him that *t* in all good things.
1Jn 2.27 as the same anointing *t* you of all

TEACHING
2Ch 15. 3 without a *t* priest, and without
Jer 32.33 them, rising up early and *t* them,
Mt 4.23 all Galilee, *t* in their synagogues,
9.35 and villages, *t* in their synagogues,
15. 9 *t* for doctrines the commandments
21.23 people came unto him as he was *t*,
26.55 sat daily with you *t* in the temple,
28.20 *T* them to observe all things
Mk 6. 6 he went round about the villages, *t*.
7. 7 *t* for doctrines the commandments
14.49 was daily with you in the temple *t*,
Lk 5.17 pass on a certain day, as he was *t*,
13.10 he was *t* in one of the synagogues
22 through the cities and villages, *t*,
21.37 day time he was *t* in the temple;
23. 5 the people, *t* throughout all Jewry,
Ac 5.25 in the temple, and *t* the people.
15.35 *t* and preaching the word of the
18.11 *t* the word of God among them.
28.31 *t* those things which concern the
Ro 12. 7 or he that teacheth, on *t*;
Col 1.28 and *t* every man in all wisdom;
3.16 *t* and admonishing one another
Tit 1.11 *t* things which they ought not, for
2.12 *T* us that, denying ungodliness

TEAR
Jdg 8. 7 I will *t* your flesh with the thorns
Ps 7. 2 Lest he *t* my soul like a lion,
35.15 they did *t* me, and ceased not:
50.22 lest I *t* you in pieces, and there be
Jer 15. 3 sword to slay, and the dogs to *t*,
16. 7 shall men *t* themselves for them
Eze 13.20 and I will *t* them from your arms,
21 Your kerchiefs also will I *t*, and
Hos 5.14 I, even I, will *t* and go away; I will
13. 8 lion: the wild beast shall *t* them.
Am 1.11 and his anger did *t* perpetually,
Na 2.12 The lion did *t* in pieces enough for
Zec 11.16 the fat, and *t* their claws in pieces.

TEARETH
Dt 33.20 *t* the arm with the crown of the
Job 16. 9 He *t* me in his wrath, who hateth
18. 4 He *t* himself in his anger: shall
Mic 5. 8 both treadeth down, and *t* in pieces,
Mk 9.18 he taketh him, he *t* him: and he
Lk 9.39 and it *t* him that he foameth again,

TEARS
2Ki 20. 5 thy prayer, I have seen thy *t*:
Est 8. 3 besought him with *t* to put away
Job 16.20 mine eye poureth out *t* unto God.
Ps 6. 6 to swim; I water my couch with *t*.
39.12 my cry; hold not thy peace at my *t*:
42. 3 My *t* have been my meat day and
56. 8 put thou my *t* into thy bottle: are
80. 5 feedest them with the bread of *t*;
5 them *t* to drink in great measure.
116. 8 mine eyes from *t*, and my feet from
126. 5 They that sow in *t* shall reap in joy.
Ec 4. 1 the *t* of such as were oppressed,
Isa 16. 9 I will water thee with my *t*, O
25. 8 Lord God will wipe away *t* from off
38. 5 heard thy prayer, I have seen thy *t*:
Jer 9. 1 and mine eyes a fountain of *t*, that
18 that our eyes may run down with *t*,
13.17 weep sore, and run down with *t*,
14.17 Let mine eyes run down with *t*
31.16 weeping, and thine eyes from *t*:
La 1. 2 night, and her *t* are on her cheeks:
2.11 Mine eyes do fail with *t*, my
18 let *t* run down like a river day and
Eze 24.16 weep, neither shall thy *t* run down.
Mal 2.13 covering...altar of the Lord with *t*,
Mk 9.24 and said with *t*, Lord, I believe;
Lk 7.38 and began to wash his feet with *t*,
44 she hath washed my feet with *t*,
Ac 20.19 humility of mind, and with many *t*,
31 every one night and day with *t*.
2Co 2. 4 I wrote unto you with many *t*; not
2Ti 1. 4 to see thee, being mindful of thy *t*,
Heb 5. 7 with strong crying and *t* unto him
12.17 he sought it carefully with *t*.
Rev 7.17 and God shall wipe away all *t* from
21. 4 and God shall wipe away all *t* from

TEDIOUS
Ac 24. 4 that I be not further *t* unto thee,

TEETH
Job 19.20 I am escaped with the skin of my *t*.
41.14 his *t* are terrible round about.
Ps 37.12 and gnasheth upon him with his *t*.
124. 6 not given us as a prey to their *t*.
Jer 31.29 the children's *t* are set on edge.
30 grape, his *t* shall be set on edge.
Eze 18. 2 the children's *t* are set on edge?
Dan 7.19 whose *t* were of iron, and his nails
Joel 1. 6 whose *t* are the *t* of a lion, and
Am 4. 6 have given you cleanness of *t*
Mt 8.12 be weeping and gnashing of *t*.
13.42, 50 be wailing and gnashing of *t*.
22.13 be weeping and gnashing of *t*.
24.51 be weeping and gnashing of *t*.
25.30 be weeping and gnashing of *t*.
27.44 with him, cast the same in his *t*.
Mk 9.18 foameth, and gnasheth with his *t*,
Lk 13.28 be weeping and gnashing of *t*,
Ac 7.54 they gnashed on him with their *t*.
Rev 9. 8 and their *t* were as...of lions.
8 were as the *t* of lions.

TEKEL

Dan 5.25 Mene, Mene, *T*, Upharsin.
27 *T*; Thou art weighed in the

TELL

Gen 15. 5 toward heaven, and *t* the stars,
29.15 *t* me, what shall thy wages be?
32.29 said, *T* me, I pray thee, thy name.
Ex 9. 1 Go in unto Pharaoh, and *t* him,
Jdg 16. 6 *T* me, I pray thee, wherein thy
Ru 3. 4 he will *t* thee what thou shalt do.
1Sa 9. 8 the man of God, to *t* us our way.
2Sa 1.20 *T* it not in Gath, publish it not in
12.22 Who can *t* whether God will be
1Ki 22.16 *t* me nothing but that which is true
Ps 26. 7 and *t* of all thy wondrous works.
Ec 6.12 for who can *t* a man what shall be
8. 7 for who can *t* him when it shall be?
10.14 a man cannot *t* what shall be; and
14 shall be after him, who can *t* him?
SS 1. 7 *T* me, O thou whom my soul loveth,
5. 8 ye *t* him, that I am sick of love.
Isa 6. 9 and *t* this people, Hear ye indeed,
Jer 23.27 they *t* every man to his neighbor,
28 hath a dream, let him *t* a dream;
Dan 2. 9 *t* me the dream, and I shall know
Joel 1. 3 *T* ye your children of it, and let
3 and let your children *t* their children,
Mt 8. 4 saith unto him, See thou *t* no man;
10.27 What I *t* you in darkness, that
16.20 should *t* no man that he was Jesus
17. 9 *T* the vision to no man, until the
18.15 *t* him his fault between thee and
17 hear them, *t* it unto the church:
21. 5 *T* ye the daughter of Sion, Behold,
24 ask you one thing, which if ye *t* me,
24 will *t* you by what authority I do
27 Jesus, and said, We cannot *t*.
27 Neither *t* I you by what authority
22. 4 *T* them which are bidden, Behold,
17 *T* us therefore, What thinkest thou?
24. 3 *T* us, when shall these things be?
26.63 *t* us whether thou be the Christ,
28. 7 *t* his disciples that he is risen from
9 And as they went to *t* his disciples,
10 go *t* my brethren that they go into
Mk 1.30 fever, and anon they *t* him of her.
5.19 *t* them how great things the Lord
7.36 them that they should *t* no man:
8.26 town, nor *t* it to any in the town.
30 that they should *t* no man of him.
9. 9 *t* no man what things they had
10.32 and began to *t* them what things
11.29 will *t* you by what authority I do
33 and said unto Jesus, We cannot *t*.
33 them, Neither do I *t* you by what
13. 4 *T* us, when shall these things be?
16. 7 *t* his disciples and Peter that he
Lk 4.25 I *t* you of a truth, many widows
5.14 And he charged him to *t* no man:
7.22 *t* John what things ye have seen
42 *T* me...which of them will love
8.56 should *t* no man what was done.
9.21 them to *t* no man that thing;
27 I *t* you of a truth, there be some
10.24 For I *t* you, that many prophets
12.51 I *t* you, Nay; but rather division:
59 I *t* thee, thou shalt not depart
13. 3, 5 I *t* you, Nay: but, except ye
27 I *t* you, I know you not whence ye
32 Go ye, and *t* that fox, Behold, I
17.34 I *t* you, in that night there shall
18. 8 I *t* you that he will avenge them
14 I *t* you, this man went down to his
19.40 I *t* you that, if these should hold
20. 2 *T* us, by what authority doest
7 they could not *t* whence it was.
8 Neither *t* I you by what authority
22.34 I *t* thee, Peter, the cock shall not
67 Art thou the Christ? *t* us. And he
67 them, If I *t* you, ye will not believe:
Jn 3. 8 but canst not *t* whence it cometh,
12 if I *t* you of heavenly things?
4.25 he is come, he will *t* us all things.
8.14 but ye cannot *t* whence I come,
45 And because I *t* you the truth, ye
10.24 If thou be the Christ, *t* us plainly.
12.22 again Andrew and Philip *t* Jesus.
13.19 Now I *t* you before it come, that,
16. 7 Nevertheless I *t* you the truth; It is
18 while? we cannot *t* what he saith.
18.34 or did others *t* it thee of me?
20.15 *t* me where thou hast laid him, and
Ac 5. 8 *T* me whether ye sold the land for
10. 6 *t* thee what thou oughtest to do.
11.14 Who shall *t* thee words, whereby
15.27 *t* you the same things by mouth.
17.21 either to *t*, or to hear some new
22.27 him, *T* me, art thou a Roman?
23.17 he hath a certain thing to *t* him.
19 him, What is that thou hast to *t* me?
22 *t* no man that thou hast shewed
2Co 12. 2 (whether in the body, I cannot *t*;
2 whether out of the body, I cannot *t*:
3 or out of the body, I cannot *t*:
Gal 4.16 enemy, because I *t* you the truth?
21 *T* me, ye that desire to be under
5.21 of the which I *t* you before, as I
Php 3.18 and now *t* you even weeping, that
Heb 11.32 time would fail me to *t* of Gedeon,
Rev 17. 7 *t* thee the mystery of the woman,

TELLEST

Ps 56. 8 Thou *t* my wanderings: put thou

TELLETH

2Sa 7.11 Also the Lord *t* thee that he will
2Ki 6.12 *t* the king of Israel the words that
Ps 41. 6 when he goeth abroad, he *t* it.
101. 7 he that *t* lies shall not tarry in my
147. 4 He *t* the number of the stars; he
Jer 33.13 the hands of him that *t* them,
Jn 12.22 Philip cometh and *t* Andrew: and

TELLING

Jdg 7.15 Gideon heard the *t* of the dream,
2Sa 11.19 an end of *t* the matters of the war
2Ki 8. 5 as he was *t* the king how he had

TEMPERANCE

Ac 24.25 as he reasoned of righteousness, *t*,
Gal 5.23 Meekness, *t*: against such there is
2Pe 1. 6 And to knowledge *t*; and to
6 and to *t* patience; and to patience

TEMPERATE

1Co 9.25 for the mastery is *t* in all things.
Tit 1. 8 of good men, sober, just, holy, *t*;
2. 2 the aged men be sober, grave, *t*,

TEMPERED

Ex 29. 2 and cakes unleavened *t* with oil,
30.35 *t* together, pure and holy:
1Co 12.24 but God hath *t* the body together,

TEMPEST

Job 9.17 For he breaketh me with a *t*, and
27.20 *t* stealeth him away in the night.
Ps 11. 6 and brimstone, and an horrible *t*:
55. 8 from the windy storm and *t*.
83.15 So persecute them with thy *t*, and
Isa 28. 2 strong one, which as a *t* of hail
29. 6 and great noise, with storm and *t*,
30.30 scattering, and *t*, and hailstones.
32. 2 the wind, and a covert from the *t*;
54.11 O thou afflicted, tossed with *t*, and
Am 1.14 a *t* in the day of the whirlwind:
Jon 1. 4 there was a mighty *t* in the sea,
12 my sake this great *t* is upon you.
Mt 8.24 there arose a great *t* in the sea,
Ac 27.18 being exceedingly tossed with a *t*,
20 and no small *t* lay on us, all hope
Heb 12.18 blackness, and darkness, and *t*,
2Pe 2.17 clouds that are carried with a *t*;

TEMPESTUOUS

Ps 50. 3 it shall be very *t* round about him.
Jon 1.11 for the sea wrought, and was *t*.
13 wrought, and was *t* against them.
Ac 27.14 there arose against it a *t* wind,

TEMPLE

1Sa 3. 3 lamp...went out in the *t* of the Lord,
2Sa 22. 7 he did hear my voice out of his *t*,
1Ch 10.10 fastened his head in...*t* of Dagon.
Ezr 4. 1 builded the *t* unto the Lord God
Neh 6.10 in the house of God, within the *t*,
10 and let us shut the doors of the *t*:
11 go into the *t* to save his life?
Ps 5. 7 will I worship toward thy holy *t*.
11. 4 The Lord is in his holy *t*, the Lord's
27. 4 of the Lord, and to inquire in his *t*.
65. 4 of thy house, even of thy holy *t*.
138. 2 I will worship toward thy holy *t*,
Isa 6. 1 lifted up, and his train filled the *t*.
66. 6 a voice from the *t*, a voice of the
Jer 7. 4 words, saying, The *t* of the Lord,
Dan 5. 3 out of the *t* of the house of God
Am 8. 3 songs of the *t* shall be howlings
Jon 2. 4 I will look again toward thy holy *t*.
Mic 1. 2 you, the Lord from his holy *t*.
Hab 2.20 But the Lord is in his holy *t*: let all
Hag 2.18 foundation of the Lord's *t* was laid,
Zec 6.12 he shall build the *t* of the Lord:
Mal 3. 1 seek, shall suddenly come to his *t*,
Mt 4. 5 setteth him on a pinnacle of the *t*,
12. 5 priests in the *t* profane...sabbath,
6 this place is one greater than the *t*.
21.12 And Jesus went into the *t* of God,
12 them that sold and bought in the *t*,
14 and the lame came to him in the *t*;
15 and the children crying in the *t*,
23 And when he was come into the *t*,
23.16 Whosoever shall swear by the *t*,
16 shall swear by the gold of the *t*,
17 or the *t* that sanctifieth the gold?
21 And whoso shall swear by the *t*,
35 slew between the *t* and the altar.
24. 1 out, and departed from the *t*:
1 to shew him the buildings of the *t*.
26.55 daily with you teaching in the *t*,
61 I am able to destroy the *t* of God,
27. 5 down the pieces of silver in the *t*.
40 Thou that destroyest the *t*, and
51 the veil of the *t* was rent in twain
Mk 11.11 into Jerusalem, and into the *t*:
15 Jesus went into the *t*, and began to
15 them that sold and bought in the *t*,
16 carry any vessel through the *t*.
27 as he was walking in the *t*, there
12.35 and said, while he taught in the *t*,
13. 1 as he went out of the *t*, one of his
3 mount of Olives over against the *t*,
14.49 daily with you in the *t* teaching,
58 destroy this *t*...made with hands,
15.29 Ah, thou that destroyest the *t*,
38 the veil of the *t* was rent in twain
Lk 1. 9 when he went into the *t* of the Lord.
21 that he tarried so long in the *t*.
22 that he had seen a vision in the *t*:
2.27 he came by the Spirit into the *t*:
37 which departed not from the *t*, but
46 three days they found him in the *t*,
4. 9 and set him on a pinnacle of the *t*,
11.51 between the altar and the *t*:
18.10 men went up into the *t* to pray;
19.45 And he went into the *t*, and began
47 And he taught daily in the *t*. But
20. 1 as he taught the people in the *t*,
21. 5 And as some spake of the *t*, how
37 day time he was teaching in the *t*;
38 in the morning to him in the *t*,
22.52 chief priests, and captains of the *t*,

53 When I was daily with you in the *t*,
23.45 veil of the *t* was rent in the midst.
24.53 And were continually in the *t*,
Jn 2.14 found in the *t* those that sold oxen
15 he drove them all out of the *t*,
19 Destroy this *t*, and in three days
20 six years was this *t* in building,
21 But he spake of the *t* of his body.
5.14 Jesus findeth him in the *t*, and
7.14 the feast Jesus went up into the *t*,
28 cried Jesus in the *t* as he taught,
8. 2 morning he came again into the *t*,
20 the treasury, as he taught in the *t*:
59 hid himself, and went out of the *t*,
10.23 Jesus walked in the *t* in Solomon's
11.56 themselves, as they stood in the *t*,
18.20 in the synagogue, and in the *t*,
Ac 2.46 daily with one accord in the *t*,
3. 1 John went up together into the *t*
2 gate of the *t*...is called Beautiful,
2 alms of them that entered...the *t*;
3 and John about to go into the *t*
8 and entered with them into the *t*,
10 alms at the Beautiful gate of the *t*:
4. 1 priests, and the captain of the *t*,
5.20 and speak in the *t* to the people
21 into the *t* early in the morning,
24 the captain of the *t* and the chief
25 put in prison are standing in the *t*,
42 daily in the *t*, and in every house,
19.27 the *t* of the great goddess Diana
21.26 with them entered into the *t*,
27 Asia, when they saw him in the *t*,
28 brought Greeks also into the *t*,
29 that Paul had brought into the *t*.)
30 Paul, and drew him out of the *t*:
22.17 while I prayed in the *t*, I was in a
24. 6 hath gone about to profane the *t*:
12 And they neither found me in the *t*
18 Asia found me purified in the *t*,
25. 8 neither against the *t*, nor yet
26.21 the Jews caught me in the *t*,
1Co 3.16 ye not that ye are the *t* of God,
17 If any man defile the *t* of God,
17 destroy; for the *t* of God is holy,
17 of God is holy, which *t* ye are.
6.19 body is the *t* of the Holy Ghost
8.10 knowledge sit at meat in the idol's *t*,
9.13 things live of the things of the *t*?
2Co 6.16 hath the *t* of God with idols?
16 for ye are the *t* of the living God;
Eph 2.21 groweth unto an holy *t* in the Lord:
2Th 2. 4 he as God sitteth in the *t* of God,
Rev 3.12 I make a pillar in the *t* of my God,
7.15 serve him day and night in his *t*:
11. 1 Rise, and measure the *t* of God,
2 the court which is without the *t*
19 the *t* of God was opened in heaven,
19 was seen in his *t* the ark of his
14.15 another angel came out of the *t*,
17 another angel came out of the *t*
15. 5 *t* of the tabernacle of the testimony
6 the seven angels came out of the *t*,
8 And the *t* was filled with smoke
8 no man was able to enter into the *t*,
16. 1 I heard a great voice out of the *t*
17 great voice out of the *t* of heaven,
21.22 I saw no *t* therein: for the Lord
22 and the Lamb are the *t* of it.

TEMPLES

Jdg 4.21 and smote the nail into his *t*, and
22 lay dead, and the nail was in his *t*.
5.26 pierced and stricken through his *t*.
SS 4. 3 *t* are like a piece of a pomegranate
6. 7 a piece of a pomegranate are thy *t*
Hos 8.14 his Maker, and buildeth *t*;
Joel 3. 5 have carried into your *t* my goodly
Ac 7.48 dwelleth not in *t* made with
17.24 dwelleth not in *t* made with hands;

Jesus drives the money changers out of the temple in this painting by Johann Platzer (1704-61).

TEMPORAL

2Co 4.18 the things which are seen are *t*;

TEMPT

Gen 22. 1 things, that God did *t* Abraham,
Ex 17. 2 me? wherefore do ye *t* the Lord?
Dt 6.16 Ye shall not *t* the Lord your God,
Isa 7.12 not ask, neither will I *t* the Lord.
Mal 3.15 that *t* God are even delivered.
Mt 4. 7 shalt not *t* the Lord thy God.
22.18 said, Why *t* ye me, ye hypocrites?
Mk 12.15 said unto them, Why *t* ye me?
Lk 4.12 shalt not *t* the Lord thy God.
20.23 and said unto them, Why *t* ye me?
Ac 5. 9 to *t* the Spirit of the Lord?
15.10 Now therefore why *t* ye God, to
1Co 7. 5 *t* you not for your incontinency.
10. 9 Neither let us *t* Christ, as some of

TEMPTATION

Ps 95. 8 in the day of *t* in the wilderness:
Mt 6.13 lead us not into *t*, but deliver
26.41 and pray, that ye enter not into *t*:
Mk 14.38 ye and pray, lest ye enter into *t*.
Lk 4.13 when the devil had ended all the *t*,
8.13 believe, and in time of *t* fall away.
11. 4 lead us not into *t*; but deliver
22.40 Pray that ye enter not into *t*.
46 rise and pray, lest ye enter into *t*.
1Co 10.13 There hath no *t* taken you but such
13 with the *t*...make a way to escape,
Gal 4.14 And my *t* which was in my flesh ye
1Ti 6. 9 will be rich fall into *t* and a snare,
Heb 3. 8 in the day of *t* in the wilderness:
Jas 1.12 is the man that endureth *t*:
Rev 3.10 will keep thee from the hour of *t*,
(See box on page 742)

TEMPTATIONS

Dt 4.34 by *t*, by signs, and by wonders,
7.19 The great *t* which thine eyes saw,
29. 3 The great *t* which thine eyes have
Lk 22.28 have continued with me in my *t*.
Ac 20.19 and *t*, which befell me by the lying
Jas 1. 2 all joy when ye fall into divers *t*;
1Pe 1. 6 in heaviness through manifold *t*:
2Pe 2. 9 how to deliver the godly out of *t*,

TEMPTED

Ex 17. 7 because they *t* the Lord, saying,
Nu 14.22 and have *t* me now these ten times,
Dt 6.16 your God, as ye *t* him in Massah.
Ps 78.18 they *t* God in their heart by asking
41 they turned back and *t* God, and
56 they *t* and provoked the most high
95. 9 When your fathers *t* me, proved me,
106.14 wilderness, and *t* God in the desert.
Mt 4. 1 wilderness to be *t* of the devil.
Mk 1.13 wilderness forty days, *t* of Satan;
Lk 4. 2 Being forty days *t* of the devil.
10.25 lawyer stood up, and *t* him,
1Co 10. 9 as some of them also *t*, and were
13 not suffer you to be *t* above that ye
Gal 6. 1 thyself, lest thou also be *t*.
1Th 3. 5 means the tempter have *t* you,
Heb 2.18 he himself hath suffered being *t*,
18 is able to succor them that are *t*.
3. 9 When your fathers *t* me, proved
4.15 was in all points *t* like as we are,
11.37 they were sawn asunder, were *t*,
Jas 1.13 say when he is *t*, I am *t* of God:
13 for God cannot be *t* with evil,
14 every man is *t*, when he is drawn

TEMPTER

Mt 4. 3 And when the *t* came to him, he
1Th 3. 5 means the *t* have tempted you,

TEMPTETH

Jas 1.13 with evil, neither *t* he any man:

TEMPTING

Mt 16. 1 and *t* desired him that he would
19. 3 came unto him, *t* him, and saying
22.35 asked him a question, *t* him,
Mk 8.11 of him a sign from heaven, *t* him.
10. 2 a man to put away his wife? *t* him.
Lk 11.16 others, *t* him, sought of him a sign
Jn 8. 6 This they said, *t* him, that they

TEN

Gen 18.32 Peradventure *t* shall be found
Lev 26. 8 you shall put *t* thousand to flight:
Nu 11.32 gathered least gathered *t* homers:

Biblical Themes

TEMPTATION

Of the fruit of the tree which is in the midst of the garden, God hath said, Ye shall not eat of it, neither shall ye touch it, lest ye die. And the serpent said unto the woman, Ye shall not surely die. . . . ye shall be as gods, knowing good and evil. Gen 3.3-5

The people did chide with Moses, and said, Give us water that we may drink. And Moses said unto them, Why chide ye with me? wherefore do ye tempt the Lord? Ex 17.2

The graven images of their gods shall ye burn with fire: thou shalt not desire the silver or gold that is on them, nor take it unto thee, lest thou be snared therein. Dt 7.25

So went Satan forth from the presence of the Lord, and smote Job with sore boils. . . . Then said his wife unto him, Dost thou still retain thine integrity? curse God, and die. But he said unto her, . . . What? shall we receive good at the hand of God, and shall we not receive evil? Job 2.7, 9-10

Harden not your heart, as in the provocation, and as in the day of temptation in the wilderness: when your fathers tempted me, proved me, and saw my work. Ps 95.8-9

My son, if sinners entice thee, consent thou not. If they say, Come with us . . . cast in thy lot among us . . . walk not thou in the way with them; refrain thy foot from their path. Pr 1.10-11, 14-15

Discretion shall preserve thee, understanding shall keep thee: to deliver thee from the way of the evil man . . . to deliver thee from the strange woman . . . which flattereth with her words. Pr 2.11-12, 16

Can a man take fire in his bosom, and his clothes not be burned? Pr 6.27

Ye have heard that it was said by them of old time, Thou shalt not commit adultery: but I say unto you, That whosoever looketh on a woman to lust after her hath committed adultery with her already in his heart. Mt 5.27-28

Lead us not into temptation, but deliver us from evil. Mt 6.13

The Pharisees came forth, and began to question with him, seeking of him a sign from heaven, tempting him. Mk 8.11

Jesus . . . was led by the Spirit into the wilderness, being forty days tempted of the devil. . . . And Jesus answered and said unto him, Get thee behind me, Satan. Lk 4.1-2, 8

Let not sin therefore reign in your mortal body, that ye should obey it in the lusts thereof. Ro 6.12

There hath no temptation taken you but such as is common to man: but God is faithful, who will not suffer you to be tempted above that ye are able; but will with the temptation also make a way to escape, that ye may be able to bear it. 1Co 10.13

We have not an high priest which cannot be touched with the feeling of our infirmities; but was in all points tempted like as we are, yet without sin. Heb 4.15

Let no man say when he is tempted, I am tempted of God: for God cannot be tempted with evil, neither tempteth he any man: but every man is tempted, when he is drawn away of his own lust, and enticed. Jas 1.13-14

Because thou hast kept the word of my patience, I also will keep thee from the hour of temptation, which shall come upon all the world, to try them that dwell upon the earth. Rev 3.10

Dt 10. 4 the *t* commandments, which the
22 Egypt with threescore and *t* persons;
1Sa 1. 8 am not I better to thee than *t* sons?
2Sa 19.43 We have *t* parts in the king, and
2Ki 20. 9 the shadow go forward *t* degrees,
10 shadow return backward *t* degrees.
2Ch 14. 1 his days the land was quiet *t* years.
Est 9.14 and they hanged Haman's *t* sons.
Job 19. 3 *t* times have ye reproached me: ye
Ps 33. 2 and an instrument of *t* strings.
90.10 our years are threescore years and *t*;
91. 7 and *t* thousand at thy right hand;
92. 3 Upon an instrument of *t* strings,
144. 9 instrument of *t* strings will I sing
SS 5.10 the chiefest among *t* thousand.
Isa 38. 8 So the sun returned *t* degrees, by
Mic 6. 7 with *t* thousands of rivers of oil?
Zec 8.23 *t* men shall take hold out of all
Mt 18.24 owed him *t* thousand talents.
20.24 the *t* heard it, they were moved
25. 1 of heaven be likened unto *t* virgins,
28 it unto him which hath *t* talents.
Mk 10.41 when the *t* heard it, they began to
Lk 14.31 able with *t* thousand to meet him
15. 8 woman having *t* pieces of silver,
17.12 met him *t* men that were lepers,
17 said, Were there not *t* cleansed?
19.13 And he called his *t* servants, and
13 and delivered them *t* pounds, and
16 thy pound hath gained *t* pounds.
17 have thou authority over *t* cities.
24 give it to him that hath *t* pounds.
25 unto him, Lord, he hath *t* pounds.)
Ac 23.23 and horsemen threescore and *t*,
25. 6 among them more than *t* days,
1Co 4.15 ye have *t* thousand instructers in
14.19 *t* thousand words in an unknown
Jude 14 with *t* thousands of his saints,
Rev 2.10 ye shall have tribulation *t* days:
5.11 was *t* thousand times *t* thousand,
12. 3 having seven heads and *t* horns,
13. 1 having seven heads and *t* horns,
1 and upon his horns *t* crowns, and
17. 3 having seven heads and *t* horns.
7 hath the seven heads and *t* horns.
12 *t* horns...thou sawest are *t* kings,
16 the *t* horns which thou sawest

TENDER

Gen 18. 7 and fetcht a calf *t* and good, and
29.17 Leah was *t* eyed; but Rachel was
33.13 knoweth that the children are *t*,
Dt 28.54 that the man that is *t* among you,
56 The *t* and delicate woman among
32. 2 as the small rain upon the *t* herb, and
2Sa 23. 4 *t* grass springing out of the earth
2Ki 22.19 Because thine heart was *t*, and
1Ch 22. 5 Solomon my son is young and *t*,
29. 1 Solomon...is yet young and *t*,
2Ch 34.27 Because thine heart was *t*, and
Job 14. 7 *t* branch thereof will not cease.
38.27 the bud of the *t* herb to spring forth?
Ps 25. 6 Remember, O Lord, thy *t* mercies
40.11 Withhold not thou thy *t* mercies
51. 1 unto the multitude of thy *t* mercies
69.16 to the multitude of thy *t* mercies.
77. 9 he in anger shut up his *t* mercies?
79. 8 let thy *t* mercies speedily prevent us:
103. 4 with lovingkindness and *t* mercies;
119.77 Let thy *t* mercies come unto me, that
156 Great are thy *t* mercies, O Lord:
145. 9 his *t* mercies are over all his works.
Pr 4. 3 *t* and only beloved in the sight of
12.10 the *t* mercies of the wicked are cruel.
27.25 and the *t* grass sheweth itself, and
SS 2.13 with the *t* grape give a good smell.
15 vines: for our vines have *t* grapes.
7.12 whether the *t* grape appear,
Isa 47. 1 thou shalt no more be called *t* and
53. 2 grow up before him as a *t* plant,
Eze 17.22 the top of his young twigs a *t* one,
Dan 1. 9 Daniel into favor and *t* love
4.15, 23 brass, in the *t* grass of the field;
Mt 24.32 When his branch is yet *t*, and
Mk 13.28 When her branch is yet *t*, and
Lk 1.78 Through the *t* mercy of our God;
Jas 5.11 is very pitiful, and of *t* mercy.

TENDERHEARTED

2Ch 13. 7 Rehoboam was young and *t*,
Eph 4.32 *t*, forgiving one another, even as

TENDETH

Pr 10.16 The labor of the righteous *t* to life:
11.19 As righteousness *t* to life: so he that
24 more than is meet, but it *t* to poverty.
14.23 the talk of the lips *t* only to penury.
19.23 The fear of the Lord *t* to life: and he

TENOR

Gen 43. 7 according to the *t* of these words:
Ex 34.27 for after the *t* of these words I have

TEN'S

Gen 18.32 I will not destroy it for *t* sake.

TENS

Ex 18.21 rulers of fifties, and rulers of *t*:
25 rulers of fifties, and rulers of *t*.
Dt 1.15 over fifties, and captains over *t*,

TENT

Gen 18. 2 he ran to meet them from the *t* door,
Jdg 4.21 Heber's wife took a nail of the *t*,

1Ch 15. 1 ark of God, and pitched for it a *t*.
Ps 78.60 the *t* which he placed among men;
Isa 40.22 them out as a *t* to dwell in:
Jer 37.10 they rise up every man in his *t*,

TENTH

Gen 28.22 I will surely give the *t* unto thee.
Nu 18.26 Lord, even a *t* part of the tithe.
Jn 1.39 day: for it was about the *t* hour.
Heb 7. 2 also Abraham gave a *t* part of all;
4 Abraham gave the *t* of the spoils.
Rev 11.13 and the *t* part of the city fell, and
21.20 a topaz; the *t*, a chrysoprasus;

TENTMAKERS

Ac 18. 3 by their occupation they were *t*.

TENTS

Gen 4.20 the father of such as dwell in *t*,
25.27 was a plain man, dwelling in *t*.
Nu 24. 5 How goodly are thy *t*, O Jacob,
2Sa 20. 1 every man to his *t*, O Israel.
1Ki 12.16 to your *t*, O Israel: now see to thine
Ezr 8.15 there abode we in *t* three days:
Ps 120. 5 that I dwell in the *t* of Kedar!
Jer 35. 7 but all your days ye shall dwell in *t*;
Hab 3. 7 I saw the *t* of Cushan in affliction:

TERAPHIM

Jdg 17. 5 and made an ephod, and *t*, and
18.14 is in these houses an ephod, and *t*,
17 image, and the ephod, and the *t*,

Jesus' temptation in the wilderness is shown in this 12th-century sculpture by Gislebertus of Autun.

18 carved image, the ephod, and the *t*,
20 and he took the ephod, and the *t*,
Hos 3. 4 without an ephod, and without *t*:

TERMED

Isa 62. 4 Thou shalt no more be *t* Forsaken;
4 thy land any more be *t* Desolate:

TERRESTRIAL

1Co 15.40 also celestial bodies, and bodies *t*:
40 and the glory of the *t* is another.

TERRIBLE

Ex 34.10 for it is a *t* thing that I will do
Dt 1.19 all that great and *t* wilderness,
7.21 is among you, a mighty God and *t*.
8.15 through...great and *t* wilderness,
10.17 a great God, a mighty, and a *t*,
21 for thee these great and *t* things,
Jdg 13. 6 of an angel of God, very *t*:
2Sa 7.23 to do for you great things and *t*,
Neh 1. 5 of heaven, the great and *t* God,
4.14 the Lord, which is great and *t*,
9.32 great, the mighty, and the *t* God,
Job 37.22 the north: with God is *t* majesty.
39.20 the glory of his nostrils is *t*.
41.14 face? his teeth are *t* round about.
Ps 45. 4 hand shall teach thee *t* things.
47. 2 For the Lord most high is *t*; he is
65. 5 By *t* things in righteousness wilt
66. 3 God, How *t* art thou in thy works!
5 he is *t* in his doing toward the
68.35 O God, thou art *t* out of thy holy
76.12 he is *t* to the kings of the earth.
99. 3 them praise thy great and *t* name;
106.22 Ham, and *t* things by the Red sea.
145. 6 speak of the might of thy *t* acts:
SS 6. 4 *t* as an army with banners.
10 and *t* as an army with banners?
Isa 13.11 lay low the haughtiness of the *t*.
18. 2 to a people *t* from their beginning
7 to a people *t* from their beginning
21. 1 from the desert, from a *t* land.
25. 3 the city of the *t* nations shall fear
4 the blast of the *t* ones is as a storm
5 the branch of the *t* ones shall be
29. 5 multitude of the *t* ones shall be as
20 For the *t* one is brought to nought,
49.25 the prey of the *t* shall be delivered:
64. 3 When thou didst *t* things which we
Jer 15.21 thee out of the hand of the *t*.
20.11 Lord is with me as a mighty *t* one:
La 5.10 an oven because of the *t* famine.
Eze 1.22 was as the color of the *t* crystal,
28. 7 upon thee, the *t* of the nations:
30.11 with him, the *t* of the nations,
31.12 the *t* of the nations, have cut him
32.12 the *t* of the nations, all of them:
Dan 2.31 thee; and the form thereof was *t*.
7. 7 a fourth beast, dreadful and *t*,
Joel 2.11 day of the Lord is great and very *t*;
31 the great and the *t* day of the Lord
Hab 1. 7 They are *t* and dreadful: their
Zep 2.11 The Lord will be *t* unto them:
Heb 12.21 so *t* was the sight, that Moses

TERRIBLENESS

Dt 26. 8 and with great *t*, and with signs,
1Ch 17.21 thee a name of greatness and *t*,
Jer 49.16 Thy *t* hath deceived thee, and the

TERRIBLY

Isa 2.19, 21 he ariseth to shake *t* the earth.
Na 2. 3 and the fir trees shall be *t* shaken.

TERRIFIED

Dt 20. 3 neither be ye *t* because of them;
Lk 21. 9 of wars and commotions, be not *t*:
24.37 But they were *t* and affrighted,
Php 1.28 in nothing *t* by your adversaries:

TERRIFIEST

Job 7.14 dreams, and *t* me through visions:

TERRIFY

Job 3. 5 let the blackness of the day *t* it.
9.34 from me, and let not his fear *t* me:
31.34 the contempt of families *t* me,
2Co 10. 9 seem as if I would *t* you by letters.

TERROR

Gen 35. 5 the *t* of God was upon the cities
Lev 26.16 I will even appoint over you *t*,
Dt 32.25 The sword without, and *t* within,
34.12 the great *t* which Moses shewed
Jos 2. 9 and that your *t* is fallen upon us,
Job 31.23 destruction from God was a *t* to
33. 7 my *t* shall not make thee afraid,
Ps 91. 5 not be afraid for the *t* by night;
Isa 10.33 hosts, shall lop the bough with *t*:
19.17 of Judah shall be a *t* unto Egypt,
33.18 Thine heart shall meditate *t*.
54.14 and from *t*; for it shall not come
Jer 17.17 Be not a *t* unto me: thou art my
20. 4 I will make thee a *t* to thyself,
32.21 strong hand,...and with great *t*;
Eze 26.17 which cause their *t* to be on all
21 I will make thee a *t*, and thou
27.36 thou shalt be a *t*, and never shalt
28.19 thou shalt be a *t*, and never shalt
32.23 which caused *t* in the land of the
24 which caused their *t* in the land of
25 their *t* was caused in the land of

Eze 32.26 they caused their *t* in the land of
27 the *t* of the mighty in the land of
30 with their *t* they are ashamed of
32 I have caused my *t* in the land of
Ro 13. 3 rulers are not a *t* to good works,
2Co 5.11 Knowing...the *t* of the Lord, we
1Pe 3.14 be not afraid of their *t*, neither be

TERRORS
Dt 4.34 stretched out arm, and by great *t*,
Job 6. 4 *t* of God do set themselves in
18.11 *T* shall make him afraid on every
14 shall bring him to the king of *t*.
20.25 out of his gall: *t* are upon him.
24.17 in the *t* of the shadow of death.
27.20 *T* take hold on him as waters, a
30.15 *T* are turned upon me: they
Ps 55. 4 the *t* of death are fallen upon me.
73.19 they are utterly consumed with *t*.
88.15 while I suffer thy *t* I am distracted.
16 over me; thy *t* have cut me off.
Jer 15. 8 it suddenly, and *t* upon the city.
La 2.22 a solemn day my *t* round about,
Eze 21.12 *t* by reason of the sword shall be

TERTIUS
Ro 16.22 I *T*, who wrote this epistle,

TERTULLUS
Ac 24. 1 with a certain orator named *T*,
2 *T* began to accuse him, saying,

TESTAMENT
Mt 26.28 For this is my blood of the new *t*,
Mk 14.24 This is my blood of the new *t*,
Lk 22.20 This cup is the new *t* in my blood,
1Co 11.25 This cup is the new *t* in my blood:
2Co 3. 6 us able ministers of the new *t*;
14 away in the reading of the old *t*;
Heb 7.22 Jesus made a surety of a better *t*.
9.15 he is the mediator of the new *t*,
15 that were under the first *t*,
16 For where a *t* is, there must also
17 For a *t* is of force after men are
18 Whereupon neither the first *t* was
20 This is the blood of the *t* which
Rev 11.19 seen in his temple the ark of his *t*:

TESTATOR
Heb 9.16 necessity be the death of the *t*.
17 strength at all while the *t* liveth.

TESTIFIED
Ex 21.29 and it hath been *t* to his owner,
Dt 19.18 hath *t* falsely against his brother;
Ru 1.21 seeing the Lord hath *t* against me,
2Sa 1.16 for thy mouth hath *t* against thee,
2Ki 17.13 Yet the Lord *t* against Israel, and
15 his testimonies which he *t* against
2Ch 24.19 Lord; and they *t* against them:
Neh 9.26 slew thy prophets which *t* against
13.15 and I *t* against them in the day
21 Then I *t* against them, and said
Jn 4.39 the saying of the woman, which *t*,
44 For Jesus himself *t*, that a prophet
13.21 he was troubled in spirit, and *t*,
Ac 8.25 they had *t* and preached the word
18. 5 *t* to the Jews that Jesus was
23.11 as thou hast *t* of me in Jerusalem,
28.23 and *t* the kingdom of God,
1Co 15.15 we have *t* of God that he raised
1Th 4. 6 also have forewarned you and *t*.
1Ti 2. 6 ransom for all, to be *t* in due time.
Heb 2. 6 But one in a certain place *t*,
1Pe 1.11 it *t* beforehand the sufferings of
1Jn 5. 9 God which he hath *t* of his Son.
3Jn 3 and *t* of the truth that is in thee,

TESTIFIETH
Hos 7.10 the pride of Israel *t* to his face:
Jn 3.32 hath seen and heard, that he *t*;
21.24 disciple which *t* of these things,
Heb 7.17 For he *t*, Thou art a priest for ever
Rev 22.20 He which *t* these things saith,

TESTIFY
Nu 35.30 one witness shall not *t* against
Dt 8.19 I *t* against you this day that ye
19.16 to *t* against him that which is
31.21 this song shall *t* against them as a
32.46 words which I *t* among you this
Neh 9.34 thou didst *t* against them.
Job 15. 6 yea, thine own lips *t* against thee.
Ps 50. 7 Israel, and I will *t* against thee:
81. 8 my people, and I will *t* unto thee:
Isa 59.12 thee, and our sins *t* against us:
Jer 14. 7 though our iniquities *t* against us,
Hos 5. 5 pride of Israel doth *t* to his face:
Am 3.13 and *t* in the house of Jacob, saith
Mic 6. 3 I wearied thee? *t* against me.
Lk 16.28 that he may *t* unto them, lest
Jn 2.25 not that any should *t* of man;
3.11 know, and *t* that we have seen;
5.39 and they are they which *t* of me.
7. 7 me it hateth, because I *t* of it,
15.26 from the Father, he shall *t* of me:
Ac 2.40 other words did he *t* and exhort,
10.42 to *t* that it is he which was
20.24 to *t* the gospel of the grace of God.
26. 5 if they would *t*, that after the
Gal 5. 3 For I *t* again to every man that is
Eph 4.17 *t* in the Lord, that ye henceforth
1Jn 4.14 and do *t* that the Father sent the
Rev 22.16 sent mine angel to *t* unto you
18 I *t* unto every man that heareth

TESTIFYING
Ac 20.21 *T* both to the Jews, and also to
Heb 11. 4 was righteous, God *t* of his gifts:
1Pe 5.12 and *t* that this is the true grace

TESTIMONIES
Dt 4.45 These are the *t*, and the statutes,
6.17 his *t*, and his statutes, which he
20 What mean the *t*, and the statutes,
1Ki 2. 3 his judgments, and his *t*, as it is
2Ki 17.15 his *t* which he testified against
23. 3 keep his commandments and his *t*
1Ch 29.19 keep thy commandments, thy *t*,
2Ch 34.31 keep his commandments, and his *t*,
Neh 9.34 thy commandments and thy *t*,
Ps 25.10 as keep his covenant and his *t*.
78.56 high God, and kept not his *t*:
93. 5 Thy *t* are very sure: holiness
99. 7 they kept his *t*, and the ordinance
119. 2 Blessed are they that keep his *t*,
14 have rejoiced in the way of thy *t*,
22 contempt; for I have kept thy *t*.
24 Thy *t* also are my delight and my
31 I have stuck unto thy *t*: O Lord,
36 Incline my heart unto thy *t*, and
46 I will speak of thy *t* also before
59 and turned my feet unto thy *t*.
79 and those that have known thy *t*.
95 me: but I will consider thy *t*.
99 for thy *t* are my meditation.
111 Thy *t* have I taken as an heritage
119 dross: therefore I love thy *t*.
125 that I may know thy *t*.
129 Thy *t* are wonderful: therefore
138 Thy *t* that thou hast commanded
144 The righteousness of thy *t* is
146 save me, and I shall keep thy *t*.
152 Concerning thy *t*, I have known of
157 yet do I not decline from thy *t*.
167 My soul hath kept thy *t*; and I
168 I have kept thy precepts and thy *t*:
Jer 44.23 nor in his statutes, nor in his *t*;

TESTIMONY
Ex 16.34 so Aaron laid it up before the *T*,
26.34 mercy seat upon the ark of the *t*
31.18 two tables of *t*, tables of stone,
34.29 the two tables of *t* in Moses' hand,
Nu 1.50 Levites over the tabernacle of *t*,
Ps 19. 7 the *t* of the Lord is sure, making
119.88 so shall I keep the *t* of thy mouth.
132.12 and my *t* that I shall teach them,
Isa 8.16 Bind up the *t*, seal the law among
Mt 8. 4 commanded, for a *t* unto them.
10.18 a *t* against them and the Gentiles.
Mk 1.44 commanded, for a *t* unto them.
6.11 your feet for a *t* against them.
13. 9 for my sake, for a *t* against them.
Lk 5.14 commanded, for a *t* unto them.
9. 5 your feet for a *t* against them.
21.13 And it shall turn to you for a *t*.
Jn 3.32 and no man receiveth his *t*.
33 He that hath received his *t* hath
5.34 But I receive not *t* from man: but
8.17 law, that the *t* of two men is true.
21.24 and we know that his *t* is true.
Ac 13.22 to whom also he gave *t*, and said,
14. 3 which gave *t* unto the word of his
22.18 not receive thy *t* concerning me.
1Co 1. 6 Even as the *t* of Christ was
2. 1 declaring unto you the *t* of God.
2Co 1.12 is this, the *t* of our conscience,
2Th 1.10 our *t* among you was believed)
2Ti 1. 8 ashamed of the *t* of our Lord,
Heb 3. 5 a *t* of those things which were to be
11. 5 had this *t*, that he pleased God.
Rev 1. 2 God, and of the *t* of Jesus Christ,
9 God, and for the *t* of Jesus Christ.
6. 9 God, and for the *t* which they held:
11. 7 they shall have finished their *t*,
12.11 Lamb, and by the word of their *t*;
17 God, and have the *t* of Jesus Christ.
15. 5 the tabernacle of the *t* in heaven
19.10 brethren that have the *t* of Jesus:
10 *t* of Jesus is the spirit of prophecy.

TETRARCH
Mt 14. 1 Herod the *t* heard of the fame of
Lk 3. 1 and Herod being *t* of Galilee, and
1 his brother Philip *t* of Ituraea and
1 and Lysanias the *t* of Abilene,
19 Herod the *t*, being reproved by
9. 7 Herod the *t* heard of all that was
Ac 13. 1 been brought up with Herod the *t*,

THADDAEUS
Mt 10. 3 Lebbaeus, whose surname was *T*;
Mk 3.18 the son of Alphaeus, and *T*, and

THANK
1Ch 16. 4 to *t* and praise the Lord God of
7 first this psalm to *t* the Lord
23.30 morning to *t* and praise the Lord,
29.13 our God, we *t* thee, and praise thy
2Ch 29.31 *t* offerings into the house of the
31 brought...sacrifices and *t* offerings;
33.16 peace offerings and *t* offerings,
Dan 2.23 I *t* thee, and praise thee, O thou
Mt 11.25 and said, I *t* thee, O Father, Lord
Lk 6.32 which love you, what *t* have ye?
33 do good to you, what *t* have ye?
34 ye hope to receive, what *t* have ye?
10.21 and said, I *t* thee, O Father, Lord
17. 9 he *t* that servant because
18.11 God, I *t* thee, that I am not as
Jn 11.41 I *t* thee that thou hast heard me.
Ro 1. 8 I *t* my God through Jesus Christ
7.25 I *t* God through Jesus Christ our
1Co 1. 4 I *t* my God always on your behalf,
14 I *t* God that I baptized none of you,
14.18 I *t* my God, I speak with tongues
Php 1. 3 *t* my God upon every remembrance
1Th 2.13 this cause also *t* we God without
2Th 1. 3 We are bound to *t* God always for
1Ti 1.12 And I *t* Christ Jesus our Lord,
2Ti 1. 3 I *t* God, whom I serve from my
Phm 4 I *t* my God, making mention of

THANKED

2Sa 14.22 bowed himself, and *t* the king:
Ac 28.15 saw, he *t* God, and took courage.
Ro 6.17 But, God be *t*, that ye were the

THANKFUL

Ps 100. 4 be *t* unto him, and bless his name.
Ro 1.21 him not as God, neither were *t*;
Col 3.15 called in one body; and be ye *t*.

THANKFULNESS

Ac 24. 3 most noble Felix, with all *t*.

THANKING

2Ch 5.13 heard in praising and *t* the Lord;

THANKS

1Ch 16. 8 Give *t* unto the Lord, call upon his
34 O give *t* unto the Lord; for he is
Neh 12.24 to praise and to give *t*, according
Ps 6. 5 in the grave who shall give thee *t*?
30.12 I will give *t* unto thee for ever.
35.18 thee *t* in the great congregation:
75. 1 Unto thee, O God, do we give *t*,
92. 1 good thing to give *t* unto the Lord,
105. 1 O give *t* unto the Lord; call upon
136. 2 O give *t* unto the God of gods: for
Dan 6.10 prayed, and gave *t* before his God,
Mt 15.36 and gave *t*, and brake them,
26.27 And he took the cup, and gave *t*,
Mk 8. 6 took the seven loaves, and gave *t*,
14.23 when he had given *t*, he gave it to
Lk 2.38 gave *t* likewise unto the Lord,
17.16 his face at his feet, giving him *t*:
22.17 And he took the cup, and gave *t*,
19 And he took bread, and gave *t*,
Jn 6.11 when he had given *t*, he distributed
23 after that the Lord had given *t*:)
Ac 27.35 gave *t* to God in presence of them
Ro 14. 6 to the Lord, for he giveth God *t*;
6 he eateth not, and giveth God *t*.
16. 4 unto whom not only I give *t*, but
1Co 10.30 of for that for which I give *t*?
11.24 when he had given *t*, he brake it,
14.16 say Amen at thy giving of *t*,
17 thou verily givest *t* well, but the
15.57 But *t* be to God, which giveth us
2Co 1.11 *t* may be given by many on our
2.14 Now *t* be unto God, which always
8.16 But *t* be to God, which put the
9.15 *T* be unto God for his unspeakable
Eph 1.16 Cease not to give *t* for you,
5. 4 convenient: but rather giving of *t*.
20 Giving *t* always for all things
Col 1. 3 We give *t* to God and the Father
12 Giving *t* unto the Father, which
3.17 giving *t* to God and the Father by
1Th 1. 2 We give *t* to God always for you
3. 9 For what *t* can we render to God
5.18 In every thing give *t*: for this is
2Th 2.13 are bound to give *t* alway to God
1Ti 2. 1 intercessions, and giving of *t*,
Heb 13.15 of our lips giving *t* to his name.
Rev 4. 9 *t* to him that sat on the throne,
11.17 We give thee *t*, O Lord God

THANKSGIVING

Lev 7.12 If he offer it for a *t*, then he shall
12 with the sacrifice of *t* unleavened
13 bread with the sacrifice of *t* of his
15 his peace offerings for *t* shall be
22.29 offer a sacrifice of *t* unto the Lord,
Neh 11.17 principal to begin the *t* in prayer:
12. 8 Mattaniah, which was over the *t*,
46 songs of praise and *t* unto God.
Ps 26. 7 may publish with the voice of *t*,
50.14 Offer unto God *t*; and pay thy vows
69.30 song, and will magnify him with *t*.
95. 2 us come before his presence with *t*,
100. 4 Enter into his gates with *t*, and
107.22 them sacrifice the sacrifices of *t*,
116.17 I will offer to thee the sacrifice of *t*,
147. 7 Sing unto the Lord with *t*; sing
Isa 51. 3 gladness shall be found therein, *t*,
Jer 30.19 out of them shall proceed *t* and the
Am 4. 5 offer a sacrifice of *t* with leaven,
Jon 2. 9 unto thee with the voice of *t*;
2Co 4.15 through the *t* of many redound to
9.11 which causeth through us *t* to God.
Php 4. 6 by prayer and supplication with *t*
Col 2. 7 taught, abounding therein with *t*.
4. 2 and watch in the same with *t*;
1Ti 4. 3 to be received with *t* of them which
4 be refused, if it be received with *t*:
Rev 7.12 and wisdom, and *t*, and honor,
(See box on page 746)

THANKSGIVINGS

Neh 12.27 both with *t*, and with singing,
2Co 9.12 also by many *t* unto God;

THANKWORTHY

1Pe 2.19 this is *t*, if a man for conscience

THEATER

Ac 19.29 rushed with one accord into the *t*.
31 not adventure himself into the *t*.

THEFT

Ex 22. 3 then he shall be sold for his *t*.
4 If the *t* be certainly found in his

THEFTS

Mt 15.19 fornications, *t*, false witness,
Mk 7.22 *T*, covetousness, wickedness,
Rev 9.21 of their fornication, nor of their *t*.

THEIRS

Gen 15.13 a stranger in a land that is not *t*,
34.23 and every beast of *t* be ours?

***The title of tetrarch** was conferred by Caesar Augustus on two of King Herod's sons, Herod Antipas and Philip, as part of the political reorganization of the Holy Land following their father's death in 4 B.C. Herod Antipas (called "Herod the tetrarch" in the Gospels) governed Galilee and Perea, while Philip's tetrarchy lay north and east of the Sea of Galilee and included the city rebuilt (and renamed) by him, Caesarea Philippi. A third son of King Herod, Archelaus, ruled as "ethnarch" over Judea, Samaria, and Idumea until A.D. 6, when Augustus deposed him and consolidated the territories as the province of Judea, ruled directly by Roman governors—the third of whom, serving from A.D. 26 to 36, was Pontius Pilate.*

BIBLICAL THEMES

THANKSGIVING

When thou hast eaten and art full, then thou shalt bless the Lord thy God for the good land which he hath given thee. Dt 8.10

And Mordecai wrote these things, and sent letters . . . to stablish this among them, that they should keep . . . the days wherein the Jews rested from their enemies, and the month which was turned unto them from sorrow to joy, and from mourning into a good day: that they should make them days of feasting and joy. . . . and that these days of Purim should not fail from among the Jews, nor the memorial of them perish from their seed. Est 9.20-22, 28

Make a joyful noise unto the Lord, all ye lands. . . . Enter into his gates with thanksgiving, and into his courts with praise: be thankful unto him, and bless his name. For the Lord is good. Ps 100.1, 4-5

Oh that men would praise the Lord for his goodness, and for his wonderful works to the children of men! Ps 107.8

What shall I render unto the Lord for all his benefits toward me? I will take the cup of salvation, and call upon the name of the Lord. Ps 116.12-13

And the shepherds returned, glorifying and praising God for all the things that they had heard and seen. Lk 2.20

And one of them, when he saw that he was healed, turned back, and with a loud voice glorified God, and fell down on his face at his feet, giving him thanks: and he was a Samaritan. And Jesus answering said, Were there not ten cleansed? but where are the nine? Lk 17.15-17

He took bread, and gave thanks, and brake it. Lk 22.19

He that eateth, eateth to the Lord, for he giveth God thanks; and he that eateth not, to the Lord he eateth not, and giveth God thanks. Ro 14.6

What hast thou that thou didst not receive? now if thou didst receive it, why dost thou glory, as if thou hadst not received it? 1Co 4.7

Thanks be to God, which giveth us the victory through our Lord Jesus Christ. 1Co 15.57

Giving thanks always for all things unto God and the Father in the name of our Lord Jesus Christ. Eph 5.20

Continue in prayer, and watch in the same with thanksgiving. Col 4.2

In every thing give thanks: for this is the will of God in Christ Jesus concerning you. 1Th 5.18

Every creature of God is good, and nothing to be refused, if it be received with thanksgiving: for it is sanctified by the word of God and prayer. 1Ti 4.4-5

By him therefore let us offer the sacrifice of praise to God continually, that is, the fruit of our lips giving thanks to his name. Heb 13.15

And when those beasts give glory and honor and thanks to him that sat on the throne, who liveth for ever and ever, the four and twenty elders fall down before him . . . and cast their crowns before the throne, saying, Thou art worthy, O Lord, to receive glory and honor and power: for thou hast created all things, and for thy pleasure they are and were created. Rev 4.9-11

Gen 43.34 was five times so much as any of *t*.
Ex 29. 9 the priest's office shall be *t* for a
Lev 18.10 for *t* is thine own nakedness.
Nu 16.26 and touch nothing of *t*, lest ye be
18. 9 from the fire: every oblation of *t*,
9 every meat offering of *t*, and every
9 and every sin offering of *t*, and
9 every trespass offering of *t*, which
Jos 21.10 Levi, had: for *t* was the first lot.
1Ch 6.54 the Kohathites: for *t* was the lot.
2Ch 18.12 I pray thee, be like one of *t*, and
Jer 44.28 whose words shall stand, mine, or *t*.
Eze 7.11 of their multitude, nor of any of *t*:
44.29 dedicated thing in Israel shall be *t*.
Hab 1. 6 the dwellingplaces that are not *t*.
Mt 5. 3, 10 for *t* is the kingdom of heaven.
1Co 1. 2 Christ our Lord, both *t* and ours:
2Ti 3. 9 manifest unto...men, as *t* also

THEN

Gen 4.26 *t* began men to call upon the name
12. 6 the Canaanite was *t* in the land.
19.24 *T* the Lord rained upon Sodom and
42.34 *t* shall I know that ye are no spies,
Ex 6. 1 *T* the Lord said unto Moses, Now
18.23 *t* thou shalt be able to endure, and all
Lev 26. 4 *T* I will give you rain in due season,
18 *t* I will punish you seven times more
42 *T* will I remember my covenant with
Nu 11.10 *T* Moses heard the people weep
22.31 *T* the Lord opened the eyes of
Dt 6.12 *T* beware lest thou forget the Lord,
8.10 *t* thou shalt bless the Lord thy God
30. 3 That *t* the Lord thy God will turn thy
32.15 *t* he forsook God which made him,
Jos 14.12 *t* I shall be able to drive them out,
Jdg 4. 8 If thou wilt go with me, *t* I will go:
6.21 *T* the angel of the Lord put forth the
11.29 *T* the Spirit of the Lord came upon
1Sa 3.10 *T* Samuel answered, Speak; for thy
12. 8 *t* the Lord sent Moses and Aaron,
26.21 *T* said Saul, I have sinned: return,
28.16 Wherefore *t* dost thou ask of me,
2Sa 15.33 *t* thou shalt be a burden unto me:
1Ki 8.34, 36 *T* hear thou in heaven, and
39 *T* hear thou in heaven thy
20.39 *t* shall thy life be for his life, or else
2Ki 7. 9 *T* they said one to another, We do
2Ch 6.23 *T* hear thou from heaven, and do,
Neh 2.18 *T* I told them of the hand of my God
Est 4. 4 *T* was the queen exceedingly
Job 4.15 *T* a spirit passed before my face; the
7.14 *T* thou scarest me with dreams, and
9.29 If I be wicked, why *t* labor I in vain?
10.14 If I sin, *t* thou markest me, and thou
13.20 *t* will I not hide myself from thee.
22 *T* call thou, and I will answer: or let
22.24 *T* shalt thou lay up gold as dust, and
25. 4 How *t* can man be justified with
29.18 *T* I said, I shall die in my nest, and I
30.26 looked for good, *t* evil came unto
34.29 hideth his face, who *t* can behold
36.18 *t* a great ransom cannot deliver thee.
41.10 up: who *t* is able to stand before me?
Ps 19.13 *t* shall I be upright, and I shall be
27.10 forsake me, *t* the Lord will take me
43. 4 *T* will I go unto the altar of God,
51.13 *T* will I teach transgressors thy ways:
55. 6 for *t* would I fly away, and be at rest.
12 me; *t* I could have borne it:
12 *t* I would have hid myself from him:
67. 6 *T* shall the earth yield her increase;
73.17 of God; *t* understood I their end.
124. 3 *T* they had swallowed us up quick,
4 *T* the waters had overwhelmed us,
126. 2 *T* was our mouth filled with
Pr 11. 2 When pride cometh, *t* cometh
18. 3 cometh, *t* cometh also contempt,
Ec 2.13 *T* I saw that wisdom excelleth folly,
4. 7 *T* I returned, and I saw vanity under
9.16 *T* said I, Wisdom is better than
12. 7 *T* shall the dust return to the earth
Isa 6. 5 *T* said I, Woe is me! for I am
6 *T* flew one of the seraphims unto
8 us? *T* said I, Here am I; send me.
11 *T* said I, Lord, how long? And he
40.18 To whom *t* will ye liken God? or
44.15 *T* shall it be for a man to burn: for he
49. 4 *T* I said, I have labored in vain, I
58. 8 *T* shall thy light break forth as
Jer 18. 3 *T* I went down to the potter's house,
25.17 *T* took I the cup at the Lord's hand,
36.10 *T* read Baruch in the book the words
Eze 3.12 *T* the spirit took me up, and I heard
6.13 *T* shall ye know that I am the Lord,
8. 5, 8, 12 *T* said he unto me, Son of man,
10. 4 *T* the glory of the Lord went up from
Dan 10. 9 *t* was I in a deep sleep on my face,
12 *T* said he unto me, Fear not, Daniel:
Hos 11. 1 Israel was a child, *t* I loved him, and
Am 6.10 *T* shall he say, Hold thy tongue: for
7. 2 *t* I said, O Lord God, forgive, I
Jon 1. 5 *T* the mariners were afraid, and
2. 1 *T* Jonah prayed unto the Lord his
Zec 1. 9 *T* said I, O my Lord, what are these?
7. 4 *T* came the word of the Lord of hosts
Mt 2. 7 *T* Herod, when he had privily
3.13 *T* cometh Jesus from Galilee to
4. 1 *T* was Jesus led up of the spirit
5.24 and *t* come and offer thy gift.
7.23 *t* will I profess unto them, I never
12.12 How much *t* is a man better than
28 *t* the kingdom of God is come
17.26 unto him, *T* are the children free.
19.25 saying, Who *t* can be saved?
22.43 How *t* doth David in spirit call
24.14 nations; and *t* shall the end come.
25.34 *T* shall the King say unto them on

27.22 What shall I do *t* with Jesus
26 *T* released he Barabbas unto
Mk 4.13 and how *t* will ye know all parables?
10.26 themselves, Who *t* can be saved?
12.37 Lord; and whence is he *t* his son?
13.26 *t* shall they see the Son of man
Lk 2.28 *T* took he him up in his arms,
6.42 *t* shalt thou see clearly to pull out
11.13 If ye *t*, being evil, know how to give
12.28 If *t* God so clothe the grass, which
18.26 heard it said, Who *t* can be saved?
20. 5 say, Why *t* believe ye him not?
44 calleth...Lord, how is he *t* his son?
22.70 all, Art thou *t* the Son of God?
24.25 *T* he said unto them, O fools, and
45 *T* opened he their understanding,
Jn 1.25 Why baptizest thou *t*, if thou be
4.35 four months, and *t* cometh harvest?
7.30 *T* they sought to take him: but no
8.28 *t* shall ye know that I am he,
31 *t* are ye my disciples indeed;
9.19 born blind? how *t* doth he now see?
12. 3 *T* took Mary a pound of ointment
7 *T* said Jesus, Let her alone:
18.33 *T* Pilate entered into the judgment
36 world, *t* would my servants fight,
19. 5 *T* came Jesus forth, wearing the
40 *T* took they the body of Jesus,
20.21 *T* said Jesus to them again, Peace
Ac 3. 6 *T* Peter said, Silver and gold have
7.33 *T* said the Lord to him, Put off thy
8.29 *T* the Spirit said unto Philip, Go
9.31 *T* had the churches rest
16.29 *T* he called for a light, and
17.22 *T* Paul stood in the midst of Mars'
19. 3 Unto what *t* were ye baptized?
25.10 *T* said Paul, I stand at Caesar's
Ro 3. 1 What advantage *t* hath the Jew?
9 What *t*? are we better than they?
5. 9 Much more *t*, being now justified
6.18 Being *t* made free from sin, ye
7.16 If *t* I do that which I would not, I
7.17 *t* it is no more I that do it, but sin
8.17 if children, *t* heirs; heirs of God,
10.17 So *t* faith cometh by hearing, and
11. 6 if by grace, *t* is it no more of works:
12. 6 Having *t* gifts differing according
14.16 Let not *t* your good be evil spoken
1Co 3. 5 Who *t* is Paul, and who is
13.12 a glass, darkly; but *t* face to face:
12 *t* shall I know even as also I am
15.13 of the dead, *t* is Christ not risen:
2Co 5.14 if one died for all, *t* were all dead:
12.10 am weak, *t* am I strong.
Gal 5.16 This I say *t*, Walk in the Spirit,
Col 3. 1 If ye *t* be risen with Christ, seek
1Th 5. 3 *t* sudden destruction cometh upon
1Ti 2.13 For Adam was first formed, *t* Eve.
Heb 4.14 Seeing *t* that we have a great
10. 7 *T* said I, Lo, I come (in the

THENCEFORTH

Lev 22.27 and *t* it shall be accepted for an
2Ch 32.23 the sight of all nations from *t*.
Mt 5.13 it is *t* good for nothing, but to be
Jn 19.12 *t* Pilate sought to release

THEOPHILUS

Lk 1. 3 thee in order, most excellent *T*,
Ac 1. 1 treatise have I made, O *T*, of all

THESSALONIANS

Ac 20. 4 and of the *T*, Aristarchus and
1Th 1. 1 unto the church of the *T* which
2Th 1. 1 unto the church of the *T* in God

THESSALONICA

Ac 17. 1 they came to *T*, where was a
11 were more noble than those in *T*,
13 the Jews of *T* had knowledge
27. 2 Aristarchus, a Macedonian of *T*,
Php 4.16 For even in *T* ye sent once and
2Ti 4.10 world, and is departed into *T*;

THICK

Ex 10.22 there was a *t* darkness in all the
19. 9 Lo, I come unto thee in a *t* cloud,
16 and a *t* cloud upon the mount,
20.21 Moses drew near unto the *t* darkness
Lev 23.40 and the boughs of *t* trees, and
Dt 4.11 darkness, clouds, and *t* darkness.
5.22 the cloud, and of the *t* darkness,
32.15 art waxen fat, thou art grown *t*,
2Sa 18. 9 under the *t* boughs of a great oak,
22.12 waters, and *t* clouds of the skies.
1Ki 7. 6 and the *t* beam were before them.
26 And it was an hand breadth *t*,
8.12 he would dwell in the *t* darkness.
2Ki 8.15 he took a *t* cloth, and dipped it in
2Ch 6. 1 he would dwell in the *t* darkness.
Neh 8.15 and branches of *t* trees, to make
Job 15.26 upon the *t* bosses of his bucklers:
22.14 *T* clouds are a covering to him,
26. 8 up the waters in his *t* clouds;
37.11 by watering he wearieth the *t* cloud:
38. 9 *t* darkness a swaddlingband for it,
Ps 18.11 dark waters and *t* clouds of the
12 before him his *t* clouds passed,
74. 5 lifted up axes upon the *t* trees.
Isa 44.22 blotted out, as a *t* cloud, thy
Eze 6.13 green tree, and under every *t* oak,
8.11 and a *t* cloud of incense went up.
19.11 was exalted among the *t* branches,
20.28 high hill, and all the *t* trees,
31. 3 his top was among the *t* boughs.
10 up his top among the *t* boughs,
14 up their top among the *t* boughs,
41.12 of the building was five cubits *t*
25 *t* planks upon the face of the
26 of the house, and *t* planks.
Joel 2. 2 day of clouds and of *t* darkness,
Hab 2. 6 that ladeth himself with *t* clay!
Zep 1.15 a day of clouds and *t* darkness,
Lk 11.29 the people were gathered *t* together,

THICKER

1Ki 12.10 finger shall be *t* than my father's
2Ch 10.10 finger shall be *t* than my father's

THICKET

Gen 22.13 a ram caught in a *t* by his horns:
Jer 4. 7 The lion is come up from his *t*,

THICKETS

1Sa 13. 6 hide themselves in caves, and in *t*,
Isa 9.18 shall kindle in the *t* of the forests,
10.34 shall cut down the *t* of the forest
Jer 4.29 they shall go into the *t*, and climb

THICKNESS

2Ch 4. 5 the *t* of it was an handbreadth,
Jer 52.21 and the *t* thereof was four fingers:
Eze 41. 9 The *t* of the wall, which was for
42.10 chambers were in the *t* of the wall

THIEF

Ex 22. 2 If a *t* be found breaking up, and
7 if a *t* be found, let him pay double.
8 If the *t* be not found, then the
Dt 24. 7 selleth him; then that *t* shall die;
Job 24.14 needy, and in the night is as a *t*.
30. 5 (they cried after them as after a *t*;)
Ps 50.18 When thou sawest a *t*, then thou
Pr 6.30 Men do not despise a *t*, if he steal
29.24 Whoso is partner with a *t* hateth
Jer 2.26 As the *t* is ashamed when he is
Hos 7. 1 the *t* cometh in, and the troop of
Joel 2. 9 enter in at the windows like a *t*.
Zec 5. 4 shall enter into the house of the *t*,
Mt 24.43 in what watch the *t* would come,
26.55 Are ye come out as against a *t*
Mk 14.48 Are ye come out, as against a *t*,
Lk 12.33 where no *t* approacheth, neither
39 what hour the *t* would come,
22.52 Be ye come out, as against a *t*,
Jn 10. 1 way, the same is a *t* and a robber.
10 The *t* cometh not, but for to steal,
12. 6 but because he was a *t*, and had a
1Th 5. 2 Lord so cometh as a *t* in the night.
4 day should overtake you as a *t*.
1Pe 4.15 you suffer as a murderer, or as a *t*,
2Pe 3.10 Lord will come as a *t* in the night;
Rev 3. 3 watch, I will come on thee as a *t*,
16.15 Behold, I come as a *t*. Blessed is

THIEVES

Isa 1.23 rebellious, and companions of *t*:
Jer 48.27 unto thee? was he found among *t*?
49. 9 if *t* by night, they will destroy till
Ob 5 If *t* came to thee, if robbers by
Mt 6.19 where *t* break through and steal:
20 where *t* do not break through nor
21.13 but ye have made it a den of *t*.
27.38 there two *t* crucified with him;
44 The *t* also, which were crucified
Mk 11.17 but ye have made it a den of *t*.
15.27 And with him they crucify two *t*;
Lk 10.30 to Jericho, and fell among *t*,
36 unto him that fell among the *t*?
19.46 but ye have made it a den of *t*.
Jn 10. 8 that ever came before me are *t*
1Co 6.10 Nor *t*, nor covetous, nor drunkards,

THIGH

Gen 24. 2 pray thee, thy hand under my *t*:
9 his hand under the *t* of Abraham
32.25 he touched the hollow of his *t*;
25 hollow of Jacob's *t* was out of joint,
31 him, and he halted upon his *t*.
32 which is upon the hollow of the *t*,
32 touched the hollow of Jacob's *t* in
47.29 I pray thee, thy hand under my *t*,
Nu 5.21 the Lord doth make thy *t* to rot,
22 thy belly to swell, and thy *t* to rot:
27 shall swell, and her *t* shall rot:
Jdg 3.16 under his raiment upon his right *t*.
21 took the dagger from his right *t*,
15. 8 And he smote them hip and *t* with
Ps 45. 3 Gird thy sword upon thy *t*, O most
SS 3. 8 man hath his sword upon his *t*
Isa 47. 2 bare the leg, uncover the *t*,
Jer 31.19 instructed, I smote upon my *t*:
Eze 21.12 smite therefore upon thy *t*.
24. 4 good piece, the *t*, and the shoulder;
Rev 19.16 and on his *t* a name written,

THIN

Gen 41. 6 seven *t* ears and blasted with the
7 And the seven *t* ears devoured the
23 behold, seven ears, withered, *t*,
24 the *t* ears devoured the seven good
27 the seven *t* and ill favored kine
Ex 39. 3 they did beat the gold into *t* plates,
Lev 13.30 and there be in it a yellow *t* hair;
1Ki 7.29 certain additions made of *t* work.
Isa 17. 4 the glory of Jacob shall be made *t*,

THINE

Gen 14.23 that I will not take any thing that is *t*,
22.12 Lay not *t* hand upon the lad, neither
31.32 discern thou what is *t* with me,
Ex 13.16 and for frontlets between *t* eyes:
14.16 and stretch out *t* hand over the sea,
Nu 22.30 Am not I *t* ass, upon which thou hast
Dt 4.39 consider it in *t* heart, that the Lord
20.13 God hath delivered it into *t* hands,
28.32 *t* eyes shall look, and fail with
32 there shall be no might in *t* hand.
34 shalt be mad for the sight of *t* eyes
29. 3 temptations which *t* eyes have seen,
30. 2 with all *t* heart, and with all thy soul;
10 the Lord thy God with all *t* heart,
Jos 17.18 But the mountain shall be *t*; for it is

Jdg 19. 5 Comfort *t* heart with a morsel of
Ru 2.10 Why have I found grace in *t* eyes,
3. 9 answered, I am Ruth *t* handmaid:
1Sa 16. 1 fill *t* horn with oil, and go, I will send
2Ki 8. 8 Take a present in *t* hand, and go,
19.16 Lord, bow down *t* ear, and hear:
20. 1 Set *t* house in order; for thou shalt
15 What have they seen in *t* house?
1Ch 12.18 *T* are we, David, and on thy side,
17.17 was a small thing in *t* eyes, O God;
29.11 *T*, O Lord, is the greatness, and the
11 is in the heaven and in the earth is *t*;
11 *t* is the kingdom, O Lord, and thou
12 and in *t* hand is power and might;
12 and in *t* hand it is to make great, and
14 and of *t* own have we given thee.
16 build thee an house for *t* holy name
16 cometh of *t* hand, and is all *t* own.
2Ch 6.40 Now, my God, let,...*t* eyes be open,
19. 3 hast prepared *t* heart to seek God.
Job 2. 6 he is in *t* hand; but save his life.
7. 8 *t* eyes are upon me, and I am not.
10. 3 despise the work of *t* hands,
11. 4 is pure, and I am clean in *t* eyes.
6 of thee less than *t* iniquity deserveth.
14 If iniquity be in *t* hand, put it far
13.21 Withdraw *t* hand far from me: and
Ps 6. 1 O Lord, rebuke me not in *t* anger,
10.12 O God, lift up *t* hand: forget not the
16.10 wilt thou suffer *t* Holy One to see
17. 6 incline *t* ear unto me, and hear my
26. 6 so will I compass *t* altar, O Lord:
31. 2 Bow down *t* ear to me; deliver me
5 Into *t* hand I commit my spirit: thou
38. 3 in my flesh because of *t* anger;
71. 2 incline *t* ear unto me, and save me.
74.22 Arise, O God, plead *t* own cause:
84. 3 she may lay her young, even *t* altars,
86. 1 Bow down *t* ear, O Lord, hear me:
90. 7 For we are consumed by *t* anger, and
11 Who knoweth the power of *t* anger?
91. 8 Only with *t* eyes shalt thou behold
93. 5 holiness becometh *t* house, O Lord,
103. 3 Who forgiveth all *t* iniquities; who
104.28 thou openest *t* hand, they are filled
110. 1 until I make *t* enemies thy footstool.
119.173 Let *t* hand help me; for I have chosen
139.16 *T* eyes did see my substance, yet
145.16 Thou openest *t* hand, and satisfiest
Pr 3. 5 Trust in the Lord with all *t* heart;
7 Be not wise in *t* own eyes: fear the
27 it is in the power of *t* hand to do it.
6.21 Bind them continually upon *t* heart,
7. 2 live; and my law as the apple of *t* eye.
22.17 Bow down *t* ear, and hear the words
25.21 If *t* enemy be hungry, give him bread
Ec 5. 6 and destroy the work of *t* hands?
SS 6. 5 Turn away *t* eyes from me, for they
8. 6 Set me as a seal upon *t* heart, as a seal
Isa 6. 7 *t* iniquity is taken away, and thy sin
33.17 *T* eyes shall see the king in...beauty:
37.17 Incline *t* ear, O Lord, and hear; open
17 hear; open *t* eyes, O Lord, and see:
38. 1 Set *t* house in order: for thou shalt
54. 5 For thy Maker is *t* husband; the Lord
60. 4 Lift up *t* eyes round about, and see:
20 the Lord shall be *t* everlasting light,
63.19 We art *t*: thou never barest rule
Jer 2.22 yet *t* iniquity is marked before me,
4.14 wash *t* heart from wickedness,
34. 3 *t* eyes shall behold the eyes of the
La 2.16 *t* enemies have opened their mouth
18 rest; let not the apply of *t* eye cease.
19 pour out *t* heart like water before
Eze 3.24 me, Go, shut thyself within *t* house.
16.30 How weak is *t* heart, saith the Lord
28. 2 thou set *t* heart as the heart of God:
4 thy wisdom and with *t* understanding
6 hast set *t* heart as the heart of God;
33. 8 but his blood will I require at *t* hand.
40. 4 me, Son of man, behold with *t* eyes,
Dan 9.18 O my God, incline *t* ear, and hear;
19 defer not, for *t* own sake, O my God:
Jon 1. 8 What is *t* occupation? and whence
Mt 5.25 Agree with *t* adversary quickly,
43 thy neighbor, and hate *t* enemy.
6.13 *t* is the kingdom, and the power,
22 if therefore *t* eye be single, thy
23 But if *t* eye be evil, thy whole body
12.13 to the man, Stretch forth *t* hand.
20.14 Take that *t* is, and go thy way: I
15 Is *t* eye evil, because I am good?
22.44 till I make *t* enemies thy footstool?
Mk 3. 5 the man, Stretch forth *t* hand.
9.47 if *t* eye offend thee, pluck it out:
12.36 till I make *t* enemies thy footstool.
Lk 4. 7 wilt worship me, all shall be *t*.
6.41 not the beam that is in *t* own eye?
7.44 I entered into *t* house, thou gavest
11.34 therefore when *t* eye is single, thy
34 but when *t* eye is evil, thy body also
12.19 take *t* ease, eat, drink, and be merry.
15.31 with me, and all that I have is *t*.
19.42 but now they are hid from *t* eyes.
20.43 I make *t* enemies thy footstool.
22.42 not my will, but *t*, be done.
Jn 9.10 unto him, How were *t* eyes opened?
17. 6 *t* they were, and thou gavest them
9 thou has given me; for they are *t*.
10 And all mine are *t*, and
10 and *t* are mine: and I am
Ac 8.37 If thou believest with all *t* heart,
13.35 shalt not suffer *t* Holy One to see
Ro 10. 9 shalt believe in *t* heart that God
12.20 Therefore if *t* enemy hunger, feed
Heb 1.10 heavens are the works of *t* hands:
13 I make *t* enemies thy footstool?
Rev 3.18 and anoint *t* eyes with eyesalve,

THING

Gen 1.24 and creeping *t*, and beast of the earth
26 over every creeping *t* that creepeth
31 God saw every *t* that he had made,
18.14 Is any *t* too hard for the Lord?
21.11 And the *t* was very grievous in
24.50 The *t* proceedeth from the Lord:
41.28 This is the *t* which I have spoken
32 because the *t* is established by God,
Ex 1.18 Why have ye done this *t*, and have
2.14 and said, Surely this *t* is known.
16.14 there lay a small round *t*, as small as
18.11 in the *t* wherein they dealt proudly
17 The *t* that thou doest is not good.
18 for this *t* is too heavy for thee;
20. 4 or any likeness of any *t* that is in
17 ass, nor any *t* that is thy neighbor's.
Lev 2. 3, 10 it is a *t* most holy of the offerings
5. 2 Or if a soul touch any unclean *t*,
12. 4 she shall touch no hallowed *t*, nor
13.48 a skin, or in any *t* made of skin;
27.23 that day, as a holy *t* unto the Lord.
Nu 4.15 but they shall not touch any holy *t*,
16. 9 Seemeth it but a small *t* unto you,
13 it a small *t* that thou hast brought us
Dt 1.14 *t* which thou hast spoken is good
13.14 if it be truth, and the *t* certain,
32.47 For it is not a vain *t* for you;
Jdg 6.29 another, Who hath done this *t*?
11.25 art thou any *t* better than Balak
37 father, Let this *t* be done for me:
1Sa 3.11 Behold, I will do a *t* in Israel, at
12.16 stand and see this great *t*,
2Sa 2. 6 because ye have done this *t*.
7.19 yet a small *t* in thy sight, O Lord
13. 2 hard for him to do any *t* to her.
33 the king take the *t* to his heart,
1Ki 1.27 Is this *t* done by my lord the king,
3.10 that Solomon had asked this *t*.
10. 3 was not any *t* hid from the king,
12.24 to his house; for this *t* is from me.
30 And this *t* became a sin: for the
2Ki 2.10 he said, Thou hast asked a hard *t*:
3.18 but a light *t* in the sight of the Lord:
5.13 had bid thee do some great *t*,
18 Lord pardon thy servant in this *t*.
7. 2 windows in heaven, might this *t* be?
11. 5 This is the *t* that ye shall do; A
1Ch 2. 7 who transgressed in the *t*, accursed.
17.17 yet this was a small *t* in thine eyes,
Est 2. 4 And the *t* pleased the king; and he
Ps 2. 1 and the people imagine a vain *t*?
27. 4 One *t* have I desired of the Lord, that
33.17 An horse is a vain *t* for safety:
92. 1 It is a good *t* to give thanks unto the
150. 6 *t* that hath breath praise the Lord.
Pr 4. 7 Wisdom is the principal *t*; therefore
18.22 findeth a wife findeth a good *t*,
Ec 1. 9 The *t* that hath been, it is that which
9 and there is no new *t* under the sun.
3. 1 To every *t* there is a season, and a
8. 1 knoweth the interpretation of a *t*?
15 a man hath no better *t* under the sun,
9. 5 but the dead know not any *t*,
12.14 every secret *t*, whether it be good,
Isa 7.13 Is it a small *t* for you to weary men,
40.15 he taketh up the isles as a very little *t*.
43.19 Behold, I will do a new *t*; now it shall
55.11 prosper in the *t* whereto I sent it.
64. 6 But we are all as an unclean *t*, and
Jer 2.10 and see if there be such a *t*.
31.22 Lord hath created a new *t* in the
32.27 is there any *t* too hard for me?
La 2.13 What *t* shall I take to witness for
13 what *t* shall I liken to thee, O
Eze 8.17 Is it a light *t* to the house of Judah
16.47 but, as if that were a very little *t*,
Am 6.13 Ye which rejoice in a *t* of nought,
Mt 8.33 and told every *t*, and what was
19.16 Good Master, what good *t* shall I do,
Mk 1.27 themselves, saying, What *t* is this?
10.21 said unto him, One *t* thou lackest:
16. 8 neither said they any *t* to any man;
Lk 1.35 also that holy *t* which shall be born
2.15 see this *t* which is come to pass,
6. 9 unto them, I will ask you one *t*;
8.17 neither any *t* hid, that shall not be
10.42 But one *t* is needful: and Mary
18.22 unto him, Yet lackest thou one *t*:
20. 3 them, I will also ask you one *t*;
Jn 1. 3 was not any *t* made that was made.
46 any good *t* come out of Nazareth?
5.14 more, lest a worse *t* come unto thee.
9.25 one *t* I know, that, whereas I was
18.34 Sayest thou this *t* of thyself, or did
Ac 5. 4 conceived this *t* in thine heart?
19.32 Some therefore cried one *t*, and
26. 8 be thought a *t* incredible with you,
26 this *t* was not done in a corner.
Ro 7.18 is, in my flesh,) dwelleth no good *t*:
8.33 Who shall lay any *t* to the charge of
13. 6 continually upon this very *t*.
8 Owe no man any *t*, but to love one
1Co 1. 5 in every *t* ye are enriched by him,
2. 2 not to know any *t* among you,
4. 3 very small *t* that I should be judged
10.19 say I then? that the idol is any *t*,
2Co 2.10 To whom ye forgive any *t*, I forgive
6. 3 Giving no offense in any *t*, that
Eph 4.28 with his hands the *t* which is good,
6. 8 whatsoever good *t* any man doeth,
Heb 10.29 an unholy *t*, and hath done despite
31 It is a fearful *t* to fall into the hands
11.40 God having provided some better *t*
Jas 1. 7 he shall receive any *t* of the Lord.
1Pe 4.12 some strange *t* happened unto you:
1Jn 2. 8 which *t* is true in him and in you:

THINGS

Gen 7.23 and the creeping *t*, and the fowl of
20. 8 and told all these *t* in their ears:
Lev 2. 8 offering that is made of these *t* unto
4. 2 *t* which ought not to be done,
2Sa 7.21 hast thou done all these great *t* to

23. 5 covenant, ordered in all t and sure:
17 These t did these three mighty men.
24.12 saith the Lord, I offer thee three t;
1Ch 4.22 And these are ancient t.
21.10 saith the Lord, I offer thee three t:
29. 2 God the gold for t to be made of
17 I have willingly offered all these t:
Job 5. 9 doeth great t, and unsearchable;
6. 7 The t that my soul refused to touch
30 cannot my taste discern perverse t?
9.10 Which doeth great t past finding out;
12. 3 who knoweth not such t as these?
22 discovereth deep t out of darkness,
41.30 sharp pointed t upon the mire.
34 He beholdeth all high t: he is a king
42. 3 t too wonderful for me, which I knew
Ps 8. 6 thou hast put all t under his feet:
15. 5 He that doeth these t shall never be
57. 2 God that performeth all t for me.
86.10 thou art great, and doest wondrous t:
87. 3 Glorious t are spoken of thee, O city
98. 1 song; for he hath done marvellous t:
103. 5 satisfieth thy mouth with good t;
119.18 behold wondrous t out of thy law.
126. 2 The Lord hath done great t for them.
3 The Lord hath done great t for us;
Pr 2.12 the man that speaketh froward t;
6.16 These six t doth the Lord hate: yea,
16. 4 The Lord hath made all t for himself:
24.23 These t also belong to the wise. It is
30. 7 Two t have I required of thee; deny
Ec 1. 8 All t are full of labor: man
7.15 All t have I seen in the days of my
25 seek out wisdom, and the reason of t,
9. 2 All t come alike to all: there is one
3 is an evil among all t that are done
10.19 merry: but money answereth all t.
Isa 12. 5 Lord; for he hath done excellent t:
25. 1 for thou hast done wonderful t; thy
6 make unto all people a feast of fat t,
29.16 Surely your turning of t upside down
38.16 O Lord, by these t men live,
16 in all these t is the life of my spirit:
41.22 let them shew the former t, what
23 Shew the t that are to come
42. 9 Behold, the former t are come to
43. 9 declare this, and shew us former t?
18 Remember ye not the former t,
44. 7 and the t that are coming, and shall
24 I am the Lord that maketh all t;
45. 7 create evil: I the Lord do all these t.
19 I declare t that are right.
46. 9 Remember the former t of old: for I
66. 2 For all those t hath mine hand made,
Jer 2. 8 and walked after t that do not profit.
5. 9 Shall I not visit for these t? saith the
25 your sins have withholden good t
13.22 Wherefore come these t upon me?
17. 9 The heart is deceitful above all t, and
31. 5 and shall eat them as common t.
45. 5 And seekest thou great t for thyself?
La 1. 7 all her pleasant t that she had in the
10 out his hand upon all her pleasant t:
16 For these t I weep; mine eye, mine
Eze 5.11 sanctuary with all thy detestable t,
17.12 Know ye not what these t mean?
42.13 the Lord shall eat the most holy t:
Dan 2.10 that asked such t at any magician,
22 He revealeth the deep and secret t:
12. 7 people, all these t shall be finished.
8 what shall be the end of these t?
Joel 2.20 up, because he hath done great t,
21 rejoice: for the Lord will do great t.
Ob 6 How are the t of Esau searched out!
6 how are his hidden t sought up!
Zec 4.10 who hath despised the day of small t?
Mt 1.20 But while he thought on these t,
2. 3 Herod the king had heard these t,
4. 9 All these t will I give thee, if thou
6. 8 knoweth what t ye have need of,
33 all these t shall be added unto you.
34 take thought for the t of itself.
11. 4 shew John again those t which ye do
25 hast hid these t from the wise and
12.34 can ye, being evil, speak good t?
13. 3 he spake many t unto them in
51 Have ye understood all these t?
52 out of his treasure t new and old.
56 then hath this man all these t?
15.18 those t which proceed out of the
20 These are the t which defile a man:
16.21 and suffer many t of the elders and
23 savorest not the t that be of God,
19.20 All these t have I kept from my
26 but with God all t are possible.
22. 4 all t are ready: come unto the
21 Caesar the t which are Caesar's;
21 unto God the t that are God's.
24. 2 unto them, See ye not all these t?
3 Tell us, when shall these t be?
25.21 thou hast been faithful over a few t,
21 I will make thee ruler over many t:
Mk 1.44 those t which Moses commanded,
4. 2 taught them many t by parables,
5.19 tell them how great t the Lord hath
26 And had suffered many t of many
6. 2 whence hath this man these t?
7. 4 many other t there be, which they
15 but the t which come out of him,
37 saying, He hath done all t well: he
8.31 the Son of man must suffer many t,
33 savorest not the t that be of God,
33 of God, but the t that be of men.
9. 9 tell no man what t they had seen,
23 t are possible to him that believeth.
10.27 for with God all t are possible.
11.11 had looked round about upon all t,
28 what authority doest thou these t?
12.17 to Caesar the t that are Caesar's,
17 and to God the t that are God's.
13. 4 Tell us, when shall these t be?
14.36 Father, all t are possible unto thee;
Lk 1. 1 in order a declaration of those t
3 had perfect understanding of all t
49 mighty hath done to me great t;
53 hath filled the hungry with good t;
2.18 wondered at those t which were told
19 But Mary kept all these t, and
20 praising God for all the t that they
7. 9 Jesus heard these t, he marvelled
22 tell John what t ye have seen and
8. 8 when he had said these t, he cried,
39 how great t God hath done unto
9. 9 who is this, of whom I hear such t?
22 Son of man must suffer many t,
10. 1 After these t the Lord appointed
22 All t are delivered to me of my
23 eyes which see the t that ye see:
11.27 as he spake these t, a certain
41 give alms of such t as ye have;
12.15 of the t which he possesseth,
20 then whose shall those t be, which
14. 6 not answer him again to these t.
17 Come; for all t are now ready.
16.14 were covetous, heard all these t:
25 thy lifetime receivedst thy good t,
25 and likewise Lazarus evil t: but now
18.22 Now when Jesus heard these t,
27 t which are impossible with men are
20. 2 authority doest thou these t?
25 Caesar the t which be Caesar's,
25 and unto God the t which be God's.
21. 6 As for these t which ye behold,
7 Master, but when shall these t be?
31 when ye see these t come to pass,
22.37 the t concerning me have an end.
23. 8 because he had heard many t of him;
31 if they do these t in a green tree,
48 beholding the t which were done,
24. 9 and told all these t unto the eleven,
19 And he said unto them, What t? And
26 not Christ to have suffered these t,
27 scriptures the t concerning himself.
44 that all t must be fulfilled, which
Jn 1. 3 All t were made by him; and without
50 thou shalt see greater t than these.
2.16 Take these t hence; make not
3. 9 unto him, How can these t be?
12 If I have told you earthly t, and ye
35 and hath given all t into his hand.
8.26 I have many t to say and to judge of
13. 3 Father had given all t into his hands,
14.25 These t have I spoken unto you,
26 he shall teach you all t, and bring all
26 and bring all t to your remembrance,
16. 1 These t have I spoken unto you,
12 I have yet many t to say unto you,
15 All t that the Father hath are mine:
19.24 these t therefore the soldiers did.
28 that all t were now accomplished,
21. 1 After these t Jesus shewed himself
17 unto him, Lord, thou knowest all t;
24 disciple which testifieth of these t,
Ac 1. 3 t pertaining to the kingdom of God:
4.20 speak the t which we have seen and
32 his own; but they had all t common.
7. 1 the high priest, Are these t so?
9.16 shew him how great t he must suffer
12.17 said, Go shew these t unto James,
14.15 Sirs, why do ye these t? We also
17. 8 the city, when they heard these t.
25 to all life, and breath, and all t;
21.12 And when we heard these t, both
25 themselves from t offered to idols,
Ro 1.20 invisible t of him from the creation
20 understood by the t that are made,
2. 1 thou that judgest doest the same t.
6.21 What fruit had ye then in those t
21 for the end of those t is death.
8. 5 the flesh do mind the t of the flesh;
5 after the Spirit the t of the Spirit.
28 we know that all t work together for
31 What shall we then say to these t?
32 not with him also freely give us all t?
37 in all these t we are more than
38 nor t present, nor t to come,
10. 5 man which doeth those t shall live
15 and bring glad tidings of good t!
12.16 Mind not high t, but condescend to
17 Provide t honest in the sight of all
14. 2 one believeth that he may eat all t:
20 All t indeed are pure; but it is evil
1Co 1.27 hath chosen the foolish t of the world
27 hath chosen the weak t of the world
28 God chosen, yea, and t which are
2. 9 t which God hath prepared for them
11 what man knoweth the t of a man,
11 so the t of God knoweth no man,
13 comparing spiritual t with spiritual.
3.21 glory in men. For all t are yours;
6. 3 much more t that pertain to this life?
12 All t are lawful unto me, but all
12 unto me, but all t are not expedient:
12 all t are lawful for me, but I will not
8. 1 Now as touching t offered unto idols,
6 God, the Father, of whom are all t,
9. 8 Say I these t as a man? or saith not
22 I am made all t to all men, that I
10. 6 Now these t were our examples,
23 All t are lawful for me, but all
23 but all t are not expedient:
23 all t are lawful for me, but all
23 are lawful for me, but all t edify not,
13. 7 Beareth all t, believeth all t,
7 hopeth all t, endureth all t.
11 became a man, I put away childish t.
15.27 For he hath put all t under his feet.
2Co 1.13 For we write none other t unto you,
4. 2 have renounced the hidden t of
15 For all t are for your sakes, that the
18 we look not at the t which are seen,
18 but at the t which are not seen:
18 the t which are seen are temporal;

2Co 4.18 the *t* which are not seen are eternal.
5.10 every one may receive the *t* done in
17 behold, all *t* are become new.
Gal 1.20 Now the *t* which I write unto you,
3. 4 Have ye suffered so many *t* in vain?
5.17 that ye cannot do the *t* that ye would.
Eph 1.10 together in one all *t* in Christ,
22 And hath put all *t* under his feet, and
3. 9 who created all *t* by Jesus Christ:
Php 1.10 ye may approve *t* that are excellent;
2. 4 Look not every man on his own *t*,
4 but every man also on the *t* of others.
10 knee should bow, of *t* in heaven,
14 Do all *t* without murmurings and
4. 8 brethren, whatsoever *t* are true,
13 I can do all *t* through Christ which
Col 1.16 For by him were all *t* created, that
2.17 Which are a shadow of *t* to come;
3. 1 Christ, seek those *t* which are above,
2 Set your affection on *t* above,
20 Children, obey your parents in all *t*:
1Th 2.14 have suffered like *t* of your own
5.21 Prove all *t*; hold fast that which is
1Ti 3.11 not slanderers sober, faithful in all *t*.
6. 2 benefit. These *t* teach and exhort.
11 thou, O man of God, flee these *t*;
17 who giveth us richly all *t* to enjoy;
Tit 1. 5 set in order the *t* that are wanting,
15 Unto the pure all *t* are pure: but unto
Heb 1. 2 whom he hath appointed heir of all *t*,
2. 1 earnestly to the *t* which we have
8 put all *t* in subjection under his feet.
6. 9 we are persuaded better *t* of you,
10. 1 having a shadow of good *t* to come,
11. 1 faith is the substance of *t* hoped
1 for, the evidence of *t* not seen.
13. 5 be content with such *t* as ye have:
18 in all *t* willing to live honestly.
1Pe 1.12 unto us they did minister the *t*,
4. 7 But the end of all *t* is at hand: be ye
11 that God in all *t* may be glorified
Rev 1. 1 servants *t* which must shortly come
2 Christ, and of all *t* that he saw.
2. 1 These *t* saith he that holdeth the
14 But I have a few *t* against thee,
4. 1 these *t* which must be hereafter.
11 for thou hast created all *t*, and for
20.12 *t* which were written in the books,
21. 4 for the former *t* are passed away.
5 said, Behold, I will make all *t* new.
7 that overcometh shall inherit all *t*;
22. 6 the *t* which must shortly be done.
8 And I John saw these *t*, and
18 If any man shall add unto these *t*,
19 the *t* which are written in this book.

THINK

Gen 40.14 *t* on me when it shall be well
Neh 5.19 *T* upon me, my God, for good,
Ec 8.17 though a wise man *t* to know it,
Isa 10. 7 so, neither doth his heart *t* so;
Dan 7.25 and *t* to change times and laws:
Jon 1. 6 if so be that God will *t* upon us,
Mt 3. 9 *t* not to say within yourselves,
5.17 *T* not that I am come to destroy
6. 7 they *t* that they shall be heard for
9. 4 Wherefore *t* ye evil in your hearts?
10.34 *T* not that I am come to send
18.12 How *t* ye? if a man have an
21.28 what *t* ye? A certain man had
22.42 Saying, What *t* ye of Christ? whose
24.44 in such an hour as ye *t* not the Son
26.66 What *t* ye? They answered and
Mk 14.64 heard the blasphemy: what *t* ye?
Lk 12.40 cometh at an hour when ye *t* not.
13. 4 *t* ye that they were sinners above
Jn 5.39 in them ye *t* ye have eternal life:
45 Do not *t* that I will accuse you to
11.56 What *t* ye, that he will not come to
16. 2 will *t* that he doeth God service.
Ac 13.25 Whom *t* ye that I am? I am not
17.29 not to *t* that the Godhead is like
26. 2 I *t* myself happy, king Agrippa,
Ro 12. 3 not to *t* of himself more highly
3 more highly than he ought to *t*;
3 but to *t* soberly, according as God
1Co 4. 6 not to *t* of men above that which is
9 For I *t* that God hath set forth us
7.36 if any man *t* that he behaveth
40 I *t* also that I have the Spirit of
8. 2 if any man *t* that he knoweth any
12.23 which we *t* to be less honorable,
14.37 If any man *t* himself to be a
2Co 3. 5 to *t* any thing as of ourselves;
10. 2 I *t* to be bold against some, which
2 which *t* of us as if we walked
7 let him of himself *t* this again,
11 Let such an one *t* this, that, such
11.16 say again, Let no man *t* me a fool;
12. 6 man should *t* of me above that
19 *t* ye that we excuse ourselves unto
Gal 6. 3 if a man *t* himself to be something,
Eph 3.20 above all that we ask or *t*,
Php 1. 7 is meet for me to *t* this of you all,
4. 8 be any praise, *t* on these things.
Jas 1. 7 that man *t* that he shall receive
4. 5 Do ye *t* that the scriptures saith in
1Pe 4. 4 *t* it strange that ye run not with them
12 *t* it not strange concerning the fiery
2Pe 1.13 Yea, I *t* it meet, as long as I am in

THIRD

Gen 1.13 and the morning were the *t* day.
50.23 children of the *t* generation:
Ex 19.11 *t* day the Lord will come down in
Dt 26.12 tithes of thine increase the *t* year,
1Ki 18. 1 Lord came to Elijah in the *t* year,
34 And he said, Do it the *t* time.
Mt 16.21 and be raised again the *t* day.
17.23 and the *t* day he shall be raised
20. 3 And he went out about the *t* hour,
19 and the *t* day he shall rise again.
22.26 also, and the *t*, unto the seventh.
26.44 and prayed the *t* time, saying the
27.64 be made sure until the *t* day,
Mk 9.31 he is killed, he shall rise the *t* day.
10.34 and the *t* day he shall rise again.
12.21 he any seed: and the *t* likewise.
14.41 he cometh the *t* time, and saith
15.25 And it was the *t* hour, and they
Lk 9.22 be slain, and be raised the *t* day.
12.38 watch, or come in the *t* watch,
13.32 and the *t* day I shall be perfected.
18.33 and the *t* day he shall rise again.
20.12 And again he sent a *t*: and they
31 And the *t* took her; and in like
23.22 And he said unto them the *t* time,
24. 7 crucified, and the *t* day rise again.
21 to day is the *t* day since these
46 to rise from the dead the *t* day:
Jn 2. 1 the *t* day there was a marriage
21.14 *t* time that Jesus shewed himself
17 He saith unto him the *t* time,
17 he said unto him the *t* time,
Ac 2.15 it is but the *t* hour of the day.
10.40 Him God raised up the *t* day, and
20. 9 and fell down from the *t* loft,
23.23 at the *t* hour of the night;
27.19 And the *t* day we cast out with
1Co 15. 4 he rose again the *t* day according
2Co 12. 2 an one caught up to the *t* heaven.
14 *t* time I am ready to come to you;
13. 1 is the *t* time I am coming to you.
Rev 4. 7 and the *t* beast had a face as a man,
6. 5 when he had opened the *t* seal,
5 I heard the *t* beast say, Come and
8. 7 the *t* part of trees was burnt up,
8 the *t* part of the sea became blood;
9 the *t* part of the creatures which
9 *t* part of the ships were destroyed.
10 And the *t* angel sounded, and there
10 fell upon the *t* part of the rivers,
11 the *t* part of the waters became
12 the *t* part of the sun was smitten,
12 and the *t* part of the moon, and the
12 moon, and the *t* part of the stars;
12 *t* part of them was darkened, and
12 the day shone not for a *t* part of it,
9.15 year, for to slay the *t* part of men.
18 three was the *t* part of men killed,
11.14 behold, the *t* woe cometh quickly.
12. 4 tail drew the *t* part of the stars of
14. 9 And the *t* angel followed them,
16. 4 *t* angel poured out his vial upon
21. 9 the *t*, a chalcedony; the fourth, an

THIRST

Ex 17. 3 our children and our cattle with *t*?
Dt 28.48 hunger, and in *t*, and in nakedness,
29.19 heart, to add drunkenness to *t*:
Jdg 15.18 and now shall I die for *t*, and fall
2Ch 32.11 yourselves to die by famine and...*t*,
Neh 9.15 for them out of the rock for their *t*,
20 and gavest them water for their *t*.
Job 24.11 their winepresses, and suffer *t*.
Ps 69.21 in my *t* they gave me vinegar to
104.11 the wild asses quench their *t*.
Isa 5.13 their multitude dried up with *t*.
41.17 and their tongue faileth for *t*,
49.10 They shall not hunger nor *t*;
50. 2 there is no water, and dieth for *t*.
Jer 2.25 unshod, and thy throat from *t*:
48.18 down from thy glory, and sit in *t*;
La 4. 4 to the roof of his mouth for *t*:
Hos 2. 3 like a dry land, and slay her with *t*.
Am 8.11 famine of bread, nor a *t* for water,
13 virgins and young men faint for *t*.
Mt 5. 6 hunger and *t* after righteousness:
Jn 4.13 drinketh...this water shall *t* again:
14 that I shall give him shall never *t*;
15 give me this water, that I *t* not,
6.35 that believeth on me shall never *t*.
7.37 If any man *t*, let him come unto
19.28 might be fulfilled, saith, I *t*.
Ro 12.20 feed him; if he *t*, give him drink:
1Co 4.11 both hunger, and *t*, and are naked,
2Co 11.27 watchings often in hunger and *t*,
Rev 7.16 no more, neither *t* any more;

THIRSTETH

Ps 42. 2 My soul *t* for God, for the living
63. 1 my soul *t* for thee, my flesh longeth
143. 6 my soul *t* after thee, as a thirsty
Isa 55. 1 Ho, every one that *t*, come ye to

THIRSTY

Jdg 4.19 a little water to drink; for I am *t*.
2Sa 17.29 is hungry, and weary, and *t*,
Ps 63. 1 longeth for thee in a dry and *t* land,
107. 5 Hungry and *t*, their soul fainted
143. 6 soul thirsteth after thee, as a *t* land.
Pr 25.21 and if he be *t*, give him water to
25 As cold waters to a *t* soul, so is good
Isa 21.14 brought water to him that was *t*,
29. 8 or as when a *t* man dreameth, and,
32. 6 will cause the drink of the *t* to fail.
35. 7 and the *t* land springs of water:
44. 3 pour water upon him that is *t*,
65.13 shall drink, but ye shall be *t*:
Eze 19.13 wilderness, in a dry and *t* ground.
Mt 25.35 I was *t*, and ye gave me drink:
37 fed thee? or *t*, gave thee drink?
42 I was *t*, and ye gave me no drink:

THIRTY

Dan 6. 7 of any God or man for *t* days,
12 of any God or man within *t* days,
12.12 hundred and five and *t* days.
Zec 11.12 for my price *t* pieces of silver.
13 and I took the *t* pieces of silver,
Mt 13.23 hundredfold, some sixty, some *t*.
26.15 with him for *t* pieces of silver.
27. 3 brought again the *t* pieces of silver

9 they took the *t* pieces of silver, the
Mk 4. 8 forth, some *t*, and some sixty, and
Lk 3.23 began to be about *t* years of age,
Jn 5. 5 had an infirmity *t* and eight years.
6.19 about five and twenty or *t* furlongs,
Gal 3.17 four hundred and *t* years after,

THISTLE
Hos 10. 8 *t* shall come up on their altars;

THISTLES
Gen 3.18 and *t* shall it bring forth to thee;
Job 31.40 Let *t* grow instead of wheat,
Mt 7.16 grapes of thorns, or figs of *t*?

THOMAS
Mt 10. 3 *T*, and Matthew the publican;
Mk 3.18 *T*, and James the son of Alphaeus,
Lk 6.15 *T*, James the son of Alphaeus,
Jn 11.16 said *T*, which is called Didymus,
14. 5 *T* saith unto him, Lord, we know
20.24 But *T*, one of the twelve, called
26 were within, and *T* with them:
27 Then saith he to *T*, Reach hither
28 *T* answered and said unto him,
29 *T*, because thou hast seen me,
21. 2 Peter, and *T* called Didymus,
Ac 1.13 *T*, Bartholomew, and Matthew,

THONGS
Ac 22.25 as they bound him with *t*, Paul

THORN
Job 41. 2 or bore his jaw through with a *t*?
Pr 26. 9 As a *t* goeth up into the hand of a
Isa 55.13 of the *t* shall come up the fir tree,
Eze 28.24 grieving *t* of all that are round
Hos 10. 8 the *t* and the thistle shall come up
Mic 7. 4 upright is sharper than a *t* hedge:
2Co 12. 7 was given to me a *t* in the flesh,

THORNS
Gen 3.18 *T* also and thistles shall it bring
Ex 22. 6 If fire break out, and catch in *t*, so
Nu 33.55 in your eyes, and *t* in your sides,
Jos 23.13 in your sides, and *t* in your eyes,
Jdg 2. 3 but they shall be as *t* in your sides,
8. 7 I will tear your flesh with the *t*
16 and *t* of the wilderness and briers,
2Sa 23. 6 be all of them as *t* thrust away,
2Ch 33.11 took Manasseh among the *t*,
Job 5. 5 and taketh it even out of the *t*,
Ps 58. 9 Before your pots can feel the *t*, he
118.12 they are quenched as the fire of *t*:
Pr 15.19 slothful man is as an hedge of *t*:
22. 5 *T* and snares are in the way of
24.31 all grown over with *t*, and nettles

THOMAS

One of the twelve disciples; given special prominence by John, who calls him Didymus (meaning "twin"); urges fellow disciples to accompany Jesus and die with him (Jn 11.16); questions Jesus about where he is going and how to know the way (Jn 14.5); is absent from group of disciples to whom Jesus appears after Resurrection, and does not believe them; his doubts not resolved until he sees Jesus and is invited to touch his wounds, an invitation that elicits his confession of faith, "My Lord and my God" (Jn 20.28); revered in later tradition by churches of Syria, Parthia, and India; sometimes believed to have been the "twin" of Jesus.

Ec 7. 6 as the crackling of *t* under a pot,
SS 2. 2 As the lily among *t*, so is my love
Isa 5. 6 there shall come up briers and *t*:
7.19 upon all *t*, and upon all bushes.
23 it shall even be for briers and *t*.
24 the land shall become briers and *t*.
25 thither the fear of briers and *t*:
9.18 it shall devour the briers and *t*,
10.17 shall burn and devour his *t* and his
27. 4 set the briers and *t* against me in
32.13 people shall come up *t* and briers;
33.12 *t* cut up shall they be burned in the
34.13 *t* shall come up in her palaces,
Jer 4. 3 ground, and sow not among *t*.
12.13 have sown wheat, but shall reap *t*:
Eze 2. 6 though briers and *t* be with thee,
Hos 2. 6 I will hedge up thy way with *t*,
9. 6 *t* shall be in their tabernacles.
Na 1.10 while they be folden together as *t*,
Mt 7.16 Do men gather grapes of *t*, or figs
13. 7 And some fell among *t*;
7 the *t* sprung up, and choked them:
22 also that received seed among the *t*
27.29 when they had platted a crown of *t*,
Mk 4. 7 And some fell among *t*,
7 and the *t* grew up, and choked it,
18 are they which are sown among *t*;
15.17 platted a crown of *t*, and put it
Lk 6.44 of *t* men do not gather figs, nor of
8. 7 And some fell among *t*;
7 *t* sprang up with it, and choked it.
14 that which fell among *t* are they,
Jn 9. 2 the soldiers platted a crown of *t*,
5 Jesus forth, wearing the crown of *t*,
Heb 6. 8 that which beareth *t* and briers is

THOUGHT
Gen 20.11 I *t*, Surely the fear of God is not
38.15 saw her, he *t* her to be an harlot;
48.11 I had not *t* to see thy face:
50.20 as for you, ye *t* evil against me;
Ex 32.14 the evil which he *t* to do unto his
Nu 24.11 I *t* to promote thee unto great
33.56 unto you, as I *t* to do unto them.
Dt 15. 9 be not a *t* in thy wicked heart,
19.19 as he had *t* to have done unto his
Jdg 15. 2 I verily *t* that thou hadst utterly
20. 5 by night, and *t* to have slain me:
Ru 4. 4 I *t* to advertise thee, saying, Buy
1Sa 1.13 Eli *t* she had been drunken.
9. 5 for the asses, and take *t* for us.
18.25 Saul *t* to make David fall by the
20.26 for he *t*, Something hath befallen
2Sa 4.10 who *t* that I would have given him a
13. 2 Amnon *t* it hard for him to do
14.13 hast thou *t* such a thing against
19.18 and to do what he *t* good.
21.16 new sword, *t* to have slain David.
2Ki 5.11 I *t*, He will surely come out to me,
2Ch 11.22 for he *t* to make him king.
32. 1 and *t* to win them for himself.
Neh 6. 2 But they *t* to do me mischief.
Est 3. 6 *t* scorn to lay hands on Mordecai
6. 6 Now Haman *t* in his heart, To
Job 12. 5 despised in the *t* of him that is at
42. 2 no *t* can be withholden from
Ps 48. 9 We have *t* of thy lovingkindness,
49.11 Their inward *t* is, that their houses
64. 6 the inward *t* of every one of them,
73.16 When I *t* to know this, it was too
119.59 I *t* on my ways, and turned my
139. 2 thou understandest my *t* afar off.
Pr 24. 9 The *t* of foolishness is sin: and
30.32 or if thou hast *t* evil, lay thine
Ec 10.20 not the king, no not in thy *t*;
Isa 14.24 Surely as I have *t*, so shall it come
Jer 18. 8 the evil that I *t* to do unto them.
Eze 38.10 and thou shalt think an evil *t*:
Dan 4. 2 I *t* it good to shew the signs
6. 3 king *t* to set him over the whole
Am 4.13 declareth unto man what is his *t*,

Zec 1. 6 the Lord of hosts *t* to do unto us,
8.14 As I *t* to punish you, when your
15 again have I *t* in these days to do
Mal 3.16 Lord, and that *t* upon his name.
Mt 1.20 But while he *t* on these things,
6.25 Take no *t* for your life, what ye
27 you by taking *t* can add one cubit
28 And why take ye *t* for raiment?
31 take no *t*, saying, What shall we
34 Take...no *t* for the morrow:
34 morrow shall take *t* for the things
10.19 take no *t* how or what ye shall
Mk 13.11 take no *t* beforehand what ye
14.72 And when he *t* thereon, he wept.
Lk 7. 7 neither *t* I myself worthy to come
9.47 perceiving the *t* of their heart,
12.11 take ye no *t* how or what thing ye
17 And he *t* within himself, saying,
22 Take no *t* for your life, what ye
25 you with taking *t* can add to his
26 is least, why take ye *t* for the rest?
19.11 they *t* that the kingdom of God
Jn 11.13 they *t* that he had spoken of taking
13.29 some of them *t*, because Judas had
Ac 8.20 thou hast *t* that the gift of God
22 *t* of thine heart may be forgiven
10.19 While Peter *t* on the vision, the
12. 9 the angel; but *t* he saw a vision.
15.38 Paul *t* not good to take him with
26. 8 should it be *t* a thing incredible
9 I verily *t* with myself, that I
1Co 13.11 as a child, I *t* as a child:
2Co 9. 5 I *t* it necessary to exhort the
10. 5 every *t* to the obedience of Christ;
Php 2. 6 *t* it not robbery to be equal with
1Th 3. 1 we *t* it good to be left at Athens
Heb 10.29 shall he be *t* worthy, who hath

THOUGHTS
Gen 6. 5 the *t* of his heart was only evil
Jdg 5.15 there were great *t* of heart.
1Ch 28. 9 all the imaginations of the *t*:
29.18 of the *t* of the heart of thy people,
Job 4.13 *t* from the visions of the night,
17.11 broken off, even the *t* of my heart.
20. 2 do my *t* cause me to answer,
21.27 I know your *t*, and the devices
Ps 10. 4 after God: God is not in all his *t*.
33.11 *t* of his heart to all generations.
40. 5 and thy *t* which are to us-ward:
56. 5 all their *t* are against me for evil.
92. 5 thy works! and thy *t* are very deep.
94.11 The Lord knoweth the *t* of man,
19 In the multitude of my *t* within
119.113 I hate vain *t*: but thy law do I
139.17 How precious...are thy *t* unto me,
23 heart: try me, and know my *t*:
146. 4 in that very day his *t* perish.
Pr 12. 5 The *t* of the righteous are right:
15.26 *t* of the wicked are an abomination
16. 3 and thy *t* shall be established.
21. 5 The *t* of the diligent tend only to
Isa 55. 7 and the unrighteous man his *t*:
8 For my *t* are not your *t*, neither
9 your ways, and my *t* than your *t*.
59. 7 blood: their *t* are *t* of iniquity;
65. 2 was not good, after their own *t*;
66.18 For I know their works and their *t*:
Jer 4.14 How long shall thy vain *t* lodge
6.19 people, even the fruit of their *t*,
23.20 have performed the *t* of his heart:
29.11 I know the *t* that I think toward
11 *t* of peace, and not of evil, to
Dan 2.29 O king, thy *t* came into thy mind
30 mightest know the *t* of thy heart.
4. 5 *t* upon my bed and the visions
19 one hour, and his *t* troubled him.
5. 6 changed, and his *t* troubled him,
10 let not thy *t* trouble thee, nor
Mic 4.12 they know not the *t* of the Lord,
Mt 9. 4 And Jesus knowing their *t* said,

Mt 12.25 Jesus knew their *t*, and said unto
15.19 out of the heart proceed evil *t*,
Mk 7.21 the heart of men, proceed evil *t*,
Lk 2.35 *t* of many hearts may be revealed.
5.22 But when Jesus perceived their *t*,
6. 8 he knew their *t*, and said to the
11.17 knowing their *t*, said unto them,
24.38 and why do *t* arise in your hearts?
Ro 2.15 and their *t* the mean while
1Co 3.20 Lord knoweth the *t* of the wise,
Heb 4.12 a discerner of the *t* and intents of
Jas 2. 4 and are become judges of evil *t*?

THOUSAND

Gen 20.16 thy brother a *t* pieces of silver:
Lev 26. 8 of you shall put ten *t* to flight:
Dt 1.11 make you a *t* times so many more
7. 9 commandments to a *t* generations;
32.30 How should one chase a *t*, and two
30 and two put ten *t* to flight, except
Jos 23.10 One man of you shall chase a *t*: for
1Ki 4.32 And he spake three *t* proverbs:
32 and his songs were a *t* and five.
19.18 Yet I have left me seven *t* in Israel,
Job 9. 3 he cannot answer him one of a *t*.
33.23 one among a *t*, to shew unto man
Ps 50.10 mine, and the cattle upon a *t* hills.
84.10 a day in thy courts is better than a *t*.
90. 4 For a *t* years in thy sight are but as
91. 7 A *t* shall fall at thy side, and ten
7 and ten *t* at thy right hand; but it
105. 8 he commanded to a *t* generations.
Ec 7.28 one man among a *t* have I found;
SS 5.10 ruddy, the chiefest among ten *t*.
Isa 30.17 One *t* shall flee at the rebuke of one;
60.22 A little one shall become a *t*, and a
Jon 4.11 sixscore *t* persons that cannot
Mt 14.21 had eaten were about five *t* men,
15.38 they that did eat were four *t* men,
16. 9 the five loaves of the five *t*,
10 the seven loaves of the four *t*,
18.24 which owed him ten *t* talents.
Mk 5.13 (they were about two *t*;) and were
6.44 the loaves were about five *t* men.
8. 9 that had eaten were about four *t*:
19 brake the five loaves among five *t*,
20 And when the seven among four *t*,
Lk 9.14 For they were about five *t* men.
14.31 be able with ten *t* to meet him
31 cometh against him with twenty *t*?
Jn 6.10 sat down, in number about five *t*.
Ac 2.41 unto them about three *t* souls.
4. 4 of the men was about five *t*.
19.19 and found it fifty *t* pieces of silver,
21.38 four *t* men that were murderers?
Ro 11. 4 reserved to myself seven *t* men,
1Co 4.15 ye have ten *t* instructers in Christ,
10. 8 fell in one day three and twenty *t*.
14.19 ten *t* words in an unknown tongue.
2Pe 3. 8 day is with the Lord as a *t* years,
8 years, and a *t* years as one day.
Rev 5.11 of them was ten *t* times ten *t*,
7. 4 forty and four *t* of all the tribes
5 tribe of Juda were sealed twelve *t*.
5 of Reuben were sealed twelve *t*.
5 tribe of Gad were sealed twelve *t*.
6 tribe of Aser were sealed twelve *t*.
6 of Nepthalim were sealed twelve *t*.
6 of Manasses were sealed twelve *t*.
7 of Simeon were sealed twelve *t*.
7 tribe of Levi were sealed twelve *t*.
7 of Issachar were sealed twelve *t*.
8 of Zabulon were sealed twelve *t*.
8 of Joseph were sealed twelve *t*.
8 of Benjamin were sealed twelve *t*.
9.16 horsemen were two hundred *t t*:
11. 3 a *t* two hundred and threescore
13 were slain of men seven *t*:
12. 6 a *t* two hundred and threescore
14. 1 him an hundred forty and four *t*,
3 the hundred and forty and four *t*,
20 of a *t* and six hundred furlongs.
20. 2 Satan, and bound him a *t* years,
3 till the *t* years should be fulfilled:
4 and reigned with Christ a *t* years.
5 until the *t* years were finished.
6 and shall reign with him a *t* years.
7 when the *t* years are expired, Satan
21.16 with the reed, twelve *t* furlongs.

THOUSANDS

Gen 24.60 be thou the mother of *t* of millions,
Ex 20. 6 shewing mercy unto *t* of them that
34. 7 Keeping mercy for *t*, forgiving
1Sa 18. 7 Saul hath slain his *t*,
7 and David his ten *t*.
Ps 3. 6 not be afraid of ten *t* of people,
68.17 thousand, even *t* of angels;
119.72 unto me than *t* of gold and silver.
Jer 32.18 shewest loving kindness unto *t*,
Dan 7.10 thousand *t* ministered unto him,
Mic 5. 2 thou be little among the *t* of Judah,
6. 7 the Lord be pleased with *t* of rams,
7 or with ten *t* of rivers of oil? shall
Ac 21.20 *t* of Jews there are which believe;
Jude 14 cometh with ten *t* of his saints,
Rev 5.11 times ten thousand, and *t* of *t*;

THREAD

Gen 14.23 take from a *t* even to a shoelatchet,
38.28 bound upon his hand a scarlet *t*,
30 that had the scarlet *t* upon his hand:
Jos 2.18 shalt bind this line of scarlet *t*
Jdg 16. 9 as a *t* of tow is broken when it
12 them from off his arms like a *t*.
SS 4. 3 Thy lips are like a *t* of scarlet, and

THREATEN

Ac 4.17 let us straitly *t* them, that they

THREATENED

Ac 4.21 So when they had further *t* them,
1Pe 2.23 again; when he suffered, he *t* not;

THREATENING

Eph 6. 9 things unto them, forbearing *t*:

THREATENINGS

Ac 4.29 And now, Lord, behold their *t*: and
9. 1 And Saul, yet breathing out *t* and

THREE

Gen 40.10 And in the vine were *t* branches:
12 The *t* branches are *t* days:
13 within *t* days shall Pharaoh lift
18 thereof: The *t* baskets are *t* days:
Ex 8.27 *t* days' journey into the wilderness,
Dt 16.16 *T* times in a year shall all thy
17. 6 of two witnesses, or *t* witnesses,
19.15 or at the mouth of *t* witnesses,
Jdg 7. 7 By the *t* hundred men that lapped
16.15 hast mocked me these *t* times,
1Sa 20.20 I will shoot *t* arrows on the side
2Sa 23.16 the *t* mighty men brake through
17 things did these *t* mighty men.
1Ki 17.21 himself upon the child *t* times,
2Ki 17. 5 to Samaria, and besieged it *t* years.
18.10 at the end of *t* years they took it:
Est 4.16 neither eat nor drink *t* days, night
Job 2.11 Job's *t* friends heard of all this evil
32. 1 these *t* men ceased to answer Job,
3 against his *t* friends was his wrath
5 answer in the mouth of these *t* men,
Pr 30.15 *t* things that are never satisfied,
18 *t* things which are too wonderful
21 For *t* things the earth is disquieted,
29 There be *t* things which go well,
Dan 3.23 these *t* men, Shadrach, Meshach,
6.10 upon his knees *t* times a day,
13 maketh his petition *t* times a day.
Am 1. 3 For *t* transgressions of Damascus,
4. 7 were yet *t* months to the harvest:
Jon 1.17 belly of the fish *t* days and *t* nights.
3. 3 great city of *t* days' journey.
Mt 12.40 as Jonas was *t* days and *t* nights
40 *t* days and *t* nights in the heart of
13.33 and hid in *t* measures of meal,
15.32 they continue with me now *t* days,
17. 4 let us make here *t* tabernacles;
18.16 in the mouth of two or *t* witnesses
20 two or *t* are gathered together in
26.61 of God, and to built it in *t* days.
27.40 and buildest it in *t* days, save
63 alive, After *t* days I will rise again.
Mk 8. 2 have now been with me *t* days,
31 killed, and after *t* days rise again.
9. 5 and let us make *t* tabernacles; one
14. 5 for more than *t* hundred pence,
58 within *t* days I will build another
15.29 temple, and buildest it in *t* days,
Lk 1.56 abode with her about *t* months,
2.46 after *t* days they found him in the
4.25 shut up *t* years and six months,
9.33 and let us make *t* tabernacles; one
10.36 Which now of these *t*, thinkest
11. 5 unto him, Friend, lend me *t* loaves;
12.52 *t* against two, and two against *t*.
13. 7 these *t* years I come seeking fruit
21 took and hid in *t* measures of meal,
Jn 2. 6 containing two or *t* firkins apiece.
19 and in *t* days I will raise it up.
20 and wilt thou rear it up in *t* days?
12. 5 ointment sold for *t* hundred pence,
21.11 fishes, an hundred and fifty and *t*:
Ac 2.41 them about *t* thousand souls.
5. 7 about the space of *t* hours after,
7.20 up in his father's house *t* months:
9. 9 And he was *t* days without sight,
10.19 unto him, Behold, *t* men seek thee.
11.10 And this was done *t* times: and all
11 *t* men already come unto the house
17. 2 *t* sabbath days reasoned with them
19. 8 boldly for the space of *t* months,
20. 3 And there abode *t* months. And
31 the space of *t* years I ceased not
25. 1 after *t* days he ascended from
28. 7 and lodged us *t* days courteously.
11 And after *t* months we departed in
12 Syracuse, we tarried there *t* days.
15 as Appii forum, and The *t* taverns:
17 after *t* days Paul called the chief
1Co 10. 8 in one day *t* and twenty thousand.
13.13 faith, hope, charity, these *t*;
14.27 let it be by two, or at the most by *t*,
29 Let the prophets speak two or *t*,
2Co 13. 1 mouth of two or *t* witnesses shall
Gal 1.18 Then after *t* years I went up to
1Ti 5.19 but before two or *t* witnesses.
Heb 10.28 mercy under two or *t* witnesses:
11.23 was hid *t* months of his parents,
Jas 5.17 space of *t* years and six months.
1Jn 5. 7 are *t* that bear record in heaven,
7 Holy Ghost: and these *t* are one.
8 are *t* that bear witness in earth,
8 blood: and these *t* agree in one.
Rev 6. 6 *t* measures of barley for a penny;
8.13 of the trumpet of the *t* angels,
9.18 By these *t* was the third part of
11. 9 dead bodies *t* days and an half,
11 after *t* days and an half the Spirit
16.13 I saw *t* unclean spirits like frogs
19 great city was divided into *t* parts,
21.13 On the east *t* gates;
13 on the north *t* gates;
13 on the south *t* gates;
13 and on the west *t* gates.

THREEFOLD

Ec 4.12 a *t* cord is not quickly broken.

THRESH

Isa 41.15 thou shalt *t* the mountains, and
Jer 51.33 threshingfloor, it is time to *t* her:

Mic 4.13 Arise and *t*, O daughter of Zion:
Hab 3.12 thou didst *t* the heathen in anger.

THRESHETH
1Co 9.10 he that *t* in hope should be partaker

THREW
2Sa 16.13 *t* stones at him, and cast dust.
2Ki 9.33 her down. So they *t* her down:
2Ch 31. 1 *t* down the high places and the
Mk 12.42 widow, and she *t* in two mites,
Lk 9.42 devil *t* him down, and tare him.
Ac 22.23 clothes, and *t* dust into the air,

THRICE
Ex 34.23 *T* in the year shall all your
24 Lord thy God *t* in the year.
2Ki 13.18 And he smote *t*, and stayed.
19 thou shalt smite Syria but *t*.
Mt 26.34, 75 crow, thou shalt deny me *t*.
Mk 14.30, 72 twice, thou shalt deny me *t*.
Lk 22.34 shalt *t* deny that thou knowest
61 cock crow, thou shalt deny me *t*.
Jn 13.38 crow, till thou hast denied me *t*.
Ac 10.16 This was done *t*: and the vessel
2Co 11.25 *T* was I beaten with rods, once
25 *t* I suffered shipwreck, a night
12. 8 this thing I besought the Lord *t*,

THROAT
Ps 5. 9 their *t* is an open sepulcher; they
69. 3 weary of my crying: my *t* is dried:
115. 7 neither speak they through their *t*.
Pr 23. 2 And put a knife to thy *t*, if thou
Jer 2.25 unshod, and thy *t* from thirst:
Mt 18.28 and took him by the *t*, saying,
Ro 3.13 Their *t* is an open sepulcher;

THRONE
Gen 41.40 only in the *t* will I be greater
Ex 11. 5 of Pharaoh that sitteth upon his *t*,
12.29 of Pharaoh that sat on his *t*
Dt 17.18 sitteth upon the *t* of his kingdom,
1Sa 2. 8 make them inherit the *t* of glory:
2Sa 3.10 to set up the *t* of David over Israel
7.13 will stablish the *t* of his kingdom
16 thy *t* shall be established for ever.
14. 9 the king and his *t* be guiltless.
1Ki 1.13 me, and he shall sit upon my *t*?
37 Solomon, and make his *t* greater
37 than the *t* of my lord king David.
10. 9 thee, to set thee on the *t* of Israel:
22.10 king of Judah sat each on his *t*,
19 I saw the Lord sitting on his *t*,
2Ki 10. 3 sons, and set him on his father's *t*,
13.13 and Jeroboam sat upon his *t*:
1Ch 17.12 and I will stablish his *t* for ever.
29.23 Solomon sat on the *t* of the Lord
2Ch 6.10 and am set on the *t* of Israel, as
16 sight to sit upon the *t* of Israel;
18. 9 Judah sat either of them on his *t*,
Ps 9. 4 thou satest in the *t* judging right.
11. 4 temple, the Lord's *t* is in heaven:
45. 6 Thy *t*, O God, is for ever and ever:
89. 4 build up thy *t* to all generations.
94.20 the *t* of iniquity have fellowship
97. 2 are the habitation of his *t*.
103.19 hath prepared his *t* in the heavens;
Isa 6. 1 saw also the Lord sitting upon a *t*,
14.13 exalt my *t* above the stars of God:
16. 5 in mercy shall the *t* be established:
22.23 a glorious *t* to his father's house.
66. 1 The heaven is my *t*, and the earth
Jer 1.15 set every one his *t* at the entering
14.21 do not disgrace the *t* of thy glory:
17.12 A glorious high *t* from the
La 5.19 *t* from generation to generation.
Dan 5.20 he was deposed from his kingly *t*,
7. 9 his *t* was like the fiery flame, and
Mt 5.34 by heaven; for it is God's *t*:
19.28 man shall sit in the *t* of his glory,
25.31 shall he sit upon the *t* of his glory:
Ac 2.30 raise up Christ to sit on his *t*;
7.49 Heaven is my *t*, and earth is my
Heb 1. 8 Thy *t*, O God, is for ever and ever:
4.16 come boldly unto the *t* of grace,
Rev 1. 4 Spirits which are before his *t*;
3.21 will I grant to sit with me in my *t*.
20.11 I saw a great white *t*, and him that
22. 1 proceeding out of the *t* of God and
3 the *t* of God and of the Lamb shall

THRONES
Ps 122. 5 For there are set *t* of judgment,
5 the *t* of the house of David.
Isa 14. 9 raised up from their *t* all the kings
Eze 26.16 sea shall come down from their *t*,
Dan 7. 9 I beheld till the *t* were cast down,
Mt 19.28 ye also shall sit upon twelve *t*,
Lk 22.30 sit on *t* judging the twelve tribes
Col 1.16 whether they be *t*, or dominions,
Rev 20. 4 I saw *t*, and they sat upon them,

THRONG
Mk 3. 9 multitude, lest they should *t* him.
Lk 8.45 the multitude *t* thee and press

THRONGED
Mk 5.24 people followed him, and *t* him.
Lk 8.24 But as he went the people *t* him.

THRONGING
Mk 5.31 Thou seest the multitude *t* thee,

THROUGHLY
Job 6. 2 Oh that my grief were *t* weighed,
Ps 51. 2 Wash me *t* from mine iniquity,
Jer 7. 5 if ye *t* amend your ways and your
Mt 3.12 he will *t* purge his floor, and gather
Lk 3.17 he will *t* purge his floor, and will
2Co 11. 6 been *t* made manifest among
2Ti 3.17 *t* furnished unto all good works.

THROUGHOUT
Ex 34. 3 let any man be seen *t* all the mount;
35. 3 kindle no fire *t* your habitations
1Sa 13. 3 Saul blew the trumpet *t* all the land,
19 smith found *t* all the land of Israel:
2Ch 16. 9 run to and fro *t* the whole earth,
Ps 72. 5 and moon endure, *t* all generations.
102.24 thy years are *t* all generations.
145.13 dominion endureth *t* all generations.
Mt 4.24 And his fame went *t* all Syria:
Mk 1.28 fame spread abroad *t* all the region
39 in their synagogues *t* all Galilee,
14. 9 be preached *t* the whole world,
Lk 1.65 *t* all the hill country of Judea.
4.25 great famine was *t* all the land;
7.17 of him went forth *t* all Judea,
17 and *t* all the region round about.
8. 1 he went *t* every city and village,
39 and published *t* the whole city how
23. 5 the people, teaching *t* all Jewry,
Jn 19.23 seam, woven from the top *t*.
Ac 8. 1 scattered abroad *t* the regions of
9.31 had the churches rest *t* all Judea
32 as Peter passed *t* all quarters, he
42 And it was known *t* all Joppa;
10.37 which was published *t* all Judea,
11.28 be great dearth *t* all the world:
13.49 was published *t* all the region.
14.24 after they had passed *t* Pisidia,
16. 6 when they had gone *t* Phrygia
19.26 but almost *t* all Asia, this Paul
24. 5 among all the Jews *t* the world,
26.20 and *t* all the coast of Judea,
Ro 1. 8 is spoken of *t* the whole world.
9.17 might be declared *t* all the earth.
2Co 8.18 is in the gospel *t* all the churches;
Eph 3.21 church by Christ Jesus *t* all ages,
1Pe 1. 1 to the strangers scattered *t* Pontus,

THROW
Jdg 2. 2 ye shall *t* down their altars:
6.25 *t* down the altar of Baal that thy
2Sa 20.15 battered the wall, to *t* it down.
2Ki 9.33 And he said, *T* her down. So
Jer 1.10 and to destroy, and to *t* down,
31.28 to *t* down, and to destroy, and to
Eze 16.39 shall *t* down thine eminent place,
Mic 5.11 and *t* down all thy strong holds:
Mal 1. 4 They shall build, but I will *t* down;

THROWN
Ex 15. 1, 21 rider hath he *t* into the sea.
Jdg 6.32 because he hath *t* down his altar.
2Sa 20.21 his head shall be *t* to thee over
1Ki 19.10, 14 covenant, *t* down thine altars,
Jer 31.40 nor *t* down any more for ever.
33. 4 which are *t* down by the mounts,
50.15 are fallen, her walls are *t* down:
La 2. 2 he hath *t* down in his wrath the
17 hath *t* down, and hath not pitied:
Eze 29. 5 leave thee *t* into the wilderness,
38.20 the mountains shall be *t* down,
Na 1. 6 and the rocks are *t* down by him.
Mt 24. 2 another, that shall not be *t* down.
Mk 13. 2 another, that shall not be *t* down.
Lk 4.35 the devil had *t* him in the midst,
21. 6 another, that shall not be *t* down.
Rev 18.21 that great city Babylon be *t* down,

THRUST
Ex 11. 1 he shall surely *t* you out hence
12.39 because they were *t* out of Egypt,
Nu 22.25 she *t* herself unto the wall, and
25. 8 tent, and *t* both of them through,
35.20 But if he *t* him of hatred, or hurl
22 *t* him suddenly without enmity,
Dt 13. 5 to *t* thee out of the way which
10 to *t* thee away from the Lord thy
15.17 *t* it through his ear unto the door,
33.27 he shall *t* out the enemy from
Jdg 3.21 right thigh, and *t* it into his belly:
6.38 *t* the fleece together, and wringed
9.41 Zebul *t* out Gaal and his brethren,
54 his young man *t* him through,
11. 2 they *t* out Jephthah, and said
1Sa 11. 2 I may *t* out all your right eyes,
31. 4 and *t* me through therewith;
4 come and *t* me through,
2Sa 2.16 and *t* his sword in his fellow's side;
18.14 and *t* them through the heart of
23. 6 be all of them as thorns *t* away,
1Ki 2.27 So Solomon *t* out Abiathar from
2Ki 4.27 Gehazi came near to *t* her away.
1Ch 10. 4 and *t* me through therewith;
2Ch 26.20 and they *t* him out from thence;
Ps 118.13 Thou hast *t* sore at me that I
Isa 13.15 that is found shall be *t* through;
14.19 are slain, *t* through with a sword,
Jer 51. 4 that are *t* through in her streets.
Eze 16.40 *t* thee through with their swords.
34.21 ye have *t* with side and with
46.18 to *t* them out of their possession;
Joel 2. 8 Neither shall one *t* another; they
Zec 13. 8 begat him shall *t* him through
Lk 4.29 rose up and *t* him out of the city,
5. 3 would *t* out a little from the land.
10.15 heaven, shall be *t* down to hell.
13.28 of God, and you yourselves *t* out.
Jn 20.25 nails, and *t* my hand into his side,
27 thy hand, and *t* it into my side:
Ac 7.27 his neighbor wrong *t* him away,
39 not obey, but *t* him from them,
16.24 *t* them into the inner prison,
37 and now do they *t* us out privily?
27.39 it were possible, to *t* in the ship.
Heb 12.20 stoned, or *t* through with a dart:
Rev 14.15 *T* in thy sickle, and reap: for
16 cloud *t* in his sickle on the earth;
18 *T* in thy sharp sickle, and gather
19 the angel *t* in his sickle into the

THRUSTETH
Job 32.13 God *t* him down, not man.

THUNDER
Ex 9.23 the Lord sent *t* and hail, and the
29 and the *t* shall cease, neither shall
1Sa 2.10 of heaven shall he *t* upon them:
7.10 the Lord thundered with a great *t*
12.17 Lord, and he shall send *t* and rain;
18 the Lord sent *t* and rain that day:
Job 26.14 but the *t* of his power who can
28.26 a way for the lightning of the *t*:
38.25 or a way for the lightning of *t*;
39.19 hast thou clothed his neck with *t*?
25 the *t* of the captains, and the
40. 9 thou *t* with a voice like him?
Ps 77.18 voice of thy *t* was in the heaven:
81. 7 thee in the secret place of *t*:
104. 7 voice of thy *t* they hasted away.
Isa 29. 6 visited of the Lord of hosts with *t*,
Mk 3.17 Boanerges,...The sons of *t*:
Rev 6. 1 I heard, as it were the noise of *t*,
14. 2 waters, and as a voice of a great *t*:

THUNDERED
1Sa 7.10 the Lord *t* with a great thunder
2Sa 22.14 The Lord *t* from heaven, and
Ps 18.13 The Lord also *t* in the heavens,
Jn 12.29 and heard it, said that it *t*:

THUNDERETH
Job 37. 4 *t* with the voice of his excellency;
5 God *t* marvellously with his voice;
Ps 29. 3 the God of glory *t*: the Lord is

THUNDERINGS
Ex 9.28 be no more mighty *t* and hail;
20.18 And all the people saw the *t*, and
Rev 4. 5 lightnings and *t* and voices:
8. 5 and there were voices, and *t*, and
11.19 were lightnings, and voices, and *t*,
19. 6 and as the voice of mighty *t*,

THUNDERS
Ex 9.33 *t* and hail ceased, and the rain
34 and the hail and the *t* were ceased,
19.16 that there were *t* and lightnings,
Rev 10. 3 cried, seven *t* uttered their voices.
4 seven *t* had uttered their voices,
4 things which the seven *t* uttered,
16.18 were voices, and *t*, and lightnings;

THYSELF
Gen 14.21 the persons, and take the goods to *t*.
Ex 10. 3 thou refuse to humble *t* before me
28 take heed to *t*, see my face no more;
18.14 why sittest thou *t* alone, and all the
Lev 19.18 thou shalt love thy neighbor as *t*:
Dt 4. 9 Only take heed to *t*, and keep thy
Ru 3. 3 Wash *t* therefore, and anoint thee,
1Sa 19. 2 abide in a secret place, and hide *t*:
2Sa 22.26 merciful thou wilt shew *t* merciful,
26 upright man thou wilt shew *t* upright.
27 With the pure thou wilt shew *t* pure;
27 froward thou wilt shew *t* unsavory.
1Ki 2. 2 strong therefore, and shew *t* a man;
3.11 *t* understanding to discern
2Ki 22.19 thou hast humbled *t* before the Lord,
2Ch 1.11 asked wisdom and knowledge for *t*,
Job 10.16 thou shewest *t* marvellous upon me.
15. 8 dost thou restrain wisdom to *t*?
40.10 Deck *t* now with majesty and
10 and array *t* with glory and beauty.
Ps 18.26 With the pure thou wilt shew *t* pure;
26 froward thou wilt shew *t* froward.
35.23 Stir up *t*, and awake to my judgment,
37. 1 Fret not *t* because of evildoers,
4 Delight *t* also in the Lord; and he
7 fret not *t* because of him who
8 fret not *t* in any wise to do evil.
55. 1 and hide not *t* from my supplication.
89.46 long, Lord? wilt thou hide *t* forever?
104. 2 Who coverest *t* with light as with a
Pr 24.19 Fret not *t* because of evil men.
27. 1 Boast not *t* of to morrow; for thou
Ec 7.16 over much; neither make *t* over wise:
16 wise: why shouldest thou destroy *t*?
22 thou *t* likewise hast cursed others.
Isa 45.15 Verily thou art a God that hidest *t*,
58. 7 thou hide not *t* from thine own flesh?
14 Then shalt thou delight *t* in the Lord;
Jer 20. 4 I will make thee a terror to *t*, and to
47. 6 put up *t* into thy scabbard, rest, and
La 2.18 give *t* no rest; let not the apple of
3.44 Thou hast covered *t* with a cloud,
Eze 22. 4 defiled *t* in thine idols which thou
Dan 10.12 and to chasten *t* before thy God, thy
Hos 13. 9 O Israel, thou hast destroyed *t*; but
Ob 4 Though thou exalt *t* as the eagle,
Mt 4. 6 be the Son of God, cast *t* down:
5.33 Thou shalt not forswear *t*, but shalt
8. 4 shew *t* to the priest, and offer the
19.19 Thou shalt love thy neighbor as *t*.
22.39 Thou shalt love thy neighbor as *t*.
27.40 buildest it in three days, save *t*.
Mk 1.44 shew *t* to the priest, and offer for
12.31 Thou shalt love thy neighbor as *t*.
15.30 Save *t*, and come down from the
Lk 4. 9 of God, cast *t* down from hence:
23 me this proverb, Physician, heal *t*:
5.14 but go, and shew *t* to the priest,
6.42 when thou *t* beholdest not the beam
7. 6 unto him, Lord, trouble not *t*: for
10.27 thy mind; and thy neighbor as *t*.
17. 8 and gird *t*, and serve me, till I have
23.37 be the king of the Jews, save *t*.
39 If thou be Christ, save *t* and us.
Jn 1.22 sent us. What sayest thou of *t*?
7. 4 these things, shew *t* to the world.
8.13 him, Thou bearest record of *t*;
53 are dead: whom makest thou *t*?
10.33 thou, being a man, makest *t* God.
14.22 that thou wilt manifest *t* unto us,
18.34 Sayest thou this thing of *t*, or did
21.18 thou wast young, thou girdest *t*,
Ac 8.29 Go near, and join *t* to this chariot.
12. 8 him, Gird *t*, and bind on thy sandals.
16.28 Do *t* no harm: for we are all here.
21.24 take, and purify *t* with them,
24 that thou *t* also walkest orderly,
24. 8 *t* mayest take knowledge of all
26. 1 Thou art permitted to speak for *t*.
24 a loud voice, Paul, thou art beside *t*;
Ro 2. 1 another, thou condemnest *t*;
5 treasures up unto *t* wrath against
19 thou *t* art a guide of the blind,
21 another, teachest thou not *t*?
13. 9 Thou shalt love thy neighbor as *t*.
14.22 thou faith? have it to *t* before God.
Gal 5.14 Thou shalt love thy neighbor as *t*.
6. 1 considering *t*, lest thou also be
1Ti 3.15 to behave *t* in the house of God,
4. 7 exercise *t* rather unto godliness.
15 these things; give *t* wholly to them;
16 Take heed unto *t*, and unto the
16 doing this thou shalt both save *t*,
5.22 of other men's sins: keep *t* pure.
6. 5 godliness: from such withdraw *t*.
2Ti 2.15 Study to show *t* approved unto
Tit 2. 7 showing *t* a pattern of good works:
Jas 2. 8 Thou shalt love thy neighbor as *t*,

TIBERIAS
Jn 6. 1 of Galilee, which is the sea of *T*.
23 there came other boats from *T*
21. 1 to the disciples at the sea of *T*;

TIBERIUS
Lk 3. 1 year of the reign of *T* Caesar,

TIDINGS
Gen 29.13 when Laban heard the *t* of Jacob
Ex 33. 4 when the people heard these evil *t*,
1Sa 4.19 heard the *t* that the ark of God
11. 4 and told the *t* in the ears of the
5 him the *t* of the men of Jabesh.
6 upon Saul when he heard those *t*,
27.11 nor woman alive, to bring *t* to Gath,
2Sa 4. 4 five years old when the *t* came
10 thinking to have brought good *t*,
10 have given him a reward for his *t*:
13.30 that *t* came to David, saying,
18.19 me now run, and bear the king *t*,
20 Thou shalt not bear *t* this day,
20 but thou shalt bear *t* another day:
20 but this day thou shalt bear no *t*,
22 seeing that thou hast no *t* ready?
25 be alone, there is *t* in his mouth,
26 the king said, He also bringeth *t*.
27 man, and cometh with good *t*.
31 Cushi said, *T*, my lord the king:
1Ki 1.42 valiant man, and bringest good *t*.
2.28 Then *t* came to Joab: for Joab
14. 6 for I am sent to thee with heavy *t*.
2Ki 7. 9 this day is a day of good *t*, and we
1Ch 10. 9 to carry *t* unto their idols, and to
Ps 112. 7 He shall not be afraid of evil *t*:
Isa 40. 9 O Zion, that bringest good *t*, get
9 O Jerusalem, that bringest good *t*,
41.27 one that bringeth good *t*.
52. 7 feet of him that bringeth good *t*,
7 that bringeth good *t* of good, that
61. 1 to preach good *t* unto the meek;
Jer 20.15 man who brought *t* to my father,
37. 5 Jerusalem heard *t* of them.
49.23 Arpad: for they have heard evil *t*:
Eze 21. 7 that thou shalt answer, For the *t*:
Dan 11.44 But *t* out of the east and out of the
Na 1.15 feet of him that bringeth good *t*,
Lk 1.19 thee, and to shew thee these glad *t*.
2.10 I bring you good *t* of great joy,
8. 1 shewing the glad *t* of the kingdom
Ac 11.22 *t* of these things came unto the
13.32 And we declare unto you glad *t*,
21.31 *t* came unto the chief captain of
Ro 10.15 and bring glad *t* of good things!
1Th 3. 6 and brought us good *t* of your faith

TIE
1Sa 6. 7 no yoke, and *t* the kine to the cart,
Pr 6.21 and *t* them about thy neck.

TIED
Ex 39.31 And they *t* unto it a lace of blue,
1Sa 6.10 milch kine, and *t* them to the cart,
2Ki 7.10 but horses *t*, and asses *t*, and the
Mt 21. 2 straightway ye shall find an ass *t*,
Mk 11. 2 ye shall find a colt *t*, whereon
4 and found the colt *t* by the door
Lk 19.30 your entering ye shall find a colt *t*,

TILING
Lk 5.19 let him down through the *t* with

TILL
Gen 2. 5 was not a man to *t* the ground.
3.19 *t* thou return unto the ground;
23 to *t* the ground from whence he
Ex 15.16 *t* thy people pass over, O Lord,
16 *t* the people pass over, which thou
Dt 17. 5 stone them with stones, *t* they die.
Ru 1.13 tarry for them *t* they were grown?
1Sa 10. 8 shalt thou tarry, *t* I come to thee,
22. 3 *t* I know what God will do for me.
2Sa 3.35 or ought else, *t* the sun be down.
9.10 servants, shall *t* the land for him.
Job 7.19 alone *t* I swallow down my spittle?
8.21 *T* he fill thy mouth with laughing,
14. 6 *t* he shall accomplish, as an
12 *t* the heavens be no more, they
Ec 2. 3 *t* I might see what was that good
Isa 5. 8 field to field, *t* there be no place,
11 until night, *t* wine inflame them!
22.14 not be purged from you *t* ye die,

30.17 *t* ye be left as a beacon upon the top
62. 7 give him no rest, *t* he establish,
Jer 7.32 bury in Tophet, *t* there be no place.
49.37 them, *t* I have consumed them:
52. 3 *t* he had cast them out from his
11 in prison *t* the day of his death.
La 3.50 *T* the Lord look down, and behold
Eze 4. 8 *t* thou hast ended the days of thy
28.15 *t* iniquity was found in thee.
34.21 *t* ye have scattered them abroad;
Hos 5.15 *t* they acknowledge their offense,
10.12 *t* he come and rain righteousness
Mt 1.25 not *t* she had brought forth her
5.18 *T* heaven and earth pass, one jot
18 pass from the law, *t* all be fulfilled.
16.28 *t* they see the Son of man coming
18.21 and I forgive him? *t* seven times?
23.39 *t* ye shall say, Blessed is he that
24.34 pass, *t* all these things be fulfilled.
Mk 6.10 abide *t* ye depart from that place.
9. 1 *t* they have seen the kingdom of
Lk 1.80 *t* the day of his shewing unto
9.27 *t* they see the kingdom of God.
12.50 straitened *t* it be accomplished!
59 *t* thou hast paid the very last mite.
Jn 13.38 crow, *t* thou hast denied me thrice.
21.22, 23 If I will that he tarry *t* I come,
1Co 11.26 the Lord's death *t* he come.
15.25 *t* he hath put all enemies under
Eph 4.13 *T* we all come in the unity of the
Heb 10.13 *t* his enemies be made his footstool.
Rev 2.25 have already hold fast *t* I come.
20. 3 *t* the thousand years shall be

TILLAGE
Pr 13.23 Much food is in the *t* of the poor:

TILLER
Gen 4. 2 but Cain was a *t* of the ground.

TILLEST
Gen 4.12 When thou *t* the ground, it shall

TILLETH
Pr 12.11 He that *t* his land shall be
28.19 He that *t* his land shall have plenty

TIMAEUS
Mk 10.46 blind Bartimaeus, the son of *T*,

TIMBER
Hab 2.11 beam out of the *t* shall answer it.
Zec 5. 4 the *t* thereof and the stones thereof.

TIMBREL
Ex 15.20 of Aaron, took a *t* in her hand;
Job 21.12 They take the *t* and harp, and
Ps 81. 2 a psalm, and bring hither the *t*,
149. 3 sing praises unto him with the *t*
150. 4 Praise him with the *t* and dance:

TIMBRELS
Ex 15.20 women went out after her with *t*
Jdg 11.34 came out to meet him with *t* and
2Sa 6. 5 harps, and on psalteries, and on *t*,
1Ch 13. 8 and with psalteries, and with *t*,
Ps 68.25 were the damsels playing with *t*.

BIBLICAL THEMES

TIME

In the beginning God created the heaven and the earth. Gen 1.1

God called the light Day, and the darkness he called Night. And the evening and the morning were the first day. Gen 1.5

And on the seventh day God ended his work which he had made; and he rested on the seventh day. Gen 2.2

The eternal God is thy refuge, and underneath are the everlasting arms. Dt 33.27

We are strangers before thee, and sojourners, as were all our fathers: our days on the earth are as a shadow, and there is none abiding. 1Ch 29.15

Is there not an appointed time to man upon earth? are not his days also like the days of an hireling? . . . When I lie down, I say, When shall I arise, and the night be gone? and I am full of tossings to and fro unto the dawning of the day. . . . My days are swifter than a weaver's shuttle, and are spent without hope. Job 7.1, 4, 6

My times are in thy hand. Ps 31.15

Lord, thou hast been our dwelling place in all generations. Before the mountains were brought forth, or ever thou hadst formed the earth and the world, . . . thou art God. . . . A thousand years in thy sight are but as yesterday when it is past, and as a watch in the night. Ps 90.1-2, 4

Boast not thyself of to morrow; for thou knowest not what a day may bring forth. Pr 27.1

To every thing there is a season, and a time to every purpose under the heaven: a time to be born, and a time to die; a time to plant, and a time to pluck up that which is planted; . . . a time to love, and a time to hate; a time of war, and a time of peace. Ec 3.1-2, 8

Behold, I will make thee know what shall be in the last end of the indignation: for at the time appointed the end shall be. Dan 8.19

Take therefore no thought for the morrow: for the morrow shall take thought for the things of itself. Sufficient unto the day is the evil thereof. Mt 6.34

He answered and said unto them, When it is evening, ye say, It will be fair weather: for the sky is red. And in the morning, It will be foul weather to day: for the sky is red and lowring. O ye hypocrites, ye can discern the face of the sky; but can ye not discern the signs of the times? Mt 16.2-3

Heaven and earth shall pass away: but my words shall not pass away. Mk 13.31

Take ye heed, watch and pray: for ye know not when the time is. . . . Ye know not when the master of the house cometh, at even, or at midnight, or at the cockcrowing, or in the morning. Mk 13.33, 35

Jesus said unto them, Verily, verily, I say unto you, Before Abraham was, I am. Jn 8.58

God that made the world and all things therein . . . hath determined the times before appointed. Ac 17.24, 26

The time is short . . . the fashion of this world passeth away. 1Co 7.29, 31

One day is with the Lord as a thousand years, and a thousand years as one day. 2Pe 3.8

I am Alpha and Omega, the beginning and the ending, saith the Lord, which is, and which was, and which is to come. Rev 1.8

They need no candle, neither light of the sun; for the Lord God giveth them light: and they shall reign for ever and ever. Rev 22.5

TIME
Gen 4. 3 And in process of *t* it came to pass,
18.10 thee according to the *t* of life;
14 At the *t* appointed I will return
21. 2 at the set *t* of which God had
47.29 the *t* drew nigh that Israel must
Ex 2.23 it came to pass in process of *t*,
9. 5 And the Lord appointed a set *t*,
13.14 thy son asketh thee in *t* to come,
21.19 he shall pay for the loss of his *t*,
Nu 10. 6 When ye blow an alarm the second *t*,
20.15 we have dwelt in Egypt a long *t*;
Dt 1. 9 I spake unto you at that *t*, saying,
5. 5 between the Lord and you at that *t*,
6.20 thy son asketh thee in *t* to come,
Jdg 3.29 slew of Moab at that *t* about ten
10.14 you in the *t* of your tribulation.
Ru 4. 7 the manner in former *t* in Israel
1Sa 1. 4 the *t* was that Elkanah offered,
3. 2 And it came to pass at that *t*, when
8 Lord called Samuel again the third *t*.
9.13 for about this *t* ye shall find him.
16 To morrow about this *t* I will
2Sa 2.11 the *t* that David was king in
20. 5 he tarried longer than the set *t*
18 They were wont to speak in old *t*,
2Ki 3. 6 went out of Samaria the same *t*,
5.26 Is it a *t* to receive money, and to
1Ch 9.20 was the ruler over them in *t* past,
20. 1 the *t* that kings go out to battle,
2Ch 7. 8 at the same *t* Solomon kept the
18.34 *t* of the sun going down he died.
35.17 kept the passover at that *t*,
Ezr 4.10, 11 side the river, and at such a *t*.
17 the river, Peace, and at such a *t*.
7.12 perfect peace, and at such a *t*.
Job 6.17 What *t* they wax warm, they
7. 1 appointed *t* to man upon earth?
9.19 who shall set me a *t* to plead?

Job 14.13 thou wouldest appoint me a set *t*,
14 days of my appointed *t* will I wait,
15.32 shall be accomplished before his *t*,
22.16 Which were cut down out of *t*,
Ps 4. 7 in the *t* that their corn and their
21. 9 a fiery oven in the *t* of thine anger:
27. 5 *t* of trouble he shall hide me in
41. 1 will deliver him in *t* of trouble.
69.13 thee, O Lord, in an acceptable *t*:
89.47 Remember how short my *t* is:
102.13 for the *t* to favor her, yea,
13 her, yea, the set *t*, is come.
121. 8 and thy coming in from this *t* forth,
Pr 25.13 cold of snow in the *t* of harvest,
Ec 1.10 it hath been already of old *t*,
3. 1 a *t* to every purpose under the
2 A *t* to be born, and a *t* to die;
2 a *t* to plant, and a *t* to pluck up that
3 A *t* to kill, and a *t* to heal;
3 a *t* to break down, and a *t* to build
4 A *t* to weep, and a *t* to laugh;
4 a *t* to mourn, and a *t* to dance;
7 A *t* to rend, and a *t* to sew;
8 A *t* to love, and a *t* to hate;
8 a *t* of war, and a *t* of peace.
11 every thing beautiful in his *t*:
7.17 shouldest thou die before thy *t*?
8. 5 man's heart discerneth both *t* and
6 to every purpose there is *t* and
SS 2.12 *t* of the singing of birds is come,
Isa 11.11 shall set his hand again the second *t*
45.21 hath declared this from ancient *t*?
49. 8 an acceptable *t* have I heard thee,
60.22 I the Lord will hasten it in his *t*.
Jer 1.13 Lord came unto me the second *t*,
2.20 For of old *t* I have broken thy yoke,
28 save thee in the *t* of thy trouble:
14. 8 the saviour thereof in *t* of trouble,
50. 4 and in that *t*, saith the Lord,
27 day is come, the *t* of their visitation.
Eze 4.10 from *t* to *t* shalt thou eat it.
7. 7 the *t* is come, the day of trouble
16. 8 behold, thy *t* was the *t* of love;
30. 3 it shall be the *t* of the heathen.
Dan 2. 8 certainty that ye would gain the *t*,
8.17 at the *t* of the end shall be the
19 the *t* appointed the end shall be.
12. 1 at that *t* shall Michael stand up,
1 and there shall be a *t* of trouble,
7 be for a *t*, times, and an half;
9 and sealed till the *t* of the end.
Am 5.13 shall keep silence in that *t*;
13 for it is an evil *t*.
Hab 2. 3 vision is yet for an appointed *t*,
Hag 1. 2 people say, The *t* is not come,
4 Is it *t* for you, O ye, to dwell in
Zec 10. 1 rain in the *t* of the latter rain;
14. 7 that at evening *t* it shall be light.
Mt 1.11 about the *t* they were carried
2. 7 of them diligently what *t* the star
4. 6 lest at any *t* thou dash thy foot
17 that *t* Jesus began to preach,
5.21 that it was said by them of old *t*,
25 lest at any *t* the adversary deliver
8.29 hither to torment us before the *t*?
12. 1 that *t* Jesus went on the sabbath
14. 1 At that *t* Herod the tetrarch heard
15 place, and the *t* is now past;
16.21 From that *t* forth began Jesus to
18. 1 At the same *t* came the disciples
21.34 when the *t* of the fruit drew near,
24.21 beginning of the world to this *t*,
26.16 from that *t* he sought opportunity
18 The Master saith, My *t* is at hand;
42 He went away again the second *t*,
44 away again, and prayed the third *t*,
Mk 1.15 The *t* is fulfilled, and the kingdom
6.35 and now the *t* is far passed:
11.13 for the *t* of figs was not yet.
13.19 which God created unto this *t*,
33 for ye know not when the *t* is.
14.41 he cometh the third *t*, and saith unto
72 And the second *t* the cock crew.
Lk 1.10 were praying without at the *t* of
57 Now Elisabeth's full *t* came that
4. 5 of the world in a moment of *t*.
11 lest at any *t* thou dash thy foot
8.13 and in *t* of temptation fall away.
9.51 the *t* was come that he should be
12.56 is it that ye do not discern this *t*?
13.35 until the *t* come when ye shall say,
16.16 *t* the kingdom of God is preached,
18.30 manifold more in this present *t*,
19.44 knewest not the *t* of thy visitation.
20. 9 into a far country for a long *t*.
21. 8 Christ; and the *t* draweth near:
Jn 1.18 No man hath seen God at any *t*;
3. 4 second *t* into his mother's womb,
5. 6 had been now a long *t* in that case,
6.66 From that *t* many of his disciples
7. 6 unto them, My *t* is not yet come:
6 come: but your *t* is alway ready.
8 feast; for my *t* is not yet full come.
14. 9 Have I been so long *t* with you,
16. 2 yea, the *t* cometh, that whosoever
4 when the *t* shall come, ye may
25 the *t* cometh, when I shall no more
21.14 now the third *t* that Jesus shewed
16 saith to him again the second *t*,
17 He saith unto him the third *t*, Simon,
Ac 1. 6 thou at this *t* restore again the
7.13 And at the second *t* Joseph was
17 the *t* of the promise drew nigh,
12. 1 Now about that *t* Herod the king
Ro 3.26 I say, at this *t* his righteousness:
5. 6 in due *t* Christ died for…ungodly.
8.18 sufferings of this present *t* are not
13.11 And that, knowing the *t*, that now
11 it is high *t* to awake out of sleep:
1Co 4. 5 judge nothing before the *t*, until
7. 5 except it be with consent for a *t*,
29 this I say, brethren, the *t* is short:
15. 8 me also, as of one born out of due *t*.
2Co 6. 2 I have heard thee in a *t* accepted,
2 now is the accepted *t*; behold, now
Gal 1.13 heard of my conversation in *t* past
4. 2 until…*t* appointed of the father.
4 the fulness of the *t* was come,
Eph 2. 2 in *t* past ye walked according to
5.16 Redeeming the *t*, because the days
2Th 2. 6 that he might be revealed in his *t*.
1Ti 2. 6 for all, to be testified in due *t*.
6.19 foundation against the *t* to come,
2Ti 4. 3 the *t* will come when they will not
Heb 1. 1 spake in *t* past unto the fathers
9. 9 a figure for the *t* then present, in
28 shall he appear the second *t* without
1Pe 1. 5 ready to be revealed in the last *t*.
4. 2 should live the rest of his *t* in the
17 the *t* is come that judgment must
5. 6 that he may exalt you in due *t*:
1Jn 2.18 Little children, it is the last *t*:
4.12 No man hath seen God at any *t*.
Jude 18 should be mockers in the last *t*,
Rev 1. 3 therein: for the *t* is at hand.
14.15 for the *t* is come for thee to reap;
22.10 of this book: for the *t* is at hand.

TIMES

Gen 27.36 hath supplanted me these two *t*:
31. 7 me, and changed my wages ten *t*;
Jos 6. 4 ye shall compass the city seven *t*,
1Ki 8.59 cause of his people Israel at all *t*,
17.21 himself upon the child three *t*,
18.43 And he said, Go again seven *t*.
2Ki 4.35 and the child sneezed seven *t*, and
5.10 Go and wash in Jordan seven *t*,
14 dipped himself seven *t* in Jordan,
19.25 of ancient *t* that I have formed it?
1Ch 12.32 men that had understanding of the *t*,
Est 1.13 to the wise men, which knew the *t*,
Job 19. 3 ten *t* have ye reproached me:
24. 1 seeing *t* are not hidden from the
Ps 9. 9 oppressed, a refuge in *t* of trouble.
10. 1 hidest thou thyself in *t* of trouble?
31. 5 My *t* are in thy hand: deliver me
34. 1 I will bless the Lord at all *t*: his
62. 8 Trust in him at all *t*; ye people,
119.20 hath unto thy judgments at all *t*.
164 Seven *t* a day do I praise thee
Jer 8. 7 heaven knoweth her appointed *t*:
Dan 1.20 he found them ten *t* better than all
2.21 changeth the *t* and the seasons:
3.19 heat the furnace one seven *t* more
6.10 upon his knees three *t* a day,
13 maketh his petition three *t* a day.
7.10 ten thousand *t* ten thousand stood
25 and think to change *t* and laws:
12. 7 shall be for a time, *t*, and an half;
Mt 16. 3 can ye not discern…signs of the *t*?
18.21 me, and I forgive him till seven *t*?
22 I say not unto thee, Until seven *t*:
22 but, Until seventy *t* seven.
Lk 17. 4 trespass against thee seven *t* in a
21.24 the *t* of the Gentiles be fulfilled.
Ac 1. 7 you to know the *t* or the seasons,
3.19 when the *t* of refreshing shall
21 until the *t* of restitution of all
17.26 determined…*t* before appointed,
30 the *t* of this ignorance God winked
2Co 11.24 five *t* received I forty stripes save
Eph 1.10 the dispensation of the fulness of *t*
1Th 5. 1 of the *t* and the seasons, brethren,
1Ti 4. 1 latter *t* some shall depart from
2Ti 3. 1 the last days perilous *t* shall come.
Heb 1. 1 who at sundry *t* and in divers
1Pe 1.20 manifest in these last *t* for you,
Rev 5.11 was ten thousand *t* ten thousand,
12.14 for a time, and *t*, and half a time,

TIMON

Ac 6. 5 *T*, and Parmenas, and Nicolas a

TIMOTHEUS

Ac 16. 1 disciple was there, named *T*,
17.14 but Silas and *T* abode there still.
15 a commandment unto Silas and *T*
18. 5 when Silas and *T* were come from
19.22 ministered unto him, *T* and
20. 4 and Gaius of Derbe, and *T*;
Ro 16.21 *T* my workfellow, and Lucius,
1Co 4.17 this cause have I sent unto you *T*,
16.10 if *T* come, see that he may be with
2Co 1.19 even by me and Silvanus and *T*,
Php 1. 1 Paul and *T*, the servants of Jesus
2.19 Jesus to send *T* shortly unto you,
Col 1. 1 the will of God, and *T* our brother,
1Th 1. 1 Silvanus, and *T*, unto the church
3. 2 sent *T*, our brother, and minister
6 But now when *T* came from you
2Th 1. 1 Silvanus, and *T*, unto the church

TIMOTHY

2Co 1. 1 *T* our brother, unto the church
1Ti 1. 2 Unto *T*, my own son in the faith:
18 charge I commit unto thee, son *T*,
6.20 O *T*, keep that which is committed
2Ti 1. 2 To *T*, my dearly beloved son:
Phm 1 and *T* our brother, unto Philemon
Heb 13.23 our brother *T* is set at liberty;

TINGLE

1Sa 3.11 every one that heareth it shall *t*.
2Ki 21.12 heareth of it, both his ears shall *t*.
Jer 19. 3 whosoever heareth, his ears shall *t*.

TINKLING

Isa 3.16 and making a *t* with their feet:
18 of their *t* ornaments about their feet;
1Co 13. 1 as sounding brass, or a *t* cymbal.

TIP

Lk 16.24 may dip the *t* of his finger in water,

TITHE
Lev 27.30 all the *t* of the land, whether of
32 concerning the *t* of the herd, or of
Nu 18.26 Lord, even a tenth part of the *t*.
Dt 12.17 within thy gates the *t* of thy corn,
14.22 truly *t* all the increase of thy seed,
23 *t* of thy corn, of thy wine, and of
28 forth all the *t* of thine increase
2Ch 31. 5 the *t* of all things brought they in
6 brought in the *t* of oxen and sheep,
6 the *t* of holy things which were
Neh 10.38 the Levites shall bring up the *t* of
13.12 brought all Judah the *t* of the corn
Mt 23.23 for ye pay *t* of mint and anise
Lk 11.42 ye *t* mint and rue and all manner

TITHES
Gen 14.20 hand. And he gave him *t* of all.
Lev 27.31 will at all redeem ought of his *t*,
Nu 18.24 But the *t* of the children of Israel,
26 the *t* which I have given you from
28 offering unto the Lord of all your *t*,
Dt 12. 6 your *t*, and heave offerings of your
11 your *t*, and the heave offering of
26.12 the *t* of thine increase the third
2Ch 31.12 brought in the offerings and the *t*
Neh 10.37 the *t* of our ground unto the
37 have the *t* in all the cities of our
38 Levites, when the Levites take *t*:
38 bring up the tithe of the *t* unto
12.44 for the first fruits, and for the *t*,
13. 5 the vessels, and the *t* of the corn,
Am 4. 4 and your *t* after three years:
Mal 3. 8 robbed thee? In *t* and offerings.
10 ye all the *t* into the storehouse,
Lk 18.12 week, I give *t* of all that I possess.
Heb 7. 5 to take *t* of the people according to
6 from them received *t* of Abraham,
8 And here men that die receive *t*;
9 receiveth *t*, payed *t* in Abraham.

TITHING
Dt 26.12 made an end of *t* all the tithes
12 third year, which is the year of *t*,

TITLE
2Ki 23.17 said, What *t* is that that I see?
Jn 19.19 And Pilate wrote a *t*, and put it
20 This *t* then read many of the Jews:

TITLES
Job 32.21 let me give flattering *t* unto man.
22 For I know not to give flattering *t*;

TITTLE
Mt 5.18 one *t* shall in no wise pass from
Lk 16.17 pass, than one *t* of the law to fail.

TITUS
2Co 2.13 I found not *T* my brother:
7. 6 comforted us by the coming of *T*;
13 the more joyed we for the joy of *T*,
14 boasting, which I made before *T*,
8. 6 Insomuch that we desired *T*, that
16 care into the heart of *T* for you.
23 Whether any do inquire of *T*, he
12.18 I desired *T*, and with him I sent
18 brother. Did *T* make a gain of you?
Gal 2. 1 and took *T* with me also.
3 But neither *T*, who was with me,
2Ti 4.10 to Galatia, *T* unto Dalmatia.
Tit 1. 4 To *T*, mine own son after the

TOGETHER
Gen 1.10 gathering *t* of the waters called he
3. 7 and they sewed fig leaves *t*, and
Nu 8. 9 gather...the children of Israel *t*:
Dt 22.10 plow with an ox and an ass *t*.
Jdg 20. 1 was gathered *t* as one man,
11 the city, knit *t* as one man.
2Sa 14. 6 and they two strove *t* in the field,
16 would destroy me and my son *t*
1Ki 5.12 and they two made a league *t*.
22. 6 of Israel gathered the prophets *t*,
Neh 6. 7 therefore, and let us take counsel *t*.
10 Let us meet *t* in the house of God,
12.28 the singers gathered themselves *t*,
Est 4.16 Go, gather *t* all the Jews that are
Job 3.18 There the prisoners rest *t*; they
10. 8 have made me and fashioned me *t*
16.10 gathered themselves *t* against me.
17.16 pit, when our rest *t* is in the dust.
34.15 All flesh shall perish *t*, and man
38. 7 When the morning stars sang *t*,
40.13 Hide them in the dust *t*; and bind
Ps 2. 2 and the rulers take counsel *t*,
33. 7 He gathereth the waters of the sea *t*
34. 3 me, and let us exalt his name *t*.
50. 5 Gather my saints *t* unto me;
85.10 Mercy and truth are met *t*;
122. 3 as a city that is compact *t*:
133. 1 is for brethren to dwell *t* in unity!
Pr 22. 2 The rich and poor meet *t*: the Lord is
Ec 3. 5 and a time to gather stones *t*;
4. 5 fool foldeth his hands *t*, and eateth
11 if two lie *t*, then they have heat:
Isa 1.18 Come now, and let us reason *t*, saith
11. 6 the young lion and the fatling *t*;
7 their young ones shall lie down *t*:
34. 4 the heavens shall be rolled *t* as
40. 5 and all flesh shall see it *t*:
41.19 and the pine, and the box tree *t*:
43. 9 Let all the nations be gathered *t*,
46. 2 They stoop, they bow down *t*;
52. 9 Break forth into joy, sing *t*, ye
60. 4 all they gather themselves *t*, they
65.25 The wolf and the lamb shall feed *t*,
Eze 37. 7 bones came *t*, bone to his bone.
Joel 3.11 gather yourselves *t* round about:
Am 3. 3 Can two walk *t*, except they be
Zec 12. 3 people of the earth be gathered *t*
Mt 13.30 Let both grow *t* until the harvest:
18.20 three are gathered *t* in my name,
19. 6 What therefore God hath joined *t*,
24.28 will the eagles be gathered *t*.
Mk 10. 9 What therefore God hath joined *t*,
13.27 gather *t* his elect from the four
Lk 5.15 great multitudes came *t* to hear,
17.37 will the eagles be gathered *t*.
Jn 20. 7 but wrapped *t* in a place by itself.
Ac 3. 1 Peter and John went up *t*
12.12 many were gathered *t* praying.
14.27 and had gathered the church *t*,
15. 6 And the apostles and elders came *t*
19.19 arts brought their books *t*,
20. 7 disciples came *t* to break bread,
Ro 8.28 that all things work *t* for good
15.30 strive *t* with me in your prayers
1Co 1.10 that ye be perfectly joined *t* in the
3. 9 For we are laborers *t* with God:
7. 5 come *t* again, that Satan
11.18 when ye come *t* in the church, I
2Co 6. 1 We then, as workers *t* with him,
14 Be ye not unequally yoked *t* with
Eph 2. 5 hath quickened us *t* with Christ,
21 all the building fitly framed *t*
4.16 the whole body fitly joined *t* and
1Th 4.17 remain shall be caught up *t* with
5.11 Wherefore comfort yourselves *t*,
Heb 10.25 the assembling of ourselves *t*,
Rev 6.14 as a scroll when it is rolled *t*;

TOIL
Gen 5.29 our work and *t* of our hands,
41.51 hath made me forget all my *t*,
Mt 6.28 they *t* not, neither do they spin:
Lk 12.27 grow: they *t* not, they spin not;

TOILED
Lk 5. 5 Master, we have *t* all the night,

TOILING
Mk 6.48 And he saw them *t* in rowing; for

TOKEN
Gen 9.12 This is the *t* of the covenant which
13 *t* of a covenant between me and
17 This is the *t* of the covenant, which
17.11 *t* of the covenant betwixt me and
Ex 3.12 this shall be a *t* unto thee, that I
12.13 the blood shall be to you for a *t*
13.16 shall be for a *t* upon thine hand,
Nu 17.10 be kept for a *t* against the rebels;
Jos 2.12 father's house, and give me a true *t*:
Ps 86.17 Shew me a *t* for good; that they
Mk 14.44 betrayed him had given them a *t*,
Php 1.28 to them an evident *t* of perdition,
2Th 1. 5 a manifest *t* of the righteous
3.17 which is the *t* in every epistle:

TOLD
Gen 3.11 Who *t* thee that thou wast naked?
40. 9 chief butler *t* his dream to Joseph,
41. 8 and Pharaoh *t* them his dream;
Nu 11.24 *t* the people the words of the Lord,
Jdg 6.13 miracles which our fathers *t* us
16. 2 it was *t* the Gazites, saying, Samson
10, 13 hast mocked me, and *t* me lies:
15 hast not *t* me wherein thy great
17 That he *t* her all his heart, and
Ru 3.16 she *t* her all that the man had done
1Sa 3.13 *t* him that I will judge his house
18 Samuel *t* him every whit, and hid
23. 1 they *t* David, saying, Behold, the
13 was *t* Saul that David was escaped
27. 4 *t* Saul that David was fled to Gath:
2Sa 1. 5 unto the young man that *t* him,
17.17 and a wench went and *t* them;
18 a lad saw them, and *t* Absalom:
1Ki 1.23 they *t* the king, saying, Behold
10. 3 Solomon *t* her all her questions:
7 and, behold, the half was not *t* me:
2Ki 1. 7 meet you, and *t* you these words?
4. 7 she came and *t* the man of God.
2Ch 2. 2 Solomon *t* out threescore and ten
9. 2 Solomon *t* her all her questions:
6 of thy wisdom was not *t* me:
Neh 2.12 neither *t* I any man what my God
Job 15.18 wise men have *t* from their fathers,
37.20 Shall it be *t* him that I speak? if a
Ps 44. 1 our fathers have *t* us, what work
90. 9 we spend our years as a tale that is *t*.
Isa 7. 2 And it was *t* the house of David,
40.21 not been *t* you from the beginning?
52.15 that which had not been *t* them
Dan 4. 7 and I *t* the dream before them;
Hab 1. 5 not believe, though it be *t* you.
Mt 8.33 into the city, and *t* every thing,
12.48 and said unto him that *t* him,
14.12 buried it, and went and *t* Jesus.
18.31 *t* unto their Lord all that was done.
24.25 Behold, I have *t* you before.
26.13 done, be *t* for a memorial of her.
28. 7 shall ye see him: lo, I have *t* you.
Mk 5.14 *t* it in the city, and in the country.
16 they that saw it *t* them how it
33 him, and *t* him all the truth.
6.30 *t* him all things, both what they
9.12 he answered and *t* them, Elias
16.10 *t* them that had been with him,
13 they went and *t* it unto the residue:
Lk 1.45 which were *t* her from the Lord.
2.17 was *t* them concerning this child.
18 were *t* them by the shepherds.
20 and seen, as it was *t* unto them.
8.20 it was *t* him by certain which said,
34 went and *t* it in the city and in the
36 which saw it *t* them by what means
9.10 *t* him all that they had done.
36 and *t* no man in those days any of
13. 1 some that *t* him of the Galileans,
18.37 they *t* him, that Jesus of Nazareth
24. 9 *t* all these things unto the eleven,
10 *t* these things unto the apostles.
35 *t* what things were done in the

Jn 3.12 If I have *t* you earthly things, and
4.29 *t* me all things that ever I did:
39 He *t* me all that ever I did.
51 and *t* him, saying, Thy son liveth.
5.15 and *t* the Jews that it was Jesus,
8.40 a man that hath *t* you the truth,
9.27 I have *t* you already, and ye did
10.25 them, I *t* you, and ye believed not:
11.46 and *t* them what things Jesus had
14. 2 it were not so, I would have *t* you.
29 have *t* you before it come to pass,
16. 4 But these things have I *t* you,
4 remember that I *t* you of them.
18. 8 I have *t* you that I am he:
20.18 *t* the disciples that she had seen
Ac 5.22 the prison, they returned, and *t*
25 Then came one and *t* them, saying,
9. 6 be *t* thee what thou must do.
12.14 *t* how Peter stood before the gate.
16.36 keeper of the prison *t* this saying
38 serjeants *t* these words unto the
22.10 it shall be *t* thee of all things
26 he went and *t* the chief captain,
23.16 entered into the castle, and *t* Paul.
30 it was *t* me how that the Jews
27.25 it shall be even as it was *t* me.
2Co 7. 7 when he *t* us your earnest desire,
13. 2 I *t* you before, and foretell you,
Gal 5.21 as I have also *t* you in time past,
Php 3.18 walk of whom I have *t* you often,
1Th 3. 4 we *t* you before that we should
2Th 2. 5 with you, I *t* you these things?
Jude 18 that they *t* you there should be

TOMB

Job 21.32 grave, and shall remain in the *t*.
Mt 27.60 laid it in his own new *t*, which he
Mk 6.29 up his corpse, and laid it in a *t*.

TOMBS

Mt 8.28 with devils, coming out of the *t*,
23.29 ye build the *t* of the prophets,
Mk 5. 2 there met him out of the *t* a man
3 had his dwelling among the *t*; and
5 and in the *t*, crying and cutting
Lk 8.27 abode in my house, but in the *t*.

TONGS

Isa 6. 6 which he had taken with the *t*
44.12 smith with the *t* both worketh in

TONGUE

Gen 10. 5 every one after his *t*, after their
Ex 4.10 slow of speech, and of a slow *t*.
Dt 28.49 whose *t* thou shalt not understand;
Jdg 7. 5 lappeth of the water with his *t*,
Ezr 4. 7 letter was written in the Syrian *t*,
Job 5.21 be hid from the scourge of the *t*:
6.24 Teach me, and I will hold my *t*:
30 Is there iniquity in my *t*? cannot
20.12 though he hide it under his *t*;
29.10 their *t* cleaved to the roof of their
Ps 5. 9 sepulcher; they flatter with their *t*.
12. 3 the *t* that speaketh proud things:
4 said, With our *t* will we prevail;
15. 3 He that backbiteth not with his *t*,
34.13 Keep thy *t* from evil, and thy lips
39. 1 my ways, that I sin not with my *t*:
45. 1 my *t* is the pen of a ready writer.
51.14 my *t* shall sing aloud of thy
52. 2 Thy *t* deviseth mischiefs; like a
73. 9 their *t* walketh through the earth.
119.172 My *t* shall speak of thy word: for
126. 2 laughter, and our *t* with singing:
137. 6 let my *t* cleave to the roof of my
139. 4 For there is not a word in my *t*,
Pr 6.17 A proud look, a lying *t*, and hands
24 of the *t* of a strange woman.
10.20 *t* of the just is as choice silver:
12.18 but the *t* of the wise is health.
19 but a lying *t* is but for a moment.
15. 2 The *t* of the wise useth knowledge
4 A wholesome *t* is a tree of life: but
17. 4 a liar giveth ear to a naughty *t*.
18.21 and life are in the power of the *t*:
21. 6 lying *t* is a vanity tossed to and fro
23 keepeth his mouth and his *t*
25.15 and a soft *t* breaketh the bone.
Isa 3. 8 their *t* and their doings are against
30.27 and his *t* as a devouring fire:
35. 6 hart, and the *t* of the dumb sing:
45.23 knee shall bow, every *t* shall swear.
50. 4 hath given me the *t* of the learned,
Jer 9. 5 have taught their *t* to speak lies,
8 Their *t* is an arrow shot out; it
18.18 and let us smite him with the *t*,
La 4. 4 *t* of the sucking child cleaveth to
Mic 6.12 their *t* is deceitful in their mouth.
Zec 14.12 their *t* shall consume away in their
Mk 7.33 and he spit, and touched his *t*;
35 and the string of his *t* was loosed,
Lk 1.64 and his *t* loosed, and he spake, and
16.24 his finger in water, and cool my *t*;
Ac 1.19 field is called in their proper *t*,
2. 8 hear we every man in our own *t*,
26 heart rejoice, and my *t* was glad;
Ro 14.11 and every *t* shall confess to God.
1Co 14. 2 he that speaketh in an unknown *t*
14 For if I pray in an unknown *t*, my
Php 2.11 every *t* should confess that Jesus
Jas 1.26 be religious, and bridleth not his *t*,
3. 5 Even so the *t* is a little member,
6 the *t* is a fire, a world of iniquity:
8 But the *t* can no man tame; it is
1Pe 3.10 let him refrain his *t* from evil,
Rev 5. 9 out of every kindred, and *t*, and
14. 6 every nation, and kindred, and *t*,
16.16 in the Hebrew *t* Armageddon.

TONGUES

Gen 10.20, 31 their families, after their *t*,
Ps 31.20 in a pavilion from the strife of *t*.
55. 9 Destroy, O Lord, and divide their *t*:
78.36 they lied unto him with their *t*.
140. 3 sharpened their *t* like a serpent;
Isa 66.18 that I will gather all nations and *t*;
Jer 9. 3 they bend their *t* like their bow for
23.21 that use their *t*, and say, He saith.
Mk 16.17 they shall speak with new *t*;
Ac 2. 3 there appeared unto them cloven *t*
4 began to speak with other *t*, as the
11 we do hear them speak in our *t* the
10.46 For they heard them speak with *t*,
19. 6 they spake with *t*, and prophesied.
Ro 3.13 with their *t* they have used deceit;
1Co 12.10 spirits; to another divers kinds of *t*;
10 to another the interpretation of *t*:
28 governments, diversities of *t*.
30 do all speak with *t*? do all
13. 1 Though I speak with the *t* of men
8 fail; whether there be *t*, they shall
14. 5 I would that ye all spake with *t*,
5 than he that speaketh with *t*,
6 if I come unto you speaking with *t*,
18 I speak with *t* more than ye all:
21 With men of other *t* and other lips
22 Wherefore *t* are for a sign, not to
23 and all speak with *t*, and there
39 and forbid not to speak with *t*.
Rev 7. 9 kindreds, and people, and *t*, stood
10.11 many peoples, and nations, and *t*,
11. 9 of the people and kindreds and *t*
13. 7 all kindreds, and *t*, and nations.
16.10 and they gnawed their *t* for pain,
17.15 and multitudes, and nations, and *t*.

TOOK

Gen 2.15 And the Lord God *t* the man, and
21 and he *t* one of his ribs, and
3. 6 she *t* of the fruit thereof, and did
5.24 and he was not; for God *t* him.
22. 3 *t* two of his young men with him,
6 Abraham *t* the wood of the burnt
6 he *t* the fire in his hand, and a
10 and *t* the knife to slay his son.
13 and Abraham went and *t* the ram,
31.23 And he *t* his brethren with him,
45 And Jacob *t* a stone, and set it up
37.24 they *t* him, and cast him into a pit:
31 they *t* Joseph's coat, and killed a
Ex 2. 1 and *t* to wife a daughter of Levi.
3 she *t* for him an ark of bulrushes,
34. 4 and *t* in his hand the two tables of
34 *t* the vail off, until he came out.
Nu 1.17 And Moses and Aaron *t* these men
23. 7 And he *t* up his parable, and said,
Jos 2. 4 woman *t* the two men, and hid
6.12 priests *t* up the ark of the Lord.
7. 1 of Judah, *t* of the accursed thing:
21 then I coveted them, and *t* them;
Jdg 1.13 Caleb's younger brother, *t* it:
16. 3 *t* the doors of the gate of the city,
12 Delilah therefore *t* new ropes,
29 Samson *t* hold of the two middle
1Sa 1.24 him, she *t* him up with her,
5. 1 the Philistines *t* the ark of God,
3 they *t* Dagon, and set him in his
16.13 Then Samuel *t* the horn of oil,
23 that David *t* an harp, and played
17.20 and *t*, and went, as Jesse had
40 And he *t* his staff in his hand,
19.13 Michal *t* an image, and laid it in
2Sa 1.10 I *t* the crown that was upon his
12. 4 but *t* the poor man's lamb, and
2Ki 2. 8 Elijah *t* his mantle, and wrapped
13 He *t* up also the mantle of Elijah
1Ch 2.19 Caleb *t* unto him Ephrath, which
10. 4 So Saul *t* a sword, and fell upon it.
17. 7 I *t* thee from the sheepcote, even
2Ch 5. 4 and the Levites *t* up the ark.
33.11 *t* Manasseh among the thorns,
15 And he *t* away the strange gods,
34.33 Josiah *t* away all the abominations
Job 1.15 fell upon them, and *t* them away;
2. 8 And he *t* him a potsherd to scrape
Ps 18.16 He sent from above, he *t* me, he
22. 9 art he that *t* me out of the womb:
Ec 2.20 to despair of all the labor which I *t*
Jer 13. 7 *t* the girdle from the place where
25.17 *t* I the cup at the Lord's hand, and
36.14 Baruch...*t* the roll in his hand,
Eze 3.12 Then the spirit *t* me up, and I
14 spirit lifted me up, and *t* me away,
11.24 Afterwards the spirit *t* me up,
33. 5 of the trumpet, and *t* not warning;
Am 7.15 And the Lord *t* me as I followed the
Jon 1.15 So they *t* up Jonah, and cast him
Zec 11. 7 I *t* unto me two staves; the one I
10 I *t* my staff, even Beauty, and cut
13 And I *t* the thirty pieces of silver,
Mt 1.24 him, and *t* unto him his wife:
2.14 he *t* the young child and his
8.17 saying, Himself *t* our infirmities,
14.12 disciples came, and *t* up the body,
20 they *t* up of the fragments that
16. 9, 10 and how many baskets ye *t* up?
22 Then Peter *t* him, and began to
18.28 and *t* him by the throat, saying,
22. 6 And the remnant *t* his servants,
15 *t* counsel how they might entangle
25. 1 ten virgins, which *t* their lamps,
3 foolish *t* their lamps, and *t* no oil
4 the wise *t* oil in their vessels with
35 I was a stranger, and ye *t* me in:
26.26 Jesus *t* bread, and blessed it, and
27 And he *t* the cup, and gave thanks,
27. 1 and elders of the people *t* counsel
9 they *t* the thirty pieces of silver,
24 he *t* water, and washed his hands
31 they *t* the robe off from him, and
Mk 1.31 he came and *t* her by the hand,
8. 6 he *t* the seven loaves, and gave
23 he *t* the blind man by the hand,

32 Peter *t* him, and began to rebuke
9.27 But Jesus *t* him by the hand, and
36 he *t* a child, and set him in the
10.16 he *t* them up in his arms, put his
32 he *t* again the twelve, and began
14.22 Jesus *t* bread, and blessed, and
15.20 they *t* off the purple from him,
46 *t* him down, and wrapped him in
Lk 2.28 Then *t* he him up in his arms,
9.10 And he *t* them, and went aside
47 *t* a child, and set him by him,
10.34 him to an inn, and *t* care of him.
35 he *t* out two pence, and gave them
20.29 the first *t* a wife, and died without
22.17 he *t* the cup, and gave thanks,
19 And he *t* bread, and gave thanks,
24.30 he *t* bread, and blessed it, and
43 he *t* it, and did eat before them.
Jn 5. 9 was made whole, and *t* up his bed,
6.11 And Jesus *t* the loaves; and when
8.59 *t* they up stones to cast at him:
11.41 *t* away the stone from the place
12. 3 Then *t* Mary a pound of ointment
13 *T* branches of palm trees, and
13. 4 and *t* a towel, and girded himself.
19. 1 Pilate therefore *t* Jesus, and
16 they *t* Jesus, and led him away.
Ac 1.16 was guide to them that *t* Jesus.
4.13 they *t* knowledge of them, that
15.39 Barnabas *t* Mark, and sailed unto
27.35 *t* bread, and gave thanks to God
28.15 he thanked God, and *t* courage.
1Co 11.23 in which he was betrayed *t* bread:
25 the same manner also he *t* the cup,
Php 2. 7 *t* upon him the form of a servant,
Col 2.14 and *t* it out of the way, nailing
Heb 2.14 himself likewise *t* part of the
16 he *t* not on him the nature of
Rev 5. 7 *t* the book out of the right hand
8. 5 the angel *t* the censer, and filled it
10.10 I *t* the little book out of the
18.21 a mighty angel *t* up a stone like a

TOOTH
Ex 21.24 Eye for eye, *t* for *t*, hand for
27 if he smite out his manservant's *t*,
27 or his maidservant's *t*; he shall let
Lev 24.20 for breach, eye for eye, *t* for *t*:
Dt 19.21 *t* for *t*, hand for hand, foot for foot.
Pr 25.19 time of trouble is like a broken *t*,
Mt 5.38 An eye for an eye, and a *t* for a *t*:

TOOTH'S
Ex 21.27 shall let him go free for his *t* sake.

TOP
Gen 28.12 and the *t* of it reached to heaven:
Ex 19.20 Lord called Moses up to the *t* of
28.32 there shall be an hole in the *t* of it,
Nu 21.20 to the *t* of Pisgah, which looketh
1Ki 18.42 Elijah went up to the *t* of Carmel;
Ps 102. 7 sparrow alone upon the house *t*.
Pr 23.34 he that lieth upon the *t* of a mast.
Isa 2. 2 established in the *t* of…mountains,
La 2.19 for hunger in the *t* of every street.
Eze 26.14 will make thee like the *t* of a rock:
Mt 27.51 in twain from the *t* to the bottom;
Mk 15.38 in twain from the *t* to the bottom.
Jn 19.23 seam, woven from the *t* throughout.
Heb 11.21 leaning upon the *t* of his staff.

TOPAZ
Ex 28.17 first row shall be a sardius, a *t*,
39.10 first row was a sardius, a *t*, and
Job 28.19 *t* of Ethiopia shall not equal it,
Eze 28.13 sardius, *t*, and the diamond,
Rev 21.20 the eighth, beryl; the ninth, a *t*;

TOPS
Gen 8. 5 were the *t* of the mountains seen.
2Sa 5.24 going in the *t* of the mulberry trees,
1Ki 7.16 to set upon the *t* of the pillars:
2Ki 19.26 herb, as the grass on the house *t*,
1Ch 14.15 in the *t* of the mulberry trees,
Job 24.24 cut off as the *t* of the ears of corn.
Isa 2.21 into the *t* of the ragged rocks,
15. 3 on the *t* of their houses, and in
Eze 6.13 in all the *t* of the mountains, and
Hos 4.13 upon the *t* of the mountains,
Joel 2. 5 chariots on the *t* of mountains shall

TORCH
Zec 12. 6 and like a *t* of fire in a sheaf;

TORCHES
Na 2. 3 chariots shall be with flaming *t*
4 they shall seem like *t*, they shall
Jn 18. 3 with lanterns and *t* and weapons.

TORMENT
Mt 8.29 art thou come hither to *t* us before
Mk 5. 7 thee by God, that thou *t* me not.
Lk 8.28 high? I beseech thee, *t* me not.
16.28 they also come into this place of *t*.
1Jn 4.18 out fear, because fear hath *t*.
Rev 9. 5 their *t* was as the *t* of a scorpion,
14.11 the smoke of their *t* ascendeth up
18. 7 so much *t* and sorrow give her:
10 Standing afar off for…fear of her *t*,
15 stand afar off for the fear of her *t*,

TORMENTED
Mt 8. 6 home sick of the palsy, grievously *t*.
Lk 16.24 tongue; for I am *t* in this flame.
25 he is comforted, and thou art *t*.
Heb 11.37 being destitute, afflicted, *t*;
Rev 9. 5 that they should be *t* five months:
11.10 these two prophets *t* them that
14.10 he shall be *t* with fire and brimstone
20.10 shall be *t* day and night for ever

TORMENTORS
Mt 18.34 wroth, and delivered him to the *t*,

TORMENTS
Mt 4.24 taken with divers diseases and *t*,
Lk 16.23 hell he lift up his eyes, being in *t*,

TORN
Gen 31.39 That which was *t* of beasts I
44.28 Surely he is *t* in pieces; and I
Ex 22.13 If it be *t* in pieces, then let him
13 not make good that which was *t*.
31 ye eat any flesh that is *t* of beasts
Lev 7.24 fat of that which is *t* with beasts,
17.15 or that which was *t* with beasts,
22. 8 dieth of itself, or is *t* with beasts,
1Ki 13.26 unto the lion, which hath *t* him,
28 eaten the carcass, nor *t* the ass.
Isa 5.25 carcasses were *t* in the midst of
Jer 5. 6 out thence shall be *t* in pieces:
Eze 4.14 dieth of itself, or is *t* in pieces;
44.31 any thing that is dead of itself, or *t*,
Hos 6. 1 for he hath *t*, and he will heal us;
Mal 1.13 and ye brought that which was *t*,
Mk 1.26 the unclean spirit had *t* him,

TORTURED
Heb 11.35 and others were *t*, not accepting

TOSS
Isa 22.18 violently turn and *t* thee like a
Jer 5.22 the waves thereof *t* themselves,

TOSSED
Ps 109.23 I am *t* up and down as the locust.
Pr 21. 6 a vanity *t* to and fro of them that
Isa 54.11 O thou afflicted, *t* with tempest, and
Mt 14.24 the midst of the sea, *t* with waves:
Ac 27.18 exceedingly *t* with a tempest,
Eph 4.14 *t* to and fro, and carried about
Jas 1. 6 sea driven with the wind and *t*.

TOUCH
Gen 3. 3 it, neither shall ye *t* it, lest ye die.
20. 6 suffered I thee not to *t* her.
Ex 19.12 the mount, or *t* the border of it:
13 There shall not an hand *t* it, but he
Lev 5. 2 Or if a soul *t* any unclean thing,
3 Or if he *t* the uncleanness of man,
6.27 *t* the flesh thereof shall be holy:
7.21 soul that shall *t* any unclean thing,
11. 8 and their carcass shall ye not *t*;
31 whosoever doth *t* them, when they
12. 4 she shall *t* no hallowed thing, nor
Nu 4.15 but they shall not *t* any holy thing,
16.26 *t* nothing of theirs, lest ye be
Dt 14. 8 flesh, nor *t* their dead carcass.
Jos 9.19 now therefore we may not *t* them.
Ru 2. 9 men that they shall not *t* thee?
2Sa 14.10 and he shall not *t* thee any more.
18.12 that none *t* the young man Absalom.
23. 7 man that shall *t* them must be
1Ch 16.22 *T* not mine anointed, and do my
Job 1.11 and *t* all that he hath, and he will
2. 5 and *t* his bone and his flesh, and he
5.19 in seven there shall no evil *t* thee.
6. 7 things that my soul refused to *t* are
Ps 105.15 *T* not mine anointed, and do my
144. 5 *t* the mountains, and they shall
Isa 52.11 from thence, *t* no unclean thing;
Jer 12.14 that *t* the inheritance which I have
La 4.14 men could not *t* their garments.
15 it is unclean; depart, depart, *t* not:
Hag 2.12 and with his skirt do *t* bread, or
13 by a dead body *t* any of these,
Mt 9.21 If I may but *t* his garment, I shall
14.36 might only *t* the hem of his garment:
Mk 3.10 they pressed upon him for to *t* him,
5.28 If I may *t* but his clothes, I shall be
6.56 *t* if it were but the border of his
8.22 him, and besought him to *t* him.
10.13 to him, that he should *t* them:
Lk 6.19 whole multitude sought to *t* him:
11.46 *t* not the burdens with one of your
18.15 also infants, that he would *t* them:
Jn 20.17 Jesus saith unto her, *T* me not;
1Co 7. 1 is good for a man not to *t* a woman.
2Co 6.17 *t* not the unclean thing; and I will
Col 2.21 (*T* not; taste not; handle not;
Heb 11.28 destroyed the firstborn shall *t*
12.20 And if so much as a beast *t* the

TOUCHED
Gen 26.29 us no hurt, as we have not *t* thee,
32.25 him, he *t* the hollow of his thigh;
32 he *t* the hollow of Jacob's thigh
Lev 22. 6 The soul which hath *t* any such
Nu 19.18 and upon him that *t* a bone, or one
31.19 and whosoever hath *t* any slain,
Jdg 6.21 *t* the flesh and…unleavened cakes;
1Sa 10.26 of men, whose hearts God had *t*.
1Ki 6.27 the wing of the one *t* the one wall,
27 the other cherub *t* the other wall;
27 their wings *t* one another in the
19. 5 then an angel *t* him, and said unto
7 and *t* him, and said, Arise and eat;
2Ki 13.21 let down, and *t* the bones of Elisha,
Est 5. 2 near, and *t* the top of the scepter.
Job 19.21 for the hand of God hath *t* me.
Isa 6. 7 and said, Lo, this hath *t* thy lips;
Jer 1. 9 forth his hand, and *t* my mouth.
Eze 3.13 creatures that *t* one another,
Dan 8. 5 earth, and *t* not the ground:
18 but he *t* me, and set me upright.
9.21 *t* me about the time of the evening
10.10 an hand *t* me, which set me upon
16 of the sons of men *t* my lips:
18 *t* me one like the appearance of a
Mt 8. 3 put forth his hand, and *t* him,
15 he *t* her hand, and the fever left her:
9.20 and *t* the hem of his garment:
29 Then *t* he their eyes, saying,
14.36 many as *t* were made perfectly

BIBLICAL THEMES

TRADITION

The Lord God of your fathers, the God of Abraham, the God of Isaac, and the God of Jacob, hath sent me unto you: this is my name for ever, and this is my memorial unto all generations. Ex 3.15

Inquire, I pray thee, of the former age, and prepare thyself to the search of their fathers: (for we are but of yesterday, and know nothing, because our days upon earth are a shadow:) shall not they teach thee, and tell thee, and utter words out of their heart? Job 8.8-10

He established a testimony in Jacob, and appointed a law in Israel, which he commanded our fathers, that they should make them known to their children: that the generation to come might know them, even the children which should be born; who should arise and declare them to their children: that they might set their hope in God, and not forget the works of God, but keep his commandments. Ps 78.5-7

Remove not the old landmark; and enter not into the fields of the fatherless. Pr 23.10

Say not thou, What is the cause that the former days were better than these? Ec 7.10

This people draw near me with their mouth, and with their lips do honor me, but have removed their heart far from me, and their fear toward me is taught by the precept of men. Isa 29.13

Look unto the rock whence ye are hewn, and to the hole of the pit whence ye are digged. Isa 51.1

Thus saith the Lord, Stand ye in the ways, and see, and ask for the old paths, where is the good way, and walk therein, and ye shall find rest for your souls. Jer 6.16

Think not that I am come to destroy the law, or the prophets: I am not come to destroy, but to fulfil. Mt 5.17

No man putteth new wine into old bottles: else the new wine doth burst the bottles, and the wine is spilled . . . but new wine must be put into new bottles. Mk 2.22

The Pharisees and scribes asked him, Why walk not thy disciples according to the tradition of the elders . . . ? He answered and said unto them, . . . laying aside the commandment of God, ye hold the tradition of men. . . . Full well ye reject the commandment of God, that ye may keep your own tradition. Mk 7.5-6

And the scribes and Pharisees watched him, whether he would heal on the sabbath day. . . . Then said Jesus unto them, I will ask you one thing; Is it lawful on the sabbath days to do good, or to do evil? to save life, or to destroy it? And looking round about upon them all, he said unto the man, Stretch forth thy hand. Lk 6.7, 9-10

Our fathers worshipped in this mountain; and ye say, that in Jerusalem is the place where men ought to worship. Jesus saith unto her, . . . the hour cometh, when ye shall neither in this mountain, nor yet at Jerusalem, worship the Father. Ye worship ye know not what: we know what we worship. Jn 4.20-22

[They] set up false witnesses, which said, This man ceaseth not to speak blasphemous words against this holy place, and the law: for we have heard him say, that this Jesus of Nazareth shall destroy this place, and shall change the customs which Moses delivered us. Ac 6.13-14

I now write unto you . . . that ye may be mindful of the words which were spoken before by the holy prophets, and of the commandment of us the apostles of the Lord and Saviour. 2Pe 3.1-2

Remember therefore how thou hast received and heard, and hold fast, and repent. Rev 3.3

Mt 17. 7 Jesus came and *t* them, and said,
20.34 on them, and *t* their eyes:
Mk 1.41 put forth his hand, and *t* him, and
5.27 the press behind, and *t* his garment.
30 press, and said, Who *t* my clothes?
31 thee, and sayest thou, Who *t* me?
6.56 as many as *t* him were made whole.
7.33 ears, and he spit, and *t* his tongue;
Lk 5.13 he put forth his hand, and *t* him,
7.14 And he came and *t* the bier: and
8.44 and *t* the border of his garment:
45 And Jesus said, Who *t* me? When
45 thee, and sayest thou, Who *t* me?
46 Jesus said, Somebody hath *t* me:
47 people for what cause she had *t* him,
22.51 And he *t* his ear, and healed him.
Ac 27. 3 And the next day we *t* at Sidon.
Heb 4.15 *t* with...feeling of our infirmities;
12.18 unto the mount that might be *t*,

TOUCHETH

Gen 26.11 He that *t* this man or his wife
Ex 19.12 whosoever *t* the mount shall be
29.37 whatsoever *t* the altar shall be holy.
30.29 whatsoever *t* them shall be holy.
Lev 6.18 every one that *t* them shall be holy.
7.19 the flesh that *t* any unclean thing
11.24 whosoever *t* the carcass of them
26 one that *t* them shall be unclean.
27 whoso *t* their carcass shall be
36 which *t* their carcass shall be
39 he that *t* the carcass thereof shall
15. 5 whosoever *t* his bed shall wash his
7 And he that *t* the flesh of him that
10 whosoever *t* any thing that was
11 whomsoever he *t* that hath the
12 that he *t* which hath the issue,
19 whosoever *t* her shall be unclean
21 whosoever *t* her bed shall wash his
22 whosoever *t* any thing that she
23 when he *t* it, he shall be unclean
27 whosoever *t* these things shall be
22. 4 whoso *t* any thing that is unclean
5 Or whosoever *t* any creeping thing,
Nu 19.11 He that *t* the dead body of any man
13 Whosoever *t* the dead body of any
16 And whosoever *t* one that is slain
21 he that *t* the water of separation
22 unclean person *t* shall be unclean;
22 the soul that *t* it shall be unclean
Jdg 16. 9 of tow is broken when it *t* the fire.
Job 4. 5 it *t* thee, and thou art troubled.
Ps 104.32 he *t* the hills, and they smoke.
Pr 6.29 *t* her shall not be innocent.
Eze 17.10 wither, when the east wind *t* it?
Hos 4. 2 they break out, and blood *t* blood.
Am 9. 5 God of hosts is he that *t* the land,
Zec 2. 8 he that *t* you *t* the apple of his eye.
Lk 7.39 manner of woman this is...*t* him:
1Jn 5.18 and that wicked one *t* him not.

TOUCHING

Gen 27.42 Behold, thy brother Esau, as *t* thee,
Nu 8.26 do unto the Levites *t* their charge.
1Sa 20.23 And as *t* the matter which thou and I
2Ki 22.18 As *t* the words which thou hast
Ezr 7.24 that *t* any of the priests and Levites,
Job 37.23 *T* the Almighty, we cannot find him
Ps 45. 1 things which I have made *t* the king:
Isa 5. 1 a song of my beloved *t* his vineyard.
Jer 1.16 them *t* all their wickedness,
21.11 And *t* the house of the king of Judah,
22.11 For thus saith the Lord *t* Shallum
Eze 7.13 the vision is *t* the whole multitude
Mt 18.19 shall agree on earth as *t* any thing
22.31 as *t* the resurrection of the dead,
Mk 12.26 And as *t* the dead, that they rise:
Lk 23.14 no fault in this man *t* those things
Ac 5.35 ye intend to do as *t* these men.
21.25 As *t* the Gentiles which believe,
24.21 *T* the resurrection of the dead I
26. 2 *t*...the things whereof I am accused
Ro 11.28 but as *t* the election, they are
1Co 8. 1 as *t* things offered unto idols,
16.12 As *t* our brother Apollos, I greatly
2Co 9. 1 as *t* the ministering to the saints,
Php 3. 5 Hebrews; as *t* the law, a Pharisee;
6 *t* the righteousness which is in the
Col 4.10 Barnabas, (*t* whom ye received
1Th 4. 9 *t* brotherly love ye need not that
2Th 3. 4 have confidence in the Lord *t* you,

TOWEL

Jn 13. 4 and took a *t*, and girded himself.
5 wipe them with the *t* wherewith

TOWER

Gen 11. 4 to, let us build us a city and a *t*,
5 down to see the city and the *t*,
2Sa 22. 3 my high *t*, and my refuge, my
51 He is the *t* of salvation for his
Ps 18. 2 of my salvation, and my high *t*.
144. 2 my high *t*, and my deliverer;
Pr 18.10 name of the Lord is a strong *t*:
SS 4. 4 Thy neck is like the *t* of David

Isa 2.15 And upon every high *t*, and upon
5. 2 and built a *t* in the midst of it,
Mic 4. 8 And thou, O *t* of the flock, the
Hab 2. 1 my watch, and set me upon the *t*,
Mt 21.33 a winepress in it, and built a *t*,
Mk 12. 1 place for the winefat, and built a *t*,
Lk 13. 4 upon whom the *t* in Siloam fell,
14.28 which of you, intending to build a *t*,

TOWN
Hab 2.12 him that buildeth a *t* with blood,
Mt 10.11 city or *t* ye shall enter,
Mk 8.23 the hand, and led him out of the *t*;
26 saying, Neither go into the *t*, nor
26 nor tell it to any in the *t*.
Lk 5.17 were come out of every *t* of Galilee,
Jn 7.42 out of the *t* of Bethlehem, where
11. 1 the *t* of Mary and her sister Martha.
30 Jesus was not yet come into the *t*,

TOWNCLERK
Ac 19.35 And when the *t* had appeased the

TOWNS
Mk 1.38 Let us go into the next *t*, that I
8.27 into the *t* of Caesarea Philippi:
Lk 9. 6 went through the *t*, preaching the
12 they may go into the *t* and country

TRADE
Gen 34.10 dwell and *t* ye therein, and get
21 dwell in the land, and *t* therein;
46.32 for their *t* hath been to feed cattle;
34 Thy servants' *t* hath been about
Rev 18.17 sailors, and as many as *t* by sea,

TRADED
Eze 27.12 tin, and lead, they *t* in thy fairs.
13 they *t* the persons of men and
14 house of Togarmah *t* in thy fairs
17 *t* in thy market wheat of Minnith,
Mt 25.16 talents went and *t* with the same.

TRADING
Lk 19.15 much every man had gained by *t*.

TRADITION
Mt 15. 2 transgress the *t* of the elders?
3 commandment of God by your *t*?
6 of God of none effect by your *t*.
Mk 7. 3 eat not, holding the *t* of the elders.
5 according to the *t* of the elders,
8 ye hold the *t* of men, as the
9 that ye may keep your own *t*.
13 God of none effect through your *t*,
Col 2. 8 vain deceit, after the *t* of men,
2Th 3. 6 not after the *t* which he received
1Pe 1.18 received by *t* from your fathers;

TRADITIONS
Gal 1.14 zealous of the *t* of my fathers.
2Th 2.15 hold the *t*...ye have been taught,

TRAIN
1Ki 10. 2 to Jerusalem with a very great *t*,
Pr 22. 6 *T* up a child in the way he should
Isa 6. 1 up, and his *t* filled the temple.

TRAITOR
Lk 6.16 Iscariot, which was also the *t*.

TRAITORS
2Ti 3. 4 *T*, heady, highminded, lovers of

TRAMPLE
Ps 91.13 dragon shalt thou *t* under feet.
Isa 63. 3 anger, and *t* them in my fury;
Mt 7. 6 lest they *t* them under their feet,

TRANCE
Nu 24. 4, 16 into a *t*, but having his eyes open:
Ac 10.10 they made ready, he fell into a *t*,
11. 5 and in a *t* I saw a vision, A certain
22.17 prayed in the temple, I was in a *t*;

TRANSFERRED
1Co 4. 6 I have in a figure *t* to myself and

TRANSFIGURED
Mt 17. 2 And was *t* before them: and his
Mk 9. 2 and he was *t* before them.

TRANSFORMED
Ro 12. 2 ye *t* by the renewing of your mind,
2Co 11.14 Satan himself is *t* into an angel
15 *t* as...ministers of righteousness;

TRANSFORMING
2Co 11.13 *t* themselves into the apostles of

TRANSGRESS
Nu 14.41 do ye *t* the commandment of the
1Sa 2.24 ye make the Lord's people to *t*.
2Ch 24.20 Why *t* ye the commandments of
Neh 1. 8 If ye *t*, I will scatter you abroad
13.27 to *t* against our God in marrying
Ps 17. 3 that my mouth shall not *t*.
25. 3 ashamed which *t* without cause.
Pr 28.21 a piece of bread that many will *t*.
Jer 2.20 and thou saidst, I will not *t*;
Eze 20.38 and them that *t* against me:
Am 4. 4 Come to Beth-el, and *t*; at Gilgal
Mt 15. 2 thy disciples *t* the tradition of the
3 do ye also *t* the commandment
Ro 2.27 and circumcision dost *t* the law?

TRANSGRESSED
Dt 26.13 I have not *t* thy commandments,
Jos 7.11 and they have also *t* my covenant
15 because he hath *t* the covenant of
23.16 When ye have *t* the covenant of the
Jdg 2.20 this people hath *t* my covenant
1Sa 14.33 he said, Ye have *t*: roll a great
15.24 for I have *t* the commandment of
1Ki 8.50 wherein they have *t* against thee,
2Ki 18.12 their God, but *t* his covenant,
1Ch 2. 7 Israel, who *t* in...thing accursed.
5.25 *t* against the God of their fathers,
2Ch 12. 2 they had *t* against the Lord,
26.16 for he *t* against the Lord his God,
28.19 naked, and *t* sore against the Lord.
36.14 people, *t* very much after all the
Ezr 10.10 Ye have *t*, and have taken strange
13 many that have *t* in this thing.
Isa 24. 5 because they have *t* the laws,
43.27 thy teachers have *t* against me.
66.24 the men that have *t* against me:
Jer 2. 8 the pastors also *t* against me, and
29 ye all have *t* against me, saith the
3.13 hast *t* against the Lord thy God,
33. 8 whereby they have *t* against me.
34.18 the men that have *t* my covenant,
La 3.42 We have *t* and have rebelled:
Eze 2. 3 their fathers have *t* against me,
18.31 transgressions, whereby ye have *t*;
Dan 9.11 Yea, all Israel have *t* thy law,
Hos 6. 7 they like men have *t* the covenant:
7.13 because they have *t* against me:
8. 1 because they have *t* my covenant,
Zep 3.11 wherein thou hast *t* against me:
Lk 15.29 neither *t* I at any time thy

TRANSGRESSETH
Pr 16.10 his mouth *t* not in judgment.
Hab 2. 5 Yea also, because he *t* by wine,
1Jn 3. 4 Whosoever committeth sin *t*
2Jn 9 Whosoever *t*, and abideth not in

TRANSGRESSION
Ex 34. 7 forgiving iniquity and *t* and sin,
Nu 14.18 forgiving iniquity and *t*, and by no
1Ch 9. 1 carried away to Babylon for their *t*.
10.13 So Saul died for his *t* which he
Ezr 10. 6 he mourned because of the *t* of
Job 7.21 why dost thou not pardon my *t*,
8. 4 he have cast them away for their *t*;
13.23 make me to know my *t* and my sin.
14.17 My *t* is sealed up in a bag, and
33. 9 I am clean without *t*, I am
Ps 19.13 shall be innocent from the great *t*.
32. 1 Blessed is he whose *t* is forgiven,
107.17 Fools because of their *t*, and
Pr 17. 9 He that covereth a *t* seeketh love;
19.11 and it is his glory to pass over a *t*.
29. 6 *t* of an evil man there is a snare:
22 and a furious man aboundeth in *t*.
Isa 53. 8 for the *t* of my people was he
58. 1 and shew my people their *t*, and
Mic 1. 5 What is the *t* of Jacob? is it not
3. 8 to declare unto Jacob his *t*, and to
6. 7 shall I give my firstborn for my *t*,
Ac 1.25 from which Judas by *t* fell, that
Ro 4.15 for where no law is, there is no *t*.
5.14 after the similitude of Adam's *t*,
1Ti 2.14 woman being deceived was in the *t*.
Heb 2. 2 every *t* and disobedience received
1Jn 3. 4 the law: for sin is the *t* of the law.

TRANSGRESSIONS
Ex 23.21 not; for he will not pardon your *t*:
Job 31.33 If I covered my *t* as Adam, by
Ps 25. 7 not the sins of my youth, nor my *t*:
39. 8 Deliver me from all my *t*: make
51. 1 thy tender mercies blot out my *t*.
3 For I acknowledge my *t*: and my
65. 3 as for our *t*, thou shalt purge them
103.12 hath he removed our *t* from us.
Isa 43.25 blotteth out thy *t* for mine own
44.22 blotted out, as a thick cloud, thy *t*,
50. 1 your *t* is your mother put away.
53. 5 But he was wounded for our *t*, he
La 1.14 yoke of my *t* is bound by his hand:
Eze 18.22 All his *t* that he hath committed,
31 Cast away from you all your *t*,
Am 1. 3 For three *t* of Damascus, and for
5.12 your manifold *t* and your mighty
Mic 1.13 the *t* of Israel were found in thee.
Gal 3.19 It was added because of *t*, till the
Heb 9.15 the *t* that were under the first

TRANSGRESSOR
Pr 21.18 and the *t* for the upright.
22.12 overthroweth the words of the *t*.
Isa 48. 8 wast called a *t* from the womb.
Gal 2.18 I destroyed, I make myself a *t*.
Jas 2.11 kill, thou art become a *t* of the law.

TRANSGRESSORS
Ps 37.38 But the *t* shall be destroyed
51.13 Then will I teach *t* thy ways; and
59. 5 be not merciful to any wicked *t*.
119.158 I beheld the *t*, and was grieved;
Pr 2.22 and the *t* shall be rooted out of it.
11. 3 the perverseness of *t* shall destroy
6 *t* shall be taken in their own
13. 2 the soul of the *t* shall eat violence.
15 favor: but the way of *t* is hard.
23.28 and increaseth the *t* among men.
26.10 the fool, and rewardeth *t*.
Isa 1.28 the destruction of the *t* and of the
46. 8 men: bring it again to mind, O ye *t*.
53.12 and he was numbered with the *t*;
12 and made intercession for the *t*.
Dan 8.23 when the *t* are come to the full,
Hos 14. 9 them: but the *t* shall fall therein.
Mk 15.28 And he was numbered with the *t*.
Lk 22.37 And he was reckoned among the *t*:
Jas 2. 9 and are convinced of the law as *t*.

TRANSLATE
2Sa 3.10 To *t* the kingdom from the house

TRANSLATED
Col 1.13 hath *t* us into the kingdom of his

Heb 11. 5 By faith Enoch was *t* that he
5 not found, because God had *t* him:

TRANSLATION
Heb 11. 5 for before his *t* he had this

TRANSPARENT
Rev 21.21 was pure gold, as it were *t* glass.

TRAP
Job 18.10 and a *t* for him in the way.
Ps 69.22 for their welfare, let it become a *t*.
Jer 5.26 they set a *t*, they catch men.
Ro 11. 9 table he made a snare, and a *t*,

TRAVAIL
Ps 48. 6 and pain, as of a woman in *t*.
Ec 3.10 I have seen the *t*, which God hath
4. 4 I considered all *t*, and every right
8 is also vanity, yea, it is a sore *t*.
Isa 23. 4 I *t* not, nor bring forth children,
53.11 He shall see of the *t* of his soul,
Jer 13.21 sorrows take thee, as a woman in *t*?
Mic 4. 9 have taken thee as a woman in *t*.
Jn 16.21 A woman...in *t* hath sorrow,
Gal 4.19 I *t* in birth again until Christ be
1Th 2. 9 brethren, our labor and *t*:
5. 3 as *t* upon a woman with child;
2Th 3. 8 wrought with labor and *t* night

TRAVAILED
Gen 35.16 Rachel *t*, and she had hard labor,
38.28 it came to pass, when she *t*, that
1Sa 4.19 dead, she bowed herself and *t*;
Isa 66. 7 Before she *t*, she brought forth;
8 for as soon as Zion *t*, she brought

TRAVAILEST
Gal 4.27 forth and cry, thou that *t* not:

TRAVAILETH
Job 15.20 wicked man *t* with pain all his
Ps 7.14 he *t* with iniquity, and hath
Isa 13. 8 be in pain as a woman that *t*:
21. 3 as the pangs of a woman that *t*:
Jer 31. 8 and her that *t* with child together:
Mic 5. 3 she which *t* hath brought forth:
Ro 8.22 and *t* in pain together until now.

TRAVAILING
Isa 42.14 now will I cry like a *t* woman; I
Hos 13.13 The sorrows of a *t* woman shall
Rev 12. 2 being with child cried, *t* in birth,

TRAVEL
Nu 20.14 all the *t* that hath befallen us:
La 3. 5 compassed me with gall and *t*.
Ac 19.29 Macedonia, Paul's companions in *t*,
2Co 8.19 chosen of the churches to *t* with us

TRAVELLED
Ac 11.19 Stephen *t* as far as Phenice, and

TRAVELLER
2Sa 12. 4 there came a *t* unto the rich man,
Job 31.32 but I opened my doors to the *t*.

TRAVELLING
Isa 21.13 O ye *t* companies of Dedanim.
63. 1 *t* in the greatness of his strength?
Mt 25.14 is as a man *t* into a far country,

TREACHEROUS
Isa 21. 2 *t* dealer dealeth treacherously
24.16 *t* dealers have dealt treacherously
16 the *t* dealers have dealt very
Jer 3. 7 And her *t* sister Judah saw it.
8 yet her *t* sister Judah feared not,
10 her *t* sister Judah hath not
11 herself more than *t* Judah.
9. 2 adulterers, an assembly of *t* men.
Zep 3. 4 prophets are light and *t* persons:

TREACHEROUSLY
Isa 21. 2 the treacherous dealer dealeth *t*,
33. 1 wast not spoiled; and dealest *t*,
1 thou shalt make an end to deal *t*,
Jer 12. 1 are all they happy that deal very *t*?
La 1. 2 her friends have dealt *t* with her,
Hos 5. 7 have dealt *t* against the Lord:
Mal 2.15 deal *t* against the wife of his youth.

TREAD
Dt 11.24 the soles of your feet shall *t* shall
Job 40.12 *t* down the wicked in their place.
Ps 7. 5 let him *t* down my life upon the
44. 5 will we *t* them under that rise up
60.12 it is that shall *t* down our enemies.
91.13 shalt *t* upon the lion and adder:
108.13 it is that shall *t* down our enemies.
Isa 1.12 this at your hand, to *t* my courts?
10. 6 *t* them down like the mire of
16.10 treaders shall *t* out no wine in
63. 3 for I will *t* them in mine anger,
Jer 48.33 none shall *t* with shouting; their
Eze 34.18 ye must *t* down with your feet the
Hos 10.11 and loveth to *t* out the corn;
Mal 4. 3 And ye shall *t* down the wicked;
Lk 10.19 you power to *t* on serpents and
Rev 11. 2 holy city shall they *t* under foot

TREADETH
Dt 25. 4 the ox when he *t* out the corn.
Job 9. 8 and *t* upon the waves of the sea.
Isa 41.25 morter, and as the potter *t* clay.
63. 2 like him that *t* in the winefat?
Am 4.13 *t* upon the high places of the earth,
Mic 5. 6 and when he *t* within our borders.
8 *t* down, and teareth in pieces,
1Co 9. 9 of the ox that *t* out the corn.
1Ti 5.18 muzzle the ox that *t* out the corn.
Rev 19.15 and he *t* the winepress of the

TREASURE
Gen 43.23 hath given you *t* in your sacks:
Ex 1.11 they built for Pharaoh *t* cities,
19. 5 then ye shall be a peculiar *t* unto me
Dt 28.12 shall open unto thee his good *t*,
1Ch 29. 8 to the *t* of the house of the Lord,
Ezr 2.69 their ability unto the *t* of the work
5.17 be search made in the king's *t*
7.20 it out of the king's *t* house.
Neh 7.70 gave to the *t* a thousand drams of
71 gave to the *t* of the work twenty
10.38 to the chambers, into the *t* house.
Ps 17.14 whose belly thou fillest with thy hid *t*:
135. 4 himself, and Israel for his peculiar *t*.
Pr 15. 6 house of the righteous is much *t*:
16 Lord than great *t* and trouble
21.20 There is *t* to be desired and oil in
Ec 2. 8 the peculiar *t* of kings and of the
Isa 33. 6 the fear of the Lord is his *t*.
Eze 22.25 they have taken the *t* and
Dan 1. 2 vessels into the *t* house of his god.
Hos 13.15 spoil the *t* of all pleasant vessels.
Mt 6.21 where your *t* is, there will your
12.35 good *t* of the heart bringeth forth
35 evil *t* bringeth forth evil things.
13.44 heaven is like unto *t* hid in a field;
52 out of his *t* things new and old.
19.21 and thou shalt have *t* in heaven:
Mk 10.21 and thou shalt have *t* in heaven:
Lk 6.45 good *t* of his heart bringeth forth
45 evil *t* of his heart bringeth forth
12.21 he that layeth up *t* for himself,
33 *t* in the heavens that faileth not,
34 where your *t* is, there will your
18.22 and thou shalt have *t* in heaven:
Ac 8.27 who had the charge of all her *t*,
2Co 4. 7 we have this *t* in earthen vessels,
Jas 5. 3 heaped *t* together for the last

TREASURES
Dt 33.19 the seas, and of *t* hid in the sand.
1Ki 15.18 in the *t* of the house of the Lord,
2Ki 20.15 among my *t* that I have not shewed
2Ch 5. 1 among the *t* of the house of God.
Job 3.21 and dig for it more than for hid *t*;
38.22 entered into the *t* of the snow?
22 or hast thou seen the *t* of the hail,
Pr 2. 4 and searchest for her as for hid *t*;
10. 2 *T* of wickedness profit nothing: but
21. 6 The getting of *t* by a lying tongue
Isa 2. 7 neither is there any end of their *t*;
45. 3 I will give thee the *t* of darkness,
Jer 10.13 bringeth forth the wind out of his *t*.
41. 8 we have *t* in the field, of wheat,
51.16 bringeth forth the wind out of his *t*.
Mic 6.10 Are there yet the *t* of wickedness
Mt 2.11 and when they had opened their *t*,
6.19 not up for yourselves *t* upon earth,
20 lay up for yourselves *t* in heaven,
Col 2. 3 whom are hid all the *t* of wisdom
Heb 11.26 greater riches than the *t* in Egypt:

TREASUREST
Ro 2. 5 *t* up unto thyself wrath against

TREASURY
Jos 6.19 shall come into the *t* of the Lord.
24 into the *t* of the house of the Lord.
Jer 38.11 the house of the king under the *t*,
Mt 27. 6 lawful for to put them into the *t*,
Mk 12.41 And Jesus sat over against the *t*,
41 the people cast money into the *t*:
43 all they which have cast into the *t*:
Lk 21. 1 men casting their gifts into the *t*.
Jn 8.20 These words spake Jesus in the *t*,

TREATISE
Ac 1. 1 The former *t* have I made, O

TREE
Gen 1.12 *t* yielding fruit, whose seed was in
2. 9 *t* of knowledge of good and evil.
3. 1 Ye shall not eat of every *t* of the
6 woman saw that the *t* was good
6 a *t* to be desired to make one wise,
11 Hast thou eaten of the *t*, whereof I
12 she gave me of the *t*, and I did eat.
40.19 thee, and shall hang thee on a *t*;
Dt 20.19 (for the *t* of the field is man's life)
21.23 not remain all night upon the *t*,
Jdg 9. 9 But the olive *t* said unto them,
1Ki 14.23 high hill, and under every green *t*.
19. 4 and sat down under a juniper *t*:
Job 14. 7 For there is hope of a *t*, if it be cut
19.10 hope hath he removed like a *t*.
24.20 wickedness shall be broken as a *t*.
Ps 1. 3 be like a *t* planted by the rivers
37.35 himself like a green bay *t*,
Pr 3.18 She is a *t* of life to them that lay
11.30 fruit of the righteous is a *t* of life;
SS 7. 7 thy stature is like to a palm *t*,
Isa 36.16 his vine, and every one of his fig *t*,
40.20 chooseth a *t* that will not rot;
55.13 the thorn shall come up the fir *t*,
13 brier shall come up the myrtle *t*:
60.13 shall come unto thee, the fir *t*,
13 the pine *t*, and the box together,
65.22 as the days of a *t* are the days of
Jer 10. 3 one cutteth a *t* out of the forest,
Eze 15. 2 What is the vine *t* more than any *t*,
34.27 *t* of the field shall yield her fruit,
Dan 4.20 The *t* that thou sawest, which grew,
Hos 14. 6 and his beauty shall be as the olive *t*,
8 I am like a green fir *t*. From me
Mic 4. 4 under his vine and under his fig *t*;
Hab 3.17 the fig *t* shall not blossom,
Hag 2.19 the olive *t*, hath not brought forth:
Mt 3.10 every *t* which bringeth not forth
7.17 good *t* bringeth forth good fruit;
17 corrupt *t* bringeth forth evil fruit.
18 good *t* cannot bring forth evil fruit,
18 a corrupt *t* bring forth good fruit.

19 every *t* that bringeth not forth
12.33 Either make the *t* good, and his
33 or else make the *t* corrupt, and his
33 for the *t* is known by his fruit.
13.32 among herbs, and becometh a *t*,
21.19 when he saw a fig *t* in the way, he
19 presently the fig *t* withered away.
20 How soon is the fig *t* withered
21 do this which is done to the fig *t*,
24.32 Now learn a parable of the fig *t*;
Mk 11.13 seeing a fig *t* afar off having leaves,
20 the fig *t* dried up from the roots.
21 fig *t*...thou cursedst is withered
13.28 Now learn a parable of the fig *t*;
Lk 3. 9 every *t* therefore which bringeth
6.43 good *t* bringeth not forth corrupt
43 corrupt *t* bring forth good fruit.
44 every *t* is known by his own fruit.
13. 6 certain man had a fig *t* planted
7 come seeking fruit on this fig *t*,
19 it grew, and waxed a great *t*;
17. 6 ye might say unto this sycamine *t*,
19. 4 climbed up into a sycomore *t* to
21.29 Behold the fig *t*, and all the trees;
23.31 they do these things in a green *t*,
Jn 1.48 when thou wast under the fig *t*, I
50 thee, I saw thee under the fig *t*,
Ac 5.30 whom ye slew and hanged on a *t*.
10.39 whom they slew and hanged on a *t*:
13.29 they took him down from the *t*,
Ro 11.17 and thou, being a wild olive *t*,
17 of the root and fatness of the olive *t*;
24 cut out of the olive *t* which is wild
24 to nature into a good olive *t*:
24 be graffed into their own olive *t*?
Gal 3.13 is every one that hangeth on a *t*:
Jas 3.12 Can the fig *t*, my brethren, bear
1Pe 2.24 our sins in his own body on the *t*,
Rev 2. 7 will I give to eat of the *t* of life,
6.13 a fig *t* casteth her untimely figs,
7. 1 nor on the sea, nor on any *t*.
9. 4 any green thing, neither any *t*;
22. 2 the river, was there the *t* of life,
2 leaves of the *t* were for the healing
14 may have right to the *t* of life, and

TREES

Gen 3. 2 We may eat of the fruit of the *t*
8 God amongst the *t* of the garden.
Lev 19.23 planted all manner of *t* for food,
Jdg 9.10 And the *t* said to the fig tree, Come
Job 40.21 He lieth under the shady *t*, in the
Ps 74. 5 lifted up axes upon the thick *t*.
96.12 shall all the *t* of the wood rejoice
104.16 The *t* of the Lord are full of sap;
17 the stork, the fir *t* are her house.
Isa 55.12 all the *t* of the field shall clap their
61. 3 might be called *t* of righteousness;
Hos 2.12 I will destroy her vines and her fig *t*,
Joel 1.19 hath burned all the *t* of the field.
Mt 3.10 axe is laid unto the root of the *t*:
21. 8 cut down branches from the *t*, and
Mk 8.24 and said, I see men as *t*, walking.
11. 8 cut down branches off the *t*, and
Lk 3. 9 axe is laid unto the root of the *t*:
21.29 Behold the fig tree, and all the *t*;
Jn 12.13 Took branches of palm *t*, and
Jude 12 *t* whose fruit withereth, without
Rev 7. 3 earth, neither the sea, nor the *t*,
8. 7 the third part of *t* was burnt up,
11. 4 These are the two olive *t*, and the

TREMBLE

Dt 2.25 and shall *t*, and be in anguish
20. 3 faint, fear not, and do not *t*,
Ezr 10. 3 those that *t* at the commandment
Job 9. 6 place, and the pillars thereof *t*.
26.11 The pillars of heaven *t* and are
Ps 60. 2 Thou hast made the earth to *t*;
99. 1 Lord reigneth; let the people *t*:
114. 7 *T*, thou earth, at the presence of
Ec 12. 3 the keepers of the house shall *t*,
Isa 5.25 the hills did *t*, and their carcasses
14.16 the man that made the earth to *t*,
32.11 *T*, ye women that are at ease; be
64. 2 nations may *t* at thy presence!
66. 5 of the Lord, ye that *t* at his word;
Jer 5.22 will ye not *t* at my presence,
10.10 at his wrath the earth shall *t*,
33. 9 they shall fear and *t* for all the
51.29 the land shall *t* and sorrow: for
Eze 26.16 shall *t* at every moment, and be
18 Now shall the isles *t* in the day of
32.10 they shall *t* at every moment,
Dan 6.26 men *t* and fear before the God of
Hos 11.10 children shall *t* from the west.
11 shall *t* as a bird out of Egypt, and
Joel 2. 1 all the inhabitants of the land *t*:
10 before them; the heavens shall *t*:
Am 8. 8 Shall not the land *t* for this, and
Hab 3. 7 curtains of the land of Midian did *t*.
Jas 2.19 the devils also believe, and *t*.

TREMBLED

Gen 27.33 And Isaac *t* very exceedingly,
Ex 19.16 the people that was in the camp *t*.
Jdg 5. 4 earth *t*, and the heavens dropped,
1Sa 4.13 his heart *t* for the ark of God.
14.15 and the spoilers, they also *t*,
16. 4 elders of the town *t* at his coming,
28. 5 was afraid, and his heart greatly *t*.
2Sa 22. 8 Then the earth shook and *t*; the
Ezr 9. 4 every one that *t* at the words of
Ps 18. 7 Then the earth shook and *t*; the
77.18 the world: the earth *t* and shook.
97. 4 the world: the earth saw, and *t*.
Jer 4.24 the mountains, and, lo, they *t*,
8.16 the whole land *t* at the sound of
Dan 5.19 *t* and feared before him:
Hab 3.10 mountains saw thee, and they *t*:
16 When I heard, my belly *t*; my
16 I *t* in myself, that I might rest in
Mk 16. 8 for they *t* and were amazed:
Ac 7.32 Then Moses *t*, and durst not
24.25 Felix *t*, and answered, Go thy

TREMBLETH

Job 37. 1 At this also my heart *t*, and is
Ps 104.32 He looketh on the earth, and it *t*:
119.120 My flesh *t* for fear of thee; and
Isa 66. 2 contrite spirit, and *t* at my word.

TREMBLING

Ex 15.15 *t* shall take hold upon them;
Dt 28.65 shall give thee there a *t* heart,
1Sa 13. 7 and all the people followed him *t*.
14.15 And there was *t* in the host, in
15 quaked: so it was a very great *t*.
Ezr 10. 9 *t* because of this matter, and for
Job 4.14 Fear came upon me, and *t*, which
21. 6 and *t* taketh hold on my flesh.
Ps 2.11 Lord with fear, and rejoice with *t*.
55. 5 Fearfulness and *t* are come upon
Isa 51.17 drunken the dregs of the cup of *t*,
22 out of thine hand the cup of *t*,
Jer 30. 5 We have heard a voice of *t*, of
Eze 12.18 drink thy water with *t* and with
26.16 shall clothe themselves with *t*;
Dan 10.11 this word unto me, I stood *t*.
Hos 13. 1 When Ephraim spake *t*, he
Zec 12. 2 I will make Jerusalem a cup of *t*
Mk 5.33 But the woman fearing and *t*,
Lk 8.47 she came *t*, and falling down
Ac 9. 6 he *t* and astonished said, Lord,
16.29 and sprang in, and came *t*,
1Co 2. 3 and in fear, and in much *t*.
2Co 7.15 with fear and *t* ye received him.
Eph 6. 5 with fear and *t*, in singleness of
Php 2.12 your own salvation with fear and *t*.

TRENCH

1Sa 17.20 he came to the *t*, as the host was
26. 5 Saul lay in the *t*, and the people
7 Saul lay sleeping within the *t*, and
2Sa 20.15 the city, and it stood in the *t*:
1Ki 18.32 and he made a *t* about the altar,
35 and he filled the *t* also with water.
38 up the water that was in the *t*.
Lk 19.43 enemies shall cast a *t* about thee,

TRESPASS

Gen 31.36 What is my *t*? what is my sin, that
50.17 the *t* of thy brethren, and their
17 forgive the *t* of thy servants of the
Lev 5.15 If a soul commit a *t*, and sin
7. 5 unto the Lord: it is a *t* offering.
7 sin offering is, so is the *t* offering:
Nu 5. 6 commit, to do a *t* against the Lord,
Jos 22.20 Achan the son of Zerah commit a *t*
1Ki 8.31 any man *t* against his neighbor,
2Ki 12.16 *t* money and sin money was not
2Ch 28.13 our *t* is great, and there is fierce
Ezr 9. 2 rulers hath been chief in this *t*.
6 *t* is grown up unto the heavens.
Eze 17.20 will plead with him there for his *t*
20.27 have committed a *t* against me.
Mt 18.15 if thy brother shall *t* against thee,
Lk 17. 3 If thy brother *t* against thee, rebuke
4 if he *t* against thee seven times in

TRESPASSED

Lev 5.19 certainly *t* against the Lord.
26.40 trespass which they *t* against me,
Nu 5. 7 unto him against whom he hath *t*.
Dt 32.51 Because ye *t* against me among
2Ch 26.18 the sanctuary; for thou hast *t*;
29. 6 For our fathers have *t*, and done
30. 7 *t* against the Lord God of their
33.23 but Amon *t* more and more.
Ezr 10. 2 We have *t* against our God, and
Eze 17.20 that he hath *t* against me.
18.24 in his trespass that he hath *t*,
39.23 because they *t* against me,
26 whereby they have *t* against me,
Dan 9. 7 that they have *t* against thee.
Hos 8. 1 my covenant, and *t* against my law.

TRESPASSES

Ezr 9.15 we are before thee in our *t*: for
Ps 68.21 as one as goeth on still in his *t*.
Eze 39.26 and all their *t* whereby they have
Mt 6.14 For if ye forgive men their *t*, your
15 But if ye forgive not men their *t*,
15 will your Father forgive your *t*.
18.35 not every one his brother their *t*.
Mk 11.25 heaven may forgive you your *t*.
26 which is in heaven forgive your *t*.
2Co 5.19 not imputing their *t* unto them;
Eph 2. 1 who were dead in *t* and sin;
Col 2.13 him, having forgiven you all *t*;

TRESPASSING

Lev 6. 7 all that he hath done in *t* therein.
Eze 14.13 land sinneth against me by *t*

TRIAL

Job 9.23 laugh at the *t* of the innocent.
Eze 21.13 Because it is a *t*, and what if the
2Co 8. 2 How that in a great *t* of affliction
Heb 11.36 others had *t* of cruel mockings
1Pe 1. 7 That the *t* of your faith, being
4.12 the fiery *t* which is to try you,

TRIBES

Gen 49.28 All these are the twelve *t* of Israel:
Dt 29.10 captains of your *t*, your elders,
Jos 11.23 to their divisions by their *t*.
13. 7 for an inheritance unto the nine *t*,
1Sa 15.17 made the head of the *t* of Israel,
2Ch 6. 5 no city among all the *t* of Israel
Ps 105.37 one feeble person among their *t*.
122. 4 the *t* go up, the *t* of the Lord,
Hos 5. 9 among the *t* of Israel have I made
Hab 3. 9 according to the oaths of the *t*,

Mt 19.28 judging the twelve *t* of Israel.
24.30 shall all the *t* of the earth mourn,
Lk 22.30 judging the twelve *t* of Israel.
Ac 26. 7 Unto which promise our twelve *t*,
Jas 1. 1 the twelve *t* which are scattered
Rev 7. 4 all the *t* of the children of Israel.
21.12 are the names of the twelve *t* of

TRIBULATION

Dt 4.30 When thou art in *t*, and all these
Jdg 10.14 deliver you in the time of your *t*.
1Sa 26.24 and let him deliver me out of all *t*.
Mt 13.21 for when *t* or persecution ariseth
24.21 For then shall be great *t*, such as
29 after the *t* of those days shall the
Mk 13.24 after that *t*, the sun...be darkened,
Jn 16.33 In the world ye shall have *t*: but
Ac 14.22 through much *t* enter into the
Ro 2. 9 *T* and anguish upon every soul of
5. 3 knowing that *t* worketh patience;
8.35 shall *t*, or distress, or persecution,
12.12 Rejoicing in hope; patient in *t*;
2Co 1. 4 Who comforteth us in all our *t*,
7. 4 I am exceeding joyful in all our *t*.
1Th 3. 4 before that we should suffer *t*;
2Th 1. 6 *t* to them that trouble you;
Rev 1. 9 your brother, and companion in *t*,
2. 9 thy works, and *t*, and poverty,
10 and ye shall have *t* ten days:
22 adultery with her into great *t*,
7.14 they which came out of great *t*,

TRIBULATIONS

1Sa 10.19 of all your adversities and your *t*;
Ro 5. 3 only so, but we glory in *t* also;
Eph 3.13 that ye faint not at my *t* for you,
2Th 1. 4 persecutions and *t* that ye endure:

TRIBUTE

Gen 49.15 and became a servant unto *t*.
Nu 31.37 the Lord's *t* of the sheep was six
Dt 16.10 a *t* of a freewill offering of thine
Ezr 4.13 then will they not pay toll, *t*, and
7.24 lawful to impose toll, *t*, or custom,
Neh 5. 4 borrowed money for the king's *t*,
Pr 12.24 but the slothful shall be under *t*.
Mt 17.24 they that receive *t* money came
24 said, Doth not your master pay *t*?
25 of the earth take custom or *t*?
22.17 Is it lawful to give *t* unto Caesar,
19 Shew me the *t* money. And they
Mk 12.14 Is it lawful to give *t* to Caesar, or
Lk 20.22 lawful for us to give *t* unto Caesar,
23. 2 and forbidding to give *t* to Caesar,
Ro 13. 6 For for this cause pay ye *t* also:
7 *t* to whom *t* is due; custom to

TRIED

Dt 21. 5 controversy and every stroke be *t*:
2Sa 22.31 perfect; the word of the Lord is *t*:
Job 23.10 when he hath *t* me, I shall come
34.36 is that Job may be *t* unto the end,
Ps 12. 6 as silver *t* in a furnace of earth,
17. 3 thou hast *t* me, and shalt find
18.30 perfect: the word of the Lord is *t*:
66.10 thou hast *t* us, as silver is *t*.
105.19 came: the word of the Lord *t* him.
Isa 28.16 a stone, and a *t* stone, a precious
Jer 12. 3 me, and *t* mine heart toward thee:
Dan 12.10 purified, and made white, and *t*;
Zec 13. 9 and will try them as gold is *t*:
Heb 11.17 when he was *t*, offered up Isaac:
Jas 1.12 for when he is *t*, he shall receive
1Pe 1. 7 though it be *t* with fire, might be
Rev 2. 2 thou hast *t* them which say they
10 you into prison, that ye may be *t*;
3.18 to buy of me gold *t* in the fire,

TRIEST

1Ch 29.17 my God, that thou *t* the heart, and
Jer 11.20 that *t* the reins and the heart,
20.12 that *t* the righteous, and seest the

TRIETH

Job 34. 3 For the ear *t* words, as the mouth
Ps 7. 9 for the righteous God *t* the hearts
11. 5 The Lord *t* the righteous: but the
Pr 17. 3 for gold: but the Lord *t* the hearts.
1Th 2. 4 but God, which *t* our hearts.

TRIMMED

2Sa 19.24 dressed his feet, nor *t* his beard,
Mt 25. 7 virgins arose, and *t* their lamps.

TRIUMPH

2Sa 1.20 daughters of the uncircumcised *t*.
Ps 25. 2 let not mine enemies *t* over me.
41.11 mine enemy doth not *t* over me.
47. 1 unto God with the voice of *t*.
60. 8 Philistia, *t* thou because of me.
92. 4 I will *t* in the works of thy hands.
94. 3 how long shall the wicked *t*?
106.47 holy name, and to *t* in thy praise.
108. 9 my shoes; over Philistia will I *t*.
2Co 2.14 always causeth us to *t* in Christ,

TRIUMPHED

Ex 15. 1 the Lord, for he hath *t* gloriously:
21 the Lord, for he hath *t* gloriously;

TRIUMPHING

Job 20. 5 That the *t* of the wicked is short,
Col 2.15 of them openly, *t* over them in it.

TROAS

Ac 16. 8 passing by Mysia came down to *T*,
11 Therefore loosing from *T*, we
20. 5 going before tarried for us at *T*.
6 came unto them to *T* in five days;
2Co 2.12 I came to *T* to preach Christ's
2Ti 4.13 cloke that I left at *T* with Carpus,

TRODDEN

Dt 1.36 give the land that he hath *t* upon,
Jos 14. 9 land whereon thy feet have *t* shall
Jdg 5.21 soul, thou hast *t* down strength.
Job 22.15 old way which wicked men have *t*?
28. 8 The lion's whelps have not *t* it, nor
Ps 119.118 hast *t* down all them that err
Isa 5. 5 thereof, and it shall be *t* down:
14.19 the pit; as a carcass *t* under feet.
18. 2 a nation meted out and *t* down,
7 nation meted out and *t* under foot,
25.10 Moab shall be *t* down under him,
10 straw is *t* down for the dunghill.
28. 3 of Ephraim, shall be *t* under feet;
18 then ye shall be *t* down by it.
63. 3 I have *t* the winepress alone; and
18 our adversaries have *t* down thy
Jer 12.10 they have *t* my portion under foot,
La 1.15 hath *t* under foot all my mighty
15 the Lord hath *t* the virgin, the
Eze 34.19 which ye have *t* with your feet;
Dan 8.13 and the host to be *t* under foot?
Mic 7.10 shall she be *t* down as the mire of
Mt 5.13 out, and to be *t* under foot of men.
Lk 8. 5 it was *t* down, and the fowls of the
21.24 Jerusalem shall be *t* down of the
Heb 10.29 who hath *t* under foot the Son of
Rev 14.20 winepress was *t* without the city,

TROOP

Gen 30.11 And Leah said, A *t* cometh: and
49.19 Gad, a *t* shall overcome him: but
1Sa 30. 8 Shall I pursue after this *t*? shall I
2Sa 2.25 after Abner, and became one *t*,
3.22 and Joab came from pursuing a *t*,
22.30 by thee I have run through a *t*: by
23.11 were gathered together into a *t*,
13 the *t* of the Philistines pitched in
Ps 18.29 by thee I have run through a *t*;
Isa 65.11 that prepare a table for that *t*,
Jer 18.22 bring a *t* suddenly upon them:
Hos 7. 1 the *t* of robbers spoileth without.
Am 9. 6 and hath founded his *t* in the earth;

TROOPS

Job 6.19 The *t* of Tema looked, the
19.12 His *t* come together, and raise up
Jer 5. 7 assembled themselves by *t* in the
Hos 6. 9 as *t* of robbers wait for a man,
Mic 5. 1 Now gather thyself in *t*,
1 O daughter of *t*: he hath laid
Hab 3.16 he will invade them with his *t*.

TROUBLE

Jos 7.25 us? the Lord shall *t* thee this day.
2Ki 19. 3 This day is a day of *t*, and of
Job 3.26 neither was I quiet; yet *t* came.
5. 6 doth *t* spring out of the ground;
7 Yet man is born unto *t*, as the
14. 1 is of few days, and full of *t*.
15.24 *T* and anguish shall make him
34.29 quietness, who then can make *t*?
Ps 3. 1 how are they increased that *t* me!
9. 9 oppressed, a refuge in times of *t*.
10. 1 hidest thou thyself in times of *t*?
20. 1 Lord hear thee in the day of *t*;
27. 5 in the time of *t* he shall hide me
46. 1 strength, a very present help in *t*.
50.15 And call upon me in the day of *t*:
77. 2 day of my *t* I sought the Lord:
107. 6, 13 cried unto the Lord in their *t*,
116. 3 upon me: I found *t* and sorrow.
Pr 11. 8 The righteous is delivered out of *t*,
12.13 but the just shall come out of *t*.
15. 6 in the revenues of the wicked is *t*.
Isa 1.14 they are a *t* unto me; I am weary
22. 5 For it is a day of *t*, and of
46. 7 answer, nor save him out of his *t*.
Jer 8.15 a time of health, and behold *t*!
La 1.21 mine enemies have heard of my *t*;
Dan 5.10 let not thy thoughts *t* thee, nor let
Na 1. 7 good, a strong hold in the day of *t*;
Mt 26.10 them, Why *t* ye the woman?
Mk 14. 6 said, Let her alone; why *t* ye her?
Lk 7. 6 unto him, Lord, *t* not thyself:
8.49 is dead; *t* not the Master.
11. 7 shall answer and say, *T* me not:
Ac 15.19 sentence is, that we *t* not them,
16.20 Jews, do exceedingly *t* our city,
20.10 *T* not yourselves; for his life is
1Co 7.28 such shall have *t* in the flesh:
2Co 1. 4 comfort them which are in any *t*,
8 our *t* which came to us in Asia,
Gal 1. 7 but there be some that *t* you, and
5.12 were even cut off which *t* you.
6.17 henceforth let no man *t* me:
2Th 1. 6 tribulation to them that *t* you;
2Ti 2. 9 Wherein I suffer *t*, as an evil doer,
Heb 12.15 of bitterness springing up *t* you,

TROUBLED

Gen 41. 8 the morning that his spirit was *t*;
45. 3 for they were *t* at his presence.
1Sa 16.14 evil spirit from the Lord *t* him.
Job 4. 5 it toucheth thee, and thou art *t*.
21. 4 why should not my spirit be *t*?
23.15 Therefore am I *t* at his presence:
Ps 46. 3 the waters thereof roar and be *t*,
77. 3 I remembered God, and was *t*:
104.29 Thou hidest thy face, they are *t*:
Pr 25.26 the wicked is as a *t* fountain,
Isa 57.20 But the wicked are like the *t* sea,
Dan 2. 1 wherewith his spirit was *t*, and
5. 9 Then was king Belshazzar greatly *t*,
Zec 10. 2 they were *t*, because there was no
Mt 2. 3 had heard these things, he was *t*,
14.26 they were *t*, saying, It is a spirit;
24. 6 see that ye be not *t*: for all these
Mk 6.50 For they all saw him, and were *t*.
13. 7 and rumors of wars, be ye not *t*:
Lk 1.12 when Zacharias saw him, he was *t*,
29 she was *t* at his saying, and cast
10.41 careful and *t* about many things:
24.38 Why are ye *t*? and why do
Jn 5. 4 into the pool, and *t* the water:

7 have no man, when the water is *t*,
11.33 groaned in the spirit,...was *t*,
12.27 Now is my soul *t*; and what shall
13.21 he was *t* in spirit, and testified,
14. 1 Let not your heart be *t*: ye believe
27 Let not your heart be *t*, neither let
Ac 15.24 out from us have *t* you with words,
17. 8 they *t* the people and the rulers of
2Co 4. 8 We are *t* on every side, yet not
7. 5 rest, but we were *t* on every side;
2Th 1. 7 And to you who are *t* rest with us,
2. 2 or be *t*, neither by spirit, nor by
1Pe 3.14 afraid of their terror, neither be *t*;

TROUBLES

Dt 31.17 evils and *t* shall befall them;
21 evils and *t* are befallen them,
Job 5.19 He shall deliver thee in six *t*: yea,
Ps 25.17 The *t* of my heart are enlarged: O
22 Israel, O God, out of all his *t*.
34. 6 him, and saved him out of all his *t*.
17 delivereth them out of all their *t*.
71.20 hast shewed me great and sore *t*,
88. 3 For my soul is full of *t*: and my
Pr 21.23 tongue keepeth his soul from *t*.
Isa 65.16 because the former *t* are forgotten,
Mk 13. 8 and there shall be famines and *t*:

TROUBLEST

Mk 5.35 dead: why *t* thou the Master any

TROUBLETH

1Sa 16.15 an evil spirit from God *t* thee.
1Ki 18.17 him, Art thou he that *t* Israel?
Job 22.10 about thee, and sudden fear *t* thee;
23.16 heart soft, and the Almighty *t* me:
Pr 11.17 he that is cruel *t* his own flesh.
29 that *t* his own house shall inherit
15.27 is greedy of gain *t* his own house;
Dan 4. 9 is in thee, and no secret *t* thee,
Lk 18. 5 yet because this widow *t* me,
Gal 5.10 but he that *t* you shall bear his

TROUBLING

Job 3.17 There the wicked cease from *t*;
Jn 5. 4 the *t* of the water stepped in was

TROUBLOUS

Dan 9.25 and the wall, even in *t* times.

TROW

Lk 17. 9 were commanded him? I *t* not.

TRUCEBREAKERS

2Ti 3. 3 Without natural affection, *t*, false

TRUE

Gen 42.11 we are *t* men, thy servants are no
31 We are *t* men; we are no spies:
1Ki 10. 6 It was a *t* report that I heard in
22.16 tell me nothing but that which is *t*
2Ch 15. 3 Israel hath been without the *t* God,
Ps 19. 9 the judgments of the Lord are *t*
119.160 Thy word is *t* from the beginning:
Pr 14.25 A *t* witness delivereth souls: but a
Jer 10.10 But the Lord is the *t* God, he is the
42. 5 Lord be a *t* and faithful witness
Dan 3.24 said unto the king, *T*, O king,
6.12 The thing is *t*, according to the
Mt 22.16 Master, we know that thou art *t*,
Mk 12.14 Master, we know that thou art *t*,
Lk 16.11 commit to your trust the *t* riches?
Jn 1. 9 That was the *t* Light, which lighteth
3.33 hath set to his seal that God is *t*.
4.23 when the *t* worshippers shall
37 herein is that saying *t*, One soweth,
5.31 of myself, my witness is not *t*.
32 which he witnesseth of me is *t*.
6.32 my Father giveth you the *t* bread
7.18 glory that sent him, the same is *t*,
28 but he that sent me is *t*, whom ye
8.13 of thyself; thy record is not *t*.
14 record of myself, yet my record is *t*:
16 yet if I judge, my judgment is *t*:
17 that the testimony of two men is *t*.
26 he that sent me is *t*; and I speak to
10.41 that John spake of this man were *t*.
15. 1 I am the *t* vine, and my Father is
17. 3 might know thee the only *t* God,
19.35 it bear record, and his record is *t*:
35 he knoweth that he saith *t*, that ye
21.24 and we know that his testimony is *t*.
Ac 12. 9 that it was *t* which was done by the
Ro 3. 4 let God be *t*, but every man a liar;
2Co 1.18 But as God is *t*, our word toward
6. 8 report: as deceivers, and yet *t*;
Eph 4.24 righteousness and *t* holiness.
Php 4. 3 I intreat thee also, *t* yokefellow,
8 brethren, whatsoever things are *t*,
1Th 1. 9 idols to serve the living and *t* God;
1Ti 3. 1 This is a *t* saying, If a man desire
Tit 1.13 This witness is *t*. Wherefore
Heb 8. 2 sanctuary, and of the *t* tabernacle,
9.24 which are the figures of the *t*;
10.22 Let us draw near with a *t* heart in
1Pe 5.12 that this is the *t* grace of God
2Pe 2.22 them according to the *t* proverb,
1Jn 2. 8 which thing is *t* in him and in you:
8 past, and the *t* light now shineth.
5.20 that we may know him that is *t*,
20 and we are in him that is *t*, even in
20 This is the *t* God, and eternal life.
3Jn 12 and ye know that our record is *t*.
Rev 3. 7 saith he that is holy, he that is *t*,
14 the faithful and *t* witness, the
6.10 How long, O Lord, holy and *t*,
15. 3 just and *t* are thy ways, thou King
16. 7 *t* and righteous are thy judgments.
19. 2 *t* and righteous are his judgments:
9 me, These are the *t* sayings of God.
11 him was called Faithful and *T*,
21. 5 for these words are *t* and faithful.
22. 6 These sayings are faithful and *t*:

TRULY

Ps 62. 1 *T* my soul waiteth upon God:
73. 1 *T* God is good to Israel, even to
116.16 O Lord, *t* I am thy servant;
Ec 11. 7 *T* the light is sweet, and a pleasant
Jer 3.23 *T* in vain is salvation hoped for
10.19 but I said, *T* this is a grief, and I
Mic 3. 8 *t* I am full of power by the spirit
Mt 9.37 The harvest *t* is plenteous, but
17.11 Elias *t* shall first come, and
27.54 saying, *T* this was the Son of God.
Mk 14.38 The spirit *t* is ready, but the flesh
15.39 *T* this man was the Son of God.
Lk 10. 2 The harvest *t* is great, but the
11.48 *T* ye bear witness that ye allow
20.21 teachest the way of God *t*:
22.22 *t* the Son of man goeth, as it was
Jn 4.18 thy husband: in that saidst thou *t*.
20.30 many other signs *t* did Jesus
Ac 1. 5 For John *t* baptized with water;
3.22 For Moses *t* said unto the fathers,
5.23 The prison *t* found we shut with
2Co 12.12 *T* the signs of an apostle were
Heb 7.23 they *t* were many priests, because
11.15 And *t*, if they had been mindful of
1Jn 1. 3 *t* our fellowship is with...Father,

TRUMP

1Co 15.52 twinkling of an eye, at the last *t*:
1Th 4.16 archangel, and with the *t* of God:

TRUMPET

Ex 19.13 when the *t* soundeth long, they
Jos 6. 5 when ye hear the sound of the *t*,
Neh 4.18 he that sounded the *t* was by me.
Ps 47. 5 the Lord with the sound of a *t*.
81. 3 Blow up the *t* in the new moon, in
150. 3 Praise him with the sound of the *t*:
Isa 58. 1 spare not, lift up thy voice like a *t*,
Jer 6.17 Hearken to the sound of the *t*.
Eze 33. 3 blow the *t*, and warn the people;
6 if the watchman...blow not the *t*,
Joel 2.15 Blow the *t* in Zion, sanctify a fast,
Zep 1.16 A day of *t* and alarm against the
Zec 9.14 and the Lord God shall blow the *t*,
Mt 6. 2 alms, do not sound a *t* before thee,
24.31 angels with a great sound of a *t*,
1Co 14. 8 if the *t* give an uncertain sound,
15.52 for the *t* shall sound, and the dead
Heb 12.19 And the sound of a *t*, and the voice
Rev 1.10 behind me a great voice, as of a *t*,
4. 1 as it were of a *t* talking with me;
8.13 voices of the *t* of the three angels,
9.14 to the sixth angel which had the *t*,

TRUMPETERS

2Ki 11.14 the princes and the *t* by the king,
2Ch 5.13 as the *t* and singers were as one,
29.28 singers sang, and the *t* sounded:
Rev 18.22 musicians, and of pipers, and *t*,

TRUMPETS

Lev 23.24 a sabbath a memorial of blowing of *t*,
Nu 29. 1 it is a day of blowing the *t* unto you.
Jos 6. 6 priests bear seven *t* of rams' horns
Jdg 7.19 and they blew the *t*, and brake the
Job 39.25 He saith among the *t*, Ha, ha; and
Ps 98. 6 With *t* and sound of cornet make
Rev 8. 2 and to them were given seven *t*.
6 the seven *t* prepared themselves to

TRUST

Jdg 9.15 and put your *t* in my shadow:
2Sa 22. 3 God of my rock; in him will I *t*:
31 a buckler to all them that *t* in him.
2Ki 18.22 me, We *t* in the Lord our God:
Job 8.14 whose *t* shall be a spider's web.
13.15 he slay me, yet will I *t* in him:
Ps 5.11 that put their *t* in thee rejoice:
7. 1 my God, in thee do I put my *t*:
11. 1 In the Lord put I my *t*: how say
20. 7 Some *t* in chariots, and some in
25. 2 O my God, I *t* in thee: let me
20 ashamed; for I put my *t* in thee.
37. 3 *T* in the Lord, and do good; so
5 *t* also in him; and he shall bring it
40. 4 man that maketh the Lord his *t*,
44. 6 For I will not *t* in my bow, neither
52. 8 I *t* in the mercy of God for ever and
56.11 In God have I put my *t*: I will not
62. 8 *T* in him at all times; ye people,
10 *T* not in oppression, and become
71. 1 In thee, O Lord, do I put my *t*: let
91. 2 fortress: my God; in him will I *t*.
115.11 Ye that fear the Lord, *t* in the Lord:
118. 8, 9 It is better to *t* in the Lord than
125. 1 They that *t* in the Lord shall be as
146. 3 Put not your *t* in princes, nor in
Pr 3. 5 *T* in the Lord with all thine heart;
Isa 26. 4 *T* ye in the Lord for ever: for in
42.17 ashamed, that *t* in graven images,
50.10 let him *t* in the name of the Lord,
59. 4 they *t* in vanity, and speak lies;
Jer 7. 4 *T* ye not in lying words,
28.15 thou makest this people to *t* in a lie.
Eze 16.15 thou didst *t* in thine own beauty,
33.13 if he *t* to his own righteousness,
Mic 7. 5 *T* ye not in a friend, put ye not
Zep 3.12 shall *t* in the name of the Lord.
Mt 12.21 in his name shall the Gentiles *t*.
Mk 10.24 for them that *t* in riches to enter
Lk 16.11 commit to your *t* the true riches?
Jn 5.45 you, even Moses, in whom ye *t*.
Ro 15.12 in him shall the Gentiles *t*.
24 for I *t* to see you in my journey,
1Co 16. 7 but I *t* to tarry a while with you,
2Co 1. 9 that we should not *t* in ourselves,
10 in whom we *t* that he will yet
13 I *t* ye shall acknowledge even to

2Co 3. 4 such *t* have we through Christ to
5.11 I *t* also are made manifest in
10. 7 If any man *t* to himself that he
13. 6 I *t* that ye shall know that we are
Php 2.19 But I *t* in the Lord Jesus to send
24 I *t* in the Lord that I also myself
3. 4 whereof he might *t* in the flesh,
1Th 2. 4 to be put in *t* with the gospel,
1Ti 1.11 which was committed to my *t*.
4.10 because we *t* in the living God,
6.17 nor *t* in uncertain riches, but in
20 that which is committed to thy *t*,
Phm 22 for I *t* that through your prayers
Heb 2.13 again, I will put my *t* in him.
13.18 we *t* we have a good conscience,
2Jn 12 but I *t* to come unto you, and
3Jn 14 But I *t* I shall shortly see thee,

TRUSTED
Dt 32.37 gods, their rock in whom they *t*,
Jdg 11.20 Sihon *t* not Israel to pass through
20.36 they *t* unto the liers in wait which
2Ki 18. 5 He *t* in the Lord God of Israel; so
Ps 13. 5 But I have *t* in thy mercy; my
22. 4 Our fathers *t* in thee: they *t*, and
5 they *t* in thee, and were not
8 He *t* on the Lord that he would
26. 1 I have *t* also in the Lord; therefore
28. 7 my heart *t* in him, and I am helped:
31.14 But I *t* in thee, O Lord: I said,
33.21 because we have *t* in his holy name.
41. 9 own familiar friend, in whom I *t*,
52. 7 but *t* in the abundance of his riches.
78.22 in God, and *t* not in his salvation:
Isa 47.10 For thou hast *t* in thy wickedness:
Jer 13.25 forgotten me, and *t* in falsehood.
48. 7 because thou hast *t* in thy works
49. 4 that *t* in her treasures, saying,
Dan 3.28 his servants that *t* in him, and
Zep 3. 2 she *t* not in the Lord; she drew
Mt 27.43 He *t* in God; let him deliver him
Lk 11.22 him all his armor wherein he *t*,
18. 9 unto certain which *t* in themselves
24.21 we *t* that it had been he which
Eph 1.12 of his glory, who first *t* in Christ.
13 In whom ye also *t*, after that ye
1Pe 3. 5 holy women also, who *t* in God,

TRUSTEST
2Ki 18.19 confidence is this wherein thou *t*?
21 thou *t* upon the staff of this bruised
19.10 God in whom thou *t* deceive thee,
Isa 36. 4 confidence is this wherein thou *t*?
6 thou *t* in the staff of this broken
37.10 Let not thy God, in whom thou *t*,

TRUSTETH
Job 40.23 he *t* that he can draw up Jordan
Ps 21. 7 For the king *t* in the Lord, and
32.10 but he that *t* in the Lord, mercy
34. 8 blessed is the man that *t* in him.
57. 1 for my soul *t* in thee: yea, in the
84.12 blessed is the man that *t* in thee.
86. 2 save thy servant that *t* in thee.
115. 8 so is every one that *t* in them.
135.18 so is every one that *t* in them.
Pr 11.28 He that *t* in his riches shall fall:
16.20 whoso *t* in the Lord, happy is he.
28.26 He that *t* in his own heart is a fool:
Isa 26. 3 on thee: because he *t* in thee.
Jer 17. 5 Cursed be the man that *t* in man,
7 Blessed is the man that *t* in...Lord,
Hab 2.18 the maker of his work *t* therein,
1Ti 5. 5 indeed, and desolate, *t* in God,

TRUSTING
Ps 112. 7 his heart is fixed, *t* in the Lord.

TRUSTY
Job 12.20 removeth away the speech of the *t*,

BIBLICAL THEMES

TRUTH AND FALSEHOOD

Thou shalt not bear false witness. Ex 20.16

Therefore have I uttered that I understood not; things too wonderful for me, which I knew not. . . . I have heard of thee by the hearing of the ear: but now mine eye seeth thee. Job 42.3, 5

Lord, who shall abide in thy tabernacle? . . . He that walketh uprightly, and worketh righteousness, and speaketh the truth in his heart. Ps 15.1-2

Let not mercy and truth forsake thee: bind them about thy neck; write them upon the table of thine heart. Pr 3.3

The getting of treasures by a lying tongue is a vanity tossed to and fro of them that seek death. Pr 21.6

Your iniquities have separated between you and your God, and your sins have hid his face from you, that he will not hear. . . . your lips have spoken lies, your tongue hath muttered perverseness. None calleth for justice, nor any pleadeth for truth: they trust in vanity, and speak lies; they conceive mischief, and bring forth iniquity. Isa 59.2-4

They that observe lying vanities forsake their own mercy. Jon 2.8

Beware of false prophets, which come to you in sheep's clothing, but inwardly they are ravening wolves. Mt 7.15

The next day . . . the chief priests and Pharisees came together unto Pilate, saying, Sir, we remember that that deceiver said, while he was yet alive, After three days I will rise again. Command therefore that the sepulcher be made sure until the third day, lest his disciples come by night, and steal him away, and say unto the people, He is risen from the dead. Mt 27.62-64

Many bare false witness against him, but their witness agreed not together. Mk 14.56

If ye continue in my word, then are ye my disciples indeed; and ye shall know the truth, and the truth shall make you free. Jn 8.31-32

Jesus answered, . . . To this end was I born, and for this cause came I into the world, that I should bear witness unto the truth. Every one that is of the truth heareth my voice. Pilate saith unto him, What is truth? Jn 18.37-38

Thou hast not lied unto men, but unto God. Ac 5.4

Let us keep the feast, not with old leaven, neither with the leaven of malice and wickedness; but with the unleavened bread of sincerity and truth. 1Co 5.8

Am I therefore become your enemy, because I tell you the truth? Gal 4.16

That we henceforth be no more children, tossed to and fro, and carried about with every wind of doctrine, by the sleight of men, and cunning craftiness, whereby they lie in wait to deceive; but speaking the truth in love, may grow up into him in all things. Eph 4.14-15

Stand therefore, having your loins girt about with truth. Eph. 6.14

The church of the living God, the pillar and ground of the truth. 1Ti 3.15

In hope of eternal life, which God, that cannot lie, promised before the world began. Tit 1.2

If we say that we have no sin, we deceive ourselves, and the truth is not in us. If we confess our sins, he is faithful and just to forgive us our sins. 1Jn 1.8-9

The fearful, and unbelieving, . . . and idolaters, and all liars, shall have their part in the lake which burneth with fire and brimstone. Rev 21.8

TRUTH
Ex 18.21 such as fear God, men of *t*, hating
Dt 32. 4 a God of *t* and without iniquity,
2Ch 18.15 that thou say nothing but the *t*
31.20 and right and *t* before the Lord
Ps 15. 2 and speaketh the *t* in his heart.
25. 5 Lead me in thy *t*, and teach me:
31. 5 hast redeemed me, O Lord God of *t*.
33. 4 and all his works are done in *t*.
40.11 and thy *t* continually preserve me.
43. 3 O send out thy light and thy *t*: let
51. 6 thou desirest *t* in the inward parts:
61. 7 O prepare mercy and *t*, which may
85.10 Mercy and *t* are met together;
11 *T* shall spring out of the earth;
100. 5 his *t* endureth to all generations.
108. 4 and thy *t* reacheth unto the clouds.
111. 8 and are done in *t* and uprightness.
117. 2 the *t* of the Lord endureth for ever.
138. 2 thy lovingkindness and for thy *t*:
Pr 3. 3 Let not mercy and *t* forsake thee:
12.19 The lip of *t* shall be established
16. 6 By mercy and *t* iniquity is purged:
20.28 Mercy and *t* preserve the king: and
23.23 Buy the *t*, and sell it not; also
Isa 25. 1 of old are faithfulness and *t*.

59. 4 for justice, nor any pleadeth for *t*:
14 for *t* is fallen in the street, and
15 *t* faileth; and he that departeth
61. 8 I will direct their work in *t*, and I
Jer 5. 3 Lord, are not thine eyes upon the *t*?
26.15 for of a *t* the Lord hath sent me
Dan 2.47 Of a *t* it is, that your God is a God
10.21 which is noted in the scripture of *t*:
Hos 4. 1 because there is no *t*, nor mercy,
Zec 8. 3 Jerusalem shall be called a city of *t*;
8 God, in *t* and in righteousness.
16 Speak ye every man the *t* to his
16 execute the judgment of *t* and
Mal 2. 6 The law of *t* was in his mouth, and
Mt 14.33 Of a *t* thou art the Son of God.
15.27 she said, *T*, Lord: yet the dogs
22.16 and teachest the way of God in *t*,
Mk 5.33 before him, and told him all the *t*.
12.14 but teachest the way of God in *t*:
32 Well, Master, thou hast said the *t*:
Lk 4.25 I tell you of a *t*, many widows were
9.27 But I tell you of a *t*, there be some
12.44 Of a *t* I say unto you, that he will
21. 3 Of a *t* I say unto you, that this poor
22.59 Of a *t* this fellow also was with
Jn 1.14 of the Father,) full of grace and *t*.
17 grace and *t* came by Jesus Christ.
3.21 he that doeth *t* cometh to the light,
4.23 the Father in spirit and in *t*:
24 must worship him in spirit and in *t*.
5.33 and he bare witness unto the *t*.
6.14 This is of a *t* that prophet that
7.40 said, Of a *t* this is the Prophet.
8.32 And ye shall know the *t*, and the
32 and the *t* shall make you free.
40 a man that hath told you the *t*,
44 beginning, and abode not in the *t*,
44 because there is no *t* in him.
45 because I tell you the *t*, ye believe
46 And if I say the *t*, why do ye not
14. 6 I am the way, the *t*, and the life:
17 Even the Spirit of *t*; whom the
15.26 the Father, even the Spirit of *t*,
16. 7 Nevertheless I tell you the *t*; It is
13 when he, the Spirit of *t*, is come, he
13 he will guide you into all *t*: for he
17.17 Sanctify them through thy *t*:
17 thy word is *t*.
19 might be sanctified through the *t*.
18.37 I should bear witness unto the *t*.
37 Every one that is of the *t* heareth
38 Pilate saith unto him, What is *t*?
Ac 4.27 of a *t* against thy holy child Jesus,
10.34 Of a *t* I perceive that God is no
26.25 forth the words of *t* and soberness.
Ro 1.18 who hold the *t* in unrighteousness;
25 Who changed the *t* of God into a lie,
2. 2 judgment of God is according to *t*
8 contentious, and do not obey the *t*,
20 knowledge and of the *t* in the law.
3. 7 if the *t* of God hath more abounded
9. 1 I say the *t* in Christ, I lie not, my
15. 8 the circumcision for the *t* of God,
1Co 5. 8 unleavened bread of sincerity and *t*.
13. 6 in iniquity, but rejoiceth in the *t*;
2Co 4. 2 but by manifestation of the *t*
6. 7 By the word of *t*, by the power of
7.14 as we spake all things to you in *t*,
11.10 As the *t* of Christ is in me, no man
12. 6 not be a fool; for I will say the *t*:
13. 8 nothing against the *t*, but for the *t*.
Gal 2. 5 the *t* of the gospel might continue
14 according to the *t* of the gospel,
3. 1 you, that ye should not obey the *t*,
4.16 enemy, because I tell you the *t*?
5. 7 you that ye should not obey the *t*?
Eph 1.13 after that ye heard the word of *t*,
4.15 speaking the *t* in love, may grow
21 taught by him, as the *t* is in Jesus:
5. 9 goodness and righteousness and *t*;)
6.14 having your loins girt about with *t*,
Php 1.18 whether in pretence, or in *t*, Christ
Col 1. 5 in the word of the *t* of the gospel;
6 and knew the grace of God in *t*:
1Th 2.13 but as it is in *t*, the word of God,
2Th 2.10 they received not the love of the *t*,
12 be damned who believed not the *t*,
13 of the Spirit and belief of the *t*:
1Ti 2. 4 come unto the knowledge of the *t*.
7 (I speak the *t* in Christ, and lie not;)
3.15 God, the pillar and ground of the *t*.
6. 5 corrupt minds,...destitute of the *t*.
2Ti 2.15 rightly dividing the word of *t*.
18 Who concerning the *t* have erred,
3. 7 to come to the knowledge of the *t*.
8 Moses, so do these also resist the *t*:
Tit 1. 1 of the *t* which is after godliness;
14 of men, that turn from the *t*.
Heb 10.26 received the knowledge of the *t*,
Jas 1.18 will begat he us with the word of *t*,
3.14 glory not, and lie not against the *t*.
5.19 if any of you do err from the *t*, and
1Pe 1.22 purified your souls in obeying the *t*
2Pe 1.12 and be established in the present *t*.
2. 2 the way of *t* shall be evil spoken of.
1Jn 1. 6 darkness, we lie, and do not the *t*:
8 ourselves, and the *t* is not in us.
2. 4 is a liar, and the *t* is not in him.
21 know it, and that no lie is of the *t*.
3.18 in tongue; but in deed and in *t*.
4. 6 Hereby know we the spirit of *t*, and
5. 6 witness, because the Spirit is *t*.
2Jn 1 her children, whom I love in the *t*;

TRUTH'S

Ps 115. 1 for thy mercy, and for thy *t* sake.
2Jn 2 For the *t* sake, that dwelleth in us,

TRY

Jdg 7. 4 and I will *t* them for thee there:
2Ch 32.31 God left him, to *t* him, that he
Job 7.18 morning, and *t* him every moment?
12.11 Doth not the ear *t* words? and the
Ps 11. 4 his eyelids *t* the children of men.
26. 2 me; *t* my reins and my heart.
139.23 *t* me, and know my thoughts:
Jer 6.27 thou mayest know and *t* their way.
9. 7 I will melt them, and *t* them;
17.10 Lord search the heart, I *t* the reins,
La 3.40 Let us search and *t* our ways,
Dan 11.35 fall, to *t* them, and to purge, and
Zec 13. 9 and will *t* them as gold is tried:
1Co 3.13 the fire shall *t* every man's work
1Pe 4.12 fiery trial which is to *t* you,
1Jn 4. 1 *t* the spirits whether they are of
Rev 3.10 *t* them that dwell upon the earth.

TRYING

Jas 1. 3 *t* of your faith worketh patience.

TUMULT

1Sa 4.14 What meaneth the noise of this *t*?
2Sa 18.29 I saw a great *t*, but I knew not
2Ki 19.28 against me and thy *t* is come up
Ps 65. 7 waves, and the *t* of the people.
74.23 the *t* of those that rise up against
83. 2 For, lo, thine enemies make a *t*:
Isa 33. 3 the noise of the *t* the people fled;
37.29 thy *t*, is come up into mine ears,
Jer 11.16 with the noise of a great *t* he hath
Hos 10.14 shall a *t* arise among thy people,
Am 2. 2 and Moab shall die with *t*, with
Zec 14.13 a great *t* from the Lord shall be
Mt 27.24 but that rather a *t* was made, he
Mk 5.38 and seeth the *t*, and them that
Ac 21.34 not know the certainty for the *t*,
24.18 neither with multitude, nor with *t*.

TUMULTS

Am 3. 9 the great *t* in the midst thereof,
2Co 6. 5 in imprisonments, in *t*, in labors,
12.20 strifes,...whisperings, swellings, *t*:

TURN

Ex 3. 3 I will now *t* aside, and see this
Lev 19. 4 *T* ye not unto idols, nor make to
Nu 22.23 Balaam smote the ass, to *t* her
Dt 4.30 if thou *t* to the Lord thy God,
13.17 Lord may *t* from the fierceness of
14.25 Then shalt thou *t* it into money,
30. 3 Lord thy God will *t* thy captivity,
10 *t* unto the Lord thy God with all
Ru 1.12 *T* again, my daughter, go your
1Sa 15.25 pardon my sin,...*t* again with me,
2Ki 17.13 *T* ye from your evil ways, and
2Ch 30. 6 *t* again unto the Lord God of
9 not *t* away his face from you,
Job 14. 6 *T* from him, that he may rest, till
24. 4 They *t* the needy out of the way:
34.15 and man shall *t* again unto dust.
Ps 4. 2 long will ye *t* my glory into shame?
40. 4 proud, nor such as *t* aside to lies.
80. 3 *T* us again, O God, and cause thy
119.37 *T* away mine eyes from
126. 4 *T* again our captivity, O Lord, as
Pr 4.27 *T* not to the right hand nor to
Ec 3.20 the dust, and all *t* to dust again.
Isa 1.25 And I will *t* my hand upon thee,
10. 2 *t* aside the needy from judgment,
14.27 out, and who shall *t* it back?
29.21 and *t* aside the just for a thing of
58.13 *t* away thy foot from the sabbath,
Jer 3.14 *T*, O backsliding children, saith
13.16 he *t* it into the shadow of death,
18. 8 *t* from their evil, I will repent of
25. 5 *T* ye again now every one from
31.13 I will *t* their mourning into joy,
La 3.35 To *t* aside the right of a man
5.21 *T* thou us unto thee, O Lord, and
Eze 3.19 he *t* not from his wickedness, nor
Dan 9.13 we might *t* from our iniquities,
11.18 shall he *t* his face unto the isles,
12. 3 they that *t* many to righteousness, as
Hos 5. 4 their doings to *t* unto their God:
14. 2 you words, and *t* to the Lord:
Joel 2.12 *t* ye even to me with all your heart,
Am 2. 7 and *t* aside the way of the meek:
5. 7 Ye who *t* judgment to wormwood,
12 they *t* aside the poor in the gate
8.10 will *t* your feasts into mourning,
Jon 3. 9 can tell if God will *t* and repent,
Mic 7.19 He will *t* again, he will have
Zep 3. 9 *t* to the people a pure language,
Zec 1. 3 *T* ye unto me, saith the Lord of
3 I will *t* unto you, saith the Lord of
4 *T* ye now from your evil ways,
Mal 3. 5 that *t* aside the stranger from his
Mt 5.39 cheek, *t* to him the other also.
42 borrow of thee *t* not thou away.
7. 6 feet, and *t* again and rend you.
Mk 13.16 is in the field not *t* back again
Lk 1.16 Israel shall he *t* to the Lord their
17 to *t* the hearts of the fathers to the
10. 6 it: if not, it shall *t* to you again.
17. 4 and seven times in a day *t* again
21.13 it shall *t* to you for a testimony.
Ac 13. 8 *t* away the deputy from the faith.
46 life, lo, we *t* to the Gentiles.
14.15 ye should *t* from these vanities
26.18 to *t* them from darkness to light,
20 they should repent and *t* to God,
Ro 11.26 *t* away ungodliness from Jacob:
2Co 3.16 when it shall *t* to the Lord,
Gal 4. 9 how *t* ye again to the weak and
Php 1.19 that this shall *t* to my salvation
2Ti 3. 5 power thereof: from such *t* away.
4. 4 they shall *t* away their ears from
Tit 1.14 of men, that *t* from the truth.
Heb 12.25 we *t* away from him that speaketh
Jas 3. 3 and we *t* about their whole body.

2Pe 2.21 to *t* from the holy commandment
Rev 11. 6 over waters to *t* them to blood,

TURNED

Gen 3.24 flaming sword which *t* every way,
Ex 3. 4 Lord saw that he *t* aside to see,
7.15 the rod which was *t* to a serpent
Nu 14.43 ye are *t* away from the Lord,
22.23 the ass *t* aside out of the way,
Dt 9.15 *t* and came down from the mount,
31.18 that they are *t* unto other gods.
1Sa 6.12 *t* not aside to the right hand or to
2Sa 1.22 the bow of Jonathan *t* not back,
2Ki 5.12 So he *t* and went away in a rage.
Neh 13. 2 God *t* the curse into a blessing.
Job 19.19 whom I loved are *t* against me.
30.15 Terrors are *t* upon me: they pursue
31 My harp also is *t* to mourning, and
37.12 is *t* round about by his counsels:
38.14 It is *t* as clay to the seal; and they
41.22 sorrow is *t* into joy before him.
42.10 the Lord *t* the captivity of Job,
Ps 66. 6 He *t* the sea into dry land: they
20 which hath not *t* away my prayer,
119.59 *t* my feet unto thy testimonies.
126. 1 the Lord *t* again the captivity of
Isa 10. 4 For all this his anger is not *t* away.
34. 9 streams...shall be *t* into pitch,
53. 6 have *t* every one to his own way;
59.14 judgment is *t* away backward,
Jer 4. 8 anger of the Lord is not *t* back
5.25 Your iniquities have *t* away these
La 1.20 mine heart is *t* within me; for I
3. 3 Surely against me is he *t*;
11 He hath *t* aside my ways, and
5.15 our dance is *t* into mourning.
Dan 9.16 anger and thy fury be *t* away
10.16 vision my sorrows are *t* upon me,
Hos 7. 8 people; Ephraim is a cake not *t*.
Joel 2.31 The sun shall be *t* into darkness,
Am 6.12 for ye have *t* judgment into gall,
Jon 3.10 that they *t* from their evil way;
Hab 2.16 Lord's right hand shall be *t* unto
Hag 2.17 yet ye *t* not to me, saith the Lord.
Mt 2.22 *t* aside into the parts of Galilee:
9.22 But Jesus *t* him about, and when
16.23 But he *t*, and said unto Peter, Get
Mk 5.30 *t* him about in the press, and said,
8.33 when he had *t* about and looked on
Lk 2.45 they *t* back again to Jerusalem,
7. 9 *t* him about, and said unto the
44 he *t* to the woman, and said unto
9.55 But he *t*, and rebuked them, and
10.23 And he *t* him unto his disciples,
14.25 him: and he *t*, and said unto them,
17.15 *t* back, and with a loud voice
22.61 Lord *t*, and looked upon Peter.
Jn 1.38 Then Jesus *t*, and saw them
16.20 your sorrow shall be *t* into joy.
20.14 she *t* herself back, and saw Jesus
16 She *t* herself, and saith unto him,
Ac 2.20 The sun shall be *t* into darkness,
7.39 hearts *t* back again into Egypt,
42 Then God *t*, and gave them up to
9.35 Saron saw him, and *t* to the Lord.
11.21 believed, and *t* unto the Lord.
15.19 among the Gentiles are *t* to God:
16.18 grieved, *t* and said to the spirit,
17. 6 that have *t* the word upside down
19.26 and *t* away much people,
1Th 1. 9 and how ye *t* to God from idols to
1Ti 1. 6 have *t* aside unto vain jangling;
5.15 are already *t* aside after Satan.
2Ti 1.15 are in Asia be *t* away from me;
4. 4 truth, and shall be *t* unto fables.
Heb 11.34 *t* to flight the armies of the aliens.
12.13 which is lame be *t* out of the way;
Jas 3. 4 *t* about with a very small helm,
4. 9 let...laughter be *t* to mourning,
2Pe 2.22 dog is *t* to his own vomit again;

Rev 1.12 I *t* to see the voice that spake with
12 And being *t*, I saw seven golden

TURNEST

1Ki 2. 3 and whithersoever thou *t* thyself:
Job 15.13 thou *t* thy spirit against God,
Ps 90. 3 Thou *t* man to destruction; and

TURNETH

Lev 20. 6 the soul that *t* after such as have
Dt 29.18 whose heart *t* away this day from
Ps 107.33 He *t* rivers into a wilderness, and
35 He *t* the wilderness into a standing
146. 9 the way of the wicked he *t* upside
Pr 15. 1 A soft answer *t* away wrath: but
26.14 As the door *t* upon his hinges, so
Isa 44.25 that *t* wise men backward, and
Eze 18.24, 26 *t* away from his righteousness,
27 man *t* away from his wickedness
33.12 day that he *t* from his wickedness;
Am 5. 8 and *t* the shadow of death into

TURNING

2Ki 21.13 wiping it, and *t* it upside down.
2Ch 26. 9 gate, and at the *t* of the wall,
36.13 heart from *t* unto the Lord God
Neh 3.19 the armory at the *t* of the wall.
20 from the *t* of the wall unto the door
24 of Azariah unto the *t* of the wall,
25 over against the *t* of the wall,
Pr 1.32 the *t* away of the simple shall slay
Isa 29.16 your *t* of things upside down
Eze 41.24 two leaves apiece, two *t* leaves;
Mic 2. 4 *t* away he hath divided our fields.
Lk 23.28 But Jesus *t* unto them said,
Jn 21.20 Peter, *t* about, seeth the disciple
Ac 3.26 in *t* away every one of you from
9.40 *t* him to the body said, Tabitha,
Jas 1.17 variableness, neither shadow of *t*.
2Pe 2. 6 *t* the cities of Sodom...into ashes
Jude 4 *t* the grace of our God into

TURTLE

SS 2.12 the voice of the *t* is heard in our
Jer 8. 7 and the *t* and the crane and the

TURTLEDOVE

Gen 15. 9 old, and a *t*, and a young pigeon.
Lev 12. 6 pigeon, or a *t*, for a sin offering,
Ps 74.19 O deliver not the soul of thy *t* unto

TURTLEDOVES

Lev 1.14 he shall bring his offering of *t*,
5. 7 two *t*, or two young pigeons, unto
11 But if he be not able to bring two *t*,
Lk 2.24 A pair of *t*, or two young pigeons.

TWAIN

1Sa 18.21 my son in law in the one of the *t*.
2Ki 4.33 and shut the door upon them *t*,
Isa 6. 2 wings; with *t* he covered his face,
2 and with *t* he covered his feet,
2 and with *t* he did fly.
Jer 34.18 when they cut the calf in *t*, and
Eze 21.19 both *t* shall come forth out of one
Mt 5.41 thee to go a mile, go with him *t*.
19. 5 wife: and they *t* shall be one flesh?
6 Wherefore they are no more *t*, but
21.31 Whether of them *t* did the will of
27.21 Whether of the *t* will ye that I
51 the veil of the temple was rent in *t*
Mk 10. 8 And they *t* shall be one flesh: so
8 so then they are no more *t*, but one
15.38 the veil of the temple was rent in *t*
Eph 2.15 make in himself of *t* one new man,

TWELFTH

Rev 21.20 a jacinth; the *t*, an amethyst.

TWELVE

Ex 24. 4 according to the *t* tribes of
Jos 4. 9 Joshua set up *t* stones in the

Mt 9.20 with an issue of blood *t* years,
10. 1 called unto him his *t* disciples,
2 the names of the *t* apostles are
5 These *t* Jesus sent forth, and
11. 1 of commanding his *t* disciples,
14.20 that remained *t* baskets full.
19.28 ye also shall sit upon *t* thrones,
28 judging the *t* tribes of Israel.
20.17 took the *t* disciples apart in the
26.14 Then one of the *t*, called Judas
20 was come, he sat down with the *t*.
47 lo, Judas, one of the *t*, came, and
53 me more than *t* legions of angels?
Mk 3.14 he ordained *t*, that they should be
4.10 that were about him with the *t*
5.25 had an issue of blood *t* years,
42 for she was of the age of *t* years.
6. 7 And he called unto him the *t*, and
43 they took up *t* baskets full of the
8.19 ye up? They say unto him, *T*.
9.35 And he sat down, and called the *t*,
10.32 he took again the *t*, and began to
11.11 went out unto Bethany with the *t*.
14.10 Judas Iscariot, one of the *t*, went
17 evening he cometh with the *t*.
20 It is one of the *t*, that dippeth
43 spake, cometh Judas, one of the *t*,
Lk 2.42 when he was *t* years old, they
6.13 of them he chose *t*, whom also he
8. 1 of God: and the *t* were with him,
42 daughter, about *t* years of age,
43 having an issue of blood *t* years,
9. 1 he called his *t* disciples together,
12 then came the *t*, and said unto
17 that remained to them *t* baskets.
18.31 Then he took unto him the *t*, and
22. 3 being of the number of the *t*.
14 and the *t* apostles with him.
30 judging the *t* tribes of Israel.
47 one of the *t*, went before them,
Jn 6.13 filled *t* baskets with the fragments
67 Then said Jesus unto the *t*, Will ye
70 Have not I chosen you *t*, and one
71 betray him, being one of the *t*.
11. 9 Are there not *t* hours in the day?
20.24 But Thomas, one of the *t*, called
Ac 6. 2 Then the *t* called the multitude of
7. 8 and Jacob begat the *t* patriarchs.
19. 7 And all the men were about *t*.
24.11 yet but *t* days since I went up to
26. 7 Unto which promise our *t* tribes,
1Co 15. 5 seen of Cephas, then of the *t*:
Jas 1. 1 to the *t* tribes which are scattered
Rev 7. 5 of Juda were sealed *t* thousand.
12. 1 upon her head a crown of *t* stars:
21.12 great and high, and had *t* gates,
12 at the gates *t* angels, and names
12 of the *t* tribes of the children of
14 wall of the city had *t* foundations,
14 the names of the *t* apostles of the
16 with the reed, *t* thousand furlongs.
21 the *t* gates were *t* pearls; every
22. 2 life, which bare *t* manner of fruits,

TWENTY

Gen 18.31 there shall be *t* found there.
Lev 27. 3 male from *t* years old even unto
Ps 68.17 chariots of God are *t* thousand,
Eze 4.10 shall be by weight, *t* shekels a day:
Lk 14.31 against him with *t* thousand?
Jn 6.19 about five and *t* or thirty furlongs,
Ac 1.15 were about an hundred and *t*,)
27.28 sounded, and found it *t* fathoms:
1Co 10. 8 in one day three and *t* thousand.
Rev 4. 4 the throne were four and *t* seats:
4 I saw four and *t* elders sitting,
10 The four and *t* elders fall down
5. 8 the four and *t* elders fell down
14 the four and *t* elders fell down
11.16 four and *t* elders, which sat before
19. 4 the four and *t* elders and the four

TWENTY'S

Gen 18.31 I will not destroy it for *t* sake.

TWICE

Gen 41.32 was doubled unto Pharaoh *t*;
Ex 16. 5 *t* as much as they gather daily.
22 they gathered *t* as much bread,
Nu 20.11 with his rod he smote the rock *t*:
1Sa 18.11 avoided out of his presence *t*.
1Ki 11. 9 which had appeared unto him *t*,
2Ki 6.10 saved himself...not once nor *t*.
Neh 13.20 without Jerusalem once or *t*.
Job 33.14 For God speaketh once, yea *t*, yet
40. 5 Once have I spoken;...yea, *t*; but I
42.10 gave Job *t* as much as he had
Ps 62.11 *t* have I heard this; that power
Ec 6. 6 he live a thousand years *t* told,
Mk 14.30 before the cock crow *t*, thou shalt
72 Before the cock crow *t*, thou shalt
Lk 18.12 I fast *t* in the week, I give tithes of
Jude 12 without fruit, *t* dead, plucked up

TWILIGHT

1Sa 30.17 David smote them from the *t*
2Ki 7. 5 they rose up in the *t*, to go unto
7 they arose and fled in the *t*, and
Job 3. 9 the stars of the *t* thereof be dark;
24.15 of the adulterer waiteth for the *t*,
Pr 7. 9 In the *t*, in the evening, in the
Eze 12. 6 and carry it forth in the *t*:
7 I brought it forth in the *t*, and I
12 bear upon his shoulder in the *t*,

TWINKLING

1Co 15.52 In a moment, in the *t* of an eye,

TWO

Gen 1.16 And God made *t* great lights;
6.19 *t* of every sort shalt thou bring
7. 9 There went in *t* and *t* unto Noah
29.16 Laban had *t* daughters: the name
Ex 2.13 *t* men of the Hebrews strove
12. 7 and strike it on the *t* side posts
16.22 much bread, *t* omers for one man:
29 on the sixth day the bread of *t* days;
31.18 *t* tables of testimony, tables of
34. 4 in his hand the *t* tables of stone.
Dt 5.22 he wrote them in *t* tables of stone,
1Sa 23.18 they *t* made a covenant before
1Ki 3.25 said, Divide the living child in *t*,
2Ki 2. 6 leave thee. And they *t* went on.
8 they *t* went over on dry ground.
24 forth *t* she bears out of the wood,
5.23 said, Be content, take *t* talents.
1Ch 11.22 he slew *t* lionlike men of Moab:
Job 13.20 Only do not *t* things unto me: then
Pr 30. 7 *T* things have I required of thee;
Ec 4. 9 *T* are better than one; because
11 Again, if *t* lie together, then they
Eze 1.11 *t* wings of every one were joined
21.19 son of man, appoint thee *t* ways,
37.22 they shall be no more *t* nations,
22 they be divided into *t* kingdoms
Hos 6. 2 After *t* days will he revive us: in the
Am 3. 3 Can *t* walk together, except they
12 out of the mouth of the lion *t* legs,
Zec 4.14 These are the *t* anointed ones,
11. 7 And I took unto me *t* staves; the
Mt 2.16 from *t* years old and under,
4.18 saw *t* brethren, Simon called
21 thence, he saw other *t* brethren,
6.24 No man can serve *t* masters: for
8.28 met him *t* possessed with devils,
9.27 *t* blind men followed him, crying,
10.10 neither *t* coats, neither shoes, nor
29 *t* sparrows sold for a farthing?
11. 2 Christ, he sent *t* of his disciples,
14.17 here but five loaves, and *t* fishes.
19 the five loaves, and the *t* fishes,
18. 8 having *t* hands or *t* feet to be cast
9 having *t* eyes to be cast into hell
16 then take with thee one or *t* more,
16 the mouth of *t* or three witnesses
19 if *t* of you shall agree on earth as
20 For where *t* or three are gathered
20.21 Grant that...my *t* sons may sit,
24 indignation against the *t* brethren.
30 *t* blind men sitting by the way side,
21. 1 Olives, then sent Jesus *t* disciples,
28 A certain man had *t* sons; and he
22.40 On these *t* commandments hang
24.40 Then shall *t* be in the field; the
41 *T* women shall be grinding at the
25.15 he gave five talents, to another *t*,
17 likewise, he that had received *t*,
17 he also gained the other *t*.
22 that had received *t* talents came
22 thou deliveredst unto me *t* talents:
22 I have gained *t* other talents
26. 2 that after *t* days is the feast of the
37 Peter and the *t* sons of Zebedee,
60 At the last came *t* false witnesses,
27.38 the *t* thieves crucified with him,
Mk 5.13 (they were about *t* thousand:)
6. 7 to send them forth by *t* and *t*;
9 sandals; and not put on *t* coats.
37 *t* hundred pennyworth of bread,
38 knew, they say, Five, and *t* fishes.
41 the five loaves and the *t* fishes,
41 *t* fishes divided he among them all.
9.43 than having *t* hands to go into hell,
45 having *t* feet to be cast into hell,
47 having *t* eyes to be cast into hell
11. 1 he sendeth forth *t* of his disciples,
4 in a place where *t* ways met;
12.42 widow, and she threw in *t* mites,
14. 1 After *t* days was the feast of the
13 he sendeth forth *t* of his disciples,
15.27 with him they crucify *t* thieves;
16.12 in another form unto *t* of them,
Lk 2.24 turtledoves, or *t* young pigeons.
3.11 He that hath *t* coats, let him impart
5. 2 saw *t* ships standing by the lake:
7.19 calling unto him *t* of his disciples
41 creditor which had *t* debtors:
9. 3 neither have *t* coats apiece.
13 more but five loaves and *t* fishes;
16 took the five loaves and the *t* fishes,
30 there talked with him *t* men,
32 the *t* men that stood with him.
10. 1 seventy others, and sent them *t*
1 and sent them...*t* before his face
35 he departed, he took out *t* pence,
12. 6 five sparrows sold for *t* farthings,
52 three against *t*, and *t* against
15.11 he said, A certain man had *t* sons:
16.13 No servant can serve *t* masters:
17.34 there shall be *t* men in one bed;
35 *T* women shall be grinding
36 *T* men shall be in the field; the
18.10 *T* men went up into the temple to
19.29 Olives, he sent *t* of his disciples,
21. 2 widow casting in thither *t* mites.
22.38 Lord, behold, here are *t* swords.
23.32 there were also *t* other, malefactors,
24. 4 *t* men stood by them in shining
13 *t* of them went that same day to a
Jn 1.35 John stood, and *t* of his disciples;
37 the *t* disciples heard him speak,
40 One of the *t* which heard John
2. 6 containing *t* or three firkins apiece.
4.40 them: and he abode there *t* days.
43 after *t* days he departed thence,
6. 7 *T* hundred pennyworth of bread
9 barley loaves, and *t* small fishes:
8.17 that the testimony of *t* men is true.
11. 6 he abode *t* days still in the same
19.18 crucified him, and *t* other with him,
20.12 And seeth *t* angels in white sitting,
21. 2 and *t* other of his disciples.
8 but as it were *t* hundred cubits,)
Ac 1.10 *t* men stood by them in white
23 they appointed *t*, Joseph called
24 of these *t* thou hast chosen,
7.29 of Madian, where he begat *t* sons.
9.38 they sent unto him *t* men, desiring
10. 7 called *t* of his household servants,
12. 6 was sleeping between *t* soldiers,
6 bound with *t* chains: and the
19.10 continued by the space of *t* years;
22 he sent into Macedonia *t* of them
34 the space of *t* hours cried out,
21.33 him to be bound with *t* chains;
23.23 he called unto him *t* centurions,
23 Make ready *t* hundred soldiers to
23 spearmen *t* hundred, at the third
24.27 after *t* years Porcius Festus came
27.37 *t* hundred threescore and sixteen
41 into a place where *t* seas met,
28.30 Paul dwelt *t* whole years in his
1Co 6.16 for *t*, saith he, shall be one flesh.
14.27 let it be by *t*, or at the most by
29 Let the prophets speak *t* or three,
2Co 13. 1 the mouth of *t* or three witnesses
Gal 4.22 Abraham had *t* sons, the one by a
24 for these are the *t* covenants; the
Eph 5.31 wife, and they *t* shall be one flesh.
Php 1.23 For I am in a strait betwixt *t*,
1Ti 5.19 but before *t* or three witnesses.
Heb 6.18 That by *t* immutable things, in
10.28 mercy under *t* or three witnesses:
Rev 2.12 the sharp sword with *t* edges;
9.12 there come *t* woes more hereafter.
16 *t* hundred thousand thousand:
11. 2 under foot forty and *t* months.
3 give power unto my *t* witnesses,
3 *t* hundred and threescore days,
4 These are the *t* olive trees, and
4 the *t* candlesticks standing before
10 these *t* prophets tormented them
12. 6 thousand *t* hundred and threescore
14 given *t* wings of a great eagle,
13. 5 to continue forty and *t* months.
11 and he had *t* horns like a lamb,

TWOEDGED

Ps 149. 6 and a *t* sword in their hand;
Pr 5. 4 wormwood, sharp as a *t* sword.
Heb 4.12 and sharper than any *t* sword,
Rev 1.16 of his mouth went a sharp *t* sword:

TWOFOLD

Mt 23.15 make him *t* more the child of hell

TYRANNUS

Ac 19. 9 daily in the school of one *T*.

TYRE

1Ki 5. 1 Hiram king of *T* sent his servants
2Ch 2.11 the king of *T* answered in writing,
Ps 45.12 daughter of *T* shall be there with
Isa 23. 1 The burden of *T*. Howl, ye ships
15 *T* shall be forgotten seventy years,
Mt 11.21 had been done in *T* and Sidon,
22 be more tolerable for *T* and Sidon
15.21 into the coasts of *T* and Sidon.
Mk 3. 8 they about *T* and Sidon, a great
7.24 into the borders of *T* and Sidon,
31 departing from the coasts of *T* and
Lk 6.17 from the sea coast of *T* and Sidon,
10.13 works had been done in *T* and
14 be more tolerable for *T* and Sidon
Ac 12.20 highly displeased with them of *T*
21. 3 sailed into Syria, and landed at *T*:
7 we had finished our course from *T*,

TYRUS

Eze 26.15 Thus saith the Lord God to *T*;
27. 3 O *T*, thou hast said, I am of perfect
8 thy wise men, O *T*, that were in
28.12 a lamentation upon the king of *T*,
Am 1. 9 For three transgressions of *T*, and
Zec 9. 3 *T* did build herself a strong hold,

U

UNADVISEDLY
Ps 106.33 so that he spake *u* with his lips.

UNAWARES
Gen 31.20 Jacob stole away *u* to Laban
26 thou hast stolen away *u* to me,
Nu 35.11 which killeth any person at *u*.
15 that killeth any person *u* may flee
Dt 4.42 should kill his neighbor *u*,
Jos 20. 3 slayer that killeth any person *u*
9 killeth any person at *u* might flee
Ps 35. 8 destruction come upon him at *u*;
Lk 21.34 and so that day come upon you *u*.
Gal 2. 4 of false brethren *u* brought in,
Heb 13. 2 some have entertained angels *u*.
Jude 4 there are certain men crept in *u*,

UNBELIEF
Mt 13.58 works there because of their *u*.
17.20 said unto them, Because of your *u*:
Mk 6. 6 he marvelled because of their *u*.
9.24 Lord, I believe; help thou mine *u*.
16.14 upbraided them with their *u* and
Ro 3. 3 shall their *u* make the faith of God
4.20 at the promise of God through *u*;
11.20 because of *u* they were broken off,
23 also, if they abide not still in *u*,
30 obtained mercy through their *u*:
1Ti 1.13 because I did it ignorantly in *u*.
Heb 3.12 be in any of you an evil heart of *u*,
19 they could not enter in because of *u*.

UNBELIEVERS
Lk 12.46 him his portion with the *u*.
1Co 6. 6 with brother, and that before the *u*.
14.23 in those that are unlearned, or *u*,
2Co 6.14 unequally yoked together with *u*:

UNBELIEVING
Ac 14. 2 the *u* Jews stirred up the Gentiles,
1Co 7.14 the *u* husband is sanctified by the
14 *u* wife is sanctified by the husband:
15 But if the *u* depart, let him depart.
Tit 1.15 are defiled and *u* is nothing pure;
Rev 21. 8 But the fearful, and *u*, and the

UNCERTAIN
1Co 14. 8 For if the trumpet gave an *u* sound,
1Ti 6.17 nor trust in *u* riches, but in the

UNCERTAINLY
1Co 9.26 I therefore so run, not as *u*; so fight

UNCHANGEABLE
Heb 7.24 ever, hath an *u* priesthood.

UNCIRCUMCISED
Gen 17.14 And the *u* man child whose flesh
34.14 give our sister to one that is *u*;
Ex 6.12 hear me, who am of *u* lips?
30 I am of *u* lips, and how shall
12.48 for no *u* person shall eat thereof.
Lev 19.23 shall count the fruit thereof as *u*:
23 three years shall it be as *u* unto
26.41 if then their *u* hearts be humbled,
Jos 5. 7 for they were *u*, because
Jdg 14. 3 to take a wife of the *u* Philistines?
15.18 and fall into the hand of the *u*?
1Sa 14. 6 over unto the garrison of these *u*:
17.26 who is this *u* Philistine, that he
31. 4 lest these *u* come and thrust me
2Sa 1.20 the daughters of the *u* triumph.
1Ch 10. 4 lest these *u* come and abuse me.
Isa 52. 1 into thee the *u* and the unclean.
Jer 6.10 ear is *u*, and they cannot hearken:
9.25 which are circumcised with the *u*,
26 for all these nations are *u*, and
26 house of Israel are *u* in the heart.
Eze 28.10 Thou shalt die the deaths of the *u*
31.18 thou shalt lie in the midst of the *u*
32.19 down, and be thou laid with the *u*.
21 they lie *u*, slain by the sword.
24 are gone down *u* into the nether
27 the mighty that are fallen of the *u*,
28 be broken in the midst of the *u*,
29 they shall lie with the *u*, and with
44. 7 *u* in heart, and *u* in flesh, to be
9 stranger, *u* in heart, nor *u* in flesh,
Ac 7.51 Ye stiffnecked and *u* in heart and
11. 3 Thou wentest in to men *u*,
Ro 4.11 which he had yet being *u*:
1Co 7.18 let him not become *u*.

UNCLEAN
Lev 5. 2 Or if a soul touch any *u* thing,
10.10 unholy, and between *u* and clean;
11. 8 ye not touch; they are *u* to you.
26 cheweth the cud, are *u* unto you:
13.44 He is a leprous man, he is *u*:
Nu 19.22 whatsoever the *u* person toucheth
Job 14. 4 bring a clean thing out of an *u*?
Ec 9. 2 and to the clean, and to the *u*;
Isa 6. 5 because I am a man of *u* lips, and
5 in the midst of a people of *u* lips:
35. 8 the *u* shall not pass over it; but it
64. 6 But we are all as an *u* thing, and
Zec 13. 2 *u* spirit to pass out of the land.
Mt 10. 1 gave them power against *u* spirits,
12.43 the *u* spirit is gone out of a man,
Mk 1.23 synagogue a man with an *u* spirit;
26 And when the *u* spirit had torn him,
27 commandeth he even the *u* spirits,
3.11 *u* spirits, when they saw him, fell
5. 2 of the tombs a man with an *u* spirit,
8 Come out of the man, thou *u* spirit.
13 the *u* spirits went out, and entered
6. 7 gave them power over *u* spirits;
7.25 young daughter had an *u* spirit,
Lk 4.33 which had a spirit of an *u* devil,
36 power he commandeth the *u* spirits,
6.18 that were vexed with *u* spirits:
9.42 Jesus rebuked the *u* spirit, and
11.24 the *u* spirit is gone out of a man,
Ac 5.16 which were vexed with *u* spirits:
8. 7 For *u* spirits, crying with loud voice,
10.14 any thing that is common or *u*.
28 not call any man common or *u*.
Ro 14.14 that there is nothing *u* of itself:
14 any thing to be *u*, to him it is *u*.
1Co 7.14 else were your children *u*; but
2Co 6.17 Lord, and touch not the *u* thing;
Eph 5. 5 nor *u* person, nor covetous man,
Rev 16.13 I saw three *u* spirits like frogs
18. 2 a cage of every *u* and hateful bird.

UNCLEANNESS
Nu 5.19 if thou hast not gone aside to *u*.
Dt 24. 1 he hath found some *u* in her:
Mt 23.27 of dead men's bones, and of all *u*.
Ro 1.24 God also gave them up to *u* through
6.19 yielded your members servants to *u*
2Co 12.21 and have not repented of the *u* and
Gal 5.19 are these; Adultery, fornication, *u*,
Eph 4.19 to work all *u* with greediness.
5. 3 But fornication, and all *u*, or
Col 3. 5 upon the earth; fornication, *u*,
1Th 2. 3 not of deceit, nor of *u*, nor in guile:
4. 7 For God hath not called us unto *u*,
2Pe 2.10 after the flesh in the lust of *u*,

UNCLOTHED
2Co 5. 4 not for that we would be *u*, but

UNCOMELY
1Co 7.36 behaveth himself *u* toward a virgin,
12.23 our *u* parts have more abundant

UNCONDEMNED
Ac 16.37 They have beaten us openly *u*,
22.25 a man that is a Roman, and *u*?

UNCORRUPTIBLE
Ro 1.23 changed the glory of the *u* God

UNCOVER
Lev 10. 6 *U* not your heads, neither rend
18. 6 kin to him, to *u* their nakedness:
7 of thy mother, shalt thou not *u*:
7 thou shalt not *u* her nakedness.
8 thy father's wife shalt thou not *u*:
21.10 shall not *u* his head, nor rend his
Nu 5.18 Lord, and *u* the woman's head,
Ru 3. 4 and *u* his feet, and lay thee down
Isa 47. 2 and grind meal: *u* thy locks,
2 make bare the leg, *u* the thigh,
Zep 2.14 for he shall *u* the cedar work.

UNCOVERED
Mk 2. 4 they *u* the roof where he was:
1Co 11. 5 or prophesieth with her head *u*
13 that a woman pray unto God *u*?

UNCTION
1Jn 2.20 ye have an *u* from the Holy One,

UNDEFILED
Ps 119. 1 Blessed are the *u* in the way,
SS 5. 2 sister, my love, my dove, my *u*:
6. 9 My dove, my *u* is but one; she is
Heb 7.26 who is holy, harmless, *u*, separate
13. 4 is honorable in all, and the bed *u*:
Jas 1.27 Pure religion and *u* before God
1Pe 1. 4 an inheritance incorruptible, and *u*,

UNDER
Gen 1. 7 which were *u* the firmament
9 waters *u* the heaven be gathered
Dt 4.11 near and stood *u* the mountain;
12. 2 the hills, and *u* every green tree:
28.23 earth that is *u* thee shall be iron.
29.20 blot out his name from *u* heaven.
Jdg 1. 7 gathered their meat *u* my table:
9.29 to God this people were *u* my hand!
2Sa 22.10 and darkness was *u* his feet.
37 Thou hast enlarged my steps *u* me;
1Ki 4.25 man *u* his vine and *u* his fig tree,
13.14 and found him sitting *u* an oak:
18.23, 23 lay it on wood, and put no fire *u*:
19. 4 and sat down *u* a juniper tree:
Job 40.21 He lieth *u* the shady trees, in the
41.30 Sharp stones are *u* him: he
Ps 8. 6 thou hast put all things *u* his feet:
17. 8 hide me *u* the shadow of thy wings,
91. 1 shall abide *u* the shadow of the
Ec 1. 9 there is no new thing *u* the sun.
2.11 and there was no profit *u* the sun.
19 shewed myself wise *u* the sun.
3. 1 time to every purpose *u* the heaven:
4. 3 evil work that is done *u* the sun.
7 and I saw vanity *u* the sun.
7. 6 the crackling of thorns *u* the pot,
9.13 wisdom have I seen also *u* the sun,
SS 4.11 honey and milk are *u* thy tongue;
Isa 28.15 *u* falsehood have we hid ourselves:
Jer 27. 8 will not put their neck *u* the yoke
La 4.20 *U* his shadow we shall live among
5. 5 Our necks are *u* persecution: we
Eze 20.37 I will cause you to pass *u* the rod,
31.17 that dwelt *u* his shadow in the midst

Hos 14. 7 They that dwell *u* his shadow shall
Jon 4. 5 booth, and sat *u* it in the shadow,
Mic 4. 4 man *u* his vine and *u* his fig tree;
Zec 3.10 *u* the vine and *u* the fig tree.
Mt 2.16 from two years old and *u*,
5.13 and to be trodden *u* foot of men.
15 a candle, and put it *u* a bushel,
8. 8 thou shouldest come *u* my roof:
9 For I am a man *u* authority,
9 having soldiers *u* me: and I say
23.37 her chickens *u* her wings, and
Mk 4.21 to be put *u* a bushel, or *u* a bed?
32 air may lodge *u* the shadow of it.
6.11 shake off the dust *u* your feet for
Lk 7. 6 thou shouldest enter *u* my roof:
8 I also am a man set *u* authority,
8 having *u* me soldiers, and I say
8.16 a vessel, or putteth it *u* a bed;
13.34 gather her brood *u* her wings,
17.24 out of the one part *u* heaven,
24 unto the other part *u* heaven;
Jn 1.48 when thou wast *u* the fig tree, I
50 thee, I saw thee *u* the fig tree,
Ac 2. 5 out of every nation *u* heaven.
4.12 none other name *u* heaven given
23.12 and bound themselves *u* a curse,
Ro 3. 9 Gentiles, that they are all *u* sin;
13 the poison of asps is *u* their lips:
19 saith to them who are *u* the law:
6.14 ye are not *u* the law, but *u* grace.
7.14 but I am carnal, sold *u* sin.
16.20 bruise Satan *u* your feet shortly.
1Co 6.12 not be brought *u* the power of any.
9.20 that are *u* the law, as *u* the law,
21 to God, but *u* the law to Christ,)
10. 1 all our fathers were *u* the cloud,
Gal 3.10 works of the law are *u* the curse:
22 hath concluded all *u* sin, that
4. 2 is *u* tutors and governors until the
4 made of a woman, made *u* the law,
21 ye that desire to be *u* the law, do ye
5.18 of the Spirit, ye are not *u* the law.
Heb 2. 8 all things in subjection *u* his feet.
8 see not yet all things put *u* him.
7.11 *u* it the people received the law,)
10.28 mercy *u* two or three witnesses:
29 trodden *u* foot the Son of God,
1Pe 5. 6 *u* the mighty hand of God,
Jude 6 in everlasting chains *u* darkness
Rev 5. 3 nor in earth, neither *u* the earth,
6. 9 I saw *u* the altar the souls of them
12. 1 the sun, and the moon *u* her feet,

UNDERGIRDING

Ac 27.17 up, they used helps, *u* the ship;

UNDERNEATH

Dt 33.27 *u* are the everlasting arms:

UNDERSTAND

Gen 11. 7 may not *u* one another's speech.
41.15 canst *u* a dream to interpret it:
2Ki 18.26 the Syrian language; for we *u* it:
1Ch 28.19 Lord made me *u* in writing by his
Neh 8. 7 caused the people to *u* the law:
Job 6.24 me to *u* wherein I have erred.
23. 5 and *u* what he would say unto me.
26.14 thunder of his power who can *u*?
32. 9 neither do the aged *u* judgment.
Ps 14. 2 see if there were any that did *u*,
19.12 Who can *u* his errors? cleanse
53. 2 see if there were any that did *u*,
92. 6 not; neither doth a fool *u* this.
119.100 I *u* more than the ancients, because
Pr 1. 6 To *u* a proverb, and the
2. 5 shalt thou *u* the fear of the Lord,
9 Then shalt thou *u* righteousness,
8. 5 O ye simple, *u* wisdom: and, ye
14. 8 of the prudent is to *u* his way:
19.25 and he will *u* knowledge.
20.24 how can a man then *u* his own way?
28. 5 Evil men *u* not judgment: but they
5 they that seek the Lord *u* all things.
29.19 for though he *u* he will not answer.
Isa 6. 9 people, Hear ye indeed, but *u* not;
10 and *u* with the heart, and convert,
28. 9 whom shall he make to *u* doctrine?
33.19 tongue, that thou canst not *u*.
Jer 9.12 is the wise man, that may *u* this?
Dan 8.16 make this man to *u* the vision.
17 he said unto me. *U*, O son of man:
10.11 *u* the words that I speak unto thee,
12.10 but the wise shall *u*.
Hos 14. 9 is wise, and he shall *u* these things?
Mic 4.12 Lord, neither *u* they his counsel:
Mt 13.13 they hear not, neither do they *u*.
14 ye shall hear, and shall not *u*;
15 and should *u* with their heart, and
15.10 and said unto them, Hear, and *u*:
17 Do not ye yet *u*, that whatsoever
16. 9 Do ye not yet *u*, neither remember
11 How is it that ye do not *u* that I
24.15 place, (whoso readeth, let him *u*:)
Mk 4.12 hearing they may hear, and not *u*;
7.14 unto me every one of you, and *u*:
8.17 perceive ye not yet, neither *u*? have
21 them, How is it that ye do not *u*?
13.14 (let him that readeth *u*,) then let
14.68 not, neither *u* I what thou sayest.
Lk 8.10 see, and hearing they might not *u*.
24.45 that they might *u* the scriptures,
Jn 8.43 Why do ye not *u* my speech? even
12.40 nor *u* with their heart, and be
Ac 24.11 Because that thou mayest *u*, that
28.26 ye shall hear, and shall not *u*;
27 *u* with their heart, and should be
Ro 15.21 they that have not heard shall *u*.
1Co 12. 3 Wherefore I give you to *u*, that no
13. 2 of prophecy, and *u* all mysteries.
Eph 3. 4 *u* my knowledge in mystery of
Php 1.12 I would ye should *u*, brethren,
Heb 11. 3 Through faith we *u* that the
2Pe 2.12 speak evil of things that they *u* not;

UNDERSTANDEST

Job 15. 9 what *u* thou, which is not in us?
Ps 139. 2 thou *u* my thought afar off.
Jer 5.15 not, neither *u* what they say.
Ac 8.30 said, *U* thou what thou readest?

UNDERSTANDETH

1Ch 28. 9 and *u* all the imaginations of the
Job 28.23 God *u* the way thereof, and he
Ps 49.20 Man that is in honor, and *u* not,
Pr 8. 9 They are all plain to him that *u*,
14. 6 knowledge is easy unto him that *u*.
Jer 9.24 that he *u* and knoweth me, that I
Mt 13.19 word of the kingdom, and *u* it not,
23 he that heareth the word, and *u* it;
Ro 3.11 There is none that *u*, there is none
1Co 14. 2 for no man *u* him; howbeit in the
16 seeing he *u* not what thou sayest?

UNDERSTANDING

Ex 35.31 spirit of God, in wisdom, in *u*,
Dt 1.13 Take you wise men, and *u*, and
1Sa 25. 3 and she was a woman of good *u*,
1Ki 3. 9 Give...thy servant an *u* heart
4.29 God gave Solomon wisdom and *u*
2Ch 26. 5 who had *u* in the visions of God:
Job 12. 3 But I have *u* as well as you; I am
20 taketh away the *u* of the aged.
20. 3 of my *u* causeth me to answer.
28.28 and to depart from evil is *u*.
32. 8 of the Almighty giveth them *u*.
Ps 32. 9 or as the mule, which have no *u*:
119.34 Give me *u*, and I shall keep thy
99 more *u* than all my teachers:
104 Through thy precepts I get *u*:
130 light; it giveth *u* unto the simple.
Pr 2. 2 and apply thine heart to *u*;
4. 5 Get wisdom, get *u*: forget it not;
7 and with all thy getting get *u*.
8. 5 and, ye fools, be ye of an *u* heart.
14.29 is slow to wrath is of great *u*:
16.16 *u* rather to be chosen than silver!
18. 2 A fool hath no delight in *u*, but
19. 8 he that keepeth *u* shall find good.
28.11 the poor that hath *u* searcheth him
16 The prince that wanteth *u* is also
Isa 11. 2 spirit of wisdom and *u*, the spirit
27.11 on fire: for it is a people of no *u*:
40.28 there is no searching of his *u*.
Jer 51.15 stretched out the heaven by his *u*.
Dan 1. 4 in knowledge, and *u* science,
17 Daniel had *u* in all visions and
5.14 *u* and excellent wisdom is found in
Ob 7 under thee: there is none *u* in him.
Mt 15.16 said, Are ye also yet without *u*?
Mk 7.18 them, Are ye so without *u* also?
12.33 all the heart, and with all the *u*,
Lk 1. 3 having had perfect *u* of all things
2.47 him were astonished at his *u*
24.45 Then opened he their *u*, that they
Ro 1.31 Without *u*, covenantbreakers,
1Co 1.19 to nothing the *u* of the prudent.
14.14 prayeth, but my *u* is unfruitful.
15 and I will pray with the *u* also:
15 and I will sing with the *u* also.
19 rather speak five words with my *u*,
20 Brethren, be not children in *u*:
20 be ye children, but in *u* be men.
Eph 1.18 eyes of your *u* being enlightened;
4.18 Having the *u* darkened, being
5.17 *u* what the will of the Lord is.
Php 4. 7 peace of God, which passeth all *u*,
Col 1. 9 in all wisdom and spiritual *u*;
2. 2 riches of the full assurance of *u*,
1Ti 1. 7 *u* neither what they say, nor
2Ti 2. 7 Lord give thee *u* in all things.
1Jn 5.20 is come, and hath given us an *u*,
Rev 13.18 him that hath *u* count the number

UNDERSTOOD

Gen 42.23 knew not that Joseph *u* them;
Dt 32.29 they were wise, that they *u* this,
1Sa 4. 6 they *u* that the ark of the Lord
26. 4 *u* that Saul was come in very deed.
2Sa 3.37 all the people and all Israel *u* that
Neh 8.12 *u* the words that were declared
13. 7 *u* of the evil that Eliashib did for
Job 13. 1 this, mine ear hath heard and *u* it.
42. 3 have I uttered that I *u* not;
Ps 73.17 of God; then *u* I their end.
81. 5 I heard a language that I *u* not.
106. 7 Our fathers *u* not thy wonders in
Isa 40.21 ye not *u* from the foundations of
44.18 They have not known nor *u*: for he
Dan 8.27 at the vision, but none *u* it.
9. 2 I Daniel *u* by books the number of
10. 1 and he *u* the thing, and had
12. 8 And I heard, but I *u* not: then said
Mt 13.51 them, Have ye *u* all these things?
16.12 Then *u* they how that he bade
17.13 the disciples *u* that he spake unto
26.10 When Jesus *u* it, he said unto
Mk 9.32 But they *u* not that saying, and
Lk 2.50 *u* not the saying which he spake
9.45 they *u* not this saying, and it was
18.34 And they *u* none of these things:
Jn 8.27 *u* not that he spake to them of
10. 6 *u* not what things they were which
12.16 These things *u* not his disciples at
Ac 7.25 his brethren would have *u* how
25 deliver them: but they *u* not.
23.27 having *u* that he was a Roman.
34 when he *u* that he was of Cilicia;
Ro 1.20 *u* by the things that are made,
1Co 13.11 I *u* as a child, I thought as a child:
14. 9 by the tongue words easy to be *u*,
2Pe 3.16 are some things hard to be *u*,

UNDO
Isa 58. 6 to *u* the heavy burdens, and to let
Zep 3.19 that time I will *u* all that afflict

UNDONE
Nu 21.29 thou art *u*, O people of Chemosh:
Jos 11.15 he left nothing *u* of all that the
Isa 6. 5 Woe is me! for I am *u*; because
Mt 23.23 done, and not to leave the other *u*.
Lk 11.42 done, and not to leave the other *u*.

UNFEIGNED
2Co 6. 6 by the Holy Ghost, by love *u*,
1Ti 1. 5 of a good conscience, and of faith *u*:
2Ti 1. 5 the *u* faith that is in thee, which
1Pe 1.22 Spirit unto *u* love of the brethren,

UNFRUITFUL
Mt 13.22 the word, and he becometh *u*.
Mk 4.19 choke the word, and it becometh *u*.
1Co 14.14 but my understanding is *u*.
Eph 5.11 with the *u* works of darkness,
Tit 3.14 necessary uses, that they be not *u*.
2Pe 1. 8 nor *u* in the knowledge of our Lord

UNGODLINESS
Ro 1.18 revealed from heaven against all *u*
11.26 and shall turn away *u* from Jacob:
2Ti 2.16 for they will increase unto more *u*.
Tit 2.12 denying *u* and worldly lusts, we

UNGODLY
2Sa 22. 5 floods of *u* men made me afraid;
2Ch 19. 2 Shouldest thou help the *u*, and
Job 16.11 God hath delivered me to the *u*,
34.18 wicked? and to princes, Ye are *u*?
Ps 1. 1 walketh not in the counsel of the *u*,
4 The *u* are not so: but are like the
5 *u* shall not stand in the judgment,
6 but the way of the *u* shall perish.
3. 7 hast broken the teeth of the *u*.
18. 4 floods of *u* men made me afraid.
43. 1 cause against an *u* nation:
73.12 these are the *u*, who prosper in
Pr 16.27 An *u* man diggeth up evil: and in
19.28 An *u* witness scorneth judgment:
Ro 4. 5 on him that justifieth the *u*, his
5. 6 in due time Christ died for the *u*.
1Ti 1. 9 for the *u* and for sinners, for
1Pe 4.18 where shall the *u* and the sinner
2Pe 2. 5 in the flood upon the world of the *u*;
6 unto those that after should live *u*;
3. 7 judgment and perdition of *u* men.
Jude 4 *u* men, turning the grace of our God
15 to convince all that are *u* among
15 all their *u* deeds which they have
15 which they have *u* committed,
15 speeches which *u* sinners have
18 walk after their own *u* lusts.

UNHOLY
Lev 10.10 difference between holy and *u*,
1Ti 1. 9 for *u* and profane, for murderers of
2Ti 3. 2 to parents, unthankful, *u*,
Heb 10.29 he was sanctified, an *u* thing,

UNICORN
Nu 23.22 as it were the strength of an *u*.
24. 8 as it were the strength of an *u*:
Job 39. 9 Will the *u* be willing to serve thee,
10 Canst thou bind the *u* with his
Ps 29. 6 Lebanon and Sirion like a young *u*.
92.10 thou exalt like the horn of an *u*:

UNICORNS
Dt 33.17 his horns are like the horns of *u*:
Ps 22.21 heard me from the horns of the *u*.
Isa 34. 7 the *u* shall come down with them,

UNITY
Ps 133. 1 brethren to dwell together in *u*!
Eph 4. 3 to keep the *u* of the Spirit in the
13 we all come in the *u* of the faith,

UNJUST
Ps 43. 1 me from the deceitful and *u* man.
Pr 11. 7 and the hope of *u* men perisheth.
28. 8 *u* gain increaseth his substance,
29.27 An *u* man is an abomination to
Zep 3. 5 not; but the *u* knoweth no shame.
Mt 5.45 rain on the just and on the *u*.
Lk 16. 8 the lord commended the *u* steward,
10 is *u* in the least is *u* also in much.
18. 6 said, Hear what the *u* judge saith.
11 as other men are, extortioners, *u*,
Ac 24.15 of the dead, both of the just and *u*.
1Co 6. 1 go to law before the *u*, and not
1Pe 3.18 suffered for sins, the just for the *u*,
2Pe 2. 9 to reserve the *u* unto the day of
Rev 22.11 He that is *u*, let him be *u* still:

UNJUSTLY
Ps 82. 2 How long will ye judge *u*, and
Isa 26.10 of uprightness will he deal *u*,

UNKNOWN
Ac 17.23 this inscription, To The *U* God.
1Co 14. 2 he that speaketh in an *u* tongue
4 in an *u* tongue edifieth himself;
13 that speaketh in an *u* tongue pray
14 if I pray in an *u* tongue, my spirit
19 ten thousand words in an *u* tongue.
27 If any man speak in an *u* tongue, let
2Co 6. 9 As *u*, and yet well known; as dying,
Gal 1.22 was *u* by face unto the churches of

UNLAWFUL
Ac 10.28 an *u* thing for a man that is a Jew
2Pe 2. 8 day to day with their *u* deeds:)

UNLEARNED
Ac 4.13 that they were *u* and ignorant men,
1Co 14.16 the *u* say Amen at thy giving of
23 there come in those that are *u*,
24 one that believeth not, or one *u*,
2Ti 2.23 foolish and *u* questions avoid,
2Pe 3.16 that are *u* and unstable wrest,

UNLEAVENED
Gen 19. 3 did bake *u* bread, and they did
Ex 12.15 Seven days shall ye eat *u* bread;
23.15 shalt keep the feast of *u* bread:
Eze 45.21 seven days; *u* bread shall be eaten.
Mt 26.17 first day of the feast of *u* bread
Mk 14. 1 of the passover, and of *u* bread:
12 the first day of *u* bread, when they
Lk 22. 1 Now the feast of *u* bread drew nigh,
7 Then came the day of *u* bread,
Ac 12. 3 (Then were the days of *u* bread.)
20. 6 Philippi after the days of *u* bread,
1Co 5. 7 ye may be a new lump, as ye are *u*.
8 the *u* bread of sincerity and truth.

UNLOOSE
Mk 1. 7 not worthy to stoop down and *u*.
Lk 3.16 whose shoes I am not worthy to *u*:
Jn 1.27 shoe's latchet I am not worthy to *u*.

UNMARRIED
1Co 7. 8 say therefore to the *u* and widows,
11 and if she depart, let her remain *u*,
32 He that is *u* careth for the things
34 The *u* woman careth for the things

UNMERCIFUL
Ro 1.31 natural affection, implacable, *u*:

UNMINDFUL
Dt 32.18 Rock that begat thee thou art *u*,

UNMOVEABLE
Ac 27.41 stuck fast, and remained *u*,
1Co 15.58 brethren, be ye stedfast, *u*,

UNPERFECT
Ps 139.16 did see my substance, yet being *u*;

UNPREPARED
2Co 9. 4 come with me, and find you *u*,

UNPROFITABLE
Job 15. 3 Should he reason with *u* talk? or
Mt 25.30 cast ye the *u* servant into outer
Lk 17.10 you, say, We are *u* servants:
Ro 3.12 way, they are together become *u*;
Tit 3. 9 the law; for they are *u* and vain.
Phm 11 Which in time past was to thee *u*,
Heb 13.17 with grief: for that is *u* for you.

UNPROFITABLENESS
Heb 7.18 for the weakness and *u* thereof.

UNPUNISHED
Pr 11.21 hand, the wicked shall not be *u*:
17. 5 is glad at calamities shall not be *u*.
19. 5, 9 A false witness shall not be *u*,
Jer 25.29 name, and should ye be utterly *u*?
29 Ye shall not be *u*: for I will call for
30.11 will not leave thee altogether *u*.

UNQUENCHABLE
Mt 3.12 will burn up the chaff with *u* fire.
Lk 3.17 the chaff he will burn with fire *u*.

UNREASONABLE
Ac 25.27 seemeth to me *u* to send a prisoner,
2Th 3. 2 delivered from *u* and wicked men:

UNRIGHTEOUS
Ex 23. 1 the wicked to be an *u* witness.
Job 27. 7 riseth up against me as the *u*.
Ps 71. 4 the hand of the *u* and cruel man.
Isa 10. 1 unto them that decree *u* decrees,
55. 7 way, and the *u* man his thoughts:
Lk 16.11 not been faithful in the *u* mammon,
Ro 3. 5 Is God *u* who taketh vengeance?
1Co 6. 9 *u* shall not inherit the kingdom of
Heb 6.10 God is not *u* to forget your work

UNRIGHTEOUSNESS
Lev 19.15 Ye shall do no *u* in judgment:
35 Ye shall do no *u* in judgment, in
Ps 92.15 my rock, and there is no *u* in him.
Jer 22.13 that buildeth his house by *u*,
Lk 16. 9 friends of the mammon of *u*;
Jn 7.18 the same is true, and no *u* is in him.
Ro 1.18 all ungodliness and *u* of men,
18 of men, who hold the truth in *u*;
29 Being filled with all *u*, fornication,
2. 8 but obey *u*, indignation and wrath,
3. 5 if our *u* commend the righteousness
6.13 as instruments of *u* unto sin:
9.14 we say then? Is there *u* with God?
2Co 6.14 hath righteousness with *u*?
2Th 2.10 deceivableness of *u* in them that
12 not the truth, but had pleasure in *u*.
Heb 8.12 For I will be merciful to their *u*,
2Pe 2.13 And shall receive the reward of *u*,
15 Bosor, who loved the wages of *u*;
1Jn 1. 9 sins, and to cleanse us from all *u*.
5.17 All *u* is sin: and there is a sin not

UNRULY
1Th 5.14 brethren, warn them that are *u*,
Tit 1. 6 children not accused of riot or *u*.
10 there are many *u* and vain talkers
Jas 3. 8 it is an *u* evil, full of deadly poison.

UNSAVORY
Job 6. 6 Can that which is *u* be eaten

UNSEARCHABLE
Job 5. 9 doeth great things and *u*;
Ps 145. 3 praised; and his greatness is *u*.
Pr 25. 3 and the heart of kings is *u*.
Ro 11.33 how *u* are his judgments, and his
Eph 3. 8 Gentiles the *u* riches of Christ;

UNSEEMLY
Ro 1.27 with men working that which is *u*,
1Co 13. 5 Doth not behave itself *u*, seeketh not

UNSKILFUL
Heb 5.13 every one that useth milk is *u* in

UNSPEAKABLE
2Co 9.15 Thanks be unto God for his *u* gift.
12. 4 into paradise, and heard *u* words,
1Pe 1. 8 with joy *u* and full of glory:

UNSPOTTED
Jas 1.27 to keep himself *u* from the world.

UNSTABLE
Gen 49. 4 *U* as water, thou shalt not excel;
Jas 1. 8 A double minded man is *u* in all
2Pe 2.14 cease from sin; beguiling *u* souls:
3.16 that are unlearned and *u* wrest,

UNSTOPPED
Isa 35. 5 and the ears of the deaf shall be *u*.

UNTAKEN
2Co 3.14 remaineth the same vail *u*

UNTHANKFUL
Lk 6.35 is kind unto the *u* and to the evil.
2Ti 3. 2 disobedient to parents, *u*, unholy,

UNTIL
Gen 26.13 and grew *u* he became very great:
32.24 with him *u* the breaking of the day.
49.10 his feet, *u* Shiloh come;
Ex 12.10 nothing of it remain *u*...morning;
34.34 he took the vail off, *u* he came out.
Nu 14.19 people, from Egypt even *u* now.
Dt 3.20 *U* the Lord have given rest unto
Jos 4.23 *u* ye were passed over, as the Lord
2Ki 7. 3 another, Why sit we here *u* we die?
1Ch 19. 5 at Jericho *u* your beards be grown,
Neh 7. 3 be opened *u* the sun be hot;
8. 3 gate from the morning *u* midday,
Job 14.13 me secret, *u* thy wrath be past,
26.10 *u* the day and night come to an
Ps 57. 1 *u* these calamities be overpast.
73.17 *U* I went into the sanctuary of God;
104.23 and to his labor *u* the evening.
110. 1 *u* I make thine enemies thy
112. 8 *u* he see his desire upon his
132. 5 *U* I find out a place for the Lord,
Pr 7.18 take our fill of love *u* the morning:
SS 2.17 *U* the day break, and the shadows
4. 6 *U* the day break, and the shadows
Isa 32.15 *U* the spirit be poured upon us
62. 1 *u* the righteousness...go forth as
Jer 37.21 *u* all the bread in the city were
Dan 7.22 *U* the Ancient of days came, and
25 *u* a time...times and the dividing
Mic 7. 9 *u* he plead my cause, and execute
Mt 1.17 *u* the carrying away into Babylon
2.13 be thou there *u* I bring thee word:
15 was there *u* the death of Herod:
11.12 days of John the Baptist *u* now
13 and the law prophesied *u* John.
13.30 both grow together *u* the harvest:
17. 9 *u* the Son of man be risen again
18.22 say not unto thee, *U* seven times:
22 times: but, *U* seventy times seven.
24.38 *u* the day that Noe entered into
26.29 *u* that day when I drink it new
27.64 be made sure *u* the third day,
Mk 14.25 *u* that day that I drink it new
15.33 the whole land *u* the ninth hour.
Lk 1.20 *u* the day that these things shall be
13.35 *u* the time...when ye shall say,
15. 4 after that which is lost, *u* he find it?
16.16 and the prophets were *u* John:
17.27 *u* the day that Noe entered into
21.24 *u* the times of the Gentiles be
22.16 *u* it be fulfilled in the kingdom of
18 *u* the kingdom of God shall come.
23.44 over all the earth *u* the ninth hour.
24.49 *u* ye be endued with power from
Jn 2.10 hast kept the good wine *u* now.
9.18 *u* they called the parents of him
Ac 1. 2 *U* the day in which he was taken
2.35 *U* I make thy foes thy footstool.
3.21 *u* the times of restitution of all
13.20 fifty years, *u* Samuel the prophet.
Ro 5.13 (For *u* the law sin was in the world:
8.22 travaileth in pain together *u* now.
11.25 *u* the fulness of the Gentiles
1Co 4. 5 *u* the Lord come, who both will
2Co 3.14 *u* this day remaineth the same vail
Gal 4. 2 *u* the time appointed of the father.
19 again *u* Christ be formed in you,
Eph 1.14 *u*...redemption of the purchased
Php 1. 5 gospel from the first day *u* now;
6 it *u* the day of Jesus Christ:
1Ti 6.14 *u* the appearing of our Lord
Heb 1.13 *u* I make thine enemies thy
9.10 them *u* the time of reformation.
2Pe 1.19 *u* the day dawn, and the day star
1Jn 2. 9 brother, is in darkness even *u* now.
Rev 6.11 *u* their fellowservants also and
17.17 *u* the words of God...be fulfilled.
20. 5 *u*...thousand years were finished.

UNTIMELY
Job 3.16 an hidden *u* birth I had not been;
Ps 58. 8 like the *u* birth of a woman, that
Ec 6. 3 that an *u* birth is better than he.
Rev 6.13 as a fig tree casteth her *u* figs,

UNTOWARD
Ac 2.40 from this *u* generation.

UNWASHEN
Mt 15.20 to eat with *u* hands defileth not a
Mk 7. 2 defiled, that is...with *u*, hands,
5 elders, but eat bread with *u* hands?

UNWISE
Dt 32. 6 O foolish people and *u*?
Hos 13.13 he is an *u* son; for he should
Ro 1.14 both to the wise, and to the *u*.
Eph 5.17 Wherefore be ye not *u*, but

UNWORTHILY
1Co 11.27 and drink this cup of the Lord, *u*,
29 For he that eateth and drinketh *u*,

UNWORTHY
Ac 13.46 *u* of everlasting life,
1Co 6. 2 *u* to judge the smallest matters?

UPBRAID
Jdg 8.15 with whom ye did *u* me, saying,
Mt 11.20 Then began he to *u* the cities

UPBRAIDED
Mk 16.14 and *u* them with their unbelief

UPBRAIDETH
Jas 1. 5 to all men liberally, and *u* not;

UPHARSIN
Dan 5.25 written, Mene, Mene, Tekel, *U*.

UPHOLD
Ps 51.12 and *u* me with thy free spirit.
54. 4 Lord is with them that *u* my soul.
119.116 *U* me according unto thy word,
Pr 29.23 but honor shall *u* the humble in
Isa 41.10 I will *u* thee with the right hand of
42. 1 Behold my servant, whom I *u*;
63. 5 I wondered...there was none to *u*:
Eze 30. 6 They also that *u* Egypt shall fall;

UPHOLDETH
Ps 37.17 but the Lord *u* the righteous.
24 for the Lord *u* him with his hand.
63. 8 after thee: thy right hand *u* me.
145.14 Lord *u* all that fall, and raiseth

UPHOLDING
Heb 1. 3 *u* all things by the word of his

UPPER
Dt 24. 6 the nether or the *u* millstone to
2Ki 18.17 stood by the conduit of the *u* pool,
2Ch 32.30 also stopped the *u* watercourse of
Isa 36. 2 stood by the conduit of the *u* pool
Mk 14.15 shew you a large *u* room furnished
Lk 22.12 shew you a large *u* room furnished:
Ac 1.13 they went up into an *u* room,
9.37 they laid her in an *u* chamber.
39 brought him into the *u* chamber:
19. 1 having passed through the *u* coasts
20. 8 many lights in the *u* chamber,

UPPERMOST
Gen 40.17 *u* basket there was of all manner
Isa 17. 6 berries in the top of the *u* bough,
9 a forsaken bough, and an *u* branch,
Mt 23. 6 love the *u* rooms at feasts, and
Mk 12.39 and the *u* rooms at feasts:
Lk 11.43 love the *u* seats in...synagogues,

UPRIGHT
Gen 37. 7 lo, my sheaf arose, and also stood *u*;
2Sa 22.26 merciful, and with the *u* man
26 thou wilt shew thyself *u*.
Job 1. 1 and that man was perfect and *u*,
12. 4 just *u* man is laughed to scorn.
17. 8 *U* men shall be astonied at this,
Ps 7.10 God, which saveth the *u* in heart.
18.23 I was also *u* before him, and I
19.13 then shall I be *u*, and I shall be
25. 8 Good and *u* is the Lord: therefore
33. 1 for praise is comely for the *u*.
37.18 Lord knoweth the days of the *u*:
64.10 and all the *u* in heart shall glory.
119.137 O Lord, and *u* are thy judgments.
Pr 2.21 For the *u* shall dwell in the land,
10.29 of the Lord is strength to the *u*:
13. 6 keepeth him that is *u* in the way:
14.11 tabernacle of the *u* shall flourish.
15. 8 the prayer of the *u* is his delight.
16.17 The highway of the *u* is to depart
28.10 the *u* shall have good things in
29.27 is *u* in the way is abomination to
Ec 7.29 found, that God had made man *u*:
12.10 that which was written was *u*,
Isa 26. 7 thou, most *u*, dost weigh the path
Dan 10.11 I speak unto thee, and stand *u*:
Mic 7. 2 and there is none *u* among men:
Ac 14.10 a loud voice, Stand *u* on thy feet.

UPRIGHTLY
Ps 15. 2 He that walketh *u*, and worketh
58. 1 do ye judge *u*, O ye sons of men?
75. 2 the congregation I will judge *u*.
84.11 withhold from them that walk *u*.
Pr 2. 7 is a buckler to them that walk *u*.
10. 9 He that walketh *u* walketh surely:
15.21 man of understanding walketh *u*.
28.18 Whoso walketh *u* shall be saved:
Isa 33.15 righteously, and speaketh *u*;
Am 5.10 they abhor him that speaketh *u*.
Mic 2. 7 do good to him that walketh *u*?
Gal 2.14 they walked not *u* according to

UPRIGHTNESS
Dt 9. 5 or for the *u* of thine heart, dost
1Ki 3. 6 and in *u* of heart with thee;
9. 4 in integrity of heart, and in *u*,
1Ch 29.17 the heart, and hast pleasure in *u*.
17 *u* of mine heart I have willingly
Job 4. 6 thy hope, and the *u* of thy ways?
33. 3 shall be of the *u* of my heart:
23 thousand, to shew unto man his *u*:
Ps 9. 8 judgment to the people in *u*.

Ps 25.21 Let integrity and *u* preserve me;
111. 8 ever, and are done in truth and *u*.
119. 7 I will praise thee with *u* of heart,
143.10 good; lead me into the land of *u*.
Pr 2.13 Who leave the paths of *u*, to walk
14. 2 He that walketh in his *u* feareth
28. 6 is the poor that walketh in his *u*,
Isa 26. 7 The way of the just is *u*: thou,
10 land of *u* will he deal unjustly,
57. 2 beds, each one walking in his *u*.

UPRISING
Ps 139. 2 my downsitting and mine *u*,

UPROAR
1Ki 1.41 noise of the city being in an *u*?
Mt 26. 5 there be an *u* among the people.
Mk 14. 2 lest there be an *u* of the people.
Ac 17. 5 and set all the city on an *u*,
19.40 called in question for this day's *u*,
20. 1 And after the *u* was ceased, Paul
21.31 that all Jerusalem was in an *u*.
38 before these days madest an *u*,

UPSIDE
2Ki 21.13 wiping it, and turning it *u*
Ps 146. 9 of the wicked he turneth *u* down.
Isa 24. 1 waste, and turneth it *u* down,
29.16 your turning of things *u* down shall
Ac 17. 6 that have turned the world *u* down

UPWARD
Nu 3.15 every male from a month old and *u*
2Ki 19.30 root downward, and bear fruit *u*.
Job 5. 7 unto trouble, as the sparks fly *u*.
Ec 3.21 the spirit of man that goeth *u*,
Isa 8.21 king and their God, and look *u*.
37.31 root downward, and bear fruit *u*:
38.14 mine eyes fail with looking *u*:

UR
Gen 11.28 his nativity, in *U* of the Chaldees.
31 with them from *U* of the Chaldees,
15. 7 thee out of *U* of the Chaldees.
1Ch 11.35 the Hararite, Eliphal the son of *U*,
Neh 9. 7 him forth out of *U* of the Chaldees

URGE
Lk 11.53 the Pharisees began to *u* him

USE
2Sa 1.18 children of Judah the *u* of the bow:
Jer 31.23 shall *u* this speech in the land of
46.11 in vain shalt thou *u* many medicines;
Eze 12.23 more *u* it as a proverb in Israel;
16.44 shall *u* this proverb against thee,
21.21 of the two ways, to *u* divination:
Mt 5.44 them which despitefully *u* you,
6. 7 when ye pray, *u* not vain repetitions,
Lk 6.28 them which despitefully *u* you,
Ac 14. 5 to *u* them despitefully, and to
Ro 1.26 did change the natural *u* into that
27 leaving...natural *u* of the woman,
1Co 7.21 mayest be made free, *u* it rather.
31 they that *u* this world, as not
2Co 1.17 thus minded, did I *u* lightness?
3.12 we *u* great plainness of speech:
13.10 being present I...*u* sharpness,
Gal 5.13 *u* not liberty for an occasion to the
Eph 4.29 is good to the *u* of edifying,
1Ti 1. 8 is good, if a man *u* it lawfully;
3.10 let them *u* the office of a deacon,
5.23 *u* a little wine for thy stomach's
2Ti 2.21 and meet for the master's *u*,
1Pe 4. 9 *U* hospitality one to another

USED
Lev 7.24 may be *u* in any other use:
Jdg 14.10 beast, for so *u* the young men to do.
20 whom he had *u* as his friend.
2Ki 17.17 *u* divination and enchantments.
2Ch 33. 6 times, and *u* enchantments,
6 and *u* witchcraft, and dealt with a
Jer 2.24 A wild ass *u* to the wilderness,
Eze 22.29 of the land have *u* oppression,
35.11 envy which thou hast *u* out of thy
Hos 12.10 multiplied visions, and *u* similitudes,
Mk 2.18 and of the Pharisees *u* to fast:
Ac 8. 9 in the same city *u* sorcery,
19.19 of them also which *u* curious arts
Ro 3.13 their tongues they have *u* deceit;
1Co 9.12 we have not *u* this power;
15 But I have *u* none of these things:
1Th 2. 5 time *u* we flattering words,
1Ti 3.13 that have *u* the office of a deacon

USES
Tit 3.14 good works for necessary *u*,

USING
Col 2.22 Which all are to perish with the *u*;)
1Pe 2.16 not *u* your liberty for a cloke of

USURER
Ex 22.25 thou shalt not be to him as an *u*,

USURP
1Ti 2.12 nor to *u* authority over the man,

USURY
Ex 22.25 shalt thou lay upon him *u*.
Lev 25.36 Take thou no *u* of him, or increase:
37 not give him thy money upon *u*,
Dt 23.19 not lend upon *u* to thy brother;
20 a stranger thou mayest lend upon *u*;
20 thou shalt not lend upon *u*:
Neh 5. 7 Ye exact *u*, every one of his
10 I pray you, let us leave off this *u*.
Ps 15. 5 putteth not out his money to *u*,
Pr 28. 8 He that by *u* and unjust gain
Isa 24. 2 as with the taker of *u*, so with
2 so with the giver of *u* to him.
Jer 15.10 I have neither lent on *u*, nor men
10 nor men have lent to me on *u*;
Eze 18. 8 thou hath not given forth upon *u*,
13 Hath given forth upon *u*, and hath
Mt 25.27 have received mine own with *u*.
Lk 19.23 have required mine own with *u*?

UTMOST
Gen 49.26 the *u* bound of the everlasting hills:
Nu 22.36 Arnon, which is in the *u* coast.
41 might see the *u* part of the people.
Dt 34. 2 the land of Judah, unto the *u* sea,
Jer 9.26 and all that are in the *u* corners,
Joel 2.20 his hinder part toward the *u* sea,
Lk 11.31 from the *u* parts of the earth to

UTTER
Jdg 5.12 Deborah: awake, awake, *u* a song:
1Ki 20.42 I appointed to *u* destruction,
Job 8.10 and *u* words out of their heart?
15. 2 a wise man *u* vain knowledge,
27. 4 nor my tongue *u* deceit.
33. 3 lips shall *u* knowledge clearly.
Ps 78. 2 I will *u* dark sayings of old:
106. 2 Who can *u* the mighty acts of the
119.171 My lips shall *u* praise, when
Pr 14. 5 but a false witness will *u* lies.
23.33 heart shall *u* perverse things.
Ec 5. 2 hasty to *u* any thing before God:
Isa 32. 6 and to *u* error against the Lord,
Jer 25.30 *u* his voice from his holy
Eze 24. 3 *u* a parable unto the rebellious
Joel 3.16 and *u* his voice from Jerusalem;
Mt 13.35 *u* things which have been kept
1Co 14. 9 except ye *u* by the tongue words
2Co 12. 4 it is not lawful for a man to *u*.

UTTERANCE
Ac 2. 4 tongues, as the Spirit gave them *u*.
1Co 1. 5 ye are enriched by him, in all *u*,
2Co 8. 7 in faith, and *u*, and knowledge,
Eph 6.19 that *u* may be given unto me, that
Col 4. 3 would open unto us a door of *u*,

UTTERED
Nu 30. 6 vowed, or *u* ought out of her lips,
Jdg 11.11 Jephthah *u* all his words before
2Sa 22.14 and the most High *u* his voice.
Neh 6.19 me, and *u* my words to him.
Job 26. 4 To whom hast thou *u* words? and
42. 3 have I *u* that I understood not;
Ps 46. 6 he *u* his voice, the earth melted.
66.14 Which my lips have *u*, and my
Jer 48.34 Jahaz, have they *u* their voice,
51.55 waters, a noise of their voice is *u*:
Hab 3.10 the deep *u* his voice, and lifted up
Ro 8.26 with groanings which cannot be *u*.
Heb 5.11 things to say, and hard to be *u*,
Rev 10. 3 seven thunders *u* their voices.

UTTERETH
Job 15. 5 For thy mouth *u* thine iniquity,
Ps 19. 2 Day unto day *u* speech, and night
Pr 1.20 she *u* her voice in the streets:
21 the city she *u* her words, saying,
10.18 and he that *u* a slander, is a fool.
29.11 A fool *u* all his mind: but a wise
Jer 10.13 When he *u* his voice, there is a
Mic 7. 3 he *u* his mischievous desire:

UTTERLY
Ex 22.17 father *u* refuse to give her unto him,
Nu 15.31 that soul shall be *u* cut off;
Jos 10. 1 taken Ai, and had *u* destroyed it;
Jdg 21.11 Ye shall *u* destroy every male,
1Sa 15. 3 and *u* destroy all that they have,
Ps 119. 8 thy statutes: O forsake me not *u*.
Isa 6.11 man, and the land be *u* desolate,
24.19 The earth is *u* broken down, the
40.30 and the young men shall *u* fall:
Jer 14.19 Hast thou *u* rejected Judah? hath
23.39 behold, I, even I, will *u* forget you,
La 5.22 But thou hast *u* rejected us; thou
Am 9. 8 I will not *u* destroy the house of
1Co 6. 7 there is *u* a fault among you,
2Pe 2.12 and shall *u* perish in their own
Rev 18. 8 she shall be *u* burned with fire:

UTTERMOST
Dt 11.24 unto the *u* sea shall your coast be.
Jos 15. 5 of the sea at the *u* part of Jordan:
Neh 1. 9 out unto the *u* part of the heaven,
Ps 2. 8 and the *u* parts of the earth for thy
139. 9 dwell in the *u* parts of the sea;
Mt 5.26 till thou hast paid the *u* farthing.
12.42 from the *u* parts of the earth
Mk 13.27 from the *u* part of the earth
27 to the *u* part of heaven.
Ac 1. 8 unto the *u* part of the earth.
24.22 I will know the *u* of your matter.
1Th 2.16 wrath is come upon them to the *u*.
Heb 7.25 able also to save them to the *u*

VAGABOND

Gen 4.12 a *v* shalt thou be in the earth.
14 a fugitive and a *v* in the earth;
Ac 19.13 Then certain of the *v* Jews,

VAGABONDS

Ps 109.10 Let his children be continually *v*,

VAIL

Gen 24.65 therefore she took a *v*, and
Ex 27.21 of the congregation without the *v*,
30. 6 the *v* that is by the ark of the
34.34 took the *v* off, until he came out.
35 Moses put the *v* upon his face
Lev 16. 2 holy place within the *v* before the
Isa 25. 7 *v* that is spread over all nations.
2Co 3.13 which put a *v* over his face, that
14 the same *v* untaken away in the
14 which *v* is done away in Christ.
15 read, the *v* is upon their heart.
16 Lord, the *v* shall be taken away.

VAIN

Ex 5. 9 let them not regard *v* words.
20. 7 name of the Lord thy God in *v*;
7 guiltless that taketh his name in *v*.
Job 9.29 wicked, why then labor I in *v*?
15. 2 a wise man utter *v* knowledge, and
27.12 then are ye thus altogether *v*?
Ps 2. 1 and the people imagine a *v* thing?
33.17 An horse is a *v* thing for safety:
60.11 trouble: for *v* is the help of man.
73.13 I have cleansed my heart in *v*,
89.47 hast thou made all men in *v*?
108.12 trouble: for *v* is the help of man.
127. 1 they labor in *v* that build it:
1 the watchman waketh but in *v*.
2 It is *v* for you to rise up early, to
Pr 1.17 Surely in *v* the net is spread in
30. 9 and take the name of my God in *v*.
Isa 1.13 Bring no more *v* oblations;
45.19 Seek ye me in *v*: I the Lord speak
Mal 3.14 have said, It is *v* to serve God:
Mt 6. 7 when ye pray, use not *v* repetitions,
15. 9 But in *v* they do worship me,
Mk 7. 7 Howbeit in *v* they do worship me,
Ac 4.25 and the people imagine *v* things?
Ro 1.21 became *v* in their imaginations,
1Co 15.14 risen, then is our preaching *v*,
14 and your faith is also *v*.
58 your labor is not in *v* in the Lord.
Gal 2. 2 I should run, or had run, in *v*.
21 the law, then Christ is dead in *v*.
5.26 Let us not be desirous of *v* glory,
Php 2.16 not run in *v*, neither labored in *v*.
Col 2. 8 through philosophy and *v* deceit.
1Ti 6.20 avoiding profane and *v* babblings,
Jas 1.26 own heart, this man's religion is *v*.
4. 5 think that the scripture saith in *v*,

VAINGLORY

Php 2. 3 be done through strife or *v*;

VAINLY

Col 2.18 *v* puffed up by his fleshly mind,

VALE

Gen 14. 3 together in the *v* of Siddim,
8 with them in the *v* of Siddim;
10 *v* of Siddim was full of slimepits;
37.14 sent him out of the *v* of Hebron,
Dt 1. 7 in the hills, and in the *v*, and in
Jos 10.40 of the south, and of the *v*, and of
1Ki 10.27 sycomore trees that are in the *v*,
2Ch 1.15 sycomore trees that are in the *v*
Jer 33.13 in the cities of the *v*, and in the

VALIANT

1Ki 1.42 Come in; for thou art a *v* man,
Isa 10.13 the inhabitants like a *v* man:
Jer 46.15 Why are thy *v* men swept away?
Heb 11.34 waxed *v* in fight, turned to flight

VALIANTLY

Ps 60.12 Through God we shall do *v*: for
108.13 Through God we shall do *v*: for he
118.15, 16 right hand of the Lord doeth *v*.

VALLEY

Gen 26.19 Isaac's servants digged in the *v*,
Jos 7.26 place was called, The *v* of Achor,
10.12 and thou, Moon, in the *v* of Ajalon.
Jdg 16. 4 loved a woman in the *v* of Sorek,
1Ch 11.15 encamped in the *v* of Rephaim.
Ps 23. 4 through the *v* of the shadow of
84. 6 Who passing through the *v* of Baca
Isa 22. 1 The burden of the *v* of vision.
40. 4 Every *v* shall be exalted, and
Jer 21.13 O inhabitant of the *v*, and rock of
Hos 2.15 the *v* of Achor for a door of hope:
Lk 3. 5 Every *v* shall be filled, and every

VALLEYS

Dt 11.11 possess it, is a land of hills and *v*,
1Ki 20.28 hills, but he is not God of the *v*,
Ps 65.13 *v* also are covered over with corn;

VALUE

Lev 27. 8 priest, and the priest shall *v* him;
8 that vowed shall the priest *v* him.
12 And the priest shall *v* it, whether
Job 13. 4 lies, ye are all physicians of no *v*.
Mt 10.31 of more *v* than many sparrows.
27. 9 of the children of Israel did *v*;
Lk 12. 7 of more *v* than many sparrows.

VALUED

Lev 27.16 barley seed shall be *v* at fifty shekels
Job 28.16 be *v* with the gold of Ophir,
19 neither shall it be *v* with pure gold.
Mt 27. 9 the price of him that was *v*,

VANISH

Job 6.17 time they wax warm, they *v*:
Isa 51. 6 heavens shall *v* away like smoke,
1Co 13. 8 be knowledge, it shall *v* away.
Heb 8.13 waxeth old is ready to *v* away.

VANISHED

Jer 49. 7 the prudent? is their wisdom *v*?
Lk 24.31 and he *v* out of their sight.

VANISHETH

Job 7. 9 As the cloud is consumed and *v*
Jas 4.14 for a little time, and then *v* away.

VANITIES

Dt 32.21 me to anger with their *v*:
1Ki 16.13, 26 of Israel to anger with their *v*.
Ps 31. 6 hated them that regard lying *v*:
Ec 1. 2 Vanity of *v*, saith the Preacher,
2 Preacher, vanity of *v*: all is vanity.
5. 7 words there are also divers *v*:
12. 8 Vanity of *v*, saith the preacher; all
Jer 8.19 images, and with strange *v*?
10. 8 the stock is a doctrine of *v*.
14.22 any among the *v* of the Gentiles
Jon 2. 8 that observe lying *v* forsake their
Ac 14.15 from these *v* unto the living God,

VANITY

Job 7.16 let me alone; for my days are *v*.
31. 5 If I have walked with *v*, or if my
Ps 4. 2 how long will ye love *v*, and seek
24. 4 hath not lifted up his soul unto *v*,
39.11 a moth: surely every man is *v*.
62. 9 Surely men of low degree are *v*,
94.11 thoughts of man, that they are *v*.
119.37 mine eyes from beholding *v*;
Pr 21. 6 treasures by a lying tongue is a *v*
22. 8 that soweth iniquity shall reap *v*:
Ec 1. 2 *V* of vanities, saith the Preacher,
2 saith the Preacher, *v* of vanities;
2 saith the Preacher,...all is *v*.
14 all is *v* and vexation of spirit.
2.11 all was *v* and vexation of spirit,
21 This also is *v* and a great evil.
12. 8 *V* of vanities, saith the preacher;
Isa 40.23 the judges of the earth as *v*.
44. 9 a graven image are all of them *v*,
Jer 51.18 They are *v*, the work of errors:
Hab 2.13 weary themselves for very *v*?
Zec 10. 2 For the idols have spoken *v*, and
Ro 8.20 creature was made subject to *v*,
Eph 4.17 walk, in the *v* of their mind,
2Pe 2.18 speak great swelling words of *v*.

VAPOR

Job 36.27 rain according to the *v* thereof:
33 the cattle also concerning the *v*.
Ac 2.19 blood, and fire, and *v* of smoke:
Jas 4.14 a *v*, that appeareth for a little time,

VARIABLENESS

Jas 1.17 with whom is no *v*, neither

VARIANCE

Mt 10.35 a man at *v* against his father,
Gal 5.20 *v*, emulations, wrath, strife,

VAUNTETH

1Co 13. 4 charity *v* not itself, is not puffed

VEHEMENT

SS 8. 6 of fire, which hath a most *v* flame.
Jon 4. 8 that God prepared a *v* east wind;
2Co 7.11 yea, what fear, yea, what *v* desire,

VEHEMENTLY

Mk 14.31 But he spake the more *v*, If I
Lk 6.48 stream beat *v* upon that house,
49 which the stream did beat *v*,
11.53 Pharisees began to urge him *v*,
23.10 scribes stood and *v* accused him.

VEIL

SS 5. 7 the keepers...took away my *v*
Mt 27.51 *v* of the temple was rent in twain
Mk 15.38 *v* of the temple was rent in twain
Lk 23.45 *v* of the temple was rent in twain
Heb 6.19 entereth into that within the *v*;
9. 3 after the second *v*, the tabernacle
10.20 consecrated for us, through the *v*,

VENGEANCE

Dt 32.35 To me belongeth *v*, and
Ps 94. 1 Lord God, to whom *v* belongeth;
149. 7 To execute *v* upon the heathen,
Isa 35. 4 your God will come with *v*, even
61. 2 Lord, and the day of *v* of our God;
Jer 50.28 declare in Zion the *v* of the Lord
28 Lord our God, the *v* of his temple.
Eze 25.15 taken *v* with a despiteful heart,
Na 1. 2 will take *v* on his adversaries,
Lk 21.22 For these be the days of *v*, that
Ac 28. 4 the sea, yet *v* suffereth not to live.
Ro 3. 5 Is God unrighteous who taketh *v*?
12.19 *V* is mine; I will repay, saith the
2Th 1. 8 In flaming fire taking *v* on them

Heb 10.30 *V* belongeth unto me, I will
Jude 7 suffering the *v* of eternal fire.

VENOMOUS
Ac 28. 4 saw the *v* beast hang on his hand,

VENTURE
1Ki 23.34 a certain man drew a bow at a *v*,
2Ch 18.33 a certain man drew a bow at a *v*,

VERILY
Gen 42.21 We are *v* guilty concerning our
Ps 37. 3 the land, and *v* thou shalt be fed.
58.11 *V* there is a reward for the
11 *v* he is a God that judgeth in the
Isa 45.15 *V* thou art a God that hidest
Mt 18. 3 *V* I say unto you, Except ye be
Mk 9.12 Elias *v* cometh first, and restoreth
Lk 4.24 *V* I say unto you, No prophet is
Ac 19. 4 John *v* baptized with the baptism
Heb 12.10 For they *v* for a few days chastened
1Pe 1.20 Who *v* was foreordained before the
1Jn 2. 5 him *v* is the love of God perfected:

VERITY
Ps 111. 7 The works of his hands are *v* and
1Ti 2. 7 of the Gentiles in faith and *v*.

VERMILION
Jer 22.14 with cedar, and painted with *v*.
Eze 23.14 of the Chaldeans pourtrayed with *v*,

VESSEL
Nu 5.17 take holy water in an earthen *v*;
1Ki 17.10 I pray thee, a little water in a *v*,
Ps 2. 9 them in pieces like a potter's *v*.
31.12 out of mind: I am like a broken *v*.
Isa 30.14 it as the breaking of the potters' *v*
66.20 bring an offering in a clean *v* into
Jer 18. 4 And the *v* that he made of clay was
18 so he made it again another *v*, as
19.11 as one breaketh a potter's *v*, that
51.34 he hath made me an empty *v*, he
Mk 11.16 carry any *v* through the temple.
Lk 8.16 a candle, covereth it with a *v*,
Jn 19.29 there was set a *v* full of vinegar:
Ac 9.15 he is a chosen *v* unto me, to bear
10.11 a certain *v* descending unto him,
16 the *v* was received up again into
11. 5 saw a vision, A certain *v* descend,
Ro 9.21 lump to make one *v* unto honor,
1Th 4. 4 to possess his *v* in sanctification
2Ti 2.21 he shall be a *v* unto honor,
1Pe 3. 7 unto the wife, as unto the weaker *v*,

VESSELS
Ex 39.40 and all the *v* of the service of the
1Ch 22.19 the holy *v* of God, into the house
2Ch 24.14 made *v* for the house of the Lord,
36.19 destroyed all the goodly *v* thereof.
Neh 10.39 where are the *v* of the sanctuary,
Dan 1. 2 part of the *v* of the house of God:
Mt 13.48 gathered the good into *v*, but cast
25. 4 wise took oil in their *v* with their
Mk 7. 4 cups, and pots, and brazen *v*, and
Ro 9.22 *v* of wrath fitted to destruction:
23 of his glory on the *v* of mercy,
2Co 4. 7 have this treasure in earthen *v*,
2Ti 2.20 are not only *v* of gold and of silver,
Heb 9.21 and all the *v* of the ministry.
Rev 2.27 as the *v* of a potter shall they be
18.12 wood, and all manner *v* of ivory,
12 manner *v* of most precious wood,

VESTMENTS
2Ki 10.22 forth *v* for all the worshippers
22 And he brought them forth *v*.

VESTRY
2Ki 10.22 unto him that was over the *v*,

VESTURE
Dt 22.12 upon the four quarters of thy *v*,
Ps 22.18 them, and cast lots upon my *v*.
102.26 as a *v* shalt thou change them,
Mt 27.35 and upon my *v* did they cast lots.
Jn 19.24 and for my *v* they did cast lots.
Heb 1.12 as a *v* shalt thou fold them up,
Rev 19.13 clothed with a *v* dipped in blood:
16 on his *v* and on his thigh a name

VEX
Ex 22.21 Thou shalt neither *v* a stranger,
Lev 18.18 take a wife to her sister, to *v* her,
19.33 in your land, ye shall not *v* him.
Nu 25.17 *V* the Midianites, and smite
18 For they *v* you with their wiles,
33.55 shall *v* you in the land wherein
2Sa 12.18 how will he then *v* himself,
2Ch 15. 6 God did *v* them with all adversity.
Job 19. 2 How long will ye *v* my soul, and
Ps 2. 5 and *v* them in his sore displeasure.
Isa 7. 6 us go up against Judah, and *v* it,
11.13 and Judah shall not *v* Ephraim.
Eze 32. 9 I will also *v* the hearts of many
Hab 2. 7 and awake that shall *v* thee,
Ac 12. 1 hands to *v* certain of the church.

VEXATION
Dt 28.20 shall send upon thee cursing, *v*,
Ec 1.14 all is vanity and *v* of spirit.
17 that this also is *v* of spirit.
2.11 all was vanity and *v* of spirit,
17 for all is vanity and *v* of spirit.
22 labor, and of the *v* of his heart,
26 also is vanity and *v* of spirit.
4. 4 This is also vanity and *v* of spirit.
6 full with travail and *v* of spirit.
16 this also is vanity and *v* of spirit.
6. 9 this is also vanity and *v* of spirit.
Isa 9. 1 shall not be such as was in her *v*,
28.19 shall be a *v* only to understand
65.14 and shall howl for *v* of spirit.

VEXED
Nu 20.15 Egyptians *v* us, and our fathers:
Jdg 2.18 that oppressed them and *v* them.
10. 8 they *v* and oppressed the children
16.16 so that his soul was *v* unto death;
1Sa 14.47 he turned himself, he *v* them.
2Sa 13. 2 Amnon was so *v*, that he fell sick
2Ki 4.27 for her soul is *v* within her:
Neh 9.27 of their enemies, who *v* them:
Job 27. 2 Almighty, who hath *v* my soul;
Ps 6. 2 heal me; for my bones are *v*.
3 My soul is also sore *v*: but thou
10 enemies be ashamed and sore *v*:
Isa 63.10 rebelled, and *v* his holy Spirit:
Eze 22. 5 which art infamous and much *v*.
7 in thee have they *v* the fatherless
29 and have *v* the poor and needy:
Mt 15.22 is grievously *v* with a devil.
17.15 for he is lunatick, and sore *v*:
Lk 6.18 that were *v* with unclean spirits:
Ac 5.16 which were *v* with unclean spirits:
2Pe 2. 7 *v* with the filthy conversation of
8 *v* his righteous soul from day to

VIALS
Rev 5. 8 and golden *v* full of odors, which
15. 7 seven golden *v* full of the wrath of
16. 1 pour out the *v* of the wrath of God
17. 1 angels which had the seven *v*,
21. 9 the seven *v* full of the seven last

VICTORY
2Sa 19. 2 the *v* that day was turned into
23.10 the Lord wrought a great *v* that
12 and the Lord wrought a great *v*.
1Ch 29.11 and the glory, and the *v*, and the
Ps 98. 1 holy arm, hath gotten him the *v*,
Isa 25. 8 He will swallow up death in *v*;
Mt 12.20 he send forth judgment unto *v*.
1Co 15.54 Death is swallowed up in *v*.
55 thy sting? O grave, where is thy *v*?
57 *v* through our Lord Jesus Christ.
1Jn 5. 4 the *v* that overcometh the world,
Rev 15. 2 had gotten the *v* over the beast,

VICTUAL
Ex 12.39 prepared for themselves any *v*.
Jdg 20.10 to fetch *v* for the people, that they
1Ki 4.27 those officers provided *v* for king
2Ch 11.11 captains in them, and store of *v*,
23 he gave them *v* in abundance.

VICTUALS
Gen 14.11 and Gomorrah, and all their *v*,
Lev 25.37 nor lend him thy *v* for increase.
Dt 23.19 usury of money, usury of *v*, usury
Jos 1.11 people, saying, Prepare you *v*;
9.11 Take *v* with you for the journey,
14 And the men took up their *v*, and
Jdg 7. 8 the people took *v* in their hand,
17.10 and a suit of apparel, and thy *v*.
1Sa 22.10 and gave him *v*, and gave him
1Ki 4. 7 provided *v* for the king and his
11.18 appointed him *v*, and gave him
Neh 10.31 ware or any *v* on the sabbath day
13.15 in the day wherein they sold *v*.
Jer 40. 5 captain of the guard gave him *v*
44.17 for then had we plenty of *v*, and
Mt 14.15 villages, and buy themselves *v*.
Lk 9.12 about, and lodge, and get *v*:

VIEW
Jos 2. 1 Go *v* the land, even Jericho.
7. 2 saying, Go up and *v* the country.
2Ki 2. 7 went, and stood to *v* afar off:
15 prophets...were to *v* at Jericho

VIGILANT
1Ti 3. 2 husband of one wife, *v*, sober, of
1Pe 5. 8 Be sober, be *v*; because your

VILE
Dt 25. 3 thy brother should seem *v* unto
Jdg 19.24 this man do not so *v* a thing.
1Sa 3.13 his sons made themselves *v*, and
15. 9 but every thing that was *v* and
2Sa 6.22 I will yet be more *v* than thus,
Job 18. 3 and reputed *v* in your sight?
40. 4 I am *v*; what shall I answer thee?
Ps 15. 4 eyes a *v* person is contemned;
Isa 32. 5 The *v* person shall be no more
6 the *v* person will speak villany,
Jer 15.19 forth the precious from the *v*,
29.17 will make them like *v* figs, that
La 1.11 and consider; for I am become *v*.
Dan 11.21 estate shall stand up a *v* person,
Na 1.14 make thy grave; for thou art *v*.
3. 6 filth upon thee, and make thee *v*,
Ro 1.26 gave them up unto *v* affections:
Php 3.21 Who shall change our *v* body,
Jas 2. 2 in also a poor man in *v* raiment:

VILLAGE
Mt 21. 2 Go into the *v* over against you,
Mk 11. 2 Go your way into the *v* over against
Lk 8. 1 went throughout every city and *v*,
9.52 entered into a *v* of the Samaritans,
56 them. And they went to another *v*.
10.38 that he entered into a certain *v*:
17.12 And as he entered into a certain *v*,
19.30 Go ye into the *v* over against you;
24.13 same day to a *v* called Emmaus,
28 And they drew nigh unto the *v*,

VILLAGES
Lev 25.31 houses of the *v* which have no wall
Est 9.19 Therefore the Jews of the *v*, that
Ps 10. 8 in the lurking places of the *v*:
Isa 42.11 the *v* that Kedar doth inhabit:

Biblical Themes

VIGILANCE

The Lord called Samuel: and he answered, Here am I. 1Sa 3.4

They which builded on the wall, and they that bare burdens . . . every one with one of his hands wrought in the work, and with the other hand held a weapon. . . . And he that sounded the trumpet was by me. Neh 4.17-18

Awake, why sleepest thou, O Lord? arise, cast us not off for ever. Wherefore hidest thou thy face, and forgettest our affliction and our oppression? Ps 44.23-24

He that keepeth thee will not slumber. Behold, he that keepeth Israel shall neither slumber nor sleep. Ps 121.3-4

Except the Lord keep the city, the watchman waketh but in vain. Ps 127.1

My soul waiteth for the Lord more than they that watch for the morning. Ps 130.6

How long wilt thou sleep, O sluggard? when wilt thou arise out of thy sleep? Yet a little sleep, a little slumber, a little folding of the hands to sleep: so shall thy poverty come as one that travelleth, and thy want as an armed man. Pr 6.9-11

I stand continually upon the watchtower. Isa 21.8

Watchman, what of the night? Watchman, what of the night? The watchman said, The morning cometh, and also the night: if ye will inquire, inquire ye: return, come. Isa 21.11-12

Whosoever heareth the sound of the trumpet, and taketh not warning; if the sword come, and take him away, his blood shall be upon his own head. Eze 33.4

I will stand upon my watch, and set me upon the tower, and will watch to see what he will say unto me. Hab 2.1

And he cometh unto the disciples, and findeth them asleep, and saith unto Peter, What, could ye not watch with me one hour? Watch and pray, that ye enter not into temptation: the spirit indeed is willing, but the flesh is weak. Mt 26.40-41

Watch ye therefore: for ye know not when the master of the house cometh, at even, or at midnight, or at the cockcrowing, or in the morning. Mk 13.35

Blessed are those servants, whom the lord when he cometh shall find watching. Lk 12.37

If the goodman of the house had known what hour the thief would come, he would have watched, and not have suffered his house to be broken through. Be ye therefore ready also: for the Son of man cometh at an hour when ye think not. Lk 12.39-40

Now it is high time to awake out of sleep: for now is our salvation nearer than when we believed. Ro 13.11

Let us not sleep, as do others; but let us watch and be sober. 1Th 5.6

We desire that every one of you do shew the same diligence to the full assurance of hope unto the end: that ye be not slothful, but followers of them who through faith and patience inherit the promises. Heb 6.11-12

Be sober, be vigilant; because your adversary the devil, as a roaring lion, walketh about, seeking whom he may devour. 1Pe 5.8

I stand at the door, and knock: if any man hear my voice, and open the door, I will come in to him. Rev 3.20

Behold, I come as a thief. Blessed is he that watcheth, and keepeth his garments, lest he walk naked, and they see his shame. Rev 16.15

Mt 9.35 went about all the cities and *v*,
14.15 that they may go into the *v*, and
Mk 6. 6 And he went round about the *v*,
36 and into the *v*, and buy themselves
56 he entered, into the *v*, or cities, or
Lk 13.22 he went through the cities and *v*,
Ac 8.25 preached the gospel in many *v*

VINE

Gen 40. 9 dream, behold, a *v* was before me;
10 And in the *v* were three branches:
1Ki 4.25 every man under his *v* and under
Ps 80. 8 hast brought a *v* out of Egypt:
128. 3 Thy wife shall be as a fruitful *v* by
Isa 34. 4 as the leaf falleth off from the *v*,
36.16 and eat ye every one of his *v*, and
Jer 2.21 degenerate plant of a strange *v*
8.13 there shall be no grapes on the *v*,
Joel 1. 7 He hath laid my *v* waste, and
Mic 4. 4 sit every man under his *v* and
Mal 3.11 neither shall your *v* cast her fruit
Mt 26.29 henceforth of this fruit of the *v*,
Mk 14.25 drink no more of the fruit of the *v*,
Lk 22.18 I will not drink of the fruit of the *v*,
Jn 15. 1 I am the true *v*, and my Father is
4 of itself, except it abide in the *v*;
5 I am the *v*, ye are the branches: He
Jas 3.12 bear olive berries? either a *v*, figs?

Rev 14.18 gather the clusters of the *v* of
19 and gathered the *v* of the earth,

VINEDRESSERS

2Ki 25.12 the land to be *v* and husbandmen.
Isa 61. 5 shall be your plowmen and your *v*.
Jer 52.16 the land for *v* and for husbandmen.
Joel 1.11 howl, O ye *v*, for the wheat and for

VINEGAR

Nu 6. 3 no *v* of wine, or *v* of strong drink,
Ru 2.14 bread, and dip thy morsel in the *v*.
Ps 69.21 my thirst they gave me *v* to drink.
Pr 10.26 As *v* to the teeth, and as smoke to
25.20 and as *v* upon nitre, so is he that
Mt 27.34 *v* to drink mingled with gall:
48 took a spunge, and filled it with *v*,
Mk 15.36 ran and filled a spunge full of *v*,
Lk 23.36 coming to him, and offering him *v*,
Jn 19.29 there was set a vessel full of *v*:
29 and they filled a spunge with *v*,
30 When Jesus...had received the *v*,

VINEYARD

Gen 9.20 husbandman, and he planted a *v*:
Lev 19.10 And thou shalt not glean thy *v*,
Dt 23.24 thou comest into thy neighbor's *v*,
1Ki 21. 1 that Naboth the Jezreelite had a *v*,
2 Give me thy *v*, that I may have it
6 I will not give thee my *v*.
Ps 80.15 the *v* which thy right hand hath
Pr 31.16 fruit of her hands she planteth a *v*.
SS 1. 6 but mine own *v* have I not kept.
Isa 5. 1 song of my beloved touching his *v*.
3 I pray you, betwixt me and my *v*.
4 have been done more to my *v*,
Mt 20. 1 to hire laborers into his *v*.
2 a day, he sent them into his *v*.
4 unto them; Go ye also into the *v*,
7 unto them, Go ye also into the *v*;
8 the lord of the *v* saith unto his
21.28 said, Son, go work to day in my *v*.
33 householder, which planted a *v*,
39 cast him out of the *v*, and slew him.
40 the lord therefore of the *v* cometh,
41 and will let out his *v* unto other
Mk 12. 1 A certain man planted a *v*, and set
2 husbandmen of the fruit of the *v*.
8 him, and cast him out of the *v*.
9 shall therefore the lord of the *v* do?
9 and will give the *v* unto others.
Lk 13. 6 man had a fig tree planted in his *v*;
7 said he unto the dresser of his *v*,
20. 9 A certain man planted a *v*, and let
10 give him of the fruit of the *v*:
13 Then said the lord of the *v*, What
15 So they cast him out of the *v*, and
15 shall the lord of the *v* do unto
16 and shall give the *v* to others.
1Co 9. 7 who planteth a *v*, and eateth not of

VINEYARDS

Nu 22.24 the Lord stood in a path of the *v*,
Dt 6.11 *v* and olive trees, which thou
Neh 5. 3 We have mortgaged our lands, *v*,
Job 24.18 he beholdeth not the way of the *v*.
Isa 16.10 in the *v* there shall be no singing,
Am 5.11 ye have planted pleasant *v*, but ye
9.14 and they shall plant *v*, and drink
Zep 1.13 they shall plant *v*, but not drink

VINTAGE

Lev 26. 5 threshing shall reach unto the *v*,
5 the *v* shall reach unto the sowing
Jdg 8. 2 better than the *v* of Abi-ezer?
Job 24. 6 they gather the *v* of the wicked.
Isa 16.10 made their *v* shouting to cease.
24.13 grapes when the *v* is done.
32.10 for the *v* shall fail, the gathering
Jer 48.32 summer fruits and upon thy *v*.
Mic 7. 1 as the grapegleanings of the *v*:
Zec 11. 2 the forest of the *v* is come down.

VIOL
Isa 5.12 And the harp, and the *v*, the
Am 6. 5 That chant to the sound of the *v*,

VIOLENCE
Gen 6.11 and the earth was filled with *v*.
Ps 11. 5 him that loveth *v* his soul hateth.
73. 6 *v* covereth them as a garment.
Isa 53. 9 because he had done no *v*,
60.18 *V* shall no more be heard in thy
Am 6. 3 cause the seat of *v* to come near;
Mic 2. 2 covet fields, and take them by *v*;
Hab 2.17 the *v* of Lebanon shall cover thee,
Zep 3. 4 they have done *v* to the law.
Mt 11.12 kingdom of heaven suffereth *v*,
Lk 3.14 Do *v* to no man, neither accuse
Ac 5.26 and brought them without *v*:
21.35 the soldiers for the *v* of the people.
24. 7 with great *v* took him away out of
27.41 broken with the *v* of the waves.
Heb 11.34 Quenched the *v* of fire, escaped
Rev 18.21 *v* shall that great city Babylon be

VIOLENT
2Sa 22.49 delivered me from the *v* man.
Ps 7.16 *v* dealing shall come down upon
18.48 hast delivered me from the *v* man.
86.14 the assemblies of *v* men have
140. 1, 4 preserve me from the *v* man;
11 evil shall hunt the *v* man to
Pr 16.29 A *v* man enticeth his neighbor, and
Ec 5. 8 *v* perverting of judgment and
Mt 11.12 and the *v* take it by force.

VIOLENTLY
Gen 21.25 servants had *v* taken away.
Lev 6. 4 restore that which he took *v*
Dt 28.31 thine ass shall be *v* taken away
Job 20.19 he hath *v* taken away an house
24. 2 they *v* take away flocks, and feed
Isa 22.18 *v* turn and toss thee like a ball
La 2. 6 *v* taken away his tabernacle,
Mt 8.32 of swine ran *v* down a steep place
Mk 5.13 the herd ran *v* down a steep place
Lk 8.33 the herd ran *v* down a steep place

VIOLS
Isa 14.11 the grave, and the noise of thy *v*:
Am 5.23 will not hear the melody of thy *v*.

VIPER
Isa 30. 6 the *v* and fiery flying serpent,
59. 5 is crushed breaketh out into a *v*.
Ac 28. 3 there came a *v* out of the heat,

VIPERS
Mt 3. 7 O generation of *v*, who hath
12.34 O generation of *v*, how can ye,
23.33 ye generation of *v*, how can ye
Lk 3. 7 O generation of *v*, who hath

VIRGIN
Gen 24.16 was very fair to look upon, a *v*,
Lev 21.14 he shall take a *v* of his own people
2Ki 19.21 The *v* the daughter of Zion hath
Isa 7.14 Behold, a *v* shall conceive, and
37.22 The *v*, the daughter of Zion, hath
47. 1 O *v* daughter of Babylon, sit on
62. 5 For as a young man marrieth a *v*,
Jer 18.13 the *v* of Israel hath done a very
Am 5. 2 The *v* of Israel is fallen; she shall
Mt 1.23 Behold, a *v* shall be with child,
Lk 1.27 To a *v* espoused to a man whose
1Co 7.28 if a *v* marry, she hath not sinned.
34 also between a wife and a *v*.
36 himself uncomely toward his *v*,
37 his heart that he will keep his *v*,
2Co 11. 2 you as a chaste *v* to Christ.

VIRGINITY
Lev 21.13 he shall take a wife in her *v*.
Jdg 11.37 bewail my *v*, I and my fellows.
Lk 2.36 husband seven years from her *v*;

VIRGIN'S
Lk 1.27 and the *v* name was Mary.

VIRGINS
Ex 22.17 according to the dowry of *v*.
La 2.10 the *v* of Jerusalem hang down
Am 8.13 the fair *v* and young men faint for
Mt 25. 1 of heaven be likened unto ten *v*,
7 all those *v* arose, and trimmed
11 Afterward came also the other *v*,
Ac 21. 9 same man had four daughters, *v*,
1Co 7.25 Now concerning *v* I have no
Rev 14. 4 with women; for they are *v*.

VIRTUE
Mk 5.30 that *v* had gone out of him,
Lk 6.19 for there went *v* out of him, and
8.46 perceive that *v* has gone out of me.
Php 4. 8 there be any *v*, and if there be any
2Pe 1. 3 that hath called us to glory and *v*:
5 diligence, add to your faith *v*;
5 and to *v* knowledge:

VIRTUOUS
Ru 3.11 know that thou art a *v* woman.
Pr 12. 4 A *v* woman is a crown to her
31.10 Who can find a *v* woman? for her

VISAGE
Isa 52.14 his *v* was so marred more than
La 4. 8 Their *v* is blacker than a coal;
Dan 3.19 the form of his *v* was changed

VISIBLE
Col 1.16 that are in earth, *v* and invisible,

VISION
Gen 15. 1 Lord came unto Abram in a *v*,
Nu 24. 4, 16 saw the *v* of the Almighty,
1Sa 3. 1 those days; there was no open *v*.
Job 20. 8 chased away as a *v* of the night.
33.15 in a *v* of the night, when deep
Ps 89.19 thou spakest in *v* to thy holy one,
Pr 29.18 Where there is no *v*, the people
Isa 22. 5 God of hosts in the valley of *v*,
Jer 14.14 they prophesy unto you a false *v*
23.16 they speak a *v* of their own heart,
La 2. 9 also find no *v* from the Lord.
Eze 11.24 brought me in a *v* by the Spirit of
Dan 7. 2 and said, I saw in my *v* by night,
8. 2 I saw in a *v*, and I was by the river
15 even I Daniel, had seen the *v*, and
17 the time of the end shall be the *v*.
26 wherefore shut thou up the *v*; for
10. 7 And I Daniel alone saw the *v*: for
Ob 1 The *v* of Obadiah. Thus saith the
Na 1. 1 The book of the *v* of Nahum the
Hab 2. 2 Write the *v*, and make it plain
Zec 13. 4 be ashamed every one of his *v*,
Mt 17. 9 Tell the *v* to no man, until the
Lk 1.22 he had seen a *v* in the temple:
24.23 they had also seen a *v* of angels,
Ac 9.10 and to him said the Lord in a *v*,
12 seen in a *v* a man named Ananias
10. 3 He saw in a *v* evidently about the
17 what this *v* which he had seen
19 While Peter thought on the *v*, the
11. 5 and in a trance I saw a *v*, a certain
12. 9 angel; but thought he saw a *v*.
16. 9 a *v* appeared to Paul in the night;
10 And after he had seen the *v*,
18. 9 Lord to Paul in the night by a *v*,
26.19 disobedient unto the heavenly *v*:
Rev 9.17 I saw the horses in the *v*, and

VISIONS
2Ch 26. 5 understanding in the *v* of God:
Job 7.14 and terrifiest me through *v*:
Eze 1. 1 were opened, and I saw *v* of God.
13.16 which see *v* of peace for her, and
Dan 4. 5 and the *v* of my head trouble me.

Joel 2.28 your young men shall see *v*:
Ac 2.17 and your young men shall see *v*,
2Co 12. 1 I will come to *v* and revelations

VISIT
Gen 50.24 God will surely *v* you, and bring
Ex 32.34 the day when I *v* I will *v* their sin
Ps 89.32 Then will I *v* their transgression
106. 4 people: O *v* me with thy salvation;
Jer 5. 9, 29 Shall I not *v* for these things?
14.10 their iniquity, and *v* their sins.
La 4.22 he will *v* thine iniquity, O daughter
Am 3.14 shall *v* the transgressions of Israel
Zep 2. 7 the Lord their God shall *v* them,
Ac 7.23 to *v* his brethren the children of
15.14 God at the first did *v* the Gentiles,
36 Let us go again and *v* our brethren
Jas 1.27 To *v* the fatherless and widows in

VISITATION
Job 10.12 thy *v* hath preserved my spirit.
Isa 10. 3 And what will ye do in the day of *v*,
Jer 10.15 time of their *v* they shall perish.
50.27 day is come, the time of their *v*.
Hos 9. 7 The days of *v* are come, the days
Mic 7. 4 of thy watchmen and thy *v* cometh;
Lk 19.44 knewest not the time of thy *v*.
1Pe 2.12 behold, glorify God in the day of *v*.

VISITED
Ex 3.16 I have surely *v* you, and seen that
Ru 1. 6 the Lord had *v* his people in giving
Ps 17. 3 thou hast *v* me in the night; thou
Isa 24.22 after many days shall they be *v*.
Jer 6. 6 Jerusalem: this is the city to be *v*;
Zec 10. 3 the Lord of hosts hath *v* his flock
Mt 25.36 I was sick, and ye *v* me: I was in
43 and in prison, and ye *v* me not.
Lk 1.68 hath *v* and redeemed his people,
78 dayspring from on high hath *v* us,
7.16 and, That God hath *v* his people.

VISITEST
Ps 8. 4 the son of man, that thou *v* him?
65. 9 Thou *v* the earth, and waterest it:
Heb 2. 6 the son of man, that thou *v* him?

VISITING
Ex 20. 5 *v* the iniquity of the fathers upon
34. 7 *v* the iniquity of the fathers upon
Nu 14.18 *v* the iniquity of the fathers upon
Dt 5. 9 *v* the iniquity of the fathers upon

VOCATION
Eph 4. 1 walk worthy of the *v* wherewith

VOICE
Gen 3. 8 they heard the *v* of the Lord God
10 I heard thy *v* in the garden, and
17 hearkened unto the *v* of thy wife,
4.10 *v* of thy brother's blood crieth unto
22.18 because thou hast obeyed my *v*.
27.22 The *v* is Jacob's *v*, but the hands
38 And Esau lifted up his *v*, and wept.
Ex 5. 2 should obey his *v* to let Israel go?
15.26 hearken to the *v* of the Lord thy
19.19 and God answered him by a *v*.
23.21 Beware of him, and obey his *v*.
24. 3 all the people answered with one *v*,
32.18 *v* of them that shout for mastery,
Lev 5. 1 hear the *v* of swearing, and is a
Nu 20.16 he heard our *v*, and sent an angel,
Dt 4.12 no similitude; only ye heard a *v*,
33 *v* of God speaking out of the midst
5.26 hath heard the *v* of the living God
21.18 will not obey the *v* of his father,
18 or the *v* of his mother, and that,
20 rebellious, he will not obey our *v*;
30. 8 return and obey the *v* of the Lord,
Jos 6.10 nor make any noise with your *v*,
24.24 we serve, and his *v* will we obey.

Jdg 18.25 Let not thy *v* be heard among us,
Ru 1. 9 they lifted up their *v*, and wept.
1Sa 24.16 said, Is this thy *v*, my son David?
2Sa 19.35 any more the *v* of singing men
22. 7 he did hear my *v* out of his temple,
14 and the most High uttered his *v*.
1Ki 18.26 But there was no *v*, nor any that
19.12 and after the fire a still small *v*.
2Ki 4.31 there was neither *v*, nor hearing.
18.28 a loud *v* in the Jews' language,
Job 3. 7 solitary, let no joyful *v* come therein.
18 hear not the *v* of the oppressor.
4.16 there was silence, and I heard a *v*,
30.31 organ into the *v* of them that weep.
37. 4 After it a *v* roareth: he thundereth
5 marvellously with his *v*; great
38.34 thou lift up thy *v* to the clouds,
40. 9 thou thunder with a *v* like him?
Ps 3. 4 I cried unto the Lord with my *v*,
5. 3 My *v* shalt thou hear in the
18. 6 he heard my *v* out of his temple,
13 and the Highest gave his *v*;
19. 3 where their *v* is not heard.
26. 7 with the *v* of thanksgiving,
28. 2 Hear the *v* of my supplications,
29. 4 The *v* of the Lord is powerful; the
4 the *v* of the Lord is full of majesty.
5 *v* of the Lord breaketh the cedars;
9 *v* of the Lord maketh the hinds to
31.22 heardest the *v* of my supplications
42. 4 with the *v* of joy and praise, with a
46. 6 he uttered his *v*, the earth melted.
58. 5 not hearken to the *v* of charmers,
64. 1 Hear my *v*, O God, in my prayer:
68.33 lo, he doth send out his *v*,
77. 1 I cried unto God with my *v*, even
93. 3 the floods have lifted up their *v*;
95. 7 hand. To day if ye will hear his *v*,
103.20 hearkening unto the *v* of his word.
104. 7 at the *v* of thy thunder they hasted
116. 1 Lord, because he hath heard my *v*
141. 1 give ear unto my *v*, when I cry
142. 1 I cried unto the Lord with my *v*;
Pr 1.20 she uttereth her *v* in the streets:
5.13 not obeyed the *v* of my teachers,
8. 1 understanding put forth her *v*?
4 and my *v* is to the sons of man.
27.14 blesseth his friend with a loud *v*,
Ec 5. 3 a fool's *v* is known by multitude of
6 should God be angry at thy *v*,
12. 4 he shall rise up at the *v* of the bird,
SS 2. 8 The *v* of my beloved! behold, he
12 the *v* of the turtle is heard in our
14 me hear thy *v*; for sweet is thy *v*,
5. 2 *v* of my beloved that knocketh,
Isa 6. 4 moved at the *v* of him that cried,
8 Also I heard the *v* of the Lord,
13. 2 exalt the *v* unto them, shake the
28.23 Give ye ear, and hear my *v*;
31. 4 he will not be afraid of their *v*, nor
40. 3 The *v* of him that crieth in the
6 The *v* said, Cry. And he said,
9 tidings, lift up thy *v* with strength;
42. 2 nor cause his *v* to be heard in the
48.20 with a *v* of singing declare ye, tell
52. 8 Thy watchmen shall lift up the *v*;
65.19 the *v* of weeping shall be no more
66. 6 a *v* from the temple,
Jer 4.31 the *v* of the daughter of Zion, that
6.23 their *v* roareth like the sea; and
7.23 Obey my *v*, and I will be your God,
34 the *v* of the bridegroom, and
34 the *v* of the bride: for the land
16. 9 the *v* of the bridegroom, and
9 and the *v* of the bride.
25.36 A *v* of the cry of the shepherds, and
30.19 the *v* of them that make merry:
31.15 A *v* was heard in Ramah.
44.23 have not obeyed the *v* of the Lord,
46.22 *v* thereof shall go like a serpent;
48. 3 A *v* of crying shall be from

La 3.56 Thou hast heard my *v*: hide not
Eze 1.24 waters, as the *v* of the Almighty,
28 and I heard a *v* of one that spake.
3.12 behind me a *v* of a great rushing,
23.42 a *v* of a multitude being at ease
33.32 song of one that hath a pleasant *v*,
43. 2 and his *v* was like a noise of many
Dan 4.31 there fell a *v* from heaven, saying,
Am 1. 2 and utter his *v* from Jerusalem;
Jon 2. 9 thee with the *v* of thanksgiving;
Mic 6. 1 and let the hills hear thy *v*.
9 The Lord's *v* crieth unto the city,
Na 2. 7 lead her as with the *v* of doves,
13 *v* of thy messengers shall no more
Hab 3.10 the deep uttered his *v*, and lifted
Zep 2.14 their *v* shall sing in the windows;
Zec 6.15 diligently obey the *v* of the Lord
11. 3 *v* of the howling of the shepherds;
Mt 2.18 In Rama was there a *v* heard,
3. 3 *v* of one crying in the wilderness,
17 And lo a *v* from heaven, saying,
12.19 any man hear his *v* in the streets.
17. 5 and behold a *v* out of the cloud,
27.46 Jesus cried with a loud *v*, saying,
50 he had cried again with a loud *v*,
Mk 1. 3 *v* of one crying in the wilderness,
11 And there came a *v* from heaven,
26 cried with a loud *v*, he came out of
5. 7 cried with a loud *v*, and said, What
9. 7 a *v* came out of the cloud, saying,
15.34 hour Jesus cried with a loud *v*,
37 Jesus cried with a loud *v*, and gave
Lk 1.42 And she spake out with a loud *v*,
44 *v* of thy salutation sounded in mine
3. 4 *v* of one crying in the wilderness,
22 a *v* came from heaven, which said,
4.33 devil, and cried out with a loud *v*,
8.28 with a loud *v* said, What have I to
9.35 there came a *v* out of the cloud,
36 when the *v* was past, Jesus was
11.27 certain woman...lifted up her *v*,
17.15 and with a loud *v* glorified God,
19.37 praise God with a loud *v* for all the
23.46 when Jesus had cried with a loud *v*,
Jn 1.23 *v* of one crying in the wilderness,
3.29 because of the bridegroom's *v*:
5.25 shall hear the *v* of the Son of God:
28 are in the graves shall hear his *v*,
37 Ye have neither heard his *v* at any
10. 3 openeth; and the sheep hear his *v*:
4 follow him: for they know his *v*.
5 they know not the *v* of strangers.
16 and they shall hear my *v*; and
27 My sheep hear my *v*, and I know
11.43 he cried with a loud *v*, Lazarus,
12.28 Then came there a *v* from heaven,
30 This *v* came not because of me,
18.37 that is of the truth heareth my *v*.
Ac 2.14 lifted up his *v*, and said unto them,
4.24 they lifted up their *v* to God with
7.31 the *v* of the Lord came unto him,
57 Then they cried out with a loud *v*,
60 cried with a loud *v*, Lord, lay not
8. 7 spirits, crying with loud *v*, came
9. 4 and heard a *v* saying unto him,
7 hearing a *v*, but seeing no man.
10.13 there came a *v* to him, Rise, Peter;
15 the *v* spake unto him again the
11. 7 And I heard a *v* saying unto me,
9 But the *v* answered me again from
12.14 And when she knew Peter's *v*, she
22 is the *v* of a god, and not of a man.
14.10 Said with a loud *v*, Stand upright
16.28 Paul cried with a loud *v*, saying,
19.34 one *v* about the space of two hours
22. 7 heard a *v* saying unto me, Saul,
9 heard not the *v* of him that spake
14 shouldest hear the *v* of his mouth.
24.21 Except it be for this one *v*, that I
26.10 death, I gave my *v* against them.
14 I heard a *v* speaking unto me, and

24 Festus said with a loud *v*, Paul,
1Co 14.11 if I know not the meaning of the *v*,
19 that by my *v* I might teach others
Gal 4.20 you now, and to change my *v*;
1Th 4.16 with the *v* of the archangel, and
Heb 3. 7 saith, To day if ye will hear his *v*,
15 said, To day if ye will hear his *v*,
4. 7 said, To day if ye will hear his *v*,
12.19 of a trumpet, and the *v* of words;
19 which *v* they that heard entreated
26 Whose *v* then shook the earth:
2Pe 1.17 came such a *v* to him from the
18 this *v* which came from heaven we
2.16 dumb ass speaking with man's *v*
Rev 1.10 and heard behind me a great *v*, as
12 I turned to see the *v* that spake
15 his *v* as the sound of many waters.
3.20 if any man hear my *v*, and open
4. 1 the first *v* which I heard was as it
5. 2 angel proclaiming with a loud *v*,
11 I heard the *v* of many angels round
12 Saying with a loud *v*, Worthy is the
6. 6 I heard a *v* in the midst of the four
7 I heard the *v* of the fourth beast
10 And they cried with a loud *v*,
7. 2 he cried with a loud *v* to the four
10 And cried with a loud *v*, saying,
8.13 saying with a loud *v*, Woe, woe,
9.13 I heard a *v* from the four horns of
10. 3 cried with a loud *v*, as when a lion
4 I heard a *v* from heaven saying
7 days of the *v* of the seventh angel,
8 *v* which I heard from heaven spake
11.12 they heard a great *v* from heaven
12.10 I heard a loud *v* saying in heaven,
14. 2 And I heard a *v* from heaven, as
2 as the *v* of many waters, and
2 and as the *v* of a great thunder:
2 heard the *v* of harpers harping
7 Saying with a loud *v*, Fear God,
9 them, saying with a loud *v*,
13 I heard a *v* from heaven saying
15 loud *v* to him that sat on the cloud,
16. 1 a great *v* out of the temple saying
17 a great *v* out of the temple of
18. 2 he cried mightily with a strong *v*,
4 I heard another *v* from heaven,
22 the *v* of harpers, and musicians,
23 the *v* of the bridegroom and of the
19. 1 I heard a great *v* of much people
5 And a *v* came out of the throne.
6 it were the *v* of a great multitude,
6 and as the *v* of many waters,
6 as the *v* of mighty thunderings,
17 and he cried with a loud *v*, saying
21. 3 a great *v* out of heaven saying,

VOICES

Jdg 21. 2 lifted up their *v*, and wept sore;
1Sa 11. 4 people lifted up their *v*, and wept.
Lk 17.13 And they lifted up their *v*, and
23.23 And they were instant with loud *v*,
23 *v* of them and of the chief priests
Ac 13.27 nor yet the *v* of the prophets which
14.11 they lifted up their *v*, saying in the
22.22 and then lifted up their *v*, and said,
1Co 14.10 so many kinds of *v* in the world,
Rev 4. 5 lightnings and thunderings and *v*:
8. 5 and there were *v*, and thunderings,
13 of the other *v* of the trumpet of
10. 3 seven thunders uttered their *v*.
4 seven thunders had uttered their *v*,
11.15 and there were great *v* in heaven,
19 lightnings, and *v*, and thunderings,
16.18 there were *v*, and thunders, and

VOID

Gen 1. 2 the earth was without form, and *v*;
Nu 30.12 made them *v* on the day he heard
12 her husband hath made them *v*;
13 or her husband may make it *v*.

Nu 30.15 make them *v* after that he hath
Dt 32.28 For they are a nation *v* of counsel,
1Ki 22.10 in a *v* place in the entrance of the
2Ch 18. 9 sat in a *v* place at the entering in
Ps 89.39 made *v*...covenant of thy servant.
119.126 for they have made *v* thy law.
Pr 7. 7 a young man *v* of understanding,
10.13 of him that is *v* of understanding.
11.12 He that is *v* of wisdom despiseth
12.11 vain persons is *v* of understanding.
17.18 A man *v* of understanding striketh
24.30 of the man *v* of understanding;
Isa 55.11 it shall not return unto me *v*, but
Jer 4.23 and, lo, it was without form, and *v*;
19. 7 make *v* the counsel of Judah and
Na 2.10 She is empty, and *v*, and waste:
Ac 24.16 conscience *v* of offense toward God,
Ro 3.31 make *v* the law through faith?
4.14 faith is made *v*, and the promise
1Co 9.15 man should make my glorying *v*.

VOLUME
Ps 40. 7 in the *v* of the book it is written
Heb 10. 7 (in the *v* of the book it is written

VOLUNTARILY
Eze 46.12 peace offerings *v* unto the Lord,

VOLUNTARY
Lev 1. 3 offer it of his own *v* will at the
7.16 offering be a vow, or a *v* offering,
Eze 46.12 shalt prepare a *v* burnt offering
Col 2.18 you of your reward in a *v* humility

VOMIT
Job 20.15 and he shall *v* them up again:
Pr 23. 8 thou hast eaten shalt thou *v* up,
25.16 thou be filled therewith, and *v* it.
26.11 a dog returneth to his *v*, so a fool
Isa 19.14 drunken man staggereth in his *v*.
28. 8 For all tables are full of *v* and
Jer 48.26 Moab also shall wallow in his *v*, and
2Pe 2.22 dog is turned to his own *v* again;

VOMITED
Jon 2.10 it *v* out Jonah upon the dry land.

VOW
Gen 28.20 Jacob vowed a *v*, saying, If God
Nu 6. 2 *v* of a Nazarite, to separate
21. 2 Israel vowed a *v* unto the Lord,
30. 2 If a man *v*...unto the Lord,
13 Every *v*, and every binding oath to
Dt 23.18 of the Lord thy God for any *v*:
21 thou shalt *v*...unto the Lord
Jdg 11.30 Jephthah vowed a *v* unto the Lord,
2Sa 15. 7 pray thee, let me go and pay my *v*,
Ps 65. 1 unto thee shall the *v* be performed.
Ec 5. 4 When thou vowest a *v* unto God,
5 that thou shouldest *v* and not pay.
Isa 19.21 a *v* unto the Lord, and perform it.
Ac 18.18 head in Cenchrea: for he had a *v*.
21.23 four men which have a *v* on them;

VOWED
Gen 28.20 And Jacob *v* a vow, saying, If God
Lev 27. 8 according to his ability that *v* shall
Nu 6.21 law of the Nazarite who hath *v*, and
21 according to the vow which he *v*,
21. 2 And Israel *v* a vow unto the Lord,
30. 6 at all an husband, when she *v*.
8 shall make her vow which she *v*,
10 if she *v* in her husband's house,
Dt 23.23 as thou hast *v* unto the Lord thy
Jdg 11.30 Jephthah *v* a vow unto the Lord,
39 to his vow which he had *v*:
1Sa 1.11 And she *v* a vow, and said, O Lord,
2Sa 15. 7 I have *v* unto the Lord, in Hebron.
8 thy servant *v* a vow while I abode
Ps 132. 2 *v* unto the mighty God of Jacob;
Ec 5. 4 pay that which thou hast *v*.

Biblical Themes

VOWS

Sojourn in this land, and I will be with thee, and will bless thee . . . and I will perform the oath which I sware unto Abraham thy father. Gen 26.3

And Jacob vowed a vow, saying, If God will be with me, and will keep me in this way that I go . . . so that I come again to my father's house in peace; then shall the Lord be my God. Gen 28.20-21

Thou shalt not take the name of the Lord thy God in vain; for the Lord will not hold him guiltless that taketh his name in vain. Ex 20.7

Jephthah vowed a vow unto the Lord, and said, If thou shalt without fail deliver the children of Amnon into mine hands, then . . . whatsoever cometh forth of the doors of my house to meet me . . . I will offer it up for a burnt offering. . . . and, behold, his daughter came out to meet him with timbrels and with dances: and she was his only child. Jdg 11.30-31, 34

And [Hannah] vowed a vow, and said, O Lord of hosts, if thou wilt indeed look on the affliction of thine handmaid, and remember me, and . . . give unto thine handmaid a man child, then I will give him unto the Lord all the days of his life. 1Sa 1.11

Praise waiteth for thee, O God, in Sion: and unto thee shall the vow be performed. Ps 65.1

Vow, and pay unto the Lord your God: let all that be round about him bring presents unto him that ought to be feared. Ps 76.11

I will pay my vows unto the Lord now in the presence of all his people. Ps 116.14

Be not rash with thy mouth, and let not thine heart be hasty to utter any thing before God: for God is in heaven, and thou upon earth: therefore let thy words be few. . . . Better is it that thou shouldest not vow, than that thou shouldest vow and not pay. Ec 5.2, 5

They have spoken words, swearing falsely in making a covenant: thus judgment springeth up as hemlock in the furrows of the field. Hos 10.4

Ye have heard that it hath been said by them of old time, Thou shalt not forswear thyself, but shalt perform unto the Lord thine oaths: but I say unto you, Swear not at all; neither by heaven; for it is God's throne: nor by the earth; for it is his footstool. . . . But let your communication be, Yea, yea; Nay, nay: for whatsoever is more than these cometh of evil. Mt 5.33-35, 37

[Peter] began to curse and to swear, saying, I know not this man of whom ye speak. And the second time the cock crew. Mk 14.71-72

When God made promise to Abraham, because he could swear by no greater, he sware by himself. . . . For men verily swear by the greater: and an oath for confirmation is to them an end of all strife. Wherein God, willing more abundantly to shew . . . the immutability of his counsel, confirmed it by an oath. Heb 6.13, 16-17

The tongue can no man tame; it is an unruly evil, full of deadly poison. Therewith bless we God, even the Father; and therewith curse we men, which are made after the similitude of God. Out of the same mouth proceedeth blessing and cursing. My brethren, these things ought not so to be. Jas 3.8-10

Above all things, my brethren, swear not, neither by heaven, neither by the earth, neither by any other oath: but let your yea be yea: and your nay, nay; lest ye fall into condemnation. Jas 5.12

The Lord is not slack concerning his promise. 2Pe 3.9

Jer 44.25 perform our vows that we have *v*,
Jon 2. 9 I will pay that that I have *v*.

VOWS
Lev 22.18 offer his oblation for all his *v*,
Job 22.27 thee, and thou shall pay thy *v*.
Ps 22.25 I will pay my *v* before them that
50.14 and pay thy *v* unto the most High:
61. 8 that I may daily perform my *v*.
116.14, 18 I will pay my *v* unto the Lord
Pr 7.14 me; this day have I payed my *v*.
Jer 44.25 will surely perform our *v* that we
Jon 1.16 sacrifice unto the Lord, and made *v*.
Na 1.15 thy solemn feasts, perform thy *v*:

VOYAGE
Ac 27.10 I perceive that this *v* will be with

VULTURE
Lev 11.14 the *v*, and the kite after his kind;
Dt 14.13 the kite, and the *v* after his kind,

VULTURE'S
Job 28. 7 which the *v* eye hath not seen:

VULTURES
Isa 34.15 the *v* also be gathered, every

WAGES
Gen 29.15 tell me, what shall thy *w* be?
30.28 Appoint me thy *w*, and I will give
31. 7 and changed my *w* ten times;
8 The speckled shall be thy *w*:
41 hast changed my *w* ten times.
Ex 2. 9 me, and I will give thee thy *w*.
Lev 19.13 *w* of him that is hired shall not
Jer 22.13 neighbor's service without *w*,
Eze 29.18 yet had he no *w*, nor his army, for
19 and it shall be the *w* for his army.
Hag 1. 6 and he that earneth *w* earneth
6 earneth *w* to put it into a bag
Mal 3. 5 that oppress the hireling in his *w*,
Lk 3.14 and be content with your *w*.
Jn 4.36 And he that reapeth receiveth *w*,
Ro 6.23 For the *w* of sin is death; but the
2Co 11. 8 other churches, taking *w* of them,
2Pe 2.15 loved the *w* of unrighteousness;

WAGGING
Mt 27.39 by reviled him, *w* their heads,
Mk 15.29 by railed on him, *w* their heads,

WAIL
Eze 32.18 *w* for the multitude of Egypt,
Mic 1. 8 Therefore I will *w* and howl, I
Rev 1. 7 kindreds of the earth shall *w*

WAILED
Mk 5.38 and them that wept and *w* greatly.

WAILING
Est 4. 3 and fasting, and weeping, and *w*;
Jer 9.10 will I take up a weeping and *w*,
18 haste, and take up a *w* for us,
19 a voice of *w* is heard out of Zion,
20 and teach your daughters *w*,
Eze 7.11 neither shall there be *w* for them.
27.31 bitterness of heart and bitter *w*.
32 in their *w* they shall take up a
Am 5.16 *W* shall be in all streets; and
16 as are skilful of lamentation to *w*.
17 And in all vineyards shall be *w*:
Mic 1. 8 I will make a *w* like the dragons,
Mt 13.42, 50 be *w* and gnashing of teeth.
Rev 18.15 of her torment, weeping and *w*,
19 cried, weeping and *w*, saying,

WAIT
Nu 3.10 shall *w* on their priest's office:
Jos 8.13 liers in *w* on the west of the city,
2Ki 6.33 I *w* for the Lord any longer?
Job 14.14 of my appointed time will I *w*,
17.13 If I *w*, the grave is mine house:
Ps 10. 9 he lieth in *w* to catch the poor: he
25. 3 none that *w* on thee be ashamed:
5 on thee do I *w* all the day.
21 preserve me; for I *w* on thee.
27.14 *W* on the Lord: be of good
14 thine heart: *w*, I say, on the Lord.
37. 7 Lord, and *w* patiently for him:
34 *W* on the Lord, and keep his way,
39. 7 And now, Lord, what *w* I for?
52. 9 and I will *w* on thy name; for it is
62. 5 My soul, *w* thou only upon God;
69. 3 eyes fail while I *w* for my God.
6 Let not them that *w* on thee,
71.10 and they that lay *w* for my soul
104.27 These *w* all upon thee; that thou
123. 2 so our eyes *w* upon the Lord our
130. 5 I *w* for the Lord, my soul doth *w*,
145.15 The eyes of all *w* upon thee; and
Pr 12. 6 the wicked are to lie in *w* for blood:
20.22 *w* on the Lord, and he shall save
23.28 She also lieth in *w* as for a prey,
Isa 30.18 therefore will the Lord *w*, that he
18 blessed are all they that *w* for him.
40.31 they that *w* upon the Lord shall
42. 4 and the isles shall *w* for his law.
49.23 not be ashamed that *w* for me.
51. 5 the isles shall *w* upon me, and on
59. 9 *w* for light, but behold obscurity;
60. 9 Surely the isles shall *w* for me,
Jer 9. 8 but in heart he layeth his *w*.
14.22 therefore we will *w* upon thee: for
La 3.10 was unto me as a bear lying in *w*,
25 Lord is good unto them that *w*
26 quietly *w* for the salvation of the
Hos 6. 9 as troops of robbers *w* for a man,
12. 6 and *w* on thy God continually.
Mic 7. 7 *w* for the God of my salvation:
Hab 2. 3 though it tarry, *w* for it; because
Mk 3. 9 a small ship should *w* on him
Lk 11.54 Laying *w* for him, and seeking to
12.36 like...men that *w* for their lord,
Ac 1. 4 *w* for the promise of the Father,
20. 3 the Jews laid *w* for him,
19 by the lying in *w* of the Jews:
23.16 son heard of their lying in *w*,
21 for there lie in *w* for him of them
30 the Jews laid *w* for the man,
25. 3 laying *w* in the way to kill
Ro 8.25 then do we with patience *w* for it.
12. 7 let us *w* on our ministering:
1Co 9.13 they which *w* at the altar are
Gal 5. 5 *w* for the hope of righteousness by
Eph 4.14 whereby they lie in *w* to deceive;
1Th 1.10 And to *w* for his Son from heaven,

WAITED
Gen 49.18 I have *w* for thy salvation, O Lord.
1Ch 6.32 and then they *w* on their office
Job 15.22 and he is *w* for of the sword.
29.23 And they *w* for me as for the rain;
30.26 when I *w* for light, there came
32.11 Behold, I *w* for your words; I
Ps 40. 1 I *w* patiently for the Lord; and he
Isa 25. 9 we have *w* for him, we will be glad
26. 8 O Lord, have we *w* for thee;
Zec 11.11 poor of the flock that *w* upon me
Mk 15.43 also *w* for the kingdom of God,
Lk 1.21 And the people *w* for Zacharias,
23.51 himself *w* for the kingdom of God.
Ac 10. 7 them that *w* on him continually;
24 And Cornelius *w* for them, and
17.16 while Paul *w* for them at Athens,
1Pe 3.20 of God *w* in the days of Noah,

WAITETH
Job 24.15 the adulterer *w* for the twilight,
Ps 33.20 Our soul *w* for the Lord: he is
62. 1 Truly my soul *w* upon God: from
65. 1 Praise *w* for thee, O God, in Sion:
130. 6 My soul *w* for the Lord more than
Pr 27.18 he that *w* on his master shall be
Isa 64. 4 prepared for him that *w* for him.
Dan 12.12 Blessed is he that *w*, and cometh to
Mic 5. 7 man, nor *w* for the sons of men.
Ro 8.19 *w* for the manifestation of the
Jas 5. 7 husbandman *w* for the precious

WAITING
Nu 8.25 cease *w* upon the service thereof,
Pr 8.34 gates, *w* at the posts of my doors.
Lk 2.25 *w* for the consolation of Israel:
8.40 him: for they were all *w* for him.
Jn 5. 3 *w* for the moving of the water.
Ro 8.23 *w* for the adoption, to wit, the
1Co 1. 7 *w* for the coming of our Lord Jesus
2Th 3. 5 and into the patient *w* for Christ.

WAKE
Jer 51.39, 57 a perpetual sleep, and not *w*,
Joel 3. 9 *w* up the mighty men, let all the
1Th 5.10 whether we *w* or sleep, we should

WAKENED
Joel 3.12 Let the heathen be *w*, and come
Zec 4. 1 a man that is *w* out of his sleep,

WAKENETH
Isa 50. 4 he *w* morning by morning,
4 *w* mine ear to hear as the learned.

WAKETH
Ps 127. 1 the watchman *w* but in vain.
SS 5. 2 I sleep, but my heart *w*: it is the

WAKING
Ps 77. 4 Thou holdest mine eyes *w*: I am

WALK
Gen 17. 1 *w* before me, and be thou perfect.
24.40 The Lord, before whom I *w*, will
48.15 fathers Abraham and Isaac did *w*,
Ex 16. 4 whether they will *w* in my law, or
18.20 the way wherein they must *w*,
Lev 26. 3 If ye *w* in my statutes, and keep
12 I will *w* among you, and will be
21 ye *w* contrary unto me, and will
24 will I also *w* contrary unto you,
Dt 8.19 *w* after other gods, and serve
13. 4 Ye shall *w* after the Lord your God,
Jos 18. 8 Go and *w* through the land, and
Jdg 5.10 in judgment, and *w* by the way.
1Ki 2. 4 to *w* before me in truth with all
8.61 Lord our God, to *w* in his statutes,
16.31 a light thing for him to *w* in the
Ps 12. 8 The wicked *w* on every side,
23. 4 though I *w* through the valley
26.11 for me, I will *w* in mine integrity:
56.13 I may *w* before God in the light
84.11 from them that *w* uprightly.
86.11 O Lord; I will *w* in thy truth:
116. 9 I will *w* before the Lord in the
119.45 I will *w* at liberty: for I seek thy
143. 8 know the way wherein I should *w*;
Pr 2.13 to *w* in the ways of darkness;
20 thou mayest *w* in the way of good
Ec 4.15 the living which *w* under the sun,
Isa 2. 3 ways, and we will *w* in his paths:
5 let us *w* in the light of the Lord.
30.21 This is the way, *w* ye in it, when
35. 9 but the redeemed shall *w* there:
40.31 and they shall *w*, and not faint.
50.11 *w* in the light of your fire, and in
59. 9 brightness, but we *w* in darkness.
Jer 6.16 is the good way, and *w* therein,
7. 6 *w* after other gods to your hurt:
16.12 *w* every one after the imagination
18.12 we will *w* after our own devices,
26. 4 hearken to me, to *w* in my law,
Eze 20.19 *w* in my statutes, and keep my
Hos 11.10 They shall *w* after the Lord: he
14. 9 right, and the just shall *w* in them:
Am 3. 3 Can two *w* together, except they
Mic 4. 2 ways, and we will *w* in his paths:
5 will *w* in the name of the Lord our
6. 8 and to *w* humbly with thy God?
Na 2. 5 they shall stumble in their *w*;
Zep 1.17 that they shall *w* like blind men,
Zec 6. 7 *w* to and fro through the earth:
Mt 9. 5 thee; or to say, Arise, and *w*?
11. 5 and the lame *w*, the lepers are
15.31 the lame to *w*, and the blind to see:
Mk 2. 9 Arise, and take up thy bed, and *w*?
7. 5 Why *w* not thy disciples according

Walking with Jesus on the water, Peter loses faith and begins to sink (Mt 14) in this 19th-century drawing.

Lk 5.23 thee; or to say, Rise up and *w*?
7.22 how that the blind see, the lame *w*,
11.44 the men that *w* over them are not
13.33 I must *w* to day, and to morrow.
20.46 which desire to *w* in long robes,
24.17 ye have one to another, as ye *w*,
Jn 5. 8 him, Rise, take up thy bed, and *w*.
11 unto me, Take up thy bed, and *w*.
12 thee, Take up thy bed, and *w*?
7. 1 for he would not *w* in Jewry,
8.12 me shall not *w* in darkness,
11. 9 If any man *w* in the day, he
10 But if a man *w* in the night, he
12.35 *W* while ye have the light, lest
Ac 3. 6 Christ of Nazareth rise up and *w*.
12 we had made this man to *w*?
14.16 all nations to *w* in their own ways.
21.21 neither to *w* after the customs.
Ro 4.12 also *w* in the steps of that faith
6. 4 should *w* in newness of life.
8. 1 who *w* not after the flesh, but
4 who *w* not after the flesh, but
13.13 Let us *w* honestly, as in the day:
1Co 3. 3 are ye not carnal, and *w* as men?
7.17 called every one, so let him *w*.
2Co 5. 7 (For we *w* by faith, not by sight:)
6.16 dwell in them, and *w* in them;
10. 3 For though we *w* in the flesh, we
Gal 5.16 *W* in the Spirit, and ye shall not
25 Spirit, let us also *w* in the Spirit.
6.16 many as *w* according to this rule,
Eph 2.10 that we should *w* in them.
4. 1 that ye *w* worthy of the vocation
17 *w* not as other Gentiles *w*,
5. 2 *w* in love, as Christ also hath loved
8 in the Lord: *w* as children of light:
15 See then that ye *w* circumspectly,
Php 3.16 let us *w* by the same rule, let us
17 mark them which *w* so as ye have
18 (For many *w*, of whom I have told
Col 1.10 That ye might *w* worthy of the
2. 6 Jesus the Lord, so *w* ye in him:
4. 5 *W* in wisdom toward them that
1Th 2.12 That ye would *w* worthy of God,
4. 1 ye ought to *w* and to please God,
12 *w* honestly toward them that are
2Th 3.11 which *w* among you disorderly,
2Pe 2.10 them that *w* after the flesh in the
1Jn 1. 6 with him, and *w* in darkness,
7 But if we *w* in the light, as he is in
2. 6 in him ought himself also so to *w*,
2Jn 6 we *w* after his commandments.
6 the beginning, ye should *w* in it.
3Jn 4 hear that my children *w* in truth.
Jude 18 *w* after their own ungodly lusts.
Rev 3. 4 they shall *w* with me in white:
9.20 neither can see, nor hear, nor *w*:
16.15 lest he *w* naked, and they see his
21.24 are saved shall *w* in the light of it:

WALKED

Gen 5.22 Enoch *w* with God after he begat
6. 9 generations, and Noah *w* with God.
Ex 14.29 children of Israel *w* upon dry land
Lev 26.40 they have *w* contrary unto me;
Jos 5. 6 *w* forty years in the wilderness,
Jdg 2.17 the way which their fathers *w* in,
1Sa 8. 3 And his sons *w* not in his ways,
2Sa 2.29 and his men *w* all that night
2Ki 16. 3 But he *w* in the way of the kings
17. 8 *w* in the statutes of the heathen,
19 *w* in the statutes of Israel which
22 children of Israel *w* in all the sins
1Ch 17. 6 I have *w* with all Israel,
Job 29. 3 his light I *w* through darkness;
Ps 55.14 and *w* unto the house of God in
Isa 9. 2 people that *w* in darkness have
38. 3 how I have *w* before thee in truth
Jer 2. 8 *w* after things that do not profit.
11. 8 *w* every one in the imagination of
16.11 have *w* after other gods, and have
Zec 6. 7 *w* to and fro through the earth.
Mal 3.14 *w* mournfully before the Lord
Mt 14.29 he *w* on the water, to go to Jesus.
Mk 1.16 Now as he *w* by the sea of Galilee,
5.42 the damsel arose, and *w*, for she
16.12 form unto two of them, as they *w*,
Jn 1.36 looking upon Jesus as he *w*, he
5. 9 whole, and took up his bed, and *w*:
6.66 back, and *w* no more with him.
7. 1 these things Jesus *w* in Galilee:
10.23 Jesus *w* in the temple in Solomon's
11.54 *w* no more openly among the
Ac 3. 8 he leaping up stood, and *w*, and
14. 8 mother's womb, who never had *w*:
10 on thy feet. And he leaped and *w*.
2Co 10. 2 as if we *w* according to the flesh.
12.18 you? *w* we not in the same spirit?
18 spirit? *w* we not in the same steps?
Gal 2.14 they *w* not uprightly according to
Eph 2. 2 in time past ye *w* according to the
Col 3. 7 In the which ye also *w* some time,
1Pe 4. 3 we *w* in lasciviousness, lusts,
1Jn 2. 6 also so to walk, even as he *w*.

WALKEDST

Jn 21.18 and *w* whither thou wouldest:

WALKEST

Dt 6. 7 and when thou *w* by the way,
11.19 and when thou *w* by the way,
1Ki 2.42 out, and *w* abroad any whither,
Isa 43. 2 when thou *w* through the fire,
Ac 21.24 *w* orderly, and keepest the law.
Ro 14.15 meat, now *w* thou not charitably.
3Jn 3 thee, even as thou *w* in the truth.

WALKETH

Dt 23.14 Lord thy God *w* in the midst of
Job 18. 8 own feet, and he *w* upon a snare.
22.14 and he *w* in the circuit of heaven.
Ps 1. 1 that *w* not in the counsel of the
15. 2 He that *w* uprightly, and worketh
39. 6 Surely every man *w* in a vain shew:
91. 6 the pestilence that *w* in darkness;
104. 3 who *w* upon the wings of the wind:
128. 1 the Lord; that *w* in his ways.
Pr 14. 2 He that *w* in his uprightness
19. 1 the poor that *w* in his integrity,
20. 7 The just man *w* in his integrity:
Ec 2.14 but the fool *w* in darkness: and I
Isa 50.10 that *w* in darkness, and hath no
Jer 10.23 in man that *w* to direct his steps.
Mic 2. 7 do good to him that *w* uprightly?
Mt 12.43 he *w* through dry places, seeking
Lk 11.24 he *w* through dry places, seeking
Jn 12.35 he that *w* in darkness knoweth
2Th 3. 6 every brother that *w* disorderly,
1Pe 5. 8 *w* about, seeking whom he may
1Jn 2.11 *w* in darkness, and knoweth not
Rev 2. 1 who *w* in the midst of the seven

WALKING

Gen 3. 8 of the Lord God *w* in the garden
Dt 2. 7 he knoweth thy *w* through this
1Ki 3. 3 *w* in the statutes of David his
16.19 in *w* in the way of Jeroboam, and
Job 1. 7 and from *w* up and down in it.
2. 2 and from *w* up and down in it.
31.26 or the moon *w* in brightness;
Ec 10. 7 and princes *w* as servants upon the
Isa 3.16 *w* and mincing as they go, and
20. 2 he did so, *w* naked and barefoot.
57. 2 each one *w* in his uprightness.
Jer 6.28 revolters, *w* with slanders:
Dan 3.25 loose, *w* in the midst of the fire,
Mic 2.11 man *w* in the spirit and falsehood
Mt 4.18 Jesus, *w* by the sea of Galilee,
14.25 went unto them, *w* on the sea.
26 the disciples saw him *w* on the sea,
Mk 6.48 cometh unto them, *w* upon the sea,
49 when they saw him *w* upon the sea,
8.24 up, and said, I see men as trees, *w*.

11.27 and as he was *w* in the temple,
Lk 1. 6 *w* in all the commandments and
Jn 6.19 they see Jesus *w* on the sea, and
Ac 3. 8 into the temple, *w*, and leaping,
9 saw him *w* and praising God:
9.31 *w* in the fear of the Lord, and in
2Co 4. 2 not *w* in craftiness, nor handling
2Pe 3. 3 scoffers, *w* after their own lusts,
2Jn 4 found of thy children *w* in truth,
Jude 16 *w* after their own lusts;

WALL
Gen 49. 6 selfwill they digged down a *w*.
Ex 14.22, 29 waters were a *w* unto them
Nu 22.25 Balaam's foot against the *w*:
Jos 2.15 and she dwelt upon the *w*.
6.20 shout, that the *w* fell down flat,
1Sa 19.10 he smote the javelin into the *w*:
25.16 *w* unto us both by night and day,
1Ki 3. 1 the *w* of Jerusalem round about.
4.33 that springeth out of the *w*:
6.27 other cherub touched the other *w*:
20.30 *w* fell upon twenty and seven
2Ki 4.10 chamber, I pray thee, on the *w*;
14.13 brake down the *w* of Jerusalem
Neh 2.17 let us build up the *w* of Jerusalem,
5.16 I continued in the work of this *w*,
6.15 *w* was finished in the twenty and
12.27 dedication of the *w* of Jerusalem
Ps 62. 3 as a bowing *w* shall ye be, and as
Pr 18.11 as an high *w* in his own conceit.
Isa 5. 5 break down the *w* thereof, and it
25. 4 ones is as a storm against the *w*.
59.10 We grope for the *w* like the blind,
La 2.18 O *w* of the daughter of Zion, let
Eze 8. 8 me, Son of man, dig now in the *w*:
38.20 every *w* shall fall to the ground.
Am 5.19 and leaned his hand on the *w*,
7. 7 upon a *w* made by a plumbline,
Hab 2.11 the stone shall cry out of the *w*,
Zec 2. 5 will be unto her a *w* of fire round
Ac 9.25 let down by the *w* in a basket.
23. 3 shall smite thee, thou whited *w*:
2Co 11.33 a basket was I let down by the *w*,
Eph 2.14 broken down the middle *w* of
Rev 21.12 And had a *w* great and high, and
14 the *w* of the city had twelve
15 gates thereof, and the *w* thereof.
17 And he measured the *w* thereof,
18 building of the *w*...was of jasper:
19 foundations of the *w* of the city

WALLED
Lev 25.29 sell a dwelling house in a *w* city,
30 *w* city shall be established for ever
Nu 13.28 and the cities are *w*, and very
Dt 1.28 are great and *w* up to heaven;

WALLOW
Jer 6.26 sackcloth, and *w* thyself in ashes:
25.34 *w* yourselves in the ashes, ye
48.26 Moab also shall *w* in his vomit,
Eze 27.30 shall *w* themselves in ashes:

WALLOWED
Mk 9.20 on the ground and *w* foaming.

WALLOWING
2Pe 2.22 was washed to her *w* in the mire.

WALLS
2Ch 3. 7 and graved cherubims on the *w*.
8. 5 fenced cities, with *w*, gates, and
Ezr 4.13 be builded, and the *w* set up again,
Neh 4. 7 the *w* of Jerusalem were made up,
Ps 51.18 build thou the *w* of Jerusalem.
122. 7 Peace be within thy *w*, and
Isa 26. 1 salvation will God appoint for *w*
60.10 of strangers shall build up thy *w*,
18 thou shalt call thy *w* Salvation,
62. 6 I have set watchmen upon thy *w*,
Jer 52.14 brake down all the *w* of Jerusalem
Eze 26. 9 set engines of war against thy *w*,
Mic 7.11 the day that thy *w* are to be built,
Heb 11.30 By faith the *w* of Jericho fell

WANDER
Gen 20.13 me to *w* from my father's house,
Nu 14.33 children shall *w* in the wilderness
32.13 he made them *w* in the wilderness
Dt 27.18 he that maketh the blind to *w* out
Job 12.24 causeth them to *w* in a wilderness
38.41 unto God, they *w* for lack of meat.
Ps 55. 7 then would I *w* far off, and remain
59.15 them *w* up and down for meat,
107.40 them to *w* in the wilderness,
119.10 not *w* from thy commandments.
Isa 47.15 shall *w* every one to his quarter;
Jer 14.10 Thus have they loved to *w*, they
48.12 that shall cause him to *w*, and
Am 8.12 And they shall *w* from sea to sea,

WANDERED
Gen 21.14 and *w* in the wilderness of
Jos 14.10 of Israel *w* in the wilderness:
Ps 107. 4 They *w* in the wilderness in a
Isa 16. 8 they *w* through the wilderness:
La 4.14 They have *w* as blind men in the
15 when they fled away and *w*, they
Eze 34. 6 My sheep *w* through all the
Am 4. 8 or three cities *w* unto one city,
Heb 11.37 they *w* about in sheepskins and
38 they *w* in deserts, and in

WANDERERS
Jer 48.12 that I will send unto him *w*,
Hos 9.17 shall be *w* among the nations.

WANDERETH
Job 15.23 He *w* abroad for bread, saying,
Pr 21.16 The man that *w* out of the way of
27. 8 As a bird that *w* from her nest, so
8 so is a man that *w* from his place.
Isa 16. 3 outcasts; bewray not him that *w*.
Jer 49. 5 none shall gather up him that *w*.

WANDERING
Gen 37.15 behold, he was *w* in the field:
Pr 26. 2 As the bird by *w*, as the swallow
Ec 6. 9 the eyes than the *w* of the desire:
Isa 16. 2 as a *w* bird cast out of the nest,
1Ti 5.13 *w* about from house to house;
Jude 13 *w* stars, to whom is reserved the

WANDERINGS
Ps 56. 8 Thou tellest my *w*: put thou my

WANT
Dt 28.48 nakedness, and in *w* of all things:
57 shall eat them for *w* of all things
Jdg 18.10 a place where there is no *w* of
19.19 there is no *w* of any thing.
Job 24. 8 embrace...rock for *w* of a shelter.
30. 3 For *w* and famine they were
31.19 seen any perish for *w* of clothing,
Ps 23. 1 is my shepherd; I shall not *w*.
34. 9 is no *w* to them that fear him.
10 Lord shall not *w* any good thing.
Pr 6.11 and thy *w* as an armed man.
10.21 but fools die for *w* of wisdom.
13.23 is destroyed for *w* of judgment.
25 the belly of the wicked shall *w*.
14.28 but in the *w* of people is the
21. 5 every one that is hasty only to *w*.
22.16 to the rich, shall surely come to *w*.
24.34 and thy *w* as an armed man.
Isa 34.16 shall fail, none shall *w* her mate:
Jer 33.17 never *w* a man to sit upon the
18 Levites *w* a man before me to offer
35.19 not *w* a man to stand before me for
La 4. 9 for *w* of the fruits of the field.
Eze 4.17 they may *w* bread and water, and
Am 4. 6 and *w* of bread in all your places:
Mk 12.44 she of her *w* did cast in all that
Lk 15.14 land; and he began to be in *w*.
2Co 8.14 may be a supply for their *w*,
14 also may be a supply for your *w*:
9.12 only supplieth the *w* of the saints,
Php 4.11 Not that I speak in respect of *w*:

WANTED
Jer 44.18 we have *w* all things, and have
Jn 2. 3 when they *w* wine, the mother of
2Co 11. 9 I was present with you, and *w*, I

WANTETH
Dt 15. 8 for his need, in that which he *w*.
Pr 9. 4 for him that *w* understanding,
16 as for him that *w* understanding,
10.19 of words there *w* not sin: but
28.16 The prince that *w* understanding
Ec 6. 2 so that he *w* nothing for his soul
SS 7. 2 round goblet, which *w* not liquor:

WANTING
2Ki 10.19 and all his priests; let none be *w*:
19 whosoever shall be *w*, he shall not
Pr 19. 7 with words, yet they are *w* to him.
Ec 1.15 which is *w* cannot be numbered.
Dan 5.27 in the balances, and art found *w*.
Tit 1. 5 set in order the things that are *w*,
3.13 that nothing be *w* unto them.
Jas 1. 4 be perfect and entire, *w* nothing.

WANTON
Isa 3.16 stretched forth necks and *w* eyes,
1Ti 5.11 begun to wax *w* against Christ,
Jas 5. 5 pleasure on the earth, and been *w*;

WANTONNESS
Ro 13.13 not in chambering and *w*, not in
2Pe 2.18 through much *w*, those that were

WANTS
Jdg 19.20 let all thy *w* lie upon me; only
Php 2.25 and he that ministered to my *w*.

WAR
Ex 15. 3 The Lord is a man of *w*: the Lord
32.17 There is a noise of *w* in the camp.
Dt 4.34 signs, and by wonders, and by *w*,
21.10 When thou goest forth to *w*
24. 5 new wife, he shall not go out to *w*,
Jos 6. 3 compass the city, all ye men of *w*,
1Sa 17.33 and he a man of *w* from his youth.
2Sa 1.27 and the weapons of *w* perished!
17. 8 thy father is a man of *w*, and will
22.35 He teacheth my hands to *w*; so
1Ki 22. 1 continued three years without *w*
1Ch 5.22 slain, because the *w* was of God.
2Ch 26.13 that made *w* with mighty power,
Job 10.17 changes and *w* are against me.
38.23 against the day of battle and *w*?
Ps 18.34 He teacheth my hands to *w*, so
27. 3 though *w* should rise against me,
55.21 butter, but *w* was in his heart:
68.30 thou the people that delight in *w*.
120. 7 but when I speak, they are for *w*.
Pr 20.18 and with good advice make *w*.
24. 6 counsel thou shalt make thy *w*:
Ec 3. 8 a time of *w*, and a time of peace.
8. 8 there is no discharge in that *w*;
9.18 is better than weapons of *w*: but
Isa 2. 4 neither shall they learn *w* any
Jer 6. 4 Prepare ye *w* against her; arise,
21. 4 I will turn back the weapons of *w*
Eze 32.27 to hell with their weapons of *w*:
39.20 mighty men, and with all men of *w*,
Joel 2. 7 shall climb the wall like men of *w*;
3. 9 Prepare *w*, wake up the mighty
Mic 4. 3 neither shall they learn *w* any
Lk 14.31 to make *w* against another king,
23.11 Herod with his men of *w* set him

BIBLICAL THEMES

WAR

The Lord is a man of war. . . . Thy right hand, O Lord, is become glorious in power: thy right hand, O Lord, hath dashed in pieces the enemy. Ex 15.3, 6

Thou comest to me with a sword, and with a spear, and with a shield: but I come to thee in the name of the Lord of hosts. . . . This day will the Lord deliver thee into mine hand; and I will smite thee, and take thine head from thee. . . . And all this assembly shall know that the Lord saveth not with sword and spear: for the battle is the Lord's. 1Sa 17.45-47

How are the mighty fallen in the midst of the battle! . . . How are the mighty fallen, and the weapons of war perished! 2Sa 1.25, 27

Shall the sword devour for ever? knowest thou not that it will be bitterness in the latter end? 2Sa 2.26

He maketh wars to cease unto the end of the earth; he breaketh the bow, and cutteth the spear in sunder; he burneth the chariot in the fire. Ps 46.9

Rebuke the company of spearmen . . . scatter thou the people that delight in war. Ps 68.30

They shall beat their swords into plowshares, and their spears into pruninghooks: nation shall not lift up sword against nation, neither shall they learn war any more. Isa 2.4

Like as the lion and the young lion roaring on his prey, when a multitude of shepherds is called forth against him, he will not be afraid of their voice . . . so shall the Lord of hosts come down to fight for mount Zion. Isa 31.4

The spoilers are come upon all high places through the wilderness: for the sword of the Lord shall devour from the one end of the land even to the other end of the land: no flesh shall have peace. Jer 12.12

O thou sword of the Lord, how long will it be ere thou be quiet? put up thyself into thy scabbard, rest, and be still. Jer 47.6

And in that day . . . I will break the bow and the sword and the battle out of the earth, and will make them to lie down safely. Hos 2.18

Prepare war, wake up the mighty men, let all the men of war draw near . . . beat your plowshares into swords, and your pruninghooks into spears: let the weak say, I am strong. Assemble yourselves, and come. Joel 3.9-11

Think not that I am come to send peace on earth: I came not to send peace, but a sword. Mt 10.34

When ye shall hear of wars and rumors of wars, be ye not troubled: for such things must needs be. . . . nation shall rise against nation, and kingdom against kingdom . . . and there shall be famines and troubles. . . . But in those days, after that tribulation, the sun shall be darkened, and the moon shall not give her light. . . . And then shall they see the Son of man coming in the clouds with great power and glory. Mk 13.7-8, 24, 26

He must reign, till he hath put all enemies under his feet. The last enemy that shall be destroyed is death. 1Co 15.25-26

The weapons of our warfare are not carnal, but mighty through God to the pulling down of strong holds. 2Co 10.4

Fight the good fight of faith. 1Ti 6.12

And there was war in heaven: Michael and his angels fought against the dragon. . . . And the great dragon was cast out, that old serpent, called the Devil . . . he was cast out into the earth, and his angels were cast out with him. And I heard a loud voice saying in heaven, Now is come salvation. Rev 12.7, 9-10

2Co 10. 3 flesh, we do not *w* after the flesh:
1Ti 1.18 them mightest *w* a good warfare;
Jas 4. 1 lusts that *w* in your members?
2 ye fight and *w*, yet ye have not,
1Pe 2.11 lusts, which *w* against the soul;
Rev 11. 7 pit shall make *w* against them,
12. 7 there was *w* in heaven: Michael
17 went to make *w* with the remnant
13. 4 who is able to make *w* with him?
7 him to make *w* with the saints,
17.14 These...make *w* with the Lamb,
19.11 he doth judge and make *w*.
19 to make *w* against him that sat

WARD

Gen 40. 3 he put them in *w* in the house of
4 and they continued a season in *w*.
7 with him in the *w* of his lord's
41.10 put me in *w* in the captain of the
42.17 he put them altogether into *w*
Lev 24.12 they put him in *w*, that the mind
Nu 15.34 they put him in *w*, because it was
2Sa 20. 3 put them in *w*, and fed them,
1Ch 12.29 kept the *w* of the house of Saul.
25. 8 And they cast lots, *w* against
8 against *w*, as well the small as the
26.16 of the going up, *w* against *w*.
Neh 12.24 the man of God, *w* over against *w*.
25 porters keeping the *w* at the
45 porters kept the *w* of their God,
45 and the *w* of the purification,
Isa 21. 8 I am set in my *w* whole nights:
Jer 37.13 a captain of the *w* was there,
Eze 19. 9 they put him in *w* in chains,
Ac 12.10 past the first and the second *w*,

WARE

Neh 10.31 the people of the land bring *w* or
13.16 brought fish, and all manner of *w*,
20 sellers of all kind of *w* lodged
Lk 8.27 devils long time, and *w* no clothes,
Ac 14. 6 They were *w* of it, and fled unto
2Ti 4.15 Of whom be thou *w* also; for he

WARES

Jer 10.17 Gather up thy *w* out of the land,
Eze 27.16, 18 of the *w* of thy making:
33 thy *w* went forth out of the seas,
Jon 1. 5 forth the *w* that were in the ship

WARFARE

1Sa 28. 1 their armies together for *w*,
Isa 40. 2 her, that her *w* is accomplished,
1Co 9. 7 Who goeth a *w* any time at his
2Co 10. 4 weapons of our *w* are not carnal,
1Ti 1.18 by them mightest war a good *w*;

WARM

2Ki 4.34 the flesh of the child waxed *w*.
Job 6.17 What time they wax *w*, they
37.17 How thy garments are *w*, when
Ec 4.11 but how can one be *w* alone?
Isa 44.15 will take thereof, and *w* himself,
16 Aha, I am *w*, I have seen the fire:
47.14 there shall not be a coal to *w* at,
Hag 1. 6 clothe you, but there is none *w*;

WARMED

Job 31.20 he were not *w* with the fleece of
Mk 14.54 and *w* himself at the fire.
Jn 18.18 was cold: and they *w* themselves:
18 stood with them, and *w* himself.
25 Simon Peter stood and *w* himself.
Jas 2.16 in peace, be ye *w* and filled;

WARMETH

Job 39.14 the earth, and *w* them in dust,
Isa 44.16 yea, he *w* himself, and saith, Aha,

WARMING

Mk 14.67 when she saw Peter *w* himself,

WARN

2Ch 19.10 *w* them that they trespass not
Eze 3.18 nor speakest to *w* the wicked
19 Yet if thou *w* the wicked, and he
21 if thou *w* the righteous man, that
33. 3 the trumpet, and *w* the people;
7 my mouth, and *w* them from me.
8 dost not speak to *w* the wicked
9 if thou *w* the wicked of his way to
Ac 20.31 I ceased not to *w* every one night
1Co 4.14 but as my beloved sons I *w* you.
1Th 5.14 *w* them that are unruly, comfort

WARNED

2Ki 6.10 of God told him and *w* him of,
Ps 19.11 by them is thy servant *w*: and in
Eze 3.21 shall surely live, because he is *w*;
33. 6 trumpet, and the people be not *w*;
Mt 2.12 being *w* of God in a dream that
22 being *w* of God in a dream, he
3. 7 *w* you to flee from the wrath to
Lk 3. 7 *w* you to flee from the wrath to
Ac 10.22 *w* from God by an holy angel to
Heb 11. 7 being *w* of God of things not seen

WARNING

Jer 6.10 whom shall I speak, and give *w*,
Eze 3.17 mouth, and give them *w* from me.

18 givest him not *w*, nor speakest
20 because thou hast not given him *w*,
33. 4 of the trumpet, and taketh not *w*;
5 of the trumpet, and took not *w*;
5 taketh *w* shall deliver his soul.
Col 1.28 *w* every man, and teaching every

WARRETH
2Ti 2. 4 No man that *w* entangleth himself

WARRING
Ro 7.23 *w* against the law of my mind,

WARRIOR
Isa 9. 5 battle of the *w* is with confused

WARS
Nu 21.14 in the book of the *w* of the Lord,
Jdg 3. 1 had not known all the *w* of Canaan;
2Sa 8.10 for Hadadezer had *w* with Toi.
1Ki 5. 3 the *w* which were about him on
1Ch 22. 8 abundantly, and hast made great *w*:
2Ch 12.15 there were *w* between Rehoboam
16. 9 henceforth thou shalt have *w*.
27. 7 the acts of Jotham, and all his *w*,
Ps 46. 9 maketh *w* to cease unto the end of
Mt 24. 6 shall hear of *w* and rumors of *w*:
Mk 13. 7 shall hear of *w* and rumors of *w*,
Lk 21. 9 ye shall hear of *w* and commotions,
Jas 4. 1 whence come *w* and fightings

WASH
Gen 18. 4 *w* your feet, and rest yourselves
24.32 water to *w* his feet, and the men's
Ex 2. 5 daughter of Pharaoh came...to *w*
Ru 3. 3 *W* thyself therefore, and anoint
2Ki 5.10 Go and *w* in Jordan seven times,
12 may I not *w* in them, and be clean?
13 he saith to thee, *W*, and be clean?
2Ch 4. 6 the sea was for the priests to *w* in.
Job 9.30 If I *w* myself with snow water, and
Ps 26. 6 I will *w* mine hands in innocency:
51. 2 *W* me throughly from mine
7 *w* me, and I shall be whiter than
Isa 1.16 *W* you, make you clean; put away
Jer 4.14 *w* thine heart from wickedness,
Mt 6.17 anoint thine head, and *w* thy face;
15. 2 *w* not their hands when they eat
Mk 7. 3 except they *w* their hands oft, eat
4 except they *w*, they eat not.
Lk 7.38 began to *w* his feet with tears,
Jn 9. 7 him, Go, *w* in the pool of Siloam,
11 Go to the pool of Siloam, and *w*:
13. 5 and began to *w* the disciples' feet,
6 him, Lord, dost thou *w* my feet?
8 him, Thou shalt never *w* my feet.
8 If I *w* thee not, thou hast no part
10 needeth not save to *w* his feet,
14 also ought to *w* one another's feet.
Ac 22.16 be baptized, and *w* away thy sins,
(See illustration on page 786)

WASHED
Gen 43.24 water, and they *w* their feet;
31 And he *w* his face, and went out,
49.11 he *w* his garments in wine, and
Ex 40.31 Aaron and his sons *w* their hands
2Sa 12.20 David arose from the earth, and *w*,
Job 29. 6 When I *w* my steps with butter,
Ps 73.13 and *w* my hands in innocency.
Isa 4. 4 Lord shall have *w* away the filth
Eze 16. 4 thou *w* in water to supple thee;
Mt 27.24 *w* his hands before the multitude,
Lk 7.44 she hath *w* my feet with tears,
11.38 he had not first *w* before dinner.
Jn 9. 7 and *w*, and came seeing.
11 I went and *w*, and I received sight.
15 mine eyes, and I *w*, and do see.
13.10 He that is *w* needeth not save to
12 So after he had *w* their feet, and
14 and Master, have *w* your feet;
Ac 9.37 whom when they had *w*, they laid
16.33 of the night, and *w* their stripes;
1Co 6.11 but ye are *w*, but ye are sanctified,
1Ti 5.10 if she have *w* the saints' feet, if
Heb 10.22 and our bodies *w* with pure water.
2Pe 2.22 sow that was *w* to her wallowing
Rev 1. 5 *w* us from our sins in his own
7.14 and have *w* their robes, and made

WASHING
Mk 7. 4 received to hold, as the *w* of cups,
8 of men, as the *w* of pots and cups:
Lk 5. 2 of them, and were *w* their nets.
Eph 5.26 cleanse it with the *w* of water by
Tit 3. 5 by the *w* of regeneration, and

WASHINGS
Heb 9.10 in meats and drinks, and divers *w*,

WAST
Gen 3.11 Who told thee that thou *w* naked?
19 ground; for out of it *w* thou taken:
Dt 5.15 *w* a servant in the land of Egypt,
1Sa 15.17 When thou *w* little in thine own
Job 15. 7 or *w* thou made before the hills?
38. 4 Where *w* thou when I laid the
Isa 43. 4 Since thou *w* precious in my sight,
Eze 16. 5 thou *w* cast out in the open field,
7 whereas thou *w* naked and bare.
28.15 from the day that thou *w* created,
Mt 26.69 Thou also *w* with Jesus of Galilee,
Mk 14.67 thou also *w* with Jesus of Nazareth.
Jn 1.48 when thou *w* under the fig tree,
9.34 Thou *w* altogether born in sins, and
21.18 When thou *w* young, thou girdedst
Rev 5. 9 for thou *w* slain, and hast redeemed
11.17 God Almighty, which art, and *w*,
16. 5 Lord, which art, and *w*, and shalt

WASTE
Lev 26.31 And I will make your cities *w*,
33 be desolate, and your cities *w*.
Nu 21.30 we have laid them *w* even unto
Dt 32.10 and in the *w* howling wilderness;
1Ki 17.14 The barrel of meal shall not *w*,
2Ki 19.25 to lay *w* fenced cities into ruinous
1Ch 17. 9 of wickedness *w* them any more,
Neh 2. 3 of my fathers' sepulchers, lieth *w*,
17 how Jerusalem lieth *w*, and the
Job 30. 3 in former time desolate and *w*.
38.27 satisfy the desolate and *w* ground;
Ps 79. 7 and laid *w* his dwelling place.
80.13 boar out of the wood doth *w* it,
Isa 5. 6 I will lay it *w*: it shall not be
17 *w* places of the fat ones shall
15. 1 in the night Ar of Moab is laid *w*,
1 the night Kir of Moab is laid *w*,
23. 1 for it is laid *w*, so that there is no
14 for your strength is laid *w*.
24. 1 and maketh it *w*, and turneth it
33. 8 The highways lie *w*, the
34.10 to generation it shall lie *w*;
37.18 Assyria have laid *w* all the nations,
26 be to lay *w* defensed cities into
42.15 I will make *w* mountains and
49.17 they that made thee *w* shall go
19 thy *w* and thy desolate places,
51. 3 he will comfort all her *w* places;
52. 9 ye *w* places of Jerusalem:
58.12 thee shall build the old *w* places:
61. 4 they shall repair the *w* cities, the
64.11 our pleasant things are laid *w*.
Jer 2.15 yelled, and they made his land *w*:
4. 7 and thy cities shall be laid *w*,
27.17 should this city be laid *w*?
46.19 Noph shall be *w* and desolate
49.13 a reproach, a *w*, and a curse;
50.21 *w* and utterly destroy after them,
Eze 5.14 Moreover I will make thee *w*,
6. 6 dwellingplaces...shall be laid *w*,
6 your altars may be laid *w* and
12.20 are inhabited shall be laid *w*,
19. 7 palaces, and he laid *w* their cities;
26. 2 be replenished, now she is laid *w*:
29. 9 of Egypt shall be desolate and *w*;
10 of Egypt utterly *w* and desolate,
12 among the cities that are laid *w*
30.12 I will make the land *w*, and all
35. 4 I will lay thy cities *w*, and thou
36.35 the *w* and desolate and ruined
38 so shall the *w* cities be filled with
38. 8 which have been always *w*:
Joel 1. 7 He hath laid my vine *w*, and
Am 7. 9 of Israel shall be laid *w*;

War was a recurrent scourge in biblical times; here Ahab defeats the Syrians (1Ki 20) in a Doré engraving.

Am 9.14 and they shall build the *w* cities,
Mic 5. 6 shall *w* the land of Assyria with
Na 2.10 She is empty, and void, and *w*:
3. 7 thee, and say, Nineveh is laid *w*:
Zep 3. 6 I made their streets *w*, that none
Hag 1. 4 houses, and this house lie *w*?
9 Because of mine house that is *w*,
Mal 1. 3 mountains and his inheritance *w*
Mt 26. 8 To what purpose is this *w*?
Mk 14. 4 Why was this *w* of the ointment

WASTED

Nu 14.33 carcasses be *w* in the wilderness.
24.22 the Kenite shall be *w*, until
Dt 2.14 the men of war were *w* out from
1Ki 17.16 And the barrel of meal *w* not,
1Ch 20. 1 *w* the country of the children of
Ps 137. 3 they that *w* us required of us
Isa 6.11 cities be *w* without inhabitant,
19. 5 the river shall be *w* and dried up.
60.12 those nations shall be utterly *w*.
Jer 44. 6 and they are *w* and desolate, as
Eze 30. 7 the midst of the cities that are *w*.
Joel 1.10 The field is *w*, the land mourneth;
10 land mourneth; for the corn is *w*:
Lk 15.13 there *w* his substance with riotous
16. 1 unto him that he had *w* his goods.
Gal 1.13 the church of God, and *w* it:

WASTER

Pr 18. 9 brother to him that is a great *w*.
Isa 54.16 I have created the *w* to destroy.

WASTES

Isa 61. 4 And they shall build the old *w*,
Jer 49.13 cities thereof shall be perpetual *w*.
Eze 33.24 those *w* of the land of Israel
27 they that are in the *w* shall fall by
36. 4 to the desolate *w*, and to the cities
10 and the *w* shall be builded:
33 cities, and the *w* shall be builded.

WASTETH

Job 14.10 But man dieth, and *w* away:
Ps 91. 6 destruction that *w* at noonday.
Pr 19.26 He that *w* his father, and

WATCH

Gen 31.49 the Lord *w* between me and thee,
Jdg 7.19 they had but newly set the *w*:
Job 7.12 that thou settest a *w* over me?
14.16 dost thou not *w* over my sin?
Ps 90. 4 it is past, and as a *w* in the night.
130. 6 than they that *w* for the morning:
141. 3 Set a *w*, O Lord, before my mouth;
Hab 2. 1 I will stand upon my *w*, and set
Mt 14.25 fourth *w* of the night Jesus went
24.42 *W* therefore: for ye know not
43 in what *w* the thief would come,
25.13 *W* therefore, for ye know neither
26.38 tarry ye here, and *w* with me.
40 could ye not *w* with me one hour?
41 *W* and pray, that ye enter not into
27.65 Ye have a *w*: go your way, make
66 sealing the stone, and setting a *w*.
28.11 some of the *w* came into the city,
Mk 6.48 about the fourth *w* of the night
13.33 Take ye heed, *w* and pray: for ye
34 and commanded the porter to *w*.
35 *W* ye therefore: for ye know not
37 I say unto you I say unto all, *W*.
14.34 unto death: tarry ye here, and *w*.
37 couldest not thou *w* one hour?
38 *W* ye and pray, lest ye enter into
Lk 2. 8 keeping *w* over their flock by
12.38 if he shall come in the second *w*,
38 or come in the third *w*, and find
21.36 *W* ye therefore, and pray always,
Ac 20.31 Therefore *w*, and remember, that
1Co 16.13 *W* ye, stand fast in the faith, quit
Col 4. 2 *w* in the same with thanksgiving;
1Th 5. 6 others; but let us *w* and be sober.
2Ti 4. 5 But *w* thou in all things, endure
Heb 13.17 they *w* for your souls, as they that
1Pe 4. 7 sober, and *w* unto prayer.
Rev 3. 3 If therefore thou shalt not *w*, I

WATCHED

Mt 24.43 he would have *w*, and would not
27.36 sitting down they *w* him there;
Mk 3. 2 they *w* him, whether he would
Lk 6. 7 the scribes and Pharisees *w* him,
12.39 he would have *w*, and not have
14. 1 the sabbath day, that they *w* him.
20.20 they *w* him, and sent forth spies,
Ac 9.24 they *w* the gates day and night to

WATCHER

Dan 4.13 a *w* and an holy one came down
23 the king saw a *w* and an holy one

WATCHERS

Jer 4.16 that *w* come from a far country,
Dan 4.17 matter is by the decree of the *w*,

WATCHES

Neh 7. 3 *w* of the inhabitants of Jerusalem,
12. 9 were over against them in the *w*.

The washing of Jesus' feet by the woman who was a sinner (Lk 7.36-50), depicted by the 15th-century Dutch artist Dirk Bouts.

Ps 63. 6 meditate on thee in the night *w*.
119.148 Mine eyes prevent the night *w*,
La 2.19 beginning of the *w* pour out thine

WATCHETH

Ps 37.32 The wicked *w* the righteous, and
Eze 7. 6 the end is come: it *w* for thee;
Rev 16.15 Blessed is he that *w*, and keepeth

WATCHFUL

Rev 3. 2 Be *w*, and strengthen the things

WATCHING

1Sa 4.13 sat upon a seat by the wayside *w*:
Pr 8.34 heareth me, *w* daily at my gates,
La 4.17 in our *w* we have watched for a
Mt 27.54 they that were with him, *w* Jesus,
Lk 12.37 lord when he cometh shall find *w*:
Eph 6.18 and *w* thereunto with all

WATCHINGS

2Co 6. 5 in tumults, in labors, in *w*, in
11.27 painfulness, in *w* often, in hunger

WATCHMAN

2Sa 18.25 And the *w* cried, and told the king.
26 and the *w* called unto the porter,
Ps 127. 1 city, the *w* waketh but in vain.
Isa 21.11, 11 *W*, what of the night?
12 The *w* said, The morning cometh,
Eze 33. 7 thee a *w* unto the house of Israel;

WATCHMAN'S

Eze 33. 6 blood will I require at the *w* hand.

WATCHMEN

Isa 56.10 His *w* are blind: they are all
Jer 6.17 I set *w* over you, saying, Hearken
Mic 7. 4 the day of thy *w* and thy visitation

WATCHTOWER

Isa 21. 5 the table, watch in the *w*, eat,
8 I stand continually upon the *w* in

WATER

Gen 2.10 went out of Eden to *w* the garden;
26.20 herdmen, saying, The *w* is ours:
49. 4 Unstable as *w*, thou shalt not excel;
Ex 7.21 not drink of the *w* of the river;
17. 2 said, Give us *w* that we may drink.
23.25 shall bless thy bread, and thy *w*;
Nu 20.10 we fetch you *w* out of this rock?
11 and the *w* came out abundantly,
13 This is the *w* of Meribah; because
Dt 2.28 and give me *w* for money, that I
8. 7 good land, a land of brooks and *w*,
11. 4 he made the *w* of the Red sea to
11 drinketh *w* of the rain of heaven:
29.11 wood unto the drawer of thy *w*:
Jos 2.10 dried up the *w* of the Red sea for
7. 5 people melted, and became as *w*.
Jdg 4.19 Give me,...a little *w* to drink;
5.25 He asked *w*, and she gave him
7. 5 Every one that lappeth of the *w*
2Sa 14.14 and are as *w* spilt on the ground,
1Ki 13.22 Eat no bread, and drink no *w*;
14.15 Israel, as a reed is shaken in the *w*,
18.33 Fill four barrels with *w*, and pour
35 he filled the trench also with *w*.
19. 6 coals, and a cruse of *w* at his head.
22.27 affliction and with *w* of affliction.
2Ki 3.11 poured *w* on the hands of Elijah.
20 and the country was filled with *w*.
22 and the sun shone upon the *w*,
1Ch 11.17 of the *w* of the well of Bethlehem,
Job 8.11 can the flag grow without *w*?
14. 9 through the scent of *w* it will bud,
15.16 which drinketh iniquity like *w*?
22. 7 not given *w* to the weary to drink,
34. 7 who drinketh up scorning like *w*?
Ps 1. 3 a tree planted by the rivers of *w*,
6. 6 I *w* my couch with my tears.
22.14 I am poured out like *w*, and all
42. 1 hart panteth after the *w* brooks.
63. 1 and thirsty land, where no *w* is;
65. 9 the river of God, which is full of *w*:
66.12 went through fire and through *w*:
72. 6 as showers that *w* the earth.
79. 3 Their blood have they shed like *w*
Pr 20. 5 the heart of man is like deep *w*;
25.21 he be thirsty, give him *w* to drink:
27.19 As in *w* face answereth to face, so
Ec 2. 6 I made me pools of *w*,
Isa 1.22 dross, thy wine mixed with *w*:
30 and as a garden that hath no *w*.
3. 1 bread, and the whole stay of *w*,
12. 3 draw *w* out of the wells of salvation.
16. 9 I will *w* thee with my tears, O
27. 3 I will *w* it every moment: lest
32. 2 as rivers of *w* in a dry place, as
35. 7 and the thirsty land springs of *w*:
41.17 When the poor and needy seek *w*,
18 make the wilderness a pool of *w*,
44. 3 pour *w* upon him that is thirsty,
58.11 like a spring of *w*, whose waters
Jer 2.13 broken cisterns, that can hold no *w*.
38. 6 in the dungeon there was no *w*,
La 3.48 eye runneth down with rivers of *w*
5. 4 We have drunken our *w* for money;
Eze 4.16 and they shall drink *w* by measure,
17 That they may want bread and *w*,
7.17 and all knees shall be weak as *w*.
17. 7 he might *w* it by the furrows of
21. 7 and all knees shall be weak as *w*:
32. 6 also *w* with thy blood the land
36.25 will I sprinkle clean *w* upon you,
Joel 3.18 and shall *w* the valley of Shittim.
Am 8.11 famine of bread, not a thirst for *w*,
Jon 3. 7 let them not feed, nor drink *w*:
Mt 3.11 I indeed baptize you with *w* unto
16 went up straightway out of the *w*:
10.42 these little ones a cup of cold *w*
14.28 bid me come unto thee on the *w*.
29 he walked on the *w*, to go to Jesus.
17.15 into the fire, and oft into the *w*.
27.24 he took *w*, and washed his hands
Mk 1. 8 I indeed have baptized you with *w*:
10 coming up out of the *w*, he saw
9.41 you a cup of *w* to drink in my name,
14.13 you a man bearing a pitcher of *w*:
Lk 3.16 all, I indeed baptize you with *w*;
7.44 thou gavest me no *w* for my feet:
8.23 they were filled with *w*, and were in
24 wind and the raging of the *w*:
25 commandeth even the winds and *w*,
16.24 may dip the tip of his finger in *w*,
22.10 meet you, bearing a pitcher of *w*;
Jn 1.26 them, saying, I baptize with *w*:
31 am I come baptizing with *w*.
33 he that sent me to baptize with *w*,
2. 7 them, Fill the waterpots with *w*.
9 tasted the *w* that was made wine,
9 servants which drew the *w* knew;)
3. 5 Except a man be born of *w* and of
23 because there was much *w* there:
4. 7 a woman of Samaria to draw *w*:
10 he would have given thee living *w*.
11 then hast thou that living *w*?
13 Whosoever drinketh of this *w* shall
14 whosoever drinketh of the *w* that I
14 *w* that I shall give him shall be in
14 him a well of *w* springing up into
15 Sir, give me this *w*, that I thirst
46 Galilee, where he made the *w* wine.
5. 3 waiting for the moving of the *w*.
4 into the pool, and troubled the *w*:
4 first after the troubling of the *w*
7 when the *w* is troubled, to put me
7.38 belly shall flow rivers of living *w*.
13. 5 that he poureth *w* into a bason,
19.34 came there out blood and *w*.
Ac 1. 5 For John truly baptized with *w*;
8.36 way, they came unto a certain *w*:
36 See, here is *w*; what doth hinder
38 they went down both into the *w*.
39 they were come up out of the *w*,
10.47 Can any man forbid *w*, that these
11.16 said, John indeed baptized with *w*;
Eph 5.26 the washing of *w* by the word,
1Ti 5.23 Drink no longer *w*, but use a little
Heb 9.19 of calves and of goats, with *w*, and
10.22 our bodies washed with pure *w*.
Jas 3.11 at the same place sweet *w* and bitter?
12 both yield salt *w* and fresh.
1Pe 3.20 is, eight souls were saved by *w*.
2Pe 2.17 These are wells without *w*, clouds
3. 5 standing out of the *w* and in the *w*:
6 being overflowed with *w*, perished:
1Jn 5. 6 is he that came by *w* and blood,
6 not by *w* only, but by *w* and blood.
8 earth, the spirit, and the *w*, and
Jude 12 clouds they are without *w*, carried
Rev 12.15 out of his mouth *w* as a flood
16.12 and the *w* thereof was dried up,
21. 6 the fountain of the *w* of life freely.
22. 1 shewed me a pure river of *w* of life,
17 will, let him take the *w* of life freely.

WATERED

Gen 2. 6 *w* the whole face of the ground.
13.10 that it was well *w* everywhere,
29. 2 out of that well they *w* the flocks:
3 the well's mouth, and *w* the sheep,
10 *w* the flock of Laban his mother's
Ex 2.17 helped them, and *w* their flock.
19 enough for us, and *w* the flock.
Pr 11.25 watereth shall be *w* also himself.
Isa 58.11 and thou shalt be like a *w* garden,
Jer 31.12 their soul shall be as a *w* garden;
1Co 3. 6 I have planted, Apollos *w*; but

WATEREST

Ps 65. 9 Thou visitest the earth, and *w* it:
10 Thou *w* the ridges thereof

WATERETH

Ps 104.13 He *w* the hills from his chambers:
Pr 11.25 he that *w* shall be watered also
Isa 55.10 *w* the earth, and maketh it bring
1Co 3. 7 any thing, neither he that *w*;
8 planteth and he that *w* are one:

WATERING

Gen 30.38 in the gutters in the *w* troughs
Job 37.11 by *w* he wearieth the thick cloud:
Lk 13.15 stall, and lead him away to *w*?

WATERPOT

Jn 4.28 The woman then left her *w*, and

WATERPOTS

Jn 2. 6 were set there six *w* of stone,
7 unto them, Fill the *w* with water.

WATERS

Gen 1. 2 moved upon the face of the *w*.
6 firmament in the midst of the *w*,
6 and let it divide the *w* from the *w*.
10 together of the *w* called he Seas:
20 Let the *w* bring forth abundantly
6.17 bring a flood of *w* upon the earth,
7. 7 ark, because of the *w* of the flood.
18 *w* prevailed, and were increased
18 ark went upon the face of the *w*.
8. 1 the earth, and the *w* asswaged;
11 Noah knew that the *w* were abated
Ex 14.21 dry land, and the *w* were divided.
15.10 they sank as lead in the mighty *w*.
23 could not drink of the *w* of Marah,
25 the *w* were made sweet:
Jos 4. 7 the *w* of Jordan were cut off before
23 God dried up the *w* of Jordan from

2Ki 2. 8 smote the *w*, and they were divided
19.24 have digged and drunk strange *w*,
Neh 9.11 as a stone into the mighty *w*.
Job 14.19 The *w* wear the stones: thou
22.11 and abundance of *w* cover thee.
26. 8 He bindeth up the *w* in his thick
27.20 Terrors take hold on him as *w*,
38.30 The *w* are hid as with a stone,
Ps 18.16 me, he drew me out of many *w*.
23. 2 he leadeth me beside the still *w*.
29. 3 voice of the Lord is upon the *w*:
33. 7 He gathereth the *w* of the sea
46. 3 Though the *w* thereof roar and be
69. 1 the *w* are come in unto my soul.
73.10 and *w* of a full cup are wrung out
77.16 *w* saw thee, O God, the *w* saw thee;
78.16 caused *w* to run down like rivers.
93. 4 mightier than the noise of many *w*,
105.29 He turned their *w* into blood, and
41 the rock, and the *w* gushed out;
107.23 ships, that do business in great *w*;
124. 4 Then the *w* had overwhelmed us,
5 proud *w* had gone over our soul.
148. 4 ye *w* that be above the heavens.
Pr 5.15 Drink *w* out of thine own cistern,
9.17 Stolen *w* are sweet, and bread
25.25 As cold *w* to a thirsty soul, so is
30. 4 hath bound the *w* in a garment?
Ec 11. 1 Cast thy bread upon the *w*: for
SS 4.15 a well of living *w*, and streams
8. 7 Many *w* cannot quench love,
Isa 8. 6 the *w* of Shiloah that go softly,
11. 9 the Lord, as the *w* cover the sea.
17.12 like the rushing of mighty *w*!
19. 5 And the *w* shall fail from the sea,
28.17 *w* shall overflow the hiding place.
32.20 Blessed...ye that sow beside all *w*,
33.16 be given him; his *w* shall be sure.
35. 6 the wilderness shall *w* break out,
40.12 measured the *w* in the hollow of
43. 2 When thou passest through the *w*,
16 sea, and a path in the mighty *w*;
20 because I give *w* in the wilderness,
55. 1 that thirsteth, come ye to the *w*,
57.20 whose *w* cast up mire and dirt.
Jer 2.13 forsaken...the fountain of living *w*,
9. 1 Oh that my head were *w*, and mine
10.13 is a multitude of *w* in the heavens,
14. 3 have sent their little ones to the *w*:
17. 8 shall be as a tree planted by the *w*,
13 the Lord, the fountain of living *w*.
47. 2 *w* rise up out of the north, and
51.13 O thou that dwellest upon many *w*,
La 3.54 *W* flowed over mine head; then I
Eze 26.19 thee, and great *w* shall cover thee;
31. 4 The *w* made him great, the deep
32. 2 troubledst the *w* with thy feet, and
47. 1 *w* issued out from under the
Am 5.24 But let judgment run down as *w*,
Jon 2. 5 The *w* compassed me about, even
Mic 1. 4 as the *w* that are poured down a
Hab 2.14 of the Lord, as the *w* cover the sea.
Mt 8.32 the sea, and perished in the *w*.
Mk 9.22 him into the fire, and into the *w*,
2Co 11.26 in perils of *w*, in perils of robbers,
Rev 1.15 his voice as the sound of many *w*.
7.17 them unto living fountains of *w*:
8.10 and upon the fountains of *w*;
11 and the third part of the *w* became
11 and many men died of the *w*,
11. 6 have power over *w* to turn them to
14. 2 heaven, as the voice of many *w*.
7 the sea, and the fountains of *w*.
16. 4 upon...rivers and fountains of *w*;
5 I heard the angel of the *w* say,
17. 1 whore that sitteth upon many *w*:
15 The *w* which thou sawest, where
19. 6 and as the voice of many *w*,

WATERSPOUTS

Ps 42. 7 unto deep at the noise of thy *w*:

WATERSPRINGS

Ps 107.33 and the *w* into dry ground;
35 and dry ground into *w*.

WAVE

Jas 1. 6 is like a *w* of the sea driven with

WAVERETH

Jas 1. 6 he that *w* is like a wave of the sea

WAVERING

Heb 10.23 profession of our faith without *w*;
Jas 1. 6 let him ask in faith, nothing *w*.

WAVES

2Sa 22. 5 the *w* of death compassed me,
Job 9. 8 treadeth upon the *w* of the sea.
38.11 here shall thy proud *w* be stayed?
Ps 42. 7 all thy *w* and thy billows are gone
65. 7 of the seas, the noise of their *w*,
88. 7 hast afflicted me with all thy *w*.
89. 9 when the *w* thereof arise, thou
93. 3 voice; the floods lift up their *w*.
4 yea, than the mighty *w* of the sea.
107.25 which lifteth up the *w* thereof.
29 so that the *w* thereof are still.
Isa 48.18 righteousness as the *w* of the sea:
51.15 divided the sea, whose *w* roared:
Jer 5.22 the *w* thereof toss themselves, yet
31.35 the sea when the *w* thereof roar;
51.42 with the multitude of the *w*
55 her *w* do roar like great waters,
Eze 26. 3 the sea causeth his *w* to come up.
Jon 2. 3 billows and thy *w* passed over me.
Zec 10.11 and shall smite the *w* in the sea,
Mt 8.24 the ship was covered with the *w*:
14.24 midst of the sea, tossed with *w*:
Mk 4.37 the *w* beat into the ship, so that it
Lk 21.25 the sea and the *w* roaring;
Ac 27.41 broken with the violence of the *w*.
Jude 13 Raging *w* of the sea, foaming out

WAX

Ex 22.24 And my wrath shall *w* hot, and I
32.10 that my wrath may *w* hot against
11 why doth thy wrath *w* hot against
22 not the anger of my lord *w* hot:
Lev 25.47 if a sojourner or stranger *w* rich
47 that dwelleth by him *w* poor,
1Sa 3. 2 his eyes began to *w* dim, that he
Job 6.17 What time they *w* warm, they
14. 8 Though the root thereof *w* old in
Ps 22.14 my heart is like *w*; it is melted in
68. 2 as *w* melteth before the fire, so let
97. 5 The hills melted like *w* at the
102.26 them shall *w* old like a garment;
Isa 17. 4 the fatness of his flesh shall *w* lean.
29.22 neither shall his face now *w* pale.
50. 9 they all shall *w* old as a garment;
51. 6 earth shall *w* old like a garment,
Jer 6.24 our hands *w* feeble: anguish hath
Mic 1. 4 shall be cleft, as *w* before the fire,
Mt 24.12 the love of many shall *w* cold.
Lk 12.33 yourselves bags which *w* not old,
1Ti 5.11 to *w* wanton against Christ,
2Ti 3.13 and seducers shall *w* worse and
Heb 1.11 all shall *w* old as doth a garment;

WAXED

Gen 18.12 After I am *w* old shall I have
41.56 the famine *w* sore in the land of
Ex 32.19 Moses' anger *w* hot, and he cast
Nu 11.23 Is the Lord's hand *w* short? thou
Dt 8. 4 Thy raiment *w* not old upon thee,
32.15 But Jeshurun *w* fat, and kicked:
Mt 13.15 For this people's heart is *w* gross,
Lk 1.80 child grew, and *w* strong in spirit,
2.40 child grew, and *w* strong in spirit,
13.19 and it grew, and *w* a great tree;
Ac 13.46 Then Paul and Barnabas *w* bold,
28.27 the heart of this people is *w* gross,
Heb 11.34 made strong, *w* valiant in fight,
Rev 18. 3 merchants of the earth are *w* rich

WAXETH

Ps 6. 7 it *w* old because of all mine
Heb 8.13 and *w* old is ready to vanish

WAXING

Php 1.14 *w* confident by my bonds, are

WAY

Gen 3.24 sword which turned every *w*,
24 to keep the *w* of the tree of life.
18.16 them to bring them on the *w*.
19 they shall keep the *w* of the Lord,
33 And the Lord went his *w*, as soon
24.27 I being in the *w*, the Lord led me
42 thou do prosper my *w* which I go:
Ex 2.12 he looked this *w* and that *w*,
30.18 *w* of the wilderness of the Red sea:
21 of a cloud, to lead them the *w*;
18. 8 had come upon them by the *w*,
20 the *w* wherein they must walk,
33. 3 lest I consume thee in the *w*.
13 shew me now thy *w*, that I may
Nu 13.17 Get you up this *w* southward, and
20.17 we will go by the king's high *w*,
22.22 stood in the *w* for an adversary
23 angel of the Lord standing in the *w*,
23 the ass turned aside out of the *w*,
Dt 1. 2 Horeb by the *w* of mount Seir
8. 2 *w* which the Lord thy God led thee
11.19 when thou walkest by the *w*, when
30 the *w* where the sun goeth down,
Jos 1. 8 thou shalt make thy *w* prosperous,
23.14 I am going the *w* of all the earth:
Jdg 2.17 *w* which their fathers walked in,
22 they will keep the *w* of the Lord
18. 5 *w* which we go shall be prosperous.
6 the Lord is your *w* wherein ye go.
1Sa 1.18 woman went her *w*, and did eat,
9. 6 shew us our *w* that we should go.
8 to the man of God, to tell us our *w*.
2Sa 2.24 the *w* of the wilderness of Gibeon.
22.31 As for God, his *w* is perfect;
33 and he maketh my *w* perfect.
1Ki 1.49 rose up, and went every man his *w*.
22.24 Which *w* went the Spirit of
Neh 9.12 to give them light in the *w* wherein
19 them by day, to lead them in the *w*;
Job 3.23 given to a man whose *w* is hid,
8.19 Behold, this is the joy of his *w*,
12.24 a wilderness where there is no *w*.
16.22 go the *w* whence I shall not return.
17. 9 righteous...shall hold on his *w*,
18.10 and a trap for him in the *w*.
19. 8 He hath fenced up my *w* that I
23.10 he knoweth the *w* that I take:
36.23 Who hath enjoined him his *w*?
Ps 1. 1 nor standeth in the *w* of sinners,
6 knoweth the *w* of the righteous:
6 the *w* of the ungodly shall perish.
18.30 As for God, his *w* is perfect:
25. 8 will he teach sinners in the *w*.
27.11 Teach me thy *w*, O Lord, and lead
37. 5 Commit thy *w* unto the Lord;
7 of him who prospereth in his *w*,
34 Wait on the Lord, and keep his *w*,
67. 2 thy *w* may be known upon earth,
80.12 they which pass by the *w* do pluck
86.11 Teach me thy *w*, O Lord; I will
119. 1 Blessed are the undefiled in the *w*,
9 shall a young man cleanse his *w*?
29 Remove from me the *w* of lying:
30 I have chosen the *w* of truth: thy
33 Teach me,...the *w* of thy statutes;
101 my feet from every evil *w*,
139.24 if there be any wicked *w* in me,
24 and lead me in the *w* everlasting.
143. 8 cause me to know the *w* wherein
Pr 1.15 walk not thou in the *w* with them;

3.23 shalt thou walk in thy *w* safely,
4.11 taught thee in the *w* of wisdom;
14 go not in the *w* of evil men.
19 *w* of the wicked is as darkness:
7. 8 and he went the *w* to her house,
27 Her house is the *w* to hell, going
10.17 He is in the *w* of life that keepeth
29 The *w* of the Lord is strength to
12.15 The *w* of a fool is right in his own
28 In the *w* of righteousness is life;
13. 6 him that is upright in the *w*:
15 but the *w* of transgressors is hard.
15. 9 *w* of the wicked is an abomination
19 The *w* of the slothful man is
19 the *w* of the righteous man is
24 The *w* of life is above to the wise,
20.14 but when he is gone his *w*, then he
24 man then understand his own *w*?
22. 5 snares are in the *w* of the froward:
6 Train up a child in the *w* he should
26.13 man saith, There is a lion in the *w*;
30.19 The *w* of an eagle in the air; the
19 *w* of a serpent upon a rock; the
19 *w* of a ship in the midst of the sea;
19 and the *w* of a man with a maid.
Ec 9. 7 Go thy *w*, eat thy bread with joy,
10. 3 he that is a fool walketh by the *w*,
11. 5 not what is the *w* of the spirit,
Isa 3.12 err, and destroy the *w* of thy paths.
28. 7 strong drink are out of the *w*;
30.11 Get you out of the *w*, turn
21 This is the *w*, walk ye in it,
35. 8 an highway shall be there, and a *w*,
8 shall be called The *w* of holiness;
40. 3 Prepare ye the *w* of the Lord,
27 My *w* is hid from the Lord, and my
43.16 which maketh a *w* in the sea, and
51.10 a *w* for the ransomed to pass over?
53. 6 turned every one to his own *w*;
55. 7 Let the wicked forsake his *w*, and
59. 8 The *w* of peace they knew not; and
Jer 2.17 God, when he led thee by the *w*?
33 trimmest thou thy *w* to seek love?
5. 4 they know not the *w* of the Lord,
10. 2 Learn not the *w* of the heathen,
23 that the *w* of man is not in himself:
12. 1 doth the *w* of the wicked prosper?
21. 8 the *w* of life, and the *w* of death.
26. 3 turn every man from his evil *w*,
Eze 3.18 the wicked from his wicked *w*,
18.25 say, The *w* of the Lord is not equal.
25 Is not my *w* equal? are not your
29 The *w* of the Lord is not equal.
21.16 Go thee one *w* or other, either on
21 stood at the parting of the *w*,
33. 8 to warn the wicked from his *w*,
Hos 2. 6 I will hedge up thy *w* with thorns,
13. 7 as a leopard by the *w* will I observe
Am 2. 7 and turn aside the *w* of the meek:
Jon 3. 8 turn every one from his evil *w*,
Na 1. 3 Lord hath his *w* in the whirlwind
Mal 2. 8 But ye are departed out of the *w*;
Mt 2.12 into their own country another *w*.
3. 3 Prepare ye the *w* of the Lord,
7.13 and broad is the *w*, that leadeth to
14 and narrow is the *w*, which leadeth
10. 5 Go not into the *w* of the Gentiles,
11.10 shall prepare thy *w* before thee.
13. 4 some seeds fell by the *w* side,
20. 4 will give you. And they went their *w*.
14 Take that thine is, and go thy *w*:
21. 8 spread their garments in the *w*;
19 when he saw a fig tree in the *w*,
32 came...in the *w* of righteousness,
22.16 and teachest the *w* of God in truth,
27.65 go your *w*, make it as sure as ye can.
Mk 1. 2 shall prepare thy *w* before thee.
3 Prepare ye the *w* of the Lord,
4. 4 he sowed, some fell by the *w* side,
9.33 it that ye disputed...by the *w*?
10.17 when he was gone forth into the *w*,
21 go thy *w*, sell whatsoever thou hast,
32 in the *w* going up to Jerusalem;
52 Go thy *w*; thy faith hath made thee
11. 2 Go your *w* into the village over
4 they went their *w*, and found the colt
8 spread their garments in the *w*:
8 trees, and strawed them in the *w*.
12.12 and they left him, and went their *w*.
14 teachest the *w* of God in truth:
16. 7 But go your *w*, tell his disciples and
Lk 1.79 guide our feet into the *w* of peace.
3. 4 Prepare ye the *w* of the Lord,
5.19 find by what *w* they might bring him
7.22 Go your *w*, and tell John what things
27 shall prepare thy *w* before thee.
8. 5 he sowed, some fell by the *w* side;
10. 4 and salute no man by the *w*.
17.19 Arise, go thy *w*: thy faith hath made
19. 4 to see him: for he was to pass that *w*.
36 they spread their clothes in the *w*.
Jn 1.23 Make straight the *w* of the Lord,
4.28 and went her *w* into the city,
50 unto him, Go thy *w*; thy son liveth.
8.21 I go my *w*, and ye shall seek me,
9. 7 went his *w* therefore, and washed,
10. 1 but climbeth up some other *w*,
14. 4 I go ye know, and the *w* ye know.
5 and how can we know the *w*?
6 I am the *w*, the truth, and the life:
16. 5 now I go my *w* to him that sent me;
18. 8 ye seek me, let these go their *w*:
Ac 8.26 *w* that goeth...from Jerusalem
39 and he went on his *w* rejoicing.
9. 2 that if he found any of this *w*,
15 Go thy *w*: for he is a chosen
27 how he had seen the Lord in the *w*,
16.17 shew unto us the *w* of salvation.
18.25 instructed in the *w* of the Lord;
26 him the *w* of God more perfectly.
24.14 after the *w* which they call heresy,
25 answered, Go thy *w* for this time;
26.13 I saw in the *w* a light from heaven,
Ro 3. 2 Much every *w*: chiefly, because
17 *w* of peace have they not known:
1Co 10.13 temptation...make a *w* to escape,
12.31 I unto you a more excellent *w*.
Php 1.18 every *w*, whether in pretence, or
Col 2.14 took it out of the *w*, nailing it to
1Th 3.11 Christ, direct our *w* unto you.
Heb 5. 2 on them that are out of the *w*;
9. 8 the *w* into the holiest of all was
10.20 By a new and living *w*, which he
Jas 1.24 beholdeth himself, and goeth his *w*,
5.20 the sinner from the error of his *w*
2Pe 2. 2 *w* of truth shall be evil spoken of.
3. 1 minds by *w* of remembrance:
Jude 11 they have gone in the *w* of Cain,
Rev 16.12 the *w* of the kings of the east

WAYFARING

Jdg 19.17 he saw a *w* man in the street of
2Sa 12. 4 the *w* man that was come unto him;
Isa 33. 8 lie waste, the *w* man ceaseth:
35. 8 the *w* men, though fools,
Jer 9. 2 a lodging place of *w* men;
14. 8 as a *w* men that turneth aside to

WAYS

Gen 19. 2 rise up early, and go on your *w*.
Dt 5.33 walk in all the *w* which the Lord
8. 6 to walk in his *w*, and to fear him.
28. 7 way, and flee before thee seven *w*.
29 thou shalt not prosper in thy *w*:
2Sa 22.22 For I have kept the *w* of the Lord,
2Ki 17.13 Turn ye from your evil *w*, and
2Ch 6.30 every man according unto all his *w*,
27. 6 prepared his *w* before the Lord
Job 4. 6 and the uprightness of thy *w*?
13.15 maintain mine own *w* before him.
22. 3 that thou makest thy *w* perfect?
28 the light shall shine upon thy *w*.
24.13 they know not the *w* thereof, nor
23 yet his eyes are upon their *w*.
31. 4 Doth not he see my *w*, and count
34.11 man to find according to his *w*.
21 his eyes are upon the *w* of man,
40.19 He is the chief of the *w* of God:
Ps 10. 5 His *w* are always grievous;
18.21 For I have kept the *w* of the Lord,
25. 4 Shew me thy *w*, O Lord; teach me
39. 1 I said, I will take heed to my *w*,
51.13 will I teach transgressors thy *w*;
81.13 and Israel had walked in my *w*!
84. 5 in whose heart are the *w* of them.
95.10 and they have not known my *w*:
103. 7 He made known his *w* unto Moses,
139. 3 and art acquainted with all my *w*.
145.17 The Lord is righteous in all his *w*,
Pr 1.19 the *w* of every one that is greedy of
2.13 to walk in the *w* of darkness;
3. 6 In all thy *w* acknowledge him,
17 Her *w* are *w* of pleasantness, and
5. 6 path of life, her *w* are moveable,
6. 6 consider her *w*, and be wise:
8.32 blessed are they that keep my *w*.
16. 2 All the *w* of a man are clean in his
7 When a man's *w* please the Lord,
25 the end thereof are the *w* of death.
17.23 to pervert the *w* of judgment.
Ec 11. 9 and walk in the *w* of thine heart,
SS 3. 2 in the broad *w* I will seek him
Isa 2. 3 and he will teach us of his *w*, and
42.24 for they would not walk in his *w*,
45.13 and I will direct all his *w*:
55. 8 neither are your *w* my *w*, saith
9 so are my *w* higher than your *w*,
58. 2 daily, and delight to know my *w*,
66. 3 they have chosen their own *w*, and
Jer 2.23 swift dromedary traversing her *w*;
6.16 Stand ye in the *w*, and see, and ask
7. 3 Amend your *w* and your doings,
12.16 diligently learn the *w* of my people,
16.17 For mine eyes are upon all their *w*:
23.12 as slippery *w* in the darkness:
La 1. 4 The *w* of Zion do mourn, because
11 He hath turned aside my *w*, and
40 Let us search and try our *w*, and
Eze 7. 3 will judge thee according to thy *w*,
18.23 that he should return from his *w*,
25 equal? are not your *w* unequal?
21.19 son of man, appoint thee two *w*,
Dan 4.37 are truth, and his *w* judgment:
Hos 4. 9 I will punish them for their *w*,
14. 9 for the *w* of the Lord are right, and
Joel 2. 7 shall march every one on his *w*,
Hab 3. 6 did bow: his *w* are everlasting.
Hag 1. 5, 7 Lord of hosts; Consider your *w*.
Mal 2. 9 as ye have not kept my *w*, but
Mt 8.33 fled, and went their *w* into the city,
22. 5 made light of it, and went their *w*,
Mk 11. 4 in a place where two *w* met;
Lk 1.76 face of the Lord to prepare his *w*;
3. 5 the rough *w* shall be made smooth;
10. 3 Go your *w*: behold, I send you forth
Jn 11.46 them went their *w* to the Pharisees,
Ac 2.28 made known to me the *w* of life;
14.16 all nations to walk in their own *w*.
Jas 1. 8 man is unstable in all his *w*.
11 the rich man fade away in his *w*.
Rev 15. 3 just and true are thy *w*, thou King

WAYSIDE

1Sa 4.13 Eli sat upon a seat by the *w*
Ps 140. 5 have spread a net by the *w*;

WEAK

Nu 13.18 whether they be strong or *w*,
Jdg 16. 7, 11 then shall I be *w*, and be as
17 I shall become *w*, and be like any
2Sa 3.39 And I am this day *w*, though
17. 2 while he is weary and *w* handed,
2Ch 15. 7 and let not your hands be *w*:

BIBLICAL THEMES

WEAKNESS AND STRENGTH

The Lord is my strength and song. Ex 15.2

[Delilah] made him sleep upon her knees; and she called for a man . . . to shave off the seven locks of his head; and she began to afflict him, and his strength went from him. Jdg 16.19

Samson called unto the Lord, and said, O Lord God, remember me, I pray thee, and strengthen me, I pray thee, only this once, O God. Jdg 16.28

The Lord is with you, while ye be with him; and if ye seek him, he will be found of you. . . . Be ye strong therefore, and let not your hands be weak: for your work shall be rewarded. 2Ch 15.2, 7

O our God . . . we have no might against this great company that cometh against us; neither know we what to do: but our eyes are upon thee. 2Ch 20.12

Behold . . . thou hast strengthened the weak hands. Thy words have upholden him that was falling, and thou hast strengthened the feeble knees. But now it is come upon thee, and thou faintest; it toucheth thee, and thou art troubled. Job 4.3-5

What is my strength, that I should hope? . . . Is my strength the strength of stones? or is my flesh of brass? Job 6.11-12

Out of the mouth of babes and sucklings hast thou ordained strength. Ps 8.2

Cast thy burden upon the Lord, and he shall sustain thee. Ps 55.22

The race is not to the swift, nor the battle to the strong. Ec 9.11

Thou hast been a strength to the poor, a strength to the needy in his distress, a refuge from the storm, a shadow from the heat. Isa 25.4

Strengthen ye the weak hands, and confirm the feeble knees. Say to them that are of a fearful heart, Be strong, fear not: behold, your God will come with vengeance . . . he will come and save you. Isa 35.3-4

The rain descended, and the floods came, and the winds blew, and beat upon that house; and it fell not: for it was founded upon a rock. Mt 7.25

The spirit indeed is willing, but the flesh is weak. Mt 26.41

He hath shewed strength with his arm; he hath scattered the proud in the imagination of their hearts. He hath put down the mighty from their seats, and exalted them of low degree. Lk 1.51-52

When we were yet without strength, in due time Christ died for the ungodly. Ro 5.6

We then that are strong ought to bear the infirmities of the weak, and not to please ourselves. Ro 15.1

The foolishness of God is wiser than men; and the weakness of God is stronger than men. . . . not many mighty, not many noble, are called: but God hath chosen the foolish things of the world to confound the wise; and God hath chosen the weak things of the world to confound the things which are mighty. 1Co 1.25-27

[The Lord] said unto me, My grace is sufficient for thee: for my strength is made perfect in weakness. . . . Therefore I take pleasure in infirmities, in reproaches, in necessities, in persecutions, in distresses for Christ's sake: for when I am weak, then am I strong. 2Co 12.9-10

Thou hast a little strength, and hast kept my word, and hast not denied my name. . . . Behold, I come quickly: hold that fast which thou hast, that no man take thy crown. Rev 3.8, 11

Job 4. 3 hast strengthened the *w* hands.
Ps 6. 2 upon me, O Lord; for I am *w*:
109.24 My knees are *w* through fasting;
Isa 14.10 Art thou also become *w* as we?
35. 3 Strengthen ye the *w* hands, and
Eze 7.17 all knees shall be *w* as water.
16.30 How *w* is thine heart, saith the
21. 7 all knees shall be *w* as water:
Joel 3.10 let the *w* say, I am strong.
Mt 26.41 is willing, but the flesh is *w*.
Mk 14.38 truly is ready, but the flesh is *w*.
Ac 20.35 ye ought to support the *w*,
Ro 4.19 being not *w* in faith, he considered
8. 3 in that it was *w* through the flesh,
14. 1 Him that is *w* in the faith receive
2 another, who is *w*, eateth herbs.
21 or is offended, or is made *w*.
15. 1 to bear the infirmities of the *w*,
1Co 1.27 chosen the *w* things of the world
4.10 we are *w*, but ye are strong;
8. 7 their conscience being *w* is defiled.
9 stumblingblock to them that are *w*.
10 the conscience of him which is *w*
11 shall the *w* brother perish,
12 and wound their *w* conscience,
9.22 To the *w* became I as *w*,
22 that I might gain the *w*: I am
11.30 many are *w* and sickly among you,
2Co 10.10 but his bodily presence is *w*, and
11.21 as though we had been *w*.
29 Who is *w*, and I am not *w*? who is
12.10 for when I am *w*, then am I strong.
13. 3 which to you-ward is not *w*, but is
4 For we also are *w* in him, but we
9 when we are *w*, and ye are strong:
Gal 4. 9 to the *w* and beggarly elements,
1Th 5.14 support the *w*, be patient toward

WEAKER

2Sa 3. 1 house of Saul waxed *w* and *w*.
1Pe 3. 7 the wife, as unto the *w* vessel,

WEAKNESS

1Co 1.25 *w* of God is stronger than men.
2. 3 I was with you in *w*, and in fear,
15.43 it is sown in *w*; it is raised in power:
2Co 12. 9 my strength is made perfect in *w*.
13. 4 though he was crucified through *w*,
Heb 7.18 for the *w* and unprofitableness
11.34 out of *w* were made strong,

WEALTH

Dt 8.17 mine hand hath gotten me this *w*.
2Ch 1.11 not asked riches, *w*, or honor,
Job 31.25 rejoiced because my *w* was great,
Ps 49. 6 They that trust in their *w*, and
10 perish, and leave their *w* to others.
112. 3 *W* and riches...be in his house:
Pr 10.15 rich man's *w* is his strong city:
13.11 *W* gotten by vanity shall be
22 the *w* of the sinner is laid up for
19. 4 *W* maketh many friends; but the
Ec 5.19 God hath given riches and *w*,
Ac 19.25 that by this craft we have our *w*.
1Co 10.24 his own, but every one another's *w*.

WEAPON

Nu 35.18 smite him with an hand *w* of
Dt 23.13 shalt have a paddle upon thy *w*;
2Ch 23.10 man having his *w* in his hand,
Neh 4.17 and with the other hand held a *w*.
Job 20.24 He shall flee from the iron *w*, and
Isa 54.17 No *w* that is formed against thee
Eze 9. 1 with his destroying *w* in his hand.
2 man a slaughter *w* in his hand;

WEAPONS

Gen 27. 3 therefore take, I pray thee, thy *w*,
Dt 1.41 girded on every man his *w* of war,
Jdg 18.11 six hundred men appointed with *w*
16 men appointed with their *w* of war,
17 that were appointed with *w* of war.
1Sa 21. 8 my sword nor my *w* with me,
2Sa 1.27 fallen, and the *w* of war perished!
2Ki 11. 8 every man with his *w* in his hand:
11 every man with his *w* in his hand,
2Ch 23. 7 every man with his *w* in his hand;
Ec 9.18 Wisdom is better than *w* of war:
Isa 13. 5 and the *w* of his indignation, to
Jer 21. 4 I will turn back the *w* of war that
22. 7 against thee, every one with his *w*:
50.25 forth the *w* of his indignation:
51.20 art my battle axe and *w* of war:
Eze 32.27 down to hell with their *w* of war:
39. 9 shall set on fire and burn the *w*,
10 for they shall burn the *w* with fire:
Jn 18. 3 with lanterns and torches and *w*.
2Co 10. 4 *w* of our warfare are not carnal,

WEAR

Ex 18.18 Thou wilt surely *w* away, both
Dt 22. 5 woman shall not *w* that which
11 not *w* a garment of divers sorts,
1Sa 2.28 incense, to *w* an ephod before me?
22.18 persons that did *w* a linen ephod.
Est 6. 8 brought which the king useth to *w*,
Job 14.19 The waters *w* the stones: thou

Isa 4. 1 bread, and *w* our own apparel:
Dan 7.25 *w* out the saints of the most High,
Zec 13. 4 *w* a rough garment to deceive:
Mt 11. 8 they that *w* soft clothing are in
Lk 9.12 when the day began to *w* away,

WEARETH
Jas 2. 3 to him that *w* the gay clothing,

WEARIED
Gen 19.11 *w* themselves to find the door.
Isa 43.23 offering, nor *w* thee with incense.
24 hast *w* me with thine iniquities.
47.13 Thou art *w* in the multitude of
57.10 *w* in the greatness of thy way:
Jer 4.31 soul is *w* because of murderers.
12. 5 and they have *w* thee, then how
5 thou trustedst, they *w* thee,
Eze 24.12 She hath *w* herself with lies, and
Mic 6. 3 wherein have I *w* thee? testify
Mal 2.17 *w* the Lord with your words.
17 ye say, Wherein have we *w* him?
Jn 4. 6 being *w* with his journey, sat
Heb 12. 3 ye be *w* and faint in your minds.

WEARINESS
Ec 12.12 much study is a *w* of the flesh.
Mal 1.13 said also, Behold, what a *w* is it!
2Co 11.27 In *w* and painfulness, in

WEARING
1Sa 14. 3 priest in Shiloh, *w* an ephod.
Jn 19. 5 Jesus forth, *w* the crown of thorns,
1Pe 3. 3 plaiting the hair, and of *w* of gold,

WEARY
Gen 27.46 I am *w* of my life because of the
2Sa 23.10 Philistines until his hand was *w*,
Job 3.17 and there the *w* be at rest.
10. 1 My soul is *w* of my life; I will
16. 7 But now he hath made me *w*:
22. 7 not given water to the *w* to drink,
Ps 6. 6 I am *w* with my groaning; all the
69. 3 I am *w* of my crying: my throat
Pr 3.11 neither be *w* of his correction:
25.17 lest he be *w* of thee, and so hate
Isa 5.27 None shall be *w* nor stumble
7.13 but will ye *w* my God also?
28.12 ye may cause the *w* to rest;
32. 2 shadow of a great rock in a *w* land.
40.28 earth, fainteth not, neither is *w*?
30 the youths shall faint and be *w*,
31 they shall run, and not be *w*; and
43.22 thou hast been *w* of me, O Israel.
46. 1 they are a burden to the *w* beast.
50. 4 word in season to him that is *w*:
Jer 6.11 the Lord; I am *w* with holding in:
15. 6 thee, I am *w* with repenting.
20. 9 I was *w* with forbearing, and I
31.25 For I have satiated the *w* soul,
Hab 2.13 the people shall *w* themselves for
Lk 18. 5 her continual coming she *w* me.
Gal 6. 9 And let us not be *w* in well doing:
2Th 3.13 brethren, be not *w* in well doing.

WEATHER
Job 37.22 Fair *w* cometh out of the north:
Pr 25.20 taketh away a garment in cold *w*,
Mt 16. 2 evening, ye say, It will be fair *w*:
3 morning, It will be foul *w* to day:

WEAVE
Isa 19. 9 and they that *w* networks, shall be
59. 5 eggs, and *w* the spider's web:

WEAVER
Ex 35.35 and in fine linen, and of the *w*,
Isa 38.12 I have cut off like a *w* my life: he

WEAVER'S
1Sa 17. 7 of his spear was like a *w* beam;
2Sa 21.19 of whose spear was like a *w* beam.

Biblical Themes

WEALTH AND POVERTY

When thou hast eaten and art full, then thou shalt bless the Lord thy God for the good land which he hath given thee. Dt 8.10

The poor shall never cease out of the land: therefore I command thee, saying, Thou shalt open thine hand wide unto thy brother, to thy poor, and to thy needy, in thy land. Dt 15.11

The Lord maketh poor, and maketh rich: he bringeth low, and lifteth up. He raiseth up the poor out of the dust . . . to set them among princes. 1Sa 2.7-8

The Lord sent Nathan unto David. And he . . . said unto him, There were two men in one city; the one rich, and the other poor. The rich man had exceeding many flocks and herds: but the poor man had nothing, save one little ewe lamb. . . . And there came a traveller unto the rich man, and he spared to take of his own flock and of his own herd . . . but took the poor man's lamb, and dressed it for the man that was come to him. And David's anger was greatly kindled. . . . And Nathan said to David, Thou art the man. 2Sa 12.1-5, 7

If I have made gold my hope . . . if I rejoiced because my wealth was great . . . this also were an iniquity to be punished . . . for I should have denied the God that is above. Job 31.24-25, 28

A little that a righteous man hath is better than the riches of many wicked. Ps 37.16

A good name is rather to be chosen than great riches. Pr 22.1

Give me neither poverty nor riches . . . lest I be full, and deny thee . . . or lest I be poor, and steal, and take the name of my God in vain. Pr 30.8-9

Ye have sown much, and bring in little; ye eat, but ye have not enough; ye drink, but ye are not filled with drink; ye clothe you, but there is none warm; and he that earneth wages earneth wages to put it into a bag with holes. Hag 1.6

Lay not up for yourselves treasures upon earth, where moth and rust doth corrupt, and where thieves break through and steal: but lay up for yourselves treasures in heaven . . . for where your treasure is, there will your heart be also. . . . Ye cannot serve God and mammon. Mt 6.19-21, 24

How hard is it for them that trust in riches to enter into the kingdom of God! it is easier for a camel to go through the eye of a needle, than for a rich man to enter into the kingdom of God. Mk 10.24-25

He hath put down the mighty from their seats, and exalted them of low degree. He hath filled the hungry with good things; and the rich he hath sent empty away. Lk 1.52-53

Blessed be ye poor: for yours is the kingdom of God. Blessed are ye that hunger now: for ye shall be filled. . . . But woe unto you that are rich! for ye have received your consolation. Woe unto you that are full! for ye shall hunger. Lk 6.20-21, 24-25

Though he was rich, yet for your sakes he became poor, that ye through his poverty might be rich. 2Co 8.9

We brought nothing into this world, and it is certain we can carry nothing out. And having food and raiment let us be therewith content. But they that will be rich fall into temptation and a snare. . . . For the love of money is the root of all evil. 1Ti 6.7-10

1Ch 11.23 hand was a spear like a *w* beam;
20. 5 spear staff was like a *w* beam.
Job 7. 6 days are swifter than a *w* shuttle,

WEB
Jdg 16.13 locks of my head with the *w*.
14 pin of the beam, and with the *w*.
Job 8.14 whose trust shall be a spider's *w*.
Isa 59. 5 eggs, and weave the spider's *w*:

WEBS
Isa 59. 6 *w* shall not become garments,

WEDDING
Mt 22. 3 them that were bidden to the *w*:
8 The *w* is ready, but they which
10 the *w* was furnished with guests.
11 which had not on a *w* garment:
12 in hither not having a *w* garment?
Lk 12.36 when he will return from the *w*;
14. 8 thou art bidden of any man to a *w*,

WEDLOCK
Eze 16.38 as women that break *w* and shed

WEEK
Gen 29.27 Fulfil her *w*, and we will give thee
28 Jacob did so, and fulfilled her *w*:
Dan 9.27 the covenant with many for one *w*:
27 and in the midst of the *w* he shall
Mt 28. 1 toward the first day of the *w*,
Mk 16. 2 the morning the first day of the *w*,
9 risen early the first day of the *w*,
Lk 18.12 I fast twice in the *w*, I give tithes

Lk 24. 1 Now upon the first day of the *w*,
Jn 20. 1 the first day of the *w* cometh Mary
19 being the first day of the *w*, when
Ac 20. 7 And upon the first day of the *w*,
1Co 16. 2 Upon the first day of the *w* let every

WEEKS

Ex 34.22 thou shalt observe the feast of *w*,
Lev 12. 5 then she shall be unclean two *w*,
Nu 28.26 after your *w* be out, ye shall have
Dt 16. 9 Seven *w* shalt thou number unto
9 begin to number the seven *w* from
10 keep the feast of *w* unto the Lord
16 in the feast of *w*, and in the feast
2Ch 8.13 in the feast of *w*, and in the feast
Jer 5.24 us the appointed *w* of the harvest.
Dan 9.24 Seventy *w* are determined upon
25 the Prince shall be seven *w*,
25 and threescore and two *w*: the
26 threescore and two *w* shall Messiah
10. 2 Daniel was mourning three full *w*.
3 till three whole *w* were fulfilled.

WEEP

Gen 23. 2 mourn for Sarah, and to *w* for her.
43.30 and he sought where to *w*; and he
Nu 11.10 people *w* throughout their families,
13 for they *w* unto me, saying, Give
1Sa 11. 5 What aileth the people that they *w*?
30. 4 until they had no more power to *w*.
2Sa 1.24 daughters of Israel, *w* over Saul,
12.21 thou didst fast and *w* for the child,
2Ch 34.27 rend thy clothes, and *w* before me;
Neh 8. 9 Lord your God; mourn not, nor *w*.
Job 27.15 death: and his widows shall not *w*.
30.25 Did not I *w* for him that was in
31 organ into the voice of them that *w*.
Ec 3. 4 A time to *w*, and a time to laugh;
Isa 15. 2 to Dibon, the high places, to *w*:
22. 4 I will *w* bitterly, labor not to
30.19 thou shalt *w* no more: he will be
33. 7 the ambassadors of peace shall *w*
Jer 9. 1 that I might *w* day and night for
13.17 my soul shall *w* in secret places for
17 and mine eye shall *w* sore, and
22.10 *W* ye not for the dead, neither
10 *w* sore for him that goeth away:
48.32 will *w* for thee with the weeping of
La 1.16 For these things I *w*; mine eye,
Eze 24.16 neither shalt thou mourn nor *w*,
23 ye shall not mourn nor *w*; but ye
27.31 shall *w* for thee with bitterness
Joel 1. 5 Awake, ye drunkards, and *w*; and
2.17 *w* between the porch and the altar,
Mic 1.10 ye it not at Gath, *w* ye not at all:
Zec 7. 3 Should I *w* in the fifth month,
Mk 5.39 Why make ye this ado, and *w*?
Lk 6.21 Blessed are ye that *w* now: for ye
25 now! for ye shall mourn and *w*.
7.13 on her, and said unto her, *W* not.
8.52 he said, *W* not; she is not dead,
23.28 Daughters of Jerusalem, *w* not for
28 but *w* for yourselves, and for your
Jn 11.31 She goeth unto the grave to *w*
16.20 you, That ye shall *w* and lament,
Ac 21.13 What mean ye to *w* and to break
Ro 12.15 rejoice, and *w* with them that *w*.
1Co 7.30 they that *w*, as though they wept
Jas 4. 9 Be afflicted, and mourn, and *w*:
5. 1 *w* and howl for your miseries that
Rev 5. 5 *W* not: behold, the Lion of the tribe
18.11 merchants of the earth shall *w*

WEEPEST

1Sa 1. 8 to her, Hannah, why *w* thou?
Jn 20.13, 15 unto her, Woman, why *w* thou?

WEEPETH

2Sa 19. 1 *w* and mourneth for Absalom.
2Ki 8.12 And Hazael said, Why *w* my lord?
Ps 126. 6 He that goeth forth and *w*, bearing
La 1. 2 She *w* sore in the night, and her

WEEPING

Nu 25. 6 were *w* before the door of the
Dt 34. 8 days of *w* and mourning for Moses
2Sa 3.16 husband went with her along *w*
15.30 they went up, *w* as they went up.
Ezr 3.13 the noise of the *w* of the people:
10. 1 *w* and casting himself down
Est 4. 3 and fasting, and *w*, and wailing;
Job 16.16 My face is foul with *w*, and on my
Ps 6. 8 Lord hath heard the voice of my *w*.
30. 5 *w* may endure for a night, but joy
102. 9 and mingled my drink with *w*,
Isa 15. 3 one shall howl, *w* abundantly.
5 Luhith with *w* shall they go it up;
16. 9 I will bewail with the *w* of Jazer
22.12 did the Lord God of hosts call to *w*,
65.19 voice of *w* shall be no more heard
Jer 3.21 *w* and supplications of the
9.10 will I take up a *w* and wailing,
31. 9 They shall come with *w*, and with
15 Ramah, lamentation, and bitter *w*;
15 Rahel *w* for her children refused
16 Refrain thy voice from *w*, and
41. 6 them, *w* all along as he went:
48. 5 Luhith continual *w* shall go up;
32 weep for thee with the *w* of Jazer:
50. 4 of Judah together, going and *w*:
Eze 8.14 there sat women *w* for Tammuz.
Joel 2.12 fasting, and with *w*, and with
Mal 2.13 with tears, with *w*, and with crying
Mt 2.18 lamentation, and *w*, and great
18 Rachel *w* for her children, and
8.12 shall be *w* and gnashing of teeth.
Lk 7.38 stood at his feet behind him *w*,
13.28 shall be *w* and gnashing of teeth,
Jn 11.33 When Jesus therefore saw her *w*,
33 Jews also *w* which came with her,
20.11 stood without at the sepulchre *w*:
Ac 9.39 and all the widows stood by him *w*,
Php 3.18 often, and now tell you even *w*,
Rev 18.15 fear of her torment, *w* and wailing,
19 *w* and wailing, saying, Alas, alas

WEIGH

1Ch 20. 2 and found it to *w* a talent of gold,
Ezr 8.29 ye *w* them before the chief of the
Ps 58. 2 ye *w* the violence of your hands
Isa 26. 7 dost *w* the path of the just.
46. 6 *w* silver in the balance, and hire
Eze 5. 1 then take thee balances to *w*, and

WEIGHED

1Sa 2. 3 and by him actions are *w*.
17. 7 spear's head *w* six hundred shekels
Job 6. 2 that my grief were throughly *w*,
31. 6 Let me be *w* in an even balance,
Isa 40.12 and *w* the mountains in scales,
Dan 5.27 Thou art *w* in the balances, and
Zec 11.12 they *w* for my price thirty pieces

WEIGHT

Job 28.25 To make the *w* for the winds; and
Pr 11. 1 Lord: but a just *w* is his delight.
16.11 A just *w* and balance are the
Eze 4.10 thou shalt eat shall be by *w*.
Jn 19.39 aloes, about an hundred pound *w*.
2Co 4.17 exceeding and eternal *w* of glory;
Heb 12. 1 let us lay aside every *w*, and the
Rev 16.21 every stone about the *w* of a talent:

WEIGHTIER

Mt 23.23 omitted the *w* matters of the law,

WEIGHTY

Pr 27. 3 A stone is heavy, and the sand *w*;
2Co 10.10 his letters, say they, are *w* and

WELL

Gen 4. 7 If thou doest *w*, shalt thou not be
7 if thou doest not *w*, sin lieth at the
12.13 it may be *w* with me for thy sake;
24.16 she went down to the *w*, and filled
29. 6 And he said unto them, Is he *w*?
6 And they said, He is *w*: and,
40.14 think on me when it shall be *w*
Ex 4.14 I know that he can speak *w*.
Nu 11.18 for it was *w* with us in Egypt:
21.17 Spring up, O *w*; sing ye unto it:
Dt 4.40 that it may go *w* with thee, and
Jdg 14. 3 for me; for she pleaseth me *w*.
Ru 3. 1 thee, that it may be *w* with thee?
1Sa 20. 7 If he say thus, It is *w*; thy servant
2Sa 23.15 the water of the *w* of Bethlehem,
2Ki 4.26 is it *w* with thy husband?
26 is it *w* with the child?
26 And she answered, It is *w*.
7. 9 said one to another, We do not *w*:
1Ch 11.17 the water of the *w* of Bethlehem,
2Ch 12.12 and also in Judah things went *w*.
Ps 49.18 when thou doest *w* to thyself.
78.29 So they did eat, and were *w* filled:
84. 6 the valley of Baca make it a *w*;
128. 2 be, and it shall be *w* with thee.
139.14 and that my soul knoweth right *w*.
Pr 5.15 running waters out of thine own *w*.
10.11 of a righteous man is a *w* of life:
11.10 When it goeth *w* with the
14.15 the prudent man looketh *w* to his
30.29 There be three things which go *w*,
Ec 8.12 be *w* with them that fear God,
SS 4.15 of gardens, a *w* of living waters,
Isa 1.17 Learn to do *w*; seek judgment,
3.10 that it shall be *w* with him:
Eze 33.32 and can play *w* on an instrument:
Jon 4. 4 Lord, Doest thou *w* to be angry?
9 thou *w* to be angry for the gourd?
Zec 8.15 I thought in these days to do *w*
Mt 3.17 Son, in whom I am *w* pleased.
12.12 is lawful to do *w* on the sabbath
18 in whom my soul is *w* pleased:
15. 7 *w* did Esaias prophesy of you,
17. 5 Son, in whom I am *w* pleased;
25.21 *W* done, thou good and faithful
23 him, *W* done, good and faithful
Mk 1.11 Son, in whom I am *w* pleased.
7. 6 *W* hath Esaias prophesied of
9 Full *w* ye reject the commandment
37 He hath done all things *w*:
12.28 that he had answered them *w*,
32 *W*, Master, thou hast said the
Lk 1. 7 were now *w* stricken in years.
18 and my wife *w* stricken in years.
3.22 Son; in thee I am *w* pleased.
6.26 all men shall speak *w* of you!
13. 9 And if it bear fruit, *w*; and if not,
19.17 unto him, *W*, thou good servant:
20.39 said, Master, thou hast *w* said.
Jn 2.10 and when men have *w* drunk,
4. 6 Now Jacob's *w* was there. Jesus
6 his journey, sat thus on the *w*:
11 to draw with, and the *w* is deep:
12 father Jacob, which gave us the *w*,
14 a *w* of water springing up into
17 Thou hast *w* said, I have no
8.48 Say we not *w* that thou art a
11.12 Lord, if he sleep, he shall do *w*.
13.13 Master and Lord: and ye say *w*;
18.23 but if *w*, why smitest thou me?
Ac 10.33 thou hast *w* done that thou art
47 the Holy Ghost as *w* as we?
15.29 ye shall do *w*. Fare ye *w*.
16. 2 was *w* reported of by the brethren
25.10 wrong, as thou very *w* knowest.
28.25 *W* spake the Holy Ghost by
Ro 2. 7 by patient continuance in *w* doing
11.20 *W*; because of unbelief they
1Co 7.37 he will keep his virgin, doeth *w*.
38 giveth her in marriage doeth *w*;
1Pe 2.14 for the praise of them that do *w*.
15 that with *w* doing ye may put to
20 when ye do *w*, and suffer for it, ye
3. 6 ye are, as long as ye do *w*, and

17 ye suffer for *w* doing, than for evil
2Pe 1.17 Son, in whom I am *w* pleased.
19 ye do *w* that ye take heed, as unto

WELLBELOVED
SS 1.13 A bundle of myrrh is my *w* unto
Isa 5. 1 Now will I sing to my *w* a song of
1 My *w* hath a vineyard in a very
Mk 12. 6 yet therefore one son, his *w*, he
Ro 16. 5 Salute my *w* Epaenetus, who is the
3Jn 1 The elder unto the *w* Gaius, whom

WELLPLEASING
Php 4.18 a sacrifice acceptable, *w* to God.
Heb 13.21 you that which is *w* in his sight,

WELLS
Gen 26.15 the *w* which his father's servants
18 Isaac digged again the *w* of water,
Ex 15.27 where were twelve *w* of water,
Nu 20.17 we drink of the water of the *w*:
Dt 6.11 *w* digged, which thou diggest not,
2Ki 3.19 and stop all *w* of water, and mar
25 they stopped all the *w* of water,
2Ch 26.10 the desert, and digged many *w*:
Neh 9.25 *w* digged, vineyards, and
Isa 12. 3 water out of the *w* of salvation.
2Pe 2.17 These are *w* without water,

WELLSPRING
Pr 16.22 Understanding is a *w* of life unto
18. 4 and the *w* of wisdom as a flowing

WENT
Gen 4.16 Cain *w* out from the presence of
7. 9 There *w* in two and two unto Noah
8.19 their kinds, *w* forth out of the ark.
22. 3 *w* unto the place of which God had
Ex 15.19 Israel *w* on dry land in the midst
19. 3 Moses *w* up unto God, and the
14 Moses *w* down from the mount
34. 4 and *w* up unto mount Sinai,
34 *w* in before the Lord to speak
Dt 1.31 in all the way that ye *w*, until ye
Jdg 2.17 they *w* a whoring after other gods,
4.18 Jael *w* out to meet Sisera, and said
16. 1 Then *w* Samson to Gaza, and
Ru 1.19 So they two *w* until they came to
21 I *w* out full, and the Lord hath
1Sa 3. 3 ere the lamp of God *w* out in the
9. 9 when a man *w* to inquire of God,
2Sa 16.13 and cursed as he *w*, and threw
18.33 as he *w*, thus he said, O my son
1Ki 19. 8 *w* in the strength of that meat
21 *w* after Elijah, and ministered
2Ki 2. 6 leave thee. And they two *w* on.
8 they two *w* over on dry ground.
11 Elijah *w* up by a whirlwind into
5.11 Naaman was wroth, and *w* away,
12 So he turned and *w* away in a rage.
26 *W* not mine heart with thee, when
Job 1.12 Satan *w* forth from the presence
Ps 42. 4 I *w* with them to the house of
73.17 Until I *w* into the sanctuary of
106.32 it *w* ill with Moses for their sakes:
Pr 24.30 I *w* by the field of the slothful,
Isa 8. 3 I *w* unto the prophetess; and she
Jer 13. 7 Then I *w* to Euphrates, and
18. 3 I *w* down to the potter's house,
Eze 3.14 I *w* in bitterness, in the heat of my
11.23 glory of the Lord *w* up from the
31.15 day when he *w* down to the grave
39.23 *w* into captivity for their iniquity:
Jon 2. 6 I *w* down to the bottoms of the
Mt 2. 9 saw in the east, *w* before them,
4.23 And Jesus *w* about all Galilee,
11. 8 what *w* ye out for to see? A man
14.23 he *w* up into a mountain apart to
19.22 that saying, he *w* away sorrowful:
21.12 Jesus *w* into the temple of God,
30 and said, I go, sir: and *w* not.
25.25 *w* and hid thy talent in the earth:
26.39 he *w* a little farther, and fell on
75 And he *w* out, and wept bitterly.
27. 5 and *w* and hanged himself.
58 He *w* to Pilate, and begged the
Mk 12. 1 and *w* into a far country.
Lk 1. 9 he *w* into the temple of the Lord.
2. 3 all *w* to be taxed, every one into
7.25, 26 But what *w* ye out for to see?
18.10 Two men *w* up into the temple to
22.39 *w*, as he was wont, to the mount
62 Peter *w* out, and wept bitterly.
Jn 8. 1 Jesus *w* unto the mount of Olives.
9 *w* out one by one, beginning at
9.11 I *w* and washed, and I received
13. 3 come from God, and *w* to God;
18.29 Pilate then *w* out unto them, and
20. 5 clothes lying; yet *w* he not in.
Ac 8.38 they *w* down both into the water,
39 and he *w* on his way rejoicing.
10.38 who *w* about doing good, and
26.12 as I *w* to Damascus with authority
28.14 days: and so we *w* toward Rome.
Ro 10.18 their sound *w* into all the earth,
Gal 1.17 but I *w* into Arabia, and returned
2. 2 And I *w* up by revelation, and
Heb 11. 8 obeyed; and he *w* out,
8 not knowing whither he *w*.
1Pe 3.19 he *w* and preached unto the
1Jn 2.19 They *w* out from us, but they were
19 they *w* out, that they might be made

WENTEST
Gen 49. 4 thou *w* up to thy father's bed;
Jdg 5. 4 Lord, when thou *w* out of Seir,
8. 1 when thou *w* to fight with the
1Sa 10. 2 asses which thou *w* to seek are
2Sa 7. 9 with thee whithersoever thou *w*,
16.17 why *w* thou not with thy friend?
19.25 Wherefore *w* not thou with me,
Ps 68. 7 thou *w* forth before thy people,
Isa 57. 7 even thither *w* thou up to offer
9 thou *w* to the king with ointment,
Jer 2. 2 thou *w* after me in the wilderness,
31.21 even the way which thou *w*:
Hab 3.13 Thou *w* forth for the salvation of
Ac 11. 3 Thou *w* in to men uncircumcised,

WEPT
Gen 21.16 and lift up her voice, and *w*.
27.38 Esau lifted up his voice, and *w*.
29.11 and lifted up his voice, and *w*.
33. 4 neck, and kissed him: and they *w*.
37.35 Thus his father *w* for him.
42.24 himself about from them, and *w*;
43.30 into his chamber, and *w* there.
45. 2 And he *w* aloud:
14 brother Benjamin's neck, and *w*;
14 and Benjamin *w* upon his neck.
15 his brethren, and *w* upon them:
46.29 and *w* on his neck a good while.
50. 1 and *w* upon him, and kissed him.
17 Joseph *w* when they spake unto
Ex 2. 6 child: and, behold, the babe *w*.
Nu 11. 4 children of Israel also *w* again,
18 ye have *w* in the ears of the Lord,
20 and have *w* before him, saying,
14. 1 cried; and the people *w* that night.
Dt 1.45 returned and *w* before the Lord;
34. 8 the children of Israel *w* for Moses
Jdg 2. 4 people lifted up their voice, and *w*.
14.16 And Samson's wife *w* before him,
17 she *w* before him the seven days,
20.23 and *w* before the Lord until even,
26 came unto the house of God, and *w*,
21. 2 lifted up their voices, and *w* sore;
Ru 1. 9 they lifted up their voice, and *w*.
14 lifted up their voice, and *w* again:
1Sa 1. 7 therefore she *w*, and did not eat.
10 prayed unto the Lord, and *w* sore.
11. 4 people lifted up their voices, and *w*.
20.41 *w* one with another, until David
24.16 Saul lifted up his voice, and *w*.
30. 4 him lifted up their voice and *w*,
2Sa 1.12 they mourned, and *w*, and fasted
3.32 and *w* at the grave of Abner;
32 of Abner; and all the people *w*.
34 all the people *w* again over him.
12.22 child was yet alive, I fasted and *w*:
13.36 and lifted up their voice and *w*:
36 and all his servants *w* very sore.
15.23 all the country *w* with a loud voice,
30 mount Olivet, and *w* as he went up,
18.33 the chamber over the gate, and *w*:
2Ki 8.11 ashamed: and the man of God *w*.
13.14 and *w* over his face, and said, O my
20. 3 thy sight. And Hezekiah *w* sore.
22.19 rent thy clothes, and *w* before me;
Ezr 3.12 their eyes, *w* with a loud voice;
10. 1 for the people *w* very sore.
Neh 1. 4 words, that I sat down and *w*,
8. 9 For all the people *w*, when they
Job 2.12 they lifted up their voice, and *w*;
Ps 69.10 When I *w*, and chastened my soul
137. 1 we *w*, when we remembered Zion.
Isa 38. 3 thy sight. And Hezekiah *w* sore.
Hos 12. 4 he *w*, and made supplication unto
Mt 26.75 And he went out, and *w* bitterly,
Mk 5.38 them that *w* and wailed greatly.
14.72 when he thought thereon, he *w*.
16.10 with him, as they mourned and *w*.
Lk 7.32 to you, and ye have not *w*.
8.52 all *w*, and bewailed her: but he
19.41 he beheld the city, and *w* over it,
22.62 Peter went out, and *w* bitterly.
Jn 11.35 Jesus *w*.
20.11 and as she *w*, she stooped down,
Ac 20.37 And they all *w* sore, and fell on
1Co 7.30 that weep, as though they *w* not;
Rev 5. 4 And I *w* much, because no man

WEST
Ps 103.12 As far as the east is from the *w*,
107. 3 from the east, and from the *w*,
Isa 43. 5 east, and gather thee from the *w*;
Mt 8.11 shall come from the east and *w*,
24.27 east, and shineth even unto the *w*;
Lk 12.54 ye see a cloud rise out of the *w*,
13.29 from the east, and from the *w*,
Ac 27.12 toward the south *w* and north
12 toward the south...and north *w*.
Rev 21.13 gates; and on the *w* three gates.

WET
Job 24. 8 They are *w* with the showers of
Dan 4.15, 23 be *w* with the dew of heaven,
25 *w* thee with the dew of heaven,
33 and his body was *w* with the dew
5.21 and his body was *w* with the dew

WHALE
Job 7.12 Am I a sea, or a *w*, that thou
Eze 32. 2 and thou art as a *w* in the seas:

WHALE'S
Mt 12.40 and three nights in the *w* belly;

WHALES
Gen 1.21 And God created great *w*, and

WHAT
Gen 3.13 *W* is this that thou hast done?
31.36 *W* is my trespass? *w* is my sin,
37.26 *W* profit is it if we slay our brother,
42.28 *W* is this that God hath done
Ex 3.13 shall say to me, *W* is his name?
12.26 you, *W* mean ye by this service?
16.15 manna: for they wist not *w* it was.
32. 1 we wot not *w* is become of him.
Nu 21.14 *W* he did in the Red sea, and in
Dt 7.18 remember *w* the Lord thy God
10.12 *w* doth the Lord thy God require

Jos 4. 6 *W* mean ye by these stones?
Jdg 14.18 down, *W* is sweeter than honey?
18 *w* is stronger than a lion? And he
2Sa 16.10 *W* have I to do with you, ye sons
1Ki 3. 5 God said, Ask *w* I shall give thee.
19. 9, 13 *W* doest thou here, Elijah?
2Ki 2. 9 Elisha, Ask *w* I shall do for thee.
8.14 to him, *W* said Elisha to thee?
9.18, 19 *W* hast thou to do with peace?
2Ch 10.16 *W* portion have we in David?
Job 6.17 *W* time they wax warm, they vanish:
25 *w* doth your arguing reprove?
7.17 *W* is man, that thou shouldest
21.15 *W* is the Almighty, that we
15 *w* profit should we have, if we pray
22.17 *w* can the Almighty do for them?
27. 8 *w* is the hope of the hypocrite,
31. 2 *w* portion of God is there from
14 *W* then shall I do when God
34. 4 know among ourselves *w* is good.
7 *W* man is like Job, who drinketh
35. 3 and, *W* profit shall I have, if I be
40. 4 I am vile; *w* shall I answer thee?
Ps 8. 4 *W* is man, that thou art mindful
34.12 *W* man is he that desireth life,
39. 7 Lord, *w* wait I for? my hope is in
56. 4 I will not fear *w* flesh can do
11 not be afraid *w* man can do unto
85. 8 hear *w* God the Lord will speak:
116.12 *W* shall I render unto the Lord
144. 3 Lord, *w* is man, that thou takest
Pr 27. 1 knowest not *w* a day may bring
Ec 1. 3 *W* profit hath a man of all his
2.22 For *w* hath man of all his labor,
6. 8 *w* hath the poor, that knoweth to
11 vanity, *w* is man the better?
12 who knoweth *w* is good for man in
12 can tell a man *w* shall be after him
10.14 a man cannot tell *w* shall be;
11. 5 not *w* is the way of the spirit,
Isa 1.11 To *w* purpose is the multitude of
5. 4 *W* could have been done more to
21.11 Seir, Watchman, *w* of the night?
40. 6 *W* shall I cry? All flesh is grass,
45. 9 fashioneth it, *W* makest thou?
10 unto his father, *W* begettest thou?
10 *W* hast thou brought forth?
Jer 23.28 *W* is the chaff to the wheat? saith
33 *W* is the burden of the Lord?
24. 3 *W* seest thou, Jeremiah? And I
La 2.13 *w* thing shall I liken to thee,
13 *w* shall I equal to thee, that I may
5. 1 O Lord, *w* is come upon us:
Eze 8. 6 Son of man, seest thou *w* they do?
19. 2 *W* is thy mother? A lioness: she
Am 4.13 unto man *w* is his thought, that
Jon 1. 6 him, *W* meanest thou, O sleeper?
8 *W* is thine occupation? and
8 comest thou? *w* is thy country?
11 *W* shall we do unto thee, that the
Mic 6. 1 Hear ye now *w* the Lord saith;
3 people, *w* have I done unto thee?
8 shewed thee, O man, *w* is good;
8 *w* doth the Lord require of thee,
Na 1. 9 *W* do ye imagine against the
Hab 2. 1 and *w* I shall answer when I am
Zec 4.11 *W* are these two olive trees upon
Mal 1.13 also, Behold, *w* a weariness is it!
3.14 *w* profit is it that we have kept
Mt 5.46 which love you, *w* reward have ye?
47 only, *w* do ye more than others?
6.31 saying, *W* shall we eat? or,
8.27 saying, *W* manner of man is this,
29 *W* have we to do with thee, Jesus,
10.19 that same hour *w* ye shall speak.
27 *W* I tell you in darkness, that
19. 6 *W* therefore God hath joined
20.15 me to do *w* I will with mine own?
22 and said, Ye know not *w* ye ask.
22.42 *W* think ye of Christ? whose son is
27. 4 *W* is that to us? see thou to that.
22 *W* shall I do then with Jesus
23 said, Why, *w* evil hath he done?
Mk 1.24 *w* have we to do with thee, thou
4.41 *W* manner of man is this, that
10. 9 *W* therefore God hath joined
13. 4 *w* shall be the sign when all these
14. 8 She hath done *w* she could: she is
36 not *w* I will, but *w* thou wilt.
Lk 3.10 him, saying, *W* shall we do then?
4.34 *w* have we to do with thee, thou
36 saying, *W* a word is this! for with
8.25 *W* manner of man is this!
10.25 *w* shall I do to inherit eternal life?
26 *W* is written in the law? how
23.22 Why, *w* evil hath he done? I have
34 them; for they know not *w* they do.
24.19 he said unto them, *W* things?
Jn 1.21 him, *W* then? Art thou Elias?
2. 4 Woman, *w* have I to do with thee?
4.22 Ye worship ye know not *w*: we
27 *W* seekest thou? or, Why talkest
18.35 thee unto me: *w* hast thou done?
38 Pilate saith unto him, *W* is truth?
19.22 *W* I have written I have written.
Ac 4. 7 By *w* power, or by *w* name,
10. 4 was afraid, and said, *W* is it, Lord?
15 *W* God hath cleansed, that call not
Heb 2. 6 *W* is man, that thou art mindful
11.32 *w* shall I more say? for the time
Jas 1.24 forgetteth *w* manner of man he
2.14 *W* doth it profit, my brethren,
4.14 For *w* is your life? It is even a

WHATSOEVER

Gen 8.19 and *w* creepeth upon the earth,
Ex 29.37 *w* toucheth the altar shall be holy.
Dt 2.37 *w* the Lord our God forbad us.
Ezr 7.23 *W* is commanded by the God
Job 41.11 *w* is under the whole heaven is mine.
Ps 1. 3 and *w* he doeth shall prosper.
Ec 8. 3 for he doeth *w* pleaseth him.
9.10 *W* thy hand findeth to do, do it
Mt 5.37 *w* is more than these cometh of evil.
7.12 *w* ye would that men should
14. 7 to give her *w* she would ask.
16.19 *w* thou shalt bind on earth
19 *w* thou shalt loose on earth shall
20. 4 and *w* is right I will give you.
21.22 *w* ye shall ask in prayer,
28.20 things *w* I have commanded you:
Mk 7.18 *w* thing from without entereth
Jn 2. 5 *W* he saith unto you, do it.
11.22 *w* thou wilt ask of God, God
14.13 *w* ye shall ask in my name,
15.14 friends, if ye do *w* I command
16.23 *W* ye shall ask the Father in
Ro 14.23 faith: for *w* is not of faith is sin.
15. 4 *w* things were written aforetime
1Co 10.27 *w* is set before you, eat, asking
31 *w* ye do, do all to the glory of God.
Gal 6. 7 *w* a man soweth, that shall he
Php 4. 8 brethren, *w* things are true,
Col 3.23 *w* ye do, do it heartily, as
1Jn 3.22 *w* we ask, we receive of him.
Rev 21.27 *w* worketh abomination, or maketh

WHEAT

Gen 30.14 went in the days of *w* harvest,
Ex 9.32 the *w* and the rie were not smitten
34.22 the firstfruits of *w* harvest, and the
Nu 18.12 best of the wine, and of the *w*,
Dt 8. 8 A land of *w*, and barley, and
32.14 with the fat of kidneys of *w*;
Jdg 6.11 his son Gideon threshed *w* by the
15. 1 after, in the time of *w* harvest,
Ru 2.23 barley harvest and of *w* harvest;
1Sa 6.13 were reaping their *w* harvest in
12.17 Is it not *w* harvest to day? I will
2Sa 4. 6 they would have fetched *w*;
17.28 vessels, and *w*, and barley, and
1Ki 5.11 twenty thousand measures of *w*
1Ch 21.20 Now Ornan was threshing *w*.
23 and the *w* for the meat offering;
2Ch 2.10 thousand measures of beaten *w*,
15 the *w*, and the barley, the oil, and
27. 5 and ten thousand measures of *w*,
Ezr 6. 9 *w*, salt, wine, and oil, according
7.22 and to an hundred measures of *w*,
Job 31.40 Let thistles grow instead of *w*,
Ps 81.16 them also with the finest of *w*.
147.14 filleth thee with the finest of the *w*.
Pr 27.22 bray a fool in a mortar among *w*
SS 7. 2 an heap of *w* set about with lilies.
Isa 28.25 cast in the principal *w*, and the
Jer 12.13 They have sown *w*, but shall reap
23.38 What is the chaff to the *w*? saith
31.12 for *w*, and for wine, and for oil,
41. 8 in the field, of *w*, and of barley,
Eze 4. 9 Take thou also unto thee *w*, and
27.17 traded in thy market *w* of Minnith,
45.13 part of an ephah of an homer of *w*,
Joel 1.11 for the *w* and for the barley;
2.24 the floors shall be full of *w*, and
Am 5.11 ye take from him burdens of *w*:
8. 5 sabbath, that we may set forth *w*,
6 yea, and sell the refuse of the *w*?
Mt 3.12 and gather his *w* into the garner;
13.25 and sowed tares among the *w*,
29 ye root up also the *w* with them.
30 but gather the *w* into my barn.
Lk 3.17 will gather the *w* into his garner;
16. 7 said, An hundred measures of *w*.
22.31 you, that he may sift you as *w*:
Jn 12.24 a corn of *w* fall into the ground
Ac 27.38 and cast out the *w* into the sea.
1Co 15.37 it may chance of *w*, or of some
Rev 6. 6 A measure of *w* for a penny, and
18.13 and oil, and fine flour, and *w*,

WHEATEN

Ex 29. 2 of *w* flour shalt thou make them.

WHEEL

1Ki 7.32 height of a *w* was a cubit and half
33 was like the work of a chariot *w*:
Ps 83.13 God, make them like a *w*; as the
Pr 20.26 and bringeth the *w* over them.
Ec 12. 6 or the *w* broken at the cistern.
Isa 28.27 neither is a cart *w* turned about
28 break it with the *w* of his cart,
Eze 1.15 behold one *w* upon the earth by
16 it were a *w* in the middle of a *w*.
10. 9 cherubim, one *w* by one cherub,
9 another *w* by another cherub:
10 a *w* had been in the midst of a *w*.
13 unto them in my hearing, O *w*.

WHEELS

Ex 14.25 took off their chariot *w*, that they
Jdg 5.28 why tarry the *w* of his chariots?
1Ki 7.30 And every base had four brasen *w*,
32 under the borders were four *w*;
32 axletrees of the *w* were joined to
33 work of the *w* was like the work of
Isa 5.28 and their *w* like a whirlwind:
Jer 18. 3 he wrought a work on the *w*.
47. 3 and at the rumbling of his *w*, the
Eze 1.16 appearance of the *w* and their
19 creatures went, the *w* went by them:
19 the earth, the *w* were lifted up.
20 the *w* were lifted up over against
20 of the living creature was in the *w*.
21 *w* were lifted up over against them:
21 of the living creature was in the *w*.
3.13 noise of the *w* over against them,
10. 2 Go in between the *w*, even under
6 Take fire from between the *w*,
6 went in, and stood beside the *w*.
9 the four *w* by the cherubims,
9 appearance of the *w* was as the
12 the *w* were full of eyes round about,
12 even the *w* that they four had,

13 As for the *w*, it was cried unto
16 cherubims went, the *w* went by
16 the same *w* also turned not from
19 out, the *w* also were beside them,
11.22 wings, and the *w* beside them; and
23.24 with chariots, wagons, and *w*,
26.10 of the horsemen, and of the *w*,
Dan 7. 9 flame, and his *w* as burning fire.
Na 3. 2 the noise of the rattling of the *w*,

WHEN

Gen 3. 6 *w* the woman saw that the tree was
42. 1 *w* Jacob saw that there was corn in
45.27 *w* he saw the wagons that Joseph had
47.15 *w* money failed in the land of Egypt,
Ex 2.11 *w* Moses was grown, that he went
12.13 *w* I see the blood, I will pass over
17.11 pass, *w* Moses held up his hand,
11 and *w* he let down his hand,
32. 1 *w* the people saw that Moses delayed
34.29 *w* Moses came down from mount
Lev 10.20 *w* Moses heard that, he was content.
Nu 11.25 that, *w* the spirit rested upon them,
15.18 *W* ye come into the land whither I
21. 8 *w* he looketh upon it, shall live.
Dt 12.10 But *w* ye go over Jordan, and dwell
28 *w* thou doest that which is good
15. 4 *w* there shall be no poor among
22. 8 *W* thou buildest a new house,
24. 5 *W* a man hath taken a new wife,
Jos 23.16 *W* ye have transgressed the covenant
Jdg 2.18 *w* the Lord raised them up judges,
5.31 the sun *w* he goeth forth in his might.
16.18 *w* Delilah saw that he had told her all
1Sa 3.12 *w* I begin, I will also make an end.
5. 2 *W* the Philistines took the ark of
12.12 *w* the Lord your God was your king.
16.16 *w* the evil spirit from God is upon
26.20 as *w* one doth hunt a partridge in
2Sa 22. 5 *W* the waves of death compassed
1Ki 8.30 and *w* thou hearest, forgive.
19.13 *w* Elijah heard it, that he wrapped
2Ki 2. 1 *w* the Lord would take up Elijah into
5. 8 *w* Elisha the man of God had heard
13 *w* he saith to thee, Wash, and be
1Ch 11. 2 time past, even *w* Saul was king,
2Ch 6.21 heaven; and *w* thou hearest, forgive.
27 *w* thou hast taught them the good
9. 1 *w* the queen of Sheba heard of the
Job 1. 6 was a day *w* the sons of God came
3.22 glad, *w* they can find the grave?
17.16 *w* our rest together is in the dust.
27. 8 *w* God taketh away his soul?
29. 3 *W* his candle shined upon my head,
4 *w* the secret of God was upon my
30.26 *w* I waited for light, there came
37.15 Dost thou know *w* God disposed
38. 4 wast thou *w* I laid the foundations
7 *W* the morning stars sang together,
Ps 4. 1 Hear me *w* I call, O God of my
3 the Lord will hear *w* I call unto him.
8. 3 *W* I consider thy heavens, the
14. 7 *w* the Lord bringeth back the
27. 8 *W* thou saidst, Seek ye my face; my
10 *W* my father and my mother
49.17 *w* he dieth he shall carry nothing
63. 6 *W* I remember thee upon my bed,
90. 4 are but as yesterday *w* it is past,
92. 7 *W* the wicked spring as the grass.
94. 8 and ye fools, *w* will ye be wise?
102.16 *W* the Lord shall build up Zion,
120. 7 but *w* I speak, they are for war.
122. 1 I was glad *w* they said unto me, Let
124. 2 our side, *w* men rose up against us:
126. 1 *W* the Lord turned again the
137. 1 we wept, *w* we remembered Zion.
139.15 *w* I was made in secret, and
18 *w* I awake, I am still with thee.
Pr 1.27 *W* your fear cometh as desolation,
6. 9 *w* wilt thou arise out of thy sleep?
21.11 *w* the wise is instructed, he receiveth
23. 1 *W* thou sittest to eat with a ruler,
24.17 Rejoice not *w* thine enemy falleth,
28. 1 The wicked flee *w* no man pursueth:
12 *w* the wicked rise, a man is hidden.
30.22 and a fool *w* he is filled with meat;
Ec 4.10 woe to him that is alone *w* he falleth;
8. 7 can tell him *w* it shall be?
10.16 to thee, O land, *w* thy king is a child,
12. 4 *w* the sound of the grinding is low,
Isa 1.12 *W* ye come to appear before me,
52. 8 *w* the Lord shall bring again Zion.
53. 2 and *w* we shall see him, there is no
10 *w* thou shalt make his soul an
57.20 troubled sea, *w* it cannot rest,
58. 7 *w* thou seest the naked, that thou
Jer 6.14 Peace, peace; *w* there is no peace.
31.23 *w* I shall bring again their captivity;
36.13 *w* Baruch read the book in the ears
Eze 5.15 *w* I shall execute judgments in thee
16 *W* I shall send upon them the evil
8. 7 *w* I looked, behold a hole in the wall.
22.28 God, *w* the Lord hath not spoken.
31.16 *w* I cast him down to hell with them
33. 8 *W* I say unto the wicked, O wicked
18 *W* the righteous turneth from his
35.14 *W* the whole earth rejoiceth, I will
37.13 *w* I have opened your graves, O my
Dan 6.10 *w* Daniel knew that the writing was
Hos 7. 1 *W* I would have healed Israel, then
11. 1 *W* Israel was a child, then I
Am 3. 4 roar in the forest, *w* he hath no prey?
8. 5 *W* will the new moon be gone,
Mic 2. 1 *w* the morning is light, they practice
7. 8 *w* I sit in darkness, the Lord shall be
Na 3.17 *w* the sun ariseth they flee away, and
Hab 2. 1 I shall answer *w* I am reproved.
Zec 8.14 *w* your fathers provoked me to
Mal 3. 2 and who shall stand *w* he appeareth?
17 that day *w* I make up my jewels;
Mt 2. 1 *w* Jesus was born in Bethlehem of
8 *w* ye have found him, bring me
10 *W* they saw the star, they rejoiced
4. 2 *w* he had fasted forty days and forty
6. 3 *w* thou doest alms, let not thy left
7 *w* ye pray, use not vain repetitions,
10.19 *w* they deliver you up, take no
13.32 *w* it is grown, it is the greatest
16. 2 *W* it is evening, ye say, it will be fair
19.28 *w* the Son of man shall sit in the
24. 3 Tell us, *w* shall these things be?
25.31 *W* the Son of man shall come in
37 *w* saw we thee an hungred, and
28.17 *w* they saw him, they worshipped
Mk 1.26 *w* the unclean spirit had torn him,
2. 5 *W* Jesus saw their faith, he said
8.19 *W* I brake the five loaves among
38 *w* he cometh in the glory of his
12.25 For *w* they shall rise from the dead,
13. 4 Tell us, *w* shall these things be?
33 for ye know not *w* the time is.
16. 9 *w* Jesus was risen early in the first
Lk 1.22 *w* he came out, he could not speak
4.13 *w* the devil had ended all the
6.26 *w* all men shall speak well of you:
9.26 *w* he shall come in his own glory,
10.35 *w* I come again, I will repay
11. 2 *W* ye pray, say, Our Father which
17.30 the day *w* the Son of man is revealed.
21. 7 *w* shall these things be? and what
24.23 *w* they found not his body, they
Jn 1.48 *w* thou was under the fig tree, I saw
3. 4 How can a man be born *w* he is old?
7.27 *w* Christ cometh, no man knoweth
31 *W* Christ cometh, will he do more
13. 1 *w* Jesus knew that his hour was come
15.26 *w* the Comforter is come, whom I
19.23 *w* they had crucified Jesus, took
20.20 disciples glad, *w* they saw the Lord.
Ac 2. 1 *w* the day of Pentecost was
Ro 5. 6 *w* we were yet without strength, in
13 sin is not imputed *w* there is no law.
7.21 *w* I would do good, evil is present
1Co 9.27 *w* I have preached to others, I myself
11.24 *w* he had given thanks, he brake it,
13.10 *w* that which is perfect is come,
11 *W* I was child, I spake as a child,
11 *w* I became a man, I put away
Gal 1.15 But *w* it pleased God, who
4. 4 But *w* the fulness of the time was
8 *w* ye knew not God, ye did service
Eph 1.20 *w* he raised him from the dead, and
Col 3. 4 *W* Christ, who is our life, shall
2Th 1.10 *W* he shall come to be glorified
Heb 1. 3 *w* he had by himself purged our sins,
6.13 *w* God made promise to Abraham,
1Pe 2.20 *w* ye do well, and suffer for it, ye
5. 4 *w* the chief Shepherd shall appear,
Rev 1.17 *w* I saw him, I fell at his feet as
20. 7 *w* the thousand years are expired,

WHENCE

Gen 16. 8 Sarai's maid, *w* comest thou?
42. 7 he said unto them, *W* come ye?
Dt 9.28 land *w* thou broughtest us out
Job 1. 7 said unto Satan, *W* comest thou?
10.21 Before I go *w* I shall not return,
28.20 *W* then cometh wisdom? and
Ps 121. 1 the hills, from *w* cometh my help.
Ec 1. 7 the place from *w* the rivers come,
Isa 30. 6 *w* come the young and the old lion,
51. 1 look unto the rock *w* ye are hewn,
1 the hole of the pit *w* ye are digged.
Jon 1. 8 and *w* comest thou? what is thy
Na 3. 7 *w* shall I seek comforters for thee?
Mt 12.44 my house from *w* I came out;
13.27 thy field? from *w* hath it tares?
54 *W* hath this man this wisdom,
Mk 6. 2 *w* hath this man these things?
12.37 Lord; and *w* is he then his son?
Lk 1.43 And *w* is this to me, that the
11.24 unto my house *w* I came out.
Jn 1.48 unto him, *W* knowest thou me?
2. 9 wine, and knew not *w* it was:
4.11 *w* then hast thou that living water?
6. 5 *W* shall we buy bread, that these
7.27 Howbeit we know this man *w* he is:
27 cometh, no man knoweth *w* he is.
28 know me, and ye know *w* I am:
8.14 for I know *w* I came, and whither
19. 9 saith unto Jesus, *W* art thou?
Php 3.20 *w* also we look for the Saviour,
Jas 4. 1 *w* come wars and fightings
Rev 2. 5 therefore from *w* thou art fallen,

WHENSOEVER

Gen 30.41 *w* the stronger cattle did conceive,
Mk 14. 7 *w* ye will ye may do them good:
Ro 15.24 *W* I take my journey into

WHERE

Gen 3. 9 and said unto him, *W* art thou?
4. 9 unto Cain, *W* is Abel thy brother?
18. 9 unto him, *W* is Sarah thy wife?
Ex 2.20 *w* is he? why is it that ye have
20.21 the thick darkness *w* God was.
24 *w* I record my name I will come
Dt 32.37 *W* are their gods, their rocks in
Jdg 9.38 *W* is now thy mouth, wherewith
18.10 *w* there is no want of any thing.
Ru 1.16 and *w* thou lodgest, I will lodge:
17 *W* thou diest, will I die, and there
2Sa 9. 4 the king said unto him, *W* is he?
2Ki 2.14 said, *W* is the Lord God of Elijah?
18.34 *W* are the gods of Hamath, and
Est 7. 5 Who is he, and *w* is he, that durst
Job 9.24 thereof; if not, *w*, and who is he?
10.22 order, and *w* the light is as darkness.
12.24 in a wilderness *w* there is no way.
23. 3 Oh that I knew *w* I might find him!
28.12 But *w* shall wisdom be found?
12 and *w* is...understanding?
35.10 *W* is God my maker, who giveth

Job 38. 4 *W* wast thou when I laid the
19 *W* is the way *w* light dwelleth?
Ps 19. 3 language, *w* their voice is not heard.
26. 8 the place *w* thine honor dwelleth.
42. 3 say unto me, *W* is thy God?
63. 1 a dry and thirsty land, *w* no water is;
79.10 *W* is their God? let him be known
115. 2 heathen say, *W* is now their God?
Pr 11.14 *W* no counsel is, the people fall: but
14. 4 *W* no oxen are, the crib is clean: but
15.17 is a dinner of herbs *w* love is,
26.20 *W* no wood is, the fire goeth out:
20 *w* there is no talebearer, the strife
29.18 *W* there is no vision the people
Isa 10. 3 and *w* will ye leave your glory?
19.12 *W* are they?...thy wise men?
33.18 *W* is the scribe? *w* is the receiver?
50. 1 *W* is the bill of your mother's
63.11 *w* is he that put his holy Spirit
66. 1 and *w* is the place of my rest?
Jer 2. 6 *W* is the Lord that brought us up
6 through, and *w* no man dwelt?
8 priests said not, *W* is the Lord?
17.15 *W* is the word of the Lord? let it
37.19 *W* are now your prophets which
Hos 13.10 *w* is any other that may save thee
Joel 2.17 among the people, *W* is their God?
Mic 7.10 unto me, *W* is the Lord thy God?
Mal 2.17 or, *W* is the God of judgment?
Mt 2. 2 *W* is he that is born King of the
8.20 man hath not *w* to lay his head.
18.20 For *w* two or three are gathered
Mk 9.44, 46 *W* their worm dieth not, and
13.14 standing *w* it ought not, (let him
14.14 saith, *W* is the guestchamber,
Lk 8.25 said unto them, *W* is your faith?
22. 9 him, *W* wilt thou that we prepare?
11 thee, *W* is the guestchamber,
Jn 1.38 Master,) *w* dwellest thou?
3. 8 The wind bloweth *w* it listeth, and
7.34 *w* I am, thither ye cannot come.
8.19 said unto him, *W* is thy Father?
11.34 And said, *W* have ye laid him?
12.26 and *w* I am, there shall also my
14. 3 that *w* I am, there ye may be also.
18. 1 *w* was a garden, into the which he
19.18 *W* they crucified him, and two
20. 2 we know not *w* they have laid
Ac 16.13 *w* prayer was wont to be made;
Ro 3.27 *W* is boasting then? It is
5.20 But *w* sin abounded, grace did
1Co 1.20 *W* is the wise? *w* is the scribe?
12.17 were an eye, *w* were the hearing?
15.55 O death, *w* is thy sting? O grave,
55 sting? O grave, *w* is thy victory?
2Co 3.17 and *w* the Spirit of the Lord is,
Gal 4.15 *W* is then the blessedness ye
Php 4.12 every *w* and in all things I
Col 3.11 *W* there is neither Greek nor
1Pe 4.18 *w* shall the ungodly and the
2Pe 3. 4 *W* is the promise of his coming?
Rev 2.13 dwellest, even *w* Satan's seat is:
11. 8 *w* also our Lord was crucified.

WHEREBY

Nu 5. 8 *w* an atonement shall be made for
Dt 7.19 *w* the Lord thy God brought thee
Jer 33. 8 iniquities, *w* they have sinned,
Eze 18.31 *w* ye have transgressed; and
39.26 *w* they have trespassed against
Lk 1.18 *W* shall I know this? for I
Ac 4.12 men, *w* we must be saved.
Ro 8.15 *w* we cry, Abba, Father.
Eph 4.14 *w* they lie in wait to deceive;
30 *w* ye are sealed unto the day
Heb 12.28 grace, *w* we may serve God
1Jn 2.18 *w* we know that it is the last time

WHEREFORE

Gen 26.27 unto them, *W* come ye to me,
31.30 yet, *w* hast thou stolen my gods?
Ex 14.15 *W* criest thou unto me? speak
Nu 11.11 *W* hast thou afflicted thy servant?
14. 3 *w* hath the Lord brought us into
21.27 *W* they that speak in proverbs
22.32 *W* hast thou smitten thine ass
2Sa 12.23 now he is dead, *w* should I fast?
16.10 then say, *W* hast thou done so?
Job 3.20 *W* is light given to him that is in
13.24 *W* hidest thou thy face, and
18. 3 *W* we are counted as beasts, and
21. 7 *W* do the wicked live, become old,
42. 6 *W* I abhor myself, and
Ps 49. 5 *W* should I fear in the days of evil,
Ec 4. 2 *W* I praised the dead which are
5. 6 *w* should God be angry at thy
Isa 55. 2 *W* do ye spend money for that
58. 3 *W* have we fasted, say they, and
3 *w* have we afflicted our soul, and
Jer 22. 8 *W* hath the Lord done thus
La 5.20 *W* dost thou forget us forever,
Mal 2.15 *w* one? That he might seek a
Mt 6.30 *W*, if God so clothe the grass of
14.31 faith, *w* didst thou doubt?
26.50 Friend, *w* art thou come?
Ac 10.21 is the cause *w* ye are come?
Ro 1.24 *W* God also gave them up to
7.12 *W* the law is holy, and the
Gal 3.24 *W* the law was our schoolmaster
Php 2. 9 *W* God also hath highly exalted
1Th 4.18 *W* comfort one another with
Heb 11.16 *w* God is not ashamed to be called
12. 1 *W* seeing we also are compassed
13.12 *W* Jesus also, that he might
1Pe 1.13 *W* gird up the loins of your mind,
Rev 17. 7 *W* didst thou marvel? I will tell

WHERESOEVER

Lev 13.12 to his foot, *w* the priest looketh;
2Ki 8. 1 and sojourn *w* thou canst sojourn:
12. 5 *w* any breach shall be found.
1Ch 17. 6 *W* I...walked with all Israel,
Jer 40. 5 go *w* it seemeth convenient
Dan 2.38 *w* the children of men dwelt,
Mt 24.28 *w* the carcass is, there will
26.13 *W* this gospel shall be
Mk 9.18 *w* he taketh him, he teareth
14. 9 *W* this gospel shall be
14 *w* he shall go in, say ye to the
Lk 17.37 *W* the body is, thither will the

WHEREWITH

Ex 16.32 may see the bread *w* I have fed you
Nu 30. 4 her bond *w* she hath bound her soul
Dt 15.14 *w* the Lord thy God hath blessed
Jdg 6.15 my Lord, *w* shall I save Israel?
2Sa 21. 3 *w* shall I make the atonement,
Job 15. 3 with speeches *w* he can do no good?
Ps 79.12 *w* they have reproached thee, O
119.42 *w* to answer him that reproacheth
Isa 28.12 *w* ye may cause the weary to rest;
La 1.12 *w* the Lord hath afflicted me in the
Mic 6. 6 *W* shall I come before the Lord,
Mt 5.13 savor, *w* shall it be salted?
Mk 9.50 saltness, *w* will ye season it?
Lk 14.34 savor, *w* shall it be seasoned?
Gal 5. 1 liberty *w* Christ hath made us free,

WHEREWITHAL

Ps 119. 9 *w* shall a young man cleanse his way
Mt 6.31 drink? or, *W* shall we be clothed?

WHET

Dt 32.41 If I *w* my glittering sword, and
Ps 7.12 he turn not, he will *w* his sword;
64. 3 Who *w* their tongue like a sword,
Ec 10.10 blunt, and he do not *w* the edge,

WHETHER

Gen 18.21 see *w* they have done altogether
27.21 *w* thou be my very son Esau or not.
37.14 *w* it be well with thy brethren, and
32 now *w* it be thy son's coat or no.
Dt 4.32 *w* there hath been any such thing as
13. 3 to know *w* ye love the Lord with
Jdg 2.22 *w* thy will keep the way of the Lord
2Sa 12.22 Who can tell *w* God will be gracious
1Ki 20.18 *W* they be come out for peace,
Job 34.29 *w* it be done against a nation, or
33 *w* thou refuse, or *w* thou choose;
Ec 2.19 *w* he shall be a wise man or a fool?
11. 6 knowest not *w* shall prosper,
6 or *w* they both shall be alike good.
Jer 30. 6 and see *w* a man doth travail with
42. 6 *W* it be good, or *w* it be evil, we
Eze 2. 5 *w* they...hear, or *w* they will forbear,
Mt 9. 5 *w* is easier, to say, Thy sins be
21.31 *W* of them twain did the will of
23.17 for *w* is greater, the gold, or the
Mk 2. 9 *W* it is easier to say to the sick of
15.36 *w* Elias will come to take him down.
Lk 3.15 *w* he were the Christ, or not;
5.23 *W* is easier, to say, Thy sins be
6. 7 *w* he would heal on the sabbath
22.27 *w* is greater, he that sitteth at
23. 6 asked *w* the man were a Galilean.
Jn 7.17 of the doctrine, *w* it be of God,
9.25 *W* he be a sinner or no, I know
Ac 1.24 *w* of these two thou hast
4.19 *W* it be right in the sight of God
Ro 6.16 ye obey; *w* of sin unto death,
14. 8 *w* we live, we live unto the
1Co 1.16 I know not *w* I baptized any other.
3.22 *W* Paul, or Apollos, or Cephas, or
12.13 body, *w* we be Jews or Gentiles,
26 And *w* one member suffer, all the
13. 8 *w* there be prophecies, they shall
1Th 5.10 *w* we wake or sleep, we should live
1Jn 4. 1 try the spirits *w* they are of God:

WHILE

Gen 8.22 *W* the earth remaineth, seedtime
Ex 33.22 thee with my hand *w* I pass by:
Nu 23.15 offering, *w* I meet the Lord yonder.
1Sa 9.27 but stand thou still a *w*, that I
2Sa 7.19 house for a great *w* to come.
12.22 *W* the child was yet alive, I fasted
2Ch 15. 2 Lord is with you, *w* ye be with him;
Job 20.23 shall rain it upon him *w* he is eating.
Ps 37.10 yet a little *w*, and the wicked shall
42.10 *w* they say daily unto me, Where is
49.18 Though *w* he lived he blest his soul:
69. 3 mine eyes fail *w* I wait for my God.
88.15 *w* I suffer thy terrors I am distracted.
104.33 to my God *w* I have my being.
146. 2 *W* I live will I praise the Lord: I
Pr 8.26 *W* as yet he had not made the
19.18 Chasten thy son *w* there is hope,
31.15 She riseth also *w* it is yet night,
Ec 12. 2 *W* the sun or the light or the
Isa 55. 6 Seek ye the Lord *w* he may be found,
6 call ye upon him *w* he is near:
Jer 15. 9 is gone down *w* it was yet day:
Hag 2. 6 it is a little *w*, and I will shake the
Mt 13.21 in himself, but dureth for a *w*:
25 *w* men slept his enemy came
25. 5 *W* the bridegroom tarried they all
27.63 deceiver said, *w* he was yet alive,
28.13 and stole him away *w* we slept.
Mk 6.31 into a desert place, and rest a *w*:
14.32 Sit ye here, *w* I shall pray.
Lk 9.34 *W* he thus spake, there came a
14.32 *w* the other is yet a great way off, he
22.60 *w* he yet spake, the cock crew.
24.32 *w* he opened to us the scriptures?
44 *w* I was yet with you, that all things
Jn 7.33 Yet a little *w* am I with you, and
9. 4 of him that sent me, *w* it is day:
12.35 *w* ye have the light, lest darkness
36 *W* ye have light, believe in the
13.33 children, yet a little *w* I am with you.
16.16 A little *w*, and ye shall not see me:
16 again, a little *w*, and ye shall see me,

Ac 1. 9 *w* they beheld, he was taken up;
10.19 *W* Peter thought on the vision, the
20.11 talked a long *w*, even till break of
Ro 5. 8 *w* we were yet sinners, Christ died
2Co 4.18 *W* we look not at the things which
Heb 3.13 daily, *w* it is called To day;

WHILST

Jdg 6.31 put to death *w* it is yet morning:
Neh 6. 3 the work cease, *w* I leave it,
Job 32.11 *w* ye searched out what to say.
Ps 141.10 own nets, *w* that I withal escape.
Jer 17. 2 *W* their children remember their
2Co 5. 6 *w* we are at home in the body, we are
7.15 *w* he remembereth the obedience
Heb 10.33 *w* ye were made a gazingstock both
33 *w* ye became companions of them

WHIP

Pr 26. 3 A *w* for the horse, a bridle for the
Na 3. 2 The noise of a *w*, and the noise of

WHIPS

1Ki 12.11 father hath chastised with you *w*,
14 father also chastised you with *w*,
2Ch 10.11, 14 my father chastised you with *w*,

WHIRLETH

Ec 1. 6 it *w* about continually, and

WHIRLWIND

2Ki 2.11 Elijah went up by a *w* into heaven.
Job 37. 9 Out of the south cometh the *w*:
38. 1 Lord answered Job out of the *w*,
Pr 1.27 your destruction cometh as a *w*;
Isa 40.24 the *w* shall take them away as
Jer 23.19 a *w* of the Lord is gone forth in
Dan 11.40 shall come against him like a *w*,
Hos 8. 7 wind, and they shall reap the *w*:
Na 1. 3 the Lord hath his way in the *w*
Hab 3.14 came out as a *w* to scatter me:
Zec 7.14 But I scattered them with a *w*

WHIRLWINDS

Isa 21. 1 As *w* in the south pass through;
Zec 9.14 and shall go with *w* of the south.

WHISPER

Ps 41. 7 All that hate me *w* together
Isa 29. 4 and thy speech shall *w* out of the

WHISPERER

Pr 16.28 and a *w* separateth chief friends.

WHISPERERS

Ro 1.29 debate, deceit, malignity; *w*,

WHISPERINGS

2Co 12.20 *w*, swellings, tumults:

WHIT

Dt 13.16 and all the spoil thereof every *w*,
1Sa 3.18 And Samuel told him every *w*,
Jn 7.23 I have made a man every *w* whole
13.10 wash his feet, but is clean every *w*:
2Co 11. 5 not a *w* behind the very chiefest

WHITE

Gen 49.12 wine, and his teeth *w* with milk.
Nu 12.10 Miriam became leprous, *w* as snow:
Est 8.15 king in royal apparel of blue and *w*,
Job 6. 6 any taste in the *w* of an egg?
Ec 9. 8 Let thy garments be always *w*;
Isa 1.18 they shall be as *w* as snow;
Dan 11.35 to purge, and to make them *w*,
12.10 shall be purified, and made *w*, and
Mt 5.36 not make one hair *w* or black.
17. 2 his raiment was *w* as the light.
28. 3 and his raiment *w* as snow:
Mk 9. 3 shining, exceeding *w* as snow;
3 as no fuller on earth can *w* them.
16. 5 side, clothed in a long *w* garment;
Lk 9.29 his raiment was *w* and glistering.
Jn 4.35 for they are *w* already to harvest.
20.12 And seeth two angels in *w* sitting,
Ac 1.10 two men stood by them in *w*
Rev 1.14 His head and his hairs were *w* like
14 as *w* as snow; and his eyes were as
2.17 will give him a *w* stone, and in the
3. 4 and they shall walk with me in *w*:
5 shall be clothed in *w* raiment;
18 *w* raiment, that thou mayest be
4. 4 sitting, clothed in *w* raiment; and
6. 2 And I saw, and behold a *w* horse:
11 *w* robes were given unto every one
7. 9 clothed with *w* robes, and palms
13 which are arrayed in *w* robes?
14 made them *w* in the blood of the
14.14 I looked, and behold a *w* cloud,
15. 6 clothed in pure and *w* linen,
19. 8 arrayed in fine linen, clean and *w*:
11 opened and behold a *w* horse;
14 followed him upon *w* horses,
14 clothed in fine linen, *w* and clean.
20.11 I saw a great *w* throne, and him

WHITED

Mt 23.27 for ye are like unto *w* sepulchers,
Ac 23. 3 God shall smite thee, thou *w* wall:

WHITER

Ps 51. 7 me, and I shall be *w* than snow.
La 4. 7 snow, they were *w* than milk,

WHITHER

Gen 16. 8 camest thou? and *w* wilt thou go?
20.13 every place *w* we shall come,
28.15 thee in all places *w* thou goest,
32.17 Whoso art thou? and *w* goest thou?
37.30 child is not; and I, *w* shall I go?
Ex 21.13 a place *w* he shall flee.
34.12 inhabitants of the land *w* thou
Lev 18. 3 *w* I bring you, shall ye not do:
20.22 *w* I bring you to dwell therein,
Nu 13.27 unto the land *w* thou sentest us,
15.18 into the land *w* I bring you,
35.25 of his refuge, *w* he was fled:
26 of his refuge, *w* he was fled;
Dt 1.28 *W* shall we go up? our brethren
3.21 unto all the kingdoms *w* thou
4. 5 the land *w* ye go to possess it.
14 *w* ye go over to possess it.
27 *w* the Lord shall lead you.
6. 1 the land *w* ye go to possess it:
7. 1 land *w* thou goest to possess
11. 8 the land, *w* ye go to possess it;
10 *w* thou goest in to possess it,
11 the land, *w* ye go to possess it,
29 land *w* thou goest to possess
12.29 *w* thou goest to possess them,
21.14 then thou shalt let her go *w* she will;
23.12 *w* thou shalt go forth abroad:
20 land *w* thou goest to possess
28.21 *w* thou goest to possess it.
37 nations *w* the Lord shall lead
63 land w thou goest to possess
30. 1, 3 *w* the Lord thy God hath
16 land *w* thou goest to possess
18 *w* thou passest over Jordan to
31.13 *w* ye go over Jordan to possess
16 *w* they go to be among them,
32.47 *w* ye go over Jordan to possess
50 in the mount *w* thou goest up,
Jos 2. 5 out: *w* the men went I wot not:
Jdg 19.17 *W* goest thou? and whence comest
Ru 1.16 for *w* thou goest, I will go:
1Sa 10.14 and to his servant, *W* went ye?
27.10 *W* have ye made a road to day?
2Sa 2. 1 And David said, *W* shall I go up?
13.13 *w* shall I cause my shame to go?
15.20 seeing I go *w* I may, return
17.18 in his court; *w* they went down.
1Ki 2.36 and go not forth thence any *w*.
42 out, and walkest abroad any *w*,
8.47 the land *w* they were carried
18.10 *w* my lord hath not sent to
12 shall carry thee *w* I know
21.18 *w* he is gone down to possess
2Ki 5.25 he said, Thy servant went no *w*.
2Ch 6.37 the land *w* they carried
38 *w* they have carried them captives,
10. 2 *w* he had fled from the presence of
Neh 2.16 And the rulers knew not *w* I went,
Ps 122. 4 *W* the tribes go up, the tribes of
139. 7 *W* shall I go from thy spirit?
7 or *w* shall I flee from thy presence?
Ec 9.10 in the grave, *w* thou goest.
SS 6. 1 *W* is thy beloved gone, O thou
1 *w* is thy beloved turned aside? that
Isa 20. 6 *w* we flee for help to be
Jer 8. 3 places *w* I have driven them,
15. 2 unto thee, *W* shall we go forth?
16.15 lands *w* he had driven them:
19.14 Tophet, *w* the Lord had sent him
22.12 the place *w* they have led him
23. 3 countries *w* I have driven them,
8 countries *w* I had driven them;
24. 9 all places *w* I shall drive them.
29. 7 city *w* I have caused you to be
14 the places *w* I have driven you,
18 nations *w* I have driven them:
30.11 nations *w* I have driven them:
32.37 *w* I have driven them in mine
40. 4 *w* it seemeth good and convenient
45. 5 in all places *w* thou goest.
46.28 nations *w* I have driven thee:
49.36 nation *w* the outcasts of Elam
Eze 1.12 *w* the spirit was to go, they
4.13 Gentiles, *w* I will drive them.
6. 9 nations *w* they shall be carried
10.11 to the place *w* the head looked
12.16 among the heathen *w* they
29.13 people *w* they were scattered:
36.20 unto the heathen, *w* they went,
21, 22 the heathen, *w* they went.
37.21 the heathen, *w* they be gone,
47. 9 live *w* the river cometh.
Dan 9. 7 *w* thou hast driven them,
Joel 3. 7 the place *w* ye have sold them,
Zec 2. 2 Then said I, *W* goest thou? And
5.10 me, *W* do these bear the ephah?
Lk 10. 1 place, *w* he himself would come.
24.28 nigh unto the village, *w* they went:
Jn 3. 8 whence it cometh, and *w* it goeth:
6.21 was at the land *w* they went.
7.35 *W* will he go, that we shall not
8.14 I know whence I came, and *w* I go;
14 tell whence I come, and *w* I go;
21 sins: *w* I go, ye cannot come.
22 he saith, *W* I go, ye cannot come.
12.35 darkness knoweth not *w* he goeth.
13.33 Jews, *W* I go, ye cannot come;
36 said unto him, Lord, *w* goest thou?
36 *W* I go, thou canst not follow me
14. 4 *w* I go ye know, and the way ye
5 we know not *w* thou goest; and
16. 5 of you asketh me, *W* goest thou?
18.20 temple, *w* the Jews always resort;
21.18 and walkedst *w* thou wouldest:
18 carry thee *w* thou wouldest not.
Heb 6.20 *W* the forerunner is...entered,
11. 8 went out, not knowing *w* he went.
1Jn 2.11 and knoweth not *w* he goeth,

WHITHERSOEVER

Jos 1. 9 God is with thee *w* thou goest.
1Sa 18. 5 David went out *w* Saul sent him,
Eze 1.20 *W* the spirit was to go, they
Mt 8.19 will follow thee *w* thou goest.
Mk 6.56 And *w* he entered, into
Lk 9.57 I will follow thee *w* thou goest.
1Co 16. 6 me on my journey *w* I go.
Jas 3. 4 helm, *w* the governor listeth,
Rev 14. 4 follow the Lamb *w* he goeth.

WHOLE

Gen 2. 6 and watered the *w* face of the
11 the *w* land of Havilah,
13 the *w* land of Ethiopia.
7.19 that were under the *w* heaven,
8. 9 were on the face of the *w* earth:
9.19 them was the *w* earth overspread.
11. 1 the *w* earth was of one language,
4 upon the face of the *w* earth.
13. 9 Is not the *w* land before thee?
47.28 the *w* age of Jacob was an hundred
Ex 12. 6 *w* assembly of the congregation
16. 2 the *w* congregation of the children
3 to kill this *w* assembly
10 the *w* congregation of the children
19.18 and the *w* mount quaked greatly.
29.18 thou shalt burn the *w* ram
Lev 3. 9 the fat thereof, and the *w* rump,
4.12 Even the *w* bullock shall he
13 the *w* congregation of Israel sin
7.14 offer one out of the *w* oblation
8.21 and Moses burnt the *w* ram
10. 6 the *w* house of Israel, bewail the
25.29 may redeem it within a *w* year
Nu 3. 7 charge of the *w* congregation
8. 9 shalt gather the *w* assembly
10. 2 of a *w* piece shalt thou make
11.20 But even a *w* month, until it
21 that they may eat a *w* month,
14. 2 the *w* congregation said unto
29 according to your *w* number, from
20. 1 *w* congregation, into the desert of
22 the *w* congregation, journeyed
Dt 2.25 that are under the *w* heaven,
Jos 5. 8 in the camp, till they were *w*.
11.23 So Joshua took the *w* land,
Job 5.18 woundeth, and his hands make *w*.
34.13 who hath disposed the *w* world?
37. 3 directeth it under the *w* heaven,
41.11 is under the *w* heaven is mine.
Ps 9. 1 thee, O Lord, with my *w* heart;
72.19 *w* earth be filled with his glory;
111. 1 praise the Lord with my *w* heart,
119. 2 that seek him with the *w* heart.
69 thy precepts with my *w* heart.
Ec 12.13 the conclusion of the *w* matter:
13 for this is the *w* duty of man.
Isa 1. 5 *w* head is sick, and the *w* heart
3. 1 the staff, the *w* stay of bread,
6. 3 the *w* earth is full of his glory.
14. 7 The *w* earth is at rest, and is quiet:
Jer 1.18 brasen walls against the *w* land,
12.11 the *w* land is made desolate,
32.41 my *w* heart and with my *w* soul.
Mic 4.13 unto the Lord of the *w* earth.
Zec 4.10 to and fro through the *w* earth.
Mal 3. 9 robbed me, even the *w* nation.
Mt 5.29, 30 thy *w* body should be cast into
6.22 thy *w* body shall be full of light.
23 *w* body shall be full of darkness.
8.32 the *w* herd of swine ran violently
34 the *w* city came out to meet Jesus:
9.12 that be *w* need not a physician,
21 touch his garment, I shall be *w*.
22 thy faith hath made thee *w*.
13. 2 *w* multitude stood on the shore.
16.26 if he shall gain the *w* world, and
26.13 shall be preached in the *w* world,
Mk 2.17 They that are *w* have no need of
3. 5 hand was restored *w* as the other.
4. 1 the *w* multitude was by the sea
8.36 if he shall gain the *w* world, and
10.52 way; thy faith hath made thee *w*.
Lk 1.10 the *w* multitude of the people
5.31 that are *w* need not a physician;
6.10 hand was restored *w* as the other.
19 *w* multitude sought to touch him:
9.25 if he gain the *w* world, and lose
11.34 thy *w* body also is full of light;
36 *w* body therefore be full of light,
13.21 of meal, till the *w* was leavened.
17.19 thy faith hath made thee *w*.
21.35 dwell on the face of the *w* earth.
Jn 4.53 believed, and his *w* house.
5. 4 *w* of whatsoever disease he had.
6 unto him. Wilt thou be made *w*?
14 him, Behold, thou art made *w*:
11.50 and that the *w* nation perish not.
Ac 4. 9 by what means he is made *w*;
9.34 Jesus Christ maketh thee *w*:
Ro 1. 8 spoken of throughout the *w* world.
8.22 that the *w* creation groaneth
1Co 5. 6 little leaven leaveneth the *w* lump?
Eph 3.15 *w* family in heaven and earth is
4.16 the *w* body fitly joined together
6.11 Put on the *w* armor of God, that ye
1Th 5.23 your *w* spirit and soul and body
1Jn 2. 2 also for the sins of the *w* world.
5.19 the *w* world lieth in wickedness.

WHOLESOME

Pr 15. 4 A *w* tongue is a tree of life: but
1Ti 6. 3 and consent not to *w* words, even

WHORE

Dt 22.21 to play the *w* in her father's house:
23.18 shalt not bring the hire of a *w*,
Pr 23.27 For a *w* is a deep ditch; and a
Eze 16.28 hast played the *w* also with the
Rev 17. 1 judgment of the great *w* that
15 where the *w* sitteth, are peoples,
16 these shall hate the *w*, and shall
19. 2 for he hath judged the great *w*,

WHOREDOM

Gen 38.24 behold, she is with child by *w*.
Lev 19.29 lest the land fall to *w*, and the
20. 5 to commit *w* with Molech, from
Nu 25. 1 people began to commit *w* with
Jer 3. 9 through the lightness of her *w*,
13.27 the lewdness of thy *w*, and thine
Eze 16.17 and didst commit *w* with them,
33 unto thee on every side for thy *w*.
20.30 commit ye *w* after their
23. 8 and poured their *w* upon her.
17 and they defiled her with their *w*,
27 thy *w* brought from the land of
43. 7 they, nor their kings, by their *w*,
9 Now let them put away their *w*,
Hos 1. 2 land hath committed great *w*,
4.10 they shall commit *w*, and shall not
11 *W* and wine and new wine take
13 your daughters shall commit *w*,
14 daughters when they commit *w*,
18 have committed *w* continually:
5. 3 O Ephraim, thou committest *w*,
6.10 there is the *w* of Ephraim, Israel

WHORING

Ex 34.15 and they go a *w* after their gods,
16 daughters go a *w* after their gods,
16 thy sons go a *w* after their gods.
Lev 17. 7 after whom they have gone a *w*.
20. 5 off, and all that go a *w* after him,
6 wizards, to go a *w* after them, I
Nu 15.39 after which ye used to go a *w*:
Dt 31.16 and go a *w* after the gods of the
Jdg 2.17 but they went a *w* after other gods,
8.27 all Israel went thither a *w* after it:
33 again, and went a *w* after Baalim,
1Ch 5.25 and went a *w* after the gods of the
2Ch 21.13 inhabitants of Jerusalem...go a *w*,
Ps 73.27 all them that go a *w* from thee.
106.39 went a *w* with their own inventions.
Eze 6. 9 which go a *w* after their idols:
23.30 hast gone a *w* after the heathen,
Hos 4.12 gone a *w* from under their God,
9. 1 thou hast gone a *w* from thy God,

WHOSE

Gen 1.11 *w* seed is in itself, upon the earth:
7.22 in *w* nostrils was the breath of life,
32.17 *W* art thou? and whither goest
Ex 34.14 the Lord, *w* name is Jealous, is a
Dt 19. 1 *w* land the Lord thy God giveth
Ru 2. 5 the reapers, *W* damsel is this?
1Sa 12. 3 his anointed: *w* ox have I taken?
3 or *w* ass have I taken?
1Ch 12. 8 *w* faces were like the faces of lions,
20. 5 *w* spear staff was like a weaver's
Ezr 1. 5 all them *w* spirit God had raised,
Job 12.10 In *w* hand is the soul of every living
26. 4 and *w* spirit came from thee?
Ps 32. 1 Blessed is he *w* transgression is
1 is forgiven, *w* sin is covered.
2 and in *w* spirit there is no guile.
33.12 is the nation *w* God is the Lord;
78. 8 *w* spirit was not stedfast with God.
84. 5 is the man *w* strength is in thee;
5 in *w* heart are the ways of them.
144.15 is that people, *w* God is the Lord.
Isa 23. 7 city, *w* antiquity is of ancient days?
8 city, *w* merchants are princes,
26. 3 peace, *w* mind is stayed on thee:
28. 1 *w* glorious beauty is a fading flower,
51. 7 the people in *w* heart is my law;
57.15 *w* name is Holy; I dwell in the
Jer 17. 7 the Lord, and *w* hope the Lord is.
44.28 know *w* words shall stand, mine,
46.18 king, *w* name is the Lord of hosts,
Eze 3. 6 *w* words...canst not understand.
21.25 *w* day is come, when iniquity shall
Dan 2.11 gods, *w* dwelling is not with flesh.
3.27 *w* bodies the fire had no power,
4.34 *w* dominion is an everlasting
5.23 the God in *w* hand thy breath is,
7.27 *w* kingdom is an everlasting
Jon 1. 7 for *w* cause this evil is upon us.
Mic 5. 2 *w* goings forth have been from of
Zec 6.12 the man *w* name is The Branch;
Mt 3.11 *w* shoes I am not worthy to bear;
12 *W* fan is in his hand, and he will
10. 3 *w* surname was Thaddaeus;
22.20 *W* is this image and
28 *W* wife shall she be of the seven?
42 think ye of Christ? *w* son is he?
Mk 1. 7 latchet of *w* shoes I am not worthy
7.25 *w* young daughter had an unclean
12.16 them, *W* is this image and
23 *w* wife shall she be of them? for
Lk 1.27 to a man *w* name was Joseph,
2.25 Jerusalem, *w* name was Simeon;
3.16 *w* shoes I am not worthy to
17 *W* fan is in his hand, and he will
6. 6 *w* right hand was withered.
12.20 *w* shall those things be, which
13. 1 *w* blood Pilate had mingled with
20.24 *W* image and superscription
33 *w* wife of them is she?
24.18 *w* name was Cleopas, answering
Jn 1. 6 sent from God, *w* name was John.
27 *w* shoe's latchet I am not worthy
4.46 *w* son was sick at Capernaum.
6.42 *w* father and mother we know?
10.12 *w* own the sheep are not, seeth the
11. 2 hair, *w* brother Lazarus was sick.
18.26 his kinsman *w* ear Peter cut off,
19.24 but cast lots for it, *w* it shall be:
20.23 *W* soever sins ye remit, they are
23 *w* soever sins ye retain, they are
Ac 7.58 young man's feet, *w* name was Saul.
10. 5 Simon, *w* surname was Peter:
6 tanner, *w* house is by the sea side:
32 Simon, *w* surname is Peter;
11.13 Simon, *w* surname is Peter;
12.12 of John, *w* surname was Mark;
25 them John, *w* surname was Mark.
13. 6 a Jew, *w* name was Bar-jesus:
25 *w* shoes of his feet I am not
15.37 them John, *w* surname was Mark.
16.14 *w* heart the Lord opened, that she
18. 7 *w* house joined hard to the
27.23 God, *w* I am, and whom I serve,

Job 36. 6 preserveth not the life of the *w*:
17 fulfilled the judgment of the *w*:
Ps 7. 9 wickedness of the *w* come to an
11 God is angry with the *w* every day.
17. 9 the *w* that oppress me, from my
13 deliver my soul from the *w*, which
27. 2 When the *w*, even mine enemies
28. 3 Draw me not away with the *w*,
32.10 Many sorrows shall be to the *w*:
37. 7 who bringeth *w* devices to pass.
12 The *w* plotteth against the just,
21 The *w* borroweth, and payeth not
35 I have seen the *w* in great power,
68. 2 *w* perish at the presence of God.
73. 3 I saw the prosperity of the *w*.
94. 3 Lord, how long shall the *w*, how
3 how long shall the *w* triumph?
112.10 The *w* shall see it, and be grieved;
10 the desire of the *w* shall perish.
119.53 of the *w* that forsake thy law.
155 Salvation is far from the *w*: for
139.19 Surely thou wilt slay the *w*, O God:
24 see if there be any *w* way in me,
141. 4 to practice *w* works with men
10 Let the *w* fall into their own nets,
Pr 2.14 in the frowardness of the *w*;
3.25 neither of the desolation of the *w*,
33 the Lord is in the house of the *w*:
4.14 Enter not into the path of the *w*,
19 The way of the *w* is as darkness:
5.22 iniquity shall take the *w* himself,
10. 3 away the substance of the *w*.
7 but the name of the *w* shall rot.
20 the heart of the *w* is little worth.
28 expectation of the *w* shall perish.
11. 5 *w* shall fall by his own wickedness.
10 the *w* perish, there is shouting.
13. 5 a *w* man is loathsome, and cometh
9 the lamp of the *w* shall be put out.
15. 6 in the revenues of the *w* is trouble.
28 mouth of the *w* poureth out evil
29 The Lord is far from the *w*: but he
20.26 A wise king scattereth the *w*, and
21. 4 and the plowing of the *w*, is sin.
10 The soul of the *w* desireth evil:
28. 1 *w* flee when no man pursueth:
12 when the *w* rise, a man is hidden.
15 is a *w* ruler over the poor people.
Ec 3.17 judge the righteous and the *w*:
7.15 a *w* man that prolongeth his life
17 Be not over much *w*, neither be
8.10 And so I saw the *w* buried, who
13 it shall not be well with the *w*,
Isa 3.11 Woe unto the *w*! it shall be ill
5.23 Which justify the *w* for reward,
53. 9 And he made his grave with the *w*,
55. 7 Let the *w* forsake his way, and the
57.20 the *w* are like the troubled sea,
21 no peace, saith my God, to the *w*.
Jer 2.33 also taught the *w* ones thy ways.
5.26 among my people are...*w* men:
28 they overpass the deeds of the *w*:
12. 1 doth the way of the *w* prosper?
17. 9 all things, and desperately *w*:
Eze 3.18 When I say unto the *w*, Thou shalt
18 to warn the *w* from his *w* way,
11. 2 and give *w* counsel in this city:
18.20 wickedness of the *w* shall be upon
21 if the *w* will turn from all his sins
23 pleasure...that the *w* should die?
33. 8 When I say unto the *w*, O *w* man,
8 *w* man shall die in his iniquity;
15 If the *w* restore the pledge, give
Dan 12.10 tried; but the *w* shall do wickedly:
10 none of the *w* shall understand;
Mic 6.10 wickedness in the house of the *w*,
11 them pure with the *w* balances,
Na 1. 3 and will not at all acquit the *w*:
Hab 1. 4 *w* doth compass about the
13 when the *w* devoureth the man
Mt 12.45 other spirits more *w* than himself,
45 be also unto this *w* generation.
16. 4 A *w* and adulterous generation
18.32 O thou *w* servant, I forgave thee
Lk 11.26 other spirits more *w* than himself;
19.22 will I judge thee, thou *w* servant.
Ac 2.23 *w* hands have crucified and slain:
Eph 6.16 quench all the fiery darts of the *w*.
Col 1.21 enemies in your mind by *w* works,
2Th 2. 8 then shall that *W* be revealed,
2Pe 2. 7 the filthy conversation of the *w*:
1Jn 2.13 ye have overcome the *w* one.

WICKEDLY

Gen 19. 7 I pray you, brethren, do not so *w*.
Dt 9.18 doing *w* in the sight of the Lord,
Jdg 19.23 nay, I pray you, do not so *w*;
1Sa 12.25 if ye shall still do *w*, ye shall be
2Sa 22.22 have not *w* departed from my God.
24.17 have sinned, and I have done *w*:
2Ki 21.11 done *w* above all...the Amorites
2Ch 6.37 done amiss, and have dealt *w*;
20.35 king of Israel, who did very *w*:
22. 3 mother was his counsellor to do *w*.
Neh 9.33 done right, but we have done *w*:
Job 13. 7 Will ye speak *w* for God? and
34.12 Yea, surely God will not do *w*,
Ps 18.21 have not *w* departed from my God.
73. 8 speak *w* concerning oppression:
74. 3 hath done *w* in the sanctuary.
106. 6 iniquity, we have done *w*.
139.20 For they speak against thee *w*,
Dan 9. 5 have done *w*, and have rebelled,
15 we have sinned, we have done *w*.
11.32 such as do *w* against the covenant
12.10 tried; but the wicked shall do *w*:
Mal 4. 1 all that do *w*, shall be stubble:

WICKEDNESS

Gen 6. 5 saw that the *w* of man was great
Dt 9. 4, 5 but for the *w* of these nations
17. 2 wrought *w* in the sight of the Lord
Jdg 9.56 God rendered the *w* of Abimelech,
20. 3 Israel, Tell us, how was this *w*?
1Sa 12.17 and see that your *w* is great,
24.13 *W* proceedeth from the wicked:
1Ki 1.52 but if *w* shall be found in him,
21.25 which did sell himself to work *w*
Job 4. 8 that plow iniquity, and sow *w*,
20.12 Though *w* be sweet in his mouth,
22. 5 Is not thy *w* great? and thine
35. 8 Thy *w* may hurt a man as thou art;
Ps 5. 4 not a God that hath pleasure in *w*:
7. 9 Oh let the *w* of the wicked come
55.11 *W* is in the midst thereof: deceit
15 for *w* is in their dwellings, and
58. 2 Yea, in heart ye work *w*; ye
84.10 than to dwell in the tents of *w*.
Pr 4.17 For they eat the bread of *w*, and
8. 7 *w* is an abomination to my lips.
10. 2 Treasurers of *w* profit nothing:
11. 5 wicked shall fall by his own *w*.
13. 6 but *w* overthroweth the sinner.
26.26 his *w* shall be shewed before the
Ec 3.16 of judgment, that *w* was there;
7.15 that prolongeth his life in his *w*.
25 and to know the *w* of folly, even
Isa 9.18 For *w* burneth as the fire: it shall
47.10 For thou hast trusted in thy *w*:
Jer 1.16 against them touching all their *w*,
2.19 Thine own *w* shall correct thee,
4.14 wash thine heart from *w*, that
6. 7 waters, so she casteth out her *w*:
8. 6 no man repented him of his *w*,
14.16 I will pour their *w* upon them.
20 We acknowledge, O Lord, our *w*,
44. 3 of their *w*...they have committed
9 ye forgotten the *w* of your fathers,
9 and the *w* of the kings of Judah,
La 1.22 Let all their *w* come before thee;
Eze 3.19 and he turn not from his *w*, nor
7.11 is risen up into a rod of *w*:
31.11 I have driven him out for his *w*.
33.12 as for the *w* of the wicked, he
12 day that he turneth from his *w*;
19 But if the wicked turn from his *w*,
Hos 7. 1 discovered, and the *w* of Samaria:
3 make the king glad with their *w*,
9.15 All their *w* is in Gilgal: for there I
15 for the *w* of their doings I will
Joel 3.13 fats overflow; for their *w* is great.
Jon 1. 2 for their *w* is come up before me.
Mic 6.10 treasures of *w* in the house of the
Zec 5. 8 And he said, This is *w*. And he
Mal 1. 4 shall call them, The border of *w*,
3.15 yea, they that work *w* are set up;
Mt 22.18 But Jesus perceived their *w*, and
Mk 7.22 Thefts, covetousness, *w*, deceit,
Lk 11.39 part is full of ravening and *w*.
Ac 8.22 Repent therefore of this thy *w*,
25. 5 man, if there be any *w* in him.
Ro 1.29 *w*, covetousness, maliciousness;
1Co 5. 8 with the leaven of malice and *w*;
Eph 6.12 against spiritual *w* in high places,
1Jn 5.19 and the whole world lieth in *w*.

WIDE

Dt 15. 8 open thine hand *w* unto him,
11 thine hand *w* unto thy brother,
1Ch 4.40 the land was *w*, and quiet,
Job 29.23 opened their mouth *w* as for the
30.14 as a *w* breaking in of waters:
Ps 35.21 opened their mouth *w* against
81.10 open thy mouth *w*, and I will fill
104.25 So is this great and *w* sea,
Pr 13. 3 he that openeth *w* his lips shall have
21. 9 a brawling woman in a *w* house.
25.24 brawling woman and in a *w* house.
Isa 57. 4 against whom make ye a *w* mouth,
Jer 22.14 I will build me a *w* house and
Na 3.13 the gates...shall be set *w* open
Mt 7.13 for *w* is the gate, and broad is the

WIDOW

Gen 38.11 Remain a *w* at thy father's house,
Ex 22.22 Ye shall not afflict any *w*, or
Lev 21.14 A *w*, or a divorced woman, or
22.13 But if the priest's daughter be a *w*,
Nu 30. 9 But every vow of a *w*, and of her
Dt 10.18 judgment of the fatherless and *w*,
14.29 and the fatherless, and the *w*,
16.11, 14 and the fatherless, and the *w*,
24.19 for the fatherless, and for the *w*:
20, 21 for the fatherless, and for the *w*.
26.12 stranger, the fatherless, and the *w*,
13 to the fatherless, and to the *w*,
27.19 of the stranger, fatherless, and *w*.
2Sa 14. 5 answered, I am indeed a *w* woman,
1Ki 11.26 name was Zeruah, a *w* woman,
17. 9 commanded a *w* woman there to
10 the *w* woman was there gathering
20 evil upon the *w* with whom I
Job 24.21 not: and doeth not good to the *w*.
31.16 caused the eyes of the *w* to fail;
Ps 94. 6 They slay the *w* and the stranger,
109. 9 be fatherless, and his wife a *w*.
146. 9 he relieveth the fatherless and *w*:
Pr 15.25 will establish the border of the *w*.
Isa 1.17 the fatherless, plead for the *w*.
23 the cause of the *w* come unto them.
47. 8 I shall not sit as a *w*, neither shall I
Jer 7. 6 stranger, the fatherless, and the *w*,
22. 3 stranger, the fatherless, nor the *w*,
La 1. 1 how is she become as a *w*! she that
Eze 22. 7 they vexed the fatherless and the *w*.
44.22 shall they take for their wives a *w*,
22 or a *w* that had a priest before.
Zec 7.10 And oppress not the *w*, nor the
Mal 3. 5 the hireling in his wages, the *w*,
Mk 12.42 And there came a certain poor *w*,
43 That this poor *w* hath cast more in,
Lk 2.37 a *w* of about fourscore and four
4.26 Sidon, unto a woman that was a *w*.

7.12 of his mother, and she was a *w*:
18. 3 And there was a *w* in that city;
5 Yet because this *w* troubleth me, I
21. 2 *w* casting in thither two mites.
3 *w* hath cast in more than they all:
1Ti 5. 4 if any *w* have children or nephews,
5 that is a *w* indeed, and desolate,
9 not a *w* be taken into the number
Rev 18. 7 I sit a queen, and am no *w*, and

WIDOWHOOD

Gen 38.19 and put on the garments of her *w*.
2Sa 20. 3 the day of their death, living in *w*.
Isa 47. 9 day, the loss of children, and *w*:
54. 4 remember the reproach of thy *w*

WIDOW'S

Gen 38.14 And she put her *w* garments off
Dt 24.17 nor take the *w* raiment to pledge:
1Ki 7.14 was a *w* son of the tribe of Naphtali,
Job 24. 3 they take the *w* ox for a pledge.
29.13 I caused the *w* heart to sing for joy.

WIDOWS

Ex 22.24 and your wives shall be *w*, and
Job 22. 9 Thou hast sent *w* away empty, and
27.15 in death: and his *w* shall not weep.
Ps 68. 5 the fatherless, and a judge of the *w*,
78.64 and their *w* made no lamentation.
Isa 9.17 mercy on their fatherless and *w*:
10. 2 people, that *w* may be their prey,
Jer 15. 8 Their *w* are increased to me above
18.21 bereaved of their children, and be *w*;
49.11 alive; and let thy *w* trust in me.
La 5. 3 fatherless, our mothers are as *w*.
Eze 22.25 made her many *w* in the midst
Lk 4.25 many *w* were in Israel in the days
Ac 6. 1 their *w* were neglected in the daily
9.39 all the *w* stood by him weeping,
41 he had called the saints and *w*,
1Co 7. 8 therefore to the unmarried and *w*,
1Ti 5. 3 Honor *w* that are *w* indeed.
11 But the younger *w* refuse: for
16 or woman that believeth have *w*,
16 relieve them that are *w* indeed.
Jas 1.27 fatherless and *w* in their affliction,

WIDOWS'

Mt 23.14 for ye devour *w* houses, and for a
Mk 12.40 Which devour *w* houses, and for a
Lk 20.47 Which devour *w* houses, and for a

WIFE

Gen 2.24 and shall cleave unto his *w*:
25 both naked, the man and his *w*,
3. 8 Adam and his *w* hid themselves
Dt 24. 1 When a man hath taken a *w*, and
5 When a man hath taken a new *w*,
25. 5 the *w* of the dead shall not marry
2Sa 12.10 me, and hast taken the *w* of Uriah
Job 19.17 My breath is strange to my *w*,
31.10 Then let my *w* grind unto another,
Ps 128. 3 Thy *w* shall be as a fruitful vine by
Pr 5.18 and rejoice with the *w* of thy youth.
18.22 Whoso findeth a *w* findeth a good
19.13 contentions of a *w* are a continual
14 and a prudent *w* is from the Lord.
Ec 9. 9 Live joyfully with the *w* whom thou
Mt 1. 6 of her that had been the *w* of Urias;
20 not to take unto thee Mary thy *w*:
24 him, and took unto him his *w*:
19. 3 lawful for a man to put away his *w*
5 mother, and shall cleave to his *w*:
9 Whosoever shall put away his *w*,
22.24 his brother shall marry his *w*, and
28 whose *w* shall she be of the seven?
27.19 seat, his *w* sent unto him, saying,
Mk 6.17 sake, his brother Philip's *w*:
10. 2 for a man to put away his *w*?
7 and mother, and cleave to his *w*;
12.19 die, and leave his *w* behind him,
19 that his brother should take his *w*,
23 rise, whose *w* shall she be of them?
Lk 1. 5 his *w* was of the daughters of
13 *w* Elisabeth shall bear thee a son,
18 and my *w* well stricken in years.
24 days his *w* Elisabeth conceived,
2. 5 taxed with Mary his espoused *w*,
3.19 Herodias his brother Philip's *w*,
17.32 Remember Lot's *w*.
20.28 any man's brother die, having a *w*,
33 whose *w* of them is she?
Jn 19.25 sister, Mary the *w* of Cleophas,
Ac 5. 1 Ananias, with Sapphira his *w*,
18. 2 from Italy, with his *w* Priscilla;
24.24 Felix came with his *w* Drusilla,
1Co 5. 1 one should have his father's *w*.
7. 2 let every man have his own *w*, and
3 husband render unto the *w* due
3 also the *w* unto the husband.
4 *w* hath not power of her own body,
4 power of his own body, but the *w*.
14 husband is sanctified by the *w*,
14 *w* is sanctified by the husband:
27 Art thou bound unto a *w*? seek not
27 loosed from a *w*? seek not a *w*.
Eph 5.23 the husband is the head of the *w*,
28 that loveth his *w* loveth himself.
31 and shall be joined unto his *w*,
33 so love his *w* even as himself; and
33 the *w* see that she reverence her
Rev 19. 7 his *w* hath made herself ready.
21. 9 shew thee the bride, the Lamb's *w*.

WIFE'S

Gen 3.20 And Adam called his *w* name Eve;
20.11 they will slay me for my *w* sake.
Mt 8.14 house, he saw his *w* mother laid,
Mk 1.30 Simon's *w* mother lay sick of a
Lk 4.38 And Simon's *w* mother was taken

WILD

Gen 16.12 And he will be a *w* man; his hand
Job 6. 5 *w* ass bray when he hath grass?
Ps 50.11 the *w* beasts of the field are mine.
104.11 the *w* asses quench their thirst.
18 hills are a refuge for the *w* goats;
Isa 5. 2 and it brought forth *w* grapes.
4 grapes, brought it forth *w* grapes?
Jer 2.24 A *w* ass used to the wilderness,
Mt 3. 4 his meat was locusts and *w* honey
Mk 1. 6 he did eat locusts and *w* honey;
13 and was with the *w* beasts;
Ac 10.12 *w* beasts, and creeping things,
11. 6 *w* beasts, and creeping things, and
Ro 11.17 being a *w* olive tree, wert graffed
24 the olive tree which is *w* by nature,

WILDERNESS

Gen 16. 7 by a fountain of water in the *w*,
Ex 3.18 three days' journey into the *w*, that
13.18 the way of the *w* of the Red sea:
14.11 taken us away to die in the *w*?
Lev 16.10 him go for a scapegoat into the *w*.
Nu 14. 2 would God we had died in this *w*!
21. 5 us up out of Egypt to die in the *w*?
32.13 them wander in the *w* forty years,
Dt 1.19 all that great and terrible *w*,
8.16 Who fed thee in the *w* with manna,
Jos 5. 6 Israel walked forty years in the *w*,
Job 24. 5 the *w* yieldeth food for them and
38.26 the *w*, wherein there is no man;
39. 6 Whose house I have made the *w*,
Ps 78.19 Can God furnish a table in the *w*?
52 guided them in the *w* like a flock.
102. 6 I am like a pelican of the *w*: I am
107. 4 wandered in...*w* in a solitary way;
33 He turneth rivers into a *w*, and the
136.16 led his people through the *w*:
Pr 21.19 It is better to dwell in the *w*, than
SS 3. 6 is this that cometh out of the *w*
Isa 14.17 That made the world a *w*, and
32.15 high, and the *w* be a fruitful field,
16 judgment shall dwell in the *w*,
35. 1 *w* and the solitary place...be glad
6 in the *w* shall waters break out,
40. 3 voice of him that crieth in the *w*,
41.18 I will make the *w* a pool of water,
43.19 I will even make a way in the *w*,
20 because I give waters in the *w*,
Jer 51.43 a desolation, a dry land, and a *w*,
La 4.19 they laid wait for us in the *w*.
Eze 20.13 rebelled against me in the *w*:
17 I make an end of them in the *w*.
Hos 13. 5 I did know thee in the *w*, in the land
15 Lord shall come up from the *w*,
Joel 2.22 for the pastures of the *w* do spring,
Mt 3. 1 preaching in the *w* of Judea,
3 The voice of one crying in the *w*,
4. 1 Jesus led up of the spirit in the *w*
11. 7 What went ye out into the *w* to see?
15.33 we have so much bread in the *w*,
Mk 1. 3 The voice of one crying in the *w*,
4 John did baptize in the *w*, and
12 the spirit driveth him into the *w*.
13 he was there in the *w* forty days,
8. 4 men with bread here in the *w*?
Lk 3. 2 the son of Zacharias in the *w*.
4 The voice of one crying in the *w*,
4. 1 was led by the Spirit into the *w*,
5.16 he withdrew himself into the *w*,
7.24 went ye out into the *w* for to see?
8.29 was driven of the devil into the *w*.)
15. 4 leave the ninety and nine in the *w*,
Jn 1.23 the voice of one crying in the *w*,
3.14 lifted up the serpent in the *w*,
6.49 fathers did eat manna in the *w*,
11.54 unto a country near to the *w*,
Ac 7.30 in the *w* of mount Sina an angel
36 Red sea, and in the *w* forty years.
38 he, that was in the church in the *w*
42 the space of forty years in the *w*?
44 the tabernacle of witness in the *w*,
13.18 suffered he their manners in the *w*.
21.38 leddest out into the *w* four
1Co 10. 5 for they were overthrown in the *w*.
2Co 11.26 in the city, in perils in the *w*,
Heb 3. 8 in the day of temptation in the *w*:
17 whose carcasses fell in the *w*?
Rev 12. 6 And the woman fled into the *w*.
14 that she might fly into the *w*,
17. 3 me away in the spirit into the *w*:

WILES

Nu 25.18 For they vex you with their *w*,
Eph 6.11 stand against the *w* of the devil.

WILFULLY

Heb 10.26 For if we sin *w* after that we have

WILL

Gen 3.16 I *w* greatly multiply thy sorrow and
6. 7 I *w* destroy man whom I have
8.21 I *w* not again curse the ground any
12. 2 I *w* make of thee a great nation.
18.14 At the time appointed I *w* return
Ex 3.12 he said, Certainly I *w* be with thee;
6. 7 I *w* be to you a God: and ye shall
12.12 I *w* pass through the land of Egypt
16. 4 I *w* rain bread from heaven for you;
22.23 all unto me, I *w* surely hear their cry;
Lev 26.33 I *w* scatter you among the heathen,
Nu 9. 8 and I *w* hear what the Lord
14 *w* keep the passover unto the Lord;
Dt 5.11 Lord *w* not hold them guiltless that
10. 2 I *w* write on the tables the words
18.15 God *w* raise up unto thee a Prophet
Jos 1. 5 was with Moses, so I *w* be with thee:
24.15 choose you this day whom ye *w*
Jdg 2. 1 I *w* never break my covenant with
Ru 1.16 for whither thou goest, I *w* go: and
16 and where thou lodgest, I *w* lodge:
1Sa 2.35 And I *w* raise me up a faithful priest,

2Sa 14.17 the Lord thy God *w* be with thee.
22. 3 God of my rock; in him *w* I trust:
1Ki 12.11 heavy yoke, I *w* add to your yoke:
11 but I *w* chastise you with scorpions.
2Ki 4.30 as thy soul liveth, I *w* not leave thee.
Neh 2.20 The God of heaven, he *w* prosper us;
Job 2. 4 that a man hath *w* he give for his life.
8.20 God *w* not cast away a perfect man,
13. 7 *W* ye speak wickedly for God?
15 Though he slay me, yet *w* I trust him:
19. 2 How long *w* ye vex my soul,
35.13 Surely God *w* not hear vanity,
Ps 4. 2 *w* ye turn my glory into shame?
6 that say, Who *w* shew us any good?
8 I *w* both lay me down in peace,
6. 9 the Lord *w* receive my prayer.
23. 4 shadow of death, I *w* fear no evil:
6 I *w* dwell in the house of the Lord for
26. 6 I *w* wash mine hands in innocency:
6 so *w* I compass thine altar, O Lord:
40. 8 I delight to do thy *w*, O my God:
63. 1 art my God; early *w* I seek thee:
89.34 My covenant *w* I not break,
91. 2 I *w* say of the Lord, He is my refuge
2 my God; in him *w* I trust.
121. 1 I *w* lift up mine eyes unto the hills,
Pr 1. 5 A wise man *w* hear,
26.27 rolleth a stone, it *w* return upon him.
Isa 1.15 hands, I *w* hide mine eyes from you;
7. 9 If ye *w* not believe, surely ye shall
25. 8 He *w* swallow up death in victory;
8 Lord God *w* wipe away tears from
35. 4 your God *w* come with vengeance,
40.18 To whom then *w* ye liken God? or
43.19 Behold, I *w* do a new thing; now it
66.12 I *w* extend peace to her like a river,
Jer 3.15 I *w* give you pastors according to
7.23 Obey my voice, and I *w* be your
20. 4 I *w* make thee a terror to thyself,
23.33 I *w* even forsake you, saith the Lord.
27. 8 nation *w* I punish, saith the Lord,
30.11 yet *w* I not make a full end of thee:
17 For I *w* restore health unto thee,
31.31 I *w* make a new covenant with the
34 I *w* remember their sin no more.
32.38 be my people, and I *w* be their God:
49.19 and who *w* appoint me the time?
51.22 *w* I break in pieces man and woman.
La 3.24 my soul; therefore *w* I hope in him.
31 For the Lord *w* not cast off for ever:
Eze 3.26 I *w* make thy tongue cleave to the
18.31 for why *w* ye die, O house of Israel?
33. 8 his blood *w* I require at thine hand.
36.25 *w* I sprinkle clean water upon you,
27 I *w* put my spirit within you, and
Dan 11. 2 And now *w* I shew thee the truth.
Hos 1. 7 *w* save them by the Lord their God,
2.18 I *w* break the bow and the sword
6. 1 he hath torn us, and he *w* heal us;
2 in the third day he *w* raise us up,
13.14 O grave, I *w* be thy destruction:
Am 3. 2 I *w* punish you for all your iniquities.
4 *W* a lion roar in the forest, when he
8. 5 When *w* the new moon be gone,
9 *w* cause the sun to go down at noon
Hag 2. 6 I *w* shake the heavens, and the earth,
7 I *w* fill this house with glory, saith
Mal 1.10 neither *w* I accept an offering at your
3. 1 Behold, I *w* send my messenger,
4. 5 I *w* send you Elijah the prophet
Mt 3.12 and he *w* throughly purge his floor,
6.10 Thy *w* be done in earth, as it is in
24 for either he *w* hate the one, and love
7.21 he that doeth the *w* of my Father
8. 3 him, saying, I *w*; be thou clean.
12. 7 I *w* have mercy, and not sacrifice,
50 do the *w* of my Father which is in
16.18 upon this rock I *w* build my church;
18.14 so it is not the *w* of your Father
20. 4 and whatsoever is right I *w* give you.
15 me to do what I *w* with mine own?
26.15 unto them, What *w* ye give me,
39 nevertheless not as I *w*, but as
42 except I drink it, thy *w* be done.
27.63 alive, After three days I *w* rise again.
Mk 1.17 *w* make you to become fishers of
41 saith unto him, I *w*; be thou clean.
14.36 nevertheless not what I *w*, but
Lk 2.14 peace, good *w* toward men.
5.13 him, saying, I *w*: be thou clean.
11. 2 Thy *w* be done, as in heaven, so
15.18 I *w* arise and go to my father,
22.42 nevertheless not my *w*, but thine,
67 If I tell you, ye *w* not believe:
23.25 but he delivered Jesus to their *w*.
Jn 1.13 *w* of the flesh, nor of the *w* of man,
2.19 and in three days I *w* raise it up.
34 is to do the *w* of him that sent me,
5.30 because I seek not mine own *w*,
14. 3 I *w* come again, and receive you
17.24 Father, I *w* that they also, whom
21.22, 23 If I *w* that he tarry till I come,
Ac 2.17 God, I *w* pour out my Spirit upon all
18.21 again unto you, if God *w*.
21.14 The *w* of the Lord be done.
Ro 7.18 for to *w* is present with me; but
12. 2 acceptable, and perfect, *w* of God.
1Co 4.19 if the Lord *w*,
Php 2.13 both to *w* and to do of his good
1Th 5.18 for this is the *w* of God in Christ
1Ti 2. 8 I *w* therefore that men pray
Heb 1. 5 I *w* be to him a Father, and he shall
13. 6 I *w* not fear what man shall do unto
21 in every good work to do his *w*,
Jas 1.18 Of his own *w* begat he us with the
2Pe 1.21 not in old time by the *w* of man:
1Jn 2.17 he that doeth the *w* of God abideth
Rev 2.10 and I *w* give thee a crown of life.
28 And I *w* give him the morning star.
3. 3 what hour I *w* come upon thee.
21. 7 and I *w* be his God, and he shall be

WILLING

Gen 24. 5 the woman will not be *w* to follow
8 woman will not be *w* to follow thee,
Ex 35. 5 whosoever is of a *w* heart, let him
21 one whom his spirit made *w*,
22 as many as were *w* hearted,
29 of Israel brought a *w* offering
29 whose heart made them *w* to
1Ch 28. 9 perfect heart and with a *w* mind:
21 workmanship every *w* skilful
29. 5 who then is *w* to consecrate his
Job 39. 9 Will the unicorn be *w* to serve thee,
Ps 110. 3 Thy people shall be *w* in the day
Isa 1.19 If ye be *w* and obedient, ye shall eat
Mt 1.19 *w* to make her a publick example,
26.41 the spirit indeed is *w*, but the
Mk 15.15 Pilate, *w* to content the people,
Lk 10.29 But he, *w* to justify himself, said
22.42 Father, if thou be *w*, remove this
23.20 Pilate...*w* to release Jesus, spake
Jn 5.35 ye were *w* for a season to rejoice
Ac 24.27 *w* to shew the Jews a pleasure,
25. 9 *w* to do the Jews a pleasure,
27.43 But the centurion, *w* to save Paul,
Ro 9.22 if God, *w* to show his wrath, and
2Co 5. 8 *w* rather to be absent from the
8. 3 power they were *w* of themselves;
12 For if there be first a *w* mind,
1Th 2. 8 were *w* to have imparted unto you,
1Ti 6.18 to distribute, *w* to communicate;
Heb 6.17 *w* more abundantly to shew unto
13.18 in all things *w* to live honestly.
2Pe 3. 9 not *w* that any should perish,

WILLINGLY

Ex 25. 2 every man that giveth it *w* with
Jdg 5. 2 the people *w* offered themselves.
9 that offered themselves *w* among
8.25 answered, We will *w* give them.
1Ch 29. 6 of the king's work, offered *w*,
9 rejoiced, for that they offered *w*,
9 with perfect heart they offered *w*
14 should be able to offer so *w* after
17 I have *w* offered all these things:
17 present here, to offer *w* unto thee.
2Ch 17.16 *w* offered himself unto the Lord;
35. 8 princes gave *w* unto the people,
Ezr 1. 6 beside all that was *w* offered.
3. 5 that *w* offered a freewill offering
7.16 offering *w* for the house of their God
Neh 11. 2 that *w* offered themselves to dwell at
Pr 31.13 and worketh *w* with her hands.
La 3.33 For he doth not afflict *w*, nor
Hos 5.11 because he *w* walked after the
Jn 6.21 they *w* received him into the ship:
Ro 8.20 subject to vanity, not *w*, but
1Co 9.17 For if I do this thing *w*, I
Phm 14 it were of necessity, but *w*.
1Pe 5. 2 thereof, not by constraint, but *w*;
2Pe 3. 5 For this they *w* are ignorant of,

WILLOW

Eze 17. 5 waters, and set it as a *w* tree.

WILLOWS

Lev 23.40 thick trees, and *w* of the brook;
Job 40.22 the *w* of the brook compass him
Ps 137. 2 We hanged our harps upon the *w*
Isa 15. 7 carry away to the brook of the *w*.
44. 4 grass, as *w* by the water courses.

WILT

Gen 18.23 *W* thou also destroy the righteous
Ex 4.13 the hand of him whom thou *w* send.
8.21 if thou *w* not let my people go,
32.32 now, if thou *w* forgive their sin-;
Jos 7. 9 *w* thou do unto thy great name?
1Sa 16. 1 How long *w* thou mourn for Saul,
2Sa 22.26 thou *w* shew thyself merciful,
28 the afflicted people thou *w* save:
Est 5. 3 her, What *w* thou, queen Esther?
Job 5. 1 to which of the saints *w* thou turn?
10. 9 and *w* thou bring me into dust again?
14 and thou *w* not acquit me from mine
Ps 13. 1 How long *w* thou forget me,
16.10 For thou *w* not leave my soul in hell;
10 *w* thou suffer thine Holy One to see
11 Thou *w* shew me the path of life:
18.28 thou *w* light my candle: the Lord my
51.17 heart, O God, thou *w* not despise.
79. 5 Lord? *w* thou be angry for ever?
85. 5 *W* thou be angry with us for ever?
88.10 *W* thou shew wonders to the dead?
101. 2 O when *w* thou come unto me? I will
Pr 6. 9 How long *w* thou sleep, O sluggard?
Isa 26. 3 Thou *w* keep him in perfect peace,
Jer 12. 5 *w* thou do in the swelling of Jordan?
13.27 *w* thou not be made clean?
Mt 4. 9 if thou *w* fall down and worship me.
7. 4 *w* thou say to thy brother, Let me
8. 2 Lord, if thou *w*, thou canst make
13.28 *W* thou then that we go and
15.28 be it unto thee even as thou *w*.
17. 4 if thou *w*, let us make here three
19.17 but if thou *w* enter into life, keep
21 If thou *w* be perfect, go and sell
20.21 he said unto her, What *w* thou?
26.17 Where *w* thou that we prepare for
39 not as I will, but as thou *w*.
Mk 1.40 If thou *w*, thou canst make me
6.22 Ask of me whatsoever thou *w*, and
10.51 What *w* thou that I should do unto
14.12 Where *w* thou that we go and
36 not what I will, but what thou *w*.
Lk 4. 7 If thou therefore *w* worship me, all
5.12 Lord, if thou *w*, thou canst make
9.54 *w* thou that we command fire to
18.41 What *w* thou that I shall do unto
22. 9 Where *w* thou that we prepare?
Jn 2.20 and *w* thou rear it up in three days?
5. 6 him, *W* thou be made whole?

11.22 whatsoever thou *w* ask of God,
13.38 *W* thou lay down thy life for my
14.22 that thou *w* manifest thyself unto us,
Ac 1. 6 *w* thou at this time restore again the
2.27 thou *w* not leave my soul in hell,
27 neither *w* thou suffer thine Holy One
7.28 *W* thou kill me as thou diddest
9. 6 Lord, what *w* thou have me to do?
13.10 *w* thou not cease to perverse the
25. 9 *W* thou go up to Jerusalem, and
Ro 9.19 Thou *w* say then unto me, Why doth
11.19 Thou *w* say then, The branches were
13. 3 *W* thou then not be afraid of the
Phm 21 thou *w* also do more than I say.
Jas 2.20 But *w* thou know, O vain man,

WIN

2Ch 32. 1 thought to *w* them for himself.
Php 3. 8 but dung, that I may *w* Christ.

WIND

Gen 8. 1 God made a *w* to pass over the
Ex 10.13 Lord brought an east *w* upon the
14.21 sea to go back by a strong east *w*
1Ki 18.45 was black with clouds and *w*,
19.11 and strong *w* rent the mountains,
11 but the Lord was not in the *w*:
11 and after the *w* an earthquake;
Job 1.19 a great *w* from the wilderness,
6.26 is desperate, which are as *w*?
7. 7 O remember that my life is *w*:
30.15 they pursue my soul as the *w*:
Ps 1. 4 chaff which the *w* driveth away.
18.10 he did fly upon the wings of the *w*.
42 small as the dust before the *w*:
103.16 For the *w* passeth over it, and it is
104. 3 walketh upon the wings of the *w*:
135. 7 bringeth the *w* out of his treasuries.
148. 8 stormy *w* fulfilling his word:
Pr 11.29 his own house shall inherit the *w*:
27.16 hideth her hideth the *w*, and
30. 4 hath gathered the *w* in his fists?
Ec 1. 6 *w* goeth toward the south, and
6 *w* returneth again according to the
5.16 he that hath labored for the *w*?
11. 4 observeth the *w* shall not sow;
Isa 7. 2 the wood are moved with the *w*.
26.18 have as it were brought forth *w*;
27. 8 he stayeth his rough *w*
41.16 and the *w* shall carry them away,
29 molten images are *w* and confusion.
64. 6 iniquities, like the *w*, have taken
Jer 2.24 snuffeth up the *w* at her pleasure;
5.13 And the prophets shall become *w*,
10.13 forth the *w* out of his treasures.
22.22 The *w* shall eat up all thy pastors,
Eze 5. 2 part thou shalt scatter in the *w*;
37. 9 he unto me, Prophesy unto the *w*,
Hos 4.19 The *w* hath bound her up in her
8. 7 they have sown the *w*, and they
Am 4.13 mountains, and createth the *w*,
Mt 11. 7 to see. A reed shaken with the *w*?
14.24 with waves: for the *w* was contrary.
30 But when he saw the *w* boisterous,
32 come into the ship, the *w* ceased.
Mk 4.37 And there arose a great storm of *w*,
39 And he arose, and rebuked the *w*,
39 the *w* ceased, and there was a great
41 even the *w* and the sea obey him?
Lk 7.24 to see? A reed shaken with the *w*?
8.23 down a storm of *w* on the lake;
24 rebuked the *w* and the raging of
Jn 3. 8 The *w* bloweth where it listeth,
Ac 2. 2 heaven as of a rushing mighty *w*,
Eph 4.14 about with every *w* of doctrine,
Rev 6.13 when she is shaken of a mighty *w*.
7. 1 the *w* should not blow on the earth,

WINDING

1Ki 6. 8 and they went up with *w* stairs
Eze 41. 7 a *w* about still upward to the side
7 *w* about of the house went still

Jesus makes wine out of water for the wedding at Cana (Jn 2); engraving by Julius Schnorr von Carolsfeld.

WINDOW

Gen 6.16 A *w* shalt thou make to the ark,
8. 6 Noah opened the *w* of the ark
26. 8 the Philistines looked out at a *w*,
Jos 2.15 down by a cord through the *w*:
18 bind this line of...thread in the *w*
21 she bound the scarlet line in the *w*.
Jdg 5.28 of Sisera looked out at a *w*,
1Sa 19.12 let David down through a *w*:
2Sa 6.16 daughter looked through a *w*,
2Ki 9.30 her head, and looked out at a *w*.
32 And he lifted up his face to the *w*,
13.17 And he said, Open the *w* eastward.
1Ch 15.29 looking out at a *w* saw king David
Pr 7. 6 at the *w* of my house I looked
Ac 20. 9 sat in a *w* a certain young man
2Co 11.33 through a *w* in a basket was I let

WINDOWS

Gen 7.11 and the *w* of heaven were opened.
8. 2 and the *w* of heaven were stopped,
1Ki 6. 4 he made *w* of narrow lights.
7. 4 And there were *w* in three rows,
5 posts were square, with the *w*:
2Ki 7. 2 Lord would make *w* in heaven,
19 Lord should make *w* in heaven,
Ec 12. 3 that look out of the *w* be darkened,
SS 2. 9 he looketh forth at the *w*,
Isa 24.18 for the *w* from on high are opened,
54.12 I will make thy *w* of agates, and
60. 8 and as the doves to their *w*?
Jer 9.21 For death is come up into our *w*,
22.14 chambers, and cutteth him out *w*;
Eze 40.16 narrow *w* to the little chambers,
16 and *w* were round about inward:
22 And their *w*, and their arches, and
25 were *w* in it and in the arches
25 thereof round about, like those *w*:
29 were *w* in it and in the arches
33 were *w* therein and in the arches
36 and the *w* to it round about:
41.16 The door posts, and the narrow *w*,
16 and from the ground up to the *w*,
16 and the *w* were covered;
26 were narrow *w* and palm trees
Dan 6.10 his *w* being open in his chamber
Joel 2. 9 shall enter in at the *w* like a thief.
Zep 2.14 their voice shall sing in the *w*;
Mal 3.10 will not open you the *w* of heaven,

WINDS

Job 28.25 To make the weight for the *w*;
Jer 49.32 I will scatter into all *w* them that
36 upon Elam will I bring the four *w*
36 scatter them toward all those *w*;
Eze 5.10 of thee will I scatter into all the *w*.
12 scatter a third part into all the *w*,
17.21 shall be scattered toward all *w*:
37. 9 Come from the four *w*, O breath,
Dan 7. 2 the four *w* of the heaven strove
8. 8 ones toward the four *w* of heaven.
11. 4 toward the four *w* of heaven;
Zec 2. 6 as the four *w* of the heaven,
Mt 7.25, 27 the floods came, and the *w* blew,
8.26 and rebuked the *w* and the sea.
27 even the *w* and the sea obey him!
24.31 together his elect from the four *w*,
Mk 13.27 together his elect from the four *w*,
Lk 8.25 commandeth even the *w* and water,
Ac 27. 4 because the *w* were contrary.
Jas 3. 4 are driven of fierce *w*, yet are they
Jude 12 without water, carried about of *w*;
Rev 7. 1 holding the four *w* of the earth,

WINE

Gen 9.21 And he drank of the *w*, and was
24 Noah awoke from his *w*, and knew
27.25 he brought him *w*, and he drank.
28 earth, and plenty of corn and *w*:
37 corn and *w* have I sustained him:
Lev 10. 9 Do not drink *w* nor strong drink,
Nu 6. 3 He shall separate himself from *w*
20 that the Nazarite may drink *w*.
Dt 7.13 of thy land, thy corn, and thy *w*,

Dt 16.13 gathered in thy corn and thy *w*:
28.39 but shalt neither drink of the *w*,
Jdg 9.13 Should I leave my *w*, which
Neh 2. 1 the king, that *w* was before him:
10.37 of *w* and of oil, unto the priests,
Ps 4. 7 their corn and their *w* increased.
75. 8 thee is a cup, and the *w* is red;
104.15 *w* that maketh glad the heart of
Pr 3.10 shall burst out with new *w*.
4.17 and drink the *w* of violence.
20. 1 *W* is a mocker, strong drink is
31. 4 it is not for kings to drink *w*;
Ec 2. 3 mine heart to give myself unto *w*,
9. 7 drink thy *w* with a merry heart;
10.19 for laughter, and *w* maketh merry:
SS 1. 2 for thy love is better than *w*.
4.10 much better is thy love than *w*!
Isa 1.22 dross, thy *w* mixed with water:
51.21 and drunken, but not with *w*:
55. 1 buy *w* and milk without money
Jer 13.12 bottle shall be filled with *w*:
25.15 Take the *w* cup of this fury at my
35. 2 chambers, and give them *w* to drink.
5 and I said unto them, Drink ye *w*.
6 they said, We will drink no *w*:
51. 7 the nations have drunken of her *w*;
Hos 2. 8 know that I gave her corn, and *w*,
9. 2 and the new *w* shall fail in her.
Joel 1. 5 and howl, all ye drinkers of *w*,
10 the new *w* is dried up, the oil
3. 3 sold a girl for *w*, that they might
Am 2. 8 drink the *w* of the condemned in
12 ye gave the Nazarites *w* to drink;
Mt 9.17 men put new *w* into old bottles:
17 and the *w* runneth out, and the
17 they put new *w* into new bottles,
Mk 2.22 putteth new *w* into old bottles;
22 the new *w* doth burst the bottles,
22 and the *w* is spilled, and the
22 but new *w* must be put into new
Lk 1.15 drink neither *w* nor strong drink;
5.37 putteth new *w* into old bottles;
37 the new *w* will burst the bottles,
38 But new *w* must be put into new
39 also having drunk old *w* straightway
7.33 eating bread nor drinking *w*;
10.34 his wounds, pouring in oil and *w*,
Jn 2. 3 when they wanted *w*, the mother
3 saith unto him, They have no *w*.
9 tasted the water that was made *w*,
4.46 where he made the water *w*.
Ac 2.13 said, These men are full of new *w*.
Eph 5.18 And be not drunk with *w*, wherein
1Ti 3. 3 Not given to *w*, no striker, not
5.23 use a little *w* for thy stomach's
1Pe 4. 3 lusts, excess of *w*, revellings,
Rev 6. 6 thou hurt not the oil and the *w*.
14. 8 drink of the *w* of the wrath of her
10 drink of the *w* of the wrath of God,
16.19 the cup of the *w* of the fierceness
17. 2 drunk with the *w* of her fornication.
18. 3 ...
20 and blood came out of the *w*, even
19.15 treadeth the *w* of the fierceness.

WINEBIBBER

Mt 11.19 and a *w*, a friend of publicans and
Lk 7.34 and a *w*, a friend of publicans and

WINEPRESS

Nu 18.27 and as the fulness of the *w*.
30 and as the increase of the *w*.
Dt 15.14 out of thy floor, and out of thy *w*:
Jdg 6.11 Gibeon threshed wheat by the *w*,
7.25 Zeeb they slew at the *w* of Zeeb,
2Ki 6.27 of the barnfloor, or out of the *w*?
Isa 5. 2 of it, and also made a *w* therein:
63. 3 I have trodden the *w* alone; and
La 1.15 the daughter of Judah, as in a *w*.
Hos 9. 2 The floor and the *w* shall not feed
Mt 21.33 and digged a *w* in it, and built a
Rev 14.19 great *w* of the wrath of God.
20 *w* was trodden without the city,

WINES

Isa 25. 6 a feast of *w* on the lees, of fat
6 of *w* on the lees well refined.

WING

1Ki 6.24 was the one *w* of the cherub,
24 cubits the other *w* of the cherub:
24 uttermost part of the one *w* unto
27 *w* of the one touched the one wall,
27 *w* of the other cherub touched the
2Ch 3.11 one *w* of the one cherub was five
11 other *w* was likewise five cubits,
11 reaching to the *w* of the other
12 one *w* of the other cherub was five
12 and the other *w* was five cubits
12 joining to...*w* of the other cherub.
Isa 10.14 there was none that moved the *w*,
Eze 17.23 it shall dwell all fowl of every *w*;

WINGED

Gen 1.21 and every *w* fowl after his kind:
Dt 4.17 likeness of any *w* fowl that flieth in

WINGS

Ex 19. 4 and how I bare you on eagles' *w*,
37. 9 the cherubims spread out their *w*
2Sa 22.11 was seen upon the *w* of the wind.
Ps 17. 8 hide me under the shadow of thy *w*,
36. 7 trust under the shadow of thy *w*.
55. 6 said, Oh that I had *w* like a dove!
63. 7 the shadow of thy *w* will I rejoice.
68.13 *w* of a dove covered with silver,
104. 3 walketh upon the *w* of the wind:
139. 9 If I take the *w* of the morning, and
Pr 23. 5 for riches...make themselves *w*;
Isa 6. 2 the seraphims: each one had six *w*;
40.31 shall mount up with *w* as eagles;
Eze 1. 6 faces, and every one had four *w*.
Dan 7. 4 was like a lion, and had eagle's *w*:
Mal 4. 2 arise with healing in his *w*;
Mt 23.37 her chickens under her *w*,
Lk 13.34 gather her brood under her *w*,
Rev 4. 8 four beasts had each of them six *w*
9. 9 sound of their *w* was as the sound
12.14 given two *w* of a great eagle,

WINK

Job 15.12 away? and what do thy eyes *w* at,
Ps 35.19 them *w* with the eye that hate me

WINKED

Ac 17.30 times of this ignorance God *w* at;

WINKETH

Pr 6.13 He *w* with his eyes, he speaketh
10.10 He that *w* with the eye causeth

WINNETH

Pr 11.30 life; and he that *w* souls is wise.

WINTER

Gen 8.22 cold and heat, and summer and *w*,
Ps 74.17 thou hast made summer and *w*.
SS 2.11 the *w* is past, the rain is over and
Isa 18. 6 the beasts...shall *w* upon them.
Am 3.15 I will smite the *w* house with the
Zec 14. 8 in summer and in *w* shall it be.
Mt 24.20 that your flight may not be in *w*,
Mk 13.18 that your flight may not be in *w*.
Jn 10.22 of the dedication, and it was in *w*.
Ac 27.12 haven was not commodious to *w* in,
12 attain to Phenice, and there to *w*;
1Co 16. 6 I will abide, yea, and *w* with you,
2Ti 4.21 thy diligence to come before *w*.
Tit 3.12 for I have determined there to *w*.

WINTERED

Ac 28.11 which had *w* in the isle, whose

WIPE

2Ki 21.13 and I will *w* Jerusalem as a man
Neh 13.14 *w* not out my good deeds that I
Isa 25. 8 Lord God will *w* away tears from
Lk 7.38 did *w* them with the hairs of her
10.11 on us, we do *w* off against you:
Jn 13. 5 and to *w* them with the towel
Rev 7.17 God shall *w* away all tears from
21. 4 God shall *w* away all tears from

WIPED

Pr 6.33 his reproach shall not be *w* away.
Lk 7.44 *w* them with the hairs of her head.
Jn 11. 2 and *w* his feet with her hair,
12. 3 and *w* his feet with her hair:

WISDOM

Ex 28. 3 I have filled with the spirit of *w*,
31. 3 with the spirit of God, in *w*,
36. 1 in whom the Lord put *w* and
Dt 4. 6 is your *w* and your understanding
34. 9 of Nun was full of the spirit of *w*;
1Ki 2. 6 Do therefore according to thy *w*,
4.29 And God gave Solomon *w* and
30 Solomon's *w* excelled the *w* of all
10. 4 Sheba had seen all Solomon's *w*,
7 thy *w* and prosperity exceedeth
2Ch 1.10 Give me now *w* and knowledge,
12 *W* and knowledge is granted unto
Job 4.21 go away? they die, even without *w*.
11. 6 would shew thee the secrets of *w*,
12. 2 people, and *w* shall die with you.
16 With him is strength and *w*: the
28.12 But where shall *w* be found?
18 for the price of *w* is above rubies.
28 the fear of the Lord, that is *w*;
32. 7 multitude of years shall teach *w*.
13 should say, We have found out *w*:
38.36 hath put *w* in the inward parts?
37 Who can number the clouds in *w*?
39.17 God hath deprived her of *w*,
Ps 37.30 of the righteous speaketh *w*,
49. 3 My mouth shall speak of *w*; and
51. 6 thou shalt make me to know *w*.
90.12 we may apply our hearts unto *w*.
104.24 in *w* hast thou made them all:
111.10 the Lord is the beginning of *w*:
136. 5 him that by *w* made the heavens:
Pr 1. 2 To know *w* and instruction;
3 To receive the instruction of *w*,
7 fools despise *w* and instruction.
2. 2 thou incline thine ear unto *w*,
6 For the Lord giveth *w*: out of his
3.13 Happy is the man that findeth *w*,
19 Lord by *w* hath founded the earth;
4. 5 Get *w*, get understanding: forget
7 *W* is the principal thing;
7. 4 Say unto *w*, Thou art my sister;
8. 1 Doth not *w* cry? and understanding
11 For *w* is better than rubies; and
14 Counsel is mine, and sound *w*:
9. 1 *W* hath builded her house, she
10 of the Lord is the beginning of *w*:
10.13 hath understanding *w* is found:
21 but fools die for want of *w*.
14. 6 A scorner seeketh *w*, and findeth
16.16 better is it to get *w* than gold!
19. 8 getteth *w* loveth his own soul:
23. 4 be rich: cease from thine own *w*.
24. 3 Through *w* is an house builded;
7 *W* is too high for a fool: he
31.26 She openeth her mouth with *w*;
Ec 1.13 search out by *w* concerning all
16 my heart had great experience of *w*
18 For in much *w* is much grief:
2. 3 acquainting mine heart with *w*;
13 Then I saw that *w* excelleth folly,
7.11 *W* is good with an inheritance:
12 *w* giveth life to them that have it.
23 All this have I proved by *w*:
8. 1 a man's *w* maketh his face to

16 I applied mine heart to know *w*,
9.10 nor device, nor knowledge, nor *w*,
18 *W* is better than weapons of war:
Isa 10.13 hand I have done it, and by my *w*;
11. 2 the spirit of *w* and understanding,
29.14 *w*, of their wise men shall perish,
Jer 8. 9 the Lord; and what *w* is in them?
10.12 hath established the world by his *w*,
Dan 1. 4 and skilful in all *w*, and cunning
2.14 answered with counsel and *w* to
21 he giveth *w* unto the wise, and
5.11 light and understanding and *w*,
14 and excellent *w* is found in thee.
Mic 6. 9 the man of *w* shall see thy name:
Mt 11.19 But *w* is justified of her children.
12.42 earth to hear the *w* of Solomon;
13.54 Whence hath this man *w*, and
Mk 6. 2 *w* is this which is given unto him,
Lk 1.17 disobedient to the *w* of the just;
2.40 strong in spirit, filled with *w*:
52 Jesus increased in *w* and stature,
7.35 *w* is justified of all her children.
21.15 For I will give you a mouth and *w*,
Ac 6. 3 full of the Holy Ghost and *w*,
7.10 gave him favor and *w* in the sight
1Co 1.17 not with *w* of words, lest the cross
19 I will destroy the *w* of the wise,
20 made foolish the *w* of this world?
21 the world by *w* knew not God,
30 who of God is made unto us *w*,
2. 1 with excellency of speech or of *w*,
4 with enticing words of man's *w*,
6 yet not the *w* of this world, nor of
7 we speak the *w* of God in a
7 even the hidden *w*, which God
3.19 *w* of this world is foolishness with
12. 8 given by the Spirit the word of *w*;
2Co 1.12 not with fleshly *w*, but by the grace
Jas 1. 5 If any of you lack *w*, let him ask
3.13 his works with meekness of *w*.
15 This *w* descendeth not from above,
17 But the *w* that is from above is
Rev 5.12 and *w*, and strength, and honor,
13.18 Here is *w*. Let him that hath

WISE

Gen 3. 6 tree to be desired to make one *w*,
41. 8 and all the *w* men thereof:
33 look out a man discreet and *w*,
Ex 7.11 Pharaoh also called the *w* men
23. 8 the gift blindeth the *w*, and
Dt 1.13 Take you *w* men, and
4. 6 is a *w* and understanding people.
16.19 a gift doth blind the eyes of the *w*,
32.29 O that they were *w*, that they
Job 5.13 He taketh the *w* in their own
9. 4 He is *w* in heart, and mighty in
11.12 vain man would be *w*, though
17.10 cannot find one *w* man among you.
22. 2 he that is *w* may be profitable
32. 9 Great men are not always *w*:
34. 2 Hear my words, O ye *w* men;
34 and let a *w* man hearken unto me.
Ps 2.10 Be *w* now therefore, O ye kings:
19. 7 is sure, making *w* the simple.
36. 3 he hath left off to be *w*, and to do
37. 8 fret not thyself in any *w* to do evil.
94. 8 and ye fools, when will ye be *w*?
107.43 Whoso is *w*, and will observe
Pr 1. 5 *w* man will hear, and will increase
5 man...shall attain unto *w* counsels:
6 the words of the *w*, and their dark
3. 7 Be not *w* in thine own eyes: fear
6. 6 consider her ways, and be *w*:
9. 8 rebuke a *w* man, and he will love
12 If thou be *w*, thou shalt be *w* for
10. 1 A *w* son maketh a glad father:
19 he that refraineth his lips is *w*.
11.29 be servant to the *w* of heart.
30 and he that winneth souls is *w*.
13. 1 A *w* son heareth his father's
14 law of the *w* is a fountain of life,
15. 2 the *w* useth knowledge aright:
7 lips of the *w* disperse knowledge:
16.14 death: but a *w* man will pacify it.
21 *w* in heart shall be called prudent:
18.15 the ear of the *w* seeketh knowledge.
20. 1 is deceived thereby is not *w*.
26 A *w* king scattereth the wicked,
26. 5 lest he be *w* in his own conceit.
28. 7 Whoso keepeth the law is a *w* son:
Ec 2.14 The *w* man's eyes are in his head;
16 how dieth the *w* man? as the fool.
7. 4 heart of the *w* is in the house of
16 neither make thyself over *w*:
23 I said, I will be *w*; but it was far
9. 1 that the righteous, and the *w*, and
12. 9 because the preacher was *w*, he
11 The words of the *w* are as goads,
Isa 5.21 unto them that are *w* in their own
19.11 the *w* counsellers of Pharaoh is
12 are they? where are thy *w* men?
Jer 4.22 they are *w* to do evil, but to do
9.12 Who is the *w* man, that may
23 the *w* man glory in his wisdom,
Dan 2.12 destroy all the *w* men of Babylon.
13 that the *w* men should be slain;
12. 3 And they that be *w* shall shine
Hos 14. 9 Who is *w*, and he shall understand
Mt 1.18 of Jesus Christ was on this *w*:
2. 1 there came *w* men from the east

Wise men from the East come to behold the infant Jesus (Mt 2) in this painting by the 15th-century artist Hans Memling.

Mt 2. 7 he had privily called the *w* men,
16 diligently inquired of the *w* men.
10.16 be ye therefore *w* as serpents, and
42 you, he shall in no *w* lose his reward.
11.25 hast hid these things from the *w*
23.34 unto you prophets, and *w* men,
24.45 then is a faithful and *w* servant,
25. 2 And five of them were *w*, and five
4 But the *w* took oil in their vessels
Mk 14.31 thee, I will not deny thee in any *w*.
Lk 10.21 hast hid these things from the *w*
12.42 is that faithful and *w* steward,
18.17 child shall in no *w* enter therein.
Jn 6.37 cometh to me I will in no *w* cast out.
Ro 1.14 both to the *w*, and to the unwise.
22 Professing themselves to be *w*,
12.16 Be not *w* in your own conceits.
1Co 1.19 I will destroy the wisdom of the *w*,
20 Where is the *w*? where is the scribe
27 of the world to confound the *w*:
3.10 as a *w* masterbuilder, I have laid
18 become a fool, that he may be *w*.
20 knoweth the thoughts of the *w*,
4.10 sake, but ye are *w* in Christ:
6. 5 there is not a *w* man among you?
Eph 5.15 not as fools, but as *w*,
Jude 25 To the only *w* God our Saviour,

WISELY

Ex 1.10 Come on, let us deal *w* with them;
1Sa 18. 5 sent him, and behaved himself *w*:
14 And David behaved himself *w*
15 that he behaved himself very *w*,
30 David behaved himself more *w*
2Ch 11.23 And he dealt *w*, and dispersed of
Ps 58. 5 charmers, charming never so *w*.
64. 9 they shall *w* consider of his doing.
101. 2 behave myself *w* in a perfect way.
Pr 16.20 He that handleth a matter *w* shall
21.12 The righteous man *w* considereth
28.26 but whoso walketh *w*, he shall be
Ec 7.10 for thou dost not inquire *w*
Lk 16. 8 steward, because he had done *w*:

WISER

1Ki 4.31 For he was *w* than all men: than
Job 35.11 and maketh us *w* than the fowls
Ps 119.98 commandments hast made me *w*
Pr 9. 9 a wise man, and he will be yet *w*:
26.16 sluggard is *w* in his own conceit
Eze 28. 3 Behold, thou art *w* than Daniel;
Lk 16. 8 *w* than the children of light.
1Co 1.25 foolishness of God is *w* than men;

WISH

Job 33. 6 I am according to thy *w* in God's
Ps 40.14 and put to shame that *w* me evil.
73. 7 have more than heart could *w*.
Ro 9. 3 could *w* that myself were accursed
2Co 13. 9 and this also we *w*, even your
3Jn 2 I *w* above all things that thou

WISHED

Jon 4. 8 and *w* in himself to die, and said,
Ac 27.29 of the stern, and *w* for the day.

WIST

Ex 16.15 for they *w* not what it was.
34.29 Moses *w* not that the skin of his
Lev 5.17 though he *w* it not, yet is he guilty,
18 wherein he erred and *w* it not,
Jos 2. 4 me, but I *w* not whence they were:
8.14 he *w* not that there were liers in
Jdg 16.20 *w* not that the Lord was departed
Mk 9. 6 For he *w* not what to say; for they
14.40 neither *w* they what to answer
Lk 2.49 *w* ye not that I must be about my
Jn 5.13 that was healed *w* not who it was:
Ac 12. 9 *w* not that it was true which was
23. 5 Then said Paul, I *w* not, brethren,

WITCH

Ex 22.18 Thou shalt not suffer a *w* to live.
Dt 18.10 of times, or an enchanter, or a *w*,

WITCHCRAFT

1Sa 15.23 For rebellion is as the sin of *w*,
2Ch 33. 6 used enchantments, and used *w*,
Gal 5.20 Idolatry, *w*, hatred, variance,

WITCHCRAFTS

2Ki 9.22 Jezebel and her *w* are so many?
Mic 5.12 will cut off *w* out of thine hand;
Na 3. 4 the mistress of *w*, that selleth
4 and families through her *w*.

WITHDRAW

1Sa 14.19 unto the priest, *W* thine hand.
Job 9.13 If God will not *w* his anger, the
13.21 *W* thine hand far from me: and
33.17 he may *w* man from his purpose,
Pr 25.17 *W* thy foot from thy neighbor's
Ec 7.18 also from this *w* not thine hand:
Isa 60.20 neither shall thy moon *w* itself:
Joel 2.10 and the stars shall *w* their shining:
3.15 and the stars shall *w* their shining.
2Th 3. 6 *w* yourselves from every brother
1Ti 6. 5 godliness: from such *w* thyself.

WITHDRAWN

Dt 13.13 *w* the inhabitants of their city,
SS 5. 6 but my beloved had *w* himself,
La 2. 8 not *w* his hand from destroying:
Eze 18. 8 hath *w* his hand from iniquity,
Hos 5. 6 he hath *w* himself from them.
Lk 22.41 And he was *w* from them about a

WITHDREW

Neh 9.29 and *w* the shoulder, and
Eze 20.22 Nevertheless I *w* mine hand,
Mt 12.15 it, he *w* himself from thence:
Mk 3. 7 Jesus *w* himself with his disciples
Lk 5.16 he *w* himself into the wilderness,
Gal 2.12 he *w* and separated himself,

WITHER

Ps 1. 3 his leaf also shall not *w*; and
37. 2 grass, and *w* as the green herb.
Isa 19. 6 up: the reeds and flags shall *w*.
7 sown by the brooks, shall *w*,
40.24 blow upon them, and they shall *w*,
Jer 12. 4 and the herbs of every field *w*,
Eze 17. 9 cut off the fruit thereof, that it *w*?
9 *w* in all the leaves of her spring,
10 shall it not utterly *w*, when the
10 *w* in the furrows where it grew.
Am 1. 2 and the top of Carmel shall *w*.

WITHERED

Gen 41.23 seven ears, *w*, thin, and blasted
Ps 102. 4 heart is smitten, and *w* like grass;
Isa 15. 6 for the hay is *w* away, the grass
27.11 When the boughs thereof are *w*,
La 4. 8 it is *w*, it is become like a stick.
Eze 19.12 strong rods were broken and *w*;
Joel 1.12 all the trees of the field, are *w*:
12 joy is *w* away from the sons of men.
17 broken down; for the corn is *w*.
Am 4. 7 piece whereupon it rained not *w*.
Jon 4. 7 and it smote the gourd that it *w*.
Mt 12.10 a man which had his hand *w*.
13. 6 they had no root, they *w* away.
21.19 And presently the fig tree *w* away.
20 How soon is the fig tree *w* away!
Mk 3. 1 man there which had a *w* hand.
3 the man which had the *w* hand,
4. 6 because it had no root, it *w* away.
11.21 which thou cursedst is *w* away.
Lk 6. 6 a man whose right hand was *w*.
8 man which had the *w* hand, Rise
8. 6 it *w*...because it lacked moisture.
Jn 5. 3 halt, *w*, waiting for the moving of
15. 6 cast forth as a branch, and it *w*;

WITHERETH

Job 8.12 down, it *w* before any other herb.
Ps 90. 6 the evening it is cut down, and *w*.
129. 6 which *w* afore it groweth up:
Isa 40. 7, 8 The grass *w*, the flowers fadeth:
Jas 1.11 burning heat, but it *w* the grass,
1Pe 1.24 The grass *w*, and the flower
Jude 12 trees whose fruit *w*, without fruit,

WITHHELD

Gen 20. 6 I also *w* thee from sinning
22.12 seeing thou hast not *w* thy son,
16 hast not *w* thy son, thine only son:
30. 2 who hath *w* from thee the fruit of
Job 31.16 If I have *w* the poor from their
Ec 2.10 I *w* not my heart from any joy;

WITHHOLD

Gen 23. 6 shall *w* from thee his sepulcher,
2Sa 13.13 for he will not *w* me from thee.
Job 4. 2 can *w* himself from speaking?
Ps 40.11 *W* not thou thy tender mercies
84.11 good thing will he *w* from them
Pr 3.27 *W* no good from them to whom it
23.13 *W* not correction from a child:
Ec 11. 6 in the evening *w* not thine hand:
Jer 2.25 *W* thy foot from being unshod,

WITHHOLDETH

Job 12.15 he *w* the waters, and they dry up:
Pr 11.24 is that *w* more than is meet,
26 He that *w* corn, the people shall
2Th 2. 6 what *w* that he might be revealed

WITHIN

Gen 18.26 Sodom fifty righteous *w* the city,
Lev 25.30 redeemed *w* the space of a...year,
Dt 5.14 thy stranger that is *w* thy gates;
15.22 Thou shalt eat it *w* thy gates: the
Jdg 9.51 was a strong tower *w* the city,
14.12 declare it me *w* the seven days
1Sa 25.37 that his heart died *w* him, and
2Sa 7. 2 ark of God dwelleth *w* curtains.
Neh 6.10 the house of God, *w* the temple,
Job 6. 4 arrows of the Almighty are *w* me,
32.18 the spirit *w* me constraineth me.
Ps 40. 8 God: yea, thy law is *w* my heart.
42. 6 God, my soul is cast down *w* me:
11 why art thou disquieted *w* me?
43. 5 why art thou disquieted *w* me?
51.10 and renew a right spirit *w* me.
103. 1 all that is *w* me, bless his holy
122. 2 Our feet shall stand *w* thy gates,
7 Peace be *w* thy walls, and prosperity
7 walls, and prosperity *w* thy palaces.
8 I will now say, Peace be *w* thee.
Ec 9.14 was a little city, and a few men *w* it;
Isa 26. 9 my spirit *w* me will I seek thee
63.11 he that put his holy Spirit *w* him?
La 1.20 mine heart is turned *w* me; for I
Eze 11.19 and I will put a new spirit *w* you;
Dan 6.12 of any God or man *w* thirty days,
Jon 2. 7 When my soul fainteth *w* me I
Zec 12. 1 formeth the spirit of man *w* him.
Mt 3. 9 think not to say *w* yourselves,
9. 3 of the scribes said *w* themselves,
21 For she said *w* herself, If I may
23.25 *w* they are full of extortion and
26 first that which is *w* the cup and
27 are *w* full of dead men's bones,
28 but *w* ye are full of hypocrisy and
Mk 2. 8 they so reasoned *w* themselves,
7.21 from *w*, out of the heart of men,
23 All these evil things come from *w*,
14. 4 had indignation *w* themselves,
58 *w* three days I will build another
Lk 3. 8 begin not to say *w* yourselves, We
7.39 he spake *w* himself, saying, This
49 him began to say *w* themselves,
11. 7 he from *w* shall answer and say,
40 make that which is *w* also?

12.17 And he thought *w* himself, saying,
16. 3 Then the steward said *w* himself,
17.21 the kingdom of God is *w* you.
18. 4 but afterward he said *w* himself,
19.44 ground, and thy children *w* thee;
24.32 Did not our heart burn *w* us, while
Jn 20.26 days again his disciples were *w*,
Ac 5.23 had opened, we found no man *w*.
Ro 8.23 we ourselves groan *w* ourselves,
1Co 5.12 do not ye judge them that are *w*?
2Co 7. 5 were fightings, *w* were fears.
Heb 6.19 entereth into that *w* the vail;
Rev 4. 8 and they were full of eyes *w*:
5. 1 on the throne a book written *w*

WITHOUT

Gen 1. 2 earth was *w* form, and void:
Lev 4.12 shall he carry forth *w* the camp
10.12 eat it *w* leaven beside the altar:
Dt 25. 5 shall not marry *w* unto a stranger:
32. 4 a God of truth and *w* iniquity,
25 The sword *w*, and terror within
Ru 4.14 left thee this day *w* a kinsman,
2Ch 15. 3 Israel hath been *w* the true God,
Ezr 6. 9 it be given them day by day *w* fail:
Job 4.21 away? they die, even *w* wisdom.
6. 6 is unsavory be eaten *w* salt?
7. 6 shuttle, and are spent *w* hope.
12.25 They grope in the dark *w* light,
35.16 multiplieth words *w* knowledge.
39.16 her labor is in vain *w* fear;
42. 3 that hideth counsel *w* knowledge?
Ps 25. 3 which transgress *w* cause.
69. 4 They that hate me *w* a cause are
Pr 1.20 Wisdom crieth *w*; she uttereth
3.30 Strive not with a man *w* cause,
11.22 fair woman which is *w* discretion.
Isa 5.14 opened her mouth *w* measure:
52. 3 ye shall be redeemed *w* money.
55. 1 and milk *w* money and *w* price.
Dan 2.34 a stone was cut out *w* hands,
Mt 5.22 angry with his brother *w* a cause
13.34 *w* a parable spake he not unto
57 A prophet is not *w* honor, save
15.16 Are ye also yet *w* understanding?
Mk 1.45 city, but was *w* in desert places:
4.11 unto them that are *w*, all these
6. 4 A prophet is not *w* honor, but in
14.58 will build another made *w* hands.
Lk 1.10 praying *w* at the time of incense.
74 enemies might serve him *w* fear,
6.49 a man that *w* a foundation built
22.35 When I sent you *w* purse, and
Jn 1. 3 *w* him was not any thing made
8. 7 He that is *w* sin among you, let
19.23 now the coat was *w* seam, woven
20.11 Mary stood *w* at the sepulcher
Ro 1. 9 *w* ceasing I make mention of you
31 *w* natural affection, implacable,
3. 3 make the faith of God *w* effect?
28 by faith *w* the deeds of the law.
5. 6 For when we were yet *w* strength,
7. 8 For *w* the law sin was dead.
10.14 how shall they hear *w* a preacher?
1Co 4. 8 ye have reigned as kings *w* us:
5.12 do to judge them also that are *w*?
13 But them that are *w* God judgeth.
6.18 that a man doeth is *w* the body;
2Co 7. 5 *w* were fightings, within were
10.13 boast of things *w* our measure,
Eph 1. 4 and *w* blame before him in love:
3.21 throughout all ages, world *w* end.
Phm 14 *w* thy mind would I do nothing;
Heb 4.15 tempted like as we are, yet *w* sin.
11. 6 *w* faith it is impossible to please
Jas 2.13 he shall have judgment *w* mercy,
18 shew me thy faith *w* thy works,
20 man, that faith *w* works is dead?
26 as the body *w* the spirit is dead,
1Pe 1.17 who *w* respect of persons judgeth

WITHSTAND

Nu 22.32 I went out to *w* thee, because thy
2Ch 13. 7 and could not *w* them.
8 to *w* the kingdom of the Lord
20. 6 so that none is able to *w* thee?
Est 9. 2 and no man could *w* them; for
Ec 4.12 against him, two shall *w* him;
Dan 11.15 the arms of the south shall not *w*,
15 shall there be any strength to *w*.
Ac 11.17 what was I, that I could *w* God?
Eph 6.13 ye may be able to *w* in the evil day,

WITNESS

Gen 21.30 that they may be a *w* unto me,
31.44 be for a *w* between me and thee.
48 heap is a *w* between me and thee
50 see, God is *w* betwixt me and thee.
Ex 20.16 shalt not bear false *w* against thy
Nu 5.13 and there be no *w* against her,
17. 7 the Lord in the tabernacle of *w*.
Dt 4.26 I call heaven and earth to *w*
17. 6 at the mouth of one *w* he shall not
31.19 that this song may be a *w* for me
Jos 22.27 But that it may be a *w* between us,
24.27 this stone shall be a *w* unto us;
1Sa 12. 3 *w* against me before the Lord,
5 The Lord is *w* against you, and
Job 16. 8 which is a *w* against me:
19 my *w* is in heaven, and my record
29.11 the eye saw me, it gave *w* to me:
Ps 89.37 and as a faithful *w* in heaven.
Pr 6.19 A false *w* that speaketh lies, and
14. 5 A faithful *w* will not lie: but a false
25 A true *w* delivereth souls: but a
25 but a deceitful *w* speaketh lies.
Isa 3. 9 countenance doth *w* against them;
55. 4 given him for a *w* to the people,
Jer 29.23 I know, and am a *w*, saith the Lord.
42. 5 The Lord be a true and faithful *w*
Mic 1. 2 the Lord God be *w* against you,
Mal 2.14 the Lord hath been *w* between
Mt 15.19 thefts, false *w*, blasphemies:
19.18 steal, Thou shalt not bear false *w*,
24.14 preached in all the world for a *w*
26.59 sought false *w* against Jesus,
62 is it which these *w* against thee?
Mk 10.19 Do not bear false *w*, Defraud not,
14.55 sought for *w* against Jesus
15. 4 many things they *w* against thee.
Lk 4.22 all bear him *w*, and wondered at
11.48 Truly ye bear *w* that ye allow the
Jn 1. 7 The same came for a *w*, to bear
8 was sent to bear *w* of that Light.
15 John bear *w* of him, and cried,
5.31 If I bear *w* of myself,
32 is another that beareth *w* of me;
36 have greater *w* than that of John:
36 works that I do, bear *w* of me,
37 hath sent me, hath borne *w* of me.
18.23 spoken evil, bear *w* of the evil:
37 I should bear *w* unto the truth.
Ac 1.22 be a *w* with us of his resurrection.
14.17 he left not himself without *w*,
15. 8 knoweth the hearts, bare them *w*,
Ro 1. 9 For God is my *w*, whom I serve
Heb 2. 4 God also bearing them *w*, both
10.15 the Holy Ghost also is a *w* to us:
Jas 5. 3 the rust of them shall be a *w*
1Jn 1. 2 we have seen it, and bear *w*,
5. 6 And it is the Spirit that beareth *w*,
8 are three that bear *w* in earth,
9 the *w* of God is greater:
Rev 1. 5 Christ, who is the faithful *w*,
3.14 the faithful and the true *w*, the
20. 4 beheaded for the *w* of Jesus,

WITNESSES

Dt 17. 6 At the mouth of two *w*,
Jos 24.22 Ye are *w* against yourselves that
Ru 4. 9 Ye are *w* this day, that I have
11 and the elders, said, We are *w*.
Ps 27.12 false *w* are risen up against me,
Isa 8. 2 took unto me faithful *w* to record,
43. 9 let them bring forth their *w*, that
10 Ye are my *w*, saith the Lord, and
Jer 32.10 evidence, and sealed it, and took *w*
25 the field for money, and take *w*;
Mt 18.16 in the mouth of two or three *w*
23.31 ye be *w* unto yourselves, that
26.60 though many false *w* came, yet
Mk 14.63 What need we any further *w*?
Lk 24.48 And ye are *w* of these things.
Ac 1. 8 and ye shall be *w* unto me both in
2.32 raised up, whereof we all are *w*.
3.15 from the dead; whereof we are *w*.
13.31 who are his *w* unto the people.
1Th 2.10 Ye are *w*, and God also, how holily
Heb 10.28 mercy unto two or three *w*:
12. 1 about with so great a cloud of *w*,
Rev 11. 3 I will give power unto my two *w*,

WITNESSETH

Jn 5.32 witness which he *w* of me is true.
Ac 20.23 the Holy Ghost *w* in every city,

WITNESSING

Ac 26.22 *w* both to small and great, saying

WIT'S

Ps 107.27 man, and are at their *w* end.

WIVES

Gen 4.19 Lamech took unto him two *w* the
6. 2 them *w* of all which they chose.
18 wife, and thy sons' *w* with thee.
Nu 14. 3 that our *w* and our children should
32.26 Our little ones, our *w*, our flocks,
Dt 3.19 But your *w*, and your little ones,
17.17 Neither shall he multiply *w* to
21.15 If a man have two *w*, one beloved,
1Sa 1. 2 And he had two *w*; the name of the
30. 3 and their *w*, and their sons, and
5 David's two *w* were taken captives,
18 away: and David rescued his two *w*.
2Ch 11.21 of Absalom above all his *w* and
23 And he desired many *w*.
Ezr 10. 2 have taken strange *w* of the people
3 with our God to put away all the *w*,
44 All these had taken strange *w*: and
Neh 4.14 daughters, your *w*, and your houses.
13.23 Jews that had married *w* of Ashdod,
Jer 6.12 with their fields and *w* together:
8.10 will I give their *w* unto others,
Eze 44.22 shall they take for their *w* a widow,
Mt 19. 8 suffered you to put away your *w*:
Lk 17.27 they drank, they married *w*, they
Ac 21. 5 on our way, with *w* and children,
1Co 7.29 have *w* be as though they had none;
Eph 5.22 *W*, submit yourselves unto your
25 Husbands, love your *w*, even as
28 to love their *w* as their own bodies.
1Pe 3. 1 ye *w*, be in subjection to your own
1 won by the conversation of the *w*;

WIVES'

1Ti 4. 7 refuse profane and old *w* fables,

WIZARD

Lev 20.27 or that is a *w*, shall surely be put
Dt 18.11 spirits, or a *w*, or a necromancer.

WIZARDS

Lev 19.31 neither seek after *w*, to be defiled
20. 6 and after *w*, to go a whoring after
1Sa 28. 3 spirits, and the *w*, out of the land.
9 spirits, and the *w*, out of the land:
2Ki 21. 6 dealt with familiar spirits and *w*:
23.24 with familiar spirits, and the *w*,
2Ch 33. 6 with a familiar spirit, and with *w*:
Isa 8.19 unto *w* that peep, and that mutter:
19. 3 have familiar spirits, and to the *w*.

Biblical Themes

WOMAN

So God created man in his own image, in the image of God created he him; male and female created he them.
Gen 1.27

But for Adam there was not found an help meet for him. And the Lord God caused a deep sleep to fall upon Adam . . . and he took one of his ribs . . . and the rib . . . made he a woman, and brought her unto the man. And Adam said, This is now bone of my bones, and flesh of my flesh: she shall be called Woman, because she was taken out of Man.
Gen 2.20-23

And when the woman saw that the tree was good for food, and that it was pleasant to the eyes, and a tree to be desired to make one wise, she took of the fruit thereof, and did eat, and gave also unto her husband with her; and he did eat.
Gen 3.6

Unto the woman he said, I will greatly multiply thy sorrow and thy conception; in sorrow thou shalt bring forth children; and thy desire shall be to thy husband, and he shall rule over thee.
Gen 3.16

Who can find a virtuous woman? for her price is far above rubies. The heart of her husband doth safely trust in her. . . . she will do him good and not evil all the days of her life. . . . She is like the merchants' ships; she bringeth her food from afar. She riseth also while it is yet night, and giveth meat to her household. . . . She girdeth her loins with strength, and strengtheneth her arms. . . . She stretcheth out her hand to the poor. . . . Strength and honor are her clothing; and she shall rejoice in time to come. She openeth her mouth with wisdom; and in her tongue is the law of kindness. . . . Give her of the fruit of her hands; and let her own works praise her in the gates.
Pr 31.10-12, 14-15, 17, 20, 25-26, 31

Can a woman forget her sucking child, that she should not have compassion on the son of her womb? yea, they may forget, yet will I not forget thee.
Isa 49.15

O woman, great is thy faith: be it unto thee even as thou wilt.
Mt 15.28

When Elisabeth heard the salutation of Mary . . . she spake out with a loud voice, and said, Blessed art thou among women, and blessed is the fruit of thy womb.
Lk 1.41-42

The twelve were with him, and certain women, which had been healed of evil spirits and infirmities, Mary called Magdalene . . . and Joanna . . . and Susanna, and many others, which ministered unto him.
Lk 8.1-3

And it came to pass, as he spake . . . a certain woman of the company lifted up her voice, and said unto him, Blessed is the womb that bare thee.
Lk 11.27

There followed him a great company of . . . women, which also bewailed and lamented him. But Jesus . . . said, Daughters of Jerusalem, weep not for me, but weep for yourselves, and for your children.
Lk 23.27-28

The man is not of the woman: but the woman of the man. . . . Nevertheless neither is the man without the woman, neither the woman without the man. . . . For as the woman is of the man, even so is the man also by the woman; but all things of God.
1Co 11.8, 11-12

There is neither Jew nor Greek, there is neither bond nor free, there is neither male nor female: for ye are all one in Christ Jesus.
Gal 3.28

When the fulness of the time was come, God sent forth his Son, made of a woman.
Gal 4.4

WOE

1Sa 4. 8 *W* unto us! who shall deliver us
Job 10.15 If I be wicked, *w* unto me; and if I
Isa 3. 9 *W* unto their soul! for they have
11 *W* unto the wicked! it shall be ill
6. 5 said I, *W* is me! for I am undone:
45. 9 *W* unto him that striveth with his
Jer 6. 4 *W* unto us! for the day goeth away,
23. 1 *W* be unto the pastors that
Eze 13. 3 *W* unto the foolish prophets,
18 *W* to the women that sew pillows
34. 2 *W* be to the shepherds of Israel
Am 5.18 *W* unto you that desire the day
6. 1 *W* to them that are at ease in
Mic 2. 1 *W* to them that devise iniquity,
Hab 2.12 *W* to him that buildeth a town
19 *W* unto him that saith to the wood,
Mt 11.21 *W* unto thee, Chorazin!
21 *w* unto thee, Bethsaida! for if the
18. 7 *W* unto the world because of
7 but *w* to that man by whom the
23.13 *w* unto you, scribes and Pharisees,
16 *W* unto you, ye blind guides,
24.19 *w* unto them that are with child,
26.24 *w* unto that man by whom the Son
Mk 13.17 *w* to them that are with child, and
14.21 *w* to that man by whom the Son of
Lk 6.24 But *w* unto you that are rich!
25 *W* unto you that are full! for ye
25 *W* unto you that laugh now! for
11.42 But *w* unto you, Pharisees! for ye
46 *W* unto you also, ye lawyers!
1Co 9.16 *w* is unto me, if I preach not the
Rev 8.13 *W*, *w*, *w*, to the inhabiters of the
9.12 One *w* is past; and, behold, there
11.14 The second *w* is past; and,
14 behold, the third *w* cometh quickly.
12.12 *W* to the inhabiters of the earth

WOES

Rev 9.12 there come two *w* more hereafter.

WOLF

Gen 49.27 Benjamin shall ravin as a *w*:
Isa 11. 6 *w* also shall dwell with the lamb,
65.25 The *w* and the lamb shall feed
Jer 5. 6 and a *w* of the evenings shall spoil
Jn 10.12 seeth the *w* coming, and leaveth
12 and the *w* catcheth them, and

WOLVES

Eze 22.27 are like *w* ravening the prey,
Hab 1. 8 more fierce than the evening *w*:
Zep 3. 3 her judges are evening *w*; they
Mt 7.15 but inwardly they are ravening *w*.
10.16 forth as sheep in the midst of *w*:
Lk 10. 3 send you forth as lambs among *w*.
Ac 20.29 grievous *w* enter in among you,

WOMAN

Gen 2.22 made he a *w*, and brought her
23 she shall be called *W*, because she
3. 2 *w* said unto the serpent, We may
6 the *w* saw that the tree was good
12 The *w* whom thou gavest to be
13 *w* said, The serpent beguiled me,
15 put enmity between thee and the *w*,
24.39 Peradventure the *w* will not follow
Nu 5.22 And the *w* shall say, Amen, amen.
26 cause the *w* to drink the water.
Jdg 9.54 men say not of me, A *w* slew him.
13. 3 of the Lord appeared unto the *w*,
14. 1 and saw a *w* in Timnath of the
Ru 3. 8 and, behold, a *w* lay at his feet.
1Sa 1.15 lord, I am a *w* of a sorrowful spirit:
20.30 son of the perverse rebellious *w*,
25. 3 she was a *w* of good understanding,
28. 7 a *w* that hath a familiar spirit,
1Ki 17.10 widow *w* was...gathering of sticks:
24 the *w* said to Elijah, Now by this
2Ki 8. 5 the *w*, whose son he had restored
Job 14. 1 Man that is born of a *w* is of few
31. 9 heart have been deceived by a *w*,
Ps 58. 8 like the untimely birth of a *w*,
Pr 9.13 A foolish *w* is clamorous: she is
11.16 A gracious *w* retaineth honor:
22 fair *w* which is without discretion.
12. 4 A virtuous *w* is a crown to her
14. 1 Every wise *w* buildeth her house:
23.27 and a strange *w* is a narrow pit.
25.24 a brawling *w* in a wide house.
30.23 an odious *w* when she is married;
31.10 Who can find a virtuous *w*? for
Isa 26.17 Like as a *w* with child, that draweth
49.15 Can a *w* forget her sucking child,
Jer 31.22 earth, A *w* shall compass a man.
Hos 3. 1 love a *w* beloved of her friend,
Mt 5.28 whosoever looketh on a *w* to lust
9.20 a *w*, which was diseased with an
22 the *w* was made whole from that
15.22 a *w* of Canaan came out of the
28 unto her, O *w*, great is thy faith:
26.7 him a *w* having an alabaster box of
10 unto them, Why trouble ye the *w*?
26.13 that this *w* hath done, be told for
Mk 5.25 certain *w*, which had an issue of
33 But the *w* fearing and trembling,
10.12 if a *w* shall put away her husband,
12.22 seed: last of all the *w* died also.
14. 3 came a *w* having an alabaster box
Lk 4.26 unto a *w* that was a widow.
7.37 behold, a *w* in the city, which was
39 what manner of *w* this is that

44 said unto Simon, Seest thou this *w*?
46 this *w* hath anointed my feet with
50 he said to the *w*, Thy faith hath
10.38 a certain *w* named Martha
11.27 certain *w* of the company lifted up
13.11 there was a *w* which had a spirit
12 *W*, thou art loosed from thine
15. 8 what *w* having ten pieces of silver,
22.57 him, saying, *W*, I know him not.
Jn 2. 4 *W*, what have I to do with thee?
4. 7 a *w* of Samaria to draw water:
21 *W*, believe me, the hour cometh,
42 said unto the *w*, Now we believe,
8. 3 brought unto him a *w* taken in
4 this *w* was taken in adultery,
10 *W*, where are…thine accusers?
16.21 A *w* when she is in travail hath
19.26 his mother, *W*, behold thy son!
20.13, 15 unto her, *W*, why weepest thou?
Ro 1.27 leaving the natural use of the *w*,
7. 2 *w* which hath an husband is bound
1Co 7. 1 good for a man not to touch a *w*.
2 every *w* have her own husband.
11. 3 the head of the *w* is the man;
7 but the *w* is the glory of the man.
8 For the man is not of the *w*;
8 but the *w* of the man.
9 was the man created for the *w*;
9 but the *w* for the man.
13 a *w* pray unto God uncovered?
15 if a *w* have long hair, it is a glory
Gal 4. 4 sent forth his Son, made of a *w*,
1Th 5. 3 as travail upon a *w* with child;
1Ti 2.11 Let the *w* learn in silence with
12 I suffer not a *w* to teach, nor to
Rev 2.20 thou sufferest that *w* Jezebel.
12. 1 a *w* clothed with the sun, and the
4 *w* which was ready to be delivered,
13 *w* which brought forth the man
17. 3 a *w* sit upon a scarlet colored
6 I saw the *w* drunken with the
7 tell thee the mystery of the *w*,
18 *w* which thou sawest is that great

WOMANKIND

Lev 18.22 not lie with mankind, as with *w*:

WOMAN'S

Gen 38.20 his pledge from the *w* hand:
Ex 21.22 according as the *w* husband will
Lev 24.11 Israelitish *w* son blasphemed the
Nu 5.18 uncover the *w* head, and put the
25 jealousy offering out of the *w* hand,
Dt 22. 5 shall a man put on a *w* garment:
1Ki 3.19 And this *w* child died in the night;

WOMB

Gen 25.23 Two nations are in thy *w*, and two
24 behold, there were twins in her *w*.
29.31 Leah was hated, he opened her *w*:
30. 2 from thee the fruit of the *w*?
22 to her, and opened her *w*.
38.27 that, behold, twins were in her *w*.
49.25 of the beasts, and of the *w*:
Ex 13. 2 whatsoever openeth the *w* among
Nu 8.16 instead of such as open every *w*,
12.12 he cometh out of his mother's *w*.
Dt 7.13 will also bless the fruit of thy *w*,
Jdg 13. 5 be a Nazarite unto God from the *w*:
7 be a Nazarite to God from the *w*
16.17 unto God from my mother's *w*:
Ru 1.11 there yet any more sons in my *w*,
1Sa 1. 5 but the Lord had shut up her *w*.
6 the Lord had shut up her *w*.
Job 1.21 came I out of my mother's *w*, and
3.10 not up the doors of my mother's *w*,
11 Why died I not from the *w*? why
10.18 brought me forth out of the *w*?
19 carried from the *w* to the grave.
24.20 The *w* shall forget him; the worm
31.15 that made me in the *w* make him?
15 did not one fashion us in the *w*?
18 guided her from my mother's *w*;)
38. 8 as if it had issued out of the *w*?
29 Out of whose *w* came the ice?
Ps 22. 9 art he that took me out of the *w*:
10 I was cast upon thee from the *w*:
58. 3 wicked are estranged from the *w*:
71. 6 have I been holden up from the *w*:
110. 3 from the *w* of the morning:
127. 3 the fruit of the *w* is his reward.
139.13 has covered me in my mother's *w*.
Pr 30.16 The grave; and the barren *w*;
31. 2 son? and what, the son of my *w*?
Ec 5.15 As he came forth of his mother's *w*,
11. 5 the bones do grow in the *w* of her
Isa 13.18 have no pity on the fruit of the *w*;
44. 2 thee, and formed thee from the *w*,
24 he that formed thee from the *w*,
46. 3 which are carried from the *w*:
48. 8 called a transgressor from the *w*.
49. 1 Lord hath called me from the *w*;
5 formed me from the *w* to be his
15 compassion on the son of her *w*?
66. 9 cause to bring forth, and shut the *w*?
Jer 1. 5 thou camest forth out of the *w* I
20.17 he slew me not from the *w*;
17 her *w* to be always great with me.
18 I forth out of the *w* to see labor
Eze 20.26 the fire all that openeth the *w*,
Hos 9.11 from the birth, and from the *w*,
14 give them a miscarrying *w* and
16 even the beloved fruit of their *w*.
12. 3 his brother by the heel in the *w*,
Mt 19.12 so born from their mother's *w*:
Lk 1.15 Ghost, even from his mother's *w*.
31 thou shalt conceive in thy *w*, and
41 the babe leaped in her *w*; and
42 and blessed is the fruit of thy *w*.
44 the babe leaped in my *w* for joy.
2.21 before he was conceived in the *w*.
23 Every male that openeth the *w*
11.27 Blessed is the *w* that bare thee,
Jn 3. 4 second time into his mother's *w*,
Ac 3. 2 man lame from his mother's *w* was
14. 8 a cripple from his mother's *w*,
Ro 4.19 yet the deadness of Sarah's *w*:
Gal 1.15 me from my mother's *w*, and

WOMBS

Gen 20.18 Lord had fast closed up all the *w*
Lk 23. 29 and the *w* that never bare, and

WOMEN

Gen 24.11 the time that *w* go out to draw water.
Ex 2. 7 call to thee a nurse of the Hebrew *w*,
Jos 8.35 congregation of Israel, with the *w*,
2Sa 1.26 wonderful, passing the love of *w*.
19.35 voice of singing men and singing *w*?
Ezr 10. 1 great congregation of men and *w*
Neh 13.26 him did outlandish *w* cause to sin.
Est 2. 8 custody of Hegai, keeper of the *w*.
17 king loved Esther above all the *w*,
Job 42.15 all the land were no *w* found so fair
Pr 22.14 mouth of strange *w* is a deep pit:
Ec 2. 8 I gat me men singers and *w* singers,
SS 1. 8 know not, O thou fairest among *w*,
Isa 3.12 oppressors, and *w* rule over them.
4. 1 seven *w* shall take hold of one man,
32. 9 Rise up, ye *w* that are at ease; hear
Jer 9.20 hear the word of the Lord, O ye *w*,
44.24 and to all the *w*, Hear the word
Eze 8.14 there sat *w* weeping for Tammuz.
13.18 Woe to the *w* that sew pillows to all
23.10 and she became famous among *w*;
Zec 8. 4 men and old *w* dwell in the streets
Mt 11.11 Among them that are born of *w*
14.21 five thousand men, beside *w* and
15.38 four thousand men, beside *w* and
24.41 Two *w* shall be grinding at the mill;
27.55 many *w* were there beholding
28. 5 answered and said unto the *w*,
Mk 15.40 were also *w* looking on afar off:
41 other *w* which came up with him
Lk 1.28 blessed art thou among *w*.
42 said, Blessed art thou among *w*,
7.28 Among those that are born of *w*
8. 2 certain *w*, which had been healed
17.35 Two *w* shall be grinding together;
23.27 company of people, and of *w*,
49 *w* that followed him from Galilee,
55 the *w* also, which came with him
24.10 and other *w* that were with them,
22 and certain *w* also of our company
24 it even so as the *w* had said:
Ac 1.14 and supplication, with the *w*,
5.14 multitudes both of men and *w*.)
8. 3 haling men and *w* committed them
12 were baptized, both men and *w*.
9. 2 whether they were men or *w*, he
13.50 the devout and honorable *w*,
16.13 spake unto the *w* which resorted
17. 4 and of the chief *w* not a few.
12 honorable *w* which were Greeks,
22. 4 into prisons both men and *w*.
Ro 1.26 their *w* did change the natural use
1Co 14.34 *w* keep silence in the churches:
35 for *w* to speak in the church.
Php 4. 3 help those *w* which labored with me
1Ti 2. 9 *w* adorn themselves in modest
10 (which becometh *w* professing
5. 2 The elder *w* as mothers; the younger
14 therefore that the younger *w* marry,
2Ti 3. 6 captive silly *w* laden with sins,
Tit 2. 3 The aged *w* likewise, that they be
4 may teach the young *w* to be sober,
Heb 11.35 *W* received their dead raised to
1Pe 3. 5 in the old time the holy *w* also,
Rev 9. 8 they had hair as the hair of *w*
14. 4 which were not defiled with *w*;

WON

1Ch 26.27 Out of the spoils *w* in battles did they
Pr 18.19 brother offended is harder to be *w*
1Pe 3. 1 may without the word be *w*

WONDER

Dt 13. 1 and giveth thee a sign of a *w*,
2 the sign or the *w* come to pass,
28.46 upon thee for a sign and for a *w*,
2Ch 32.31 inquire of the *w* that was done
Ps 71. 7 I am as a *w* unto many; but thou
Isa 20. 3 for a sign and *w* upon Egypt
29. 9 Stay yourselves, and *w*; cry ye
14 even a marvellous work and a *w*:
Jer 4. 9 and the prophets shall *w*.
Hab 1. 5 and regard, and *w* marvellously:
Ac 3.10 and they were filled with *w* and
13.41 Behold, ye despisers, and *w*,
Rev 12. 1 appeared a great *w* in heaven;
3 appeared another *w* in heaven;
17. 8 that dwell on the earth shall *w*,

WONDERED

Isa 59.16 *w* that there was no intercessor:
63. 5 *w* that there was none to uphold:
Zec 3. 8 thee: for they are men *w* at:
Mt 15.31 Insomuch that the multitude *w*,
Mk 6.51 beyond measure, and *w*.
Lk 2.18 that heard it *w* at those things
4.22 and *w* at the gracious words which
8.25 they being afraid *w*, saying one to
9.43 they *w* every one at all things
11.14 dumb spake; and the people *w*.
24.41 they yet believed not for joy, and *w*,
Ac 7.31 Moses saw it, he *w* at the sight:
8.13 and *w*, beholding the miracles
Rev 13. 3 and all the world *w* after the beast.
17. 6 her, I *w* with great admiration.

WONDERFUL

Dt 28.59 the Lord will make thy plagues *w*,
2Sa 1.26 thy love to me was *w*, passing the

2Ch 2. 9 am about to build shall be *w* great.
Job 42. 3 things too *w* for me, which I knew
Ps 40. 5 thy *w* works which thou hast done,
78. 4 and his *w* works that he hath done.
107. 8, 15, 21, 31 *w* works to the children of
111. 4 his *w* works to be remembered:
119.129 Thy testimonies are *w*:
139. 6 Such knowledge is too *w* for me;
Pr 30.18 be three things which are too *w*
Isa 9. 6 and his name shall be called *W*,
25. 1 for thou hast done *w* things; thy
28.29 which is *w* in counsel, and
Jer 5.30 *w* and horrible thing is committed
Mt 7.22 name done many *w* works?
21.15 saw the *w* things that he did,
Ac 2.11 our tongues the *w* works of God.

WONDERFULLY

1Sa 6. 6 he had wrought *w* among them,
Ps 139.14 for I am fearfully and *w* made:
La 1. 9 therefore she came down *w*: she
Dan 8.24 and he shall destroy *w*, and shall

WONDERING

Gen 24.21 the man *w* at her held his peace,
Lk 24.12 *w* in himself at that which was
Ac 3.11 is called Solomon's, greatly *w*.

WONDERS

Ex 3.20 smite Egypt with all my *w* which
4.21 do all those *w* before Pharaoh,
7. 3 and my *w* in the land of Egypt.
11. 9 that my *w* may be multiplied in
10 did all these *w* before Pharaoh:
15.11 fearful in praises, doing *w*?
Dt 4.34 by signs, and by *w*, and by war,
6.22 And the Lord shewed signs and *w*,
7.19 and the *w*, and the mighty hand,
26. 8 and with signs and with *w*:
34.11 the *w*, which the Lord sent him to
Jos 8. 5 the Lord will do *w* among you.
1Ch 16.12 his *w*, and the judgments of his
Neh 9.10 signs and *w* upon Pharaoh,
17 neither were mindful of thy *w*
Job 9.10 out; yea, and *w* without number.
Ps 77.11 I will remember thy *w* of old.
14 Thou art the God that doest *w*:
78.11 His *w* that he had shewed them.
43 and his *w* in the field of Zoan:
88.10 Wilt thou shew *w* to the dead?
12 Shall thy *w* be known in the dark?
89. 5 And the heavens shall praise thy *w*,
96. 3 heathen, his *w* among all people.
105. 5 his *w*, and the judgments of his
27 them, and *w* in the land of Ham.
106. 7 Our fathers understood not thy *w*
107.24 the Lord, and his *w* in the deep.
135. 9 Who sent tokens and *w* into the
136. 4 To him who alone doeth great *w*:
Isa 8.18 for *w* in Israel from the Lord
Jer 32.20 signs and *w* in the land of Egypt,
21 with signs, and with *w*, and with a
Dan 4. 2 *w* that the high God hath wrought
3 and how mighty are his *w*!
6.27 he worketh signs and *w* in heaven
12. 6 shall it be to the end of these *w*?
Joel 2.30 And I will shew *w* in the heavens
Mt 24.24 and shall shew great signs and *w*;
Mk 13.22 rise, and shall shew signs and *w*.
Jn 4.48 Except ye see signs and *w*, ye will
Ac 2.19 And I will shew *w* in heaven above,
22 you by miracles and *w* and signs,
43 and many *w* and signs were done
4.30 and that signs and *w* may be done
5.12 were many signs and *w* wrought
6. 8 did great *w* and miracles among
7.36 that he had shewed *w* and signs
14. 3 granted signs and *w* to be done
15.12 declaring what miracles and *w* God
Ro 15.19 Through mighty signs and *w*, by
2Co 12.12 signs, and *w*, and mighty deeds.
2Th 2. 9 all power and signs and lying *w*,
Heb 2. 4 witness, both with signs and *w*,
Rev 13.13 And he doeth great *w*, so that he

WONDROUS

1Ch 16. 9 him, talk ye of all his *w* works.
Job 37.14 and consider the *w* works of God.
16 *w* work of him which is perfect
Ps 26. 7 and tell of all thy *w* works.
71.17 have I declared thy *w* works.
72.18 of Israel, who only doeth *w* things.
75. 1 name is near thy *w* works declare.
78.32 and believed not for his *w* works.
86.10 thou art great, and doest *w* things:
105. 2 him: talk ye of all his *w* works.
106.22 *W* works in the land of Ham, and
119.18 behold *w* things out of thy law.
27 so shall I talk of thy *w* works.
145. 5 of thy majesty, and of thy *w* works.
Jer 21. 2 us according to all his *w* works,

WONT

Ex 21.29 ox were *w* to push with his horn
Nu 22.30 was I ever *w* to do so unto thee?
1Sa 30.31 and his men were *w* to haunt.
2Sa 20.18 They were *w* to speak in old time,
Dan 3.19 seven times more than it was *w*
Mt 27.15 governor was *w* to release unto
Mk 10. 1 and, as he was *w*, he taught them
Lk 22.39 and went, as he was *w*, to
Ac 16.13 where prayer was *w* to be made;

WOOD

Gen 6.14 Make thee an ark of gopher *w*;
22. 3 clave the *w* for the burnt offering,
7 he said, Behold the fire and the *w*:
9 laid him on the altar upon the *w*.
Ex 7.19 both in vessels of *w*, and in vessels
25. 5 and badgers' skins, and shittim *w*,
10 shall make an ark of shittim *w*:
26.15 for the tabernacle of shittim *w*
Lev 1. 7 lay the *w* in order upon the fire:
Dt 4.28 work of men's hands, *w* and stone,
28.36 thou serve other gods, *w* and stone.
29.11 hewer of thy *w* unto the drawer
Jos 9.21 but let them be hewers of *w* and
2Sa 6. 5 of instruments made of fir *w*,
24.22 instruments of the oxen for *w*.
1Ki 6.15 covered them on the inside with *w*,
18.23, 23 and lay it on *w*, and put no fire
1Ch 16.33 shall the trees of the *w* sing out
29. 2 of iron, and *w* for things of *w*;
2Ch 2.16 And we will cut *w* out of Lebanon,
Neh 8. 4 the scribe stood upon a pulpit of *w*,
Ps 80.13 boar out of the *w* doth waste it,
96.12 shall all the trees of the *w* rejoice.
Pr 26.20 Where no *w* is, there the fire
Ec 2. 6 the *w* that bringeth forth trees:
10. 9 and he that cleaveth *w* shall be
Isa 7. 2 as the trees of the *w* are moved
45.20 set up the *w* of their graven image.
La 5. 4 for money; our *w* is sold unto us.
Eze 15. 3 *w* be taken thereof to do any work?
24.10 Heap on *w*, kindle the fire,
Hab 2.19 him that saith to the *w*, Awake;
1Co 3.12 precious stones, *w*, hay, stubble;
2Ti 2.20 silver, but also of *w* and of earth;
Rev 9.20 and brass, and stone,and of *w*:
18.12 and scarlet, and all thyine *w*,
12 manner vessels of most precious *w*,

WOOL

Jdg 6.37 will put a fleece of *w* in the floor;
2Ki 3. 4 thousand rams, with the *w*.
Ps 147.16 He giveth snow like *w*: he
Pr 31.13 She seeketh *w*, and flax, and
Isa 1.18 like crimson, they shall be as *w*.
51. 8 the worm shall eat them like *w*:
Eze 27.18 the wine of Helbon, and white *w*.
34. 3 fat, and ye clothe you with the *w*,
44.17 and no *w* shall come upon them,
Dan 7. 9 hair of his head like the pure *w*:
Hos 2. 5 my *w* and my flax, mine oil and
9 will recover my *w* and my flax
Heb 9.19 and scarlet *w* and hyssop, and
Rev 1.14 and his hairs were white like *w*,

WOOLLEN

Lev 13.47 whether it be a *w* garment, or a
48 warp, or woof; of linen, or of *w*;
52 warp or woof, in *w* or in linen,
59 leprosy in a garment of *w* or linen,
19.19 garment mingled of linen and *w*
Dt 22.11 sorts, as of *w* and linen together.

WORD

Gen 15. 1 *w* of the Lord came unto Abram
30.34 it might be according to thy *w*.
37.14 the flocks; and bring me *w* again.
Ex 8.10 he said, Be it according to thy *w*:
13 did according to the *w* of Moses;
9.20 He that feared the *w* of the Lord
Nu 3.16, 51 according to the *w* of the Lord,
15.31 hath despised the *w* of the Lord,
22. 8 I will bring you *w* again, as the
38 *w* that God putteth in my mouth,
30. 2 he shall not break his *w*, he shall
Dt 1.22 bring us *w* again by what way we
8. 3 but by every *w* that proceedeth out
18.20 presume to speak a *w* in my name,
30.14 But the *w* is very nigh unto thee,
Jos 1.13 Remember the *w* which Moses
14. 7 I brought him *w* again as it was
10 the Lord spake this *w* unto Moses,
1Ki 2. 4 Lord may continue his *w* which he
23 spoken this *w* against his own life.
42 The *w* that I have heard is good.
8.20 Lord hath performed his *w* that he
26 let thy *w*, I pray thee, be verified,
13. 1 by the *w* of the Lord unto Beth-el:
9 charged me by the *w* of the Lord,
18. 1 *w* of the Lord came to Elijah
2Ki 1.16 God in Israel to inquire of his *w*?
3.12 The *w* of the Lord is with him.
7. 1 said, Hear ye the *w* of the Lord;
20. 4 the *w* of the Lord came to him,
19 Good is the *w* of the Lord which
2Ch 6.10 hath performed his *w* that he hath
10.15 the Lord might perform his *w*,
Ezr 1. 1 *w* of the Lord by the mouth of
6.11 that whosoever shall alter this *w*,
Ps 17. 4 *w* of thy lips I have kept me from
18.30 the *w* of the Lord is tried: he is a
33. 4 For the *w* of the Lord is right;
56. 4 In God I will praise his *w*, in God I
68.11 The Lord gave the *w*: great was
105. 8 the *w* which he commanded to a
19 Until the time that his *w* came:
28 they rebelled not against his *w*.
107.20 He sent his *w*, and healed them,
119. 9 heed thereto according to thy *w*.
11 Thy *w* have I hid in mine heart,
16 statutes: I will not forget thy *w*.
25 quicken...me according to thy *w*.
38 Stablish thy *w* unto thy servant,
74 because I have hoped in thy *w*.
82 Mine eyes fail for thy *w*, saying,
105 Thy *w* is a lamp unto my feet, and
116 Uphold me according unto thy *w*,
133 Order my steps in thy *w*: and let not
140 Thy *w* is very pure: therefore thy
139. 4 there is not a *w* in my tongue,
147.15 earth: his *w* runneth very swiftly.
148. 8 stormy wind fulfilling his *w*:
Pr 12.25 but a good *w* maketh it glad.
13.13 despiseth the *w* shall be destroyed:
14.15 The simple believeth every *w*:
15.23 and a *w* spoken in due season,
25.11 A *w* fitly spoken is like apples of
30. 5 Every *w* of God is pure: he is a
Ec 8. 4 Where the *w* of a king is, there is
Isa 1.10 Hear the *w* of the Lord, ye rulers

16.13 is the *w* that the Lord hath spoken
24. 3 for the Lord hath spoken this *w*.
36.21 peace, and answered him not a *w*:
40. 8 *w* of our God shall stand for ever.
55.11 So shall my *w* be that goeth forth
Jer 1. 2 To whom the *w* of the Lord came
4, 11 the *w* of the Lord came unto me,
17.15 Where is the *w* of the Lord? let it
18. 1 *w* which came to Jeremiah from
23.18 hath perceived and heard his *w*?
29 Is not my *w* like as a fire? saith the
36 every man's *w* shall be his burden;
37. 6 *w* of the Lord unto the prophet
38.21 *w* that the Lord hath shewed me:
Eze 1. 3 *w* of the Lord came expressly
37. 4 dry bones, hear the *w* of the Lord.
Dan 3.28 and have changed the king's *w*,
Hos 1. 1 The *w* of the Lord that came unto
2 of the *w* of the Lord by Hosea.
Joel 1. 1 *w* of the Lord that came to Joel
2.11 he is strong that executeth his *w*:
Am 3. 1 Hear this *w* that the Lord hath
8.12 and fro to seek the *w* of the Lord,
Zep 1. 1 *w* of the Lord which came unto
2. 5 The *w* of the Lord is against you;
Zec 1. 1, 7 *w* of the Lord unto Zechariah,
9. 1 The burden of the *w* of the Lord
Mal 1. 1 The burden of the *w* of the Lord
Mt 2. 8 bring me *w* again, that I may
4. 4 by every *w* that proceedeth out of
8. 8 but speak the *w* only, and my
16 he cast out the spirits with his *w*,
12.32 speaketh a *w* against the Son of
36 every idle *w* that men shall speak,
13.19 one heareth the *w* of the kingdom,
21 ariseth because of the *w*,
22 thorns is he that heareth the *w*;
22 choke the *w*, and he becometh
23 ground is he that heareth the *w*,
18.16 every *w* may be established.
26.75 remembered the *w* of Jesus,
Mk 2. 2 he preached the *w* unto them.
4.14 The sower soweth the *w*.
15 the way side, where the *w* is sown;
20 such as hear the *w*, and receive it,
33 parables spake he the *w* unto them,
7.13 Making the *w* of God of none
16.20 and confirming the *w* with signs
Lk 1. 2 and ministers of the *w*;
38 be it unto me according to thy *w*.
2.29 in peace, according to thy *w*:
3. 2 the *w* of God came unto John the
4. 4 alone, but by every *w* of God.
32 for his *w* was with power.
36 saying, What a *w* is this! for with
5. 1 upon him to hear the *w* of God,
5 at thy *w* I will let down the net.
8.11 is this: The seed is the *w* of God.
12 away the *w* out of their hearts,
13 they hear, receive the *w* with joy:
10.39 sat at Jesus' feet, and heard his *w*.
11.28 that hear the *w* of God, and keep it.
12.10 speak a *w* against the Son of man,
24.19 mighty in deed and *w* before God
Jn 1. 1 In the beginning was the *W*,
1 and the *W* was with God,
1 and the *W* was God.
14 the *W* was made flesh, and dwelt
5.24 He that heareth my *w*, and
38 ye have not his *w* abiding in you:
8.31 If ye continue in my *w*, then are
37 because my *w* hath no place in you,
43 even because ye cannot hear my *w*.
10.35 unto whom the *w* of God came,
14.24 the *w* which ye hear is not mine,
15. 3 *w* which I have spoken unto you.
25 that the *w* might be fulfilled that
17. 6 me; and they have kept thy *w*.
17 through thy truth: thy *w* is truth.
Ac 2.41 received his *w* were baptized:
4. 4 them which heard the *w* believed;
29 boldness they may speak thy *w*,
31 spake the *w* of God with boldness.
6. 2 that we should leave the *w* of God,
4 and to the ministry of the *w*.
7 And the *w* of God increased; and
8. 4 went every where preaching the *w*.
10.36 The *w* which God sent unto the
37 That *w*, I say, ye know, which
12.24 the *w* of God grew and multiplied.
13. 5 they preached the *w* of God in the
26 to you is the *w* of this salvation
14. 3 which gave testimony unto the *w*
15. 7 should hear the *w* of the gospel,
17.11 received the *w* with all readiness
13 *w* of God was preached of Paul
19.10 in Asia heard the *w* of the Lord
20 So mightily grew the *w* of God and
Ro 9. 6 Not as though the *w* of God hath
9 For this is the *w* of promise, At
10. 8 *w* is nigh thee, even in thy mouth,
15.18 obedient, by *w* and deed,
1Co 4.20 the kingdom of God is not in *w*,
12. 8 given by the Spirit the *w* of wisdom;
14.36 came the *w* of God out from you?
2Co 1.18 our *w* toward you was not yea and
2.17 many, which corrupt the *w* of God:
Gal 5.14 all the law is fulfilled in one *w*,
Eph 1.13 after that ye heard the *w* of truth,
6.17 the Spirit, which is the *w* of God:
Col 1. 5 heard before in the *w* of the truth
17 whatsoever ye do in *w* or deed, do
Heb 1. 3 all things by the *w* of his power,
2. 2 For if the *w* spoken by angels was
4. 2 *w* preached did not profit them,
12 For the *w* of God is quick, and
6. 5 have tasted the good *w* of God,
1Pe 1.23 by the *w* of God, which liveth and
25 *w* of the Lord endureth for ever.
2. 2 desire the sincere milk of the *w*,
1Jn 1. 1 have handled, of the *W* of life:
3.18 children, let us not love in *w*,
5. 7 the Father, the *W*, and the Holy
Rev 1. 2 Who bare record of the *w* of God,
6. 9 that were slain for the *w* of God,
19.13 his name is called The *W* of God,

WORD'S

2Sa 7.21 For thy *w* sake, and according to
Mk 4.17 persecution ariseth for...*w* sake,

WORDS

Gen 24.30 when he heard the *w* of Rebekah
44. 6 he spake unto them these same *w*.
7 Wherefore saith my lord these *w*?
Ex 4.15 him, and put *w* in his mouth:
20. 1 God spake all these *w*, saying,
24. 3 the people all the *w* of the Lord,
4 Moses wrote all the *w* of the Lord,
34. 1 the *w* that were in the first tables,
27 unto Moses, Write thou these *w*:
Nu 11.24 told the people the *w* of the Lord,
Dt 1. 1 the *w* which Moses spake unto all
11.18 lay up these my *w* in your heart
13. 3 hearken unto the *w* of that prophet,
16.19 and pervert the *w* of the righteous.
29. 1 These are the *w* of the covenant,
32. 1 hear, O earth, the *w* of my mouth.
46 observe to do, all the *w* of this law.
Jos 1.18 and will not hearken unto thy *w*
8.34 he read all the *w* of the law,
24.26 Joshua wrote these *w* in the book
Jdg 2. 4 angel of the Lord spake these *w*
2Sa 3. 8 wroth for the *w* of Ish-bosheth,
23. 1 Now these be the last *w* of David.
1Ki 1.14 in after thee, and confirm thy *w*.
22.13 *w* of the prophets declare good
2Ki 1. 7 to meet you, and told you these *w*?
22.11 king had heard the *w* of the book
13 the *w* of this book that is found:
1Ch 17.15 According to these *w*, and
25. 5 the king's seer in the *w* of God,
2Ch 9. 6 I believed not their *w*, until I came,
18.12 the *w* of the prophets declare good
Ezr 7.11 of the *w* of the commandments
9. 4 trembled at the *w* of the God of
Neh 1. 1 The *w* of Nehemiah the son of
8. 9 when they heard the *w* of the law.
Job 4. 4 Thy *w* have upholden him that
6. 3 therefore my *w* are swallowed up.
10 concealed the *w* of the Holy One.
25 How forcible are right *w*! but what
11. 2 the multitude of *w* be answered?
12.11 Doth not the ear try *w*? and the
15.13 lettest such *w* go out of thy mouth?
16. 3 Shall vain *w* have an end?
19. 2 and break me in pieces with *w*?
33. 1 and hearken to all my *w*.
3 My *w* shall be of the uprightness
34. 2 Hear my *w*, O ye wise men; and
3 For the ear trieth *w*, as the mouth
35 and his *w* were without wisdom.
37 and multiplieth his *w* against God.
38. 2 counsel by *w* without knowledge?
41. 3 will he speak soft *w* unto thee?
Ps 5. 1 Give ear to my *w*, O Lord, consider
12. 6 The *w* of the Lord are pure *w*:
19. 4 their *w* to the end of the world.
14 Let the *w* of my mouth, and the
36. 3 The *w* of his mouth are iniquity
64. 3 shoot their arrows, even bitter *w*:
107.11 rebelled against the *w* of God,
119.57 have said that I would keep thy *w*.
103 sweet are thy *w* unto my taste!
130 entrance of thy *w* giveth light;
Pr 1. 2 to perceive the *w* of understanding;
6 the *w* of the wise, and their dark
2. 1 My son, if thou wilt receive my *w*,
4. 4 Let thine heart retain my *w*:
20 My son, attend to my *w*; incline
10.19 multitude of *w* there wanteth not
12. 6 *w* of the wicked are to lie in wait
15. 1 but grievous *w* stir up anger.
16.24 Pleasant *w* are as an honeycomb,
18. 4 The *w* of the man's mouth are as
8 *w* of a talebearer are as wounds,
22.12 the *w* of the transgressor.
21 the certainty of the *w* of truth;
23. 8 vomit up, and lose thy sweet *w*.
9 will despise the wisdom of thy *w*.
Ec 1. 1 The *w* of the Preacher, the son of
10.12 The *w* of a wise man's mouth are
14 A fool also is full of *w*: a man
12.10 sought to find out acceptable *w*:
10 was upright, even *w* of truth.
11 The *w* of the wise are as goads,
Isa 29.11 as the *w* of a book that is sealed,
31. 2 evil, and will not call back his *w*:
32. 7 to destroy the poor with lying *w*,
36. 5 thou, (but they are but vain *w*) I
13 Hear ye the *w* of the great king,
41.26 there is none that heareth your *w*.
51.16 I have put my *w* in thy mouth,
Jer 1. 1 *w* of Jeremiah the son of Hilkiah,
5.14 I will make my *w* in thy mouth fire,
7. 4 Trust ye not in lying *w*, saying,
11. 2 Hear ye the *w* of this covenant,
23. 9 because of the *w* of his holiness.
36 perverted the *w* of the living God,
29. 1 *w* of the letter that Jeremiah
23 have spoken lying *w* in my name,
36. 2 write...all the *w* that I have spoken
8 in the book the *w* of the Lord
10 in the book the *w* of Jeremiah
17 write all these *w* at his mouth?
32 *w* of the book which Jehoiakim
Eze 2. 6 them, neither be afraid of their *w*,
7 thou shalt speak my *w* unto them,
3. 4 and speak with my *w* unto them.
6 *w* thou canst not understand.
33.31 they hear thy *w*, but they will not
32 for they hear thy *w*, but they do
Dan 2. 9 corrupt *w* to speak before me,

BIBLICAL THEMES

WORK

The Lord God took the man, and put him into the garden of Eden to dress it and to keep it. Gen 2.15

Because thou hast hearkened unto the voice of thy wife, and hast eaten of the tree . . . cursed is the ground for thy sake; in sorrow shalt thou eat of it all the days of thy life . . . in the sweat of thy face shalt thou eat bread, till thou return unto the ground. Gen 3.17, 19

And they made their lives bitter with hard bondage, in morter, and in brick, and in all manner of service in the field. Ex 1.14

Six days shall work be done, but on the seventh day there shall be to you an holy day, a sabbath of rest to the Lord. Ex 35.2

Thou shalt not oppress an hired servant that is poor and needy . . . at his day thou shalt give him his hire, neither shall the sun go down upon it. Dt 24.14-15

Is it good unto thee that thou shouldest oppress, that thou shouldest despise the work of thine hands. . . ? Job 10.3

Except the Lord build the house, they labor in vain that build it. Ps 127.1

He that tilleth his land shall be satisfied with bread. Pr 12.11

In all labor there is profit: but the talk of the lips tendeth only to penury. Pr 14.23

I looked on all the works that my hands had wrought, and on the labor that I had labored to do: and, behold, all was vanity and vexation of spirit. . . . I hated all my labor which I had taken under the sun: because I should leave it unto the man that shall be after me. And who knoweth whether he shall be a wise man or a fool? Ec 2.11, 18-19

There is nothing better for a man, than that he should eat and drink, and that he should make his soul enjoy good in his labor. Ec 2.24

Whatsoever thy hand findeth to do, do it with thy might; for there is no work, nor device, nor knowledge, nor wisdom, in the grave. Ec 9.10

They shall build houses, and inhabit them; and they shall plant vineyards, and eat the fruit of them. They shall not build, and another inhabit; they shall not plant, and another eat. . . . They shall not labor in vain. Isa 65.21-23

The harvest truly is plenteous, but the laborers are few; pray ye therefore the Lord . . . that he will send forth laborers into his harvest. Mt 9.37-38

Come unto me, all ye that labor and are heavy laden, and I will give you rest. Take my yoke upon you, and learn of me. . . . For my yoke is easy, and my burden is light. Mt 11.28-30

Labor not for the meat which perisheth, but for that meat which endureth unto everlasting life. . . . Then said they unto him, What shall we do, that we might work the works of God? Jesus answered and said unto them, This is the work of God, that ye believe on him whom he hath sent. Jn 6.27-29

Every man's work shall be made manifest . . . and the fire shall try every man's work of what sort it is. 1Co 3.13

Remembering without ceasing your work of faith, and labor of love, and patience of hope in our Lord. 1Th 1.3

Study . . . to do your own business, and to work with your own hands . . . that ye may walk honestly toward them that are without, and that ye may have lack of nothing. 1Th 4.11-12

Dan 7.11 great *w* which the horn spake:
25 great *w* against the most High,
10. 6 his *w* like the voice of a multitude.
12 before thy God, thy *w* were heard,
Hos 6. 5 slain them by the *w* of my mouth:
14. 2 Take with you *w*, and turn to the
Am 1. 1 The *w* of Amos, who was among
8.11 but of hearing the *w* of the Lord:
Mal 2.17 wearied the Lord with your *w*.
Mt 10.14 nor hear your *w*, when ye depart
12.37 by thy *w* thou shalt be justified,
37 by thy *w* thou shalt be condemned.
24.35 but my *w* shall not pass away.
26.44 third time, saying the same *w*.
Mk 8.38 be ashamed of me and of my *w*
10.24 disciples were astonished at his *w*.
12.13 Herodians, to catch him in his *w*.
13.31 but my *w* shall not pass away.
Lk 1.20 because thou believest not my *w*,
9.26 be ashamed of me and of my *w*,
20.20 they might take hold of his *w*,
21.33 but my *w* shall not pass away.
24. 8 And they remembered his *w*,
11 their *w* seemed to them as idle
Jn 3.34 hath sent speaketh the *w* of God:
5.47 how shall ye believe my *w*?
6.63 the *w* that I speak unto you, they
68 go? thou hast the *w* of eternal life.
10.21 the *w* of him that hath a devil.
12.47 And if any man hear my *w*, and
48 and receiveth not my *w*, hath one
14.10 *w* that I speak unto you I speak
23 man love me, he will keep my *w*:
15. 7 my *w* abide in you, ye shall ask
Ac 2.14 unto you, and hearken to my *w*:
22 Ye men of Israel, hear these *w*;
6.11 blasphemous *w* against Moses,
7.22 was mighty in *w* and in deeds.
20.35 remember the *w* of the Lord Jesus,
26.25 but speak forth the *w* of truth
Ro 10.18 *w* unto the ends of the world.
16.18 good *w* and fair speeches deceive
1Co 1.17 not with wisdom of *w*, lest the
2. 4 with enticing *w* of man's wisdom,
14. 9 tongue *w* easy to be understood,
19 five *w* with my understanding,
19 thousand *w* in an unknown tongue.
2Co 12. 4 and heard unspeakable *w*, which
Col 2. 4 beguile you with enticing *w*.
1Ti 4. 6 nourished up in the *w* of faith and
6. 3 and consent not to wholesome *w*,
4 about questions and strifes of *w*,
2Ti 1.13 Hold fast the form of sound *w*,
2.14 strive not about *w* to no profit,
Heb 12.19 a trumpet, and the voice of *w*;
2Pe 2. 3 with feigned *w* make merchandise
18 speak great swelling *w* of vanity,
Rev 1. 3 that hear the *w* of this prophecy,
17.17 the *w* of God shall be fulfilled.
21. 5 for these *w* are true and faithful.

WORK

Gen 2. 2 the seventh day God ended his *w*
3 in it he had rested from all his *w*
Ex 5.18 Go therefore now, and *w*; for
12.16 no manner of *w* shall be done in
20. 9 thou labor, and do all thy *w*:
10 in it thou shalt not do any *w*, thou
23.12 Six days thou shalt do thy *w*, and
31.15 Six days may *w* be done; but in
32.16 the tables were the *w* of God, and
36. 1 understanding to know how to *w*
4 wrought all the *w* of the sanctuary,
37.29 to the *w* of the apothecary.
40.33 gate. So Moses finished the *w*.
Lev 23. 7, 8 ye shall do no servile *w* therein.
Dt 4.28 serve gods, the *w* of men's hands,
32. 4 He is the Rock, his *w* is perfect:
1Sa 14. 6 be that the Lord will *w* for us:
1Ki 21.20 *w* evil in the sight of the Lord.
25 did sell himself to *w* wickedness
2Ch 2.14 man of Tyre, skilful to *w* in gold,
18 overseers to set the people a *w*.
Ezr 4.24 ceased the *w* of the house of God
Neh 4. 6 for the people had a mind to *w*.
19 The *w* is great and large, and we
6. 3 I am doing a great *w*, so that I
16 this *w* was wrought of our God.
Job 1.10 hast blessed the *w* of his hands,
7. 2 looketh for the reward of his *w*:
10. 3 despise the *w* of thine hands,
24. 5 desert, go they forth to their *w*;
34.19 they all are the *w* of his hands.
Ps 8. 3 thy heavens, the *w* of thy fingers,
62.12 to every man according to his *w*.
77.12 I will meditate also of all thy *w*,
90.16 thy *w* appear unto thy servants,
17 establish thou the *w* of our hands
17 *w* of our hands establish thou it.
102.25 heavens are the *w* of thy hands.
104.23 Man goeth forth unto his *w* and
119.126 It is time for thee, Lord, to *w*:
Pr 11.18 wicked worketh a deceitful *w*:
16.11 the weights of the bag are his *w*.
18. 9 He also that is slothful in his *w*
21. 8 as for the pure, his *w* is right.
Ec 2.17 *w* that is wrought under the sun
3.17 every purpose and for every *w*.
7.13 Consider the *w* of God: for who
8.17 Then I beheld all the *w* of God,
Isa 2. 8 worship the *w* of their own hands,
29.16 the *w* say of him that made it,
32.17 the *w* of righteousness shall be

40.10 with him, and his *w* before him.
49. 4 Lord, and my *w* with my God.
64. 8 and we all are the *w* of thine hand.
Jer 10.15 are vanity, and the *w* of errors:
17.24 sabbath day, to do no *w* therein;
La 4. 2 the *w* of the hands of the potter!
Mic 5.13 worship the *w* of thine hands.
Hab 3. 2 revive thy *w* in the midst of the
Mt 7.23 from me, ye that *w* iniquity.
21.28 Son, go *w* to day in my vineyard.
26.10 hath wrought a good *w* upon me.
Mk 6. 5 he could there do no mighty *w*,
13.34 servants, and to every man his *w*,
14. 6 she hath wrought a good *w* on me.
Lk 13.14 days in which men ought to *w*:
Jn 4.34 that sent me, and to finish his *w*.
5.17 worketh hitherto, and I *w*.
6.28 that we might *w* the works of God?
29 This is the *w* of God, that ye
30 believe thee? what dost thou *w*?
7.21 I have done one *w*, and ye all
9. 4 I must *w* the works of him that
4 night cometh, when no man can *w*.
10.33 For a good *w* we stone thee not;
Ro 2.15 shew the *w* of the law written in
8.28 all things *w* together for good to
9.28 For he will finish the *w*, and cut
28 short *w* will the Lord make upon
1Co 3.13 man's *w* shall be made manifest:
13 fire shall try every man's *w*
9. 1 are not ye my *w* in the Lord?
Php 1. 6 which hath begun a good *w* in you
2.12 *w* out your own salvation with
2Th 1.11 and the *w* of faith with power:
3.10 that if any would not *w*, neither
Heb 6.10 forget your *w* and labor of love,
Rev 22.12 man according as his *w* shall be.

WORKERS

2Ki 23.24 Moreover the *w* with familiar spirits,
1Ch 22.15 and *w* of stone and timber, and
Job 31. 3 punishment to the *w* of iniquity?
34. 8 in company with the *w* of iniquity,
22 where the *w* of iniquity may hide
Ps 5. 5 thou hatest all *w* of iniquity.
6. 8 from me, all ye *w* of iniquity;
14. 4 the *w* of iniquity no knowledge?
28. 3 with the *w* of iniquity, which speak
36.12 There are the *w* of iniquity fallen:
37. 1 against the *w* of iniquity.
53. 4 the *w* of iniquity no knowledge?
59. 2 Deliver me from the *w* of iniquity,
64. 2 insurrection of the *w* of iniquity:
92. 7 all the *w* of iniquity do flourish;
9 *w* of iniquity shall be scattered.
94. 4 *w* of iniquity boast themselves?
16 for me against the *w* of iniquity?
125. 5 them forth with the *w* of iniquity:
141. 9 and the gins of the *w* of iniquity.
Pr 10.29 shall be to the *w* of iniquity.
21.15 shall be to the *w* of iniquity.
Lk 13.27 from me, all ye *w* of iniquity.
1Co 12.29 teachers? are all *w* of miracles?
2Co 6. 1 We then, as *w* together with him,
11.13 are false apostles, deceitful *w*,
Php 3. 2 Beware of dogs, beware of evil *w*,

WORKETH

Job 33.29 these things *w* God oftentimes
Ps 15. 2 and *w* righteousness, and speaketh
101. 7 He that *w* deceit shall not dwell
Pr 11.18 The wicked *w* a deceitful work:
26.28 and a flattering mouth *w* ruin.
31.13 and *w* willingly with her hands.
Ec 3. 9 What profit hath he that *w* in that
Isa 44.12 with the tongs both *w* in the coals,
12 *w* it with the strength of his arms:
64. 5 rejoiceth and *w* righteousness,
Dan 6.27 *w* signs and wonders in heaven
Jn 5.17 My Father *w* hitherto, and I work.
Ac 10.35 *w* righteousness, is accepted with
Ro 2.10 peace, to every man that *w* good,
4. 4 to him that *w* is the reward not
5 But to him that *w* not, but
15 Because the law *w* wrath: for
5. 3 knowing...tribulation *w* patience;
13.10 Love *w* no ill to his neighbor:
1Co 12. 6 the same God which *w* all in all.
11 *w* that one and the selfsame Spirit,
16.10 he *w* the work of the Lord, as I
2Co 4.12 So then death *w* in us, but life in
17 *w* for us a far more exceeding
7.10 godly sorrow *w* repentance unto
10 the sorrow of the world *w* death.
Gal 3. 5 Spirit, and *w* miracles among you,
5. 6 but faith which *w* by love.
Eph 1.11 purpose of him who *w* all things
2. 2 spirit that now *w* in the children
3.20 to the power that *w* in us,
Php 2.13 is God which *w* in you both to will
Col 1.29 working, which *w* in me mightily.
1Th 2.13 which effectually *w* also in you
Jas 1. 3 trying of your faith *w* patience.
20 *w* not the righteousness of God.
Rev 21.27 whatsoever *w* abomination, or

WORKING

Ps 52. 2 like a sharp rasor, *w* deceitfully.
74.12 *w* salvation in the midst of the
Isa 28.29 in counsel, and excellent in *w*.
Eze 46. 1 east shall be shut the six *w* days;
Mk 16.20 the Lord *w* with them, and
Ro 1.27 men *w* that which is unseemly,
7.13 *w* death in me by that which is
1Co 4.12 labor, *w* with our own hands:
9. 6 have not we power to forbear *w*?
12.10 To another the *w* of miracles;
Eph 1.19 to the *w* of his mighty power,
3. 7 me by the effectual *w* of his power.
4.16 to the effectual *w* in the measure
28 *w* with his hands the thing which
Php 3.21 according to the *w* whereby he is
Col 1.29 striving according to his *w*, which
2Th 2. 9 coming is after the *w* of Satan
3.11 *w* not at all, but are busybodies.
Heb 13.21 his will, *w* in you that which is
Rev 16.14 the spirits of devils, *w* miracles,

WORKMAN

Ex 35.35 engraver, and of the cunning *w*,
38.23 an engraver, and a cunning *w*,
SS 7. 1 work of the hands of a cunning *w*,
Isa 40.19 The *w* melteth a graven image,
20 seeketh unto him a cunning *w* to
Jer 10. 3 the work of the hands of the *w*,
9 from Uphaz, the work of the *w*,
Hos 8. 6 the *w* made it; therefore it is not
Mt 10.10 for the *w* is worthy of his meat.
2Ti 2.15 a *w* that needeth not to be

WORKMANSHIP

Ex 31. 3 and in all manner of *w*,
5 to work in all manner of *w*,
35.31 and in all manner of *w*;
2Ki 16.10 according to all the *w* thereof.
1Ch 28.21 be with thee for all manner of *w*
Eze 28.13 *w* of thy tabrets and of thy pipes
Eph 2.10 For we are his *w*, created in

WORKMEN

2Ki 12.14 But they gave that to the *w*,
15 money to be bestowed on *w*:
1Ch 22.15 are *w* with thee in abundance,
25. 1 number of the *w* according
2Ch 24.13 So the *w* wrought, and the
34.10 *w* that had the oversight
10 *w* that wrought in the house
17 and to the hand of the *w*.
Ezr 3. 9 and *w* in the house of God:
Isa 44.11 and the *w*, they are of men:
Ac 19.25 with the *w* of like occupation,

WORK'S

1Th 5.13 highly in love for their *w* sake.

WORKS

Dt 15.10 God shall bless thee in all thy *w*,
Jdg 2. 7 seen all the great *w* of the Lord,
1Ki 13.11 *w* that the man of God had done
1Ch 16.12 Remember his marvellous *w* that he
Neh 9.35 turned they from their wicked *w*.
Ps 8. 6 dominion over the *w* of thy hands
9. 1 shew forth all thy marvellous *w*.
46. 8 Come, behold the *w* of the Lord,
66. 5 Come and see the *w* of God: he is
77.11 remember the *w* of the Lord:
78. 7 God, and not forget the *w* of God,
92. 5 O Lord, how great are thy *w*!
104.24 O Lord, how manifold are thy *w*!
107.24 These see the *w* of the Lord, and
31 his wonderful *w* to the children
139.14 marvellous are thy *w*; and that
143. 5 I meditate on all thy *w*; I muse
145. 4 shall praise thy *w* to another,
9 tender mercies are over all his *w*.
10 All thy *w* shall praise thee, O
Pr 16. 3 commit thy *w* unto the Lord,
31.31 her own *w* praise her in the gates.
Ec 2. 4 I made me great *w*; I builded me
3.22 man should rejoice in his own *w*;
9. 7 for God now accepteth thy *w*.
11. 5 thou knowest not the *w* of God
Isa 41.29 all vanity; their *w* are nothing:
Dan 9.14 our God is righteous in all his *w*
Jon 3.10 And God saw their *w*, that they
Mt 5.16 that they may see your good *w*,
7.22 name done many wonderful *w*?
11. 2 in the prison the *w* of Christ,
20 most of his mighty *w* were done.
13.54 this wisdom, and these mighty *w*?
16.27 every man according to his *w*.
23. 3 but do not ye after their *w*:
5 *w* they do for to be seen of men:
Mk 6. 2 even such mighty *w* are wrought
14 mighty *w* do shew forth...in him.
Jn 5.20 shew him greater *w* than these,
36 *w* which the Father hath given me
6.28 that we might work the *w* of God?
7. 3 may see the *w* that thou doest.
7 of it, that the *w* thereof are evil.
8.39 ye would do the *w* of Abraham.
9. 3 *w* of God should be made manifest
4 work the *w* of him that sent me,
10.25 *w* that I do in my Father's name,
32 Many good *w* have I shewed you
32 which of those *w* do ye stone me?
37 If I do not the *w* of my Father,
38 ye believe not me, believe the *w*:
14.10 dwelleth in me, he doeth the *w*.
12 the *w* that I do shall he do also;
12 greater *w* than these shall he do;
15.24 the *w* which none other man did,
Ac 2.11 tongues the wonderful *w* of God.
9.36 this woman was full of good *w* and
15.18 Known unto God are all his *w*
26.20 and do *w* meet for repentance.
Ro 3.27 By what law? of *w*? Nay: but by
4. 2 if Abraham were justified by *w*,
11. 6 by grace, then is it no more of *w*:
13. 3 rulers are not a terror to good *w*,
12 cast off the *w* of darkness, and
2Co 11.15 end shall be according to their *w*.
Gal 2.16 not justified by the *w* of the law,
3. 2 Received ye the Spirit by the *w* of
5.19 the *w* of the flesh are manifest,
Eph 2. 9 Not of *w*, lest any man should
10 in Christ Jesus unto good *w*,
1Ti 2.10 godliness) with good *w*.
6.18 that they be rich in good *w*, ready
2Ti 1. 9 calling, not according to our *w*,
4.14 reward him according to his *w*:
Heb 1.10 heavens are the *w* of thine hands:
9.14 purge your conscience from dead *w*

Heb 10.24 provoke unto love and to good *w*:
Jas 2.14 say he hath faith, and have not *w*?
17 so faith, if it hath not *w*, is dead,
18 shew me thy faith without thy *w*,
18 I will shew thee my faith by my *w*.
21 Abraham our father justified by *w*
22 and by *w* was faith made perfect?
25 Rahab the harlot justified by *w*,
26 so faith without *w* is dead also.
Rev 2. 2 I know thy *w*, and thy labor, and
19 faith, and thy patience, and thy *w*;
23 one of you according to your *w*.
14.13 and their *w* do follow them.
15. 3 Great and marvellous are thy *w*,
20.12 in the books, according to their *w*.
13 every man according to their *w*.

WORKS'

Jn 14.11 believe me for the very *w* sake.

WORLD

1Sa 2. 8 and he hath set the *w* upon them.
2Sa 22.16 the foundations of the *w* were
1Ch 16.30 the *w* also shall be stable, that it
Job 34.13 or who hath disposed the whole *w*?
Ps 9. 8 shall judge the *w* in righteousness,
19. 4 their words to the end of the *w*.
24. 1 the *w*, and they that dwell therein.
33. 8 inhabitants of the *w* stand in awe
50.12 for the *w* is mine, and the fulness
90. 2 hadst formed the earth and the *w*,
93. 1 the *w* also is stablished, that it
96.13 judge the *w* with righteousness,
98. 7 the *w*, and they that dwell therein.
9 righteousness shall he judge the *w*,
Ec 3.11 he hath set the *w* in their heart,
Isa 13.11 I will punish the *w* for their evil,
14.17 That made the *w* as a wilderness,
24. 4 *w* languisheth and fadeth away,
45.17 nor confounded *w* without end.
Jer 10.12 established the *w* by his wisdom.
La 4.12 and all the inhabitants of the *w*,
Na 1. 5 the *w*, and all that dwell therein.
Mt 4. 8 him all the kingdoms of the *w*,
5.14 Ye are the light of the *w*. A city
12.32 forgiven him, neither in this *w*,
32 neither in the *w* to come.
13.22 the word; and the care of this *w*,
49 So shall it be at the end of the *w*:
16.26 if he shall gain the whole *w*, and
18. 7 Woe unto the *w* because of
24. 3 coming, and of the end of the *w*?
21 not since the beginning of the *w*
25.34 you from the foundation of the *w*:
26.13 shall be preached in the whole *w*,
Mk 4.19 And the cares of this *w*, and the
8.36 if he shall gain the whole *w*, and
10.30 and in the *w* to come eternal life.
16.15 Go ye into all the *w*, and preach
Lk 1.70 have been since the *w* began:
4. 5 unto him all the kingdoms of the *w*
9.25 if he gain the whole *w*, and lose
11.50 shed from the foundation of the *w*,
18.30 in the *w* to come life everlasting.
20.34 The children of this *w* marry, and
35 accounted worthy to obtain that *w*,
Jn 1. 9 every man that cometh into the *w*.
10 He was in the *w*,
10 and the *w* was made by him,
10 and the *w* knew him not.
29 which taketh away the sin of the *w*.
3.16 For God so loved the *w*, that he
17 Son into the *w* to condemn the *w*;
17 the *w* through him might be saved.
19 that light is come into the *w*, and
4.42 the Christ, the Saviour of the *w*.
8.12 saying, I am the light of the *w*:
23 am from above: ye are of this *w*;
23 I am not of this *w*.
12.19 behold, the *w* is gone after him.
25 that hateth his life in this *w* shall
31 Now is the judgment of this *w*:
47 to judge the *w*, but to save the *w*.
13. 1 he should depart out of this *w* unto
1 loved his own which were in the *w*,
14.17 whom the *w* cannot receive,
27 not as the *w* giveth, give I unto you.
30 for the prince of this *w* cometh,
31 *w* may know that I love the Father;
15.18 If the *w* hate you, ye know that it
19 but because ye are not of the *w*,
19 I have chosen you out of the *w*,
16. 8 he will reprove the *w* of sin, and of
20 lament, but the *w* shall rejoice:
21 joy that a man is born into the *w*.
28 I leave the *w*, and go to the Father.
33 In the *w* ye shall have tribulation:
33 cheer; I have overcome the *w*.
17. 5 I had with thee before the *w* was.
9 I pray not for the *w*, but for them
11 And now I am no more in the *w*,
18 As thou hast sent me into the *w*,
18 so have I also sent them into the *w*.
23 *w* may know...thou hast sent me,
18.20 I spake openly to the *w*; I ever
36 My kingdom is not of this *w*:
37 for this cause came I into the *w*,
Ac 3.21 holy prophets since the *w* began.
17. 6 have turned the *w* upside down
Ro 1. 8 spoken of throughout the whole *w*.
3. 6 then how shall God judge the *w*?
5.12 by one man sin entered into the *w*,
1Co 1.20 where is the disputer of this *w*?
20 foolish the wisdom of this *w*?
3.18 you seemeth to be wise in this *w*,
19 wisdom of this *w* is foolishness
22 or the *w*, or life, or death, or
7.31 And they that use this *w*, as not
31 fashion of this *w* passeth away.
2Co 1.12 had our conversation in the *w*,
5.19 reconciling the *w* unto himself,
7.10 sorrow of the *w* worketh death.
Gal 1. 4 deliver us from the present evil *w*,
6.14 whom the *w* is crucified unto me,
14 and I unto the *w*.
Eph 1. 4 before the foundation of the *w*,
3. 9 the beginning of the *w* hath been
21 throughout all ages, *w* without end.
6.12 rulers of the darkness of this *w*,
Heb 1. 6 in the firstbegotten into the *w*,
2. 5 put in subjection the *w* to come,
Jas 1.27 himself unspotted from the *w*.
2. 5 the poor of this *w* rich in faith,
3. 6 tongue is a fire, a *w* of iniquity:
4. 4 the friendship of the *w* is enmity
2Pe 1. 4 the corruption that is in the *w*
2. 5 And spared not the old *w*, but
5 flood upon the *w* of the ungodly;
1Jn 2. 2 also for the sins of the whole *w*.
15 Love not the *w*, neither
17 And the *w* passeth away, and the
3. 1 therefore the *w* knoweth us not,
4. 1 prophets are gone out into the *w*.
9 his only begotten Son into the *w*,
5. 4 born of God overcometh the *w*:
Rev 3.10 which shall come upon all the *w*,
11.15 kingdoms of this *w* are become

WORLDLY

Tit 2.12 denying ungodliness and *w* lusts,
Heb 9. 1 service, and a *w* sanctuary.

WORLD'S

1Jn 3.17 But whoso hath this *w* good,

WORLDS

Heb 1. 2 by whom also he made the *w*;
11. 3 the *w* were framed by the word of

WORM

Job 17.14 to the *w*, Thou art my mother,
24.20 the *w* shall feed sweetly on him;
25. 6 How much less man, that is a *w*?
6 the son of man, which is a *w*?
Ps 22. 6 But I am a *w*, and no man;
Isa 66.24 for their *w* shall not die, neither
Jon 4. 7 But God prepared a *w* when the
Mk 9.44, 46 Where their *w* dieth not,
48 Where their *w* dieth not,

WORMS

Ex 16.20 and it bred *w*, and stank:
Dt 28.39 grapes; for the *w* shall eat them.
Job 7. 5 My flesh is clothed with *w* and
19.26 after my skin *w* shall destroy this
21.26 dust, and the *w* shall cover them.
Isa 14.11 under thee, and the *w* cover thee.
Mic 7.17 of their holes like *w* of the earth:
Ac 12.23 he was eaten of *w*, and gave up

WORMWOOD

Dt 29.18 a root that beareth gall and *w*;
Pr 5. 4 But her end is bitter as *w*, sharp
Jer 9.15 them, even this people, with *w*,
23.15 I will feed them with *w*, and make
La 3.15 hath made me drunken with *w*.
19 my misery, the *w* and the gall.
Am 5. 7 Ye who turn judgment to *w*, and
Rev 8.11 the name of the star is called *W*:
11 part of the waters became *w*;

WORSE

Gen 19. 9 now will we deal *w* with thee,
2Sa 19. 7 that will be *w* unto thee than all
1Ki 16.25 did *w* than all that were before
2Ki 14.12 Judah was put to the *w* before
1Ch 19.16, 19 were put to the *w* before Israel,
2Ch 6.24 thy people Israel be put to the *w*
25.22 Judah was put to the *w* before
33. 9 to do *w* than the heathen, whom
Jer 7.26 they did *w* than their fathers.
16.12 have done *w* than your fathers;
Dan 1.10 faces *w* liking than the children
Mt 9.16 garment, and the rent is made *w*.
12.45 of that man is *w* than the first.
27.64 last error shall be *w* than the first.
Mk 2.21 the old, and the rent is made *w*.
5.26 bettered, but rather grew *w*,
Lk 11.26 of that man is *w* than the first.
Jn 2.10 well drunk, then that which is *w*:
5.14 lest a *w* thing come unto thee.
1Co 8. 8 if we eat not, are we the *w*.
11.17 not for the better, but for the *w*.
1Ti 5. 8 faith, and is *w* than an infidel.
2Ti 3.13 and seducers shall wax *w* and *w*,
2Pe 2.20 the latter end is *w* with them than

WORSHIP

Gen 22. 5 and the lad will go yonder and *w*,
Ex 34.14 For thou shalt *w* no other god:
Dt 11.16 and serve other gods, and *w* them;
26.10 and *w* before the Lord thy God:
1Sa 1. 3 went up out of his city yearly to *w*
15.30 that I may *w* the Lord thy God.
1Ch 16.29 *w* the Lord in the beauty of
Ps 5. 7 will I *w* toward thy holy temple.
29. 2 *w* the Lord in the beauty of
66. 4 All the earth shall *w* thee, and
95. 6 O come, let us *w* and bow down:
96. 9 O *w* the Lord in the beauty of
138. 2 I will *w* toward thy holy temple,
Isa 27.13 shall *w* the Lord in the holy mount
46. 6 a god: they fall down, yea, they *w*.
Eze 46. 2 *w* at the threshold of the gate:
Dan 3. 5 fall down and *w* the golden image
28 might not serve nor *w* any god,
Mic 5.13 more *w* the work of thine hands.
Zep 1. 5 them that *w* the host of heaven
Zec 14.16 from year to year to *w* the King,
17 unto Jerusalem to *w* the King,
Mt 2. 2 the east, and are come to *w* him.
8 that I may come and *w* him also.
4. 9 if thou wilt fall down and *w* me.

10 Thou shalt *w* the Lord thy God,
15. 9 But in vain do they *w* me, teaching
Mk 7. 7 Howbeit in vain do they *w* me,
Lk 4. 7 If thou therefore wilt *w* me,
8 Thou shalt *w* the Lord thy God,
14.10 have *w* in the presence of them
Jn 4.20 the place where men ought to *w*.
21 yet at Jerusalem, *w* the Father.
22 Ye *w* ye know not what:
22 we know what we *w*: for salvation
23 shall *w* the Father in spirit and in
23 the Father seeketh such to *w* him.
24 is a Spirit: and they that *w* him
24 must *w* him in spirit and in truth.
12.20 that came up to *w* at the feast:
Ac 7.42 them up to *w* the host of heaven;
43 which ye made to *w* them:
8.27 had come to Jerusalem for to *w*,
17.23 Whom therefore ye ignorantly *w*,
18.13 fellow persuadeth men to *w* God
24.11 I went up to Jerusalem for to *w*.
14 so *w* I the God of my fathers,
1Co 14.25 down on his face he will *w* God,
Php 3. 3 which *w* God in the spirit, and
Col 2.23 indeed a shew of wisdom in will *w*,
Heb 1. 6 let all the angels of God *w* him.
Rev 3. 9 to come and *w* before thy feet,
4.10 and *w* him that liveth for ever and
9.20 that they should not *w* devils, and
11. 1 altar, and them that *w* therein.
13. 8 dwell upon the earth shall *w* him,
12 dwell therein to *w* the first beast,
15 not *w* the image of the beast
14. 7 and *w* him that made heaven, and
9 If any man *w* the beast and his
11 who *w* the beast and his image,
15. 4 shall come and *w* before thee;
19.10 And I fell at his feet to *w* him.
10 *w* God: for the testimony of Jesus
22. 8 I fell down to *w* before the feet of
9 the sayings of this book: *w* God.

WORSHIPPED

Gen 24.26 down his head, and *w* the Lord.
52 heard their words, he *w* the Lord,
Ex 32. 8 them a molten calf, and have *w* it.
Dt 17. 3 and served other gods, and *w* them,
1Sa 15.31 after Saul; and Saul *w* the Lord.
2Sa 15.32 top of the mount, where he *w* God,
1Ki 16.31 went and served Baal, and *w* him.
2Ki 21. 3 and *w* all the host of heaven, and
2Ch 29.28 And all the congregation *w*, and
Neh 9. 3 and *w* the Lord their God.
Jer 1.16 *w* the works of their own hands.
Eze 8.16 they *w* the sun toward the east.
Dan 3. 7 fell down and *w* the golden image
Mt 2.11 mother, and fell down and *w* him:
8. 2 there came a leper and *w* him,
9.18 came a certain ruler, and *w* him,
14.33 were in the ship came and *w* him,
15.25 Then came she and *w* him, saying,
18.26 fell down, and *w* him, saying, Lord,
28. 9 held him by the feet, and *w* him.
17 they *w* him: but some doubted.
Mk 5. 6 Jesus afar off, he ran and *w* him,
15.19 and bowing their knees *w* him.
Lk 24.52 And they *w* him, and returned to
Jn 4.20 Our fathers *w* in this mountain;
9.38 Lord, I believe. And he *w* him.
Ac 10.25 fell down at his feet, and *w* him.
16.14 Thyatira, which *w* God, heard us;
17.25 Neither is *w* with men's hands,
18. 7 named Justus, one that *w* God,
Ro 1.25 and *w* and served the creature
2Th 2. 4 all that is called God, or that is *w*;
Heb 11.21 and *w*, leaning upon the top of
Rev 5.14 and *w* him that liveth for ever and
7.11 throne on their faces, and *w* God,
11.16 fell upon their faces, and *w* God,
13. 4 *w* the dragon which gave power
4 and they *w* the beast, saying, Who

16. 2 and upon them which *w* his image.
19. 4 four beasts fell down and *w* God
20 beast, and them that *w* his image.
20. 4 which had not *w* the beast, neither

WORSHIPPER

Jn 9.31 but if any man be a *w* of God, and
Ac 19.35 a *w* of the great goddess Diana,

WORSHIPPERS

2Ki 10.19 he might destroy the *w* of Baal.
21 all the *w* of Baal came, so that
22 vestments for all the *w* of Baal.
23 said unto the *w* of Baal, Search,
23 the Lord, but the *w* of Baal only.
Jn 4.23 true *w* shall worship the Father
Heb 10. 2 the *w* once purged should have

WORSHIPPETH

Neh 9. 6 and the host of heaven *w* thee.
Isa 44.15 yea, he maketh a god, and *w* it;
17 he falleth down unto it, and *w* it,
Dan 3. 6 whoso falleth not down and *w*
11 And whoso falleth not down and *w*,
Ac 19.27 whom all Asia and the world *w*.

WORSHIPPING

2Ki 19.37 *w* in the house of Nisroch his god,
2Ch 20.18 fell before the Lord, *w* the Lord.
Isa 37.38 *w* in the house of Nisroch his god,
Mt 20.20 *w* him, and desiring a certain
Col 2.18 humility and *w* of angels,

WORTH

Gen 23. 9 money as it is *w* he shall give it
Lev 27.23 unto him the *w* of thy estimation,
Dt 15.18 been *w* a double hired servant
2Sa 18. 3 thou art *w* ten thousand of us:
1Ki 21. 2 give thee the *w* of it in money.
Job 24.25 and make my speech nothing *w*?
Pr 10.20 the heart of the wicked is little *w*.
Eze 30. 2 God; Howl ye, Woe *w* the day!

WORTHY

Gen 32.10 I am not *w* of the least of all the
Dt 17. 6 is *w* of death to be put to death;
1Sa 26.16 ye are *w* to die, because ye have
2Sa 22. 4 the Lord, who is *w* to be praised:
1Ki 1.52 will shew himself a *w* man,
Ps 18. 3 the Lord, who is *w* to be praised:
Jer 26.11 saying, This man is *w* to die;
16 This man is not *w* to die: for he
Mt 3.11 whose shoes I am not *w* to bear:
8. 8 I am not *w* that thou shouldest
10.10 for the workman is *w* of his meat.
11 shall enter, inquire who in it is *w*;
13 if the house be *w*, let your peace
13 if it be not *w*, let your peace return
37 more than me is not *w* of me:
37 more than me is not *w* of me.
38 followeth after me, is not *w* of me.
22. 8 which were bidden were not *w*.
Mk 1. 7 shoes I am not *w* to stoop down
Lk 3. 8 therefore fruits *w* of repentance,
16 shoes I am not *w* to unloose:
7. 4 he was *w* for whom he should do
6 I am not *w* that thou shouldest
7 thought I myself *w* to come
10. 7 for the laborer is *w* of his hire.
12.48 did commit things *w* of stripes,
15.19 am no more *w* to be called thy son:
21 am no more *w* to be called thy son.
20.35 accounted *w* to obtain that world,
21.36 accounted *w* to escape all these
23.15 nothing *w* of death is done unto
Jn 1.27 latchet I am not *w* to unloose.
Ac 5.41 were counted *w* to suffer shame
13.25 of his feet I am not *w* to loose.
23.29 laid to his charge *w* of death
24. 2 very *w* deeds are done unto this
25.11 committed any thing *w* of death,

25 had committed nothing *w* of death,
26.31 nothing *w* of death or of bonds.
Ro 1.32 such things are *w* of death,
8.18 time are not *w* to be compared
Eph 4. 1 that ye walk *w* of the vocation
Col 1.10 might walk *w* of the Lord unto
1Th 2.12 That ye would walk *w* of God, who
2Th 1. 5 may be counted *w* of the kingdom
11 count you *w* of this calling,
1Ti 1.15 saying, and *w* of all acceptation,
4. 9 saying and *w* of all acceptation.
5.17 be counted *w* of double honor,
18 The laborer is *w* of his reward.
6. 1 their own masters *w* of all honor,
Heb 3. 3 man was counted *w* of more glory
10.29 shall he be thought *w*, who hath
11.38 (Of whom the world was not *w*:)
Jas 2. 7 they blaspheme that *w* name
Rev 3. 4 with me in white: for they are *w*.
4.11 Thou art *w*, O Lord, to receive
5. 2 Who is *w* to open the book, and to
4 no man was found *w* to open and
9 Thou art *w* to take the book, and
12 *W* is the lamb that was slain to
16. 6 blood to drink; for they are *w*.

WOT

Gen 21.26 I *w* not who hath done this thing:
44.15 *w* ye not that such a man as I can
Ex 32. 1, 23 *w* not what is become of him.
Nu 22. 6 I *w* that he whom thou blessest is
Jos 2. 5 whither the men went I *w* not:
Ac 3.17 I *w* that through ignorance ye
7.40 we *w* not what is become of him.
Ro 11. 2 *W* ye not what the scripture saith
Php 1.22 yet what I shall choose I *w* not.

WOULD

Ex 8.32 neither *w* he let the people go.
Nu 11.29 Lord *w* put his spirit upon them!
14. 2 *W* God that we had died in the
2 *w* God we...died in the wilderness!
22.29 I *w* there were a sword in mine
Dt 1.45 Lord *w* not hearken to your voice,
28.67 say, *W* God it were even!
67 say, *W* God it were morning!
32.29 they *w* consider their latter end!
Jos 7. 7 *w* to God we had been content,
2Sa 18.33 *w* God I had died for thee, O
23.15 that one *w* give me drink of the water
16 nevertheless he *w* not drink
17 therefore he *w* not drink it. These
1Ki 13.33 whosoever *w*, he consecrated him,
2Ki 5. 3 for he *w* recover him of his leprosy.
7. 2 Lord *w* make windows in heaven,
1Ch 11.17 that one *w* give me drink of the water
18 but David *w* not drink of it, but
19 Therefore he *w* not drink it.
2Ch 15.13 whosoever *w* not seek the Lord God
Job 5. 8 I *w* seek unto God,
8 and unto God *w* I commit my cause:
6. 8 that God *w* grant me the thing that
9 that it *w* please God to destroy me;
10 I *w* harden myself in sorrow: let
9.15 I were righteous, yet *w* I not answer,
15 I *w* make supplication to my judge.
35 Then *w* I speak, and not fear him;
11. 5 But oh that God *w* speak, and open
13. 3 Surely I *w* speak to the Almighty,
23. 4 I *w* order my cause before him, and
5 he *w* answer me, and understand
5 understand what he *w* say unto me.
31.35 that the Almighty *w* answer me, and
36 Surely I *w* take it upon my shoulder,
37 as a prince *w* I go near unto him.
Ps 50.12 If I were hungry, I *w* not tell thee:
51.16 not sacrifice; else *w* I give it: thou
55. 6 for then *w* I fly away, and be at rest.
81.11 and Israel *w* none of me.
107. 8, 15, 21, 31 men *w* praise the Lord for
Pr 1.25 counsel, and *w* none of my reproof:

Pr 1.30 They *w* none of my counsel: they
Jer 10. 7 Who *w* not fear thee, O King of
Eze 13. 6 hope that they *w* confirm the word.
Dan 5.19 before him: whom he *w* he slew;
Hos 11. 7 most High, none at all *w* exalt him.
Jon 3.10 he had said that he *w* do unto them;
4. 5 see what *w* become of the city.
Zec 7.13 so they cried, and I *w* not hear,
Mt 7.12 ye *w* that men should do to you,
8.34 he *w* depart out of their coasts.
12. 7 ye *w* not have condemned the
18.30 he *w* not: but went and cast him
23.37 *w* I have gathered thy children
37 under her wings, and ye *w* not!
27.15 people a prisoner, whom they *w*.
34 tasted thereof, he *w* not drink.
Mk 3.13 and calleth unto him whom he *w*:
7.24 and *w* have no man know it:
9.30 he *w* not that any man should
10.36 What *w* ye that I should do for you?
11.16 And *w* not suffer that any man
Lk 6.31 ye *w* that men should do to you,
7.39 *w* have known who and what
9.53 as though he *w* go to Jerusalem.
13.34 *w* I have gathered thy children
34 under her wings, and ye *w* not!
18. 4 And he *w* not for a while: but
19.40 the stones *w* immediately cry out.
24.28 as though he *w* have gone further.
Jn 5.46 Moses, ye *w* have believed me:
7. 1 for he *w* not walk in Jewry,
8.42 God were your Father, ye *w* love
12.21 him, saying, Sir, we *w* see Jesus.
14. 2 if it were not so, I *w* have told you.
Ac 2.30 he *w* raise up Christ to sit on his
7.25 brethren *w* have understood that
16.27 sword, and *w* have killed himself,
26.29 I *w* to God, that not only thou,
Ro 1.13 Now I *w* not have you ignorant,
5. 7 good man some *w* even dare to die.
7.15 for what I *w*, that I do not; but
16 If then I do that which I *w* not,
19 For the good that I *w* I do not:
19 the evil which I *w* not, that I do.
20 Now if I do that I *w* not, it is no
21 when I *w* do good, evil is present
1Co 2. 8 they *w* not have crucified the Lord of
7. 7 I *w* that all men were even as I
14. 5 I *w* that ye all spake with tongues,
Gal 2.10 they *w* that we should remember the
Col 2. 1 For I *w* that ye knew what great
4. 3 that God *w* open unto us a door of
1Th 2.12 That ye *w* walk worthy of God, who
Heb 11.32 the time *w* fail me to tell of Gideon,
2Jn 12 I *w* not write with paper and ink:
3Jn 10 forbiddeth them that *w*, and casteth
Rev 3.15 hot: I *w* thou wert cold or hot.

WOULDEST

Dt 8. 2 thou *w* keep his commandments,
2Ki 5.13 great thing, *w* thou not have done it?
1Ch 4.10 Oh that thou *w* bless me indeed, and
Neh 2. 5 that thou *w* send me unto Judah,
Job 14.13 O that thou *w* hide me in the grave,
13 that thou *w* keep me secret, until thy
13 that thou *w* appoint me a set time,
Isa 64. 1 Oh that thou *w* rend the heavens,
1 that thou *w* come down, that the
Lk 16.27 *w* send him to my father's house:
Jn 4.10 *w* have asked of him, and he would
11.40 if thou *w* believe, thou shouldest see
21.18 and walkedst whither thou *w*:
18 carry thee whither thou *w* not.
Ac 23.20 thee that thou *w* bring down Paul
24. 4 thou *w* hear us of thy clemency
Heb 10. 5 Sacrifice and offering thou *w* not,
8 and offering for sin thou *w* not,

WOUND

Ex 21.25 burning, *w* for *w*, stripe for stripe.
Dt 32.39 I make alive; I *w*, and I heal:
1Ki 22.35 the blood ran out of the *w* into
Job 34. 6 my *w* is incurable without
Ps 68.21 But God shall *w* the head of his
110. 6 he shall *w* the heads over many
Pr 6.33 A *w* and dishonor shall he get;
20.30 blueness of a *w* cleanseth...evil:
Isa 30.26 and healeth the stroke of their *w*.
Jer 10.19 me for my hurt! my *w* is grievous:
15.18 perpetual, and my *w* incurable,
30.12 incurable, and thy *w* is grievous.
14 thee with the *w* of an enemy,
Hos 5.13 sickness, and Judah saw his *w*,
13 heal you, nor cure you of your *w*.
Ob 7 bread have laid a *w* under thee:
Mic 1. 9 her *w* is incurable; for it is come
Na 3.19 of thy bruise; thy *w* is grievous:
Jn 19.40 and *w* it in linen clothes with the
Ac 5. 6 the young men arose, *w* him up,
1Co 8.12 and *w* their weak conscience, ye
Rev 13. 3 and his deadly *w* was healed:
12 beast, whose deadly *w* was healed.
14 which had the *w* by a sword, and

WOUNDED

Dt 23. 1 He that is *w* in the stones,
Jdg 9.40 many were overthrown and *w*,
1Sa 17.52 the *w* of the Philistines fell down
31. 3 he was sore *w* of the archers.
2Sa 22.39 consumed them, and *w* them.
1Ki 20.37 so that in smiting he *w* him.
22.34 me out of the host; for I am *w*.
2Ki 8.28 and the Syrians *w* Joram.
1Ch 10. 3 and he was *w* of the archers.
2Ch 18.33 out of the host; for I am sore *w*.
35.23 Have me away; for I am sore *w*.
Job 24.12 and the soul of the *w* crieth out:
Ps 18.38 *w* them that they were not able
64. 7 arrow; suddenly shall they be *w*.
69.26 grief of those whom thou hast *w*.
109.22 and my heart is *w* within me.
Pr 7.26 For she hath cast down many *w*:
18.14 but a *w* spirit who can bear?
SS 5. 7 me, they smote me, they *w* me;
Isa 51. 9 cut Rahab, and *w* the dragon?
53. 5 he was *w* for our transgressions,
Jer 30.14 I have *w* thee with the wound of
37.10 there remained but *w* men among
51.52 all her land the *w* shall groan.
La 2.12 swooned as the *w* in the streets
Eze 26.15 sound of thy fall, when the *w* cry,
28.23 the *w* shall be judged in the midst
30.24 groanings of a deadly *w* man.
Joel 2. 8 the sword, they shall not be *w*.
Zec 13. 6 was *w* in the house of my friends.
Mk 12. 4 and *w* him in the head, and sent him
Lk 10.30 *w* him, and departed, leaving
20.12 and they *w* him also, and cast
Ac 19.16 fled out of that house naked and *w*.
Rev 13. 3 his heads as it were *w* to death;

WOUNDING

Gen 4.23 for I have slain a man to my *w*,

WOUNDS

2Ki 8.29 to be healed in Jezreel of the *w*
9.15 to be healed in Jezreel of the *w*
2Ch 22. 6 healed in Jezreel because of the *w*
Job 9.17 multiplieth my *w* without cause.
Ps 38. 5 My *w* stink and are corrupt
147. 3 in heart, and bindeth up their *w*.
Pr 18. 8 words of a talebearer are as *w*,
23.29 who hath *w* without cause? who
26.22 words of a talebearer are as *w*,
27. 6 Faithful are the *w* of a friend;
Isa 1. 6 but *w*, and bruises, and putrifying
Jer 6. 7 me continually is grief and *w*.
30.17 and I will heal thee of thy *w*, saith
Zec 13. 6 What are these *w* in thine hands?
Lk 10.34 went to him, and bound up his *w*,

WOVEN

Ex 28.32 it shall have a binding of *w* work
39.22 the robe of the ephod of *w* work,
27 of fine linen of *w* work for Aaron,
Jn 19.23 seam, *w* from the top throughout.

WRAP

Isa 28.20 than that he can *w* himself in it.
Mic 7. 3 desire: so they *w* it up.

WRAPPED

Gen 38.14 her with a vail and *w* herself,
1Sa 21. 9 *w* in a cloth behind the ephod:
1Ki 19.13 that he *w* his face in his mantle,
2Ki 2. 8 his mantle, and *w* it together,
Job 8.17 His roots are *w* about the heap,
40.17 the sinews of his stones are *w*
Eze 21.15 it is *w* up for the slaughter.
Jon 2. 5 the weeds were *w* about my head.
Mt 27.59 he *w* it in a clean linen cloth,
Mk 15.46 him down, and *w* him in the linen,
Lk 2. 7 and *w* him in swaddling clothes,
12 the babe *w* in swaddling clothes,
23.53 it down, and *w* it in linen,
Jn 20. 7 but *w* together in a place by itself.

WRATH

Gen 49. 7 and their *w*, for it was cruel:
Ex 32.12 Turn from thy fierce *w*, and repent
Nu 11.33 *w* of the Lord was kindled against
16.46 is *w* gone out from the Lord;
Dt 9. 7 provokedst the Lord thy God to *w*
32.27 that I feared the *w* of the enemy,
2Ch 12.12 *w* of the Lord turned from him,
Ezr 10.14 fierce *w* of our God for this matter
Est 7.10 Then was the king's *w* pacified.
Job 5. 2 For *w* killeth the foolish man,
14.13 me secret, until thy *w* be past,
16. 9 He teareth me in his *w*, who hateth
21.20 drink of the *w* of the Almighty.
30 be brought forth to the day of *w*.
32. 3 his three friends was his *w* kindled,
Ps 2.12 when his *w* is kindled but a little.
37. 8 Cease from anger, and forsake *w*:
38. 1 O Lord, rebuke me not in thy *w*:
78.31 The *w* of God came upon them,
79. 6 Pour out thy *w* upon the heathen
88. 7 Thy *w* lieth hard upon me, and
90. 7 and by thy *w* are we troubled.
11 according to thy fear, so is thy *w*.
Pr 11. 4 Riches profit not in the day of *w*:
12.16 A fool's *w* is presently known:
14.29 He that is slow to *w* is of great
15. 1 A soft answer turneth away *w*:
27. 3 a fool's *w* is heavier than them
4 *W* is cruel, and anger is
30.33 forcing of *w* bringeth forth strife.
Isa 60.10 in my *w* I smote thee, but in my
Jer 10.10 at his *w* the earth shall tremble,
La 3. 1 seen affliction by the rod of his *w*.
Hos 5.10 I will pour out my *w* upon them
Zep 1.15 That day is a day of *w*, a day of
Zec 8.14 your fathers provoked me to *w*,
Mt 3. 7 you to flee from the *w* to come?
Lk 3. 7 you to flee from the *w* to come?
4.28 these things, were filled with *w*.
21.23 the land, and *w* upon his people.
Jn 3.36 but the *w* of God abideth on him.
Ac 19.28 these sayings, they were full of *w*,
Ro 1.18 For the *w* of God is revealed from
2. 5 heart treasurest up unto thyself *w*
5 against the day of *w* and
8 unrighteousness, indignation...*w*,
4.15 Because the law worketh *w*: for
5. 9 be saved from *w* through him.
9.22 What if God, willing to shew his *w*,
22 vessels of *w* fitted to destruction:
12.19 but rather give place unto *w*:
13. 4 to execute *w* upon him that doeth
5 needs be subject, not only for *w*,
Gal 5.20 hatred, variance, emulations, *w*,

Eph 2. 3 were by nature the children of *w*,
4.26 the sun go down upon your *w*:
31 and *w*, and anger, and clamor,
5. 6 things cometh the *w* of God
6. 4 provoke not your children to *w*:
Col 3. 6 things' sake the *w* of God cometh
8 anger, *w*, malice, blasphemy,
1Th 1.10 delivered us from the *w* to come.
2.16 for the *w* is come upon them to
5. 9 God hath not appointed us to *w*,
1Ti 2. 8 hands, without *w* and doubting.
Heb 3.11 So I sware in my *w*, They shall
4. 3 As I have sworn in my *w*, If they
11.27 not fearing the *w* of the king:
Jas 1.19 hear, slow to speak, slow to *w*:
20 For the *w* of man worketh not the
Rev 6.16 and from the *w* of the Lamb:
17 the great day of his *w* has come;
11.18 were angry, and thy *w* is come,
12.12 having great *w*, because he
14. 8 wine of the *w* of her fornication.
10 drink of the wine of the *w* of God,
19 great winepress of the *w* of God.
15. 1 in them is filled up the *w* of God.
7 golden vials full of the *w* of God,
16. 1 pour out the vials of the *w* of God
19 wine of the fierceness of his *w*.
18. 3 wine of the *w* of her fornication,
19.15 fierceness and *w* of Almighty God.

WRATHFUL
Ps 69.24 thy *w* anger take hold of them.
Pr 15.18 A *w* man stirreth up strife: but

WREST
Ex 23. 2 after many to *w* judgment:
6 shalt not *w* the judgment of thy
Dt 16.19 Thou shalt not *w* judgment; thou
Ps 56. 5 Every day they *w* my words:
2Pe 3.16 are unlearned and unstable *w*,

WRESTLE
Eph 6.12 For we *w* not against flesh

WRESTLED
Gen 30. 8 have I *w* with my sister, and I
32.24 there *w* a man with him until the
25 was out of a joint, as he *w* with him.

WRETCHED
Ro 7.24 O *w* man that I am! who shall
Rev 3.17 and knowest not that thou art *w*,

WRETCHEDNESS
Nu 11.15 sight; and let me not see my *w*.

WRINKLE
Eph 5.27 spot, or *w*, or any such thing;

WRITE
Ex 17.14 *W* this for a memorial in a book,
34. 1 will *w* upon these tables the words
Nu 17. 3 *w* Aaron's name upon the rod of
Dt 11.20 shalt *w* them upon the door posts
24. 1, 3 *w* her a bill of divorcement,
Pr 3. 3 *w* them upon the table of thine
Isa 10.19 be few, that a child may *w* them.
Jer 31.33 parts, and *w* it in their hearts;
Hab 2. 2 *W* the vision, and make it plain
Mk 10. 4 to *w* a bill of divorcement,
Lk 1. 3 very first, to *w* unto thee in order,
16. 6 and sit down quickly, and *w* fifty.
7 Take thy bill, and *w* fourscore.
Jn 1.45 in the law, and the prophets, did *w*,
19.21 *W* not, The King of the Jews;
Ac 15.20 But that we *w* unto them, that
25.26 I have no certain thing to *w* unto
26 had, I might have somewhat to *w*.
1Co 4.14 I *w* not these things to shame you,
14.37 that the things that I *w* unto you
2Co 1.13 we *w* none other things unto you,
2. 9 For to this end also did I *w*, that I
9. 1 is superfluous for me to *w* to you:
13. 2 I *w* to them which heretofore have
10 I *w* these things being absent, lest
Gal 1.20 the things which I *w* unto you,
Php 3. 1 To *w* the same things to you,
1Th 4. 9 ye need not that I *w* unto you:
5. 1 I have no need that I *w* unto you.
2Th 3.17 token in every epistle: so I *w*.
1Ti 3.14 These things *w* I unto thee,
Heb 8.10 mind, and *w* them in their hearts:
10.16 and in their minds will I *w* them;
2Pe 3. 1 beloved, I now *w* unto you;
1Jn 1. 4 And these things *w* we unto you,
2. 1 these things *w* I unto you, that ye
7 I *w* no new commandment unto
8 new commandment I *w* unto you,
12 I *w* unto you, little children,
13 I *w* unto you, fathers, because ye
13 I *w* unto you, young men, because
13 I *w* unto you, little children,
2Jn 12 Having many things to *w* unto you,
12 I would not *w* with paper and ink:
3Jn 13 I had many things to *w*, but I will
13 not with ink and pen *w* unto thee:
Jude 3 to *w* unto you of the common
3 needful for me to *w* unto you,
Rev 1.11 What thou seest, *w* in a book,
19 *W* the things which thou hast
2. 1 angel of the church of Ephesus *w*;
8 angel of the church in Smyrna *w*;
12 of the church in Pergamos *w*;
18 angel of the church in Thyatira *w*;
3. 1 angel of the church in Sardis *w*;
7 of the church in Philadelphia *w*;
12 I will *w* upon him the name of my
12 I will *w* upon him my new name.
14 the church of the Laodiceans *w*;
10. 4 their voices, I was about to *w*:
4 thunders uttered, and *w* them not.
14.13 *W*, Blessed are the dead which die
19. 9 *W*, Blessed are they which are
21. 5 *W*: for these words are true

WRITER
Jdg 5.14 they that handle the pen of the *w*.
Ps 45. 1 my tongue is the pen of a ready *w*.

WRITING
Ex 32.16 the *w* was the *w* of God, graven
Dt 31.24 an end of *w* the words of this law
1Ch 28.19 Lord made me understand in *w*
2Ch 36.22 his kingdom, and put it also in *w*,
Dan 5. 7 Whosoever shall read this *w*,
6. 9 king Darius signed the *w* and the
10 Daniel knew that the *w* was signed,
Mt 5.31 let him give her a *w* of divorcement:
19. 7 to give a *w* of divorcement, and
Lk 1.63 And he asked for a *w* table, and
Jn 19.19 And the *w* was, Jesus Of Nazareth

WRITINGS
Jn 5.47 if ye believe not his *w*, how shall

WRITTEN
Ex 24.12 commandments which I have *w*;
31.18 stone, *w* with the finger of God.
32.15 tables were *w* on both their sides;
Dt 9.10 stone *w* with the finger of God;
29.20 the curses that are *w* in this book
30.10 statutes which are *w* in this book
Jos 10.13 not this *w* in the book of Jasher?
1Ki 2. 3 as it is *w* in the law of Moses,
2Ki 23.24 which were *w* in the book of Hilkiah
1Ch 29.29 *w* in the book of Samuel the seer,
2Ch 9.29 not *w* in the book of Nathan the
12.15 not *w* in the book of Shemaiah the
13.22 *w* in the story of the prophet Iddo.
16.11 *w* in the book of the kings of Judah
20.34 they are *w* in the book of Jehu
27. 7 *w* in the book of the kings of Israel
32.32 they are *w* in the vision of Isaiah
Ezr 4. 7 letter was *w* in the Syrian tongue,
6. 2 a roll, and therein was a record *w*:
Est 1.19 *w* among the laws of the Persians
Job 19.23 Oh that my words were now *w*!
31.35 that mine adversary had *w* a book.
Ps 40. 7 volume of the book it is *w* of me,
139.16 thy book all my members were *w*,
Isa 4. 3 one that is *w* among the living
Jer 25.13 even all that is *w* in this book,
Eze 2.10 and it was *w* within and without:
10 there was *w* therein lamentations,
Mal 3.16 and a book of remembrance was *w*
Mt 2. 5 for thus it is *w* by the prophet,
4. 4 It is *w*, Man shall not live by
6 for it is *w*, He shall give his angels
7 It is *w* again, Thou shalt not tempt
10 for it is *w*, Thou shalt worship the
11.10 For this is he, of whom it is *w*,
26.24 Son of man goeth as it is *w* of him:
31 it is *w*, I will smite the shepherd,
27.37 up over his head his accusation *w*,
Mk 1. 2 As it is *w* in the prophets, Behold,
9.12 how it is *w* of the Son of man, that
11.17 it not *w*, My house shall be called
Lk 2.23 (As it is *w* in the law of the Lord,
4. 4 It is *w*, That man shall not live by
8 it is *w*, Thou shalt worship the
10 it is *w*, He shall give his angels
7.27 This is he, of whom it is *w*, Behold,
10.20 your names are *w* in heaven.
18.31 things that are *w* by the prophets
21.22 that all things...*w* may be fulfilled.
22.37 that is *w* must yet be accomplished
Jn 2.17 remembered that it was *w*,
6.31 as it is *w*, He gave them bread
15.25 be fulfilled that is *w* in their law,
19.20 it was *w* in Hebrew, and Greek,
22 What I have *w* I have *w*.
20.30 which are not *w* in this book:
31 these are *w*, that ye might believe
21.25 if they should be *w* every one, I
Ac 1.20 it is *w* in the book of Psalms,
7.42 it is *w* in the book of the prophets,
13.29 had fulfilled all that was *w* of him,
Ro 1.17 as it is *w*, The just shall live by
2.15 work of the law *w* in their hearts,
12.19 for it is *w*, Vengeance is mine;
2Co 3. 2 Ye are our epistle *w* in our hearts,
3 ministered by us, *w* not with ink,
7 *w* and engraven in stones,
Rev 1. 3 those things which are *w* therein:
2.17 and in the stone a new name *w*,
13. 8 names are not *w* in the book of life
14. 1 Father's name *w* in their foreheads.
19.12 had a name *w*, that no man knew,
20.12 things which were *w* in the books,
15 was not found *w* in the book of life
21.12 and names *w* thereon, which are
27 are *w* in the Lamb's book of life.

WRONG
Gen 16. 5 unto Abram, My *w* be upon thee:
Ex 2.13 he said to him that did the *w*,
Dt 19.16 against him that which is *w*;
Jdg 11.27 doest me *w* to war against me:
1Ch 12.17 there is no *w* in mine hands,
16.21 suffered no man to do them *w*:
Est 1.16 the queen hath not done *w* to the
Job 19. 7 Behold, I cry out of *w*, but I am
Ps 105.14 suffered no man to do them *w*:
Jer 22. 3 and do no *w*, do no violence
13 and his chambers by *w*;
La 3.59 O Lord, thou hast seen my *w*:
Hab 1. 4 *w* judgment proceedeth.
Mt 20.13 Friend, I do thee no *w*: didst not
Ac 7.24 And seeing one of them suffer *w*,
26 why do ye *w* one to another?
27 he that did his neighbor *w* thrust
18.14 matter of *w* or wicked lewdness,
25.10 to the Jews have I done no *w*,

1Co 6. 7 Why do ye not rather take *w*? why
8 Nay, ye do *w*, and defraud, and that
2Co 7.12 for his cause that had done the *w*,
12 for his cause that suffered *w*, but
12.13 to you? forgive me this *w*.
Col 3.25 But he that doeth *w* shall receive
25 for the *w* which he hath done:

WRONGED

2Co 7. 2 we have *w* no man, we have
Phm 18 If he hath *w* thee, or oweth thee

WRONGETH

Pr 8.36 against me *w* his own soul:

WRONGFULLY

Job 21.27 which ye *w* imagine against me.
Ps 35.19 mine enemies *w* rejoice over me:
38.19 that hate me *w* are multiplied.
69. 4 being mine enemies *w*, are
119.86 they persecute me *w*; help thou
Eze 22.29 oppressed the stranger *w*.
1Pe 2.19 God endure grief, suffering *w*.

WROTE

Ex 24. 4 Moses *w* all the words of the
34.28 he *w* upon the tables the words of
Dt 4.13 *w* them upon two tables of stone.
31. 9 Moses *w* this law, and delivered it
22 Moses therefore *w* this song the
Jos 24.26 Joshua *w* these words in the book
2Ch 32.17 *w* also letters to rail on the Lord
Est 8. 5 which he *w* to destroy the Jews
Jer 36.18 I *w* them with ink in the book.
51.60 Jeremiah *w* in a book all the evil
Dan 5. 5 saw the part of the hand that *w*.
Mk 10. 5 your heart he *w* you this precept.
12.19 Master, Moses *w* unto us, If a
Lk 1.63 and *w*, saying, His name is John.
20.28 Master, Moses *w* unto us, If any
Jn 5.46 have believed me: for he *w* of me.
8. 6 with his finger *w* on the ground,
8 down, and *w* on the ground.
19.19 And Pilate *w* a title, and put it on
21.24 these things, and *w* these things:
Ac 15.23 they *w* letters by them after this
18.27 the brethren *w*, exhorting the
23.25 he *w* a letter after this manner:
Ro 16.22 I Tertius, who *w* this epistle,
1Co 5. 9 I *w* unto you in an epistle not to
7. 1 the things whereof ye *w* unto me:
2Co 2. 3 And I *w* this same unto you, lest,
4 I *w* unto you with many tears;
7.12 though I *w* unto you, I did it not
Eph 3. 3 (as I *w* afore in few words,
Phm 21 in thy obedience I *w* unto thee,
2Jn 5 though I *w* a new commandment
3Jn 9 I *w* unto the church: but

WROTH

Gen 4. 5 And Cain was very *w*, and his
6 said unto Cain, Why art thou *w*?
Ex 16.20 and Moses was *w* with them.
Nu 31.14 Moses was *w* with the officers of
Dt 1.34 words, and was *w*, and sware,
3.26 the Lord was *w* with me for your
9.19 the Lord was *w* against you to
2Sa 22. 8 and shook, because he was *w*.
2Ki 5.11 Naaman was *w*, and went away,
2Ch 28. 9 of your fathers was *w* with Judah,
Ps 18. 7 were shaken, because he was *w*.
78.21 the Lord heard this, and was *w*:
59 When God heard this, he was *w*,
89.38 hast been *w* with thine anointed.
Isa 47. 6 I was *w* with my people, I have
54. 9 that I would not be *w* with thee,
57.16 ever, neither will I be always *w*:
17 I hid me, and was *w*, and he went
64. 5 thou art *w*; for we have sinned:
9 Be not *w* very sore, O Lord,
La 5.22 thou art very *w* against us.
Mt 2.16 was exceeding *w*, and sent forth,
18.34 his lord was *w*, and delivered
22. 7 the king heard thereof, he was *w*:
Rev 12.17 dragon was *w* with the woman,

WROUGHT

Ex 36. 4 *w* all the work of the sanctuary,
Nu 23.23 and of Israel, What hath God *w*!
1Sa 6. 6 *w* wonderfully among them,
11.13 Lord hath *w* salvation in Israel.
14.45 *w* this great salvation in Israel?
45 for he hath *w* with God this day.
2Sa 18.13 I should have *w* falsehood against
1Ki 16.25 But Omri *w* evil in the eyes of the
Neh 4.17 one of his hands *w* in the work,
6.16 that this work was *w* of our God.
Job 12. 9 the hand of the Lord had *w* this?
36.23 can say, thou hast *w* iniquity?
Ps 31.19 thou hast *w* for them that trust in
68.28 that which thou hast *w* for us.
139.15 curiously *w* in the lowest parts of
Ec 2.11 the works that my hands had *w*,
Isa 26.12 also hast *w* all our works in us.
41. 4 Who hath *w* and done it, calling
Jer 18. 3 he *w* a work on the wheels.
Eze 20. 9, 14, 22 *w* for my name's sake,
Dan 4. 2 the high God hath *w* toward me.
Jon 1.11 unto us, for the sea *w*, and was
Mt 20.12 These last have *w* but one hour,
26.10 she hath *w* a good work upon me.
Mk 6. 2 mighty works are *w* by his hands?
14. 6 she hath *w* a good work on me.
Jn 3.21 manifest, that they are *w* in God.
Ac 5.12 and wonders *w* among the people;
15.12 God had *w* among the Gentiles
18. 3 he abode with them, and *w*:
19.11 God *w* special miracles by the
21.19 God had *w* among the Gentiles by
Ro 7. 8 *w* in me all manner of
15.18 which Christ hath not *w* by me,
2Co 5. 5 that hath *w* us for the selfsame
7.11 what carefulness it *w* in you, yea,
12.12 signs of an apostle were *w* among
Gal 2. 8 (For he that *w* effectually in
Eph 1.20 Which he *w* in Christ, when he
2Th 3. 8 *w* with labor and travail night
Heb 11.33 *w* righteousness, obtained
Jas 2.22 thou how faith *w* with his works,
1Pe 4. 3 have *w* the will of the Gentiles,
2Jn 8 not those things which we have *w*,
Rev 19.20 the false prophet that *w* miracles

YEA

2Ki 2. 3, 5 *Y*, I know it; hold...your peace.
Job 22.25 *Y*, the Almighty shall be thy
33.14 For God speaketh once, *y* twice, yet
34.12 *Y*, surely God will not do
Ps 84. 2 My soul longeth, *y*, even fainteth
3 *Y*, the sparrow hath found an
90.17 *y*, the work of our hands establish
116. 5 righteous: *y*, our God is merciful.
Isa 44. 8 *y*, there is no God; I know not any.
15 *y*, he maketh a god, and
Jer 8. 7 *Y*, the stork in the heaven
Mt 5.37 let your communication be, *Y*, *y*;
9.28 They said unto him, *Y*, Lord.
Lk 14.26 *y*, and his own life also, he cannot
Jn 16.32 the hour cometh, *y*, is now come,
21.15, 16 *Y*, Lord; thou knowest that I
Ac 5. 8 And she said, *Y*, for so much.
Ro 3. 4 *y*, let God be true, but every man a
8.34 died, *y* rather, that is risen again,
2Co 1.17 that with me there should be *y y*,
18 toward you was not *y* and nay.
19 not *y* and nay, but in him was *y*.
20 the promises of God in him are *y*,
Jas 5.12 your *y* be *y*, and your nay, nay;
Rev 14.13 *Y*, saith the Spirit, that they may

YEAR

Gen 47.18 When that *y* was ended, they came
Ex 34.23 Thrice in the *y* shall all your
Lev 25. 4 the seventh *y* shall be a sabbath
5 it is a *y* of rest unto the land.
11 A jubile shall that fiftieth *y* be
Dt 24. 5 but he shall be free at home one *y*,
2Ch 8.13 solemn feasts, three times in the *y*,
Est 9.27 to their appointed time every *y*;
Job 3. 6 be joined unto the days of the *y*,
Ps 65.11 crownest the *y* with thy goodness;
Isa 6. 1 In the *y* that king Uzziah died I
61. 2 the acceptable *y* of the Lord,
63. 4 and the *y* of my redeemed is come.
Lk 2.41 parents went to Jerusalem every *y*
3. 1 fifteenth *y* of the reign of Tiberius
4.19 the acceptable *y* of the Lord.
13. 8 Lord, let it alone this *y* also, till I
Jn 11.49 being the high priest that same *y*,
51 but being high priest that *y*, he
18.13 was the high priest that same *y*.
Ac 11.26 that a whole *y* they assembled
18.11 he continued there a *y* and six
2Co 8.10 but also to be forward a *y* ago.
9. 2 Achaia was ready a *y* ago;
Heb 9. 7 the high priest alone once every *y*,
25 into the holy place every *y* with
10. 1 they offered *y* by *y* continually,
3 again made of sins every *y*.
Jas 4.13 and continue there a *y*, and buy
Rev 9.15 and a day, and a month, and a *y*,

YEAR'S

Ex 34.22 feast of ingathering at the *y* end.

YEARS

Gen 5.21 Enoch lived sixty and five *y*, and
22 Methuselah three hundred *y*,
7. 6 Noah was six hundred *y* old when
17. 1 Abram was ninety *y* old and nine.
25. 8 old age, an old man, and full of *y*;
29.18 will serve thee seven *y* for Rachel
41.26 The seven good kine are seven *y*;
27 wind shall be seven *y* of famine.
Ex 16.35 of Israel did eat manna forty *y*,
23.10 And six *y* thou shalt sow thy land,
Lev 25. 3 Six *y* thou shalt sow thy field,
Nu 32.13 wander in the wilderness forty *y*,
Dt 8. 2 thy God led thee these forty *y*
Jdg 5.31 And the land had rest forty *y*.
1Sa 4.15 Eli was ninety and eight *y* old;
2Sa 19.32 aged man, even fourscore *y* old:
1Ki 17. 1 shall not be dew nor rain these *y*,
Job 10. 5 of man? are thy *y* as man's days,
15.20 the number of *y* is hidden to the
32. 7 and multitude of *y* should teach
36.26 number of his *y* be searched out.
Ps 90. 4 For a thousand *y* in thy sight are
9 we spend our *y* as a tale that is
10 The days of our *y* are threescore *y*
10 of strength they be fourscore *y*,
15 the *y* wherein we have seen evil.
95.10 Forty *y* long was I grieved with
102.27 same, and thy *y* shall have no end.
Pr 4.10 and the *y* of thy life shall be many.
Ec 11. 8 But if a man live many *y*, and
Isa 38.15 I shall go softly all my *y* in the
Joel 2.25 restore to you the *y* that the locust
Am 2.10 led you forty *y* through the
Hab 3. 2 thy work in the midst of the *y*,
Zec 1.12 these threescore and ten *y*?
7. 3 as I have done these so many *y*?
Mt 2.16 from two *y* old and under,
9.20 with an issue of blood twelve *y*,
Mk 5.25 had an issue of blood twelve *y*,
42 for she was of the age of twelve *y*.
Lk 1. 7 both were now well stricken in *y*.
18 and my wife well stricken in *y*.
2.36 had lived with an husband seven *y*
37 of about fourscore and four *y*,
42 when he was twelve *y* old, they
3.23 began to be about thirty *y* of age,
4.25 shut up three *y* and six months,
8.42 daughter, about twelve *y* of age,
43 having an issue of blood twelve *y*,
12.19 much goods laid up for many *y*;
13. 7 these three *y* I come seeking fruit
11 had a spirit of infirmity eighteen *y*,
16 hath bound, lo, these eighteen *y*,
15.29 Lo, these many *y* do I serve thee,
Jn 2.20 Forty and six *y* was this temple in
5. 5 had an infirmity thirty and eight *y*.
8.57 Thou art not yet fifty *y* old, and
Ac 4.22 the man was above forty *y* old,
7. 6 entreat them evil four hundred *y*.
23 And when he was full forty *y* old,
30 And when forty *y* were expired,
36 and in the wilderness forty *y*.
42 space of forty *y* in the wilderness?
9.33 which had kept his bed eight *y*,
13.18 And about the time of forty *y*
20 space of four hundred and fifty *y*,
21 Benjamin, by the space of forty *y*.
19.10 continued by the space of two *y*;
20.31 the space of three *y* I ceased not
24.10 thou hast been of many *y* a judge
17 after many *y* I came to bring alms
27 after two *y* Porcius Festus came
28.30 Paul dwelt two whole *y* in his own
Ro 4.19 he was about an hundred *y* old,
15.23 a great desire these many *y* to
2Co 12. 2 in Christ above fourteen *y* ago,
Gal 1.18 Then after three *y* I went up to
2. 1 fourteen *y* after I went up again
3.17 four hundred and thirty *y* after,
4.10 and months, and times, and *y*.
1Ti 5. 9 number under threescore *y* old,
Heb 1.12 the same, and thy *y* shall not fail.
3. 9 me, and saw my works forty *y*.
17 whom was he grieved forty *y*?
11.24 when he was come to *y*,
Jas 5.17 earth by the space of three *y* and
2Pe 3. 8 is with the Lord as a thousand *y*,
8 and a thousand *y* as one day.
Rev 20. 2 and bound him a thousand *y*,
3 the thousand *y* should be fulfilled:
4 reigned with Christ a thousand *y*.
5 until the thousand *y* were finished.
6 shall reign with him a thousand *y*.
7 when the thousand *y* are expired,

YELLOW

Lev 13.30 and there be in it a *y* thin hair;
32 and there be in it no *y* hair,
36 the priest shall not seek for *y* hair;
Ps 68.13 and her feathers with *y* gold.

YES

Mt 17.25 He saith, *Y*. And when he was
Mk 7.28 and said unto him, *Y*, Lord:
Ro 3.29 Gentiles? *Y*, of the Gentiles also:
10.18 *Y*, verily, their sound went into

YESTERDAY

Job 8. 9 (For we are but of *y*, and know
Ps 90. 4 years in thy sight are but as *y*
Jn 4.52 *Y* at the seventh hour the fever
Ac 7.28 as thou diddest the Egyptian *y*?
Heb 13. 8 Jesus Christ the same *y*, and to day,

YET

Gen 18.32 and I will speak *y* but this once:
37. 5 and they hated him *y* the more.
40.23 *Y* did not the chief butler remember
45. 3 am Joseph; doth my father *y* live?
28 Joseph my son is *y* alive: I will go
Ex 10. 7 knowest thou not *y* that Egypt is
Lev 26.24 you *y* seven times for your sins.
Dt 9.29 *Y* they are thy people and thine
12. 9 not as *y* come to the rest
Jdg 7. 4 The people are *y* too many;
10.13 *Y* ye have forsaken me, and served
Ru 1.11 are there *y* any more sons in my
1Sa 3. 7 Samuel did not *y* know the Lord,
16.11 There remaineth *y* the youngest,
2Sa 12.18 while the child was *y* alive, we
1Ki 8.28 *Y* have thou respect unto the prayer
19.18 *Y* I have left me seven thousand in
2Ki 13.23 them from his presence as *y*.
17.13 *Y* the Lord testified against Israel,
2Ch 6.26 *y* if they pray toward this place, and
18. 7 There is *y* one man, by whom we
24.19 *Y* he sent prophets to them, to bring
Ezr 3. 6 temple of the Lord was not *y* laid.
9. 9 *y* our God hath not forsaken us in
Est 5.13 *Y* all this availeth me nothing,
Job 3.26 neither was I quiet; *y* trouble came.
5. 7 *Y* man is born to trouble, as the
8. 7 *y* thy latter end should greatly
13.15 he slay me, *y* will I trust in him:
19.26 body, *y* in my flesh shall I see God:
24.12 *y* God layeth not folly to them.
29. 5 the Almighty was *y* with me,
Ps 2. 6 *Y* have I set my king upon my holy
37.10 For *y* a little while, and the
25 *y* have I not seen the righteous
42. 5 I shall *y* praise him for the help
11 for I shall *y* praise him, who is
43. 5 for I shall *y* praise him, who is
94. 7 *Y* they say, The Lord shall not see,
119.141 *y* do not I forget thy precepts.
138. 6 *y* hath he respect unto the lowly:
139.16 my substance, *y* being unperfect;
Pr 6.10 *Y* a little sleep, a little slumber,
13. 7 maketh himself rich, *y* hath nothing:
7 himself poor, *y* hath great riches.
24.33 *Y* a little sleep, a little slumber,
Ec 1. 7 run into the sea; *y* the sea is not full;
4. 3 both they, which have not *y* been,
6. 6 twice told, *y* hath he seen no good:
8.17 to seek it out, *y* he shall not find it;

Ec 8.17 *y* shall he not be able to find it.
Isa 10.22 *y* a remnant of them shall return:
25 For *y* a very little while, and the
28. 4 is *y* in his hand he eateth it up.
49.15 may forget, *y* will I not forget thee.
53. 4 *y* we did esteem him stricken,
7 afflicted, *y* he opened not his mouth:
10 *Y* it pleased the Lord to bruise him;
57.10 *y* saidst thou not, There is no hope:
65.24 while they are *y* speaking, I will
Jer 2. 9 Wherefore I will *y* plead with you,
11 their gods, which are *y* no gods?
22 *y* thine iniquity is marked before me,
32 *y* my people have forgotten me days
15. 9 sun is gone down while it is *y* day:
23.21 not sent these prophets, *y* they ran:
Eze 3.19 *Y* if thou warn the wicked, and he
6. 8 *Y* will I leave a remnant, that ye may
8.18 a loud voice, *y* will I not hear them.
18.25 *Y* ye say, The way of the Lord is not
26.21 *y* shalt thou never be found again,
28. 2 *y* thou art a man, and not God,
Hos 1. 4 for *y* a little while, and I will
13. 4 *Y* I am the Lord thy God from the
Am 4. 6 *y* have ye not returned unto me,
Jon 3. 4 *Y* forty days, and Nineveh shall
Hab 3.18 *Y* I will rejoice in the Lord, I will
Hag 2.17 *y* ye turned out to me, saith the
Zec 1.17 the Lord shall *y* comfort Zion,
Mal 1. 2 *Y* ye say, Wherein hast thou loved
3. 8 rob God? *Y* have ye robbed me.
Mt 6.26 *y* your heavenly Father feedeth
15.17 Do ye not *y* understand, that
27 *y* the dogs eat of the crumbs
19.20 from my youth up: what lack I *y*?
24. 6 come to pass, but the end is not *y*.
26.35 die with thee, *y* will I not deny
27.63 said, while he was *y* alive,
Mk 7.28 *y* the dogs under the table eat
13. 7 be; but the end shall not be *y*.
14.29 all shall be offended, *y* will not I.
Lk 3.20 Added *y* this above all, that he
11. 8 *y* because of his importunity he
12.27 *y* I say unto you, that Solomon in all
14.22 commanded, and *y* there is room.
18.22 him, *Y* lackest thou one thing:
22.60 while he *y* spake, the cock crew.
Jn 2. 4 thee? mine hour is not *y* come.
4.35 There are *y* four months, and
7. 6 unto them, My time is not *y* come:
33 *Y* a little while am I with you,
39 the Holy Ghost was not *y* given;
8.57 Thou art not *y* fifty years old, and
9.30 and *y* he hath opened mine eyes.
11.25 though he were dead, *y* shall he live:
12.35 *Y* a little while is the light with
16.12 I have *y* many things to say unto
20. 9 as *y* they knew not the scripture,
29 have not seen, and *y* have believed.
Ac 8.16 as *y* he was fallen upon none of
Ro 4.11 which he had *y* being uncircumcised:
5. 6 we were *y* without strength,
7 *y* peradventure for a good man
8 while we were *y* sinners, Christ
8.24 man seeth, why doth he *y* hope for?
9.19 me, Why doth he *y* find fault?
1Co 3. 3 For ye are *y* carnal: for whereas
15 shall be saved; *y* so as by fire.
7.10 *y* not I, but the Lord, Let not the
12.20 many members, *y* but one body.
15.10 *y* not I, but the grace of God which
17 is vain; ye are *y* in your sins.
2Co 6. 8 report: as deceivers, and *y* true;
9 As unknown, and *y* well known;
10 As sorrowful, *y* alway rejoicing;
10 as poor, *y* making many rich;
10 nothing, and *y* possessing all things.
8. 9 *y* for your sakes he became poor,
Gal 2.20 *y* not I, but Christ liveth in me:
Col 2. 5 *y* am I with you in the spirit,
Heb 4.15 tempted like as we are, *y* without sin.

Biblical Themes

YOUTH

These words, which I command thee this day, shall be in thine heart: and thou shalt teach them diligently unto thy children. Dt 6.6-7

His bones are full of the sin of his youth, which shall lie down with him in the dust. Job 20.11

Out of the mouth of babes and sucklings hast thou ordained strength. Ps 8.2

Remember not the sins of my youth, nor my transgressions . . . remember thou me for thy goodness' sake, O Lord. Ps 25.7

Lo, children are an heritage of the Lord: and the fruit of the womb is his reward. As arrows are in the hand of a mighty man; so are children of the youth. Ps 127.3-4

Even a child is known by his doings, whether his work be pure, and whether it be right. Pr 20.11

Train up a child in the way he should go: and when he is old, he will not depart from it. Pr 22.6

Foolishness is bound in the heart of a child; but the rod of correction shall drive it far from him. Pr 22.15

Better is a poor and a wise child than an old and foolish king. Ec 4.13

Rejoice, O young man, in thy youth; and let thy heart cheer thee in the days of thy youth, and walk in the ways of thine heart, and in the sight of thine eyes: but know thou, that for all these things God will bring thee into judgment. Therefore remove sorrow from thy heart, and put away evil from thy flesh: for childhood and youth are vanity. Ec 11.9-10

Remember now thy Creator in the days of thy youth, while the evil days come not . . . while the sun, or the light, or the moon, or the stars, be not darkened. Ec 12.1-2

And a little child shall lead them. Isa 11.6

A little one shall become a thousand, and a small one a strong nation. Isa 60.22

It is good for a man that he bear the yoke in his youth. La 3.27

Jesus called a little child unto him, and set him in the midst of them, and said, Verily I say unto you, Except ye be converted, and become as little children, ye shall not enter into the kingdom of heaven. Mt 18.2-3

And they brought young children to him, that he should touch them: and his disciples rebuked those that brought them. But when Jesus saw it, he was much displeased, and said unto them, Suffer the little children to come unto me, and forbid them not: for of such is the kingdom of God. Verily I say unto you, Whosoever shall not receive the kingdom of God as a little child, he shall not enter therein. And he took them up in his arms, put his hands upon them, and blessed them. Mk 10.13-16

When I was a child, I spake as a child, I understood as a child, I thought as a child: but when I became a man, I put away childish things. 1Co 13.11

Children, obey your parents. . . . And, ye fathers, provoke not your children to wrath. Eph 6.1, 4

Let no man despise thy youth; but be thou an example of the believers. 1Ti 4.12

11. 4 by it he being dead *y* speaketh.
1Pe 4.16 *Y* if any man suffer as a Christian,
1Jn 3. 2 not *y* appear what we shall be:
Rev 17. 8 that was, and is not, and *y* is.
10 one is, and the other is not *y* come;
12 have received no kingdom as *y*;

YIELD

Gen 4.12 not henceforth *y* unto thee fruits.
49.20 fat, and he shall *y* royal dainties.
Lev 19.25 it may *y* unto you the increase
25.19 And the land shall *y* her fruit,
26. 4 and the land shall *y* her increase,
4 trees of the field shall *y* their fruit.
20 your land shall not *y* her increase.
20 the trees of the land *y* their fruits.
Dt 11.17 and that the land *y* not her fruit;
2Ch 30. 8 *y* yourselves unto the Lord,
Ps 67. 6 shall the earth *y* her increase;
85.12 and our land shall *y* her increase.
107.37 which may *y* fruits of increase.
Pr 7.21 fair speech she caused him to *y*,
Isa 5.10 of vineyard shall *y* one bath,
10 seed of an homer shall *y* an ephah.
Eze 34.27 tree of the field shall *y* her fruit,
27 and the earth shall *y* her increase,
36. 8 and *y* your fruit to my people of
Hos 8. 7 stalk: the bud shall *y* no meal:
7 if so be it *y*, the strangers shall
Joel 2.22 and the vine do *y* their strength.
Hab 3.17 fail, and the field shall *y* no meat:
Mk 4. 8 and did *y* fruit that sprang up
Ac 23.21 But do not thou *y* unto them:
Ro 6.13 Neither *y* ye your members as

13 but *y* yourselves unto God, as
16 ye *y* yourselves servants to obey,
19 so now *y* your members servants
Jas 3.12 no fountain both *y* salt water and

YIELDED
Gen 49.33 *y* up the ghost, and was gathered
Nu 17. 8 blossoms, and *y* almonds.
Dan 3.28 king's word, and *y* their bodies,
Mt 27.50 with a loud voice, *y* up the ghost.
Mk 4. 7 and choked it, and it *y* no fruit.
Ac 5.10 at his feet, and *y* up the ghost:
Ro 6.19 have *y* your members servants
Rev 22. 2 and *y* her fruit every month:

YIELDETH
Neh 9. 3 it *y* much increase unto the kings
Job 24. 5 the wilderness *y* food for them and
Pr 12.12 the root of the righteous *y* fruit.
Heb 12.11 afterward it *y* the peaceable fruit

YIELDING
Gen 1.11 forth grass, the herb *y* seed,
11 fruit tree *y* fruit after his kind,
12 and herb *y* seed after his kind,
12 and the tree *y* fruit, whose seed
29 is the fruit of a tree *y* seed;
Ec 10. 4 for *y* pacifieth great offenses.
Jer 17. 8 neither shall cease from *y* fruit.

YOKE
Gen 27.40 break his *y* from off thy neck.
Lev 26.13 I have broken the bands of your *y*,
Nu 19. 2 and upon which never came *y*:
Dt 28.48 shall put a *y* of iron upon thy neck,
1Ki 12. 4 Thy father made our *y* grievous:
11 I will add to your *y*: my father
2Ch 10.10 Thy father made our *y* heavy,
11 will put more to your *y*: my father
Isa 9. 4 hast broken the *y* of his burden,
La 1.14 The *y* of my transgressions is
Mt 11.29 Take my *y* upon you, and learn of
30 For my *y* is easy, and my burden
Lk 14.19 I have bought five *y* of oxen,
Ac 15.10 *y* upon the neck of the disciples,
Gal 5. 1 again with the *y* of bondage.
1Ti 6. 1 many servants as are under the *y*

YOKED
2Co 6.14 *y* together with unbelievers:

YOKEFELLOW
Php 4. 3 true *y*, help those women which

YONDER
Gen 22. 5 lad will go *y* and worship,
Nu 16.37 and scatter thou the fire *y*;
23.15 offering, while I meet the Lord *y*.
32.19 inherit with them on *y* side Jordan,
2Ki 4.25 Behold, *y* is that Shunammite:
Mt 17.20 Remove hence to *y* place;
26.36 Sit ye here, while I go and pray *y*.

YOUNG
Ex 23.26 There shall nothing cast their *y*, nor
Lev 22.28 kill it and her *y* both in one day.
Dt 22. 6 not take the dam with the *y*:
28.50 old, nor shew favor to the *y*:
57 toward her *y* one that cometh out
32.11 fluttereth over her *y*, spreadeth
Jos 6.23 *y* men that were spies went in,
Jdg 9.54 his *y* man thrust him through, and
17.12 and the *y* man became his priest,
1Sa 9. 2 Saul, a choice *y* man, and a goodly:
2Sa 18.12 none touch the *y* man Absalom.
29 said, Is the *y* man Absalom safe?
32 do thee hurt, be as that *y* man is.
2Ki 9. 4 even the *y* man the prophet,
1Ch 22. 5 Solomon my son is *y* and tender,
2Ch 10.14 after the advice of the *y* men,
13. 7 when Rehoboam was *y* and
34. 3 while he was yet *y*, he began to
Job 19.18 Yea, *y* children despised me;
29. 8 The *y* men saw me, and hid
38.41 when his *y* ones cry unto God,
39.16 is hardened against her *y* ones,
Ps 34.10 The *y* lions do lack, and suffer
37.25 I have been *y*, and now am old;
84. 3 where she may lay her *y*, even
104.21 The *y* lions roar after their prey,
119. 9 shall a *y* man cleanse his way?
147. 9 and to the *y* ravens which cry.
Pr 20.29 glory of *y* men is their strength:
30.17 out, and the *y* eagles shall eat it.
Ec 11. 9 Rejoice, O *y* man, in thy youth;
SS 2. 9 beloved is like a roe or a *y* hart:
Isa 11. 7 *y* ones shall lie down together:
23. 4 neither do I nourish up *y* men,
30. 6 riches upon the shoulders of *y* asses,
40.11 gently lead those that are with *y*.
30 the *y* men shall utterly fall:
Jer 31.12 the *y* of the flock and of the herd:
13 both *y* men and old together:
49.26 her *y* men shall fall in her streets,
La 2.21 *y* and the old lie on the ground
4. 4 the *y* children ask bread, and no man
Eze 17. 4 off the top of his *y* twigs, and
Joel 2.28 your *y* men shall see visions:
Am 2.11 and of your *y* men for Nazarites.
8.13 virgins and *y* men faint for thirst.
Mt 2. 8 search diligently for the *y* child;
9 stood over where the *y* child was.
11 the *y* child with Mary his mother,
13 take the *y* child and his mother,
13 seek the *y* child to destroy him.
14 he took the *y* child and his mother
20 take the *y* child and his mother,
20 which sought the *y* child's life.
21 took the *y* child and his mother,
19.20 The *y* man saith unto him, All
22 the *y* man heard that saying, he
Mk 7.25 *y* daughter had an unclean spirit,
10.13 they brought *y* children to him,
14.51 followed him a certain *y* man,
51 and the *y* men laid hold on him:
16. 5 say a *y* man sitting on the right
Lk 2.24 of turtledoves, or two *y* pigeons.
7.14 *Y* man, I say unto thee, Arise.
Jn 12.14 when he had found a *y* ass, sat
21.18 When thou wast *y*, thou girdedst
Ac 2.17 and your *y* men shall see visions,
5. 6 the *y* men arose, wound him up,
10 *y* men came in, and found her
7.19 they cast out their *y* children,
58 their clothes at a *y* man's feet,
20. 9 a certain *y* man named Eutychus,
12 they brought the *y* man alive,
23.17 this *y* man unto the chief captain:
18 prayed me to bring this *y* man
22 then let the *y* man depart,
Tit 2. 4 teach the *y* women to be sober,
6 *Y* men likewise exhort to be
1Jn 2.13 I write unto you, *y* men, because
14 written unto you, *y* men, because

YOUNGER
Gen 29.16 and the name of the *y* was Rachel.
26 to give the *y* before the firstborn.
Job 30. 1 *y* than I have me in derision,
Lk 15.12 the *y* of them said to his father,
13 the *y* son gathered all together,
22.26 among you, let him be as the *y*;
Ro 9.12 her, The elder shall serve the *y*.
1Ti 5. 1 and the *y* men as brethren;
2 the *y* as sisters, with all purity.
11 But the *y* widows refuse: for when
14 therefore that the *y* women marry,
1Pe 5. 5 ye *y*, submit yourselves unto the

YOUNGEST
Gen 42.13 the *y* is this day with our father,
34 bring your *y* brother unto me:
44.23 Except your *y* brother come down
1Sa 16.11 said, There remaineth yet the *y*,
17.14 And David was the *y*: and the

YOURS
Gen 45.20 the good of all the land of Egypt is *y*.
Jos 2.14 Our life for *y*, if ye utter not this our
2Ch 20.15 for the battle is not *y*, but God's.
Lk 6.20 poor: for *y* is the kingdom of God.
Jn 15.20 my saying, they will keep *y* also.
1Co 3.21 in men. For all things are *y*;
22 or things to come; all are *y*;
8. 9 means this liberty of *y* become a
16.18 have refreshed my spirit and *y*:
2Co 12.14 for I seek not *y*, but you: for the

YOUTH
Gen 8.21 of man's heart is evil from his *y*;
46.34 cattle from our *y* even until now,
Jdg 8.20 feared, because he was yet a *y*.
1Sa 17.33 with him: for thou art but a *y*,
33 and he a man of war from his *y*.
55 host, Abner, whose son is this *y*?
1Ki 18.12 servant fear the Lord from my *y*.
Job 13.26 to possess the iniquities of my *y*.
20.11 bones are full of the sin of his *y*,
29. 4 As I was in the days of my *y*,
30.12 Upon my right hand rise the *y*;
33.25 shall return to the days of his *y*:
36.14 They die in *y*, and their life is
Ps 25. 7 Remember not the sins of my *y*,
71. 5 thou art my trust from my *y*.
17 thou hast taught me from my *y*:
88.15 and ready to die from my *y* up:
89.45 The days of his *y* hast thou
103. 5 thy *y* is renewed like the eagle's.
110. 3 thou hast the dew of thy *y*.
127. 4 man; so are children of the *y*.
129. 1 have they afflicted me from my *y*,
144.12 be as plants grown up in their *y*;
Pr 2.17 forsaketh the guide of her *y*,
5.18 rejoice with the wife of thy *y*.
Ec 11. 9 Rejoice, O young man, in thy *y*;
10 for childhood and *y* are vanity.
12. 1 thy Creator in the days of thy *y*,
Isa 47.12 thou hast labored from thy *y*;
54. 4 shalt forget the shame of thy *y*,
Jer 2. 2 the kindness of thy *y*, the love
3. 4 father, thou art the guide of my *y*?
22.21 been thy manner from thy *y*,
31.19 I did bear the reproach of my *y*.
32.30 done evil before me from their *y*:
48.11 hath been at ease from his *y*,
La 3.27 that he bear the yoke in his *y*.
Eze 4.14 from my *y* up even till now have I
16.22, 43 remembered the days of thy *y*,
Hos 2.15 sing there, as in the days of her *y*,
Joel 1. 8 for the husband of her *y*.
Zec 13. 5 me to keep cattle from my *y*.
Mt 19.20 have I kept from my *y* up:
Mk 10.20 these have I observed from my *y*.
Lk 18.21 these have I kept from my *y* up.
Ac 26. 4 My manner of life from my *y*,
1Ti 4.12 Let no man despise thy *y*; but be

YOUTHFUL
2Ti 2.22 Flee also *y* lusts: but follow

YOUTHS
Pr 7. 7 I discerned among the *y*, a young
Isa 40.30 the *y* shall faint and be weary,

YOU-WARD
2Co 1.12 and more abundantly to *y*.
13. 3 which to *y* is not weak, but is
Eph 3. 2 grace...which is given me to *y*:

Z

ZABULON
Mt 4.13 borders of *Z* and Nephthalim:
15 The land of *Z*, and the land of
Rev 7. 8 Of the tribe of *Z* were sealed

ZACCHEUS
Lk 19. 2 there was a man named *Z*,
5 and unto him, *Z*, make haste,
8 *Z* stood, and said unto the Lord;

ZACHARIAS
Mt 23.35 blood of *Z* son of Barachias,
Lk 1. 5 a certain priest named *Z*, of the
12 And when *Z* saw him, he was
13 angel said unto him, Fear not, *Z*:
18 And *Z* said unto the angel,
21 And the people waited for *Z*,
40 And entered into the house of *Z*,
59 they called him *Z*, after the name
67 And his father *Z* was filled with
3. 2 came unto John the son of *Z*
11.51 of Abel unto the blood of *Z*,

ZEAL
2Sa 21. 2 slay them in his *z* to the children
2Ki 10.16 and see my *z* for the Lord.
19.31 *z* of the Lord of hosts shall do this.
Ps 69. 9 *z* of thine house hath eaten me up;
119.139 My *z* hath consumed me, because
Isa 9. 7 The *z* of the Lord of hosts will
37.32 *z* of the Lord of hosts shall do this.
59.17 and was clad with *z* as a cloke.
63.15 where is thy *z* and thy strength,
Eze 5.13 I the Lord have spoken it in my *z*,
Jn 2.17 *z* of thine house hath eaten me
Ro 10. 2 record that they have a *z* of God,
2Co 7.11 yea, what *z*, yea, what revenge!
9. 2 your *z* hath provoked very many.
Php 3. 6 Concerning *z*, persecuting the
Col 4.13 that he hath a great *z* for you,

ZEALOUS
Nu 25.11 while he was *z* for my sake
13 because he was *z* for his God, and
Ac 21.20 and they are all *z* of the law:
22. 3 and was *z* toward God, as ye all
1Co 14.12 as ye are *z* of spiritual gifts,

ZEDEKIAH

Last king of Judah, early 6th century B.C.; placed on the throne by Nebuchadnezzar to succeed the exiled Jehoiachin, his nephew (2Ki 24); despite the warnings of Jeremiah (Jer 27), later rebels against Babylon, and Jerusalem is besieged (2Ki 24–25); sends to inquire of Jeremiah concerning the outcome and is told the city will fall (Jer 21); makes a covenant freeing slaves but revokes it when the siege is temporarily lifted (Jer 34); secretly consults Jeremiah when he is cast into a dungeon and instructs that he be held and provided for in the prison court (Jer 37–38); when city walls are breached, flees toward Jericho but is captured and witnesses death of his sons before his eyes are put out and he is taken in chains to Babylon (2Ki 25; Jer 39); is also condemned by Ezekiel for breaking his covenant of submission to Nebuchadnezzar (Eze 21).

Gal 1.14 *z* of the traditions of my fathers.
Tit 2.14 a peculiar people, *z* of good works.
Rev 3.19 be *z* therefore, and repent.

ZEALOUSLY
Gal 4.17 They *z* affect you, but not well;
18 good to be *z* affected always in a

ZEBEDEE
Mt 4.21 James the son of *Z*, and John his
21 in a ship with *Z* their father,
10. 2 James the son of *Z*, and John his
26.37 him Peter and the two sons of *Z*,
Mk 1.19 he saw James the son of *Z*, and
20 left their father *Z* in the ship
3.17 And James the son of *Z*, and John
10.35 James and John, the sons of *Z*,
Lk 5.10 James, and John, the sons of *Z*,
Jn 21. 2 and the sons of *Z*, and two other

ZEBEDEE'S
Mt 20.20 came...the mother of *Z* children
27.56 and the mother of *Z* children.

ZEDEKIAH
2Ki 24.17 stead, and changed his name to *Z*.
18 *Z* was twenty and one years old
20 that *Z* rebelled against the king
25. 2 unto the eleventh year of king *Z*
7 slew the sons of *Z* before his eyes,
7 put out the eyes of *Z*, and bound
Jer 1. 3 eleventh year of *Z* the son of
21. 1 king *Z* sent unto him Pashur the
3 them, Thus shall ye say to *Z*:
7 I will deliver *Z* king of Judah,
24. 8 will I give *Z* the king of Judah,
27. 3 come to Jerusalem unto *Z* king of
12 I spake also to *Z* king of Judah
28. 1 in the beginning of the reign of *Z*
29. 3 (whom *Z* king of Judah sent unto
21 and of *Z* the son of Maaseiah,
22 The Lord make thee like *Z* and
32. 1 the Lord in the tenth year of *Z*
3 For *Z* king of Judah had shut him
4 *Z* king of Judah shall not escape
5 And he shall lead *Z* to Babylon,
34. 2 Go and speak to *Z* king of Judah,
4 of the Lord, O *Z* king of Judah;
6 spake all these words unto *Z* king
8 the king *Z* had made a covenant
21 *Z* king of Judah and his princes
36.12 and *Z* the son of Hananiah,
37. 1 king *Z* the son of Josiah reigned
38. 5 *Z* the king said, Behold, he is in
14 Then *Z* the king sent, and took
15 Jeremiah said unto *Z*, If I declare
16 So *Z* the king sware secretly unto
17 Then said Jeremiah unto *Z*, Thus
19 *Z* the king said unto Jeremiah, I
24 said *Z* unto Jeremiah, Let no man
39. 1 ninth year of *Z* king of Judah,
2 And in the eleventh year of *Z*,
4 when *Z* the king of Judah saw
5 and overtook *Z* in the plains of
6 king of Babylon slew the sons of *Z*

ZELOTES
Lk 6.15 of Alpheus, and Simon called *Z*,
Ac 1.13 Simon *Z*, and Judas the brother

ZENAS
Tit 3.13 Bring *Z* the lawyer and Apollos

ZERUBBABEL
Ezr 2. 2 Which came with *Z*: Jeshua,
3. 2 priests, and *Z* the son of Shealtiel,

ZERUBBABEL

Leader of postexilic community in Jerusalem, 6th century B.C.; grandson of Jehoiachin (1Ch 3), one of Judah's last kings; among the first to return to Judah from Babylonia (Ezr 2); initially serves under Sheshbazzar, also a royal prince (Ezr 1), but is later himself named "governor of Judah" (Hag 1); together with Joshua the priest, takes initiative in rebuilding of the temple in 537 B.C. (Ezr 3); resists subtle attempt by Judah's adversaries to thwart the project (Ezr 4); when more direct opposition does halt the building, is again in forefront of renewed efforts in 520 B.C. (Ezr 5); prophets Haggai and Zechariah predict his completion of the work, which occurs in 516 B.C. (Zec 4); by virtue of his royal descent, he becomes focus of more long-term messianic hopes (Hag 2; Zec 6); these hopes are not realized, however, and Davidic line ceases to play important role in Judah's history, although descendants of Zerubbabel are listed in 1Ch 3.

8 began *Z* the son of Shealtiel,
4. 2 Then they came to *Z*, and to the
3 But *Z*, and Jeshua, and the rest
5. 2 rose up *Z* the son of Shealtiel,
Hag 1. 1 by Haggai the prophet unto *Z* the
2. 2 Speak now to *Z* the son of
21 Speak to *Z*, governor of Judah,
23 will I take thee, O *Z*, my servant,
Zec 4. 6 is the word of the Lord unto *Z*,
7 before *Z* thou shalt become a
9 The hands of *Z* have laid the
10 plummet in the hand of *Z* with

ZION
2Sa 5. 7 David took the strong hold of *Z*:
1Ki 8. 1 of the city of David, which is *Z*.
2Ki 19.21 daughter of *Z* hath despised thee,
31 they that escape out of mount *Z*:
1Ch 11. 5 David took the castle of *Z*,
2Ch 5. 2 of the city of David, which is *Z*.
Ps 2. 6 my king upon my holy hill of *Z*.
9.11 to the Lord, which dwelleth in *Z*:
14 in the gates of the daughter of *Z*:
14. 7 of Israel were come out of *Z*!
20. 2 and strengthen thee out of *Z*;
48. 2 of the whole earth, is mount *Z*,
11 Let mount *Z* rejoice, let the
12 Walk about *Z*, and go round
50. 2 Out of *Z* the perfection of beauty,
51.18 good in thy good pleasure unto *Z*:
53. 6 of Israel were come out of *Z*!
69.35 For God will save *Z*, and will
76. 2 and his dwelling place in *Z*.
78.68 the mount *Z* which he loved.
87. 2 The Lord loveth the gates of *Z*
97. 8 *Z* heard, and was glad; and the
99. 2 The Lord is great in *Z*; and he is
102.13 arise, and have mercy upon *Z*:
16 when the Lord shall build up *Z*,
110. 2 the rod of thy strength out of *Z*:
125. 1 in the Lord shall be as mount *Z*,
126. 1 turned again the captivity of *Z*,
128. 5 The Lord shall bless thee out of *Z*:
129. 5 and turned back that hate *Z*.
132.13 For the Lord hath chosen *Z*;

BIBLICAL THEMES

ZEAL

And they came to the place which God had told him of; and Abraham built an altar there, and laid the wood in order, and bound Isaac his son, and laid him on the altar upon the wood. And Abraham stretched forth his hand, and took the knife to slay his son. Gen 22.9-10

Caleb stilled the people before Moses, and said, Let us go up at once, and possess it; for we are well able to overcome it. Nu 13.30

And they brought forth the images out of the house of Baal, and burned them. And they brake down the image of Baal, and brake down the house of Baal, and made it a draft house unto this day. Thus Jehu destroyed Baal out of Israel. 2Ki 10.26-28

I am become a stranger unto my brethren, and an alien unto my mother's children. For the zeal of thine house hath eaten me up; and the reproaches of them that reproached thee are fallen upon me. Ps 69.8-9

Whatsoever thy hand findeth to do, do it with thy might. Ec 9.10

Also I heard the voice of the Lord, saying, Whom shall I send, and who will go for us? Then said I, Here am I; send me. Isa 6.8

He put on righteousness as a breastplate, and an helmet of salvation upon his head; and he put on the garments of vengeance for clothing, and was clad with zeal as a cloke. Isa 59.17

Where is thy zeal and thy strength, the sounding of thy bowels and of thy mercies toward me? are they restrained? Isa 63.15

The kingdom of heaven is like unto a merchant man, seeking goodly pearls: who, when he had found one pearl of great price, went and sold all that he had, and bought it. Mt 13.45-46

Woe unto you, scribes and Pharisees, hypocrites! for ye compass sea and land to make one proselyte, and when he is made, ye make him twofold more the child of hell than yourselves. Mt 23.15

I indeed baptize you with water; but one mightier than I cometh . . . he shall baptize you with the Holy Ghost and with fire. Lk 3.16

No man, having put his hand to the plow, and looking back, is fit for the kingdom of God. Lk 9.62

When he had made a scourge of small cords, he drove them all out of the temple . . . and poured out the changers' money, and overthrew the tables; and said . . . Take these things hence; make not my Father's house an house of merchandise. Jn 2.15-16

Then Simon Peter having a sword drew it, and smote the high priest's servant, and cut off his right ear. Jn 18.10

As for Saul, he made havock of the church, entering into every house, and haling men and women committed them to prison. Ac 8.3

If the trumpet give an uncertain sound, who shall prepare himself to the battle? 1Co 14.8

Whatsoever ye do, do it heartily, as to the Lord, and not unto men. Col 3.23

See that ye love one another with a pure heart fervently. 1Pe 1.22

I know thy works, that thou art neither cold nor hot: I would thou wert cold or hot. So then because thou art lukewarm, and neither cold nor hot, I will spue thee out of my mouth. Rev 3.15-16

Behold, I come quickly; and my reward is with me, to give every man according as his work shall be. Rev 22.12

133. 3 upon the mountains of *Z*:
134. 3 and earth bless thee out of *Z*.
135.21 Blessed be the Lord out of *Z*,
137. 1 we wept, when we remembered *Z*.
3 Sing us one of the songs of *Z*.
146.10 reign for ever, even thy God, O *Z*,
147.12 O Jerusalem; praise thy God, O *Z*.
149. 2 let the children of *Z* be joyful in
SS 3.11 Go forth, O ye daughters of *Z*, and
Isa 1. 8 daughter of *Z* is left as a cottage
27 *Z* shall be redeemed with
2. 3 for out of *Z* shall go forth the law,
3.16 the daughters of *Z* are haughty,
4. 3 to pass, that he that is left in *Z*,
4 the filth of the daughters of *Z*,
8.18 hosts, which dwelleth in mount *Z*.
10.12 his whole work upon mount *Z*
24 O my people that dwellest in *Z*,
12. 6 and shout, thou inhabitant of *Z*:
14.32 That the Lord hath founded *Z*,
18. 7 of the Lord of hosts, the mount *Z*.
24.23 of hosts shall reign in mount *Z*,
28.16 I lay in *Z* for a foundation a stone,
29. 8 be, that fight against mount *Z*.
30.19 shall dwell in *Z* at Jerusalem:
31. 4 come down to fight for mount *Z*,
9 the Lord, whose fire is in *Z*,
33. 5 he hath filled *Z* with judgment
14 The sinners in *Z* are afraid;
20 Look upon *Z*, the city of our
34. 8 for the controversy of *Z*.
35.10 and come to *Z* with songs and
37.22 daughter of *Z*, hath despised thee,
32 they that escape out of mount *Z*:
40. 9 O *Z*, that bringest good tidings,
41.27 The first shall say to *Z*, Behold,
46.13 place salvation in *Z* for Israel my
49.14 *Z* said, The Lord hath forsaken
51. 3 For the Lord shall comfort *Z*:
11 and come with singing unto *Z*;
16 say unto *Z*, Thou art my people,
52. 1 awake; put on thy strength, O *Z*;
2 thy neck, O captive daughter of *Z*.
7 saith unto *Z*, Thy God reigneth!
8 the Lord shall bring again *Z*.
59.20 the Redeemer shall come to *Z*,
60.14 The *Z* of the Holy One of Israel.
61. 3 unto them that mourn in *Z*,
62.11 Say ye to the daughter of *Z*,
64.10 *Z* is a wilderness, Jerusalem a
66. 8 for as soon as *Z* travailed, she
Jer 3.14 family, and I will bring you to *Z*:
4. 6 Set up the standard toward *Z*:
31 the voice of the daughter of *Z*,
6. 2 have likened the daughter of *Z* to
23 war against thee, O daughter of *Z*.
8.19 Is not the Lord in *Z*? is not her
9.19 voice of wailing is heard out of *Z*,
14.19 Judah? hath thy soul lothed *Z*?
26.18 *Z* shall be plowed like a field, and
30.17 This is *Z*, whom no man seeketh
31. 6 let us go up to *Z* unto the Lord
12 come and sing in the height of *Z*,
50. 5 They shall ask the way to *Z* with
28 to declare in *Z* the vengeance of the
51.10 declare in *Z* the work of the Lord
24 evil that they have done in *Z*
35 shall the inhabitant of *Z* say;
La 1. 4 The ways of *Z* do mourn, because
6 from the daughter of *Z* all her
17 *Z* spreadeth forth her hands, and
2. 1 covered the daughter of *Z* with a
4 tabernacle of the daughter of *Z*:
6 and sabbaths to be forgotten in *Z*,
10 The elders of the daughter of *Z* sit
13 thee, O virgin daughter of *Z*?
18 O wall of the daughter of *Z*, let
4. 2 The precious sons of *Z*,
11 and hath kindled a fire in *Z*,
5.11 They ravished the women in *Z*,
Joel 2. 1 Blow ye the trumpet in *Z*, and
15 Blow the trumpet in *Z*, sanctify
23 Be glad then, ye children of *Z*,
32 for in mount *Z* and in Jerusalem
3.16 Lord also shall roar out of *Z*,
17 the Lord your God dwelling in *Z*,
21 for the Lord dwelleth in *Z*.
Am 1. 2 The Lord will roar from *Z*, and
6. 1 Woe to them that are at ease in *Z*,
Ob 17 upon mount *Z* shall be deliverance,
21 come up on mount *Z* to judge
Mic 1.13 of the sin to the daughter of *Z*:
3.10 They build up *Z* with blood, and
12 shall *Z* for your sake be plowed
4. 2 for the law shall go forth of *Z*,
7 shall reign over them in mount *Z*
8 strong hold of the daughter of *Z*,
11 and let our eye look upon *Z*.
13 and thresh, O daughter of *Z*:
Zep 3.14 Sing, O daughter of *Z*; shout,
16 and to *Z*, Let not thine hands be
Zec 1.14 jealous for Jerusalem and for *Z*
17 and the Lord shall yet comfort *Z*,
2. 7 Deliver thyself, O *Z*, that dwellest
10 and rejoice, O daughter of *Z*:
8. 2 jealous for *Z* with great jealousy,
3 I am returned unto *Z*, and will
9. 9 Rejoice greatly, O daughter of *Z*;
13 and raised up thy sons, O *Z*,

Words That Have Changed In Meaning

This list of archaic and obsolete words and phrases has been prepared to help the reader understand more readily the meaning of the King James Version. Of course, not all of these words and phrases are inappropriate in all contexts; each expression, therefore, is followed by a list of those passages in which misunderstanding is likely to occur. In each instance the boldface word or phrase represents the King James text. This is followed by the more meaningful alternative. Where there is more than one alternative, each is given and the corresponding passages are listed. Though this list is not exhaustive, it does provide the reader with a handy reference to most expressions that are likely to produce difficulty in comprehending the meaning of the King James Version.

A

abased humbled, Mt 23.12; Lk 14.11; 18.14
abide await, Ac 20.23
accursed devoted, Jos 6.17, 18; 7.1, 11, 12, 13, 15; 22.20; 1Ch 2.7
admiration wonder, Rev 17.6
advanced appointed, 1Sa 12.6
advertise advise, Nu 24.14 / reveal to, Ru 4.4
affections passions, Gal 5.24
alleging proving, Ac 17.3
allow(ed) (eth) approve(d), Lk 11.48; Ro 14.22; 1Th 2.4 / accept, Ac 24.15 / knoweth, Ro 7.15
amazement terror, 1Pe 3.6
ambassage embassy, Lk 14.32
amend mend, Jn 4.52
approved (approving) proved (proving), 2Co 6.4; 7.11
armholes elbows, Eze 13.18
assayed (assaying) attempted (attempting), Ac 9.26; 16.7; Heb 11.29; Dt 4.34; 1Sa 17.39
attendance attention, 1Ti 4.13
audience hearing, Gen 23.10, 13, 16; 1Sa 25.24; Neh 13.1

B

barren bereaved, SS 4.2; 6.6
bed couch, SS 1.16 / litter, SS 3.7
behaved stilled, Ps 131.2
behind lacking, Col 1.24
belly body, Ps 31.9
bewitched amazed, Ac 8.9,11
bewrayeth betrays, Mt 26.73 / reveals, Pr 29.24
bloody blood-thirsty, Ps 5.6; 26.9; 139.19
bottles wineskins, Mt 9.17, Mk 2.22; Lk 5.37, 38
bottles of wine wineskins, Jos 9.13; 1Sa 1.24; 10.3; 16.20; 2Sa 16.1; Job 32.19 / heat of wine, Hos 7.5
bound landmark, Hos 5.10
bowels heart, Gen 43.30; 1Ki 3.26; Ps 109.18; SS 5.4; Isa 16.11; 63.15; Jer 31.20; La 1.20; 2.11; Phm 12.20; 1Jn 3.17 / hearts, Col 3.12; Phm 7 / affections, 2Co 6.12; Php 2.1 / anguish, Jer 4.19 / tender mercies, Php 1.8
box jar, Mt 26.7; Mk 14.3; Lk 7.37
branch song, Isa 25.5
breaking up breaking in, Ex 22.2

C

careful anxious, Lk 10.41; Php 4.6
carefully anxiously, Mic 1.12 / diligently, Php 2.28
carriage(s) baggage, Isa 10.28, 46.1; Ac 21.15
certify advise, 2Sa 15.28
charger platter, Mt 14.8, 11; Mk 6.25, 28
charitably in love, Ro 14.15
charity love, 1Co 8.1; 13.1-4, 8, 13; 14.1; 16.14; Col 3.14; 1Th 3.6; 2Th 1.3; 1Ti 1.5; 2.15; 4.12; 2Ti 2.22; 3.10; Tit 2.2; 1Pe 4.8; 5.14; 2Pe 1.7; 3Jn 6; Jude 12; Rev 2.19
clean completely, Jos 3.17; 4.1, 11; Ps 77.8; Isa 24.19
comeliness majesty, Eze 16.14
comely seemly, Ps 33.1; Ec 5.18; 1Co 7.35; 11.13 / stately, Pr 30.29
communicate unto share with, Gal 6.6; Php 4.14, 15; 1Ti 6.18; Heb 13.16
communication companionship, 1Co 15.33 / fellowship, Phm 6
concluded shut up, Ro 11.32; Gal 3.22
conscience consciousness, 1Co 8.7; Heb 10.2
convenient needful, Pr 30.8 / fitting, Ro 1.28; Eph 5.4; Phm 8
conversation in the way, Ps 37.14; 50.23 / citizenship, Php 3.20 / life, 1Pe 1.15 / way of life, 2Co 1.12; Gal 1.13; Eph 2.3; 4.22; Php 1.27; 1Ti 4.12; Heb 13.5, 7; Jas 3.13; 1Pe 1.18; 2.12; 3.1, 2, 16; 2Pe 2.7; 3.11
convert turn, Isa 6.10
corrupt, are scoff, Ps 73.8
curious skillfully woven, Ex 28.8, 27, 28; 29.5; 35.32; 39.5, 20,21; Lev 8.7
curse devoted thing, Jos 6.18

D

darling dear life, Ps 22.20; 35.17
darts weapons, 2Ch 32.5
daysman umpire, Job 9.33
defense gold, Job 22.25
delicately cheerfully, 1Sa 15.32 / luxuriously, Lk 7.25
deliciously wantonly, Rev 18.7, 9
delight delicate living, Pr 19.10
desolate condemned, Ps 34.21, 22 / found guilty, Isa 24.6
destroy hold guilty, Ps 5.10
devils satyrs, 2Ch 11.15
direct their work give them their recompense, Isa 61.8
discomfited, be become tributary, Isa 31.8
discover(ed) disclose(d), 1Sa 14.11 / uncover(ed), Lev 20.18; 2Sa 22.16; Ps 18.15; Is 57.8; Eze 13.14; 16.57; 23.10, 18, 29 / removed, Isa 22.8
ditch reservoir, Isa 22.11
doctors teachers, Lk 2.46
doctrine the message, Isa 28.9
doubtful anxious, Lk 12.29

E

Easter the Passover, Ac 12.4
ensue pursue, 1Pe 3.11
entreat(ed) treat(ed), Mt 22.6;Lk 18.32; 20.11; Ac 7.6,19; 27.3; 1Th 2.2
erred through, have reel with, Isa 28.7
estate council, Ac 22.5
estates men, Mk 6.21
evidently openly, Gal 3.1 / clearly, Ac 10.3

F

fame report, Mt 4.24; 9.26, 31; 14.1; Mk 1.28; Lk 4.14, 37; 5.15
fast close, Ru 2.23
feeble-minded fainthearted, 1Th 5.14
fetch(ed) a compass make (made) a circuit, 2Sa 5.23; 2Ki 3.9; Ac 28.13 / turn about, Nu 34.5
flood river, Jos 24.2, 3, 14, 15
floor the threshing floor, Hos 9.2; Mic 4.12
flowers impurity, Lev 15.24, 33
folk in nations for, Jer 51.58
forward earnest, 2Co 8.17 / ready, 2Co 8.10 / eager, Gal 2.10
free willing, Ps 51.12
freely for nought, Nu 11.5
froward wayward, Pr 4.24 / crooked, Pr 8.8; 17.20 / perverse, Dt 32.20; 2Sa 22.27; Job 5.13; Ps 18.26; 101.4; Pr 2.12, 15; 3.32; 6.12; 8.13; 10.31; 11.20; 16.28, 30; 17.20; 22.5
furnished filled, Mt 22.10

G

gender breed, Lev 19.19
glistering glistening, 1Ch 29.2; Lk 9.29
go beyond transgress, 1Th 4.6
goodman my husband, Pr 7.19 / master, Mt 20.11; 24.43; Mk 14.14; Lk 12.39; 22.11
governor pilot, Jas 3.4
grave engrave, Ex 28.9,36; 2Ch 2.7
grief sickness, Jer 6.7
grudge (grudging) grumble (grumbling), Jas 5.9; 1Pe 4.9 / tarry all night, Ps 59.15
guide companion, Ps 55.13
guilty bound, Mt 23.18

H

habitations pastures, Am 1.2
hardly with difficulty, Mt 19.23
hardly bestead sore distressed, Isa 8.21
hasted hastened, Gen 18.7; Job 31.5 / urged, Ex 5.13
heresies factions, 1Co 11.19; Gal 5.20; 2Pe 2.1
heretick factious, Tit 3.10

I

imagination stubbornness, Dt 29.19; Jer 7.24; 9.14; 11.8; 13.10; 16.12; 18.12
imagine devise, Hos 7.15
influences, sweet cluster, Job 38.31
instant insistent, Lk 23.23 / constant, Ro 12.12 / urgent, 2Ti 4.2
instantly diligently, Lk 7.4 / earnestly, Ac 26.7
instrument weapon, Isa 54.16
inward familiar, Job 19.19
isle(s) coastland(s), Isa 20.6; 23.2; 24.15

J

Jewry Judea, Lk 23.5; Jn 7.1

judgment justice, Pr 21.14; Am 5.15, 24; Mic 3.9 / by reason of injustice, Pr 13.23
juniper-roots broom roots, Job 30.4

K

keep under buffet, 1Co 9.27
kindle burn, Jer 33.18

L

lade load, Lk 11.46
lay to make, Isa 28.17
leasing lies, Ps 5.6 / falsehood, Ps 4.2
lent granted, Ex 12.36
let hindered, Ro 1.13 / restrain, 2Th 2.7
lewd wicked, Ac 17.5
lewdness villainy, Ac 18.14
lightness vain boasting, Jer 23.32
listed would, Mt 17.12; Mk 9.13
listeth willeth, Jn 3.8; Jas 3.4
Lucifer Daystar, Isa 14.12
lunatick epileptic, Mt 4.24; 17.15

M

mad foolish, Ec 7.7
maid virgin, Dt 22.14, 17; Job 31.1
mean obscure, Pr 22.29
meat meal, Lev 6.14 / food, Gen 1.30; Jdg 1.7; 14.14; 1Ki 19.8; Job 34.3; 38.41; Ps 42.3; 69.21; 74.14; 78.25; 104.27; 145.15; Pr 23.3; 30.22; 31.15; Isa 65.25; Eze 16.19; 47.12; Dan 1.8; Hab 3.17; Mt 3.4; 6.25; 10.10; 15.37; 24.45; 25.35; Mk 8.8; Lk 3.11; 8.55; 9.13; 12.23, 42; 24.41; Jn 4.8, 32, 34; 6.27, 55; 21.5; Ac 2.46; 9.19; 16.34; 27.33, 34, 36; Ro 14.15, 17, 20; 1Co 3.2; 8.8, 13; 10.3; Col 2.16; Heb 5.12, 14; 12.16
mete measure, Ex 16.18; Ps 60.6
minished diminished, Ps 107.39
minister attendant, Lk 4.20
motions passions, Ro 7.5

N

naturally truly, Php 2.20
naughtiness wickedness, Jas 1.21
nephews grandchildren, 1Ti 5.4
nether lower, Dt 24.6

O

observed him kept him safe, Mk 6.20
occupied used, Ex 38.24
occupied in traded for, Eze 27.16, 19, 22
offend be held guilty, Jer 2.3
oil olive olive oil, Ex 27.20; 30.24; Lev 24.2; 2Ki 18.32 / olive trees, Dt 8.8
open frequent, 1Sa 3.1
organs pipe, Ps 150.4
overcharge(d) overburden(ed), Lk 21.34; 2Co 2.5

P

part share, 1Sa 30.24
particularly in detail, Ac 21.19; Heb 9.5
pastor(s) ruler(s), Jer 2.8 / shepherds, Jer 3.15; 10.21; 12.10; 22.22; 23.1
perish be ruined, Mt 9.17; Lk 5.37
pitiful merciful, 1Pe 3.8
plain quiet, Gen 25.27
platted plaited, Mt 27.29; Mk 15.17; Jn 19.2
polluted (polluting) profaned (profaning), Isa 47.6; 56.2, 6
possessed formed, Ps 139.13
pots sheepfolds, Ps 68.13
power striven, Gen 32.28
presently immediately, Mt 21.19
pressed out of oppressed beyond, 2Co 1.8
prevent(ed) come before, Job 41.11; Ps 88.13; Am 9.10 / receive, Job 3.12 / precede, 1Th 4.15 / spoke first to, Mt 17.25 / met, Isa 21.14 / came upon, 2Sa 22.6, 19; Job 30.27; Ps 18.5, 18 / anticipate(d), Ps 119.147
prevent meet, Ps 59.10; 79.8
printed inscribed, Job 19.23
privily secretly, Ps 10.8; 11.2
profited advanced, Gal 1.14
profiting progress, 1Ti 4.15
proper own, Ac 1.19, 1Co 7.7 / beautiful, Heb 11.23
prove(d) test(ed), Dan 1.12, 14
purely thoroughly, Isa 1.25

Q

quick alive, Lev 13.10; Nu 16.30; Ps 55.15; 124.3 / living, Heb 4.12
quit guiltless, Jos 2.20
quit you acquit yourselves, 1Co 16.13

R

record witness, Jn 1.19; Ac 20.26; 2Co 1.23; Php 1.8
regard preserve, Pr 5.2
removed, be sway, Isa 24.20 / give way, Isa 22.25
reprobate refuse, Jer 6.30
reprove decide, Isa 11.4
respect, had looked, Heb 11.26
rest, take my be silent, Isa 18.4
restrain limit, Job 15.8
roaring groaning, Ps 22.1
robbery violence, Pr 21.7
rod shoot, Isa 11.1
room stead, 1Ki 5.5
room, in the place, Mt 2.22; Lk 14.9, 10; Ac 24.27; 1Co 14.16 / seat, Lk 14.8
rooms seats, Lk 14.7

S

scrip wallet, 1Sa 17.40 / bag, Mt 10.10; Mk 6.8; Lk 9.3; 10.4; 22.35, 36
secret counsel, Pr 3.32
senators elders, Ps 105.22
sentence judgment, Ac 15.19
settle ledge, Eze 43.14, 17, 20; 45.19
sever distinguish, Ex 9.4
several particular, Mt 25.15
shamefacedness propriety, 1Ti 2.9
shoot pass, Ex 36.33
sides innermost parts, Jon 1.5
sincere pure, 1Pe 2.2
skill, can (could) has (had) skill, 1Ki 5.6; 2Ch 2.7, 8; 34.12
smell take no delight in, Am 5.21
snuffed up the wind pant for air, Jer 14.6
sore fierce, 1Sa 14.52; 2Sa 2.17
sorrowful loathsome, Job 6.7
sorrows cords, Ps 18.4, 5
spirit breath, Isa 40.7 / wind, Ec 11.5
spoiling bereaving, Ps 35.12
stay rely, Isa 30.12; 50.10 / uphold, Pr 28.17
stem stock, Isa 11.1
strain at strain out, Mt 23.24
strait narrow, 2Ki 6.1
strange foreign, Ac 26.11
strangers of visitors from, Ac 2.10
strength stronghold, Isa 25.4
strike put, Ex 12.7
string bond, Mk 7.35
study strive, 1Th 4.11; 2Ti 2.15
stuff baggage, 1Sa 10.22; 25.13; 30.24

T

table(s) tablet(s), Lk 1.63; 2Co 3.3
tablets armlets, Ex 35.22
tabret(s) timbrel(s), Gen 31.27; 1Sa 10.5; 18.6; Job 17.6; Isa 24.8; 30.32; Jer 31.4; Eze 28.13
take no thought be not anxious, Mt 6.25, 28, 31, 34; Lk 12.11, 22, 26
tale number, Ex 5.8, 18; 1Sa 18.27; 1Ch 9.28
temperance self-control, Ac 24.25; Gal 5.23; 2Pe 1.6
temperate self-controlled, 1Co 9.25; Tit 1.8
told counted, 2Ch 2.2
translate(d) transfer(red), 2Sa 3.10; Col 1.13; Heb 11.5
trow think, Lk 17.9
turning away backsliding, Pr 1.32
turtle turtledove, SS 2.12; Jer 8.7

U

uncomely unseemly, 1Co 7.36
unicorn(s) wild ox (oxen), Nu 23.22; 24.8; Dt 33.17; Job 39.9, 10; Ps 22.21; 29.6; 92.10; Isa 34.7
unperfect unformed, Ps 139.16
untoward crooked, Ac 2.40
usury interest, Isa 24.2; Mt 25.27; Lk 19.23

V

vagabond wandering, Ac 19.13
vain lying, Ex 5.9
vale lowland, Dt 1.7
vanity falsehood, Ps 24.4
vehement sultry, Jn 4.8
vengeance justice, Ac 28.4
victory, in forever, Isa 25.8
virtue power, Mk 5.30; Lk 6.19; 8.46
void an open, 1Ki 22.10
volume roll, Heb 10.7

W

wanted lacked in, Jn 2.3
ware wary, 2Ti 4.15 / aware, Ac 14.6
waster destroyer, Pr 18.9
wealth good, 1Co 10.24
whale monster, Eze 32.2
whole healed, Jos 5.8
wist knew, Ex 16.15; 34.29; Lev 5.17, 18; Jos 2.4; 8.14; Jdg 16.20; Mk 9.6; 14.40; Lk 2.49; Jn 5.13; Ac 12.9; 23.5
wood forest, Isa 7.2
work recompense, Isa 40.10; 49.4
worship honor, Lk 14.10
wot know, Gen 21.26; 44.15; Ex 32.1, 23; Nu 22.6; Jos 2.5; Ac 3.17; 7.40; Ro 11.2; Phm 1.22
wounds dainty morsels, Pr 26.22
wrap weave together, Mic 7.3

A Chronology of the Biblical World

Date	LOWER MESOPOTAMIA, IRAN	UPPER MESOPOTAMIA	ANATOLIA, ARMENIA
	Sumerian city-states; Sumer, Akkad, Ur. Early Sumerian dynasties, c. 2850-2360.		Troy founded.
2500 B.C.	Sargon unites Mesopotamia; creates Akkadian empire, c. 2360-2180; penetrates to Syria; rules from sea to sea. Akkadian dynasty collapses, as Gutians invade Mesopotamia; dark age.	Hurrians (Horites) settle, extend influence from Lake Van to Euphrates.	Hittites settle in Anatolia, establish early Hittite kingdom.
2000	Third dynasty of Ur, c. 2060-1950; engulfed by Amorites, Elam. Amorite invaders establish dynasty in Babylon, 1830-c. 1531.	Assyrian establish trading posts in Anatolia, extend power.	
1800	Hammurabi reunifies Mesopotamia, issues Babylonian law code; his empire collapses under barbarian invasions.	Amorite state of Mari, defeated by Hammurabi, 1697. Hurrians penetrate to north Syria, Canaan, dominate Assyria, form KINGDOM OF MITANNI, 1500-1380. they control upper Mesopotamia to Mediterranean, threaten Egypt.	Hittites expand south, destroy Babylon, c. 1531, form HITTITE EMPIRE, 1450-1200. Hittites extend boundaries to north Syria, battle Assyrians, displaced by Sea Peoples.
1600	Kassites migrate from east, rule in Babylon, c. 1600-1150; dark age.		
1400		Mitanni defeated by Hittites, 1366. Assyria controls Mesopotamia to Euphrates; Adad-nirari I, 1308-1276, defeats Kassites, calls himself "King of Everything."	Urartu (Hurrians) form kingdom of Van, 1270. Sack of Troy, c. 1250.
1200	Elamites expand into Mesopotamia. Babylon conquered by Assyrians. Chaldeans infiltrate settle in south.	Period of Assyrian weakness. Tiglath-pileser I, 1116-1078, establishes Assyrian empire, occupies Syria and Phoenicia, halts Phrygian invasion, calls himself "King of the Four World Regions." Invading Arameans break Assyrian power.	Invading Phrygians replace Hittites, dominate Anatolia, submit to Assyrian expansion, Cimmerian invasions, 690; power transferred to Lydians.
1000			
900		Assyrian resurgence and westward expansion restores empire. Shalmaneser III, 859-825, attempts to extend empire, defeated by an alliance at battle of Qarqar on the Orontes, 854.	Urartu expansion to borders of Phrygia and Assyria, c. 840; control Armenia; weakened by Cimmerian invasion; Assyrian raid, 714; Scythian invasion, fall to Medes, 612.
800		Tiglath-pileser III restores Assyrian power, 745, battles Urartu, extends power to mid-Anatolia, 738, Galilee, Damascus, 734-732, king of Babylon, 729; Israel and Judah pay tribute.	
700	Elam crushed by Assyria, 640; rise of Persia. Chaldean dynasty rules in Babylon, 626-539. Babylonians conquer Nineveh, 612; overthrow Assyrian empire.	ASSYRIAN EMPIRE reaches to Egypt. Empire collapses from decay, civil war.	Medes form confederacy, c. 700, with Babylon conquer Assyria, 612, rule upper Mesopotamia, 625-550.
600	NEO-BABYLONIAN EMPIRE, 612-539. Persians conquer Babylon, 539, seize empire to Egypt's border. PERSIAN EMPIRE, 539-331		Lydians take over Phrygia, expand to border Media at the Halys, 585. Cyrus of Persia overthrows Medes, 550, conquers Lydia, 547; Persians rule Asia Minor to Egypt. PERSIAN RULE 547-333
500			
400	Alexander the Great defeats Persians at Issus, 333, Gaugamela, 331; Greeks take Persian empire; Alexander dies in Babylon, 323; his generals divide empire. Seleucids rule Mesopotamia, seize western Asia Minor, 281, lose eastern provinces as Parthia, Bactria declare independence, c. 250.		HELLENISTIC RULE 333-65 B.C. Celts invade, 279, settle Galatia. Emergence of Pergamum during Seleucid weakness. Antiochus III defeated by Romans at Magnesia, 190, surrenders Anatolia (Asia Minor), 189.
300			
200	Parthians take Media, c. 150, Babylon, Mesopotamia from Seleucids, 141.		Pergamum bequeathed to Rome, 133. Asia Minor under Roman rule, 65. Armenians seize Seleucid remnants, rule Syria, 83-69.
100	Parthians invade Syria-Palestine, 40, defend Mesopotamia against Roman expansion eastward, repulse Romans at Euphrates; Crassus slain at Carrhae, 53; Antony defeated, 36; Parthia retains control of the East.		
0	Trajan invades Armenia; takes Mesopotamia from Parthia, 115; Hadrian abandons eastern conquests, 117.		
100 A.D.			

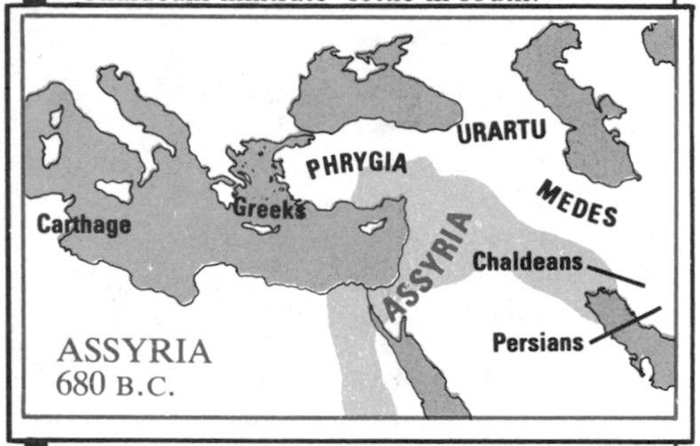

ASSYRIA
680 B.C.

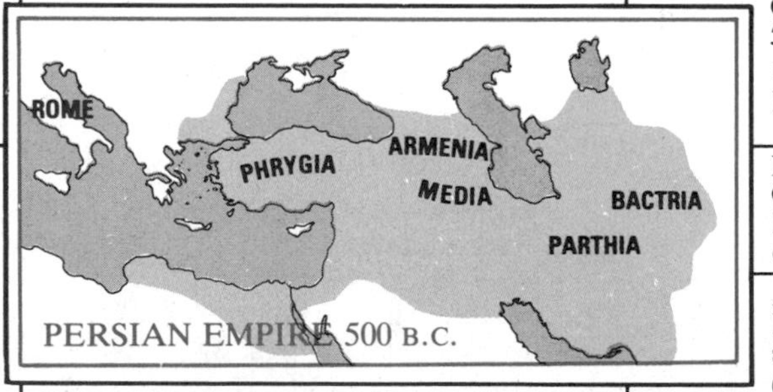

PERSIAN EMPIRE 500 B.C.

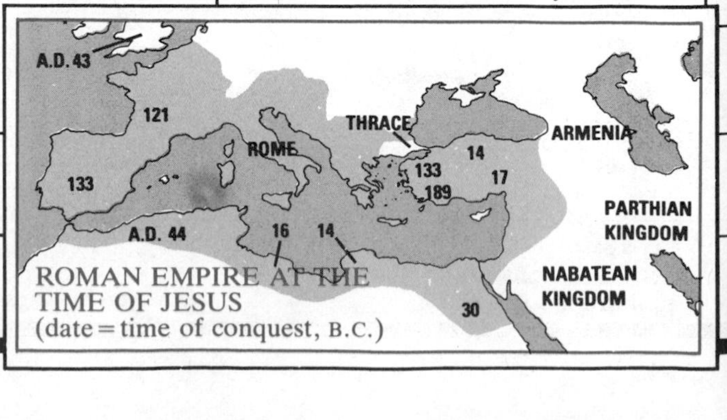

ROMAN EMPIRE AT THE TIME OF JESUS
(date = time of conquest, B.C.)

EGYPT	HOLY LAND	AEGEAN AND WESTERN MEDITERRANEAN	
Old Kingdom, c. 2664-2180; pyramids at Giza built during 4th dynasty, c. 2614-2502.			2500 B.C.
Middle Kingdom, c. 2052-1786.		Rise of Minoan sea empire on Crete, destroyed by volcano, c. 1470, and fire.	2000
	Abraham arrives in land of Canaan; Isaac, Jacob, Joseph.		1800
Hyksos rule, c. 1700-1550, Egypt; introduce war chariots. Hebrews in Egypt. c. 1700-1290.	Fortified towns in Palestine.		1600
New Kingdom, c. 1554-1075. Thutmose III, c. 1490-1436, wins battle of Megiddo, c. 1469, takes north Syria from Mitanni.	Hurrian (Mitanni) invasion.		1400
Akhenaton, c. 1366-1349, worships one god; succeeded by Tutankhamen, c. 1348-1339. Seti I, c. 1305-1290, Ramses II, c. 1290-1224, extend border of Egypt northward.	Moses leads Exodus of Jews from Egypt. Joshua leads conquest of Canaan. Rise of Phoenician city-states, c. 1200.	Sea Peoples destroy Mycenaean civilization.	1200
Ramses III, c. 1183-1152, defeats Sea Peoples. During power void following invasions, Israelites form kingdom of David.	Philistines settle coastal plain. Period of Judges. Saul named first king of Israel, c. 1020.		1000
Libyan dynasty, c. 935-725. Shishak, c. 935-914, robs temple, c. 918.	David rules Judah, c. 1000-993; captures Jerusalem and rules united kingdom of Israel, c. 993-961; Solomon, c. 961-922. Beginning of divided monarchy, c. 922. House of Omri rules Israel, 876-842.		900
Osorkon II, c. 860-833, allies with Syria-Palestine, defeats Shalmaneser III at Qarqar.	Revolt of Jehu, 842. Israel pays tribute to Assyria, 841. Renaissance of Israel under Jeroboam II, 786-746, and Judah under Uzziah, 783-742. Assyrians capture Samaria; end of kingdom of Israel, 721.	Phoenecians found Carthage on North African coast, 814.	800
Attempt to aid Israel defeated by Assyrians at Raphia, 716. Ethiopian dynasty, c. 736-657.	Sennacherib attacks Judah, 701.	Legendary founding of Rome, 753;	700
Assyria conquers Egypt, c. 664; Saite dynasty, c. 664-525. Vassal kings assume authority, annex Syria-Palestine during Assyrian decline.	Babylonians take Jerusalem, end of kingdom of Judah, 587; Babylonian captivity.	Italy dominated by Etruscan kings.	600
Cambyses of Persia conquers Egypt, first Persian period, 525-404.	Edict of Cyrus, 538; Jews return to Holy Land; Nehemiah builds Temple; Ezra brings the Law.	Roman republic founded, 509.	500
Rebellion and independence from Persia, 404-341.		Greeks defeat Persians at Marathon, 490, Thermopylae, Salamis, 480. Golden Age of Greece.	400
Second Persian period, 341-332. Alexander welcomed as Egypt's liberator, founds Alexandria, 332. Ptolemies begin Egyptian rule, establish naval supremacy and outposts on coastal Anatolia.	Alexander conquers Tyre, 332.	Rise of Rome; dominates Italy, 270. Philip II of Macedonia unites Greek states, 338. Alexander seizes Persia and east, 334-326. HELLENISTIC EMPIRES	300
	Four Syrian Wars, 276-217; power struggle between Seleucids and Ptolemies to control Syria and Phoenicia.	First Punic War between Rome and Carthage, 264-241. Hannibal crosses Alps at start of Second Punic War, 218-201. Carthage destroyed by Rome at end of Third Punic War, 149-146.	200
Antiochus IV invades Egypt, 168, checked by Romans who dominate east.	Battle of Paneas, 198; Seleucids rule Holy Land. Beginning of Maccabean revolt, 167.	Rome rules in western Mediterranean. Julius Caesar conquers Gaul, Britain, 58-51. Caesar, Crassus, Pompey form first triumvirate, 60. Caesar assassinated, 44.	100
Julius Caesar secures throne for Cleopatra VII, 48. Octavian defeats Antony and Cleopatra at battle of Actium, 31. Cleopatra suicide, 30, end of Ptolemaic reign. Octavian captures Alexandria, Egypt made a Roman province.	John Hyrcanus II, High Priest, 134-104. Hasmoneans rule Judea, 104-37. Pompey captures Jerusalem, extends Roman rule to Holy Land, 63. Parthians invade, put Antigonus II on throne, 40-37. Herod the Great, 37-4.	ROMAN EMPIRE Reign of Octavian as Augustus Caesar, 27 B.C.–A.D. 14. Reigns of Tiberius, 14-37, Caligula, 37-41, Claudius, 41-54.	0
	Life of Jesus, c. 7 B.C.–A.D. 29. Pontius Pilate, governor of Judea, 26-36. Paul begins missionary journeys, c. 44, taken to Rome, 60, where he is martyred.	Reign of Nero, 54-68; Christians persecuted after Roman fire, 64. Reigns of Vespasian, 69-79, Titus, 79-81. Persecution of Christians reaches peak during reign of Diocletian, 284-305.	100 A.D.
	First Jewish revolt against Rome, 66-73. Second (Bar Kokhba) Jewish revolt against Rome, 132-135, ends in complete Roman victory; Jews dispersed.	Constantine wins battle of Milvian Bridge, 312, issues Edict of Milan, 313.	

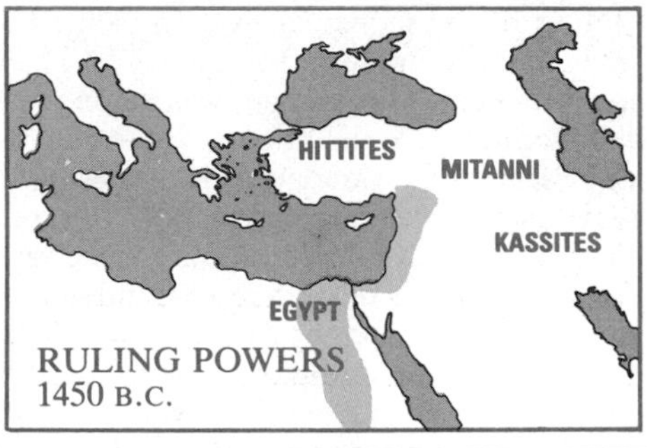

The Jewish Calendar

The Jewish calendar as it exists today developed over a period of many centuries and, like ancient Israel itself, was influenced in various ways by the world around it. In the age of the Patriarchs, most systems of reckoning time were linked to the agricultural cycle and framed by a few basic reference points: the changing of the seasons and the movements of the sun and moon. In Hebrew tradition, each new day began at sunset (following the sequence given in Gen 1.5: "And the evening and the morning were the first day"). The week, also following the Creation narrative, was made up of seven days, and the month was equal to one cycle of the moon, about 29 1/2 days. But lunar calendars did not mesh properly with the observed solar year: 12 cycles of the moon added up to about 354 days, 11 short of the yearly total. Since various holidays were fixed in the Bible by both month and season, it was especially important to correct the discrepancy. Without an adjustment, for example, the springtime month specified for the Passover feast would soon arrive in the winter, then in the fall, and so on. The adjustment came to be made by adding a 13th month, called Adar II, every second or third year.

Another difficulty had to do with the year's starting point. Some systems fixed it at the vernal equinox and others at the autumnal equinox, and much confusion and controversy would later arise from the fact that at different times the Israelites used both methods. During the period of the monarchy a fall new year was observed, possibly inherited from a system previously used by the Canaanites. But by the 7th century B.C. the spring new year of the Babylonian calendar, along with Babylonian names for the months, had been widely adopted and continued to be used after the return from the Exile. The conflicts between these two systems are reflected in the Old Testament, which in different passages places the start of the year in both spring and fall. Not until well after the biblical era—in the 4th century A.D.—did rabbinical authorities establish the basic Hebrew calendar that has remained in effect since then. As the table below indicates, they resolved the conflicts by preserving elements of both systems. The Bible refers to months more often by number than by either their Babylonian or earlier Canaanite-derived names. Since the numbering always begins in the spring, even when a fall new year is mentioned, the rabbinical calendar followed this sequence, establishing Nisan as the first month but observing the religious new year in the autumn month of Tishri (while continuing to calculate the reigns of kings on the basis of a spring new year, as later Old Testament compilers had done).

The most ancient feast in Jewish tradition is Passover, celebrating the deliverance from slavery in Egypt. The Passover meal—known as a Seder, held on the 15th Nisan (and often repeated the next evening)—had taken on something like its present-day form by New Testament times, and was the occasion of the Last Supper shared by Jesus and his disciples as recounted in the three synoptic Gospels.

Shavuot, or the Feast of Weeks, comes seven weeks and one day after Passover, when the first grain was harvested in early summer (it is also called the Feast of First Fruits). This feast was later connected with the traditional date on which Moses received the Law on Mount Sinai. Its significance in the New Testament grows out of the latter tradition: the Christian Pentecost, observed seven weeks after Easter, commemorates the descent of the Holy Spirit upon the apostles.

New Year's Day, Rosh Hashanah, comes in early autumn with the 1st Tishri and inaugurates ten days of penitence known as the Days of Awe, culminating in the solemn fast of Yom Kippur, the Day of Atonement. On this day in ancient times, a goat chosen by lot to carry all the people's sins—a "scapegoat"—was driven into the wilderness in accordance with Mosaic law (Lev 16.8-10).

Beginning less than a week after Yom Kippur, Succoth—the seven-day Feast of Booths—commemorates the Israelites' wanderings in the wilderness, during which they lived in temporary shelters: "I made the children of Israel to dwell in booths, when I brought them out of the land of Egypt" (Lev 23.32). Succoth was also an agricultural holiday marking the fall harvest, observed as the Feast of Ingathering (Ex 23.16).

The eight-day celebration of Hanukkah—known as the Feast of the Dedication, or the Feast of Lights—begins on the 25th Kislev and commemorates the victory of the Maccabees over Antiochus IV of Syria and the rededication of the temple in Jerusalem in 164 B.C. The full story of this historic event is told in 2 Maccabees in the Apocrypha.

Coming on 14th Adar, the joyous holiday of Purim commemorates the rescue of the Jews from extermination in the lands ruled by Ahasuerus (Xerxes) of Persia, the dramatic tale recounted in the Book of Esther.

Month	Equivalent Western Months	Holidays	Dates
Nisan	Mar/Apr	Passover	15th Nisan for a week
Iyyar	Apr/May		
Sivan	May/June	Shavuot (Feast of Weeks)	6th Sivan
Tammuz	June/July		
Av	July/Aug		
Elul	Aug/Sept	Rosh Hashana (New Year's Day)	1st Tishri
Tishri	Sept/Oct	Yom Kippur (Day of Atonement)	10th Tishri
Heshvan	Oct/Nov	Succoth (Feast of Booths)	15th-21st Tishri
Kislev	Nov/Dec	Hanukkah (Feast of the Dedication)	25th Kislev for 8 days
Tevet	Dec/Jan		
Shevat	Jan/Feb		
Adar	Feb/Mar	Purim	14th Adar

Biblical Weights and Measures

*Thou shalt not have in thy bag divers weights,
a great and a small. . . . thou shalt have a perfect
and just weight, a perfect and just measure shalt thou have:
that thy days may be lengthened in the land which
the Lord thy God giveth thee. (Dt 25.13, 15)*

Weights and measures in the ancient world were calculated in common, everyday terms. Weights might be determined in grains of cereal, for example, and measures as the distance from the elbow to the tip of the finger. In time, stones and pieces of metal came to be used to calculate the equivalencies between different items. Probably the earliest instrument for weighing objects was the primitive balance scale with two pans suspended from the ends of a beam. Biblical weights and measures were based chiefly on those of Mesopotamia and Egypt. There was no single standard and sometimes two were used: thus a cubit has been estimated at 17.4 inches (the short, or common, cubit) and at 20.4 inches (known as Ezekiel's cubit). In New Testament times, a talent could mean a specific weight or any large weight or large sum of money.

Then, as now, the accuracy of amounts quoted in business dealings could not necessarily be taken for granted—a point raised in the Book of Proverbs: "A false balance is an abomination to the Lord: but a just weight is his delight" (Pr 11.1).

OLD TESTAMENT WEIGHTS	*U.S. system*	*Metric system*
talent (60 minas)	75.558 lb	34.227 kg
mina (50 shekels)	20.148 oz	571.175 grams
shekel (2 bekas)	176.29 grains	11.423 grams
beka, ½ shekel (10 gerahs)	88.14 grains	5.711 grams
gerah	8.81 grains	0.570 grams
NEW TESTAMENT WEIGHTS		
talent (Hebrew talent)	75.558 lb	34.227 kg
pound (Hebrew mina)	20.148 oz	571.175 grams
pound (Latin libra)	0.719 lb	325.707 grams
OLD TESTAMENT MEASURES OF CAPACITY		
Dry measure		
homer, measure, cor (2 lethechs)	6.524 bu	229.892 L
lethech (5 ephahs)	3.262 bu	114.946 L
ephah, measure (3 seahs)	20.878 qt	22.986 L
measure (3⅓ omers)	6.959 qt	7.661 L
omer, 1/10 ephah (1 4/5 kabs)	2.087 qt	2.297 L
kab	1.159 qt	1.276 L
Liquid measure		
measure, cor (10 baths)	60.738 gal	229.893 L
bath (6 hins)	6.073 gal	22.986 L
hin (3 kabs)	1.012 gal	3.830 L
kab (4 logs)	1.349 qt	1.276 L
log	0.674 pt	0.318 L
NEW TESTAMENT MEASURES OF CAPACITY		
measure (Hebrew bath)	6.073 gal	22.986 L
measure (Hebrew cor)	6.524 bu	229.892 L
measure (Hebrew seah)	6.959 qt	7.661 L
measure	10.3 gal	38.985 L
quart	0.98 dry qt	1.078 L
bushel (Latin modius)	7.68 dry qt	8.455 L
pot (Latin sextarius)	0.96 dry pt	0.528 L
	or 1.12 fluid pt	0.529 L
OLD TESTAMENT MEASURES OF LENGTH		
cubit (2 spans)	17.49 in.	44.424 cm
span (3 handbreadths)	8.745 in.	22.212 cm
handbreadth (4 fingers)	2.915 in.	7.404 cm
finger	0.728 in.	1.849 cm
NEW TESTAMENT MEASURES OF LENGTH		
cubit	c. 18 in.	45 cm
fathom	c. 72 in.	182 cm
furlong, stadia, or the equivalent in miles	c. 606 ft	184 m
mile	c. 4,879 ft	1,486 m

Adapted from the New Oxford Annotated Bible

Genealogies and Dynasties

There are certain passages in the Bible that readers through the ages have doubtless been tempted to skip over: the lists of genealogies and dynasties, often running to great length, that have little apparent bearing on the Bible's central teachings. But in fact these records were of major significance to the compilers and interpreters of the Scriptures. Familial lines of descent provided vital links to the past, chains of continuity and legitimacy that were especially important in a world in which religious and political authority were so closely intertwined. Presented here are charts of four ancestral or royal lines, each from a different era, each playing an essential role in the ongoing history of the Holy Land.

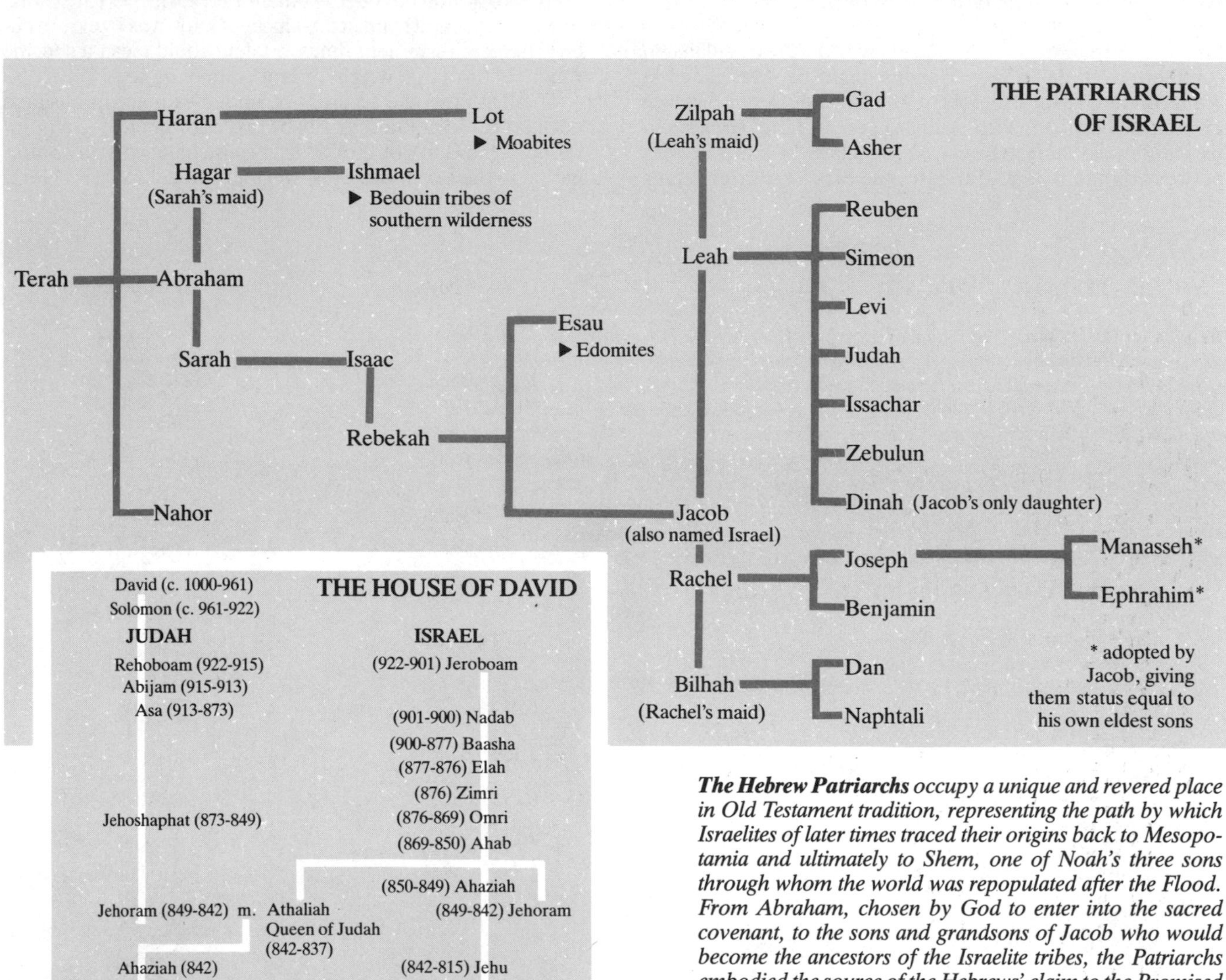

The Hebrew Patriarchs *occupy a unique and revered place in Old Testament tradition, representing the path by which Israelites of later times traced their origins back to Mesopotamia and ultimately to Shem, one of Noah's three sons through whom the world was repopulated after the Flood. From Abraham, chosen by God to enter into the sacred covenant, to the sons and grandsons of Jacob who would become the ancestors of the Israelite tribes, the Patriarchs embodied the source of the Hebrews' claim to the Promised Land and the foundation on which ancient Israel was built.*

The kingdom created by David *was divided after the death of his son Solomon, but David's heirs continued to rule the southern kingdom of Judah until Jerusalem fell to the Babylonians in 597 B.C. The sole interruption was the 5-year reign of Queen Athaliah, who usurped the throne after the death of her husband, Jehoram, in 842. By contrast, power in the northern kingdom of Israel was gained more often by intrigue and bloodshed than by dynastic inheritance. The Gospels of Matthew and Luke contain genealogies linking Jesus to David by family descent. The two lists differ, but both were meant to establish Jesus' legal claim to the throne of David—an important issue, since Old Testament prophets had foretold that the Messiah would be a "son of David," a descendant of the Davidic line.*

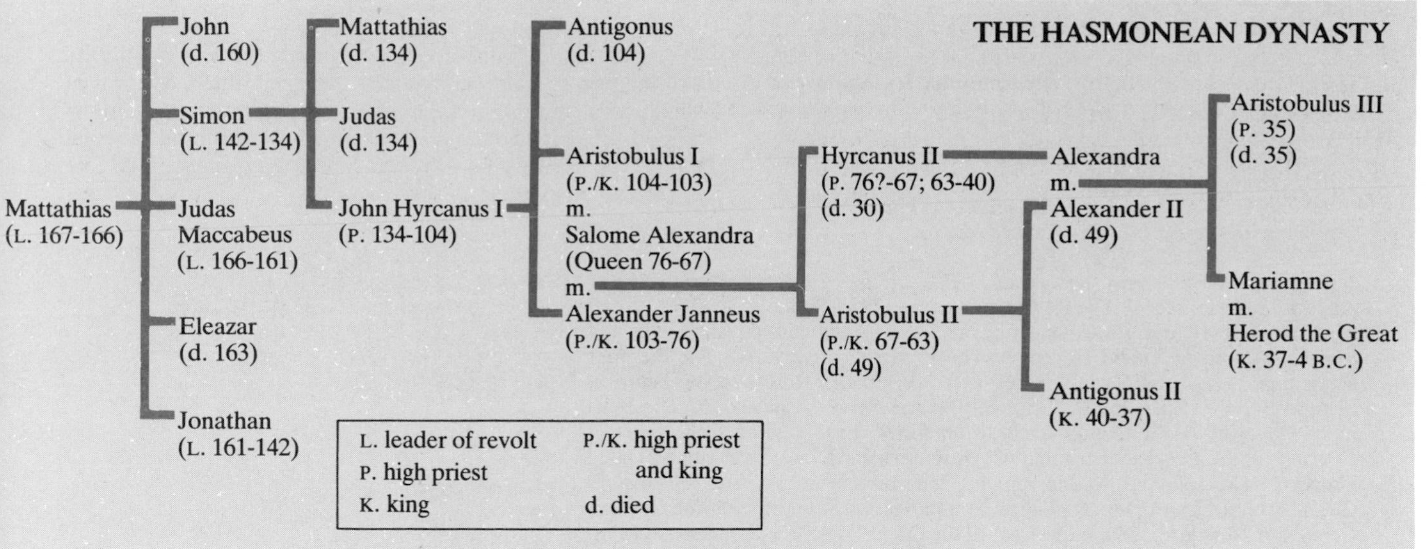

The Maccabees burst onto the stage of Israelite history in the 2nd century B.C., during the most intense and brutal campaign of religious repression the Jews had ever known. The oppressor was the Syrian despot Antiochus IV, and those who led the uprising against him were a family headed by Mattathias Hasmoneas, an aging priest from the town of Modein near Jerusalem. On Mattathias' death, leadership was assumed by one of his five sons, Judas—soon nicknamed Maccabeus, "the Hammer"—under whose brilliant guidance the rebels successfully defied Syrian attempts to crush their resistance and erase the culture of their ancestors. Judas' brothers continued the fight after his death in battle in 161, and their descendants went on to rule Israel as priest-kings until the advent of the Romans. The Golden Age of the Hasmonean dynasty marked Israel's last period of independence as a nation until the creation of modern Israel almost 2,000 years later.

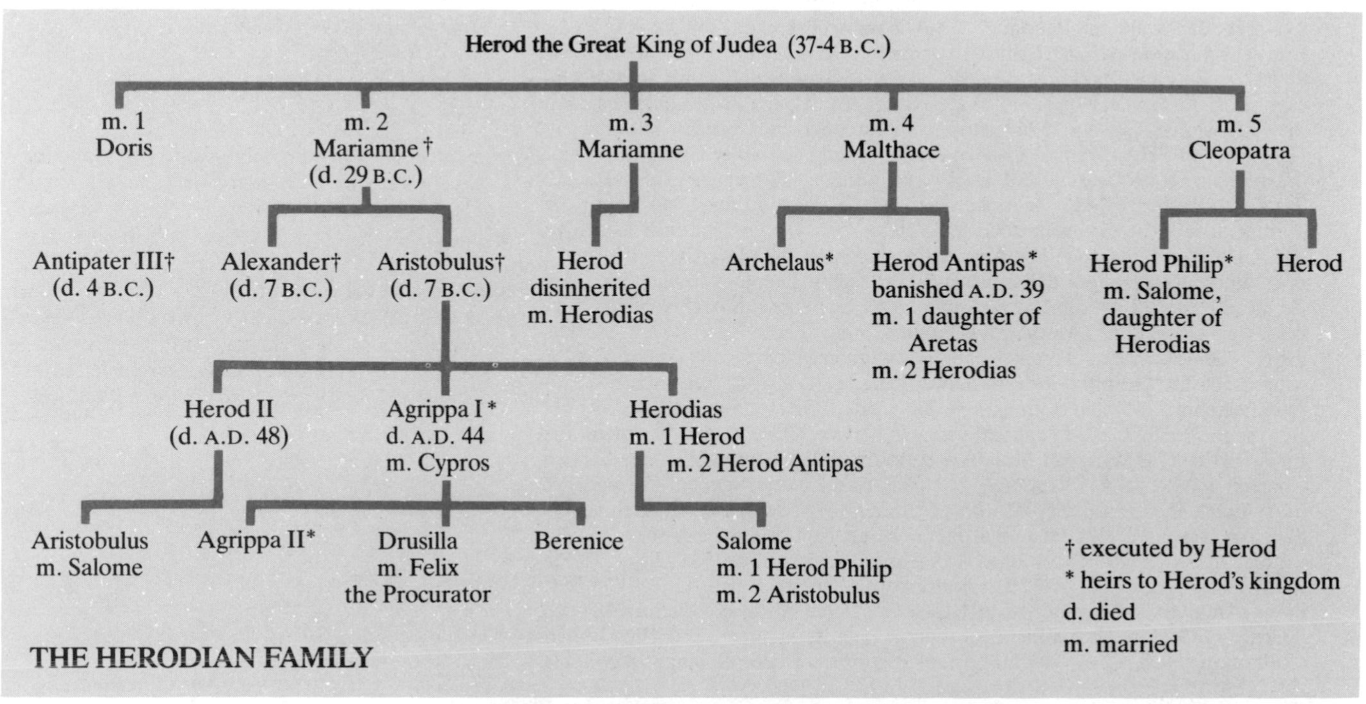

The legacy of King Herod was everywhere visible in the Holy Land of New Testament times, from the monumental building projects that transformed his realm—above all the rebuilding of the temple in Jerusalem—to the power his heirs continued to wield in the 1st century A.D. Though dependent on the approval of his Roman overlords and despised as an Idumean usurper by his Jewish subjects, Herod in many ways fit the classic mold of the ancient world's warrior-kings: bold and courageous in battle, shrewd in political maneuverings, utterly ruthless in dealing with rivals (including members of his own family), and grandiose in his conception of the role destined for him in history.

Credits and Acknowledgments

The editors wish to thank the American Bible Society for permission to adapt the glossary appearing on pp. 824-825 of words that have changed in meaning.

Maps adapted from original artwork by H. Shaw Borst, Inc. (397, 424, 706, 745) and by George Buctel (58, 97, 515, 566).
Inset maps (826-827) and cosmos diagram (41 *bottom*) by Kenneth Chaya.
Jerusalem illustration (408) by Victor Lazarro.

3 The Granger Collection, New York. **6** The Granger Collection, New York. **11** Alinari/Art Resource. **12** The Bettmann Archive. **13** *left* Shrine of the Book, Israel Museum, Jerusalem; *right* Courtesy of the Israel Department of Antiquities and Museums/Photo by David Harris. **39** The Bettmann Archive. **40** The Pierpont Morgan Library. **41** *top* Scala/Art Resource. **43** Scala/Art Resource. **46** Historical Pictures Service, Chicago. **47** Historical Pictures Service, Chicago. **57** The Bettmann Archive. **62** Courtauld Institute Galleries, London, Lee Collection. **71** Courtesy of the Israel Department of Antiquities and Museums/Photo by David Harris. **76** The John and Mable Ringling Museum of Art, Sarasota, Florida. **79** Courtesy of the Israel Department of Antiquities and Museums. **85** The Granger Collection, New York. **96** *top* Courtesy of the Oriental Institute, University of Chicago; *bottom* The Bettmann Archive. **100** The Bettmann Archive. **104** Paulus Leeser. **115** Culver Pictures. **133** The Rockefeller Archaeological Museum, Jerusalem/Erich Lessing Photo/Magnum. **145** *top* Alinari/Art Resource; *bottom* Lucia Woods/Photo Researchers. **146** The Granger Collection, New York. **159** Scala/Art Resource. **160** E. Borowski Collection, Israel Museum, Jerusalem/Erich Lessing Photo/Magnum. **175** The Bettmann Archive. **189** Scala/Art Resource. **191** Borromeo/Art Resource. **195** Alinari/Art Resource. **200** The Bettmann Archive. **222** The Bettmann Archive. **227** The Bettmann Archive. **231** Alinari/Art Resource. **235** SEF/Art Resource. **236** The Granger Collection, New York. **251** Alinari/Art Resource. **253** George Holton/Photo Researchers. **258** The Bettmann Archive. **266** Frances Mortimer/Rapho/Photo Researchers. **280** Culver Pictures. **287** Alinari/Art Resource. **296** Scala/Art Resource. **314** The Bettmann Archive. **315** National Gallery of Art, Washington, Samuel H. Kress Collection/Art Resource. **316** Biblioteca Vaticana/Madeline Grimoldi Archives. **320** The Bettmann Archive. **329** Alinari/Art Resource. **331** SEF/Art Resource. **341** George Holton/Photo Researchers. **354** Scala/Art Resource. **355** Alinari/Art Resource. **358** Sotheby Parke-Bernet/Art Resource. **367** British Information Services/Photo Researchers. **369** Snark/Art Resource. **371** Scala/Art Resource. **373** Historical Pictures Service, Chicago. **379** The Jewish Museum/Art Resource. **385** Culver Pictures. **388** Historical Pictures Service, Chicago. **396** Historical Pictures Service, Chicago. **400** Josse/Art Resource. **404** The Granger Collection, New York. **406** Mary Evans Picture Library/Photo Researchers. **412** Alinari/Art Resource. **420** Scala/Art Resource. **429** Scala/Art Resource. **435** Historical Pictures Service, Chicago. **444** Photo Researchers. **460** The Granger Collection, New York. **475** The Bettmann Archive. **494** Alinari/Art Resource. **506** Alinari/Art Resource. **508** Mary Evans Picture Library/Photo Researchers. **510** Courtesy of Biblical Archaeology Review/Photos by Zev Radovan. **512** Alinari/Art Resource. **517** The Bettmann Archive. **520** Giraudon/Art Resource. **537** Mary Evans Picture Library/Photo Researchers. **545** Historical Pictures Service, Chicago. **558** The Bettmann Archive. **559** Alinari/Art Resource. **564** The Granger Collection, New York. **570** Scala/Art Resource. **578** Photo Researchers. **579** The Bettmann Archive. **582** The Bettmann Archive. **595** The Bettmann Archive. **596** Historical Pictures Service, Chicago. **618** Historical Pictures Service, Chicago. **621** Scala/Art Resource. **622** Historical Pictures Service, Chicago. **629** Scala/Art Resource. **652** Historical Pictures Service, Chicago. **653** Mary Evans Picture Library/Photo Researchers. **661** The Bettmann Archive. **665** SEF/Art Resource. **678** Historical Pictures Service, Chicago. **686** Scala/Art Resource. **707** Alinari/Art Resource. **717** Alinari/Art Resource. **731** Historical Pictures Service, Chicago. **735** Historical Pictures Service, Chicago. **741** The Bettmann Archive. **743** Rapho/Photo Researchers. **782** Historical Pictures Service, Chicago. **785** Mary Evans Picture Library/Photo Researchers. **786** The Granger Collection, New York. **803** Historical Pictures Service, Chicago. **805** Scala/Art Resource.